MOTOR
AUTO REPAIR MANUAL

38th Edition

First Printing

TL
152
M815
1975

Editor
Louis C. Forier, S.A.E.

Managing Editor
Larry Solnik, S.A.E.

Associate Editors
Michael Kromida · Dan Irizarry

Editorial Assistants
Warren Schildknecht · Connie Nevers

Published by

MOTOR

250 West 55th St., New York, N. Y. 10019

The Automotive Business Magazine

Printed in the U.S.A. © Copyright 1974 by The Hearst Corporation

ISBN 0-910992-34-7

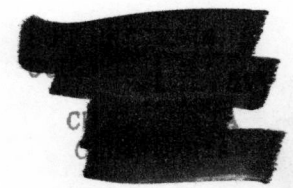

Books Published by MOTOR

> The nature of the automobile we know today makes it economically impractical to cover all phases of servicing in one book. A brief descriptive list of all titles is provided below for your convenience.

Auto Repair Manual

This most-widely used and respected book of its kind covers 2,300 car models of 37 series of American-make cars from 1969-75. Also includes tune-up and front end specs on models from 1946-68. The big 1975 edition has more than 1,300 double-size pages featuring 55,000 essential service specifications and over 300 quick-check specification charts, 225,000 service and repair facts, and over 3,000 "how-to-do-it" pictures.

Foreign Car Repair Manual

Published in three volumes by country of origin (English & Italian, Japanese & French, German & Swedish). For the "Foreign Car" owner who is totally involved with his car and is interested in Do-It-Yourself car repairs; the maintenance of peak performance . . . and in saving money. Also included is a section (not available elsewhere) on parts and tool availability that guides the car owner as to where he can buy the parts and special tools needed to keep his car in top running condition.

Truck Repair Manual

Service and repair is surprisingly easy with this new edition that covers 2,800 Truck Models, 1962 through 1975. Over 1,300 pages of step-by-step instructions, 2,000 cutaway pictures, 3,000 service and repair facts, specs and adjustments. Covers all popular makes of trucks. Manual also gives specs for gasoline and diesel engines used in off-highway equipment and farm tractors.

Auto Engines & Electrical Systems

Ideal basic book for car buffs, students, engineers, mechanics. Over 700 pages, 1,300 pictures and diagrams explain the workings of engines, fuel and electrical systems. Special chapters on the Rotary and Turbine engines.

Automobile Trouble Shooter

This new hardback edition is a must for the glove compartment or tool box of every do-it-yourself car enthusiast. A handy guide to finding out what's wrong, it pinpoints over 2,000 causes of car trouble. A new section on excessive fuel consumption points out conditions which greatly affect fuel economy; tells how to fashion your own gas mileage tester to check your driving habits. The trip planning section advises the owner of items he should carry in case of emergencies. Important today, when so many are heading for the backwoods country where there may be no assistance.

INDEX

This Edition Covers Mechanical Specifications and Service Procedures on 1969-75 Models
*For your convenience in locating this section, a black bar has been positioned beneath all odd page numbers.

───── CAR INFORMATION SECTION—1 ─────

AMERICAN MTRS. ..1-2
Ambassador • American
AMX • DPL • Gremlin
Hornet • Javelin • Matador
Rambler • Rebel • Rogue

BUICK 1-47
Apollo • Centurion • Century
Electra • Gran Sport • Le Sabre
Regal • Riviera
Skylark • Special
Wagons • Wildcat

BUICK SKYHAWK .1-245

CADILLAC 1-89

CHECKER MTRS. 1-131

CHEVROLET 1-144
Bel Air • Biscayne
Camaro • Caprice
Chevelle • Impala
Monte Carlo • Nova
Wagons

**CHEVROLET
MONZA 2+2** ...1-245

**CHEVROLET
VEGA** 1-220

CHRYSLER 1-275

CORVETTE 1-144

DODGE 1-275
Challenger • Charger
Coronet • Dart
Demon • Monaco
Polara • Swinger

FORD (Full Size) ..1-355
Custom • Galaxie
LTD • XL • Wagons

**FORD (Compact &
Inter.)** 1-400
Elite • Fairlane
Falcon • Granada
Maverick • Mustang
Torino

FORD MUSTANG II .1-462

FORD PINTO 1-462

IMPERIAL 1-275

LINCOLN 1-532
Continental • Mark III-IV

**MERCURY (Full
Size)** 1-355
Brougham • Marauder
Marquis • Monterey
Wagons

**MERCURY (Compact &
Inter.)** 1-400
Comet • Cougar
Cyclone • GT • Monarch
Montego • Wagons

OLDSMOBILE 1-565
Cutlass • Delta 88
F-85 • 4-4-2 • 98
Omega • Royale
Super 88 • Toronado
Vista Cruiser

OLDS STARFIRE 1-245

PLYMOUTH 1-275
Barracuda • Belvedere
Duster • Fury • GTX
Roadrunner • Satellite
Scamp • Signet
Valiant • VIP

PONTIAC 1-629
Bonneville • Catalina
Executive • Firebird • GrandAm
Grand Prix • Grandville
GTO • Le Mans
Sprint • Tempest
T-37 • Ventura II • Wagons

PONTIAC ASTRE ..1-220

THUNDERBIRD ...1-504

Tune Up Data and Wheel Alignment for 1946-68 Models:—Page1-679

Foreign Car Tune Up Data:—Page 1-706

Flasher Locations:—Page 1-715

Car Warranties:—Page 1-717

How to Push and Tow Automatic Drive Cars:—Inside Back Cover

Decimal and Millimeter Equivalents and Tap Drill Sizes:—Inside Back Cover

───── GENERAL SERVICE INFORMATION SECTION—2* ─────

Air Conditioning 2-20
Air Cushion Restraint System .2-367
Alternator Service 2-69
Anti-Skid Brake Systems 2-162
Automatic Level Controls ...2-39
Auto. Trans. Quick Service ..2-231
Brake, Hydraulic System 2-123
Brakes, Anti-Skid 2-162
Brakes, Disc Type 2-133
Carburetor Service 2-372
Dash Gauges 2-50
Disc Brakes 2-133

Distributors, Standard 2-525
Distributors, Transistor 2-535
Electronic Ignition 2-535
Emission Control Systems ...2-545
Fans, Variable Speed 2-38
Fuel Pumps 2-369
Headlamps, Concealed 2-46
Headlight Aiming 2-45
Hydraulic Brake System 2-123
Ignition Coils and Resistors ..2-521
Instruments, Dash 2-50
Overdrive Service 2-175

Seat Belt Interlock Systems ..2-311
Starting Motors 2-54
Starting Switches 2-67
Steering Gears, Manual 2-170
Transmissions, Manual Shift:
    Three Speed 2-177
    Four Speed 2-199
Transmisssions, Automatic:
    Quick Service 2-231
Trouble Shooting 2-1
Tune Up Service 2-517
Universal Joints 2-117

AMERICAN MOTORS

OLD CAR SPECIFICATIONS: For 1946-68 Tune Up and Wheel Alignment Specifications see main index.

INDEX OF SERVICE OPERATIONS

ACCESSORIES

PAGE NO.

Air Conditioning 2-20
Automatic Level Controls 2-39
Blower Motor Remove 1-23
Clock Troubles 2-11
Heater Core, Replace 1-22
Power Seat Troubles 2-18
Power Top Troubles 2-18
Power Window Troubles 2-18
Radio, Replace 1-21
Speed Controls, Adjust 1-24

BRAKES

Anti-Skid Brakes 2-162
Brake Troubles, Mechanical 2-17
Disc Brake Service 2-133
Hydraulic System Service 2-123
Master Cylinder, Replace 1-43
Parking Brake, Adjust 1-43
Service Brakes, Adjust 1-41

CLUTCH

Clutch Pedal, Adjust 1-32
Clutch, Replace 1-32
Clutch Troubles 2-12

COOLING SYSTEM

Cooling System Troubles 2-6
Variable Speed Fans 2-38
Water Pump, Replace 1-31

ELECTRICAL

Alternator Service 2-69
Blower Motor Remove 1-23
Dash Gauge Service 2-50
Distributor, Replace 1-15
Distributor Service:
  Standard 2-525
  Breakerless Inductive Discharge ... 1-15
Headlight Aiming 2-45
Horn Sounder, Remove 1-19
Ignition Coils and Resistors 2-521
Ignition Lock 1-18
Ignition Switch, Replace 1-18
Ignition Timing 2-518
Instrument Cluster, Removal 1-19
Light Switch, Replace 1-18
Neutral Safety Switch, Replace 1-19
Seat Belt Interlock Systems 2-311
Starter Service 2-54
Starter, Replace 1-18
Starter Switch Service 2-67
Stop Light Switch, Replace 1-18
Turn Signal Switch, Replace 1-19
Turn Signal Troubles 2-11
Windshield Wiper Motor, Replace 1-20
Windshield Wiper Troubles 2-19

ENGINE

PAGE NO.

Camshaft 1-28
Crankshaft Rear Oil Seal 1-29
Cylinder Head, Replace 1-25
Engine Markings 1-24
Engine Mounts 1-24
Engine, Replace 1-24
Engine Troubles 2-1
Main Bearings, Replace 1-29
Piston Pins, Replace 1-29
Piston Rings, Replace 1-29
Piston and Rod, Assemble 1-29
Pistons, Replace 1-29
Rocker Arms 1-25
Rod Bearings, Replace 1-29
Timing Case Cover, Replace 1-27
Timing Chain, Replace 1-28
Valve Arrangement 1-25
Valve Guides 1-26
Valve Lifters 1-27

ENGINE LUBRICATION

Emission Control Systems 2-545
Oil Pan, Replace 1-30
Oil Pump, Replace 1-30

FUEL SYSTEM

Carburetor Adjustment and Specs. ... 2-372
Emission Control Systems 2-545
Fuel Pump, Replace 1-31
Fuel Pump Service 2-369
Fuel System Troubles 2-2

PROPELLER SHAFT & U JOINTS

Propeller Shaft 1-41
Universal Joint Service 2-117

REAR AXLE & SUSPENSION

Axle Shaft, Bearing and Seal 1-41
Coil Springs, Replace 1-43
Control Arms & Bushings, Replace ... 1-43
Leaf Springs, Replace 1-43
Rear Axle Description 1-39
Rear Axle Troubles 2-16
Shock Absorber, Replace 1-43

SPECIFICATIONS

Alternator 1-12
Belt Tension 1-31
Brakes 1-14
Capacities 1-13
Carburetors 2-372
Cooling System 1-13
Crankshaft and Bearings 1-10

Distributors 1-8
Engine Tightening Torque 1-10
Fuel Pump Pressure 1-31
General Engine Specs. 1-5
Ignition Coils and Resistors 2-521
Pistons, Rings and Pins 1-10
Rear Axle 1-11
Starting Motors 1-12
Tune Up 1-6
Valve Lift 1-25
Valves 1-8
Valve Timing 1-25
Wheel Alignment 1-11

STEERING GEAR

Horn Sounder, Removal 1-19
Ignition Lock 1-18
Mechanical Gear, Replace 1-46
Mechanical Gear Service 2-170
Mechanical Gear Troubles 2-17
Power Gear, Replace 1-46
Steering Wheel, Replace 1-19

SUSPENSION, FRONT

Ball Joints, Replace 1-45
Ball Joints, Check for Wear 1-45
Spring, Replace 1-46
Lubrication 1-44
Shock Absorber, Replace 1-45
Suspension, Description of 1-44
Toe-In, Adjust 1-44
Wheel Alignment, Adjust 1-44
Wheel Bearings, Adjust 1-45
Wheel Bearings, Replace 1-45

TRANSMISSIONS

Three Speed Manual:
  Replace 1-33
  Repairs 2-177
  Linkage, Adjust 1-33
Four Speed Manual:
  Replace 1-33
  Repairs 2-199
  Linkage, Adjust 1-33
Automatic Units 2-231
  1975 Linkage 1-33
Overdrive Service 1-34, 2-175

TUNE UP

Service 2-517
Specifications 1-6

WINDSHIELD WIPER

Wiper Arms 1-20
Wiper Blades 1-20
Wiper Linkage, Replace 1-21
Wiper Motor, Replace 1-20
Wiper Switch, Replace 1-21
Wiper Troubles 2-19

American Motors

ENGINE IDENTIFICATION

6-199 & 6-232 (1969): The engine code number is located on a machined pad adjacent to the distributor. The letter contained in the code number identifies the cubic inch displacement of the engine. The letter "J" denotes the 199 engine with 8.5 compression ratio. The letter "L" denotes the 232 engine with 8.5 compression ratio.

6-199 & 6-232 (1970): The engine code number is located on a machined pad adjacent to the distributor. The letter "A" denotes the 199 engine. The letter "E" denotes the 232 engine with 1 barrel carburetor while the letter "G" denotes the 232 engine with 2 barrel carburetor.

6-232 & 6-258 (1971-74): The engine code is located on a pad between number two and three cylinders. The letter "A" denotes the 258 engine. The letter "E" denotes the 232 engine.

V8-287 & 327: The engine code number is located on a tag attached to the alternator mounting bracket. The letter contained in the code denotes the size of the cylinder bore and compression ratio. The letter "E" denotes the

4" bore with 8.7 compression ratio (327 engine). The letter "F" denotes the 4" bore with 9.7 compression ratio (327 engine). The letter "G" denotes the 3¾" bore with 8.7 compression ratio (287 engine).

V8-290, 343 & 390 (1969): The engine code is located on a plate attached to the front of the right-hand rocker arm cover. The letter "H" four-barrel carburetor. The letter "Z" is for the 243 engine with four-barrel carburetor; "S" for two-barrel carburetor. The letter "W" is for the 390 engine with two-barrel carburetor in 1968 and four-barrel in 1969; "X" with four-barrel carburetor in 1968.

V8-304, 360, 390, & 401 (1970-74): The engine code is located on a tag attached to the right bank rocker cover. The letter "H" denotes the 304 engine. The letter "N" denotes the 360 engine with 2 barrel carburetor while the letter "P" denotes the 360 engine with 4 barrel carburetor. The letter "X" denotes the 390 engine. The letter "Z" denotes the 401 engine.

GRILLE IDENTIFICATION

1969 Javelin

1969 AMX

1969 Rambler

1969 Rebel

1969 Ambassador

1970-72 Hornet

1970 Rebel

1970 Ambassador

1970 AMX

1970 Javelin

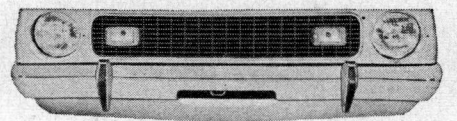
1970-72 Gremlin

1971 Javelin

GRILLE IDENTIFICATION—Continued

1971-72 AMX

1971-72 Ambassador

1971 Matador

1972 Javelin

1972 Matador

1973 Gremlin

1973 Hornet

1973 Javelin

1973 AMX

1973 Matador

1973 Ambassador

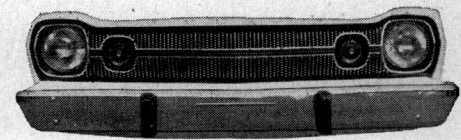

1974 Hornet

1974 Javelin

1974 Ambassador

1974 AMX

1974 Matador 4 Door

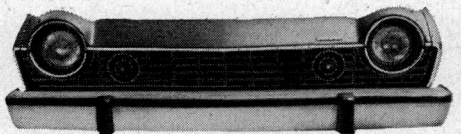

1974-75 Matador 2 Door

1975 Matador 4 Door

1974-75 Gremlin

1974-75 Gremlin X

1975 Hornet

GENERAL ENGINE SPECIFICATIONS

Year	Engine	Carburetor	Bore and Stroke	Piston Displacement, Cubic Inches	Compression Ratio	Maximum Brake H.P. @ R.P.M.	Maximum Torque Lbs. Ft. @ R.P.M.	Normal Oil Pressure Pounds
1969	128 Horsepower.............6-199	1 Barrel	3.75 x 3.00	199	8.5	128 @ 4400	182 @ 1600	75
	145 Horsepower.............6-232	1 Barrel	3.75 x 3.50	232	8.5	145 @ 4300	215 @ 1600	75
	155 Horsepower.............6-232	2 Barrel	3.75 x 3.50	232	8.5	155 @ 4400	222 @ 1600	75
	200 Horsepower.............V8-290	2 Barrel	3.75 x 3.28	290	9.0	200 @ 4600	285 @ 2800	75
	225 Horsepower.............V8-290	4 Barrel	3.75 x 3.28	290	10.0	225 @ 4700	300 @ 3200	75
	235 Horsepower.............V8-343	2 Barrel	4.08 x 3.28	343	9.0	235 @ 4400	345 @ 2600	75
	280 Horsepower.............V8-343	4 Barrel	4.08 x 3.28	343	10.2	280 @ 4800	365 @ 3000	75
	315 Horsepower.............V8-390	4 Barrel	4.165 x 3.574	390	10.2	315 @ 4600	425 @ 3200	75
1970	128 Horsepower.............6-199	1 Barrel	3.75 x 3.00	199	8.5	128 @ 4400	182 @ 1600	75
	145 Horsepower.............6-232	1 Barrel	3.75 x 3.50	232	8.5	145 @ 4300	215 @ 1600	75
	155 Horsepower.............6-232	2 Barrel	3.75 x 3.50	232	8.5	155 @ 4400	222 @ 1600	75
	210 Horsepower.............V8-304	2 Barrel	3.75 x 3.44	304	9.0	210 @ 4400	305 @ 2800	75
	245 Horsepower.............V8-360	2 Barrel	4.08 x 3.44	360	9.0	245 @ 4400	365 @ 2400	75
	290 Horsepower.............V8-360	4 Barrel	4.08 x 3.44	360	10.0	290 @ 4800	395 @ 3200	75
	325 Horsepower.............V8-390	4 Barrel	4.156 x 3.574	390	10.0	325 @ 5000	420 @ 3200	75
	340 Horsepower①............V8-390	4 Barrel	4.165 x 3.574	390	10.0	340 @ 5100	430 @ 3600	75
1971	135 Horsepower.............6-232	1 Barrel	3.75 x 3.50	232	8.0	135 @ 4000	210 @ 1600	75
	150 Horsepower.............6-258	1 Barrel	3.75 x 3.90	258	8.0	150 @ 3800	240 @ 1800	75
	210 Horsepower.............V8-304	2 Barrel	3.75 x 3.44	304	8.4	210 @ 4400	300 @ 2600	75
	245 Horsepower.............V8-360	2 Barrel	4.08 x 3.44	360	8.5	245 @ 4400	365 @ 2600	75
	285 Horsepower.............V8-360	4 Barrel	4.08 x 3.44	360	8.5	285 @ 4800	390 @ 3200	75
	330 Horsepower.............V8-401	4 Barrel	4.17 x 3.68	401	9.5	330 @ 5000	430 @ 3400	75
1972	100 Horsepower②............6-232	1 Barrel	3.75 x 3.50	232	8.0	100 @ 3600	185 @ 1800	75
	110 Horsepower②............6-258	1 Barrel	3.75 x 3.895	258	8.0	110 @ 3500	195 @ 2000	75
	150 Horsepower②............V8-304	2 Barrel	3.75 x 3.44	304	8.3	150 @ 4200	245 @ 2500	75
	175 Horsepower②............V8-360	2 Barrel	4.08 x 3.44	360	8.3	175 @ 4000	285 @ 2400	75
	195 Horsepower②............V8-360	4 Barrel	4.08 x 3.44	360	8.3	195 @ 4400	295 @ 2900	75
	220 Horsepower②③...........V8-360	4 Barrel	4.08 x 3.44	360	8.3	220 @ 4400	315 @ 3100	75
	255 Horsepower②............V8-401	4 Barrel	4.165 x 3.68	401	8.5	255 @ 4600	345 @ 3300	75
1973	100 Horsepower②............6-232	1 Barrel	3.75 x 3.50	232	8.0	100 @ 3600	185 @ 1800	75
	110 Horsepower②............6-258	1 Barrel	3.75 x 3.895	258	8.0	110 @ 3500	195 @ 2000	75
	150 Horsepower②............V8-304	2 Barrel	3.75 x 3.44	304	8.4	150 @ 4200	245 @ 2500	75
	175 Horsepower②............V8-360	2 Barrel	4.08 x 3.44	360	8.5	175 @ 4000	285 @ 2400	75
	195 Horsepower②............V8-360	4 Barrel	4.08 x 3.44	360	8.5	195 @ 4400	295 @ 2900	75
	220 Horsepower②③...........V8-360	4 Barrel	4.08 x 3.44	360	8.5	220 @ 4400	315 @ 3100	75
	255 Horsepower②............V8-401	4 Barrel	4.165 x 3.68	401	8.5	255 @ 4600	345 @ 3300	75
1974	100 Horsepower②............6-232	1 Barrel	3.75 x 3.50	232	8.0	100 @ 3600	185 @ 1800	75
	110 Horsepower②............6-258	1 Barrel	3.75 x 3.90	258	8.0	110 @ 3500	195 @ 2000	75
	150 Horsepower②............V8-304	2 Barrel	3.75 x 3.44	304	8.4	150 @ 4200	245 @ 2500	75
	175 Horsepower②............V8-360	2 Barrel	4.08 x 3.44	360	8.5	175 @ 4000	285 @ 2400	75
	195 Horsepower②............V8-360	4 Barrel	4.08 x 3.44	360	8.5	195 @ 4400	295 @ 2900	75
	220 Horsepower②③...........V8-360	4 Barrel	4.08 x 3.44	360	8.5	220 @ 4400	315 @ 3100	75
	255 Horsepower②............V8-401	4 Barrel	4.165 x 3.68	401	8.5	235 @ 4600	335 @ 3200	75
1975	100 Horsepower.............6-232	1 Barrel	3.75 x 3.50	232	8.0	100 @ 3600	185 @ 1800	37-75
	110 Horsepower.............6-258	1 Barrel	3.75 x 3.90	258	8.0	110 @ 3500	195 @ 2000	37-75
	150 Horsepower.............V8-304	2 Barrel	3.75 x 3.44	304	8.4	150 @ 4200	245 @ 2500	37-75
	175 Horsepower.............V8-360	2 Barrel	4.08 x 3.44	360	8.25	175 @ 4000	285 @ 2400	37-75
	195 Horsepower.............V8-360	4 Barrel	4.08 x 3.44	360	8.25	195 @ 4400	295 @ 2900	37-75
	220 Horsepower.............V8-360	4 Barrel	4.08 x 3.44	360	8.25	220 @ 4400	315 @ 3100	37-75

①—Rebel Machine.
②—Ratings are net (as installed in the vehicle).
③—With dual exhausts.

TUNE UP SPECIFICATIONS

OLD CAR SPECIFICATIONS: For 1946-68 Tune Up Specifications see main index.

★When using a timing light, disconnect vacuum hose or tube at distributor and plug opening in hose or tube so idle speed will not be affected.

●When checking compression, lowest cylinder must be within 80 percent of highest.

▲Before removing wires from distributor cap, determine location of the No. 1 wire in cap,
as distributor position may have been altered from that shown at the end of this chart.

Year	Spark Plug		Distributor		Ignition Timing★			Carb. Adjustments					
	Type	Gap Inch	Point Gap Inch	Dwell Angle Deg.	Firing Order Fig. ▲	Timing BTDC ①	Mark Fig.	Hot Idle Speed③		Air Fuel Ratio		Idle CO%	
								Std. Trans.	Auto. Trans.②	Std. Trans.	Auto. Trans.	Std. Trans.	Auto. Trans.
1969													
6-199, 232 Std. Tr.	N14Y	.035	.016	31–34	A	TDC	D	600⑤	—	—	—	—	—
6-199, 232 Auto. Tr.	N14Y	.035	.016	31–34	A	5°	D	—	525D⑥	—	—	—	—
V8-290, 343, 390	N12Y	.035	.016	29–31	B	TDC	C	650⑤	550D⑥	—	—	—	—
1970													
6-199, 232	N14Y	.035	.016	31–34	A	3°	D	600	550D	14.0 to 1	14.0 to 1	—	—
V8-304, 360, 390	N12Y	.035	.016	29–31	B	5°④	C	650	600D	14.0 to 1	14.0 to 1	—	—
1971													
6-232 Std. Tr.	N12Y	.035	.016	31–34	A	3°	D	700	—	14.0 to 1	14.0 to 1	—	—
6-232 Auto. Tr.	N12Y	.035	.016	31–34	A	5°	D	—	600D	14.0 to 1	14.0 to 1	—	—
6-258	N12Y	.035	.016	31–34	A	5°	D	700	600D	14.0 to 1	14.0 to 1	—	—
V8-304, 360, 401	N12Y	.035	.016	29–31	B	2½°	C	750	650D	14.0 to 1	14.0 to 1	—	—
1972													
6-232 Exc. Calif.	N12Y	.035	.016	31–34	A	5°	D	600	550D	14.0 to 1	14.0 to 1	—	—
6-232 Calif.	N12Y	.035	.016	31–34	A	3°	D	700	600D	14.0 to 1	14.0 to 1	—	—
6-258 Exc. Calif.	N12Y	.035	.016	31–34	A	5°	D	600	550D	14.0 to 1	14.0 to 1	—	—
6-258 Calif.	N12Y	.035	.016	31–34	A	3°	D	700	600D	14.0 to 1	14.0 to 1	—	—
V8-304 Exc. Calif.	N12Y	.035	.016	29–31	B	5°	C	750	650D	13.5 to 1	14.0 to 1	—	—
V8-304 Calif.	N12Y	.035	.016	29–31	B	5°	C	750	700D	13.5 to 1	14.0 to 1	—	—
V8-360	N12Y	.035	.016	29–31	B	5°	C	750	700D	14.0 to 1	14.0 to 1	—	—
V8-401 Exc. Calif.	N12Y	.035	.016	29–31	B	5°	C	700	650D	13.5 to 1	13.5 to 1	—	—
V8-401 Calif.	N12Y	.035	.016	29–31	B	5°	C	700	700D	14.0 to 1	14.0 to 1	—	—
1973													
6-232	N12Y	.035	.016	31–34	A	5°	D	700⑦	600D⑧	—	—	⑨	⑨
6-258	N12Y	.035	.016	31–34	A	3°	D	700⑦	600D⑧	—	—	⑨	⑨
V8-304	N12Y	.035	.016	29–31	B	5°	C	750	700D	—	—	0.5–1.0	0.5–1.0
V8-360	N12Y	.035	.016	29–31	B	5°	C	750	700D	—	—	0.5–1.0	0.5–1.0
V8-401	N12Y	.035	.016	29–31	B	5°	C	750	700D	—	—	0.5–1.0	0.5–1.0
1974													
6-232 L/EGR	N12Y	.035	.016	31–34	A	5°	D	700	600D	—	—	⑨	⑨
6-232 W/EGR	N12Y	.035	.016	31–34	A	5°	D	600	550D	—	—	⑨	⑨
6-232 Calif.	N12Y	.035	.016	31–34	A	5°	D	600	700D	—	—	⑨	⑨
6-258 L/EGR	N12Y	.035	.016	31–34	A	3°	D	550	700D	—	—	⑨	⑨
6-258 W/EGR	N12Y	.035	.016	31–34	A	3°	D	550	600D	—	—	⑨	⑨
6-258 Calif.	N12Y	.035	.016	31–34	A	3°	D	600	700D	—	—	⑨	⑨
V8-304	N12Y	.035	.016	29–31	B	⑩	C	750	700D	—	—	0.5–1.0	0.5–1.0
V8-360	N12Y	.035	.016	29–31	B	5°	C	750	700D	—	—	0.5–1.0	0.5–1.0
V8-401	N12Y	.035	.016	29–31	B	5°	C	750	700D	—	—	0.5–1.0	0.5–1.0

Continued

TUNE UP SPECIFICATIONS—Continued

OLD CAR SPECIFICATIONS: For 1946-68 Tune Up Specifications see main index.

★When using a timing light, disconnect vacuum hose or tube at distributor and plug opening in hose or tube so idle speed will not be affected.

●When checking compression, lowest cylinder must be within 80 percent of highest.

▲Before removing wires from distributor cap, determine location of the No. 1 wire in cap, as distributor position may have been altered from that shown at the end of this chart.

Year	Spark Plug		Distributor		Ignition Timing★			Carb. Adjustments					
	Type	Gap Inch	Point Gap Inch	Dwell Angle Deg.	Firing Order Fig. ▲	Timing BTDC ①	Mark Fig.	Hot Idle Speed③		Air Fuel Ratio		Idle CO%	
								Std. Trans.	Auto. Trans.②	Std. Trans.	Auto. Trans.	Std. Trans.	Auto. Trans.
1975													
6-232, 258	N12Y	.035	—	—	A	5°	E	600	550D	—	—	—	—
6-232, 258 Calif.	N12Y	.035	—	—	A	3°	E	600	700D	—	—	—	—
V8-304	N12Y	.035	—	—	B	5°	C	750	700D	—	—	—	—
V8-360	N12Y	.035	—	—	B	5°	C	—	700D	—	—	—	—

①—BTDC: Before top dead center.
②—D: Drive. N: Neutral.
③—Where two speeds are listed, lower speed indicates idle solenoid disconnected.
④—V8-390 with distributor 1111948 set at TDC.
⑤—If air conditioned turn A/C switch full on.
⑦—Set Matador wagon at 600 R.P.M.
⑧—Set Matador at 650D.
⑨—W/Air Guard 0.5–1.0%. W/O Air Guard 1.0–1.5%.
⑩—Exc. Calif. auto. trans., 5° BTDC; Calif. auto. trans., 2½° BTDC.

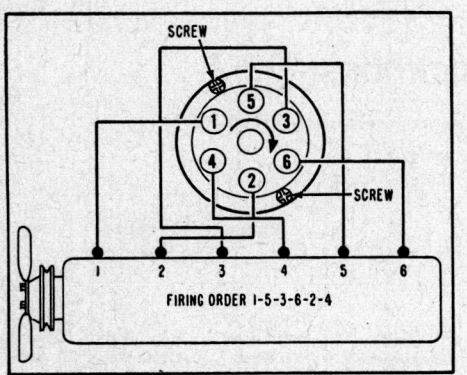

Fig. A

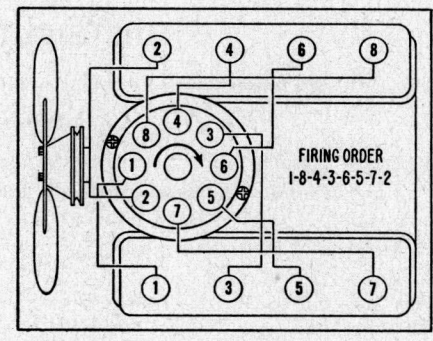

Fig. B

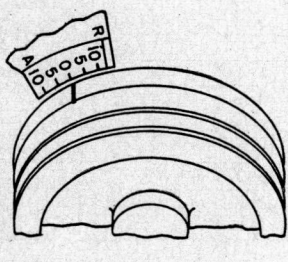

Fig. C

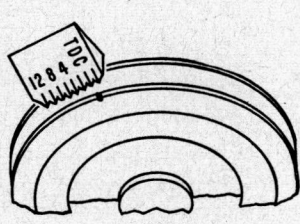

Fig. D

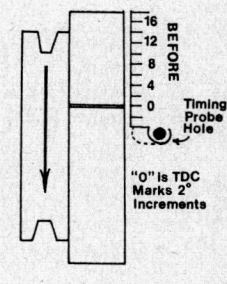

Fig. E

VALVE SPECIFICATIONS

Year	Model	Valve Lash		Valve Angles		Valve Spring Installed Height	Valve Spring Pressure Lbs. @ In.	Stem Clearance		Stem Diameter	
		Int.	Exh.	Seat	Face			Intake	Exhaust	Intake	Exhaust
1969	6-199, 232	Hydraulic③	Hydraulic③	④	②	1 13/16	195 @ 1 7/16	.001–.003	.001–.003	.3715–.3725	.3715–.3725
	8-290, 343, 390	Hydraulic③		①	⑤	1 13/16	200 @ 1 25/64	.001–.003	.001–.003	.3715–.3725	.3715–.3725
1970	6-199, 232	Hydraulic③		④	②	1 13/16	195 @ 1 7/16	.001–.003	.001–.003	.3715–.3725	.3715–.3725
	V8-304, 360, 390	Hydraulic③		①	⑦	1 13/16	200 @ 1 25/64	.001–.003	.001–.003	.3715–.3725	.3715–.3725
	8-390⑥	Hydraulic③		①	⑦	1 13/16	189 @ 1 23/64	.001–.003	.001–.003	.3715–.3725	.3715–.3725
1971	6-232, 258	Hydraulic③		⑦	②	1 13/16	195 @ 1 7/16	.001–.003	.001–.003	.3715–.3725	.3715–.3725
	V8-304, 360, 401	Hydraulic③		①	⑤	1 13/16	189 @ 1 23/64	.001–.003	.001–.003	.3715–.3725	.3715–.3725
1972	6-232, 258	Hydraulic③		⑦	②	1 13/16	195 @ 1 7/16	.001–.003	.001–.003	.3715–.3725	.3715–.3725
	V8-304, 360, 401	Hyrdaulic③		①	⑤	1 13/16	218 @ 1 23/64	.001–.003	.001–.003	.3715–.3725	.3715–.3725
1973	6-232, 258	Hydraulic③		⑦	②	1 13/16	195 @ 1 7/16	.001–.003	.001–.003	.3715–.3725	.3715–.3725
	V8-304, 360, 401	Hydraulic③		⑦	②	1 13/16	218 @ 1 23/64	.001–.003	.001–.003	.3715–.3725	.3715–.3725
1974	6-232, 258	Hydraulic③		⑦	②	⑧	⑨	.001–.003	.001–.003	.3715–.3725	.3715–.3725
	V8-304, 360, 401	Hydraulic③		⑦	②	⑧	⑩	.001–.003	.001–.003	.3715–.3725	.3715–.3725
1975	6-232, 258	Hydraulic③		⑦	②	⑧	⑨	.001–.003	.001–.003	.3715–.3725	.3715–.3725
	V8-304, 360	Hydraulic③		⑦	②	⑧	⑩	.001–.003	.001–.003	.3715–.3725	.3715–.3725

①—Intake 30°, exhaust 45°.
②—Intake 29°, exhaust 44°.
③—No adjustment.
④—Intake 30°, exhaust 44°.
⑤—Intake 29°, exhaust 44½°.

⑥—Rebel Machine.
⑦—Intake 30°, exhaust 44½°.
⑧—With valve rotator, 1⅝"; less valve rotator, 1 13/16".

⑨—With valve rotator, 218 lbs. @ 1 3/16"; less valve rotator, 195 lbs. @ 1 7/16".
⑩—With valve rotator, 213 lbs. @ 1 3/16"; less valve rotator, 213 lbs. @ 1 23/64.

DISTRIBUTOR SPECIFICATIONS

★If unit is checked on vehicle, double the RPM and degrees to get crankshaft figures.

Breaker arm spring tension 17–21.

Distributor Part No.①	Centrifugal Advance Degrees @ RPM of Distributor					Vacuum Advance		Distributor Retard	
	Advance Starts	Intermediate Advance			Full Advance	Inches of Vacuum to Start Plunger	Max. Adv. Dist. Deg. @ Vacuum	In. of Mercury Start Retard	Max. Retard Dist. Deg. @ Vacuum
1969-70									
1110444	2–3 @ 450	8–10 @ 1000	—	—	14 @ 2000	5–7	11 @ 17	—	—
1110481	0–2 @ 450	7–9 @ 1050	—	—	13 @ 2250	5–7	11 @ 17	5	4½ @ 14
1111191	0–1 @ 450	7.5–9.5 @ 1000	—	—	15 @ 2200	8–10	12 @ 20.5	—	—
1111472	0–1 @ 450	7.5–9.5 @ 1000	—	—	15 @ 2200	4–6	12 @ 19½	—	—
1111473	0–1 @ 400	0–2.5 @ 450	8.5–10.5 @ 800	—	16 @ 2200	8–10	12 @ 20.5	—	—
1111948	0–1 @ 400	0–2.5 @ 450	8.5–10.5 @ 800	—	16 @ 2200	4–6	12 @ 19.5	—	—
1111987	0–2 @ 450	6–8 @ 750	—	—	13 @ 2000	5–7	9½ @ 14.5	5	5½ @ 14
1111988	0–2 @ 500	5–7 @ 825	—	—	14 @ 2100	5–7	9½ @ 14.5	5	5½ @ 14
1112018	0–2 @ 500	4.5–6.5 @ 800	—	—	14 @ 2200	—	—	5	5½ @ 14
1971-72									
1110340	0–2 @ 450	7–9 @ 950	8–10 @ 1200	8.5–11.5 @ 1500	13.5 @ 2000	5–7	11.5 @ 17	—	—
1110497	0–5 @ 500	5–7 @ 950	7.5–9.5 @ 1200	9–11 @ 1500	14 @ 2000	5–7	9 @ 11	—	—
1111948	0–2.5 @ 450	8.9–10.5 @ 800	9–11.5 @ 1100	11–13 @ 1500	15 @ 2000	5–6	12.5 @ 19	—	—
1112028	0–2 @ 450	7–9 @ 1100	9.5–11.5 @ 1500	11–13 @ 1750	14.5 @ 2000	5–6	12.5 @ 19	—	—
1112111	0–2 @ 550	7.5–9.5 @ 1100	9.5–11.5 @ 1300	10.5–12 @ 1500	15 @ 2000	5–7	9 @ 16	—	—
1112112	0–1.5 @ 500	3.5–5.5 @ 750	7.5–9.5 @ 1000	9.5–11.5 @ 1500	14 @ 2000	5–7	8¼ @ 12½	—	—

Continued

DISTRIBUTOR SPECIFICATIONS—Continued

★ If unit is checked on vehicle, double the RPM and degrees to get crankshaft figures.

Breaker arm spring tension 17–21.

Distributor Part No.①	Centrifugal Advance Degrees @ RPM of Distributor					Vacuum Advance		Distributor Retard	
	Advance Starts	Intermediate Advance			Full Advance	Inches of Vacuum to Start Plunger	Max. Adv. Dist. Deg. @ Vacuum	In. of Mercury Start Retard	Max. Retard Dist. Deg. @ Vacuum
1973									
1110522	0–2.5 @ 500	4.5–6.5 @ 800	7–9 @ 1000	9–11 @ 1500	14 @ 2200	5–7	9 @ 13¼	—	—
1110523	0–1 @ 550	2–4.5 @ 750	6.5–8.5 @ 1000	9–11 @ 1500	15 @ 2200	5–7	9 @ 13¼	—	—
1112112	0–1.5 @ 500	3.5–5.5 @ 750	7.5–9.5 @ 1000	9.5–11.5 @ 1500	14 @ 2000	5–7	8¼ @ 12½	—	—
1112179	0–1 @ 400	4.5–6.5 @ 750	8–9.75 @ 1000	10¾–12¼ @ 1500	17 @ 2200	5–7	8¼ @ 12½	—	—
1112214	0–2¼ @ 450	6¾–8¾ @ 750	8–10 @ 1000	11–13 @ 1500	17 @ 2200	4–6	8¼ @ 13	—	—
1112215	0–3¼ @ 400	5–7 @ 750	6¼–8½ @ 1000	9½–11½ @ 1500	16 @ 2300	4–6	8¼ @ 13	—	—
1974									
1110528	0–2 @ 600	3–5.5 @ 800	6–8.5 @ 1000	6.5–9 @ 1500	15 @ 2200	5–7	9 @ 13	—	—
1110529	0–2 @ 500	4.5–7 @ 800	7–9 @ 1000	7–9.5 @ 1500	14 @ 2300	5–7	9 @ 13	—	—
1112112	0–2 @ 500	4.5–6.5 @ 800	7.5–9.5 @ 1000	9¾–11¾ @ 1500	14 @ 2200	5–7	8¼ @ 12¾	—	—
1112179	0–2 @ 500	4.5–6.5 @ 750	8–10 @ 1000	12.5–13.5 @ 1600	17 @ 2200	5–7	8¼ @ 12¾	—	—
1112214	0–2.5 @ 500	6.5–8.5 @ 700	—	11–13 @ 1500	17 @ 2200	4–6	8¼ @ 13	—	—
1112215	0–1.5 @ 400	4–6¾ @ 600	6.5–8.5 @ 1000	10–12 @ 1600	16 @ 2200	4–6	8¼ @ 13	—	—
1975									
3224746	0–1½ @ 400	5–7 @ 750	6½–8½ @ 1000	—	9¼–14 @ 1500	—	16¾ @ 1000	—	—
3224965	0–1 @ 400	4½–6 @ 750	8–10 @ 1000	—	11–13 @ 1500	—	18 @ 1000	—	—
3224966	0–2½ @ 450	6¼–8¾ @ 750	8¼–10¼ @ 1000	—	11–13 @ 1500	—	18¼ @ 1000	—	—
3224968	0–1 @ 500	2–4½ @ 750	6½–8½ @ 1500	—	6–9 @ 1500	—	17½ @ 1000	—	—
3224969	0–2 @ 500	3½–6 @ 750	7–9 @ 1000	—	7–9½ @ 1500	—	18 @ 1000	—	—

①—Stamped on distributor housing plate.

PISTONS, PINS, RINGS, CRANKSHAFT & BEARINGS

Year	Model	Piston Clearance Top of Skirt	Ring End Gap①		Wrist-pin Diameter	Rod Bearings		Main Bearings		Thrust on Bear. No.	Shaft End Play
			Comp.	Oil		Shaft Diameter	Bearing Clearance	Shaft Diameter	Bearing Clearance		
1969	6-199, 232	.0005–.0013	.010	.015	.9306	2.0934–2.0955	.001–.002	2.4981–2.5001	.001–.002	3	.0015–.007
	V8-290	.001–.0018	.010	.015	.9306	2.0934–2.0955	.001–.002	②	.001–.002	3	.003–008
	V8-343	.0012–.002	.010	.015	.9306	2.0934–2.0955	.001–.002	②	.001–.002	3	.003–.008
	V8-390	.001–.0018	.010	.015	1.000	2.2471–2.2492	.001–.002	②	.001–.002	3	.003–.008
1970	6-199, 232	.0005–.0013	.010	.015	.9306	2.0934–2.0955	.001–.002	2.4981–2.5001	⑤	3	.0015–.007
	V8-304	.001–.0018	.010	.015	.9306	2.0934–2.0955	.001–.002	④	⑤	3	.003–.008
	V8-360	.0012–.002	.010	.015	.9306	2.0934–2.0955	.001–.002	④	⑤	3	.003–.008
	V8-390	.0012–.002	.010	.015	1.000	2.2402–2.2471	.001–.002	④	⑤	3	.003–.008
	V8-390③	.001–.0018	.010	.015	1.000	2.2402–2.2471	.001–.002	④	⑤	3	.003–.008

Continued

PISTONS, PINS, RINGS, CRANKSHAFT & BEARINGS—Continued

Year	Model	Piston Clearance Top of Skirt	Ring End Gap① Comp.	Oil	Wrist-pin Diameter	Rod Bearings Shaft Diameter	Bearing Clearance	Main Bearings Shaft Diameter	Bearing Clearance	Thrust on Bear. No.	Shaft End Play
1971	6-232, 258	.0005–.0013	.010	.015	.9306	2.0934–2.0955	.001–.002	2.4986–2.5001	.001–.002	3	.0015–.007
	V8-304	.001–.0018	.010	.015	.9306	2.0934–2.0955	.001–.002	④	⑤	3	.003–008
	V8-360	.0012–.002	.010	.015	.9306	2.0934–2.0955	.001–.002	④	⑤	3	.003–.008
	V8-401	.001–.0018	.010	.015	1.000	2.2471–2.2485	.001–.002	④	⑤	3	.003–.008
1972-73	6-232, 258	.0009–.0017	.010	.010	.9306	2.0934–2.0955	.001–.002	2.4986–2.5001	.001–.002	3	.0015–.007
	V8-304	.001–.0018	.010	.010	.9306	2.0934–2.0955	.001–.002	④	⑤	3	.003–.008
	V8-360	⑥	.010	.015	.9306	2.0934–2.0955	.001–.002	④	⑤	3	.003–.008
	V8-401	⑦	.010	.015	1.000	2.2464–2.2485	.001–.002	④	⑤	3	.003–.008
1974	6-232, 250	.0009–.0017	.010	.010	.9304	2.0934–2.0955	.001–.003	2.4986–2.5001	.001–.003	3	.0015–.0065
	V8-304	.0010–.0018	.010	.010	.9308	2.0934–2.0955	.001–.003	④	.001–.003	3	.003–.008
	V8-360	.0012–.0020	.010	.015	.9308	2.0934–2.0955	.001–.003	④	.001–.003	3	.003–.008
	V8-401	.0010–.0018	.010	.015	1.0009	2.2464–2.2485	.001–.003	④	.001–.003	3	.003–.008
1975	6-232, 258	.0009–.0017	.010	.010	.9306	2.0934–2.0955	.001–.003	2.4986–2.5001	.001–.003	3	.0015–.0065
	V8-304	.001–.0018	.010	.010	.9310	2.0934–2.0955	.001–.003	④	.001–.003	3	.003–.008
	V8-360	.0012–.002	.010	.015	.9310	2.0934–2.0955	.001–.003	④	.001–.003	3	.003–.008

①—Fit rings in tapered bores for clearance listed in tightest portion of ring travel.
②—Rear main 2.7464–2.7479", others 2.7469–2.7489".
③—Rebel machine.
④—Rear main 2.7479–2.7464", others 2.7489–2.7474".
⑤—Rear main .002–.003", others .001–.002".
⑥—Except police, .0012–.002". Police, .0016–0024".
⑦—Except police, .001–.0018". Police, .0014–.0022".

ENGINE TIGHTENING SPECIFICATIONS★

★Torque specifications are for clean and lightly lubricated threads only. Dry or dirty threads produce increased friction which prevents accurate measurement of tightness.

Year	Engine Model	Spark Plugs Ft. Lbs.	Cylinder Head Bolts Ft. Lbs.	Intake Manifold Ft. Lbs.	Exhaust Manifold Ft. Lbs.	Rocker Arm Shaft Bracket Ft. Lbs.	Rocker Arm Cover Ft. Lbs.	Connecting Rod Cap Bolts Ft. Lbs.	Main Bearing Cap Bolts Ft. Lbs.	Flywheel to Crankshaft Ft. Lbs.	Vibration Damper or Pulley Ft. Lbs.
1969	6-199, 232	25–30	80–85	20–25	20–25	—	45–55①	26–30	75–85	100–110	50–60
1970	6-199, 232, 258	25–30	75–85	20–25	20–25	—	45–55①	26–30	75–85	100–110	50–60
1971–72	6-232, 258	25–30	80–85	20–25	20–25	—	45–55①	26–30	75–85	100–110	50–60
1973–74	6-232, 258	25–30	105	23	23	—	50①	28	80	105	55
1975	6-232, 258	28	105	23	23	—	50①	28	80	105	55
1969	V8-290, 343	25–30	90–100	40–45	30–35	65–70②	20–30①	26–30	95–105	100–110	50–60
1970–71	V8-304, 360	25–30	105–115	40–45	30–35	65–70②	20–30①	26–30	95–105	100–110	50–60
1972	V8-304, 360	25–30	105–115	40–45	30–35	65–70②	45–55①	26–30	95–105	100–110	50–60
1973–74	V8-304, 360	28	110	43	25	67②	50①	28	100	105	55
1969	V8-390	25–30	90–100	40–45	30–35	65–70②	20–30①	35–40	95–105	100–110	50–60
1970–71	V8-390, 401	25–30	105–115	40–45	30–35	65–70②	20–30①	35–40	95–105	100–110	50–60
1972	V8-401	25–30	105–115	40–45	30–35	65–70②	45–55①	35–40	95–105	100–110	50–60
1973–74	V8-401	28	110	43	25	67②	50①	38	100	105	55
1975	V8-304, 360	28	110	43	25	—	50①	28	100	105	55

①—Inch pounds.　②—Rocker arm stud.

REAR AXLE SPECIFICATIONS

Year	Model	Carrier Type ②	Ring Gear & Pinion Backlash		Pinion Bearing Preload			Differential Bearing Preload		
			Method	Adjustment	Method	New Bearings Inch-Lbs.	Used Bearings Inch-Lbs.	Method	New Bearings Inch-Lbs.	Used Bearings Inch-Lbs.
1969	6 Cyl.	Integral	Shims	.005–.009	Shims	15–25①	15–25①	Shims	.008	.008
	V8s	Integral	Shims	.005–.009	Spacer	17–28①	17–28①	Shims	.008	.008
1970	7⁷⁄₁₆″ Dr. Gr.	Integral	Shims	.005–.009	Sleeve	15–25①	15–25①	Shims	.008	.008
	8⅞″ Dr. Gr.	Integral	Shims	.005–.009	Sleeve	17–28①	17–28①	Shims	.008	.008
1971–75	7⁹⁄₁₆″ Dr. Gr.	Integral	Shims	.005–.009	Sleeve	15–25①	15–25①	Shims	.008	.008
	8⅞″ Dr. Gr.	Integral	Shims	.005–.009	Sleeve	17–28①	17–28①	Shims	.008	.008

①—Adjust at drive pinion flange nut with inch-pound torque wrench.　②—Axle shaft end play .006″.

WHEEL ALIGNMENT SPECIFICATIONS

OLD CAR SPECIFICATIONS: For 1946–68 Wheel Alignment Specifications see main index.

Year	Model	Caster Angle, Degrees		Camber Angle, Degrees				Toe-In. Inch	Toe-Out on Turns, Deg.①	
		Limits	Desired	Limits		Desired			Outer Wheel	Inner Wheel
				Left	Right	Left	Right			
1969	Rebel, Amb.	0 to −1	−½	−⅜ to +⅜	−⅜ to +⅜	Zero	Zero	⅛	22	25
	Others②	−½ to +½	Zero	−⅜ to +⅜	−⅜ to +⅜	Zero	Zero	⅛	22	25
	Others③	+½ to +1½	+¾	−⅜ to +⅜	−⅜ to +⅜	Zero	Zero	⅛	22	25
1970	Man. Steer.④	−½ to +½	Zero	−⅜ to +⅜	−⅜ to +⅜	Zero	Zero	¹⁄₁₆–³⁄₁₆	22	25
	Power Steer.④	+½ to 1½	+1	−⅜ to +⅜	−⅜ to +⅜	Zero	Zero	¹⁄₁₆–³⁄₁₆	22	25
	Javelin	+½ to +1½	+1	−⅜ to +⅜	−⅜ to +⅜	Zero	Zero	¹⁄₁₆–³⁄₁₆	22	25
1971	All Models	+½ to +1½	+1	−⅜ to +⅜	−⅜ to +⅜	Zero	Zero	¹⁄₁₆–³⁄₁₆	22	25
1972	All Models	—	+1	—	—	+⅜	+⅛	⅛	22	25
1973–75	Hornet, Gremlin	−½ to +½	Zero	+⅛ to +⅝	0 to +½	+⅜	+⅛	⅛	22	25
	Others	+½ to +1½	+1	+⅛ to +⅝	0 to +½	+⅜	+⅛	⅛	22	25

①—Incorrect toe-out when other adjustments are correct, indicates bent steering arms.　③—Power Steering.
②—Manual steering.　④—Except Javelin.

ALTERNATOR SPECIFICATIONS

Year	Alternator								Regulator			
				Rated Output		Field Current				Regulator Test @ 120°F.		
	Make	Model	Ground Polarity	Amperes	Volts	Amperes ①	Volts		Model	Ampere Load	Altern. R.P.M.	Volts
1969–71	Amer. Mtrs.	3195534	Negative	35	15	2.4–2.5	10		3195003②	10	2000	13.7–14.5
	Motorola	A-12NAM 456	Negative	35	14.2	2.0–2.6	—		R2AM 4②	10	2000	13.7–14.5
	Motorola	A-12NAM 606	Negative	55	15	1.8–2.4	—		R2AM 4②	10	2000	13.7–14.5
1972	Motorola	—	Negative	37	—	1.8–2.5	—		8RB2005②	10	2000	13.4–13.9
	Motorola	—	Negative	55	—	1.8–2.5	—		8RB2005②	10	2000	13.4–13.9
1973	Motorola	—	Negative	37	—	1.8–2.5	—		8RD2001②	10	2000	13.4–13.9
	Motorola	—	Negative	51	—	1.8–2.5	—		8RD2001②	10	2000	13.4–13.9
	Motorola	—	Negative	62	—	1.8–2.5	—		8RD2001②	10	2000	13.4–13.9
1974–75	Motorola	—	Negative	37	—	1.8–2.5	—		8RH2003	10	2000	13.1–14.3
	Motorola	—	Negative	51	—	1.8–2.5	—		8RH2003	10	2000	13.1–14.3
	Motorola	—	Negative	62	—	1.8–2.5	—		8RH2003	10	2000	13.1–14.3
1975	Delco	—	Negative	37	—	—	—		—	—	—	—
	Delco	—	Negative	55	—	—	—		—	—	—	—
	Delco	—	Negative	61	—	—	—		—	—	—	—

①—Excessive current drawn indicates shorted field winding. No current draw indicates an open winding.
②—Regulator is a sealed assembly, requiring no adjustments.

STARTING MOTOR SPECIFICATIONS

Year	Part No. ②	Rotation ①	Brush Spring Tension, Ounces	No Load Test			Torque Test		
				Amperes	Volts	R.P.M.	Amperes	Volts	Torque, Lbs. Ft.
1969–70	C7FF-11001-B	C	40	65	12	9250	500	4.5	—
	C9FF-11001-A	C	40	65	12	9250	500	4.5	—
1971	—	C	40	65	12	9250	600	3.4	13
1972	—	C	40	65	12	9250	600	4.5	13
1973–75	—	C	40	65	12	9250	600	3.4	13

①—As viewed from drive end. C—Clockwise. ②—Stamped on plate riveted to side of housing.

COOLING SYSTEM & CAPACITY DATA

★NOTE: Alcohol should not be used in Rambler engines having aluminum components in contact with the coolant. When only water is used a good corrosion inhibitor must be added to the system. Failure to use an inhibited coolant may result in severe corrosion damage to the cooling system components.

Year	Model or Engine	Cooling Capacity, Qts.			Radiator Cap Relief Pressure, Lbs.		Thermo. Opening Temp. ①	Fuel Tank Gals.	Engine Oil Refill Qts. ②	Transmission Oil			Rear Axle Oils Pint
		No Heater	With Heater	With A/C	With A/C	No A/C				3 Speed Pints	4 Speed Pints	Auto. Trans. Qts. ⑩	
1969	6-199, 232	9½	10½	10½	14	14	195⑪	⑫	4	1½⑬	—	9	3
	V8-290	13	14	14	14	14	195	⑫	4	3	2½	⑭	4
	V8-343, 390	12	13	13	14	14	195	⑫	4	—	2½	11	4
1970	6-199, 232	9½	10½	10½	14	14	195	⑮	4	1½⑬	—	9½	3
	V8-304	13	14	14	14	14	195	⑮	4	3	2½	9½	4
	V8-360, 390	12	13	13	14	14	195	⑮	4	—	2½	10	4
1971	6-232	9½	10½	10½	14	14	205	③	4	*1½⑬	—	9½	④
	6-258	9½	10½	10½	14	14	205	③	4	2½	—	9½	④
	V8-304	13	14	14	14	14	195	③	4	2½	2½	9½	4
	V8-360, 401	12	13	13	14	14	195	③	4	3	2½	10	4
1972	6-232	9½	10½	10½	14	14	205	⑤	4	1½⑬	—	8½	④
	6-258	9½	10½	10½	14	14	205	⑤	4	1½⑬	—	8½	④
	V8-304	13	14	14	14	14	195	⑤	4	3	2½	9½	4
	V8-360, 401	12	13	13	14	14	195	⑤	4	3	2½	9½	4
1973	6-332, 258	9½	10½	10½	14	14	205	⑥	4	2½	2½	8½	⑦
	V8-304	13	14	14	14	14	195	⑥	4	2½	2½	9½	⑦
	V8-360, 401	12	13	13	14	14	195	⑥	4	2½	2½	9½	⑦
1974	6-232, 258	10	11	11½	14	14	205	⑯	4	2½	—	8½	⑦
	6-232, 258 Mat. 2 Dr. Coupe	10	11	13½⑰	14	14	205	⑯	4	2½	—	8½	⑦
	V8-304 Hornet, Gremlin	15	16	16	14	14	195	⑯	4	2½	—	8½	⑦
	V8-304 Mat., Amb.	15½	16½	16½	14	14	195	⑯	4	2½	—	8½	⑦
	V8-304, Mat. 2 Dr. Coupe	17½	18½⑰	18½⑰	14	14	195	⑯	4	2½	—	8½	⑦
	V8-304 Javelin	—	15	15½	14	14	195	⑯	4	1½	—	8½	⑦
	V8-360 Hornet	14	15	15	14	14	195	⑯	4	1½	—	9½	⑦
	V8-360, 401 Matador	14½	15½	15½⑰	14	14	195	⑯	4	—	—	9½	⑦
	V8-360, 401 Mat. 2 Dr. Coupe	16½	17½⑰	17½⑰	14	14	195	⑯	4	1½	—	9½	⑦
	V8-360, 401 Javelin	14	15	15	14	14	195	⑯	4	—	2½	9½	⑦
	V8-360, 401 Ambassador	14½	15½	15½	14	14	195	⑯	4	1½	—	9½	⑦
1975	6-232-258	—	11.0	⑧	14	14	195	⑨	4	—	—	8½	⑦
	Gremlin, Hornet V8-304	—	16	16	14	14	195	⑨	4	—	—	8½	⑦
	Matador V8-304	—	16½⑰	16½⑰	14	14	195	⑨	4	—	—	8½	⑦
	Matador V8-304	—	18½	18½	14	14	195	24½	4	—	—	8½	⑦
	Hornet V8-360	—	15	15	14	14	195	17	4	—	—	9½	⑦
	Matador V8-360	—	15½⑰	15½⑰	14	14	195	⑨	4	—	—	9½	⑦
	Matador V8-360	—	17½	17½	14	14	195	24½	4	—	—	9½	⑦

① —With alcohol-type anti-freeze use a 170° unit.

② —Add one quart with filter change.

③ —Gremlin, 21; Hornet & Javelin, 16; Ambassador wagons & Matador 3 seat wagon, 17; all others, 19½.

④ —Matador & Ambassador, 4; all others, 3.

⑤ —Hornet, 16; Gremlin, 21; Javelin; 16; Matador & Ambassador sedans, 19½; Matador 2 seat wagons, 19½; Matador 3 seat wagons, 21½; Ambassador wagons, 21½.

⑥ —Hornet, 16; Gremlin, 21; Javelin, 16; Matador & Amb. sedans, 19½; Matador 2 seat wagon, 19½; Matador 3 seat wagon, 20; Ambassador wagon, 20. All Others 21½.

⑦ —7 7/16" axle, 3 pints. 8 7/8" axle, 4 pints.

⑧ —Matador 2 dr. coupe 13½ qts., all others 11½ qts.

⑨ —Gremlin 21 gals., Hornet 17 gals., Matador 24½, wagon 21 gals.

⑩ —Approximate. Make final check with dipstick.

⑪ —Rambler Rogue with 6-232 uses 205°.

⑫ —Rambler 16.
AMX and Javelin 19.
Rebel 3-seat wagon and Amb. wagon 19.

⑬ —Fully synchronized 2½.

⑭ —With 2 barrel carb. 9; with 4 barrel carb. 11.

⑮ —Rebel and Ambassador sedans, 21½, Rebel 2 seat wagons, 21½. All others 19. California vehicles about 2 gal. less.

⑯ —Hornet & Javelin, 16; Gremlin, 21; Matador Sedan & 2 Dr. Coupe, 24¾; Ambassador Sedan, 24¾; Mat. & Amb. Wagons, 21.

⑰ —Add two quarts with coolant recovery system.

BRAKE SPECIFICATIONS

Year	Model	Brake Drum Inside Diameter	Wheel Cylinder Bore Diameter			Master Cylinder Bore Diameter		
			Disc Brake	Front Drum Brake	Rear Drum Brake	Disc Brakes	Drum Brakes	Power Brakes
1969	American, Javelin 6-Cyl.	9	—	1⅛	¹⁵⁄₁₆	—	1	1
	Rebel (Except Wagon) 6-Cyl.	9	—	1⅛	¹⁵⁄₁₆④	—	1	1
	All V8s & Rebel 6 Wagon	10	—	1³⁄₁₆③	¹⁵⁄₁₆④	—	1	1
	All V8s with Disc Brakes	10	2	—	1	1	—	1
1970	Gremlin	9	—	1⅛	¹⁵⁄₁₆	—	1	1
	Hornet, Javelin 6-Cyl.	9	—	1⅛	¹⁵⁄₁₆	—	1	1
	Ambassador, Rebel 6-Cyl.	10	—	1⅛	¹⁵⁄₁₆	—	1	1
	AMX, Hornet, Javelin V8	10	—	—	—	—	1	1
	Rebel V8	10	—	—	—	—	1	1
	All with Disc Brakes	10	2	—	1	1	—	1
1971	Gremlin	9	—	1⅛	⅞	—	1	1
	Hornet, Javelin 6-Cyl.	9	—	1⅛	⅞	—	1	1
	Matador, Amb. 6-Cyl.	10	—	1³⁄₃₂	¹⁵⁄₁₆	—	1	1
	Hornet, Javelin V8	10	2¾	1³⁄₁₆	⅞	⑤	1	1
	Matador, Amb. V8	10	2¾	1³⁄₁₆	¹⁵⁄₁₆⑥	1⅛	1	1
1972	Gremlin 6-Cyl.	9	2¾	1⅛	¹³⁄₁₆	1①	1	1
	Gremlin V8	9	2¾	1³⁄₁₆	⅞	1¹⁄₁₆	1	1
	Hornet, Javelin 6-Cyl.	9	2¾	1⅛	⅞	1①	1	1
	Hornet, Javelin V8	10	2¾	1³⁄₁₆	⅞	1①	1	1
	Matador, Amb. 6-Cyl.	10	2¾	1³⁄₃₂	¹⁵⁄₁₆	1⅛	1	1
	Matador, Amb. V8	10	2¾	1³⁄₁₆	¹⁵⁄₁₆	1⅛	1	1
1973	Gremlin 6-Cyl.	9	2¾	1⅛	¹³⁄₁₆	1¹⁄₁₆	1	1
	Gremlin V8	10	2¾	1³⁄₁₆	⅞	1¹⁄₁₆	1	1
	Hornet, Javelin 6-Cyl.	9	2¾	1⅛	⅞	1¹⁄₁₆	1	1
	Hornet, Javelin V8	10	2¾	1³⁄₁₆	⅞	1¹⁄₁₆	1	1
	Matador 6-Cyl.	10	2¾	1³⁄₃₂	¹⁵⁄₁₆	1¹⁄₁₆	1	②
	Matador, Amb. V8	10	2¾	1³⁄₃₂	¹⁵⁄₁₆	1⅛	1	②
1974	Gremlin 6-Cyl.	9	2¾	1⅛	¹³⁄₁₆	1⅛①	1	1
	Gremlin V8	10	2¾	1³⁄₁₆	⅞	1⅛①	1	1
	Hornet, Javelin 6-Cyl.	9	2¾	1⅛	⅞	1	1	1
	Hornet, Javelin V8	10	2¾	1³⁄₁₆	⅞	1	1	1
	Matador, Ambassador	10	2¾	1³⁄₃₂	¹⁵⁄₁₆	1⅛①	1	1
	Station Wagons	10	2¾	1³⁄₃₂	¹⁵⁄₁₆	1⅛①	1	1
1975	Gremlin 6-Cyl.	9	3.1	1⅛	⅞	1¹⁄₁₆	1	1
	Hornet 6-Cyl.	9	3.1	1⅛	¹³⁄₁₆	1¹⁄₁₆	1	1
	Gremlin, Hornet V8	10	3.1	1³⁄₁₆	⅞	1¹⁄₁₆	1	1
	Matador	10	3.1	—	⅞	1¹⁄₁₆	—	1⅛

①—Non power disc brakes 1¹⁄₁₆".
④—⅞" on Rambler, Javelin and AMX.
②—Power drum 1", power disc 1⅛".
⑤—Manual 1¹⁄₁₆", power 1".
③—³⁄₃₂" on V8-343, 390 wagons.
⑥—1" on wagons.

Electrical Section

DISTRIBUTOR, REPLACE

1. Disconnect distributor primary wire from coil terminal.
2. Remove distributor cap and rotor. *Mark position of rotor arm on distributor housing so distributor can be installed in same position.*
3. Remove vacuum line from distributor.
4. Remove distributor hold-down clamp.
5. Note relative position of distributor in block, then work it out of the engine.

Installation

1. Turn rotor about ⅛ of a turn counterclockwise past the mark previously placed on the distributor housing.
2. Push the distributor down into the block with the housing in the normal "installed" position. *On gear-driven distributors, it may be necessary to move the rotor slightly to start gear into mesh with camshaft gear, but rotor should line up with mark when distribuor is down in place.*
3. Tighten distributor clamp screw snugly and connect vacuum line, primary wire to coil, and install cap.

V8 Note

If the engine was disturbed while the distributor was removed from the engine, first crank the engine to bring No. 1 piston up on its compression stroke and continue cranking until the timing mark is adjacent to the timing indicator. Then rotate the distributor cam until the rotor is in position to fire No. 1 cylinder. Install the distributor as outlined above and set the ignition timing as directed elsewhere in this manual.

BREAKERLESS INDUCTIVE DISCHARGE (BID) IGNITION SYSTEM

Description

The BID ignition system incorporates four major units; an electronic control unit, ignition coil, distributor and high tension wires, Fig. 1. The electronic control unit is a solid-state, moisture resistant module with the components sealed in a potting compound to resist vibration and environmental conditions. Since the control unit has an internal current regulator, a resistance wire or ballast resistor is not necessary in the primary circuit. Battery voltage is applied to the ignition coil positive terminal when the ignition switch is in the "On" or "Start" position, therefore, an ignition system bypass is not required in this system. The primary

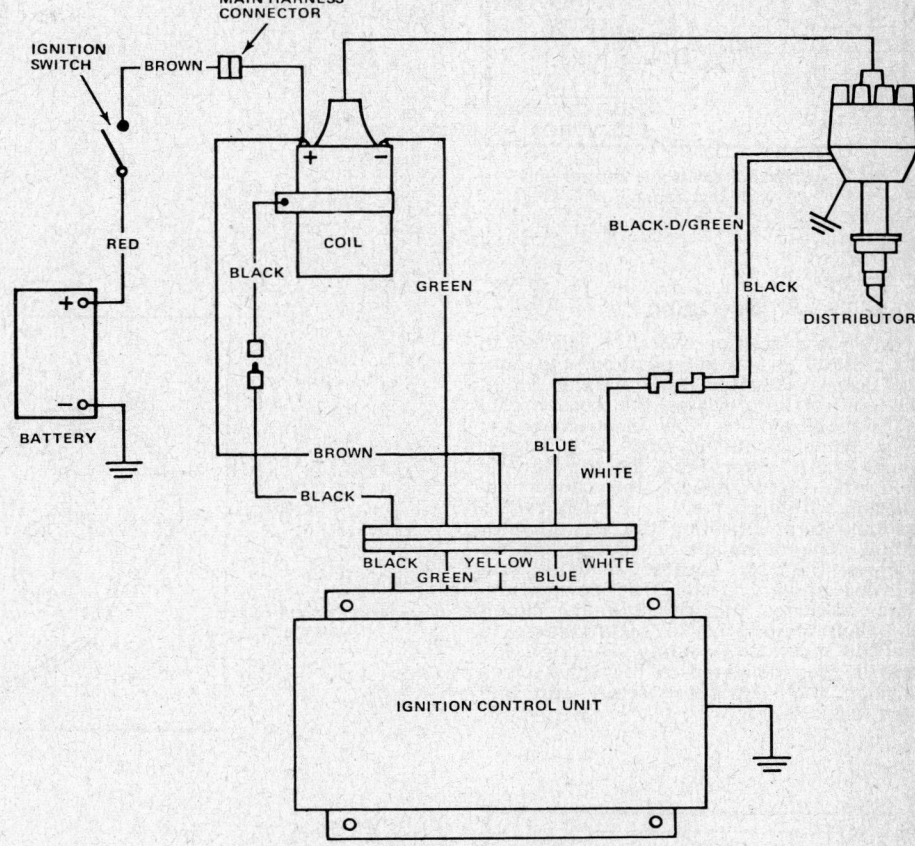

Fig. 1 BID ignition system wiring

coil circuit is electronically regulated by this unit.

The ignition coil is of standard construction and requires no special service. The function of the ignition coil in the BID ignition system is the same as for conventional ignition systems.

The distributor is conventional except the contact points, condenser and cam are replaced by a sensor and trigger wheel, and since no wearing occurs between the trigger wheel and sensor, dwell angle remains constant and requires no adjustment. The sensor is a small coil of fine wire and receives an alternating current signal from the electronic control unit. The senor develops an electromagnetic field used to detect the presence of metal which are the leading edges of the trigger wheel teeth.

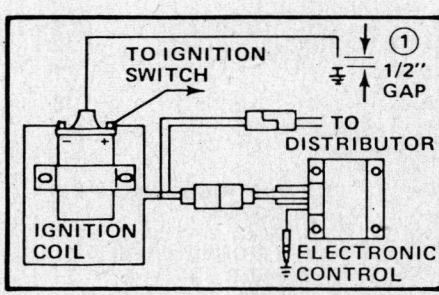

Fig. 2 Checking spark at coil wire

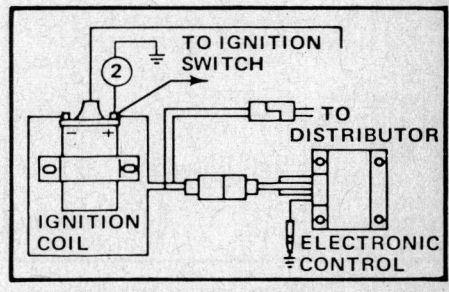

Fig. 3 Checking battery to ignition coil wiring

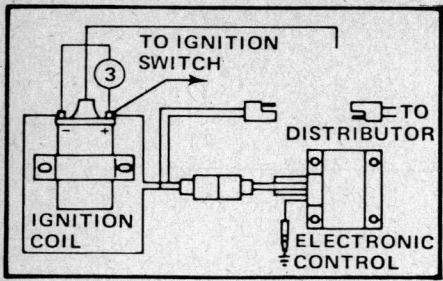

Fig. 4   Checking electronic control unit with test lamp

Operation

When the ignition switch is placed in the "Start" or "Run" position, the control unit is activated. An oscillator within the control unit excites the sensor coil, in turn developing the electromagnetic field. When a leading edge of a trigger wheel tooth enters the electromagnetic field, the tooth reduces the sensor oscillation strength to a predetermined level, in turn activating the demodulator circuit. The demodulator circuit controls a power transistor located in series with the coil primary circuit. The power transistor switches the coil primary circuit off, thereby inducing a high voltage in the coil secondary winding. The high voltage is then delivered to the spark plugs through the distributor rotor, cap and high tension wires.

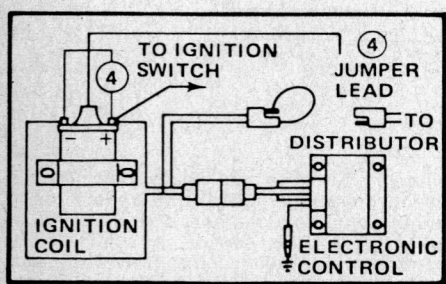

Fig. 5   Checking electronic control unit with test lamp & jumper wire

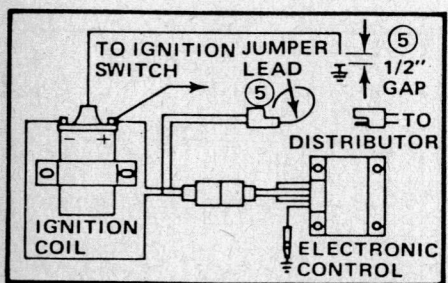

Fig. 6   Checking spark at coil wire with electronic control leads shorted

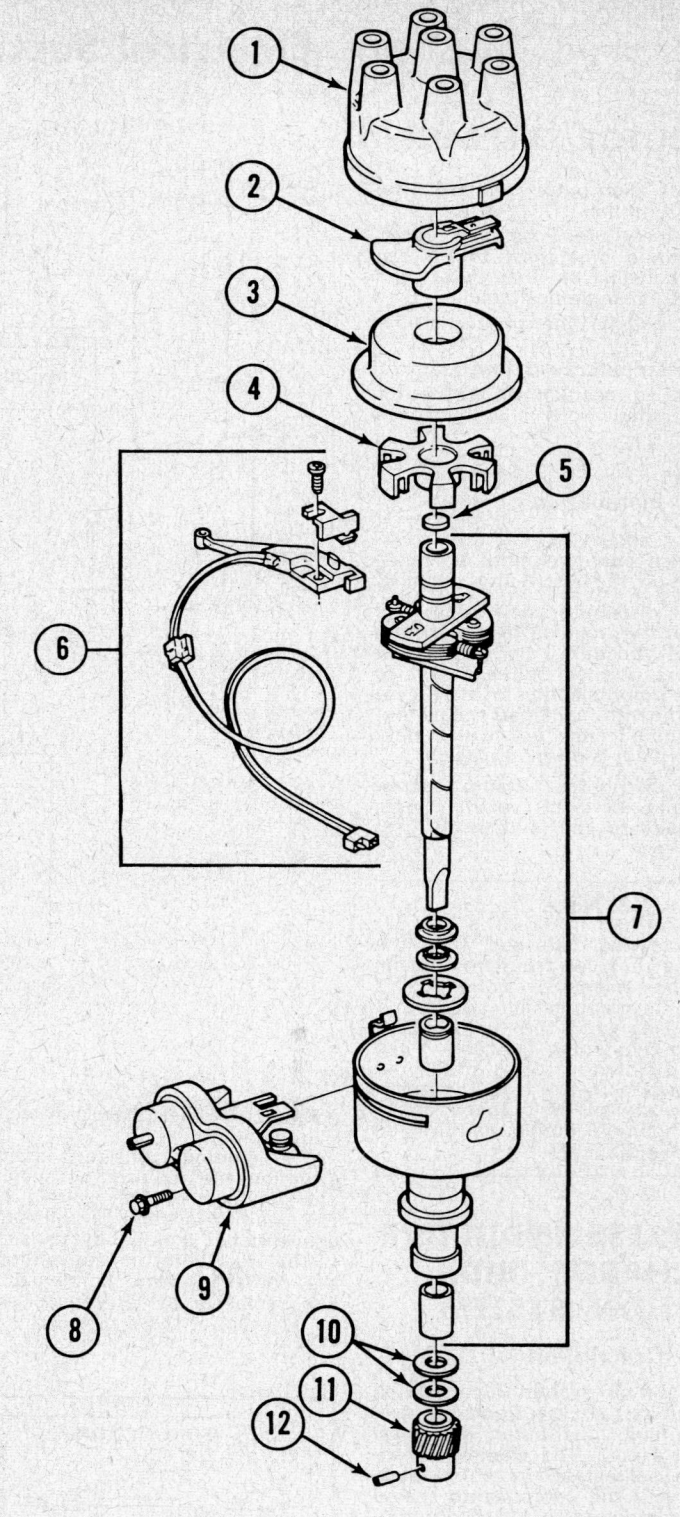

1. DISTRIBUTOR CAP
2. ROTOR
3. DUST SHIELD
4. TRIGGER WHEEL
5. FELT
6. SENSOR ASSEMBLY
7. HOUSING
8. VACUUM CONTROL SCREW
9. VACUUM CONTROL
10. SHIM
11. DRIVE GEAR
12. PIN

Fig. 7   BID distributor, exploded view

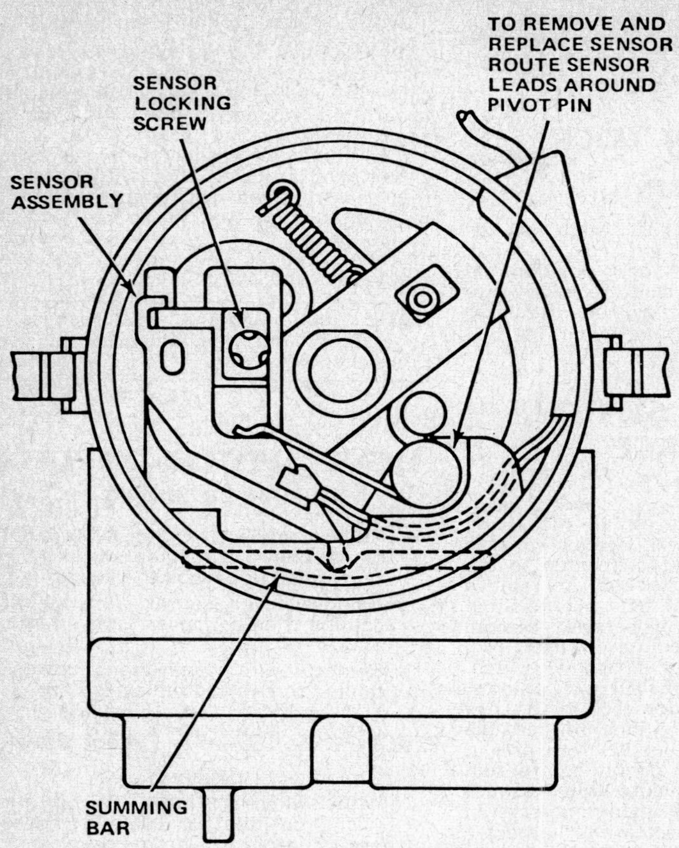

SENSOR
ASSEMBLY

SENSOR
LOCKING
SCREW

TO REMOVE AND
REPLACE SENSOR
ROUTE SENSOR
LEADS AROUND
PIVOT PIN

SUMMING
BAR

Fig. 8   Sensor installation

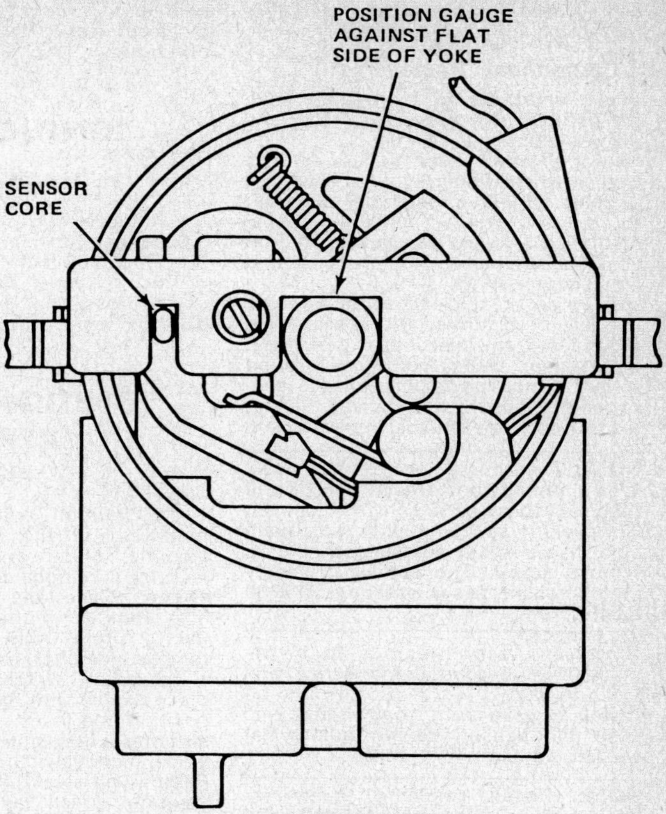

SENSOR
CORE

POSITION GAUGE
AGAINST FLAT
SIDE OF YOKE

Fig. 9   Positioning sensor

Troubleshooting

Ensure all electrical connections are correct before proceeding with the following checks.

1. Disconnect coil wire from distributor, hold wire approximately ½ inch from a suitable ground and crank engine, Fig. 2. If spark jumps between the coil wire and the ground, system is satisfactory.

2. If no spark occurs in step No. 1, connect a No. 57 test lamp between coil positive terminal and the ground, Fig. 3. Turn ignition switch to "On" and "Start" positions. If test lamp does not light in both positions, check ignition switch and wiring between battery and ignition coil.

3. If test lamp lights in both ignition switch positions, connect test lamp across ignition coil terminals, disconnect distributor connector and turn ignition switch to "On" position, Fig. 4. If test lamp does not light, check electronic for proper ground.

4. If test lamp lights in step No. 3, connect a jumper wire across electronic control lead terminals, Fig. 5. If test lamp remains lit, replace electronic control unit.

5. If test lamp goes out in step No. 4, remove test lamp and hold coil wire approximately ½ inch from a suitable ground. Intermittantly short the electronic control lead terminals and check for spark at coil wire gap, Fig. 6. If no spark occurs, replace ignition

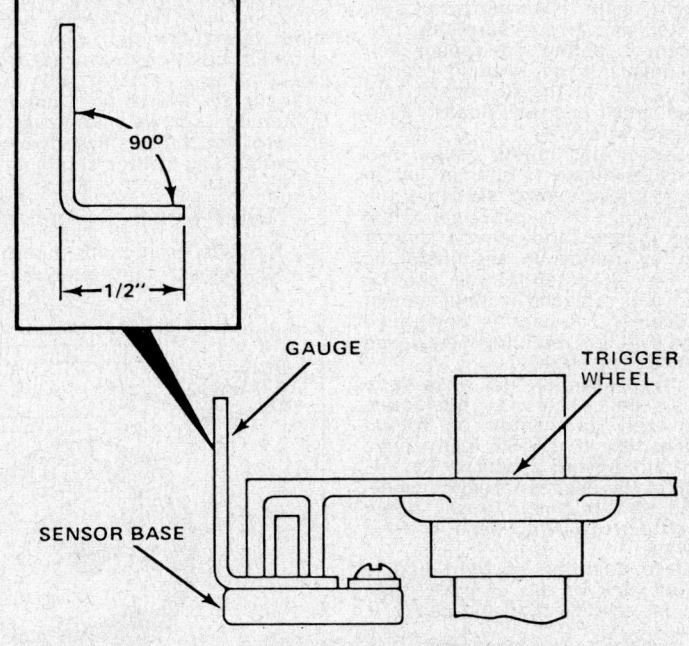

90°

1/2"

GAUGE

TRIGGER
WHEEL

SENSOR BASE

Fig. 10   Trigger wheel installation

coil. If spark occurs, the sensor is faulty and must be replaced.

Component Replacement

1. Place distributor in a suitable holding fixture and remove cap, rotor and dust shield, Fig. 7.
2. Using a small gear puller, remove trigger wheel. Ensure puller jaws are gripping trigger wheel inner shoulder to prevent trigger wheel damage. Also, use a thick flat washer or nut as a spacer and do not press against small center shaft.
3. Loosen sensor locking screw approximately three turns, lift sensor lead grommet from distributor bowl and pull sensor leads from slot around sensor spring pivot pin. Release sensor spring, ensure spring clears sensor leads and slide sensor from bracket.

NOTE: The sensor locking screw utilizes a tamper proof head design and requires tool J-25097 for removal. However, if special tool is not available, use a small needlenose plier to remove screw. The service (replacement) sensor has a standard slotted head screw.

4. If vacuum control unit is to be replaced, remove retaining screw and vacuum unit.
5. Install new vacuum control unit and assemble sensor, sensor guide, flat washer and retaining screw.

NOTE: Install retaining screw far enough to hold assembly together and ensure it does not protrude past bottom of sensor.

6. If vacuum control has been replaced and original sensor is being used, replace special head screw with standard slotted head screw.
7. Install sensor assembly on vacuum chamber bracket, ensuring tip of sensor located properly in summing bar. Place sensor spring on sensor and route sensor leads around spring pivot pin, Fig. 8. Install sensor lead grommet and position leads away from trigger wheel.
8. Install sensor positioning gauge over yoke, ensure gauge is against flat of shaft, and move sensor sideways until gauge can be positioned. Snug retaining screw and check sensor position by removing and installing gauge, Fig. 9. When gauge can be removed and replaced without sensor side movement, sensor is positioned properly. Tighten retaining screw and check sensor position.
9. Place trigger wheel on yoke and check if sensor core is positioned approximately in center of trigger wheel legs. Bend a .050 inch gauge wire to dimension specified in Fig. 10, and place between trigger wheel legs and sensor base. Press trigger wheel onto yoke until legs contact gauge wire.
10. Apply 3 to 5 drops of light engine oil to felt wick in top of yoke, then install dust shield, rotor and cap.

STARTER, REPLACE

To remove starter, disconnect cable from battery. Disconnect cable and solenoid lead wire from solenoid switch. Remove starter attaching bolts and take off starter.

IGNITION LOCK
1970-75

1. Remove turn signal switch as described further on.
2. Place key lock in "Lock" position and using a small flat blade screwdriver to depress the lock cylinder retaining tab, remove the lock cylinder, Fig. 11.

IGNITION SWITCH, REPLACE
1970-75

The ignition switch on all models is mounted on the lower section of the steering column and is connected to the lock by a remote control rod. To remove switch, place key in Off-Lock position and remove mounting screws. Disconnect switch from remote control rod, remove wire harness and remove switch.

To install switch on 1970-71 models, place switch and ignition lock in Off-Lock position and insert a 3/32 inch drill into the switch aligning hole, Fig. 12. With drill in place, install switch on remote control rod. Remove all slack by sliding switch toward steering wheel. Install mounting screws, remove drill and connect wiring harness.

To install switch on 1972-75 models equipped with standard steering column, move slider to extreme left position (left side of switch pointing inward toward steering column). Place actuator rod in slider hole and install switch on column. Tighten retaining screws.

To install switch on 1972-75 models equipped with tilt steering column, move slider to extreme right position (right side of switch pointing downward from steering wheel). Place actuator rod in slider hole and install switch on column without tightening screws. Remove lash from actuator rod by pushing downward lightly on switch and tighten retaining screws.

1969 Rebel & Ambassador

1. Remove escutcheon nut from switch.
2. Disconnect wires and remove switch.

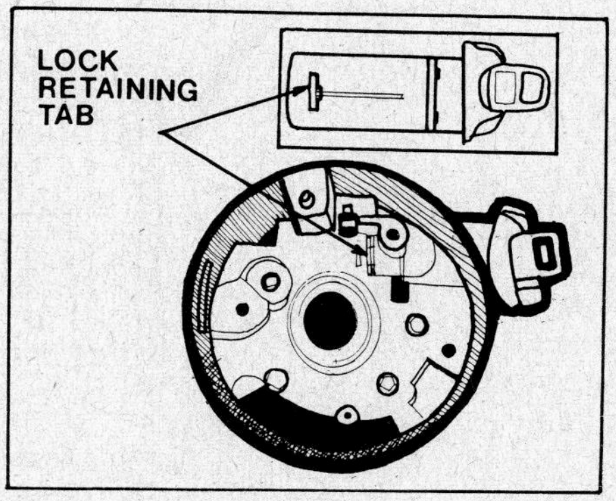

1969 AMX, Javelin & Rambler

Remove ignition switch from rear of instrument panel by holding switch escutcheon while pressing switch assembly toward instrument panel and turning counterclockwise.

The multi-wire connector on the switch should be removed after the switch is removed from the instrument panel. The multi-wire connector is locked to the switch by plastic fingers which are part of the connector and must be released before removing the connector.

NOTE: The AMX and Javelin have a separate ground wire added to the ignition switch plate.

LIGHT SWITCH, REPLACE
1971-74 Javelin

1. Remove knob from toggle switch by depressing a small spring steel retaining tab up toward the handle.
2. Remove seven screws from steering column lower cover and remove cover.
3. Remove wire connections, two retaining screws and remove switch.

1969-70 & 1971-75 Except Javelin

1. Disconnect a battery cable.
2. With switch in full "Off" position ("On" position for 1969-75 models) press button on side or top of switch to release shaft and knob assembly.
3. Remove switch mounting sleeve nut.
4. Disconnect wire harness connector.
5. Reverse procedure to install. Position switch so that shaft is lined up properly before tightening.

STOP LIGHT SWITCH, REPLACE
1972-75

1. Disconnect wire connector from

Fig. 11   Lock cylinder removal

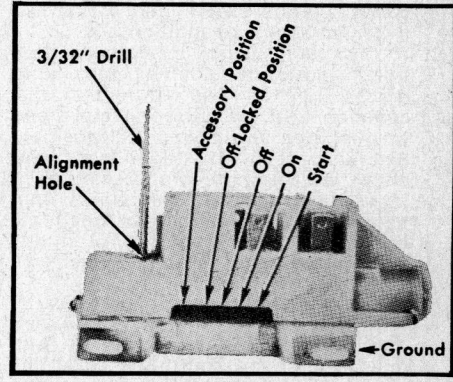

Fig. 12   Ignition switch alignment. 1970-75 (typical)

switch.

2. Remove brake pedal pivot bolt, nylon retaining rings, sleeve and remove switch.
3. When installing switch, be sure dimple on switch is opposite the bushing collar, Fig. 13.

1969-71

The switch is a mechanical, pedal operated switch. When replacing, be sure switch is adjusted so it is in "off" position when pedal is pulled back to stop. If switch is "on", check for binding linkage or improperly adjusted "Cruise Command" switch.

NEUTRAL SAFETY SWITCH
1972-75

A non-adjustable combination neutral safety and back-up light switch is located at the lower left hand side of the automatic transmission case.

1969-71 Console Type

The switch is located on the right side of the selector shaft under the console. It also functions as a back-up light switch, therefore, the following adjustments will automatically adjust the back-up light switch for proper contact when the shift lever is in the "R" position.

1. Remove selector knob from shaft.
2. Unfasten and lift console up and over selector shaft.
3. Place selector lever in neutral.
4. Use a 3/32" drill as an aligning pin. Insert the pin in the hole on the face of the switch. If necessary, move switch until pin enters freely into hole in switch toggle. *Switch toggle must enter into slot of actuating tab.*
5. Secure two screws that fasten switch to pivot bracket and remove aligning pin.
6. When switch is adjusted properly, engine will start only in Park or Neutral.

1969-71 Steering Column Type

The neutral safety switch also functions as a back-up light switch (when the car is so equipped). Therefore, the following adjustments will automatically adjust the back-up light switch for proper contact when the gear selector lever is in the "R" position.

1. Loosen two screws that secure switch to steering jacket tube.
2. Place selector lever in "N".
3. Using a 3/32" drill as an aligning pin, insert the pin in the hole on the face of the switch. If necessary, rotate the switch until the pin enters freely in the hole in the switch toggle.
4. Tighten the switch screws and remove aligning pin.

TURN SIGNAL SWITCH, REPLACE
1970-75

1. Disconnect negative battery cable.

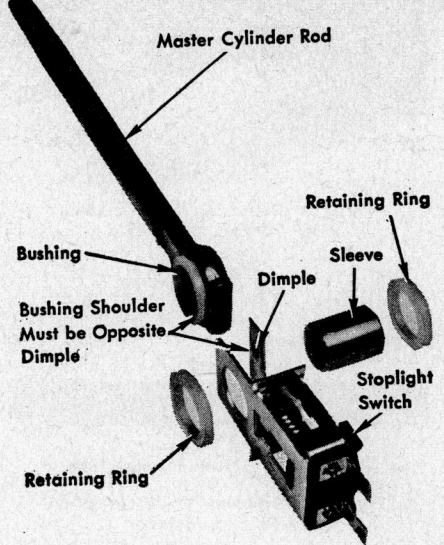

Fig. 13   Spotlight switch. 1972-75 (typical)

2. Remove steering wheel.
3. Loosen anti-theft cover retaining screws and lift cover from column. *It is not necessary to remove these screws completely as they are held on the cover by plastic retainers.*
4. Using a suitable tool, depress lock plate and pry out snap ring from steering shaft groove.
5. Remove tool, lock plate, cancelling cam, upper bearing preload spring and thrust washer.
6. Place directional signal lever in right turn position and remove lever.
7. Depress hazard warning light switch and remove the button by turning in a counterclockwise direction.
8. Remove directional signal wire harness from mounting bracket on lower column. On Shift Command, column shift, use a stiff wire to depress lock tab which retains the shift quadrant light wire in connector block.
9. Remove directional signal switch screws and remove switch, Fig. 14.

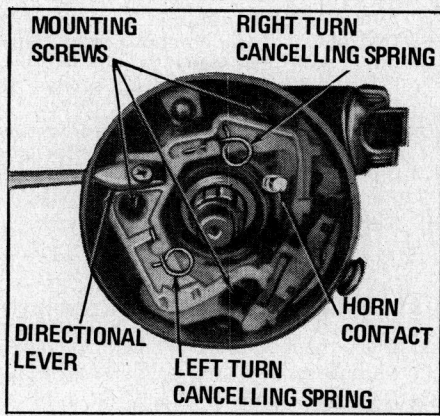

Fig. 14   Turn signal switch. 1970-75

1969 All

1. Disconnect battery ground cable then remove steering wheel using a suitable puller.
2. Remove cancelling cam, turn signal switch lever, hazard warning knob and light shield (if equipped).
3. Remove plastic trim covering column support plate. Remove signal switch wiring harness protector from lower side of column. Do not remove column support plate.
4. Disconnect signal switch connector from main harness and remove terminals from switch harness. Do not cut switch harness wires.
5. Remove turn signal cover, switch retaining screws and switch.
6. Reverse procedure to install.

HORN SOUNDER & STEERING WHEEL

Disconnect battery. Remove horn button or ring. This is retained by screws from under the steering wheel on some models and is rubber mounted and can be pulled up on others. Remove steering wheel with a puller. Note line up of dash marks on steering shaft and wheel and align these marks when wheel is installed.

INSTRUMENT CLUSTER
1974 Matador & Ambassador

1. Disconnect battery ground cable.
2. Remove radio knobs, attaching nuts and bezel retaining screws.
3. Tilt bezel forward and disconnect wiring.
4. Remove bezel, then remove clock or economy fuel gauge (if used) attaching screws, pull assembly away from cluster and disconnect bulbs and electrical leads. If equipped with fuel economy gauge, disconnect vacuum line and remove assembly.
5. Using clock opening, disconnect speedometer cable from instrument cluster, and disconnect gear selector dial cable from steering column.
6. Remove cluster mounting screws, disconnect any remaining electrical connections and remove cluster.

1972-75 Hornet & Gremlin

1. Disconnect battery ground cable.
2. Remove package tray, if so equipped, to gain access to wiper control and speedo cable.
3. Remove wiper control knob and spanner nut. To remove control knob, rotate knob until slot in neck of knob is visible. Insert a small diameter tool in slot and apply pressure toward knob to release pressure on spring metal clip. Remove knob.
4. Remove speedometer cable.

5. Remove four top and two side screws from instrument panel and tilt panel forward slightly to gain access to light switch and connectors.
6. Remove headlight switch knob, retaining nut and switch.
7. Cover steering column with a cloth to prevent scratches and disconnect harness connectors and remove cluster.

1972-73 Matador & Ambassador

1. Disconnect battery ground cable.
2. Remove screws from cluster overlay. Remove radio knobs and remove cluster overlay.
3. Remove screws securing cluster to panel.
4. Disconnect speedo cable and harness connector plug and remove cluster.

1971 Hornet & Gremlin

1. If so equipped, the package tray must be removed to gain access to speedometer cable, light switch and wiper control.
2. Disconnect battery.
3. Remove wiper control knob and spanner nut.
4. Disconnect speedometer cable at rear of cluster.
5. Remove top and side screws from cluster overlay.
6. Partially remove cluster from instrument panel to gain access to harness connectors. **NOTE:** If equipped with low fuel warning system, remove relay mounting screw at lower left side of panel and remove complete system with the cluster.

1971 Matador & Ambassador

1. Disconnect battery and remove screws from cluster overlay.
2. Remove A/C thermostat control knob if so equipped.
3. Remove overlay.
4. Remove screws securing cluster to panel.
5. Disconnect speedometer cable from behind panel.
6. Remove cluster disconnect plug and flasher unit.
7. Remove low fuel warning relay mounting screw at lower side of panel, if so equipped.
8. Remove cluster assembly.

1971-74 Javelin

1. Disconnect battery.
2. Cover painted surface of column with a cloth.
3. Remove the top, side and lower screws around bezel.
4. If equipped with radio, remove control knobs and retaining nuts.
5. Remove knobs from four instrument panel switches.
6. If equipped with A/C, release the speedometer cable hold-down clip on wheelhouse panel to allow movement of cable.
7. Move bezel and cluster out of opening far enough to reach in and disconnect speedometer cable, wire

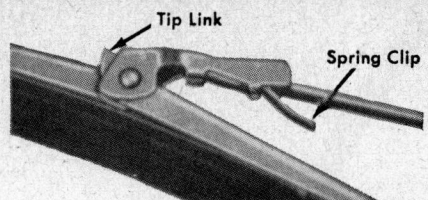

Fig. 15 Removing wiper blade. 1969-75 Exc. Matador X

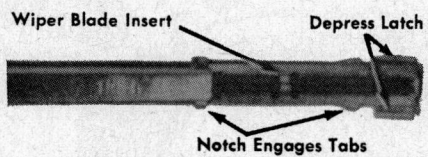

Fig. 16 Removing blade element. 1969-75 Exc. Matador X

harness plug and wire connections.
8. The cluster can be removed from bezel by removing eight screws and the clock set knob.

1970 Hornet & Gremlin

1. Disconnect negative battery cable.
2. Cover steering column to prevent scratching and remove package tray if so equipped.
3. Disconnect speedometer cable.
4. Remove control knobs and retaining nuts from wiper and headlight switch.
5. Remove bezel retaining screws and remove bezel and cluster toward the center of the car as an assembly.
6. Disconnect all wires and lamps from rear of cluster.

1969 Rambler

1. Disconnect battery.
2. Remove cigar lighter and ignition switch.
3. Remove W/S wiper switch knob.
4. Remove light switch knob and shaft.
5. Remove flasher unit.
6. Disconnect speedometer cable housing at rear of cluster.
7. Remove two Phillips head screws at top of cluster overlay.
8. Partially remove cluster from instrument panel to gain access for removal of cluster pin plug.
9. Remove cluster assembly.
10. Reverse procedure to install.

1969 Except Rambler
1970 Except Hornet & Gremlin

1. Disconnect battery.
2. Remove screws from cluster overlay.
3. Remove overlay.
4. Remove screws securing cluster to instrument panel.

5. Remove pin plug and cluster.
6. Disconnect speedometer cable and parking brake light.

IMPORTANT: Spring metal grounding clip is required between cluster and Weather-eye controls. Also between clock or tachometer of AMX, Javelin. Be sure to install clip upon assembly of cluster if it was removed.

W/S WIPER BLADES

1974-75 Matador X

Insert an appropriate tool into spring release opening of blade saddle, depress spring clip and pull blade from arm. To install, push blade saddle onto pin so spring engages pin.

1969-75 Exc. Matador X

The wiper blade assembly can be removed from the wiper arm by lifting the blade off the windshield and tipping the blade to arm connecting link toward the glass. This will disengage the embossing tab on the top of the arm out of the hole in the link.

At the same time, slide the blade away from the end of the arm so the embossing does not index with the hole. Then push the spring tab, Fig. 15, downward away from the depression in the bottom side of the arm and slide the blade off the arm.

The blade element can be removed by compressing the blade latch and sliding it from the bridge, Fig. 16. When installing, the metal backing must engage the tabs on the bridge.

W/S WIPER ARMS

The wiper arms are set on the serrated pivot shafts and held securely by spring tension on the arm. To remove the arm, lift the arm against the spring tension and with a screwdriver, slide the cap away from the serrated pivot shaft.

NOTE: Arms are marked "R" or "L" on the underside of the arm to designate right or left arm.

W/S WIPER MOTOR, REPLACE

1974-75 Matador X

1. Remove wiper arms and cowl screen.
2. Remove retaining clip from linkage drive arm and disconnect electrical connectors from motor.
3. Remove wiper motor retaining screws and wiper motor.

NOTE: If output arm contacts dash panel, preventing wiper motor removal, hand turn output arm so arm clears dash opening.

4. Before installing motor, be sure output arm is in park position.

1973-75 Exc. Matador X

1. Remove wiper arms and blades.
2. Remove four screws holding motor to dash.
3. Separate harness connector at the motor.
4. Pull motor and linkage out of opening to expose the drive link to crank stud retaining clip. Raise up the lock tab of the clip with a flat bladed screwdriver and slide clip off stud.

1969-72 Rebel, Ambassador & Matador

1. Remove wiper arms and blades and cowl air intake cover.
2. Slide link to motor retainer clip off motor arm stud which is accessible through cowl top opening. Remove link from motor.
3. On vacuum type motor, disconnect control cable and hose from motor, then remove motor and mounting plate from dash panel.
4. On models with electric wiper, disconnect switch-to-motor female connectors at switch and remove through main wire harness grommet. Remove wiper motor and mounting plate.

AMX & Javelin; 1969-72 Rambler, AMX, Javelin, Gremlin & Hornet

1. To remove wiper motor, remove four screws holding motor to dash panel.
2. Remove hose and control cable from vacuum type motor. On electric motors, separate wiper harness plug under instrument panel.
3. Tilt motor and slide link-to-motor retaining clip off of stud and remove motor.

W/S WIPER TRANSMISSION, REPLACE

1974-75 Matador X

1. Remove wiper arms and cowl screen.
2. Remove clip securing left linkage arm to drive arm.
3. Remove left pivot shaft body to cowl retaining screws and remove left arm and pivot shaft body through cowl opening.
4. Remove clip securing drive arm from motor arm crankpin.
5. Remove right pivot shaft body to cowl retaining screws and remove right arm and pivot shaft body through cowl opening.

1969-75 Rebel, Ambassador & Matador Exc. Matador X

1. Remove wiper arms and blades.
2. Remove cowl air intake cover.
3. Disconnect link-to-motor retainer and link from wiper arm through cowl top opening.
4. Close hood and remove two cap-screws holding each pivot shaft body to cowl top.

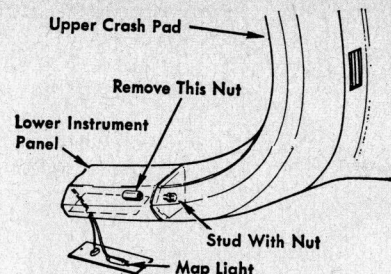

Fig. 17   Location of hidden stud nut. 1972-74 Javelin

5. Remove both pivot body and link assemblies as a unit through cowl top opening.
6. Pivot shaft bodies may than be removed by sliding retainer off stud.

NOTE

When installing pivot shaft bodies to cowl top, the assist spring must be in a position to engage rubber sleeved stud on vacuum wiper. There are no assist springs on electric wipers.

AMX & Javelin; 1969-74 Rambler, AMX, Javelin, Hornet & Gremlin

1. Remove wiper arms and blades.
2. Remove pivot shaft-to-cowl top nuts.
3. Remove wiper motor.
4. Slide pivot shaft body and link assembly to the left to clear right pivot shaft opening and move assembly to the right side of car to remove as a unit.

NOTE

When installing pivot shafts to cowl top, flat side of pivot shaft indexes flat side of hole in cowl top when pivot shaft is in up position.

W/S WIPER CONTROL, REPLACE

1974-75 All Except Javelin

1. Locate small notch at base of knob and insert a small screwdriver and apply pressure to release spring and pull knob from shaft.
2. Remove slotted trim nut from front of switch.
3. Push switch through instrument panel then disconnect wiring harness and remove switch.

1973 Except Javelin

1. Remove knob and slotted trim nut from front of switch.
2. Push switch through instrument panel, disconnect harness and remove switch.

1973-74 Javelin

1. Remove control knob.
2. Access can be gained to switch screws by removing steering column cover.

1972 Ambassador & Matador

The control is mounted behind the instrument panel with two sheet metal screws. These are accessible after removing the cardboard shield. Then disconnect washer and wiper motor wires from switch.

1970-71 Ambassador, Rebel & Matador

1. Disconnect negative battery cable.
2. Cover steering column to prevent scratching.
3. If so equipped, remove package tray and disconnect speedometer cable.
4. Remove control knob and retaining nut from the wiper control.
5. On vacuum wiper systems, disconnect control at the wiper motor.
6. Remove instrument cluster retaining screws and pull out cluster as a unit.
7. Remove vacuum wiper control.
8. On electrical systems, disconnect the electrical connections to the switch and remove switch.

1969 All, 1970-72 AMX, Javelin, Hornet & Gremlin

1. Remove control knob. The knob is retained either by a set screw or by a spring retainer. The spring retainer is released as follows: turn knob fully to right and insert Allen wrench in notch at small end of knob. Push toward shaft to raise spring out of groove and at same time pull knob off shaft.
2. On all models, after the knob has been removed, disconnect control cable from motor on vacuum wipers. On electric wipers, disconnect three female connectors from switch. Remove French nut to disengage switch from instrument panel.

NOTE: On vacuum wipers the control cable must be installed with the washer at the end of the control wire inserted in slot in slide valve. The conduit must butt against the shoulders of the anchoring slot and be fastened securely to assure positive opening and closing of the valve for efficient operation.

RADIO

NOTE: When installing radio, be sure to adjust antenna trimmer for peak performance.

1974 Ambassador & 1974-75 Matador

1. Remove radio knobs, retaining nuts and bezel.
2. Loosen upper radio retaining screw and lift radio disengaging bracket from screw, and pull radio forward.

3. Disconnect antenna lead, electrical wiring and remove radio.

1971-74 Javelin

To remove the radio, the entire crash pad will have to be removed.
1. Disconnect battery ground cable.
2. Remove the six attaching screws that lie next to lower edge of windshield.
3. Remove radio knobs and retaining nuts.
4. Open right door and remove two panel attaching screws at door pillar area.
5. Remove the five attaching screws in the upper flange of the cluster bezel. Remove moulding attaching screws and assist handle at lower right finish panel.

NOTE: On 1972-74 remove map light to gain access to hidden stud nut which retains crash pad to lower instrument panel, Fig. 17.

6. Remove entire panel top cover to expose radio and speaker.
7. Disconnect and remove speaker except on 1971 models with FM radio. Slide radio back and lift up to disconnect speaker and bulb wires.
8. Remove radio input wire from fuse panel. Tie a heavy string to wire before removing radio to assist in dressing wire back through wiring and duct assemblies.
9. Remove radio.

1971-73 Matador & Ambassador

1. The radio is retained to the cluster by three screws adjacent to the face of the radio.
2. Disconnect battery.
3. Disconnect antenna and speaker leads from radio.
4. Remove instrument cluster overlay.
5. Remove radio lead from fuse panel.
6. Remove radio mounting screws and remove radio.

1970-75 Hornet & Gremlin

1. Disconnect battery.
2. Remove package tray if so equipped.
3. Remove ash tray and bracket.
4. Remove radio knobs and shaft nuts.
5. Remove bezel retaining screws and bezel.
6. Disconnect antenna, speaker and power lead.
7. Remove radio.

1970 AMX & Javelin

1. Disconnect battery.
2. Remove four bezel retaining screws.
3. Remove knobs and shaft nuts.
4. Remove bezel.
5. Removing retaining screw from rear or radio.
6. Disconnect leads and remove radio.

1969 Javelin & AMX

1. Remove the ash tray.
2. Remove the retaining bolt in the ash tray which is threaded into the radio. With AM-Tapeplayer combi-

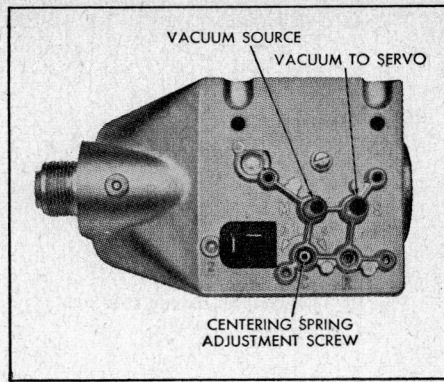

Fig. 22 Centering spring adjustment. 1969-75

nation this bolt is not used. A retaining nut is used on the rear of the radio and must be removed.
3. Remove the shaft retaining nuts.
4. Disconnect all leads from radio and tip the rear of the radio up and to the toe board and remove from the rear edge of the panel.

NOTE: If equipped with A/C the air discharge duct must be removed to gain clearance.

1969 Rambler

1. Disconnect battery and remove antenna lead from radio.
2. Disconnect power lead from radio and unplug radio-to-speaker cable.

3. Remove control knobs and control shaft bushing retainer nuts.
4. Remove ash tray.
5. Remove Phillips head screw which is threaded into cage nut on radio.
6. Radio can now be removed toward back and down from panel.

NOTE: If equipped with A/C it will be necessary to remove the glove box.

1969-70 Rebel & Ambassador

1. The radio is retained to the instrument cluster by four screws adjacent to the face of the radio and a brace rod from the rear of the radio down to the instrument panel flange.
2. Disconnect the battery.
3. Disconnect antenna, power, ground and speaker leads from radio.
4. Remove instrument panel overlay.
5. Remove radio mounting screws and remove radio.

NOTE: Leads attached to radio must be drawn carefully through the opening while removing the radio to prevent damage to the wiring.

HEATER CORE REMOVAL

1974 Ambassador & 1974-75 Matador, Fig. 18

1. Disconnect battery ground cable.
2. Drain about 2 quarts of coolant then disconnect heater hoses and plug ends of hoses and core openings.

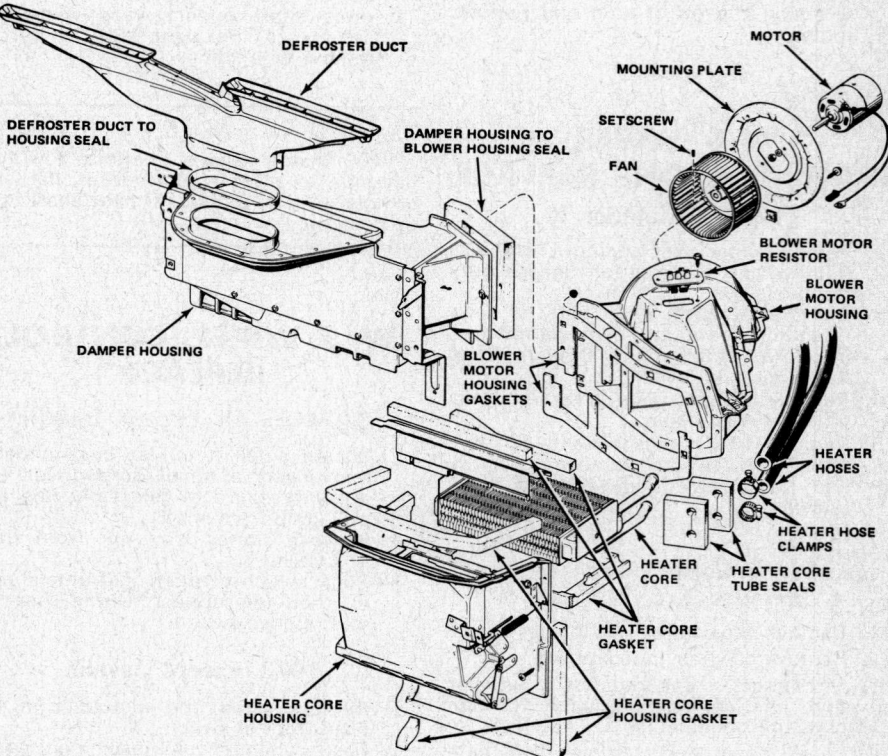

Fig. 18   Heater and blower housing assembly. 1974 Ambassador & 1974-75 Matador

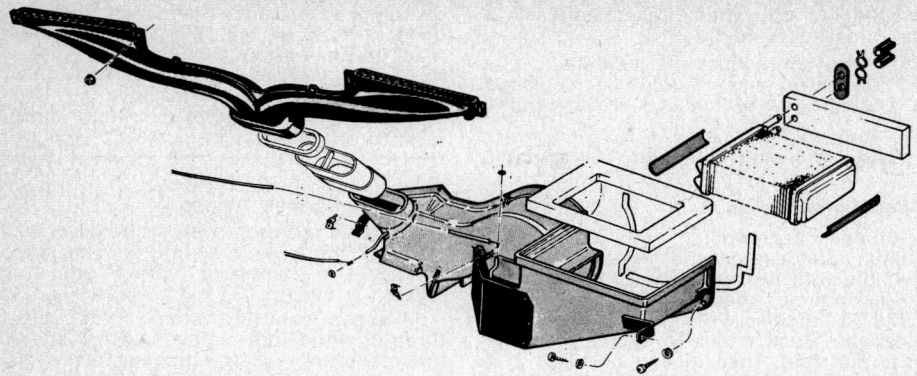

Fig. 19   Heater core and housing assembly. 1969 Rambler, 1969-70 AMX and Javelin

3. Remove lower instrument finish panel and glove box.
4. Disconnect control cables and vacuum motor hoses.
5. Remove retaining screws and remove heater core housing assembly.

1971-74 Javelin

1. Drain 2 qts. of water from cooling system and disconnect hoses from core tubes in engine compartment. Install corks in hoses and core tubes.
2. Disconnect blower motor wires.
3. Remove ground wire from dash panel ground stud and remove ground stud nut and washer.
4. Remove instrument panel top cover, right side mouldings, assist handle, lower right finish panel and right hand panel support brace.
5. Disconnect air vent cable at heater housing.
6. Remove heater housing attaching screws in front compartment.
7. After removal of housing assembly the heater core can be removed.

1970-75 Hornet & Gremlin

1. Open heater valve and drain about 2 qts. from cooling system.

2. Disconnect heater hoses and plug heater core tubes.
3. Remove blower motor and fan.
4. Remove package tray if so equipped.
5. Disconnect wire connector at resistor.
6. Remove instrument panel bezel, outlet and duct.
7. Disconnect control cables from damper levers.
8. Remove right side windshield pillar moulding and the instrument panel upper attaching screws and right side cap screw at the door hinge post.
9. Remove right side kick panel and heater housing attaching screws.
10. Pull the right side of the instrument panel slightly rearward and remove the housing.

1969 Rambler, 1969-70 AMX & Javelin, Fig. 19

1. Open heater water valve and drain about 2 qts from cooling system.
2. After disconnecting hoses from heater core, install cork plugs in hoses and core tubes.
3. Disconnect blower motor wires and ground wire to dash panel.
4. Remove glove box and its door. On

AMX and Javelin, it is necessary to remove glove box hinge bracket.
5. Disconnect outside air control cable at damper lever.
6. Remove three heater housing attaching screws in front compartment and lift out heater core and blower housing assembly.
7. Heater core is now accessible for removal.

1969-73 Rebel, Ambassador & Matador, Fig. 20

1. Disconnect outside air damper cable at heater housing under dash.
2. Drain system and disconnect hoses.
3. Remove two lower attaching nuts for blower housing in engine compartment.
4. Remove glove box and door in order to remove remaining heater housing screws and lower heater and core housing as an assembly.
5. Slide heater core out of housing.

BLOWER MOTOR REMOVE

1974 Ambassador & 1974-75 Matador, Fig. 18

1. Disconnect blower motor wiring.
2. Remove blower motor attaching screws and remove blower motor.

1969-73 Rebel, Matador & Ambassador, Fig. 21

1. Remove heater valve from blower housing. It is not necessary to disconnect hoses and cable.
2. In engine compartment, unfasten blower housing from dash panel.
3. After blower housing is removed, the fan and motor are accessible.

1969-75 Except Rebel, Matador & Ambassador

1. Working in engine compartment, disconnect blower motor wire.

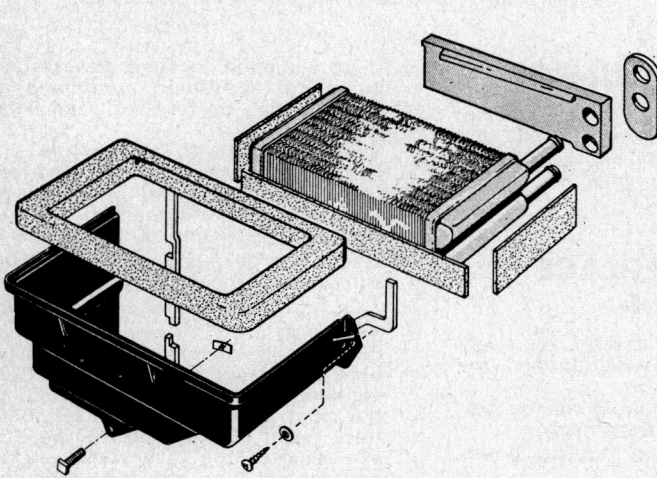

Fig. 20   Heater core assembly. 1969-73 Ambassador and Rebel

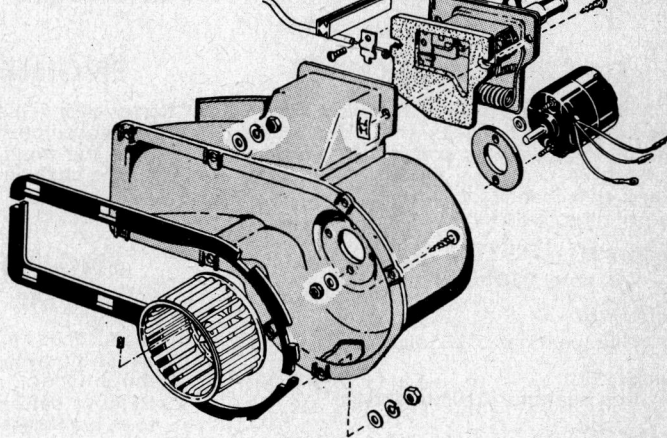

Fig. 21   Blower motor and housing assembly. 1969-73 Ambassador and Rebel

2. Remove three retaining nuts for blower scroll cover to which blower assembly is attached and remove blower motor and fan.

SPEED CONTROL
1969-75

Brake Release Switch, Adjust

1. Disconnect multiple connector at regulator.
2. Turn ignition switch to accessory position.
3. Using a test lamp, ground one test lamp lead and touch the other to terminal No. 2 in harness connector.
4. Adjust switch so that lamp will light when brake pedal is fully released and will go out when brake pedal is depressed ⅜ inch.
5. If switch cannot be adjusted, it is defective and should be replaced. Install new switch and repeat Step 4.
6. Remove test lamp, turn off ignition key and plug connector to regulator.

Chain Linkage, Adjust

Chain linkage should never be taut. To adjust, start engine and set carburetor at hot idle with anti-stall plunger backed off so as not to affect idle speed and on 1973-75 models, disconnect idle stop solenoid. Hook chain to accelerator linkage, pull taut, then loosen one ball at a time until a slight chain deflection is obtained without moving carburetor throttle or servo. After chain has been adjusted, bend servo hook tabs together and chain must be free in hook.

NOTE: Whenever adjusting chain linkage, be sure chain does not hold carburetor throttle open.

Centering Springs, Adjust

If speed control system holds speed three or more mph higher than selected speed, turn centering spring adjusting screw (C) toward (S) 1/32" or less, Fig. 22.

If speed control system holds speed three or more mph below selected speed, turn centering spring adjusting screw (C) toward (F) 1/32" or less. *Do not move adjustment screw (R).*

Engine Section

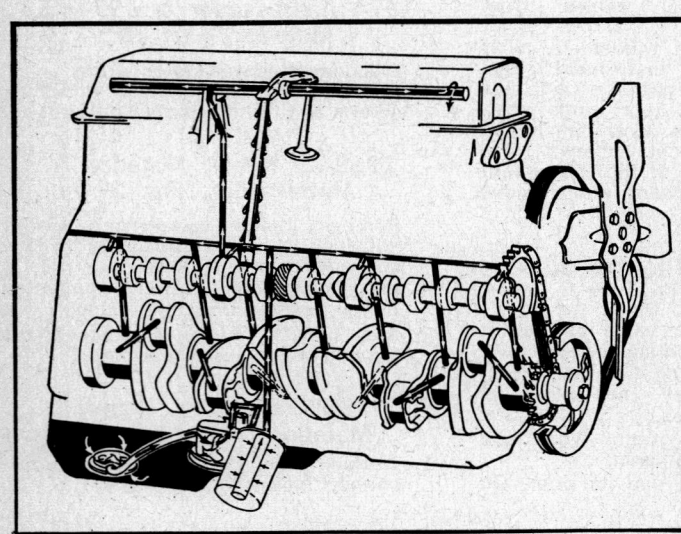

Engine oiling system. 1969-72 & early 1974 6-199, 232, 258 engines

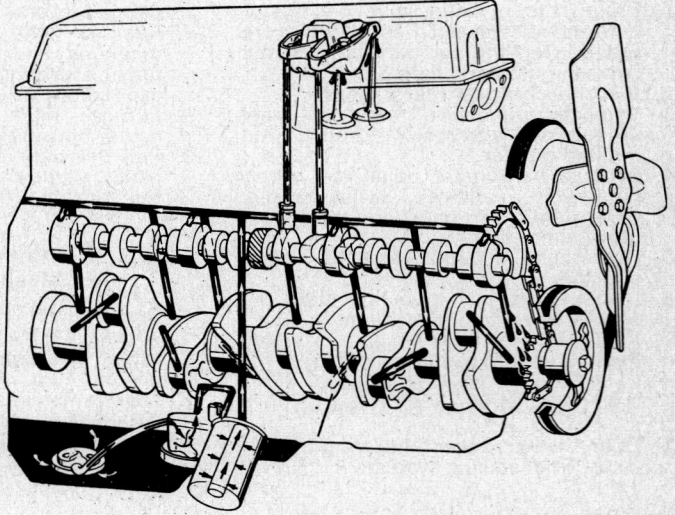

Engine oiling system. 1973, late 1974 & 1975 6-232, 258

ENGINE MARKINGS

A letter code is used to denote size of the bore, main bearings and rod bearings. On V8 engines, this code is stamped on the engine code tag. On six cylinder engines, this code is located on a boss above the oil filter. This letter code is as follows:

Letter "B"
   Cyl. bore .010" oversize

Letter "M"
   Main bearings .010" undersize

Letter "P"
   Rod bearings .010" undersize

Letter "C"
   Camshaft block bore .010" oversize

Letters "PM"
   Main and rod bearings .010" undersize

ENGINE MOUNTS

Removal or replacement of any cushion can be accomplished by supporting the weight of the engine or transmission at the area of the cushion to be replaced, Fig. 1.

ENGINE REPLACE
All Models

1. Mark hood hinge location on hood panel to aid in installation and remove hood.
2. Remove battery and drain cooling system, crankcase and transmission.
3. Disconnect all wiring, tubing, hoses and linkage.
4. Disconnect exhaust pipe.
5. Remove radiator and air cleaner.
6. If so equipped, remove power steering pump, Air Guard pump and air conditioning compressor and condenser.
7. Support engine with lifting fixture.
8. Remove rear crossmember and disconnect torque tube, where used, from transmission extension.
9. Disconnect speedometer cable.
10. Disconnect gearshift linkage. On floor shift units, remove gear selector lever.

NOTE: On pre-1970 units, the selector lever is removed by removing boot then removing the two attaching bolts. On 1970-74 models, remove the boot then insert a .015"-.020" thick feeler blade alongside the driver's side of the lever between the spring steel barb and the lower part of the shaft lever.

11. Disconnect front engine support cushions from engine and lift engine forward and upward through hood opening while supporting driveshaft.

CYLINDER HEAD

Tighten cylinder head bolts a little at a time in three steps in the sequence shown in the illustrations. Final tightening should be to the torque specifications listed in the *Engine Tightening* table.

V8-290, 304, 343, 360, 390, 401

The cylinder block has two locating dowels on each bank to assist in lining up and holding the cylinder head and gasket in position during installation.

IMPORTANT: The No. 7 bolt shown in Fig. 2, second from front on the left bank, must have the threads sealed to prevent coolant leakage. Permatex No. 2 or equivalent is recommended.

6-199, 6-232, 258 Engines

IMPORTANT: The cylinder head bolt located at the left front corner of the head (No. 11, Fig. 3) must have the threads sealed to prevent coolant leakage. Permatex No. 2 or equivalent is recommended.

VALVE ARRANGEMENT
Front to Rear

All V8s . . . . E-I-I-E-E-I-I-E
6-199, 232, 258 . . . . . E-I-I-E-I-E-E-I-E-I-I-E

VALVE LIFT SPECS.

Year	Engine	Intake	Exhaust
1969-71 & Early 1974	Six	.381	.381
Late 1974[2] & 1975	Six	.372	.372
1972-73	Six	.372	.372
1969-75	V8's exc. 401 & 1970 390	.425[1]	.425[1]
1970	V8-390	.457[1]	.457[1]
1971-74	V8-401	.457[1]	.457[1]

[1]Hi-Perf. cam, .477.
[2]Beginning with engine build date code 704 (A or E) 04.

VALVE TIMING
Intake Opens Before TDC

Year	Engine	Degrees
1969-73 & Early 1974	Six	12½
Late 1974[1] & 1975	Six	12.12
1969	V8-290, 343	18½
1969	V8-390	18½
1970	V8 Exc. Machine	18½
1970	Machine	18

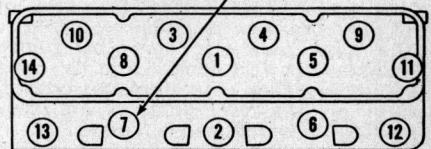

Engine oiling system. V8-290, 304, 343, 360, 390, 401 engines

| 1971-75 | V8-304, 360 | 14¾ |
| 1971-74 | V8-401 | 25.57 |

[1]Beginning with engine build date code 704 (A or E) 04.

ROCKER ARMS
V8-290, 304, 343, 360, 390, 401

These engines have individually mounted rocker arms consisting of a rocker arm retaining stud, rocker arm pivot ball,

Fig. 2 Cylinder head tightening sequence on V8-290, 304, 343, 360, 390 & 401. The No. 7 bolt indicated (second from front on left bank only) must be sealed to prevent coolant leakage

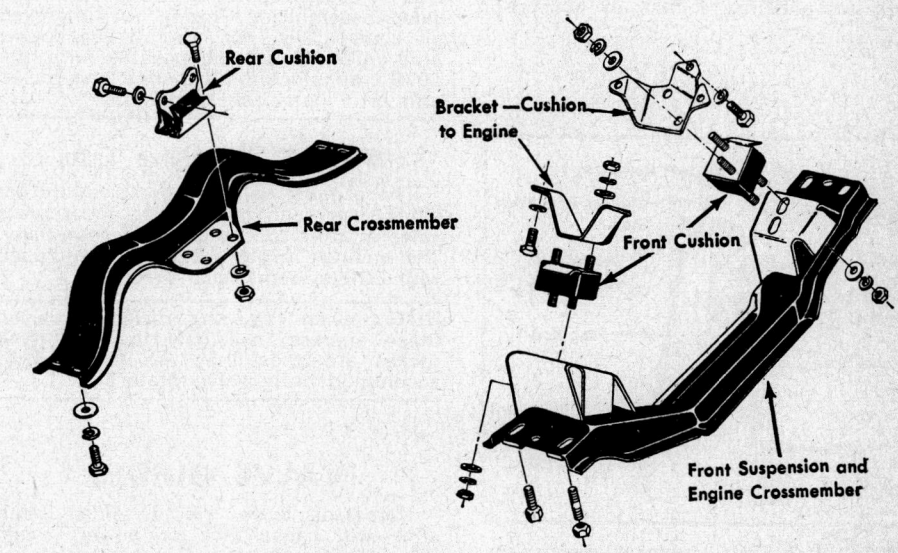

Fig. 1 Typical V8 engine mounts

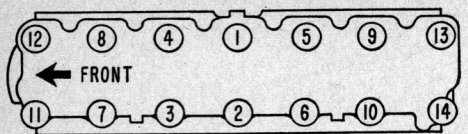

Fig. 3 Cylinder head tightening sequence 6-199, 232, 258 engines. The No. 11 bolt must be sealed to prevent coolant leakage

rocker arm and retaining nut to operate each valve, Fig. 4. The 1973 V8-304 and all 1974-75 V8 engines have the intake and exhaust rocker arms pivoting on a bridged pivot assembly which is secured to the cylinder head by two cap screws, Fig. 4A.

The rocker arm studs are threaded into the cylinder head. The threads are of such design to cause an interference fit; therefore, care must be taken that replacement studs be installed until the hexagon head is flush with the cylinder head and torqued to 65-70 ft-lbs.

The push rods are hollow, serving as oil galleries for lubricating each individual rocker arm assembly. Prior to installing, the push rods should be cleaned thoroughly, inspected for wear and deposits which may restrict the flow of oil to the rocker arm assembly.

The push rods also serve as guides to maintain correct rocker arm to valve stem relationship; therefore, a contact pattern on the push rods where they contact the cylinder head is normal.

When installing the rocker arm retaining nut, it is important that they be tightened until bottomed, using a torque of 20-25 ft-lbs.

Lubrication to each rocker arm is supplied by the corresponding hydraulic valve lifter. A metering system located in each valve lifter consists of a stepped lower surface on the push rod cap that contacts a flat plate, causing a restriction, Fig. 5. The restriction meters the amount of oil flow through the push rod cap, hollow push rod, and upper valve train components. A loss of lubrication

to the rocker arm could be caused by a restricted or plugged push rod or a defective hydraulic valve lifter.

CAUTION: Correct installation of push rods in these engines is critical and more than normal care must be taken upon installation. When placing the push rods through the guide hole in the cylinder head, it is important that the push rod end is inserted in the plunger cap socket. It is possible that the push rod may seat itself on the edge of the plunger cap which will restrict valve lifter rotation and lubrication to rocker arms.

It is recommended that, just prior to installation of the cylinder head covers, the engine be operated and the supply of lubrication to each rocker arm be visually inspected. If inspection reveals that an individual rocker arm is not being supplied with lubrication, the push rod and/or valve lifter must be inspected to determine the cause.

6-199, 6-232, 258 Engines

On 1969-72 and early 1974 engines, the pressure supply for each rocker arm is obtained from No. 3 camshaft bearing location where the camshaft meters the flow of oil from the main lubricating gallery through a groove in the camshaft bearing surface to a gallery extending upwards to the cylinder head gasket surface, Fig. 6. On 1973, late 1974 and 1975 232, 258, oil is supplied through the valve lifters and hollow push rods. On 1969-72 and early 1974 199, 232 and 258, install the rocker arm shaft with oil holes facing down toward the cylinder head, Fig. 7. The 1973, late 1974 and 1975 232, 258 engines have the intake and exhaust rocker arms pivoting on a bridged pivot assembly which is secured to the cylinder head by two cap screws, Fig. 4A.

NOTE: The new rocker arms used on late 1974 engines (beginning with build date code 704 (A or E) 04, have been redesigned with the oil hole on the push rod end relocated, pointing away from the valve assemblies allowing for improved oil control, Fig. 4B. Also, these rocker arms are not interchangeable with the 1973 type, since the camshaft and rocker arm ratio has been modified.

6-232 & 258 Valve Train

The exhaust valve train on certain engines, has been modified to incorporate valve rotators to improve valve durability. The engines involved are those equipped with EGR systems less Air Guard.

NOTE: When replacing rocker arms on these engines, use only the cast type rocker arms, as they are designed to accommodate the valve rotators.

VALVE GUIDES

Excessive valve stem-to-guide clearance will cause lack of power, rough idling and noisy valves, and may cause valve breakage. Insufficient clearance

Fig. 4A Rocker arms, push rod and pivot assembly. 1973, late 1974 & 1975 6-232, 258, 1973 V8-304 and all 1974-75 V8's

will result in noisy and sticky functioning of valves and disturb engine smoothness of operation.

Valve stem-to-guide clearances are listed in the *Engine Valve Specifications* table. By using a micrometer and a suitable telescope hole gauge, check the diameter of the valve stem in three places (top, center and bottom). Insert telescope hole gauge in valve guide bore, measuring at the center. Subtract the highest reading of valve stem diameter from valve guide bore center diameter to obtain valve-to-guide clearance. If clearance is not within specified limits, use the next oversize valve and ream bore to fit. Valves with oversize stems are available in .003", .015" and .030".

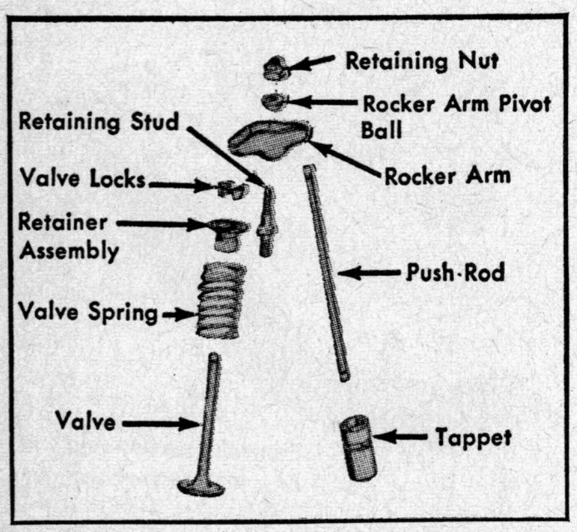

Fig. 4 Valve train on 1969-73 V8-290, 343, 360, 390, 401 and 1969-72 V8-304 engines

[Diagram labels:]
Retaining Nut
Rocker Arm Pivot Ball
Retaining Stud
Valve Locks
Rocker Arm
Retainer Assembly
Push-Rod
Valve Spring
Valve
Tappet

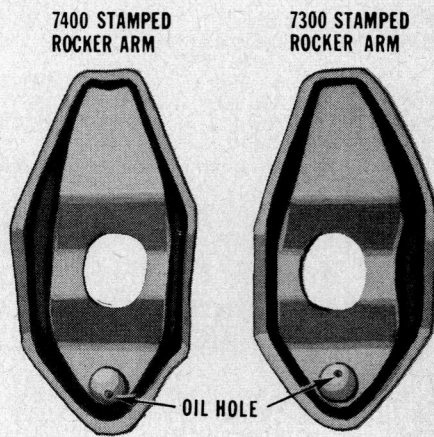

7400 STAMPED ROCKER ARM   7300 STAMPED ROCKER ARM

OIL HOLE

Fig. 4B 1973 (7300) and 1974 (7400) rocker arm identification

Hydraulic Lifters

Valve lifters may be removed from their bores after removing the rocker arms and push rods. Adjustable pliers with taped jaws may be used to remove lifters that are stuck due to varnish, carbon, etc. Fig. 8 illustrates the type of lifter used.

TIMING CHAIN COVER
6-199, 232, 258

1. Remove drive belts, fan and pulley.
2. Remove vibration damper.
3. Remove oil pan-to-timing chain cover screws and cover-to-block screws.
4. Raise the cover and pull the oil pan front seal up enough to pull the retaining nibs from the holes in the cover.
5. Remove timing chain cover gasket from block. Cut off seal tab flush with front face of cylinder block. Clean gasket surfaces.
6. Remove oil seal.
7. Place gasket in position on cylinder block. Install new oil pan front seal, cut off protruding tab of seal to match portion of the original seal.
8. Insert suitable aligning tool in cover seal bore and on crankshaft. Install cover-to-oil pan screws and tighten lightly. Install cover screws and tighten.
9. Retighten all screws and install new cover seal.

V8-290, 304, 343, 360, 390, 401

The timing chain cover is a die casting incorporating an oil seal at the vibration damper hub, Fig. 9. The crankshaft front seal is installed from the back side of the cover, therefore, it is necessary to remove the cover when replacement of the seal is required. To remove cover, proceed as follows:
1. Drain cooling system completely.
2. Remove lower radiator hose and by-pass hose from cover.
3. Remove distributor, fuel pump, drive belts, fan and hub assembly and vibration damper, using a suitable puller.

NOTE: It is not necessary to disconnect power steering or discharge air conditioning system (if equipped). Remove units from their mounting brackets and place them aside.

4. Remove two front oil pan bolts and the eight hex head bolts retaining the cover to the cylinder block.
5. Pull cover forward until free from locating dowel pins.
6. Remove used seal and clean seal bore and gasket surface of cover.
7. Apply sealing compound to outer surface of seal and a film of Lubri-plate or equivalent to seal lips. Drive seal into cover bore until seal contacts outer flange of cover.

Installation of Cover
1. Prior to installation of cover, remove lower dowel pin from cylinder block.
2. Using a sharp knife or razor blade, cut oil pan gasket flush with cylinder block on both sides of oil pan.
3. Cut corresponding pieces of gasket from the replacement oil pan gasket set. Cement gasket to cover. Install replacement Neoprene oil pan seal into cover and align cork gasket tabs to the pan seal.
4. Apply a strip of sealing compound to both the cut-off oil pan gaskets at the oil pan to cylinder block location.

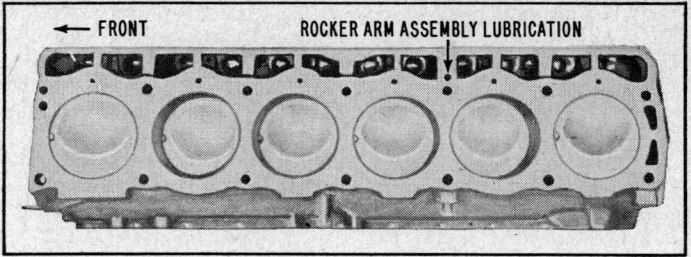
Fig. 6 Rocker arm lubrication gallery. 1969-72 & early 1974 6-199, 232, 258 engines

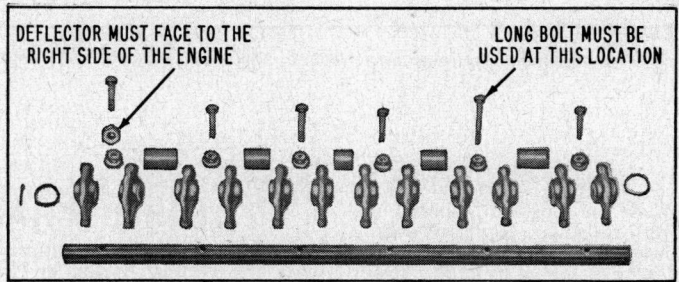
Fig. 7 Rocker arm assembly. 1969-72 & early 1974 6-199, 232, 258 engines

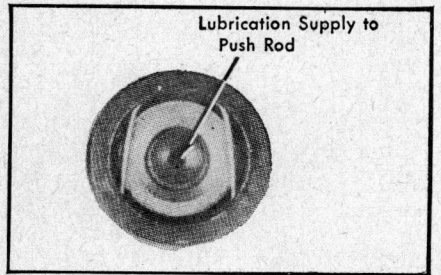
Fig. 5 Hydraulic lifter identification. V8-290, 304, 343, 360, 390, 401 engines

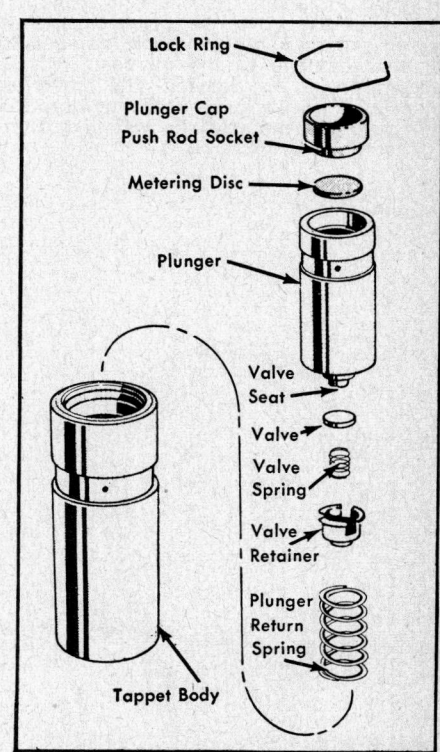
Fig. 8 Hydraulic valve lifter

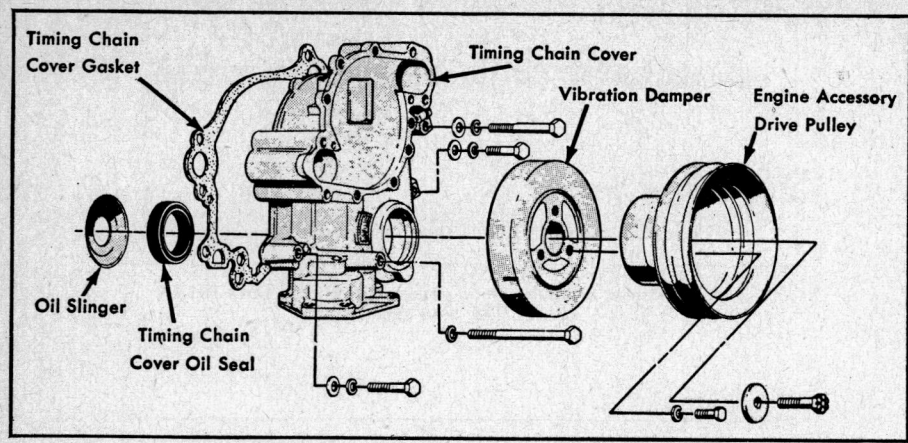

Fig. 9 Timing chain cover assembly. V8-290, 304, 343, 360, 390, 401 engines

CAMSHAFT

6-199, 232, 258

1. Remove cylinder head.
2. Remove value lifters.
3. Remove radiator and, if so equipped, air conditioning condenser.
4. Remove timing chain cover.
5. Rotate crankshaft until timing marks on sprockets are aligned, Fig. 11.
6. Remove sprockets and chain.
7. Lower front bumper by removing forward back bar-to-side sill bolts.
8. Remove crankshaft.

5. Place cover in position, install oil pan bolts in cover, tighten evenly and slowly until cover aligns with upper dowel. Then install lower dowel through cover. Drive dowel in corresponding hole in cylinder block.
6. Install cover attaching bolts and torque to 20-30 ft-lbs.

Six Cylinder

When installing the cover it is important that the cover be properly aligned when installing the vibration damper to prevent damage to the oil seal. This is accomplished by leaving the cover-to-block cap screws loose until the vibration damper has been partially installed. Then tighten the cover screws.

TIMING CHAIN

When installing a timing chain, see that the timing marks on the sprockets are in line as shown in Figs. 10, 10A and 11.

NOTE: All V8-360 and 401 heavy duty engines (Fleet) built after April 22, 1974 use a new double row roller type timing chain to improve timing chain durability. This new timing chain is available as a service replacement item and should be installed when timing chain failures occur to eliminate recurrence of the problem. Installation of the new timing chain requires the use of a new heavy duty camshaft sprocket and crankshaft sprocket.

V8-290, 304, 343, 360, 390, 401

1. Disconnect battery ground cable.
2. Disconnect transmission cooler lines at radiator if so equipped.
3. Remove radiator.
4. Remove distributor, wires and coil.
5. Remove intake manifold and carburetor as an assembly.
6. Remove cylinder head covers, loosen rocker arms and remove push rods and lifters.
7. Dismount power steering pump.
8. Remove fan and hub, fuel pump and heater hose at water pump.
9. Remove alternator.
10. Remove vibration damper and pulley and lower radiator hose at water pump.
11. Remove timing chain cover, distributor-oil pump drive gear, fuel pump eccentric sprockets and chain.
12. Remove hood latch support bracket upper retaining screws and move bracket as required to allow removal of camshaft.

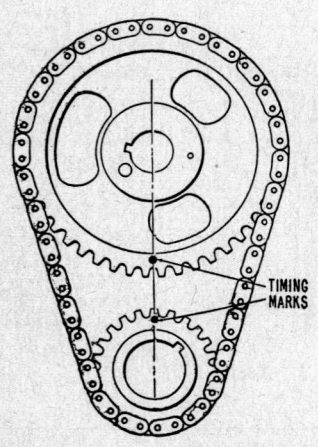

Fig. 10 Valve timing. V8 engines

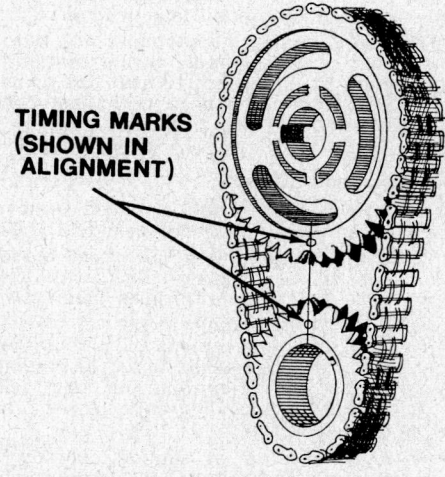

Fig. 10A Valve timing. V8-360 & 401 with double row roller timing chain

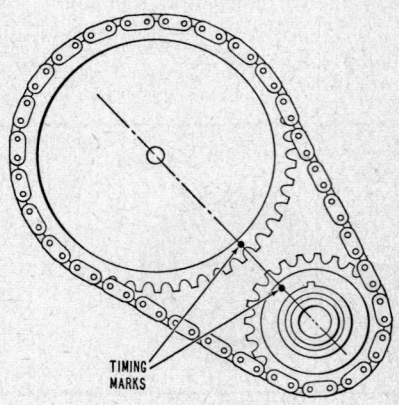

Fig. 11 Valve timing. 6-199, 232, 258 engines

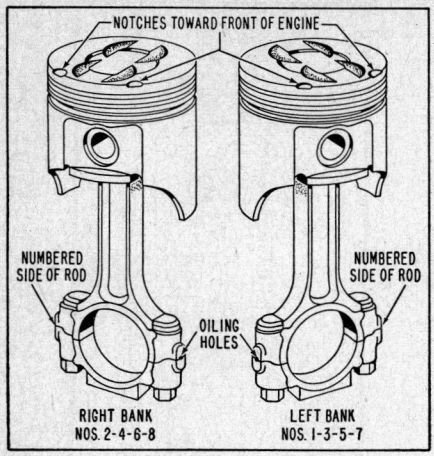

Fig. 12   Piston and rod assembly.
1969 Low Compression V8-290, 343

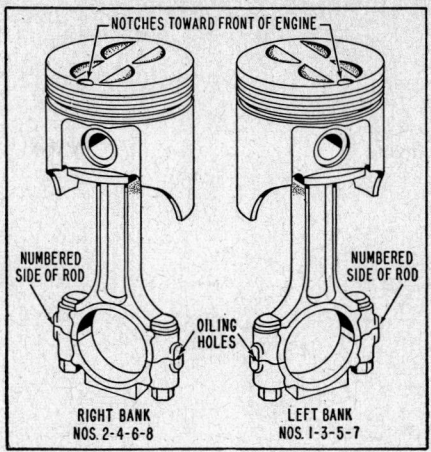

Fig. 13   Piston and rod assembly.
1969 High Comp. V8-343

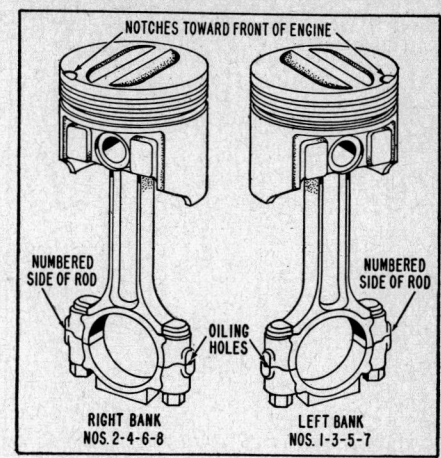

Fig. 14   Piston and rod assembly.
1969 V8-390

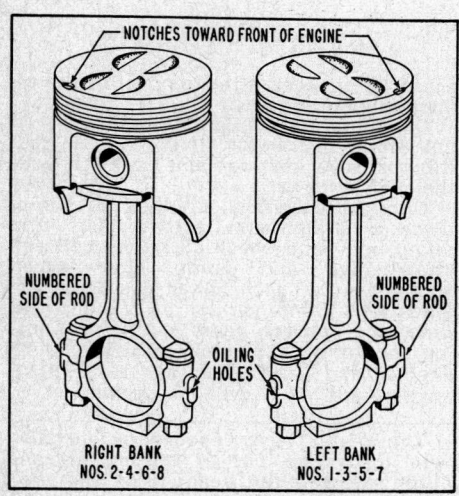

Fig. 15   Piston and rod assembly.
1969 V8-290 High Comp.

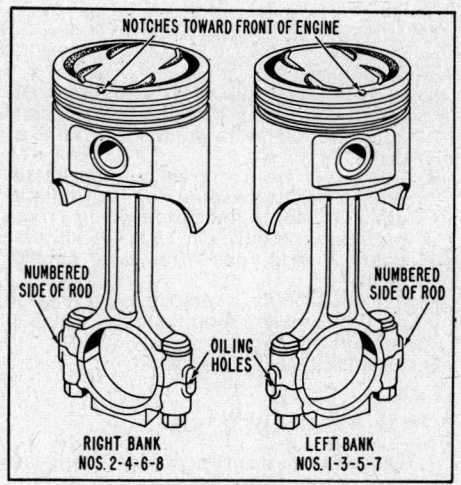

Fig. 16   Piston and rod assembly.
1970 V8-304

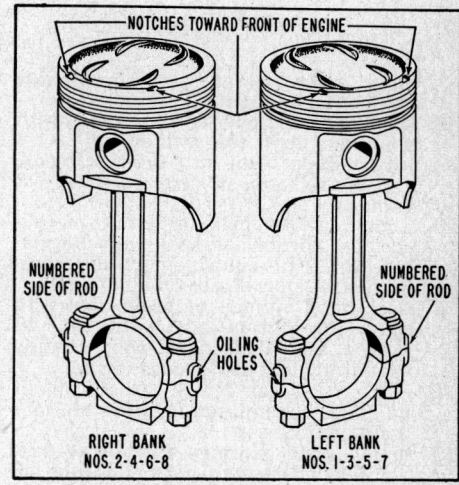

Fig. 17   Piston and rod assembly.
1970-74 V8-360 Std. Compression
and 1971-74 V8-304

PISTONS & RODS, ASSEMBLE

V8 Engines

Assemble piston to connecting rod as shown in Figs. 12 to 19.

Overhead Valve 6-Cyl.

Pistons are marked with a depression notch on the top perimeter, Fig. 20. When installed in the engine this notch must be toward the front of the engine. Always assemble rods and caps with the cylinder numbers facing the camshaft side of engine.

PISTONS, PINS & RINGS

Pistons are furnished in standard sizes and oversizes of .002, .005. .010 and .020".

Piston pins are furnished in oversizes of .003 and .005".

Piston rings are available in .020" oversizes.

MAIN & ROD BEARINGS

Both main and rod bearings are supplied in undersizes of .001, .002, .010 and .012".

CRANKSHAFT REAR OIL SEAL

199, 232, 290, 304, 343, 360, 390, 401 Engines

1. To replace the seal, Fig. 21, remove oil pan and scrape oil pan surfaces clean.
2. Remove rear main bearing cap.
3. Remove and discard old seals.
4. Clean cap throughly.
5. Loosen all remaining main bearing cap screws.
6. With a brass drift and hammer, tap upper seal until sufficient seal is protruding to permit pulling seal out completely with pliers.

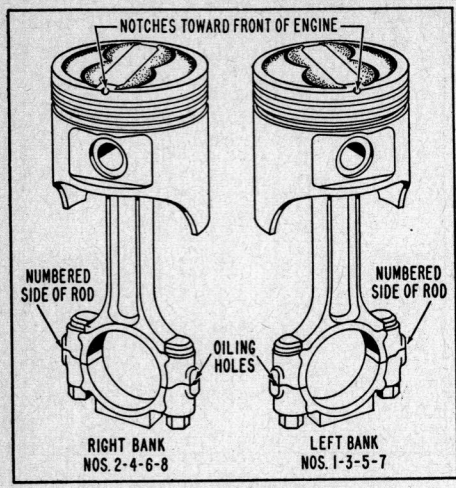

Fig. 18 Piston and rod assembly.
1970 V8-360 High Compression

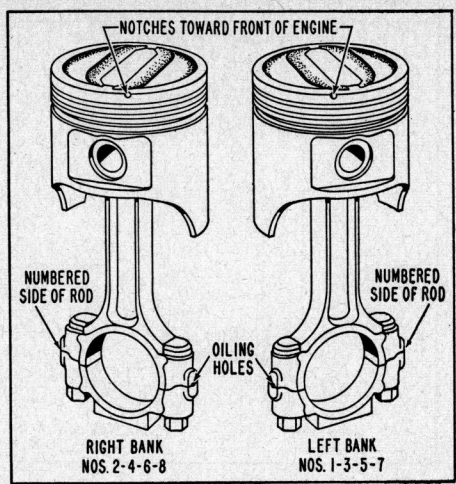

Fig. 19 Piston and rod assembly.
1970-74 V8-390, 401

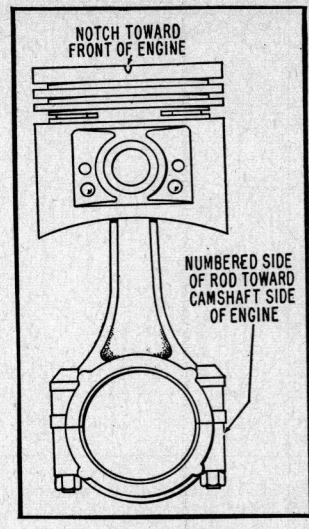

Fig. 20 Piston and rod assembly.
6-199, 232, 258 engines

7. Wipe seal surface of crankshaft clean, then oil lightly.
8. Coat back surface of upper seal with soap, and lip of seal with engine oil.
9. Install upper seal into cylinder block. *Lip of seal must face to front of engine.*
10. Coat cap and cylinder block mating surface portion of seal with Permatex No. 2 or equivalent, being careful not to apply sealer on lip of seal.
11. Coat back surface of lower seal with soap, and lip of seal with No. 40 engine oil. Place into cap, seating seal firmly into seal recess in cap.
12. Place Permatex No. 2 or equivalent on both chamfered edges of rear main bearing cap.
13. Install main bearings and install cap. Tighten all caps to correct torque as listed in the *Engine Tightening Specifications* table.
14. Cement oil pan gasket to cylinder block with tongue of gasket at each end coated with Permatex or equivalent before installing into rear main bearing cap at joint of tongue and oil pan front neoprene seal.
15. Coat oil pan rear seal with soap. Place into recess of rear main bearing cap, making certain seal is firmly and evenly seated.
16. Install oil pan and tighten drain plug securely.

OIL PAN
1969 V8; 1970-75 All

1. Disconnect battery ground cable.
2. Support engine with lifting fixture, Fig. 22.
3. Raise car and support on side sills.
4. Disconnect engine mounts at engine brackets.
5. Disconnect idler arm at sill. Disconnect body ground cables if so

equipped.
6. Loosen sway bar if so equipped. On 1969 V8 except Ambassador, disconnect shock absorbers at lower control arms.
7. Remove front crossmember-to-sill bolts, pull crossmember down and place 2"x4"x6" blocks between crossmember and sills. On 1971-74 V8, disconnect strut rods from lower control arms.
8. On six cylinder, remove right engine mount bracket from engine. On V8, remove starter.
9. Drain and remove oil pan.

1969 Six

1. Disconnect front cushions from engine bracket.
2. Remove right bracket from engine.
3. Disconnect ground strap.
4. Remove cylinder head cover and air cleaner.
5. Disconnect fan shroud if so equipped.
6. Raise engine as far as possible.
7. Disconnect stabilizer bar from side sill if so equipped.
8. Loosen strut rod bolts at lower control arms.
9. Remove crossmember-to-side sill bolts.
10. With weight of car on wheels pry down crossmember, use wooden blocks to hold crossmember down.
11. Drain engine oil, remove oil pan.

OIL PUMP
6-199, 6-232, 258 & V8s

The oil pump on six cylinder models is located in the oil pan thus necessitating removal of the pan to gain access to the pump. The pump on V8 engines is an integral part of the timing case cover and

it can be serviced after removal of the oil filter adapter body.

Oil pump removal or replacement will not affect distributor timing as the distributor drive gear remains in mesh with the camshaft gear.

Upon disassembly of the oil pump, place a straightedge across gears and pump body and check clearance between straightedge and pump body which should be .003 inch for all 6 cylinder engines and .004 inch for all V8 engines. Clearance between gears and pump housing should be .003 inch for 1969-71 V8 engines and .0005-.0025 for 1972-75 V8 engines and all 6 cylinder engines.

The pump cover should be installed with the pump out of the engine and pump checked for freedom of operation before installation.

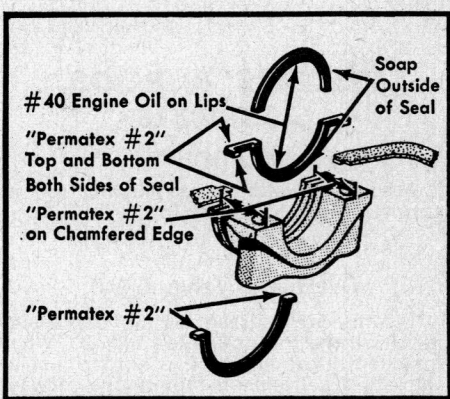

Fig. 21 Rear main bearing sealing. 199, 232, 290, 304, 343, 360, 390, 401 engines

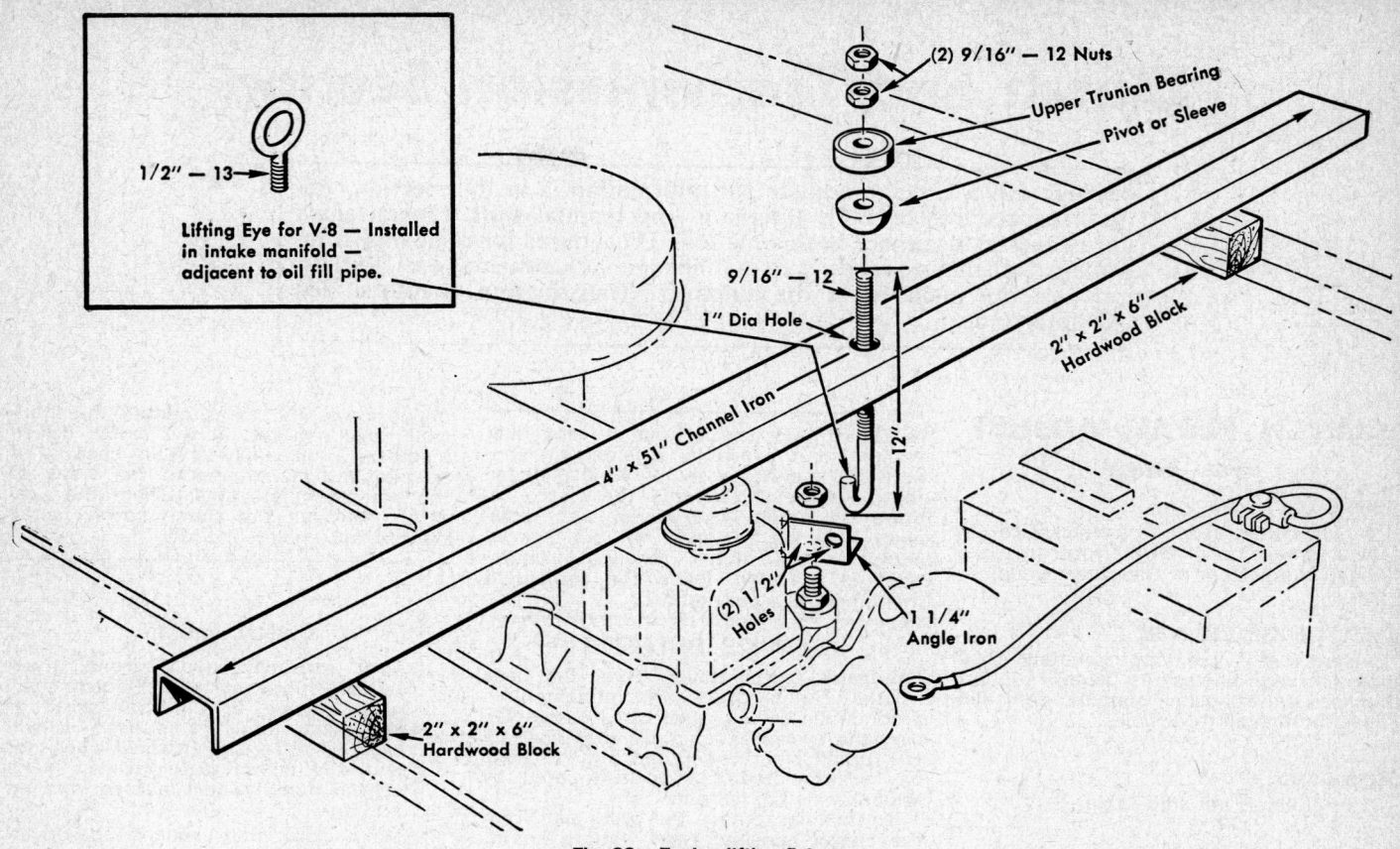

1/2" — 13 →

Lifting Eye for V-8 — Installed in intake manifold — adjacent to oil fill pipe.

(2) 9/16" — 12 Nuts

Upper Trunion Bearing

Pivot or Sleeve

9/16" — 12

1" Dia Hole

4" x 51" Channel Iron

2" x 2" x 6" Hardwood Block

12"

(2) 1/2" Holes

1 1/4" Angle Iron

2" x 2" x 6" Hardwood Block

Fig. 22   Engine lifting fixture

The oil pressure relief valve, which is built into the pump, is not adjustable, the correct pressure being built into the relief valve spring.

BELT TENSION DATA

	New Lbs.	Used Lbs.
1969-70—		
Air Condition	125-145	90-110
Fan and Alternator	125-145	90-110
Power Steering	125-145	90-110
1971-72—		
Air Condition	125-145	105-125
Fan and Alternator—		
Exc. V8 With A/C	125-145	90-110
V8 With A/C	125-145	105-125
Power Steering—		
Exc. V8 With A/C	125-145	90-110
V8 With A/C	125-145	105-120
1973-74—		
Air Condition	125-155	105-130
Air Pump—		
Exc. 6 cyl. With A/C	125-155	90-115
6 cyl. With A/C (1/4 inch belt)	40-50	35-40
Fan and Alternator—		
Exc. V8 With A/C	125-155	90-115
V8 With A/C	125-155	105-130
Power Steering—		
Exc. V8 With A/C	125-145	90-110
V8 with A/C	125-145	105-120
1975		
Air Condition	125-155	105-130
Air Pump—		
Exc. 6 cyl. With A/C	125-155	90-115
6 cyl. With A/C (1/4 inch belt)	40-50	35-40
Fan and Power Steering	125-155	90-115

WATER PUMP

1. Disconnect battery ground cable.
2. Drain cooling system and disconnect radiator and heater hoses from pump.
3. Remove drive belts.

NOTE: On some models it will be necessary to remove alternator front bracket and place alternator aside, without disconnecting wires.

4. Remove fan shroud attaching bolts, then remove fan, hub and shroud.
5. Remove water pump and gasket.

FUEL PUMP PRESSURE

Year	Engine	Pressure lbs.
1969-75	Six cyl.	4-5½
1969-75	V8	5-6½

FUEL PUMP, REPLACE

1. Remove all gasket material from the pump and block gasket surfaces. Apply sealer to both sides of new gasket.
2. Position gasket on pump flange and hold pump in position against its mounting surface. Make sure rocker arm is riding on camshaft eccentric.
3. Press pump tight against its mounting. Install retaining screws and tighten them alternately.
4. Connect fuel lines. Then operate engine and check for leaks.

SERVICE NOTE: Before installing the pump, it is good practice to crank the engine so that the nose of the camshaft eccentric is out of the way of the fuel pump rocker arm when the pump is installed. In this way there will be the least amount of tension on the rocker arm, thereby easing the installation of the pump.

Clutch and Transmission Section

NOTE: 1975 Linkage adjustment information is in this section. Repair procedures on both automatic and manual shift transmissions are covered elsewhere in this manual. Procedures for removing automatic transmissions as well as linkage adjustments on 1969-74 models are included in the automatic transmission chapters. See Chapter Index.

CLUTCH PEDAL, ADJUST
Pedal Height

1969 6-199

Adjust clutch pedal stop bracket to obtain a dimension of 6½" from the bare floor to the bottom of the clutch pedal.

1969-71 6-232, 258 & V8

Insert a 5/16" pin, approximately 4½" long, through holes in pedal support bracket. Adjust pedal support until pin slides through all three holes.

1970 6-199

This clutch is not adjustable.

Pedal Free Play

In order to provide sufficient free movement of the clutch release bearing when the clutch is engaged and pedal fully released, free pedal play should be ⅞" to 1⅛" with desired free play of 1⅛" for 1973-75 and 1" for 1969-72.

Adjustment for free pedal play is made by varying the length of the beam or link to the release lever rod. Lengthening this rod reduces pedal travel; shortening it increases pedal play, Fig. 1.

CLUTCH, REPLACE
Removal

1. Remove transmission as described further on.
2. Remove starter, clutch housing, throwout lever, wave washer, bearing and sleeve assembly.

NOTE: Mark clutch cover, pressure plate and flywheel to insure correct alignment during installation.

3. Remove clutch cover and pressure plate assembly.

NOTE: When removing clutch cover and pressure plate assembly from flywheel, loosen screws evenly until spring tension is released, as cover could be warped by improper removal, resulting in clutch chatter when reassembled.

NOTE: Unless special clutch rebuilding equipment is available, it is recommended that the clutch assembly be exchanged for a rebuilt unit should the clutch require rebuilding. The driven disc, however, may be replaced without special equipment. If clutch rebuilding equipment is available, follow the equipment manufacturer's instructions.

SERVICE BULLETIN

Lubricates Clutch Cover: Three felt pads in the clutch cover are lubricated in production before they are assembled over the eyebolts. A squeak that may occur during clutch operation after mileage has accumulated can be eliminated by relubricating the felt pads.

To do this, remove the cover pan from the clutch housing. Next, with a squirt-type oil can, carefully apply a mixture of heavy oil and mineral spirits to the three felt pads. Use only a small amount of lubricant, and make certain the lubricant does not get on the clutch driven member. Then apply a thin coating of a suitable light grease to the sides of the pressure plate lugs, where the lugs extend through the clutch cover. Install the pan to complete the job.

Clutch, Install

1. Very sparingly apply front wheel bearing lubricant to the clutch shaft pilot bearing in the crankshaft. If too much lubricant is used, it will run out of face of flywheel when hot and ruin driven plate facings. Make certain that flywheel surface is clean and dry.
2. Make sure that splines in driven plate hub are clean, and apply a light coating of lubriplate. Driven plate facings must be clean and dry.

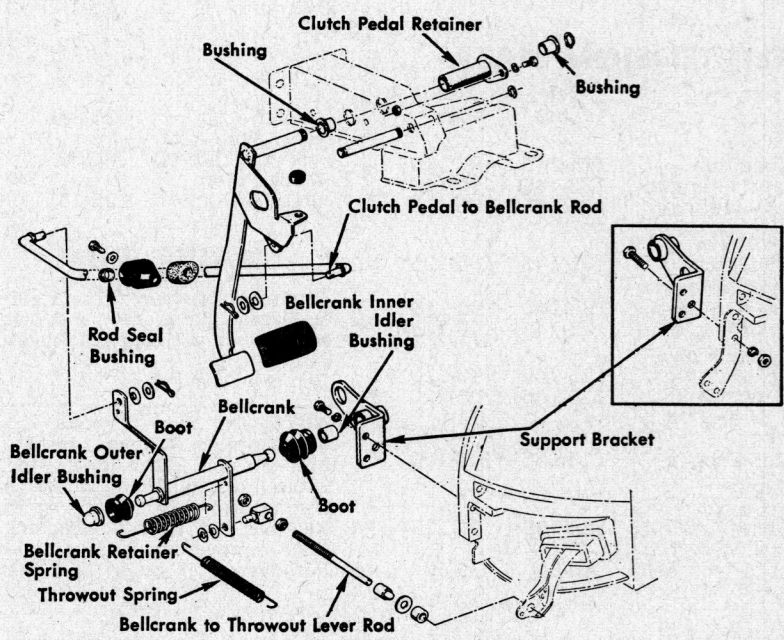

Fig. 1 Typical clutch linkage

3. Place driven plate on pressure plate, then place clutch assembly in position on flywheel, being sure to align marks made on flywheel and cover before removal.
4. Install cover bolts with washers but do not tighten.
5. Insert a spare clutch shaft through hub of driven plate and into pilot bearing.
6. Tighten each clutch cover bolt several turns at a time to draw cover evenly to flywheel and avoid distortion of cover.
7. While tightening cover bolts, move clutch shaft from side to side to center driven plate with pilot bearing. If driven plate is not centered, it will be difficult to slide the transmission into place. Make sure all cover bolts are uniformly tightened.
8. Remove aligning clutch shaft and install transmission, clutch linkage and adjust clutch pedal free play.

MANUAL TRANS.
Three Speed, Replace
1971-75

NOTE: On cars equipped with floor shift, remove bezel, boot and shift selector lever.

IMPORTANT: It is necessary to open the hood to avoid damage to the hood and air cleaner whenever the rear crossmember is removed.

1. Raise the vehicle.
2. Mark rear universal joint yoke and bearing prior to removal to insure proper alignment at time of installation.
3. Disconnect propeller shaft from rear axle.
4. Slide front universal joint yoke from transmission.
5. Unfasten and lower exhaust pipes on V8 models.
6. Support the engine and detach rear support cushion from transmission.
7. Remove bolts securing rear crossmember to side sills and remove rear crossmember.
8. Disconnect speedo cable, back up light switch wires and any other wiring.
9. Disconnect column shift rods and reverse lock up rod.
10. Lower engine until clearance is obtained to permit transmission removal.

NOTE: Care must be taken not to damage clutch shaft, pilot bushing or clutch disc.

1969-70
1. Raise car and support engine.
2. Mark rear U-joint yoke to aid in assembly, and disconnect propeller shaft from rear axle.
3. Slide front U-joint from transmission mainshaft.
4. Remove screws from rear engine support cushion at extension housing.

5.. Remove bolts that secure rear crossmember to sills and remove crossmember.

NOTE: Before removing rear member on Javelin and AMX with power steering, open hood to avoid damage from pump reservoir wing nut.

6. Disconnect speedometer cable and shift rods from transmission.
7. On models with floor shift, remove shift lever bezel, boot, retainer and shift lever.
8. When removing transmission, use guide pins in place of two lower cap screws so as not to damage clutch shaft.

Four Speed, Replace
1969 All Models
1. Remove chrome trim ring that secures rubber boot to floor pan and slide boot up on shift lever.
2. Unfasten and remove shift lever from cross shaft (2 capscrews).
3. Raise vehicle.
4. Unfasten and remove exhaust pipes from exhaust manifolds.
5. Jack up or support engine.
6. Unfasten rear engine support cushion from crossmember.
7. Unfasten and remove crossmember.

NOTE: Before removing crossmember on Javelin and AMX models with power steering, open hood to avoid damage from pump reservoir wing nut.

8. Remove propeller shaft.
9. Disconnect speedometer cable from transmission.
10. Lower engine until adequate clearance is obtained to permit transmission removal.
11. Reverse procedure to install.

1970-75 All Models
The procedure to remove the transmission is the same as that given previously for the three speed transmission.

MANUAL TRANS. SHIFT LINKAGE
1969-75 Three Spd. Floor Shift

NOTE: For 1969 models, omit Steps 1-4.

1. Loosen reverse trunnion nuts.
2. Shift transmission into reverse and lock steering column.

NOTE: It may be necessary to move the lower column shift lever upward until it is in the locked position.

3. Tighten lower trunnion lock nut until it contacts the trunnion then tighten upper lock nut while holding trunnion centered in lever.
4. Unlock steering column.
5. Shift transmission into neutral.

6. Loosen 2-3 lever attaching nut and adjusting bolt.
7. With 1st-Reverse shift rod in neutral, align the 2-3 shift rod so the shift notch is exactly aligned with the 1st-Reverse shift notch. Tighten adjusting bolt and attaching nut.
8. On 1970-72 units, shift transmission into reverse and lock steering column. Column must lock without any binding.

1969-75 Three Spd. Column Shift

NOTE: For 1969 models, omit Steps 1-3.

1. With shift rods disconnected from levers, place column lever in reverse position and lock column.
2. Place transmission levers in reverse position and adjust shift rod trunnion for a free pin fit in the lever. Tighten trunnion. Unlock column.
3. Shift transmission into neutral.
4. Insert a $3/16$" drill bit through the aligning holes of the two shift levers, shift gate and the bracket on the jacket tube.
5. With the shift levers in the neutral position, carefully adjust the trunnions to a free fit in the shift levers and secure the trunnion in this position with the lock nuts. Use care when tightening the lock nuts so a binding condition does not exist.

1969-75 Four Speed

NOTE: On some units, it is necessary to lower the rear of the transmission before adjusting the linkage.

1. Loosen the transmission shift lever nuts (two on each lever) and loosen the lock nuts on the reverse shift rod at the trunnion.
2. Install a $1/4$" drill bit through the selector lever retainer, through the levers, spacer plate, and through the aligning hole in the mounting bracket.
3. This is the neutral position. Place all three transmission levers in the neutral position.
4. Adjust the trunnion on the reverse shift rod to enter freely into the reverse lever. Lock the check nuts on the reverse rod and secure with washer and cotter pin.
5. Tighten the lower nuts of the shift levers first, being careful not to move the outer levers out of position.
6. Tighten the upper "hug nuts" to 10 ft. lbs. Do not overtighten or the shift shafts could be broken. Remove the aligning pin.

1975 AUTO. TRANS. LINKAGE ADJUST

Linkage adjustments for the 1975 models are the same as for 1974 models and can be found elsewhere in this manual. Beginning with 1972 American Motors uses the Torque Command Transmission.

OVERDRIVE

DESCRIPTION

The overdrive is an additional gear unit located between the transmission and propeller shaft, Fig. 1, and provides a higher overall gear ratio than normally provided by the drive gear and pinion. The overdrive permits highway cruising at a lower engine speed than in a normal third gear. This unit reduces engine-to-rear axle ratio approximately 25%, thus providing a transmission ratio in overdrive third gear of .75 to 1.00.

The overdrive is a hydraulically operated unit and its actuation is controlled by a solenoid valve. This solenoid valve is activated by a control switch mounted on the steering column. A governor speed switch, operated by the speedometer cable, determines cut-in and cut-out speeds for the unit. The overdrive may be engaged when the vehicle is above the governor cut-in speed of 38 MPH and in third gear only. A third gear switch installed in the transmission prevents overdrive engagement in any other gear.

NOTE: California vehicles require a TCS switch which is open when the transmission is in third gear. To complete the overdrive control circuit, but also prevent overdrive operation in any gear except third gear, a third gear relay is connected to the TCS switch. This relay performs the same function as the third gear switch and is closed only when the transmission is in third gear.

The overdrive is engaged by activating the control switch and until the switch is deactivated or the vehicle decelerates to below the governor cut-out speed of 32 MPH, the overdrive remains engaged. A kickdown switch is incorporated into the control circuit, Fig. 2. This switch, mounted on the carburetor base, is actuated by throttle linkage. When the throttle is fully opened, the switch is actuated and "Opens" the control circuit, in turn de-energizing the solenoid valve and disengaging the overdrive. When the throttle returns from the wide open position, the switch "Closes" the control circuit, re-energizing the solenoid and re-engaging the overdrive.

An indicator lamp, connected electrically to the solenoid valve, is provided to indicate overdrive engagement.

Hydraulic system pressure is developed by a cam operated plunger-type pump, Fig. 3, and is driven by the transmission output shaft through a drive key. The pump obtains oil from the air cooled sump, through the oil pan filter, and pumps it through the non-return valve and pressure filter to the clutch apply pistons, solenoid valve and relief valve assembly. A spring loaded piston within the relief valve assembly provides smooth engagement and disengagement under all operating conditions. When the overdrive is disengaged, a residual system pressure of 20 to 40

PSI is maintained. The system pressure with the overdrive engaged is 520 to 540 PSI and is maintained by the relief valve.

DIAGNOSIS

Overdrive Will Not Engage

1. Low lubricant level.
2. Open wire or switch in electrical control circuit.
3. Plugged oil pan or pressure filters, plugged or sticking pump non-return valve assembly.
4. Sticking relief valve piston.
5. Broken relief valve assembly or piston springs.
6. Plugged control orifice.
7. Solenoid valve sticking, grounded or open.
8. Sticking or worn sliding clutch.
9. Broken or weak clutch return springs.
10. Leaking clutch apply piston seals, or internal case leaks.
11. Damaged or worn gear components.
12. Pump body misaligned with oil feed slot in case bore.
13. Pump plunger of body worn excessively.

Overdrive Will Not Disengage

CAUTION: This condition requires immediate correction, as extensive damage may result if vehicle is moved in reverse.

1. Closed switch or short in electrical circuit.
2. Solenoid valve stuck or shorted.
3. Relief valve piston stuck or spring broke.
4. Control orifice plugged.

5. Sliding clutch sticking.
6. Damaged or seized gear components.

Slow Disengagement and/or Overdrive Freewheels On Overrun

1. Solenoid valve oil feed holes plugged or valve sticking.
2. Control orifice plugged.
3. Overrunning clutch worn or seized.
4. Worn or damaged sun gear or sliding clutch hub.
5. Worn or damaged friction material on sliding clutch.
6. Worn or damaged brake ring.
7. Relief valve piston sticking.

Overdrive Slips When Engaging

1. Low lubricant level.
2. Plugged oil pan or pressure filter.
3. Sticking or plugged non-return valve.
4. Broken spring on relief valve assembly.
5. Control orifice stuck.
6. Solenoid valve sticking.
7. Oil feed holes plugged.
8. Loose wire at solenoid terminal.
9. Worn clutch apply piston seals or worn friction material on sliding clutch.
10. Internal leak in case.
11. Worn pump plunger or body.
12. Damaged or worn gear components.
13. Pump body not aligned with oil feed slot in case bore.
14. Annulus gear clutch surface worn, burned, or galled.

Shudders, Chatters When Backing Up (Overdrive Disengaged)

1. Loose or defective engine and transmission support cushions.

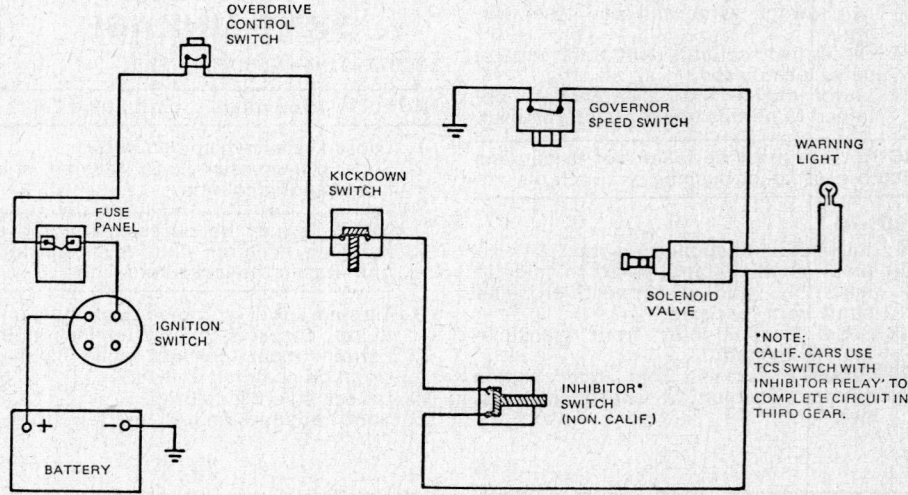

Fig. 2 Overdrive electrical control circuit

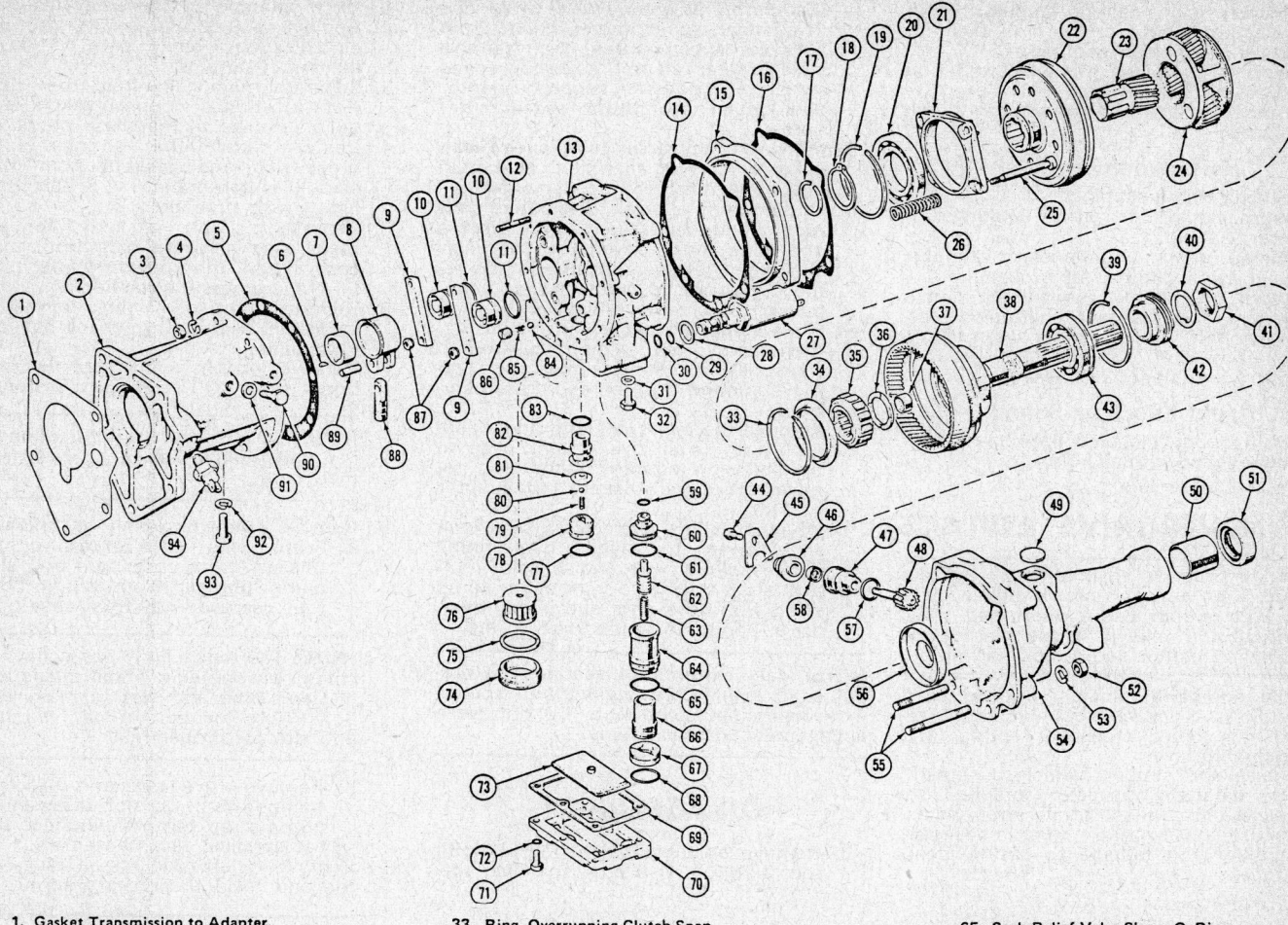

1. Gasket Transmission to Adapter
2. Adapter, Transmission
3. Nut, Self Locking, Main Case Stud
4. Washer, Lock
5. Gasket, Main Case to Transmission Adaptor
6. Key, Pump Strap Cam Drive
7. Cam, Pump Strap
8. Strap, Pump
9. Bar, Clutch Piston Apply
10. Piston, Clutch Apply
11. Seal, Clutch Apply Piston O-Ring
12. Stud, Main Case to Transmission Adapter
13. Main Case
14. Gasket, Clutch Brake Ring (front)
15. Brake Ring, Clutch
16. Gasket, Clutch Brake Ring (rear)
17. Ring, Sun Gear Snap
18. Ring Lock, Sliding Clutch
19. Ring, Thrust Bearing Snap
20. Bearing, Thrust
21. Cover, Thrust Bearing
22. Clutch, Sliding
23. Sun Gear
24. Assembly, Pinion Carrier
25. Bolt, Thrust Bearing Cover (4 reqd.)
26. Spring, Clutch Return (4 reqd.)
27. Solenoid Valve
28. Washer, Solenoid Valve
29. Seal, Solenoid Valve O-Ring
30. Seal, Solenoid Valve O-Ring
31. Gasket, Main Case Pressure Plug
32. Plug, Main Case Pressure

33. Ring, Overrunning Clutch Snap
34. Slinger, Overrunning Clutch Oil
35. Assembly, Overrunning Clutch
36. Washer, Mainshaft Thrust
37. Bushing, Mainshaft Support (Included in Mainshaft)
38. Main Shaft and Annulus Gear
39. Ring, Mainshaft Bearing Snap
40. Washer, Speedometer Drive Gear Tab
41. Nut, Speedometer Drive Gear Lock
42. Gear, Speedometer Drive
43. Bearing, Mainshaft
44. Bolt, Speedometer Adapter Clamp
45. Clamp, Speedometer Adapter
46. Adapter, Speedometer to Governor Speed Switch
47. Adapter, Speedometer Driven Gear
48. Gear, Speedometer Driven
49. Plug, Expansion
50. Bushing, Rear Case (Included in Case)
51. Seal, Rear Case Oil
52. Nut, Self Locking, Main Case to Rear Case Stud
53. Washer, Lock
54. Rear Case
55. Stud, Main Case to Rear Case
56. Washer, Disc (not removed: included in rear case)
57. Seal, Speedometer Adapter O-Ring
58. Seal, Speedometer Adaptor Oil
59. Seal, Relief Valve Body O-Ring (Inner)
60. Body, Relief Valve
61. Seal, Relief Valve Body O-Ring (Outer)
62. Assembly, Relief Valve and Spring
63. Spring, Relief Valve Residual Pressure
64. Sleeve, Relief Valve

65. Seal, Relief Valve Sleeve O-Ring
66. Piston, Relief Valve
67. Plug, Relief Valve Piston
68. Seal, Relief Valve Piston Plug O-Ring
69. Gasket, Oil Pan
70. Oil Pan
71. Bolt, Oil Pan
72. Washer, Lock
73. Filter, Oil Pan
74. Plug, Pressure Filter
75. Washer, Pressure Filter (Aluminum)
76. Filter, Pressure
77. Seal, Pump Body O-Ring
78. Plug, Pump Body
79. Spring, Non-return Valve Ball-seat
80. Ball, Non-return Valve Check
81. Seat, Non-return Valve
82. Body, Pump Plunger
83. Seal, Pump Plunger Body O-Ring
84. Ball, Lubrication Relief Valve Check
85. Spring, Lubrication Relief Valve
86. Plug, Lubrication Relief Valve
87. Nut, Self Locking, Clutch Piston Apply Bar
88. Plunger, Pump
89. Pin, Pump Plunger
90. Bolt, Gearshift Lever Retainer to Adapter
91. Washer, Lock
92. Washer, Lock
93. Bolt, Rear Support Cushion to Adapter
94. Switch, Back-up Light

Fig. 1 Overdrive unit, exploded view

2. Transmission clutch slipping, incorrectly adjusted.
3. Weak clutch return springs.
4. Worn or damaged friction material on sliding clutch.
5. Burned or galled annulus gear clutch surface.

Noisy When Engaged

1. Sliding clutch slipping.
2. Worn, galled or pitted bearings or rear bushing.
3. Pinion gears or mainshaft annulus gear teeth chipped or broken.
4. Worn or chipped overrunning clutch rollers, or clutch race in annulus gear.
5. Mainshaft thrust washer worn, broken or missing.
6. Sun gear chipped or missing.

Light Knocking Sound

1. Pump body installed improperly (flat not aligned with oil hole).

OVERDRIVE REPLACE

NOTE: In order to ease removal, operate vehicle, then engage and disengage overdrive with clutch pedal depressed. This procedure will relieve torque loading on overrunning clutch and pinion carrier.

1. On floorshift vehicles, remove gearshift lever bezel, boot, insulator, retaining bolts, crossover spring, and gearshift lever.
2. Raise and support vehicle on hoist.
3. On catalytic converter equipped vehicles, disconnect converter from exhaust pipes, and lower converter, muffler and tailpipe to obtain clearance.

4. Disconnect solenoid valve wires and disconnect speedometer cable from governor speed switch, then remove speedometer clamp, governor speed switch, speedometer support, adaptor and driven gear from speedometer bore.
5. Mark rear universal joint and pinion yoke for correct alignment at installation and remove propeller shaft.
6. On floorshift vehicles, disconnect shift rods at transmission shifter levers and slide rods forward out of gearshift lever retainer bushings, then remove retainer to transmission adapter bolts and remove retainer.
7. Place a support under clutch housing, then remove rear support cushion to transmission adaptor bolts and remove support cushion and crossmember.
8. Remove the eight locknuts and washers from overdrive main case-to-transmission adaptor studs and remove overdrive. Discard old adaptor gasket.
9. When installing overdrive, use a long screwdriver to align overrunning clutch splines with transmission output shaft splines, then align pump strap with drive cam and install overdrive. Torque locknuts to 18 ft. lbs.

NOTE: Make certain that transmission output shaft splines are aligned with splines in overrunning clutch hub. Do not force engagement when installing.

DISASSEMBLY

1. Remove solenoid valve, Fig. 1, with tool J-25304. Use only specified tool

since solenoid damage may result.
2. Remove and discard nuts securing clutch piston apply bars to thrust bearing cover pins.
3. Separate main case from rear case. Note location of copper gaskets used on main case to rear case studs.
4. Remove clutch return springs, clutch brake ring and gaskets from main case. If clutch brake ring is stuck, tap lightly with a mallet.
5. Remove oil pan, gasket, filter and main case pressure plug from main case, Fig. 4, then pressure filter plug, filter and aluminum washer.
6. Remove pump body plug, non-return valve ball seat spring, check ball and valve seat.
7. Remove clutch apply pistons from bores, then "O" rings from pistons.

NOTE: Do not remove lubrication relief valve plug, spring or ball from main case.

8. Remove pump assembly as follows:
   a. Push pump body upward until it unseats from case bore and slide pump plunger from pump body, then remove body from case bore.

NOTE: The pump body has a flat machined on one side which aligns with oil feed hole and slot in main case bore. Note location of oil feed hole and slot for proper reassembly.

   b. Remove drive cam and key from pump strap. Do not disassemble pump strap and plunger since they are serviced as an assembly.
9. Remove relief valve piston plug, piston and residual pressure spring.

NOTE: The residual pressure spring is the only loose spring in the relief valve assembly.

10. With a magnet or needlenose plier, remove relief valve and spring assembly. Do not remove calibrated spring from relief valve piston.
11. Using tool J-25307, remove relief valve sleeve and body as follows:
    a. Install hooked end of tool through relief valve body bore and hook tool over inner edge of body. Slide tool barrel downward, securing tool, and pull valve body and sleeve from case bore.
    b. Remove and discard "O" rings from valve body, sleeve and plug.
12. Remove sliding clutch, sun gear and thrust bearing cover from main shaft annulus gear in rear case, then remove pinion carrier from main shaft annulus gear.
13. Remove sun gear snap ring, sliding clutch ring lock and push sun gear from sliding clutch hub.
14. Install tool J-25315 into sliding clutch hub and tap end of tool to drive clutch hub from thrust bearing. Remove thrust bearing snap ring and press bearing from cover.
15. Remove overrunning clutch snap ring and brass oil slinger. Install tool J-25308 into main shaft annulus gear bore, reach through tool and pull overrunning clutch into tool and re-

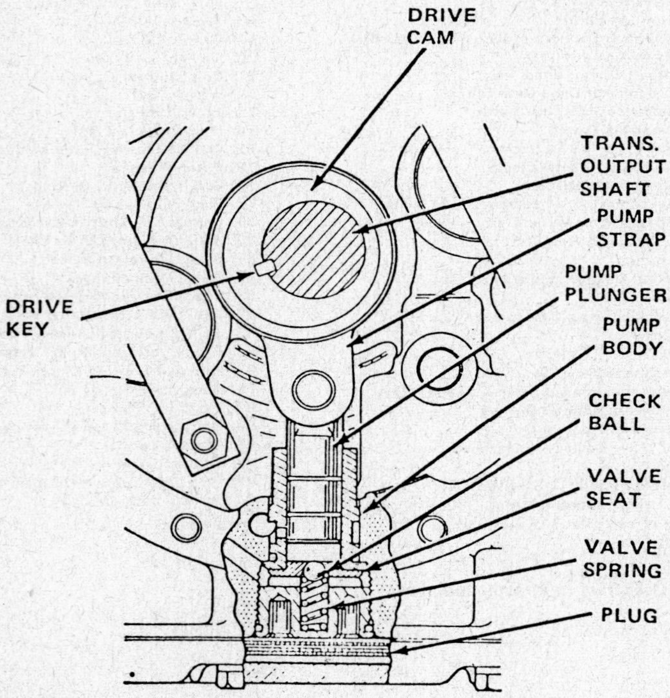

Fig. 3 Overdrive unit oil pump assembly

DRIVE CAM

TRANS. OUTPUT SHAFT

PUMP STRAP

PUMP PLUNGER

PUMP BODY

CHECK BALL

VALVE SEAT

VALVE SPRING

PLUG

DRIVE KEY

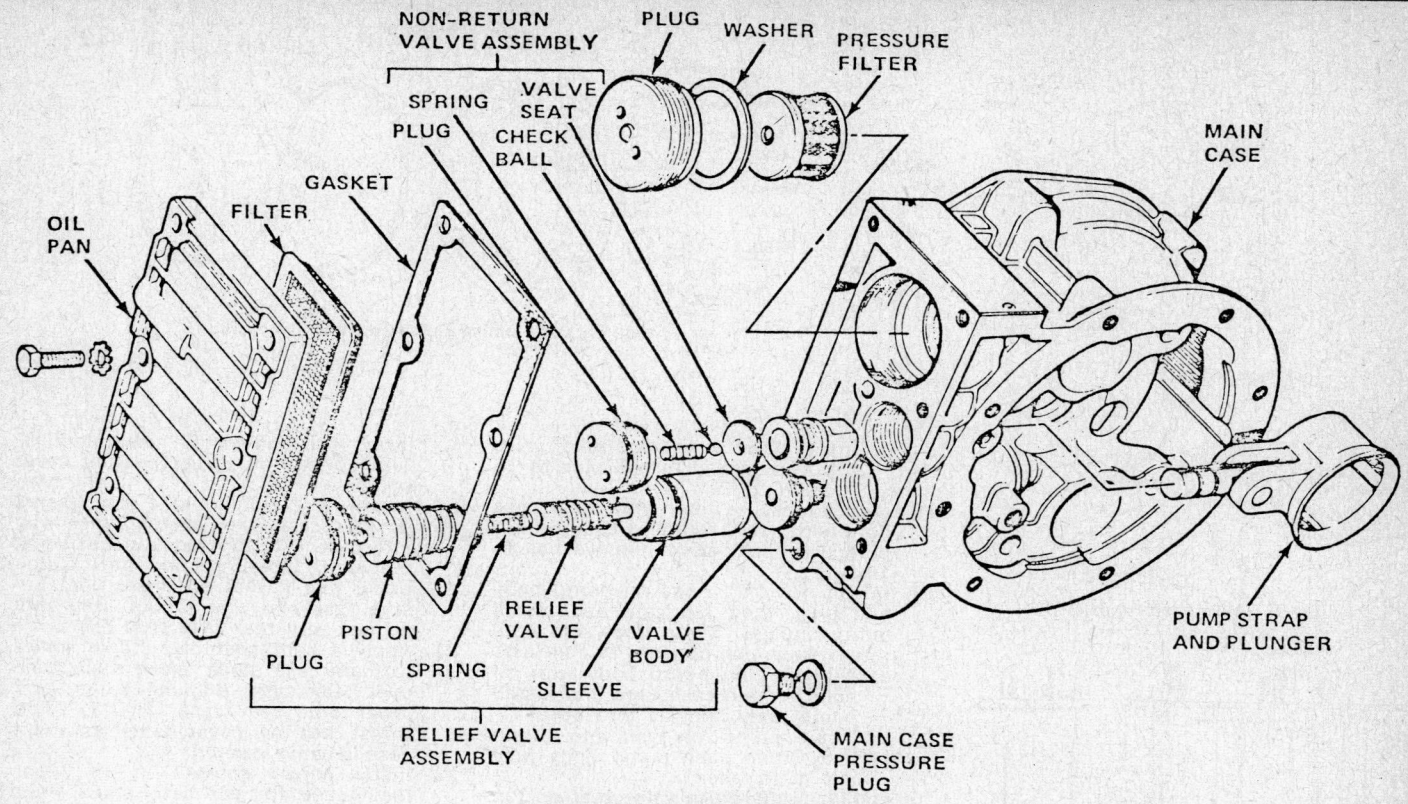

Fig. 4 Overdrive main case components

move tool and overrunning clutch to-gether. Remove main shaft thrust washer from main shaft annulus gear recess. Remove overrunning clutch from tool and disassemble.
16. Remove rear case expansion plug.
17. Place rear case on wooden blocks, expand main shaft bearing snap ring and tap main shaft out from rear case, Fig. 5.
18. Remove speedometer drive gear lock nut, tab washer and drive gear, then main shaft bearing.
19. Pry rear case oil seal from case and remove main shaft bearing snap ring from machined groove in rear case.

NOTE: Do not remove disc washer or rear bushing from rear case since they are not serviceable and are available as part of the rear case.

ASSEMBLY

1. Lubricate and install main shaft bearing on main shaft with the groove facing toward rear of main shaft.
2. Install speedometer drive gear with shoulder side of gear facing toward main shaft bearing, tab washer and drive gear lock nut on main shaft. Torque lock nut to 55 ft. lbs. while holding main shaft secure, then bend drive gear washer against lock nut in two places, securing lock nut.

3. Install main shaft bearing snap ring into rear case machined groove, place main shaft in upright position and lower rear case onto main shaft. Tap end of case to start main shaft bearing into counterbore of case, expand snap ring and tap case until bearing fully seats in counterbore and snap ring in bearing groove.
4. Lubricate and install rear case oil seal, then new rear case expansion plug.
5. Lubricate and install main shaft thrust washer into main shaft annulus gear recess.
6. Assembly overrunning clutch, Fig. 6, as follows:
   a. Insert longest hub spring hooked end into cage locating hole.
   b. Hold cage stationary and rotate hub against spring.
7. Place assembled cage and hub into tool J-25308 with cage open end facing outward. Install clutch rollers into cage slots through gate in tool while rotating cage in clockwise direction.
8. Lubricate and install overrunning clutch assembly in main shaft annulus gear bore. Remove tool J-25308 and install brass oil slinger with shoulder facing outward, then overrunning clutch snap ring, ensuring snap ring fully seats in groove.
9. Lubricate and install pinion carrier into main shaft annulus gear.
10. Press thrust bearing into thrust bearing cover, then install thrust bearing snap ring.
11. Position thrust bearing and cover on

sliding clutch hub and tap cover to start bearing onto hub. Invert assembly and install tool J-25315 into clutch hub and drive hub into thrust bearing.
12. Install sun gear into sliding clutch hub, then sliding clutch lock ring with sharp edge facing upward and sun gear snap ring.
13. Install sliding clutch assembly onto main shaft annulus gear while engaging sun gear in pinion gears. Ensure sliding clutch fully seats on the annulus and the sun gear is fully engaged in pinion gears.

NOTE: To aid installation, rotate main shaft while engaging sun gear.

14. Lubricate and install clutch apply pistons with new "O" rings into main case bores with piston counterbored ends facing outward.
15. Install new "O" rings on relief valve body, sleeve and valve piston plug, then install relief valve assembly as follows:
   a. Install valve body into main case bore.
   b. Align valve sleeve oil hole with oil hole in bore and insert sleeve into bore with "O" ring end facing upward until sleeve and valve body are seated.
   c. Install relief valve and spring assembly into valve body, then residual pressure spring into the assembly.

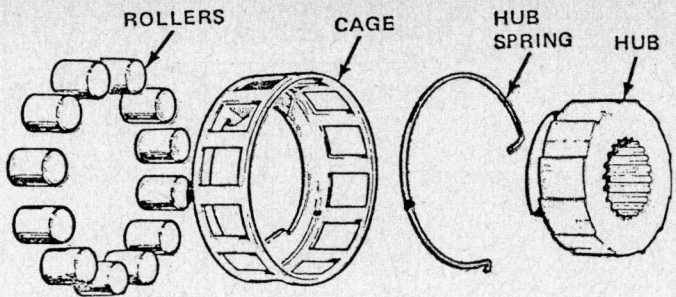

Fig. 6   Overrunning clutch assembly

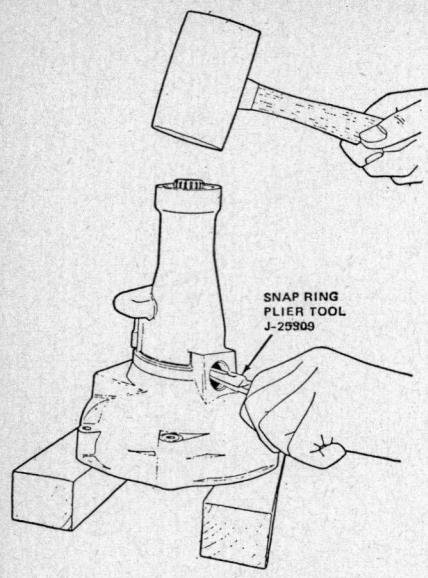

Fig. 5   Main shaft removal

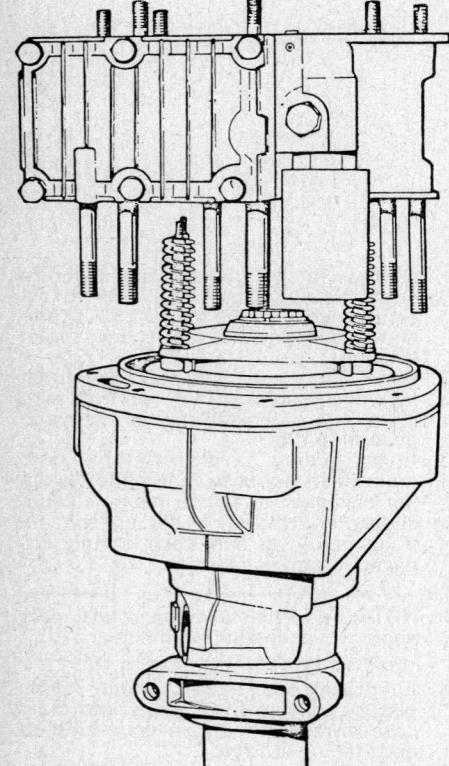

Fig. 7   Installing main case on rear case

d. Install valve piston and relief valve piston plug and torque plug to 16 ft. lbs.

16. Install pressure filter into main case bore and install torque pressure filter plug with new aluminum washer to 16 ft. lbs.

17. Install new "O" rings on pump body and plug, then lubricate and install pump plunger, pump body and non-return valve components as follows:
   a. Align flat on pump body with oil hole in main case bore and install pump body halfway into bore.
   b. Insert pump plunger into pump body, then push pump body fully into main case.
   c. Place non-return valve seat on top of pump body with check ball seat facing upward, then place check ball onto valve seat.
   d. Place non-return valve spring into pump body plug and install assembly. Torque plug to 16 ft. lbs.

18. Install main case pressure plug, gasket, oil pan filter, oil pan gasket and oil pump cover on main case. Torque oil pan bolts to 6 ft. lbs. and pressure plug to 13 ft. lbs.

19. Place rear case assembly in a soft jawed vise and install new clutch return springs on thrust bearing cover bolts.

20. Install first clutch brake ring gasket on rear case, then clutch brake ring into case with tapered surface facing rearward. Install second new clutch brake ring gasket on brake ring. Ensure gaskets and brake ring are aligned with rear case stud holes.

21. Apply a light coat of suitable sealer to main case studs, place main case over rear case, aligning studs, and lower onto rear case, Fig. 7. Align thrust bearing cover bolts as main case is being lowered.

22. Install copper gaskets on the upper main case to rear case studs, four lockwashers on remaining studs and nuts and all studs. Torque nuts to 11 ft. lbs.

23. Install clutch apply bars on thrust bearing cover bolts and torque attaching nuts to 8 ft. lbs.

24. Install solenoid valve with tool J-25304.

25. Lubricate and install oil pump drive cam and drive key on transmission output shaft and secure with snap ring.

Rear Axle, Propeller Shaft & Brakes

REAR AXLES

Fig. 1 illustrates the rear axle assembly used on these cars. When necessary to overhaul the unit, refer to the *Rear Axle Specifications* table in this chapter.

DESCRIPTION

Except Twin Grip

In these rear axles, Fig. 1, the drive pinion is mounted in two tapered roller bearings. These bearings are preloaded by a washer behind the front bearing. The pinion is positioned by shims located in front of the rear bearing. The differential is supported in the carrier by two tapered roller side bearings. These bearings are preloaded by shims located between the bearings and carrier housing. The differential assembly is positioned for proper ring gear and pinion backlash by varying the position of these shims. The differential case houses two side gears in mesh with two pinions mounted on a pinion shaft which is held in place by a lock pin. The side gears and pinions are backed by thrust washers.

It is not necessary to remove the rear axle assembly. However, the underbody should be washed to prevent particles of road dirt from contaminating the parts.

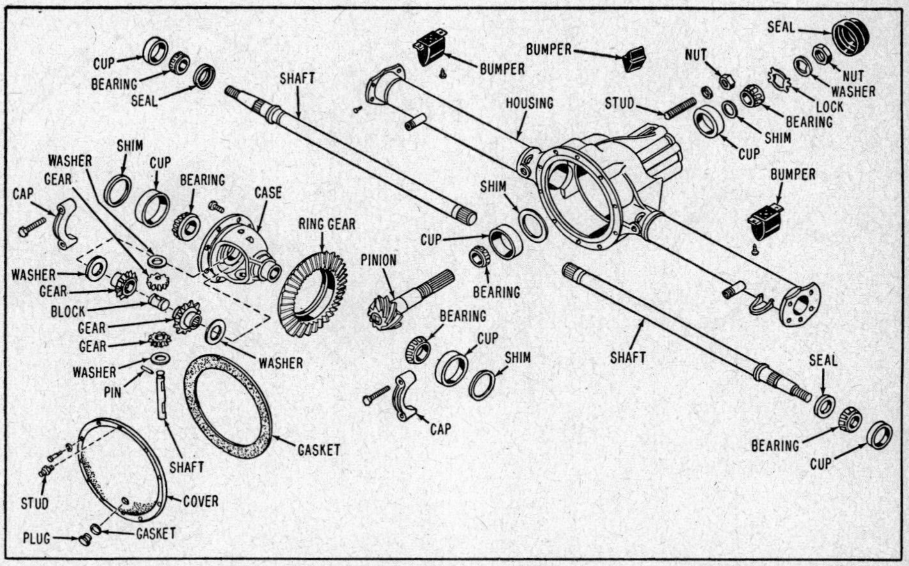

Fig. 1   Rear axle assembly, except Twin Grip. For 1969-75 V8s the pinion bearing preload is adjusted by means of a collapsible spacer instead of the shim shown

Twin Grip

Conventional type differentials divide torque equally between both wheels, causing the wheel with the least traction to slip first. Twin Grip locking type differential, Fig. 2, provides the torque of the slipping wheel to the driving wheel. Unlike the positive lock type, this unit will release before excessive driving force can be directed to one rear wheel.

Locking action on the 7⁹⁄₁₆ inch axle, is accomplished through cone brakes which are spring loaded to allow adequate driving force at the high traction wheel and at the same time not interfere with steering characteristics or differential action. Under extremely unbalanced traction conditions, wheel spin may occur if over-acceleration is attempted. This spinning produces a whirring sound caused by clutch cone overrun. This spinning condition or sound does not indicate a unit failure.

NOTE: Twin Grip differentials used on 7⁹⁄₁₆ inch axles, are serviced as an assembly only.

Locking action on 8⅞ inch axles, is accomplished through multiple disc clutch packs between the differential gears and case. The concentrically grooved clutch discs are splined to the differential gears and are engaged primarily by spring preload pressure on the clutch discs. The locking action is increased by reaction between the differential gears and pinions when torque and traction increase. When turning corners, the wheel travel differential torque will overcome clutch spring load and permit normal differential action.

REAR AXLE & PROP. SHAFT, REPLACE

1969-75 Hornet, Rambler, AMX, Javelin & Gremlin

1. Remove axle shaft nuts prior to raising the car weight from the wheels.
2. Remove the axle housing cover to drain the lubricant.
3. Raise and support the rear of the body.
4. Remove the rear wheels and rear wheel hubs and drums.
5. Disconnect rear parking brake cables at equalizer.
6. Remove the brake support plates.

NOTE: Retain the shims located between the left support plate and axle tube for use on reassembly.

7. Remove the axle shafts from the axle.
8. Mark the universal joint yoke and bearing before separating to insure same alignment at time of assembly. Disconnect the propeller shaft at the rear universal joint.
9. Disconnect the rear shocks at the axle.
10. Disconnect the brake line at the body floor pan bracket.
11. Remove the rear spring U bolts and the axle may now be removed.

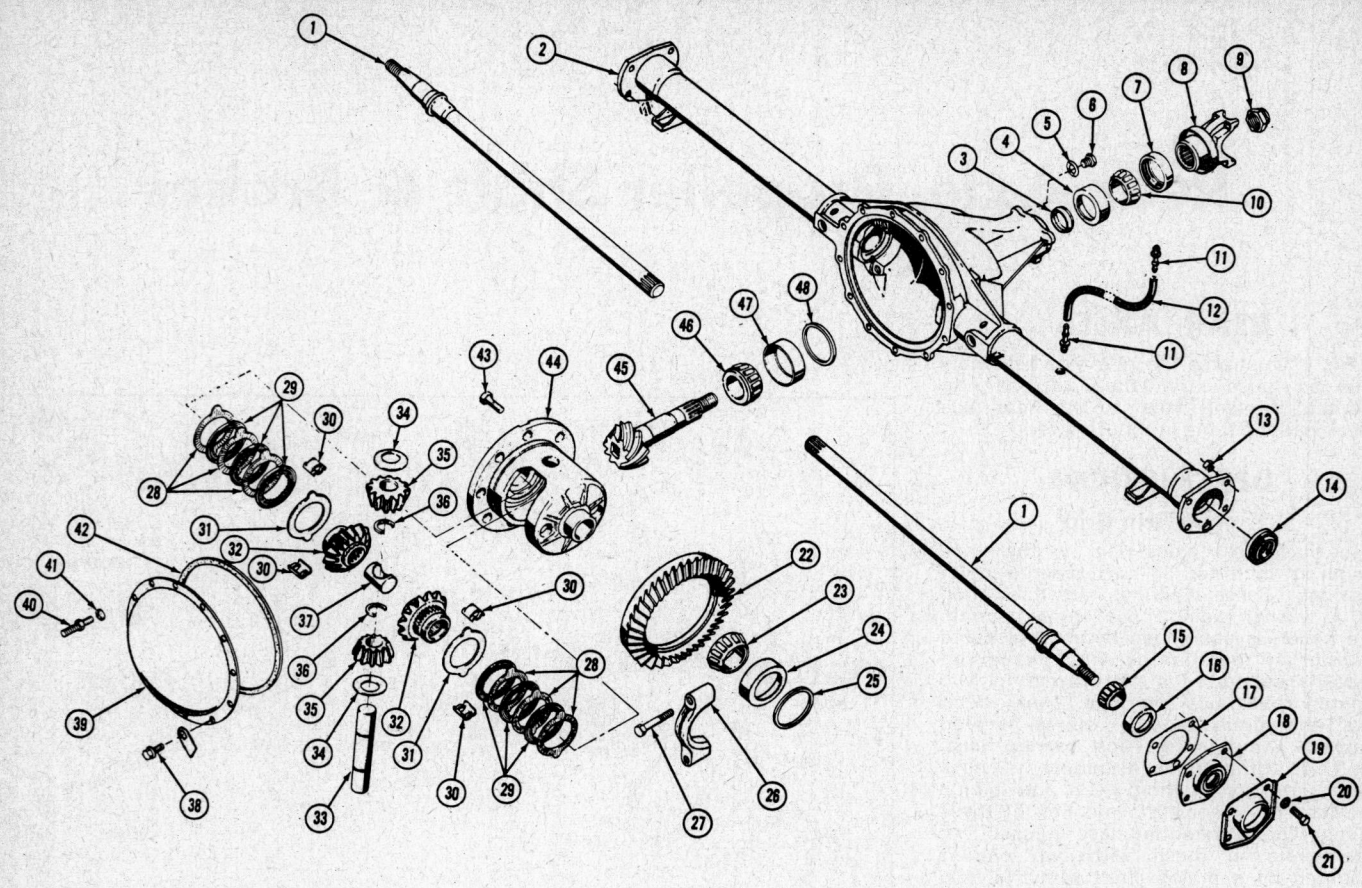

Fig. 2 Twin Grip rear axle assembly

1. AXLE SHAFT
2. REAR AXLE HOUSING
3. FRONT COLLAPSIBLE SPACER
5. FILLER PLUG GASKET
6. FILLER PLUG
7. PINION OIL SEAL
8. UNIVERSAL JOINT YOKE
9. PINION NUT
10. FRONT PINION BEARING
11. BREATHER (2)
12. BREATHER HOSE
13. NUT
14. AXLE SHAFT INNER OIL SEAL
15. AXLE SHAFT BEARING
16. AXLE SHAFT BEARING CUP
17. AXLE SHAFT BEARING SHIM

18. AXLE SHAFT OIL SEAL
19. AXLE SHAFT OIL SEAL RETAINER
20. WASHER
21. BOLT
22. DRIVE GEAR
23. DIFFERENTIAL BEARING
24. DIFFERENTIAL BEARING CUP
25. DIFFERENTIAL BEARING SHIM
26. DIFFERENTIAL BEARING CAP
27. BOLT
28. CLUTCH ASSEMBLY PLATES
29. CLUTCH ASSEMBLY DISCS
30. CLUTCH ASSEMBLY RETAINER CLIP
31. CLUTCH ASSEMBLY BELLEVILLE SPRING
32. DIFFERENTIAL GEAR
33. DIFFERENTIAL PIONION SHAFT

34. DIFFERENTIAL PINION THRUST WASHER
35. DIFFERENTIAL PINION GEAR
36. DIFFERENTIAL PINION SHAFT SNAP RING
37. DIFFERENTIAL PINION SHAFT THRUST BLOCK
38. BOLT
39. HOUSING COVER
40. STUD
41. WASHER
42. HOUSING COVER GASKET
43. BOLT
44. DIFFERENTIAL CASE
45. DRIVE PINION
46. REAR PINION BEARING
47. REAR PINION BEARING CUP
48. PINION DEPTH ADJUSTING SHIM

1969-75 Rebel, Ambassador & Matador

1. Remove axle shaft nuts prior to raising the car weight from the wheels.
2. Raise and support the rear of the car.
3. Remove the axle housing cover and drain the lubricant.
4. Mark the rear universal joint and bearing and disconnect the propeller shaft at the rear universal joint.
5. Disconnect the parking brake cable at the equalizer.

   NOTE: The left cable is routed to upper long end of equalizer. Disconnect the brake lines at the support plates.

6. Remove the wheels, hubs, drums, support plates, seals, axle shafts and bearings.
7. Support the axle assembly and disconnect the shocks at the axle tubes.
8. Lower axle assembly until it is supported by the control arms.
9. Pull one axle tube down and remove the spring. Pull the other axle tube and remove the other spring.
10. Support the axle assembly and disconnect the upper control arms at the axle housing.
11. Disconnect the lower control arms at the axle tubes and the axle may now be removed.

AXLE SHAFTS

The hub and drum are separate units, and the hub and axle shaft are serrated to mate and fit together on the taper. Both are punched marked to insure correct assembly, Fig. 3. The axle shaft and bearing may be removed as follows:

1. Remove rear wheel, drum and hub, then disconnect parking brake cable at equalizer.
2. Disconnect brake tube from wheel cylinder and remove brake support plate assembly, oil seal and axle shims from axle shaft.

   NOTE: Axle shaft end play shims are located on the left side only.

3. Using suitable puller, pull axle shaft and bearing from axle tube, then remove and discard inner oil seal.

NOTE: The bearing cone must be pressed off the shaft, using an arbor press.

When installing hub onto axle, install two well lubricated thrust washers and axle shaft nut. Tighten axle shaft nut until hub is installed to the dimensions shown in Fig. 3. Remove axle shaft nut and one thrust washer. Reinstall axle shaft nut and tighten to 250 ft. lbs. If cotter pin hole is not aligned, tighten the nut to the next castellation and install cotter pin.

NOTE

Do not use an original hub on a replacement axle shaft; use a new hub. A new hub may be installed on an original axle shaft providing the serrations on the shaft are not worn or damaged. Be certain that the hub and axle shaft are punch marked to insure proper alignment on installation. A replacement hub, which is not serrated, can be installed and serrations will be cut in the hub when installed on the shaft due to the difference in hardness of the shaft and the hub.

Assembly

Replace the parts in the reverse order of their removal. If the old parts are replaced and the shims have not been disturbed, the axle shaft end play should be correct when the parts are assembled. However, if a new shaft, bearing, differential carrier or housing has been installed, it will be necessary to check the end play.

The end play can be checked when all parts have been replaced except the wheel and hub. To make this check, rap each axle shaft after the nuts are tight to be sure the bearing cups are seated. Then place a dial indicator so that its stem contacts the end of the shaft and work the shaft in and out to determine the amount of existing end play. If an adjustment is necessary, remove the outer oil seal and brake support and add or remove shims as required. When making this adjustment, an equal thickness of shims should be removed or added on each side of the axle housing to maintain a central position of the differential thrust block.

NOTE

The application of a bead of sealing material such as "Pliobond" or "Permatex" to the outer diameter of axle tube flange and the brake support contact area is recommended. The sealing material will be used in addition to the gasket for improved sealing.

PROPELLER SHAFT VIBRATION

With the use of an electronic wheel balancer, the propeller shaft can be balanced as follows:

1. Raise and support the rear of the car at the axle and remove rear wheels.
2. Place electronic pick up unit under axle housing as close as possible to pinion yoke. Use crayon or chalk to mark four equally spaced horizontal lines on the propeller shaft. To aid in identifying lines, it is suggested they be of unequal length.
3. Operate the car in gear at the speed of greatest vibration. Locate the heavy spot.

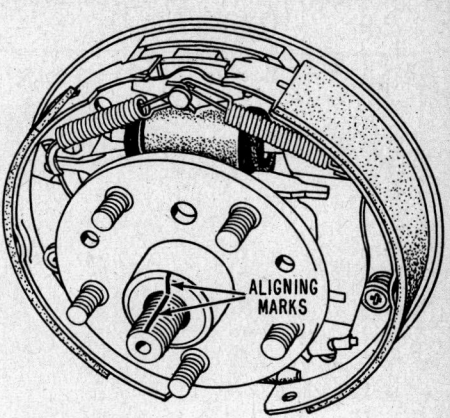

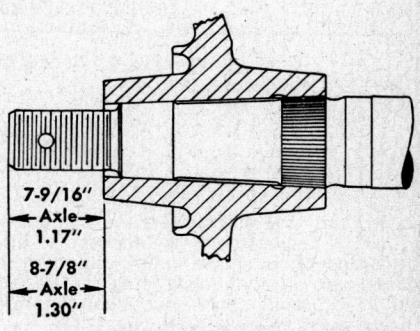

Fig. 3 Installing hub on axle shaft

NOTE: Do not operate in gear for long periods as overheating may occur.

4. Place two worm type hose clamps on propeller shaft with heads of clamps located 180° from heavy spot noted previously. Slide clamps as far to rear as possible.
5. Again operate car in gear and if vibration still exists move both clamp heads an equal distance in opposite directions toward the heavy spot until balancer indicator remains within acceptable range of scale.
6. Replace rear wheels and road test car.

BRAKE ADJUSTMENTS

1969-75 Self-Adjusting Brakes

These brakes, Figs. 4 and 5 have self-adjusting mechanisms that assure correct lining-to-drum clearances at all times. The automatic adjusters operate only when the brakes are applied as the car is moving rearward.

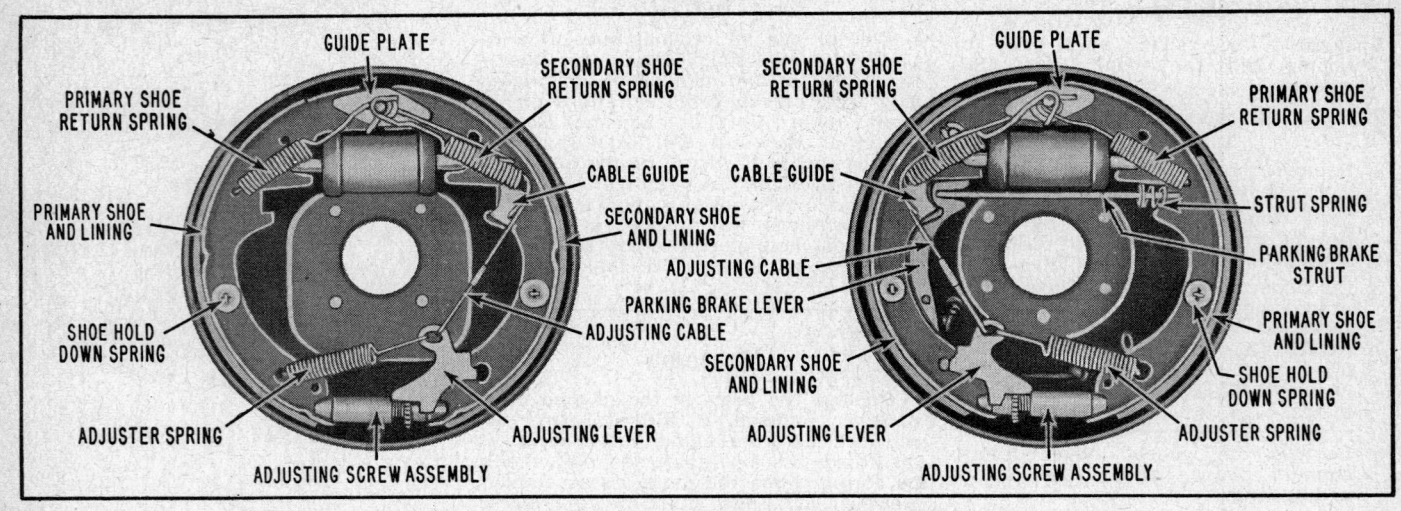

Fig. 4 Bendix Duo-Servo Brake. Left view is a left front brake. Right view is a right rear brake

Although the brakes are self-adjusting, an initial adjustment is necessary after the brake shoes have been relined or replaced, or when the length of the star wheel adjusting screw has been changed during some other service operation.

Frequent usage of an automatic transmission forward range to halt reverse vehicle motion may prevent the automatic adjusters from functioning, thereby inducing low pedal heights. Should low pedal heights be encountered on these models, it is recommended that numerous forward and reverse stops be made until satisfactory pedal height is obtained.

NOTE

If a low pedal condition cannot be corrected by making numerous stops (provided the hydraulic system is free of air) it indicates that the self-adjusting mechanism is not functioning. Therefore, it will be necessary to remove the brake drum, clean, free up and lubricate the adjusting mechanisms. Then adjust the brakes as follows, being sure the parking brake is fully released.

Adjustment

1. When the brake parts have been installed in their correct position, initially adjust the star wheel assemblies to a point where $3/16$" to $1/4$" of threads are exposed between star wheel and star wheel nut on Series 10, $3/8$" of threads exposed on American, Ambassador and Rebel models.
2. Following the initial adjustment and final assembly, check the brake pedal height to insure brake operation. Then drive the car forward and reverse, making 10 to 15 brake applications prior to road testing. This action balances the adjustment of the four brake units and raises the brake pedal.

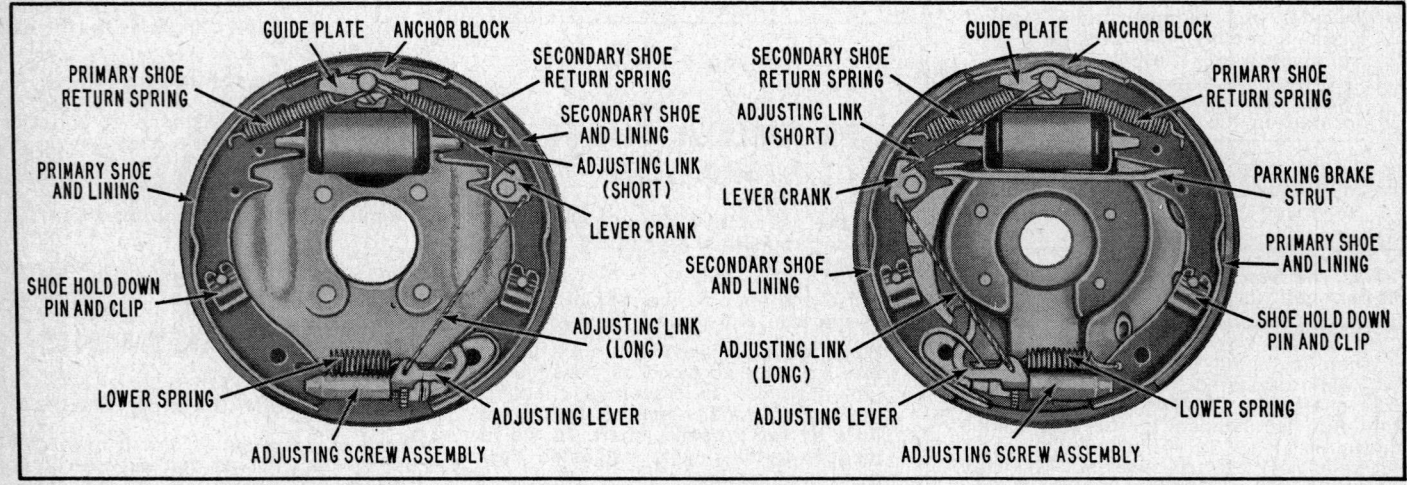

Fig. 5 Wagner Compound Shoe-Type Brake. Left view is a left front brake. Right view is a right rear brake

PARKING BRAKE, ADJUST
1969 Rambler

1. With service brakes properly adjusted, pull parking brake handle to the third notch from the released position.
2. Tighten the parking brake cable at the equalizer to a point where the rear wheels are locked from forward rotation.
3. Release brake handle and check for rear brake drag—wheels should rotate freely.

1969 Except Rambler; 1970-75 All

1. With service brakes properly adjusted, set parking brake pedal on the first notch from fully released position.
2. Tighten parking brake cable at equalizer to a point where the rear wheels are locked in forward rotation.
3. Release pedal and check for rear wheel drag—wheels should rotate freely.

BRAKE MASTER CYLINDER, REPLACE

To remove the master cylinder, disconnect the brake lines from the connections on the master cylinder. Unfasten the cylinder from its mounting and remove from the car.

Install in the reverse order of removal and bleed the brake system.

Rear Suspension

SHOCK ABSORBER, REPLACE

1. With the rear axle supported properly, disconnect lower end of shock absorber from stud on mounting bracket.
2. On models with leaf springs, upper attaching nut is accessible from trunk. On models with coil springs, remove upper mounting bracket from underbody.
3. Reverse procedure to install.

LEAF SPRINGS, REPLACE

1. Support rear axle, removing tension from springs.
2. Disconnect lower end of shock absorber from stud on mounting bracket.
3. Remove "U" bolts securing spring plate and spring to axle tube.
4. Disassemble rear shackle and remove eye bolt from spring forward mounting bracket.
5. Reverse procedure to install. Replace bushings as necessary.

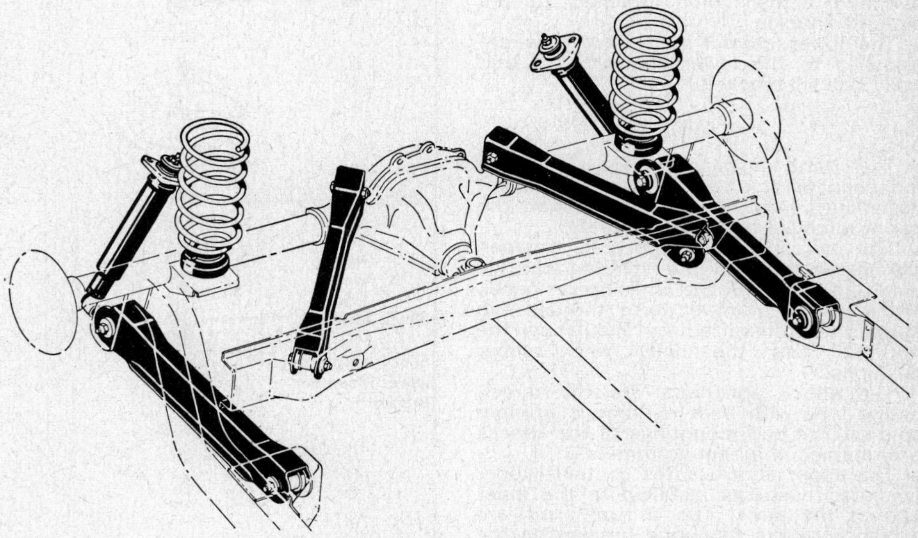

COIL SPRINGS, REPLACE

1. Support vehicle at frame and support rear axle with a suitable jack.
2. Disconnect shock absorbers from lower mountings and lower the axle as far as possible, Fig. 1.

Fig. 1   Coil spring suspension (typical)

3. Remove spring by pulling downward on axle tube.
4. Reverse procedure to install.

CONTROL ARMS & BUSHINGS, REPLACE

NOTE: Replace control arms one at a time to prevent axle assembly misalignment, making installation difficult.

Upper Control Arms

1. Support vehicle at frame.
2. Remove control arm bolts from frame crossmember and axle tube bracket.
3. To replace axle tube bracket bushings, refer to Figs. 2 & 3.
4. Reverse procedure to install.

Lower Control Arms

1. Remove control arm mount bolts from frame and axle tube brackets.

2. Reverse procedure to install.

NOTE: Lower control arm bushings are not serviceable.

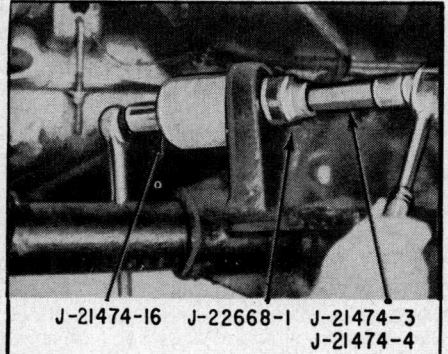

J-21474-16   J-22668-1   J-21474-3
J-21474-4

Fig. 2   Upper control arm rear bushing removal

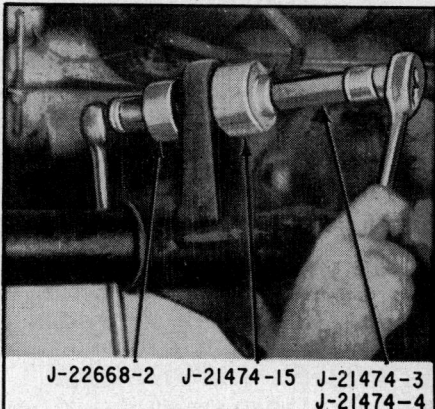

J-22668-2   J-21474-15   J-21474-3
J-21474-4

Fig. 3   Upper control arm rear bushing installation

American Motors

Front End and Steering Section

1970-75

The front suspension, Fig. 1, is an independent linked type, with the coil springs located between seats in the wheel house panels and seats attached to the upper control arms.

Direct acting telescoping shock absorbers are located inside the coil springs.

Each upper control arm assembly has two rubber bushings attached to the wheel house panel and a ball joint attached to the steering knuckle.

Each lower control arm has a rubber bushing attached to the front crossmember and a ball joint attached to the steering knuckle.

The lower control arm strut rods are attached to the lower control arms and body side sill brackets.

1969

The front suspension, Fig. 2, is an independent link type. The right and left assemblies may be disassembled on the car or removed for bench overhaul.

The coil springs are located between the upper seats of the steering knuckle pins and a seat in the wheelhouse panel. Transmission of road noise through the springs is minimized by insulating the springs from the body with rubber cushions.

The shock absorbers are the direct-acting type with built-in rebound bumper control. The end mountings of the shocks are retained in rubber grommets.

The upper control arms contain rubber insulated bushings installed in the inner end of the arms. The control arms are attached to the mounting bracket on the wheelhouse panel and the trunnion at the outer end.

The lower control arms are attached to a removable crossmember at the pivot ends. The outer ends are attached to the steering knuckle pin with a ball joint stud.

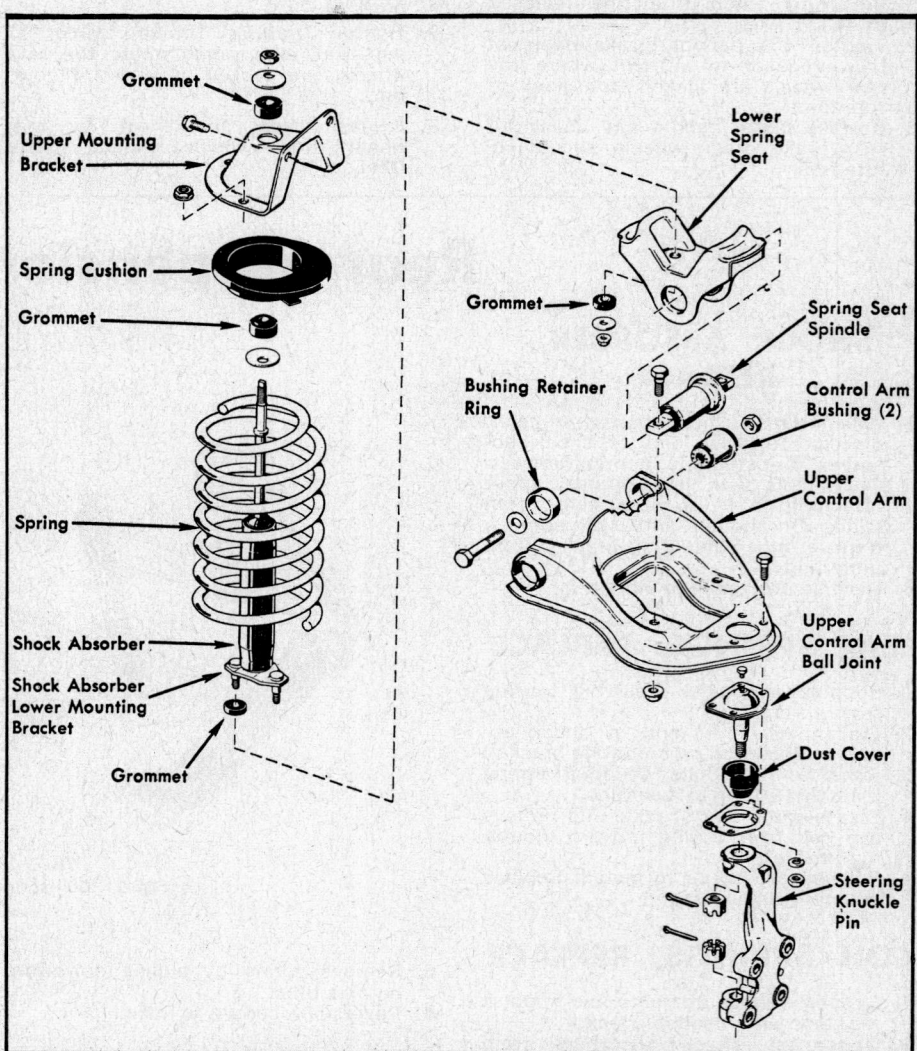

Fig. 1   1970-75 front suspension. Lower control arm (not shown) is the same as used on previous models

LUBRICATION

All 1969-75 models are equipped with plugs which must be removed and hand-operated grease gun used with special grease to lubricate the suspension at 24,000-mile intervals or two years, whichever occurs first under normal driving conditions.

Under severe driving conditions, such as dusty or extreme wet conditions, earlier lubrication is recommended. Under these conditions the suspension system should be inspected every 12,000 miles or one year whichever occurs first, and lubricated as required.

WHEEL ALIGNMENT
1969-74 All

Caster is obtained by moving the two adjusting nuts on the threaded strut rod, Fig. 2. One nut is on each side of the

mounting bracket. Therefore, moving the nuts on the rod will move the lower control arm to front or rear for desired caster angle. After adjustment, torque nuts to 85 ft. lbs. on all 1969-73 models. On 1974-75 models, torque adjusting nuts to 65 ft. lbs. and locknut to 55 ft. lbs.

Camber is obtained by turning on the eccentric lower control arm bolt, Fig. 3. After adjustment, torque lock nut to 95 ft-lbs.

TOE-IN, ADJUST

To adjust toe-in, loosen the clamps at both ends of the adjustable tubes on each tie rod. Turn the tubes an equal amount until the toe-in is correct. Turning the right tube in the direction the wheels re-

volve when the car is going forward increases the toe-in and turning the left tube in the opposite direction increases toe-in. To decrease toe-in turn the right tube backward and the left tube forward. It is important that both tubes be turned an equal amount in order to maintain the correct position of the steering wheel. When adjustment is complete, tighten all clamp bolts.

NOTE: In performing service operations on the steering linkage or when adjusting toe-in, be sure to square the tie rod ball sockets on the studs and align the tie rod stud in the center, or slightly above center, of the cross tube opening, before tightening the steering linkage adjusting

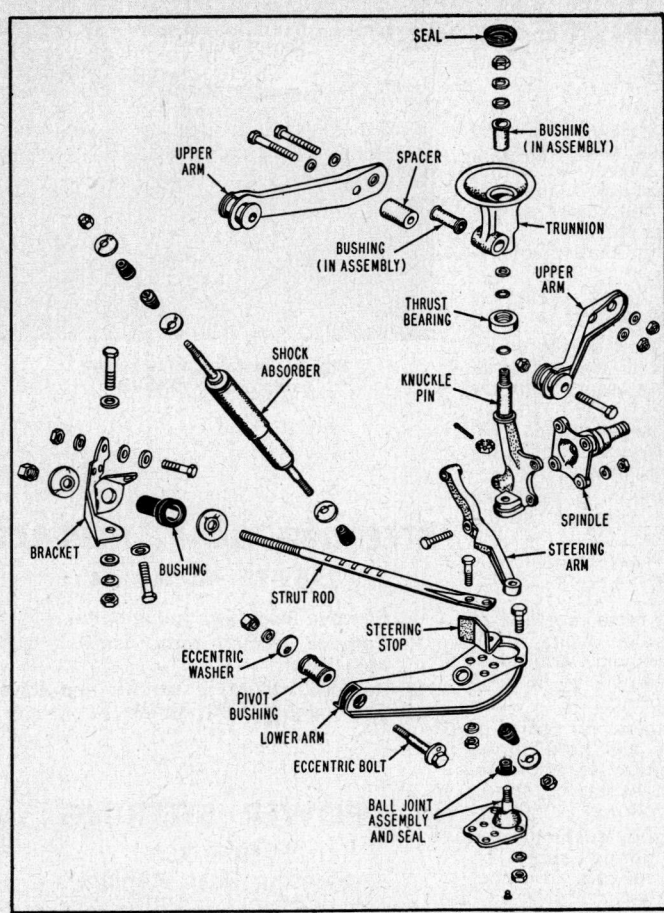

Fig. 2 Front suspension. 1969 (typical)

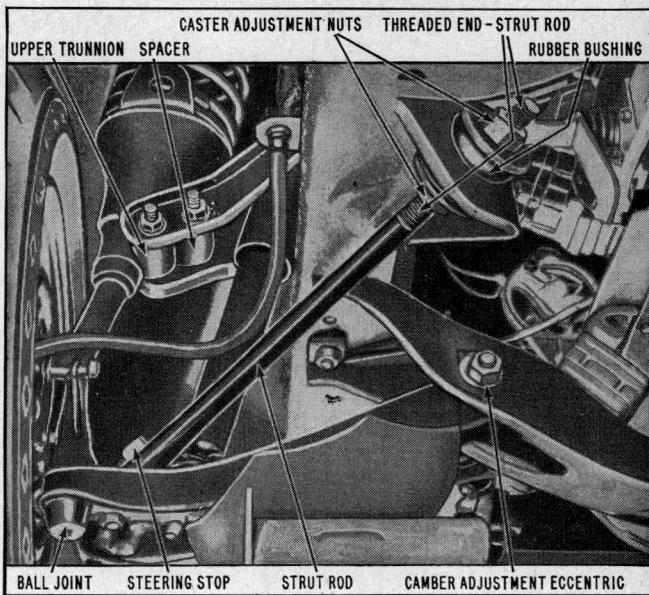

Fig. 3 Front suspension (rear view) showing caster and camber adjustments. 1969-74 All (typical)

tube. This will prevent the stud from contacting the side of the cross tube opening, which would otherwise result in noise problems or damage.

WHEEL BEARINGS, ADJUST

1969-75

1. To adjust bearings, tighten spindle nut to 22 ft-lbs torque while rotating the wheel to seat bearings.
2. Then loosen spindle nut 1/3 turn and with wheel rotating, retorque spindle nut to 12 inch pound on 1969-72 and 2-10 inch pound on 1973-75.
3. Place the nut retainer on spindle nut with the slots of the retainer aligned with the cotter pin hole on the spindle.
4. Install cotter pin and dust cap.

WHEEL BEARINGS, REPLACE

(Disc Brakes)

1. Remove two thirds of the total fluid capacity of the master cylinder res-

ervoir to prevent fluid overflow when the caliper pistons are pushed back on their bores.
2. Raise car and remove front wheels.
3. Disconnect hydraulic tube from mounting bracket. Do not disconnect any hydraulic fitting.
4. Holding the lower edge of the caliper, remove the lower bolt. Any shims that fall out at this point should be labeled to insure that they be replaced in their original position.
5. Holding the upper edge of the caliper, remove the upper bolt, tag these shims.
6. Hang caliper from upper suspension to prevent strain being placed on brake hose.
7. Remove spindle nut and hub and disc assembly. Grease retainer and inner bearing can now be removed.

CHECKING BALL JOINTS FOR WEAR

1969-75

Before checking ball joints for wear, make sure the front wheel bearings are properly adjusted and that the control arms are tight.

Referring to Fig. 4, raise wheel with a jack placed under the frame as shown. Then test by moving the wheel up and down to check axial play, and rocking it at the top and bottom to measure radial play.

The upper ball joint should be replaced if total travel when rocking wheel and tire exceeds .160".

The lower ball joint is spring loaded and should be replaced if there is any noticeable lateral shake.

BALL JOINTS, REPLACE

NOTE: Upper and lower ball joint can be replaced using the following procedure.

1. Drill out the rivets that attach ball joint to control arm.
2. Remove two strut rod mounting bolts.
3. Remove steering knuckle arm and stud nut and remove ball joint from knuckle pin with a suitable ball joint remover.
4. When installing new ball joints, note that two bolts, lockwashers and nuts are furnished to replace rivets that were removed.

SHOCK ABSORBER, REPLACE

1970-75

After disconnecting shock absorber from wheelhouse panel at top and lower spring seat at the bottom, withdraw shock absorber out of top of wheelhouse.

Fig. 4   Checking ball joints for wear. 1969-74

1969

After disconnecting the shock from the wheelhouse panel at the top and from the lower control arm at the bottom, collapse the unit, work to one side and remove from out of the lower control arm.

Reverse the foregoing procedure to install.

SPRING, REPLACE
1970-75

1. Remove shock absorber.
2. Install spring compressor (J-23474) through upper spring seat opening, Fig. 5. Place tool lower attaching screws through shock absorber mounting holes in the lower spring seat. Install tool lower retainer.
3. Remove lower spring seat pivot retaining nuts.
4. Tighten compressor until spring is compressed approximately 1".
5. Raise and support front of car under frame allowing control arms to fall free of lower spring seat. Remove wheel.
6. Pull lower spring seat away from car. Loosen compressor and allow lower spring seat to come out.
7. When all spring tension is released, remove tool lower retainer spring seat and spring.

1969

1. To remove a spring, raise rear end of car opposite from side from which spring is to be removed. Additional pressure may be gained by leaning on fender over the spring.
2. Install hooks in holes on ears of spring seats. Hooks will hold spring in compressed position to allow removal from vehicle. A service spring may be installed as follows:
3. Install upper and lower cushions and upper and lower spring seats on spring. Align holes in ears of upper and lower spring seats.
4. Compress spring by suitable means (arbor press or hydraulic jack) and install hook on spring seats. Spring can then be installed on spring support.

CAUTION: Lip of lower spring seat must engage seat support to prevent spring from shifting during operation.

5. Hooks are released from spring seat by raising opposite near end of vehicle.

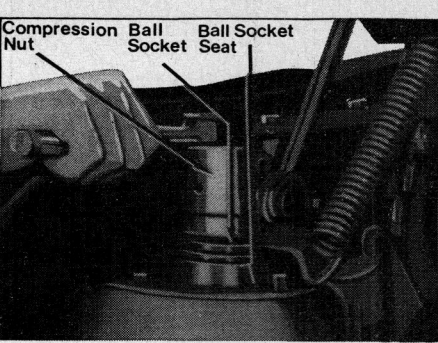

Fig. 5   Installation of spring compressor. 1970-75

STEERING GEAR, REPLACE
1969-75 All Models

1. Remove flexible coupling bolts.
2. Remove pitman arm, using a suitable puller.
3. Remove mounting screws and lower steering gear from vehicle.

POWER STEERING
1969-75
Steering Gear, Replace

1. Disconnect pressure and return hoses from gear. Raise hoses above pump level to keep oil from draining out of pump.
2. Remove flexible coupling bolt nuts, noting the different nut sizes to insure correct assembly.
3. Remove pitman arm with a suitable puller.
4. Remove gear attaching bolts.
5. Slide lower shaft free of coupling flange, then remove gear.
6. Reverse procedure to install.

BUICK
All Intermediate & Full Size Models

OLD CAR SPECIFICATIONS: For 1946-68 Tune Up and Wheel Alignment Specifications see main index.

INDEX OF SERVICE OPERATIONS

PAGE NO.

ACCESSORIES

Air Conditioning 2-20
Air Cushion Restraint System 2-367
Automatic Level Controls 2-39
Blower Motor, Replace 1-72
Clock Troubles 2-11
Heater Core, Replace 1-69
Power Top Troubles 2-18
Power Window Troubles 2-18
Radio, Replace 1-69
Speed Controls, Adjust 1-72

BRAKES

Anti-Skid Brakes 2-162
Brake Troubles, Mechanical 2-17
Disc Brake Service 2-133
Hydraulic System Service 2-123
Master Cylinder, Replace 1-83
Parking Brake, Adjust 1-83
Power Brake Unit, Replace 1-83
Service Brakes, Adjust 1-82

CLUTCH

Clutch Pedal, Adjust 1-78
Clutch, Replace 1-79
Clutch Troubles 2-12

COOLING SYSTEM

Belt Tension Data 1-78
Cooling System Troubles 2-6
Variable Speed Fans 2-38
Water Pump, Replace 1-78

ELECTRICAL

Alternator Service 2-69
Back-up Light Switch, Replace 1-63
Blower Motor, Replace 1-72
Clutch Start Switch 1-63
Dash Gauge Service 2-50
Distributor, Replace 1-62
Distributor Service:
   Standard .2-525
   Transistorized 2-535
Electrical Troubles 2-8
Headlamps, Concealed Type 2-46
Headlight Aiming 2-45
High Energy Ignition Systems 1-62
Horn Sounder, Remove 1-64
Ignition Coils and Resistors 2-521
Ignition Lock, Replace 1-62
Ignition Switch, Replace 1-62
Ignition Timing 2-518
Instrument Cluster Removal 1-64
Light Switch Replace 1-62
Neutral Start Switch, Replace 1-63
Radio, Replace 1-69
Seat Belt Interlock System 2-311
Starter Service 2-54
Starter, Replace 1-62
Starter Switch Service 2-67
Stop Light Switch, Replace 1-63
Turn Signal Switch, Replace 1-63

PAGE NO.

Turn Signal Troubles 2-11
Windshield Wiper Motor, Replace 1-68
Windshield Wiper Troubles 2-19

ENGINE

Camshaft, Replace 1-76
Crankshaft Rear Oil Seal 1-77
Cylinder Head, Replace 1-73
Engine Identification 1-50
Engine Mounts, Replace 1-73
Engine, Replace 1-73
Engine Troubles 2-1
Main Bearings 1-77
Oil Pan, Replace 1-77
Piston Pins 1-76
Piston Rings 1-76
Piston and Rod, Assemble 1-76
Pistons 1-76
Rocker Arm Service 1-73
Rod Bearings 1-77
Timing Case Cover, Replace 1-75
Timing Chain, Replace 1-76
Valve Arrangement 1-74
Valve Guides 1-74
Valve Lifters 1-75

ENGINE LUBRICATION

Emission Control Systems 2-545
Oil Pump 1-77

FUEL SYSTEM

Carburetor Adjustments and Specs 2-372
Emission Control Systems 2-545
Fuel Pump, Replace 1-78
Fuel Pump Service 2-369
Fuel System Troubles 2-2
Fuel Pump Pressure 1-78

PROPELLER SHAFT & U JOINTS

Propeller Shaft 1-81
Universal Joint Service 2-117

REAR AXLE & SUSPENSION

Axle Shaft, Bearing and Seal 1-81
Control Arms, Replace 1-84
Coil Springs, Replace 1-84
Leaf Springs, Replace 1-83
Rear Axle, Replace 1-80
Rear Axle Description 1-79
Rear Axle Specifications 1-56
Rear Axle Troubles 2-16
Shock Absorber, Replace 1-83
Stabilizer Bar, Replace 1-85
Track Bar & Bushing, Replace 1-84

SPECIFICATIONS

Alternator 1-57
Belt Tension 1-78
Brakes 1-59
Capacities 1-60

PAGE NO.

Carburetors 2-372
Cooling System 1-60
Crankshaft and Bearings 1-56
Distributors 1-55
Engine Tightening Torque 1-57
Fuel Pump Pressure 1-78
General Engine Specs. 1-50
Ignition Coils and Resistors 2-521
Pistons, Rings and Pins 1-56
Rear Axle 1-56
Starting Motor 1-54
Tune Up 1-52
Valves 1-54
Valve Lift 1-74
Valve Timing 1-74
Wheel Alignment 1-59

STEERING GEAR

Horn Sounder Removal 1-64
Ignition Lock, Replace 1-62
Manual Gear, Replace 1-88
Manual Gear Service 2-170
Manual Gear Troubles 2-17
Power Gear, Replace 1-88
Steering Wheel, Replace 1-64

SUSPENSION, FRONT

Ball Joints, Replace 1-87
Ball Joints, Check for Wear 1-87
Coil Spring, Replace 1-88
Shock Absorber, Replace 1-88
Suspension, Description of 1-86
Toe-In, Adjust 1-87
Wheel Alignment, Adjust 1-87
Wheel Bearings, Adjust 1-87
Wheel Bearings, Replace 1-87

TRANSMISSIONS

Three Speed Manual:
   Replace 1-79
   Repairs .2-177
   Linkage, Adjust 1-79
Four Speed Manual:
   Replace 1-79
   Repairs .2-199
   Linkage, Adjust 1-79
Automatic Units 2-231
   Linkage, 1975 1-79

TUNE UP

Service 2-517
Specifications 1-52

WINDSHIELD WIPER

Wiper Arms, Replace 1-67
Wiper Blades, Replace 1-67
Wiper Linkage, Replace 1-68
Wiper Motor, Replace 1-68
Wiper Switch, Replace 1-68
Wiper Troubles 2-19

GRILLE IDENTIFICATION

1969 Sportwagon, Special

1969 Skylark

1969 Gran Sport

1969 LeSabre

1969 Wildcat

1969 Electra

1969 Riviera

1970 Skylark, Sportwagon

1970 Gran Sport

1970 LeSabre

1970 Estate Wagon

1970 Wildcat

1970 Electra

1970 Riviera

1971 Skylark

1971 Gran Sport 400

1971 Gran Sport Stage 1

1971 LeSabre

1971 Centurion

1971 Electra

1971 Riviera

1972 Skylark

1972 Skylark Custom

1972 Gran Sport

GRILLE IDENTIFICATION—Continued

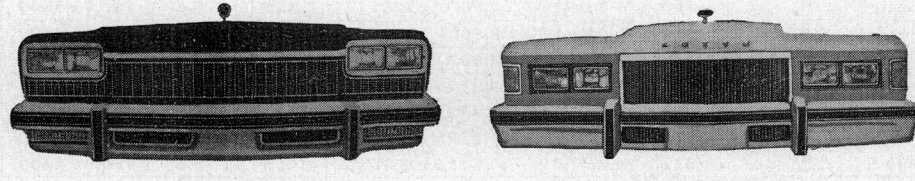

1972 LeSabre    1972 Centurion    1972 Electra

1972 Riviera    1973 Apollo    1973 Century

1973 Regal    1973 LeSabre & Centurion    1973 Electra

1973 Riviera    1974 Apollo    1974 Century

1974 Regal    1974 LeSabre    1974 Electra & Estate Wagon

1974 Riviera    1975 Apollo    1975 Skylark

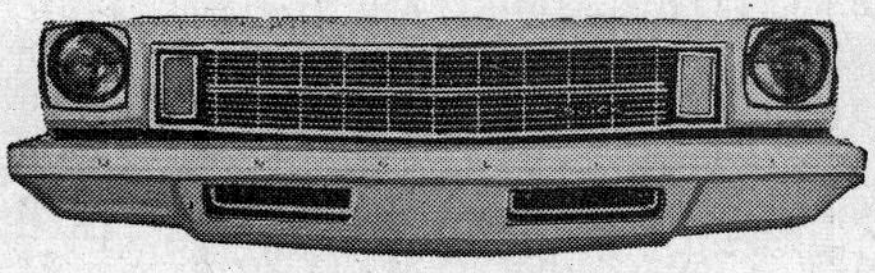

1975 Century    1975 Regal    1975 LeSabre

1975 Electra   1975 Riveria

ENGINE IDENTIFICATION

Buick engines are stamped with two different sets of numbers. One is the engine production code which identifies the engine and its approximate production date. The other is the engine serial number which is the same number that is found on the vehicle identification plate. To identify an engine, look for the production code prefix letters, then refer to the following table for its identification.

On Six 250 code is stamped on cylinder block next to distributor.

On 1969-74 V8 350, 400, 430, 455 on left bank cylinder head.

On 1975 models the fifth digit in the VIN denotes the engine used.

Engine	Code Prefix
1969 6-250	....
V8-350 2 Bar. Carb.	..........RO
V8-350 4 Bar. Carb.	..........RP

Engine	Code Prefix
V8-400	....................RR
V8-430	....................RD
1970 6-250	....
V8-350 2 Bar. Carb.	..........SO
V8-350 4 Bar. Carb.	........SB, P
V8-455	..............SF, R, S
1971 6-250	....
V8-350 2 Bar. Carb.	..........TC, TO
V8-350 4 Bar. Carb.	........TB, TP
V8-455	..............TA, R, S
1972 V8-350 2 Bar. Carb.	..........WC
V8-350 4 Bar. Carb.	..........WB
V8-455	....................WF
V8-455 (Stage I)	..........WS
V8-455 (Riviera G.S.)	..........WA

Engine	Code Prefix
1973 6-250	....
V8-350 2 Bar. Carb.	XC
V8-350 4 Bar. Carb.	..........XB
V8-455	....................XF
V8-455 (Stage 1)	..........XS
V8-455 (Riviera G.S.)	..........XA
1974 6-250 Auto. Trans.	....CCW, CCX
6-250 Manual Trans.	........CCR
V8-350 2 Bar. Carb.	....ZC, ZP
V8-350 4 Bar. Carb.	......ZB, ZM
V8-455 2 Bar. Carb.	..........ZI
V8-455 4 Bar. Carb.	......ZF, ZK
V8-455 (Stage 1)	..........ZA, ZS
1975 V6-231	C
6-250	....................D
V8-260	....................F
V8-350 2 Bar. Carb.	..........H
V8-350 4 Bar. Carb.	..........J
V8-400	....................S
V8-455	....................T

GENERAL ENGINE SPECIFICATIONS

Year	Engine	Carburetor	Bore and Stroke	Piston Displacement, Cubic Inches	Compression Ratio	Maximum Brake H.P. @ R.P.M.	Maximum Torque Lbs. Ft. @ R.P.M.	Normal Oil Pressure Pounds
1969	155 Horsepower..............①6-250	1 Barrel	3.875 x 3.53	250	8.5	155 @ 4200	235 @ 1600	30-45
	230 Horsepower..............V8-350	2 Barrel	3.800 x 3.85	350	9.0	230 @ 4400	350 @ 2400	37
	280 Horsepower..............V8-350	4 Barrel	3.800 x 3.85	350	10.25	280 @ 4600	375 @ 3200	37
	340 Horsepower..............V8-400	4 Barrel	4.040 x 3.90	400	10.25	340 @ 5000	440 @ 3200	40
	360 Horsepower..............V8-430	4 Barrel	4.1875 x 3.90	430	10.25	360 @ 5000	475 @ 3200	40
1970	155 Horsepower..............①6-250	1 Barrel	3.875 x 3.53	250	8.5	155 @ 4200	235 @ 1600	30-45
	260 Horsepower..............V8-350	2 Barrel	3.800 x 3.85	350	9.0	260 @ 4600	360 @ 2600	37
	285 Horsepower..............V8-350	4 Barrel	3.800 x 3.85	350	9.0	285 @ 4600	375 @ 3000	37
	315 Horsepower..............V8-350	4 Barrel	3.800 x 3.85	350	10.25	315 @ 4800	410 @ 3200	37
	350 Horsepower..............V8-455	4 Barrel	4.3125 x 3.90	455	10.00	350 @ 4600	510 @ 2800	40
	360 Horsepower..............V8-455	4 Barrel	4.3125 x 3.90	455	10.00	360 @ 4600	510 @ 2800	40
	370 Horsepower..............V8-455	4 Barrel	4.3125 x 3.90	455	10.00	370 @ 4600	510 @ 2800	40
1971	145 Horsepower..............①6-250	1 Barrel	3.875 x 3.53	250	8.5	145 @ 4000	235 @ 2400	30-45
	230 Horsepower..............V8-350	2 Barrel	3.800 x 3.85	350	8.5	230 @ 4400	350 @ 2400	37
	260 Horsepower..............V8-350	4 Barrel	3.800 x 3.85	350	8.5	260 @ 4600	360 @ 3000	37
	315 Horsepower..............V8-455	4 Barrel	4.3125 x 3.90	455	8.5	315 @ 4400	450 @ 2800	40
	330 Horsepower..............V8-455	4 Barrel	4.3125 x 3.90	455	8.5	330 @ 4600	455 @ 2800	40
	345 Horsepower..............V8-455	4 Barrel	4.3125 x 3.90	455	8.5	345 @ 5000	460 @ 3000	40
1972	150 Horsepower②..............V8-350	2 Barrel	3.800 x 3.85	350	8.5	150 @ 3800	265 @ 2400	37
	155 Horsepower②..............V8-350	2 Barrel	3.800 x 3.85	350	8.5	155 @ 3800	270 @ 2400	37
	175 Horsepower②..............V8-350	4 Barrel	3.800 x 3.85	350	8.5	175 @ 3800	270 @ 2400	37
	180 Horsepower②..............V8-350	4 Barrel	3.800 x 3.85	350	8.5	180 @ 3800	275 @ 2400	37
	190 Horsepower②..............V8-350	4 Barrel	3.800 x 3.85	350	8.5	190 @ 4000	285 @ 2800	37
	195 Horsepower②..............V8-350	4 Barrel	3.800 x 3.85	350	8.5	195 @ 4000	290 @ 2800	37
1972	225 Horsepower②..............V8-455	4 Barrel	4.3125 x 3.90	455	8.5	225 @ 4000	360 @ 2600	40
	250 Horsepower②..............V8-455	4 Barrel	4.3125 x 3.90	455	8.5	250 @ 4000	375 @ 2800	40
	260 Horsepower②..............V8-455	4 Barrel	4.3125 x 3.90	455	8.5	260 @ 4400	380 @ 2800	40
	270 Horsepower②..............V8-455	4 Barrel	4.3125 x 3.90	455	8.5	270 @ 4400	390 @ 3000	40

Continued

GENERAL ENGINE SPECIFICATIONS—Continued

Year	Engine	Carburetor	Bore and Stroke	Piston Displacement, Cubic Inches	Compression Ratio	Maximum Brake H.P. @ R.P.M.	Maximum Torque Lbs. Ft. @ R.P.M.	Normal Oil Pressure Pounds
1973	100 Horsepower②............6-250①	1 Barrel	3.875 x 3.53	250	8.25	100 @ 3600	175 @ 1600	40
	150 Horsepower②............V8-350	2 Barrel	3.800 x 3.85	350	8.5	150 @ 3800	265 @ 2400	37
	175 Horsepower②............V8-350	4 Barrel	3.800 x 3.85	350	8.5	175 @ 3800	270 @ 2400	37
	190 Horsepower②............V8-350	4 Barrel	3.800 x 3.85	350	8.5	190 @ 4000	285 @ 2800	37
	225 Horsepower②............V8-455	4 Barrel	4.3125 x 3.90	455	8.5	225 @ 4000	360 @ 2600	40
	250 Horsepower②............V8-455	4 Barrel	4.3125 x 3.90	455	8.5	250 @ 4000	375 @ 2800	40
	260 Horsepower②............V8-455	4 Barrel	4.3125 x 3.90	455	8.5	260 @ 4400	380 @ 2800	40
	270 Horsepower②............V8-455	4 Barrel	4.3125 x 3.90	455	8.5	270 @ 4400	390 @ 3000	40
1974	100 Horsepower②............6-250①	1 Barrel	3.875 x 3.53	250	8.25	100 @ 3600	175 @ 1600	40
	150 Horsepower②............V8-350	2 Barrel	3.800 x 3.85	350	8.5	150 @ 3600	270 @ 2000	37
	165 Horsepower②..........V8-350③	2 Barrel	3.800 x 3.85	350	8.5	165 @ 3800	285 @ 2000	37
	175 Horsepower②............V8-350	4 Barrel	3.800 x 3.85	350	8.5	175 @ 3800	260 @ 2000	37
	195 Horsepower②..........V8-350③	4 Barrel	3.800 x 3.85	350	8.5	195 @ 4000	280 @ 2000	37
	175 Horsepower②............V8-455	2 Barrel	4.3125 x 3.90	455	8.5	175 @ 3400	355 @ 2000	40
	190 Horsepower②..........V8-455③	2 Barrel	4.3125 x 3.90	455	8.5	190 @ 3600	370 @ 2000	40
	210 Horsepower②............V8-455	4 Barrel	4.3125 x 3.90	455	8.5	210 @ 3600	335 @ 2200	40
	230 Horsepower②..........V8-455③	4 Barrel	4.3125 x 3.90	455	8.5	230 @ 3800	355 @ 2200	40
	245 Horsepower②..........V8-455④	4 Barrel	4.3125 x 3.90	455	8.5	245 @ 4000	360 @ 2400	40
	255 Horsepower②..........V8-455④	4 Barrel	4.3125 x 3.90	455	8.5	255 @ 4400	370 @ 2800	40
1975	Horsepower②............6-250①	1 Barrel	3.875 x 3.53	250	8.0			36—41
	110 Horsepower②............V6-231	2 Barrel	3.80 x 3.40	231	8.0	110 @ 4000	175 @ 2000	37
	Horsepower②..........V8-260⑤	2 Barrel	3.80 x 3.385	260	8.5			
	145 Horsepower②............V8-350	2 Barrel	3.80 x 3.85	350	8.0	145 @ 3200	270 @ 2000	37
	165 Horsepower②............V8-350	4 Barrel	3.80 x 3.85	350	8.0	165 @ 3800	260 @ 2200	37
	Horsepower②..........V8-400⑥	2 Barrel	4.12 x 3.75	400	7.6			55—60
	Horsepower②..........V8-400⑥	4 Barrel	4.12 x 3.75	400	7.6			55—60
	205 Horsepower②............V8-455	4 Barrel	4.3125 x 3.90	455	7.9	205 @ 3800	345 @ 2000	40

①—See Chevrolet chapter for service procedures on this engine.
②—Net Rating—As installed in vehicle.
③—Dual exhaust.
④—Stage 1.
⑤—See Oldsmobile chapter for service procedures on this engine.
⑥—See Pontiac chapter for service procedure on this engine.

TUNE UP SPECIFICATIONS

OLD CAR SPECIFICATIONS: For 1946–68 Tune Up Specifications see main index.

★When using a timing light, disconnect vacuum hose or tube at distributor and plug opening in tube or hose so idle speed will not be affected.

●When checking compression, lowest cylinder must be within 80 percent of highest.

▲Before removing wires from distributor cap, determine location of the No. 1 wire in cap, as distributor position may have been altered from that shown at the end of this chart.

| Year | Spark Plug | | Distributor | | Ignition Timing★ | | | Carb. Adjustments | | | | | |
| | Type | Gap Inch | Point Gap Inch | Dwell Angle Deg. | Firing Order Fig. ▲ | Timing BTDC ① | Mark Fig. | Hot Idle Speed | | Air Fuel Ratio | | Idle CO % | |
								Std. Trans.	Auto. Trans. ②	Std. Trans.	Auto. Trans.	Std. Trans.	Auto. Trans.
1969													
6-250⑧ Std. Tr.	R46N	.035	.019	32	A	TDC	C	700	—	—	—	—	—
6-250⑧ Auto. Tr.	R46N	.035	.019	32	A	4°	C	—	500D④	—	—	—	—
V8-350	R45TS	.030	.016	30	B	TDC⑨	E	700	600D	—	—	—	—
V8-400 Std. Tr.	R44TS	.030	.016	30	B	2½° ATDC	E	700	—	—	—	—	—
V8-400 Auto. Tr.	R44TS	.030	.016	30	B	TDC	E	—	600D	—	—	—	—
V8-400 G.S. Stage 1	R44TS	.030	.016	30	B	10°	E	700	600D	—	—	—	—
V8-430	R44TS	.030	.016	30	B	TDC	E	—	550D	—	—	—	—
1970													
6-250⑧	R46N	.035	.019	32	A	⑥	C	700	550D	—	—	—	—
V8-350	R45TS	.030	.016	30	B	6°	F	700	600D	—	—	—	—
V8-455	R44TS	.030	.016	30	B	6°⑩	F	700	600D	—	—	—	—
1971													
6-250⑧	R46TS	.035	.019	32	A	4°	D	550	500D	—	—	—	—
V8-350 Std. Tr.	R45TS	.030	.016	30	B	6°	F	800	—	—	—	—	—
V8-350 Auto. Tr.	R45TS	.030	.016	30	B	⑪	F	—	600D	—	—	—	—
V8-455 Std. Tr.	R44TS	.030	.016	30	B	6°	F	700	—	—	—	—	—
V8-455 Auto. Tr.	R44TS	.030	.016	30	B	4°	F	—	600D	—	—	—	—
V8-455 Stage 1	R44TS	.030	.016	30	B	10°	F	700	600D	—	—	—	—
1972													
V8-350	R45TS	.040	.016	30	B	4°	F	800	650D	—	—	—	—
V8-455	R45TS	.040	.016	30	B	4°	F	900	650D	—	—	—	—
V8-455 Stage 1	R45TS	.040	.016	30	B	⑦	F	900	650D	—	—	—	—
1973													
6-250⑧	R46T	.035	.019	31–34	A	6°	D	700	600D	—	—	—	—
V8-350	R45TS	.040	.016	30	B	4°	F	800	650D	—	—	—	—
V8-455	R45TS	.040	.016	30	B	4°	F	900	650D	—	—	—	—
V8-455 Stage I	R45TS	.040	.016	30	B	10°	F	900	650D	—	—	—	—
1974													
6-250⑧	R46T	.035	.019	31–34	A	③	D	950	600D	—	—	—	—
V8-350	R45TS	.040	.016	29–31	B	4°	F	—	650D	—	—	—	—
V8-455	R45TS	.040	.016	29–31	B	⑤	F	—	650D	—	—	—	—
1975													
6-250⑧	R46TX	.060	—	—	—	10°	D	800	600D	—	—	—	—
V6-231	R44SX	.060	—	—	G	12°	H	800	700D	—	—	—	—
V8-260⑫	R46SX	.080	—	—	—	16°	I	—	600D	—	—	—	—
V8-350	R45TSX	.060	—	—	—	12°	F	—	600D	—	—	—	—
V8-400 2 B. Carb.⑬	R46TSX	.060	—	—	—	16°	J	—	650D	—	—	—	—
V8-400 4 B. Carb.⑬	R45TSX	.060	—	—	—	16°	J	—	650D	—	—	—	—
V8-455	R45TSX	.060	—	—	—	12°	F	—	600D	—	—	—	—

Continued

TUNE UP NOTES

①—BTDC: Before top dead center.
②—D: Drive. N: Neutral.
③—Manual trans., 8° BTDC; auto. trans., 6° BTDC.
④—If air conditioned, turn A/C switch to "Full On" position.
⑤—Exc. intermediate model Stage 1 eng., 4° BTDC; intermediate model Stage 1 eng., 10° BTDC.
⑥—Std. trans. TDC: Auto. Trans. 4°.
⑦—Manual trans., 8°; Automatic trans., 10°.
⑧—See Chevrolet chapter for service procedures on this engine.
⑨—5° BTDC for LeSabre.
⑩—Early Gran Sport models set at TDC.
⑪—4 Barrel carburetors and all LeSabres 4°; All others 10°.
⑫—See Oldsmobile chapter for service procedures on this engine.
⑬—See Pontiac chapter for service procedures on this engine.

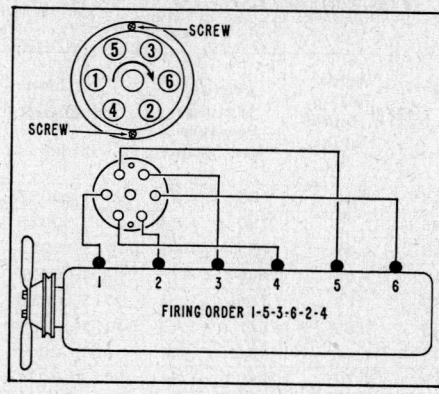

Fig. A

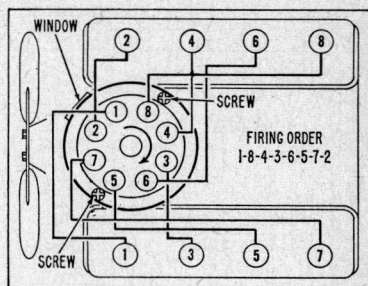

Fig. B

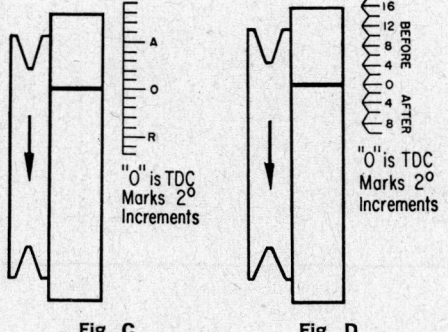

Fig. C   Fig. D

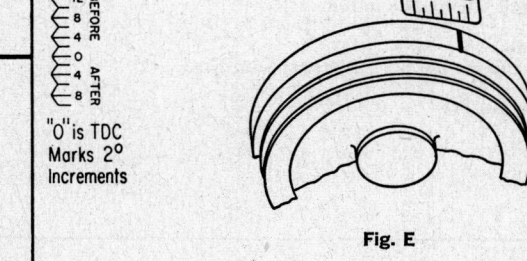

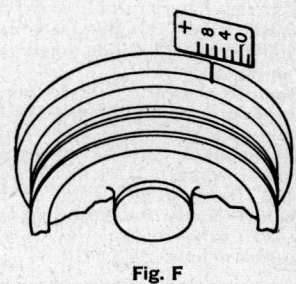

Fig. E

Fig. F

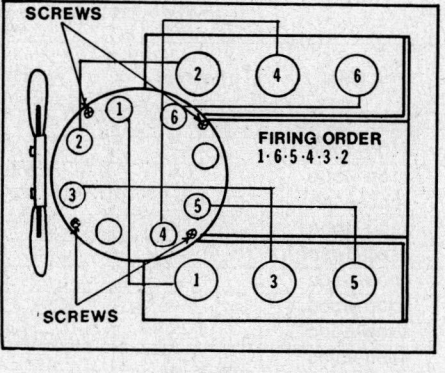

Fig. G

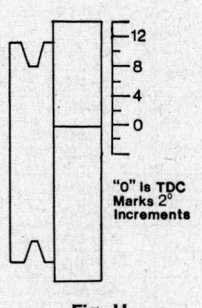

Fig. H

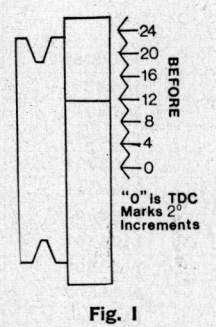

Fig. I

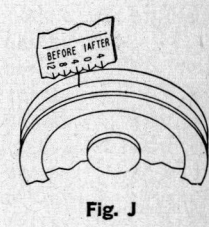

Fig. J

VALVE SPECIFICATIONS

Year	Model	Valve Lash Int.	Valve Lash Exh.	Valve Angles Seat	Valve Angles Face	Valve Spring Installed Height [3]	Valve Spring Pressure Lbs. @ In.	Stem Clearance Intake	Stem Clearance Exhaust	Stem Diameter Intake	Stem Diameter Exhaust
1969	6-250[4]	1 Turn[5]		46	45	1.66	185 @ 1.27	.001–.0027	.001–.0027	.3410–.3417	.3410–.3417
	V8-350	Hydraulic[6]		45	45	1.72	180 @ 1.34	.0015–.0035	.0015–.0035[1]	.3720–.3730	.3720–.3730[2]
	V8-400, 430	Hydraulic[6]		45	45	1.89	177 @ 1.45	.0015–.0035	.0015–.0035[1]	.3720–.3730	.3720–.3730[2]
1970–71	6-250[4]	1 Turn[5]		46	45	1.66	185 @ 1.27	.001–.0027	.001–.0027	.3410–.3417	.3410–.3417
	V8-350	Hydraulic[6]		45	45	1.72	180 @ 1.34	.0015–.0035	.0015–.0035[1]	.3720–.3730	.3720–.3730[2]
	V8-455	Hydraulic[6]		45	45	1.89	177 @ 1.45	.0015–.0035	.0015–.0035[1]	.3720–.3730	.3720–.3730[2]
1972–74	6-250[4]	1 Turn[5]		46	45	1.66	186 @ 1.27	.001–.0027	.001–.0027	.3410–.3417	.3410–.3417
	V8-350	Hydraulic[6]		45	45	1.72	180 @ 1.34	.0015–.0035	.0015–.0032[1]	.3720–.3730	.3723–.3730[2]
	V8-455	Hydraulic[6]		45	45	1.89	177 @ 1.45	.0015–.0035	.0015–.0032[1]	.3720–.3730	.3723–.3730[2]
1975	6-250	1 Turn[5]		46	45	1.66	186 @ 1.27	.001–.0027	.001–.002	.3410–.3417	.3410–.3417
	V6-231	Hydraulic[6]		45	45	1.727	168 @ 1.327	.0015–.0032	.0015–.0032	.3402–.3412	.3405–.3412
	V8-260[7]	Hydraulic[6]		[8]	[9]	1.67	187 @ 1.27	.001–.0027	.0015–.0032	.3425–.3432	.3420–.3427
	V8-350	Hydraulic[6]		45	45	1.727	177 @ 1.45	.0015–.0035	.0015–.0032	.3720–.3730	.3723–.3730
	V8-400[10]	Hydraulic[6]		[11]	[12]	—	—	.0016–.0033	.0021–.0038	.3412–.3419	.3407–.3414
	V8-455	Hydraulic[6]		45	45	1.89	177 @ 1.45	.0015–.0035	.0015–.0032	.3770–.3730	.3723–.3730

[1]—Plus or minus .001". Guide tapers top to bottom with larger dimension at bottom.
[2]—Plus or minus .0005". Guide tapers top to bottom with larger dimension at top.
[3]—Outer spring.
[4]—See Chevrolet chapter for service procedures on this engine.
[5]—Turn rocker arm stud nut until all lash is eliminated, then tighten nut the additional turn listed.
[6]—No adjustment.
[7]—See Oldsmobile Chapter for service procedures on this engine.
[8]—Intake, 45°; exhaust, 31°.
[9]—Intake 44°; exhaust, 30°.
[10]—See Pontiac Chapter for service procedure on this engine.
[11]—Intake, 30°; exhaust, 45°.
[12]—Intake, 29°; exhaust 44°.

STARTING MOTOR SPECIFICATIONS

Year	Model	Starter Number	Brush Spring Tension Oz[1]	Free Speed Test Amps.	Free Speed Test Volts	Free Speed Test R.P.M.	Resistance Test[3] Amps.[1]	Resistance Test[3] Volts
1969–70	6-250	1108365	35	49–87[2]	10.6	6200–10700	290–425[3]	4.2
	V8-350	1108391	35	55–85[2]	9	3100–4900	—	—
	V8-400, 430, 455	1108392	35	48–74[2]	9	4100–6300	—	—
1971	V8-455	1108392	35	45–80[2]	9	4000–6500	—	—
1971–73	V8-350	1108391	35	80[2]	9	3500–6000	—	—
1971–74	6-250	1108365	35	50–80[2]	9	5500–10500	—	—
1972–73	V8-455	1108392	35	45–80[2]	9	4000–6500	—	—
1973	V8-350	1108503	35	55–80[2]	9	3500–6000	—	—
1974	V8-350	1108506	35	55–80[2]	9	3500–6000	—	—
	V8-455	1108507	35	45–80[2]	9	4000–6500	—	—
1975	6-250	1108365	35	50–80	9	5500–10500	—	—
	V6-231	1108770	35	55–80	9	3500–6000	—	—
	V8-260		35	55–80	9	3500–6000	—	—
	V8-350	1108762	35	55–80	9	3500–6000	—	—
	V8-400		35	65–95	9	7500–10500	—	—
	V8-455	1108763	35	45–80	9	4000–6500	—	—

[1]—Minimum.   [2]—Includes solenoid.
[3]—Check capacity of motor by using a 500 ampere meter and a carbon pile rheostat to control voltage. Apply volts listed across motor with armature locked. Current should be as listed.

DISTRIBUTOR SPECIFICATIONS

★Note: If unit is checked on the vehicle, double the RPM and degrees to get crankshaft figures.

Breaker arm spring tension—19–23.

Distributor Part No.①	Centrifugal Advance Degrees @ RPM of Distributor					Vacuum Advance	
	Advance Starts	Intermediate Advance			Full Advance	Inches of Vacuum to Start Plunger	Max. Adv. Dist. Deg. @ Vacuum
1969							
1110463	0–1 @ 500	9½–11½ @ 975	—	—	17 @ 2100	6–8	12 @ 17
1110464	0–1 @ 500	7½–9½ @ 950	—	—	15 @ 2100	6–8	12 @ 17
1111334	0–1 @ 600	8½–10½ @ 900	—	—	15 @ 2300	6–8	9 @ 16
1111335	0–1 @ 600	9½–11½ @ 900	—	—	17 @ 2300	6–8	9 @ 16
1111938	0–1 @ 475	9½–11½ @ 975	—	—	17 @ 2300	6–8	9 @ 16
1970							
1111962	0–1 @ 600	4½–6½ @ 900	—	—	12 @ 2300	6–8	9 @ 16
1111984	0–1 @ 600	9½–11½ @ 900	—	—	17 @ 2300	6–8	9 @ 16
1111986	0–1 @ 475	9½–11½ @ 975	—	—	17 @ 2300	6–8	9 @ 16
1112006	0–1 @ 600	8½–10½ @ 900	—	—	15 @ 2300	6–8	9 @ 16
1971							
1110489	0–1 @ 500	4–6 @ 1150	—	—	11 @ 2050	6–8	12 @ 16
1112006	0–1 @ 550	3½–5½ @ 1000	—	—	10 @ 2300	6–8	9 @ 16
1112037	0–1 @ 800	2½–3½ @ 925	—	—	7 @ 2300	6–8	9 @ 16
1112077	0–1 @ 800	7–9 @ 1000	—	—	10 @ 1500	6–8	10 @ 16
1112080	0–1 @ 800	6–8 @ 1050	—	—	9 @ 1450	6–8	9 @ 16
1972							
1112016	0 @ 350	4½–6½ @ 900	—	—	12 @ 2300	6–8	9 @ 16
1112109	0 @ 400	4½–6½ @ 900	—	—	8 @ 1500	6–8	9 @ 16
1112110	0 @ 500	6–8 @ 1050	—	—	9 @ 1450	6–8	9 @ 13
1973							
1112016	0 @ 350	4½–6½ @ 900	—	—	12 @ 2300	6–8	9 @ 16
1112109	0 @ 375	5½–7½ @ 900	—	—	9 @ 1450	6–8	9 @ 16
1112110	0 @ 375	6–8 @ 1050	—	—	10 @ 1500	6.5–8.5	9.5 @ 13
1110499	0 @ 550	7 @ 1150	—	—	11½ @ 2100	6	11 @ 14
1974							
1110499	0–1 @ 550	7 @ 1150	—	—	10½ @ 2050	6	11 @ 14
1112520②	0–1 @ 450	7–9 @ 1200	—	—	10 @ 1500	6.5–8.5	9.5 @ 13
1112521②	0–1 @ 400	4½–6½ @ 900	—	—	12 @ 2300	6–8	9 @ 16
1112541	0–1 @ 450	5½–7½ @ 900	—	—	12 @ 1800	6–8	9 @ 16
1112542	0–1 @ 450	7–9 @ 1050	—	—	14 @ 2050	6.5–8.5	9.5 @ 13
1112802②	0–1 @ 450	5½–7½ @ 900	—	—	12 @ 1800	6–8	9 @ 16
1112803②	0–1 @ 450	7–9 @ 1050	—	—	14 @ 2050	6.5–8.5	9.5 @ 13
1975							
V6-231②	0 @ 500	5 @ 1000	—	—	8 @ 2050	6	9 @ 10
6-250②	0 @ 550	3½ @ 1150	—	—	8 @ 2100	4	13 @ 15½
V8-260②	0 @ 325	9½ @ 1200	—	—	14 @ 2200	4	12 @ 15
V8-350②	—	2–4 @ 1050	—	—	7 @ 2250	7½	8 @ 11½
V8-400②	0 @ 600	2 @ 700	—	—	8 @ 2200	7	13½ @ 13½
V8-455②	—	4½–6 @ 1500	—	—	9 @ 2200	5	7.1 @ 11

①—Stamped on distributor housing plate.
②—High Energy Ignition.

PISTONS, PINS, RINGS, CRANKSHAFT & BEARINGS

Year	Engine	Piston Clearance	Ring End Gap① Comp.	Ring End Gap① Oil	Wrist-pin Diameter	Rod Bearings Shaft Diameter	Rod Bearings Bearing Clearance	Main Bearings Shaft Diameter	Main Bearings Bearing Clearance	Thrust on Bear. No.	Shaft End Play
1969	6-250②	.0005–.0011	.010	.015	.9271	1.999–2.000	.0007–.0027	2.3004	.0003–.0029	7	.002–.006
	V8-350	.0008–.0014	.013	.015	.9393	2.0000	.0002–.0023	2.9995	.0004–.0015	3	.003–.009
	V8-400, 430	.0007–.0013	.013	.015	.9993	2.249–2.250	.0002–.0023	3.2500	.0007–.0018	3	.003–.009
1970	6-250②	.0005–.0011	.010	.015	.9271	1.999–2.000	.0007–.0027	2.3004	.0003–.0029	7	.002–.006
	V8-350	.0008–.0014	.013	.015	.9393	2.0000	.0002–.0023	2.9995	.0004–.0015	3	.003–.009
	V8-455	.0010–.0022	.013	.015	.9993	2.249–2.250	.0002–.0023	3.2500	.0007–.0018	3	.003–.009
1971–74	6-250②	.0005–.0015	.010	.015	.927	1.999–2.000	.0007–.0027	2.3004	.0003–.0029	7	.002–.006
	V8-350	.0008–.0020	.010	.015	.9393	2.000	.0002–.0023	③	.0004–.0015	3	.003–.009
	V8-455	.0010–.0016	.013	.015	.9993	2.249–2.250	.0002–.0023	3.250	.0007–.0018	3	.003–.009
1975	6-250②	.0005–.0015	.010	.015	.927	1.999–2.000	.0007–.0027	2.2999	.0003–.0029	7	.002–.006
	V6-231	.0008–.0014	.013	.015	.9391	2.000	.0002–.0023	2.4995	.0004–.0015	2	.004–.008
	V8-260④	.001–.002	.010	.015	.9805	2.1238–2.1248	.0004–.0033	⑤	.0005–.0021⑥	3	.004–.008
	V8-350	.008–.0014	.013	.015	.9394	1.999–2.000	.0005–.0026	2.9995	.0004–.0015	3	.003–.009
	V8-400⑦	.003–.005	⑧	.035	.9802	2.25	.0005–.0025	3.00	.0002–.0017	4	.0035–.0085
	V8-455	.001–.0016	.013	.015	.991	2.249–2.250	.0005–.0026	3.250	.0007–.0018	3	.003–.009

①—Fit rings in tapered bores for clearance given in tightest portion of ring travel. Clearances specified are minimum gaps.
②—See Chevrolet Chapter for service procedures on this engine.
③—1971–73, 2.9995 inch; 1974, 3.00 inch.
④—See Oldsmobile Chapter for service procedures on this engine.
⑤—No. 1: 2.4988–2.4998 inch; Nos. 2, 3, 4, 5: 2.4985–2.4995 inch.
⑥—Rear, .0015–.0031 inch.
⑦—See Pontiac Chapter for service procedures on this engine.
⑧—No. 1, .019; No. 2, .015.

REAR AXLE SPECIFICATIONS

Year	Model	Carrier Type	Ring Gear & Pinion Backlash Method	Ring Gear & Pinion Backlash Adjustment	Pinion Bearing Preload Method	Pinion Bearing Preload Adjustment New Bearings Inch-Lbs.	Pinion Bearing Preload Adjustment Used Bearings Inch-Lbs.	Differential Bearing Preload Method	Differential Bearing Preload Adjustment New Bearings Inch-Lbs.	Differential Bearing Preload Adjustment Used Bearings Inch-Lbs.
1969–70	43-44-45000	Integral	Shims	.006–.008	Spacer	20–25①	10–15①	Shims	35–40②	20–25②
	46-48-49000	Integral	Shims	.007–.009	Spacer	25–30①	10–15①	Shims	35–40②	25–30②
1971–74	All Exc. Apollo	Integral	Shims	.006–.008	Spacer	20–25①	10–15①	Shims	35–40②	20–25②
1973	Apollo	Integral	Shims	.005–.008	Spacer	15–30	5–10	Shims	.010	.010
1974	Apollo	Integral	Shims	.006–.008	Spacer	20–25①	10–15①	Shims	30–40②	20–25②
1975	All	Integral	Shims	.006–.008	Spacer	20–25①	10–15①	—	—	—

①—Measured with torque wrench at pinion flange nut.
②—Total preload measured with torque wrench at pinion flange nut with new seal installed.

ENGINE TIGHTENING SPECIFICATIONS*

★Torque specifications are for clean and lightly lubricated threads only. Dry or dirty threads produce increased friction which prevents accurate measurement of tightness.

Year	Engine	Spark Plugs Ft. Lbs. ③	Cylinder Head Bolts Ft. Lbs.	Intake Manifold Ft. Lbs.	Exhaust Manifold Ft. Lbs.	Rocker Arm Shaft Bracket Ft. Lbs.	Rocker Arm Cover Ft. Lbs.	Connecting Rod Cap Bolts Ft. Lbs.	Main Bearing Cap Bolts Ft. Lbs.	Flywheel to Crankshaft Ft. Lbs.	Vibration Damper or Pulley Ft. Lbs.
1969	6-250	25	95	①	①	—	5	35	65	60	②
	V8-350	15	75	55	18	30	4	35	95	60	140 min.
	V8-400, 430	15	100	55	18	30	4	45	110	60	200 min.
1970	6-250	25	95	①	①	—	5	35	65	60	②
	V8-350	15	75	55	18	25	4	35	95	60	120 min.
	V8-455	15	100	55	18	25	4	45	110	58	200 min.
1971-72	V8-350	15	75	55	18	25	4	35	95	60	120 min.
	V8-455	15	100	65	18	25	4	45	110	58	200 min.
1973	6-250	15	95	35	30	—	4	35	65	60	②
	V8-350	15	80	55	18	30	4	35	115	60	140 min.
	V8-455	15	100	65	18	30	4	45	115	60	200 min.
1974	6-250	15	95	35	30	—	4	35	65	60	②
	V8-350	15	80	45	28	30	4	40	115	60	140 min.
	V8-455	15	100	45	28	30	4	45	115	60	200 min.
1975	6-250	25	—	—	—	—	—	—	—	—	—
	V6-231	15	75	45	25	30	5	40	115	55	—
	V8-260	15	85	40	25	—	7	42	④	60	310
	V8-350	25	—	—	—	—	—	—	—	—	—
	V8-400	25	—	—	—	—	—	—	—	—	—
	V8-455	25	—	—	—	—	—	—	—	—	—

①—End clamps 20, center bolts 30. ②—Pressed on. ③—Dry threads. ④—Nos. 1, 2, 3, 4—80 ft. lbs., No. 5—120 ft. lbs.

ALTERNATOR & REGULATOR SPECIFICATIONS

Year	Alternator			Cold Output @ 14 Volts		Regulator	Field Relay			Voltage Regulator		
	Model	Rated Hot Output Amps.	Field Current 12 Volts @ 80 F.	2000 R.P.M. Amps.	5000 R.P.M. Amps.	Model	Air Gap In.	Point Gap In.	Closing Voltage	Air Gap In.	Point Gap In.	Voltage @ 125° F.
1969	1100762	37	2.2-2.6	25	35	1119515	.015	.030	1.5-3.2	.067	.014	13.6-14.4
	1100761	37	2.2-2.6	25	35	1119515	.015	.030	1.5-3.2	.067	.014	13.6-14.4
	1100802	55	2.2-2.6	32	50	1119515	.015	.030	1.5-3.2	.067	.014	13.6-14.4
	1100691	42	2.2-2.6	28	40	1119515	.015	.030	1.5-3.2	.067	.014	13.6-14.4
	1100774	55	2.2-2.6	32	50	1119515	.015	.030	1.5-3.2	.067	.014	13.6-14.4
1970	1100761	37	2.2-2.6	7①	29②	1119515	.015	.030	1.5-3.2	.067	.014	13.6-14.4
	1100888	37	2.2-2.6	7①	29②	1119515	.015	.030	1.5-3.2	.067	.014	13.6-14.4
	1100691	42	2.2-2.6	9①	32②	1119515	.015	.030	1.5-3.2	.067	.014	13.6-14.4
	1100774	55	2.2-2.6	9①	44②	1119515	.015	.030	1.5-3.2	.067	.014	13.6-14.4
	1100892	55	2.2-2.6	9①	44②	1119515	.015	.030	1.5-3.2	.067	.014	13.6-14.4
	1100860	61	2.2-2.6	12①	47②	1119515	.015	.030	1.5-3.2	.067	.014	13.6-14.4
1971	1100891	—	2.2-2.6	—	—	1119515	.015	.030	1.5-3.2	.067	.014	13.6-14.4
	1100905	37	2.2-2.6	7①	29②	1119515	.015	.030	1.5-3.2	.067	.014	13.6-14.4
	1100924	55	4.0-4.5	9①	44②	1116384	—	—				13.5-14.5
	1100926	42	4.0-4.5	9①	32②	1116384	—	—				13.5-14.5

Continued

ALTERNATOR & REGULATOR SPECIFICATIONS—Continued

Year	Alternator					Regulator						
	Model	Rated Hot Output Amps.	Field Current 12 Volts @ 80 F.	Cold Output @ 14 Volts		Model	Field Relay			Voltage Regulator		
				2000 R.P.M. Amps.	5000 R.P.M. Amps.		Air Gap In.	Point Gap In.	Closing Voltage	Air Gap In.	Point Gap In.	Voltage @ 125° F.
1971	1100931	42	2.2–2.6	9①	44②	1119515	.015	.030	1.5–3.2	.067	.014	13.6–14.4
	1100932	—	2.2–2.6	12①	47②	1119515	.015	.030	1.5–3.2	.067	.014	13.6–14.4
	1100933	63	2.8–3.2	13①	51②	1119519	.015	.030	1.5–3.2	.067	.014	—
	1100943	42	2.2–2.6	9①	32②	1119515	.015	.030	1.5–3.2	.067	.014	13.6–14.4
1972	1102449	37	2.2–2.6	7①	29②	1119515	.015	.030	1.5–3.2	.067	.014	13.5–14.5
	1102443	42	2.2–2.6	9①	32③	1119515	.015	.030	1.5–3.2	.067	.014	13.5–14.5
	1102448	55	2.2–2.6	9①	44③	1119515	.015	.030	1.5–3.2	.067	.014	13.5–14.5
	1102442	55	2.2–2.6	9①	44③	1119515	.015	.030	1.5–3.2	.067	.014	13.5–14.5
	1102450	61	2.2–2.6	12①	47②	1119515	.015	.030	1.5–3.2	.067	.014	13.5–14.5
	1102447	63	2.8–3.2	13①	51③	1119519	.015	.030	1.5–3.2	.067	.014	13.5–14.5
1973	1100497	37	4.0–4.5	13③	37	Integral	—	—	—	—	—	13.5–14.5
	1100925	63	4.0–4.5	36③	58	Integral	—	—	—	—	—	13.5–14.5
	1100926	42	4.0–4.5	15③	37	Integral	—	—	—	—	—	13.5–14.5
	1100946	55	4.0–4.5	19③	50	Integral	—	—	—	—	—	13.5–14.5
	1100947	37	4.0–4.5	12③	32	Integral	—	—	—	—	—	13.5–14.5
	1100948	61	4.0–4.5	24③	55	Integral	—	—	—	—	—	13.5–14.5
	1101018	80	4.0–4.5	40③	74	Integral	—	—	—	—	—	13.5–14.5
1974	1100497	37	4.0–4.5	13③	37	Integral	—	—	—	—	—	13.5–14.5
	1100925	63	4.0–4.5	36③	58	Integral	—	—	—	—	—	13.5–14.5
	1100926	42	4.0–4.5	15③	37	Integral	—	—	—	—	—	13.5–14.5
	1100946	55	4.0–4.5	—	50	Integral	—	—	—	—	—	13.5–14.5
	1100947	37	4.0–4.5	12③	32	Integral	—	—	—	—	—	13.5–14.5
	1100948	61	4.0–4.5	24③	55	Integral	—	—	—	—	—	13.5–14.5
	1101018	80	4.0–4.5	—	74	Integral	—	—	—	—	—	13.5–14.5
1975	1102388	37	—	—	—	Integral	—	—	—	—	—	13.6–14.2
	1102389	42	—	—	—	Integral	—	—	—	—	—	13.6–14.2
	1102390	55	—	—	—	Integral	—	—	—	—	—	13.6–14.2
	1102391	61	—	—	—	Integral	—	—	—	—	—	13.6–14.2
	1102394	37	—	—	—	Integral	—	—	—	—	—	13.6–14.2
	1102495	55	—	—	—	Integral	—	—	—	—	—	13.6–14.2
	1102939	63	—	—	—	Integral	—	—	—	—	—	13.6–14.2

①—At 500 engine R.P.M.   ②—At 1500 engine R.P.M.   ③—At 600 engine R.P.M.

WHEEL ALIGNMENT SPECIFICATIONS

OLD CAR SPECIFICATIONS: For 1946–68 Wheel Alignment Specifications see main index.

Year	Model	Caster Angle, Degrees		Camber Angle, Degrees				Toe-In. Inch	Toe-Out on Turns, Deg.	
		Limits	Desired	Limits		Desired			Outer Wheel	Inner Wheel
				Left	Right	Left	Right			
1969–70	Intermediates	−1 to 0	−½	0 to +1	0 to +1	+½	+½	⅛–¼	18½	20
	Le Sabre	+¼ to +1¼	+¾	−½ to +½	−½ to +½	0	0	7/32–5/16	19½	20
	Estate Wagon	+¼ to +1¼	+¾	−½ to +½	−½ to +½	0	0	7/32–5/16	19½	20
	Wildcat	+¼ to +1¼	+¾	−½ to +½	−½ to +½	0	0	7/32–5/16	19½	20
	Electra 225	+¼ to +1¼	+¾	−½ to +½	−½ to +½	0	0	7/32–5/16	19½	20
	Riviera	+½ to +1½	+1	−¼ to +¾	−¼ to +¾	+¼	+¼	5/32–¼	16¾	20
1971	Intermediates	−1 to 0	−½	0 to +1	0 to 1	+½	+½	⅛–¼	18½	20
	Others	+½ to +1½	+1	−¼ to +¾	−¼ to +¾	+¼	+¼	⅛–¼	18½	20
1972	Intermediates	−1 to 0	−½	0 to +1	0 to +1	+½	+½	⅛–¼	18½	20
	Others	+½ to +1½	+1	0 to +1	0 to +1	+½	+½	⅛–¼	18½	20
1973	Apollo	0 to +1	+½	−¼ to +¾	−¼ to +¾	+¼	+¼	⅛–¼	—	—
	Intermediates①	−½ to −1½	−1	+½ to +1½	0 to +1	+1	+½	0–⅛	③	20
	Intermediates②	−½ to +½	0	+½ to +1½	0 to +1	+1	+½	0–⅛	③	20
	Others	+½ to +1½	+1	+½ to +1½	0 to +1	+1	+½	0–⅛	18½	20
1974	Apollo	0 to +1	+½	−¼ to +¾	−¼ to +¾	+¼	+¼	⅛–¼	—	20
	Intermediates	−½ to +½	0	+½ to +1½	0 to +1	+1	+½	0–⅛	③	20
	Others	+½ to +1½	+1	+½ to +1½	0 to +1	+1	+½	0–⅛	18½	20
1975	Apollo, Skylark①	−½ to −1½	−1	+¼ to +1¼	+¼ to +1¼	+¾	+¾	0–⅛	—	—
	Apollo, Skylark②	+½ to +1½	+1	+¼ to +1¼	+¼ to +1¼	+¾	+¾	0–⅛	—	—
	Century	+1½ to +2½	+2	+½ to +1½	0 to +1	+1	+½	0–⅛	—	—
	Others	+1 to +2	+1½	+½ to +1½	0 to +1	+1	+½	0–⅛	—	—

①—Manual steering. ②—Power steering.
③—Manual steering & all Sta. Wag.—right turn, 19 3/16°; left turn, 18 13/16°: power steering Exc. Sta. Wag.—right turn, 19°; left turn, 18 11/16°.

BRAKE SPECIFICATIONS

Year	Model	Brake Drum Inside Diameter	Wheel Cylinder Bore Diameter			Master Cylinder Bore Diameter		
			Front Disc Brake	Front Drum Brake	Rear Drum Brake	With Disc Brakes	With Drum Brakes	With Power Brakes
1969	Special, Skylark	9.495–9.505	—	1⅛	⅞	1⅛	1.00	①
	Sportwagon	9.495–9.505	—	1⅛	1.00	1⅛	1.00	①
	GS-350, GS-400	9.495–9.505	—	1⅛	⅞	1⅛	1.00	①
	LeSabre, Wildcat, Electra	11.997–12.022	2 15/16	1 3/16	1.00	1⅛	1.00	①
	Riviera	11.997–12.022	2 15/16	1 3/16	15/16	1⅛	1.00	①
1970	Skylark, GS, GS-455	9.495–9.505	—	1⅛	⅞	1⅛	1.00	①
	Sportwagon	9.495–9.505	—	1⅛	⅞	1⅛	1.00	①
	Le Sabre, Wildcat, Electra, Wagon	11.997–12.022	2 15/16	1 3/16	1.00	1⅛	1.00	①
	Riviera	11.997–12.022	2 15/16	1 3/16	15/16	1⅛	1.00	①
1971–72	Skylark, GS, GS-455	9.495–9.505	—	1⅛	⅞	1⅛	1.00	①
	Sportwagon	9.495–9.505	—	1⅛	⅞	1⅛	1.00	①
	Le Sabre, Centurion, Electra	10.997–11.007	2 15/16	—	15/16	1⅛	—	①
	Estate Wagon	11.997–12.007	2 15/16	—	15/16	1⅛	—	①
	Riviera	10.997–11.007	2 15/16	—	15/16	1⅛	—	①

Continued

BRAKE SPECIFICATIONS—Continued

Year	Model	Brake Drum Inside Diameter	Wheel Cylinder Bore Diameter			Master Cylinder Bore Diameter		
			Front Disc Brake	Front Drum Brake	Rear Drum Brake	With Disc Brakes	With Drum Brakes	With Power Brakes
1973–74	Apollo	9.50	$2^{15}/_{16}$	$1\frac{1}{8}$	$\frac{7}{8}$	$1\frac{1}{8}$	1.00	①
	Century, Luxus, Regal	9.495–9.505	$2^{15}/_{16}$	—	$\frac{7}{8}$	$1\frac{1}{8}$	—	$1\frac{1}{8}$
	Century Wagon	10.997–11.007	$2^{15}/_{16}$	—	$^{15}/_{16}$	$1\frac{1}{8}$	—	$1\frac{1}{8}$
	LeSabre, Centurion, Electra, Riviera	10.997–11.007	$2^{15}/_{16}$	—	$^{15}/_{16}$	$1\frac{1}{8}$	—	$1\frac{1}{8}$
	Estate Wagon	11.997–12.007	$2^{15}/_{16}$	—	1	$1\frac{1}{8}$	—	$1\frac{1}{8}$
1975	Apollo, Skylark	9.50	$2^{15}/_{16}$	—	$\frac{7}{8}$	$1\frac{1}{8}$	—	$1\frac{1}{8}$
	Century, Regal, Custom	9.494–9.505	$2^{15}/_{16}$	—	$\frac{7}{8}$	$1\frac{1}{8}$	—	②
	Century Wagon	10.997–11.007	$2^{15}/_{16}$	—	$\frac{7}{8}$	$1\frac{1}{8}$	—	$1\frac{1}{8}$
	LeSabre	—	$2^{15}/_{16}$	—	$^{15}/_{16}$	$1\frac{1}{8}$	—	$1\frac{1}{8}$
	Electra, Riviera	10.997–11.007	$2^{15}/_{16}$	—	$^{15}/_{16}$	$1\frac{1}{8}$	—	$1\frac{1}{8}$
	Estate Wagon	11.997–12.007	$2^{15}/_{16}$	—	1	$1\frac{1}{8}$	—	$1\frac{1}{8}$

①—Drum brakes 1″, disc brakes $1\frac{1}{8}$″.
②—Manual brakes, 1.00 inch; power brakes, $1\frac{1}{8}$ inch.

COOLING SYSTEM & CAPACITY DATA

Year	Model or Engine	Cooling Capacity, Qts.			Radiator Cap Relief Pressure, Lbs.		Thermo. Opening Temp.	Fuel Tank Gals.	Engine Oil Refill Qts. ①	Transmission Oil			Rear Axle Oil Pints
		No Heater	With Heater	With A/C	With A/C	No A/C				3 Speed Pints	4 Speed Pints	Auto. Trans. Qts. ⑬	
1969	6-250	10.0	11.3	13.0	15	15	195	20	4	$3\frac{3}{8}$	—	⑫	2.9
	V8-350⑪	12.6	13.5	13.5	15	15	190	20	4	$3\frac{3}{8}$	—	⑭	2.9
	GS-350	12.6	13.5	13.5	15	15	190	20	4	3.4	3	⑮	2.9
	GS-400	15.3	16.2	16.7	15	15	190	20	4	3.5	3	⑯	2.9
	V8-350⑩	12.3	13.2	13.6	15	15	190	25	4	3.5	—	⑰	2.9
	V8-430	16.0	16.7	17.0	15	15	190	25	4	—	—	⑱	$4\frac{1}{4}$
	Riviera	16.0	16.7	17.0	15	15	190	21	4	—	—	⑱	$4\frac{1}{4}$
1970	6-250	—	16.04	16.04	15	15	190	20	4	$3\frac{1}{2}$	3	⑮	3
	V8-350⑪	—	16.45	16.52	15	15	190	20⑱	4	$3\frac{1}{2}$	3	⑮	3
	GS-455	—	19.17	19.67	15	15	190	20	4	4	3	⑯	3
	V8-350⑩	—	16.20	16.55	15	15	190	25⑲	4	$3\frac{1}{2}$	—	⑮	3
	V8-455	—	19.70	20.0	15	15	190	25⑲	4	$3\frac{1}{2}$	—	⑯	$4\frac{1}{4}$
	Riviera	—	19.70	20.0	15	15	190	21	4	—	—	⑯	$4\frac{1}{4}$
1971	6-250	—	16.04	16.04	15	15	195	20	4	$3\frac{1}{2}$	—	⑮	$4\frac{1}{4}$
	V8-350⑪	—	16.5	16.5	15	15	190	20⑱	4	$3\frac{1}{2}$	3	⑮	$4\frac{1}{4}$
	GS-455	—	19.0	19.5	15	15	190	20	4	$3\frac{1}{2}$	3	⑯	$4\frac{1}{4}$
	V8-350⑩	—	16.2	16.55	15	15	190	25⑲	4	$3\frac{1}{2}$	—	⑮	$4\frac{1}{4}$
	V8-455	—	19.7	20.0	15	15	190	25⑲	4	$3\frac{1}{2}$	—	⑯	$5\frac{1}{2}$
	Riviera	—	19.7	20.0	15	15	190	21	4	—	—	⑯	$5\frac{1}{2}$
1972	V8-350⑪	—	16.45	16.85	15	15	190	20⑱	4	$3\frac{1}{2}$	3	⑮	②
	V8-350⑩	—	18.9	19.3	15	15	190	25	4	$3\frac{1}{2}$	—	⑮	②
	GS-455	—	16.2	16.3	15	15	190	20	4	$3\frac{1}{2}$	3	⑯	②
	V8-455	—	18.7	19.0	15	15	190	25⑲	4	—	—	⑯	②

Continued

COOLING SYSTEM & CAPACITY DATA—Continued

Year	Model or Engine	Cooling Capacity, Qts.			Radiator Cap Relief Pressure, Lbs.		Thermo. Opening Temp.	Fuel Tank Gals.	Engine Oil Refill Qts. ①	Transmission Oil			Rear Axle Oil Pints
		No Heater	With Heater	With A/C	With A/C	No A/C				3 Speed Pints	4 Speed Pints	Auto. Trans. Qts. ⑬	
1973	6-250	—	14.0	14.0	15	15	195	21	4	3½	—	⑮	②
	V8-350 Apollo	—	19.5	20.0	15	15	190	21	4	3½	—	⑮	②
	V8-350⑪	—	16.45	16.85	15	15	190	22	4	3½	—	⑮	②
	V8-350⑩	—	18.9	19.3	15	15	190	26	4	—	—	⑮	②
	GS-455	—	16.2	16.6	15	15	190	22	4	3½	—	⑯	②
	V8-455	—	18.7	19.0	15	15	190	26③	4	—	—	⑯	②
1974	6-250	—	14.0	14.0	15	15	195	21	4	3½	—	⑮	②
	V8-350 Apollo	—	16.5	17.0	15	15	190	21	4	3½	—	⑮	②
	V8-350⑪	—	17.3	④	15	15	190	22	4	—	—	⑮	②
	V8-350⑩	—	17.3	17.2	15	15	190	26	4	—	—	⑮	②
	V8-455⑪	—	19.4	19.9	15	15	190	22	4	—	—	⑯	②
	V8-455⑥	—	19.6	19.8⑤	15	15	190	26③	4	—	—	⑯	②
1975	6-250	—	16.3	16.4	15	15	190	21	4	3½	—	⑮	4.25
	V6-231⑦	—	16.5	16.6	15	15	190	21	4	3½	—	⑮	4.25
	V6-231⑪	—	15.3	15.3	15	15	190	22	4	3½	—	⑮	4.25
	V8-260⑦	—	22.4	22.9	—	—	195	21	4	3½	—	⑮	4.25
	V8-350⑦	—	17.9	18.6	15	15	190	21	4	—	—	⑮	4.25
	V8-350⑪	—	16.9	17.2	15	15	190	22	4	3½	—	⑮	4.25
	V8-350⑩	—	16.9	17.2	15	15	190	26	4	—	—	⑮	4.25
	V8-400	—	—	—	—	—	195	26	5	—	—	⑮	—
	V8-455	—	19.6	20⑤	15	15	190	26③	4	—	—	⑯	5.4

①—Add one quart with filter change.
②—8½ inch axle, 4¼ pts.; 8⅞ inch axle, 5¼ pts.; 9⅜ inch axle, 5½ pts.
③—Estate Wagon 22 gallons.
④—With 20 inch fan shroud, 17.6 qts.; with 22 inch fan shroud, 17.2 qts.
⑤—With heavy duty cooling system 21.6 qts.
⑥—Estate Wagon, Electra & Riviera.
⑦—Apollo & Skylark.
⑩—LeSabre.
⑪—Intermediates
⑫—Total 9½ qts. Oil pan only 2½ qts.
⑬—Approximate. Make final check with dipstick.
⑭—Two speed unit 9½ qts. total. Oil pan only 2½ qts. Three speed unit 10 qts. total. Oil pan only 3 qts.
⑮—Total 10 qts. pan only 3 qts. O ‖
⑯—Total 11½ qts. Oil pan only 3½ qts.
⑰—Two speed unit 9½ qts. total. Oil pan only 2½ qts. Three speed unit 11½ qts. total. Oil pan only 3½ qts.
⑱—Sportwagon 23 gallons.
⑲—Estate Wagon 24 gallons.

Electrical Section

1975 HIGH ENERGY IGNITION SYSTEM (H.E.I.)

Service procedures for the V6 and V8 H.E.I. distributors are found in the "Electronic Ignition System" section of the "Tune Up Service" chapter. Service procedures for the H.E.I. distributor used on the 6-250 engine differ slightly since the ignition coil is mounted externally.

On all 1975 H.E.I. distributors, a special RFI rotor is used to further reduce radio interference.

DISTRIBUTOR, REPLACE

1. Disconnect primary wire from distributor and disconnect hose from vacuum control unit.

   NOTE: On H.E.I. systems, disconnect feed and module connectors from distributor cap.

2. Remove distributor cap.
3. Crank engine until distributor rotor is in position to fire No. 1 cylinder and the timing mark (see *Tune Up Chart*) is aligned with the timing indicator.
4. Remove distributor clamp and lift out distributor.

NOTE: Before installation of either a new or repaired distributor apply a few drops of engine oil to the drain hole near the lower end of the housing and apply oil to the oiler on the housing. Rotate the distributor shaft several times by hand to distribute the oil and to make sure that the shaft turns freely.

1. Check to make sure that the timing mark is aligned with the timing indicator with No. 1 piston on the compression stroke in position to fire.
2. Place a new seal on distributor housing.
3. Rotate distributor cam in direction of arrow on cam until rotor is in position to fire No. 1 cylinder.
4. Rotate oil pump shaft with screwdriver to align slot in shaft with tongue on lower end of distributor shaft.
5. Install distributor in crankcase with vacuum control pointing to right side of engine, in position to connect to vacuum hose.
6. Install distributor clamp and bolt with lockwasher, leaving bolt just loose enough to permit movement of distributor.
7. Rotate distributor housing until breaker points just start to open and tighten clamp bolt. This will permit starting engine for setting timing.
8. Connect pipe to vacuum control and primary wire to terminal stud.
9. Install distributor cap. If spark plug wires are disconnected from cap make certain that wires are connected in accordance with firing order.

10. Check and set ignition timing.

NOTE: When using a timing light to adjust ignition timing, the connection should be made at the No. 1 spark plug. Forcing foreign objects through the boot at the No. 1 terminal of the distributor cap will damage the boot and could cause engine misfiring.

STARTER, REPLACE

To remove the starter, disconnect battery cable from battery. Disconnect cable and solenoid lead wire from solenoid switch. Remove flywheel inspection cover. Remove starter attaching bolts and remove starter.

LIGHT SWITCH, REPLACE
1969-75

CAUTION: On vehicles equipped with an Air Cushion Restraint System, turn ignition switch to "Lock," disconnect battery ground cable and tape end, thereby deactivating system.

1. Disconnect battery ground cable.
2. On 1969-72 intermediate models equipped with A/C, remove left hand duct.

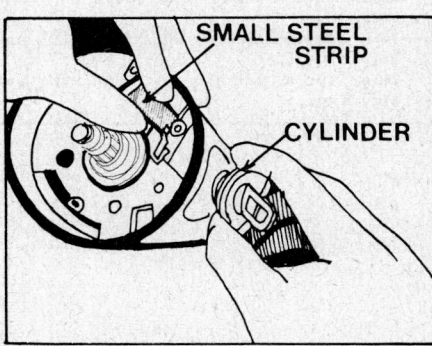

SMALL STEEL STRIP

CYLINDER

Fig. 1   Ignition lock. 1969-75

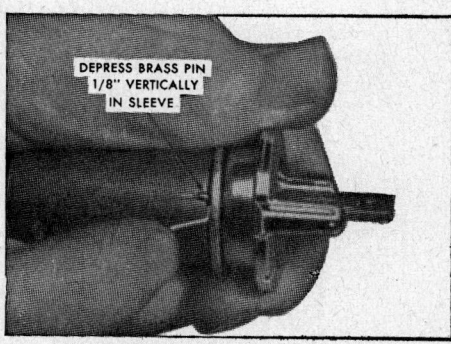

DEPRESS BRASS PIN 1/8" VERTICALLY IN SLEEVE

Fig. 2   Ignition lock disassembly

3. On 1971-75 full size models, remove left hand trim panel.
4. On all models, pull switch knob to full "On" position, depress latch button on rear of switch and pull knob and rod from switch. Remove switch escutcheon or retaining nut, if used.
5. Pull switch down, disconecct electrical connector and remove switch.

NOTE: On 1975 Full Size Models, remove switch from mounting bracket.

6. Reverse procedure to install.

IGNITION LOCK
1969-75

1. Follow procedure to remove turn signal switch as described further on.
2. The lock cylinder may be removed in any position from "accessory" to "run." However, the "accessory" position is desired because of its positive position.
3. Place a thin tool (small screw-driver or knife blade) into the slot next to the switch mounting screw boss (right hand slot) and depress spring latch at bottom of slot which releases lock Fig. 1, Remove lock.
4. To separate the lock from the cylinder, Fig. 2, use a paper clip or similar quality wire, place a 90 deg. bend about 1/8" from one end of the wire.
5. Using the wire as described in step 4, depress the plunger pin (above the stake mark) approx. 1/8" vertically in sleeve housing, at the same time exert light upward pressure on the lock assembly, rotate the cylinder counter-clockwise until it pops up from the sleeve assembly.

IGNITION SWITCH, REPLACE
1969-75

CAUTION: On vehicles equipped with an Air Cushion Restraint System, turn ignition switch to "Lock" position, disconnect battery ground cable and tape end, thereby deactivating system.

The ignition switch is located on the top of the steering column under the instrument panel. To replace it the steering column must be lowered as follows:

1. Disconnect shift indicator link.
2. Remove nuts securing bracket to dash panel and carefully lower column.
3. Disconnect electrical connector from switch. Ensure switch is in "Accessory" position on 1969-73 models, Fig. 3, or "Off-Unlock" position on 1974-75 models.
4. Remove two screws securing switch and remove switch.

Fig. 3   Ignition switch in "Lock" position. 1969-75

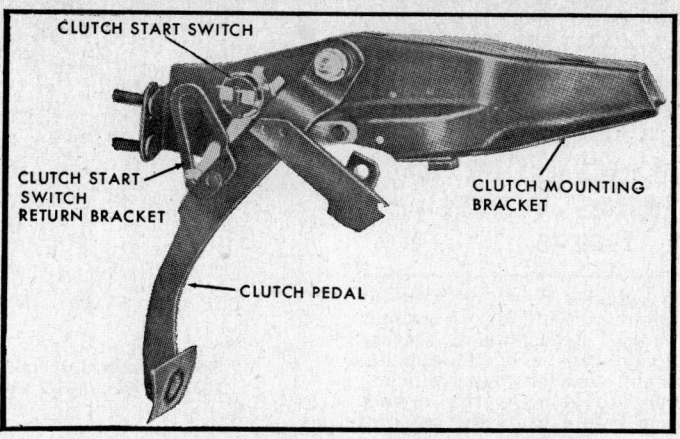

Fig. 4   Clutch start switch in start position. 1969-75

5. On 1969-73 models, position switch and lock in the "Lock" position for installation, Fig. 8. On 1974-75 models, the switch and lock are placed in the "Off-Unlock" position.
6. Fit actuator rod into switch and assemble to column.
7. Complete assembly in reverse of removal procedure.

STOP LIGHT SWITCH, REPLACE

1969-75

The stop lights are controlled by a mechanical switch mounted on the brake pedal bracket. This spring loaded switch makes contact whenever the brake pedal is applied. When the brake pedal is released it depresses the switch to open the contacts and turn brake lights off.

CLUTCH START SWITCH

1969-75

A clutch start switch is installed on all manual transmission cars. The switch is mounted on the clutch pedal bracket and it prevents the car from being started until the clutch pedal is depressed, Fig. 4.

TURN SIGNAL SWITCH, REPLACE

1969-75

CAUTION: On vehicles equipped with an Air Cushion Restraint System, turn ignition switch to "Lock," disconnect battery ground cable and tape end, thereby deactivating system.

As shown in Fig. 5, the assembly is a turn signal switch and hazard warning switch. It is mounted in a housing at the upper end of the steering column mast jacket, just below the steering wheel. Therefore to get at the switch the steering wheel will have to be removed. Also, on models equipped with tilt steering columns, it is necessary to lower the column assembly from instrument panel.
1. Disconnect battery ground cable.
2. Remove steering wheel and lock plate cover. On tilt columns, remove tilt lever.
3. With a suitable compressor, compress lock plate and spring, then remove snap ring from shaft.
4. Remove lock plate, cancelling cam, preload spring and thrust washer.
5. Remove turn signal lever and hazard warning switch knob.
6. Disconnect switch wiring connector and wrap a piece of tape around connector upper end and wiring harness, preventing snagging when removing switch.
7. Remove three switch retaining screws and switch.
8. Reverse procedure to install.

NEUTRAL START & BACK-UP LIGHT SWITCH

To check operation of switch after adjustments are made as outlined below, proceed as follows:
1. With shift lever in Park starter should operate.
2. With shift lever in Reverse back-up lights should light but starter should not operate.
3. With shift lever in Neutral starter should operate but back-up lights should be out.
4. With shift lever in Drive, starter should not operate and back-up lights should be out.

1969-75

1. Place shift lever in Drive (Neutral for 1972-74).
2. Attempt to insert a 3/32" or a No. 42 drill through gauging hole in switch body into inner hole in sliding part of switch, Fig. 6.

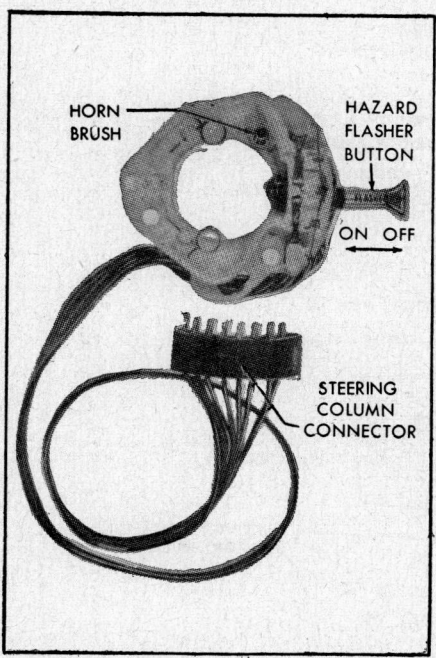

Fig. 5   Turn signal and hazard warning flasher switch assembly. 1969-75

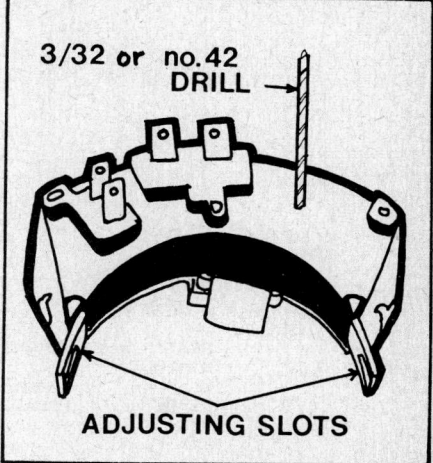

Fig. 6   Adjusting neutral safety switch. 1969-75

3. If drill does not enter inner hole, loosen two switch mounting screws and slide switch body as required to allow drill to enter inner hole. Tighten screws and remove drill.

HORN SOUNDER & STEERING WHEEL
1969-75

CAUTION: On vehicles equipped with an Air Cushion Restraint System, turn ignition switch to "Lock," disconnect battery ground cable and tape end, thereby deactivating system. Also, on these vehicles, it is necessary to remove the drivers cushion module before removing steering wheel. With tool J-24628-2, remove the module to steering wheel screws, lift module and disconnect horn wire. Then, with tool J-24628-3, disconnect module wire connector from slip ring.

1. Remove horn cap or actuator bar.
2. On 1975 models, remove steering wheel nut retainer.
3. On all models, back off nut until flush with top of steering shaft.
4. Use a suitable puller to remove wheel.

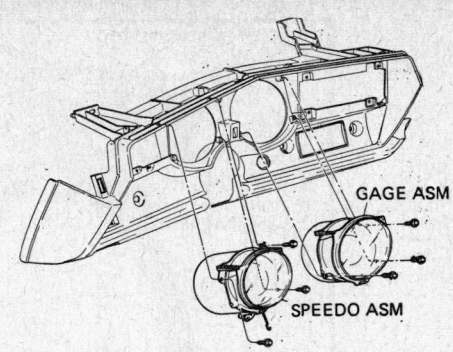

Fig. 7   Speedometer & telltale assembly. 1973-75 Century & Regal

INSTRUMENT CLUSTER

CAUTION: On vehicles equipped with an Air Cushion Restraint System, turn ignition switch to "Lock," disconnect battery ground cable and tape end, thereby deactivating system.

1975 Full Size

1. Disconnect battery ground cable.
2. Remove instrument cluster bezel and lens.
3. Remove screws securing speedometer head assembly and pull assembly from housing.
4. Remove screws securing fuel gauge assembly and pull assembly from housing.
5. Reverse procedure to install.

1973-75 Apollo & Skylark

1. Disconnect battery ground cable.
2. Disconnect heater or A/C control panel from the instrument panel carrier.
3. Remove radio control knobs, bezels and nuts, leaving the radio attached to the instrument panel reinforcement.
4. Disconnect instrument panel pad from the carrier and disconnect the shift quadrant indicator cable at the shift bowl. On automatic transmission equipped vehicles remove the two nuts securing the steering column to instrument panel.
5. Remove toe plate cover and discon-

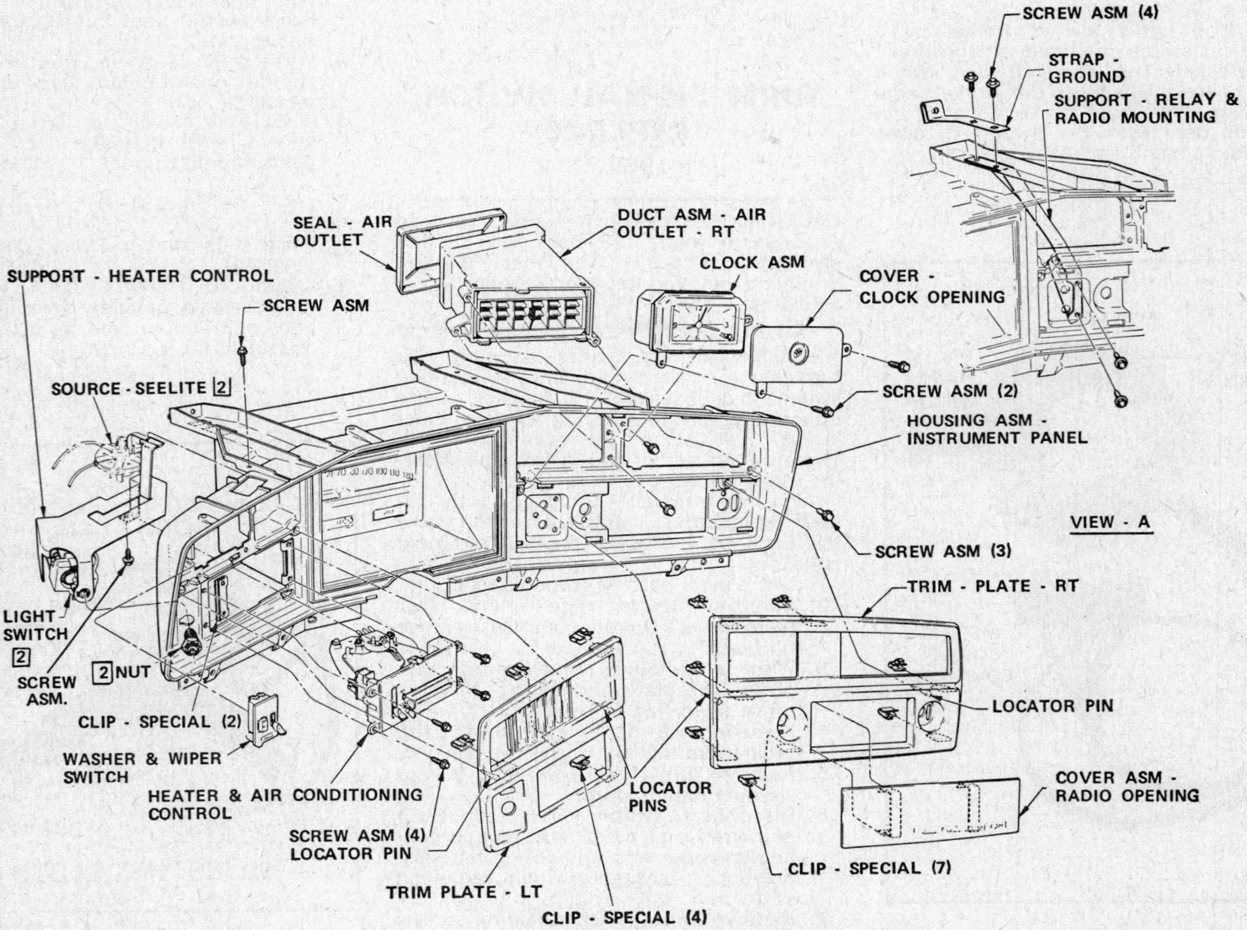

Fig. 8   Instrument cluster trim panels. 1971-72 full size models

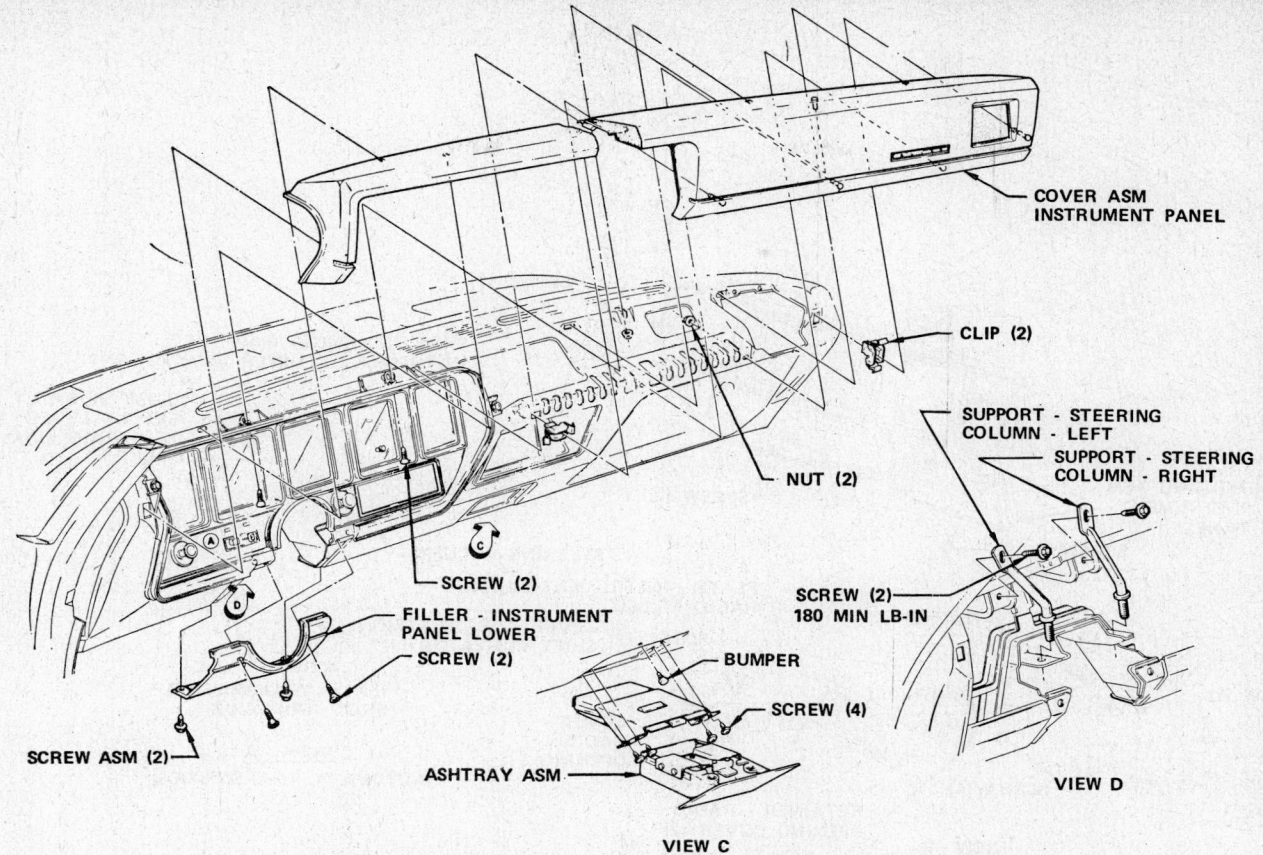

COVER ASM INSTRUMENT PANEL

CLIP (2)

SUPPORT - STEERING COLUMN - LEFT

SUPPORT - STEERING COLUMN - RIGHT

NUT (2)

SCREW (2)

FILLER - INSTRUMENT PANEL LOWER

SCREW (2)

SCREW (2) 180 MIN LB-IN

SCREW ASM (2)

BUMPER

SCREW (4)

ASHTRAY ASM

VIEW C

VIEW D

Fig. 9   Instrument panel cover. 1969-72 intermediate models

nect from cowl.

6. Lower steering column from instrument panel and use a protective cover (such as shop towel).
7. Disconnect the ground wire from left side of instrument panel pad followed by the speedometer cable.
8. With carrier and cluster assembly tilted rearward, disconnect printed circuit and cluster ground connectors.
9. Rest assembly on top of column and disconnect cluster from carrier assembly.
10. Reverse procedure to install.

1973-75 Century & Regal

Speedometer Cluster

1. Disconnect battery ground cable.
2. Place transmission selector lever in "L" position and disconnect shift indicator cable from steering column.
3. Pry trim plate from instrument panel.
4. Remove speedometer retaining screws, Fig. 7, disconnect speedometer cable and wiring connector, then remove speedometer.
5. Reverse procedure to install.

Fuel Gauge & Telltale Assembly

1. Disconnect battery ground cable.
2. Pry trim plate from instrument panel.
3. Remove retaining screws, Fig. 7, disconnect wiring connectors, then remove assembly.

NOTE: If equipped with temperature and oil pressure gauges and one gauge of the assembly is defective, all three gauges must be replaced since the cluster is serviced as an assembly.

4. Reverse procedure to install.

1971-74 Full Size

1. Disconnect battery ground cable.
2. On 1971-72 models, it is necessary to remove the cluster trim panels, Fig. 8, as follows:
   Left Trim Panel—pull headlight knob out to last detent and depress clip on back of knob to remove. Pull trim panel out and pull wires out of connectors.
   Right Trim Panel—Remove radio knobs and escutcheons. Remove trip set and speed alert knobs, if equipped. Pull trim panel out and pull wire from connector.
3. *Speedometer* removal is accomplished as follows: Remove lower instrument panel filler panel. Disconnect shift pointer cable with shift lever in L1. Remove speedo face glass by removing two screws on top of glass and remove speedometer by removing three screws on speedo face.

4. *Fuel & Temperature Gauges:* After removal of speedometer these gauges can be removed by pulling out of connector.

1969-72 Intermediates

CAUTION: If equipped with Cruise Control, disconnect speedometer cable from transducer to prevent damage when cluster housing is pulled back.

1. Remove glove box (9 screws).
2. Remove instrument panel upper cover (2 screws thru cluster housing and 2 nuts above glove box opening). Pull cover rearward to disengage three guide pins from clips, Fig. 9.
3. Remove steering column opening filler (4 screws). On air conditioned units, drop left plastic duct by removing 2 screws and disconnecting inner end from center distribution duct.
4. Lower steering column by removing 2 nuts and disconnecting shift indicator link. Pad column to avoid marring paint.
5. Pull cluster housing back after removing eight screws, Fig. 10. Rest housing on column and rotate so back of cluster is visible.
6. Disconnect speedometer cable and wires from cluster. On air conditioned units, disconnect left air hose

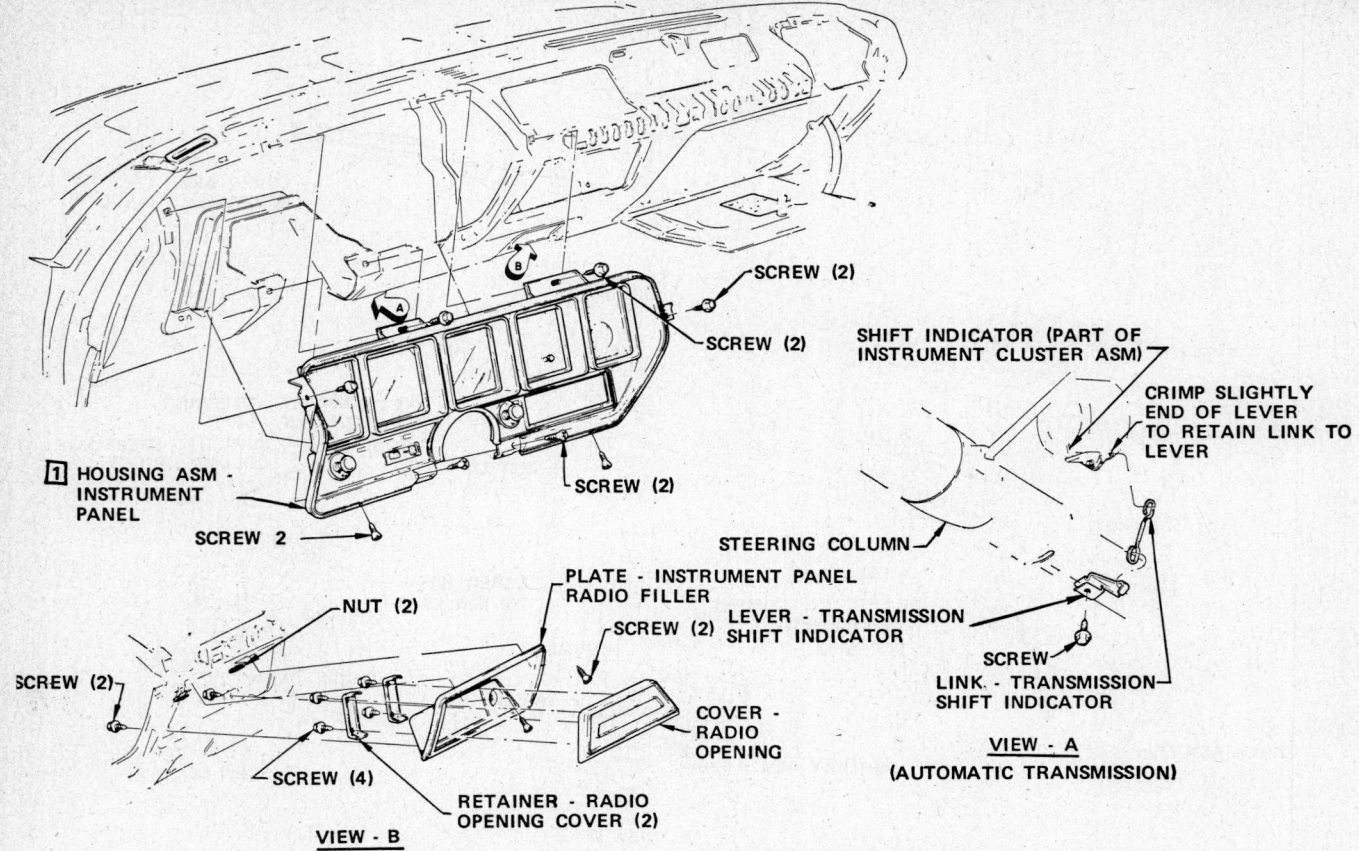

SCREW (2)

SHIFT INDICATOR (PART OF
INSTRUMENT CLUSTER ASM)

SCREW (2)

CRIMP SLIGHTLY
END OF LEVER
TO RETAIN LINK TO
LEVER

1 HOUSING ASM -
INSTRUMENT
PANEL

SCREW 2

SCREW (2)

STEERING COLUMN

PLATE - INSTRUMENT PANEL
RADIO FILLER

NUT (2)

SCREW (2)

LEVER - TRANSMISSION
SHIFT INDICATOR

SCREW

SCREW (2)

LINK - TRANSMISSION
SHIFT INDICATOR

COVER -
RADIO
OPENING

SCREW (4)

RETAINER - RADIO
OPENING COVER (2)

VIEW - A
(AUTOMATIC TRANSMISSION)

VIEW - B

Fig. 10   Instrument panel housing. 1969-72 intermediate models

from left outlet by twisting "quick-connect" coupling counterclockwise. Disconnect heater control panel.

7. Remove cluster by removing cluster to housing screws, Fig. 11.
8. Reverse above procedure to install.

1969-70 Full Size Exc. Riviera

CAUTION: If equipped with Cruise Control, disconnect speedometer cable from transducer to prevent damage when cluster housing is pulled back.

1. Remove lower instrument panel filler (4 screws), then slide filler forward and down.
2. Remove glove box (5 screws).

NOTE: Do not remove glove box door as it comes off with cover along with ash tray assembly.

3. Remove instrument panel cover (2 nuts above glove box opening and 3 screws thru cluster housing) and remove all screws along bottom edge of cover.
4. Lower steering column by removing two nuts and disconnecting shift indicator link. Pad column to avoid marring paint.
5. Pull cluster housing back after re-

moving eight screws. Rest housing on column and rotate so back of housing is visible.

6. Disconnect speedometer cable and wires.
7. Disconnect heater-air conditioner control panel.

NOTE: Do not disturb cables and vacuum hoses or adjustment will be required after reassembly.

8. Remove instrument cluster (6 cluster to housing screws).
9. Reverse procedure to install.

1969-70 Riviera

CAUTION: If equipped with Cruise Control the upper speedometer cable must be disconnected from the transducer before cluster housing is pulled back.

1. Remove instrument compartment body (8 screws).
2. Remove four nuts at right underside of dash and four screws at housing. Pull instrument panel upper cover rearward to remove.
3. Remove steering column filler (2 screws). If column shift, disconnect shift quadrant link wire at steering

column. Remove two nuts from column mounting bracket and one nut from column wedge. Lower steering column.

4. Remove two nuts from lower edge of instrument panel housing at steering column. Remove four screws across upper edge of instrument panel housing.
5. Remove one nut at lower left side of instrument housing.
6. Remove ash receiver (4 screws).
7. Remove one nut at lower right side of instrument housing.
8. Remove two screws at heater control installation and separate from instrument panel housing.
9. Protect steering column so panel housing will not mar column when housing is tilted back.
10. Disconnect from cluster the speedometer cable, two wiring harness clips, printed circuit connector (all from above).

NOTE: If equipped with Cruise Control, disconnect speedometer cable at Cruise Control transducer located at rear of engine compartment. This will allow instrument housing to be pulled rearward.

11. Disconnect from instrument housing the clock connector and two clock

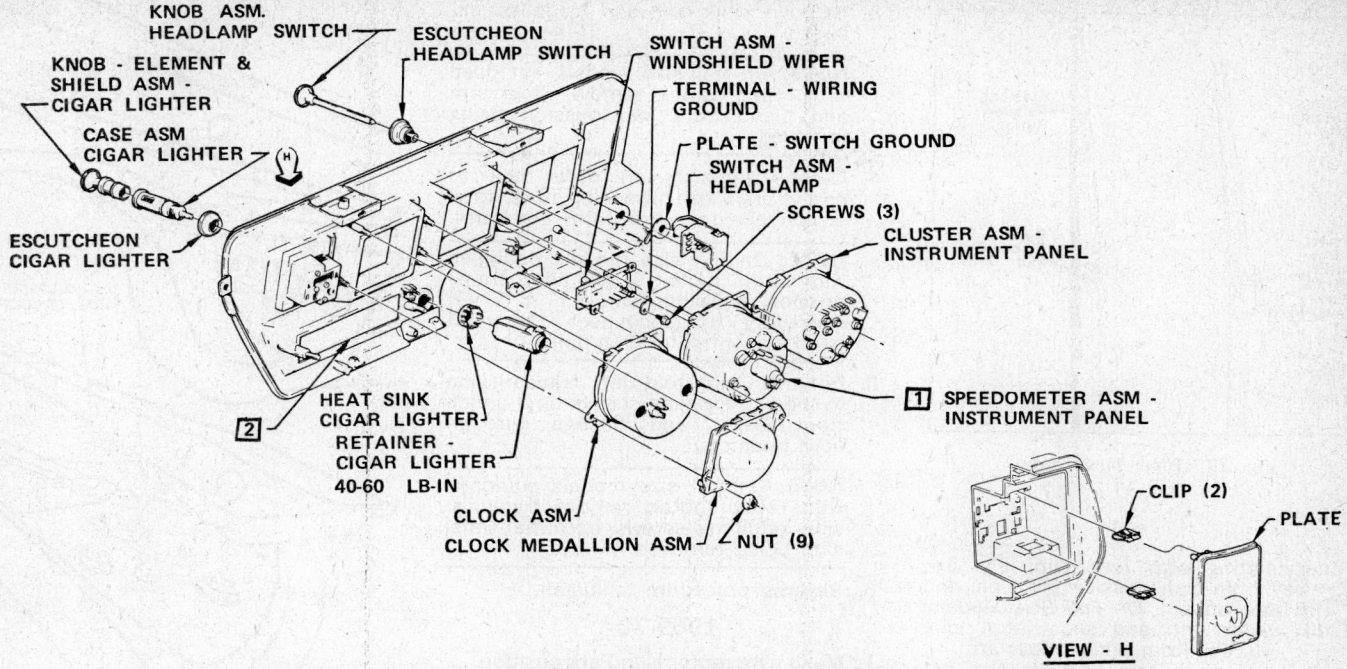

KNOB ASM.
HEADLAMP SWITCH
ESCUTCHEON
HEADLAMP SWITCH
KNOB - ELEMENT &
SHIELD ASM -
CIGAR LIGHTER
SWITCH ASM -
WINDSHIELD WIPER
TERMINAL - WIRING
GROUND
CASE ASM
CIGAR LIGHTER
PLATE - SWITCH GROUND
SWITCH ASM -
HEADLAMP
ESCUTCHEON
CIGAR LIGHTER
SCREWS (3)
CLUSTER ASM -
INSTRUMENT PANEL
HEAT SINK
CIGAR LIGHTER
RETAINER -
CIGAR LIGHTER
40-60 LB-IN
SPEEDOMETER ASM -
INSTRUMENT PANEL
CLOCK ASM
CLOCK MEDALLION ASM
NUT (9)
CLIP (2)
PLATE
VIEW - H

Fig. 11   Instrument cluster. 1970-72 intermediate models (Typical of 1969 models)

bulbs, Cruise Control switch connector, courtesy light connector, W/S wiper-washer switch connector, antenna and accessory switch connectors, cluster ground wire, A/C hose and headlight connector (all from above).

12. Remove instrument panel housing.
13. Separate panel housing from cluster (6 screws), Fig. 12.
14. Reverse procedure to install.

W/S WIPER BLADES

Two methods are used to retain wiper blades to wiper arms, Fig. 13. One method uses a press type release tab. When the release tab is depressed the blade assembly can be slid off the wiper arm pin. The other method uses a coil spring retainer. A screw driver must be inserted on top of the spring and the spring pushed downward. The blade assembly can then be slid off the wiper arm pin. Two methods are also used to retain the blade element in the blade assembly, Fig. 13. One method uses a press type release button. When the button is depressed, the two piece blade assembly can be slid off the blade element. The other method uses a spring type retainer clip in the end of the blade element. When the retainer clip is squeezed together, the blade element can be slid out of the blade assembly.

NOTE: To be sure of correct installation, the element release button, or the spring element retaining clip should be at the end of the wiper blade assembly nearest the wiper transmission.

W/S WIPER ARMS
With Rectangular Motor

1. Wiper motor must be in park position.
2. Use suitable tool to minimize the possibility of windshield or paint finish damage during arm removal.
3. Remove arm by prying up with tool to disengage arm from serrated transmission shaft.

4. To install arm to transmission rotate the required distance and direction so that blades rest in proper position.

With Round Motor

1. Wiper motor must be in park position.
2. Raise hood to gain access to wiper arm.
3. *On Intermediate Models:* lift arm off transmission shaft. On left arm, slide

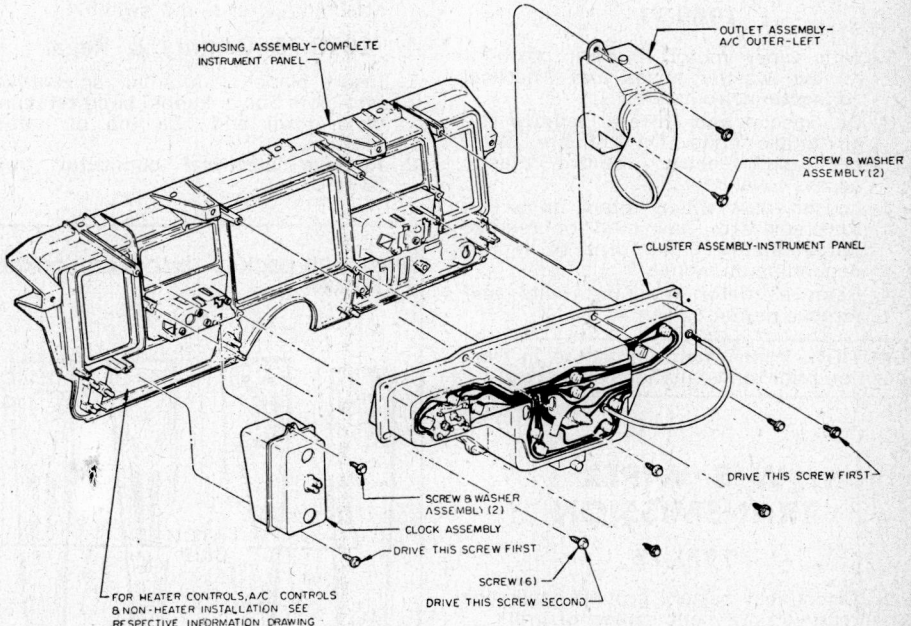

HOUSING ASSEMBLY-COMPLETE
INSTRUMENT PANEL
OUTLET ASSEMBLY—
A/C OUTER-LEFT
SCREW & WASHER
ASSEMBLY (2)
CLUSTER ASSEMBLY-INSTRUMENT PANEL
DRIVE THIS SCREW FIRST
SCREW & WASHER
ASSEMBLY (2)
CLOCK ASSEMBLY
DRIVE THIS SCREW FIRST
SCREW (6)
DRIVE THIS SCREW SECOND
FOR HEATER CONTROLS, A/C CONTROLS
& NON-HEATER INSTALLATION SEE
RESPECTIVE INFORMATION DRAWING

Fig. 12   Instrument cluster. 1969-70 Riviera

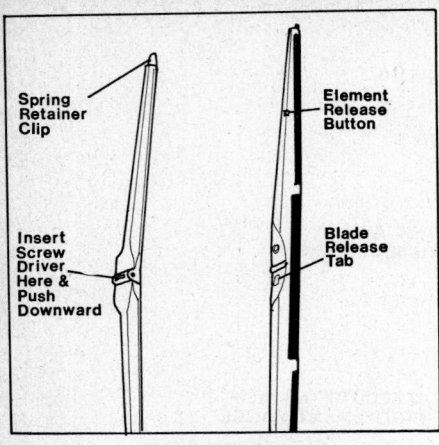

Fig. 13 Wiper blade assy

articulating arm lock clip, Fig. 14, away from transmission pivot pin and lift arm off pin. *On Full Size Models:* lift wiper arm and slide latch clip, Fig. 15, out from under wiper arm.
4. Release wiper arm and lift arm assembly off transmission shaft.

W/S WIPER MOTOR, REPLACE
1972-74

1. Disconnect battery and remove cowl screen.
2. Loosen nuts on wiper drivelink to motor cranking arm and slip drivelink off cranking arm.
3. Disconnect washer hoses and electrical connections.
4. Unfasten motor and remove.

1969-71

1. With wiper motor in Park position, remove washer hoses and electrical connections from motor.
2. On Special and Riviera, remove the air intake grille. On LeSabre, Wildcat and Electra, remove plastic access cover.
3. Loosen nuts which retain drive link to crank arm ball stud or remove nut retaining crank arm to motor, depending on model.
4. Remove motor retaining bolts and remove motor.

CAUTION: Wiper motor must be in Park position prior to installation on the cowl.

W/S WIPER TRANSMISSION
1971-75

1. Disconnect battery ground cable and remove cowl bent screen or grille.
2. Disconnect wiper motor electrical connector.

3. Remove wiper arm and blade assemblies.

NOTE: On full size models equipped with round motor, remove wiper arm and blade from transmission being removed.

4. Loosen transmission drive link to motor crankarm attaching nuts, then disconnect drive link from crankarm.

NOTE: On full size models equipped with round motor, if left hand transmission is being removed, it is not necessary to disconnect the right hand transmission drive link.

5. Remove right and left transmission to body retaining screws and guide transmission and linkage through cowl opening.

NOTE: On full size models equipped with round motor, remove transmission retaining screws from transmission being removed.

6. Reverse procedure to install.

1969-70

1. Make sure motor is in Park position.
2. Remove arm and blade assemblies.
3. Remove air intake grille or screen (if equipped).
4. Disconnect drive rod from motor crank.
5. Remove transmission retaining nuts or bolts and lower drive rods into plenum chamber.
6. Remove transmission assemblies through cowl opening.

W/S WIPER SWITCH, REPLACE
1973-75 Apollo & Skylark

1. Remove electrical connector, three attaching screws and switch.

1973-75 Century & Regal

1. Insert blade of a small screwdriver into slots above knobs, bend retaining clips down and pull top of switch outward.
2. Remove electrical connector from switch.

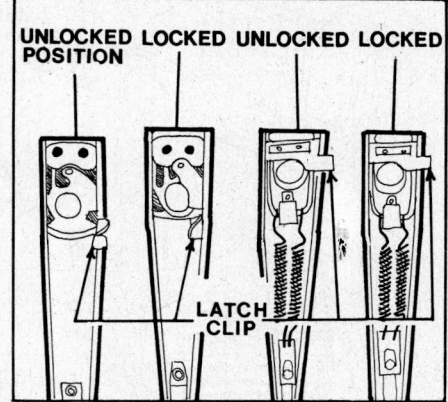

Fig. 15 Wiper arm latch clips

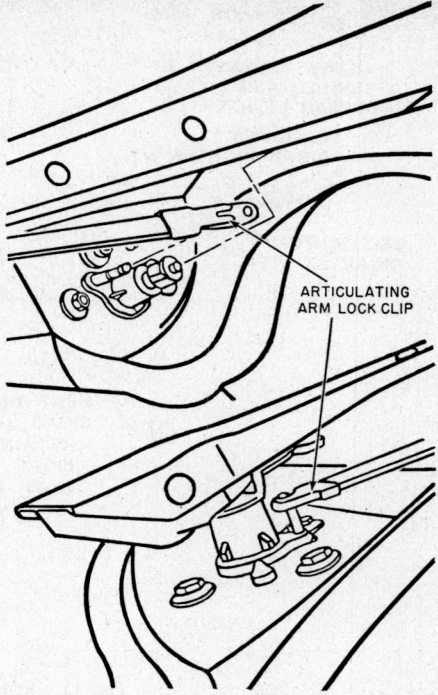

Fig. 14 Articulating arm lock clips

1971-75 Senior Models

CAUTION: On vehicles equipped with an Air Cushion Restraint System, turn ignition switch to "Lock," disconnect battery ground cable and tape end, thereby deactivating system.

1. Remove left trim panel as outlined under the "Instrument Cluster, 1971-74 Full Size" procedure.
2. Using a screwdriver, depress switch retaining clips and remove switch.
3. Disconnect seelite cable and electrical connector.
4. Reverse procedure to install.

1970 LeSabre, Estate Wagon, Wildcat & Electra

1. Remove lower instrument panel filler (4 screws) then slide filler forward and down.
2. Lower steering column by removing two nuts and disconnecting shift indicator link.
3. Unplug connector from switch.
4. Remove wiper knob.
5. Remove switch (two screws).

1969 LeSabre, Wildcat & Electra

1. Pry wiper-washer switch from cluster housing.
2. Remove switch by unplugging switch connector.
3. Reverse procedure to install.

1969-72 Special & Skylark

1. If air conditioned, remove two screws at left A/C distribution duct and remove duct.

2. Remove steering column filler (4 screws).
3. Unplug connectors from wiper-washer switches.
4. Remove screws from switches and pull switches down.
5. Reverse procedure to install.

1969-70 Riviera

1. Pull instrument panel housing assembly out to rest on column and knees.
2. Unplug connectors from wiper-washer switches.
3. Unfasten and pull switches out (2 screws).
4. Reverse procedure to install.

RADIO, REPLACE

NOTE: When installing radio, be sure to adjust antenna trimmer for peak performance.

1975 Senior Models

CAUTION: On vehicles equipped with an Air Cushion Restraint System, turn ignition switch to "Lock," disconnect battery ground cable and tape end, thereby deactivating system.

1. Disconnect battery ground cable.
2. Pry out lower right instrument panel trim.
3. Remove radio knobs, escutcheons and retaining nuts from control shafts.
4. Remove plastic trim plate.
5. Disconnect leads from radio and remove rear radio attaching nut, then pull radio from panel.
6. Reverse procedure to install.

1974 Senior Models with Air Cushion Restraint System

1. Turn ignition switch to "Lock" and disconnect battery ground cable and tape end.
2. Remove both lower instrument panel cover trim plates.
3. Disconnect parking brake release cable, then remove lower left instrument panel cover retaining screws and cover.
4. Remove two horizontal screws below instrument panel, four screws from upper horizontal surface of instrument panel, two outer screws from glove box door hinge and screw from instrument panel cover right side.
5. Disconnect leads from radio.
6. Release four clips behind instrument panel by grasping tongue of right hand side clip, squeezing and pulling forward.
7. Remove radio knobs, escutcheons and instrument panel trim plate.
8. Remove retaining nuts from control shafts and power antenna relay retaining screws.
9. Loosen left radio support nut, remove right radio support nut and lower radio from instrument panel.
10. Reverse procedure to install.

1973-75 Apollo & Skylark

1. Remove radio knobs, bezels, nuts and side brace screw.
2. Disconnect antenna and leads.
3. Remove radio from under dash.
4. Reverse procedure to install.

1973-75 Century & Regal

1. Remove radio knobs and escutcheons. If equipped with center air duct assembly control, remove screws.
2. Disconnect antenna and leads.
3. Remove radio support nut.
4. Remove attaching nuts and slide radio to front of car and downward.
5. Reverse procedure to install.

1972-74 Senior Models less Air Cushion Restraint System

1. Remove knobs and escutcheons. If equipped with trip-set and speed alert, unscrew the cone shaped knobs.
2. Remove right trim panel.
3. Remove retaining nuts from shafts.
4. Remove ash tray and separate connectors and antenna lead in from radio.

1971 Senior Models

1. Remove right trim panel as described previously.
2. Remove ash tray assembly.
3. Disconnect antenna lead-in and radio connector.
4. Loosen radio side brace.
5. Remove radio retaining nuts on front of panel.
6. Disconnect center A/C duct behind ash tray.
7. Remove radio.

1970 LeSabre, Estate Wagon, Wildcat & Electra

1. Remove instrument panel lower filler (4 screws) then slide filler forward and down.
2. Remove radio ground strap screws.
3. Remove radio knobs, escutcheons, hex nuts and lower radio downward.

NOTE: On air condition cars, remove center distributor duct for clearance.

4. Disconnect antenna and leads and remove radio.

1969-72 Special & Skylark

1. Remove radio knobs, escutcheons and two hex nuts.
2. Remove filler plate (2 screws).
3. Remove ash tray and slide (4 screws).
4. Remove radio support (2 screws). If air conditioned, remove center distributor duct.
5. Remove two nuts attaching radio face to instrument panel and move radio downward.
6. Disconnect antenna lead and wiring and remove radio.

7. Reverse procedure to install.

1969 LeSabre, Wildcat & Electra

1. On A/C models, remove center distribution duct.
2. Remove right instrument trim panel and remove screw in bottom of radio.
3. Remove radio knobs and escutcheons and nuts. Unplug antenna lead and wires from radio.
4. Remove radio downward.
5. Reverse procedure to install.

1969-70 Riviera

1. Remove ash tray assembly (4 screws).
2. Remove radio knobs, escutcheons and hex nuts.
3. Unplug antenna and leads from radio.
4. Remove radio downward through ash tray opening.
5. Reverse procedure to install.

HEATER CORE REMOVAL

After draining radiator and disconnecting heater hoses, proceed as follows:

1973-75 Apollo & Skylark

Without Air Conditioning

1. Disconnect battery ground cable and drain radiator.
2. Disconnect heater hoses from core and plug hoses and core openings to prevent coolant spillage.
3. Remove core case retaining nuts from engine side of dash, Fig. 16.
4. Remove glove compartment and door.
5. Using a 1/4 inch twist drill, drill out lower right hand heater case stud from inside vehicle.
6. Pull heater core and case assembly from dash.
7. Disconnect heater cables and blower motor resistor connector from case, then remove heater core and case assembly from vehicle.
8. Remove core tube seal and retaining strips, then heater core from case.
9. Reverse procedure to install.

With Air Conditioning

1. Disconnect battery ground cable and drain radiator.
2. Disconnect upper heater hose and plug hose and core openings. Remove accessible heater core and case attaching nuts.
3. Remove right front fender skirt bolts, lower skirt and disconnect lower heater hose from core tube. Plug hose and core openings.
4. Remove lower right hand heater core and case attaching nuts, Fig. 16.
5. Remove glove compartment and door.
6. Remove right hand kick panel recirculation vacuum diaphragm.
7. Remove heater outlet from bottom of heater case, then cold air distributor duct.

8. Remove heater case extension screws, then separate extension from heater case.
9. Disconnect heater cables and electrical connectors from heater case, then remove heater core and case assembly. Separate core from case.
10. Reverse procedure to install.

1973-75 Century & Regal

Without Air Conditioning

1. Disconnect control cables from door levers.
2. Remove four nuts securing heater to dash, Fig. 17.
3. Remove screw securing defroster outlet to heater.
4. Work heater assembly rearward until studs clear dash.

With Air Conditioning

1. Disconnect control cables from temperature door guides and vacuum hoses from actuator diaphragms.
2. Remove resistor assembly and reach through opening and remove one attaching nut to dash. Remove one attaching nut to dash directly over transmission and two attaching nuts to upper and lower inboard evaporator case half.
3. From inside car remove one screw in lower righthand corner on passenger side.
4. Remove lower attaching outlets and work assembly rearward until studs clear dash.

GASKET
SEALER (CEMENT)
SEAL
CORE PIPES
HEATER CORE AND CASE ASSEMBLY
EVAPORATOR ASSEMBLY
STUDS
DEFROSTER NOZZLE
STUD
HEATER CASE EXTENSION (DISTRIBUTOR ASSEMBLY)
DISTRIBUTOR DUCT (COLD AIR)
SEALER (CEMENT)
GASKET
HEATER OUTLET DUCT

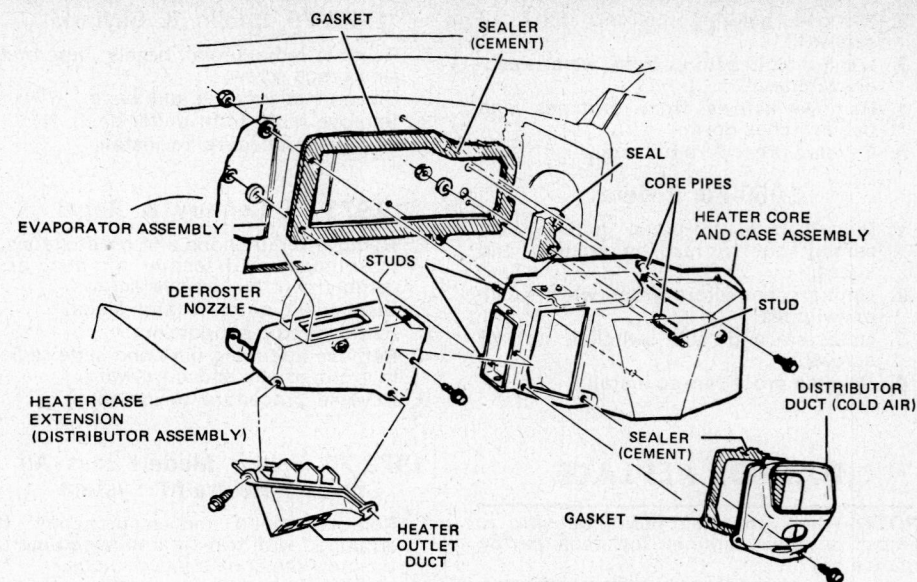

Fig. 16 Heater core. 1973-75 Apollo & Skylark (Typical)

1969-72 Special & Skylark

Without Air Conditioning

1. Remove right front fender skirt.
2. Disconnect control cables from lever of defroster door and outside air inlet door on heater.
3. Disconnect temperature control cable

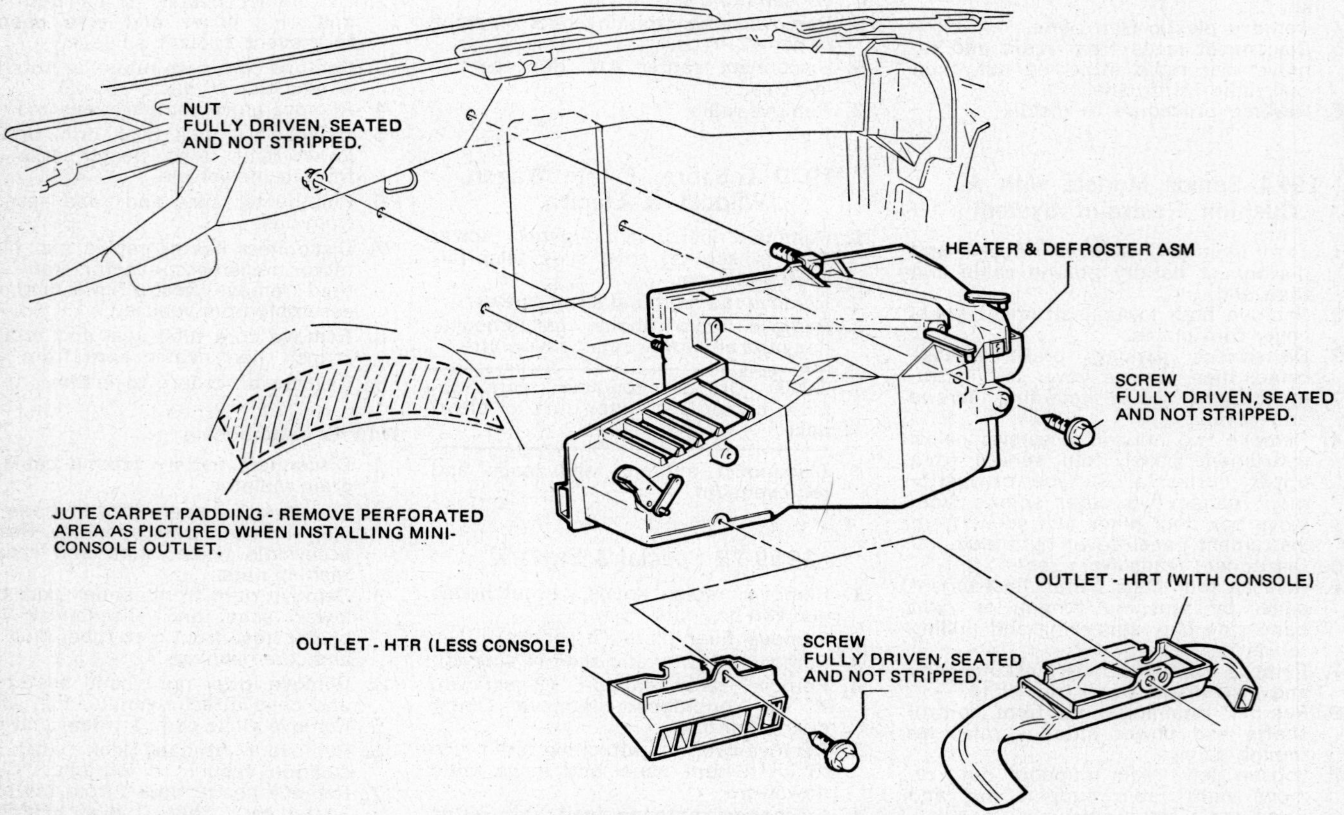

NUT
FULLY DRIVEN, SEATED AND NOT STRIPPED.
HEATER & DEFROSTER ASM
SCREW
FULLY DRIVEN, SEATED AND NOT STRIPPED.
JUTE CARPET PADDING - REMOVE PERFORATED AREA AS PICTURED WHEN INSTALLING MINI-CONSOLE OUTLET.
OUTLET - HRT (WITH CONSOLE)
OUTLET - HTR (LESS CONSOLE)
SCREW
FULLY DRIVEN, SEATED AND NOT STRIPPED.

Fig. 17 Heater core. 1973-75 intermediate models (Typical)

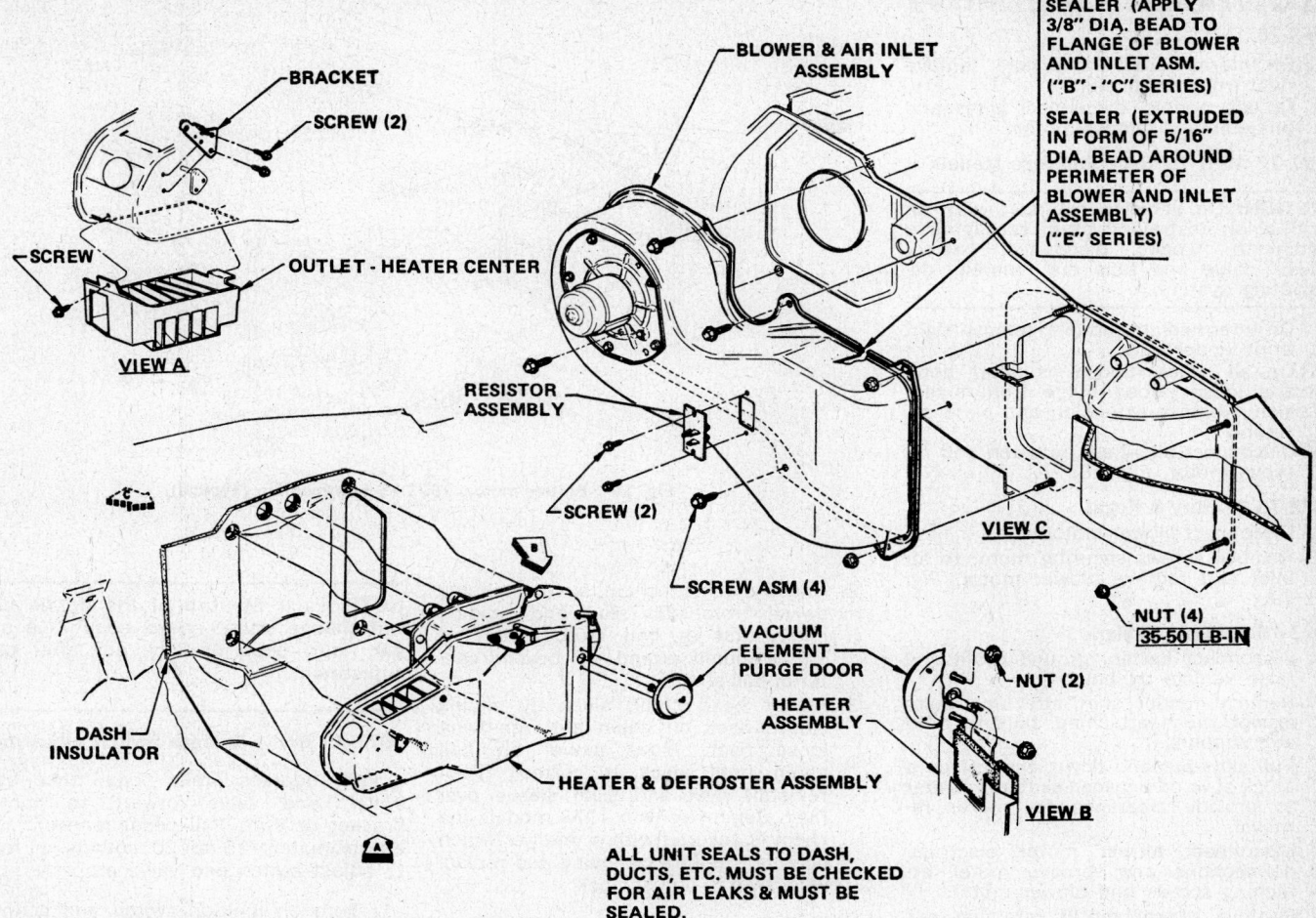

SEALER (APPLY 3/8" DIA. BEAD TO FLANGE OF BLOWER AND INLET ASM. ("B"-"C" SERIES)

SEALER (EXTRUDED IN FORM OF 5/16" DIA. BEAD AROUND PERIMETER OF BLOWER AND INLET ASSEMBLY) ("E" SERIES)

BRACKET
SCREW (2)
SCREW
OUTLET - HEATER CENTER
VIEW A

BLOWER & AIR INLET ASSEMBLY

RESISTOR ASSEMBLY
SCREW (2)
SCREW ASM (4)
VIEW C
NUT (4)
35-50 LB-IN

DASH INSULATOR

VACUUM ELEMENT PURGE DOOR
HEATER ASSEMBLY
NUT (2)
VIEW B

HEATER & DEFROSTER ASSEMBLY

ALL UNIT SEALS TO DASH, DUCTS, ETC. MUST BE CHECKED FOR AIR LEAKS & MUST BE SEALED.

Fig. 18   Heater core & blower motor. 1971-74 full size models (Typical)

from lever of temperature door on heater.
4. Remove attaching nuts from heater studs.
5. Remove connector from blower motor resistor.
6. Remove screws from lower part of defroster outlet to top of heater.
7. Work heater rearward until studs clear dash and remove.
8. Reverse procedure to install.

With Air Conditioning
1. Remove instrument panel cover with right side A/C outlet and hose attached.
2. Remove center A/C duct, left A/C outlet duct, A/C distributor duct and defroster assembly.
3. Disconnect defroster and temperature control wires.
4. Unfasten and remove air conditioner-heater assembly from dash.
5. Heater core can now be removed from assembly.

1972-75 All Senior Models
1969-71 LeSabre, Wildcat & Electra

CAUTION: On vehicles equipped with an Air Cushion Restraint System, turn ignition

switch to "Lock," disconnect battery ground cable and tape end, thereby de-activating system.

Without Air Conditioning
1. Disconnect vacuum hoses from defroster door and outside air inlet door actuator diaphrams and control cable from temperature door lever.
2. Unfasten connector from blower motor resistor.
3. Remove nuts securing heater to dash, Fig. 18.
4. Remove screws securing defroster outlet adapter to heater and raise adapter away from heater.
5. Work heater rearward until studs clear dash and remove.
6. Reverse procedure to install.

With Air Conditioning
1. Remove instrument panel cover with center A/C outlet and right A/C outlet and hose attached.
2. Remove center A/C duct, A/C distributor duct and defroster outlet manifold assembly.
3. Disconnect defroster and temperature control wires and pink hose

from mode door diaphragm.
4. Unfasten and remove air conditioner-heater assembly from dash.
5. Heater core can now be removed from assembly.

1969-71 Riviera

Without Air Conditioning
1. Remove right front fender.
2. Disconnect blower motor wire and resistor connectors.
3. Disconnect temperature door cable.
4. Disconnect vacuum hoses attached to outside door and vent heater door vacuum diaphrams.
5. Remove screws securing blower and heater assembly to dash and remove.
6. Reverse procedure to install.

With Air Conditioning
1. Disconnect temperature door control cable and blower resistor connector.
2. Unfasten and remove air conditioner-heater assembly from dash.
3. Remove air distributor duct and heater core.

BLOWER MOTOR REMOVE

1969-70

1. On Intermediates and Riviera, remove right front fender skirt.
2. On all models, disconnect wires and unfasten and remove motor.

1971-72 All & 1973-74 Full Size Models

CAUTION: On vehicles equipped with an Air Cushion Restraint System, turn ignition switch to "Lock", disconnect battery ground cable and tape end, thereby de-activating system.

1. On Intermediate models, remove right front fender skirt.
2. On all other models, support hood and loosen hood hinge from extension. Remove extension and plate assembly.
3. Disconnect all wires, unfasten and remove motor, Fig. 18.

1973-75 Century & Regal

1. Disconnect blower motor wire.
2. Remove screws securing motor to air inlet and remove blower motor, Fig. 19.

1973-75 Apollo & Skylark

1. Disconnect battery ground cable and raise vehicle on hoist.
2. Remove fender skirt attaching bolts except those attaching skirt to radiator support.
3. Pull skirt out and down, then place a block of wood between skirt and fender to provide clearance for motor removal.
4. Disconnect blower motor electrical connections and remove motor attaching screws and blower motor.
5. Remove blower motor retaining nut and separate impeller from motor.
6. Reverse procedure to install.

SPEED CONTROL

1969-75 Cruise Master

Bead Chain Adjustment

1. Adjust engine hot idle speed and mixture, then shut off engine.

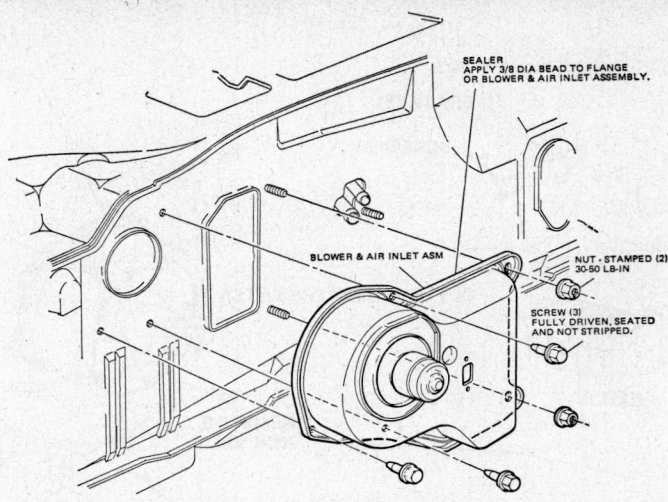

Fig. 19   Blower motor. 1973-75 intermediate (Typical)

2. Check slack in chain by unsnapping swivel from ball stud and holding chain taut at ball stud; center of swivel should extend $\frac{1}{8}''$ beyond center of ball stud.
3. Adjust bead chain slack by sliding sleeve back on chain and removing loose rivet. Move swivel on ball chain until slack is correct. Then reinstall rivet and slide sleeve over rivet. Beginning with 1973 models the chain is secured with a retainer which does not require removing and replacing a rivet to adjust slack.

Cruise Speed Adjustment

The cruise speed adjustment can be set as follows:

1. If car cruises below engagement speed, screw orifice tube on transducer outward.
2. If car cruises above engagement speed, screw orifice tube inward.

NOTE: Each $\frac{1}{4}$ turn of the orifice tube will change cruise speed about one mile per hour. Snug up lock nut after each adjustment.

1971-75 Brake Release Switch Adjustment

Fully depress brake pedal, then push switch and valve forward to contact bracket or arm. Pull pedal rearward with approximately 15 to 20 pounds of force to adjust switch and valve properly.

1. Turn on ignition switch and connect a test light between one terminal of brake release switch and ground; select terminal where light goes out when pedal is depressed.
2. Loosen screw that retains switch to pedal support bracket. Position switch so circuit opens (light goes out) when pedal is depressed $\frac{1}{4}''$. Tighten screw and recheck.

Engine Section

NOTE: For service see Chevrolet Chapter for 6-250; Oldsmobile Chapter for V8-260 and Pontiac Chapter for V8-400.

ENGINE MOUNTS REPLACE

1. Raise car and provide frame support at front of car.
2. Support weight of engine at forward edge of pan.
3. Remove mount to engine block bolts. Raise engine slightly and remove mount to mount bracket bolt and nut. Remove mount.
4. Reverse above procedure to install and torque to specifications as shown on Figs. 1 thru 9.

ENGINE, REPLACE

1. Remove hood and drain radiator.
2. Remove fan shroud, radiator and air cleaner.
3. If equipped with A/C, disconnect compressor brackets and position out of way.
4. Remove power steering from bracket and position out of way.
5. Disconnect all hoses, linkages and electrical connections from engine.
6. Disconnect exhaust pipes and remove converter cover.
7. Remove flywheel to converter or pressure plate bolts, engine to transmission bolts and motor mount bolts.
8. Support transmission and remove engine.

CYLINDER HEADS

Some cylinder head gaskets are coated

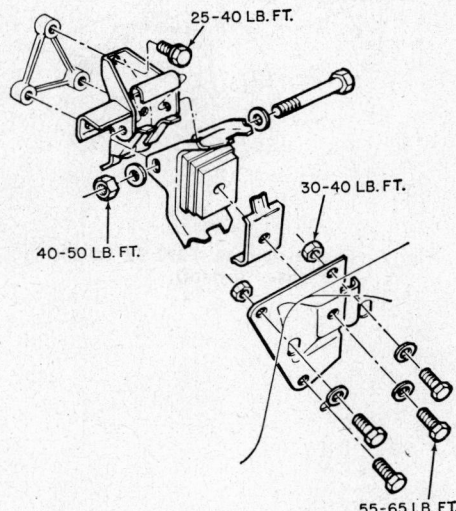

Fig. 1 Engine mounts. 1969-70 Six

with a special lacquer to provide a good seal once the parts have warmed up. Do not use any additional sealer on such gaskets. If the gasket does not have this lacquer coating, apply suitable sealer to both sides.

1969-75

1. Drain coolant and disconnect battery.
2. Remove intake manifold.
3. When removing right cylinder head, remove Delcotron and/or A/C com-

pressor with mounting bracket and move out of the way. *Do not disconnect hoses from air compressor.*
4. When removing left cylinder head, remove oil dipstick, power steering pump and move out of the way with hoses attached.
5. Disconnect exhaust manifold from head to be removed.
6. Remove rocker arm shaft and lift out push rods. On 1973-75 Apollo models equipped with V8-350 engines. To replace left cylinder head, disconnect power brake unit hose at rear of cylinder head. Remove left front engine mount bolt and loosen right front engine mount bolt. Raise engine until exhaust manifold clears steering gear.
7. Remove cylinder head.
8. Reverse procedure to install and tighten bolts gradually and evenly in the sequence shown in Figs. 10 and 11.

ROCKER ARMS

1970-75, V8-350, 455 & 1975 V6-231

A nylon retainer is used to retain the rocker arm. Break them below their heads with a chisel, Fig. 13, or pry out with channel locks. On 1970-72 engines, install rocker arms so the external rib on each pair of arms point away from the rocker arm shaft bolt, Fig. 14. On 1973-75 engines, production rocker arms can be installed in any sequence since the arms are identical, however, replacement arms are identified with a stamping, right (R) and left (L).

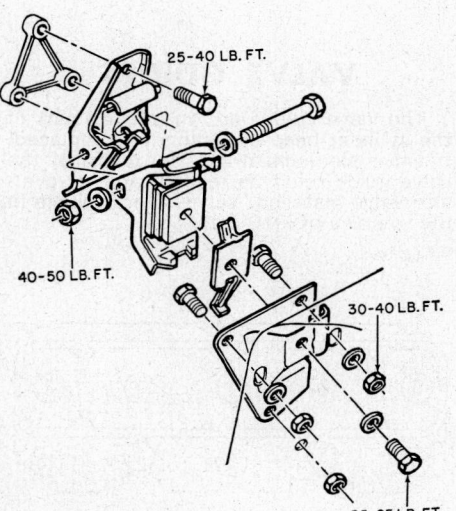

Fig. 2 Engine mounts. 1971 Six

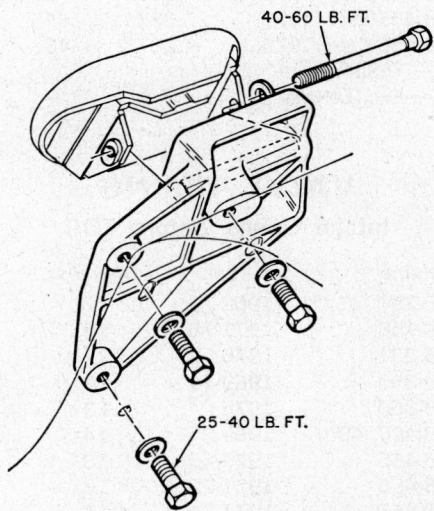

Fig. 3 Engine mounts

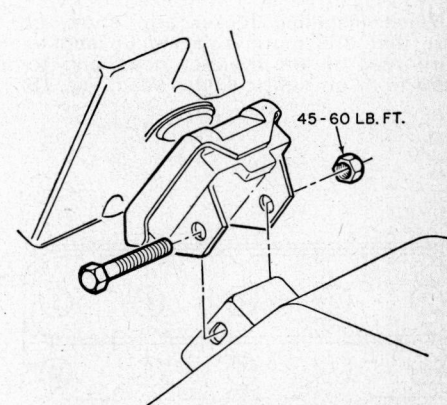

Fig. 4 Engine mounts. 1969-70 LeSabre V8-350

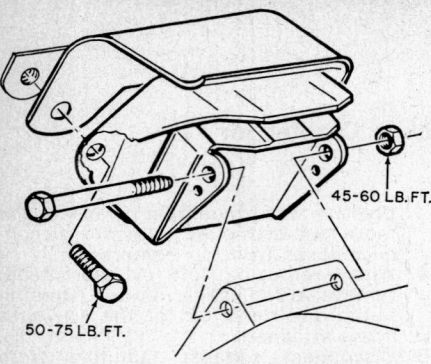

Fig. 5   Engine mounts. 1969 Wildcat, Electra, Riviera V8-400, 430; 1970 V8-455 LeSabre & Riviera

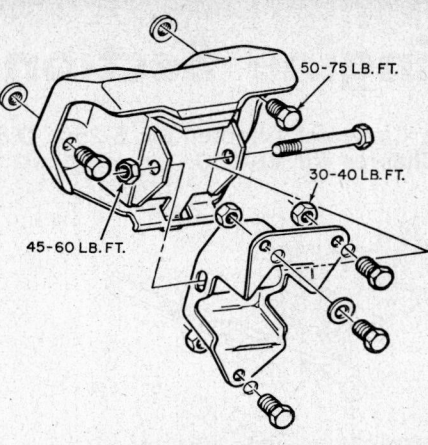

Fig. 7   Engine mounts. 1971-72 V8-350 (Exc. Skylark)

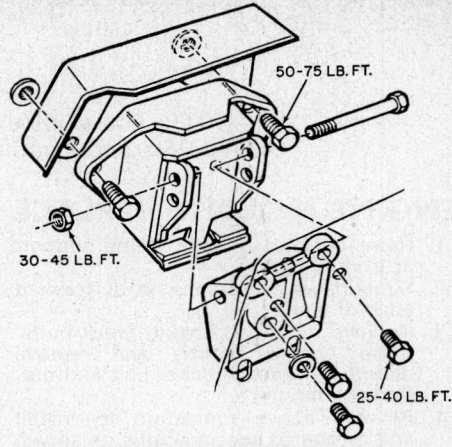

Fig. 8   Engine mounts. 1969-70 Special & Skylark V8-400; 1971-72 Skylark and all 1973-74 with V8-455. Typical

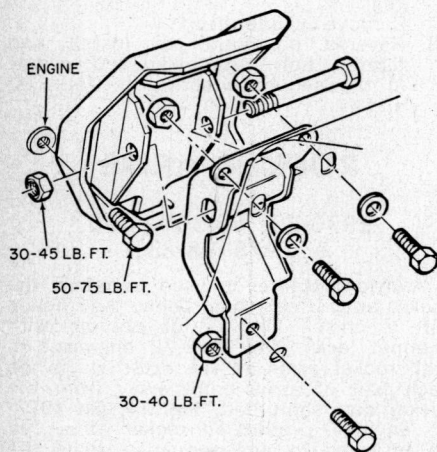

Fig. 6   Engine mounts. 1969-72 Skylark and all 1973-74 with V8-350. Typical

VALVE ARRANGEMENT
Front to Rear

V8-350, 400, 430, 455 . . . . . E-I-I-E-E-I-I-E

VALVE LIFT SPECS.

Engine	Year	Intake	Exhaust
6-250	1969-74	.3880	.3880
6-250	1975	.3880	.4051
V6-231	1975	.4011	.3768
V8-350	1969	.3766	.3840
V8-400, 430	1969	.4187	.4482
V8-350	1970-75	.3818	.3984
V8-455	1970	.3873	.4584
V8-455	1971-72	.3873	.456
V8-455	1973-74	.3873	.455
V8-455[1]	1975	.3873	.445
V8-455[2]	1975	.3873	.403

[1]—LeSabre.
[2]—Exc. LeSabre.

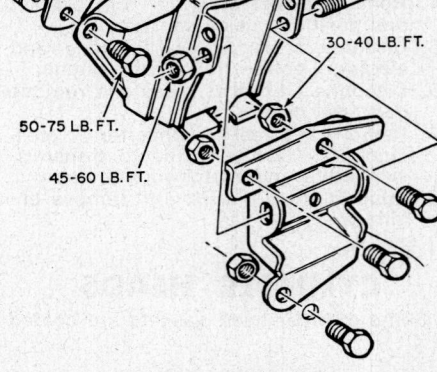

Fig. 9   Engine mounts. 1971 V8-455 Riviera; 1972 V8-455 (Exc. Skylark)

1969 V8-350, 400, 430

When installing rocker arm shaft, be sure that drill mark is facing up and toward rear of left cylinder head and toward front on right cylinder head, Fig. 15.

VALVE GUIDES

The valve guides are an integral part of the cylinder head and cannot be replaced. If valve stem clearance is excessive, the valve guide must be reamed and an oversize valve installed. Valves are available in the oversize of .010 inch.

VALVE TIMING
Intake Opens Before TDC

Engine	Year	Degrees
6-250	1969-70	62
6-250	1971-75	16
V6-231	1975	17
V8-350	1969-74	24
V8-350	1975	19
V8-400, 430	1969	14
V8-455	1970	18
V8-455	1971-72	12
V8-455	1973-74	14
V8-455	1975	10

Fig. 10   Cylinder head tightening sequence. 1969 V8-350, 400, 430

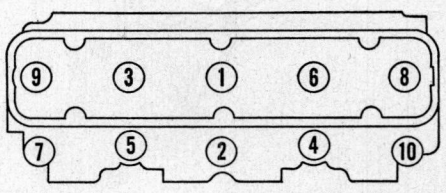

Fig. 11   Cylinder head tightening sequence. 1970-75 V8-350, 455

Fig. 12   Intake manifold tightening sequence. V8-350, 400, 430, 455

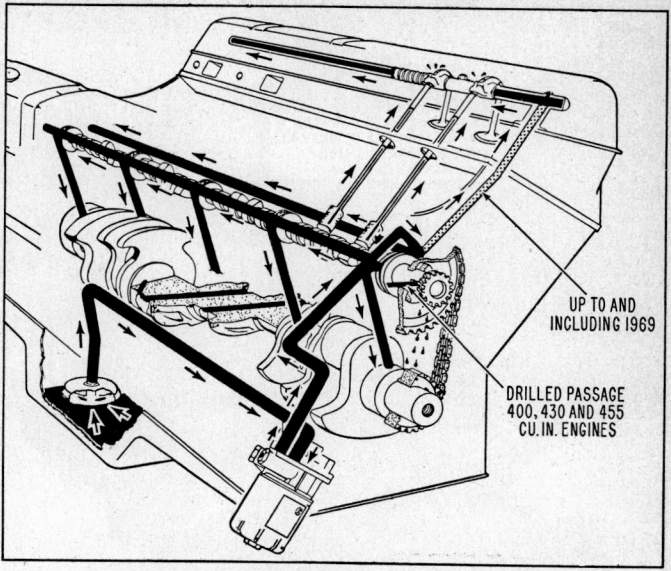

Engine lubrication system.   350, 400, 430, 455

UP TO AND INCLUDING 1969

DRILLED PASSAGE 400, 430 AND 455 CU. IN. ENGINES

HYDRAULIC VALVE LIFTERS

Failure of an hydraulic valve lifter, Fig. 16, is generally caused by an inadequate oil supply or dirt. An air leak at the intake side of the oil pump or too much oil in the engine will cause air bubbles in the oil supply to the lifters, causing them to collapse. This is a prob-

DRILL MARK- (REAR) LEFT BANK (FRONT) RIGHT BANK

ROCKER ARM

EACH PAIR MUST BE OFFSET

Fig. 15   Rocker arms positioned on shaft. 1969 V8-350, 400, 430

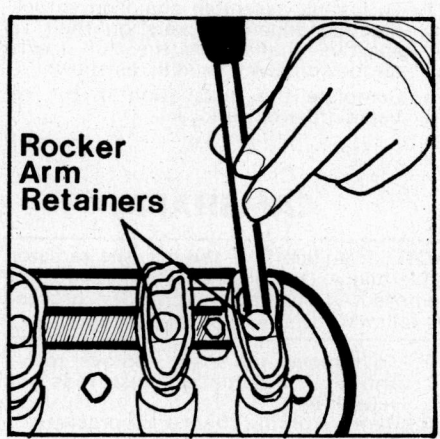

Rocker Arm Retainers

Fig. 13   Removing nylon retainer. 1970-74 V8-350, 455 & 1975 V6-231

able cause of trouble if several lifters fail to function, but air in the oil is an unlikely cause of failure of a single unit.

The valve lifters may be lifted out of their bores after removing the rocker arms, push rods and intake manifold. Adjustable pliers with taped jaws may be used to remove lifters that are stuck due to varnish, carbon, etc. Fig. 16 illustrates the type of lifter used.

NOTE: 1974-75 in production .010" oversize lifters are being used for oversize lifter bores. The lifter bore will be marked with an "O" and the lifter will have two grooves in the lifter body. When replacing lifters, check bores for oversize markings.

TIMING CHAIN COVER
V6-231 & V8-350, 400, 430, 455

1. Drain cooling system and remove radiator.
2. Remove fan, pulleys and belts.
3. Remove crankshaft pulley and reinforcement.

4. If equipped with power steering, remove any pump bracket bolts attached to timing chain cover and loosen and remove any other bolts necessary that will allow pump and brackets to be moved out of the way.
5. Remove fuel pump.
6. Remove Delcotron and brackets.
7. Remove distributor cap and pull spark plug wire retainers off brackets on rocker arm cover. Swing distrib-

ROCKER ARM   EXTERNAL RIB

Fig. 14   Rocker arm positioned on shaft. 1970-72 V8-350, 455

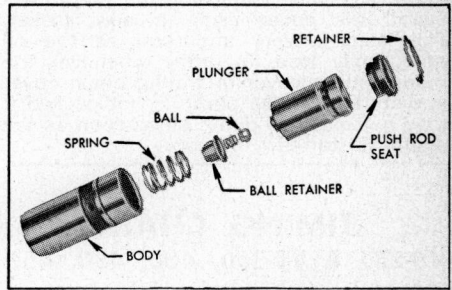

RETAINER PLUNGER BALL SPRING BALL RETAINER PUSH ROD SEAT BODY

Fig. 16   Hydraulic valve lifter parts

Fig. 17 Timing chain cover installation. V8-400, 430, 455

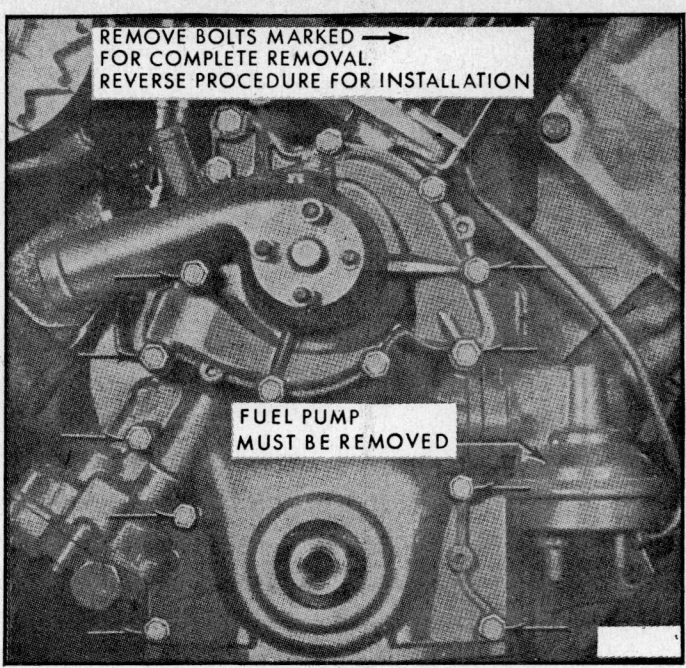

Fig. 18 Timing chain cover installation. V8-350

utor cap with wires attached out of the way. Disconnect distributor primary lead. On 400, 430, remove coil.
8. Remove distributor. *If chain and sprockets are not to be disturbed, note position of distributor rotor for installation in the same position.*
9. Loosen and slide clamp on thermostat by-pass hose rearward.
10. Remove bolts attaching chain cover to block.
11. On V6-231 and V8-350 engines, remove two oil pan-to-chain cover bolts and remove cover.
12. On 400, 430, 455 engines, remove four oil pan-to-chain cover bolts. *Do not remove the five bolts attaching water pump to chain cover.* Remove cover, using care to avoid damaging oil pan gasket.
13. Reverse procedure to install, noting data shown in Figs. 17 and 18.

IMPORTANT

Remove the oil pump cover and pack the space around the oil pump gears completely full of vaseline. There must be no air space left inside the pump. Reinstall the cover using a new gasket. This step is very important as the oil pump may lose its prime whenever the pump, pump cover or timing chain cover is disturbed. If the pump is not packed it may not begin to pump oil as soon as the engine is started.

TIMING CHAIN
V6-231 & V8-350, 400, 430, 455

1. With the timing case cover removed as outlined above, temporarily install the vibration damper bolt and wash-

er in end of crankshaft.
2. Turn crankshaft so sprockets are positioned as shown in Fig. 19. Use a sharp rap on a wrench handle to start the vibration damper bolt out without disturbing the position of the sprockets.
3. On V8-400, 430 and 455, remove the oil pan.
4. Remove oil slinger.
5. On V6-231 and V8-350 remove camshaft distributor drive gear and fuel pump eccentric. On V8-400, 430 and 455, remove sprocket bolts.
6. Use two large screwdrivers to al-

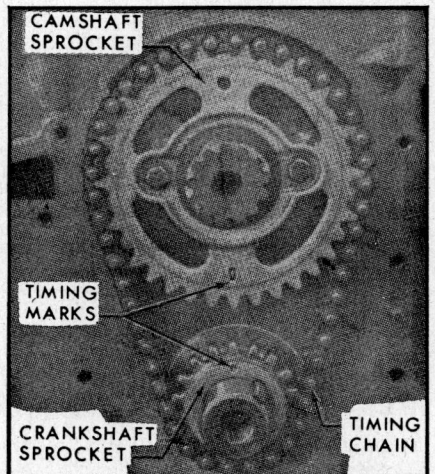

Fig. 19 Valve timing marks.
V6-231 & V8-350, 400, 430, 455

ternately pry the camshaft sprocket then the crankshaft sprocket forward until the camshaft sprocket is free. Then remove camshaft sprocket and chain, and crankshaft sprocket off crankshaft.
7. To install, assemble chain on sprockets and slide sprockets on their respective shafts with the "0" marks on the sprockets lined up as shown.
8. Complete the installation in the reverse order of removal.

CAMSHAFT

NOTE: If engine is in the car, the radiator, grille and A/C components will have to be removed. If engine is out of car, proceed as follows:

1. To remove camshaft, remove rocker arm shaft assemblies, push rods and valve lifters.
2. Remove timing chain and sprockets.
3. Slide camshaft out of engine, using care not to mar the bearing surfaces.

PISTONS & RODS, ASSEMBLE

Rods and pistons should be assembled and installed as shown in Figs. 20 and 20A.

PISTONS, PINS & RINGS

Pistons are available in standard sizes and oversizes of .001, .005, .010, .020

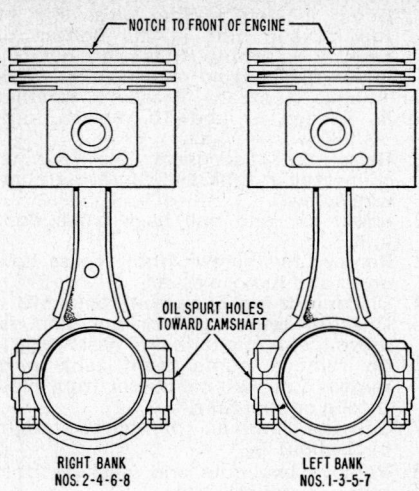

Fig. 20 Pistons and rod assembly.
1969-72 350, 400, 430, 455

Rings are furnished in standard sizes and oversizes of .010, .020 and .030 inch.
Piston pins are supplied in standard sizes and oversizes of .003 and .005 inch.

MAIN & ROD BEARINGS

Main bearings are available in standard sizes and undersizes of .001, .002, .003 and .010 inch.
Rod bearings are furnished in standard sizes and undersizes of .001, .002 and .010", Fig. 21.

CRANKSHAFT OIL SEAL

A braided oil seal is pressed into the upper and lower grooves behind the rear main bearing.

OIL PAN

6-250 Exc. 1973-75 Apollo

To remove oil pan it is necessary to

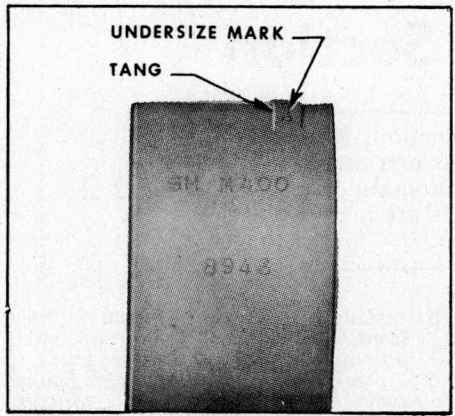

Fig. 21 Location of undersize mark on main and rod bearing shell

---

remove the engine from the chassis.

1975 V6-231

1. Support vehicle on hoist and drain oil.
2. Remove transmission dust cover and exhaust crossover pipe.
3. Remove oil pan bolts and allow pan to drop.

NOTE: To remove oil pan, front wheels must be turned to the left, also the crankshaft may have to be turned to provide clearance.

4. Reverse procedure to install.

1973-75 Apollo 6-250

Refer to the 1973-75 Six cylinder procedure in the Chevrolet Chapter.

1970-75 V8-350, 455

NOTE: On 1973-75 Intermediate models, it is no longer necessary to disconnect the idler arm. Otherwise, proceed as follows:

1. Disconnect battery and drain oil.
2. Remove fan shroud to radiator tie bar screws.
3. Remove air cleaner and disconnect linkage to throttle.
4. Raise and support car on stands.
5. With manual transmission, loosen clutch equalizer bracket to frame bolts. Disconnect crossover pipe at engine.
6. With automatic transmission, remove lower flywheel housing. Remove shift linkage attaching bolt and swing out of way. Disconnect crossover pipe at engine. Disconnect idler arm at frame and push steering linkage forward to crossmember. Remove front engine mount bolts and raise engine by placing jack under crankshaft pulley mounting.

NOTE: If car is air conditioned, at this point it will be necessary to place a support under right side of transmission prior to raising engine to prevent transmission from cocking to the right when raised.

7. Remove oil pan. It may be necessary to position crankshaft so 1 and 2 crankpin and counterweight will not interfere with front of pan.

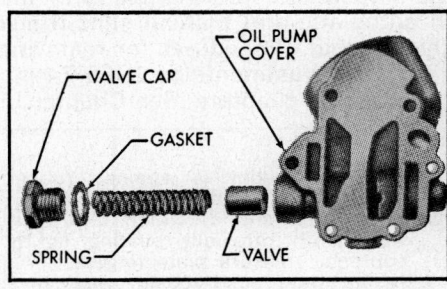

Fig. 22 Oil pump cover and by-pass valve. V6-231 & V8-350, 400, 430, 455

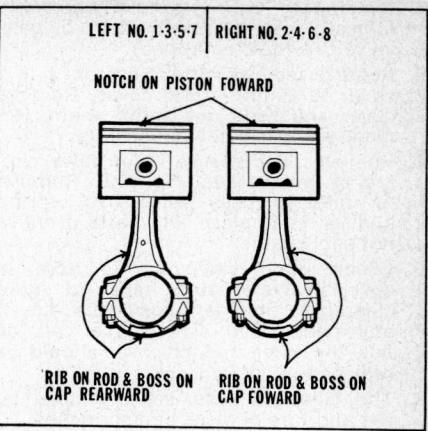

Fig. 20A Piston and rod assembly. 1973-75 350, 455

1969 V8-350, 400, 430

1. Disconnect battery and drain oil.
2. Raise and support car on stands.
3. With manual transmission, loosen clutch equalizer bracket-to-frame bolts. Remove exhaust crossover pipe, and front engine mounting bolts. Remove fan shroud-to-radiator tie bar screws.
4. With automatic transmission, remove lower flywheel housing. Remove shift linkage attaching bolts and swing out of the way (LeSabre only). Remove front engine mounting bolts. Remove fan shroud-to-radiator tie bar screws.
5. Raise engine by placing jack under crankshaft pulley mounting.
6. Unfasten and remove pan.
7. Reverse procedure to install. loosen clutch equalizer bracket-to-frame bolts. Remove lower flywheel housing, exhaust crossover pipe, front engine mount bolts and fan shroud-to-radiator tie bar screws.

OIL PUMP

V6-231 & V8-350, 400, 430, 455

1. To remove pump, take off oil filter.

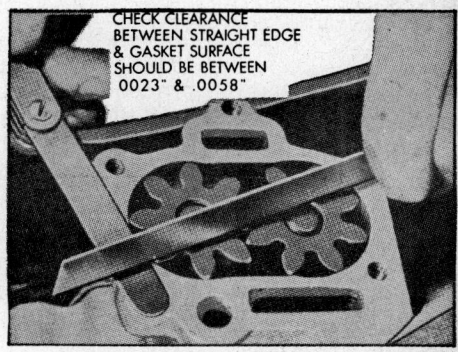

Fig. 23 Checking oil pump gear and clearance. V6-231 & V8-350, 400, 430, 455

2. Disconnect wire from oil pressure indicator switch in filter by-pass valve cap (if so equipped).
3. Remove screws attaching oil pump cover to timing chain cover. Remove cover and slide out pump gears. Replace any parts not serviceable.
4. Remove oil pressure relief valve cap, spring and valve, Fig. 22. Remove oil filter by-pass valve cap, spring and valve. Replace any parts of valve not serviceable.
5. Check relief valve in its bore in cover. Valve should have no more clearance than an easy slip fit. If any perceptible side shake can be felt, the valve and/or cover should be replaced.
6. The filter by-pass valve should be flat and free of nicks and scratches.

Assembly & Installation

1. Lubricate and install pressure relief valve and spring in bore of pump cover. Install cap and gasket. Torque cap to 30-35 ft-lbs.
2. Install filter by-pass valve flat in its seat in cover. Install spring, cap and gasket. Torque cap to 30-35 ft-lbs.
3. Install pump gears and shaft in pump body section of timing chain cover to check gear end clearance. Check clearance as shown in Fig. 23. If clearance is less than .0018" check timing chain cover for evidence of wear.
4. If gear end clearance is satisfactory, remove gears and pack gear pocket *full* of vaseline, not chassis lube.
5. Reinstall gears so vaseline is forced into every cavity of gear pocket and between teeth of gears. *Unless pump is packed with vaseline, it may not prime itself when engine is started.*
6. Install cover and tighten screws alternately and evenly. Final tightening is 10-15 ft-lbs. torque. Install filter on nipple.

BELT TENSION DATA

1975—	New lbs.
Air Condition V6-231	150
Air Pump V6-231	70
1969-74—	
Air Condition	100
Generator	80
Power Steering—	
Exc. V8-Models	80
V8-Models	90

WATER PUMP, REPLACE

Drain cooling system, being sure to drain into a clean container if antifreeze solution is to be saved. Remove the fan belt and disconnect all hoses from water pump. Remove water pump.

FUEL PUMP PRESSURE

Year	Engine	Pressure, Lbs.
1969-71	6-250	4-5
1973	6-250	4-5
1974	6-250	3½-4½
1975	6-250	4-5
1975	V6-231	4¼-5¾
1969-70	V8-350	4¼-5¾
1969	V8-400 (Exc. Stage I)	5½-7
1969	V8-400 Stage I	6-8
1969	V8-430	5½-7
1970	V8-455	4¼-5¾
1971	V8 All	4¼-5¾
1972-74	V8-350	3
1972-74	V8-455	4½
1975	V8 All	4¼-5¾

FUEL PUMP, REPLACE

1969-70 Riviera Electric Pump

These models have a turbine type electric pump located at the lower end of the fuel pick-up pipe in the bottom of the tank. This pump runs continuously whenever the engine is running thus maintaining a steady pressure whether fuel is needed or not. To replace, proceed as follows:

1. Raise car, disconnect two terminal connector at tank and remove ground wire screw.
2. Lower car and pull back trunk floor mat.
3. Remove five screws from access hole cover and remove cover.
4. Disconnect fuel hose from tank unit.
5. Unscrew retaining cam ring and remove fuel pump-tank unit assembly.
6. To remove pump from tank unit, remove flat wire conductor from plastic clip on fuel tube.
7. Squeeze clamp and pull pump straight back about ½".
8. Remove two nuts and washers from pump terminals.
9. Squeeze clamp and pull pump straight back, take care to prevent bending of circular support bracket.
10. Reverse procedure to install.

All Models-Mechanical Pump

NOTE: Before installing the pump, it is good practice to crank the engine so that the nose of the camshaft eccentric is out of the way of the fuel pump rocker arm when the pump is installed. In this way there will be the least amount of tension on the rocker arm, thereby easing the installation of the pump.

1. Remove all gasket material from the pump and block gasket surfaces. Apply sealer to both sides of new gasket.
2. Position gasket on pump flange and hold pump in position against its mounting surface. Make sure rocker arm is riding on camshaft eccentric.
3. Press pump tight against its mounting. Install retaining screws and tighten them alternately.
4. Connect fuel lines. Then operate engine and check for leaks.

Clutch and Transmission Section

NOTE: 1975 linkage adjustment information is in this section. Repair procedures on both automatic and manual shift transmissions are covered elsewhere in this manual. Procedures for removing automatic transmissions as well as linkage adjustments on 1969-74 models are included in the automatic transmission chapters. See Chapter Index.

CLUTCH PEDAL, ADJUST

1975 Apollo, Skylark & Century

1. Disconnect return spring from clutch fork.
2. Rotate clutch lever and shaft assembly until pedal is against rubber bumper on dash brace.
3. Push outer end of clutch fork rearward until throwout bearing lightly contacts pressure plate fingers.
4. Install lower push rod in gauge hole and increase length until all lash is removed.
5. Install swivel or rod in hole furthest from centerline of lever and shaft assembly, then install retainer.
6. Tighten lock nut and spacer against swivel and connect clutch fork return spring.
7. Check clutch pedal free travel which should be 55/64 inch to 1 29/64 inch.

1969-74

Adjust linkage to provide ⅝" to ⅞" pedal free play. On LeSabre, Wildcat and G.S. 400 units, remove swivel retainer, disconnect swivel from equalizer arm and turn swivel to obtain proper adjustment. On other units, loosen lock nut and turn rod. When proper clearance is reached, tighten lock nut.

CLUTCH, REPLACE
1969-75

1. Remove transmission.
2. Remove pedal return spring from clutch fork. *On LeSabre, Wildcat and G.S. 400, disconnect rod assembly from clutch fork.*
3. Remove flywheel housing.
4. Remove clutch throw-out bearing from clutch fork.
5. Disconnect clutch fork from ball stud by moving it toward center of flywheel housing.
6. Mark clutch cover and flywheel so it can be installed in the same position.
7. Loosen clutch cover to flywheel bolts one turn at a time to avoid bending of clutch cover flange until spring pressure is released.
8. Support pressure plate and cover assembly while removing last bolts, then remove pressure plate and driven plate.
9. Reverse procedure to install being sure to line up marks made in removal.

3 SPEED TRANS. REPLACE
All 1969-75

1. Disconnect speedometer cable from driven gear fitting.
2. Disconnect shift control rods from shifter levers at transmission.
3. Remove propeller shaft.

4. Support rear of engine and remove transmission crossmember.
5. Remove two top transmission attaching bolts and insert guide pins in these holes.
6. Remove two lower bolts and slide transmission straight back and out of vehicle.
7. Reverse procedure to install.

3 SPEED TRANS. SHIFT LINKAGE
1969-75

Column Shift

1. Place column selector lever in Reverse detent, making sure the steering column selector plate engages lower most column lever (1st-reverse).
2. Loosen 1st-reverse adjusting clamp.
3. Shift transmission lever into reverse and tighten the 1st-reverse clamp to 17-23 ft-lbs.
4. Shift transmission levers into neutral and loosen 2nd-3rd clamp.
5. Install ³⁄₁₆" diameter rod through 2nd-3rd lever selector plate and the 1st-reverse lever and alignment plate.
6. Tighten 2nd-3rd shift rod clamp to 17-23 ft-lbs.

Floor Shift

1. Place transmission levers in Neutral.
2. Loosen shift rod adjusting clamp bolts on shifter assembly.
3. Insert ¼" drill rod through shift assembly and shift levers.
4. Tighten clamp bolts to 17-23 ft-lbs.
5. To adjust back drive linkage, shift transmission into Reverse. *This must be done using selector lever inside the car.* Loosen clamp bolt.
6. Push back drive rod up against stop in steering column. Tighten clamp bolt.

4 SPEED TRANS. REPLACE
1969-73 G.S. 350, 400, 455

1. Disconnect speedometer cable and remove driven gear.
2. Disconnect shift control rods from transmission.
3. Remove propeller shaft.
4. Support rear of engine and remove transmission support.
5. Remove two top transmission-to-flywheel housing bolts and insert guide pins.
6. Remove two lower bolts.
7. Slide transmission back and out.
8. Reverse procedure to install.

4 SPEED TRANS. SHIFT LINKAGE
1969-73 G.S. 350, 400, 455

Floor Shift

1. Place transmission in neutral.
2. Adjust all three shift rods so a ¼" drill rod can be installed through shifter assembly and shift levers.
3. Tighten swivel nuts to 17-23 ft-lbs.
4. On 1969-73 models, using shift handle inside car only, shift transmission into Reverse, loosen clamp bolt and push back drive rod up against stop in steering column. Tighten clamp bolt.

1975 AUTO. TRANS. LINKAGE ADJUST

This adjustment is the same as that described for previous models and is found elsewhere in this manual.

Rear Axle, Propeller Shaft & Brakes

REAR AXLES

Figure 1 illustrates the type rear axle assemblies used on Buicks. When necessary to overhaul any of these units, refer to the *Rear Axle Specifications* table in this chapter.

NOTE: Canadian built Specials and Skylarks may use a "C" type axle. This design axle employs "C" locks to retain the axle shafts. Service on this type axle is

covered in the Chevrolet section of this manual.

1969-75 All

In this rear axle, Fig. 1, the drive pinion is mounted in two tapered roller bearings which are preloaded by two selected spacers at assembly. The pinion is positioned by shims located between a shoulder on the drive pinion and the rear bearing. The front bearing is held in place by a large nut.

The differential is supported in the

carrier by two tapered roller side bearings. These are preloaded by inserting shims between the bearings and the pedestals. The differential assembly is positioned for proper ring gear and pinion backlash by varying these shims. The ring gear is bolted to the case. The case houses two side gears in mesh with two pinions mounted on a pinion axle which is anchored in the case by a spring pin. The pinions and side gears are backed by thrust washers.

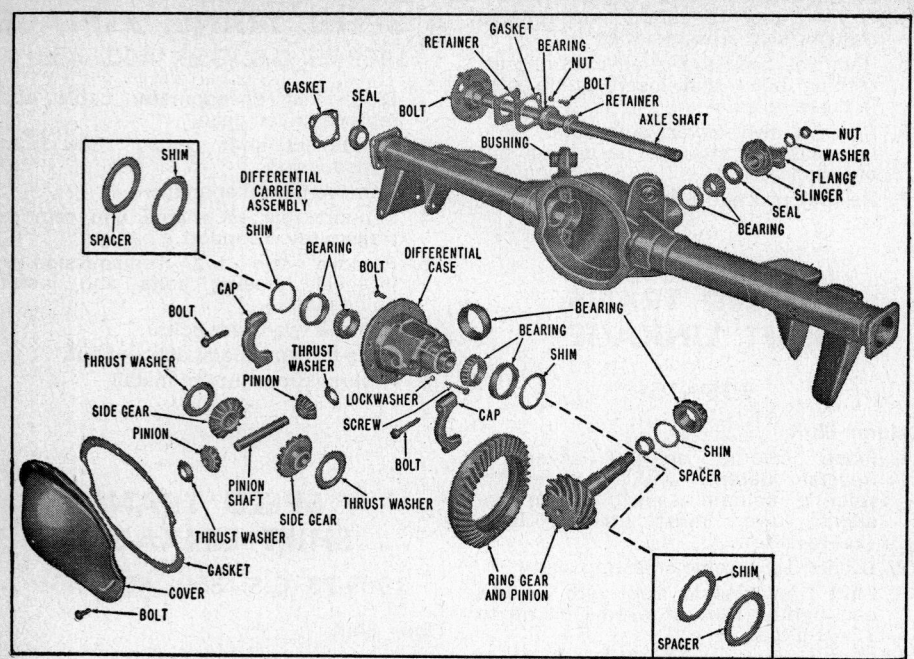

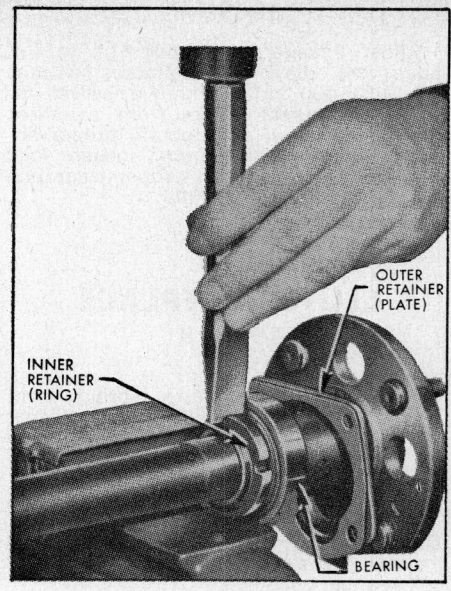

Fig. 2 Removing axle shaft bearing retainer

Fig. 1 Rear axle assembly. Roller bearings are used in the axle shafts of some 1969-74 models

REAR AXLE ASSEMBLY, REPLACE

1970-75

It is not necessary to remove the rear axle assembly for any normal repairs but if the housing must be replaced the assembly may be removed as follows:

1. Raise car high enough and support

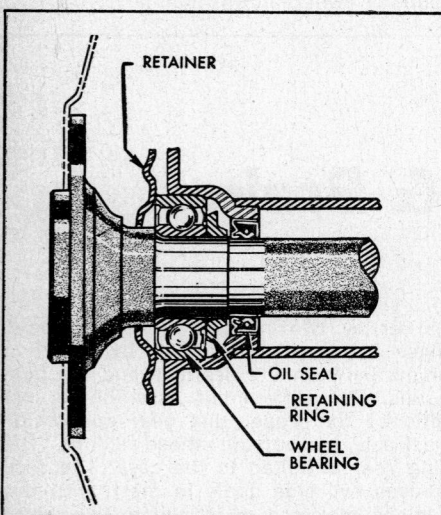

Fig. 3 Axle shaft bearing and oil seal. 1969-75 Senior Series except Estate Wagon

using jack stands under both frame side rails.
2. Mark rear universal joint and flange for proper reassembly and disconnect rear joint.
3. Push propeller shaft as far forward as possible and wire up out of way.
4. Disconnect parking brake cables and rear brake hose. Cover brake hose opening to prevent entrance of dirt.
5. Support axle with jack and disconnect shock absorbers at lower ends.
   On 1971-75 Estate Wagons, disconnect exhaust system right side by removing exhaust hanger screw at rear frame crossmember. On Apollo and 1971-75 Estate Wagons, remove leaf spring as outlined under "Leaf Spring, Replace" procedure in the Rear Suspension section.
6. On 1969-70 Riviera, disconnect track bar at axle housing.
7. Disconnect upper control arms at axle housing.
8. Disconnect lower control arms and remove axle assembly.

1969 All

It is not necessary to remove the rear axle assembly for any normal repairs. The axle shafts and carrier assembly can easily be removed from the vehicle, leaving the axle housing in place.

1. Raise rear end of car with rear axle hanging on shock absorbers.
2. Mark rear universal joint and pinion flange for proper reassembly. *These parts are carefully balanced in production and assembled with heavy sides opposite. For this reason they should be reassembled the same way.*

3. Disconnect rear universal joint from pinion flange by removing two U-bolts. Wire propeller shaft to exhaust pipe to support it out of the way.
4. Remove rear wheels and brake drums.
5. Remove axle shafts as outlined below.
6. Remove all cover bolts and break cover loose at the bottom to allow lubricant to drain.
7. Remove carrier assembly by prying or by use of a slide hammer.
8. Reverse foregoing procedure to install the carrier assembly, being sure to connect the rear universal joint to the pinion flange according to the alignment marks made previously.

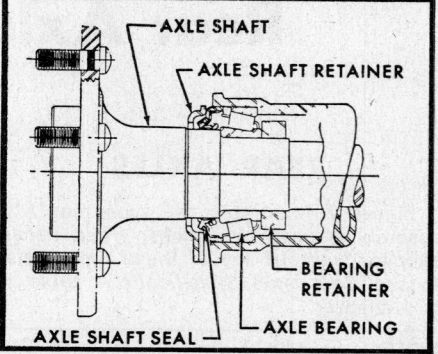

Fig. 4 Axle shaft, bearing and oil seal. 1969-75 Intermediate Series and 1970-75 Estate Wagon

AXLE SHAFT, REPLACE
1969-75

IMPORTANT

Design allows for axle shaft end play of .018″ on all 1969-72 and 1973-75 "B" and "O" axles. On 1973-75 "C", "G" and "K" axles, allowable end play is .022″ and .032″ on "P" axles. These axles may be identified by the third letter located on the right rear tube on the forward side. This end play can be checked with the wheel and brake drum removed by measuring the difference between the end of the housing and the axle shaft flange while moving the axle shaft in and out by hand.

End play over this is excessive. Compensating for all the end play by inserting a shim inboard of the bearing in the housing is not recommended since it ignores the end play of the bearing itself, and may result in improper seating of the gasket or backing plate against the housing. If end play is excessive, the axle shaft and bearing assembly should be removed and the cause of the excessive end play determined and corrected.

Removing Axle Shaft

1971-75 C, G, K & P Axles

1. Remove wheels and brake drums.
2. Remove bolts and differential cover and allow lubricant to drain.
3. Remove pinion shaft lock bolt and pinion shaft then push axle shafts inward, remove C-lock and axle shaft.

1969-70 All & 1971-75 B & O Axles

1. Remove wheels and brake drums.
2. Remove retainer plate nuts. Pull retainers clear of bolts and reinstall two opposite nuts to hold brake backing plate in place.
3. Pull axle shaft assembly using a puller.

Replacing Axle Shaft Bearings & Seals

1971-75 C, G, K & P Axles

To remove the axle shaft bearing and seal, use Remover Tool J-23689 and to install, use Installer Tool J-23690.

1969-70 All & 1971-75 B & O Axles

1. Place axle shaft in a vise so that the retainer ring rests on vise jaws. Use a chisel and a hammer to crack the ring, Fig. 2.
2. Press bearing off shaft and remove seal. Inspect seal running surface for bad spots and replace if necessary, Figs. 3 and 4.

   NOTE: Before installing seal, apply grease between seal lips to avoid damaging the seal.

3. Press bearing against shoulder on shaft and retainer ring against bearing using Installer tool J-21022 for intermediate models and J-8609 for full size models.

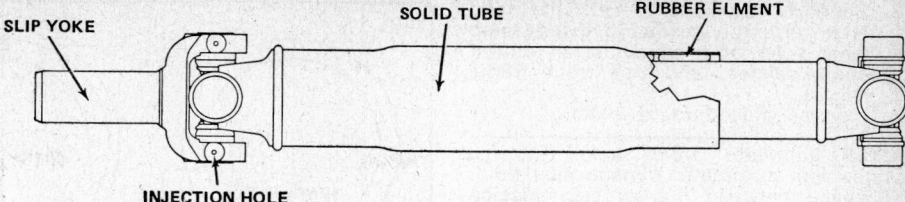

Fig. 5   Propeller shaft used with 1975 V6-231 engines

Axle Shaft, Install

1. Apply a coat of wheel bearing grease in wheel bearing and seal recess.
2. For 1969-70 all and B & O axles, apply a coat of wheel bearing grease on seal surface of shaft and install shaft.

   NOTE: If Posi-Traction, use only positive traction lubricant.

3. For C, G, K and P axles:
   a. Install axle shaft through seal and bearing and through side gear as far in as possible.

      NOTE: Do not let shaft drag across seal lip and apply grease between seal lips.

   b. Install C-lock and move axle shaft outward to bottom C-lock in recess of side gear.
   c. Install pinion shaft and torque lock bolt to 15 ft. lbs.
   d. Install gasket and cover and torque bolts to 30 ft. lbs. After 20 minutes, retorque bolts to 30 ft. lbs.
   e. Install correct type and amount of lubricant.
4. Install retainer nuts and torque to 35 ft. lbs. on Century models and 55 ft. lbs. on all other models.
5. Install drum and wheel and torque nuts to 70-75 ft. lbs.

PROPELLER SHAFT

NOTE

When service is required, the propeller shaft must be removed from the car as a complete assembly. While handling it out of the car, the assembly must be supported on a straight line as nearly as possible to avoid jamming or bending any of the parts.

The propeller shaft used on 1975 vehicles equipped with V6-231 engines are constructed of concentric steel tubes with rubber elements between them, Fig. 5.

1969-75 Exc. 1969-70 Riviera

NOTE: Two attachment methods are used to secure the propeller shaft to the pinion flange or end yoke, a pair of bolted straps or a set of bolted flanges.

1. Scribe alignment marks between propeller shaft and pinion flange or end yoke to aid reassembly.
2. Remove strap or flange bolts at rear of propeller shaft. Tape bearing cups to prevent loss of needle bearings.
3. Slide shaft assembly rearward, disengaging front yoke from transmission output shaft splines and lower from vehicle.
4. Reverse procedure to install.

NOTE: Apply grease (Grade EP 1) to internal splines of front yokes having a .060 inch vent hole (automatic transmission models). Apply engine oil to same area of front yokes without vent holes (manual transmission models).

1969-70 Riviera

1. Scribe alignment marks between rear flange and pinion flange to aid reassembly.
2. Remove center bearing support attaching bolts and the four CV joint to pinion flange bolts, Fig. 6.

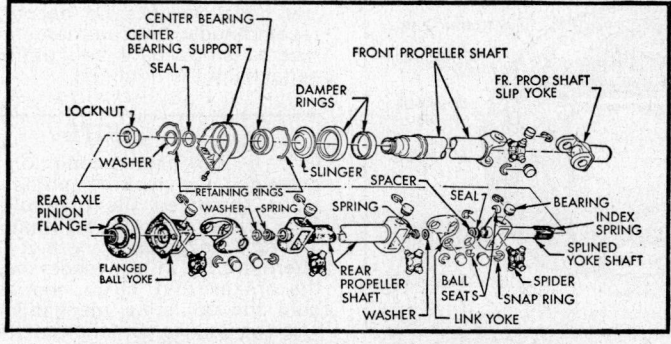

Fig. 6   Propeller shaft assembly. 1969-70 Riviera

3. Support rear of propeller shaft and slide assembly rearward, disengaging front yoke from transmission output shaft splines, and out from frame tunnel.
4. Reverse procedure to install.

NOTE: Lubricate front yoke internal splines with automatic transmission fluid. Fill space between lips of transmission seal with wheel bearing grease and coat seal surface of front U-joint with same grease.

PROPELLER SHAFT BALANCE

A wheel balancer of the type equipped with a strobe light can be used to facilitate balancing of the driveshaft. The pick-up unit should be placed directly under the nose of the rear axle carrier and as far forward as possible.

1. Place car on twin post lift so rear of car is supported on the rear axle housing and rear wheels are free to rotate.
2. Remove both rear wheels and tire assemblies and reinstall wheel lug nuts with flat side next to drum.
3. Mark and number driveshaft at four points 90° apart at rear of shaft just forward of balance weights.
4. Place strobe light pick-up under nose of differential.
5. With car running in gear at car speed where unbalance is at its peak, allow driveline to stabilize by holding at constant speed. Point strobe light at spinning shaft and note position of one of the reference marks.
6. Shut off engine and position shaft so reference mark will be in position noted when car was running.

CAUTION: Do not run car on hoist for extended periods due to danger of overheating transmission or engine.

7. When strobe light flashed, the heaviest point of the shaft was down. To balance shaft it will be necessary to apply weight 180° away. Screw type hose clamps can be used as weights as shown in Fig. 7.

REAR U-JOINT ANGLE

If drive line shudder, roughness, vibra-

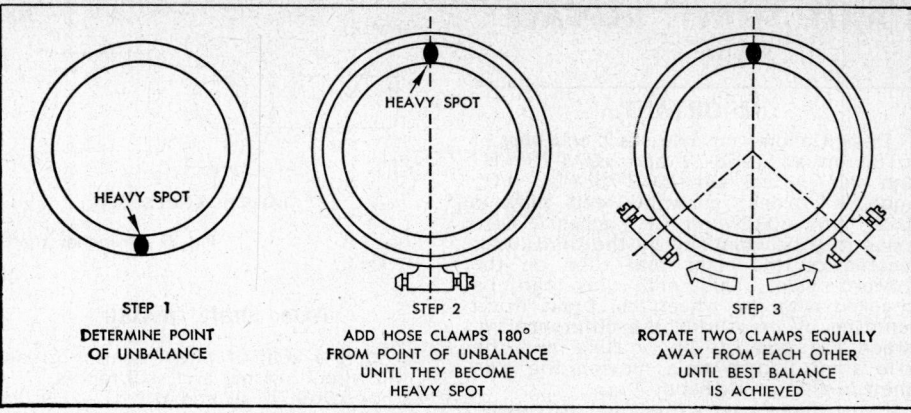

Fig. 7   Positioning hose clamps to balance shaft

tion, or rumble is experienced, it may be due to incorrect rear universal joint angle and this angle should be checked. Also, if there is a severe rear end collision, or if the axle housing or any control arms are replaced, the rear universal joint angle should be checked and corrected if necessary. To make the check, however, special Alignment Set No. J-8973 must be used. Inasmuch as this equipment is not likely to be found in general repair shops, it is recommended that a Buick dealer having this equipment do the work.

BRAKE ADJUSTMENTS
1969-75 Self-Adjusting Brakes

These brakes, Fig. 8, have self-adjusting shoe mechanisms that assure correct lining-to-drum clearances at all times. The automatic adjusters operate only when the brakes are applied as the car is moving rearward or when the car comes to an uphill stop.

Although the brakes are self-adjusting, an initial adjustment is necessary after the brake shoes have been relined or replaced, or when the length of the adjusting screw has been changed during some other service operation.

Frequent usage of an automatic transmission forward range to halt reverse vehicle motion may prevent the automatic adjusters from functioning, thereby inducing low pedal heights. Should low pedal heights be encountered, it is recommended that numerous forward and reverse stops be made until satisfactory pedal height is obtained.

NOTE

If a low pedal condition cannot be corrected by making numerous reverse stops (provided the hydraulic system is free of air) it indicates that the self-adjusting mechanism is not functioning. Therefore, it will be necessary to remove the brake drum, clean, free up and lubricate the adjusting mechanism. Then adjust the brakes as follows, being sure the parking brake is fully released.

Adjustment

1. Remove adjusting hole cover from backing plate. Turn brake adjusting screw to expand shoes until wheel can just be turned by hand.
2. Using suitable tool to hold actuator away from adjuster, Fig. 9, back off adjuster 30 notches. If shoes still drag, back off one or two additional notches.

NOTE: Brakes should be free of drag when adjuster has been backed off approximately 12 notches. Heavy drag at this point indicates tight parking brake cables.

3. Install adjusting hole cover and check parking brake adjustment.

CAUTION

If finger movement will not turn the screw, free it up. If this is not done, the actuator will not turn the screw during subsequent vehicle operation. Lubricate the screw with oil

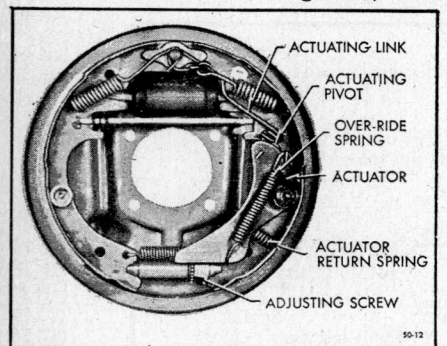

Fig. 8   Left rear wheel brake. 1969-75

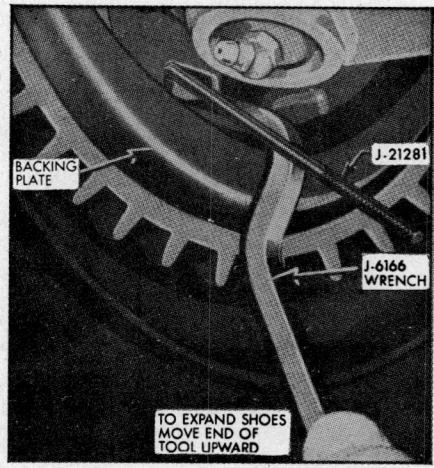

Fig. 9   Adjusting drum brakes. 1969-75

and coat with wheel bearing grease. Any other adjustment procedure may cause damage to the adjusting screw with consequent self-adjuster problems.

4. Install wheel and drum, and adjusting hole cover. Adjust brakes on remaining wheels in the same manner.
5. If pedal height is not satisfactory, drive the vehicle and make sufficient reverse stops until proper pedal height is obtained.

PARKING BRAKE, ADJUST
1969-75 All

Need for parking brake adjustment is indicated if the service brake operates with good pedal reserve but the parking brake pedal can be depressed more than eight ratchet clicks for intermediate models and sixteen for full size models, under heavy foot pressure. After making sure that the service brakes are properly adjusted, adjust the parking brake as follows:

1. Depress parking brake exactly three ratchet clicks on all except Apollo and 1974-75 Estate Wagon, two ratchet clicks on Apollo and six ratchet clicks on the 1974-75 Estate Wagon.
2. Loosen jam nut, and tighten adjusting nut until rear wheels can just be turned rearward using both hands but are locked when forward motion is attempted.
3. Tighten jam nut and release parking brake. Rear wheels should turn freely in either direction with no brake drag.

MASTER CYLINDER, REPLACE
1969-75

1. Disconnect brake pipes from master cylinder and tape end of pipes to prevent entrance of dirt.
2. On manual brakes, disconnect brake pedal from master cylinder push rod.
3. Remove two nuts holding master cylinder to dash or power cylinder and remove master cylinder from car.

POWER BRAKE UNIT
1969-75

1. Disconnect brake pipes from master cylinder and tape ends of pipes to prevent entrance of dirt. Disconnect vacuum hose from cylinder.
2. Remove four nuts holding power unit to dash.
3. Remove retainer and washer from brake pedal pin and disengage push rod eye or clevis.
4. Remove power unit from car.

Rear Suspension

SHOCK ABSORBER, REPLACE

1. With the rear axle supported properly, disconnect shock absorber from lower mounting bracket.
2. Disconnect shock absorber upper end from underbody attachment.
3. Reverse procedure to install.

LEAF SPRINGS & BUSHINGS, REPLACE
1973-75 Apollo & Skylark

1. Support vehicle at frame and rear axle, relieving tension from spring.
2. Disconnect shock absorber from lower mounting.

3. Loosen spring front mount bolt.
4. Remove spring front mounting bracket attaching screws, lower axle and remove bracket.
5. Disconnect parking brake cable from spring plate bracket.
6. Remove "U" bolts and spring plate.
7. Support spring, remove front mount bolt and disassemble rear shackle.
8. Replace rear shackle and spring eye bushings as necessary, Figs. 1 and 2.
9. Reverse procedure to install.

1971-75 Estate Wagon

1. Support vehicle at frame and support rear axle, removing tension from springs.
2. Disconnect shock absorbers from lower mounting bracket and the exhaust system right side from hanger and support system, Fig. 3.
3. Remove "U" bolts and lower spring plates.
4. Disconnect spring at front and rear attachments.
5. Reverse procedure to install.

LEAF SPRING SERVICE
1973-75 Apollo & Skylark

NOTE: The spring leaves are not serviced separately, however, the spring leaf inserts may be replaced.

1. Clamp spring in a vise and remove spring clips.
2. File peened end of center bolt to permit nut removal, remove nut and open vise slowly, allowing spring to expand.

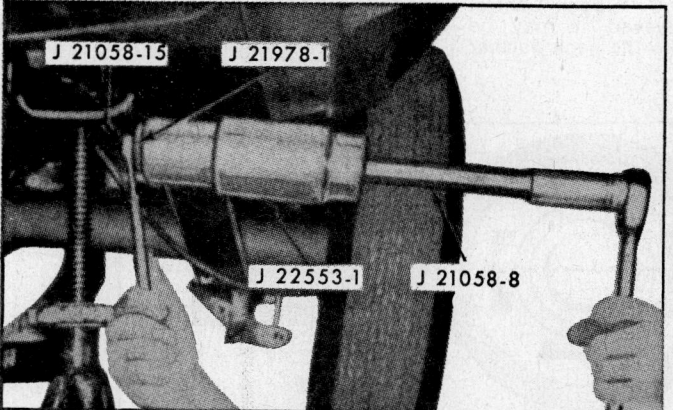

Fig. 1 Leaf spring bushings removal. 1973-75 Apollo & Skylark

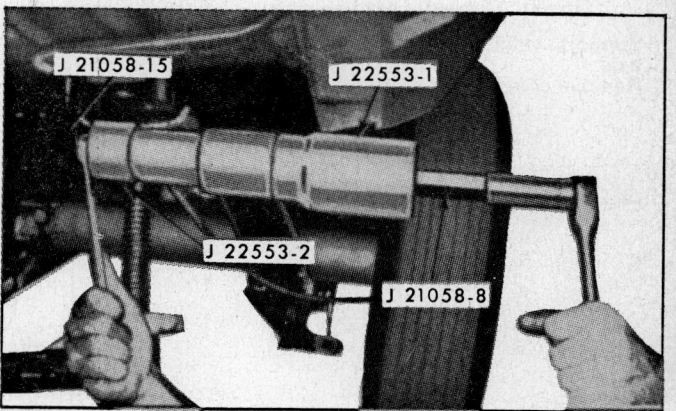

Fig. 2 Leaf spring bushings installation. 1973-75 Apollo & Skylark

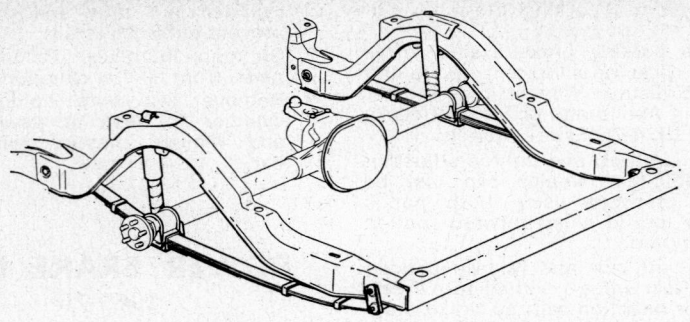

Fig. 3   Leaf spring suspension (typical)

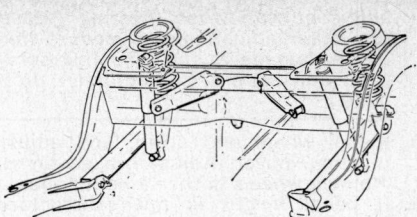

Fig. 4   Coil spring suspension.
Except 1969-70 Riviera

3. Replace spring leaf inserts as necessary.
4. Use a drift to align center bolt holes, compress spring in vise and install new center bolt and nut. Peen end of bolt to retain nut.
5. Align springs and bend spring clips into position.

NOTE: Overtightening of spring clips will cause spring binding.

COIL SPRINGS, REPLACE

1. Support vehicle at frame and support rear axle with a suitable jack.
2. On 1969-72 models, place an alignment mark between rear universal joint and pinion flange for use during installation. Disconnect and slide drive shaft just far enough forward to clear rear companion flange and support drive shaft.
3. Disconnect shock absorbers from lower mounting bracket, Fig. 4, and the brake lines from wheel cylinders.
4. Lower jack fully extending springs and remove springs.
5. Reverse procedure to install, Fig. 5.

CONTROL ARMS, REPLACE

NOTE: Remove and replace one control arm at a time as axle assembly may slip sideways, making installation difficult.

Upper Control Arms

1. Support vehicle at frame and rear axle.
2. Remove control arm mount bolts from

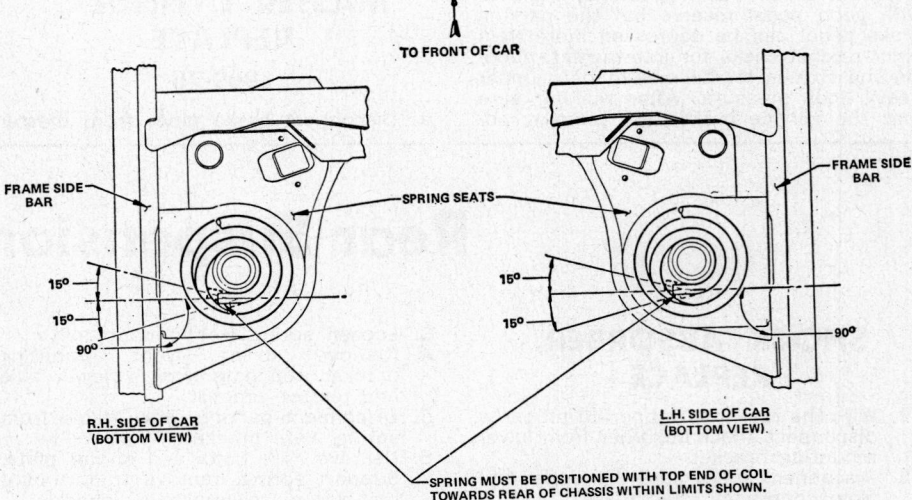

Fig. 5   Coil spring installation

frame and axle housing attachments, Fig. 4.
3. Reverse procedure to install.

NOTE: Control arm bolts must be tightened with vehicle at curb height.

Lower Control Arm

Lower control arms may be removed and replaced using the "Upper Control Arms" procedure. However, it may be necessary to reposition the jack farther

forward under carrier to aid in removing rear mount bolt. Also, a brass drift may be needed to remove mount bolts.

TRACK BAR BUSHING, REPLACE

1969-70 Riviera

1. Support rear axle so vehicle weight will be on springs.

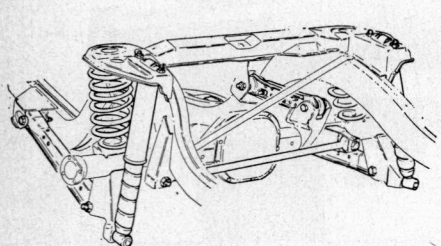

Fig. 6   Rear suspension. 1969-70 Riviera

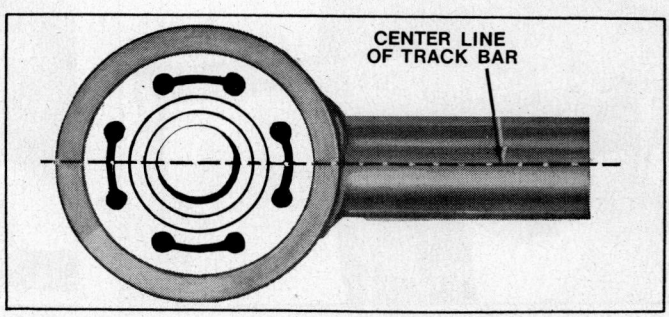

Fig. 7   Track bar bushing installation. 1969-70 Riviera

2. Remove track bar attaching bolts from brackets on frame and axle housing, Fig. 6.
3. Reverse procedure to install.
4. If bushing is damaged follow replacement procedure below:
   a. Remove enough material from bushing flange by grinding or some other suitable means so track bar eye is supported by press plate.
   b. Press out bushing from side with no flange using a ram with an outside diameter of $1\frac{7}{8}$ inch.
   c. Press new bushing into eye by pressing on flanged side until flange contacts eye of track bar. Bushing must be installed so slots in rubber bushing are in line with centerline of track bar, Fig. 7.

STABILIZER BAR, REPLACE

1973-75 Apollo & Skylark

1. Support vehicle at rear axle.
2. Disconnect stabilizer bar from spring plate brackets, Fig. 8.
3. Disconnect stabilizer bar from body brackets.
4. Reverse procedure to install. Tighten attaching bolts with vehicle at curb height.

1969-75 Exc. Apollo

1. Support vehicle at rear axle.
2. Remove stabilizer bar attaching bolts from brackets on lower control arms, Fig. 9.
3. Reverse procedure to install.

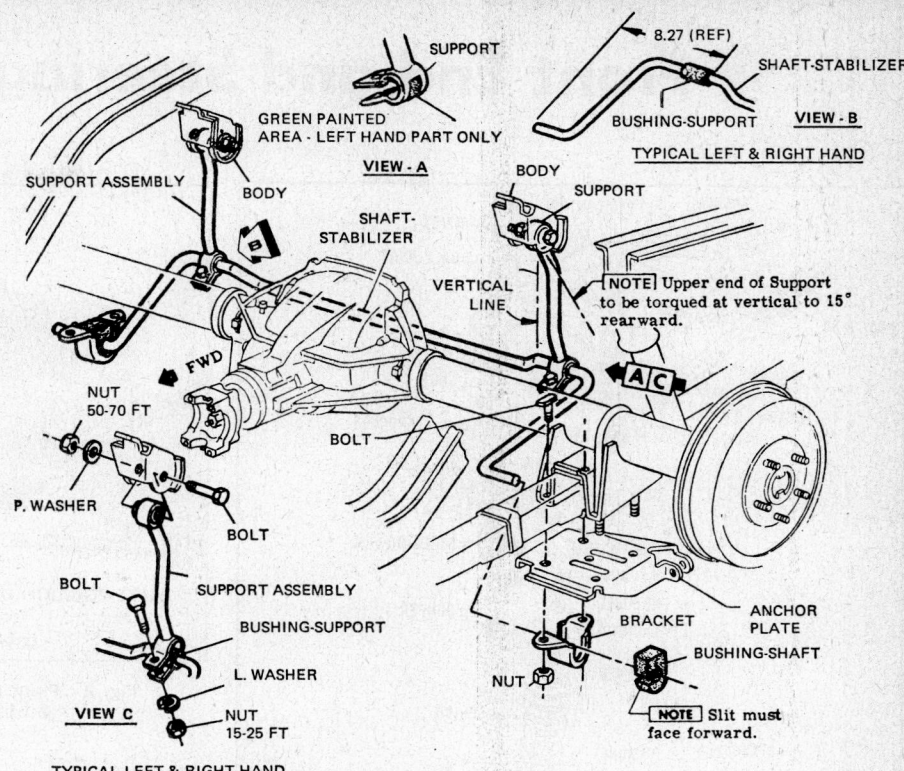

Fig. 8 Stabilizer bar installation. 1973-75 Apollo & Skylark

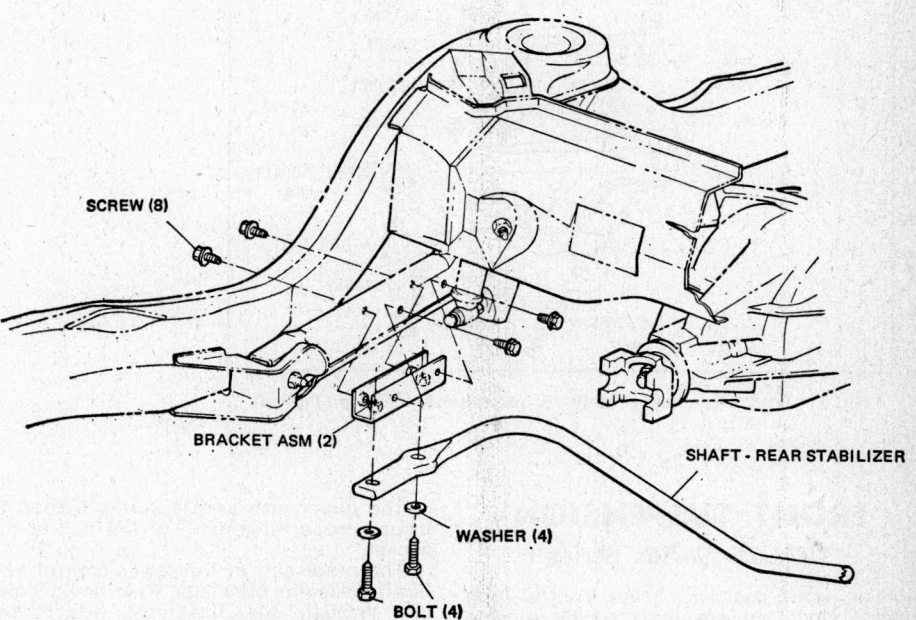

Fig. 9 Stabilizer bar installation exc. 1973-75 Apollo

Front End and Steering Section

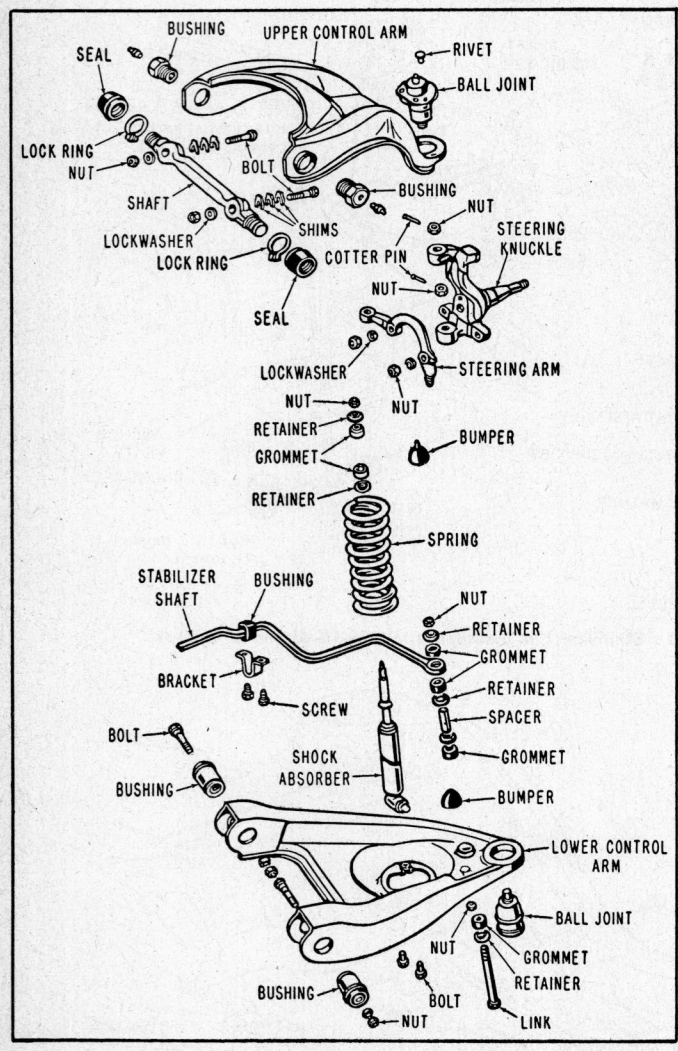

Fig. 1 Front suspension. 1969-75 intermediate models (Typical)

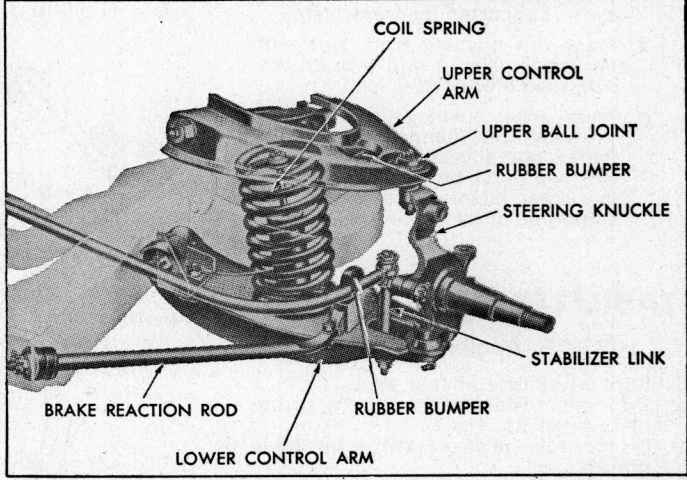

Fig. 2 Front suspension. 1969-70 Senior Series. Rubber bushings are used at upper shaft ends

FRONT SUSPENSION

1971-75 Senior Series

The strut rod and lower control arm used previously are replaced by a wide span lower control arm. The brake reaction rod is no longer used.

1969-75 Intermediate Models

NOTE: Rubber bushings are used at the upper shaft ends in place of the threaded steel bushings shown in Fig. 1.

A ball joint is riveted to the outer end of the upper arm and is spring loaded to insure proper alignment of the ball in the socket.

The inner end of the lower control arm has pressed-in bushings. Two bolts, passing through the bushings, attach the arm to the frame. The lower ball joint is a press fit in the arm and attaches to the steering knuckle with a castellated nut that is retained with a cotter pin.

Rubber seals are provided on upper and lower shafts and at ball socket assemblies to exclude dirt and moisture from bearing surfaces. Grease fittings are provided at all bearing locations.

SERVICE BULLETIN

Wheel Bolt Replaced: Wheel bolts should not be pressed out of a front hub. A shoulder is formed on each bolt by a swaging operation when the bolts are pressed into the hub and drum during manufacture. Pressing out a swaged bolt enlarges the bolt hole in the hub and drum, making it impossible to install the new bolt tightly.

The method recommended to remove the bolt is to secure the hub and drum in a vise, and mark the center of the bolt head with a center punch. Drill a $\frac{1}{8}$ in. pilot hole in the head of the bolt, and then redrill with a $\frac{9}{16}$ in. bit. Use a chisel to cut off a portion of the bolt head, and then drive out the bolt with a drift. Press the new wheel bolt into place to complete the job.

1969-70 Senior Series

Referring to Fig. 2, the lower control arm assembly consists of two stamped steel plates welded together. The inner ends of the lower control arms are bolted to the frame front crossmember through rubber bushings. The outer end of each arm is connectd to the steering knuckle with a ball joint assembly pressed into the lower control arm and bolted to the steering knuckle. The lower ball joint can be removed for service replacement. Position of the lower control arms is maintained by a brake reaction rod mounted between the lower control arm and frame.

To resist fore and aft movement of the lower control arm in relation to the frame, two solid steel brake reaction rods are positioned between the lower control arms and front of frame side rails. The forward ends of the rods are rubber mounted to hold securely to the frame bracket with nuts and cotter pins. The rearward end of the brake reaction rod attaches to the lower control arm with two bolts.

Special hardened flat washers are used under the bolts and nuts to aid in maintaining required torque. The brake reaction rod must be properly installed and secured prior to checking caster and camber.

The upper control arms consist of a single stamped steel plate. Two replaceable hardened steel bushings are threaded into the inner end of each assembly. 1969 models use rubber bushings at these locations. A ball joint is positioned through the outer end of each arm.

NOTE

The upper ball joint is pressed into the control arm and is serviced only as part of the control arm-ball joint assembly.

IMPORTANT

The front suspension is initially lubricated with a special lubricant (Buick Specification No. 742). Every 6000 miles or six months, whichever occurs first, this lubricant or its equivalent should be used. If lubricants other than this type is used the lubrication interval should be shortened and should not exceed 2000 miles.

WHEEL ALIGNMENT
1969-75

Caster and camber are adjusted by shimming at the upper control arm shaft attaching points.

Adding shims at the front locations will change caster toward negative with practically no change in camber. Adding shims at the rear locations will change caster toward positive and camber toward negative. Adding equal shims at both front and rear locations will not change caster but will change camber toward negative.

To adjust, loosen both front and rear bolts to free shims for removal or addition. The maximum dimension for one shim pack is .600 inch for 1969-72 full models and .750 inch for 1969-72 intermediate models and all 1973-75 models. After installing or removing shims, torque shaft nuts to 50 ft. lbs on 1969-72 intermediate models; 75 ft. lbs. on 1969-72 full size models and all 1973-75 models except Apollo and 45-55 ft. lbs. on 1973-75 Apollo & Skylark.

TOE-IN, ADJUST
1969-75

IMPORTANT

Car must be at curb weight and running height; bounce front end and allow it to settle at running height. Steering gear and front wheel bearings must be properly adjusted with no looseness at tie rod ends. The car should be moved forward one complete revolution of the wheels before the toe-in check and adjustment is started and the car should never be moved backward while making the check and adjustment.

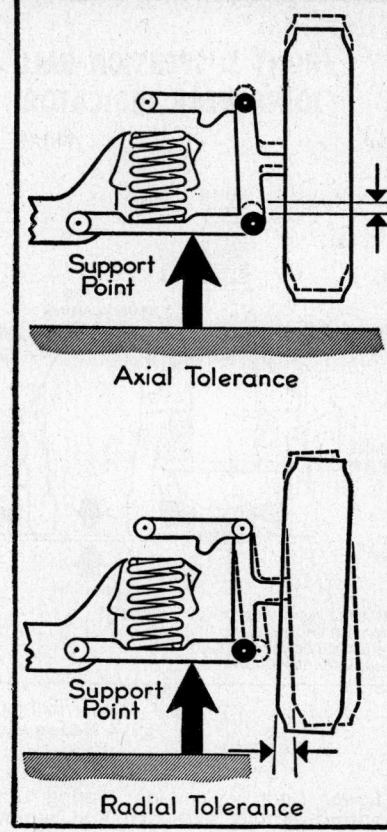

Fig. 3   Checking ball joints for wear

With front wheels in the straight ahead position, toe-in is adjusted by turning the tie rod adjusting sleeves as required. Left and right adjusting sleeves must be turned exactly the same amount but in opposite directions in order to maintain front wheels in straight ahead position when steering wheel is in straight ahead position.

IMPORTANT

The steering knuckle and steering arm "rock" or tilt as front wheel rises and falls. Therefore, it is vitally important to position the bottom face of the tie rod end parallel with the machined surface at the outer end of the steering arm when tie rod length is adjusted. Severe damage and possible failure can result unless this precaution is taken. The tie rod sleeve clamps must be straight down to 45° forward to provide clearance.

WHEEL BEARINGS, ADJUST
1969-75

1. Hand spin wheel in a forward direction and while wheel is spinning, snug up spindle nut to 19 ft. lbs. to fully seat bearings.
2. Back off nut ¼ to ½ turn.
3. Snug up spindle nut by hand. Do

not install cotter pin if hole in spindle lines up with a slot in spindle nut.
4. Loosen spindle nut 1/12 to 1/6 turn then insert cotter pin.
5. With bearings properly adjusted, on 1969-73 models the end play must be .002-.006 inch. On 1974-75 models the end play must be .001 to .005 inch.

WHEEL BEARINGS, REPLACE
(Disc Brakes)

1. Raise car and remove front wheels.
2. Remove tube support bracket bolt. Do not disconnect hydraulic tube or hose.
3. Remove cliper to mounting bracket bolts. Hang caliper from upper suspension.

NOTE: Do not place strain on brake line.

4. Remove spindle nut and hub and disc assembly. Inner wheel bearing and grease retainer can now be removed.

CHECKING BALL JOINTS FOR WEAR

If loose ball joints are suspected, first be sure front wheel bearings are properly adjusted and that control arms are tight. Then check ball joints as follows: Referring to Fig. 3, raise the wheel with a jack placed under the lower control arm at the point shown. Then test by moving the wheel up and down to check axial play, and rocking it at the top and bottom to measure radial play.

1. Upper ball joint should be replaced if there is any noticeable looseness at this joint.
2. Lower ball joint should be replaced if radial play exceeds .250".
3. Lower ball joint should be replaced if axial play between lower control arm and spindle exceeds the following tolerances:

1969-70 Senior Series	.100"
1969-72 Intermediate Models	.070"
1971-72 Senior Series	①
1973 Intermediate Models	②
1973-75 Senior Series	③
1974-75 Intermediate Models	③

①—With ball joint dislodged from steering knuckle, install stud nut. Rotating torque should be 2-10 ft. lbs.
②—No looseness.
③—Visually inspect wear indicator. See Fig. 4.

BALL JOINTS, REPLACE

NOTE: On all models the upper ball joint is spring-loaded in its socket. If the ball stud has any perceptible shake or if it can be twisted with the fingers, the ball joint should be replaced.

On all models except 1973-75 Century and Regal, the lower ball joint is not spring-loaded and depends upon car weight to load the ball. The lower ball joint should never be replaced merely because it "feels" loose when in an unloaded condition.

Upper ball joints on 1969-70 full size models are pressed into the control arm and are not serviced separately. Upper ball joints on 1969-70 intermediate models and all 1971-74 models are riveted to the control arm and can be replaced.

Lower ball joints on all 1969-74 models are pressed into the control arm and can be replaced with a suitable ball joint tool.

CAUTION: When servicing lower ball joints, be sure to support lower control arm with a suitable jack. If lower control arm is not supported and steering knuckle is disconnected from control arm, the heavily compressed front spring will be completely released.

SHOCK ABSORBER, REPLACE

Unfasten shock absorber top and bottom and remove it through the spring seat. Check shock absorber for obvious physical damage or oil leakage. Push and pull shock absorber in an upright position. If smooth hydraulic resistance is not present in both directions, replace shock absorber.

SPRING, REPLACE

1. Raise car and support with jack stands under frame. Remove wheel with hub and drum.
2. Disconnect stabilizer link from lower control arm and remove shock absorber.
3. Support lower control arm with a suitable floor jack to take up tension of front spring. Disconnect lower control arm ball joint stud from steering knuckle.

CAUTION: Be sure lower control arm is properly supported before disconnecting ball stud.

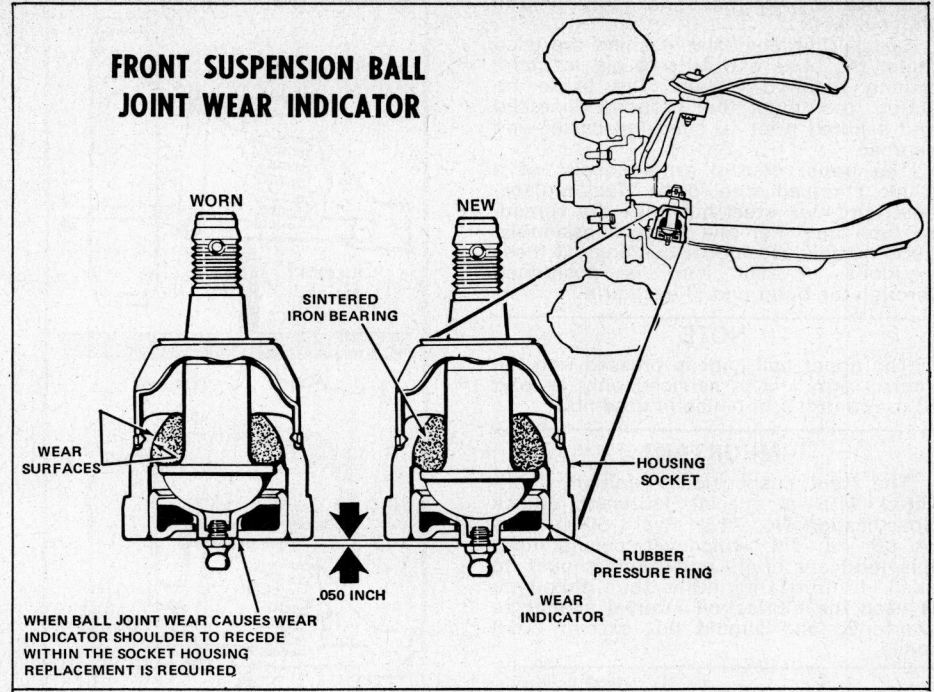

FRONT SUSPENSION BALL JOINT WEAR INDICATOR

WORN NEW

SINTERED IRON BEARING

WEAR SURFACES

HOUSING SOCKET

RUBBER PRESSURE RING

.050 INCH

WEAR INDICATOR

WHEN BALL JOINT WEAR CAUSES WEAR INDICATOR SHOULDER TO RECEDE WITHIN THE SOCKET HOUSING REPLACEMENT IS REQUIRED

Fig. 4 Lower ball joint check. 1973 Full Size Models, 1974 Models exc. Apollo & all 1975 Models

4. Lower floor jack under spring until spring is fully extended and remove spring.
5. Complete the installation in the reverse order of removal.

MANUAL STEERING GEAR, REPLACE

1969-75 All Models

1. Remove two nuts or pinch bolt securing lower coupling to steering shaft flange.
2. Use a suitable puller to remove pitman arm.
3. Unfasten gear (3 bolts) from frame and remove from car.

POWER STEERING, REPLACE

1969-75

1. Disconnect pressure and return line hoses at steering gear and elevate ends of hoses higher than pump to prevent oil from draining out of pump.
2. Remove pinch bolt securing coupling to steering gear.
3. Jack up car and remove pitman shaft nut, then use a suitable puller to remove pitman arm.
4. On Senior models, remove sheet metal baffle that covers frame-to-gear attaching bolts.
5. Loosen the three frame-to-steering gear bolts and remove steering gear.

CADILLAC

OLD CAR SPECIFICATIONS: For 1946-68 Tune Up and Wheel Alignment Specifications see main index.

INDEX OF SERVICE OPERATIONS

PAGE NO.

ACCESSORIES

Air Conditioning 2-20
Automatic Level Controls 2-39
Blower Motor Removal 1-103
Clock Troubles 2-11
Heater Core, Replace 1-102
Power Seat Troubles 2-18
Power Top Troubles 2-18
Power Window Troubles 2-18
Radio, Replace 1-100
Speed Controls, Adjust 1-103

BRAKES

Anti-Skid Brakes 2-162
Brake Troubles, Mechanical 2-17
Disc Brake Service 2-133
Hydraulic System Service 2-123
Parking Brake, Adjust 1-120
Power Brake, Replace 1-121
Service Brakes, Adjust 1-120
Vacuum Release Parking Brake 1-121

COOLING SYSTEM

Belt Tension Data 1-109
Cooling System Troubles 2-6
Variable Speed Fans 2-38
Water Pump, Replace 1-110

ELECTRICAL

Alternator Service 2-69
Blower Motor, Replace 1-103
Dash Gauge Service 2-50
Distributor, Replace 1-96
Distributor Service:
  Standard 2-525
  Transistorized 2-535
Electrical Troubles 2-8
Headlamp Aiming 2-45
Headlamps, Concealed Type 2-46
Horn Sounder, Remove 1-99
Ignition Coils and Resistors 2-521
Ignition Lock, Replace 1-97
Ignition Switch, Replace 1-97
Ignition Timing 2-518
Instrument Cluster Removal 1-99
Light Switch, Replace 1-97
Neutral Start Switch, Replace 1-98
Radio, Replace 1-100
Starter Service 2-54
Starter, Replace 1-96
Starter Switch Service 2-67
Stop Light Switch, Replace 1-97
Turn Signal Switch, Replace 1-98
Turn Signal Troubles 2-11
Windshield Wiper Motor, Replace 1-102
Windshield Wiper Troubles 2-19

ENGINE

Camshaft, Replace 1-108
Crankshaft Rear Oil Seal 1-109
Cylinder Head, Replace 1-106
Engine Mounts, Replace 1-105
Engine, Replace 1-105
Engine Troubles 2-1

Main Bearings 1-109
Piston Pins 1-109
Piston Rings 1-108
Piston and Rod, Assemble 1-108
Pistons 1-108
Rocker Arms 1-106
Rod Bearings 1-109
Timing Case Cover, Replace 1-106
Timing Case Oil Seal 1-107
Timing Chain, Replace 1-107
Valve Arrangement 1-106
Valve Guides 1-106
Valve Lifters 1-106

ENGINE LUBRICATION

Emission Control Systems 2-545
Oil Pan, Replace 1-109
Oil Pump Repairs 1-109

FRONT DRIVE AXLE

C. V. U-Joint Service 1-118
Drive Axles, Replace 1-117
Drive Link Belt 1-111
Final Drive Description 1-115
Final Drive, Replace 1-119
Output Shaft, Replace 1-119

FUEL SYSTEM

Carburetor Adjustment and Specs. 2-372
Emission Control Systems 2-545
Fuel Pump, Replace 1-100
Fuel Pump Service 2-369
Fuel System Troubles 2-2
Fuel Pump Pressure 1-110

PROPELLER SHAFT & U JOINTS

Propeller Shaft 1-114
Universal Joint Service 2-117

REAR AXLE & SUSPENSION

Axle Shaft, Bearing and Seal 1-112
Coil Springs, Replace 1-122
Control Arms & Bushings, Replace 1-123
Leaf Springs, Replace 1-122
Rear Axle Troubles 2-16
Shock Absorber, Replace 1-122

SPECIFICATIONS

Alternator 1-94
Belt Tension 1-109
Brakes 1-95
Capacities 1-94
Carburetors 2-372
Cooling System 1-94
Crankshaft and Bearings 1-95
Distributors 1-91
Engine Tightening Torque 1-95

PAGE NO.

Fuel Pump Pressure 1-110
General Engine Specs. 1-91
Ignition Coils and Resistors 2-521
Pistons, Rings and Pins 1-95
Starting Motors 1-93
Tune Up 1-92
Valves 1-93
Valve Lift 1-106
Valve Timing 1-106
Wheel Alignment 1-93

STEERING GEAR

Horn Sounder Removal 1-99
Ignition Lock, Replace 1-97
Mechanical Gear Service 2-170
Mechanical Gear Troubles 2-17
Power Gear, Replace 1-130
Steering Wheel, Replace 1-99

SUSPENSION, FRONT

Ball Joints, Replace:
  Standard Cars 1-126
  Eldorado 1-129
Ball Joints, Check for Wear:
  Standard Cars 1-126
  Eldorado 1-129
Coil Spring, Replace 1-127
Lubrication 1-124
Shock Absorber, Replace 1-126
Standing Height, Adjust 1-127
Suspension, Description of:
  Standard Cars 1-124
  Eldorado 1-127
Tie-Strut & Bushings, Replace 1-127
Toe-In, Adjust:
  Standard Cars 1-125
  Eldorado 1-128
Torsion Bar, Replace 1-129
Wheel Alignment, Adjust:
  Standard Cars 1-124
  Eldorado 1-128
Wheel Bearings, Adjust 1-125
Wheel Bearings:
  Standard Cars 1-125
  Eldorado 1-128

TRANSMISSIONS

Automatic Units 2-231
Drive Link Belt 1-111
Linkage, 1975 1-110

TUNE UP

Service 2-517
Specifications 1-92

WINDSHIELD WIPER

Wiper Arms 1-101
Wiper Blades 1-101
Wiper Linkage, Replace 1-102
Wiper Motor, Replace 1-102
Wiper Switch, Replace 1-102
Wiper Troubles 2-19

CADILLAC

VEHICLE IDENTIFICATION NUMBER LOCATION: On 1969-75 models it is located on rear upper portion of cylinder block, behind intake manifold and on left side of transmission.

ENGINE UNIT NUMBER LOCATION: On 1969-75 at rear of cylinder block.

GRILLE IDENTIFICATION

1969 Eldorado

1969 Except Eldorado

1970 Eldorado

1970 Except Eldorado

1971 Except Eldorado

1971 Eldorado

1972 Eldorado

1972 Except Eldorado

1973 Except Eldorado

1973 Eldorado

1974 Eldorado

1974 Except Eldorado

1975 Eldorado

1975 Except Eldorado

GENERAL ENGINE SPECIFICATIONS

Year	Engine	Carburetor	Bore and Stroke	Piston Displacement, Cubic Inches	Compression Ratio	Maximum Brake H.P. @ R.P.M.	Maximum Torque Lbs. Ft. @ R.P.M.	Normal Oil Pressure Pounds
1969	375 Horsepower.............V8-472	4 Barrel	4.3000 x 4.060	472	10.50	375 @ 4400	525 @ 3000	30–35
1970	375 Horsepower.............V8-472	4 Barrel	4.3000 x 4.060	472	10.00	375 @ 4400	525 @ 3000	35–40
	400 Horsepower.............V8-500	4 Barrel	4.3000 x 4.304	500	10.00	400 @ 4400	550 @ 3000	35–40
1971	345 Horsepower.............V8-472	4 Barrel	4.3000 x 4.060	472	8.50	345 @ 4400	500 @ 2800	35–40
	365 Horsepower.............V8-500	4 Barrel	4.3000 x 4.304	500	8.50	365 @ 4400	535 @ 2800	35–40
1972–73	220 Horsepower①...........V8-472	4 Barrel	4.300 x 4.060	472	8.50	220 @ 4000	365 @ 2400	35–40
	235 Horsepower①...........V8-500	4 Barrel	4.300 x 4.304	500	8.50	235 @ 3800	385 @ 2400	35–40
1974	205 Horsepower①...........V8-472	4 Barrel	4.300 x 4.060	472	8.25	205 @ 3600	365 @ 2000	35–40
	210 Horsepower①...........V8-500	4 Barrel	4.300 x 4.304	500	8.25	210 @ 3600	380 @ 2000	35–40
1975	190 Horsepower.............V8-500	4 Barrel	4.300 x 4.304	500	8.5	190 @ 3600	360 @ 2000	35–40

①—Net rating—as installed in the vehicle.

DISTRIBUTOR SPECIFICATIONS

★Note: If unit is checked on the vehicle, double the RPM and degrees to get crankshaft figures.

Breaker arm spring tension—19-23.

Distributor Part No.①	Advance Starts	Centrifugal Advance Degrees @ RPM of Distributor			Full Advance	Vacuum Advance	
		Intermediate Advance				Inches of Vacuum to Start Plunger	Max. Adv. Dist. Deg. @ Vacuum
1111262	0–2¼ @ 400	3¼–7¼ @ 800	4¾–8½ @ 1000	6¼–10 @ 1200	16 @ 2000	10–12	13¼–15¼ @ 11¼
1111939	0–2¼ @ 400	5.15–7.15 @ 800	7.40–9.40 @ 1000	8.40–10.30 @ 1200	14 @ 2000	8–10	11.30–12.60 @ 13
1112065	0–1 @ 400	3–5 @ 800	4¾–6¾ @ 1000	6–8 @ 1200	13 @ 2000	8–10	11.30–12.60 @ 13
1112108	0–1 @ 400	3–5 @ 800	4¾–6¾ @ 1000	6–8 @ 1200	13 @ 2000	8–10	11.30–12.60 @ 13
1112219	0 @ 400	—	4½–6½ @ 950	—	13 @ 2000	5–7	12 @ 13
1112835	0 @ 400	5 @ 600	—	—	10 @ 2500	5	16 @ 11.5
1112836	0 @ 400	5 @ 600	—	—	10 @ 2500	7	16 @ 13.5
1112837	0 @ 400	4 @ 600	—	—	9 @ 2500	5	16 @ 11.5
1112838	0 @ 400	4 @ 600	—	—	9 @ 2500	7	16 @ 13.5
1112839	0 @ 400	5 @ 600	—	—	10 @ 2500	5	16 @ 11.5
1112840	0 @ 400	5 @ 600	—	—	10 @ 2500	7	16 @ 13.5
1112841	0 @ 400	4 @ 600	—	—	9 @ 2500	5	16 @ 11.5
1112842	0 @ 400	4 @ 600	—	—	9 @ 2500	7	16 @ 13.5
1112845	1 @ 500	—	—	—	12 @ 2000	5	16 @ 11.5
1112855	1 @ 500	—	—	—	12 @ 2000	5	16 @ 11.5
1112892②	−½–0 @ 330	−1–2¼ @ 450	3–5 @ 600	5–7 @ 1400	10 @ 3000	6.5	9.5–10.5 @ 14
1112954②	−½–0 @ 330	−1–2¼ @ 450	3–5 @ 600	5–7 @ 1400	10 @ 3000	5.5	13.5–14.5 @ 16

①—Stamped on distributor housing plate.
②—High energy ignition.

CADILLAC

TUNE UP SPECIFICATIONS

OLD CAR SPECIFICATIONS: For 1946-68 Tune Up Specifications see main index.

★When using a timing light, disconnect vacuum hose or tube at distributor and plug opening in hose or tube so idle speed will not be affected.

●When checking compression, lowest cylinder must be within 80 percent of highest.

▲Before removing wires from distributor cap, determine location of No. 1 wire in cap, as distributor position may have been altered from that shown at the end of this chart.

| Year | Spark Plug | | Distributor | | Ignition Timing★ | | | Carb. Adjustments | | | | | |
| | Type | Gap Inch | Point Gap Inch | Dwell Angle Deg. | Firing Order Fig. ▲ | Timing BTDC ① | Mark Fig. | Hot Idle Speed | | Air Fuel Ratio | | Idle "CO" % | |
								Std. Trans.	Auto. Trans. ②	Std. Trans.	Auto. Trans.	Std. Trans.	Auto. Trans.
1969	R44N	.035	③	30	C	5°	B	—	550D④	—	—	—	—
1970	R46N	.035	③	30	C	7½°	A	—	600D④	—	—	—	—
1971–72	R46N	.035	③	30	C	8°	D	—	600D④	—	—	—	—
1973	R46N	.035	③	30	C	8°	D	—	600D④	—	—	—	.5
1974	R45NS	.035	③	30	C	10°	D	—	600D④	—	—	—	.4
1975	R45NSX	.060	—		C	6°	D	—	600D	—	—	—	—

①—BTDC: Before top dead center.
②—D: Drive. N: Neutral.
③—Turn adjusting screw in (clockwise) until engine begins to misfire; then back screw out ½ turn.
④—When making adjustments, air conditioner must be turned off (if equipped). Also, hose must be disconnected at vacuum release cylinder. The hot idle compensator must be closed; this can be done by pressing finger or eraser end of pencil on compensator.

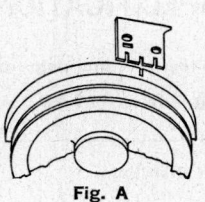

Fig. A

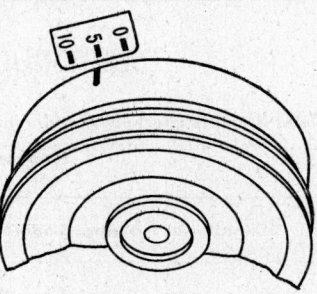

Fig. B

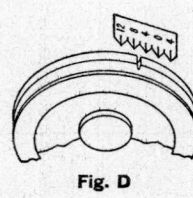

Fig. D

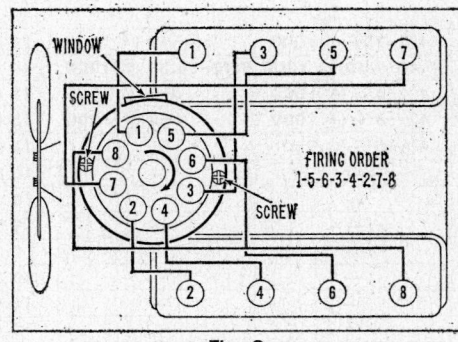

Fig. C

STARTING MOTOR SPECIFICATIONS

Year	Model	Starter Number	Brush Spring Tension Oz①	Free Speed Test			Resistance Test③	
				Amps.	Volts	R.P.M.	Amps.	Volts
1969–70; 1972	Std. Cars	1108381	35	70–99②	10.6	7800–12000	435–455②	3.0
	Eldorado	1108352	35	70–99②	10.6	7800–12000	435–455②	3.0
1971	Std. Cars	1108371	35	65–95②	—	7000–10500	—	—
	Eldorado	1107389	35	70–99②	10.6	7800–12000	435–535②	3.0
1973	Std. Cars	1108371	35	65–95②	—	7000–10500	—	—
	Eldorado	1108352	35	70–99②	10.6	7800–12000	435–535②	3.0
1974	Std. Cars	1108521	35	65–95②	—	7000–10500	—	—
	Eldorado	1108522	35	70–99②	10.6	7800–12000	435–535②	3.0
1975	All	—	35	65–95②	9	7000–10500	—	—

①—Minimum.   ②—Includes solenoid.

③—Check capacity of motor by using a 500-ampere meter and a carbon pile rheostat to control voltage. Apply volts listed across motor with armature locked. Current should be as listed.

VALVE SPECIFICATIONS

Year	Model	Valve Lash	Valve Angles		Valve Spring Installed Height	Valve Spring Pressure Lbs. @ In.	Stem Clearance		Stem Diameter	
			Seat	Face			Intake	Exhaust	Intake	Exhaust
1969–70	All	Hydraulic①	45	44	1¹⁵⁄₁₆	160 @ 1½	.0005–.0025	.001–.0025	.3415–.3425	.3415–.3420
1971	All	Hydraulic①	45	44	1¹⁵⁄₁₆	160 @ 1½	.0005–.0025	.001–.0025	.3413–.3420	.3415–.3420
1972–75	All	Hydraulic①	45	44	1⁶¹⁄₆₄	168 @ 1½	.0010–.0027	.0012–.0027	.3413–.3420	.3413–.3418

①—No adjustment.

WHEEL ALIGNMENT SPECIFICATIONS

OLD CAR SPECIFICATIONS: For 1946-68 Wheel Alignment Specifications see main index.

Year	Model	Caster Angle, Degrees		Camber Angle, Degrees				Toe-In. Inch	Toe-Out on Turns, Deg.	
		Limits	Desired	Limits		Desired			Outer Wheel	Inner Wheel
				Left	Right	Left	Right			
1969–70	Eldorado	−1½ to −2½	−2	+⅜ to −⅜	+⅜ to −⅜	Zero	Zero	0 to ⅛	18⅙	20
	All Others	−½ to −1½	−1	+⅜ to −⅜	+⅜ to −⅜	Zero	Zero	⅛ to ¼	18⅙	20
1971–72	Eldorado	−½ to −1½	−1	+⅜ to −⅜	+⅜ to −⅜	Zero	Zero	0 to ¹⁄₁₆	—	—
	All Others	−½ to −1½	−1	+⅜ to −⅜	−⅝ to +⅛	Zero	−¼	⅛ to ¼	—	—
1973	Eldorado	−½ to +½	Zero	−⅜ to +⅜	−⅜ to +⅜	Zero	Zero	0 to ¹⁄₁₆	—	—
	Others	−½ to −1½	−1	−⅜ to +⅜	−⅝ to +⅛	Zero	−¼	⅛ to ¼	—	—
1974	Eldorado	−½ to +½	Zero	−⅜ to +⅜	−⅝ to +⅛	Zero	−¼	0 to ¹⁄₁₆	—	—
	Series 75	−½ to +½	Zero	−⅜ to +⅜	−⅝ to +⅛	Zero	−¼	¹⁄₁₆ to ³⁄₁₆	—	—
	Others	−½ to −1½	−1	−⅜ to +⅜	−⅝ to +⅛	Zero	−¼	¹⁄₁₆ to ³⁄₁₆	—	—
1975	Series 75	−1½ to −½	−1	−⅜ to +⅜	−⅝ to +⅛	Zero	−¼	0–¹⁄₁₆	—	—
	Others	−½ to +½	Zero	−⅜ to +⅜	−⅝ to +⅛	Zero	−¼	0–¹⁄₁₆	—	—

CADILLAC

ALTERNATOR & REGULATOR SPECIFICATIONS

Year	Alternator					Regulator							
				Output @ 14 Volts			Field Relay			Voltage Regulator		
	Model	Rated Hot Output Amps.	Field Current 12 Volts @ 80° F.	2000 R.P.M. Amps.	5000 R.P.M. Amps.	Model	Air Gap In.	Point Gap In.	Closing Voltage	Air Gap In.	Point Gap In.	Voltage @ 125 F.
1969–70	1100742	63	2.8–3.2	35	59	1119519	.015	.030	1.5–2.7	.067	.014	13.5–14.3
	1100696	42	2.2–2.6	28	40	1119515	.015	.030	2.3–3.7	.060	.014	13.5–14.4
	1100694	55	2.2–2.6	32	50	1119515	.015	.030	2.3–3.7	.060	.014	13.5–14.4
1971–74	1100558	42	2.2–2.6	—	—	1119515	.015	.030	2.3–3.7	.060	.014	13.8–14.8
	1100940	42	4.0–4.5	—	—	—	—	—	—	—	—	—
	1100557	63	2.8–3.2	—	—	1119519	—	—	—	—	—	13.8–14.8
	1100937	63	4.0–4.5	—	—	—	—	—	—	—	—	—
	1101015	80	4.0–4.5	—	—	—	—	—	—	—	—	—
1975	—	63	4.0–4.5	—	—	Integral	—	—	—	—	—	—
	—	63	4.0–4.5	—	—	Integral	—	—	—	—	—	—
	—	80	4.0–4.5	—	—	Integral	—	—	—	—	—	—
	—	80	4.0–4.5	—	—	Integral	—	—	—	—	—	—
	—	145	4.0–4.5	—	—	Integral	—	—	—	—	—	—

COOLING SYSTEM & CAPACITY DATA

Year	Model or Engine	Cooling Capacity, Qts.			Radiator Cap Relief Pressure, Lbs.		Thermo. Opening Temp. [1]	Fuel Tank Gals.	Engine Oil Refill Qts. [3]	Transmission Oil			Rear Axle Oil Pints
		No Heater	With Heater	With A/C	With A/C	No. A/C				3 Speed Pints	4 Speed Pints	Auto. Trans. Qts. [10]	
1969	Eldorado	—	20.3	20.8	15	15	195	24	5	—	—	[9]	4½ [14]
	Series 75	—	23.8 [13]	23.8 [13]	15	15	195	20	4	—	—	[8]	5
	Others	—	20.3 [11]	20.8 [12]	15	15	195	26	4	—	—	[8]	5
1970	Eldorado	—	21.3	21.3	15	15	180	24 [15]	5	—	—	[16]	4½ [14]
	Series 75	—	21.8	21.8	15	15	180	26 [15]	4	—	—	[17]	5
	Others	—	21.3	21.3	15	15	180	26 [15]	4	—	—	[17]	5
1971–72	Eldorado	—	21.3	21.8	15	15	180	27	5	—	—	[16]	4 [14]
	Series 75	—	—	24.8	15	15	180	27	4	—	—	[17]	5
	Others	—	21.3	21.8	15	15	180	27	4	—	—	[17]	5
1973–74	Eldorado	—	21.3	23.8	15	15	180	27	5	—	—	[16]	4 [14]
	Series 75	—	—	26.8	15	—	180	27	4	—	—	[17]	5
	Others	—	21.3	23.8	15	15	180	27	4	—	—	[17]	5
1975	Eldorado	—	23	23	15	15	177	27½	5	—	—	[9]	4 [14]
	Series 75	—	25.8	25.8	15	15	177	27½	4	—	—	[17]	5
	Others	—	23	23	15	15	177	27½	4	—	—	[17]	5

[1]—For permanent anti-freeze.
[3]—Add one quart with filter change.
[8]—Oil pan 2 qts. Total capacity 12½ qts.
[9]—Oil pan 5 qts. Total capacity 13 qts.
[10]—Approximate. Make final check with dipstick.
[11]—1969, 21.3 qts.
[12]—1969, 21.8 qts.
[13]—1969, 24.8 qts.
[14]—Front drive axle.
[15]—California vehicles approx. 2 gallons less.
[16]—Oil pan 6 qts. Total capacity 13½ qts.
[17]—Oil pan 4 qts. Total capacity 12½ qts.

BRAKE SPECIFICATIONS

Year	Model	Brake Drum Inside Diameter	Wheel Cylinder Bore Diameter			Master Cylinder Bore Diameter		
			Disc Brake	Front Drum Brake	Rear Drum Brake	Disc Brakes	Drum Brakes	Power Brakes
1969–70	Series 75	12	2¾	—	⅞	1	—	1
	Eldorado	11	2 15/16	—	⅞	1	—	1
	All Others	12	2¾	—	13/16	1	—	1
1971–75	Eldorado	11	2 15/16	—	15/16	1⅛	—	1⅛
	Others	12	2 15/16	—	15/16	1⅛	—	1⅛

PISTONS, PINS, RINGS, CRANKSHAFT & BEARINGS

Year	Model	Fitting Pistons		Ring End Gap①		Wrist-pin Diameter	Rod Bearings		Main Bearings			
		Shim To Use	Pounds Pull On Scale	Comp.	Oil		Shaft Diameter	Bearing Clearance	Shaft Diameter	Bearing Clearance	Thrust on Bear. No.	Shaft End Play
1969–70	All	②	②	.013	.015	.9995	2.500	.0005–.0028	3.250	.0003–.0026	3	.002–.012
1971–75	All	②	②	.013	.015	.9995	2.500	.0005–.0028	3.250	.0001–.0026	3	.002–.012

①—Fit rings in tapered bores for clearance given in tightest portion of ring travel.

②—See text under "Pistons".

ENGINE TIGHTENING SPECIFICATIONS★

★Torque specifications are for clean and lightly lubricated threads only. Dry or dirty threads produce increased friction which prevents accurate measurement of tightness.

Year	Spark Plugs Ft. Lbs.	Cylinder Head Bolts Ft. Lbs.	Intake Manifold Ft. Lbs.	Exhaust Manifold Ft. Lbs.	Rocker Arm Shaft Bracket Ft. Lbs.	Rocker Arm Cover Ft. Lbs.	Connecting Rod Cap Bolts Ft. Lbs.	Main Bearing Cap Bolts Ft. Lbs.	Flex Plate to Crankshaft Ft. Lbs.	Vibration Damper or Pulley Ft. Lbs.
1969–75	25	115	30	35	—	24①	40	90	75	17

①—Inch pounds. Retorque after engine has been run.

Electrical Section

DISTRIBUTOR, REPLACE

1. Remove distributor cap.
2. On vehicles without H.E.I. system, disconnect primary wire from coil. On vehicles equipped with H.E.I. system, disconnect harness connector from side of distributor cap.
3. Disconnect vacuum advance pipe or hose from distributor.
4. Crank engine until rotor is pointing to No. 1 spark plug wire position on cap.
5. Remove distributor hold-down nut and clamp.
6. Lift distributor from engine.
7. Note that the rotor will turn slightly as the drive gear becomes disengaged from the camshaft gear. Therefore, when installing the distributor, the rotor should be turned slightly counter-clockwise from No. 1 spark plug position to insure proper engagement of gears. When properly installed, rotor should point directly to No. 1 spark plug position.

STARTER, REPLACE

1972-75

1. Disconnect battery ground cable at battery.
2. On Eldorado, disconnect starter harness at connector at right rear of engine.
3. Raise front end of car.
4. On all except 1972-73 Eldorado models, disconnect battery lead at starter solenoid and disconnect neutral switch wire and coil feed wire at starter solenoid terminals.
5. On all except 1974 Eldorado and H.E.I. equipped vehicles, disconnect interlock relay wire and solenoid wire at starter solenoid terminals.
6. On Eldorado, remove spring clip securing wire to solenoid housing.

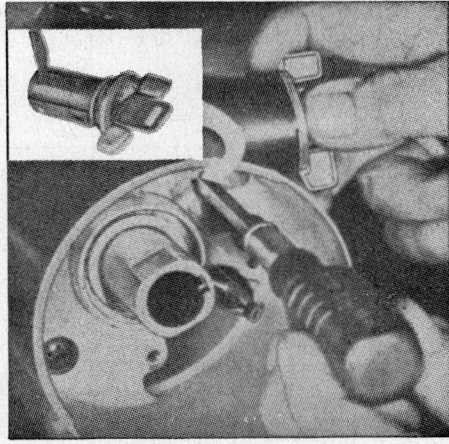

Fig. 1 Lock cylinder removal

7. Remove screw and nut securing support bracket to starter and crankcase.
8. Unfasten starter motor from crankcase and remove starter by pulling it forward, then toward RH front wheel and up over steering linkage toward rear of car.

1969-71

1. Disconnect ground strap at battery.
2. Raise and support front end of car.
3. Disconnect battery lead at starter solenoid terminal.
4. Disconnect neutral safety switch wire and coil feed wire at starter solenoid.
5. Remove spring clip securing wires to solenoid housing.
6. Unfasten starter (2 screws) and remove starter by pulling it forward and then lowering it straight down.
7. Reverse procedure to install.

IGNITION LOCK

CAUTION: On vehicles equipped with an Air Cushion Restraint system, turn ignition switch to "Lock," disconnect battery ground cable and tape end, thereby deactivating system.

1. Follow procedure to remove the turn signal switch as described further on.
2. Turn ignition switch to the "On" or "Run" position.
3. Insert a small screw-driver into slot next to the switch mounting screw boss, Fig. 1. Gently tap on screwdriver until screw-driver breaks through thin wall casting. Depress lock cylinder retaining tab with screw-driver and remove cylinder.
4. To separate the lock from the cylinder Fig. 2, use a paper clip or similar quality wire, place a 90 deg. bend about ⅛" from one end of the wire.
5. Using the wire as described in step 4, depress the plunger pin (above the stake mark) approx. ⅛" vertically in sleeve housing, at the same time exert light pressure on the lock assembly, rotate the cylinder counter-clockwise until it pops up from the sleeve assembly.

IGNITION SWITCH, REPLACE

CAUTION: On vehicles equipped with an Air Cushion Restraint system, turn ignition switch to "Lock," disconnect battery ground cable and tape end, thereby deactivating system.

1969-75

1. Disconnect battery cable and position ignition key in "Lock".
2. Remove steering column lower cover.
3. Loosen two upper column support nuts and allow column to drop as far

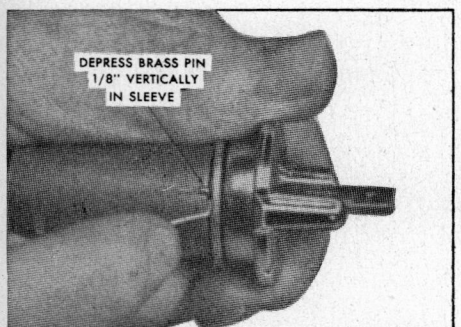

Fig. 2 Lock cylinder disassembly

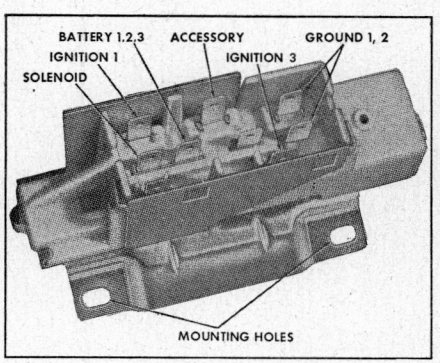

Fig. 3 Ignition switch. 1969-72

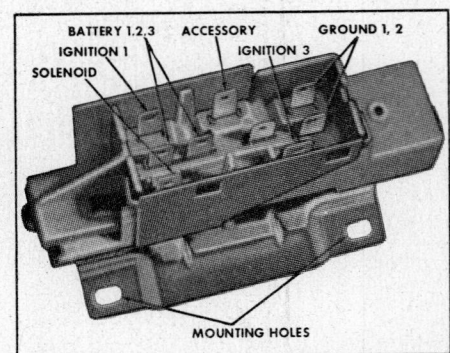

Fig. 4 Ignition switch. 1973-75

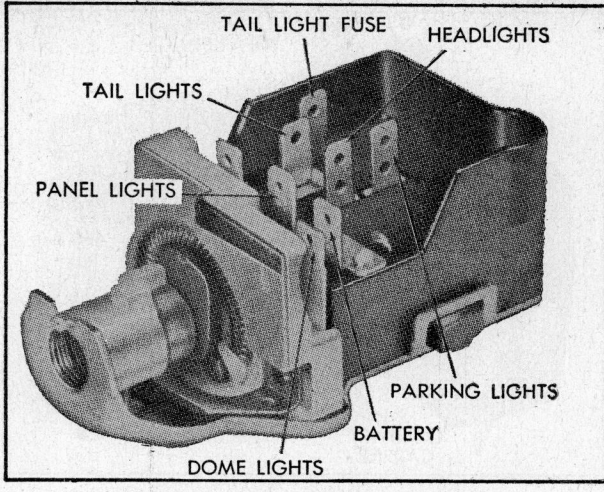

Fig. 5   Headlight switch. 1969

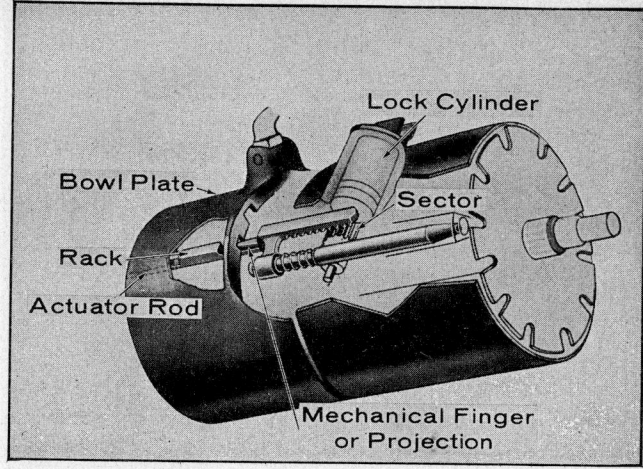

Fig. 6   Mechanical neutral start system late 1973 with Standard column and all 1974-75 models

as possible without removing the nuts.

NOTE: Do not remove nuts as column may bend under its own weight.

4. Disconnect switch connector and remove switch, Figs. 3 and 4.
5. When reassembling, make sure the ignition key is in the "Lock" position. Assemble switch on actuator rod. Hold rod stationary and move switch towards bottom of column then back off one detent on standard steering column models. On models with tilt column, move switch toward upper end of column and back off one detent.

LIGHT SWITCH, REPLACE

CAUTION: On vehicles equipped with an Air Cushion Restraint system, turn ignition switch to "Lock," disconnect battery ground cable and tape end, thereby deactivating system.

1974-75

1. Disconnect battery ground cable.
2. Remove steering column lower cover.
3. Disconnect headlamp electrical connector and lower bulb.
4. Pull knob to "ON" position, depress spring loaded button and remove knob and shaft, escutcheon and washer.
5. Remove case to instrument support screw.
6. Lower switch assembly, disconnect upper bulb and remove switch.

1970-73

1. Remove steering column lower cover.
2. Unfasten wiring harness retainer running below switch.
3. Depress button on top of switch and remove knob and rod.

4. Remove screw with ground wire at bottom of switch housing.
5. Pull switch down and rearward and disconnect wire and bulbs.
6. Remove hex head sleeve securing switch to housing case and remove switch.

1969

1. Remove instrument panel top cover and steering column lower cover.
2. Remove left A/C duct and outlet and disconnect wiring harness below headlight switch.
3. Depress button on top of switch and remove knob and rod assembly.
4. Remove attaching screws, pull switch rearward and disconnect bulbs and wires and remove switch, Fig. 5.

STOP LIGHT SWITCH
1970-74

The stoplight is retained to the brake pedal bracket. To adjust, pull the brake pedal fully up to its stop. This action automatically adjusts the switch.

1969

1. Disconnect two leads wires from switch on brake pedal flange.
2. Remove locking nut from switch.
3. Remove stop light switch.
4. Reverse procedure to install.

NOTE: Adjust switch action so that stop light is on when brake pedal is depressed 1/2". Loosen front and rear nuts that hold switch and move switch up or down until this action is obtained. Tighten switch lock nuts securely to prevent loss of adjustment.

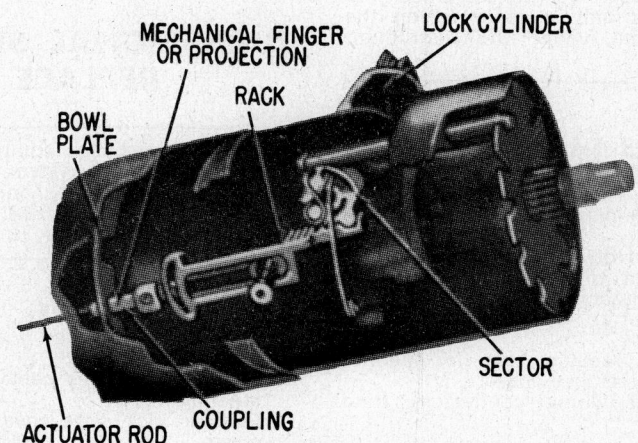

Fig. 7   Mechanical neutral switch system with Tilt-Telescope column. 1974-75

Fig. 8 Mechanical neutral start system in Park position

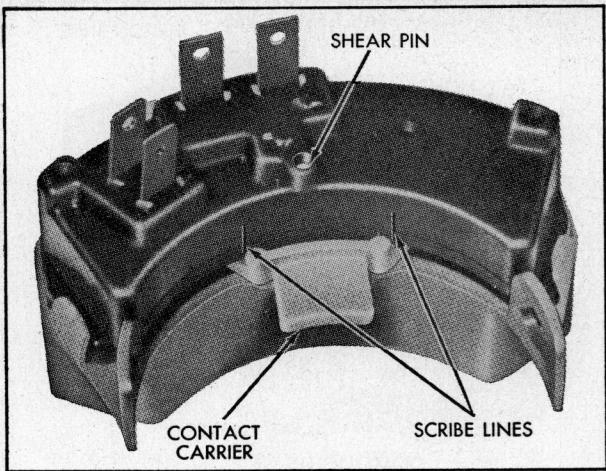

Fig. 9 Switch in neutral position. 1969-72

NEUTRAL START SWITCH

1973 Late Std. Column & All 1974-75 Models

Actuation of the ignition switch is prevented by a mechanical lockout system, Figs. 6 and 7, which prevents the lock cylinder from rotating when the selector lever is out of Park or Neutral. When the selector lever is in Park or Neutral, the slots in the bowl plate and the finger on the actuator rod align allowing the finger to pass through the bowl plate in turn actuating the ignition switch, Fig. 8. If the selector lever is in any position other than Park or Neutral, the finger contacts the bowl plate when the lock cylinder is rotated, thereby preventing full travel of the lock cylinder.

NOTE: On all models incorporating an electric neutral start switch, this switch plus the back-up light switch and parking brake vacuum release valve are combined into one unit. This unit is mounted on the steering column under the instrument panel.

1969-73 Exc. Late 1973 W/Std. Column

1. Place transmission shift lever in neutral.
2. Remove switch from column, being careful not to disturb neutral position of contact carrier, Fig. 9.
3. Mark neutral position of contact carrier.
4. Mark top vacuum hose for identification and remove hoses.
5. Disconnect wiring connectors from switch.

Installation
1. Place transmission shift lever in neutral detent.
2. Connect wires to switch.
3. Move contact carrier on switch to neutral position as marked during removal.

NOTE: If necessary to install a new switch, the switch will be secured in neutral by a shear pin. Do not break pin.

4. Install switch on steering column, aligning contact carrier blade with slot in shift tube.
5. Secure switch to steering column with two mounting nuts, making sure that shift lever is in neutral detent while this operation is performed.
6. Connect vacuum hoses to switch as marked during removal.
7. Switch should now be properly adjusted. If new switch was installed, a slightly greater effort to position the shift lever in any position besides neutral will be necessary to break the shear pin.

TURN SIGNAL SWITCH, REPLACE

CAUTION: On vehicles equipped with an Air Cushion Restraint system, turn ignition switch to "Lock", disconnect battery ground cable and tape end, thereby deactivating system.

1974-75

Standard column
1. Disconnect battery cable and remove steering wheel.
2. Remove lock plate cover screws and cover.
3. With a suitable compressor, compress lock plate and spring and remove snap ring from shaft.
4. Remove lock plate, cancelling cam, preload spring and thrust washer.
5. Remove steering lower cover and the signal lever.
6. On car equipped with cruise control proceed as follows:
   a. Disconnect cruise control wire from harness.
   b. Remove harness protector from cruise control.
   c. Wrap wire around turn signal lever until lever is disconnected. Do not remove wire from column.
7. On all models remove bolts at upper support.
8. Remove four screws securing upper mounting bracket to column and remove bracket.
9. Disconnect turn signal harness and remove wires from plastic protector.
10. Remove screw securing turn signal switch to column and pull switch out.

Tilt & Telescope Wheel
1. Disconnect battery cable.
2. Remove steering wheel and slide rubber sleeve from steering shaft.
3. Remove plastic retainer from C-ring.
4. With a suitable compressor, thread bolt into steering shaft lock hole.
5. Compress preload spring and remove C-ring.
6. Remove compressor and remove lock plate, horn contact carrier and preload spring.
7. Remove steering lower cover and the signal lever.
8. On cars equipped with cruise control proceed as follows:
   a. Disconnect cruise control wire from harness.
   b. Remove harness protector from cruise control.
   c. Wrap wire around turn signal lever until lever is disconnected. Do not remove wire from column.
9. On all models remove bolts at upper support.
10. Remove four screws securing upper mounting bracket to column and remove bracket.

11. Disconnect turn signal harness and remove wires from plastic protector.
12. Remove screw securing turn signal switch to column and pull switch out.

1969-73

Standard Wheel

1. Remove battery cable.
2. Remove steering wheel.
3. Remove lock plate cover screws and cover.
4. With a suitable compressor, compress lock plate and spring and remove snap ring from shaft.
5. Remove lock plate, cancelling cam, preload spring and thrust washer.
6. Remove turn signal lever.
7. Disconnect switch wiring connector and wrap a piece of tape around connector and harness to facilitate removal.
8. Remove upper mounting bracket from column.
9. Remove three retaining screws and remove switch. Reverse procedure to install.

Tilt & Telescope Wheel

1. Disconnect battery cable and remove steering wheel and rubber bump stop.
2. With a suitable tool, compress upper steering shaft pre-load spring and remove C-ring, Fig. 10.
3. Remove compressor, lock plate, horn contact, and upper shaft pre-load spring.
4. Disconnect switch wiring connector and wrap a piece of tape around connector and harness to facilitate removal.
5. Remove upper mounting bracket and switch wiring protector.
6. Position shift bowl in "Park" and remove turn signal lever.
7. On Eldorado, disconnect switch and Cruise Control connectors on column and attach a piece of piano wire to connector on Cruise Control harness, unscrew signal lever and gently pull Cruise Control harness up through and out of column. Secure piano wire in column to aid in reassembly.
8. Push hazard warning flasher button in then unscrew and remove button.
9. Remove retaining screws and remove switch.
10. Reverse procedure to install. On Eldorado, use the piece of piano wire previously installed to draw the Cruise Control harness through the column.

HORN SOUNDER & STEERING WHEEL

1969-75

CAUTION: On vehicles equipped with an Air Cushion Restraint system, turn ignition switch to "Lock," disconnect battery ground cable and tape end, thereby deactivating system.

1. Disconnect battery ground cable.
2. On vehicles equipped with Air Cushion Restraint System, remove the driver

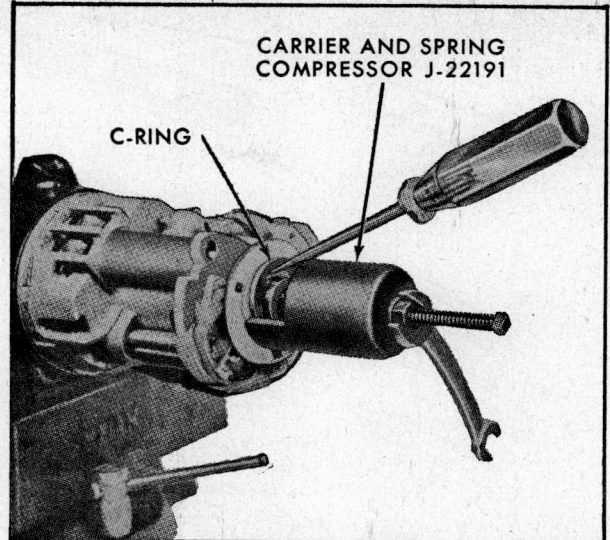

Fig. 10   Removing C-ring. 1969-73

module attaching screws using tool J-24628-2. On vehicles not equipped with Air Cushion Restraint System, remove three screws from back of spokes and lift pad assembly from wheel.
3. On tilt and telescope wheels remove three screws securing lever and knob assembly to flange and screw assembly. Unscrew flange and screw assembly from steering shaft and remove. Remove lever and knob assembly.
4. On standard wheels, scribe an alignment mark on wheel hub in line with slash mark on steering shaft to be used upon installation.

5. Loosen steering shaft nut, apply a suitable puller to loosen wheel; then remove puller, nut and wheel.
6. Remove three screws securing three contact wires to wheel.
7. Reverse procedure to install.

INSTRUMENT CLUSTER

CAUTION: On vehicles equipped with an Air Cushion Restraint system, turn ignition switch to "Lock," disconnect battery ground cable and tape end, thereby deactivating system.

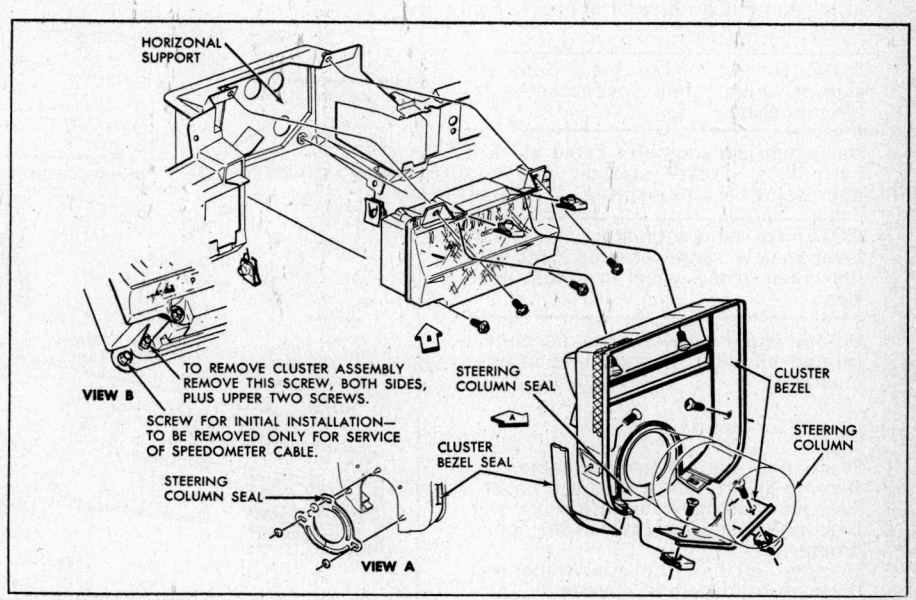

Fig. 11   Instrument panel cluster. 1974

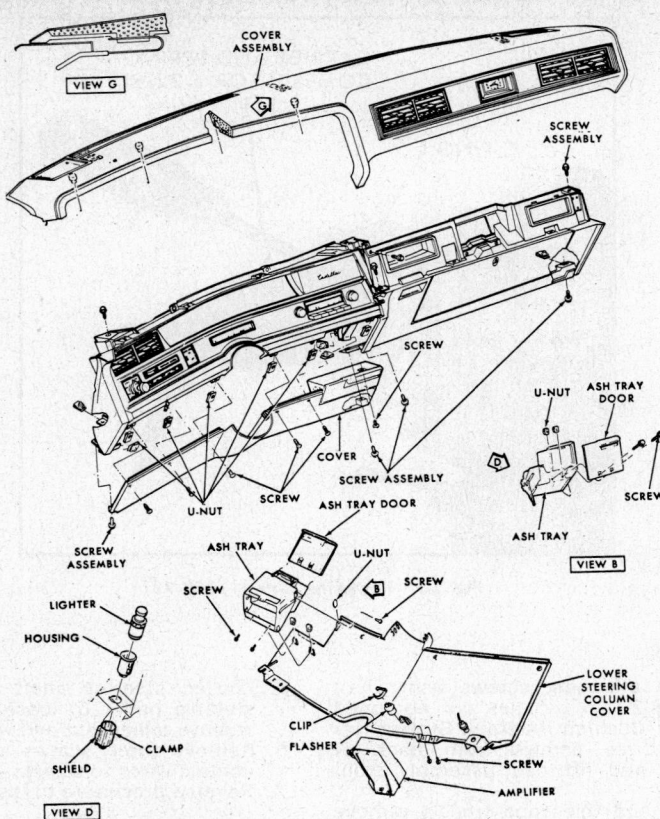

Fig. 12 Instrument panel cover. 1971-73

back of cluster and position out of way.

8. Remove screw securing shift pointer to column and remove pointer, Fig. 12.
9. Remove four screws (2 upper and 2 lower) securing cluster to bezel.
10. Move cluster back and to right. Tip right hand corner of cluster upward and remove cluster out through top of panel.

1969-70

1. Disconnect battery cable.
2. Remove instrument panel top cover, clock, radio and steering column lower cover.
3. Remove shift indicator pointer.
4. Remove odometer reset knob by pulling if off shaft.
5. Remove four cluster-to-bezel screws, Fig. 13.
6. Move cluster forward and to the right. Tip right hand corner of cluster downward and remove cluster from under panel.

RADIO, REPLACE

NOTE: When installing radio, be sure to adjust antenna trimmer for peak performance.

1974-75

CAUTION: On vehicles equipped with an Air Cushion Restraint system, turn ignition switch to "Lock," disconnect battery ground cable and tape end, thereby de-activating system.

1. Disconnect battery ground cable.

1974-75

1. Disconnect battery ground cable.
2. Remove cluster bezel and with shift lever in "Park" remove screw securing shift indicator cable to steering column.
3. Remove four screws securing cluster to instrument horizontal support, Fig. 11.

NOTE: Do not remove the 2 outboard screws which retain speedometer cable mounting.

4. Disengage speedometer cable at neck by pulling cluster straight out and depressing retaining spring.

NOTE: To remove cluster, place shift lever in low range and on cars with tilt wheel, place wheel in lowest position.

5. Rotate cluster downward, disconnect printed circuit connector and remove cluster.

1971-73

1. Disconnect battery ground cable.
2. Remove instrument panel top cover.
3. Remove steering column lower cover.
4. Disconnect speedo cable from speedometer.
5. Remove left hand air conditioner outlet hose from behind cluster.
6. Disconnect cluster connector.
7. Disengage wiring harness from clip at

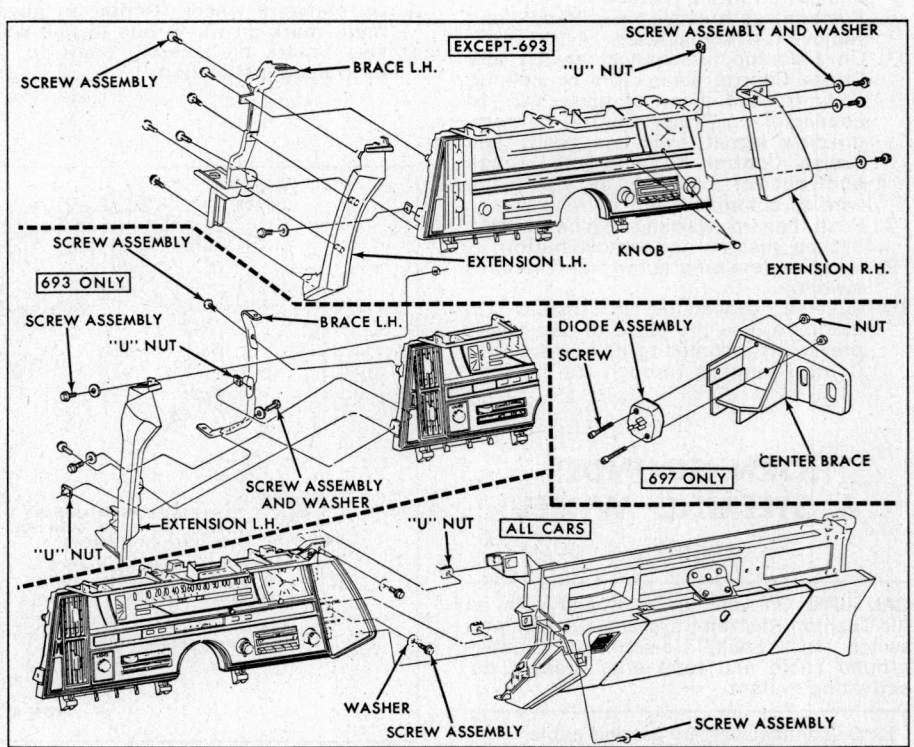

Fig. 13 Instrument panel. 1969-70 (Typical)

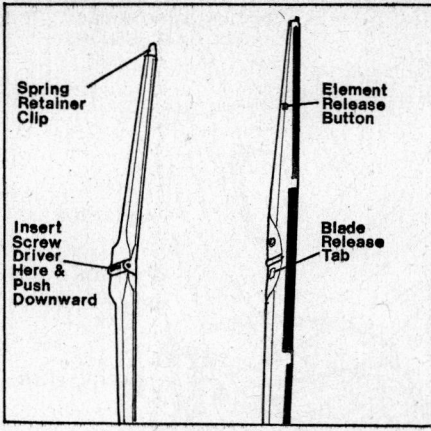

Spring Retainer Clip

Element Release Button

Insert Screw Driver Here & Push Downward

Blade Release Tab

Fig. 14 Wiper Blades

2. Remove ash tray, radio knobs, washers, control rings and nuts.
3. Remove radio to lower support brace nut from rear and rotate brace to the right.
4. Disconnect wires, antenna lead and the dial bulb from radio.
5. Lower left hand side of radio and remove radio through the ash tray opening.

1970-73

1. Remove steering column lower cover.
2. If necessary, remove defroster hose from behind radio.
3. Remove radio knobs, washers and control rings.
4. Remove spanner nuts that hold shafts to panel.
5. Disconnect wires and antenna lead from radio.
6. Remove two hex head screws that hold lower support bracket to radio and instrument panel center support and remove bracket.

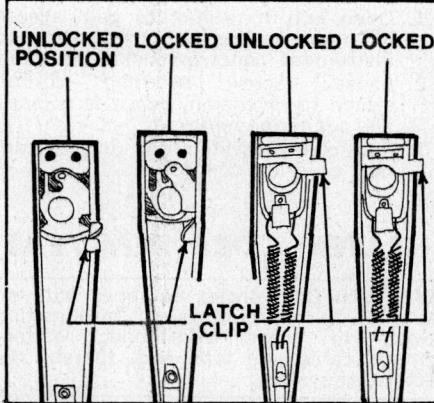

UNLOCKED LOCKED UNLOCKED LOCKED POSITION

LATCH CLIP

Fig. 16 Wiper arm removal. 1971-75

7. Pull radio back from panel to disengage shafts and lower to gain access to dial bulb.
8. Disconnect dial bulb and remove radio.

1969

1. Remove steering column lower cover. If necessary, remove defroster hose from behind radio.
2. Remove radio knobs, springs and rings.
3. Remove spanner nuts that hold radio control shafts to instrument panel.
4. Remove screw on right side that secures radio to bracket and loosen screw that secures bracket to brace.
5. Pull radio rearward to disengage control shafts and drop radio slightly to gain access to wiring connectors.
6. On AM/FM Stereo radio, disconnect audio-amplifier unit connector.
7. Disconnect antenna lead-in cable and connector at radio.
8. Disconnect light bulb socket from radio.
9. Disconnect foot control cable plug from radio if equipped.
10. On stereo radio, remove tape securing speaker leads: Two pieces on instrument panel cluster and two pieces at instrument panel frame above glove box door.
11. Remove radio.

W/S WIPER BLADES

Two methods are used to retain wiper blades to wiper arms, Fig. 14. One method uses a press type release tab. When the release tab is depressed the blade assembly can be slid off the wiper arm pin. The other method uses a coil spring retainer. A screw driver must be inserted on top of the spring and the spring pushed downward. The blade assembly can then slide off the wiper arm pin. Two methods are also used to retain the blade element in the blade assembly, Fig. 14. One method uses a press type release button. When the button is depressed, the two piece blade assembly can be slid off the blade element. The other method uses a spring type retainer clip in the end of the blade element. When the retainer clip is squeezed together, the blade element can be slid out of the blade assembly.

NOTE: To be sure of correct installation, the element release button, or the spring element retaining clip should be at the end of the wiper blade assembly nearest the wiper transmission.

W/S WIPER ARMS
1969-70

1. Open hood to gain access to wiper arms.
2. Lift wiper arms off windshield and in-

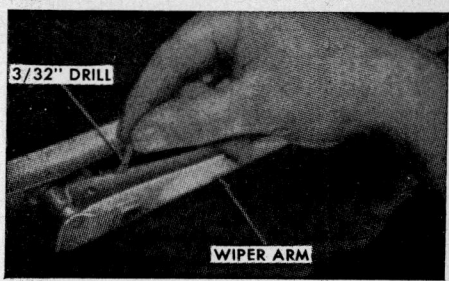

3/32" DRILL

WIPER ARM

Fig. 15 Wiper arm removal. 1969-70

sert a 3/32" drill (#43) in hole behind wiper arm, Fig. 15.
3. Release wiper arm, leaving drill in hole, and lift wiper arm assembly off transmission shaft.
4. On left side, slide drag link clip toward end of arm enough to disengage drag link from pivot pin and remove wiper arm and drag link from vehicle.

CAUTION: Do not remove drill installed in step 2.

5. To install left wiper arm, position drag link on pivot pin and secure by sliding retainer down to pivot pin until it locks.
6. Install wiper arm on transmission shaft.
7. Pull up on wiper arm and remove drill from hole in wiper arm assembly.

NOTE: When installing wiper arm and blade assemblies, be sure to "overpark" the arm and blade assemblies below the windshield so that a proper return to park position will result.

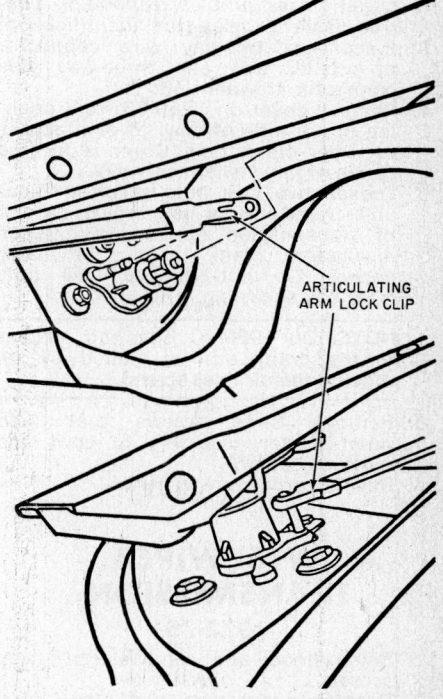

ARTICULATING ARM LOCK CLIP

Fig. 17 Articulating arm lock clip

1971-75

1. Raise hood to gain access to wiper arms.
2. Lift wiper arm and slide latch clip, Fig. 16, out from under wiper arm.
3. Release wiper arm and lift wiper arm assembly off transmission shaft.
4. On left arm, slide articulating arm lock clip away from transmission pivot pin, Fig. 17, and lift arm off pin.
5. To install left wiper arm assembly, position the articulating arm over the transmission pivot pin and slide the lock clip toward the pivot pin until it locks in place on the pin. Install the left wiper arm assembly to the transmission shaft aligning the keyway to the shaft.
6. Align keyway in right wiper arm assembly to transmission shaft and install arm assembly to shaft.
7. Lift the wiper arm assemblies and slide latch clips under the arms. Release wiper arms and check wipe pattern and park position.

W/S WIPER MOTOR
1972-75

1. Raise hood and remove cowl screen.
2. Reach opening and loosen transmission drive link to crank arm nuts.
3. Remove transmission drive link from motor crankarm.
4. Disconnect wiring and washer hoses.
5. Remove motor attaching screws.
6. Remove motor while guiding crankarm through hole.

1969-71

1. Disconnect battery ground cable.
2. Disconnect three washer hoses from washer control valve. *Mark small outlet hoses and corresponding control valve nozzles for identification.*
3. Disconnect two-way wire connector at washer unit and three-way wire connector at wiper unit.
4. Remove cover on 1969-70 from opening in left side of cowl to gain access to wiper crank arm. *Cover is located above wiper-washer assembly.*
5. Loosen two lock nuts securing wiper unit crank arm to ball socket on end of transmission drive linkage, then disengage crank arm from ball socket. *Do not remove lock nuts from ball sockets.*

NOTE: On 1969-70 Eldorado, access to the crank arm is gained by removing the air inlet screen.

6. Remove three screws that hold wiper-washer assembly to cowl and remove assembly.
7. Reverse procedure to install.

W/S WIPER TRANSMISSION
1972-75

1. Raise hood and remove cowl vent screen.
2. Remove wiper arm and blade from transmission to be removed.

3. Loosen attaching nuts securing transmission drive link to motor crankarm.

NOTE: If only left side is to be removed, it will not be necessary to loosen nuts securing right drive link to motor crankarm.

4. Disconnect transmission drive link from crankarm.
5. Remove attaching screws securing transmission to body.
6. Remove transmission and linkage assembly through plenum chamber opening.

1969-71 Except Eldorado

1. Remove both wiper arms.
2. Remove six clips securing rubber hood seal to cowl and position seal out of the way.
3. Remove cowl ventilator screen (12 screws).
4. Unfasten left wiper transmission from cowl (3 screws).
5. Repeat Step 4 for right side.
6. Allow transmissions, linkage and bellcrank to lie in cowl plenum.
7. Remove ball socket cover (2 screws). Cover is located on top of cowl directly behind wiper-washer assembly.
8. Loosen two lock nuts securing crank arm to ball socket on end of drive linkage, then disengage crank arm from ball socket. Do not remove locknuts from ball socket studs.
9. Slide linkage to one side to allow one end of linkage to be drawn out through opening in cowl and remove linkage.
10. Reverse procedure to install.

1969-71 Eldorado

1. Remove both wiper arms.
2. Remove cowl air inlet screen.

3. Remove access hole cover from opening in center of cowl to gain access to wiper unit crank arm.
4. Remove lock nut securing crank arm to ball socket stud.
5. Remove three transmission mounting screws on right and left transmissions.
6. Disengage ball socket stud at wiper unit and remove transmissions and linkages as a complete assembly.
7. Reverse procedure to install.

W/S WIPER SWITCH
1974-75

1. Remove left hand climate control outlet grille.
2. Remove screw securing switch to instrument panel.
3. Pull control switch and electrical connector out and disconnect from panel.

1969-73

1. Open left front door to gain access to screw securing control switch to instrument panel extension on door.
2. Loosen screw securing control switch to extension. *Screw is trapped and cannot be removed.*
3. Pull control switch out and disconnect electrical connector.

HEATER CORE REMOVAL

CAUTION: On vehicles equipped with an Air Cushion Restraint system, turn ignition switch to "Lock," disconnect battery ground cable and tape end, thereby deactivating system.

After draining radiator and disconnecting heater hoses proceed as follows:

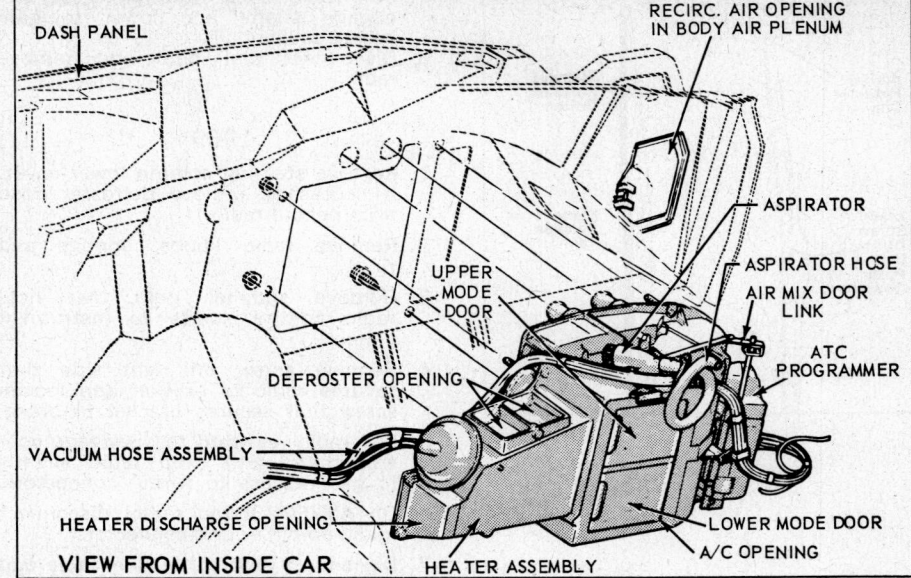

Fig. 18 Heater core. 1971-75 (Typical)

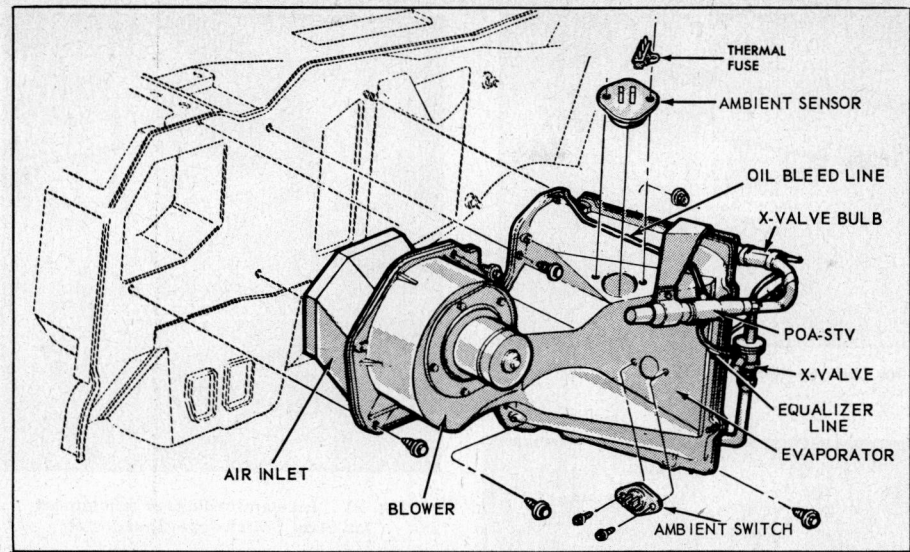

THERMAL FUSE

AMBIENT SENSOR

OIL BLEED LINE

X-VALVE BULB

POA-STV

X-VALVE

EQUALIZER LINE

EVAPORATOR

AIR INLET

BLOWER

AMBIENT SWITCH

Fig. 19 Blower motor. 1971-75 (Typical)

1971-75

With Air Conditioning

1. Remove instrument panel top cover.
2. Remove right and left outlet A/C hoses and center outlet connector. On 1974 models, remove right and left outlet A/C hoses from A/C distributor.

NOTE: On 1974-75 models, remove center outlet support and connector from position between cowl and horizontal support.

3. Remove two screws securing A/C distributor to heater case and remove distributor.
4. Remove one screw securing defroster nozzle to heater case and remove nozzle from under clips and out of car.
5. Remove glove compartment liner.
6. Disconnect vacuum hoses at recirc door, water valve, control head and supply hose.
7. Disconnect aspirator hose from in-car sensor.
8. Remove instrument panel center vertical brace.
9. Remove instrument panel horizontal brace.
10. Remove four nuts securing heater case to cowl on engine side of dash, Fig. 18.
11. Remove heater case from position under panel being careful to hold case as upright as possible to avoid spilling coolant.
12. Remove rubber seal from around core water nipples.
13. Remove screw and clip from under seal.
14. Remove two screws and clip from opposite end of case and remove core.

Without Air Conditioning

1. Remove instrument panel top cover.
2. Remove two screws and position center ventilation duct and sleeve out

of way.
3. Remove vacuum hoses from diverter door and defroster door vacuum actuators.
4. Remove Bowden cable from temperature door arm and remove screw securing cable to heater case. Reposition cable out of way.
5. Remove two screws and nuts securing heater case to cowl and pull case away from cowl.
6. Remove heater case from position under panel being careful to hold in upright position to avoid spilling coolant.
7. Remove two screws and retainer at each side of core securing core to case and remove core.

1969-70 All Models

With Air Conditioning

1. Working in engine compartment, disconnect vacuum hoses and wiring from servo units being sure to mark them for proper installation.
2. On 1969 models remove fender to cowl tie struts. If car is equipped with Auto Level Control position left tie strut with compressor attached.
3. To gain access to the Heater & Air Modulator assembly, remove the vacuum storage tank and disconnect master switch, control cables and vacuum hoses again being sure to mark them for ease of assembly.
4. Unfasten and remove Heater & Air Modulator assembly from engine compartment.
5. The heater core can now be removed from this assembly.

1969-70 Except Eldorado

Without Air Conditioning

1. Blower motor and heater-blower assembly must be removed to get at the heater core. To do this, first disconnect electrical connector to blower on cowl in engine compart-

ment. Then remove five screws securing blower motor to its case and remove motor.
2. Disconnect cable at temperature valve at pivot point on heater and remove cable clamp.
3. Remove screw securing vacuum manifold to heater and move manifold and hoses out of the way.
4. Remove seven screws securing bottom of heater to cowl and six screws securing top of heater to cowl, and take out heater assembly.
5. To remove heater core, remove four screws (two each side) that secure wire retaining clamp to heater blower case and remove clamps.
6. Heater core can now be pulled out of case and rubber grommets removed from inlet and outlet fittings.

1969-70 Eldorado

Without Air Conditioning

1. Before removing heater blower and motor, disconnect rubber cooling hose from nipple on blower motor.
2. The left cowl-to-fender shield strut rod must also be removed before taking out heater-blower assembly.

BLOWER MOTOR REPLACE

1969-70

1. Disconnect battery ground cable.
2. Remove screw securing antenna bracket to wheel housing.
3. Remove cooling hose from nipple and blower motor.
4. Disconnect feed wire at motor.
5. Unfasten motor, rotate 180° and remove.

1971-75

CAUTION: On vehicles equipped with an Air Cushion Restraint system, turn ignition switch to "Lock," disconnect battery ground cable and tape end, thereby deactivating system.

1. Disconnect battery ground cable.
2. Remove cooling hose from nipple and blower.
3. Disconnect electrical connector at lead to motor.
4. Unfasten and remove motor, Fig. 19.

SPEED CONTROL

1970-75

Bead Chain Adjustment

1. Adjust engine hot idle speed and mixture, then shut off engine.
2. Check slack in chain by unsnapping swivel from ball stud and holding chain taut at ball stud; center of swivel should extent 1/8" beyond center of ball stud.
3. Adjust bead chain slack by sliding sleeve back on chain and removing

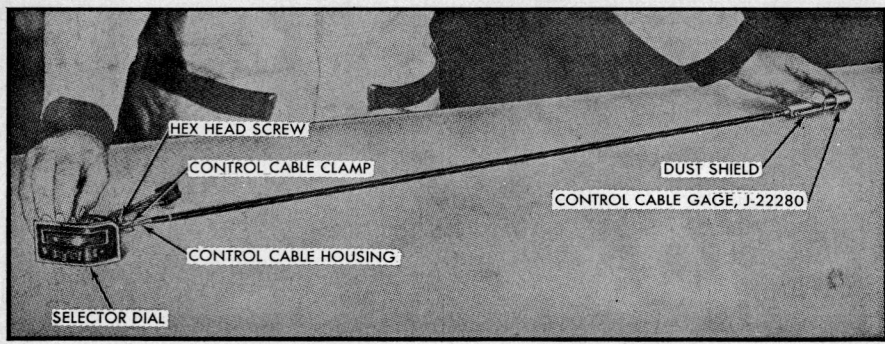

Fig. 20 Control cable adjustment for Slide Switch Speedostat

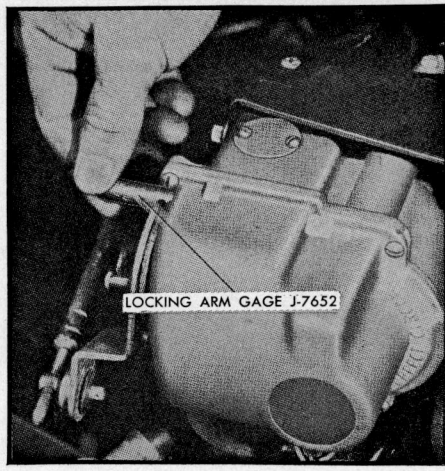

Fig. 21 Accelerator linkage adjustment for Slide Switch type Speedostat

loose rivet. Move swivel on ball chain until slack is correct. Then reinstall rivet and slide sleeve over rivet. On late models, install bead chain with second ball on the inboard slot of the throttle plate clip.

Cruise Speed Adjustment

The cruise speed adjustment can be set as follows:
1. If car cruises below engagement speed, screw orifice tube on transducer outward.
2. If car cruises above engagement speed, screw orifice tube inward.

NOTE: Each ¼ turn of the orifice tube will change cruise speed about one mile per hour. Snug up lock nut after each adjustment.

Brake Release Switch Adjustment

1. Turn on ignition switch and connect a test light between one terminal of brake release switch and ground; select terminal where light goes out when pedal is depressed.
2. Loosen screw that retains switch to pedal support bracket. Position switch so circuit opens (light goes out) when pedal is depressed ¼". Tighten screw and recheck.

Control Cable Adjustment, 1969

The cable is preset at the factory and should not require adjustment unless a new cable is installed. This adjustment must be performed off the car as follows:
1. Remove the selector assembly.
2. Rotate selector dial to low speed position until it is positioned against its stop but do not force beyond its stop.
3. Position assembly flat on workbench

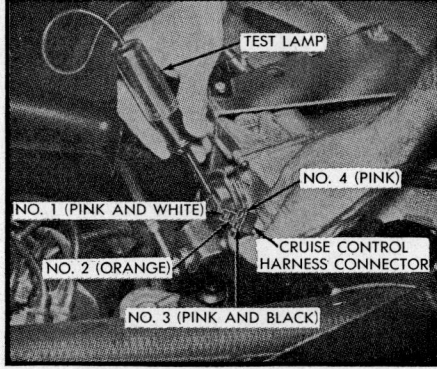

Fig. 22 Electrical connections on Slide Switch type Speedostat

and make certain there are no kinks in cable.
4. Loosen hex head set screw at cable clamp on selector control.
5. Pull cable housing until it is approximately half-way out of cable clamp. Position control cable gauge shown in Fig. 20 in end of dust shield. Hold dust shield and gauge and push toward selector control assembly until gauge bottoms. While holding in this position, tighten set screw at cable clamp.

Accelerator Linkage

1. Adjust throttle rod.
2. Start engine and operate at slow idle with transmission lever in "Park".
3. Separate linkage from exterior arm.
4. Adjust trunnion so that when it is installed through exterior arm, the

stop stud will be aligned with locating notch and throttle valves will be closed.
5. Install washer on trunnion and secure with cotter pin.

NOTE: Due to the angle at which the trunnion enters hole in exterior arm, it is necessary to rotate the exterior arm slightly forward when inserting the trunnion. Repeat this operation until proper alignment is obtained. Be careful not to turn trunnion too far back or throttle valves will unseat and cause an incorrect adjustment. Insert the gauge shown in Fig. 21 (or small diameter pipe) over stop stud to check alignment.

Brake Release Switch

1. Turn on ignition but do not start engine.
2. Momentarily move slide switch to AUTO position until red indicator light glows.
3. Using a test lamp, ground one lead and touch the other lead to terminal No. 4, Fig. 22.
4. Loosen mounting screw securing release switch to brake pedal mounting bracket.
5. Adjust release switch so that lamp will light when brake pedal is fully released, and will go out when brake pedal is depressed about ¼ inch. Tighten switch mounting screw. If switch cannot be adjusted, it is defective and should be replaced.

Engine Section

ENGINE MOUNTS

1971-75 Except Eldorado

1. On 1973-75 vehicles, open hood and remove radiator cover.
2. Raise and support vehicle on hoist.
3. Remove two through bolts from mount to be replaced, Fig. 1.
4. If left hand (driver side) mount is being replaced, remove nut and washer from both mounts.
5. If right hand (passenger side) mount is being replaced, remove nut and washer from left hand mount and loosen right hand nut until no threads are visible on stud.
6. Support car with stands at each front frame horn.
7. Apply pressure (hoist, jack, etc.) to oil pan. Apply pressure over entire bottom with no concentration of pressure due to bumps or knobs on lift.
8. Raise engine until mount may be removed.

CAUTION: Amount engine may be raised is limited due to clearance between fan and shroud. Use caution when raising engine to avoid damage to these components.

1973-75 Eldorado

Left Front Mount

1. Remove radiator cover and disconnect battery ground cable.
2. Raise car and remove nut and washer from mount stud.
3. Remove capscrew securing transmission cooler lines to final drive bracket.
4. Remove screw securing top of steering gear flex coupling shroud to frame.
5. Remove nut from large through bolt securing top of engine mount and top of final drive bracket to engine.
6. Remove nut from lower engine mount through bolt.

NOTE: Attach box end wrench to nut, then use pry bar between wrench and engine.

7. Remove remaining screw securing flex coupling shroud to frame and remove shroud.
8. Remove cross bar bolt, nut and washers securing bottom of final drive bracket to final drive. Remove bracket by tipping back and to left of car.
9. Using block of wood and jack stand, lift engine from frame at crankshaft pulley to relieve load on engine mount bolts and remove bolts from mount.
10. Loosen, but do not remove, nut and washer from right engine mount stud.
11. Raise engine enough to remove mount. Work mount down and forward between fuel pump and frame.

Right Front Mount

1. Remove radiator cover.
2. Remove nut and washer securing left engine mount to frame.
3. Raise car and remove nut and washer securing right mount to frame.
4. Reach between right mount and oil

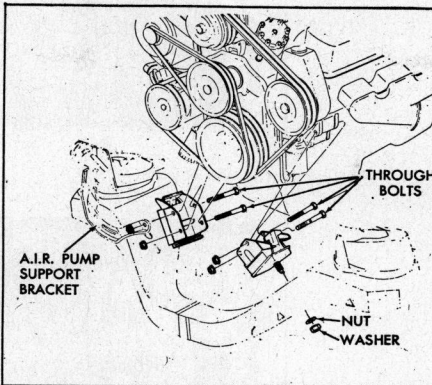

Fig. 1 Front engine mounts

pump to attach open end wrench to nut on lower bolt securing mount to engine. Holding this wrench in place, remove lower mounting bolt from rear, using ratchet, U-joint socket and 18" extension.
5. Work end wrench up between oil pump and crankshaft pulley and position wrench in a straight vertical position to engage nut on upper mounting bolt. Holding wrench in place, use same tools as in Step 4 to remove upper mounting bolt.

NOTE: If nut is impossible to engage, an alternative is to first perform the following Step, then use a 5" extension and a 9/16" crowfoot adapter and engage tool on nut by slipping between oil pump and A.I.R. pump.

6. Place jackstand under crankshaft pulley and, using wood block to avoid damage to pulley, either raise engine or lower chassis to remove mount.

CAUTION: When separating engine and chassis, observe relative position of frame rail and right drive axle tripot housing. Interference between these parts requires removal of right drive axle before mount can be removed. Furthermore, if tri-pot housing does clear the frame, vertical movement is limited by presence of fuel lines. Do not allow tri-pot housing to contact fuel lines.

7. Work mount free and pull rearward over tri-pot housing to remove.

1971-72 Eldorado

1. Remove fan and then raise car.
2. Remove nuts securing engine mount to crossmember.
3. Position a stand under crankshaft pulley and lower car until mount studs are disengaged from frame.

CAUTION: Transmission cooler lines and fuel lines must receive special handling to avoid damage.

4. Remove bolts securing mount to adapter and remove mount.

ENGINE, REPLACE

1970-75

1. Disconnect battery ground cable.
2. Remove hood and carburetor air cleaner with hoses.
3. Disconnect carburetor linkage at pedal lever.
4. Disconnect Cruise Control vacuum hoses if so equipped.
5. Remove clamp securing upper radiator hose to cradle.
6. Disconnect and/or remove all necessary wiring, pipes, hoses, linkage, etc.
7. Remove fan and A/C compressor.
8. Partially remove power steering pump, laying it aside so hoses are above fluid level in reservoir.
9. Drain radiator and disconnect hoses.
10. Proceed with steps 13 through 32 as described for 1969 models.

1969

NOTE: Disregard optional equipment items mentioned in the following if the car being serviced is not so equipped.

1. Disconnect battery ground cable.
2. Remove hood, air cleaner and automatic level control hoses.
3. Disconnect carburetor linkage at pedal lever.
4. Disconnect Cruise Control linkage.
5. Remove radiator shroud and clamp securing radiator upper hoses to cradle.
6. Disconnect and/or remove all necessary wiring, pipes, hoses, linkage, etc.
7. Remove fan. On Eldorado, remove studs from water pump shaft hub.
8. Remove Cruise Control power head.
9. Remove A/C compressor.
10. Partially remove power steering pump, laying it aside so that pressure and return hoses are above the fluid level in pump reservoir.
11. Position power steering cooler out of the way.
12. Loosen A.I.R. pump and remove belt.
13. Remove water pump pulley and alternator.
14. Remove two upper transmission-to-engine screws. Right screw secures transmission dipstick and modulator line to engine.
15. Remove A/C power servo from heater air selector. On cars other than Eldorado, remove blower relay and master switch from heater air selector.
16. Remove dust shield-to-cowl tie struts.
17. Position a lifting bracket to rear intake manifold attaching screws on Cruise Control cars. Bracket is in place on all others.
18. Raise car and place on jack stands.
19. Remove front engine mount nuts.

20. Remove oil filter.
21. On Eldorado, remove right output shaft.
22. Unfasten starter and allow it to hang by its cables.
23. Remove converter inspection pan.
24. Disconnect exhaust pipes from manifolds.
25. Place a jack under exhaust pipes to support system while engine is removed.
26. Support transmission with a jack.
27. Remove four lower transmission-to-engine screws.
28. Remove three screws securing converter to flex plate.
29. With lifting rig attached, pry engine forward while raising it as far as possible.
30. Lower transmission and again raise engine.
31. Remove flex plate and lift engine free of car.
32. Reverse procedure to install.

CYLINDER HEAD, REPLACE
1969-75

1. Remove intake manifold.
2. Drain coolant from radiator.
3. Disconnect ground strap at rear of cylinder heads from cowl on 1969-73 models.
4. Disconnect wiring connector for high engine temperature warning system from sending unit at rear of left cylinder head.
5. Remove alternator if working on right cylinder head, or partially remove power steering pump if working on left cylinder head.
6. Remove A.I.R. manifold from both cylinder heads if equipped.
7. Unfasten wiring harness from cylinder head and position out of the way.
8. Unfasten exhaust manifold from cylinder head.
9. Remove rocker arm cover.
10. Remove rocker arm assemblies and lift out push rods.
11. Unfasten and lift off cylinder head.
12. After carefully removing all gasket material from mating surfaces of head and block, position new gasket over dowels and install cylinder head in reverse order of removal, being sure to install the screws as indicated in Fig. 2.

VALVE ARRANGEMENT
Front to Rear

All Models . . . . E-I-I-E-I-I-E

VALVE LIFT SPECS.

Engine	Year	Intake	Exhaust
V8-472	1969-71	.440	.454
V8-500	1970-71	.440	.454
V8-472	1972-73	.490	.490

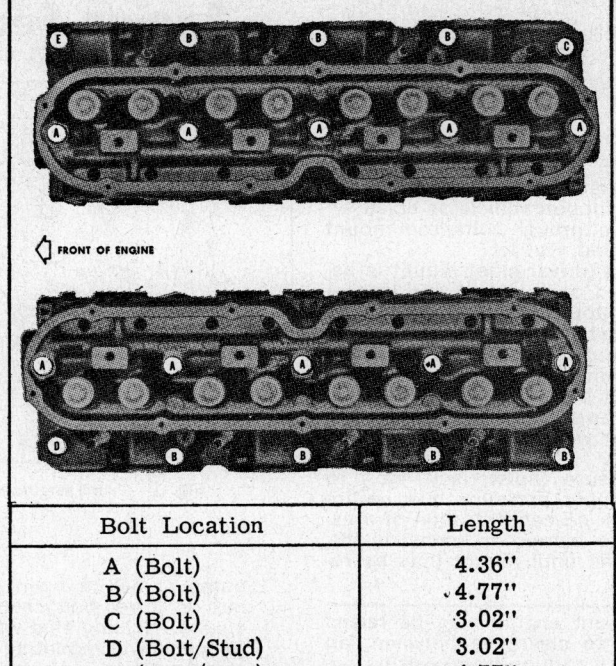

Bolt Location	Length
A (Bolt)	4.36"
B (Bolt)	4.77"
C (Bolt)	3.02"
D (Bolt/Stud)	3.02"
E (Bolt/Stud)	4.77"

Fig. 2   Location and length of cylinder head screws. 1969-75

V8-500	1972-73	.490	.490
V8-472	1974	.457	.473
V8-500	1974-75	.475	.473

VALVE TIMING
Intake Opens Before TDC

Engine	Year	Degrees
V8-472	1969-70	18
V8-472	1971	38
V8-500	1970	18
V8-500	1971-73	34
V8-472	1972-73	34
V8-472	1974	21
V8-500	1974-75	21

ROCKER ARMS
1969-75

When disassembling the rocker arm assembly, be sure to keep the supports and rocker arms in order so they can be installed in the exact same position.

Install rocker arms on supports and place supports in retainers as shown in Fig. 3. *Be sure that the "EX" on support is positioned toward the exhaust valve and "IN" toward the intake valve.*

Place capscrews through the reinforcements, supports and retainers and position assemblies on cylinder head. Make sure that push rods are properly seated in the lifter seats and in the rocker arms. Lubricate rocker arm bearing surfaces before assembling in order to prevent wear.

VALVE GUIDES

Check valve stem to valve guide clearance, clearance should be no more than .005 inch. Service valves are available in standard (.343 inch) and .003, .006 and .013 inch oversizes. If clearance is found to be excessive, valve guide should be reamed out to next oversize using appropriate reamer, and a corresponding oversize valve installed. On some engines, valves with a .003 inch oversize diameter and .003 inch oversize valve guides are installed at the factory. Engines so fitted will be identified by a "3" stamped on the cylinder head gasket surface inline with the oversize valve.

VALVE LIFTERS

The valve lifters may be lifted out of their bores after removing the rocker arms, push rods and intake manifold. Adjustable pliers with taped jaws may be used to remove lifters that are stuck due to varnish, carbon, etc. Fig. 4 illustrates the type of lifter used.

ENGINE FRONT COVER
1969-75

1. On Eldorado models, remove engine from vehicle.
2. Remove harmonic balancer.
3. Loosen starter sufficiently to gain access to oil pan screws and lower front of oil pan until it clears front studs.

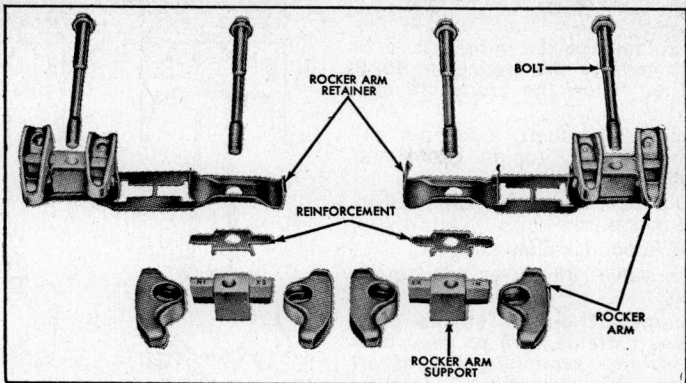

Fig. 3   Rocker arm components disassembled. 1969-75

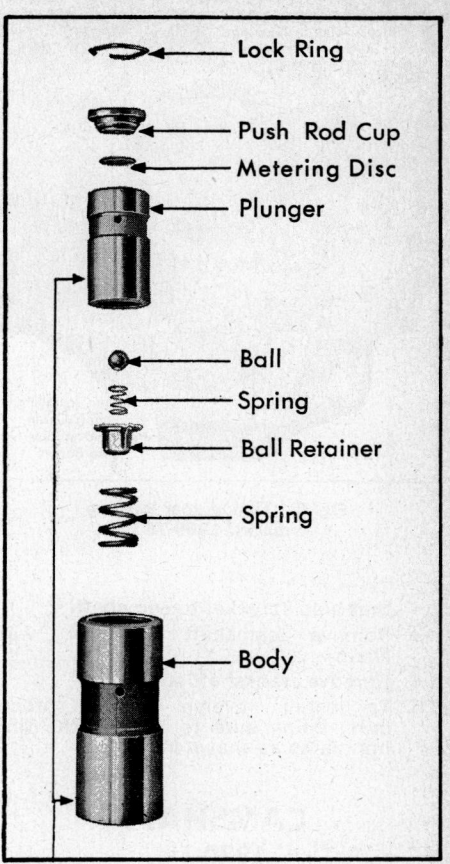

Fig. 4   Hydraulic valve lifter

4. Drain radiator and remove lower hose from water pump.
5. Remove the 10 screws securing front cover to the cylinder block and remove cover with water pump as an assembly.
6. Reverse removal procedure, to install, referring to Fig. 5.

FRONT COVER OIL SEAL
1970-75
1. Remove vibration damper.

2. With a thin blade screw driver or similar tool, pry out front cover oil seal.

3. Lubricate new seal and fill cavity with wheel bearing grease. Position seal on end of crankshaft with garter spring side toward engine.

4. Using a suitable installer drive seal into cover until it bottoms against cover.

1969
1. Disconnect battery ground cable.
2. Remove carburetor air cleaner.
3. Raise front of car.
4. Remove alternator drive belt.
5. Remove air pump drive belt.
6. Remove power steering pump belt.
7. Working under car, remove four screws that hold crankshaft pulley to vibration damper. Place scribe marks on pulley and damper for proper installation.
8. Remove plug from end of crankshaft.
9. Use a suitable puller to remove vibration damper.
10. Pry out seal.
11. Lubricate new oil seal by filling cavity between lips with wheel bearing grease. Position seal on end of crankshaft with garter spring side toward engine.
12. Using a suitable seal installer, drive seal into front cover until it bottoms against cover.

TIMING CHAIN
1. Remove engine front cover as outlined above.
2. Remove two capscrews and washers

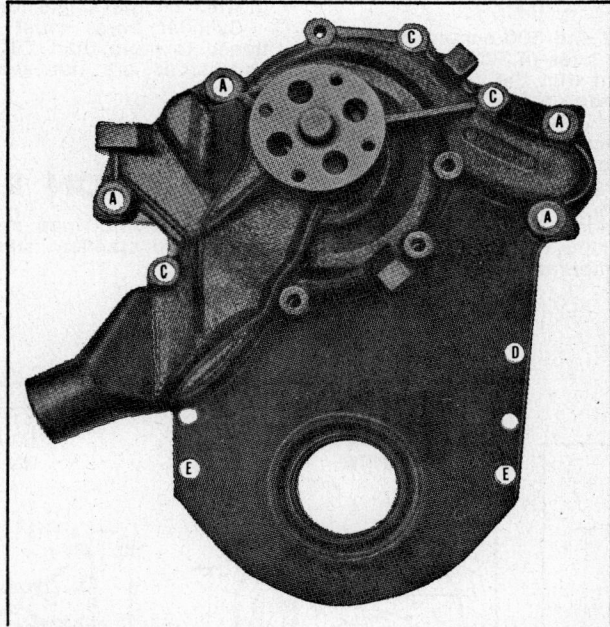

Key	(No.)	Size	Torque
A	(4)	3/8-16 x 1-3/8	25 Foot-Pounds
C	(3)	5/16-18 x 1-1/4	15 Foot-Pounds
D	(1)	5/16-18 x 5/8	15 Foot-Pounds
E	(2)	3/8-16 x 5/8	25 Foot-Pounds

Fig. 5   Engine front cover attaching screws. 1969-75

Dowel Holes in Camshaft and Sprocket Must Line Up

When Installing Timing Chain, Marks Must Line Up, As Shown

Fig. 6   Timing gear locating marks. 1969-75

1969

In order to replace the camshaft, it is necessary to remove the engine on 1969 Eldorado. Then follow the procedure outlined below.

1. To remove camshaft, take off engine front cover, timing chain and sprockets.
2. If equipped with air conditioner, remove condenser.
3. Remove hood lock plate support.
4. Remove valve lifters as previously outlined.
5. Slide camshaft out of engine carefully. *Use extreme care to keep cam lobes from scratching camshaft bearings.*
6. When installing camshaft, apply a coating of rear axle lubricant to camshaft bearing journals and camshaft lobes.

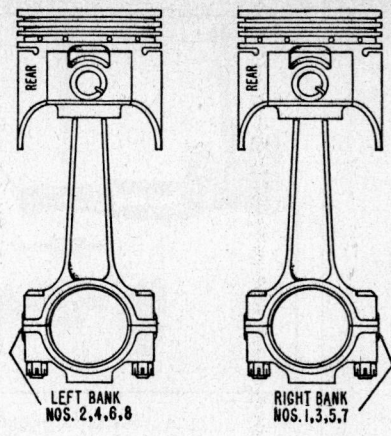

LEFT BANK NOS. 2,4,6,8

RIGHT BANK NOS. 1,3,5,7

Fig. 7   1969-75 piston and rod assembly

that hold sprocket to camshaft.

3. Remove camshaft sprocket with chain.
4. Remove crankshaft sprocket.
5. To install, reverse removal procedure, being sure to line up the timing marks as shown in Fig. 6.

CAMSHAFT
1970-75

1. Remove engine front cover.
2. Remove distributor and oil pump.
3. Remove oil slinger from crankshaft.
4. Remove fuel pump and fuel pump eccentric.
5. Unfasten and remove camshaft sprocket with chain attached.
6. Remove valve lifters as previously outlined.
7. Remove radiator.
8. Carefully slide camshaft forward until it is out of engine.

PISTONS & RODS ASSEMBLE

On all engines, assemble and install the piston and rod assemblies as shown in Fig. 7.

PISTONS
1969-75

The V8-472 and 500 engines both have identical bore sizes (4.300 inch), therefore it is important that the correct piston be installed for the engine being worked on. Refer to Figs. 7A and 7B, for correct piston identification.

Pistons should be measured for size as shown in Fig. 8. Cylinders should be measured $1\frac{1}{8}$" from the top, crosswise to the cylinder block. The clearance should be .0006-.0010" in this position at room temperature (70°F). Subtract

.0001" from measurement for every 6° above 70°.

An identification letter is stamped on the valve lifter compartment cover next to lower inside edge of cylinder head. The letters are in groups of two for adjacent cylinders (such as "A" "B") midway between the two cylinders. This letter denotes the cylinder size as shown in Fig. 9. The table indicates ten piston sizes to match ten bore sizes. This makes it possible to maintain the proper clearance between block and piston.

If double letters (such as "AA" "BB") appear, it indicates that the cylinder has been bored .010" over the diameter indicated by the single letter in the chart.

Cylinder bores must not be reconditioned to more than .0100 inch oversize, as pistons are not available over this range.

PISTON RINGS

Replacement rings are available from Cadillac in standard size and .010" oversize.

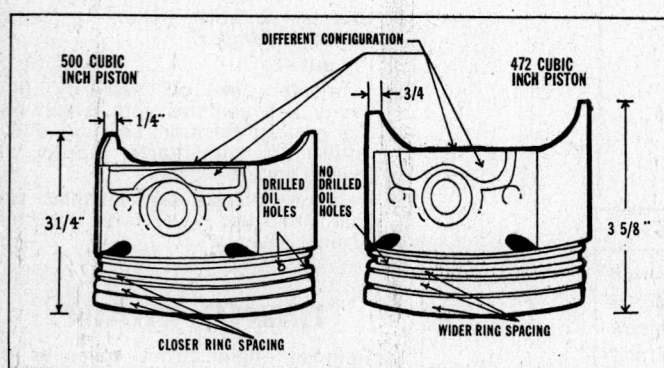

Fig. 7A   Piston identification. 1970-73 V8-472 and 500

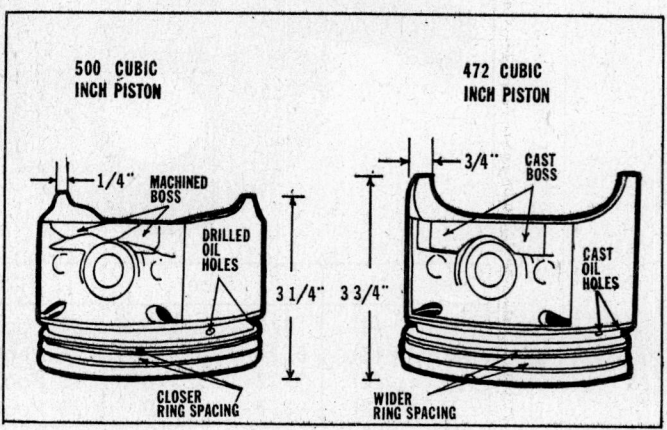

Fig. 7B   Piston identification. 1974 V8-472 and 1974-75 V8-500

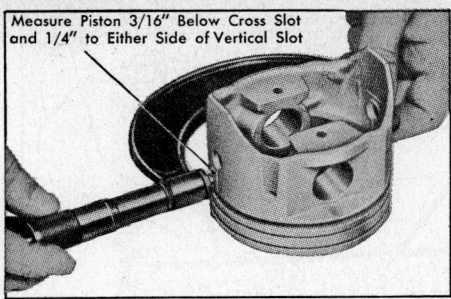

Fig. 8   Measuring piston diameter. 1969-75

Cylinder and piston sizes (as indicated by letters stamped on the cylinder head gasket surface). The letters are in groups of two for adjacent cylinders (such as "H" and "B") midway between the two cylinders. The letters denote the cylinder piston sizes as shown below).

Letter	Cylinder Size (Diameter in Inches)	Piston Size (Diameter in Inches)
A	4.3000 - 4.3002	4.2992 - 4.2994
B	4.3002 - 4.3004	4.2994 - 4.2996
C	4.3004 - 4.3006	4.2996 - 4.2998
D	4.3006 - 4.3008	4.2998 - 4.3000
E	4.3008 - 4.3010	4.3000 - 4.3002
H	4.3010 - 4.3012	4.3002 - 4.3004
J	4.3012 - 4.3014	4.3004 - 4.3006
K	4.3014 - 4.3016	4.3006 - 4.3008
L	4.3016 - 4.3018	4.3008 - 4.3010
M	4.3018 - 4.3020	4.3010 - 4.3012
AA	4.3100 - 4.3102	4.3092 - 4.3094
BB	4.3102 - 4.3104	4.3094 - 4.3096
CC	4.3104 - 4.3106	4.3096 - 4.3098
DD	4.3106 - 4.3108	4.3098 - 4.3100
EE	4.3108 - 4.3110	4.3100 - 4.3102
HH	4.3110 - 4.3112	4.3102 - 4.3104
JJ	4.3112 - 4.3114	4.3104 - 4.3106
KK	4.3114 - 4.3116	4.3106 - 4.3108
LL	4.3116 - 4.3118	4.3108 - 4.3110
MM	4.3118 - 4.3120	4.3110 - 4.3112

Fig. 9   Cylinder and piston sizes. 1969-75

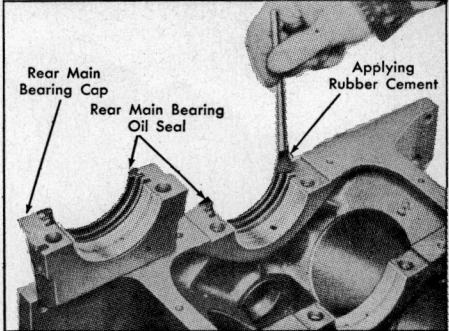

Fig. 10   Rear main bearing cap and seal. 1969-75

PISTON PINS

Piston pins are a matched fit with the piston and are not available separately. Piston pins are pressed in the connecting rods and will not become loose enough to cause a knock or tapping until after very high mileages. In such cases a new piston and pin assembly should be installed.

MAIN & ROD BEARINGS

Main and rod bearings are supplied by Cadillac in standard sizes only.

CRANKSHAFT OIL SEAL
1969-75

The two seal halves are identical and can be used in either the lower or upper location. However, both seal halves are pre-lubricated with a film of wax for break-in. Do not remove or damage this film. Fig. 10 shows the construction of the main bearing cap and seal.

To install the lower half of the seal into the bearing cap, slide either end of seal into position at one end of bearing cap and place tool on seal land at other end of bearing, Fig. 11. Make sure seal is positioned over bearing ridge and lip of seal is facing forward (car position).

Hold thumb over end of seal that is flush with split line to prevent it from slipping upward, and push seal into seated position by applying pressure to the other end. Make sure seal is pressed down firmly and is flush on each side to avoid possibility of a leak at seal split line. Avoid pressing on lip as damage to sealing edge could result.

To install upper half of seal in cylinder block (with crankshaft in car), position "shoehorn" tool on land of block. Start seal into groove in block with lip facing forward and rotate seal into position. Do not press on lip or sealing edge may be damaged. Both ends of seal must be flush at seal split line to avoid leaks. If necessary, Lubriplate or its equivalent may be used to facilitate installation of both upper and lower seal halves. Do not use silicone or a leak may result.

OIL PAN, REPLACE
1969-75 Except Eldorado

NOTE: For easier removal of the oil pan past the stabilizer bar, first remove the two front dowel studs from the block by running a jam nut on each stud to lock the pan nut on the stud. Working over the front frame crossmember, use a socket to remove the stud with the two nuts attached.

1. Disconnect battery ground cable.
2. Drain engine oil.

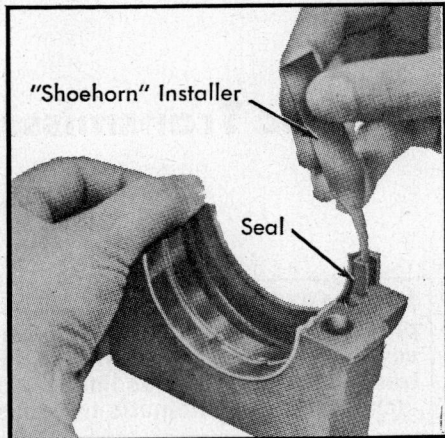

Fig. 11   Installing rear main bearing oil seal. 1969-75

3. Remove "Y" exhaust pipe at exhaust manifold.
4. Remove starter.
5. Unfasten and lower idler arm support.
6. Disconnect pitman arm at center link and lower steering linkage.
7. Remove transmission lower cover.
8. Unfasten and lower oil pan.

NOTE: To align the oil pan at the rear and prevent damage from the flywheel teeth during installation, first locate the oil pan on the crankcase with two screws at mid-point. Then install two screws at the rear while checking gasket alignment.

1969-75 Eldorado

To remove the oil pan it is necessary to remove the engine as described previously.

OIL PUMP
1969-75

1. Raise car and remove oil filter.
2. Remove five screws securing pump to engine. The screw nearest the pressure regulator should be removed last, allowing the pump to come down with screw.
3. Remove pump drive shaft.
4. Reverse procedure to install, being sure to pack the pump with petrolatum.

BELT TENSION DATA

	New Lbs.	Used Lbs.
1969-73—		
Air Condition	100	55-70
A.I.R. Pump	100	55-70
Generator	100	55-70
Power Steering	100	55-70
1974-75—		
Air Condition	170	120
A.I.R. Pump	170	120
Generator	100	70
Power Steering	170	120

Fig. 12 Water pump attaching screws. 1969-75

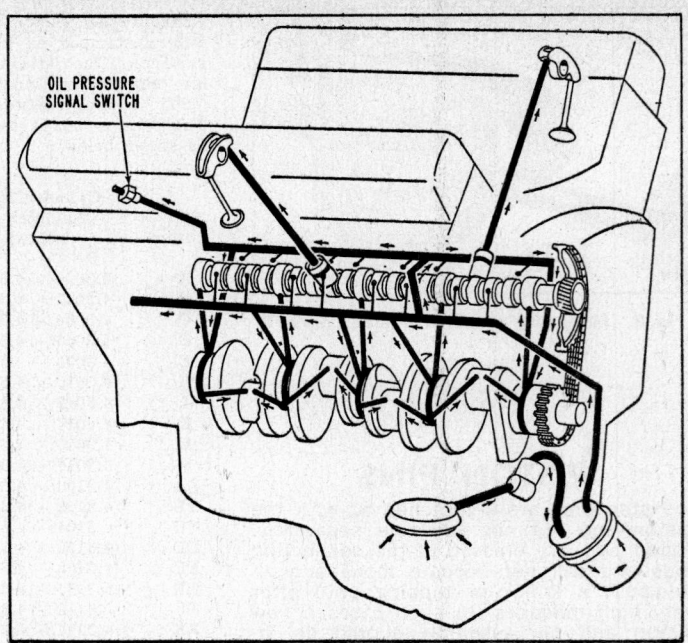

OIL PRESSURE SIGNAL SWITCH

Engine oiling system. 1969-75

WATER PUMP, REPLACE
1969-75

1. Disconnect battery ground cable.
2. Drain radiator and remove fan shroud.
3. Remove fan assembly. *On A/C cars, be sure to keep the fan clutch in the "on car" position when removed to prevent leakage of silicone fluid into clutch mechanism.*
4. Remove all drive belts.
5. Pull pump pulley off shaft.
6. Disconnect water inlet from pump.
7. Unfasten and remove pump from front cover.
8. Reverse procedure to install, being sure to install bolts as shown in Fig. 12.

FUEL PUMP PRESSURE

Year	Engine	Pressure, Lbs.
1969-75	All	$5\frac{1}{4}$-$6\frac{1}{2}$

FUEL PUMP, REPLACE
1969-75

1. Raise car and disconnect fuel line at pump and plug line.
2. Disconnect fuel pipe to fuel filter at pump.
3. Remove mounting screw on upper pump flange.
4. Remove nut from mounting stud at lower pump flange.
5. Tipping pump upward, pull pump straight out from engine and remove.
6. Reverse procedure to install.

Automatic Transmission

1975 AUTO. TRANS. LINKAGE ADJUSTMENTS

Linkage adjustment procedures for 1975 models are the same as those for 1974 models as outlined elsewhere in this manual.

NOTE: 1975 linkage adjustment information is in this section. Repair procedures on both automatic and manual shift transmissions are covered elsewhere in this manual. Procedures for removing automatic transmissions as well as linkage adjustments on 1969-74 models are included in the automatic transmission chapters. See Chapter Index.

Eldorado Drive Link Belt

LINK BELT OR SPROCKETS

Removal

After removal of transmission as described elsewhere in this manual, proceed as follows:

1. Remove sprocket housing cover attaching bolts and cover.
2. Remove sprocket bearing retaining snap rings from retaining grooves in support housing located under drive and driven sprockets, Fig. 1.

   NOTE: Do not remove the snap rings from beneath the sprockets, leave them in a loose position between the sprockets and the bearing assemblies.

3. Remove drive and driven sprockets, link belt, bearings and shafts simultaneously by alternately pulling upwards and driven support housing, Fig. 2.

   NOTE: If sprockets and link belt are difficult to remove, place a small piece of masonite, or similar material between the sprocket and a short pry bar. Alternately pry upward under each sprocket. Do not pry on links or aluminum case, Fig. 3.

4. Remove link belt from drive and driven sprockets.

Installation

1. Place link belt around the drive and driven sprockets so that the links engage the teeth of the sprockets, colored guide link which has etched numerals facing link cover.

Fig. 1   Removing or installing retaining rings

2. Simultaneously place link belt, drive and driven sprockets into support housing, Fig. 1.
3. Using a plastic mallet, gently seat the sprocket bearing assemblies into the support housings.
4. Install sprocket assembly to support housing snap rings, Fig. 2.
5. Install new case to cover and plate assembly sprocket housing gasket.

NOTE: Important: One sprocket cover housing attaching bolt is 1/4 inch longer. This bolt must be installed in the tapped hole located directly over the cooler fittings on the transmission case.

6. Install sprocket housing cover and plate assembly and eighteen attaching bolts. Torque bolts to 8 ft. lbs.

Fig. 2   Removing or installing sprockets and link assembly

Fig. 3   Removing tight sprockets

Rear Axle, Propeller Shaft & Brakes

REAR AXLE
1969-75 Eldorado

The rear axle used on these models is a welded assembly of the beam type with a drop center. The rear wheel spindles are a press fit and bolted to the rear axle assembly, Fig. 1. As shown, tapered roller bearings are used in the rear wheels. These bearings do not require regularly scheduled repacking. When major brake service work is to be performed, however, it is recommended that the bearings be cleaned and repacked.

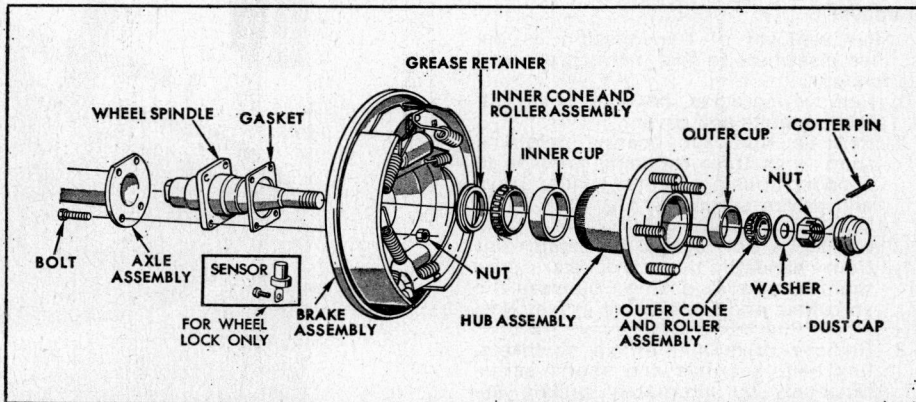

Fig. 1   Rear wheel spindle disassembled. 1969-75 Eldorado (typical)

Wheel Bearing Adjustment

Adjustment of the rear wheel bearings should be made while revolving the wheel at least three times the speed of the nut rotation when taking torque readings.
1. Check to make sure that hub is completely seated on wheel spindle.
2. While rotating wheel, tighten spindle nut to 30 ft-lbs. Make certain all parts are properly seated and that threads are free.
3. Back nut off ½ turn, then retighten nut to 2 ft. lbs. and install cotter pin.
4. If cotter pin cannot be installed in either of the two holes in the spindle, with the nut at 2 ft. lbs., back nut off until cotter pin can be installed.
5. The rear hub must be rotated at least three revolutions during tightening of spindle nut. The final adjustment to be 2 ft. lbs. to provide .004" bearing end play.
6. Peen end of cotter pin snug against side of nut. If it can be moved with a finger, vibration may cause it to wear and break.

Wheel Spindle, Replace

1. Raise and support rear of car and remove hub.
2. Disconnect brake line at wheel cylinder.
3. Unfasten and remove brake backing plate and position out of the way.
4. Place jack under rear axle.
5. Remove four nuts from center spring clamp and lower rear axle until spindle is accessible.
6. Remove lower spring insulator from rear axle.
7. Drive spindle out of rear axle.

Installation

1. Start new spindle, with keyway up, into axle and install four backing plate to spindle nuts.
2. Progressively tighten nuts until spindle is fully seated and then remove attaching nuts and bolts.
3. Position lower spring insulator to rear axle.
4. Position rear axle to center spring clamp, making sure that spring aligning pin locates into axle. See that lower insulator is properly posi-

tioned and that center spring clamp bolts engage rear axle mounting holes.
5. Install four nuts securing center spring clamp to rear axle, tightening to 30 ft-lbs.
6. Install new gasket on wheel spindle.
7. Install brake backing plate and tighten nuts to 40 ft-lbs.
8. Connect brake line to wheel cylinder, tightening fitting to 14 ft-lbs.
9. Install rear hub.

Rear Axle, Replace

1. Raise and support rear of car with jack stands at rear frame pads ahead of rear wheel opening.
2. Remove rear wheels and hubs.
3. Disconnect brake lines at wheel cylinders.
4. Disconnect parking brake cable at equalizer.
5. Disconnect rubber brake hose at underbody connector.
6. Disconnect overtravel lever link from bracket on rear axle.
7. Remove spring guides retaining parking brake cable to center spring clamp.
8. If rear axle is being replaced, remove brake backing plates.
9. Supporting rear axle at center with a jack, remove eight nuts (4 each side) from center spring clamp assemblies.
10. Lower rear axle with jack and remove from car.
11. Remove lower spring insulators from rear axle.
12. If rear axle is being replaced, remove bolt securing brake line junction fitting to axle. Remove brake line, overtravel lever link bracket, and drive spindles from axle.
13. Reverse procedure to install.

1970-75 Standard Cars

This axle design, Fig. 1A, uses two tapered roller bearings and a straight roller straddle bearing to support the pinion and provide rigidity. Adjustment of the pinion is done by the use of shims at the pinion retainer to differential carrier connection. Pinion-ring gear backlash adjustment of .005-.010" is accomplished through the use of a shim located to the left of the left side bearing. The differential preload is adjusted by means of an adjuster nut that is retained under the right side bearing cap which in addition to the shim provides the correct backlash.

The rear wheel bearing is called a "unit bearing". It is a tapered roller bearing that is completely assembled as a unit.

Differential Removal

1. Raise car on a hoist.
2. Remove wheel shields, discs, wheels and brake drums.
3. Remove four nuts that secure retainer and backing to rear axle housing.
4. Attach a suitable to axle shaft and remove axle shafts.
5. Install two nuts on backing plate mounting studs to prevent plates from falling and damaging brake lines.
6. Remove two attaching screws and lockwashers that secure differential carrier nose bumper arm.
7. Support propeller shaft with a chain and disconnect shaft at axle flange.
8. Place a drain pan under differential and remove axle housing cover.
9. Remove five pinion retainer to carrier screws and loosen remaining screw.

CAUTION: Do not remove remaining screw.

10. Install guide pins, Fig. 2.
11. Position drain pan under pinion retainer and attach puller.
12. Using slide hammer, unseat pinion from carrier, removing remaining screw and slide pinion assembly over guide pins and out of carrier.
13. Remove adjuster lock tab, bearing caps, adjuster nut and remove carrier case.

Axle Shaft, Replace

1. Raise car and remove wheel and brake drum.
2. Remove axle retaining nuts and lockwashers.
3. Attach slide type puller and remove axle shaft.

NOTE: When removing axle shaft, the bearing may separate leaving the outer race in the housing. This is normal and does not indicate failure. If the bearing is to be replaced, make sure the old bearing outer race is removed from the housing.

Removing Bearings

1. On 1969-70 models, drill holes into bearing retainer, Fig. 2A, not more than 1/2 inch deep to prevent axle shaft damage.
2. On all models, using a cold chisel, notch retainer next to bearing, being careful not to damage bearing.

NOTE: On 1969-70 vehicles where retainer is drilled, the retainer need not be completely split. Drive chisel into retainer only until retainer can be slipped off shaft. On 1971-75 vehicles where it is not recommended that the bearing retainer be drilled, the bearing retainer must be completely split by driving chisel into retainer until it separates.

3. Stand axle upright on flanged end and using two screwdrivers pry seal away from bearing.
4. Position shaft in a press and press shaft out of bearing.

Installing Bearing

1. Install bearing cover on shaft with raised side of cover against shaft flange, Fig. 3.
2. Install seal protector on shaft with small end of protector toward splined end of shaft, Fig. 3A.
3. Lubricate lip of seal and install by pressing down over protector. Seal is properly installed when the lip of the seal clears the large end of the protector.
4. Position bearing on shaft with narrow ring of bearing facing flanged end of shaft.
5. Press bearing on shaft until bearing bottoms against shoulder on shaft.
6. Position retainer on shaft with chamfer on retainer next to bearing.
7. Press retainer on shaft until retainer bottoms against bearing.

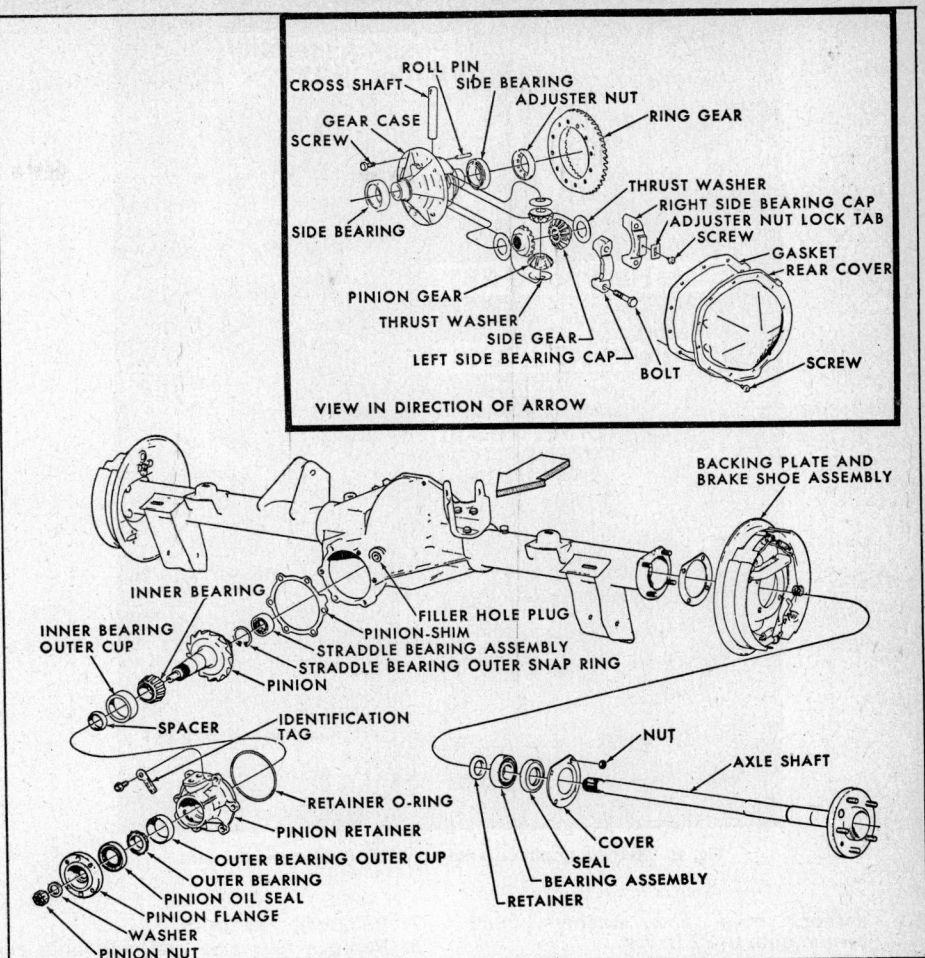

Fig. 1A   Rear axle assembly. 1970-75 standard cars

1969 Standard Cars

The design of the rear axle carrier assembly is shown in Fig. 3B. The axle shafts are supported at the outer ends by ball bearings which are lubricated from the differential carrier. The axle shaft oil seals are an integral part of the bearings and they are not serviceable separately from the bearing. An "O" ring seal is located in the grooved outer surface of the bearing.

Any service on the differential carrier assembly, except drive pinion oil seal or yoke replacement, should be handled by replacement of the complete assembly. No disassembly or adjustment of this unit should be attempted because special equipment is used at the factory for selection of mating parts and setting side bearing preload.

Whenever a carrier is removed because of scored gears, worn bearings, or any failure which causes dirt or metal chips, it will be necessary to remove the housing from the car for thorough cleaning before the new carrier is installed. Also check axle shaft bearings for metal chips and clean if necessary.

In case of lubricant leakage between differential carrier and axle housing, check first to make sure that the nuts are tightened to the recommended torque of 37 ft. lbs. If tightening the nuts does not stop the leak, an extra gasket should be installed, using a non-hardening sealer. The additional sealing effect of the extra gasket should prevent further leakage. If a replacement differential is installed, the special lubricant shipped with the new differential must be used.

Removal

1. Disconnect rear universal joint at pinion yoke. Use suction gun to remove grease from differential carrier.
2. Remove axle shafts as outlined below.
3. Remove nuts and washers that hold carrier to axle housing and remove entire assembly with gasket.

Installation

NOTE: Use a new carrier-to-housing gasket and new "O" ring seals on axle shaft bearings.

1. Place gasket on housing, install

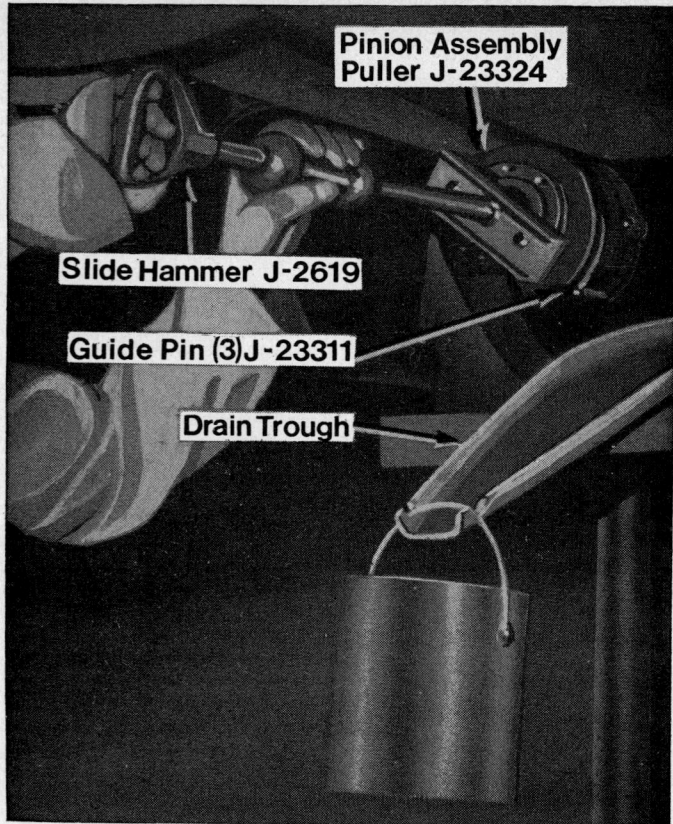

Fig. 2   Removing pinion assembly. 1970-75 standard cars

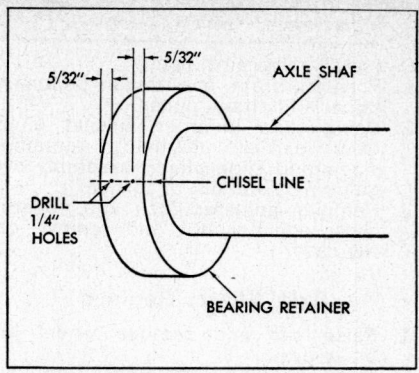

Fig. 2A   Removing bearing retainer. 1969-70 standard cars

Install Axle Shaft

1. Apply film of differential lube to wheel bearing bore in axle housing after checking for burrs and nicks.
2. Use a new "O" ring seal on wheel bearing and install axle shaft (shorter one on left side), being careful not to damage "O" ring seal.
3. Install brake backing plate and bearing retainer.
4. Install nuts and lockwashers on housing bolts and tighten by inserting socket wrench through rear axle flange.
5. Install brake drum and wheel.

PROPELLER SHAFT

Two Piece Type

Removal

1. With car raised, remove two center bearing support-to-frame bolts.
2. Remove U-bolts and locks at rear axle pinion.
3. Slide propeller shaft and front yoke off transmission output shaft and through frame tunnel section, removing it at the rear. *Slide spare yoke into transmission extension housing to prevent oil from leaking out.*

carrier, nuts and washers, and torque nuts to 37 ft. lbs.
2. Install axle shafts as explained below.
3. Install lubricant in differential to filler plug level.
4. Connect rear universal joint at pinion yoke.

Axle Shaft, Replace

1. Raise car and remove wheel.

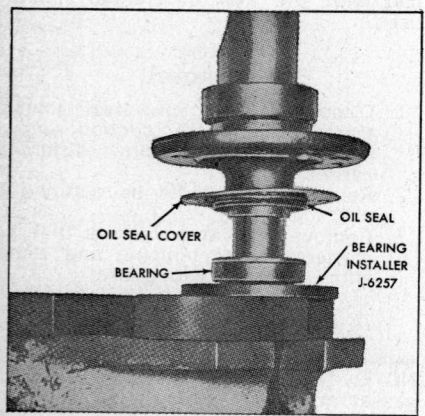

Fig. 3   Installing wheel bearing. 1970-75 standard cars

2. Remove brake drum.
3. Remove four axle retaining nuts and lockwashers.
4. Using slide hammer type puller, remove axle shaft.

Removing Bearings

1. Using a chisel and hammer, groove spacer next to bearing. The spacer need not be split. Drive chisel into spacer only enough to allow spacer to be slipped from shaft.

NOTE: On Eldorado models, before notching retainer, drill two ¼" holes along chisel line. Be sure not to drill any deeper than ½" as axle shaft may be damaged.

2. Press shaft through bearing. *If bearing has been removed because of failure, inspect axle housing and differential carrier for metal chips and, if necessary, clean thoroughly.*

Installing Bearing

1. Install new bearing on shaft so that bearing seal is toward flange end of shaft.
2. Press bearing on shaft so that it is located 3.180" from outer surface of axle shaft flange to inner end of bearing inner race.
3. Install oil ring seal on bearing.

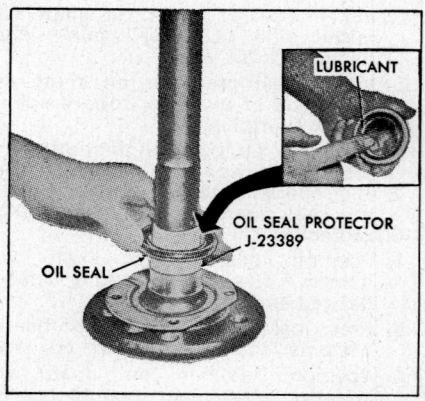

Fig. 3A   Installing rear wheel oil seal. 1970-75 standard cars

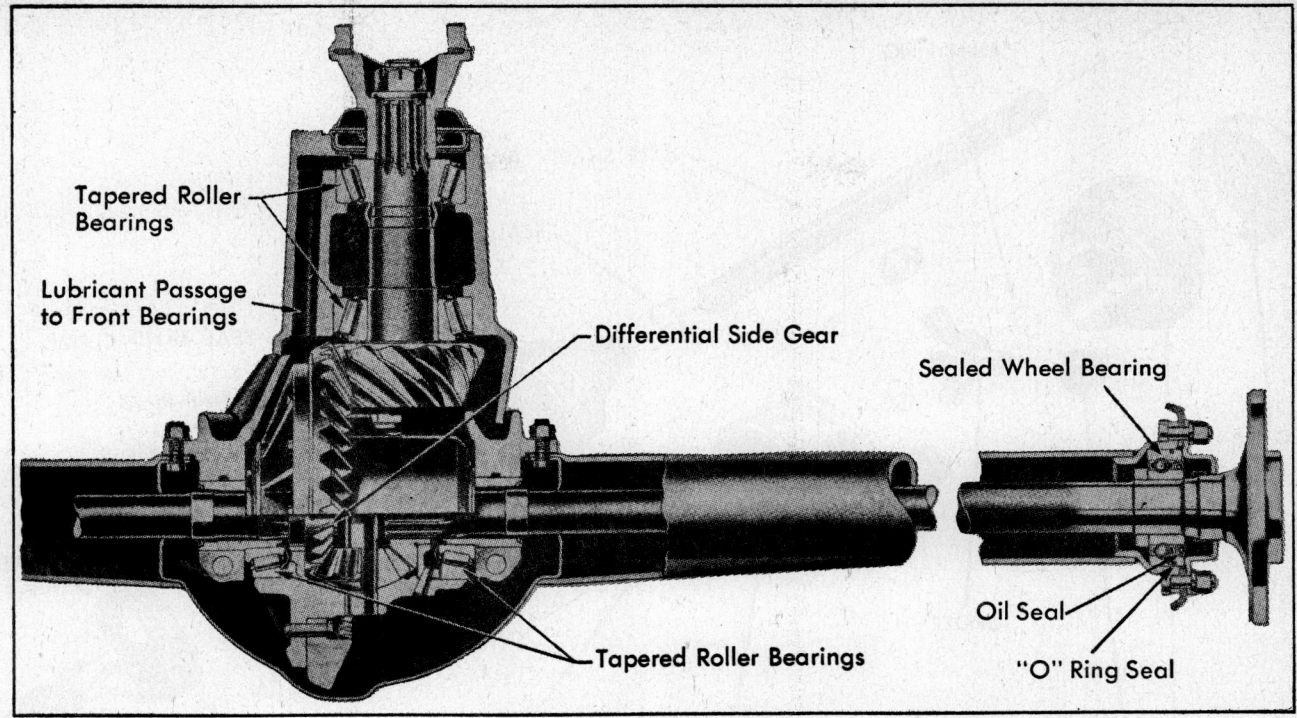

Fig. 3B   Rear axle assembly. 1969 standard cars

Installation

1. Lubricate front propeller shaft yoke with automatic transmission oil and remove spare yoke from transmission extension housing that had been installed to prevent oil leaking out.
2. Slide propeller shaft and front yoke through frame tunnel section and into transmission output shaft being careful not to nick yoke. *Be sure to reinstall any shims that may have been removed from between propeller shaft center support and frame tunnel.*
3. Install two center bearing support-to-frame bolts. Install U-bolts and locks at rear axle pinion and torque U-bolt nuts to 15 ft. lbs.

IMPORTANT

If drive line shudder, roughness, vibration or rumble is experienced, it may be due to misalignment of the propeller shaft assembly. To make this check, however, a special Propeller Shaft Alignment Gauge Set. No. J-8905 must be used. Inasmuch as this equipment is not likely to be found in general repair shops, it is recommended that a Cadillac dealer having this equipment do the work.

One Piece Type

Removal
1. Raise car on hoist.
2. Remove flange attaching bolts and lower propeller shaft.

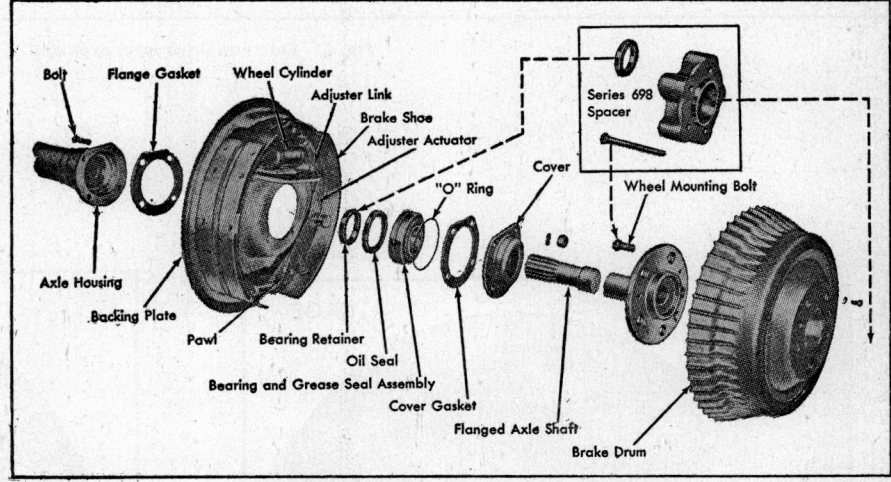

Fig. 4   Rear wheel disassembled. 1969

NOTE: Do not allow shaft to hang on front constant velocity joint.

3. Push shaft forward so rear universal joint flange clears pinion shaft, then remove shaft by pulling rearward to disengage slip yoke. Install spare yoke into transmission extension housing to prevent loss of oil.

Installation
1. Remove spare yoke and insert front yoke of propeller shaft into extension housing, engaging transmission shaft splines.
2. Install rear flange attaching bolts and torque to 65 ft. lbs.
3. Check transmission oil.

ELDORADO DRIVE AXLES
General Description

Each drive axle, Fig. 5, consists of an axle shaft, with a ball type constant velocity joint at the outboard end and a tri-pot type at the inboard end. The torsional damper on the right hand shaft is not serviceable and must be replaced as a unit.

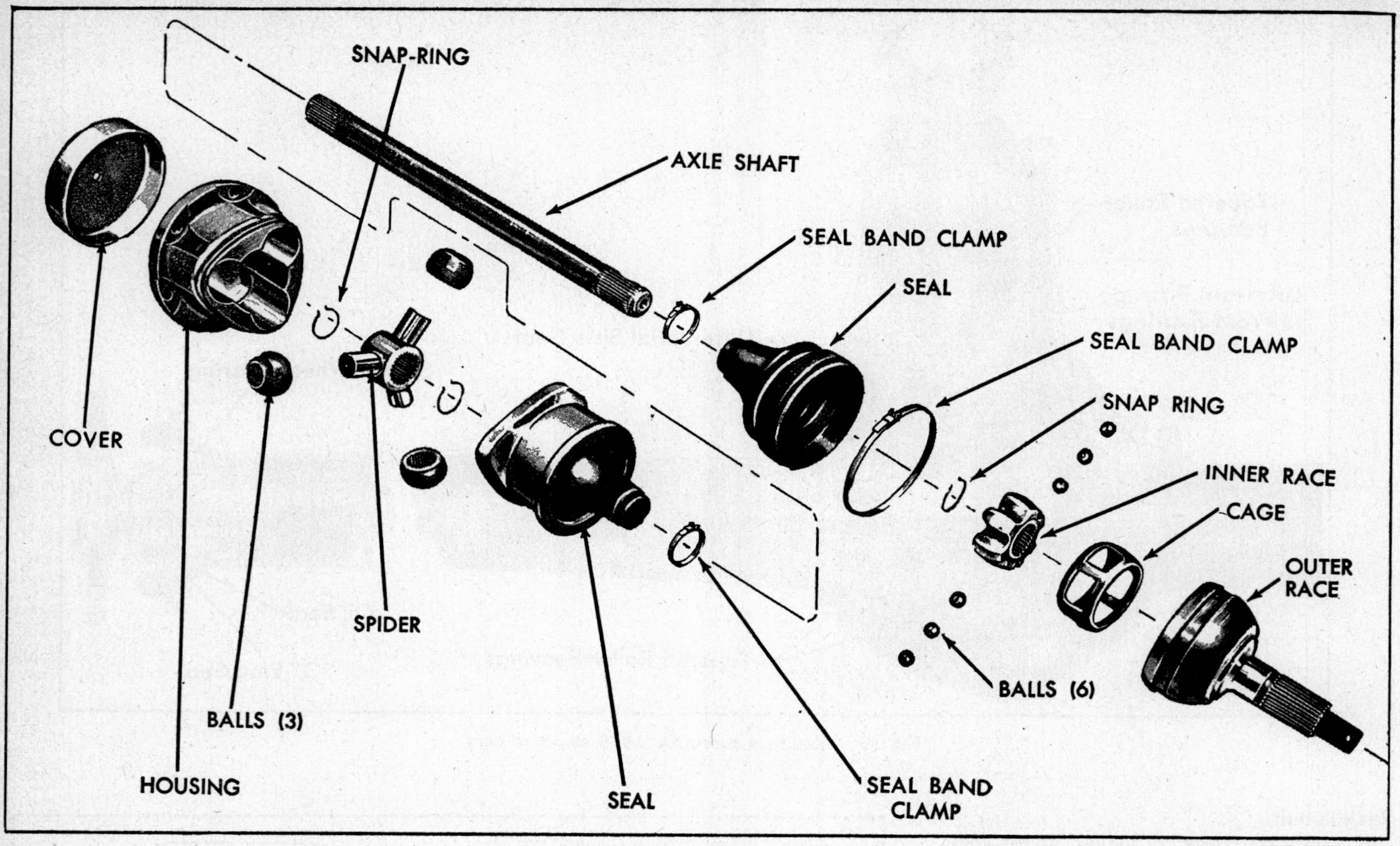

SNAP-RING

AXLE SHAFT

SEAL BAND CLAMP

SEAL

SEAL BAND CLAMP

SNAP RING

INNER RACE

CAGE

OUTER RACE

COVER

SPIDER

BALLS (6)

BALLS (3)

HOUSING

SEAL

SEAL BAND CLAMP

Fig. 5   Eldorado drive axle, exploded

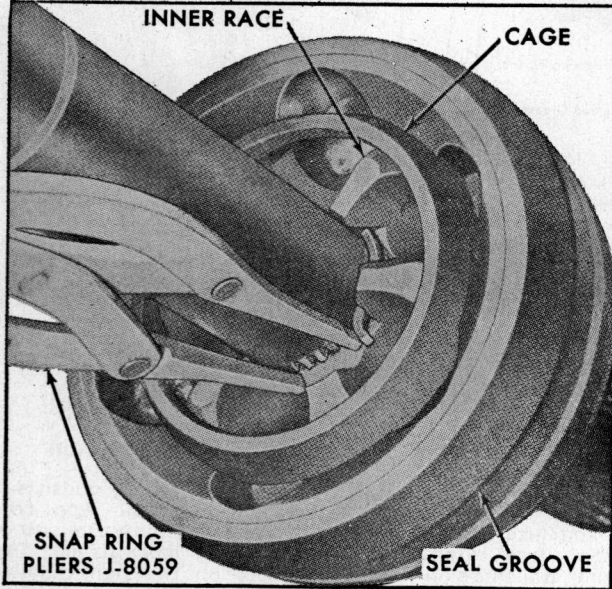

INNER RACE

CAGE

SNAP RING PLIERS J-8059

SEAL GROOVE

Fig. 6   Removing outer joint from axle

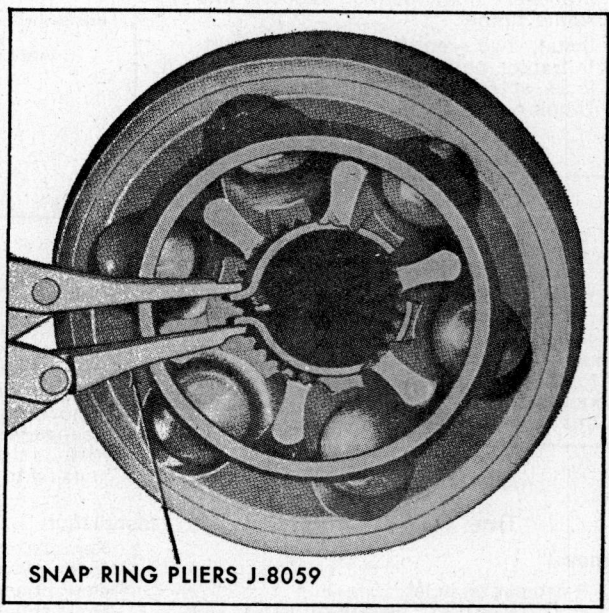

SNAP RING PLIERS J-8059

Fig. 7   Removing and installing inner snap ring

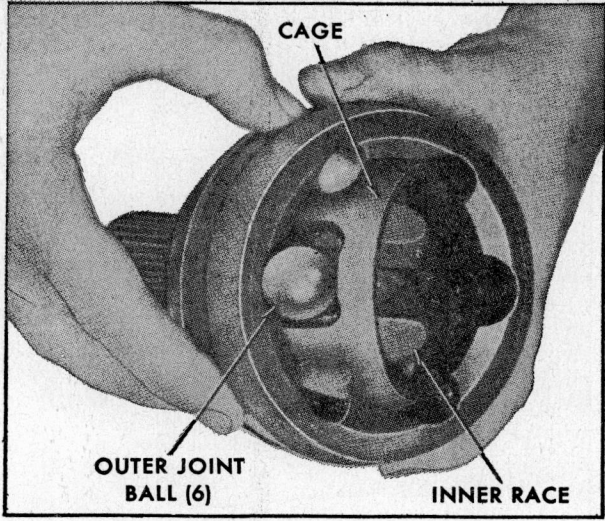

Fig. 8   Removing balls from outer joint

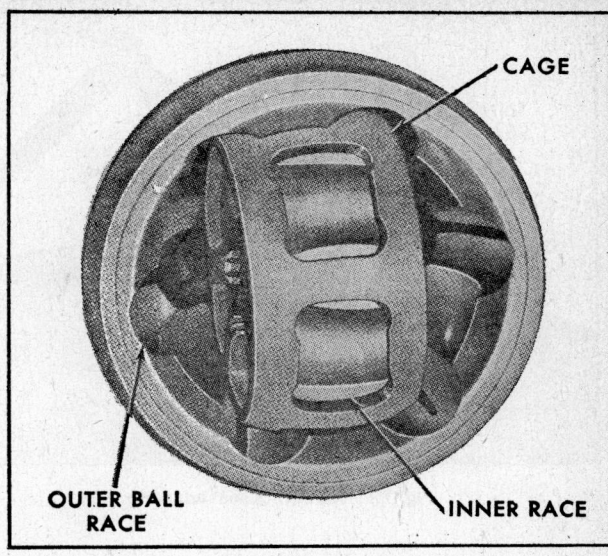

Fig. 9   Removing cage and inner race

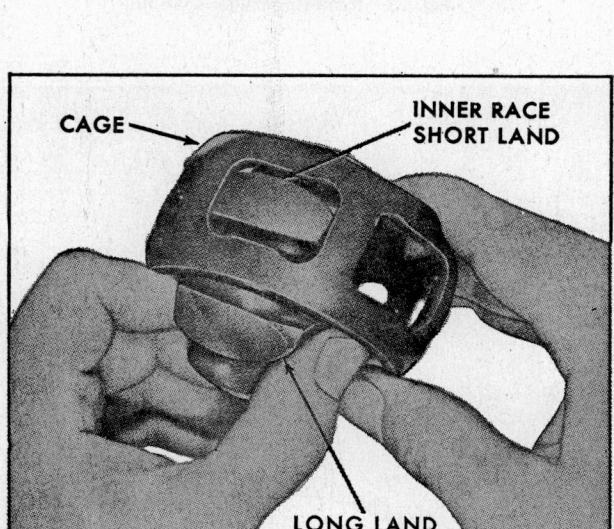

Fig. 10   Removing inner race from cage

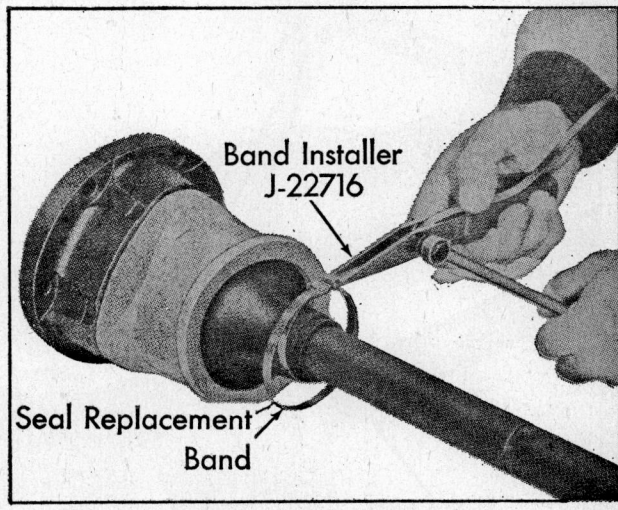

Fig. 11   Installing new seal clamp

The inboard joint is not only flexible to operate at various angles, but can also move in and out as required by suspension movement.

Right Drive Axle

1. Disconnect negative battery cable.
2. Raise car and remove wheel. Remove drive axle spindle nut.
3. Using a block of wood and a hammer, tap on end of drive axle to unseat axle at hub assembly.

NOTE: Install a short piece of rubber hose on the lower control arm torsion bar connector to prevent damage to the drive axle seals.

4. Remove six drive axle-to-output shaft screws and lock washers.
5. Remove two output shaft support-to-engine bolts and one support-to-brace self tapping screw.
6. Rotate inboard end of drive axle rearward toward starter.
7. Slide shaft straight out toward side of car and remove output shaft from underside of car.
8. Remove drive axle by rotating axle inboard and toward front of car.
9. Reverse procedure to install.

NOTE: When attaching right hand output shaft support to the engine, do not allow the shaft and support assembly to hang in the final drive unit. Install support bolts and washers loosely and by

moving the flange end of the shaft up and down, and back and forth, find the center location. Hold shaft in this position and tighten bolts to 50 ft-lbs.

Left Drive Axle

Perform steps 1-4 of removal of right axle then proceed as follows:
1. Loosen shock absorber upper mounting bolt.
2. Remove stabilizer bar link bolt cotter pin and nut.
3. Remove upper ball joint cotter pin and nut. Using a hammer, strike knuckle to disengage upper ball joint then remove ball joint stud from knuckle and brake line clip from stud.

1-117

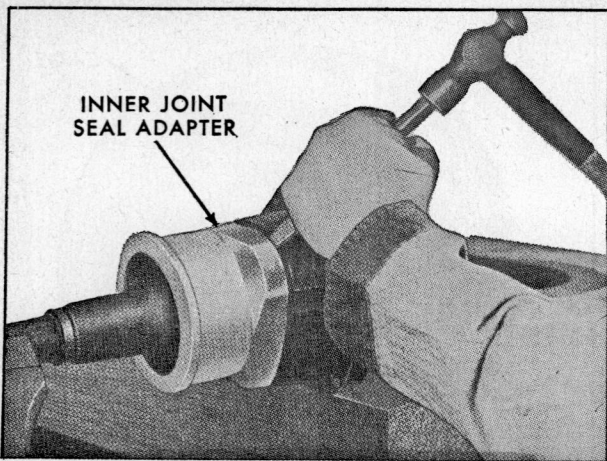

Fig. 12 Removing seal adapter

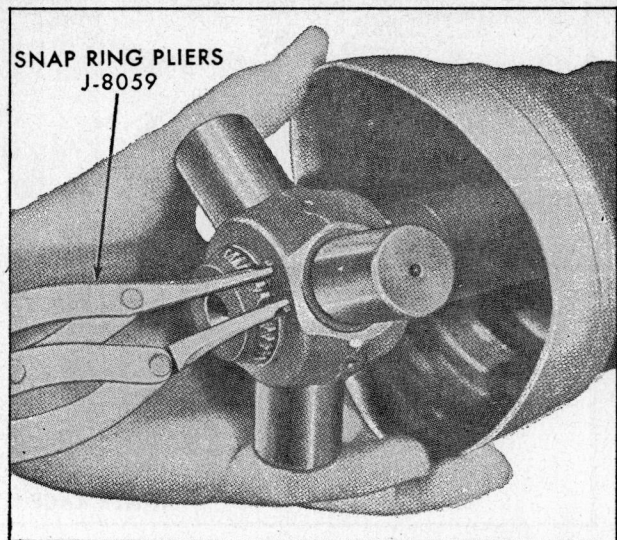

Fig. 13 Removing spider snap ring

Fig. 14 Installing seal adapter on joint housing

Fig. 15 Rubber hose location

4. Remove brake hose bracket from frame.
5. Carefully tip disc and knuckle assembly out at upper end to extent of brake hose.

NOTE: Wire assembly to upper control arm so brake does not support weight of knuckle assembly.

6. Rotate inner end of drive axle toward front of car.

7. Guide drive axle out of knuckle and remove axle from car.
8. Reverse procedure to install, being careful not to damage brake line when installing upper ball joint stud.

Outer Constant Velocity Joint

1. Remove inner and outer seal clamps by cutting with a chisel and slide seal down axle shaft to gain access to joint.
2. Wipe excess grease from joint and spread snap ring and slide joint off spline, Fig. 6.
3. Remove inner race snap ring, Fig. 7.
4. Hold constant velocity joint in one hand then tilt cage and inner race so that one ball can be removed, Fig. 8. Continue until all balls have been removed.

NOTE: It may be necessary to tap

the outer cage to rotate it.

5. Turn cage 90° with slot in cage aligned with short land on outer race and lift cage out of race, Fig. 9.
6. Turn short land of inner race 90° in line with hole in cage. Lift land on inner race up through hole in cage, then turn up and out to separate, Fig. 10.
7. Reverse procedure to install, using new seal clamps, Fig. 11. Cut off excess strap.

Inner Constant Velocity Joint

1. Remove small seal clamp bank by cutting it with a chisel.
2. Remove large end of seal from joint housing by prying up crimped edge on seal adapter. Drive seal adapter and seal off of joint housing with hammer and chisel, Fig. 12.

NOTE: Use care when removing seal adapter not to damage it or the seal.

3. Slide seal and adapter down axle shaft until joint is exposed.

NOTE: Do not allow spider leg balls to fall off by accident as adapter is moved.

4. Remove spider leg balls.
5. Remove spider outer snap ring, Fig. 13.
6. Tap spider assembly from shaft.

7. Reverse procedure to install, being sure to stake seal adapter to joint housing, Fig. 14.

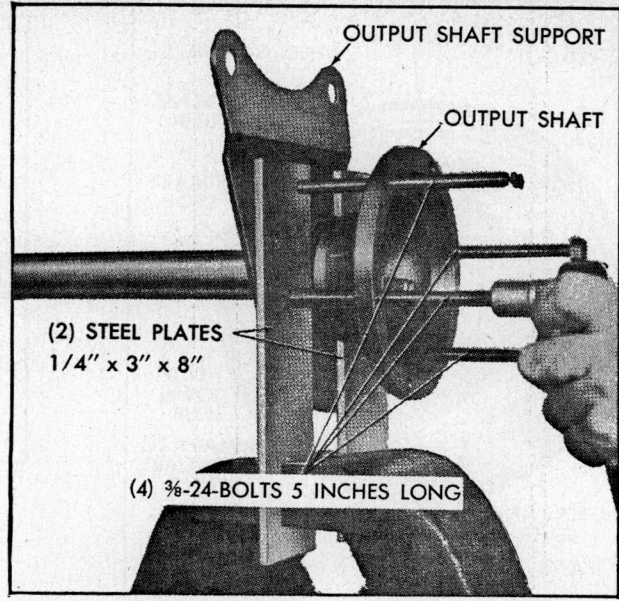

Fig. 16   Removing right hand output shaft support and bearing

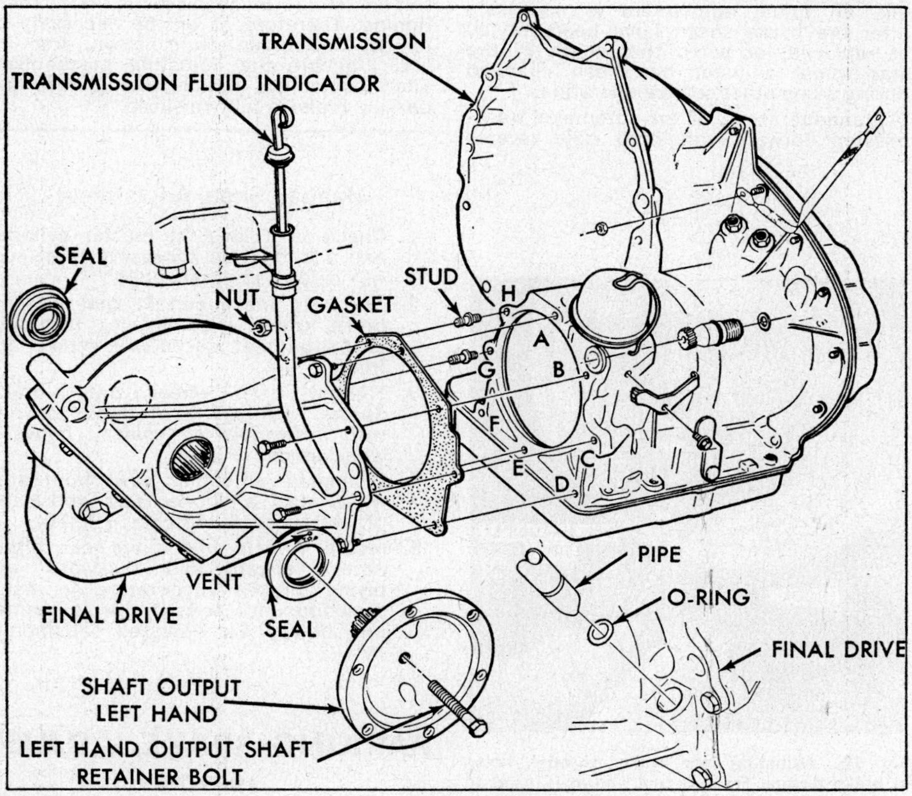

Right Hand Output Shaft

1. Disconnect negative battery cable.
2. Raise car and install a short length of rubber hose on lower control arm torsion bar connector, Fig. 15.
3. Remove six drive axle-to-output shaft bolts and lock washers.
4. Remove output shaft support mounting bolts.
5. Rotate inboard end of drive axle rearward.
6. Pull output shaft out until it clears final drive then lower splined end and remove from car.

Right Hand Output Shaft Bearing, Replace

1. Remove output shaft as described above.
2. Remove three output shaft bearing retainer-to-support bolts.
3. Using two fabricated steel plates and four 3/8 x 24 bolts five inches long illustrated in Fig. 16, tighten bolts alternately to press out bearing.

Left Hand Output Shaft

1. Remove left drive axle.
2. Remove output shaft retaining bolt and pull shaft out of final drive.

Final Drive, Replace

The final drive unit is not serviced but is replaced as a unit.
1. Disconnect negative battery cable.
2. Remove approximately one gallon of fluid from transmission then remove transmission filler tube and plug tube hole.
3. Remove bolts "A" and "B" and nut "H", Fig. 17.
4. Remove bolt securing transmission oil cooler lines to final drive.
5. Remove nut from large through bolt,

Fig. 17   Final drive attachment

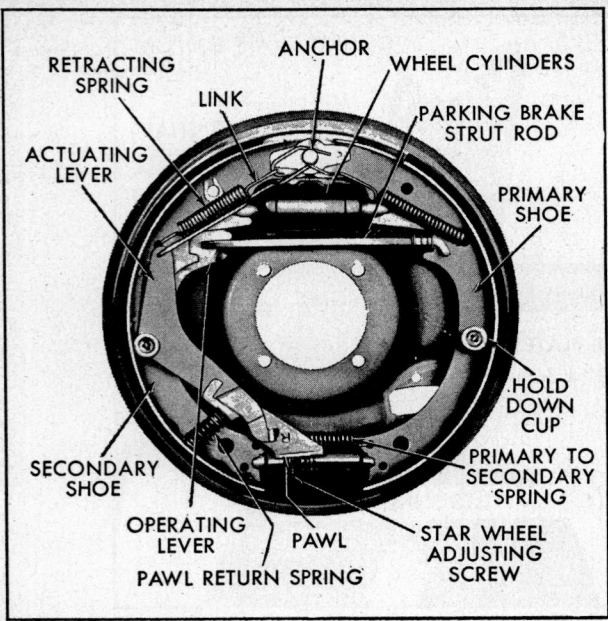

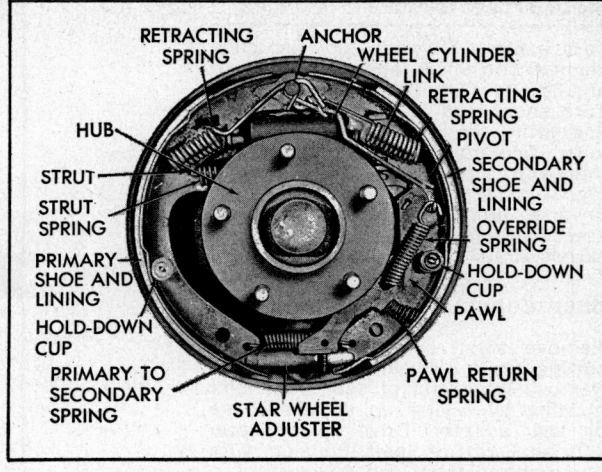

Fig. 18A Rear drum brake. 1969-73 Eldorado

Fig. 18 Rear drum brake. 1974-75 all and 1969-73 Exc. Eldorado

final drive support bracket to final drive.

6. Disconnect left front engine mount support bracket from engine. And final drive support bracket from left front engine mount support.
7. Remove right output shaft as outlined above.
8. Remove six left output shaft-to-drive axle bolts and lock washers.
9. Loosen final drive cover screws and drain fluid, then remove cover.
10. Compress left hand inner constant velocity joint and secure drive axle to frame with a piece of wire to provide clearance.
11. Remove final drive support bracket.
12. Remove remaining final drive-to-transmission bolts and nut "G".
13. Disengage final drive splines from transmission.

NOTE: To avoid damage to seals, final drive unit should be supported by a suitable jack and proper alignment must be maintained throughout removal.

14. Remove final drive unit from underside of car by sliding unit toward front of car, permitting ring gear to rotate up over steering linkage and work unit free from car.
15. Reverse procedure to install, being very careful to maintain proper final drive-to-transmission alignment to prevent seal damage.

BRAKE ADJUSTMENTS
1969-75 Self-Adjusting Brakes

These brakes, Figs. 18, 18A, have self-

adjusting shoe mechanisms that assure correct lining-to-drum clearances at all times. The automatic adjusters operate only when the brakes are applied as the car is moving rearward or when the car comes to an uphill stop.

Although the brakes are self-adjusting, an initial adjustment is necessary after the brake shoes have been relined or replaced, or when the length of the star wheel adjuster has been changed during some other service operation.

Frequent usage of an automatic transmission forward range to halt reverse

Fig. 19 Adjusting rear brakes through holes in brake drums. Hooked tool shown is used to hold pawl free of star wheel while adjusting rear brakes on 1969-71 models

vehicle motion may prevent the automatic adjusters from functioning, thereby inducing low pedal heights. Should low pedal heights be encountered, it is recommended that numerous forward and reverse stops be made with a moderate pedal effort until satisfactory pedal height is obtained.

NOTE

If a low pedal height condition cannot be corrected by making numerous reverse stops (provided the hydraulic system is free of air) it indicates that the self-adjusting mechanism is not functioning. Therefore, it will be necessary to remove the brake drum, clean, free up and lubricate the adjusting mechanism. Then adjust the brakes, being sure the parking brake is fully released.

Manual Shoe Adjustment

1. Check fluid level in master cylinder and add fluid as necessary to a level $\frac{1}{4}$" below top of reservoir.
2. Check to make certain that parking brake cable and linkage, including levers on rear secondary shoes, are free.
3. Tighten star wheel until brake drums can just be rotated forward with a two-foot bar placed between wheel studs.
4. Disengage adjusting pawl from star wheel with a hooked tool and back off star wheel 40 notches, Fig. 19.
5. Install wheels and drive car alternately forward and backward, applying brakes moderately in each direction until pedal travel is normal and brakes are adjusted satisfactorily.

PARKING BRAKE, ADJUST
1969-75

1. With service brakes properly adjust-

ed, lubricate parking brake linkage at equalizer and cable stud with heat-resistant lubricant, and check for free movement of cables.

2. Depress parking brake pedal about 1-3/4" from full released position.
3. Raise rear wheels off floor.
4. Hold brake cable and stud from turning and tighten equalizer nut until a slight drag is felt on either wheel (going forward). After each turn of equalizer nut, check to see if either wheel begins to drag.
5. Release parking brake. No brake drag should be felt at either rear wheel. Operate several times to check adjustment. After adjustment is completed, parking brake pedal should travel 1-3/4" to 2-3/4".

VACUUM RELEASE PARKING BRAKE

1969-75

The foot-operated parking brake is mounted on the cowl to the left of the steering column. It incorporates a vacuum release, Fig. 21, operated by a vacuum diaphragm that is connected to the parking brake mechanism. When the transmission selector is moved into any Drive position, a vacuum valve in the neutral safety switch opens, allowing diaphragm to be actuated by engine vacuum.

The diaphragm is connected by a link to a release mechanism on the parking brake. Vacuum acting on the diaphragm unlocks the parking brake pedal, permitting it to return to the release position by spring action. Any abnormal leaks in the vacuum release system will prevent proper brake release. A manual release is provided and may be used if the automatic release is inoperative or if manual release is desired at any time.

Testing Vacuum Release

1. If the mechanism is inoperative, first check for damaged or kinked vacuum hoses and for loose hose connections at the diaphragm, vacuum release valve at neutral safety switch, and at engine manifold connection.
2. Check adjustment of neutral safety switch and operation of vacuum release valve.
3. Check diaphragm piston travel by running engine and moving transmission selector lever from drive to neutral. The manual release lever should move up and down as vacuum

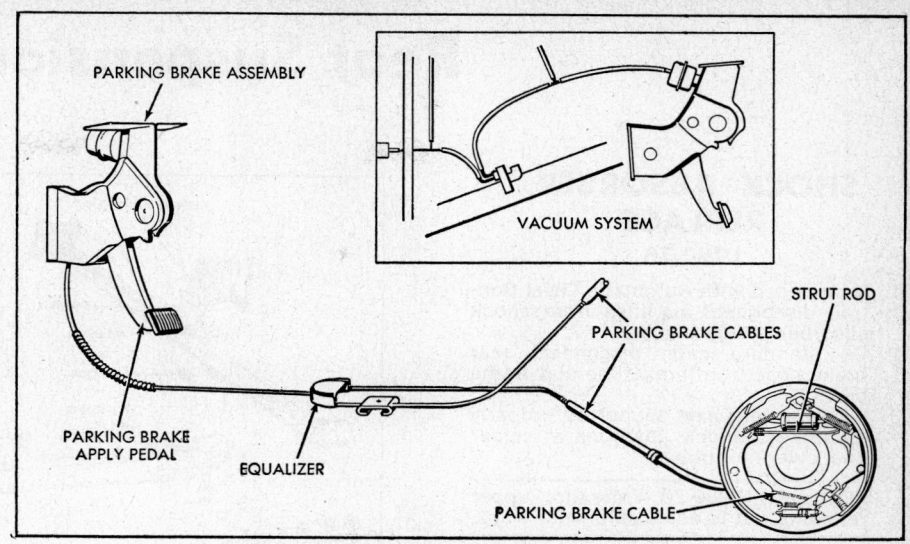

Fig. 21   Parking brake linkage. 1969-75 (typical)

is applied and released. If no movement is observed, or if movement is slow (more than 1 or 2 seconds to complete the full stroke) diaphragm is leaking and should be replaced.
4. Check brake release with vacuum applied. If diaphragm piston completes full stroke but does not release brake, a malfunction of the pedal assembly is indicated, and the complete parking brake assembly should be replaced.
5. Check operation of parking brake with engine off. Parking brake should remain engaged regardless of transmission selector lever position. If not, replace parking brake assembly.

POWER BRAKE, REPLACE

Service Bulletin

A sign of brake fluid dampness below the master cylinder at the power brake unit or on wheel cylinders at the bottom of the boot, does not necessarily indicate that these cylinders are leaking.

A small amount of fluid leakage at these areas can occur due to the creeping action of a very light film of fluid on the cylinder bores around the seals. This action provides proper seal lubrication.

In addition, normal brake heat will produce a slight escape of lubricant from the impregnated, porous-metal wheel cylinder pistons.

Normal dampness at the master cylinder or wheel cylinders is not easily distinguishable from a definite leak. Therefore, this condition must be checked carefully.

If there is sufficient dampness to form a "teardrop" of fluid at the bottom of the master cylinder or on the bottom of the wheel cylinders at the boot area, the rate of fluid seepage is too high and the cause should be determined and corrected.

1969-75

1. Disconnect hydraulic lines from master cylinder on power unit. Cap line fittings to prevent dirt entering system.
2. Disconnect vacuum hose from vacuum check valve on power unit. Remove steering column lower cover.
3. Remove cotter pin and spring spacer that attach power unit push rod to brake pedal relay lever.
4. Unfasten and remove power unit from cowl.

CADILLAC

Rear Suspension

SHOCK ABSORBER, REPLACE
1969-75

1. If equipped with Automatic Level Control, disconnect air lines from shock absorber fittings.
2. On standard cars, disconnect rear brake hose from brake line and frame bracket.
3. With the rear axle supported properly disconnect shock absorber at upper and lower mountings.

NOTE: On 1969-70 Eldorado, upper retaining nut is accessible from trunk.

4. Reverse procedure to install.

NOTE: 1969-70 Eldorado models incorporate horizontal shock absorbers in addition to the conventional type, Fig. 1. To replace, remove front and rear attaching bolts and lift unit from vehicle.

COIL SPRINGS, REPLACE
1971-75

1. Support vehicle at frame and support rear axle with a suitable jack.

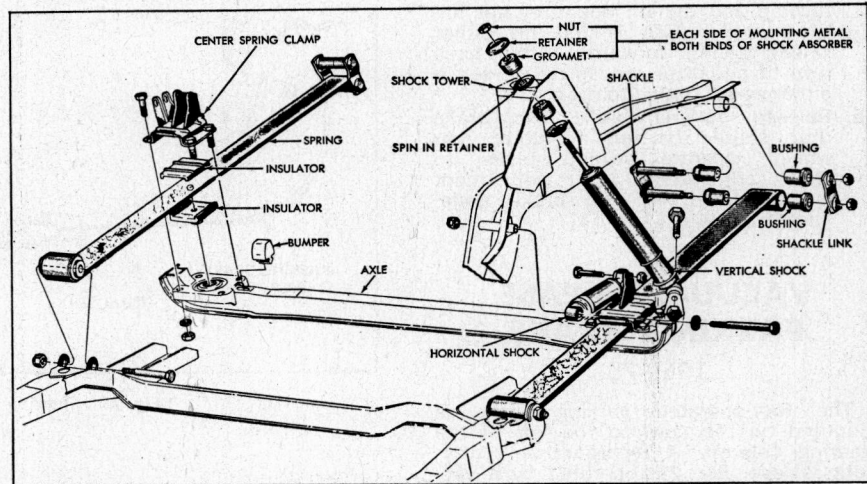

Fig. 1   1969-70 Eldorado rear suspension

2. If equipped with Automatic Level Control, disconnect overtravel lever link and place lever in center position.
3. Disconnect shock absorbers from lower mountings and rear brake hose from brake line.

4. On standard cars, disconnect propeller shaft from differential pinion flange.
5. Remove upper control arm rear mount bolt and lift arm from axle bracket, Figs. 2 and 3.
6. Lower axle assembly slowly until springs are free.

NOTE: When lowering axle assembly, use care to prevent axle from rotating, as springs may snap from the seats. If necessary, compress springs by hand to remove.

7. Reverse procedure to install. Note spring positions, Figs. 4 and 5. Tighten control arm bolt with vehicle at curb height.

1969-70 Except Eldorado

1. Perform steps 1, 2, 3 and 5 as outlined in above procedure and remove rear wheels.

NOTE: Install a second jack under differential carrier nose to aid removal of control arm bolt.

2. Remove screw securing parking brake cable strap.
3. Remove jack from carrier nose and lower axle assembly.
4. Install a jack under lower control arm rear mounting on side opposite spring being removed and raise jack until spring can be removed.
5. Reverse procedure to install. Tighten control arm bolt with vehicle at curb height.

LEAF SPRING, REPLACE
1969-70 Eldorado

1. Support vehicle at frame and support

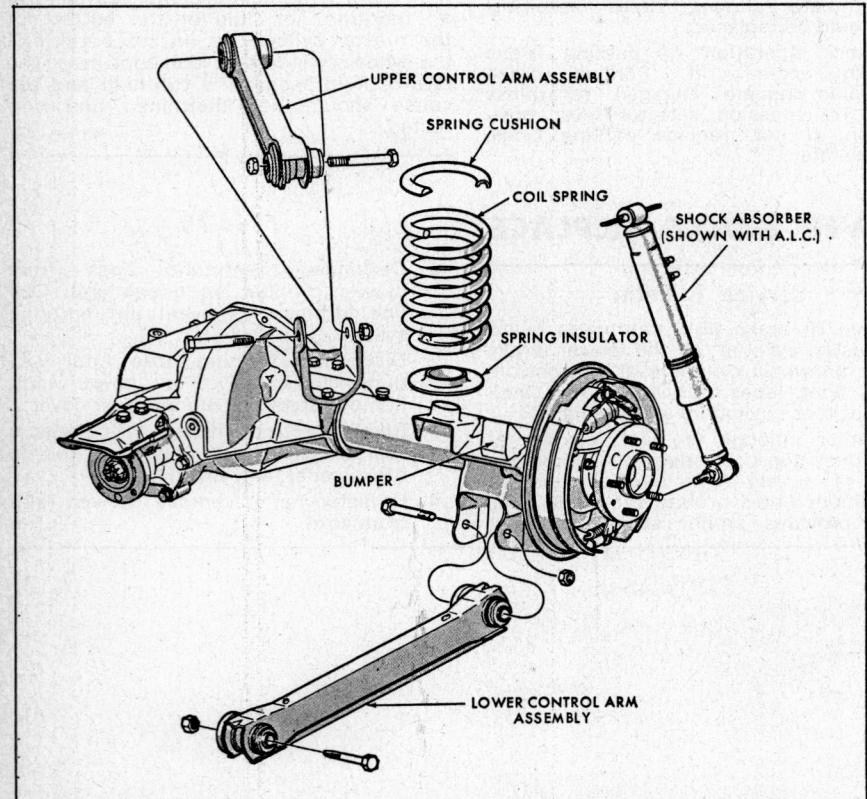

Fig. 2   1969-75 rear suspension (typical). Except Eldorado

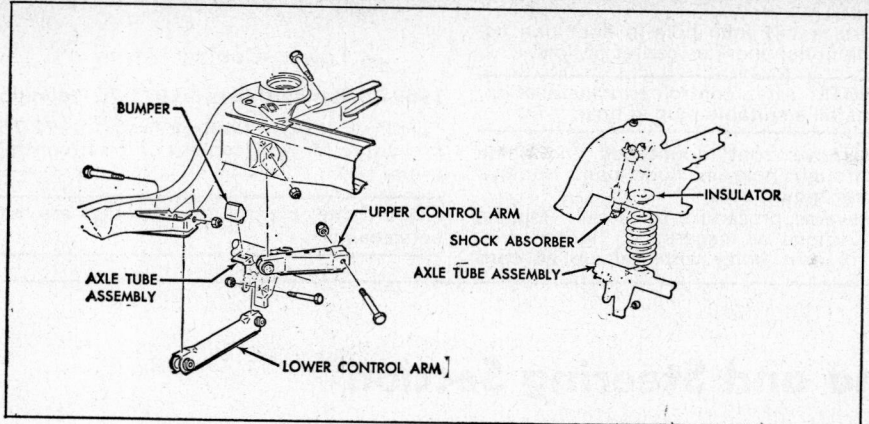

Fig. 3 1971-75 Eldorado rear suspension

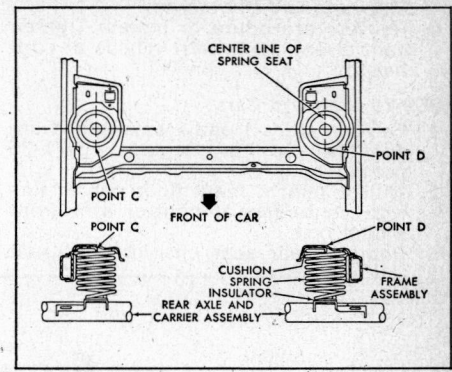

Fig. 4 Coil spring installation.
1969-75 Except Eldorado

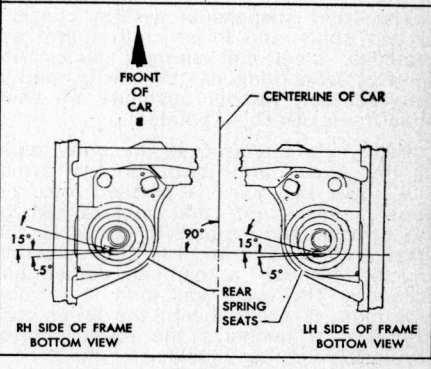

Fig. 5 Coil spring installation.
1971-75 Eldorado

rear axle with a suitable jack.

2. Remove Automatic Level Control over-travel lever link from axle bracket.

3. Remove nut from spring front bracket bolt. Do not remove nut.

4. Remove rear shackle outerlink, Fig. 1.

5. Remove nuts and lockwashers from center spring clamp and shift clamp to a side.

6. Lower axle so tension is removed from spring and disassemble rear shackle.

7. Remove bolt from spring front bracket.

8. Reverse procedure to install. Replace bushings as necessary. Tighten rear shackle nuts and spring front bracket bolt with vehicle at curb height.

CONTROL ARMS & BUSHINGS, REPLACE

NOTE: Replace one control arm at a time as axle assembly may slip sideways, making installation difficult.

Upper Control Arms

1971-75

1. Perform steps 1 and 2 as outlined under "Coil Springs, Replace" 1971-75 procedure. On Eldorado disconnect shock absorbers from lower mountings.

2. Remove control arm front and rear mount bolts.

3. On Eldorado, replace axle bracket bushing as required, Figs. 6 and 7. New bushing is installed with flanged

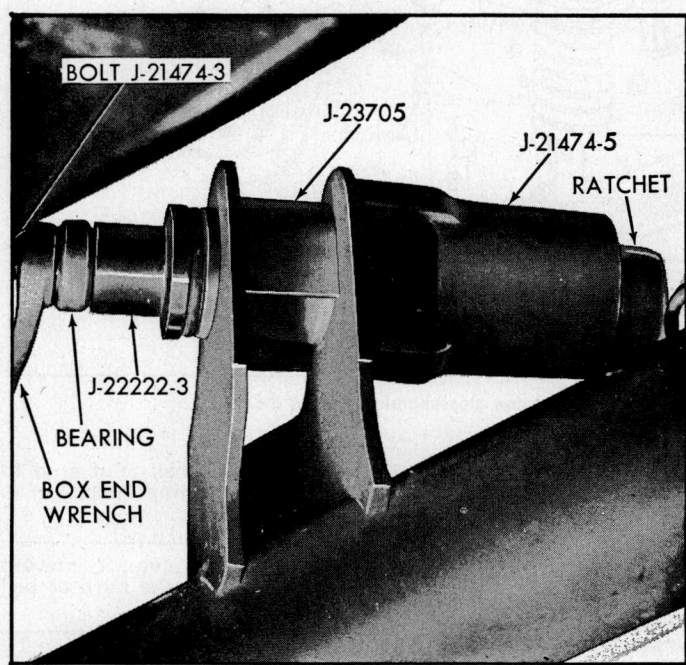

Fig. 6 Upper control arm axle bracket bushing removal, 1971-75 Eldorado

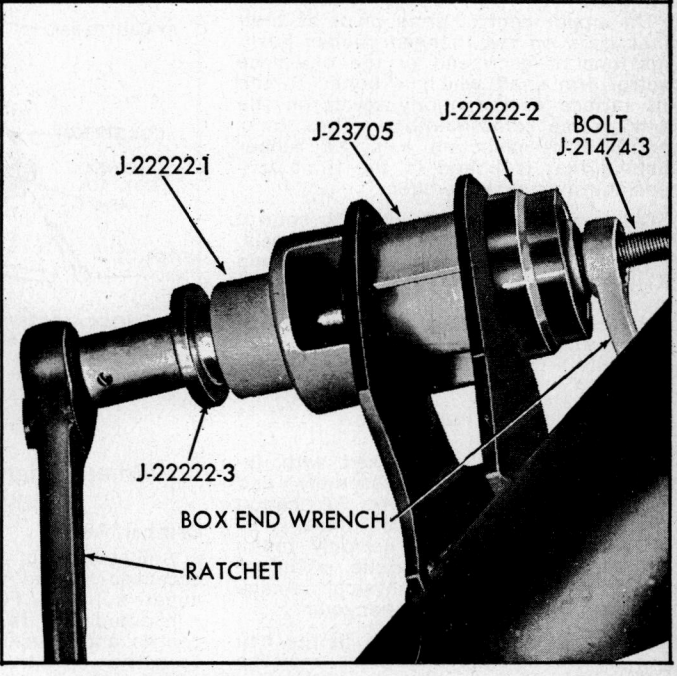

Fig. 7 Upper control arm axle bracket bushing installation, 1971-75 Eldorado

side outboard of bracket.

4. Reverse procedure to install. Tighten control arm bolts with vehicle at curb height.

1969-70 Standard Cars

1. Perform steps 1 and 2 as outlined under "Coil Springs, Replace" 1971-75 procedure.
2. With a punch, mark floor pan in line with centerline of control arm front mount bolt.
3. Remove rear seat cushion and seat back.
4. Drill a 1¼ inch hole in floor pan using punch mark as center of hole.

NOTE: After control arm installation, install a suitable plug in hole.

5. Remove front mount bolt and guide through hole in floor pan. Remove rear mount bolt.
6. Reverse procedure to install. Replace bushings as necessary. Tighten control arm bolts with vehicle at curb height.

Lower Control Arms

1969-75 Standard Cars & 1971-75 Eldorado

Follow "Upper Control Arms" 1971-75 procedure for replacement of lower control arms.

NOTE: Lower control arm bushings are not serviceable.

Front End and Steering Section

FRONT SUSPENSION 1969-75 STANDARD CARS

The front suspension system consists of two upper and lower control arm assemblies, steel coil springs, shock absorbers, front diagonal tie struts, and a stabilizer bar. Rubber bushings are used at all frame attaching points.

Ball joints are used at the outer ends of the upper and lower control arms. The upper ball joint is pressed into the upper control arm and tack-welded to the arm at two points. It connects the upper control arm to the steering knuckle through a camber adjustment eccentric. The lower ball joint, a tension type joint, is pressed into the lower control arm. It connects the lower control arm to the steering knuckle.

Beginning with 1970 models the steering knuckle is a combination steering knuckle, brake caliper support and steering arm.

The upper control arms pivot at their inner ends on two flanged rubber bushings, one at each end of the one-piece control arm shaft which is bolted to the top surface of the spring tower on the front frame crossmember. The lower control arms pivot on a single rubber bushing that is bolted to the front suspension frame crossmember.

Diagonal tie struts are used to control the fore and aft movement of the wheels. The struts are bolted to the outer ends of the lower control arms and extend through the frame crossmember. Rubber bushings and a steel spacer are used at the frame mount.

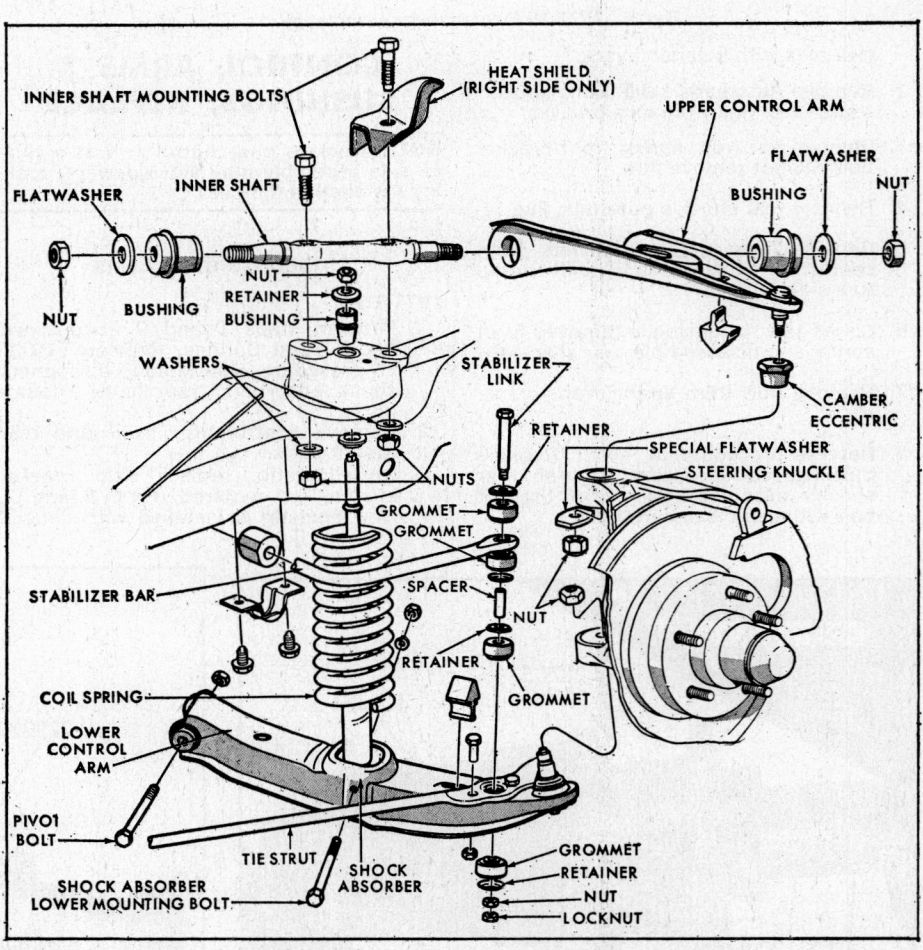

Fig. 1   Front suspension disassembled. Except Eldorado

Lubrication

The ball joints are packed with lubricant and sealed at assembly and should not require further lubrication throughout their service life under normal driving conditions. The only maintenance they normally require is an inspection of the seals for physical damage each time the engine oil is changed.

Service plugs are provided in the ball joint covers so that the joints may be packed in the event a seal should become damaged and require replacement. Both the seals and plugs are serviceable.

Wheel Alignment, 1969-75 Standard Cars

Camber, Adjust

Adjustment is made at the camber eccentric located in the steering knuckle upper support, Fig. 2. The upper ball joint stud fits through the camber eccentric and knuckle support. Turning the eccentric repositions the upper ball joint stud.

To adjust camber, loosen locknut on ball joint stud one turn and strike steering knuckle in area of ball joint stud to free eccentric from steering knuckle, Fig. 1A.

CAUTION: Use extreme care to prevent striking and damaging brake hose or ball joint seal.

Using adjustable wrench shown in Fig. 3, turn eccentric as required to obtain the camber specifications listed in the Wheel Alignment chart. The final position of the

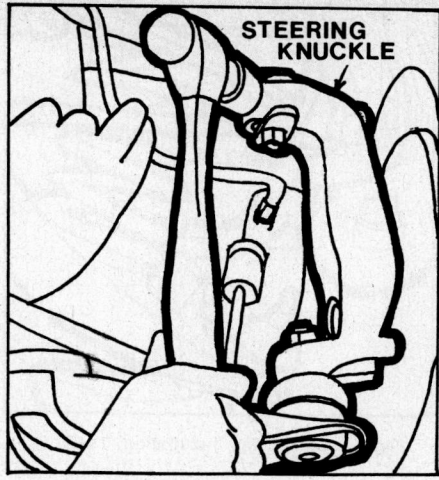

Fig. 1A Loosening camber eccentric

stud should be in the rear portion of the camber eccentric in order to keep steering angle correct. After proper adjustment has been established, torque stud nut to 60 ft. lbs.

NOTE

If the camber eccentric is too tight to be adjusted a tool can easily be made by cutting a piece of $7/16''$ diameter steel rod about 20'' long, chamfering it on one end and rounding it off on the other end.

If the eccentric must be freed for a camber adjustment, position the car on a wheel alignment machine, backing off the self-locking nut on the ball joint stud one turn, and thread a standard nut halfway on the stud. Insert the rounded end of the tool inside the nut and against the bottom of the stud. Then pound on the end of the tool with a heavy hammer to break the camber eccentric loose.

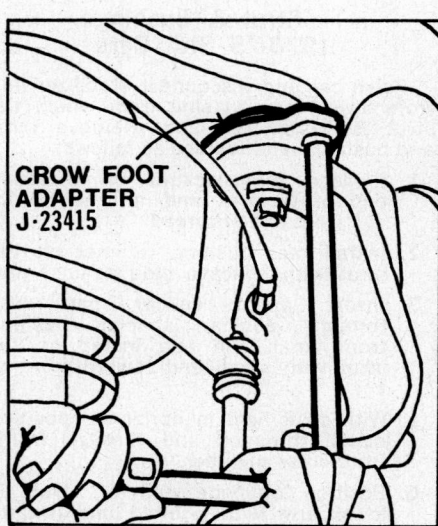

Fig. 3 Adjusting camber. 1969-75

In cases where the eccentric is to be removed but comes loose from the stud instead of the knuckle, place a washer against the bottom of the eccentric and drive the eccentric out from below, using the same tool as described above. When the eccentric must be removed in this manner, inspect it for damage and replace if necessary.

Caster, Adjust

Adjustment is made by turning the retaining nuts on the forward ends of the tie-struts at the frame front crossmember, Fig. 4. To gain access to the retaining nuts, it is necessary to remove the splash shield.

Proper caster adjustment is obtained by shortening or lengthening the struts between the lower suspension arms and the frame front crossmember. To provide more negative caster, lengthen the struts by loosening the front bushing retaining nuts and tightening the rear bushing retaining nuts. One turn of the nuts results in approximately $1/2°$ change in caster.

To provide more positive caster, shorten the struts by loosening the rear bushing retaining nuts and tightening the front bushing retaining nuts.

After proper adjustment has been made, tighten front retaining nuts to 60 ft. lbs., being sure to hold the rear nut with a wrench so as not to disturb the adjustment.

Toe-In, Adjust

Toe-in is adjusted by turning the tie rod adjusters at the outer ends of each tie rod after loosening the clamp bolts. (Both right and left pivot ends have right-hand threads.) Be sure to turn both adjusters an equal amount so that the relation of the steering gear high spot to the straight ahead position of the front wheels will not be changed.

When adjustment has been completed according to the specification listed in the *Wheel Alignment* chart, tighten nuts on clamp bolts to 20 ft. lbs. torque.

NOTE

Make certain that both inner and outer tie rod ball pivots are centered in their respective housings prior to tightening the tie rod adjusting clamps.

If the tie rods are not properly positioned, a binding condition may occur, resulting in poor return of wheels to the straight ahead position.

Each tie rod should be checked after adjustment by grasping the center of the tie rod and rotating it fore and aft. The movement should be equal in both directions. If not, it indicates that the pivot studs are not properly positioned.

Wheel Bearings, Adjust

Service Bulletin

Looseness at a front wheel does not necessarily indicate worn bearings or a

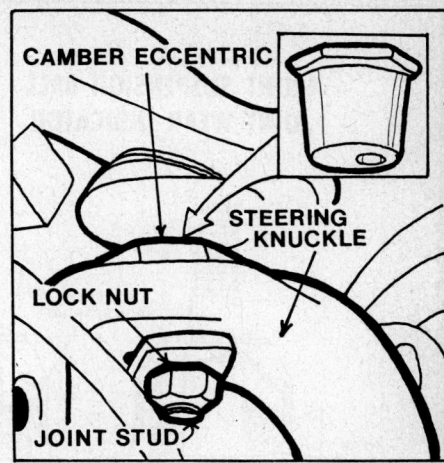

Fig. 2 Camber adjustment eccentric. 1969-75

loose spindle nut, since the tapered roller bearings used on front wheels of all standard Cadillacs should not be preloaded and normally can have up to .004'' end play.

1. While rotating wheel and tire assembly, tighten spindle nut to 30 ft. lbs. for 1969-71 vehicles and 15 ft. lbs. for 1972-75 vehicles, making certain that hub is fully seated on spindle.
2. Back off spindle nut until free, and on 1969-71 vehicles, retorque nut to 6 ft. lbs. On 1972-75 vehicles tighten nut finger tight.
3. Install new cotter pin. If pin cannot be installed, back off nut to next hole and install pin.

NOTE: Cotter pin must be tight after installation, as vibration can break pin.

Wheel Bearings, Replace

1972-75

1. Remove caliper retaining bolts, then slide caliper off disc and using a length of wire, attach caliper to upper control arm.

NOTE: Never allow caliper to hang from brake hose.

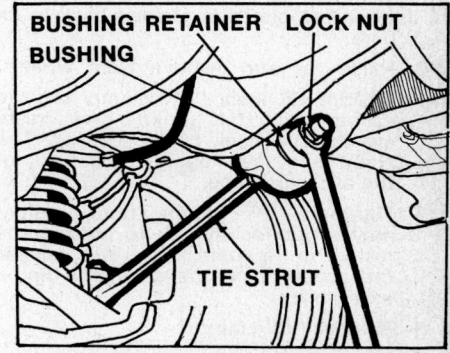

Fig. 4 Adjusting caster. 1969-75

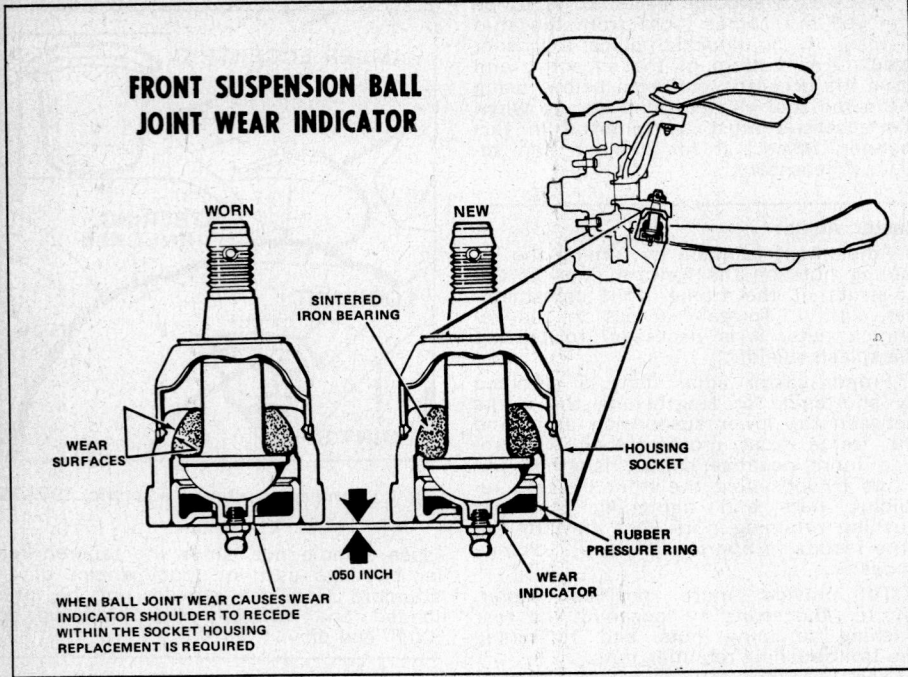

FRONT SUSPENSION BALL JOINT WEAR INDICATOR

WORN — NEW

SINTERED IRON BEARING

WEAR SURFACES

HOUSING SOCKET

.050 INCH

RUBBER PRESSURE RING

WEAR INDICATOR

WHEN BALL JOINT WEAR CAUSES WEAR INDICATOR SHOULDER TO RECEDE WITHIN THE SOCKET HOUSING REPLACEMENT IS REQUIRED

Fig. 5   Ball joint wear indicator. 1974-75 except Eldorado

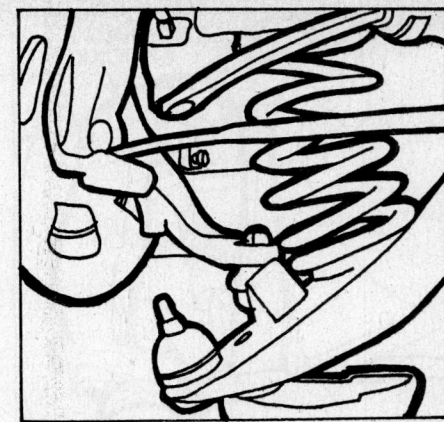

Fig. 6   Coil spring installation. 1969-75

2. Remove dust cap, cotter pin, spindle nut, washer and outer bearing assembly.
3. Remove hub and disc assembly, being careful to avoid damage to spindle threads or grease seal.
4. Remove inner bearing grease seal and bearing assembly.

NOTE: Inner and outer bearing cups are press fit in hub and can be driven out from the opposite side using a brass drift. Tap alternately on opposite sides to prevent cocking cup and damaging hub.

1969-71

1. Remove two thirds of the total fluid capacity in the front master cylinder reservoir to prevent fluid overflow when the piston is pushed back in its bore.
2. Raise car and remove front wheels.
3. Position 7 inch "C" clamp on the caliper so that solid side rests against the back of the caliper. The screw end rests against the back of the outboard shoe.
4. Tighten "C" clamp until caliper moves out far enough to bottom the piston in its bore. This will release the pressure on the shoe and lining assemblies.
5. Remove "C" clamp.
6. Remove two bolts which hold caliper to support plate.

NOTE: It is not necessary to remove brake hose from caliper during this operation.

7. Slide caliper off of disc. Do not allow caliper to hang from brake hose.
8. Remove spindle nut and hub and disc assembly. Grease retainer and inner bearing can now be removed.

Checking Ball Joints For Wear 1969-75 Std. Cars

Upper Ball Joint

Using the regular ball joint stud nut and a second nut as a lock nut, turn joint in its socket with a torque wrench. If the torque is not within the limits of 2 to 4 ft-lbs, the joint should be replaced.

Lower Ball Joint, 1969-73

The lower ball joint is designed to turn freely in its socket and cannot be checked with a torque wrench. It should be checked by noting the amount of free play as the joint is worked vertically in its socket. Free play should not exceed 1/16". Replace joint if it exceeds this limit.

Lower Ball Joint, 1974 exc. Eldorado

Beginning in 1974 models, a wear indicator is built in the ball joint. Remove dirt deposits around service plug and observe position of nipple. Refer to Fig. 5, for wear tolerance.

Ball Joints, Replace

The upper ball joints are pressed into the upper control arm and tack-welded to the arm. Therefore, the upper ball joints are supplied only with the upper control arm. The lower ball joints are pressed into the lower control arms but they are replaceable.

Shock Absorber, Replace

The shock absorbers are removed through the bottom of the lower control arm after unfastening it at the top and bottom.

To install, place the retainer and rubber grommet on the upper stem and fully extend the shock absorber rod. Insert the shock absorber up into the coil spring and guide the stem through the tower in the crossmember. Then place the lower end in position on the lower control arm. Install bolt, washer and nut and torque nut to 90-110 ft. lbs. Fasten shock absorber at top.

Tie-Strut & Bushings 1970-75 Std. Cars

Raise car and disconnect stabilizer link from lower arm on side from which tie-strut is to be removed. Remove strut and bushings and replace as follows:

1. Replace rear locknut on threaded end of tie-strut and run nut about 3/4" from end of thread.
2. Install rear bushing retainer on tie-strut with concave side against nut.
3. Insert metal spacer part way through conical shaped bushing from small end and install on tie-strut with small end toward front of car.
4. With strut held in horizontal position install threaded end through frame front cross member.
5. Position opposite end of strut on lower arm with pointed end inward, and install attaching bolts and nuts loosely.

6. Install front bushing on end of strut, cupped side toward frame, and slide bushing against cross member.
7. Install front bushing retainer on strut with concave side against bushing.
8. Start new locknut on threaded end of strut and connect stabilizer link to lower arm.
9. Lower car and with car weight on all four wheels, position front bushing on metal spacer and tighten locknut on front end of strut to 35 ft. lbs.
10. Tighten tie-strut to lower arm nuts and bolts to 55 ft. lbs.

Tie-Strut & Bushings 1969 Std. Cars

Raise car and jack up under frame side rails. Remove splash shield and disconnect stabilizer link from lower control arm on side tie-strut is to be removed. Remove strut and bushings. Then replace as follows:
1. Insert spacer in rear bushing and install bushing and spacer in frame through rear side of crossmember.
2. Install nut on tie-strut and run nut to bottom of thread.
3. Install rear bushing retainer on strut with concave side toward nut.
4. With strut held in horizontal position, install threaded end of strut through rear bushing in frame crossmember.
5. Install front bushing on end of strut and slide bushing into position in frame crossmember. Front bushing should lock in rear bushing.
6. Install front bushing retainer on threaded end of strut with flat side against bushing. Start front nut on end of strut but do not tighten.
7. Secure opposite end of strut to lower control arm and torque bolts to 55 ft. lbs.
8. Connect stabilizer link.
9. Lower car and with car weight on all four wheels, tighten front nut to 55-70 ft. lbs.
10. Tighten rear nut, compressing bushing until retainer bottoms on metal spacer in bushing.
11. Adjust caster as outlined previously.
12. Install splash shield.

Coil Spring, Replace

1. Disconnect shock absorber at upper end.
2. Raise front of car and place jack stands under frame side rails.
3. Disconnect stabilizer link from side from which spring is to be removed.
4. Disconnect tie strut at lower arm.
5. Remove shock absorber.
6. Remove wheel and brake drum.
7. Place a floor jack under outer end of lower control arm, then separate lower ball joint from steering knuckle.
8. Lower floor jack and remove spring, Fig. 6.
9. Reverse procedure to install.

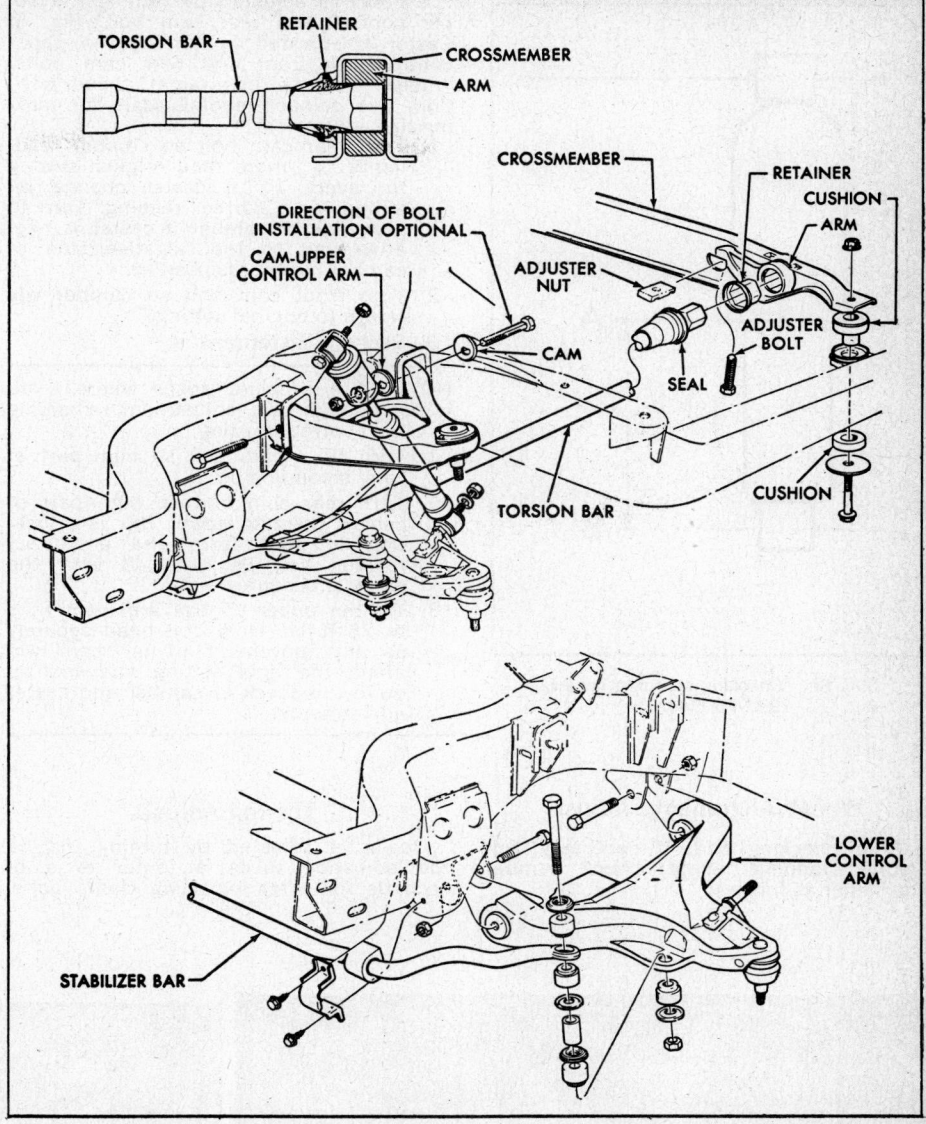

Fig. 7 Front suspension disassembled. 1969-75 Eldorado

ELDORADO FRONT SUSPENSION

The front suspension consists of two upper and two lower control arms, a stabilizer bar, shock absorbers and a right and left torsion bar, Fig. 7. Torsion bars are used instead of the conventional coil springs. The front end of the torsion bar is attached to the lower control arm. The rear of the torsion bar is mounted into an adjustable arm in the torsion bar crossmember. The standing height of the car is controlled by this adjustment.

Standing Height, Adjust

The standing height must be checked and adjusted if necessary before checking and adjusting front wheel alignment.

The standing height is controlled by the adjustment setting of the torsion bar adjusting bolt, Fig. 7. Clockwise rotation of the bolt increases standing height; counterclockwise rotation decrease standing height.

To check height on 1969-70 vehicles measure from top of the upper shock absorber mounting bolt to the top of the lower shock mount bolt. As shown in Fig. 8, this dimension should be 14.6". If dimensions are not correct, adjust as required.

To check height on 1971-75 vehicles, measure from lower edge of front shock absorber dust tube (A) to centerline of lower attachment (B), Fig. 8A, this dimension between (A) and (B) should be 8-$8\frac{1}{4}$ inch on 1971-73 vehicles, and $8\frac{3}{16}$-$8\frac{7}{16}$ inch on 1974-75 vehicles.

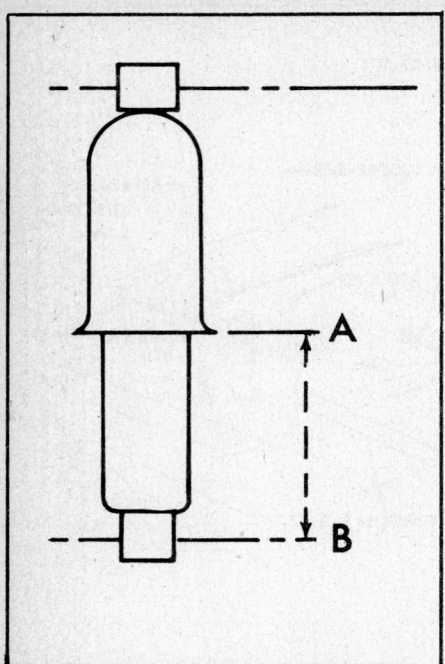

Fig. 8A Checking standing height.
1971-75 Eldorado

Camber is adjusted by turning the upper control arm rear cam bolt, Fig. 9. Caster is adjusted by turning the upper control arm front and rear cam bolts. Wheels must be in straight ahead position. Use camber reading scale for making this adjustment.

1. Turn rear cam bolt so camber reading is $\frac{1}{4}°$ more than original setting for every 1° of caster change required for a correct reading. Turn to plus side of camber if caster is negative and to the negative side of camber if caster is positive.
2. Turn front cam bolt so camber will return to original setting.
3. Recheck caster reading.

NOTE: If a problem arises where there is not enough cam adjustment remaining to obtain correct reading:

1. Turn front cam bolt so high part of cam is pointing up.
2. Turn rear cam bolt so high part of cam is pointing down. This is a location to start from and a correct reading can be obtained with the above procedure.
3. Tighten upper control arm cam nuts to 75 ft-lbs. Hold bolt head securely as any movement of the cam will affect the final setting and will require a recheck of camber and caster adjustments.

Wheel Alignment, Adjust

After checking and, if necessary, adjusting standing height, check camber and caster as follows:

Toe-In, Adjust

Toe-in is adjusted by turning the tie rod adjusting tubes at outer ends of each tie rod after loosening clamp bolts.

Readings should be taken only when front wheels are straight ahead and steering gear is on its high spot.

1. Center steering wheel, raise car and check wheel run-out.
2. Loosen tie rod adjuster nuts and adjust tie rods to obtain the specified toe-in.
3. Tighten tie rod adjuster nuts to 20 ft-lbs.
4. Position adjuster clamps so that opening of clamps are facing up. Interference with front suspension components could occur while turning if clamps are facing down.

Wheel Bearing & Steering Knuckle, Replace

1. Raise and support vehicle under lower control arms.
2. Remove drive axle nut and washer and remove wheel and tire assembly.
3. Remove brake hose clip from ball joint and replace nut, then remove brake caliper off disc, and using a length of wire support caliper on suspension.

NOTE: Do not allow caliper to hang from brake hose as this could cause damage and premature failure of hose.

4. Mark hub and disc assembly for alignment during assembly and remove disc, then strike steering knuckle in area of upper ball joint until upper ball joint is loose.

Fig. 8 Checking standing height. 1969-70 Eldorado

Fig. 9 Caster-camber cam locations. 1969-75 Eldorado

Fig. 10   Horizontal check for ball joint wear. 1969-75 Eldorado

CAUTION: Use extreme care to prevent striking and damaging brake hose or ball joint seal.

5. Place a short length of rubber hose over lower control arm torsion bar connector to avoid damage to inboard tri-pot joint seal when hub and knuckle are removed.
6. Using appropriate puller, disconnect tie rod end, upper and lower ball joints and remove steering knuckle and hub assembly, Fig. 12.

Ball Joints

Vertical Check for Wear
1. Raise car and position jack stands under lower control arms as near as possible to each ball joint.
2. Clamp vise grips on end of drive axle and position a dial indicator so that dial indicator ball rests on vise grip.
3. Place a pry bar between lower control arm and outer race and pry down on bar. Reading must not exceed ⅛".

Horizontal Check for Wear
1. With car raised as above, position dial indicator as shown in Fig. 10.
2. Grasp front wheel and push in on bottom of tire while pulling out at top. Read dial gauge, then reverse push-pull procedure.
3. Horizontal deflection on gauge should not exceed ⅛" at wheel rim. This procedure checks both the upper and lower ball joints.

Upper Ball Joint, Replace
1. Remove upper control arm and grind head off three rivets. Using a hammer and punch, drive out rivets.
2. Install new ball joint, securing it in place with three bolts and nuts contained in the kit.
3. Install upper control arm and lubricate ball joint fitting until grease escapes between seal and steering knuckle, Fig. 11.

Lower Ball Joint, Replace
1. Remove lower control arm and cut off two rivet heads from sides of control arm. Grind off head of rivet at bottom of control arm, then drive rivet out of arm.
2. Install service ball joint, securing it to control arm with bolts and nuts contained in kit.

Fig. 11   Repacking upper ball joint. 1969-75 Eldorado

Torsion Bar, Replace
1. Raise and place car on jack stands.
2. Remove wheel, the install one or two nuts to prevent drum from falling off car.
3. Remove hub cotter pin, nut and washer, and brake line clip attached to frame.
4. Place jack under lower control arm on side torsion bar is to be removed.
5. Disconnect upper ball joint and remove nut and brake line clip.
6. Disconnect shock absorber at lower end.
7. Pull tie rod from steering knuckle.

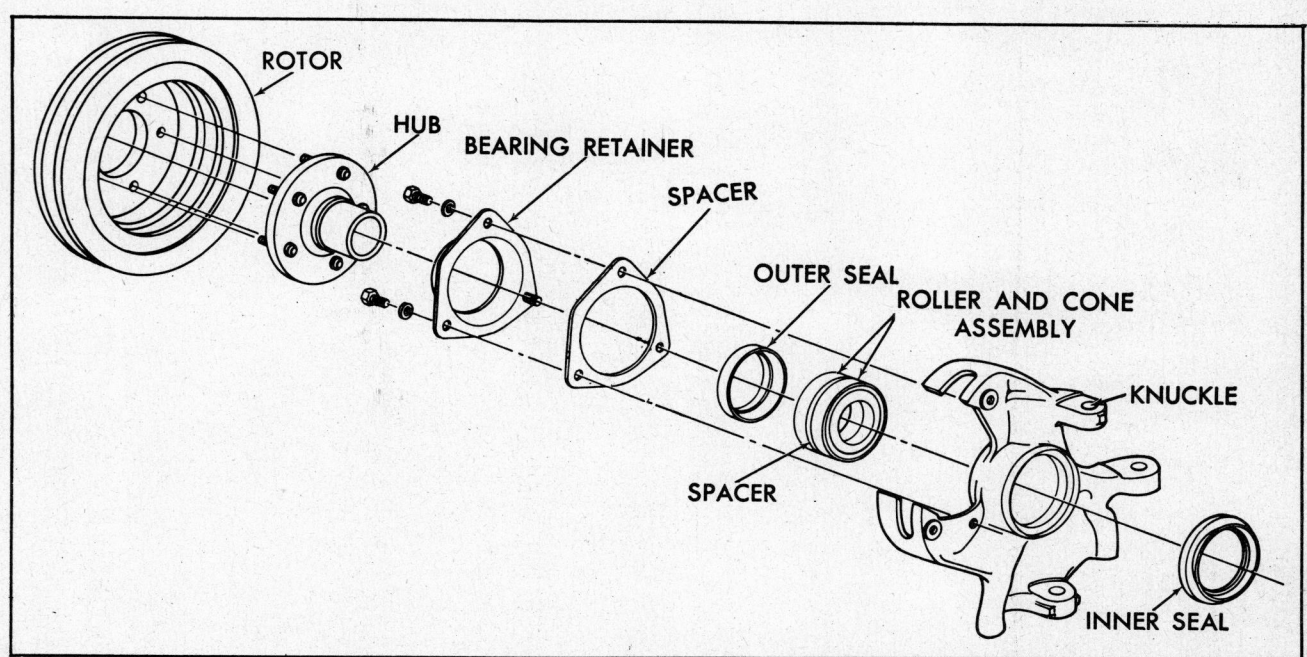

Fig. 12   Wheel bearing and steering knuckle assembly. Eldorado

8. Disconnect stabilizer bar.
9. Disconnect lower ball joint.
10. Disengage brake backing plate from drive axle and wire it to upper control arm.
11. Remove lower control arm-to-frame attaching nuts. *Do not remove bolts yet.*
12. Lower jack from under lower control arm. The torsion bar is now unloaded and lower control arm is hanging free.
13. Remove torsion bar adjusting bolt.
14. Pull down on outer end of lower control arm with one hand, while reaching back with the other hand to remove torsion bar adjusting nut from frame crossmember.
15. Remove lower control arm-to-frame attaching bolts and disengage arm from frame mounts.
16. Slide lower control arm off torsion bar and slide bar out of frame crossmember retainer and remove from car.

Inspection

1. Check rubber seal for damage and replace if necessary.
2. A new retainer must be used when torsion bar is replaced.
3. Check torsion bar for nicks, scratches or dents. If any of these conditions exist the torsion bar must be replaced.

Installation

1. Lubricate both ends of bar for about 3" with lubriplate.
2. Lubricate bar retainer in crossmember.
3. Place torsion bar in retainer. *Torsion bar ends are marked and must be installed as indicated as it is possible to reverse bar when installing.*
4. Lubricate lower control arm torsion bar connector and position control arm on bar. *When installing control arm, make sure that arm is installed in the "on car position" and is level. Also check torsion bar, making certain that it is fully seated in crossmember.*
5. With a jack, raise lower control arm and install in chassis mounts. Do not tighten nuts yet.
6. Pull down on lower control arm with one hand, and with the other hand, install torsion bar lock nut through chassis crossmember and under arm.
7. Lubricate adjusting bolt with E.P. chassis lube and install bolt. Do not tighten bolt yet.
8. Install brake backing plate.
9. Install lower ball joint, tighten nut to 40 ft-lbs and install cotter pin.
10. Install upper ball joint to steering knuckle.
11. Complete the installation and lower car. Tighten nuts that were left loose. Finally, check standing height and wheel alignment as outlined previously.

POWER STEERING, REPLACE

1969-75 Standard Cars

1. Disconnect pressure and return line hoses at steering gear. Have container ready to catch dripping oil. Secure hoses in raised position to prevent loss of fluid.
2. Raise car and use a puller to disconnect pitman arm from steering linkage.
3. Remove screw that holds flexible coupling to steering shaft.
4. Unfasten gear from frame side rail, lower gear down and out of car with pitman arm attached.
5. Reverse procedure to install.

1969-75 Eldorado

1. Disconnect hydraulic hoses at rear of pump reservoir. Cap pump fittings to prevent drainage of fluid from pump. Also, cap or tape hose fittings. If equipped with steering pump cooler, disconnect return hose at cooler.
2. Pull pitman arm from drag link.
3. Remove two bolts holding flexible coupling together.
4. Unfasten gear from frame and move gear forward and down out of car.
5. Reverse procedure to install. Check fluid level and bleed hydraulic system as outlined for standard cars.

CHECKER MOTORS

OLD CAR SPECIFICATIONS: For 1946-68 Tune Up and Wheel Alignment Specifications see main index.

INDEX OF SERVICE OPERATIONS

ACCESSORIES
PAGE NO.

Air Conditioning 2-20
Automatic Level Controls 2-39
Blower Motor, Replace 1-139
Clock Troubles 2-11
Heater Core, Replace 1-140
Power Top Troubles 2-18
Power Window Troubles 2-18
Radio, Replace 1-39

BRAKES

Anti-Skid Brakes 2-162
Brake Troubles, Mechanical 2-17
Disc Brake Service 2-133
Hydraulic System Service 2-123
Master Cylinder, Replace 1-141
Parking Brake, Adjust 1-141
Power Brake Unit, Replace 1-141
Service Brakes, Adjust 1-141

CLUTCH

Clutch Pedal, Adjust 1-140
Clutch, Replace 1-140
Clutch Troubles 2-12

COOLING SYSTEM

Cooling System Troubles 2-6
Variable Speed Fans 2-38

ELECTRICAL

Alternator Service 2-69
Blower Motor, Replace 1-139
Dash Gauge Service 2-50
Distributor, Replace 1-139
Distributor Service:
    Standard 2-525
    Transistorized 2-535
Electrical Troubles 2-8
Headlight Aiming 2-45
Ignition Coils and Resistors 2-521
Ignition Lock, Replace 1-139
Ignition Switch, Replace 1-139
Instrument Cluster, Removal 1-139
Light Switch, Replace 1-139
Neutral Safety Switch, Replace 1-139
Starter Service 2-54
Starter, Replace 1-139
Starter Switch Service 2-67
Stop Light Switch, Replace 1-139

Turn Signal Switch, Replace 1-139
Turn Signal Troubles 2-11
Windshield Wiper Motor, Replace 1-139
Windshield Wiper Troubles 2-19

ENGINE
PAGE NO.

Engine Identification 1-132
Engine, Service 1-140
Engine Troubles 2-1

ENGINE LUBRICATION

Emission Control Systems 2-545

FUEL SYSTEM

Carburetor Adjustments and Specs. .. 2-372
Emission Control Systems 2-545
Fuel Pump Service 2-369
Fuel System Troubles 2-2

PROPELLER SHAFT & U JOINTS

Propeller Shaft 1-141
Universal Joint Service 2-117

REAR AXLE

Axle Shaft 1-141
Rear Axle, Replace 1-141
Rear Axle Specifications 1-137
Rear Axle Troubles 2-16

SPECIFICATIONS

Alternator 1-135
Brakes 1-138
Capacities 1-137
Carburetors 2-372
Cooling System 1-137
Crankshaft and Bearings 1-135
Distributors 1-134
Engine Tightening Torque 1-136
General Engine Specs. 1-132
Ignition Coils and Resistors 2-521
Pistons, Rings and Pins 1-135
Rear Axle 1-137
Starting Motors 1-136
Tune Up 1-133

Valves 1-135
Wheel Alignment 1-136

STEERING GEAR
PAGE NO.

Horn Sounder Removal 1-139
Ignition Lock, Replace 1-139
Mechanical Gear, Replace 1-143
Mechanical Gear Service 2-170
Mechanical Gear Troubles 2-17
Power Gear, Replace 1-143
Steering Wheel, Replace 1-139

SUSPENSION, FRONT

Ball Joints, Replace 1-143
Ball Joints, Check for Wear 1-142
Coil Spring, Replace 1-143
Lubrication 1-142
Shock Absorber, Replace 1-143
Suspension, Description of 1-142
Toe-In, Adjust 1-142
Wheel Alignment, Adjust 1-142
Wheel Bearings, Adjust 1-142
Wheel Bearings, Replace 1-142

SUSPENSION, REAR

Helper Spring, Replace 1-141
Leaf Spring, Replace 1-141
Shock Absorber, Replace 1-141

TRANSMISSIONS

Three Speed Manual:
    Replace 1-140
    Repairs 2-177
    Linkage, Adjust 1-140
Automatic Units 2-231
    Linkage 1-140
Overdrive Service 2-175

TUNE UP

Service 2-517
Specifications 1-133

WINDSHIELD WIPER

Wiper Arms, Replace 1-139
Wiper Blades, Replace 1-139
Wiper Linkage, Replace 1-139
Wiper Motor, Replace 1-139
Wiper Troubles 2-19

SERIAL NUMBER LOCATION: Plate on left front door pillar, cowl left side above master cylinder or top of left side instrument panel

ENGINE NUMBER LOCATION

SIX CYL.: Pad at front righthand side of cylinder block at rear of distributor

V8 ENGINES: Pad at front righthand side of cylinder block

ENGINE IDENTIFICATION CODE

Engines are identified in the following table by the code letter or letters immediately following the engine serial number.

CODE	TRANS.	ENGINE
1969		
6BG	①	6-250
6BH	②	6-250
6BS	①	V8-327
6BT	②	V8-327
6BV	②	V8-350③
6BV	①	V8-350④
6BX	②	V8-350
1970		
1CE	①	6-250
2CA	①	V8-350④
2CB	②	V8-350④
2CC	②	V8-350③
2CD	②	V8-350

① —Std. trans.

CODE	TRANS.	ENGINE
1971		
CAD	②	6-250
2DI	②	V8-350
2DJ	①	V8-350④
2DK	②	V8-350④
1972		
CBK	②	6-250
EAJ	②	6-250⑤
EBS	②	V8-350
EBT	②	V8-350④
EBW	②	V8-350④⑤

② —Auto. trans.
③ —High performance.

CODE	TRANS.	ENGINE
1973		
EBD	②	6-250
ECH	②	6-250
ECJ	②	V8-350
ECK	②	V8-350④
EDA	②	V8-350
EDB	②	V8-350④
1974		
4SB	②	6-250
4SC	②	6-250⑤
4WD	②	V8-350
4WF	②	V8-350④

④ —Aerobus.
⑤ —California.

GENERAL ENGINE SPECIFICATIONS

Note: See Chevrolet chapter for engine service procedures.

Year	Engine	Car-buretor	Bore and Stroke	Piston Dis-place-ment, Cubic Inches	Com-pres-sion Ratio	Maximum Brake H.P. @ R.P.M.	Maximum Torque Lbs. Ft. @ R.P.M.	Normal Oil Pressure Pounds
1969	155 Horsepower...6-250	1 Barrel	3.875 x 3.53	250	8.5	155 @ 4200	235 @ 1600	30-45
	235 Horsepower...V8-327	2 Barrel	4.001 x 3.25	327	9.0	235 @ 4800	325 @ 2800	30-45
	215 Horsepower...V8-350	2 Barrel	4.001 x 3.48	350	8.1	215 @ 4400	320 @ 2400	30-45
	300 Horsepower...V8-350	4 Barrel	4.001 x 3.48	350	10.25	300 @ 4800	380 @ 3200	30-45
1970	155 Horsepower...6-250	1 Barrel	3.875 x 3.53	250	8.5	155 @ 4200	235 @ 1600	30-45
	215 Horsepower...V8-350	2 Barrel	4.001 x 3.48	350	8.1	215 @ 4400	320 @ 2400	30-45
	250 Horsepower...V8-350	2 Barrel	4.001 x 3.48	350	9.0	250 @ 4800	345 @ 2800	30-45
1971	145 Horsepower...6-250	1 Barrel	3.875 x 3.53	250	8.5	145 @ 4200	230 @ 1600	30-45
	215 Horsepower...V8-350	2 Barrel	4.001 x 3.48	350	8.1	215 @ 4000	335 @ 2800	30
	245 Horsepower...V8-350	2 Barrel	4.001 x 3.48	350	8.5	245 @ 4800	350 @ 2800	35-45
1972	110 Horsepower①...6-250	1 Barrel	3.875 x 3.53	250	8.5	110 @ 3800	185 @ 1600	30-45
	165 Horsepower①...V8-350	2 Barrel	4.001 x 3.48	350	8.5	165 @ 4000	280 @ 2400	35-45
	175 Horsepower①...V8-350	4 Barrel	4.001 x 3.48	350	8.5	175 @ 4000	280 @ 2400	35-45
1973	100 Horsepower①...6-250	1 Barrel	3.875 x 3.53	250	8.25	100 @ 3800	175 @ 1600	40
	145 Horsepower①...V8-350	2 Barrel	4.001 x 3.48	350	8.5	145 @ 4000	255 @ 2400	40
	155 Horsepower①...V8-350	4 Barrel	4.001 x 3.48	350	8.5	155 @ 4000	255 @ 2400	40
1974	100 Horsepower①...6-250	1 Barrel	3.875 x 3.53	250	8.25	100 @ 3600	175 @ 1800	40
	145 Horsepower①...V8-350	2 Barrel	4.000 x 3.48	350	8.5	145 @ 3800	250 @ 2200	40
	155 Horsepower①...V8-350	4 Barrel	4.000 x 3.48	350	8.5	155 @ 3800	250 @ 2400	40

① —Ratings are net—As installed in vehicle.

TUNE UP SPECIFICATIONS

★ When using a timing light, disconnect vacuum hose or tube at distributor and plug opening in hose or tube so idle speed will not be affected.

● When checking compression, lowest cylinder must be within 80 percent of highest.

▲ Before removing wires from distributor cap, determine location of the No. 1 wire in cap, as distributor position may have been altered from that shown at the end of this chart.

Year	Spark Plug		Distributor		Ignition Timing ★			Carb. Adjustments					
	Type	Gap Inch	Point Gap Inch	Dwell Angle Deg.	Firing Order Fig. ▲	Timing BTDC ①	Mark Fig.	Hot Idle Speed		Air Fuel Ratio		Idle "CO" %	
								Std. Trans.	Auto. Trans. ②	Std. Trans.	Auto. Trans.	Std. Trans.	Auto. Trans.
1969													
6-250 ③	R46N	.035	⑤	31–34	A	TDC	C	700	—	—	—	—	—
6-250 ④	R46N	.035	⑤	31–34	A	4	C	—	500D	—	—	—	—
V8-327 ③	R44	.035	⑤	28–32	B	2 ATC	C	700	—	—	—	—	—
V8-327 ④	R44	.035	⑤	28–32	B	2	C	—	600D	—	—	—	—
V8-350 ⑥	CR43	.035	⑤	28–32	B	4	C	—	600D	—	—	—	—
V8-350 ⑦	R44	.035	⑤	28–32	B	4	C	—	600D	—	—	—	—
1970													
6-250	R46T	.035	⑤	31–34	A	4	C	700	600D	—	—	—	—
V8-350	R44	.035	⑤	28–32	B	4	C	—	600D	—	—	—	—
1971													
6-250	R46TS	.035	⑤	31–34	A	4	D	700	600D	—	—	—	—
V8-350 ⑧	R44TS	.035	⑤	29–31	B	6	D	—	550D	—	—	—	—
V8-350 ⑨	R44T	.035	⑤	29–31	B	4	D	—	550D	—	—	—	—
1972													
6-250	R46T	.035	⑤	31–34	A	4	D	—	600D	—	—	—	—
V8-350 ⑧	R44T	.035	⑤	29–31	B	6	D	—	600D	—	—	—	—
V8-350 ⑨	R44T	.035	⑤	29–31	B	8	D	—	600D	—	—	—	—
1973													
6-250	R46T	.035	⑤	31–34	A	6	D	—	600D	—	—	—	—
V8-350 ⑧	R44T	.035	⑤	29–31	B	8	D	—	600D	—	—	—	—
V8-350 ⑨	R44T	.035	⑤	29–31	B	12	D	—	600D	—	—	—	—
1974													
6-250	R46T	.035	⑤	31–34	A	6	D	—	600D	—	—	—	—
V8-350	R44T	.035	⑤	29–31	B	8	D	—	600D	—	—	—	—

①—BTDC: Before top dead center.
②—D: Drive. N: Neutral.
③—Std. Trans.
④—Auto. Trans.

⑤—New points, .019", used, .016". On V8's, turn adjusting screw in (clockwise) until engine misfires, then back off ½ turn.
⑥—215 H.P.

⑦—300 H.P.
⑧—Marathon & Taxicab.
⑨—Aerobus.

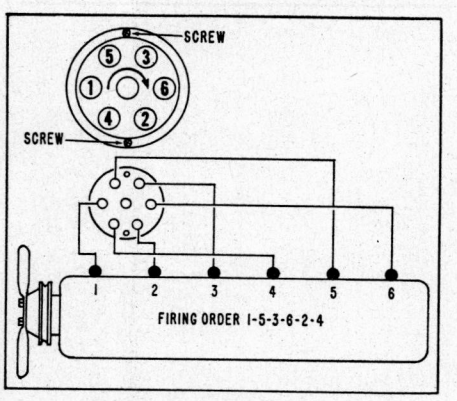

Fig. A

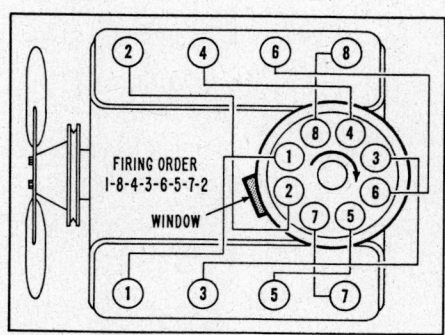

Fig. B

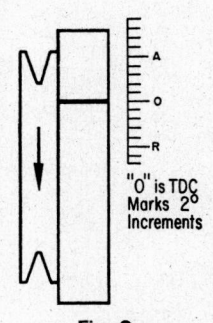

Fig. C

Fig. D

DISTRIBUTOR SPECIFICATIONS

★Note: If unit is checked on vehicle, double the RPM and degrees to get crankshaft figures.

Distributor Part No.①	Advance Starts	Centrifugal Advance Degrees @ RPM of Distributor				Vacuum Advance	
		Intermediate Advance			Full Advance	Inches of Vacuum to Start Plunger	Max. Adv. Dist. Deg. @ Vacuum
1969							
1110469	0 @ 500	3 @ 600	8½ @ 975	—	14 @ 2100	6	7½ @ 12
1110470	0 @ 500	5 @ 580	10½ @ 975	—	16 @ 2100	6	7½ @ 12
1111338	0 @ 450	4½ @ 625	8½ @ 1000	—	16 @ 2500	—	—
1111482	0 @ 500	5 @ 700	—	—	16 @ 2150	6	7½ @ 12
1111483	0 @ 450	6 @ 1000	—	—	14 @ 2150	6	7½ @ 12
1111489	0 @ 450	4½ @ 650	7½ @ 850	—	13 @ 2350	10	5 @ 17
1970							
1110482	0 @ 500	5 @ 700	—	—	16 @ 2150	6	7½ @ 12
1111495	0 @ 375	1 @ 525	7 @ 1000	—	14 @ 2050	8	7½ @ 15½
1112002	0 @ 450	1 @ 550	4 @ 700	—	16 @ 2200	7	12 @ 17
1971							
1112048	0 @ 600	—	5 @ 850	—	10 @ 1900	8	8 @ 17
1971-72							
1110489	0 @ 475	1 @ 635	7 @ 1150	—	12 @ 2050	8	11½ @ 16
1112005	0 @ 400	1 @ 600	6 @ 1100	—	12 @ 2150	8	10 @ 17
1972							
1112047	0 @ 650	—	6 @ 1200	—	9 @ 2100	8	8 @ 17
1973							
1110499	0 @ 550	—	—	—	11½ @ 2100	6	11 @ 14
1112094	0 @ 600	—	—	—	7 @ 2100	6	7½ @ 14
1112168	0 @ 500	6 @ 1500	—	—	9 @ 2100	4	8 @ 7
1974							
1110499	0 @ 550	—	—	—	11½ @ 2100	6	11 @ 14
1112093	0 @ 550	5½ @ 1200	—	—	9 @ 2100	6	7½ @ 13½
1112844	0 @ 500	—	—	—	9 @ 2100	4	7 @ 7

①—Stamped on distributor housing cover.

VALVE SPECIFICATIONS

Year	Engine Model	Valve Lash Int.	Valve Lash Exh.	Valve Angles Seat	Valve Angles Face	Valve Spring Installed Height	Valve Spring Pressure Lbs. @ In.	Stem Clearance Intake	Stem Clearance Exhaust	Stem Diameter Intake	Stem Diameter Exhaust
1969	8-327, 350	Hydraulic①		46	45	1.70	200 @ 1.25	.001–.0027	.001–.0027	.3410–.3417	.3410–.3417
1969–74	6-250	Hydraulic①		46	45	1.66	186 @ 1.27	.001–.0027	.0015–.0032	.3410–.3417	.3410–.3417
1970	8-350	Hydraulic①		46	45	1.70	200 @ 1.25	.001–.0027	.0012–.0029	.3410–.3417	.3410–.3417
1971–72	8-350	Hydraulic①		46	45	1.70	200 @ 1.25	.001–.0027	.001–.0027	.3410–.3417	.3410–.3417
1973–74	8-350	Hydraulic①		46	45	1.66	189 @ 1.20	.001–.0027	.0012–.0029	.3410–.3417	.3410–.3417

①—No adjustment.

PISTONS, PINS, RINGS, CRANKSHAFT & BEARINGS

Year	Engine Model	Piston Clearance	Ring End Gap① Comp.	Ring End Gap① Oil	Wrist-pin Diameter	Rod Bearings Shaft Diameter	Rod Bearings Bearing Clearance	Main Bearings Shaft Diameter	Main Bearings Bearing Clearance	Main Bearings Thrust on Bear. No.	Main Bearings Shaft End Play
1969–72	6-250	.0015–.0025	.010	.015	.9272	1.999–2.000	.0007–.0027	2.2983–2.2993	.0003–.0029	7	.002–.006
1973	6-250	.0015–.0025	.010	.015	.9272	1.9928–2.000	.0007–.0027	2.2983–2.2993	.0003–.0029	7	.002–.006
1969	8-327	.0005–.0011	.013	.015	.9272	2.099–2.100	.0007–.0028	2.4479–2.4488	③	5	.003–.011
1969	8-350	.0005–.0011	.013	.015	.9272	2.099–2.100	.0007–.0028	2.4479–2.4488	③	5	.003–.011
1970	8-350	.0007–.0013	④	.015	.9272	2.099–2.100	.0007–.0028	②	⑤	5	.002–.006
1971	8-350	.0007–.0017	.010	.015	.9272	2.099–2.100	.0013–.0035	②	⑥	5	.002–.006
1972	8-350	.0007–.0017	.010	.015	.9272	2.099–2.100	.0013–.0035	⑦	⑥	5	.002–.006
1973–74	8-350	.0007–.0017	④	.015	.9272	2.099–2.100	.0013–.0035	⑦	⑥	5	.002–.006

①—Fit rings in tapered bores to the clearance listed in tightest portion of ring travel. Clearance specified are mimimum gaps.
②—No. 1, 2, 3, 4: 2.4484–2.4493; No. 5: 2.4479–2.4488.
③—No. 1, 2, 3, 4: .0008–.0020; No. 5: .0018–.0034.
④—Top ring, .010; lower ring, .013.
⑤—No. 1: .0003–.0015; No. 2, 3, 4: .0006–.0018; No. 5: .0008–.0028.
⑥—No. 1: .0008–.0020; No. 2, 3, 4: .0011–.0023; No. 5: .0017–.0033.
⑦—No. 1: 2.4484–2.4493; No. 2, 3, 4: 2.4481–2.4490; No. 5: 2.4475–2.4488.

ALTERNATOR SPECIFICATIONS

Year	Make	Model	Ground Polarity	Alternator Rated Output Amperes	Alternator Rated Output Volts	Alternator Field Current Amperes ①	Alternator Field Current Volts	Regulator② Model	Regulator Test @ 120°F Ampere Load	Regulator Test @ 120°F Altern. R.P.M.	Regulator Test @ 120°F Volts
1969–70	Motorola	8AL-2001	Negative	35	15	1.8–2.4	12.6	R2CC1	10	1500	13.7–14.5
1969–74	Motorola	8AL-2002	Negative	55	15	1.8–2.4	12.6	8RD2009	10	2000	13.4–13.9

①—Excessive current drain indicates shorted field windings.
②—Regulator is a sealed assembly, requiring no adjustments.

ENGINE TIGHTENING SPECIFICATIONS*

★Torque specifications are for clean and lightly lubricated threads only. Dry or dirty threads produce increased friction which prevents accurate measurement of tightness.

Year	Engine Model	Spark Plugs Ft. Lbs.	Cylinder Head Bolts Ft. Lbs.	Intake Manifold Ft. Lbs.	Exhaust Manifold Ft. Lbs.	Rocker Arm Stud Ft. Lbs.	Rocker Arm Cover Ft. Lbs.	Connecting Rod Cap Bolts Ft. Lbs.	Main Bearing Cap Bolts Ft. Lbs.	Flywheel to Crankshaft Ft. Lbs.	Vibration Damper or Pulley Ft. Lbs.
1969-70	6-230, 250	25①	95	②	②	—	55③	35	65	60	④
1971-74	6-250	15	95	②	②	—	45③	35	65	60	60
1969	8-327	25	65	30	20	—	55③	⑥	80	60	60
1969-70	8-350	25	65	30	20⑤	—	55③	45	75	60	60
1971-74	8-350	15	65	30	20⑤	50	45③	45	75⑦	60	60

①—1970 6-250, 15 ft. lbs.
②—End clamp bolts 20 ft. lbs.; center bolts, 30 ft. lbs.
③—Inch lbs.
④—Pressed on.
⑤—Inside bolts, 30 ft. lbs.
⑥—⅜ inch bolts, 45 ft. lbs.; 11⁄32 inch bolts, 35 ft. lbs.
⑦—Outer bolts on engines with 4 bolt caps, 65 ft. lbs.

STARTING MOTOR SPECIFICATIONS

Year	Engine	Starter Number	Brush Spring Tension Oz.①	Free Speed Test			Resistance Test③	
				Amps.②	Volts	R.P.M.①	Amps.	Volts
1969	6-230, 250	1108360	35	55–80	9	3500–6000	—	—
	V8-327, 350	1108361	35	65–100	10.6	3600–5100	300–360	3.5
	V8-307, 327	1108367	35	49–87	10.6	6200–10700	290–425	4.2
	V8-307, 327	1108368	35	50–80	9	5500–10500	—	—
1969-73	6-230, 250	1108365	35	49–87	10.6	6200–10700	290–425	4.2
1970	V8-350	1108420	35	65–95	9	7500–10500	—	—
1971-74	V8-350	1108361	35	65–100	10.6	3600–5100	300–360	3.5
1973-74	6-250	1108480	35	50–80	9	5500–10500	—	—
1973-74	V8-350	1108430	35	65–95	9	7500–10500	—	—

①—Minimum.
②—Includes solenoid.
③—Check capacity of motor by using a 500 ampere meter and a carbon pile rheostat to control voltage. Apply the volts listed across motor with armature locked. Current should be as listed.

WHEEL ALIGNMENT SPECIFICATIONS

Year	Model	Caster Angle, Degrees		Camber Angle, Degrees				Toe-In Inch	Toe-Out on Turns, Deg.①	
		Limits	Desired	Limits		Desired			Outer Wheel	Inner Wheel
				Left	Right	Left	Right			
1969-74	Aerobus	+2	+2	+1 to +2	+1 to +2	+1½	+1½	⅛ to ³⁄₁₆	—	—
1969-74	Exc. Aerobus	+2	+2	0 to +1	0 to +1	+½	+½	¹⁄₁₆ to ⅛	—	—

①—Incorrect toe-out when other adjustments are correct, indicates bent steering arms.

REAR AXLE SPECIFICATIONS

Year	Model	Carrier Type	Ring Gear & Pinion Backlash		Pinion Bearing Preload			Differential Bearing Preload		
			Method	Adjustment	Method	New Bearings Inch-Lbs.	Used Bearings Inch-Lbs.	Method	New Bearings Inch-Lbs.	Used Bearings Inch-Lbs.
1969-74	44	Integral	Shims	.005–.010	Shims	20–40①	10–20①	Shims	.015	.015
1969-74	62	Integral	Shims	.005–.009	Shims	20–40①	10–20①	Shims	.015	.015

①—Use inch-pound torque wrench on pinion shaft nut.

COOLING SYSTEM & CAPACITY DATA

Year	Model or Engine	Cooling Capacity, Qts.			Radiator Cap Relief Pressure, Lbs.		Thermo. Opening Temp. ①	Fuel Tank Gals.	Engine Oil Refill Qts. ②	Transmission Oil			Rear Axle Oil Pints
		No Heater	With Heater	With A/C	With A/C	No A/C				3 Speed Pints	4 Speed Pints	Auto. Trans. Qts.③	
1969	6-250	11	12	12	13	13	195	23	4	2.6	—	8½	3
1969	V8-350④	16	17	17	13	13	195	23	4	2.6	—	8½	3
1969	V8-350⑤	—	17⑥	17⑥	13	13	180	23	4	2.6	—	8½	6
1970	6-250	11	12	12	13	13	195	23	4	—	—	8½	3
1970	V8-350④	16	17	17	13	13	195	23	4	—	—	8½	3
1970	V8-350⑤	—	17	17	13	13	180	23	4	—	—	8½	6
1971	6-250	—	12	12	13	13	195	21½	4	—	—	8½	3
1971	V8-350④	—	17	17	13	13	195	21½	4	—	—	8½	3
1971	V8-350⑤	—	21	21	13	13	195	23	4	—	—	8½	6
1972-74	6-250	—	12	12	15	15	195	21½	4	—	—	⑦	3
1972-74	V8-350④	—	17	17	15	15	195	21½	4	—	—	⑦	3
1972-74	V8-350⑤	—	21	21	15	15	195	21½	4	—	—	⑦	6

①—For permanent type anti-freeze.
②—Add one quart with filter change.
③—Approximate. Make final check with dipstick.
④—Marathon & Taxicab.
⑤—Aerobus.
⑥—Add 9 qts. with underseat heaters.
⑦—Exc. late 1973, 8½ qts. Late 1973, Turbo Hydra-Matic, 9 qts.

BRAKE SPECIFICATIONS

Year	Model	Brake Drum Inside Diameter	Wheel Cylinder Bore Diameter			Master Cylinder Bore Diameter		
			Disc Brake	Front Drum Brake	Rear Drum Brake	Disc Brakes	Drum Brakes	Power Brakes
1969–70	All Exc. Aerobus	11	$2\frac{15}{16}$	$1\frac{1}{8}$	$\frac{15}{16}$	$1\frac{1}{8}$	1	1
	Aerobus	11	—	$1\frac{1}{8}$	1	—	—	1
1971–74	All Exc. Aerobus	11	$2\frac{15}{16}$	—	$\frac{15}{16}$	$1\frac{1}{8}$	—	1
	Aerobus	11	—	$1\frac{1}{8}$	1	—	—	1

DISC BRAKE ROTOR SPECIFICATIONS

Year	Nominal Thickness	Minimum Thickness	Thickness Variation Parallelism	Run-out (T.I.R.)	Finish (Micro-in.)
1969–70	1.240	1.215	.0007	.004	20–60
1971–73	1.290	1.215	.0007	.005	20–60

Electrical Section

DISTRIBUTOR

Refer to the Chevrolet chapter for removal and installation procedures.

STARTER, REPLACE

Refer to the Chevrolet chapter for replacement procedure.

IGNITION LOCK

Refer to the Chevrolet chapter for replacement procedure.

IGNITION SWITCH, REPLACE

Refer to the Chevrolet chapter for replacement procedure.

LIGHT SWITCH, REPLACE

1969-74 All

1. Disconnect battery ground cable.
2. Pull switch knob to "ON" position, reach under instrument panel and depress shaft retainer, then pull knob and shaft from switch.
3. Remove ferrule nut and switch from instrument panel and disconnect wiring.
4. Reverse procedure to install.

STOP LIGHT SWITCH, REPLACE

1969-74 All

1. Disconnect electrical connector from switch on brake pedal support.
2. Remove retaining nut, if so equipped, then remove switch from bracket.
3. Install and adjust new switch so stop lights are actuated when brake pedal is depressed 3/8 inch from fully released position.

NEUTRAL SAFETY SWITCH, REPLACE

Refer to the Chevrolet chapter, "1971-73 Column Shift" and "1969-70 Column Shift" for replacement procedures.

TURN SIGNAL SWITCH, REPLACE

Refer to the Chevrolet chapter, "1969-75" replacement procedures.

HORN SOUNDER & STEERING WHEEL

Refer to the Chevrolet chapter, "1969 Deluxe & 1970-75 Standard Wheel" procedures.

INSTRUMENT CLUSTER

1969-74 All

1. Disconnect battery ground cable.
2. Remove instrument cluster retaining screws.
3. Pull cluster forward, disconnect wiring and remove instrument cluster.
4. Reverse procedure to install.

W/S WIPER BLADES

Two methods are used to retain wiper blades to wiper arms, Fig. 1. One method uses a press type release tab. When the release tab is depressed the blade assembly can be slid off the wiper arm pin. The other method uses a coil spring retainer. A screwdriver must be inserted on top of the spring and the spring pushed downward. The blade assembly can then be slid off the wiper arm pin. Two methods are also used to retain the blade element in the blade assembly, Fig. 1. One method uses a press type release button. When the button is depressed the two piece blade assembly can be slid off the blade element. The other method uses a spring type retainer clip in the end of the blade element. When the retainer clip is squeezed together, the blade element can be slid out of the blade assembly.

NOTE: To be sure of correct installation, the element release button, or the spring element retaining clip should be at the end of the wiper blade assembly nearest the wiper transmission.

W/S WIPER ARMS

1. Wiper motor must be in park position.
2. Use suitable tool to minimize the possibility of windshield or paint finish damage during arm removal.
3. Remove arm by prying up with tool to disengage arm from serrated transmission shaft.
4. To install arm to transmission shaft rotate the required distance and direction so that the blades rest in proper position.

W/S WIPER MOTOR

1. Remove nut and lock washer through center hole of pivot arm drive disc and separate drive disc from motor.
2. Remove bolts securing motor to cowl, lower transmission and disconnect motor electrical connector.
3. Remove motor from vehicle.

W/S WIPER TRANSMISSION

1. Perform step 1 as outlined under "W/S Wiper Motor".
2. Remove retaining clip from stud and disconnect right hand arm from transmission.
3. Remove wiper arm assemblies, outside linkage nut and transmission and linkage from under dash.

RADIO, REPLACE

1. Remove inner and outer knobs and right hand shaft insert.
2. Remove mounting nuts, escutcheon inserts and escutcheon.
3. Disconnect antenna, speaker and power feed leads.
4. Remove mounting nut from bracket and remove radio.

BLOWER MOTOR, REMOVAL

1. Disconnect wiring from motor.
2. Remove blower to heater housing screws and remove blower motor.

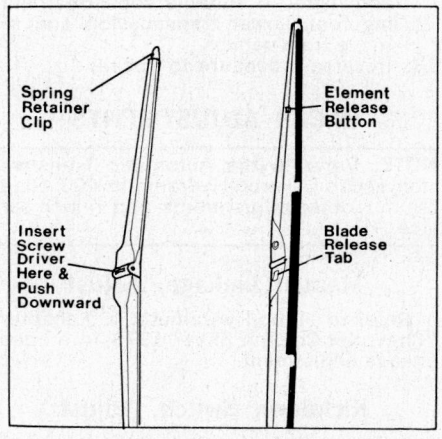

Spring Retainer Clip

Element Release Button

Insert Screw Driver Here & Push Downward

Blade Release Tab

Fig. 1   Wiper blades

HEATER CORE, REMOVAL

1. Disconnect resistor wires and remove heater core cover.
2. Disconnect heater hoses from core and plug hoses and core openings.
3. Slide heater core from housing.

Engine Section

Refer to Chevrolet Chapter for Engine Service Procedures.

Clutch and Transmission Section

CLUTCH PEDAL, ADJUST

Proper clutch pedal adjustment is obtained by adjusting the length of the throwout lever rod. Clutch pedal free travel for all models is 1 to 1⅜ inch.

CLUTCH, REPLACE

Refer to Chevrolet chapter for replacement procedure.

THREE SPEED TRANSMISSION, REPLACE

1. Support vehicle on jack stands and remove propeller shaft.
2. Disconnect shift linkage and speedometer cable from transmission.
3. Support transmission, remove transmission to clutch housing bolts, slide transmission rearward and lower transmission from vehicle.
4. Reverse procedure to install.

THREE SPEED SHIFT LINKAGE, ADJUST

1. Disconnect shift rods from shift arms on steering column.
2. Position shift arms parallel one above another, check shift lever movement through the steering column.
3. Hold shift arms in straight position and adjust one shift rod between shift arm and transmission lever.
4. Insert a wedge between the 2nd and 3rd selector lever and selector gate and check for proper cross-over. If necessary, adjust lower steering column bearing by loosening screws, forcing bearing upward and adding shims if necessary.
5. Check adjustment for proper cross-over and gear engagement.

TURBO-HYDRAMATIC 400, REPLACE

Late 1973-74

1. Disconnect battery negative cable and raise vehicle.
2. Remove filler tube and drain transmission.
3. Support engine and remove converter underpan.
4. Remove converter to flywheel bolts.
5. Disconnect speedometer cable, kickdown switch wiring and shift linkage.
6. Disconnect vacuum modulator line and remove vacuum modulator.
7. Disconnect oil cooler lines.
8. Reinstall vacuum modulator with retaining bolt finger tight.
9. Disconnect parking brake cable from frame lever and on all models except Aerobus, remove parking brake lever bracket.
10. Remove propeller shaft.
11. Place a jack under transmission and remove rear engine support.
12. Lower engine and transmission slightly and remove engine to transmission bolts. Move transmission rearward and install a suitable converter holding tool. Lower transmission and remove from vehicle.
13. Reverse procedure to install.

IN-CAR ADJUSTMENTS

NOTE: Refer to the Automatic Transmission section, Turbo-Hydramatic 400 chapter, for other adjustments and minor service.

Manual Linkage, Adjust

Refer to Turbo-Hydramatic 400 chapter, "Chevrolet Column Shift" 1973-74 manual linkage adjustment.

Kickdown Switch, Adjust

Adjust switch, located under accelerator pedal, so plunger is depressed when carburetor throttle is in the wide open position.

WARNER AUTOMATIC, REPLACE

1969-Early 1973

1. Support vehicle on jack stands.
2. Remove filler tube from pan, then drain transmission.
3. Disconnect speedometer cable from transmission and remove vacuum line from vacuum control unit.
4. Disconnect electrical wiring and oil cooler lines from transmission.
5. Remove propeller shaft.
6. Support transmission, remove transmission to engine bolts and slide transmission rearward, disengaging transmission from converter. Remove transmission from vehicle.
7. Remove converter.
8. Reverse procedure to install.

IN-CAR ADJUSTMENTS

NOTE: Refer to the Automatic Transmission section, "American Motors Shift-Command" chapter, for other adjustments and minor service.

Manual Linkage, Adjust

Refer to Turbo-Hydramatic 400 chapter, "Chevrolet Column Shift" 1969-72 manual linkage adjustment.

Kickdown Switch, Adjust

Adjust switch by loosening the two nuts on the switch and turn the upper nut clockwise or counter-clockwise so plunger is depressed by the accelerator pedal when carburetor throttle is in the wide open position.

Rear Axle, Propeller Shaft & Brakes

REAR AXLE, REPLACE

1. Support vehicle at frame and rear axle, relieving tension from springs and remove rear wheels.
2. Disconnect parking brake cable at equalizer and brake line at axle tube connector.
3. Disconnect shock absorbers from lower mountings.
4. Place an alignment mark between rear propeller shaft yoke, universal joint and pinion flange yoke for alignment during assembly. Disconnect propeller shaft from pinion flange.
5. Remove axle shafts and brake support plates.
6. Remove leaf spring "U" bolts and spring plates.
7. Remove axle assembly from vehicle.
8. Reverse procedure to install.

AXLE SHAFT

1969-74 All

1. Raise vehicle and remove wheel and brake drum.
2. Remove axle shaft flange dust cap, then brake backing plate attaching nuts or screws.
3. Using a suitable puller, remove axle shaft.
4. Remove bearing cup and inner axle shaft seal with a suitable puller.
5. Reverse procedure to install.

PROPELLER SHAFT

Marathon and Taxicab models use a one piece propeller shaft while the Aerobus has a two piece shaft. Universal joints must be lubricated every 2500 miles with a suitable lithium soap base grease. When lubricating these joints, lubricant must flow from all four bearing seals.

BRAKE ADJUSTMENTS

Refer to the Chevrolet chapter for brake adjustments on the Marathon and Taxicab models.

Refer to the Chrysler chapter for brake adjustments on Aerobus models.

PARKING BRAKE, ADJUST

Depress parking brake pedal approximately ½ inch, then remove slack from cable at clevis. Check cable adjustment to ensure against brake drag.

MASTER CYLINDER, REPLACE

Disconnect hydraulic lines from master cylinder. Remove bolts securing master cylinder to mounting.

POWER BRAKE UNIT

Refer to the Chevrolet chapter for replacement procedures.

Rear Suspension Section

SHOCK ABSORBER, REPLACE

1. With rear axle properly supported, remove nuts securing shock absorber to spring plate bracket, Fig. 1.
2. Remove nuts securing shock absorber to upper mounting bracket.
3. Reverse procedure to install.

LEAF SPRING, REPLACE

1. Support vehicle at frame and rear axle, removing tension from spring.
2. Disconnect shock absorber from spring plate mounting bracket.
3. Remove "U" bolt nuts, spring plate and "U" bolts.
4. Disassemble rear shackle.
5. Remove nuts securing spring front mounting bracket to the frame, pull spring assembly rearward and remove from vehicle. Remove spring front mounting bracket from spring.
6. Reverse procedure to install.

HELPER SPRING, REPLACE

1. Perform steps 1 to 3 as outlined under "Leaf Spring, Replace" procedure.
2. Remove rubber bumper "U" bolt nuts, plate, "U" bolt and rubber bumper, Fig. 2.
3. Reverse procedure to install.

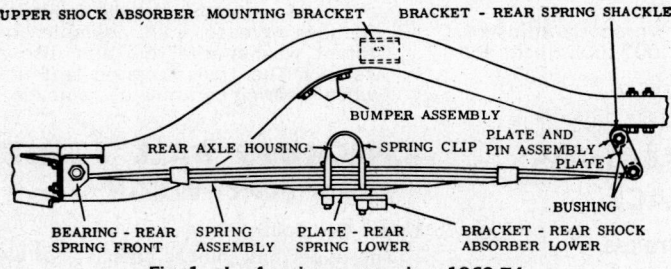

Fig. 1 Leaf spring suspension. 1969-74

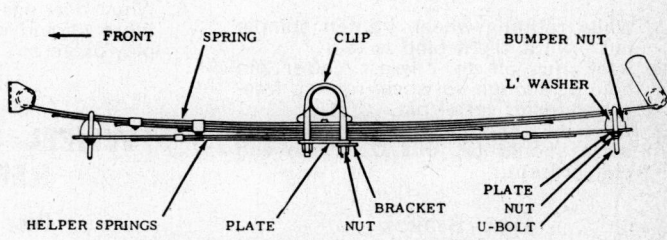

Fig. 2 Helper spring installation. 1969-74

Front End and Steering Section

FRONT SUSPENSION

All front suspension systems incorporate independent coil springs riding on the lower control arms. Ball joints connect the upper and lower control arms to the steering knuckles, Figs. 1 and 2.

LUBRICATION

Lubrication is recommended at 2,500 mile intervals with a suitable lithium base grease. When lubricating the ball joints, the joint must be unloaded.

WHEEL ALIGNMENT

Caster and camber adjustments are made by means of shims between the upper control arm shaft and the frame. Shims may be added, subtracted or transferred to change the readings as follows:

Caster, Adjust

Transfer shims from front to rear or rear to front. The transfer of one shim (.06 inch) from rear to front will increase positive caster by $\frac{1}{2}°$. In any case, the total thickness of the shim pack should not exceed .562 inch.

Camber, Adjust

Add or subtract shims at both bolts (front and rear). Adding one shim (.06 inch) at front and rear bolts will increase positive camber by $\frac{1}{4}°$.

TOE-IN, ADJUST

Toe-in can be adjusted by loosening the clamp bolts at each end of the tie rods and turning each tie rod to increase or decrease its length as necessary until proper toe-in is obtained with the steering gear on the high point for straight ahead driving and the steering wheel centered.

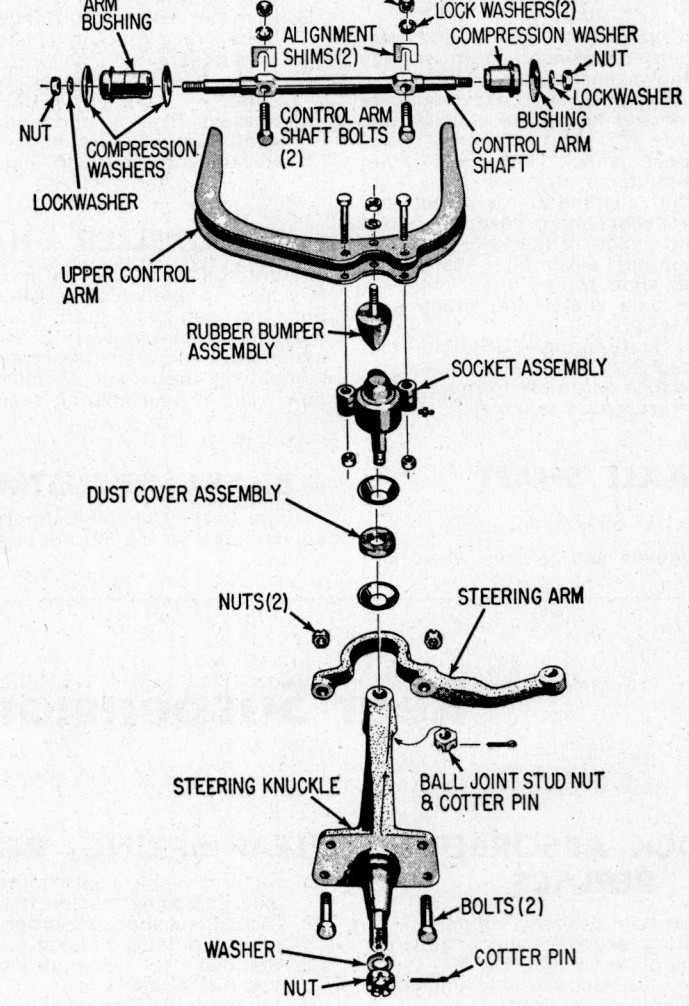

Fig. 1   Upper control arm & steering knuckle installation. 1969-74 All

WHEEL BEARINGS, ADJUST

Drum Brakes

1. While rotating wheel, tighten spindle nut until a slight bind is felt.
2. Back nut off to nearest cotter pin hole or enough so wheel rotates freely and insert cotter pin.
3. When bearings are properly adjusted, there should be .001-.010 inch end play present.

Disc Brakes

1. While rotating wheel, snug-up spindle nut.
2. Back nut off, then snug-up nut by hand.
3. Loosen nut to nearest cotter pin hole and insert cotter pin.
4. When bearings are properly adjusted, there should be .001-.005 inch end play present.

WHEEL BEARINGS, REPLACE

Disc Brakes

1. Raise front of vehicle and remove front wheels.
2. Remove brake caliper mounting bolts and caliper. Once caliper is removed, support caliper away from disc to avoid damage to hydraulic brake line.
3. Remove grease cup, spindle nut, thrust washer and hub and disc assembly. The grease retainer and inner wheel bearing can now be removed.

CHECKING BALL JOINTS FOR WEAR

Upper Ball Joint

The upper ball joint is checked for wear by measuring the amount of torque required to rotate the ball stud in the assembly. To make this type of check, it is necessary to remove the stud from the steering knuckle.

Install a nut on the ball stud and using a torque wrench, turn the stud. Acceptable torque for an upper ball joint is 28-40 inch lbs. If torque readings are excessively low or high, replace the ball joint.

Lower Ball Joint

The lower ball joint is checked for wear by measuring the amount of "pull" required to move the ball stud in the assembly. This check is made with the stud removed from the steering knuckle.

With a spring scale attached to the stud cotter pin hole, pull the spring scale until the stud moves and note the reading. The specified "pull" for an acceptable lower ball joint is 8 lbs. If reading is lower than specified, replace the ball joint.

UPPER BALL JOINT, REPLACE

1. Support vehicle at lower control arm and remove wheel.
2. Remove cotter pin from ball stud and loosen stud nut.
3. Lightly tap ball stud to loosen stud and remove stud nut.
4. Remove bolts securing ball joint to control arm.
5. Install new ball joint and torque bolts to 20-30 ft. lbs.
6. Assemble ball joint to steering knuckle and torque stud nut to 80 foot pounds and install cotter pin.

LOWER BALL JOINT, REPLACE

1. Support vehicle at lower control arm and remove wheel.
2. If equipped with disc brakes, remove caliper assembly.
3. Perform steps 2, 3 and 4 as outlined in above procedure.
4. Install new ball joint and torque bolts to 20-30 ft. lbs.
5. Raise control arm with jack until ball stud contacts spindle, install and torque stud nut to 100 ft. lbs.

SHOCK ABSORBER, REPLACE

1. Support vehicle at lower control arm.
2. Remove shock absorber upper mounting nuts.
3. Remove shock absorber mounting plate to lower control arm bolts. After shock absorber is removed, disconnect mounting plate from shock absorber.
4. Reverse procedure to install.

COIL SPRING, REPLACE

1. Support vehicle at frame and lower control arm with a suitable jack.
2. Disconnect stabilizer bar from lower

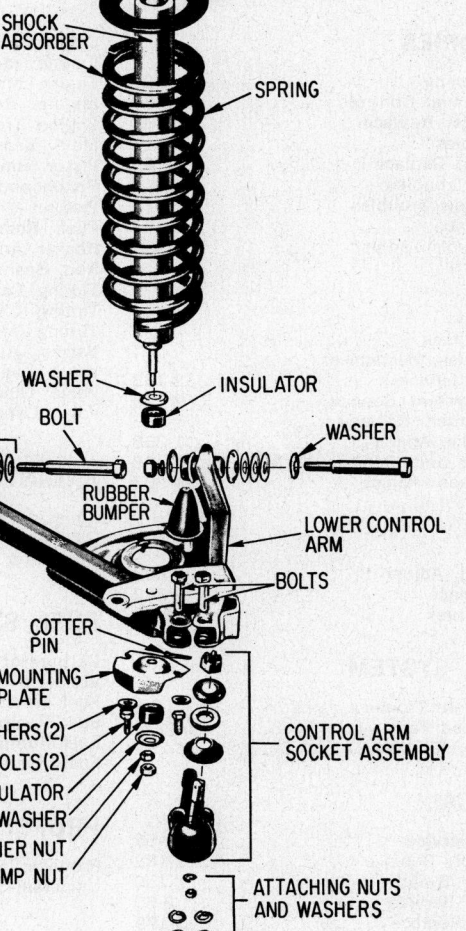

control arm and loosen lower ball joint stud nut two turns. Lightly tap steering knuckle to loosen ball stud, then remove stud nut.
3. Lower jack slowly until tension is relieved from spring and remove spring and insulator.

NOTE: Install a safety chain through coil spring and lower control arm to prevent injury or damage if spring slips from mounting.

STEERING GEAR, REPLACE

1. Remove pitman arm nut and washer

Fig. 2   Lower control arm, coil spring & shock absorber installation. 1969-74 All

from sector shaft and mark position of arm on shaft.
2. With a suitable puller, remove pitman arm from sector shaft.
3. Remove steering shaft coupling bolts and steering gear to frame bolts. Remove steering gear.

INTEGRAL POWER STEERING

To remove gear assembly, disconnect pressure and return hoses, cap hoses and steering gear outlet ports, then follow procedure as outlined under "Steering Gear, Replace".

CAMARO · CHEVELLE · CHEVROLET
CORVETTE · MONTE CARLO · NOVA

OLD CAR SPECIFICATIONS: For 1946-68 Tune Up and Wheel Alignment Specifications see main index.

INDEX OF SERVICE OPERATIONS

PAGE NO.

ACCESSORIES

Air Conditioning 2-20
Automatic Level Controls 2-39
Blower Motor, Replace 1-188
Clock Troubles 2-11
Heater Core, Replace 1-189
Power Top Troubles 2-18
Power Window Troubles 2-18
Radio, Replace 1-187
Speed Controls, Adjust 1-190

BRAKES

Anti-Skid Brakes 2-162
Brake Troubles, Mechanical 2-17
Disc Brake Service 2-133
Hydraulic System Service 2-123
Master Cylinder, Replace 1-208
Parking Brake, Adjust 1-208
Power Brake Unit, Replace 1-208
Service Brakes, Adjust 1-207

CLUTCH

Clutch Pedal, Adjust 1-202
Clutch, Replace 1-202
Clutch Troubles 2-12

COOLING SYSTEM

Cooling System Troubles 2-6
Variable Speed Fans 2-38
Water Pump, Replace 1-201

ELECTRICAL

Alternator Service 2-69
Blower Motor, Replace 1-188
Clutch Start Switch 1-180
Dash Gauge Service 2-50
Distributor, Replace 1-179
Distributor Service:
   Standard 2-525
   Transistorized 2-535
Electrical Troubles 2-8
Headlamps, Concealed Type 2-46
Headlight Aiming 2-45
Horn Sounder 1-181
Ignition Coils and Resistors 2-521
Ignition Lock, Replace 1-179
Ignition Switch, Replace 1-179
Instrument Cluster Removal 1-182
Light Switch, Replace 1-180
Neutral Safety Switch, Replace 1-180
Seat Belt Interlock Systems 2-311
Starter Service 2-54
Starter, Replace 1-179
Starter Switch Service 2-67
Stop Light Switch, Replace 1-180
Turn Signal Switch, Replace 1-181
Turn Signal Troubles 2-11
Windshield Wiper Motor, Replace 1-186
Windshield Wiper Troubles 2-19

ENGINE

Camshaft, Replace 1-197
Crankshaft Rear Oil Seal 1-198

PAGE NO.

Cylinder Head, Replace 1-191
Engine Identification 1-145
Engine Mounts, Replace 1-191
Engine, Replace 1-191
Engine Troubles 2-1
Main Bearings 1-197
Piston Rings 1-197
Piston and Rod, Assemble 1-197
Pistons 1-197
Push Rods 1-194
Rocker Arm Studs 1-193
Rod Bearings 1-197
Timing Case Cover, Replace 1-195
Timing Chain 1-197
Timing Gears, Replace 1-196
Valves, Adjust 1-192
Valve Arrangement 1-193
Valve Guides 1-195
Valve Lifters 1-195

ENGINE LUBRICATION

Emission Control Systems 2-545
Oil Pan, Replace 1-198
Oil Pump 1-200

FUEL SYSTEM

Carburetor Adjustments and Specs. . . . 2-372
Emission Control Systems 2-545
Fuel Pump Pressure 1-201
Fuel Pump, Replace 1-201
Fuel Pump Service 2-369
Fuel System Troubles 2-2

PROPELLER SHAFT & U JOINTS

Propeller Shaft 1-207
Universal Joint Service 2-117

REAR AXLE & SUSPENSION

Axle Shaft, Bearing and Seal 1-207
Coil Springs, Replace 1-209
Control Arms & Bushings, Replace 1-210
Corvette Rear Wheel Alignment 1-209
Leaf Springs & Bushings, Replace 1-209
Rear Axle Description 1-205
Rear Axle Specifications 1-163
Rear Axle Troubles 2-16
Shock Absorber, Replace 1-209
Stabilizer Bar, Replace 1-211
Strut Rod, Replace 1-213
Suspension Crossmember & Isolation
   Mount, Replace 1-214
Suspension Tie Rod & Bushing, Replace . 1-211
Torque Control Arms & Bushings,
   Replace 1-213

SPECIFICATIONS

Alternator 1-173
Belt Tension Data 1-201
Brakes 1-170
Capacities 1-175
Carburetors 2-372

PAGE NO.

Cooling System 1-175
Crankshaft and Bearings 1-168
Distributors 1-164
Engine Tightening Torque 1-171
Fuel Pump Pressure 1-201
General Engine Specs. 1-152
Ignition Coils and Resistors 2-521
Pistons, Rings and Pins 1-168
Rear Axle 1-163
Starting Motors 1-172
Tune Up 1-154
Valve Lift Specs. 1-193
Valve Timing 1-194
Valves 1-167
Wheel Alignment 1-174

STEERING GEAR

Horn Sounder Removal 1-181
Ignition Lock, Replace 1-179
Mechanical Gear, Replace 1-218
Mechanical Gear Service 2-170
Mechanical Gear Troubles 2-17
Power Gear Replace 1-218
Steering Wheel, Replace 1-181

SUSPENSION, FRONT

Ball Joints, Replace 1-217
Ball Joints, Check for Wear 1-216
Coil Spring, Replace 1-218
Lubrication 1-215
Shock Absorber, Replace 1-217
Suspension, Description of 1-215
Toe-In, Adjust 1-216
Wheel Alignment, Adjust 1-215
Wheel Bearings, Adjust 1-216
Wheel Bearings, Replace 1-216

TRANSMISSIONS

Three Speed Manual:
   Replace 1-203
   Repairs 2-177
   Linkage, Adjust 1-203
Four Speed Manual:
   Replace 1-203
   Repairs 2-199
   Linkage, Adjust 1-205
Automatic Units 2-231
   Linkage, 1975 1-205
Overdrive Service 2-175

TUNE UP

Service 2-517
Specifications 1-154

WINDSHIELD WIPER

Wiper Arms, Replace 1-185
Wiper Blades, Replace 1-185
Wiper Linkage, Replace 1-186
Wiper Motor, Replace 1-186
Wiper Switch, Replace 1-187
Wiper Troubles 2-19

SERIAL NUMBER LOCATION: Plate on left front door pillar or top of left side instrument panel

ENGINE NUMBER LOCATION

4 & 6 CYL.: Pad at front righthand side of cylinder block at rear of distributor | **V8 ENGINES:** Pad at front righthand side of cylinder block

ENGINE IDENTIFICATION CODE

Engines are identified in the following table by the code letter or letters immediately following the engine serial number.

CAMARO

CODE			CODE			CODE		
AM	6-230 with M/T	1969	CJY	6-250	1975	CNC	8-307 with M/T	1970
AN	6-230 with P/G, T/D	1969	CJZ	6-250	1975	CND	8-307 with 4 sp. tr.	1970
AO	6-230 with T/H	1969	CKG	8-307 with M/T	1972	CNE	8-307 with P/G	1970
AP	6-230 with A/C	1969	CKH	8-307 with P/G	1972	CNF	8-307 with T/H	1970
AQ	6-230 with P/G, T/D, A/C	1969	CHB	8-307 with M/T	1973	CNI	8-350 with M/T, 250 H.P.	1970
AR	6-230 with A/C, T/H	1969	CHH	8-307 with T/H	1973	CNJ	8-350 with M/T, 300 H.P.	1970
BB	6-250 with P/G, T/D	1969	CHJ	8-307 with M/T & E.E.C.	1973	CNK	8-350 with P/G, 300 H.P.	1970
BC	6-250 with P/G, T/D, A/C	1969	CHK	8-307 with T/H & E.E.C.	1973	CNM	8-350 with P/G, 250 H.P.	1970
BD	6-250 with T/H	1969	CKO	8-400 with M/T, 375 H.P.	1970	CNN	8-350 with T/H, 250 H.P.	1970
BE	6-250 with M/T	1969	CKT	8-350 with T/H, 255 H.P.	1972	CRE	8-350 with T/H, 300 H.P.	1970
BF	6-250 with A/C	1969	CKB	8-350 165 H.P.	1972	CRF	6-250 with M/T	1970
BH	6-250 with T/H, A/C	1969	CKK	8-350 with M/T, 175, 200 H.P.	1972	CRG	6-250 with M/T	1970
CAA	6-250 with M/T	1971	CKD	8-350 with T/H, 175, 200 H.P.	1972	CSD	6-250 with P/G, E.E.C.	1972
CAB	6-250 with P/G	1971	CKS	8-350 with M/T, 255 H.P.	1972	CTB	8-350 with M/T, 320 H.P.	1970
CAY	8-307 with M/T, E.E.C.	1972	CLJ	8-350 with 4 sp. tr. & 245 H.P.	1973	CTC	8-350 with T/H, 320 H.P.	1970
CAZ	8-307 with P/G, E.E.C.	1972	CLK	8-350 with T.H. 400	1973	CTK	8-307 with T/H	1972
CBA	6-250 with M/T, E.E.C.	1972	CKA	8-350 4 sp. tr. & 145 H.P.	1973	CTW	8-400 with M/T, 350 H.P.	1970
CBG	6-250 with M/T	1972	CKU	8-350 with T/H	1973	CTX	8-400 with M/T, 350 H.P.	1970
CBJ	6-250 with P/G	1972	CKB	8-350 with M/T & 175 H.P.	1973	CTY	8-400 with T/H, 375 H.P.	1970
CCA	6-250 with T/H	1973	CKW	8-350 with T/H & 145 H.P.	1973	DA	8-307 with M/T	1969
CCB	6-250 with E.E.C.	1973	CLL	8-350 with T/H 400 & E.E.C.	1973	DC	8-307 with P/G	1969
CCC	6-250 with E.E.C.	1973	CLM	8-350 with M/T & E.E.C. & 245 H.P.	1973	DD	8-307 with T/H	1969
CCD	6-250 with M/T & E.E.C.	1973	CKX	8-350 with T/H, E.E.C. & 145 H.P.	1973	DE	8-307 with 4 sp. tr.	1969
CCR	6-250 with M/T	1974	CKY	8-350 with M/T, E.E.C. & 145 H.P.	1973	DZ	8-302 with 4 BC	1969
CCW	6-250 with T/H, E.E.C.	1974	CKD	8-350 with T/H, E.E.C. & 175 H.P.	1973	FA	8-327 with M/T	1969
CCX	6-250 with T/H	1974	CKH	8-350 with M/T, E.E.C. & 175 H.P.	1973	FB	8-327 with P/G	1969
CCA	8-307	1971				FC	8-327 with T/H	1969
CCG	6-250 with M/T	1970	CMA	8-307 with T/H, E.E.C.	1972	FH	8-327 with T/H	1969
CCK	6-250 with T/H, taxi & police	1970	CMA	8-350 with T/H	1974	HA	8-350 with M/T	1969
CCL	6-250 with M/T, taxi & police	1970	CMC	8-350 with M/T	1974	HB	8-350 with T/H	1969
CCM	6-250 with P/G, taxi & police	1970	CKB	8-350 with M/T, 185 H.P.	1974	HC	8-350 with 2 BC	1969
CCZ	6-250 with M/T	1970	CKH	8-350 with 4 BC, M/T	1974	HD	8-350 with 2 BC, T/H	1969
CDM	6-250 with M/T, AIR	1972	CKH	8-350 with M/T, E.E.C., 185 H.P.	1974	HE	8-350 with P/G	1969
CDL	6-250 with P/G, AIR	1972	CLJ	8-350 with M/T, 245 H.P.	1974	HF	8-350 with 2 BC, P/G	1969
CGB	8-350 with P/G, 250 H.P.	1971	CKU	8-350 with T/H, 185 H.P.	1974	HQ	8-350 with M/T	1969
CGB	8-350 with P/G	1972	CKD	8-350 with 4BC, T/H	1974	HR	8-350 with M/T	1969
CGK	8-350 with M/T, 300 H.P.	1971	CKD	8-350 with T/H, E.E.C., 185 H.P.	1974	HS	8-350 with T/H	1969
CGL	8-350 with T/H, 300 H.P.	1971	CLK	8-350 with 4BC, T/H	1974	JB	8-396 with P/G	1969
CGP	8-350 with M/T, 360 H.P.	1971	CLD	8-400 with T/H, 350 H.P.	1971	JF	8-396 with HPE	1969
CGR	8-350 with T/H, 360 H.P.	1971	CLC	8-400 with M/T, 350 H.P.	1971	JG	8-396 with SHPE	1969
CJD	8-350 with T/H, 270 H.P.	1971	CMU	8-350	1975	JH	8-396 with SHPE	1969
CJF	8-396 with M/T, 350 H.P.	1970	CRC	8-350	1975	JI	8-396 with HPE, T/H	1969
CJG	8-350 with M/T, 270 H.P.	1971	CMF	8-350	1975	JJ	8-396 with M/T, A/H	1969
CJH	8-396 with M/T, 375 H.P.	1970	CMH	8-350	1975	JL	8-396 with SHPE, T/H	1969
CJI	8-396 with T/H, 350 H.P.	1970	CRX	8-350	1975	JM	8-396 with A/H, T/H	1969
CJL	8-396 with T/H, 375 H.P.	1970	CHW	8-350	1975	JU	8-396 with M/T	1969
CJL	6-250	1975	CHS	8-350	1975	KA	8-396 with SHPE, M/T	1969
CJM	6-250	1975	CHT	8-350	1975	KC	8-396 with SHPE, M/T	1969
CJR	6-250	1975				KE	8-396 with A/H, M/T	1969
CJT	6-250	1975				CLA	8-400 with M/T	1972
CJU	6-250	1975				CLB	8-400 with T/H	1972
CJF	6-250	1975						

Continued

ENGINE IDENTIFICATION CODE—Continued

CHEVROLET

CODE		
BA	6-250 with M/T	1969
BG	6-250 with M/T, A/C	1969
CAA	6-250 with M/T	1971
CAB	6-250 with P/G, T/D	1971
CAC	6-250 with M/T, taxi & police	1971
CAD	6-250 with P/G, taxi & police	1971
CAT	8-400 with T/H	1972
CBH	6-250 with M/T, taxi & police	1972
CBJ	6-250 with P/G	1972
CBK	6-250 with P/G, taxi & police	1972
CNJ	6-250 with M/T	1972
CCL	6-250 with M/T	1973
CCM	6-250 with M/T, E.E.C.	1973
CCM	6 cyl. with P/G, taxi & police	1970
CCG	6 cyl. with M/T	1970
CCH	6 cyl. with M/T	1970
CCK	6 cyl. T/H, taxi & police	1970
CCZ	6 cyl. with M/T	1970
CCL	6 cyl. with M/T, taxi & police	1970
CAR	8-350 with T/H, taxi & police	1972
CDB	8-350 with T/H, E.E.C.	1972
CDL	6-250 with P/G, AIR	1972
CDL	8-400 with T/H, Police	1972
CDM	8-400 with T/H, Police, E.E.C.	1972
CKB	8-350 with T/H	1972
CSH	8-350 with T/H, taxi & police	1972
CSJ	8-350 with M/T	1972
CJH	8-350 with M/T, Police, 270 H.P.	1971
CKL	8-350 with T/H & 145 H.P.	1973
CKS	8-350 with T/H, 145 H.P., taxi & police	1973
CKK	8-350 with T/H, 145 H.P., E.E.C.	1973
CLT	8-350 with T/H, 145 H.P., E.E.C.	1973
CLU	8-350 with T/H & 145 H.P.	1973
CLW	8-350 with T/H, 145 H.P., E.E.C., police	1973
CLX	8-350 with T/H, 145 H.P., police	1973
CKR	8-350 with T/H, E.E.C., 175 H.P., police	1973
CKD	8-350 with T/H, E.E.C. & 175 H.P.	1973
CKJ	8-350 with T/H & 175 H.P.	1973
CLR	8-400 with M/T, Police, 300 H.P.	1971
CMK	8-350 with 4BC, E.E.C., taxi & police	1974
CMA	8-350 with E.E.C., taxi & police	1974
CMD	8-350 with taxi & police	1974
CMH	8-350 with 4BC, E.E.C., police	1974
CMJ	8-350 with 4BC, police	1974
CMJ	8-350	1975
CKD	8-350 with 4BC, E.E.C.	1974
CGA	8-350, with M/T, 245 H.P.	1971
CGB	8-350, with P/G, 245 H.P.	1971

CODE		
CGC	8-350 with M/T, 245 H.P.	1971
CGJ	8-350 with T/H, taxi & police, 245 H.P.	1971
CJB	8-350 with M/T, police, 275 H.P.	1971
CKP	8-400 with T/H	1972
CLB	8-400 with M/T	1972
CLR	8-400 with M/T, police	1972
CRU	8-350	1975
CRW	8-454 T/H, AIR	1972
CRW	8-350	1975
CRY	8-454 with T/H, AIR, Police	1972
CRY	8-350	1975
CSA	8-400	1975
CSA	8-400 with T/H	1973
CSB	8-400 with T/H, police	1973
CSC	8-400 with T/H, E.E.C., police	1973
CSD	8-400 with T/H & E.E.C.	1973
CSK	8-400 with T/H	1973
CSL	8-400 with T/H, E.E.C., police	1973
CSM	8-400 with T/H & police	1973
CTC	8-400 with 4BC, E.E.C., 180 H.P.	1974
CTD	8-400 with 4BC, 180 H.P.	1974
CTK	8-400 with 4BC, E.E.C., 180 H.P., police	1974
CTJ	8-400 with 4BC, 180 H.P., police	1974
CTA	8-400 with 150 H.P.	1974
CTB	8-400 with 150 H.P., police	1974
CLK	8-400 with T/H, 255 H.P.	1971
CLP	8-400 with T/H, 300 H.P.	1971
CPD	8-454 with M/T, 365 H.P.	1971
CPG	8-454 with M/T, police, 365 H.P.	1971
CPD	8-454 with T/H	1972
CPG	8-454 with T/H, police	1972
CTL	8-400	1975
CTM	8-400	1975
CTU	8-400	1975
CTW	8-400	1975
CTY	8-400	1975
CTZ	8-400	1975
CWD	8-454 with T/H, E.E.C.	1973
CWJ	8-454 with T/H, E.E.C., police	1973
CWK	8-454 with T/H, police	1973
CWL	8-454 with T/H	1973
CWU	8-454 with police	1974
CWW	8-454 with E.E.C., police	1974
CWY	8-454 with E.E.C.	1974
CXA	8-454	1974
CRF	6 cyl. with M/T	1970
CRG	6 cyl. with M/T	1970
CND	8-350 with M/T, 250 H.P.	1970
CNP	8-350 with M/T, taxi & police, 250 H.P.	1970
CNQ	8-350 with M/T, 300 H.P.	1970

CODE		
CNR	8-350 with T/H, 300 H.P.	1970
CNS	8-350 with P/G, police, 300 H.P.	1970
CNT	8-350 with T/H, police, 300 H.P.	1970
CNU	8-350 with P/G, 250 H.P.	1970
CNV	8-350 with T/H, 250 H.P.	1970
CNW	8-350 P/G, taxi & police, 250 H.P.	1970
CNX	8-350 T/H, taxi & police, 250 H.P.	1970
CGR	8-400 with M/T, 265 H.P.	1970
CGV	8-454 with M/T, 345 H.P.	1970
CGS	8-454 M/T, police, 345 H.P.	1970
CGT	8-454 with M/T, police, 390 H.P.	1970
CGU	8-454 with M/T, 390 H.P.	1970
CXX	8-454	1975
CXY	8-454	1975
FA	8-327 with M/T	1969
FB	8-327 with P/G	1969
FC	8-327 with T/H	1969
FH	8-327 with M/T	1969
FJ	8-327 with M/T	1969
FK	8-327 with P/G	1969
FL	8-327 with T/H	1969
GE	8-327 with P/G	1969
HD	8-350 with 2 bar. carb., M/T, T/M	1969
HF	8-350 with 2 bar. carb., P/G	1969
HG	8-350 with M/T	1969
HH	8-350 with T/H	1969
HI	8-350 with 2 BC	1969
HJ	8-350 with 2 BC, T/H	1969
HK	8-350 with P/G	1969
HL	8-350 with 2 BC, P/G	1969
HM	8-350 with 2 BC, T/H	1969
HN	8-350 with T/H	1969
HP	8-350 with M/T	1969
HT	8-350 with M/T	1969
HU	8-350 with P/G	1969
HY	8-350 with T/H	1969
IA	8-350 with T/H	1969
JN	8-396 with 2 BC, M/T	1969
JQ	8-396 with 2 BC, T/H	1969
JT	8-396 with M/T	1969
LA	8-427 with HPE	1969
LB	8-427 with 4 BC	1969
LC	8-427 with HPE, T/H	1969
LD	8-427 with SHPE, M/T	1969
LE	8-427 with 4 BC, T/H	1969
LH	8-427 with HPE	1969
LI	8-427 with T/H	1969
LS	8-427 with SHPE, T/H	1969
MA	8-427 with M/T	1969
MC	8-427 with HPE, M/T	1969
MD	8-427 with SHPE, M/T	1969

CHEVELLE & MONTE CARLO

CODE		
AD	6-230 with T/H	1969
AM	6-230 with M/T	1969
AN	6-230 with P/G, T/D	1969
AP	6-230 with A/C	1969
AQ	6-230 with P/G, T/D, A/C	1969
AR	6-230 with T/H, A/C	1969
BB	6-250 with P/G, T/D	1969
BC	6-250 with P/G, T/D, A/C	1969
BD	6-250 with T/H	1969
BE	6-250 with M/T	1969
BF	6-250 with A/C	1969

CODE		
BH	6-250 with T/H, A/C	1969
CAA	6-250 with M/T	1971
CBA	6-250 with M/T, E.E.C.	1972
CBD	6-250 with M/T, Taxi, E.E.C.	1972
CBG	6-250 with M/T	1972
CBJ	6-250 with P/G	1972
CBK	6-250 with P/G, Taxi	1972
CSD	6-250 with P/G, E.E.C.	1972
CCA	6-250 with T/H	1973
CCB	6-250 with T/H, E.E.C.	1973
CCC	6-250 with M/T	1973

CODE		
CCD	6-250 with M/T, E.E.C.	1973
CCR	6-250 with M/T	1974
CCW	6-250 with T/H, E.E.C.	1974
CCX	6-250 with T/H	1974
CCK	6-250	1974
CCA	8-307 with M/T	1971
CCM	6-250 P/G, police & taxi	1970
CCK	6-250 T/H, police & taxi	1970
CCL	6-250 M/T, police & taxi	1970

Continued

ENGINE IDENTIFICATION CODE—Continued

CHEVELLE & MONTE CARLO—Continued

CODE			CODE			CODE		
CAR	8-350 with T/H, Police, E.E.C.	1972	CLJ	8-400 with M/T	1972	CRR	8-454 with T/H, 450 H.P.	1970
CAY	8-307 with M/T, E.E.C.	1972	CLK	8-400 with T/H	1972	CRS	8-454 T/H alum. heads, 450 H.P.	1970
CAZ	8-307 with P/G, E.E.C.	1972	CLL	8-400 with 4 sp. tr.	1972	CRT	8-454 with M/T, 390 H.P.	1970
CDA	8-350 with M/T	1972	CLR	8-400 with M/T, police	1972	CRT	8-350	1975
CDB	8-350 with P/G	1972	CLS	8-400 with M/T	1972	CRU	8-350	1975
CDD	8-350 with T/H	1972	CMA	8-307 with T/H, E.E.C.	1972	CRU	8-454 with HDC, 390 H.P.	1970
CDG	8-350 with M/T	1972	CMD	8-350 with T/H, E.E.C.	1972	CRV	8-454 with M/T, 450 H.P.	1970
CJD	8-350 with T/H, 270 H.P.	1971	CMF	8-350	1975	CRW	8-454 M/T, alum. heads, 450 H.P.	1970
CJJ	8-350 with M/T, 270 H.P.	1971	CMH	8-350	1975	CRW	8-454 with T/H, AIR	1972
CJL	6-250	1975	CMJ	8-350	1975	CRX	8-350	1975
CLM	6-250	1975	CMU	8-350	1975	CRX	8-454 with T/H, AIR	1972
CJR	6-250	1975	CTC	8-400 with T/H, E.E.C., 180 H.P.	1974	CRX	8-454 with HDC, 450 H.P.	1970
CJT	6-250	1975	CTA	8-400 with T/H, 150 H.P.	1974	CRY	8-454 HDC, alum. heads, 450 H.P.	1970
CJU	6-250	1975	CNC	8-307 with M/T	1970	CSM	8-400	1975
CJF	6-250	1975	CND	8-307 with 4 sp. tr.	1970	CSH	8-350 with T/H, Police	1972
CJZ	6-250	1975	CNE	8-307 with P/G	1970	CTA	8-400 M/T, AIR, Taxi & Police	1972
CKA	8-350 with M/T	1972	CNF	8-307 with T/H	1970	CTB	8-400 T/H, AIR	1972
CKA	8-350 with M/T, 145 H.P.	1973	CNI	8-350 with M/T, 250 H.P.	1970	CTH	8-400 HDC, AIR	1972
CKL	8-350 with T/H, 145 H.P.	1973	CNJ	8-350 with M/T, 300 H.P.	1970	CTJ	8-400 T/H, AIR, Taxi & Police	1972
CKB	8-350 with M/T, 145 H.P.	1973	CNK	8-350 with P/G, 300 H.P.	1970	CTK	8-307 with M/T	1972
CKB	8-350 with P/G	1972	CPA	8-454 with M/T, 365 H.P.	1971	CTL	8-350 with T/H	1972
CKC	8-350 with M/T, E.E.C., 145 H.P.	1973	CPG	8-454 with M/T, 365 H.P.	1971	CTL	8-400	1975
CKD	8-350 with T/H	1972	CPP	8-454 with M/T, 460 H.P.	1971	CTU	8-400	1975
CKK	8-350 with T/H, E.E.C., 145 H.P.	1973	CPR	8-454 with T/H, 460 H.P.	1971	CTX	8-400	1975
CKH	8-350 with M/T, E.E.C., 175 H.P.	1973	CPA	8-454 with M/T	1972	CXW	8-454	1975
CKD	8-350 with T/H, E.E.C., 175 H.P.	1973	CPD	8-454 with T/H	1972	DA	8-307 with M/T	1969
CKJ	8-350 with T/H, 175 H.P.	1973	CWC	8-454 with M/T, E.E.C.	1973	DC	8-307 with P/G	1969
CKK	8-350 with M/T	1972	CWD	8-454 with T/H, E.E.C.	1973	DD	8-307 with T/H	1969
CLR	8-400 with M/T, Police	1971	CWA	8-454 with M/T	1973	DE	8-307 with 4 sp. tr.	1969
CLS	8-400 with M/T	1971	CWB	8-454 with T/H	1973	HA	8-350 with M/T	1969
CMC	8-350 with M/T	1974	CWA	8-454 with M/T	1974	HB	8-350 with T/H	1969
CMA	8-350 with T/H	1974	CWX	8-454 with T/H	1974	HC	8-350 with 2 BC	1969
CKH	8-350 with 4BC, M/T	1974	CWD	8-454 with T/H, E.E.C.	1974	HD	8-350 with 2 BC, T/H	1969
CKD	8-350 with 4BC, T/H	1974	CRE	8-350 with M/T, 300 H.P.	1970	HE	8-350 with P/G	1969
CGA	8-350 with M/T, 245 H.P.	1971	CNM	8-350 with P/G, 250 H.P.	1970	HF	8-350 with 2 BC, P/G	1969
CGB	8-350 with P/G, 245 H.P.	1971	CTW	8-396 with T/H, 350 H.P.	1970	HP	8-350 with M/T	1969
CGK	8-350 with M/T, 270 H.P.	1971	CTX	8-396 with M/T, 350 H.P.	1970	HR	8-350 with M/T, P/G	1969
CGL	8-350 with T/H, 270 H.P.	1971	CTY	8-396 with T/H, 375 H.P.	1970	HS	8-350 with T/H	1969
CKG	8-307 with M/T	1972	CTZ	8-396 with HDC, 350 H.P.	1970	JA	8-396 with M/T	1969
CKH	8-307 with P/G	1972	CKN	8-400 with T/H, 325 H.P.	1970	JC	8-396 with HPE	1969
CHA	8-307 with T/H	1973	CKD	8-396 with M/T, 375 H.P.	1970	JD	8-396 with SHPE	1969
CHB	8-307 with M/T	1973	CKP	8-396, with T/H, A/H, 375 H.P.	1970	JE	8-396 with HPE, T/H	1969
CHC	8-307 with T/H, E.E.C.	1973	CKQ	8-396 with HDC, 375 H.P.	1970	JK	8-396 with M/T	1969
CLA	8-400 with M/T, 330 H.P.	1971	CKR	8-400 with M/T, 4BC, 330 H.P.	1970	JV	8-396 with M/T	1969
CLB	8-400 with T/H, 300 H.P.	1971	CKS	8-400 with HDC, 4BC, 330 H.P.	1970	KB	8-396 with HPE, M/T	1969
CLJ	8-400 with M/T, 255 H.P.	1971	CKT	8-396 with T/H, 375 H.P.	1970	KD	8-396 with SHPE, M/T	1969
CLK	8-400 with T/H, 255 H.P.	1971	CKU	8-396 with HDC, 375 H.P.	1970	KF	8-396 with SHPE, T/H	1969
CLL	8-400 with M/T, 300 H.P.	1971	CZX	8-400 with M/T, 265 H.P.	1970	KG	8-396 with M/T	1969
CLP	8-400 with T/H, 300 H.P.	1971	CRH	8-400 with T/H, 265 H.P.	1970	KH	8-396 with T/H	1969
CLA	8-400 with M/T	1972	CRN	8-454 with M/T, 390 H.P.	1970	KI	8-396 with M/T	1969
CLB	8-400 with T/H	1972	CRQ	8-454 with T/H, 390 H.P.	1970			

Continued

ENGINE IDENTIFICATION CODE—Continued
CHEVY NOVA

CODE		
AA	4-153 with M/T	1969
AB	4-153 with T/D, P/G	1969
AM	6-230 with M/T	1969
AN	6-230 with P/G, T/D	1969
AO	6-230 with T/H	1969
AP	6-230 with A/C	1969
AR	6-230 with T/H, A/C	1969
AQ	6-230 with T/D, P/G, A/C	1969
BB	6-250 with P/G, T/D	1969
BC	6-250 with P/G, T/D, A/C	1969
BD	6-250 with T/H	1969
BE	6-250 with M/T	1969
BF	6-250 with A/C	1969
BH	6-250 with T/H, A/C	1969
CAA	6-250 with M/T	1971
CAB	6-250 with P/G, T/D	1971
CAL	6-250 with M/T, Taxi	1972
CAY	8-307 with T/H	1972
CAZ	8-307 with M/T, E.E.C.	1972
CBA	6-250 with M/T, E.E.C.	1972
CBG	6-250 with M/T	1972
CBJ	6-250 with P/G, T/D	1972
CBK	6-250 with P/G, Taxi	1972
CBL	6-250 with P/G, AIR	1972
CBM	6-250 with M/T, AIR	1972
CCA	6-250 with P/G	1973
CCB	6-250 with P/G, E.E.C.	1973
CCC	6-250 with M/T	1973
CCD	6-250 with M/T, E.E.C.	1973
CCR	6-250 with M/T	1974
CCW	6-250 with T/H, E.E.C.	1974
CCX	6-250 with T/H	1974
CCK	6-250	1974
CCA	8-307 with M/T	1971
CCA	4-153 with M/T	1970
CCB	4-153 with T/D	1970
CCC	8-307 with P/G	1971
CCD	6-230 with T/D	1970
CCM	6-250 with P/G, police & taxi	1970
CCG	6-250 with M/T	1970
CCK	6-250 with T/H, police & taxi	1970
CCL	6-250 with M/T, police & taxi	1970
CCS	6-250	1975
CCT	6-250	1975
CCU	6-250	1975
CCW	6-250	1975
CCZ	6-250 with M/T	1970
CDA	8-350 with M/T, E.E.C.	1972
CDD	8-350 with T/H, E.E.C.	1972
CDG	8-350 with P/G, E.E.C.	1972
CGB	8-350 with P/G	1972
CGC	8-262	1975
CGD	8-262	1975
CGF	8-262	1975
CGH	8-262	1975
CHW	8-350	1975
CJF	6-250	1975
CJL	6-250	1975
CJM	6-250	1975
CJR	6-250	1975
CJS	6-250	1975
CJT	6-250	1975
CJU	6-250	1975
CJW	6-250	1975
CJX	6-250	1975
CJZ	6-250	1975
CKA	8-350 with M/T, 165 H.P.	1972
CKB	8-350 with T/H, 165 H.P.	1972
CKD	8-350 with T/H	1972
CKK	8-350	1972
CKA	8-350 with M/T, 145 H.P.	1973
CKU	8-350 with T/H, 175 H.P.	1973
CKB	8-350 with T/H, 175 H.P.	1973
CKW	8-350 with T/H, 145 H.P.	1973
CKC	8-350 with M/T, E.E.C., 145 H.P.	1973
CKK	8-350 with T/H, E.E.C., 145 H.P.	1973
CKD	8-350 with T/H, E.E.C., 175 H.P.	1973
CKH	8-350 with M/T, E.E.C., 175 H.P.	1973
CMC	8-350 with M/T	1974
CMA	8-350 with T/H	1974
CKB	8-350 with M/T, 185 H.P.	1974
CKH	8-350 with 4BC, M/T	1974
CKH	8-350 with M/T, E.E.C., 185 H.P.	1974
CKU	8-350 with T/H, 185 H.P.	1974
CKD	8-350 with 4 BC, T/H, E.E.C.	1974
CGB	8-350 with P/G, 250 H.P.	1971
CGK	8-350 with M/T, 300 H.P.	1971
CGL	8-350 with T/H, 300 H.P.	1971
CKG	8-307 with M/T	1972
CKH	8-307 with P/G	1972
CHB	8-307 with M/T	1973
CHH	8-307 with T/H	1973
CHC	8-307 with T/H, E.E.C.	1973
CHD	8-307 with M/T, E.E.C.	1973
CKO	8-400 with M/T, 375 H.P.	1970
CKP	8-400 T/H, alum. heads, 375 H.P.	1970
CKQ	8-400 with HDC, 375 H.P.	1970
CKR	8-400 with M/T, 330 H.P.	1970
CKS	8-400 with HDC, 330 H.P.	1970
CKT	8-400 M/T, alum. heads, 375 H.P.	1970
CKU	8-400 HDC, alum. heads, 375 H.P.	1970
CMA	8-307 with P/G, E.E.C.	1972
CMD	8-350 with T/H, AIR	1972
CMF	8-350	1975
CMH	8-350	1975
CMU	8-350	1975
CNC	8-307 with M/T	1970
CND	8-307 with 4 sp. tr.	1970
CNE	8-307 with P/G	1970
CNF	8-307 with T/H	1970
CNI	8-350 with M/T, 250 H.P.	1970
CNJ	8-350 with M/T, 300 H.P.	1970
CNK	8-350 with P/G, 300 H.P.	1970
CNM	8-350 with P/G, 250 H.P.	1970
CNN	8-350 with T/H, 250 H.P.	1970
CPT	8-454 with T/H	1971
CPS	8-454 with M/T	1971
CRC	8-350	1975
CRE	8-350 with T/H, 300 H.P.	1970
CRF	6-250 with M/T	1970
CRK	8-350 with T/H, AIR	1972
CRL	8-350 with M/T, AIR	1972
CRX	8-350	1975
CTB	8-350 with M/T, 320 H.P.	1970
CTC	8-350 with T/H, 320 H.P.	1970
CTK	8-307 with T/H	1972
CTL	8-350 with T/H	1972
CTW	8-400 with T/H, 350 H.P.	1970
CTX	8-400 with M/T, 350 H.P.	1970
CTY	8-400 with T/H, 375 H.P.	1970
CTZ	8-400 with HDC, 350 H.P.	1970
CZF	8-262	1975
CZH	8-262	1975
CZJ	8-262	1975
CZK	8-262	1975
CZL	8-262	1975
CZM	8-262	1975
CZY	8-262	1975
CZZ	8-262	1975
DA	8-307 with M/T	1969
DC	8-307 with P/G	1969
DD	8-307 with T/H	1969
DE	8-307 with 4 sp. tr.	1969
HA	8-350 with M/T	1969
HB	8-350 with T/H	1969
HC	8-350 with 2 BC	1969
HD	8-350 with 2 BC, T/H	1969
HE	8-350 with P/G	1969
HF	8-350 with 2 BC, P/G	1969
HQ	8-350 with P/G	1969
HR	8-350 with P/G	1969
HS	8-350 with T/H	1969
JF	8-396 with HPE	1969
JH	8-396 with SHPE	1969
JI	8-396 with HPE, T/H	1969
JL	8-396 with SHPE, T/H	1969
JM	8-396 with T/H	1969
JU	8-396 with P/G	1969
KA	8-396 with SHPE	1969
KC	8-396 with SHPE	1969
KE	8-396 with M/T	1969

Continued

ENGINE IDENTIFICATION CODE—Continued

CORVETTE

CODE			CODE			CODE		
CHA	8-350	1975	CDH	8-350 with 4 sp. trs., E.E.C., 200 H.P.	1972	CTM	8-350 with T/H	1970
CHB	8-350	1975	CKX	8-350 with T/H 400, 200 H.P.	1972	CTN	8-350 with HPE	1970
CHC	8-350	1975	CDJ	8-350 with T/H 400, E.E.C., 200 H.P.	1972	CTO	8-350 with HPE, A/C	1970
CHR	8-350	1975				CTP	8-350 with HPE, T/I	1970
CHU	8-350	1975	CKY	8-350 with 4 sp. trs., 255 H.P.	1972	CTQ	8-350 with HPE, T/I, A/C	1970
CHZ	8-350	1975	CKZ	8-350 with H.D. 4 sp. trs., 255 H.P.	1972	CTR	8-350 with SHPE	1970
CKZ	8-350 with M/T	1974	CRT	8-350 with 4 sp. trs., A.I.R., 255 H.P.	1972	CTU	8-350 with SHPE, T/I	1970
CLB	8-350 with M/T, E.E.C.	1974	CRS	8-350 with T/H 400, A.I.R., 255 H.P.	1972	CTV	8-350 with SHPE, T/I, 4 sp. tr.	1970
CLR	8-350 with M/T, 245 H.P.	1974				CZL	8-454 with H/D	1970
CLA	8-350 with T/H	1974	CPH	8-454 with 4 sp. trs.	1972	CZN	8-454 with H/D, T/H	1970
CLC	8-350 with T/H, E.E.C.	1974	CPJ	8-454 with T/H-400	1972	CZU	8-454 with HPE	1970
CLD	8-350 with T/H, 245 H.P.	1974	CSR	8-454 with A.I.R.	1972	HW	8-350 with HPE	1969
CKZ	8-350 with M/T, 175 H.P.	1973	CSS	8-454 with A.I.R.	1972	HX	8-350 with HPE, A/C	1969
CLA	8-350 with T/H	1973	CGS	8-350 with M/T, 300 H.P.	1971	HY	8-350 with M/T	1969
CLR	8-350 with M/T, 250 H.P.	1973	CGT	8-350 with T/H, 270 H.P.	1971	HZ	8-350 with T/H	1969
CLB	8-350 with M/T, E.E.C., 175 H.P.	1973	CGW	4-454 with 4 BC HPE, T/H	1970	LL	8-427 with HPE, T/H	1969
CLC	8-350 with T/H, E.E.C., 175 H.P.	1973	CGW	8-350 with M/T, 350 H.P.	1971	LM	8-427 with HPE	1969
CLS	8-350 with M/T, E.E.C., 250 H.P.	1973	CGX	8-350 with M/T, 350 H.P.	1971	LN	8-427 with HPE, T/H, 3 Carbs.	1969
CLD	8-350 with T/H, 250 H.P.	1973	CGY	8-350 with M/T, 330 H.P.	1971	LO	8-427 with HD	1969
CLH	8-350 with T/H, E.E.C., 250 H.P.	1973	CGZ	8-350 with M/T, 330 H.P.	1971	LP	8-427 with A/H	1969
CWM	8-454 with M/T	1974	CPH	8-454 with M/T, 365 H.P.	1971	LQ	8-427 with HPE, 3 Carbs.	1969
CWR	8-454 with T/H	1974	CPJ	8-454 with T/H, 365 H.P.	1971	LR	8-427 with SHPE, 3 Carbs.	1969
CWS	8-454 with T/H, E.E.C.	1974	CPW	8-454 with M/T, 425 H.P.	1971	LT	8-427 with SHPE, 3 Carbs., HDC	1969
CWS	8-454 with T/H, E.E.C.	1973	CPX	8-454 with T/H, 425 H.P.	1971	LU	8-427 with A/H, HDC	1969
CWT	8-454 with M/T, E.E.C.	1973	CPK	8-454 with M/T, 460 H.P.	1970	LV	8-427 with T/H	1969
CWM	8-454 with M/T	1973	CPL	8-454 with T/H, 460 H.P.	1971	LW	8-427 with A/H, T/H	1969
CWR	8-454 with T/H	1973	CRI	8-454 with HPE, T/I	1970	LX	8-427 with SHPE, 3 Carbs, T/H	1969
CKW	8-350 with 4 sp. trs., 200 H.P.	1972	CTL	8-350 with M/T	1970			

NOTES

A/C: Air Conditioned
A/H: Aluminum Heads
A/S: Air suspension
AIR: Air injection reactor
A/T: Automatic transmission
4BC: Four barrel carburetor
E.E.C.: Exhaust emission control.
F/I: Fuel injection

H/D: Heavy Duty
HDC: Heavy duty clutch
HPE: High performance engine
H/L: Hydraulic lifters
M/T: Manual transmission
O/D: Overdrive
P/G: Powerglide

P/S: Power steering
P/V: Positive crankcase ventilation
SHPE: Special high perf. engine
S.S.: Super Sport
T/D: Torque Drive
T/H: Turbo Hydramatic
T/I: Transistor ignition

CHEVROLET—Exc. Monza 2+2 & Vega

GRILLE IDENTIFICATION

1969 Camaro

1969 Camaro S. S.

1969 Chevy Nova

1969 Chevelle

1969 Chevelle S. S.

1969 Chevrolet

1969 Corvette

1970 Chevrolet

1970-72 Chevy Nova

1970-71 Camaro

1970-71 Camaro S. S.

1970 Monte Carlo

1970 Chevelle

1970 Chevelle S. S.

1970-72 Corvette

1971 Chevelle

1971 Chevelle S. S.

1971 Monte Carlo

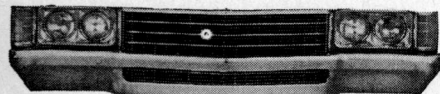
1971 Bel Air & Impala

1971 Caprice & Estate Wagon

1972 Camaro

1972 Chevelle

1972 Monte Carlo

1972 Bel Air & Impala

1972 Caprice & Estate Wagon

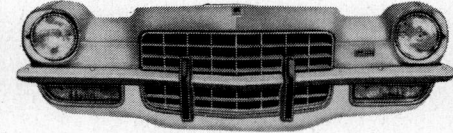
1973 Camaro

1973 Chevy Nova

GRILLE IDENTIFICATION—Continued

1973 Chevelle Malibu

1973 Chevelle Laguna

1973 Monte Carlo

1973 Bel Air & Impala

1973 Caprice & Estate Wagon

1973-74 Corvette

1974 Camaro

1974 Chevelle Malibu

1974 Chevelle Laguna

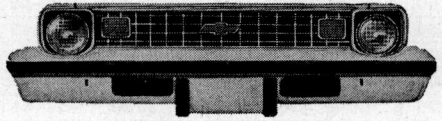
1974 Chevy Nova

1974 Monte Carlo

1974 Bel Air & Impala

1974 Caprice & Estate Wagon

1975 Camaro

1975 Chevelle

1975 Nova

1975 Nova Custom

1975 Monte Carlo

1975 Bel Air & Impala

1975 Caprice & Estate Wagon

1975 Corvette

CHEVROLET—Exc. Monza 2+2 & Vega

GENERAL ENGINE SPECIFICATIONS

Year	Engine	Car-buretor	Bore and Stroke	Piston Dis-place-ment, Cubic Inches	Com-pres-sion Ratio	Maximum Brake H.P. @ R.P.M.	Maximum Torque Lbs. Ft. @ R.P.M.	Normal Oil Pressure Pounds
1969	90 Horsepower.............4-153	1 Barrel	3.875 x 3.25	153	8.50	90 @ 4000	152 @ 2400	30–45
	140 Horsepower.............6-230	1 Barrel	3.875 x 3.25	230	8.50	140 @ 4400	220 @ 1600	30–45
	155 Horsepower.............6-250	1 Barrel	3.875 x 3.53	250	8.50	155 @ 4200	235 @ 1600	30–45
	290 Horsepower.............V8-302	4 Barrel	4.000 x 3.00	302	11.00	290 @ 5800	290 @ 4200	30–45
	200 Horsepower.............V8-307	2 Barrel	3.875 x 3.25	307	9.00	200 @ 4600	300 @ 2400	30–45
	210 Horsepower.............V8-327	2 Barrel	4.001 x 3.25	327	9.00	210 @ 4600	320 @ 2400	30–45
	235 Horsepower.............V8-327	2 Barrel	4.001 x 3.25	327	9.00	235 @ 4800	325 @ 2800	30–45
	255 Horsepower.............V8-350	4 Barrel	4.001 x 3.48	350	9.00	255 @ 4800	365 @ 3200	30–45
	300 Horsepower.............V8-350	4 Barrel	4.001 x 3.48	350	10.25	300 @ 4800	380 @ 3200	30–45
	350 Horsepower.............V8-350	4 Barrel	4.001 x 3.48	350	11.00	350 @ 5600	380 @ 3600	30–45
	370 Horsepower.............V8-350	4 Barrel	4.001 x 3.48	350	11.00	370 @ 5800	380 @ 4000	30–45
	265 Horsepower.............V8-396	2 Barrel	4.094 x 3.76	396	9.00	265 @ 4800	400 @ 2800	30–35
	325 Horsepower.............V8-396	4 Barrel	4.094 x 3.76	396	10.25	325 @ 4800	410 @ 3200	30–35
	350 Horsepower.............V8-396	4 Barrel	4.094 x 3.76	396	10.25	350 @ 5200	415 @ 3400	30–35
	375 Horsepower.............V8-396	4 Barrel	4.094 x 3.76	396	11.00	375 @ 5600	415 @ 3600	30–35
	335 Horsepower.............V8-427	4 Barrel	4.251 x 3.76	427	10.25	335 @ 4800	470 @ 3200	30–35
	390 Horsepower.............V8-427	4 Barrel	4.251 x 3.76	427	10.25	390 @ 5400	460 @ 3600	30–35
	400 Horsepower.............V8-427	4 Barrel	4.251 x 3.76	427	10.25	400 @ 5400	460 @ 3600	30–35
	425 Horsepower.............V8-427	4 Barrel	4.251 x 3.76	427	11.00	425 @ 5600	460 @ 4000	30–35
	430 Horsepower.............V8-427	4 Barrel	4.251 x 3.76	427	12.00	430 @ 5200	450 @ 4000	30–35
	435 Horsepower.............V8-427	3 Carbs.	4.251 x 3.76	427	11.00	435 @ 5800	460 @ 4000	30–35
1970	90 Horsepower.............4-153	1 Barrel	3.875 x 3.25	153	8.50	90 @ 4000	152 @ 2400	30–45
	140 Horsepower.............6-230	1 Barrel	3.875 x 3.25	230	8.50	140 @ 4400	220 @ 1600	30–45
	155 Horsepower.............6-250	1 Barrel	3.875 x 3.53	250	8.50	155 @ 4200	235 @ 1600	30–45
	200 Horsepower.............V8-307	2 Barrel	3.875 x 3.25	307	9.00	200 @ 4600	300 @ 2400	30–45
	250 Horsepower.............V8-350	2 Barrel	4.001 x 3.48	350	9.00	250 @ 4800	345 @ 2800	30–45
	300 Horsepower.............V8-350	4 Barrel	4.001 x 3.48	350	10.25	300 @ 4800	380 @ 3200	30–45
	350 Horsepower.............V8-350	4 Barrel	4.001 x 3.48	350	11.00	350 @ 5600	380 @ 3600	30–45
	360 Horsepower.............V8-350	4 Barrel	4.001 x 3.48	350	11.00	360 @ 6000	380 @ 4000	35–45
	370 Horsepower.............V8-350	4 Barrel	4.001 x 3.48	350	11.00	370 @ 6000	380 @ 4000	30–45
	350 Horsepower.............V8-396	4 Barrel	4.125 x 3.76	①	10.25	350 @ 5200	415 @ 3400	30–35
	375 Horsepower.............V8-396	4 Barrel	4.125 x 3.76	①	11.00	375 @ 5600	415 @ 3600	30–35
	265 Horsepower.............V8-400	2 Barrel	4.125 x 3.75	400	9.00	265 @ 4400	400 @ 2400	30–35
	330 Horsepower.............V8-400	4 Barrel	4.125 x 3.75	400	10.25	330 @ 4800	410 @ 3200	30–35
	345 Horsepower.............V8-454	4 Barrel	4.251 x 4.00	454	10.25	345 @ 4400	500 @ 3000	30–35
	360 Horsepower.............V8-454	4 Barrel	4.251 x 4.00	454	10.25	360 @ 4400	500 @ 3200	30–35
	390 Horsepower.............V8-454	4 Barrel	4.251 x 4.00	454	10.25	390 @ 4800	500 @ 3400	30–35
	450 Horsepower.............V8-454	4 Barrel	4.251 x 4.00	454	11.25	450 @ 5600	500 @ 3600	30–35
	460 Horsepower.............V8-454	4 Barrel	4.251 x 4.00	454	11.25	460 @ 5600	490 @ 3000	30–35
1971	145 Horsepower.............6-250	1 Barrel	3.875 x 3.53	250	8.50	145 @ 4200	230 @ 1600	30–45
	200 Horsepower.............V8-307	2 Barrel	3.875 x 3.25	307	8.50	200 @ 4600	300 @ 2400	30–45
	245 Horsepower.............V8-350	2 Barrel	4.00 x 3.48	350	8.50	245 @ 4800	350 @ 2800	35–45
	270 Horsepower.............V8-350	4 Barrel	4.00 x 3.48	350	8.50	270 @ 4800	360 @ 3200	35–45
	330 Horsepower.............V8-350	4 Barrel	4.00 x 3.48	350	9.0	330 @ 5600	360 @ 4000	35–45
	255 Horsepower.............V8-400	2 Barrel	4.125 x 3.76	400	8.50	255 @ 4400	390 @ 2400	35–45
	300 Horsepower.............V8-396	4 Barrel	4.126 x 3.76	①	8.50	300 @ 4800	400 @ 3200	35–45
	365 Horsepower.............V8-454	4 Barrel	4.251 x 4.00	454	8.50	365 @ 4800	465 @ 3200	35–45
	425 Horsepower.............V8-454	4 Barrel	4.251 x 4.00	454	9.0	425 @ 5600	475 @ 4000	35–45
1972	110 Horsepower②.............6-250	1 Barrel	3.875 x 3.53	250	8.50	110 @ 3800	185 @ 1600	30–45
	130 Horsepower②.............V8-307	2 Barrel	3.875 x 3.25	307	8.50	130 @ 4000	230 @ 2400	30–45
	165 Horsepower②.............V8-350	2 Barrel	4.00 x 3.48	350	8.50	165 @ 4000	280 @ 2400	35–45
	175 Horsepower②.............V8-350	4 Barrel	4.00 x 3.48	350	8.50	175 @ 4000	280 @ 2400	35–45
	200 Horsepower②.............V8-350	4 Barrel	4.00 x 3.48	350	8.50	200 @ 4400	300 @ 2800	35–45
	255 Horsepower②.............V8-350	4 Barrel	4.00 x 3.48	350	9.0	255 @ 5600	280 @ 4000	35–45
	170 Horsepower②.............V8-400	2 Barrel	4.126 x 3.75	400	8.50	170 @ 3400	325 @ 2000	35–45

GENERAL ENGINE SPECIFICATIONS—Continued

Year	Engine	Car-buretor	Bore and Stroke	Piston Displacement, Cubic Inches	Compression Ratio	Maximum Brake H.P. @ R.P.M.	Maximum Torque Lbs. Ft. @ R.P.M.	Normal Oil Pressure Pounds
1972	210 Horsepower②............V8-402	4 Barrel	4.126 x 3.76	402	8.50	210 @ 4400	320 @ 2400	35—45
	240 Horsepower②............V8-402	4 Barrel	4.126 x 3.76	402	8.50	240 @ 4400	345 @ 3200	35—45
	230 Horsepower②............V8-454	4 Barrel	4.251 x 4.00	454	8.50	230 @ 4000	360 @ 3200	35—45
	270 Horsepower②............V8-454	4 Barrel	4.251 x 4.00	454	8.50	270 @ 4000	390 @ 3200	35—45
1973	100 Horsepower②..............6-250	1 Barrel	3.875 x 3.53	250	8.25	100 @ 3800	175 @ 1600	40
	115 Horsepower②............V8-307	2 Barrel	3.875 x 3.25	307	8.50	115 @ 4000	205 @ 2000	40
	145 Horsepower②............V8-350	2 Barrel	4.00 x 3.48	350	8.50	145 @ 4000	255 @ 2400	40
	175 Horsepower②............V8-350	4 Barrel	4.00 x 3.48	350	8.50	175 @ 4000	270 @ 2400	40
	190 Horsepower②............V8-350	4 Barrel	4.00 x 3.48	350	8.50	190 @ 4400	270 @ 2800	40
	245 Horsepower②............V8-350	4 Barrel	4.00 x 3.48	350	9.0	245 @ 5200	280 @ 4000	40
	250 Horsepower②............V8-350	4 Barrel	4.00 x 3.48	350	9.0	250 @ 5200	285 @ 4000	40
	150 Horsepower②............V8-400	2 Barrel	4.126 x 3.75	400	8.50	150 @ 3200	295 @ 2000	40
	215 Horsepower②............V8-454	4 Barrel	4.251 x 4.00	454	8.50	215 @ 4000	345 @ 2400	40
	245 Horsepower②............V8-454	4 Barrel	4.251 x 4.00	454	8.50	245 @ 4000	375 @ 2800	40
	275 Horsepower②............V8-454	4 Barrel	4.251 x 4.00	454	8.50	275 @ 4000	395 @ 2800	40
1974	100 Horsepower②..............6-250	1 Barrel	3.875 x 3.53	250	8.25	100 @ 3600	175 @ 1800	40
	145 Horsepower②............V8-350	2 Barrel	4.00 x 3.48	350	8.50	145 @ 3600	250 @ 2200	40
	160 Horsepower②............V8-350	4 Barrel	4.00 x 3.48	350	8.50	160 @ 3800	250 @ 2400	40
	185 Horsepower②............V8-350	4 Barrel	4.00 x 3.48	350	8.50	185 @ 4000	270 @ 2600	40
	195 Horsepower②............V8-350	4 Barrel	4.00 x 3.48	350	8.50	195 @ 4400	275 @ 2800	40
	245 Horsepower②............V8-350	4 Barrel	4.00 x 3.48	350	9.0	245 @ 5200	280 @ 4000	40
	250 Horsepower②............V8-350	4 Barrel	4.00 x 3.48	350	9.0	250 @ 5200	285 @ 4000	40
	150 Horsepower②............V8-400	2 Barrel	4.125 x 3.75	400	8.50	150 @ 3200	295 @ 2000	40
	180 Horsepower②............V8-400	4 Barrel	4.125 x 3.75	400	8.50	180 @ 3800	290 @ 2400	40
	235 Horsepower②............V8-454	4 Barrel	4.250 x 4.00	454	8.50	235 @ 4000	360 @ 2800	45
	270 Horsepower②............V8-454	4 Barrel	4.250 x 4.00	454	8.50	270 @ 4400	380 @ 2800	45
1975	105 Horsepower②..............6-250	1 Barrel	3.875 x 3.53	250	8.25	105 @ 3800	185 @ 1200	36—41
	110 Horsepower②............V8-262	2 Barrel	3.671 x 3.10	262	8.5	110 @ 3600	200 @ 2000	32—40
	145 Horsepower②............V8-350	2 Barrel	4.00 x 3.48	350	8.5	145 @ 3800	250 @ 2200	32—40
	155 Horsepower②............V8-350	4 Barrel	4.00 x 3.48	350	8.5	155 @ 3800	250 @ 2400	32—40
	165 Horsepower②............V8-350	4 Barrel	4.00 x 3.48	350	8.5	165 @ 3800	255 @ 2400	32—40
	205 Horsepower②............V8-350	4 Barrel	4.00 x 3.48	350	9.0	205 @ 4800	255 @ 3600	32—40
	175 Horsepower②............V8-400	4 Barrel	4.125 x 3.75	400	8.5	175 @ 3600	305 @ 2000	42—46
	215 Horsepower②............V8-454	4 Barrel	4.251 x 4.00	454	8.15	215 @ 4000	350 @ 2400	42—46

①—Marketed as 396 cu. in. but actually 402 cu. in.   ②—Ratings are net—As installed in the vehicle.

CHEVROLET—Exc. Monza 2+2 & Vega

TUNE UP SPECIFICATIONS

OLD CAR SPECIFICATIONS: For 1946-68 Tune Up Specifications see main index.

★When using a timing light, disconnect vacuum hose or tube at distributor and plug opening in hose or tube so idle speed will not be affected.

●When checking compression, lowest cylinder must be within 80 percent of highest.

▲Before removing wires from distributor cap, determine location of the No. 1 wire in cap, as distributor position may have been altered from that shown at the end of this chart.

Year	Spark Plug		Distributor		Ignition Timing★			Carb. Adjustments					
	Type	Gap Inch	Point Gap Inch	Dwell Angle Deg.	Firing Order Fig. ▲	Timing BTDC ①	Mark Fig.	Hot Idle Speed③		Air Fuel Ratio		Idle "CO" %	
								Std. Trans.	Auto. Trans. ②	Std. Trans.	Auto. Trans.	Std. Trans.	Auto. Trans.
CAMARO													
1969													
6-230, 250⑱	R46N	.035	④	31–34	D	TDC	A	700⑱	—	—	—	—	—
6-230, 250⑲	R46N	.035	④	31–34	D	4°	A	—	550D⑱	—	—	—	—
8-302	R43	.035	④	28–32	E	4°	A	900⑱	—	—	—	—	—
8-307	R45S	.035	④	28–32	E	2°	A	700⑱	600D⑱	—	—	—	—
8-327, 210 H.P.⑱	R45S	.035	④	28–32	E	2° ATC	A	700⑱	—	—	—	—	—
8-327, 210 H.P.⑲	R45S	.035	④	28–32	E	2°	A	—	600D⑱	—	—	—	—
8-350, 255 H.P.⑱	R44	.035	④	28–32	E	TDC	A	700⑱	—	—	—	—	—
8-350, 255 H.P.⑲	R44	.035	④	28–32	E	4°	A	—	600D⑱	—	—	—	—
8-350, 300 H.P.⑱	R44	.035	④	28–32	E	TDC	A	700⑱	—	—	—	—	—
8-350, 300 H.P.⑲	R44	.035	④	28–32	E	4°	A	—	600D⑱	—	—	—	—
8-396, 325 H.P.	R44N	.035	④	28–32	E	4°	A	800⑱	600D⑱	—	—	—	—
8-396, 350 H.P.⑱	R43N	.035	④	28–32	E	TDC	A	800⑱	—	—	—	—	—
8-396, 350 H.P.⑲	R43N	.035	④	28–32	E	4°	A	—	600D⑱	—	—	—	—
8-396, 375 H.P.	R43N	.035	④	28–32	E	4°	A	750⑱	700D⑱	—	—	—	—
1970													
6-250 Std. Tr.	R46T	.035	④	31–34	D	TDC	A	750	—	—	—	—	—
6-250 Auto. Tr.	R46T	.035	④	31–34	D	4°	A	—	600D/400	—	—	—	—
8-307 Std. Tr.	R43	.035	④	29–31	E	2°	A	700	—	—	—	—	—
8-307 Auto. Tr.	R43	.035	④	29–31	E	8°	A	—	600D/450	—	—	—	—
8-350, 250 H.P.⑱	R44	.035	④	29–31	E	TDC	A	750	—	—	—	—	—
8-350, 250 H.P.⑲	R44	.035	④	29–31	E	4°	A	—	600D/450	—	—	—	—
8-350, 300 H.P.⑱	R44	.035	④	29–31	E	TDC	A	700	—	—	—	—	—
8-350, 300 H.P.⑲	R44	.035	④	29–31	E	4°	A	—	600D	—	—	—	—
8-350, 360 H.P.	R43	.035	④	29–31	E	8°	A	800	750D/500	—	—	—	—
8-396, 350 H.P.⑱㉑	R44T	.035	④	29–31	E	TDC	A	700	—	—	—	—	—
8-396, 350 H.P.⑲㉑	R44T	.035	④	29–31	E	4°	A	—	600D	—	—	—	—
8-396, 375 H.P.㉑	R43T	.035	④	29–31	E	4°	A	750	700D	—	—	—	—
8-454, 450 H.P.	R43T	.035	④	29–31	E	4°	A	750	700D	—	—	—	—
1971													
8-250	R46TS	.035	④	31–34	D	4°	B	550	550D	—	—	1.0	1.0
6-307 Std. Tr.	R45TS	.035	④	29–31	E	4°	B	550	—	—	—	0.5	—
8-307 Auto. Tr.	R45TS	.035	④	29–31	E	8°	B	—	550D	—	—	—	0.5
8-350, 245 H.P.⑱	R45TS	.035	④	29–31	E	2°	B	600	—	—	—	0.5	—
8-350, 245 H.P.⑲	R45TS	.035	④	29–31	E	6°	B	—	550D	—	—	—	0.5
8-350, 270 H.P.⑱	R44TS	.035	④	29–31	E	4°	B	600	—	—	—	1.0	—
8-350, 270 H.P.⑲	R44TS	.035	④	29–31	E	8°	B	—	550D	—	—	—	0.5
8-350, 330 H.P.⑱	R43TS	.035	④	29–31	E	8°	B	700	—	—	—	—	—
8-350, 330 H.P.⑲	R43TS	.035	④	29–31	E	12°	B	—	700D	—	—	—	—
8-396, 300 H.P.	R44TS	.035	④	29–31	E	8°	B	600	600D	—	—	1.0	1.0

Continued

TUNE UP SPECIFICATIONS—Continued

OLD CAR SPECIFICATIONS: For 1946-68 Tune Up Specifications see main index.

★When using a timing light, disconnect vacuum hose or tube at distributor and plug opening in hose or tube so idle speed will not be affected.

●When checking compression, lowest cylinder must be within 80 percent of highest.

▲Before removing wires from distributor cap, determine location of the No. 1 wire in cap, as distributor position may have been altered from that shown at the end of this chart.

Year	Spark Plug		Distributor		Ignition Timing★			Carb. Adjustments					
	Type	Gap Inch	Point Gap Inch	Dwell Angle Deg.	Firing Order Fig. ▲	Timing BTDC ①	Mark Fig.	Hot Idle Speed⑤		Air Fuel Ratio		Idle "CO" %	
								Std. Trans.	Auto. Trans. ②	Std. Trans.	Auto. Trans.	Std. Trans.	Auto. Trans.
CAMARO—Continued													
1972													
6-250	R46T	.035	④	31–34	D	4°	B	700	600D	—	—	—	—
8-307 Std. Tr.	R44T	.035	④	29–31	E	4°	B	900	—	—	—	—	—
8-307 Auto. Tr.	R44T	.035	④	29–31	E	8°	B	—	600D	—	—	—	—
8-350, 165 H.P.	R44T	.035	④	29–31	E	6°	B	900	600D	—	—	—	—
8-350, 200 H.P.⑱	R44T	.035	④	29–31	E	4°	B	800	—	—	—	—	—
8-350, 200 H.P.⑲	R44T	.035	④	29–31	E	8°	B	—	600D	—	—	—	—
8-350, 255 H.P.⑱	R44T	.035	④	29–31	E	4°	B	900	—	—	—	—	—
8-350, 255 H.P.⑲	R44T	.035	④	29–31	E	8°	B	—	700D	—	—	—	—
8-402	R44T	.035	④	29–31	E	8°	B	750	600D	—	—	—	—
1973													
6-250	R46T	.035	④	31–34	D	6°	B	700	600D	—	—	—	—
8-307 Std. Tr.	R44T	.035	④	29–31	E	4°	B	900	—	—	—	—	—
8-307 Auto. Tr.	R44T	.035	④	29–31	E	8°	B	—	600D	—	—	—	—
8-350, 145 H.P.	R44T	.035	④	29–31	E	8°	B	900	600D	—	—	—	—
8-350, 175 H.P.⑱	R44T	.035	④	29–31	E	8°	B	900	—	—	—	—	—
8-350, 175 H.P.⑲	R44T	.035	④	29–31	E	12°	B	—	600D	—	—	—	—
8-350, 245 H.P.	R44T	.035	④	29–31	E	8°	B	900	700D	—	—	—	—
1974													
6-250⑱	R46T	.035	④	31–34	D	8°	B	850	—	—	—	.3	.3
6-250⑲	R46T	.035	④	31–34	D	6°	B	—	600D	—	—	.3	.3
8-350, 145 H.P.⑱	R44T	.035	④	29–31	E	TDC	B	900	—	—	—	.5	.5
8-350, 145 H.P.⑲	R44T	.035	④	29–31	E	8°	B	—	600D	—	—	.5	.5
8-350, 160 H.P.⑱	R44T	.035	④	29–31	E	4°	B	900	—	—	—	.5	.5
8-350, 160 H.P.⑲	R44T	.035	④	29–31	E	8°	B	—	600D	—	—	.5	.5
8-350, 185 H.P.⑱	R44T	.035	④	29–31	E	8°⑥	B	900	—	—	—	.5	.5
8-350, 185 H.P.⑲	R44T	.035	④	29–31	E	8°	B	—	600D	—	—	.5	.5
8-350, 245 H.P.	R44T	.035	④	29–31	E	8°	B	900	700D	—	—	.5	.5
1975													
6-250	R46TX	.060	—	—	⑮	8°	B	850	600D	—	—	—	—
6-250⑦	R46TX	.060	—	—	⑮	10°	B	850	550D⑨	—	—	—	—
8-350 2 BBl. Carb.	R44TX	.060	—	—	㉒	6°	B	800	600D	—	—	—	—
8-350⑱	R44TX	.060	—	—	㉒	6°⑥	B	800	—	—	—	—	—
8-350⑲	R44TX	.060	—	—	㉒	8°⑧	B	—	600D	—	—	—	—

Continued

TUNE UP SPECIFICATIONS—Continued

OLD CAR SPECIFICATIONS: For 1946-68 Tune Up Specifications see main index.

★When using a timing light, disconnect vacuum hose or tube at distributor and plug opening in hose or tube so idle speed will not be affected.

●When checking compression, lowest cylinder must be within 80 percent of highest.

▲Before removing wires from distributor cap, determine location of the No. 1 wire in cap, as distributor position may have been altered from that shown at the end of this chart.

Year	Spark Plug		Distributor		Ignition Timing★			Carb. Adjustments					
	Type	Gap Inch	Point Gap Inch	Dwell Angle Deg.	Firing Order Fig. ▲	Timing BTDC ①	Mark Fig.	Hot Idle Speed③		Air Fuel Ratio		Idle "CO" %	
								Std. Trans.	Auto. Trans. ②	Std. Trans.	Auto. Trans.	Std. Trans.	Auto. Trans.
CHEVELLE & MONTE CARLO													
1969													
6-230, 250⑱	R46N	.035	④	31–34	D	TDC	A	700⑯	—	—	—	—	—
6-230, 250⑲	R46N	.035	④	31–34	D	4°	A	—	550D⑯	—	—	—	—
8-307	R45S	.035	④	28–32	E	2°	A	700⑯	600D⑱	—	—	—	—
8-350, 255 H.P.⑱	R44	.035	④	28–32	E	TDC	A	700⑱	—	—	—	—	—
8-350, 255 H.P.⑲	R44	.035	④	28–32	E	4°	A	—	600D⑯	—	—	—	—
8-350, 300 H.P.⑱	R44	.035	④	28–32	E	TDC	A	700⑯	—	—	—	—	—
8-350, 300 H.P.⑲	R44	.035	④	28–32	E	4°	A	—	600D⑯	—	—	—	—
8-396, 325 H.P.	R44N	.035	④	28–32	E	4°	A	800⑯	600D⑭	—	—	—	—
8-396, 350 H.P.⑱	R43N	.035	④	28–32	E	TDC	A	800⑯	—	—	—	—	—
8-396, 350 H.P.⑲	R43N	.035	④	28–32	E	4°	A	—	600D⑯	—	—	—	—
8-396, 375 H.P.	R43N	.035	④	28–32	E	4°	A	750⑯	750D⑱	—	—	—	—
1970													
6-250⑱	R46T	.035	④	31–34	D	TDC	A	750	—	—	—	—	—
6-250⑲	R46T	.035	④	31–34	D	4°	A	—	600D/400	—	—	—	—
8-307⑱	R43	.035	④	28–32	E	2°	A	700	—	—	—	—	—
8-307⑲	R43	.035	④	28–32	E	8°	A	—	600D/450	—	—	—	—
8-350⑱	R44	.035	④	28–32	E	TDC	A	700	—	—	—	—	—
8-350⑲	R44	.035	④	28–32	E	4°	A	—	600D	—	—	—	—
8-400, 265 H.P.⑱	R44	.035	④	28–32	E	4°	A	700	—	—	—	—	—
8-400, 265 H.P.⑲	R44	.035	④	28–32	E	8°	A	—	600D	—	—	—	—
8-400, 330 H.P.	R44T	.035	④	28–32	E	4°	A	700	600D	—	—	—	—
8-396, 350 H.P.⑱	R44T	.035	④	28–32	E	TDC	A	700	—	—	—	—	—
8-396, 350 H.P.⑲	R44T	.035	④	28–32	E	4°	A	—	600D	—	—	—	—
8-396, 375 H.P.	R43T	.035	④	28–32	E	4°	A	750	700D	—	—	—	—
8-454, 360 H.P.	R43T	.035	④	28–32	E	6°	A	700	600	—	—	—	—
8-454, 390 H.P.	R43T	.035	④	28–32	E	6°	A	700	600D	—	—	—	—
8-454, 450 H.P.	R43T	.035	④	28–32	E	4°	A	700	700D	—	—	—	—
1971													
6-250	R46TS	.035	④	31–34	D	4°	B	550	500D	—	—	1.0	1.0
8-307⑱	R45TS	.035	④	29–31	E	4°	B	550	—	—	—	0.5	
8-307⑲	R45TS	.035	④	29–31	E	8°	B	—	500D	—	—	—	0.5
8-350, 245 H.P.⑱	R45TS	.035	④	29–31	E	2°	B	600	—	—	—	0.5	
8-350, 245 H.P.⑲	R45TS	.035	④	29–31	E	6°	B	—	600D	—	—	—	0.5
8-350, 270 H.P.⑱	R44TS	.035	④	29–31	E	4°	B	600	—	—	—	1.0	—
8-350, 270 H.P.⑲	R44TS	.035	④	29–31	E	8°	B	—	600D	—	—	—	0.5
8-400	R44TS	.035	④	29–31	E	8°	B	600	600D	—	—	0.5	0.5
8-454, 365 H.P.	R43TS	.035	④	29–31	E	8°	B	600	600D	—	—	1.0	1.0
8-454, 425 H.P.⑱	R44TS	.035	④	29–31	E	8°	B	700	—	—	—	—	—
8-454, 425 H.P.⑲	R44TS	.035	④	29–31	E	12°	B	—	700D	—	—	—	—

Continued

TUNE UP SPECIFICATIONS—Continued

OLD CAR SPECIFICATIONS: For 1946-68 Tune Up Specifications see main index.

★When using a timing light, disconnect vacuum hose or tube at distributor and plug opening in hose or tube so idle speed will not be affected.

●When checking compression, lowest cylinder must be within 80 percent of highest.

▲Before removing wires from distributor cap, determine location of the No. 1 wire in cap, as distributor position may have been altered from that shown at the end of this chart.

| Year | Spark Plug | | Distributor | | Ignition Timing★ | | | Carb. Adjustments | | | | | |
| | Type | Gap Inch | Point Gap Inch | Dwell Angle Deg. | Firing Order Fig. ▲ | Timing BTDC ① | Mark Fig. | Hot Idle Speed③ | | Air Fuel Ratio | | Idle "CO" % | |
								Std. Trans.	Auto. Trans. ②	Std. Trans.	Auto. Trans.	Std. Trans.	Auto. Trans.
CHEVELLE & MONTE CARLO—Continued													
1972													
6-250	R46T	.035	④	31–34	D	4°	B	700	600D	—	—	—	—
8-307 Std. Tr.	R44T	.035	④	29–31	E	4°	B	900	—	—	—	—	—
8-307 Auto. Tr.	R44T	.035	④	29–31	E	8°	B	—	600D	—	—	—	—
8-350, 165 H.P.	R44T	.035	④	29–31	E	6°	B	900	600D	—	—	—	—
8-350, 175 H.P.⑱	R44T	.035	④	29–31	E	4°	B	800	—	—	—	—	—
8-350, 175 H.P.⑲	R44T	.035	④	29–31	E	8°	B	—	600D	—	—	—	—
8-402	R44T	.035	④	29–31	E	8°	B	750	600D	—	—	—	—
8-454	R44T	.035	④	29–31	E	8°	B	750	600D	—	—	—	—
1973													
6-250	R46T	.035	④	31–34	D	6°	B	700	600D	—	—	—	—
8-307⑱	R44T	.035	④	29–31	E	4°	B	900	—	—	—	—	—
8-307⑲	R44T	.035	④	29–31	E	8°	B	—	600D	—	—	—	—
8-350, 145 H.P.	R44T	.035	④	29–31	E	8°	B	900	600D	—	—	—	—
8-350, 175 H.P.⑱	R44T	.035	④	29–31	E	8°	B	900	—	—	—	—	—
8-350, 175 H.P.⑲	R44T	.035	④	29–31	E	12°	B	—	600D	—	—	—	—
8-454, 245 H.P.	R44T	.035	④	29–31	E	10°	B	900	600D	—	—	—	—
1974													
6-250⑱	R46T	.035	④	31–34	D	8°	B	850	—	—	—	.3	.3
6-250⑲	R46T	.035	④	31–34	D	6°	B	—	600D	—	—	.3	.3
8-350, 145 H.P.⑱	R44T	.035	④	29–31	E	TDC	B	900	—	—	—	.5	.5
8-350, 145 H.P.⑲	R44T	.035	④	29–31	E	8°	B	—	600D	—	—	.5	.5
8-350, 160 H.P.⑱	R44T	.035	④	29–31	E	4°	B	900	—	—	—	.5	.5
8-350, 160 H.P.⑲	R44T	.035	④	29–31	E	⑦	B	—	600D	—	—	.5	.5
8-350, 185 H.P.⑱	R44T	.035	④	29–31	E	8°⑥	B	900	—	—	—	.5	.5
8-350, 185 H.P.⑲	R44T	.035	④	29–31	E	8°	B	—	600D	—	—	.5	.5
8-400	R44T	.035	④	29–31	E	8°	B	—	600D	—	—	.5	.5
8-454	R44T	.035	④	29–31	E	10°	B	800	600D	—	—	.5	.5
1975													
6-250	R46TX	.060	—	—	⑮	8°	B	850	600D	—	—	—	—
6-250⑦	R46TX	.060	—	—	⑮	10°	B	850	550D⑨	—	—	—	—
8-350 2 BBl. Carb.	R44TX	.060	—	—	㉒	6°	B	800	600D	—	—	—	—
8-350⑱	R44TX	.060	—	—	㉒	6°⑥	B	800	—	—	—	—	—
8-350⑲	R44TX	.060	—	—	㉒	8°⑧	B	—	600D	—	—	—	—
8-400	R44TX	.060	—	—	㉒	8°	B	—	600D	—	—	—	—
8-454	R44TX	.060	—	—	㉒	16°	B	—	600D	—	—	—	—

Continued

TUNE UP SPECIFICATIONS—Continued

OLD CAR SPECIFICATIONS: For 1946-68 Tune Up Specifications see main index.

★When using a timing light, disconnect vacuum hose or tube at distributor and plug opening in hose or tube so idle speed will not be affected.

●When checking compression, lowest cylinder must be within 80 percent of highest.

▲Before removing wires from distributor cap, determine location of the No. 1 wire in cap, as distributor position may have been altered from that shown at the end of this chart.

Year	Spark Plug		Distributor		Ignition Timing ★			Carb. Adjustments					
	Type	Gap Inch	Point Gap Inch	Dwell Angle Deg.	Firing Order Fig. ▲	Timing BTDC ①	Mark Fig.	Hot Idle Speed③		Air Fuel Ratio		Idle "CO" %	
								Std. Trans.	Auto. Trans. ②	Std. Trans.	Auto. Trans.	Std. Trans.	Auto. Trans.
CHEVY NOVA													
1969													
4-153⑱	R46N	.035	④	31–34	F	TDC	A	750⑯	—	—	—	—	—
4-153⑲	R46N	.035	④	31–34	F	4°	A	—	600D⑯	—	—	—	—
6-230, 250⑱	R46N	.035	④	31–34	D	TDC	A	700⑯	—	—	—	—	—
6-230, 250⑲	R46N	.035	④	31–34	D	4°	A	—	550D⑯	—	—	—	—
8-307	R45S	.035	④	28–32	E	2°	A	700⑯	600D⑯	—	—	—	—
8-327, 210 H.P.⑱	R45S	.035	④	28–32	E	2° ATC	A	700⑯	—	—	—	—	—
8-350, 255 H.P.⑱	R44	.035	④	28–32	E	TDC	A	700⑯	—	—	—	—	—
8-350, 255 H.P.⑲	R44	.035	④	28–32	E	4°	A	—	600D⑯	—	—	—	—
8-350, 300 H.P.⑱	R44	.035	④	28–32	E	TDC	A	700⑯	—	—	—	—	—
8-350, 300 H.P.⑲	R44	.035	④	28–32	E	4°	A	—	600D⑯	—	—	—	—
8-396, 350 H.P.⑱	R43N	.035	④	28–32	E	TDC	A	800⑯	—	—	—	—	—
8-396, 350 H.P.⑲	R43N	.035	④	28–32	E	4°	A	—	600D⑯	—	—	—	—
8-396, 375 H.P.	R43N	.035	④	28–32	E	4°	A	750⑯	750D⑯	—	—	—	—
1970													
4-153⑱	R46N	.035	④	31–34	F	TDC	A	750	—	—	—	—	—
4-153⑲	R46N	.035	④	31–34	F	4°	A	—	650D	—	—	—	—
6-230, 250⑱	R46T	.035	④	31–34	D	TDC	A	750	—	—	—	—	—
6-230, 250⑲	R46T	.035	④	31–34	D	4°	A	—	600D/400	—	—	—	—
8-307⑱	R43	.035	④	28–32	E	2°	A	700	—	—	—	—	—
8-307⑲	R43	.035	④	28–32	E	8°	A	—	600D/450	—	—	—	—
8-350, 250 H.P.⑱	R44	.035	④	28–32	E	TDC	A	750	—	—	—	—	—
8-350, 250 H.P.⑲	R44	.035	④	28–32	E	4°	A	—	600D/450	—	—	—	—
8-350, 300 H.P.⑱	R44	.035	④	28–32	E	TDC	A	700	—	—	—	—	—
8-350, 300 H.P.⑲	R44	.035	④	28–32	E	4°	A	—	600D	—	—	—	—
8-396, 350 H.P.	R44T	.035	④	28–32	E	TDC	A	700	—	—	—	—	—
8-396, 375 H.P.⑱	R43T	.035	④	28–32	E	4°	A	750	—	—	—	—	—
8-396, 375 H.P.⑲	R43T	.035	④	28–32	E	4°	A	—	700D	—	—	—	—
1971													
6-250	R46TS	.035	④	31–34	D	4°	B	550	500D	—	—	1.0	1.0
8-307, 200 H.P.⑱	R45TS	.035	④	29–31	E	4°	B	550	—	—	—	0.5	0.5
8-307, 200 H.P.⑲	R45TS	.035	④	29–31	E	8°	B	—	550D	—	—	0.5	0.5
8-350, 245 H.P.⑱	R44TS	.035	④	29–31	E	2°	B	600	—	—	—	0.5	0.5
8-350, 245 H.P.⑲	R44TS	.035	④	29–31	E	6°	B	—	550D	—	—	0.5	0.5
8-350, 270 H.P.⑱	R44TS	.035	④	29–31	E	4°	B	600	—	—	—	1.0	—
8-350, 270 H.P.⑲	R44TS	.035	④	29–31	E	8°	B	—	550D	—	—	—	0.5
1972													
6-250	R46T	.035	④	31–34	D	4°	B	700	600D	—	—	—	—
8-307, Std. Tr.	R44T	.035	④	29–31	E	4°	B	900	—	—	—	—	—
8-307, Auto. Tr.	R44T	.035	④	29–31	E	8°	B	—	600D	—	—	—	—
8-350, 165 H.P.	R44T	.035	④	29–31	E	6°	B	900	600D	—	—	—	—
8-350, 200 H.P.⑱	R44T	.035	④	29–31	E	4°	B	800	—	—	—	—	—
8-350, 200 H.P.⑲	R44T	.035	④	29–31	E	8°	B	—	600D	—	—	—	—

Continued

TUNE UP SPECIFICATIONS—Continued

OLD CAR SPECIFICATIONS: For 1946-68 Tune Up Specifications see main index.

★When using a timing light, disconnect vacuum hose or tube at distributor and plug opening in hose or tube so idle speed will not be affected.

●When checking compression, lowest cylinder must be within 80 percent of highest.

▲Before removing wires from distributor cap, determine location of the No. 1 wire in cap, as distributor position may have been altered from that shown at the end of this chart.

Year	Spark Plug		Distributor		Ignition Timing ★			Carb. Adjustments					
	Type	Gap Inch	Point Gap Inch	Dwell Angle Deg.	Firing Order Fig. ▲	Timing BTDC ①	Mark Fig.	Hot Idle Speed③		Air Fuel Ratio		Idle "CO" %	
								Std. Trans.	Auto. Trans. ②	Std. Trans.	Auto. Trans.	Std. Trans.	Auto. Trans.
CHEVY NOVA—Continued													
1973													
6-250	R46T	.035	④	31–34	D	6°	B	700	600D	—	—	—	—
8-307 Std. Tr.	R44T	.035	④	29–31	E	4°	B	900	—	—	—	—	—
8-307 Auto. Tr.	R44T	.035	④	29–31	E	8°	B	—	600D	—	—	—	—
8-350, 145 H.P.	R44T	.035	④	29–31	E	8°	B	900	600D	—	—	—	—
8-350, 175 H.P.⑱	R44T	.035	④	29–31	E	8°	B	900	—	—	—	—	—
8-350, 175 H.P.⑲	R44T	.035	④	29–31	E	12°	B	—	600D	—	—	—	—
1974													
6-250⑱	R46T	.035	④	31–34	D	8°	B	850	—	—	—	.3	.3
6-250⑲	R46T	.035	④	31–34	D	6°	B	—	600D	—	—	.3	.3
8-350, 145 H.P.⑱	R44T	.035	④	29–31	E	TDC	B	900	—	—	—	.5	.5
8-350, 145 H.P.⑲	R44T	.035	④	29–31	E	8°	B	—	600D	—	—	.5	.5
8-350, 160 H.P.⑱	R44T	.035	④	29–31	E	4°	B	900	—	—	—	.5	.5
8-350, 160 H.P.⑲	R44T	.035	④	29–31	E	8°	B	—	600D	—	—	.5	.5
8-350, 185 H.P.⑱	R44T	.035	④	29–31	E	8°⑥	B	900	—	—	—	.5	.5
8-350, 185 H.P.⑲	R44T	.035	④	29–31	E	8°	B	—	600D	—	—	.5	.5
1975													
6-250	R46TX	.060	—	—	⑮	8°	B	850	600D	—	—	—	—
6-250⑦	R46TX	.060	—	—	⑮	10°	B	850	550D⑨	—	—	—	—
8-262	R44TX	.060	—	—	㉒	8°	G	800	600D	—	—	—	—
8-350 2 BBl. Carb.	R44TX	.060	—	—	㉒	6°	B	800	600D	—	—	—	—
8-350⑱	R44TX	.060	—	—	㉒	6°⑥	B	800	—	—	—	—	—
8-350⑲	R44TX	.060	—	—	㉒	8°⑧	B	—	600D	—	—	—	—
CHEVROLET													
1969													
6-250⑱	R46N	.035	④	31–34	D	TDC	A	700⑯	—	—	—	—	—
6-250⑲	R46N	.035	④	31–34	D	4°	A	—	550D⑯	—	—	—	—
8-327, 325 H.P.⑱	R45S	.035	④	28–32	E	2° ATC	A	700⑯	—	—	—	—	—
8-327, 235 H.P.⑲	R45S	.035	④	28–32	E	2°	A	—	600D⑯	—	—	—	—
8-350, 255 H.P.⑱	R44	.035	④	28–32	E	TDC	A	700⑯	—	—	—	—	—
8-350, 255 H.P.⑲	R44	.035	④	28–32	E	4°	A	—	600D⑯	—	—	—	—
8-350, 300 H.P.⑱	R44	.035	④	28–32	E	TDC	A	700⑯	—	—	—	—	—
8-350, 300 H.P.⑲	R44	.035	④	28–32	E	4°	A	—	600D⑯	—	—	—	—
8-396, 265 H.P.⑱	R44N	.035	④	28–32	E	TDC	A	700⑯	—	—	—	—	—
8-396, 265 H.P.⑲	R44N	.035	④	28–32	E	4°	A	—	600D⑯	—	—	—	—
8-427, 335 H.P.	R44N	.035	④	28–32	E	4°	A	800⑯	600D⑯	—	—	—	—
8-427, 390 H.P.	R43N	.035	④	28–32	E	4°	A	800⑪	600D⑪	—	—	—	—
8-427, 425 H.P.	R43N	.035	④	28–32	E	4°	A	750⑯	750D⑯	—	—	—	—

Continued

TUNE UP SPECIFICATIONS—Continued

OLD CAR SPECIFICATIONS: For 1946-68 Tune Up Specifications see main index.

★When using a timing light, disconnect vacuum hose or tube at distributor and plug opening in hose or tube so idle speed will not be affected.

●When checking compression, lowest cylinder must be within 80 percent of highest.

▲Before removing wires from distributor cap, determine location of the No. 1 wire in cap, as distributor position may have been altered from that shown at the end of this chart.

Year	Spark Plug		Distributor		Ignition Timing★			Carb. Adjustments					
								Hot Idle Speed③		Air Fuel Ratio		Idle "CO" %	
	Type	Gap Inch	Point Gap Inch	Dwell Angle Deg.	Firing Order Fig. ▲	Timing BTDC ①	Mark Fig.	Std. Trans.	Auto. Trans. ②	Std. Trans.	Auto. Trans.	Std. Trans.	Auto. Trans.
CHEVROLET—Continued													
1970													
6-250⑱	R46T	.035	④	31–34	D	TDC	A	750	—	—	—	—	—
6-250⑲	R46T	.035	④	31–34	D	4°	A	—	600D/400	—	—	—	—
8-350, 250 H.P.⑱	R44	.035	④	28–32	E	TDC	A	750	—	—	—	—	—
8-350, 250 H.P.⑲	R44	.035	④	28–32	E	4°	A	—	600D/450	—	—	—	—
8-350, 300 H.P.⑱	R44	.035	④	28–32	E	TDC	A	700	—	—	—	—	—
8-350, 300 H.P.⑲	R44	.035	④	28–32	E	4°	A	—	600D	—	—	—	—
8-400, 265 H.P.⑱	R44	.035	④	28–32	E	4°	A	700	—	—	—	—	—
8-400, 265 H.P.⑲	R44	.035	④	28–32	E	8°	A	—	600D/450	—	—	—	—
8-454, 345 H.P.	R44T	.035	④	28–32	E	6°	A	—	600D	—	—	—	—
8-454, 360 H.P.	R43T	.035	④	28–32	E	6°	A	700	600	—	—	—	—
8-454, 390 H.P.	R43T	.035	④	28–32	E	6°	A	700	600D	—	—	—	—
1971													
6-250	R46TS	.035	④	31–34	D	4°	B	550	550D	—	—	1.0	1.0
8-350, 245 H.P.⑱	R44TS	.035	④	29–31	E	2°	B	550	—	—	—	0.5	0.5
8-350, 245 H.P.⑲	R44TS	.035	④	29–31	E	6°	B	—	550D	—	—	0.5	0.5
8-350, 270 H.P.	R44TS	.035	④	29–31	E	8°	B	—	550D	—	—	1.0	0.5
8-400, 255 H.P.⑱	R44TS	.035	④	29–31	E	4°	B	550	—	—	—	0.5	0.5
8-400, 255 H.P.⑲	R44TS	.035	④	29–31	E	8°	B	—	550D	—	—	0.5	0.5
8-400, 300 H.P.	R44TS	.035	④	29–31	E	8°	B	—	600D	—	—	1.0	1.0
8-454, 365 H.P.	R43TS	.035	④	29–31	E	8°	B	—	600D	—	—	1.0	1.0
1972													
6-250	R46T	.035	④	31–34	D	4°	B	700	600D	—	—	—	—
8-350	R44T	.035	④	29–31	E	6°	B	—	600D	—	—	—	—
8-400	R44T	.035	④	29–31	E	6°	B	—	600D	—	—	—	—
8-402	R44T	.035	④	29–31	E	8°	B	—	600D	—	—	—	—
8-454	R44T	.035	④	29–31	E	8°	B	—	600D	—	—	—	—
1973													
6-250	R46T	.035	④	31–34	D	6°	B	700	600D	—	—	—	—
8-350, 145 H.P.	R44T	.035	④	29–31	E	8°	B	—	600D	—	—	—	—
8-350, 175 H.P.	R44T	.035	④	29–31	E	12°	B	—	600D	—	—	—	—
8-400	R44T	.035	④	29–31	E	8°	B	—	600D	—	—	—	—
8-454	R44T	.035	④	29–31	E	10°	B	—	600D	—	—	—	—
1974													
8-350, 145 H.P.	R44T	.035	④	29–31	E	8°	B	—	600D	—	—	.5	.5
8-350, 160 H.P.	R44T	.035	④	29–31	E	8°	B	—	600D	—	—	.5	.5
8-400	R44T	.035	④	29–31	E	8°	B	—	600D	—	—	.5	.5
8-454	R44T	.035	④	29–31	E	10°	B	—	600D	—	—	.5	.5

Continued

TUNE UP SPECIFICATIONS—Continued

OLD CAR SPECIFICATIONS: For 1946-68 Tune Up Specifications see main index.

★When using a timing light, disconnect vacuum hose or tube at distributor and plug opening in hose or tube so idle speed will not be affected.

●When checking compression, lowest cylinder must be within 80 percent of highest.

▲Before removing wires from distributor cap, determine location of the No. 1 wire in cap, as distributor position may have been altered from that shown at the end of this chart.

Year	Spark Plug		Distributor		Ignition Timing★			Carb. Adjustments					
	Type	Gap Inch	Point Gap Inch	Dwell Angle Deg.	Firing Order Fig. ▲	Timing BTDC ①	Mark Fig.	Hot Idle Speed③		Air Fuel Ratio		Idle "CO" %	
								Std. Trans.	Auto. Trans. ②	Std. Trans.	Auto. Trans.	Std. Trans.	Auto. Trans.
CHEVROLET—Continued													
1975													
8-350 2 BBl. Carb.	R44TX	.060	—	—	㉒	6°	B	—	600D	—	—	—	—
8-350	R44TX	.060	—	—	㉒	8°⑧	B	—	600D	—	—	—	—
8-400	R44TX	.060	—	—	㉒	8°	B	—	600D	—	—	—	—
8-454	R44TX	.060	—	—	㉒	16°	B	—	600D	—	—	—	—
CORVETTE													
1969													
8-350, 300 H.P.⑱	R44	.035	④	28–32	E	4°	A	700⑯	—	—	—	—	—
8-350, 300 H.P.⑲	R44	.035	④	28–32	E	4°	A	—	600D⑯	—	—	—	—
8-350, 350 H.P.	R44	.035	④	28–32	E	8°	A	750⑯	—	—	—	—	—
8-350, 370 H.P.	R43	.035	④	28–32	E	⑳	A	750⑯	—	—	—	—	—
8-427, 390 H.P.	R43N	.035	④	28–32	E	4°	A	800⑪	600D⑪	—	—	—	—
8-427, 400 H.P.	R43N	.035	④	28–32	E	4°	A	800⑪	600D⑪	—	—	—	—
8-427, 425 H.P.	R43N	.035	④	28–32	E	4°	A	750⑯	750D⑯	—	—	—	—
8-427, 430 H.P.	R43XL	.035	—	—	E	12°⑤	A	1000⑯	—	—	—	—	—
8-427, 435 H.P.	R43N	.035	—	—	E	4°	A	750⑯	750D⑯	—	—	—	—
1970													
8-350, 300 H.P.	R44	.035	④	29–31	E	4°	A	700	600	—	—	—	—
8-350, 350 H.P.	R44	.035	④	29–31	E	8°	A	750	—	—	—	—	—
8-350, 370 H.P.	R43	.035	—	—	E	8°	A	900	—	—	—	—	—
8-454, 360 H.P.	R43T	.035	④	28–32	E	6°	A	700	600	—	—	—	—
8-454, 390 H.P.	R43T	.035	④	29–31	E	6°	A	700	600	—	—	—	—
8-454, 460 H.P.	R43XL	.035	—	—	E	8°	A	700	600	—	—	—	—
1971													
8-350, 270 H.P.	R44TS	.035	④	29–31	E	8°	B	600	550D	—	—	1.0	0.5
8-350, 330 H.P.	R43TS	.035	—	—	E	8°	B	700	—	—	—	—	—
8-454, 365 H.P.	R43TS	.035	④	29–31	E	8°	B	600	600D	—	—	1.0	1.0
8-454, 425 H.P.⑱	R44TS	.035	—	—	E	8°	B	700	—	—	—	—	—
8-454, 425 H.P.⑲	R44TS	.035	—	—	E	12°	B	—	700D	—	—	—	—
1972													
8-350, 200 H.P.	R44T	.035	④	29–31	E	8°	B	800	600D	—	—	—	—
8-350, 255 H.P.	R44T	.035	④	29–31	E	4°	B	900	—	—	—	—	—
8-454	R44T	.035	④	29–31	E	8°	B	750	600D	—	—	—	—
1973													
8-350, 190 H.P.	R44T	.035	④	29–31	C	12°	B	900	600D	—	—	—	—
8-350, 250 H.P.	R44T	.035	④	29–31	C	8°	B	900	700D	—	—	—	—
8-454, 275 H.P.	R44T	.035	④	29–31	E	10°	B	900	600D	—	—	—	—

Continued

TUNE UP SPECIFICATIONS—Continued

OLD CAR SPECIFICATIONS: For 1946-68 Tune Up Specifications see main index.

★When using a timing light, disconnect vacuum hose or tube at distributor and plug opening in hose or tube so idle speed will not be affected.

●When checking compression, lowest cylinder must be within 80 percent of highest.

▲Before removing wires from distributor cap, determine location of the No. 1 wire in cap, as distributor position may have been altered from that shown at the end of this chart.

| Year | Spark Plug | | Distributor | | Ignition Timing★ | | | Carb. Adjustments | | | | | |
| | Type | Gap Inch | Point Gap Inch | Dwell Angle Deg. | Firing Order Fig. ▲ | Timing BTDC ① | Mark Fig. | Hot Idle Speed③ | | Air Fuel Ratio | | Idle "CO" % | |
								Std. Trans.	Auto. Trans. ②	Std. Trans.	Auto. Trans.	Std. Trans.	Auto. Trans.
CORVETTE—Continued													
1974													
8-350, 195 H.P.⑱	R44T	.035	④	29–31	C	8°⑥	B	900	—	—	—	.5	.5
8-350, 195 H.P.⑲	R44T	.035	④	29–31	C	8°	B	—	600D	—	—	.5	.5
8-350, 250 H.P.	R44T	.035	④	29–31	C	8°	B	900	700D	—	—	.5	.5
8-454	R44T	.035	④	29–31	E	10°	B	800	600D	—	—	.5	.5
1975													
8-350⑱	R44TX	.060	—	—	㉒	6°⑥	B	800	—	—	—	—	—
8-350⑲	R44TX	.060	—	—	㉒	6°	B	—	600D	—	—	—	—

①—BTDC: Before top dead center.
②—D: Drive. N: Neutral.
③—Where two speeds are listed, lower speed indicates idle solenoid disconnected.
④—New points, .019", used .016". On V8s, turn adjusting screw in (clockwise) until engine misfires; then back off ½ turn.
⑤—Adjust timing at 800 R.P.M.
⑥—For California set at 4° BTDC.

⑦—With integral intake manifold and all California models.
⑧—For California set at 6° BTDC.
⑨—For California 600 R.P.M.
⑪—With A/C "ON".
⑮—Firing order, 1-5-3-6-2-4; Cylinder numbering sequence, front to rear, 1-2-3-4-5-6.
⑯—With A/C "OFF".

⑱—With standard transmission.
⑲—With automatic transmission.
⑳—With distributor 1111496 set at 14°. All others set at 4°.
㉑—Marketed as 396 but actually 402 cu. in.
㉒—Firing order, 1-8-4-3-6-5-7-2; Cylinder numbering sequence, front to rear; right bank 2-4-6-8, and left bank 1-3-5-7.

Continued

TUNE-UP NOTES—Continued

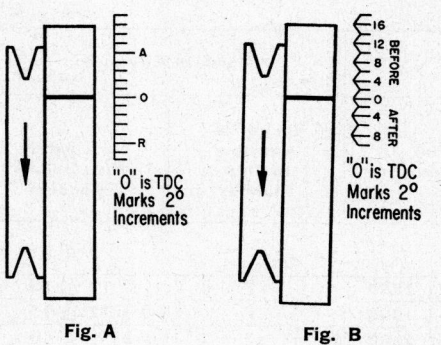

Fig. A   Fig. B

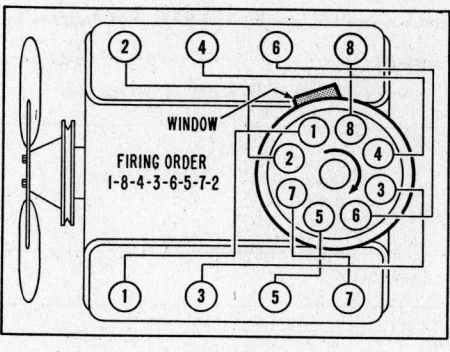

Fig. C

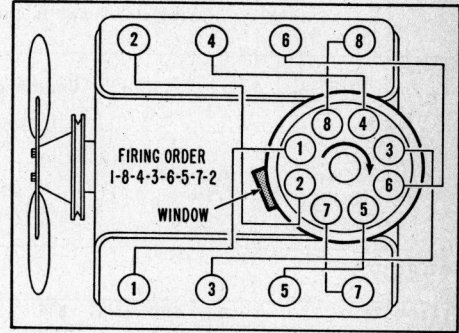

Fig. E

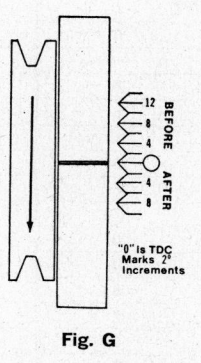

Fig. G

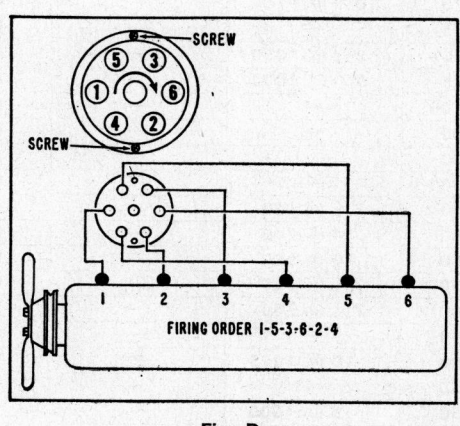

Fig. D

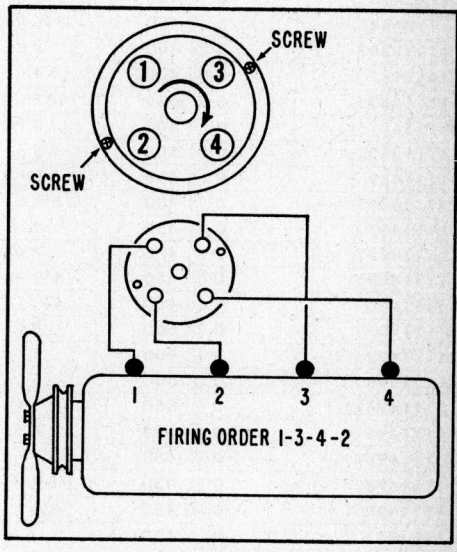

Fig. F

REAR AXLE SPECIFICATIONS

Year	Model	Carrier Type	Ring Gear & Pinion Backlash		Pinion Bearing Preload			Differential Bearing Preload		
			Method	Adjustment	Method	New Bearings Inch-Lbs.	Used Bearings Inch-Lbs.	Method	New Bearings Inch-Lbs.	Used Bearings Inch-Lbs.
1969	Exc. Corvette	Integral	Shims	.005–.008	Spacer	20–30①	5–15①	Shims	.010	.010
1969	Corvette	Integral	Shims	.005–.008	Spacer	20–25①	5–15①	Shims	.010	.010
1970	All	Integral	Shims	.005–.008	Spacer	20–25①	5–10①	Shims	.010	.010
1971–75	Corvette	Integral	Shims	.005–.008	Spacer	20–25①	5–10①	Shims	.010	.010
1971–72	Exc. Corvette	Integral	Shims	.005–.008	Spacer	25①	10①	Shims	.010	.010
1973–75	Exc. Corvette	Integral	Shims	.005–.008	Spacer	15–30①	5–10①	Shims	.010	.010

①—Use inch-pound torque wrench on pinion shaft nut.

DISTRIBUTOR SPECIFICATIONS

★Note: If unit is checked on vehicle, double the RPM and degrees to get crankshaft figures.

| Distributor Part No.① | Advance Starts | Centrifugal Advance Degrees @ RPM of Distributor | | | Vacuum Advance | |
		Intermediate Advance		Full Advance	Inches of Vacuum to Start Plunger	Max. Adv. Dist. Deg. @ Vacuum
1969-70						
1110457②	0 @ 450	8½ @ 850	—	14 @ 1850	7	12 @ 15
1110458②	0 @ 450	7 @ 850	—	12 @ 1800	7	12 @ 15
1110459②	0 @ 500	3½ @ 600	10½ @ 1050	18 @ 2300	7	11½ @ 16
1110460②	0 @ 500	8½ @ 1050	—	16 @ 2300	7	11½ @ 16
1110463②	0 @ 450	4½ @ 610	10½ @ 975	16 @ 2100	7	11½ @ 16
1110464②	0 @ 450	8½ @ 975	—	14 @ 2100	7	11½ @ 16
1111436②	0 @ 400	1 @ 540	8½ @ 1050	13 @ 2000	8	7½ @ 15
1111437②	0 @ 400	4 @ 625	9½ @ 1000	13 @ 1900	—	—
1111480②	0 @ 625	11 @ 1100	—	16 @ 2200	8	7½ @ 15
1111481②	0 @ 500	5 @ 800	—	14 @ 2150	6	7½ @ 12
1111482②	0 @ 500	5 @ 700	—	16 @ 2150	6	7½ @ 12
1111483②	0 @ 450	6 @ 1000	—	14 @ 2150	6	7½ @ 12
1111486②	0 @ 400	1½ @ 500	7½ @ 900	18 @ 2050	7	6½ @ 19
1111487②	0 @ 450	1 @ 550	4 @ 700	16 @ 2200	7	6½ @ 17
1111488②	0 @ 475	7 @ 700	10 @ 900	15 @ 2350	10	5 @ 17
1111489②	0 @ 450	4½ @ 650	7½ @ 850	13 @ 2350	10	5 @ 17
1111490②	0 @ 450	4½ @ 600	7½ @ 750	15 @ 2550	8	5 @ 17
1111491②	0 @ 500	5 @ 650	—	13 @ 2500	7	7½ @ 12
1111492②	0 @ 400	1 @ 500	10 @ 1225	16 @ 2200	6	7½ @ 12
1111493②	0 @ 500	5 @ 850	—	13 @ 2500	7	7½ @ 12
1111494②	0 @ 350	1 @ 550	6 @ 1000	14 @ 2200	6	7½ @ 12
1111496②	0 @ 600	6 @ 1000	—	10 @ 2300	7	6 @ 12
1111497②	0 @ 450	4½ @ 625	8½ @ 1000	16 @ 2500	8	7½ @ 15
1111498②	0 @ 450	6½ @ 635	10½ @ 1000	18 @ 2500	8	7½ @ 15
1111499②	0 @ 450	4½ @ 625	8½ @ 1000	16 @ 2500	6	7½ @ 12
1111925②	0 @ 400	4 @ 625	9½ @ 1000	13 @ 1900	8	7½ @ 15
1111926②	0 @ 400	4 @ 625	8½ @ 1000	13 @ 1900	7	6 @ 12
1111927	0 @ 600	8 @ 950		14½ @ 2500	—	—
1111928	0 @ 450	1 @ 550	—	15 @ 1900	8	7½ @ 15
1111949	0 @ 450	6½ @ 650	11 @ 1000	19 @ 2100	8	7½ @ 15
1111950	0 @ 450	1½ @ 550	8½ @ 950	17 @ 2150	8	7½ @ 15
1111954	0 @ 450	4 @ 600	8½ @ 1000	13 @ 1850	7	6 @ 12
1111955	0 @ 450	8½ @ 950	11 @ 1000	16 @ 2200	7	6½ @ 17
1111956	0 @ 450	5 @ 600	10½ @ 1000	16 @ 2200	7	12 @ 13
1111963	0 @ 400	1 @ 540	8½ @ 1050	13 @ 2000	8	7½ @ 15
1111971	0 @ 475	1 @ 600	6 @ 1000	10 @ 2300	7	6 @ 12
1111995	0 @ 500	1½ @ 600	5 @ 800	14 @ 2150	6	7½ @ 12
1111996	0 @ 475	7 @ 700	10 @ 900	15 @ 2350	10	7½ @ 17
1111997	0 @ 450	4½ @ 650	7½ @ 850	13 @ 2350	10	10 @ 17
1111998	0 @ 450	4½ @ 625	8½ @ 1000	16 @ 2500	8	7½ @ 15
1111999	0 @ 450	6½ @ 635	10½ @ 1000	18 @ 2500	8	7½ @ 15
1112000	0 @ 450	4½ @ 625	8½ @ 1000	16 @ 2500	6	7½ @ 12
1112001	0 @ 400	1½ @ 500	7½ @ 900	18 @ 2050	7	12 @ 17
1112002	0 @ 450	1 @ 550	4 @ 700	16 @ 2200	7	12 @ 17
1112005	0 @ 400	1 @ 600	6 @ 1100	12 @ 2150	8	10 @ 17

Continued

DISTRIBUTOR SPECIFICATIONS—Continued

★Note: If unit is checked on vehicle, double the RPM and degrees to get crankshaft figures.

Distributor Part No.①	Advance Starts	Centrifugal Advance Degrees @ RPM of Distributor				Vacuum Advance	
		Intermediate Advance			Full Advance	Inches of Vacuum to Start Plunger	Max. Adv. Dist. Deg. @ Vacuum
1971-72							
1110489③	0 @ 475	1 @ 635	7 @ 1150	—	12 @ 2050	8	11½ @ 16
1112005③	0 @ 400	1 @ 600	6 @ 1100	—	12 @ 2150	8	10 @ 17
1112038③	0 @ 530	1 @ 670	8½ @ 1200	—	12 @ 2400	8	7½ @ 15
1112039③	0 @ 340	1 @ 670	—	—	10 @ 2100	8	10 @ 17
1112042③	0 @ 440	1 @ 560	5 @ 800	7½ @ 1100	14 @ 2150	8	10 @ 17
1112044③	0 @ 420	1 @ 580	5 @ 900	7½ @ 1200	11 @ 2100	8	7½ @ 15
1112045③	0 @ 435	1 @ 670	5½ @ 1200	—	9 @ 2100	8	7½ @ 15
1112049③	0 @ 535	1 @ 665	8 @ 1125	—	12 @ 2500	8	7½ @ 15
1112050③	0 @ 435	1 @ 670	5½ @ 1200	—	9 @ 2100	8	6 @ 15
1112051③	0 @ 430	1 @ 570	7 @ 1000	—	11 @ 1950	8	10 @ 17
1112052③	0 @ 430	1 @ 670	7 @ 1000	—	11 @ 1950	8	10 @ 17
1112053③	0 @ 545	1 @ 655	11 @ 1200	—	14 @ 2750	7	6 @ 12
1112054③	0 @ 545	1 @ 660	10½ @ 1175	—	14 @ 2500	7	6 @ 12
1112055③	0 @ 500	1 @ 600	4½ @ 760	8½ @ 1150	14 @ 2250	10	9 @ 17
1112056③	0 @ 475	1 @ 635	7 @ 1150	—	12 @ 2250	10	9 @ 17
1112057③	0 @ 475	1 @ 630	8 @ 1200	—	15 @ 2200	8	10 @ 17
1112074③	0 @ 520	1 @ 680	6 @ 1100	—	10 @ 2500	8	7½ @ 15
1112075③	0 @ 650	2½ @ 750	6 @ 1200	—	8 @ 2500	7	6 @ 12
1112076③	0 @ 550	1½ @ 650	5.4 @ 795	12½ @ 1175	16 @ 2500	7	6 @ 12
1112095③	0 @ 545	1 @ 655	10½ @ 1175	—	14 @ 2500	8	7½ @ 15
1112099③	0 @ 475	1 @ 635	7 @ 1150	7 @ 1150	12 @ 2250	8	10 @ 17
1973							
1110499③	0 @ 465	1 @ 635	7 @ 1150	—	12 @ 2050	7	12 @ 15
1112093③	0 @ 550	1 @ 660	3 @ 900	5½ @ 1200	9 @ 2100	6	7½ @ 14
1112094③	0 @ 550	1 @ 775	3 @ 1205	6 @ 1650	7 @ 2100	6	7½ @ 14
1112098③	0 @ 550	1 @ 775	3 @ 1205	6 @ 1650	7 @ 2100	6	7½ @ 14
1112102③	0 @ 500	1 @ 660	5 @ 1050	—	10 @ 2100	6	7½ @ 12
1112113③	0 @ 550	1 @ 660	5½ @ 1200	—	9 @ 2100	6	10 @ 15
1112114③	0 @ 550	1 @ 670	5½ @ 1200	—	9 @ 2100	6	10 @ 15
1112148③	0 @ 600	1 @ 730	6 @ 1100	—	10 @ 2500	6	7½ @ 12
1112150③	0 @ 600	1 @ 730	6 @ 1100	—	10 @ 2500	6	7½ @ 12
1112166③	0 @ 500	1 @ 650	5 @ 1300	—	10 @ 2100	8	7½ @ 15.5
1112168③	0 @ 500	1 @ 650	5 @ 1300	—	10 @ 2100	4	7 @ 7
1112227③	0 @ 500	1 @ 600	6 @ 1100	—	12 @ 2150	6	7½ @ 12
1112230③	0 @ 500	1 @ 650	5 @ 1300	—	10 @ 2100	4	5 @ 5.8

Continued

DISTRIBUTOR SPECIFICATIONS—Continued

★Note: If unit is checked on vehicle, double the RPM and degrees to get crankshaft figures.

Distributor Part No.①	Advance Starts	Centrifugal Advance Degrees @ RPM of Distributor				Vacuum Advance	
		Intermediate Advance			Full Advance	Inches of Vacuum to Start Plunger	Max. Adv. Dist. Deg. @ Vacuum
1974							
1110499②	0 @ 550	7 @ 1150	—	—	12 @ 2050	7	12 @ 15.5
1112093③	0 @ 550	5½ @ 1200	—	—	9 @ 2100	6	7½ @ 14
1112113③	0 @ 550	5½ @ 1200	—	—	9 @ 2100	6	10 @ 15.7
1112114③	0 @ 550	5½ @ 1200	—	—	9 @ 2100	6	10 @ 15.7
1112168	0 @ 500	—	—	—	10 @ 1100	4	7 @ 8.5
1112247②	0 @ 550	5½ @ 1200	—	—	9 @ 2100	6	7½ @ 14
1112250③	0 @ 550	5½ @ 1200	—	—	9 @ 2100	10	5 @ 15.5
1112504③	0 @ 550	5½ @ 1200	—	—	9 @ 2100	8	8 @ 16
1112846	0 @ 500	—	—	—	10 @ 2100	4	15 @ 10.5
1112847	0 @ 550	5½ @ 1200	—	—	9 @ 2100	6	14 @ 8.5
1112849	0 @ 500	5 @ 900	7½ @ 1200	—	11 @ 2100	3	14 @ 8.5
1112850	0 @ 500	5 @ 900	7½ @ 1200	—	11 @ 2100	3	14 @ 8.5
1112851	0 @ 550	5½ @ 1200	—	—	9 @ 2100	3	14 @ 8.5
1112852	0 @ 600	1 @ 730	6 @ 1100	—	10 @ 2500	3	14 @ 8.5
1112853	0 @ 500	6 @ 1100	—	—	10 @ 2500	3	14 @ 8.5
1112854	0 @ 500	—	—	—	10 @ 2100	4	15 @ 10.5
1975							
1110650	0 @ 550	3½ @ 1150	—	—	8 @ 2100	4	9 @ 12
1112863	0 @ 800	3 @ 1100	—	—	7 @ 1900	4	9 @ 12
1112880	0 @ 600	6 @ 1000	—	—	11 @ 2100	4	9 @ 12
1112882	0 @ 500	4 @ 800	—	—	7½ @ 1400	8	7½ @ 15½
1112883	0 @ 550	6 @ 800	8 @ 1200	—	11 @ 2300	4	7½ @ 10
1112886	0 @ 900	—	—	—	6 @ 2100	4	9 @ 14
1112888	0 @ 550	6 @ 800	—	—	8 @ 2100	4	9 @ 12
1112933	0 @ 600	4½ @ 1000	—	—	11 @ 2000	3	8 @ 8

①—Stamped on distributor housing cover. ②—Breaker arm spring tension—19–23. ③—Breaker arm spring tension—28–32.

VALVE SPECIFICATIONS

★Adjust hydraulic lifters by tightening rocker arm stud nut just to the point where all lash is eliminated. Then turn nut the additional turns listed. See Valves Adjust text for details.

Year	Engine Model	Valve Lash ★ Int.	Valve Lash ★ Exh.	Valve Angles Seat	Valve Angles Face	Valve Spring Installed Height	Valve Spring Pressure Lbs. @ In.	Stem Clearance Intake	Stem Clearance Exhaust	Stem Diameter Intake	Stem Diameter Exhaust
1969	4-153	1 Turn⑤		46	45	1.66	175 @ 1.26	.001-.0027	.0015-.0032	.3410-.3417	.3410-.3417
	6-230	1 Turn⑤		46	45	1.66	175 @ 1.33	.001-.0027	.0015-.0032	.3410-.3417	.3410-.3417
	6-250	1 Turn⑤		46	45	1.66	186 @ 1.27	.001-.0027	.0015-.0032	.3410-.3417	.3410-.3417
	8-302	.030H	.030H	46	45	1.70	200 @ 1.25	.001-.0027	.001-.0027	.3410-.3417	.3410-.3417
	8-307, 327, 350①	1 Turn⑤		46	45	1.70	200 @ 1.25	.001-.0027	.001-.0027	.3410-.3417	.3410-.3417
	8-350, 370 H.P.	.030H	.030H	46	45	1.70	200 @ 1.25	.001-.0027	.001-.0027	.3410-.3417	.3410-.3417
	8-396, 265, 325 H.P.	1 Turn⑤		46	45	1.88	220 @ 1.46	.001-.0025	.0012-.0027	.3715-.3722	.3713-.3722
	8-396, 350	1 Turn⑤		46	45	1.88	312 @ 1.38	.001-.0025	.0012-.0027	.3715-.3722	.3713-.3722
	8-396, 375	.024H	.028H	46	45	1.88	312 @ 1.38	.001-.0025	.0012-.0027	.3715-.3722	.3713-.3722
	8-427⑥	1 Turn		46	45	1.88	312 @ 1.38	.001-.0025	.0012-.0027	.3715-.3722	.3713-.3722
	8-427, 425 H.P.	.024H	.028H	46	45	1.88	312 @ 1.38	.001-.0025	.0012-.0027	.3715-.3722	.3713-.3722
	8-427, 430 H.P.	.022H	.024H	46④	45	1.88	198 @ 1.32	.001-.0025	.0012-.0027	.3715-.3722	.3713-.3722
	8-427, 435 H.P.	.024H	.028H	46④	45	1.88	312 @ 1.38	.001-.0025	.0012-.0027	.3715-.3722	.3713-.3722
1970	4-153	1 Turn⑤		46	45	1.66	175 @ 1.26	.001-.0027	.0015-.0032	.3410-.3417	.3410-.3417
	6-230	1 Turn⑤		46	45	1.66	177 @ 1.33	.001-.0027	.0015-.0032	.3410-.3417	.3410-.3417
	6-250	1 Turn⑤		46	45	1.66	186 @ 1.27	.001-.0027	.0015-.0032	.3410-.3417	.3410-.3417
	8-307	1 Turn⑤		46	45	1.70	200 @ 1.25	.001-.0027	.0012-.0029	.3410-.3417	.3410-.3417
	8-350, 250, 300 H.P.	1 Turn⑤		46	45	1.70	200 @ 1.25	.001-.0027	.0012-.0029	.3410-.3417	.3410-.3417
	8-350, 360 H.P.	.024H	.030H	46	45	1.70	200 @ 1.25	.001-.0027	.0012-.0029	.3410-.3417	.3410-.3417
	8-350, 370 H.P.	.020H	.025H	46	45	1.70	200 @ 1.25	.001-.0027	.0012-.0029	.3410-.3417	.3410-.3417
	8-396, 350 H.P.⑦	1 Turn⑤		46	45	1.88	240 @ 1.38	.001-.0027	.0012-.0027	.3715-.3722	.3715-.3722
	8-396, 375 H.P.⑦	.024H	.028H	46	45	1.88	240 @ 1.38	.001-.0027	.0012-.0027	.3715-.3722	.3715-.3722
	8-400, 265 H.P.	1 Turn⑤		46	45	1.70	200 @ 1.25	.001-.0027	.0012-.0027	.3410-.3417	.3410-.3417
	8-400, 330 H.P.	1 Turn⑤		46	45	1.88	240 @ 1.38	.001-.0027	.0012-.0027	.3715-.3722	.3715-.3722
	8-454, 345 H.P.	1 Turn⑤		46	45	1.88	240 @ 1.38	.001-.0027	.0012-.0027	.3715-.3722	.3715-.3722
	8-454, 360, 390 H.P.	1 Turn⑤		46	45	1.88	240 @ 1.38	.001-.0027	.0012-.0027	.3715-.3722	.3715-.3722
	8-454, 450 H.P.	.024H	.028H	46	45	1.88	240 @ .138	.001-.0027	.0012-.0027	.3715-.3722	.3715-.3722
1971	6-250	1 Turn⑤		46	45	1.66	186 @ 1.27	.001-.0027	.0015-.0032	.3410-.3417	.3410-.3417
	8-307	1 Turn⑤		46	45	1.70	200 @ 1.25	.001-.0027	.001-.0027	.3410-.3417	.3410-.3417
	8-350, 245, 270 H.P.	1 Turn⑤		46	45	1.70	200 @ 1.25	.001-.0027	.001-.0027	.3410-.3417	.3410-.3417
	8-350, 330 H.P.	.024H	.030H	46	45	1.70	200 @ 1.25	.001-.0027	.001-.0027	.3410-.3417	.3410-.3417
	8-396⑦	1 Turn⑤		46	45	1.88	240 @ 1.38	.001-.0027	.001-.0027	.3715-.3722	.3715-.3722
	8-400	1 Turn⑤		46	45	1.70	200 @ 1.25	.001-.0027	.001-.0027	.3410-.3417	.3410-.3417
	8-454, 365 H.P.	1 Turn⑤		46	45	1.88	240 @ 1.38	.001-.0027	.001-.0027	.3715-.3722	.3715-.3722
	8-454, 425 H.P.	.024H	.028H	46	45	1.88	240 @ 1.38	.001-.0027	.001-.0027	.3713-.3720	.3713-.3720
1972	6-250	1 Turn⑤		46	45	1.66	186 @ 1.27	.001-.0027	.001-.0027	.3410-.3417	.3410-.3417
	8-307	1 Turn⑤		46	45	1.68	200 @ 1.17	.001-.0027	.001-.0027	.3410-.3417	.3410-.3417
	8-350, 165 H.P.	1 Turn⑤		46	45	1.70	200 @ 1.25	.001-.0027	.001-.0027	.3410-.3417	.3410-.3417
	8-350, 175, 200 H.P.	1 Turn⑤		46	45	1.70	200 @ 1.25	.001-.0027	.001-.0027	.3410-.3417	.3410-.3417
	8-350, 255 H.P.	.024H	.030H	46	45	1.70	200 @ 1.25	.001-.0027	.001-.0027	.3410-.3417	.3410-.3417
	8-400	1 Turn⑤		46	45	1.70	200 @ 1.25	.001-.0027	.001-.0027	.3410-.3417	.3410-.3417
	8-402	1 Turn⑤		46	45	1.88	215 @ 1.48	.001-.0027	.001-.0027	.3715-.3722	.3713-.3720
	8-454	1 Turn⑤		46	45	1.88	240 @ 1.38	.001-.0027	.001-.0027	.3715-.3722	.3713-.3720
1973	6-250	1 Turn⑤		46	45	1.66	186 @ 1.27	.001-.0027	.0015-.0032	.3410-.3417	.3410-.3417
	8-307	1 Turn⑤		46	45	1.61	189 @ 1.20	.001-.0027	.0012-.0029	.3410-.3417	.3410-.3417
	8-350, 145, 175 H.P.	1 Turn⑤		46	45	1.61	189 @ 1.20	.001-.0027	.0012-.0029	.3410-.3417	.3410-.3417
	8-350, 190 H.P.	1 Turn⑤		46	45	1.61	189 @ 1.20	.001-.0027	.0012-.0029	.3410-.3417	.3410-.3417
	8-350, 245, 250 H.P.	1 Turn⑤		46	45	1.70	200 @ 1.25	.001-.0027	.0012-.0029	.3410-.3417	.3410-.3417
	8-400	1 Turn⑤		46	45	1.70	200 @ 1.25	.001-.0027	.0012-.0027	.3410-.3417	.3410-.3417
	8-454	1 Turn⑤		46	45	1.88	300 @ 1.38	.001-.0027	.0012-.0027	.3715-.3722	.3715-.3722

Continued

VALVE SPECIFICATIONS—Continued

★Adjust hydraulic lifters by tightening rocker arm stud nut just to the point where all lash is eliminated. Then turn nut the additional turns listed. See Valves Adjust text for details.

Year	Engine Model	Valve Lash ★ Int.	Exh.	Valve Angles Seat	Face	Valve Spring Installed Height	Valve Spring Pressure Lbs. @ In.	Stem Clearance Intake	Exhaust	Stem Diameter Intake	Exhaust
1974	6-250	1 Turn⑤		46	45	1.66	186 @ 1.27	.001–.0027	.0015–.0032	.3410–.3417	.3410–.3417
	8-350, 145, 160 H.P.	1 Turn⑤		46	45	②	③	.001–.0027	.0012–.0029	.3410–.3417	.3410–.3417
	8-350, 185, 245 H.P.	1 Turn⑤		46	45	②	③	.001–.0027	.0012–.0029	.3410–.3417	.3410–.3417
	8-350, 250 H.P.	1 Turn⑤		46	45	1.70	200 @ 1.25	.001–.0027	.0012–.0029	.3410–.3417	.3410–.3417
	8-400	1 Turn⑤		46	45	1.70	200 @ 1.25	.001–.0027	.0012–.0027	.3410–.3417	.3410–.3417
	8-454	1 Turn⑤		46	45	1.88	300 @ 1.38	.001–.0027	.0012–.0027	.3715–.3722	.3715–.3722
1975	6-250	1 Turn⑤		46	45	1.66	186 @ 1.27	.001–.0027	.0015–.0032	.3410–.3417	.3410–.3417
	V8-262	1 Turn⑤		46	45	②	③	.001–.0027	.001–.0027	.3410–.3417	.3410–.3417
	V8-350	1 Turn⑤		46	45	②	③	.001–.0027	.0012–.0029	.3410–.3417	.3410–.3417
	V8-350⑧	1 Turn⑤		46	45	1.70	200 @ 1.25	.001–.0027	.0012–.0029	.3410–.3417	.3410–.3417
	V8-400	1 Turn⑤		46	45	1.70	200 @ 1.25	.001–.0027	.0012–.0027	.3410–.3417	.3410–.3417
	V8-454	1 Turn⑤		46	45	1.88	300 @ 1.38	.001–.0027	.0012–.0027	.3715–.3722	.3713–.3720

①—255, 300, 350 H.P.
②—Intake 1.70; exhaust 1.61.
③—Intake 200 @ 1.25; exhaust 189 @ 1.20.
④—Aluminum heads 45°.

⑤—Turn rocker arm stud nut until all lash is eliminated, then tighten nut the additional turn listed.
⑥—335, 385, 390, 400 H.P.
⑦—Marketed as 396 but actually 402 cu. in.
⑧—Corvette Hi Perf.

PISTONS, PINS, RINGS, CRANKSHAFT & BEARINGS

Year	Engine Model	Piston Clearance	Ring End Gap① Comp.	Oil	Wrist-pin Diameter	Rod Bearings Shaft Diameter	Bearing Clearance	Main Bearings Shaft Diameter	Bearing Clearance	Thrust on Bear. No.	Shaft End Play
1969–70	4-153	.0005–.0015	.010	.015	.9272	1.999–2.000	.0007–.0027	2.2983–2.2993	.0003–.0029	5	.002–.006
1969–70	6-230, 250	.0005–.0015⑪	.010	.015	.9272	1.999–2.000	.0007–.0027	2.2983–2.2993	.0003–.0029	7	.002–.006
1971–72	6-250	.0015–.0025	.010	.015	.9272	1.999–2.000	.0007–.0027	2.2983–2.2993	.0003–.0029	7	.002–.006
1973–74	6-250	.0005–.0015	.010	.015	.9272	1.9928–2.000	.0007–.0027	2.2983–2.2993	.0003–.0029	7	.002–.006
1975	6-250	.0005–.0015	.010	.015	.9272	1.9928–2.000	.007–.0027	2.2983–2.2993	.0003–.0029	7	.002–.006
1975	V8-262	.0007–.0013	⑭	.015	.9272	2.098–2.099	.0013–.0035	㉒	㊴	5	.002–.007
1969	8-302	.0024–.0030	.013	.015	.9272	1.999–2.000	.0007–.0028	2.4479–2.4488	.0008–.0030	5	.003–.011
1969	8-307	.0005–.0011	.010	.015	.9272	2.099–2.100	.0007–.0027	2.4479–2.4488	.0008–.0020	5	.003–.011
1970	8-307	.0005–.0011	.010	.015	.9272	2.099–2.100	.0007–.0028	②	㉘	5	.002–.006
1971	8-307	.0005–.0011	.010	.015	.9272	2.099–2.100	.0013–.0035	②	㊴	5	.002–.006
1972–73	8-307	.0005–.0011	.010	.015	.9272	2.099–2.100	.0013–.0035	㉒	㊴	5	.002–.006
1969	8-327	.0005–.0011	.013	.015	.9272	2.099–2.100	.0007–.0028	2.4479–2.4488	㉗	5	.003–.011
1969	8-350㉕	.0005–.0011	.013	.015	.9272	2.099–2.100	.0007–.0028	2.4479–2.4488	㉗	5	.003–.011
	8-350㉖	.0024–.0030	⑭	.015	.9272	2.099–2.100	.0007–.0028	2.4479–2.4488	㉗	5	.003–.011
1970	8-350㉕	.0007–.0013	⑭	.015	.9272	2.099–2.100	.0007–.0028	②	㉘	5	.002–.006
	8-350㉖	.0020–.0026	⑭	.015	.9272	2.009–2.100	.0007–.0028	②	㉘	5	.002–.006
	8-350㉚	.0036–.0042	⑭	.015	.9272	2.099–2.100	.0007–.0028	②	㉘	5	.002–.006

Continued

PISTONS, PINS, RINGS, CRANKSHAFT & BEARINGS—Continued

Year	Engine Model	Piston Clearance	Ring End Gap①		Wrist-pin Diameter	Rod Bearings		Main Bearings			
			Comp.	Oil		Shaft Diameter	Bearing Clearance	Shaft Diameter	Bearing Clearance	Thrust on Bear. No.	Shaft End Play
1971	8-350 ④⓪	.0007–.0017	.010	.015	.9272	2.099–2.100	.0013–.0035	②	㉙	5	.002–.006
	8-350 ④①	.0036–.0042	.010	.015	.9272	2.099–2.100	.0013–.0035	⑫	⑮	5	.002–.006
1972	8-350 ㊸	.0007–.0013	⑭	.015	.9272	2.099–2.100	.0013–.0035	㉒	㉙	5	.002–.006
	8-350 ⑬	.0036–.0042	⑭	.015	.9272	2.099–2.100	.0013–.0035	㉒	⑮	5	.002–.006
1973–75	8-350 ④①	.0007–.0013	⑭	.015	.9272	2.099–2.100	.0013–.0035	㉒	㉙	5	.002–.006
	8-350 ⑯	.0036–.0042	⑭	.015	.9272	2.099–2.100	.0013–.0035	㉒	⑮	5	.002–.006
1969	8-396 ⑰	.0010–.0018	.010	.010	.9897	2.199–2.200	.0009–.0025	⑲	⑤	5	.006–.010
	8-396 ⑱	.0036–.0044	.010	.010	.9897	2.1985–2.1995	.0014–.0030	④	⑥	5	.006–.010
1970	8-396 ⑳㉘	.0018–.0026	.010	.010	.9897	2.199–2.200	.0009–.0025	③	㉝	5	.006–.010
	8-396 ⑱㉘	.0036–.0046	.010	.010	.9897	2.1985–2.1995	.0014–.0030	⑨	㉞	5	.006–.010
1971	8-396	.0018–.0026	.010	.015	.9897	2.199–2.200	.0009–.0025	③	㊷	5	.006–.010
1970	8-400 ㉛	.0014–.0020	.010	.015	.9897	2.099–2.100	.0009–.0030	⑩	㉘	5	.002–.006
	8-400 ㉜	.0018–.0026	.010	.015	.9897	2.199–2.200	.0009–.0025	⑩	㉙	5	.002–.006
1971	8-400	.0014–.0020	.010	.015	.9272	2.099–2.100	.0013–.0035	⑩	㉙	5	.002–.006
1972–75	8-400	.0014–.0020	.010	.015	.9272	2.099–2.100	.0013–.0035	⑩	㉚	5	.002–.006
1972	8-402	.0018–.0026	.010	.010	.9897	2.199–2.200	.0009–.0025	2.7504	㊷	5	.006–.010
1969	8-427 ⑳	.0012–.0020	.010	.010	.9897	2.199–2.200	.0009–.0025	㉑	⑥	5	.006–.010
	8-427 ㉒	.0037–.0043	.010	.010	.9897	2.1985–2.1995	.0014–.0030	㉑	⑥	5	.006–.010
	8-427 ㉓	.0058–.0066	.010	.010	.9897	2.1985–2.1995	.0014–.0030	㉑	⑥	5	.006–.010
	8-427 ㉔	.0040–.0048	.010	.010	.9897	2.1985–2.1995	.0014–.0030	㉑	⑥	5	.006–.010
1970	8-454 ㉟	.0024–.0034	.010	.010	.9897	2.199–2.200	.0009–.0025	④	㊲	5	.006–.010
	8-454 ㊱	.0040–.0050	.010	.010	.9897	2.1985–2.1995	.0014–.0030	㉑	㉞	5	.006–.010
1971	8-454 ⑦	.0024–.0034	.010	.010	.9897	2.199–2.200	.0009–.0025	④	㊲	5	.006–.010
	8-454 ⑧	.0040–.0050	.010	.015	.9897	2.199–2.200	.0009–.0025	㉑	㉞	5	.006–.010
1972	8-454	.0024–.0034	.010	.010	.9897	2.199–2.200	.0009–.0025	④	㊲	5	.006–.010
1973–75	8-454	.0018–.0028	.010	.015	.9897	2.199–2.200	.0009–.0025	④	㊲	5	.006–.010

①—Fit rings in tapered bores to the clearance listed in tightest portion of ring travel. Clearances specified are minimum gaps.

②—No. 1, 2, 3, 4: 2.4484–2.4493; No. 5: 2.4479–2.4488.

③—No. 1 & 2: 2.7487–2.7496; No. 3 & 4: 2.7481–2.7490; No. 5: 2.7478–2.7488.

④—1: 2.7484–2.7493; 2, 3 & 4: 2.7481–2.7490; 5: 2.7478–2.7488.

⑤—No. 1 & 2: .0010–.0022; No. 3 & 4: .0013–.0025; No. 5: .0015–.0031.

⑥—No. 1, 2, 3 & 4: .0013–.0025; No. 5: .0015–.0031.

⑦—Except 425 H.P.

⑧—425 H.P.

⑨—No. 1, 2, 3 & 4: 2.7481–2.7490; No. 5: 2.7473–2.7483.

⑩—No. 1, 2, 3 & 4: 2.6484–2.6493; No. 5: 2.6479–2.6488.

⑪—6-250 Piston Clearance .0015–.0025.

⑫—Manual/Trans.; No. 1, 2, 3 & 4: 2.7481–2.7490; No. 5: 2.7473–2.7483. Auto/Trans.; No. 1: 2.745–2.7484;

No. 2, 3 & 4: 2.7481–2.7490; No. 5: 2.7473–2.7483.

⑬—255 H.P.

⑭—Top ring, .010, lower ring, .013".

⑮—Manual/Trans.; No. 1, 2, 3 & 4: .0013–.0025; No. 5: .0023–.0033. Auto/Trans.; No. 1: .0019–.0031; No. 2, 3 & 4: .0013–.0025; No. 5: .0023–.0033.

⑯—245, 250 H.P.

⑰—Except 375 H.P.

⑱—375 H.P.

⑲—1 & 2: 2.7484–2.7493; 3 & 4: 2.7481–2.7490; 5: 2.7478–2.7488.

⑳—335, 390, 400 H.P.

㉑—1, 2, 3 & 4: 2.7481–2.7490; 5: 2.7478–2.7488.

㉒—No. 1: 2.4484–2.4493; No. 2, 3 & 4: 2.4481–2.4490; No. 5: 2.4479–2.4488.

㉓—430 H.P.

㉔—435 H.P.

㉕—250, 255 & 300 H.P.

㉖—350 & 370 H.P.

㉗—No. 1, 2, 3, 4: .0008–.002; No. 5: .0018–.0034.

㉘—No. 1: .0003–.0015; No. 2, 3, 4: .0006–.0018; No. 5. .0008–.0023.

㉙—350 H.P.

㉚—360 & 370 H.P.

㉛—265 H.P.

㉜—330 H.P.

㉝—No. 1: .0007–.0019; No. 2, 3, 4: .0013–.0025; No. 5: .0024–.0040.

㉞—No. 1, 2, 3, 4: .0013–.0025; No. 5: .0029–.0045.

㉟—Except 450 H.P.

㊱—450 H.P.

㊲—No. 1, 2, 3, 4: .0013–.0025; No. 5: .0024–.0040.

㊳—Marketed as 396 but actually 402 cu. in.

㊴—No. 1: .0008–.0020; No. 2, 3, 4: .0011–.0023; No. 5: .0017–.0033.

㊵—245 & 270 H.P.

㊶—Except 245, 250 H.P.

㊷—No. 1: .0007–.0019; No. 2, 3, 4: .0013–.0025; No. 5: .0019–.0035.

㊸—165, 175, 200 H.P.

BRAKE SPECIFICATIONS

Year	Model	Brake Drum Inside Diameter	Wheel Cylinder Bore Diameter			Master Cylinder Bore Diameter		
			Disc Brake	Front Drum Brake	Rear Drum Brake	Disc Brakes	Drum Brakes	Power Brakes
1969	Camaro	9½	2 1/16 ④	1 1/8	7/8	—	1	1
	Chevelle	9½	2 1/16	1 1/8	7/8	1 1/8	1	1
	Nova	9½	2 1/16	1 1/8	7/8	—	1	1
	Chevrolet	11	2 1/16	1 3/16	1	1	1	1
	Corvette	—	③	—	—	1	—	1
1970–72	Camaro	9½	2 15/16	—	7/8	1 1/8	—	1 1/8
	Chevelle & Monte Carlo	9½	2 15/16	1 1/8	7/8	1 1/8	1	1
	Nova	9½	2 15/16	1 1/8	7/8	1 1/8	1	1
	Chevrolet	11 ⑦	2 15/16	1 3/16	1 ⑤	1 1/8	—	1
	Corvette	—	③	—	—	1	—	1 ②
1973–74	Camaro	9½	2 15/16	—	7/8	1	—	1 1/8
	Chevelle & Monte Carlo	9½ ⑥	2 15/16	—	7/8 ①	1	1	1 1/8
	Nova	9½	2 15/16	1 1/8	7/8	1	1	1 1/8
	Chevrolet	11 ⑦	2 15/16	—	1 ⑤	1 1/8	—	1 1/8
	Corvette	—	③	—	—	1	—	1 1/8
1975	Camaro	9½	2 15/16	—	7/8	1	—	1 1/8
	Chevelle & Monte Carlo	9½ ⑥	2 15/16	—	7/8 ①	1	—	1 1/8
	Nova	9½	2 15/16	—	7/8	1	—	1 1/8
	Chevrolet	11 ⑦	2 15/16	—	1 ⑤	1 1/8	—	1 1/8
	Corvette	—	③	—	—	1	—	1 1/8

①—Sta. Wagon 15/16".
②—1972 power brakes 1 1/8".
③—Front 1 7/8; Rear 1 3/8.
④—Front discs only. For 4 wheel disc option, see Corvette.
⑤—1971–75 Sedans and Coupes 15/16".
⑥—Sta. Wagon 11".
⑦—1971–75 Wagon, 12.

ENGINE TIGHTENING SPECIFICATIONS★

★Torque specifications are for clean and lightly lubricated threads only. Dry or dirty threads produce increased friction which prevents accurate measurement of tightness.

Year	Engine Model	Spark Plugs Ft. Lbs.	Cylinder Head Bolts Ft. Lbs.	Intake Manifold Ft. Lbs.	Exhaust Manifold Ft. Lbs.	Rocker Arm Stud Ft. Lbs.	Rocker Arm Cover Ft. Lbs.	Connecting Rod Cap Bolts Ft. Lbs.	Main Bearing Cap Bolts Ft. Lbs.	Flywheel to Crankshaft Ft. Lbs.	Vibration Damper or Pulley Ft. Lbs.
1969–70	4-153	25	95	③	③	—	55④	35	65	60	②
1969	6-230	25	95	③	③	—	55④	35	65	60	②
1970	6-230	15	95	③	③	—	55④	35	65	60	②
1969	6-250	25	95	③	③	—	55④	35	65	60	②
1970	6-250	15	95	③	③	—	55④	35	65	60	②
1971–74	6-250	15	95	③	③	—	45④	35	65	60	60
1975	6-250	15	95	⑬	30⑭	—	45④	35	65	60	60
1975	8-262	15	65	30	20①	—	45④	45	70	60	60
1969	8-302	25	65	30	20	—	55④	45	80	60	60
1969–70	8-307	25	65	30	20①	—	55④	45	75	60	②
1971–73	8-307	15	65	30	20①	—	45④	45	75⑫	60	60
1969	8-327	25	65	30	20	—	55④	⑩	80	60	60
1969–70	8-350	25	65	30	20①	—	55④	45	75	60	60
1971–74	8-350	15	65	30	20①	50	45④	45	75⑫	60	60
1975	8-350	15	65	30	20①	—	45④	45	70⑫	60	60
1969	8-396	25	80	30	20	50	50④	45	⑤	60	85
1970	8-396⑪	15	80	30	20	50	50④	50	105	65	85
1970–74	8-400⑥	25	65	30	20	—	55④	45	75	60	60
1970	8-400⑦	15	80	30	20	50	50④	50	105	65	85
1975	8-400	15	65	30	20	50	45④	45	70	60	60
1971–72	8-402	15	80	30	20	50	50④	50	105	65	85
1969	8-427	25	80⑧	30	20	50⑨	50④	45	⑤	60	85
1970–73	8-454	15	80	30	20	50	50④	50	105	65	85
1974	8-454	15	80	30	20	50	50④	50	110	65	85

①—Inside bolts 30 ft. lbs.
②—Pressed on.
③—End clamp bolts 20, center bolts 30.
④—Inch lbs.
⑤—2 bolt caps 95 ft.-lbs., 4 bolt caps 105 ft.-lbs.
⑥—Exc. 330 H.P.
⑦—330 H.P.
⑧—Aluminum Head–Short bolts 65 ft. lbs Long bolts 75 ft. lbs.
⑨—Aluminum Head–60 ft. lbs.
⑩—For 3⁄8″ bolts 45 ft.-lbs.; for 11⁄32″ bolts 35 ft.-lbs.
⑪—Marketed as 396 but actually 402 cu. in.
⑫—Outer bolts on engines with 4 bolt caps 65 ft. lbs.
⑬—Integral Intake Manifold.
⑭—Outer bolts 20 ft. lb.

STARTING MOTOR SPECIFICATIONS

Year	Model	Starter Number	Brush Spring Tension Oz①	Free Speed Test			Resistance Test③	
				Amps.	Volts	R.P.M.①	Amps.	Volts
1969	8-327, 427	1108351	35	70–99②	10.6	7800–12000	300–360	3.5
	8-327, 350	1108361	35	65–100②	10.6	3600–5100	300–360②	3.5
	4-153, 6-230, 250	1108365	35	49–87②	10.6	6200–10700	290–425②	4.2
	4-153	1108366	35	49–87②	10.6	6200–10700	290–425②	4.2
	8-307, 302, 327	1108367	35	49–87②	10.6	6200–10700	290–425②	4.2
	8-350	1108338	35	55–85②	9	3100–4900	—	—
	8-396, 427	1108418	35	65–95②	9	7500–10500	—	—
	8-327	1108382	35	53–69②	9	6400–8600	—	—
	6-250	1107372	35	55–95②	9	3000–4800	—	—
	8-427	1108400	35	65–95②	9	7500–10500	—	—
1970	4 & 6 Cyl.	1108365	35	50–80②	9	5500–10500	—	—
	6-250	1107372	35	55–95②	9	3000–4800	—	—
	8-307	1108367	35	50–80②	9	5500–10500	—	—
	8-350	1108338	35	55–80②	9	3500–6000	—	—
	8-350	1108427	35	55–80②	9	3500–6000	—	—
	8-454	1108430	35	65–95②	9	7500–10500	—	—
	8-400	1108418	35	65–95②	9	7500–10500	—	—
	8-454	1108400	35	65–95②	9	7500–10500	—	—
1971–74	6-250	1108365	35	50–80②	9	5500–10500	—	—
	8-307	1108367	35	50–80②	9	5500–10500	—	—
	8-307⑤	1108512	35	50–80②	9	5500–10500	—	—
	④	1108418	35	65–95②	9	7500–10500	—	—
	④	1108430	35	65–95②	9	7500–10500	—	—
	8-454	1108429	35	65–95②	9	7500–10500	—	—
	8-454	1108400	35	65–95②	9	7500–10500	—	—
1975	6-250	1108365	35	50–80②	9	5500–10500	—	—
	6-250	1108774	—	50–80②	9	5500–10500	—	—
	V8-262	1108512	—	55–80②	9	3500–6000	—	—
	V8-262	1108790	—	55–80②	9	3500–6000	—	—
	350, 400, 454	1108430	—	65–95②	9	7500–10500	—	—
	350, 400, 454	1108776	—	65–95②	9	7500–10500	—	—
	350, 454	1108418	—	65–95②	9	7500–10500	—	—
	350, 454	1108775	—	65–95②	9	7500–10500	—	—

①—Minimum.
②—Includes solenoid.
③—Check capacity of motor by using a 500 ampere meter and a carbon pile rheostat to control voltage. Apply the volts listed across motor with armature locked. Current should be as listed.
④—Used on V8-350, 400, 402, and 454 engines.
⑤—1973 only.

ALTERNATOR & REGULATOR SPECIFICATIONS

Year	Alternator			Output @ 14 Volts		Regulator	Field Relay			Voltage Regulator		
	Model	Rated Hot Output Amps.	Field Current 12 Volts @ 80° F.	2000 R.P.M. Amps.	5000 R.P.M. Amps.	Model	Air Gap In.	Point Gap In.	Closing Voltage	Air Gap In.	Point Gap In.	Voltage @ 125° F.
1969–70	1100825①	61	4.0–4.5	—	—	—	—	—	—	—	—	—
	1100833①	42	4.0–4.5	—	—	—	—	—	—	—	—	—
	1100834	37	2.2–2.6	—	—	1119515	.015	.030	1.5–3.2	.067	.014	13.4–14.3
	1100836	37	2.2–2.6	25	35	1119515	.015	.030	1.5–3.2	.067	.014	13.4–14.3
	1100837	37	2.2–2.6	25	35	1119515	.015	.030	1.5–3.2	.067	.014	13.4–14.3
	1100839	42	2.2–2.6	—	—	1119515	.015	.030	1.5–3.2	.067	.014	13.4–14.3
	1100841	42	2.2–2.6	—	—	1119515	.015	.030	1.5–3.2	.067	.014	13.4–14.3
	1100843	61	2.2–2.6	33	58	1119515	.015	.030	1.5–3.2	.067	.014	13.4–14.3
	1100845	61	2.2–2.6	—	—	1119515	.015	.030	1.5–3.2	.067	.014	13.4–14.3
	1100846	63	2.2–2.6	—	—	1119515	.015	.030	1.5–3.2	.067	.014	13.4–14.3
	1100847	61	2.2–2.6	—	—	1119515	.015	.030	1.5–3.2	.067	.014	13.4–14.3
	1100859①	42	4.0–4.5	—	—	—	—	—	—	—	—	—
	1100896	61	2.2–2.6	—	—	1119515	.015	.030	1.5–3.2	.067	.014	13.4–14.3
	1100897	61	2.2–2.6	—	—	1119515	.015	.030	1.5–3.2	.067	.014	13.4–14.3
	1100900①	42	—	—	—	—	—	—	—	—	—	—
	1100901①	42	—	—	—	—	—	—	—	—	—	—
	1100950①	42	—	—	—	—	—	—	—	—	—	—
1971	1100543①	42	4–4.5	—	37	—	—	—	—	—	—	—
	1100544①	61	4–4.5	—	55	—	—	—	—	—	—	—
	1100566	37	2.2–2.6	25	35	1119515	.015	.030	1.5–3.2	.067	.014	13.8–14.8
	1100567	42	2.2–2.6	28	40	1119515	.015	.030	1.5–3.2	.067	.014	13.8–14.8
	1100836	37	2.2–2.6	25	35	1119515	.015	.030	1.5–3.2	.067	.014	13.8–14.8
	1100837	37	2.2–2.6	25	35	1119515	.015	.030	1.5–3.2	.067	.014	13.8–14.8
	1100843	61	2.2–2.6	33	58	1119515	.015	.030	1.5–3.2	.067	.014	13.8–14.8
	1100917	63	2.8–3.2	35	59	1119519	.030	.030	1.5–3.2	.067	.014	13.8–14.8
	1100950①	42	4–4.5	—	37	—	—	—	—	—	—	—
1972	1100543	42	4–4.5	—	37	—	—	—	—	—	—	—
	1100544	61	4–4.5	—	55	—	—	—	—	—	—	—
	1100950	42	4–4.5	—	37	—	—	—	—	—	—	—
	1102440	37	2.2–2.6	25	35	1119515	.015	.030	1.5–3.2	.067	.014	13.5–14.4
	1102452	37	2.2–2.6	25	35	1119515	.015	.030	1.5–3.2	.067	.014	13.5–14.4
	1102453	37	2.2–2.6	25	35	1119515	.015	.030	1.5–3.2	.067	.014	13.5–14.4
	1102454	37	2.2–2.6	25	35	1119515	.015	.030	1.5–3.2	.067	.014	13.5–14.4
	1102456	37	2.2–2.6	25	35	1119515	.015	.030	1.5–3.2	.067	.014	13.5–14.4
	1102458	42	2.2–2.6	28	40	1119515	.015	.030	1.5–3.2	.067	.014	13.5–14.4
	1102459	42	2.2–2.6	28	40	1119515	.015	.030	1.5–3.2	.067	.014	13.5–14.4
	1102463	61	2.2–2.6	33	58	1119515	.015	.030	1.5–3.2	.067	.014	13.5–14.4
	1102464	63	2.8–3.2	35	59	1119519	.030	.030	1.5–3.2	.067	.014	13.5–14.5
1973	1100542	63	4–4.5	—	58	Integral	—	—	—	—	—	—
	1102346	42	4–4.5	—	37	Integral	—	—	—	—	—	—
	1102354	63	4–4.5	—	58	Integral	—	—	—	—	—	—
1973–75	1100497	37	4.4–4.9	—	36②	Integral	—	—	—	—	—	13.8–14.8
	1100934	37	4–4.5	—	32	Integral	—	—	—	—	—	13.8–14.8
	1100950	42	4–4.5	—	37	Integral	—	—	—	—	—	13.8–14.8
	1100544	61	4–4.5	—	55	Integral	—	—	—	—	—	—
	1100573	42	4–4.5	—	37	Integral	—	—	—	—	—	—
	1100597	61	4–4.5	—	55	Integral	—	—	—	—	—	—
	1102353	42	4–4.5	—	37	Integral	—	—	—	—	—	—

Continued

ALTERNATOR & REGULATOR SPECIFICATIONS—Continued

Year	Model	Rated Hot Output Amps.	Field Current 12 Volts @ 80° F.	Output @ 14 Volts 2000 R.P.M. Amps.	Output @ 14 Volts 5000 R.P.M. Amps.	Model	Field Relay Air Gap In.	Field Relay Point Gap In.	Field Relay Closing Voltage	Voltage Regulator Air Gap In.	Voltage Regulator Point Gap In.	Voltage Regulator Voltage @ 125° F.
1974-75	1100560	55	4–4.5	—	50	Integral	—	—	—	—	—	—
	1100575	55	4–4.5	—	50	Integral	—	—	—	—	—	—
	1102347	61	4–4.5	—	55	Integral	—	—	—	—	—	—
1975	1102397	37	4–4.5	—	33	Integral	—	—	—	—	—	—
	1102483	37	4–4.5	—	33	Integral	—	—	—	—	—	—
	1102493	42	4–4.5	—	38	Integral	—	—	—	—	—	—

①—Integral System.   ②—At 7000 RPM.

WHEEL ALIGNMENT SPECIFICATIONS

OLD CAR SPECIFICATIONS: For 1946-68 Wheel Alignment Specifications see main index.

Year	Model	Caster Angle, Degrees Limits	Caster Angle, Degrees Desired	Camber Angle, Degrees Limits Left	Camber Angle, Degrees Limits Right	Camber Angle, Degrees Desired Left	Camber Angle, Degrees Desired Right	Toe-In. Inch	Toe-Out on Turns, Deg.① Outer Wheel	Toe-Out on Turns, Deg.① Inner Wheel
CAMARO										
1969	All	0 to +1	+½	−¼ to +¾	−¼ to +¾	+½	+½	⅛ to ¼	—	20
1970	Z-28	−¾ to +¼	−¼	+¼ to +1¼	+¼ to +1¼	+¾	+¾	⅛ to ¼	—	—
	Others	0 to +1	+½	+½ to +1½	+½ to +1½	+1	+1	⅛ to ¼	—	—
1971-72	Z-28	−½ to +½	Zero	−1¼ to −¼	−1¼ to −¼	−¾	−¾	⅛ to ¼	—	—
	Others	−1 to +1	Zero	+¼ to +1¾	+¼ to +1¾	+1	+1	1⁄16 to 5⁄16	—	—
1973-74	Z-28	−½ to −1½	−1	+¼ to +1¼	+¼ to +1¼	+¾	+¾	⅛ to ¼	—	—
	Others	−½ to +½	Zero	+½ to +1½	+½ to +1½	+1	+1	⅛ to ¼	—	—
1975	All	−½ to ½	Zero	+½ to +1½	+½ to +1½	+1	+1	0 to ⅛	—	—
CHEVELLE & MONTE CARLO										
1969-70	S.S., M. Carlo	−1 to 0	−½	0 to +1	0 to +1	+½	+½	⅛ to ¼	18.4	20
	Others	−1½ to −½	−1	0 to +1	0 to +1	+½	+½	⅛ to ¼	18.4	20
1971	All	−½ to −1½	−1	+¼ to +1¼	+¼ to +1¼	+¾	+¾	⅛ to ¼	—	—
1972	All	−2 to 0	−1	0 to +1½	0 to +1½	+¾	+¾	1⁄16–5⁄16	—	—
1973-74	Chevelle③	−½ to −1½	−1	+½ to +1½	0 to +1	+1	+½	0 to ⅛	—	—
	Chevelle④	−½ to +½	Zero	+½ to +1½	0 to +1	+1	+½	0 to ⅛	—	—
	Monte Carlo	+4½ to +5½	+5	+½ to +1½	0 to +1	+1	+½	0 to ⅛	—	—
1975	Chevelle③	+½ to +1½	+1	+½ to +1½	0 to +1	+1	+½	0 to ⅛	—	—
	Chevelle④	+1½ to +2½	+2	+½ to +1½	0 to +1	+1	+½	0 to ⅛	—	—
	Monte Carlo	+4½ to +5½	+5	+½ to +1½	0 to +1	+1	+½	0 to ⅛	—	—
CHEVY NOVA										
1969-71	All	0 to +1	+½	−¼ to +¾	−¼ to +¾	+½	+½	⅛ to ¼	—	20
1972	All	−1 to +1½	+½	−½ to +1	−½ to +1	+¼	+¼	1⁄16–5⁄16	—	—
1973-74	All	0 to +1	+½	−¼ to +¾	−¼ to +¾	+¼	+¼	⅛ to ¼	—	—
1975	All③	−½ to −1½	−1	+¼ to +1¼	+¼ to +1¼	+¾	+¾	0 to ⅛	—	—
	All④	+½ to +1½	+1	+¼ to +1¼	+¼ to +1¼	+¾	+¾	0 to ⅛	—	—

Continued

WHEEL ALIGNMENT SPECIFICATIONS—Continued

OLD CAR SPECIFICATIONS: For 1946-68 Wheel Alignment Specifications see main index.

| Year | Model | Caster Angle, Degrees | | Camber Angle, Degrees | | | | Toe-In. Inch | Toe-Out on Turns, Deg.① | |
| | | Limits | Desired | Limits | | Desired | | | Outer Wheel | Inner Wheel |
				Left	Right	Left	Right			
CHEVROLET										
1969-70	All	+¼ to +1¼	+¾	−¼ to +¾	−¼ to +¾	+¼	+¼	⅛ to ¼	20	22½
1971	All	−1½ to −½	−1	0 to +1	0 to +1	+½	+½	⅛ to ¼	—	—
1972	All	+½ to +1½	+1	0 to +1	0 to +1	+½	+½	⅛ to ¼	—	—
1973-74	All	+½ to +1½	+1	+½ to +1½	0 to +1	+1	+½	0 to ⅛	—	—
1975	All	+1 to +2	+1½	+½ to +1½	0 to +1	+1	+½	0 to ⅛	—	—
CORVETTE										
1969-74	Manual Steer.	+½ to +1½	+1	+¼ to +1¼	+¼ to +1¼	+¾	+¾	3/16 to 5/16②	—	20
	Power Steer.	+1¾ to +2¾	+2¼	+¼ to +1¼	+¼ to +1¼	+¾	+¾	3/16 to 5/16②	—	20
	Rear Wheel Align.	—	—	−⅝ to −1⅛	−⅝ to −1⅛	−⅞	−⅞	1/32 to 3/32	—	—
1975	Manual Steer.	+½ to +1½	+1	+¼ to +1¼	+¼ to +1¼	+¾	+¾	3/16 to 5/16	—	—
	Power Steer.	+1¾ to +2¾	+2¼	+¼ to +1¼	+¼ to +1¼	+¾	+¾	3/16 to 5/16	—	—
	Rear Whl. Align.	—	—	−1 to +1	−1 to +1	−½	−½	1/16 to ⅛	—	—

①—Incorrect toe-out, when other adjustments are correct, indicates bent steering arms.
②—1971 ⅛" to ⅜".
③—Manual steering.
④—Power steering.

COOLING SYSTEM & CAPACITY DATA

| Year | Model or Engine | Cooling Capacity, Qts. | | | Radiator Cap Relief Pressure, Lbs. | | Thermo. Opening Temp. ① | Fuel Tank Gals. | Engine Oil Refill Qts. ② | Transmission Oil | | | Rear Axle Oil Pints |
		No Heater	With Heater	With A/C	With A/C	No A/C				3 Speed Pints	4 Speed Pints	Auto. Trans. Qts. ⑮	
CAMARO													
1969	6-230, 250	11	13	13	15	15	195	18	4	3⑧	3	⑲	3½
	8-327	16	17	17	15	15	195	18	4	3⑧	3	⑲	3½
	8-350	15	16	17	15	15	195	18	4	3⑧	3	⑲	3½
	8-396	22	23	23	15	15	195	18	4	3⑧	3	⑲	4
1970	6-250	11	12	13	15	15	195	19	4	3	—	⑲	3½
	8-307	14	15	16	15	15	195	19	4	3	—	⑲	3½
	8-350 Exc. 360 H.P.	15	16	16	15	15	195	19	4	—	3	⑲	3½
	8-350, 360 H.P.	15	16	16	15	15	180	19	4	—	3	⑲	3½
	8-396㉖	22	23	23	15	15	195	19	4	—	3	⑲	3½
1971	6-250	11	12	12	15	15	195	18	4	3	—	⑲	3½
	8-307	14	15	15	15	15	195	18	4	3	—	⑲	3½
	8-350 Exc. 330 H.P.	14	15	15	15	15	195	18	4	—	3	⑲	㉖
	8-350, 330 H.P.	14	15	15	15	15	180	18	4	—	3	⑲	㉖
	8-396㉖	23	24	24	15	15	195	18	4	—	3	⑲	㉖
1972	6-250	11	12	13	15	15	195	18	4	3	—	⑲	4¼
	8-307	14	15	17	15	15	195	18	4	3	—	⑲	4¼
	8-350 Exc. 255 H.P.	15	16	17	15	15	195	18	4	—	3	⑲	4¼
	8-350, 255 H.P.	15	16	17	15	15	180	18	4	—	3	⑲	4¼
	8-402	23	24	25	15	15	195	18	4	—	3	⑲	4¼

Continued

COOLING SYSTEM & CAPACITY DATA—Continued

Year	Model or Engine	Cooling Capacity, Qts.			Radiator Cap Relief Pressure, Lbs.		Thermo. Opening Temp. ①	Fuel Tank Gals.	Engine Oil Refill Qts. ②	Transmission Oil			Rear Axle Oil Pints
		No Heater	With Heater	With A/C	With A/C	No A/C				3 Speed Pints	4 Speed Pints	Auto. Trans. Qts. ⑱	
CAMARO—Continued													
1973	6-250	11	12	13	15	15	195	18	4	3	—	⑲	4¼
	V8-307	15	16	17	15	15	195	18	4	3	—	⑲	4¼
	V8-350, 145 H.P.	15	16	17	15	15	195	18	4	3	3	⑲	4¼
	V8-350, 175 H.P.	15	16	17	15	15	195	18	4	3	3	⑲	4¼
	V8-350, 245 H.P.	15	16	17	15	15	180	18	4	3	3	⑲	4¼
1974	6-250	14	14	—	15	15	195	21	4	3	—	⑦	4¼
	8-350, 145 H.P.	18	18	—	15	15	195	21	4	3	3	⑦	4¼
	8-350, 160 H.P.	18	18	—	15	15	195	21	4	3	3	⑦	4¼
	8-350, 185 H.P.	18	18	—	15	15	195	21	4	3	3	⑦	4¼
	8-350, 245 H.P.	18	18	—	15	15	180	21	4	3	3	⑦	4¼
1975	6-250	—	12½	12½	15	15	195	21	4	3	—	4⑥	4¼
	8-350	—	15½	16½	15	15	195	21	4	3	3	4⑥	4¼
	8-350, Z28	—	15½	16½	15	15	180	21	4	—	3	4⑥	4¼
CHEVELLE & MONTE CARLO													
1969	6-230, 250	11	13	13	15	15	195	20⑳	4	3⑧	—	⑲	3½
	8-307	16	17	18	15	15	195	20⑳	4	3⑧	3	⑲	3½
	8-350	15	16	17	15	15	195	20⑳	4	3⑧	3	⑲	4
	8-396	22	23	23	15	15	195	20⑳	4	3⑧	3	⑲	4
1970	6-250	11	12	13	15	15	195	20㉒	4	3⑧	—	⑲	⑨
	8-307	14	15	16	15	15	195	20㉒	4	3⑧	3	⑲	⑨
	8-350	15	16	16	15	15	195	20㉒	4	3⑧	3	⑲	⑨
	8-400	22	23	24	15	15	195	20㉒	4	3⑧	3	⑲	⑨
	8-454	21	22	23	15	15	195	20㉒	4	3⑧	3	⑲	⑨
1971	6-250	11	12	12	15	15	195	18	4	3	—	⑲	㉖
	8-307	15	16	16	15	15	195	18	4	3	—	⑲	㉖
	8-350	15	16	16	15	15	195	18	4	3	3	⑲	㉖
	8-396㉕	22	23	23	15	15	195	18	4	3	3	⑲	㉖
	8-454, 365 H.P.	21	22	22	15	15	195	18	4	—	3	⑲	㉖
	8-454, 425 H.P.	21	22	22	15	15	180	18	4	—	3	⑲	㉖
1972	6-250	11	12	12	15	15	195	㉘	4	3	—	⑲	㉙
	8-307	14	15	16	15	15	195	㉘	4	3	—	⑲	㉙
	8-350	15	16	17	15	15	195	㉘	4	3	3	⑲	㉙
	8-402	22	23	24	15	15	195	㉘	4	3	3	⑲	㉙
	8-454	22	23	24	15	15	195	㉘	4	—	3	⑲	㉙
1973	6-250	11	12	12	15	15	195	22	4	3	—	⑲	㉙
	8-307	15	16	17	15	15	195	22	4	3	3	⑲	㉙
	8-350, 145 H.P.	15	16	17	15	15	195	22	4	3	—	⑲	㉙
	8-350, 175 H.P.	15	16	17	15	15	195	22	4	—	4	⑲	㉙
	8-454	22	23	24	15	15	195	22	4	—	4	⑲	㉙
1974	6-250	—	14	14	15	15	195	22⑩	4	3	—	⑦	㉙
	8-350, 145 H.P.	—	18	18③	15	15	195	22⑩	4	3	—	⑦	㉙
	8-350, 160 H.P.	—	18	18③	15	15	195	22⑩	4	3	—	⑦	㉙
	8-400, 150 H.P.	—	18	18③	15	15	195	22⑩	4	—	—	⑦	㉙
	8-400, 180 H.P.	—	18	18③	15	15	195	22⑩	4	—	—	⑦	㉙
	8-454, 235 H.P.	—	24	18⑤	15	15	195	22⑩	4	—	3	⑦	㉙
1975	6-250	—	12½	12½	15	15	195	22⑩	4	3	—	4⑥	㉙
	8-350	—	16	17	15	15	195	22⑩	4	3	—	4⑥	㉙
	8-400	—	16	17	15	15	195	22⑩	4	—	—	4⑥	㉙
	8-454	—	23	24	15	15	195	22⑩	4	—	—	4½⑥	㉙

Continued

COOLING SYSTEM & CAPACITY DATA—Continued

Year	Model or Engine	Cooling Capacity, Qts. No Heater	With Heater	With A/C	Radiator Cap Relief Pressure, Lbs. With A/C	No A/C	Thermo. Opening Temp. [1]	Fuel Tank Gals.	Engine Oil Refill Qts. [2]	Transmission Oil 3 Speed Pints	4 Speed Pints	Auto. Trans. Qts. [15]	Rear Axle Oil Pints
CHEVY NOVA													
1969	4-153	8	9	9	15	15	195	18	4	3[8]	—	[19]	3½
	6-230, 250	11	13	13	15	15	195	18	4	3[8]	—	[19]	3½
	8-307	16	17	17	15	15	195	18	4	3[8]	3	[19]	3½
	8-350	15	16	16	15	15	195	18	4	3½	3	[19]	4
	8-396	22	23	23	15	15	195	18	4	3½	3	[19]	4
1970	4-153	8	9	9	15	15	195	18[23]	3½[11]	3	—	[19]	[9]
	6-230, 250	11	12	13	15	15	195	18[23]	4	3	—	[19]	[9]
	8-307	14	15	16	15	15	195	18[23]	4	3[8]	3	[19]	[9]
	8-350	15	16	16	15	15	195	18[23]	4	3[8]	3	[19]	[9]
1971	6-250	11	12	12	15	15	195	18	4	3	—	[19]	[26]
	8-307	15	16	16	15	15	195	18	4	3	—	[19]	[26]
	8-350	15	16	16	15	15	195	18	4	3	3	[19]	[26]
1972	6-250	11	12	12	15	15	195	16	4	3	—	[19]	4¼
	8-307	14	15	16	15	15	195	16	4	3	—	[19]	4¼
	8-350	15	16	17	15	15	195	16	4	3	3	[19]	4¼
1973	6-250	11	12	12	15	15	195	21	4	3	—	[19]	4¼
	8-307	16	15	16	15	15	195	21	4	3	—	[19]	4¼
	8-350, 145 H.P.	17	16	17	15	15	195	21	4	3	—	[19]	4¼
	8-350, 175 H.P.	17	16	17	15	15	195	21	4	—	4	[19]	4¼
1974	6-250	14	14	—	15	15	195	21	4	3	—	[7]	4¼
	8-350, 145 H.P.	18	18	—	15	15	195	21	4	3	—	[7]	4¼
	8-350, 160 H.P.	18	18	—	15	15	195	21	4	3	—	[7]	4¼
	8-350, 185 H.P.	18	18	—	15	15	195	21	4	—	3	[7]	4¼
1975	6-250	—	12½	12½	15	15	195	21	4	3	—	4[8]	4¼
	8-262	—	—	—	15	15	195	21	4	3	—	4[8]	4¼
	8-350	—	15½	16½	15	15	195	21	4	3	—	4[8]	4¼
CHEVROLET													
1969	6-250	11	12	13	15	15	195	24	4	3[8]	—	[19]	3½
	8-327	16	17	18	15	15	195	24	4	3[8]	3	[19]	3½
	8-350	14	15	16	15	15	195	24	4	3½	3	[19]	4
	8-396	22	23	23	15	15	195	24	4	3½	3	[19]	4
	8-427	21	22	22	15	15	195	24	4	3½	3	[19]	4
1970	6-250	11	12	12	15	15	195	25[24]	4	3[8]	—	[19]	[9]
	8-350, 250 H.P.	15	16	16	15	15	195	25[24]	4	3[8]	—	[19]	[9]
	8-350, 300 H.P.	15	16	17	15	15	195	25[24]	4	3[8]	—	[19]	[9]
	8-400	15	16	17	15	15	195	25[24]	4	3[8]	—	[19]	[9]
	8-454	21	22	22	15	15	Thermo	25[24]	4	3[8]	—	[19]	[9]
1971	6-250	11	12	12	15	15	195	23[27]	4	3	—	[19]	[26]
	8-350	15	16	16	15	15	195	23[27]	4	3	—	[19]	[26]
	8-396[25]	22	23	23	15	15	195	23[27]	4	—	—	[19]	[26]
	8-400	15	16	16	15	15	195	23[27]	4	3	—	[19]	[26]
	8-454	21	22	22	15	15	195	23[27]	4	—	—	[19]	[26]
1972	6-250	11	12	12	15	15	195	23[30]	4	3	—	[19]	[29]
	8-350	15	16	17	15	15	195	23[30]	4	—	—	[19]	[29]
	8-400	15	16	17	15	15	195	23[30]	4	—	—	[19]	[29]
	8-402	22	23	24	15	15	195	23[30]	4	—	—	[19]	[29]
	8-454	21	22	23	15	15	195	23[30]	4	—	—	[19]	[29]

Continued

CHEVROLET—Exc. Monza 2+2 & Vega

COOLING SYSTEM & CAPACITY DATA—Continued

Year	Model or Engine	Cooling Capacity, Qts.			Radiator Cap Relief Pressure, Lbs.		Thermo. Opening Temp. [1]	Fuel Tank Gals.	Engine Oil Refill Qts. [2]	Transmission Oil			Rear Axle Oil Pints
		No Heater	With Heater	With A/C	With A/C	No A/C				3 Speed Pints	4 Speed Pints	Auto. Trans. Qts. [16]	
CHEVROLET—Continued													
1973	6-250	11	12	12	15	15	195	[30]	4	3	—	—	[29]
	8-350, 145 H.P.	15	16	17	15	15	195	[30]	4	—	—	4	[29]
	8-350, 175 H.P.	15	16	17	15	15	195	[30]	4	—	—	4	[29]
	8-400	15	16	17	15	15	195	[30]	4	—	—	4	[29]
	8-454	22	23	24	15	15	195	[30]	4	—	—	4½	[29]
1974	8-350, 145 H.P.	18	18	—	15	15	195	26[20]	4	—	—	[7]	[29]
	8-350, 160 H.P.	18	18	—	15	15	195	26[20]	4	—	—	[7]	[29]
	8-400, 150 H.P.	18	18	—	15	15	195	26[20]	4	—	—	[7]	[29]
	8-400, 180 H.P.	18	18	—	15	15	195	26[20]	4	—	—	[7]	[29]
	8-454, 235 H.P.	24	26	—	15	15	195	26[20]	4	—	—	[7]	[29]
1975	8-350	—	16	17	15	15	195	26[20]	4	—	—	4[6]	[29]
	8-400	—	16½	17½	15	15	195	26[20]	4	—	—	4½[6]	[29]
	8-454	—	23	24	15	15	195	26[20]	4	—	—	4½[6]	[29]
CORVETTE													
1969	8-350	14	15	15	15	15	195	20	4	3	3	[21]	4
	8-427	21	22	22	15	15	195	20	5	3	3	[21]	4
1970	8-350 Exc. 370 H.P.	14	15	21	15	15	195	20	4	—	3	[4]	4
	8-350, 370 H.P.	17	18	22	15	15	180	20	4	—	3	[4]	4
	8-454	21	22	—	15	15	195	20	5	—	3	[4]	4
1971	8-350 Exc. 330 H.P.[13]	14	15	15	15	15	195	18	4	—	3	—	4
	8-350 Exc. 330 H.P.[14]	17	18	18	15	15	195	18	4	—	—	[19]	4
	8-350, 330 H.P.	17	18	18	15	15	180	18	4	—	3	[19]	4
	8-454, 365 H.P.	21	22	22	15	15	195	18	5	—	3	[19]	4
	8-454, 425 H.P.[13]	19	20	20	15	15	180	18	5	—	3	—	4
	8-454, 425 H.P.[14]	21	22	22	15	15	180	18	5	—	—	[19]	4
1972	8-350, 200 H.P.	16	17	18	15	15	195	18	4	—	3	4	4
	8-350, 255 H.P.	16	17	18	15	15	180	18	4	—	3	—	4
	8-454	22	23	24	15	15	195	18	5	—	3	4	4
1973	8-350, 190 H.P.	17	18	18	15	15	195	18	4	—	3	4	4
	8-350, 250 H.P.	17	18	18	15	15	180	18	4	—	3	4	4
	8-454, 275 H.P.	23	24	24	15	15	195	18	5	—	3	4	4
1974	8-350, 195 H.P.	17	19	—	15	15	195	18	4	—	3	[7]	4
	8-350, 250 H.P.	17	19	—	15	15	180	18	4	—	3	[7]	4
	8-454, 270 H.P.	24	24	—	15	15	195	18	4	—	3	[7]	4
1975	8-350	—	18	18	15	15	180	18	4	—	3	4[6]	4

[1]—For permanent type anti-freeze.
[2]—Add one quart with filter change.
[3]—Monte Carlo 20 qts.
[4]—Refill 1½ qts. Total capacity 7½ qts.
[5]—Monte Carlo 26 qts.
[6]—Turbo Hydramatic 250 & 350 total capacity 10 qts., T.H. 400 total capacity 11 qts.
[7]—Turbo Hydramatic 250 & 350 refill 2½ qts., T.H. 400 refill 3¾ qts.
[8]—Heavy duty unit 3½.
[9]—3¾ for 8⅛" ring gear and 4¼ for 8⅞" ring gear.
[10]—El Camino 26 gal.
[11]—Add one pint with filter change.
[13]—Standard trans.
[14]—Auto. trans.
[16]—Approximate. Make final check with dipstick.
[19]—Powerglide & Torque Drive: Refill 3 qts. Total capacity 8½ qts. Turbo-Hydramatic 350: Refill 2½ qts. Total capacity 10 qts. Turbo-Hydramatic 400: Refill 4 qts. Total capacity 11 qts.
[20]—Wagons 22 gallons.
[21]—Refill 4 qts. Total capacity 11 qts.
[22]—California vehicles about 2 gallons less.
[23]—California vehicles about 1 gallon less.
[24]—Wagons 22 gallons. California vehicles about 2 gallons less.
[25]—Marketed as 396 but actually 402 cu. in.
[26]—3½ for 8⅛" ring gear and 4 for 8⅞" ring gear.
[27]—Wagons 20 gallons.
[28]—Wagons 19 gallons; others 18 gallons.
[29]—4¼ for 8⅛" and 8½" ring gears and 4.9 for 8⅞" ring gear.
[30]—Station wagons 22 gals.; others 26 gals.

Electrical Section

1975 HIGH ENERGY IGNITION SYSTEM (H.E.I.)

Service procedures for the 1975 V8 H.E.I. distributor are found in the "Tune Up Service" chapter under Electronic Ignition Systems. Service procedures for the 6-250 H.E.I. distributor are slightly different since the ignition coil is externally mounted.

DISTRIBUTOR
Removal

1. Disconnect distributor primary wire from coil terminal.

   NOTE: On H.E.I. systems, disconnect feed and module connectors from distributor cap.

2. Remove distributor cap and rotor. *Mark position of rotor arm on distributor housing so distributor can be installed in same position.*
3. Remove vacuum line and distributor hold down clamp. On Corvette, units, remove tachometer drive cable.
4. Note relative position of distributor in block, then work it out of the engine.

Installation

1. Turn rotor about ⅛ of a turn counterclockwise past the mark previously placed on the distributor housing.
2. Push the distributor down into the block with the housing in the normal "installed" position. *It may be necessary to move the rotor slightly to start gear into mesh with camshaft gear, but rotor should line up with mark when distributor is down in place.*

NOTE: Because the lower end of the distributor shaft drives the oil pump, use extra care when installing the distributor to be sure it is completely seated and engaged in oil pump.

NOTE

If the engine was disturbed while the distributor was removed from the engine, first crank the engine to bring No. 1 piston up on its compression stroke and continue cranking until the timing mark is adjacent to the timing indicator. Then rotate the distributor cam until the rotor is in position to fire No. 1 cylinder. Install the distributor.

3. Tighten distributor clamp screw snugly and connect vacuum line, primary wire to coil, and install cap.
4. Set ignition timing.

NOTE: When using a timing light to adjust ignition timing, the connection should be made at the No. 1 spark plug. Forcing foreign objects

Fig. 1   Ignition lock removal

through the boot at the No. 1 terminal of the distributor cap will damage the boot and could cause engine misfiring.

STARTER, REPLACE
1969-75 All Models

1. Disconnect ground cable at battery.
2. Raise vehicle to working height.
3. Disconnect all wires at solenoid.

   NOTE: Reinstall terminal nuts as each wire is disconnected as thread size is different but may be mixed and stripped.

4. Loosen starter front bracket (nut on V8 and bolt on Sixes) then remove two mounting bolts.

   NOTE: On V8 engines using solenoid heat shield, remove front bracket upper bolt and detach bracket from starter.

5. Remove front bracket bolt or nut and rotate bracket clear of work area. Then lower starter from

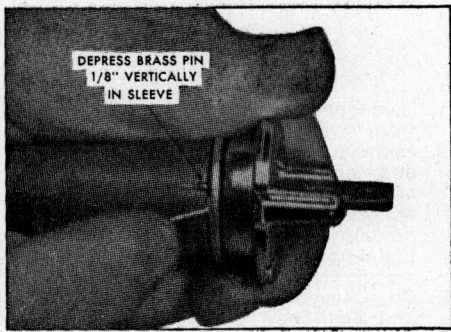

Fig. 2   Ignition lock disassembly

vehicle by lowering front end first (hold starter against bell housing and sort of roll end-over end).

6. Reverse removal procedure to install and torque mount bolts to 25-35 ft-lbs. On 1973-75 Corvette, apply a suitable sealing compound around starter where it enters engine splash shield.

IGNITION LOCK
1969-75

1. Follow the procedure to remove the turn signal switch as described further on.
2. On *1969-70* models the lock cylinder may be removed in any position from "Accessory" to "ON". However, the "LOCK" position is desired because of its positive location. On *1971-75* models the lock cylinder should be removed in the "RUN" position only.
3. Place a thin tool (small screwdriver or knife blade) into the slot, Fig. 1, next to the switch mounting screw boss (right hand slot) and depress spring latch at bottom of slot which releases lock. Remove lock.
4. To separate the lock from the cylinder, Fig. 2, use a paper clip or similar wire, place a 90° bend about ⅛" from one end of the wire.
5. Place the cylinder in "LOCK" position. Using the wire as described in step 4, depress the plunger pin (above the stake mark) about ⅛" vertically in sleeve housing, at the same time exert light upward pressure on the lock assembly, rotate the cylinder counter-clockwise until it pops up from the sleeve assembly.

IGNITION SWITCH, REPLACE
1969-75

The ignition switch is mounted on top of the mast jacket inside the brake pedal support and is actuated by a rod and rack assembly.

1. Disconnect battery cable.
2. Disconnect and lower steering column.

   NOTE: It may be necessary, on some models, to remove the upper column mounting bracket if it hinders servicing of switch.

3. The switch should be in the "Lock" position before removal. If lock cylinder has been removed, the actuating rod is pulled up to the stop then back one detent, to place it in the "Lock" position. Remove retaining screws and switch.
4. Reverse procedure to install being sure that the switch is in the "Lock" position before installing.

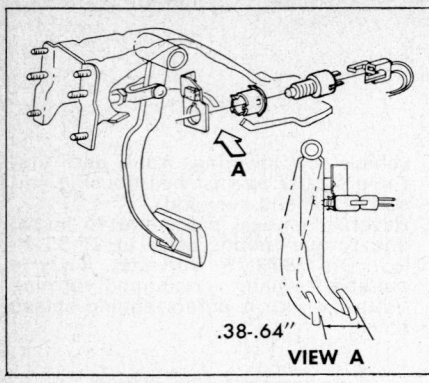

Fig. 3   Stop light switch.
1969-72 Chevelle

LIGHT SWITCH, REPLACE

1973-75 Chevelle & Monte Carlo

1. Disconnect battery ground cable.
2. Remove instrument panel pad.
3. Remove left radio speaker to one side.
4. Pull headlamp control knob to "ON" position and while standing outside vehicle on left side, reach in and behind instrument panel and depress switch retainer and pull knob and shaft assembly out.
5. Remove ferrule nut and switch from panel.

1969-75 Corvette

1. Disconnect battery cable.
2. Remove screws securing mast jacket trim covers and remove covers.
3. Remove left side console forward trim panel.
4. Lower steering column.
5. Remove screws securing left instrument panel to door opening, top of dash and left side of center instrument panel.
6. Pull cluster down and tip forward for access.
7. Depress switch shaft retainer and remove the knob and shaft assembly. Remove switch retaining bezel.
8. Disconnect vacuum hoses from switch, tagging them for assembly. Pry the connector from the switch and remove the switch.

1970-75 Camaro

1. Disconnect battery ground cable.
2. Remove steering column lower cover.
3. Reach up under cluster and depress lighting switch shaft retainer while pulling gently on shaft.
4. Remove nut securing switch to carrier.
5. Remove cluster carrier screws and tilt right side of cluster out.

NOTE: On 1970-71 models, grounding ring at cigar lighter may be disconnected to permit further carrier movement.

6. Unplug connector and remove switch.

1973-75 Chevrolet & Nova; 1969-72 Except Corvette & 1970-72 Camaro

1. Disconnect battery ground cable.

NOTE: On Chevy Nova remove the parking brake bracket and lower assembly to the floor. Heater on air conditioning control head must also be removed.

2. Pull switch knob to "ON" position.
3. Reach up under instrument panel and depress switch shaft retainer, then remove knob and shaft assembly.
4. Remove ferrule nut and switch from panel.

NOTE: Remove vacuum hoses from Camaro and Chevrolet optional headlight switches. Tag location of hoses for assembly.

5. Disconnect multi-contact connector from light switch.
6. Reverse procedure to install.

STOP LIGHT SWITCH, REPLACE

1973-75 Except Corvette

1. Disconnect wiring connector at switch.
2. Remove retaining nut, if so equipped, and unscrew switch from bracket.
3. To install: On Nova, install inboard adjusting nut, install switch through bracket and install retaining nut. On all other models, depress brake pedal and push new switch into clip until shoulder bottoms out.
4. Plug connector onto switch and check operation. Electrical contact should be made when pedal is depressed $\frac{3}{8}$" to $\frac{5}{8}$" from fully released position.

1973-75 Corvette

1. Disconnect wiring connector at switch.
2. Remove retaining nut and unscrew switch from bracket.
3. Upon installation, check for proper operation. Electrical contact should be made when pedal is depressed $\frac{1}{4}$" to $\frac{5}{8}$". Switch bracket has a slotted screw hole for adjustment.

1969-72

1. Disconnect wiring harness connector from switch, Figs. 3 and 4.
2. Remove retaining nut (if equipped) and unscrew switch from bracket.

NOTE: On Corvettes, remove screw holding switch bracket to brake pedal housing.

3. On Chevelles, depress brake pedal and push new switch into clip until shoulder bottoms out.
4. On Corvettes, align switch bracket

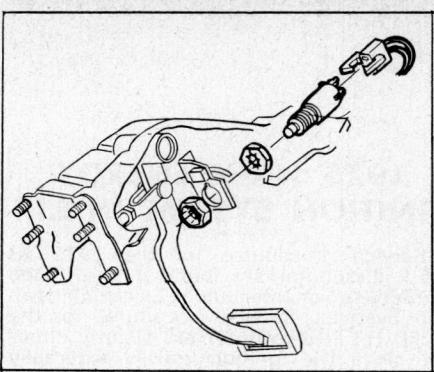

Fig. 4   Stop light switch. 1969-72 Camaro, Chevrolet and Chevy Nova

on brake pedal housing and install screw.
5. On all other models, install inboard adjusting nut, install switch through bracket and install retaining nut.
6. Plug connector onto switch.

CLUTCH START SWITCH

1969 All; 1973-75 Corvette

1. Unplug connector from switch.
2. Remove retainer from pins or link on clutch pedal arm.
3. Remove retaining screw and switch.

1970-72 All; 1973-75 Except Corvette

1. Unplug connector from switch.
2. Compress switch actuating shaft retainer and remove shaft with switch attached from switch bracket.

NEUTRAL SAFETY SWITCH, REPLACE

1971-75 Column Shift & 1974 Floor Shift Exc. Corvette

NOTE: On 1974-75 floor shift vehicles, position shift lever in "Park." Also, the new switch assembly is pinned in the "Park" position.

1. Disconnect wiring connector at switch terminals.
2. Unfasten and remove switch from mast jacket.
3. To install: position shift lever against NEUTRAL gate by rotating lower lever counterclockwise as viewed from drivers seat.
4. Assemble switch to column by inserting actuating tang in shifter tube slot.
5. Tighten screws, connect wiring connector and move selector lever out of NEUTRAL to shear pin which is part of new switch.

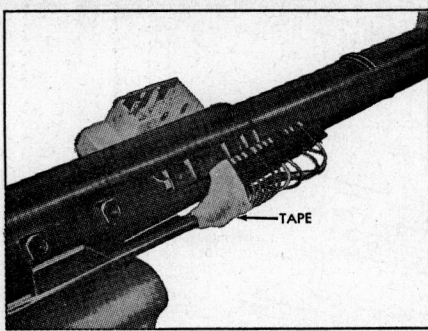

Fig. 5 Taping turn signal connector and wires. 1969-75

plate (horn contact carrier on tilt models) and remove snap ring ("C" ring on tilt models).
4. Remove lock plate, cancelling cam, spring, thrust washer and signal lever.
5. Push hazard warning knob in and unscrew knob.
6. Pull connector from bracket and wrap upper part of connector with tape to prevent snagging the wires during removal. On Tilt models, position shifter housing in "Low" position. Remove harness cover.
7. Remove retaining screws and remove switch, Figs. 5 and 6.

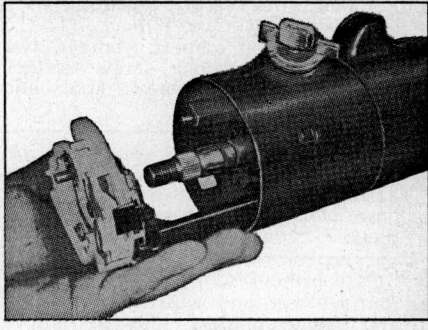

Fig. 6 Removing turn signal switch. 1969-75

1969-70 Column Shift

1. Disconnect wiring connectors at switch terminals.
2. Unfasten and remove switch from mast jacket.
3. To install, locate shift lever in "Drive" and locate lever tang against transmission selector plate.
4. If provided for, align slot in contact support with hole in switch and insert a 3/32" rod to hold support in place. Switch is now in drive position.
5. Place contact support drive slot over shifter tube drive tang and tighten screws. Remove clamp and 3/32" rod.
6. Connect wiring harness and check operation of switch.

1974 Corvette & 1969-73 All Floor Shift

1. Disconnect shift control lever arm from transmission control rod.
2. Remove shift control knob.
3. Remove trim plate.
4. Remove control assembly from seal and disconnect switch wiring.
5. Remove switch from control assembly.
6. To install, position gearshift in Drive position, align hole in contact support with hole in switch and insert a pin (3/32") to hold support in place.
7. Place contact support drive slot over drive tang and tighten switch mounting screws.
8. Connect wiring harness to switch wiring.
9. Install trim plate control knob and connect shift lever arm to transmission control rod.

TURN SIGNAL SWITCH, REPLACE

1969-75

1. Disconnect battery cable and remove steering wheel.
2. Remove cover from shaft. *The cover retaining screws need not be completely removed from the cover.*
3. Using a suitable tool, compress lock

HORN SOUNDER & STEERING WHEEL

1970-75 Cushioned Rim Wheel

1. Disconnect battery ground cable.
2. Remove two steering wheel shroud screws at underside of steering wheel and remove shroud.
3. Remove three spacer screws, spacer, plate and belleville spring.
4. Remove steering wheel nut and washer and, using a suitable puller, remove steering wheel.

NOTE: On 1975 models, remove snap ring before steering wheel nut.

1969 Deluxe Wheel
1970-75 Standard Wheel

1. Disconnect battery ground cable.
2. Remove attaching screws on underside of steering wheel, Fig. 7.
3. Lift steering wheel shroud and pull horn wires from cancelling cam tower.
4. Remove steering wheel nut and washer, and use a suitable puller to remove steering wheel.

NOTE: On 1975 models, remove snap ring before steering wheel nut.

(Fig. 7 image area)

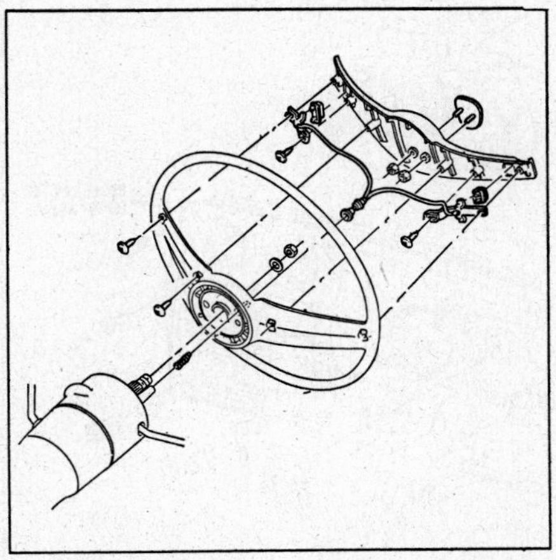

Fig. 7 Steering wheel and horn attachments. 1969-75 (typical)

1969 Standard Wheel Exc. Corvette

1. Disconnect battery ground cable.
2. Pull out horn button cap or center ornament and retainer.
3. Remove three screws from receiving cup.
4. Remove receiving cup, belleville spring, bushing and pivot ring.
5. Remove wheel nut and washer and use a suitable puller to remove wheel.

CAUTION: Turn signal control assembly must be in neutral position when assembling steering wheel to prevent damage to cancelling cam and control assembly.

1969 Simulated Wood Wheel

1. Disconnect steering column harness from chassis wiring harness at connector.
2. Disconnect battery ground cable.
3. Remove horn cap by pulling up.
4. Remove screws and contact assembly.

NOTE: If steering wheel only is to be replaced, perform Step 4. If turn signal cancelling cam is to be replaced, omit Step 4 and proceed with Steps 5 and 6.

5. Remove retaining screws and remove wheel from hub assembly.
6. Remove wheel nut and washer.
7. Use a suitable puller to remove wheel.

NOTE: Turn signal control assembly must be in neutral position when assembling the hub to prevent damage to cancelling cam and control assembly.

8. Reverse procedure to install.

1969-75 Corvette (Exc. Simulated Wood Wheel)

1. Disconnect steering column harness at wiring connector. Disconnect battery ground cable.
2. Pry off horn button cap.

3. Remove three screws securing horn contact to spacer and hub.
4. On telescoping wheels, remove two screws securing lock screw to lock knob and remove screw, knob and spacer.

   NOTE: If wheel only is to be replaced, perform Step 5. If turn signal cancelling cam is to be replaced, omit Step 5 and proceed with Steps 6 and 7.

5. Remove wheel from hub (6 screws).
6. Remove nut and washer from shaft and use a suitable puller to remove wheel and hub.

   NOTE: On 1975 models, remove snap ring before steering wheel nut.

7. Slide cancelling cam and spring off shaft.

INSTRUMENT CLUSTER
1973-75 Chevelle & Monte Carlo

1. Disconnect battery ground cable.
2. Remove radio knobs and clock stem set knob, if equipped.
3. Remove instrument bezel retaining screws, Figs. 8 and 9.
4. Pull bezel out to disconnect tail gate release or rear defogger switch, if equipped.
5. Remove instrument bezel.

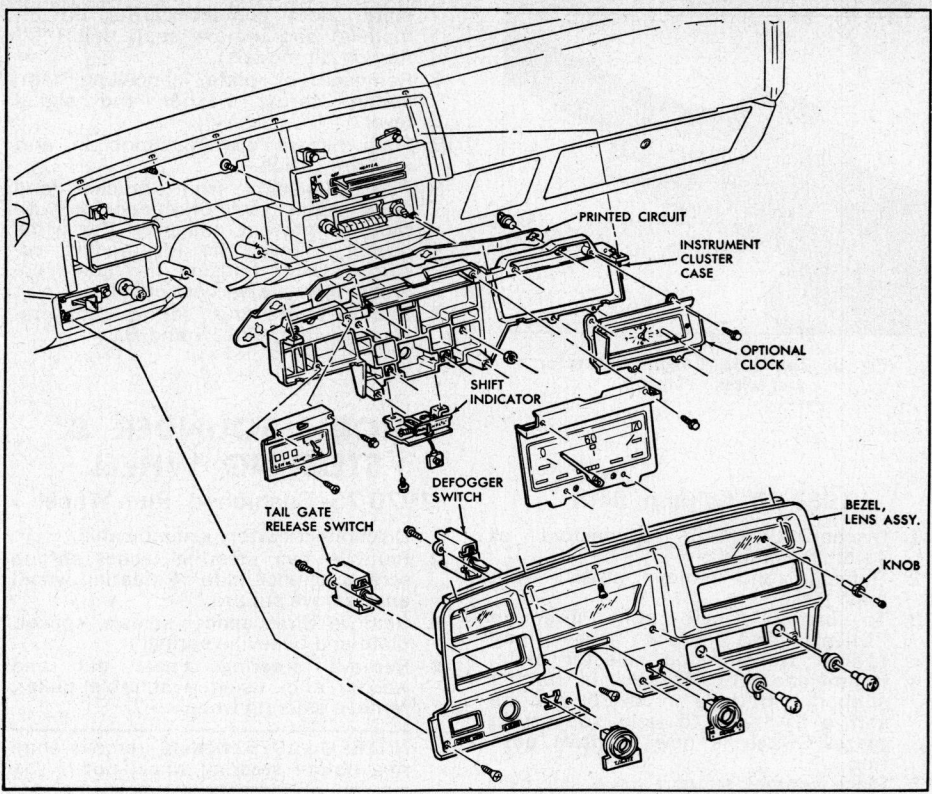

Fig. 8   Instrument cluster. 1973-75 Chevelle with standard cluster

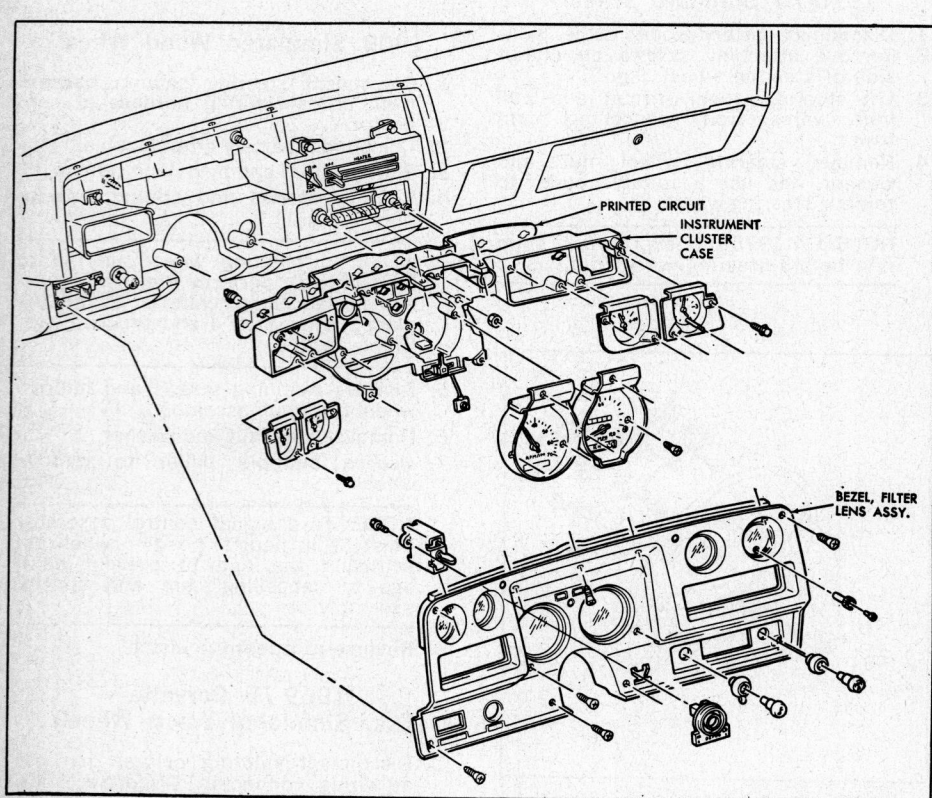

Fig. 9   Instrument cluster. 1973-75 Chevelle with optional cluster & Monte Carlo

1971-75 Chevrolet

1. Disconnect battery ground cable.
2. Remove cigar lighter knob and hidden screw in shroud where knob was.
3. Pull on headlamp switch shaft then remove hidden screw above middle of shaft.
4. Remove two screws at bottom corners of shroud and lift off shroud, Fig. 10.
5. To service instruments, remove clock stem set knob.
6. Remove lens retaining strip secured by three screws at top of lens. Be careful not to mar lens.
7. Lift off lens carefully—guide pins are on bottom of lens.
8. Gently lift up on bottom of filter housing and rotate housing up and rearward, toward technician on front seat. Top of housing should clear top of instrument carrier. Use care around PRNDL housing and lift filter assembly off. Speedometer, fuel gauge and clock can now be removed.

1970-75 Camaro

1. Disconnect battery ground cable.
2. Remove 6 screws securing trim cover beneath steering column. Two of these screws are located above the ash tray.
3. Remove headlamp switch retaining nut.
4. From behind panel, disconnect cigar

lighter and unscrew retainer. Note grounding ring.

5. From under lower edge of cluster, remove screw on either side of column, Fig. 11.
6. Remove 4 screws visible on front of carrier.
7. Remove screw retaining ground wire for wiper switch. Screw is fastened under top left corner of switch.
8. Carefully tilt carrier out of access to the connectors on headlamp and wiper switches.
9. Remove lens screws then cluster screws.
10. Disconnect shift indicator from steering column.
11. Disconnect speedometer cable and tilt cluster forward and remove remaining connectors.
12. Lift cluster out.

1970-75 Chevy Nova

1. Disconnect battery ground cable.
2. Lower steering column and apply protective covering to mast jacket to protect paint.
3. Remove three screws above front of heater control securing it to instrument cluster, Fig. 12.
4. Remove radio control knobs, washers, bezel nuts and front support at lower edge of cluster. This will allow radio to remain in panel.
5. Remove screws at top, bottom and sides of cluster securing it to panel.
6. Tilt console forward and reach behind to disconnect speedometer cable and all other connections and lift instrument panel out of carrier after removing screws.

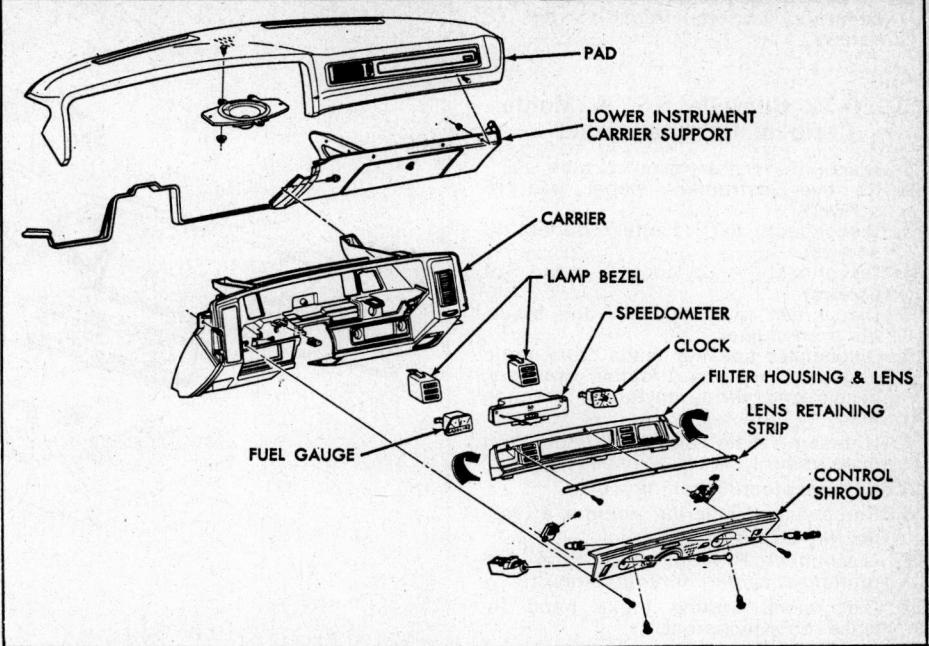

Fig. 10   Instrument cluster. 1971-75 Chevrolet

1970-72 Chevelle (W/Standard Panel)

1. Disconnect battery ground cable.
2. Lower steering column.
3. Disconnect parking brake hand release rod attachment.
4. Disconnect speedometer cable from speedometer.
5. Remove instrument panel pad (six screws), Fig. 13.
6. Disconnect radio speaker bracket from instrument panel.
7. Disconnect A/C center outlet (three screws).
8. Disconnect A/C control head (four screws).
9. Disconnect radio speaker connector from radio.
10. Remove radio knobs, washers, bezels and wiring and remove bolts from braces securing radio; roll radio out from under panel.
11. Remove six instrument panel attaching bolts and roll out instrument panel. **NOTE: Two men are needed.**
12. Pop out three telltale snap covers and remove three telltale housing attaching screws, remove telltale housing.

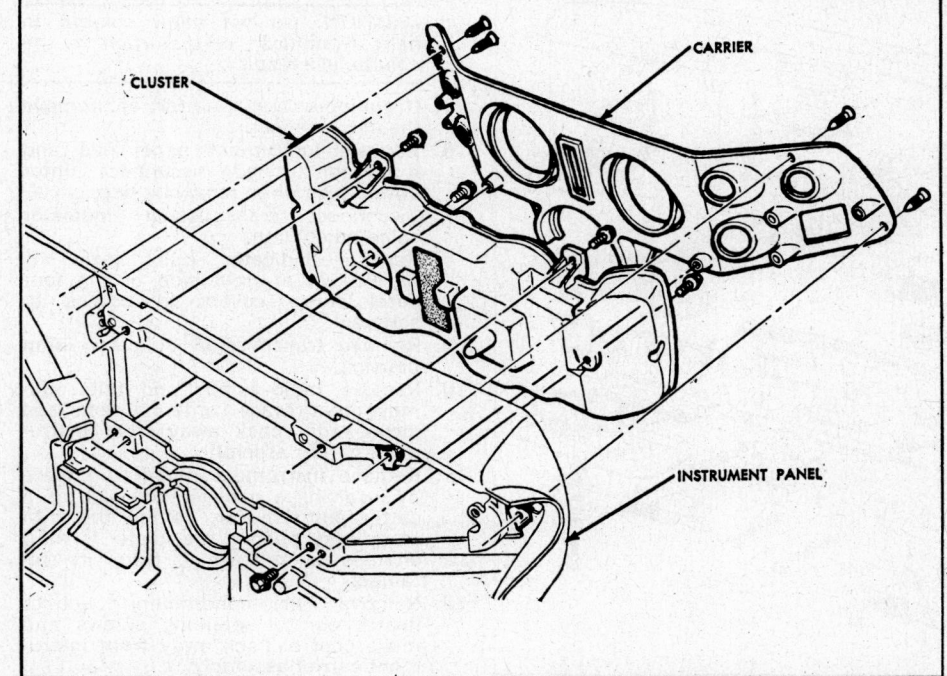

Fig. 11   Instrument cluster. 1970-75 Camaro

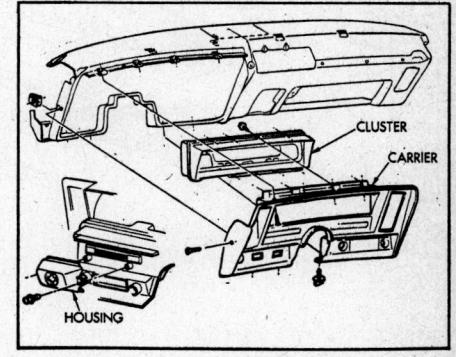

Fig. 12   Instrument cluster. 1970-75 Chevy Nova

13. Remove clock stem set knob and separate cluster from carrier (8 screws).

1970-72 Chevelle S.S. & Monte Carlo & Optional Panel

1. Disconnect battery ground cable.
2. Remove instrument panel pad (6 screws).
3. Disconnect A/C center outlet (3 screws).
4. Disconnect A/C control head (4 screws).
5. Disconnect radio speaker and brackets from cluster.
6. Disconnect speaker leads from radio and remove radio knobs, washers, bezels and wiring including antenna lead.
7. Unfasten radio and roll radio out from under instrument panel.
8. Remove steering column cover.
9. Remove two steering column attaching bolts. Note shims.
10. Disconnect PRNDL cable from column housing and lower column.
11. Disconnect parking brake hand release rod attachment.
12. Remove six instrument panel attaching bolts and roll out panel, Fig. 14.

NOTE: Two men are needed.

13. Disconnect speedometer cable.
14. Remove cluster lamp sockets, clock, fuel gauge, and all connectors from rear of panel.
15. Remove screws retaining printed circuit and lift off circuit panel.

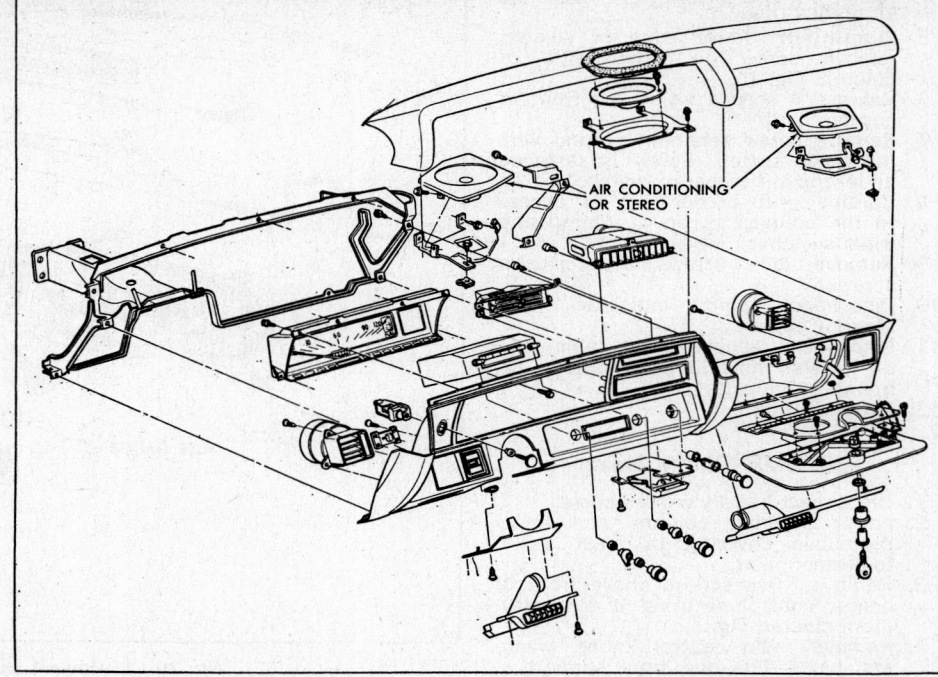

Fig. 13   Instrument cluster. 1970-72 Chevelle with standard cluster

1969-70 Chevrolet

1. Disconnect battery ground cable.
2. If air conditioned, remove lap cooler from under steering column.
3. Remove column mast jacket trim cover.
4. Lower steering column.

CAUTION: *Do not allow column to hang from dash or distortion to the column will result.*

5. If equipped with Comfortron, remove the in-car sensor.
6. Remove instrument panel pad and if air conditioned, disconnect center outlet hose when removing pad.
7. Disconnect transmission indicator cable on column.
8. Remove indicator bulb bezel by pushing in at right side of the four bezel screw covers to access to screws.
9. Remove transmission indicator lamp housing.
10. Remove radio knobs and nuts. Remove rear brace, antenna lead and move radio back away from instrument carrier assembly.
11. Remove instrument panel trim plate by inserting a hooked tool such as a cotter pin remover, behind the trim plate and pulling the plate forward enough to release it from its retainers.
12. Remove air conditioning and/or heater control retaining screws and move control back away from instrument carrier assembly.
13. Remove screws retaining instrument carrier to panel lower reinforcement

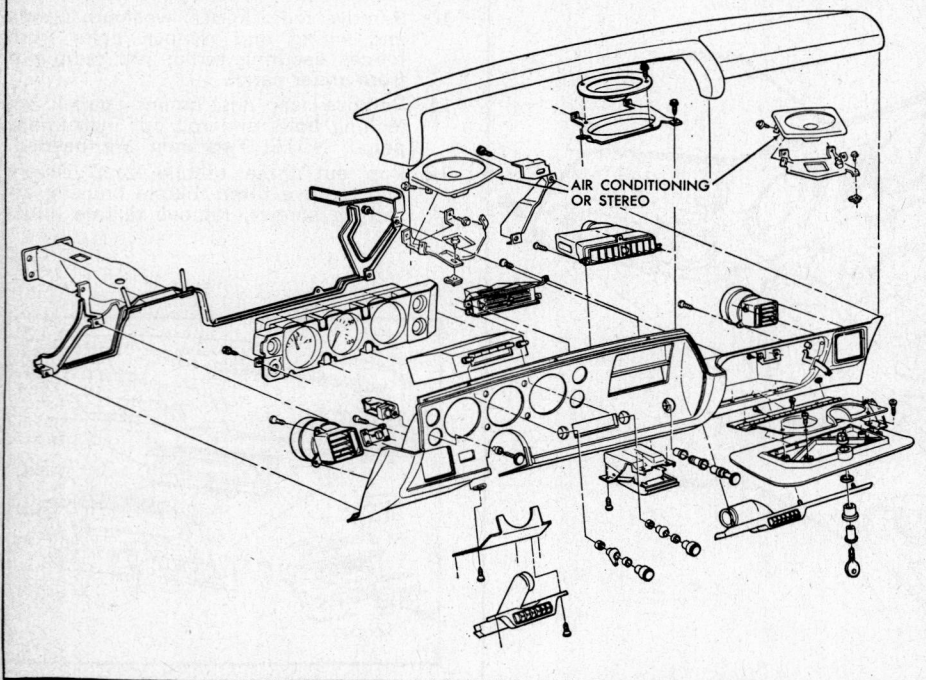

Fig. 14   Instrument cluster. 1970-72 Chevelle with optional cluster & Monte Carlo

and to parking brake pedal bracket.

14. Remove ash tray and retaining bracket.
15. Remove three screws at top of instrument carrier and tilt the carrier assembly forward.
16. Disconnect speedometer cable. Disconnect panel harness by removing six screws that hold illumination cover to rear of carrier and remove all other connections.
17. Remove carrier assembly from panel opening and remove eight screws retaining cluster to carrier.

1969 Chevelle

1. Disconnect battery ground cable.
2. Remove ash tray and retainer.
3. Remove radio knobs, nuts, electrical connections, aerial plug and radio rear support, then lift out radio.
4. Remove heater control screws, then push control head out of instrument panel.
5. Lower steering column. If equipped, remove automatic transmission indicator cable on steering column.
6. Remove instrument panel retaining screws at top, sides and bottom of panel. Also remove any attachments to underside of panel such as speedometer stem, defogger or tail gate control switch.
7. Lift loosened instrument panel up and back slightly, reach behind cluster and remove speedometer cable housing retaining nut, then support instrument panel on protected steering column.
8. Remove clips on top of instrument cluster rear cover and remove all connectors at back of cover and oil pressure pipe fitting from rear of oil pressure gauge (if so equipped).
9. Remove five screws securing twin window cluster to back of instrument panel and remove cluster.
10. Reverse procedure to install.

1969-75 Corvette

Left Hand Side
1. Disconnect battery ground cable.
2. Lower steering column.
3. Remove screws and washers securing left instrument panel to door opening, top of dash and left side of center instrument panel.
4. Unclip and remove floor console trim panel.
5. Pull cluster slightly forward to obtain clearance for removal of speedometer cable housing nut, tachometer cable housing nut, headlamp and ignition switch connectors and panel illuminating lamps.
6. Reverse procedure to install.

Center Cluster
1. Disconnect battery ground cable at battery.
2. Remove wiper switch trim plate screws and tip plate forward for access to switch connector. Lift trim plate out from cluster.
3. Unclip and remove right and left console forward trim pads to gain

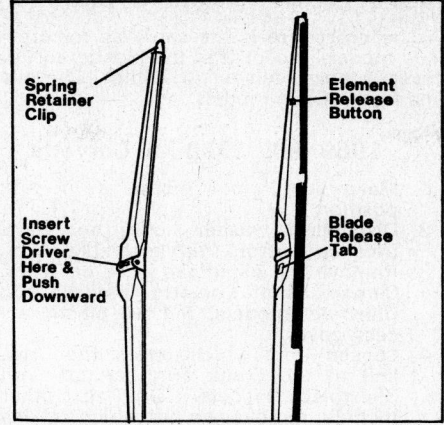

Fig. 15 Wiper blades

access to studs at lower edge of cluster.
4. Remove nuts from studs at lower edge of cluster.
5. Remove remaining screws retaining cluster to instrument panel.
6. Remove right instrument panel pad.
7. Remove radio knobs, bezel retaining nuts and one radio support bolt (from behind cluster).
8. Slide radio back towards firewall and pull cluster forward. Reach behind cluster, disconnect oil pressure line, wiring harness and bulbs.

CAUTION: The center cluster trim plate is designed to collapse under impact, Consequently, do not try to deflect the cluster plate forward to gain access to back of gauges.

9. Lift cluster assembly up and forward to remove.
10. Reverse procedure to install cluster.

1969 Camaro

1. Disconnect battery ground cable.
2. Remove instrument panel pad, A/C attachments and radio brace attachments.
3. Remove mast jacket supports at toe pan and dash, and lower column. *Both supports must be detached to prevent distortion of mast jacket.*
4. Remove cluster retaining screws from face of panel and partially remove assembly from console opening.
5. Reaching behind cluster assembly, disconnect speedometer cable, speed warning device (if equipped) and chassis harness connector at rear of panel.
6. Remove assembly from console.
7. Reverse procedure to install.

1969 Chevy Nova

1. Disconnect battery.
2. Unfasten heater control from cluster (2 screws).
3. Remove radio knobs, bezel nuts and front support at lower edge of cluster. This will allow radio to re-

main in instrument panel during cluster removal.
4. Disconnect and lower column.
5. Remove toe pan trim cover.
6. Remove bolts securing steering column retainer to toe pan. Loosen bolts securing retainer halves.
7. Remove bolts at top, bottom and sides of cluster securing it to instrument panel.
8. Remove steering column-to-dash panel bracket nuts and carefully lower column. Be careful not to jar or apply any load on column during this operation.
9. Remove ignition switch tumbler and bezel through cluster and leave hanging.
10. Tilt cluster forward and disconnect speedometer cable and necessary electrical connectors. Then remove cluster.
11. Reverse procedure to install and align steering column.

W/S WIPER BLADES

Two methods are used to retain wiper blades to wiper arms, Fig. 15. One method uses a press type release tab. When the release tab is depressed the blade assembly can be slid off the wiper arm pin. The other method uses a coil spring retainer. A screwdriver must be inserted on top of the spring and the spring pushed downward. The blade assembly can then be slid off the wiper arm pin. Two methods are also used to retain the blade element in the blade assembly, Fig. 15. One method uses a press type release button. When the button is depressed the two piece blade assembly can be slid off the blade element. The other method uses a spring type retainer clip in the end of the blade element. When the retainer clip is squeezed together, the blade element can be slid out of the blade assembly.

NOTE: To be sure of correct installation, the element release button, or the spring element retaining clip should be at the end of the wiper blade assembly nearest the wiper transmission.

W/S WIPER ARMS

Models with Rectangular Motor
1. Wiper motor must be in park position.
2. Use suitable tool to minimize the possibility of windshield or paint finish damage during arm removal.
3. Remove arm by prying up with tool to disengage arm from serrated transmission shaft.
4. To install arm to transmission shaft rotate the required distance and direction so that the blades rest in proper position.

Models with Round Motor
1. Wiper motor must be in park position.
2. Raise hood to gain access to wiper arms.
3. *Corvette only:* Remove the rubber plug from the front of the wiper door

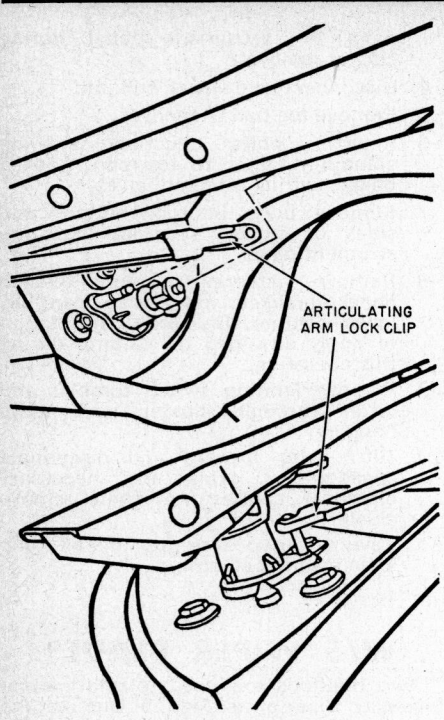

Fig. 16 Wiper articulating arm lock clip

actuator then insert a screwdriver, pushing the internal piston rearward to actuate the wiper door open.

4. Lift the wiper arm off the transmission shaft. On left arm slide the articulating arm lock clip, Fig. 16, away from the transmission pivot pin and lift arm off pin.
5. Slide latch clip, Fig. 17, out from under the wiper arm.
6. Release the wiper arm and lift assembly off transmission shaft.

W/S WIPER MOTOR

1971-75 Except Corvette

1. Raise hood and remove cowl screen or grille.
2. Disconnect wiring and washer hoses.
3. Reaching through cowl opening, loosen transmission drive link attaching nuts to motor crankarm.
4. Disconnect drive link from motor crankarm.
5. Remove motor attaching screws.
6. Remove motor while guiding crankarm through hole.

1970 Camaro

1. Remove two cowl screen attaching screws from center of cowl then pry up screen at eight clips and remove.
2. Reaching through cowl opening, loosen the two crank arm attaching nuts.
3. Remove transmission crank arm.
4. Disconnect wiring and washer hoses.
5. Remove motor attaching screws and remove motor while guiding crank arm through hole.

1970 Except Camaro & Corvette

The procedure is the same as for previous models except that the plastic access cover is now used on Chevrolet, Chevelle and Monte Carlo models.

1969 All; 1970-75 Corvette

1. Make sure wiper motor is in park position.
2. Disconnect washer hoses and electrical connectors from assembly.
3. Remove the air intake grille on Nova, Camaro and Corvette models. On Chevrolet models, remove plastic access cover.
4. Loosen nuts which retain the drive link to the crank arm ball stud on Chevrolet models. On all other models, remove the nut which retains the crank arm to the motor.
5. On Corvette, it is necessary to remove the ignition shield and distributor cap to gain access to the motor retaining screws or nuts.

NOTE: *Remove left bank spark plug wires from the cap and mark both cap and wires for aid in reinstallation.*

6. Remove three motor retaining screws or nuts and remove motor.

CAUTION: Wiper motor must be in the park position prior to installation on the cowl. Do not install a motor that was dropped or hung by the drive link.

W/S WIPER TRANSMISSION

1971-75 W/Rectangular Motor

1. Remove wiper arms and blades.
2. Raise hood and remove cowl vent screen or grille.
3. Disconnect wiring from motor.
4. Loosen, but do not remove, transmission drive link to motor crankarm attaching nuts and disconnect drive link from crankarm.
5. Remove right and left transmission to body attaching screws and guide transmission and linkage through cowl opening.

NOTE: When installing, motor must be in Park position.

1971-75 W/Round Motor

1. Raise hood and remove cowl vent screen.
2. On Chevelle, Monte Carlo and Camaro models, remove right and left wiper arm and blades.
3. On Chevrolet models, remove arm and blade only from transmission to be removed.
4. Loosen, do not remove, attaching nuts securing drive link to motor crankarm.
5. Disconnect transmission drive link from motor crankarm.
6. On Chevelle, Monte Carlo and Camaro models, remove right and left trans-

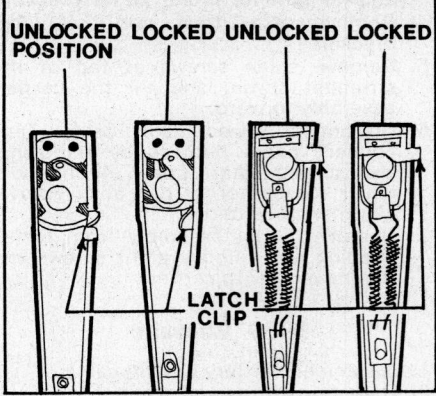

Fig. 17 Wiper arm latch clips

mission to body screws.

7. On Chevrolet models, remove attaching screws securing only the transmission to be removed.
8. Remove transmission and linkage through cowl opening.

NOTE: When installing, motor must be in Park position.

1973-75 Corvette

1. Make sure motor is in PARK position.
2. Disconnect battery ground cable.
3. Open hood and remove chamber screen.
4. Loosen nuts retaining ball sockets to crankarm and detach drive rod from crankarm.
5. Remove transmission nuts, then lift rod assemblies from chamber.
6. Remove transmission linkage from chamber.

1969-70 All & 1971-72 Corvette

1. Make sure wiper motor is in park position.
2. On Corvette only, remove rubber plug from front of wiper motor actuator, then insert a screwdriver, pushing internal piston rearward to actuate wiper door open.
3. On all models, remove wiper arm and blade assembly from one transmission. On articulated left-hand arm assemblies, remove clip retaining pinned arm to blade arm.
4. Remove air intake grille or screen (if equipped).
5. Loosen nuts retaining drive rod ball stud-to-crank arm and detach rod from arm.
6. Remove transmission retaining screws, or nuts, then lower drive rod assemblies into plenum chamber.
7. Remove transmission and linkage through cowl opening.
8. Reverse procedure to install. Make sure wiper blades are installed in the park position (plus or minus 3/8" from top of reveal molding on recessed wiper arms).

W/S WIPER SWITCH

1971-75 Chevrolet

1. Disconnect battery ground cable.
2. Remove screws securing control shroud on instrument panel. (One screw is hidden above headlight switch shaft and one is hidden above cigarette lighter knob.)
3. Lift off shroud and remove remaining screws.
4. Unplug wiper switch and remove.

1973-75 Chevelle & Monte Carlo

1. Disconnect battery ground cable.
2. Remove instrument cluster.
3. Pull electric connector off rear of wiper switch.
4. Remove screws from front of switch and lift switch out front of panel.

1970-75 Camaro

1. Disconnect battery ground cable.
2. Remove trim plate and A/C outlet from below steering column if so equipped.
3. Remove light switch.
4. Remove 6 screws securing instrument carrier. Two of these are behind the cluster on either side of steering column.

NOTE: Cigar lighter grounding ring may have to be removed with lighter housing to gain access to left side of carrier.

5. Disconnect wiper switch wiring.
6. Tilting carrier forward, reach behind and remove 3 switch retaining screws and lift out switch.

1969-70 Chevrolet
1970-72 Chevelle & Monte Carlo

1. Disconnect battery ground cable.
2. On 1969-72, remove trim plate and lap cooler outlet.
3. Disconnect and remove switch from rear of panel.
4. Reverse procedure to install.

1969 Camaro, Chevelle, Nova
1970-75 Chevy Nova

1. Disconnect battery ground cable.
2. On Chevelle, remove left air outlet and headlight switch.
3. Disconnect and remove switch from rear of panel.
4. Reverse procedure to install.

1969-75 Corvette

1. Disconnect battery ground cable.
2. Remove screws from upper part of center console marked "Corvette".
3. Disconnect and remove switch and plate.
4. Carefully pry knob from switch then remove switch from plate.

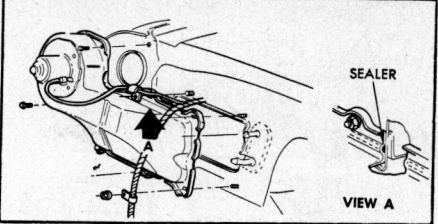

Fig. 18 Blower Motor. 1969-75 All (Typical)

5. To install, insert a small rod in the switch arm before pushing the knob on the arm outside of the trim plate then reverse the above procedure.

RADIO, REPLACE

NOTE: When installing radio, be sure to adjust antenna trimmer for peak performance.

NOTE: When installing, be sure to connect speaker before applying power to radio.

1973-75 Chevrolet

1. Disconnect battery ground cable.
2. On A/C equipped vehicles, it may be necessary to remove the lap cooler duct.
3. Turn radio knobs until slot in base in knob is visible. Depress the metal retainer and remove knobs and bezels.
4. Remove control shaft nuts and washers.
5. Remove right hand bracket to instrument panel bolt and the stud nut on left side of radio.
6. Push radio forward and then lower it far enough to gain access to electrical connections.
7. Disconnect antenna, speaker and power feed and remove radio.

1973-75 Chevelle & Monte Carlo

1. Disconnect battery ground cable.
2. On A/C vehicles, remove left lap cooler duct.
3. Pull off radio knobs and bezels.
4. Remove control shaft nuts and washers.
5. Disconnect antenna, speaker and power wires.
6. Remove radio to support bracket stud nut.
7. Push radio forward until shafts clear instrument panel and then lower from car.

1973-75 Camaro & Nova

1. Disconnect battery ground cable.
2. Pull off radio control knobs and bezels.
3. Remove control shaft nuts and washers.
4. Remove screws or nuts from radio brackets.
5. Push radio forward until shafts clear

instrument panel and lower unit enough to remove electrical connections.
6. Disconnect antenna, speaker and power leads and remove radio.

1973-75 Corvette

1. Disconnect battery ground cable.
2. Remove right instrument panel pad.
3. Disconnect speaker connectors.
4. Remove wiper switch trim plate screws and tip plate for access to switch connector. Remove switch connector and trim plate from cluster.
5. Unclip and remove right and left console forward trim pads. Remove forward most screw on right and left side of console.
6. Insert a flexible drive socket between console and metal horseshoe brace and remove nuts from two studs on lower edge of console cluster.
7. Remove remaining screws retaining cluster to instrument panel.
8. From rear of console, disconnect electric connector, brace and antenna.
9. Remove knobs and bezel retaining nuts.
10. Pull top of console rearward and separate radio from console and remove it from right side opening.

CAUTION: The center instrument cluster trim plate is designed to collapse under impact. DO NOT try to deflect the cluster plate forward to gain more access to remove radio. Also use care so as not to damage the plastic oil pressure line when pulling console forward.

1970-72 Chevelle, Chevrolet & Nova

1. Disconnect battery ground cable.
2. Remove ash tray and retainer.
3. Remove radio knobs, washers, controls, trim plate and nuts from radio bushings.
4. Remove hoses from center A/C duct if equipped.
5. Disconnect all leads to radio.
6. Remove screw from radio rear mounting bracket and lower radio.

1969 Except Corvette

1. Disconnect battery ground cable.
2. On Chevelle and Chevrolet, remove ash tray and retainer.
3. Remove radio knobs, nuts, electrical connections, rear support and lift radio out.

1969-72 Corvette

Coupe

1. Disconnect battery ground cable.
2. Remove left and right door sill plates and kick pads. Disconnect radio to speaker connectors (left and right side).
3. Remove right side dash pad.
4. Remove right and left console forward trim pads.
5. Remove one bolt securing heater floor outlet duct to center distributor assembly.
6. Remove floor outlet duct by pulling it through left hand opening.
7. From front of console, tape radio

push buttons in depressed position. From rear of console, disconnect electrical connector, brace and antenna.

8. Remove radio knobs and bezel retaining nuts. Push radio forward (towards front of car). From rear of console, tip back of radio up and remove from right side opening.
9. Reverse procedure to install.

Convertible

1. Disconnect battery cable.
2. Remove right instrument panel pad.
3. Disconnect speaker connectors.

NOTE: On some vehicles it may be necessary to remove kick panels to gain access to speaker connectors.

4. Remove wiper switch trim plate screws and tip plate for access to switch connector. Remove switch connector and trim plate from cluster assembly.
5. Unclip and remove right and left console forward trim pads. Remove forwardmost screw on each side of console.
6. Insert a flexible drive socket between the console and metal horseshoe brace, remove the nuts from the two studs on the lower edge of the console cluster.
7. Remove remaining screws retaining cluster to instrument panel.
8. From rear of console, disconnect radio connector, brace and antenna.
9. Remove radio knobs and bezel retaining nuts.
10. Pull top of console forward. Separate radio from console and remove it from the right side opening.

NOTE: The center instrument cluster trim plate is designed to collapse under impact. Consequently, do not try to deflect the cluster plate forward to gain more access to remove the radio. Also use care so as not to damage the plastic oil pressure line when pulling console forward.

BLOWER MOTOR REMOVAL

1969 Chevrolet

1. Remove battery and tray.
2. Remove all wires, hoses, etc. attached to skirt.
3. Raise front of vehicle on hoist.
4. Remove inner skirt to cowl brace.
5. Remove skirt attaching bolts.
6. Remove lower fender attaching bolt.
7. Pull lower section of fender outward slightly, pushing skirt upward and inboard. When skirt is free, lower and rest on wheel.
8. Disconnect the blower motor lead wire.
9. Remove motor attaching screws and remove motor, Fig. 18.

1969 Chevelle

1. Disconnect the battery ground cable.
2. Remove battery. Remove all heater

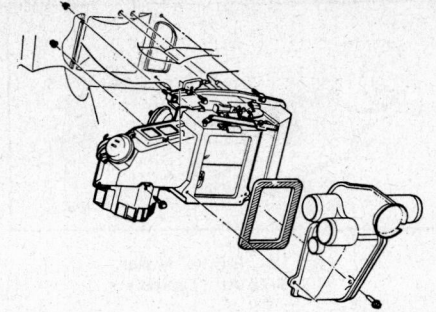

Fig. 19 Heater core. 1971-75 Chevrolet (Typical)

hoses, wires, etc. attached to the right fender skirt.
3. Raise front of vehicle on hoist.
4. Remove all skirt-to-fender attaching bolts and lower skirt on tire.
5. Disconnect blower motor wire and remove screws retaining blower motor to case. Remove blower motor, Fig. 18.

1969 Chevy Nova

1. Disconnect the battery ground cable.
2. Remove all wires, hoses, etc. attached to the right fender skirt.
3. Remove all skirt-fender screws and rest skirt on wheel.
4. Remove blower motor wire.
5. Remove blower to case attaching screws and remove blower assembly, Fig. 18.

1969 Camaro

1. Remove battery and battery tray.
2. Disconnect hoses, wiring, etc., at fender skirt.
3. Remove wheel opening trim, if so equipped.
4. Remove rocker panel moulding to fender and rear quarter panel screws and remove moulding.
5. Loosen rear lower fender to body bolt.
6. Remove all fender skirt attaching screws.
7. Pull out on lower edge of fender at rear of wheelhouse, push in on skirt until flange clears fender and then lower fender on wheel.
8. Remove the blower to case attaching screws and remove the blower assembly, Fig. 18.

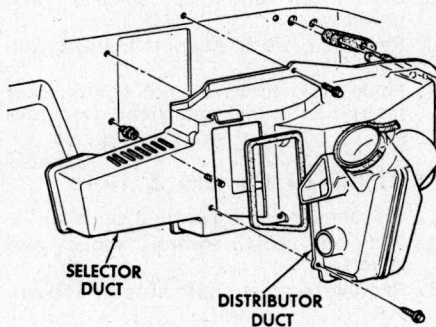

SELECTOR DUCT

DISTRIBUTOR DUCT

Fig. 20 Heater core. 1970-72 Chevelle & Monte Carlo (Typical)

1969-72 Corvette

1. Disconnect the battery ground cable, blower motor wire and the rubber air cooling tube.
2. Remove the three front sill plate moulding screws and pry out to gain access to the right splash shield retaining bolts.
3. Remove the splash shield retaining bolts and remove splash shield.
4. Remove motor to case mounting screws and lower motor assembly through splash shield opening, Fig. 18.

1970-72 Except Corvette

1. Disconnect the battery ground cable.
2. Remove all heater hoses and wires attached to the fender skirt.
3. Raise the vehicle on hoist.
4. Remove all fender skirt attaching bolts except those attaching the skirt to the radiator support.
5. Pull out then down on the fender skirt and place a block of wood between the skirt and the fender to allow room to remove the blower and motor.
6. Disconnect the blower motor cooling tube at the motor. Remove the blower-case attaching screws and remove the blower assembly.
7. Remove the blower wheel retaining nut and separate the motor and wheel, Fig. 18.

1973-75 Corvette

1. Disconnect battery ground cable.
2. Remove radiator supply tank, if so equipped.
3. Disconnect blower motor wires.
4. Remove blower motor to case mounting screws and remove motor, Fig. 18.

1973 Chevrolet & Camaro

1. Disconnect battery ground cable.
2. Remove all heater hoses and wires attached to fender skirt.
3. Raise vehicle on a hoist.
4. Remove all fender skirt attaching bolts except those attaching skirt to radiator support.
5. Pull out then down on fender skirt and place a 2" × 4" block of wood between skirt and fender to allow room to remove blower.
6. Remove blower to case screws and remove blower, Fig. 18.

1973-75 Chevelle & Monte Carlo

1. Disconnect battery ground cable.
2. Disconnect blower lead wire at motor.
3. Remove blower to case screws and remove blower, Fig. 18.

1974-75 Chevrolet, Camaro & 1973-75 Nova

1. Disconnect battery ground cable.
2. Disconnect blower lead and remove all hoses and wires connected to fender skirt then raise vehicle.
3. On all except Nova, remove all fender skirt retaining bolts except those retaining skirt to radiator support. On Nova, remove the eight rearmost fender skirt to fender retaining screws.
4. Pull out and down on fender skirt and

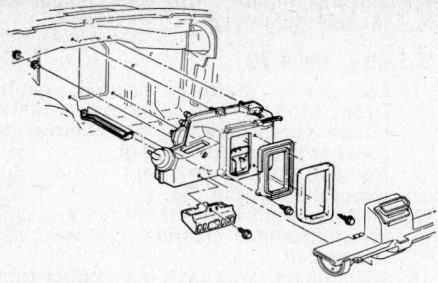

Fig. 21 Heater core. 1973-75 Chevelle & Monte Carlo (Typical)

wedge a 2x4 inch block of wood between skirt and fender to allow room for blower motor removal.

5. Remove blower to case retaining screws and remove blower assembly. Gently pry flange, since sealer will act as an adhesive, Fig. 18.

NOTE: On Nova, remove blower retaining nut and separate wheel and motor before removing through fender and skirt.

6. Reverse procedure to install.

HEATER CORE REMOVAL

L/Air Cond.

1971-75

1. Disconnect battery ground cable.
2. Drain radiator, disconnect heater hoses at core and plug openings to prevent spillage of water.
3. Remove nuts from air distributor duct studs on engine side of firewall, Figs. 19 through 24.
4. On Chevrolet and 1973-75 Chevelle and Monte Carlo, remove distributor duct retaining screw.
5. On 1971-72 Chevelle and Monte Carlo, from under dash, drill out lower right hand distributor stud with a 1/4" drill.
6. On Nova, remove glove box and door and drill out lower right hand distributor stud with a 1/4" drill.
7. On Camaro, remove glove box, radio, and defroster duct to distributor duct screw.
8. On Corvette, remove right instrument panel pad, right hand dash braces, center dash console duct and floor

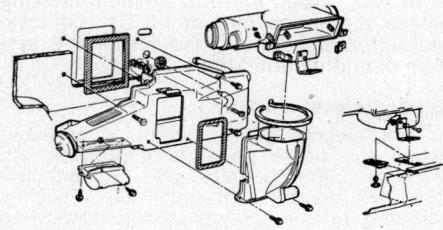

Fig. 22 Heater core. 1969-75 Chevy Nova (Typical)

outlet duct, radio and center dash console.

9. On all models, pull distributor duct from firewall being careful not to bend cable.
10. On Camaro, disconnect cable and resistor wires and remove distributor and core.
11. On all other models, remove core assembly from duct.

1969-70 All

1. Disconnect battery ground cable. Drain radiator.
2. Disconnect heater hoses and plug heater outlets to prevent coolant spillage.
3. Remove nuts from air distributor duct studs on engine side of firewall.
4. On Chevrolet and Nova, remove glove box and door assembly. On Corvette, remove right instrument panel pad, right hand dash braces, center dash console duct and floor outlet duct.
5. Except Corvette: from under dash, drill out lower right distributor stud. Corvette: remove radio and center dash console.
6. Pull distributor duct from firewall mounting, remove resistor wires and lay distributor duct on floor.

NOTE: Use care to avoid bending bowden cables.

7. Remove core from distributor duct.

W/Air Cond.

Chevrolet 1971-75 Comfortron & 1972-75 4 Seasons

1. Disconnect battery ground cable and compressor clutch connector.
2. Drain radiator and disconnect heater hoses from core. Plug hoses and core openings.
3. On 1971 Comfortron, disconnect control head vacuum hoses from in-line connector. On all 1972-75 systems, disconnect vacuum hose from vacuum check valve and push hose grommet through firewall.
4. Remove accessible screws and stud nuts from heater and air selector duct from dash side of firewall, Fig. 19.
5. On 1971 Comfortron, remove three stud nuts and on all 1972-75 systems, remove two screws and three stud nuts, accessible from engine side of dash.
6. On 1971 Comfortron, drill out lower right hand case stud from inside vehicle. On all 1972-75 systems, the last screw is accessible by removing the screws securing the fender skirt and holding skirt away from rear of wheel-well.
7. Remove lap cooler assembly, glove box door and glove box.
8. Remove floor outlet duct and instrument panel pad. On 1972-75 Comfortron, disconnect aspirator and in-car sensor connector.
9. Remove distributor duct hoses and connector, then remove distributor duct from selector. On 1971 Comfortron, remove programmer.
10. Remove defroster duct screw and move duct to gain access to selector and heater core. On 1972-75 Comfortron, disconnect in-line vacuum

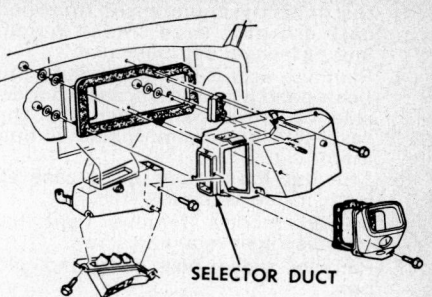

Fig. 23 Heater core. 1970-75 Camaro (Typical)

connector and line from outside air diaphragm, then disconnect electrical and vacuum connections from programmer.

11. Disconnect cables and vacuum lines from selector, then remove heater core and selector. Separate heater core from selector by removing clamp screws.

Chevrolet, 1969-71 Four Seasons

1. Disconnect battery ground cable.
2. Drain radiator and disconnect heater hoses from core. Plug openings to prevent spillage of coolant.
3. Remove nuts from selector duct studs projecting through firewall.
4. Remove glove box and door.
5. Remove center distributor duct hoses, duct cable, center distributor duct to selector duct screws and remove center duct.
6. Inside car, drill out lower right hand case stud using a 1/4" drill.
7. Remove floor distributor duct.
8. Unfasten and remove selector duct from firewall.
9. Disconnect wiring, vacuum lines and cables and remove from vehicle.
10. Scribe location of temperature door camming plate on selector duct and remove camming plate. Remove core and core housing from duct.

Chevrolet, 1969-70 Comfortron

1. Disconnect battery ground cable and drain radiator.
2. Disconnect heater hoses and plug hoses and core openings.

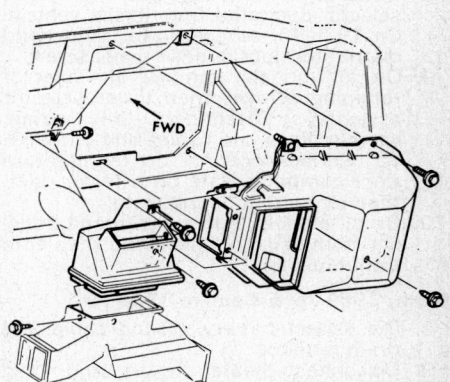

Fig. 24 Heater core. 1979-75 Corvette (Typical)

3. Disconnect vacuum hoses from under dash and push large firewall grommet into passenger compartment.
4. Remove accessible stud nuts from heater and air selector case from dash side of firewall and then the three case stud nuts from engine compartment.
5. Drill out lower right hand case stud from inside vehicle.
6. On all models remove right hand courtesy light retaining screw.
7. Remove glove box door and glove box.
8. On all models remove floor distributor duct.
9. Remove center distributor duct hoses, shut-off cables and center duct.
10. On all models disconnect power servo electrical leads, then remove power retaining screws. Tilt servo forward and remove cover screws. Disconnect vacuum line from servo diaphragm and remove vacuum head and servo cover. Disconnect link from servo and remove servo assembly.
11. Remove transducer retaining screws and without removing vacuum hoses, pull transducer to front of dash.

NOTE: One transducer retaining screw secures a ground wire.

12. Remove heater, air distributor and control head as an assembly. Remove screws securing die cast plate to air inlet side of case and disconnect temperature door linkage from door shaft. Remove die cast plate with core from case.

Chevelle & Monte Carlo, 1969-75

1. Disconnect battery ground cable and drain radiator.
2. Disconnect heater hoses from core and plug hoses and core openings.
3. Remove distributor case stud nuts projecting through firewall, Figs. 20 and 21. On 1973-75, remove resistor assembly and the last stud nut through its opening.
4. On all except 1970-72, remove glove box door and glove box.
5. On all models, remove right hand lap cooler and kick pad cover. On 1969, remove recirculating air valve.
6. On all models, disconnect center duct hoses and remove center duct to selector duct screws, then remove center duct.
7. Remove floor distributor duct.
8. On 1969-72, drill out lower right hand selector duct stud from inside vehicle. On 1973-75, remove lower right hand distributor duct to dash panel screw.
9. On all models, remove air selector retaining screws, then lower selector assembly. Disconnect all wiring, vacuum lines and cables and on 1969-72, scribe location of temperature door camming plate on selector duct, then remove camming plate.
10. On all models, remove core and housing from selector assembly, then core from housing.

Nova, 1969-75 & Camaro 1969-70

1. Disconnect battery ground cable and drain radiator.
2. Disconnect heater hoses and plug hoses and core openings to prevent coolant spillage.

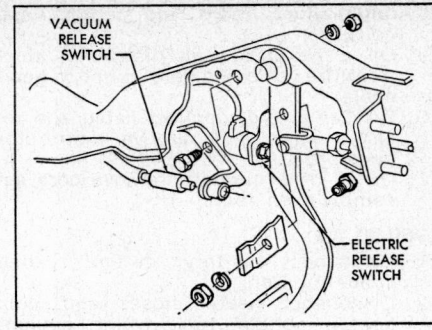

Fig. 25 Release switches and brackets. 1969-70

3. Remove accessible stud nut from air selector duct, Fig. 22.
4. On Camaro, remove right side lower rocker molding and the lower fender attaching bolts.
5. On all models, remove right hand fender skirt to fender and skirt reinforcing screws. Lower skirt to wheel and remove remaining stud nut.
6. Remove glove box door, glove box and right hand kick pad recirculating air valve.
7. Remove center and floor ducts. Remove screws securing selector duct halves together, then separate.
8. On Nova, remove selector duct right half to firewall screws and remove duct. On Camaro, remove screws securing selector duct to firewall and remove duct.
9. On all models, disconnect all wiring and cables. Scribe location of temperature camming plate on selector duct and remove plate and core.

Camaro, 1971-75

1. Disconnect battery ground cable.
2. Drain radiator and disconnect heater hoses from core. Plug openings to prevent spillage of coolant.
3. Remove nuts from distributor studs on engine side of firewall, Fig. 23.
4. Remove glove box and radio.
5. Remove defroster duct to distributor duct screw. With radio removed, the defroster duct can be pulled rearward to gain clearance for distributor duct removal.
6. Carefully pull distributor from firewall

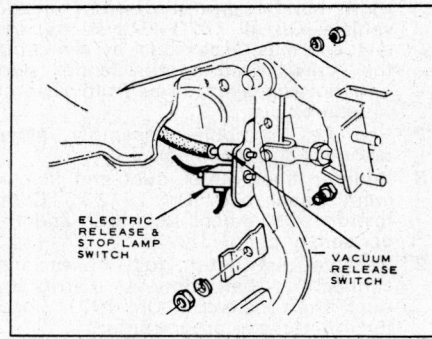

Fig. 26 Release switches and brackets. 1971-75

and disconnect wiring and cables. Remove duct and core from vehicle.

Corvette, 1969-75

1. Disconnect battery ground cable. Drain radiator and disconnect heater hoses from core. Plug openings to prevent spillage of coolant.
2. Remove nuts from engine side distributor duct, Fig. 24.
3. Remove right hand dash pad and center instrument cluster. Remove dash braces.
4. Disconnect right dash outlet duct from center duct. Remove screws attaching center duct to selector duct and remove center duct.
5. Remove screws attaching selector duct to firewall and pull selector rearward and to the right. Disconnect cables and wiring.
6. Remove selector duct from car. Remove temperature door camming plate from duct and remove core and housing.

SPEED CONTROLS
1969-75 Cruise Master

Servo Unit Adjustment

Adjust the bead chain or cable so that it is as tight as possible without holding the throttle open when the carburetor is set at its lowest idle throttle position. The cable is adjusted by turning the hex portion of servo. On 1973-75 units, the bead chain or cable is adjusted so there is 1/16 inch of lost motion in servo cable.

When connecting the bead chain or cable (engine stopped) manually set the fast idle cam at its lowest step and connect the chain so that it does not hold the idle screw off the cam. If the chain needs to be cut, cut it three beads beyond the bead that pulls the linkage.

Regulator Unit Adjustment

To remove any difference between engagement and cruising speed, one adjustment is possible. However, no adjustment should be made until the following items have been checked or serviced.
1. Bead chain or cable properly adjusted.
2. All hoses in good condition, properly attached, not leaking, pinched or cracked.
3. Regulator air filter cleaned and properly oiled.
4. Electric and vacuum switches properly adjusted.

Engagement - Cruising Speed Zeroing

If the cruising speed is lower than the engagement speed, loosen the orifice tube locknut and turn the tube outward; if higher turn the tube inward. Each 1/4 turn will alter the engagement-cruising speed difference one mph. Tighten locknut after adjustment and check the system operation at 50 mph.

Brake Release Switch

The electric brake switch is actuated when the brake pedal is depressed .25 inch on 1969-70 units, Fig. 25, and .38-.64 inch on 1971-75 units, Fig. 26. The vacuum release switch is actuated when brake pedal is moved 5/16 inch on all units.

Engine Section

Throughout the engine section there will be references to Small V8s and Mark IV V8s. These can be distinguished as follows:

Small V8s: V8-302, 307, 327, 350 and 170 H.P. and 265 H.P. V8-400.

Mark IV V8s: V8-396, other V8-400s, V8-402, 427, 454.

ENGINE MOUNTS, REPLACE

1973-75 All 6 & 1969-72 Chevy Nova 4 & 6

1. Remove nut, washer and engine mount through-bolt.
2. Raise engine to release weight from mount.
3. Remove bracket-to-mount bolt, then remove mount.
4. Install new mount on bracket.
5. Lower engine, install through-bolt and tighten all mount bolts, Figs. 1, 2 and 6.

1969-72 Camaro, Chevelle & Chevrolet 6

1. Remove nut, washer, spacer then engine mount through-bolt.
2. Raise engine to release weight from mount.
3. Remove mount, stop bracket and frame bracket assembly from crossmember, then remove stop bracket and mount from frame bracket.
4. Install stop bracket and new mount on frame bracket, then install assembly on crossmember.
5. Lower engine, install through-bolt and tighten all mount bolts, Fig. 2.

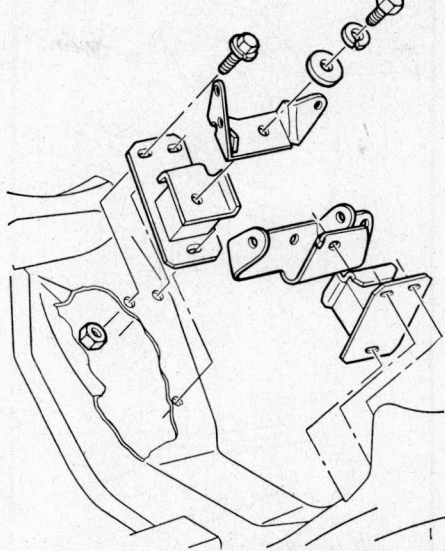

Fig. 1 Engine mounts. 1969-70 4 cyl.

1969-75 All V-8

NOTE: On some V8 engines, the mount on the right side of the engine cannot be removed without first removing the fuel pump.

1. Remove nut, washer and engine mount through-bolt.
2. Raise engine to release weight from mount.
3. Remove mount from engine.
4. Install new mount on engine.
5. Lower engine, install through-bolt and tighten all mount bolts, Figs. 3 thru 10.

ENGINE, REPLACE

NOTE: V8 engines are equipped with two strap type lifting rings, one at the right front the other at the left rear of the engine. Use of these rings eliminates the need to remove the rocker arm covers to install lifting adapters.

1969-75 Except Corvette

NOTE: The engine and transmission are removed as a unit. First disconnect and/or remove as required wires, tubes, hoses and linkage attached to engine and transmission. Then do the following:

1. Remove hood, radiator and fan. Also power steering pump and A/C compressor (if equipped).
2. Remove drive shaft.

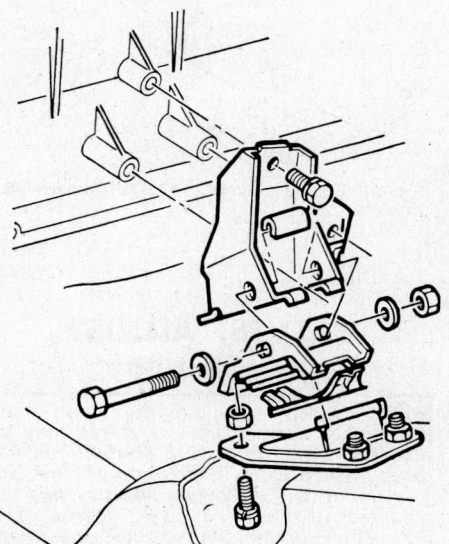

Fig. 2 Engine mounts. 1969-72 6 cyl. (typical)

3. Unfasten and lower exhaust pipes.
4. Remove rocker arm cover (s) and attach lifting device.
5. Remove front mount through bolts.
6. Raise engine to take weight off mounts, then remove rear mount bolts and crossmember. On Chevrolet models it will be necessary to remove mount from transmission before crossmember can be removed. On Chevrolet it will be necessary to remove mount from transmission and loosen rear frame cushion bolts before crossmember can be removed. On 1969-75 Camaro, it is not necessary to remove the crossmember completely; after removing the bolts, slide it back.
7. Remove engine and transmission assembly.

1969-75 Corvette

When necessary to remove the engine, it is recommended that the engine and transmission assembly be lifted from the vehicle as a unit. It takes considerably less time to remove the engine and transmission as a unit than it would to "split" the engine from the transmission in the vehicle and remove the engine alone.

CYLINDER HEAD

1969-75 Four & Six Cylinder

1. Drain cooling system and remove air cleaner.
2. Disconnect choke rod or choke cable, accelerator pedal rod at bellcrank on manifold, and fuel and vacuum lines at carburetor.
3. Disconnect exhaust pipe at manifold flange, then unfasten and remove manifolds and carburetor as an assembly.
4. Remove fuel and vacuum line retaining clip from water outlet and disconnect wire harness from temperature sending unit and coil, leaving

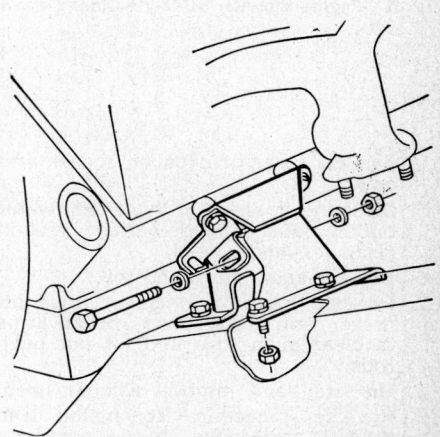

Fig. 3 Engine mounts. 1969 Chevrolet V8

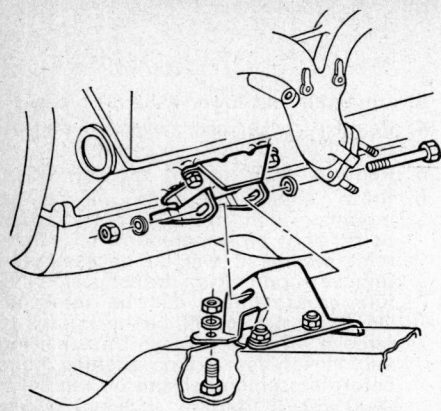

Fig. 4   Engine mounts. 1970 Chevrolet V8

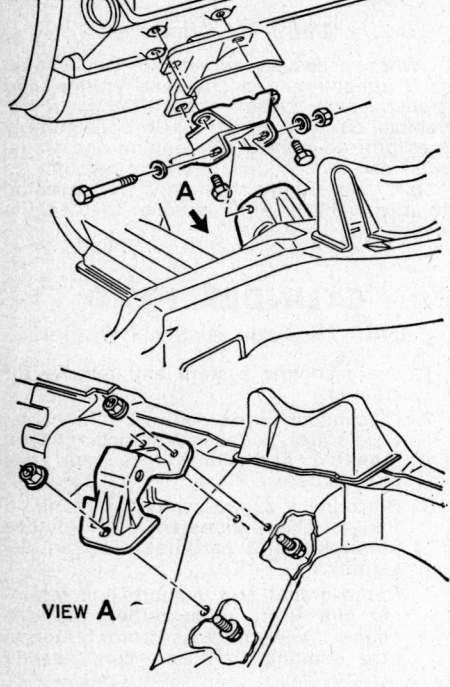

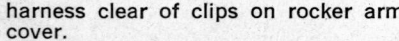

VIEW A

Fig. 5   Engine mounts. 1971-72 Chevrolet V8

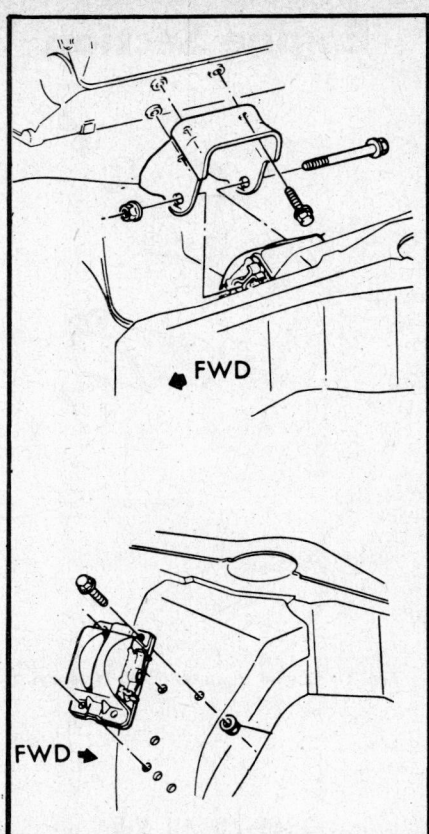

FWD

FWD ►

Fig. 6   Engine mounts. 1973-75 Except Corvette (typical)

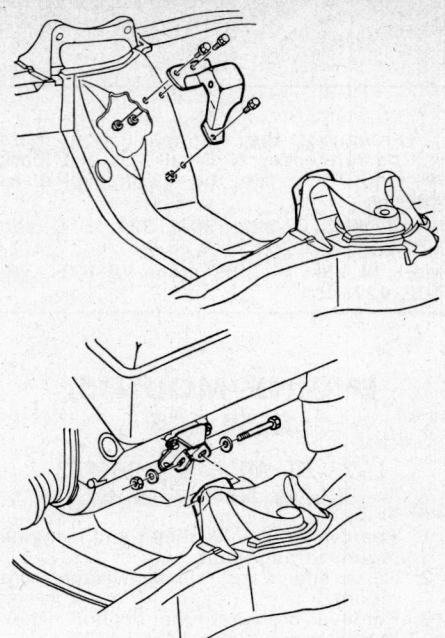

Fig. 8   Engine mounts. 1969 Camaro V8

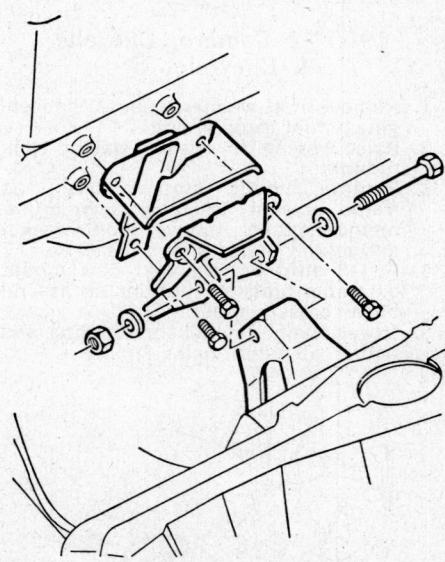

Fig. 9   Engine mounts. 1971-72 Camaro V8

harness clear of clips on rocker arm cover.

5. Disconnect radiator hose at water outlet housing and battery ground strap at cylinder head.

6. Remove spark plugs and coil.

7. Remove rocker arm cover. Back off rocker arm nuts, pivot rocker arms to clear push rods and lift out push rods.

8. Unfasten and remove cylinder head.

9. Reverse procedure to install and tighten head bolts in the sequence shown in Figs. 12 and 13.

1969-75 V8s

NOTE: On Camaro with V8-396 and air conditioning it is necessary to remove the battery, A/C compressor, radiator shroud, air injector pump and starter. As the engine must be raised 2½″ to remove the exhaust manifold it will be necessary to remove the engine mount through bolts and loosen transmission mount bolts.

When removing left head, power steering pump or air suspension compressor must be removed if so equipped.

On all other models, proceed as follows:

1. Remove intake and exhaust manifolds.

2. Remove rocker arm covers.

3. Back off rocker arm nuts, pivot rocker arms to clear push rods and remove push rods.

4. Unfasten and remove cylinder heads.

5. Reverse procedure to install and tighten head bolts in the sequence shown in Figs. 14 to 16.

VALVES, ADJUST
Hydraulic Lifters

NOTE: *After the engine has been thoroughly warmed up the valves may be adjusted with the engine shut off as follows: With engine in position to fire No. 1 cylinder the following valves may be adjusted: Exhaust 1-3-4-8, intake 1-2-5-7. Then crank the engine one more complete revolution which will bring No. 6 cylinder to the firing position at which time the following valves may be adjust-*

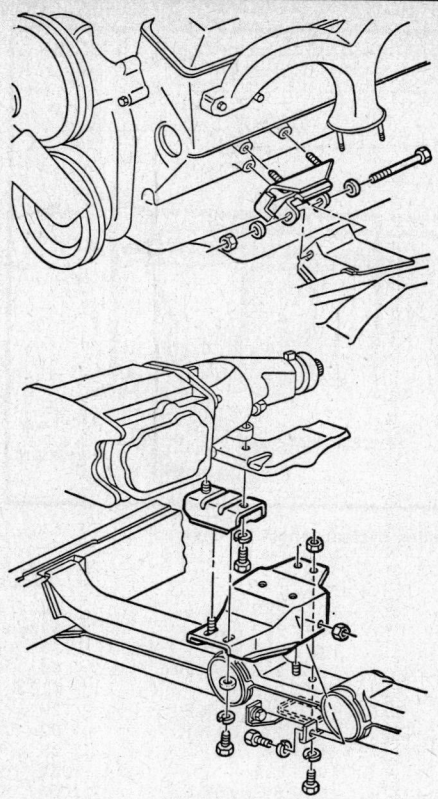

Fig. 10 Engine mounts. 1969-75 Corvette (typical)

temperature as described above, turn rocker arm stud nut as required to obtain the clearances given in *Valve Specifications* table.

VALVE ARRANGEMENT
Front to Rear

4 Cylinder	E-I-I-E-E-I-I-E
6 Cylinder	E-I-I-E-E-I-I-E-E-I-I-E
Small V8	E-I-I-E-E-I-I-E
Mark IV V8	I-E-I-E-I-E-I-E

ROCKER ARM STUDS

Rocker arm studs that have damaged threads may be replaced with standard studs. If studs are loose in the head, oversize studs (.003" or .013") may be installed after reaming the holes with a proper size reamer.
1. Remove the old stud by placing a suitable spacer, Fig. 17, over stud. Install nut and flat washer and remove stud by turning nut.
2. Ream hole for oversize stud.
3. Coat press-fit area of stud with rear axle lube. Then install new stud, Fig. 18. If tool shown is used, it should bottom on the head.

NOTE: 1970-71 V8-350 cu. in., 360 and 370 H.P. engines are equipped with threaded rocker arm studs.

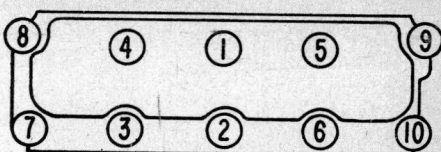

Fig. 12 Cylinder head tightening sequence. 4-153 engine

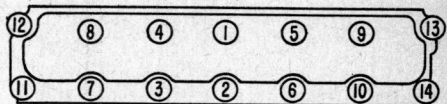

Fig. 13 Cylinder head tightening sequence. 6-230, 250

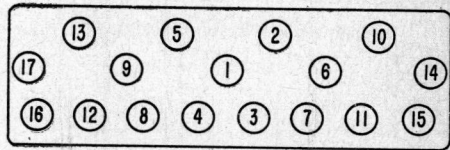

Fig. 14 Cylinder head tightening sequence. Small V8 engines

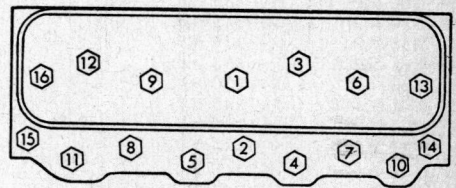

Fig. 15 Cylinder head tightening sequence. Mark IV V8 engines

ed: Exhaust 2-5-6-7, intake 3-4-6-8.

The following procedure, performed with the engine running should be done only in case readjustment is required.
1. After engine has been warmed up to operating temperature, remove valve cover and install a new valve cover gasket on cylinder head to prevent oil from running out.
2. With engine running at idle speed, back off valve rocker arm nut until rocker arm starts to clatter.
3. Turn rocker arm nut down slowly until the clatter just stops. This is the zero lash position.
4. Turn nut down ¼ additional turn and pause 10 seconds until engine runs smoothly. Repeat additional ¼ turns, pausing 10 seconds each time, until nut has been turned down the number of turns listed in the *Valve Specifications Chart* from the zero lash position.

NOTE

This preload adjustment must be done slowly to allow the lifter to adjust itself to prevent the possibility of interference between the intake valve head and top of piston, which might result in internal damage and/or bent push rods. Noisy lifters should be replaced.

Mechanical Lifters

With the engine warmed to operating

VALVE LIFT SPECS

Engine	Year	Intake	Exhaust
4-153	1969-70	.3973	.3973
6-230	1969-70	.3317	.3317
6-250	1969-74	.388	.388
	1972㉗	.388	.4051
	1974㉗	.388	.4051
	1975	.388	.4051
8-262	1975	.3727	.3900
8-302	1969	.4851	.4851
8-307	1969③⑯	.3945	.3945
	1970-73	.390	.410
	1972㉗	.4006	.4100
8-327	1969	.3945	.3945

Engine	Year	Intake	Exhaust
8-350	1969③⑯	.3945	.3945
	1969④	.4500	.4600
	1969⑰	.4851	.4851
	1970③	.390	.410
	1970④	.4500	.4600
	1970-71⑰㉒㉔	.4586	.4850
	1971㉕㉖	.390	.410
	1972-73㉘	.390	.4100
	1972㉗㉘	.4006	.4100
	1972㉘	.4586	.4850
	1974㉜	.390	.410
	1974㉜	.4500	.4600
	1975⑥	.3900	.4100
	1975⑦	.4500	.4600
8-396	1969⑨⑱	.398	.398
	1969④	.4614	.4800
	1969⑲	.5197	.5197
8-400	1970⑱	.390	.410
	1970㉒	.3983	.3983
	1970④	.4614	.480
	1971③	.3983	.430
	1972-75	.390	.410
	1972㉗	.4006	.410
8-402	1972	.3983	.430
8-427	1969⑭	.4614	.4800
	1969⑫	.4614	.4800
	1969⑮	.5917	.5917
	1969⑮	.5197	.5197
	1969⑳	.398	.398
	1969㉑	.5586	.580

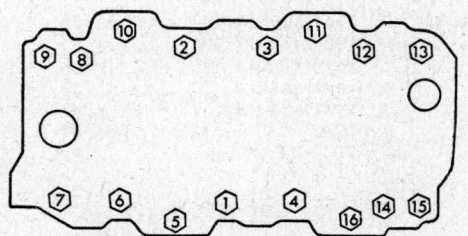

Fig. 16 Intake manifold tightening sequence. Mark IV V8 engines

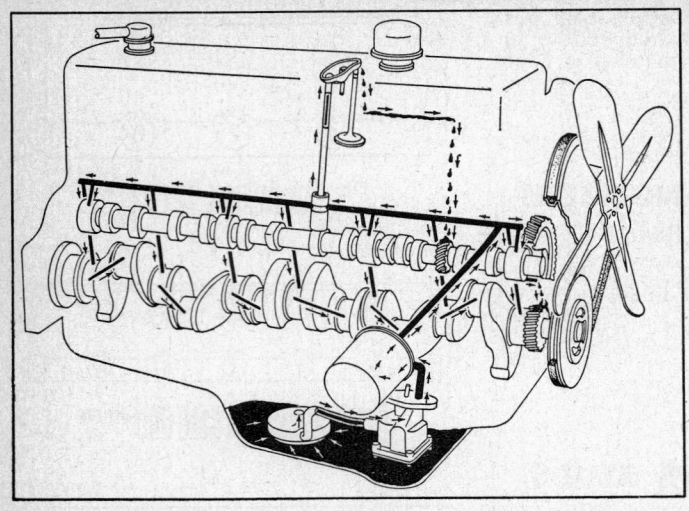

Engine oiling system. 6-230, 250. Four cylinder is similar

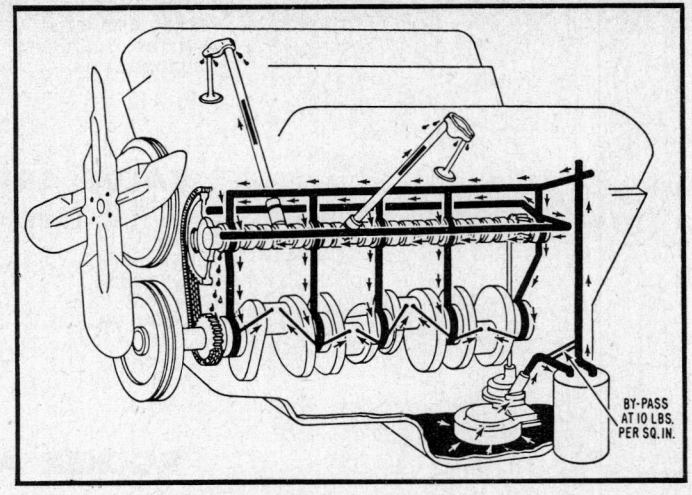

BY-PASS AT 10 LBS. PER SQ. IN.

Engine oiling system. Small V8 engines

8-454	1970⊗	.3983	.4300
	1970⑭⑤	.4614	.480
	1971⑩	.5197	.5197
	1972㉚	.4614	.480
	1972㉛	.3983	.480
	1973-75	.440	.440

②—250 H.P.	⑰—370 H.P.
③—300 H.P.	⑱—265 H.P.
④—350 H.P.	⑲—375 H.P.
⑤—365 H.P.	⑳—335 H.P.
⑥—Exc. L82 &	㉑—430 H.P.
Z28	㉒—330 H.P.
⑦—L82 & Z28	㉓—345 H.P.
⑨—325 H.P.	㉔—360 H.P.
⑩—425 H.P.	㉕—245 H.P.
⑪—340 H.P.	㉖—270 H.P.
⑫—400 H.P.	㉗—California vehicles
⑬—385 H.P.	㉘—165, 200 H.P.
⑭—390 H.P.	㉙—255 H.P.
⑮—435 H.P.	㉚—230 H.P.
⑯—255 H.P.	㉛—270 H.P.
	㉜—145, 160, 185, 195 H.P.

VALVE TIMING

Intake Opens Before TDC
All Except Corvette

Engine	Year	Degrees
4-153	1969-70	17½
6-230	1969-70	16
6-250	1969-75	16
8-262	1975	26
8-307	1968-72; 1973	28
	1972 Calif.	44
8-327	1969	28
8-350	1969-70 255, 300 H.P.	28
	1969 350 H.P.	52
	1970 250, 300 H.P.	28
	1970 360 H.P.	42½
	1971 245, 270 H.P.	28
	1971 330 H.P.	42⅔
	1972-73 165, 200 H.P.	28
	1972 165, 200 H.P. Calif.	44
	1972 255 H.P.	42⅔
	1974 145, 160, 185, 195 H.P.	28
	1974 145, 160, 185, 195 H.P. Calif.	44
	1974 245 H.P.	52
	1975 Exc. Z28	28
	1975 Z28	52
8-396	1969 265, 325 H.P.	28
	1969 350 H.P.	56
8-400	1970 265, 330 H.P.	28
	1970 350 H.P.	56
	1971 300 H.P.	28
	1972-75	28
	1972 Calif	44
	1974 Calif.	44
8-402	1972	30
8-427	1969 390, 400 H.P.	56
	1969 435 H.P.	44
8-454	1970 360 H.P.	56
	1971 365 H.P.	56
	1971 425 H.P.	44
	1972	56
	1973-75	55

Corvette

Engine	Year	Degrees
8-350	1969-70 300 H.P.	28
	1969-70 350 H.P.	52
	1970 370 H.P.	42½

	1971 270 H.P.	28
	1971 330 H.P.	42⅔
	1972 200 H.P.	28
	1972 200 H.P. Calif.	44
	1972 255 H.P.	42¾
	1973-74 195 H.P.	28
	1973-74 250 H.P.	52
	1975 Exc. L82	28
	1975 L82	52
8-427	1969 390, 400 H.P.	56
	1969 435 H.P.	44
8-454	1970 390 H.P.	56
	1970 460 H.P.	62
	1971 365 H.P.	56
	1971 425 H.P.	44
	1972	56
	1973-74	55

PUSH RODS

On engines that use push rods with a hardened insert at one end, the hardened end is identified by a color stripe and should always be installed toward the rocker arm during assembly.

Service Bulletin

On 6-cylinder engines with air conditioning, it is not necessary to remove the distributor wires, etc. to replace the valve

Fig. 17 Removing valve rocker arm stud

TOOL J-5802

Fig. 18 Installing valve rocker arm stud

TOOL J-6880

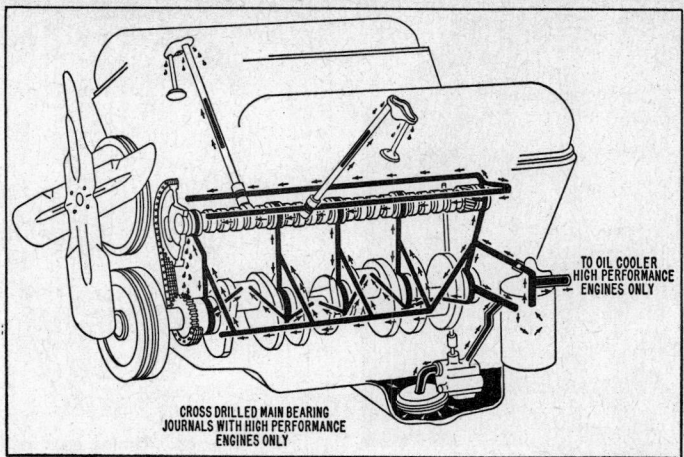

Engine lubrication. Mark IV V8 engines

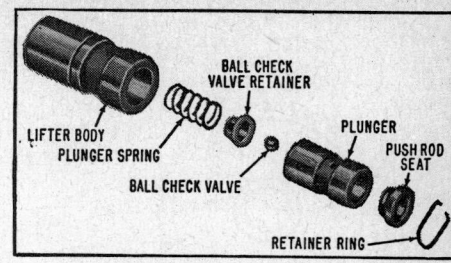

Fig. 19 Hydraulic valve lifter

push rod cover and/or gasket.
1. Remove coil and bracket from block.
2. Remove distributor hold-down clamp.
3. Lift distributor up for clearance (do not disengage from cam gear), then remove push rod cover.
4. Use new gasket and reverse procedure to install.

VALVE GUIDES

On all engines valves operate in guide holes bored in the head. If clearance becomes excessive, use the next oversize valve and ream the bore to fit. Valves with oversize stems are available in .003, .015 and .030".

HYDRAULIC LIFTERS

Valve lifters may be lifted from their bores after removing rocker arms and push rods. Adjustable pliers with taped jaws may be used to remove lifters that are stuck due to varnish, carbon, etc. Fig. 19 illustrates the type of lifter used.

TIMING CASE COVER

NOTE: On all engines the cover oil seal may be replaced without taking off the timing gear cover. After removing the vibration damper, pry out the old seal with a screwdriver. Install the new seal with the lip or open end toward inside of cover and drive it into position.

1969-75 Four & Six Cylinder

1. To remove cover, remove radiator.
2. Remove vibration damper (6-cyl.) or pulley (4-cyl.).

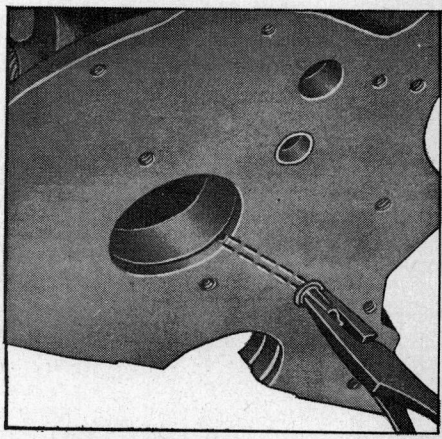

Fig. 20 Timing gear oil nozzle removal. 4-153, 6-230, 250

3. Remove oil pan.
4. Unfasten and remove cover.
5. Pry oil seal out of cover with a large screwdriver. Install new seal with open side of seal inside of cover and drive or press seal into place.
6. If oil nozzle is to be replaced, remove it with pliers as shown in Fig. 20. Drive new nozzle in place, using a suitable light plastic or rubber hammer.
7. Clean gasket surfaces.
8. Install a suitable centering tool over

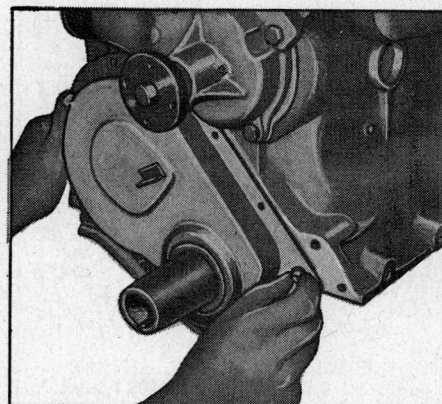

Fig. 21 Installing timing case cover. 4-153, 6-230, 250

Fig. 22 Removing camshaft gear from camshaft. 4-153 and all 6 cylinder engines

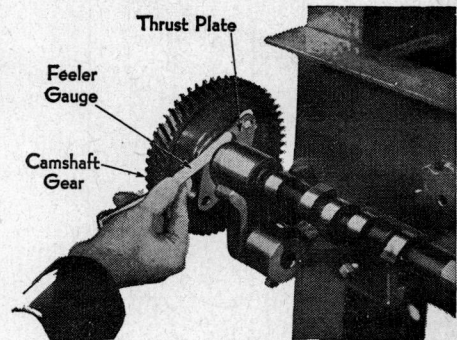

Fig. 23 Checking camshaft end play which should be .001 to .005". 4-153 and all 6 cylinder engines

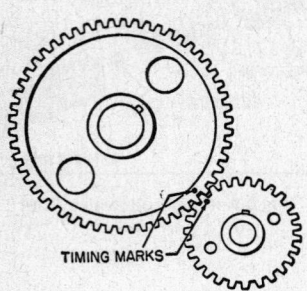

Fig. 24 Timing gear locating marks. 4-153 and all 6 cylinder engines

Fig. 25 Checking timing gear backlash with feeler gauge. Lash should be .004 to .006". 4-153 and all 6 cylinder engines

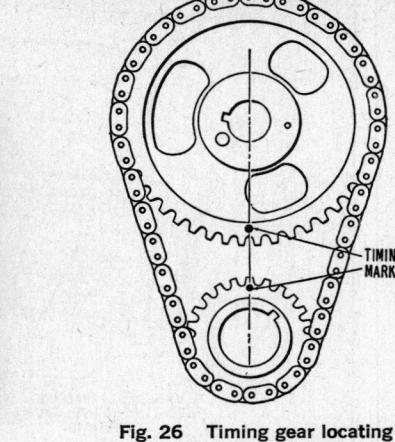

Fig. 26 Timing gear locating marks. V8 engines

end of crankshaft.

9. Coat gasket with light grease and stick it in position on block.
10. Install cover over centering tool, Fig. 21, and install cover screws, tightening them to 6 to 8 ft. lbs. *It is important that the centering tool be used to align the cover so the vibration damper installation will not damage the seal and position seal evenly around damper hub surface.*

1969-75 V8s

NOTE: The timing chain cover has been redesigned on 1974-75 small V8 engines to facilitate removal. The inner flange seal retainer has been shortened enough to clear the oil pan lip, making oil pan removal unnecessary.

Remove vibration damper, oil pan, heater hose from water pump, and water pump from cylinder block. Unfasten and remove cover and gaskets.

Pry old seal out of cover from the front with a large screwdriver. Install the new seal so the open end of the seal is toward the inside of the cover and drive it into position with a suitable driver, being sure to support cover at sealing area.

1. Make certain that the mating faces of cover and block are clean and flat.
2. Make certain oil slinger is in place against crankshaft sprocket.
3. Coat oil seal with light grease and, using a new cover gasket, install cover and gasket over dowel pins in cylinder block.
4. Install and tighten cover screws to 6-8 lb. ft. torque.
5. Install oil pan, harmonic balancer and water pump.
6. Start engine and check for leaks.

TIMING GEARS

4-153 & All 6 Cyl. Engines

When necessary to install a new camshaft gear, the camshaft will have to be removed as the gear is a pressed fit on the shaft. The camshaft is held in position by a thrust plate which is fastened to the crankcase by two capscrews which are accessible through two holes in the gear web.

Use an arbor press to remove the gear and when doing so, a suitable sleeve, Fig. 22, should be employed to support the gear properly on its steel hub.

Before installing a new gear, assemble a new thrust plate on the shaft and press the gear on just far enough so that the thrust plate has practically no clearance, yet is free to turn. The correct clearance

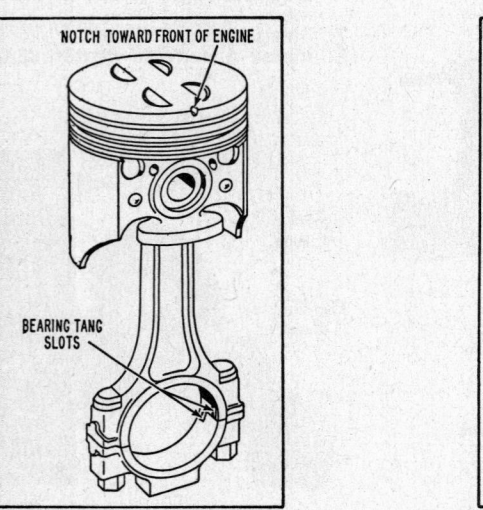

Fig. 28 Piston and rod assembly. 4-153 and 6-230 engines

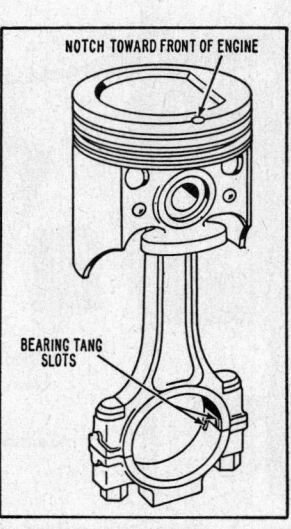

Fig. 29 Piston and rod assembly. 6-250 engine

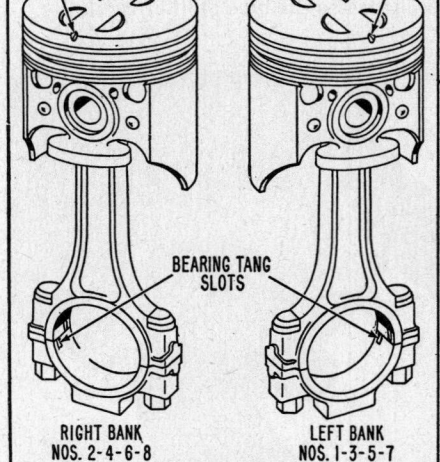

Fig. 30 V8-307, 350 and 327 (except 325 and 350 H.P.)

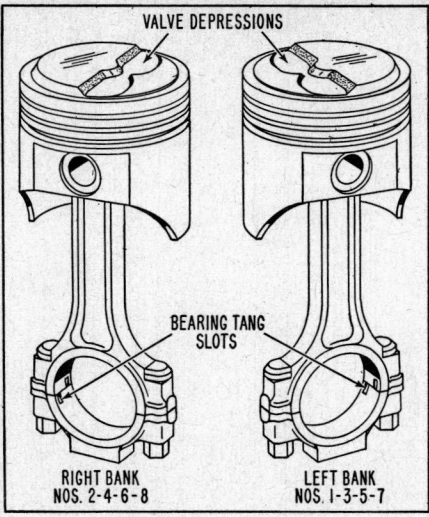

Fig. 31 V8-302, 327
(325 and 350 H.P.)

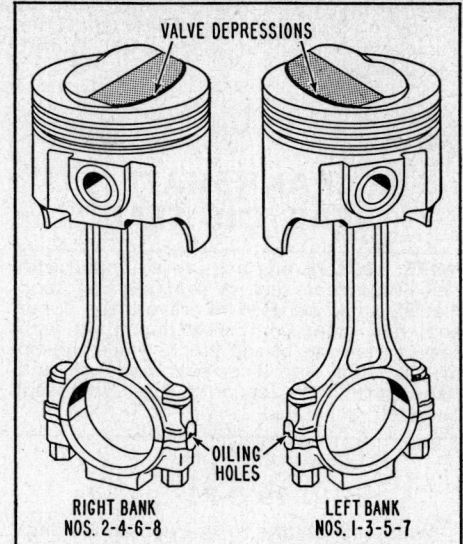

Fig. 32 V8-302, 350 Z-28
High performance

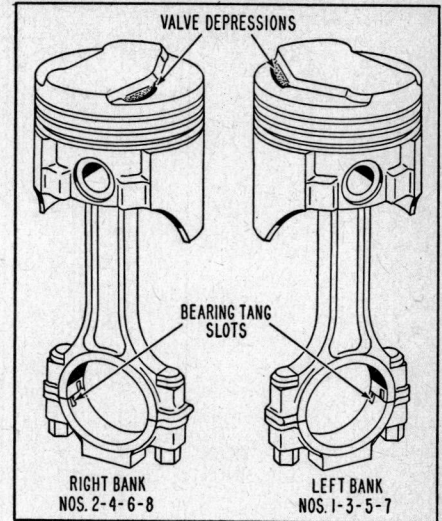

Fig. 33 V8-396, 454 engines

is from .001" to .005", Fig. 23.

The crankshaft gear can be removed by utilizing the two tapped holes in conjunction with a gear puller.

When the timing gears are installed, be sure the punch-marks on both gears are in mesh, Fig. 24. Backlash between the gears should be from .004" to .006", Fig. 25. Check the run-out of the gears, and if the camshaft gear run-out exceeds .004" or the crank gear run-out is in excess of .003", remove the gear (or gears) and examine for burrs, dirt or some other fault which may cause the run-out. If these conditions are not the cause, replace the gear (or gears).

TIMING CHAIN

V8 Engines

1. Remove timing chain cover as outlined previously.
2. Remove crankshaft oil slinger.
3. Crank engine until "O" marks on sprockets are in alignment, Fig. 26.
4. Remove three camshaft-to-sprocket bolts.
5. Remove camshaft sprocket and timing chain together. Sprocket is a light press fit on camshaft for approximately ⅛". If sprocket does not come off easily, a light blow with a plastic hammer on the lower edge of the sprocket should dislodge it.
6. If crankshaft sprocket is to be replaced, remove it with a suitable gear puller. Install new sprocket, aligning key and keyway.
7. Install chain on camshaft sprocket. Hold sprocket vertical with chain hanging below and shift around to align the "O" marks on sprockets.
8. Align dowel in camshaft with dowel hole in sprocket and install sprocket on camshaft. *Do not attempt to drive sprocket on camshaft as welch*

plug at rear of engine can be dislodged.

9. Draw sprocket onto camshaft, using the three mounting bolts. Tighten to 15-20 lb. ft. torque.
10. Lubricate timing chain and install cover.

CAMSHAFT

If necessary to replace bearings, the engine will have to be removed from the chassis. Then remove camshaft, flywheel and crankshaft. Drive out the expansion plug at the rear of the rear camshaft bearing and use suitable equipment to remove and replace the bearings.

6 Cyl. & 1969 Exc. Camaro

To remove the camshaft, remove radiator, grille, push rods, valve lifters, oil pan, vibration damper (6 cyl) or pulley (4 cyl), and timing case cover. Then pull out camshaft and gear assembly.

1969 Camaro & All 1970-75

On 1969 Camaro 6 cyl. and 1970-75 4 and 6 cylinder engines, it is recommended that the engine is first removed from the vehicle. Once the engine is removed, the camshaft is removed as outlined above.

V8 Engines

To remove the camshaft, remove valve lifters, fuel pump and its push rod, radiator, timing chain and camshaft sprocket. Install two ⁵⁄₁₆"-18 x 4" bolts in two camshaft bolt holes. Using these bolts as a puller, remove camshaft.

PISTONS & RODS, ASSEMBLE

1969-75

Assemble pistons to connecting rods as shown in Fig. 28 to 36.

PISTON OVERSIZES

4-153	.001, .020, .030, .040"
6 Cyl.	.001, .020, .030, .040"
V8-302, 307, 327, 350	.001, .020, .030"
V8-396, 310, 350 H.P.	.001, .020, .030"
V8-396 375 H.P.	.001, .030"
V8-400	.001, .020, .030"
V8-427 390 H.P.	.001, .020, .030"
V8-427, 425, 435 H.P.	.001, .030, .060"
V8-454, 230, 245 H.P.	.001, .030"
V8-454, 270, 275 H.P.	.001, .030"
V8-454 345, 390 H.P.	.001, .020, .030"
V8-454, 365, 425 H.P.	.001, .020, .030"
V8-454 450, 460 H.P.	.001, .030, .060"
V8-454 465 H.P.	.001, .030, .060"

RING OVERSIZES

4-153, 6-230, 6-250	.020, .030, .040"
V8-327, 350	.020, .030"
V8-396	.020, .030"
V8-400	.020, .030"
V8-427 390 H.P.	.020, .030"
V8-427, 425, 435 H.P.	.030, .060"
V8-454	.020, .030, .060"

MAIN & ROD BEARINGS
Undersizes

On all engines main and rod bearings are available in undersizes of .001, .002, .009, .010, .020 and .030".

SERVICE BULLETIN

Connecting rod type noise correction on

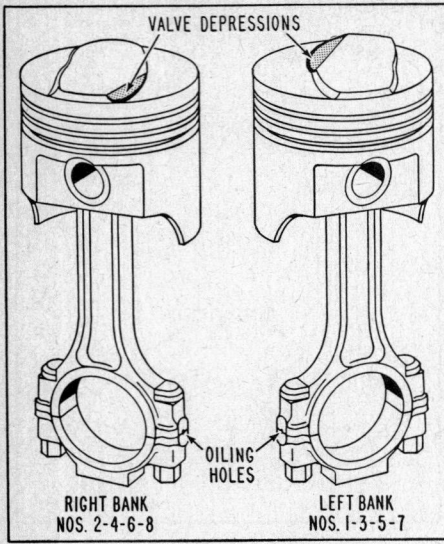

Fig. 34   V8-400 High performance

6-230 engines may be made as follows:

Remove connecting rod cap and Plastigage the bearings. If clearance is within .001 to .002", reinstall cap and retaining nuts. Then tighten nuts to the proper torque as listed in the *Engine Tightening Specifications* table.

NOTE 4-153 & All 6 Cyl.

The rear main bearing journal has no oil hole drilling. To remove the upper bearing half (bearing half with oil hole) proceed as follows after cap is removed:

1. Use a small drift punch and hammer to start the bearing rotating out of the block.
2. Use a pair of pliers (tape jaws) to hold the bearing thrust surface to the oil slinger and rotate the crankshaft to pull the bearing out.
3. To install, start the bearing (side not notched) into side of block by hand, then use pliers as before to turn bearing half into place.

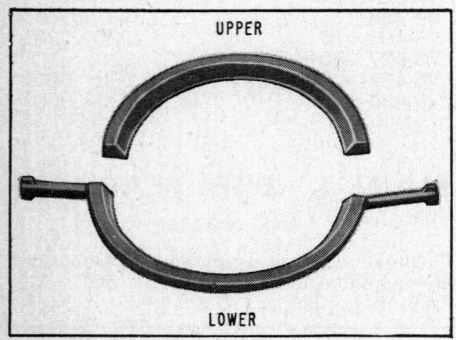

Fig. 37   Crankshaft and rear oil seal (typical)

4. The last ¼" movement may be done by holding just the slinger with the pliers or tap in place with a drift punch.

CRANKSHAFT REAR OIL SEAL

NOTE: 1971-75 engines are equipped with helix type rear seal. A seal starting tool, Fig. 38, must be used to prevent the upper seal half from coming into contact with the sharp edge of the block. Place the tip of the tool into the seal channel and "shoehorn" the seal into the upper seal channel.

1969-75

When necessary to correct an oil leak due to a defective seal, always replace the upper and lower seal halves as a unit, Fig. 37. *When installing either half, lubricate the lip portion only with engine oil, keeping oil off the parting line surface as this is treated with glue.* Always clean crankshaft surface before installing a new seal. Be careful of seal retainer tang while inserting a new seal so that it doesn't cut the seal.

1. To replace the lower seal, remove seal from groove in bearing cap, using a small screwdriver to pry it out.
2. Insert new seal and roll it in place with finger and thumb.
3. To replace the upper seal (with engine in car) use a small hammer and tap a brass pin punch on one end of the seal until it protrudes far enough to be removed with pliers.
4. Insert the new seal, gradually pushing with a hammer handle until seal is rolled into place.
5. Install bearing cap with new seal and tighten bearing cap bolts.

OIL PAN
1973-75 Six

1. Disconnect battery positive cable.
2. Remove radiator upper mounting panel or side mount bolts.
3. Place a piece of heavy cardboard between fan and radiator.
4. Disconnect fuel suction line at fuel pump.
5. Raise vehicle on a hoist and drain engine oil.
6. Disconnect and remove starter and flywheel underpan or converter housing underpan and splash shield.
7. On Nova, disconnect steering rod at idler lever and position linkage to one side for pan clearance.
8. Rotate crankshaft until timing mark on damper is at 6 o'clock.
9. Remove bolts attaching brake line to front crossmember and move brake line away from crossmember.
10. Remove through bolts from engine front mounts.
11. Remove oil pan bolts.

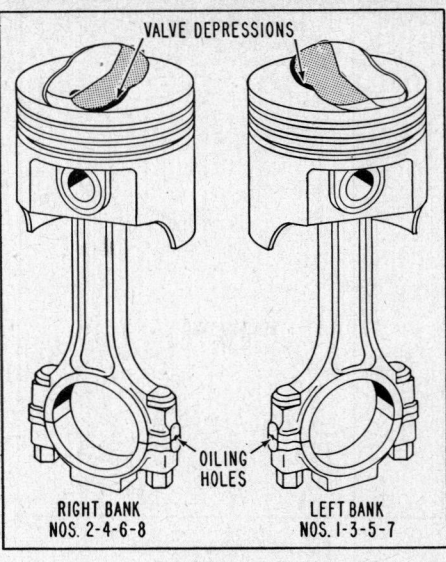

Fig. 36   V8-427 engine, 1969-70

12. On Chevrolet models, raise engine slowly until motor mount through bolts can be removed, remove bolts, then continue to raise engine about 3".
13. On Nova, remove left engine mount and frame bracket. Remove oil pan by lowering slightly and then rolling it into opening created by removal of left engine mount. Tilt front of pan upward and remove by pulling pan down and to rear.
14. On Camaro, raise engine enough to insert 2" x 4" block of wood under engine mounts. Then lower engine onto blocks and lower and remove pan.

1973-75 V8 Except Corvette

NOTE: On Chevelle equipped with V8-454 and manual transmission, it is necessary to remove the starter and the flywheel shield. Also, remove rear transmission mount to crossmember nut and raise rear of transmission.

1. Disconnect battery ground cable.
2. Remove distributor cap and fan shroud retaining bolts.

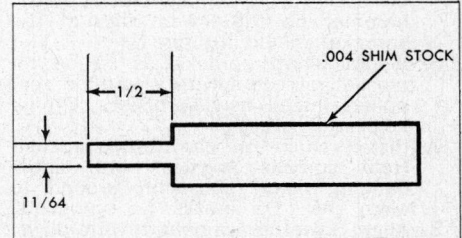

Fig. 38   Fabricated seal starting tool for helix type seal

Fig. 39   Install strap over cowl

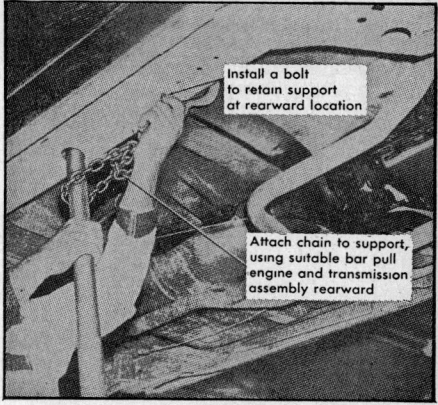

Fig. 40   Prying engine/transmission assembly rearward. 1969 Chevelle V8-307, 327, 350 with Std. Trans.

3. On Mark IV engines, place a piece of heavy cardboard between fan and radiator.
4. Raise vehicle on hoist and drain oil.
5. Disconnect exhaust or crossover pipes.
6. If equipped with automatic transmission, remove converter underpan and splash shield.
7. On Nova, disconnect steering idler lever at frame and swing linkage down for pan clearance.
8. Rotate crankshaft until timing mark on damper is at 6 o'clock.
9. On all except V8-350 and Mark IV engines with automatic transmission, disconnect starter brace at starter. Remove inboard starter bolt and loosen outboard starter bolt. Swing starter outward to gain clearance.
10. Remove both through bolts from engine front mounts.
11. Using suitable equipment, raise engine until wood blocks of 2" on Chevrolet and Nova and 3" on Chevelle and Monte Carlo can be inserted under engine mounts. Lower engine onto blocks.
12. Remove oil pan bolts and lower oil pan.

1971-72 Six

1. Disconnect battery positive cable.
2. Remove radiator upper mounting panel or side mount bolts.
3. Place a piece of heavy cardboard between fan and radiator.
4. Disconnect fuel suction line at fuel pump.
5. Raise vehicle on hoist and drain oil.
6. Disconnect and remove starter.
7. Remove either flywheel underpan or converter housing underpan and splash shield.
8. On all vehicles except Chevelle and Chevrolet, disconnect steering rod at idler lever, than position steering linkage to one side for clearance.
9. Rotate crankshaft until timing mark on damper is at 6 o'clock position.

10. Remove bolts attaching brake line to front crossmember and move brake line away from member.
11. Remove through bolts from engine front mounts.
12. Remove oil pan bolts.
13. On Chevelle and Chevrolet, raise engine slowly until motor mounts can be removed from frame brackets, remove mount and continue to raise engine until it is about three inches up.
14. On all models except Chevelle and Chevrolet, raise engine enough to insert 2" x 4" wood blocks under engine mounts, then lower engine onto blocks.
15. Lower oil pan and remove.

1971-72 V8 Except Chevelle with Mark IV Engines

1. Disconnect battery ground cable.
2. Remove distributor cap.
3. Remove fan shroud retaining bolts.
4. On Mark IV engines, place a heavy piece of cardboard between fan and radiator.
5. Raise vehicle on hoist and drain oil.
6. Disconnect exhaust or crossover pipes.
7. On vehicles with automatic transmission, remove converter housing underpan and splash shield.
8. On all models except Chevelle and Chevrolet, disconnect steering idler lever at frame and swing linkage down for clearance.
9. Rotate crankshaft until timing mark on damper is at 6 o'clock position.
10. On small V8 engines, disconnect starter brace at starter. Remove inboard starter bolt and loosen outboard starter bolt. Starter can be swung out for clearance.
11. Remove through bolts from engine front mounts.
12. Use a suitable jack and a block of wood and raise engine until blocks of wood 2" on Chevrolet and Nova and 3" on Chevelle can be inserted under

mounts. Lower engine until supported by blocks.
13. Remove oil pan.

1971-72 Chevelle with Mark IV Engines

1. Disconnect battery positive cable.
2. Remove air cleaner, dipstick and disconnect distributor cap from distributor.
3. Disconnect radiator shroud and upper mounting panel. This allows radiator to move up and down freely in later steps.
4. Place a heavy piece of cardboard between fan and radiator.
5. Disconnect engine ground straps at engine.
6. Disconnect accelerator control cable from engine.
7. Place a hook and chain over cowl, Fig. 39.
8. Raise vehicle on hoist and drain oil.
9. Remove propeller shaft and plug rear of transmission.
10. On floor shift models, remove two bolts securing shift lever to linkage. On all other models, disconnect linkage at transmission.
11. Disconnect speedometer cable and back-up lamp switch connector.
12. On manual transmissions, disconnect clutch cordon shaft at frame. On automatics, disconnect cooler lines, detent cable, rod or switch wire and modulator pipe.
13. Remove crossmember bolts and place jack under engine. Raise engine and move crossmember toward rear of car.
14. On engines with single exhaust, remove crossover pipe. On dual exhaust models, disconnect exhaust pipes.
15. Remove flywheel housing cover. Remove transmission attaching bolts and remove transmission. On manual transmission models, remove flywheel housing, throwout bearing and flywheel.
16. Remove engine mount through bolts.

17. Raise rear of engine about 4 inches. Attach each end of chain to engine using bell housing bolts or transmission mounting bolts. Lower engine jack and move to front of engine.
18. Raise front of engine and insert 2" blocks of wood under front mounts.
19. Rotate crankshaft until timing mark on damper is at 6 o'clock position.
20. Remove oil pan.

1970 Camaro

1. Disconnect battery ground cable.
2. Remove distributor cap on V8 units to prevent damage when engine is raised.
3. On Mark IV engines, remove dipstick and tube.
4. Raise car and drain crankcase.
5. Disconnect exhaust crossover pipe at manifolds if necessary.
6. Remove automatic transmission converter under pan if so equipped.
7. Rotate crankshaft so timing mark is at 6 o'clock position.
8. Remove front engine mount through bolts.
9. Raise engine and insert 3" wood blocks under engine mounts. Lower engine until it is supported by blocks.
10. Remove oil pan bolts and oil pan.

1970 Chevrolet Six

1. Disconnect battery ground cable, starter wires and starter brace attaching bolt.
2. Loosen fan belt.
3. Raise vehicle and drain crankcase.
4. Remove starter, flywheel underpan and engine mount through bolts. Rotate crankshaft so timing mark is positioned at 6 o'clock position.
5. Position fan so the widest openings between the blades are at the top and bottom.
6. Raise the front of the engine and remove the engine mounts at the frame brackets.
7. Insert 5" wood blocks between the engine mount brackets and the frame brackets.
8. Remove oil pan bolts and oil pan.

1970 Chevrolet V8, 1969 Chevrolet All, 1969 Camaro 1969-70 Chevelle V8 with Auto. Trans. Exc. V8-396 1969-70 Chevy Nova

1. Disconnect battery ground cable.
2. On V8s, lift cap off distributor to prevent damaging cap when engine is raised.
3. Remove through bolts from engine front mounts.
4. Remove fan blade and starter.
5. Disconnect cooler lines (if equipped) at transmission and remove converter housing underpan.
6. Disconnect steering linkage at idler lever and swing linkage for pan clearance.

7. Rotate crankshaft until timing mark on vibration damper is at 6 o'clock position.
8. Use a suitable jack and a block of wood to prevent damage to oil pan and raise engine enough to insert 2" x 4" wood blocks under engine mounts; then lower engine to blocks.

On 1969 Chevy Nova, attach a cantilever hoist or chain-fall to engine. If chain-fall is used, disconnect and move hood out of the way.

NOTE: If 2" x 4" wood blocks are cut 5½" long they can be used on all Chevrolet engines. The 5½" length up for 4 and 6 cylinder engines and the 4" side for V8 engines.

9. On Camaro six-cylinder models, after oil pan bolts are removed and oil pan lowered, remove the oil pump, then remove the pan. On all other models, remove the pan without removing the pump.

NOTE: On 396 and 427 engines the oil pan has three ¼"-20 attaching bolts at the crankcase front cover—one at each corner and one at lower center.

1969-70 Chevelle V8-307, 327, 350 with Std. Trans.

1. Disconnect battery positive cable and remove air cleaner. Remove distributor cap.
2. Remove radiator upper mounting panel.
3. Remove fuel pump and left rear engine mount bolt. Remove fan belt.
4. On floor shift, remove shift lever and floor plate.
5. Raise vehicle on hoist and drain oil.
6. Remove crankshaft pulley and starter motor.
7. Remove flywheel underpan, disconnect transmission linkage and remove shift bracket assembly.
8. Remove drive shaft, disconnect exhaust pipes from manifolds and remove front engine mounts to block bolts.
9. Rotate crankshaft until timing mark on harmonic balancer is at 6 o'clock position.
10. Remove bolts attaching transmission crossmember to frame. Remove two bolts attaching brake line to front crossmember and move brake line from crossmember.
11. Raise front of engine at harmonic balancer until clearance between engine mounts and block is approximately ½ inch.
12. Using a chain and bar as illustrated in Fig. 40, pull the engine/transmission assembly rearward and insert a bolt through the forward mounting hole in the crossmember and the rearward hole in the frame on each side.

NOTE: Use extreme caution during this step as the engine is "free" in the chassis.

13. Raise front of engine approximately 2 additional inches. Remove oil pan bolts and lower oil pan.
14. Remove front main bearing cap and remove oil pan.

1969-70 Chevelle V8-396

The engine must be completely disconnected from its mounts, front and rear, and the crossmember disconnected and moved rearward to allow the engine to be raised high enough to provide clearance for the oil pan to be removed. The engine therefore, must be supported by a fabricated hook and a suitable chain, hung over the cowl, Fig. 39, or by removing the hood and attaching a chain hoist to raise the engine. *Because the engine is free and the crossmember removed, use caution.*

Once the engine has been raised and secured, proceed as outlined for Chevelle V8 with auto. trans.

1969 Chevelle Six

1. Remove radiator upper mounting panel. Disconnect battery positive cable.
2. Disconnect fuel line. Raise vehicle and remove splash shield, underpan and starter motor.
3. Remove through bolts from front engine mounts.
4. Rotate crankshaft until timing mark on harmonic balancer is at 6 o'clock position.
5. Remove brake line retainer bolts at crossmember and move line out of the way. Remove oil pan bolts.
6. Raise engine slowly until engine mounts can be removed from frame brackets. Continue to raise engine until it has been raised approximately 3 inches.
7. Lower oil pan and remove.

1969-74 Corvette

1. Disconnect battery and remove oil dipstick and tube.
2. Disconnect steering linkage idler arm at frame and lower linkage.
3. Remove oil pan.
4. On high performance engines, the oil baffle must be removed before additional operations can be performed.

NOTE: On 427 engines the oil pan has three ¼"-20 bolts at the crankcase front cover—one at each corner and one at lower center.

OIL PUMP

4-153, 6-230, 6-250

The pumps used in these engines are of the positive gear type. After disassembling the pump, examine the shaft and gears for excessive wear and replace where necessary, or better still, install a new pump. When assembling the pump, be sure the ground side of the idler gear is toward the cover.

The gasket used between the pump cover and the body is special in that it controls the clearance in the pump. If the relief valve parts show wear, install new parts. Be sure that the tapered set screw which holds the pump in place is fully seated and locked with its lock nut.

V8 Engines

After removing the oil pan, unfasten pump from rear main bearing cap. Disconnect pump shaft from extension by removing clip from collar. Remove pump cover and take out idler gear, drive gear and shaft.

Should any of the following conditions be found it is advisable to replace the pump assembly.

1. Inspect pump body for cracks or wear.
2. Inspect gears for wear or damage.
3. Check shaft for looseness in housing.
4. Check inside of cover for wear that would permit oil to leak past the ends of gear.
5. Check oil pick-up screen for damage to screen, by-pass valve or body.
6. Check for oil in air chamber.

BELT TENSION DATA

	New Lbs.	Used Lbs.
1969-75—		
Air Condition	135-145	95
Air Pump—		
1969	70-80	55
1970-75	120-130	75
Fan and Power Steering	120-130	75

WATER PUMP, REPLACE
All Models

1. Drain radiator and break loose fan pulley bolts.
2. Disconnect heater hose at water pump.
3. Loosen Delcotron and remove fan belt, then unfasten and remove pump. On 6-cylinder engines, pull pump straight out of block first to prevent damage to impeller.
4. Reverse procedure to install.

FUEL PUMP PRESSURE

Year	Engine	Pressure Lbs.
Camaro		
1969	Six	3-4½
1969	V8 (Exc. V8-396)	5-6½
1969-70	V8-396	5-8½
1970-74	Six	3½-4½
1975	Six	4-5
1970-73	V8-307	5-6½
1970-74	V8-350	7-8½
1975	V8-350	7½-9
1971	V8-396	7-8½
1972	V8-402	7-8½
Chevelle & Monte Carlo		
1969-70	Six	3-4½
1969-70	V8-307, 350	5-6½
1969-70	V8-396, 400, 454	5-8½
1971-74	Six	3½-4½
1975	Six	4-5
1971-74	V8-350, 400, 454	7-8½
1975	V8-350, 400, 454	7½-9
1971-73	V8-307	5-6½
Chevy Nova		
1969-70	Four & Six	3-4½
1969-70	V8-307, 327, 350	5-6½
1969-70	V8-396	5-8½
1971-74	Six	3½-4½
1975	Six	4-5
1975	V8-262	7½-9
1971-73	V8-307	5-6½
1971-74	V8-350	7-8½
1975	V8-250	7½-9
Chevrolet		
1969-70	Six	3-4½
1969	V8-327, 350, 396	5-6½
1969	V8-427	5-8½
1970	V8-350	5-6½
1970	V8-400, 454	5-8½
1971-73	Six	3½-4½
1971-74	V8	7-8½
1975	V8	7½-9
Corvette		
1969	V8-350	5-6½
1969	V8-427	5-8½
1970	Exc. V8-454, 360 H.P.	7½-9
1970	V8-454, 360 H.P.	5-8½
1971-74	All	7-8½
1975	All	7½-9

FUEL PUMP, REPLACE
1969-75

1. Disconnect fuel lines at pump.
2. Unfasten and remove pump.
3. If push rod is to be removed on 396, 400, 427 and 454 engines, remove pipe plug, then remove push rod. On 262, 302, 307, 327, 350 and 265 H.P. V8-400, remove fuel pump adapter and gasket then remove push rod.
4. Reverse procedure to install. *On V8 engines, a pair of mechanical fingers may be used to hold fuel pump push rod up while installing pump.*

NOTE

Installation of the pump on the V8-327 engine can be performed faster by using the following means of retaining the fuel pump push rod in the engine during pump replacement.

1. Before removing the pump, remove upper bolt from engine front mount boss located to the right of the timing chain cover on the front of the engine. This bolt enters the push rod bore acting as a plug.
2. Remove the original bolt and install one that is 1¾" long. Turn it down by hand until it is stopped by the push rod. *Do not use a wrench to turn in this bolt as it may damage the push rod, necessitating its replacement.*
3. The fuel pump can then be removed without the push rod slipping from its installed position. After installing the pump, the original shorter bolt must be reinstalled to avoid oil leakage.

Service Bulletin

On Mark IV engines the access hole for removal of the fuel pump push rod is located below the fuel pump mounting bolts. This access hole, which permits removal of the push rod after the pump has been removed, has a threaded plug with a square recessed hole. The plug may be removed by using a hand-made tool. A 5/16" square end for inserting and turning the plug for removal is required. A piece of bar stock, approximately 1½" long is suggested.

Clutch and Transmission Section

> NOTE: 1975 linkage adjustment information is in this section. Repair procedures on both automatic and manual shift transmissions are covered elsewhere in this manual. Procedures for removing automatic transmissions as well as linkage adjustments on 1969-74 models are included in the automatic transmission chapters. See Chapter Index.

CLUTCH PEDAL, ADJUST

1972-75 Except Corvette

1. Disconnect return spring at clutch fork.
2. Rotate clutch lever and shaft assembly until pedal is against rubber bumper on dash brace.
3. Push outer end of clutch fork rearward until throwout bearing lightly contacts pressure plate fingers.
4. Install push rod in gauge hole and increase length until all lash is removed, Fig. 1.

NOTE: On 1973-75 Chevelle, it may be necessary to move rubber bumper rearward to obtain additional clutch pedal travel.

5. Remove swivel or rod from gauge hole and insert into lower hole on lever. Install retainer and tighten lock nut being careful not to change rod length.
6. Reinstall return spring and check pedal free travel:
   1975 Camaro & Nova, $^{55}/_{64}$" to $1^{29}/_{64}$".
   Chevelle & Monte Carlo, $^{45}/_{64}$" to $1^{5}/_{16}$".
   1972–74 Camaro, 1" to $1^{3}/_{8}$".
   Chevelle, $^{3}/_{4}$" to $1^{5}/_{16}$".
   Nova, $^{3}/_{4}$" to $1^{3}/_{8}$".
   1972–73 Chevrolet, $1^{1}/_{4}$" to $1^{3}/_{4}$".

1975 Corvette

1. Disconnect return spring between toe pan brace and cross shaft lever, Fig. 2.
2. Rotate clutch lever and shaft assembly until pedal is against dash brace rubber bumper.
3. Install swivel (C) into clutch lever hole and install retainer.
4. Loosen nuts (A) and (B), then apply a 5 pound load in direction of arrow (F) until bearing lightly contacts plate fingers.
5. Rotate nut (B) toward swivel until dimension "X" is approximately $^{3}/_{8}$ to $^{7}/_{16}$ inch, then tighten nut (A) to lock swivel against nut (B).
6. Reinstall return spring and adjust clutch pedal free travel which should be 1 to $1^{1}/_{2}$ inch.

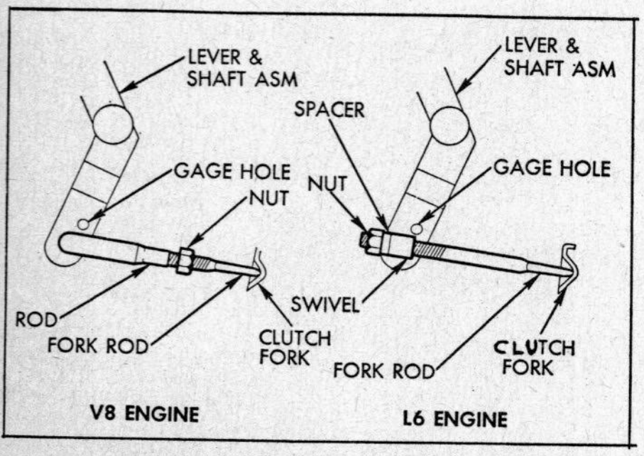

1972-74 Corvette

1. Referring to Fig. 2, disconnect spring (E) between toe pan brace and cross shaft lever.
2. With pedal against stop, loosen jam nuts sufficiently to allow adjusting rod to move against clutch fork until release bearing contacts pressure plate fingers lightly.
3. Rotate upper nut (B) against swivel and back off $4^{1}/_{2}$ turns. Tighten lower nut (A) to lock swivel against nut (B).
4. Install return spring (E) and check pedal free travel. It should be 1" to $1^{1}/_{2}$".

1969-70 Chevrolet & 1969-71 Corvette

1. Disconnect spring between clutch push rod and cross shaft lever.
2. With clutch pedal against stop, loosen jam nuts just enough to allow adjusting rod to move against the clutch fork until the release bearing contacts the pressure plate fingers lightly.
3. Rotate upper nut against swivel and back off $4^{1}/_{2}$ turns. Tighten lower nut to lock swivel against nut.
4. Install return spring and check clutch pedal free travel:
   Chevrolet 1 to $1^{1}/_{2}$".
   Corvette standard clutch $1^{1}/_{4}$ to 2".
   Corvette heavy duty clutch 2 to $2^{1}/_{2}$".

1971 Chevrolet & 1969-71 Chevelle, Camaro & Chevy Nova

1. Disconnect return spring at clutch fork.
2. With clutch pedal against stop, loosen lock nut just enough to allow the adjusting rod to be turned out off swivel and against clutch fork until release bearing contacts pressure plate fingers lightly.
3. Rotate push rod into swivel three turns and tighten lock nut.

NOTE: Nova and Camaro V8 models use a two-piece push rod. Turn adjusting rod portion of push rod three turns into rod end and tighten lock nut.

4. Reinstall return spring and check clutch pedal free travel:
   Exc. Nova, $1^{1}/_{8}$" to $1^{3}/_{4}$".
   Nova, 1" to $1^{1}/_{8}$".

CLUTCH, REPLACE

Clutch Disc Installation

On all 4 and 6-cylinder engines the clutch disc is installed with the damper springs to the flywheel side. On V8's install clutch disc with damper springs and grease slinger to transmission side.

1969-75

1. Support engine and remove transmission as outlined further on.
2. Disconnect clutch fork push rod and spring.
3. Remove flywheel housing.
4. Slide clutch fork from ball stud and remove fork from dust boot.

NOTE: Look for "X" mark on flywheel and on clutch cover. If "X" mark is not evident, prick punch marks on flywheel and clutch cover for indexing purposes during installation.

5. Loosen clutch-to-flywheel attaching bolts evenly one turn at a time until spring pressure is released. Then remove bolts and clutch assembly.
6. Reverse procedure to install.

Fig. 1 Clutch pedal adjust. Except Corvette

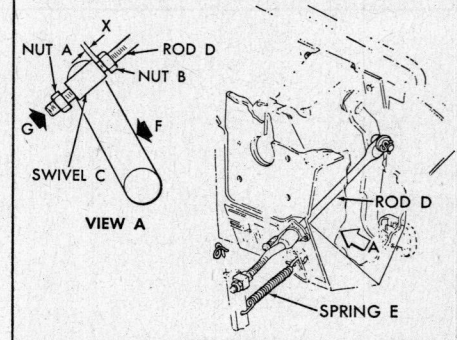

Fig. 2 Clutch pedal adjust. Corvette

THREE SPEED TRANSMISSION, REPLACE

1969 Corvette

1. Disconnect battery ground cable.
2. Remove shift ball.
3. Remove console trim plate.
4. Raise vehicle on a hoist.
5. Remove right and left exhaust pipes. *In order to remove the exhaust pipes on 8-427 engines, it will be necessary to remove the forward stud on each manifold.*
6. Disconnect and lower front of propeller shaft. Remove slip yoke from transmission.
7. Remove bolts retaining rear mounts to bracket. Raise engine, lifting transmission off mount bracket.
8. Unfasten transmission linkage mounting bracket from frame.
9. Detach gearshift from mounting bracket and remove bracket. Remove shifter mechanism with rods attached.
10. Disconnect shifter levers at transmission. Disconnect speedometer cable.
11. Unfasten and remove transmission mount bracket. Unfasten rear mount cushion and exhaust pipe yoke.
12. Unfasten transmission from clutch housing.
13. Pull transmission rearward and rotate clockwise until it is clear of clutch housing. *To allow room for transmission removal, slowly lower rear of engine until tachometer drive cable at the distributor just clears horizontal ledge across front of dash.*

CAUTION: The tachometer cable can be easily damaged by heavy contact with the dash. Slide transmission rearward out of the clutch, then tip front end of transmission down-

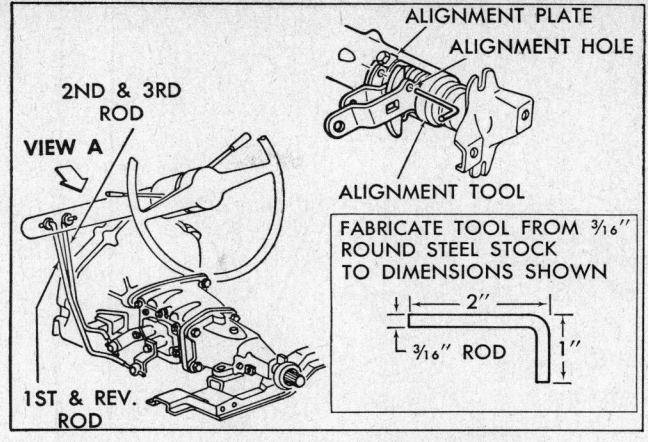

Fig. 3 Three-speed column shift linkage adjustment. 1969-74 Chevrolet, Chevy Nova, Chevelle and Camaro

ward and lower assembly from vehicle.

14. Reverse procedure to install.

1969-75 Except Corvette

NOTE: On 1975 models, it may be necessary to remove the catalytic converter and its support bracket to facilitate transmission removal.

1. On floor shift models, remove shift knob and console trim plate.
2. Disconnect speedometer cable at transmission and on floor shift models, disconnect back-up lamp switch. Disconnect T.C.S. switch wire if so equipped.
3. Remove drive shaft.
4. On 1969 Camaro, disconnect exhaust pipe at manifold.
5. Remove crossmember-to-frame attaching bolts. On floor shift models, remove crossmember-to-control lever support attaching bolts. On Chevelle, also remove control lever brace-to-crossmember attaching bolt.
6. Remove bolts retaining transmission mount to crossmember.
7. Support engine and raise slightly until crossmember may be slid rearward or removed.

NOTE: On some Camaros, it may be necessary to remove the right rear body mount bolt then, using a suitable tool, pry the right rear portion of the frame downward and insert a block of wood to maintain enough of a gap so the crossmember can be removed.

8. Remove shift levers at transmission side cover. On floor shift models, remove stabilizer-to-control lever retaining nut. Push bolt toward transmission until stabilizer rod may be disconnected.
9. Remove transmission-to-clutch housing upper retaining bolts and install

guide pins in holes, then remove lower bolts.
10. Slide transmission rearward and remove from vehicle.
11. Reverse procedure to install.

FOUR SPEED TRANSMISSION, REPLACE

1969-75 All Models

The procedure for removing this transmission is similar to that described for the "1969-75 Exc. Corvette" 3-speed unit.

THREE SPEED SHIFT LINKAGE, ADJUST

1969-75 Except Corvette

Column Shift
1. Place shift lever in "Reverse" position and ignition switch in "Lock".
2. Raise vehicle on a hoist.

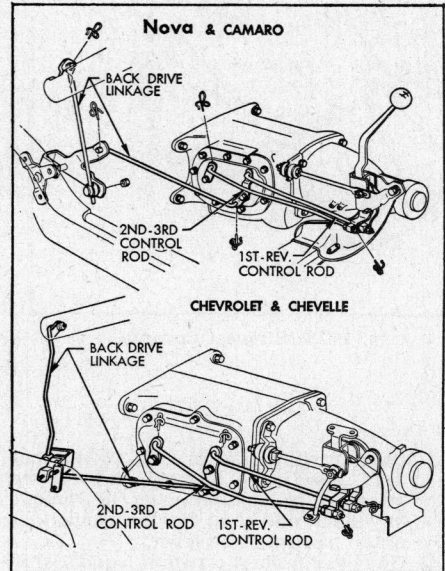

Fig. 4 3-Speed floor shift linkage. 1969-75 except Corvette (typical)

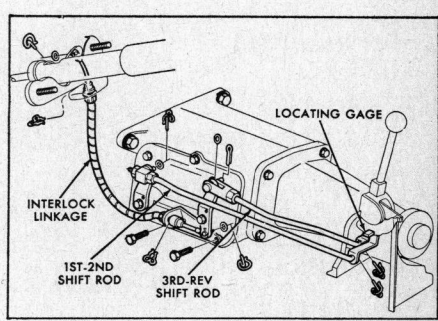

Fig. 5 3 Speed linkage. 1969-70 Corvette (typical)

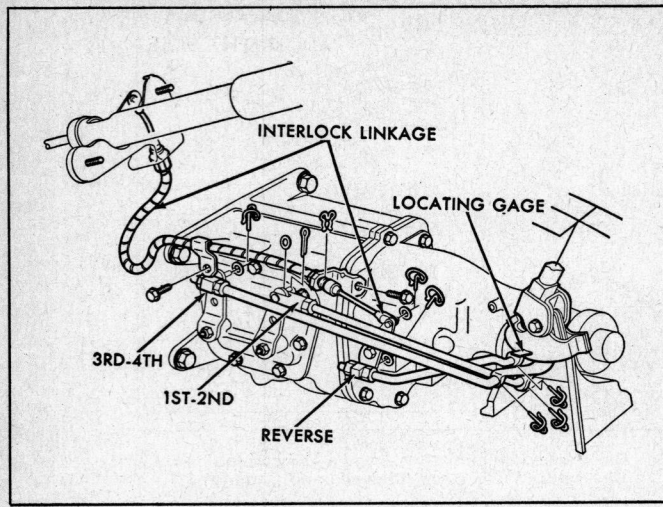

Fig. 6 4 Speed Linkage. 1969-75 Corvette (typical)

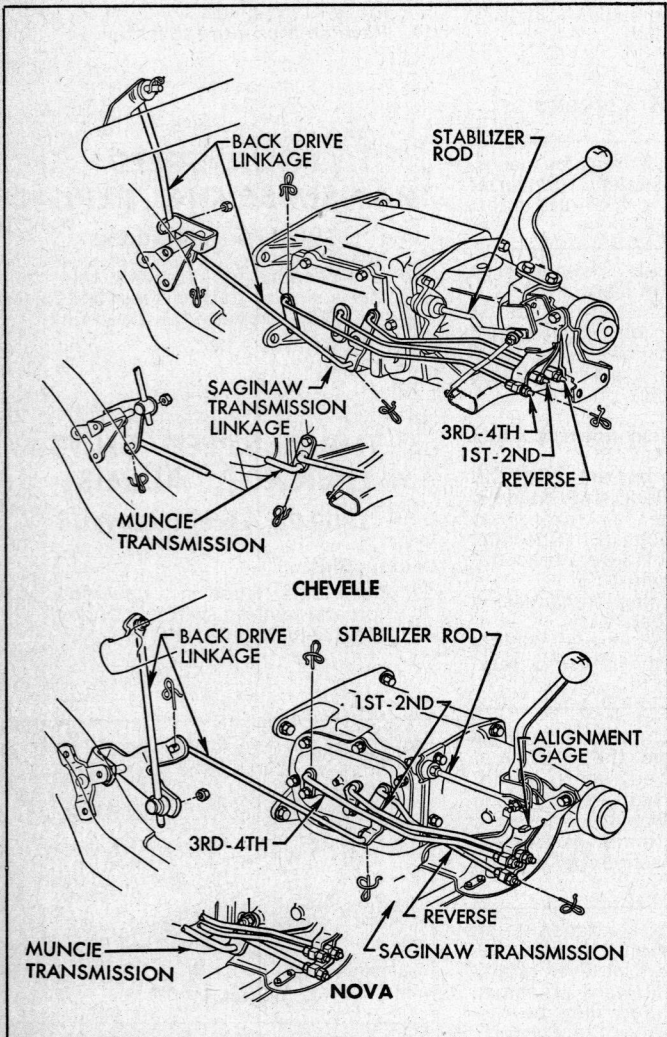

CHEVELLE

NOVA

Fig. 7 4 Speed linkage. 1969-72 except Corvette

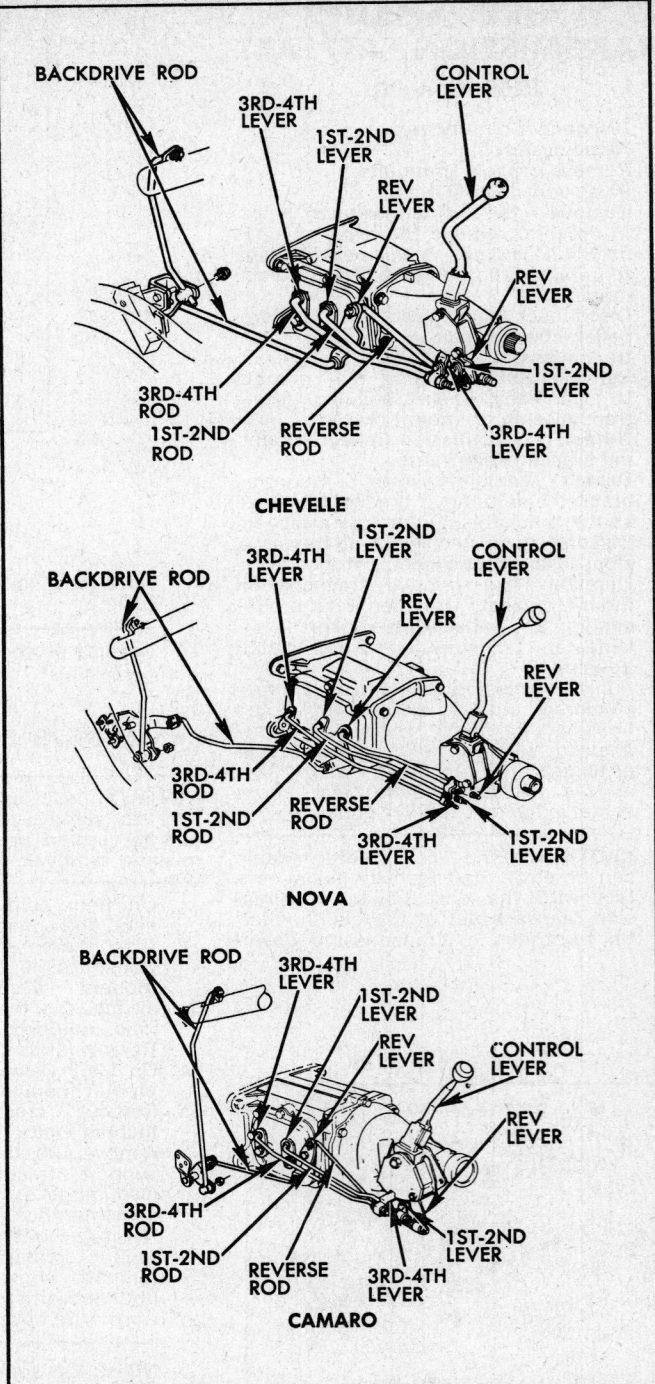

CHEVELLE

NOVA

CAMARO

Fig. 8 4 Speed linkage. 1973-75 except Corvette

3. Loosen shift control rod swivel lock nuts. Pull down slightly on 1/R rod attached to column lever to remove any slack and then tighten clevis lock nut at transmission lever.

4. Unlock ignition switch and shift column lever to "Neutral". Position column lower levers in "Neutral", align gauge holes in levers and insert

gauge pin.

NOTE: Alignment holes are on the lower side of levers on Chevelle and Nova models.

5. Support rod and swivel to prevent movement and tighten 2/3 shift control rod lock nut.
6. Remove alignment tool from column lower levers and check operation. Then place column lever in "Reverse" and check interlock control.

Floor Shift

1. Turn ignition switch to "Lock" position and raise vehicle on hoist.
2. Loosen lock nuts at swivels on both shift rods and on back drive rod, Fig. 4.
3. Set transmission shift levers in "Neutral".
4. Set shift lever in car in "Neutral" and install locating gauge into control lever bracket assembly.
5. Run 1/R shift rod nut against swivel and tighten locknut against swivel.
6. Run 2/3 shift rod against swivel and tighten locknut against swivel.
7. Remove gauge pin and shift lever into "Reverse", then pull down slightly on rod to remove any slack and tighten clevis jam nut. Ignition switch

should move freely in and out of "Lock".

1969-70 Corvette

1. Turn ignition switch to "Lock" and raise vehicle on a hoist.
2. Loosen swivel lock nuts on both shift rods and disconnect back drive cable from column lock tube lever, Fig. 5.
3. Place shift control in car into "Neutral" and insert a locking gauge (.644") in notch of lever and bracket assembly.
4. Place transmission levers into "Neutral".
5. Hold 1/R rod and lever against locating gauge and tighten locknut against swivel.
6. Hold 2/3 rod and lever against locating gauge and tighten the forward nut against swivel and then the aft. Remove locating gauge.
7. Check operation of linkage. *Caution: Shift lever must be properly centered in console to prevent fore and aft and side contact with console. Shim lever support bracket as required but be sure to maintain support to extension clearance.*
8. From inside vehicle, loosen two nuts at steering column to dash panel bracket.
9. Place transmission shift lever into "Reverse".

10. Rotate the lock tube lever counter-clockwise to remove free play. Reposition the cable bracket until the cable eye passes over the retaining pin on the bracket.
11. Hold the bracket in position and have an assistant tighten the steering column to dash panel bracket retaining nuts.
12. Reinstall the cotter pin and washer retaining the back drive cable.

FOUR SPEED SHIFT LINKAGE, ADJUST
1969-75

The procedure, Figs. 6, 7, 8, is the same as that for Three Speed transmissions described previously.

1975 AUTO. TRANS. LINKAGE, ADJUST

1975 linkages are basically the same as those used in 1974 and the adjustments are covered in the "Automatic Transmission section" in rear of this manual.

Rear Axle, Propeller Shaft & Brakes

REAR AXLE

Figs. 1 and 2 illustrate the rear axle assemblies used. When necessary to overhaul any of these units, refer to the *Rear Axle Specifications* table in this chapter.

1969-75 Corvette

In this axle, the drive pinion is mounted in two tapered roller bearings that are preloaded by a spacer. The pinion is positioned by a shim located between the head of the drive pinion and the rear pinion bearing. The front bearing is held in place by a large washer and a locking pinion nut.

The differential is supported in the carrier by two tapered roller side bearings.

The differential side bearings are preloaded by shims between the bearings and carrier housing, Fig. 2. The differential assembly is positioned for proper ring gear and pinion backlash by varying the position and thickness of these shims.

The ring gear is bolted to the case. The case houses two side gears in mesh with two pinions mounted on a pinion shaft which is held in place by a lock screw. The side gears are backed by thrust washers.

The differential side gears drive two splined yokes which are retained by snap rings located on the yoke splined end. The yokes are supported on caged needle bearings pressed into the carrier, adjacent to the differential bearings. A lip seal, pressed into the carrier outboard of the bearing, prevents oil leakage and dirt entry.

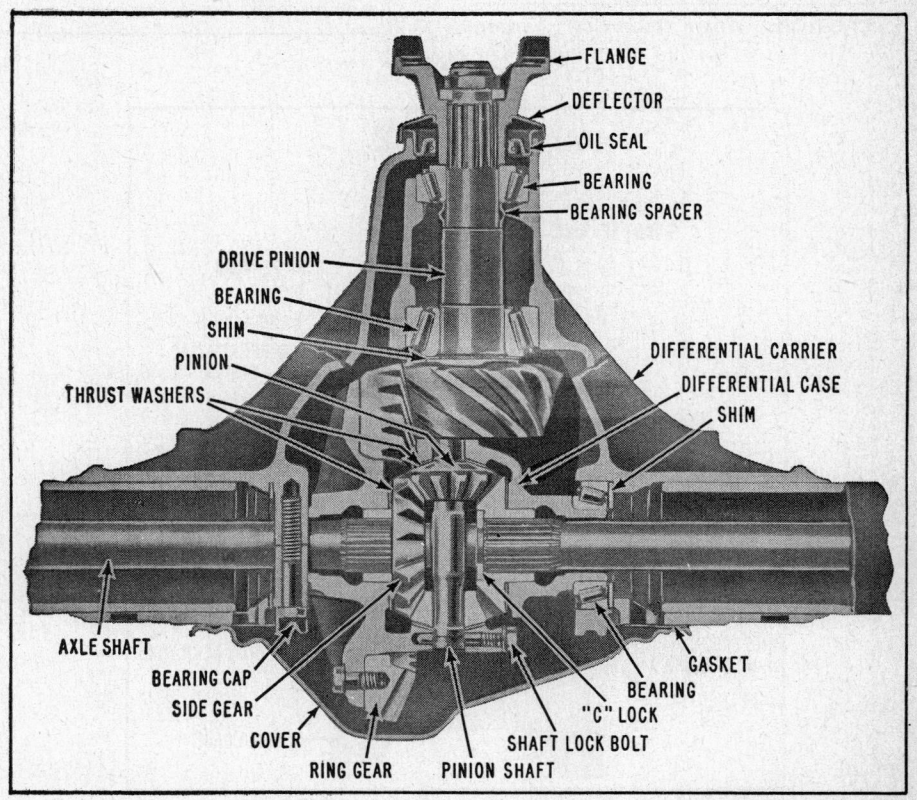

Fig. 1   Rear axle. 1969-74 Camaro, Chevrolet, Chevelle, Monte Carlo and Nova. "C" Type

On 1969 models, Positraction type differential is optional. Positraction is standard on 1970-75 units.

Remove & Replace

It is not necessary to remove the rear axle assembly for any normal repairs. The axle shafts and carrier assembly can easily be removed from the vehicle, leaving the rear axle housing in place.

Corvette 1969-75

1. Disconnect spring and spring links.
2. Disconnect axle drive shafts at carrier by removing U-bolts securing trunnion to side gear yoke, Fig. 2.
3. Disconnect carrier front support bracket at frame crossmember. Remove bolts and bracket.
4. Disconnect propeller shaft at transmission and at companion flange. Slide transmission yoke forward into transmission. Drop propeller shaft down and out toward the rear.
5. Mark camber cam and bolt relative location on strut rod bracket and loosen cam bolts, Fig. 3.
6. Remove four bolts securing bracket to carrier lower surface and drop bracket. Remove camber cam bolts and swing strut rods up and out of the way.
7. Loosen carrier-to-cover bolts gradually to allow grease to drain out.
8. With mounting bolts removed, pull carrier partially out of cover, drop nose to clear crossmember and gradually work carrier down and out.

CAUTION: *When removing carrier,* use care so as not to scrape or gouge gasket mounting surface on cover with ring gear. A deep scratch or gouge at this point may cause a lubricant leak after assembly.

9. Reverse removal procedure to install carrier, *being sure to move the camber cams to marked location before tightening nuts.*

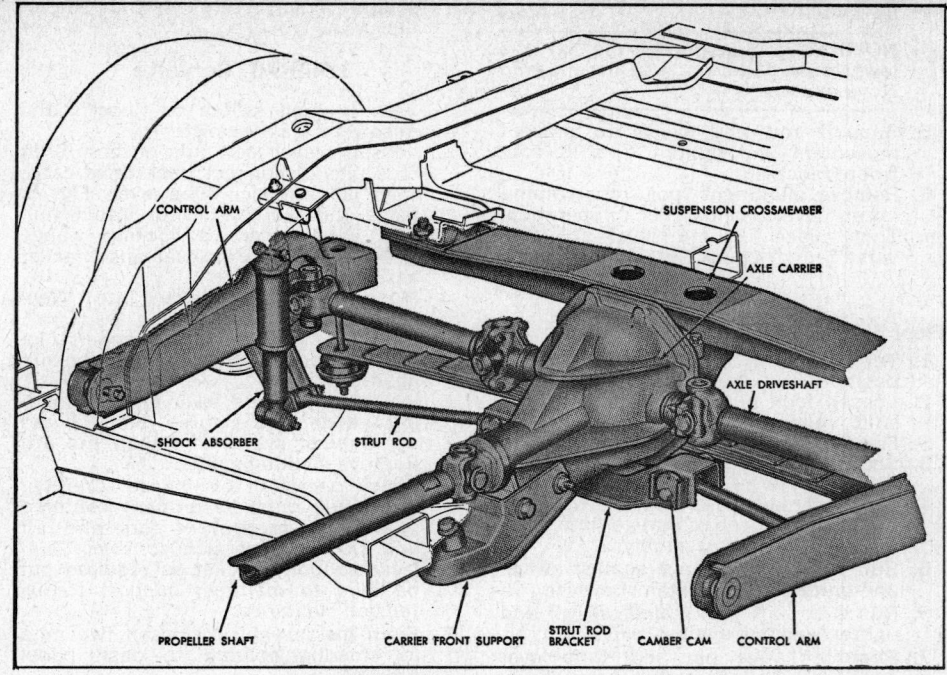

Fig. 3   Rear suspension. 1969-75 Corvette

Fig. 2   Rear axle. 1969-75 Corvette

REAR AXLE

1969-75 Camaro, Chevrolet, Chevelle, Nova & Monte Carlo

In these rear axles, Fig. 1, the rear axle housing and differential carrier are cast into an integral assembly. The drive pinion assembly is mounted in two opposed tapered roller bearings. The pinion bearings are preloaded by a spacer behind the front bearing. The pinion is positioned by a washer between the head of the pinion and the rear bearing.

The differential is supported in the carrier by two tapered roller side bearings. These bearings are preloaded by spacers located between the bearings and carrier housing. The differential assembly is positioned for proper ring gear and pinion backlash by varying these spacers. The differential case houses two side gears in mesh with two pinions mounted on a pinion shaft which is held in place by a lock pin. The side gears and pinions are backed by thrust washers.

Remove & Replace

Construction of the axle assembly is such that service operations may be performed with the housing installed in the vehicle or with the housing removed and installed in a holding fixture. The following procedure is necessary only when the housing requires replacement.

1. Raise vehicle and place stand jacks under frame side rails.
2. Remove rear wheels.
3. Support rear axle assembly with a suitable jack so that tension is relieved in springs and tie rod.
4. Disconnect tie rod at axle housing bracket.
5. Remove trunnion bearing "U" bolts from rear yoke, split universals joint, position propeller shaft to one side and tie it to frame side rail.
6. Remove axle "U" bolt nuts and allow control arm and shock absorbers to hang freely so that they do not interfere with axle. On models with leaf springs, remove spring plate nuts.
7. Disconnect hydraulic brake hose at connector on axle housing.
8. Remove brake drum and disconnect parking brake cable at lever and at flange plate. Remove brake support plate.
9. On models with coil springs, lower axle slowly to relieve tension on springs and remove axle from vehicle. On models with leaf springs, shift axle assembly to clear springs when removing from vehicle.
10. Reverse foregoing procedure to install axle assembly.

AXLE SHAFT
1969-74 Camaro, Chevrolet, Chevelle & Chevy Nova "C" Type

1. Raise vehicle and remove wheel and brake drum.
2. Drain lube from carrier and remove cover.
3. Remove differential pinion shaft lock screw and remove differential pinion shaft.
4. Pull flanged end of axle shaft toward center of vehicle and remove "C" lock from button end of shaft.
5. Remove axle shaft from housing, being careful not to damage seal.
6. Reverse foregoing procedure to install the axle shaft.

1971-75 Chevrolet "B" & "O" Type

1. Raise vehicle and remove wheel and brake drum.
2. Remove bolts attaching axle shaft retainer plate to backing plate.
3. Using a slide hammer/puller, the axle shaft can now be removed.

NOTE: You may find the wheel bearing will come out in pieces as you remove the shaft. The inner race with bearing and one retainer plate will come out with the shaft. The outer race and inner retainer plate will remain in the axle housing. These pieces can easily be removed. Even though the bearing is not in one piece it is no indication that the bearing has failed.

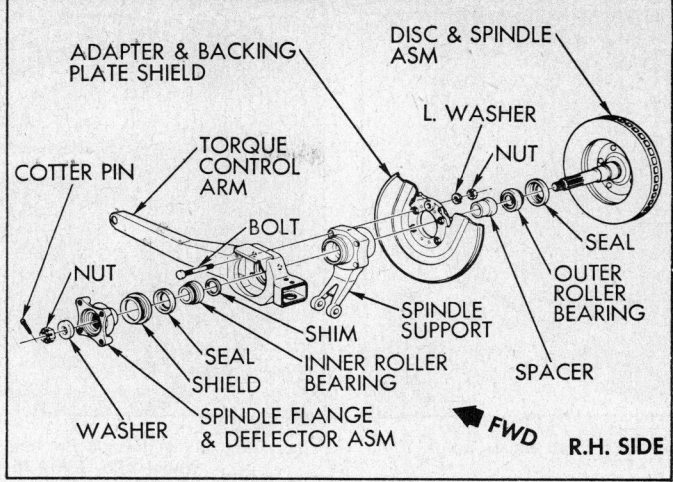

Fig. 4 Corvette rear wheel spindle

Corvette 1969-75

1. Disconnect inboard drive shaft trunnion from side gear yoke, Fig. 3.
2. Remove four bolts securing shaft flange to spindle drive flange.
3. Pry drive shaft out of outboard drive flange pilot and remove by withdrawing outboard end first.
4. If necessary, overhaul universal joints as described in the *Universal Joint* chapter.
5. Install axle shaft in reverse order of removal, *being certain to rotate yokes so that trunnion seats are phased 90 degrees apart.* Torque drive flange bolts to 70-90 ft-lbs and U-bolt nuts to 14-18 ft-lbs.

CORVETTE REAR SPINDLE

1. Referring to Fig. 4, raise vehicle and remove wheel and tire.
2. Apply parking brake to prevent spindle from turning and remove cotter pin and nut from spindle.
3. Release parking brake and remove drive spindle flange from splined end of spindle.
4. Remove brake caliper and disc.
5. Using a suitable puller, remove spindle.

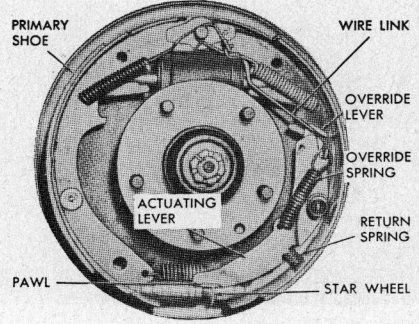

Fig. 5 Left front brake. 1969-74

6. When spindle is removed, the outer bearing will remain on the spindle. The inner bearing, tubular spacer, end play shim and both outer races will remain in the spindle support.

PROPELLER SHAFT
1969-75

These models use a one-piece propeller shaft. Powerglide models use a propeller shaft tube which incorporates rubber insulators for quieter operation. These insulators, which are bonded to the smaller tube, press fit to the larger tube.

BRAKE ADJUSTMENTS
1969-75 Self-Adjusting Brakes

These brakes, Fig. 5, have self-adjusting shoe mechanisms that assure correct lining-to-drum clearances at all times. The automatic adjusters operate only when the brakes are applied as the car is moving rearward or when the car comes to an uphill stop.

Although the brakes are self-adjusting, an initial adjustment is necessary after the brake shoes have been relined or replaced, or when the length of the adjusting screw has been changed during some other service operation.

Frequent usage of an automatic transmission forward range to halt reverse vehicle motion may prevent to automatic adjusters from functioning, thereby inducing low pedal heights. Should low pedal heights be encountered, it is recommended that numerous forward and reverse stops be made until satisfactory pedal height is obtained.

NOTE

If a low pedal condition cannot be corrected by making numerous reverse stops (provided the hydraulic system is free of air) it indicates that the self-adjusting mechanism is not functioning. Therefore

Fig. 6   Brake drum access hole

Fig. 7   Aligning drum tang with wheel hub. 1969-75

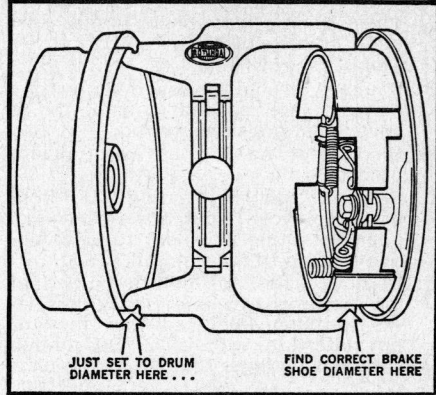

JUST SET TO DRUM DIAMETER HERE . . .

FIND CORRECT BRAKE SHOE DIAMETER HERE

Fig. 8   Use of Drum-to-Brake Shoe Clearance Gauge (J-21177)

it will be necessary to remove the brake drum, clean, free up and lubricate the adjusting mechanism. Then adjust the brakes, being sure the parking brake is fully released.

Adjustment

A lanced "knock out" area, Fig. 6, is provided in the web of the brake drum for servicing purposes in the event retracting of the brake shoes is required in order to remove the drum.

1. With brake drum off, disengage the actuator from the star wheel and rotate the star wheel by spinning or turning with a screwdriver.
2. Using the brake drum as an adjustment fixture, turn the star wheel until the drum slides over the brake shoes with a slide drag.
3. Turn the star wheel 1¼ turns to retract the brake shoes. This will allow sufficient lining-to-drum clearance so final adjustment may be made.
4. Install drum and wheel.

NOTE: If lanced area in brake drum was knocked out, be sure all metal has been removed from brake compartment. Install new hole cover in drum to prevent contamination of brakes. Make certain that drums are installed in the same position as when removed with the drum locating tang in line with the locating hole in the wheel hub, Fig. 7.

5. Make final adjustment by driving and stopping in forward and reverse until satisfactory pedal height is obtained.

NOTE: The recommended method of adjusting the brakes is by using the Drum-to-Brake Shoe Clearance Guage shown in Fig. 8 to check the diameter of the brake drum inner surface. Turn the tool to the opposite side and fit over the brake shoes by turning the star wheel until the gauge just slides over the linings. Rotate the gauge around the brake shoe lining surface to assure proper clearance.

PARKING BRAKE, ADJUST
1969-75 Except Corvette

1. Jack up both rear wheels.
2. Apply parking brake two notches from fully released position.
3. Loosen equalizer forward check nut and tighten rear nut until a light to moderate drag is felt when rear wheels are rotated.
4. Tighten check nuts securely.
5. Fully release parking brake and rotate rear wheels; no drag should be present.

1969-75 Corvette

1. With car on lift or jack stands, remove wheel. (On optional knock-off wheels, the adapter bracket must be removed to gain access to the hole in the hat section of the disc.)
2. Turn disc until the adjusting screw can be seen through hole in disc.
3. Insert a screwdriver through hole in disc and tighen adjusting screw by moving your hand away from the floor on both the left and right sides, Fig. 9.
4. Tighten until disc will not move, then

Fig. 9   Adjusting parking brake shoes. 1969-75 Corvette

back off 6 to 8 notches.
5. Apply emergency brake two notches from inside of car.
6. Tighten brake cables at equalizer to produce a light drag with wheels mounted.
7. Fully released parking brake handle and rotate rear wheels. No drag should be evident with handle released.

MASTER CYLINDER, REPLACE
1969-75

Disconnect hydraulic lines from master cylinder. Unfasten and remove cylinder from its mounting.

POWER BRAKE UNIT
1973-75

1. Remove vacuum hose from check valve and master cylinder retaining nuts.
2. Pull master cylinder forward so it clears mounting studs and move to one side. Support cylinder to avoid stress on hydraulic lines.
3. Remove power unit to dash nuts. On Chevelle and Monte Carlo, remove brake line clip from power unit.
4. Remove brake pedal push rod retainer and disconnect push rod from pin.

NOTE: On Chevelle and Monte Carlo, push brake pedal to floor. This pushes power unit away from dash, providing clearance to remove push rod.

5. Remove power unit from vehicle.

1969-72

1. Remove vacuum hose from vacuum check valve.
2. Disconnect hydraulic line at main cylinder.
3. On 1969-72 Chevelle with standard transmission, remove main cylinder

from power unit and from inside vehicle remove nuts holding unit to firewall. Push brake pedal to floor. There is now enough clearance to remove the pivot pin.

4. On all other models, disconnect push rod at brake pedal and unfasten and remove power unit.

1969-75 CORVETTE REAR WHEEL ALIGNMENT

Rear wheel camber and toe-out should be inspected and corrected if rear tires show unusual wear.

Camber, Adjust

Wheel camber is obtained by adjusting the eccentric cam and bolt assembly located at the inboard mounting of the strut rod (see Fig. 2). Place rear wheels on alignment machine and determine camber angle.

To adjust, loosen camber bolt nut and rotate cam and bolt assembly until the camber angle is within specifications listed in the front of this chapter.

Toe-Out, Adjust

Rear wheel toe-out is adjusted by inserting slotted shims of varying thickness inside the frame side member on both sides of the torque control arm pivot bushing. Shims are available in thicknesses of $1/32''$, $1/8''$ and $1/4''$.

To adjust, loosen torque arm pivot bolts until shims are free enough to remove. Position torque arm assembly to obtain toe-out of $1/32''$ to $3/32''$ per wheel. Shim gap toward vehicle centerline between end of control arm bushing and frame side inner wall.

Rear Suspension

SHOCK ABSORBER, REPLACE

1969-75 All

1. If equipped with Superlift shock absorbers, disconnect air lines from shock absorber fittings.
2. With rear axle properly supported, disconnect shock absorber from upper and lower mountings, Figs. 1, 2 and 3.
3. Reverse procedure to install.

COIL SPRINGS, REPLACE

1971-75 Chevrolet, 1969-75 Chevelle & Monte Carlo

1. Support vehicle at frame and rear axle.
2. Disconnect shock absorbers at lower mountings.
3. Lower axle until it reaches end of its travel and using a suitable tool, pry lower pigtail over retainer on axle bracket. Remove spring and insulator.
4. Reverse procedure to install. Springs must be installed with an insulator between upper seat and spring and positioned properly, Fig. 4.

1969-70 Chevrolet

1. Perform steps 1 and 2 as outlined in above procedure. Remove rear wheels.

2. Loosen rear mounting bolts on upper and lower control arms. Do not remove nuts.
3. Disconnect suspension tie rod from stud on axle tube.
4. Slightly loosen bolt retaining lower seat and spring to control arm.

CAUTION: Do not remove nut at this time. Nut should still have all threads engaged on bolt.

5. Lower axle to carry springs out of upper seats and remove nut and bolt retaining spring to lower seat.
6. Reverse procedure and install spring with an insulator between upper seat and spring.

LEAF SPRINGS & BUSHINGS, REPLACE

1971-75 125" Wheel Base Wagon

1. Support vehicle at frame and rear axle, removing tension from spring.
2. Disconnect shock absorber from lower mounting.
3. Remove rear shackle upper bolt and spring front mount bolt.
4. Support spring, remove "U" bolts, spring plate and spring. Remove rear shackle from spring.
5. Replace shackle and spring eye bushings as necessary. To replace spring eye bushing, use a press and a suitably sized piece of pipe, tubing or similar tool as a ram, press out bushing. Press in new bushing with a suitable tool pressing on outer steel shell of bushing. Bushing is correctly installed when it protrudes equally on both sides of eye.
6. Reverse procedure to install.

1969-75 Camaro & Nova

1. Perform steps 1 and 2 as outlined in above procedure.
2. Loosen spring front mount bolt.
3. Remove spring front mounting bracket attaching screws, lower axle and remove bracket.
4. Disconnect parking brake cable from spring plate bracket.

5. Remove spring plate by removing axle bracket nuts on single leaf models and the "U" bolts on multi-leaf models.
6. Support spring, remove front mount bolt and disassemble rear shackle.
7. Replace rear shackle and spring eye bushings as necessary, Figs. 5 and 6.
8. Reverse procedure to install.

1969-75 Corvette

1. Support vehicle at frame and remove rear wheels.
2. Install a "C" clamp approximately 9 inches from end of spring.
3. Place a suitable jack under spring, Fig. 7, and place a wooden block between "C" clamp and jack pad.
4. Raise jack until load is off spring link, then remove cotter pin, link nut and spring cushion. Lower jack, removing tension from spring.
5. Repeat steps 2, 3 and 4 on opposite side of spring.
6. Remove bolts from spring center clamp plate, then remove clamp plate.
7. Remove spring from vehicle, Fig. 8.
8. Reverse procedure to install.

LEAF SPRING SERVICE

NOTE: On 1971-75 models, the spring leaves are not serviced separately, how-

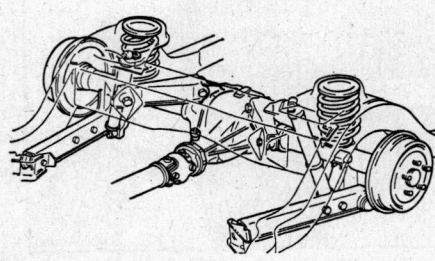

Fig. 1 Rear suspension. 1969-75 Chevrolet Chevelle & Monte Carlo (typical)

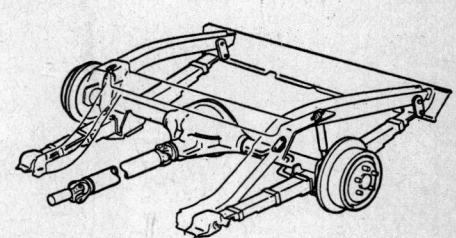

Fig. 2 Rear suspension. 1969-75 Camaro, Nova & 125" Wheelbase station wagon (typical)

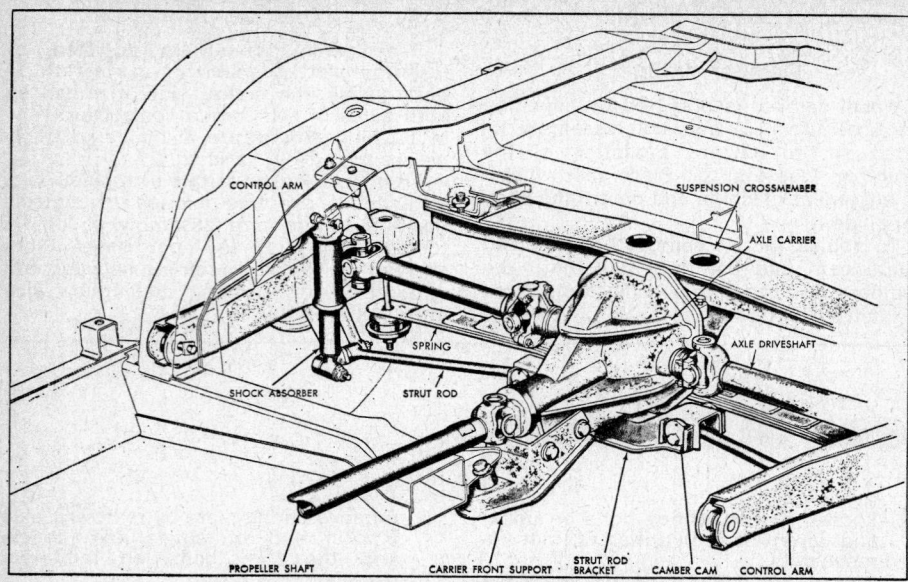

Fig. 3 Rear suspension. 1969-75 Corvette

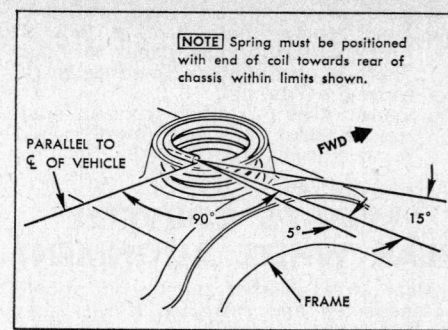

Fig. 4 Coil spring installation. 1969-75 all models

ever, the spring leaf inserts may be re-placed.

1. Clamp spring in a vise and remove spring clips.
2. File peened end of center bolt to permit nut removal, remove nut and open vise slowly, allowing spring to expand.
3. Replace spring leaves or leaf inserts.
4. On Corvette, to replace main leaf cushion retainers, chisel flared portion until retainer can be removed from leaf. Install new retainers and flare over with a hammer.
5. On all models use a drift to align center bolt holes, compress spring in vise and install new center bolt and nut. Peen end of bolt to retain nut.
6. Align springs and bend spring clips into position.

NOTE: Overtightening of spring clips will cause spring binding.

CONTROL ARMS & BUSHINGS, REPLACE

NOTE: On Chevelle, Monte Carlo & 119" wheelbase station wagons, if both upper or lower control arms are to be removed at the same time, remove coil springs as outlined previously.

Upper Control Arms

1971-75 Chevrolet, 1969-75 Chevelle, Monte Carlo

1. Support vehicle at frame and rear axle with a suitable jack.
2. Remove control arm front and rear mounting bolts.
3. Replace bushings as necessary, Figs., 9 thru 15.

NOTE: To remove bushings, Fig. 9,

use tool J-21830-2. To install bushings, Fig. 10, reverse tool J-21474-2.

4. Reverse procedure to install. Control arm bolts must be tightened with vehicle at curb height.

1969-70 Chevrolet

1. Support vehicle at rear axle.
2. Remove control arm rear mount bolt.
3. Remove bolts securing control arm forward bracket to crossmember, then remove control arm mounting bolt.
4. Replace bushings as necessary, Fig. 16.

NOTE: To remove bushings, Fig. 16, reverse tool J-21830-2 and on 1970 V8 models, omit tool J-21830-4 and use a similar tool of appropriate size.

5. Reverse procedure to install. Control arm bolts must be tightened with vehicle at curb height.

Lower Control Arms

1971-75 Chevrolet, 1969-75 Chevelle, Monte Carlo

Follow "Upper Control Arms" 1971-75 procedure for replacement of lower control arms.

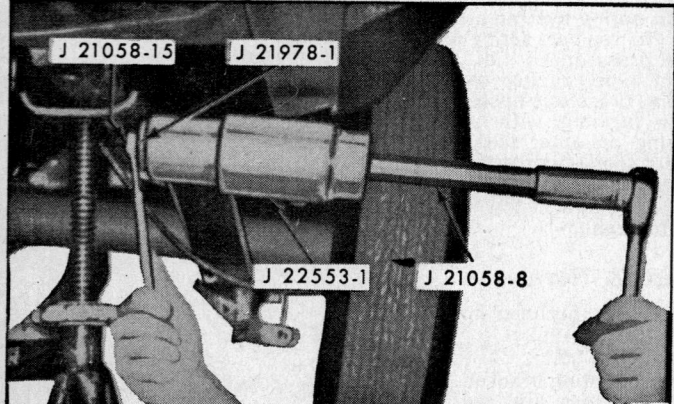

Fig. 5 Leaf spring bushings removal. 1969-75 Camaro, Nova & 125" Wheelbase station wagon

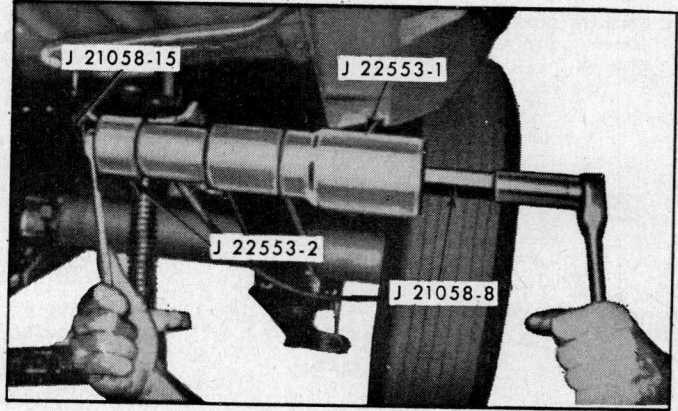

Fig. 6 Leaf springs bushing installation. 1969-75 Camaro, Nova & 125" Wheelbase station wagon

Fig. 7 Supporting leaf spring. 1969-75 Corvette

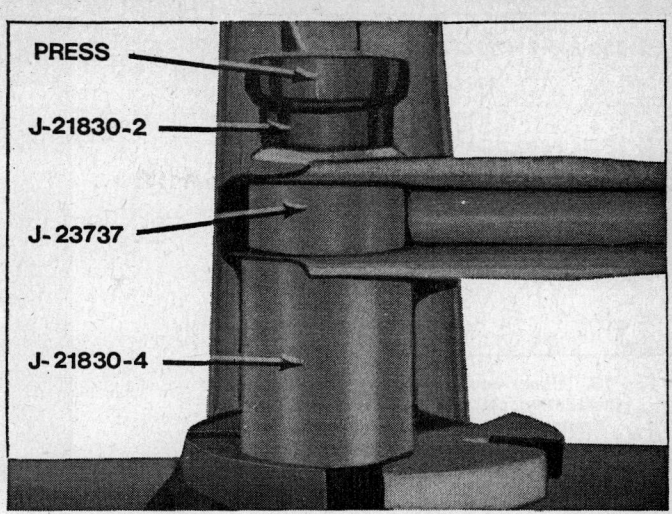

Fig. 9 Control arms front all & lower control arm rear bushings removal. 1971-75 Chevrolet

---

NOTE: To remove bushings, Fig. 9, use tool J-21830-2. To install bushings, Fig. 10, reverse tool J-21474-2.

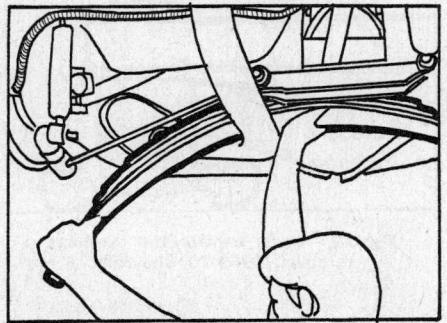

Fig. 8 Removing leaf spring. 1969-75 Corvette

1969-70 Chevrolet

1. Remove shock absorbers and coil springs as outlined previously.
2. Note control arm position in forward attachment bracket to facilitate reassembly, then disconnect control arm from front and rear mountings.
3. Replace bushings as necessary, Fig. 19.

NOTE: To remove control arm front bushings on 1969 models and 1970 6 cylinder models, substitute tool J-7574-1 for tool J-21830-2, Fig. 19. To install control arm front bushings on 1969 models and 1970 6 cylinder models, substitute tool J-7574-2 for tool J-21830-2, Fig. 19. To install control arm rear bushings and control arm front bushings on 1970 V8 models, reverse tool J-21830-2, Fig. 19.

4. Reverse procedure to install control arm.

TIE ROD & BUSHING, REPLACE
1969-71 Chevrolet

1. Support vehicle at rear axle.
2. Disconnect tie rod from left side frame bracket.
3. Disconnect tie rod from axle bracket mounting stud and replace bushing if necessary, Fig. 20.
4. Reverse procedure to install. On all models except station wagons, flanged side of bushing must be installed against frame attachment bracket.

STABILIZER BAR, REPLACE
1971-75 Chevrolet & Chevelle

1. Support vehicle at rear axle.
2. Remove bolts securing stabilizer bar

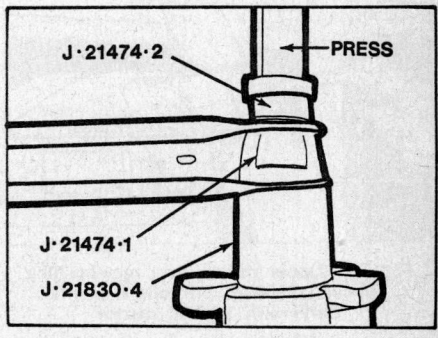

Fig. 11 Upper control arm front & all lower control arm bushings. 1969-75 Chevelle & Monte Carlo removal. Also upper control arm rear bushing removal. 1971-75 Chevrolet

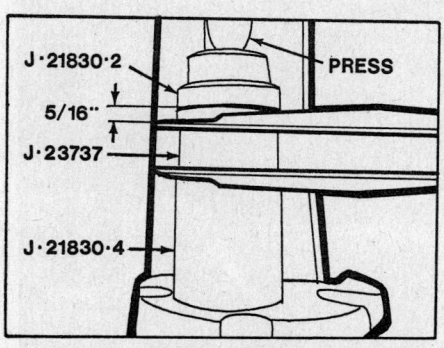

Fig. 10 Control arms front all & lower control arm rear bushings installation. 1971-75 Chevrolet

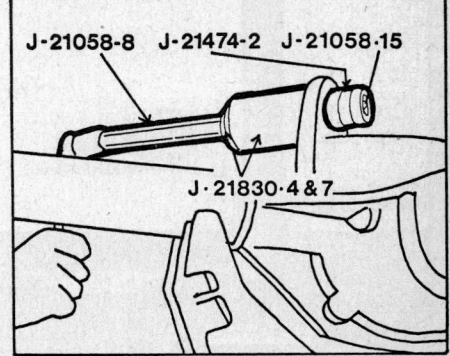

Fig. 12 Upper control arm rear bushing removal. 1969-72 Chevelle & Monte Carlo with 10 bolt carrier

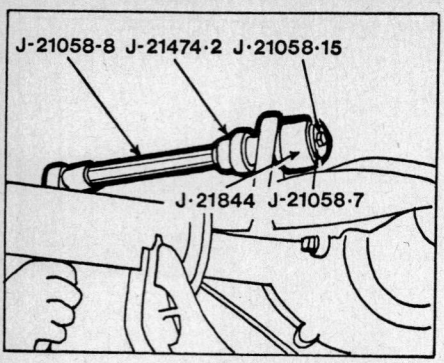

Fig. 13 Upper control arm rear bushing installation. 1969-72 Chevelle & Monte Carlo with 10 bolt carrier

Fig. 15 Upper control arm rear bushing installation. 1969-75 Chevelle & Monte Carlo with 12 bolt carrier

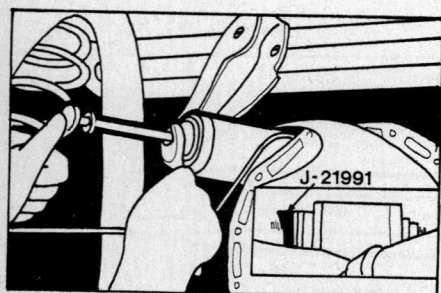

Fig. 14 Upper control arm rear bushing removal. 1969-74 Chevelle & Monte Carlo with 12 bolt carrier

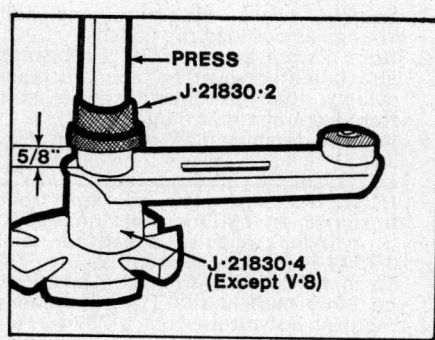

Fig. 16 Upper control arm bushings installation. 1969-70 Chevrolet

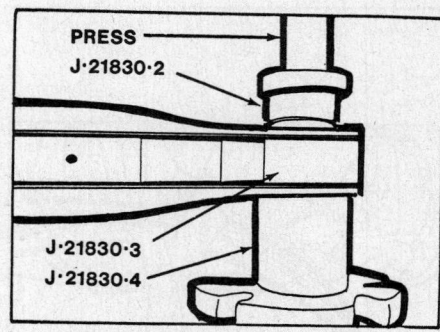

Fig. 19 Lower control arm bushings removal. 1969-70 Chevrolet

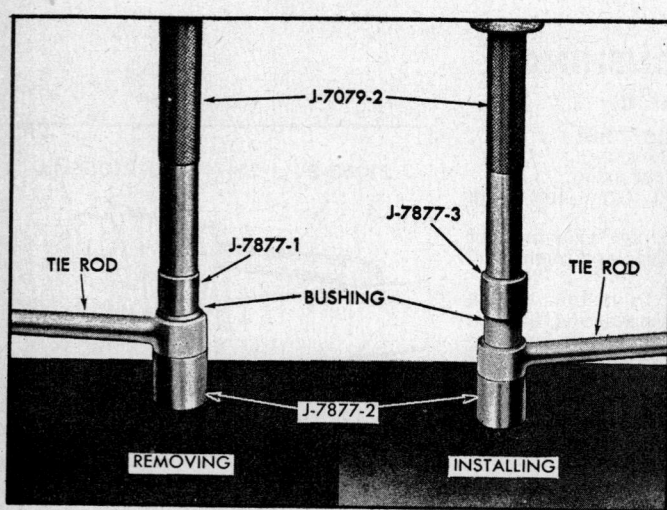

Fig. 20 Suspension tie rod bushing. 1969-71 Chevrolet, also strut rod bushing. 1969-75 Corvette replacement

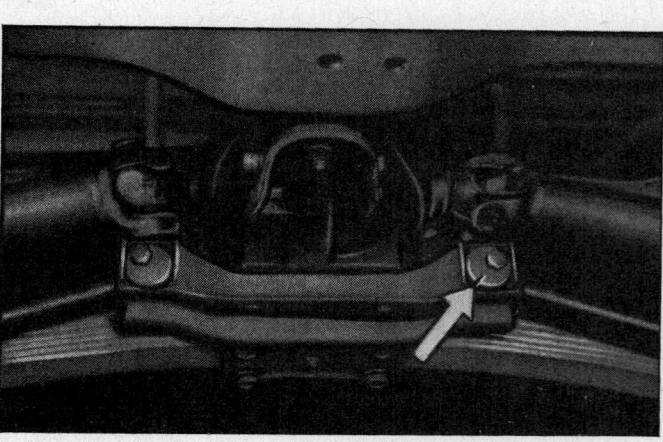

Fig. 24 Indexing camber cam & bracket. 1969-75 Corvette

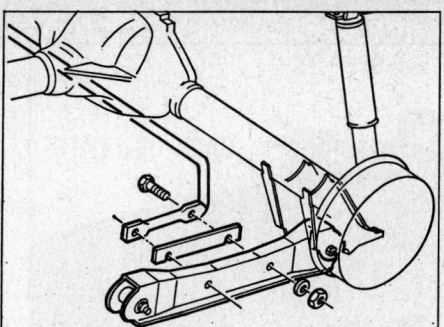

Fig. 21 Stabilizer bar installation.
1969-75 Chevrolet & Chevelle

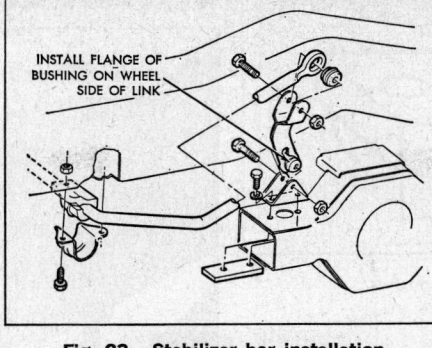

INSTALL FLANGE OF
BUSHING ON WHEEL
SIDE OF LINK

Fig. 23 Stabilizer bar installation.
1969-75 Corvette

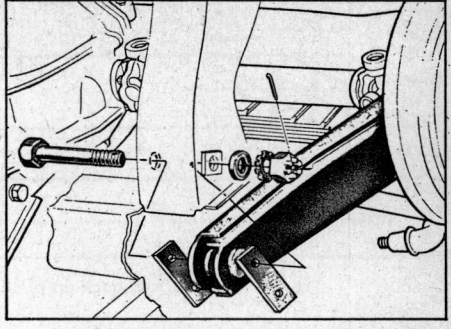

Fig. 25 Torque control arm installation.
1969-75 Corvette

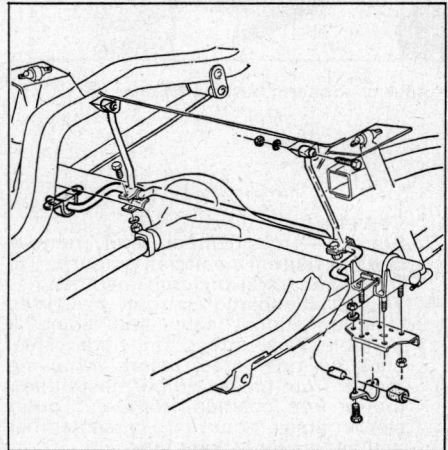

Fig. 22 Stabilizer bar installation.
1969-75 Camaro & Nova

to lower control arms, Fig. 21.
3. Reverse procedure to install. Use spacer shims, if needed, placed equally on each side of stabilizer bar. Tighten attaching bolts with vehicle at curb height.

1971-73 Camaro & Nova

1. Support vehicle at rear axle.
2. Disconnect stabilizer bar from spring plate brackets, Fig. 22.
3. Disconnect stabilizer bar from body brackets.
4. Reverse procedure to install. Tighten attaching bolts with vehicle at curb height.

1969-75 Corvette

1. Disconnect stabilizer bar from torque control arms and remove stabilizer bar frame brackets, Fig. 23.
2. Replace bushings as necessary, Fig. 23.
3. Reverse procedure to install.

STRUT ROD, REPLACE
1969-75 Corvette

1. Support vehicle at frame.

2. Disconnect shock frame from lower mounting.
3. Remove cotter pin and nut from strut rod shaft. Pull shaft toward front of vehicle and remove from bracket.
4. Mark position of camber adjusting cam to ensure proper installation, Fig. 24, and loosen camber bolt nut.
5. Remove bolts securing strut rod bracket to carrier.
6. Remove camber bolt and nut, pull strut rod out of bracket and remove bushing caps.
7. Replace bushings as necessary, Fig. 20.
8. Reverse procedure to install.

TORQUE CONTROL ARMS & BUSHINGS, REPLACE
1969-75 Corvette

1. Perform steps 1 thru 4 as outlined under "Leaf Spring, Replace" 1969-75 Corvette procedure.
2. If equipped with a stabilizer shaft, disconnect shaft at torque arms.
3. Disconnect shock absorber at lower mounting.
4. Disconnect and lower strut rod shaft.
5. Disconnect axle drive shaft from spindle flange by removing attaching bolts.

NOTE: It may be necessary to force

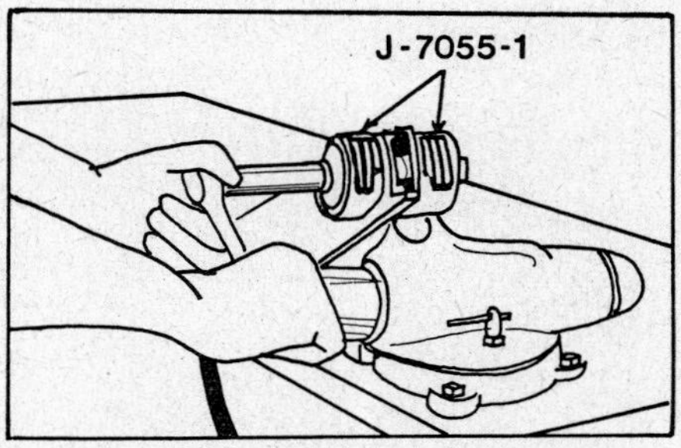

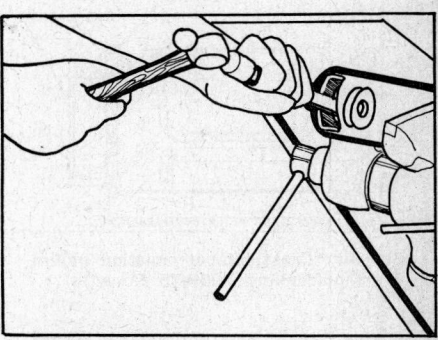

Fig. 26 Torque control arm bushing removal. 1969-75 Corvette

torque arm outboard providing clearance to lower axle drive shaft.

6. Disconnect brake line from caliper and from torque arm. Disconnect parking brake cable.
7. Remove torque arm forward mounting bolt and toe-in shims, Fig. 25, and pull torque arm out of frame attachment.
8. Replace bushings if necessary as described under "Torque Control Arm Bushing Service."
9. Reverse procedure to install.

Torque Control Arm Bushing Service

1. Using an 11/16 inch twist drill, drill out flared end of bushing retainer, remove retainer plate and retainer from bushing.
2. Spread bushing with a chisel, Fig. 26, and tap bushing from arm.

NOTE: If bushing is rusted in torque arm, torque arm may spread during bushing removal. Install a "C" clamp torque arm, preventing torque arm spreading.

3. Oil steel portion of new bushing and press bushing into arm, Fig. 27.
4. Place retainer plate over flared portion of bushing retainer and insert retainer into bushing.
5. Make a flaring tool back-up plate, Fig. 28, with 1/2 inch bolt holes.
6. Place back-up plate on flared end of bushing retainer and assemble tool to plate, Fig. 29, with 1/2 x 5 inch bolts.

J-7055-1

Fig. 27 Torque control arm bushing installation. 1969-75 Corvette

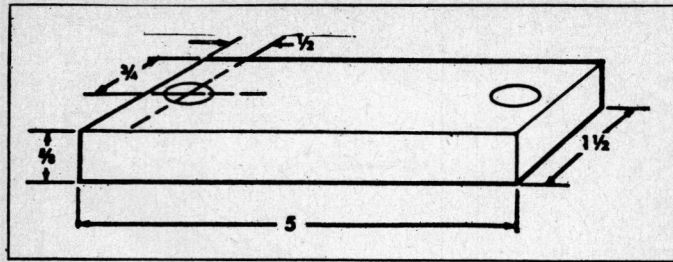

Fig. 28   Flaring tool back-up plate dimension

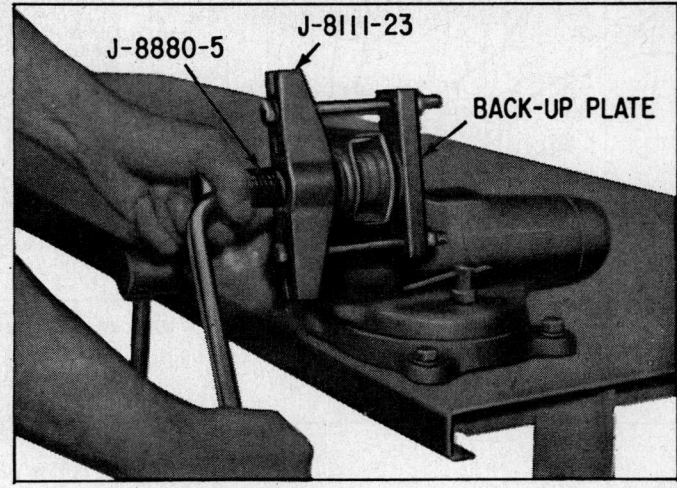

Fig. 29   Flaring torque control arm bushing retainer

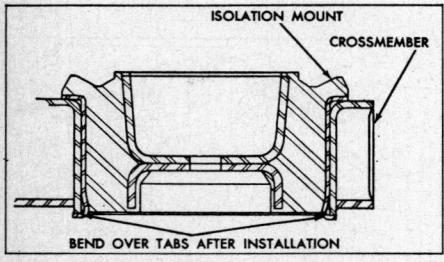

Fig. 30   Crossmember isolation mount replacement. 1969-75 Corvette

Center threaded hole in tool # J-8111-23 over unflared end of bushing retainer. Also center chamfered retainer plate over retainer tube.

7. Lubricate end of tool # J-8880-5 and thread screw into tool, flaring retainer.

CROSSMEMBER & ISOLATION MOUNT, REPLACE
1969-75 Corvette

1. Remove leaf spring as outlined under "Leaf Spring, Replace" 1969-75 Corvette procedure.
2. Remove differential carrier and cover as outlined in "Rear Axle, Propeller Shaft & Brakes" section, 1969-75 Corvette procedure.
3. Support crossmember and remove bolts securing isolation mounts to frame and lower the crossmember.
4. To replace isolation mount, straighten isolation mount tabs and using a suitable ram, press on outer steel shell or inner steel insert, removing mount from crossmember. Install new mount into position, compress outer sleeve, press mount into crossmember and bend over locking tabs, Fig. 30.
5. Reverse procedure to install crossmember.

Front End and Steering Section

FRONT SUSPENSION

All front suspension systems are basically similar, being of the S.L.A. (short-long arm) type with independent coil springs riding on the lower control arms. Ball joints connect the upper and lower control arms to the steering knuckles. See Figs. 1 and 2.

LUBRICATION

IMPORTANT

On models that have a recommended chassis lubrication period of 6000 miles, the car should be warmed up before lubricating the front suspension ball joints. If the car has been outdoors in extreme cold weather it should be allowed to warm up to at least 10°F. above zero before this job is started. Inadequate ball joint lubrication or seal damage can result should the job be done while the parts are at lower temperatures.

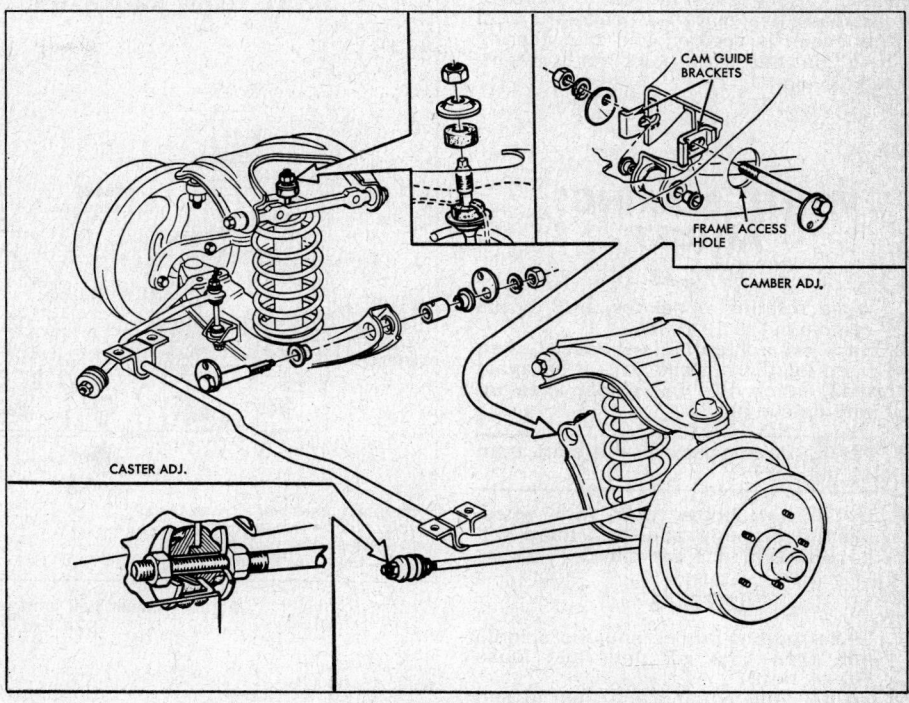

Fig. 1   Front suspension. 1969 Chevrolet

WHEEL ALIGNMENT

NOTE: Before adjusting caster and camber angles after complaint of excessive tire wear or poor handling, the front bumper should be raised and quickly released to allow car to return to its normal height.

1969 Chevrolet

The caster angle is adjusted by turning the two nuts at the front of the lower control arm strut rod, Fig. 1. Shortening this rod will increase caster, lengthening it will decrease caster.

Camber angle is adjusted by loosening the lower control arm pivot bolt and rotating the cam located on the pivot, Fig. 1. This eccentric cam action will move the lower control arm in or out, thereby varying camber.

1970-75 Chevrolet
1969-75 Chevy Nova
1969-75 Camaro
1969-75 Chevelle
1969-75 Corvette

Caster and camber adjustments are made by means of shims between the upper control arm inner support shaft and the support bracket attached to the frame. Shims may be added, subtracted or transferred to change the readings as follows:

Caster, Adjust

Transfer shims from front to rear or rear to front. The transfer of one shim to the front bolt from the rear bolt will decrease positive caster. On shim ($1/32$″) transferred from the rear bolt to the front bolt will change caster about $1/2$ degree.

Camber, Adjust

Change shims at both the front and rear of the shaft. Adding an equal number of shims at both front and rear of the support shaft will decrease positive camber. One shim ($1/32$″) at each location will move camber approximately 1/5 degree on Camaro, Chevelle and Nova, on Chevrolet and Corvette the change will be about 1/6 degree.

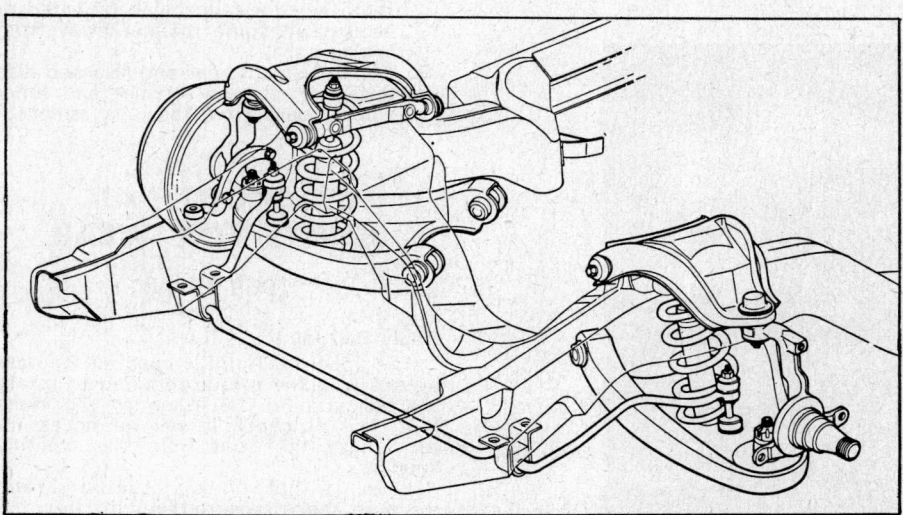

Fig. 2   Front suspension. 1969-75 Nova, 1969-75 Camaro, 1969-75 Chevelle. Typical of 1969-75 Corvette and 1970-75 Chevrolet

TOE-IN, ADJUST

Toe-in can be adjusted by loosening the clamp bolts at each end of each tie rod and turning each tie rod to increase or decrease its length as necessary until proper toe-in is secured and the steering gear is on the high point for straight-ahead driving.

WHEEL BEARINGS, ADJUST

1974-75

1. While rotating wheel forward, torque spindle nut to 12 ft. lbs.
2. Back off nut until "just loose" then hand tighten nut and back it off again until either hole in spindle lines up with hole in nut.

NOTE: Do not back off nut more than ½ flat.

3. Install new cotter pin. With wheel bearing properly adjusted, there will be .001-.005 inch end play.

1972-73

1. While rotating wheel, snug-up spindle nut, then back off until just loose (¼-½ turn).
2. Tighten nut by hand and then loosen nut so cotter pin can be installed.

NOTE: Bearing must not be even finger tight.

3. With bearing properly adjusted, there will be .001"-.008" end play.

1969-71

1. While rotating wheel, tighten spindle nut to 12 ft-lbs torque.
2. Back off adjusting nut one flat and insert cotter pin. If slot and pin hole

do not line up, back off adjusting nut an additional ½ flat or less as required to insert cotter pin.
3. Spin wheel to see that it turns freely, then spread cotter pin.
4. Bearings should have zero preload and .001 to .008" end movement when properly adjusted.

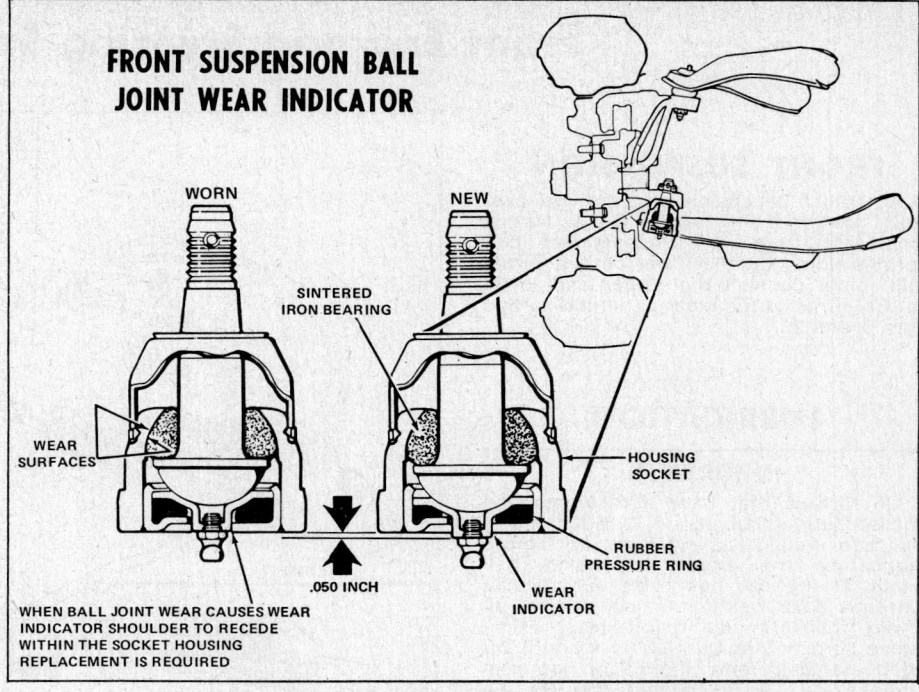

FRONT SUSPENSION BALL JOINT WEAR INDICATOR

WORN NEW

SINTERED IRON BEARING

WEAR SURFACES

HOUSING SOCKET

RUBBER PRESSURE RING

WEAR INDICATOR

.050 INCH

WHEN BALL JOINT WEAR CAUSES WEAR INDICATOR SHOULDER TO RECEDE WITHIN THE SOCKET HOUSING REPLACEMENT IS REQUIRED

Fig. 3 Lower ball joint wear indicator. 1973 Chevrolet, 1974 Exc. Nova & 1975 All

WHEEL BEARINGS, REPLACE

Disc Brakes

1. Raise car and remove front wheels.
2. Remove bolts holding brake caliper to its mounting and insert a fabricated block (1¹⁄₁₆ x 1¹⁄₁₆ x 2 inches in length) between the brake pads as the caliper is being removed. Once removed, the caliper can be wired or secured in some manner away from the disc.
3. Remove spindle nut and hub and disc assembly. Grease retainer and inner wheel bearing can now be removed.

CHECKING BALL JOINTS FOR WEAR

1969-75 All

Upper Ball Joint

The upper ball joint is checked for wear by checking the torque required to rotate the ball stud in the assembly. To make this type of check it will be necessary to remove the stud from the steering knuckle.

Install a nut on the ball stud and measure the torque required to turn the stud in the assembly with a torque wrench. Specified torque for a new ball joint is 3 to 10 ft-lbs. If torque readings

Fig. 4 Supporting coil spring. 1969-75 All except 1969-70 Chevrolet

J-23028

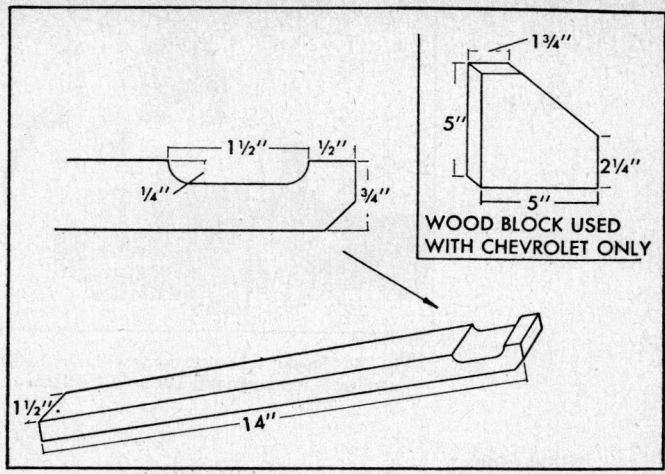

Fig. 5 Spring removal tools. 1969-70 Chevrolet

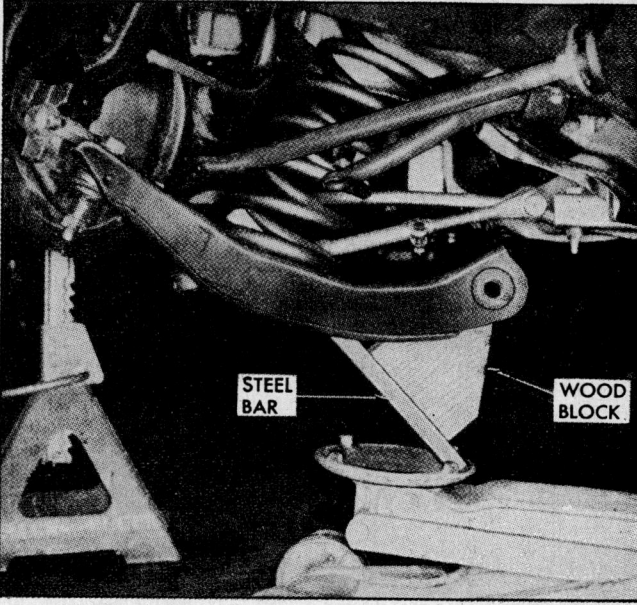

STEEL BAR **WOOD BLOCK**

Fig. 6 Removing front spring. 1969-70 Chevrolet

are excessively high or low, replace the ball joint. If excessive wear is indicated in the upper ball joint, both upper and lower ball joints should be replaced.

Lower Ball Joint

Raise car and support lower control arm so spring is compressed in the same manner as if the wheels were on the ground and check axial (up and down) play at ball joint. If play exceeds 1/16", replace the joint.

Another indication of lower ball joint excessive wear is when difficulty is experienced when lubricating the joint. If the liner has worn to the point where the lubrication grooves in the liner have been worn away, then abnormal pressure is required to force lubricant through the joint. Should this condition be evident, replace both lower ball joints.

NOTE: 1973 Chevrolet, 1974 except Nova and all 1975 models have a wear indicator built into the lower ball joint, Fig. 3.

UPPER BALL JOINT, REPLACE

1969-75 All

1. Support weight of vehicle at outer end of lower control arm.
2. Remove wheel assembly.
3. Remove nut from upper ball joint stud.
4. Remove stud from knuckle.
5. Cut off ball rivets with a chisel.
6. Enlarge ball stud attaching holes in control arm (if necessary) to accept the bolts included in the ball joint replacement kit.
7. Install and tighten new ball joint.
8. Reassemble ball joint to steering knuckle.

LOWER BALL JOINT, REPLACE

1971-75 Exc. Corvette

1. Support vehicle at frame and lower control arm with suitable jacks.
2. Remove wheel and, if equipped with disc brakes, caliper assembly.
3. Loosen ball joint stud nut not more than one turn and, using a suitable tool, press ball stud free of steering knuckle, then remove stud nut.
4. Lower the jack from under the control arm.
5. With a suitable tool, replace lower ball joint.
6. Reverse procedure to assemble.

1969-70 Chevrolet & 1969-75 Corvette

1. Support lower control arm at outer end on floor jack with hoist or jack pad clear of lower ball stud nut and seal.
2. If equipped with disc brakes, remove caliper assembly.
3. Remove upper and lower ball stud nuts, free ball studs from steering knuckle and wire knuckle and brake drum or disc assembly out of the way.
4. Being careful not to enlarge holes in control arm, cut off rivets.
5. Install new joint against underside of control arm and retain in place with special bolts supplied with replacement ball joint kit. Use only the alloy bolts supplied for this operation. The special thick headed bolt must be installed in the forward side of the control arm.
6. Tighten bolts and nut on ball stud and lubricate joint.

1969-70 Chevelle, Camaro & Nova

1. Support lower control arm at outer end of floor jack with hoist or jack pad clear of lower ball stud and remove wheel. If equipped with disc brakes, remove caliper assembly.
2. Remove upper and lower ball stud nuts, free ball studs from steering knuckle and wire knuckle and brake drum or disc assembly out of the way.
3. Use a screwdriver to pry out seal and retainer. Use a suitable extractor to push out ball joint.
4. Start replacement ball joint into control arm and use a suitable puller tool to pull the ball joint into position. Be sure to position air vent in rubber boot inboard.
5. Install stud into steering knuckle and secure in place.

SHOCK ABSORBER, REPLACE

1969-75 All

1. Hold shock upper stem from turning with a suitable wrench and remove nut and grommet.
2. Unfasten lower shock pivot from lower control arm and pull shock and mounting out through bottom of spring housing.
3. Reverse removal procedure to install. Tighten upper retaining nut until it bottoms on shoulder of stem.

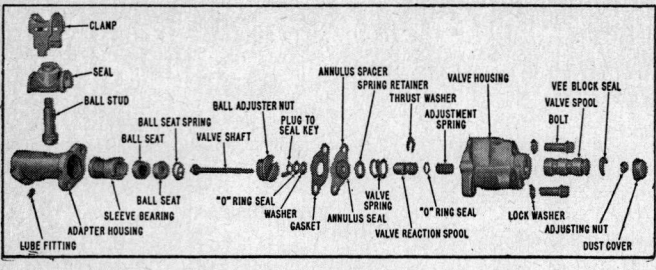

Fig. 7 Power steering control valve and adapter assembly. 1969-75 Corvette

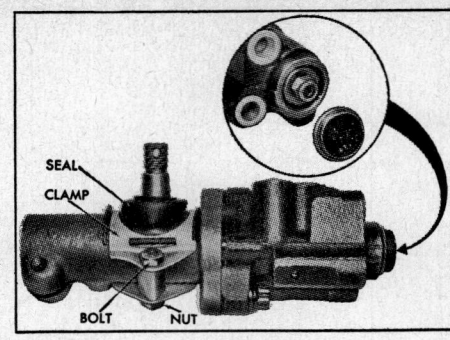

Fig. 8 Power steering control valve ball stud seal replacement. 1969-75 Corvette

COIL SPRING, REPLACE

1969-75 All Exc. 1969-70 Chevrolet

1. Remove shock absorber on 1969-70 models as outlined under "Shock Absorber, Replace" procedure. On 1971-75 models, disconnect shock absorber from lower mounting, push shock absorber through hole in lower control arm and compress into spring.
2. Support vehicle by frame so control arms hand free.
3. On 1969-70 models, remove stabilizer bar-to-lower control arm link.
4. Install a safety chain through spring and lower control arm.
5. Install tool J-23028 onto a suitable jack and position jack so control arm is supported by bushings seated in grooves of tool, Fig. 4.
6. Raise jack to relieve tension on control arm bolts and remove bolts.
7. Lower jack until tension is removed from spring, remove chain and spring from vehicle.

1969-70 Chevrolet

1. With suitable wrench, hold shock absorber upper stem from turning, then remove retaining nut, retainer and upper grommet.
2. With car supported by the frame so that control arms hang free, remove wheel assembly. Replace one wheel nut to hold brake drum.
3. Remove shock absorber, stabilizer bar-to-lower control arm link, strut rod-to-lower control arm attaching nuts and tie rod end.
4. Install a steel bar (made to the dimensions shown in Fig. 5) through shock absorber mounting hole in lower control arm so that notch seats over bottom spring coil and bar extends inboard and under inner bushing.
5. Fit a 5" wood block, Fig. 6, between bar and bushing.
6. With suitable jack or hoist, lift up slightly on end of bar to remove tension from inner pivot cam bolt, which can then be removed.
7. Lower inner end of lower control arm. Tension on spring will be removed before spring can be removed from vehicle.

8. Reverse procedure to install and check wheel alignment.

CAUTION

The spring force under compression is very great. Exercise every safety precaution when performing this operation to see that individuals and materials subject to damage are removed from the path of the spring when the control arm is being lowered. Also, the compressed spring should be relaxed immediately after lowering the control arm to reduce the time of exposure to the great compressive force.

STEERING GEAR, REPLACE

1969-75 All Models

NOTE: On models where shield is installed, remove shield from coupling.

1. Remove nuts, washers and bolts at steering coupling.
2. Remove pitman arm nut and washer from sector shaft and mark relation of arm position to shaft.
3. Use a suitable puller to remove pitman arm. On Camaro models, use care not to bend or facture brake pipe when removing steering gear.
4. Unfasten gear from frame and remove assembly.
5. Reverse procedure to install.

INTEGRAL POWER STEERING

1969-75 Exc. Corvette

To remove gear assembly, disconnect pressure and return hoses from gear housing and cap both hoses and steering gear outlets to prevent foreign material from entering system, then follow procedure as outlined under *Steering Gear, Replace.*

LINKAGE TYPE POWER STEERING

1969-75 Corvette

Power steering equipment consists of a recirculating ball type steering gear and linkage to which a hydraulic power mechanism has been added as part of the steering linkage. The hydraulic mechanism furnishes additional power to *assist* the manual operation so that the turning effort at the steering wheel is greatly reduced. The hydraulic mechanism consists of three basic units: a hydraulic pump and reservoir, a control valve, and a power cylinder.

Control Valve, Adjust

1. Disconnect cylinder rod from frame bracket.
2. With car on a hoist, start the engine. One of the following two conditions will exist:
   a. If piston rod remains retracted, turn the adjusting nut clockwise until the rod begins to move out. Then turn the nut counterclockwise until the rod just begins to move in. Now turn the nut clockwise to exactly one half the rotation needed to change the direction of shaft movement.
   b. If the rod extends upon starting the pump, move the nut counterclockwise until the rod begins to retract, then clockwise until the rod begins to move out again. Now turn the rod to exactly one half the rotation needed to change the direction of shaft movement.

Do not turn the nut back and forth more than is absolutely necessary to balance the valve.

3. Restart engine. Front wheels should not turn from center if valve has been properly balanced.

Power Cylinder Repairs

Removal
1. Disconnect two hydraulic lines at power cylinder.
2. Unfasten power cylinder rod from

brace at frame.

3. Unfasten power cylinder from relay rod bracket.
4. Remove power cylinder from car.

Inspection

1. Inspect seals for leaks around cylinder rod and if leaks are present, replace seals as follows:
2. Use a hook tool to remove retaining ring. Remove wiper ring, back-up washer, back-up ring and seal. *Piston rod seal should not be removed unless there are signs of leakage along the piston shaft at shaft seal.*
3. Examine brass fitting hose connection seats for cracks or damage and replace if necessary.
4. For service other than seat or seal replacement, replace the power cylinder.

Installation

1. Install power cylinder on car by reversing removal procedure.
2. Reconnect two hoses, fill system with fluid and bleed system as outlined below.

Filling & Bleeding System

1. Fill reservoir to proper level with Automatic Transmission Fluid and let fluid remain undisturbed for about two minutes.
2. Raise front wheels off floor.
3. Run engine at idle for two minutes.
4. Increase engine speed to about 1500 rpm.
5. Turn wheels from one extreme to the other, lightly contacting stops.
6. Lower wheels to floor and turn wheels right and left.
7. Recheck for leaks.
8. Check oil level and refill as required. Pump pressure should be 870 lbs.

Control Valve Repairs

Removal, Fig. 7

1. Loosen relay rod-to-control valve clamp.
2. Disconnect hose connections at control valve.
3. Disconnect control valve from pitman arm.
4. Unscrew control valve from relay rod.
5. Remove control valve from car.

Ball Stud Seal, Replace

In servicing the control valve, refer to Fig. 7. To replace the ball stud seal, refer to Fig. 8 and proceed as follows:

1. Remove pitman arm with a suitable puller.
2. Remove clamp by removing nut, bolt and spacer. If crimped type clamp is used, straighten clamp end and pull clamp and seal off end of stud.
3. Install new seal and clamp over stud so lips on seal mate with clamp. (A nut and bolt attachment type clamp replaces the crimped type for service, Fig. 8).
4. Center the ball stud, seal and clamp in opening in adapter housing, then install spacer, bolt and nut.

CHEVROLET VEGA • PONTIAC ASTRE

OLD CAR SPECIFICATIONS: For 1946-68 Tune Up and Wheel Alignment Specifications see main index.

INDEX OF SERVICE OPERATIONS

PAGE NO.

ACCESSORIES
Air Conditioning 2-20
Automatic Level Controls 2-39
Blower Motor, Remove 1-231
Clock Troubles 2-11
Heater Core, Replace 1-230
Power Top Troubles 2-18
Power Window Troubles 2-18
Radio, Replace 1-230

BRAKES
Anti-Skid Brakes 2-162
Brake Troubles, Mechanical 2-17
Disc Brake Service 2-133
Hydraulic System Service 2-123
Master Cylinder, Replace 1-240
Parking Brake, Adjust 1-240
Power Brake Unit, Replace 1-240
Service Brakes, Adjust 1-239

CLUTCH
Clutch Pedal, Adjust 1-236
Clutch, Replace 1-237
Clutch Troubles 2-12

COOLING SYSTEM
Cooling System Troubles 2-6
Variable Speed Fans 2-38
Water Pump, Replace 1-235

ELECTRICAL
Alternator Service 2-69
Blower Motor, Remove 1-231
Clutch Start Switch 1-228
Dash Gauge Service 2-50
Distributor, Replace 1-226
Distributor Service:
    Standard 2-525
    Transistorized 2-535
Electrical Troubles 2-8
Headlamps, Concealed Type 2-46
Headlight Aiming 2-45
Ignition Coils and Resistors 2-521
Ignition Lock, Replace 1-227
Ignition Switch, Replace 1-227
Instrument Cluster Removal 1-228
Light Switch, Replace 1-227
Neutral Safety Switch, Replace 1-228
Seat Belt Interlock Systems 2-311
Starter Service 2-54
Starter, Replace 1-227
Starter Switch Service 2-67
Stop Light Switch, Replace 1-228
Turn Signal Switch, Replace 1-228
Turn Signal Troubles 2-11
Windshield Wiper Motor, Replace 1-229
Windshield Wiper Troubles 2-19

ENGINE
Camshaft Bearings 1-233
Camshaft Cover 1-232
Camshaft, Replace 1-233
Camshaft Sprocket 1-234
Crankshaft Sprocket 1-234
Cylinder Head, Replace 1-232
Engine Front Cover 1-234
Engine Identification 1-221
Engine, Replace 1-232
Engine Mounts, Replace 1-231
Engine Troubles 2-1
Main Bearings 1-234
Piston and Rod, Assemble 1-234
Pistons 1-234
Rod Bearings 1-234
Timing Belt 1-234
Valves, Adjust 1-232
Valve Arrangement 1-232
Valve Guides 1-234

ENGINE LUBRICATION
Emission Control Systems 2-545
Oil Pan, Replace 1-235
Oil Pump 1-235

FUEL SYSTEM
Carburetor Adjustments and Specs. ... 2-372
Emission Control Systems 2-545
Fuel Pressure 1-236
Fuel Pump, Replace 1-236
Fuel Pump Service 2-369
Fuel System Troubles 2-2

PROPELLER SHAFT & U JOINTS
Propeller Shaft 1-239
Universal Joint Service 2-117

REAR AXLE & SUSPENSION
Axle Shaft, Bearing & Seal 1-239
Control Arms & Bushings, Replace ... 1-241
Coil Springs, Replace 1-241
Rear Axle Description 1-238
Rear Axle Specifications 1-226
Rear Axle Troubles 2-16
Shock Absorber, Replace 1-241
Stabilizer Bar, Replace 1-241

SPECIFICATIONS
Alternator 1-224
Belt Tension Data 1-235
Brakes 1-225
Capacities 1-226
Carburetors 2-372

PAGE NO.
Cooling System 1-226
Crankshaft and Bearings 1-225
Distributors 1-222
Engine Tightening Torque 1-224
Fuel Pump Pressure 1-236
General Engine Specs. 1-222
Ignition Coils and Resistors 2-521
Pistons, Rings and Pins 1-225
Rear Axle 1-226
Starting Motors 1-222
Tune Up 1-223
Valve Lift Specs. 1-234
Valve Timing 1-234
Valves 1-224
Wheel Alignment 1-225

STEERING GEAR
Horn Sounder Removal 1-228
Ignition Lock, Replace 1-227
Mechanical Gear, Replace 1-244
Mechanical Gear Service 2-170
Mechanical Gear Troubles 2-17
Power Gear, Replace 1-244
Steering Wheel, Replace 1-228

SUSPENSION, FRONT
Ball Joints, Replace 1-243
Ball Joints, Check for Wear 1-243
Coil Spring, Replace 1-244
Shock Absorber, Replace 1-244
Suspension, Description of 1-242
Toe-In, Adjust 1-242
Wheel Alignment, Adjust 1-242
Wheel Bearings, Adjust 1-242
Wheel Bearings, Replace 1-243

TRANSMISSIONS
Three Speed Manual:
    Repairs 2-177
    Replace 1-237
Four Speed Manual:
    Repairs 2-199
    Replace 1-237
Automatic Units 2-231
    Linkage, 1975 1-237

TUNE UP
Service 2-517
Specifications 1-223

WINDSHIELD WIPER
Wiper Arms, Replace 1-229
Wiper Blades, Replace 1-229
Wiper Motor, Replace 1-229
Wiper Switch, Replace 1-230
Wiper Troubles 2-19

SERIAL NUMBER LOCATION

On top of instrument panel, left front.

ENGINE NUMBER LOCATION

On pad at right side of cylinder block, above starter.

ENGINE IDENTIFICATION CODE

Engines are identified in the following table by the code letter or letters immediately following the engine serial number.

Code		Code		Code	
CHA with P/G, T/D	1971	CAB with P/G, T.H. 350 L/E.E.C.	1973	CAD with M/T, W/E.E.C.	1974
CHC with M/T	1971	CAH with P/G, T.H. 350 W/E.E.C.	1973	CAK with T.H. 350, W/E.E.C.	1974
CHB with P/G, T/D	1971	CAJ with M/T W/E.E.C.	1973	CAL with M/T, W/E.E.C.	1974
CHD with M/T	1971	CAC with P/G., T.H. 350 L/E.E.C.	1973	CAM 4-140	1975
CND with P/G, T/D, T.H. 350	1972	CAD with M/T L/E.E.C.	1973	CAR 4-140	1975
CNA with M/T	1972	CAK W/P.G., T.H. 350 W/E.E.C.	1973	CAS 4-140	1975
CG13 with M/T	1972	CAL W/M.T. W/E.E.C.	1973	CAT 4-140	1975
CGD with P/G, T/D	1972	CAB with T.H. 350, W/E.E.C.	1974	CBB 4-140	1975
CSK with P/G, T.H. 350	1972	CAA with M/T, W/E.E.C.	1974	CBC 4-140	1975
CNB with M/T	1972	CAH with T.H. 350, W/E.E.C.	1974		
CBM with P/G, T.H. 350	1972	CAJ with M/T, W/E.E.C.	1974		
CAA with M/T, L/E.E.C.	1973	CAC with T.H. 350, W/E.E.C.	1974		

M/T: Manual transmission
P/G: Powerglide
T/D: Torque drive

T/H: Turbo Hydramatic
L/E.E.C.: Less Exhaust Emission Control

W/E.E.C.: With Exhaust Emission Control

GRILLE IDENTIFICATION

1971-72

1973

1974

1975 Vega

1975 Astre

CHEVROLET VEGA • PONTIAC ASTRE

GENERAL ENGINE SPECIFICATIONS

Year	Engine	Carburetor	Bore and Stroke	Piston Displacement, Cubic Inches	Compression Ratio	Maximum Brake H.P. @ R.P.M.	Maximum Torque Lbs. Ft. @ R.P.M.	Normal Oil Pressure Pounds
1971–72	80 Horsepower①..............4-140	1 Barrel	3.500 x 3.625	140	8.00	80 @ 4400	121 @ 2400	40
	90 Horsepower①..............4-140	2 Barrel	3.500 x 3.625	140	8.00	90 @ 4800	121 @ 2800	40
1973	72 Horsepower①..............4-140	1 Barrel	3.500 x 3.625	140	8.00	72 @ 4400	100 @ 2000	40
	85 Horsepower①..............4-140	2 Barrel	3.500 x 3.625	140	8.00	85 @ 4800	115 @ 2400	40
1974	75 Horsepower①..............4-140	1 Barrel	3.500 x 3.625	140	8.00	75 @ 4400	115 @ 2400	40
	85 Horsepower①..............4-140	2 Barrel	3.500 x 3.625	140	8.00	85 @ 4400	122 @ 2400	40
1975	78 Horsepower①..............4-140	1 Barrel	3.500 x 3.625	140	8.00	78 @ 4200	120 @ 2000	40
	87 Horsepower①..............4-140	2 Barrel	3.500 x 3.625	140	8.00	87 @ 4400	122 @ 2800	40

①—Ratings Net—as installed in the vehicle.

DISTRIBUTOR SPECIFICATIONS

★If unit is checked on vehicle double the RPM and degrees to get crankshaft figures.

Distributor Part No.①	Centrifugal Advance Degrees @ RPM of Distributor					Vacuum Advance		Distributor Retard
	Advance Starts	Intermediate Advance			Full Advance	Inches of Vacuum To Start Plunger	Max. Adv. Dist. Deg. @ Vacuum	Max. Ret. Dist. Deg. @ Vacuum
1971-72								
1110492	0 @ 590	1 @ 800	—	—	12 @ 2000	7	12 @ 15	—
1110435	0 @ 470	1 @ 725	—	—	11 @ 2000	7	12 @ 15	—
1973-74								
1110496	0 @ 800	1 @ 875	6 @ 1600	—	11 @ 2400	7½	12 @ 15	—
1975								
1112862②	0 @ 810	2½ @ 1000	—	—	11 @ 2400	5	12 @ 12	—

①—Located on distributor housing plate.
②—High Energy Ignition.

STARTING MOTOR SPECIFICATIONS

Year	Model	Starter Number	Brush Spring Tension Oz.①	Free Speed Test			Resistance Test	
				Amps.	Volts	R.P.M.①	Amps.	Volts
1971–74	Std. Trans.	1108195	—	50–75	9	6500–10000	—	—
	Auto. Trans.	1108196	—	50–75	9	6500–10000	—	—
1975	Std. Trans.	1108771	—	50–75	9	6500–10000	—	—
	Auto. Trans.	1108772	—	50–75	9	6500–10000	—	—

①—Minimum.

TUNE UP SPECIFICATIONS

OLD CAR SPECIFICATIONS: For 1946-68 Tune Up Specifications see main index.

★When using a timing light, disconnect vacuum hose or tube at distributor and plug opening in hose or tube so idle speed will not be affected.

●When checking compression, lowest cylinder must be within 80 percent of highest.

▲Before removing wires from distributor cap, determine location of the No. 1 wire in cap, as distributor position may have been altered from that shown at the end of this chart.

| Year | Spark Plug | | Distributor | | Ignition Timing ★ | | | Carb. Adjustments | | | | | |
| | Type | Gap Inch | Point Gap Inch | Dwell Angle Deg. | Firing Order Fig. ▲ | Timing BTDC ① | Mark Fig. | Hot Idle Speed | | Air Fuel Ratio | | Idle "CO" % | |
								Std. Trans.	Auto. Trans. ②	Std. Trans.	Auto. Trans.	Std. Trans.	Auto. Trans.
1971													
80 Horsepower	R42TS	.035	③	31–34	A	6°	B	850⑤	650D⑤	—	—	2.0	2.0
90 Horsepower	R42TS	.035	③	31–34	A	④	B	1200⑤	700D⑤	—	—	2.0	2.0
1972													
80 Horsepower	R42TS	.035	③	31–34	A	6°⑦	B	850⑥	700D⑥	—	—	—	—
90 Horsepower	R42TS	.035	③	31–34	A	8°	B	1200	700D⑥	—	—	—	—
1973													
72 Horsepower	R42TS	.035	③	31–34	A	8°	B	1000	750D	—	—	—	—
85 Horsepower	R42TS	.035	③	31–34	A	10°⑨	B	1200	750D⑧	—	—	—	—
1974													
All	R42TS	.035	③	31–34	A	⑩	B	700	750D	—	—	0.5	0.5
1975													
78 Horsepower	R43TS	.060	—	—		⑪		700	550D	—	—	—	—
87 Horsepower	R43TS	.060	—	—		⑩		700	600D	—	—	—	—

①—BTDC—Before top dead center.
②—D—Drive.
③—New points .019", used .016".
④—With synchromesh trans. 6°; with automatic trans. 10°.
⑤—Solenoid disconnected.
⑥—1200 R.P.M. in California.
⑦—4° for California vehicles w/manual trans.
⑧—With Air Cond. 800 RPM.
⑨—With Auto. Trans. 12°.
⑩—Synchromesh trans. 10° BTDC; automatic trans. 12° BTDC.
⑪—Synchromesh trans. 8° BTDC, automatic trans. 10° BTDC.

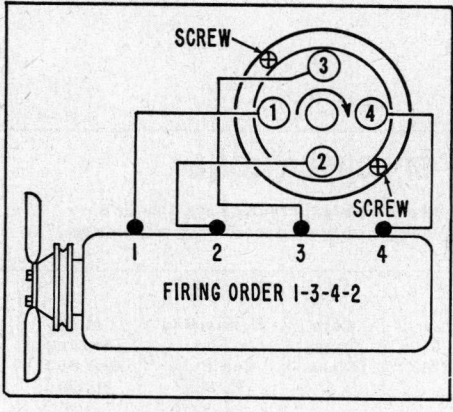

FIRING ORDER 1-3-4-2

Fig. A

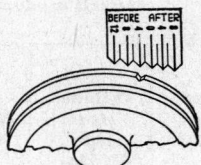

Fig. B

ALTERNATOR & REGULATOR SPECIFICATIONS

| Year | | Alternator | | | | | | Regulator | | | | | | |
| | Model | Rated Hot Output Amps. | Field Current 12 Volts @ 80 F. | Cold Output @ 14 Volts | | Model | Field Relay | | | Voltage Regulator | | |
				2000 R.P.M. Amps.	5000 R.P.M. Amps.		Air Gap In.	Point Gap In.	Closing Voltage	Air Gap In.	Point Gap In.	Voltage @ 125° F.
1971–75	1100545	32	4–4.5	—	31	—	—	—	—	—	—	—
	1100546	55	4–4.5	—	50	—	—	—	—	—	—	—
	1100559	32	4–4.5	—	31	—	—	—	—	—	—	—
	1100560	55	4–4.5	—	50	—	—	—	—	—	—	—
1975	1102500	55	4–4.5	—	50	—	—	—	—	—	—	—
	1102856	37	4–4.5	—	33	—	—	—	—	—	—	—

VALVE SPECIFICATIONS

| Year | Engine Model | Valve Lash | | Valve Angles | | Valve Spring Installed Height | Valve Spring Pressure Lbs. @ In. | Stem Clearance | | Stem Diameter | |
		Int.	Exh.	Seat	Face			Intake	Exhaust	Intake	Exhaust
1971–72	80 Horsepower	.015C	.030C	46	45	1.746	186 @ 1.29	.001–.0027	.001–.0027	.3410–.3417	.3410–.3417
	90 Horsepower	.015C	.030C	46	45	1.746	190 @ 1.31	.001–.0027	.001–.0027	.3410–.3417	.3410–.3417
1973	72 Horsepower	.015C	.030C	46	45	1.750	186 @ 1.29	.001–.0027	.001–.0027	.3410–.3417	.3410–.3417
	85 Horsepower	.015C	.030C	46	45	1.750	190 @ 1.31	.001–.0027	.001–.0027	.3410–.3417	.3410–.3417
1974	All	.015C	.030C	46	45	1.746	190 @ 1.31	.001–.0027	.001–.0027	.3410–.3417	.3410–.3417
1975	4-140 1 BBl.	.015C	.030C	46	45	1.75	186 @ 1.29	.001–.0027	.001–.0027	.3410–.3417	.3410–.3417
	4-140 2 BBl.	.015C	.030C	46	45	1.75	190 @ 1.31	.001–.0027	.001–.0027	.3410–.3417	.3410–.3417

①—Outer spring 110 @ .92; inner spring 79½ @ .875.

ENGINE TIGHTENING SPECIFICATIONS*

★Torque specifications are for clean and lightly lubricated threads only. Dry or dirty threads produce increased friction which prevents accurate measurement of tightness.

Year	Engine Model	Spark Plugs Ft. Lbs.	Cylinder Head Bolts Ft. Lbs.	Intake Manifold Ft. Lbs.	Exhaust Manifold Ft. Lbs.	Rocker Arm Stud Ft. Lbs.	Cam Cover Ft. Lbs.	Connecting Rod Cap Bolts Ft. Lbs.	Main Bearing Cap Bolts Ft. Lbs.	Flywheel to Crankshaft Ft. Lbs.	Vibration Damper or Pulley Ft. Lbs.
1971–75	4-140	15	60	30	30	—	35①	35	65	60	80

①—Inch pounds.

CHEVROLET VEGA • PONTIAC ASTRE

PISTONS, PINS, RINGS, CRANKSHAFT & BEARINGS

Year	Engine Model	Piston Clearance	Ring End Gap① Comp.	Oil	Wrist-pin-Diameter	Rod Bearings Shaft Diameter	Bearing Clearance	Main Bearings Shaft Diameter	Bearing Clearance	Thrust on Bear. No.	Shaft End Play
1971-72	4-140	.0018-.0028	④	.010	.927	1.999-2.000	.0007-.0027	2.2983-2.2992	②	4	.002-.007
1973	4-140	.0018-.0028	④	.010	.927	1.999-2.000	.0007-.0038	2.2983-2.2923	③	4	.002-.007
1974-75	4-140	.0018-.0028	④	.010	.927	1.999-2.000	.0007-.0038	2.2983-2.2993	③	4	.002-.008

①—Fit rings in tapered bores for clearance listed in tightest portion of ring travel.
②—#1 .0003-.002; others .0003-.003.
③—#1 .0003-.002; others .0003-.0027.
④—Top ring .015; lower ring .009.

WHEEL ALIGNMENT SPECIFICATIONS

OLD CAR SPECIFICATIONS: For 1946-68 Wheel Alignment Specifications see main index.

Year	Model	Caster Angle, Degrees Limits	Desired	Camber Angle, Degrees Limits Left	Right	Desired Left	Right	Toe-In. Inch	Toe-Out on Turns, Deg.① Outer Wheel	Inner Wheel
1971-73	All	−¼ to −1¼	−¾	−¼ to +¾	−¼ to +¾	+¼	+¼	3/16 to 5/16	—	—
1974	All	−1¾ to +¼	−¾	−¾ to +1¼	−¾ to +1¼	+¼	+¼	3/16 to 5/16	—	—
1975	Vega	−1¾ to +¼	−¾	−¼ to +¾	−¼ to +¾	+¼	+¼	0-⅛	—	—
	Astre	−¼ to −1¼	−¾	−¼ to +¾	−¼ to +¾	+¼	+¼	3/16 to 5/16	—	—

①—Incorrect toe-out when other adjustments are correct, indicates bent steering arms.

BRAKE SPECIFICATIONS

Year	Model	Brake Drum Inside Diameter	Wheel Cylinder Bore Diameter Disc Brake	Front Drum Brake	Rear Drum Brake	Master Cylinder Bore Diameter Disc Brakes	Drum Brakes	Power Brakes
1971-75	All	9	1⅞	—	¾	¾	—	¾

COOLING SYSTEM & CAPACITY DATA

Year	Model or Engine	Cooling Capacity, Qts.			Radiator Cap Relief Pressure, Lbs.		Thermo. Opening Temp. ①	Fuel Tank Gals.	Engine Oil Refill Qts. ②	Transmission Oil			Rear Axle Oil Pints
		No Heater	With Heater	With A/C	With A/C	No A/C				3 Speed Pints	4 Speed Pints	Auto. Trans. Qts. ③	
1971–72	4-140	5.7	6.5	6.5	15	15	195	11	3	2.4	3	③	2.5
1973	4-140	7.8	8.6	9.0	15	15	195	11	3	3	3	④	2.8
1974	4-140	—	7.6	8.0	15	15	195	16	3	3	3	4	2.8
1975	4-140	—	7	7½	15	15	195	16	3	2.4	2.4	⑤	2¼

① —For permanent type anti-freeze.
② —Add 1 quart with filter change.
③ —Refill 3 qts. Total capacity 8½ qts.
④ —Powerglide 3 qts.; turbo hydra-matic 4 qts.
⑤ —Refill 4 qts. Total capacity 10 qts.

REAR AXLE SPECIFICATIONS

Year	Model	Carrier Type	Ring Gear & Pinion Backlash		Pinion Bearing Preload			Differential Bearing Preload		
			Method	Adjustment	Method	New Bearings Inch-Lbs.	Used Bearings Inch-Lbs.	Method	New Bearings Inch-Lbs.	Used Bearings Inch-Lbs.
1971-75	All	Integral	Shims	.005–.008	Spacer	25	10	Shims	—	—

Electrical Section

1975 HIGH ENERGY IGNITION SYSTEM (H.E.I.)

Service procedure for the H.E.I. distributor are found in the "Tune-Up Service" chapter, Electronic Ignition System section. Some service procedures are slightly different since the ignition coil is externally mounted.

DISTRIBUTOR

Removal

1. Release distributor cap hold-down screws and remove cap.
2. Disconnect distributor primary lead from coil terminal.

NOTE: On H.E.I. systems, disconnect feed and module connectors from distributor cap.

3. Scribe an alignment mark on the distributor and engine in line with the rotor.
4. Remove distributor hold-down bolt and clamp and remove distributor.

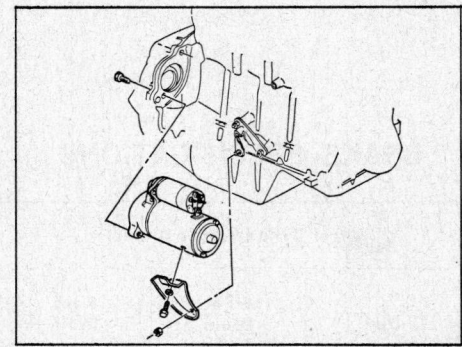

Fig. 1   Starter motor installation

CAUTION: Avoid rotating engine while distributor is removed.

Installation

1. Turn rotor about ⅛ turn in a clockwise direction past the mark previously made to locate rotor.

2. Push distributor down into position in cylinder head with distributor housing in a normal installed position.

NOTE: It may be necessary to move rotor slightly to start gear into mesh with camshaft gear, but rotor should line up with the mark when distributor is down in place.

NOTE

If the engine was disturbed while the distributor was removed, it will be necessary to crank the engine to bring No. 1 cylinder piston up on the compression stroke. Continue cranking until timing mark is adjacent to pointer. Then rotate the distributor cam until rotor is in position to fire No. 1. Install distributor in this position.

3. Tighten distributor clamp bolt and connect vacuum line, primary wire and install the cap.
4. Set ignition timing.

NOTE: When using a timing light to ad-

Fig. 2   Ignition lock removal

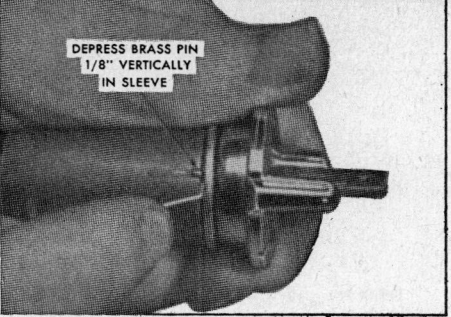

DEPRESS BRASS PIN 1/8" VERTICALLY IN SLEEVE

Fig. 3   Disassembling ignition lock

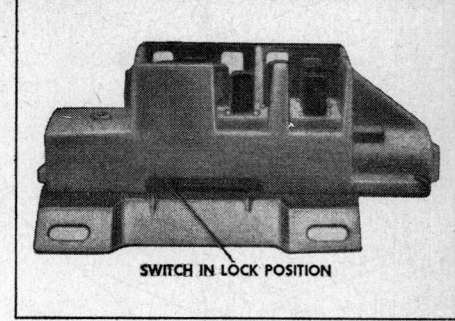

SWITCH IN LOCK POSITION

Fig. 4   Ignition switch assembly

just ignition timing, the connection should be made at the No. 1 spark plug. Forcing foreign objects through the boot at the No. 1 terminal of the distributor cap will damage the boot and could cause engine misfiring.

STARTER, REPLACE

NOTE: The following procedure may vary slightly depending on model and series of vehicle.

1. Disconnect battery ground cable at battery.
2. Disconnect all wires at solenoid terminals.

NOTE: Reinstall the nuts on the terminals as each wire is removed as thread size is different and if mixed, stripping of threads may occur.

3. Loosen starter front bracket then remove two mount bolts, Fig. 1.
4. Remove front bracket bolt and rotate bracket clear of work area then lower starter from vehicle by lowering front end first.
5. Reverse procedure to install.

IGNITION LOCK, REPLACE

1. Remove the turn signal switch as de-

scribed further on.
2. On *1971 Models* the lock cylinder may be removed in any position from "Accessory" to "On" however, the "Lock" position is recommended because of its positive position. On *1972-75 Models* the lock cylinder should be removed in the "Run" position only. Removal in any other position will damage the buzzer switch.
3. Insert a small screw driver or similar tool into the turn signal housing slot, Fig. 2. Keeping the tool to the right side of the slot, break the housing flash loose, and at the same time depress the spring latch at the lower end of the lock cylinder. With the latch depressed, the lock cylinder can be removed from the housing.
4. To separate the lock from the cylinder, Fig. 3, use a paper clip or similar quality wire, place a 90° bend about ⅛" from one end of the wire.
5. Place the cylinder in the "LOCK" position. Using the wire as described in step 4, depress the plunger pin (above the stake mark) approx. ⅛" vertically in sleeve housing, at the same time exert light upward pressure on the lock assembly, rotate the cylinder counter-clockwise until it pops up from the sleeve assembly.

IGNITION SWITCH, REPLACE

The ignition switch is mounted on the top of the steering column jacket near the front of the dash. It is located inside the channel section of the brake pedal support and is completely inaccessible without first lowering the steering column.

1. Lower the steering column and be sure it is properly supported before proceeding.
2. The switch should be positioned in Lock position before removing, Fig. 4.
3. Unfasten and remove the switch, detaching it from the actuating rod.
4. When installing, make sure the lock and the switch are in the Lock position. Then install the activating rod into the switch and fasten the switch.

LIGHT SWITCH, REPLACE

1. Disconnect ground cable at battery.
2. Pull headlamp switch knob to "ON" position.
3. Reach under instrument panel and depress switch shaft retainer button while pulling on the switch control shaft knob.
4. With a large bladed screwdriver, remove the light switch ferrule nut

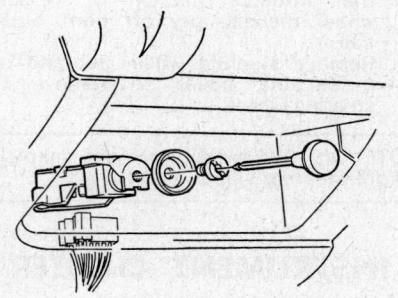

Fig. 5   Light switch replacement

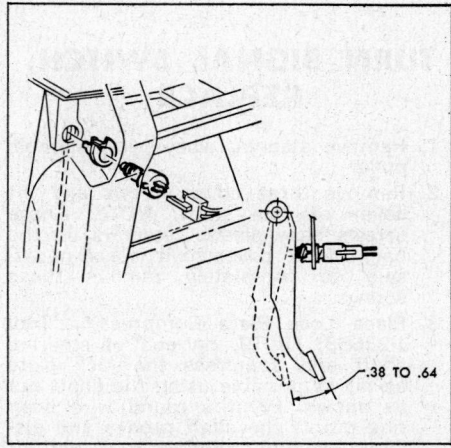

.38 TO .64

Fig. 6   Stop light switch replacement

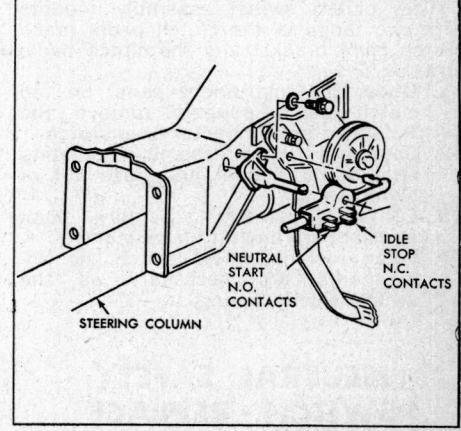

NEUTRAL START N.O. CONTACTS

IDLE STOP N.C. CONTACTS

STEERING COLUMN

Fig. 7   Clutch operated neutral start switch

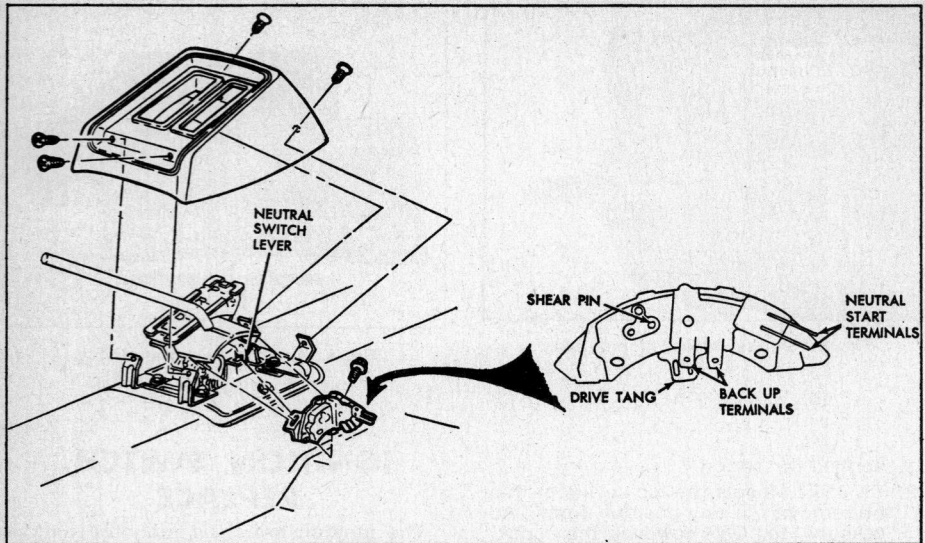

Fig. 8   Neutral safety switch installation

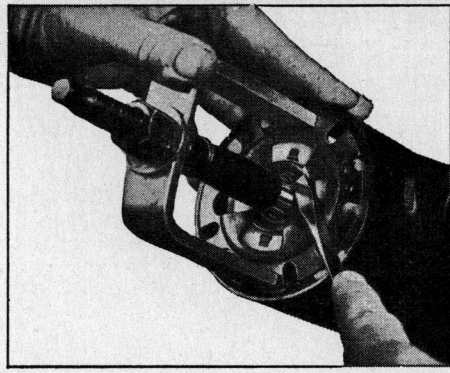

Fig. 9   Removing lock plate retaining ring

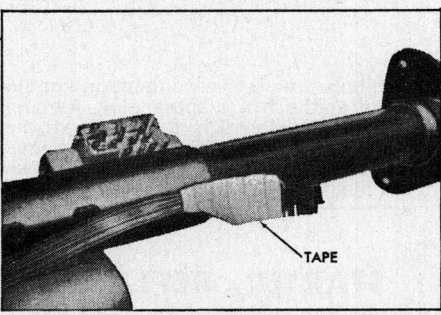

Fig. 10   Taping turn signal connector and wires

from front of instrument panel.

5. Disconnect the multi-contact connector from side of switch and remove switch.

STOP LIGHT SWITCH

1. Reach under right side of instrument panel at brake pedal support and release wiring harness connector at switch.
2. Pull switch from mounting bracket.
3. When installing switch, adjust by bringing brake pedal to normal position. Electrical contact should be made when pedal is depressed as shown in Fig. 6. To adjust, the switch may be rotated or pulled in the clip.

CLUTCH START SWITCH

NOTE: The clutch pedal must be fully depressed and the ignition switch in START position for the vehicle to start.

The clutch switch assembly mounts with two tangs to the clutch pedal brace switch pivot bracket and the clutch pedal arm, Fig. 7.

1. Under the instrument panel on the clutch pedal support remove the multi-contact connector from switch.
2. Compress switch assembly actuating shaft barb retainer and push out of clutch pedal.
3. Compress switch assembly pivot bracket barb and lift off switch.
4. When installing new switch, no adjustments are necessary as the switch is self aligning.

NEUTRAL SAFETY SWITCH, REPLACE

1. Remove four screws securing floor console, Fig. 8.
2. Disconnect electrical plugs on back-up contacts and neutral start contacts of switch assembly.
3. Place shift lever in Neutral.
4. Remove two screws securing shift indicator plate.
5. Remove two screws securing shift lever curved cover.
6. Remove two screws securing switch to lever assembly.

NOTE: Screws are hidden beneath lever cover.

7. Tilt switch to right as you lift switch out of lever hole.
8. When installing switch, make sure it is in Neutral position. When switch is installed, shifting out of Neutral will shear the switch plastic locating pin.

TURN SIGNAL SWITCH, REPLACE

1. Remove steering wheel with suitable puller.
2. Remove three cover screws and lift cover off the shaft. NOTE: These screws have plastic retainers on the back of the cover so it is not necessary to completely remove these screws.
3. Place Lock Plate Compressing Tool J-23653, Fig. 9, on end of steering shaft and compress the lock plate as far as possible using the shaft nut as shown. Pry the round wire snap ring out of the shaft groove and discard the ring. Remove tool and lift lock plate off end of shaft.

4. Slide the signal cancelling cam, upper bearing preload spring and thrust washer off the end of shaft.
5. Remove turn signal lever screw and remove the lever.
6. Push hazard warning knob in and unscrew the knob.
7. Wrap upper part of connector with tape, Fig. 10 to prevent snagging of wires during switch removal.
8. Remove three screws on switch and pull switch straight up through housing.

HORN SOUNDER & STEERING WHEEL

1. Disconnect battery ground cable.
2. On regular production steering wheel models, remove the two screws securing the steering wheel shroud from beneath the wheel and remove the shroud. On GT or optional wheel models, pry off horn button cap.
3. Remove steering wheel nut and use a suitable puller to remove the steering wheel.

NOTE: On 1975 models, remove snap ring before steering wheel nut.

INSTRUMENT CLUSTER

Standard Cluster

The instrument cluster bezel is retained by nine screws, Fig. 11. After removal of bezel, remove cluster lens-light shield combination (2 screws at top of lens and 2 screws at bottom of light shield). The lens tips out at the top and then lifts off. Instruments are then easily removed.

GT Cluster

The cluster bezel is retained by six screws, Fig. 12. After removal of bezel, remove the lens light shield (6 screws). Then lift lens and light shield straight out. Instruments are then accessible for replacement.

W/S WIPER BLADES

1. Remove the wiper blade from the arm by depressing the spring type blade clip, Fig. 13, away from the under side of the arm and slide the arm out of the blade clip.
2. To install wiper blade to wiper arm, slide tip end of arm into blade clip, until pin on tip end of arm engages hole in clip.
3. The blade element is retained in the blade assembly by a spring type retainer clip in the end of the blade element. When the retainer clip is squeezed together, the blade element can be slid out of the blade assembly.
4. When installing a blade element into a blade assembly, be certain to engage the metal insert of the element into all retaining tabs of the blade assembly.

NOTE: When properly installed, the spring type element retaining clip should be at the end of the wiper blade assembly nearest the wiper transmission.

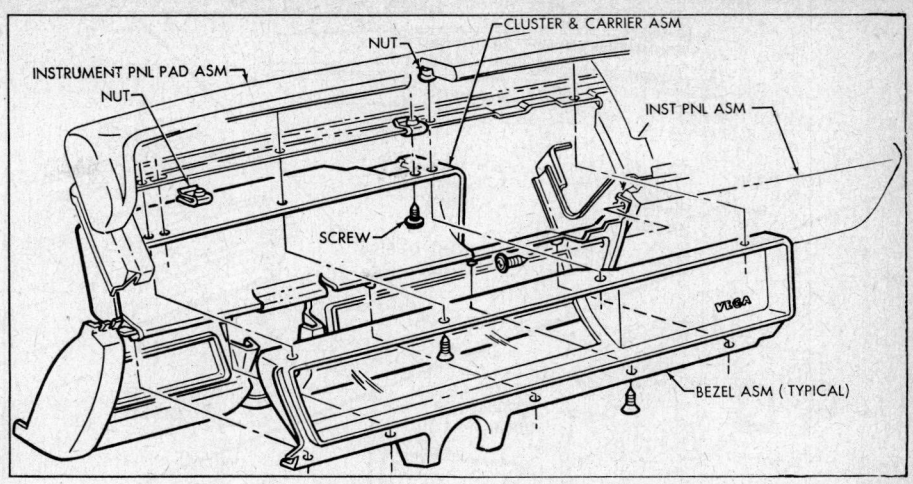

Fig. 11 Instrument panel. Standard cluster

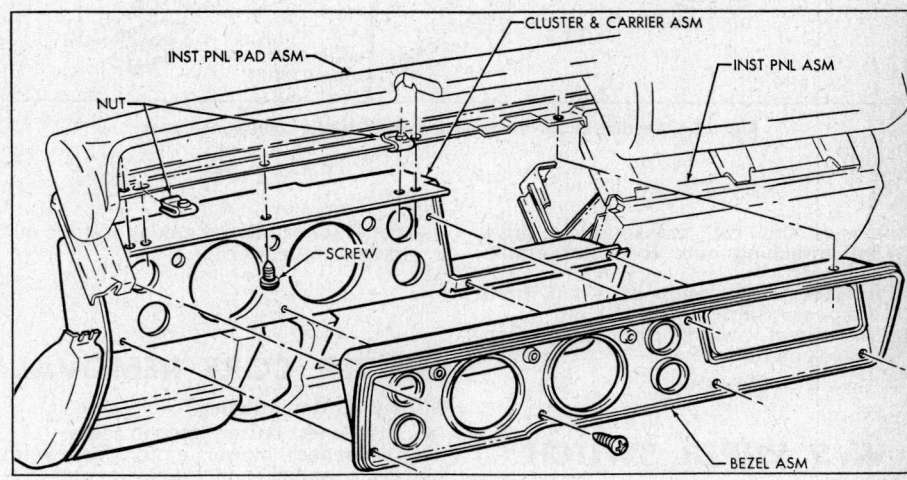

Fig. 12 Instrument panel. GT cluster

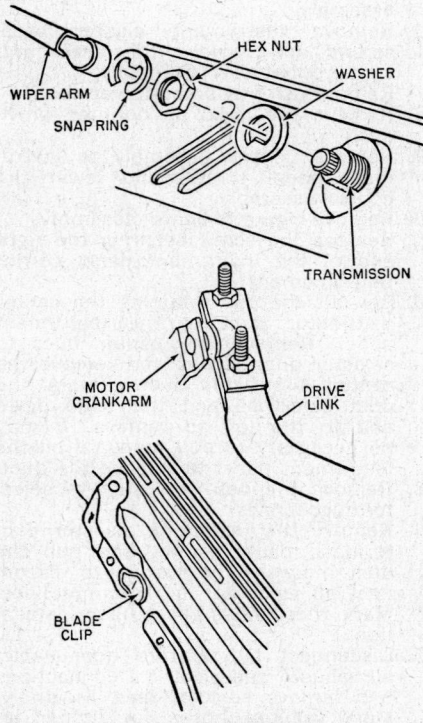

Fig. 13 Wiper blade clip

W/S WIPER ARMS

1. Wiper motor must be in park position.
2. Use suitable tool to minimize the possibility of windshield or paint finish damage during arm removal.
3. Remove arm by prying up with tool to disengage arm from serrated transmission shaft.
4. To install arm to transmission shaft rotate the required distance and direction so that blades rest in proper parked position.

CAUTION: The parked position for the left blade tip is approx. 2″ above lower windshield reveal moulding and the right blade tip within 2″ of the lower windshield reveal moulding.

W/S WIPER MOTOR

1. Raise hood.
2. Reaching through cowl opening,

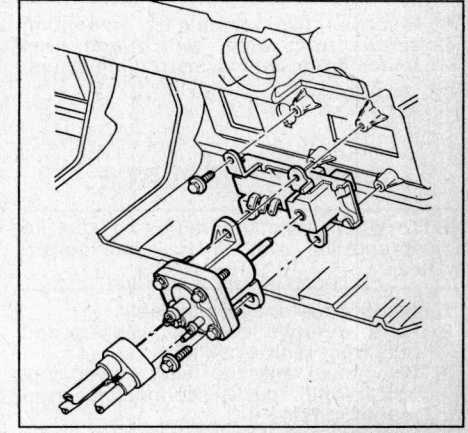

Fig. 14 Wiper-washer control switch

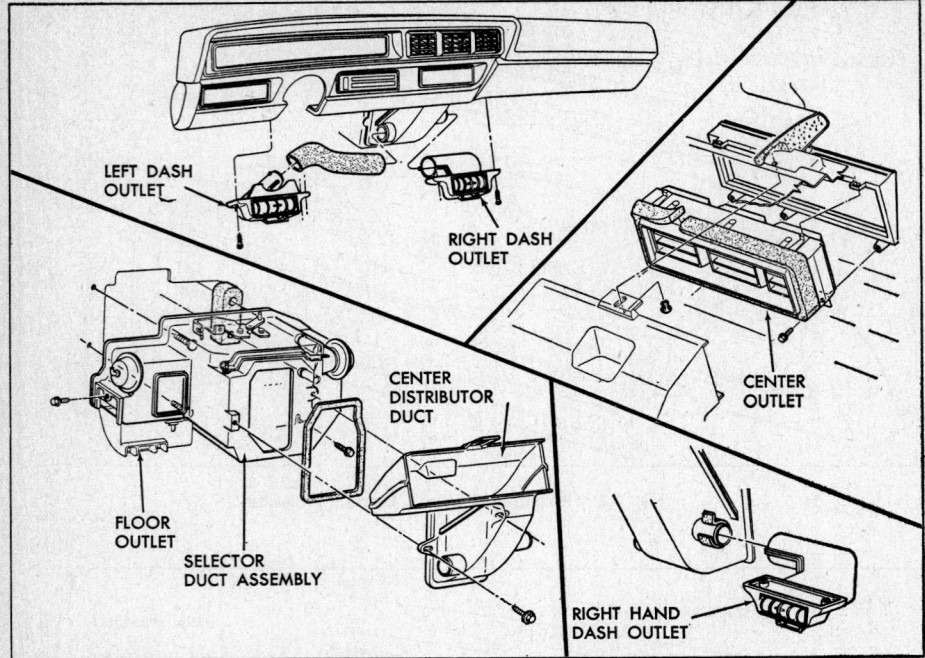

Fig. 15 Air distributor ducts and outlets on air conditioned cars

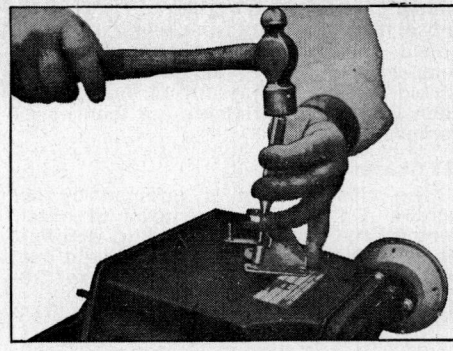

Fig. 16 Removing temperature door bell crank on air conditioned vehicles

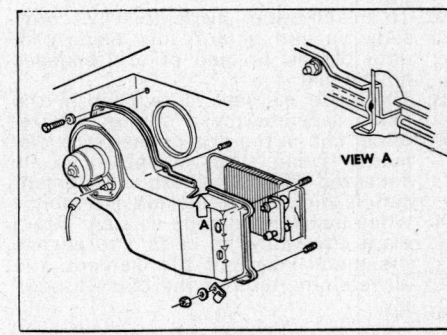

Fig. 17 Blower motor (Typical)

loosen the two transmission drive link attaching nuts to motor crankarm.
3. Remove transmission drive link from motor crankarm.
4. Disconnect wiring and unfasten motor and remove.

W/S WIPER SWITCH

1. Beneath instrument panel, unplug the headlamp switch multi-connector for clearance to wiper switch screw.
2. Unplug connector on bottom of wiper switch.
3. Remove two screws mounting washer pump, Fig. 14.

NOTE: Do not remove washer pump hoses.

4. Remove two remaining mounting screws from wiper switch and drop switch from behind instrument panel.

RADIO, REPLACE

NOTE: When installing radio, be sure to adjust antenna trimmer for peak performance.

1. Remove battery ground cable.
2. Remove knobs, controls, washers and nuts from radio bushings.
3. Disconnect antenna lead, power connector and speaker connectors from rear of radio.
4. Remove two screws securing radio mounting bracket to instrument panel lower reinforcement and lift out radio.

HEATER CORE REMOVAL

Without Air Conditioning
1. Disconnect battery ground cable.
2. Disconnect blower motor lead wire.
3. Place a pan under vehicle and disconnect heater hoses at core connections and secure ends of hoses in a raised position.
4. Remove the coil bracket to dash panel stud nut and move coil out of way.
5. Remove the blower inlet to dash panel screws and nuts and remove the blower inlet, blower motor and wheel as an assembly.
6. Remove the core retainer strap screws and remove the core.
7. When replacing core, be sure the blower inlet sealer is intact.

With Air Conditioning
1. Disconnect battery ground cable.
2. Place a pan under heater core tubes, disconnect heater hoses at the core and secure ends of hoses in a raised position. Cap or tape the core tubes to prevent coolant spillage during selector duct removal.
3. Referring to Fig. 15, remove nuts from selector duct studs on engine side of dash.
4. Disconnect left hand dash outlet flexible hose at center distributor duct.

5. Remove the right hand dash outlet assembly.
6. Remove instrument cluster bezel screws and remove the bezel and center outlet as an assembly.
7. Remove ash tray and retainer.
8. Remove the radio as outlined previously.
9. Remove control assembly to instrument panel screws and lower the control assembly.
10. Remove cigarette lighter assembly.
11. Remove the screw securing the right end of the instrument panel carrier reinforcement.
12. Pry out the clip retaining the center distributor duct to the instrument panel. Remove the center duct to selector duct screws and remove the center distributor duct. Rotate the duct clockwise and then pull down and to the left to remove. It may be necessary to pull rearward on the instrument panel to remove the duct.
13. Remove the defroster duct to selector duct screws.
14. Remove the remaining selector duct to dash panel screws and pull the duct rearward far enough to disconnect all electrical and vacuum lines. Mark these lines for proper installation.
15. Disconnect temperature door cable, all vacuum and electrical connections and remove selector duct assembly. Mark vacuum hoses for proper installation.

16. If the core must be replaced, pry off or punch out the temperature door bell crank, Fig. 16.

CAUTION: Use care to prevent bending the arm or damaging the selector case. Then remove the screws securing the backing plate and the temperature door cable retainer and remove the core and backing plate as an assembly.

BLOWER MOTOR, REPLACE

1. Disconnect the battery ground cable.
2. Disconnect the blower motor lead wire.
3. Scribe the blower motor flange to case position.
4. Remove the blower to case attaching screws and remove the blower wheel and motor assembly, Fig. 17. Pry the flange gently if the sealer acts as an adhesive.
5. Remove the blower motor wheel retaining nut and separate the motor and wheel.
6. To install, reverse steps 1 thru 5, lining up the scribe marks on the motor flange which were made at removal.

NOTE: Assemble the blower wheel to the motor with the open end of the blower away from the motor. Replace sealer at the motor flange if necessary.

Engine Section

CHECKING ENGINE MOUNTS

Raise engine to remove weight from mounts leaving a slight tension in the rubber. Observe both mounts while raising engine. Check for the following and replace if:

a. Hard rubber surface is covered with heat check cracks.
b. Rubber separated from metal plate of mount.
c. Rubber split through center.

If there is relative movement between a metal plate of the mount and its attaching points lower the engine on the mounts and tighten the screws or nuts attaching the mounts to the engine, frame, or bracket.

ENGINE MOUNTS, REPLACE

1971-75 Front

1. Raise vehicle on hoist and support front of engine to take weight off front mounts.
2. If only one mount is being replaced,

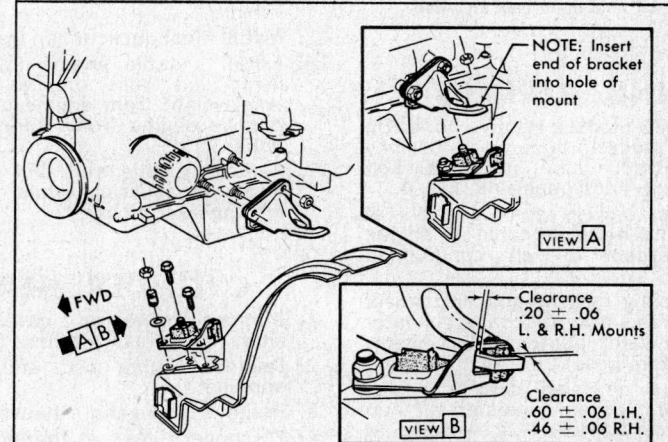

Fig. 1   Front mounts. 1971-75 (Typical)

remove the mount-to-engine bracket nut on the mount not being replaced, Fig. 1.
3. Remove the stud nut and two bolts securing mount to housing support.
4. Remove the three stud nuts securing the bracket to the engine. On the right side remove the starter brace at starter and on air conditioned equipped vehicles, remove the compressor rear lower brace at the compressor.
5. Raise front of engine to provide maximum clearance without imposing stress on other engine components.
6. Remove mount and bracket as a unit and separate by removing stud nut.

1971-75 Rear

CAUTION: The rear mount serves to locate the power train fore and aft and side to side; therefore mark relationship of rear mount to transmission support cross member to ensure proper alignment when new mount is installed.

---

1. Remove crossmember-to-mount bolts, Figs. 2 and 3.
2. Raise transmission at extension housing to release weight from mount.
3. Remove mount-to-transmission bolts, then remove mount.

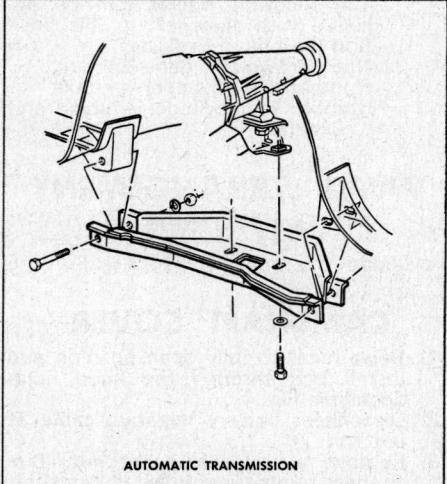

Fig. 2   Rear mount. Automatic trans

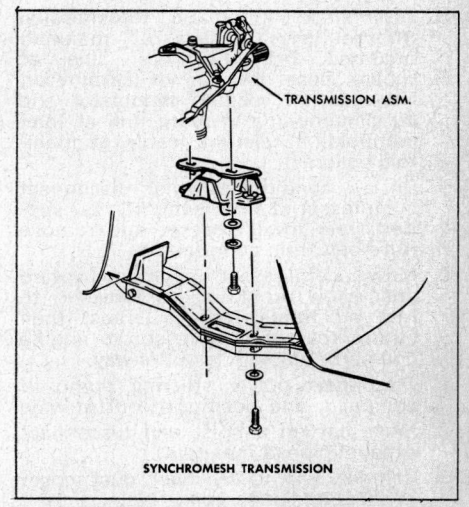

Fig. 3   Rear mount. Synchromesh trans

Fig. 4   Hood hold-open bolt installed

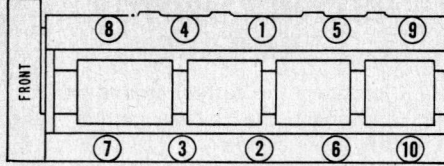

Fig. 5   Cylinder head tightening sequence

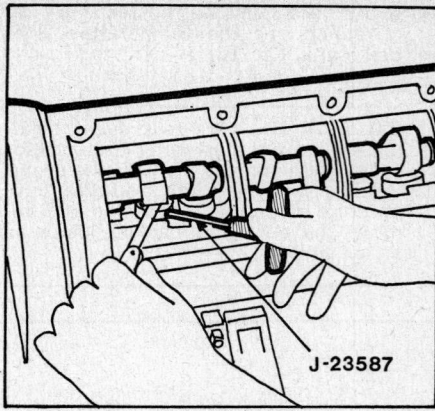

J-23587

Fig. 6   Adjusting valve lash

ENGINE, REPLACE

1. On 1973-75 models, remove hood. On 1971-72 models, raise hood to fully open position and install a bolt through the hood-open link, Fig. 4.
2. Disconnect battery positive cable at battery and negative cable at engine block (except on air conditioned vehicles).
3. Drain cooling system and disconnect hoses at radiator. Disconnect heater hoses at water pump and at heater inlet (bottom hose).
4. Disconnect emission system hoses: PCV at cam cover; cannister vacuum hose at carburetor; PCV vacuum at inlet manifold and bowl vent at carburetor.
5. Remove radiator panel or shroud and remove radiator, fan and spacer.
6. Remove air cleaner, disconnecting vent tube at base of cleaner.
7. Disconnect electrical leads at: Delcotron, ignition coil, starter solenoid, oil pressure switch, engine temperature switch, transmission controlled spark switch at transmission, transmission controlled spark solenoid and engine ground strap at cowl.
8. Disconnect: Automatic transmission throttle valve linkage at manifold mounted bellcrank, fuel line at rubber hose to rear of carburetor, transmission vacuum modulator and air conditioning vacuum line at inlet manifold, accelerator cable at manifold bellcrank.
9. On air conditioned cars, disconnect compressor at front support, rear support, rear lower bracket and remove drive belt from compressor.
10. Move compressor slightly forward and allow front of compressor to rest on frame forward brace, then secure rear of compressor to engine compartment so it is out of way.
11. Disconnect power steering pump, if equipped, and position it out of way.
12. Raise car on a hoist and disconnect exhaust pipe at manifold.
13. Remove engine flywheel dust cover or converter underpan.
14. On automatic transmission cars, re-move converter-to-flywheel retaining bolts and nuts and install coverter safety strap.
15. Remove converter housing or flywheel housing-to-engine retaining bolts.
16. Loosen engine front mount retaining bolts at frame attachment and lower vehicle.
17. Install floor jack under transmission.
18. Install suitable engine lifting equipment and raise engine slightly to take weight from engine mounts and remove engine front mount retaining bolts.
19. Remove engine and pull forward to clear transmission while slowly lifting engine from car.

CYLINDER HEAD

1. Remove engine front cover and camshaft cover as outlined further on.
2. Remove timing belt and camshaft sprocket.
3. Remove intake and exhaust manifolds.
4. Disconnect hose at thermostat housing.
5. Remove cylinder head bolts and with the aid of an assistant lift head and gasket from engine. Place head on two blocks of wood to prevent damage to valves.
6. Reverse procedure to install and tighten head bolts in sequence shown in Fig. 5.

Fig. 7   Tappet and adjusting screw assembly. Screw is threaded in all areas except in valve stem contact surface

VALVES, ADJUST

1. To adjust valves, the tappet must be on the base circle of the cam lobe. Do this as follows:
   a. Rotate camshaft timing sprocket to align timing mark on sprocket with inverted "V" notch on timing belt upper cover. The following valves can be adjusted with cam in this position (number one firing).
      Number one cylinder—Intake and Exhaust
      Number two cylinder—Intake
      Number three cylinder—Exhaust
   b. Use a feeler gauge and measure clearance between tappet and cam lobe. Adjust clearance by turning adjusting screw in tappet, Fig. 6.

   NOTE: It is mandatory that the adjusting screw, Fig. 7, be turned one complete revolution to maintain proper stem-to-screw relationship. Each revolution of screw alters clearance by .003".

   c. Rotate camshaft timing sprocket 180 degrees so timing mark is at 12 o'clock position and in line with notch on timing belt upper cover. The following valves can be adjusted with camshaft in this position (number four firing).
      Number two cylinder—Exhaust
      Number three cylinder—Intake
      Number four cylinder—Intake and Exhaust

VALVE ARRANGEMENT
Front to Rear

4-cylinder . . . . I-E-I-E-I-E-I-E

CAMSHAFT COVER

1. Raise hood to fully open position and install bolt through the hood hold-open link, Fig. 4.
2. Disconnect battery negative cable at battery.
3. Remove air cleaner wing nut. Disconnect ventilation tube at camshaft cover or at air cleaner; then remove air cleaner.

Fig. 8 Camshaft removal tool installed

Fig. 9 Depressing valve tappets

4. Remove PCV valve from grommet at front of cover.
5. Remove cover-to-cylinder head screws and withdraw cover from head.

CAMSHAFT, REMOVAL

1. Remove hood.
2. Remove camshaft timing sprocket.
3. Remove timing belt upper cover and

cam retainer and seal assembly.
4. Remove camshaft cover.
5. Disconnect fuel line at carburetor and remove idle solenoid from bracket.
6. Remove carburetor choke coil, cover and rod assembly.
7. Remove distributor.
8. Raise vehicle on a hoist, disconnect engine front mounts at body attachment, raise front of engine and install wood blocks, about 1½" thick, between engine mounts and body. Lower vehicle.
9. Install camshaft removal tool as shown in Fig. 8, to cylinder head as follows:

   a. Position tool to cylinder head so attaching holes align with cam cover lower attaching holes.
   b. Align tappet depressing levers on tool so each lever will depress both intake and exhaust valve for their respective cylinder. Lever should fit squarely in notches adjacent to valve tappets.
   c. With tool aligned, make sure screws in bottom of tool are backed off so they do not make contact with bosses beneath tool.
   d. Install hardened screws supplied with tool, to attach tool to head. Torque screws securely.
   e. Turn screws in bottom of tool downward until they just seat against corresponding bosses on head.
   f. Apply a heavy body lubricant to ball end of lever depressing screws and proceed to tighten screws to depress tappets, Fig. 9.

NOTE: Use a torque wrench to tighten screws the final few turns. About 10 ft. lbs. is required to depress tappets.

10. At this point the camshaft can be removed by sliding it forward from the head.

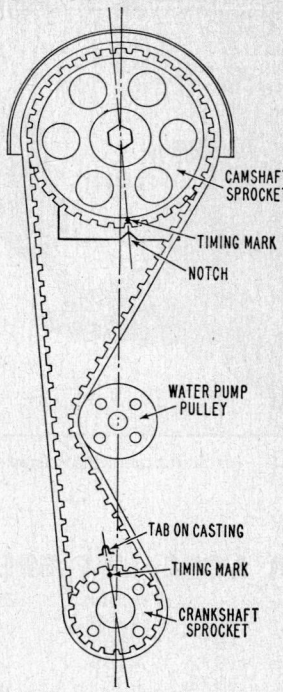

Fig. 10 Sprocket alignment marks

CAMSHAFT BEARINGS

After removal of the camshaft as described previously, the bearings can be removed without removing the camshaft end plug.

Fig. 11 Checking sprocket alignment. 1972-75

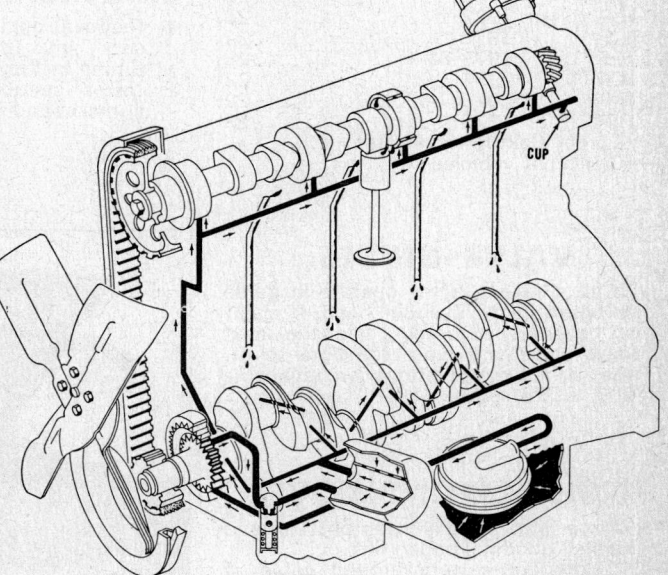

Engine lubrication system

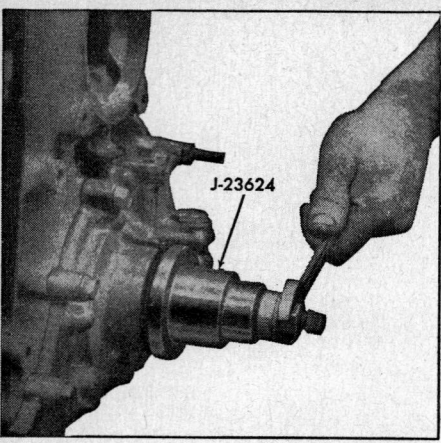

Fig. 12 Installing crankshaft front seal

CAM LOBE LIFT SPECS.

		Intake	Exhaust
80 H.P.	1971	.4199	.4301
90 H.P.	1971	.4365	.4365
80 H.P.①	1972	.4199	.4302
80 H.P.②	1972	.4367	.4379
90 H.P.	1972	.4367	.4379
72 H.P.	1973	.4199	.4302
85 H.P.	1973	.4369	.4379
75 H.P.	1974	.4199	.4302
85 H.P.	1974	.4367	.4379
78 H.P.	1975	.4199	.4302
87 H.P.	1975	.4367	.4379

①—Except California vehicles.
②—California vehicles.

VALVE TIMING
Intake Open Before TDC

80 H.P.	1971	22
90 H.P.	1971	25
80 H.P.①	1972	22
80 H.P.②	1972	28
90 H.P.	1972	28
72 H.P.	1973	22
85 H.P.	1973-74	28
75 H.P.	1974	22
78 H.P.	1975	22
87 H.P.	1975	28

①—Except California vehicles.
②—California vehicles.

VALVE GUIDES

On all engines, valves operate in guide holes bored in the cylinder head. If clearance becomes excessive, use the next oversize valve and ream toe bore to fit. Valves with oversize stems are available in .003, .015 and 030".

ENGINE FRONT COVER

1. Raise hood to fully open position and install hood hold-open bolt.
2. Disconnect battery ground cable at battery.
3. Remove fan and spacer.

4. Loosen, but do not remove, the two cover lower screws. Cover is slotted to permit easy removal.
5. Remove the two cover upper retaining screws and remove cover.

TIMING BELT & WATER PUMP

1. Remove engine front cover as previously described.
2. Remove accessory drive pulley or damper.
3. Drain coolant and loosen water pump bolts to relieve tension on belt.
4. Remove timing belt lower cover, then remove belt from sprockets.
5. Remove water pump bolts and lift off pump.

CAMSHAFT SPROCKET

After removal of timing belt, the camshaft sprocket can be removed as follows:
1. Align one hole in sprocket with bolt head behind sprocket, then using a socket on bolt head to prevent cam from turning, remove sprocket retaining bolt and withdraw sprocket from camshaft.
2. When installing, be sure timing marks are aligned as in Fig. 10.

NOTE: For 1972-75 a simplified method is provided for checking camshaft and crankshaft alignment. Proper alignment is assured by making sure hole in left rear of the timing belt upper cover is in line with the corresponding hole in the camshaft sprocket. Check alignment by inserting a pencil or other similar tool through the hole in cover. If alignment is correct, tool will also enter small hole in cam gear, Fig. 11.

CRANKSHAFT SPROCKET

1. Remove engine front cover, accessory drive pulley, timing belt and timing belt lower cover.
2. Install suitable puller to crankshaft sprocket and remove sprocket.

Fig. 14 Removing oil pan baffle

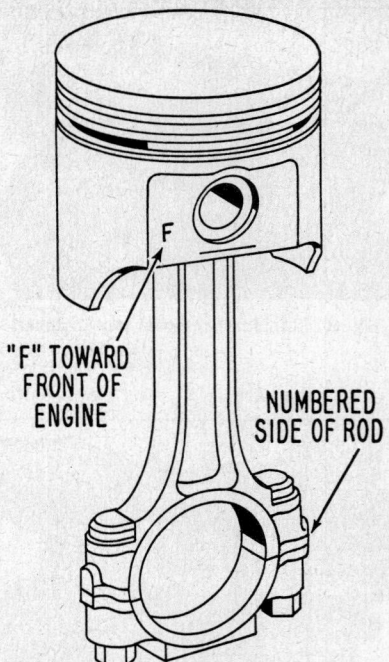

"F" TOWARD FRONT OF ENGINE

NUMBERED SIDE OF ROD

Fig. 13 Piston and rod assembly

OIL PUMP (CRANKCASE FRONT COVER) SEAL

1. Remove engine front cover, accessory drive pulley, timing belt and timing belt lower cover and crankshaft sprocket.
2. Pry old seal from front cover being careful not to damage seal housing or seal lip contact surfaces.
3. Coat seal with light engine oil and apply an approved sealing compound to outside diameter of seal.
4. Position seal, closed end outward, onto crankshaft. Then install seal into bore using tool J-23624, Fig. 12.

PISTONS & RODS, ASSEMBLE

The "F" on the front of the piston must face the front of the engine when the piston and road assembly is installed in its proper cylinder, Fig. 13.

Piston Oversizes

Oversize pistons are available in oversizes of .010 and .020 inch.

MAIN & ROD BEARINGS
Undersizes

Bearings are available in .001, .002, .010 and .020" undersizes.

NOTE: If for any reason main bearing caps

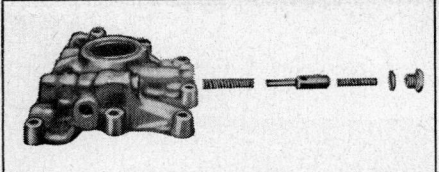

Fig. 15   Oil pump pressure regulator

Fig. 16   Checking driven gear-to-housing clearance

OIL PUMP (CRANKCASE FRONT COVER)

1. Remove engine front cover, accessory drive pulley, timing belt, timing belt lower cover and crankshaft sprocket.
2. Raise vehicle on a hoist and remove oil pan and baffle.
3. Remove bolts and stud securing oil pump to cylinder case.

Inspection

1. Clean gasket surfaces, then wash parts in approved solvent and blow out all passages.
2. Check pressure regulator for free operation, Fig. 15.
3. Inspect pump gears for nicks, broken parts and other damage.
4. Check clearance between outside diameter of driven gear and pump. Clearance should be .0038-.0068", Fig. 16.
5. Check clearance between outside diameter of drive gear and crescent. Clearance should be .0023-.0093", Fig. 17.
6. Check clearance between inside diameter of driven gear and pump crescent. Clearance should be .0068-.0148", Fig. 18.
7. Check gear end clearance. It should be .0009-.0023", Fig. 19.

NOTE: The pump gears and body are not serviced separately. If pump gears or body are worn, replacement of the entire is necessary.

Fig. 17   Checking drive gear-to-crescent clearance

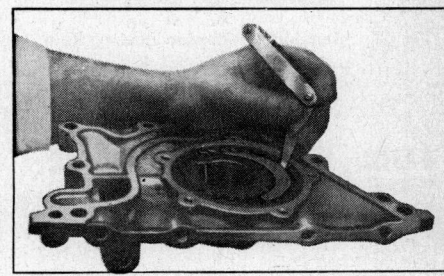

Fig. 18   Checking driven gear-to-crescent clearance

are replaced, shimming may be necessary. Laminated shims for each cap are available for service. Shim requirements will be determined by bearing clearance.

OIL PAN

1. Raise vehicle on a hoist and drain engine oil.
2. Support front of engine so weight is off front mounts, and remove frame crossmember and both front crossmember braces.
3. Disconnect idler arm at frame side rail.

NOTE: On air conditioned vehicles, disconnect idler arm at relay rod.

4. Mark relationship of steering linkage pitman arm to steering gear pitman shaft and remove pitman arm.

NOTE: Do not rotate steering gear pitman shaft while arm is disconnected as this will change steering wheel alignment.

5. Remove flywheel cover or converter underpan.
6. Remove oil pan to cylinder case screws, tap pan lightly to break sealing bond and remove oil pan.
7. Remove pick up screen to baffle support bolts, then remove support from baffle.
8. Remove bolt securing oil pan drain back tube to baffle. Then rotate baffle 90 degrees towards left side of car and remove baffle from pick up screen, Fig. 14.

BELT TENSION DATA

1971-75—	New Lbs.	Used Lbs.
Air Condition	135-145	95
A.I.R. Pump	120-130	75
Generator	120-130	75
Power Steering	120 130	75
Timing Belt	100-140	—

WATER PUMP, REPLACE

1. Raise hood to fully open position and install hold-open bolt.
2. Disconnect battery ground cable at

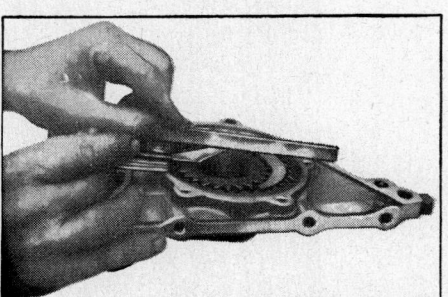

Fig. 19   Checking gear end clearance

battery.
3. Remove engine fan and spacer.
4. Loosen, but do not remove, the two cover lower screws. Cover is slotted to permit easy removal.
5. Remove the two cover upper retaining screws and remove cover.
6. Drain coolant and loosen water pump bolts to relieve tension in timing belt.
7. Remove radiator lower hose and heater hose at water pump.
8. Unfasten and remove water pump.

TIMING BELT TENSION, ADJUST

1. Drain coolant at engine block and remove fan and extension.
2. Remove engine front cover.
3. Remove water pump retaining bolts, clean gasket surfaces on block and pump. Install new gasket and loosely install water pump bolts.

NOTE: Apply an approved anti-seize compound to the water pump bolts before installation.

4. Position tool J-23564 in gauge hole adjacent to left side of pump, Fig. 20.
5. Apply 15 ft. lbs. of torque to water pump as shown in Fig. 21. Tighten water pump bolts while maintaining torque on side of pump.
6. Reinstall front cover, fan, extension and fill cooling system.

Fig. 20   Tensioning adapter locating hole

Fig. 21   Adjusting timing belt

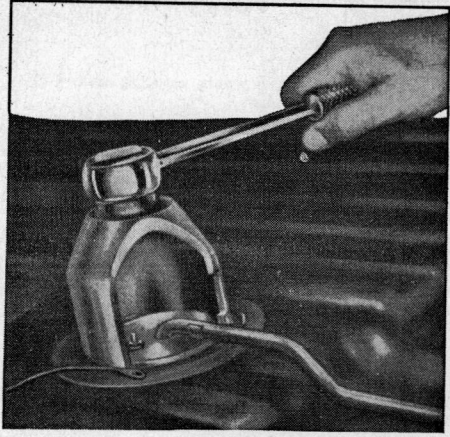

Fig. 22   Removing fuel pump and gauge unit

FUEL PUMP PRESSURE

Year	Engine	Pressure, Lbs.
1971-75	All	3-4½

FUEL PUMP, REPLACE

Removal

1. Disconnect battery ground cable.
2. Disconnect meter and pump wires at rear wiring harness connector.
3. Raise vehicle on hoist and drain fuel tank.
4. Disconnect fuel line hose at gauge unit pick up line.
5. Disconnect tank vent lines to vapor separator.
6. Remove gauge ground wire screw at underbody floorpan.
7. Remove tank straps bolts and lower tank carefully.
8. Unscrew retaining ring using spanner wrench J-22554, Fig. 22, and remove pump-tank unit assembly.

Replacement

1. Remove flat wire conductor from plastic clip on fuel tube.
2. Squeeze clamp and pull pump straight back about ½ inch.
3. Remove two nuts and lockwashers and conductor wires from pump terminals.
4. Squeeze clamp and pull pump straight back to remove it from tank unit. Take care to prevent bending of circular support bracket.
5. Slide replacement pump through circular support bracket until it rests against rubber coupling. Make sure pump has rubber isolator and saran strainer attached.
6. Attach two conductor wires to pump terminals using lockwashers and nuts being certain flat conductor is attached to terminal located on side away from float arm.
7. Squeeze clamp and push pump into rubber coupling.
8. Replace flat wire conductor in plastic clip on fuel pick up tube.
9. Install unit into tank and replace fuel tank.

Clutch & Transmission Section

CLUTCH PEDAL, ADJUST

Initial adjustment after clutch and/or cable replacement is made at two points, at the ball stud and the lower end of the cable.

1. Ball stud adjustment is made before attaching the cable as follows: using gauge J-23644, place it so flat end is against the front face of the clutch housing and the hooked end is located at the point of cable attachment on the fork, Fig. 1.
2. Turn ball stud inward until clutch release bearing lightly contacts the clutch spring levers, then install the lock nut and tighten being careful not to change the adjustment. Remove the gauge by pulling outward at the housing end.
3. To adjust the cable, place it through the hole in the fork and pull it until the clutch pedal is firmly against the rubber bumper.
4. Push the clutch fork forward until the throwout bearing lightly con-

Fig. 1   Clutch adjusting gauge in place

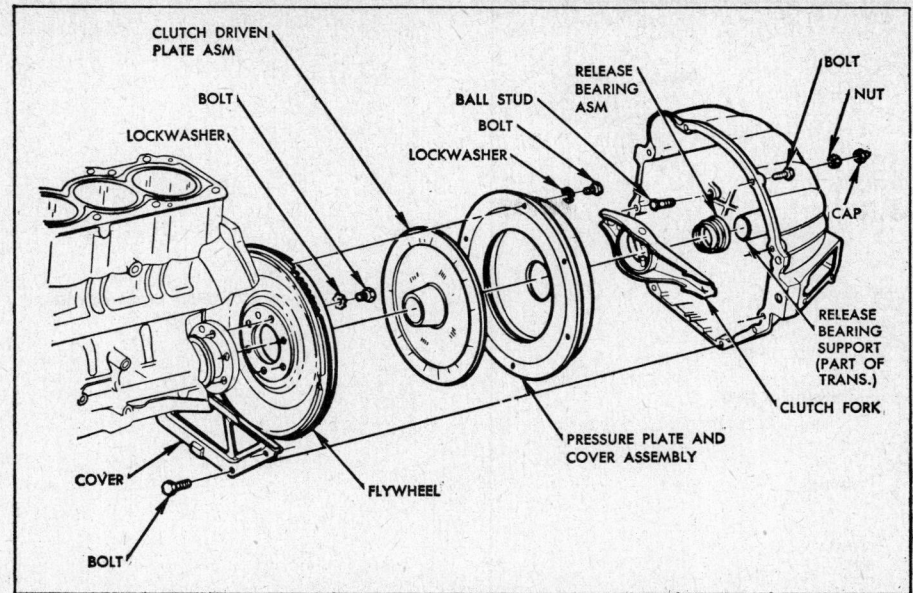

Fig. 2   1971-75 clutch & housing

Fig. 3   Gearshift lever installation

tacts the clutch spring levers, then screw the lock pin on the cable until it bottoms out on the fork. Turn it ¼ additional clockwise revolution, set pin into groove in the fork and attach return spring. This procedure will produce .90" lash at the pedal. Adjustment for normal clutch wear is accomplished by loosening the lock nut and by turning the clutch fork ball stud counterclockwise until .90" of free play is obtained at the pedal.

CLUTCH REPLACE

1. Remove transmission.
2. Remove clutch fork cover then disconnect clutch return spring and control cable from clutch fork.
3. On 1971-72 vehicles, remove main drive gear oil seal from clutch release bearing sleeve.
4. On all vehicles, remove flywheel housing lower cover and flywheel housing, Fig. 2.
5. Remove release bearing from the clutch fork and sleeve by sliding lever off ball stud and against spring force. If ball stud is to be replaced, remove cap, lock nut and stud from housing.
6. Make sure alignment marks on clutch assembly and flywheel are distinguishable.
7. Loosen clutch cover to flywheel bolts one turn at a time until spring pressure is released, to avoid bending the clutch cover flange.
8. Support the pressure plate and cover assembly while removing bolts and clutch assembly.

NOTE: Do not disassemble the clutch cover, spring and pressure plate for repairs. If defective replace complete assembly.

9. Reverse procedure to install making sure to index alignment marks.
10. After installing crossmember, loosely install retaining bolts, then the crossmember to transmission mount bolts. Tighten all retaining bolts to specifications and remove the engine support.

CAUTION: Check position of engine in front mounts and realign as necessary.

GEARSHIFT

The shift controls for both transmissions are floor mounted, Fig. 3. The shift selector shaft, Fig. 4, located inside the case with the ends extending through the case perpendicular to the mainshaft, has both side to side and angular movement.

Two intermediate shift levers, which select the gear required, are attached to the selector shaft by means of spiral pins. The side movement of the selector shaft allows the intermediate shift levers to pick up the proper shift shaft. The angular movement positions the shift shaft such that the shift forks (attached to shafts by spiral pins) move the synchronizer sleeves to obtain the required gear.

The 4-speed shift control operation is similar to the 3-speed except for the gear shift lever which has a reverse lockout feature, Fig. 5.

TRANSMISSION, REPLACE

1. Place shift lever in neutral and remove shift lever.
2. Raise vehicle on a hoist and drain lubricant.
3. Remove propeller shaft.
4. Disconnect speedo cable, TCS switch and back-up lamp switch.
5. Remove crossmember to transmission mount bolts.

Fig. 4   Shift selector shaft

6. Support engine with an appropriate jack stand and remove crossmember to frame bolts and remove crossmember.
7. Remove transmission to clutch housing upper retaining bolts and install guide pins in holes.
8. Remove lower bolts, then slide transmission rearward and remove from vehicle.

NOTE: Inspect throwout bearing support gasket located beneath lip of support. If necessary, replace gasket before installing transmission.

1975 AUTO. TRANS. LINKAGE, ADJUST

Linkage adjustments for 1975 models are the same as 1974 Turbo Hydra-matic 250 adjustments found in the Automatic Transmission section.

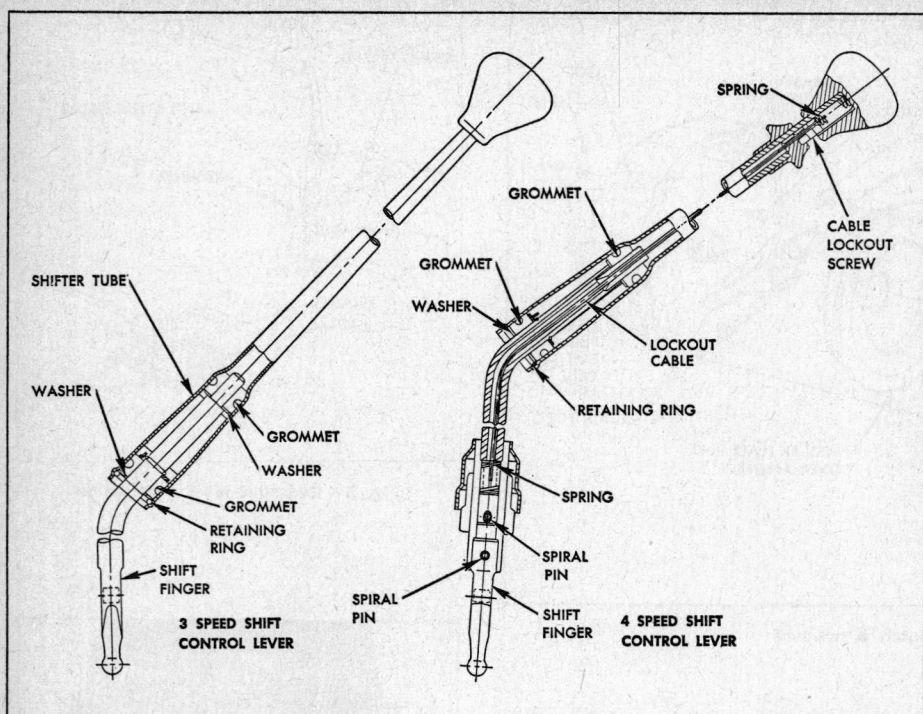

SPRING

GROMMET

GROMMET

WASHER

SHIFTER TUBE

WASHER

GROMMET

WASHER

GROMMET

RETAINING RING

SHIFT FINGER

SPIRAL PIN

3 SPEED SHIFT CONTROL LEVER

CABLE LOCKOUT SCREW

LOCKOUT CABLE

RETAINING RING

SPRING

SPIRAL PIN

SHIFT FINGER

4 SPEED SHIFT CONTROL LEVER

Fig. 5 Shift control lever cross section

Rear Axle, Propeller Shaft & Brakes

REAR AXLE
Description

The rear axle, Fig. 1, is a semi-floating type consisting of a cast carrier and large bosses on each end into which two welded steel tubes are fitted. The carrier contains an overhung hypoid pinion and ring gear. The differential is a two pinion arrangement.

The overhung hypoid drive pinion is supported by two preloaded tapered roller bearings. The pinion shaft is sealed by means of a molded, spring loaded, rubber seal. The seal is mounted on the pinion shaft flange which is splined and bolts to the hypoid pinion shaft.

The ring gear is bolted to a one piece differential case and is supported by two preloaded tapered roller bearings.

Removal

1. Raise vehicle on a hoist.
2. Place adjustable lifting device under axle.
3. Disconnect rear shock absorbers from axle and remove propeller shaft.
4. Disconnect upper control arm from axle and remove both rear wheels.
5. Remove right and left brake drums.
6. Disconnect brake lines from clips on axle tubes.
7. Remove differential cover and drain lubricant.
8. Unscrew differential lock screw, remove pinion shaft and axle shaft "C" locks. Reinstall pinion shaft and tighten lock screw to retain differential gears, Fig. 2.
9. Remove both axle shafts.
10. Remove brake backing plate retaining nuts and remove backing plates, with shoes anad brake lines attached, and wire to frame.
11. Remove right and left lower control arm pivot bolts at axle.
12. Lower axle assembly slowly until coil spring tension is released, then re-

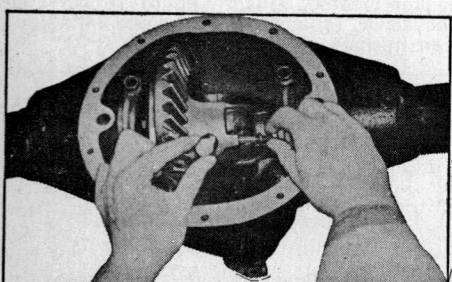

Fig. 2 Differential pinion shaft removal

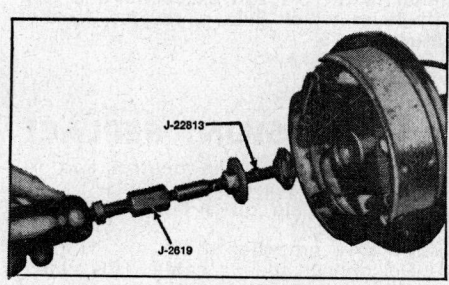

J-22813

J-2619

Fig. 3 Removing wheel bearing and seal

Fig. 4 Installation seal and wheel bearing

move axle.

AXLE SHAFT

1. Raise vehicle on a hoist and remove wheel and tire assembly and brake drum.
2. Drain lubricant from axle by removing carrier cover.
3. Unscrew pinion shaft lock screw and remove pinion shaft, Fig. 2.
4. Push flanged end of axle shaft toward center of car and remove "C" lock from button end of shaft.
5. Remove axle shaft from housing being careful not to damage seal.

Oil Seal &/or Bearing Replacement

1. If replacing seal only, remove the seal by using the button end of axle shaft. Insert the button end of shaft behind the steel case of the seal and pry seal out of bore being careful not to damage housing.
2. If replacing bearings, insert tool J-22813 into bore so tool head grasps behind bearing, Fig. 3. Slide washer against seal, or bearing, and turn nut against washer. Attach slide hammer J-2619 and remove bearing.
3. Pack cavity between seal lips with a high melting point wheel bearing lubricant. Position seal on tool J-21491 and position seal in axle housing bore, tap seal in bore just below end of housing, Fig. 4.

PROPELLER SHAFT

1. Raise vehicle on a hoist. Mark relationship of shaft to companion flange and disconnect the rear universal joint by removing trunnion bearing "U" bolts. Tape bearing cups to trunnion to prevent dropping and loss of bearing rollers.
2. Withdraw propeller shaft front yoke from transmission.
3. When installing, be sure to align marks made in removal to prevent driveline vibration.

BRAKE ADJUSTMENTS

Disc brakes are used on the front

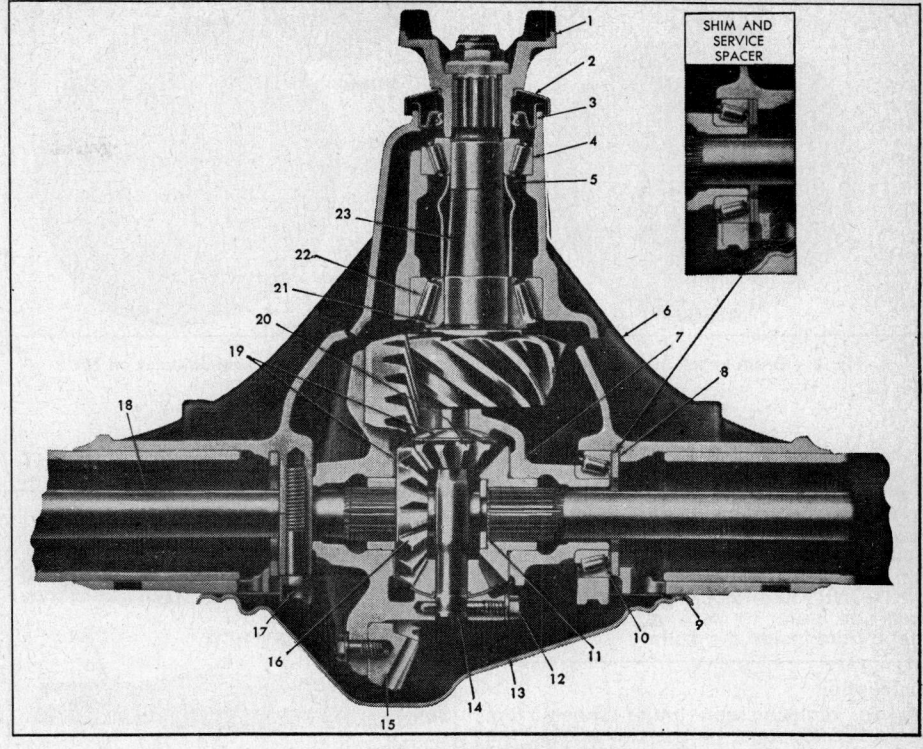

Fig. 1   Rear axle cross section

1. Companion Flange	6. Differential Carrier	11. "C" Lock	15. Ring Gear	20. Differential Pinion
2. Deflector	7. Differential Case	12. Pinion Shaft Lock Bolt	16. Side Gear	21. Shim
3. Pinion Oil Seal	8. Shim	13. Cover	17. Bearing Cap	22. Pinion Rear Bearing
4. Pinion Front Bearing	9. Gasket	14. Pinion Shaft	18. Axle Shaft	23. Drive Pinion
5. Pinion Bearing Spacer	10. Differential Bearing		19. Thrust Washer	

wheels and drum brakes, Fig. 6, are used on the rear wheels. Rear brake adjustment is not automatic. Adjustment takes place, if needed, only when the parking brake is applied. When the parking brake is applied, the strut is pushed against the front shoe and the rod is pulled against the rear shoe. As the shoes spread, a spring lock mounted within the strut and rod assembly, allows the strut and rod assembly to lengthen. When the parking brake is released, the rod connected to the rear shoe is relaxed and

brake shoe pressure on the drum is released providing running clearance. Clearance is obtained by the difference in the diameter of the rod and the diameter of the hole in the rear shoe.

NOTE: If the brake drum cannot be removed, it will be necessary to release the brake adjuster. To gain access to the adjuster, knock out the lanced area in web of brake drum, Fig. 7, using a chisel or similar tool. Release the rod from the trailing shoe by pushing in on

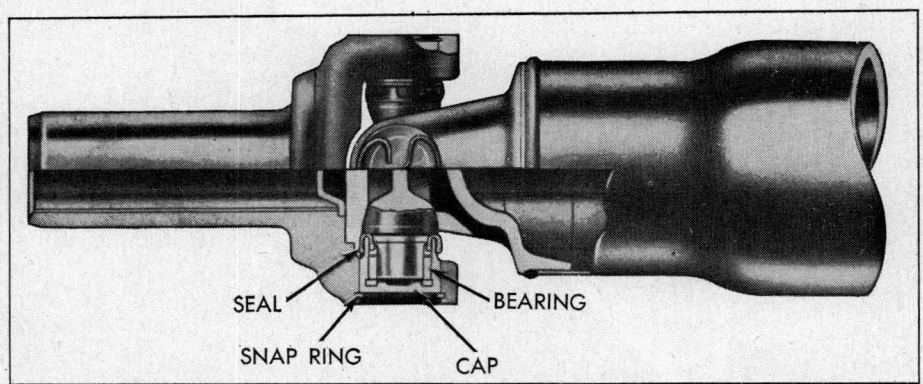

Fig. 5   Propeller shaft cross section

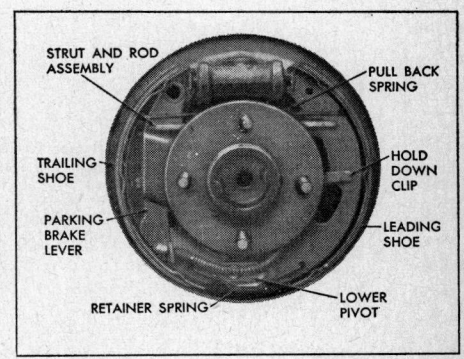

Fig. 6   Rear brake assembly

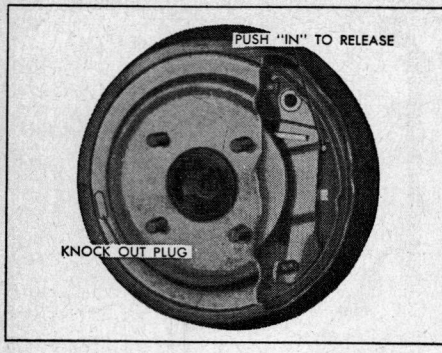

Fig. 7   Drum knock out provision

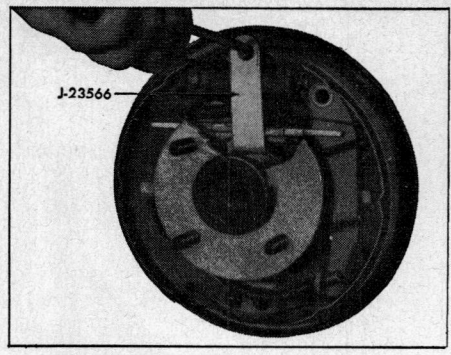

Fig. 8   Releasing adjuster on car

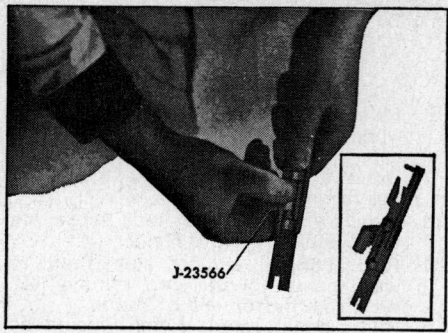

Fig. 9   Releasing adjuster off car

the rod until it is clear of the shoe. The pull back spring will then pull the shoes toward each other and the drum may be removed.

CAUTION: After knocking out the lanced area, be sure to remove the piece of metal from inside the drum.

Installation

1. To replace rear brake shoes, tool J-23566, must be used to release the adjuster, Fig. 8. The adjuster position for new shoes is shown in Fig. 10.

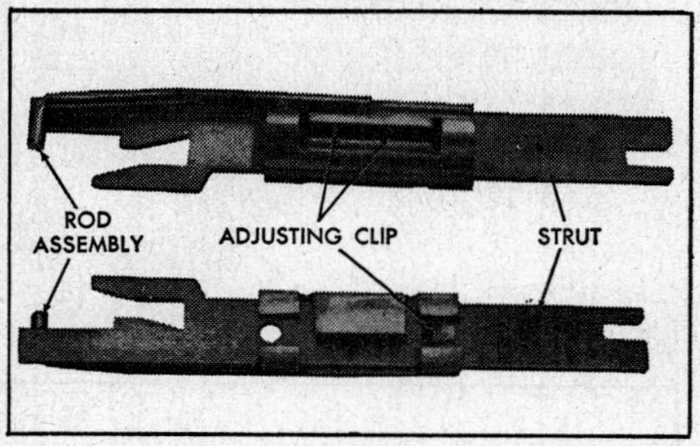

Fig. 10   Adjuster position for new shoes

PARKING BRAKE, ADJUST

1. Place vehicle on a hoist.
2. Apply parking brake one notch from fully released position and raise hoist.
3. Loosen equalizer check nut and tighten the adjusting nut until a slight drag is felt when rear wheels are rotated.
4. Tighten check nut securely.
5. Release parking brake and rotate rear wheels. No drag should be present.

MASTER CYLINDER, REPLACE

1. Disconnect cylinder push rod from brake pedal.
2. Disconnect brake lines from two outlets on cylinder and cover ends of lines to prevent entry of dirt.
3. Unfasten and remove cylinder from dash.

POWER BRAKE UNIT

1975

1. Remove the vacuum hose from check valve and then remove the master cylinder retaining nuts.
2. Remove the bolt securing the brake pipe distributor and switch assembly to fender skirt.
3. Pull master cylinder forward until it just clears mounting studs and move aside. Support cylinder to avoid stress on hydraulic lines.
4. Remove power unit to dash nuts.
5. Remove brake pedal pushrod retainer and disconnect push rod from pin.
6. Remove power unit from vehicle.

Rear Suspension

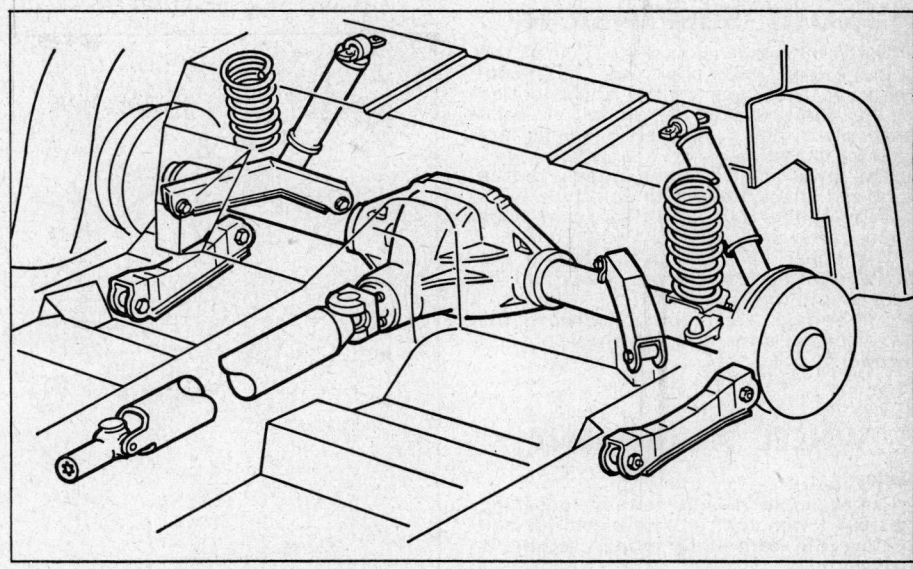

Fig. 1   Rear suspension

SHOCK ABSORBER, REPLACE

1. With the rear axle supported properly disconnect shock absorber from upper and lower mounting, Fig. 1.

   NOTE: Use a wrench to hold lower mounting stud from turning.

2. Reverse procedure to install.

COIL SPRING, REPLACE

1. Support vehicle at frame and rear axle with a suitable jack.
2. Disconnect shock absorbers from lower mountings.
3. Lower rear axle until springs can be removed.
4. Reverse procedure to install.

CONTROL ARMS & BUSHINGS, REPLACE

Upper Control Arms

1. Support vehicle at rear axle.
2. Remove control arm front and rear mount bolts.
3. Replace bushings as necessary, Fig. 2.
4. Reverse procedure to install. Control arm bolts must be tightened with vehicle at curb height.

Lower Control Arms

1. Support vehicle at rear axle.
2. Disconnect stabilizer bar, if used, from lower arms.
3. Remove control arm front and rear mount bolts.
4. Replace bushings as necessary, Fig. 2.
5. Reverse procedure to install. Control arm bolts must be tightened with vehicle at curb height.

STABILIZER BAR, REPLACE

1. Remove bolts securing stabilizer bar to lower control arms, Fig. 3.
2. Reverse procedure to install.

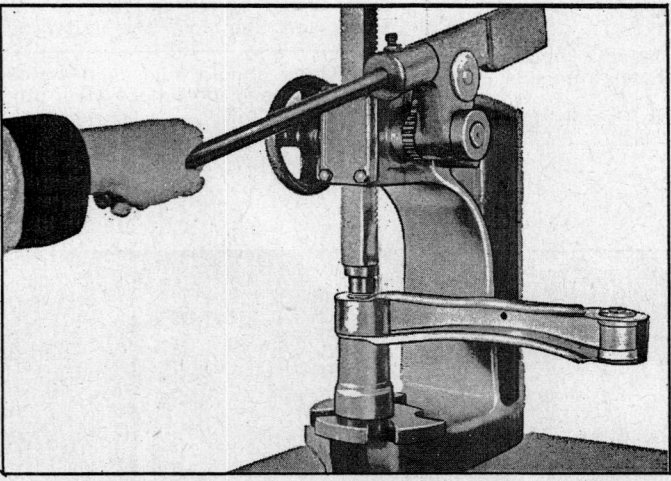

Fig. 2   Control arm bushing replacement

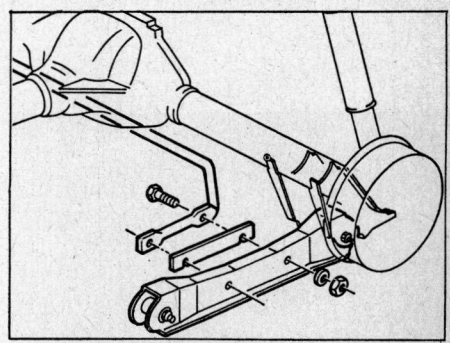

Fig. 3   Stabilizer bar installation

Front End & Steering Section

FRONT SUSPENSION

The front suspension, Fig. 1, is of the A frame type with short and long control arms. The upper control arm is bolted to the front end sheet metal at each inner pivot point. Rubber bushings are used for mounting.

The lower control arms attach to the front end sheet metal with cam type bolts through rubber bushings. The cam bolts adjust caster and camber.

The upper ball joint is riveted in the upper arm and the lower ball joint is pressed into the lower arm.

Coil springs are mounted between the lower control arms and the shock absorber tower.

WHEEL ALIGNMENT

Caster

Caster angle is adjusted by loosening the rear lower control arm pivot nut and rotating the cam until proper setting is reached.

NOTE: This eccentric cam action will tend to move the lower control arm fore or aft thereby varying the caster. Hold the cam bolt while tightening the nut.

Camber

Camber angle is adjusted by loosening the front lower control arm pivot nut and rotating the cam until setting is reached.

NOTE: This eccentric cam action will move the lower arm in or out thereby varying the setting. Hold the cam bolt head while tightening the nut.

TOE-IN, ADJUST

1. Loosen clamp bolt nut at each end of each tie rod and rotate the sleeve until proper toe-in is reached.
2. Position tie rod ball stud assembly straight on a center line through their attaching points.
3. Tighten clamp nuts.

WHEEL BEARINGS, ADJUST

1. With wheel raised, remove hub cap, dust cap and cotter pin from end of spindle.
2. While rotating wheel, tighten spindle nut to 12 ft. lbs.
3. Back off adjusting nut one flat and insert cotter pin. If slot and pin hole do not line up, back off the adjusting nut an additional $\frac{1}{2}$ flat or less as required to insert cotter pin.
4. Spin wheel to check that it rolls freely and then lock the cotter pin.

NOTE: Bearing should have zero preload and .001-.008" end movement when properly adjusted.

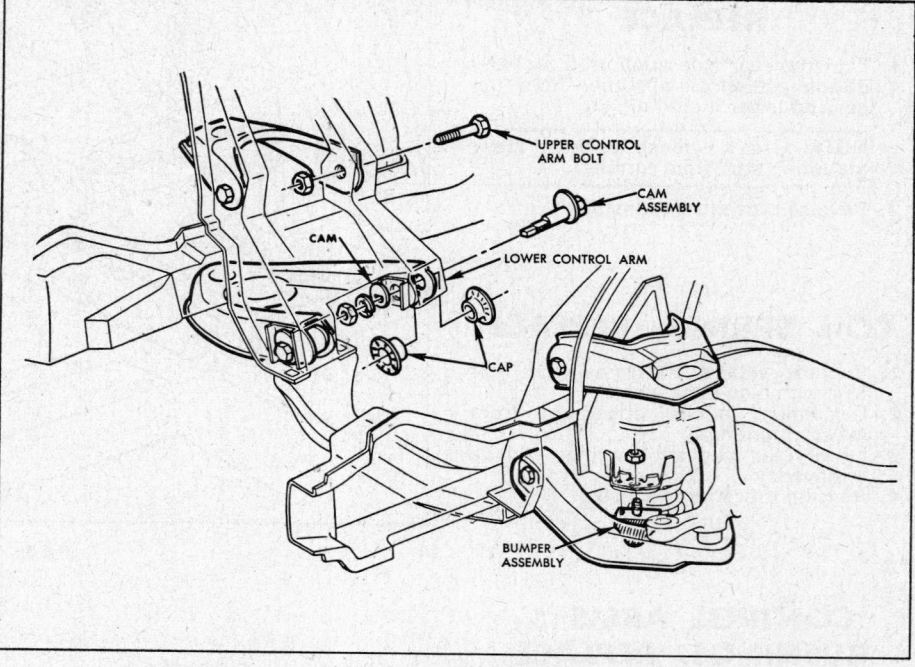

Fig. 1   Front suspension

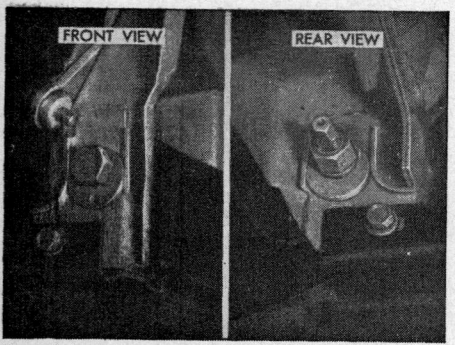

Fig. 2   Caster and camber adjustment

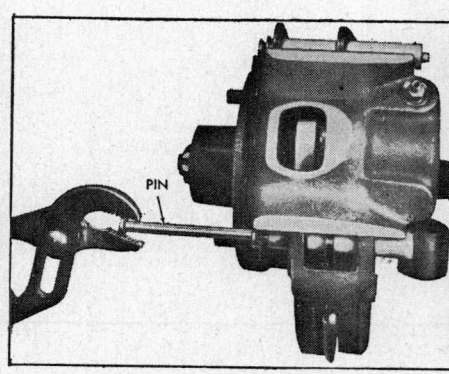

Fig. 3   Removing caliper mounting pins

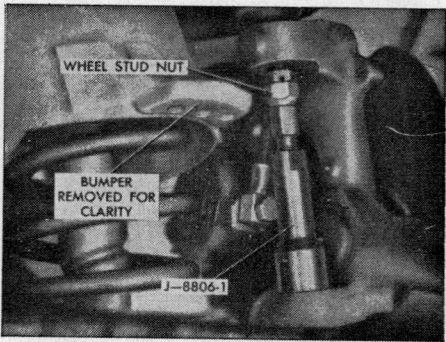

Fig. 4   Removing upper ball joint stud from knuckle

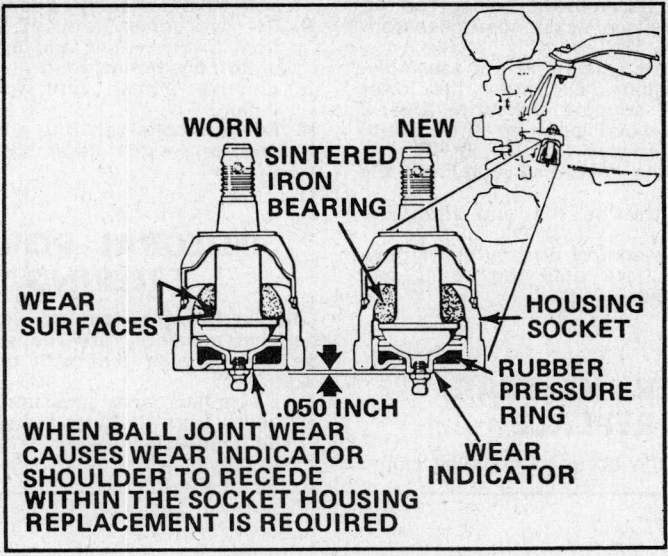

Fig. 3A Lower ball joint wear indicator

WORN   NEW
SINTERED IRON BEARING
WEAR SURFACES
HOUSING SOCKET
RUBBER PRESSURE RING
.050 INCH
WEAR INDICATOR
WHEN BALL JOINT WEAR CAUSES WEAR INDICATOR SHOULDER TO RECEDE WITHIN THE SOCKET HOUSING REPLACEMENT IS REQUIRED

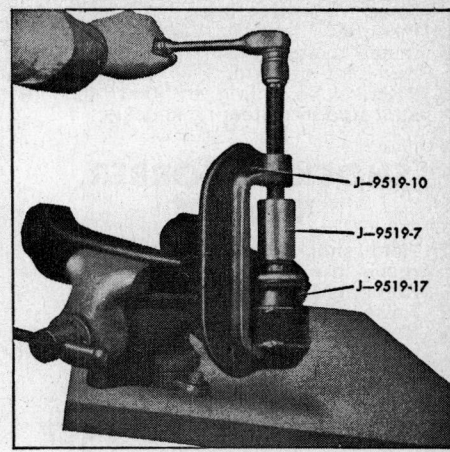

Fig. 5 Removing lower ball joint

WHEEL BEARINGS, REPLACE

1. Raise vehicle on a hoist and remove the wheel and tire assembly.
2. Remove the brake caliper from the disc by removing the mounting pins and stamped nuts, Fig. 3.
3. Remove hub grease cap, cotter pin, spindle nut and washer and remove hub and bearings.
4. Remove inner bearing by prying out the grease seal.

CHECKING BALL JOINTS FOR WEAR

Upper Ball Joint

The upper ball joint is checked for wear by checking the torque required to rotate the ball joint stud in the assembly. This is done after first dislodging the ball joint from the steering knuckle.

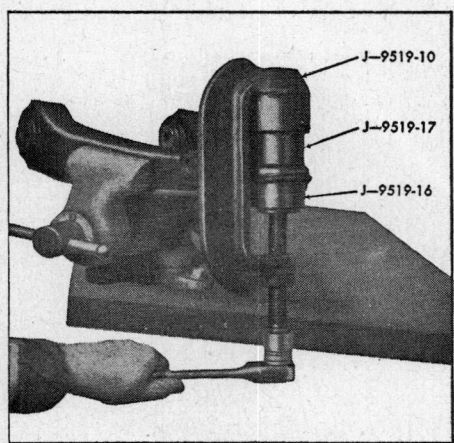

Fig. 6 Installing lower ball joint

1. Install the stud nut to the ball stud. in the seat.
2. Check the torque required to turn the ball stud.

NOTE: Specified torque for a new joint is 2 to 4 ft. lbs. rotating torque. If readings are excessively high or low, replace the joint.

Lower Ball Joint

NOTE: All 1975 vehicles use lower ball joints incorporating wear indicators, Fig. 3A.

The lower ball joint is checked for wear by checking to be sure torque is present. After dislodging ball joint from steering knuckle perform the following:
1. Install the stud nut to the ball stud.
2. Check the torque required to turn the ball stud in the seat.

NOTE: Some torque is required, if zero torque is observed, sufficient wear has taken place for replacement of the ball joint.

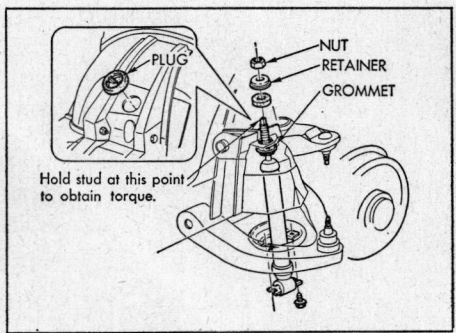

Fig. 7 Front shock absorber mountings

PLUG
NUT
RETAINER
GROMMET
Hold stud at this point to obtain torque.

UPPER BALL JOINT, REPLACE

1. Raise vehicle on a hoist and remove wheel and tire assembly.
2. Support lower control arm with a floor jack.
3. Remove upper ball stud nut and re-move ball stud from knuckle, Fig. 4.
4. Remove control arm pivot bolts and remove control arm.
5. Grind off rivets securing ball joint to arm.
6. Install new ball joint using bolts and nuts supplied in kit.

LOWER BALL JOINT, REPLACE

1. Place vehicle on hoist and support lower control arm at outer end on a jack.
2. Free lower ball stud from knuckle.
3. Using tool shown in Fig. 5, press ball joint out of control arm.
4. Position new ball joint so that grease

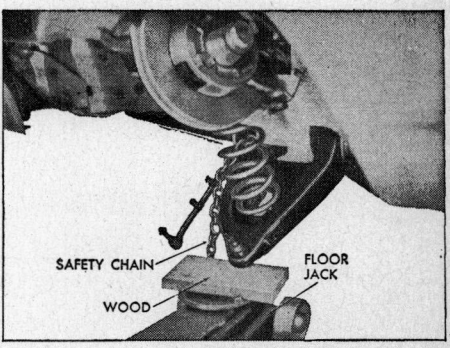

Fig. 8 Removing front coil spring

SAFETY CHAIN
WOOD
FLOOR JACK

bleed vent in rubber boot is facing inboard.
5. Install tool shown in Fig. 6 and press new joint into arm.
6. Install lube fitting in joint and install stud into steering knuckle.

SHOCK ABSORBER, REPLACE

1. Hold shock absorber stem and remove the nut, upper retainer and rubber grommet, Fig. 7.
2. Raise vehicle on a hoist.
3. Remove bolts from lower end of shock absorber and lower the shock from the vehicle.

COIL SPRING, REPLACE

1. With shock absorber removed and stabilizer bar removed, raise the vehicle and place jackstands under front braces.
2. Remove the wheel and tire assembly.
3. Place a floor jack under the lower arm and support the arm. Use a block of wood between the control arm and the jack, Fig. 8.
4. Remove the lower ball stud from the knuckle.
5. Remove the tie rod end from the knuckle.
6. Lower the control arm by slowly lowering the jack until the spring can be removed.

STEERING GEAR, REPLACE

1. Remove the pot joint coupling clamp bolt at the steering gear wormshaft.
2. Remove pitman arm nut and washer from pitman shaft and mark relation of arm position to shaft.
3. Remove pitman arm with suitable puller.
4. Remove bolts securing gear to frame and remove gear assembly.

INTEGRAL POWER STEERING

Replacement procedures for removing the gear assembly are the same as for the manual type gear with the following additions:
1. Disconnect both pressure and return hoses from the gear housing and cap both hoses and steering gear outlets to prevent entry of dirt.

CHEV. MONZA 2+2
BUICK SKYHAWK · OLDS STARFIRE

OLD CAR SPECIFICATIONS: For 1946-68 Tune Up and Wheel Alignment Specifications see main index.

INDEX OF SERVICE OPERATIONS

ACCESSORIES

PAGE NO.

Air Conditioning 2-20
Automatic Level Controls 2-39
Blower Motor, Remove 1-253
Clock Troubles 2-11
Heater Core, Replace 1-253
Power Top Troubles 2-18
Power Window Troubles 2-18
Radio, Replace 1-253

BRAKES

Anti-Skid Brakes 2-162
Brake Troubles, Mechanical 2-17
Disc Brake Service 2-133
Hydraulic System Service 2-123
Master Cylinder, Replace 1-267
Parking Brake, Adjust 1-267
Power Brake Unit, Replace 1-267
Service Brakes, Adjust 1-266

CLUTCH

Clutch Pedal, Adjust 1-264
Clutch, Replace 1-264
Clutch Troubles 2-12

COOLING SYSTEM

Cooling System Troubles 2-6
Variable Speed Fans 2-38
Water Pump, Replace 1-263

ELECTRICAL

Alternator Service 2-69
Blower Motor, Remove 1-253
Clutch Start Switch 1-252
Dash Gauge Service 2-50
Distributor, Replace 1-251
Distributor Service:
  Standard .2-525
  Transistorized 2-535
Electrical Troubles 2-8
Headlamps, Concealed Type 2-46
Headlight Aiming 2-45
Ignition Coils and Resistors 2-521
Ignition Lock, Replace 1-252
Ignition Switch, Replace 1-252
Instrument Panel Pad 1-253
Light Switch, Replace 1-252
Neutral Safety Switch, Replace 1-252
Seat Belt Interlock Systems 2-311
Starter Service 2-54
Starter, Replace 1-251
Starter Switch Service 2-67
Stop Light Switch, Replace 1-252
Turn Signal Switch, Replace 1-252
Turn Signal Troubles 2-11
Windshield Wiper Motor, Replace 1-254
Windshield Wiper Troubles 2-19

ENGINE

PAGE NO.

Camshaft Cover 1-257
Camshaft, Replace 1-257
Camshaft Sprocket 1-258
Crankshaft Sprocket 1-258
Cylinder Head, Replace 1-255
Engine Front Cover 1-257
Engine Identification 1-246
Engine, Replace 1-254
Engine Mounts, Replace 1-254
Engine Troubles 2-1
Main Bearings 1-259
Piston and Rod, Assemble 1-259
Pistons 1-259
Rocker Arms .1-255
Rocker Arm Studs 1-255
Rod Bearings 1-259
Timing Belt 1-258
Timing Chain .1-257
Valves, Adjust 1-256
Valve Arrangement 1-256
Valve Guides .1-257
Valve Lifters .1-257

ENGINE LUBRICATION

Emission Control Systems 2-545
Oil Pan, Replace 1-260
Oil Pump 1-260

FUEL SYSTEM

Carburetor Adjustments and Specs. 2-372
Emission Control Systems 2-545
Fuel Pressure 1-263
Fuel Pump, Replace 1-263
Fuel Pump Service 2-369
Fuel System Troubles 2-2

PROPELLER SHAFT & U JOINTS

Propeller Shaft 1-266
Universal Joint Service 2-117

REAR AXLE & SUSPENSION

Axle Shaft, Bearing and Seal 1-265
Control Arms & Bushings, Replace 1-268
Coil Springs, Replace 1-268
Rear Axle Description 1-265
Rear Axle Specifications 1-249
Rear Axle Troubles 2-16
Shock Absorber, Replace 1-268
Stabilizer Bar, Replace 1-268

SPECIFICATIONS

Alternator 1-249
Belt Tension Data 1-263
Brakes 1-248

PAGE NO.

Capacities 1-250
Carburetors .2-372
Cooling System 1-250
Crankshaft and Bearings 1-250
Distributors 1-248
Engine Tightening Torque 1-250
Fuel Pump Pressure 1-263
General Engine Specs. 1-246
Ignition Coils and Resistors 2-521
Pistons, Rings and Pins 1-250
Rear Axle 1-249
Starting Motors 1-249
Tune Up 1-247
Valve Lift Specs. 1-257
Valve Timing .1-257
Valves 1-248
Wheel Alignment 1-251

STEERING GEAR

Horn Sounder Removal 1-253
Ignition Lock, Replace 1-252
Mechanical Gear, Replace 1-274
Mechanical Gear Service 2-170
Mechanical Gear Troubles 2-17
Power Gear, Replace 1-274
Steering Wheel, Replace 1-253

SUSPENSION, FRONT

Ball Joints, Replace 1-272
Ball Joints, Check for Wear 1-272
Coil Spring, Replace 1-273
Shock Absorber, Replace 1-273
Suspension, Description of 1-271
Toe-In, Adjust 1-271
Wheel Alignment, Adjust 1-271
Wheel Bearings, Adjust 1-271
Wheel Bearings, Replace 1-272

TRANSMISSIONS

Four Speed Manual:
  Repairs 2-199
  Replace 1-264
Automatic Units 2-231
  Linkage, 1975 1-265

TUNE UP

Service 2-517
Specifications 1-247

WINDSHIELD WIPER

Wiper Arms, Replace 1-254
Wiper Blades, Replace 1-253
Wiper Motor, Replace 1-254
Wiper Switch, Replace 1-253
Wiper Troubles 2-19

SERIAL NUMBER LOCATION

On top of instrument panel, left front.

ENGINE NUMBER LOCATION

4 Cyl: On pad at right side of cylinder block, above starter.

ENGINE INDENTIFICATION CODE

Engines are identified in the following table by the code letter or letters immediately following the engine serial number.

Code

1975
4-410③ . . . . CAM, CAR, CAS
4-140 . . . . CAT, CBB, CBC
V6-231 Std. Tr.①④ . . . . FP
V6-231 Auto Tr.①④ . . . . FR
V6-231 Auto Tr.②④ . . . . FS

Code

V8-262 Std. Tr.③ . . . . CZA, CZB, CZC
V8-262 Std. Tr.③ . . . . CZD, CZT, CZU
V8-262 Auto. Tr.③ . . . . CZE, CZG
V8-262 Auto. Tr.③ . . . . CGA, CGJ, CGK

①—Except California.
②—California.
③—Monza.
④—Starfire.

GRILLE IDENTIFICATION

1975 Chevrolet Monza 2+2

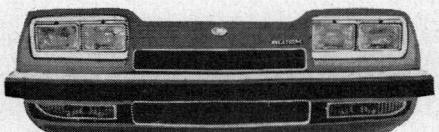

1975 Buick Skyhawk

1975 Oldsmobile Starfire

GENERAL ENGINE SPECIFICATIONS

Year	Engine	Carburetor	Bore and Stroke	Piston Displacement, Cubic Inches	Compression Ratio	Maximum Brake H.P. @ R.P.M.	Maximum Torque Lbs. Ft. @ R.P.M.	Normal Oil Pressure Pounds
1975	Horsepower 4-140	2 Barrel	3.5 x 3.625	140	8.0	—	—	40
	110 Horsepower V6-231	2 Barrel	3.8 x 3.4	231	8.0	110 @ 4000	175 @ 2000	37
	Horsepower V8-262	2 Barrel	3.67 x 3.10	262	8.5	—	—	32–40

TUNE UP SPECIFICATIONS

OLD CAR SPECIFICATIONS: For 1946–68 Tune Up Specifications see main index.

★When using a timing light, disconnect vacuum hose or tube at distributor and plug opening in hose or tube so idle speed will not be affected.

●When checking compression, lowest cylinder must be within 80 percent of highest.

▲Before removing wires from distributor cap, determine location of No. 1 wire in cap, as distributor position may have been altered from that shown at the end of this chart.

Year	Spark Plug		Distributor		Ignition Timing★			Carb. Adjustments					
	Type	Gap Inch	Point Gap Inch	Dwell Angle Deg.	Firing Order Fig. ▲	Timing BTDC ①	Mark Fig.	Hot Idle Speed		Air Fuel Ratio		Idle "CO" %	
								Std. Trans.	Auto. Trans.②	Std. Trans.	Auto. Trans.	Std. Trans.	Auto. Trans.
1975													
4-140	R43TSX	.060	—	—	④	③	B	700	750D	—	—	.5	.5
V6-231	R44SX	.060	—	—	A	12°	C	800	700D	—	—	—	—
V8-262	R44TX	.060	—	—	⑤	8°	D	800	600D	—	—	—	—

①—BTDC—Before Top Dead Center.

②—D—Drive.

③—Standard trans. 10°, Automatic trans. 12°.

④—Firing order; 1-3-4-2. Cylinder numbering sequence, front to rear; 1-2-3-4.

⑤—Firing order, 1-8-4-3-6-5-7-2. Cylinder numbering sequence, front to rear; right bank, 2-4-6-8, left bank, 1-3-5-7.

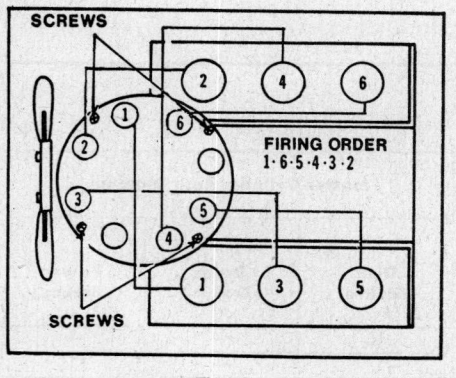

Fig. A

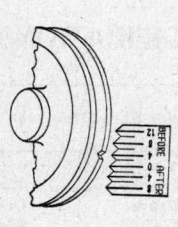

Fig. B

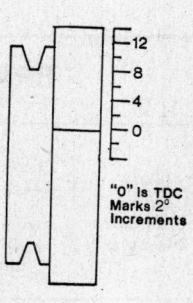

Fig. C

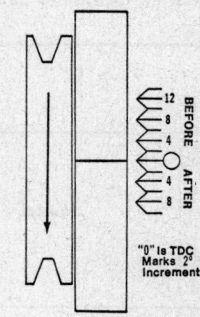

Fig. D

VALVE SPECIFICATIONS

Year	Engine Model	Valve Lash		Valve Angles		Valve Spring Installed Height	Valve Spring Pressure Lbs. @ In.	Stem Clearance		Stem Diameter	
		Int.	Exh.	Seat	Face			Intake	Exhaust	Intake	Exhaust
1975	4-140	.015C	.030C	46	45	1.75	①	.001–.0027	.001–.0027	.3410–.3417	.3410–.3417
	V6-231	Hydraulic		45	—	1.727	168 @ 1.327	.0015–.0032	.0015–.0032	.3405–.3412	.3405–.3412
	V8-262	1 Turn		46	45	②	③	.001–.0027	.001–.0027	.3410–.3417	.3410–.3417

①—Intake 190 @ 1.31, Exhaust 186 @ 1.29.
②—Intake 1.70, Exhaust 1.61.
③—Intake 189 @ 1.20, Exhaust 200 @ 1.25.

DISTRIBUTOR SPECIFICATIONS

★If unit is checked on vehicle double the RPM and degrees to get crankshaft figures.

Distributor Part No.①	Centrifugal Advance Degrees @ RPM of Distributor				Vacuum Advance		Distributor Retard
	Advance Starts	Intermediate Advance		Full Advance	Inches of Vacuum To Start Plunger	Max. Adv. Dist. Deg. @ Vacuum	Max. Ret. Dist. Deg. @ Vacuum
1975							
1112862	0 @ 810	2½ @ 1000	—	11 @ 2200	4	9 @ 12	—
1112933	0 @ 600	4½ @ 1000	—	11 @ 2000	3	8 @ 8	—
V6-231	0 @ 500	5 @ 1000	—	8 @ 2050	6	9 @ 10	—

①—Located on distributor housing plate.

BRAKE SPECIFICATIONS

Year	Model	Brake Drum Inside Diameter	Wheel Cylinder Bore Diameter			Master Cylinder Bore Diameter		
			Disc Brake	Front Drum Brake	Rear Drum Brake	Disc Brakes	Drum Brakes	Power Brakes
1975	Monza	9	1⅞	—	¾	¾	—	—
	Skyhawk, Starfire	9	1⅞	—	¾	1	—	1⅛

ALTERNATOR & REGULATOR SPECIFICATIONS

| Year | Model | Alternator | | Cold Output @ 14 Volts | | Regulator | Field Relay | | | Voltage Regulator | | |
		Rated Hot Output Amps.	Field Current 12 Volts @ 80 F.	2000 R.P.M. Amps.	5000 R.P.M. Amps.	Model	Air Gap In.	Point Gap In.	Closing Voltage	Air Gap In.	Point Gap In.	Voltage @ 125°F.
1975	1100545	32	4–4.5	—	31	Integral	—	—	—	—	—	—
	1100546	55	4–4.5	—	50	Integral	—	—	—	—	—	—
	1100549	32	4–4.5	—	31	Integral	—	—	—	—	—	—
	1100560	55	4–4.5	—	50	Integral	—	—	—	—	—	—
	1102394	37	—	—	—	Integral	—	—	—	—	—	13.6–14.2
	1102495	—	—	—	—	Integral	—	—	—	—	—	13.6–14.2
	1102500	5	4–4.5	—	50	Integral	—	—	—	—	—	—
	1102854	6	4–4.5	—	60	Integral	—	—	—	—	—	—
	1102856	3	4–4.5	—	33	Integral	—	—	—	—	—	—
	1102857	6	4–4.5	—	60	Integral	—	—	—	—	—	—

STARTING MOTOR SPECIFICATIONS

| Year | Model | Starter Number | Brush Spring Tension Oz.[1] | Free Speed Test | | | Resistance Test | |
				Amps.	Volts	R.P.M.[1]	Amps.	Volts
1975	4-140 Std. Trans.	1108771	—	50–75[2]	9	6500–10000	—	—
	4-140 Auto. Trans.	1108772	—	50–75[2]	9	6500–10000	—	—
	V6-231	1108770	35	50–80	9	3500–6000	—	—
	V8-262	1108790	—	50–80[2]	9	3500–6000	—	—

[1]—Minimum.
[2]—Includes solenoid.

REAR AXLE SPECIFICATIONS

| Year | Model | Carrier Type | Ring Gear & Pinion Backlash | | Pinion Bearing Preload | | | Differential Bearing Preload | | |
			Method	Adjustment	Method	New Bearings Inch-Lbs.	Used Bearings Inch-Lbs.	Method	New Bearings Inch-Lbs.	Used Bearings Inch-Lbs.
1975	All	Integral	Shim	.005–.008	Spacer	10–25	8–12	Shim	—	—

PISTONS, PINS, RINGS, CRANKSHAFT & BEARINGS

Year	Engine Model	Piston Clearance	Ring End Gap①		Wrist-pin-Diameter	Rod Bearings		Main Bearings			
			Comp.	Oil		Shaft Diameter	Bearing Clearance	Shaft Diameter	Bearing Clearance	Thrust on Bear. No.	Shaft End Play
1975	4-140	.0018–.0028	②	.010	.9272	1.999–2.000	.0007–.0038	2.2983–2.2993	③	4	.002–.007
	V6-231	.0013–.0035	.010	.015	.9393	2.000	.0005–.0026	2.4995	.0004–.0015	—	.006–.020.
	V8-262	.0007–.0013	④	.015	.9272	2.098–2.099	.0013–.0035	⑤	⑥	—	.002–.007

①—Fit rings in tapered bore for clearance listed in tightest portion of ring travel.
②—#1—.015", #2—.009".
③—#1—.0003–.002, #2, 3, 4 & 5—.0003–.0027.
④—#1—.010", #2—.013".
⑤—#1—2.4484–2.4493, #2, 3 & 4—2.4481–2.4490, #5—2.4479–2.4488.
⑥—#1—.0008–.0020, #2, 3 & 4—.0011–.0023, #5—.0017–.0033.

ENGINE TIGHTENING SPECIFICATIONS★

★Torque specifications are for clean and lightly lubricated threads only. Dry or dirty threads produce increased friction which prevents accurate measurement of tightness.

Year	Engine Model	Spark Plugs Ft. Lbs.	Cylinder Head Bolts Ft. Lbs.	Intake Manifold Ft. Lbs.	Exhaust Manifold Ft. Lbs.	Rocker Arm Stud Ft. Lbs.	Cam Cover Ft. Lbs. ①	Connecting Rod Cap Bolts Ft. Lbs.	Main Bearing Cap Bolts Ft. Lbs.	Flywheel to Crankshaft Ft. Lbs.	Vibration Damper or Pulley Ft. Lbs.
1975	4-140	15	60	30	30	—	35②	35	65	60	80
	V6-231	15	75	45	25	30③	5	40	115	55	—
	V8-262	15	65	30	20④	—	45③	45	70	60	60

①—Rocker arm cover ft. lbs.
②—In. lbs.
③—Rocker arm shaft to cylinder head.
④—Inside bolts 30 ft. lbs.

COOLING SYSTEM & CAPACITY DATA

Year	Model or Engine	Cooling Capacity, Qts.			Radiator Cap Relief Pressure, Lbs.		Thermo. Opening Temp. ①	Fuel Tank Gals.	Engine Oil Refill Qts. ②	Transmission Oil			Rear Axle Oil Pints
		No Heater	With Heater	With A/C	With A/C	No A/C				3 Speed Pints	4 Speed Pints	Auto. Trans. Qts. ③	
1975	4-140	—	7	7½	15	15	195	18½	3	2.4	2.4	④	2¼
	V6-231	—	13¼	13¾	15	15	190	18½	3	—	2½	④	2¾
	V8-262	—	—	—	15	15	195	18½	4	2.4	2.4	④	2¼

①—For permanent type anti freeze.
②—Add 1 qt. with filter change.
③—Approximate. Make final check with dip stick.
④—Refill 3 qts., total capacity 10 qts.

WHEEL ALIGNMENT SPECIFICATIONS

OLD CAR SPECIFICATIONS: For 1946-68 Wheel Alignment Specifications see main index.

Year	Model	Caster Angle, Degrees		Camber Angle, Degrees				Toe-In. Inch	Toe-Out on Turns, Deg.①	
		Limits	Desired	Limits		Desired			Outer Wheel	Inner Wheel
				Left	Right	Left	Right			
1975	Monza	−¼ to −1¼	−¾	−¼ to +¾	−¼ to +¾	+¼	+¼	0 to ⅛	—	—
	Skyhawk	−1¾ to +¼	−¼	0 to 1	0 to 1	+½	+½	3⁄16 to 5⁄16	—	—
	Starfire	−¼ to −1¼	−¾	−¼ to +¾	−¼ to +¾	+¼	+¼	0 to ⅛	—	—

①—Incorrect toe out when other adjustments are correct indicates bent steering arms.

Electrical Section

DISTRIBUTOR

Removal

1. Disconnect wiring connectors from distributor cap.
2. Remove distributor cap and position out of way, then disconnect vacuum advance hose.
3. Scribe a mark on engine in line with rotor, noting approximate position of distributor housing in relation to engine.
4. Remove hold-down nut and clamp and lift distributor from engine. Do not crank engine after distributor is

removed, otherwise the distributor will have to be initially timed to the engine.
5. Install distributor in reverse order of removal, making certain to align scribe marks, then start engine and adjust timing.

STARTER, REPLACE

4-140 & V8-262

1. Disconnect battery ground cable and disconnect all wires at solenoid terminals.

NOTE: Reinstall the nuts on the terminals as each wire is removed, as thread size is different and if mixed, stripping of threads may occur.

2. Loosen starter front bracket and remove the two mounting bolts.
3. Remove from bracket bolt or nut and rotate brace clear of work area, then remove starter from vehicle by lowering front end of starter first.
4. Reverse procedure to install.

V6-231

1. Disconnect battery ground cable.
2. Remove exhaust crossover pipe and transmission flywheel cover.
3. Remove transmission mount bolts, then position adjustable jack under transmission extension housing.
4. Remove right transmission support to underbody bolt, then loosen left bolt and pivot support downward.

Fig. 1   Ignition lock removal

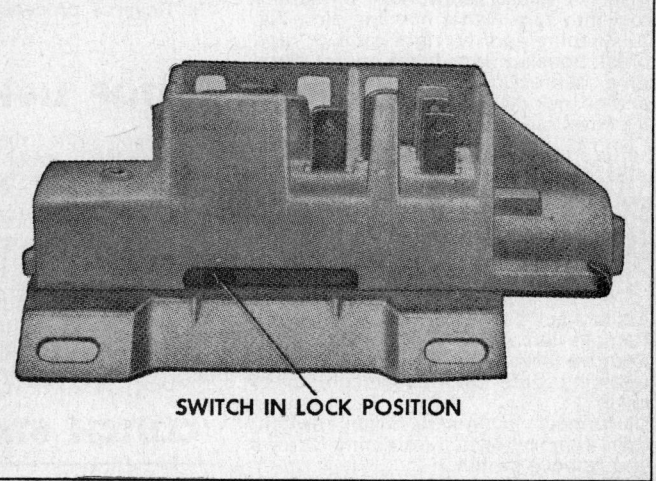

SWITCH IN LOCK POSITION

Fig. 2   Ignition switch assembly

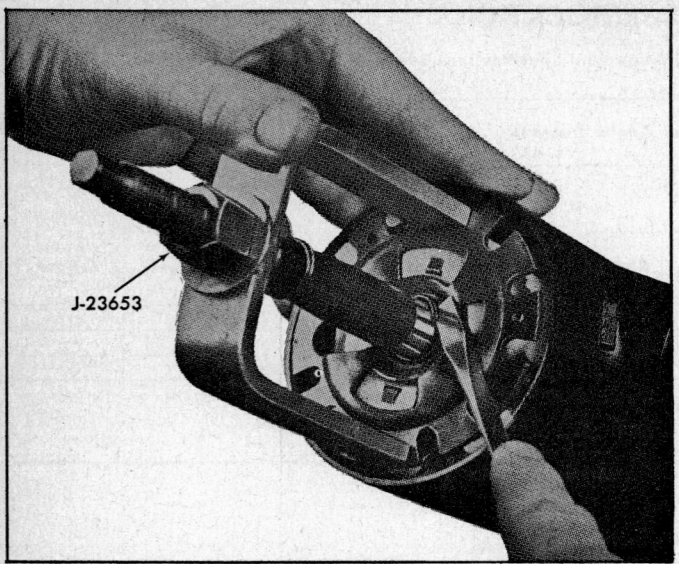

Fig. 3   Compressing lock plate and removing retaining ring

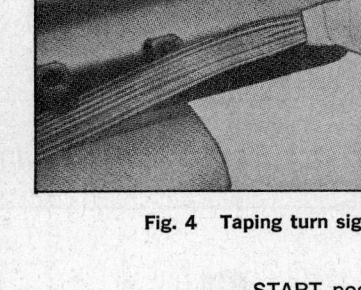

Fig. 4   Taping turn signal connector and wires

5. Lower transmission and disconnect oil cooler lines at transmission.
6. Remove the two starter attaching bolts, then lower starter and disconnect wires and remove starter.
7. Reverse procedure to install.

IGNITION LOCK, REPLACE

1. Remove steering wheel as outlined under "Horn Sounder & Steering Wheel" procedure, then *with ignition lock in "Run" position,* pull directional switch rearward far enough to slip it over end of shaft. Do not pull harness out of column.

NOTE: Do not remove buzzer switch as damage to lock cylinder will result.

2. Insert a small screwdriver or similar tool into turn signal housing slot, Fig. 1. Keeping tool to right side of slot, break housing flash loose and at same time depress spring latch at lower end of lock cylinder.
3. Remove lock cylinder from housing.

IGNITION SWITCH, REPLACE

1. Disconnect battery ground cable.
2. Remove left A/C outlet duct.
3. Remove steering column to support retaining nuts and allow column to lower.
4. Disconnect connector from switch, then remove switch retaining screws and remove switch.
5. Reverse procedure to install with ignition switch in "lock" position, Fig. 2.

NEUTRAL SAFETY SWITCH, REPLACE

1. Disconnect battery ground cable.
2. Remove console cover.
3. Disconnect connector from switch, then remove switch retaining screws and remove switch.
4. Reverse procedure to install and make certain that switch is correctly adjusted.

LIGHT SWITCH, REPLACE

1. Disconnect battery ground cable.
2. Remove left A/C duct if equipped.
3. Reaching under instrument panel, release and pull switch knob and shaft assembly out of switch.
4. Remove switch bezel retaining nut, then disconnect switch connector and remove switch.
5. Reverse procedure to install.

STOP LIGHT SWITCH

1. Reach under right side of instrument panel at brake pedal support and lease wiring harness connector at switch.
2. Pull switch from mounting bracket.
3. When installing switch, adjust by bringing brake pedal to normal position. Electrical contact should be made when pedal is depressed $3/8$ to $5/8$ inch. To adjust, the switch may be rotated or pulled in the clip.

CLUTCH START SWITCH

NOTE: The clutch pedal must be fully depressed and the ignition switch in

START position for the vehicle to start.

The clutch switch assembly mounts with two tangs to the clutch pedal brace switch pivot bracket and the clutch pedal arm.
1. Under the instrument panel on the clutch pedal support remove the multi-contact connector from switch.
2. Compress switch assembly actuating shaft barb retainer and push out of clutch pedal.
3. Compress switch assembly pivot bracket barb and lift off switch.
4. When installing new switch, no adjustments are necessary as the switch is self aligning.

TURN SIGNAL SWITCH, REPLACE

1. Remove steering wheel with suitable puller.
2. Remove three cover screws and lift cover off the shaft. **NOTE:** These screws have plastic retainers on the back of the cover so it is not necessary to completely remove these screws.
3. Place Lock Plate Compressing Tool J-23653, Fig. 3, on end of steering shaft and compress the lock plate as far as possible using the shaft nut as shown. Pry the round wire snap ring out of the shaft groove and discard the ring. Remove tool and lift lock plate off end of shaft.
4. Slide the signal cancelling cam, upper bearing preload spring and thrust washer off the end of shaft.
5. Remove turn signal lever screw and remove the lever.
6. Push hazard warning knob in and unscrew the knob.
7. Wrap upper part of connector with tape, Fig. 4 to prevent snagging of wires during switch removal.
8. Remove three screws on switch and pull switch straight up through housing, Fig. 5.

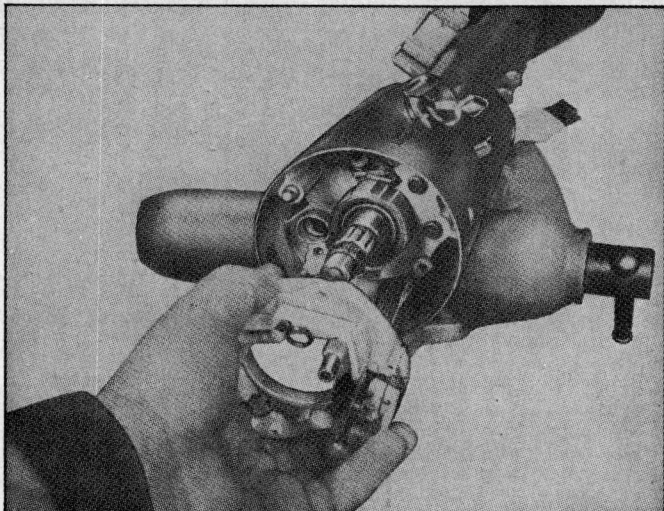

Fig. 5   Removing turn signal switch

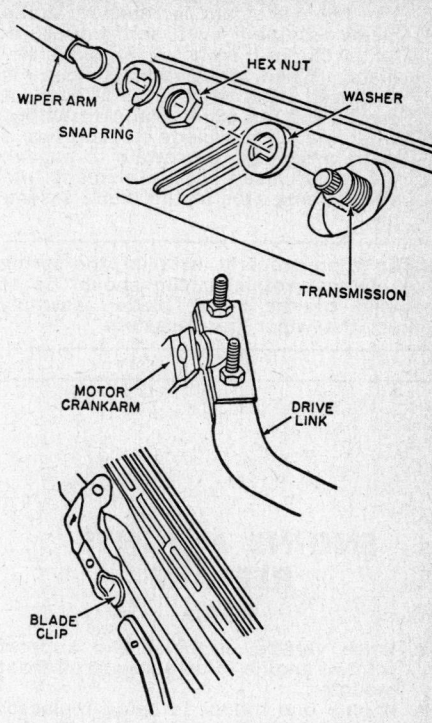

Fig. 6   Wiper blade clip location

HORN SOUNDER & STEERING WHEEL

1. Disconnect battery ground cable.
2. On regular production steering wheel models, remove the two screws securing the steering wheel shroud from beneath the wheel and remove the shroud. On optional wheels models, pry off horn button cap.
3. Remove steering wheel nut and use a suitable puller to remove the steering wheel.

RADIO, REPLACE

Monza & Skyhawk

1. Disconnect battery ground cable.
2. Remove clock stem knob, instrument panel bezel and glove box.
3. Remove instrument panel pad and radio knobs.
4. Remove the two lower screws from radio mounting bracket and remove the left lap cooler and duct, if equipped with A/C.
5. Remove two nuts from steering column mounting bracket, three screws from top of instrument panel and three bolts from instrument panel carrier reinforcement.

CAUTION: The two steering column mounting nuts are important attaching parts as they could affect the operation of the collapsible steering column. If replacement becomes necessary, they must be replaced with one of the same or equivalent part number. Also, the 15-25 ft. lb. torque must be adhered to.

6. Disconnect speedometer cable from instrument cluster, then pull complete instrument panel slightly forward and disconnect all electrical leads and antenna.
7. Remove radio from instrument panel.
8. Reverse procedure to install.

Starfire

1. Remove instrument panel pad and instrument cluster.
2. Remove radio knobs, escutcheons, washers and nuts, then remove radio support to lower dash screw.
3. Disconnect all electrical leads and antenna from radio and remove radio through instrument cluster opening.
4. Reverse procedure to install.

HEATER CORE REMOVAL

1. Disconnect battery ground cable and disconnect blower motor electrical lead.
2. Place a pan under vehicle, then disconnect heater hoses from core and secure hoses in a raised position.
3. Remove blower inlet to dash panel screws and nuts, then remove blower inlet and blower motor and wheel assembly.
4. Remove core retaining strap screws and remove core.
5. Reverse procedure to install making certain that blower inlet sealer is intact, replace as necessary.

BLOWER MOTOR, REPLACE

1. Disconnect battery ground cable and disconnect blower motor electrical leads.
2. Scribe blower motor flange to case position.
3. Remove blower motor retaining screws and remove blower motor and wheel assembly. Pry flange gently, if sealer acts as an adhesive.
4. Reverse removal procedure to install aligning scribe marks made during removal.

INSTRUMENT PANEL PAD

The instrument panel pad must be removed to service all gauges and instruments.
1. Remove glove box, then reaching through glove box opening, remove the four nuts retaining the right side of pad.
2. Remove clock set knob and instrument panel bezel.
3. Remove two screws at top of cluster, then remove four (two on Starfire) screws along lower edge of cover and remove instrument panel pad.
4. Reverse procedure to install.

W/S WIPER SWITCH

1. Disconnect battery ground cable.
2. Remove left A/C duct if equipped, then disconnect headlight from instrument panel.
3. Disconnect electrical connectors from wiper switch and seat belt buzzer and remove wiper switch.
4. Reverse procedure to remove.

W/S WIPER BLADES

1. Remove the wiper blade from the arm by depressing the spring type blade clip, Fig. 6, away from the under side of the arm and slide the arm out of the blade clip.
2. To install wiper blade to wiper arm, slide tip end of arm into blade clip, until pin on tip end of arm engages hole in clip.

3. The blade element is retained in the blade assembly by a spring type retainer clip in the end of the blade element. When the retainer clip is squeezed together, the blade element can be slid out of the blade assembly.
4. When installing a blade element into a blade assembly, be certain to engage the metal insert in the element into all retaining tabs of the blade assembly.

NOTE: When properly installed, the spring type element retaining clip should be at the end of the wiper blade assembly nearest the wiper transmission.

W/S WIPER ARMS

1. Wiper motor must be in park position.
2. Use suitable tool to minimize the possibility of windshield or paint finish damage during arm removal.
3. Remove arm by prying up with tool to disengage arm from serrated transmission shaft.
4. To install arm to transmission shaft rotate the required distance and direction so that blades rest in proper parked position.

CAUTION: The parked position for the left blade tip is approx. 2" above lower windshield reveal mounting and the right blade tip within 2" of the lower windshield reveal moulding.

W/S WIPER MOTOR

1. Raise hood.
2. Reaching through cowl opening, loosen the two transmission drive link attaching nuts to motor crankarm.
3. Remove transmission drive link from motor crankarm.
4. Disconnect wiring and unfasten motor and remove.

Engine Section

ENGINE MOUNTS, REPLACE

4-140

1. Raise vehicle on hoist and support front of engine to take weight off front mounts.
2. If only one mount is being replaced, remove the mount-to-engine bracket nut on the mount not being replaced.
3. Remove the stud nut and two bolts securing mount to housing support.
4. Remove the three stud nuts securing the bracket to the engine. On the right side remove the starter brace at starter and on air conditioned equipped vehicles, remove the compressor rear lower brace at the compressor.
5. Raise front of engine to provide maximum clearance without imposing stress on other engine components.

V6-231

1. Raise car and provide frame support at front of car.
2. Support weight of engine at forward edge of pan.
3. Remove mount to engine block bolts. Raise engine slightly and remove mount to mount bracket bolt and nut. Remove mount.
4. Reverse above procedure to install and torque to specifications as shown on Fig. 1.

ENGINE, REPLACE

4-140

1. Raise hood to fully open position and install a bolt through the hood hold-open link to hold hood in wide open position.
2. Disconnect battery positive cable at battery and negative cable at engine block (except on air conditioned vehicles).
3. Drain cooling system and disconnect hoses at radiator. Disconnect heater hoses at water pump and at heater inlet (bottom hose).
4. Disconnect emission system hoses: PCV at cam cover; cannister vacuum hose at carburetor; PCV vacuum at

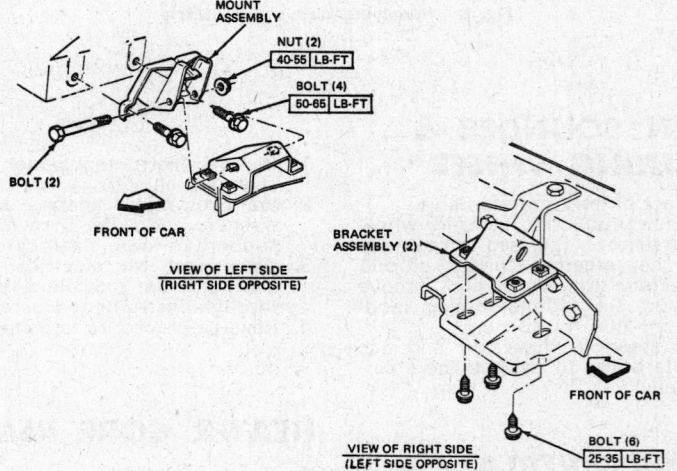

Fig. 1   Engine mounts. V6-231

inlet manifold and bowl vent at carburetor.
5. Remove radiator panel or shroud and remove radiator, fan and spacer.
6. Remove air cleaner, disconnecting vent tube at base of cleaner.
7. Disconnect electrical leads at: Delcotron, ignition coil, starter solenoid, oil pressure switch, engine temperature switch, transmission controlled spark switch at transmission, transmission controlled spark solenoid and engine ground strap at cowl.
8. Disconnect: Automatic transmission throttle valve linkage at manifold mounted bellcrank, fuel line at rubber hose to rear of carburetor, transmission vacuum modulator and air conditioning vacuum line at inlet manifold, accelerator cable at manifold bellcrank.
9. On air conditioned cars, disconnect compressor at front support, rear support, rear lower bracket and remove drive belt from compressor.
10. Move compressor slightly forward and allow front of compressor to rest on frame forward brace, then secure rear of compressor to engine compartment so it is out of way.

11. Disconnect power steering pump, if equipped, and position it out of way.
12. Raise car on a hoist and disconnect exhaust pipe at manifold.
13. Remove engine flywheel dust cover or converter underpan.
14. On automatic transmission cars, remove converter-to-flywheel retaining bolts and nuts and install coverter safety strap.
15. Remove converter housing or flywheel housing-to-engine retaining bolts.
16. Loosen engine front mount retaining bolts at frame attachment and lower vehicle.
17. Install floor jack under transmission.
18. Install suitable engine lifting equipment and raise engine slightly to take weight from engine mounts and remove engine front mount retaining bolts.
19. Remove engine and pull forward to clear transmission while slowly lifting engine from car.

V6-231

1. Remove hood and drain radiator.
2. Remove fan shroud, radiator and air cleaner.

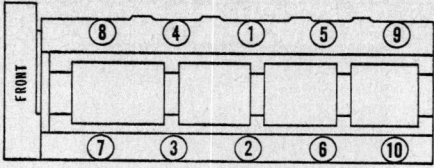

Fig. 2 Cylinder head tightening sequence. 4-140

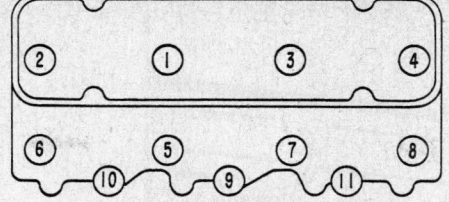

Fig. 3 Cylinder head tightening sequence. V6-231

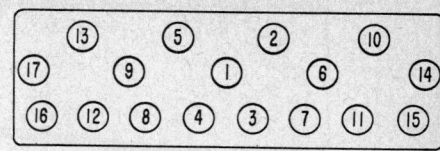

Fig. 4 Cylinder head tightening sequence. V8-262

3. If equipped with A/C, disconnect compressor brackets and position out of way.
4. Remove power steering from bracket and position out of way.
5. Disconnect all hoses, linkages and electrical connections from engine.
6. Disconnect exhaust pipes and remove converter cover.
7. Remove flywheel to converter or pressure plate bolts, engine to transmission bolts and motor mount bolts.
8. Support transmission and remove engine.

CYLINDER HEADS

Some cylinder head gaskets are coated with a special lacquer to provide a good seal once the parts have warmed up. Do not use any additional sealer on such gaskets. If the gasket does not have this lacquer coating, apply suitable sealer to both sides.

4-140

1. Remove engine front cover and camshaft cover as outlined further on.
2. Remove timing belt and camshaft sprocket.
3. Remove intake and exhaust manifolds.
4. Disconnect hose at thermostat housing.
5. Remove cylinder head bolts and with the aid of an assistant lift head and gasket from engine. Place head on

two blocks of wood to prevent damage to valves.
6. Reverse procedure to install and tighten head bolts in sequence shown in Fig. 2.

V6-231

1. Drain coolant and disconnect battery.
2. Remove intake manifold.
3. When removing right cylinder head, remove Delcotron and/or A/C compressor with mounting bracket and move out of the way. Do not disconnect hoses from air compressor.
4. When removing left cylinder head, remove oil dipstick, power steering pump and move out of the way with hoses attached.
5. Disconnect exhaust manifold from head to be removed.
6. Remove rocker arm shaft and lift out push rods.
7. Remove cylinder head.
8. Reverse procedure to install and tighten bolts gradually and evenly to specifications and in order shown in Fig. 3.

V8-262

1. Remove intake and exhaust manifolds.
2. Remove rocker arm covers.
3. Back off rocker arm nuts, pivot rocker arms to clear push rods and remove push rods.
4. Unfasten and remove cylinder heads.

5. Reverse procedure to install and tighten head bolts in sequence shown in Fig. 4.

ROCKER ARMS

V6-231

A nylon retainer is used to retain the rocker arms. Break them below their heads with a chisel, Fig. 5, or pry out with channel locks. Production rocker arms can be installed in any sequence since the arms are identical, however, replacement arms are identified with a stamping right (R) and left (L).

ROCKER ARM STUDS

V8-262

Rocker arm studs that have damaged threads may be replaced with standard studs. If studs are loose in the head, oversize studs (.003" or .013") may be installed after reaming the holes with a proper size reamer.

1. Remove old stud by placing a suitable spacer, Fig. 6 over stud. Install nut and flat washer and remove stud by turning nut.
2. Ream hole for oversize stud.
3. Coat press-fit area of stud with rear axle lube. Then install new stud, Fig. 7. If tool J-6880 shown is used, it should bottom on the head.

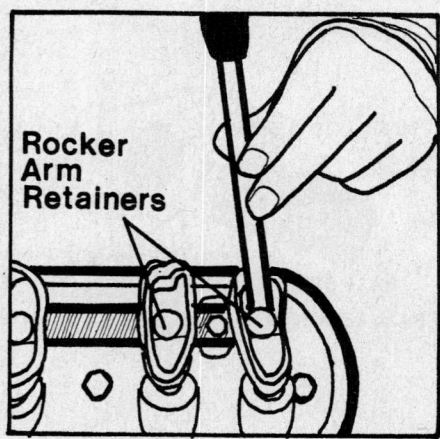

Fig. 5 Removing nylon rocker arm retainer. V6-231

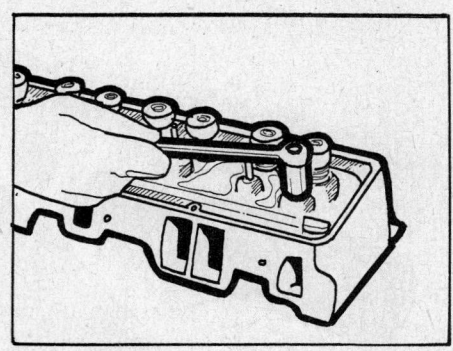

Fig. 6 Removing rocker arm stud. V8-262

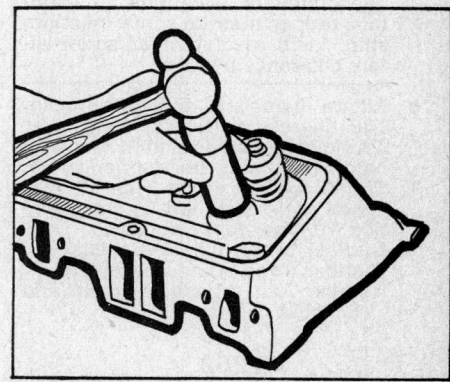

Fig. 7 Installing rocker arm stud. V8-262

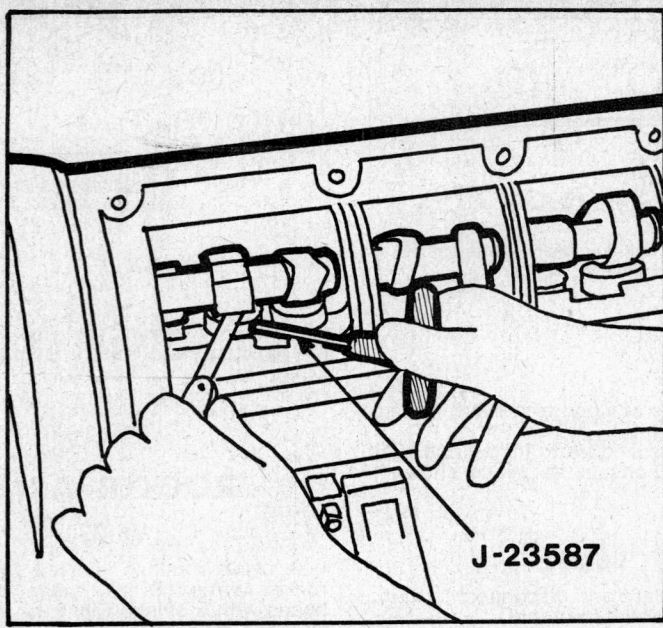

Fig. 8   Adjusting valve lash. 4-140

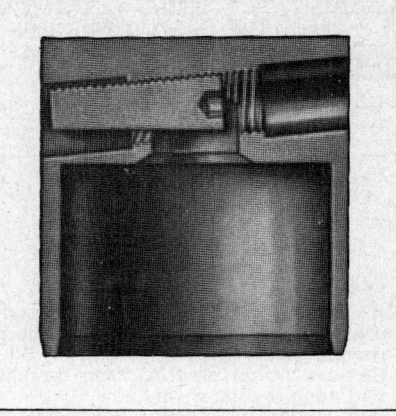

Fig. 9   Tappet and adjusting screw assembly. Screw is threaded in all areas except in valve stem contact surface. 4-140

VALVES, ADJUST

4-140

1. To adjust valves, the tappet must be on the base circle of the cam lobe. Do this as follows:
   a. Rotate camshaft timing sprocket to align timing mark on sprocket with inverted "V" notch on timing belt upper cover. The following valves can be adjusted with cam in this position (number one firing).
   Number one cylinder—Intake and Exhaust
   Number two cylinder—Intake
   Number three cylinder—Exhaust
   b. Use a feeler gauge and measure clearance between tappet and cam lobe. Adjust clearance by turning adjusting screw in tappet, Fig. 8.

NOTE: It is mandatory that the adjusting screw, Fig. 9, be turned one complete revolution to maintain proper stem-to-screw relationship. Each revolution of screw alters clearance by .003".

   c. Rotate camshaft timing sprocket 180 degrees so timing mark is at 12 o'clock position and in line with notch on timing belt upper cover. The following valves can be adjusted with camshaft in this position (number four firing).
   Number two cylinder—Exhaust
   Number three cylinder—Intake
   Number four cylinder—Intake and Exhaust

V8-262

NOTE: *After the engine has been thoroughly warmed up the valves may be ad-*

justed with the engine shut off as follows: With engine in position to fire No. 1 cylinder the following valves may be adjusted: Exhaust 1-3-4-8, intake 1-2-5-7. Then crank the engine one more complete revolution which will bring No. 6 cylinder to the firing position at which time the following valves may be adjusted: Exhaust 2-5-6-7, intake 3-4-6-8.

The following procedure, performed with the engine running should be done only in case readjustment is required.

1. After engine has been warmed up to operating temperature, remove valve cover and install a new valve cover gasket on cylinder head to prevent oil from running out.
2. With engine running at idle speed, back off valve rocker arm nut until rocker arm starts to clatter.
3. Turn rocker arm nut down slowly un-

til the clatter just stops. This is the zero lash position.
4. Turn nut down ¼ additional turn and pause 10 seconds until engine runs smoothly. Repeat additional ¼ turns, pausing 10 seconds each time, until nut has been turned down the number of turns listed in the *Valve Specifications Chart* from the zero-lash position.

NOTE

This preload adjustment must be done slowly to allow the lifter to adjust itself to prevent the possibility of interference between the intake valve head and top of piston, which might result in internal damage and/or bent push rods. Noisy lifters should be replaced.

VALVE ARRANGEMENT

Front to Rear

4-140	I-E-I-E-I-E-I-E
V8-262	E-I-I-E-E-I-I-E

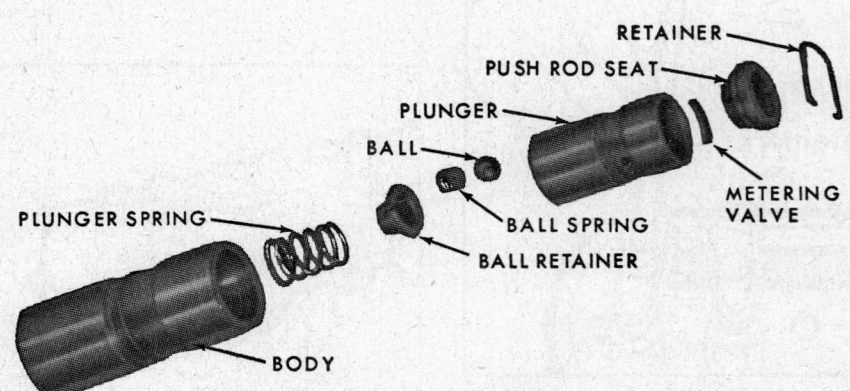

Fig. 10   Hydraulic valve lifter. V6-231 and V8-262

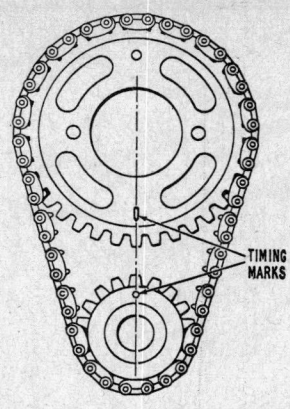

Fig. 11 Valve timing marks aligned for correct valve timing. V6-231

CAM LOBE LIFT SPECS.

	Year	Intake	Exhaust
4-140 1 bar. carb.	1975	.4199	.4302
4-140 2 bar. carb.	1975	.4367	.4379①

① .4302 on Monza 2+2.

VALVE LIFT SPECS.

Engine	Year	Intake	Exhaust
V6-231	1975	—	—
V8-262	1975	.3727	.4100

VALVE TIMING

Intake Opens Before TDC

Engine	Year	Degrees
4-140 1 bar. carb.	1975	22
4-140 2 bar. carb.	1975	28
6-231	1975	—
V8-262	1975	26

VALVE GUIDES

V6-231 & V8-262

Valve guides are an integral part of the cylinder head and are not removable. If valve stem clearance is excessive, the valve stem should be reamed to the next oversize and the appropriate oversize valves installed. Valves are available in .003, .015 and .030 inch oversize for the 4-140 and V8-262 and .010 inch for the V6-231.

HYDRAULIC VALVE LIFTERS

V6-231 & V8-262

Failure of an hydraulic valve lifter, is generally caused by an inadequate oil supply or dirt. An air leak at the intake side of the oil pump or too much oil in the engine will cause air bubbles in the oil supply to the lifters, causing them to collapse. This is a probable cause of trouble if several lifters fail to function, but air in the oil is an unlikely cause of failure of a single unit.

The valve lifters may be lifted out of their bores after removing the rocker arms, push rods and intake manifold. Adjustable pliers with taped jaws may be used to remove lifters that are stuck due to varnish, carbon, etc. Fig. 10 illustrates the type of lifter used.

CAMSHAFT COVER

4-140

1. Raise hood to fully open position and install bolt through the hood holdopen link.
2. Disconnect battery negative cable at battery.
3. Remove air cleaner wing nut. Disconnect ventilation tube at camshaft cover or at air cleaner; then remove air cleaner.
4. Remove PCV valve from grommet at front of cover.
5. Remove cover-to-cylinder head screws and withdraw cover from head.

ENGINE FRONT COVER

4-140

1. Raise hood to fully open position and install hood hold-open bolt.
2. Disconnect battery ground cable at battery.
3. Remove fan and spacer.
4. Loosen, but do not remove, the two cover lower screws. Cover is slotted to permit easy removal.
5. Remove the two cover upper retaining screws and remove cover.

V6-231

1. Drain cooling system and remove radiator.
2. Remove fan, pulleys and belts.
3. Remove crankshaft pulley and reinforcement.
4. If equipped with power steering, remove any pump bracket bolts attached to timing chain cover and loosen and remove any other bolts necessary that will allow pump and brackets to be moved out of the way.
5. Remove fuel pump.
6. Remove Delcotron and brackets.
7. Remove distributor cap and pull spark plug wire retainers off brackets on rocker arm cover. Swing distributor cap with wires attached out of the way.
8. Remove distributor. *If chain and sprockets are not to be disturbed, note position of distributor rotor for installation in the same position.*
9. Loosen and slide clamp on thermostat by-pass hose rearward.
10. Remove bolts attaching chain cover to block.
11. Remove two oil pan-to-chain cover bolts and remove cover.

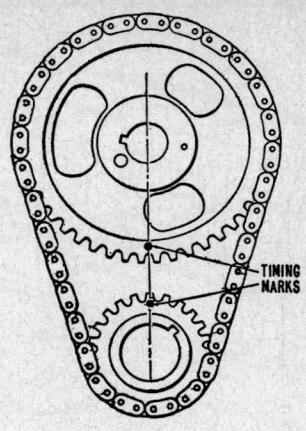

Fig. 12 Valve timing marks aligned for correct valve timing. V8-262

TIMING CHAIN

V6-231 & V8-262

1. Remove timing chain cover.
2. Turn crankshaft so that sprockets are aligned as shown in Figs. 11 and 12.
3. Remove oil slinger.
4. On V6-231, remove camshaft distributor drive gear and fuel pump eccentric, then using two large screwdrivers, alternately pry camshaft sprocket and crankshaft sprocket until camshaft is free. Remove camshaft sprocket and chain, then slide crankshaft sprocket off crankshaft.
5. On V8-262, remove three camshaft to sprocket bolts, then remove camshaft sprocket and timing chain together. Sprocket is a light fit on camshaft for about 1/8 inch, if sprocket does not come off easily, a light blow with a plastic hammer should dislodge it. If crankshaft sprocket is to be replaced, remove it with a suitable puller.
6. To install, assemble chain on sprockets with timing marks aligned as shown in Figs. 11 & 12.
7. Complete installation in reverse order of removal.

CAMSHAFT, REMOVAL

4-140

1. Remove hood.
2. Remove camshaft timing sprocket.
3. Remove timing belt upper cover and cam retainer and seal assembly.
4. Remove camshaft cover.
5. Disconnect fuel line at carburetor and remove idle solenoid from bracket.
6. Remove carburetor choke coil, cover and rod assembly.
7. Remove distributor.
8. Raise vehicle on a hoist, disconnect engine front mounts at body attachment, raise front of engine and install wood blocks, about 1½" thick, between engine mounts and body. Lower vehicle.

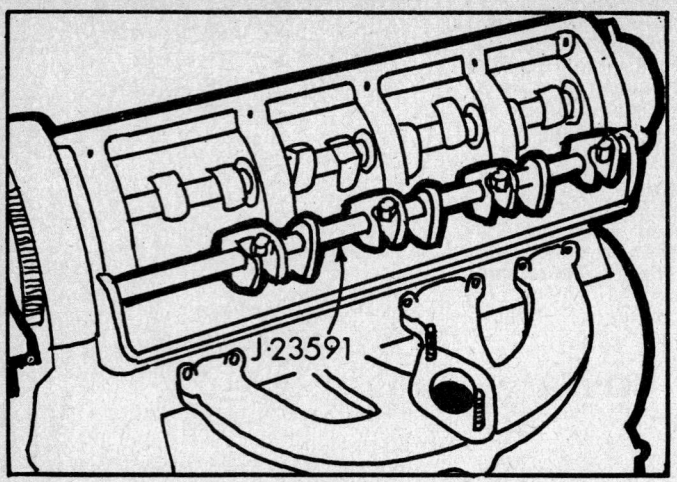

Fig. 13 Camshaft removal tool installed. 4-140

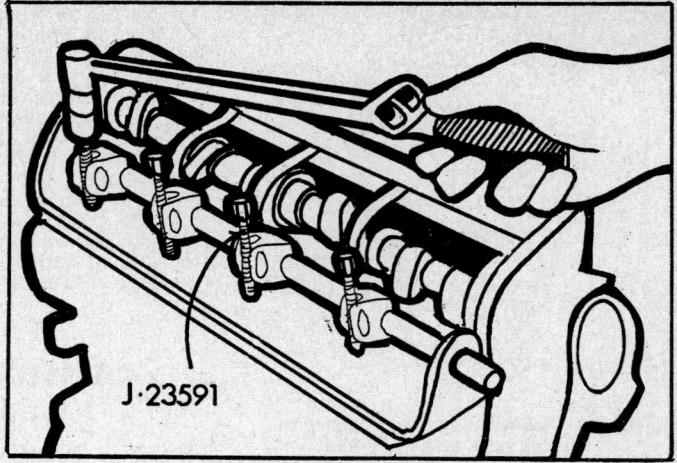

Fig. 14 Depressing valve tappets. 4-140

9. Install camshaft removal tool as shown in Fig. 13, to cylinder head as follows:
   a. Position tool to cylinder head so attaching holes align with cam cover lower attaching holes.
   b. Align tappet depressing levers on tool so each lever will depress both intake and exhaust valve for their respective cylinder. Lever should fit squarely in notches adjacent to valve tappets.
   c. With tool aligned, make sure screws in bottom of tool are backed off so they do not make contact with bosses beneath tool.
   d. Install hardened screws supplied with tool, to attach tool to head. Torque screws securely.
   e. Turn screws in bottom of tool downward until they just seat against corresponding bosses on head.
   f. Apply a heavy body lubricant to ball end of lever depressing screws and proceed to tighten screws to depress tappets, Fig. 14.

   NOTE: Use a torque wrench to tighten screws the final few turns. About 10 ft. lbs. is required to depress tappets.

10. At this point the camshaft can be removed by sliding it forward from the head.

V6-231

NOTE: If engine is in the car, the radiator, grille and A/C components will have to be removed. If engine is out of car, proceed as follows:

1. To remove camshaft, remove rocker arm shaft assemblies, push rods and valve lifters.
2. Remove timing chain and sprockets.
3. Slide camshaft out of engine, using care not to mar the bearing surfaces.

TIMING BELT & WATER PUMP
4-140

1. Remove engine front cover as previously described.
2. Remove accessory drive pulley or damper.
3. Drain coolant and loosen water pump bolts to relieve tension on belt.
4. Remove timing belt lower cover, then remove belt from sprockets.
5. Remove water pump bolts and lift off pump.

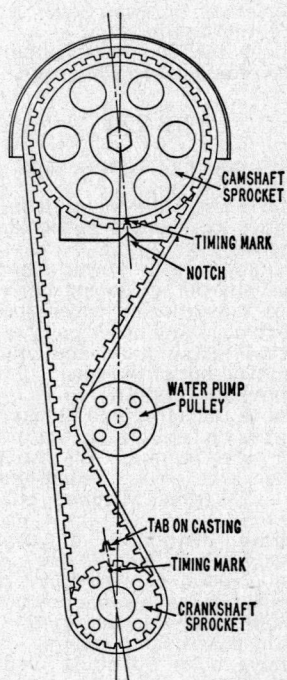

Fig. 15 Sprocket alignment marks. 4-140

CAMSHAFT SPROCKET
4-140

After removal of timing belt, the camshaft sprocket can be removed as follows:
1. Align one hole in sprocket with bolt head behind sprocket, then using a socket on bolt head to prevent cam from turning, remove sprocket retaining bolt and withdraw sprocket from camshaft.
2. When installing, be sure timing marks are aligned as in Fig. 15.

NOTE: A simplified method is provided for checking camshaft and crankshaft alignment. Proper alignment is assured by making sure hole in left rear of the timing belt upper cover is in line with the corresponding hole in the camshaft sprocket. Check alignment by inserting a pencil or other similar tool through hole in cover. If alignment is correct, the tool will enter small hole in cam gear, Fig. 16.

CRANKSHAFT SPROCKET
4-140

1. Remove engine front cover, accessory drive pulley, timing belt and timing belt lower cover.
2. Install suitable puller to crankshaft sprocket and remove sprocket.

OIL PUMP (CRANKCASE FRONT COVER) SEAL
4-140

1. Remove engine front cover, accessory drive pulley, timing belt and timing belt lower cover and crankshaft sprocket.

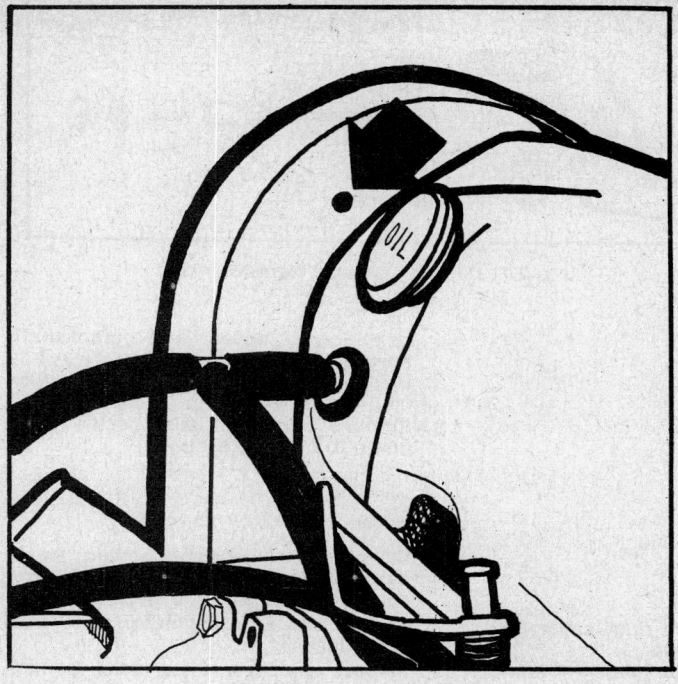

Fig. 16   Checking sprocket alignment. 4-140

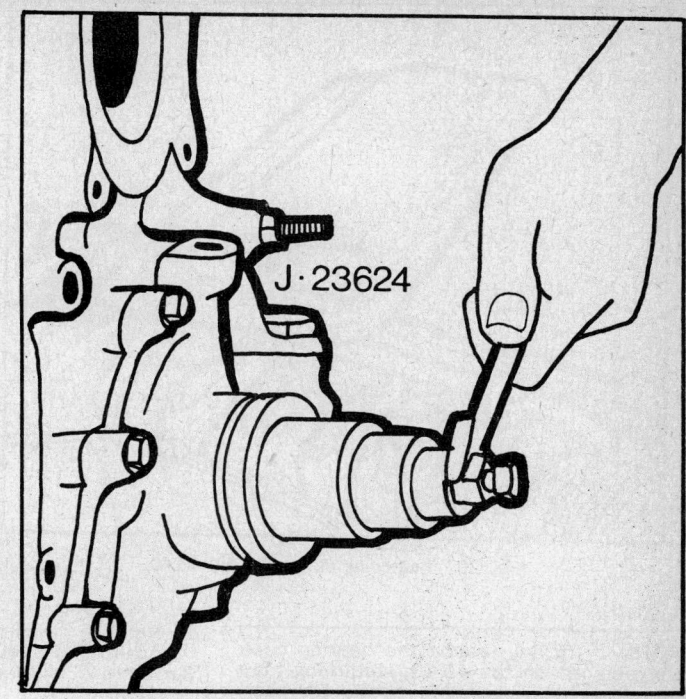

Fig. 17   Installing crankshaft front oil seal. 4-140

2. Pry old seal from front cover being careful not to damage seal housing or seal lip contact surfaces.

3. Coat seal with light engine oil and apply an approved sealing compound to outside diameter of seal.

4. Position seal, closed end outward, onto crankshaft. Then install seal into bore using tool J-23624, Fig. 17.

PISTONS & RODS, ASSEMBLE

4-140

The "F" on the front of the piston must face the front of the engine when the piston and rod assembly is installed in its proper cylinder, Fig. 18.

Oversize pistons are not available since bore reconditioning is not recommended. Production pistons are available in four size ranges so pistons can be select fitted to the bores. Cylinder bore repairs, such as glaze busting, honing or reboring will destroy the electro-chemically treated finish necessary for proper piston-to-bore operation. Therefore, if cylinder bores are unserviceable, a new cylinder case and piston assembly should be installed.

V6-231

Rods and pistons should be assembled and installed as shown in Fig. 19.

PISTONS, PINS & RINGS

V6-231 & V8-262

Pistons are available in standard sizes and oversizes of .001, .005, .010, .020 and .030 inch for the V6-231 & .001, .020 and .030 for the V8-262.

Rings are furnished in standard sizes and oversizes of .010, .020 and .030 inch for the V6-231 and .020 and .030 for the V8-262.

Pistons pins are furnished in standard sizes and oversizes of .003 and .005 inch for the V6-231.

MAIN & ROD BEARINGS

Main and rod bearings are available in standard sizes and undersizes of .001, .002, .020 and .030 inch for the 4-140, .001, .002, .003 and .010 inch for the V6-231 and .001, .002, .009, .010 and .020 inch for the V8-262.

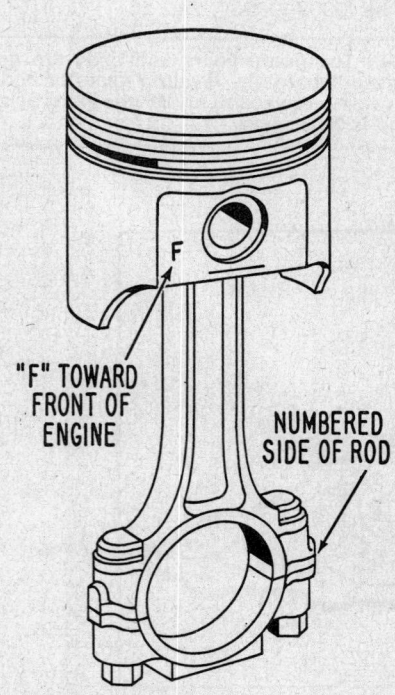

"F" TOWARD FRONT OF ENGINE

NUMBERED SIDE OF ROD

Fig. 18   Piston and rod assembly. 4-140

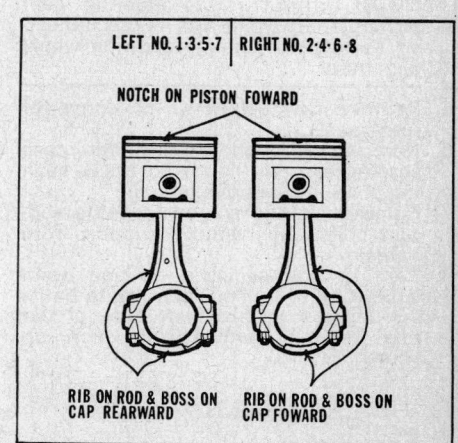

LEFT NO. 1-3-5-7 | RIGHT NO. 2-4-6-8

NOTCH ON PISTON FOWARD

RIB ON ROD & BOSS ON CAP REARWARD

RIB ON ROD & BOSS ON CAP FOWARD

Fig. 19   Piston and rod assembly. V6-231

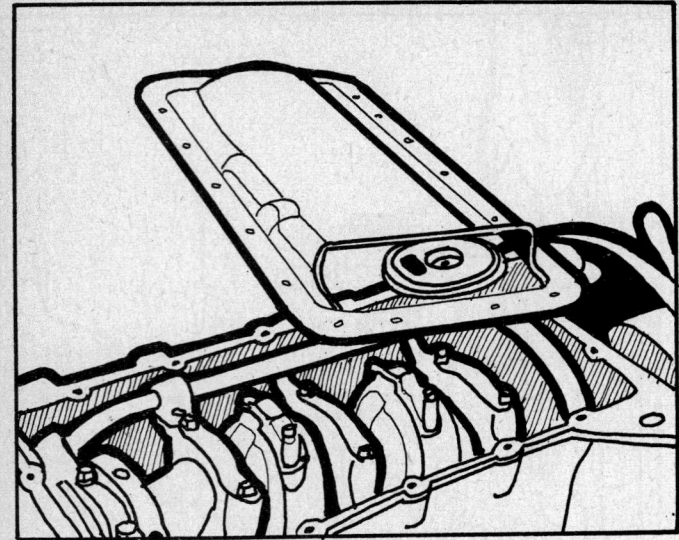

Fig. 20   Removing oil pan baffle. 4-140

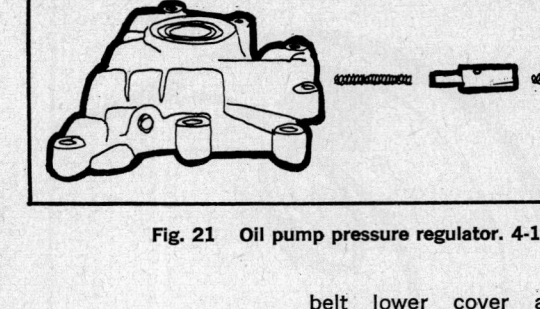

Fig. 21   Oil pump pressure regulator. 4-140

NOTE: If for any reason the bearing caps are replaced on the 4-140, shimming may be necessary. Laminated shims for each cap are available for service. Shim requirements will be determined by bearing clearance.

OIL PAN

4-140

1. Raise vehicle on a hoist and drain engine oil.
2. Support front of engine so weight is off front mounts, and remove frame crossmember and both front crossmember braces.
3. Disconnect idler arm at frame side rail.

   NOTE: On air conditioned vehicles, disconnect idler arm at relay rod.

4. Mark relationship of steering linkage pitman arm to steering gear pitman shaft and remove pitman arm.

   NOTE: Do not rotate steering gear pitman shaft while arm is disconnected as this will change steering wheel alignment.

5. Remove flywheel cover or converter underpan.
6. Remove oil pan to cylinder case screws, tap pan lightly to break sealing bond and remove oil pan.
7. Remove pick up screen to baffle support bolts, then remove support from baffle.
8. Remove bolt securing oil pan drain back tube to baffle. Then rotate baffle 90 degrees towards left side of car and remove baffle from pick up screen, Fig. 20.

V6-231

1. Support vehicle on hoist and drain oil.

2. Remove transmission dust cover and exhaust crossover pipe.
3. Remove oil pan bolts and allow pan to drop.

   NOTE: To remove oil pan, front wheels must be turned to the left, also the crankshaft may have to be turned to provide clearance.

4. Reverse removal procedure to install.

OIL PUMP (CRANKCASE FRONT COVER)

4-140

1. Remove engine front cover, accessory drive pulley, timing belt, timing belt lower cover and crankshaft sprocket.
2. Raise vehicle on a hoist and remove oil pan and baffle.
3. Remove bolts and stud securing oil pump to cylinder case.

Inspection

1. Clean gasket surfaces, then wash parts in approved solvent and blow out all passages.
2. Check pressure regulator for free operation, Fig. 21.
3. Inspect pump gears for nicks, broken parts and other damage.
4. Check clearance between outside diameter, of driven gear and pump. Clearance should be .0038-.0068", Fig. 22.
5. Check clearance between outside diameter of drive gear and crescent. Clearance should be .0023-.0093", Fig. 23.
6. Check clearance between inside diameter of driven gear and pump crescent. Clearance should be .0068-.0148", Fig. 24.
7. Check gear end clearance. It should be .0009-.0023", Fig. 25.

NOTE: The pump gears and body are not serviced separately. If pump gears or body are worn, replacement of the entire oil pump is necessary.

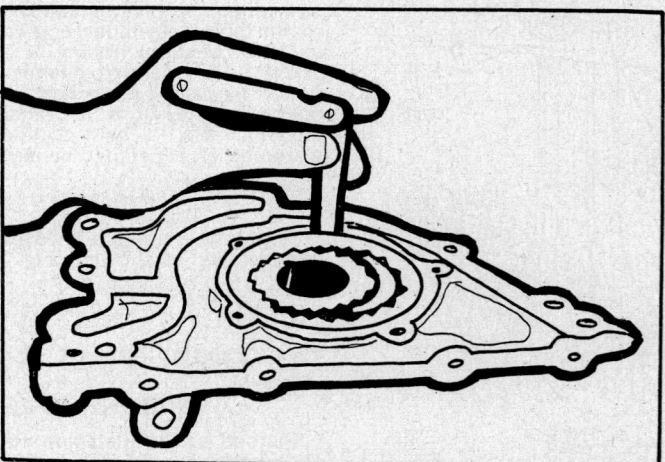

Fig. 22   Checking driven gear to housing clearance. 4-140

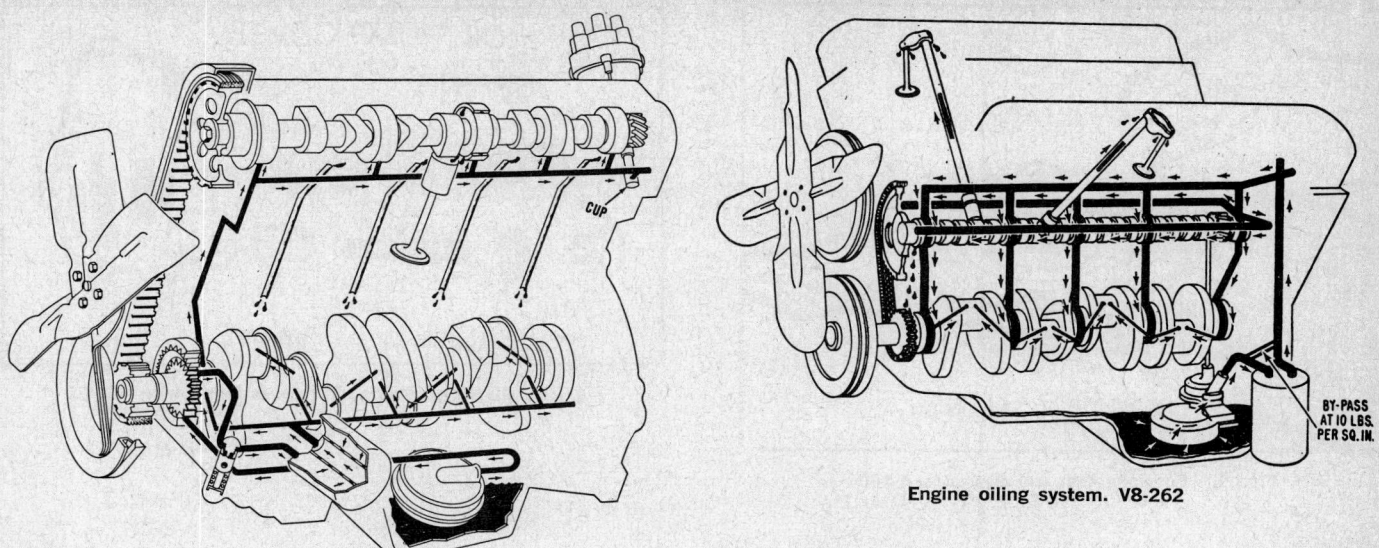

Engine oiling system. 4-140

Engine oiling system. V8-262

BY-PASS
AT 10 LBS.
PER SQ. IN.

OIL PUMP

V6-231

1. To remove pump, take off oil filter.
2. Disconnect wire from oil pressure indicator switch in filter by-pass valve cap (if so equipped).
3. Remove screws attaching oil pump cover to timing chain cover. Remove cover and slide out pump gears. Replace any parts not serviceable.
4. Remove oil pressure relief valve cap, spring and valve, Fig. 26. Remove oil filter by-pass valve cap, spring and valve. Replace any parts of valve not serviceable.
5. Check relief valve in its bore in cover. Valve should have no more clearance

than an easy slip fit. If any perceptible side shake can be felt, the valve and/or cover should be replaced.
6. The filter by-pass valve should be flat and free of nicks and scratches.

Assembly & Installation

1. Lubricate and install pressure relief valve and spring in bore of pump cover. Install cap and gasket. Torque cap to 30-35 lbs.
2. Install filter by-pass valve flat in its seat in cover. Install spring, cap and gasket. Torque cap to 30-35 ft-lbs.
3. Install pump gears and shaft in pump body section of timing chain cover to check gear end clearance. Check

clearance as shown in Fig. 27. If clearance is less than .0018" check timing chain cover for evidence of wear.
4. If gear end clearance is satisfactory, remove gears and pack gear pocket *full* of vaseline, not chassis lube.
5. Reinstall gears so vaseline is forced into every cavity of gear pocket and between teeth of gears. *Unless pump is packed with vaseline, it may not prime itself when engine is started.*
6. Install cover and tighten screws alternately and evenly. Final tightening is 10-15 ft-lbs. torque. Install filter on nipple.

V8-262

After removing the oil pan, unfasten pump from rear main bearing cap. Disconnect pump shaft from extension by removing clip from collar. Remove pump cover and take out idler gear, drive gear

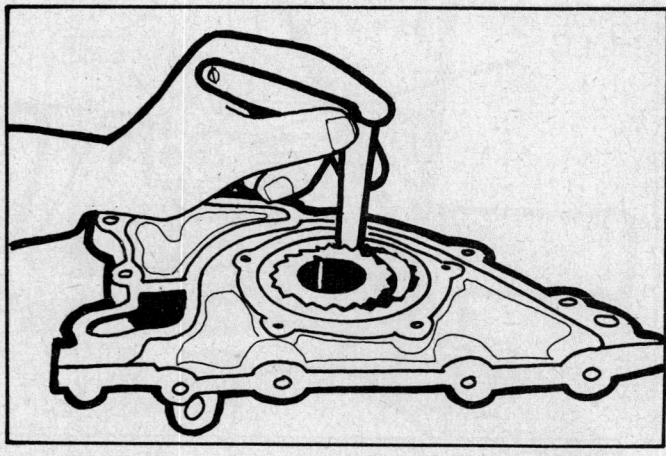

Fig. 23   Checking drive gear to crescent clearance. 4-140

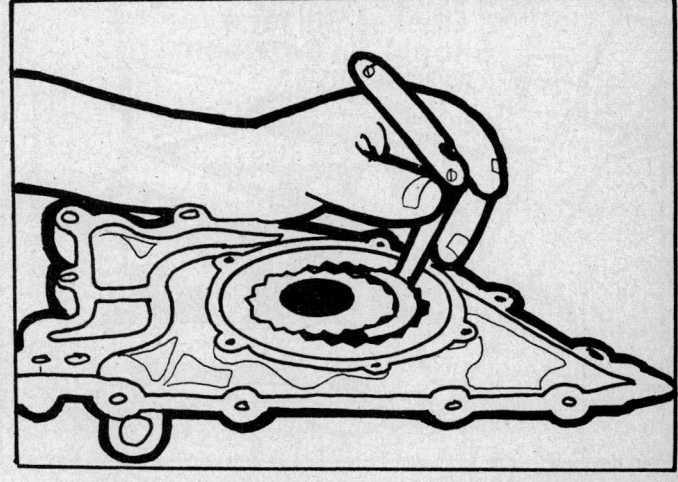

Fig. 24   Checking driven gear to crescent clearance. 4-140

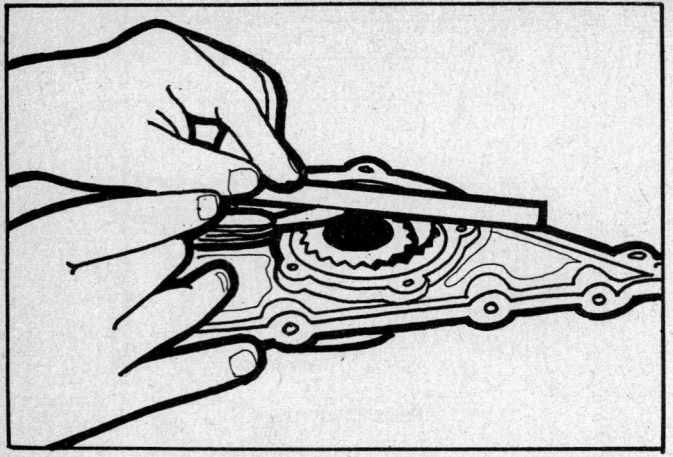

Fig. 25   Checking gear end clearance. 4-140

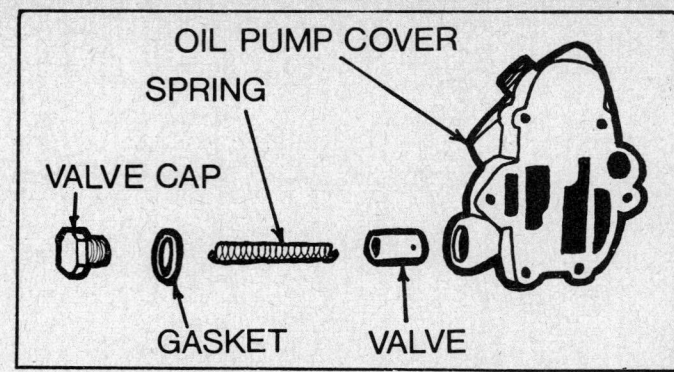

Fig. 26   Oil pump cover and pressure relief valve. V6-231

and shaft.

Should any of the following conditions be found it is advisable to replace the pump assembly.

1. Inspect pump body for cracks or wear.
2. Inspect gears for wear or damage.
3. Check shaft for looseness in housing.
4. Check inside of cover for wear that would permit oil to leak past the ends of gear.
5. Check oil pick-up screen for damage to screen, by-pass valve or body.
6. Check for oil in air chamber.

CRANKSHAFT REAR OIL SEAL

V6-231 & V8-262

NOTE: V8-262 engines are equipped with helix type rear seal. A seal starting tool

Fig. 28, must be used to prevent the upper seal half from coming into contact with the sharp edge of the block. Place the tip of the tool into the seal channel and "shoehorn" the seal into the upper seal channel.

When necessary to correct an oil leak due to a defective seal, always replace the upper and lower halves as a unit. When installing either half, lubricate the lip portion only with engine oil, keeping oil off the parting line surface as this is treated with glue. Always clean crankshaft surface before installing a new seal. Be careful of seal retainer tang while inserting a new

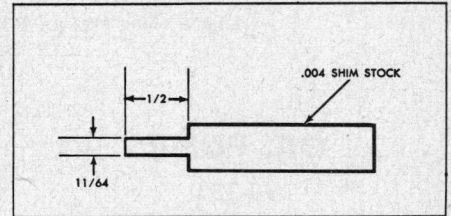

Fig. 28   Fabricated seal starting tool for helix type seal

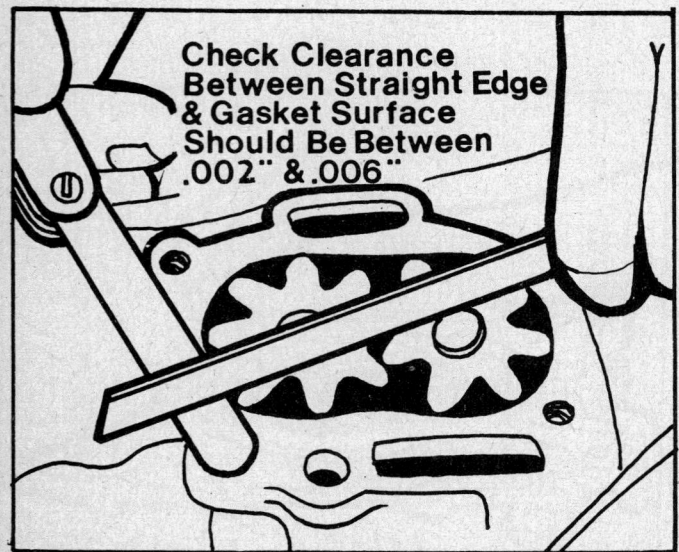

Fig. 27   Checking oil pump gear end clearance. V6-231

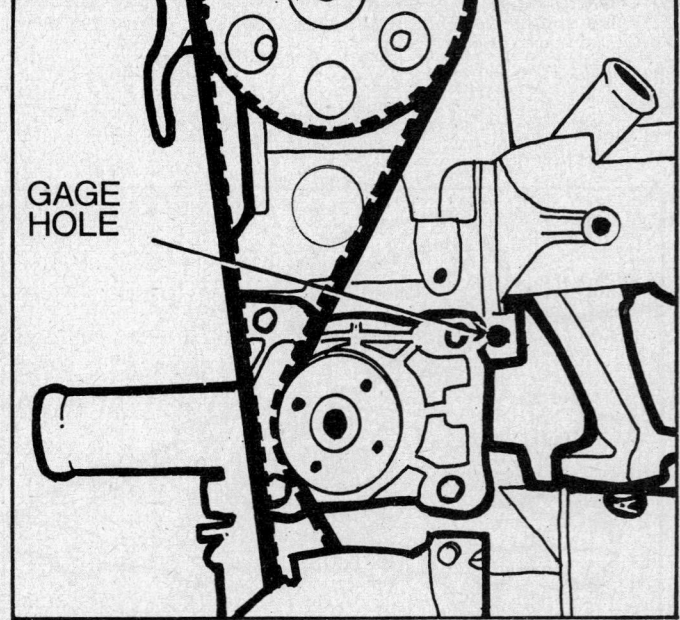

Fig. 29   Tensioning adaptor locating hole

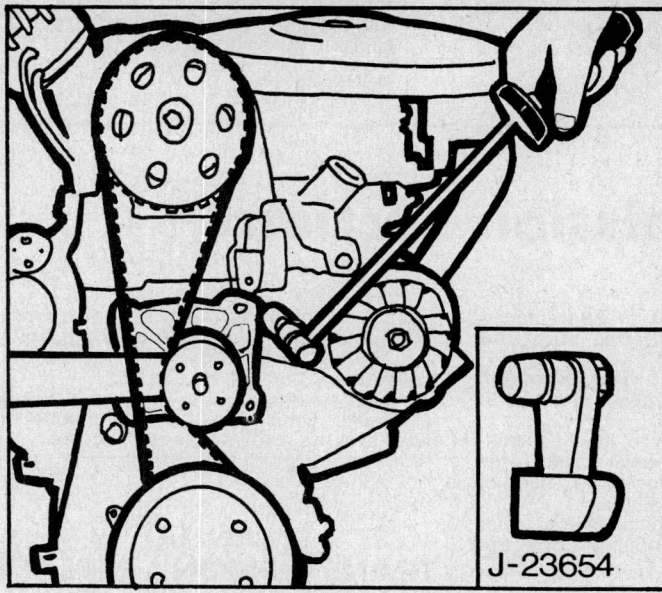

Fig. 30   Adjusting timing belt

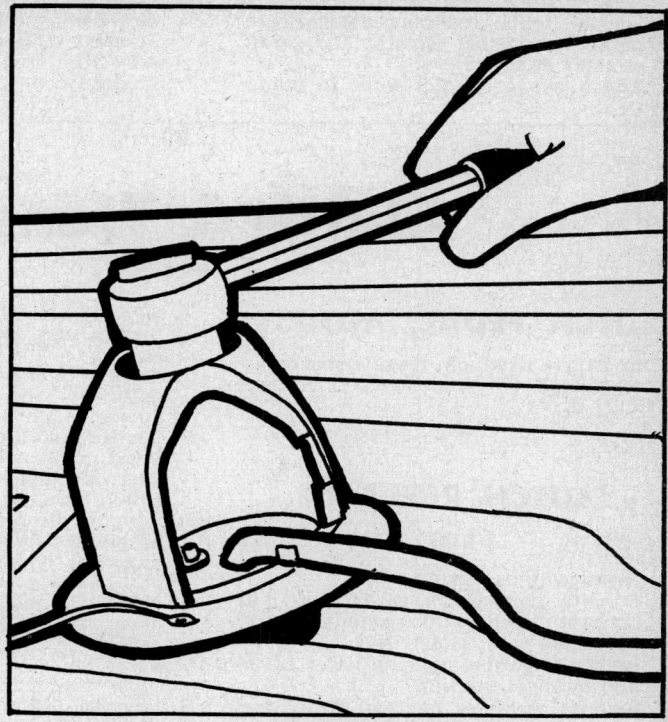

Fig. 31   Removing fuel pump and gauge unit

seal so that it doesn't cut the seal.

1. To replace the lower seal, remove seal from groove in bearing cap, using a small screwdriver to pry it out.
2. Insert new seal and roll it in place with finger and thumb.
3. To replace the upper seal (with engine in car) use a small hammer and tap a brass pin punch on one end of the seal until it protrudes far enough to be removed with pliers.
4. Insert the new seal, gradually pushing with a hammer handle until seal is rolled into place.
5. Install bearing cap with new seal and tighten bearing cap bolts.

TIMING BELT TENSION, ADJUST

4-140

1. Drain coolant at engine block and remove fan and extension.
2. Remove engine front cover.
3. Remove water pump retaining bolts, clean gasket surfaces on block and pump. Install new gasket and loosely install water pump bolts.

NOTE: Apply an approved anti-seize compound to the water pump bolts before installation.

4. Position tool J-23564 in gauge hole adjacent to left side of pump, Fig. 29.
5. Apply 15 ft. lbs. of torque to water pump as shown in Fig. 30. Tighten water pump bolts while maintaining torque on side of pump.
6. Reinstall front cover, fan, extension and fill cooling system.

BELT TENSION DATA

	New lbs.	Used lbs.
Air Condition		
4-140 & V8-262	135-145	95
V6-231	150	100
Air Pump		
4-140 & V8-262	120-130	75
V6-231	70	65
Delcotron		
4-140 & V8-262	120-130	75
V6-231	125	80
Power Steering		
4-140 & V8-262	120-130	75
V6-231	150	90
Timing Belt		
4-140	100-140	—

WATER PUMP, REPLACE

1. Raise hood to fully open position and install hold-open bolt.
2. Disconnect battery ground cable at battery.
3. Remove engine fan and spacer.
4. Loosen, but do not remove, the two cover lower screws. Cover is slotted to permit easy removal.
5. Remove the two cover upper retaining screws and remove cover.
6. Drain coolant and loosen water pump bolts to relieve tension in timing belt.
7. Remove radiator lower hose and heater hose at water pump.
8. Unfasten and remove water pump. Drain cooling system, being sure to drain into a clean container if antifreeze solution is to be saved. Remove the fan belt and disconnect all hoses from water pump. Remove water pump.

FUEL PUMP PRESSURE

Year	Engine	Pressure lbs.
1975	4-140, V6-231	3-4½
	V8-262	7-8½

FUEL PUMP, REPLACE

Removal

1. Disconnect battery ground cable.
2. Disconnect meter and pump wires at rear wiring harness connector.
3. Raise vehicle on hoist and drain fuel tank.
4. Disconnect fuel line hose at gauge unit pick up line.
5. Disconnect tank vent lines to vapor separator.
6. Remove gauge ground wire screw at underbody floorpan.
7. Remove tank straps bolts and lower tank carefully.
8. Unscrew retaining ring using spanner wrench J-22554, Fig. 31, and remove pump-tank unit assembly.

Replacement

1. Remove flat wire conductor from plastic clip on fuel tube.
2. Squeeze clamp and pull pump straight back about ½ inch.
3. Remove two nuts and lockwashers and conductor wires from pump terminals.
4. Squeeze clamp and pull pump straight back to remove it from tank unit. Take care to prevent bending of circular support bracket.
5. Slide replacement pump through cir-

cular support bracket until it rests against rubber coupling. Make sure pump has rubber isolator and saran strainer attached.
6. Attach two conductor wires to pump

terminals using lockwashers and nuts being certain flat conductor is attached to terminal located on side away from float arm.
7. Squeeze clamp and push pump into

rubber coupling.
8. Replace flat wire conductor in plastic clip on fuel pick up tube.
9. Install unit into tank and replace fuel tank.

Clutch & Transmission Section

CLUTCH PEDAL, ADJUST

The clutch used on these vehicles is cable actuated. For proper adjustment, refer to Fig. 1.

CLUTCH REPLACE
4-140

1. Remove transmission.
2. Remove clutch fork cover then disconnect clutch return spring and control cable from clutch fork.
3. Remove flywheel housing lower cover and flywheel housing.
4. Remove release bearing from the clutch fork and sleeve by sliding lever off ball stud and against spring pres-

sure. If ball stud is to be replaced, remove cap, lock nut and stud from housing.
5. Make sure alignment marks on clutch assembly and flywheel are distinguishable.
6. Loosen clutch cover to flywheel bolts one turn at a time until spring pressure is released to avoid bending clutch cover flange, Fig. 2.
7. Support the pressure plate and cover assembly while removing bolts and clutch assembly.

NOTE: Do not disassemble the clutch cover, spring and pressure plate for repairs. If defective, replace complete assembly.

8. Reverse procedure to install making sure to index alignment marks.
9. After installing crossmember, loosely

install retaining bolts, then the crossmember to transmission mount bolts. Tighten all bolts to specifications and remove the engine support.

CAUTION: Check position of engine in front mounts and realign as necessary.

MANUAL TRANSMISSION, REPLACE
4-140

1. Place shift lever in neutral and remove shift lever.
2. Raise vehicle on a hoist and drain lubricant.
3. Remove propeller shaft and torque arm.

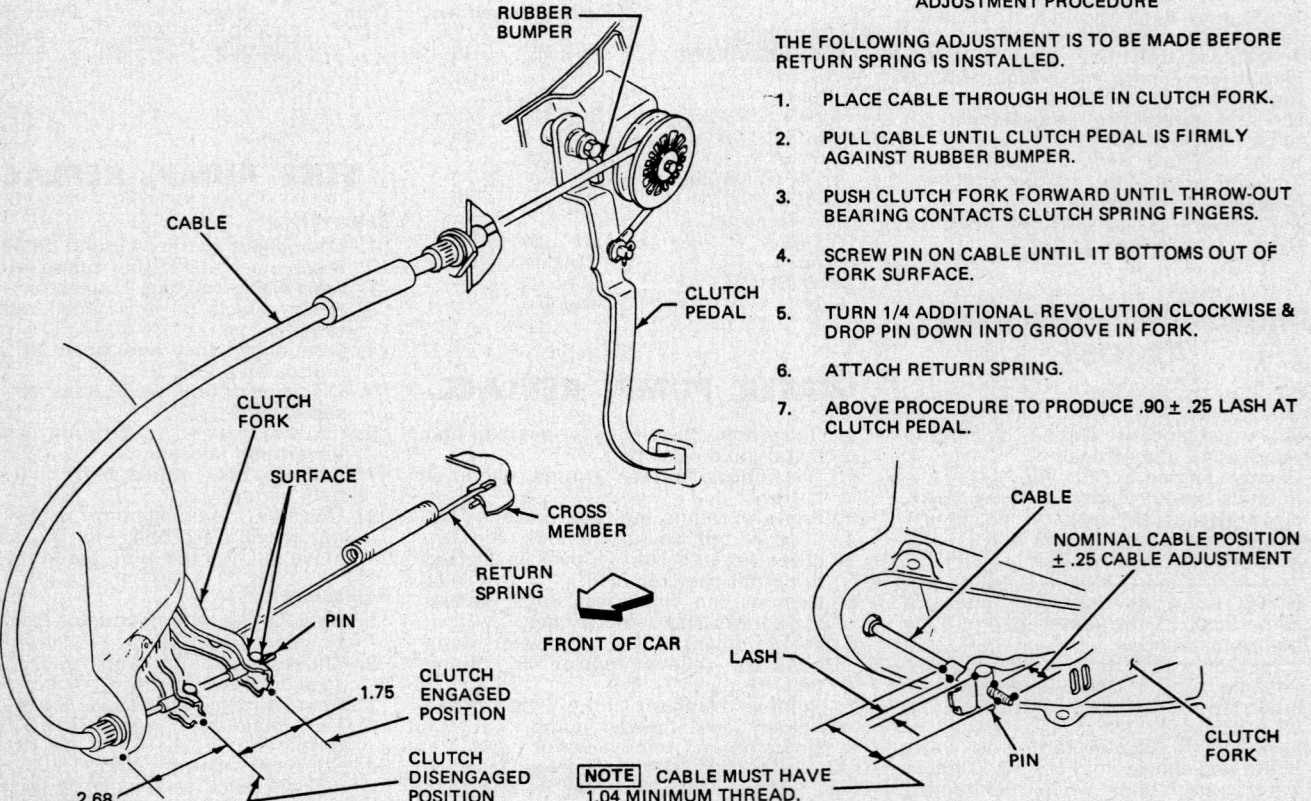

RUBBER BUMPER

ADJUSTMENT PROCEDURE

THE FOLLOWING ADJUSTMENT IS TO BE MADE BEFORE RETURN SPRING IS INSTALLED.

1. PLACE CABLE THROUGH HOLE IN CLUTCH FORK.
2. PULL CABLE UNTIL CLUTCH PEDAL IS FIRMLY AGAINST RUBBER BUMPER.
3. PUSH CLUTCH FORK FORWARD UNTIL THROW-OUT BEARING CONTACTS CLUTCH SPRING FINGERS.
4. SCREW PIN ON CABLE UNTIL IT BOTTOMS OUT OF FORK SURFACE.
5. TURN 1/4 ADDITIONAL REVOLUTION CLOCKWISE & DROP PIN DOWN INTO GROOVE IN FORK.
6. ATTACH RETURN SPRING.
7. ABOVE PROCEDURE TO PRODUCE .90 ± .25 LASH AT CLUTCH PEDAL.

CABLE
CLUTCH PEDAL
CLUTCH FORK
SURFACE
CROSS MEMBER
RETURN SPRING
PIN
FRONT OF CAR
1.75
CLUTCH ENGAGED POSITION
2.68
CLUTCH DISENGAGED POSITION

CABLE
NOMINAL CABLE POSITION ± .25 CABLE ADJUSTMENT
LASH
PIN
CLUTCH FORK

NOTE CABLE MUST HAVE 1.04 MINIMUM THREAD.

Fig. 1 Cable actuated clutch adjustment

4. Remove catalytic converter bracket from transmission and disconnect exhaust pipe and converter.
5. Disconnect speedo cable, TCS switch and back-up lamp switch.
6. Remove crossmember to transmission mount bolts.
7. Support engine with an appropriate jack stand and remove crossmember to frame bolts and remove crossmember.
8. Remove transmission to clutch housing upper retaining bolts and install guide pins in holes.
9. Remove lower bolts, then slide transmission rearward and remove from vehicle.

NOTE: Inspect throwout bearing support gasket located beneath lip of support. If necessary, replace gasket before installing transmission.

AUTO. TRANSMISSION, REPLACE

1. Disconnect battery ground cable.
2. Remove air cleaner and disconnect downshift cable from carburetor. Release parking brake.
3. Raise vehicle and remove torque arm and propeller shaft.
4. Remove catalytic converter bracket from transmission and disconnect exhaust pipe and converter.
5. Disconnect speedo cable, modulator vacuum line, shift linkage and downshift cable from transmission.
6. Support transmission with a suitable jack and disconnect transmission rear mount from crossmember, then remove crossmember.
7. Remove converter cover, then converter to flywheel bolts.

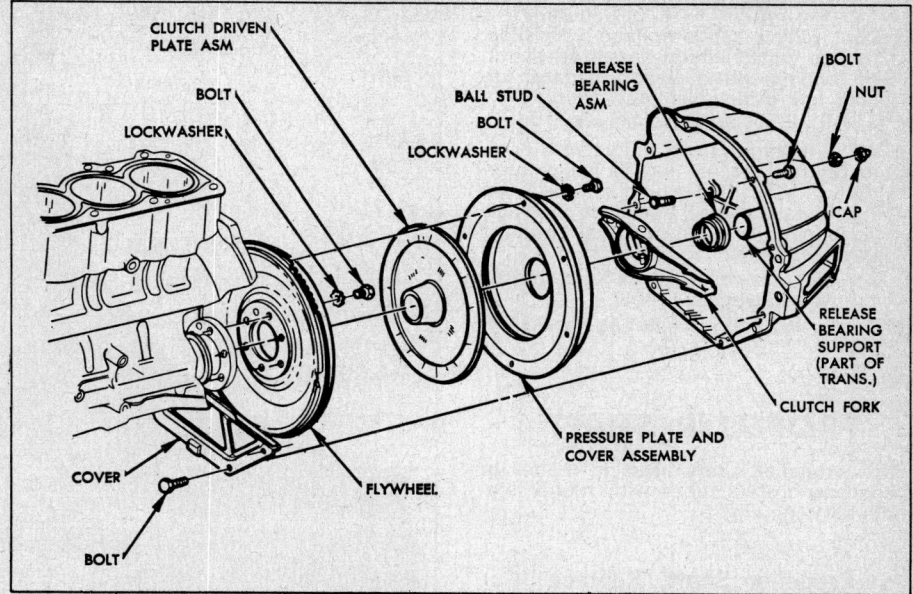

Fig. 2 Four cylinder engine clutch & components

8. Lower transmission until it is barely supported and remove transmission to engine bolts.
9. Remove oil filler tube and on V8 models, disconnect oil cooler lines.
10. Raise transmission, support engine with a suitable jack and slide transmission rearward and lower unit from vehicle.
11. Reverse procedure to install.

1975 AUTO. TRANS. LINKAGE, ADJUST

Linkage adjustments for these models are the same as the 1973-74 Vega linkage adjustments found in the "Automatic Transmission" chapter, Turbo Hydra-matic 250, 350 section.

Rear Axle, Propeller Shaft & Brakes

REAR AXLE

Description

The rear axle, Fig. 1, is a semi-floating type consisting of a cast carrier and large bosses on each end into which two welded steel tubes are fitted. The carrier contains an overhung hypoid pinion and ring gear. The differential is a two pinion arrangement.

The overhung hypoid drive pinion is supported by two preloaded tapered roller bearings. The pinion shaft is sealed by means of a molded, spring loaded, rubber seal. The seal is mounted on the pinion shaft flange which is splined and bolts to the hypoid pinion shaft.

The ring gear is bolted to a one piece differential case and is supported by two preloaded tapered roller bearings.

AXLE SHAFT

1. Raise vehicle on a hoist and remove wheel and tire assembly and brake drum.
2. Drain lubricant from axle by removing carrier cover.
3. Unscrew pinion shaft lock screw and remove pinion shaft, Fig. 2.
4. Push flanged end of axle shaft toward center of car and remove "C" lock from button end of shaft.
5. Remove axle shaft from housing being careful not to damage seal.

Oil Seal &/or Bearing Replacement

1. If replacing seal only, remove the seal by using the button end of axle shaft. Insert the button end of shaft behind the steel case of the seal and pry seal out of bore being careful not to damage housing.
2. If replacing bearings, insert tool J-22813 into bore so tool head grasps behind bearing, Fig. 3. Slide washer against seal, or bearing, and turn nut

against washer. Attach slide hammer J-2619 and remove bearing.
3. Pack cavity between seal lips with a high melting point wheel bearing lubricant. Position seal on tool J-21491 and position seal in axle housing bore, tap seal in bore just below end of housing, Fig. 4.

PINION FLANGE
Removal

1. Support vehicle and remove both rear wheels and drums.
2. Disconnect propeller shaft and support it by wiring shaft to exhaust pipe.

NOTE: Use a heavy rubber band or tape to hold bearings onto journal to prevent losing bearing rollers if tie wire has been removed.

3. Using an inch pound torque wrench, check pinion bearing pre-load.
4. Remove pinion flange.

Installation

1. Coat pinion flange splines with silactic and install pinion flange on pinion by tapping with a plastic hammer until a few threads project through.
2. Install pinion flange washer and nut.
3. While holding pinion flange with holder tighten the nut slowly while intermittantly rotating pinion to seat bearing. Check preload until it is 3-5 inch pounds more than reading obtained in step 3 under "Removal."
4. Connect propeller shaft and install drums and wheels.
5. Check and add lubricant as necessary.

PROPELLER SHAFT

The propeller shaft used is made up of concentric steel tubes with rubber elements between, Fig. 5.

Propeller Shaft, Replace

1. Raise vehicle on a hoist. Mark relationship of shaft to companion flange and disconnect the rear universal joint by removing trunnion bearing "U" bolts. Tape bearing cups to trunnion to prevent dropping and loss of bearing rollers.
2. Withdraw propeller shaft front yoke from transmission.
3. When installing, be sure to align marks made in removal to prevent driveline vibration.

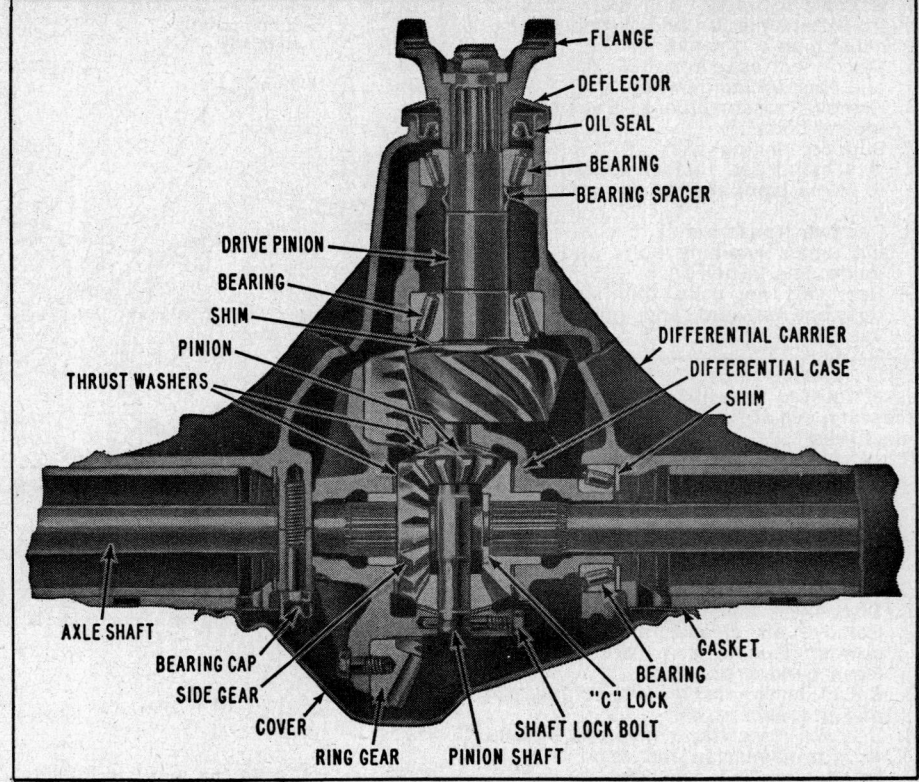

Fig. 1   Rear axle cross section

BRAKE ADJUSTMENTS

Power disc brakes are used on the front wheels and drum brakes, Fig. 6, are used on the rear wheels. Rear brake adjustment is not automatic. Adjustment takes place, if needed, only when the parking brake is applied. When the parking brake is applied, the strut is pushed against the front shoe and the rod is pulled against the rear shoe. As the shoes spread, a spring lock mounted within the strut and rod assembly, allows the strut and rod assembly to lengthen. When the parking brake is released, the rod connected to the rear shoe is relaxed and brake shoe pressure on the drum is released providing running clearance. Clearance is obtained by the difference in the diameter of the rod and the diameter of the hole in the rear shoe.

NOTE: If the brake drum cannot be removed, it will be necessary to release the brake adjuster. To gain access to the adjuster, knock out the lanced area in web of brake drum, Fig. 7, using a chisel or similar tool. Release the rod from the trailing shoe by pushing in on the rod until it is clear of the shoe. The pull back spring will then pull the shoes toward each other and the drum may be removed.

CAUTION: After knocking out the lanced area, be sure to remove the piece of metal from inside the drum.

When installing new brake shoes Fig. 8, the adjuster assembly must be released and repositioned. Position tool J-23730 so that tang of tool rests on flat portion of locks (between lock tangs) Fig. 9, then press down on adjuster locks. Work rod assembly free of adjuster locks, then when both adjuster tangs are clear of rod assembly, slide rod off lever. Sub-assemble rod assembly to strut making certain that index hole is lined up and seated Fig. 10, then slide rod assembly over adjuster locks, Fig. 11, until both locks are

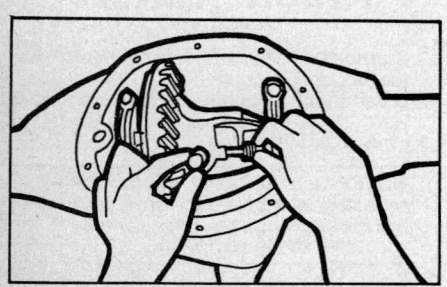

Fig. 2   Differential pinion shaft removal

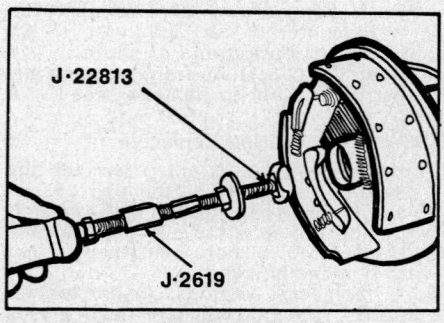

Fig. 3   Removing wheel bearing and seal

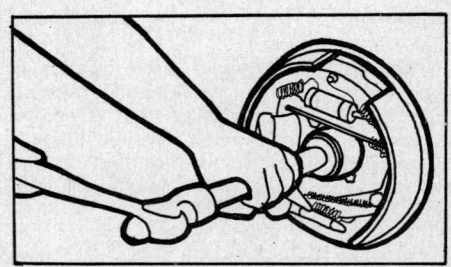

Fig. 4   Installing seal and wheel bearing

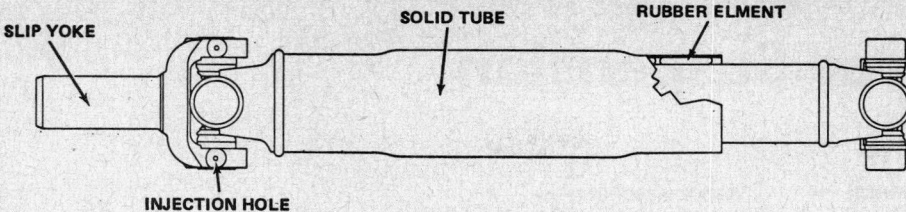

Fig. 5   Propeller shaft cross section

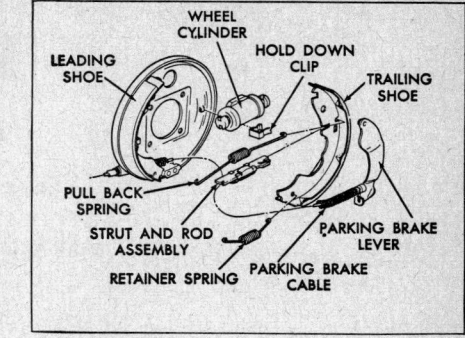

Fig. 8   Rear brake disassembled

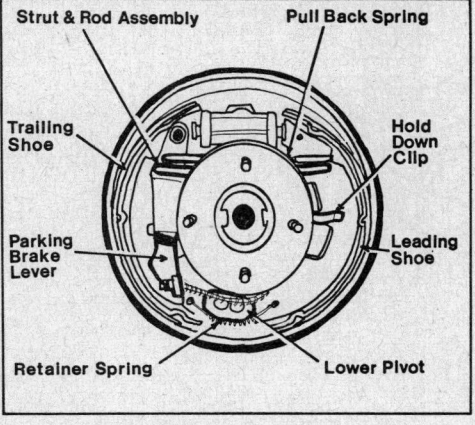

Fig. 6   Rear brake assembly

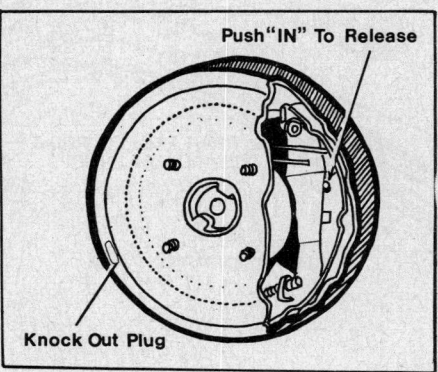

Fig. 7   Drum knock out provision

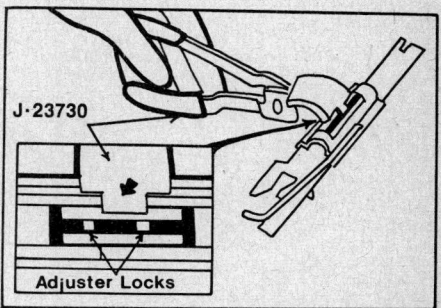

Fig. 9   Releasing adjuster locks

positioned as shown in Fig. 12. Note that adjuster lock index is about ½ covered by rod assembly.

PARKING BRAKE, ADJUST

1. Place vehicle on a hoist.
2. Apply parking brake one notch from fully released position and raise hoist.
3. Loosen equalizer check nut and tighten the adjusting nut until a slight drag is felt when rear wheels are rotated.

4. Tighten check nut securely.
5. Release parking brake and rotate rear wheels. No drag should be present.

MASTER CYLINDER, REPLACE

1. Disconnect cylinder push rod from brake pedal.
2. Disconnect brake lines from two outlets on cylinder and cover ends of lines to prevent entry of dirt.
3. Unfasten and remove cylinder from brake booster.

POWER BRAKE UNIT
1975

1. Remove the vacuum hose from check valve and then remove the master cylinder retaining nuts.
2. Remove the bolt securing the brake pipe distributor and switch assembly to fender skirt.
3. Pull master cylinder forward until it just clears mounting studs and move aside. Support cylinder to avoid stress on hydraulic lines.
4. Remove power unit to dash nuts.
5. Remove brake pedal pushrod retainer and disconnect push rod from pin.
6. Remove power unit from vehicle.

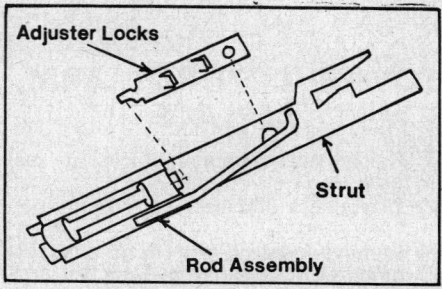

Fig. 10   Adjuster lock positioning

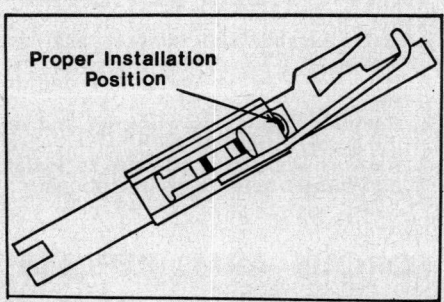

Fig. 11   Installing rod assembly

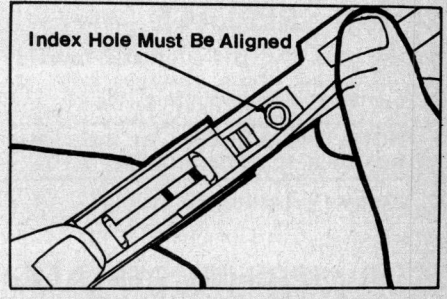

Fig. 12   Properly positioned adjuster rod assembly

Rear Suspension

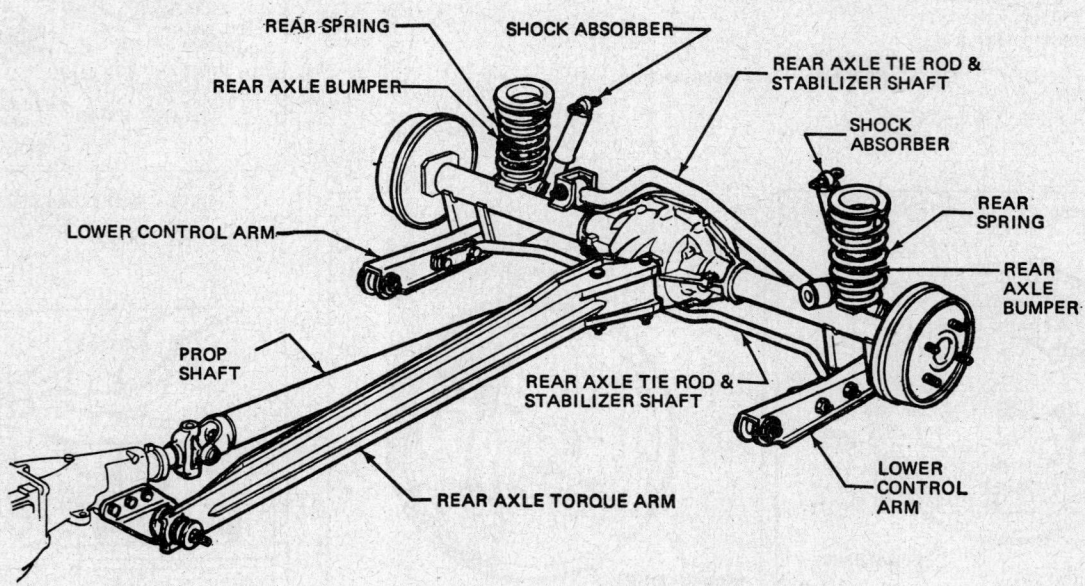

Fig. 1   Rear suspension

DESCRIPTION

This rear suspension system does not use upper control arms, instead, it uses a torque arm mounted rigidly to the differential housing at the rear and to the transmission through a rubber bushing at the front. This torque arm prevents axle housing rotation caused by starting and stopping. Along with the torque arm a track rod is used to connect the axle housing to the body to control side sway and a rear stabilizer shaft is used for improved handling, Fig. 1.

SHOCK ABSORBER, REPLACE

1. With the rear axle supported properly disconnect shock absorber from upper and lower mounting, Fig. 1.

   NOTE: Use a wrench to hold lower mounting stud from turning.

2. Reverse procedure to install.

COIL SPRING, REPLACE

1. Support vehicle at frame and rear axle with a suitable jack.

2. Disconnect shock absorbers from lower mountings.
3. Lower rear axle until springs can be removed.
4. Reverse procedure to install.

STABILIZER BAR, REPLACE

1. Remove bolts securing stabilizer bar to lower control arms, Fig. 2.
2. Reverse procedure to install and torque bolts to specifications.

TRACK ROD, REMOVAL

1. Raise vehicle and support axle assembly.
2. Remove bolts at underbody end of rod.
3. Remove bolts at axle bracket and remove track rod, Fig. 2.
4. Reverse removal procedure to install and torque bolts to specifications.

TORQUE ARM, REPLACE

1. Raise vehicle by axle assembly and support underbody with jackstands.
2. Lower axle assembly slightly and re-

move torque arm to differential bolts.
3. Disconnect mounting bracket from transmission and then remove through bolt from bracket and remove torque arm, Figs. 3 and 4.
4. To replace bushing, use an arbor press and tool J-25317-2 as a receiver and press bushing out of arm, then position new bushing in torque arm with bushing sleeve aligned with the length of the torque arm. Press bushing into place using tool J-25317-1 over bushing to properly locate bushing in arm.
5. Reverse removal procedure to install and torque nuts and bolts to specifications.

LOWER CONTROL ARM, REPLACE

1. Raise and support vehicle at rear axle.
2. Disconnect stabilizer bar from lower control arms.
3. Remove control arm front and rear mount bolts and remove control arm, Fig. 5.
4. Reverse removal procedure to install and torque bolts to specifications.

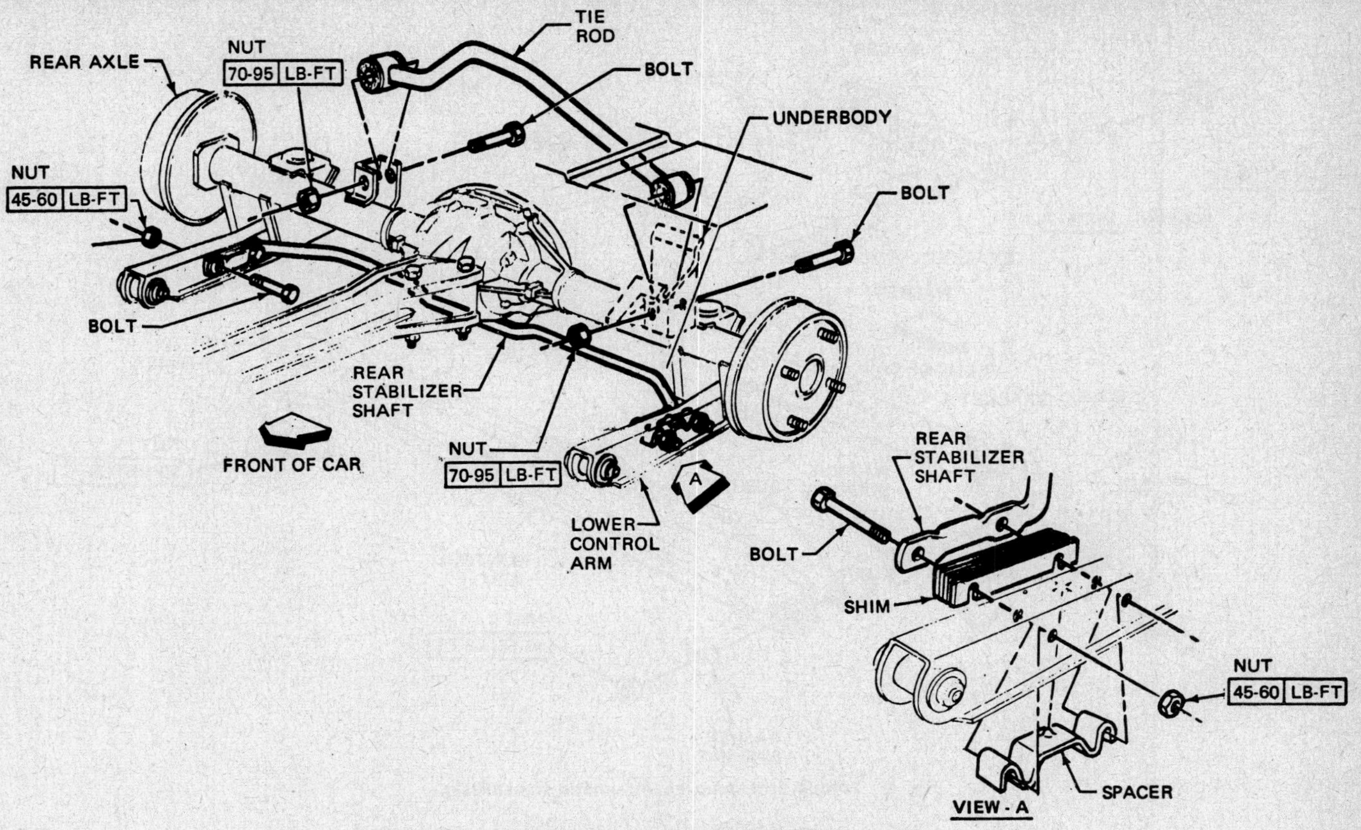

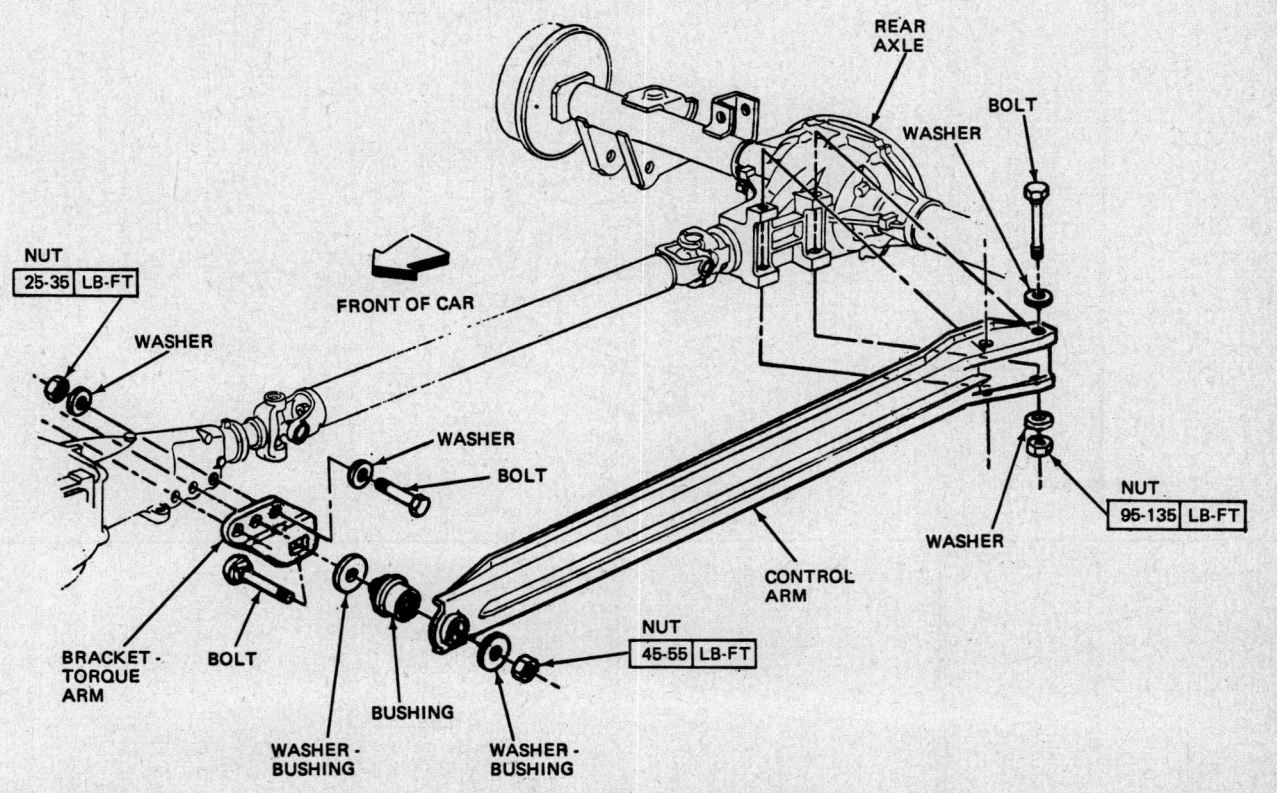

NUT 70-95 LB-FT

REAR AXLE

TIE ROD

BOLT

UNDERBODY

BOLT

NUT 45-60 LB-FT

BOLT

REAR STABILIZER SHAFT

FRONT OF CAR

NUT 70-95 LB-FT

LOWER CONTROL ARM

A

REAR STABILIZER SHAFT

BOLT

SHIM

NUT 45-60 LB-FT

VIEW - A

SPACER

Fig. 2 Track rod and stabilizer bar

REAR AXLE

BOLT

WASHER

NUT 25-35 LB-FT

WASHER

FRONT OF CAR

WASHER

BOLT

CONTROL ARM

WASHER

NUT 95-135 LB-FT

BRACKET - TORQUE ARM

BOLT

WASHER - BUSHING

BUSHING

WASHER - BUSHING

NUT 45-55 LB-FT

Fig. 3 Torque arm removal. Manual transmission

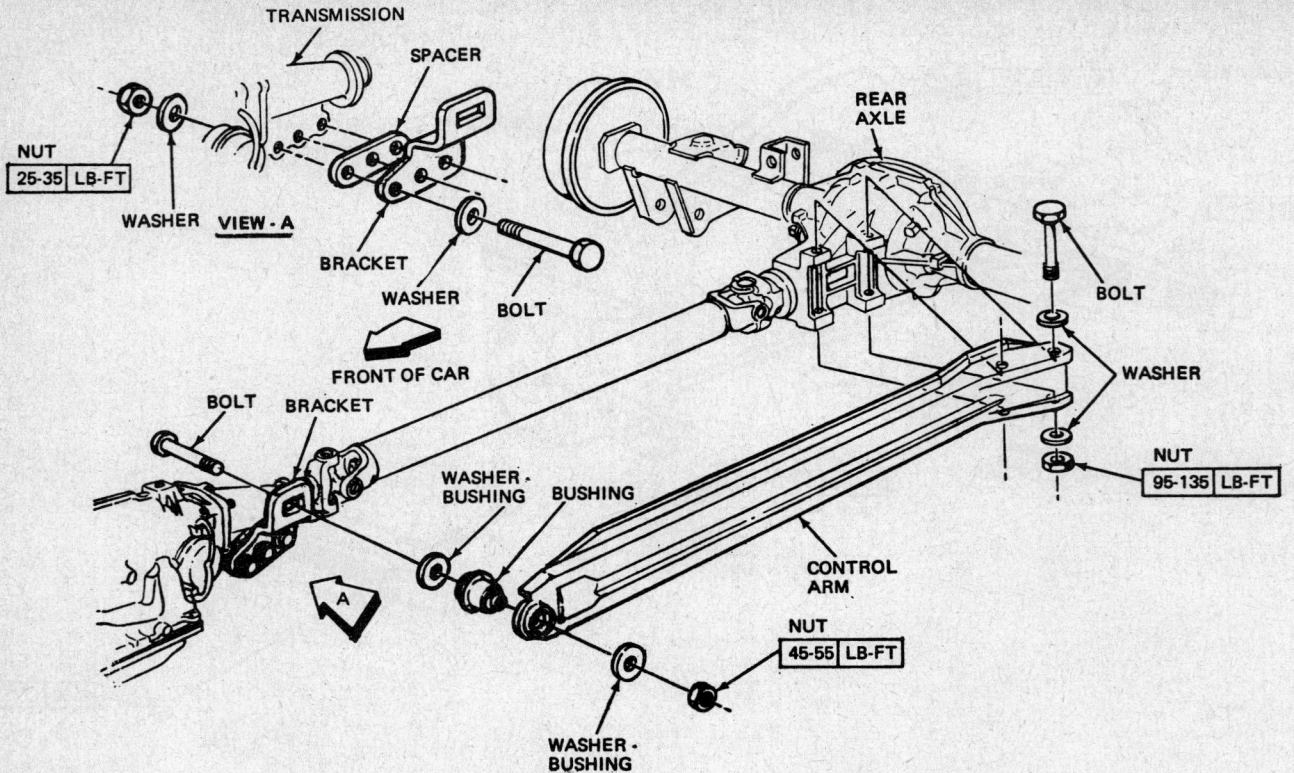

NUT 25-35 LB-FT

TRANSMISSION

SPACER

NUT

WASHER   VIEW - A

BRACKET

WASHER

BOLT

FRONT OF CAR

BOLT   BRACKET

WASHER · BUSHING   BUSHING

A

WASHER · BUSHING

REAR AXLE

BOLT

WASHER

NUT 95-135 LB-FT

CONTROL ARM

NUT 45-55 LB-FT

Fig. 4   Torque arm removal. Automatic transmission

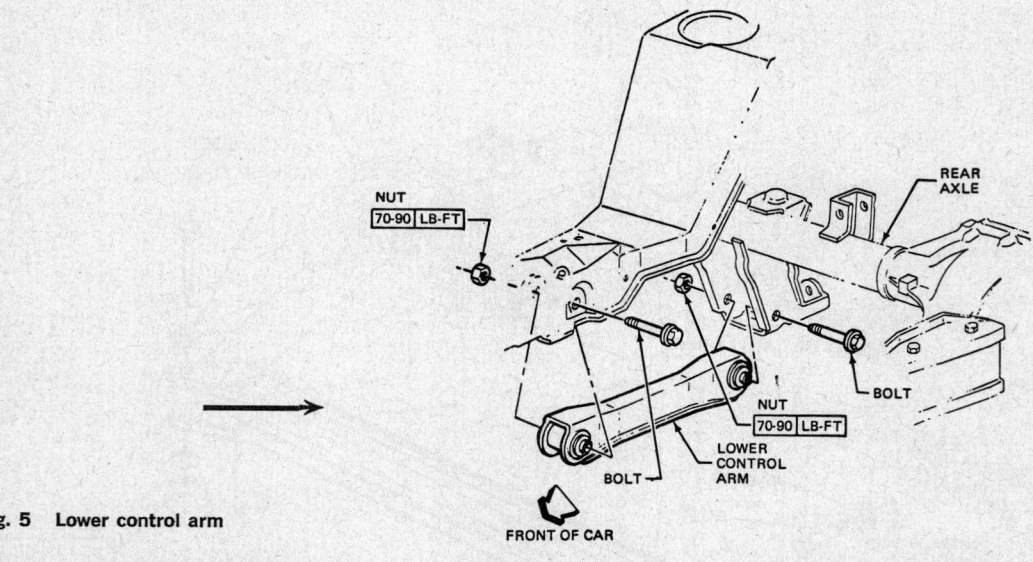

NUT 70-90 LB-FT

REAR AXLE

BOLT

NUT 70-90 LB-FT

LOWER CONTROL ARM

BOLT

FRONT OF CAR

Fig. 5   Lower control arm

Front End & Steering Section

FRONT SUSPENSION

The front suspension, Fig. 1, is of the A frame type with short and long control arms. The upper control arm is bolted to the front end sheet metal at each inner pivot point. Rubber bushings are used for mounting.

The lower control arms attach to the front end sheet metal with cam type bolts through rubber bushings. The cam bolts adjust caster and camber.

The upper ball joint is riveted in the upper arm and the lower ball joint is pressed into the lower arm.

Coil springs are mounted between the lower control arms and the shock absorber tower.

WHEEL ALIGNMENT

Caster

Caster angle is adjusted by loosening the rear lower control arm pivot nut and rotating the cam until proper setting is reached, Fig. 2.

NOTE: This eccentric cam action will tend to move the lower control arm fore or aft thereby varying the caster. Hold the cam bolt while tightening the nut.

Camber

Camber angle is adjusted by loosening the front lower control arm pivot nut and rotating the cam until setting is reached, Fig. 2.

NOTE: This eccentric cam action will move the lower arm in or out thereby varying the setting. Hold the cam bolt head while tightening the nut.

TOE-IN, ADJUST

1. Loosen clamp bolt nut at each end of each tie rod and rotate the sleeve until proper toe-in is reached.
2. Position tie rod ball stud assembly straight on a center line through their attaching points.
3. Position clamp as shown in Fig. 3 and tighten clamp nuts.

WHEEL BEARINGS, ADJUST

1. With wheel raised, remove hub cap, dust cap and cotter pin from end of spindle.
2. While rotating wheel, tighten spindle nut to 12 ft. lbs.
3. Back off adjusting nut one flat and insert cotter pin. If slot and pin hole do not line up, back off the adjusting nut an additional ½ flat or less as required to insert cotter pin.
4. Spin wheel to check that it rolls freely and then lock the cotter pin.

NOTE: Bearing should have zero preload and .001-.008″ end movement when properly adjusted.

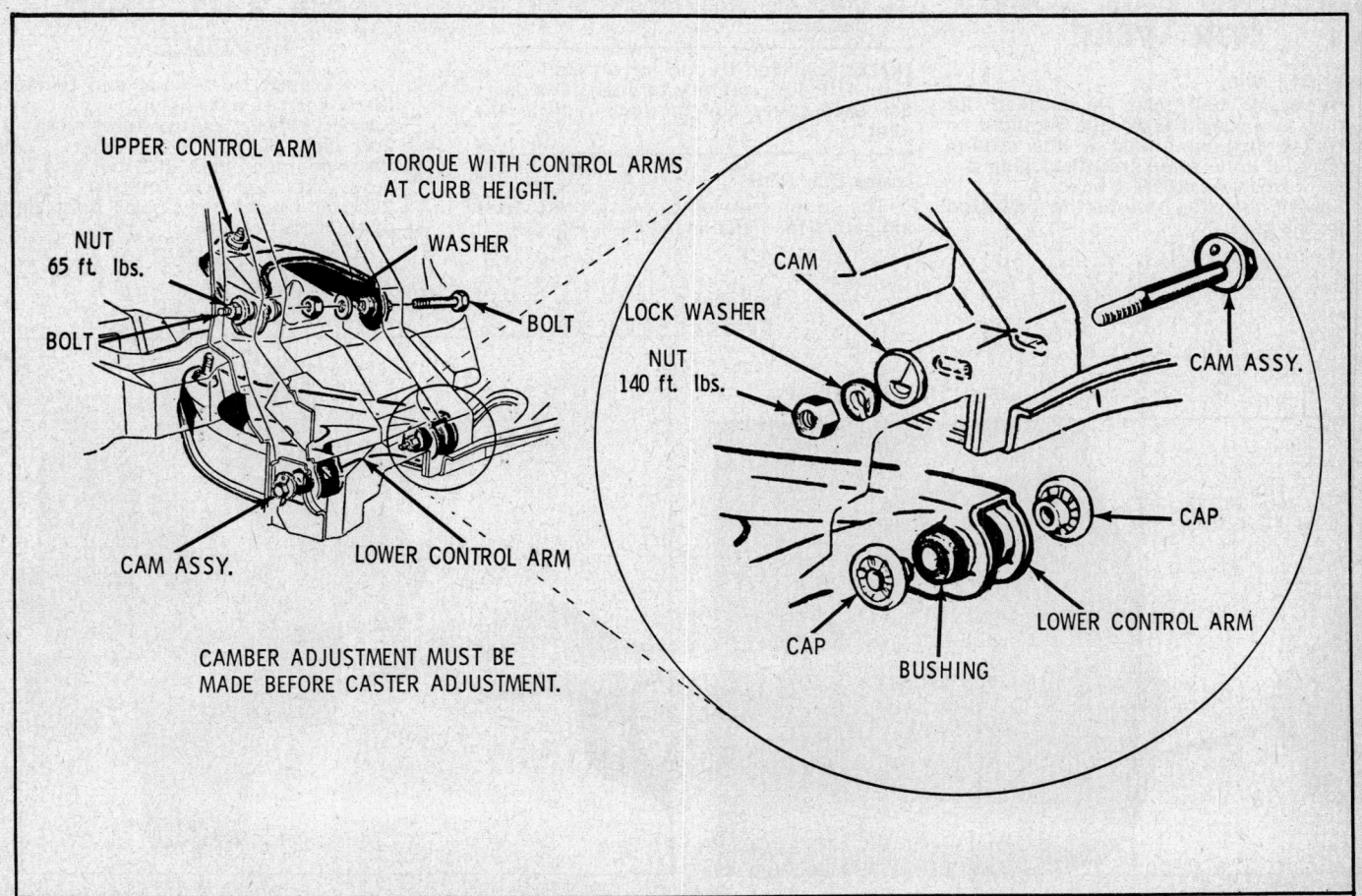

UPPER CONTROL ARM

TORQUE WITH CONTROL ARMS AT CURB HEIGHT.

NUT 65 ft. lbs.

WASHER

BOLT

BOLT

CAM ASSY.

LOWER CONTROL ARM

CAMBER ADJUSTMENT MUST BE MADE BEFORE CASTER ADJUSTMENT.

CAM

LOCK WASHER

NUT 140 ft. lbs.

CAM ASSY.

CAP

LOWER CONTROL ARM

CAP

BUSHING

Fig. 1   Front suspension

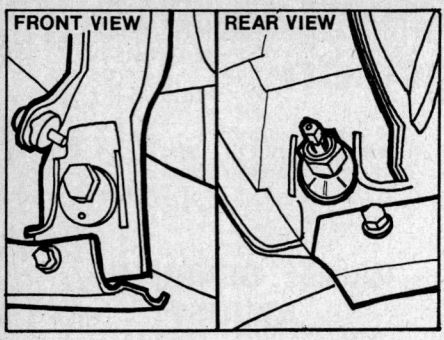

Fig. 2   Caster and camber adjustment

WHEEL BEARINGS, REPLACE

1. Raise vehicle on a hoist and remove the wheel and tire assembly.
2. Remove the brake caliper from the disc by removing the mounting pins and stamped nuts, Figs. 4 & 5.
3. Remove hub grease cap, cotter pin, spindle nut and washer and remove hub and bearings.
4. Remove inner bearing by prying out the grease seal.

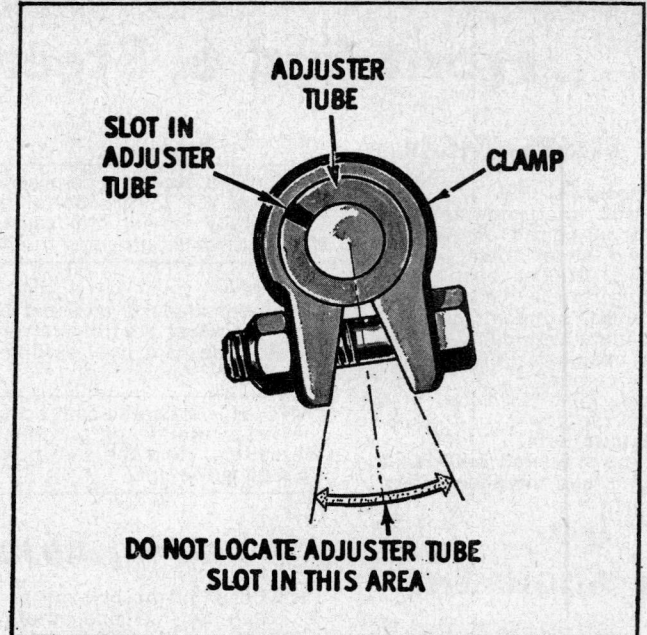

Fig. 3   Adjuster sleeve and clamp location

CHECKING BALL JOINTS FOR WEAR

Upper Ball Joint

The upper ball joint is checked for wear by checking the torque required to rotate the ball joint stud in the assembly. This is done after first dislodging the ball joint from the steering knuckle.

1. Install the stud nut to the ball stud in the seat.
2. Check the torque required to turn the ball stud.

NOTE: Specified torque for a new joint is 2 to 4 ft. lbs. rotating torque. If readings are excessively high or low, replace the joint.

Lower Ball Joint

The lower ball joints incorporate wear indicators for visual inspection, Fig. 5.

UPPER BALL JOINT, REPLACE

1. Raise vehicle on a hoist and remove wheel and tire assembly.
2. Support lower control arm with a floor jack.
3. Remove upper ball stud nut and remove ball stud from knuckle, Fig. 7.
4. Remove control arm pivot bolts and remove control arm.

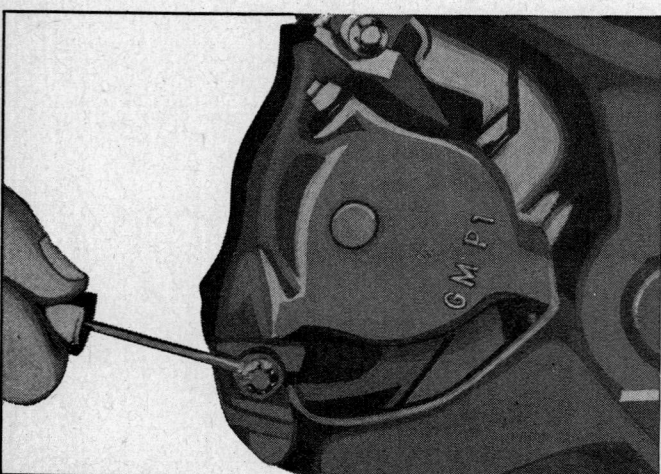

Fig. 4   Removing caliper retaining stamped nuts

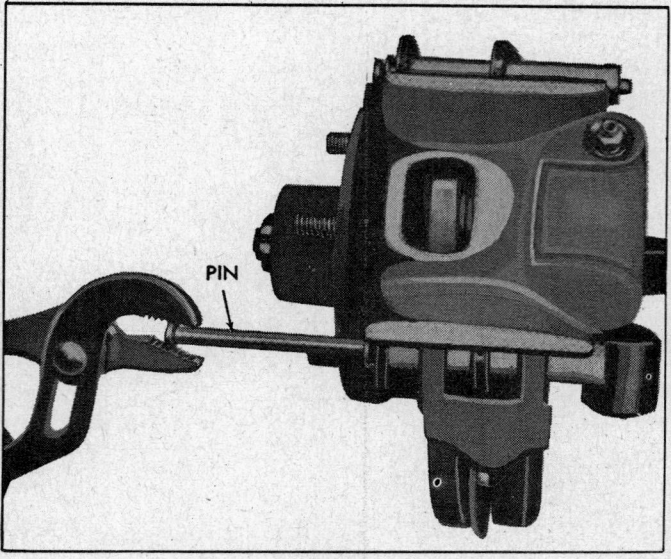

Fig. 5   Removing caliper mounting pins

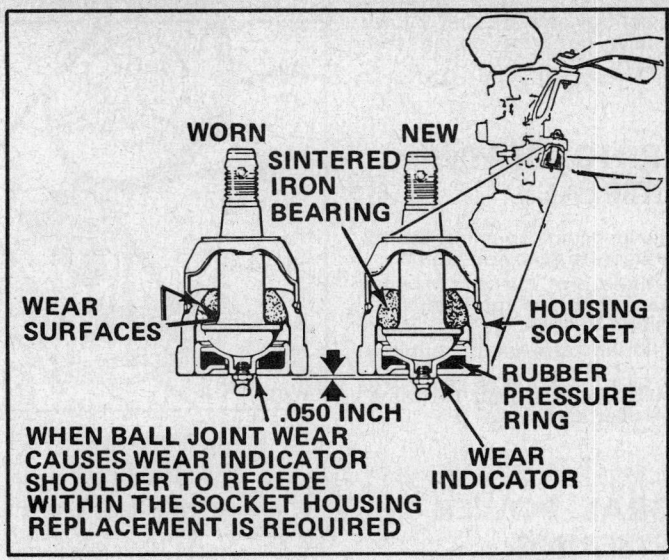

WORN | NEW

SINTERED IRON BEARING

WEAR SURFACES

HOUSING SOCKET

RUBBER PRESSURE RING

.050 INCH

WEAR INDICATOR

WHEN BALL JOINT WEAR CAUSES WEAR INDICATOR SHOULDER TO RECEDE WITHIN THE SOCKET HOUSING REPLACEMENT IS REQUIRED

Fig. 6   Lower ball joint wear indicator

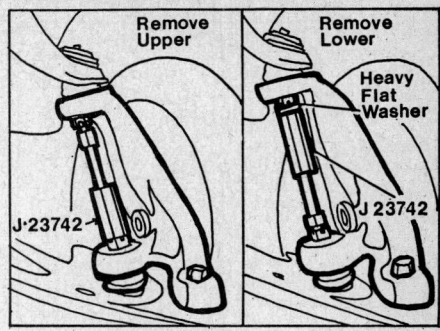

Remove Upper

Remove Lower

Heavy Flat Washer

J-23742   J 23742

Fig. 7   Removing upper and lower ball joint from steering knuckle

5. Grind off rivets securing ball joint to arm.
6. Install new ball joint using bolts and nuts supplied in kit.

LOWER BALL JOINT, REPLACE

1. Place vehicle on hoist and support lower control arm at outer end on a jack.
2. Free lower ball stud from knuckle, Fig. 7.
3. Using tool shown in Fig. 8, press ball joint out of control arm.
4. Position new ball joint so that grease bleed vent in rubber boot is facing inboard.
5. Install tool shown in Fig. 9 and press new joint into arm.
6. Install lube fitting in joint and install stud into steering knuckle.

SHOCK ABSORBER, REPLACE

1. Hold shock absorber stem and remove the nut, upper retainer and rubber grommet, Fig. 10.
2. Raise vehicle on a hoist.
3. Remove bolts from lower end of shock absorber and lower the shock from the vehicle.

COIL SPRING, REPLACE

1. With shock absorber removed and stabilizer bar removed, raise the vehicle and place jackstands under front braces.
2. Remove the wheel and tire assembly.
3. Place a floor jack under the lower

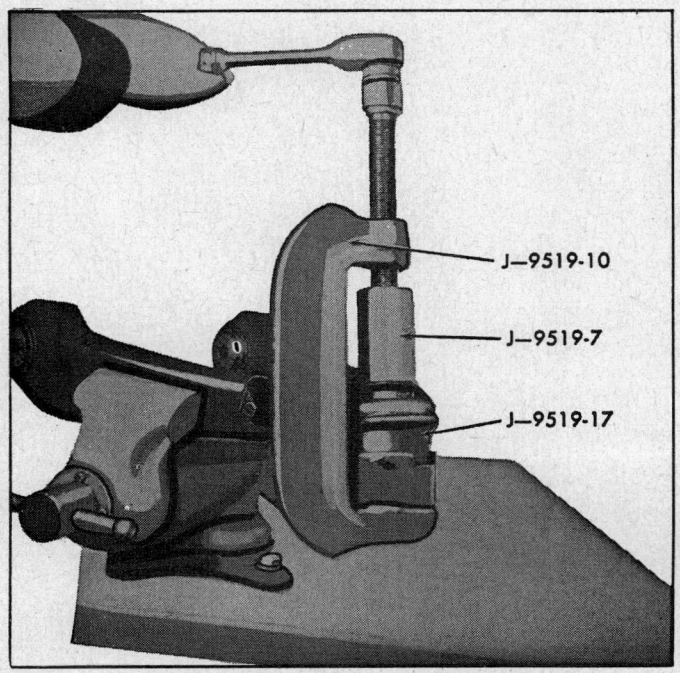

J-9519-10

J-9519-7

J-9519-17

Fig. 8   Removing lower ball joint

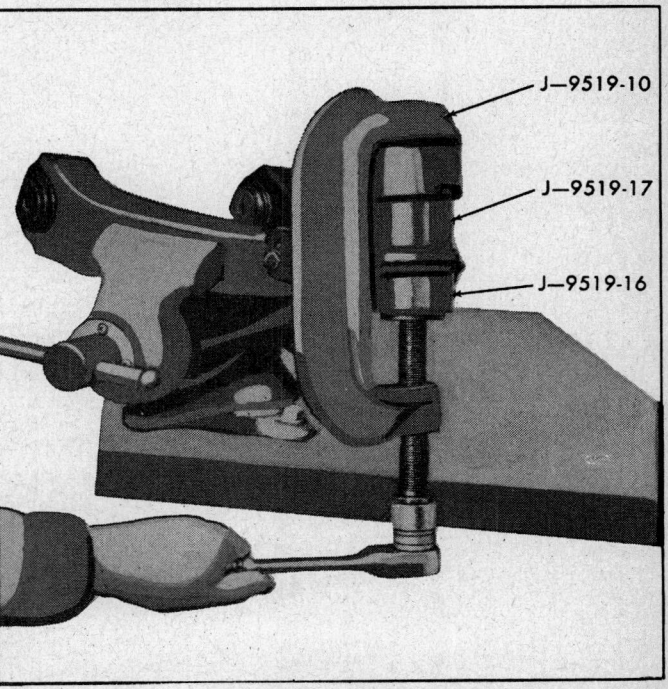

J-9519-10

J-9519-17

J-9519-16

Fig. 9   Installing lower ball joint

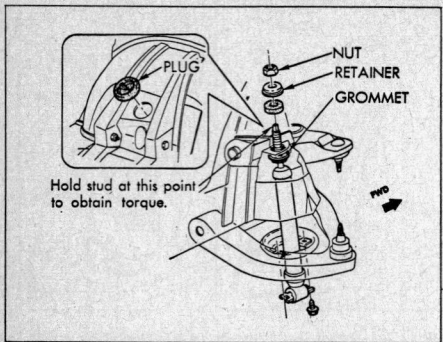

Fig. 10   Front shock absorber mountings

arm and support the arm. Use a block of wood between the control arm and the jack, Fig. 11.

4. Remove the lower ball stud from the knuckle.
5. Remove the tie rod end from the knuckle.

6. Lower the control arm by slowly lowering the jack until the spring can be removed.

STEERING GEAR, REPLACE

1. Remove the pot joint coupling clamp bolt at the steering gear wormshaft.
2. Remove pitman arm nut and washer from pitman shaft and mark relation of arm position to shaft.
3. Remove pitman arm with suitable puller.
4. Remove bolts securing gear to frame and remove gear assembly.

INTEGRAL POWER STEERING

Replacement procedures for removing the gear assembly are the same as for

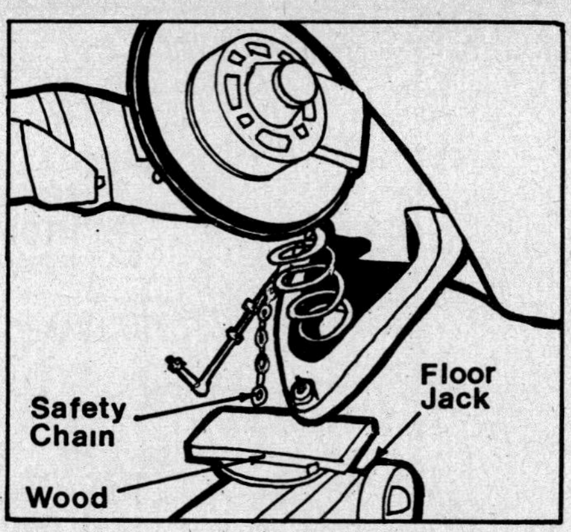

Fig. 11   Removing front coil spring

the manual type gear with the following additions:

1. Disconnect both pressure and return hoses from the gear housing and cap both hoses and steering gear outlets to prevent entry of dirt.

CHRYSLER • DODGE
IMPERIAL • PLYMOUTH

OLD CAR SPECIFICATIONS: For 1946-68 Tune Up and Wheel Alignment Specifications see main index.

INDEX OF SERVICE OPERATIONS

ACCESSORIES

Air Conditioning 2-20
Automatic Level Controls 2-39
Blower Motor, Remove 1-328
Clock Troubles 2-11
Heater Core, Replace 1-325
Power Top Troubles 2-18
Power Window Troubles 2-18
Radio, Replace .1-324
Speed Controls, Adjust 1-329

BRAKES

Anti-Skid Brakes 2-162
Brake Troubles, Mechanical 2-17
Disc Brake Service 2-133
Hydraulic System Service 2-123
Master Cylinder, Replace 1-348
Parking Brake, Adjust 1-347
Power Brake Unit, Replace 1-349
Service Brakes, Adjust 1-347
Vacuum Release Parking Brake 1-347

CLUTCH

Clutch Pedal, Adjust 1-340
Clutch, Replace 1-340
Clutch Troubles 2-12

COOLING SYSTEM

Cooling System Troubles 2-6
Variable Speed Fans 2-38
Water Pump, Replace 1-340

ELECTRICAL

Alternator Service 2-69
Blower Motor, Remove 1-328
Clutch Switch 1-311
Dash Gauge Service 2-50
Distributor, Replace 1-311
Distributor Service:
    Standard 2-525
    Transistorized 2-535
Electrical Troubles 2-8
Headlamps, Concealed Type 2-46
Headlight Aiming 2-45
Horn Sounder, Remove 1-313
Ignition Coils and Resistors 2-521
Ignition Lock, Replace 1-311
Ignition Switch, Replace 1-311
Ignition Timing .2-518
Instrument Cluster Removal 1-313
Light Switch, Replace 1-312
Neutral Safety Switch, Replace 1-313
Radio, Replace .1-324
Seat Belt Interlock Systems 2-311
Starter Service 2-54
Starter, Replace 1-311
Starter Switch Service 2-67
Stop Light Switch, Replace 1-313
Turn Signal Switch, Replace 1-313
Turn Signal Troubles 2-11

Windshield Wiper Motor, Replace 1-322
Windshield Wiper Troubles 2-19

ENGINE

Camshaft, Replace 1-337
Crankshaft Rear Oil Seal 1-338
Cylinder Head, Replace 1-332
Engine Identification 1-276
Engine Mounts, Replace 1-331
Engine, Replace 1-331
Engine Troubles 2-1
Main Bearings .1-338
Piston Pins 1-337
Piston Rings 1-337
Piston and Rod, Assemble 1-337
Pistons 1-337
Rocker Arm Service 1-334
Rod Bearings 1-338
Timing Case Cover, Replace 1-336
Timing Chain, Replace 1-336
Valve Arrangement 1-333
Valve Guide Service 1-335
Valve Lifters 1-335
Valves, Adjust .1-333

ENGINE LUBRICATION

Emission Control Systems 2-545
Oil Pan, Replace 1-338
Oil Pump, Service 1-339

FUEL SYSTEM

Carburetor Adjustments and Specs. 2-372
EGR Maintenance Reminder 1-329
Emission Control Systems 2-545
Fuel Pump, Replace 1-340
Fuel Pump Service 2-369
Fuel System Troubles 2-2

PROPELLER SHAFT & U JOINTS

Propeller Shaft .1-346
Universal Joint Service 2-117

REAR AXLE & SUSPENSION

Axle Shaft, Bearing and Seal 1-343
Leaf Springs & Bushings Replace 1-349
Rear Axle Description 1-342
Rear Axle Specifications 1-310
Rear Axle Troubles 2-16
Shock Absorber, Replace 1-349
Sway Bar, Replace 1-349

SPECIFICATIONS

Alternator 1-300
Belt Tension 1-340
Brakes 1-303
Capacities 1-305
Carburetors 2-372
Cooling System 1-305

Crankshaft and Bearings 1-299
Distributors 1-293
Engine Tightening Torque 1-301
Fuel Pump Pressure 1-340
General Engine Specs 1-282
Ignition Coils and Resistors 2-521
Pistons, Rings and Pins 1-299
Rear Axle 1-310
Starting Motors 1-300
Tune Up 1-286
Valve Lift 1-333
Valve Timing 1-334
Valves 1-297
Wheel Alignment 1-301

STEERING GEAR

Horn Sounder, Removal 1-313
Mechanical Gear, Replace 1-353
Mechanical Gear Service 2-170
Mechanical Gear Troubles 2-17
Power Gear, Replace 1-354
Steering Wheel, Replace 1-313

SUSPENSION, FRONT

Ball Joints, Check for Wear 1-352
Ball Joints, Replace 1-352
Lubrication 1-351
Riding Height, Adjust 1-353
Suspension, Description of 1-350
Toe-In, Adjust .1-352
Torsion Bar, Replace 1-353
Wheel Alignment, Adjust 1-352
Wheel Bearings, Adjust 1-352
Wheel Bearings, Replace 1-352

TRANSMISSIONS

Three Speed Manual:
    Replace 1-341
    Repairs 2-177
    Linkage, Adjust 1-341
Four Speed Manual:
    Replace 1-341
    Repairs 2-199
    Linkage, Adjust 1-342
Automatic Units 2-231
    1975 Linkage 1-342

TUNE UP

Service 2-517
Specifications 1-286

WINDSHIELD WIPER

Wiper Arms 1-322
Wiper Blades 1-322
Wiper Linkage, Replace 1-323
Wiper Motor, Replace 1-322
Wiper Switch, Replace 1-324
Wiper Troubles 2-19

CHRYSLER • DODGE • IMPERIAL • PLYMOUTH

1969-75: ON PLATE ATTACHED TO DASH PAD AND VISIBLE THROUGH WINDSHIELD.

ENGINE NUMBER LOCATION

1968-75 Six: Right front of block below cylinder head.

1969-75 V8-273, 318, 340, 360: Left front of block below cylinder head.

1969-71 V8-383 426, 440: Left side rear of block near oil pan flange.

1971-72 V8-400: Right front of block below cylinder head.

1972 V8-440: Upper left front of cylinder block.

1973-75 V8-400, 440: Upper right front of cylinder block.

ENGINE IDENTIFICATION CODE

1969-75 engines are identified by the cubic inch displacement found within the engine number stamped on the pad.

CHRYSLER GRILLE IDENTIFICATION

1969 Newport

1969 "300"

1969 New Yorker

1970 Newport

1970 "300"

1970 New Yorker

1971 Newport

1971 "300" & New Yorker

1971 New Yorker & Town Country

1972 Newport

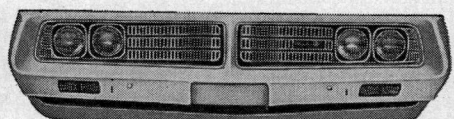
1972 New Yorker & Town Country

1973 Newport

1973 New Yorker & Town Country

1974 Newport

1974 New Yorker & Town Country

1975 Cordoba

1975 Newport

1975 New Yorker & Town Country

DODGE GRILLE IDENTIFICATION

1969 Dart

1969 Coronet

1969 Coronet "500"

1969 Charger

1969 Polara

1969 Monaco

1970 Dart

1970 Coronet, R/T, Super Bee

1970 Challenger

1970 Charger

1970 Polara

1970 Monaco

1971 Dart & Demon

1971 Challenger

1971 Charger

1971 Coronet

1971 Polara

1971 Monaco

1972 Dart

1972 Challenger

1972 Charger

1972 Coronet

1972 Polara

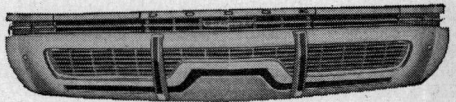

1972 Monaco

DODGE GRILLE IDENTIFICATION—Continued

1973 Dart

1973 Coronet

1973 Charger

1973 Challenger

1973 Polara

1973 Monaco

1974 Dart

1974 Challenger

1974 Charger

1974 Charger SE

1974 Coronet

1974 Monaco

1975 Dart

1975 Coronet

1975 Coronet Brougham

1975 Charger S.E.

1975 Monaco

1975 Royal Monaco

IMPERIAL GRILLE IDENTIFICATION

1969

1970

1971

1972

1973

1974

1975

PLYMOUTH GRILLE IDENTIFICATION

1969 Valiant

1969 Barracuda

1969 Belvedere, Road Runner & Satellite

1969 "GTX"

1969 Sport Satellite

1969 Fury

1969 Sport Fury & VIP

1970 Valiant & Duster

1970 Barracuda

PLYMOUTH GRILLE IDENTIFICATION—Continued

1970 Hemi 'Cuda

1970 Belvedere, Road Runner & Satellite

1970 Sport Satellite

1970 "GTX"

1970 Fury

1970 Sport Fury

1971 Valiant & Duster

1971 Duster 340

1971 Barracuda

1971 Satellite

1971 Road Runner

1971 Fury

1971 Sport Fury

1972 Valiant & Duster

1972 Barracuda

1972 Satellite

1972 Road Runner

1972 Sebring

1972 Fury

1973 Valiant & Duster

1973 Barracuda

1973 Satellite

1973 Sebring

1973 Fury

1974 Valiant & Duster

1974 Barracuda

1974 Satellite 2-Door,
Sebring & Road Runner

1974 Satellite 4-Door

1974 Fury

1975 Valiant & Duster

1975 Road Runner

1975 Fury & Custom

1975 Fury Sport

1975 Gran Fury Sport & Brougham

1975 Gran Fury

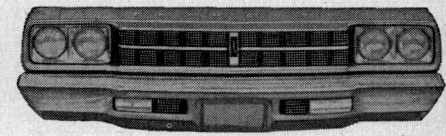

1975 Gran Fury Custom

GENERAL ENGINE SPECIFICATIONS

Year	Engine	Car-buretor	Bore and Stroke	Piston Dis-place-ment, Cubic Inches	Com-pres-sion Ratio	Maximum Brake H.P. @ R.P.M.	Maximum Torque Lbs. Ft. @ R.P.M.	Normal Oil Pressure Pounds
CHRYSLER AND IMPERIAL								
1969	290 Horsepower..............V8-383	2 Barrel	4.25 x 3.375	383	9.2	290 @ 4400	380 @ 2400	45-65
	330 Horsepower..............V8-383	4 Barrel	4.25 x 3.375	383	10.0	330 @ 5000	425 @ 3200	45-65
	350 Horsepower..............V8-440	4 Barrel	4.32 x 3.75	440	10.1	350 @ 4400	480 @ 2800	45-65
	375 Horsepower..............V8-440	4 Barrel	4.32 x 3.75	440	10.1	375 @ 4600	480 @ 3200	45-65
1970	290 Horsepower..............V8-383	2 Barrel	4.25 x 3.375	383	8.7	290 @ 4400	380 @ 2800	45-65
	330 Horsepower..............V8-383	4 Barrel	4.25 x 3.375	383	9.5	330 @ 5000	425 @ 3200	45-65
	350 Horsepower..............V8-440	4 Barrel	4.32 x 3.75	440	9.7	350 @ 4400	480 @ 2800	45-65
	375 Horsepower..............V8-440	4 Barrel	4.32 x 3.75	440	9.7	375 @ 4600	480 @ 3200	45-65
1971	275 Horsepower..............V8-383	2 Barrel	4.25 x 3.375	383	8.7	275 @ 4400	375 @ 2800	45-65
	300 Horsepower..............V8-383	4 Barrel	4.25 x 3.375	383	8.7	300 @ 4800	410 @ 3400	45-65
	190 Horsepower[1]..........V8-400	2 Barrel	4.342 x 3.375	400	8.2	190 @ 4400	310 @ 2400	45-65
	335 Horsepower..............V8-440	4 Barrel	4.32 x 3.75	440	9.0	335 @ 4400	460 @ 3200	45-65
	370 Horsepower..............V8-440	4 Barrel	4.32 x 3.75	440	9.7	370 @ 4600	480 @ 3200	45-65
1972	175 Horsepower[1]..........V8-360	2 Barrel	4.00 x 3.58	360	8.8	175 @ 4000	285 @ 2400	45-65
	190 Horsepower[1]..........V8-400	2 Barrel	4.342 x 3.375	400	8.2	190 @ 4400	310 @ 2400	45-65
	225 Horsepower[1]..........V8-440	4 Barrel	4.32 x 3.75	440	8.2	225 @ 4400	345 @ 3200	45-65
	245 Horsepower[1][2]........V8-440	4 Barrel	4.32 x 3.75	440	8.2	245 @ 4400	360 @ 3200	45-65
1973	185 Horsepower[1]..........V8-400	2 Barrel	4.34 x 3.38	400	8.2	185 @ 3600	310 @ 2400	45-65
	215 Horsepower[1]..........V8-440	4 Barrel	4.32 x 3.75	440	8.2	215 @ 3600	345 @ 2000	45-65
1974	185 Horsepower[1]..........V8-400	2 Barrel	4.34 x 3.38	400	8.2	185 @ 4000	315 @ 2400	45-65
	200 Horsepower[1]..........V8-400[4]	4 Barrel	4.34 x 3.38	400	8.2	200 @ 4400	310 @ 2400	45-65
	205 Horsepower[1]..........V8-400[3]	4 Barrel	4.34 x 3.38	400	8.2	205 @ 4400	310 @ 2400	45-65
	220 Horsepower[1]..........V8-440[4]	4 Barrel	4.32 x 3.75	440	8.2	220 @ 4000	345 @ 3200	45-65
	230 Horsepower[1]..........V8-440[3]	4 Barrel	4.32 x 3.75	440	8.2	230 @ 4000	350 @ 3200	45-65
1975	Horsepower..............V8-318	2 Barrel	3.91 x 3.31	318	8.6	—	—	30-80
	Horsepower..............V8-360	2 Barrel	4.0 x 3.58	360	8.4	—	—	30-80
	Horsepower..............V8-360	4 Barrel	4.0 x 3.58	360	8.4	—	—	30-80
	Horsepower..............V8-400	2 Barrel	4.342 x 3.375	400	8.2	—	—	30-80
	Horsepower..............V8-400	4 Barrel	4.342 x 3.375	400	8.2	—	—	30-80
	Horsepower..............V8-400	4 Barrel	4.342 x 3.375	400	8.2	—	—	30-80
	Horsepower..............V8-440	4 Barrel	4.32 x 3.75	440	8.2	—	—	30-80
	Horsepower..............V8-440	4 Barrel	4.32 x 3.75	440	8.2	—	—	30-80
DODGE								
1969	115 Horsepower..............6-170	1 Barrel	3.40 x 3.125	170	8.5	115 @ 4400	115 @ 2400	45-65
	145 Horsepower..............6-225	1 Barrel	3.40 x 4.125	225	8.4	145 @ 4000	215 @ 2400	45-65
	190 Horsepower..............V8-273	2 Barrel	3.63 x 3.31	273	9.0	190 @ 4400	260 @ 2000	45-65
	230 Horsepower..............V8-318	2 Barrel	3.91 x 3.31	318	9.2	230 @ 4400	340 @ 2400	45-65
	275 Horsepower..............V8-340	4 Barrel	4.04 x 3.31	340	10.5	275 @ 5000	340 @ 3200	45-65
	290 Horsepower..............V8-383	2 Barrel	4.25 x 3.38	383	9.2	290 @ 4400	390 @ 2800	45-65
	330 Horsepower..............V8-383	4 Barrel	4.25 x 3.38	383	10.0	330 @ 5000	425 @ 3200	45-65
	335 Horsepower..............V8-383	4 Barrel	4.25 x 3.38	383	10.0	335 @ 5000	425 @ 3400	45-65
	350 Horsepower..............V8-440	4 Barrel	4.32 x 3.75	440	10.1	350 @ 4400	480 @ 2800	45-65
	375 Horsepower..............V8-440	4 Barrel	4.32 x 3.75	440	10.1	375 @ 4600	480 @ 3200	45-65
	390 Horsepower..............V8-440	Three 2 Bar.	4.32 x 3.75	440	10.5	390 @ 4700	490 @ 3200	45-65
	425 Horsepower..............V8-426	Two 4 Bar.	4.25 x 3.75	426	10.25	425 @ 5000	490 @ 4000	45-65

Continued

GENERAL ENGINE SPECIFICATIONS—Continued

Year	Engine	Car-buretor	Bore and Stroke	Piston Dis-place-ment, Cubic Inches	Com-pres-sion Ratio	Maximum Brake H.P. @ R.P.M.	Maximum Torque Lbs. Ft. @ R.P.M.	Normal Oil Pressure Pounds
DODGE—Continued								
1970	125 Horsepower................6-198	1 Barrel	3.40 x 3.64	198	8.4	125 @ 4400	180 @ 2000	45–65
	145 Horsepower................6-225	1 Barrel	3.40 x 4.12	225	8.4	145 @ 4000	215 @ 2400	45–65
	230 Horsepower............V8-318	2 Barrel	3.91 x 3.31	318	8.8	230 @ 4400	320 @ 2000	45–65
	275 Horsepower............V8-340	4 Barrel	4.04 x 3.31	340	8.8	275 @ 5000	340 @ 3200	45–65
	290 Horsepower............V8-383	2 Barrel	4.25 x 3.38	383	8.7	290 @ 4400	390 @ 2800	45–65
	330 Horsepower............V8-383	4 Barrel	4.25 x 3.38	383	9.5	330 @ 5000	425 @ 3200	45–65
	335 Horsepower............V8-383	4 Barrel	4.25 x 3.38	383	9.5	335 @ 5200	425 @ 3400	45–65
	425 Horsepower............V8-426	Two 4 Bar.	4.25 x 3.75	426	10.2	425 @ 5000	490 @ 4000	45–65
	350 Horsepower............V8-440	4 Barrel	4.32 x 3.75	440	9.7	350 @ 4400	480 @ 2800	45–65
	375 Horsepower............V8-440	4 Barrel	4.32 x 3.75	440	9.7	375 @ 4600	480 @ 3200	45–65
	390 Horsepower............V8-440	Three 2 Bar.	4.32 x 3.75	440	10.5	390 @ 4700	490 @ 3200	45–65
1971	125 Horsepower................6-198	1 Barrel	3.40 x 3.64	198	8.4	125 @ 4400	180 @ 2000	45–65
	145 Horsepower................6-225	1 Barrel	3.40 x 4.12	225	8.4	145 @ 4000	215 @ 2400	45–65
	230 Horsepower............V8-318	2 Barrel	3.91 x 3.31	318	8.6	230 @ 4400	320 @ 2000	45–65
	275 Horsepower............V8-340	4 Barrel	4.04 x 3.31	340	10.2	340 @ 5000	340 @ 3200	45–65
	290 Horsepower............V8-340	Three 2 Bar.	4.04 x 3.31	340	10.2	290 @ 5000	340 @ 3200	45–65
	255 Horsepower............V8-360	2 Barrel	4.00 x 3.58	360	8.7	255 @ 4400	360 @ 2400	45–65
	275 Horsepower............V8-383	2 Barrel	4.25 x 3.38	383	8.5	275 @ 4400	375 @ 2800	45–65
	300 Horsepower............V8-383	4 Barrel	4.25 x 3.38	383	8.5	300 @ 4800	410 @ 3400	45–65
	425 Horsepower............V8-426	Two 4 Bar.	4.25 x 3.75	426	10.2	425 @ 5000	490 @ 4000	45–65
	335 Horsepower............V8-440	4 Barrel	4.32 x 3.75	440	9.0	335 @ 4400	460 @ 3200	45–65
	370 Horsepower............V8-440	4 Barrel	4.32 x 3.75	440	9.7	370 @ 4600	280 @ 3200	45–65
	385 Horsepower............V8-440	Three 2 Bar.	4.32 x 3.75	440	10.5	385 @ 4700	490 @ 3200	45–65
1972	100 Horsepower①..............6-198	1 Barrel	3.40 x 3.64	198	8.4	100 @ 4400	160 @ 2400	45–65
	110 Horsepower①..............6-225	1 Barrel	3.40 x 4.12	225	8.4	110 @ 4000	185 @ 2000	45–65
	150 Horsepower①..........V8-318	2 Barrel	3.91 x 3.31	318	8.6	150 @ 4000	260 @ 1600	45–65
	240 Horsepower①..........V8-340	4 Barrel	4.04 x 3.31	340	8.5	240 @ 4800	290 @ 3600	45–65
	175 Horsepower①..........V8-360	2 Barrel	4.00 x 3.58	360	8.8	175 @ 4000	285 @ 2400	45–65
	190 Horsepower①..........V8-400	2 Barrel	4.34 x 3.38	400	8.2	190 @ 4400	310 @ 2400	45–65
	255 Horsepower①②........V8-400	4 Barrel	4.34 x 3.38	400	8.2	255 @ 4800	340 @ 3200	45–65
	225 Horsepower①..........V8-440	4 Barrel	4.32 x 3.75	440	8.2	225 @ 4400	345 @ 3200	45–65
	245 Horsepower①②........V8-440	4 Barrel	4.32 x 3.75	440	8.2	245 @ 4400	360 @ 3200	45–65
	330 Horsepower①..........V8-440	Three 2 Bar.	4.32 x 3.75	440	10.3	330 @ 4800	410 @ 3600	45–65
1973	95 Horsepower①..............6-198	1 Barrel	3.40 x 3.64	198	8.4	95 @ 4000	150 @ 1600	45–65
	105 Horsepower①..............6-225	1 Barrel	3.40 x 4.12	225	8.4	105 @ 4000	185 @ 1600	45–65
	150 Horsepower①..........V8-318	2 Barrel	3.91 x 3.31	318	8.6	150 @ 3600	265 @ 2000	45–65
	240 Horsepower①..........V8-340	4 Barrel	4.04 x 3.31	340	8.5	240 @ 4800	295 @ 3600	45–65
	170 Horsepower①..........V8-360	2 Barrel	4.00 x 3.58	360	8.4	170 @ 4000	285 @ 2400	45–65
	175 Horsepower①..........V8-400	2 Barrel	4.34 x 3.38	400	8.2	175 @ 3600	305 @ 2400	45–65
	185 Horsepower①..........V8-400	2 Barrel	4.34 x 3.38	400	8.2	185 @ 3600	310 @ 2400	45–65
	260 Horsepower①..........V8-400	4 Barrel	4.34 x 3.38	400	8.2	260 @ 4800	335 @ 3600	45–65
	220 Horsepower①..........V8-440	4 Barrel	4.32 x 3.75	440	8.2	220 @ 3600	350 @ 2400	45–65
	280 Horsepower①..........V8-440	4 Barrel	4.32 x 3.75	440	8.2	280 @ 4800	380 @ 3200	45–65
1974	95 Horsepower①..............6-198	1 Barrel	3.40 x 3.64	198	8.4	95 @ 4000	145 @ 2000	45–65
	105 Horsepower①..............6-225	1 Barrel	3.40 x 4.12	225	8.4	105 @ 3600	180 @ 1600	45–65
	150 Horsepower①..........V8-318	2 Barrel	3.91 x 3.31	318	8.6	150 @ 4000	255 @ 2200	45–65
	180 Horsepower①..........V8-360③	2 Barrel	4.00 x 3.58	360	8.4	180 @ 4000	290 @ 2400	45–65

Continued

GENERAL ENGINE SPECIFICATIONS—Continued

Year	Engine	Car-buretor	Bore and Stroke	Piston Dis-place-ment, Cubic Inches	Com-pres-sion Ratio	Maximum Brake H.P. @ R.P.M.	Maximum Torque Lbs. Ft. @ R.P.M.	Normal Oil Pressure Pounds
DODGE—Continued								
1974	200 Horsepower①.........V8-360④	4 Barrel	4.00 x 3.58	360	8.4	200 @ 4000	290 @ 3200	45–65
	245 Horsepower①②.........V8-360③	4 Barrel	4.00 x 3.58	360	8.4	245 @ 4800	320 @ 3600	45–65
	185 Horsepower①..........V8-400③	2 Barrel	4.34 x 3.38	400	8.2	185 @ 4000	315 @ 2400	45–65
	200 Horsepower①..........V8-400④	4 Barrel	4.34 x 3.38	400	8.2	200 @ 4400	310 @ 2400	45–65
	205 Horsepower①..........V8-400③	4 Barrel	4.34 x 3.38	400	8.2	205 @ 4400	310 @ 2400	45–65
	250 Horsepower①②.........V8-400③	4 Barrel	4.34 x 3.38	400	8.2	250 @ 4800	330 @ 3400	45–65
	230 Horsepower①..........V8-440③	4 Barrel	4.32 x 3.75	440	8.2	230 @ 4000	350 @ 3200	45–65
	220 Horsepower①..........V8-440④	4 Barrel	4.32 x 3.75	440	8.2	220 @ 4000	345 @ 3200	45–65
	275 Horsepower①②.........V8-440	4 Barrel	4.32 x 3.75	440	8.2	275 @ 4400	375 @ 3200	45–65
1975	Horsepower..............6-225	1 Barrel	3.4 x 4.125	225	8.4	—	—	30–70
	Horsepower.............V8-318	2 Barrel	3.91 x 3.31	318	8.6	—	—	30–80
	Horsepower.............V8-360	2 Barrel	4.0 x 3.58	360	8.4	—	—	30–80
	Horsepower.............V8-360	4 Barrel	4.0 x 3.58	360	8.4	—	—	30–80
	Horsepower.............V8-360	4 Barrel	4.0 x 3.58	360	8.4	—	—	30–80
	Horsepower.............V8-400	2 Barrel	4.342 x 3.375	400	8.2	—	—	30–80
	Horsepower.............V8-400	4 Barrel	4.342 x 3.375	400	8.2	—	—	30–80
	Horsepower.............V8-400	4 Barrel	4.342 x 3.375	400	8.2	—	—	30–80
	Horsepower.............V8-440	4 Barrel	4.32 x 3.75	440	8.2	—	—	30–80
	Horsepower.............V8-440	4 Barrel	4.342 x 3.75	440	8.2	—	—	30–80
PLYMOUTH								
1969	115 Horsepower..............6-170	1 Barrel	3.40 x 3.125	170	8.5	115 @ 4400	155 @ 2400	45–65
	145 Horsepower..............6-225	1 Barrel	3.40 x 4.125	225	8.4	145 @ 4000	215 @ 2400	45–65
	190 Horsepower.............V8-273	2 Barrel	3.63 x 3.31	273	9.0	190 @ 4400	260 @ 2000	45–65
	230 Horsepower.............V8-318	2 Barrel	3.91 x 3.31	318	9.2	230 @ 4400	340 @ 2400	45–65
	275 Horsepower.............V8-340	4 Barrel	4.04 x 3.31	340	10.5	275 @ 5000	340 @ 3200	45–65
	290 Horsepower.............V8-383	2 Barrel	4.25 x 3.38	383	9.2	290 @ 4400	390 @ 2800	45–65
	330 Horsepower.............V8-383	4 Barrel	4.25 x 3.38	383	10.0	330 @ 5000	425 @ 3200	45–65
	335 Horsepower.............V8-383	4 Barrel	4.25 x 3.38	383	10.0	335 @ 5000	425 @ 3400	45–65
	350 Horsepower.............V8-440	4 Barrel	4.32 x 3.75	440	10.1	350 @ 4400	480 @ 2800	45–65
	375 Horsepower.............V8-440	4 Barrel	4.32 x 3.75	440	10.1	375 @ 4600	480 @ 3200	45–65
	390 Horsepower.............V8-440	Three 2 Bar.	4.32 x 3.75	440	10.5	390 @ 4700	490 @ 3200	45–65
	425 Horsepower.............V8-426	Two 4 Bar.	4.25 x 3.75	426	10.25	425 @ 5000	490 @ 4000	45–65
1970	125 Horsepower..............6-198	1 Barrel	3.40 x 3.64	198	8.4	125 @ 4400	180 @ 2000	45–65
	145 Horsepower..............6-225	1 Barrel	3.40 x 4.12	225	8.4	145 @ 4000	215 @ 2400	45–65
	230 Horsepower.............V8-318	2 Barrel	3.91 x 3.31	318	8.8	230 @ 4400	320 @ 2000	45–65
	275 Horsepower.............V8-340	4 Barrel	4.04 x 3.31	340	10.5	275 @ 5000	340 @ 3200	45–65
	290 Horsepower.............V8-383	2 Barrel	4.25 x 3.38	383	8.7	290 @ 4400	390 @ 2800	45–65
	330 Horsepower.............V8-383	4 Barrel	4.25 x 3.38	383	9.5	330 @ 5000	425 @ 3200	45–65
	335 Horsepower.............V8-383	4 Barrel	4.25 x 3.38	383	9.5	335 @ 5200	425 @ 3400	45–65
	425 Horsepower.............V8-426	Two 4 Bar.	4.25 x 3.75	426	10.2	425 @ 5000	490 @ 4000	45–65
	350 Horsepower.............V8-440	4 Barrel	4.32 x 3.75	440	9.7	350 @ 4400	480 @ 2800	45–65
	375 Horsepower.............V8-440	4 Barrel	4.32 x 3.75	440	9.7	375 @ 4600	480 @ 3200	45–65
	390 Horsepower.............V8-440	Three 2 Bar.	4.32 x 3.75	440	10.5	390 @ 4700	490 @ 3200	45–65
1971	125 Horsepower..............6-198	1 Barrel	3.40 x 3.64	198	8.4	125 @ 4400	180 @ 2000	45–65
	145 Horsepower..............6-225	1 Barrel	3.40 x 4.12	225	8.4	145 @ 4000	215 @ 2400	45–65
	230 Horsepower.............V8-318	2 Barrel	3.91 x 3.31	318	8.6	230 @ 4400	320 @ 2000	45–65
	275 Horsepower.............V8-340	4 Barrel	4.04 x 3.31	340	10.3	340 @ 5000	340 @ 3200	45–65
	290 Horsepower.............V8-340	Three 2 Bar.	4.04 x 3.31	340	10.2	290 @ 5000	340 @ 3200	45–65

Continued

GENERAL ENGINE SPECIFICATIONS—Continued

Year	Engine	Car-buretor	Bore and Stroke	Piston Dis-place-ment, Cubic Inches	Com-pres-sion Ratio	Maximum Brake H.P. @ R.P.M.	Maximum Torque H.P. @ R.P.M.	Normal Oil Pressure Pounds
PLYMOUTH—Continued								
1971	255 Horsepower..............V8-360	2 Barrel	4.00 x 3.58	360	8.7	255 @ 4400	360 @ 2400	45–65
	275 Horsepower..............V8-383	2 Barrel	4.25 x 3.38	383	8.5	275 @ 4400	375 @ 2800	45–65
	300 Horsepower..............V8-383	4 Barrel	4.25 x 3.38	383	8.5	300 @ 4800	410 @ 3400	45–65
	425 Horsepower..............V8-426	Two 4 Bar.	4.25 x 3.75	426	10.2	425 @ 5000	490 @ 4000	45–65
	335 Horsepower..............V8-440	4 Barrel	4.32 x 3.75	440	9.0	335 @ 4400	460 @ 3200	45–65
	370 Horsepower..............V8-440	4 Barrel	4.32 x 3.75	440	9.7	370 @ 4600	280 @ 3200	45–65
	385 Horsepower..............V8-440	Three 2 Bar.	4.32 x 3.75	440	10.5	385 @ 4700	490 @ 3200	45–65
1972	100 Horsepower①..............6-198	1 Barrel	3.40 x 3.64	198	8.4	100 @ 4400	160 @ 2400	45–65
	110 Horsepower①..............6-225	1 Barrel	3.40 x 4.12	225	8.4	110 @ 4000	185 @ 2000	45–65
	150 Horsepower①..............V8-318	2 Barrel	3.91 x 3.31	318	8.6	150 @ 4000	260 @ 1600	45–65
	240 Horsepower①..............V8-340	4 Barrel	4.04 x 3.31	340	8.5	240 @ 4800	290 @ 3600	45–65
	175 Horsepower①..............V8-360	2 Barrel	4.00 x 3.58	360	8.8	175 @ 4000	285 @ 2400	45–65
	190 Horsepower①..............V8-400	2 Barrel	4.34 x 3.38	400	8.2	190 @ 4400	310 @ 2400	45–65
	255 Horsepower①②..............V8-400	4 Barrel	4.34 x 3.38	400	8.2	255 @ 4800	340 @ 3200	45–65
	255 Horsepower①..............V8-440	4 Barrel	4.32 x 3.75	440	8.2	225 @ 4400	345 @ 3200	45–65
	245 Horsepower①②..............V8-440	4 Barrel	4.32 x 3.75	440	8.2	245 @ 4400	360 @ 3200	45–65
	330 Horsepower①..............V8-440	Three 2 Bar.	4.32 x 3.75	440	10.3	330 @ 4800	410 @ 3600	45–65
1973	95 Horsepower①..............6-198	1 Barrel	3.40 x 3.64	198	8.4	95 @ 4000	150 @ 1600	45–65
	105 Horsepower①..............6-225	1 Barrel	3.40 x 4.12	225	8.4	105 @ 4000	185 @ 1600	45–65
	150 Horsepower①..............V8-318	2 Barrel	3.91 x 3.31	318	8.6	150 @ 3600	265 @ 2000	45–65
	240 Horsepower①..............V8-340	4 Barrel	4.04 x 3.31	340	8.5	240 @ 4800	295 @ 3600	45–65
	170 Horsepower①..............V8-360	2 Barrel	4.00 x 3.58	360	8.4	170 @ 4000	285 @ 2400	45–65
	175 Horsepower①..............V8-400	2 Barrel	4.34 x 3.38	400	8.2	175 @ 3600	305 @ 2400	45–65
	185 Horsepower①..............V8-400	2 Barrel	4.34 x 3.38	400	8.2	185 @ 3600	310 @ 2400	45–65
	260 Horsepower①..............V8-400	4 Barrel	4.34 x 3.38	400	8.2	260 @ 4800	335 @ 3600	45–65
	220 Horsepower①..............V8-440	4 Barrel	4.32 x 3.75	440	8.2	220 @ 3600	350 @ 2400	45–65
	280 Horsepower①..............V8-440	4 Barrel	4.32 x 3.75	440	8.2	280 @ 4800	380 @ 3200	45–65
1974	95 Horsepower①..............6-198	1 Barrel	3.40 x 3.64	198	8.4	95 @ 4000	145 @ 2000	45–65
	105 Horsepower①..............6-225	1 Barrel	3.40 x 4.12	225	8.4	105 @ 3600	180 @ 1600	45–65
	150 Horsepower①..............V8-318	2 Barrel	3.91 x 3.31	318	8.6	150 @ 4000	255 @ 2200	45–65
	170 Horsepower①②..............V8-318	2 Barrel	3.91 x 3.31	318	8.6	170 @ 4000	265 @ 2400	45–65
	180 Horsepower①..............V8-360	2 Barrel	4.00 x 3.58	360	8.4	180 @ 4000	290 @ 2400	45–65
	200 Horsepower①..............V8-360④	4 Barrel	4.00 x 3.58	360	8.4	200 @ 4000	290 @ 3200	45–65
	245 Horsepower①②..............V8-360③	4 Barrel	4.00 x 3.58	360	8.4	245 @ 4800	320 @ 3600	45–65
	185 Horsepower①..............V8-400	2 Barrel	4.34 x 3.38	400	8.2	185 @ 4000	315 @ 2400	45–65
	205 Horsepower①..............V8-400	4 Barrel	4.34 x 3.38	400	8.2	205 @ 4400	310 @ 2400	45–65
	250 Horsepower①②..............V8-400	4 Barrel	4.34 x 3.38	400	8.2	250 @ 4800	330 @ 3400	45–65
	230 Horsepower①..............V8-440③	4 Barrel	4.32 x 3.75	440	8.2	230 @ 4000	350 @ 3200	45–65
	220 Horsepower①..............V8-440④	4 Barrel	4.32 x 3.75	440	8.2	220 @ 4000	345 @ 3200	45–65
	275 Horsepower①②..............V8-440	4 Barrel	4.32 x 3.75	440	8.2	275 @ 4400	375 @ 3200	45–65
1975	Horsepower..............6-225	1 Barrel	3.4 x 4.125	225	8.4	—	—	30–70
	Horsepower..............V8-318	2 Barrel	3.91 x 3.31	318	8.6	—	—	30–80
	Horsepower..............V8-360	2 Barrel	4.0 x 3.58	360	8.4	—	—	30–80
	Horsepower..............V8-360	4 Barrel	4.0 x 3.58	360	8.4	—	—	30–80
	Horsepower..............V8-360	4 Barrel	4.0 x 3.58	360	8.4	—	—	30–80
	Horsepower..............V8-400	2 Barrel	4.342 x 3.375	400	8.2	—	—	30–80
	Horsepower..............V8-400	4 Barrel	4.342 x 3.375	400	8.2	—	—	30–80
	Horsepower..............V8-400	4 Barrel	4.342 x 3.375	400	8.2	—	—	30–80
	Horsepower..............V8-440	4 Barrel	4.32 x 3.75	440	8.2	—	—	30–80
	Horsepower..............V8-440	4 Barrel	4.32 x 3.75	440	8.2	—	—	30–80

①—Ratings are NET—as installed in the vehicle.
②—With dual exhausts.
③—Exc. California.
④—California.

TUNE UP SPECIFICATIONS

OLD CAR SPECIFICATIONS: For 1946-68 Tune Up Specifications see main index.

★When using a timing light, disconnet vacuum hose or tube at distribtor and plug opening in hose or tube so idle speed will not be affected.

●When checking compression, lowest cylinder must be within 80 percent of highest.

▲Before removing wires from distributor cap, determine location of the No. 1 wire in cap, as distributor position may have been altered from that shown at the end of this chart.

Year	Spark Plug Type ⑦	Spark Plug Gap Inch	Distributor Point Gap Inch	Distributor Dwell Angle Deg.	Firing Order Fig. ▲	Timing BTDC ①	Mark Fig.	Hot Idle Speed Std. Trans.	Hot Idle Speed Auto. Trans. ②	Air Fuel Ratio Std. Trans.	Air Fuel Ratio Auto. Trans.	Idle "CO" % Std. Trans.	Idle "CO" % Auto. Trans.
CHRYSLER & IMPERIAL													
1969													
V8-383 Std. Tr.㉑	J14Y	.035	.017	30—35	J	TDC	F	700⑥	—	—	—	—	—
V8-383 Auto. Tr.㉑	J14Y	.035	.017	30—35	J	7½°	F	—	600⑥	—	—	—	—
V8-383 Auto. Tr.④	J11Y	.035	.017	30—35	J	5°	F	700⑥	650⑥	—	—	—	—
V8-440 Auto. Tr.	J13Y	.035	.017	30—35	J	7½°	F	—	650⑥	—	—	—	—
V8-440 Auto. Tr.㉒	J11Y	.035	.017	30—35	J	5°	F	—	650⑥	—	—	—	—
V8-440 Std. Tr.㉒	J11Y	.035	.017	⑰	J	TDC	F	700⑥	—	—	—	—	—
1970-71													
V8-360	N13Y	.035	.017	30—34	H	2½	E	750	700	14.2 to 1	14.2 to 1	—	—
V8-383 Std. Tr.㉑	J14Y	.035	.019	28½—32½	J	TDC	F	750	—	14.2 to 1	—	—	—
V8-383 Auto. Tr.㉑	J14Y	.035	.019	28½—32½	J	2½°	F	—	650N	—	14.2 to 1	—	—
V8-383 Std. Tr.④	J11Y	.035	.019	28½—32½	J	TDC	F	900	—	14.2 to 1	—	—	—
V8-383 Auto. Tr.④	J11Y	.035	.019	28½—32½	J	2½°	F	—	700N	—	14.2 to 1	—	—
V8-400 Auto. Tr.	J11Y	.035	.019	28½—32½	J	2½°	F	—	700N	—	14.2 to 1	—	—
V8-440 Auto. Tr.	J13Y	.035	.019	28½—32½	J	5°	F	—	650N	—	14.2 to 1	—	—
V8-440 Std. Tr.㉒	J11Y	.035	.019	28½—32½	J	TDC	F	900	—	14.2 to 1	—	—	—
V8-440 Auto. Tr.㉒	J11Y	.035	.019	28½—32½	J	2½°	F	—	800N	—	14.2 to 1	—	—
1972													
V8-360	N13Y	.035	.017	30—34	H	TDC	E	—	750N	14.2 to 1	14.2 to 1	—	—
V8-400	J13Y	.035	.019	28½—32½	J	5°	F	—	700N	14.2 to 1	14.2 to 1	—	—
V8-440 Chrysler	J11Y	.035	.019	28½—32½	J	10°㉗	F	—	750N㉘	14.2 to 1	14.2 to 1	—	—
V8-440 Imperial	J11Y	.035	—	—	J	10°	F	—	750N㉘	14.2 to 1	14.2 to 1	—	—
1973													
V8-400㉑	J13Y	.035	—	—	J	10°	F	—	700	—	14.2 to 1	—	—
V8-400④	J11Y	.035	—	—	J	7½°	F	—	750	—	14.2 to 1	—	—
V8-440	J11Y	.035	—	—	J	10°	F	—	700	—	14.2 to 1	—	—
1974													
V8-400㉑	J13Y	.035	—	—	J	7½°⑨	F	—	750	—	14.3	—	—
V8-400④㉔	J13Y	.035	—	—	J	5°	F	—	750	—	14.3	—	—
V8-400④㉕	J13Y	.035	—	—	J	5°	F	—	750	—	14.1	—	—
V8-440㉔	J11Y	.035	—	—	J	10°	F	—	750	—	14.3	—	—
V8-440㉕	J11Y	.035	—	—	J	10°	F	—	750	—	14.1	—	—
1975													
V8-318⑥㉔	N13Y	.035	—	—	H	2°	E	800	750N	14.3 to 1	14.3 to 1	.3⑲	.3⑲
V8-318⑥㉔	N13Y	.035	—	—	H	2°⑮	E	750	750N	—	14.3 to 1	—	.5⑳
V8-318㉕	N13Y	.035	—	—	H	TDC	E	—	750N	—	—	—	.5⑳
V8-360 2 BBl. Carb.	N12Y	.035	—	—	H	6°	E	—	750N	—	14.3 to 1	—	.3⑲
V8-360 4 BBl. Carb.㉔	N12Y	.035	—	—	H	2°	E	—	750N	—	14.3 to 1	—	.5⑳
V8-360 4 BBl. Carb.㉕	N12Y	.035	—	—	H	6°	E	—	750N	—	—	—	.5⑳
V8-400 2 BBl. Carb.	J13Y	.035	—	—	J	10°	F	—	750N	—	—	—	.3⑲
V8-400 4 BBl. Carb.	J13Y	.035	—	—	J	8°	F	—	750N	—	㉜	—	㉝
V8-440	RJ87P	.040	—	—	J	8°	F	—	750N	—	㉜	—	㉞
V8-440㉒㉔	J11Y	.035	—	—	J	10°	F	—	750N	—	14.3 to 1	—	.3⑲
V8-440㉒㉕	RJ87P	.035	—	—	J	8°	F	—	750N	—	—	—	.5⑳

TUNE UP SPECIFICATIONS—Continued

OLD CAR SPECIFICATIONS: For 1946-68 Tune Up Specifications see main index.

★When using a timing light, disconnect vacuum hose or tube at distributor and plug opening in hose or tube so idle speed will not be affected.

●When checking compression, lowest cylinder must be within 80 percent of highest.

▲Before removing wires from distributor cap, determine location of the No. 1 wire in cap, as distributor position may have been altered from that shown at the end of this chart.

Year	Spark Plug Type ⑦	Gap Inch	Point Gap Inch	Dwell Angle Deg.	Firing Order Fig. ▲	Timing BTDC ①	Mark Fig.	Hot Idle Speed Std. Trans.	Hot Idle Speed Auto. Trans. ②	Air Fuel Ratio Std. Trans.	Air Fuel Ratio Auto. Trans.	Idle "CO" % Std. Trans.	Idle "CO" % Auto. Trans.
DODGE 1969													
6-170 Std. Tr.	N14Y	.035	.020	42–47	G	5° ATC	E	750⑭	—	14.2 to 1	—	—	—
6-170 Auto. Tr.	N14Y	.035	.020	42–47	G	TDC	E	—	750N⑭	—	14.2 to 1	—	—
6-225	N14Y	.035	.020	42–47	G	TDC	E	650⑭	650N⑭	14.2 to 1	14.2 to 1	—	—
V8-273	N14Y	.035	.017	30–35	H	2½° ATC	F	700⑭	650N⑭	14.2 to 1	14.2 to 1	—	—
V8-318	N14Y	.035	.017	30–35	H	TDC	F	700⑭	650N⑭	14.2 to 1	14.2 to 1	—	—
V8-340 Std. Tr.	N9Y	.035	.017	⑰	H	TDC	F	750⑭	—	14.2 to 1	—	—	—
V8-340 Auto. Tr.	N9Y	.035	.017	30–35	H	5°	F	—	700N⑭	—	14.2 to 1	—	—
V8-383 Std. Tr.㉑	J14Y	.035	.017	30–35	J	TDC	F	700⑭	—	14.2 to 1	—	—	—
V8-383 Auto. Tr.㉑	J14Y	.035	.017	30–35	J	7½°	F	—	600N⑭	—	14.2 to 1	—	—
V8-383 Std. Tr.④	J11Y	.035	.017	30–35	J	TDC	F	700	—	14.2 to 1	—	—	—
V8-383 Auto. Tr.④	J11Y	.035	.017	30–35	J	5°	F	—	650N⑭	—	14.2 to 1	—	—
V8-383 Std. Tr.㉘	J11Y	.035	.017	⑰	J	TDC	F	700	—	14.2 to 1	—	—	—
V8-383 Auto. Tr.㉘	J11Y	.035	.017	⑰	J	5°	F	—	650N⑭	—	14.2 to 1	—	—
V8-440, 350 H.P.	J13Y	.035	.017	30–35	J	7½°	F	—	600N⑭	—	14.2 to 1	—	—
V8-440 Std. Tr.㉒	J11Y	.035	.017	⑰	J	TDC	F	700	—	14.2 to 1	—	—	—
V8-440 Auto. Tr.㉒	J11Y	.035	.017	30–35	J	5°	F	—	650N⑭	—	14.2 to 1	—	—
V8-426 Hemi.	N10Y	.035	.017	⑰	J	TDC	F	750	750N⑭	14.2 to 1	14.2 to 1	—	—
V8-440, 390H.P.	J11Y	.035	.017	⑰	J	5°	F	900	900	14.2 to 1	14.2 to 1	—	—
1970													
6-198 Std. Tr.	N14Y	.035	.020	41–46	G	2½°	C	750⑥	—	14.2 to 1	—	—	—
6-198 Auto. Tr.	N14Y	.035	.020	41–46	G	TDC	C	—	750⑥	—	14.2 to 1	—	—
6-225	N14Y	.035	.020	41–46	G	TDC	C	700⑥	650⑥	14.2 to 1	14.2 to 1	—	—
V8-318	N14Y	.035	.017	30–34	H	TDC	E	750⑥	700⑥	14.2 to 1	14.2 to 1	—	—
V8-340 Std. Tr.	N9Y	.035	.017	⑰	H	5°	E	950	—	14.2 to 1	—	—	—
V8-340 Auto. Tr.	N9Y	.035	.017	30–34	H	5°	E	—	900	—	14.2 to 1	—	—
V8-383 Std. Tr.㉑	J14Y	.035	.017	28–32	J	TDC	F	750	—	14.2 to 1	—	—	—
V8-383 Auto. Tr.㉑	J14Y	.035	.017	28–32	J	2½°	F	—	650	—	14.2 to 1	—	—
V8-383 Std. Tr.④	J11Y	.035	.017	28–32	J	TDC	F	750	—	14.2 to 1	—	—	—
V8-383 Auto. Tr.④	J11Y	.035	.017	28–32	J	2½°	F	—	750	—	14.2 to 1	—	—
V8-440, 350 H.P.	J13Y	.035	.017	28–32	J	5°	F	—	600	14.2 to 1	14.2 to 1	—	—
V8-440 Std. Tr.㉒	J11Y	.035	.017	28–32	J	TDC	F	900	—	14.2 to 1	—	—	—
V8-440 Auto. Tr.㉒	J11Y	.035	.017	28–32	J	2½°	F	—	800	—	14.2 to 1	—	—
V8-440, 390 H.P.	J11Y	.035	.017	⑰	J	5°	F	900	900	14.2 to 1	14.2 to 1	—	—
V8-426 Std. Tr.	N10Y	.035	.017	⑰	J	TDC	F	900	—	14.2 to 1	—	—	—
V8-426 Auto. Tr.	N10Y	.035	.017	⑰	J	5°	F	—	900	—	14.2 to 1	—	—
1971													
6-198	N14Y	.035	.020	41–46	G	2½°	C	800	800	14.2 to 1	14.2 to 1	—	—
6-225㉔	N14Y	.035	.020	41–46	G	TDC	C	750	750	14.2 to 1	14.2 to 1	—	—
6-225㉖	N14Y	.035	.020	41–46	G	2½°	C	750	750	14.2 to 1	14.2 to 1	—	—
V8-318	N14Y	.035	.017	30–34	H	TDC	E	750	700	14.2 to 1	14.2 to 1	—	—

Continued

TUNE UP SPECIFICATIONS—Continued

OLD CAR SPECIFICATIONS: For 1946-68 Tune Up Specifications see main index.

★When using a timing light, disconnect vacuum hose or tube at distributor and plug opening in hose or tube so idle speed will not be affected.

●When checking compression, lowest cylinder must be within 80 percent of highest.

▲Before removing wires from distributor cap, determine location of the No. 1 wire in cap, as distributor position may have been altered from that shown at the end of this chart.

| Year | Spark Plug | | Distributor | | Ignition Timing★ | | | Carb. Adjustments | | | | | |
| | Type ⑦ | Gap Inch | Point Gap Inch | Dwell Angle Deg. | Firing Order Fig. ▲ | Timing BTDC ① | Mark Fig. | Hot Idle Speed | | Air Fuel Ratio | | Idle "CO" % | |
								Std. Trans.	Auto. Trans. ②	Std. Trans.	Auto. Trans.	Std. Trans.	Auto. Trans.
DODGE—Continued													
1971													
V8-340 Std. Tr.④	N9Y	.035	.017	⑰	H	5°	E	900	—	14.2 to 1	—	—	—
V8-340 Auto. Tr.④	N9Y	.035	.017	30–34	H	5°	E	—	900	—	14.2 to 1	—	—
V8-340 Std. Tr.㉘	N9Y	.035	.017	⑰	H	2½°	E	1000	—	14.2 to 1	—	—	—
V8-340 Auto. Tr.㉘	N9Y	.035	.017	30–34	H	2½°	E	—	950	—	14.2 to 1	—	—
V8-340③	N9Y	.035	—	—	H	5°	E	900	—	14.2 to 1	14.2 to 1	—	—
V8-360	N13Y	.035	.017	30–34	H	2½°	E	750	700	14.2 to 1	14.2 to 1	—	—
V8-383 Std. Tr.㉑	J14Y	.035	.017	30–34	J	TDC	F	750	—	14.2 to 1	—	—	—
V8-383 Auto. Tr.㉑	J14Y	.035	.017	30–34	J	2½°	F	—	700	—	14.2 to 1	—	—
V8-383 Std. Tr.④	J11Y	.035	.017	30–34	J	TDC	F	750	—	14.2 to 1	—	—	—
V8-383 Auto. Tr.④	J11Y	.035	.017	30–34	J	2½°	F	—	700	—	14.2 to 1	—	—
V8-426 Std. Tr.	N10Y	.035	.017	⑰	J	TDC	F	900	—	14.2 to 1	—	—	—
V8-426 Auto. Tr.	N10Y	.035	.017	⑰	J	2½°	F	—	900	—	14.2 to 1	—	—
V8-440	J13Y	.035	.017	28½–32½	J	5°	F	—	900	14.2 to 1	14.2 to 1	—	—
V8-440 Std. Tr.㉒	J11Y	.035	.017	28½–32½	J	TDC	F	900	—	14.2 to 1	—	—	—
V8-440 Auto. Tr.㉒	J11Y	.035	.017	28½–32½	J	2½°	F	—	900	—	14.2 to 1	—	—
V8-440㉖	J11Y	.035	.017	⑰	J	5°	F	900	900	14.2 to 1	—	—	—
1972													
6-198	N14Y	.035	.020	41–46	G	2½°	C	800㉘	800N㉘	14.2 to 1	14.2 to 1	—	—
6-225	N14Y	.035	.020	41–46	G	TDC	C	750㉘	750N㉘	14.2 to 1	14.2 to 1	—	—
V8-318	N13Y	.035	.017	30–34	H	TDC	E	750	750N㉘	14.2 to 1	14.2 to 1	—	—
V8-340	N9Y	.035	—	—	H	2½°	E	900㉙	750N	14.2 to 1	14.2 to 1	—	—
V8-360	N13Y	.035	.017	30–34	H	TDC	E	—	750N	14.2 to 1	14.2 to 1	—	—
V8-400㉑	J13Y	.035	.019	28½–32½	J	5°	F	—	700N	14.2 to 1	—	—	—
V8-400 Std. Tr.④	J11Y	.035	—	—	J	2½°	F	900㉚	—	14.2 to 1	—	—	—
V8-400 Auto. Tr.④	J11Y	.035	—	—	J	10°㉗	F	—	750N	—	14.2 to 1	—	—
V8-440	J11Y	.035	.019	28½–32½	J	10°㉗	F	—	750N㉘	14.2 to 1	14.2 to 1	—	—
V8-440 Std. Tr.㉒	J11Y	.035	—	—	J	2½°	F	900㉚	—	14.2 to 1	—	—	—
V8-440 Auto. Tr.㉒	J11Y	.035	—	—	J	10°㉗	F	—	900N	—	14.2 to 1	—	—
V8-440㉘	J11Y	.035	—	—	J	2½°	F	—	900N	14.2 to 1	—	—	—
1973													
6-198	N14Y	.035	—	—	G	TDC	C	800	750N	14.2 to 1	14.2 to 1	—	—
6-225 Std. Trans.	N14Y	.035	—	—	G	2½°	C	750	—	14.2 to 1	—	—	—
6-225 Auto. Trans.	N14Y	.035	—	—	G	TDC	C	—	750N	—	14.2 to 1	—	—
8-318	N13Y	.035	—	—	H	TDC	E	750	750N	14.2 to 1	14.2 to 1	—	—
8-340 Std. Trans.	N12Y	.035	—	—	H	5°	E	900	—	14.2 to 1	—	—	—
8-340 Auto. Trans.	N12Y	.035	—	—	H	2½°⑱	E	—	750N	—	14.2 to 1	—	—
8-360	N13Y	.035	—	—	H	⑩	E	750	750N	14.2 to 1	14.2 to 1	—	—
8-400 2 Bar. Carb.	J13Y	.035	—	—	J	10°	F	700	700N	14.2 to 1	14.2 to 1	—	—
8-400 4 Bar. Carb.㉛	J11Y	.035	—	—	J	10°	F	900	—	14.2 to 1	—	—	—
8-400 4 Bar. Carb.⑫	J11Y	.035	—	—	J	7½°	F	—	750N	—	14.2 to 1	—	—
8-440 Std. Trans.	J11Y	.035	—	—	J	10°	F	800	—	14.2 to 1	—	—	—
8-440 Auto. Trans.	J11Y	.035	—	—	J	10°	F	—	700N	—	14.2 to 1	—	—

Continued

TUNE UP SPECIFICATIONS—Continued

OLD CAR SPECIFICATIONS: For 1946-68 Tune Up Specifications see main index.

★When using a timing light, disconnect vacuum hose or tube at distributor and plug opening in hose or tube so idle speed will not be affected.

●When checking compression, lowest cylinder must be within 80 percent of highest.

▲Before removing wires from distributor cap, determine location of the No. 1 wire in cap, as distributor position may have been altered from that shown at the end of this chart.

Year	Spark Plug		Distributor		Ignition Timing★			Carb. Adjustments					
	Type ⑦	Gap Inch	Point Gap Inch	Dwell Angle Deg.	Firing Order Fig. ▲	Timing BTDC ①	Mark Fig.	Hot Idle Speed		Air Fuel Ratio		Idle "CO" %	
								Std. Trans.	Auto. Trans. ③	Std. Trans.	Auto. Trans.	Std. Trans.	Auto. Trans.
DODGE—Continued													
1974													
6-198	N14Y	.035	—	—	G	2½°	C	800	750	14.3 to 1	14.3 to 1	—	—
6-225	N14Y	.035	—	—	G	TDC	C	800	750	14.3 to 1	14.3 to 1	—	—
V8-318	N13Y	.035	—	—	H	TDC	E	750	750	14.3 to 1	14.3 to 1	—	—
V8-360	N12Y	.035	—	—	H	5°⑪	E	850	850	14.3 to 1	14.3 to 1	—	—
V8-400 Auto. Trans.㉑	J13Y	.035	—	—	J	7½°⑨	F	—	750	—	14.3 to 1	—	—
V8-400 Auto. Trans.④	J13Y	.035	—	—	J	5°	F	—	750	—	14.3 to 1	—	—
V8-400 Std. Trans.㉒	J11Y	.035	—	—	J	5°	F	900	—	14.3 to 1	—	—	—
V8-400 Auto. Trans.⑯	J11Y	.035	—	—	J	5°⑬	F	—	850	—	14.3 to 1	—	—
V8-440	J11Y	.035	—	—	J	10°	F	—	850	—	14.3 to 1	—	—
1975													
6-225	BL13Y	.035	—	—	G	TDC	C	800	750N	㉜	㉜	.3⑲	㉞
V8-318⑥㉔	N13Y	.035	—	—	H	2°	E	750	750N	14.3 to 1	14.3 to 1	.3⑲	.3⑲
V8-318⑧㉔	N13Y	.035	—	—	H	2°⑮	E	—	900N	—	14.3 to 1	—	.5⑳
V8-318㉕	N13Y	.035	—	—	H	TDC	E	—	750N	—	—	—	.5⑳
V8-360 2 BBI. Carb.	N12Y	.035	—	—	H	6°	E	—	750N	—	14.3 to 1	—	.3⑲
V8-360 4 BBI. Carb.㉔	N12Y	.035	—	—	H	2°	E	—	850N	—	14.3 to 1	—	.5⑳
V8-360 4 BBI. Carb.㉕	N12Y	.035	—	—	H	6°	E	—	750N	—	—	—	.3⑲
V8-400 2 BBI. Carb.	J13Y	.035	—	—	J	10°	F	—	750N	—	14.3 to 1	—	.3⑲
V8-400 4 BBI. Carb.	J13Y	.035	—	—	J	8°	F	—	750N	—	㉜	—	㉝
V8-440	RJ87P	.040	—	—	J	8°	F	—	750N	—	㉜	—	㉞
V8-440㉒㉔	J11Y	.035	—	—	J	10°	F	—	750N	—	14.3 to 1	—	.3⑲
V8-440㉒㉔	RJ87P	.035	—	—	J	8°	F	—	750N	—	—	—	.5⑳
PLYMOUTH													
1969													
6-170 Std. Tr.	N14Y	.035	.020	42–47	G	5° ATC	E	750⑭	—	14.2 to 1	—	—	—
6-170 Auto. Tr.	N14Y	.035	.020	42–47	G	2½° ATC	E	—	750N⑭	—	14.2 to 1	—	—
6-225	N14Y	.035	.020	42–47	G	TDC	E	650⑭	650N⑭	14.2 to 1	14.2 to 1	—	—
V8-273	N14Y	.035	.017	30–35	H	2½° ATC	F	700⑭	650N⑭	14.2 to 1	14.2 to 1	—	—
V8-318	N14Y	.035	.017	30–35	H	TDC	F	700⑭	650N⑭	14.2 to 1	14.2 to 1	—	—
V8-340 Std. Tr.	N9Y	.035	.017	⑰	H	TDC	F	750⑭	—	14.2 to 1	—	—	—
V8-340 Auto. Tr.	N9Y	.035	.017	30–35	H	5°	F	—	700N⑭	—	14.2 to 1	—	—
V8-383 Std. Tr.㉑	J14Y	.035	.017	30–35	J	TDC	F	700⑭	—	14.2 to 1	—	—	—
V8-383 Auto. Tr.㉑	J14Y	.035	.017	30–35	J	7½°	F	—	600N⑭	—	14.2 to 1	—	—
V8-383 Std. Tr.④	J11Y	.035	.017	30–35	J	TDC	F	700	—	14.2 to 1	—	—	—
V8-383 Auto. Tr.④	J11Y	.035	.017	30–35	J	5°	F	—	650N⑭	—	14.2 to 1	—	—
V8-383 Std. Tr.㉓	J11Y	.035	.017	⑰	J	TDC	F	700	—	14.2 to 1	—	—	—
V8-383 Auto. Tr.㉓	J11Y	.035	.017	⑰	J	5°	F	—	650N⑭	—	14.2 to 1	—	—
V8-440, 350 H.P.	J13Y	.035	.017	30–35	J	7½°	F	—	600N⑭	14.2 to 1	14.2 to 1	—	—
V8-440 Std. Tr.㉒	J11Y	.035	.017	⑰	J	TDC	F	700	—	14.2 to 1	—	—	—
V8-440 Auto. Tr.㉓	J11Y	.035	.017	30–35	J	5°	F	—	650N⑭	—	14.2 to 1	—	—
V8-440, 390 H.P.	J11Y	.035	.017	⑰	J	5°	F	900	900⑭	14.2 to 1	14.2 to 1	—	—
V8-426 Hemi	N10Y	.035	.017	⑰	J	TDC	F	750	750⑭	14.2 to 1	—	—	—

Continued

CHRYSLER • DODGE • IMPERIAL • PLYMOUTH

TUNE UP SPECIFICATIONS—Continued

OLD CAR SPECIFICATIONS: For 1946-68 Tune Up Specifications see main index.

★When using a timing light, disconnect vacuum hose or tube at distributor and plug opening in hose or tube so idle speed will not be affected.

●When checking compression, lowest cylinder must be within 80 percent of highest.

▲Before removing wires from distributor cap, determine location of the No. 1 wire in cap, as distributor position may have been altered from that shown at the end of this chart.

| Year | Spark Plug | | Distributor | | Ignition Timing★ | | | Carb. Adjustments | | | | | |
| | Type ⑦ | Gap Inch | Point Gap Inch | Dwell Angle Deg. | Firing Order Fig. ▲ | Timing BTDC ① | Mark Fig. | Hot Idle Speed | | Air Fuel Ratio | | Idle CO % | |
								Std. Trans.	Auto. Trans. ②	Std. Trans.	Auto. Trans.	Std. Trans.	Auto. Trans.
PLYMOUTH—Continued													
1970													
6-198 Std. Tr.	N14Y	.035	.020	41–46	G	2½°	C	750⑥	—	14.2 to 1	—	—	—
6-198 Auto. Tr.	N14Y	.035	.020	41–46	G	TDC	C	—	750⑥	—	14.2 to 1	—	—
6-225	N14Y	.035	.020	41–46	G	TDC	C	700⑥	650⑥	14.2 to 1	14.2 to 1	—	—
V8-318	N14Y	.035	.017	30–34	H	TDC	E	750⑥	700⑥	14.2 to 1	14.2 to 1	—	—
V8-340 Std. Tr.	N9Y	.035	.017	⑰	H	5°	E	950	—	14.2 to 1	—	—	—
V8-340 Auto. Tr.	N9Y	.035	.017	30–34	H	5°	E	—	900	—	14.2 to 1	—	—
V8-383 Std. Tr.㉑	J14Y	.035	.017	28–32	J	TDC	F	750	—	14.2 to 1	—	—	—
V8-383 Auto. Tr.㉑	J14Y	.035	.017	28–32	J	2½°	F	—	650	—	14.2 to 1	—	—
V8-383 Std. Tr.④	J11Y	.035	.017	28–32	J	TDC	F	750	—	14.2 to 1	—	—	—
V8-383 Auto. Tr.④	J11Y	.035	.017	28–32	J	2½°	F	—	750	—	14.2 to 1	—	—
V8-440, 350 H.P.	J13Y	.035	.017	28–32	J	5°	F	—	600	14.2 to 1	14.2 to 1	—	—
V8-440 Std. Tr.㉒	J11Y	.035	.017	28–32	J	TDC	F	900	—	14.2 to 1	—	—	—
V8-440 Auto. Tr.㉒	J11Y	.035	.017	28–32	J	2½°	F	—	800	—	14.2 to 1	—	—
V8-440, 390 H.P.	J11Y	.035	.017	⑰	J	5°	F	900	900	14.2 to 1	14.2 to 1	—	—
V8-426 Std. Tr.	N10Y	.035	.017	⑰	J	TDC	F	900	—	14.2 to 1	—	—	—
V8-426 Auto. Tr.	N10Y	.035	.017	⑰	J	5°	F	—	900	—	14.2 to 1	—	—
1971													
6-198	N14Y	.035	.020	41–46	G	2½°	C	800	800	14.2 to 1	14.2 to 1	—	—
6-225㉔	N14Y	.035	.020	41–46	G	TDC	C	750	750	14.2 to 1	14.2 to 1	—	—
6-225㉕	N14Y	.035	.020	41–46	G	2½°	C	750	750	14.2 to 1	14.2 to 1	—	—
V8-318	N14Y	.035	.017	30–34	H	TDC	E	750	700	14.2 to 1	14.2 to 1	—	—
V8-340 Std. Tr.④	N9Y	.035	.017	⑰	H	5°	E	900	—	14.2 to 1	—	—	—
V8-340 Auto. Tr.④	N9Y	.035	.017	30–34	H	5°	E	—	900	—	14.2 to 1	—	—
V8-340 Std. Tr.㉖	N9Y	.035	.017	⑰	H	2½°	E	1000	—	14.2 to 1	—	—	—
V8-340 Auto. Tr.㉖	N9Y	.035	.017	30–34	H	2½°	E	—	950	—	14.2 to 1	—	—
V8-340③	N9Y	.035	—	—	H	5°	E	900	—	14.2 to 1	14.2 to 1	—	—
V8-360	N13Y	.035	.017	30–34	H	2½°	E	750	700	14.2 to 1	14.2 to 1	—	—
V8-383 Std. Tr.㉑	J14Y	.035	.017	30–34	J	TDC	F	750	—	14.2 to 1	—	—	—
V8-383 Auto. Tr.㉑	J14Y	.035	.017	30–34	J	2½°	F	—	700	—	14.2 to 1	—	—
V8-383 Std. Tr.④	J11Y	.035	.017	30–34	J	TDC	F	750	—	14.2 to 1	—	—	—
V8-383 Auto. Tr.④	J11Y	.035	.017	30–34	J	2½°	F	—	700	—	14.2 to 1	—	—
V8-426 Std. Tr.	N10Y	.035	.017	⑰	J	TDC	F	900	—	14.2 to 1	—	—	—
V8-426 Auto. Tr.	N10Y	.035	.017	⑰	J	2½°	F	—	900	—	14.2 to 1	—	—
V8-440	J13Y	.035	.017	28½–32½	J	5°	F	—	900	14.2 to 1	14.2 to 1	—	—
V8-440 Std. Tr.㉒	J11Y	.035	.017	28½–32½	J	TDC	F	900	—	14.2 to 1	—	—	—
V8-440 Auto. Tr.㉒	J11Y	.035	.017	28½–32½	J	2½°	F	—	900	—	14.2 to 1	—	—
V8-440㉖	J11Y	.035	.017	⑰	J	5°	F	900	900	14.2 to 1	—	—	—
1972													
6-198	N14Y	.035	.020	41–46	G	2½°	C	800㉘	800N㉘	14.2 to 1	14.2 to 1	—	—
6-225	N14Y	.035	.020	41–46	G	TDC	C	750㉘	750N㉘	14.2 to 1	14.2 to 1	—	—
V8-318	N13Y	.035	.017	30–34	H	TDC	E	750	750N㉘	14.2 to 1	14.2 to 1	—	—
V8-340	N9Y	.035	—	—	H	2½°	E	900㉙	750N	14.2 to 1	14.2 to 1	—	—
V8-360	N13Y	.035	.017	30–34	H	TDC	E	—	750N	14.2 to 1	14.2 to 1	—	—

Continued

TUNE UP SPECIFICATIONS—Continued

OLD CAR SPECIFICATIONS: For 1946-68 Tune Up Specifications see main index.

★When using a timing light, disconnect vacuum hose or tube at distributor and plug opening in hose or tube so idle speed will not be affected.

●When checking compression, lowest cylinder must be within 80 percent of highest.

▲Before removing wires from distributor cap, determine location of the No. 1 wire in cap, as distributor position may have been altered from that shown at the end of this chart.

Year	Spark Plug		Distributor		Ignition Timing★			Carb. Adjustments					
	Type ⑦	Gap Inch	Point Gap Inch	Dwell Angle Deg.	Firing Order Fig. ▲	Timing BTDC ①	Mark Fig.	Hot Idle Speed		Air Fuel Ratio		Idle "CO" %	
								Std. Trans.	Auto. Trans. ②	Std. Trans.	Auto. Trans.	Std. Trans.	Auto. Trans.
PLYMOUTH—Continued													
1972													
V8-400㉑	J13Y	.035	.019	28½–32½	J	5°	F	—	700N	14.2 to 1	14.2 to 1	—	—
V8-400 Std. Tr.④	J11Y	.035	—	—	J	2½°	F	900㉚	—	—	14.2 to 1	—	—
V8-400 Auto. Tr.④	J11Y	.035	—	—	J	10°㉗	F	—	750N	—	14.2 to 1	—	—
V8-440	J11Y	.035	.019	28½–32½	J	10°㉗	F	—	750N㉘	14.2 to 1	14.2 to 1	—	—
V8-440 Std. Tr.㉒	J11Y	.035	—	—	J	2½°	F	900㉚	—	14.2 to 1	—	—	—
V8-440 Auto. Tr.㉒	J11Y	.035	—	—	J	10°㉗	F	—	900N	—	14.2 to 1	—	—
V8-440㉔	J11Y	.035	—	—	J	2½°	F	—	900N	14.2 to 1	—	—	—
1973													
6-198	N14Y	.035	—	—	G	TDC	C	800	750N	14.2 to 1	14.2 to 1	—	—
6-225 Std. Trans.	N14Y	.035	—	—	G	2½°	C	750	—	14.2 to 1	—	—	—
6-225 Auto. Trans.	N14Y	.035	—	—	G	TDC	C	—	750N	—	14.2 to 1	—	—
8-318	N13Y	.035	—	—	H	TDC	E	750	750N	14.2 to 1	14.2 to 1	—	—
8-340 Std. Trans.	N12Y	.035	—	—	H	5°	E	900	—	14.2 to 1	—	—	—
8-340 Auto. Trans.	N12Y	.035	—	—	H	2½°⑱	E	—	750N	—	14.2 to 1	—	—
8-360	N13Y	.035	—	—	H	⑩	E	750	750N	14.2 to 1	14.2 to 1	—	—
8-400 2 Bar. Carb.	J13Y	.035	—	—	J	10°	F	700	700N	14.2 to 1	14.2 to 1	—	—
8-400 4 Bar. Carb.㉛	J11Y	.035	—	—	J	10°	F	900	—	14.2 to 1	—	—	—
8-400 4 Bar. Carb.⑫	J11Y	.035	—	—	J	7½°	F	—	750N	—	14.2 to 1	—	—
8-440 Std. Trans.	J11Y	.035	—	—	J	10°	F	800	—	14.2 to 1	—	—	—
8-440 Auto. Trans.	J11Y	.035	—	—	J	10°	F	—	700N	—	14.2 to 1	—	—
1974													
6-198	N14Y	.035	—	—	G	2½°	C	800	750	14.3 to 1	14.3 to 1	—	—
6-225	N14Y	.035	—	—	G	TDC	C	800	750	14.3 to 1	14.3 to 1	—	—
V8-318	N13Y	.035	—	—	H	TDC	E	750	750	14.3 to 1	14.3 to 1	—	—
V8-360	N12Y	.035	—	—	H	5°⑪	E	850	850	14.3 to 1	14.3 to 1	—	—
V8-400 Auto. Trans.㉑	J13Y	.035	—	—	J	7½°⑨	F	—	750	—	14.3 to 1	—	—
V8-400 Auto. Trans.④	J13Y	.035	—	—	J	5°	F	—	750	—	14.3 to 1	—	—
V8-400 Std. Trans.㉒	J11Y	.035	—	—	J	5°	F	900	—	14.3 to 1	—	—	—
V8-400 Auto. Trans.⑯	J11Y	.035	—	—	J	5°⑬	F	—	850	—	14.3 to 1	—	—
V8-440	J11Y	.035	—	—	J	10°	F	—	850	—	14.3 to 1	—	—
1975													
6-225	BL13Y	.035	—	—	G	TDC	C	800	750N	㉜	㉜	.3⑲	㉞
V8-318⑤㉔	N13Y	.035	—	—	H	2°	E	750	750N	14.3 to 1	14.3 to 1	.3⑲	㉞
V8-318⑧㉔	N13Y	.035	—	—	H	2°⑯	E	—	900N	—	14.3 to 1	—	.5⑳
V8-318㉕	N13Y	.035	—	—	H	TDC	E	—	750N	—	—	—	.5⑳
V8-360 2 BBl. Carb.	N12Y	.035	—	—	H	6°	E	—	750N	—	14.3 to 1	—	.3⑲
V8-360 4 BBl. Carb.㉔	N12Y	.035	—	—	H	2°	E	—	850N	—	14.3 to 1	—	.5⑳
V8-360 4 BBl. Carb.㉕	N12Y	.035	—	—	H	6°	E	—	750N	—	—	—	.5⑳
V8-400 2 BBl. Carb.	J13Y	.035	—	—	J	10°	F	—	750N	—	14.3 to 1	—	.3⑲
V8-400 4 BBl. Carb.	J13Y	.035	—	—	J	8°	F	—	750N	—	㉜	—	㉝
V8-440	RJ87P	.040	—	—	J	8°	F	—	750N	—	㉜	—	㉞
V8-440㉒㉔	J11Y	.035	—	—	J	10°	F	—	750N	—	14.3 to 1	—	.3⑲
V8-440㉒㉕	RJ87P	.035	—	—	J	8°	F	—	750N	—	—	—	.5⑳

Continued

TUNE UP NOTES

① —BTDC: Before top dead center.
② —D: Drive. N: Neutral.
③ —Electronic ignition.
④ —Four barrel carburetor.
⑤ —With catalytic converter.
⑥ —Set idle speed with air conditioning compressor operating.
⑦ —Champion.
⑧ —With air pump.
⑨ —All except Station Wagons, Station Wagons 5° BTDC.
⑩ —Dist. No. 3656780, TDC.
Dist. No. 3755336, 7½°.
Dist. No. 3755337 & 3755365, 5°.
⑪ —Calif. V8-360 Hi Perf. Manual Trans. 2½° BTDC.

⑫ —Auto. trans.
⑬ —Exc. Calif. auto. trans. & Police; Calif. auto. trans. & Police, 2½°.
⑭ —Adjust idle speed with headlights on. If air conditioned turn A/C switch to "Full On" position.
⑮ —ATDC: after top dead center.
⑯ —High performance & Police.
⑰ —Each set of points 27–32°; total dwell both sets 37–42°.
⑱ —Exc. Calif. late production; Calif. late production, TDC.
⑲ —Measured ahead of catalytic converter.
⑳ —Measured in tailpipe.
㉑ —Two barrel carburetor.
㉒ —High performance engine.

㉓ —Formula "S" and Super Bee only.
㉔ —Exc. California.
㉕ —California only.
㉖ —Three Carbs.
㉗ —California vehicles with electronic ignition 5°.
㉘ —California vehicles 700N.
㉙ —California vehicles 850.
㉚ —California vehicles 800.
㉛ —Std. trans.
㉜ —All except Calif. 14.3 to 1.
㉝ —Except Calif. .3 (see note 19), Calif. .5 (see note 19).
㉞ —Except Calif. .3 (see note 19), Calif. 1.5 (see note 20).

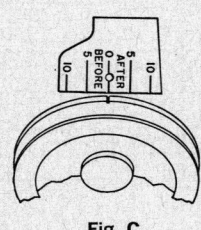

Fig. C

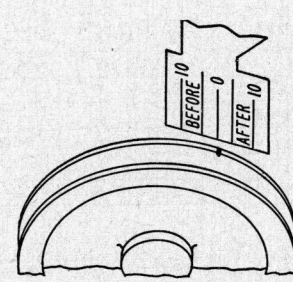

Fig. E

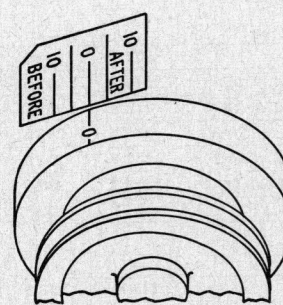

Fig. F

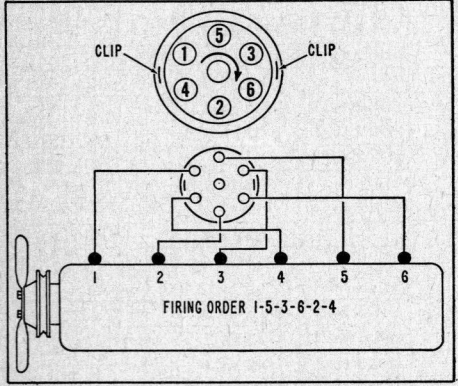

Fig. G

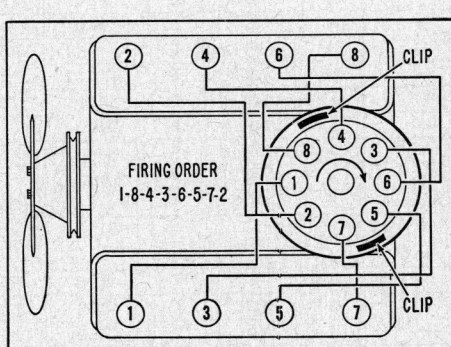

Fig. H

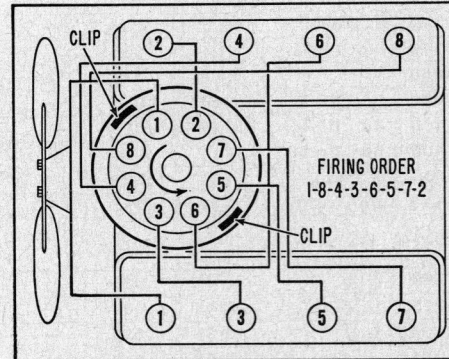

Fig. J

CHRYSLER • DODGE • IMPERIAL • PLYMOUTH

DISTRIBUTOR SPECIFICATIONS

★Note: If unit is checked on vehicle, double the RPM and degrees to get crankshaft figures.

Breaker arm spring tension—17–20.

Distributor Part No.①	Centrifugal Advance Degrees @ RPM of Distributor					Vacuum Advance		Distributor Retard
	Advance Starts	Intermediate Advance			Full Advance	Inches of Vacuum to Start Plunger	Max. Adv. Dist. Deg. @ Vacuum	Max. Retard Dist. Deg. @ Vacuum
CHRYSLER & IMPERIAL								
1969								
2875731	1–7.5 @ 550	10.5–12.5 @ 850	—	—	17 @ 2500	8	12 @ 15	—
2875742	1–9.5 @ 550	11–13 @ 800	—	—	23 @ 2350	8.5	13.5 @ 13.5	—
2875747	1–6 @ 500	8–10 @ 750	—	—	19 @ 2300	8.5	13.5 @ 13.5	—
2875758	2–7 @ 550	9–11 @ 850	—	—	16 @ 2400	10.5	12 @ 16	—
2875764	0–3.5 @ 500	6.5–8.5 @ 850	—	—	14 @ 2250	11.5	13.5 @ 16	—
2875772	1–8.5 @ 550	11.5–13.5 @ 850	—	—	19 @ 2500	10.5	12 @ 16	—
1970								
3438219	0.5–3.7 @ 650	5.7–7.7 @ 900	—	—	14 @ 2300	10.5	12 @ 15.5	2¾②
3438222	0–4.6 @ 600	5.6–7.6 @ 800	—	—	12 @ 2300	10.5	12 @ 15.5	2¾②
3438231	0–3.8 @ 550	7.5–9.5 @ 850	—	—	16 @ 2200	7.5	11.8 @ 12	2¾②
3438233	0–4.6 @ 600	5.6–7.6 @ 800	—	—	12 @ 2300	10.5	12 @ 15.5	2¾②
1971								
3438534	1–4.5 @ 600	5–7 @ 800	—	—	14 @ 2000	9	10 @ 15	—
3438544	0.5–3.5 @ 700	5–7.5 @ 900	—	—	14 @ 2000	9	10 @ 15	—
3438559	0.5–3.5 @ 700	3.5–5.5 @ 900	—	—	12 @ 2400	12	10 @ 16	—
3438572	0–3.5 @ 600	4.5–6.5 @ 800	—	—	10 @ 2200	10.5	12 @ 15.5	—
3438690	0.5–3.5 @ 650	6–8 @ 900	—	—	14 @ 2400	10.5	10 @ 15	—
3438694	0.5–4 @ 700	5–7 @ 900	—	—	10 @ 2200	10.5	12 @ 15.5	—
1972								
3656272	1–6 @ 550	8.5–10.5 @ 800	—	—	16 @ 2100	9.5	10.5 @ 15	—
3656329	1–5 @ 650	8–10 @ 900	—	—	14 @ 2000	10.5	10.5 @ 15.5	—
3656332	0.5–4 @ 650	6–8 @ 950	—	—	12 @ 2000	10.5	10.5 @ 15.5	—
3656335	1–5 @ 650	8–10 @ 900	—	—	15 @ 2250	10.5	10.5 @ 15.5	—
3656338	0.5–4 @ 650	6–8 @ 950	—	—	12.5 @ 2500	10.5	10.5 @ 15.5	—
3656341	0.5–4 @ 650	6–8 @ 950	—	—	12.5 @ 2500	10.5	10.5 @ 15.5	—
3656344	0.5–4 @ 650	6–8 @ 950	—	—	12 @ 2000	10.5	10.5 @ 15.5	—
3656347	1–5 @ 650	8–10 @ 900	—	—	15 @ 2250	10.5	10.5 @ 15.5	—
3656350	1–5 @ 650	8–10 @ 900	—	—	14 @ 2000	10.5	10.5 @ 15.5	—
3656429	1–6 @ 550	8.5–10.5 @ 800	—	—	15 @ 1900	9	10 @ 14	—
3656435	0–4 @ 600	9–11 @ 1100	—	—	15 @ 1900	9	10 @ 14	—
3656593	1–4.5 @ 550	7.5–9.5 @ 800	—	—	16 @ 1900	10.5	10.5 @ 15.5	—
3656596	1–4.5 @ 550	7.5–9.5 @ 800	—	—	15 @ 1800	10.5	10.5 @ 15.5	—
1973								
3656791	0.5–3.5 @ 550	8–10.5 @ 850	—	—	15 @ 1950	10.5	10.5 @ 15.5	—
3656802	0.5–4.0 @ 650	6–8 @ 950	—	—	12.5 @ 2500	10.5	10.5 @ 15.5	—
3755157	0.5–4.0 @ 650	6–8 @ 950	—	—	12.5 @ 2500	10.5	10.5 @ 15.5	—
1974								
3755518	0.5–3.5 @ 650	5.5–8 @ 900	—	—	12 @ 2000	8	10 @ 14	—
3755522	0.5–3 @ 650	4–6.5 @ 900	—	—	10 @ 2000	8	10 @ 14	—
3755681	1–4.5 @ 650	8.5–11 @ 950	—	—	16 @ 2150	8	10 @ 14	—

Continued

DISTRIBUTOR SPECIFICATIONS—Continued

★Note: If unit is checked on vehicle, double the RPM and degrees to get crankshaft figures.

Breaker arm spring tension—17-20.

Distributor Part No.①	Centrifugal Advance Degrees @ RPM of Distributor				Vacuum Advance		Distributor Retard
	Advance Starts	Intermediate Advance		Full Advance	Inches of Vacuum to Start Plunger	Max. Adv. Dist. Deg. @ Vacuum	Max. Retard Dist. Deg. @ Vacuum

CHRYSLER & IMPERIAL—Continued

1975

3874090	1.5–5.5 @ 550	5.5–8 @ 700	—	14 @ 2200	7	12 @ 12.5	—
3874101	.5–3 @ 600	6–8.5 @ 950	—	12 @ 2000	8	11 @ 14	—
3874110	1–3.5 @ 600	6–8.5 @ 900	—	12 @ 2000	8	11 @ 14	—
3874115	1–3.5 @ 600	6–8.5 @ 900	—	12 @ 2000	7	12 @ 12.5	—
3874173	1–3.5 @ 600	3.5–6 @ 750	—	10 @ 2000	8	11 @ 14	—
3874298	.5–3.5 @ 700	7–10 @ 1100	—	16 @ 2100	9	12.5 @ 15.5	—

①—Stamped on distributor housing.
②—Solenoid controlled.

DODGE & PLYMOUTH

1969

2875140②	2.5–9.5 @ 650	10–12 @ 850	—	16 @ 1550	10	11 @ 15	—
2875715②	1–7 @ 550	12–14 @ 900	—	19 @ 2500	8	12 @ 15	—
2875731②	1–7.5 @ 550	10.5–12.5 @ 850	—	17 @ 2500	8	12 @ 15	—
2875742②	1–9.5 @ 550	11–13 @ 800	—	23 @ 2350	8.5	13.5 @ 13.5	—
2875747②	1–6 @ 500	8–10 @ 750	—	19 @ 2300	8.5	13.5 @ 13.5	—
2875750②	1–7 @ 550	12–14 @ 900	—	19 @ 2500	8	12 @ 15	—
2875758②	2–7 @ 550	9–11 @ 850	—	16 @ 2400	10.5	12 @ 16	—
2875764②	0.5–3.5 @ 500	6.5–8.5 @ 850	—	14 @ 2250	11.5	13.5 @ 16	—
2875772②	1–8.5 @ 550	11.5–13.5 @ 850	—	19 @ 2500	10.5	12 @ 16	—
2875779②	2–6 @ 600	7–9 @ 900	—	12 @ 2000	8	10 @ 10.5	—
2875782②	1–6.5 @ 550	9.5–11.5 @ 900	—	14 @ 1800	8	10 @ 10.5	—
2875790②	2–8.5 @ 550	11.5–13.5 @ 900	—	16 @ 1900	8.5	13.5 @ 13.5	—
2875796②	1.5–6.5 @ 550	7.5–9.5 @ 850	—	19 @ 2400	10.5	10¾ @ 15	—
2875813②	2–6 @ 600	12.5–14.5 @ 1100	—	19 @ 2200	7.5	8.5 @ 10	—
2875822②	1–5 @ 550	9.5–11.5 @ 1000	—	14 @ 2000	10	7¾ @ 16	—
2875826②	1–5 @ 550	9.5–11.5 @ 1000	—	14 @ 2000	7	7¾ @ 10	—
2875846②	1–7.5 @ 550	10.5–12.5 @ 850	—	17 @ 2500	8	12 @ 15	—
2875855②	1–8 @ 550	9–11 @ 900	—	16 @ 2200	7.5	8 @ 10	—

1970

2875822②	1–5 @ 550	9.2–11.2 @ 900	—	14 @ 2000	10	7¾ @ 15	—
2875826②	1–5 @ 550	9.2–11.2 @ 900	—	14 @ 2000	7	7¾ @ 10	—
2875982②	0–5.3 @ 600	9–11 @ 850	—	14 @ 2400	11	12.5 @ 15.5	—
2875987②	0–4.5 @ 650	12.2–14.2 @ 1050	—	16 @ 1600	9	9.2 @ 13.5	—
2875989④	0–4.2 @ 600	9.7–11.7 @ 950	—	13.5 @ 1600	9	9.2 @ 13.5	—
3438219②	0.5–3.7 @ 650	5.7–7.7 @ 900	—	14 @ 2300	10.5	12 @ 15.5	—
3438222②	0–4.6 @ 600	5.6–7.6 @ 800	—	12 @ 2300	10.5	12 @ 15.5	—
3438225②	1–6 @ 550	8.5–10.5 @ 800	—	14 @ 2100	12	10¾ @ 15	—
3438231②	0–3.8 @ 550	7.5–9.5 @ 850	—	16 @ 2200	7.5	11.8 @ 12	—
3438233②	0–4.6 @ 600	5.6–7.6 @ 800	—	12 @ 2300	10.5	12 @ 15.5	—
3438237②	0–7.5 @ 525	9.3–11.3 @ 750	—	14 @ 1600	7	7¾ @ 10	—
3438255②	1–6 @ 550	8.5–10.5 @ 800	—	16 @ 2100	10.5	10¾ @ 15	—
3438314④	0–4.5 @ 650	9–11 @ 950	—	14 @ 2400	11	12.5 @ 15.5	—
3438317④	1.5–6.5 @ 700	—	—	10 @ 900	7.7	10 @ 10.5	—
3438325②	1.5–5.5 @ 650	—	—	10 @ 850	7.7	10 @ 10.5	—

Continued

DISTRIBUTOR SPECIFICATIONS—Continued

★Note: If unit is checked on vehicle, double the RPM and degrees to get crankshaft figures.

Breaker arm spring tension—17-20.

Distributor Part No.①	Centrifugal Advance Degrees @ RPM of Distributor					Vacuum Advance		Distributor Retard
	Advance Starts	Intermediate Advance			Full Advance	Inches of Vacuum to Start Plunger	Max. Adv. Dist. Deg. @ Vacuum	Max. Retard Dist. Deg. @ Vacuum
DODGE & PLYMOUTH—Continued								
1971								
2875822②	1–5 @ 550	9.2–11.2 @ 900	—	—	14 @ 2000	10	7¾ @ 15	—
2875826②	1–5 @ 550	9.2–11.2 @ 900	—	—	14 @ 2000	7	7¾ @ 10	—
2875987④	0–4.5 @ 650	12.2–14.2 @ 1050	—	—	16 @ 1600	9	9.2 @ 13.5	—
3438225②	1–6 @ 550	8.5–10.5 @ 800	—	—	16 @ 2100	12	10¾ @ 15	—
3438255②	1–6 @ 550	8.5–10.5 @ 800	—	—	16 @ 2100	10.5	10¾ @ 15	—
3438422②	1–6 @ 550	8.5–10.5 @ 800	—	—	16 @ 2100	9.5	10.5 @ 15	—
3438440②	0.5–3.5 @ 800	8–10.5 @ 1200	—	—	14 @ 2200	10	7¾ @ 15	—
3438442②	0.5–3.5 @ 800	8–10.5 @ 1200	—	—	14 @ 2200	7	7¾ @ 10	—
3438453②	0–4 @ 600	8–10.5 @ 1000	—	—	16 @ 2100	9.5	10.5 @ 15	—
3438509②	1–6.5 @ 550	8–10 @ 750	—	—	14 @ 2000	7	8.5 @ 11	—
3438517②	0.5–4 @ 600	9.5–12 @ 1000	—	—	12 @ 2100	9	10 @ 12.5	—
3438522④	0.5–4 @ 650	5.5–8.5 @ 850	—	—	12 @ 2000	7	10 @ 11	—
3438524②	2–6 @ 700	8.5–10.5 @ 900	—	—	14 @ 2000	7	7¾ @ 10	—
3438534②	1–4.5 @ 600	5–7 @ 800	—	—	14 @ 2000	9	10 @ 15	—
3438544②	0.5–3.5 @ 700	5–7.5 @ 900	—	—	14 @ 2000	9	10 @ 15	—
3438559②	0.5–3.5 @ 700	3.5–5.5 @ 900	—	—	12 @ 2400	12	10 @ 16	—
3438572②	0–3.5 @ 600	4.5–6.5 @ 800	—	—	10 @ 2200	10.5	12 @ 15.5	—
3438577④	1–3 @ 700	4.5–6.5 @ 950	—	—	6.5 @ 2200	10.5	10 @ 15	—
3438579④	0–4 @ 600	9.5–12.5 @ 1250	—	—	15 @ 1600	9	9.2 @ 13.5	—
3438615④	0.5–4 @ 700	9–11 @ 1100	—	—	15 @ 2200	7	10 @ 11	—
3438617②	0.5–4 @ 700	9–11 @ 1100	—	—	15 @ 2200	9	10 @ 12.5	—
3438690②	0.5–3.5 @ 650	6–8 @ 900	—	—	14 @ 2400	10.5	10 @ 15	—
3438694②	0.5–4 @ 700	5–7 @ 900	—	—	10 @ 2200	10.5	12 @ 15.5	—
3656151⑥	0.5–4 @ 650	5.5–8.5 @ 850	—	—	12 @ 2000	7	10 @ 11	—
1972								
3656237②	0–5 @ 550	8–10 @ 800	—	—	14 @ 2000	7	8.5 @ 11	—
3656243②	1–4.5 @ 650	8.5–10.5 @ 950	—	—	14 @ 2000	7	8.5 @ 11	—
3656252②	0.5–4.5 @ 550	9–11 @ 900	—	—	14 @ 2000	10	8 @ 15	—
3656257②	0.5–4.5 @ 550	9–11 @ 900	—	—	14 @ 2000	7	7.5 @ 9.5	—
3656260②	0.5–3.5 @ 700	9.5–11.5 @ 1150	—	—	14 @ 2000	10	8 @ 15	—
3656266②	0.5–3.5 @ 700	9.5–11.5 @ 1150	—	—	14 @ 2000	7	7.5 @ 9.5	—
3656272②	1–6 @ 550	8.5–10.5 @ 800	—	—	16 @ 2100	9.5	10.5 @ 15	—
3656275②	0–4 @ 600	9–11 @ 1000	—	—	16 @ 2100	9.5	10.5 @ 15	—
3656278②	1–5 @ 650	12–14 @ 1050	—	—	13.5 @ 2400	9	10 @ 12.5	—
3656329②	1–5 @ 650	8–10 @ 900	—	—	14 @ 2000	10.5	10.5 @ 15.5	—
3656332②	0.5–4 @ 650	6–8 @ 950	—	—	12 @ 2000	10.5	10.5 @ 15.5	—
3656335	1–5 @ 650	8–10 @ 900	—	—	15 @ 2250	10.5	10.5 @ 15.5	—
3656338	0.5–4 @ 650	6–8 @ 950	—	—	12.5 @ 2500	10.5	10.5 @ 15.5	—
3656341	0.5–4 @ 650	6–8 @ 950	—	—	12.5 @ 2500	10.5	10.5 @ 15.5	—
3656344②	0.5–4 @ 650	6–8 @ 950	—	—	12 @ 2000	10.5	10.5 @ 15.5	—
3656347	1–5 @ 650	8–10 @ 900	—	—	15 @ 2250	10.5	10.5 @ 15.5	—
3656350	1–5 @ 650	8–10 @ 900	—	—	14 @ 2000	10.5	10.5 @ 15.5	—
3656390	1–6 @ 550	8.5–10.5 @ 800	—	—	16 @ 2100	12	10.5 @ 15	—
3656429	1–6 @ 550	8.5–10.5 @ 800	—	—	15 @ 1900	9	10 @ 14	—
3656435	0–4 @ 600	9–11 @ 1100	—	—	15 @ 1900	9	10 @ 14	—
3656587	1–6 @ 550	8.5–10.5 @ 800	—	—	16 @ 2100	12	10 @ 14.5	—
3656593	1–4.5 @ 550	7.5–9.5 @ 800	—	—	16 @ 1900	10.5	10.5 @ 15.5	—
3656596	1–4.5 @ 550	7.5–9.5 @ 800	—	—	15 @ 1800	10.5	10.5 @ 15.5	—

Continued

DISTRIBUTOR SPECIFICATIONS—Continued

★Note: If unit is checked on vehicle, double the RPM and degrees to get crankshaft figures.

Distributor Part No.①	Centrifugal Advance Degrees @ RPM of Distributor					Vacuum Advance		Distributor Retard
	Advance Starts	Intermediate Advance			Full Advance	Inches of Vacuum to Start Plunger	Max. Adv. Dist. Deg. @ Vacuum	Max. Retard Dist. Deg. @ Vacuum
DODGE AND PLYMOUTH—Continued								
1973								
3755037	0.5–4.5 @ 550	9–11 @ 900	—	—	14 @ 2000	9.5	10 @ 15	—
3755042	0.5–4.5 @ 550	9–11 @ 900	—	—	14 @ 2000	7	10 @ 11	—
3755157	0.5–4.0 @ 650	6–8 @ 950	—	—	12.5 @ 2500	10.5	10.5 @ 15.5	—
3755308	0–2.5 @ 600	8–10.5 @ 1000	—	—	15.5 @ 2150	10.5	10.5 @ 15.5	—
3755336	0–2.5 @ 600	6.5–8.5 @ 900	—	—	12 @ 2000	9	12.5 @ 15	—
3755337	0–2.5 @ 600	6.5–8.5 @ 900	—	—	12 @ 2000	9	12.5 @ 15	—
3755365	0.5–4.0 @ 550	8–10 @ 800	—	—	14 @ 2000	9	12.5 @ 15	—
3656859	0–5 @ 550	8–10 @ 900	—	—	14 @ 2000	7	10 @ 11	—
3656763	1–4.5 @ 525	6.5–8.5 @ 750	—	—	15 @ 1900	9	12.5 @ 15	—
3656771	0.5–3.5 @ 600	8.5–11 @ 1000	—	—	13 @ 2000	9	10 @ 12.5	—
3656780	0.5–3.5 @ 500	10–12.5 @ 800	—	—	15 @ 1750	9	12.5 @ 15	—
3656791	0.5–3.5 @ 550	8–10.5 @ 850	—	—	15 @ 1950	10.5	10.5 @ 15.5	—
3656802	0.5–4.0 @ 650	6–8 @ 950	—	—	12.5 @ 2500	10.5	10.5 @ 15.5	—
1974								
3755037	1–4 @ 550	9–11.5 @ 900	—	—	14 @ 2000	9	8.5 @ 15.5	—
3755042	1–4 @ 550	9–11.5 @ 900	—	—	14 @ 2000	7	8.5 @ 11.5	—
3755467	0.5–3.5 @ 550	7–9.5 @ 950	—	—	14 @ 2000	9	8.5 @ 15.5	—
3755470	0.5–3.5 @ 550	7–9.5 @ 950	—	—	14 @ 2000	7	8.5 @ 11.5	—
3755475	0.5–4 @ 550	8–11.5 @ 800	—	—	14 @ 2000	7	11 @ 12.5	—
3755486	1–5 @ 600	8–10 @ 850	—	—	14 @ 2000	8	11 @ 13.5	—
3755503	0.5–4 @ 550	8–10.5 @ 850	—	—	16 @ 2200	8	10 @ 14	—
3755508	1–4.5 @ 650	8–10.5 @ 950	—	—	14 @ 2000	8	10¼ @ 16	—
3755512	0.5–3.5 @ 650	5.5–8 @ 900	—	—	12 @ 2000	8	10 @ 14	—
3755518	0.5–3.5 @ 650	5.5–8 @ 900	—	—	12 @ 2000	8	10 @ 14	—
3755522	0.5–3 @ 650	4–6.5 @ 900	—	—	12 @ 2000	8	10 @ 14	—
3755681	1–4.5 @ 650	8.5–11 @ 950	—	—	16 @ 2150	8	10 @ 14	—
3755686	0.5–4 @ 550	8–10.5 @ 850	—	—	16 @ 2200	8	10¼ @ 16	—
3656763	1.5–5.5 @ 550	6–8.5 @ 700	—	—	16 @ 2100	9	11 @ 15.5	—
3656859	0.5–4 @ 550	8–10.5 @ 800	—	—	14 @ 2000	7	8.5 @ 11.5	—
1975								
3874082	1–4.5 @ 600	8–10.5 @ 900	—	—	14 @ 2200	7	10 @ 11.5	—
3874090	1.5–5.5 @ 550	5.5–8 @ 700	—	—	14 @ 2200	7	12 @ 12.5	—
3874097	1–4.5 @ 650	8.5–11 @ 950	—	—	16 @ 2150	7	12 @ 12.5	—
3874101	.5–3 @ 600	6–8.5 @ 950	—	—	12 @ 2000	8	11 @ 14	—
3874110	1–3.5 @ 600	6–8.5 @ 900	—	—	12 @ 2000	8	11 @ 14	—
3874115	1–3.5 @ 600	6–8.5 @ 900	—	—	12 @ 2000	7	12 @ 12.5	—
3874173	1–3.5 @ 600	3.5–6 @ 750	—	—	10 @ 2000	8	11 @ 14	—
3874298	.5–3.5 @ 700	7–10 @ 1100	—	—	16 @ 2100	9	12.5 @ 15.5	—

①—Stamped on distributor housing.   ②—Breaker arm spring tension—17–20.   ③—California vehicles.
④—Breaker arm spring tension—17–21½.   ⑤—Electronic ignition.

VALVE SPECIFICATIONS

Year	Model	Valve Lash Int.	Valve Lash Exh.	Valve Angles Seat	Valve Angles Face	Valve Spring Installed Height	Valve Spring Pressure Lbs. @ In.	Stem Clearance Intake	Stem Clearance Exhaust	Stem Diameter Intake	Stem Diameter Exhaust
CHRYSLER & IMPERIAL											
1969–70	8-383, 290 H.P.	Hydraulic①		45	45	1.86	200 @ 1.43	.001–.003	.002–.004	.372–.373	.371–.372
	8-383, 330 H.P.	Hydraulic①		45	45	1.86	225 @ 1.43	.001–.003	.002–.004	.372–.373	.371–.372
	8-440, 350 H.P.	Hydraulic①		45	45	1.86	200 @ 1.43	.001–.003	.002–.004	.372–.373	.371–.372
	8-440, 375 H.P.	Hydraulic①		45	45	1.86	230 @ 1.41	.001–.003	.002–.004	.372–.373	.371–.372
1971	8-383, 270 H.P.	Hydraulic①		45	45	$1\frac{55}{64}$	200 @ $1\frac{7}{16}$	.001–.003	.002–.004	.372–.373	.371–.372
	8-383, 300 H.P.	Hydraulic①		45	45	$1\frac{55}{64}$	246 @ $1\frac{23}{64}$	.001–.003	.002–.004	.372–.373	.371–.372
	8-400	Hydraulic①		45	45	$1\frac{55}{64}$	200 @ $1\frac{7}{16}$	.001–.003	.002–.004	.372–.373	.371–.372
	8-440, 335 H.P.	Hydraulic①		45	45	$1\frac{55}{64}$	200 @ $1\frac{7}{16}$	.001–.003	.002–.004	.372–.373	.371–.372
	8-440, 370 H.P.	Hydraulic①		45	45	$1\frac{55}{64}$	246 @ $1\frac{23}{64}$	.001–.003	.002–.004	.372–.373	.371–.372
1972	8-360	Hydraulic①		45	45	1.65	195 @ 1.24	.001–.003	.002–.004	.372–.373	.371–.372
1972–74	8-400, 440	Hydraulic①		45	45	1.86	200 @ 1.42	.001–.003	.002–.004	.372–.373	.371–.372
1975	V8-318	Hydraulic		45	②	$1\frac{11}{16}$	177 @ $1\frac{5}{16}$	.001–.003	.002–.004	.372–.373	.371–.372
	V8-360	Hydraulic		45	②	$1\frac{11}{16}$	208 @ $1\frac{5}{16}$	.001–.003	.002–.004	.372–.373	.371–.372
	V8-400, 440	Hydraulic		45	45	$1\frac{55}{64}$	200 @ $1\frac{7}{16}$	.0011–.0028	④	.3723–.373	⑥
	V8-400, 440③	Hydraulic		45	45	$1\frac{55}{64}$	246 @ $1\frac{23}{64}$	.0016–.0033	⑤	.3718–.3725	⑦
DODGE & PLYMOUTH											
1969–70	6-170, 198, 225	.010H	.020H	45	②	$1\frac{11}{16}$	145 @ $1\frac{5}{16}$	.001–.003	.002–.004	.372–.373	.371–.372
	8-273, 318	Hydraulic		45	②	$1\frac{11}{16}$	177 @ $1\frac{5}{16}$	.001–.003	.002–.004	.372–.373	.371–.372
	8-340	Hydraulic①		45	②	$1\frac{11}{16}$	242 @ $1\frac{7}{32}$	.001–.003	.002–.004	.372–.373	.371–.372
	8-383, 290 H.P.	Hydraulic①		45	45	$1\frac{57}{64}$	200 @ $1\frac{7}{16}$	.001–.003	.002–.004	.372–.373	.371–.372
	8-383, 330 H.P.	Hydraulic①		45	45	$1\frac{57}{64}$	246 @ $1\frac{23}{64}$	.001–.003	.002–.004	.372–.373	.371–.372
	8-383, 335 H.P.	Hydraulic①		45	45	$1\frac{57}{64}$	246 @ $1\frac{23}{64}$	.001–.003	.002–.004	.372–.373	.371–.372
	8-440, 350 H.P.	Hydraulic①		45	45	$1\frac{57}{64}$	200 @ $1\frac{7}{16}$	.001–.003	.002–.004	.372–.373	.371–.372
	8-440, 375 H.P.	Hydraulic①		45	45	$1\frac{57}{64}$	246 @ $1\frac{23}{64}$	.001–.003	.002–.004	.372–.373	.371–.372
	8-440, 390 H.P.	Hydraulic①		45	45	$1\frac{57}{64}$	310 @ $1\frac{3}{8}$	.001–.003	.002–.004	.372–.373	.371–.372
	8-426	.028C	.032C	45	45	$1\frac{57}{64}$	280 @ $1\frac{3}{8}$	.001–.003	.002–.004	.372–.373	.371–.372
1971	6-198, 225	.010H	.020H	45	②	$1\frac{11}{16}$	145 @ $1\frac{5}{16}$	.001–.003	.002–.004	.372–.373	.371–.372
	8-318	Hydraulic		45	③	$1\frac{11}{16}$	177 @ $1\frac{5}{16}$	.001–.003	.002–.004	.372–.373	.371–.372
	8-340	Hydraulic①		45	②	$1\frac{11}{16}$	238 @ $1\frac{5}{16}$	.001–.003	.002–.004	.372–.373	.371–.372
	8-360	Hydraulic①		45	②	$1\frac{11}{16}$	177 @ $1\frac{5}{16}$	.001–.003	.002–.004	.372–.373	.371–.372
	8-383, 2 B. Carb.	Hydraulic①		45	45	$1\frac{55}{64}$	200 @ $1\frac{7}{16}$	.001–.003	.002–.004	.372–.373	.371–.372
	8-383, 4 B. Carb.	Hydraulic①		45	45	$1\frac{55}{64}$	246 @ $1\frac{23}{64}$	.001–.003	.002–.004	.372–.373	.371–.372
	8-440	Hydraulic①		45	45	$1\frac{55}{64}$	200 @ $1\frac{7}{16}$	.001–.003	.002–.004	.372–.373	.371–.372
	8-440, Hi Perf.	Hydraulic①		45	45	$1\frac{55}{64}$	246 @ $1\frac{23}{64}$	.001–.003	.002–.004	.372–.373	.371–.372
	8-440, 3 Carbs.	Hydraulic①		45	45	$1\frac{55}{64}$	246 @ $1\frac{23}{64}$	.001–.003	.002–.004	.372–.373	.371–.372
	8-426	Hydraulic①		45	45	$1\frac{55}{64}$	310 @ $1\frac{3}{8}$	.002–.004	.003–.005	.3085–.3095	.3075–.3085
1972	6-198, 225	.010H	.020H	45	②	1.65	160 @ 1.24	.001–.003	.002–.004	.372–.373	.371–.372
	8-318	Hydraulic①		45	②	1.65	189 @ 1.28	.001–.003	.002–.004	.372–.373	.371–.372
	8-340	Hydraulic①		45	②	1.65	238 @ 1.22	.001–.003	.002–.004	.372–.373	.371–.372
	8-360	Hydraulic①		45	②	1.65	195 @ 1.24	.001–.003	.002–.004	.372–.373	.371–.372
	8-400, 2 B. Carb.	Hydraulic①		45	45	1.86	200 @ 1.42	.001–.003	.002–.004	.372–.373	.371–.372
	8-400, 4 B. Carb.	Hydraulic①		45	45	1.86	246 @ 1.36	.001–.003	.002–.004	.372–.373	.371–.372
	8-440	Hydraulic①		45	45	1.86	200 @ 1.42	.001–.003	.002–.004	.372–.373	.371–.372
	8-440, Hi Perf.	Hydraulic①		45	45	1.86	246 @ 1.36	.001–.003	.002–.004	.372–.373	.371–.372
	8-440, 3 Carbs.	Hydraulic①		45	45	1.86	246 @ 1.36	.001–.003	.002–.004	.372–.373	.371–.372

Continued

VALVE SPECIFICATIONS—Continued

Year	Model	Valve Lash		Valve Angles		Valve Spring Installed Height	Valve Spring Pressure Lbs. @ In.	Stem Clearance		Stem Diameter	
		Int.	Exh.	Seat	Face			Intake	Exhaust	Intake	Exhaust

DODGE & PLYMOUTH—Continued

Year	Model	Int.	Exh.	Seat	Face	Installed Height	Pressure Lbs. @ In.	Intake	Exhaust	Intake	Exhaust
1973	6-198, 225	.010H	.020H	45	②	1.65	160 @ 1.25	.001–.003	.002–.004	.372–.373	.371–.372
	8-318	Hydraulic①		45	②	1.65	193 @ 1.25	.001–.003	.002–.004	.372–.373	.371–.372
	8-340	Hydraulic①		45	②	1.65	241 @ 1.21	.001–.003	.002–.004	.371–.372	.370–.371
	8-360	Hydraulic①		45	②	1.65	195 @ 1.24	.001–.003	.002–.004	.372–.373	.371–.372
	8-400, 2 Bar. Carb.	Hydraulic①		45	45	1.86	200 @ 1.42	.001–.003	.002–.004	.372–.373	.371–.372
	8-400, 4 Bar. Carb.	Hydraulic①		45	45	1.86	246 @ 1.36	.001–.003	.002–.004	.372–.373	.371–.372
	8-440	Hydraulic①		45	45	1.86	200 @ 1.42	.001–.003	.002–.004	.372–.373	.371–.372
1974	6-198, 225	.010H	.020H	45	②	1.65	147 @ 1⁵⁄₁₆	.001–.003	.002–.004	.372–.373	.371–.372
	8-318	Hydraulic①		45	②	1.65	177 @ 1⁵⁄₁₆	.001–.003	.002–.004	.372–.373	.371–.372
	8-360, 2 Bar. Carb.	Hydraulic①		45	②	1.65	177 @ 1⁵⁄₁₆	.001–.003	.002–.004	.372–.373	.371–.372
	8-360, 4 Bar. Carb.	Hydraulic①		45	②	1.65	238 @ 1⁵⁄₁₆	.001–.003	.002–.004	.372–.373	.371–.372
	8-400, 440	Hydraulic①		45	45	1.86	200 @ 1⁷⁄₁₆	.001–.003	.002–.004	.372–.373	.371–.372
	8-400, 440 Hi Perf.	Hydraulic①		45	45	1.86	246 @ 1²³⁄₆₄	.001–.003	.002–.004	.372–.373	.371–.372
1975	6-225	.010H	.020H	45	45	1¹¹⁄₁₆	144 @ 1⁵⁄₁₆	.001–.003	.002–.004	.372–.373	.371–.372
	V8-318	Hydraulic		45	②	1¹¹⁄₁₆	177 @ 1⁵⁄₁₆	.001–.003	.002–.004	.372–.373	.371–.372
	V8-360	Hydraulic		45	②	1¹¹⁄₁₆	208 @ 1⁵⁄₁₆	.001–.003	.002–.004	.372–.373	.371–.372
	V8-360③	Hydraulic		45	②	1¹¹⁄₁₆	238 @ 1.22	.001–.003	.002–.004	.372–.373	.371–.372
	V8-400, 440	Hydraulic		45	45	1⁵⁵⁄₆₄	200 @ 1⁷⁄₁₆	.0011–.0028	④	.3723–.373	⑥
	V8-400, 440③	Hydraulic		45	45	1⁵⁵⁄₆₄	246 @ 1²³⁄₆₄	.0016–.0033	⑤	.3718–.3725	⑦

①—No adjustment.
②—Intake 45°, exhaust 43°.
③—High Performance.
④—Hot end .0021-.0038, Cold end .0011-.0028.

⑤—Hot end .0026-.0043, Cold end .0016-.0033.
⑥—Hot end .3713-.372, Cold end .3723-.373.
⑦—Hot end .3708-.3715, Cold end .3718-.3725.

PISTONS, PINS, RINGS, CRANKSHAFT & BEARINGS

Year	Model	Piston Clearance Top of Skirt	Ring End Gap① Comp.	Oil	Wrist-pin Diameter	Rod Bearings Shaft Diameter	Bearing Clearance	Main Bearings Shaft Diameter	Bearing Clearance	Thrust on Bear. No.	Shaft End Play
CHRYSLER & IMPERIAL											
1969	8-383	.0003–.0013	.013	.015	1.0936	2.374–2.375	.001–.002	2.6245–2.6255	.0005–.0015	3	.002–.007
	8-440	.0003–.0013	.013	.015	1.0936	2.374–2.375	.001–.002	2.7495–2.7505	.0005–.0015	3	.002–.007
1970	8-383, 2 B. C.	.0003–.0012	.013	.015	1.0936	2.374–2.375	.0005–.0015	2.6245–2.6255	.0005–.0015	3	.002–.007
	8-383, 4 B. C.	.0003–.0012	.013	.015	1.0936	2.374–2.375	.001–.002	2.6245–2.6255	.0005–.0015	3	.002–.007
	8-440	.0003–.0012	.013	.015	1.0936	2.374–2.375	.001–.002	2.7495–2.7505	.0005–.0015	3	.002–.007
1971	8-383, 2 B. C.	.0003–.0012	.013	.015	1.0936	2.374–2.375	.0005–.0025	2.6245–2.6255	.0005–.0015	3	.002–.007
	8-383, 4 B. C.	.0003–.0012	.013	.015	1.0936	2.374–2.375	.0007–.0032	2.6245–2.6255	.0005–.0015	3	.002–.007
	8-400	.0003–.0013	.013	.015	1.0936	2.374–2.375	.0005–.002	2.6245–2.6255	.0005–.002	3	.002–.007
	8-440	.0003–.0012	.013	.015	1.0936	2.374–2.375	.0001–.0032	2.7495–2.7505	.0005–.0015	3	.002–.007
1972	8-360	.0005–.0015	.010	.015	.9842	2.124–2.125	.0005–.0025	2.8095–2.8105	.0005–.0025	3	.002–.010
	8-400	.0003–.0013	.013	.015	1.0936	2.374–2.375	②	2.6245–2.6255	.0005–.0025	3	.002–.010
	8-440	.0003–.0013	.013	.015	1.0936	2.374–2.375	.001–.0025	2.7495–2.7505	.0005–.0025	3	.002–.010
1973–74	8-400	.0003–.0013	.013	.015	1.0935	2.374–2.375	②	2.6245–2.6255	.0005–.0025	3	.002–.007
	8-440	.0003–.0013	.013	.015	1.0935	2.374–2.375	.001–.0025	2.7495–2.7505	.0005–.0025	3	.002–.007
1975	V8-318	.0005–.0015	.010	.015	.9482	2.124–2.125	.0005–.0025	2.4995–2.5005	.0005–.0020	3	.002–.010
	V8-360	.0005–.0015	.010	.015	.9482	2.124–2.125	.0005–.0025	2.8095–2.8105	.0005–.0020	3	.002–.010
	V8-400	.0003–.0013	.013	.015	1.0936	2.375–2.376	⑧	2.6245–2.6255	.0005–.0020	3	.002–.007
	V8-440	.0003–.0013	.013	.015	1.0936	2.375–2.376	.0004–.0029	2.7495–2.7505	.0005–.0020	3	.002–.007
DODGE & PLYMOUTH											
1969–70	6-170	.0005–.0015	.010	.010	.9008	2.1865–2.1875	.0005–.001	2.7495–2.7505	.0005–.0015	3	.002–.007
	6-198, 225	.0005–.0015	.010	.015	.9008	2.1865–2.1875	.0005–.0015	2.7495–2.7505	.0005–.0015	3	.002–.007
	8-273, 318	.0005–.0015	.010	.015	.9842	2.124–2.125	.0005–.0015	2.4995–2.5005	.0005–.0015	3	.002–.007
	8-340	.0005–.0015	.010	.015	.9842	2.124–2.125	.0005–.0020	2.4995–2.5005	.0005–.0015	3	.002–.007
	8-383, 290 H.P.	.0003–.0013	.013	.015	1.0936	2.374–2.375	.0005–.0015	2.6245–2.6255	.0005–.0015	3	.002–.007
	8-383, 330 H.P.	.0003–.0013	.013	.015	1.0936	2.374–2.375	.001–.002	2.6245–2.6255	.0005–.0015	3	.002–.007
	8-383, 335 H.P.	.0003–.0013	.013	.015	1.0936	2.374–2.375	.001–.002	2.6245–2.6255	.0005–.0015	3	.002–.007
	8-440	.0003–.0013	.013	.015	1.0936	2.374–2.375	.001–.002	2.7495–2.7505	.0005–.0015	3	.002–.007
	8-426	.0025–.0035	.013	.015	1.0311	2.374–2.375	.0015–.0025	2.7495–2.7505	.0015–.0025	3	.002–.007
1971	6-198, 225	.0005–.0015	.010	.015	.9008	2.1865–2.1875	.0005–.002	2.7495–2.7505	.0005–.002	3	.002–.007
	8-318, 340, 360	.0005–.0015	.010	.015	.9842	2.124–2.125	.0005–.002	2.4995–2.5005	.0005–.002	3	.002–.006
	8-383	.0003–.0013	.013	.015	1.0936	2.374–2.375	.0005–.002	2.6245–2.6255	.0005–.002	3	.002–.007
	8-440	.0003–.0013	.013	.015	1.0936	2.374–2.375	.0005–.002	2.7495–2.7505	.0005–.002	3	.002–.007
	8-426	.0025–.0035	.013	.015	1.0311	2.374–2.375	.0015–.0025	2.7490–2.75005	.0015–.003	3	.002–.007
1972–74	6-198, 225	.0005–.0015	.010	.015	.9008	2.1865–2.1875	.0005–.0025	2.7495–2.7505	.0005–.0025	3	.002–.010
	8-318	.0005–.0015	.010	.015	.9842	2.124–2.125	.0005–.0025	2.4995–2.5005	.0005–.0025	3	.002–.010
	8-340	.0005–.0015	.010	.015	.9842	2.124–2.125	.0005–.0030	2.4995–2.5005	.0005–.0025	3	.002–.010
	8-360	.0005–.0015	.010	.015	.9842	2.124–2.125	.0005–.0025	2.8095–2.8105	.0005–.0025	3	.002–.010
	8-400	.0003–.0013	.013	.015	1.0936	2.374–2.375	②	2.6245–2.6255	.0005–.0025	3	.002–.010
	8-440	.0003–.0013	.013	.015	1.0936	2.374–2.375	.001–.0025	2.7495–2.7505	.0005–.0025	3	.002–.010
1975	6-225	.0005–.0015	.010	.015	.9008	2.1865–2.1875	.0005–.002	2.7495–2.7505	.0005–.002	3	.002–.007
	V8-318	.0005–.0015	.010	.015	.9482	2.124–2.125	.0005–.0025	2.4995–2.5005	.0005–.002	3	.002–.010
	V8-360	.0005–.0015	.010	.015	.9482	2.124–2.125	.0005–.0025	2.8095–2.8105	.0005–.002	3	.002–.010
	V8-400	.0003–.0013	.013	.015	1.0936	2.375–2.376	⑧	2.6245–2.6255	.0005–.002	3	.002–.007
	V8-440	.0003–.0013	.013	.015	1.0936	2.375–2.376	.0004–.0029	2.7495–2.7505	.0005–.002	3	.002–.007

①—Fit rings in tapered bores for clearance listed in tightest portion of ring travel.
②—W/2 bbl. carb., .0005–.0020″; W/4 bbl. carb., .001–.0025″.
⑧—2 bbl. carb., .0002–.0022, 4 bbl. carb., .0004–.0029.

ALTERNATOR & REGULATOR SPECIFICATIONS

Year	Unit Number	Ground Polarity	Field Coil Draw Amperes	Current Output			Operating Voltage			Voltage Regulator Point Gap	Regulator Armature Air Gap
				Engine R.P.M.	Amperes	Volts	Engine R.P.M.	Volts	Voltage @ 120° ①		
1969	⑥	Negative	2.38–2.75②	1250	26③	15	1250	15	13.3–14.3	.012–.016	.048–.052
	⑦	Negative	2.38–2.75②	1250	34.5③	15	1250	15	13.3–14.3	.012–.016	.048–.052
	⑧	Negative	2.38–2.75②	1250	41③	15	1250	15	13.3–14.3	.012–.016	.048–.052
	⑨	Negative	2.38–2.75②	1250	51③	15	1250	15	13.3–14.3	.012–.016	.048–.052
1970–71	⑥	Negative	2.38–2.75②	1250	26③	15	1250	15	13.3–14.4	—	—
	⑦	Negative	2.38–2.75②	1250	34.5③	15	1250	15	13.3–14.4	—	—
	⑧	Negative	2.38–2.75②	1250	44.5③	15	1250	15	13.3–14.4	—	—
	⑨	Negative	2.38–2.75②	1250	51③	15	1250	15	13.3–14.4	—	—
1972–73	⑥	Negative	2.5–3.1②	1250	39③	15	1250	15	13.8–14.4⑩	—	—
	⑦	Negative	2.5–3.1②	1250	41③	15	1250	15	13.8–14.4⑩	—	—
	⑧	Negative	2.5–3.1②	1250	50③	15	1250	15	13.8–14.4⑩	—	—
	⑨	Negative	2.5–3.1②	1250	60③	15	1250	15	13.8–14.4⑩	—	—
1973–74	Black Tag	Negative	2.5–3.7	1250	65③	15	1250	15	13.8–14.4⑩	—	—
1974	Yellow Tag	Negative	2.5–3.7	1250	36③	15	1250	15	13.8–14.4⑩	—	—
	Red Tag	Negative	2.5–3.7	1250	41③	15	1250	15	13.8–14.4⑩	—	—
	Green Tag	Negative	2.5–3.7	1250	50③	15	1250	15	13.8–14.4⑩	—	—
	Blue or Natural Tag	Negative	2.5–3.7	1250	60③	15	1250	15	13.8–14.4⑩	—	—
1975	Yellow Tag④	Negative	2.5–3.7②	1250	36③	15	1250	15	14.23–14.43⑩	—	—
	Red Tag	Negative	2.5–3.7②	1250	40③	15	1250	15	14.23–14.43⑩	—	—
	Green Tag	Negative	2.5–3.7②	1250	47③	15	1250	15	14.23–14.43⑩	—	—
	Blue Tag	Negative	2.5–3.7②	1250	57③	15	1250	15	14.23–14.43⑩	—	—
	Natural Tag	Negative	2.5–3.7②	1250	57③	15	1250	15	14.23–14.43⑩	—	—
	Black Tag	Negative	2.5–3.7②	1250	62③	15	1250	15	14.23–14.43⑩	—	—
	Yellow Tag⑤	Negative	4.75–6②	900	84⑪	13	900	13	14.23–14.43⑩	—	—

①—For each 10 degree rise in temperature subtract .04 volt. Temperature is checked with thermometer two inches from installed voltage regulator cover.
②—Current draw at 12 volts while turning rotor shaft by hand.
③—Plus or minus three amperes. If output is low, stator or rectifier is shorted.
④—34 amp rating.
⑤—100 amp rating.
⑥—Standard with 6-cyl. engines.
⑦—Standard with V8 engines.
⑧—Heavy duty and/or air conditioning.
⑨—Special equipment.
⑩—At 80 degrees F.
⑪—Minimum output, rating 100 amps.

STARTING MOTOR SPECIFICATIONS

Year	Part No.	Rotation ①	Brush Spring Tension, Ounces	No Load Test			Torque Test		
				Amperes	Volts	R.P.M.	Amperes	Volts	Torque, Lbs. Ft.
1969–72	2095150	Clockwise	32–36	90	11	1925–2600	400–450	4	—
	2098500	Clockwise	32–36	90	11	2950	340–420	4	—
	1889100	Clockwise	32–36	78	11	3800	310–445	4	—
	2642930	Clockwise	32–36	78	11	3800	310–445	4	—
	2875560	Clockwise	32–36	90	11	1925–2600	400–450	4	—
1973	2875560	Clockwise	32–36	90	11	1925–2600	400–450	4	—
1973–74	3656575	Clockwise	32–36	90	11	②	475–550	4	—
1975	3755250	Clockwise	32–36	90	11	5700	475–550	4	—
	3755900	Clockwise	32–36	90	11	3700	475–550	4	—

①—Viewed from drive end.
②—1973 4300 R.P.M., 1974 3700–4200 R.P.M.

ENGINE TIGHTENING SPECIFICATIONS★

★Torque specifications are for clean and lightly lubricated threads only. Dry or dirty threads produce increased friction which prevents accurate measurement of tightness.

Year	Engine	Spark Plugs Ft. Lbs.	Cylinder Head Bolts Ft. Lbs.	Intake Manifold Ft. Lbs.	Exhaust Manifold Ft. Lbs.	Rocker Arm Shaft Bracket Ft. Lbs.	Rocker Arm Cover Ft. Lbs.	Connecting Rod Cap Bolts Ft. Lbs.	Main Bearing Cap Bolts Ft. Lbs.	Flywheel to Crankshaft Ft. Lbs.	Vibration Damper or Pulley Ft. Lbs.
1969–72	6-170, 198	30	65	200①	10	25	40①	45	85	55	②
1969–72	6-225	30	65	200①	10	25	40①	45	85	55	②
1969	8-273	30	85	35	30	210①	36①	45	85	55	135
1969–72	8-318	30	④	35	30	200①	36①	45	85	55	135⑤
1969–72	8-340, 360	30	95	35	30	200①	36①	45	85	55	135⑤
1969–72	8-383, 400	30	70	50	30	25	40①	45	85	55	135
1969–71	8-426 Hemi	30	75	⑧	35	30	40①	75	100	70	135
1969–72	8-440	30	70	50	30	25	40①	45	85	55	135
1973–75	6-198, 225	30	70	240①	10	25	40①	45	85	55	②
1973–75	8-318, 360	30	95	35	20	200①	40①	45	85	55	100
1973	8-340	30	95	35	20	200①	40①	45	85	55	100
1973–75	8-400, 440	30	70	40	30	25	40①	45	85	55	135

①—Inch pounds.
②—Press fit.
⑤—1971 100 ft. lbs.
⑧—Tighten 8 (4 each side) center screws to 72 inch-lbs; all others 48 inch-lbs.
④—Composition gasket 95 ft.-lbs. Steel gasket 85 ft.-lbs.

WHEEL ALIGNMENT SPECIFICATIONS

NOTE: See that riding height is correct before checking wheel alignment.

OLD CAR SPECIFICATIONS: For 1946-68 Wheel Alignment Specifications see main index.

Year	Model	Caster Angle, Degrees		Camber Angle, Degrees				Toe-In. Inch	Toe-Out on Turns, Deg.	
		Limits	Desired	Limits		Desired			Outer Wheel	Inner Wheel
				Left	Right	Left	Right			

CHRYSLER & IMPERIAL

Year	Model	Caster Limits	Caster Desired	Camber Limits Left	Camber Limits Right	Camber Desired Left	Camber Desired Right	Toe-In Inch	Outer Wheel	Inner Wheel
1969	Manual Steer.	+1/16 to −1 1/16	−1/2	+1/4 to +3/4	0 to +1/2	+1/2	+1/4	1/8	18.8①	20
	Power Steer.	+1/16 to −1 1/16②	−1/2	+1/4 to +3/4	0 to +1/2	+1/2	+1/4	1/8	18.8①	20
1970	Manual Steer.	0 to −1	−1/2	+1/4 to +3/4	0 to +1/2	+1/2	+1/4	1/8	18.8①	20
	Power Steer.	0 to −1③	−1/2	+1/4 to +3/4	0 to +1/2	+1/2	+1/4	1/8	18.8①	20
1971	Manual Steer.	0 to −1	−1/2	+1/4 to +3/4	0 to +1/2	+1/2	+1/4	1/8	—	—
	Power Steer.	+1/4 to +1 1/4③	+3/4	+1/4 to +3/4	0 to +1/2	+1/2	+1/4	1/8	—	—
1972	All	−1/16 to +1 5/16	+5/8	+1/8 to +7/8	−1/8 to +5/8	+1/2	+1/4	1/8	—	—
1973-74	All	+1/4 to +1 1/4	+3/4	+1/4 to +3/4	0 to +1/2	+1/2	+1/4	1/8	18.3	20
1975	Chry. & Imp.	−1/16 to +1 5/16	+3/4	+1/8 to +7/8	−1/8 to +5/8	+1/2	+1/4	3/32 to 5/32	—	—
	Cordoba	−1/16 to +1 5/16	+3/4	+1/8 to +7/8	−5/8 to +1/8	+1/2	−1/4	3/32 to 5/32	—	—

①—1969-70 Imperial 17.9°.
②—Imperial +3/16 to +1 5/16 with +3/4 preferred.
③—Imperial +1/4 to +1 1/4 with +3/4 preferred.

Continued

WHEEL ALIGNMENT SPECIFICATIONS—Continued

NOTE: See that riding height is correct before checking wheel alignment.

OLD CAR SPECIFICATIONS: For 1946-68 Wheel Alignment Specifications see main index.

Year	Model	Caster Angle, Degrees		Camber Angle, Degrees				Toe-In. Inch	Toe-Out on Turns, Deg.	
		Limits	Desired	Limits		Desired			Outer Wheel	Inner Wheel
				Left	Right	Left	Right			
DODGE										
1969–70	Man. Steer.①	0 to −1	−½	+¼ to +¾	0 to +½	+½	+¼	⅛	17.6	20
	Power Steer.①	+¼ to +1¼	+¾	+¼ to +¾	0 to +½	+½	+¼	⅛	17.6	20
	Man. Steer.②	0 to −1	−½	+¼ to +¾	0 to +½	+½	+¼	⅛	17.8	20
	Power Steer.②	+¼ to +1¼	+¾	+¼ to +¾	0 to +½	+½	+¼	⅛	17.8	20
	Man. Steer.③	0 to −1	−½	+¼ to +¾	0 to +½	+½	+¼	⅛	18.8	20
	Power Steer.③	0 to −1	−½	+¼ to +¾	0 to +½	+½	+¼	⅛	18.8	20
1971–73	Man. Steer.	0 to −1	−½	+¼ to +¾	0 to +½	+½	+¼	⅛	④	20
	Power Steer.	+¼ to +1¼	+¾	+¼ to +¾	0 to +½	+½	+¼	⅛	④	20
1974	Man. Steer.	−1¾ to +½	−½	0 to +1	−¼ to +¾	+½	+¼	5/32	⑤	20
	Power Steer.	−½ to +1¾	+¾	0 to +1	−¼ to +¾	+½	+¼	5/32	⑤	20
1975	Man. Steer.①	−1 5/16 to +1/16	−⅝	+⅛ to +⅞	−⅛ to +⅝	+½	+¼	1/16 to ¼	—	—
	Power Steer.①	−1/16 to +1 5/16	+⅝	+⅛ to +⅞	−⅛ to +⅝	+½	+¼	1/16 to ¼	—	—
	Man. Steer.⑥	−1 5/16 to +1/16	−½	+⅛ to +⅞	−⅛ to +⅝	+½	+¼	3/32 to 9/32	—	—
	Power Steer.⑦	−1/16 to +1 5/16	+¾	+⅛ to +⅞	−⅛ to +⅝	+½	+¼	3/32 to 9/32	—	—

①—Dart.
②—Coronet, Charger and Challenger.
③—Monaco, Polara.
④—Dart & Challenger 17.5°, 1971–72 Charger & Coronet 17.8°, 1973 Charger & Coronet 18.5°, Polara & Monaco 18.8°.
⑤—Dart 18.5°, Challenger 18.4°, Charger & Coronet 18°, Monaco 18.3°.
⑥—Coronet.
⑦—Coronet, Charger, Monaco.

Year	Model	Caster Limits	Caster Desired	Camber Limits Left	Camber Limits Right	Camber Desired Left	Camber Desired Right	Toe-In. Inch	Toe-Out Outer Wheel	Toe-Out Inner Wheel
PLYMOUTH										
1969–70	Man. Steer.	+1/16 to −1 1/16	−½	+¼ to +¾	0 to +½	+½	+¼	⅛	①	20
	Power Steer.	+3/16 to +1 5/16	+¾	+0¼ to +¾	0 to +½	+½	+¼	⅛	①	20
1971–73	Man. Steer.	0 to −1	−½	+¼ to +¾	0 to +½	+½	+¼	⅛	⑥	20
	Power Steer.	+¼ to +1¼	+¾	+¼ to +¾	0 to +½	+½	+¼	⅛	⑥	20
1974	Man. Steer.	−1¾ to +½	−½	0 to +1	−¼ to +¾	+½	+¼	5/32	②	20
	Power Steer.	−½ to +1¾	+¾	0 to +1	−¼ to +¾	+½	+¼	5/32	②	20
1975	Man. Steer.③	−5/16 to +1/16	−⅝	+⅛ to +⅞	−⅛ to +⅝	+½	+¼	1/16 to ¼	—	—
	Power Steer.③	−1/16 to +1 5/16	+⅝	+⅛ to +⅞	−⅛ to +⅝	+½	+¼	1/16 to ¼	—	—
	Man. Steer.④	−1 5/16 to +1/16	−½	+⅛ to +⅞	−⅛ to +⅝	+½	+¼	3/32 to 9/32	—	—
	Power Steer.⑤	−1/16 to +1 5/16	+¾	+⅛ to +⅞	−⅛ to +⅝	+½	+¼	3/32 to 9/32	—	—

①—Fury 17.7°, others 18°.
②—Valiant 18.5°, Barracuda 18.4°, Satellite 18°, Fury 18.3°
③—Valiant.

BRAKE SPECIFICATIONS

Year	Model	Brake Drum Inside Diameter	Wheel Cylinder Bore Diameter			Master Cylinder Bore Diameter		
			Disc Brake	Front Drum Brake	Rear Drum Brake	Disc Brakes	Drum Brakes	Power Brakes
CHRYSLER & IMPERIAL								
1969	Chrysler	11	2.750	1⅛	¹⁵⁄₁₆	1⅛	1	1
	Imperial	11	2.375	—	¹⁵⁄₁₆	1⅛	—	—
1970	All	11	2.750	1⅛	¹⁵⁄₁₆	1⅛	1	1
1971	All	11	2.750	1³⁄₁₆	¹⁵⁄₁₆	1	1	1
1972–73	All	11	2.750	—	¹⁵⁄₁₆	1¹⁄₃₂	—	1¹⁄₃₂
1974	Chrysler	11	3.10	—	¹⁵⁄₁₆	1¹⁄₃₂	—	1¹⁄₃₂
	Imperial	—	①	—	—	1¹⁄₁₆	—	1¹⁄₁₆
1975	Cordoba	10	2¾	—	¹⁵⁄₁₆	1.03	—	1.03
	Chrysler	11	3.1	—	¹⁵⁄₁₆	1.03	—	1.03
	Imperial	—	①	—	—	1.06	—	1.06

①—Front 3.10; Rear 2.60.

Year	Model	Brake Drum Inside Diameter	Disc Brake	Front Drum Brake	Rear Drum Brake	Disc Brakes	Drum Brakes	Power Brakes
DODGE								
1969	Dart 6	9	1.638	1	¹³⁄₁₆	1	1	1
	Dart V8	10	1.638	1⅛	¹⁵⁄₁₆	1	1	1
	Coronet Deluxe, 440	10	2.00	1⅛	¹⁵⁄₁₆	1⅛	1	1
	Coronet R/T, 500	11	2.00	1⅛	¹⁵⁄₁₆	1⅛	1	1
	Charger	10	2.00	1⅛	¹⁵⁄₁₆	1⅛	1	1
	Polara, Monaco	11	②	1⅛	¹⁵⁄₁₆	1⅛	1	1
1970	Dart 6	③	1.638	1	¹³⁄₁₆	1	1	1
	Dart V8	10	1.638	1⅛	¹⁵⁄₁₆	1	1	1
	Challenger	10④	2.750	1³⁄₁₆	¹⁵⁄₁₆	1⅛	1	1
	Coronet, Charger	10①	2.750	1⅛	¹⁵⁄₁₆	1⅛	1	1
	Monaco, Polara	11	2.750	1⅛	¹⁵⁄₁₆	1⅛	1	1
1971	Dart, Demon 6	9	—	1	¹³⁄₁₆	—	1	1
	Dart, Demon V8	10	1⅝	1³⁄₁₆	¹⁵⁄₁₆	1	1	1
	Challenger	10④	2.750	1³⁄₁₆	¹⁵⁄₁₆	1⅛	1	1
	Coronet, Charger	10④	2.750	1³⁄₁₆	¹⁵⁄₁₆	1⅛	1	1
	Monaco, Polara	11	2.750	1³⁄₁₆	¹⁵⁄₁₆	1	1	1
1972	Dart, Demon 6	9	—	1	¹³⁄₁₆	—	¹⁵⁄₁₆	¹⁵⁄₁₆
	Dart, Demon V8	10	1⅝	1³⁄₁₆	¹⁵⁄₁₆	1¹⁄₃₂	1¹⁄₃₂	1¹⁄₃₂
	Challenger	10	2.750	1³⁄₁₆	¹⁵⁄₁₆	1¹⁄₃₂	1¹⁄₃₂	1¹⁄₃₂
	Coronet, Charger	10④	2.750	1³⁄₁₆	¹⁵⁄₁₆	1¹⁄₃₂	1¹⁄₃₂	1¹⁄₃₂
	Monaco, Polara	11	2.750	1³⁄₁₆	¹⁵⁄₁₆	1¹⁄₃₂	1¹⁄₃₂	1¹⁄₃₂
1973	Dart, 6 cyl. (Early)	9	—	1¹⁄₁₆	¹³⁄₁₆	—	¹⁵⁄₁₆	¹⁵⁄₁₆
	Dart, 6 cyl. (Late)	10	—	1¹³⁄₁₆	¹³⁄₁₆	—	1¹⁄₃₂	1¹⁄₃₂
	Dart, V8	10	2.599	1¹⁄₁₆	¹⁵⁄₁₆	1¹⁄₃₂	1¹⁄₃₂	1¹⁄₃₂
	Challenger	10	2.750	—	¹⁵⁄₁₆	1¹⁄₃₂	1¹⁄₃₂	1¹⁄₃₂
	Coronet, Charger	10④	2.750	—	¹⁵⁄₁₆	1¹⁄₃₂	1¹⁄₃₂	1¹⁄₃₂
	Monaco, Polara	11	2.750	—	¹⁵⁄₁₆	1¹⁄₃₂	1¹⁄₃₂	1¹⁄₃₂
1974	Dart, 6 cyl.	③	—	1⅛	¹³⁄₁₆	—	1¹⁄₃₂	1¹⁄₃₂
	Dart, V8	10	2.60	—	¹⁵⁄₁₆	1¹⁄₃₂	—	¹⁵⁄₁₆
	Challenger	10	2.75	—	¹⁵⁄₁₆	1	—	1¹⁄₃₂
	Charger, Coronet Exc. Sta. Wag.	10	2.75	—	¹⁵⁄₁₆	1	—	1¹⁄₃₂
	Coronet Sta. Wag.	11	2.75	—	¹⁵⁄₁₆	1	—	1¹⁄₃₂
	Monaco, Polara	11	3.10	—	¹⁵⁄₁₆	1¹⁄₃₂	—	1¹⁄₃₂
1975	Dart 6 cyl.	③	—	1⅛	¹³⁄₁₆	—	1.03	—
	Dart V8	10	2.6	—	¹⁵⁄₁₆	1.03	—	¹⁵⁄₁₆
	Intermediate	10⑥	2.75	—	¹⁵⁄₁₆	1	—	1.03
	Monaco	11	3.1	—	¹⁵⁄₁₆	1.03	—	1.03

Continued

BRAKE SPECIFICATIONS—Continued

Year	Model	Brake Drum Inside Diameter	Wheel Cylinder Bore Diameter			Master Cylinder Bore Diameter		
			Disc Brake	Front Drum Brake	Rear Drum Brake	Disc Brakes	Drum Brakes	Power Brakes
PLYMOUTH								
1969	Valiant, Barracuda 6	9	1.638	1	$13/16$	1	1	1
	Valiant, Barracuda V8	10	1.638	$1\,1/8$	$15/16$	1	1	1
	Belvedere, Satellite	10①	2.00	$1\,1/8$	$15/16$	$1\,1/8$	1	1
	Fury, VIP	11	②	$1\,1/8$	$15/16$	$1\,1/8$	1	1
1970	Valiant, Duster 6	③	1.638	1	$13/16$	1	1	1
	Valiant, Duster V8	10	1.638	$1\,3/16$	$15/16$	1	1	1
	Barracuda	10④	2.750	$1\,3/16$	$15/16$	$1\,1/8$	1	1
	Belvedere, Satellite	10①	2.750	$1\,1/8$	$15/16$	$1\,1/8$	1	1
	Fury	11	2.750	$1\,1/8$	$15/16$	$1\,1/8$	1	1
1971	Valiant, Duster 6	9	—	1	$13/16$	—	1	1
	Valiant, Duster V8	10	$1\,5/8$	$1\,3/16$	$15/16$	1	1	1
	Barracuda	10④	2.750	$1\,3/16$	$15/16$	$1\,1/8$	1	1
	Satellite	10④	2.750	$1\,3/16$	$15/16$	$1\,1/8$	1	1
	Fury	11	2.750	$1\,3/16$	$15/16$	1	1	1
1972	Valiant, Duster 6	9	—	1	$13/16$	—	$15/16$	$15/16$
	Valiant, Duster V8	10	$1\,5/8$	$1\,3/16$	$15/16$	$1\,1/32$	$1\,1/32$	$1\,1/32$
	Barracuda	10	2.750	$1\,3/16$	$15/16$	$1\,1/32$	$1\,1/32$	$1\,1/32$
	Satellite	10④	2.750	$1\,3/16$	$15/16$	$1\,1/32$	$1\,1/32$	$1\,1/32$
	Fury	11	2.750	$1\,3/16$	$15/16$	$1\,1/32$	$1\,1/32$	$1\,1/32$
1973	Valiant, 6 cyl. (Early)	9	—	$1\,1/16$	$13/16$	—	$15/16$	$15/16$
	Valiant, 6 cyl. (Late)	10	—	$1\,3/16$	$13/16$	—	$1\,1/32$	$1\,1/32$
	Valiant, V8	10	2.599	$1\,1/16$	$15/16$	$1\,1/32$	$1\,1/32$	$1\,1/32$
	Barracuda	10	2.750	—	$15/16$	$1\,1/32$	$1\,1/32$	$1\,1/32$
	Satellite	10④	2.750	—	$15/16$	$1\,1/32$	$1\,1/32$	$1\,1/32$
	Fury	11	2.750	—	$15/16$	$1\,1/32$	$1\,1/32$	$1\,1/32$
1974	Valiant, 6 cyl.	③	—	$1\,1/8$	$13/16$	—	$1\,1/32$	$1\,1/32$
	Valiant, V8	10	2.60	—	$15/16$	$1\,1/32$	—	$15/16$
	Barracuda	10	2.75	—	$15/16$	1	—	$1\,1/32$
	Satellite Exc. Sta. Wag.	10	2.75	—	$15/16$	1	—	$1\,1/32$
	Satellite Sta. Wag.	11	2.75	—	$15/16$	1	—	$1\,1/32$
	Fury	11	3.10	—	$15/16$	$1\,1/32$	—	$1\,1/32$
1975	Valiant 6 cyl.	③	—	$1\,1/8$	$13/16$	—	1.03	—
	Valiant V8	10	2.6	—	$15/16$	1.03	—	$15/16$
	Intermediate	10⑤	2.75	—	$15/16$	1	—	1.03
	Gran Fury	11	3.1	—	$15/16$	1.03	—	1.03

①—With 383 Hi Perf., 426 or 440 engine, 11″ drums.   ②—For 1969, 2.757.   ③—Front 10″, rear 9″.   ④—Heavy duty 11″.
⑤—Wagon 11″.

COOLING SYSTEM & CAPACITY DATA

Year	Model or Engine	Cooling Capacity, Qts.			Radiator Cap Relief Pressure, Lbs.		Thermo. Opening Temp. ①	Fuel Tank Gals.	Engine Oil Refill Qts. ②	Transmission Oil			Rear Axle Oil Pints
		No Heater	With Heater	With A/C	With A/C	No A/C				3 Speed Pints	4 Speed Pints	Auto. Trans. Qts. ⑫	
CHRYSLER													
1969	8-383	—	16⑨	17	16	16	190	24③	4	6	—	9¼	4
	8-440	—	17⑨	18	16	16	190	24③	4	6	—	9¼	4
1970	8-383, 2 B. Carb.	—	14½⑨	15	16	16	195	24⑰	4	5	—	9½	4.4
	8-383, 4 B. Carb.	—	14½⑨	16	16	16	195	24⑰	4	5	—	8	4.4
	8-440	—	15½⑨	17	16	16	195④	24⑰	4	5	—	9½	4.4
1971	8-383, 2 B. Carb.	13½	14½	15	16	16	185	23	4	4¾	—	9½	4.5
	8-383, 4 B. Carb.	13½	14½	15	16	16	185	23	4	—	—	8	4.5
	8-440	14½	15½	17	16	16	185	23	4	—	—	9½	4.5
1972	8-360	14½	15½	15	16	16	185	23	4	—	—	8	4.5
	8-400	13½	14½	14	16	16	185	23	4	—	—	9½	4.5
	8-440	14½	15½	16	16	16	185	23	4	—	—	9½	4.5
1973	8-400, 440	—	16	17	16	16	185	23	4	—	—	9½	4.4
1974	8-400, 440	—	16½	16½	16	16	195	25㉗	4	—	—	9½	4.5
1975	V8-318	—	16	16	16	16	195	25½	4	—	—	9½	4½
	V8-360 Cordoba	—	16½	16½	16	16	195	25½	4	—	—	9½	4½
	V8-360 Chrysler	—	16	16	16	16	195	⑤	4	—	—	9½	4½
	V8-400	—	16½	16½	16	16	195	⑤	4	—	—	9½	4½
	V8-440	—	16	16	16	16	195	26½㉔	4㉚	—	—	9½	4½
IMPERIAL													
1969	All	—	19⑨	19	16	16	190	24	4	—	—	9¼	4
1970	All	—	17½⑨	17½	16	16	195	24	4	—	—	9½	4.4
1971–72	All	16½	17½	17½	16	16	185	23	4	—	—	9½	4.5
1973	All	—	18	18	16	16	185	23	4	—	—	9½	4.4
1974	All	—	17	17	16	16	195	25	4	—	—	9½	4.5
1975	All	—	16	16	16	16	195	26½	4	—	—	9½	4½
DODGE													
1969	Dart 6-170	—	12⑯	—	—	16	200	18	4	6½	—	7¾	2
	Dart 6-225	—	13	15	16	16	190	18	4	6½	—	7¾	2
	Dart 8-273	—	17	19	16	16	190	18	4	6	7	7¾	2
	Dart 318	—	16	18	16	16	190	18	4	6	7	7¾	2⑩
	Dart 8-340	—	16	16	16	16	190	18	4	—	7	7¾	4
	Dart 8-383	—	16	16	16	16	190	18	4	—	7	7¾⑱	4
	Coronet 6-225	—	13	15	16	16	190	19	4	6½	—	7¾	2⑦
	Coro. Charger 8-318	—	16	19	16	16	190	19	4	6	—	7¾	4
	Coro. Charger 8-383	—	16	17	16	16	190	19	4	—	7½	7¾⑱	4
	Coro. Charger 8-440	—	17	18	16	16	190	19	4	—	7½	9¼	4⑬
	Coro. Charger 8-426	—	18	—	16	16	190	19	6	—	7½	8	4⑬
	Polara, Monaco 8-318	—	16	19	16	16	190	24③	4	6	—	7¾	4
	Polara, Monaco 8-383	—	16	17	16	16	190	24③	4	6	—	7¾⑱	4
	Polara, Monaco 8-440	—	17	18	16	16	190	24③	4	—	—	9¼	4⑭
1970	Dart 6 Cyl.	12	13	13	16	16	190	18	4	6½	—	8½	2
	Dart 8-318	15	16	16	16	16	195	18	4	4¾	—	8	4
	Dart 8-340	14	15	15	16	16	190	18	4	4¾	7	8	4
	Challenger 6 Cyl.	—	13	14	16	16	190	18	4	6½	—	8½	2
	Challenger 8-318	—	16	17½	16	16	195	18	4	4¾	7	8	4
	Challenger 8-340	—	15½	15½	16	16	190	18	4	4¾	7	8	4

Continued

COOLING SYSTEM & CAPACITY DATA—Continued

Year	Model or Engine	Cooling Capacity, Qts.			Radiator Cap Relief Pressure, Lbs.		Thermo. Opening Temp. ①	Fuel Tank Gals.	Engine Oil Refill Qts. ②	Transmission Oil			Rear Axle Oil Pints
		No Heater	With Heater	With A/C	With A/C	No A/C				3 Speed Pints	4 Speed Pints	Auto. Trans. Qts. ⑫	
DODGE—Continued													
1970	Challenger 8-383	—	14½	15	16	16	190	18	4	4¾	7	8⑬	4
	Challenger 8-440	—	17	17	16	16	190	18	6	—	7	9	5½
	Challenger 8-426	—	17	17	16	16	190	18	6	—	7	8½	5½
	Coro., Charger 6-225	12	13	13	16	16	190	19	4	4¾	—	8½	2
	Coro., Charger 8-318	15	16	16	16	16	195	19	4	4¾	—	8	4
	Coro., Charger 8-383	13½	14½	15	16	16	190	19	4	4¾	7	8⑬	4
	Coro., Charger 8-440	16	17	17	16	16	190	19	6	—	7	8½	5½
	Coro., Charger 8-426	16	17	17	16	16	190	19	6	—	7	8½	5½
	Polara, Monaco 8-318	16	17	17	16	16	195	24⑰	4	4¾	—	8	4
	Polara, Monaco 8-383	13½	14½	14½	16	16	195	24⑰	4	4¾	—	9½	4
	Polara, Monaco 8-440	14½	15½	15½	16	16	195	24⑰	4	—	—	9½	4
1971	Dart 6 Cyl.	12	13	13	16	16	185	17	4	6½	—	8½	2
	Dart 8-318	15	16	16½	16	16	185	17	4	4¾	—	8½	4½
	Dart 8-340	14	15	15	16	16	185	17	4	4¾	7	8	4½
	Challenger 6 Cyl.	12	13	13	16	16	185	18	4	4¾	—	8½	2
	Challenger 8-318	15	16	16½	16	16	185	18	4	4¾	—	8½	2
	Challenger 8-340	14	15	15	16	16	185	18	4	4¾	7½	8	4½
	Challenger 8-383	13½	14½	15	16	16	185	18	4	4¾	7½	8⑬	4½
	Challenger 8-440	16⑲	17⑲	17⑳	16	16	185	18	4	—	7½	9½	5½
	Challenger 8-426	14½	15½	—	16	16	185	18	6	—	7½	8	5½
	Coro., Charger 6-225	12	13	13	16	16	185	21	4	6½	—	8½	4
	Coro., Charger 8-318	15	16	16½	16	16	185	21	4	4¾	—	8½	4
	Coro., Charger 8-383	13½	14½	15	16	16	185	21	4	4¾	7½	8⑬	4
	Coro., Charger 8-440	14½	15½	17	16	16	185	21	4	—	7½	9½	5½
	Coro., Charger 8-426	14½	15½	—	16	16	185	21	6	—	7½	8	5½
	Polara, Monaco 6-225	12	13	13	16	16	185	23	4	4¾	—	8½	4½
	Polara, Monaco 8-318	15	16	16½	16	16	185	23	4	4¾	—	8½	4½
	Polara, Monaco 8-360	14	15	15	16	16	185	23	4	4¾	—	8	4½
	Polara, Monaco 8-383	13½	14½	15	16	16	185	23	4	4¾	—	8⑬	4½
	Polara, Monaco 8-440	14½	15½	17	16	16	185	23	4	—	—	9½	4½
1972	Dart 6 Cyl.	12	13	13	16	16	185	16	4	6½	—	8½	2
	Dart 8-318	15	16	16	16	16	185	16	4	4¾	—	8½	4½
	Dart 8-340	14	15	15	16	16	185	16	4	4¾	7	8	4¼
	Challenger 6 Cyl.	12	13	13	16	16	185	18	4	4¾	—	8½	2
	Challenger 8-318	15	16	16½	16	16	185	18	4	4¾	—	8½	4½
	Challenger 8-340	14	15	14½	16	16	185	18	4	4¾	7½	8	4½
	Coro., Charger 6-225	12	13	13	16	16	185	21	4	6½	—	8½	4½
	Coro., Charger 8-318	15	16	16½	16	16	185	21	4	4¾	—	8½	4½
	Coro., Charger 8-340	14	15	14½	16	16	185	21	4	—	7½	8	4½
	Coro., Charger 8-400	13½	14½	15	16	16	185	21	4	—	7½	8⑬	4½⑭
	Coro., Charger 8-440	14	15	15	16	16	185	21	4㉖	—	7½	9½	5½
	Polara, Monaco 8-318	15	16	16½	16	16	185	23	4	—	—	8½	4½
	Polara, Monaco 8-360	14½	15½	15	16	16	185	23	4	—	—	8	4½
	Polara, Monaco 8-400	13½	14½	14	16	16	185	23	4	—	—	9½	4½
	Polara, Monaco 8-440	14½	15½	16	16	16	185	23	4	—	—	9½	4½

Continued

COOLING SYSTEM & CAPACITY DATA—Continued

Year	Model or Engine	Cooling Capacity, Qts.			Radiator Cap Relief Pressure, Lbs.		Thermo. Opening Temp. [1]	Fuel Tank Gals.	Engine Oil Refill Qts. [2]	Transmission Oil			Rear Axle Oil Pints
		No Heater	With Heater	With A/C	With A/C	No A/C				3 Speed Pints	4 Speed Pints	Auto. Trans. Qts. [12]	
DODGE—Continued													
1973	Dart 6 Cyl.	12	13	13	16	16	185	16	4	6½	—	8½	2
	Dart 8-318	15	16	18	16	16	185	16	4	4¾	—	8½	2
	Dart 8-340	15	16	16	16	16	185	16	4	4¾	7	8	4½
	Challenger 6 Cyl.	12	13	13	16	16	185	18	4	4¾	—	8½	4½
	Challenger 8-318	15	16	18	16	16	185	18	4	4¾	—	8½	4½
	Challenger 8-340	14	15	16	16	16	185	18	4	4¾	7	8	4½
	Coro, Charger 6-225	12	13	13	16	16	185	21	4	6½	—	8½	2
	Coro, Charger 8-318	15	16	18	16	16	185	21	4	4¾	7½	8½	4½
	Coro, Charger 8-340	14	15	16	16	16	185	21	4	4¾	7½	8	4½
	Coro, Charger 8-400	15	16	17	16	16	185	21	4	4¾	7½	8[21]	4½
	Coro, Charger 8-440	16	17	17	16	16	185	21	4	—	—	9½	4½
	Polara, Monaco 8-318	15	16	19	16	16	185	23	4	—	—	8½	4½
	Polara, Monaco 8-360	15	16	16	16	16	185	23	4	—	—	8½	4½
	Polara, Monaco 8-400	15[22]	16[23]	17[23]	16	16	185	23	4	—	—	9½[24]	4½
	Polara, Monaco 8-440	15[23]	16[23]	17[23]	16	16	185	23	4	—	—	9½	4½
1974	Dart 6 cyl.	—	13	14	16	16	195	16	4	6½	—	8¼	2
	Dart 8-318	—	16	17½	16	16	195	16	4	4¾	7	8¼	4½
	Dart 8-360	—	16	16	16	16	195	16	4	4¾	7	8	4½
	Challenger 8-318	—	16	17½	16	16	195	18	4	4¾	—	8¼	4½
	Challenger 8-360	—	16	16	16	16	195	18	4	4¾	7½	8	4½
	Coro., Charger 6-225	—	13	15	16	16	195	19½[26]	4	4¾	—	8¼	4½
	Coro., Charger 8-318	—	16	18	16	16	195	19½[26]	4	4¾	7½	8¼	4½
	Coro., Charger 8-360	—	16½	16½	16	16	195	19½[26]	4	—	7½	8	4½
	Coro., Charger 8-400	—	16½	16½	16	16	195	19½[26]	4	—	7½	9½[29]	4½
	Coro., Charger 8-440	—	16	16	16	16	195	19½[26]	4	—	—	8	4½
	Monaco 8-360	—	16	16	16	16	195	25[27]	4	—	—	8	4½
	Monaco 8-400	—	16½	16½	16	16	195	25[27]	4	—	—	9½	4½
	Monaco 8-440	—	16	16	16	16	195	25[27]	4	—	—	9½	4½
1975	Dart 6-225	—	13	14	16	16	195	16	4	[6]	7	8½	[8]
	Dart 8-318	—	16	17½	16	16	195	16	4	4¾	7	8½	[8]
	Dart 8-360	—	16	16	16	16	195	16	4	4¾	7	8¼	[8]
	Coronet 6-225	—	13	15	16	16	195	25½	4	4¾	—	8½	4½
	Coro., Charger 8-318	—	16	18	16	16	195	25½[11]	4	4¾	—	8½	4½
	Coro., Charger 8-360	—	16½	16½	16	16	195	25½[11]	4	—	—	9½	4½
	Coro., Charger 8-400	—	16½	16½	16	16	195	25½[11]	4	—	—	9½	4½
	Coronet 8-440	—	16	16	16	16	195	25½[11]	4[30]	—	—	8¼	4½
	Monaco 8-318	—	16	16	16	16	195	26½[27]	4	—	—	8½	4½
	Monaco 8-360	—	16	16	16	16	195	26½[27]	4	—	—	9½	4½
	Monaco 8-400	—	16½	16½	16	16	195	26½[27]	4	—	—	9½	4½
	Monaco 8-440	—	16	16	16	16	195	26½[27]	4[30]	—	—	9½	4½
PLYMOUTH													
1969	Fury, VIP 6-225	—	13	—	16	—	190	24[3]	4	6½	—	7¾	4
	Others 6-225	—	13	15	16	16	190	19	4	6½	—	7¾	2[7]
	Fury, VIP 8-318	—	16	19	16	16	190	24[3]	4	6½	—	7¾	4
	Others 8-318	—	16	19	16	16	190	19	4	6½	—	7¾	4
	Fury, VIP 8-383 2 B.C.	—	16	17	16	16	190	24[3]	4	—	7¾	9¼	4
	Others 8-383 2 B.C.	—	16	17	16	16	190	19	4	—	7½	9¼	4
	Fury, VIP 8-383 4 B.C.	—	16	17	16	16	190	24[3]	4	—	7¾	7¾	4
	Others 8-383 4 B.C.	—	16	17	16	16	190	19	4	—	7½	7¾	4

Continued

COOLING SYSTEM & CAPACITY DATA—Continued

Year	Model or Engine	Cooling Capacity, Qts.			Radiator Cap Relief Pressure, Lbs.		Thermo. Opening Temp. ①	Fuel Tank Gals.	Engine Oil Refill Qts. ②	Transmission Oil			Rear Axle Oil Pints
		No Heater	With Heater	With A/C	With A/C	No A/C				3 Speed Pints	4 Speed Pints	Auto. Trans. Qts. ⑫	

PLYMOUTH—Continued

Year	Model or Engine	No Heater	With Heater	With A/C	With A/C	No A/C	Thermo	Fuel	Oil	3 Speed	4 Speed	Auto	Rear Axle
1969	8-426 Hemi.	—	18	—	16	—	190	19	6	—	7½	8	4⑬
	Fury, VIP 8-440	—	17	18	16	16	190	24③	4	—	7¾	9¼	4
	Others 8-440	—	17	18	16	16	190	19	4	—	7½	9¼	4⑬
1970	Fury 6-225	—	12	14	16	16	190	24③	4	4¾	—	8½	4
	Others 6-225	—	12	14	16	16	190	19	4	4¾	—	8½	2
	Fury 8-318	—	16	17½	16	16	195	24③	4	4¾	—	8	4
	Others 8-318	—	16	17½	16	16	195	19	4	4¾	—	8	4
	Fury 8-383 2 B.C.	—	14½	16	16	16	190	24③	4	4¾	—	9½	4
	Others 8-383 2 B.C.	—	14½	15	16	16	190	19	4	4¾	—	9½	4
	Fury 8-383 4 B.C.	—	14½	16	16	16	190	24③	4	—	—	8	4
	Others 8-383 4 B.C.	—	14½	16	16	16	190	19	4	4¾	7	8	4
	Fury 8-440	—	15½	17	16	16	190	24③	4	—	—	9½	4
	Others 8-440	—	15½	17	16	16	190	19	4	—	7	9½	5½
	8-426 Hemi	—	17	—	16	16	190	19	6	—	7	8½	5½
1971	Fury 6-225	12	13	13	16	16	185	23	4	6½	—	8½	4½
	Others 6-225	12	13	13	16	16	185	21	4	4¾	—	8½	4
	Fury 8-318	15	16	16½	16	16	185	23	4	4¾	—	8½	4½
	Others 8-318	15	16	16½	16	16	185	21	4	4¾	—	8½	4
	Fury 8-360	14	15	15	16	16	185	23	4	4¾	—	8	4½
	Fury 8-383	13½	14½	15	16	16	185	23	4	4¾	—	8⑱	4½
	Others 8-383	13½	14½	15	16	16	185	21	4	4¾	7½	8⑱	4
	Others 8-426	14½	15½	—	16	16	185	21	6	—	7½	8½	5½
	Fury 8-440	14½	15½	17	16	16	185	23	4	—	—	9½	4½
	Others 8-440	14½	15½	17	16	16	185	21	4	—	7½	9½	5½
1972	Satellite 6-225	12	13	13	16	16	185	21	4	6½	—	8½	4½
	Satellite 8-318	15	16	16½	16	16	185	21	4	4¾	—	8½	4½
	Satellite 8-340	14	15	14½	16	16	185	21	4	4¾	7½	8	4½
	Satellite 8-400	13½	14½	15	16	16	185	21	4	4¾	7½	8⑱	4½
	Satellite 8-440	14	15	15	16	16	185	21	4㉖	—	7½	9½	5½
	Fury 8-318	15	16	16½	16	16	185	23	4	—	—	8½	4½
	Fury 8-360	14½	15½	15	16	16	185	23	4	—	—	8	4½
	Fury 8-400	13½	14½	14	16	16	185	23	4	—	—	9½	4½
	Fury 8-440	14½	15½	16	16	16	185	23	4	—	—	9½	4½
1973	Satellite 6-225	12	13	13	16	16	185	21	4	6½	—	8½	4½
	Satellite 8-318	15	16	18	16	16	185	21	4	4¾	7.5	8½	4½
	Satellite 8-340	14	15	16	16	16	185	21	4	4¾	7.5	8	4½
	Satellite 8-400	15	16	17	16	16	185	21	4	4¾	7.5	8	4½
	Satellite 8-440	16	17	17	16	16	185	21	4	—	—	9½	4½
	Fury 8-318	15	16	19	16	16	185	23	4	—	—	8½	4½
	Fury 8-360	15	16	16	16	16	185	23	4	—	—	8	4½
	Fury 8-400	15㉒	16㉓	17㉕	16	16	185	23	4	—	—	8㉑	4½
	Fury 8-440	15㉒	16㉓	17㉕	16	16	185	23	4	—	—	9½	4½
1974	Satellite 6-225	—	13	16	16	16	195	19½㉘	4	4¾	—	8½	4½
	Satellite 8-318	—	16	18	16	16	195	19½㉘	4	4¾	7½	8½	4½
	Satellite 8-360	—	16½	16½	16	16	195	19½㉘	4	—	7½	8	4½
	Satellite 8-400	—	16½	16½	16	16	195	19½㉘	4	—	7½	9㉙	4½
	Satellite 8-440	—	16	16	16	16	195	19½㉘	4	—	—	8	4½
	Fury 8-360	—	16	16	16	16	195	25㉗	4	—	—	8	4½
	Fury 8-400	—	16½	16½	16	16	195	25㉗	4	—	—	9½	4½
	Fury 8-440	—	16	16	16	16	195	25㉗	4	—	—	9½	4½

Continued

COOLING SYSTEM & CAPACITY DATA—Continued

Year	Model or Engine	Cooling Capacity, Qts.			Radiator Cap Relief Pressure, Lbs.		Thermo. Opening Temp. ①	Fuel Tank Gals.	Engine Oil Refill Qts. ③	Transmission Oil			Rear Axle Oil Pints
		No Heater	With Heater	With A/C	With A/C	No A/C				3 Speed Pints	4 Speed Pints	Auto. Trans. Qts. ⑫	
PLYMOUTH—Continued													
1975	Fury 6-225	—	13	15	16	16	195	25½⑪	4	4¾	—	8½	4½
	Fury 8-318	—	16	18	16	16	195	25½⑪	4	4¾	—	8½	4½
	Fury 8-360	—	16½	16½	16	16	195	25½⑪	4	—	—	9½	4½
	Fury 8-400	—	16½	16½	16	16	195	25½⑪	4	—	—	9½	4½
	Fury 8-440	—	16	16	16	16	195	25½⑪	4⑳	—	—	8¼	4½
	Gran Fury 8-318	—	16	16	16	16	195	26½⑳	4	—	—	8½	4½
	Gran Fury 8-360	—	16	16	16	16	195	26½⑳	4	—	—	9½	4½
	Gran Fury 8-400	—	16½	16½	16	16	195	26½⑳	4	—	—	9½	4½
	Gran Fury 8-440	—	16	16	16	16	195	26½⑳	4⑳	—	—	9½	4½
VALIANT & BARRACUDA													
1969	6-170	—	12	14	16	16	200	18	4	6½	—	7¾	2
	6-225	—	13	15	16	16	190	18	4	6½	—	7¾	2
	8-273	—	17	19	16	16	190	18	4	6½	7	7¾	4
	8-318	—	16	18	16	16	190	18	4	6½	7	9¼	4
	8-340	—	16	—	16		190	18	4	6½	7	9¼	4
	8-383 2 Bar. Carb.	—	16	—	16		190	18	4	6½	7	9¼	4
	8-383 4 Bar. Carb.	—	16	—	16		190	18	4	6½	7	7¾	4
1970	Valiant 6-198, 225	—	13	14	16	16	190	18	4	6½	—	8½	2
	Barracuda 6-225	—	13	14	16	16	190	18	4	4¾	—	8½	2
	8-318	—	16	17	16	16	195	18	4	4¾	7	8½	4
	Valiant 8-340	—	15	17	16	16	190	18	4	4¾	7	8	4
	Barracuda 8-340	—	15½	15½	16	16	190	18	4	4¾	7	8	4
	8-383 2 Bar. Carb.	—	14½	15	16	16	190	18	4	—	—	9½	4
	8-383 4 Bar. Carb.	—	14½	15	16	16	190	18	4	4¾	7	8	4
	8-440	—	17	17	16	16	190	18	6	—	7	9½	5½
	8-426	—	17	—	16	16	190	18	6	—	7	8	5½
1971	Valiant 6 Cyl.	12	13	13	16	16	185	17	4	6½	—	8½	2
	Barracuda 6 Cyl.	12	13	13	16	16	185	18	4	4¾	—	8½	2
	Valiant 8-318	15	16	16½	16	16	185	17	4	4¾	—	8½	4½
	Barracuda 8-318	15	16	16½	16	16	185	18	4	4¾	—	8½	2
	Valiant 8-340	14	15	15	16	16	185	17	4	4¾	7	8	4½
	Barracuda 8-340	14	15	15	16	16	185	18	4	4¾	7½	8	4½
	8-383	13½	14½	15	16	16	185	18	4	4¾	7½	8⑱	4½
	8-440	16⑲	17⑲	17⑳	16	16	185	18	4	—	7½	9½	5½
	8-426	14½	15½	—	16	16	185	18	6	—	7½	8	5½
1972	Valiant 6 Cyl.	12	13	13	16	16	185	16	4	6½	—	8½	2
	Barracuda 6 Cyl.	12	13	13	16	16	185	16½	4	4¾	—	8½	2
	Valiant 8-318	15	16	16	16	16	185	16	4	4¾	—	8½	4½
	Barracuda 8-318	15	16	16½	16	16	185	16½	4	4¾	—	8½	4½
	Valiant 8-340	14	15	15	16	16	185	16	4	4¾	7	8	4½
	Barracuda 8-340	14	15	14½	16	16	185	16½	4	—	7½	8	4½
1973	Valiant 6 Cyl.	12	13	13	16	16	185	16	4	6½	—	8½	2
	Valiant 8-318	15	16	18	16	16	185	16	4	4¾	—	8½	2
	Valiant 8-340	15	16	16	16	16	185	16	4	4¾	7	8	4½
	Barracuda 6 Cyl.	12	13	13	16	16	185	16½	4	4¾	7½	8	4½
	Barracuda 8-318	15	16	18	16	16	185	16½	4	4¾	—	8½	4½
	Barracuda 8-340	14	15	16	16	16	185	16½	4	4¾	7½	8	4½

Continued

COOLING SYSTEM & CAPACITY DATA—Continued

Year	Model or Engine	Cooling Capacity, Qts.			Radiator Cap Relief Pressure, Lbs.		Thermo. Opening Temp. ①	Fuel Tank Gals.	Engine Oil Refill Qts. ②	Transmission Oil			Rear Axle Oil Pints
		No Heater	With Heater	With A/C	With A/C	No A/C				3 Speed Pints	4 Speed Pints	Auto. Trans. Qts. ⑫	
VALIANT & BARRACUDA—Continued													
1974	Valiant 6-198	—	13	14	16	16	195	16	4	6½	—	8¼	2
	Valiant 6-225	—	13	14	16	16	195	16	4	6½	—	8¼	2
	Valiant 8-318	—	16	17½	16	16	195	16	4	4¾	7	8¼	4½
	Valiant 8-360	—	16	16	16	16	195	16	4	4¾	7	8	4½
	Barracuda 8-318	—	16	17½	16	16	195	16½	4	4¾	—	8¼	4½
	Barracuda 8-360	—	16	16	16	16	195	16½	4	4¾	7½	8	4½
1975	Valiant 6-225	—	13	14	16	16	195	16	4	⑥	7	8½	⑧
	Valiant V8-318	—	16	17½	16	16	195	16	4	4¾	7	8½	⑧
	Valiant V8-360	—	16	16	16	16	195	16	4	—	—	8¼	⑧

①—With alcohol type anti-freeze use a 160° unit.
②—Add one qt. with filter change.
③—Wagons 22 gals.
④—440 Hi Perf. uses 190°.
⑤—Cordoba 25½ gals., Chrysler 26½, Wagon 24 gals.
⑥—Except floor mounted 3½ pts.; floor mounted 4¾ pts.
⑦—Station Wagon 4 pints.
⑧—7¼" ring gear 2 pts.; 8¾" ring gear 4½ pts.
⑨—Add 1½ qts. for rear seat heater.
⑩—With manual transmission 4 pints.
⑪—Wagon 20 gals., Sedan Models with dual exhaust 20½ gals.
⑫—Approximate. Make final check with dipstick.
⑬—With manual trans. 5½ pints.
⑭—5½ pints for High Perf. engine.
⑮—Add 2 qts. for 22" radiator.
⑯—9¼ qts. for High Perf.
⑰—Wagons 23 gals.
⑱—With 2 bar. carb. 9½ qts.
⑲—Auto. Trans., 1½ qts. less.
⑳—Auto. Trans. 18 qts.
㉑—9½ pints with 2 Bar. Carb.
㉒—16 quarts with 4 Bar. Carb. or Hi-Perf.
㉓—17 quarts with 4 Bar. Carb. or Hi-Perf.
㉔—8 quarts with 4 Bar. Carb. or Hi-Perf.
㉕—18 quarts with 4 Bar. Carb. or Hi-Perf.
㉖—Hi Perf. uses 6 qts. plus filter.
㉗—Wagons 24 gals.
㉘—Wagons 21 gals.
㉙—Hi Perf. 8 qts.
㉚—High performance engine 5 qts.

REAR AXLE SPECIFICATIONS

Year	Model	Carrier Type	Ring Gear & Pinion Backlash		Pinion Bearing Preload			Differential Bearing Preload		
			Method	Adjustment	Method	New Bearings Inch-Lbs.	Used Bearings Inch-Lbs.	Method	New Bearings Inch-Lbs.	Used Bearings Inch-Lbs.
1969–73	All	Removable①	②	.006–.008	Shims	20–30④	10–15④	②	③	③
1969–73	Exc. Below	Integral	Shims	.004–.007	Shims	15–25④	8–12④	Shims	③	③
1969–73	⑤	Integral	Shims	.004–.009	Shims	10–20④	10–20④	Shims	③	③
1969–74	8¼" ⑥	Integral	②	.006–.008	⑦	20–35④	10–25④	②	③	③
1973–74	9¼⑥	Integral	②	.006–.008	⑦	20–35④	10–25④	②	③	③
1974	7¼"	Integral	②	.004–.006	⑦	15–25	—	②	③	③
	8¾"	Integral	②	.006–.008	⑦	20–30	—	②	③	③

①—Adjust axle shaft end play to .008–.018".
②—Threaded adjusters.
③—Preload is correct when ring gear and pinion backlash is properly adjusted.
④—Adjust by turning pinion shaft nut with an inch-pound torque wrench and seal removed.
⑤—9¼" and 9¾" axles.
⑥—"C" lock type.
⑦—Collapsible spacer.

Electrical Section

DISTRIBUTOR, REPLACE
6-170, 198, 225

The distributor rotates clockwise. To remove, take off cap, disconnect primary wire and vacuum line. Remove hold-down bolt and lift out distributor. Install in the following manner.

1. Rotate crankshaft to bring No. 1 piston up on its compression stroke, and position mark on inner edge of crankshaft pulley in line with the "O" (TDC) mark on timing chain cover.
2. With distributor gasket in position, hold distributor over mounting pad.
3. Turn rotor to a position just ahead of the No. 1 distributor cap terminal.
4. Install distributor, engaging distributor gear with drive gear on camshaft. With distributor fully seated on engine, rotor should be under No. 1 cap terminal and on conventional systems, breaker points just opening.
5. Install hold-down bolt.
6. Adjust timing with timing light.

1969-75 V8s

To remove the distributor, disconnect the vacuum control line and low tension wire and remove the cap and lock plate hold-down screw.

When installing the distributor, make sure that No. 1 piston is on top dead center on compression stroke and that the distributor rotor is in No. 1 firing position.

SERVICE BULLETIN

FUSIBLE LINK REPAIR: Alternator equipped 1969-75 cars have charging circuits protected by a fuse-type wire. This fusible link is installed on the starter relay battery terminal.

If the charging circuit becomes overloaded, the inner fuse wire of this link burns out and the insulation heats up and breaks apart. This cuts off the battery from the charging system.

In the event one of these cars has none of its electrical parts functioning, check for a burned out fusible link. After locating and correcting the short, a new fusible link should be installed. Do not allow the insulation to contact any other wiring.

In situations like this, never use an uninsulated wire as a jumper if a fusible link replacement is not available. This can cause a fire in the electrical system.

STARTER, REPLACE
Reduction Gear Type

1. To remove starter, disconnect ground cable at battery.
2. Remove cable at starter.
3. Disconnect wires at solenoid.

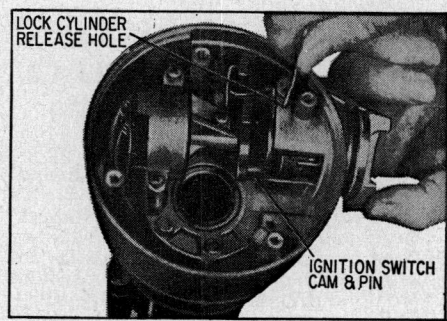

Fig. 1   Lock cylinder removal. 1970-75

4. Remove one stud nut and one bolt attaching starter motor to flywheel housing.
5. Slide transmission oil cooler bracket off stud (if so equipped).
6. Remove starter motor and removeable seal.
7. Reverse above procedure to install.

NOTE: When tightening attaching bolt and nut be sure to hold starter away from engine to insure proper alignment.

Direct Drive Type

1. Disconnect battery ground cable.
2. Remove cable at starter.
3. Disconnect lead wire from solenoid.
4. Unfasten and remove starter and removable seal.

NOTE

Noisy or erratic starter operation may be caused by lack of lubrication or deposits of foreign material on the Bendix driveshaft.

To correct this condition, remove the inspection plate at the bottom of the torque converter or clutch housing. Then apply a suitable upper-cylinder rust inhibitor or SAE 5W or SAE 10W oil to the shaft by means of a 7" piece of tubing attached to the spout of a pressure oil can. In extreme cases, it may be necessary to remove, disassemble and clean the starter.

CLUTCH SWITCH
1970-75

A clutch switch is used which necessitates depressing the clutch pedal before the engine can be started.

IGNITION SWITCH & LOCK, REPLACE
1971-75

1. Disconnect battery ground cable.
2. Remove steering column cover and remove two screws attaching wiring cover from column.
3. Disconnect wiring connectors at column.
4. Remove horn ring ornament, horn ring or rim blow switch pad and ornament if so equipped.
5. Disconnect horn wires at steering wheel hub.
6. Remove horn ring.
7. Remove steering wheel with suitable puller.
8. Remove screw attaching turn signal lever and remove lever.

NOTE: On Tilt & Tel columns, lever screws out.

9. Attach a string or fine wire to signal switch wiring before removing switch from column. When switch is removed leave wire in column jacket tube as an aid in replacement.
10. Remove screws attaching signal switch and upper bearing retainer screws and remove retainer and signal switch and flasher switch.
11. Remove screw and lift out ignition key lamp assembly.
12. Remove snap ring from upper end of steering shaft.
13. Remove three bearing housing attaching screws.
14. With tool C-3044 attached to threaded holes for signal switch retaining screws, pull bearing and housing from steering shaft.
15. Remove lower snap ring from steering shaft.
16. Remove lock plate pin retaining ring from lock plate hub.
17. Use tool C-4113 and press steering shaft lock plate pin out of shaft and plate and remove lock plate.

NOTE: Do not use hammer as damage to column may result.

18. Remove lock lever guide plate screws and plate.
19. Depress key cylinder retainer toward the cylinder to disengage it from slot in housing bore, then withdraw key cylinder from lock housing, Fig. 1.

1970 With Standard Steering Column

1. Disconnect battery ground cable.
2. Remove steering column cover and remove two screws attaching wiring cover to steering column. Disconnect wiring connectors at column.

3. Remove steering wheel.
4. Remove turn signal lever.
5. Attach a piece of fine wire to signal switch wiring before removing switch. When switch is removed, leave wire in column to aid in replacement of wire.
6. Remove turn signal switch and upper bearing retainer screws and remove switch.
7. Remove ignition key lamp retaining screws and lift out lamp.
8. Remove snap ring from upper end of column.
9. Remove three bearing housing attaching screws and with a suitable puller, pull bearing and housing from steering shaft.
10. Remove lower snap ring from steering shaft.
11. Remove lock plate retaining pin from lock plate hub. *This pin must be pressed out. Do not attempt to hammer on pin or shaft as damage to the collapsible column may result.*
12. Remove lock plate and lock lever guide.
13. Insert a small wire in access hole, depress lock cylinder retainer and withdraw cylinder, Fig. 1.
14. Remove switch retaining screws and remove switch.

1970 With Tilt-O-Scope

The ignition switch is mounted on the steering column lower cover and is actuated by a rod connected to the rack. Before removal or installation, be sure lock cylinder is in the Lock position.

1969 Polara & Monaco

1. Remove center air conditioning duct and left cooler duct.
2. Remove ignition switch bezel nut.
3. Remove ignition switch from under side of panel and disconnect main harness.

1969 Chrysler & Imperial

1. Remove switch bezel nut from front of panel.
2. Push switch into and down below panel.
3. Disconnect wiring harness multiple connector and remove switch.

1969 Charger

1. Remove lower center A/C duct and left A/C duct (if equipped).
2. Remove steering column cover for visual assist and remove ignition switch spanner.
3. Disconnect wiring connector and remove switch.

1969 Coronet & Dart

1. Remove A/C duct (if equipped).
2. Remove switch bezel.
3. On Coronet, loosen harness from clip for access.
4. Disconnect wiring connector and pull switch out from under panel.

1969 Plymouth & Valiant

1. Where necessary, remove air conditioning elbow. Remove bezel nut and lower switch behind panel far enough to remove multiple connector.
2. Before installing switch, connect multiple connector and position switch in panel.
3. Install and tighten bezel nut.

LIGHT SWITCH, REPLACE
1975, Cordoba, Coronet, Charger SE & Fury

1. Disconnect battery ground cable and fusible link.
2. Remove instrument cluster upper bezel and escutcheon mounting screw.
3. Remove switch mounting plate to cluster housing screws, pull switch from housing and disconnect electrical connector.
4. Depress release button on rear of switch and pull knob and stem from switch.
5. Remove switch escutcheon and mounting plate.
6. Reverse procedure to install.

1975 Gran Fury & Monaco

Refer to the "1974 Fury & Monaco" procedure for switch replacement.

1974-75 Chrysler Newport, New Yorker & Imperial

1. Remove headlight switch lens.
2. Remove headlight switch to mounting plate retaining nut.
3. Remove switch.

1974 Fury & Monaco

1. Remove instrument cluster bezel.
2. Remove windshield wiper switch mounting screws and headlight switch mounting screws.
3. Pull switch outwards and disconnect electrical leads, then pull switch to the "ON" position and depress release button on side of switch. Remove knob and stem from switch.
4. Remove escutcheon and mounting plate retaining nut and remove switch.

1973 Polara & Monaco

1. Remove column cover. Remove A/C duct.
2. Reach up under instrument panel and depress stem release button. At the same time remove switch stem from front panel.
3. Disconnect wiring from switch. Remove switch mounting nut and remove switch.

1973-75 Dart & Valiant

1. On 1973 models, remove fuse block attaching screw and position fuse block aside.
2. On all models, depress release button on rear of switch and remove knob and stem.

3. Remove spanner nut and drop switch below panel and disconnect wiring from switch.

1971-73 Chrysler & Imperial

1. Remove left spotcooler duct.
2. Remove headlamp switch knob and shaft by pulling the switch to on, depressing the release button on bottom of switch case, and pulling on the knob.
3. Remove headlamp sentinel and automatic dimmer control knobs if so equipped.
4. Remove headlamp switch mounting nut.
5. Remove headlamp switch from under instrument panel and disconnect wiring.

1971-74 Coronet, Charger, & 1971-72 Polara & Monaco

1. Reaching under instrument panel, disconnect wiring to switch.
2. Remove switch mounting screws and remove switch.

1971-73 Fury & 1971-74 Satellite

1. Reaching under instrument panel, disconnect switch wiring.
2. Unfasten and remove switch.

1970 Coronet & Belvedere

1. Disconnect battery ground cable.
2. Remove mounting screws and move safety relay and vent controls to one side.
3. Remove left air conditioner duct if necessary.
4. Remove two mounting screws, disconnect wire and remove switch. Place wires on switch before installing switch.

1969 Coronet, Belvedere & Satellite

1. Disconnect battery ground cable at battery.
2. Disconnect all wiring connectors from back of switches.
3. Remove switch bezel mounting screws.
4. Remove switches and bezel assembly and remove headlight switch.

NOTE: *Carefully pull trim bezel straight to avoid damaging trim pad.*

5. Reverse procedure to install.

1969-70 Monaco & Polara

1. Remove switch bezel.
2. Remove two mounting screws and remove switch.

1969-70 Chrysler & Imperial

1. Remove lamp panel.
2. Remove instrument cluster to gain access to switch.
3. Remove switch mounting screws and switch.

1969-70 Charger

1. Remove instrument cluster as described further on.
2. Disconnect wiring connector.
3. Disconnect heater vacuum hoses for accessibility.
4. Remove two switch mounting screws.
5. Reverse procedure to install.

1970-74 Barracuda, Challenger

1. Disconnect battery ground cable.
2. Remove lamp panel retaining screws and carefully slide panel out and lay it on top of instrument panel.
3. Remove bezel retaining screws and slide assembly out and disconnect wiring harness.
4. Remove switch mounting screws and remove switch.

1969-72 Valiant, 1969-72 Dart 1969 Barracuda

1. From under instrument panel, remove screw retaining fuse block to panel and move fuse block out of the way.
2. Reaching under panel, depress release button on right side of switch and pull knob out of switch.
3. Remove bezel nut and lower switch under panel to disconnect multiple connector and remove switch.
4. Reverse procedure to install. Insert switch knob into switch until a "click" is heard.

1969-70 Fury & V.I.P.

1. On models with air conditioning, remove left spot cooler hose from duct and move out of the way.
2. If necessary, remove fuse block retaining screw and move fuse block away to gain access to switch.
3. From under panel, use a magnetic screwdriver to remove two screws retaining switch to rear of panel sheet metal.
4. Move switch down from panel reinforcement far enough to disconnect multiple connector and remove switch.
5. Reverse procedure to install.

STOP LIGHT SWITCH REPLACE

1969-75 All Cars

To remove the switch, disconnect wires from switch and remove switch from its mounting. Install the new switch and connect the wires.

NEUTRAL SAFETY & BACK-UP SWITCH

1969-75 All Cars

1. Unscrew switch from transmission case, allowing fluid to drain onto a container, Fig. 2.

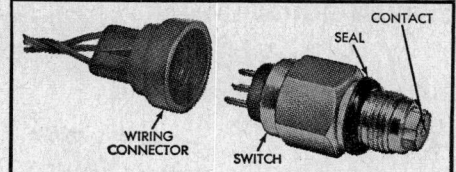

Fig. 2   Neutral safety switch

2. Move shift lever to "Park" and then to "Neutral" positions and inspect to see that switch operating lever is centered in switch opening in case.
3. Screw switch into transmission case and torque to 24 ft-lbs.
4. Add fluid to proper level.
5. Check to see that switch operates only in "Park" and "Neutral".

HORN SOUNDER & STEERING WHEEL

1969-75 All Cars

1. Disconnect ground cable at battery.
2. Remove horn ring ornament by turning counterclockwise or remove rim blow switch pad and ornament if so equipped.
3. Disconnect wires at horn switch.
4. Remove three screws attaching horn ring and switch to steering wheel, then remove horn ring and switch.
5. Remove wheel nut and use a suitable puller to remove steering wheel.

CAUTION: Do not bump or hammer on steering shaft to remove wheel as damage to shaft may result. See *Steering Gear, Replace* for other precautions.

TURN SIGNAL SWITCH

1974-75

1. Disconnect battery ground cable.
2. Remove steering wheel as previously outlined.
3. Remove turn signal lever mounting nut and lever.

NOTE: On vehicles equipped with cruise control, do not remove lever, but let lever hang.

4. Remove the switch and upper bearing retainer attaching screws, then remove retainer.

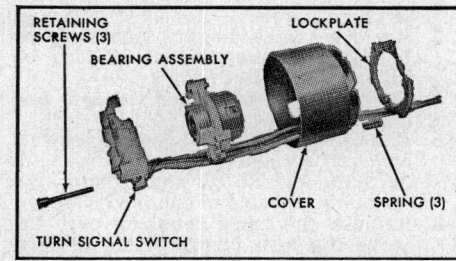

Fig. 3   Turn signal switch. 1969-74

5. Remove column cover, if equipped, and disconnect horn wire from mounting nut.
6. Remove column bracket to lower panel reinforcement attaching nuts, then bracket to column attaching nuts.
7. Remove wiring harness through from steering column and the tape securing wiring harness to column, then disconnect wiring harness connector.
8. Pull switch outward from column, guiding wires and connector through column opening, Fig. 3.

1971-73

1. Disconnect battery ground cable.
2. Remove steering column cover and remove screws attaching wiring through cover from column, Fig. 3.
3. Disconnect wiring connectors at column.
4. Remove horn ring ornament, horn ring or rim blow switch pad and ornament, if so equipped.
5. Disconnect horn wires at steering wheel hub.
6. Remove horn ring.
7. Remove steering wheel with a suitable puller.
8. Remove screw attaching turn signal lever and remove lever. On Tilt and Tel columns, the lever screws out.
9. Attach a piece of string or fine wire, to turn signal wiring before removing switch from column.
10. Remove screws attaching signal switch and upper bearing retainer screws and remove retainer and signal and flasher switch.

1969-70 All Cars

1. Disconnect battery ground cable.
2. Remove steering wheel as outlined above and remove signal operating lever.
3. Disconnect switch wiring multiple connector at steering column jacket. Remove each terminal from connector, tying them together with a piece of string or fine wire, Fig. 3.
4. Remove screws attaching turn signal switch to steering column and remove switch and wires from column. Leave string or wire in column to aid installation.
5. Reverse procedure to install, using wire or string to pull wires through column. Tighten switch lever to 30 inch pounds, steering wheel nut to 24 foot pounds.

INSTRUMENT CLUSTER REMOVAL

1975 Cordoba, Coronet, Charger SE & Fury

1. Disconnect battery ground cable.
2. Remove trim pad, radio and heater or A/C controls, Fig. 4.
3. Remove cluster housing reinforcement bracket.
4. Disconnect speedo cable, all electrical connectors and three wiring through clips from cluster.
5. Remove upper cluster bezel and instrument panel end cap.

6. Remove steering column to support bracket nuts.
7. Remove cluster housing to instrument panel retaining screws, then remove cluster.
8. Reverse procedure to install.

1975 Gran Fury & Monaco

Refer to the "1974 Fury & Monaco" procedure for instrument cluster removal.

1974-75 Chrysler Newport, New Yorker & Imperial

1. Disconnect battery ground cable.
2. Remove instrument panel upper cover, then working through top of panel, disconnect speedometer cable and printed circuit multiple connector.
3. Remove instrument cluster bezel, Fig. 5.
4. On Chrysler, remove gear selector and warning lamp bezel.
5. On all models disconnect instrument cluster lens and cluster housing from carrier.
6. Pull cluster out and disconnect two illumination and warning light modules.
7. Disconnect remaining electrical leads and remove cluster assembly.

1974 Fury & Monaco

1. Place selector lever in low position and remove ash tray and cigarette lighter.
2. Center the windshield wiper switch, rear window defogger switch, heater or A/C fan switch and the temperature control lever.
3. Remove cluster bezel retaining screws from under lower edge of bezel and pull top of cluster bezel outward to release upper spring clips, Fig. 6.
4. Disengage cluster bezel locking tabs from bezel and remove cluster bezel.

1974 Coronet, Charger & Satellite

1. Disconnect battery ground cable.
2. Remove radio.
3. Remove heater and/or air conditioner control and allow control to hang.
4. Lower steering column.
5. Disconnect speedometer cable and all electrical leads.
6. Remove the two screws attaching cluster housing to lower reinforcement.
7. Remove screws mounting cluster to panel, then disconnect cluster assembly from panel, Fig. 7.

1973-75 Dart & Valiant

1. Disconnect battery ground cable.
2. Tape steering column to prevent damage to finish and remove center A/C duct (if equipped).
3. Remove steering column cover and

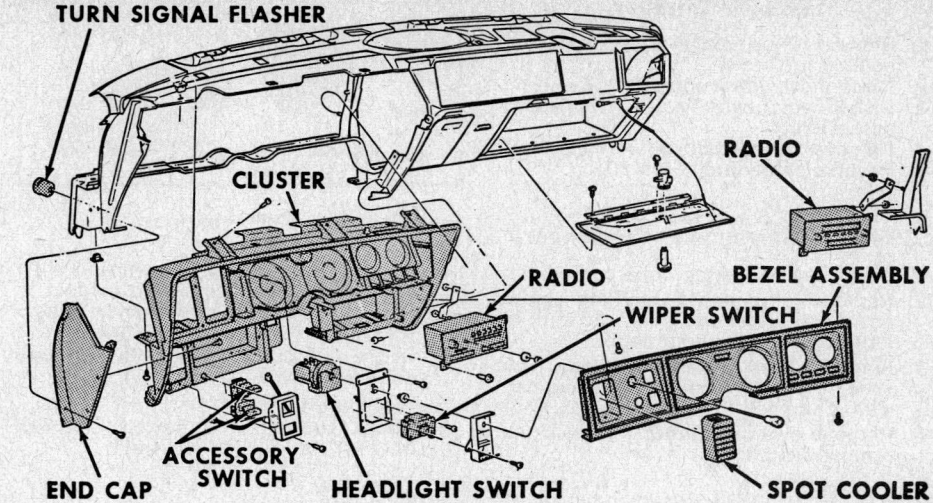

Fig. 4   Instrument cluster. 1975 Cordoba, Coronet, Charger SE & Fury

lower steering column.
4. Disconnect speedometer cable from cluster and remove six cluster to panel retaining screws.
5. Pull cluster outward, disconnect all electrical leads attached to printed circuit board and remove cluster from panel.

1973 Coronet, Charger & Satellite

1. Disconnect battery ground cable.
2. Remove radio.
3. Remove all electrical leads and all lamps on right side of instrument cluster.
4. Disconnect speedometer cable from under dash.
5. Remove heater control screws and allow control to hang.
6. Tape steering column to prevent damage to finish.
7. Lower steering column.
8. Remove cluster scews attaching cluster to panel, lower cluster out at top, and disconnect the remaining electrical leads and remove lamps from left rear of cluster, Fig. 7. Remove cluster from panel.

1973 Fury, Polara & Monaco

1. Disconnect battery ground cable.
2. Tape column to prevent damage upon removal of cluster.
3. Remove lamp panel screws and lower panel down; then place on top of instrument panel.
4. Remove screws holding hood release handle and allow handle to lay on floor.
5. Remove column cover screws and drop cover down.
6. Disconnect rear speaker fader control wiring, if equipped.
7. Snip the plastic rib that retains the vent control cable in column cover.
8. Remove the cable retaining clip. Remove the vent control cable through the opening in column cover.
9. Remove the center air conditioner

duct by removing the screw from the duct support bracket.
10. Lower the steering column, and disconnect the speedometer cable from under the dash panel.
11. Remove two hidden screws from lower edge of cluster bezel, one screw from side and one screw from top of bezel, Fig. 8.
12. Remove bezel mounting screws and roll cluster down and towards you far enough to disconnect all electrical leads and lamps.
13. Remove cluster bezel from panel.
14. Remove four cluster mounting screws. Remove cluster assembly.

1972 Fury, Polara & Monaco

1. Disconnect battery ground cable.
2. Remove lamp panel and remove column cover.
3. Lower steering column.
4. Disconnect speedometer cable.
5. Remove radio bezel.
6. Remove bezel mounting screws.
7. Roll cluster bezel down and toward you and disconnect wiring. Remove bezel, Fig. 8.

'1972 Dart & Valiant

1. Disconnect battery ground cable.
2. Disconnect speedometer cable and printed circuit board connector from under dash panel.
3. Remove column cover and loosen steering column floor plate attaching screws, remove steering column upper clamp and allow column to rest in lowered position.
4. Tape top of column to prevent damage to painted surface.
5. Remove six mounting screws from cluster, Fig. 9.
6. Before rolling cluster out of instrument panel, reach up behind and above cluster and bend three wire harness clips out of the way. Roll upper edge of cluster out far enough to disconnect wire to ammeter. Discon-

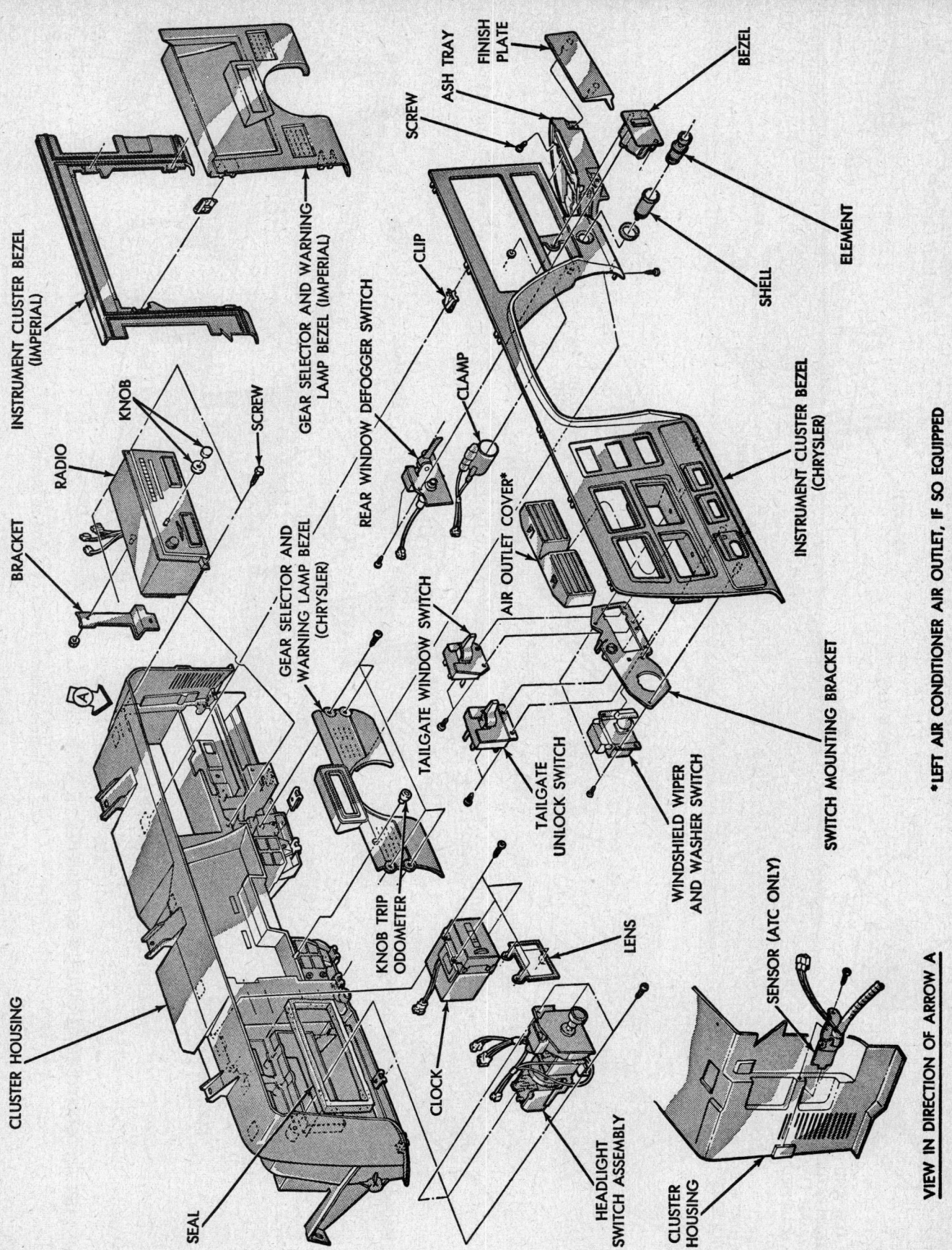

INSTRUMENT CLUSTER BEZEL (IMPERIAL)

GEAR SELECTOR AND WARNING LAMP BEZEL (IMPERIAL)

KNOB

RADIO

BRACKET

SCREW

CLIP

REAR WINDOW DEFOGGER SWITCH

CLAMP

SCREW

ASH TRAY

FINISH PLATE

BEZEL

ELEMENT

SHELL

INSTRUMENT CLUSTER BEZEL (CHRYSLER)

GEAR SELECTOR AND WARNING LAMP BEZEL (CHRYSLER)

AIR OUTLET COVER*

TAILGATE WINDOW SWITCH

TAILGATE UNLOCK SWITCH

WINDSHIELD WIPER AND WASHER SWITCH

SWITCH MOUNTING BRACKET

KNOB TRIP ODOMETER

CLUSTER HOUSING

SEAL

CLOCK

LENS

HEADLIGHT SWITCH ASSEMBLY

SENSOR (ATC ONLY)

CLUSTER HOUSING

VIEW IN DIRECTION OF ARROW A

*LEFT AIR CONDITIONER AIR OUTLET, IF SO EQUIPPED

Fig. 5 Instrument cluster. 1974-75 Chrysler Newport, New Yorker & Imperial

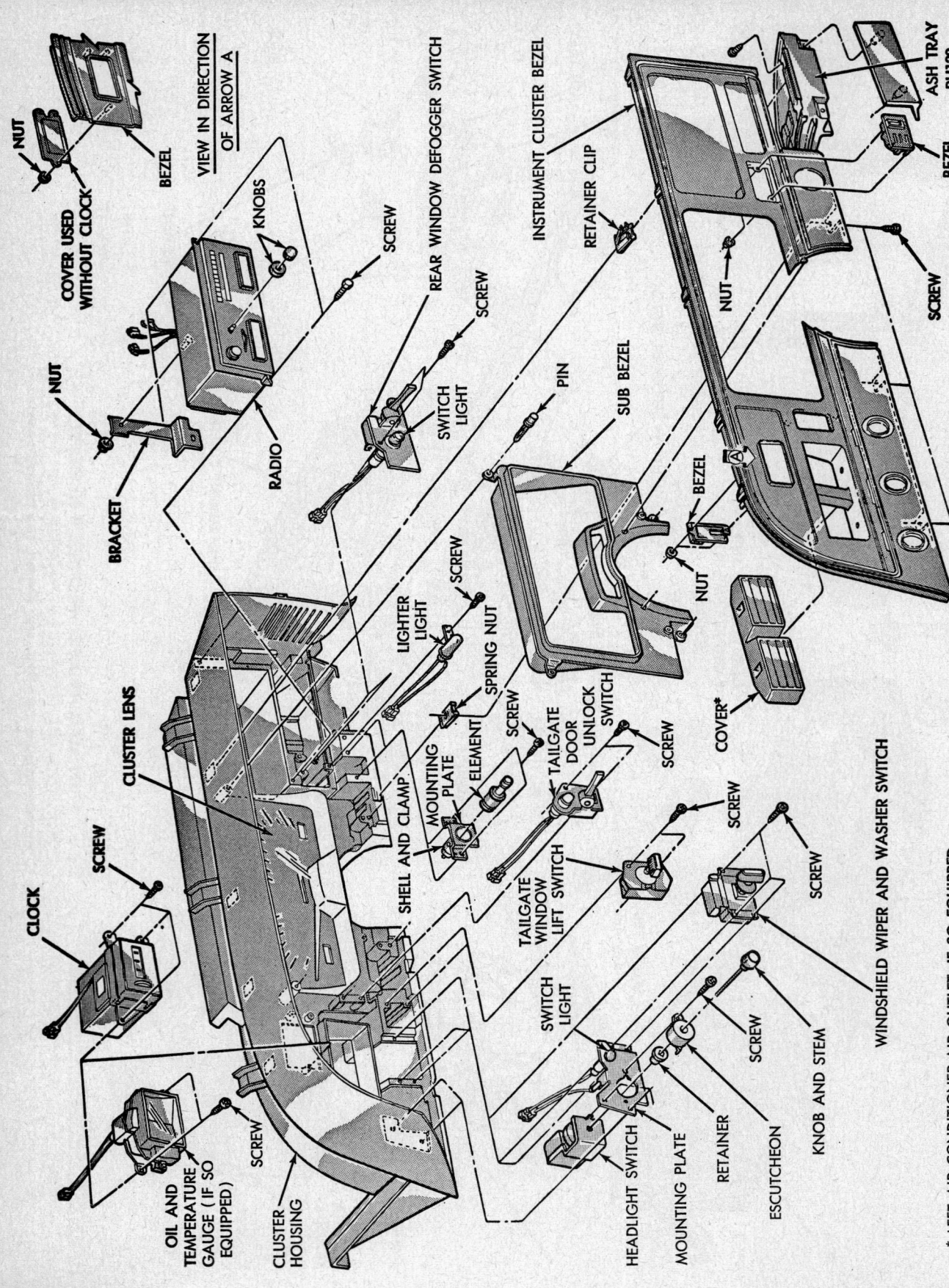

NUT

BEZEL

COVER USED WITHOUT CLOCK

VIEW IN DIRECTION OF ARROW A

KNOBS

SCREW

REAR WINDOW DEFOGGER SWITCH

SCREW

SWITCH LIGHT

NUT

RADIO

BRACKET

NUT

INSTRUMENT CLUSTER BEZEL

RETAINER CLIP

ASH TRAY PH139

BEZEL

NUT

SCREW

SUB BEZEL

PIN

BEZEL

NUT

COVER*

LIGHTER LIGHT

SCREW

SPRING NUT

MOUNTING PLATE

ELEMENT

SCREW

TAILGATE DOOR UNLOCK SWITCH

SCREW

SCREW

SCREW

CLUSTER LENS

SCREW

CLOCK

SHELL AND CLAMP

TAILGATE WINDOW LIFT SWITCH

SWITCH LIGHT

SCREW

WINDSHIELD WIPER AND WASHER SWITCH

HEADLIGHT SWITCH

MOUNTING PLATE

RETAINER

SCREW

ESCUTCHEON

KNOB AND STEM

OIL AND TEMPERATURE GAUGE (IF SO EQUIPPED)

SCREW

CLUSTER HOUSING

Fig. 6   Instrument cluster. 1974 Fury & 1974-75 Monaco

* LEFT AIR CONDITIONER AIR OUTLET, IF SO EQUIPPED

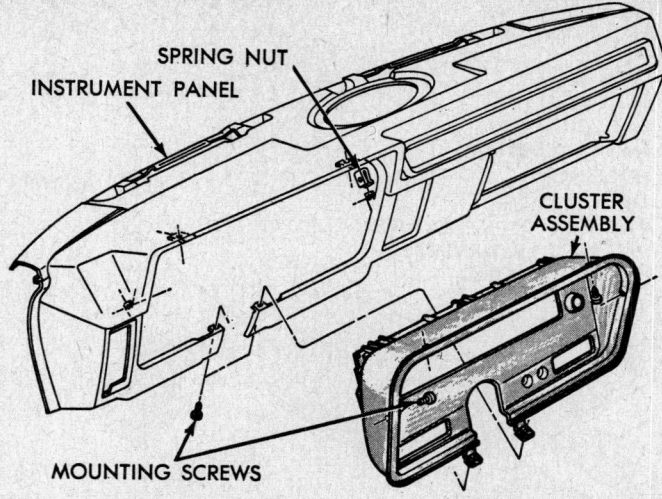

Fig. 7   Instrument cluster. 1971-74 Charger, Coronet & Satellite

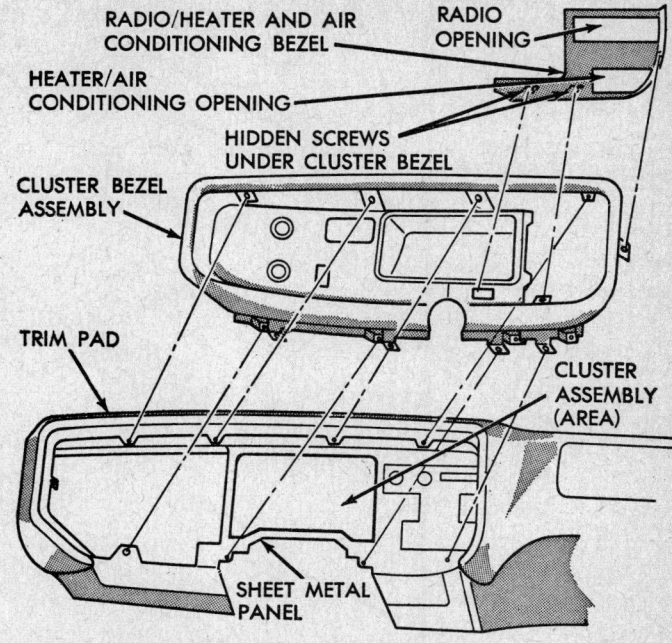

Fig. 8   Instrument cluster. 1972-73 Fury, Monaco & Polara

nect windshield wiper and headlight connectors.
7. Remove cluster assembly.

1971-73 Chrysler & Imperial

1. Remove map lamp, lamp panel end and panel.
2. Remove headlamp switch, radio and A.T.C. controls.
3. Lower steering column cover by removing four screws. Do not disconnect vent control cables.
4. Remove gearshift indicator pointer.
5. Lower steering column and allow steering wheel to rest on seat cushion.
6. Disconnect speedometer cable.
7. Remove five lower cluster mounting screws working through access holes in lower instrument panel.
8. Remove screw holding A.T.C. sensor to instrument cluster bezel and take sensor loose from bezel. On Imperial, remove clock.
9. Working over top of cluster, remove five upper cluster mounting screws, Figs. 10 through 12.
10. Carefully remove cluster by pulling it rearward in car and rolling the bottom slightly up to clear upper legs on cluster. Disconnect wiring as access is gained.

1971-72 Coronet, Charger & Satellite

1. Disconnect battery ground cable.
2. Remove ash tray, radio and heater control panel.
3. Remove upper steering column clamp and lower steering column.
4. Remove instrument cluster mounting screws.
5. Disconnect speedometer cable and wiring and remove cluster.

1971 Polara & Monaco

1. Disconnect battery ground cable.
2. Remove lamp panel and steering column cover.

3. Remove radio trim bezel.
4. Remove left trim bezel and/or spot cooler if so equipped.
5. Remove left A/C duct and center A/C connector if so equipped.
6. From under panel disconnect wiring and speedometer cable.
7. Remove gearshift indicator pointer.
8. Tape column to protect finish and remove three column upper clamp nuts and three bolts at lower support at floor.
9. Carefully lower column and allow steering wheel to rest on seat cushion.

10. Remove eight screws mounting cluster to panel and roll cluster out, disconnecting remaining wiring to high beam indicator, fuel gauge, ammeter and temperature gauge and remove cluster to padded work bench for service, Fig. 13.

1969-71 Dart

1. Disconnect battery ground cable.
2. Remove column opening cover (4 screws).

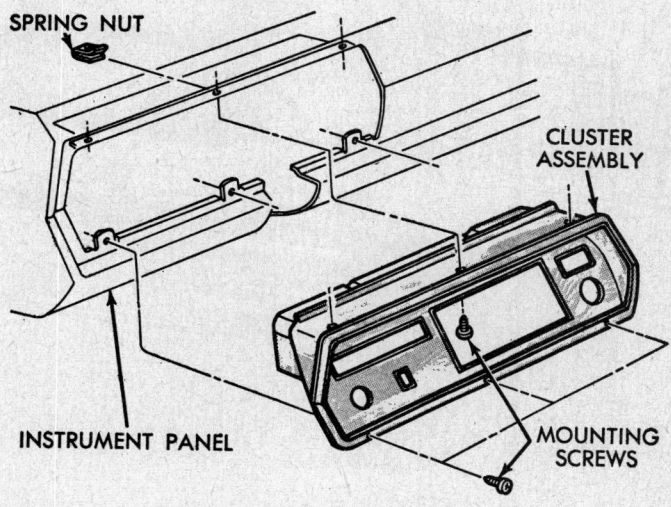

Fig. 9   Instrument cluster. 1972 Dart & Valiant

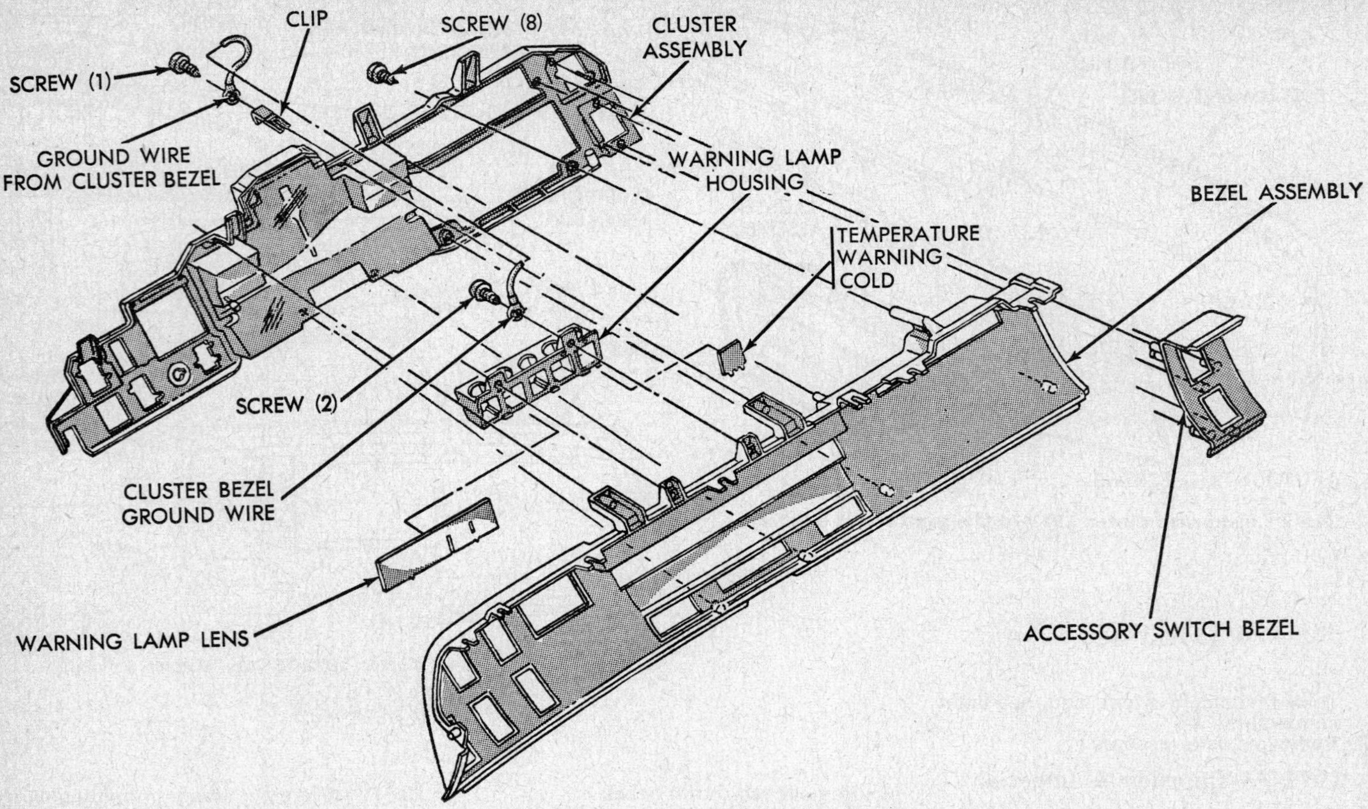

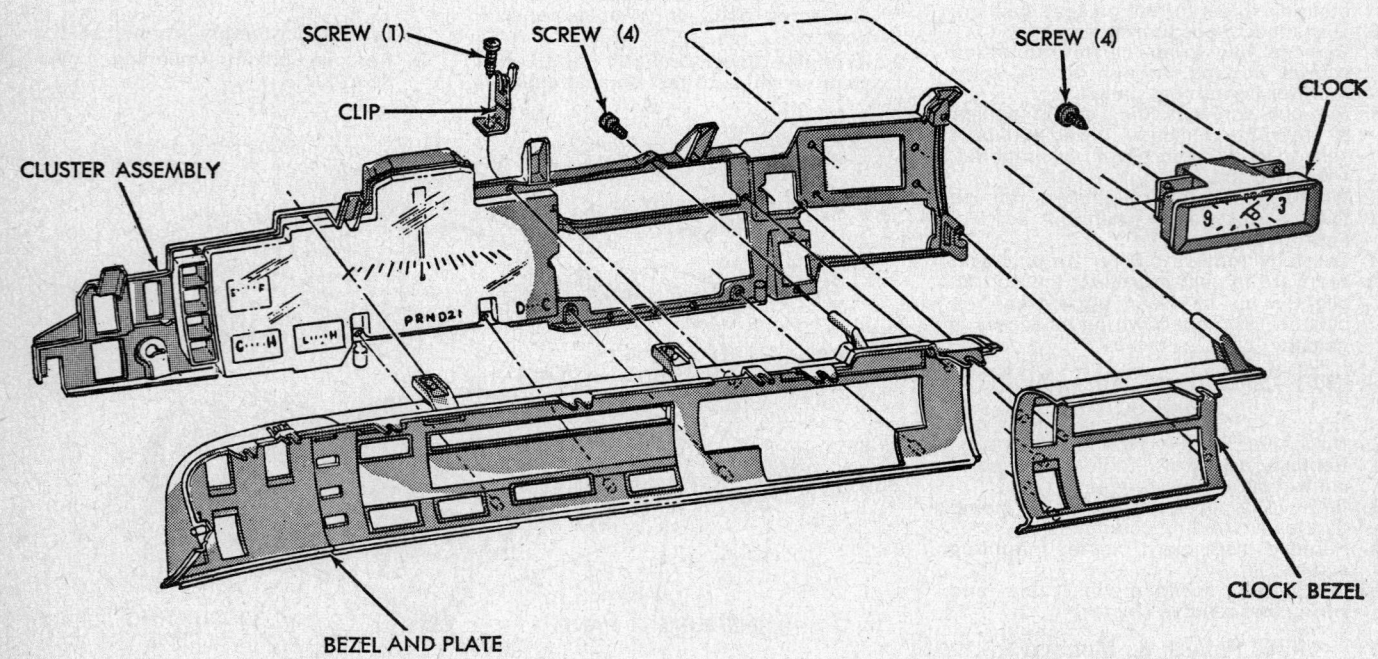

SCREW (1)

CLIP

SCREW (8)

CLUSTER ASSEMBLY

GROUND WIRE FROM CLUSTER BEZEL

WARNING LAMP HOUSING

BEZEL ASSEMBLY

TEMPERATURE WARNING COLD

SCREW (2)

CLUSTER BEZEL GROUND WIRE

WARNING LAMP LENS

ACCESSORY SWITCH BEZEL

Fig. 10   Instrument cluster. 1969-71 Chrysler (Typical)

SCREW (1)

SCREW (4)

SCREW (4)

CLOCK

CLIP

CLUSTER ASSEMBLY

PRND21

BEZEL AND PLATE

CLOCK BEZEL

Fig. 11   Instrument cluster. 1969-71 Imperial (Typical)

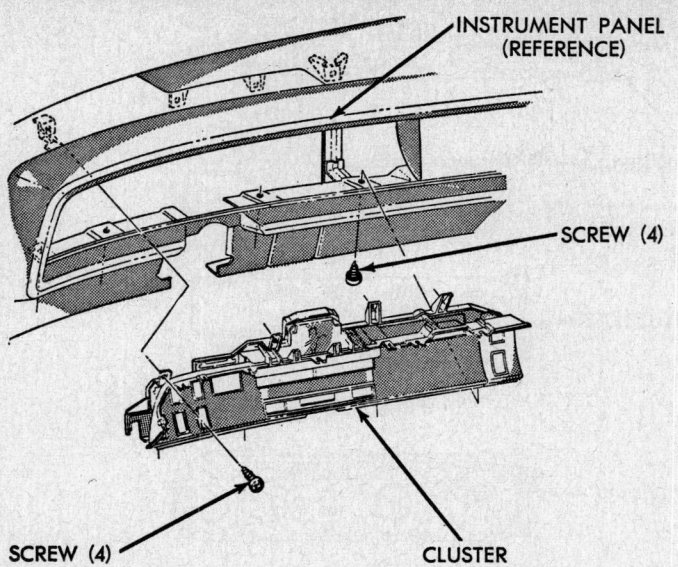

INSTRUMENT PANEL
(REFERENCE)

SCREW (4)

SCREW (4)

CLUSTER

Fig. 12   Instrument cluster. 1972 Chrysler

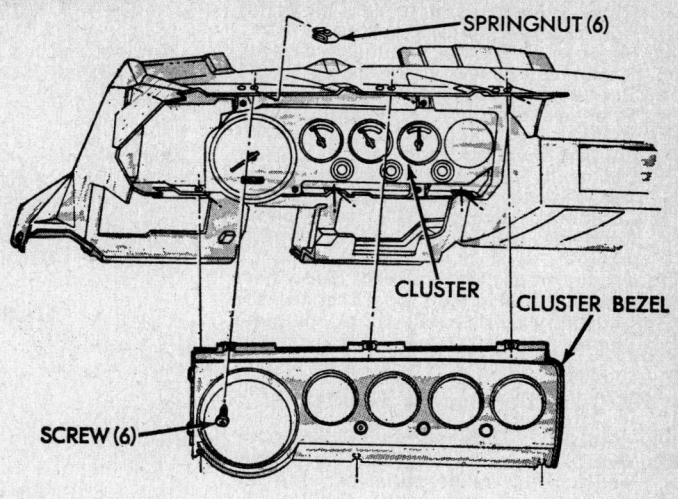

SPRINGNUT (6)

CLUSTER

CLUSTER BEZEL

SCREW (6)

Fig. 14   Instrument cluster. 1970-74 Barracuda & Challenger
with standard cluster

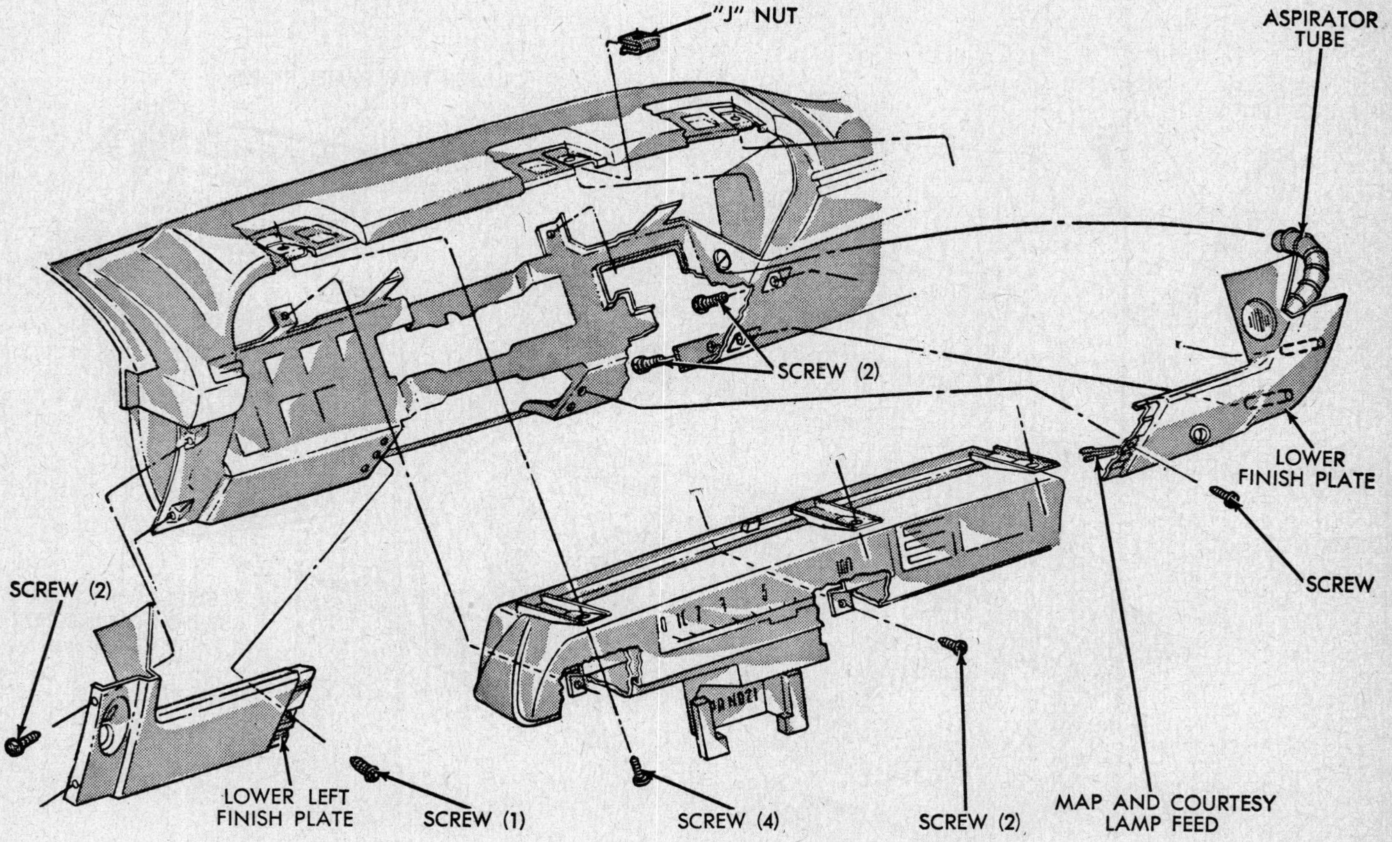

"J" NUT

ASPIRATOR
TUBE

SCREW (2)

LOWER
FINISH PLATE

SCREW

SCREW (2)

LOWER LEFT
FINISH PLATE

SCREW (1)

SCREW (4)

SCREW (2)

MAP AND COURTESY
LAMP FEED

Fig. 13   Instrument cluster. 1969-71 Monaco & Polara

3. Remove lower column plate (3 bolts) and upper mounting clamp.
4. Remove six cluster mounting screws.
5. Disconnect speedometer cable.
6. Remove fuse block (1 screw).
7. Rock cluster out and release wiring harness from spring clip at back of cluster, then continue to rock cluster out while using a screwdriver to hold harness clear of speedometer.
8. Disconnect left printed circuit board connector and brake system warning light.
9. From front of panel, disconnect right printed circuit board connector and ammeter leads, then complete cluster roll-out.

1970-74 Barracuda, Challenger

1. Disconnect battery ground cable.
2. Remove lamp panel mounting screws and carefully slide panel out and lay it on top of instrument panel. It is not necessary to disconnect wiring.
3. Remove switch bezel mounting screws and allow bezel to hang loose.
4. Remove steering column plate and disconnect column clamps and allow column to rest on seat.
5. Disconnect speedometer cable.
6. Remove six cluster bezel mounting screws, angle bezel out to clear clock button. Reach behind bezel and disconnect stereo control wiring, if so equipped.

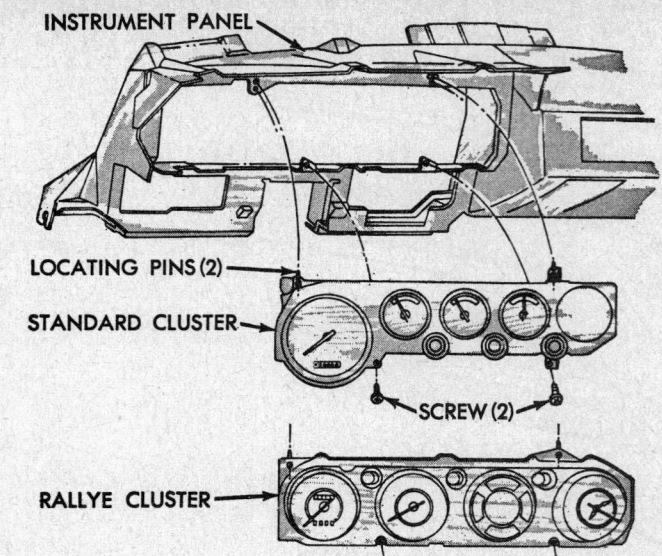

Fig. 15 Instrument cluster. 1970-74 Barracuda & Challenger with Rallye cluster

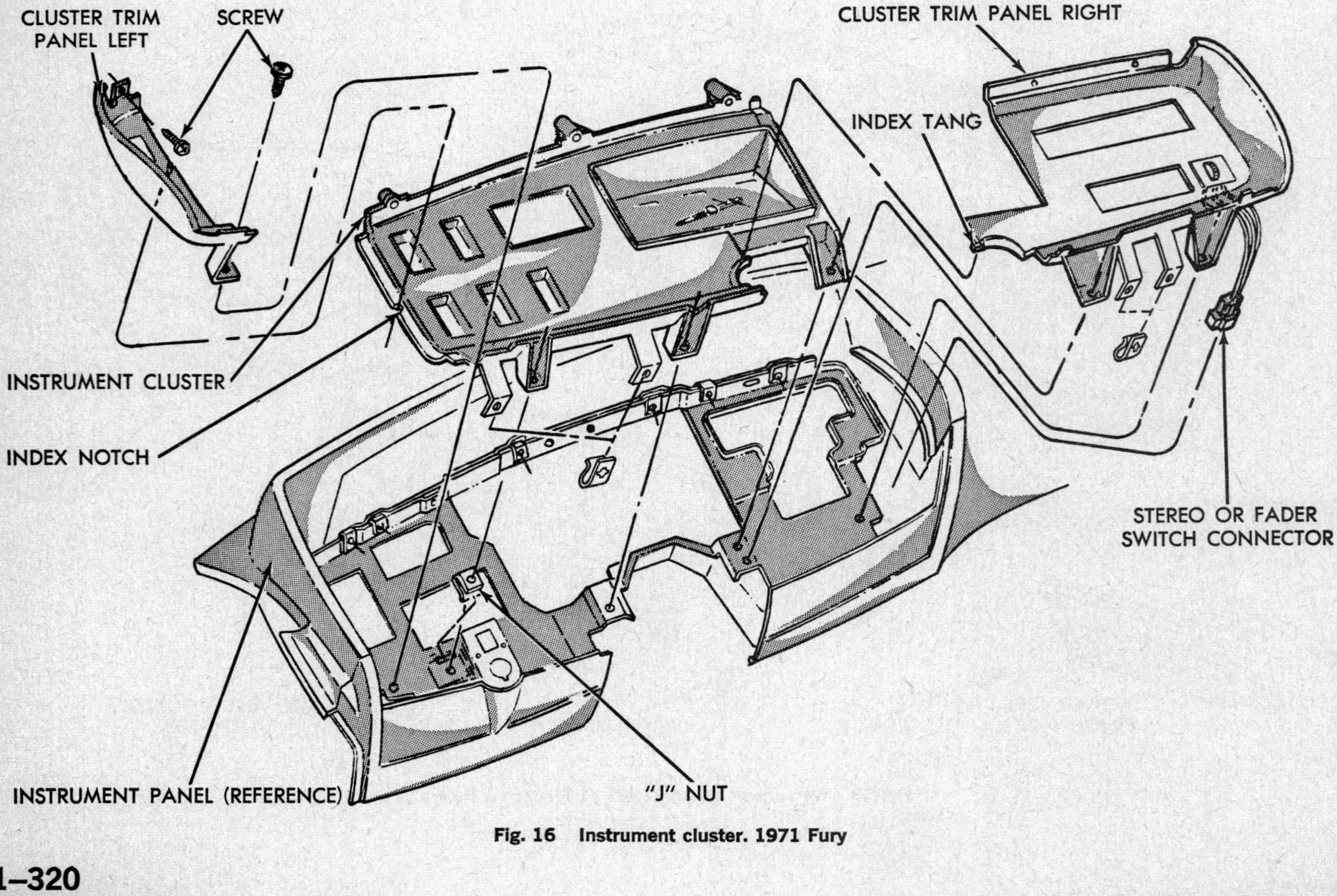

Fig. 16 Instrument cluster. 1971 Fury

CHRYSLER • DODGE • IMPERIAL • PLYMOUTH

7. On Rallye cluster, remove clock and odometer reset knobs.
8. Remove four cluster-to-panel mounting screws, disconnect wiring harnesses and remove cluster.

1969-70 Belvedere, Coronet & Satellite

1. Disconnect battery ground cable.
2. Remove steering column cover (4 screws).
3. Roll carpeting down and remove steering column cover plate (4 bolts).
4. Remove column clamp at instrument panel (2 nuts).
5. Remove upper trim molding (6 screws if equipped).
6. Remove left side trim molding (1 screw if equipped).
7. Remove left side trim plate (1 screw and 1 T-bolt, if equipped).
8. Remove radio trim plate (2 screws).
9. Remove switch bezel (4 screws).

NOTE: Steps 10-12 do not apply to 1970 models.

10. Remove ignition switch.
11. Remove A/C center opening cover (if equipped).
12. Remove lower left trim pad (6 screws from under panel and 4 screws from front of instrument panel).
13. Disconnect speedometer cable.
14. Remove six screws attaching cluster to panel, rock cluster out far enough to reach and disconnect wiring harness and connectors and remove cluster.
15. Reverse procedure to install.

1969-70 Charger

1. Disconnect battery ground cable.
2. Remove steering column opening cover (4 screws).
3. Remove steering column lower support plate (3 bolts).
4. Remove upper mounting bracket support bolts.
5. Disconnect speedometer cable.
6. Remove five screws mounting cluster to panel. A small screwdriver may be used in removing the medallion from the cluster bezel.
7. Release wire harness from retainer clips and roll cluster out of panel far enough to disconnect wiring from ammeter, switches, tachometer, clock, light bulbs and printed circuit board connectors, then complete cluster roll-out.

1969-70 Monaco & Polara

1. Disconnect battery ground cable.
2. Remove steering column cover.
3. Remove gear shift indicator from the column.
4. Remove lower column floor plate.
5. Remove upper column mounting nuts and lower steering column down to seat.
6. Remove switch and radio bezels, cluster trim pad and trim bezel.

7. Disconnect clock reset cable at the instrument panel lower reinforcement.
8. Disconnect clock lead and remove five cluster mounting screws.
9. Roll cluster out slightly and disconnect the speedometer cable.
10. Disconnect gear shift indicator lamp, main harness and alternator gauge leads and remove cluster.

1970 Chrysler

1. Disconnect battery ground cable.
2. Remove lower steering column cover.
3. Remove three outside floor plate mounting screws.
4. Remove steering column ground strap, disconnect clamp and lower steering column.
5. Remove left ash tray, radio and heater controls.
6. Remove two vent control screws and allow assembly to hang free.
7. Remove map light.
8. Remove lamp panel and lay it on top of the instrument panel.
9. From under instrument panel, remove four screws from right end accessory switch cover.
10. Disconnect speedometer cable.
11. Remove wiring harness from clip on left side of column support.
12. Remove cluster mounting screws and move cluster to right, rotating right end of cluster towards front of car and down.
13. Roll top of cluster down and rock cluster to left to gain access to wiring.
14. Disconnect wiring and roll cluster out.

1969 Chrysler

1. Disconnect battery ground cable.
2. Remove lower steering column cover and shift indicator pointer.
3. Disconnect turn signal wiring connector.
4. Remove outside floor plate mounting bolts, steering column clamp and ground strap and lower column.
5. Remove ash tray, radio and heater controls.
6. Remove vent control mounting screws and allow vent to hang free.
7. Remove map lamp and lamp panel and lay it on top of instrument panel.
8. From under panel, remove four mounting screws from right and accessory switch cover.
9. Disconnect speedometer cable, remove wiring harness from clip on column and remove cluster mounting screws.
10. Move cluster to right, rotating right end to front of car and down.
11. Roll top of cluster down and rock panel slightly left to gain access to wiring. Disconnect wiring and roll cluster out of panel.

1969-70 Imperial

1. Disconnect battery ground cable.
2. Remove ash tray, radio and heater controls.
3. Disconnect vent control cables at fresh air doors. Remove vent control mounting screws and move control to allow for lamp panel removal.
4. Remove map lamp, lamp panel cluster bezel, steering column cover,

steering column cover, shift indicator pointer, steering column clamp at instrument panel and cover screws at floor panel. Lower column.
5. Disconnect speedometer cable.
6. Remove cluster mounting screws.
7. Move cluster to right, pushing right end of cluster to front of car while turning top of cluster down, then pull left end of cluster out of panel.
8. Disconnect wiring and remove cluster.

1969-71 Fury & V.I.P.

1. Disconnect battery ground cable.
2. Remove lamp panel, steering column cover and radio trim bezel.
3. Remove left trim bezel and/or spot cooler if so equipped.
4. Remove left and center A/C duct if so equipped.
5. From under panel, disconnect leads to switches, clock and lamp assemblies and disconnect speedometer cable.
6. Remove shift indicator pointer.
7. Remove steering column upper clamp nuts, three bolts at lower support at floor and lower column. Remove cluster mounting screws, roll cluster out, disconnect leads to high beam indicator, fuel gauge, ammeter and temperature gauge and remove cluster, Fig. 16.

1969 Barracuda

1. Disconnect battery ground cable.
2. Disconnect speedometer cable and multiple connector from left printed circuit board.
3. Remove four cluster screws from underside of crash pad and four screws from lower front face of cluster.
4. Remove clock reset cable.
5. Pull cluster out far enough to reach behind and disconnect right printed circuit board multiple connector, ammeter wires, vacuum gauge hose or tachometer wire and emergency switch flasher connector.
6. Loosen A/C or heater knobs and remove from slide control. Remove A/C or heater mounting screws and move control out of the way.
7. Depress headlight switch knob release button on bottom side of switch and pull knob and shaft out of switch. Remove switch bezel and allow switch to remain connected to wire harness.
8. Pull w/s wiper knob from shaft. Remove wiper switch bezel nut and allow switch to remain connected to wire harness.
9. Roll cluster out from panel opening, face down and to the right.

1969-71 Valiant

1. Disconnect ground cable at battery.
2. Disconnect speedometer cable and printed circuit board multiple connector.
3. Loosen steering column floor plate attaching screws, remove column

upper clamp and allow column to rest in lowered position.

4. Remove six mounting screws from cluster (three in underside of cluster bezel and three in lower edge).
5. Before rolling cluster out of instrument panel, reach behind and above cluster and bend three wire harness clips out of the way. Roll upper edge of cluster out far enough to disconnect ammeter wires, emergency flasher, windshield wiper and headlight switch connectors.

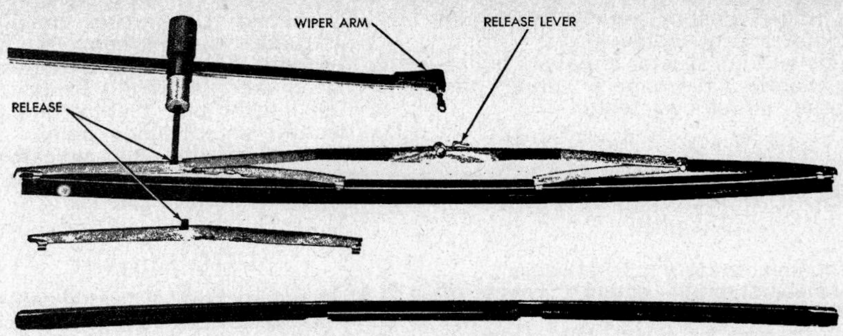

Fig. 17 Wiper blade assembly

W/S WIPER BLADES

1. Turn wiper switch "ON", move blades to a convenient position by turning the ignition switch "ON" and "OFF".
2. Lift wiper arm and blade off glass.
3. Depress release lever on center bridge and remove blade from arm, Fig. 17.
4. Depress release on end bridge (either button or lever) with screw driver to release from center bridge.
5. Pull rubber wiping element from the end bridge.
6. When replacing rubber element use caution to insure that all four bridge claws are engaged and properly positioned on filler assembly.
7. Check each release point for positive locking when installing blade and blade assembly.

W/S WIPER ARMS

CAUTION: The use of a screwdriver or other prying tool to remove an arm may distort it in a manner that will cause the arm to come off the pivot shaft in the future, regardless of how carefully it is reinstalled. *Do not* under any circumstances push or bend the spring clip in the base of the arm in an attempt to release the arm. This clip is self-releasing.

1969-75

1. Place wiper motor in park position.
2. For non-concealed wiper arms, position tool on wiper arm assembly, Fig. 18, and remove wiper arm assembly.
3. For 1969-70 with concealed wiper arms, insert a .090" dia. pin or drill into the arm, Fig. 19, and pull the wiper arm off the wiper pivot with a rocking motion.
4. For 1971-75 with concealed wiper arms, lift arm to permit the latch, Fig. 20, to be pulled out and remove the arm from the pivot using a rocking motion.

W/S WIPER MOTOR REPLACE

1971-75 with Non-Concealed Wipers

1. Disconnect battery ground cable.
2. Disconnect wiper motor harness.
3. Remove three motor mounting nuts. On vehicles without A/C it is easier to remove crank arm nut and crank arm from under instrument panel first

and omit next two steps.
4. Work motor off mounting studs far enough to gain access to crank arm mounting nut. Do not force or pry motor from studs as drive link can easily be distorted.
5. Using a ½" open end wrench, remove motor crank arm nut. Carefully pry crank arm off shaft and remove motor.

1971-75 with Concealed Wipers

1. Disconnect battery ground cable.
2. Remove wiper arm and blades.
3. Remove cowl screen.
4. Remove drive crank arm retaining nut and drive crank. Disconnect wiring to motor.
5. Unfasten and remove wiper motor.

1969-70 Chrysler & Imperial

1. Remove wiper arms and blades.
2. Remove windshield lower moulding.
3. Remove cowl grille panel.
4. Remove drive crank from motor (one nut) and disconnect wiring to motor.
5. Unfasten motor from dash panel (3 nuts) and remove motor out through cowl grille panel opening.

1970 Barracuda, Challenger

1. Disconnect battery ground cable.
2. Remove wiper arm and blade assemblies.

Fig. 18 Non-concealed wiper arm. 1969-75

3. Remove left cowl screen.
4. Remove drive crank arm nut and crank. Disconnect wiring.
5. Remove mounting nuts and remove motor.

1969 Barracuda, 1969-70 Dart, Coronet, Charger, Valiant, Belvedere & Satellite

Without Air Conditioning

1. Disconnect ground cable at battery.
2. Disconnect wiper motor wire harness at bulkhead multiple connector.
3. From under instrument panel, remove crank arm nut and arm from motor shaft.
4. Remove mounting nuts and work motor off studs.

With Air Conditioning

1. Disconnect ground cable at battery.
2. Disconnect wiper motor wire harness at bulkhead multiple connector.
3. Remove motor mounting nuts.
4. Disconnect linkage.
5. Work motor off mounting studs far enough to gain access to crank arm mounting nut. *Do not force or pry motor from studs as drive link may be distorted.*
6. Remove motor crank arm nut, pry arm off shaft and remove motor.

1969-70 Polara, Monaco •

1. Remove wiper arms and blades.
2. Remove windshield lower moulding.
3. Remove cowl grille panel.
4. Remove nut that mounts drive crank to motor. Remove drive crank and disconnect wiring at motor.
5. Unfasten motor from dash panel (3 nuts) and take motor out through cowl grille panel opening.

1969-70 Fury & V.I.P.

1. Remove wiper arms and blades.
2. Remove windshield lower moulding.
3. Remove cowl grille panel.
4. Remove nut that mounts drive crank to motor. Then remove drive crank and disconnect wiring at motor.

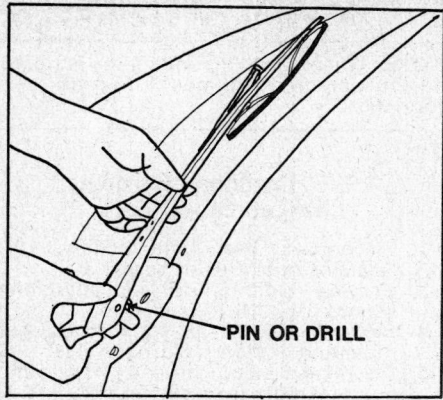

Fig. 19   Concealed wiper arm. 1969-70

5. Unfasten motor from dash panel (3 nuts) and take motor out through cowl grille panel opening.

W/S WIPER TRANSMISSION

1973-75 with Non-Concealed Wipers

1. Disconnect the battery ground cable.
2. For non A/C equipped models, remove the drive crank from the motor by removing the attaching nut (above the accelerator pedal) with a ⅜" wrench. For A/C equipped vehicles, remove the wiper motor nuts and/or bolts with ½" wrench.
3. Move wiper motor forward and to the right to gain access to the drive attaching nut. Loosen nut with a ⅜" wrench and remove the drive crank from the motor.
4. Remove the drive link and crank assembly from the left pivot by prying the link bushing from the pivot pin.

1973-75 with Concealed Wipers

1. Disconnect the battery ground cable.
2. Remove the cowl top plastic screen to gain access to the linkage assembly.
3. Remove the arm and blade assemblies.
4. Remove the drive crank from the wiper motor by removing the attaching nut with a ⅜" wrench.
5. Remove the pivot mounting screws, and the linkage assembly from the plenum chamber.

1971-72 with Non-Concealed Wipers

1. Disconnect battery ground cable.
2. If A/C equipped, remove duct supplying left spot cooler to provide access to left wiper pivot.
3. Insert a wide blade screwdriver between plastic link bushing and pivot crank arm. Gently twist screwdriver to force bushing and link free of pivot pin.
4. Remove motor mounting nuts, pull motor away from bulkhead and remove motor crank arm retaining nut. After crank arm is removed from motor shaft, remove drive link assembly

from under left side of panel.

NOTE: In heater equipped models, remove motor drive crank arm retaining nut and pry crank arm off motor shaft. Gently pry drive link and bushing from left pivot crank arm pin and withdraw assembly from under panel. Remove motor drive crank arm from drive link after removal of assembly from vehicle.

5. To remove connecting link from pivots, remove glove box, reach through opening and gently pry bushing and link from right pivot pin. Lift the link from the pivot crank arm pin and repeat operation at left pivot. Withdraw from under left side of panel. The wiper pivots can be removed if required by the removal of the ½" mounting nuts at this time.

1971-72 With Concealed Wipers

1. Remove wiper arms and blade assemblies and the cowl screen to provide access.
2. Disconnect battery ground cable.
3. Remove crank arm nut and crank arm from motor shaft.
4. Remove bolts mounting left and right pivots to body.
5. Remove links and pivots through cowl top opening. The linkage and pivots can be serviced on bench after removal from vehicle.

1969-70 Chrysler, Imperial, Polara & Monaco

To service either the drive link or the connecting link, it is necessary to remove the wiper arms and blades, windshield lower moulding and cowl grille panel to gain access to the wiper system. Before starting the installation procedure, make certain the wiper system is in the "Park" position and the battery ground cable disconnected.

1. With connecting and drive links assembled as a unit, insert links through cowl top opening and bolt pivots in position.
2. Position motor crank arm on motor shaft and tighten to 140 inch-pounds. Reconnect battery ground cable.
3. Test wiper system operation and then replace cowl screen and windshield lower moulding.
4. Using a pin or drill, install and adjust wiper arm and blade assemblies.

1970 Barracuda, Challenger, Fury

1. Disconnect battery ground cable.
2. Remove motor crank arm.
3. Remove pivot bolts and remove links and pivots through top cowl opening.

NOTE: If servicing of the mechanism on the 2-speed motor crank is required, be sure that during reassembly, the link is positioned between the ears of the cover retainer.

1969-70 Dart, Coronet, Charger, Valiant, Belvedere, Satellite & 1969 Barracuda

NOTE: On air conditioned models, after

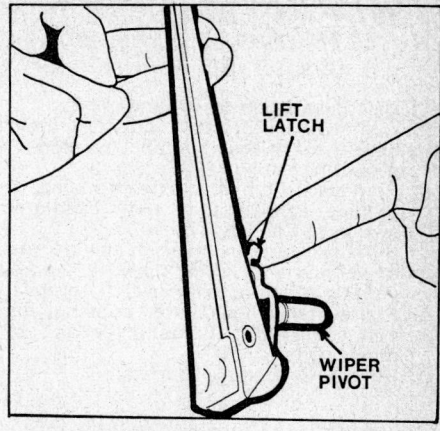

Fig. 20   Concealed wiper arm. 1971-75

disconnecting the battery ground cable, remove left spot cooler duct and carefully pry the link and bushing from the pivot pin. Remove motor mounting nuts, pull motor away from bulkhead and remove motor crank arm retaining nut and crank arm. Remove drive link assembly from under panel.

On models without air conditioning, remove crank arm from motor, remove drive link from left pivot pin and withdraw assembly from under panel. Remove crank arm from drive link after assembly is removed from vehicle. Connecting link can be removed from pivots by removing glove box and reaching through the opening to pry bushing and link from pivot pin. Withdraw from under left side of panel.

1. Install bushing on motor crank arm pin, position drive link on bushing so large side of pivot bushing faces away from drive crank arm. Large side of bushing will be on same side of link as crank arm retainer.
2. Install spring washer with convex side towards link and install retainer. *If retainer was distorted in removal, it should be replaced.*
3. In heater equipped vehicles, insert drive link assembly under left side of panel, position crank arm on motor shaft, indexing flats on shaft with flats on arm and install retaining nut.

NOTE: On air conditioned models, install drive link from under instrument panel. Install crank arm on motor shaft from engine side of bulkhead. Secure motor with three nuts. Press plastic bushing over pin on left pivot.

4. Insert connecting link into place with "R" (right side) and "L" (left side) facing instrument panel side. Press link bushings onto pivot crank pins.
5. Reconnect battery cable and test operation. Install glove box if necessary.

W/S WIPER SWITCH

1975 Cordoba, Coronet, Charger SE & Fury

1. Disconnect battery ground cable.
2. Remove instrument cluster upper bezel and the switch escutcheon mounting screw.
3. Remove switch to cluster housing retaining screws and pull headlamp switch to the "On" position.
4. Slide escutcheon on shaft toward rear of vehicle and rotate upward, thereby gaining clearance for switch removal.
5. Pull switch from cluster housing, disconnect electrical connector and remove switch.
6. Reverse procedure to install.

1975 Chrysler Newport, New Yorker, Gran Fury, Imperial & Monaco

1. Disconnect battery ground cable.
2. Remove instrument cluster bezel.
3. Remove switch mounting screws.
4. Disconnect electrical connector and remove switch from bezel.

1974 Chrysler, Fury, Imperial, Monaco

1. Remove instrument cluster bezel.
2. Remove switch mounting screws.
3. Disconnect electric leads and remove switch from bezel.

1973-74 Charger, Coronet, & Satellite

1. Remove wiper switch knob.
2. Remove wiper switch bezel nut.
3. Remove wiper switch from instrument cluster and disconnect electrical leads.

1973 Fury, Polara & Monaco

1. Remove column cover and A/C duct.
2. Remove left spot cooler duct.
3. Reach up under dash panel and disconnect wiring from switch.
4. Remove two switch mounting screws and remove switch.

1971-73 Chrysler & Imperial

1. Remove instrument cluster.
2. Remove screws securing switch and plate to cluster housing.
3. Remove the assembly.
4. Remove screws holding switch to mounting plate and remove switch.

1971-72 Fury, Polara & Monaco

1. Roll cluster down and towards you.

NOTE: It is not necessary to remove bezel assembly, only roll it far enough to gain access to switch mounting screws and wiring.

2. Disconnect leads to switch and unfasten switch.

1970-74 Barracuda, Challenger

1. Disconnect battery ground cable.
2. Remove lamp panel retaining screws and carefully slide panel out and lay it on top of instrument panel.
3. Remove bezel retaining screws and slide assembly out and disconnect wiring harness.
4. Pull control knob from shaft. Remove mounting nut and remove switch from bezel.

1970-72 Coronet & Satellite

1. Remove steering column cover.
2. Lower steering column and allow it to rest on seat.
3. Remove lower trim bezel.
4. Remove switch mounting screws and disconnect wiring. Place wires on switch before installing switch.

1969 Coronet, Belvedere & Satellite

The wiper switch is serviced in the same manner as the headlight switch.

1969-75 Dart, 1969 Barracuda & 1969-75 Valiant

1. Remove air conditioning duct (if so equipped).
2. On 1969-71 models, loosen knob set screw and on all models, pull knob from switch.
3. Remove spanner nut.
4. Remove wiring harness from clip. Disconnect wiring and remove switch.

1969-70 Polara & Monaco

The wiper switch is serviced in the same manner as the headlight switch.

1969-70 Fury & V.I.P.

1. Remove all A/C ducts from underside of panel if so equipped.
2. From under panel, disconnect electrical leads.
3. Remove two mounting screws and remove switch.

1969-70 Chrysler & Imperial

1. Remove lamp panel.
2. Remove instrument panel to gain access to switch.
3. Remove two switch mounting screws and remove switch.

1969-72 Charger

The wiper switch is serviced in the same manner as the headlight switch.

RADIO, REPLACE

NOTE: When installing radio, be sure to adjust antenna trimmer for peak performance.

1975 Cordoba, Coronet, Charger SE & Fury

1. Disconnect battery ground cable.
2. Remove lower cluster bezel.
3. Remove radio knobs and mounting screws.
4. Remove radio rear support bracket mounting nut on radio right side.
5. Disconnect electrical leads from radio and pull radio from cluster housing.
6. Reverse procedure to install.

1975 Chrysler Newport, New Yorker, Gran Fury, Imperial & Monaco

Refer to the "1974 Fury, Monaco, Chrysler & Imperial" procedure for radio replacement.

1974 Barracuda & Challenger

1. Disconnect battery ground cable.
2. Remove radio retaining screws and disconnect antenna lead.
3. Remove radio support bracket nut and move radio forward and down.
4. Disconnect electrical and speaker leads and remove radio.

1974 Charger, Coronet, & Satellite

1. Disconnect battery ground cable.
2. Remove ash tray and right radio retaining screw which is accessible through lower left corner of ash tray housing.
3. Loosen radio support bracket nut and remove radio knobs and mounting nuts.
4. Disconnect antenna and electrical leads and remove radio.

1974-75 Valiant & Dart

1. Disconnect battery ground cable.
2. If equipped with A/C, remove outlet duct assembly, ash tray and ash tray housing mounting screws.
3. Remove radio knobs, mounting nuts and radio support bracket screw.
4. Lift radio, relocate ash tray housing for additional clearance and disconnect antenna lead.
5. Move radio forward and down, disconnect electrical and speaker leads and remove radio.

1974 Fury, Monaco, Chrysler & Imperial

1. Disconnect battery ground cable.
2. Remove bezel. On Fury and Monaco, also remove sub bezel.
3. Remove lamp assembly from radio (monaural only).

4. Remove radio to panel retaining screws and instrument panel upper cover.
5. Working through top of panel, disconnect antenna lead and remove radio mounting bracket nut.
6. On monaural radio, disconnect speaker lead from speaker. On stereo radio, disconnect speaker lead from radio.
7. Pull radio out from panel and disconnect electrical lead.

1971-73 Coronet, Charger & Satellite

1. Disconnect battery ground cable.
2. Remove ash tray.
3. Remove radio knobs and mounting nuts.
4. Remove radio.

1971-73 Polara & Monaco

1. Disconnect battery ground cable.
2. Remove nine lamp panel mounting screws, lower lamp panel slightly, disconnect lamp harness from main harness and remove lamp panel.
3. Remove steering column cover and radio trim bezel.
4. Remove center lower A/C duct, if so equipped.
5. Disconnect wiring and antenna from radio.
6. Remove radio support bracket.
7. Remove radio mounting bolts.
8. Remove radio down through bottom of instrument panel carefully to avoid damage to vacuum hoses and wiring.

1969-70 Polara & Monaco

1. Disconnect battery ground cable.
2. Remove Auto-Temp. control (if so equipped).
3. Remove radio bezel and two radio mounting bolts at front of instrument panel.
4. Remove air conditioning duct (if so equipped).
5. Disconnect electrical leads, loosen radio mounting bracket stud nut and slide radio and stud towards front of car from mounting bracket. Carefully remove radio from under panel.

1969-73 Dart, Challenger, Barracuda, Valiant

1. Disconnect battery ground cable.
2. Disconnect electrical leads and remove knob.
3. From under panel, remove two radio mounting nuts and remove radio mounting bracket. Remove radio down and out from under panel.

1969-73 Chrysler & Imperial

1. Disconnect battery ground cable.
2. Remove left ash receiver and steering column cover.
3. Unscrew stereo tape reset knob if so equipped.
4. Disconnect all electrical leads.
5. Loosen defroster vacuum actuator and move it to facilitate radio removal.

6. Remove two radio mounting screws through access openings in lower panel. On search-tune radios, remove knobs bezels and nuts.
7. Remove support bracket screw from lower reinforcement. Support radio.
8. Working through ashtray opening, remove support bracket from radio.
9. Remove radio from under panel.

1969-70 Charger

1. Disconnect battery ground cable.
2. Remove radio finish plate.
3. On A/C models, remove lower center air duct, left air duct and upper center duct.
4. Remove radio mounting bracket.
5. Unfasten radio from instrument panel (2 screws).
6. Disconnect antenna and speaker leads and remove radio.

1969-72 Fury & V.I.P.

1. Disconnect battery ground cable.
2. Remove lamp panel and steering column cover.
3. Remove radio trim bezel.
4. Remove center lower A/C duct if so equipped.
5. Disconnect electrical leads.
6. Remove radio support bracket and mounting bolts.
7. Remove radio down through bottom of panel carefully to avoid damage to vacuum and electrical connections.

1969-70 Belvedere, Coronet & Satellite

1. Disconnect battery ground cable.
2. Remove radio upper trim panel.
3. Remove radio finish plate.
4. Remove radio rear mounting nut from bracket.
5. Disconnect electrical wiring and antenna lead.
6. Remove two screws from front of instrument panel and remove radio.

HEATER CORE REMOVAL

Before attempting to remove a heater core, disconnect the battery ground cable, drain the radiator and remove inlet and outlet hoses from heater assembly in engine compartment. Refer to Figs. 21 and 22.

1975 Chrysler Newport, New Yorker, Gran Fury, Imperial & Monaco

Refer to the "1974 Chrysler, Imperial, Fury & Monaco" procedure for heater core removal.

1974 Chrysler, Imperial, Fury & Monaco

1. Disconnect battery and drain radiator.
2. Disconnect heater hoses and plug

hose fittings on heater core.
3. Move front seat rearward and remove instrument panel lower cover. Unplug antenna lead from radio and disconnect upper level vent vacuum line.
4. Disconnect the upper level vent from heater housing and the mounting bracket from dash, then swing duct back.
5. Disconnect electrical connectors from blower motor resistor and control cable from clip and crank.
6. Disconnect support bracket and swing bracket out of way.
7. From engine compartment, remove five retaining nuts from studs.
8. Roll or tip housing out from under instrument panel and disconnect control cable from clip and the blend air door crank.
9. Remove core tube locating screw from between core tubes, remove housing retaining nuts, separate housing and remove core.

1971-75 Dart & Valiant

Less Air Conditioning
1. Remove heater hoses to dash panel seal and retainer plate.
2. Remove heater motor seal retainer plate and seal from dash panel.
3. Disconnect control cables from heater.
4. Remove heater motor resistor wire from resistor.
5. Remove defroster tubes from heater.
6. Disconnect heater housing support rod from outside air duct.
7. Remove heater assembly.

With Air Conditioning: 1973-75
1. Remove battery, drain radiator and disconnect heater from unit.
2. Remove core tube seal nut, bracket and seal.
3. Remove A/C duct, ash tray and housing and radio.
4. Remove heat-defrost vacuum actuator pot; let hang by rod.
5. To remove heat distribution duct, remove three screws on front cover, two on each end and work housing out of lip and remove to left side.
6. Remove left defroster duct. Remove right defroster duct and let it hang from top.
7. To remove the rear distribution housing, reach through radio opening and remove three screws top and bottom and one at left end.
8. With housing off, core will be settling loose. Separate seal and lift out.

With Air Conditioning: 1971-72
1. Disconnect battery and remove air cleaner.
2. Remove air outlet assembly, glove box and right defroster tube.
3. Disconnect wiring from resistor block, vacuum hoses from outside recirculating air door actuator, temperature control cable, evaporator temperature control switch control cable and heater core ground wire.
4. Remove screw securing heater to evaporator assembly.
5. Disconnect heater housing support rod from outside air duct.
6. Remove heater assembly.
7. Remove outside recirculating air door

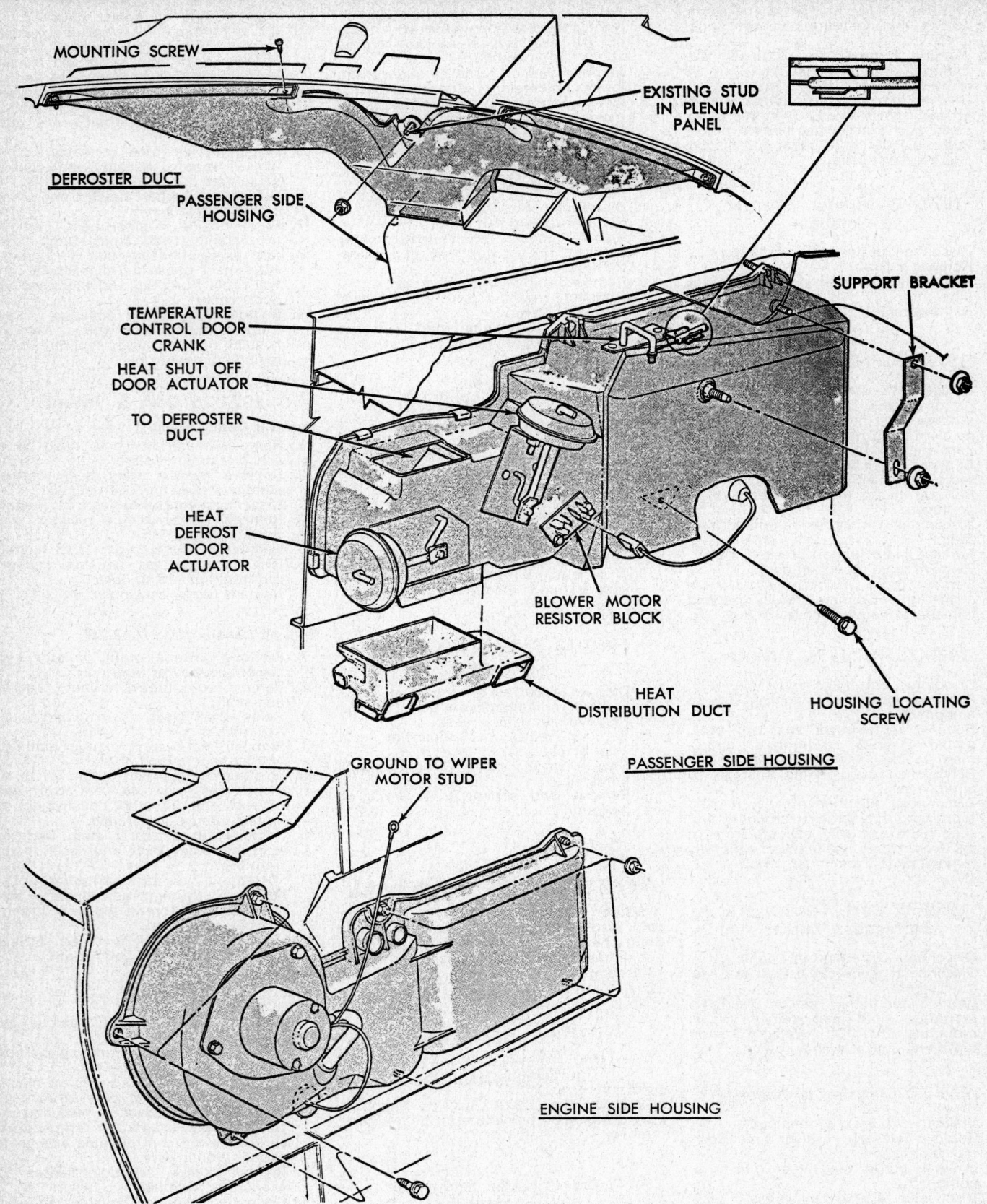

MOUNTING SCREW

EXISTING STUD
IN PLENUM
PANEL

DEFROSTER DUCT

PASSENGER SIDE
HOUSING

SUPPORT BRACKET

TEMPERATURE
CONTROL DOOR
CRANK

HEAT SHUT OFF
DOOR ACTUATOR

TO DEFROSTER
DUCT

HEAT
DEFROST
DOOR
ACTUATOR

BLOWER MOTOR
RESISTOR BLOCK

HEAT
DISTRIBUTION DUCT

HOUSING LOCATING
SCREW

PASSENGER SIDE HOUSING

GROUND TO WIPER
MOTOR STUD

ENGINE SIDE HOUSING

Fig. 21   Heater core & blower motor. 1969-75 less air conditioning (Typical)

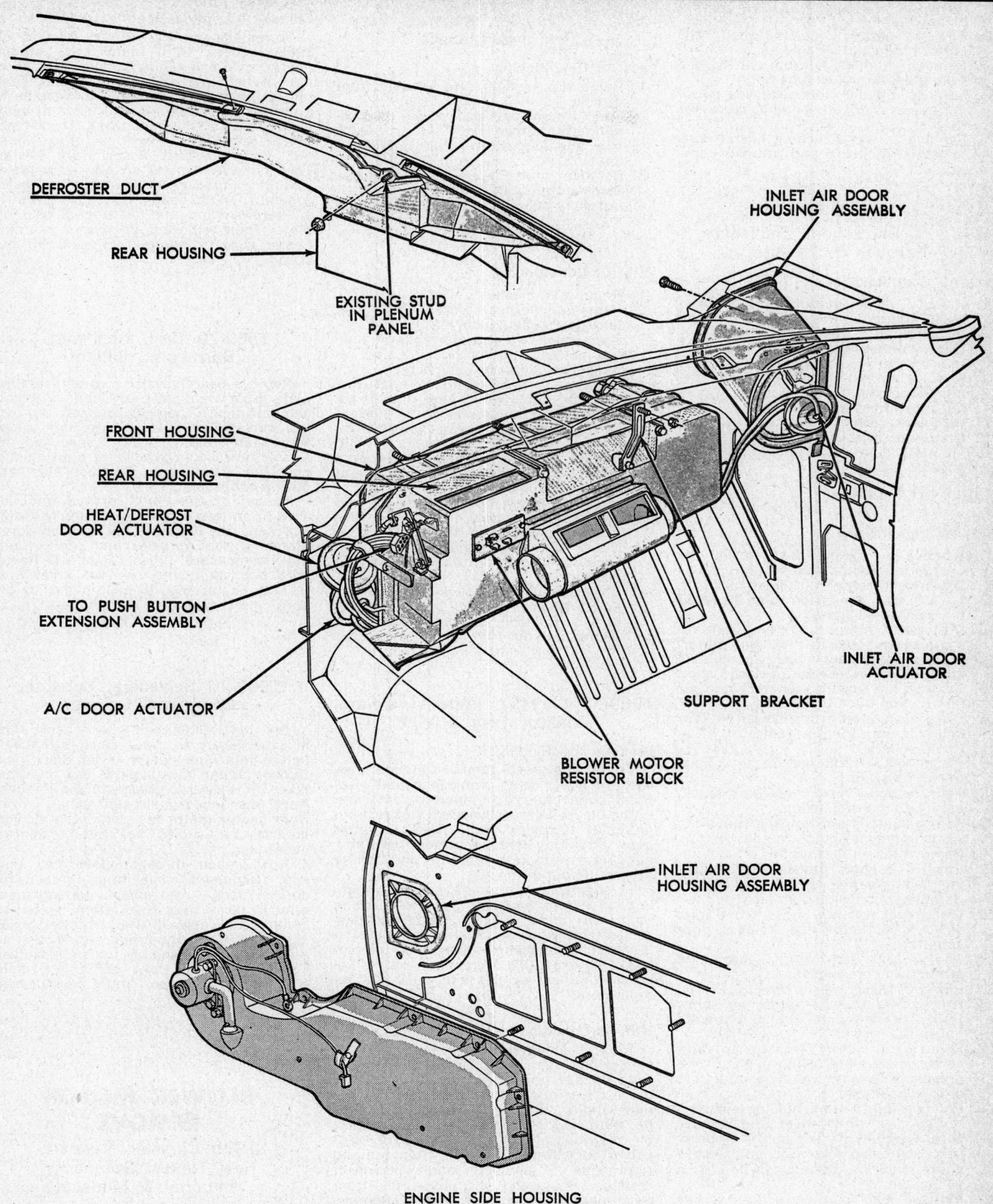

DEFROSTER DUCT

REAR HOUSING

EXISTING STUD
IN PLENUM
PANEL

INLET AIR DOOR
HOUSING ASSEMBLY

FRONT HOUSING

REAR HOUSING

HEAT/DEFROST
DOOR ACTUATOR

TO PUSH BUTTON
EXTENSION ASSEMBLY

A/C DOOR ACTUATOR

INLET AIR DOOR
ACTUATOR

SUPPORT BRACKET

BLOWER MOTOR
RESISTOR BLOCK

INLET AIR DOOR
HOUSING ASSEMBLY

ENGINE SIDE HOUSING

Fig. 22 Heater core & blower motor. 1969-75 with air conditioning (Typical)

8. Remove operating link between bell-crank and recirculating door.
9. Remove air inlet seal from either front or rear heater housing half only.
10. Remove retainer clips attaching housing halves together and separate halves.
11. Remove screws attaching heater core to heater housing and remove core.

1971-74 Barracuda, Challenger, Coronet & Satellite

Less Air Conditioning

1. Remove three mounting nuts from studs around blower motor and remove flange and air seal.
2. Unplug antenna from radio and place to one side.
3. Remove screw from housing to plenum support rod on right side of housing above fresh air opening.
4. Disconnect three air door cables.
5. Disconnect wires from blower resistor.
6. Tip unit down and out from under panel.

With Air Conditioning

1. Remove air cleaner and slowly discharge refrigerant from system.
2. Disconnect refrigerant lines at dash panel. Leave expansion valve attached to line. Cap all lines.
3. Disconnect blower motor wires and remove motor cooling tube and motor.
4. Remove glove box and appearance shield from lower edge of dash panel.
5. Remove left spot cooler duct and air distribution duct.
6. Disconnect wires from blower resistor and antenna wire from radio.
7. Remove radio.
8. Disconnect vacuum harness from back of control switch.
9. Remove water valve cable from bracket on left end of housing.
10. Remove nuts from housing mounting studs in engine compartment.
11. Remove rubber drain tube.
12. Remove support bracket from housing plenum panel.
13. Carefully remove plenum air seal.
14. Disconnect vacuum hose from inlet air door actuator and by-pass door actuator.
15. Remove air seal from heater and evaporator core tubes.
16. Remove 18 screws holding front and rear covers together and one screw from between core tubes. Separate housings.
17. Remove 3 screws from evaporator core access plate, remove plate, this provides access to two evaporator core mounting screws.
18. Remove four screws holding evaporator core to front cover and remove core. Carefully lift left half of housing seal from rear cover. Do not remove entire seal as bottom portion is a water seal.
19. Remove two core retaining screws from mounting plates and one from between core tubes in back of rear cover. Lift core out of housing.

1971-73 Chrysler, Imperial, Fury, Polara & Monaco

Less Air Conditioning

1. Remove passenger side housing from vehicle.
2. From inside housing, remove two retaining nuts from right side of heater core and four screws from outside of housing.
3. Remove core tube locating metal screw from top of housing.
4. Carefully pull heater core out of housing.

With Air Conditioning

1. Remove air cleaner.
2. Remove steering column cover and left spot cooling duct.
3. Disconnect two actuator rods at linkage on left side of housing and remove two cover retaining screws.
4. Remove screws retaining heat distribution duct. When heat duct is removed, screws or clamps in bottom lip of front cover can now be removed.
5. Remove glove box and center spot cooler, air distribution housing and right spot cooler duct.
6. From glove box opening, remove two top retaining screws and three screws from right side of housing.
7. Disconnect wires at resistor block and vacuum hoses from air inlet housing actuator.
8. Remove nut from housing end of support bracket and swing bracket up out of way. Carefully roll front cover and heater core out from under panel.

1969-70 Chrysler, Imperial, Polara, Monaco, Fury & V.I.P

Less Air Conditioning

From under dash, remove antenna lead, vacuum hoses from trunk lock and electrical connectors from blower motor resistor block. Remove vacuum hoses from defroster actuator and heater shutoff door actuator. Remove bottom retaining nut from support bracket and swing bracket up out of the way.

In engine compartment, remove retaining nuts from housing. Remove locating bolt from under bottom center of passenger side housing. Roll or tip housing out from under panel and remove temperature control cable from door crank. Remove retaining screws and nuts and remove core.

With Air Conditioning

Remove steering column cover and left spot cooler duct. Disconnect actuator rods from linkage on left side of housing. Remove cover and distribution duct screws, duct and screws from front cover lower lip. Remove glove box, center spot cooler, air distribution housing and right spot cooler duct. Remove screws from top and right side of housing and disconnect resistor wiring and vacuum hoses from recirculating housing actuator. Remove support bracket to housing nut, swing bracket up and roll front cover and heater core from under instrument panel.

Chrysler & Imperial Rear Seat Heater

To remove core from rear seat heater on 1969 models, from under car, remove heater hose and tubing support clamps at rear of floor pan and drain system. Then remove rear seat cushion and seat back. From inside car remove hoses from heater, and spare tire from trunk. Disconnect motor feed wire, fresh air intake hose and floor air duct hoses from heater. Take out three metal screws from heater mounting brackets and remove heater assembly. With heater on bench, remove 11 screws from end plate and take off plate. Then remove four screws retaining heater core to heater body and lift out core.

1969-70 Dart, Challenger, Barracuda, Valiant

Remove heater motor seal and retainer plate from right side of dash in engine compartment. Then disconnect all control cables from heater assembly, along with heater motor resistor wire and defroster tubes. Remove heater housing support rod from fresh air duct and take out heater assembly.

To get at the core, remove retaining clips from two halves of heater housing and separate halves. Then remove screw attaching seal retainer and seal around the heater core tubes. Take off heater core support clamp, remove screws attaching heater core to heater and lift out core.

1969-70 Belvedere, Satellite, Charger & Coronet

On models equipped with console shift, it is necessary to move console rearward before removing heater. After doing this, remove upper half of glove box and then take off heater-to-cowl support bracket. Next, disconnect defroster hoses, wiring from heater motor resistor, fresh air vent control, and cables for shut-off door at heater end.

Now, reach through glove box door and disconnect cable from temperature control door. From engine compartment, remove three nuts that retain heater assembly to firewall. Then rotate heater assembly until mounting studs are up and lift heater assembly from under dash. To remove core, take off heater cover from front of heater and take out core mounting screws.

BLOWER MOTOR REMOVE

1975 Chrysler Newport, New Yorker, Gran Fury, Imperial & Monaco

Refer to the "1969-74 Chrysler, Imperial, Fury, Polara & Monaco" procedure for blower motor removal.

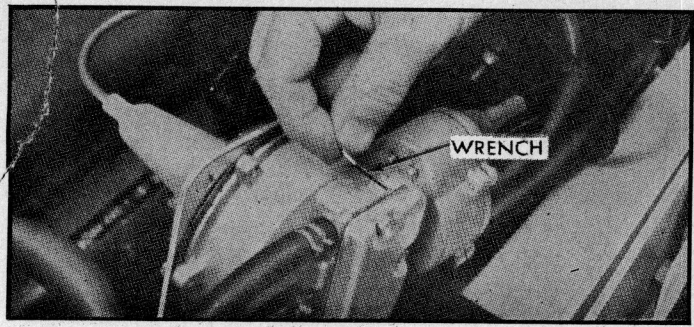

Fig. 23   Speed Control lock-in screw adjustment. 1969-75

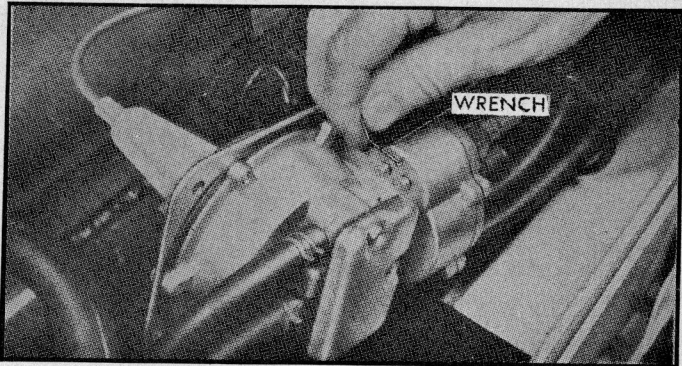

Fig. 24   Speed Control cut-in screw adjustment. 1969-70

1970-74 Challenger: 1971-74 Coronet, Charger, Barracuda & Satellite

Less Air Conditioning

The heater assembly must be removed to service the blower motor. See procedure for *Heater Core Removal* to remove assembly, then proceed to *Remove Blower Motor* as follows:

1. Disconnect blower motor lead from resistor block. Disconnect the ground wire from the mounting plate, Fig. 21.
2. Remove six screws and retaining clips holding blower motor mounting plate to housing. Separate the blower motor and mounting plate from the housing, Fig. 21.
3. Remove the blower wheel from the motor shaft.
4. Remove the two retaining nuts and separate the motor from the mounting plate. Remove the motor.

With Air Conditioning

NOTE: All service to the blower motor is made from the engine compartment side.

1. Disconnect the feed wire at the connector and the ground wire. Remove the air tube.
2. Remove three screws located on the outer surface of the mounting plate.
3. Remove the mounting plate and blower motor as an assembly, Fig. 22.

1969-74 Chrysler, Imperial, Fury, Polara & Monaco

The blower motor is mounted to the engine side housing under the right front fender between the inner fender shield and the fender, Figs. 21 and 22. The inner fender shield must be removed to service the blower motor.

1969-70 Coronet, Charger & Satellite; 1969-74 Dart & Valiant

Less Air Conditioning

The heater assembly must be removed to service the blower motor. See procedure for *Heater Core Removal* to remove assembly, then proceed to *Remove Blower Motor* as follows:

1. Disconnect lead wire from the blower

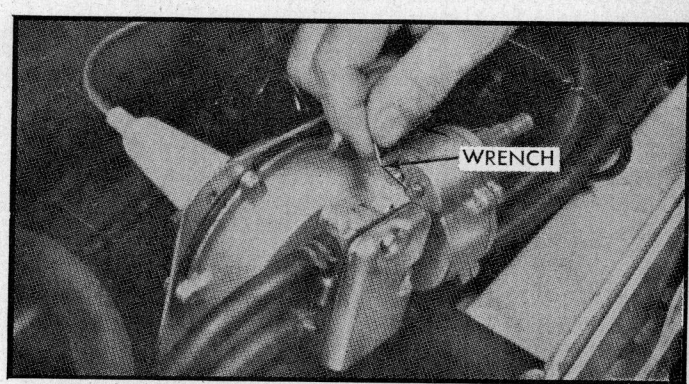

Fig. 25   Speed Control cut-out screw adjustment. 1969-70

motor to the heater assembly.
2. Remove motor cooler tube.
3. Remove heater backplate assembly from heater.
4. Remove fan from motor shaft. Remove blower motor from backplate, Fig. 21.

With Air Conditioning

NOTE: All service to the blower motor is made from the engine compartment side.

1. Disconnect the feed wire at the connector and the ground wire. Remove the air tube.
2. Remove three screws located on the outer surface of the mounting plate.
3. Remove the mounting plate and blower motor as an assembly, Fig. 22.

EGR MAINTENANCE REMINDER SYSTEM

This reminder system on 1975 vehicles uses a warning light in the instrument cluster, to alert the driver of the vehicle at 15,000 mile intervals to have the EGR

system checked for the following:
1. Vacuum hose leakage
2. EGR valve operation
3. CCEGR valve operation
4. Timer and solenoid operation
5. Intake manifold and EGR valve flow passages

Once the EGR system has been properly serviced, the reminder system must be reset for the next 15,000 mile interval and to turn off the warning light. If the EGR switch has to be replaced before a 15,000 mile interval, the EGR system maintenance check must be performed and the new switch installed.

SPEED CONTROLS
1969-75 Speed Control

Servo Adjustments

There are three adjustment set screws in the servo housing, Figs. 23, 24 and 25. The adjustment of these set screws have been factory set and under normal conditions there should be no need for altering the factory setting during the life of the vehicle.

Need for adjustment can be determined only after accurate diagnosis of the system operation. If adjustment is found to be necessary, perform the appropriate adjustment outlined below; if screw is loose stake side of servo housing adjacent to screw to insure a snug fit.

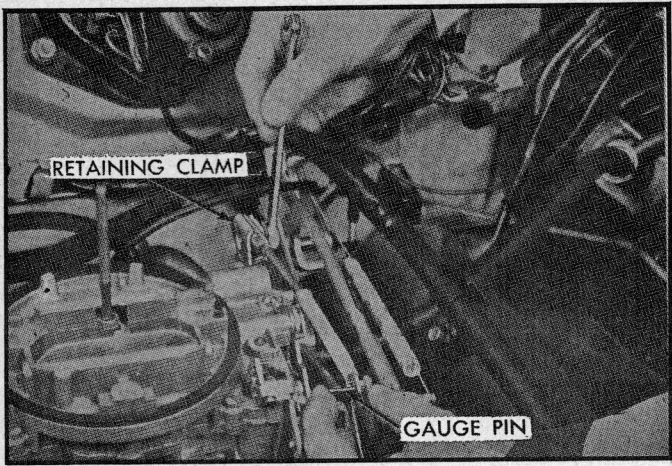

Fig. 26   Speed Control servo cable
throttle adjustment. 1969-75

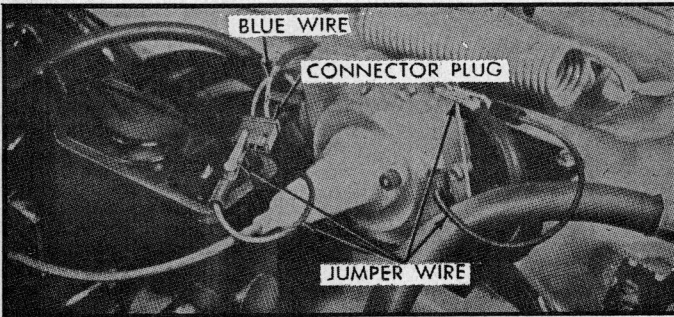

Fig. 27   Speed Control brake switch adjustment. 1969-70

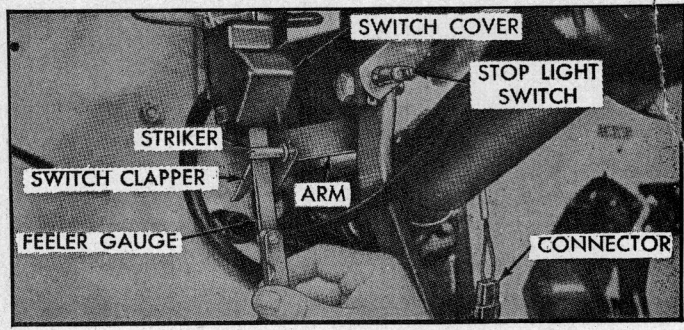

Fig. 28   Checking clapper and striker pin clearance
on intermediate size cars. 1969 Speed Control

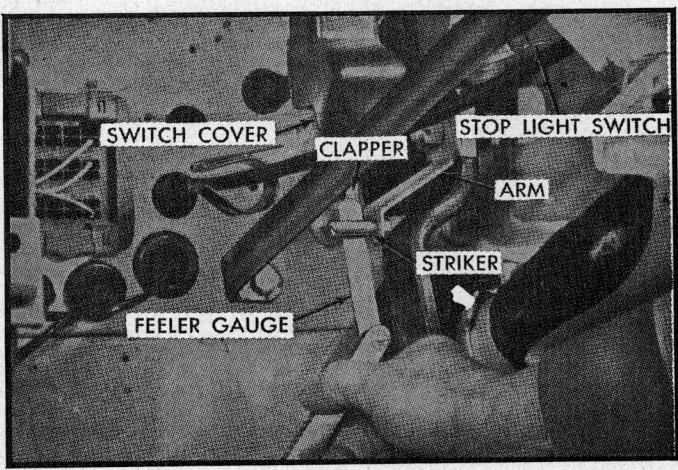

Fig. 29   Checking clapper and striker pin clearance
on full size cars. 1969 Speed Control

Lock-in Screw Adjustment, Fig. 23

Lock-in accuracy will be affected by poor engine performance (need for tune-up), loaded gross weight of car (trailering), improper slack in control cable. After the foregoing items have been considered and the speed sags or drops more than 2 to 3 mph when the speed control is activated, the lock-in adjusting screw should be turned counter-clockwise approximately 1/4 turn per one mph correction required.

If a speed increase of more than 2 to 3 mph occurs, the lock-in adjusting screw should be turned clockwise 1/4 turn per one mph correction required.

CAUTION: This adjustment must not exceed two turns in either direction or damage to the unit may occur.

Cut-in Speed Adjustment, Fig. 24

This adjustment regulates the minimum road speed at which the low speed inhibit switch allows the speed control to be activated. This should range from 25 to 33 mph. If cut-in speed is too low, turn set screw counter-clockwise. If too high, turn set screw clockwise. Make adjustments in 1/8 turn increments; total adjust-

ment must not exceed two turns.

Cut-out Adjustment, Fig. 25

This adjustment affects the road speed at which the system is deactivated during deceleration. Turning the screw clockwise increases road speed at which the system deactivates (cuts out). A counter-clockwise adjustment decreases the cut-out speed. The desired cut-out speed should occur approximately 5 mph below the cut-in setting. Make adjustments in 1/8 turn increments; total adjustment must not exceed two turns.

Throttle Cable Adjustment, Fig. 26

Optimum servo performance is obtained with a given amount of free play in the throttle control cable. To obtain proper free play, insert a 1/16" diameter pin between forward end of slot in cable end of carburetor linkage pin (hair pin clip removed from linkage pin). With choke in full open position and carburetor at curb idle, pull cable back toward dash panel without moving carburetor linkage until all free play is removed. Tighten cable clamp bolt to 45 inch-pounds, remove 1/16"

pin and install hair pin clip.

Brake Switch Adjustment, 1969

1. Disconnect harness connector at speed control servo and run a jumper wire from the blue wire terminal of connector to a good ground, Fig. 27.
2. Turn ignition key to accessory position, depress and release turn signal lever push button and check clearance between engaged actuator arm and striker pin on brake pedal, Figs. 28 and 29. Clearance should be .070" to .100".
3. If clearance is not correct, loosen striker pin attaching nut and move pin to obtain this clearance. Then tighten nut securely, insuring that the adjusted clearance is maintained.

NOTE: Before making the low speed inhibit switch adjustment, check speedometer cables to assure proper core length so that both cable drive ends are properly engaged in servo shaft keyways without binding. Also be sure that cable ferrule nuts are properly positioned on servo pilot diameters and nuts properly tightened.

Brake Switch Adjustment, 1970
1. Loosen switch bracket.
2. Insert .140"-.150" spacer gauge between brake push rod and switch with pedal in free position.
3. Push switch bracket assembly toward

brake push rod until plunger is fully depressed and switch contacts spacer.
4. Tighten bracket bolt to 100 in-lbs. and remove spacer.

Brake Switch Adjustment, 1971-75
This procedure is the same as that for

1970 models, but the spacer must be .110 inch for 1971-73 models, .120 inch for 1974-75 Charger, Coronet and Satellite models and .130 inch for 1974-75 Fury, Dart, Chrysler and Imperial models.

Engine Section

ENGINE MOUNTS REPLACE

1969-75 Exc. V8-426

1. Disconnect throttle linkage at transmission and at carburetor.
2. Raise hood and position fan to clear radiator hose and radiator top tank.
3. Remove torque nuts from insulator studs.
4. Raise engine just enough to remove front engine mount.
5. Reverse above to install.

1969-71 V8-426

1. Disconnect throttle linkage from bellcrank at rear of engine.
2. Position fan to clear radiator top tank and hoses.
3. Remove engine mount to frame bolts; on the right side disconnect flexible line and fitting from fuel pump and move line to side; on left side remove splash shield.
4. Raise engine and remove engine mounts wth brackets. Remove insulators from brackets.
5. Reverse above to install.

ENGINE, REPLACE

1969-75 Chrysler & Imperial

In addition to the usual items such as fuel lines, linkage, propeller shaft, etc., perform the following:
1. Scribe a line on hinge brackets on hood to assure proper adjustments when installing. Then remove hood.
2. Remove battery, drain cooling system, remove all hoses, fan shroud, disconnect oil cooler lines and remove radiator.
3. Attach lifting fixture.
4. Disconnect torque converter drive plate from engine.
5. Support transmission in its normal position in relation to the vehicle, to insure ease of installation.
6. Remove engine front mounting bolts Then raise and work engine out of chassis.

Dodge & Plymouth 1969-75 V8s

1. Scribe hood hinge outlines on hood and remove hood.
2. Drain cooling system and remove battery.
3. Remove fan shroud (if equipped) and radiator.

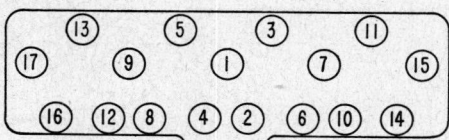

Fig. 1   Cylinder head tightening sequence. V8s with distributor at front of engine

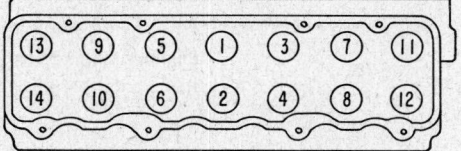

Fig. 2   Cylinder head tightening sequence. 6-170, 198, 225

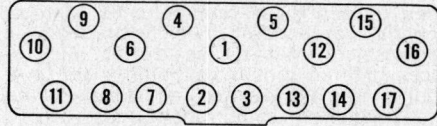

Fig. 3   Cylinder head tightening sequence. V8-426 HP2 engine

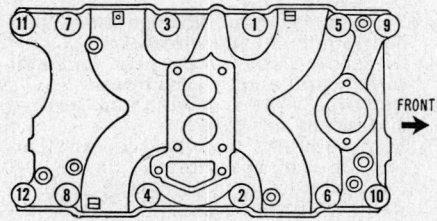

Fig. 4   Intake manifold tightening sequence. V8-273, late 318 & 340, 360

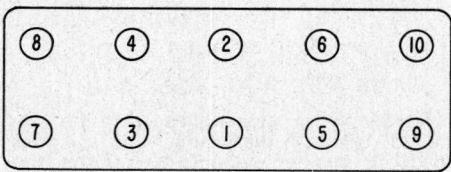

Fig. 5   Cylinder head tightening sequence. V8s with distributor at rear of engine

4. Disconnect fuel lines and wiring to engine.
5. Remove carburetor. Attach engine lifting fixture to carburetor flange studs on intake manifold.
6. Remove engine front mounting nuts.
7. Disconnect exhaust pipes at manifold.
8. On manual transmission equipped vehicles disconnect propeller shaft, tie out of the way and disconnect wires and linkage at transmission.
9. On manual transmission equipped vehicles attach engine support fixture, remove engine rear crossmember and remove transmission.
10. On automatic transmission equipped vehicles disconnect torque converter drive plate from engine. Support transmission in its normal position in relation to the vehicle, to insure ease of installation.
11. Lift engine out of chassis.

1969-75 6-170, 198, 225

1. Scribe hood hinge outlines on hood and remove hood.
2. Drain cooling system and remove battery and carburetor air cleaner.
3. Disconnect transmission cooler lines at radiator (if equipped).
4. Remove radiator and hoses.
5. Remove outlet vent pipe or closed vent system and rocker arm cover.
6. Disconnect fuel lines, carburetor linkage and wiring to engine.
7. Disconnect exhaust pipe at manifold.
8. Remove converter cover plate.
9. On manual transmission equipped vehicles disconnect propeller shaft, tie out of the way and disconnect wires and linkage at transmission.
10. On manual transmission equipped vehicles attach engine support fixture, remove engine rear crossmember and remove transmission.
11. On automatic transmission equipped vehicles disconnect torque converter drive plate from engine. Support transmission in its normal position in relation to the vehicle, to insure ease of installation.
12. Attach lifting fixture to cylinder head and attach chain hoist.
13. Remove engine support and front engine mounting bolts and lift engine from chassis.

CYLINDER HEAD

1969-75 Chrysler & Imperial

Some cylinder head gaskets are coated with a special lacquer to provide a good seal once the parts have warmed up. Do not use any additional sealer on such gaskets. If the gasket does not have this lacquer coating, apply suitable sealer to both sides.

1. Drain cooling system and disconnect battery ground cable.
2. Remove alternator or generator, carburetor air cleaner and fuel line.
3. Disconnect accelerator linkage.
4. Remove vacuum control tube at carburetor and distributor.
5. Disconnect heat indicator sending unit wire.
6. Remove spark plugs.
7. Remove intake manifold, ignition coil and carburetor as a unit.
8. Remove valve lifter chamber cover.
9. Remove rocker arm covers.
10. Remove exhaust manifolds.
11. Remove rocker arm assemblies.
12. Remove push rods.
13. Remove head attaching bolts and take off heads.
14. Installing the heads is a matter of reversing the removal procedure. Tighten attaching bolts in the sequence shown in Fig. 1.

1969-75 Dodge & Dart Six

1. Drain cooling system.
2. Remove carburetor air cleaner and fuel line.
3. Disconnect accelerator linkage.
4. Remove vacuum control tube at carburetor and distributor.
5. Disconnect spark plug wires, heater hose and clamp holding by-pass hose.
6. Disconnect heat indicator sending unit wire.
7. Disconnect exhaust pipe at manifold.
8. Remove intake and exhaust manifold and carburetor as a unit.
9. Remove closed vent system and rocker arm cover.
10. Remove rocker arms and push rods.
11. Remove head bolts and lift off head.
12. Install the head in the reverse order of removal, and tighten the bolts in the sequence shown in Fig. 2.
13. *When installing the manifolds, loosen the three bolts holding the intake and exhaust manifolds together. This is required to maintain proper alignment.* Install intake and exhaust manifolds with cup side of the conical washers against the manifolds.

Dodge V8-273, 318, 340, 360

NOTE: The intake manifold attaching bolts on some engines are tilted upward about 30 degrees at an angle to the manifold-to-cylinder head gasket face. The purpose of this design is to provide more effective sealing at the cylinder block end gaskets. If the intake manifold is removed the installation should be such that the bolt

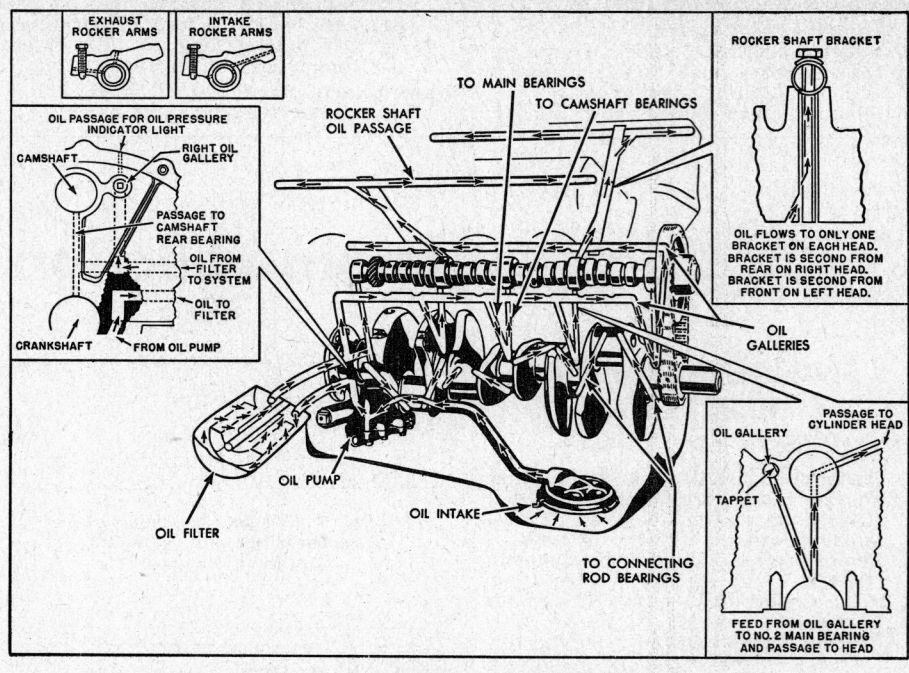

Engine oiling system, V8-273, 318, 340, 360

tightening is done evenly and in the sequence shown in Fig. 4.

With gaskets in place start all bolts, leaving them loose. Run bolts 1 through 4 down so the heads just touch manifold. Then tighten these four bolts to 25 foot-pounds torque. After checking to see that gaskets are properly seated at all surfaces, tighten remaining bolts to 25 foot-pounds. Finally tighten all bolts in the sequence shown to 35 foot-pounds.

1. Drain cooling system and disconnect battery ground cable.
2. Remove alternator, carburetor air cleaner and fuel line. Disconnect accelerator linkage.
3. Remove vacuum advance hose and distributor cap and wires.
4. Disconnect coil wires, heat indicator wire, heater and by-pass hoses.
5. Remove closed ventilation system and rocker arm covers.
6. Remove intake manifold, coil and carburetor as an assembly.
7. Remove exhaust manifolds.
8. Remove rocker arm and shaft assemblies. Remove push rods.
9. Remove head bolts and lift off cylinder heads.
10. Reverse procedure to install heads and tighten bolts in sequence shown in Fig. 5.

V8-383, 400, 426, 440

Rocker arm assemblies can be removed without disturbing the cylinder heads or cooling system. To remove the heads, proceed as follows:
1. Drain cooling system, remove air cleaner, fuel line from pump and carburetor, distributor vacuum tube and

generator.
2. Disconnect throttle linkage at carburetor, distributor cap, coil wires, heat indicator sending unit wire and heater hoses at engine.
3. Remove spark plugs and cables, and engine vent pipe or closed vent system.
4. Remove intake manifold, carburetor and coil as an assembly.
5. Remove exhaust manifolds.
6. Remove cylinder head covers and spark plug cable support brackets.
7. Remove rocker shaft assemblies. *Do not remove bolts from end brackets.*
8. Remove push rods and valve lifter chamber cover.
9. Remove attaching bolts and lift off heads.

NOTE: V8-426 Hemi-Charger engines, in addition to the regular cylinder head bolts, have four stud nuts holding the heads in place. These stud nuts must be removed from inside the tappet chamber before any attempt is made to remove the head.

10. Reverse the foregoing procedure to install the heads and tighten bolts in the sequence shown in Figs. 1 and 3.

V8-426 Hemi-Charger Engine

Cylinder head bolt torque is critical on this engine and in order to obtain proper cylinder head gasket compression, Lubriplate should be applied to the bolt threads and between the bolt head and hardened washer.

NOTE: Care must be taken so as not to get any of the Lubriplate between the hardened washer and bolt boss as this can cause excessive bolt tension and may result in head bolt breakage.

Plymouth 6-170, 198, 225

1. To remove head, drain cooling system.
2. Remove carburetor air cleaner and fuel line.
3. Disconnect accelerator linkage.
4. Remove vacuum control tube at carburetor and distributor.
5. Disconnect spark plug wires, heater hose and clamp holding by-pass hose.
6. Disconnect heat indicator sending unit wire.
7. Disconnect exhaust pipe at manifold.
8. Remove intake and exhaust manifold and carburetor as a unit.
9. Remove vent system and rocker arm cover.
10. Remove thermostat housing and thermostat.
11. Remove rocker arms and push rods.
12. Remove head bolts and lift off head.
13. Check all surfaces of head with a straightedge if there is any reason to suspect leakage. *Cylinder head warpage should not exceed .005" lengthwise or .003" crosswise.* If there is any reason to suspect restricted water passages, the large recessed screw plug in the rear of the head can be removed.
14. Clean the oil return passages in the head and block.
15. Install the head in the reverse order of removal and tighten the bolts in the sequence shown in Fig. 1 and to the torque listed in the *Engine Torque* table.
16. *When installing the manifolds, loosen the three bolts holding the intake manifold to the exhaust manifold. This is required to maintain proper alignment.* Install intake and exhaust manifold with carburetor with the cup side of the conical washers against the manifolds.

Plymouth 1969-75 V8s

NOTE, V8-273: The intake manifold attaching bolts on this engine are tilted upward about 30 degrees at an angle to the manifold-to-cylinder head gasket face. The purpose of this design is to provide more effective sealing at the cylinder block end gaskets. If the manifold is removed the installation should be such that the bolt tightening is done evenly and in the sequence shown in Fig. 4.

With gaskets in place start all bolts, leaving them loose. Run bolts 1 through 4 down so heads just touch manifold. Then tighten these four bolts to 60 inch-pounds torque. After checking to see that gaskets are properly seated at all surfaces, tighten remaining bolts to 60 inch-pounds. Finally, tighten all bolts to 270 inch-pounds.

1. Drain cooling system. Remove air cleaner, fuel line, alternator and distributor vacuum line.
2. Disconnect throttle linkage, coil wires, heat indicator sending unit wire, and heater hoses at engine.

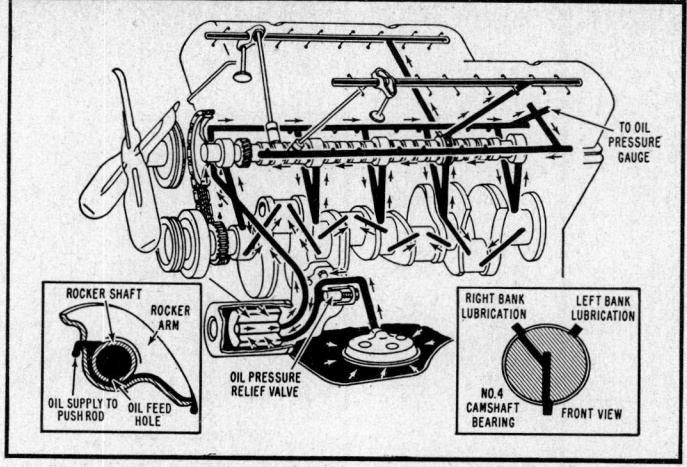

Engine oiling system. V8-383, 400, 426, 440 engines

3. Remove distributor cap and spark plug cables.
4. Remove intake manifold, coil and carburetor as an assembly.
5. On 383, 440, 426 engines, remove valve lifter chamber cover and spark plugs located under exhaust manifolds.
6. On all engines, remove rocker arm covers, closed vent system and exhaust manifolds.
7. On 383, 440, 426 engines, remove rocker arms and shaft assemblies. Lift out push rods and place them in a suitable holder in their respective slots. *On 318 engines, push rods and rocker arms are removed with cylinder head.*
8. Remove head bolts from each head and lift off heads.
9. Reverse the removal procedure to install the heads and tighten head bolts in the sequence shown in the diagrams and to the torque listed in the *Engine Tightening Specifications* table.

V8-426 HEMI-CHARGER: Cylinder head bolt torque is critical on this engine and in order to obtain proper cylinder head gasket compression, Lubriplate should be applied to the bolt threads and between bolt head and hardened washer.

NOTE: Care must be taken so as not to get any Lubriplate between hardened washer and bolt boss as this can cause excessive bolt tension and may result in head bolt breakage.

VALVES, ADJUST

6-170, 198, 225

Before the final valve lash adjustment is made, operate the engine for 30 minutes at a fast idle to stabilize engine temperatures.

Before starting the adjustment procedure, make two chalk marks on the vibration damper. Space the marks approximately 120° apart (⅓ of circumference) so that with the timing mark the damper is divided into three equal parts. Adjust the valves for No. 1 cylinder. Repeat the procedure for the remaining valves, turning the crankshaft ⅓ turn in the direction of normal rotation while adjusting the valves in the firing order sequence of 153624.

V8s With Mechanical Lifters

Engines with mechanical lifters can be identified by the rocker arm adjusting screws. These screws are self-locking and when turning them during the process of adjustment they should indicate some resistance to turning (a minimum of 3 lb. ft. tension). If any screw turns too easily it should be replaced and, if necessary, the rocker arm as well.

Valve clearances should be set up after the engine is warmed up to operating temperature and to the clearances listed in the *Valve Specifications* table.

VALVE ARRANGEMENT

Front to Rear

```
8-318:
  Right Bank . . . . . . . . . . . . I-E-I-E-I-E-I-E
  Left Bank . . . . . . . . . . . . . E-I-E-I-E-I-E-I
8-273, 340, 360 . . . . . . . . . E-I-I-E-E-I-I-E
8-383, 426, 400, 440 . . . . . . E-I-I-E-E-I-I-E
6-170, 198, 225 . . . . . E-I-E-I-E-I-I-E-I-E-I-E
```

VALVE LIFT SPECS

Engine	Year	Intake	Exhaust
6-170	1969	.395	.395
6-198	1970	.395	.395
	1971-74	.406	.414

Engine	Year		
6-225	1969-70	.395	.395
	1971-75	.406	.414
8-273	1969	.373	.399
8-318	1969-75	.373	.399
8-340	1969-73	.429	.444
8-360	1971-74	.410	.412
	1974②	.429	.444
	1975		
	Exc. Hi Perf.	.410	.410
	1975 Hi Perf.	.429	.444
8-383	1969-71①⑥	.425	.435
	1969-71②⑨	.450	.458
8-400	1972-74①	.434	.430
	1972-73②	.449	.464
	1974②	.450	.464
	1975 All	.434	.430
8-426	1969	.467	.473
	1970-71	.490	.481
8-440	1969-71⑨	.425	.435
	1969-71⑬	.450	.458
	1972	.434	.430
	1972-73⑬	.449	.464
	1972-73⑭	.449	.464
	1974-75	.434	.430
	1974⑬	.450	.464

①—2 bar. carb. ②—4 bar. carb.
③—340 H.P.
⑥—330 H.P. ⑦—360 H.P.
⑧—Exc. 330 H.P. ⑨—Exc. 330 H.P.
⑩—Exc. Hi. Perf.
⑬—Hi Perf.
⑭—3 Carbs.

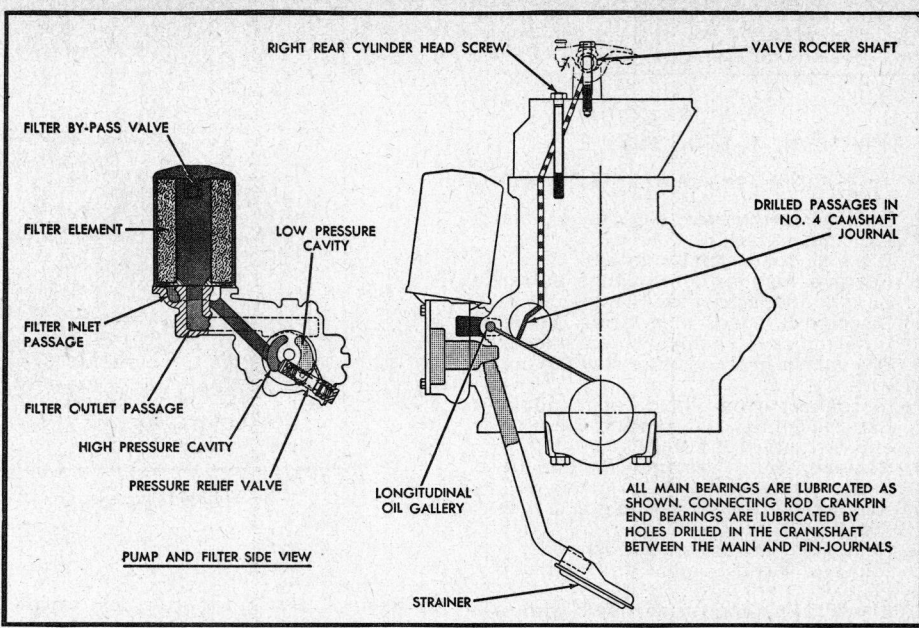

Engine oiling system. 6-170, 198, 225

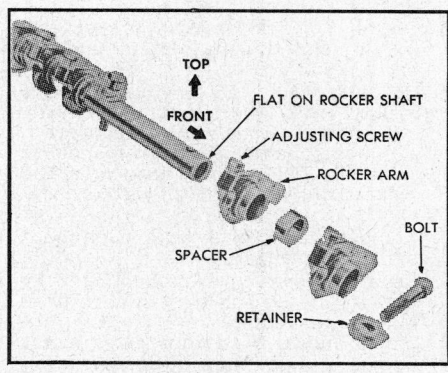

Fig. 6 Rocker arm and shaft assembly. 6-170, 198, 225

8-400	1972-74 2 bar. carb.	18
	1972-74 4 bar. carb.	21
	1975 All	18
8-426	1969-71	36
8-440	1969-75 L/Hi. Perf.	18
	1969-74 W/Hi. Perf.	21

①—2 bar. carb. & 330 H.P.
②—4 bar. carb. exc. 330 H.P.

VALVE TIMING SPECS.

Intake Opens Before TDC

Engine	Year	Degrees
6-170	1969	10
6-198	1970	10
	1971-74	16
6-225	1969-70	10
	1971-75	16
8-273	1969	10
8-318	1969-75	10
8-340	1969-73	22
8-360	1971-74	16
	1974 4 B. C.	20
	1975 Exc. Hi Perf.	18
	1975 Hi Perf.	22
8-383	1969-71①	18
	1969-71②	21

ROCKER ARMS

6-170, 198, 225

1. To remove rocker arms, take off head cover outlet tube.
2. Remove rocker arm cover.
3. Remove rocker shaft bolts and retainers.
4. Lift off rocker arms and shaft.

Inspection

Clean all parts with a suitable solvent. Be sure the inside of the shaft is clean and the oil holes are open. The drilled oil hole in the bore of the rocker arm must be open to the trough and valve end of the arms. The trough also feeds oil to the adjusting screw and push rod.

The shaft should be free from excessive wear in arm contact areas. The shaft should be smooth in retainer contact areas. The adjusting screws in the rocker arms should have a uniform round end. The drag torque should be smooth and uniform. The retainers should be smooth and undamaged in the shaft contact area.

Fig. 7 Notches at end of both rocker arm shafts must face toward center of engine. V8-273 and 1969-75 V8-318, 340, 360

Assemble and Install

1. Referring to Fig. 6, note flat on forward end of rocker shaft which denotes the upper side of the shaft. Rocker arms must be put on the shaft with the adjusting screw to the right side of the engine. Place one of the small retainers on the one long bolt and install the bolt in the rear hole in the shaft from the top side.

2. Install one rocker arm and one spacer; then two rocker arms and a spacer. Continue in same sequence until all rocker arms and spacers are on the shaft.

3. Place a bolt and small retainer in front hole in shaft.

4. Place a bolt and the one *wide* retainer through the center hole in the shaft with six rocker arms on each side of center.

5. Install remaining bolts and retainers, separating the four pairs of rocker arms.

6. Locate the assembly on the cylinder head and position rocker arm adjusting screws in push rods.

7. Tighten bolts finger tight, bringing retainers in contact with the shaft *between rocker arms.*

8. Tighten bolts to specified torque.

9. After running engine to normal operating temperature, adjust valve lash to specifications.

10. Complete the job by installing the remaining parts removed.

V8-273, & 1969-75 V8-318, 340, 360

To provide correct lubrication for the rocker arms on these engines, the rocker shafts have a small notch machined at one end, Fig. 7, and these notches must always face inward toward the center of the engine when installed. In other words, the notched end must be toward the rear of the engine on the right bank, and to the front of the engine on the left bank.

Rocker arms must be correctly positioned on the shaft prior to installation on cylinder head. A good way to do this is to place each rocker arm on the shaft so the adjusting screw is on the same side as the

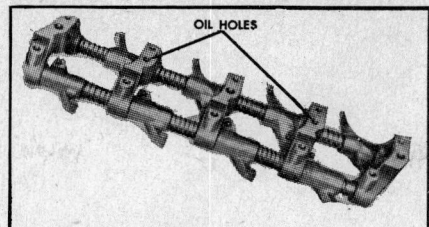

Fig. 8 Rocker arm shaft assembly. V8-426 HP2 engine

notch of the shaft when the rocker arm is right side up.

It is also important when installing the rocker shaft assembly on the cylinder head to position the short retainers at each end and in the center, and to place long retainers in the two remaining positions.

V8-383, 400, 426, 440

1. Install rocker shafts so that the $\frac{3}{16}''$ diameter rocker arm lubrication holes point downward into rocker arm, and so that the 15 degree angle of these holes point outward toward valve end of rocker arm, Figs. 8 and 9. The 15 degree angle is determined from the center line of the bolt holes through the shaft which are used to attach the shaft assembly to the cylinder head.

2. On all engines, install rocker arms and shaft assembly, making sure to install long stamped steel retainers in No. 2 and 4 positions.

NOTE: Use extreme care in tightening the bolts so that valve lifters have time to bleed down to their operating length. Bulged lifter bodies, bent push rods and permanent noisy operation may result if lifters are forced down too rapidly.

3. Installation should be as shown in Fig. 10.

426 Hemi-Charger Service Note

This engine has three different rocker shaft brackets and it is very important that they are positioned as shown in Fig. 11. Because the oil feed holes in the cylinder block are the number 2 and 4 positions, and the number 1 and 3 positions do not have cylinder head gasket beads, mis-location of the brackets can cause either of the following conditions:

1. No. 1 and 3 brackets installed in No. 2 and 4 positions will cause a dry cylinder head.

2. No. 2 and 4 brackets installed in No. 1 and 3 positions will cause a cylinder head gasket leak.

VALVE GUIDES
Non-Removable Type

Valves operate in guide holes bored directly in the cylinder head. When valve stem-to-guide clearance becomes excessive, valves with oversize stems of .005" .015" and .030" are available for service replacement. When necessary to install valves with oversize stems the valve bores should be reamed to provide the proper operating clearance.

VALVE LIFTERS
6-170, 198, 225

After taking off rocker arm and shaft assembly, lift out push rods. The valve lifters may then be removed with a suitably long magnet rod. If the lifters cannot be removed with the magnet rod, a special tool (C-3661) may be used, Fig. 13. Insert the tool through the push rod opening in the cylinder head and into lifter. Turn the handle to expand the tool in the lifter, then with a twisting motion remove the lifter from its bore.

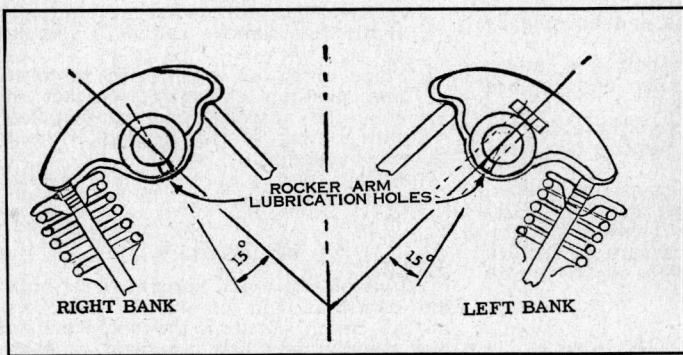

Fig. 9 Rocker arm shaft installation. V8-383, 400, 426, 440

Fig. 10 Rocker arm and shaft assembly installed. 8-273, 383, 400, 426, 440

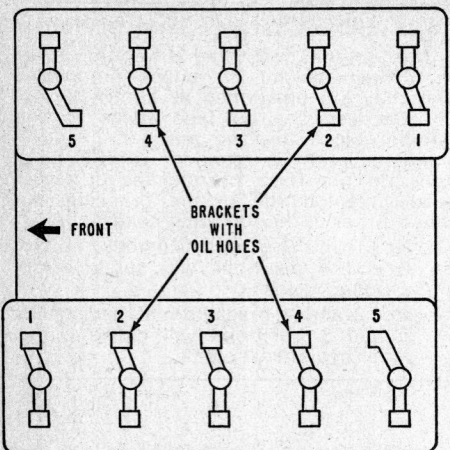

Fig. 11 Valve rocker shaft bracket locations. V8-426 Hemi-Charger engine

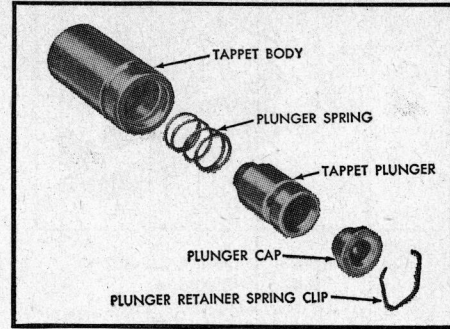

Fig. 12 Hydraulic valve lifter

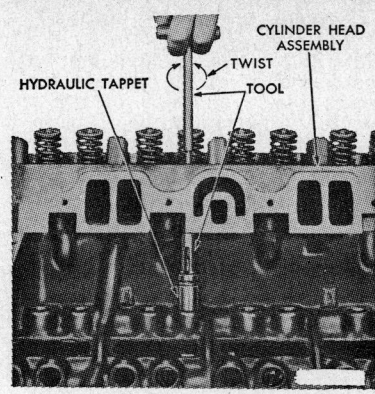

Fig. 13 Removing stuck valve lifter

NOTE

In the aluminum engine, the valve lifters operate in machined bores in the engine and may be rebored to accommodate oversize lifters of .001", .008" and .030".

HYDRAULIC LIFTERS
Lifter, Replace

Chrysler Tool is available for this operation. To remove the lifter, insert the tool in the lifter body. (This portion of the tool can be used to remove lifters without a varnish build-up around the bottom of the body.) Lift the lifter out of the bore, Fig. 12. If they are struck proceed as follows:

Slide the puller portion of the tool through the cylinder head push rod holes and seat it firmly in the top of the lifter. Insert the puller pin through the body and tool shaft in the holes provided, Fig. 13. Grasp the tool handle and pull the lifter out of the bore as shown.

Checking Hydraulic Lifter Static Clearance

After performing a valve grind job or replacing a cylinder head the hydraulic lifters should be collapsed and the valve stem-to-rocker arm clearance checked. Each lifter should be checked individually to guard against differences in machining or wear variables.

Valve stem-to-rocker arm clearance should check within the limits given in the *Valve Specifications* chart. If the actual measured clearance is less than the minimum specified, very likely the valve has been ground down too much and a new valve should be installed.

When the actual measured clearance is more than the maximum specified, the valve face should be ground down further to bring it at or below the maximum static clearance specified.

To check the clearance a special spanner-type tool is commercially available to apply pressure on the rocker arm to bleed down the hydraulic lifter until the plunger is completely bottomed. Of course, checking must be done with the lifter on the heel of the cam. If the special tool is not available, a stiff rod, such as a socket extension, and a length of wire can be used to collapse the lifter. Wire one end of the rod to the rocker arm as close to the valve stem as possible and apply pressure to the other end until the lifter is collapsed.

TIMING CHAIN COVER

NOTE: In order to replace the cover oil seal the cover must be removed from the engine.

6-170, 198, 225

1. To remove cover, drain cooling system and remove radiator and fan.
2. Remove vibration damper with a puller.
3. Loosen oil pan bolts to allow clearance and remove chain case cover.
4. Reverse above procedure to install cover.

V8-383, 400, 426, 440

1. Drain cooling system.
2. Remove radiator, fan and belt.
3. Remove water pump and housing as an assembly.
4. Remove crankshaft bolt and pulley from vibration damper and remove damper with a puller.
5. Remove key from crankshaft. On V8-426 Hemi-Charger, remove two front pan bolts.
6. Remove chain case cover and gasket. *Use extreme caution to avoid damaging the oil pan gasket; if damaged it will be necessary to remove the oil pan in order to install a new pan gasket.*

V8-273, 318, 340, 360

1. Remove radiator, fan and belt.

2. Remove water pump and housing as a unit.
3. Remove crankshaft pulley.
4. Remove key from crankshaft.
5. Remove fuel pump.
6. Remove chain case cover and gasket, *using extreme caution to avoid damaging oil pan gasket otherwise oil pan will have to be removed. It is normal to find particles of neoprene collected between crankshaft seal retainer and oil slinger.*

TIMING CHAIN
6-170, 198, 225

1. After removing chain case cover as outlined above, take off camshaft sprocket attaching bolt.
2. Remove chain with camshaft sprocket.
3. Clean all parts and dry with compressed air.
4. Inspect timing chain for broken or damaged links. Inspect sprockets for cracks and chipped, worn or damaged teeth.

Installation

1. Turn crankshaft so sprocket timing mark is toward and directly in line with centerline of camshaft.
2. Temporarily install camshaft sprocket. Rotate camshaft to position sprocket timing mark toward and directly in line with centerline of crankshaft; then remove camshaft sprocket.
3. Place chain on crankshaft sprocket and position camshaft sprocket in chain so sprocket can be installed with timing marks aligned without moving camshaft, Fig. 15.
4. Install parts removed in reverse order of removal.

V8 Engines

To install chain and sprockets, lay both the camshaft and crankshaft sprockets on the bench. Position the sprockets so that the timing marks are next to each other. Place the chain on both sprockets, then push the gears apart as far as the

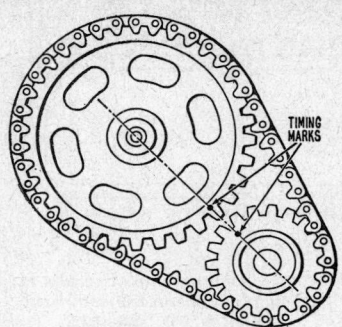

Fig. 15   Valve timing marks aligned for correct valve timing. All Sixes

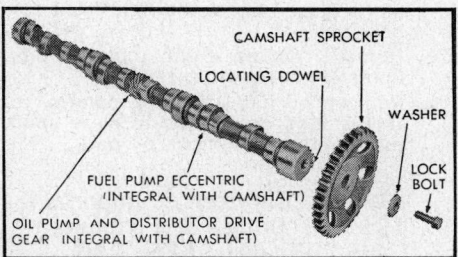

Fig. 17   Camshaft and related parts. 6-170, 198, 225

Fig. 19   Piston and rod assembly. 6-170, 198, 225 engines with cast iron block. On aluminum block engines assemble rod to piston with oil hole toward left side of engine

chain will permit. Use a straightedge to form a line through the exact centers of both gears. The timing marks must be on this line, Fig. 16.

This is the same procedure as in previous models, except that now the alignment is done on the bench rather than on the engine.

Slide the chain with both sprockets on the camshaft and crankshaft at the same time; then recheck the alignment.

CAMSHAFT & BEARINGS
6-170, 198, 225

The camshaft is supported by four precision type, steel backed, babbitt-lined bearings. Rearward thrust is taken by the rear face of the sprocket hub contacting the front of the engine block.

The camshaft, Fig. 17, can be removed after removing the grille, radiator and timing chain. To remove the camshaft bearings, the torque converter (or flywheel) must also be removed.

1. Remove valve lifters, oil pump and distributor.
2. Slide camshaft out of engine.
3. Remove welch plug back of rear camshaft bearing.
4. Remove bearings with suitable puller equipment.
5. Install new bearings, being sure the oil holes in bearings line up with the corresponding oil holes in the crankcase.

V8 Engines

To remove the camshaft, remove all valve lifters, timing chain and sprockets. Remove distributor and oil pump-distributor drive gear. Remove fuel pump and see that push rod has moved away from eccentric drive cam. Withdraw the camshaft from the engine, using care to see that the cam lobes do not damage the camshaft bearings.

If camshaft bearings are to be replaced, it is recommended that the engine be removed from the chassis and the crankshaft taken out in order that any chips or foreign material may be removed from the oil passages.

PISTON & ROD, ASSEMBLE
6-170, 198, 225

Piston and rod assemblies must be installed as shown in Fig. 19.

V8 Engines

When installing piston and rod assemblies in the cylinders, the compression ring gaps should be diametrically opposite one another and not in line with the oil ring gap. The oil ring expander gap should be toward the outside of the "V" of the engine. The oil ring gap should be turned toward the inside of the engine "V".

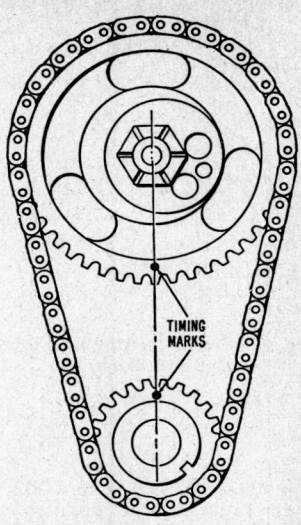

Fig. 16   Valve timing marks aligned for correct valve timing. All V8s

Immerse the piston head and rings in clean engine oil and, with a suitable piston ring compressor, insert the piston and rod assembly into the bore. Tap the piston down into the bore, using the handle of a hammer.

Assembly the pistons to the rods as shown in Fig. 20.

PISTONS, PINS & RINGS

Pistons are available in standard sizes and the following oversizes: V8-440: 005, .020". All others: .005, .020, .040".

Pins are available in the following

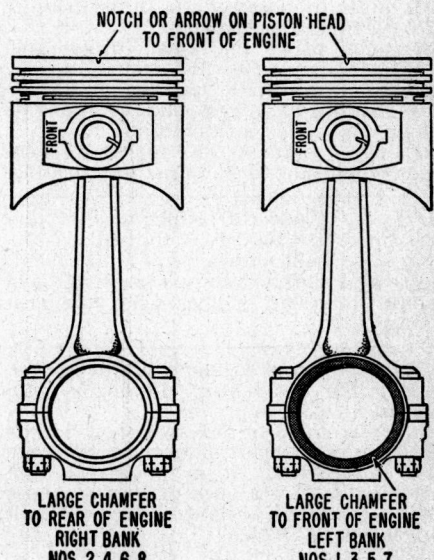

Fig. 20   Piston and rod assembly, V8. On V8-426 Hemi, bearing tangs must face outboard

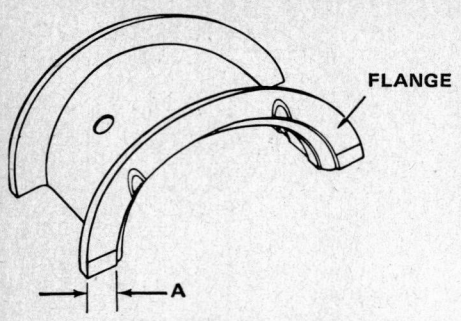

Fig. 20A   Main bearing with small thrust wall flange (A)

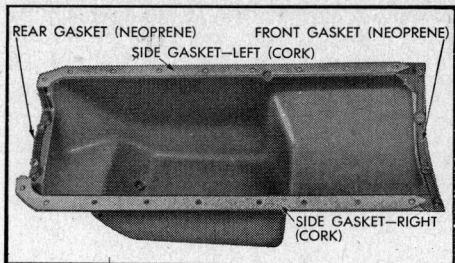

Fig. 21   Location of oil pan gaskets. 6-170, 198, 225

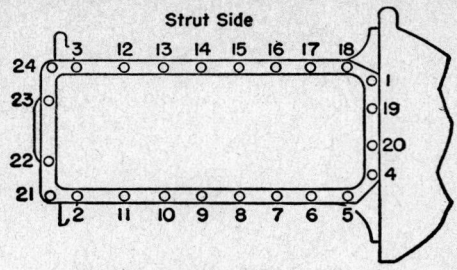

Fig. 22   Tighten oil pan screws to 200 inch pounds in the sequence shown. 6-170, 198, 225

oversizes: V8-273, 318, 426, .003, .008". Not furnished on all other engines.

Rings are available in the following oversizes: 1969 Six and all V8s, std. to .009, .020-.029, .040-.049".

MAIN & ROD BEARINGS

Main bearings are furnished in standard sizes and the following undersizes: 1969-75 Six, .001, .002, .010". 1969-75 V8s, .001, .002, .003, .010, .012".

Rod bearings are furnished in standard sizes and the following undersizes: Six, .001, .002, .003, .010". V8s, .001, .002, .003, .010, .012".

NOTE

Some 1974 V8-400 and V8-440 engines were built with low thrust wall cylinder blocks. These engines require a small thrust wall or flange (No. 3) crankshaft main bearing. The dimension "A" in Fig. 20A, must be noted if the thrust bearing (No. 3) is to be replaced.

Engines using the small thrust wall (flange) bearing, Fig. 20A, can be identified by the yellow "X" painted on the engine identification pad and also engine will be date coded 8-12 on the pad.

All other 1974 V8-400 and V8-440 engines require the large thrust wall bearing.

NOTE: Some 400 CID 2-BBL engines (engine number 4T400-1-03 through 4T400-108) were built with a forged crankshaft requiring a different torque converter and damper than the engines using the cast crankshaft.

This forged crankshaft is normally used only in the 400-4-BBL, HP engine with manual transmission.

If replacement of the crankshaft, torque converter, crankshaft damper or short engine is required, it is important that matching parts are used otherwise severe engine vibration will result, (Consult Chrysler Parts Dept.).

The cast crankshaft engine can be easily identified since it has the letter "E" stamped on the engine numbering pad following the built date.

CRANKSHAFT REAR OIL SEAL

SERVICE BULLETIN

V8-273, 318 SEAL: When oil seal replacement is necessary on these engines, thoroughly clean the bearing cap and block to assure proper seating of the cap. Install a new rope seal in the conventional manner. Then apply an All Purpose cement (Mopar 1316241) on the joint face on the ends of the rope and $\frac{1}{4}$" to each side of the rubber side gaskets. Do not use sealer on the rope where it contacts the crankshaft or near the bearing shell.

SERVICE BULLETIN

V8-383 SIDE SEALS: The side seals used with the crankshaft rear bearing retainer on these engines should be installed in the retainer as rapidly as possible as they are made from a material that expands rapidly when oiled. Apply mineral spirits or kerosene to the seals and install them in the grooves immediately. Install seal retainer and torque to 30 ft-lbs. Failure to pre-oil seals will result in an oil leak.

OIL PAN

CAUTION: *Engine oil pan bolts on all V8-383, 426, 440 engines are $\frac{13}{16}$" long with the exception of two bolts at the rear center of the oil pan. The two rear center bolts are $\frac{9}{16}$" long and thread into the aluminum seal retainer. Do not use longer bolts than $\frac{9}{16}$" at this location as they will bottom in the aluminum seal retainer and, if forced in may strip the threads and damage the seal retainer, causing an oil leak.*

1973-75 Six

1. Drain radiator, disconnect battery and radiator hoses and remove oil dipstick.
2. Remove shroud attaching screws, separate shroud from radiator and position rearward on engine.
3. Raise vehicle and drain oil pan.
4. Remove center link from steering arm and idler arm ball joints.

5. Support front of engine with a jack stand placed under the right front corner of oil pan.
6. Remove engine front mount bolts. Raise engine approx. 1½ to 2".
7. Remove oil pan attaching screws, rotate engine crankshaft to clear counterweights and remove oil pan.

1969-75 Chrysler & Imperial
1969-75 Dodge & Plymouth
V8-383, 400, 426, 440

1. Disconnect battery cable and drain crankcase.
2. Raise car on hoist and disconnect steering linkage from idler arm and pitman arm.
3. Remove outlet vent pipe and disconnect exhaust pipe branches from manifolds.
4. Remove clamp attaching exhaust pipe to extension and remove exhaust pipe.
5. Remove converter dust shield.
6. Remove oil pan bolts and turn flywheel until counterweight and connecting rods at the front end of crankshaft are at their highest position to provide clearance, and lower the pan. Turn the pan to clear oil screen and suction pipe.
7. On some 1974-75 models, it may be necessary to release motor mounts and raise engine approximately 3 inches.

1969-72 Dart & Valiant Six

1. Raise car and drain oil pan.
2. Use a puller to remove steering and idler arm ball joints from steering linkage center link.
3. Remove dust shield and engine mount stud nuts.
4. Lower vehicle and remove horns and mounting brackets, then disconnect battery ground cable.
5. Raise engine from 1½ to 2 inches, using a lifting rig.
6. Again raise vehicle, then remove oil pan.
7. When installing pan, refer to Figs. 21 and 22.

1969-72 Dodge & Plymouth Six

1. Remove oil dipstick, disconnect battery ground cable. Raise vehicle and drain oil.

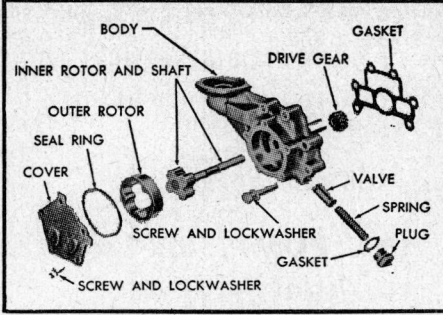

Fig. 23   Oil pump. 6-170, 198, 6-225

OIL PUMP REPAIRS

6-170, 198, 225

To disassemble, remove the pump cover seal ring, Fig. 23. Press off the drive gear, supporting the gear to keep load off aluminum body. Remove rotor and shaft and lift out outer pump rotor. Remove oil pressure relief valve plug and lift out spring and plunger. Remove oil pressure sending unit.

Inspection

1. The rotor contact area and the bores for the shaft and valve in the pump body should be smooth, free from scratches, scoring or excessive wear.
2. The pump cover should be smooth, flat and free from scoring or ridges. Lay a straightedge across the cover. If a .0015″ feeler gauge can be inserted under the straightedge, the cover should be replaced.
3. All surfaces of the outer rotor should be smooth and uniform, free from ridges, scratches or uneven wear. Discard a rotor less than .649″ thick and/or less than 2.469″ in diameter.
4. The inner rotor and shaft assembly should be smooth, free from scoring and uneven wear. Discard rotors less than .649″ thick.
5. Place outer rotor in pump body and measure clearance between rotor and body. Discard pump body if clearance is more than .014″.
6. Install inner rotor and shaft in pump body. Shaft should turn freely but without side play. If clearance between rotor teeth is more than .010″, replace both rotors.
7. Measure rotor end clearance. If feeler gauge of more than .004″ can be inserted between straightedge and rotors, install a new pump body.
8. The oil pressure relief valve should be smooth, free from scratches or scoring, and should be a free fit in its bore.
9. Relief valve springs are painted either gray, red or brown to denote free lengths of 2.19, 2.29 and 2.39 inches. Rather than change the length, replace a spring with one of the same color.

Assemble and Install

1. With pump rotors in body, press drive gear on shaft, flush with end of shaft.
2. Install seal ring in groove in body and install cover. Tighten bolts to 10 ft. lbs. Test pump for free turning.
3. Install oil pressure relief valve spring. Use new washer (gasket) and tighten plug securely.
4. If pump shaft turns freely, remove pump cover and outer rotor before installation of pump on engine.
5. Install oil pressure sending unit and tighten to 60 inch lbs. (5 ft. lbs.)
6. Using a new gasket, install pump on engine and tighten bolts to 200 inch lbs. (16 ft. lbs.)

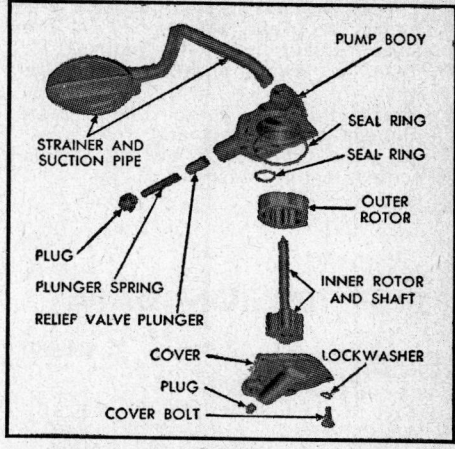

Fig. 24   Oil pump. V8-383, 426, 440

7. Install oil filter reservoir on pump. Install filter element and tighten cover nuts to 25 ft. lbs.
8. Connect oil pressure sending unit wire.
9. Complete the installation by reversing steps as given under Oil Pump, Replace.

V8 Engines

After removing the pump from the engine it should be disassembled, cleaned and inspected for wear, Fig. 24.

1. Remove the cotter pin holding the oil strainer to the oil suction pipe. Then remove the pipe from the pump body.
2. Remove the pump cover and discard the oil seal ring.
3. Remove pump rotor and shaft and lift out rotor body.
4. Remove oil pressure relief valve plug and lift out the spring and plunger.
5. Wash all parts in cleaning solvent and inspect carefully for damage or wear.
6. The mating face of the oil pump cover should be smooth. If it is scratched or grooved, the cover should be replaced with a new one.
7. Check for excessive cover-to-rotor wear by laying a straight edge across the cover surface. If a .0015″ feeler gauge can be inserted between cover and straight edge, the cover should be discarded and a new one installed.
8. Slide rotor body and rotor into pump body and then place a straight edge across the face of the pump body between the bolt holes. If a feeler gauge of less than .003″ or more than .006″ can be inserted between the rotors and straight edge, install a new pump body.
9. Remove the pump rotor and shaft, leaving rotor body in pump cavity. Press rotor body to one side with the fingers and measure the clearance between rotor and pump bodies. If it is more than .014″, install a new pump body.

2. Use a puller to remove steering and idler arm ball joints from steering center link. Remove dust shield.
3. Remove oil pan bolts, rotate engine crankshaft to clear counterweights, then remove oil pan.
4. When installing pan, refer to Figs. 21 and 22.

1969-75 V8-273, 318, 340, 360

1. Disconnect battery ground cable.
2. Remove oil level dipstick.
3. Raise vehicle and drain oil.
4. Remove engine-to-torque converter left housing brace.
5. Remove steering and idler arm ball joints from steering center link.
6. Remove exhaust crossover pipe from exhaust manifolds and leave it hang without disconnecting it from muffler.
7. On some models it will be necessary to remove crossover pipe.
8. On some 1974-75 models, it may be necessary to release motor mounts and raise engine approximately 3 inches.
9. Unfasten and remove oil pan.

OIL PUMP, REPLACE

1969-75 Six Cylinder

1. Drain radiator and disconnect upper and lower hoses.
2. Remove fan shroud (if equipped).
3. Raise vehicle on a hoist, support front of engine with a jack stand place under right front corner of engine oil pan. *Do not support engine at crankshaft pulley or vibration damper.*
4. Remove front engine mounts.
5. Raise engine 1½ to 2 inches.
6. Remove oil filter, pump attaching bolts and remove pump assembly.

V8 Engines

On 273, 318, 340, 360 engines, remove oil pump from rear main bearing cap.

On 383, 400, 426, 440 engines, unfasten oil pump from engine and remove pump and filter assembly from bottom of engine.

10. Check the clearance between the pump rotor and rotor body. If the measurement is more than .014", install a new pump rotor and rotor body.

11. Check the oil pump relief valve plunger for scoring and free operation in its bore. If the plunger is scored, install a new one.

BELT TENSION DATA

	New[1]	Used[1]
1969-70—		
Air Condition—		
Exc. Six Cylinder	1/8	3/16
Six Cylinder	3/32	1/8
Alternator—		
With A/C—		
Exc. V8-273, 318 & 340	3/16	9/32
V8-273, 318 & 340	1/8	3/16
Without A/C—		
Six Cylinder	3/16	9/32
V8-273, 318 & 340	1/8	3/16
V8-383, 426 Hemi & 440	3/32	3/16
Fan	1/16	3/32
Power Steering	3/32	5/32
1971-75 All	120[2]	70[2]

[1]—Deflection measured in inches.
[2]—Belt tension in ft. lbs.

WATER PUMP, REPLACE

CAUTION: When it becomes necessary to remove a fan clutch of the silicone type, the assembly must be supported in the vertical position to prevent leaks of silicone fluid from the clutch mechanism. This loss of fluid will render the fan clutch inoperative.

Drain cooling system, and on air conditioned cars only remove upper half of fan shroud. Loosen power steering pump or idler pulley, and generator. Remove all belts, fan, space and pulley.

On air conditioned cars, remove pulley from water pump fan hub, loosen all nuts from fan and remove the fan drive.

On some air conditioned cars, it may be necessary to remove the compressor bracket and/or air pump bracket and tie the compressor and/or air pump out of the way.

On all models, remove bolts holding water pump body to housing and remove water pump.

Service Bulletin

CORE HOLE PLUG SIZES: When replacing a cup-type core hole plug in an engine, the size of the hole in the cylinder head, water jacket or rear bearing bore for the camshaft should be checked. At these locations a 1/16" oversize hole is sometimes bored in production and an oversize core plug installed.

Core plugs 1/16" oversize are available for replacement should they be required at these locations.

FUEL PUMP PRESSURE

Year	Engine	Pressure Lbs.
CHRYSLER & IMPERIAL		
1969-71	All	3½-5
1972	V8-360	5-7
1972-75	V8-400	3½-5
1972-75	V8-440 Chrysler	3½-5
1972-73	V8-440 Imperial	5½-7
1974-75	V8-440 Imperial	3½-5

DODGE & PLYMOUTH

1969-75	Six	3½-5
1969-75	V8-273, 318, 340, 360	5-7
1969-71	V8-383	3½-5
1969-71	V8-440 (Exc. Hi-Perf.)	3½-5
1969-71	V8-440 Hi-Perf.	6-7½
1969-71	V8-326	7-8½
1972-75	V8-440, 440[1]	3½-5

[1]V8-440 Hi-Perf. 6-7½ lbs.

FUEL PUMP, REPLACE

Electric Fuel Pump

The 1972 Imperial equipped with an Air Injection pump employs a Bendix electric fuel pump. It is mounted on the left side of the frame in the kick up area about even with the front of the fuel tank. When replacing the pump it must be mounted so that the outlet is higher than the inlet. This is critical to pump operation.

Mechanical Fuel Pump

SERVICE NOTE: Before installing the pump, it is good practice to crank the engine so that the nose of the camshaft eccentric is out of the way of the fuel pump rocker arm when the pump is installed. In this way there will be the least amount of tension on the rocker arm, thereby easing the installation of the pump.

1. Remove all gasket material from the pump and block gasket surfaces. Apply sealer to both sides of new gasket.
2. Position gasket on pump flange and hold pump in position against its mounting surface. Make sure rocker arm is riding on camshaft eccentric.
3. Press pump tight against its mounting. Install retaining screws and tighten them alternately.
4. Connect fuel lines. Then operate engine and check for leaks.

Clutch and Transmission Section

NOTE: 1975 linkage adjustment information is in this section. Repair procedures on both automatic and manual shift transmissions are covered elsewhere in this manual. Procedures for removing automatic transmissions as well as linkage adjustments on 1969-74 models are included in the automatic transmission chapters. See Chapter Index.

CLUTCH PEDAL, ADJUST
1969-75 All Cars

1. Inspect condition of clutch pedal rubber stop, if stop is damaged install a new one.
2. Where necessary, disconnect interlock clutch rod at transmission end.
3. Adjust linkage by turning self-locking adjusting nut to provide 5/32" free movement at outer end of fork. This movement will provide the prescribed one-inch free play at pedal.
4. Assemble interlock clutch rod (if used) to transmission pawl.

CLUTCH, REPLACE

Unless special clutch rebuilding equipment is available, it is recommended that the clutch assembly be exchanged for a rebuilt unit should the clutch require rebuilding. The driven disc, however, may be replaced without special equipment. If clutch rebuilding equipment is available, follow the equipment manufacturer's instructions.

Removal

1. Remove transmission and clutch pan.
2. Pull out release bearing and sleeve.
3. Mark clutch cover and flywheel so they may be assembled in the same

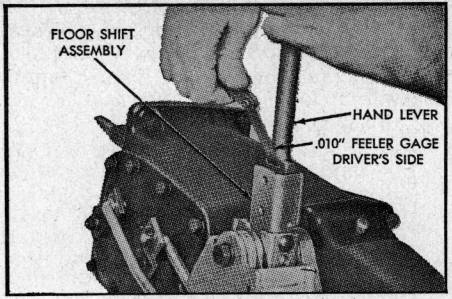

Fig. 1   Removing floor shift handle. 1969-75

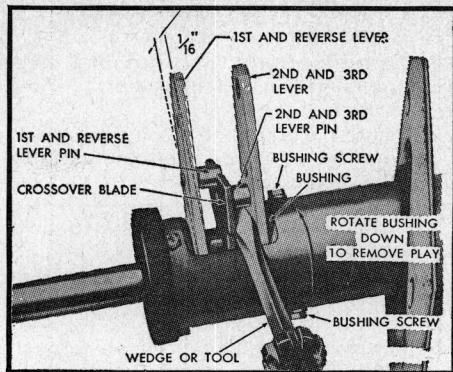

Fig. 2   Gearshift lever adjustment. 1969 Three Speed Transmission

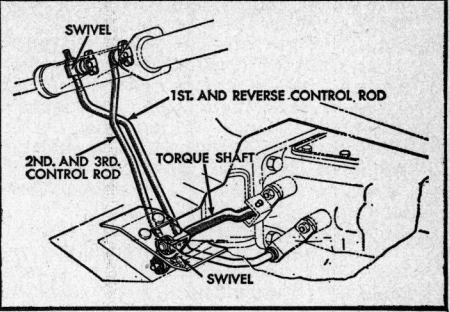

Fig. 3   Gearshift controls. 1969-75 Three Speed Transmission

relative position and thus maintain original balance.

4. Remove cap screws which retain clutch cover to flywheel. Loosen each screw a few turns in succession until cover is free.

5. Clutch assembly and driven disc may now be removed from the housing.

Installation

1. Coat the pilot bearing in crankshaft with wheel bearing grease.
2. Clean surfaces of flywheel and pressure plate, making certain no oil or grease remains on these parts.
3. Hold cover plate and disc in place and insert a special clutch aligning tool or a spare clutch shaft through the hub of the disc and into the crankshaft pilot bearing.
4. Bolt clutch cover loosely to flywheel, being sure marks previously made are lined up.
5. To avoid distortion of clutch cover, tighten cover bolts a few turns each in progression until all are tight. The final tightening should be 15-20 ft-lbs. for 5/16" bolts and 30 ft-lbs. for 3/8" bolts.
6. Install transmission by guiding it into place with guide studs inserted in the two top holes of the housing.
7. Adjust clutch pedal free travel.

THREE SPEED TRANSMISSION, REPLACE

1969-71 Chrysler, 1969-75 Dodge & Plymouth

1. Drain lubricant from transmission.
2. Disconnect propeller shaft, speedometer cable and housing and gearshift control rods.
3. Remove speedometer cable with hand so that housing is not crushed.
4. Disconnect back-up lamp switch leads (if so equipped) and if necessary, loosen exhaust system for clearance.
5. Support engine with a jack or suitable fixture against underside of oil pan flange.
6. Raise engine slightly and disconnect

extension housing from removable center crossmember.

7. Support transmission with a suitable jack. Then tap out four long bolts and remove center crossmember. Remove bolts that attach transmission to clutch housing.
8. Slide transmission rearward until clutch shaft clears clutch disc before lowering transmission. Lower and remove transmission.
9. Reverse removal procedure to install.

FOUR SPEED TRANSMISSION, REPLACE

1969-75 Dodge & Plymouth

1. Remove console and shift components.

NOTE: On 1969 models, the shift lever is removed by using a .010" feeler gauge as shown in Fig. 1 to release internal spring clip. When re-installing lever, push it down into shift unit far enough for spring to click and lock lever in place.

2. Drain fluid from transmission.

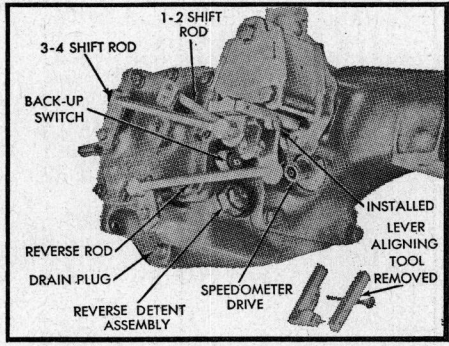

Fig. 4   Gearshift linkage adjustment. 1969 four speed transmission

3. Disconnect propeller shaft at rear universal joint and carefully pull yoke out of extension housing. *Be careful not to scratch or nick ground surface on sliding spline yoke during removal and installation of shaft.*
4. Disconnect speedometer cable and stop light switch leads.
5. Disconnect left-hand exhaust pipe (dual exhaust) from manifold.
6. Disconnect parking cable where necessary.
7. Support rear of engine with a jack.
8. Raise engine slightly and disconnect extension housing from removable center crossmember.
9. Support transmission with a suitable jack and remove center crossmember.
10. Remove transmission-to-clutch housing bolts.
11. Slide transmission rearward and out of vehicle.
12. Reverse procedure to install.

SHIFT LINKAGE, ADJUST THREE SPEED TRANS.

1969-75

1. With 2-3 control rod disconnected from lever on steering column and 1st-reverse rod disconnected from transmission lever, position both transmission levers in neutral.

NOTE: The neutral detent balls must be engaged to make this adjustment. To check this, start engine (clutch disengaged) then release clutch slowly.

2. Inspect fore and aft movement of shift levers in steering column. If movement at outer end of levers exceeds 1/16", loosen two upper bushing screws, Fig. 2, and rotate bushing downward until all free play of levers has been removed. Then retighten bushing screws.
3. Wedge a screwdriver between crossover blade and the 2-3 lever so that

crossover blade is engaged with both lever crossover pins.

4. Adjust length of 2-3 control rod until stud shaft of control rod and swivel enters hole in column lever, Fig. 3. Install washer and clip and tighten swivel lock nut. During the above setting the 2-3 control rod should be adjusted also to position selector lever on column 5°-10° above horizontal.

5. Slide clamp and swivel (on end of 1st-reverse control rod) either in or out until swivel stub shaft enters hole in transmission lever, Fig. 3. Install washers and clip. Determine middle backlash position in linkage, then tighten control rod lock nut.

6. Remove screwdriver from crossover blade and lever. Then move selector lever through all positions to check adjustments and to insure crossover smoothness.

SHIFT LINKAGE, ADJUST FOUR SPEED TRANS.

1969-75 Four Speed Trans.

NOTE: 1970-75 floor shift linkages incorporate a transmission lock rod. This rod is adjusted after the shift linkage as follows:

1. Loosen rod swivel clamp bolt.
2. Place transmission in reverse.
3. Align steering column locating slots and install a suitable tool to hold position.
4. Tighten clamp bolt. Column should now lock in reverse but not in any other gear.

1. Install lever alignment tool to hold levers in neutral, Fig. 4.
2. Shift transmission into neutral, then disconnect all control rods from transmission levers.
3. Insert lever alignment tool through slots in levers, making sure it is through all levers and against the back plate.
4. Adjust length of control rods so they enter transmission levers freely without any rearward or forward movement.
5. Secure adjustment and remove tool.
6. Check linkage for ease of shifting into all gears and for crossover smoothness.

1975 AUTO. TRANS. LINKAGE, ADJUST

Column Shift

1. Place gearshift lever in PARK and

lock steering column with key.
2. Move control lever on transmission all the way to rear (PARK).
3. Set adjustable rod to proper length with no load in either direction.
4. Check as follows:
   a. Shift effort must be free and detents feel crisp. All gate stops must be positive.
   b. Detent position must be close enough to gate stops in neutral and drive to assure that hand lever will not remain out of detent when placed against gate and then released.
   c. Key start must occur with shift lever held down against PARK gate.

Console Shift

1. At steering column upper end, line up locating slots in bottom of shift housing and bearing housing. Install suitable tool to hold alignment and lock column with ignition key.
2. Place console lever in PARK and move shift control lever on transmission all the way to rear (PARK).
3. Set adjustable rods to proper length with no load applied in either direction.
4. Check adjustment as described above for column shift.

Rear Axle, Propeller Shaft & Brakes

NOTE: Figs. 1 and 2 illustrate the various rear axle assemblies used on these cars. When necessary to overhaul any of these units, refer to the *Rear Axle Specifications* table in this chapter.

INTEGRAL TYPE REAR AXLE

Two types of integral carrier axles are used. In both types, the drive pinion is mounted in two opposing tapered roller bearings which are preloaded by a spacer positioned between them.

In the unit shown in Fig. 1, used from 1969 through 1975, the differential is supported by two tapered roller side bearings. These bearings are preloaded by spacers located between the bearings and carrier housing. The differential assembly is positioned for ring and pinion backlash by varying these spacers.

Axle shafts in this unit are held in place by retainers at the outer ends of the shafts. These retainers are bolted

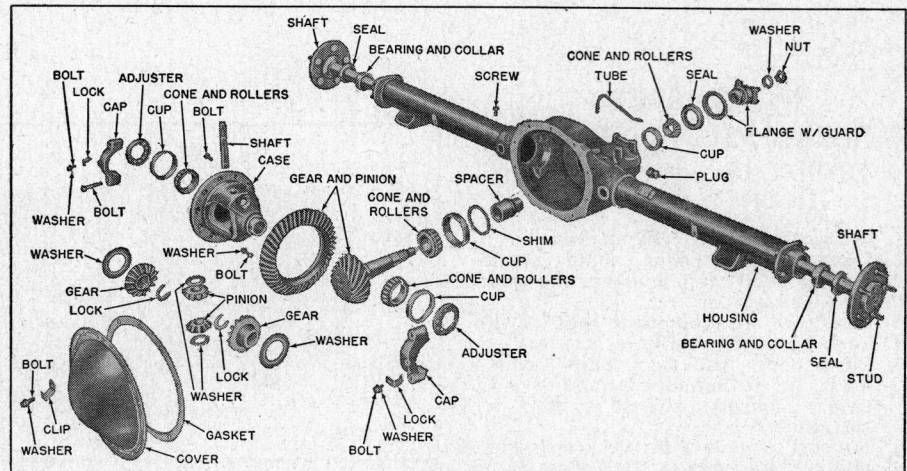

Fig. 2   Integral "C" washer type rear axle. 1969-75

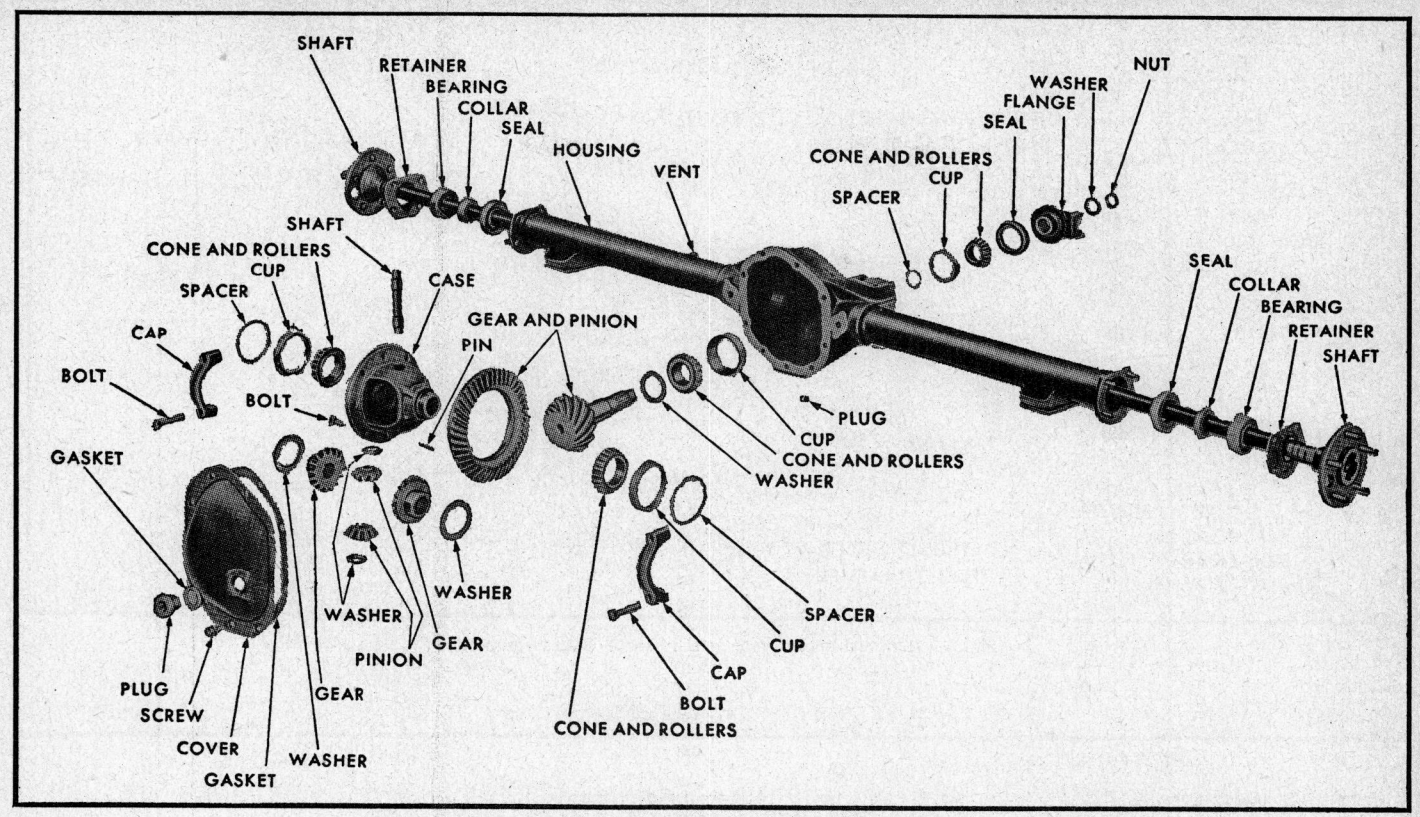

Fig. 1   Integral rear axle. 1969-75

through the brake backing plates to the rear axle tubes.

In the unit shown in Fig. 2, introduced in 1969, the differential is also supported by two tapered roller bearings. A threaded differential bearing adjuster is located in each bearing pedestal cap to eliminate differential side play, adjust and maintain ring and pinion backlash and provide a means of obtaining differential bearing preload.

Axles are retained by means of a "C" washer which is installed into a groove in the inner end of the axle shaft inside the differential unit.

On both these units, a removable stamped steel cover, bolted to the rear of the carrier, permits inspection and service of the differential without removal of the complete axle assembly from the vehicle.

Axle Shaft, Renew (Fig. 1 Type)

1. With wheel removed, remove clips holding brake drum on wheel studs and remove drum.
2. Disconnect brake lines at wheel cylinders.
3. Using access hole in axle flange, remove retainer nuts from end of housing.
4. Remove axle shaft and brake assembly, using a slide hammer-type puller.
5. Remove brake assembly from axle shaft with care to avoid damaging shaft in seal contact area.

6. Remove oil seal from axle housing.
7. *Remove axle shaft bearings only when necessary. Removal of bearings makes them unfit for further use.*
8. *Axle shaft end play is pre-set and not adjustable. End play is accomplished by the amount of end play built into the bearings. The two axle housing brake support plate gaskets on each side are used for sealing purposes only. Always replace the gaskets once they have been removed.*
9. Press bearing and collar on shaft firmly against shoulders on shaft.

Fig. 3   Location of "C" washer locks

10. Install new oil seal in housing.
11. Install brake assembly on axle housing and carefully slide axle shaft through oil seal and into side gear splines.
12. Tap end of axle shaft lightly to position axle shaft bearing into bearing bore and attach retainer plate to housing.
13. Install brake drums and wheels.

Axle Shaft, Renew (Fig. 2 Type)

1. With wheel and brake drum removed, or caliper and rotor assembly removed, loosen differential housing cover and drain lubricant. Remove cover.
2. Turn differential case to make pinion shaft lock screw accessible and remove lock screw and shaft.
3. Push axle shaft inward toward center of car and remove "C" washer from groove in axle shaft, Fig. 3.
4. Remove axle shaft from housing, being careful not to damage the axle bearing, which will remain in the housing.
5. The axle bearing and/or seal can now be removed if necessary.
6. Reverse procedure to install.

REMOVABLE CARRIER TYPE

In these rear axles, Figs. 4 and 5, the drive pinion is mounted in two tapered

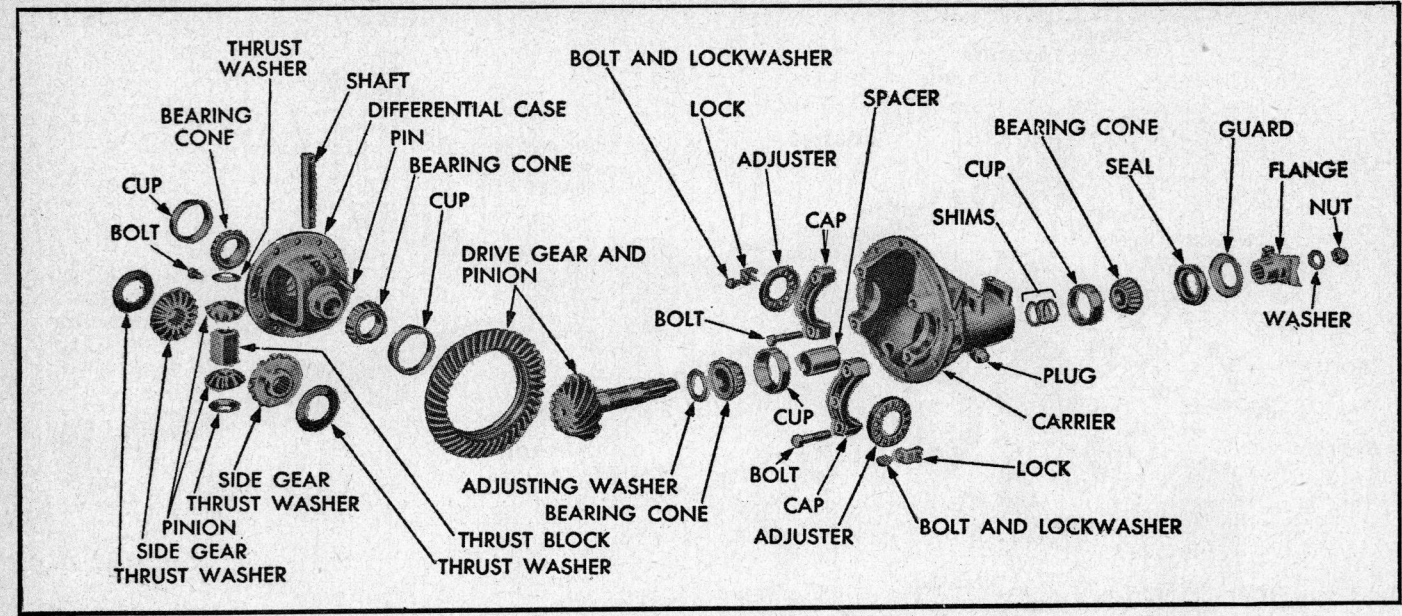

Fig. 4 Removable type rear axle assembly with large pinion

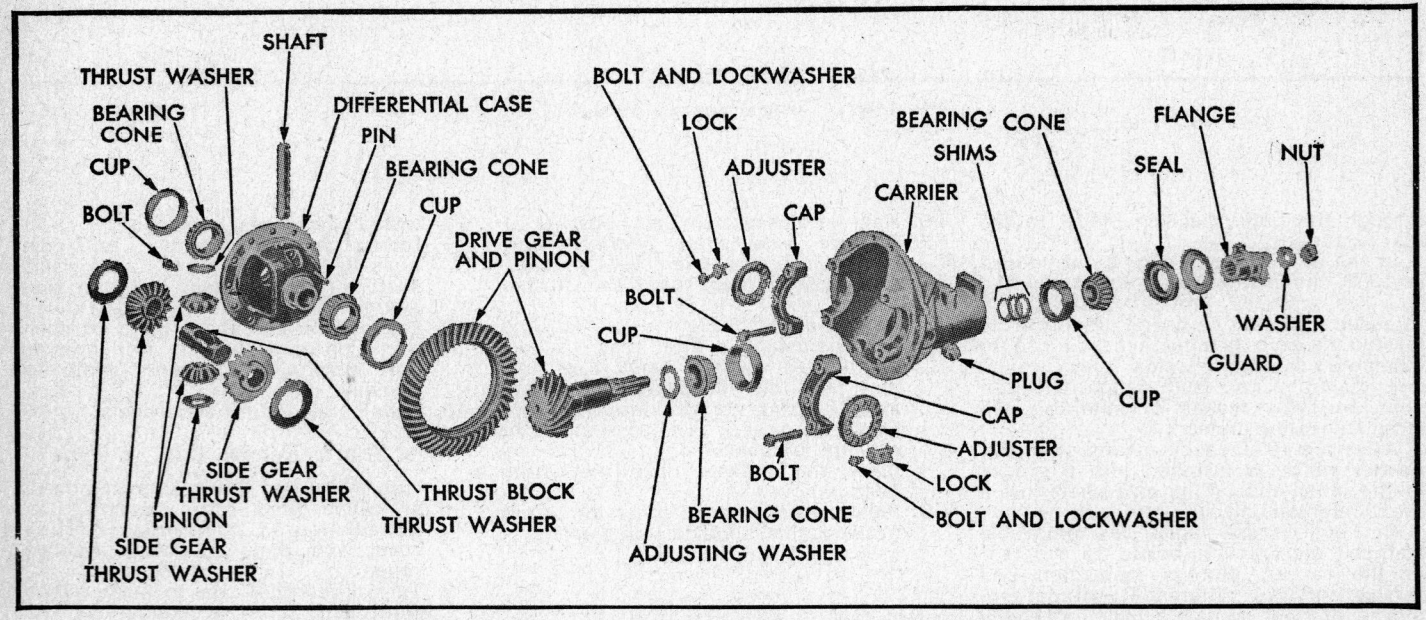

Fig. 5 Removable type rear axle assembly with small pinion

roller bearings. The bearings are preloaded by a spacer and shims behind the front bearing. The drive pinion is positioned by an adjusting washer between the head of the drive pinion and the rear pinion bearing. The front bearing is held in place by a large washer and nut.

The differential is supported in the carrier by two tapered roller side bearings. These bearings are preloaded by two threaded ring nuts between the bearings and the pedestals. The differential assembly is positioned for proper ring

gear and pinion backlash by varying the adjustment of these ring nuts. The differential case houses two side gears in mesh with two pinions mounted on a pinion shaft which is held in place by a lock pin. The side gears and pinions are backed up by thrust washers. Side thrust of the wheels is transferred from one axle shaft to the other by means of a thrust block in the center of the differential case.

Carrier, Remove & Replace

It is not necessary to remove the rear

axle assembly for any normal repairs. The axle shafts and carrier assembly can easily be moved from the vehicle, leaving the rear axle housing in place.

1. Remove axle shafts as outlined below.
2. Disconnect rear universal joint and move propeller shaft out of the way. Support shaft to relieve strain on the front universal joint.
3. Remove lubricant from axle housing with a suction gun.
4. Remove attaching nuts and lift car-

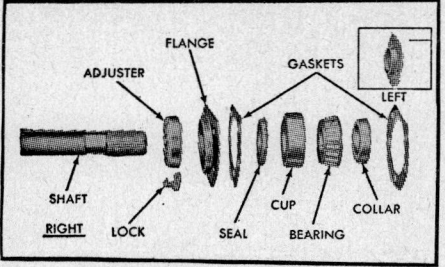

Fig. 6   Axle shaft disassembled

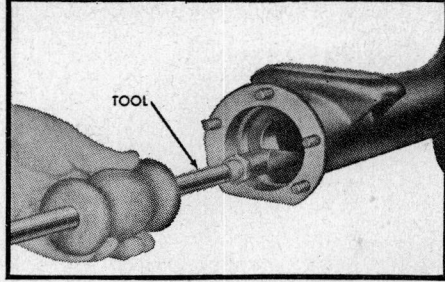

Fig. 8   Removing inner oil seal

Fig. 10   Notching bearing retainer collar

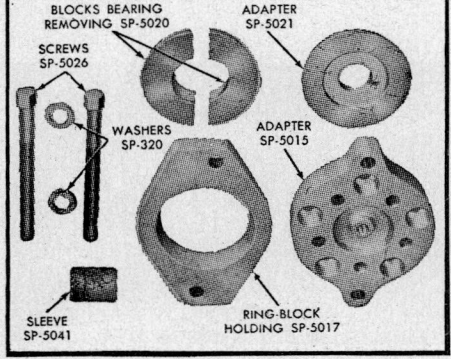

Fig. 7   Tool set for removing axle shaft

Fig. 9   Installing inner oil seal

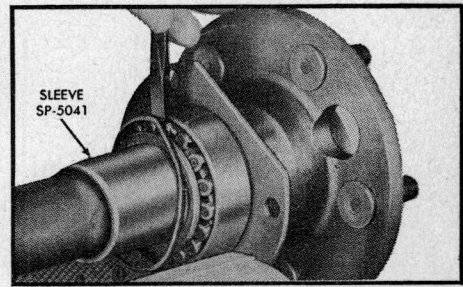

Fig. 11   Removing roller retainer

rier assembly out of axle housing.

5. Reverse removal procedure to install.

Axle Shaft, Renew (1969-70)

1. With wheels removed, remove clips holding brake drum on axle shaft studs and remove brake drum.
2. Using access hole in axle shaft flange, remove retainer nuts. The right shaft with threaded adjuster in retainer plate will have a lock under one of the studs that should be removed at this time, Fig. 6.
3. Remove parking brake strut.
4. Attach axle shaft remover tool, Fig. 7, to axle shaft flange and remove axle shaft. Remove brake assembly and foam gaskets.
5. Remove oil seal, Fig. 8.

Fig. 12   Flange ground off inner bearing cone

6. Wipe axle shaft housing seal bore clean and install a new seal, Fig. 9.

Disassembly

To prevent the possibility of damaging axle shaft seal surface, slide a protective sleeve over seal surface next to bearing collar, Fig. 10.

1. Position axle shaft bearing collar on a heavy vise and, using a chisel, cut deep grooves into retaining collar at 90-degree intervals, as shown in Fig. 10. This will enlarge bore of collar and permit it to be driven off axle shaft.
2. Remove bearing roller retainer flange by cutting off lower edge with a chisel, Fig. 11.
3. Grind a section off flange of inner bearing cone, Fig. 12, and remove bearing rollers, Fig. 13.
4. Pull bearing roller retainer down as far as possible and cut with side cutters and remove, Fig. 14.
5. Remove roller bearing cup and protective sleeve from axle shaft.

CAUTION: Sleeve should not be used as a protector for the seal journal when pressing off bearing cone as it was not designed for this purpose.

6. To avoid scuffing seal journal when bearing cone is being removed, it should be protected by a single wrap of .002" shim stock held in place by a rubber band, Fig. 15.
7. Remove bearing cone with tool set shown in Fig. 7. Tighten bolts of tool alternately until cone is removed, Fig. 16.
8. Remove seal in bearing retainer plate

and replace with a new seal.

Assembly

1. Install retainer plate and seal on axle shaft.
2. Install new axle shaft bearing cup, cone and collar on shaft, using tool shown in Fig. 17. Tighten bolts of tool alternately until bearing and collar are seated properly.
3. Inspect axle shaft seal journal for scratches and polish with #600 crocus cloth if necessary.
4. Lubricate wheel bearings with approved grease.

Installation

1. Clean axle shaft flange face and install new gasket followed by brake support plate on left side of axle housing.

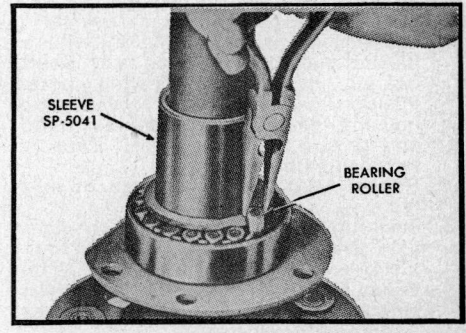

Fig. 13   Removing bearing rollers

Fig. 14 Cutting out bearing retainer

Fig. 17 Installing bearing and collar

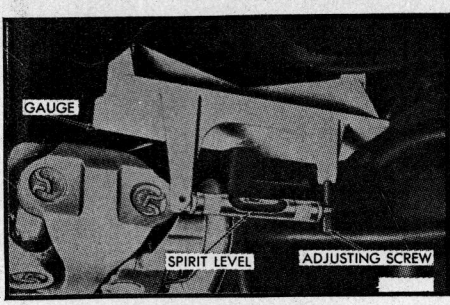

Fig. 19 Measuring rear axle angle. 1969-70 Imperial

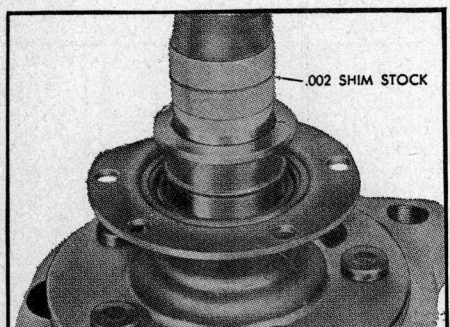

Fig. 15 Seal journal protection

Fig. 18 Measuring axle shaft end play

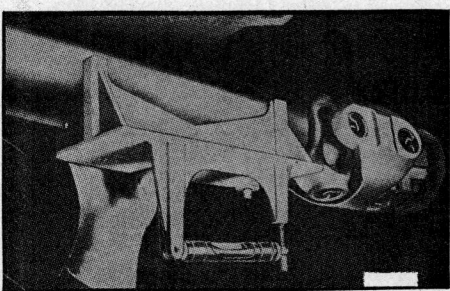

Fig. 20 Measuring propeller shaft angle. 1969-70 Imperial

Fig. 16 Removing bearing cone

2. Install foam gasket on studs of axle housing and slide shaft through oil seal and engage splines in differential side gear.
3. Tap end of axle shaft lightly with a plastic mallet to position axle shaft bearing in housing bearing bore. Position retainer plate over axle housing studs. Install retainer nuts and torque to 30-35 ft-lbs. Start by tightening bottom nut.
4. Repeat Step 1 on right side of axle housing.
5. Back off threaded adjuster on right axle shaft until inner face of adjuster is flush with inner face of retainer plate. Carefully slide axle shaft through oil seal and engage splines in differential side gears.
6. Repeat Step 3.

Axle Shaft End Play

When setting end play both rear wheels must be off the ground, otherwise a false end play setting will occur.

1. Using a dial indicator mounted as shown in Fig. 18, turn the adjuster clockwise until both wheel bearings are seated and there is zero end play in axle shafts. Back off adjuster counterclockwise four notches to establish an axle shaft end play of .013-.023".
2. Tap end of axle shaft lightly with a plastic mallet to seat right wheel bearing cup against adjuster, and rotate axle shaft several revolutions so that a true end play reading is indicated.
3. Remove one retainer plate nut and install adjuster lock. If tab on lock does not mate with notch in adjuster, turn adjuster slightly until it does. Install nut and torque to 30-35 ft-lbs.
4. Recheck axle shaft end play. If not within prescribed limits, repeat adjustment procedure.
5. Remove dial indicator and install brake drum, drum retaining clips and wheel.

PROPELLER SHAFT
One Piece Shaft, 1969

1. Remove both rear universal joint

roller and bushing assembly clamps from pinion yoke. Do not disturb retaining strap holding roller assemblies on cross.
2. If equipped with sliding yoke front joint, lower front of vehicle slightly to prevent loss of transmission oil and pull drive shaft out as an assembly. If equipped with ball and trunnion front joint, disconnect joint from transmission.
3. To install sliding yoke type, carefully slide yoke into splines on transmission output shaft. For ball and trunnion type, connect front universal to transmission flange and torque retaining nuts to 35 ft. lbs.
4. Align rear of propeller shaft with pinion yoke and position roller and bushing assemblies into seats of pinion yoke.
5. Install bushing clamps and tighten clamp bolts to 170 inch lbs.

PROP. SHAFT ANGLES
One Piece Shaft, 1969-75

Front Joint Angle
1. Position spirit level gauge and adapter at left side of engine so that adapter pins contact flat surface of engine oil pan flange adjacent to vertical wall of oil pan.
2. Set position of bubble in spirit level.
3. Remove adapter and position gauge firmly along underside of propeller shaft, Fig. 20.

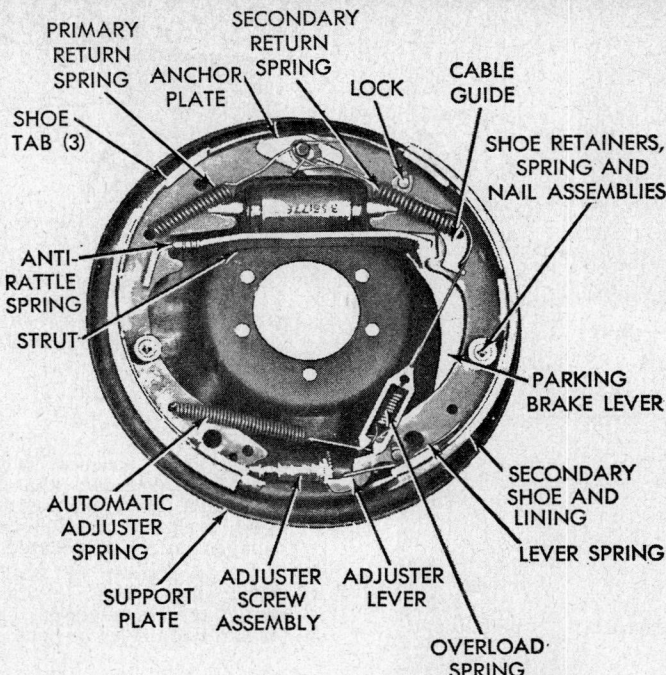

Fig. 21   Left rear brake (10-11 inch). 1969-75

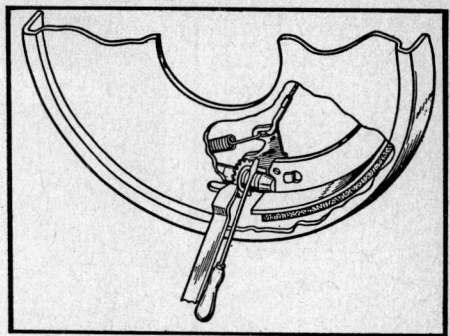

Fig. 22   Releasing brake lever with screwdriver while adjusting star wheel

4. Observe position of bubble. Reading should not exceed 2 degrees. If bubble is slightly forward of tolerance, the angle is smaller than specified and need not be corrected. If bubble is rearward of tolerance, angle must be corrected. To reduce angle by one graduation, install a ⅛″ shim between transmission extension housing and rear engine mount.

Rear Joint Angle

1. Remove pinion bumper plate and position gauge on machined pads with locating pin in rear bolt hole, Fig. 19.
2. Set bubble in spirit level.
3. Remove gauge from carrier and position it firmly along underside of propeller shaft, Fig. 20.
4. Observe position of the bubble. Reading should not exceed 2 degrees. Rear joint angle is corrected by installing wedge type shims between both rear springs and axle housing pads. If bubble is too far forward, insert shim with thick end toward front of car. If bubble is too far rearward, thick end of shim goes to rear of car.

BRAKE ADJUSTMENTS
1969-75 Self Adjusting Brakes

These brakes, Fig. 21, have self-adjusting shoe mechanisms that assure correct lining-to-drum clearances at all times. The automatic adjusters operate only when the brakes are applied as the car is moving rearward or when the car comes to an uphill stop.

Although the brakes are self-adjusting, an initial adjustment is necessary when the brake shoes have been relined or replaced, or when the length of the star wheel adjuster has been changed during some other service operation.

Frequent usage of an automatic transmission forward range to halt reverse vehicle motion may prevent the automatic adjusters from functioning, thereby inducing low pedal heights. Should low pedal heights be encountered, it is recommended that numerous forward and reverse stops be made until satisfactory pedal height is obtained.

Service Note

If a low pedal height condition cannot be corrected by making numerous reverse stops (provided the hydraulic system is free of air) it indicates that the self-adjusting mechanism is not functioning. Therefore, it will be necessary to remove the drum, clean, free up and lubricate the adjusting mechanism. Then adjust the brakes, being sure the parking brake is fully released.

Adjustment

1. Each backing plate has two adjusting hole covers; remove the rear cover and turn the adjusting screw upward with a screwdriver or other suitable tool to expand the shoes until a slight drag is felt when the drum is rotated.
2. Remove the drum.
3. While holding the adjusting lever out of engagement with the adjusting screw, Fig. 22; back off the ad- justing screw about one turn with the fingers.

NOTE: *If finger movement will not turn the screw, free it up. If this is not done, the adjusting lever will not turn the screw during subsequent vehicle operation. Lubricate the screw with oil and coat with wheel bearing grease.*

4. Install wheel and drum, and adjusting hole cover. Adjust brakes on remaining wheels in the same manner.
5. If pedal height is not satisfactory, drive the vehicle and make sufficient reverse stops until proper pedal height is obtained.

PARKING BRAKE, ADJUST

Exc. 1974-75 Imperial

1. Release parking brake lever and loosen cable adjusting nut to be sure cable is slack.
2. With rear wheel brakes properly adjusted, tighten cable adjusting nut until a slight drag is felt when the rear wheels are rotated. Then loosen the cable adjusting nut until both rear wheels can be rotated freely.
3. To complete the operation, back off an additional two turns of the cable adjusting nut.
4. Apply and release parking brake several times to be sure rear wheels are not dragging when cable is in released position.

1974-75 Imperial

Adjust parking brake by rotating adjuster wheel with tool C-4223, Fig. 23, until brakes seat against drums, then back off adjuster wheel 12 clicks to prevent brake drag.

VACUUM RELEASE PARKING BRAKE

The parking brake is pedal applied

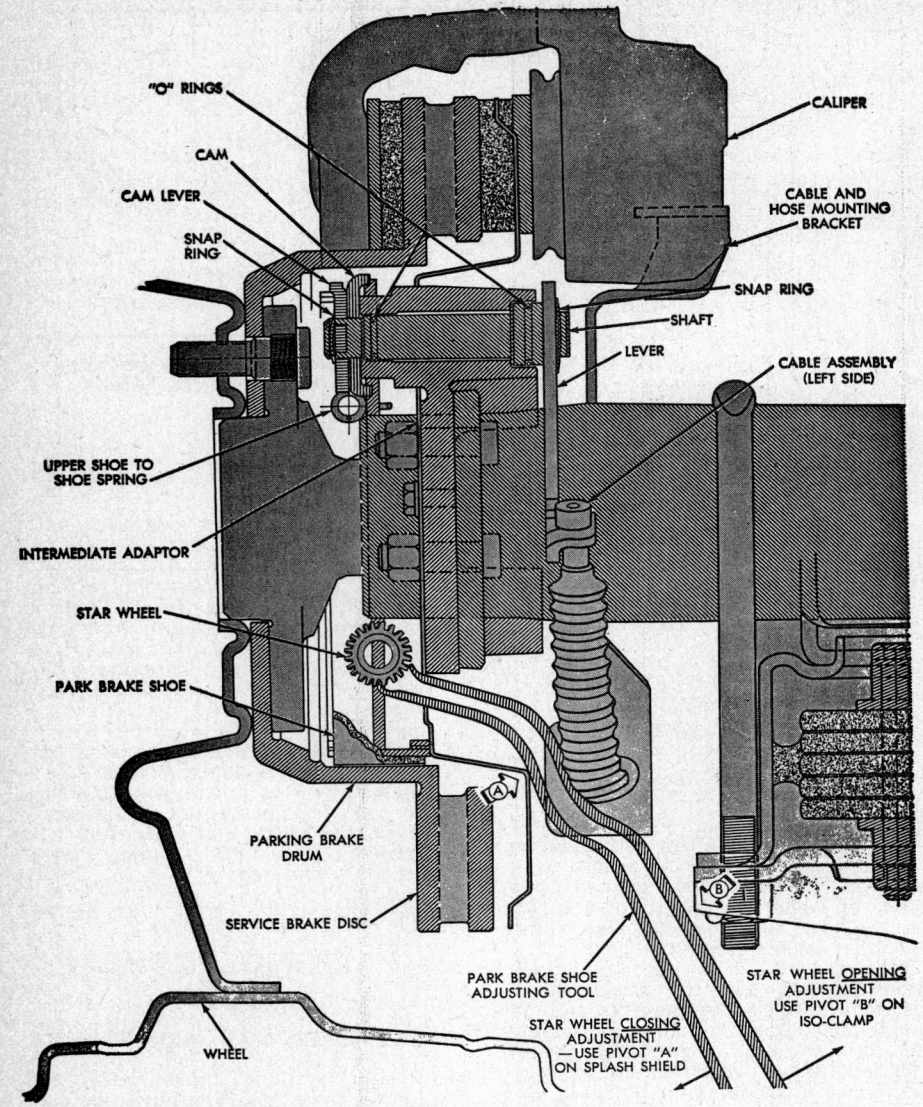

"O" RINGS
CAM
CAM LEVER
SNAP RING
UPPER SHOE TO SHOE SPRING
INTERMEDIATE ADAPTOR
STAR WHEEL
PARK BRAKE SHOE
PARKING BRAKE DRUM
SERVICE BRAKE DISC
WHEEL
CALIPER
CABLE AND HOSE MOUNTING BRACKET
SNAP RING
SHAFT
LEVER
CABLE ASSEMBLY (LEFT SIDE)
PARK BRAKE SHOE ADJUSTING TOOL
STAR WHEEL CLOSING ADJUSTMENT —USE PIVOT "A" ON SPLASH SHIELD
STAR WHEEL OPENING ADJUSTMENT USE PIVOT "B" ON ISO-CLAMP

Fig. 23   Rear wheel disc brake drum type parking brake shoe adjustment. 1974-75 Imperial

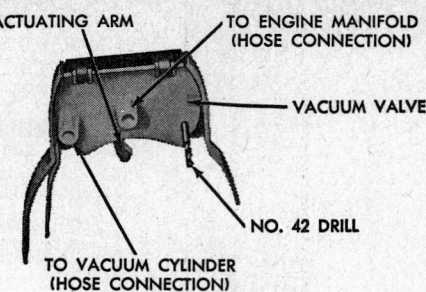

ACTUATING ARM
TO ENGINE MANIFOLD (HOSE CONNECTION)
VACUUM VALVE
NO. 42 DRILL
TO VACUUM CYLINDER (HOSE CONNECTION)

Fig. 24   Parking brake vacuum release valve. 1969-75 (typical)

replaced.

4. Check brake release with vacuum applied. If vacuum chamber piston completes full stroke but does not release brake, a malfunction of the pedal assembly is indicated.

5. Check operation of parking brake with engine off. Parking brake should remain engaged regardless of transmission selector position.

Parking Brake Vacuum Valve, Replace

1. With engine off, place shift lever in drive, remove vacuum hoses and retaining screws and remove valve from steering column.

2. To install, move actuating arm on valve against spring to extreme position or until locating holes line up and install a #42 drill in hole, Fig. 23.

3. Place shift lever in park and install valve but do not tighten screws. Rotate valve clockwise until actuating arm contacts tab in steering column then tighten screws.

4. Remove drill and install vacuum hoses making sure that hose from engine manifold is attached to center fitting on valve, Fig. 24.

5. Start engine and check that parking brake can be set in neutral and park and will release in reverse and drive positions.

and released by a vacuum chamber. When the engine is started and vacuum is developed, energy is then available to release the parking brake. This is controlled by the transmission push buttons or shift linkage. When the transmission is in "Neutral", vacuum is cut off from the release chamber and there is no action of the parking brake pedal.

When the transmission is shifted into a drive gear (forward or reverse), the vacuum control valve is opened, actuating the vacuum release chamber mounted on the parking brake assembly.

NOTE: *In the event of engine failure and no vacuum, the brake may be released by a manual release lever mounted on the left side of the parking brake pedal assembly. This assembly prevents the vehicle from being driven with the parking brake in the applied position.*

Testing Vacuum Release

1. If the mechanism is inoperative, first check for damaged or kinked vacuum hoses and for loose hose connections at the vacuum chamber, vacuum release valve at neutral safety switch, and at engine manifold connection.

2. Check adjustment of neutral safety switch and operation of vacuum release valve.

3. Check vacuum chamber piston travel by running engine and shifting transmission selector from drive to neutral. The manual release lever should move up and down as vacuum is applied and released. If no movement is observed or if movement is slow (more than 1 or 2 seconds to complete full stroke), the vacuum chamber is leaking and should be

BRAKE MASTER CYLINDER, REPLACE

1969-75 All Cars

1. Disconnect front and rear brake tubes from master cylinder (residual pressure valves will keep cylinder from draining).

2. Remove nuts that attach master cylinder to cowl panel and/or power brake unit.

3. Disconnect pedal push rod (manual brakes) from brake pedal.

4. Slide master cylinder straight out from cowl panel and/or power brake unit.

5. Reverse procedure to install.

POWER BRAKE

1969-75 Bendix Booster

1. Disconnect brake line(s) from master cylinder.
2. Remove vacuum hose from booster.
3. From under dash, remove brake pedal and push rod attaching bolt.
4. Remove four booster attaching nuts and lift booster from vehicle.
5. Installation is made in the reverse order of removal. Bleed system and check booster operation.

1969-75 Midland-Ross Booster

1. With engine shut off, apply brake several times to balance the internal pressure of the booster.
2. Disconnect hydraulic line at master cylinder and vacuum hose from booster.
3. From underneath dash, remove bolt from plunger and brake pedal linkage.
4. Remove four attaching bolts and lift off booster and master cylinder.

Rear Suspension

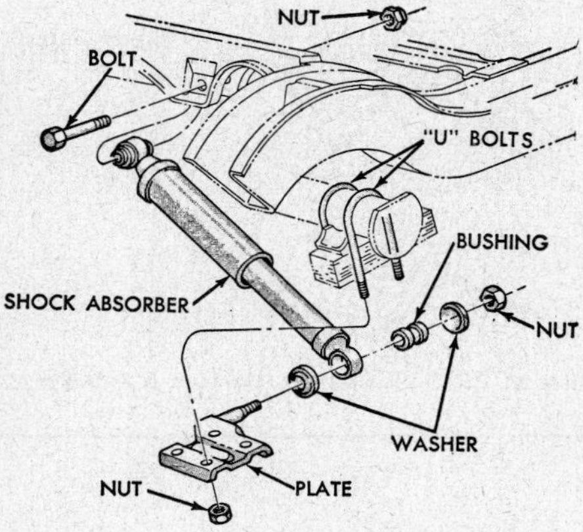

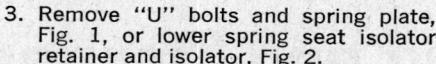

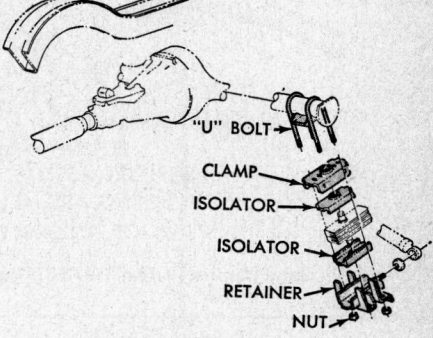

Fig. 2   Rear spring isolator

LEAF SPRINGS & BUSHINGS, REPLACE

1. Support rear axle, relieving tension from spring.

   NOTE: 1974-75 Full Size Models are equipped with preloaded "tension" type springs and a spring stretcher (C-4211) must be used during spring removal.

2. Disconnect shock absorber from lower mounting.

   NOTE: On 1968 Imperial, disconnect track bar from axle stud.

3. Remove "U" bolts and spring plate, Fig. 1, or lower spring seat isolator retainer and isolator, Fig. 2.
4. Remove spring front hanger to body mount bracket nuts, Fig. 3.
5. Remove rear shackle bolts, lower spring, thus pulling spring front hanger bolts out of holes.
6. Remove front hanger and rear shackle from spring. To replace eye bushings, refer to Fig. 4. Bushing replacement is accomplished in one operation.
7. Reverse procedure to install.

Leaf Spring Service

To replace interliners, remove spring alignment clips and on all models except Imperial, discard alignment clips. Separate spring leaves with a screwdriver or other suitable tool and remove interliners. Thoroughly clean spring surfaces before installation of new interliners.

To replace zinc interleaves, clamp spring in a vise and remove center bolt. Open vise carefully, allowing spring to expand. Interleaves can now be serviced. Install a drift through spring center bolt holes and clamp spring in a vise. Remove drift and install center bolt.

Fig. 1   Spring plate (typical)

SHOCK ABSORBER, REPLACE

To replace shock absorber, support rear axle properly and disconnect shock absorber at upper and lower mountings. On 1970-75 Barracuda and Challenger, the upper nut is accessible from trunk.

SWAY BAR, REPLACE

1. Remove nuts, retainers and rubber insulators from sway bar upper links, Figs. 5 and 6.
2. Disconnect sway bar brackets from frame.
3. Remove link from support assembly and replace insulators.
4. Reverse procedure to install.

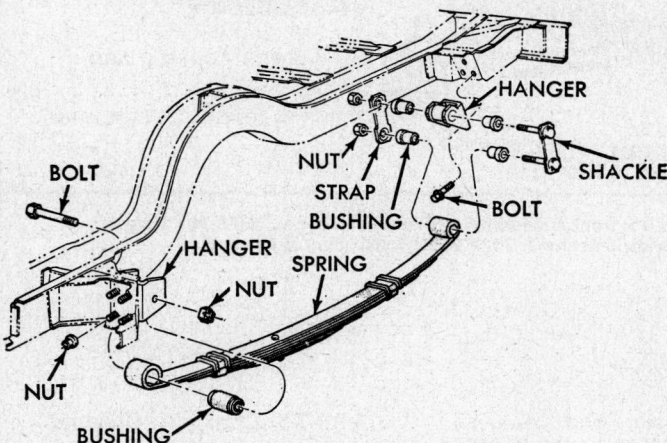

Fig. 3   Rear spring (typical)

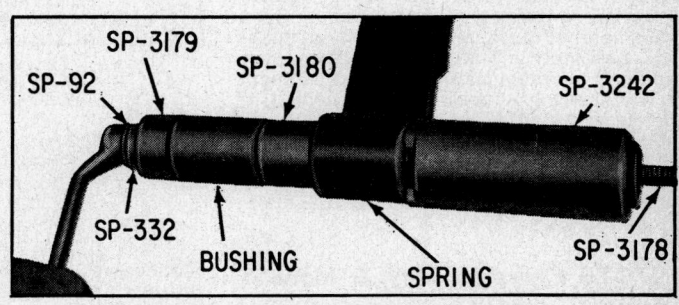

Fig. 4   Spring front bushing replacement

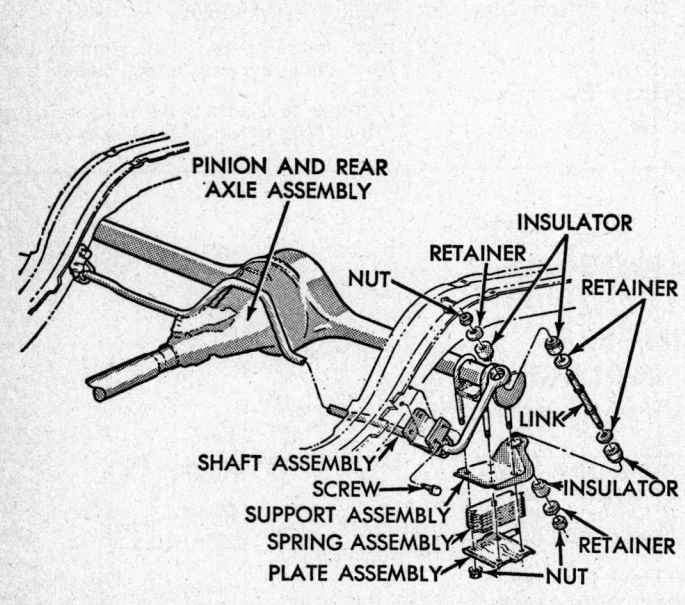

Fig. 5 Sway bar installation. 1973-75 Barracuda & Challenger

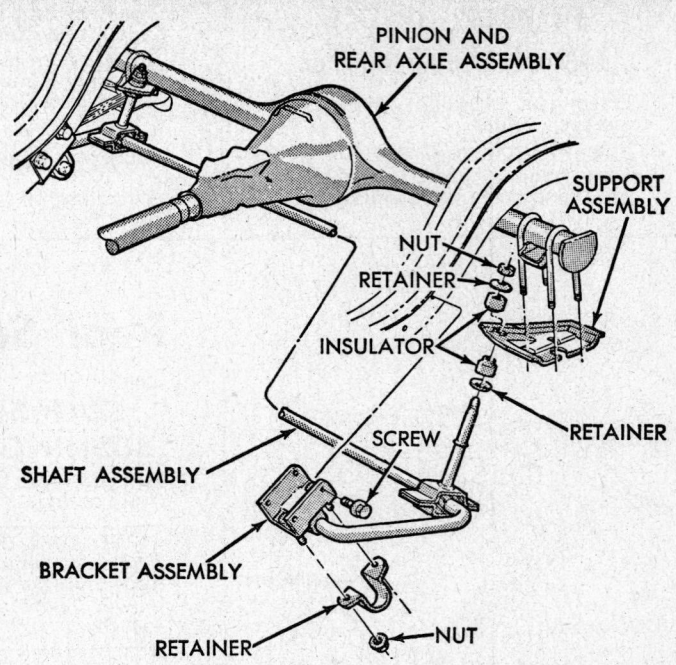

Fig. 6 Sway bar installation. 1973-75 Charger, Coronet & Satellite

Front End and Steering Section

FRONT SUSPENSION

All Cars Except Imperial & 1973-75 Charger, Coronet & Satellite

This suspension, Fig. 1, consists of two torsion bar springs (right and left), two sets of upper and lower control arms, four ball joints and two struts.

The front ends of the torsion bar springs engage the lower control arms at the inner pivot points. The rear end of the torsion bars engage adjustable anchor and cam assemblies that are supported by brackets welded to the frame side rails and a removable crossmember.

The upper control arms are mounted on removable brackets that are bolted to the frame side rails. The lower control arms are attached to the frame front crossmember by a pivot shaft and bushing assembly. The pivot shafts are mounted in replaceable rubber bushings.

The steering knuckles are connected to the upper and lower control arms by means of ball joints. To prevent the possibility of fore and aft movement of the lower control arms, a strut is attached to the front crossmember and to the lower control arm.

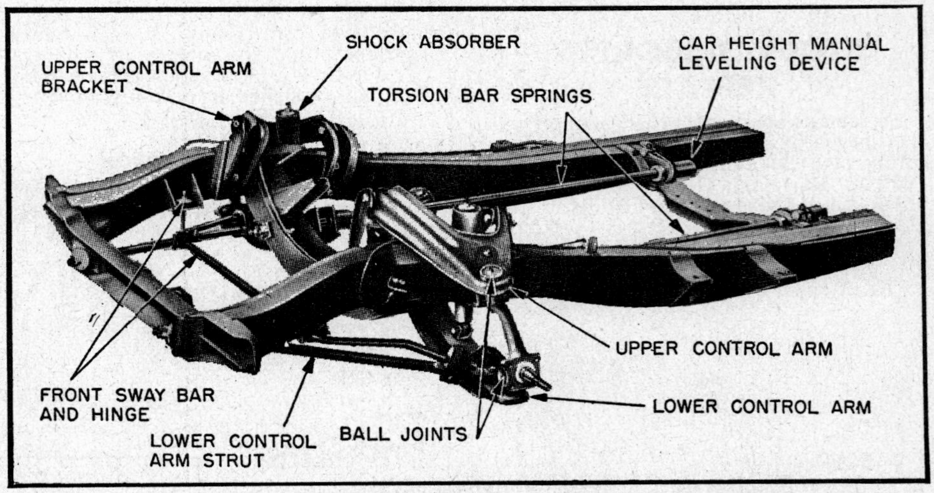

Fig. 1 Torsion bar front suspension. All except Imperial, 1973-75 Charger, Coronet, Satellite & 1974-75 Chrysler, Fury & Monaco

1974-75 Chrysler, Fury & Monaco

This suspension has new lower control arms with pressed in ball joints and more serviceable struts. Caster and camber settings are made by loosening the upper control arm pivot bar bolt nuts and adjusting as necessary.

1973-75 Charger, Coronet & Satellite

This suspension has a rubber mounted

crossmember, a torsion bar crossmember, more serviceable struts and a lower control arm with screw in ball joints for 1973 and pressed in for 1974-75 models. Caster and camber settings are made by loosening the upper control arm pivot bar bolt nuts and adjusting as necessary.

1969-75 Imperial

The front suspension has a front "K" crossmember that is isolated from the stub frame by four rubber bushing type isolators. The torsion bar rear anchor crossmember is isolated from the stub frame crossmember by two sandwich type rubber insulators. The front anchors are part of the lower control arms and provide the means of adjusting the vehicle front height. The upper control arm is mounted on a pivot bar and the *front wheel alignment is set by the adjustment of two vertically mounted cam bolts*, Fig. 2.

LUBRICATION

1969-75

All ball joints and torsion bars are effectively sealed against road splash by tightly fitted balloon type flexible type seals. The ball joints are semi-permanently lubricated with special lubricant, and should not under normal conditions require lubrication before 32,000 miles.

All ball joints, tie rod end seals and protectors should be inspected at all oil change periods. Damaged seals must be replaced to prevent lubricant leakage or contamination and subsequent component failure.

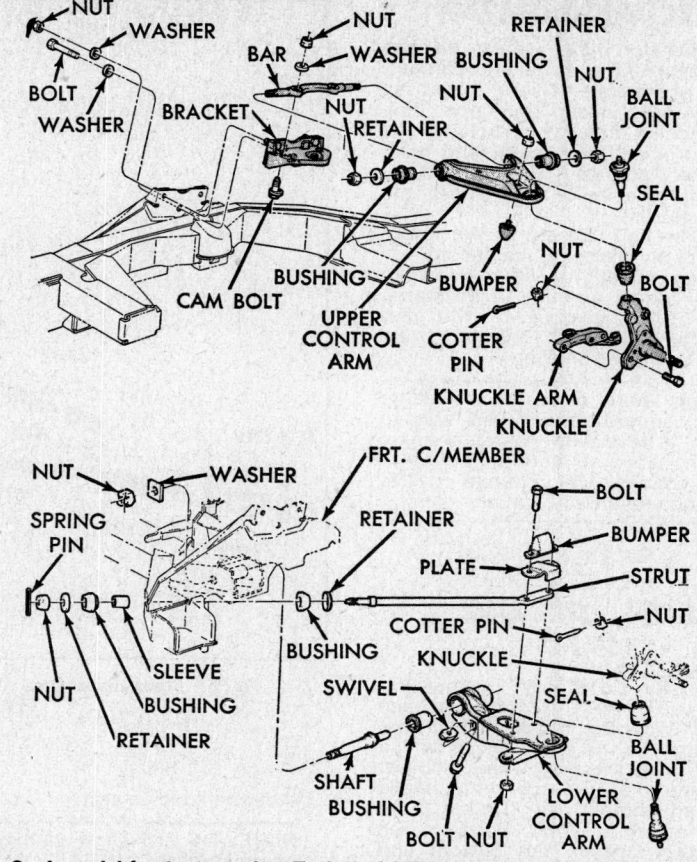

Fig. 2   Imperial front suspension. Typical of 1973-75 Charger, Coronet, Satellite & 1974-75 Chrysler, Fury & Monaco

WARNING

Do not use pressure type lubrication equipment as the pressure may damage the balloon type seals. Use a hand type lubrication gun filled only with the special lubricant specified for the job. Fill each unit slowly to avoid rupturing the seal.

Every 32,000 miles remove the plug from the ball joint and install a grease fitting. Using a hand gun, pump the grease into the unit until the seal balloons—indicating fullness. Remove the grease fitting and reinstall the plug.

Fig. 3   Camber and caster adjusting bolts. All except Imperial, 1973-75 Charger, Coronet, Satellite & 1974-75 Chrysler, Fury & Monaco

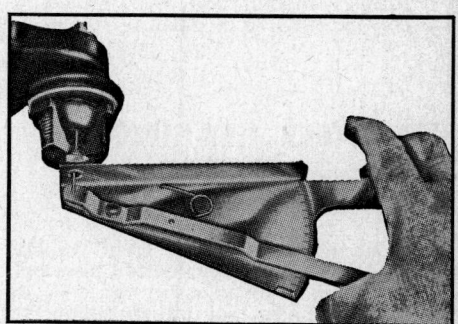

Fig. 4   Scale used to check lower ball joint for wear (tool C-3911)

WHEEL ALIGNMENT

Front suspension height must be correct before measuring caster and camber. After using a suitable solvent to loosen any rust, carefully loosen the upper control arm attaching nuts while holding the bolts from turning. Once caster and camber have been adjusted, Fig. 3, a very small turn of the bolts will affect the gauge readings.

Turning one bolt affects caster more than camber. By bringing caster to approximate specifications, then turning both bolts an equal amount in the same direction to bring camber to the preferred specification, will usually bring caster to the preferred setting.

NOTE: Turning both cams in the same direction an equal amount will change camber with little or no caster change. Turning both cams an equal amount in opposite directions will change caster with little or no change of camber.

TOE-IN, ADJUST
1969-75

With the front wheels in straight ahead position, loosen the clamps at each end of both adjusting tubes. Adjust toe-in by turning the tie rod sleeve which will "center" the steering wheel spokes. If the steering wheel was centered, make the toe-in adjustment by turning both sleeves an equal amount. Position the clamps so they are on the bottom and tighten bolts to 15 ft. lbs.

WHEEL BEARINGS, ADJUST

1. Tighten adjusting nut to 8 ft. lbs. on 1969-72 models and 20-25 ft. lbs. on 1973-75 models, while rotating wheel.
2. On 1969-72 models, place nut lock on nut with one pair of slots aligned with cotter pin hole and back off adjusting nut lock assembly one slot and install cotter pin.
3. On 1973-75 models, back off nut to completely release bearing preload, then finger tighten adjusting nut and install cotter pin.
4. The resulting adjustment should be zero (no preload) to .003 inch on 1969-72 models and .0001-.003 end play for 1973-75 models.

WHEEL BEARINGS, REPLACE

(Disc Brakes)

1. Raise car and remove front wheels.
2. Remove grease cap, cotter pin, lock nut and bearing adjusting nut.
3. Remove bolts that attach caliper to steering knuckle.
4. Slowly slide caliper up and away from disc and support caliper on

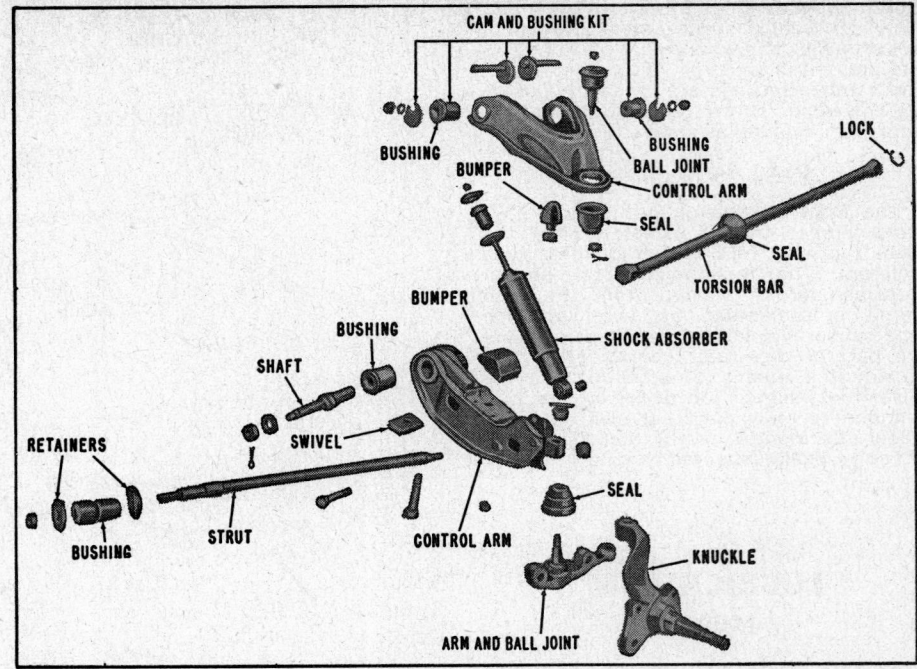

Fig. 5 Front suspension. All except Imperial, 1973-75 Charger, Coronet, Satellite & 1974-75 Chrysler, Fury & Monaco

steering knuckle arm.

NOTE: Do not allow caliper to hang by brake hose.

5. Remove thrust washer and outer bearing cone. Remove hub and disc assembly. Grease retainer and inner bearing can now be removed.

CHECKING BALL JOINTS FOR WEAR

If loose ball joints are suspected, first make sure the front wheel bearings are properly adjusted and that the control arms are tight.

Fig. 4 illustrates tool No. C-3911 which has been developed to measure accurately lower ball joint wear and to eliminate needless replacement of ball

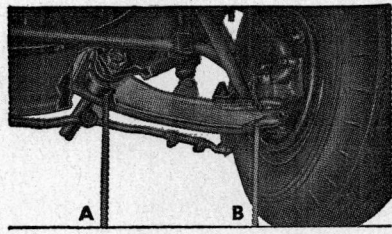

Fig. 6 Measuring front suspension height (typical)

joints not excessively worn. Checking procedure is as follows:

1. Raise front of vehicle at lower control arms to bring wheels clear of floor.

CAUTION—*Lower control arms must be supported sufficiently outboard so that the rebound bumper is not compressed in order to unload lower ball joint.*

2. Remove ball joint plug and screw threaded fitting of tool into ball joint hole until it is firmly seated as shown.
3. Raise and lower wheel by hand or with a pry bar and note free play indicated on scale of tool. The scale should not read more than .070 inch for all except 1974-75 intermediates and .040 inch for 1974-75 intermediates.
4. Replacement for excessive wear is necessary only when movement of the gauge arm exceeds the above.

NOTE: On Imperial, 1973-75 Charger, Coronet and Satellite and 1975 Chrysler, Fury and Monaco, the lower ball joints are pre-loaded (zero axial end play). Therefore, if any up and down movement is observed on all except 1974-75 models, the ball joint and lower control arm should be replaced. The ball joint is a press fit and requires very high removing and installing forces. If movement is in excess of .020 inch on the 1974-75 models, the ball joint assembly should be replaced.

BALL JOINTS, REPLACE

On 1969-75 Imperial, the upper ball

joint is threaded into the control arm and the lower ball joint is serviced as an assembly with the lower control arm. On all other models, the upper ball joint is threaded into the control arm whereas the lower ball joint is furnished as an assembly with the steering arm.

Use a suitable tool to press the ball joints from the steering knuckles, and when installing a ball joint, be sure to start it squarely into the control arm threads.

TORSION BAR, REPLACE

The torsion bars are not interchangeable side for side. The bars are marked either right or left by an "R" or an "L" stamped on one end of the bar. The general procedure for replacing a torsion bar is as follows:

Removal

1. Remove upper control arm rebound bumper.
2. If vehicle is to be raised on a hoist, make sure it is lifted on the body only so suspension is in full rebound position (no load).
3. Release all load from torsion bar by turning anchor adjusting bolt counterclockwise.

NOTE: On 1969-75 Imperial models load on *both* torsion bars will have to be released by turning the anchor adjusting bolts counterclockwise. This is necessary because the rubber isolator rear crossmember would be under load and could possibly cause severe damage or personal injury.

4. Slide rear anchor balloon seal off of rear anchor and remove lock ring from anchor.
5. Remove torsion bar, by sliding bar out through rear of rear anchor. Use care not to damage balloon seal when it is removed from torsion bar.

Inspection

1. Inspect balloon seal for damage and replace if necessary.
2. Inspect torsion bar for scores or nicks. Dress down all scratches and nicks to remove sharp edges, then paint repaired areas with a rust preventive.
3. Remove all foreign material from hex openings in anchors and from hex ends of torsion bars.
4. Inspect adjusting bolt and swivel and replace if there is any sign of corrosion or other damage. Lubricate for easy operation.

Installation

1. Insert torsion bar through rear anchor.
2. Slide balloon seal over torsion bar with cupped end toward rear of bar.
3. Coat both ends of torsion bar with a long mileage lubricant.
4. Slide torsion bar in hex opening of lower control arm.
5. Install lock ring, making sure it is seated in groove.
6. Pack annular opening in rear anchor completely full of a long mileage lubricant.
7. Position lip of balloon seal in groove

of anchor. *On 1969-75 Imperial models, install balloon seal clamp.*
8. On all models except 1969-75 Imperial, turn adjusting bolt clockwise to place a load on torsion bar. *On 1969-75 Imperial, turn both adjusting bolts clockwise to place a load on both torsion bars.*
9. Lower vehicle to floor and adjust front suspension height.
10. Install upper control arm rebound bumper.

RIDING HEIGHT, ADJUST

Before taking measurements, grasp the bumpers at the center (rear bumper first) and jounce the car up and down several times. Jounce the car at the front bumper the same number of times and release the bumper at the same point in the cycle each time.

1. Measure from the ball joint to the floor (measurement "B"), and from the control arm torsion bar spring anchor housing to the floor (measurement "A"), Fig. 6.
2. Subtract "B" from "A". The distance should be as listed below (plus or minus $\frac{1}{8}$").
3. Measure the other side in the same manner.
4. Adjust by turning the torsion bar anchor adjusting nut *clockwise to increase* the height and *counterclockwise to decrease* the height. The difference from side-to-side should not exceed $\frac{1}{8}$".
5. After adjusting, jounce the car and recheck the measurements on both sides, even if only one side may have been adjusted.

Dodge & Dart

1969-70	Dart	2⅛"
	Challenger	1³⁄₁₆"
	Coronet, Charger	1⅞"
	Polara, Monaco	1⅜"
1971-72	Dart 4 Dr.	2⅛"
	Dart 2 Dr.	1⅝"
	Challenger	1"
	Coronet, Charger	1⅝"
	Polara, Monaco	1⅜"
1973-75	Dart 4 Dr.	2⅛"
	Dart 2 Dr.	1⅞"
	Challenger	1⅛"
	Coronet & Charger	1⅞"
	Polara & Monaco	1½"

Plymouth

1969-70	Belvedere, Satellite, Roadrunner	1⅞"
	Fury, V.I.P.	1⅜"
1971-72	Satellite	1⅝"
	Fury	1⅜"
1973-75	Satellite	1⅞"
	Fury	1½"

Valiant

1969	Barracuda	1⅜"
	Valiant	2⅛"
1970	Barracuda	1³⁄₁₆"
	Valiant	2⅛"
1971-72	Valiant 4 Dr.	2⅛"
	Valiant 2 Dr.	1⅝"
	Barracuda	1"

1974-75	Valiant 4 Dr.	2⅛"
	Valiant 2 Dr.	1⅞"
	Barracuda	1"

Chrysler & Imperial

1969-72	Chrysler	1⅛"
	Imperial	1¾"
1973-75	Chrysler	1¼"
	Imperial	1¾"

MANUAL STEERING GEAR, REPLACE
1970-75

CAUTION: To avoid damage to the energy absorbing steering column, it is recommended that the steering column be completely detached from floor and instrument panel before steering gear is removed.

1. Use a suitable puller to remove steering arm from under vehicle.
2. Remove gear to frame retaining bolts and remove gear.

1969 Chrysler, Monaco, Polara

1. Use a suitable puller to remove steering arm.
2. Disconnect transmission gear selector linkage (if column mounted).
3. Remove pin from coupling clamp at upper end of steering gear worm shaft.
4. To provide sufficient clearance at coupling, loosen column jacket-to-instrument panel clamp bolts enough to disengage tab on clamp from slot in column jacket. Slide column up far enough to disengage coupling from worm shaft.
5. Raise carpet and remove column lower support plate-to-floor pan bolts.
6. Remove three gear housing mounting bolts and remove gear from under vehicle.

1969-70 Dodge & Plymouth (Except Monaco & Polara)

1. Perform Steps 1 through 4 as described above for other 1969-70 models.
2. Then on Dart and Valiant with 273 engines, from under vehicle remove left front engine mount stud nut and washer. Using a suitable jack, raise engine about 1½ inches. Remove starter. After removing the three steering gear mounting bolts, lower gear through opening.
3. On models with 426 engine, remove battery and battery tray. Remove left front engine mount stud nut and washer. Using a suitable jack, raise engine about 1½ inches. After removing the three gear mounting bolts, rotate gear forward between cylinder head and shock absorber tower, and up through opening left

by battery tray removal.

4. On models with 273, 318, 340, 383 and 440 engines (except Dart and Valiant), remove the three steering gear mounting bolts and lower gear from under vehicle.

5. On all 6-cylinder models, remove steering gear mounting bolts and remove gear through engine compartment.

POWER STEERING, REPLACE

1969-75 Imperial

1. Disconnect battery ground cable.
2. Disconnect pressure and return hoses at steering gear and fasten ends of hoses above oil level in pump reservoir.
3. Remove rubber coupling heat shield.
4. Remove two capscrews attaching rubber coupling to upper flange of steering column shaft.
5. Remove roll pin from pot coupling.
6. Move upper end of intermediate shaft until rubber coupling clears upper flange and carefully tap lower coupling up and off steering gear worm shaft.
7. Using a suitable puller, remove steering gear arm.
8. Disconnect exhaust pipe at ball coupling and exhaust manifold flanges and remove pipe.
9. Disconnect transmission cooler lines from transmission and clamp at starter flange bolt.
10. Remove two steering gear mounting bolts and stud nut. Then remove gear from under vehicle.

1969-75 Chrysler, Plymouth & Dodge

1. Disconnect battery ground cable.
2. Remove column coupling-to-worm shaft roll pin.
3. Loosen column jacket clamp nuts enough to allow column to be pulled up two inches. On some models it will be necessary to remove column finish plate to get at the clamp.
4. Remove three bolts in lower column support plate at floor pan.
5. Tap coupling and column upward and lift off end of worm shaft.
6. Disconnect pressure and return hoses at gear. Fasten hose ends above fluid level in pump.
7. Use a suitable puller to remove steering arm.
8. Remove gear-to-frame bolts and remove gear from vehicle as follows:
9. On six-cylinder models, remove gear from top of engine compartment.
10. Dart and Valiant with 8-273 engine, remove left front engine mount stud nut. Using suitable jack, raise engine slightly to provide clearance between left exhaust manifold and body sheet metal. Remove starter and then take steering gear out from under vehicle.
11. Dodge and Plymouth with 8-426 engine, remove battery and battery tray. From top side of engine compartment, remove left engine mount insulator stud nut, through bolt and bracket upper bolt. Jack up left side of engine about 1½". Separate engine from engine mount and allow insulator to rest on frame. Rotate steering gear (worm shaft end) up between cylinder head and shock absorber tower and out through battery tray opening.
12. On all other models remove gear from under vehicle.

FORD & MERCURY
Full Size Models

INDEX OF SERVICE OPERATIONS

PAGE NO.

ACCESSORIES

Air Conditioning	2-20
Automatic Level Controls	2-39
Blower Motor, Replace	1-378
Clock Troubles	2-11
Heater Core, Replace	1-376
Power Top Troubles	2-18
Power Window Troubles	2-18
Radio, Replace	1-376
Speed Controls, Adjust	1-378

BRAKES

Anti-Skid Brakes	2-162
Brake Troubles, Mechanical	2-17
Disc Brake Service	2-133
Hydraulic System Service	2-123
Master Cylinder, Replace	1-395
Parking Brake, Adjust	1-395
Power Brake Unit, Replace	1-396
Service Brakes, Adjust	1-393
Vacuum Release Parking Brake Unit	1-395

CLUTCH

Clutch Pedal, Adjust	1-390
Clutch, Replace	1-390
Clutch Troubles	2-12

COOLING SYSTEM

Cooling System Troubles	2-6
Variable Speed Fans	2-38
Water Pump, Replace	1-388

ELECTRICAL

Alternator Service	2-69
Blower Motor, Replace	1-378
Dash Gauge Service	2-50
Distributor, Replace	1-370
Distributor Service:	
Standard	2-525
Transistorized	2-535
Electrical Troubles	2-8
Headlamps, Concealed Type	2-46
Headlight Aiming	2-45
Horn Sounder	1-373
Ignition Coils and Resistors	2-521
Ignition Lock, Replace	1-370
Ignition Switch, Replace	1-371
Ignition Timing	2-518
Instrument Cluster Removal	1-373
Light Switch, Replace	1-371
Neutral Safety Switch, Replace	1-372
Seat Belt Interlock Systems	2-311
Starter Service	2-54
Starter, Replace	1-370
Starter Switch Service	2-67
Stop Light Switch, Replace	1-372
Turn Signal Switch, Replace	1-372
Turn Signal Troubles	2-11
Windshield Wiper Motor, Replace	1-375
Windshield Wiper Troubles	2-19

PAGE NO.

ENGINE

Camshaft, Replace	1-384
Camshaft Bearings	1-385
Crankshaft Rear Oil Seal	1-386
Cylinder Head, Replace	1-379
Engine Identification	1-356
Engine Mounts	1-378
Engine, Replace	1-379
Engine Troubles	2-1
Main Bearings	1-385
Piston Pins	1-385
Piston Rings	1-385
Piston and Rod, Assemble	1-385
Pistons	1-385
Rocker Arm Service	1-382
Rocker Arm Stud	1-383
Rod Bearings	1-385
Timing Case Cover, Replace	1-383
Timing Chain, Replace	1-384
Timing Gears, Replace	1-384
Valves, Adjust	1-382
Valve Arrangement	1-381
Valve Guides	1-382
Valve Lifters	1-383

ENGINE LUBRICATION

Emission Control Systems	2-545
Oil Pan, Replace	1-386
Oil Pump Repairs	1-388

FUEL SYSTEM

Carburetor Adjustments and Specs.	2-372
1975 Carburetors	1-716
Emission Control Systems	2-545
Fuel Pump, Replace	1-389
Fuel Pump Service	2-369
Fuel System Troubles	2-2

PROPELLER SHAFT & U JOINTS

Propeller Shaft	1-393
Universal Joint Service	2-117

REAR AXLE & SUSPENSION

Axle Shaft, Bearing and Seal	1-393
Coil Springs, Replace	1-397
Control Arms, Replace	1-397
Rear Axle Description	1-391
Rear Axle Troubles	2-16
Shock Absorber, Replace	1-397
Track Bar, Replace	1-397

SPECIFICATIONS

Alternator	1-367
Belt Tension Data	1-388
Brakes	1-368
Capacities	1-368
Carburetors	2-372
Cooling System	1-368

PAGE NO.

Crankshaft and Bearings	1-365
Distributors	1-362
Engine Tightening Torque	1-366
Fuel Pump Pressure	1-389
General Engine Specs.	1-357
Ignition Coils and Resistors	2-521
Pistons, Rings and Pins	1-365
Rear Axle	1-368
Starting Motors	1-365
Tune Up	1-359
Valve Lift	1-381
Valve Timing	1-382
Valves	1-364
Wheel Alignment	1-366

STEERING GEAR

Horn Sounder Removal	1-373
Mechanical Gear, Replace	1-399
Mechanical Gear Service	2-170
Mechanical Gear Troubles	2-17
Power Gear, Replace	1-399

SUSPENSION, FRONT

Ball Joints, Replace	1-399
Ball Joints, Check for Wear	1-398
Coil Spring, Replace	1-399
Lubrication	1-397
Shock Absorber, Replace	1-399
Suspension, Description of	1-397
Toe-In, Adjust	1-398
Wheel Alignment, Adjust	1-398
Wheel Bearings, Adjust	1-398
Wheel Bearings, Replace	1-398

TRANSMISSIONS

Three Speed Manual:	
Replace	1-390
Repairs	2-177
Linkage, Adjust	1-390
Four Speed Manual:	
Replace	1-390
Repairs	2-199
Linkage, Adjust	1-391
Automatic Units	2-231
1975 Linkage	1-391

TUNE UP

Service	2-517
Specifications	1-359

WINDSHIELD WIPER

Wiper Arms	1-375
Wiper Blades	1-375
Wiper Linkage, Replace	1-376
Wiper Motor, Replace	1-375
Wiper Switch, Replace	1-375
Wiper Troubles	2-19

ENGINE & SERIAL NUMBER LOCATION
Plate On Left Front Door Pillar

ENGINE IDENTIFICATION
★Serial number on Vehicle Warranty Plate
Engine code for 1969-75 is the last letter in the serial number.

Year	Engine	Engine Code★	Year	Engine	Engine Code★	Year	Engine	Engine Code★	Year	Engine	Engine Code★
1969–70	6-240	V	1971	V8-302①	F	1972	V8-351①	H	1974-75	V8-351	H
	V8-302①	F		V8-351①	H		V8-351④	Q		V8-400	S
	V8-351 (W)①	H		V8-390①	Y		V8-400	S		V8-460	A
	V8-390①	Y		V8-400①	S		V8-429	N			
	V8-390⑥	X		V8-429①	K	1973	V8-351	H			
	V8-429①	K		V8-429②	N		V8-400	S			
	V8-429②	N	1972	6-240	V		V8-429	N			
1971	6-240	V		V8-302①	F		V8-460	A			

①—Two barrel carburetor.
②—Four barrel carburetor.
③—Two 4 barrel carburetors.
④—Four barrel special.
⑤—Premium fuel.
⑥—Two barrel special.

GRILLE IDENTIFICATION

1969 Ford Custom, Galaxie

1969 Ford "LTD", XL, Squire

1969 Mercury Monterey

1969 Mercury Marauder, Marquis

1970 Ford Custom, Galaxie

1970 Ford "LTD", XL, Squire

1970 Mercury Marauder, Marquis

1970 Mercury Monterey

1971 Ford Custom, Galaxie

1971 Ford "LTD", Squire

1971 Mercury Brougham, Marquis

1971 Mercury Monterey

1972 Ford Custom, Galaxie

1972 Ford "LTD", Squire

1972 Mercury Monterey

GRILLE IDENTIFICATION—Continued

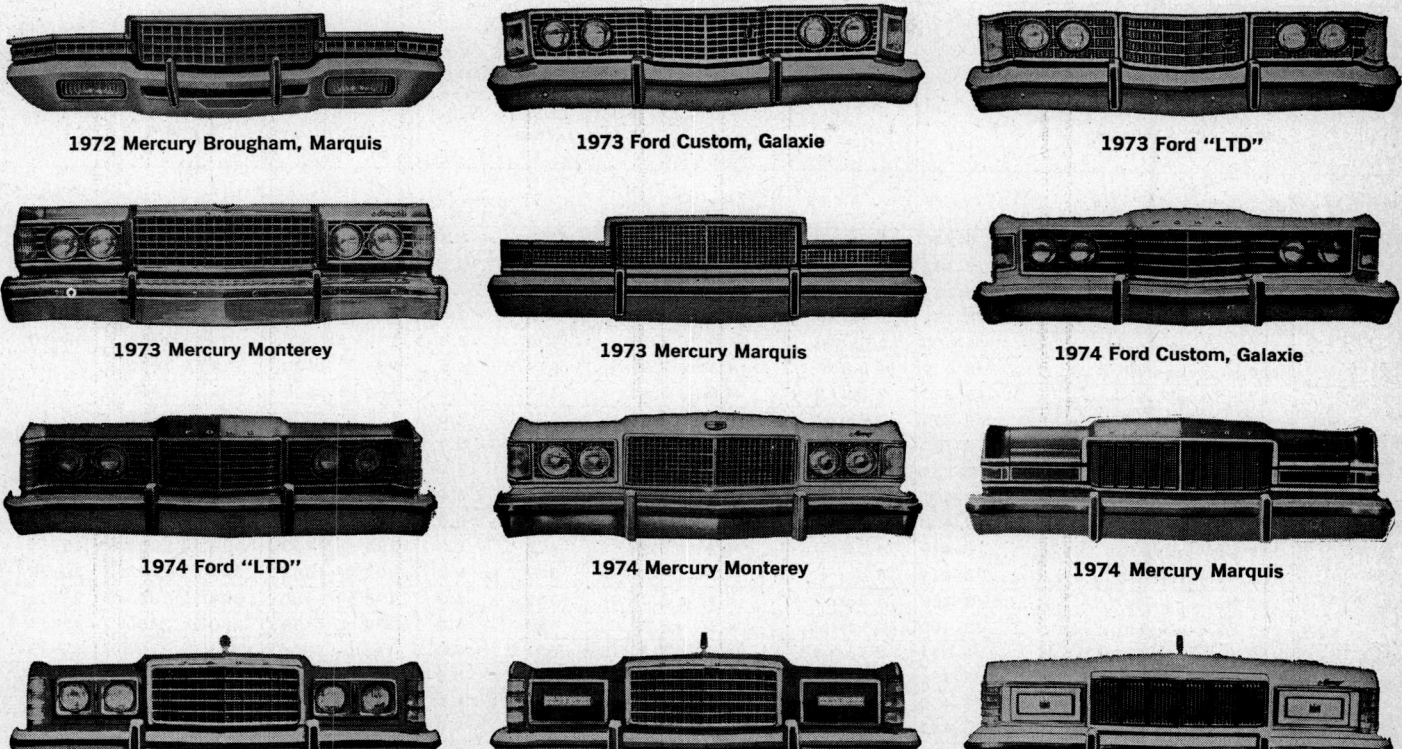

1972 Mercury Brougham, Marquis	1973 Ford Custom, Galaxie	1973 Ford "LTD"
1973 Mercury Monterey	1973 Mercury Marquis	1974 Ford Custom, Galaxie
1974 Ford "LTD"	1974 Mercury Monterey	1974 Mercury Marquis
1975 Ford "LTD"	1975 Ford "LTD" Landau	1975 Mercury

GENERAL ENGINE SPECIFICATIONS

Year	Engine	Carburetor	Bore and Stroke	Piston Displacement, Cubic Inches	Compression Ratio	Maximum Brake H.P. @ R.P.M.	Maximum Torque Lbs. Ft. @ R.P.M.	Normal Oil Pressure Pounds
FORD								
1969–70	150 Horsepower..............6-240	1 Barrel	4.00 x 3.18	240	9.2	150 @ 4000	234 @ 2200	35–60
	210 Horsepower............V8-302	2 Barrel	4.00 x 3.00	302	9.5	210 @ 4400	295 @ 2400	35–60
	250 Horsepower............V8-351	2 Barrel	4.00 x 3.50	351	9.5	250 @ 4600	355 @ 2600	35–60
	270 Horsepower............V8-390	2 Barrel	4.05 x 3.78	390	9.5	270 @ 4400	390 @ 2600	35–60
	320 Horsepower............V8-429	2 Barrel	4.36 x 3.59	429	10.5	320 @ 4400	460 @ 2200	35–60
	360 Horsepower............V8-429	4 Barrel	4.36 x 3.59	429	11.0	360 @ 4600	476 @ 2800	35–60
1971	140 Horsepower..............6-240	1 Barrel	4.00 x 3.18	240	8.9	140 @ 4000	230 @ 2200	35–60
	210 Horsepower............V8-302	2 Barrel	4.00 x 3.00	302	9.0	210 @ 4600	296 @ 2600	35–60
	240 Horsepower............V8-351	2 Barrel	4.00 x 3.50	351	9.0	240 @ 4600	350 @ 2600	35–60
	255 Horsepower............V8-390	2 Barrel	4.05 x 3.78	390	8.6	255 @ 4400	376 @ 2600	35–60
	260 Horsepower............V8-400	2 Barrel	4.00 x 4.00	400	9.0	260 @ 4400	400 @ 2200	35–60
	320 Horsepower............V8-429	2 Barrel	4.36 x 3.59	429	10.5	320 @ 4400	460 @ 2200	35–60
	360 Horsepower............V8-429	4 Barrel	4.36 x 3.59	429	10.5	360 @ 4600	480 @ 2800	35–60

Continued

GENERAL ENGINE SPECIFICATIONS—Continued

Year	Engine	Carburetor	Bore and Stroke	Piston Displacement, Cubic Inches	Compression Ratio	Maximum Brake H.P. @ R.P.M.	Maximum Torque Lbs. Ft. @ R.P.M.	Normal Oil Pressure Pounds
FORD—Continued								
1972	103 Horsepower① 6-240	1 Barrel	4.00 x 3.18	240	8.5	103 @ 3800	170 @ 2200	35–60
	140 Horsepower① V8-302	2 Barrel	4.00 x 3.00	302	8.5	140 @ 4000	239 @ 2000	35–60
	153 Horsepower① V8-351	2 Barrel	4.00 x 3.50	351	8.3	153 @ 3800	266 @ 2000	35–60
	163 Horsepower① V8-351	2 Barrel	4.00 x 3.50	351	8.6	163 @ 3800	277 @ 2000	35–60
	172 Horsepower① V8-400	2 Barrel	4.00 x 4.00	400	8.4	172 @ 4000	298 @ 2200	35–60
	208 Horsepower① V8-429	4 Barrel	4.36 x 3.59	429	8.5	208 @ 4400	322 @ 2800	35–60
1973	154 Horsepower① V8-351	2 Barrel	4.00 x 3.50	351	8.0	154 @ 3800	256 @ 2400	45–65
	157 Horsepower① V8-351	2 Barrel	4.00 x 3.50	351	8.0	157 @ 4000	246 @ 2400	45–75
	158 Horsepower① V8-351	2 Barrel	4.00 x 3.50	351	8.0	158 @ 3800	264 @ 2400	45–65
	161 Horsepower① V8-351	2 Barrel	4.00 x 3.50	351	8.0	161 @ 4000	254 @ 2400	45–75
	167 Horsepower① V8-400	2 Barrel	4.00 x 4.00	400	8.0	167 @ 3600	312 @ 2200	45–75
	171 Horsepower① V8-400	2 Barrel	4.00 x 4.00	400	8.0	171 @ 3600	314 @ 2000	45–75
	198 Horsepower① V8-429	4 Barrel	4.36 x 3.59	429	8.0	198 @ 4400	320 @ 2800	35–65
	202 Horsepower① V8-429	4 Barrel	4.36 x 3.59	429	8.0	202 @ 4400	320 @ 2800	35–65
	198 Horsepower① V8-460	4 Barrel	4.36 x 3.85	460	8.0	198 @ 4400	328 @ 2800	35–65
	202 Horsepower① V8-460	4 Barrel	4.36 x 3.85	460	8.0	202 @ 4400	330 @ 2800	35–65
1974	162 Horsepower① V8-351	2 Barrel	4.00 x 3.50	351	8.0	162 @ 4000	275 @ 2200	45–75
	163 Horsepower① V8-351	2 Barrel	4.00 x 3.50	351	8.0	163 @ 4200	278 @ 2000	45–65
	170 Horsepower① V8-400	2 Barrel	4.00 x 4.00	400	8.0	170 @ 3400	330 @ 2000	45–75
	195 Horsepower① V8-460	4 Barrel	4.36 x 3.85	460	8.0	195 @ 3800	335 @ 2600	35–65
	275 Horsepower① V8-460	4 Barrel	4.36 x 3.85	460	8.8	275 @ 4400	395 @ 2800	35–65
1975	148 Horsepower① V8-351	2 Barrel	4.00 x 3.50	351	8.0	148 @ 3800	243 @ 2400	45–75
	150 Horsepower① V8-351	2 Barrel	4.00 x 3.50	351	8.0	150 @ 3800	244 @ 2800	45–75
	158 Horsepower① V8-400	2 Barrel	4.00 x 4.00	400	8.0	158 @ 3800	276 @ 2000	45–75
	144 Horsepower① V8-400	2 Barrel	4.00 x 4.00	400	8.0	144 @ 3600	255 @ 2200	45–75
	218 Horsepower① V8-460	4 Barrel	4.36 x 3.85	460	8.0	218 @ 4000	369 @ 2600	35–65
MERCURY								
1969–70	270 Horsepower V8-390	2 Barrel	4.05 x 3.78	390	9.5	270 @ 4400	390 @ 2600	35–60
	280 Horsepower (1969) V8-390	2 Barrel	4.05 x 3.78	390	10.5	280 @ 4400	403 @ 2600	35–60
	320 Horsepower V8-429	2 Barrel	4.36 x 3.59	429	10.5	320 @ 4400	460 @ 2200	35–60
	360 Horsepower V8-429	4 Barrel	4.36 x 3.59	429	11.0	360 @ 4600	476 @ 2800	35–60
1971	240 Horsepower V8-351	2 Barrel	4.00 x 3.50	351	9.0	240 @ 4600	350 @ 2600	35–60
	260 Horsepower V8-400	2 Barrel	4.00 x 4.00	400	9.0	260 @ 4400	400 @ 2200	35–60
	320 Horsepower V8-429	2 Barrel	4.36 x 3.59	429	10.5	320 @ 4400	460 @ 2200	35–60
	360 Horsepower V8-429	4 Barrel	4.36 x 3.59	429	10.5	360 @ 4600	480 @ 2800	35–60
1972	153 Horsepower① V8-351	2 Barrel	4.00 x 3.50	351	8.3	153 @ 3800	266 @ 2000	35–60
	163 Horsepower① V8-351	2 Barrel	4.00 x 3.50	351	8.6	163 @ 3800	277 @ 2000	35–60
	172 Horsepower① V8-400	2 Barrel	4.00 x 4.00	400	8.4	172 @ 4000	298 @ 2200	35–60
	208 Horsepower① V8-429	4 Barrel	4.36 x 3.59	429	8.5	208 @ 4400	322 @ 2800	35–60
	200 Horsepower① V8-460	4 Barrel	4.36 x 3.85	460	8.5	200 @ 4400	326 @ 2800	35–75
1973	157 Horsepower① V8-351	2 Barrel	4.00 x 3.50	351	8.0	157 @ 4000	246 @ 2400	45–75
	161 Horsepower① V8-351	2 Barrel	4.00 x 3.50	351	8.0	161 @ 4000	254 @ 2400	45–75
	167 Horsepower① V8-400	2 Barrel	4.00 x 4.00	400	8.0	167 @ 3600	312 @ 2200	45–75
	171 Horsepower① V8-400	2 Barrel	4.00 x 4.00	400	8.0	171 @ 3600	314 @ 2000	45–75
	198 Horsepower① V8-429	4 Barrel	4.36 x 3.59	429	8.0	198 @ 4400	320 @ 2800	35–65
	202 Horsepower① V8-429	4 Barrel	4.36 x 3.59	429	8.0	202 @ 4400	320 @ 2800	35–65
	198 Horsepower① V8-460	4 Barrel	4.36 x 3.85	460	8.0	198 @ 4400	328 @ 2800	35–65
	202 Horsepower① V8-460	4 Barrel	4.36 x 3.85	460	8.0	202 @ 4400	330 @ 2800	35–65
1974	170 Horsepower① V8-400	2 Barrel	4.00 x 4.00	400	8.0	170 @ 3400	330 @ 2000	45–75
	195 Horsepower① V8-460	4 Barrel	4.36 x 3.85	460	8.0	195 @ 3800	335 @ 2600	35–65
	275 Horsepower① V8-460	4 Barrel	4.36 x 3.85	460	8.8	275 @ 4400	395 @ 2800	35–65

Continued

GENERAL ENGINE SPECIFICATIONS—Continued

Year	Engine	Car-buretor	Bore and Stroke	Piston Dis-place-ment, Cubic Inches	Com-pres-sion Ratio	Maximum Brake H.P. @ R.P.M.	Maximum Torque Lbs. Ft. @ R.P.M.	Normal Oil Pressure Pounds
MERCURY—Continued								
1975	148 Horsepower①............V8-351	2 Barrel	4.00 x 3.50	351	8.0	148 @ 3800	243 @ 2400	45–75
	150 Horsepower①............V8-351	2 Barrel	4.00 x 3.50	351	8.0	150 @ 3800	244 @ 2800	45–75
	144 Horsepower①............V8-400	2 Barrel	4.00 x 4.00	400	8.0	144 @ 3600	255 @ 2200	45–75
	158 Horsepower①............V8-400	2 Barrel	4.00 x 4.00	400	8.0	158 @ 3800	276 @ 2000	45–75
	218 Horsepower①............V8-460	4 Barrel	4.36 x 3.85	460	8.0	218 @ 4000	369 @ 2600	35–65

①—Ratings are NET—as installed in the vehicle.

TUNE UP SPECIFICATIONS

OLD CAR SPECIFICATIONS: For 1946-68 Tune Up Specifications see main index.

★When using a timing light, disconnect vacuum hose or tube at distributor and plug opening in tube or hose so idle speed will not be affected.

●When checking compression, lowest cylinder must be within 75% of the highest.

▲Before removing wires from distributor cap, determine location of the No. 1 wire in cap, as distributor position may have been altered from that shown at the end of this chart.

Year	Spark Plug Type ⑤	Spark Plug Gap Inch	Distributor Point Gap Inch	Distributor Dwell Angle Deg.	Ignition Timing Firing Order Fig. ▲	Ignition Timing Timing BTDC ①	Mark Fig.	Hot Idle Speed Std. Trans.	Hot Idle Speed Auto. Trans. ②	Air Fuel Ratio Std. Trans.	Air Fuel Ratio Auto. Trans.	Idle "CO" % Std. Trans.	Idle "CO" % Auto. Trans.
1969													
6-240	BF-42	.034	.027	35–40	C	6°	D	775/500⑭	500D	—	13.9 to 1	—	—
V8-302 Std. Tr.	BF-42	.034	.021	24–29	B	6°	F	650	—	14.0 to 1	—	1.8	—
V8-302 Auto. Tr.	BF-42	.034	.017	26–31	B	6°	F	—	550D	—	13.8 to 1	—	2.2
V8-351	BF-42	.034	.017	26–31	A	6°	F	650	550D	14.0 to 1	14.0 to 1	1.8	1.6
V8-390	BF-42	.034	.017	26–31	B	6°	E	650	550D	14.0 to 1	14.4 to 1	1.6	1.1
V8-390⑮	BF-42	.034	.021	24–29	B	6°	E	—	550D	14.0 to 1	14.4 to 1	1.8	0.5
V8-429	BF-42	.034	.017	26–31	B	6°	E	—	550D	14.0 to 1	14.4 to 1	1.8	1.2
1970													
6-240	BF-42	.035	⑰	⑰	C	6°	D	775/500⑭	500④	14.45 to 1	14.70 to 1	—	—
V8-302	BF-42	.035	.021	24–29	B	6°	F	775/500⑭	575④	14.0 to 1	13.8 to 1	0.34	0.44
V8-351	BF-42	.035	.021	24–29	A	6°	F	775/500⑭	575④	⑩	⑩	0.30	0.14
V8-390 Std. Tr.	BF-42	.035	.021	24–29	B	6°	E	775/500⑭	—	14.1 to 1	—	0.12	—
V8-390 Auto. Tr.	BF-42	.035	.017	26–31	B	6°	E	—	600/500⑭	—	14.4 to 1	—	0.12
V8-429⑦	BF-42	.035	.021	24–29	B	4°	E	—	600/500⑭	13.5 to 1	13.5 to 1	0.20	0.20
V8-429⑧	BF-42	.035	⑬	⑬	B	4°	E	700	600	14.5 to 1	14.5 to 1	0.75	0.75
1971													
6-240	BRF-42	.034	.027	35–40	C	6°	G	800/500⑭	500	14.5 to 1	14.5 to 1	1.0	0.5
V8-302 L/Air Cond.	BRF-42	.034	.021	24–29	B	6°	H	800/500⑭	575	12.5 to 1	12.5 to 1	0.3	0.4
V8-302 w/Air Cond.	BRF-42	.034	.021	24–29	B	6°	H	800/500⑭	600/500⑭	12.5 to 1	12.5 to 1	0.3	0.4
V8-351 L/Air Cond.⑪	BRF-42	.034	.021	24–29	A	6°	H	700/500⑭	575	13.50 to 1	13.90 to 1	1.1	0.5
V8-351 w/Air Cond.⑪	BRF-42	.034	.021	24–29	A	6°	H	700/500⑭	600/500⑭	13.50 to 1	13.90 to 1	1.1	0.5
V8-351⑫	ARF-42	.034	.021	24–29	A	6°	H	775/500⑭	600/500⑭	14.30 to 1	14.40 to 1	0.2	0.2
V8-390	BRF-42	.034	.021	24–29	B	6°	H	—	600/500⑭	—	—	—	—

Continued

TUNE UP SPECIFICATIONS—Continued

OLD CAR SPECIFICATIONS: For 1946-68 Tune Up Specifications see main index.

★When using a timing light, disconnect vacuum hose or tube at distributor and plug opening in tube or hose so idle speed will not be affected.

●When checking compression, lowest cylinder must be within 75% of the highest.

▲Before removing wires from distributor cap, determine location of the No. 1 wire in cap, as distributor position may have been altered from that shown at the end of this chart.

Year	Spark Plug		Distributor		Ignition Timing ★			Carb. Adjustments					
								Hot Idle Speed		Air Fuel Ratio		Idle "CO" %	
	Type ⑤	Gap Inch	Point Gap Inch	Dwell Angle Deg.	Firing Order Fig. ▲	Timing BTDC ①	Mark Fig.	Std. Trans.	Auto. Trans.②	Std. Trans.	Auto. Trans.	Std. Trans.	Auto. Trans.
1971—Continued													
V8-400	ARF-42	.034	.021	24–29	A	③	H	—	600/500⑭	14.5 to 1	14.5 to 1	—	0.7
V8-429⑦ L/Air Cond.	BRF-42	.034	.021	24–29	B	6°	H	—	590	14.5 to 1	14.5 to 1	—	0.2
V8-429⑦ w/Air Cond.	BRF-42	.034	.021	24–29	B	6°	H	—	600/500⑭	14.5 to 1	14.5 to 1	—	0.2
V8-429⑥	BRF-42	.034	.021	24–29	B	4°	H	700	600	14.50 to 1	14.50 to 1	0.2	0.2
1972													
6-240	BRF-42	.034	.027	35–39	C	6°	G	—	500	—	—	—	0.5
V8-302 w/Air Cond.	BRF-42	.034	.017	26–30	B	6°	H	800/500	600/500⑭	—	—	—	0.19
V8-302 L/Air Cond.	BRF-42	.034	.017	26–30	B	6°	H	—	575	—	—	—	0.19
V8-351 w/Air Cond.⑪	BRF-42	.034	.017	26–30	A	6°	H	—	600/500⑭	—	—	—	0.15
V8-351 L/Air Cond.⑪	BRF-42	.034	.017	26–30	A	6°	H	—	575	—	—	—	0.15
V8-351⑫	ARF-42	.034	.017	26–30	A	6°	H	—	700/500⑭	—	—	—	0.50
V8-351 Calif.⑫	ARF-42	.034	.017	26–30	A	6°	H	—	625/500⑭	—	—	—	0.50
V8-400	ARF-42	.034	.017	26–30	A	⑧	H	—	625/500⑭	—	—	—	0.10
V8-429	BRF-42	.034	.017	26–30	B	10°	H	—	600/500⑭	—	—	—	0.03
1973													
V8-351⑪	BRF-42	.034	.017	26–30	A	6°	H	—	600	—	—	—	0.5⑨
V8-351⑪	ARF-42	.034	.017	26–30	A	10°	H	—	600	—	—	0.5⑨	0.5⑨
V8-400	ARF-42	.034	.017	26–31	A	6°	H	—	625	—	—	—	0.5⑨
V8-429	ARF-42	.034	.017	26–30	B	10°	H	—	600	—	—	—	0.5⑨
V8-460	ARF-42	.034	.017	26–30	B	10°	H	—	650	—	—	—	0.4⑨
1974													
V8-351⑪	BRF-42	.044	.017	26–30	A	6°	H	—	600	—	—	—	—
V8-351⑪⑱	BRF-42	.044	—	—	A	6°	H	—	600	—	—	—	—
V8-351⑫	ARF-42	.044	.017	26–30	A	14°	H	—	650	—	—	—	—
V8-351⑫⑱	ARF-42	.044	—	—	A	14°	H	—	650	—	—	—	—
V8-400⑱	ARF-42	.044	—	—	A	12°	H	—	625	—	—	—	—
V8-460⑱	ARF-52	.054	—	—	B	⑯	H	—	⑯	—	—	—	.25
1975													
V8-351	ARF-42	.044	—	—	A	14°	H	—	700D	—	—	—	—
V8-400	ARF-42	.044	—	—	A	12°	H	—	625D	—	—	—	—
V8-460	ARF-52	.044	—	—	B	14°	H	—	650D	—	—	—	—

Continued

TUNE UP SPECIFICATIONS—Continued

①—BTDC: Before top dead center.
②—D: Drive. N: Neutral.
③—California vehicles 6°; all others 10°.
④—With headlights on and A/C off.
⑤—Autolite.
⑥—Four barrel carburetor.
⑦—Two barrel carburetor.
⑧—California vehicles 6°; all others 8°.
⑨—For Calif. 0.2%.

⑩—With 2 Bar. Carb.—14.0 to 1, with 4 Bar. Carb.—14.5 to 1.
⑪—Windsor engine.
⑫—Cleveland engine.
⑬—Dual diaphragm dist., .021 gap, 24°-29° dwell. Single diaphragm .017 gap, 26°-31° dwell.

⑭—Higher figure is with throttle modulator energized.
⑮—Premium fuel.
⑯—Exc. Police Interceptor 14° at 650, Police Interceptor 10° at 700.
⑰—Dual diaphragm dist., .027 gap, 35°-40° dwell. Single diaphragm dist., .025 gap, 37°-42° dwell.
⑱—Breakerless distributor.

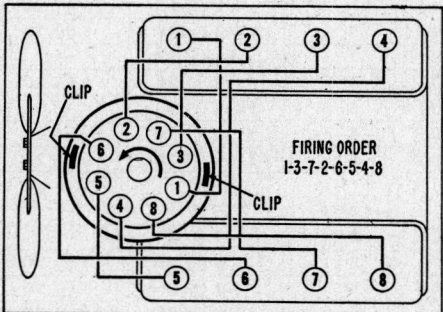

Fig. A

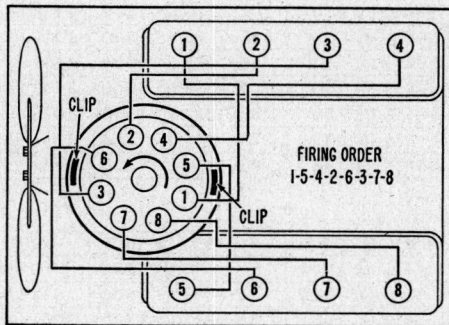

Fig. B

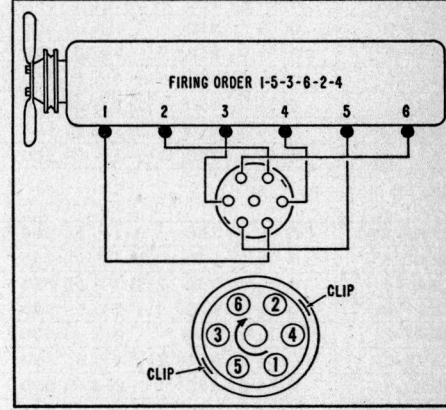

Fig. C

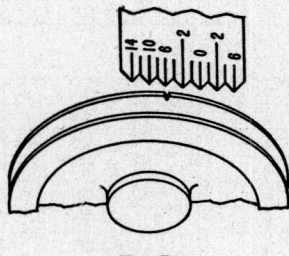

Fig. D

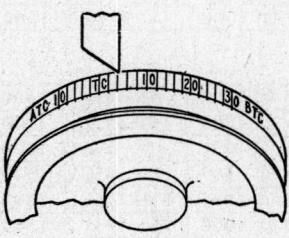

Fig. E

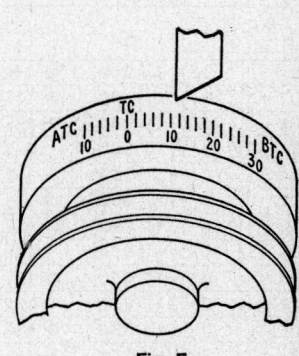

Fig. F

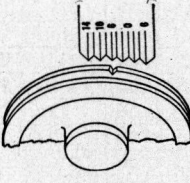

Fig. G

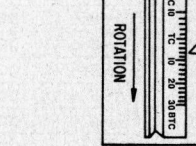

Fig. H

DISTRIBUTOR SPECIFICATIONS

★Note: If unit is checked on vehicle, double the RPM and degrees to get crankshaft figures.
Breaker arm spring tension—17–21.

Distributor Part No.①	Advance Starts	Intermediate Advance			Full Advance	Inches of Vacuum to Start Plunger	Max. Adv. Dist. Deg. @ Vacuum	Max. Retard Dist. Deg. @ Vacuum
1969								
C7AF-AA	0-½ @ 350	0-1½ @ 500	4¼-6¼ @ 750	7½-9¾ @ 1500	12 @ 2000	5	11½ @ 20	—
C8AF-A	0-½ @ 350	0-1½ @ 750	2¼-4½ @ 1000	6-8 @ 1500	10 @ 2000	5	8 @ 25	6 @ 20
C8AF-B	0-½ @ 350	1¾-3¾ @ 750	2¾-5 @ 1000	4½-6¾ @ 1500	8¾ @ 2000	5	9 @ 25	6 @ 20
C8AF-E	0-½ @ 350	0-1¾ @ 500	4½-6¾ @ 750	8-10 @ 1500	12½ @ 2000	5	11 @ 25	6 @ 20
C8AF-R	0-½ @ 350	0-2 @ 500	4¾-6¾ @ 750	7¾-10 @ 1500	12¼ @ 2000	5	12½ @ 25	6 @ 20
C8VF-A	0-½ @ 350	2½-4½ @ 750	6½-8½ @ 1000	8-10¼ @ 1500	11½ @ 2000	5	12 @ 25	—
C8VF-C	0-½ @ 350	2¼-4¼ @ 750	6½-8½ @ 1000	8-10¼ @ 1500	11½ @ 2000	5	12 @ 25	6 @ 20
C9AF-J	0-½ @ 350	½-2½ @ 500	2¼-4¼ @ 750	5¾-8¼ @ 1500	10¾ @ 2000	5	12½ @ 20	—
C9AF-N	0-½ @ 350	1¾-3¾ @ 500	5½-7½ @ 750	7¼-9½ @ 1500	10¾ @ 2000	5	11½ @ 20	—
C9AF-R	0-½ @ 350	1¾-3¾ @ 500	5½-7½ @ 750	7¼-9½ @ 1500	10¾ @ 2000	5	11½ @ 20	6 @ 20
1970								
C7AF-AA	0-½ @ 350	0-1½ @ 500	4¼-6¼ @ 750	7½-9¾ @ 1500	12 @ 2000	5	11½ @ 25	—
C8AF-A	0-½ @ 350	0-1½ @ 750	2¼-4½ @ 1000	6-8 @ 1500	10 @ 2000	5	8 @ 25	6 @ 20
C8AF-B	0-½ @ 350	1¾-3¾ @ 750	2¾-5 @ 1000	4½-6¾ @ 1500	8¾ @ 2000	5	9 @ 25	6 @ 20
C8AF-M	0-½ @ 350	½-2½ @ 500	2¼-4¼ @ 750	5¾-8¾ @ 1500	10¾ @ 1500	5	12½ @ 25	6 @ 20
C8AF-R	0-½ @ 350	0-2 @ 500	4¾-6¾ @ 750	7¾-10 @ 1500	12¼ @ 2000	5	12½ @ 25	6 @ 20
C8VF-C	0-½ @ 350	2¼-4½ @ 750	6½-8½ @ 1000	9-10¼ @ 1500	11½ @ 2000	5	12 @ 25	6 @ 20
C9AF-Y	0-½ @ 350	2-4 @ 500	6¾-8¾ @ 750	8½-10¾ @ 1500	12 @ 2000	5	8½ @ 25	6 @ 20
D0AF-AC	0-½ @ 350	0-2 @ 500	4¼-6¼ @ 750	7½-9¾ @ 1500	12¼ @ 2000	5	9½ @ 25	6 @ 20
D0AF-H	0-½ @ 350	0-2 @ 500	4¼-6¼ @ 750	7½-9¾ @ 1500	12¼ @ 2000	5	8 @ 25	6 @ 20
D0AF-M	0-½ @ 350	2¼-4½ @ 750	6½-8½ @ 1000	9-10¼ @ 1500	11½ @ 2000	5	12 @ 25	6 @ 20
D0AF-T	0-½ @ 350	0-1¾ @ 750	6-8 @ 1000	7¼-9¼ @ 1500	10¾ @ 2000	5	11½ @ 25	3½ @ 20
D0AF-Y	0-½ @ 350	0-1¾ @ 750	6-8 @ 1000	8-10¼ @ 1500	12½ @ 2000	5	11 @ 25	6 @ 20
D0AF-Z	0-½ @ 350	2¼-4¼ @ 750	6½-8½ @ 1000	8-10 @ 1500	11½ @ 2000	5	11 @ 25	—
1971								
C8AF-B	0-½ @ 350	1¾-3¾ @ 750	2¾-5 @ 1000	4½-6¾ @ 1500	8¾ @ 2000	5	9 @ 25	7 @ 20
C8VF-C	0-½ @ 350	0-1½ @ 500	2¼-4½ @ 750	6½-8½ @ 1000	11½ @ 2000	5	12 @ 25	7 @ 20
D1AF-CA	0-½ @ 350	0-1½ @ 500	1-3¼ @ 1000	6-8 @ 1500	10 @ 2000	5	8 @ 25	7 @ 20
D1AF-GA	0-½ @ 350	0-2 @ 500	4½-6¼ @ 750	7½-9¾ @ 1500	12 @ 2000	5	7 @ 25	7 @ 20
D1AF-HA	0-½ @ 350	0-1½ @ 500	4¾-7 @ 750	9½-11¾ @ 1500	14 @ 2000	5	9½ @ 25	7 @ 20
D1AF-KB	0-½ @ 350	0-1½ @ 750	5¼-8 @ 1000	9¾-11¾ @ 1500	14½ @ 2000	5	9½ @ 25	7 @ 20
D1AF-LB	0-½ @ 350	1¼-4½ @ 500	7¾-9¾ @ 750	11½-13½ @ 1500	16¼ @ 2000	5	9 @ 25	4 @ 20
D1MF-FA	0-½ @ 350	0-½ @ 500	2¼-4¼ @ 750	8-10¼ @ 1500	11½ @ 2000	5	11 @ 25	7 @ 20
D1OF-GA	0-½ @ 350	0-1½ @ 500	3¼-5¼ @ 750	8¼-10½ @ 1500	12½ @ 2000	5	11 @ 25	4 @ 20
D0AF-AE	0-½ @ 350	0-2 @ 750	5¼-8 @ 1000	7¼-9¼ @ 1500	10¾ @ 2000	5	2½ @ 25	7 @ 20
D0AF-Y	0-½ @ 350	0-1¾ @ 750	6-8 @ 1000	8-10 @ 1500	12½ @ 2000	5	11 @ 25	7 @ 20
D0OF-U	0-½ @ 350	1¼-3¼ @ 500	5¼-7¼ @ 750	8¼-10½ @ 1500	12¾ @ 2000	5	12½ @ 25	—
1972								
D2AF-BA	0-1 @ 500	1½-4 @ 750	3-5 @ 1000	4½-7 @ 1500	8½ @ 2000	5	9½ @ 20	7 @ 20
D2AF-CA	0-½ @ 500	0-1½ @ 750	4½-6½ @ 1000	7-9½ @ 1500	11 @ 2000	5	5½ @ 20	7 @ 20
D2AF-KA	1-3 @ 500	5½-7½ @ 750	6½-8½ @ 1000	8½-10½ @ 1500	12½ @ 2000	5	13 @ 20	7 @ 20
D2AF-PA	0-1 @ 500	1½-4 @ 750	6½-8½ @ 1000	8½-11 @ 1500	13½ @ 2000	5	9½ @ 20	7 @ 20
D2AF-RA	½-2½ @ 500	2-4 @ 750	3½-5½ @ 1000	6½-9 @ 1500	12 @ 2000	5	13½ @ 20	4 @ 20
D2AF-SA	½-2½ @ 500	2-4 @ 750	3½-5½ @ 1000	6½-9 @ 1500	12 @ 2000	5	13½ @ 20	4 @ 20
D2MF-EA	0-1 @ 500	2-4 @ 750	4½-6½ @ 1000	6-8 @ 1500	9½ @ 2000	5	11½ @ 20	4 @ 20
D2MF-FA	0-1 @ 500	2-4 @ 750	4½-6½ @ 1000	6-8 @ 1500	9½ @ 2000	5	11½ @ 20	4 @ 20
D2SF-EA	0-1 @ 500	0-1½ @ 750	2½-4½ @ 1000	4½-6½ @ 1500	8½ @ 2000	5	—	—
D2ZF-AA	0-1½ @ 500	2-4 @ 750	4½-6½ @ 1000	8-10 @ 1500	12½ @ 2000	5	12½ @ 20	7 @ 20
D2ZF-CA	0-1 @ 500	3½-5½ @ 750	6½-8½ @ 1000	8½-10½ @ 1500	12½ @ 2000	5	10 @ 20	4 @ 20

Continued

DISTRIBUTOR SPECIFICATIONS—Continued

★Note: If unit is checked on vehicle, double the RPM and degrees to get crankshaft figures.

Breaker arm spring tension—17–21.

Distributor Part No.①	Centrifugal Advance Degrees @ RPM of Distributor					Vacuum Advance		Distributor Retard
	Advance Starts	Intermediate Advance			Full Advance	Inches of Vacuum to Start Plunger	Max. Adv. Dist. Deg. @ Vacuum	Max. Retard Dist. Deg. @ Vacuum
1973								
D3AF-AA	0–1½ @ 500	4–6 @ 750	6–8 @ 1000	10–12½ @ 1500	16½ @ 2000	5	13 @ 20	—
D3ZF-CA	0–1 @ 500	3–5½ @ 750	4½–6½ @ 1000	6½–9 @ 1500	11½ @ 2000	5	13 @ 20	—
D3ZF-GA	0–1 @ 500	0–2½ @ 750	2–4 @ 1000	5½–7½ @ 1500	11 @ 2000	5	12½ @ 20	—
D3AF-BA	0–1½ @ 500	3½–5½ @ 750	5½–7½ @ 1000	8½–11 @ 1500	14½ @ 2000	5	13 @ 20	—
D3MF-GA	0–1 @ 500	0–2 @ 750	1½–3½ @ 1000	4½–7 @ 1500	10½ @ 2000	5	13½ @ 20	—
D3MF-DA	0–1 @ 500	1½–4 @ 750	5½–7½ @ 1000	7½–9 @ 1500	10½ @ 2000	5	11 @ 20	—
D3SF-BA	0–1 @ 500	½–2½ @ 750	5½–8 @ 1000	10–12 @ 1500	13½ @ 2000	5	11 @ 20	—
D3VF-CA	0–1 @ 500	0–1½ @ 750	4–6 @ 1000	6–8 @ 1500	10 @ 2000	5	11 @ 20	—
D3MF-BA	0–1 @ 500	0–1½ @ 750	3½–5½ @ 1000	7½–10 @ 1500	11 @ 2000	5	7 @ 20	—
D3VF-AA	0–1 @ 500	0–1½ @ 750	3–5 @ 1000	4–6 @ 1500	7½ @ 2000	5	11 @ 20	—
D3VF-BA	0–1 @ 500	0–2½ @ 750	5–7 @ 1000	7½–10 @ 1500	12 @ 2000	5	7 @ 20	—
1974								
D3AF-AA	0–1½ @ 500	4–6 @ 750	6–8¼ @ 1000	10–12½ @ 1500	15¼ @ 2000	5	13¼ @ 20	—
D3ZF-GA	0–1 @ 500	0–2½ @ 750	2¼–4¼ @ 1000	5½–7½ @ 1500	9½ @ 2000	5	12½ @ 20	—
D4OE-CA	0–½ @ 500	0–1½ @ 750	2–4 @ 1000	5½–7½ @ 1500	9¼ @ 2000	5	13½ @ 20	—
D4VE-CA	0–½ @ 500	0–½ @ 750	3–5 @ 1000	7–9 @ 1500	9½ @ 2000	5	11¼ @ 20	—
1975								
D4AE-AA	0–2 @ 520	4½–7½ @ 800	10–12½ @ 1500	—	15¼ @ 2000	4	12¾ @ 17	—
D4OE-EA	0–2 @ 520	4½–7½ @ 800	10–12½ @ 1500	—	15¼ @ 2000	4	12¾ @ 17	—
D4VE-CA	−1½–+½ @ 800	3–5 @ 1000	—	—	19 @ 2000	4	19¾ @ 14	—

①—Basic part No. 12127.

VALVE SPECIFICATIONS

Year	Engine Model	Valve Lash Int.	Valve Lash Exh.	Valve Angles Seat	Valve Angles Face	Valve Spring Installed Height	Valve Spring Pressure Lbs. @ In.	Stem Clearance Intake	Stem Clearance Exhaust	Stem Diameter Intake	Stem Diameter Exhaust
1969	6-240	1 Turn⑤		45	44	1 9/16	80 @ 1.70	.001–.0027	.001–.0027	.3416–.3423	.3416–.3423
	8-302	1 Turn⑤		45	44	1 5/8	75 @ 1.66	.001–.0027	.0015–.0032	.3416–.3423	.3411–.3418
	8-351	1 Turn⑤		45	44	1 25/32	83 @ 1.79	.001–.0027	.0015–.0032	.3416–.3423	.3411–.3418
	8-390	.100–.200④		45	44	1 7/8	90 @ 1.82	.001–.0027	.0015–.0032	.3711–.3718	.3706–.3713
	8-429	1 Turn⑤		45	44	1 13/16	80 @ 1.81	.001–.0027	.001–.0027	.3416–.3423	.3416–.3423
1970	6-240	1 Turn⑤		45	44	1 9/16	80 @ 1.70	.001–.0027	.001–.0027	.3416–.3423	.3416–.3423
	8-302	.067–.167⑤		45	44	1 5/8	75 @ 1.66	.001–.0027	.0015–.0032	.3416–.3423	.3411–.3418
	8-351	.083–.183⑤		45	44	1 25/32	83 @ 1.79	.001–.0027	.0015–.0032	.3416–.3423	.3411–.3418
	8-390	.100–.200④		①	44	1 7/8	90 @ 1.82	.001–.0027	.0015–.0032	.3711–.3718	.3706–.3713
	8-429	.075–.175④		45	44	1 51/64	80 @ 1.81	.001–.0027	.001–.0027	.3416–.3423	.3416–.3423
1971–72	6-240	1 Turn⑤		45	44	1 9/16	80 @ 1.70	.001–.0027	.001–.0027	.3416–.3423	.3416–.3423
	8-302	.090–.190⑤		45	44	1 5/8	75 @ 1.66	.001–.0027	.0015–.0032	.3416–.3423	.3411–.3418
	8-351③	.100–.200⑤		45	44	1 25/32	83 @ 1.79	.001–.0027	.001–.0027	.3416–.3423	.3411–.3418
	8-351⑥	.100–.200⑤		45	44	1 13/16	80 @ 1.82	.001–.0027	.0015–.0032	.3416–.3423	.3411–.3418
	8-390	.100–.200④		45	44	1 7/8	90 @ 1.82	.001–.0027	.0015–.0032	.3711–.3718	.3706–.3713
	8-400	.100–.200④		45	44	1 13/16	80 @ 1.82	.001–.0027	.0015–.0032	.3416–.3423	.3411–.3418
	8-429	⑦④		45	44	1 51/64	80 @ 1.81	.001–.0027	.001–.0027	.3416–.3423	.3416–.3423
1973	8-351③	.106–.156⑤		45	44	1 25/32	79 @ 1.79	.0010–.0027	.0015–.0032	.3416–.3423	.3411–.3418
	8-351⑥	.100–.150⑤		45	44	1 53/64	84 @ 1.82	.0010–.0027	.0015–.0032	.3416–.3423	.3411–.3418
	8-400	.100–.150⑤		45	44	1 53/64	84 @ 1.82	.0010–.0027	.0015–.0032	.3416–.3423	.3411–.3418
	8-429	.075–.125④		45	44	1 13/16	79 @ 1.78	.0010–.0027	.0010–.0027	.3416–.3423	.3416–.3423
	8-460	.105–.155④		45	44	1 13/16	79 @ 1.78	.0010–.0027	.0010–.0027	.3416–.3423	.3416–.3423
1974	8-351③	.106–.156④		45	44	1 51/64	75 @ 1.79	.0010–.0027	.0015–.0032	.3416–.3423	.3411–.3418
	8-351⑥	.100–.150④		45	44	1 13/16	80 @ 1.82	.0010–.0027	.0015–.0032	.3416–.3423	.3411–.3418
	8-400	.100–.150④		45	44	1 13/16	80 @ 1.82	.0010–.0027	.0015–.0032	.3416–.3423	.3411–.3418
	8-460	.075–.125④		45	44	1 13/16	80 @ 1.81	.0010–.0027	.0010–.0027	.3416–.3423	.3416–.3423
1975	V8-351	—		45	45	1.82	⑧	.001–.0027	.0015–.0032	.3416–.3423	.3411–.3418
	V8-400	—		45	45	1.82	⑧	.001–.0027	.0015–.0032	.3416–.3423	.3411–.3418
	V8-460	.075–.125		45	45	1.81	253 @ 1.33	.001–.0027	.0015–.0032	.3416–.3423	.3416–.3423

①—Intake 30°, exhaust 45°.
③—Windsor engine.
④—Clearance specified is obtainable at valve stem tip with lifter collapsed. See "Valves, Adjust" text.
⑤—See text under Valves, Adjust for procedure.
⑥—Cleveland engine.
⑦—1971, .155; 1972, .075–.125.
⑧—Intake 210 @ 1.39, Exhaust 226 @ 1.39.

PISTONS, PINS, RINGS, CRANKSHAFT & BEARINGS

Year	Engine Model	Piston Clearance	Ring End Gap① Comp.	Ring End Gap① Oil	Wrist-pin Diam-eter	Rod Bearings Shaft Diameter	Rod Bearings Bearing Clearance	Main Bearings Shaft Diameter	Main Bearings Bearing Clearance	Thrust on Bear. No.	Shaft End Play
1969–73	6-240	.0014–.0022	.010	.015	.9121	2.1228–2.1236	.0008–.0015	2.3982–2.3990	.0005–.0015	5	.004–.008
	8-302	.0018–.0026	.010	.015	.9121	2.1228–2.1236	.0008–.0015	2.2482–2.2490	.0005–.0015	3	.004–.008
	8-351②	.0018–.0026	.010	.015	.912	2.3103–2.3110	.0008–.0015	2.9994–3.0002	.0013–.0025	3	.004–.008
	8-351③	.0014–.0022	.010	.015	.912	2.3103–2.3110	.0008–.0026	2.7484–2.7492	.0009–.0026	3	.004–.008
	8-390	.0015–.0023	.010	.015	.975	2.4380–2.4388	.0008–.0015	2.7484–2.7492	.0013–.0025	3	.004–.010
	8-400	.0014–.0022	.010	.015	.975	2.3103–2.3111	.0008–.0026	2.9994–3.0002	.0009–.0026	3	.004–.010
	8-427	.0030–.0038	.018	.015	.975	2.4380–2.4388	.0008–.0015	2.7484–2.7492	.0005–.0015	3	.004–.010
	8-428	.0015–.0023	.010	.015	.975	2.4380–2.4388	.0008–.0015	2.7484–2.7492	.0005–.0015	3	.004–.010
	8-429	.0014–.0022	.010	.015	1.041	2.4992–2.5000	.0008–.0015	2.9994–3.0002	.0005–.0015	3	.004–.008
	8-460	.0014–.0022	.010	.015	1.040	2.4992–2.5000	.0008–.0015	2.9994–3.0002	.0005–.0015	3	.004–.008
1974	8-351②	.0018–.0026	.010	.015	.912	2.3103–2.3111	.0008–.0026	2.9994–3.0002	.0008–.0026	3	.004–.008
	8-351③	.0014–.0022	.010	.015	.912	2.3103–2.3111	.0008–.0026	2.7482–2.7492	.0009–.0026	3	.004–.008
	8-400	.0014–.0022	.010	.015	.975	2.3103–2.3111	.0008–.0026	2.9994–3.0002	.0009–.0026	3	.004–.008
	8-460	.0022–.0030	.010	.015	1.040	2.4992–2.5000	.0008–.0026	2.9994–3.0002	④	3	.004–.008
1975	V8-351	.0014–.0022	.010	.015	.9752	2.3107	.0008–.0026	2.9988	.0009–.0026	3	.004–.008
	V8-400	.0014–.0022	.010	.015	.9752	2.3107	.0008–.0026	2.9988	.0009–.0026	3	.004–.008
	V8-460	.0013–.0023	.010	.015	1.0401	2.4992–2.500	.0008–.0028	2.9998	⑤	3	.004–.008

①—Fit rings in tapered bores for clearance listed in tightest portion of ring travel.
②—Windsor engine.
③—Cleveland engine.
④—#1, .0004–.0020; others, .0012–.0028.
⑤—No. 1—.0004–.0022; #2, 3, 4, 5—.0009–.0027.

STARTING MOTOR SPECIFICATIONS

Year	Model	Ident. No.	Rotation	Brush Spring Tension Ounces	No Load Test Amperes	No Load Test Volts	No Load Test R.P.M.	Torque Text Amperes	Torque Text Volts	Torque Ft. Lbs.
1969–70	6-240, 8-302, 351	C7AF-B	C	40	70	12	9500	670	5.0	15.5
	6-240, 8-302, 351	C9ZF-A	C	40	70	12	9500	670	5.0	15.5
	8-390	C7AF-C	C	40	70	12	9500	670	5.0	15.5
	8-429	C9AF-A	C	40	70	12	10000	700	5.0	15.5
1971	6-240, 8-302, 351	D0AF-B	C	40	70	12	9500	670	5.0	15.5
	8-390	D0AF-A	C	40	70	12	9500	670	5.0	15.5
	8-429	C9AF-A	C	40	70	12	10000	700	5.0	15.5
1972-73	6-240, 8-302, 351	D2AF-CA	C	40	70	12	9500	670	5.0	15.5
	8-429, 460	D2AF-AA	C	40	70	12	10000	700	5.0	15.5
1974	8-351	D2AF-CA	C	—	—	—	—	—	—	—
	8-400	D4AF-BA	C	—	—	—	—	—	—	—
	8-460	D4AF-AA	C	80	90	12	—	—	—	—
1975	V8-351	D2AF-AA	C	—	—	—	—	—	—	—
	V8-400	D5AF-BB	C	—	—	—	—	—	—	—
	V8-460	D5AF-AB	C	—	—	—	—	—	—	—

FORD & MERCURY — Full Size Models

ENGINE TIGHTENING SPECIFICATIONS*

★Torque specifications are for clean and lightly lubricated threads only. Dry or dirty threads produce increased friction which prevents accurate measurement of tightness.

Year	Engine Model	Spark Plugs Ft. Lbs.	Cylinder Head Bolts Ft. Lbs.	Intake Manifold Ft. Lbs.	Exhaust Manifold Ft. Lbs.	Rocker Arm Shaft Bracket Ft. Lbs.	Rocker Arm Cover Ft. Lbs.	Connecting Rod Cap Bolts Ft. Lbs.	Main Bearing Cap Bolts Ft. Lbs.	Flywheel to Crank-shaft Ft. Lbs.	Vibration Damper or Pulley Ft. Lbs.
1969–72	6-240	15–20	70–75	23–28	23–28	—	7–9	40–45	60–70	75–85	130–150
1969–72	V8-302	15–20	65–72	23–25	12–16	—	3–5	19–24	60–70	75–85	70–90
1969–72	V8-351	15–20	95–100	23–25	18–24	—	3–5	40–45	95–105	75–85	70–90
1969–71	V8-390	15–20	80–90	32–35	18–24	40–45	4–7	40–45	95–105	75–85	70–90
1971–72	V8-400	15–20	95–105	②	12–16	18–25①	3–5	40–45	95–105	75–85	70–90
1969–72	V8-429	15–20	130–140	25–30	28–33	65–75①	5–6	40–45	95–105	75–85	70–90
1973	V8-351③	15–20	105–112	23–25	18–24	17–23①	3–5	40–45	95–105	75–85	100–130
	V8-351④	15–20	95–105	②	12–22	18–25①	3–5	40–45	⑤	75–85	70–90
	V8-400	15–20	95–105	②	12–16	18–25①	3–5	40–45	⑤	75–85	70–90
	V8-429, 460	15–20	130–140	25–30	28–33	18–25①	5–6	40–45	95–105	75–85	70–90
1974	V8-351③	15–20	105–112	19–27	18–24	17–23①	3–5	40–45	95–105	75–85	100–130
	V8-351④	15–20	95–105	⑥	12–22	18–25①	3–5	40–45	⑤	75–85	70–90
	V8-400	15–20	95–105	⑥	12–16	18–25①	3–5	40–45	⑤	75–85	70–90
	V8-460	15–20	130–140	22–32	28–33	18–25①	5–6	40–45	95–105	75–85	70–90

①—Rocker arm stud to cylinder head. ②—5/16″ bolts 21–25 ft. lbs. 3/8″ bolts 27–33 ft. lbs. 1/4″ bolts 6–9 ft. lbs. ③—Windsor engine. ④—Cleveland engine. ⑤—1/2″ bolts 95–105 ft. lbs. 3/8″ bolts 35–45 ft. lbs. ⑥—5/16″ bolts, 22–32, 3/8″ bolts, 17–25, 1/4″ bolts, 6–9.

WHEEL ALIGNMENT SPECIFICATIONS

OLD CAR SPECIFICATIONS: For 1946-68 Wheel Alignment Specifications see main index.

Year	Model	Caster Angle, Degrees Limits	Caster Angle, Degrees Desired	Camber Angle, Degrees Limits Left	Camber Angle, Degrees Limits Right	Camber Angle, Degrees Desired Left	Camber Angle, Degrees Desired Right	Toe-In. Inch	Toe-Out on Turns, Deg.① Outer Wheel	Toe-Out on Turns, Deg.① Inner Wheel
1969	All	0 to +2	+1	−1/4 to +1 1/4	−1/4 to +1 1/4	+1/2	+1/2	3/16	②	20
1970–72	All	0 to +2	+1	−1/4 to +1 1/4	−1/4 to +1 1/4	+1/2	+1/2	3/16	19 1/8	20
1973	All	0 to +4	+2	−1 to +1	−1 to +1	0	0	3/16	18 3/4	20
1974–75	All	0 to +4	+2	−1/2 to +1 1/2	−3/4 to +1 1/4	+1/2	+1/4	3/16	18 3/4	20

①—Incorrect toe-out, when other adjustments are correct, indicates bent steering arms.
②—Manual steering 18.96°; Power steering 19.14°.

ALTERNATOR & REGULATOR SPECIFICATIONS

Year	Make or Model	Current Rating		Field Current @ 75°F.		Voltage Regulator				Field Relay	
		Amperes	Volts	Amperes	Volts	Part No. (10316)	Voltage @ 75°F.	Contact Gap	Armature Air Gap	Armature Air Gap	Closing Voltage @ 75°F.
1969	C6AF-10300-A	55	15	2.8–3.3	12	C3SZ-B	13.5–15.3	②	②	②	2.3–4.2
	C6AF-10300-B	42	15	2.8–3.3	12	C3SZ-B	13.5–15.3	②	②	②	2.3–4.2
	C6AF-10300-F	55	15	2.8–3.3	12	C3SZ-B	13.5–15.3	②	②	②	2.3–4.2
	C6AF-10300-G	55	15	2.8–3.3	12	C3SZ-B	13.5–15.3	②	②	②	2.3–4.2
	C7AF-10300-A	65	15	2.9	12	C3SZ-B	14.3–15.1	.045–.052	.010–.015	.015	3.0–4.0
	C9AF-10300-A	42	15	2.8–3.3	12	C3SZ-B	13.5–15.3	②	②	②	2.3–4.2
1970–72	D0ZF-10300-B	38	15	2.4	12	C3SZ-B	13.5–15.3	②	②	②	2.0–4.2
	D0AF-10300-C	42	15	2.9	12	C3SZ-B	13.5–15.3	②	②	②	2.0–4.2
	D0AF-10300-F	42	15	2.9	12	C3SZ-B	13.5–15.3	②	②	②	2.0–4.2
	D0AF-10300-G	42	15	2.9	12	C3SZ-B	13.5–15.3	②	②	②	2.0–4.2
	D0AF-10300-E	55	15	2.9	12	C3SZ-B	13.5–15.3	②	②	②	2.0–4.2
	D0AF-10300-H	55	15	2.9	12	C3SZ-B	13.5–15.3	②	②	②	2.0–4.2
	D0ZF-10300-A	55	15	2.9	12	C3SZ-B	13.6–15.1	.018–.020	.042–.052	.011–.018	6.2–7.2
	D0ZF-10300-C	55	15	2.9	12	C3SZ-B	13.6–15.1	.018–.020	.042–.052	.011–.018	6.2–7.2
	D0SF-10300-A	55	15	2.9	12	C3SZ-B	13.6–15.1	.018–.020	.042–.052	.011–.018	6.2–7.2
	D1ZF-10300-AA	55	15	2.9	12	C3SZ-B	13.5–15.3	②	②	②	2.0–4.2
	D1AF-10300-AA	61	15	2.9	12	C3SZ-B	13.5–15.3	②	②	②	2.0–4.2
	D1AF-10300-BA	65	15	2.9	12	C3SZ-B	13.5–15.3	②	②	②	2.0–4.2
	D0AF-10300-A ③	65	15	2.9	12	—	—	—	—	—	—
	C5TF-10300-K	65	15	2.9	12	—	—	—	—	—	—
1973	Orange ①	42	15	2.9	12	D3TZ-A	13.5–15.3	—	—	—	2½–4
	Red ①	55	15	2.9	12	D3TZ-A	13.5–15.3	—	—	—	2½–4
	Green ①	61	15	2.9	12	D3TZ-A	13.5–15.3	—	—	—	2½–4
	All	70	15	2.9	12	D3TZ-A	13.5–15.3	—	—	—	2½–4
	All	90	15	2.9	12	D3TZ-A	13.5–15.3	—	—	—	2½–4
1974	Purple ①	38	15	2.9	12	D4TZ-A	—	—	—	—	—
	Orange ①	42	15	2.9	12	D4TZ-A	—	—	—	—	—
	Red ①	55	15	2.9	12	D4TZ-A	—	—	—	—	—
	Green ①	61	15	2.9	12	D4TZ-A	—	—	—	—	—
	All	70	15	2.9	12	D4TZ-A	—	—	—	—	—
	All	90	15	2.9	12	D4TZ-A	—	—	—	—	—
1975	D3VF-10300-AB	90	—	—	—	D4TF-AA	13.5–15.3	—	—	—	2.5–4
	D3OF-10300-AA	70	—	—	—	D4TF-AA	13.5–15.3	—	—	—	2.5–4
	D3OF-10300-BA	55	—	—	—	D4AF-AA	13.5–15.3	—	—	—	2.5–4
	D3OF-10300-EA	61	—	—	—	D4AF-AA	13.5–15.3	—	—	—	2.5–4
	D3OF-10300-FA	42	—	—	—	D4AF-AA	13.5–15.3	—	—	—	2.5–4
	D32F-10300-BA	61	—	—	—	D4AF-AA	13.5–15.3	—	—	—	2.5–4
	D4LF-10300-AA	55	—	—	—	D4AF-AA	13.5–15.3	—	—	—	2.5–4
	D4LF-10300-CA	55	—	—	—	D4AF-AA	13.5–15.3	—	—	—	2.5–4
	D4OF-10300-AA	42	—	—	—	D4AF-AA	13.5–15.3	—	—	—	2.5–4
	D4OF-10300-BA	55	—	—	—	D4AF-AA	13.5–15.3	—	—	—	2.5–4
	D4OF-10300-DA	61	—	—	—	D4AF-AA	13.5–15.3	—	—	—	2.5–4
	D4OF-10300-EA	70	—	—	—	D4TF-AA	13.5–15.3	—	—	—	2.5–4
	D42F-10300-BA	61	—	—	—	D4AF-AA	13.5–15.3	—	—	—	2.5–4

①—Identification tag.　②—Not adjustable.　③—Integral regulator.

FORD & MERCURY — Full Size Models

REAR AXLE SPECIFICATIONS

Year	Model	Carrier Type	Ring Gear & Pinion Backlash Inch	Nominal Pinion Locating Shim, Inch	Pinion Bearing Preload				Differential Bearing Preload	Pinion Nut Torque Ft.-Lbs.①
					New Bearings With Seal Inch-Lbs.	Used Bearings With Seal Inch-Lbs.	New Bearings Less Seal Inch-Lbs.	Used Bearings Less Seal Inch-Lbs.		
1969-73	④	Integral	.008–.012	.030	22–32	8–14	—	—	.008–.012⑥	140
	Others	Removable	.008–.012	.015	22–32⑤	8–14	—	—	.008–.012③	⑦
1974	—	Integral	.008–.012	.030	17–27	8–14	—	—	.008–.012⑥	140
	—	Removable	.008–.012	.015	17–27⑤	8–14	—	—	.008–.012③	⑧

①—If torque cannot be obtained, install new spacer.
③—Case spread with new bearings; with used bearings .005–.008".
④—8-302 engine with two-barrel carburetor and 6-240 engine.
⑤—Solid spacer 13–33 inch-lbs.
⑥—Case spread with new bearing; with used bearings .006–.010".
⑦—Collapsible spacer 175 ft. lbs.; solid spacer 200 ft. lbs.
⑧—Collapsible spacer 170 ft. lbs.; solid spacer 200 ft. lbs.

BRAKE SPECIFICATIONS

Year	Model	Brake Drum Inside Diameter	Wheel Cylinder Bore Diameter			Master Cylinder Bore Diameter		
			Front Disc Brake	Front Drum Brake	Rear Brake	With Disc Brakes	With Drum Brakes	With Power Brakes
1969–72	All Passenger Cars	11.03	2.755	1.125	.938	1.00	1.00	1.00
	All Wagons	11.03	2.755	1.094	.938	1.00	1.00	1.00
1973	All Passenger Cars	11.03	3.100	1.125	1.00	1.00	1.00	1.00
	All Wagons	11.03	3.100	0.875	0.875	1.00	1.00	1.00
1974	All	11.03	3.100	—	1.00	1.00	1.00	1.00
1975	All①	11.03	3.1	—	1	1	—	1
	All②		3.1	—	—	1⅛	—	1⅛

①—Except 4 wheel disc brakes with hydro boost.
②—With 4 wheel disc brakes with hydro boost.

COOLING SYSTEM & CAPACITY DATA

Year	Model or Engine	Cooling Capacity, Qts.			Radiator Cap Relief Pressure, Lbs.		Thermo. Opening Temp. ①	Fuel Tank Gals.	Engine Oil Refill Qts. ②	Transmission Oil			Rear Axle Oil Pints
		No Heater	With Heater	With A/C	With A/C	No A/C				3 Speed Pints	4 Speed Pints	Auto. Trans. Qts. ③	

FORD

1969	6-240	12	13	13	12–15	12–15	195	24⑥	4	3½	4	⑬	4½
	8-302	14	15	15	12–15	12–15	195	24⑥	4	3½	4	⑬	4½
	8-390	19½	20½	20½	12–15	12–15	195	24⑥	4	3½	4	⑫	5
	8-429	19½	20½	20½	12–15	12–15	195	24⑥	4	3½	4	12¾	5
1970	6-240	13½	14½	14½	12–15	12–15	195	24⑩	4	3½	4	⑬	4½
	8-302	13½	14½	14½	12–15	12–15	195	24⑩	4	3½	4	⑬	4½
	8-351	15½	16½	16½	12–15	12–15	195	24⑩	4	3½	4	⑬	5
	8-390	19	20	20	12–15	12–15	195	24⑩	4	3½	4	⑬	5
	8-429	17½	18½	18½	12–15	12–15	195	24⑩	4	3½	4	12¾	5

Continued

COOLING SYSTEM & CAPACITY DATA—Continued

Year	Model or Engine	Cooling Capacity, Qts.			Radiator Cap Relief Pressure, Lbs.		Thermo. Opening Temp. ①	Fuel Tank Gals.	Engine Oil Refill Qts. ②	Transmission Oil			Rear Axle Oil Pints
		No Heater	With Heater	With A/C	With A/C	No A/C				3 Speed Pints	4 Speed Pints	Auto. Trans. Qts. ③	
FORD—Continued													
1971	6-240	13	14	14	12-15	12-15	195	23⑩	4	3½	4	⑬	⑤
	8-302	14	15	15	12-15	12-15	195	23⑩	4*	3½	4	⑬	⑤
	8-351	15¼	16¼	16¼	12-15	12-15	195	23⑩	4	3½	4	11	5
	8-390	19	20	20	12-15	12-15	195	23⑩	4	3½	4	12¾	5
	8-400	16½	17½	18¼	12-15	12-15	195	23⑩	4	3½	4	12¾	5
	8-429	18	19	19	12-15	12-15	195	23⑩	4	3½	4	12¾	5
1972	6-240	13¼	14¼	14¼	12-15	12-15	195	22④	4	—	—	⑬	⑤
	8-302	14¼	15¼	15¼	12-15	12-15	195	22④	4	—	—	⑬	⑤
	8-351	15½	16½	16½	12-15	12-15	195	22④	4	—	—	⑬	5
	8-400	16¾	17¾	18¼	12-15	12-15	195	22④	4	—	—	12¾	5
	8-429	17¾	18¾	20	12-15	12-15	195	22④	4	—	—	12¾	5
1973	8-351⑧	14½	15½	16¼	12-15	12-15	195	22④	4	—	—	10¼	4
	8-351⑨	15½	16½	17	12-15	12-15	195	22④	4	—	—	10¼	4
	8-400	17	18	18	12-15	12-15	195	22④	4	—	—	12½	⑥
	8-429	18½	19½	19½	12-15	12-15	195	22④	4	—	—	12½	5
1974	8-351⑧	15.3	16½	17.2	12-16	12-16	191	22④	4	—	—	⑪	⑥
	8-351⑨	15.3	16½	16½	12-16	12-16	191	22④	4	—	—	⑭	⑥
	8-400	17	18	18½	12-16	12-16	191	22④	4	—	—	⑭	⑥
	8-460	18.4	19½	19½	12-16	12-16	191	22④	4	—	—	12½	⑥
1975	8-351	—	17.1	17.6	12-16	12-16	191	24.2④	3½	—	—	⑪	⑥
	8-400	—	17.1	17.6	12-16	12-16	191	24.2④	3½	—	—	⑬	⑥
	8-460	—	18.5	18.5⑮	12-16	12-16	191	24.2④	4⑯	—	—	⑬	⑥
MERCURY													
1969	All	19½	20½	20½	12-15	12-15	195	24⑧	4	3½	—	12¾	5
1970	8-390	19	20	20	12-15	12-15	195	24⑩	4	3½	—	12¾	5
	8-429	17½	18½	18½	12-15	12-15	195	24⑩	4	3½	—	12¾	5
1971	8-351	15¼	16¼	16¼	12-15	12-15	195	23⑩	4	3½	—	11	5
	8-400	16½	17½	18¼	12-15	12-15	195	23⑩	4	3½	—	12¾	5
	8-429	18	19	19	12-15	12-15	195	23⑩	4	3½	—	12¾	5
1972	8-351	15¼	16¼	16¾	12-15	12-15	195	22½⑦	4	—	—	11	5
	8-400	16.6	17.6	18.3	12-15	12-15	195	22½⑦	4	—	—	12¾	5
	8-429	17.8	18.8	19½	12-15	12-15	195	22½⑦	4	—	—	12¾	5
1973	8-351⑧	14½	15½	16¼	12-15	12-15	195	22④	4	—	—	10¼	⑥
	8-351⑨	15½	16½	17	12-15	12-15	195	22④	4	—	—	10¼	⑥
	8-400	17	18	18	12-15	12-15	195	22④	4	—	—	12½	⑥
	8-429, 460	18½	19½	19½	12-15	12-15	195	22④	4	—	—	12½	⑥
1974	8-351⑧	15.3	16½	17	12-16	12-16	191	22④	4	—	—	10½	⑥
	8-400	17	18	18½	12-16	12-16	191	22④	4	—	—	⑬	⑥
	8-460	18.4	19½	19½	12-16	12-16	191	22④	4	—	—	12½	⑥
1975	8-400	—	17.1	17.6	12-16	12-16	191	24.2④	3½	—	—	⑬	⑥
	8-460	—	18.5	18.5⑮	12-16	12-16	191	24.2④	4⑯	—	—	⑬	⑥

①—For alcohol type anti-freeze use a 160° unit.
②—Add one quart with filter change.
③—Approximate. Make final check with dipstick.
④—Station Wagons 21 gals.
⑤—WER axles 4, all others 5.
⑥—Station Wagons 20 gals.
⑦—Station Wagons 21½ gallons.
⑧—Cleveland engine.
⑨—Windsor engine.
⑩—Station Wagon 22 gals.
⑪—C4 10½ qts., FMX 11 qts.
⑫—Three spd. 11 qts., C6 13 qts.
⑬—FMX 11 qts., C6 12½ qts.
⑭—FMX 11 qts., C6 12½ qts., CW 11⅛ qts.
⑮—Medium duty 19 qts., Heavy duty and Police 20 qts.
⑯—Police Models 6 qts.

Electrical Section

DISTRIBUTOR, REPLACE
Removal

1. To remove the distributor, disconnect the primary wire and vacuum control pipe. On some models the work may be made easier if the acceleration pull back spring is disconnected.
2. Remove distributor cap.
3. Scribe a mark on the distributor body indicating the position of the rotor, and scribe another mark on the body and engine block indicating position of distributor body in block. These marks can be used as guides when installing distributor in a correctly timed engine.
4. Remove hold down screw or screws and lift distributor out of block. *Do not crank engine while distributor is removed or the initial timing operation will have to be performed.*

Installation

If the crankshaft has not been disturbed, install the distributor, using the scribed marks previously made on the distributor body and engine block as guides.

If the crankshaft has been rotated while the distributor was removed from the engine, it will be necessary to retime the engine. Crank the engine to bring No. 1 piston on top dead center of its compression stroke. Align the timing mark on the vibration damper or pulley with the timing pointer (see *Tune Up* chart). Install the distributor so that the rotor points to the No. 1 spark plug wire terminal in the distributor cap.

NOTE: On all overhead valve engines, make sure the oil pump intermediate shaft properly engages the distributor shaft. It may be necessary to crank the engine with the starter, after the distributor drive gear is properly engaged, in order to engage the oil pump intermediate shaft.

STARTER REPLACE

SERVICE BULLETIN

STARTER PROBLEMS: If the starter is noisy or if it locks up, before condemning the starter, loosen the three mounting bolts enough to hand fit the starter properly into the pilot plate. Then tighten the mounting bolts, starting with the top bolt.

1969-75 Ford & Mercury

1. Disconnect cable at starter terminal.
2. Remove screws and take off starter.
3. Reverse procedure to install and torque bolts to 15-20 ft. lbs.

IGNITION LOCK, REPLACE
1970-75

1. Disconnect battery ground cable.
2. *Units with Fixed Steering Columns:* Remove steering wheel and trim pad. Insert a .090 inch wire pin in the hole located inside the column halfway down the lock cylinder housing, Fig. 1. *Units with Tilt Steering Columns:* Insert wire pin in the hole located on the outside of the flange casting next to the emergency flasher button, Fig. 1.
3. Place the gear shift lever in *PARK* (with automatic trans) or *REVERSE* (with manual trans) position, and turn the lock cylinder with the ignition key to *RUN* position.
4. Depress the wire pin while pulling up on the lock cylinder to remove. Remove the wire pin.
5. To install insert the lock cylinder into housing in the flange casting, and turn the key to *OFF* position. Be certain that the cylinder is fully inserted before turning to the *OFF* position. This action will extend the cylinder retaining pin into the cylinder housing.
6. Turn the key to check for correct operation in all positions.
7. Install the steering wheel and trim pad on fixed column units.
8. Connect the battery ground cable.

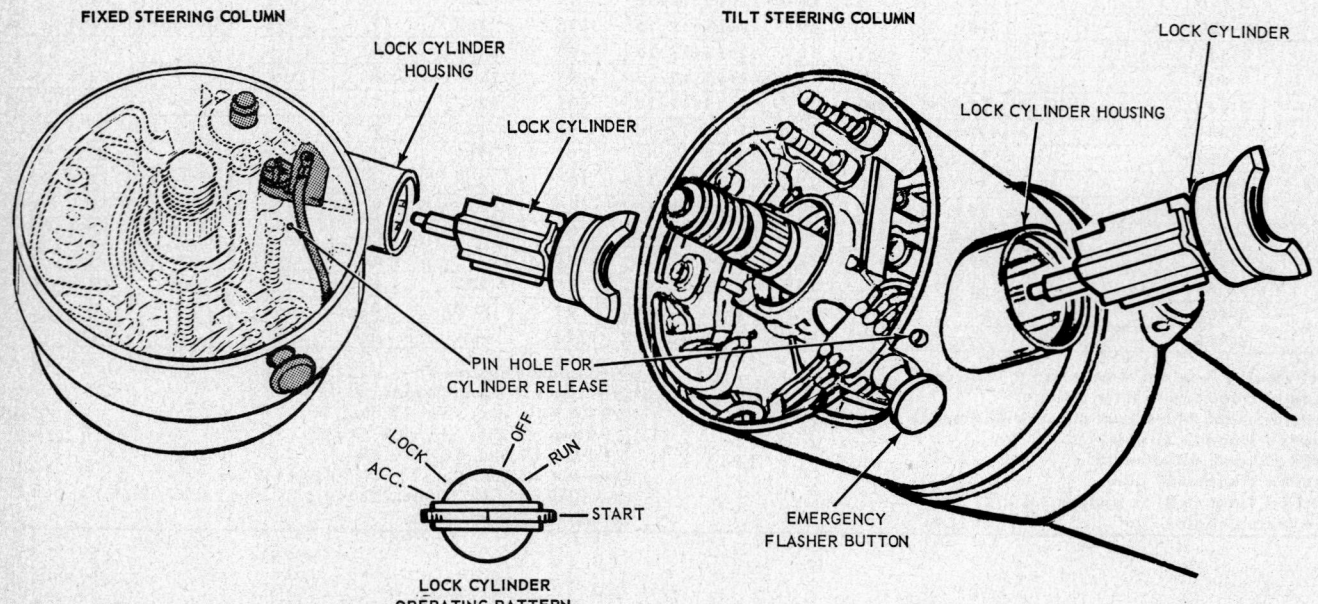

Fig. 1   Ignition Lock. 1970-75

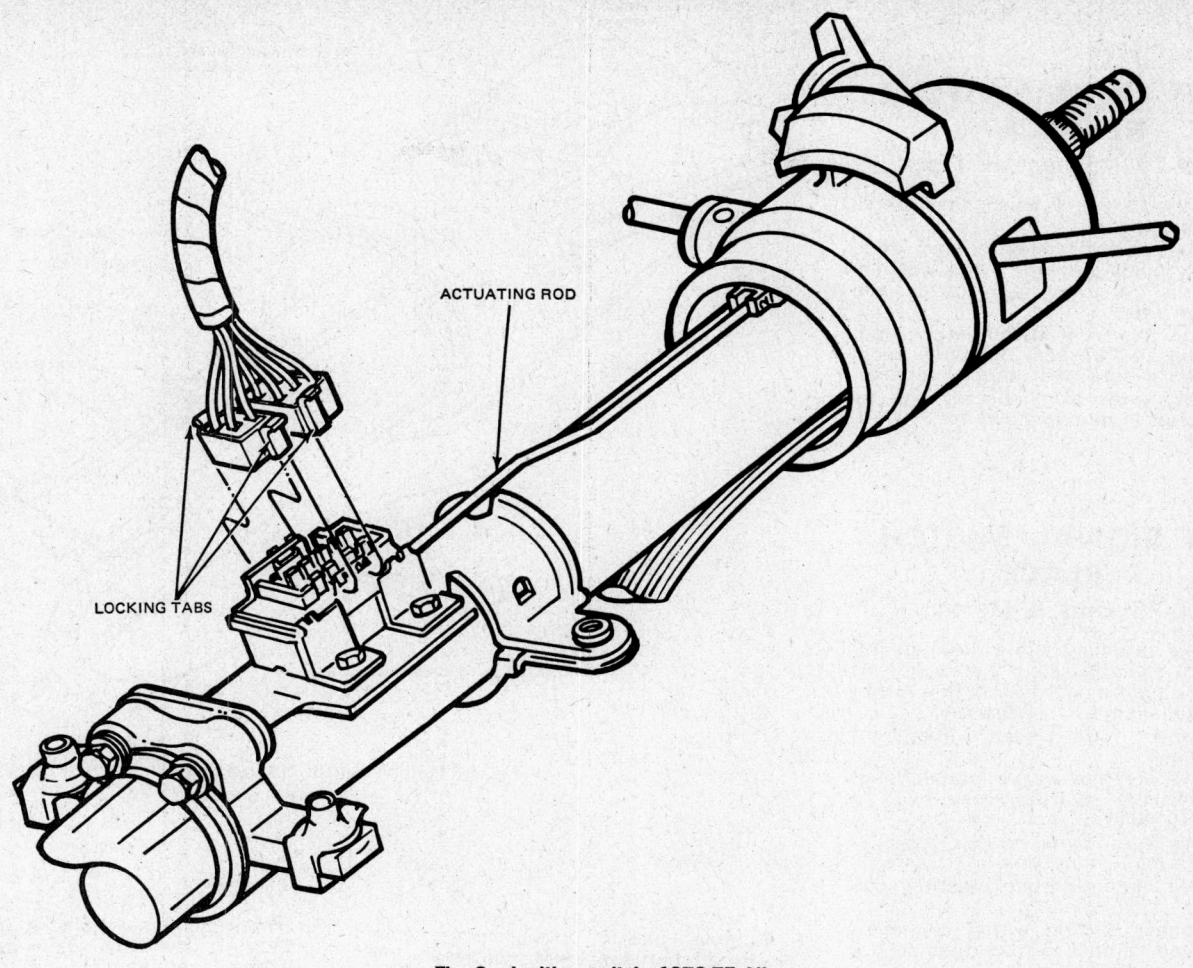

ACTUATING ROD

LOCKING TABS

Fig. 2   Ignition switch. 1972-75 All

IGNITION SWITCH, REPLACE

1970-75 Ford & Mercury

1. Remove steering column shroud and lower steering column from brake support bracket.
2. Disconnect battery cable.
3. Disconnect switch wiring and remove two switch retaining nuts. Disconnect switch from actuator and remove switch, Figs. 2 and 3.
4. Move shift lever to Park position on automatic transmissions and Reverse on standard transmission units. Place ignition key in Lock position and remove the key.

NOTE: New replacement switches are pinned in the Lock position by a plastic shipping pin inserted in a locking hole in the switch. For an existing switch, pull plunger out as far as it will go then back one detent to Lock position and insert a $3/32''$ drill in locking hole to retain switch in Lock position.

5. With locking pin in place, install switch on steering column, determine mid position of actuator lash and tighten retaining bolts.
6. Remove locking pin.

1969 Ford & Mercury

1. Disconnect battery ground cable.
2. Insert ignition key in switch. Turn key to accessory position and insert a wire pin in hole on ignition switch. Slightly depress pin while turning counterclockwise past the accessory position; this will release lock cylinder from switch. Pull lock cylinder from switch with the key, Fig. 4.
3. Remove bezel nut retaining switch to instrument panel and lower switch.
4. Depress tabs securing multiple connector from switch and remove switch.
5. Reverse procedure to install.

LIGHT SWITCH, REPLACE

All Except 1970 Mercury

1. Disconnect battery ground cable.

2. On 1973-75 models, remove wiper switch knob.
3. With headlight switch "On" on all models, depress release button on switch housing and remove knob and shaft, Fig. 5.
4. On 1969 Mercury, remove wiring harness bracket screws from switch and remove bracket.
5. On all models remove bezel nut from light switch and on 1973-75 models, remove lower finish panel.
6. On 1972-75 Mercury and 1972 Ford models, remove three mounting plate screws.
7. Disconnect electrical connector. If equipped with concealed headlamps, disconnect vacuum hoses from switch and remove switch.

1970 Mercury

1. Disconnect battery ground cable.
2. From behind instrument panel, disconnect wiring plug and vacuum hoses if so equipped from switch.
3. Remove four retaining screws and pull switch out from behind instrument panel.

STOP LIGHT SWITCH, REPLACE

1969-75 Mechanical Type

1. Referring to Fig. 6, disconnect wires at connector.
2. Remove hairpin retainer and slide switch, push rod and nylon washers and bushing away from pedal, and remove switch.
3. Position the new switch, push rod, bushing and washers on brake pedal pin and secure with hairpin retainer.
4. Connect wires at connector and install wires in retaining clip.

TURN SIGNAL SWITCH, REPLACE

1970-75 Ford & Mercury

1. Remove retaining screw from underside of steering wheel spoke and lift off the pad horn switch/trim cover and medallion as an assembly.
2. Disconnect horn switch wires from terminals.
3. Remove steering wheel retaining nut and remove steering wheel with a suitable puller.
4. Remove turn signal switch lever by unscrewing it from column.
5. Remove shroud from steering column.
6. Disconnect column wiring connector plug and remove screws that secure switch to column.
7. On tilt column models, remove wires and terminals from column wiring plug.

NOTE: *Record the color code and position of each wire before removing it from plug. A hole provided in the flange casting on fixed column models makes it unnecessary to separate wires from plug. The plug with wires installed can be guided through the hole.*

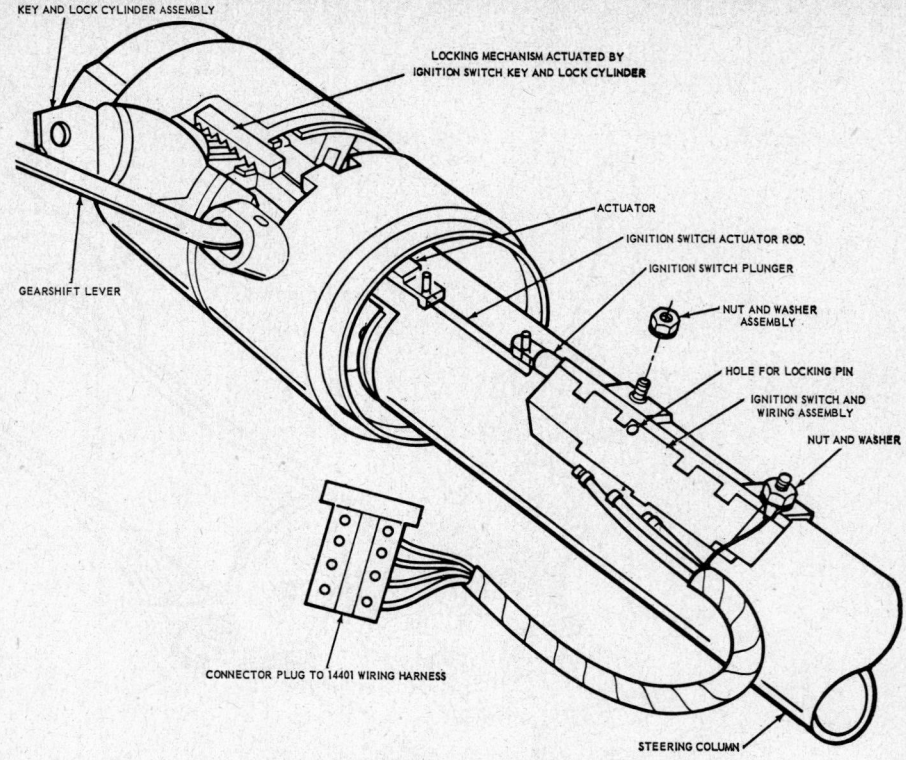

Fig. 3   Ignition switch. 1970-71 All

8. Remove plastic cover sleeve from wiring harness and remove the switch from top of column.
On vehicles equipped with speed control, transfer the ground brush located in the turn signal cancelling cam to the new switch assembly.

1969 Ford & Mercury

Removal
1. Disconnect battery ground cable.
2. Remove horn button and steering wheel.
3. Remove turn indicator handle.
4. Unscrew and remove turn indicator switch from steering column tube.
5. Disconnect connector blocks at the column.
6. From lower portion of column, remove cover from wiring and tie a cord to the wire ends. Remove switch from top of column, feeding wiring and cord up the column.

Installation
1. Attach the wire ends of a new turn indicator switch to the cord and feed wires down through steering column. Remove cord and install cover.

2. Install connector blocks in column. Plug in electrical leads and secure wiring in retaining clip.
3. Install switch to steering column tube and install indicator handle.
4. Install steering wheel and horn button, and connect battery cable.

NEUTRAL SAFETY SWITCH

1970-75 Ford & Mercury

Column Shift
The neutral safety switch has been

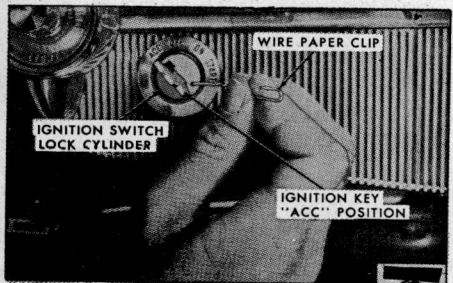

Fig. 4   Ignition switch lock.
1969 Ford and Mercury

Fig. 5   Light switch. Ford and Mercury. Typical

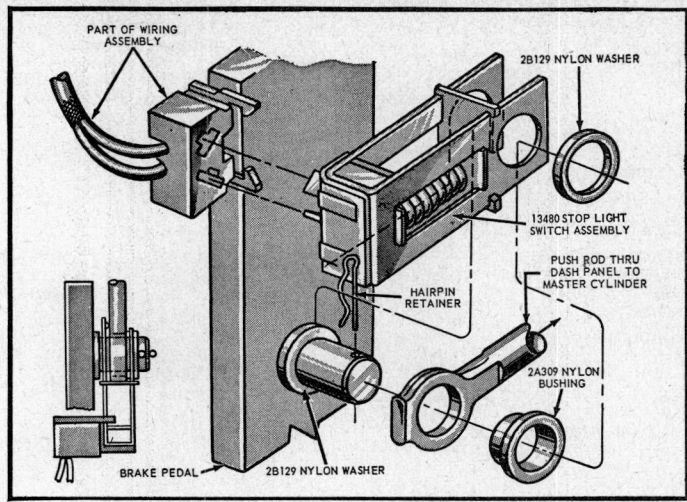

Fig. 6 Mechanical stop light switch. 1969-75 Ford and Mercury

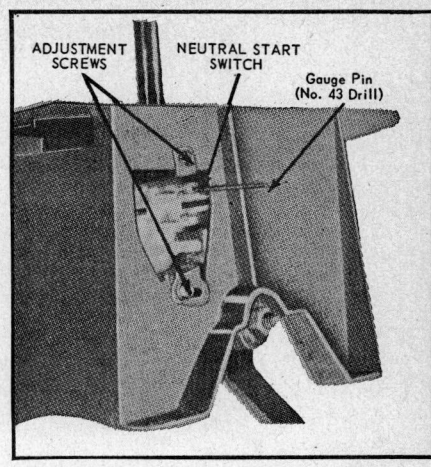

Fig. 7 Neutral safety switch (console shift). 1969 with C4 and C6 transmissions

eliminated and is replaced by a series of steps designed into the steering column selector lever hub casting.

Console Shift

1. Remove four screws and plates securing selector lever handle to the lever. Remove handle and detent control.
2. Remove two screws from rear of console top panel. Pull panel back to unhook it from front of console and remove panel.
3. Loosen two switch attaching screws.
4. Move selector lever back and forth until gauge pin (No. 43 drill) can be fully inserted into gauge pin holes.
5. Place selector lever firmly against the stop of the neutral detent position.
6. Slide switch forward or rearward as required until the switch lever contacts the selector lever actuator. If an adjustment cannot be made, loosen the actuating lever attaching screw and adjust the lever.
7. Tighten switch attaching screws and if actuator lever was adjusted tighten the actuator bolt.
8. Turn ignition key to ACC position and place selector lever in the reverse position and check operation of back-up lights. Turn key off.
9. Place console top panel on console and install screws.
10. Position selector lever detent control and handle on selector lever and secure with plates and screws.

1969 Ford & Mercury

Column Shift

To adjust the switch proceed as follows:

1. Place transmission selector lever against the stop of the neutral detent.
2. Loosen two retaining screws on the steering column.
3. With the selector lever against neutral stop, rotate the switch until a start in neutral position is obtained.

Then tighten the two screws.

4. With the switch properly adjusted in neutral, place the selector lever in the "1" position and push the park reset button, located on the right side of the switch, to the left until it stops.

NOTE: The park reset must be performed whenever the switch has been adjusted.

1969 C4 & C6 Units

Console Shift, Fig. 7

1. Remove selector lever handle.
2. Unfasten and position console to one side.
3. Loosen adjusting screws.
4. Move selector lever back and forth until gauge pin (#43 drill) can be fully inserted into gauge pin holes.
5. Place transmission selector lever firmly against stop of neutral detent position.
6. Slide combination neutral start and back-up light switch forward or rearward as required until switch actuating lever contacts selector lever.
7. Tighten switch attaching screws, remove gauge pin and check for starting in Park position.

HORN SOUNDER, REPLACE

Rim-Blow Type

The rubber insert and copper strip assembly is not replaceable on all 1970-71 vehicles and the 1972-75 vehicles with speed control. If a new insert assembly is required the entire steering wheel must be replaced.

1. Remove the pad from the steering

wheel (three screws).
2. Remove medallion from the pad.
3. After removing the steering wheel nut the wheel can be removed from the shaft with a wheel puller.

Except Rim-Blow Type

1. Disconnect battery ground cable.
2. Remove steering column pad (2 screws).
3. Push down and turn horn ring and remove ring and spring.
4. Reverse procedure to install.

INSTRUMENT CLUSTER

1973-75 Ford & Mercury

1. Disconnect the battery ground cable.
2. Remove two steering column cover screws and remove the cover.
3. Remove two instrument cluster trim cover attaching screws and remove cover, Fig. 7A.
4. Reach behind the cluster and disconnect the cluster feed plug from its receptacle.
5. Disconnect the speedometer cable.
6. Remove the screw attaching the transmission indicator cable to the steering column.
7. Remove the four cluster attaching screws and remove the cluster assembly.

1971-72 Ford

Instrument Cluster

1. Disconnect battery ground cable.
2. Remove instrument panel pad.
3. Disconnect speedometer cable and all electrical connections to the instrument cluster.
4. Remove four cluster attaching screws (two at bottom and two at top), and lift the cluster from the instrument panel.

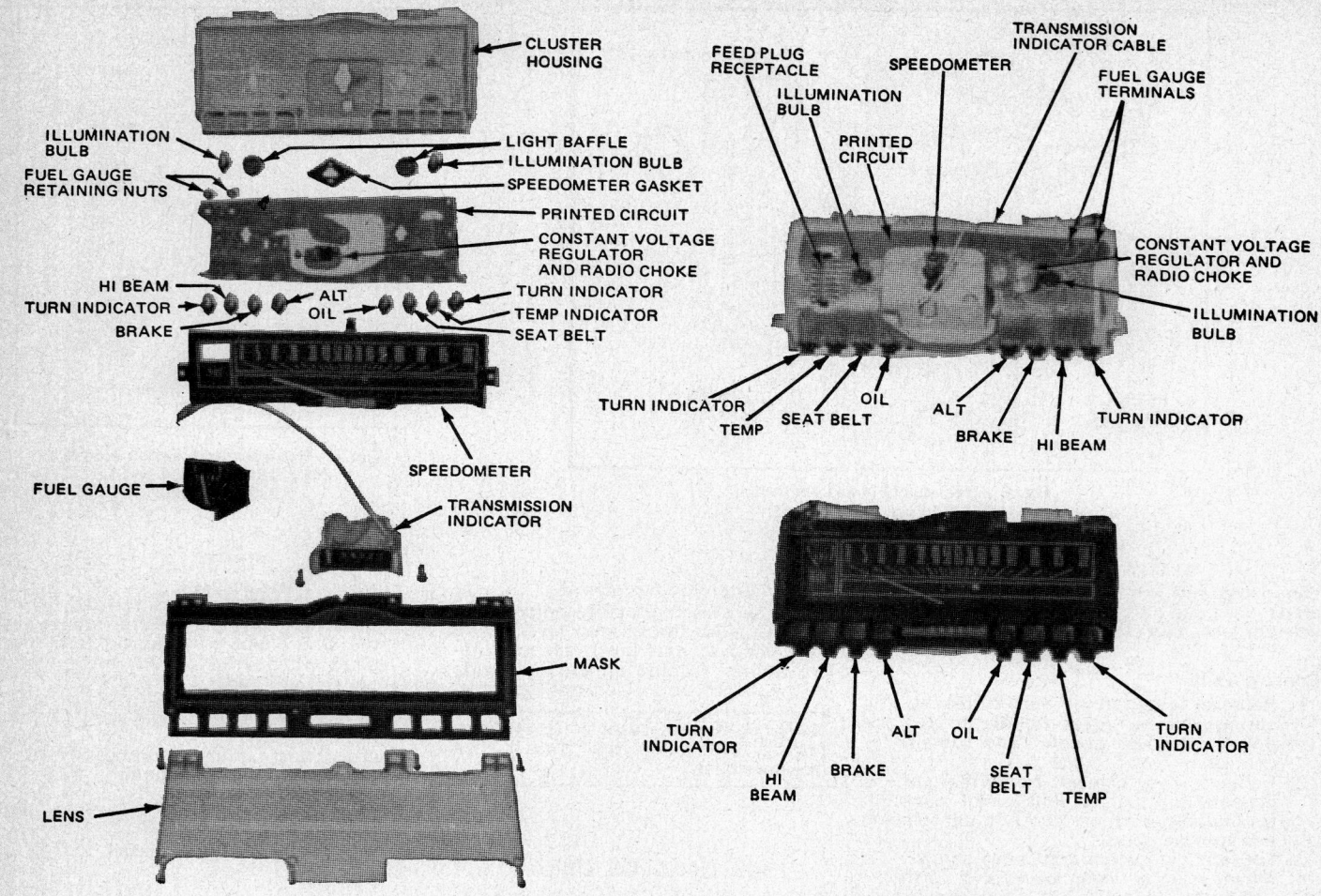

Fig. 7A Instrument cluster. 1973-75 Ford & Mercury

Fuel Gauge & Speedometer
1. Remove instrument cluster as described above.
2. Remove lights, wiper-washer and clock reset knobs.
3. Remove eight screws attaching lens, shield and mask to cluster.
4. Remove two screws attaching speedometer to cluster.
5. To remove fuel gauge, remove two terminal nuts.

1971-72 Mercury

Instrument Cluster
1. Disconnect battery ground cable.
2. Remove instrument panel pad.
3. Disconnect speedometer cable and all wires from back of cluster.
4. Remove four screws from lower edge of cluster and remove cluster.

Fuel Gauge & Speedometer
1. Remove cluster as described above.
2. Remove seven screws attaching the cluster housing and lens and inner mask and the cluster mask.

3. To remove speedometer, remove two screws from rear of cluster housing.
4. To remove fuel gauge, remove terminal nuts and gauge attaching screw.

1969-70 Ford

Fuel Gauge & Speedometer
1. From passenger side of instrument panel, remove lighter element and all of the control knobs, and then remove the cluster trim cover (10 screws).
2. Remove the attaching screws and the lens.
3. Remove attaching screws and lift the mask from the speedometer and fuel gauge.
4. Remove spring washers and nuts (one at each side) and the attaching screw at the bottom, then remove fuel gauge from the studs.
5. Remove attaching screws and pull speedometer head out of cluster far enough to reach the cable disconnect.
6. To disengage the cable, press on the flat surface of the disconnect and at the same time pull the cable from the head.

7. Remove the speedometer.
8. Reverse the procedure to install.

Instrument Cluster
1. Remove the instrument panel pad (20 screws).
2. From behind cluster disconnect all electrical connections to cluster.
3. Disconnect heater, air conditioner and speedometer cables.
4. Remove lighter element and all control knobs from passenger side of cluster.
5. Remove cluster trim cover (10 screws).
6. Remove eight mounting screws and withdraw cluster from panel.
7. Reverse procedure to install.

1969-70 Mercury

Instrument Cluster
1. Remove wiper knob and bezel, cigar lighter element and the finish panel.
2. Remove instrument panel pad.
3. Remove wiper nut and the bracket (3 screws) from left end of pad support.

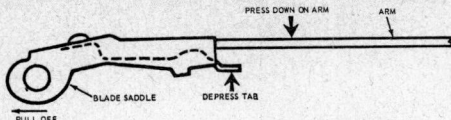

Fig. 8   Trico bayonet type blade

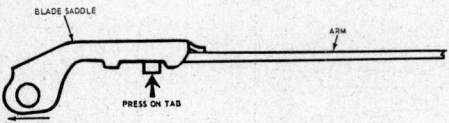

Fig. 9   Anco bayonet type blade

4. Remove lighter socket and bracket from right end of pad support.
5. Remove five pad support-to-instrument panel screws and three lower left panel-to-instrument panel screws and then remove pad support and lower panel as an assembly.
6. From behind cluster, disconnect all electrical connections to cluster and speedometer cable.
7. Remove the cluster assembly from panel (6 screws).
8. Reverse procedure to install.

Fuel Gauge & Speedometer

After removal of cluster as described above, the speedometer and fuel gauge can be removed from the cluster.

W/S WIPER BLADES

NOTE: Trico and Anco blades are used and both come in two types Bayonet type and Side Saddle Pin type.

Bayonet Type: To remove the *Trico* type press down on the arm to unlock the top stud. Depress the tab on the saddle, Fig. 8, and pull the blade from the arm. To remove the *Anco* type press inward on the tab, Fig. 9, and pull the blade from the arm. To install a new blade assembly slide the blade saddle over the end of the wiper arm so that the locking stud snaps into place.

Side Saddle Pin Type: To remove the pin type (Trico or Anco) insert an appropriate tool into the spring release opening of the blade saddle, depress the spring clip and pull the blade from the arm, Fig. 10. To install, push the blade saddle on to the pin so that the spring clip engages the pin. To replace the rubber element in a *Trico* blade squeeze the latch lock release and pull the element out of the lever jaws, Fig. 11. Remove *Anco* element by depressing the latch pin, Fig. 11, and sliding the element out of the yoke jaws. To install insert the element through the yoke or lever jaws. Be sure the element is engaged at all points.

W/S WIPER ARMS

Swing the arm and blade assembly away from the windshield and insert a 3/32" inch pin through the pin hole as shown in Fig. 12. Swinging the assembly away from the windshield will release the spring loaded attaching clip in the arm from the pivot shaft. Inserting the pin will hold it in the released position. The arm can now be pulled off the pivot shaft. *Do not* pry off with a screw driver. Leave the pin in the arm until after installation. A new replacement arm comes with a pin already installed to hold it in released position. Make sure the pivot shaft is in park position when installing new assembly. Push the arm onto the pivot shaft. Lock the arm to the pivot shaft by removing the pin.

W/S WIPER MOTOR
1971-75 Ford & Mercury

1. Disconnect battery ground cable.
2. Remove wiper arm and blade assemblies from pivot shafts.
3. Remove left cowl screen (four screws) for access.
4. Disconnect linkage drive arm from the motor output crankpin by removing retaining clip.
5. From engine side of dash, remove two wire connectors from motor.
6. Remove three bolts that retain motor to dash and remove motor. If output arm catches on dash during removal, handturn the arm clockwise so it will clear opening in the dash. Before installing motor, be sure output arm is in park position.

1969-70 Ford & Mercury

1. Remove wiper arm and blade assemblies from pivot shafts.
2. Remove cowl top grille (10 screws).
3. Disconnect linkage drive arm from motor output arm crankpin by removing clip.
4. Disconnect wire push-on connectors from motor.
5. From engine side of dash, remove bolts retaining motor to dash and remove motor. If output arm catches on dash during removal, hand turn the arm clockwise so it will clear opening in dash.
6. When installing motor, align output arm with opening in dash and turn the arm clockwise as necessary.

W/S WIPER SWITCH
1973-75 All

1. Disconnect battery ground cable.
2. Remove wiper and headlight switch knobs.
3. Remove headlight switch bezel, trim panel retaining screw and trim panel.
4. Remove wiper switch retaining screws, pull switch rearward, disconnect connector and remove switch.

1972 All

1. Disconnect battery ground cable.
2. Remove instrument panel pad.
3. On Mercury models, remove nut and bezel.

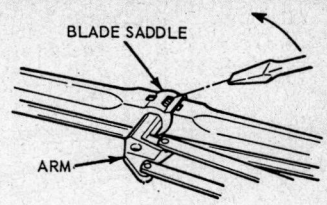

BLADE REMOVAL

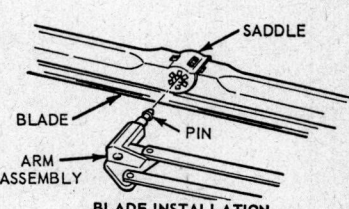

BLADE INSTALLATION

Fig. 10   Pin type blade

4. Remove three mounting plate retaining screws and remove switch and mounting plate.

1971 Ford & Mercury

1. Disconnect battery ground cable.
2. Remove instrument panel pad and instrument cluster.
3. Remove three switch attaching screws and remove switch.

1970 Ford

1. Disconnect battery ground cable and remove two piece cover from steering column (2 screws).
2. To allow removal of cluster trim cover, remove radio, wiper, washer, interval, heater and defogger switch knobs and lighter element.
3. Remove screw that retains the PRND21 dial cable to column and loosen set screw that retains the cable pin in the shaft housing.
4. Remove retaining screws and cluster trim cover assembly.
5. Remove the two screws that retain switch to cluster, lower the switch and disconnect multiple connector and hoses.

1969 Ford

1. To allow removal of cluster trim cover, remove the radio, wiper, washer, interval and heater switch knobs and the lighter element.
2. Remove retaining screws and cluster trim cover assembly.
3. Remove screws that retain the switch to the cluster, lower switch and disconnect multiple connector and vacuum hose from switch.

1969-70 Mercury

1. Remove wiper knob and bezel from switch shaft.
2. Remove nut that retains switch to bracket.
3. Lower switch from behind panel and

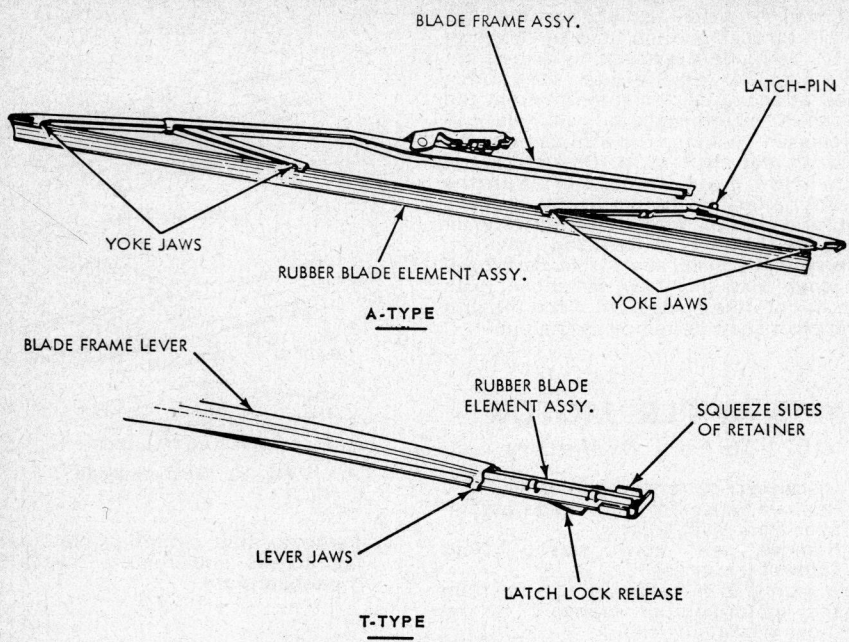

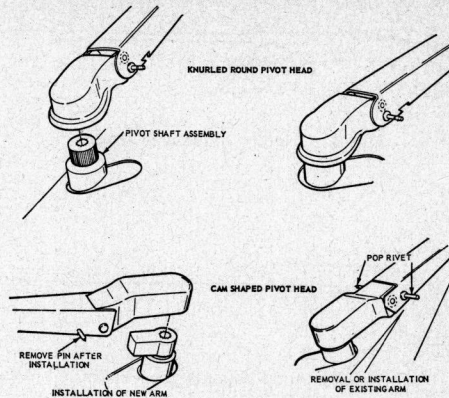

Fig. 12   Wiper arms

Fig. 11   Wiper blade element

ment panel.
2. Remove three nuts retaining front of radio to cluster.
3. Remove screw retaining the rear support to the bottom of the radio.
4. Pull radio from cluster and disconnect wires from chassis.

1969-70 Mercury

1. Disconnect battery ground cable.
2. Remove control knobs from radio.
3. Disconnect all wires from radio and remove nut attaching the rear support to the back of the radio.
4. Remove nut attaching the front edge of radio to instrument panel and remove radio.
5. Remove nut from radio control shaft.

disconnect multiple connector and vacuum hoses from the switch.

W/S WIPER TRANSMISSION

1971-75 Ford & Mercury

1. Disconnect battery and remove wiper arm and blade assemblies from pivot shafts.
2. Remove cowl screens for access to linkage.
3. Disconnect the left linkage arm from the drive arm by removing the clip.
4. Remove the three bolts retaining the left pivot shaft assembly to the cowl.
5. Remove the left arm and pivot shaft assembly through the cowl opening.
6. Disconnect linkage drive arm from motor crankpin by removing the clip.
7. Remove three bolts that connect drive arm pivot shaft assembly to the cowl and remove the pivot shaft drive arm and right arm as an assembly.

1969-70 Ford & Mercury

1. Remove wiper arm and blades from pivot shafts.
2. Remove cowl top grille.
3. The right pivot shaft and link on Mercury has to be removed before the left assembly or drive arm can be removed. Remove three retaining screws at right pivot shaft and disconnect the right link from the plate on the inner side of the dash panel by removing the clip. Lift the pivot

assembly out of cowl opening.
4. Remove three retaining screws at the left pivot shaft and disconnect the left link from the plate and lift out of cowl opening.
5. Reverse the procedure to install.

RADIO, REPLACE

NOTE: When installing radio, be sure to adjust antenna trimmer for peak performance.

1973-75 Ford & Mercury

1. Disconnect battery ground cable.
2. Remove radio knobs and instrument panel bezel.
3. Remove mounting plate retaining screws and pull radio disengaging it from rear bracket.
4. Disconnect antenna and electrical wires and remove radio.

1971-72 Ford & Mercury

1. Disconnect battery ground cable.
2. Remove radio and fader knobs.
3. Remove radio bezel.
4. Remove upper and lower rear radio support bolts and brackets.
5. Disconnect power, antenna and speaker.
6. Remove two nuts retaining radio to instrument panel and remove radio.

1969-70 Ford

1. Remove the trim cover from instru-

HEATER CORE REMOVAL

1973-75 Ford & Mercury with Air Cond.

1. Drain cooling system.
2. Disconnect heater hoses from core tubes.
3. Remove heater core cover plate and gasket.
4. Pull heater core and mounting gasket up out of case.
5. Remove core mounting gasket. Remove heater core.

1969-75 Ford & Mercury less Air Cond.

1. Drain cooling system and disconnect heater hoses from the core.
2. Remove the core cover and gasket and remove the heater core.

1969-72 Ford & Mercury with Air Cond.

1. Drain cooling system.
2. Remove carburetor air cleaner.
3. Remove vacuum manifold from dash panel.
4. Disconnect heater hoses, remove core cover and remove the core.

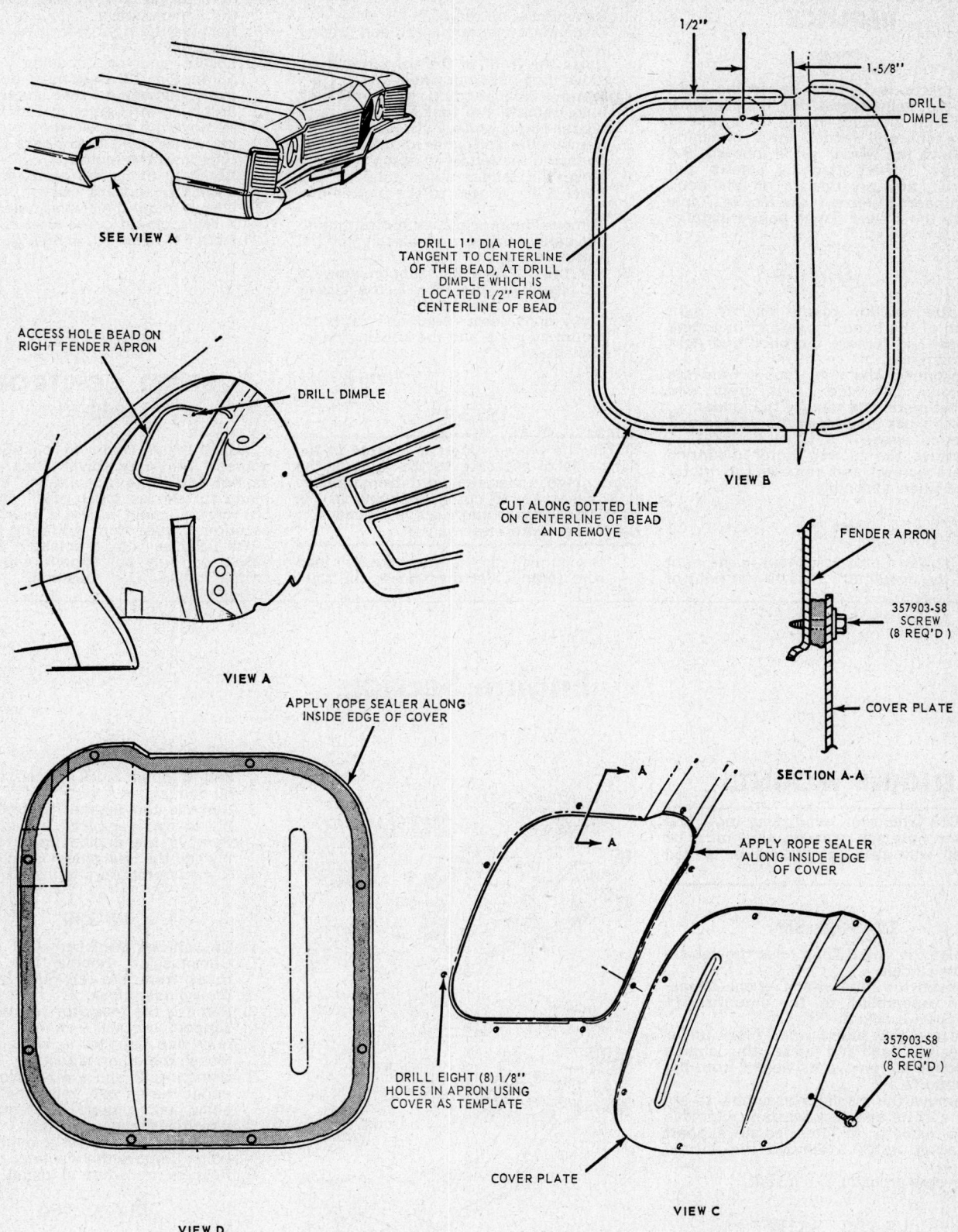

SEE VIEW A

DRILL 1" DIA HOLE TANGENT TO CENTERLINE OF THE BEAD, AT DRILL DIMPLE WHICH IS LOCATED 1/2" FROM CENTERLINE OF BEAD

1/2"

1-5/8"

DRILL DIMPLE

VIEW B

ACCESS HOLE BEAD ON RIGHT FENDER APRON

DRILL DIMPLE

CUT ALONG DOTTED LINE ON CENTERLINE OF BEAD AND REMOVE

FENDER APRON

357903-S8 SCREW (8 REQ'D)

COVER PLATE

SECTION A-A

VIEW A

APPLY ROPE SEALER ALONG INSIDE EDGE OF COVER

APPLY ROPE SEALER ALONG INSIDE EDGE OF COVER

A
A

357903-S8 SCREW (8 REQ'D)

DRILL EIGHT (8) 1/8" HOLES IN APRON USING COVER AS TEMPLATE

COVER PLATE

VIEW D

VIEW C

Fig. 13   Blower motor access. 1973-75 Ford & Mercury

BLOWER MOTOR, REPLACE

1969

The motor is located under the right fender. To gain access for replacement, remove the battery, right front wheel, vacuum tank and fender apron attaching bolts. Move the fender apron inboard. Remove the blower attaching screws and vent hose, and pry upward on the hood hinge support to remove the blower. Apply sealer to the blower flange before installation.

1970

1. Scribe location marks on the right side of the hood, hinge and mounting panel and remove the hood and right hood hinge.
2. Disconnect the right fender from the apron, cowl side panel, front end sheet metal and remove the fender.
3. Disconnect the blower motor lead and ground wires.
4. Remove the blower motor mounting plate screws and remove the motor and wheel assembly.

1971-72

The blower motor is located in the right side of the evaporator case to the right of the hood hinge under the right front fender.

1. Remove the battery.
2. Disconnect the motor lead and ground wires.
3. Raise the front of the vehicle and remove the right front wheel.
4. Remove the vacuum tank retaining nuts, remove the tank from the right fender apron, and set it to one side.
5. Remove the 15 fender apron retaining bolts and the fender-to-apron brace.
6. Move the fender apron inboard and lower it for access to the blower motor.
7. Remove the four blower motor mounting plate screws, and disconnect the motor vent hose.
8. Pry the hood hinge support upward for clearance and remove the blower motor and wheel assembly.
9. Apply body sealer between the motor mounting plate and the housing on installation.

1973-75

NOTE: The blower motor is located in the right side of the case to the right of the hood hinge under the right front fender. It is necessary to cut an opening in the right front fender apron to gain access to the blower motor assembly.

1. Disconnect the blower motor lead wire (orange) at the rear of the right hood hinge.
2. Remove the ground wire (black) from the upper cowl.
3. Remove the right front tire and wheel assembly.
4. Locate and cut opening in fender apron, Fig. 13. Care must be taken to avoid damage to the heater case by drill push-through or over-travel.
5. Remove the four blower motor mounting screws and disconnect the cooler tube from the motor.
6. Carefully move the motor and wheel assembly forward out of the heater case through the access hole.
7. A replacement cover plate is available from Ford part no. #18A475.

SPEED CONTROLS
1969-75

Adjust bead chain to obtain .06-.25" actuator arm free travel when engine is at hot idle. The adjustment should be made to take as much slack as possible out of the chain without restricting the carburetor lever from returning to idle.

On vehicles with a solenoid anti-diesel valve, perform adjustment with ignition switch in the "ON" position.

Engine Section

ENGINE MOUNTS

CAUTION: Whenever self-locking mounting bolts and nuts are removed, they must be replaced with new self-locking bolts and nuts.

1969-72 Six

1. Raise the hood. Then raise the vehicle with a hoist.
2. Loosen the nuts attaching the insulator assemblies to the intermediate support brackets, Fig. 1.
3. Place a jack and a wood block under the oil pan and raise the engine enough to remove its weight from the supports.
4. Remove the insulator assembly to engine bolts and lock washers. Remove the insulator to intermediate support bracket nut(s). Remove the insulator(s).
5. Reverse procedure to install.

V8-302, 351W

1. Remove the nut and through bolt attaching the insulator to the support bracket, Fig. 2.
2. Raise the engine slightly with a jack

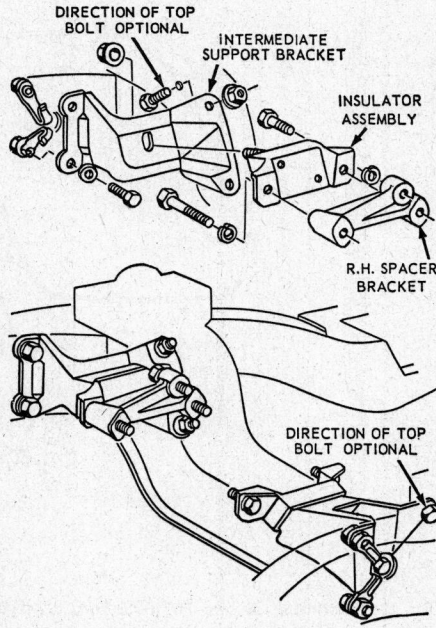

Fig. 1   Engine mount. 1969-72 Six

and a wood block placed under the oil pan.
3. Remove the engine insulator assembly to cylinder block attaching bolts. Remove the engine insulator assembly and the heat shield, if so equipped.
4. Reverse procedure to install.

V8-390

1. On vehicles equipped with automatic transmission, remove the oil cooler tubes from the retaining bracket on the cylinder block.
2. Remove the insulator to intermediate support bracket lock nut, Fig. 3. If only one support is being removed, loosen the other support.
3. Using a jack and a wood block placed under the oil pan, raise the engine to allow just enough clearance for removal of the insulator(s).
4. Remove the insulator to engine locking bolts. Remove the insulator(s).
5. Reverse procedure to install.

V8-429, 460

1. Block rear wheels and set parking brake. Raise front of vehicle with floor jack and install safety stands.
2. Position jack under the front area of the oil pan. Place a wood block be-

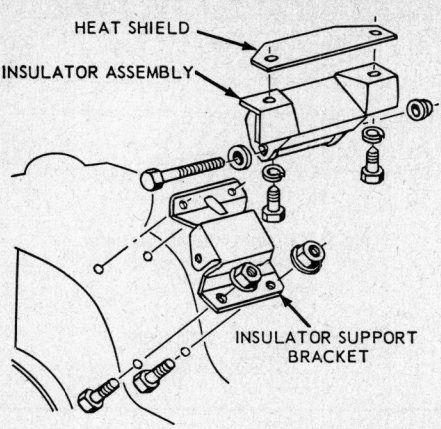

Fig. 2 Engine mount. V8-302, 351W

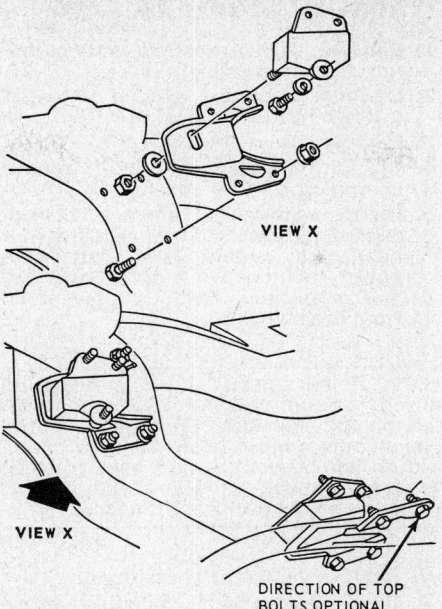

Fig. 3 Engine mount. V8-390

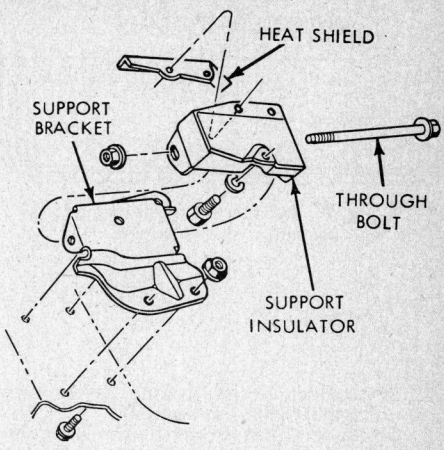

Fig. 4 Engine mount. 1969-71 V8-429

tween the jack and oil pan. Raise the jack just enough to support the engine.
3. Remove the nut through bolt that attaches the front support insulator to the lower support bracket, Figs. 4, 5.
4. Remove the bolts attaching the support insulator and heat shield to the cylinder block. Replace the insulator on one side before proceding to the other insulator.
5. Reverse procedure to install.

V8-351C, 351M, 400

1. Remove the fan shroud attaching bolts. Remove the transmission oil cooler lines from the retaining bracket on the block.
2. Remove the through bolt and lock nut attaching the insulator support bracket, Fig. 6. Remove the bolt and nut on the opposite mount to prevent distortion of the insulator.
3. Raise the engine slightly with a jack

and a wood block placed under the oil pan.
4. Remove the engine insulator assembly to cylinder block attaching bolts and lockwashers.
5. Remove the engine insulator assembly and heat shield, if equipped.
6. Reverse procedure to install.

ENGINE, REPLACE

NOTE: Because of engine compartment tolerances, the engine should not be removed and installed with the transmission attached.

1. Drain cooling system and crankcase.
2. Remove radiator and air cleaner.
3. Remove hood.
4. Remove fuel and vacuum lines and all hoses, wires and linkage attached to engine.
5. Disconnect exhaust pipe from manifolds.
6. Remove starter and automatic transmission filler tube (if equipped).
7. Remove converter or flywheel housing lower cover.
8. Remove clutch release linkage (if equipped).
9. Support transmission with jack.
10. Unfasten coverter or flywheel housing from engine.
11. Remove engine mounting bolts and lift engine out of chassis.

CYLINDER HEAD REPLACE

Tighten cylinder head bolts a little at a time in three steps in the sequence

shown in the illustrations. Final tightening should be to the torque specifications listed in the *Engine Tightening* table. After bolts have been tightened to specifications, *they should not be disturbed.*

In instances where cylinder head gasket leakage is hard to control, aluminum paint can be applied to the gasket as a sealer. Spray one coat of the aluminum paint on both sides of the gasket and allow the paint to dry. Then spray a second coat on both sides and, while the paint is still wet, install the gasket. Torque the head and manifold bolts to specifications to complete the job.

1969-72 6-240 Engine

1. Drain cooling system and remove air cleaner.

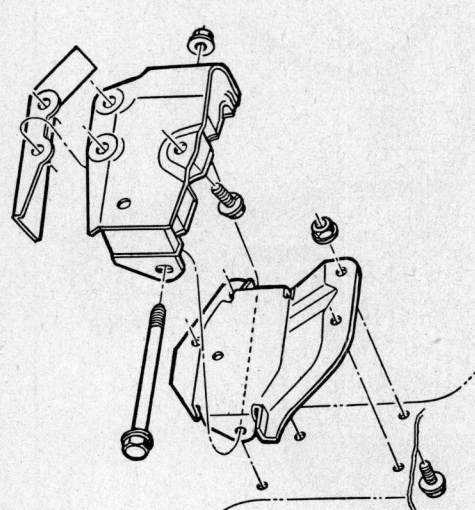

Fig. 5 Engine mount. 1972-74 V8-429, 460

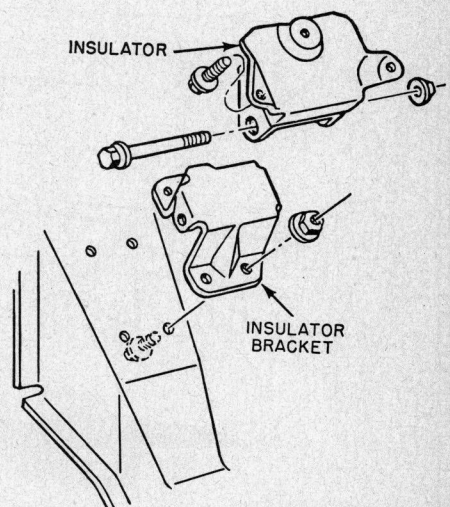

Fig. 6 Engine mount. V8-351C, 351M, 400

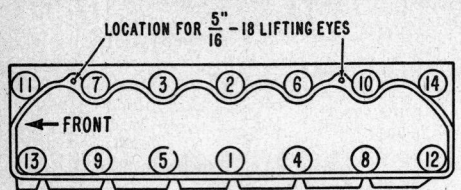

LOCATION FOR 5/16 — 18 LIFTING EYES

← FRONT

Fig. 7 Cylinder head tightening sequence. 6-240 engine

1969-75 V8-302, 351, 400

1. Remove intake manifold and carburetor as an assembly.
2. Disconnect battery ground cable at cylinder head.
3. Remove rocker arm cover.
4. On air conditioned cars, remove compressor.
5. On car with power steering, disconnect pump bracket from left cylinder head and remove drive belt. Wire power steering pump out of the way and in position that will prevent oil from draining out.

NOTE: If left cylinder head is being removed on an engine equipped with Thermactor Exhaust Emission Control System, disconnect hose from air manifold on left head. If a right head is to be removed, remove air pump and bracket and disconnect hose on right head.

6. Remove generator or alternator.
7. Disconnect exhaust manifold at exhaust pipes.
8. Loosen rocker arm stud nuts so that rocker arms can be rotated to the side.
9. Remove push rods, keeping them in sequence so they may be returned to their original locations.
10. Unfasten and remove cylinder head.
11. Reverse removal procedure to install the head. Tighten cylinder head down in the sequence shown in Fig. 8.

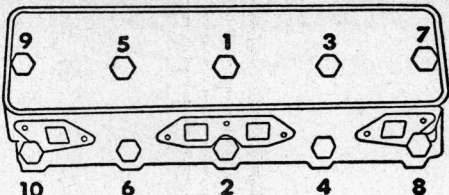

Fig. 8 Cylinder head tightening sequence. V8 engines

1969-75 V8-390, 429, 460

NOTE

When installing intake manifold attaching bolts on these engines, apply a liberal coat of oil resistant sealer to the underside of bolt heads or to the bolt head bosses on the intake manifold. Failure to do so can result in oil leakage.

---

1. Remove intake manifold, carburetor and radiator supply tank as an assembly.

NOTE: If equipped with Thermactor Exhaust Emission Control System, disconnect air lines and hoses as necessary for accessibility. Then remove intake manifold, positive crankcase vent system components (if applicable), carburetor and thermostat housing (or radiator supply tank) as an assembly.

---

2. Disconnect exhaust pipes from ex-

2. Disconnect hoses, tubing, wires and linkage attached to head.
3. Grasp crankcase ventilation regulator valve and pull it from rocker arm cover. Disconnect crankcase vent hose from inlet tube on intake manifold and remove hose and valve.

NOTE: If equipped with Thermactor Exhaust Emission Control System, disconnect air pump outlet hose at air manifold assembly. Remove air manifold. Disconnect anti-backfire valve air and vacuum lines at intake manifold.

4. Remove rocker arm cover. Loosen rocker arm stud nuts so that rocker arms can be rotated to one side.
5. Remove push rods and identify them so they can be installed in their original locations.
6. Disconnect exhaust pipe from engine.
7. Remove head bolts.
8. Install cylinder head lifting eyes in locations shown in Fig. 7.
9. Lift head with intake and exhaust manifolds from engine.
10. Reverse procedure to install and tighten head down in the sequence shown in Fig. 7.

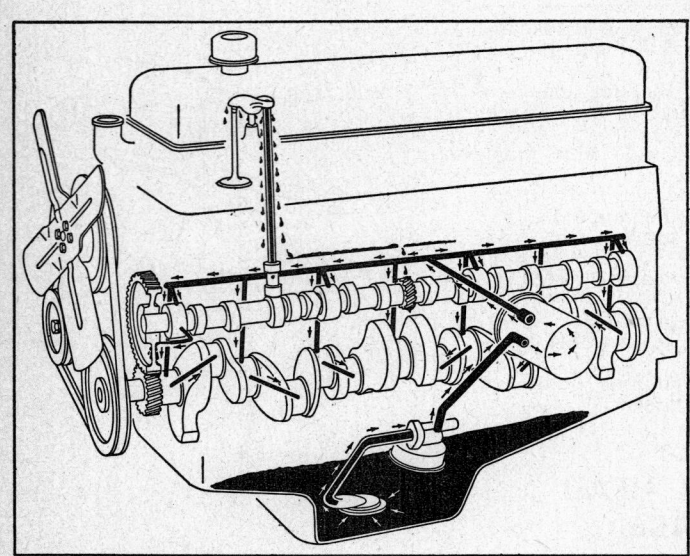

Engine oiling system. 6-240 engine

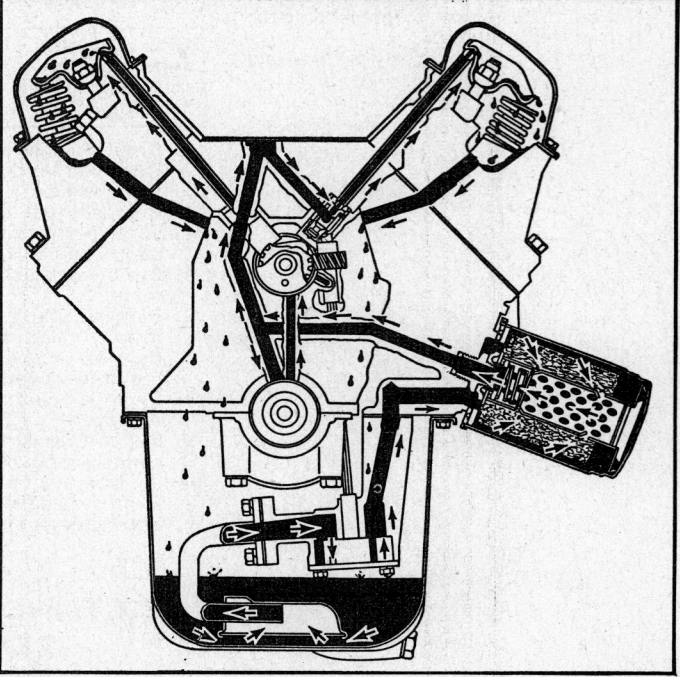

Engine oiling system. V8-302, 351, 400

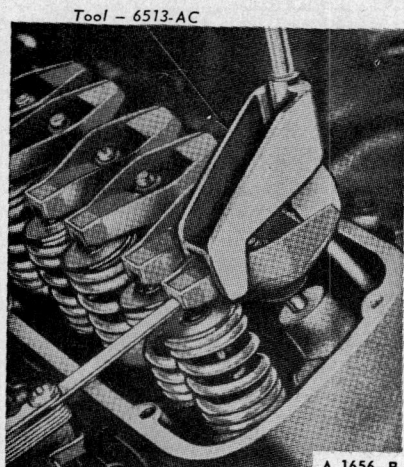

Fig. 9 Checking valve clearance on models with hydraulic lifters

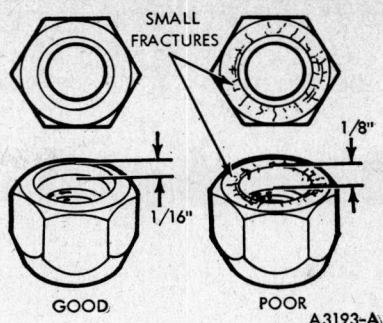

Fig. 10 Inspection of rocker arm stud nut. V8-302, 351W

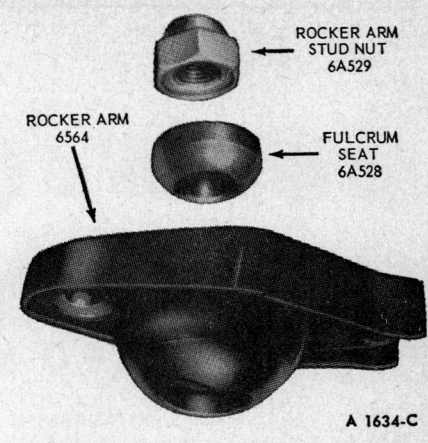

Fig. 11 Valve rocker arm parts. V8-302, 351W

haust manifolds.
3. Remove bolts and lift off head.
4. Install cylinder heads in the reverse order of removal and tighten bolts in the sequence shown in Fig. 8.

NOTE

If a noise is encountered after the cylinder head is installed on six-cylinder engines, check for interference between push rod and push rod hole in cylinder head. If interference exists check push rod for straightness. If push rod is straight, then the cylinder head has not been aligned properly during its installation. The use of cylinder head guide pins (one at each end) on cylinder head installation will insure correct head alignment.

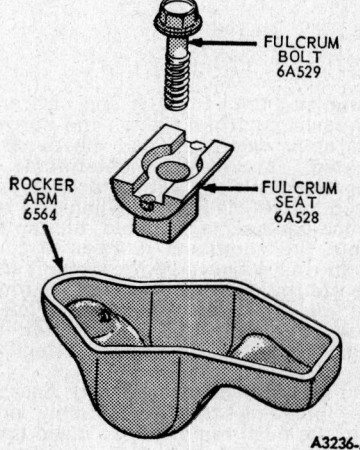

Fig. 12 Rocker arm and related parts. V8-351C, 351M & 1972-75 V8-400, 429, 460

VALVE ARRANGEMENT
Front to Rear

6-240	E-I-E-I-E-I-E-I-E-I-E-I
302, 351, 429 Right	I-E-I-E-I-E-I-E
302, 351, 429 Left	E-I-E-I-E-I-E-I
361, 390	E-I-E-I-E-I-E-I
400, 460 Right	I-E-I-E-I-E-I-E
400, 460 Left	E-I-E-I-E-I-E-I

VALVE LIFT SPECS.

Engine	Year	Intake	Exhaust
6-240	1969-71	.376	.400
	1972	.400	.400
8-302	1969-72	.368	.381
8-351	1969-75 [5]	.418	.448
	1971-75 [5]	.407	.407

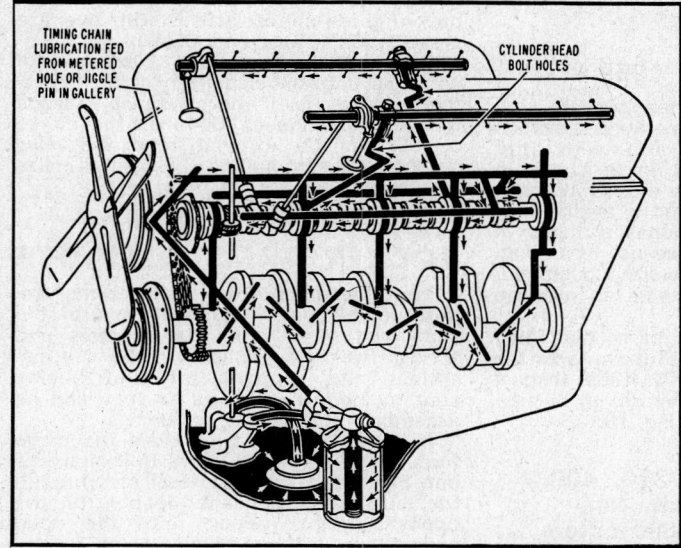

Engine oiling system. V8-390

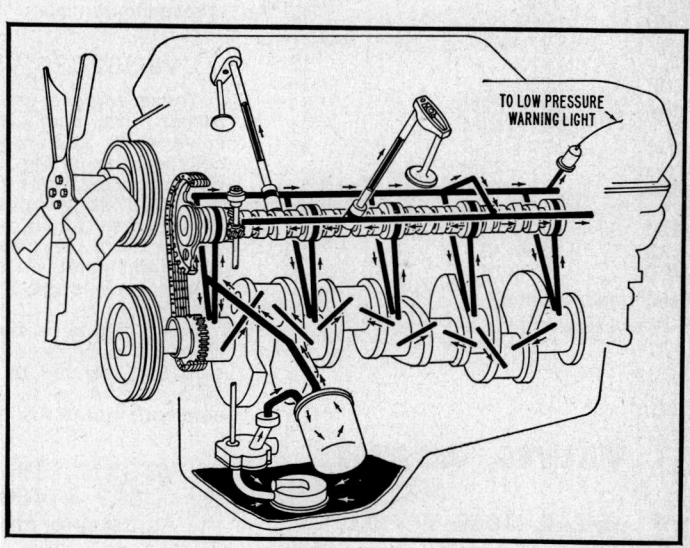

Engine oiling system. V8-429, 460

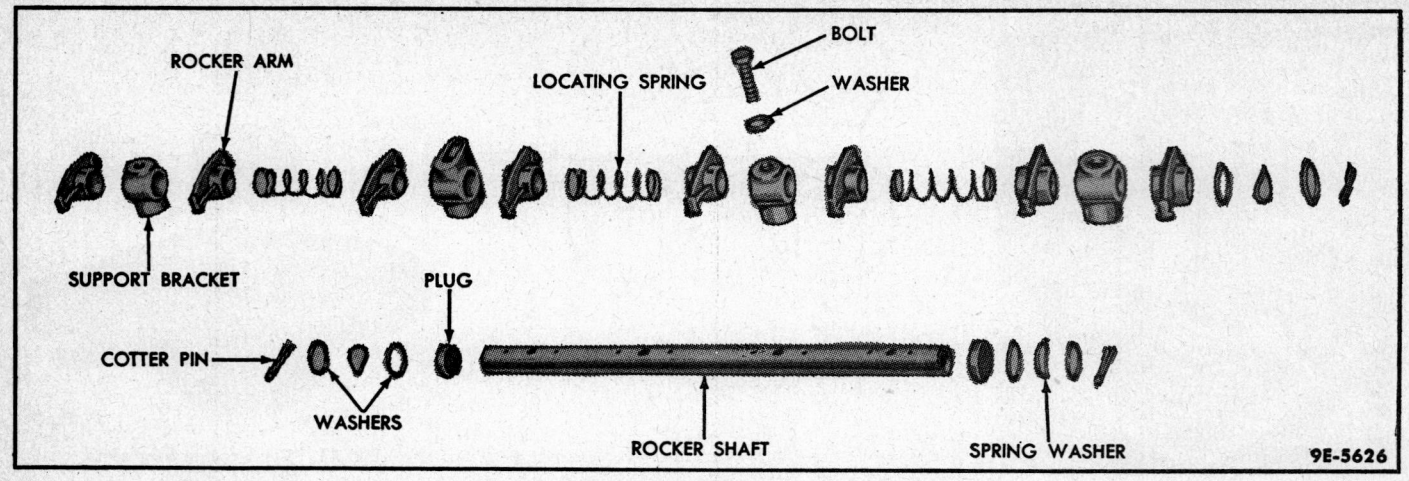

Fig. 13   Rocker arm shaft assembly. V8-390 engine

8-390	1969-71①	.427	.430
	1969②	.440	.440
	1969④	.440	.440
8-400	1971	.427	.433
	1972	.422	.427
	1973	.427	.433
	1974-75	.427	.433
8-429	1969-73	.443	.486
8-460	1973	.440	.480
	1974-75	.442	.486

①—2 bar. carb. ②—4 bar. carb.
④—2 bar. carb.-premium fuel.
⑤—Windsor engine.
⑥—Cleveland engine.

VALVE TIMING

Intake Opens Before TDC

Engine	Year	Degrees
6-240	1969	12
	1970-71	10
	1972	18
8-302	1969-72	16
8-351	1969-72①	11
	1971-73②	12
	1974-75①	15
	1974-75②	19½
8-390	1969-71 Reg. Fuel	13
	1969 Prem. Fuel	16
8-400	1971-75	17
8-429	1969-73	16
8-460	1974-75	8

①—Windsor engine.
②—Cleveland engine.

VALVES, ADJUST

6-240, 1969 V8-302

With the piston at top dead center of its compression stroke, loosen the rocker arm stud nut until there is end clearance in the push rod. Then tighten the nut just to the point where all end clearance is eliminated. This may be determined by moving the push rod with the fingers as the stud nut is tightened. When the end clearance has been eliminated, tighten the stud nut the additional number of turns listed in the *Valve Specifications Table.* Operate the engine and check for rough engine idle or noisy lifters. Valve clearance set too tight will cause rough engine idle; if set too loose, noisy lifters will result.

If an adjustment is necessary because of the foregoing conditions, apply pressure on the push rod slowly to bleed down the valve lifter until the plunger is completely bottomed. While holding the lifter in the fully collapsed position, check the available clearance between rocker arm and valve stem tip. If clearance is not within specifications, turn the rocker arm stud nut clockwise to decrease the clearance and counterclockwise to increase clearance.

V8-302, 351W & 1969-429

These engines use a new positive stop rocker arm stud. If clearance between valve stem and rocker arm, with lifter collapsed, as in Fig. 9, is not as shown in *Valve Specifications* table a .060" shorter or a .060" longer push rod is available to compensate for dimensional changes in valve train. If clearance is less than specified, install an undersized push rod. If clearance is greater install an oversize push rod.

Valve clearance should be correct when stud nut is tightened until it contacts the stop and torqued to 18-22 ft-lbs. Inspect stud nuts to be sure they are in acceptable condition for re-use, Fig. 10.

V8-351C, 351M, 390, 400, 429 & 460 With Non-Adjustable Hydraulic Lifters

For these engines a .060" shorter push rod (color coded white) or a .060" longer push rod (color coded yellow) are available for service to provide a means of compensating for dimensional changes in the valve mechanism.

To check the clearance, bring the piston of the cylinder being checked on top dead center of the compression stroke. Then with hydraulic lifter collapsed, Fig. 9 check the clearance between valve stem and rocker arm. If the clearance is less than the minimum listed in the *Valve Specifications* table, the .060" shorter push rod should be used. If the clearance is more than the maximum specified, the .060" longer push rod should be used.

VALVE GUIDES

Overhead Valve Engines

Valve guides in these engines are an integral part of the head and, therefore, cannot be removed. For service, guides can be reamed oversize to accommodate one of three service valves with oversize stems (.003", .015" and .030").

Check the valve stem clearance of each valve (after cleaning) in its respective valve guide. If the clearance exceeds the service limits of .004" on the intake or .005" on the exhaust, ream the valve guides to accommodate the next oversize diameter valve.

ROCKER ARMS & SHAFTS

To disassemble the rocker arms, remove cotter pins from each end of the shaft and remove the flat washers and spring washers. Slide rocker arms, springs and supports off shaft, being sure to identify all parts so they can be assembled in the same position.

If it is necessary to remove the plugs from each end of the shaft, drill or pierce one plug, then insert a steel rod through the plug and knock out the plug on the opposite end. Working from the open end, knock out the remaining plug.

Assemble the rocker arms and related parts as indicated by Fig. 13.

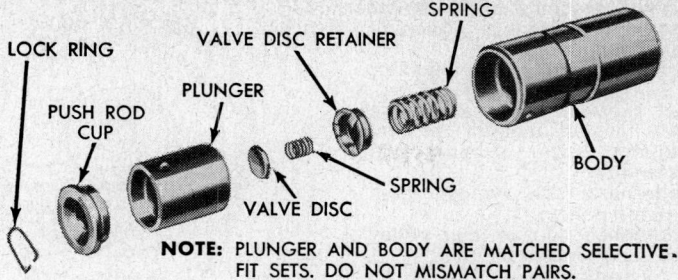

LOCK RING
PUSH ROD CUP
PLUNGER
VALVE DISC RETAINER
SPRING
BODY
SPRING
VALVE DISC

NOTE: PLUNGER AND BODY ARE MATCHED SELECTIVE. FIT SETS. DO NOT MISMATCH PAIRS.

Fig. 14   Hydraulic valve lifter disassembled (typical)

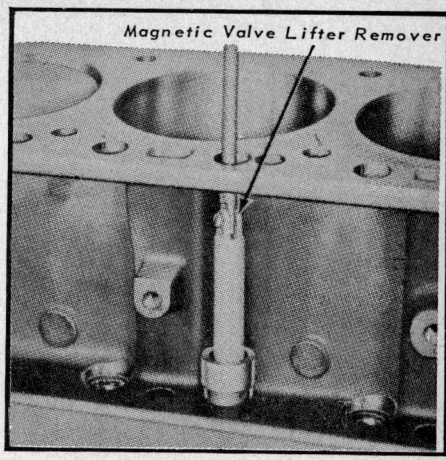

Magnetic Valve Lifter Remover

Fig. 15   Removing valve lifter. 6-240 engine

ROCKER ARM STUD
6-240, 1969 V8-302

If necessary to replace a rocker arm stud, a kit is available which contains a stud remover, a stud installer, and two reamers, one .006" and the other 015".

Rocker arm studs that are broken or have damaged threads may be replaced with standard studs. Loose studs in the head may be replaced with .006", .010" or .015" oversize studs which are available for service. *The standard studs have no identification marks, whereas the .006" oversize stud has two grooves around the pilot end of the stud. The .015" oversize stud has a step produced by the increased diameter of the stud approximately 1 5/32" from the pilot end.*

When going from a standard size stud to a .010 or .015" oversize stud, always use a .006" reamer before finish reaming with a .010" or .015" reamer.

If a stud is broken off flush with the stud boss, use an easy-out to remove the broken stud, following the instructions of the tool manufacturer.

V8-302 & V8-351W

A new type positive stop rocker arm stud and nut eliminates the need for adjusting valve lash.

Installation

1. Position the piston of the cylinder to be worked on at TDC compression stroke.
2. Locate stud properly with tool T69P-6049D. Make sure tool bottoms on the head.
3. Lubricate rocker arm components and place rocker arm and fulcrum on the stud.
4. Thread nut onto the stud until it contacts the shoulder then tighten nut to 18-22 ft-lbs.

V8-351C, 351M & 1972-75 V8-400, 429, 460

The rocker arm is supported by a fulcrum bolt which fits through the fulcrum seat and threads into the cylinder head. To disassemble, remove the bolt, oil de-

flector, fulcrum seat and rocker arm.

1969-71 V8-429

The rocker arm support studs are threaded into the cylinder head and can be replaced as follows:
1. Position the piston of the cylinder being worked on the TDC compression stroke.
2. Thread the rocker arm stud into the head until the shoulder contacts the head. Tighten to the torque specified in the *Engine Tightening Table*.
3. Lubricate rocker arm components and position the arm and the fulcrum on the stud.
4. Thread the nut until it contacts the shoulder, then tighten to 18-22 ft. lbs.

HYDRAULIC VALVE LIFTERS

The internal parts of each hydraulic valve lifter assembly are a matched set. If these are mixed, improper valve operation may result. Therefore, disassemble, inspect and test each assembly separately to prevent mixing the parts.

Fig. 14 illustrates the type of hydraulic lifter used. See the *Trouble Shooting Chapter* under the heading *Engine Noises* for causes of hydraulic valve lifter noise.

Hydraulic Lifters, Replace
6-240 Engine

1. Remove valve rocker arm cover.
2. Remove valve push rod cover.
3. Loosen rocker arm stud nuts until rocker arms can be disengaged from push rods.
4. Remove push rods, keeping them in a rack so they may be installed in their original location.
5. Remove valve lifters, using the tool shown in Fig. 15 (or equivalent). Place lifters in a rack so they may be installed in their original location.

V8-302, 351, 400, 429, 460
1. Remove intake manifold and related parts.

2. Remove rocker arm covers.
3. Loosen rocker arm stud nuts or bolts and rotate rocker arms to the side.
4. Lift out push rods, keeping them in sequence in a rack so they may be installed in their original location.
5. Using a magnet rod, remove valve lifters and place them in sequence in a rack so they may be installed in their original location.

All V8s With Rocker Arm Shafts
1. Remove intake manifold.
2. Remove rocker arms and shafts.
3. Remove push rods, keeping them in a rack in sequence so they may be installed in their original location.
4. Remove valve lifters with a magnet rod and place them in a rack in sequence so they may be installed in original location.
5. Reverse procedure to install.

TIMING CASE COVER

NOTE: To replace the seal in the timing gear cover, it is necessary to remove the cover as outlined below.

1969-75 V8-302, 351, 400
1. Drain cooling system and oil pan.
2. Disconnect lower radiator hose from water pump.
3. Disconnect heater hose from water pump and slide water pump bypass hose clamp toward pump.
4. Unfasten and position alternator and bracket out of way.
5. If equipped with power steering or air conditioning, remove the drive belts.
6. Remove the fan, spacer, pulley and drive belt.
7. Remove crankshaft pulley and vibration damper.
8. Disconnect fuel pump outlet line from pump and remove pump retaining bolts and lay pump to one

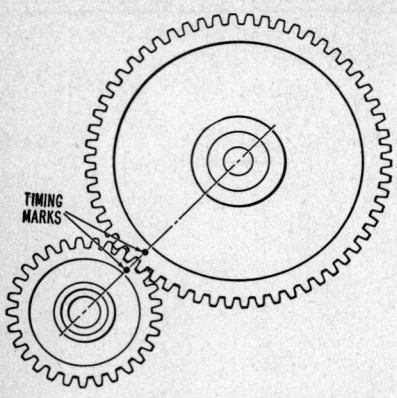

Fig. 16 Timing marks aligned for correct valve timing. 6-240 engine

side with flex line attached.
9. Remove oil dipstick and the oil pan to front cover attaching bolts.
10. Unfasten and remove the cylinder front cover and water pump as an assembly.
11. Reverse the foregoing to install.

1969-71 V8-390

1. Drain cooling system and oil pan.
2. Disconnect battery ground cable.
3. Disconnect transmission cooler lines from radiator if so equipped and disconnect water hoses from radiator and remove radiator.
4. Remove heater hose from water pump and remove hose from choke housing clamp.
5. Slide water pump bypass hose clamp toward engine.
6. If equipped with power steering, remove pump bracket bolts and position pump to left side to prevent fluid from draining.
7. If air conditioned, remove compressor mounting bolts and lay compressor out of way.
8. Unfasten and position alternator and bracket out of way.
9. Remove water pump and fan assembly.
10. If air conditioned, unfasten condenser attaching bolts and position condenser forward.
11. Remove compressor drive belt and if Thermactor equipped remove the air pump drive belt and the accessory drive pulley.
12. Remove crankshaft pulleys and vibration damper.
13. Disconnect fuel pump outlet line at pump and remove pump attaching bolts and lay pump to one side with flex line attached.
14. Remove crankshaft sleeve.
15. Unfasten and remove the front cover.
16. Reverse the foregoing to install.

V8-429, 460

1. Drain cooling system and oil pan.

---

2. Remove bolts attaching fan to water pump and remove screws attaching radiator shroud to radiator.
3. Remove fan assembly and radiator shroud.
4. Disconnect radiator hoses at engine and cooler lines at radiator and remove radiator upper support and radiator assembly.
5. Loosen alternator and remove drive belt with pump pulley.
6. If air conditioned, loosen idler pulley and remove compressor support.
7. Remove vibration damper from crankshaft.
8. Disconnect power steering lines at pump and unfasten and remove the pump.
9. Loosen bypass hose at pump and disconnect heater return tube at pump.
10. Disconnect and plug fuel inlet line at pump and disconnect fuel outlet line from pump. Unfasten and remove fuel pump.
11. Unfasten and remove cylinder front cover.
12. Reverse procedure to install.

1969-72 6-240

1. Drain cooling system and oil pan.
2. Disconnect automatic transmission oil cooler lines from radiator.
3. Remove radiator.
4. Remove power steering drive belt. Unfasten and position power steering pump and bracket out of the way.
5. Remove fan, spacer, belt and pulley.
6. Remove vibration damper.
7. Remove oil pan, oil pump screen and inlet tube.
8. Unfasten and remove front cover.
9. Reverse procedure to install.

TIMING GEARS
1969-72 6-240 Engine

CAUTION

When the camshaft and crankshaft lose their timing relationship through removal of the timing gears, interference may occur between crankshaft and cam lobes. Therefore, to prevent possible damage to the camshaft lobes, do not rotate the camshaft or crankshaft in the engine without the timing gears installed.

1. To remove gears, remove cylinder front cover and camshaft.
2. Remove oil slinger from crankshaft.
3. Use a puller to remove crankshaft gear.
4. Press gear off camshaft and remove thrust plate, spacer and key.
5. Reverse procedure to install, being sure timing marks are aligned as shown in Fig. 16.

NOTE: Be sure the camshaft gear and spacer are tight against the shoulder on camshaft and that the

---

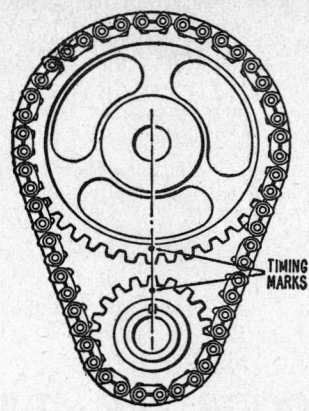

Fig. 17 Timing marks aligned for correct valve timing. V8s

thrust plate can be moved freely.

TIMING CHAIN
V8-302, 351, 400

After removing the cover as outlined above, remove the crankshaft front oil slinger. Crank the engine until the timing marks are aligned as shown in Fig. 17. Remove crankshaft sprocket retaining bolt and washer. Slide both sprockets and chain forward and remove them as an assembly.

Reverse the order of the foregoing procedure to install the chain and sprockets, being sure the timing marks are aligned.

V8-390, 429, 460

1. To remove the chain, first take off the front cover as outlined previously.
2. Crank engine until timing marks on camshaft sprocket is adjacent to timing mark on crankshaft sprocket, Fig. 17.
3. Remove camshaft sprocket cap screw and fuel pump eccentric.
4. Slide both sprockets and chain forward and remove as an assembly.
5. Reverse foregoing procedure to install the chain, being sure to align the timing marks as shown.

CAMSHAFT, REPLACE
1969-72 6-240 Engine

1. To remove camshaft, remove radiator and grille.
2. Remove rocker arm cover. Loosen rocker arm stud nuts and move rocker arms to one side and take out push rods. Place push rods in a rack so they can be installed in their original location.
3. Remove valve push rod cover and take out valve lifters. Place valve

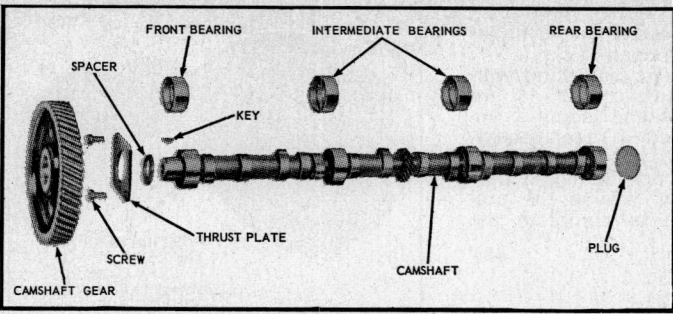

Fig. 18   Camshaft and related parts. 6-240 engine

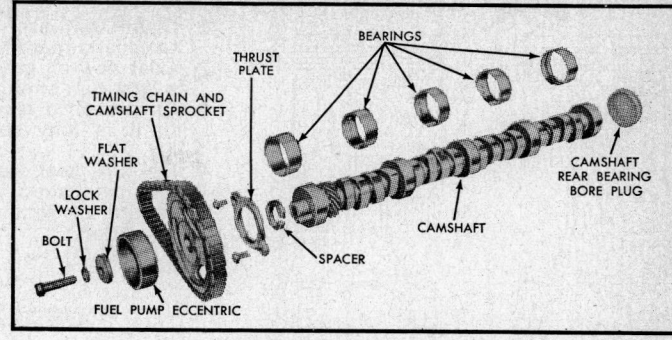

Fig. 19   Camshaft and related parts. V8-302

lifters in a rack so they may be installed in their original location.
4. Remove cylinder front cover.
5. Turn crankshaft to align timing marks as shown in Fig. 16.
6. Carefully remove camshaft with gear attached, Fig. 18.
7. Reverse procedure to install.

V8-302, 351, 400

1. To remove camshaft, remove cylinder front cover and timing chain.
2. Remove distributor cap and spark plug wires, then remove distributor.
3. Disconnect automatic transmission oil cooler lines from radiator and remove radiator.
4. Remove intake manifold and carburetor as an assembly.
5. Remove rocker arm covers.
6. Loosen rocker arm stud nuts or bolts and rotate rocker arms to one side.
7. Remove push rods, keeping them in sequence in a rack so they may be installed in their original location.
8. Using a magnet, remove valve lifters and place them in a rack in sequence so they may be installed in their original location.
9. Remove camshaft thrust plate, Fig. 19, and carefully pull camshaft from engine, using care to avoid damaging camshaft bearings.
10. Reverse procedure to install.

V8-390, 429, 460

1. Remove timing chain cover, chain, sprockets and intake manifold.
2. Remove grille and distributor.
3. Remove rocker arm assembly.
4. Remove push rods.
5. Position an inspection light through push rod opening and into valve push rod valley. Remove valve lifters with a magnet through push rod openings. *It may be necessary in some cases to transfer the lifter over to an adjoining push rod opening in order to remove it.*
6. Remove oil pan.
7. Slide camshaft out of engine, Fig. 20.

CAMSHAFT BEARINGS

When necessary to replace camshaft

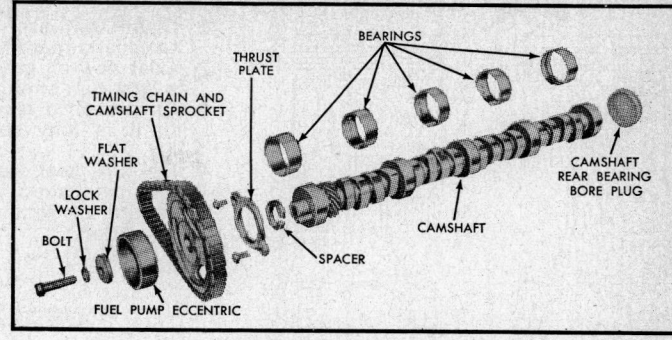

Fig. 20   Camshaft and related parts. V8-390, 400, 429, 460
NOTE: Spacer not used on all models

bearings, the engine will have to be removed from the vehicle and the plug at the rear of the cylinder block will have to be removed in order to utilize the special camshaft bearing removing and installing tools required to do this job. If properly installed, camshaft bearings require no reaming—nor should this type bearing be reamed or altered in any manner in an attempt to fit bearings.

PISTON & ROD, ASSEMBLE

All V8's

Assemble the pistons to the rods as shown in Fig. 21.

All Sixes

Piston heads are marked for location on the forward side, Fig. 22. Rods and caps are numbered on the same side as the piston they serve.

PISTONS, PINS & RINGS

SERVICE BULLETIN
Piston and Pin Replacement: When servicing engines using press fit piston pins, the piston and pin must be replaced as an assembly if either does not meet specifications. These components are not serviced separately for the principle reason that excess clearances are usually caused by piston wear rather than pin wear. Elimination of excessive clearance by using oversize pins may result in fracture of the connecting rod.

Pistons and rings are available in standard sizes and oversizes of .003, .020, .030 and .040 inch.
Oversizes piston pins of .001 and .002" are available on 6-240 and V8-390 only.

MAIN & ROD BEARINGS

Main and rod bearings are available in standard sizes and the following undersizes:
V8-302, 390, 400, 429, 460: .002, .010, .020, .030, .040".
All other engines: .002, .010, .020, .030".

NOTE
Main and rod bearings are a selective

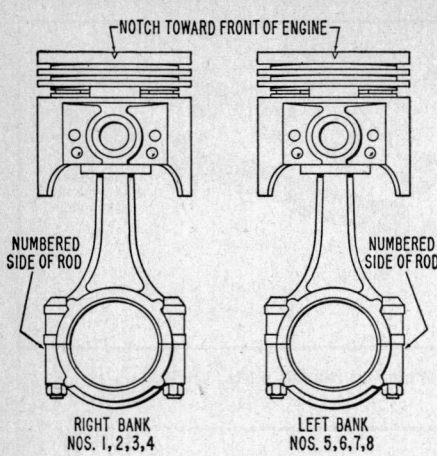

NOTCH TOWARD FRONT OF ENGINE

NUMBERED SIDE OF ROD

NUMBERED SIDE OF ROD

RIGHT BANK NOS. 1, 2, 3, 4

LEFT BANK NOS. 5, 6, 7, 8

Fig. 21 Piston and rod assembly. All V8 engines

fit. Do not file or lap bearing caps or use bearing shims to obtain proper bearing clearance. Selective fit bearings are available for service in standard sizes only. Standard bearings are divided into two sizes and are identified by a daub of red or blue paint. Red marked bearings increase the clearance; blue marked bearings decrease clearance. When replacing standard bearings with new bearings, it is good practice first to try to obtain the proper clearance with two blue bearing halves.

CRANKSHAFT OIL SEAL
1969-72 6-240 Engine

NOTE: If crankshaft rear oil seal replacement is the only operation being performed, it can be done in the vehicle. If the oil seal is being replaced in conjunction with a rear main bearing replacement, the engine must be removed from the vehicle. To replace the seal only, proceed as follows:

1. Remove starting motor.
2. Disconnect transmission from engine and slide it back. On manual shift transmission, remove clutch assembly.
3. Remove flywheel and engine rear cover plate.
4. Use an awl to punch two holes in crankshaft rear oil seal. Punch holes on opposite sides of crankshaft and just above bearing cap-to-cylinder block split line. Insert a sheet metal screw in each hole.
5. Use two large screwdrivers or pry bars and pry against both screws at the same time to remove seal. It may be necessary to place small blocks of wood against cylinder block to provide a fulcrum point for pry bars. Use caution to avoid scratching or otherwise damaging crankshaft oil seal surfaces.

Installation

1. Clean oil seal recess in cylinder block and rear main bearing cap.
2. Coat new oil seal and crankshaft with a light film of engine oil.
3. Start seal in recess and install it until it is fully seated in seal recess, Fig. 23.
4. Be sure seal was not damaged during installation and reverse the procedure of removal to complete the operation.

V8-302, 351

A braided oil seal is pressed into the upper and lower grooves behind the rear main bearing. Directly in front of this seal is an oil slinger which deflects the oil back into the oil pan. Should the braided seal require replacement, the installation of the lower half is accomplished as follows:

With the bearing cap and lower bearing half removed, install a new seal so that both ends protrude above the cap. Tap the seal down into position or roll it snugly in its groove with a smooth rounded tool. Then cut off the protruding end of the seal with sharp knife or razor blade.

V8-302, 351 NOTE

The crankshaft rear seal is in contact with the outer surface of the flywheel flange rather than on the main bearing journal. In this design, the front face of the flange is exposed to crankcase splash. Therefore, to eliminate the possibility of oil leaks through the threaded holes in the flange, the flywheel attaching capscrews must be coated with an oil resistant sealer.

V8-302, 351, 390, 400, 429, 460

A new rubber split-lip rear crankshaft oil seal is released for service. This seal can be installed without removal of the crankshaft and also eliminates the necessity of seal installation tools.

1. Remove oil pan.
2. Remove rear main bearing cap.
3. Loosen remaining bearing caps, allowing crankshaft to drop down about $1/32$".
4. Remove old seals from both cylinder block and rear main bearing cap. Use a brass rod to drift upper half of seal from cylinder block groove. Rotate crankshaft while drifting to facilitate removal.
5. Carefully clean seal groove in block with a brush and solvent. Also clean seal groove in bearing cap. Remove the oil seal retaining pin from the bearing cap if so equipped. *The pin is not used with the split-lip seal.*
6. Dip seal halves in clean engine oil.
7. Carefully install upper seal half in its groove with undercut side of seal toward front of engine, Fig. 24, by

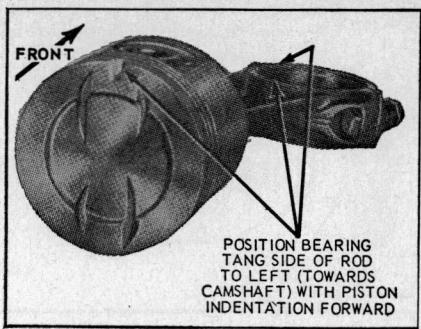

POSITION BEARING TANG SIDE OF ROD TO LEFT (TOWARDS CAMSHAFT) WITH PISTON INDENTATION FORWARD

Fig. 22 Piston and rod assembly. 1969-72 6-240 engine

rotating it on shaft journal of crankshaft until approximately $3/8$" protrudes below the parting surface. *Be sure no rubber has been shaved from outside diameter of seal by bottom edge of groove.*

8. Retighten main bearing caps and torque to specifications.
9. Install lower seal in main bearing cap with undercut side of seal toward front of engine, and allow seal to protrude about $3/8$" above parting surface to mate with upper seal upon cap installation.
10. Apply suitable sealer to parting faces of cap and block. Install cap and torque to specifications.

NOTE: If difficulty is encountered in installing the upper half of the seal in position, lightly lap (sandpaper) the side of the seal opposite the lip side using a medium grit paper. After sanding, the seal must be washed in solvent, then dipped in clean engine oil prior to installation.

SERVICE BULLETIN

A revised crankshaft rear oil seal has been released for service. This new seal may be received when ordering an oil pan gasket kit and is installed in the same manner as described previously, Fig. 25.

OIL PAN, REPLACE
1969-72 6-240 Engine

1. Drain crankcase and cooling system.
2. Remove radiator.
3. Disconnect flexible fuel line at fuel pump.
4. With automatic transmission disconnect kickdown rod at bellcrank.
5. With manual shift transmission, disconnect clutch linkage.
6. Raise car and remove starter.
7. Remove engine front support retaining nuts.
8. Raise transmission, remove rear support insulator and lower transmission to crossmember.
9. Raise engine and place 3" thick wood blocks between both front support insulators and intermediate support brackets.
10. Remove oil pan bolts and oil pump retaining bolts.

11. Remove oil pump from block and lay it in bottom of oil pan.
12. Rotate crankshaft as required to remove oil pan.
13. Remove inlet tube and screen from pump.

Installation

1. After cleaning, install inlet tube and screen on oil pump, using a new gasket.
2. Clean gasket surfaces of oil pump, pan and block.
3. Remove rear main bearing cap-to-oil pan seal and cylinder front cover-to-oil pan seal. Clean seal grooves.
4. Apply oil-resistant sealer in cavities between bearing cap and cylinder block, Fig. 26.
5. Install new side gaskets on oil pan with oil-resistant sealer.
6. Position a new cylinder front cover seal on oil pan.
7. Place oil pump assembly in pan. Position pan under engine. Install oil pump with new gasket on cylinder block. Install oil pan and tighten screws securely.
8. Complete the operation by reversing the removal procedure.

1969 V8-302, 351

1. Drain crankcase and remove dip-stick.
2. Unfasten and position oil pan on No. 2 crossmember.
3. Remove one of the inlet tube retaining bolts and loosen the other. This

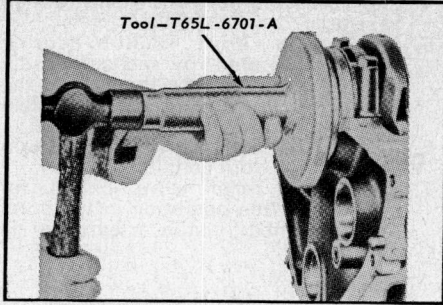

Fig. 23   Crankshaft rear oil seal installation. 6-240 engine

allows inlet tube to be positioned out of the way when removing oil pan.
4. Crank engine as required to obtain clearance and remove oil pan.
5. Remove oil pump inlet tube and screen.

Installation

1. Position oil inlet tube and loosely install one retaining bolt.
2. Clean gasket surfaces of block and pan.
3. Coat block surface and oil pan gasket with sealer. Position pan gaskets on cylinder block.
4. Position front seal on cylinder front cover, being sure tabs on seal are over oil pan gasket.
5. Position rear oil pan seal on rear main bearing cap, being sure tabs on seal are over oil pan gasket.
6. Place pan on No. 2 crossmember and install other inlet tube retaining bolt.
7. Complete installation in reverse order of removal.

1970-75 V8-302, 351C, 351W, 351M, 400

1. Drain oil pan and remove dip stick.
2. Remove fan shroud bolts and place shroud over fan.
3. On V8-351C, 351M, 400 engines, remove starter.
4. On all engines, remove engine front mount to chassis bolts, raise engine and install wood blocks between mounts and chassis, then lower engine onto the wood blocks.
5. On V8-302, 351W engines, disconnect stabilizer bar from lower control arms and position stabilizer bar and control arms to permit oil pan removal. Also, on all models with automatic transmission, position oil cooler lines aside for pan removal.
6. Remove oil pan bolts and oil pan.

Installation

1. Coat all gasket surfaces with a suitable sealer and install gaskets on engine.
2. On V8-351C, 351M, 400 engines, install pan seal on cylinder front cover and pan rear seal on rear main bearing cap.
3. On all engines, install oil pan. Torque

¼ inch bolts to 7-9 ft. lbs.; V8-302, 351W, 5/16 inch bolts to 9-11 ft. lbs.; V8-351C, 351M, 400, 5/16 inch bolts to 11-13 ft. lbs.
4. On V8-302, 351W engines, connect stabilizer bar to lower control arms and torque bolts to 6-12 ft. lbs.
5. On all engines, raise engine, remove wood blocks, lower engine and install front mount to chassis bolts.
6. Install starter, if removed, fan shroud and dip stick.

1969-71 V8-390 & 1969-75 429, 460

1. Drain oil pan.
2. On V8-429, 460 engines, remove starter.
3. On 1969-71 engines, disconnect stabilizer bar at connecting links and pull ends down. On 1972-75 engines disconnect sway bar and pull forward on struts.
4. Remove fan shroud bolts, place shroud on fan and remove oil filter.

NOTE: *To allow clearance for removal of oil pan, remove the front engine mount nuts. Then position floor jack under front leading edge of oil pan (use wood block between pan and jack). Raise engine about 1¼" and insert a 1" block of wood between insulators and frame crossmember. Then remove floor jack.*

5. Remove oil pan screws and lower pan to crossmember.
6. Crank engine to obtain necessary clearance between crankshaft counterweight and rear of oil pan. Then remove pan.

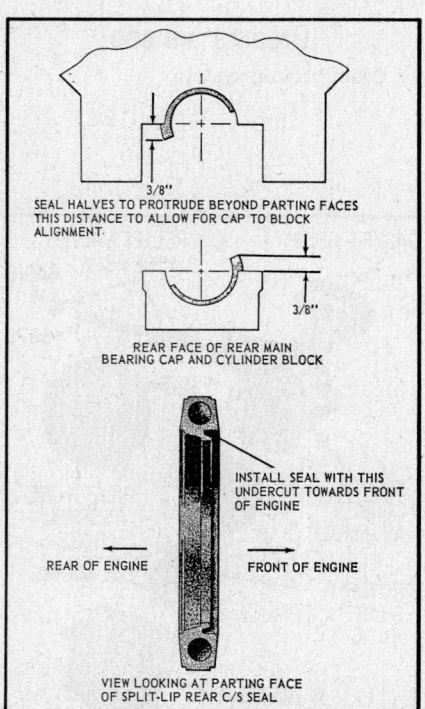

SEAL HALVES TO PROTRUDE BEYOND PARTING FACES THIS DISTANCE TO ALLOW FOR CAP TO BLOCK ALIGNMENT.

3/8"

3/8"

REAR FACE OF REAR MAIN BEARING CAP AND CYLINDER BLOCK

INSTALL SEAL WITH THIS UNDERCUT TOWARDS FRONT OF ENGINE

REAR OF ENGINE ← → FRONT OF ENGINE

VIEW LOOKING AT PARTING FACE OF SPLIT-LIP REAR C/S SEAL

Fig. 24   Split-lip rear crankshaft seal installation on V8-351, 390, 400, 429, 460

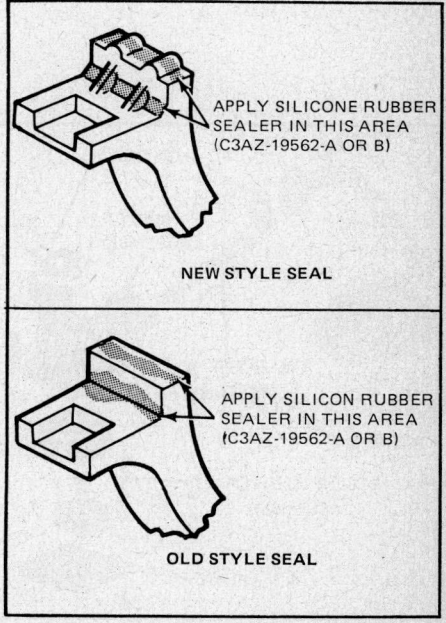

APPLY SILICONE RUBBER SEALER IN THIS AREA (C3AZ-19562-A OR B)

NEW STYLE SEAL

APPLY SILICON RUBBER SEALER IN THIS AREA (C3AZ-19562-A OR B)

OLD STYLE SEAL

Fig. 25   Crankshaft rear oil seals

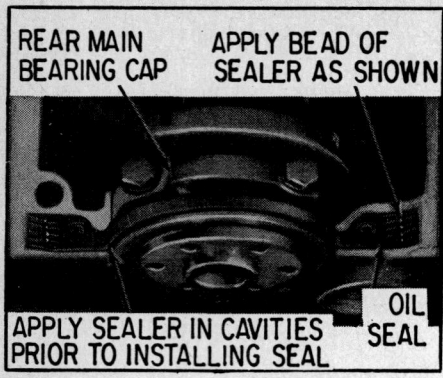

Fig. 26 Oil pan rear seal installation. 6-240 engine

and rotor are furnished only as an assembly.

5. Check the drive shaft-to-housing bearing clearance by measuring the O.D. of the shaft and the I.D. of the housing bearing. The recommended clearance limits are .0015-.0029".
6. Inspect the relief valve spring for a collapsed or worn condition.
7. Check the relief valve piston for scores and free operation in the bore. The specified piston clearance is .0015-0029".

BELT TENSION DATA

	New Lbs.	Used Lbs.
1969-75 All	140	110

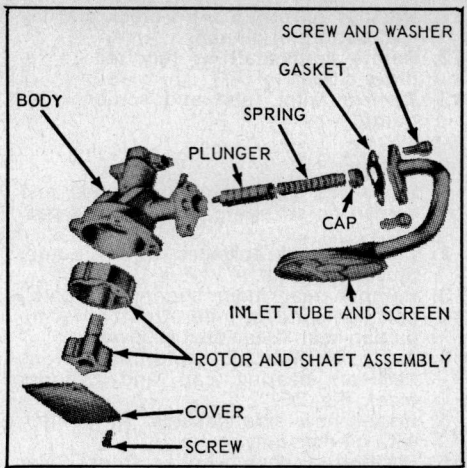

Fig. 27 Oil pump. 6-240 engine

OIL PUMP REPAIRS

Figs. 27, 28, 29, 30

1. With all parts clean and dry, check the inside of the pump housing and the outer race and rotor for damage or excessive wear.
2. Check the mating surface of the pump cover for wear. If this surface is worn, scored or grooved, replace the cover.
3. Measure the clearance between the outer race and housing. This clearance should be .006-.013 inch on 1969-73 engines and .001-.013 inch on 1974-75 engines.
4. With the rotor assembly installed in the housing, place a straight edge over the rotor assembly and housing. Measure the clearance between the straight edge and the rotor and outer race. Recommended limits are .0011-.0041". The outer race, shaft

WATER PUMP, REPLACE

1969-72 Six

1. Drain cooling system.
2. Loosen and remove alternator, power steering and air conditioning belts.
3. Disconnect radiator lower hose and heater hose at pump.
4. Remove fan, spacer, pulley and belt.
5. Unfasten and remove the water pump.

1969-75 V8-351, 400, 429, 460

1. Drain cooling system, remove fan shroud, fan and all belts.
2. Disconnect alternator bracket and position bracket out of way.
3. Remove power steering pump, A/C compressor and position units out of way.
4. Remove A/C compressor bracket and disconnect hoses from water pump.

5. Remove water pump and remove separator plates from pump.

1969-73 V8-302, 351, 400

1. Drain cooling system.
2. Remove power steering drive belt (if equipped). If air conditioned, remove compressor belt.
3. Disconnect radiator lower hose and heater hose at water pump.
4. Remove drive belt, fan, spacer or fan drive clutch and pulley.
5. Unfasten and remove water pump from cylinder front cover.

1969-73 V8-390

1. Drain cooling system.

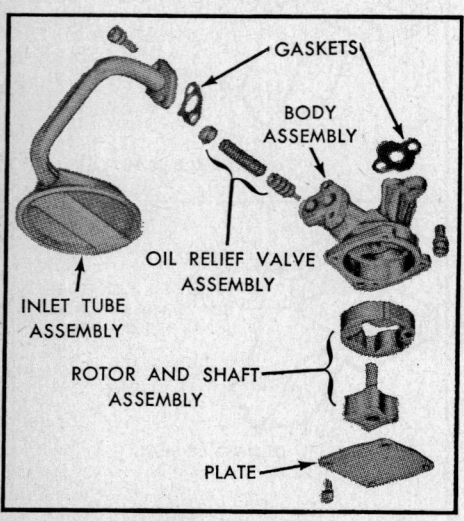

Fig. 28 Oil pump. V8-302, 351, 351W

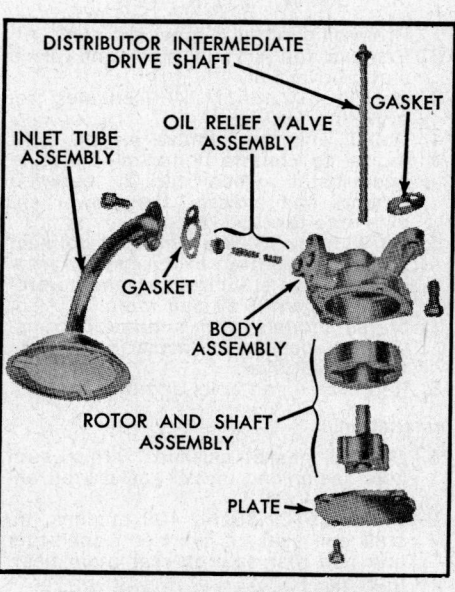

Fig. 29 Oil pump. V8-390, 429, 460

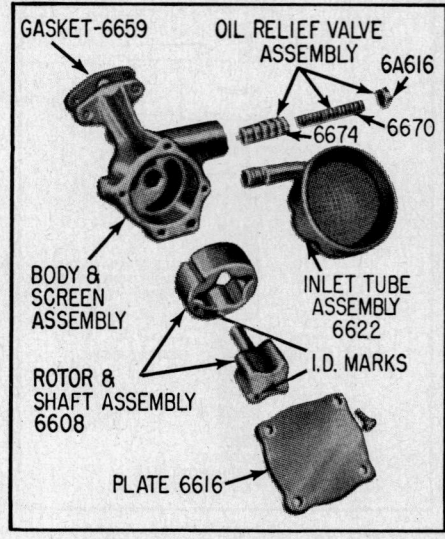

Fig. 30 Oil pump assembly. V8-351C, 351M and 400

2. Remove power steering drive belt (if equipped). If air conditioned, remove compressor drive belt.
3. Disconnect radiator lower hose and heater hose at water pump.
4. Remove radiator upper support and fan guard.
5. Remove fan belt or belts, fan, spacer or fan drive clutch and pulley.
6. Unfasten and remove water pump.

FUEL PUMP PRESSURE

Year	Engine	Pressure Lbs.
1969-72	6-240	4-6
1969	All V8	4½-6½

1970-71	V8 exc. 302	5-7
1970-71	V8-302	4-6
1972-75	V8 exc. 1974-75 460	5-7
1974	V8-460 Calif.	5.7-7.7
1974	V8-460 exc. Calif.	5-7
1975	V8-460	5.7-7.7

FUEL PUMP, REPLACE

1. Remove all gasket material from the pump and block gasket surfaces. Apply sealer to both sides of new gasket.
2. Position gasket on pump flange and hold pump in position against its mounting surface. Make sure rocker arm is riding on camshaft eccentric.
3. Press pump tight against its mounting. Install retaining screws and tighten them alternately.
4. Connect fuel lines. Then operate engine and check for leaks.

NOTE: Before installing the pump, it is good practice to crank the engine so that the nose of the camshaft eccentric is out of the way of the fuel pump rocker arm when the pump is installed. In this way there will be the lease amount of tension on the rocker arm, thereby easing the installation of the pump.

Clutch and Transmission Section

> NOTE: 1975 linkage adjustment information is in this section. Repair procedures on both automatic and manual shift transmissions are covered elsewhere in this manual. Procedures for removing automatic transmissions as well as linkage adjustments on 1969-74 models are included in the automatic transmission chapters. See Chapter Index.

CLUTCH PEDAL, ADJUST
1969-71

1. Disconnect clutch release lever spring from release lever.
2. Loosen release lever rod locknut and adjusting nut.
3. Move clutch release lever rearward until release bearing lightly touches pressure plate release fingers.
4. Adjust adapter length until adapter seats in release lever pocket.
5. Insert a .194" feeler against the back face of rod adapter and tighten the adjusting nut finger tight against the feeler gauge.
6. Tighten locknut against adjusting nut being careful not to disturb adjustment.
7. Remove feeler gauge.
8. Install release lever spring and check pedal free travel. Travel should be 7/8" to 1 1/8".

CLUTCH, REPLACE
1969-71

1. Remove transmission as outlined.
2. On cars with aluminum clutch housing, remove starter. Unfasten housing from engine and move housing back just far enough to clear pressure plate, then move it to the right to free the pivot from clutch equalizer bar. Be careful not to lose bushing or disturb linkage or assist spring.
3. Remove flywheel housing cover (cast iron housings only).
4. Remove release lever return spring. Then slide release bearing and hub off release lever (cast iron housings only).
5. Loosen pressure plate attaching bolts gradually and evenly to release spring tension. If same clutch is being installed, first mark clutch cover and flywheel so installation may be made in same position.
6. Remove clutch and driven plate.

MANUAL SHIFT TRANS.

Transmission Replace

Three Speed Units
1. Raise car and drain lube from transmission.

2. Mark drive shaft so that it may be installed in the same relative position.
3. Disconnect drive shaft from U-joint flange and slide it out of extension housing.
4. Disconnect speedometer cable.
5. Disconnect shift rods from levers at transmission.
6. Disconnect parking brake cable at equalizer.
7. Unfasten extension from rear support.
8. Raise engine high enough to remove weight from frame crossmember.
9. Support transmission with a jack and detach it from flywheel housing.
10. Slide transmission back and out of car.
11. Reverse removal procedure to install transmission.

Four Speed Units
1. Remove transmission gearshift lever boot retainer. Working under boot, remove shift lever retaining bolts and remove lever. The remaining shift linkage may be left on the transmission during removal.

2. Raise car and disconnect drive shaft from rear U-joint flange and remove drive shaft.
3. Disconnect speedometer cable.
4. Disconnect parking brake cable at equalizer bar and raise rear of engine.
5. Unfasten extension housing from engine rear support.
6. Raise transmission slightly with a jack. Disconnect and remove crossmember and engine rear support as a unit.
7. Unfasten transmission from clutch housing and install guide pins in the two lower holes.
8. Remove transmission. If necessary, lower engine to gain enough clearance for removal of transmission.
9. Reverse removal procedure to install.

SHIFT LINKAGE, ADJUST
1969-71 3 Speed Units

1. Place selector lever in neutral.

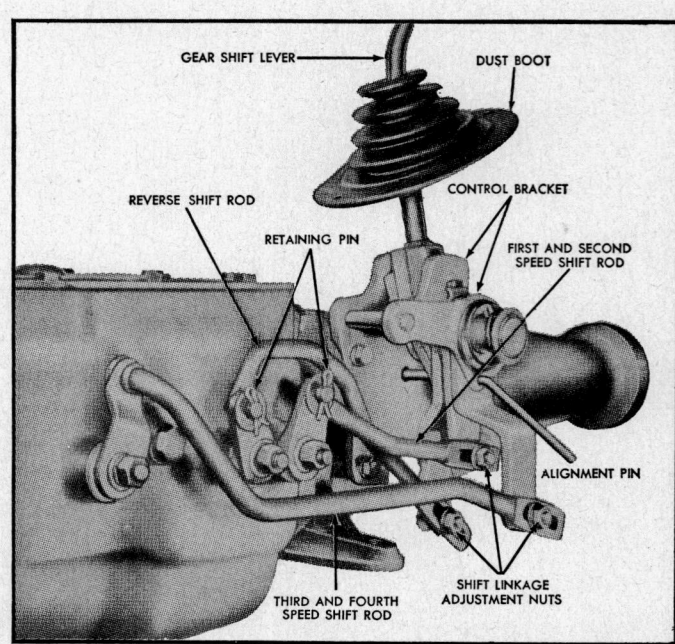

Fig. 1   Shift linkage. 1969-71 four speed transmission

2. Loosen the two shift rod adjusting nuts.
3. Insert a 3/16" drill shank through the low-reverse and 2-3 shift levers at steering column. It may be necessary to align levers to insert drill.
4. Tighten adjusting nuts.
5. Remove drill gauge.
6. Start engine and move shift lever to each position to be sure it operates freely.

1969-71 4 Speed Units

1. Loosen three shift linkage adjustment nuts.
2. Install a 1/4" diameter alignment tool through control bracket and levers as shown in Fig. 1.

NOTE: An alignment tool can be made from 1/4" diameter drill rod bent to an "L" shape. The extensions should be 1 1/2" and 3 3/4" from elbow. Short end of tool should be inserted into control bracket and linkage holes until it bottoms.

---

3. Tighten three linkage adjusting nuts and then remove alignment tool.
4. Check shift lever for smooth cross-over.

NOTE: On 1970-71 models, a transmission lock rod is incorporated in the shift linkage. This link must be adjusted AFTER the shift linkage is properly adjusted.

1. Place shift lever in Neutral and loosen lock rod adjustment nut.
2. Align the hole in the steering column socket casting with the column alignment mark and insert a .180" dia. gauge rod. The column casting must not rotate with the gauge rod installed.
3. Tighten rod lock nut and check for proper operation.

1975 AUTO. TRANS. LINKAGE, ADJUST

Linkage adjustment procedures are the same as those described for 1974 models described elsewhere in this manual.

Rear Axle, Propeller Shaft & Brakes

REAR AXLES

Figs. 1 and 3 illustrate the rear axle assemblies used on these cars. When necessary to overhaul either of these units, refer to the *Rear Axle Specifications* table in this chapter.

Integral Carrier Type

The gear set consists of a ring gear and an overhung drive pinion which is supported by two opposed tapered roller bearings, Fig. 1. The differential case is a one-piece design with openings allowing assembly of the internal parts and lubricant flow. The differential pinion shaft is retained with a threaded bolt (lock) assembled to the case.

The roller type wheel bearings have no inner race, and the rollers directly contact the bearing journals of the axle shafts. The axle shafts do not use an inner and outer bearing retainer. Rather, they are held in the axle by means of C-locks, Fig. 2. These C-locks also fit into a machined recess in the differential side gears within the differential case. There is no retainer bolt access hole in the axle shaft flange.

Axle Shaft, Bearing & Oil Seal

1. Raise car on hoist and remove wheels.
2. Drain differential lubricant.
3. Remove brake drums.
4. Remove differential housing cover.
5. Position safety stands under rear frame member and lower hoist to allow axle to lower as far as possible.
6. Working through differential case opening, remove pinion shaft lock bolt and pinion shaft.
7. Push axle shaft(s) inward toward center of axle housing and remove C-lock(s) from housing, Fig. 2.
8. Remove axle shaft, using extreme care to avoid contact of shaft seal lip with any portion of axle shaft ex-

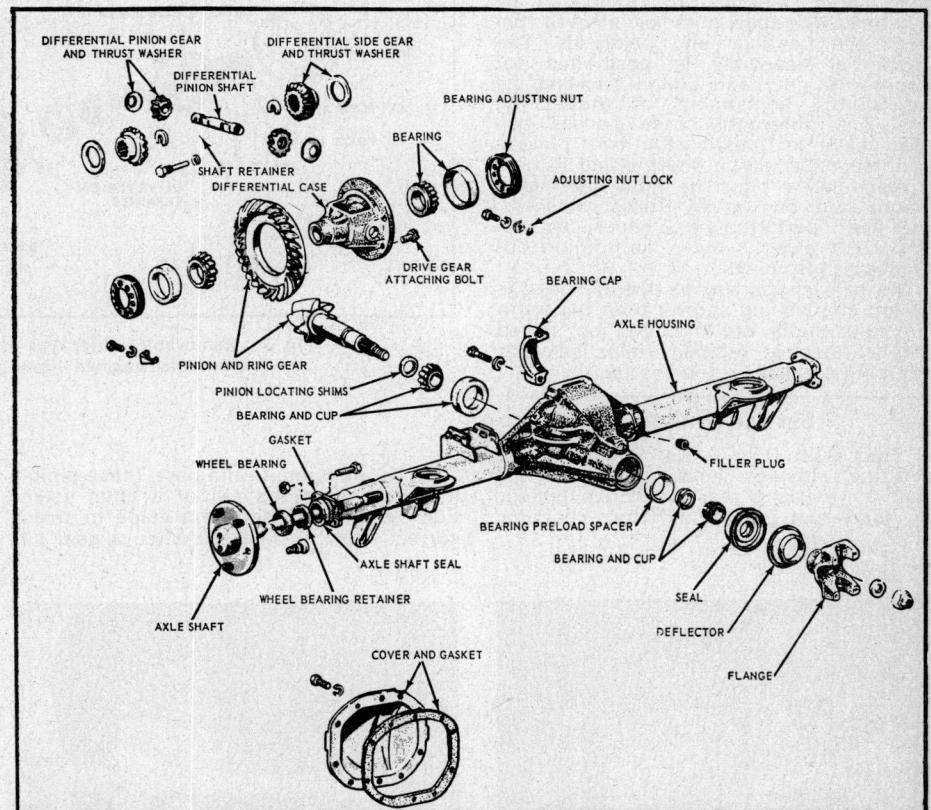

Fig. 1   Integral type rear axle assembly

cept seal journal.
9. Use a hook-type puller to remove seal and bearing, Fig. 7.
10. Reverse procedure to install, using suitable driving tools, Fig. 8, to install seal and bearing. New seals are pre-packed with lubricant and do not require oil soaking before installation.

Removable Carrier Type

In these axles, Fig. 3, the drive pinion is straddle-mounted by two opposed tapered roller bearings which support the pinion shaft in front of the drive pinion gear, and straight roller bearing that supports the pinion shaft at the rear of the pinion gear. The drive pinion

Fig. 2   Axle shaft C-locks. 1969-75 Ford integral type axle

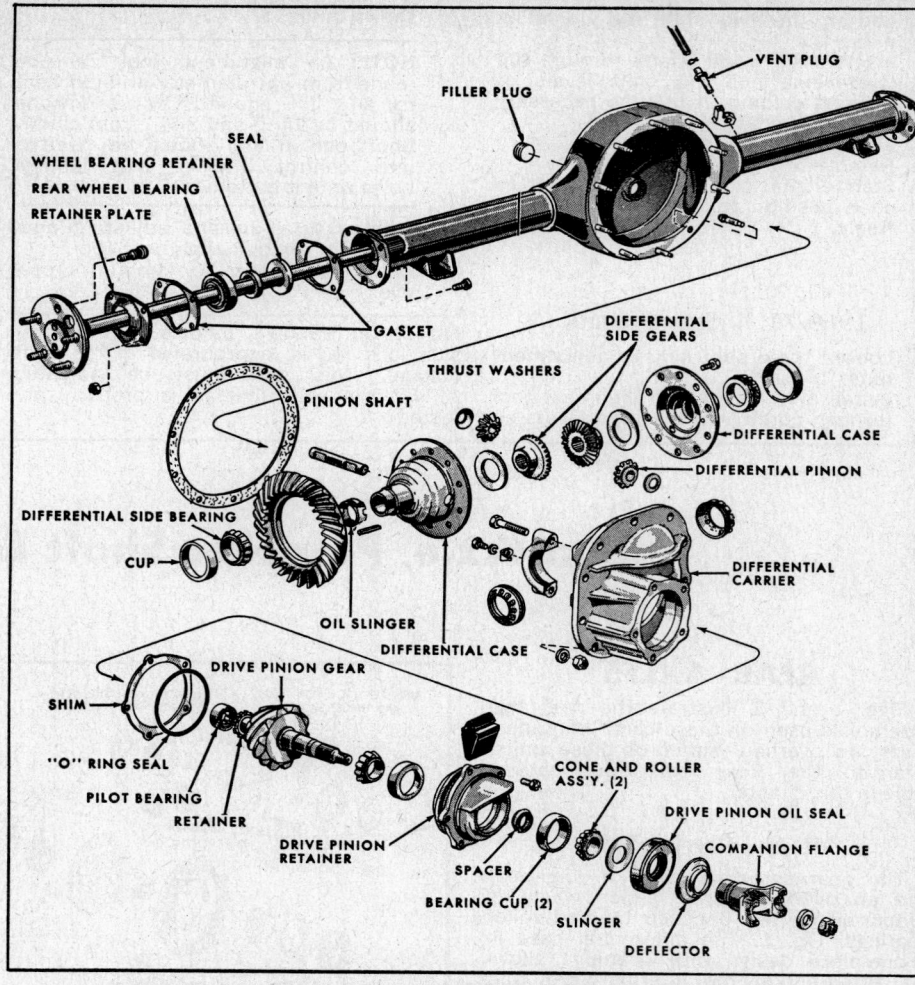

Fig. 3   Removable carrier type of rear axle assembly. On some high performance engines a four-pinion differential is also used

is assembled in a pinion retainer that is bolted to the differential carrier. The tapered roller bearings are preloaded by a collapsible spacer between the bearings. The pinion is positioned by a shim or shims located between the drive pinion retainer and the differential carrier.

The differential is supported in the carrier by two tapered roller side bearings. These bearings are preloaded by two threaded ring nuts or sleeves between the bearings and pedestals. The differential assembly is positioned for proper ring gear and pinion backlash by varying the adjustment of these ring nuts. The differential case houses two side gears in mesh with two pinions mounted on a pinion shaft which is held in place by a pin. The side gears and pinions are backed by thrust washers. With high performance engines, an optional rear axle having a four-pinion differential is also used.

The axle shafts are of unequal length, the left shaft being shorter than the right. The axle shafts are mounted on sealed ball bearings or tapered roller bearings which are pressed on the shafts.

Service Bulletin

All Ford Built Rear Axles: Recent manufacturing changes have eliminated the need for marking rear axle drive pinions for individual variations from nominal shim thicknesses. In the past, these pinion markings, with the aid of a shim selection table, were used as a guide to select correct shim thicknesses when a gear set or carrier assembly replacement was performed.

With the elimination of pinion markings, use of the shim selection table is

Fig. 4   Removing nuts from rear bearing retainer

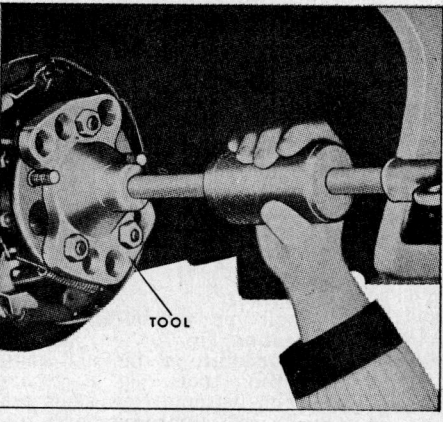

Fig. 5   Removing axle shaft with slide hammer-type puller

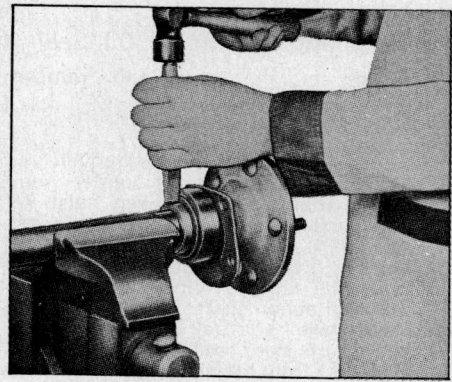

Fig. 6   Splitting bearing inner retainer for bearing removal

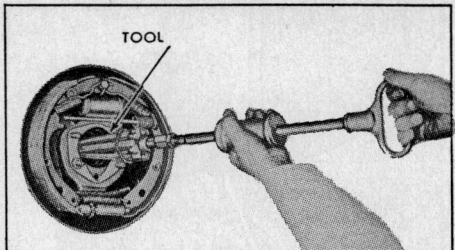

Fig. 7 Using hook-type tool to remove oil seal

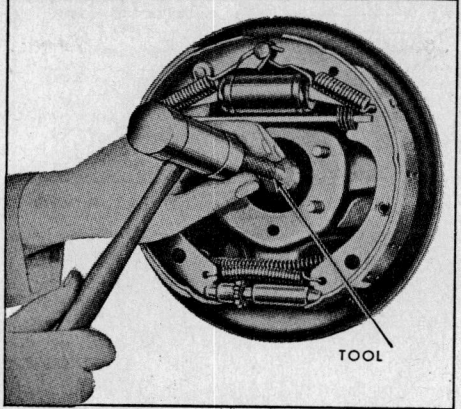

Fig. 8 Using special driver to install oil seal

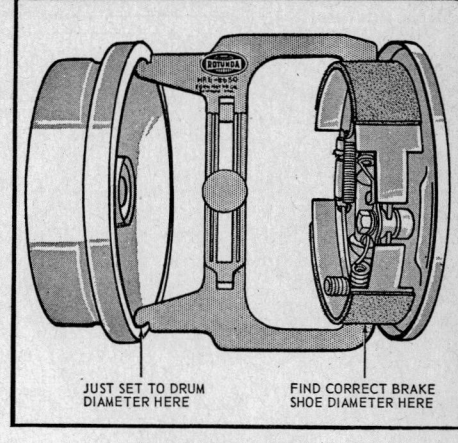

JUST SET TO DRUM DIAMETER HERE   FIND CORRECT BRAKE SHOE DIAMETER HERE

Fig. 9 Brake adjustment gauge

no longer possible and the methods outlined below must be used.

1. Measure the thickness of the original pinion depth shim removed from the axle. Use the same thickness upon installation of the replacement carrier or drive pinion. If any further shim change is necessary, it will be indicated in the tooth pattern check.
2. If the original shim is lost, substitute a nominal shim for the original and use the tooth pattern check to determine if further shim changes are required.

Axle Shaft, Bearing & Seal

1. Remove wheel assembly.
2. Remove brake drum or caliper.
3. Working through hole provided in axle shaft flange, Fig. 4, remove nuts that secure bearing retainer.
4. Pull axle shaft out of housing. If bearing is a tight fit in axle housing, use a slide hammer-type puller, Fig. 5. *Brake carrier plate must not be dislodged. Install one nut to hold plate in place after axle shaft is removed.*

NOTE: On 1974-75 models, remove brake carrier plate.

5. If axle shaft bearing is to be replaced, drill a ¼ inch hole not more than ⁵⁄₁₆ inch deep in retainer ring surface and then nick it deeply in several places and slide bearing retain off, Fig. 6.
6. Press bearing from axle shaft.
7. Inspect machined surfaces of axle shaft and housing for rough spots that would affect the sealing action of the oil seal. Carefully remove any burrs or rough spots.
8. Press new bearing on shaft until it seats firmly against shoulder on shaft.
9. Press inner bearing retainer on shaft until it seats firmly against bearing.
10. If oil seal is to be replaced, use a hook-type tool to pull it out of the housing, Fig. 7. Wipe a small amount of oil resistant sealer on outer edge of seal before it is installed, Fig. 8.

Installation

NOTE: On models equipped with rear disc brakes, ensure disc brake adapters are

installed in the correct position and are identified with a stamping.

1. On 1974-75 models, place a new gasket on each side of brake carrier plate and slide axle shaft into housing.
2. On all models start the splines into the differential side gear and push the shaft in until bearing bottoms in housing.
3. Install retainer and tighten nuts to 30-40 ft. lbs.
4. Install brake drum and wheel.

PROPELLER SHAFT

Remove & Replace

1. Disconnect rear U-joint from drive pinion flange.
2. Pull dirve shaft toward rear of car until front U-joint yoke clears transmission extension housing and output shaft.
3. Install a suitable tool, such as a seal driver, in seal to prevent lube from leaking from transmission.
4. Before installing, check U-joints for freedom of movement. If a bind has resulted from misalignment after overhauling the U-joints, tap the ears of the drive shaft sharply to relieve the bind.
5. If rubber seal installed on end of transmission extension housing is damaged, install a new seal.
6. On a manual shift transmission, lubricate yoke spline with conventional transmission lubricant. On an automatic transmission, lubricate yoke spline with special spline lubricant. *This spline is sealed so that transmission fluid does not "wash" away spline lubricant.*
7. Install yoke on transmission output shaft.
8. Install U-bolts and nuts which attach U-joint to pinion flange. Tighten U-bolts evenly to prevent binding U-joint bearings.

BRAKE ADJUSTMENTS

1. Use the brake shoe adjustment gauge shown in Fig. 9 to obtain the drum inside diameter as shown. Tighten the adjusting knob on the gauge to hold this setting.
2. Place the opposite side of the gauge over the brake shoes and adjust the shoes by turning the adjuster screw until the gauge just slides over the linings. Rotate the gauge around the lining surface to assure proper lining diameter adjustment and clearance.
3. Install brake drum and wheel. Final adjustment is accomplished by making several firm reverse stops, using the brake pedal.

Self-Adjusting Brakes

These brakes, Fig. 10, have self-adjusting shoe mechanisms that assure correct lining-to-drum clearances at all times. The automatic adjusters operate only when the brakes are applied as the car is moving rearward or when the car comes to an uphill stop.

Although the brakes are self-adjusting, an initial adjustment is necessary after the brake shoes have been relined or replaced, or when the length of the star wheel adjuster has been changed during some other service operation.

Frequent usage of an automatic transmission forward range to halt reverse vehicle motion may prevent the automatic adjusters from functioning, thereby inducing low pedal heights. Should low pedal heights be encountered, it is recommended that numerous forward and reverse stops be performed with a firm pedal effort until satisfactory pedal height is obtained.

NOTE

If a low pedal height condition cannot be corrected by making numerous reverse stops (provided the hydraulic system is free of air), it indicates that the self-adjusting mechanism is not functioning. Therefore, it will be necessary

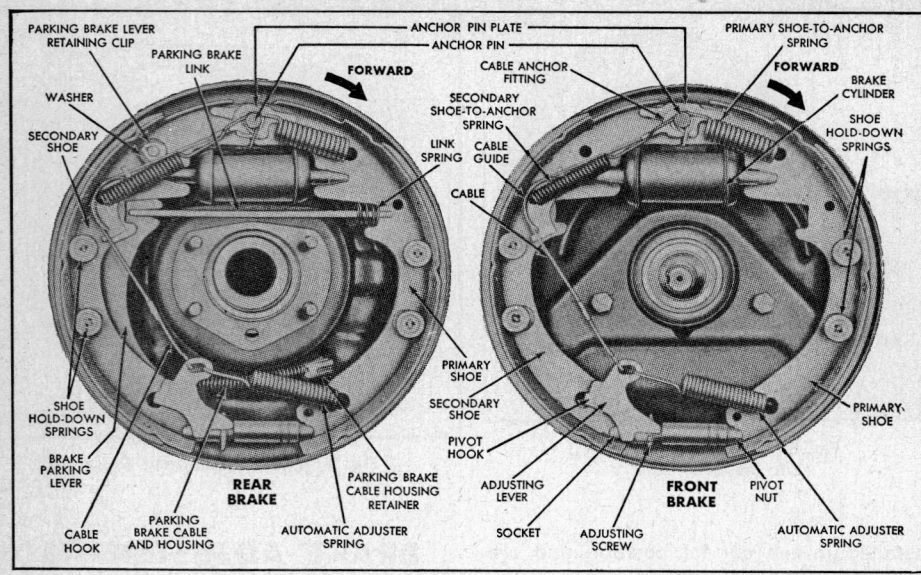

Fig. 10   Right front and rear drum brakes

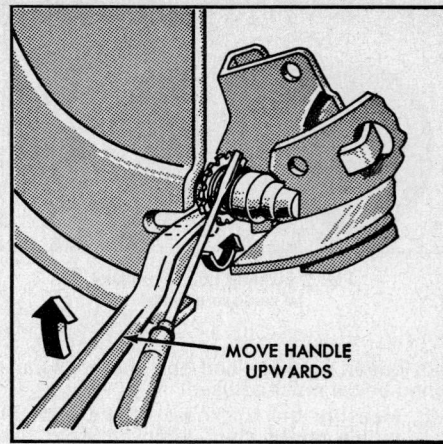

Fig. 11   Backing off brake adjustment by disengaging adjusting lever with screwdriver

to remove the brake drums, clean, free up and lubricate the adjusting mechanism. Then adjust the brakes, being sure the parking brake is fully released.

Initial Adjustment

1. Remove adjusting hole cover from brake backing plate and, from the backing plate side, turn the adjusting screw upward with a screwdriver or other suitable tool to expand the shoes until a slight drag is felt when the drums are rotated.

2. Remove the drum.

3. While holding the adjusting lever out of engagement with the adjusting screw, Fig. 11, back off the adjusting screw about one full turn with the fingers.

NOTE: If finger movement will not turn the screw, free it up. If this is not done, the adjusting lever will not turn the screw during vehicle operation. Lubricate the screw with oil and coat with wheel bearing grease. Any other adjustment procedure may cause damage to the adjusting screw with consequent self-adjuster problems.

4. Install wheel and drum, and adjusting hole cover. Adjust brakes on remaining wheels in the same manner.

5. If pedal height is not satisfactory, drive the vehicle and make sufficient reverse stops with a firm pedal effort until proper pedal height is obtained.

REAR WHEEL DISC BRAKE & PARKING BRAKE SERVICE
Mercury

Sliding caliper rear disc brakes are used on some 1975 models, Fig. 12. The caliper is basically the same as the larger front wheel caliper, however, a parking brake mechanism and a larger inner brake shoe anti-rattle spring has been added, Fig. 13. A hydraulically powered brake booster (Hydroboost) provides the power assist for this four wheel disc system.

The parking brake lever, located at the rear of the caliper, is actuated by a cable system similar to rear drum brake applications. When the parking brake is applied, the cable rotates the lever and operating shaft. Three steel balls, placed in pockets between the opposing heads of the operating shaft and thrust screw, roll between ramps formed in the pockets and force the

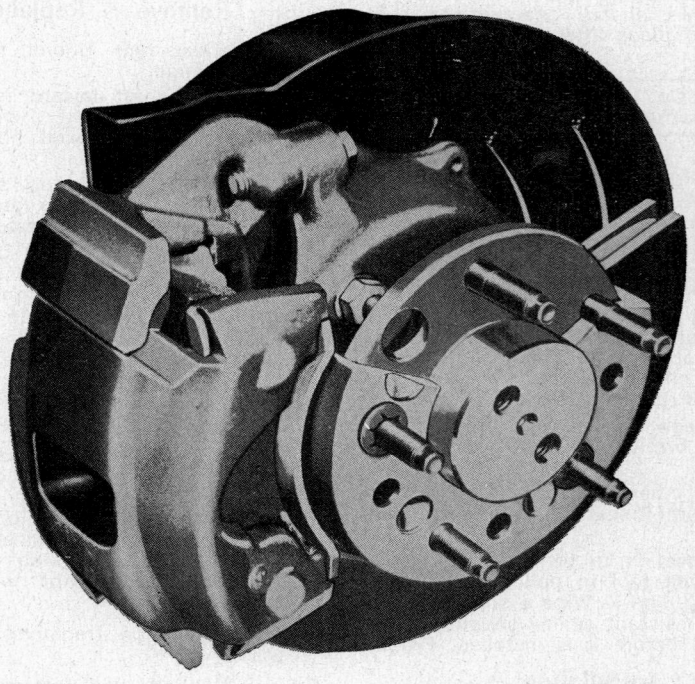

Fig. 12   Rear disc brake. 1975 Mercury

thrust screw away from the operating shaft, in turn, driving the caliper piston and brake shoe assembly against the rotor. An automatic adjuster in the assembly compensates for lining wear and maintains proper clearance in the parking brake mechanism.

The cast iron rotors are ventilated by curved fins located between the braking surfaces and are designed to cause the rotor to act as an air pump when the vehicle is traveling forward. The rotors are not interchangeable and are identified by a Right or Left marking cast inside the hat section of the rotor. The rotor is secured to the axle flange in the same manner as a rear brake drum. A splash shield is bolted to a forged axle adapter to protect the inboard rotor surface.

NOTE: Refer to the "Lincoln Continental" chapter, "Transmission, Rear Axle, Propeller Shaft and Brake" section for service procedures.

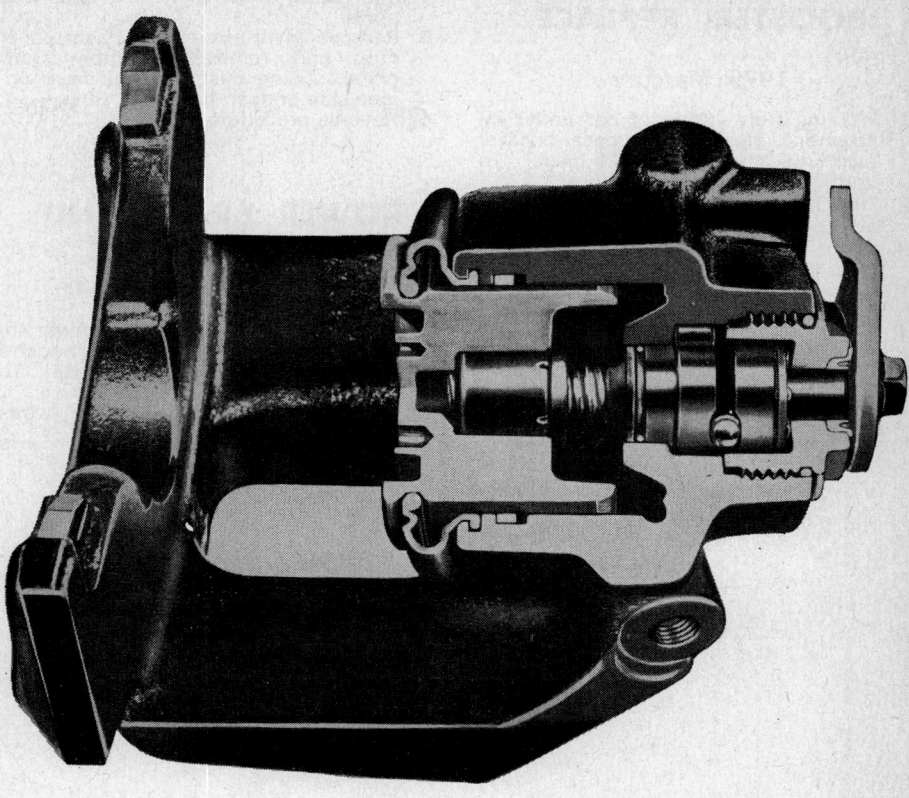

Fig. 13   Caliper housing cutaway to show parking brake mechanism

PARKING BRAKE, ADJUST

Check parking brake cables when brakes are fully released. If cables are loose, adjust as follows:

1969-75 Ford & Mercury

1. Make sure parking brake is released.
2. Place transmission in neutral and raise the vehicle.
3. Tighten the adjusting nut against the cable equalizer to cause rear brakes to drag.
4. Then loosen the adjusting nut until the rear wheels are fully released. There should be no drag.
5. Lower vehicle and check operation.

VACUUM RELEASE PARKING BRAKE

The vacuum power unit will release the parking brakes automatically when the shift lever is moved into any drive position with the engine running. The brakes will not release automatically, however, when the shift lever is in neutral or park position with the engine running, or in any position with the engine off.

The power unit piston rod is attached to the release lever. Since the release lever pivots against the pawl, a slight movement of the release lever will disengage the pawl from the ratchet, allowing the brakes to release. The release lever pivots on a rivet pin in the pedal mount.

As shown in Fig. 14, hoses connect the power unit and the engine manifold to a vacuum release valve in the transmission neutral safety switch. Moving the transmission selector lever into any drive position with the engine running will open

the release valve to connect engine manifold vacuum to one side of the actuating piston in the power unit. The pressure differential thus created will cause the piston and link to pull the release lever.

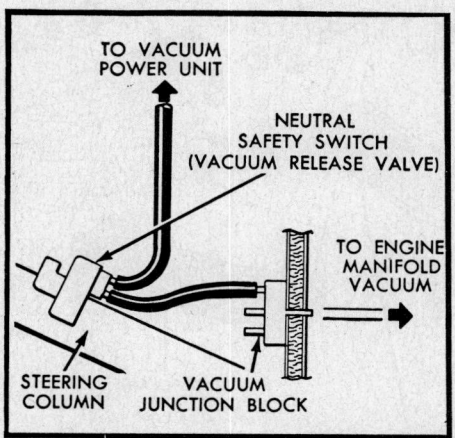

Fig. 14   Connections for automatic parking brake release. Typical

MASTER CYLINDER, REPLACE

1969-75 Ford & Mercury

Less Power Brakes

1. Working from inside of car beneath instrument panel, disconnect master cylinder push rod from brake pedal.
2. Disconnect stop light switch wires at connector. Remove hairpin retainer. Slide stop light switch off brake pedal pin just enough to clear end of pin, then lift switch straight upward from pin.
3. Slide master cylinder push rod, nylon washers and bushings from pedal pin.
4. Remove brake tubes from both outlet ports of master cylinder.
5. Unfasten and remove master cylinder from dash panel.

With Power Brakes

1. Disconnect brake lines from master cylinder.
2. Remove nuts retaining master cylinder to brake booster.
3. Remove master cylinder.

HYDRO-BOOST BRAKE BOOSTER, REPLACE

1975 Mercury

1. Working from inside of car under instrument panel, disconnect booster push rod link from brake pedal. To do this, proceed as follows:
2. Disconnect stop light switch wires at connector. Remove hairpin retainer. Slide switch off brake pedal pin just far enough for switch outer hole to clear pin. Then lift switch straight upward from pin. Slide master cylinder push rod and nylon washers and bushing off brake pedal pin.
3. Open hood and disconnect brake line at master cylinder outlet fitting.
4. Disconnect the pressure, steering gear and return lines, then plug lines and ports.
5. Remove Hydro-Boost to dash panel nuts and remove assembly from panel, sliding push rod link from engine side of dash panel.
6. Reverse procedure to install.

POWER BRAKE UNIT REPLACE

1969-75 Ford & Mercury

1. Working from inside of car under instrument panel, disconnect booster push rod link from brake pedal. To do this, proceed as follows:
2. Disconnect stop light switch wires at connector. Remove hairpin retainer. Slide switch off brake pedal pin just far enough for switch outer hole to clear pin. Then lift switch straight upward from pin. Slide master cylinder push rod and nylon washers and bushing off brake pedal pin.
3. Open hood and disconnect brake line at master cylinder outlet fitting.
4. Disconnect vacuum hose from booster unit. If equipped with automatic transmission disconnect transmission vacuum unit hose.
5. Remove four attaching nuts and remove booster and bracket from dash panel, slide push rod link out from engine side of dash panel. Remove four spacers.
6. Remove push rod link boot from dash panel.
7. Reverse procedure to install.

Rear Suspension

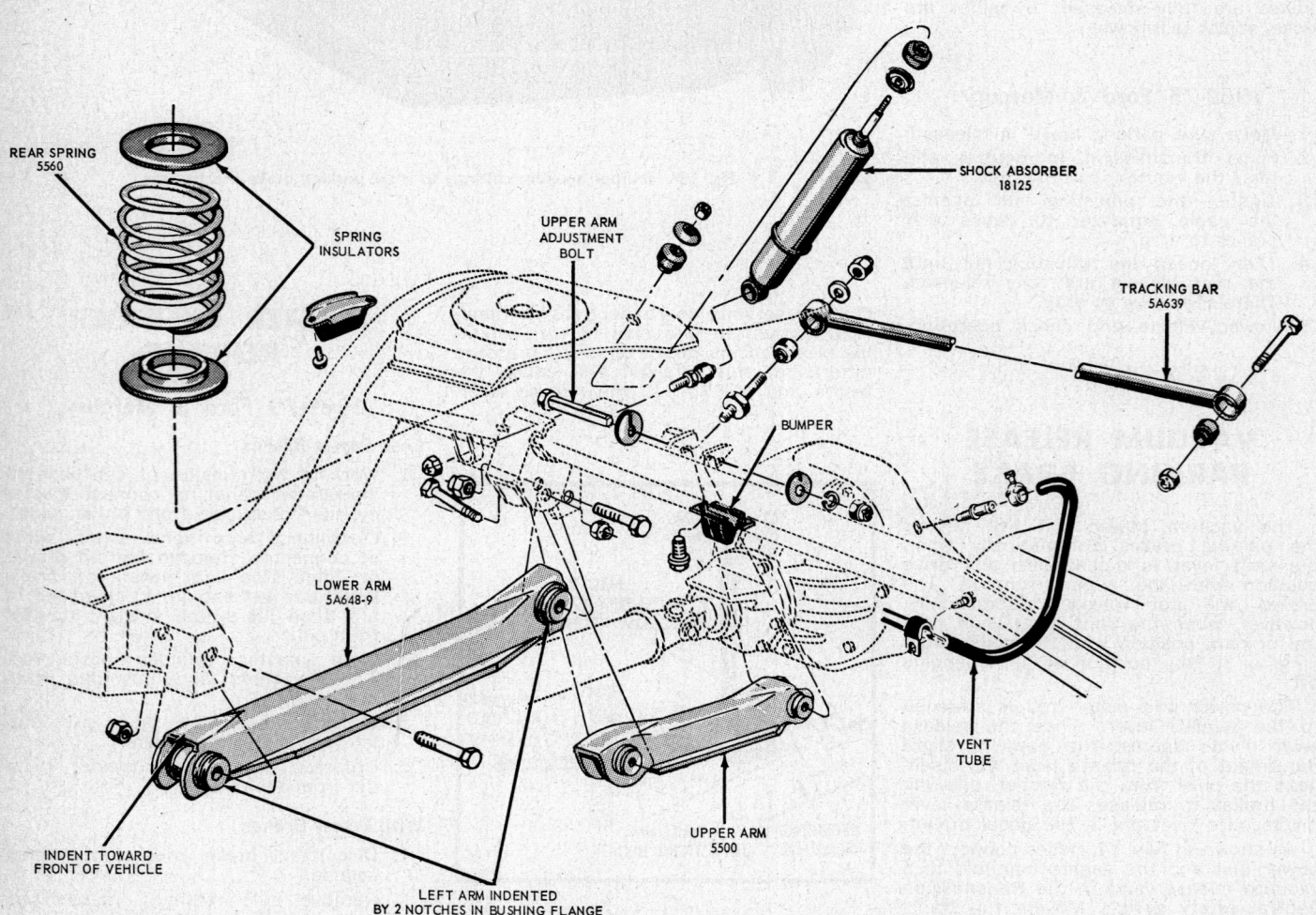

Fig. 1   Rear suspension (typical)

SHOCK ABSORBER, REPLACE

1. With the rear axle supported properly disconnect shock absorber at upper mounting and compress it to clear hole in spring seat.
2. Disconnect shock absorber from stud on axle bracket.
3. Reverse procedure to install.

COIL SPRING, REPLACE

1. Raise rear of vehicle and support at frame. Support rear axle with a suitable jack.
2. Disconnect shock absorbers at lower mountings.

3. On 1973-75 models, disconnect brake line from rear brake hose and remove hose to bracket clip.
4. Lower axle to remove springs.
5. Reverse procedure to install. Install an insulator between upper and lower seats and the spring.

CONTROL ARMS, REPLACE

NOTE: On 1972-75 models, lower arms must be replaced in pairs.

1. Raise rear of vehicle and support at frame. Support axle with a suitable jack.

2. Disconnect track bar from frame mounting bracket.
3. Lower axle and install a second jack under differential pinion nose.
4. Disconnect control arm from axle bracket. On upper arms, disconnect arm from crossmember and on lower arms, disconnect arm from frame attachment bracket.
5. Reverse procedure to install.

TRACK BAR, REPLACE

1. Remove cover from track bar axle attachment and disconnect track bar from mounting stud.
2. Disconnect track bar from frame side rail.
3. Reverse procedure to install.

Front End and Steering Section

FRONT SUSPENSION
1969-75

Referring to Fig. 1, the construction of the front suspension differs from earlier models in that the lower control arm pivots on a bolt in the front crossmember. The struts, which are connected between the lower control arms and frame crossmember, prevent the control arms from moving forward and backward.

LUBRICATION
1969-75

Ball joints are prelubricated with a special lubricant. The lubricating interval is 36,000 miles. At these intervals, remove the plugs, apply the special lubricant, remove the fittings and replace the plugs.

SERVICE BULLETIN

Some uninformed service people recommend that conventional grease fittings be installed and that the car be lubricated every 1000 miles. This is completely unnecessary and, in fact, may cause damage to the lubrication points.

The use of conventional lubricants not only can do damage to the special seals but is incompatible with the special lubricant. Moreover, after the special sealing plugs have been replaced by conventional grease fittings, dirt and water can enter and cause excessive wear, rendering the units unfit for further service.

SERVICE BULLETIN, 1969-75

BALL JOINT LUBE: The ball joint seals on these models have been redesigned to provide improved sealing and longer life. The new seals can be damaged and the sealing characteristics destroyed if

Fig. 1 Front suspension. 1969-75 Ford & Mercury

excessive lubricant is used. Specifications call for the addition of only 10 grams (level teaspoon) of lubricant to the ball joints at 36,000 miles intervals. The initial application of 10 grams of lubricant insures forcing grease into the bearing area and still allows for three subsequent lubrications of 10 grams each without ballooning the seals and resultant premature failure.

For the above reasons the ball joint seals on new cars might appear to be collapsed and give the mistaken impression that additional lubricant is required.

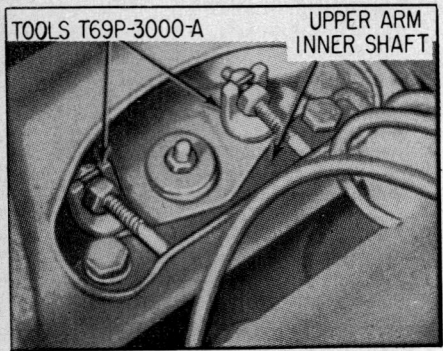

Fig. 2 Adjusting caster and camber.
1969-75 Ford and Mercury

This is not the case and under no circumstances should more than 10 grams of lubricant be added to the ball joints at the 36,000 mile intervals.

SERVICE BULLETIN

1969-75 STEERING LINKAGE LUBE: The steering linkage on these models should be lubricated at intervals of 36,000 miles. Normal breathing of socket joints permits moisture condensation within the joint. Moisture inside the joint assembly will cause no appreciable damage and the joint will function normally. However, if the moisture is concentrated in the bearing grease grooves and is frozen at the time of attempted lubrication, grease cannot flow and pressure greasing may damage the joint.

Do not attempt to lubricate the steering linkage on these vehicles if it has set in temperatures lower than 20 deg. above zero F. The vehicle should be allowed to warm up in a heated garage for 30 minutes or until the joints accept lubrication.

IMPORTANT: A torch must not be used to heat joints because this quantity of heat will melt the nylon bearing within the joint.

WHEEL ALIGNMENT

SERVICE BULLETIN

WHEEL BALANCING DIFFERS: On cars with disc brakes, dynamic balancing of the wheel-and-tire assembly on the car should not be attempted without first pulling back the shoe and lining assemblies from the rotor. If this is not done, brake drag may burn out the motor on the wheel spinner.

The drag can be eliminated by removing the wheel, taking out the two bolts holding the caliper splash shield, and detaching the shield. Then push the pistons into their cylinder bores by applying steady pressure on the shoes on each side of the rotor for at least a minute. If necessary, use waterpump pliers to apply the pressure.

After the pistons have been retracted, reinstall the splash shield and wheel. The

wheel-and-tire assembly can then be dynamically balanced in the usual way. After the balancing job has been completed, be sure to pump the brake pedal several times until the shoes are seated and a firm brake pedal is obtained.

1969-75 Ford & Mercury

Caster and camber can be adjusted by loosening the bolts that attach the upper suspension arm to the shaft at the frame side rail, and moving the arm assembly in or out in the elongated bolt holes, Fig. 2. Since any movement of the arm affects both caster and camber, both factors should be balanced against one another when making the adjustment.

NOTE: Install the tool with the pins in the frame holes and the hooks over the upper arm inner shaft. Tighten the hook nuts snug before loosening the upper arm inner shaft attaching bolts.

Caster, Adjust

1. Tighten the tool front hook nut or loosen the rear hook nut as required to increase caster to the desired angle.
2. To decrease caster, tighten the rear hook nut or loosen the front hook nut as required.

NOTE: The caster angle can be checked without tightening the inner shaft retaining bolts.

3. Check the camber angle to be sure it did not change during the caster adjustment and adjust if necessary.
4. Tighten the upper arm inner shaft retaining bolts and remove tool.

Camber, Adjust

1. Loosen both inner shaft retaining bolts.
2. Tighten or loosen the hook nuts as necessary to increase or decrease camber.
3. Recheck caster and readjust if necessary.

TOE-IN, ADJUST

Position the front wheels in their straight-ahead position. Then turn both tie rod adjusting sleeves an equal amount until the desired toe-in setting is obtained.

WHEEL BEARINGS, ADJUST

1. With wheel rotating, tighten adjusting nut to 17-25 ft. lbs.
2. Back off adjusting nut ½ turn and retighten nut to 10-15 inch lbs.
3. Place nut lock on nut so that castellations on lock are aligned with cotter pin hole in spindle and install cotter pin.
4. Check front wheel rotation, if it rotates noisily or rough, clean, inspect or replace wheel bearings as necessary.

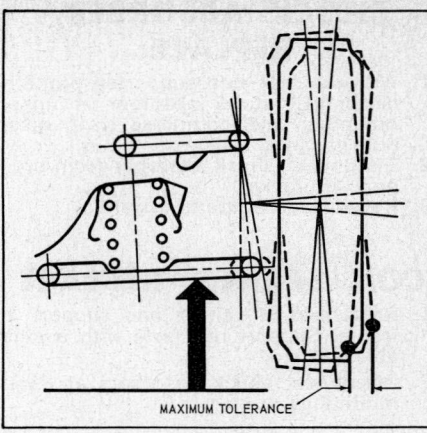

Fig. 3 Measuring lower ball joint radial play, which should not exceed ¼"

WHEEL BEARINGS, REPLACE

(Disc Brakes)

1. Raise car and remove front wheels.
2. Remove caliper mounting bolts.

NOTE: It is not necessary to disconnect the brake lines for this operation.

3. Slide caliper off of disc, inserting a spacer between the shoes to hold them in their bores after the caliper is removed. Position caliper assembly out of the way.

NOTE: Do not allow caliper to hang by brake hose.

4. Remove hub and disc assembly. Grease retainer and inner bearing can now be removed.

CHECKING BALL JOINTS FOR WEAR
Upper Ball Joint

1. Raise car on floor jacks placed beneath lower control arms.
2. Grasp lower edge of tire and move wheel in and out.
3. As wheel is being moved in and out, observe upper end of spindle and upper arm.
4. Any movement between upper end of spindle and upper arm indicates ball joint wear and loss of preload. If any such movement is observed, replace upper ball joint.

NOTE: During the foregoing check, the lower ball joint will be unloaded and may move. Disregard all such movement of the lower ball joint. Also, do not mistake loose wheel bearings for a worn ball joint.

Lower Ball Joint

1. Raise car on jacks placed under lower control arms as shown in Fig. 3. This will unload ball joints.
2. Adjust wheel bearings.
3. Attach a dial indicator to lower control arm and position so that its plunger rests against the inner side of the wheel rim adjacent to the lower ball joint.
4. Grasp tire at top and bottom and slowly move it in and out as shown in Fig. 3.
5. If reading on dial indicator exceeds ¼″, replace lower ball joint.

SHOCK ABSORBER, REPLACE

To remove a shock absorber, unfasten it at the top and bottom and lower it through the opening in the lower control arm.

COIL SPRING, REPLACE

1. Raise vehicle and support front end of frame with jack stands.
2. Disconnect shock absorber from lower arm, collapse shock absorber into the spring and place a jack under the lower arm for support, Fig. 4.
3. Remove strut and rebound bumper bolts and disconnect lower end of sway bar stud from lower arm.
4. Remove the nut and bolt retaining the inner end of the lower arm to the crossmember.
5. Carefully lower jack to relieve spring pressure on lower arm, then remove the spring.

BALL JOINTS, REPLACE

The ball joints are riveted to the upper and lower control arms. The ball joints can be replaced on the car by removing the rivets and retaining the new ball joint to the control arm with the attach-

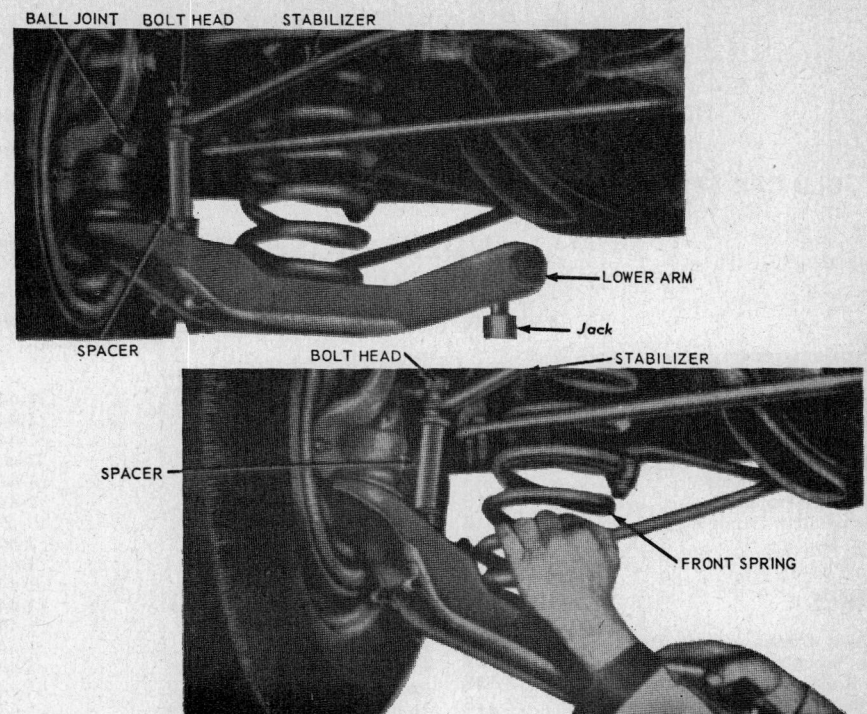

Fig. 4   Replacing coil spring. 1969-75

ing bolts, nuts and washers furnished with the ball joint kit.

When removing a ball joint, use a suitable pressing tool to force the ball joint out of the spindle.

STEERING GEAR, REPLACE
1969-71 Ford & Mercury

1. Remove flex coupling retaining bolts.
2. Remove pitman arm to sector shaft nut and lock washer.
3. Using suitable puller, remove pitman arm from sector shaft.

NOTE: On vehicles equipped with manual transmission, it may be necessary to disconnect the clutch linkage, and on vehicles equipped with V8 engines, it may be necessary to lower the exhaust system.

4. Remove steering gear retaining bolts and remove gear.

POWER STEERING GEAR
1969-75 Ford & Mercury

1. Disconnect pressure and return lines from steering gear. Plug lines and ports in gear to prevent entry of dirt.
2. Remove two bolts that secure flex coupling to steering gear and to column.
3. Raise car and remove sector shaft nut.
4. Use a puller to remove pitman arm.
5. If car has a standard transmission, remove clutch release lever retracting spring to provide clearance for gear removal.
6. Support steering gear, then remove attaching bolts.
7. Work steering gear free of flex coupling and remove it from car.
8. Reverse procedure to install.

FORD & MERCURY
Compact & Intermediate Models

NOTE: The 1974-75 Ford Mustang II & Pinto is located elsewhere in this manual.

OLD CAR SPECIFICATIONS: For 1946-68 Tune Up and Wheel Alignment Specifications see main index.

INDEX OF SERVICE OPERATIONS

PAGE NO.

ACCESSORIES

Air Conditioning 2-20
Automatic Level Controls 2-39
Blower Motor, Replace 1-436
Clock Troubles 2-11
Heater Core, Replace 1-433
Power Top Troubles 2-18
Power Window Troubles 2-18
Radio, Replace 1-432

BRAKES

Anti-Skid Brakes 2-162
Brake Troubles, Mechanical 2-17
Disc Brake Service 2-133
Hydraulic System -Service 2-123
Master Cylinder, Replace 1-456
Parking Brake, Adjust 1-456
Power Brake Unit, Replace 1-456
Service Brakes, Adjust 1-455

CLUTCH

Clutch Pedal, Adjust 1-450
Clutch, Replace 1-451
Clutch Troubles 2-12

COOLING SYSTEM

Cooling System Troubles 2-6
Variable Speed Fans 2-38
Water Pump, Replace 1-450

ELECTRICAL

Alternator Service 2-69
Blower Motor, Replace 1-436
Dash Gauge Service 2-50
Distributor, Replace 1-422
Distributor Service:
    Standard 2-525
    Transistorized 2-535
Electrical Troubles 2-8
Headlamps, Concealed Type 2-46
Headlight Aiming 2-45
Horn Sounder, Remove 1-426
Ignition Coils & Resistors 2-521
Ignition Lock, Replace 1-422
Ignition Switch, Replace 1-422
Ignition Timing 2-518
Instrument Cluster Removal 1-426
Light Switch, Replace 1-424
Neutral Safety Switch, Replace ... 1-424
Seat Belt Interlock Systems 2-311
Starter Service 2-54
Starter, Replace 1-422
Starter Switch Service 2-67
Stop Light Switch, Replace 1-424
Turn Signal Switch, Replace 1-425
Turn Signal Troubles 2-11
Windshield Wiper Motor, Replace ... 1-431
Windshield Wiper Troubles 2-19

PAGE NO.

ENGINE

Camshaft, Replace 1-448
Crankshaft Rear Oil Seal 1-448
Cylinder Head, Replace 1-443
Engine Identification 1-401
Engine Mounts 1-438
Engine, Replace 1-441
Engine Troubles 2-1
Main Bearings 1-448
Piston Pins 1-448
Piston Rings 1-448
Piston and Rod, Assemble 1-448
Pistons 1-448
Rocker Arm Service 1-446
Rocker Arm Stud 1-446
Rod Bearings 1-448
Timing Case Cover, Replace 1-447
Timing Chain, Replace 1-447
Valve Arrangement 1-444
Valve Guides 1-446
Valve Lifters 1-447
Valves, Adjust 1-445

ENGINE LUBRICATION

Emission Control Systems 2-545
Oil Pan, Replace 1-449
Oil Pump, Replace 1-450
Oil Pump, Repairs 1-450

FUEL SYSTEM

Carburetor Adjustments and Specs. 2-372
1975 Carburetors 1-716
Emission Control Systems 2-545
Fuel Pump, Replace 1-450
Fuel Pump Service 2-369
Fuel System Troubles 2-2

PROPELLER SHAFT & U JOINTS

Propeller Shafts 1-454
Universal Joint Service 2-117

REAR AXLE & SUSPENSION

Axle Shaft Bearing and Seal 1-454
Coil Spring, Replace 1-456
Control Arms, Replace 1-457
Leaf Springs & Bushings, Replace ... 1-456
Rear Axle Description 1-452
Rear Axle Troubles 2-16
Shock Absorber, Replace 1-456
Stabilizer Bar, Replace 1-457

SPECIFICATIONS

Alternator 1-416
Belt Tension 1-450
Brakes 1-420
Capacities 1-418
Carburetors 2-372

PAGE NO.

Cooling System 1-418
Crankshaft and Bearings 1-415
Distributors 1-409
Engine Tightening Torque 1-416
Fuel Pump Pressure 1-450
General Engine Specs. 1-404
Ignition Coils and Resistors 2-521
Pistons, Rings and Pins 1-415
Rear Axle 1-421
Starting Motors 1-413
Tune Up 1-406
Valve Lift 1-444
Valve Timing 1-444
Valves 1-413
Wheel Alignment 1-417

STEERING GEAR

Horn Sounder Removal 1-426
Mechanical Gear, Replace 1-461
Mechanical Gear Service 2-170
Mechanical Gear Troubles 2-17
Power Steering 1-461
Steering Wheel, Replace 1-426

SUSPENSION, FRONT

Ball Joints, Replace 1-461
Ball Joints, Check for Wear 1-460
Coil Spring, Replace 1-461
Lubrication 1-458
Shock Absorber, Replace 1-461
Suspension, Description of 1-458
Toe-In, Adjust 1-459
Wheel Alignment, Adjust 1-459
Wheel Bearings, Adjust 1-459
Wheel Bearings, Replace 1-460

TRANSMISSIONS

Three Speed Manual:
    Replace 1-451
    Repairs 2-177
    Linkage, Adjust 1-451
Four Speed Manual:
    Replace 1-451
    Repairs 2-199
    Linkage, Adjust 1-452
Automatic Units 2-231
1975 Linkage 1-452

TUNE UP

Service 2-517
Specifications 1-406

WINDSHIELD WIPER

Wiper Arms 1-431
Wiper Blades 1-430
Wiper Linkage, Replace 1-431
Wiper Motor, Replace 1-431
Wiper Switch, Replace 1-432
Wiper Troubles 2-19

Compact & Intermediate Models — FORD & MERCURY

ENGINE & SERIAL NUMBER LOCATION: Vehicle warranty plate on rear face of left front door.

ENGINE IDENTIFICATION: Engine code is last letter in serial number on vehicle warranty plate.

Year	Engine	Engine Code	Year	Engine	Engine Code
1969	6-170	U	1972	6-170	U
	6-200	T		6-200	T
	6-250	L		6-250	L
	V8-302①	F		V8-302	F
	V8-351①	H		V8-351①	H
	V8-351②	M		V8-351②	Q
	V8-390②	S		V8-351⑥	R
	V8-427②	W		V8-400	S
	V8-428	Q		V8-429	N
	V8-428⑧	R	1973-74	6-200	T
1970	6-170	U		6-250	L
	6-200	T		8-302	F
	6-250	L		8-351①	H
	V8-302	F		8-351②	Q
	V8-302 "Boss"	G		8-351⑥	R
	V8-351①	H		8-400	S
	V8-351②	M		8-429	N
	V8-428 CJ	Q		8-460	A
	V8-428 CJ⑧	R		8-460⑨	C
	V8-429	N	1975	6-200	T
	V8-429 CJ	C		6-250	L
	V8-429 "Boss"	Z		8-302	F
1971	6-170	U		8-351	H
	6-200	T		8-400	S
	6-250	L		8-460	A
	V8-302	F		8-460⑨	C
	V8-302 H.O.	G			
	V8-351①	H			
	V8-351②	M			
	V8-351②	Q (GT)			
	V8-429 CJ	C			
	V8-429 SCJ	J			

①—Two barrel carburetor.
②—Four barrel carburetor.
④—With transistorized ignition.
⑤—Premium fuel.
⑥—High Performance.
⑦—Special.
⑧—Ram Air.
⑨—Police Interceptor.

GRILLE IDENTIFICATION

1969 Montego and Cyclone

1969 Fairlane, Cobra

1969 Torino GT

1969, 1970 (Early) Falcon

1969 Cougar

1969 Mustang

1970 Torino/Fairlane & 1970 (Late) Falcon

1970 Torino Cobra

1970 Torino GT

FORD & MERCURY — Compact & Intermediate Models

GRILLE IDENTIFICATION—Continued

1970 Cougar

1970 Cyclone

1970 Montego

1970-72 Maverick

1970 Mustang

1970 Mustang Mach 1

1971-72 Maverick Grabber

1971 Cyclone

1971 Montego

1971-72 Cougar

1971-72 Comet

1971-72 Cougar XR7

1971-72 Mustang

1971-72 Mustang Mach 1

1971 Torino

1972 Torino

1972 Gran Torino

1972 Montego

1972 Montego GT

1973 Comet

1973 Cougar

1973 Maverick

1973 Montego

1973 Mustang

GRILLE IDENTIFICATION—Continued

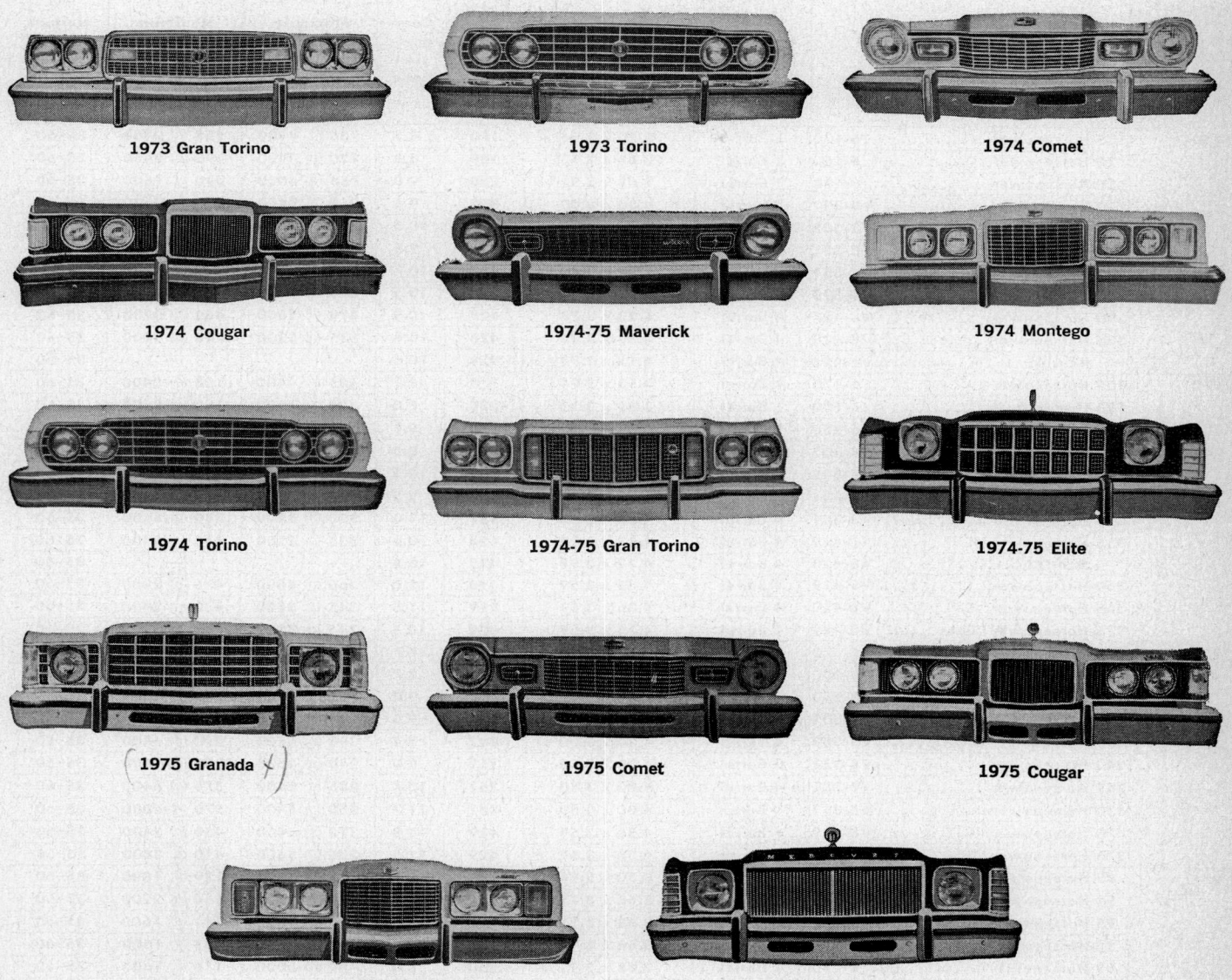

1973 Gran Torino

1973 Torino

1974 Comet

1974 Cougar

1974-75 Maverick

1974 Montego

1974 Torino

1974-75 Gran Torino

1974-75 Elite

1975 Granada

1975 Comet

1975 Cougar

1975 Montego

1975 Monarch

GENERAL ENGINE SPECIFICATIONS

Year	Engine	Car-buretor	Bore and Stroke	Piston Dis-place-ment, Cubic Inches	Com-pres-sion Ratio	Maximum Brake H.P. @ R.P.M.	Maximum Torque Lbs. Ft. @ R.P.M.	Normal Oil Pressure Pounds
1969	105 Horsepower.............6-170	1 Barrel	3.50 x 2.94	170	9.1	105 @ 4400	158 @ 2400	35–60
	120 Horsepower.............6-200	1 Barrel	3.68 x 3.13	200	8.8	120 @ 4400	190 @ 2400	35–60
	155 Horsepower.............6-250	1 Barrel	3.68 x 3.91	250	9.0①	155 @ 4000	240 @ 1600	35–60
	210 Horsepower.........V8-302	2 Barrel	4.00 x 3.00	302	9.5	210 @ 4400	295 @ 2400	35–60
	290 Horsepower "H.O."......V8-302	4 Barrel	4.00 x 3.00	302	10.5	290 @ 5800	290 @ 4300	35–60
	250 Horsepower.........V8-351	2 Barrel	4.00 x 3.50	351	9.5	250 @ 4600	355 @ 2600	35–60
	290 Horsepower.........V8-351	4 Barrel	4.00 x 3.50	351	10.7	290 @ 4800	385 @ 3200	35–60
	320 Horsepower.........V8-390	4 Barrel	4.05 x 3.78	390	10.5	320 @ 4800	427 @ 3200	35–60
	390 Horsepower.........V8-427	4 Barrel	4.23 x 3.78	427	10.9	390 @ 5600	460 @ 3200	35–60
	335 Horsepower.........V8-428	4 Barrel	4.13 x 3.98	428	10.6	335 @ 5200	440 @ 3400	35–60
	Ram Air.............V8-428	4 Barrel	4.13 x 3.98	428	10.6	—	—	35–60
1970	105 Horsepower.............6-170	1 Barrel	3.50 x 2.94	170	9.1	105 @ 4400	158 @ 2400	35–60
	120 Horsepower.............6-200	1 Barrel	3.68 x 3.13	200	8.8	120 @ 4400	190 @ 2400	35–60
	155 Horsepower.............6-250	1 Barrel	3.68 x 3.91	250	9.1	155 @ 4000	240 @ 1600	35–60
	210 Horsepower.........V8-302	2 Barrel	4.00 x 3.00	302	9.5	210 @ 4400	295 @ 2400	35–60
	290 Horsepower "BOSS"......V8-302	4 Barrel	4.00 x 3.00	302	10.5	290 @ 5800	290 @ 4300	35–60
	250 Horsepower.........V8-351	2 Barrel	4.00 x 3.50	351	9.5	250 @ 4600	355 @ 2600	35–60
	300 Horsepower.........V8-351	4 Barrel	4.00 x 3.50	351	11.0	300 @ 5400	380 @ 3400	35–60
	335 Horsepower "CJ".......V8-428	4 Barrel	4.13 x 3.98	428	10.6	335 @ 5200	440 @ 3400	35–60
	Ram Air.............V8-428	4 Barrel	4.13 x 3.98	428	10.6	—	—	35–60
	360 Horsepower.........V8-429	4 Barrel	4.36 x 3.59	429	11.0	360 @ 4600	476 @ 2800	35–60
	345 Horsepower "CJ".......V8-429	4 Barrel	4.36 x 3.59	429	11.5	345 @ 5800	450 @ 3400	35–60
	375 Horsepower "Boss"......V8-429	4 Barrel	4.36 x 3.59	429	10.5	375 @ 5200	450 @ 3400	20–60
1971	100 Horsepower.............6-170	1 Barrel	3.50 x 2.94	170	8.7	100 @ 4200	148 @ 2600	35–60
	115 Horsepower.............6-200	1 Barrel	3.68 x 3.13	200	8.7	115 @ 4000	180 @ 2200	35–60
	145 Horsepower.............6-250	1 Barrel	3.68 x 3.91	250	9.0	145 @ 4000	232 @ 1600	35–60
	210 Horsepower.........V8-302	2 Barrel	4.00 x 3.00	302	9.0	210 @ 4600	296 @ 2600	35–60
	290 Horsepower H.O.........V8-302	4 Barrel	4.00 x 3.00	302	9.4	290 @ 5800	290 @ 4300	35–60
	240 Horsepower.........V8-351	2 Barrel	4.00 x 3.50	351	9.0	240 @ 4600	350 @ 2600	35–60
	285 Horsepower.........V8-351	4 Barrel	4.00 x 3.50	351	10.7	285 @ 5400	370 @ 3400	35–60
	330 Horsepower.........V8-351	4 Barrel	4.00 x 3.50	351	11.7	330 @ 5400	370 @ 4000	35–60
	370 Horsepower "CJ".......V8-429	4 Barrel	4.36 x 3.59	429	11.3	370 @ 5400	450 @ 3400	35–60
	375 Horsepower "SCJ".......V8-429	4 Barrel	4.36 x 3.59	429	11.5	375 @ 5600	450 @ 3400	35–60
1972	82 Horsepower②.............6-170	1 Barrel	3.50 x 2.94	170	8.3	82 @ 4400	129 @ 1800	35–60
	91 Horsepower②.............6-200	1 Barrel	3.68 x 3.13	200	8.3	91 @ 4000	154 @ 2200	35–60
	95 Horsepower②.............6-250	1 Barrel	3.68 x 3.91	250	8.0	95 @ 3600	181 @ 1600	35–60
	98 Horsepower②.............6-250	1 Barrel	3.68 x 3.91	250	8.0	98 @ 3600	183 @ 1600	35–60
	99 Horsepower②.............6-250	1 Barrel	3.68 x 3.91	250	8.0	99 @ 3600	184 @ 1600	35–60
	140 Horsepower②.........V8-302	2 Barrel	4.00 x 3.00	302	8.5	140 @ 4000	230 @ 2200	35–60
	141 Horsepower②.........V8-302	2 Barrel	4.00 x 3.00	302	8.5	141 @ 4000	242 @ 2000	35–60
	143 Horsepower②.........V8-302	2 Barrel	4.00 x 3.00	302	8.5	143 @ 4000	242 @ 2000	35–60
	161 Horsepower②.........V8-351	2 Barrel	4.00 x 3.50	351	8.6	161 @ 4000	276 @ 2000	35–60
	164 Horsepower②.........V8-351	2 Barrel	4.00 x 3.50	351	8.6	164 @ 4000	276 @ 2000	35–85
	177 Horsepower②.........V8-351	2 Barrel	4.00 x 3.50	351	8.6	177 @ 4000	284 @ 2000	35–85
	248 Horsepower② "CJ".......V8-351	4 Barrel	4.00 x 3.50	351	8.6	248 @ 5400	299 @ 3800	50–70
	262 Horsepower②.........V8-351	4 Barrel	4.00 x 3.50	351	8.6	262 @ 5400	299 @ 3600	35–85
	266 Horsepower②.........V8-351	4 Barrel	4.00 x 3.50	351	8.6	266 @ 5400	301 @ 3600	35–85
	168 Horsepower②.........V8-400	2 Barrel	4.00 x 4.00	400	8.4	168 @ 4200	297 @ 2200	35–85
	205 Horsepower③.........V8-429	4 Barrel	4.36 x 3.59	429	8.5	205 @ 4400	322 @ 2600	35–60
1973	84 Horsepower.............6-200	1 Barrel	3.68 x 3.13	200	8.3	84 @ 3600	151 @ 1800	30–50
	88 Horsepower②.............6-250	1 Barrel	3.68 x 3.91	250	8.0	88 @ 3200	196 @ 1600	35–60
	92 Horsepower②.............6-250	1 Barrel	3.68 x 3.91	250	8.0	92 @ 3200	197 @ 1600	35–60
	95 Horsepower②.............6-250	1 Barrel	3.68 x 3.91	250	8.0	95 @ 3200	199 @ 1600	35–60

Continued

GENERAL ENGINE SPECIFICATIONS—Continued

Year	Engine	Car-buretor	Bore and Stroke	Piston Dis-place-ment, Cubic Inches	Com-pres-sion Ratio	Maximum Brake H.P. @ R.P.M.	Maximum Torque Lbs. Ft. @ R.P.M.	Normal Oil Pressure Pounds
1973	135 Horsepower② V8-302	2 Barrel	4.00 x 3.00	302	8.0	135 @ 4200	228 @ 2200	35–60
	136 Horsepower② V8-302	2 Barrel	4.00 x 3.00	302	8.0	136 @ 4200	232 @ 2200	35–60
	137 Horsepower② V8-302	2 Barrel	4.00 x 3.00	302	8.0	137 @ 4200	230 @ 2200	35–60
	138 Horsepower② V8-302	2 Barrel	4.00 x 3.00	302	8.0	138 @ 4200	234 @ 2200	35–60
	154 Horsepower② V8-351	2 Barrel	4.00 x 3.50	351	8.0	154 @ 4000	246 @ 2400	35–60
	156 Horsepower② V8-351	2 Barrel	4.00 x 3.50	351	8.0	156 @ 3800	260 @ 2400	35–60
	159 Horsepower② V8-351	2 Barrel	4.00 x 3.50	351	8.0	159 @ 4000	250 @ 2400	35–60
	246 Horsepower② V8-351	4 Barrel	4.00 x 3.50	351	8.0	246 @ 5400	312 @ 3600	35–60
	264 Horsepower② V8-351	4 Barrel	4.00 x 3.50	351	8.0	264 @ 5400	314 @ 3600	35–60
	163 Horsepower② V8-400	2 Barrel	4.00 x 4.00	400	8.0	163 @ 3800	300 @ 2000	35–60
	168 Horsepower② V8-400	2 Barrel	4.00 x 4.00	400	8.0	168 @ 3800	310 @ 2000	35–60
	197 Horsepower② V8-429	4 Barrel	4.36 x 3.59	429	8.0	197 @ 4400	320 @ 2600	35–60
	201 Horsepower② V8-429	4 Barrel	4.36 x 3.59	429	8.0	201 @ 4400	322 @ 2600	35–60
	274 Horsepower V8-460	4 Barrel	4.36 x 3.85	460	8.8	274 @ 4600	392 @ 2800	35–65
1974	84 Horsepower② 6-200	1 Barrel	3.68 x 3.13	200	8.0	84 @ 3800	150 @ 1800	30–50
	91 Horsepower② 6-250	1 Barrel	3.68 x 3.91	250	8.0	91 @ 3200	190 @ 1600	40–60
	140 Horsepower② V8-302	2 Barrel	4.00 x 3.00	302	8.0	140 @ 3800	230 @ 2600	40–60
	162 Horsepower② V8-351	2 Barrel	4.00 x 3.50	351	8.0	162 @ 4000	275 @ 2200	40–65
	163 Horsepower② V8-351	2 Barrel	4.00 x 3.50	351	8.0	163 @ 4200	278 @ 2000	45–75
	255 Horsepower② V8-351	4 Barrel	4.00 x 3.50	351	8.0	255 @ 5600	290 @ 3400	45–75
	170 Horsepower② V8-400	2 Barrel	4.00 x 4.00	400	8.0	170 @ 3400	330 @ 2000	45–75
	195 Horsepower② V8-460	4 Barrel	4.36 x 3.85	460	8.0	195 @ 3800	335 @ 2600	35–65
	220 Horsepower②③ V8-460	4 Barrel	4.36 x 3.85	460	8.0	220 @ 4000	355 @ 2600	35–65
	260 Horsepower② V8-460	4 Barrel	4.36 x 3.85	460	8.0	260 @ 4400	355 @ 2700	35–65
1975	Horsepower② 6-200	1 Barrel	3.683 x 3.126	200	8.3	—	—	40–60
	70 Horsepower②⑤ 6-250	1 Barrel	3.682 x 3.910	250	8.0	70 @ 2800	175 @ 1400	40–60
	72 Horsepower②④ 6-250	1 Barrel	3.682 x 3.910	250	8.0	72 @ 2900	180 @ 1400	40–60
	122 Horsepower②⑤ V8-302	2 Barrel	4.00 x 3.00	302	8.0	122 @ 3800⑥	208 @ 1800⑦	45–65
	129 Horsepower②⑧ V8-302	2 Barrel	4.00 x 3.00	302	8.0	129 @ 3800⑧	220 @ 1800⑨	45–65
	148 Horsepower②④ V8-351M	2 Barrel	4.00 x 3.50	351	8.0	148 @ 3800	243 @ 2400	45–75
	150 Horsepower②⑤ V8-351M	2 Barrel	4.00 x 3.50	351	8.0	150 @ 3800	244 @ 2800	45–75
	143 Horsepower②⑩ V8-351W	2 Barrel	4.00 x 3.50	351	8.1	143 @ 3600⑩	255 @ 2200⑪	45–65
	154 Horsepower②⑫ V8-351W	2 Barrel	4.00 x 3.50	351	8.1	154 @ 3800⑫	268 @ 2200	45–65
	144 Horsepower②⑤ V8-400	2 Barrel	4.00 x 4.00	400	8.0	144 @ 3600	255 @ 2200	35–65
	158 Horsepower②④ V8-400	2 Barrel	4.00 x 4.00	400	8.0	158 @ 4000	276 @ 2000	35–65
	216 Horsepower②④ V8-460	4 Barrel	4.36 x 3.85	460	8.0	216 @ 4000	366 @ 2600	35–65
	217 Horsepower②⑤ V8-460	4 Barrel	4.36 x 3.85	460	8.0	217 @ 4000	365 @ 2600	35–65

①—Mustang "E" Model, 9.5.
②—Ratings are NET—as installed in the vehicle.
③—Cougar XR-7 requires A/C in California.
④—Except California.
⑤—California.
⑥—Comet & Maverick, California vehicles rated at 115 H.P. @ 3600 RPM.

⑦—California vehicles rated at 203 @ 1400 RPM.
⑧—Granada & Monarch, California vehicles rated at 115 H.P. @ 3600 RPM.
⑨—California vehicles rated at 203 @ 1800 RPM.

⑩—Granada, Monarch, Torino & Elite, California vehicles rated at 153 H.P. @ 3400 RPM.
⑪—California vehicles rated at 270 @ 2400 RPM.
⑫—Cougar & Montego, not available in California.

TUNE UP SPECIFICATIONS

OLD CAR SPECIFICATIONS: For 1946-68 Tune Up Specifications see main index.

★When using a timing light, disconnect vacuum hose or tube at distributor and plug opening in hose or tube so idle speed will not be affected.

●When checking compression, lowest cylinder must be within 75% of the highest.

▲Before removing wires from distributor cap, determine location of the No. 1 wire in cap, as distributor position may have been altered from that shown at the end of this chart.

Year	Spark Plug		Distributor		Ignition Timing★			Carb. Adjustments					
	Type	Gap Inch	Point Gap Inch	Dwell Angle Deg.	Firing Order Fig. ▲	Timing BTDC ①	Mark Fig.	Hot Idle Speed③		Air Fuel Ratio		Idle "CO" %	
								Std. Trans.	Auto. Trans.②	Std. Trans.	Auto. Trans.	Std. Trans.	Auto. Trans.
1969													
6-170	BF-82	.034	.027	35–40	H	6°	G	750	550D	13.80 to 1	13.60 to 1	2.2	2.6
6-200	BF-82	.034	.027	35–40	H	6°	G	750	550D	14.50 to 1	14.00 to 1	0.9	1.8
6-250 Less Air Cond.	BF-82⑱	.034	.025	37–42	H	6°	G	700	550D	14.0 to 1	13.5 to 1	1.8	2.8
6-250 With Air Cond.	BF-82⑱	.034	.025	37–42	H	6°	G	700/500⑥	550/450D⑥	14.0 to 1	13.5 to 1	1.8	2.8
V8-302 Std. Trans.	BF-42	.034	.021	24–29	E	6°	C	650	—	14.0 to 1	—	1.8	—
V8-302 Auto. Trans.	BF-42	.034	.017	26–31	E	6°	C	—	550D	—	13.8 to 1	—	2.2
V8-302 "H.O."	AF-32	.030	.020	30–33	E	16°	C	800	—	—	—	—	—
V8-351 2 B. Carb.	BF-42	.034	.017	26–31	F	6°	C	650	550D	14.0 to 1	14.0 to 1	1.8	1.8
V8-351 4 B. Carb.	BF-32	.034	.017	26–31	F	6°	C	650	550D	14.0 to 1	14.3 to 1	1.8	1.2
V8-390 Std. Trans.	BF-42	.034	.017	26–31	E	6°	B	700	—	㉖	—	㉗	—
V8-390 Auto. Trans.	BF-32	.034	.017	26–31	E	6°	B	—	550D	—	㉖	—	㉔
V8-427	BF-32	.034	.017	26–31	E	6°	C	—	600D	—	—	—	—
V8-428	BF-32	.034	.017	26–31	E	6°	B	700	650D	14.1 to 1	14.1 to 1	1.6	1.6
1970													
6-170	BF-82	.035	.027	35–40	H	6°	G	750	550	14.45 to 1	14.45 to 1	1.0	1.0
6-200	BF-82	.035	.027	35–40	H	6°	G	750	550	14.45 to 1	14.20 to 1	1.0	1.5
6-250	BF-82	.035	.027	35–40	H	6°	G	800/500⑥	500	14.20 to 1	14.20 to 1	1.5	1.5
V8-302	BF-42	.035	.021	24–29	E	6°	C	800/500⑥	600/500D⑥	14.0 to 1	13.80 to 1	0.34	0.44
V8-302 "BOSS"	AF-32	.034	.020	30–33	E	16°	C	800/500⑥	—	13.50 to 1	—	2.80	—
V8-351⑦⑯	AF-42	.034	⑪	⑪	F	6°	C	700/500⑥	600/500D⑥	14.0 to 1	14.0 to 1	0.30	0.14
V8-351⑦⑰ Std. Tr.	BF-42	.034	⑪	⑪	F	6°	C	700/500⑥	—	14.0 to 1	—	0.30	—
V8-351⑦⑰ Auto. Tr.	BF-42	.034	⑪	⑪	F	10°	C	700/500⑥	—	—	14.0 to 1	—	0.14
V8-351⑧	AF-32	.034	⑪	⑪	F	6°	C	800/500⑥	600/500D⑥	14.44 to 1	14.45 to 1	0.90	0.75
V8-428	BF-32	.034	⑪	⑪	E	6°	B	800/500⑥	600/500D⑥	13.8 to 1	14.3 to 1	2.15	0.95
V8-429 Auto. Trans.⑧	BF-42	.034	⑪	⑪	E	4°	C	700/500⑥	700/500⑥	—	14.45 to 1	—	0.75
V8-429 "CJ"	AF-32	.034	⑪	⑪	E	10°	C	700	600	14.4 to 1	14.45 to 1	0.35	0.35
V8-429 "BOSS"	AF-32	.034	.020	30–33	E	10°	D	700	—	14.2 to 1	—	2.3	—
1971													
6-170	BRF-82	.034	.027	35–40	H	6°	A	750③	—	14.5 to 1	14.5 to 1	1.0	1.0
6-200	BRF-82	.034	.027	35–40	H	6°	A	750③	550D③	14.5 to 1	14.2 to 1	1.0	1.5
6-250	BRF-82	.034	⑤	⑤	H	6°	A	750/500⑥	600/500D⑥	14.2 to 1	14.2 to 1	1.5	1.5
V8-302	BRF-42	.034	.021	24–29	E	6°	I	800/500⑥	600/500D⑥	14.5 to 1	14.5 to 1	0.3	0.4
V8-302 H.O.	AF-32	.034	.020	30–33	E	16°	I	800/500⑥	—	14.5 to 1	14.5 to 1	0.3	0.4
V8-351⑦	ARF-42	.034	⑪	⑪	F	6°	I	700/500⑥	600D	14.5 to 1	14.5 to 1	0.2	0.2
V8-351⑧	ARF-42	.034	.021	24–29	F	6°	I	800/500⑥	600D	14.5 to 1	—	1.1	—
V8-429 "CJ"	AF-32	.034	.021	24–29	E	10°	C	700/500⑥	650/500D⑥	14.5 to 1	14.5 to 1	0.3	0.3
V8-429 "SCJ"	AF-32	.034	.021	24–29	E	10°	C	650/500⑥	700/500D⑥	14.5 to 1	14.5 to 1	0.3	0.3

Continued

TUNE UP SPECIFICATIONS—Continued

OLD CAR SPECIFICATIONS: For 1946-68 Tune Up Specifications see main index.

★When using a timing light, disconnect vacuum hose or tube at distributor and plug opening in hose or tube so idle speed will not be affected.

●When checking compression, lowest cylinder must be within 75% of the highest.

▲Before removing wires from distributor cap, determine location of the No. 1 wire in cap, as distributor position may have been altered from that shown at the end of this chart.

Year	Spark Plug Type	Gap Inch	Point Gap Inch	Dwell Angle Deg.	Firing Order Fig. ▲	Timing BTDC (1)	Mark Fig.	Hot Idle Speed(3) Std. Trans.	Hot Idle Speed(3) Auto. Trans.(2)	Air Fuel Ratio Std. Trans.	Air Fuel Ratio Auto. Trans.	Idle "CO" % Std. Trans.	Idle "CO" % Auto. Trans.
1972													
6-170	BRF-82	.034	.027	35–39	H	6°	A	750	—	—	—	1.2	1.2
6-200 Less Air Cond.	BRF-82	.034	.027	35–39	H	6°	A	750	550D	—	—	0.8	—
6-200 With Air Cond.	BRF-82	.034	.027	35–39	H	6°	A	800/500(6)	600/500D(6)	—	—	—	1.2
6-250	BRF-82	.034	.027	35–39	H	6°	A	550	550D	—	—	1.0	1.0
6-250	BRF-82	.034	.027	35–39	H	6°	A	750/500(6)	600/500D(6)	—	—	1.0	1.0
V8-302	BRF-42	.034	.017	26–30	E	6°	I	575	575D	—	—	—	0.19
V8-302	BRF-42	.034	.017	26–30	E	6°	I	800/500(6)	600/500D(6)	—	—	—	0.19
V8-351(7)	ARF-42	.034	.017	26–30	F	6°	I	750/500(6)	575/500D(6)	—	—	0.50	0.50
V8-351(7) Calif.	ARF-42	.034	.017	26–30	F	6°	I	—	625/500D(6)	—	—	0.50	0.50
V8-351(8) Std. Tr.	ARF-42	.034	.020	26–30	F	16°	I	1000/500(6)	—	—	—	0.5	—
V8-351(8) Auto. Tr.	ARF-42	.034	.017	26–30	F	16°(13)	I	—	700/500D(6)	—	—	—	0.5
V8-351(8) Auto. Tr. Calif.	ARF-42	.034	.017	26–30	F	16°	I	—	800/500D(6)	—	—	—	0.5
V8-351 H.O.	ARF-42	.034	.020	26–30	F	10°	I	1000/500(6)	—	—	—	—	—
V8-400	ARF-42	.034	.017	26–30	F	(12)	I	—	625/500D(6)	—	—	—	0.10
V8-429	BRF-42	.034	.017	26–30	E	10°	I	—	600/500D(6)	—	—	0.3	0.3
1973													
6-200	BRF-82	.034	.027	35–39	H	6°	C	800	650D	—	—	—	—
6-250	BRF-82	.034	.025	33–39	H	6°	A	750	600D	—	—	0.5	0.5
8-302	BRF-42	.034	.017	24–30	E	6°	I	800	650D	—	—	0.5(19)	0.5(19)
8-351(7)(23)	BRF-42	.034	.017	24–30	F	6°	I	—	625D	—	—	0.5(19)	0.5(19)
8-351(7)(22)	ARF-42	.034	.017	24–30	F	10°	I	—	625D	—	—	0.5(19)	0.5(19)
8-351(8)	ARF-42	.034	(21)	(9)	F	(20)	I	900	700D	—	—	0.6(19)	0.5(19)
8-400	ARF-42	.034	.017	24–30	F	6°	I	—	625D	—	—	—	0.5(19)
8-429	ARF-42	.034	.017	24–30	E	18°	I	—	600D	—	—	—	0.5(19)
8-460	ARF-42	.034	.017	24–30	E	14°	I	—	600D	—	—	—	0.4(19)
1974													
6-200	BRF-82	.034	.025	33	H	6°	A	750	550D	—	—	—	—
6-200(14)	BRF-82	.034	—	—	H	6°	A	750	550D	—	—	—	—
6-250	BRF-82	.034	.025	33	H	6°	A	600	600D	—	—	—	—
6-250(14)	BRF-82	.034	—	—	H	6°	A	600	600D	—	—	—	—
8-302	BRF-42	.034	.017	26–30	E	6°	I	850	575D	—	—	—	.5
8-302(14)	BRF-42	.034	—	—	E	6°	I	850	575D	—	—	—	.5
8-351(7)(23)	BRF-42	.034	.017	26–30	F	6°	I	—	600D	—	—	—	.4
8-351(7)(23)(14)	BRF-42	.034	—	—	F	6°	I	—	600D	—	—	—	.4
8-351(7)(22)	ARF-42	.044	.017	26–30	F	10°	I	—	650D	—	—	—	.5
8-351(7)(22)(14)	ARF-42	.044	—	—	F	10°	I	—	650D	—	—	—	.5
8-351(8)	ARF-42	.034	.017(21)	26–31	F	(20)	I	900	800D	—	—	—	—
8-351(8)(14)	ARF-42	.034	—	—	F	(20)	I	900	800D	—	—	—	—
8-400(14)	ARF-42	.044	—	—	F	(10)	I	—	625D	—	—	—	—
8-460(14)	ARF-52	.054	—	—	E	(15)	I	—	650D	—	—	—	.25

Continued

TUNE UP SPECIFICATIONS—Continued

OLD CAR SPECIFICATIONS: For 1946–68 Tune Up Specifications see main index.

★When using a timing light, disconnect vacuum hose or tube at distributor and plug opening in hose or tube so idle speed will not be affected.

●When checking compression, lowest cylinder must be within 75% of the highest.

▲Before removing wires from distributor cap, determine location of the No. 1 wire in cap, as distributor position may have been altered from that shown at the end of this chart.

Year	Spark Plug		Distributor		Ignition Timing★			Carb. Adjustments					
	Type	Gap Inch	Point Gap Inch	Dwell Angle Deg.	Firing Order Fig. ▲	Timing BTDC ①	Mark Fig.	Hot Idle Speed③		Air Fuel Ratio		Idle "CO"%	
								Std. Trans.	Auto. Trans.②	Std. Trans.	Auto. Trans.	Std. Trans.	Auto. Trans.
1975													
6-200⑭	BRF-82	.044	—	—	H	6°	A	750	600D	—	—	—	—
6-250⑭	BRF-82	.044	—	—	H	6°	A	750	600D	—	—	—	—
V8-302⑭	ARF-42	.044	—	—	E	6°	I	900	650D	—	—	—	—
V8-351④⑭	ARF-42	.044	—	—	F	14°	I	—	650D	—	—	—	—
V8-351⑭㉓	ARF-42	.044	—	—	F	—	I	—	650D	—	—	—	—
V8-400⑭	ARF-42	.044	—	—	F	12°	I	—	650D	—	—	—	—
V8-460⑭	ARF-52	.044	—	—	E	14°	I	—	650D	—	—	—	—

①—BTDC: Before top dead center.
②—D: Drive.
③—For A/C add 50 R.P.M. Set with headlamps on high beam and A/C off.
④—Modified Engine.
⑤—Dual diaphragm .027 gap, 35–40 dwell. Single diaphragm .025 gap, 37–42 dwell.
⑥—Higher figure is with throttle solenoid energized.
⑦—With two barrel carburetor.
⑧—With four barrel carburetor.

⑨—Manual trans. 32–35, Auto. trans. 24–30.
⑩—Cougar 12°, all others 6°.
⑪—Dual diaphragm .021 gap, 24°–29° dwell. Single diaphragm .017 gap, 26°–31° dwell.
⑫—Exc. Calif. 8°, Calif. 6°.
⑬—Cougar with 12 inch converter 10° BTDC.
⑭—Breakerless distributor.
⑮—Cougar 14°, all others 10°.
⑯—Fairlane & Montego.
⑰—Mustang & Cougar
⑱—Mustang "E" BF-92.

⑲—For California 0.2%.
⑳—Manual trans. 16° BTDC, Auto. trans. 18° BTDC.
㉑—Manual trans. .020, Auto. trans. .017.
㉒—Cleveland engine.
㉓—Windsor engine.
㉔—2 Bar. Carb. 1.1, 4 Bar. Carb. 0.5.
㉕—2 Bar. Carb. 14.1 to 1, 4 Bar Carb. 14.0 to 1.
㉖—2 Bar. Carb. 14.4 to 1, 4 Bar Carb. 14.8 to 1.
㉗—2 Bar. Carb. 1.6, 4 Bar. Carb. 1.8.

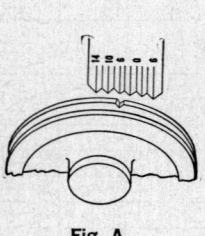

Fig. A

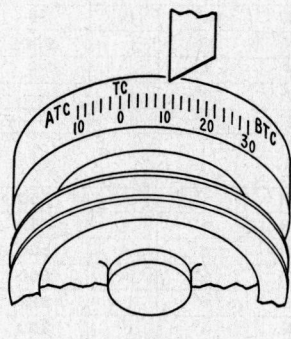

Fig. B

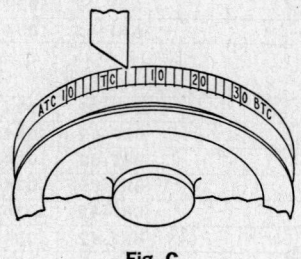

Fig. C

Continued

TUNE UP NOTES—Continued

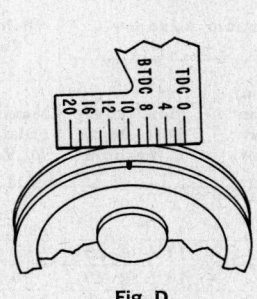

Fig. D

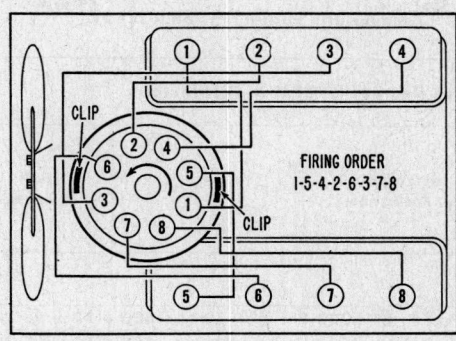

FIRING ORDER
1-5-4-2-6-3-7-8

Fig. E

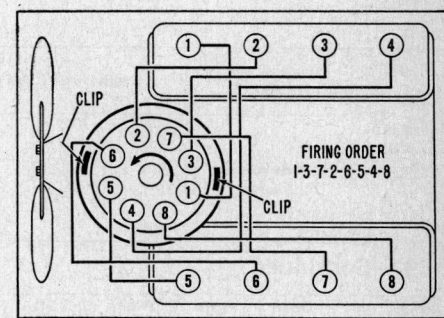

FIRING ORDER
1-3-7-2-6-5-4-8

Fig. F

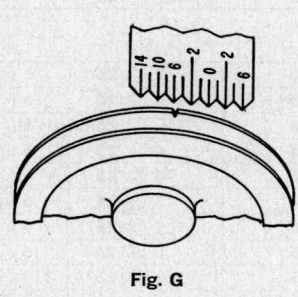

Fig. G

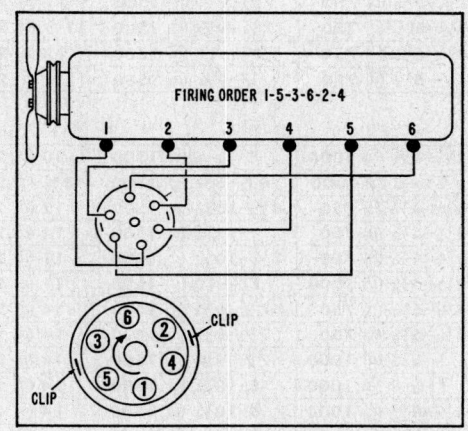

FIRING ORDER 1-5-3-6-2-4

Fig. H

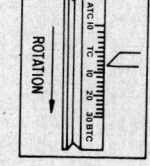

Fig. I

DISTRIBUTOR SPECIFICATIONS

★Note: If unit is checked on vehicle, double the RPM and degrees to get crankshaft figures.

Breaker arm spring tension—17–21.

| Distributor Part No.① | Centrifugal Advance Degrees @ RPM of Distributor | | | | Vacuum Advance | | Distributor Retard |
	Advance Starts	Intermediate Advance		Full Advance	Inches of Vacuum to Start Plunger	Max. Adv. Dist. Deg. @ Vacuum	Max. Retard Dist. Deg. @ Vacuum
1969							
C7AF-AC	0–½ @ 350	0–2 @ 500	4¾–6¾ @ 750	7¾–10 @ 1500	12¼ @ 2000	5	12½ @ 20	—
C8AF-E	0–½ @ 350	0–1¾ @ 500	4½–6¾ @ 750	8–10¼ @ 1500	12½ @ 2000	5	11 @ 25	6 @ 20
C8DF-C	0–½ @ 350	0–2 @ 500	3¼–5¼ @ 750	8¼–10½ @ 1500	12 @ 2000	5	12½ @ 25	6 @ 20
C8DF-D	0–½ @ 350	0–1¼ @ 500	2¾–4¾ @ 750	9–11¼ @ 1500	14 @ 2000	5	11 @ 25	6 @ 20
C8DF-J	0–½ @ 350	0–1½ @ 500	3¼–5¼ @ 750	9½–11¾ @ 1500	14¾ @ 2000	5	11 @ 25	6 @ 20
C8OF-H	0–½ @ 350	¾–2¾ @ 500	7½–9½ @ 750	9½–11¾ @ 1500	13½ @ 2000	5	9½ @ 25	3½ @ 20
C8OF-J	0–½ @ 350	¾–2¾ @ 500	7½–9½ @ 750	9¾–12 @ 1500	13½ @ 2000	5	11 @ 20	—

Continued

DISTRIBUTOR SPECIFICATIONS—Continued

★Note: If unit is checked on vehicle, double the RPM and degrees to get crankshaft figures.

Breaker arm spring tension—17–21.

Distributor Part No.①	Centrifugal Advance Degrees @ RPM of Distributor					Vacuum Advance		Distributor Retard
	Advance Starts	Intermediate Advance			Full Advance	Inches of Vacuum to Start Plunger	Max. Adv. Dist. Deg. @ Vacuum	Max. Retard Dist. Deg. @ Vacuum
1969—Continued								
C9AF-K	0–½ @ 350	2¾–4¾ @ 750	5¾–7¾ @ 1000	7¾–10 @ 1500	12¼ @ 2000	5	11½ @ 25	—
C9AF-N	0–½ @ 350	1¾–3¾ @ 500	5½–7½ @ 750	7¼–9½ @ 1500	10¾ @ 2000	5	11½ @ 20	6 @ 20
C9DF-B	0–½ @ 350	0–1½ @ 500	4½–6½ @ 750	9–11¼ @ 1500	13¾ @ 2000	5	8 @ 25	—
C9OF-M	0–½ @ 350	0–2 @ 500	4¼–6¼ @ 750	7½–9¾ @ 1500	12¼ @ 2000	5	8 @ 20	—
C9OF-N	0–½ @ 350	0–2 @ 500	3¾–5¾ @ 750	7½–9¾ @ 1500	11 @ 2000	5	10½ @ 20	—
C9OF-R	0–½ @ 350	0–2 @ 500	4½–6½ @ 750	7¼–9½ @ 1500	11½ @ 2000	5	8½ @ 20	—
C9OF-T	0–½ @ 350	¼–2½ @ 500	4¾–6¾ @ 750	8¾–11 @ 1500	12 @ 2000	5	12½ @ 20	—
C9OF-U	0–½ @ 350	1¼–3¼ @ 500	4½–6½ @ 750	7–9¼ @ 1500	11¾ @ 2000	5	12½ @ 20	—
1970								
C8AF-A	0–½ @ 350	0–1½ @ 750	2¼–4½ @ 1000	6–8 @ 1500	10 @ 2000	5	8 @ 25	6 @ 20
C8AF-B	0–½ @ 350	1¾–3¾ @ 750	2¾–5 @ 1000	4½–6¾ @ 1500	8¾ @ 2000	5	9 @ 25	6 @ 20
C9AF-Y	0–½ @ 350	2–4 @ 500	6¾–8¾ @ 750	8½–10¾ @ 1500	12 @ 2000	5	8½ @ 25	6 @ 20
C9DF-B	0–½ @ 350	0–1½ @ 500	4½–6½ @ 750	9–11¼ @ 1500	14 @ 2050	5	8 @ 25	6 @ 20
C9ZF-D	0–½ @ 350	0–1½ @ 500	2¾–4¾ @ 750	8¼–10½ @ 1500	11 @ 2000	5	10 @ 25	6 @ 20
C9ZF-E	0–½ @ 350	0–1¾ @ 750	2½–4¾ @ 1000	7¾–10 @ 1500	11 @ 2000	5	7 @ 25	6 @ 20
D0AF-AC	0–½ @ 350	0–2 @ 500	4¼–6¼ @ 750	7½–9¾ @ 1500	14 @ 2375	5	9½ @ 25	6 @ 20
D0AF-H	0–½ @ 350	0–2 @ 500	4¼–6¼ @ 750	7½–9¾ @ 1500	14 @ 2375	5	8 @ 25	6 @ 20
D0AF-T	0–½ @ 350	0–1¾ @ 750	6–8 @ 1000	7¼–9¼ @ 1500	14 @ 3150	5	11½ @ 25	3½ @ 20
D0AF-Y	0–½ @ 350	0–1¾ @ 750	6–8 @ 1000	8–10¼ @ 1500	14 @ 2325	5	11 @ 25	6 @ 20
D0AF-Z	0–½ @ 350	2¼–4¼ @ 750	6½–8½ @ 1000	8–10¼ @ 1500	14 @ 2950	5	11 @ 25	—
D0DF-C	0–½ @ 350	½–2½ @ 500	4¾–6¾ @ 750	10–12¼ @ 1500	16 @ 2800	5	7 @ 25	6 @ 20
D0DF-E	0–½ @ 350	¼–2½ @ 750	7–9 @ 1000	9¾–12 @ 1500	19 @ 2650	5	11 @ 25	6 @ 20
D0OF-A	0–½ @ 350	½–2½ @ 500	6–8 @ 750	10–12¼ @ 1500	16 @ 2175	5	9 @ 25	6 @ 20
D0OF-AB	0–½ @ 350	0–1¾ @ 500	4¾–6¾ @ 750	8¼–10½ @ 1500	12 @ 2000	5	8½ @ 25	6 @ 20
D0OF-T	0–½ @ 350	0–1½ @ 500	2–4 @ 750	4½–6½ @ 1000	14 @ 2300	5	12½ @ 25	6 @ 20
D0OF-U	0–½ @ 350	1¼–3¼ @ 500	5¼–7¼ @ 750	8¼–10½ @ 1500	14 @ 2275	5	12½ @ 25	—
D0OF-V	0–½ @ 350	¾–2¾ @ 750	3¾–5¾ @ 1000	8½–10¾ @ 1500	14 @ 2300	5	10½ @ 25	6 @ 20
D0OF-Z	0–½ @ 350	3–5 @ 750	5½–7½ @ 1000	6¾–9 @ 1500	10¼ @ 2000	5	10½ @ 25	3½ @ 20
D0ZF-C	0–½ @ 350	5–7 @ 750	8¾–10¼ @ 1000	9¾–12 @ 1500	14 @ 2150	5	11 @ 25	3½ @ 20
D0ZF-G	0–½ @ 350	4¼–6¼ @ 750	6¾–8¾ @ 1000	8¾–11 @ 1500	14 @ 2075	5	9½ @ 25	—
1971								
C9DF-B	0–½ @ 350	4½–6½ @ 750	7–9 @ 1000	9–11¼ @ 1500	14 @ 2050	5	8 @ 25	7 @ 20
D0AF-Y	0–½ @ 350	0–1¾ @ 750	6–8 @ 1000	8–10¼ @ 1500	14 @ 2325	5	11 @ 25	7 @ 20
D0DF-C	0–½ @ 350	½–2½ @ 500	9–11 @ 1000	10–12¼ @ 1500	16 @ 2800	5	7 @ 25	7 @ 20
D0OF-AA	0–½ @ 350	0–1½ @ 500	5–7¼ @ 750	10¼–12½ @ 1500	16 @ 2200	5	8½ @ 25	7 @ 20
D0OF-AC	0–½ @ 350	0–1¾ @ 750	5½–8 @ 1000	7¼–9¼ @ 1500	13 @ 2500	5	5 @ 25	7 @ 20
D0OF-G	0–½ @ 350	3–5 @ 750	5½–7½ @ 1000	6¾–8¾ @ 1500	13 @ 2500	5	10½ @ 25	7 @ 20
D0OF-T	0–½ @ 350	2–4 @ 750	4½–6½ @ 1000	7¾–10 @ 1500	14 @ 2300	5	12½ @ 25	7 @ 20
D0OF-U	0–½ @ 350	1¼–3¼ @ 500	6¼–8¼ @ 1000	8¼–10½ @ 1500	14 @ 2275	5	12½ @ 25	—
D0OF-V	0–½ @ 350	¾–2¾ @ 750	3¾–5¾ @ 1000	8½–10¾ @ 1500	14 @ 2300	5	10½ @ 25	7 @ 20
D1AF-NA	0–½ @ 350	3–7 @ 750	8–10 @ 1000	10½–12½ @ 1500	14 @ 2500	5	8½ @ 25	7 @ 20
D1DF-BB	0–½ @ 350	0–¾ @ 500	3–5 @ 750	9½–11¾ @ 1500	14 @ 2500	5	7½ @ 25	7 @ 20
D1DF-EA	0–½ @ 350	0–1¾ @ 750	5½–8 @ 1000	7¼–9¼ @ 1500	13 @ 2500	5	11½ @ 25	7 @ 20
D1DF-FA	0–½ @ 350	0–2 @ 500	3¼–5 @ 750	9–11 @ 1500	14 @ 2500	5	8 @ 25	7 @ 20
D1DF-GA	0–½ @ 350	0–¾ @ 750	3¼–5¾ @ 1000	9–11¼ @ 1500	14 @ 2500	5	7 @ 25	7 @ 20
D1OF-AB	0–½ @ 350	0–1½ @ 500	3½–5¼ @ 750	7–9¼ @ 1500	14 @ 2500	5	7½ @ 25	—
D1OF-BB	0–½ @ 350	0–1 @ 750	3½–5½ @ 1000	7–9¼ @ 1500	14 @ 2500	5	7½ @ 25	—

Continued

DISTRIBUTOR SPECIFICATIONS—Continued

★Note: If unit is checked on vehicle, double the RPM and degrees to get crankshaft figures.

Breaker arm spring tension—17–21.

Distributor Part No.①	Centrifugal Advance Degrees @ RPM of Distributor					Vacuum Advance		Distributor Retard
	Advance Starts	Intermediate Advance			Full Advance	Inches of Vacuum to Start Plunger	Max. Adv. Dist. Deg. @ Vacuum	Max. Retard Dist. Deg. @ Vacuum
1971—Continued								
D1OF-CA	0-½ @ 350	0-1½ @ 500	3¼-5¼ @ 750	7-9¼ @ 1500	14 @ 2500	5	10 @ 25	7 @ 20
D1OF-GA	0-½ @ 350	3¼-5¼ @ 750	6½-8¾ @ 1000	8¼-10½ @ 1500	13 @ 2500	5	11 @ 25	4 @ 20
D1OF-LA	0-½ @ 350	½-3¼ @ 750	5¼-7¼ @ 1000	6¾-9 @ 1500	18 @ 2500	5	10½ @ 25	7 @ 20
D1OF-PA	0-½ @ 350	0-1½ @ 500	4½-6½ @ 750	10½-12¾ @ 1500	14 @ 2500	5	11 @ 25	—
D1ZF-AA	0-½ @ 350	0-1½ @ 750	2¾-4¾ @ 1000	8¾-10 @ 1500	11 @ 2500	5	2½ @ 25	7 @ 20
D1ZF-EA	0-½ @ 350	1-3 @ 750	4-6 @ 1000	9½-12 @ 1500	15 @ 2500	5	10½ @ 25	7 @ 20
D1ZF-FA	0-½ @ 350	1¼-3½ @ 750	4¼-6¼ @ 1000	10-12 @ 1500	16½ @ 2500	5	8½ @ 25	—
1972								
D2AF-RA	½-2½ @ 500	2-4 @ 750	3½-5½ @ 1000	6½-9 @ 1500	12 @ 2000	5	13½ @ 20	4 @ 20
D2AF-SA	½-2½ @ 500	2-4 @ 750	3½-5½ @ 1000	6½-9 @ 1500	12 @ 2000	5	13½ @ 20	4 @ 20
D2AF-CA	0-½ @ 500	0-1½ @ 750	4½-6½ @ 1000	7-9½ @ 1500	11 @ 2000	5	5½ @ 20	7 @ 20
D2AF-KA	1-3 @ 500	5½-7½ @ 750	6½-8½ @ 1000	8½-10½ @ 1500	12½ @ 2000	5	13 @ 20	7 @ 20
D2DF-AA	0-2 @ 500	4½-6½ @ 750	7-9 @ 1000	9-11½ @ 1500	13½ @ 2000	5	7½ @ 20	7 @ 20
D2DF-BA	0-2 @ 500	4½-6½ @ 750	7-9 @ 1000	9-11½ @ 1500	13½ @ 2000	5	7½ @ 20	7 @ 20
D2DF-CA	0-1 @ 500	3-5 @ 750	7½-9½ @ 1000	9½-12 @ 1500	12½ @ 2000	5	7½ @ 20	7 @ 20
D2DF-EA	0-1 @ 500	3-5 @ 750	7½-9½ @ 1000	9½-12 @ 1500	12½ @ 2000	5	7½ @ 20	7 @ 20
D2DF-DA	½-2½ @ 500	5-7 @ 750	9-11 @ 1000	10½-12½ @ 1500	13½ @ 2000	5	7½ @ 20	4 @ 20
D2DF-FA	0-1 @ 500	0-1½ @ 750	4½-7 @ 1000	10½-12½ @ 1500	13½ @ 2000	5	7½ @ 20	4 @ 20
D22F-LA	0-½ @ 500	0-1½ @ 750	2½-4½ @ 1000	8-10 @ 1500	13½ @ 2000	5	12½ @ 20	4 @ 20
D22F-HA	0-1 @ 500	1½-3½ @ 750	4½-6½ @ 1000	10-12 @ 1500	14½ @ 2000	5	9½ @ 20	—
D2MF-EA	0-1 @ 500	2-4 @ 750	4½-6½ @ 1000	6-8 @ 1500	9½ @ 2000	5	11½ @ 20	4 @ 20
D2MF-FA	0-1 @ 500	2-4 @ 750	4½-6½ @ 1000	6-8 @ 1500	9½ @ 2000	5	11½ @ 20	4 @ 20
D2OF-PA	0-2½ @ 500	6-8 @ 750	7½-9½ @ 1000	10-12½ @ 1500	15 @ 2000	5	9½ @ 20	7 @ 20
D2OF-DA	0-1½ @ 500	5-7 @ 750	5½-7½ @ 1000	7-9 @ 1500	10½ @ 2000	5	9½ @ 20	7 @ 20
D2OF-EA	0-1 @ 500	1½-3½ @ 750	4-6 @ 1000	7-9 @ 1500	10½ @ 2000	5	9½ @ 20	4 @ 20
D2OF-HA	0-1 @ 500	0-2 @ 750	5-7 @ 1000	7½-9½ @ 1500	11 @ 2000	5	5½ @ 20	7 @ 20
D2OF-JA	0-1 @ 500	0-2 @ 750	5-7 @ 1000	7½-9½ @ 1500	11 @ 2000	5	5½ @ 20	7 @ 20
D2OF-RA	0-½ @ 500	0-1½ @ 750	4½-6½ @ 1000	7-9½ @ 1500	11 @ 2000	5	5½ @ 20	7 @ 20
D2ZF-EA	0-½ @ 500	0-1 @ 750	1-3 @ 1000	5½-8 @ 1500	13 @ 2000	5	5½ @ 20	7 @ 20
D2ZF-AA	0-1½ @ 500	2¼-4¼ @ 750	4½-6½ @ 1000	8-10 @ 1500	12½ @ 2000	5	12½ @ 20	7 @ 20
D2ZF-CA	0-1 @ 500	3½-5½ @ 750	6½-8½ @ 1000	8½-10½ @ 1500	12½ @ 2000	5	10 @ 20	4 @ 20
D2ZF-FA	0-½ @ 500	0-1 @ 750	1-3 @ 1000	5½-8 @ 1500	13 @ 2000	5	5½ @ 20	7 @ 20
D2ZF-GC	0-½ @ 500	0-1 @ 750	0-2 @ 1000	4½-6½ @ 1500	11 @ 2000	5	9½ @ 20	—
D2ZF-HA	0-1 @ 500	1½-3½ @ 750	4½-6½ @ 1000	10-12 @ 1500	14½ @ 2000	5	9½ @ 20	—
D2ZF-JA	0-1 @ 500	0-1½ @ 750	2½-4½ @ 1000	7½-9½ @ 1500	13 @ 2000	5	11½ @ 20	7 @ 20
1973								
D3AF-AA	0-1½ @ 500	4-6 @ 750	6-8 @ 1000	10-12½ @ 1500	16½ @ 2000	5	13 @ 20	—
D3AF-BA	0-1½ @ 500	3½-5½ @ 750	5½-7½ @ 1000	8½-11 @ 1500	14½ @ 2000	5	13 @ 20	—
D3MF-BA	0-1 @ 500	0-1½ @ 750	3½-5½ @ 1000	7½-10 @ 1500	11 @ 2000	5	7 @ 20	—
D3MF-DA	0-1 @ 500	1½-4 @ 750	5½-7½ @ 1000	7½-9 @ 1500	10½ @ 2000	5	11 @ 20	—
D3MF-GA	0-1 @ 500	0-2 @ 750	1½-3½ @ 1000	4½-7 @ 1500	10½ @ 2000	5	13½ @ 20	—
D3OF-AA	0-1½ @ 500	6½-8½ @ 750	7-9 @ 1000	8-10½ @ 1500	11½ @ 2000	5	9 @ 20	4 @ 20
D3OF-BA	0-1½ @ 500	4-6 @ 750	4½-6½ @ 1000	6-8 @ 1500	10 @ 2000	5	9 @ 20	4 @ 20
D3OF-DA	0-1 @ 500	0-1½ @ 750	4-6 @ 1000	7-9½ @ 1500	11 @ 2000	5	5 @ 20	7 @ 20
D3OF-EA	0-1 @ 500	0-1½ @ 750	4-6 @ 1000	7-9½ @ 1500	11 @ 2000	5	5 @ 20	4 @ 20
D3OF-FA	0-1 @ 500	0-1½ @ 750	1-3 @ 1000	5½-8 @ 1500	13 @ 2000	5	5 @ 20	7 @ 20
D3OF-GA	0-1 @ 500	0-1½ @ 750	1-3½ @ 1000	6-8½ @ 1500	13½ @ 2000	5	5 @ 20	—
D3OF-HA	0-1 @ 500	0-2½ @ 750	2-4½ @ 1000	5½-8½ @ 1500	12 @ 2000	5	5 @ 20	—

Continued

DISTRIBUTOR SPECIFICATIONS—Continued

★Note: If unit is checked on vehicle, double the RPM and degrees to get crankshaft figures.

Breaker arm spring tension—17–21.

Distributor Part No.①	Centrifugal Advance Degrees @ RPM of Distributor					Vacuum Advance		Distributor Retard
	Advance Starts	Intermediate Advance			Full Advance	Inches of Vacuum to Start Plunger	Max. Adv. Dist. Deg. @ Vacuum	Max. Retard Dist. Deg. @ Vacuum
1973—Continued								
D3OF-JA	0–1 @ 500	0–2½ @ 750	2–4½ @ 1000	5½–8½ @ 1500	12 @ 2000	5	5 @ 20	—
D3OF-LA	0–1½ @ 500	4½–6½ @ 750	6–8 @ 1000	8–10½ @ 1500	12 @ 2000	5	9 @ 20	4 @ 20
D3OF-PA	0–1 @ 500	0–2½ @ 750	2–4½ @ 1000	6–8½ @ 1500	12½ @ 2000	5	5 @ 20	4 @ 20
D3OF-RA	0–1½ @ 500	3½–5½ @ 750	5½–7½ @ 1000	6½–8½ @ 1500	10 @ 2000	5	9½ @ 20	4 @ 20
D3SF-BA	0–1 @ 500	½–2½ @ 750	5½–8 @ 1000	10–12 @ 1500	13½ @ 2000	5	11 @ 20	—
D3UF-GA	0–1 @ 500	0–2½ @ 750	2–4½ @ 1000	5½–8½ @ 1500	12 @ 2000	5	5 @ 20	4 @ 20
D3VF-CA	0–1 @ 500	0–1½ @ 750	4–6 @ 1000	6–8 @ 1500	10 @ 2000	5	11 @ 20	—
D3ZF-CA	0–1 @ 500	3½–5½ @ 750	4½–6½ @ 1000	6½–9 @ 1500	11½ @ 2000	5	13 @ 20	—
D3ZF-GA	0–1 @ 500	0–2½ @ 750	2½–4 @ 1000	5½–7½ @ 1500	11 @ 2000	5	12½ @ 20	—
1974								
D3AF-AA	0–1½ @ 500	4–6 @ 750	6–8¼ @ 1000	10–12½ @ 1500	16½ @ 2000	5	13¼ @ 20	—
D3BF-DA	0–1¼ @ 500	2½–4½ @ 750	5½–7½ @ 1000	8½–10½ @ 1500	12 @ 2000	5	11¼ @ 20	5–7 @ 20
D3DF-FA	0–1½ @ 500	1½–3½ @ 750	4½–6½ @ 1000	6½–9 @ 1500	9¼ @ 2000	5	9¼ @ 20	2–4 @ 20
D3DF-HA	0–1½ @ 500	3½–5½ @ 750	7½–9½ @ 1000	9½–11½ @ 1500	11¼ @ 2000	5	7¼ @ 20	—
D3DF-KA	0–1½ @ 500	4½–6½ @ 750	7½–9½ @ 1000	8½–11 @ 1500	11¼ @ 2000	5	7¼ @ 20	2–4 @ 20
D3OF-FA	0–1 @ 500	0–1½ @ 750	1–3 @ 1000	5½–8½ @ 1500	13 @ 2000	5	5¼ @ 20	5–7 @ 20
D3OF-GA	0–1 @ 500	0–1½ @ 750	1–3½ @ 1000	6½–8½ @ 1500	13½ @ 2000	5	5¼ @ 20	—
D3OF-HB	0–1½ @ 500	½–3 @ 750	2½–5 @ 1000	6½–9 @ 1500	13½ @ 2000	5	11¼ @ 20	—
D3OF-RA	0–1½ @ 500	3½–5½ @ 750	5½–7½ @ 1000	6½–8½ @ 1500	10 @ 2000	5	9¼ @ 20	2–4 @ 20
D3UF-EA	0–1¼ @ 500	2½–4½ @ 750	5½–7½ @ 1000	9–11 @ 1500	14½ @ 2000	5	9¼ @ 20	5–7 @ 20
D3ZF-GA	0–1 @ 500	0–2½ @ 750	2¼–4¼ @ 1000	5½–7½ @ 1500	11 @ 2000	5	12½ @ 20	—
D4AE-AA	0–½ @ 500	0–2 @ 750	2½–4½ @ 1000	5½–7½ @ 1500	11 @ 2000	5	12½ @ 20	—
D4AE-HA	0–1½ @ 500	5–7 @ 750	6–8 @ 1000	8–10½ @ 1500	12½ @ 2000	5	9½ @ 20	5–7 @ 20
D4DE-FA	0–1½ @ 500	4½–6½ @ 750	7½–9½ @ 1000	9–11 @ 1500	12½ @ 2000	5	7¼ @ 20	2–4 @ 20
D4DE-LA	0–1½ @ 500	4–6 @ 750	4½–6½ @ 1000	6–8 @ 1500	9½ @ 2000	5	9 @ 20	2–4 @ 20
D4DE-MA	0–½ @ 500	½–2½ @ 750	3½–5½ @ 1000	7½–9½ @ 1500	13½ @ 2000	5	11½ @ 20	—
D4DE-NA	0–1½ @ 500	3½–5½ @ 750	5½–7½ @ 1000	6½–8½ @ 1500	10 @ 2000	5	9¼ @ 20	2–4 @ 20
D4DE-RA	0–1½ @ 500	3½–5½ @ 750	5½–7½ @ 1000	6½–8½ @ 1500	10½ @ 2000	5	9¼ @ 20	2–4 @ 20
D4OE-CA	0–½ @ 500	0–1½ @ 750	2–4 @ 1000	5½–7½ @ 1500	10½ @ 2000	5	13½ @ 20	—
D4VE-CA	0–½ @ 500	0–½ @ 750	3–5 @ 1000	7–9 @ 1500	10½ @ 2000	5	11¼ @ 20	—
1975								
D3ZF-GA	0–2 @ 775	2–4 @ 975	5.4–7.7 @ 1500	—	10¾ @ 2500	6	13¼ @ 24	—
D4OE-EA	0–2 @ 520	4½–7½ @ 800	10–12½ @ 1500	—	17¾ @ 2000	4	13 @ 17	—
D4VE-CA	0–2 @ 825	4–6 @ 1025	7–9¼ @ 1500	8⅓–11¼ @ 2000	12½ @ 2500	4	11¾ @ 14.6	—
D5AE-BA	0–2½ @ 975	—	3¾–6¼ @ 1500	—	11¼ @ 2150	4	13¼ @ 13	—
D5AE-DA	0–2½ @ 975	—	3¾–6¼ @ 1500	—	11¼ @ 2150	4.3	15¼ @ 13	—
D5AE-EA	0–2½ @ 975	—	3¾–6¼ @ 1500	—	11¼ @ 2150	3	13¼ @ 11	—
D5DE-HA	0–2 @ 550	3½–5½ @ 1000	7–9¼ @ 1500	10½–13 @ 2000	16½ @ 2500	4½	13¼ @ 19	—

①—Basic part No. 12127.

STARTING MOTOR SPECIFICATIONS

Year	Engine Model	Part No.	Brush Spring Tension, Ounces	No Load Test			Torque Test		
				Amperes	Volts	R.P.M.	Amperes	Volts	Torque Lbs. Ft.
1969–72	6-170, 200	C6OZ-A	40	70	12	8500	460	6	9
	6-170	C2DZ-A	40	70	12	8500	460	6	9
	6-200	C3OZ-C	40	70	12	9500	670	5	15½
	6-250	C2OZ-A	40	70	12	9500	670	5	15½
	8-302, 351	C2OZ-A	40	70	12	9500	670	5	15½
	8-302, 351	C5TZ-A	40	70	12	9500	670	5	15½
	8-390, 427	C3OZ-C	40	70	12	9500	670	5	15½
	8-428	C8AZ-A	40	70	12	11000	700	5	15½
	8-429	C8VY-C	40	70	12	10000	700	5	15½
1973	6-200	D2ZF-BA	40	70	12	8500	460	6	9
	6-250	D2AF-CA	40	70	12	9500	670	5	15½
	8-302	D2ZF-AA	40	70	12	9500	670	5	15½
	8-351	D2AF-DA	40	70	12	9500	670	5	15½
	8-351	D2AF-CA	40	70	12	9500	670	5	15½
	8-400	DZAF-AA	40	70	12	9500	670	5	15½
	8-429	DZAF-EA	40	70	12	10000	700	5	15½
1974	6-200	D2ZF-BA	③	④	12	8500	⑤	5	⑥
	6-250	D2AF-CA	③	④	12	9500	⑤	5	⑥
	8-302, 351	D2AF-CA	③	④	12	9500	⑤	5	⑥
	8-400	D2AF-AA	③	④	12	9500	⑤	5	⑥
	8-460	D2AF-EA	80	90	12	—	—	—	—
1975	6-200	D2ZF-BA	③	④	12	—	⑤	5	⑥
	6-250	D5OF-AA	③	④	12	—	⑤	5	⑥
	8-302, 351①	D5OF-AA	③	④	12	—	⑤	5	⑥
	8-351②, 400	D2AF-AA	③	④	12	—	⑤	5	⑥
	8-460	D5AF-AB	80	90	12	—	—	—	—

①—Windsor.
②—Modified.
③—4" diameter starter 40 oz., 4½" diameter starter 80 oz.
④—4" diameter starter 70 amps, 4½" diameter starter 80 amps.
⑤—4" diameter starter 460 amps, 4½" diameter starter 670 amps.
⑥—4" diameter starter 9 ft. lbs., 4½" diameter starter 15½ ft. lbs.

VALVE SPECIFICATIONS

Year	Engine	Valve Lash		Valve Angles		Valve Spring Installed Height	Valve Spring Pressure Lbs. @ In.	Stem Clearance		Stem Diameter, Standard	
		Int.	Exh.	Seat	Face			Intake	Exhaust	Intake	Exhaust
1969	6-170	.066–.117④		45	44	1⁹⁄₁₆	150 @ 1.22	.0008–.0025	.001–.0027	.3100–.3107	.3098–.3105
	6-200, 250	.095–.195④		45	44	1⁹⁄₁₆	150 @ 1.22	.0008–.0025	.001–.0027	.3100–.3107	.3098–.3105
	8-302	1 Turn①		45	44	1⁵⁄₈	180 @ 1.23	.001–.0027	.0015–.0032	.3416–.3423	.3411–.3418
	8-302 "H.O."	.025H	.025H	45	44	1¹³⁄₁₆	315 @ 1.32	.001–.0027	.0015–.0032	.3416–.3423	.3411–.3418
	8-351	1 Turn①		45	44	1²⁵⁄₃₂	215 @ 1.34	.001–.0027	.0015–.0032	.3416–.3423	.3411–.3418
	8-390	.100–.200④		45	44	1⅞	220 @ 1.38	.001–.0027	.0015–.0032	.3711–.3718	.3706–.3713
	8-427	.100–.200④		⑦	⑫	1¹³⁄₁₆	270 @ 1.32	.001–.0027	.0015–.0032	.3711–.3718	.3706–.3713
	8-428	.100–.200④		45	44	1¹³⁄₁₆	270 @ 1.32	.001–.0027	.0015–.0032	.3711–.3718	.3706–.3713
1970	6-170	.066–.117④		45	44	1⁹⁄₁₆	150 @ 1.22	.0008–.0025	.001–.0027	.3100–.3107	.3098–.3105
	6-200, 250	.095–.195④		45	44	1⁹⁄₁₆	150 @ 1.22	.0008–.0025	.001–.0027	.3100–.3107	.3098–.3105
	8-302	.067–.167④		45	44	1⁵⁄₈	180 @ 1.23	.001–.0027	.0015–.0032	.3416–.3423	.3411–.3418
	8-302 "BOSS"	.025H	.025H	45	44	1¹³⁄₁₆	315 @ 1.32	.001–.0027	.0015–.0032	.3416–.3423	.3411–.3418
	8-351⑧	.083–.183④		45	44	1²⁵⁄₃₂	215 @ 1.34	.001–.0027	.0015–.0032	.3416–.3423	.3411–.3418
	8-351⑨⑩	.100–.200④		45	44	1¹³⁄₁₆	210 @ 1.42	.001–.0027	.0015–.0032	.3416–.3423	.3411–.3418
	8-351⑨⑪	.100–.200④		45	44	1¹³⁄₁₆	285 @ 1.32	.001–.0027	.0015–.0032	.3416–.3423	.3411–.3418
	8-428	.100–.200④		45	44	1¹³⁄₁₆	270 @ 1.32	.001–.0027	.0015–.0032	.3711–.3718	.3706–.3713

Continued

VALVE SPECIFICATIONS—Continued

Year	Engine Model	Valve Lash Int.	Valve Lash Exh.	Valve Angles Seat	Valve Angles Face	Valve Spring Installed Height	Valve Spring Pressure Lbs. @ In.	Stem Clearance Intake	Stem Clearance Exhaust	Stem Diameter Standard Intake	Stem Diameter Standard Exhaust
1970	8-429 "CJ"	.019H	.019H	[7]	[12]	$1\frac{13}{16}$	306 @ 1.36	.001-.0024	.002-.0034	.3416-.3423	.3416-.3418
	8-429 "SCJ"	.019H	.019H	[7]	[12]	$1\frac{13}{32}$	306 @ 1.36	.001-.0024	.002-.0034	.3711-.3718	.3701-.3708
	8-429 "BOSS"	.013C	.013C	[7]	[13]	$1\frac{13}{32}$	315 @ 1.32	.001-.0024	.002-.0034	.3711-.3718	.3701-.3708
1971	6-170	.066-.117[4]		45	44	$1\frac{9}{16}$	150 @ 1.22	.0008-.0025	.001-.0027	.3100-.3107	.3098-.3105
	6-200	.079-.144[4]		45	44	$1\frac{9}{16}$	150 @ 1.22	.0008-.0025	.001-.0027	.3100-.3107	.3098-.3105
	6-250	.095-.145[4]		45	44	$1\frac{9}{16}$	150 @ 1.22	.0008-.0025	.001-.0027	.3100-.3107	.3098-.3105
	8-302	.090-.190[4]		45	44	$1\frac{5}{8}$	180 @ 1.23	.001-.0027	.001-.0027	.3416-.3423	.3411-.3418
	8-302 H.O.	.025H	.025H	45	44	$1\frac{13}{16}$	315 @ 1.32	.001-.0027	.001-.0027	.3416-.3423	.3411-.3418
	8-351[8]	.100-.200[4]		45	44	$1\frac{25}{32}$	215 @ 1.34	.001-.0027	.001-.0027	.3416-.3423	.3411-.3418
	8-351[9][10]	.100-.200[4]		45	44	$1\frac{13}{16}$	210 @ 1.42	.001-.0027	.001-.0027	.3416-.3423	.3411-.3418
	8-351[9][11]	.100-.200[4]		45	44	$1\frac{13}{16}$	285 @ 1.32	.001-.0027	.001-.0027	.3416-.3423	.3411-.3418
	8-429	.075-.155[4]		45	44	$1\frac{13}{32}$	315 @ 1.32	.001-.0027	.001-.0027	.3416-.3423	.3416-.3423
1972	6-170	.100-.150[4]		45	45	$1\frac{19}{32}$	150 @ 1.22	.0008-.0025	.001-.0027	.3100-.3107	.3098-.3105
	6-200	.100-.150[4]		45	45	$1\frac{19}{32}$	150 @ 1.22	.0008-.0025	.001-.0027	.3100-.3107	.3098-.3105
	6-250	.100-.150[4]		45	45	$1\frac{37}{64}$	150 @ 1.22	.0008-.0025	.001-.0027	.3100-.3107	.3098-.3105
	6-250 Calif.	.100-.150[4]		45	45	$1\frac{37}{64}$	146 @ 1.20	.0008-.0025	.001-.0027	.3100-.3107	.3098-.3105
	8-302	.090-.140[4]		45	45	$1\frac{11}{16}$	200 @ 1.31	.001-.0027	.0015-.0032	.3416-.3423	.3411-.3418
	8-351[10]	.106-.156[4]		45	45	$1\frac{13}{16}$	210 @ 1.42	.001-.0027	.0015-.0032	.3416-.3423	.3411-.3418
	8-351[11]	.100-.150[4]		45	45	$1\frac{13}{16}$	277 @ 1.34	.001-.0027	.0015-.0032	.3416-.3423	.3411-.3418
	8-351 H.O.	.025H	.025H	45	45	$1\frac{5}{8}$	315 @ 1.32	.001-.0027	.0015-.0032	.3416-.3423	.3411-.3418
	8-400	.100-.150[4]		45	45	$1\frac{13}{16}$	226 @ 1.39	.001-.0027	.0015-.0032	.3416-.3423	.3411-.3418
	8-429	.075-.125[4]		45	45	$1\frac{13}{16}$	229 @ 1.33	.001-.0027	.0015-.0032	.3416-.3423	.3411-.3418
1973	6-200	.079-.129[4]		45	45	$1\frac{19}{32}$	150 @ 1.22	.0008-.0025	.001-.0027	.3100-.3107	.3098-.3105
	6-250	.095-.145[4]		45	44	$1\frac{37}{64}$	149 @ 1.20	.0008-.0025	.001-.0027	.3100-.3107	.3098-.3105
	8-302	.090-.140[4]		45	44	$1\frac{11}{16}$	200 @ 1.31	.001-.0027	.0015-.0032	.3416-.3423	.3411-.3418
	8-351[8]	.106-.156[4]		45	44	$1\frac{25}{32}$	200 @ 1.34	.001-.0027	.0015-.0032	.3416-.3423	.3411-.3418
	8-351[9][10]	.100-.150[4]		45	44	$1\frac{53}{64}$	210 @ 1.42	.001-.0027	.0015-.0032	.3416-.3423	.3411-.3418
	8-351[9][11]	.100-.150[4]		45	44	$1\frac{53}{64}$	285 @ 1.32	.001-.0027	.0015-.0032	.3416-.3423	.3411-.3418
	8-400	.100-.150[4]		45	44	$1\frac{53}{64}$	226 @ 1.39	.001-.0027	.0015-.0032	.3416-.3423	.3411-.3418
	8-429	.075-.125[4]		45	44	$1\frac{13}{16}$	169 @ 1.39	.001-.0027	.001-.0027	.3416-.3423	.3416-.3423
	8-460	.105-.155[4]		45	44	$1\frac{25}{32}$	169 @ 1.39	.0010-.0027	.0010-.0027	.3416-.3423	.3416-.3423
1974	6-200	.079-.129[4]		45	44	$1\frac{37}{64}$	146 @ 1.20	.0008-.0025	.0010-.0027	.3100-.3107	.3098-.3105
	6-250	.095-.195[4]		45	44	$1\frac{37}{64}$	146 @ 1.20	.0008-.0025	.0010-.0027	.3100-.3107	.3098-.3105
	8-302	.090-.140[4]		45	44	[6]	[14]	.0010-.0027	.0015-.0032	.3416-.3423	.3411-.3418
	8-351[9][10]	.100-.150[4]		45	44	$1\frac{53}{64}$	226 @ 1.42	.0010-.0027	.0015-.0032	.3416-.3423	.3411-.3418
	8-351[8][10]	.106-.156[4]		45	44	$1\frac{51}{64}$	200 @ 1.34	.0010-.0027	.0015-.0032	.3416-.3423	.3411-.3418
	8-351[11]	.100-.150[4]		45	44	$1\frac{53}{64}$	280 @ 1.34	.001-.0027	.0015-.0032	.3416-.3423	.3411-.3418
	8-400	.100-.150[4]		45	44	$1\frac{53}{64}$	226 @ 1.39	.0010-.0027	.0015-.0032	.3416-.3423	.3411-.3418
	8-460	.075-.125[4]		45	44	$1\frac{53}{64}$	253 @ 1.33	.0010-.0027	.0010-.0027	.3416-.3423	.3416-.3423
1975	6-200	.079-.209		45	45	$1\frac{19}{32}$	[2]	.0008-.0025	.001-.0027	.3100-.3107	.3098-.3105
	6-250	.079-.209		45	45	[3]	155 @ 1.20	.0008-.0025	.001-.0027	.3100-.3107	.3098-.3105
	V8-302	.090-.190		45	45	[13]	[14]	.001-.0027	.0015-.0032	.3416-.3423	.3411-.3418
	V8-351[8]	.106-.206		45	45	$1\frac{51}{64}$	200 @ 1.34	.001-.0027	.0015-.0032	.3416-.3423	.3411-.3418
	V8-351[8], 400	.100-.200		45	45	$1\frac{53}{64}$	226 @ 1.39	.001-.0027	.0015-.0032	.3416-.3423	.3411-.3418
	V8-460	.075-.175		45	45	$1\frac{53}{64}$	315 @ 1.32	.001-.0027	.001-.0027	.3416-.3423	.3416-.3423

[1]—Tighten rocker arm adjusting screw to eliminate all push rod end clearance, then tighten screw the number of turns listed.
[2]—Intake 156 @ 1.20, exhaust 148 @ 1.23.
[3]—Intake $1\frac{19}{32}$, exhaust $1\frac{9}{16}$.
[4]—Clearance is obtained at valve stem tip with hydraulic lifter collapsed. If clearance is less than the minimum install an undersize push rod; if clearance is greater than the maximum install an oversize push rod.
[5]—Modified engine.
[6]—Intake $1\frac{11}{16}$, exhaust $1\frac{9}{16}$.
[7]—Intake 30°, Exhaust 45°.
[8]—Windsor engine.
[9]—Cleveland engine.
[10]—2 barrel carb.
[11]—4 barrel carb.
[12]—Intake 29°, exhaust 44°.
[13]—Intake $1\frac{45}{64}$, exhaust $1\frac{39}{64}$.
[14]—Intake 200 @ 1.31, exhaust 200 @ 1.22.

PISTONS, PINS, RINGS, CRANKSHAFT & BEARINGS

Year	Engine	Piston Clearance	Ring End Gap① Comp.	Ring End Gap① Oil	Wrist-pin Diameter	Rod Bearings Shaft Diameter	Rod Bearings Bearing Clearance	Main Bearings Shaft Diameter	Main Bearings Bearing Clearance	Thrust on Bear. No.	Shaft End Play
1969	6-170, 200	.0014–.0020	.010	.015	.912	2.1232–2.1240	.0008–.0015	2.2482–2.2490	.0005–.0015	④	.004–.008
	6-250	.0014–.0020	.010	.015	.912	2.1232–2.1240	.0008–.0015	2.3982–2.3990	.0005–.0015	5	.004–.008
	8-302	.0018–.0026	.010	.015	.912	2.1228–2.1236	.0008–.0015	2.2482–2.2490	.0005–.0015	3	.004–.008
	8-302 "H.O."	.0034–.0042	.010	.015	.912	2.1222–2.1230	.001–.0028	2.2482–2.2490	.0005–.0015	3	.004–.008
	8-351	.0018–.0026	.010	.015	.912	2.3103–2.3110	.0008–.0015	2.9994–3.0002	.0013–.0025	3	.004–.008
	8-390	.0015–.0023	.010	.015	.975	2.4380–2.4388	.0008–.0015	2.7484–2.7492	.001–.002	3	.004–.010
	8-427, 428	.0030–.0038	.018	.015	.975	2.4380–2.4388	.002–.003	2.7484–2.7492	.001–.002	3	.004–.010
1970–71	6-170, 200	.0014–.0020	.010	.015	.912	2.1232–2.1240	.0008–.0026	2.2482–2.2490	.0005–.0025	④	.004–.010
	6-250	.0014–.0020	.010	.015	.912	2.1232–2.1240	.0008–.0026	2.3982–2.3990	.0005–.0025	5	.004–.008
	8-302	.0018–.0026	.010	.015	.912	2.1228–2.1236	.0008–.0026	2.2482–2.2400	.0005–.0025	3	.004–.008
	8-302 "BOSS"	.0034–.0042	.010	.015	.912	2.1222–2.1230	.001–.0028	2.2482–2.2490	.0005–.0015	3	.004–.008
	8-351②	.0018–.0026	.010	.015	.912	2.3103–2.3110	.0008–.0026	2.9994–3.0002	.0013–.0025	3	.004–.008
	8-351③	.0014–.0022	.010	.015	.912	2.3103–2.3110	.0008–.0026	2.7484–2.7492	.0013–.0029	3	.004–.008
	8-428	.003–.0038	.018	.015	.975	2.4380–2.4388	.002–.003	2.7484–2.7492	.001–.002	3	.004–.010
	8-429 "CJ"	.003–.0038	.010	.010	1.040	2.4992–2.5000	.001–.0015	2.9994–3.0002	.0005–.0025	3	.004–.008
	8-429 "BOSS"	.003–.0038	.010	.010	1.040	2.4992–2.5000	.0008–.0026	2.9994–3.0002	.0009–.0025	3	.004–.008
1972	6-170	.0013–.0026	.008	.015	.912	2.1232–2.1240	.0002–.0024	2.2482–2.2490	.0007–.0026	3	.004–.008
	6-200	.0014–.0020	.008	.015	.912	2.1232–2.1240	.0002–.0024	2.2482–2.2490	.0007–.0026	5	.004–.008
	6-250	.0013–.0021	.008	.015	.912	2.1232–2.1240	.0008–.0024	2.3982–2.3990	.0005–.0022	5	.004–.008
	8-302	.0018–.0026	.010	.015	.912	2.1232–2.1240	.0008–.0026	2.2482–2.2490	.0005–.0024	3	.004–.008
	8-351⑤	.0014–.0022	.010	.015	.912	2.3103–2.3110	.0008–.0026	2.7484–2.7492	.0009–.0026	3	.004–.010
	8-351⑥	.0018–.0026	.010	.015	.912	2.3103–2.3110	.0011–.0026	2.7484–2.7492	.0011–.0028	3	.004–.010
	8-400	.0014–.0022	.010	.015	.975	2.3103–2.3110	.0008–.0026	2.9994–3.0002	.0009–.0026	3	.004–.008
	8-429	.0014–.0022	.010	.015	.975	2.4992–2.5000	.0008–.0028	2.9994–3.0002	⑦	3	.004–.008
1973	6-200	.0014–.0020	.008	.015	.912	2.1232–2.1240	.0002–.0024	2.2482–2.2490	.0007–.0026	5	.004–.008
	6-250	.0013–.0021	.008	.015	.912	2.1232–2.1240	.0008–.0024	2.3982–2.3990	.0008–.0024	5	.004–.008
	8-302	.0018–.0026	.010	.015	.912	2.1228–2.1236	.0008–.0026	2.2482–2.2490	.0005–.0024	3	.004–.008
	8-351⑤②	.0018–.0026	.010	.015	.912	2.3103–2.3111	.0008–.0026	2.9994–3.0002	.0008–.0026	3	.004–.008
	8-351⑤③	.0014–.0022	.010	.015	.912	2.3103–2.3111	.0008–.0026	2.7484–2.7492	.0009–.0026	3	.004–.010
	8-351⑥	.0034–.0042	.010	.015	.912	2.3103–2.3111	.0011–.0026	2.7484–2.7492	.0011–.0028	3	.004–.010
	8-351⑥⑧	.0034–.0042	.010	.015	.912	2.3103–2.3111	.0011–.0026	2.7484–2.7492	.0011–.0028	3	.004–.010
	8-400	.0014–.0022	.010	.015	.975	2.3103–2.3111	.0008–.0026	2.9994–3.0002	.0009–.0026	3	.004–.008
	8-429	.0014–.0022	.010	.015	.975	2.4992–2.5000	.0008–.0028	2.9994–3.0002	⑦	3	.004–.008
	8-460	.0014–.0022	.010	.015	1.040	2.4992–2.5000	.0008–.0028	2.9994–3.0002	.0005–.0025	3	.004–.008
1974	6-200	.0013–.0021	.008	.015	.912	2.1232–2.1240	.0008–.0024	2.2482–2.2490	.0007–.0026	5	.004–.008
	6-250	.0013–.0021	.008	.015	.912	2.1232–2.1240	.0008–.0024	2.3982–2.3990	.0005–.0022	5	.004–.008
	8-302	.0018–.0026	.010	.015	.912	2.1228–2.1236	.0008–.0026	2.2482–2.2490	⑩	3	.004–.008
	8-351⑤②	.0018–.0026	.010	.015	.912	2.3103–2.3111	.0008–.0026	2.9994–3.0002	.0008–.0026	3	.004–.008
	8-351⑤③	.0014–.0022	.010	.015	.912	3.3103–2.3111	.0008–.0026	2.7484–2.7492	.0009–.0026	3	.004–.008
	8-351⑥③	.0018–.0026	.010	.015	.912	2.3103–2.3111	.0011–.0026	2.7484–2.7492	.0011–.0028	3	.004–.008
	8-400	.0014–.0022	.010	.015	.975	2.3103–2.3111	.0008–.0026	2.9994–3.0002	.0009–.0026	3	.004–.008
	8-460	.0022–.0030	.010	.015	1.040	2.4992–2.5000	.0008–.0028	2.9994–3.0002	⑦	3	.004–.008
1975	6-200	.0013–.0021	.008	.015	.9121	2.136	.0008–.0026	2.2486	.0007–.0024	5	.004–.008
	6-250	.0013–.0021	.008	.015	.9121	2.136	.0008–.0024	2.3986	.0005–.0022	5	.004–.008
	8-302	.0018–.0026	.010	.015	.9121	2.136	.0008–.0026	2.2486	.0005–.0024	3	.004–.008
	8-351②	.0018–.0026	.010	.015	.9121	2.3207	.0008–.0026	2.9998	.0008–.0026	3	.004–.008
	8-351③, 400	.0014–.0022	.010	.015	.9751	2.3207	.0008–.0026	2.9998	.0009–.0026	3	.004–.008
	8-460	.0014–.0022	.010	.015	1.040	2.4992–2.5000	.0008–.0028	2.9998	⑦	3	.004–.008

①—Fit rings in tapered bores for clearance listed in tightest portion of ring travel.
②—Windsor engine.
③—Cleveland engine.
④—No. 3 in 6–170, No. 5 on 6–200.
⑤—Two barrel carburetor.
⑥—Four barrel carburetor.
⑦—No. 1, .0004–.0020; others, .0012–.0028.
⑧—Hi-Perf engine.
⑨—Modified engine.
⑩—No. 1, .0001–.0020, No. 2, 3, 4, 5, .0005–.0024.

ENGINE TIGHTENING SPECIFICATIONS★

★Torque specifications are for clean and lightly lubricated threads only. Dry or dirty threads produce increased friction which prevents accurate measurement of tightness.

Year	Engine	Spark Plugs Ft. Lbs.	Cylinder Head Bolts Ft. Lbs.	Intake Manifold Ft. Lbs.	Exhaust Manifold Ft. Lbs.	Rocker Arm Shaft Bracket Ft. Lbs.	Rocker Arm Cover Ft. Lbs.	Connecting Rod Cap Bolts Ft. Lbs.	Main Bearing Cap Bolts Ft. Lbs.	Flywheel to Crank-shaft Ft. Lbs.	Vibration Damper or Pulley Ft. Lbs.
1969–72	6 Cyl.	15–20	70–75	—	13–18	30–35	3–5	③	60–70	75–85	85–100
	8-302④	15–20	65–72	23–25	12–16	—	3–5	19–24	60–70	75–85	100–130
	8-302⑤	5–10	65–72	⑥	12–16	—	3–5	40–45	60–70⑦	75–85	70–90
	8-351	15–20	95–100	23–25	18–24	—	3–5	40–45	95–105	75–85	70–90
	8-390	15–20	80–90	32–35	18–24	40–45	4–7	40–45	95–105	75–85	70–90
	8-400	10–15	95–105	⑥	⑥	—	3–5	40–45	95–105	75–85	70–90
	8-427	15–20	90–100	32–35	18–24	40–45	4–7	53–58	95–105	75–85	70–90
	8-428	15–20	80–90	32–35	18–24	—	4–7	53–58	95–105	75–85	70–90
	8-429	15–20⑧	130–140	25–30	28–33	—	2½–4	40–45	95–105	75–85	75–90
1973	6 Cyl.	15–20	70–75	—	13–18	30–35	3–5	21–26	60–70	75–85	85–100
	8-302	15–20	65–72	23–25	12–16	17–23⑨	3–5	19–24	60–70	75–85	70–90
	8-351⑩	15–20	105–112	23–25	18–24	17–23⑨	3–5	40–45	95–105	75–85	100–130
	8-351⑪	15–20	95–105	⑫	12–22	18–25	3–5	40–45	⑬	75–85	70–90
	8-400	10–15	95–105	⑫	12–16	18–25	3–5	40–45	⑬	75–85	70–90
	8-429	15–20	130–140	25–30	28–33	18–25	5–6	40–45	95–105	75–85	70–90
1974	6 Cyl.	15–20	70–75	—	13–18	30–35	3–5	③	60–70	75–85	85–100
	8-302	15–20	65–72	19–27	12–16	17–23⑨	3–5	19–24	60–70	75–85	70–90
	8-351⑩	15–20	105–112	19–27	18–24	17–23⑨	3–5	40–45	95–105	75–85	100–130
	8-351⑪	15–20	95–105	⑭	12–22	18–25	3–5	40–45	⑬	75–85	70–90
	8-400	10–15	95–105	⑭	12–16	18–25	3–5	40–45	⑬	75–85	70–90
	8-460	15–20	130–140	22–32	28–33	18–25	5–6	40–45	95–105	75–85	70–90

③—6-170, 200 is 19–24; 6-250 is 21–26.
④—Except "H.O."
⑤—"H.O."
⑥—5/16 Bolts, 23–25, 3/8 Bolts, 28–32, ¼ Bolt, 6–9
⑦—Outer bolts on caps 2, 3 & 4—35–40.

⑧—"CJ", "SCJ", "BOSS" use 5–10 ft.-lbs.
⑨—Rocker arm stud nut.
⑩—Windsor engine.
⑪—Cleveland engine.

⑫—5/16" bolts, 21–25, 3/8" bolts, 27–33, ¼" bolt, 6–9.
⑬—½" bolts, 95–105, 3/8" bolts, 35–45.
⑭—5/16" bolts, 22–32, 3/8" bolts, 17–25, ¼" bolts, 6–9.

ALTERNATOR & REGULATOR SPECIFICATIONS

Year	Make or Model	Current Rating①		Field Current @ 75°F.		Voltage Regulator②				Field Relay	
		Amperes	Volts	Amperes	Volts	Basic Part No. (10316)	Voltage @ 75°F.	Contact Gap	Armature Air Gap	Armature Air Gap	Closing Voltage @ 75°F.
1969	C5TF-10300-K	38	15	2.4	12	C3SZ-B	13.5–15.3	④	④	④	2.3–4.2
	C6AF-10300-B	42	15	2.8–3.3	12	C3SZ-B	13.5–15.3	④	④	④	2.3–4.2
	C6AF-10300-F	55	15	2.8–3.3	12	C3SZ-B	13.5–15.3	④	④	④	2.3–4.2
	C6AF-10300-G	55	15	2.8–3.3	12	C3SZ-B	13.5–15.3	④	④	④	2.3–4.2
	C6DF-10300-A	38	15	2.4	12	C3SZ-B	13.5–15.3	④	④	④	2.3–4.2
	C7AF-10300-A	65	15	2.9	12	C3SZ-B	13.5–15.3	④	④	④	2.3–4.2
	C9AF-10300-A	42	15	2.8–3.3	12	C3SZ-B	13.5–15.3	④	④	④	2.3–4.2
	C9AF-10300-B	55	15	2.8–3.3	12	C3SZ-B	13.5–15.3	④	④	④	2.3–4.2
	C9AF-10300-C	42	15	2.8–3.3	12	C3SZ-B	13.5–15.3	④	④	④	2.3–4.2
	C9SF-10300-A	55	15	2.8–3.3	12	C3SZ-B	13.5–15.3	④	④	④	2.3–4.2
	C9ZF-10300-B	55	15	2.8–3.3	12	C3SZ-B	13.5–15.3	④	④	④	2.3–4.2
	C9ZF-10300-C	55	15	2.8–3.3	12	C3SZ-B	13.5–15.3	④	④	④	2.3–4.2
1970–72	D0ZF-10300-B	38	15	2.4	12	C3SZ-B	13.5–15.3	④	④	④	2.0–4.2
	D0AF-10300-C	42	15	2.9	12	C3SZ-B	13.5–15.3	④	④	④	2.0–4.2
	D0AF-10300-F	42	15	2.9	12	C3SZ-B	13.5–15.3	④	④	④	2.0–4.2
	D0AF-10300-G	42	15	2.9	12	C3SZ-B	13.5–15.3	④	④	④	2.0–4.2
	D0AF-10300-E	55	15	2.9	12	C3SZ-B	13.5–15.3	④	④	④	2.0–4.2

Continued

ALTERNATOR & REGULATOR SPECIFICATIONS—Continued

Year	Make or Model	Current Rating①		Field Current @ 75°F.		Basic Part No. (10316)	Voltage Regulator②			Field Relay	
		Amperes	Volts	Amperes	Volts		Voltage @ 75°F.	Contact Gap	Armature Air Gap	Armature Air Gap	Closing Voltage @ 75°F.
1970–72	D0AF-10300-H	55	15	2.9	12	C3SZ-B	13.5–15.3	④	④	④	2.0–4.2
	D0ZF-10300-A	55	15	2.9	12	C3SZ-B	13.6–15.1	.018–.020	.042–.052	.011–.013	6.2–7.2
	D0ZF-10300-C	55	15	2.9	12	C3SZ-B	13.6–15.1	.018–.020	.042–.052	.011–.013	6.2–7.2
	D0SF-10300-A	55	15	2.9	12	C3SZ-B	13.6–15.1	.018–.020	.042–.052	.011–.013	6.2–7.2
	D0LF-10300A⑤	55	15	2.9	12	C8SZ-A	—	—	—	—	—
	D1ZF-10300AA	55	15	2.9	12	C3SZ-B	13.5–15.3	④	④	④	2.0–4.2
	D1AF-10300AA	61	15	2.9	12	C3SZ-B	13.5–15.3	④	④	④	2.0–4.2
	D0AF-10300A⑤	65	15	2.9	12	C3SZ B	—	—	—	—	—
1973	Purple	38	15	2.9	12	D3TZ-A	13.5–15.3	④	④	④	2.5–4.0
	Orange	42	15	2.9	12	D3TZ-A	13.5–15.3	④	④	④	2.5–4.0
	Red	55	15	2.9	12	D3TZ-A	—	④	④	④	2.5–4.0
	Green	61	15	2.9	12	D3TZ-A	13.5–15.3	④	④	④	2.5–4.0
	Green	70	15	2.9	12	D3TZ-A	13.5–15.3	④	④	④	2.5–4.0
1974–75	Purple	38	15	2.9	12	D4TZ-A	—	—	—	—	—
	Orange	42	15	2.9	12	D4TZ-A	—	—	—	—	—
	Red	55	15	2.9	12	D4TZ-A	—	—	—	—	—
	Green	61	15	2.9	12	D4TZ-A	—	—	—	—	—
	All	70	15	2.9	12	D4TZ-A	—	—	—	—	—
	All	90	15	2.9	12	D4TZ-A	—	—	—	—	—

①—Current rating stamped on housing. ②—Voltage regulation stamped on cover. ④—Not adjustable.
⑤—Integral regulator alternator.

WHEEL ALIGNMENT SPECIFICATIONS

OLD CAR SPECIFICATIONS: For 1946-68 Wheel Alignment Specifications see main index.

Year	Model	Caster Angle, Degrees		Camber Angle, Degrees				Toe-In. Inch	Toe-Out on Turns, Deg	
		Limits	Desired	Limits Left	Limits Right	Desired Left	Desired Right		Outer Wheel	Inner Wheel
1969	Falcon	−1¾ to +¼	−¾	−½ to +1	−½ to +1	+¼	+¼	3/16	18.1③	20
	Fairlane	−1¾ to +¼	−¾	−½ to +1	−½ to +1	+¼	+¼	3/16	18.1③	20
	Montego	−1¾ to +¼	−¾	−½ to +1	−½ to +1	+¼	+¼	3/16	18.1③	20
	Mustang	−¾ to +1¼	+¼	+¼ to +1¾	+¼ to +1¾	+¾	+¾	3/16	18.68	20
	Cougar	−¾ to +1¼	+¼	+¼ to +1¾	+¼ to +1¾	+¾	+¾	3/16	18.68	20
1970	Maverick	−1½ to +½	−½	−½ to +1	−½ to +1	+¼	+¼	¼	18.48	20
	Falcon	−1¾ to +¾	+¾	−½ to +1	−½ to +1	+¼	+¼	3/16	17.32④	20
	Torino	−1¾ to +¾	+¾	−½ to +1	−½ to +1	+¼	+¼	3/16	17.32④	20
	Montego	−1¾ to +¾	+¾	−½ to +1	−½ to +1	+¼	+¼	3/16	17.32④	20
	Mustang	−1 to +1	Zero	+¼ to +1¾	+¼ to +1¾	+1	+1	3/16	16.68	20
	Cougar	−1 to +1	Zero	+¼ to +1¾	+¼ to +1¾	+1	+1	3/16	16.68	20
1971	Maverick	−2½ to +1½	−½	−¾ to +1¼	−¾ to +1¼	+¼	+¼	3/16	18.48	20
	Torino	−2¾ to +1¼	+¾	−¾ to +1¼	−¾ to +1¼	+¼	+¼	3/16	17.32④	20
	Mustang	−2 to +2	Zero	−½ to +1½	−½ to +1½	+¾	+¾	3/16	18.68	20
	Comet	−2½ to +1½	−½	−¾ to +1¼	−¾ to +1¼	+¼	+¼	3/16	18.48	20
	Montego	−2¾ to +1¼	+¾	−¾ to +1¼	−¾ to +1¼	+¼	+¼	3/16	17.32④	20
	Cougar	−2 to +2	Zero	−½ to +1½	−½ to +1½	+¾	+¾	3/16	18.68	20

Continued

WHEEL ALIGNMENT SPECIFICATIONS—Continued

OLD CAR SPECIFICATIONS: For 1946-68 Wheel Alignment Specifications see main index.

Year	Model	Caster Angle, Degrees		Camber Angle, Degrees				Toe-In. Inch	Toe-Out on Turns, Deg.	
				Limits		Desired				
		Limits	Desired	Left	Right	Left	Right		Outer Wheel	Inner Wheel
1972	Maverick	−2½ to +1½	−½	−¾ to +1¼	−¾ to +1¼	+¼	+¼	3/16	18.21⑤	20
	Torino	−1¼ to +2¾	+¾	−¼ to +1¾	−¼ to +1¾	+¾	+¾	3/16	17.73	20
	Mustang	−2 to +2	Zero	−½ to +1½	−½ to +1½	+½	+½	3/16	17.72	20
	Comet	−2½ to +1½	−½	−¾ to +1¼	−¾ to +1¼	+¼	+¼	3/16	18.21⑤	20
	Montego	−1¼ to +2¾	+¾	−¼ to +1¼	−¼ to +1¾	+¾	+¾	3/16	17.73	20
	Cougar	−2 to +2	Zero	−½ to +1½	−½ to +1½	+½	+½	3/16	17.72	20
1973	Maverick	−2½ to +1½	−½	−¾ to +1¼	−¾ to +1¼	+¼	+¼	¼	18.21⑤	20
	Torino	−¾ to +2¼	+¾	−¼ to +1¾	−¼ to +1¾	+¾	+¾	⅜	17.73	20
	Mustang	−2 to +2	0	−½ to +1½	−½ to +1½	+½	+½	¼	17.72	20
	Comet	−2½ to +1½	−½	−¾ to +1¼	−¾ to +1¼	+¼	+¼	¼	18.21⑤	20
	Montego	−¾ to +2¼	+¾	−¼ to +1¾	−¼ to +1¾	+¾	+¾	⅜	17.73	20
	Cougar	−2 to +2	0	−½ to +1½	−½ to +1½	+½	+½	¼	17.72	20
1974	Maverick	−2½ to +1½	−½	−¾ to +1¼	−¾ to +1¼	+¼	+¼	3/16	18.16⑥	20
	Torino	+½ to +3½	+2	−⅜ to +1⅝	−⅞ to +1⅛	+⅝	+⅛	⅛	18.11	20
	Comet	−2½ to +1½	−½	−¾ to +1¼	−¾ to +1¼	+¼	+¼	3/16	18.16⑥	20
	Montego	+½ to +3½	+2	−⅜ to +1⅝	−⅞ to +1⅛	+⅝	+⅛	⅛	18.11	20
	Cougar	+½ to +3½	+2	−⅜ to +1⅝	−⅞ to +1⅛	+⅝	+⅛	⅛	18.84	20
1975	Maverick	−2½ to +1½	−½	−¾ to +1¼	−¾ to +1¼	+¼	+¼	3/16	18.36①	20
	Granada	−2½ to +1½	−½	−¾ to +1¼	−¾ to +1¼	+¼	+¼	3/16	18.43②	20
	Torino	+2½ to +5½	+4	−⅜ to +1⅝	−⅞ to +1⅛	+⅝	+⅛	⅛	18.06	20
	Comet	−2½ to +1½	−½	−¾ to +1¼	−¾ to +1¼	+¼	+¼	3/16	18.36①	20
	Monarch	−2½ to +1½	−½	−¾ to +1¼	−¾ to +1¼	+¼	+¼	3/16	18.43②	20
	Montego	+2½ to +5½	+4	−⅜ to +1⅝	−⅞ to +1⅛	+⅝	+⅛	⅛	18.06	20
	Cougar	+2½ to +5½	+4	−⅜ to +1⅝	−⅞ to +1⅛	+⅝	+⅛	⅛	18.06	20

①—Power steering 18.13°.
②—Power steering 18.20°.
③—Power steering 17⅞°.
④—Power steering 17.81°.
⑤—Manual Steering 18.44°.
⑥—Manual Steering 18.39°.

COOLING SYSTEM & CAPACITY DATA

Year	Model or Engine	Cooling Capacity, Qts.			Radiator Cap Relief Pressure, Lbs.		Thermo. Opening Temp. ①	Fuel Tank Gals.	Engine Oil Refill Qts. ②	Transmission Oil			Rear Axle Oil Pints
		No Heater	With Heater	With A/C	With A/C	No A/C				3 Speed Pints	4 Speed Pints	Auto. Trans. Qts. ⑨	
1969	6-170, 200	8½	9½	9½	12–15	12–15	190	⑥	3½	3½	4	8	2½
	6-250	9	10	10	12–15	12–15	190	⑥	3½	3½	4	9	4
	8-302	14	15	15	12–15	12–15	190	⑥	4	3½	4	9	4
	8-351	14	15	15	12–15	12–15	190	⑥	4	3½	4	11	5
	8-390	19½	20½	20½	12–15	12–15	190	⑥	4	3½	4	12¾	5
	8-427	19½	20½	20½	12–15	12–15	190	⑥	5	3½	4	12¾	5
	8-428	19½	20½	20½	12–15	12–15	190	⑥	4	3½	4	12¾	5
1970	6-170, 200	9	10	10	12–15	12–15	190	⑫	3½	3½	4	8	2½
	6-250	10½	11½	11½	12–15	12–15	190	⑫	3½	3½	4	9	4
	8-302	14½	15½	15½	12–15	12–15	190	⑫	4	3½	4	9	4
	8-351	15½	16½	16½	12–15	12–15	190	⑫	4	3½	4	⑬	5
	8-428	19	20	20	12–15	12–15	190	⑫	4	3½	4	12¾	5

Continued

COOLING SYSTEM & CAPACITY DATA—Continued

Year	Model or Engine	Cooling Capacity, Qts.			Radiator Cap Relief Pressure, Lbs.		Thermo. Opening Temp. ①	Fuel Tank Gals.	Engine Oil Refill Qts. ②	Transmission Oil			Rear Axle Oil Pints
		No Heater	With Heater	With A/C	With A/C	No A/C				3 Speed Pints	4 Speed Pints	Auto. Trans. Qts. ⑨	
1970	8-429	17½	18½	18½	12-15	12-15	190	⑫	4	3½	4	12¾	5
	8-429 "CJ"	18½	19½	19½	12-15	12-15	190	⑫	4.	3½	4	12¾	5
	8-429 "BOSS"⑩	18½	19½	19½	12-15	12-15	190	⑫	4	—	4	—	5
	8-429 "BOSS"⑪	18½	19½	19½	12-15	12-15	190	⑫	6	—	4	—	5
1971	6-170	8¼	9¼	9¼	12-15	12-15	190	16	3½	3½	—	8	4
	6-200, 250③	7½	8½	8½	12-15	12-15	190	16	3½	3½	—	8	4
	6-250	7½	8½	8½	12-15	12-15	190	⑭	3½	3½	—	9	4
	8-302	14	15	15	12-15	12-15	190	⑭	4	3½	4	9	4
	8-351	15¼	16¼	16¼	12-15	12-15	190	⑭	4	3½	4	⑬	5
	8-429	18½	19½	19½	12-15	12-15	190	⑭	6	3½	4	12¾	5
1972	Maverick 6-170	8¼	9¼	9¼	12-15	12-15	190	15	3½	3½	—	8	4
	Comet 6-170	8	9	9	12-15	12-15	190	15	3½	3½	—	8	4
	Maverick 6-200	8	9	9	12-15	12-15	190	15	3½	3½	—	8	4
	Comet 6-200	7¾	8¾	9	12-15	12-15	190	15	3½	3½	—	8	4
	Maverick 6-250	9	10	10	12-15	12-15	190	15	3½	3½	—	8	4
	Comet 6-250	8¾	9¾	9¾	12-15	12-15	190	15	3½	3½	—	8	4
	Torino 6-250	10½	11½	12	12-15	12-15	190	⑮	3½	3½	—	9	4
	Montego 6-250	10½	11½	11½	12-15	12-15	190	⑯	3½	3½	—	9	4
	Mustang 6-250	10¼	11¼	11¼	12-15	12-15	190	19½	3½	3½	—	9	4
	8-302③	12½	13½	14¼	12-15	12-15	190	15	4	3½	—	9	4
	Torino 8-302	14¼	15¼	16¼	12-15	12-15	190	⑮	4	3½	4	9	4
	Montego 8-302	14¼	15¼	15¼	12-15	12-15	190	⑯	4	3½	4	9	4
	Mustang 8-302	14¼	15¼	15½	12-15	12-15	190	19½	4	3½	4	9	4
	Torino 8-351	14½	15½	15¾	12-15	12-15	190	⑮	4	3½	4	11	5
	Montego 8-351	14½	15½	15⅞	12-15	12-15	190	⑯	4	3½	4	11	5
	Mustang 8-351	14¾	15¾	15¾	12-15	12-15	190	19½	4⑦	3½	4	11	5
	Cougar 8-351	14¾	15¾	15¾	12-15	12-15	190	16½	4	3½	4	⑧	5
	Torino 8-400	16¾	17¾	17¾	12-15	12-15	190	⑮	4	—	4	12¾	5
	Montego 8-400	16¾	17¾	17¾	12-15	12-15	190	⑯	4	—	4	12¾	5
	Torino 8-429	17¾	18¾	20	12-15	12-15	190	⑮	4	—	4	12¾	5
	Montego 8-429	17⅞	18⅞	18⅞	12-15	12-15	190	⑯	4	—	4	12¾	5
1973	Maverick 6-200	8	9	9	12-16	12-16	190	15	4	3½	—	8	4
	Maverick 6-250	8¾	9¾	9¾	12-15	12-15	190	15	3½	3½	—	8	4
	Comet 6-250	8¾	9¾	9¾	12-15	12-15	190	15	3½	3½	—	8	4
	Torino 6-250	10½	11½	11½	12-15	12-15	190	⑰	3½	3½	4	9	4
	Montego 6-250	10½	11½	11½	12-15	12-15	190	⑰	3½	3½	4	9	4
	Mustang 6-250	10¼	11¼	11¼	12-15	12-15	190	19½	3½	—	4	9	4
	8-302③	12½	13½	14¼	12-15	12-15	190	15	4	3½	—	9	4
	Torino 8-302	14¼	15¼	15¾	12-15	12-15	190	⑰	4	3½	4	9	4
	Montego 8-302	14¼	15¼	15¾	12-15	12-15	Thermo.	⑰	4	3½	4	9	4
	Mustang 8-302	14¼	15¼	15¼	12-15	12-15	190	19½	4	—	4	9	4
	Torino 8-351	14¾	15¾	16¾	12-15	12-15	190	⑰	4	3½	4	⑲	5
	Montego 8-351	14¾	15¾	16¾	12-15	12-15	190	⑰	4	3½	4	10½	5
	Mustang 8-351	14¾	15¾	15¾	12-15	12-15	190	19½	4	—	4	⑳	5
	Cougar 8-351	14¾	15¾	15¾	12-15	12-15	190	19½	4	—	4	⑳	5
	Montego 8-400	16¾	17¾	17¾	12-15	12-15	190	⑰	4	—	4	12½	5
	Torino 8-400	16¾	17¾	17¾	12-15	12-15	190	⑰	4	—	4	⑲	5
	Montego 8-429	17¾	18¾	18¾	12-15	12-15	190	⑰	4	—	4	12¾	5
	Torino 8-429	17¾	18¾	18¾	12-15	12-15	190	⑰	4	—	4	12½	5
	8-460⑩	18.5	19.5	19.5	12-16	12-16	190	⑰	6	—	—	13	5

Continued

COOLING SYSTEM & CAPACITY DATA—Continued

Year	Model or Engine	Cooling Capacity, Qts.			Radiator Cap Relief Pressure, Lbs.		Thermo. Opening Temp. ①	Fuel Tank Gals.	Engine Oil Refill Qts. ②	Transmission Oil			Rear Axle Oil Pints
		No Heater	With Heater	With A/C	With A/C	No A/C				3 Speed Pints	4 Speed Pints	Auto. Trans. Qts. ⑨	
1974	6-200③	8.0	9.0	9.0	12-16	12-16	191	15	4	3½	—	8	4
	6-250③	8.7	9½	9½	12-16	12-16	191	15	4	3½	—	9	4
	6-250⑩	—	11.9		12-16	12-16	191	26½	4	3½	—	10¼	4
	8-302③	12.4	13½	14¼	12-16	12-16	191	15	4	3½	—	9	4
	8-302⑩	14.2	15½	15½	12-16	12-16	191	④	4	3½	—	⑤	4
	8-351C⑩	14.8	16	16½	12-16	12-16	191	④	4	—	—	10¼	4
	Cougar 8-351C	14.9	16	16½	12-16	12-16	191	26½	4	—	—	㉓	5
	8-351 W⑩	15.3	16½	16½	12-16	12-16	191	④	4	—	—	㉓	4
	Cougar 8-351 W	15.3	16½	16½	12-16	12-16	191	26½	4	—	—	㉓	5
	8-351 "CJ"⑩	14.7	16½	16½	12-16	12-16	191	④	4	—	4	㉓	4
	Cougar 8-351 "CJ"	14.9	16½	16½	12-16	12-16	191	26½	4	—	—	㉓	5
	8-400⑩	16.7	17¾	18.3	12-16	12-16	191	④	4	—	—	㉓	5
	8-460⑩	18.4	19	19½	12-16	12-16	191	④	4	—	—	㉓	5
	Cougar 400	—	17½	18½	12-16	12-16	191	26½	4	—	—	㉓	5
	Cougar 460	—	19	19½	12-16	12-16	191	26½	6	—	—	㉓	5
1975	6-250③	—	9.7	9.7	12-16	12-16	191	16	4	3½	—	㉓	4
	6-250⑱	—	10.5	10.7	12-16	12-16	191	19.2	4	3½	—	㉓	4
	8-302③	—	13.5	14.1	12-16	12-16	191	16	3½	3½	—	㉓	4
	8-302⑱	—	14.4	14.6	12-16	12-16	191	19.2	3½	3½	—	㉓	4
	8-351W⑱	—	15.7	16.7	12-16	12-16	191	19.2	3½	—	—	㉓	4
	8-351W㉒	—	15.9	16.2	12-16	12-16	191	④	3½	—	—	㉓	—
	8-351M㉒	—	17.1	18	12-16	12-16	191	④	3½	—	—	㉓	—
	8-400㉒	—	17.1	17.5	12-16	12-16	191	④	3½	—	—	㉓	—
	8-460㉒	—	19.2	19.7	12-16	12-16	191	④	4	—	—	㉓	—

①—Use with permanent type anti-freeze.
②—Add 1 qt. with filter change.
③—Maverick and Comet.
④—Sta. Wagons 21 gals.; others 26½ gals.
⑤—C4 9 quarts, FMX 11 quarts.
⑥—Falcon cars and Mustang 16, Cougar 17, Fairlane, Montego and Falcon Wagons 20.
⑦—H.O., 5.
⑧—12" converter, 12¾; others, 11.
⑨—Approximate. Make final check with dipstick.
⑩—Torino & Montego.
⑪—Mustang & Cougar.
⑫—Early Falcon cars & Maverick 16, Mustang, Cougar, Fairlane, Late Falcon & Montego cars 22, Fairlane, Falcon & Montego wagons 19. Subtract 2 gals. for California cars.
⑬—C4 10¼, FMX 11, C6 12¾.
⑭—Torino, Montego, Mustang & Cougar cars, 20. Station wagons, 18.
⑮—Sedans, 22½; wagons, 20½.
⑯—Sedans, 23; wagons, 21.
⑰—Sta. Wagons 20½ gals.; others 22½ gals.
⑱—Granada and Monarch.
⑲—12½" converter, 12½; others, 10½.
⑳—With 2 Bar. Carb. 11; with 4 Bar. Carb. & 10¼" converter, 10¾; others 12¾.
㉑—C4 10 quarts, FMX 11 quarts, C6 12½ quarts.
㉒—Torino, Montego and Cougar.
㉓—C4—10¼ qts., C6—10½ qts., FMX 11 qts.

BRAKE SPECIFICATIONS

Year	Model	Brake Drum Inside Diameter	Wheel Cylinder Bore Diameter			Master Cylinder Bore Diameter		
			Front Disc Brake	Front Drum Brake	Rear Brake	With Disc Brakes	With Drum Brakes	With Power Brakes
1969-70	Falcon & Maverick 6 Cyl. Cars②	9.00	2.381	1.062	.844	.9375	1.00	.9375
	Falcon V8 Cars	10.00	2.381	1.094	.906	.9375	1.00	.9375
	Falcon Wagons	10.00	2.381	1.125	.938	.9375	1.00	.9375
	Mustang 6 Cyl.	9.00	2.381	1.062	.844	1.00	1.00	1.00
	Mustang & Cougar 8-302	10.00	2.381	1.125	.875	1.00	1.00	1.00
	Mustang & Cougar 8-351, 390	10.00	2.381	1.094	.813	1.00	1.00	1.00
	Montego & Fairlane 6-250, 8-302①③	10.00	2.381	1.125	.096	.9375	1.00	.9375
	Montego & Fairlane 8-351, 390	10.00	2.381	1.094	.875	.9375	1.00	.9375
	Montego & Fairlane Conv. (Exc. 8-351, 390)	10.00	2.381	1.094	.906	.9375	1.00	.9375
	Montego & Fairlane Wagons (Exc. 8-390)	10.00	2.381	1.094	.938	.9375	1.00	.9375

Continued

BRAKE SPECIFICATIONS—Continued

Year	Model	Brake Drum Inside Diameter	Wheel Cylinder Bore Diameter			Master Cylinder Bore Diameter		
			Front Disc Brake	Front Drum Brake	Rear Brake	With Disc Brakes	With Drum Brakes	With Power Brakes
1971	Maverick & Comet 6 Cyl.	9.00	—	1.062	.844	—	1.00	.9375
	Maverick & Comet V8	10.00	—	1.125	.875	—	1.00	.9375
	Torino & Montego Cars	10.00	2.381	1.125	.906	.9375	1.00	.9375
	Torino & Montego Wagons	10.00	2.381	1.125	.968	.9375	1.00	.9375
	Mustang & Cougar 6-250, 8-302	10.00	2.381	1.125	.875	.9375	1.00	1.00
	Mustang & Cougar 8-351, 429	10.00	2.381	1.125	.906	.9375	1.00	1.00
1972	Maverick & Comet 6 Cyl.	9.00	—	1.062	.844	—	1.00	.9375
	Maverick & Comet V8	10.00	—	1.125	.875	—	1.00	.9375
	Torino & Montego	10.00	3.100	—	1.00	1.00	1.00	1.00
	Mustang & Cougar 6-250, 8-302	10.00	2.381	1.125	.875	1.00	1.00	1.00
	Mustang & Cougar 8-351	10.00	2.381	1.125	.906	1.00	1.00	1.00
1973	Maverick & Comet	10.00	—	1.125	.875	—	1.00	—
	Montego & Torino	10.00	3.100	—	1.00	1.00	1.00	1.00
	Mustang & Cougar	10.00	2.380	1.125	.875	.9375	1.00	1.00
1974	Maverick & Comet	10.00	2.600	1.125	.875	.9375	.9375	—
	Montego & Torino	④	3.100	—	1.00	1.00	1.00	1.00
	Cougar	9.00	3.100	—	.875	1.00	.9375	.9375
1975	Maverick & Comet	10.00	2.6	1.125	.843	.938	.938	.938
	Granada & Monarch	10.00	2.6	—	.938	.938	—	.938
	Torino, Montego, Cougar	10.00	3.1	—	1.00	1.00	—	1.00

①—Except convertible.
②—Includes only early 1970 Falcons.
③—Includes late 1970 Falcons.
④—Exc. Sta. Wagons 10.00, Sta. Wagons 11.0.

REAR AXLE SPECIFICATIONS

Year	Model	Carrier Type	Ring Gear & Pinion Backlash Inch	Nominal Pinion Locating Shim, Inch	Pinion Bearing Preload				Differential Bearing Preload	Pinion Nut Torque Ft.-Lbs.①
					New Bearings With Seal Inch-Lbs.	Used Bearings With Seal Inch-Lbs.	New Bearings Less Seal Inch-Lbs.	Used Bearings Less Seal Inch-Lbs.		
1969		Integral	.008–.012	.017	17–27	6–12	—	—	.008–.012③	140
		Removable	.008–.012	④	⑤	8–14	—	—	.008–.012⑥	175
1970–71		Integral	.008–.012	.030	22–32	8–14	—	—	.008–.012②	140
		Removable	.008–.012	④	20–30	8–14	—	—	.008–.012⑥	175
1972		Removable	.008–.012	.015⑦	20–30⑧	8–14	—	—	.008–.012⑥	⑨
1973		Removable	.008–.012	.015⑦	17–27⑧	8–14	—	—	.008–.012⑥	⑨
1974		Removable	.008–.012	.015⑦	17–27⑧	8–14⑩	—	—	.008–.012⑪	⑨

①—If torque cannot be obtained, install new spacer.
②—Case spread with new bearings. With used bearings .006–.010".
③—Case spread with new bearings. With used bearings .003–.005".
④—With 7¾" and 8" ring gear .022". With 8¾" and 9" ring gear .015.
⑤—With 7¾" and 8" ring gear 17–32 inch-lbs. With 8¾" and 9" ring gear 22–32 inch-lbs.
⑥—Case spread with new bearings. With used bearings .005–.008".
⑦—With 8" ring gear .002".
⑧—Solid spacer 13–33 inch-lbs.
⑨—With collapsible spacer 170 ft. lbs., with solid spacer 200 ft. lbs.
⑩—With 6¾" ring gear 6–12 inch-lbs.
⑪—Case spread with new bearings. With used bearings for 6¾" ring gear .003–.005, 8" and 9" ring gear .005–.008.

Electrical Section

DISTRIBUTOR, REPLACE

1. To remove the distributor, disconnect the primary wire and vacuum control pipe.
2. Remove distributor cap.
3. Scribe a mark on the distributor body indicating the position of the rotor, and scribe another mark on the body and engine block indicating position of distributor body in block. These marks can be used as guides when installing distributor in a correctly timed engine.
4. Remove hold down screw or screws and lift distributor out of block. *Do not crank engine while distributor is removed or the initial timing operation will have to be performed.*

Installation

If the crankshaft has not been disturbed, install the distributor, using the scribed marks previously made on the distributor body and engine block as guides.

If the crankshaft has been rotated while the distributor was removed from the engine, it will be necessary to retime the engine. Crank the engine to bring No. 1 piston on top dead center of its compression stroke. Align the timing mark on the crankshaft pulley with the timing pointer (see *Tune Up* chart). Install the distributor so that the rotor points to the No. 1 spark plug wire terminal in the distributor cap.

Make sure the oil pump intermediate shaft properly engages the distributor shaft. It may be necessary to crank the engine with the starter, after the distributor drive gear is properly engaged, in order to engage the oil pump intermediate shaft.

STARTER, REPLACE
1969-75

1. Raise car on hoist.
2. Disconnect cable at starter terminal.
3. On all models, unfasten and remove starter.

NOTE: On engines equipped with a solenoid actuated starter, turn wheel to full right and remove the idler arm to frame bolts. On some 1973-75 models, it may be necessary to turn wheels aside to aid starter removal. Also, on 1969-70 Montego with V8 engine and power steering and 1970 models equipped with a V8-428 engine, disconnect and lower the idler arm.

NOISY STARTER OR STARTER LOCKUP: If either of these situations occur, loosen the three mounting bolts enough to hand fit the starter properly into pilot plate. Then tighten starter mounting bolts, starting with top bolt. Starter should not be replaced until it has been proven noisy after proper alignment has been established by the above method.

IGNITION LOCK, REPLACE
1970-75

1. Disconnect the battery ground cable.
2. *Units With Fixed Steering Columns:* Remove steering wheel and trim pad. Insert a wire .090 inch pin into the hole inside the column halfway down the lock cylinder housing, Fig. 1. *Units with Tilt Steering Columns:* Insert wire pin in the hole located on the outside of the flange casting next to the emergency flasher button, Fig. 1.
3. Place the gear shift lever in *Park* (with automatic trans) or *Reverse* (with manual trans) position, and turn the lock cylinder with the ignition key to *Run* position.
4. Depress the wire pin while pulling up on the lock cylinder to remove. Remove the wire pin.
5. To install insert the lock cylinder into housing in the flange casting, and turn the key to *Off* position. Be certain that the cylinder is fully inserted before turning to the *Off* position. This action will extend the cylinder retaining pin into the cylinder housing.
6. Turn the key to check for correct operation in all positions.
7. Install the steering wheel and trim pad on fixed column units.
8. Connect the battery ground cable.

IGNITION SWITCH, REPLACE
1970-75 All (Except Early 1970 Maverick)

1. Remove steering column shroud and lower steering column from brake support bracket.
2. Disconnect battery cable.
3. Disconnect switch wiring and remove two switch retaining nuts. Disconnect

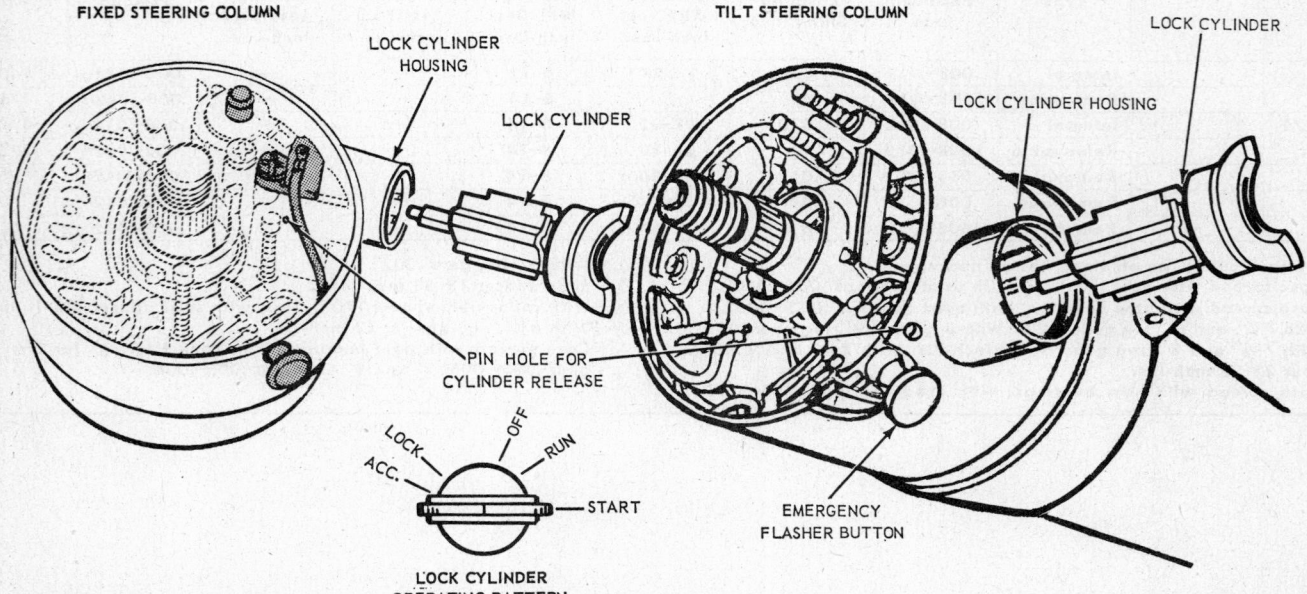

FIXED STEERING COLUMN

LOCK CYLINDER HOUSING

LOCK CYLINDER

TILT STEERING COLUMN

LOCK CYLINDER

LOCK CYLINDER HOUSING

PIN HOLE FOR CYLINDER RELEASE

LOCK

OFF

RUN

ACC.

START

LOCK CYLINDER OPERATING PATTERN

EMERGENCY FLASHER BUTTON

Fig. 1 Ignition lock

switch from actuator and remove switch, Figs. 2 and 3.

4. Move shift lever to Park position on automatic transmissions and Reverse on standard transmission units. Place ignition key in Lock position and remove the key.

NOTE: New replacement switches are pinned in the Lock position by a plastic shipping pin inserted in a locking hole in the switch. For an existing switch, pull plunger out as far as it will go then back one detent to Lock position and insert a 3/32" drill in locking hole to retain switch in Lock position.

5. With locking pin in place, install switch on steering column, determine mid position of actuator lash and tighten retaining bolts.

6. Remove locking pin.

1969 All & Early 1970 Maverick

1. Disconnect battery ground cable.

Fig. 2 Ignition switch installation. 1970-71 Montego & Torino, 1970-73 Mustang, 1970-75 Comet, Cougar & late 1970, 1971-75 Maverick ➡

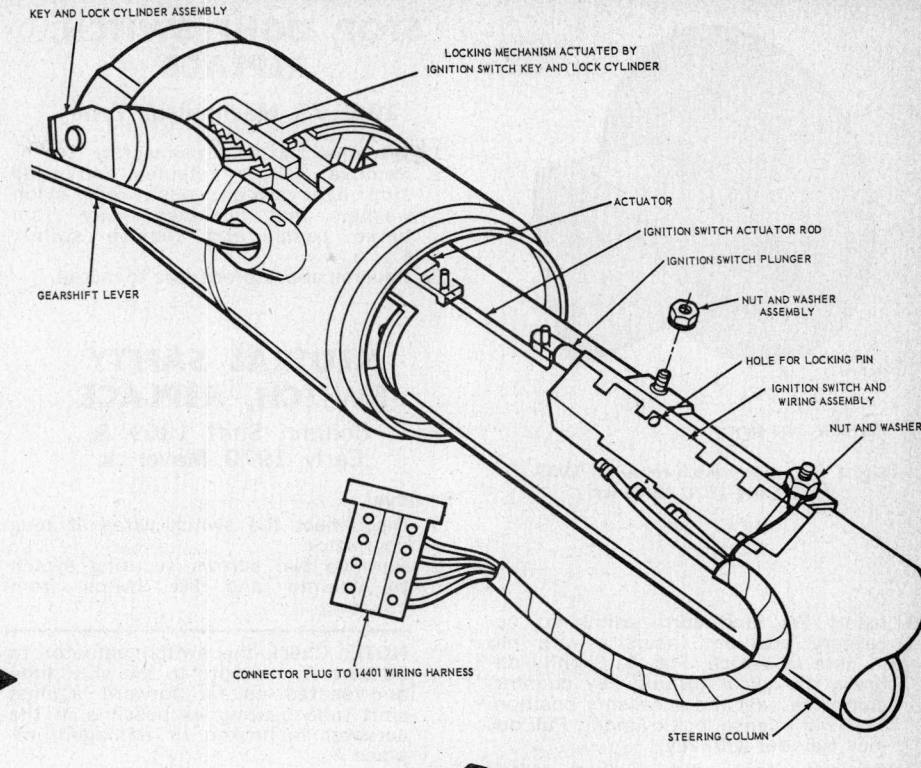

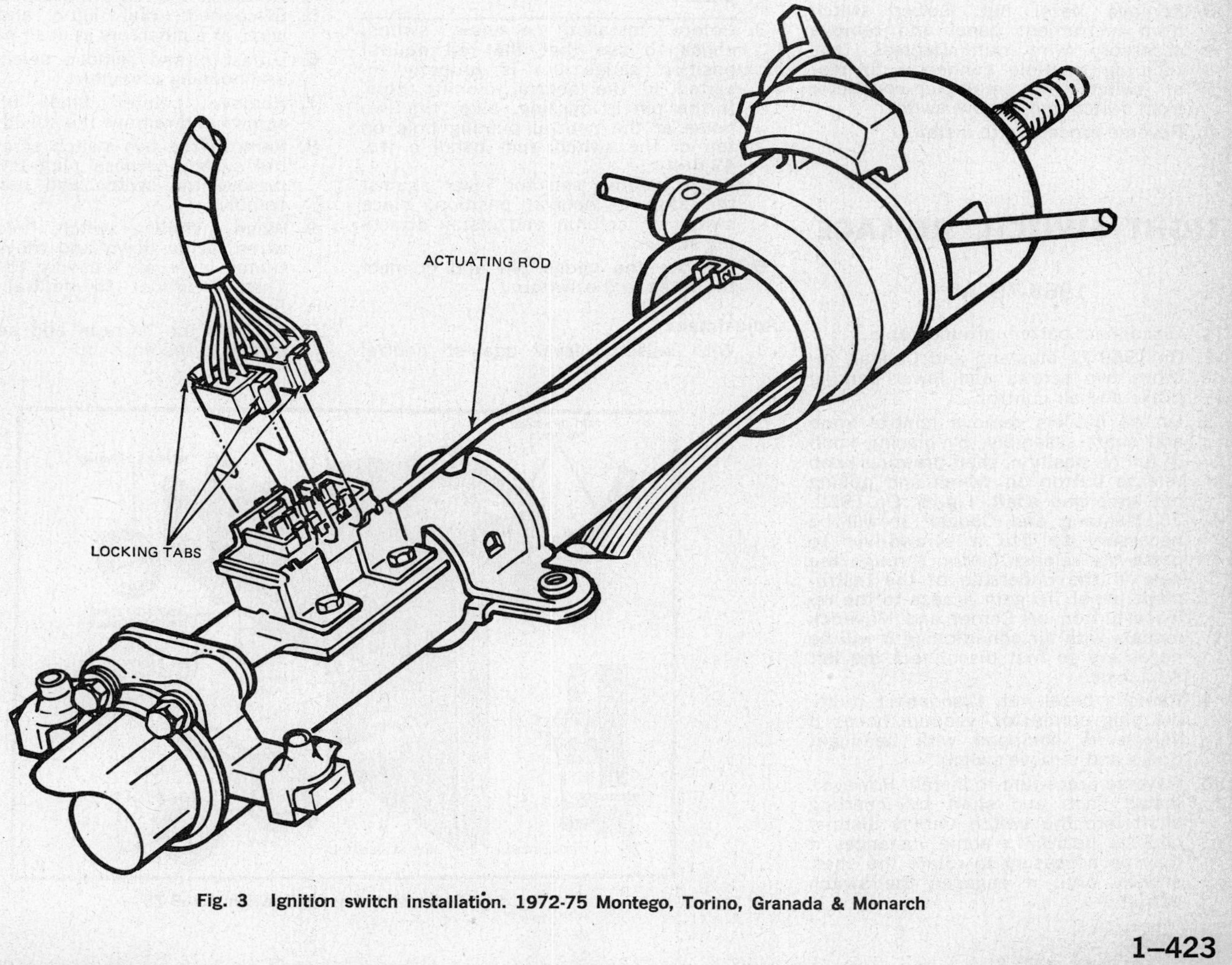

Fig. 3 Ignition switch installation. 1972-75 Montego, Torino, Granada & Monarch

RELEASE–PIN HOLE

Fig. 4   Ignition switch removal. 1969 All & Early 1970 Maverick

2. Insert key and turn switch to accessory position. Insert a wire pin in hole in switch, Fig. 4. Slightly depress pin while turning key counterclockwise past the accessory position. This will release lock cylinder. Pull out lock cylinder with key.
3. Remove bezel nut. Lower switch from instrument panel and remove accessory wire nut. Depress tabs securing multiple connector to rear of switch. Pull multiple connector from switch and remove switch.
4. Reverse procedure to install.

LIGHT SWITCH, REPLACE

1969-75 All

1. Disconnect battery ground cable.
2. On 1969-71 Mustang and Cougar, remove two screws and lower parking brake and air control.
3. On all models remove control knob and shaft assembly, by placing knob in full on position, then pressing knob release button on switch and pulling out knob and shaft, Fig. 5. On 1972-73 Mustang and Cougar, it will be necessary to use a screwdriver to press the release button through the hole in the underside of the instrument panel. To gain access to the release button on Comet and Maverick models with air conditioning it will be necessary to first disconnect the left A/C duct.
4. Remove bezel nut. Disconnect multiple plug connector, vacuum hoses if vehicle is equipped with headlight doors and remove switch.
5. Reverse procedure to install. However, install knob and shaft by inserting shaft into the switch until a distinct click is heard. In some instances it may be necessary to rotate the shaft slightly until it engages the switch carrier.

STOP LIGHT SWITCH, REPLACE

1969-75 Mechanical Type

1. Disconnect wires at connector.
2. Remove hairpin retainer and slide stop light switch, push rod, nylon washers and bushings away from brake pedal, and remove switch, Fig. 6.
3. Reverse above procedure to install.

NEUTRAL SAFETY SWITCH, REPLACE
Column Shift 1969 & Early 1970 Maverick

Removal

1. Disconnect the switch wires at plug connector.
2. Remove two screws securing switch to column and lift switch from column.

NOTE: Check the switch actuator to be sure it is secure to the shift tube and seated as far forward against shift tube bearing as possible. If the actuator is broken or damaged, replace it.

3. Before installing a new switch, check to see that the red neutral position gauge pin is properly inserted in the neutral pinning hole. If the pin is missing, align the two holes at the neutral pinning hole on top of the switch and install a No. 43 drill.
4. While holding selector lever against the stop in neutral position, place switch on column and install attaching screws.
5. Remove the gauge pin and connect the wires to the switch.

Adjustment

1. With selector lever against neutral

KNOB RELEASE BUTTON

Fig. 5   Light switches. Typical

stop, loosen two switch retaining screws.
2. Rotate switch until a start is obtained and tighten switch screws.
3. Place selector lever in "1" position and push the park reset button, located on right side of switch, to the left until it stops.

1969-73 Mustang, 1969-75 Cougar, 1972-75 Montego & Torino Console

Removal & Adjustment

1. Place selector lever in neutral.
2. Raise car and remove manual lever control rod attaching nut.
3. Lower car and remove selector lever handle.
4. Unfasten and remove dial housing.
5. Disconnect dial light and switch wires at connectors at dash panel.
6. Unfasten and remove selector lever and housing assembly.
7. Remove pointer back up shield screws and remove the shield.
8. Remove the two switch screws, push the switch harness plug inward and remove the switch and harness assembly.
9. When installing switch, hold it with wires facing down and move the actuator lever all the way to the left. Then return it to neutral positon, Fig. 7.
10. Position the harness and secure the switch to the housing.

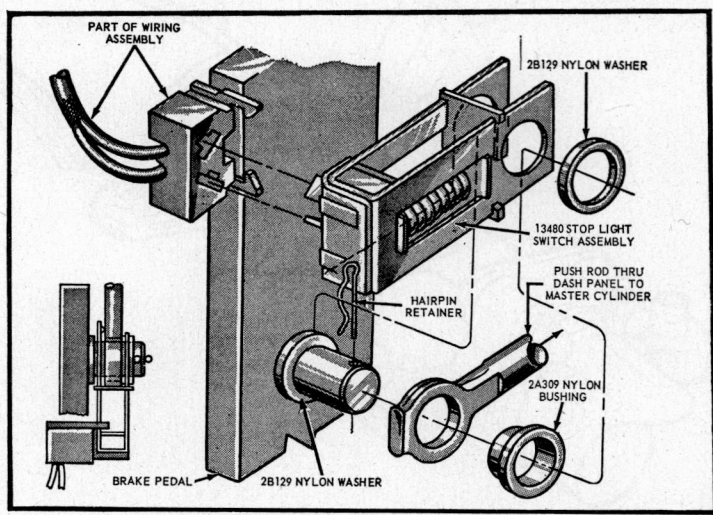

PART OF WIRING ASSEMBLY

2B129 NYLON WASHER

13480 STOP LIGHT SWITCH ASSEMBLY

PUSH ROD THRU DASH PANEL TO MASTER CYLINDER

HAIRPIN RETAINER

2A309 NYLON BUSHING

BRAKE PEDAL

2B129 NYLON WASHER

Fig. 6   Mechanical stop light switch. 1969-75

11. Install pointer back up shield.
12. Position selector lever and housing assembly on console and fasten.
13. Connect dial light and switch wires.
14. Install dial housing and selector lever handle.
15. Raise car and attach manual lever control rod.
16. Lower car and check operation of switch in Park position.

1969-70 Montego, Comet, Fairlane & 1970-71 Montego & Torino

Console Shift, Fig. 8

1. Remove handle from selector lever.
2. Remove trim panel from top of console.
3. Remove cover and dial indicator as a unit.
4. Unfasten and remove selector lever retainer from housing (6 screws).
5. Unfasten switch from lever housing (2 screws). Disconnect wires at plug connector and remove switch.
6. With selector lever in neutral, move lever back and forth until gauge pin (#43 drill) can be fully inserted in gauge pin holes, Fig. 8.
7. Place transmission selector lever firmly against stop of neutral detent position.
8. Slide combination neutral start and back-up light switch forward or rearward as required until switch actuating lever contacts selector lever.
9. Tighten switch screws and remove gauge pin.
10. Complete installation in reverse order of removal.

1971-75 Maverick, Comet

Transmission Mounted Switch, Fig. 9

1. Remove downshift linkage rod from transmission downshift lever.
2. Apply penetrating oil to downshift lever shaft and nut; then remove downshift outer lever.
3. Remove switch attaching bolts.
4. Disconnect multiple wire connector and remove switch from transmission.
5. Install new switch.
6. With transmission manual lever in neutral, rotate switch and install gauge pin (#43 drill) into gauge pin holes.
7. Tighten switch attaching bolts and remove gauge pin.
8. Complete the installation in reverse order of removal.

TURN SIGNAL SWITCH, REPLACE

1971-75

1. Remove retaining screw from underside of steering wheel spokes and lift off pad horn switch/trim cover and medallion as an assembly.
2. Disconnect horn switch wires from terminals.
3. Remove steering wheel retaining nut and remove steering wheel with suitable puller.
4. Remove turn signal switch lever by unscrewing it from steering column.
5. Remove shroud from under steering column.
6. Disconnect steering column wiring connector plugs and remove screws that secure switch to column.
7. On tilt column, remove wires and terminals from column plug. *NOTE: Record color code and position of wires before removing. A hole provided in the flange casting on fixed columns makes it unnecessary to*

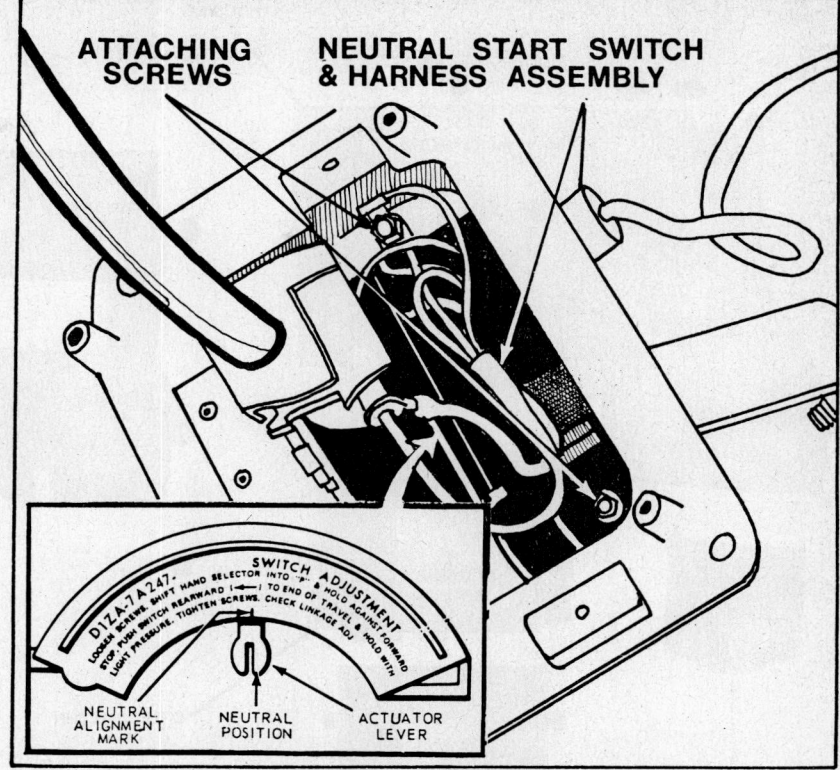

Fig. 7 Neutral switch. 1969-73 Mustang, 1969-75 Cougar, 1972-75 Montego & Torino with console

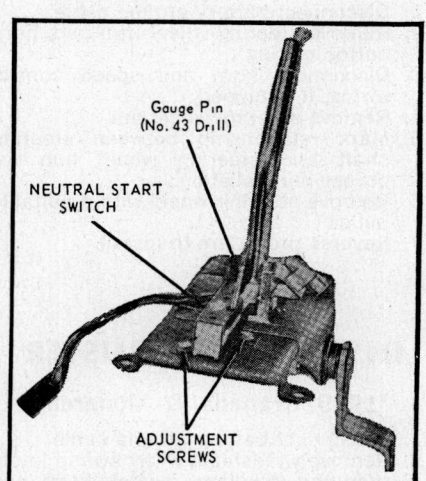

Fig. 8 Neutral safety switch (console shift). 1969-71 Comet, Fairlane and Montego

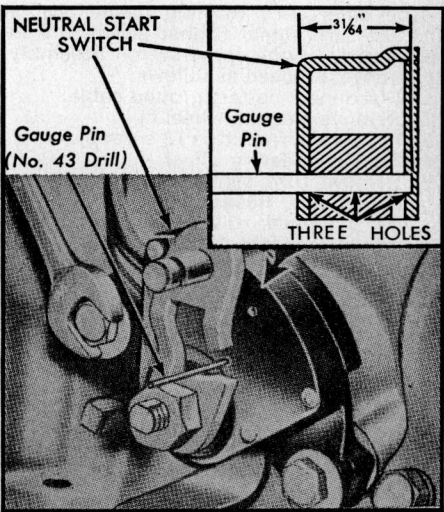

Fig. 9 Neutral safety switch. 1971-75 Maverick, Comet

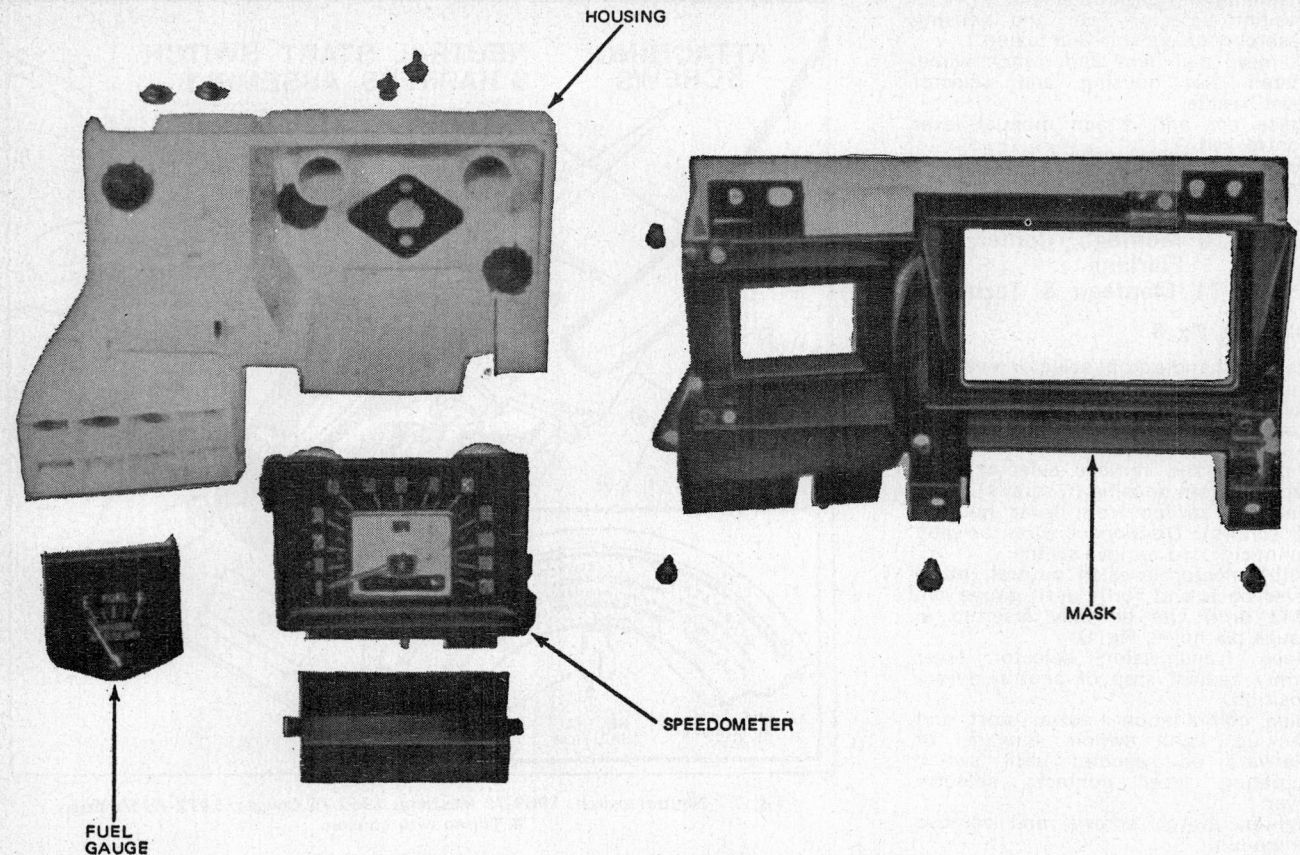

Fig. 10   Instrument cluster. 1975 Granada & Monarch

separate wires from plug as the plug with wires can be guided through hole.

8. Remove plastic cover sleeve from wiring harness and remove switch from top of column.

1969-70

The emergency warning flasher switch and the turn signal flasher switch are integral parts of the same switch assembly. To remove, proceed as follows:

1. Disconnect battery ground cable.
2. Remove steering wheel hub.
3. Remove horn button (3 screws).
4. Remove steering wheel.
5. Remove turn signal switch lever and emergency flasher control knob. If so equipped, disconnect set speed switch wiring connector.
6. Remove steering column upper collar (2 screws).
7. Disconnect turn signal switch wiring multiple connector near bottom of steering column. It may be necessary to lower hand brake control and left air vent control on some Mustang and Cougar models to provide access to turn signal wiring connector.
8. Remove wires and terminals from connector blocks. This can be done by depressing the tab on the wire terminal with an awl or with an empty ball point pen refill cartridge, then pull wire and terminal from connector block. Record color code and

location of each wire before removing it from connector block.

9. Tape wires together and attach a piece of heavy cord to the wires to help pull them through steering column during installation.
10. Remove plastic cover from over wires.
11. Push lower steering column collar down. Remove wiring retainer clip.
12. Remove switch from steering column (2 screws) and pull switch and wiring out of column.
13. Reverse procedure to install.

HORN SOUNDER

The horn button or ring used on some models may be removed by twisting the button or ring counter-clockwise. The horn switch on some models is part of the trim cover assembly and if defective, the trim cover must be replaced. The horn sounder on 1970-75 rim-blow steering wheels equipped with speed control cannot be replaced and if defective, the steering wheel assembly must be replaced. On 1972-75 rim-blow steering wheels without speed control, the horn sounder (plastic strip and copper insert) may be replaced using the following procedure:

1. Remove trim pad and disconnect lead wires.
2. Remove plastic cover and lift out horn

insert on inner diameter of steering wheel.

3. Reverse procedure to install.

STEERING WHEEL

1. Disconnect battery ground cable.
2. Remove steering wheel trim pad, horn button or ring.
3. Disconnect horn and speed control wiring, if equipped.
4. Remove steering wheel nut.
5. Mark relationship between steering shaft and steering wheel hub for proper reinstallation.
6. Remove steering wheel with a suitable puller.
7. Reverse procedure to install.

INSTRUMENT CLUSTER

1975 Granada & Monarch

1. Disconnect battery ground cable.
2. Remove windshield wiper switch knob, then the headlamp switch knob and shaft assembly and bezel.
3. Remove front and lower cluster cover screws, then the steering column shroud, Fig. 10.

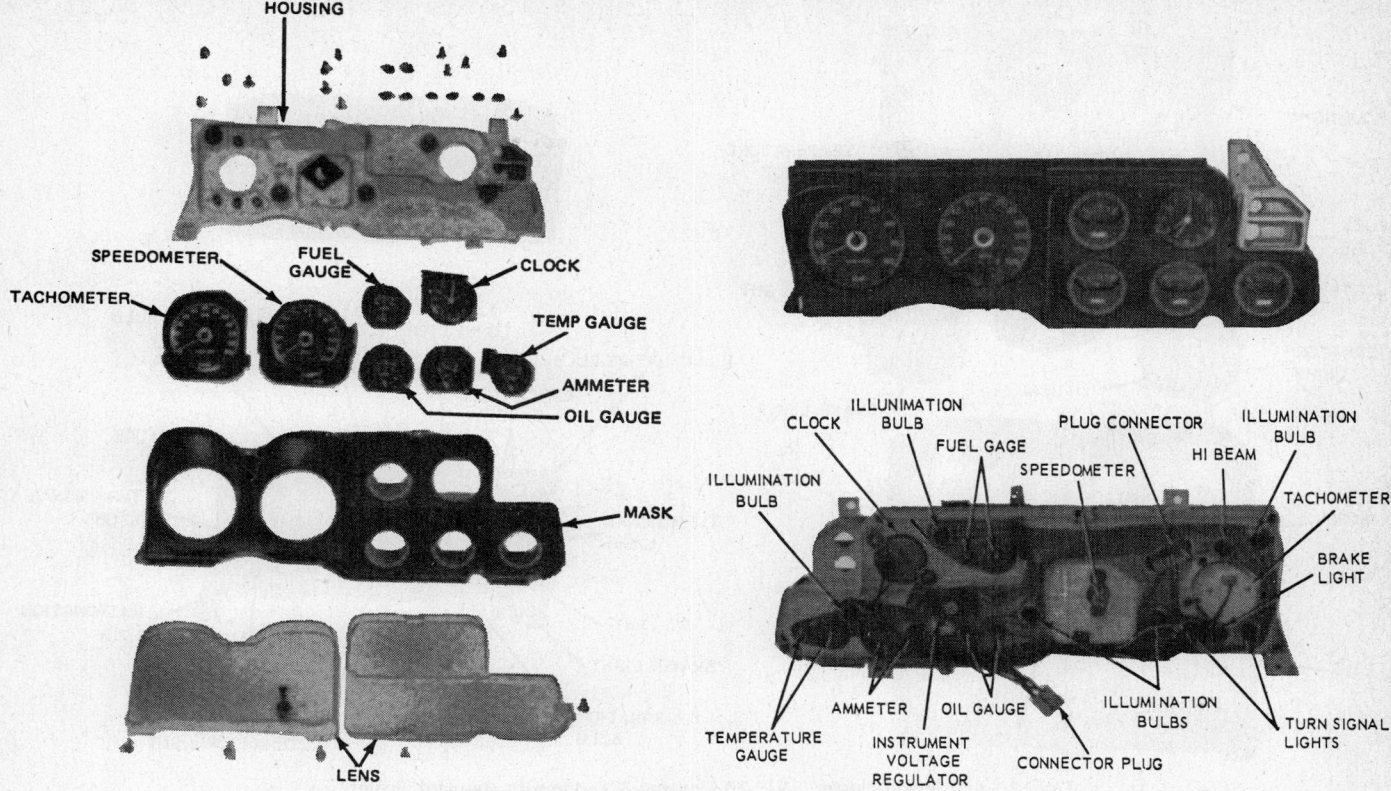

Fig. 11   Instrument cluster. 1974-75 Cougar; 1972-75 Montego & Torino with performance cluster

4. Using a right angle screwdriver, pry along edges of finish panel, thereby removing stud from retainers, and remove finish panel.
5. Disconnect automatic transmission indicator cable and speedo cable.
6. Remove cluster to instrument panel screws, pull cluster out and disconnect feeder plug from printed circuit, then remove cluster.

1974-75 Cougar XR7

1. Disconnect battery ground cable.
2. Remove upper and lower retaining screws from cluster trim cover and remove the cover, Fig. 11.
3. Remove two upper and two lower screws retaining cluster to the panel.
4. Pull cluster away from panel and disconnect speedo cable.
5. Disconnect cluster feed plug from receptable in printed circuit.
6. Remove PARK light socket from receptable (if so equipped).
7. Disconnect overlay harness connector and remove cluster.

1972-75 Torino & Montego

Standard Cluster

1. Disconnect battery ground cable.
2. Remove upper and lower retaining screws from instrument cluster trim cover and remove the cover, Fig. 12.
3. Remove upper and two lower screws retaining instrument cluster to panel.

4. Pull cluster away from panel and disconnect speedo cable.
5. Disconnect cluster feed plug from printed circuit.
6. Remove "Belts and Park" light sockets from receptacles, if so equipped.
7. Remove cluster.

Performance Cluster

1. Disconnect battery ground cable.
2. Remove upper and lower retaining screws from cluster trim cover and remove the cover, Fig. 11.
3. Remove two upper and two lower screws retaining cluster to the panel.
4. Pull cluster away from panel and disconnect speedo cable.
5. Disconnect cluster feed plug from receptacle in printed circuit.
6. Disconnect clock and tachometer wire loom at connector.
7. Remove cluster.

1972-73 Cougar XR7

1. Disconnect battery ground cable.
2. Remove instrument panel pad, radio bezel retaining screws and the heater-A/C control screws.
3. Disconnect the cluster front cover.
4. Remove oil pressure and ammeter connectors.
5. Disconnect map light and the two bulb sockets from auxiliary gauge assembly.
6. Remove cluster front cover and disconnect speedometer cable.
7. Remove cluster to instrument panel

screws.
8. Disconnect cluster feed plug from the printed circuit.
9. Disconnect tachometer and remove cluster.

1971-73 Mustang

1. Disconnect battery ground cable.
2. Remove instrument panel end finish panel and the cluster opening finish panel.
3. Remove four cluster attaching screws and pull cluster away from instrument panel.
4. Disconnect speedometer cable and wiring.

1971-73 Cougar

1. Disconnect battery ground cable.
2. Remove instrument panel pad.
3. Remove four screws attaching cluster to instrument panel, Fig. 13.
4. Disconnect speedometer cable and wiring and remove cluster.

1969-70 Mustang & Cougar

1. Disconnect battery ground cable.
2. Remove instrument panel pad for access to cluster mounting screws.
3. Remove six screws retaining cluster to panel and withdraw cluster slightly.

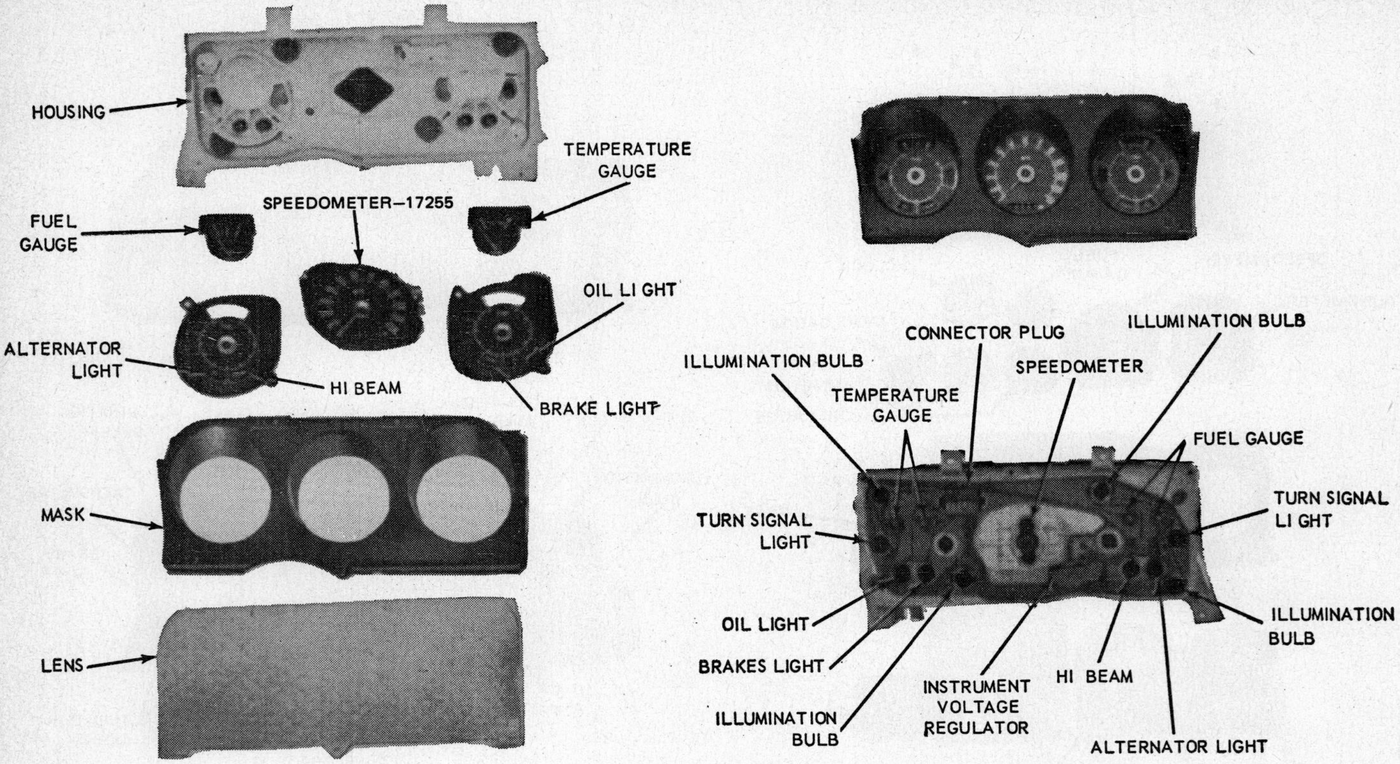

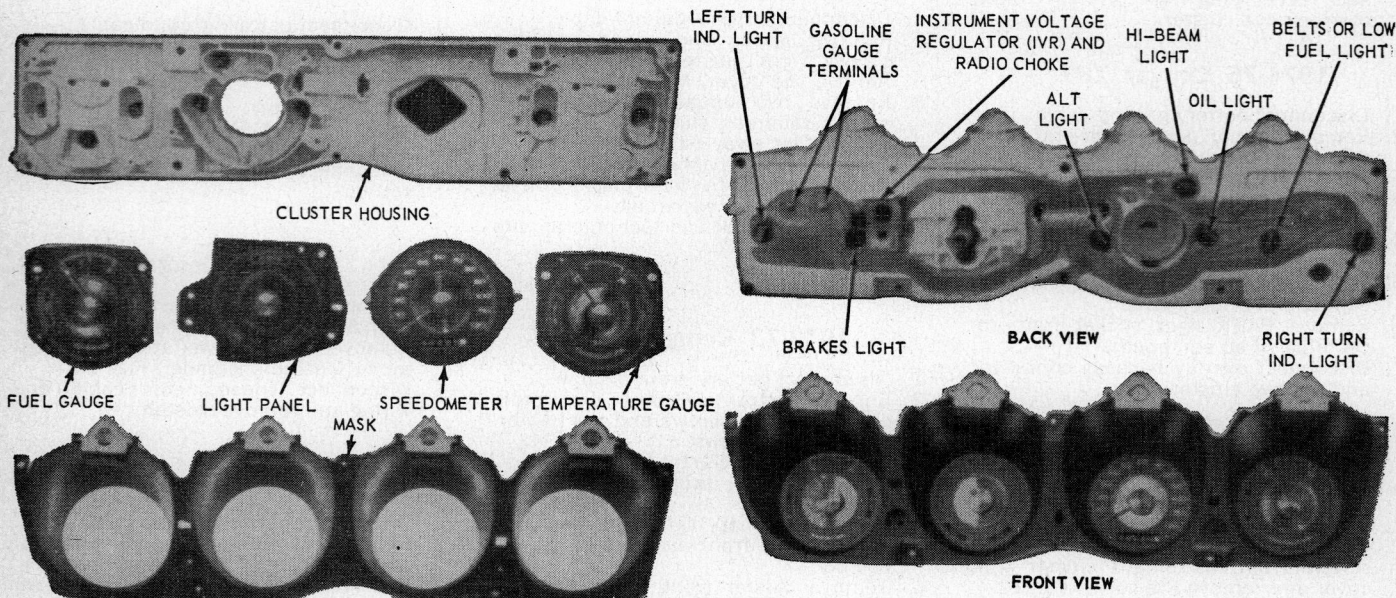

Fig. 12   Instrument cluster. 1972-75 Montego & Torino with standard cluster

4. Disconnect plug to printed circuit and tachometer if so equipped.
5. Disconnect speedometer cable by pressing on knurled surface of plastic connector and pulling cable away from head.
6. The cluster can now be removed from the panel.
7. Reverse the foregoing to install.

1969-71 Fairlane/Torino Late 1970 Falcon

1. Disconnect battery ground cable.

Fig. 13   Instrument cluster. 1971-73 Cougar (Typical)

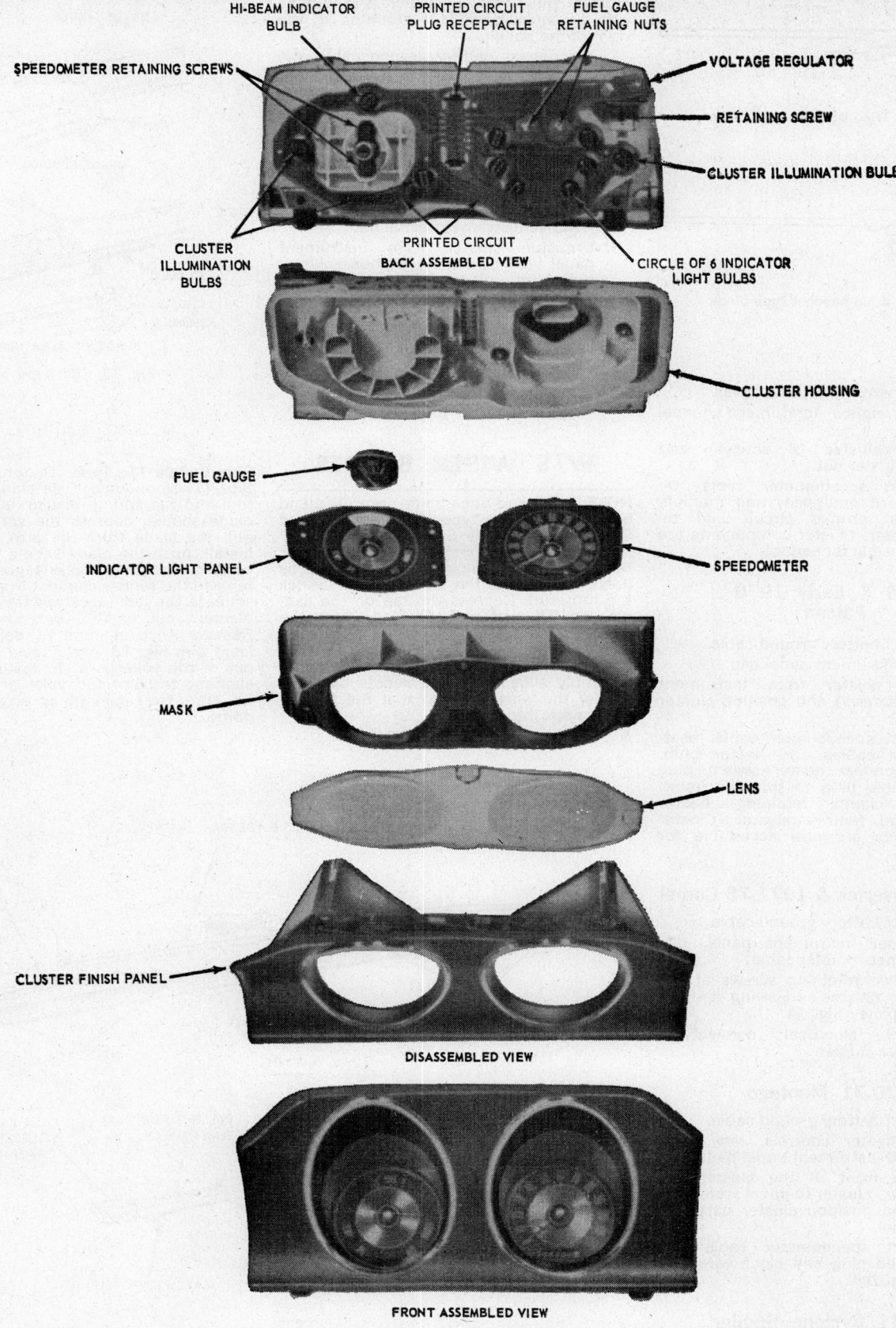

HI-BEAM INDICATOR BULB

PRINTED CIRCUIT PLUG RECEPTACLE

FUEL GAUGE RETAINING NUTS

SPEEDOMETER RETAINING SCREWS

VOLTAGE REGULATOR

RETAINING SCREW

CLUSTER ILLUMINATION BULB

CLUSTER ILLUMINATION BULBS

PRINTED CIRCUIT
BACK ASSEMBLED VIEW

CIRCLE OF 6 INDICATOR LIGHT BULBS

CLUSTER HOUSING

FUEL GAUGE

INDICATOR LIGHT PANEL

SPEEDOMETER

MASK

LENS

CLUSTER FINISH PANEL

DISASSEMBLED VIEW

FRONT ASSEMBLED VIEW

Fig. 14   Instrument cluster. 1971-75 Comet & Maverick

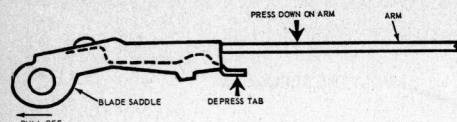

Fig. 15   Trico bayonet type blade

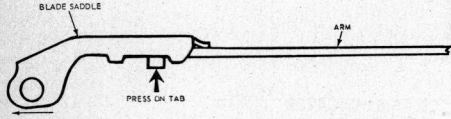

Fig. 16   Anco bayonet type blade

2. Remove instrument panel cover.
3. Remove right instrument panel shield.
4. Unfasten cluster (5 screws) and position cluster out.
5. Disconnect speedometer cable, tachometer (if equipped) and multiple plug from printed circuit and remove cluster. Cluster components are now accessible for service.

1969 & Early 1970 Falcon

1. Disconnect battery ground cable.
2. Remove instrument panel pad.
3. Unfasten cluster from instrument panel (5 screws) and position cluster out.
4. Disconnect speedometer cable, heater control cables and heater bulb. Also disconnect heater switch plug and multiple plug to printed circuit. Remove clamp retaining heater cables and remove cluster. Cluster components are now accessible for service.

1970-75 Maverick & 1971-75 Comet

1. Disconnect battery ground cable.
2. From under instrument panel, disconnect speedometer cable.
3. Remove two retaining screws at the top of the cluster and swing it down from the panel, Fig. 14.
4. Disconnect electrical connections and remove cluster.

1970-71 Montego

1. Disconnect battery ground cable.
2. Remove heater controls, left finish panels and instrument panel pad.
3. From the front of the cluster, remove four cluster-to-panel retaining screws and position cluster part way out of panel.
4. Disconnect speedometer cable and cluster feed plug and clock wire and remove cluster.

1970-71 Cyclone Spoiler

In addition to the main instrument cluster, the Cyclone Spoiler is equipped with an auxiliary cluster mounted to the right of the panel.

1. Disconnect battery ground cable and remove panel pad.
2. From the inner side of the pad assembly, remove cluster-to-pad retaining nuts and remove cluster.

1969 Comet & Montego

1. Disconnect battery ground cable.
2. Remove instrument panel pad.
3. Unfasten cluster from instrument panel (8 screws). Position cluster out and disconnect speedometer cable. Also disconnect multiple plug to cluster, multiple plug to convenience control lights (if equipped), heater control cables and switch.
4. Disconnect clock (if equipped) and remove cluster. Cluster components are now accessible for service.

W/S WIPER BLADES

NOTE: Trico and Anco blades are used and both come in two types Bayonet type and Side Saddle Pin type.

Bayonet Type: Remove the Trico type by pressing down on the arm, this will unlock the top stud. Depress the tab on the saddle, Fig. 15, and pull the blade from the arm. To remove the Anco type press inward on the tab, Fig. 16, and pull the blade from the arm. To install a new blade assembly slide the blade saddle over the end of the wiper arm so that the locking stud snaps into place.

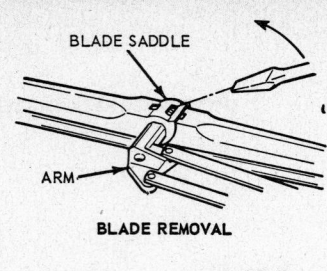

BLADE REMOVAL

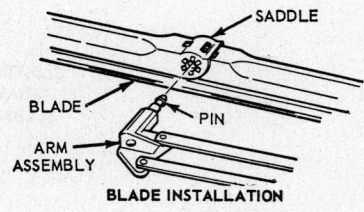

BLADE INSTALLATION

Fig. 17   Pin type blade

Side Saddle Pin Type: To remove the pin type (Trico or Anco) insert an appropriate tool into the spring release opening of the blade saddle, depress the spring clip and pull the blade from the arm, Fig. 17. To install, push the blade saddle onto the pin so that the spring clip engages the pin. To replace the rubber element in a *Trico* blade squeeze the latch lock release and pull the element out of the lever jaws, Fig. 18. Remove *Anco* element by depressing the latch pin, Fig. 18, and sliding the element out of the yoke jaws. To install insert the element through the yoke or lever jaws. Be sure the element is engaged at all points.

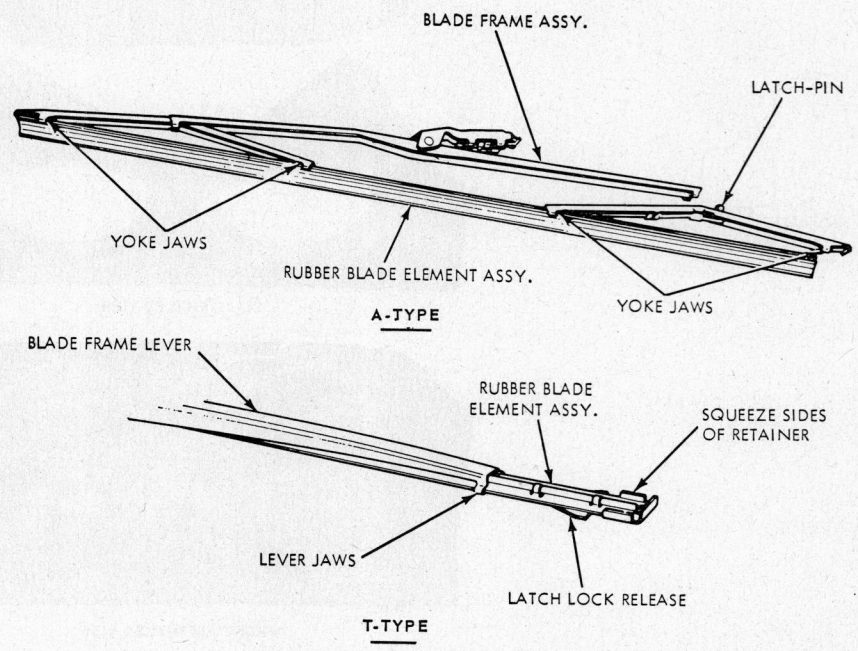

Fig. 18   Wiper blade element

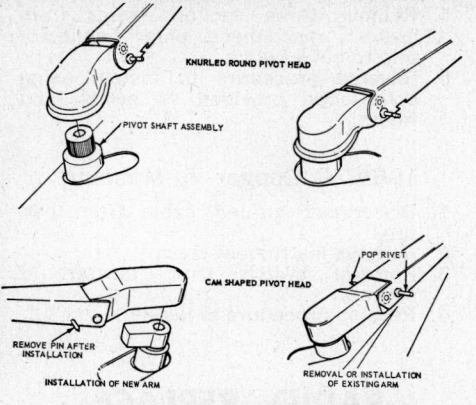

Fig. 19   Wiper arm (Exc. 1972-75 Montego, Torino & 1974-75 Cougar)

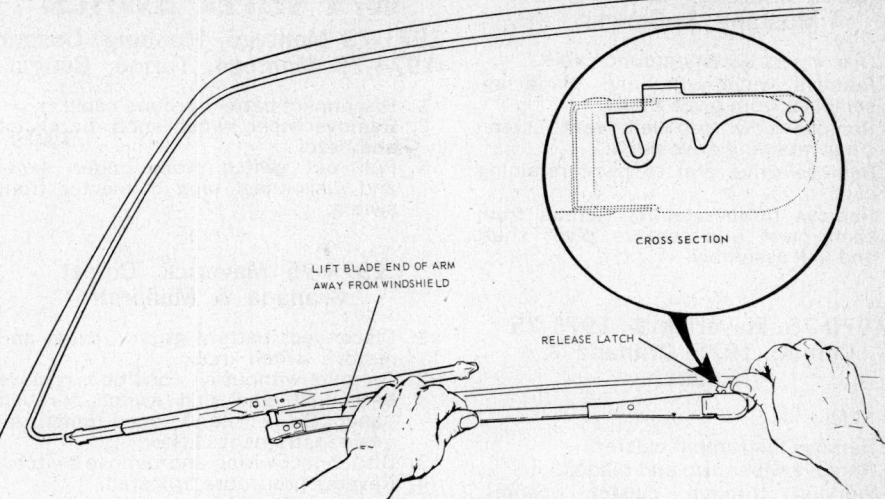

Fig. 20   Wiper arm. 1972-75 Montego, Torino & 1974-75 Cougar

W/S WIPER ARMS

1970-71 Fairlane, Torino, Montego; 1971-73 Cougar; 1972-73 Mustang

Swing the arm and blade assembly away from the windshield and insert a 3/32" pin through the pin hole as shown in Fig. 19. Swinging the assembly away from the windshield will release the spring loaded attaching clip in the arm from the pivot shaft. Inserting the pin will hold it in the released position. The arm can now be pulled off the pivot shaft. *Do not pry* off with a screwdriver. Leave the pin in the arm until after installation. A new replacement arm comes with a pin already installed to hold it in released position. Make sure the pivot shaft is in parked position when installing new assembly. Push the arm onto the pivot shaft. Lock the arm to the pivot shaft by removing the pin.

1970 Falcon, Cougar, Mustang; 1970-75 Comet, Maverick, Granada & Monarch

NOTE: These models do not have a pin and hole arrangement to hold the attaching clip in the released position.

To remove, swing the arm and blade assembly away from the windshield to release the spring loaded attaching clip in the arm from the pivot. Hold in this position and pull the arm off the pivot shaft. To install, hold the arm and blade assembly in the swing out position and push the arm on to the pivot shaft. The arm will lock to the pivot when it is moved back against the windshield.

1972-75 Montego, Torino & 1974-75 Cougar

Raise the blade end of the arm off of the windshield and move the slide latch, Fig. 20, away from the pivot shaft. This action will unlock the wiper arm from the pivot shaft and hold the blade end of the arm off the glass at the same time. The wiper arm can now be pulled off of the pivot shaft without the aid of any tools.

W/S WIPER MOTOR

1972-75 Torino, Montego & 1974-75 Cougar

Procedure for removal is the same as for 1971 Ford & Mercury Full Size Models and can be found in that car chapter.

1971 Montego & 1971-73 Mustang & Cougar

1. Disconnect battery ground cable.
2. Disconnect wiper motor wiring connector.
3. Remove cowl top left vent screen.
4. Remove wiper link retaining clip from wiper motor arm.
5. Remove three motor retaining bolts and remove wiper and bracket.

1970-75 Maverick & 1971-75 Comet

1. Remove instrument cluster.
2. On air conditioned units, remove center connector and duct assembly.
3. Working through cluster opening, disconnect two pivot shaft links from motor drive arm by removing retaining clip.
4. Disconnect wiring and remove mounting bolts and remove motor through cluster opening.

1969-70 Cougar & Mustang

1. Remove wiper arm and blades.
2. Disconnect washer hose at "T" fitting (left side) on the cowl grille.
3. Remove cowl top grille.
4. Disconnect motor ground wire at forward edge of plenum chamber.

5. Disconnect motor harness at plug and push it back into plenum chamber.
6. Disconnect linkage drive arm from motor output arm crankpin by removing clip.
7. Remove three bolts that retain motor to bracket and rotate motor output arm 180° and remove the motor.

NOTE: Before installing motor, rotate arm 180° and before connecting linkage to motor, turn on ignition to ACC position to allow motor to go into park position.

1969-70 Montego, Comet, Fairlane, Falcon & 1970-71 Torino

1. Disconnect wiper motor wiring connector.
2. Remove wiper arms and blades.
3. Remove cowl top grille panel.
4. Remove wiper link clip from motor arm.
5. Unfasten and remove wiper motor and mounting bracket (4 bolts).
6. Reverse procedure to install.

W/S WIPER TRANSMISSION

1972-75 Torino, Montego & 1974-75 Cougar

1. Disconnect battery ground cable.
2. Remove wiper arm and blade assemblies.
3. Remove cowl screen. Screen snaps into cowl and the arm stop is integral with the screen.
4. Disconnect linkage drive arm from motor by removing retaining clip.
5. Remove pivot shaft retaining bolts and remove linkage and pivot shaft assemblies.

1971 Montego & 1971-73 Mustang & Cougar

1. Disconnect battery ground cable.
2. Remove wiper arm and blade assemblies from pivot shafts.
3. Remove cowl top left vent screen (four retaining drive pins).
4. Remove drive arm to pivot retaining clip.
5. Remove three retaining screws from each pivot and remove pivot shaft and link assembly.

1970-75 Maverick & 1971-75 Comet, 1975 Granada & Monarch

Left Side:

1. Remove instrument cluster.
2. Remove wiper arm and blade.
3. Working through cluster opening, disconnect both pivot shaft links from motor drive arm by removing retaining clip.
4. Remove three pivot shaft assembly retaining bolts and remove assembly through cluster opening.

Right Side:

1. Disconnect battery ground cable and remove wiper blade and arm.
2. On air conditioned units, remove right duct assembly.
3. From under the instrument panel, disconnect first left then right pivot shaft link from motor drive arm.
4. Reaching between utility shelf and instrument panel, remove pivot shaft retaining bolts and lower assembly out from under panel.

1969-70 Cougar & Mustang

1. Remove arm and blade assemblies from pivot shafts.
2. Disconnect washer hose at "T" fitting on cowl grille.
3. Remove cowl top grille.
4. Disconnect linkage drive arm from motor output arm crankpin by removing clip.
5. Disconnect right link from right arm and pivot shaft and remove the arm and pivot shaft assembly.
6. Unfasten and remove the left arm and pivot shaft and lift out to the right: the pivot shaft and arm, left link and linkage drive arm as one assembly.

NOTE: When installing the linkage, install the left pivot shaft and linkage first.

1969-70 Montego, Comet, Fairlane, Falcon & 1970-71 Torino

1. Remove wiper arms and blades.
2. Remove cowl top grille panel.
3. Remove drive arm to pivot clip and remove pivot shaft and link assembly.
4. Reverse procedure to install.

W/S WIPER SWITCH

1971-73 Montego, Mustang, Cougar 1974-75 Montego, Torino, Cougar

1. Disconnect battery ground cable.
2. Remove wiper switch knob, bezel nut and bezel.
3. Pull out switch from under panel and disconnect plug connector from switch.

1974-75 Maverick, Comet, Granada & Monarch

1. Disconnect battery ground cable and remove switch knob.
2. On units without air condition, remove bezel nut and pull switch through panel. On air conditioned units, remove instrument cluster.
3. Disconnect wiring and remove switch.
4. Reverse procedure to install.

1970-73 Maverick & 1971-73 Comet

1. On air conditioned units, remove left AC duct.
2. Release control knob retaining spring by pressing in through slot in knob and pull knob from shaft.
3. Remove switch retaining nut and lower switch from under instrument panel.
4. Disconnect switch wiring and remove switch.

1969-73 Fairlane & Torino Late 1970 Falcon

1. Disconnect battery ground cable.
2. Remove switch control knob and bezel nut.
3. Unplug and remove switch.
4. Reverse procedure to install.

1969 & Early 1970 Falcon

1. Disconnect ground cable from battery.
2. Remove switch knobs and unplug connectors at switch.
3. Unfasten (2 screws) and remove switch from under instrument panel.
4. Separate washer switch from wiper switch (2 screws).
5. Reverse procedure to install.

1969-70 Montego, Comet

Standard Wiper

1. Disconnect battery ground cable.
2. Remove switch knob, nut and bezel.
3. Pull switch out from instrument panel.
4. Disconnect plug connector from switch and remove switch.
5. Reverse procedure to install.

Intermittent Wipers

1. Disconnect ground cable from battery.
2. Remove set screws and remove control knob.
3. Remove bezel nut and bezel.
4. Lower switch assembly.

5. Remove three vacuum hoses from switch, disconnect plug connector and remove switch.
6. Reverse procedure to install, using color code provided on switch and hoses.

1969-70 Cougar & Mustang

1. Disconnect ground cable from battery.
2. Remove instrument cluster.
3. Remove switch from cluster (2 screws).
4. Reverse procedure to install.

RADIO, REPLACE

NOTE: When installing radio, be sure to adjust antenna trimmer for peak performance.

1975 Granada & Monarch

1. Disconnect battery ground cable.
2. Remove headlamp switch.
3. Remove knobs from heater and A/C control, windshield wiper switch and radio.
4. Remove instrument panel applique.
5. Disconnect antenna lead.
6. Remove radio bezel to instrument panel screws, then pull radio and bezel out to disconnect remaining electrical leads and remove radio from panel.
7. Remove rear support bracket and bezel from radio.
8. Reverse procedure to install.

1974 Comet & Maverick

1. Disconnect battery ground cable.
2. Remove radio knobs, discs, control shaft nuts and washers.
3. Remove radio rear support attaching nut.
4. Remove radio from bezel and from rear support.
5. Reverse procedure to install.

1969-73 Cougar, Mustang, Maverick & 1971-73 Comet

1. Disconnect battery ground cable.
2. Pull control knobs, discs and sleeve from radio shafts.
3. Remove radio applique panel from dash.
4. Remove right and left finish panels.
5. Remove two mounting plate attaching screws.
6. Pull radio out of panel and disconnect wires.
7. Remove mounting plate and rear support from radio.
8. Reverse procedure to install.

1969-73 Fairlane, Falcon, Montego 1974 Montego, Torino, Cougar

1. Disconnect battery ground cable.
2. Pull off radio control knobs.
3. Remove radio support to instrument panel attaching screw.
4. Remove bezel nuts from radio control shafts, then lower radio and disconnect speaker, power and an-

tenna wire from radio.
5. Reverse procedure to install.

HEATER CORE REMOVAL

1975 Granada & Monarch

Less Air Conditioning

1. Drain cooling system and disconnect heater hoses from heater core.
2. Remove glove box and the right and floor air distribution ducts.
3. Disconnect heater control cables and wiring harness from blower motor.
4. Remove push nut securing defroster duct to heater case and one nut securing the vent duct to upper cowling.
5. Remove heater case to dash panel nuts, then the heater case and vent duct assembly.
6. Remove core cover and seal, then slide core from case, Fig. 21.

With Air Conditioning

1. Disconnect battery ground cable and drain coolant system, then disconnect heater hoses from core at engine side of dash panel.

   NOTE: Easier access may be obtained by first disconnecting suction hose and moving it out of the way.

2. Remove heat distribution duct from instrument panel, seat belt interlock module and glove box liner, then loosen right door sill scuff plate and remove right cowl side from trim panel.
3. Loosen instrument panel to right cowl side bolt and remove instrument panel brace bolt at lower rail under glove box.
4. Remove defroster nozzle by removing instrument panel crash pad, removing radio speaker or radio cowl panel brace, removing four nozzle to cowl bracket screws and lifting defroster nozzle upward through crash panel, Fig. 22.
5. Disconnect vacuum hoses from A/C-Defrost and A/C-Heat door motors and remove vacuum harness to plenum clip screw, then remove the two A/C-Heat mounting nuts and swing door rearward on crankarm.
6. Remove two plenum to left mounting bracket screws and remove the two screws and three clips securing plenum to evaporator case.
7. Swing bottom of plenum away from evaporator case and disengage S-clip on forward flange of plenum, then raise plenum to clear tabs on top of evaporator case.
8. Move plenum to left as far as possible (about 4 inches), pulling rearward on instrument panel to gain clearance.

   NOTE: Use extreme care when pulling back on instrument panel to avoid cracking plastic panel. Also, there is very little clearance between plenum and wiper motor assembly.

9. Using tab molded into rear heater core seal, pull heater core to left, then as rear surface of heater core clears evaporator case, pull core rearward and downward to clear instrument panel.

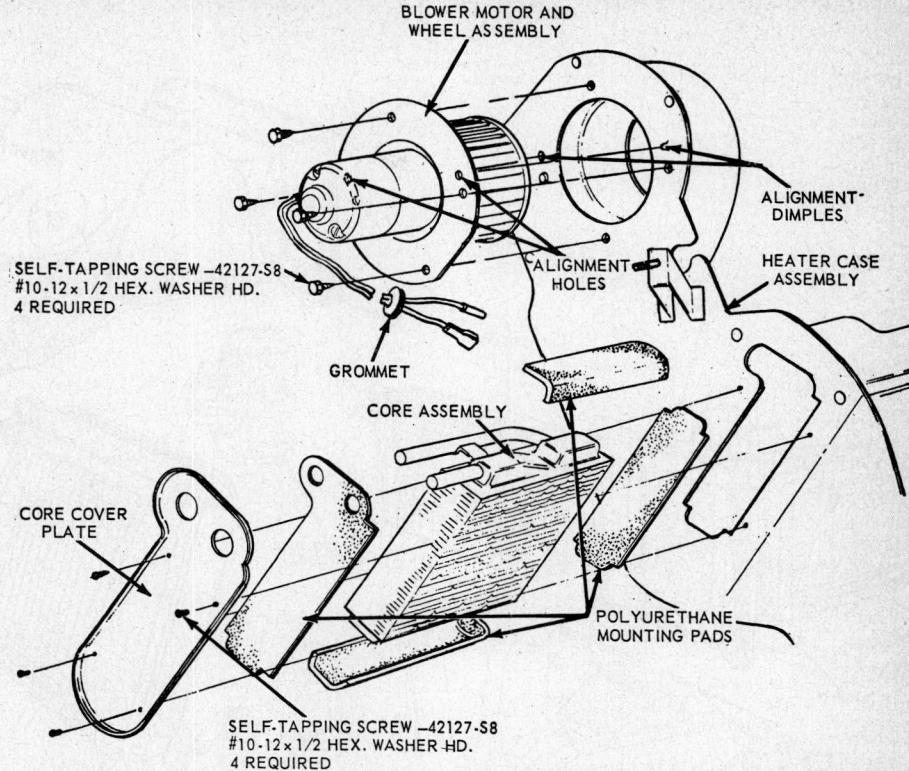

Fig. 21 Heater core & blower motor less air conditioning. 1969-70 Fairlane, Falcon & Maverick; 1969-75 Montego & Torino; 1971-73 Mustang; 1971-75 Cougar; 1975 Granada & Monarch

10. Reverse procedure to install, making certain that heater core tube to dash panel seal is in place between evaporator case and dash panel.

1972-75 Torino, Montego & 1974-5 Cougar

Less Air Conditioning

Removal of the core is done the same as for previous models and is described further on, Fig. 21.

With Air Conditioning

1. Drain engine coolant and disconnect heater hoses from core.
2. Remove glove box.
3. Remove heater air outlet register from plenum assembly (2 snap clips).
4. Remove temperature control cable assembly mounting screw, and disconnect the end of the cable from the blend door crank arm (1 spring nut).
5. Remove the blue and red vacuum hoses from the high-low door vacuum motor; the yellow hose from the panel-defrost door motor, and the brown hose at the inline tee connector to the temperature by-pass door motor.
6. Disconnect wiring connector from resistor.
7. Remove ten screws from around flange of plenum case and remove rear case half of the plenum, Fig. 23.
8. Remove mounting nut from heater core tube support bracket.
9. Remove heater core.

NOTE: During installation of heater core, be sure to apply body sealer around the case flanges to provide a positive seal. Also make sure core mounting gasket is properly installed.

1971-75 Comet & Maverick

Less Air Conditioning

1. Disconnect battery ground cable and drain engine cooling system.
2. Disconnect blower motor ground wire from fender apron at engine side of dash.
3. Disconnect heater hoses at engine block.
4. Remove heater assembly to dash panel mounting nuts.
5. On 1971-73 units, disconnect ignition switch and plate from package tray and remove package tray from instrument panel.
6. On 1974-75 units, remove glove compartment and on all models remove right cowl trim panel.
7. Remove cable retaining clips and the push nuts at door crank arms. Disconnect control cables from crank arms.
8. Remove defroster air duct from left side of heater assembly.
9. Disconnect motor lead from resistor assembly on bottom of heater.
10. Remove heater case to instrument panel support bracket mounting screw.
11. Pull heater hoses through dash panel and disconnect hoses from heater core.
12. Separate halves of heater and remove core, Fig. 24.

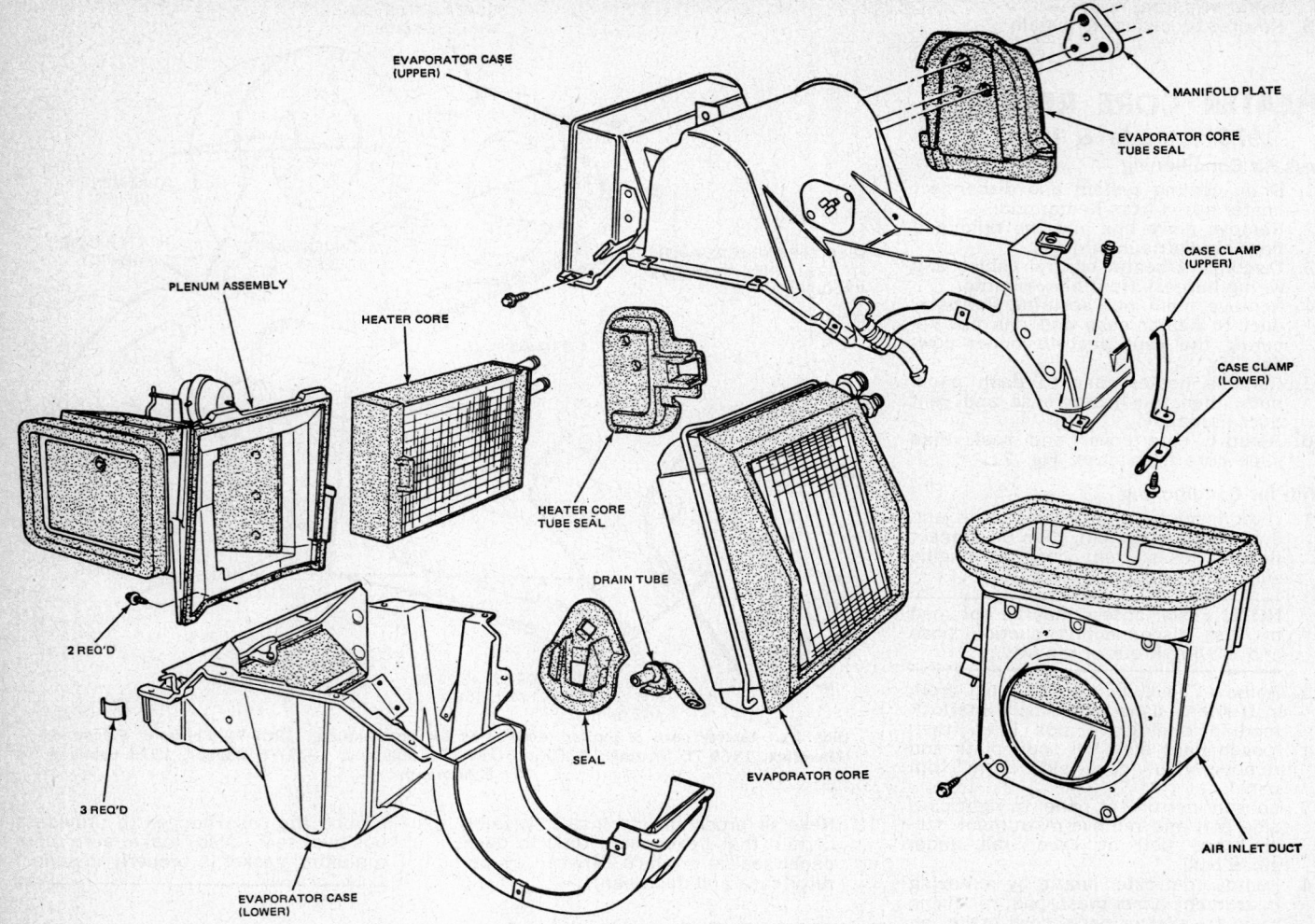

EVAPORATOR CASE (UPPER)

MANIFOLD PLATE

EVAPORATOR CORE TUBE SEAL

PLENUM ASSEMBLY

HEATER CORE

CASE CLAMP (UPPER)

CASE CLAMP (LOWER)

HEATER CORE TUBE SEAL

DRAIN TUBE

2 REQ'D

SEAL

EVAPORATOR CORE

3 REQ'D

AIR INLET DUCT

EVAPORATOR CASE (LOWER)

Fig. 22 Heater core. 1975 Granada & Monarch with air conditioning.

With Air Conditioning

1. Disconnect battery ground cable, remove air cleaner and drain cooling system.
2. Connect gauge set to compressor and discharge system.
3. Disconnect evaporator core tubes and tape ends to keep out foreign material and disconnect heater hoses from heater core tubes.
4. Remove A/C assembly-to-dash panel stud nuts.
5. On 1971-73 units, remove utility shelf from lower edge of instrument panel, the right cowl trim panel, utility bracket and remove radio.
6. On 1974 units, remove right cowl trim panel and remove glove compartment.
7. On all models disconnect right and left A/C air ducts.
8. Remove floor distribution duct from blower. Disconnect vacuum hoses from door motor and the vacuum harness multiple connector.
9. Disconnect temperature control cable from door crank arm on evaporator.
10. Remove screw that retains evaporator to cowl upper support and remove A/C rearward and away from dash panel.

11. Disconnect wire connectors from A/C thermostat switch on the evaporator housing and also the resistor on blower housing.
12. Disconnect blower motor ground wire from wiper mounting bracket and lower the blower and evaporator housing removing it from vehicle.
13. Separate halves of evaporator housing and remove water valve vacuum switch.
14. Remove temperature blend door shaft, frames and door from lower half of evaporator housing.
15. Lift heater core out of lower housing and remove pads from core.

1971-73 Mustang & Cougar

1. Drain coolant and remove heater hoses from core.
2. Remove glove box and right vent air duct assembly.
3. Disconnect control cables from heater case.
4. Remove heater case assembly (4 heater case-to-dash panel mounting stud nuts).
5. Remove heater core cover and pad and remove core from case.

1969-70 Cougar & Mustang

Less Air Conditioning

1. Disconnect battery ground cable and drain cooling system.
2. Remove instrument panel pad.
3. Remove glove box liner and door.
4. Remove air distribution duct from heater.
5. Disconnect control cables from heater.
6. Disconnect wires from blower motor resistor.
7. Remove right courtesy light from underside of dash, if so equipped.
8. Remove heater support to dash panel screw.
9. Disconnect vacuum hoses and remove power vent air duct.
10. Disconnect blower motor ground wire in engine compartment.
11. Disconnect heater hoses from heater at dash.
12. In engine compartment, remove heater retaining nuts.
13. Remove instrument panel-to-cowl panel attaching screws.
14. Remove instrument panel right side brace.
15. Pull heater assembly and right side of instrument panel rearward and

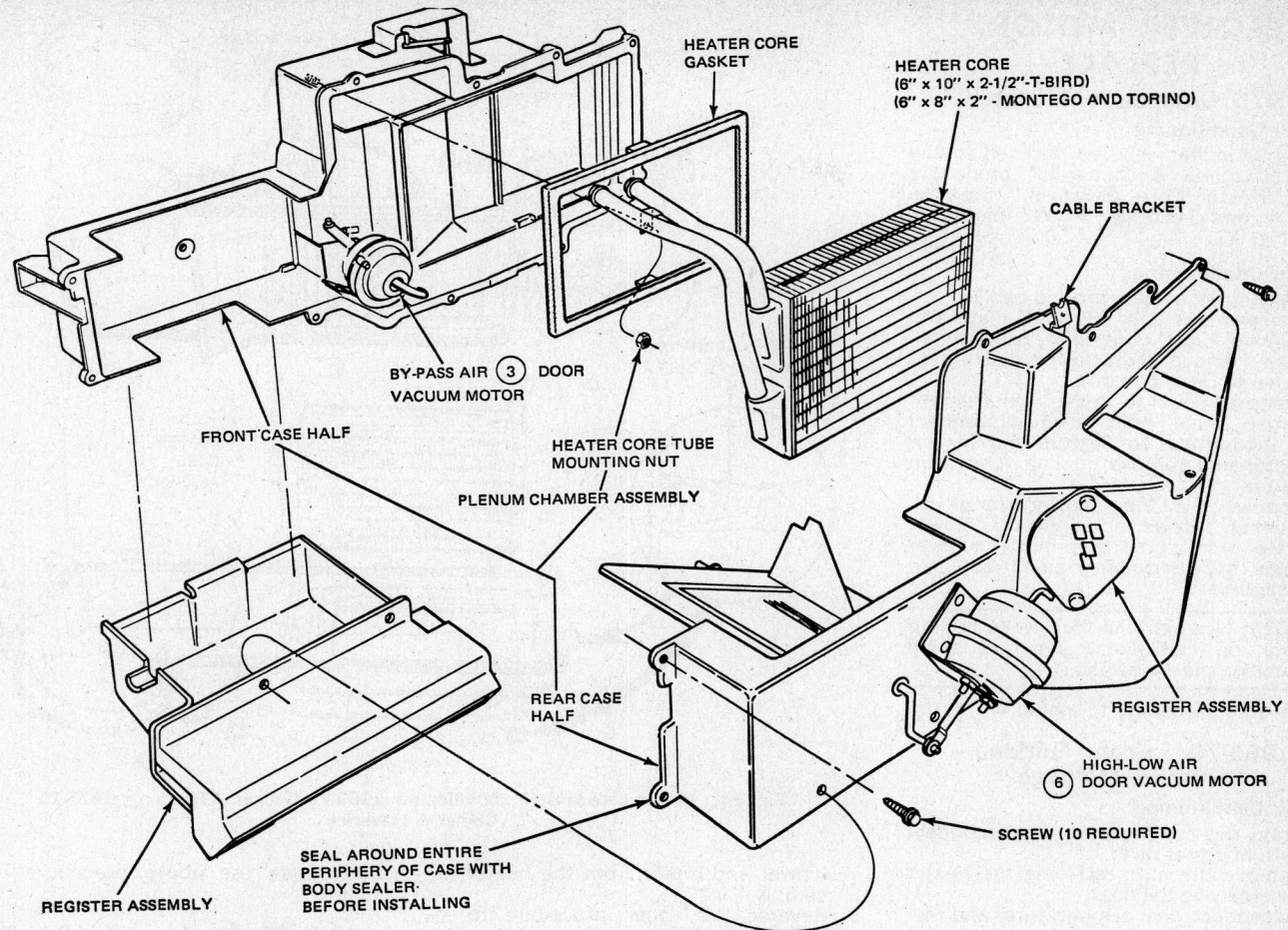

HEATER CORE GASKET

HEATER CORE
(6" x 10" x 2-1/2"-T-BIRD)
(6" x 8" x 2" - MONTEGO AND TORINO)

CABLE BRACKET

BY-PASS AIR ③ DOOR
VACUUM MOTOR

FRONT CASE HALF

HEATER CORE TUBE
MOUNTING NUT

PLENUM CHAMBER ASSEMBLY

REAR CASE
HALF

REGISTER ASSEMBLY

HIGH-LOW AIR
⑥ DOOR VACUUM MOTOR

SCREW (10 REQUIRED)

SEAL AROUND ENTIRE
PERIPHERY OF CASE WITH
BODY SEALER
BEFORE INSTALLING

REGISTER ASSEMBLY

Fig. 23 Heater core with air conditioning. 1972-75 Montego & Torino; 1974-75 Cougar

remove heater assembly.
16. Remove air inlet seal from heater.
17. Separate halves of heater and re-move core, Fig. 24.

With Air Conditioning

1. Disconnect battery ground cable and remove air cleaner.
2. Connect gauge set to compressor valves and isolate compressor.
3. Drain cooling system and remove heat shield from expansion valve.
4. Disconnect low pressure hose and service valve from compressor.
5. Disconnect high pressure hose at quick disconnect.
6. Remove straps retaining refrigerant hoses to the dash-to-fender apron supports.
7. Disconnect heater hoses from heater core.
8. Remove upper and lower seal re-tainers and remove hose seal.
9. From engine side of dash, remove evaporator housing mounting nuts and blower housing mounting nut.
10. Remove instrument panel pad.
11. Remove instrument cluster.
12. Disconnect vacuum hoses from re-heat door and outside recirc door vacuum motors.

13. Disconnect vacuum hoses from water valve vacuum switch.
14. Disconnect control cable from tem-perature blend door.
15. Disconnect wires from thermostat switch.
16. Remove right and left air ducts from defrost plenum chamber.
17. Remove defrost plenum chamber.
18. Remove instrument panel right side brace.
19. Remove evaporator housing upper rear support bracket-to-cowl screw.
20. Remove blower housing-to-cowl screws.
21. Move blower housing to left away from evaporator housing.
22. Cover the carpet and pull drain tube from hole in floor.
23. Remove instrument panel-to-cowl screws from right side.
24. Remove instrument panel finish cov-er from around steering column.
25. Unfasten instrument panel from steering column support.
26. Remove instrument panel-to-cowl screws from left side.
27. Position instrument panel back and remove evaporator housing.
28. Separate halves of evaporator hous-ing.
29. Remove water valve vacuum switch.

30. Remove temperature blend door shaft, frames and door from lower half of evaporator housing.
31. Remove heater core from evaporator lower housing and remove pads from core.
32. Reverse procedure to install.

1969-70 Fairlane, Falcon, Comet, Montego, Maverick
1971 Montego & Torino

1. Drain cooling system and disconnect both heater hoses at dash.
2. Unfasten heater from dash.
3. Disconnect temperature and de-froster cables at heater.
4. Disconnect wires from resistor, and blower motor wires and clip retain-ing heater to defroster nozzle.
5. Remove glove box.
6. Remove bolt and nut retaining right air duct control to instrument panel.
7. Remove nuts retaining right air duct and remove duct.
8. Take heater assembly to bench. Then remove heater core cover and pad and lift out core.

BLOWER MOTOR, REPLACE

1975 Granada & Monarch

Less Air Conditioning

Remove heater case as outlined in the "1975 Granada & Monarch" procedure under "Heater Core, Removal," then remove screws securing blower motor to case, Fig. 21.

With Air Conditioning

1. Disconnect battery ground cable.
2. Loosen right door sill scuff plate and remove right cowl side trim panel, then remove right lower instrument panel to cowl side bolt.
3. Remove cowl to loosen instrument panel brace bolt, then disconnect wiring harness connectors from blower motor and remove cooling tube from motor.
4. Remove the four blower motor attaching screws and remove blower motor from scroll by pulling on lower edge of instrument panel to gain clearance.

NOTE: Use extreme care when pulling back on instrument panel to avoid cracking plastic panel.

5. Reverse procedure to install.

1969-70 Falcon, Fairlane, Comet & Montego

Less Air Conditioning

1. Drain the cooling system. Disconnect both hoses at dash.
2. Remove the nuts retaining the heater assembly to the dash.
3. Disconnect the temperature and defroster cables to the dash.
4. Disconnect the wires from the resistor, and disconnect the blower motor wires and the clip retaining the heater assembly to the defroster nozzle.
5. Remove the glove box.
6. Remove the bolt and nut retaining the right air duct control to the instrument panel. Remove the nuts retaining the right air duct and remove the duct assembly.
7. Remove the heater assembly to a bench. Remove the blower mounting screws and remove the motor and wheel assembly.
8. Reverse above procedure to install.

With Air Conditioning

1. Remove the glove box.
2. Remove the right hand fresh air duct. Disconnect the vacuum line from the actuator and position it out of the way.
3. Disconnect the plug from the resistor block and remove the resistor block.
4. Remove the blower motor cover and remove the motor and blower wheel.
5. Reverse above procedure to install.

1969-70 Cougar & Mustang

Less Air Conditioning

1. Follow the procedure to remove the heater core as described previously.
2. Remove the heater assembly from the vehicle.
3. Disconnect the blower motor wire from the resistor.
4. Remove the four blower and motor mounting plate nuts, and remove the

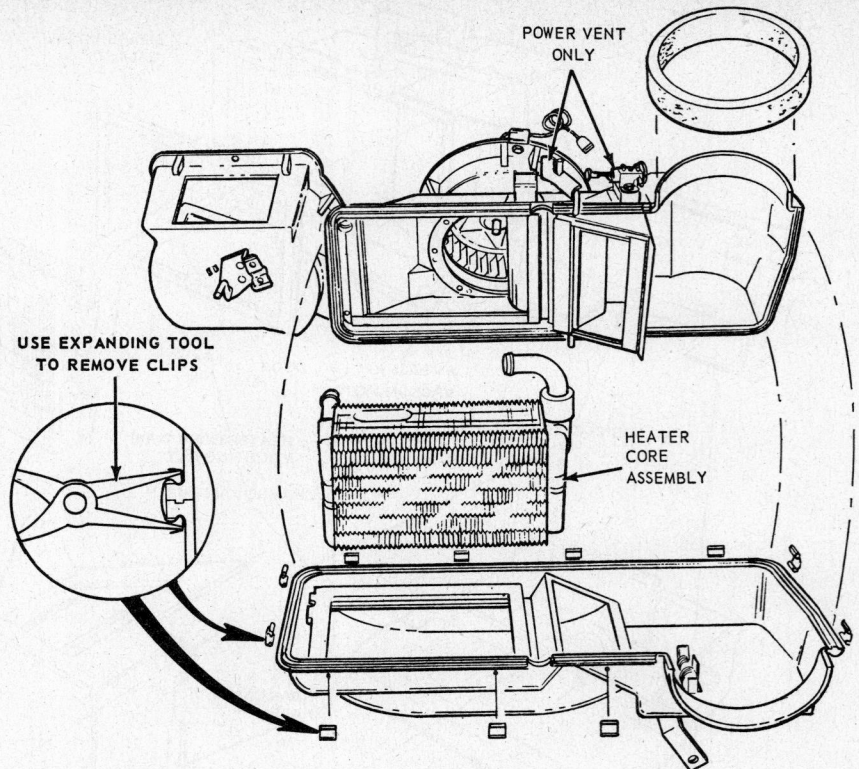

Fig. 24 Heater core less air conditioning. 1969-70 Cougar & Mustang; 1971-75 Comet & Maverick

blower and motor from the heater assembly.
5. Reverse the above procedure to install.

With Air Conditioning

1. Remove the accelerator pedal assembly.
2. Remove the lower air distribution duct.
3. Disconnect the blower motor cooling tube and wiring.
4. Remove the four blower mounting plate attaching screws, and remove the blower and motor.
5. Reverse the above procedure to install.

1970 Maverick

Less Air Conditioning

Follow procedure shown for 1970 Falcon, Fairlane, Montego.

With Air Conditioning

1. Remove the radio. Disconnect the ignition switch from the package tray.
2. Remove the package tray and disconnect both left and right duct assemblies.
3. Remove the air distribution duct from the blower housing.
4. Remove the lower nut retaining the blower housing to the evaporator assembly. Rotate the blower housing until it disengages from the evaporator housing, and disconnect the vacuum hoses at the motor on the blower housing. Disconnect the resistor assembly and the blower ground wire and remove the blower.

5. Reverse the above procedure to install.

1971-73 Mustang & 1971-75 Cougar, Montego, Torino

Less Air Conditioning

1. Follow the procedure to remove the heater core as described previously.
2. Remove the heater assembly from the vehicle, and place it on a bench.
3. Remove the four mounting screws and remove the blower motor and wheel assembly from the blower, Fig. 21.
4. Reverse the above procedure to install.

With Air Conditioning: 1971-73 Mustang & Cougar

1. Remove the blower housing mounting bracket stud nut, from the engine side of the dash panel.
2. Remove the two blower housing-to-instrument panel support mounting screws.
3. Remove the floor air distribution duct (three plastic buttons).
4. Disconnect the blower motor ground wire (black) from the upper cowl.
5. Disconnect the blower motor lead wire (orange-black) from the resistor.
6. Rotate the blower motor housing to a diagonal position.
7. Remove the four blower motor mounting plate screws, and remove the blower motor and wheel as an assembly.

With Air Conditioning: 1971 Montego & Torino

1. Remove the glove box.
2. Remove the right hand fresh air duct.

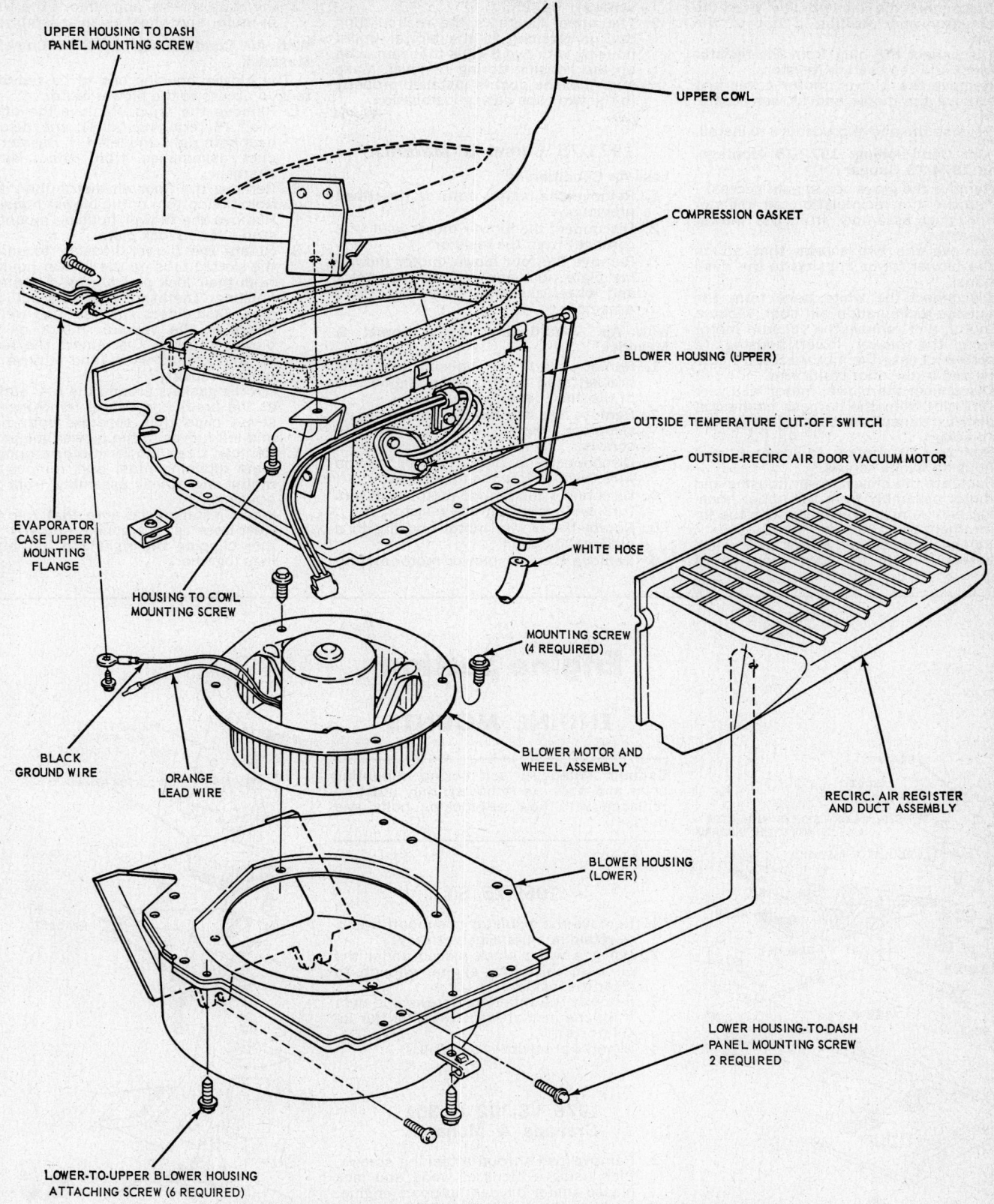

Fig. 25   Blower motor with air conditioning. 1972-75 Montego & Torino; 1974-75 Cougar

Disconnect the vacuum line from the actuator and position it out of the way.

3. Disconnect the plug from the resistor block and remove the resistor.
4. Remove the blower motor cover and remove the motor and blower assembly.
5. Reverse the above procedure to install.

With Air Conditioning: 1972-75 Montego, Torino 1974-75 Cougar

1. Remove the glove box to gain access.
2. Remove the recirculation air register and duct assembly from the blower assembly.
3. Remove the two screws that attach the blower lower housing to the dash panel.
4. Disconnect the white hose from the outside-recirculation air door vacuum motor, and remove the vacuum motor from the blower lower housing (2 screws). Leave the motor actuator connected to the door crank arm.
5. Disconnect the blower motor lead wire (orange) from the harness connector, and disconnect the motor ground wire (black).
6. Remove six upper to lower blower housing flange screws.
7. Separate the blower lower housing and motor assembly from the upper housing and remove it from under the instrument pad.
8. Remove the blower motor and wheel assembly from the lower housing (4 screws), Fig. 25.
9. The upper flange of the recirculating duct is retained to the blower upper housing with two S-clips that remained on the housing during removal. Make sure that the duct is installed properly in the two clips during installation.

1971-75 Comet & Maverick

Less Air Conditioning

1. Remove the heater core as described previously.
2. Disconnect the blower motor lead wire (orange) from the resistor.
3. Remove the four blower motor mounting plate nuts and remove the motor and wheel assembly from the heater assembly.

With Air Conditioning: 1971 Comet & Maverick

1. Remove the blower housing mounting bracket stud nut from the engine side of the dash panel.
2. Remove the two blower housing-to-instrument panel support mounting screws.
3. Disconnect the blower motor ground wire (black) from the upper cowl.
4. Disconnect the blower motor lead wire (orange-black) from the resistor.
5. Rotate the blower motor housing to a diagonal position.
6. Remove the four blower motor mounting plate screws, and remove the blower motor and wheel as an assembly.

With Air Conditioning: 1972-75 Comet & Maverick

The blower housing has to be removed to gain access to the blower motor.

1. Remove the radio. Remove the utility shelf (5 retaining bolts), and disconnect both right and left A/C register air duct assemblies from the plenum chamber.
2. Remove the floor air distribution duct from the bottom of the blower housing. Remove the blower housing mounting stud nut and lock plate.
3. Rotate the blower housing to unlock the slotted tabs on the blower housing from their lock pins on the evaporator housing. There are two tabs and two pins. Disconnect the red and yellow hoses at the vacuum motor on the blower housing. Disconnect the resistor and ground wires, and remove the blower housing.
4. Cut the gaskets around the A/C outlets at the break line before removing the seven clips that separate both right and left halves of the blower housing.
5. Remove three blower motor mounting plate retaining nuts, and remove the motor and wheel assembly from the housing.
6. When installing be sure that the A/C Heat-Door is positioned properly before clipping the right and left housings together.

Engine Section

ENGINE MOUNTS

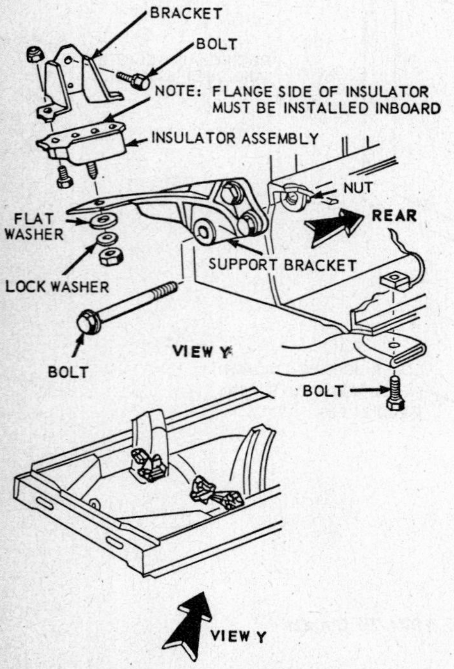

Caution: Whenever self-locking mounting bolts and nuts are removed, they must be replaced with new self-locking bolts and nuts.

1969-75 Six

1. Remove the insulator to support bracket retaining nuts, Figs. 1 thru 7.
2. Using a wood block placed under the oil pan, raise the engine enough to clear the insulator.
3. Remove the retaining screws and nuts from the insulator(s). Remove the insulator(s).
4. Reverse procedure to install.

1975 V8-302 & 351 Granada & Monarch

1. Remove pan shroud attaching screws, then using a block of wood and jack placed under oil pan, support engine.
2. Remove through bolt attaching motor mount to crossmember, Fig. 8.
3. Remove engine mount to engine attaching bolts and remove engine mount and heat shield (if used).
4. Reverse procedure to install.

Fig. 1 Engine mounts. 1969-70 Mustang 6-170, 200

BRACKET
BOLT
NOTE: FLANGE SIDE OF INSULATOR MUST BE INSTALLED INBOARD
INSULATOR ASSEMBLY
NUT
REAR
FLAT WASHER
LOCK WASHER
SUPPORT BRACKET
VIEW Y
BOLT
BOLT
VIEW Y

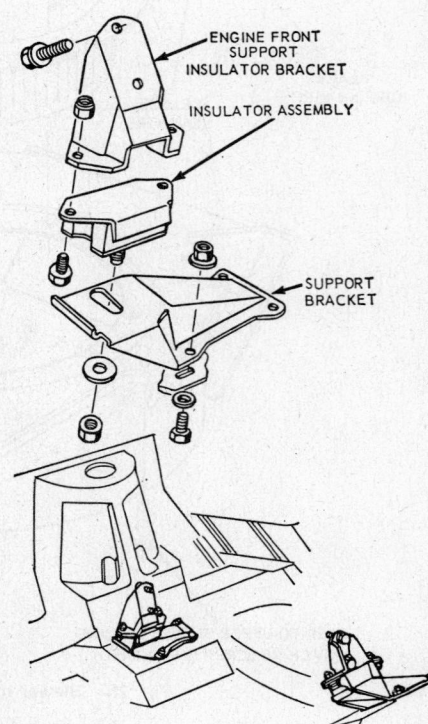

Fig. 2 Engine mounts. 1969-70 Fairlane, Falcon, Montego, Comet 6-170, 200

ENGINE FRONT SUPPORT INSULATOR BRACKET
INSULATOR ASSEMBLY
SUPPORT BRACKET

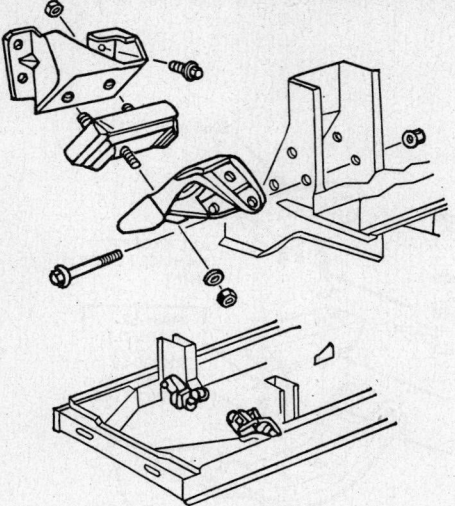

Fig. 3 Engine mounts. 1969-71 Mustang 6-250

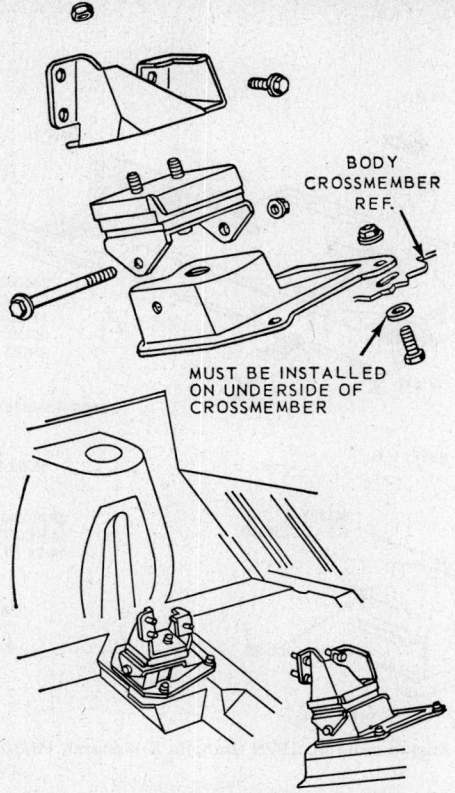

BODY CROSSMEMBER REF.

MUST BE INSTALLED ON UNDERSIDE OF CROSSMEMBER

Fig. 4 Engine mounts. 1969-71 Fairlane, Falcon, Montego, Torino 6-250

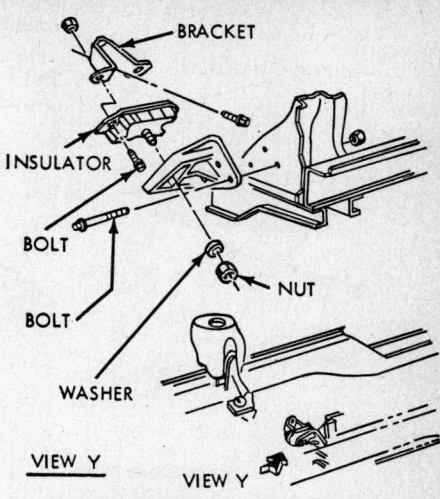

BRACKET

INSULATOR

BOLT

BOLT

NUT

WASHER

VIEW Y

VIEW Y

Fig. 5 Engine mounts. 1970-72 Comet, Maverick & All 1973-75 Six

1969-75 V8-289, 302, 351, 400 Exc. Granada & Monarch

1. Raise the engine with a jack and wood block placed under the oil pan.
2. Remove bolts and washers attaching engine mount to engine, Fig. 9 thru 12.
3. Remove bolts and washers attaching engine mount brackets to side support.
4. Remove engine mount bracket assembly.
5. Detach engine mount from bracket by removing long bolts and nuts.

1969 V8-390, 428

1. On vehicles with automatic transmission, remove the oil cooler lines, and retaining bracket on the cylinder block.
2. Remove the insulator to intermediate

support bracket nut and lock washer, Fig. 14. If only one support is being removed, loosen the other support.
3. Using a jack and a wood block placed under the oil pan, raise the engine to allow just enough clearance for the removal of the insulator(s).
4. Remove the insulator to engine bolts and lock washers. Remove the insulator.
5. Reverse procedure to install.

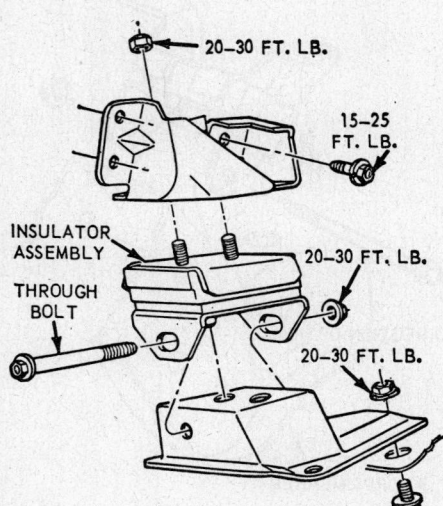

20–30 FT. LB.

15–25 FT. LB.

INSULATOR ASSEMBLY

THROUGH BOLT

20–30 FT. LB.

20–30 FT. LB.

Fig. 6 Engine mounts. 1972 Mustang 6-250

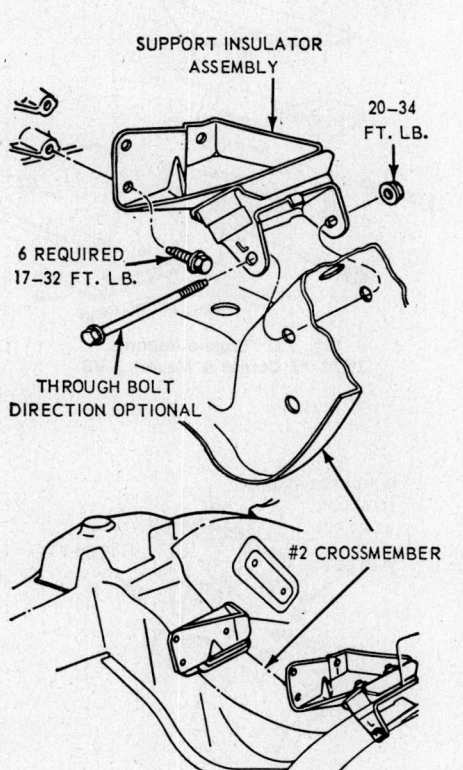

SUPPORT INSULATOR ASSEMBLY

20–34 FT. LB.

6 REQUIRED 17–32 FT. LB.

THROUGH BOLT DIRECTION OPTIONAL

#2 CROSSMEMBER

Fig. 7 Engine mounts. 1972 Torino & Montego 6-250

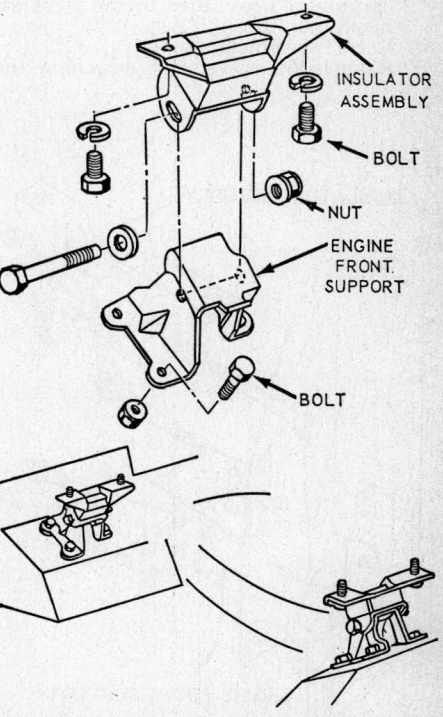

INSULATOR ASSEMBLY

BOLT

NUT

ENGINE FRONT SUPPORT

BOLT

Fig. 9 Engine mounts. 1969-71 V8-289, 302, 351 Fairlane/Torino Falcon, Montego & Comet

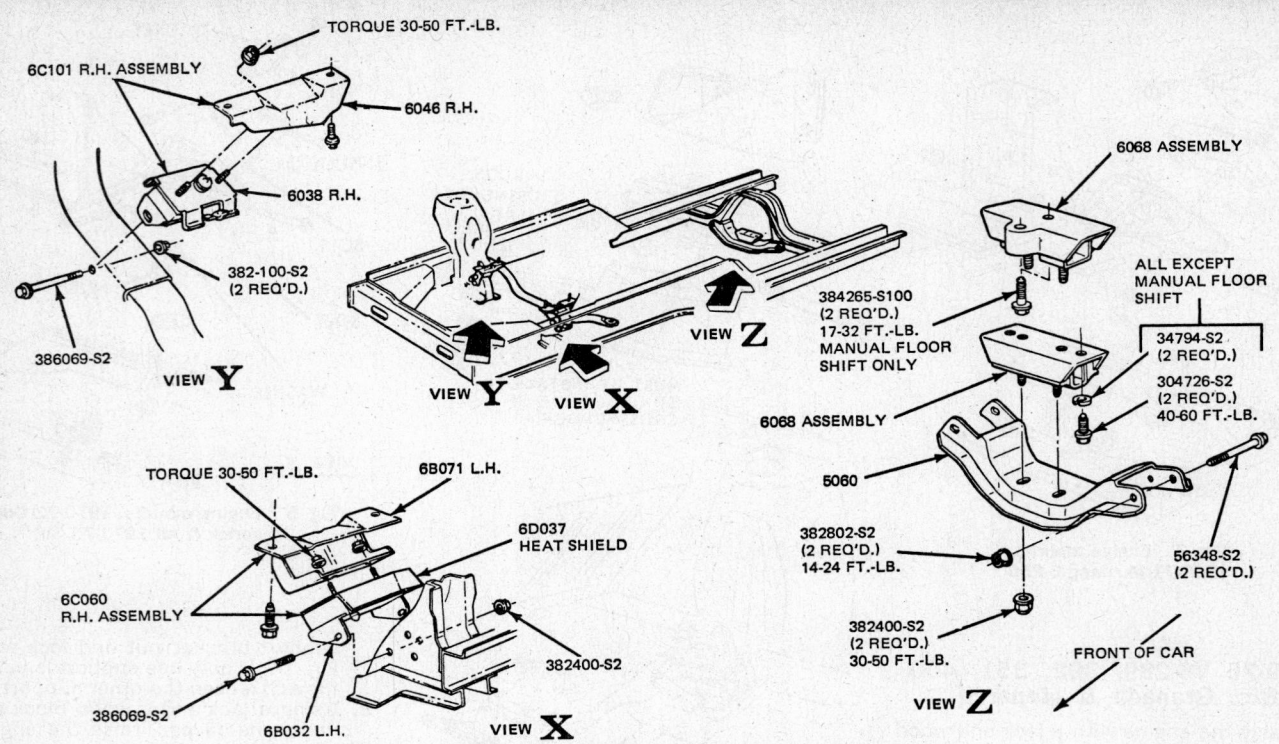

TORQUE 30-50 FT.-LB.
6C101 R.H. ASSEMBLY
6046 R.H.
6038 R.H.
382-100-S2 (2 REQ'D.)
386069-S2
VIEW Y

VIEW Y
VIEW X

6068 ASSEMBLY
ALL EXCEPT MANUAL FLOOR SHIFT
384265-S100 (2 REQ'D.) 17-32 FT.-LB. MANUAL FLOOR SHIFT ONLY
VIEW Z
6068 ASSEMBLY
34794-S2 (2 REQ'D.)
304726-S2 (2 REQ'D.) 40-60 FT.-LB.
5060
382802-S2 (2 REQ'D.) 14-24 FT.-LB.
56348-S2 (2 REQ'D.)
382400-S2 (2 REQ'D.) 30-50 FT.-LB.
FRONT OF CAR
VIEW Z

TORQUE 30-50 FT.-LB.
6B071 L.H.
6D037 HEAT SHIELD
6C060 R.H. ASSEMBLY
382400-S2
386069-S2
6B032 L.H.
VIEW X

Fig. 8 Engine mounts. 1975 Granada & Monarch V8-302 & 351

1970 V8-428 Cobra Jet
1. Remove the air cleaner.
2. Remove the attaching bolts to radiator shroud and leave it loose to allow fan clearance when raising the engine.
3. Remove the upper nut attaching the carburetor heat stove to the right exhaust manifold.
4. Raise the vehicle.
5. Remove the lower nut attaching the

carburetor heat stove to the right exhaust manifold. Rotate the stove up and around the front of the manifold and position it under the battery carrier, out of the way.
6. Disconnect the power steering oil cooler lines at the engine oil filter adapter.
7. Remove the power steering line retainer and position lines out of the way.
8. Place a floor jack under the engine.
9. Place a wood block between the oil pan and the jack and raise the engine slightly.

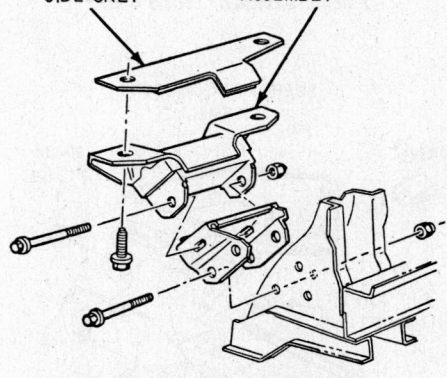

L.H. SIDE ONLY
INSULATOR ASSEMBLY

Fig. 11 Engine mounts. 1971-75 Comet & Maverick V8

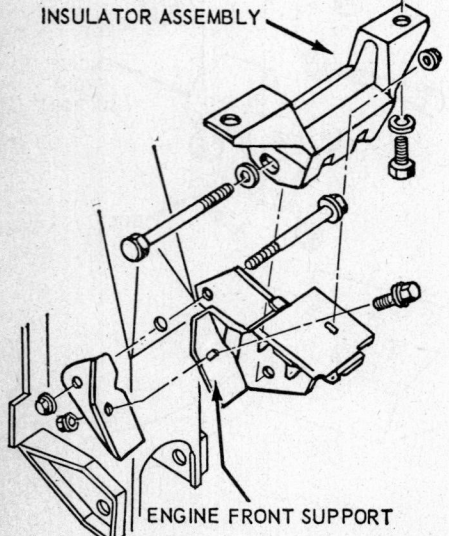

INSULATOR ASSEMBLY
ENGINE FRONT SUPPORT

Fig. 10 Engine mounts. 1969-73 Cougar & Mustang V8-289, 302, 351

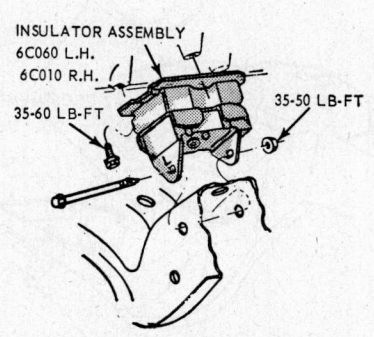

INSULATOR ASSEMBLY
6C060 L.H.
6C010 R.H.
35-60 LB-FT
35-50 LB-FT

Fig. 11A Engine mounts. 1973-75 Torino & Montego V8-400

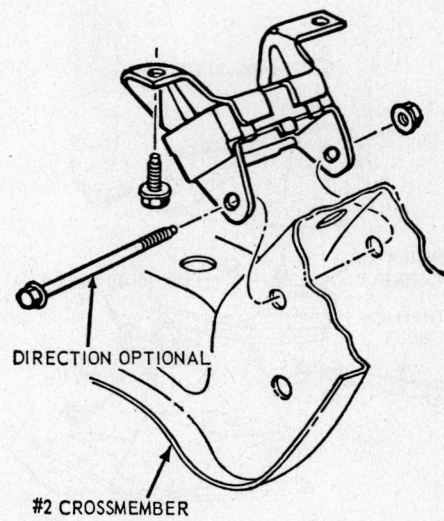

DIRECTION OPTIONAL
#2 CROSSMEMBER

Fig. 12 Engine Mounts. 1972-75 Torino & Montego V8-302, 351 & 1974-75 Cougar V8-351C

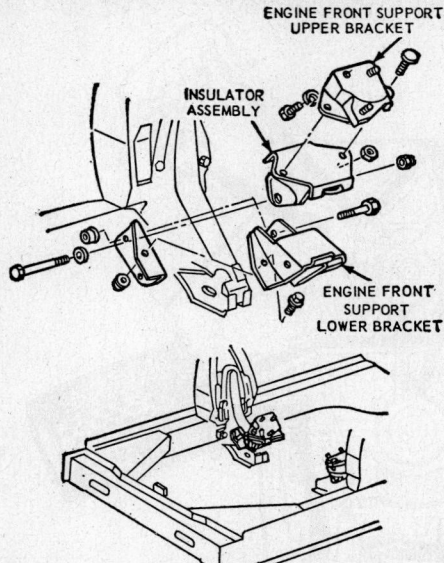

Fig. 13 Engine mounts. 1970 V8-428 "CJ"

10. Remove the engine support to chassis thru bolt and nut on either or both sides, Fig. 13.
11. Remove nuts and bolts attaching the engine support bracket to the chassis on either or both sides. Raise the engine.
12. Remove the nuts attaching the engine support insulators to the engine brackets and remove the insulators.

1970-71 V8-429

1. Block the rear wheels and set the park-

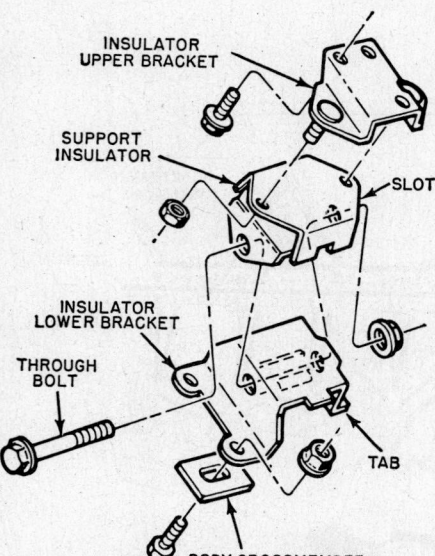

Fig. 15 Engine mounts. V8-429 1970 Fairlane & Montego, 1971 Cougar, Montego, Mustang & Torino

ing brake. Raise the front of the vehicle with a floor jack and install safety stands.
2. Remove the two nuts attaching the upper insulator bracket to the insulator, Fig. 15.
3. Place a jack under the front area of the oil pan. Position a wood block between the jack and the oil pan. Raise the engine enough to take the load off the through-bolt.
4. Remove the through bolt and raise the engine to a point where the insulator can be removed from the lower bracket.
5. Remove the two nuts that attach the insulator to the insulator upper bracket and remove the insulator.

1972-75 V8-429, 460

1. Remove the fan shroud attaching screws and support the engine using a jack and block of wood under the oil pan.
2. Remove the through bolt and nut attaching the insulator to the frame crossmember.
3. Remove the insulator to upper bracket attaching nuts, Fig. 16.
4. Raise the engine enough to remove the insulator and heat shield if so equipped.
5. If necessary, the upper bracket can now be removed by removal of the three screws holding the bracket to the cylinder block.

ENGINE, REPLACE
1969-75 Six-Cylinder

NOTE: The engine is removed from the chassis, leaving the transmission in place. First disconnect and/or remove as required wires, tubes, hoses and linkage attached to engine. Then do the following:

1. Remove hood, radiator, fan and pulley.
2. Remove starting motor.
3. On cars with manual shift transmission, remove clutch equalizer shaft and arm bracket.
4. Remove flywheel or converter housing-to-engine upper bolts through access holes in underbody.
5. Disconnect engine right and left mount at underbody bracket.
6. Remove flywheel or converter housing cover.
7. Remove flywheel or converter housing-to-engine lower bolts.
8. Support transmission and flywheel or converter housing with a jack.
9. Attach a lifting rig to engine and remove it from vehicle.

1969-75 V8-390, 427, 428, 429, 460

NOTE: The engine is removed from the vehicle, leaving the transmission in place. First disconnect and/or remove as required wires, tubes, hose and linkage attached to engine. Then do the following:

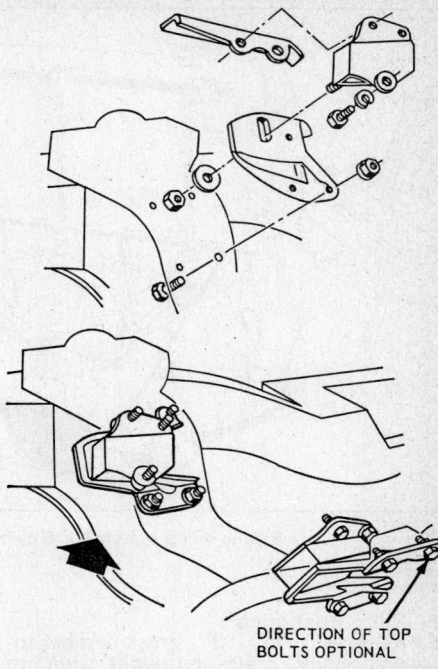

Fig. 14 Engine mounts. 1969 V8-390, 428 Cougar, Fairlane, Montego & Mustang

1. Drain cooling system and crankcase.
2. Remove hood, radiator and ignition coil.
3. If air conditioned, unfasten air compressor from its mounting and position it out of the way, leaving refrigerant lines attached.
4. Unfasten and wire power steering pump to hood left hinge in a position that will prevent oil from draining out.

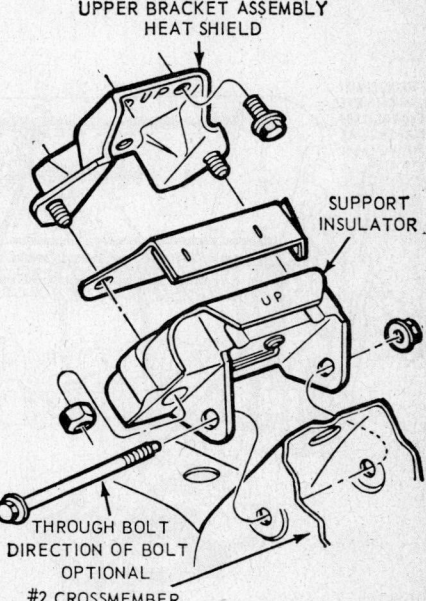

Fig. 16 Engine mounts. 1972-75 V8-429 460 Torino & Montego

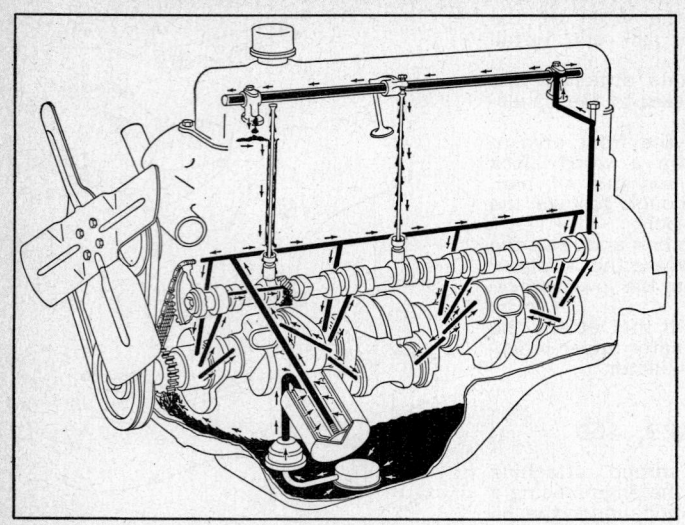

Engine oiling system for 6 cylinder engines

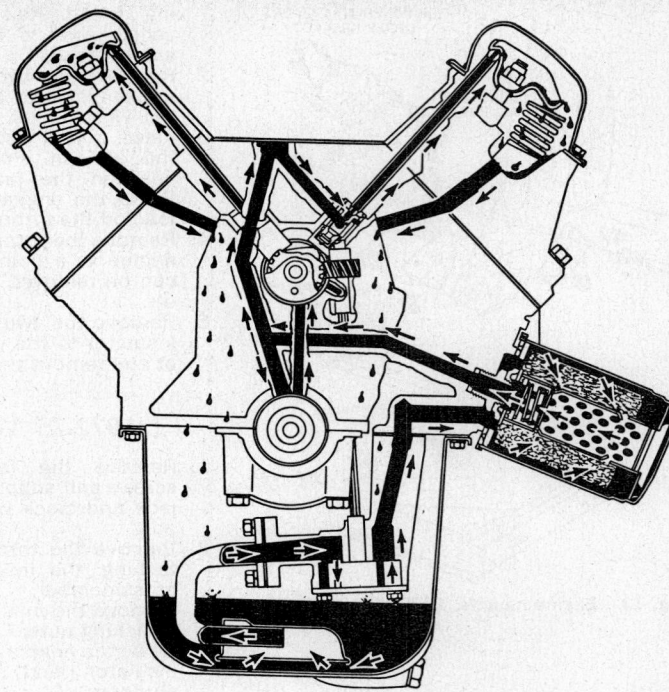

Engine oiling system. V8-289, 302, 351, 400

5. Raise front of car.
6. Remove No. 2 crossmember-to-underbody brace on right side to provide clearance for starter removal. Remove starter and dust seal and transmission fluid filler tube bracket.
7. Remove engine intermediate support bracket-to-crossmember retaining nut on right and left engine front supports.
8. Remove converter housing cover.
9. Remove flywheel-to-converter nuts.
10. Secure converter to housing.
11. Remove converter housing-to-engine lower bolts.
12. Lower car and support transmission.
13. Remove converter housing upper bolts.
14. Remove front fender-to-upper dash braces.
15. Lift engine out of chassis.

1969-75 V8-289, 302, 351, 400

NOTE: The engine is removed from the vehicle, leaving the transmission in place. First disconnect and/or remove as required wires, tubes, hose and linkage attached to engine. Then do the following:

1. Drain cooling system and crankcase.
2. Remove oil filter, hood, radiator, fan and pulley.
3. Remove air cleaner and intake duct.

4. If air conditioned, unfasten and position air compressor out of the way.
5. Remove and position power steering pump to one side.
6. If equipped with Thermactor Exhaust Emission Control System, remove air pump air filter if it is not connected to engine.
7. Remove flywheel-to-converter housing upper bolts.
8. Raise front of car and remove starter and dust seal.

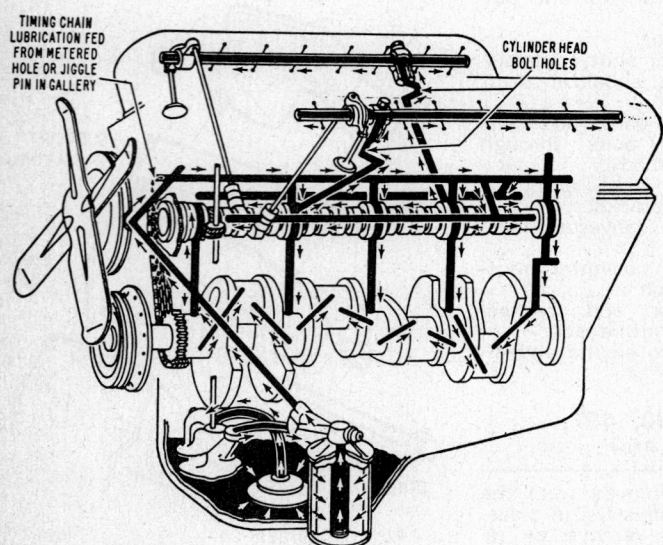

Engine oiling system. V8-390, 427, 428

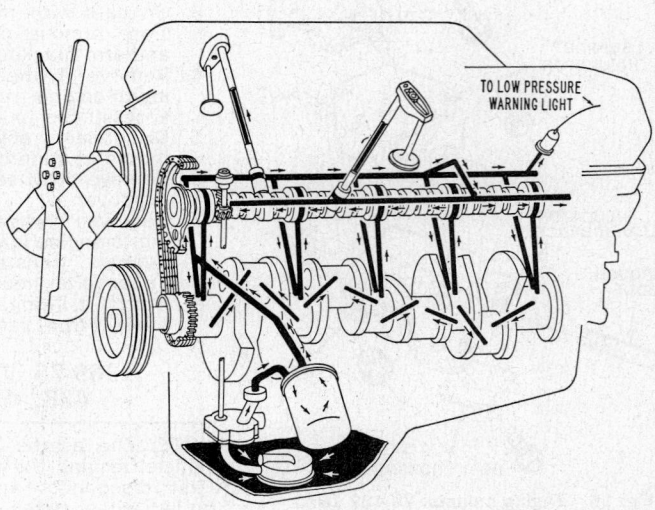

Engine oiling system. V8-429, 460

Fig. 17 Cylinder head tightening sequence. Six cylinder

9. Disconnect engine support insulators at brackets on frame underbody.
10. Remove remaining flywheel or converter housing-to-engine bolts.
11. Lower car, then support transmission.
12. Attach a lifting rig to engine and remove from vehicle.

CYLINDER HEAD, REPLACE

Tighten cylinder head bolts a little at a time in three steps in the sequence shown in the illustrations. Final tightening should be to the torque specifications listed in the *Engine Tightening* table. After tightening the bolts to specifications, *they should not be disturbed.*

1969-75 Six-Cylinder

1. Drain cooling system and remove air cleaner.
2. Unfasten exhaust pipe from manifold and pull it down.
3. Disconnect accelerator rod from carburetor.
4. Disconnect fuel inlet line at fuel filter hose, and distributor vacuum line at carburetor.
5. Disconnect coolant lines at carburetor spacer. Remove radiator upper hose at outlet housing.
6. Disconnect distributor vacuum line at distributor. Disconnect carburetor fuel inlet line at fuel pump. Remove lines as an assembly.
7. Disconnect spark plug wires at plugs and temperature sending unit wire at sending unit.
8. Remove crankcase ventilation system. Remove hoses from Thermactor system as necessary for accessability.
9. Remove valve rocker arm cover.
10. Remove rocker arm shaft assembly.
11. Remove valve push rods.
12. Remove remaining cylinder head bolts and lift off head.
13. Reverse procedure to install and tighten head bolts in the sequence shown in Fig. 17.

1969-75 V8-289, 302, 341, 400

1. Remove intake manifold and carburetor as an assembly.
2. Disconnect battery ground cable at cylinder head.
3. If left head is being removed, remove air compressor (if equipped). Also remove and wire power steering pump out of the way. If equipped with Thermactor System, disconnect hose from air manifold on left cylinder head.
4. If right head is to be removed, remove alternator mounting bracket bolt and spacer, ignition coil and air cleaner inlet duct.
5. If right head is to be removed on an engine with Thermactor System, remove air pump from bracket. Disconnect hose from air manifold.
6. Disconnect exhaust manifolds at exhaust pipes.

NOTE: On V8-351, separate the exhaust manifolds from the heads first in order to gain access to the lower row of cylinder head attaching bolts.

7. Remove rocker arm covers. If equip-

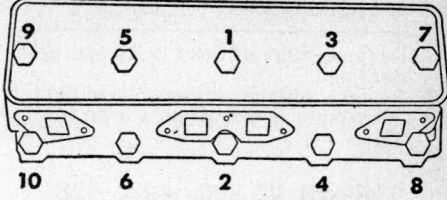

Fig. 18 Cylinder head tightening. V8 engines

ped with Thermactor System, remove check valve from air manifold.
8. Loosen rocker arm nuts so rocker arms can be rotated to one side. Remove push rods.
9. Remove head bolts and lift head off block.
10. Reverse removal procedure to install and tighten head bolts in the sequence shown in Fig. 18.

1969-75 V8-429 & 460

1. Remove intake manifold and carburetor as an assembly and disconnect exhaust pipes from manifold.
2. Loosen A/C belt if equipped and remove alternator.
3. If equipped with A/C, isolate compressor at service valves and disconnect valves and hoses from compressor. Remove compressor attaching bolts and position unit out of way.
4. If not equipped with A/C, remove power steering retaining bolts and position unit out of way.
5. Remove valve covers. On 1969-71, back off adjusting nuts, turn rocker arms to one side and remove push rods. On 1972-75, remove rocker arm bolts, rocker arms, oil deflectors, fulcrums and push rods.

NOTE: Remove all parts in sequence so that they are installed in their

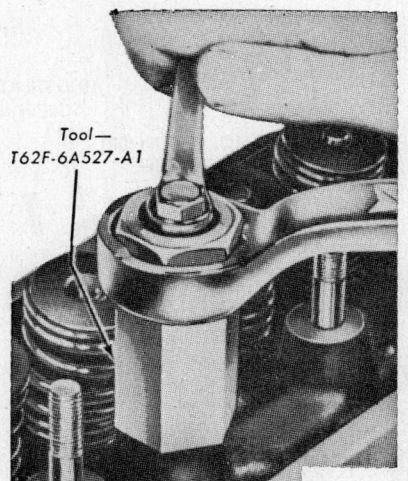

Fig. 19 Rocker arm stud removal. 6 cylinder and V8 engines with pressed-in rocker arm studs

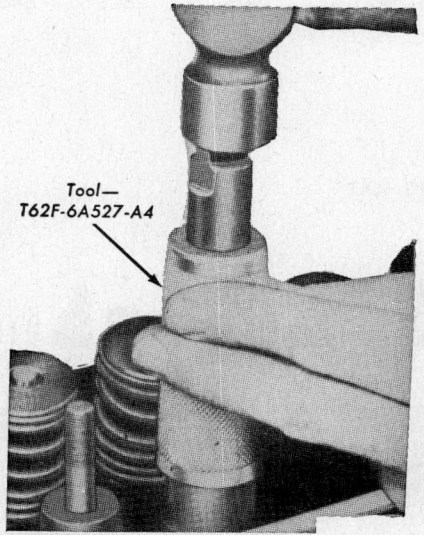

Fig. 20 Conventional type rocker arm stud installation. 6 cylinder and V8 engines with pressed-in studs

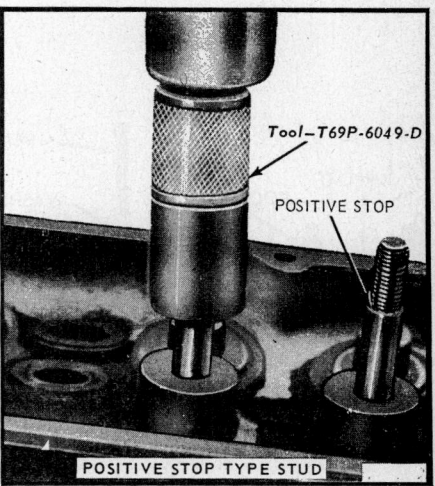

Fig. 21 Positive stop type rocker arm stud installation. 6 cylinder and V8 engines with pressed-in studs

original positions.

6. Remove cylinder head bolts and cylinder head.
7. Reverse removal procedure and tighten head bolts in sequence shown in Fig. 18.

1969-70 V8-390, 427, 428

1. If equipped with Thermactor System, disconnect air hoses as necessary for accessability, and position them out of the way.
2. Remove intake manifold and carburetor as an assembly.
3. Remove rocker arms and push rods. Keep all parts in sequence so they can be installed in the same locations.
4. Disconnect exhaust manifolds at exhaust pipes.
5. If left head is being removed, remove ignition coil and engine identification tag, and remove power steering pump mounting bolt from right cylinder head.
6. Remove head bolts and take off head.
7. Reverse procedure to install and tighten head bolts in the sequence shown in Fig. 18.

VALVE ARRANGEMENT

Front to Rear

Sixes	E-I-I-E-I-E-E-I-E-I-I-E
8-289, 302 Right	I-E-I-E-I-E-I-E
8-289, 302 Left	E-I-E-I-E-I-E-I
8-351, 400 Right	I-E-I-E-I-E-I-E
8-351, 400 Left	E-I-E-I-E-I-E-I
V8-390, 427, 428	E-I-E-I-E-I-E-I-E
V8-429, 460 Right	I-E-I-E-I-E-I-E
V8-429, 460 Left	E-I-E-I-E-I-E-I

VALVE LIFT SPECS.

Engine	Year	Intake	Exhaust
6-170	1969-72	.348	.348
6-200	1969-72	.348	.348
6-200	1973-75	.380	.348
6-250	1969-73	.368	.368
6-250[6]	1972-73	.380	.348
6-250	1974-75	.380	.348
8-302	1969-72	.368	.381
8-302	1973	.370	.382
8-302	1974-75	.368	.380
8-302 "H.O."	1969-71	.477	.477
8-351[4]	1969-75	.418	.448
8-351[5][1]	1970-74	.407	.407
8-351M[1][7]	1975	.406	.406
8-351[5][2]	1970-71	.427	.427
8-351[5][2]	1971	.427	.453
8-351[5][2]	1972	.480	.488
8-351[5][2]	1973	.481	.490
8-351[5][2]	1974	.480	.490
8-351[5][2][3]	1973	.490	.490
8-390[2]	1969	.481	.490
8-400	1972	.422	.427
8-400	1973	.427	.433
8-400	1974	.428	.433
8-400[8]	1975	.428	.443
8-400[9]	1975	.427	.433
8-427	1969	.481	.490
8-428	1969-70	.481	.490
8-429 "CJ"	1970-71	.515	.515
8-429 "SCJ"	1970-71	.500	.500
8-429 "BOSS"	1970	.478	.505
8-429	1972	.442	.486
8-429	1973	.437	.480
8-460	1973	.482	.500
8-460	1974-75	.442	.486
8-460	1975	.482	.500

[1]—Two bar. carb. [2]—Four bar. carb.
[3]—Hi Perf. engine.
[4]—Windsor engine.
[5]—Cleveland engine.
[6]—California engine.
[7]—Modified.
[8]—Cougar.
[9]—Torino.
[10]—Police Interceptor.

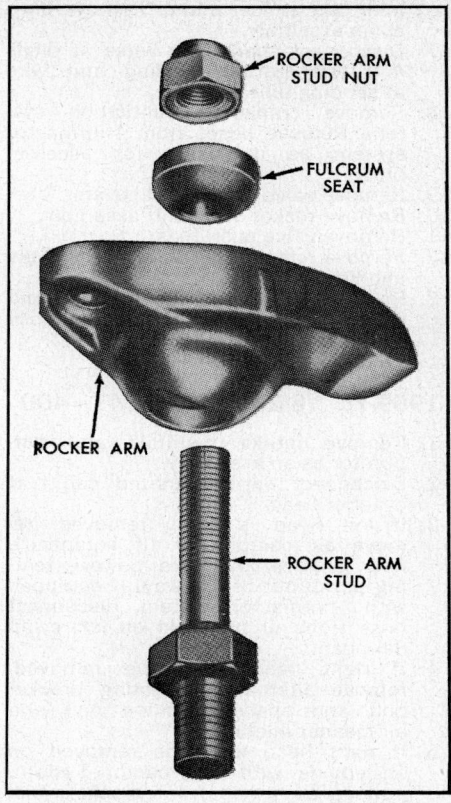

Fig. 22 Valve rocker arm and stud. High Performance V8-289 H.O., V8-302 & 1969-70 V8-429 Except "BOSS"

VALVE TIMING
Intake Opens Before TDC

Engine	Year	Degrees
6-170	1969-72	9
6-200	1969-72	9
	1974-75	28
6-250	1969-72	10
	1972[6]	16

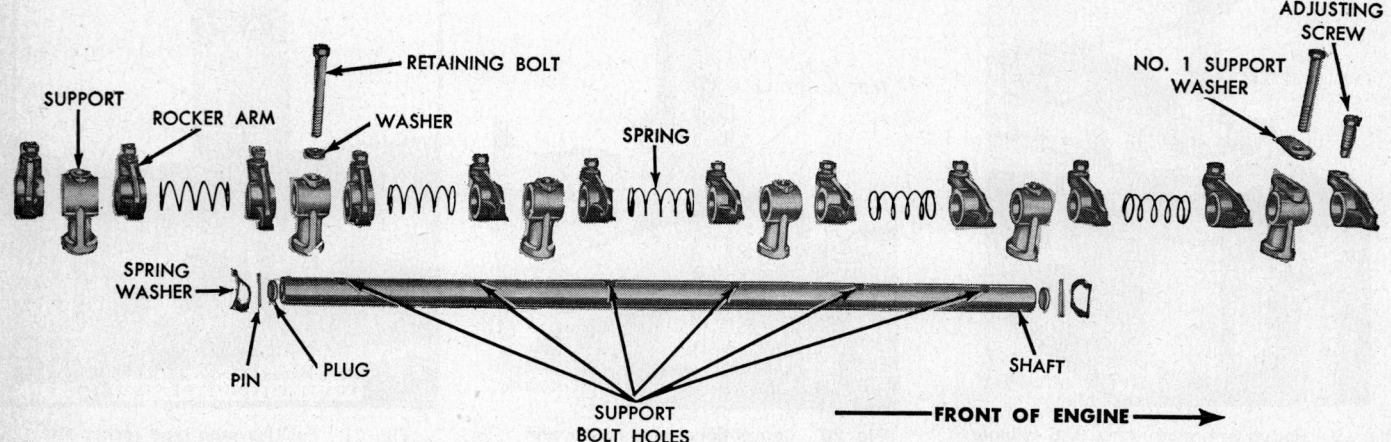

Fig. 23 Rocker arm shaft assembly. Six cylinder engines

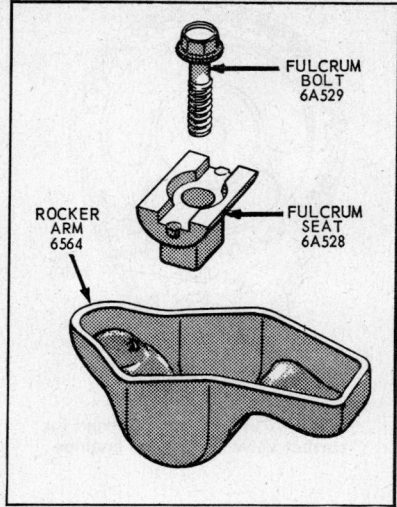

Fig. 24 Rocker assembly. 1970-74 V8-351C,
351M, 400 & 1971-75 V8-429, 460

6-250	1973	17
	1974-75	26
8-302	1969-72	16
8-302 "H.O."	1969	40
8-302 "BOSS"	1970-71	34
8-302[7]	1973-74	16
8-302[4]	1973-75	20
8-351[5]	1969-71	11
	1974-75	15
8-351[3][1]	1970-73	12
	1974	19½
8-351[2][1]	1970	14
8-351[2][1]	1971-73	18
8-351[2]	1974	14
8-351[8]	1975	19.5
8-390	1969	16
8-400	1972-75	17
8-427	1969	18
8-428	1969-70	18
8-429	1972-73	8
8-429 "CJ"	1970-71	32
8-429 "SCJ"	1970-71	40.5

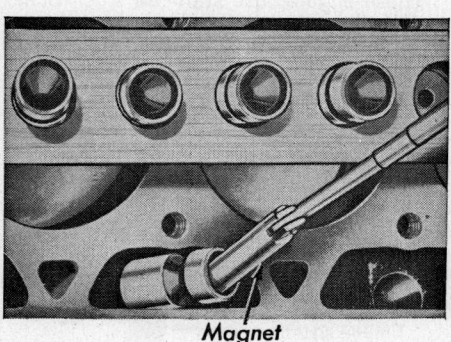

Magnet

Fig. 25 Removing valve lifter
with magnetic rod

8-429 "BOSS"	1970	40
8-460	1973-75	8
8-460[9]	1974-75	18

[1]—Cleveland engine.
[2]—Four bar. carb. [3]—Two bar. carb.
[4]—Auto. trans.
[5]—Windsor engine.
[6]—California engine.
[7]—Std. trans.
[8]—Modified.
[9]—Police Interceptor.

VALVES, ADJUST
Six Cylinder

The procedure used to check the valve clearance is to rotate the crankshaft with an auxiliary starter switch until the No. 1 piston is near TDC at the end of the compression stroke. At this point the following valves can be checked:

No. 1 Intake	No. 3 Exhaust
No. 1 Exhaust	No. 4 Intake
No. 2 Intake	No. 5 Exhaust

After the clearance of these valves have been checked, rotate the crankshaft until the No. 6 piston is on TDC at the end of its compression stroke (1 revolution of the crankshaft) and check the following valves:

No. 2 Exhaust	No. 5 Intake
No. 3 Intake	No. 6 Intake
No. 4 Exhaust	No. 6 Exhaust

Non-Adjustable Rocker Arm:

1. Position cylinder to be checked at T.D.C.
2. Apply pressure on the push rod end of the rocker arm until the tappet plunger is completely bottomed.
3. Hold rocker arm in this position and check the clearance between rocker arm and valve stem.
4. If the clearance is not within limits, install the appropriate undersize or oversize push rod, which are available in .060" undersize and .060" oversize.

Mechanical Valve Lifters

Before the final lash adjustment is made, operate the engine for 30 minutes at a fast idle to stabilize engine temperatures. To set the lash accurately, use only a step-type feeler gauge. For example, to obtain the correct setting if the clearance is .019", the .018" portion of the gauge should slip between valve tip and rocker arm but the "no go" end (.020") should not.

V8-289, Early 302 w/Hydraulic Lifters

1. Turn crankshaft to position No. 1 piston at TDC of the compression stroke. With the piston in this position, adjust the following valves to obtain the clearances listed in the Valve Specifications table.

No. 1 Intake	No. 4 Exhaust
No. 1 Exhaust	No. 5 Exhaust
No. 2 Exhaust	No. 7 Exhaust
No. 3 Intake	No. 8 Intake

2. Turn crankshaft to position No. 6 piston on TDC of the compression

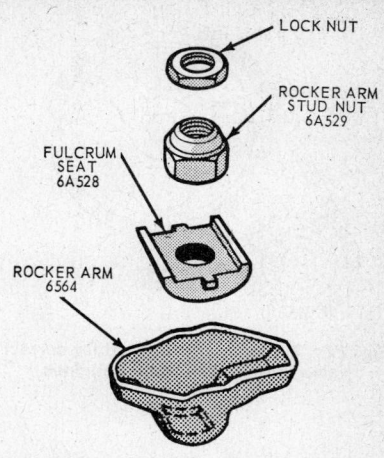

Fig. 24A Rocker assembly.
1969-71 V8-302 "BOSS"

stroke, and adjust the following valve clearances, using the same procedure as in Step 1.

No. 2 Intake	No. 6 Intake
No. 3 Exhaust	No. 6 Exhaust
No. 4 Exhaust	No. 7 Exhaust
No. 5 Intake	No. 8 Exhaust

V8-302 "BOSS", V8-429 "SCJ"

The valves in these engines use mechanical lifters which are adjusted in the conventional manner to the clearance listed in the Valve Specifications table.

Late V8-302 w/Hydraulic Lifters, V8-351 "Windsor" Engine

These engines incorporate a positive stop rocker arm stud and nut. Thread nut onto stud until it contacts the stud then tighten nut to 18-22 ft-lbs.

V8-351 "Cleveland" Engine V8-351M, 390, 400, 427, 428, 429, "CJ", 460

For these engines, a .060" longer or a

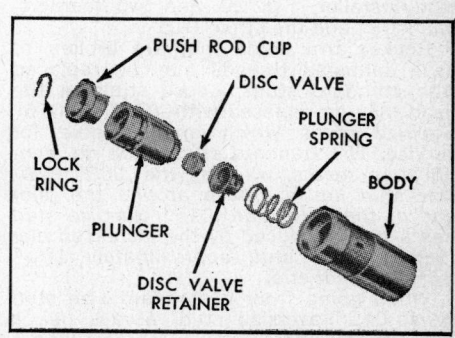

Fig. 26 Hydraulic valve lifter

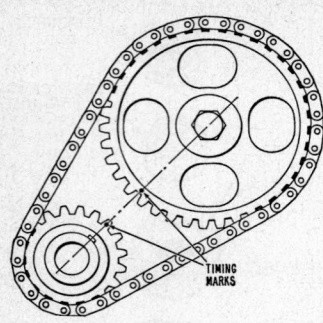

Fig. 27 Timing marks aligned for correct valve timing. Six cylinder engines

.060" shorter push rod is available to provide a means of compensating for dimensional changes in the valve train.

To check the clearance, bring the piston of the cylinder being checked on top dead center of the compression stroke. Then with hydraulic lifter collapsed, check the clearance between valve stem and rocker arm. If the clearance is less than the minimum, the .060" shorter push rod should be used. If clearance is more than the maximum the .060" longer push rod should be used.

V8-429 "BOSS"

The valve clearance should be set only with the engine cold.

1. Remove rocker arm covers and position No. 1 piston at TDC of its compression stroke.
2. Torque rocker arm shaft nuts for No. 1 cylinder to specifications then adjust valve lash.
3. Rotate crankshaft 90° to bring No. 5 piston to TDC and repeat adjustment for that cylinder.
4. Proceed through the firing order (1-5-4-2-6-3-7-8) until all valves have been adjusted.

ROCKER ARM STUD
V8-289, 302, 351W

If necessary to replace a rocker arm stud, a rocker arm stud kit is available and contains a stud remover, Fig. 19, a stud installer, Fig. 20, and two reamers, one .003" and the other .015".

Rocker arm studs that are broken or have damaged threads may be replaced with standard studs. Loose studs in the head may be replaced with .003" or .015" oversize studs which are available for service. *The standard studs have no identification marks, whereas the .003" oversize stud has a groove around the pilot end of the stud. The .015" oversize stud has a step produced by the increased diameter of the stud approximately 1⁵⁄₃₂" from the pilot end.*

When going from a standard size stud to a .015" oversize stud, always use a .003" reamer before finish reaming with a .015" reamer.

If a stud is broken off flush with the stud boss, use an easy-out to remove the broken stud, following the instructions of the tool manufacturer.

Late V8-302 w/Hydraulic Lifters & V8-351 "Windsor" Engine

A new type positive stop rocker arm stud and nut eliminates the need of adjusting valve lash.

Installation

1. Position the piston of the cylinder being worked on at TDC compression stroke.
2. Locate stud properly with tool T69P-6049D, Fig. 21. Make sure tool bottoms on the head.
3. Lubricate rocker arm components and place rocker arm and fulcrum on the stud.
4. Thread nut onto the stud until it contacts the shoulder, then tighten nut to 18-22 ft lbs.

High Performance V8-289, 302 & 1969-71 V8-429 Except "BOSS"

Threaded rocker arm studs are used in these engines, Fig. 22. To remove stud, remove rocker arm cover, lock nut, if used, stud nut, fulcrum seat and rocker arm. Unscrew stud from cylinder head.

Installation:

1. Apply water resistant sealer to threads.
2. Install push rod guide if used, stud and torque 60-70 ft-lbs. for V8-289, 85 ft-lbs. for V8-302, and 65-75 for V8-429.
3. Lubricate and install rocker arm, fulcrum and stud nut.
4. With engine warmed up, adjust valve lash and install lock nut where used.

VALVE GUIDES

Valve guides consist of holes bored in the cylinder head. For service the guide holes can be reamed oversize to accommodate valves with oversize stems of .003, .015 and .030".

ROCKER ARM SERVICE
6 Cylinder Engines

1. To disassemble, remove pin and

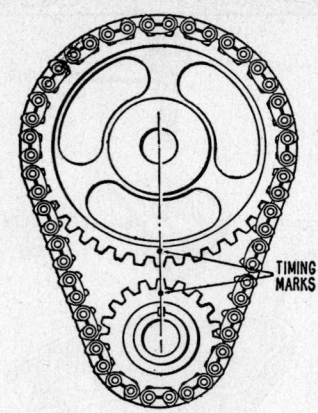

Fig. 28 Timing marks aligned for correct valve timing. V8 engines

spring washer from each end of rocker shaft, Fig. 23.
2. Slide rocker arms, springs and supports off the shaft, being sure to identify location of parts for reassembly.
3. If it is necessary to remove the plugs from the shaft ends, drill or pierce the plug on one end. Then use a steel rod to knock out the plug on the opposite end. Working from the open end, knock out the remaining plug.

Assemble

1. Lubricate all parts with engine oil. Apply Lubriplate to the rocker arm pads.
2. If plugs were removed from shaft ends, use a blunt tool or large diameter pin punch and install a plug (cup side out) in each end of shaft.
3. Install spring washer and pin on one end of shaft.
4. Install rocker arms, supports and springs in order shown in Fig. 23. *Be sure oil holes in shaft are facing downward.*
5. Complete the assembly by installing remaining spring washer and pin.

1970-75 V8-351C, 351M, 400 & 1972-74 V8-429, 460

These engines use stamped steel rocker arms retained by a fulcrum seat, Fig.

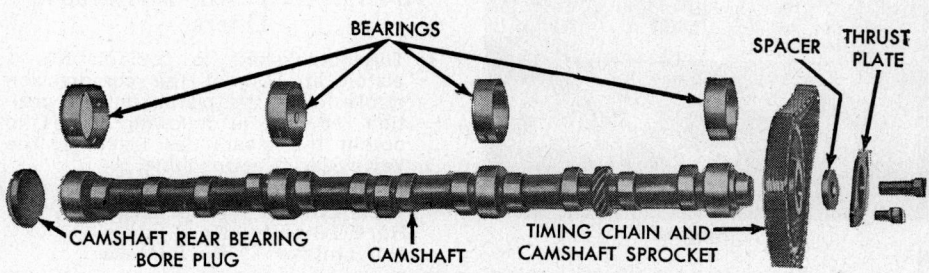

Fig. 29 Camshaft and related parts. Six cylinder engines

24. The fulcrum seat bolts directly to the cylinder head and guides the rocker arm.

1969-71 V8-302 "BOSS"

These engines use stamped steel rocker arms mounted on their own studs and retained by a fulcrum seat, stud nut and locknut, Fig. 24A. To remove rocker arm, remove valve cover, then remove locknut, fulcrum and seat and rocker arm.

V8-390, 427, 428, 429 Except "BOSS" & 460

See Ford-Mercury chapter.

V8-429 "BOSS"

Each rocker arm is mounted on its own shaft which in turn is mounted on a pedestal on the cylinder head. All valves and shafts are independent of each other.

VALVE LIFTERS, REPLACE

6 Cylinder Engines

When necessary to replace valve lifters, remove cylinder head and related parts as outlined previously. Then, using a magnet rod, Fig. 25, remove and install one lifter at a time to be sure they are placed in their original bores.

When installing, apply Lubriplate to each lifter foot and coat the remainder of lifter with oil before installation.

V8 Engines

1. Remove intake manifold.
2. Remove rocker arm covers. On engines with stud-mounted rocker

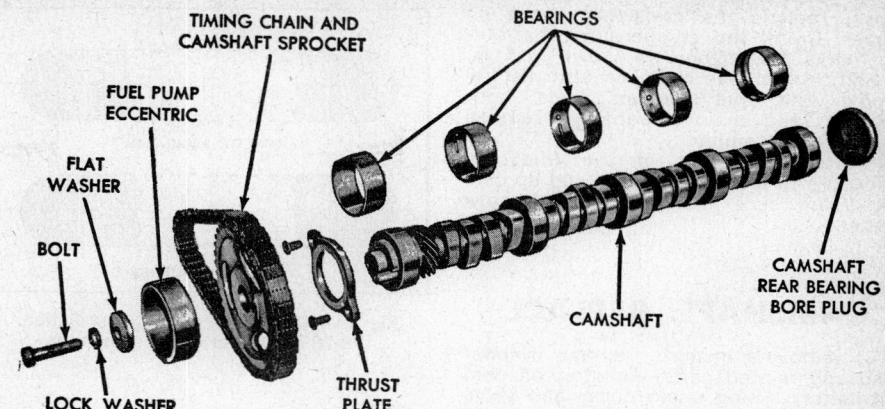

Fig. 30 Camshaft and related parts. V8 engines

arms, loosen stud nuts and rotate rocker arms to one side. On other engines, remove rocker arms and shafts.
3. Remove push rods in sequence so they can be installed in their original bores.
4. Using a magnet rod, Fig. 25, remove the lifters and place them in a numbered rack so they can be installed in their original bores. *If the lifters are stuck in their bores by excessive varnish, etc., it may be necessary to use a plier-type tool to remove them. Rotate the lifter back and forth to loosen it from the gum or varnish.*
5. The internal parts of each lifter are matched sets. Do not intermix parts. Keep the assemblies intact until they are to be cleaned, Fig. 26.

TIMING CASE COVER

NOTE: On all except V8-351 "Cleveland" engine; if necessary to replace cover oil seal, the cover and oil pan must be removed.

6 Cylinder Engines

1. Drain cooling system and crankcase.
2. Remove radiator, fan and pulley.
3. Use puller to remove damper.
4. Remove front cover and gasket.
5. Remove crankshaft oil slinger.
6. Drive seal out of cover with a pin punch and clean out recess in cover.
7. Coat a new seal with grease and drive it in until fully seated in recess. Check seal after installation to be sure spring is properly positioned in seal.
8. Reverse removal procedure to install.

V8 Engines

1. To remove cover, drain cooling system and crankcase. Remove air cleaner and disconnect battery ground cable.
2. Remove water hose as necessary.
3. Remove generator support bolt at water pump, and loosen generator

mounting bolts.
4. Remove fan, spacer and pulley.
5. Remove power steering drive belt (if equipped). If air conditioned, remove compressor drive belt.
6. Remove crankshaft pulley and adapter.
7. Remove fuel pump and lay it to one side with flexible fuel line attached.
8. Remove oil level dipstick tube bracket and oil filler tube bracket.
9. Remove oil pan-to-front cover bolts.
10. Remove cover and water pump as an assembly.
11. Drive out cover seal with a pin punch. Clean out recess in cover.
12. Coat a new seal with grease and drive seal in until it is fully seated in recess. Check seal after installation to be sure spring is properly positioned in seal.
13. Reverse removal procedure to install cover.

TIMING CHAIN

After removing the cover as outlined

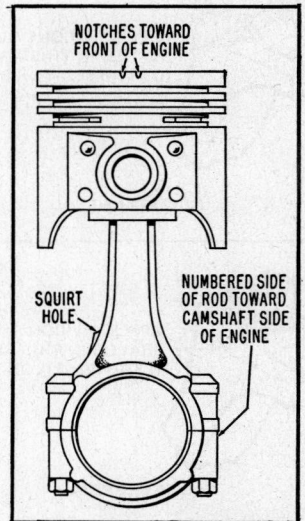

Fig. 31 Piston and rod assembly. Six cylinder engines

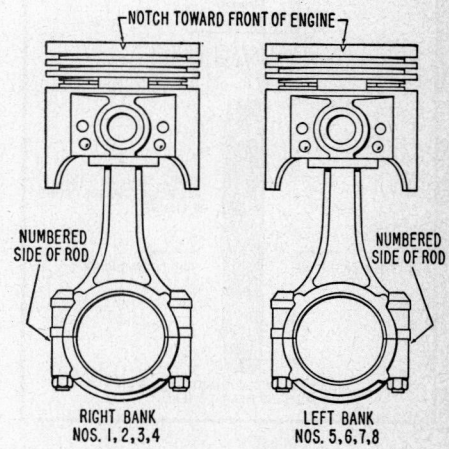

Fig. 32 Piston and rod assembly. V8s

above, remove the crankshaft front oil slinger. Crank the engine until the timing marks are aligned as shown in Figs. 27 and 28. Remove camshaft sprocket retaining bolt and washer. Slide both sprockets and chain forward and remove them as an assembly.

Reverse the order of the foregoing procedure to install the chain and sprockets, being sure the timing marks are aligned.

CAMSHAFT, REPLACE

To remove camshaft, remove cylinder head and related parts, radiator, oil pan, distributor, timing chain cover and valve lifters.

Remove timing chain and sprockets, camshaft thrust plate, and pull camshaft out of engine. If thrust plate shows signs of wear, install a new one, Figs. 29, 30.

SERVICE NOTE: On Mustang models, in addition to the above, it is necessary to remove the front bumper and grille center support bracket. Also remove the bolts from the left side of upper and lower stone shields. If necessary, loosen the bolts on the right side of the stone shields and raise the stone shields out of the way to remove the camshaft.

PISTON & ROD ASSEMBLY

When installed, piston and rod as-

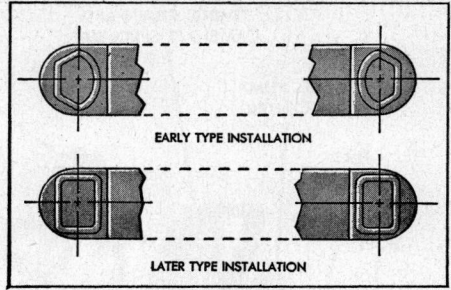

Fig. 34   Connecting rod bolt installation. V8-289 with four barrel carburetor

sembly should have the notch or arrow in piston head toward front of engine with connecting rod numbers positioned as shown in Figs. 31 and 32.

SERVICE NOTE: On V8-289 engine with four-barrel carburetor two types of connecting rod bolts have been used. These bolts must be installed as shown in Fig. 34 to be properly seated and eliminate the possibility of bolt loosening and eventual failure.

PISTONS, PINS & RINGS

Pistons and rings are furnished in standard sizes and oversizes of .020, .030 and .040". On 6-200 and V8-289 engines, .060" oversizes are also available.

Oversize pins are not furnished.

SERVICE BULLETIN

PISTON & PIN REPLACEMENT: When servicing engines using press fit piston pins, the piston and pin must be replaced as an assembly if either does not meet specifications. These components are not serviced separately for the principle reason that excess clearances are usually caused by piston wear rather than pin wear. Elimination of excess clearance by using oversize pins may result in fracture of the connecting rod.

MAIN & ROD BEARINGS

NOTE: Some High Output engines are equipped with an oil baffle tray connected to the main bearing caps. This baffle must be removed to service main and rod bearings.

SERVICE BULLETIN

UNDERSIZE CRANKSHAFTS: Crankshafts with .010" undersize rod and/or main journals are now authorized for use in all 1967 engines. All assemblies containing undersize crankshafts are identified on the cylinder block date stamp pad with a letter M for .010" undersize main journals and/or a letter P for undersize crankpin (rod) journals. These crankshafts can appear in

both production and service engines, and short block assemblies. Bearing clearances will remain the same as for standard crankshafts. All rod and/or main journals will be ground undersize if any one of the rod and/or main journals are undersize. This avoids mixing of standard and undersize bearings in the same engine. Three possible combinations can exist on crankshafts with undersize bearing journals:

1. All rod journals .010" undersize with standard main bearing journals.
2. All rod journals standard with .010" undersize main bearing journals.
3. Both rod and main bearing journals .010" undersize.

CRANKSHAFT OIL SEAL

Braided Type

To replace both upper and lower halves, engine and crankshaft must be removed. To replace lower half only, proceed as follows:

1. Remove oil pan and rear main bearing cap.
2. Remove seal and clean groove and cap and block mating surfaces. Preform new seal to approximate radius of cap.
3. Insert seal in cap, seating the center first and allowing seal to extend equally at both ends.
4. Using seating tool, firmly seat seal in groove and cut off ends flush with cap.
5. Apply sealer to cap at rear of the top mating surfaces. Do not apply sealer forward of the oil slinger groove.
6. Install cap and torque to specification.

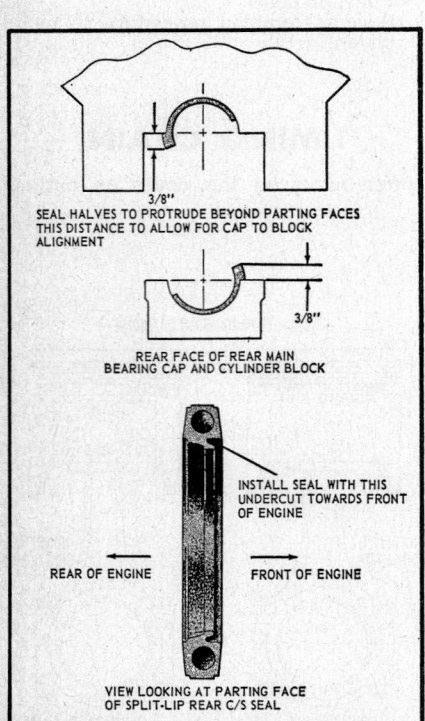

SEAL HALVES TO PROTRUDE BEYOND PARTING FACES THIS DISTANCE TO ALLOW FOR CAP TO BLOCK ALIGNMENT

3/8"

3/8"

REAR FACE OF REAR MAIN BEARING CAP AND CYLINDER BLOCK

INSTALL SEAL WITH THIS UNDERCUT TOWARDS FRONT OF ENGINE

REAR OF ENGINE   FRONT OF ENGINE

VIEW LOOKING AT PARTING FACE OF SPLIT-LIP REAR C/S SEAL

Fig. 35   New split-lip crankshaft rear seal installation

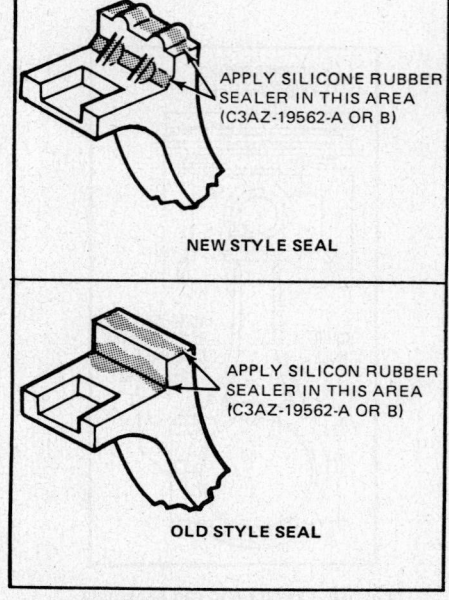

APPLY SILICONE RUBBER SEALER IN THIS AREA (C3AZ-19562-A OR B)

NEW STYLE SEAL

APPLY SILICON RUBBER SEALER IN THIS AREA (C3AZ-19562-A OR B)

OLD STYLE SEAL

Fig. 35A   Crankshaft oil seals

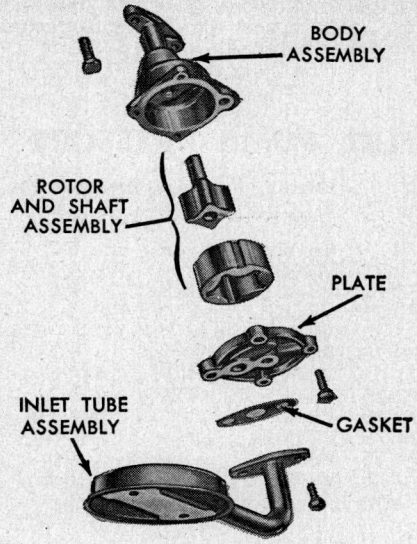

Fig. 36 Oil pump assembly. Six cylinder engines

Split Lip Type

1. Remove oil pan.
2. Remove rear bearing cap.
3. Loosen remaining bearing caps, allowing crankshaft to drop down about $1/32$".
4. Remove old seals from both cylinder block and rear main bearing cap. Use a brass rod to drift upper half of seal from cylinder block groove. Rotate crankshaft while drifting to facilitate removal.
5. Carefully clean seal groove in block with a brush and solvent. Also clean seal groove in bearing cap. Remove the oil seal retaining pin from the bearing cap if so equipped. *The pin is not used with the split-lip seal.*
6. Dip seal halves in clean engine oil.
7. Carefully install upper seal half in its groove with undercut side of seal toward front of engine, Fig. 35, by rotating it on shaft journal of crankshaft until approximately $3/8$" protrudes below the parting surface. *Be sure no rubber has been shaved from outside diameter of seal by bottom edge of groove.*
8. Retighten main bearing caps and torque to specifications.
9. Install lower seal in main bearing cap with undercut side of seal toward front of engine, and allow seal to protrude about $3/8$" above parting surface to mate with upper seal upon cap installation.
10. Apply suitable sealer to parting faces of cap and block. Install cap and torque to specifications.

NOTE: If difficulty is encountered in installing the upper half of the seal in position, lightly lap (sandpaper) the side of the seal opposite the lip side using a medium grit paper. After sanding, the seal must be washed in solvent, then

---

dipped in clean engine oil prior to installation.

SERVICE BULLETIN

A new crankshaft rear oil seal has been released for service. This new seal may be received when ordering an oil pan gasket kit and is installed in the same manner as described above, Fig. 35A.

OIL PAN, REPLACE

1969-75 V8-390, 427, 428, 429, 460

1. If equipped with air conditioning, remove fan shroud from radiator and position it over fan.
2. Disconnect stabilizer bar and pull ends down.

NOTE: To allow for clearance for removal of oil pan, remove engine front support insulator-to-intermediate support bracket nuts. Install a block of wood on a floor jack and position the jack under the front leading edge of the oil pan. Raise the engine about $1\frac{1}{4}$" and insert a 1" block of wood between insulators and frame crossmember; then remove floor jack.

3. Unfasten and lower oil pan to crossmember.
4. Crank engine to obtain necessary clearance between crankshaft counterweight and rear of oil pan. Remove upper bolt and loosen lower bolt on inlet tube.
5. Position inlet tube out of the way and remove oil pan.
6. Reverse procedure to install.

1969-75 Sixes

1. Remove oil level dipstick and fly-

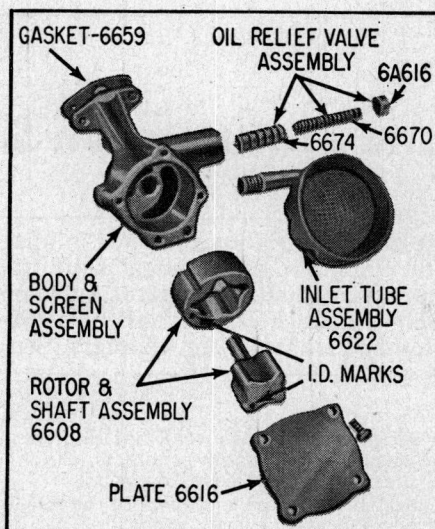

Fig. 37A Oil pump assembly. V8-351C, 351M & 400

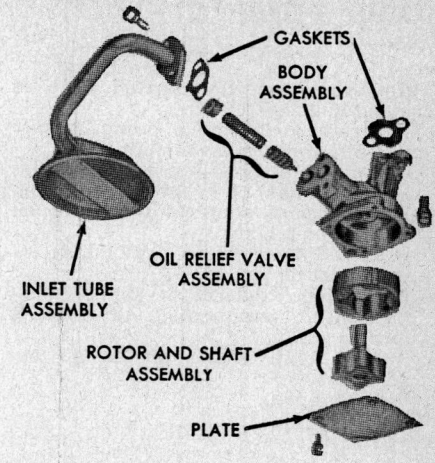

Fig. 37 Oil pump assembly. V8-289, 302, 351W

---

wheel housing inspection cover.
2. On a Mustang, disconnect stabilizer bar and pull it downward out of the way. Remove one bolt and loosen the other on the No. 2 crossmember and lower it out of the way.
3. Remove oil pan and gasket.
4. Reverse procedure to install.

1970-73 Mustang & 1970-75 Cougar V8-351C, 351M, 400

1. Remove oil dipstick and drain crankcase.
2. Remove starter.
3. Remove sway bar retaining bolts and No. 2 crossmember (under engine)-to-chassis bolts.
4. Remove oil pan bolts, turn crankshaft for maximum clearance and remove oil pan.

1970-75 Fairlane, Montego & Torino V8-351C, 351M & 400

1. Remove dipstick, remove fan shroud retaining bolts and position shroud over fan.
2. Raise car and drain crankcase.
3. Remove starter.
4. Disconnect and lower sway bar.
5. Remove front engine support through bolts, raise engine and place wood blocks between supports and brackets.
6. Remove oil pan bolts and lower oil pan.

1969-73 V8-289, 302, 351 "Windsor" Engine

1. Drain crankcase and remove oil level dipstick.
2. Lower stabilizer bar. On a Mustang the idler arm will also have to be lowered.
3. Remove oil pan bolts and crank engine as required to obtain clearance for removal of pan.

OIL PUMP REPLACE
6 Cylinder Engines

1. Remove oil pan and related parts as directed above.
2. Unfasten and remove pump, gasket and intermediate drive shaft.
3. Prime pump by filling either the inlet or outlet port with engine oil. Rotate pump shaft to distribute oil within pump body.
4. Position intermediate drive shaft into distributor socket.
5. Position new gasket on pump housing. Insert intermediate drive shaft into oil pump.
6. Install pump and shaft as an assembly.
7. Install oil pan.

V8-289, 302, 351, 400

1. Remove oil pan as outlined above.
2. Remove pump inlet tube and screen.
3. Remove pump retaining bolts and remove pump, gasket and intermediate shaft.
4. To install, position intermediate drive shaft into distributor socket. With shaft seated in socket, stop on shaft should touch roof of crankcase. Remove shaft and position stop as necessary.
5. With new gasket on pump housing and stop properly positioned, insert intermediate shaft into oil pump. Install pump and shaft as a unit. *Do not force pump into position if it will not seat readily. The drive shaft hex may be misaligned with distributor shaft. To align, rotate shaft into new position.*

V8-390, 427, 428, 429, 460

1. Remove oil pan as outlined above.
2. Remove oil pump screws, oil pump and intermediate shaft.

3. Remove inlet tube and screen from pump and discard gasket.
4. Prime pump by filling either inlet or outlet port with engine oil. Rotate pump shaft to distribute oil within pump body.
5. Position new gasket on pump housing.
6. Insert intermediate drive shaft into oil pump.
7. Install pump and shaft as a unit.
8. Complete installation in reverse order of removal.

OIL PUMP REPAIRS
V8-390, 427, 428, 429

See Ford-Mercury Full Size Car chapter for an illustration and service procedure for the oil pump used on this engine.

V8-289, 302, 351, 400 & All Sixes

Referring to Figs. 36, 37 and 37A, disassemble pump. To remove the oil pressure relief valve, insert a self-threading sheet metal screw of the proper diameter into the oil pressure relief valve chamber cap and pull cap out of chamber. Remove spring and plunger.

The inner rotor and shaft and the outer race are serviced as an assembly. One part should not be replaced without replacing the other.

Install the pump cover and tighten to 6-9 ft. lbs. torque.

BELT TENSION DATA

	New	Used
1969-75 All	140	110

WATER PUMP, REPLACE

Drain cooling system and disconnect radiator lower hose and heater hose at water pump. Remove drive belt, fan and pulley (also spacer on V8's). Unfasten and remove pump.

FUEL PUMP PRESSURE

Year	Engine	Pressure Lbs.
1969-75	Six Cyl.	4½-6½
1969	V8	4½-6½
1970	V8-429	5-7
1970-71	V8-429 "CJ"	6½-8½ ①
1970-71	V8-302 exc. "Boss"	4-6
1970-71	V8-302 "Boss", V8-428, V8-429 "Boss" "SCJ"	4½-6½
1970-75	V8-351C	5-7
1971	V8-429 "CJ"	4½-6½
1972-75	V8-302, 400, 429	5-7
1973-75	V8-460	5½-7½
1974-75	V8-302	4½-5½
1974-75	V8-351W	4-6
1974-75	V8-351C, 351M, 400	5½-6½

①—With fuel return line inoperative.

FUEL PUMP, REPLACE

1. Remove all gasket material from pump and block gasket surfaces. Apply sealer to both sides of new gasket.
2. Position gasket on pump flange and hold pump in position against its mounting surface. Make sure rocker arm is riding on camshaft eccentric.
3. Press pump tight against its mounting. Install retaining screws and tighten them alternately.
4. Connect fuel lines. Then operate engine and check for leaks.

NOTE: Before installing the pump, it is good practice to crank the engine so that the nose of the camshaft eccentric is out of the way of the fuel pump rocker arm when the pump is installed. In this way there will be the least amount of tension on the rocker arm, thereby easing installation of the pump.

Clutch and Transmission Section

NOTE: 1975 linkage adjustment information is in this section. Repair procedures on both automatic and manual shift transmissions are covered elsewhere in this manual. Procedures for removing automatic transmissions as well as linkage adjustments on 1969-74 models are included in the automatic transmission chapters. See Chapter Index.

CLUTCH PEDAL, ADJUST
1969-75

1. Disconnect clutch return spring from release lever.
2. Loosen release lever rod lock nut.

3. Move release lever rearward until release bearing lightly contacts clutch pressure plate release fingers.
4. Adjust adapter length until adapter seats in release lever pocket.
5. Insert the proper feeler gauge (see below) against back face of rod adapter, then tighten lock nut finger

tight against feeler gauge.

1973-75 Exc. Comet & Maverick	.194"
1973-75 Comet & Maverick	.136"
1972	.194"
1969-71 except 8-390 engine	.136"
1969-71 8-390 engine	.178"

6. Remove feeler gauge. Hold lock nut

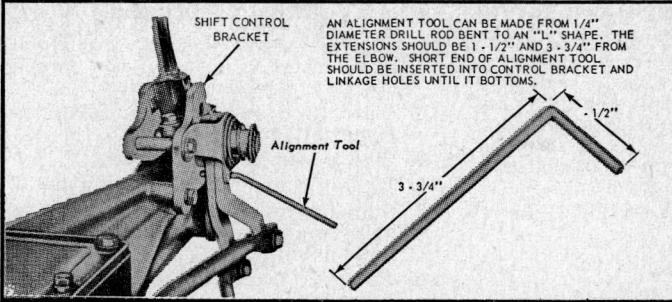

Fig. 1   Gearshift linkage. Typical 1969-75

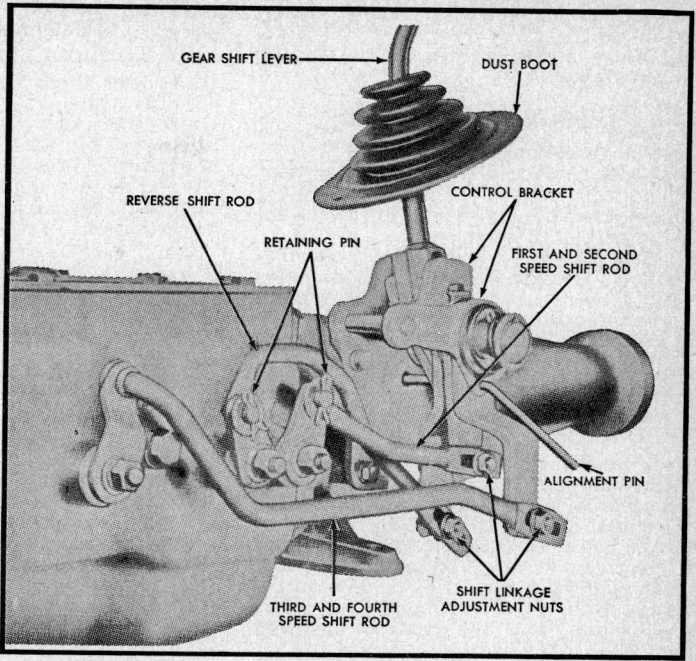

Fig. 2   Ford four speed shift linkage. Typical 1969-75

in position and tighten adapter against nut.

7. Install release spring and check for free travel of pedal which is $\frac{7}{8}$" to $1\frac{1}{8}$".

SERVICE BULLETIN

CLUTCH ROD INTERFERENCE: High clutch pedal effort and/or binding on acceleration may exist on some 1969 Cougar and Montego V8-351 with 3 or 4 speed manual transmission due to the clutch release rod contacting the flywheel housing during acceleration. If evidence of this condition exists, grind off flywheel housing cover flush with clutch housing.

CLUTCH, REPLACE

1. Remove transmission as outlined further on.
2. Remove release lever retracting spring. Then slide release bearing and hub off release lever.
3. Remove inspection cover on 6-170 engine and flywheel housing on either engine.
4. Loosen clutch cover attaching bolts a little at a time until spring tension is relieved. *If the same cover and pressure plate is to be installed, mark the cover and flywheel so that the pressure plate can be installed in the same position.*
5. Remove cover, pressure plate and clutch disc.
6. Remove clutch release lever from housing.
7. Reverse removal procedure to install the clutch and adjust the pedal as outlined previously.

THREE SPEED TRANS. REPLACE

1969-75

1. Raise and support vehicle on a hoist or safety stands.
2. Disconnect electrical connectors from transmission.
3. Mark drive shaft so that it may be installed in the same position then disconnect it from rear U joint and remove it from output shaft.

NOTE: Plug extension housing to prevent loss of lubricant.

4. Disconnect speedometer cable and shift linkages from transmission.
5. On 1969-72 Ford and Mercury models, disconnect parking brake cable from equalizer lever and remove lever from crossmember. Remove the extension housing to engine rear support bolts.
6. On 1971-72 intermediate models, raise transmission with suitable jack and remove engine rear support nuts. Remove the crossmember and rear support insulator.
7. Support engine and remove transmission.

NOTE: Do not depress clutch pedal with transmission removed.

FOUR SPEED TRANS. REPLACE

1969-75 Ford Design

1. Raise vehicle and support on hoist or safety stands.
2. Disconnect electrical connectors from transmission.
3. Mark driveshaft so that it may be installed in the same position then disconnect it from rear U joint and remove it from output shaft.
4. Disconnect speedometer cable from transmission and parking brake cable from equalizer lever and remove lever from crossmember.
5. Remove hairpin retainer from parking brake cable and remove cable from crossmember.

6. Remove the shift rods from the shift levers and remove the shift control.
7. Support engine with suitable jack and remove rear support bolts then raise engine enough to relieve weight from crossmember and remove crossmember bolts and crossmember.
8. Support transmission with suitable jack and remove transmission bolts and transmission.

NOTE: Do not depress clutch pedal with transmission removed.

GEARSHIFT LINKAGE

NOTE: *If the transmission shifts hard or will not engage, the gearshift levers may need adjusting at the cross-over. Move the shift lever through all positions to see that the cross-over operation is smooth. If not, adjust as follows:*

1972-75 Torino & Montego Column Shift

1. Working inside car, loosen clamp nut holding gearshift tube and shaft.
2. Loosen shift rod adjusting nuts at transmission.
3. Remove plastic covers over gearshift lever assembly and insert $\frac{1}{4}$" rod.
4. Set gearshift lever in Neutral in the 2-3 plane and torque clamp nut inside car to 12-18 ft. lbs.
5. Set transmission levers in Neutral and insert $\frac{1}{4}$" rod in locator holes in lower end of steering column.
6. Torque shift rod adjusting nuts using care to prevent motion between the rods and the studs on transmission levers.

7. Remove alignment pins and install covers.
8. Check operation to assure smooth crossover.

1969-71 Column Shift

1. Place shift lever in neutral.
2. Loosen two gearshift rod adjustment nuts.
3. See that transmission shift levers are in neutral position.
4. Insert a $3/16''$ diameter rod through holes in both levers and both holes in lower casting. It may be necessary to align levers to insert tool.
5. Tighten shift rod adjustment nuts.
6. Remove alignment tool and check operation of shift levers.

1969-75 3 Speed Floor Shift

NOTE: 1970-75 floor shift linkages incorporate a transmission lock rod. This rod must be adjusted AFTER the shift linkage has been adjusted. With shift lever in Neutral and lock rod adjustment nut loose, align hole in steering column socket casting with alignment mark and insert a .180" dia. rod. The casting must not rotate with the rod in this position. Tighten lock rod adjustment nut.

1. Loosen three shift linkage adjusting nuts. Install a $1/4''$ diameter alignment pin through control bracket and levers, Fig. 1.
2. Tighten three linkage adjusting nuts and remove alignment pin.
3. Check gearshift lever for smooth crossover.

1974-75 4 Speed

1. Disconnect shift rods from shift levers.
2. Install alignment pin in shift control, Fig. 2.
3. Turn reverse lever clockwise into gear to make sure forward gears are in neutral.
4. Attach forward speed shift rods on levers and rotate reverse lever counterclockwise until it stops then attach reverse rod on reverse lever.
5. Attach column lock rod and remove alignment pin.
6. Adjust transmission lock rod as outlined for 1970-75 three speed units.

1969-73 4 Speed

1. Loosen shift linkage adjustment nuts. Install a $1/4''$ dia. rod through control bracket and lever holes.
2. Disconnect reverse gear shift rod from shift lever.
3. Shift transmission into reverse.
4. Tighten 1-2 and 3-4 shift rod nuts.
5. Connect reverse shift rod to lever, shift reverse lever to neutral position and tighten nut.
6. Remove alignment tool and check operation.
7. On 1970-73 units, adjust transmission lock rod as outlined for 1970-75 three speed units.

1975 AUTO. TRANS. LINKAGE, ADJUST

NOTE: All 1975 vehicles, use the same procedure as previous models and can be found elsewhere in this book.

Rear Axle, Propeller Shaft & Brakes

REAR AXLES

Figs. 1 and 2 illustrate the rear axle assemblies used on these cars. When necessary to overhaul either of these units, refer to the *Rear Axle Specifications* table in this chapter.

Integral Carrier Type, Fig. 1

In these axles, Fig. 1, the rear axle housing and differential carrier are cast into an integral assembly. The drive pinion assembly is mounted on two opposed tapered roller bearings. Spacers are used and are located between the front and rear bearing cones. Ring gear and pinion tooth contact is adjusted by shims between the rear bearing cone and pinion gear.

The differential carrier assembly is mounted on two opposed tapered roller bearings. The bearings are retained in the housing by removable caps. Differential bearing preload and drive gear backlash is adjusted by threaded ring nuts or sleeves located behind each differential bearing cup.

All service operations on the differential case assembly and the drive pinion assembly can be performed with the housing in the vehicle. The axle shafts and bearings can be pulled out of the housing ends. The differential assembly and then the drive pinion can be removed from the housing after the cover is removed from the rear face of the carrier casting.

Service Bulletin

All Ford Built Rear Axles: Recent manufacturing changes have eliminated the

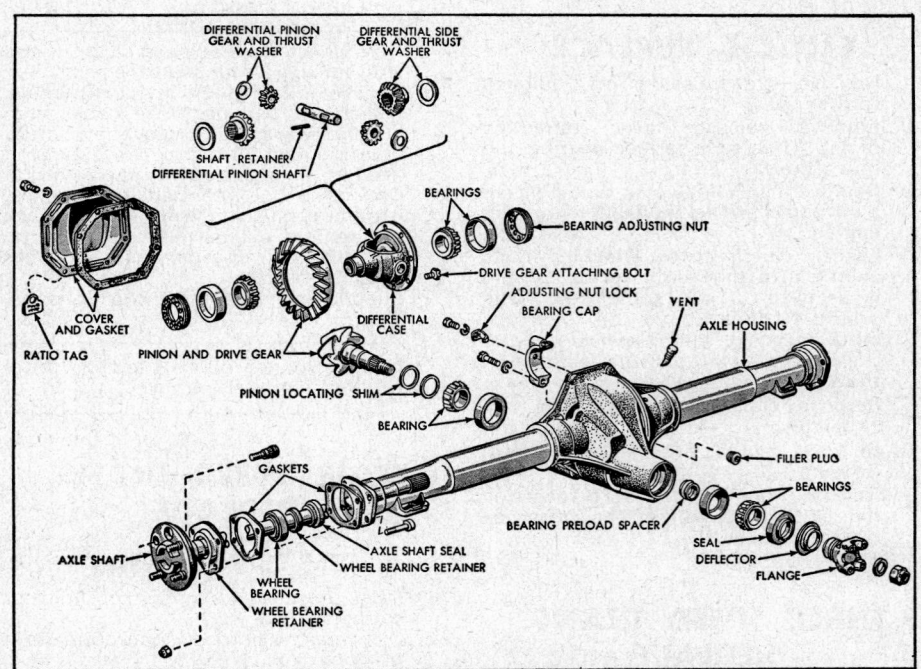

Fig. 1   Disassembled view of integral carrier type rear axle assembly

need for marking rear axle drive pinions for individual variations from nominal shim thicknesses. In the past, these pinion markings, with the aid of a shim selection table, were used as a guide to select correct shim thicknesses when a gear set or carrier assembly replacement was performed.

With the elimination of pinion markings, use of the shim selection table is no

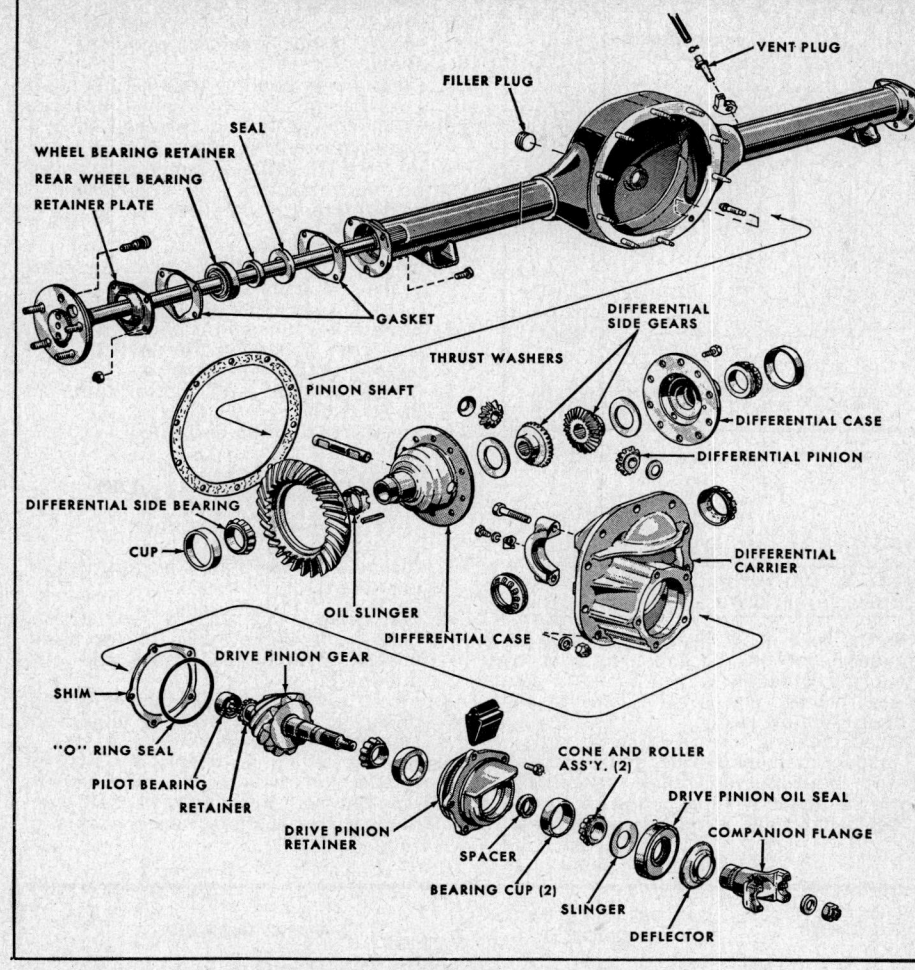

Fig. 2   Rear axle assembly with removable carrier

Fig. 3   Removing nuts from wheel bearing retainer

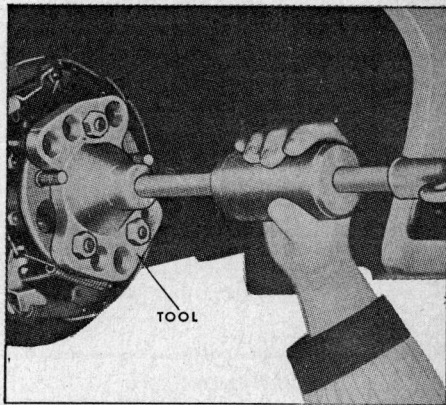

Fig. 4   Removing axle shaft with slide hammer-type puller

longer possible and the methods outlined below must be used.

1. Measure the thickness of the original pinion depth shim removed from the axle. Use the same thickness upon installation of the replacement carrier or drive pinion. If any further shim change is necessary, it will be indicated in the tooth pattern check.

2. If the original shim is lost, substitute a nominal shim for the original and use the tooth pattern check to determine if further shim changes are required.

Removable Carrier Type

In these axles, Fig. 2, the drive pinion is straddle-mounted by two opposed tapered roller bearings which support the pinion shaft in front of the drive pinion gear, and a straight roller bearing that

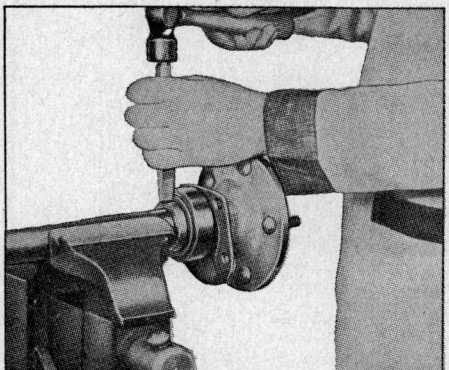

Fig. 5   Splitting bearing inner retainer for bearing removal

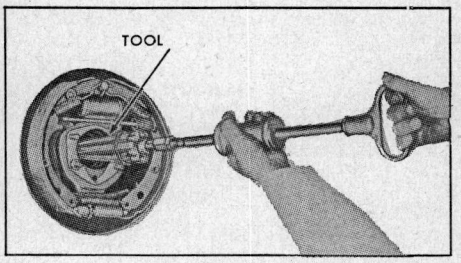

Fig. 6   Using hook-type tool to remove oil seal

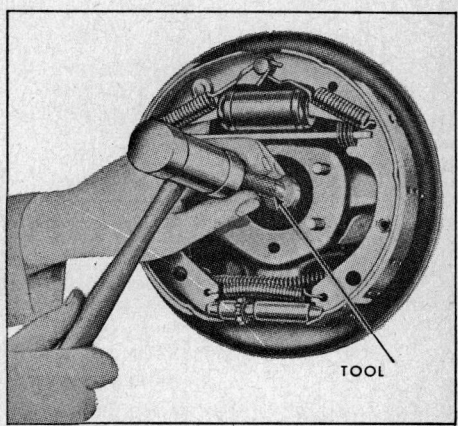

Fig. 7   Using special driver to install oil seal

supports the pinion shaft at the rear of the pinion gear. The drive pinion is assembled in a pinion retainer that is bolted to the differential carrier. The tapered roller bearings are preloaded by a collapsible spacer between the bearings. The pinion is positioned by a shim or shims located between the drive pinion retainer and the differential carrier.

The differential is supported in the carrier by two tapered roller side bearings. These bearings are preloaded by two threaded ring nuts or sleeves between the bearings and the pedestals. The differential assembly is positioned for proper ring gear and pinion backlash by varying the adjustment of these ring nuts. The differential case houses two side gears in mesh with two pinions mounted on a pinion shaft which held in place by a pin. The side gears and pinions are backed by thrust washers.

The axle shafts are of unequal length, the left shaft being shorter than the right. The axle shafts are mounted in sealed ball bearings which are pressed on the shafts.

Axle Shaft, Replace

1. Remove wheel assembly.
2. Remove brake drum from flange.
3. Working through hole provided in axle shaft flange, Fig. 3, remove nuts that secure wheel bearing retainer.
4. Pull axle shaft out of housing. If bearing is a tight fit in axle housing use a slide hammer-type puller, Fig. 4. *Brake carrier plate must not be dislodged. Install one nut to hold the plate in place after axle shaft is removed.*

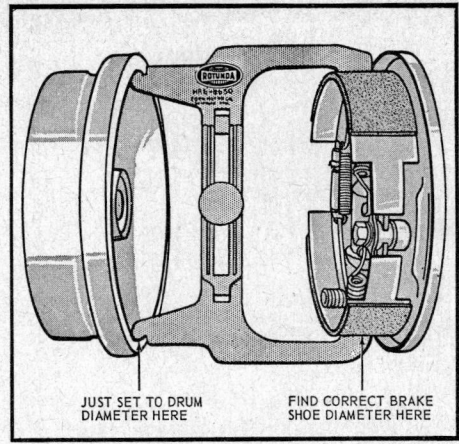

JUST SET TO DRUM DIAMETER HERE **FIND CORRECT BRAKE SHOE DIAMETER HERE**

Fig. 8   Revised brake adjustment

moved.

NOTE: On 1974-75 models, remove brake carrier plate.

5. If the axle shaft bearing is to be replaced, loosen the inner retainer by nicking it deeply with a chisel in several places, Fig. 5. The bearing will then slide off easily.
6. Press bearing from axle shaft.
7. Inspect machined surface of axle shaft and housing for rough spots that would affect sealing action of the oil seal. Carefully remove any burrs or

rough spots.
8. Press new bearing on shaft until it seats firmly against shoulder on shaft.
9. Press inner bearing retainer on shaft until it seats firmly against bearing.
10. If oil seal is to be replaced, use a hook-type tool to pull it out of housing, Fig. 6. Wipe a small amount of oil resistant sealer on outer edge of seal before it is installed, Fig. 7.

Installation

1. On 1974-75 models, place a new gasket on each side of brake carrier plate and slide axle shaft into housing.
2. Start the splines into the differential side gear and push the shaft in until bearing bottoms in housing.
3. Install retainer and tighten nuts to 30-40 ft. lbs.
4. Install brake drum and wheel.

PROPELLER SHAFT
Remove & Replace

1. Disconnect rear U-joint from drive pinion flange.
2. Pull drive shaft toward rear of car until front U-joint yoke clears transmission extension housing and output shaft.
3. Install a suitable tool, such as a seal driver, in seal to prevent lube from leaking from transmission.
4. Before installing, check U-joints for freedom of movement. If a bind has resulted from misalignment after overhauling the U-joints, tap the ears of

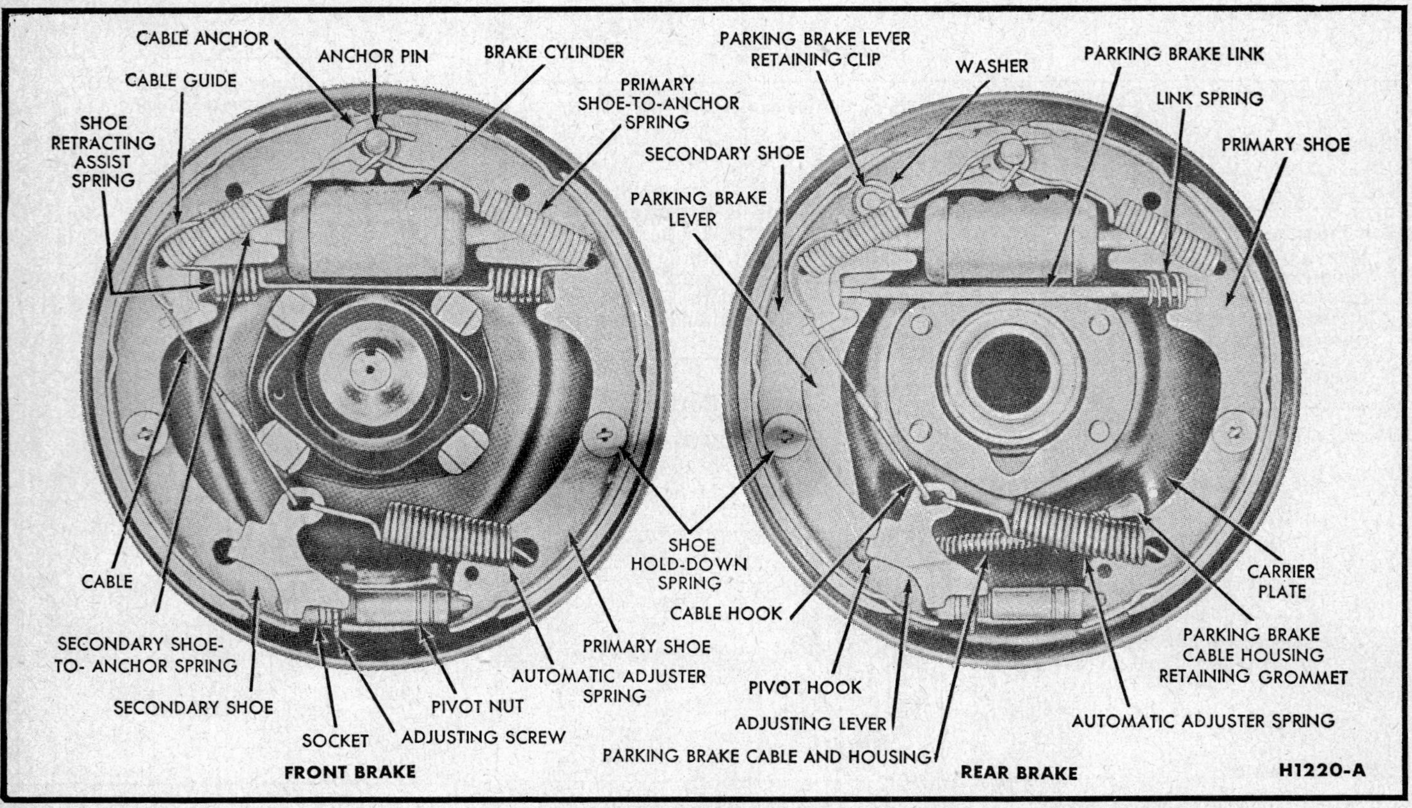

FRONT BRAKE labels: CABLE ANCHOR, CABLE GUIDE, ANCHOR PIN, BRAKE CYLINDER, PRIMARY SHOE-TO-ANCHOR SPRING, SHOE RETRACTING ASSIST SPRING, CABLE, SECONDARY SHOE-TO-ANCHOR SPRING, SECONDARY SHOE, SOCKET, PIVOT NUT, ADJUSTING SCREW, AUTOMATIC ADJUSTER SPRING, PRIMARY SHOE, SHOE HOLD-DOWN SPRING

REAR BRAKE labels: PARKING BRAKE LEVER RETAINING CLIP, SECONDARY SHOE, PARKING BRAKE LEVER, WASHER, PARKING BRAKE LINK, LINK SPRING, PRIMARY SHOE, CARRIER PLATE, PARKING BRAKE CABLE HOUSING RETAINING GROMMET, AUTOMATIC ADJUSTER SPRING, PARKING BRAKE CABLE AND HOUSING, ADJUSTING LEVER, PIVOT HOOK, CABLE HOOK

H1220-A

Fig. 9   Right front and rear brake mechanism. 1969-75 V8s

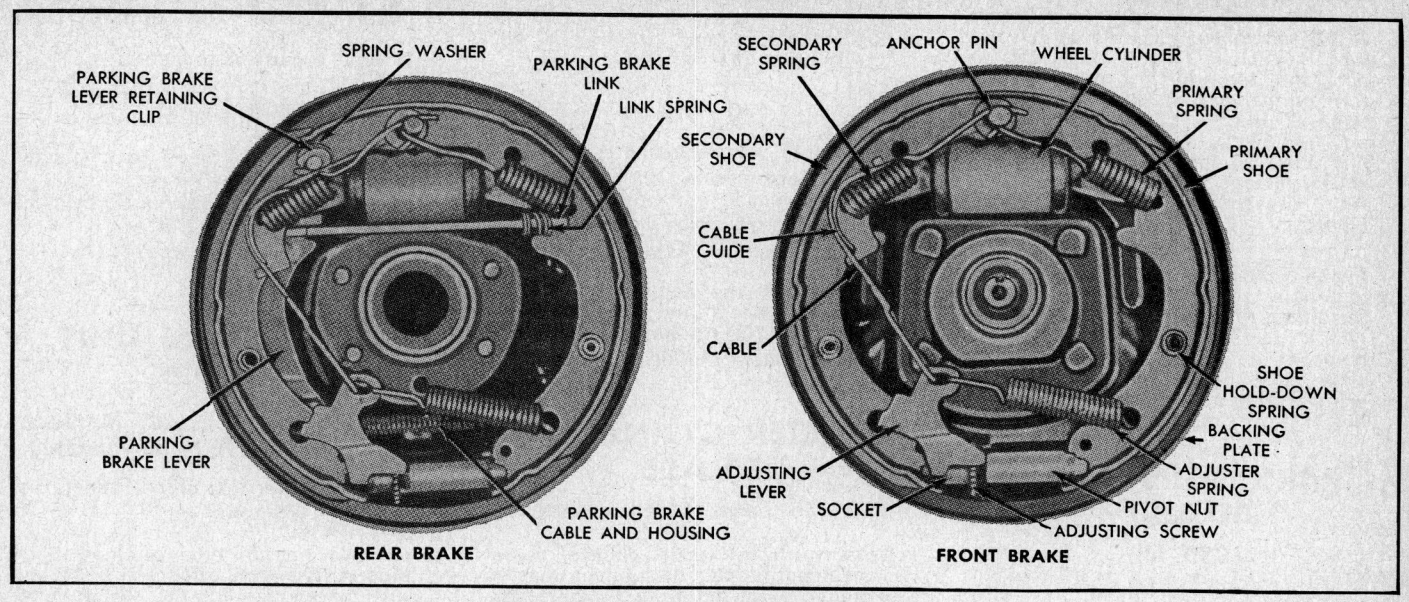

PARKING BRAKE LEVER RETAINING CLIP · SPRING WASHER · PARKING BRAKE LINK · LINK SPRING · SECONDARY SPRING · ANCHOR PIN · WHEEL CYLINDER · PRIMARY SPRING · PRIMARY SHOE · SECONDARY SHOE · CABLE GUIDE · CABLE · PARKING BRAKE LEVER · PARKING BRAKE CABLE AND HOUSING · ADJUSTING LEVER · SOCKET · ADJUSTING SCREW · PIVOT NUT · ADJUSTER SPRING · BACKING PLATE · SHOE HOLD-DOWN SPRING

REAR BRAKE   **FRONT BRAKE**

Fig. 10   **Right front and rear brakes. 1969-75 Six-Cylinder models**

the drive shaft sharply to relieve the bind.

5. If rubber seal installed on end of transmission extension housing is damaged, install a new seal.
6. On a manual shift transmission, lubricate yoke spline with conventional transmission grease. On an automatic transmission, lubricate yoke spline with special spline grease. *This spline is sealed so that transmission fluid does not "wash" away spline lubricant.*
7. Install yoke on transmission output shaft.
8. Install U-bolts and nuts which attach U-joint to pinion flange. Tighten U-bolts evenly to prevent binding U-joint bearings.

BRAKE ADJUSTMENTS

SERVICE BULLETIN

REVISED BRAKE ADJUSTMENT PROCEDURE: Some models use a new front and rear brake backing plate which omits the adjusting slot for manual brake adjustment. The backing plates have a partially stamped knock-out slot for use ONLY when the brake drums cannot be removed in a normal manner. The open slot is then covered with a rubber plug as used in the past to prevent contamination of the brakes.

When servicing a vehicle requiring a brake adjustment, the metal knock-out plugs should NOT be removed. Rather the drums should be removed and brakes inspected for a malfunction.

Although the brakes are self-adjusting, an initial adjustment will be necessary after a brake repair, such as relining or replacement. The initial adjustment can be obtained by the new procedure which follows:

1. Use the brake shoe adjustment gauge

shown in Fig. 8 to obtain the drum inside diameter as shown. Tighten the adjusting knob on the gauge to hold this setting.
2. Place the opposite side of the gauge over the brake shoes and adjust the shoes by turning the adjuster screw until the gauge just slides over the linings. Rotate the gauge around the lining surface to assure proper lining diameter adjustment and clearance.
3. Install brake drum and wheel. Final adjustment is accomplished by making several firm reverse stops, using the brake pedal.

Self-Adjusting Brakes

These brakes, Figs. 9 and 10, have

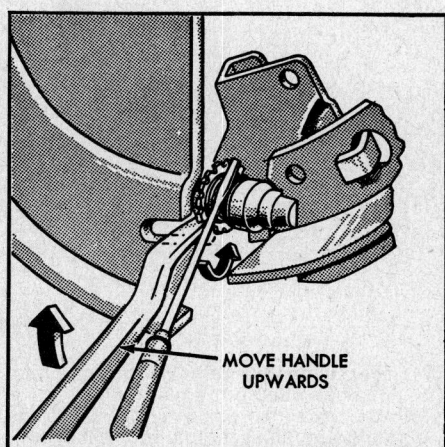

MOVE HANDLE UPWARDS

Fig. 11   **Backing off brake adjustment by disengaging adjusting lever with screwdriver**

self-adjusting shoe mechanisms that assure correct lining-to-drum clearances at all times. The automatic adjusters operate only when the brakes are applied as the car is moving rearward or when the car comes to an uphill stop.

Although the brakes are self-adjusting, an initial adjustment in necessary after the brake shoes have been relined or replaced, or when the length of the star wheel adjuster has been changed during some other service operation.

Frequent usage of an automatic transmission forward range to halt reverse vehicle motion may prevent the automatic adjusters from functioning, thereby inducing low pedal heights. Should low pedal heights be encountered, it is recommended that numerous forward and reverse stops be made until satisfactory pedal height is obtained.

NOTE

If a low pedal condition cannot be corrected by making numerous reverse stops (provided the hydraulic system is free of air) it indicates that the self-adjusting mechanism is not functioning. Therefore, it will be necessary to remove the brake drum, clean, free up and lubricate the adjusting mechanism. Then adjust the brake, being sure the parking brake is fully released.

Adjustment

1. Remove adjusting hole cover from the brake backing plate and, from the backing plate side, turn the adjusting screw with a screwdriver or other suitable tool to expand the shoes until a slight drag is felt when the drum is rotated.
2. Remove the drum.
3. While holding the adjusting lever out of engagement with the adjusting screw, Fig. 11, back off the adjusting screw about ¾ turn with the fingers.

NOTE—*If finger movement will not turn the screw, free it up. If this is not done, the adjusting lever will not turn during subsequent vehicle operation. Lubricate the screw with oil and coat with wheel bearing grease. Any other adjustment procedure may cause damage to the adjusting screw with consequent self-adjuster problems.*

4. Install wheel and drum, and adjusting hole cover. Adjust brakes on remaining wheels in the same manner.
5. If pedal height is not satisfactory, drive the vehicle and make sufficient reverse stops until proper pedal height is obtained.

PARKING BRAKE, ADJUST

1969 All

1. Fully release parking brake.
2. Pull brake handle out to third notch from fully released position.
3. Raise vehicle and remove wheel cover.
4. Turn locking adjustment nut forward against cable guide on equalizer until there is 100 ft-lbs breakaway torque at rear wheel when turning rear wheels in direction of forward rotation with a torque wrench. This torque measurement must be made relative to the centerline of the wheel.
5. Release parking brake and make sure brake shoes return to fully released position and no drag is felt when turning rear wheels.

1970-75 All

1. Make sure parking brake is released.
2. Place transmission in neutral and raise the vehicle.
3. Tighten the adjusting nut against the cable equalizer to cause rear brakes to drag.
4. Then loosen the adjusting nut until the rear wheels are fully released. There should be no drag.
5. Lower vehicle and check operation.

MASTER CYLINDER, REPLACE

1969-75 Less Power Brakes

1. Working from inside vehicle below instrument panel, disconnect master cylinder push rod from brake pedal.
2. Disconnect stop light switch wires, remove hairpin retainer and slide stop light switch off brake pedal pin just far enough to clear end of pin. Then lift switch straight upward from pin.
3. Slide master cylinder push rod with nylon washers and bushings from brake pedal pin.
4. Remove brake tubes from outlet ports of master cylinder.
5. Remove lock nuts that secure master cylinder to dash panel and lift cylinder forward and upward from vehicle.
6. Reverse procedure to install.

1969-75 Power Brakes

1. Disconnect brake lines from master cylinder.
2. Remove nuts retaining master cylinder to brake booster.
3. Remove master cylinder.

POWER BRAKE UNIT, REPLACE

1969-75 Comet, Cougar, Montego & Fairlane & 1969-73 Mustang

1. Working under instrument panel, disconnect stop light switch wires at connector.
2. Remove hairpin type retainer. Slide stop light switch off brake pedal pin just far enough for the switch outer hole to clear the pin, then lower switch away from pin.
3. Slide master cylinder push rod link and nylon washers and bushing off brake pedal pin.
4. Disconnect brake line from master cylinder.
5. Disconnect vacuum hose from booster at check valve.
6. Unfasten and remove booster and bracket assembly from dash panel, sliding push rod link out from engine side of dash panel.

Rear Suspension

SHOCK ABSORBER, REPLACE

To replace shock absorber, support rear axle properly and disconnect shock absorber at upper and lower mountings. On all models except convertibles and 1971-73 Comet and Maverick, the upper nut is accessible from inside trunk. On 1969-71 Montego, Torino and all Cougar, Mustang Models access cover must be removed from trunk floor panel. On convertibles the upper attachment access cover is accessible by removing the rear seat.

LEAF SPRINGS & BUSHINGS REPLACE

All Exc. 1972-75 Montego, Torino

1. Raise rear of vehicle and support at frame. Support axle with a suitable jack.
2. Disconnect shock absorbers from lower mountings.

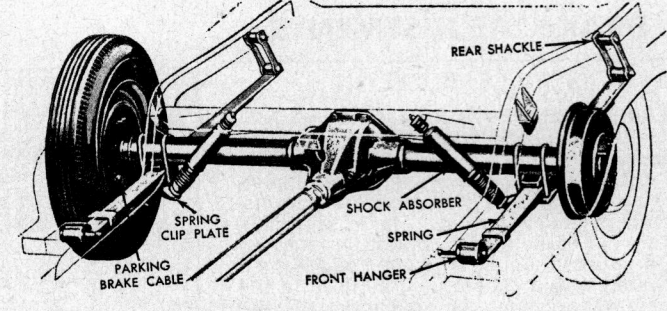

Fig. 1   Leaf spring suspension (typical)

3. Lower jack and remove spring plate "U" bolts and spring plate, Fig. 1.
4. Raise axle to remove weight from spring and disassemble rear shackle.
5. Remove spring front mount bolt.
6. Replace spring front eye bushings as necessary, Figs. 2 and 3.
7. Reverse procedure to install.

COIL SPRING, REPLACE

1972-75 Montego & Torino

1. Raise rear of vehicle and support at frame. Support axle with a suitable jack.
2. Disconnect shock absorbers from lower mountings.

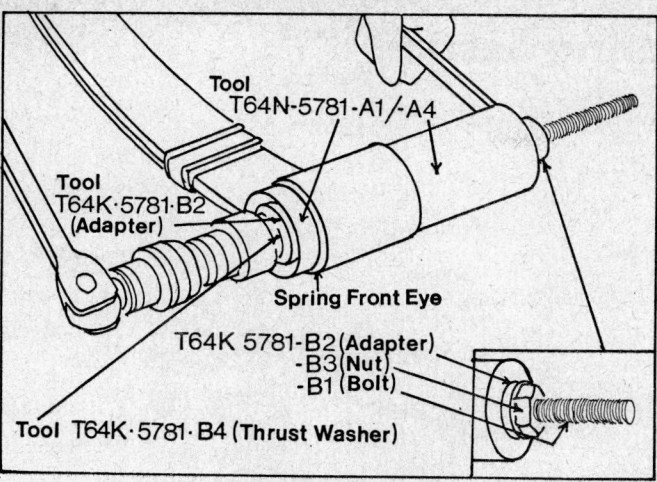

Fig. 2 Spring front bushing removal

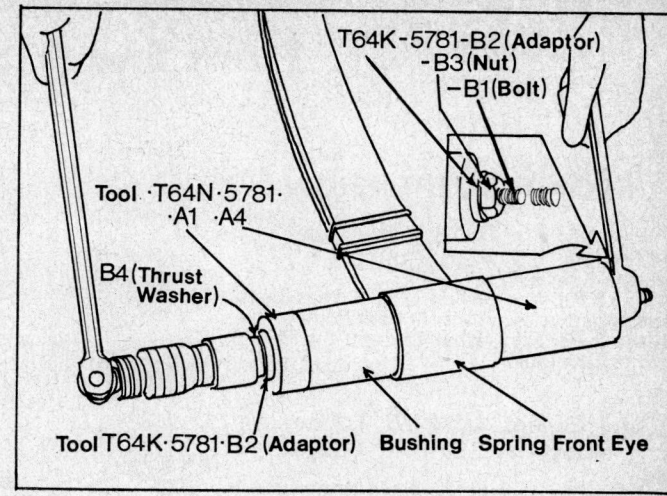

Fig. 3 Spring front bushing installation

3. Lower axle to remove springs.
4. Reverse procedure to install. Install an insulator between upper and lower seats and spring.

CONTROL ARMS, REPLACE

1972-75 Montego & Torino

NOTE: Upper and lower control arms must be replaced in pairs.

1. Raise rear of vehicle and support at frame. Support axle with a suitable jack. Also support differential pinion nose.
2. Disconnect control arm from axle bracket. On upper arms, disconnect arm from crossmember and on lower arms, disconnect arm from frame attachment bracket, Fig. 4.
3. Reverse procedure to install.

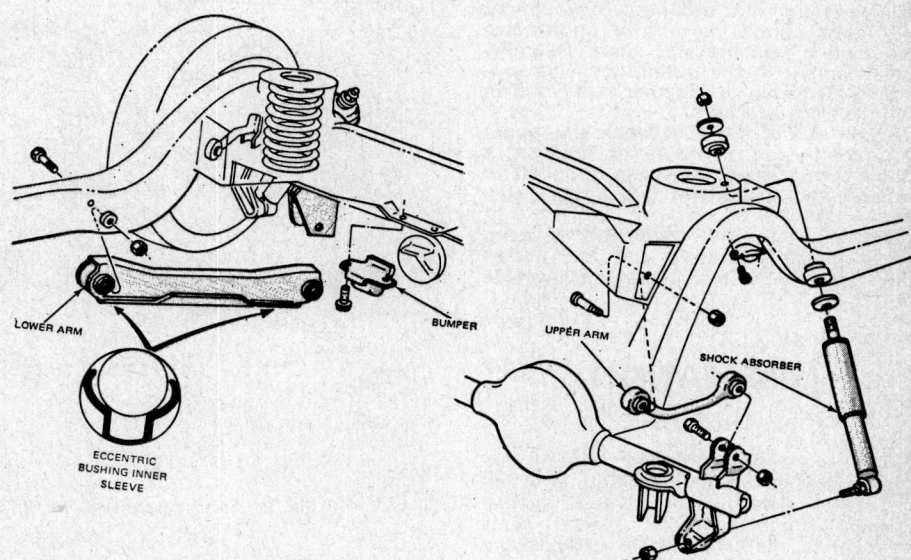

Fig. 4 Rear suspension, 1972-75 Montego & Torino

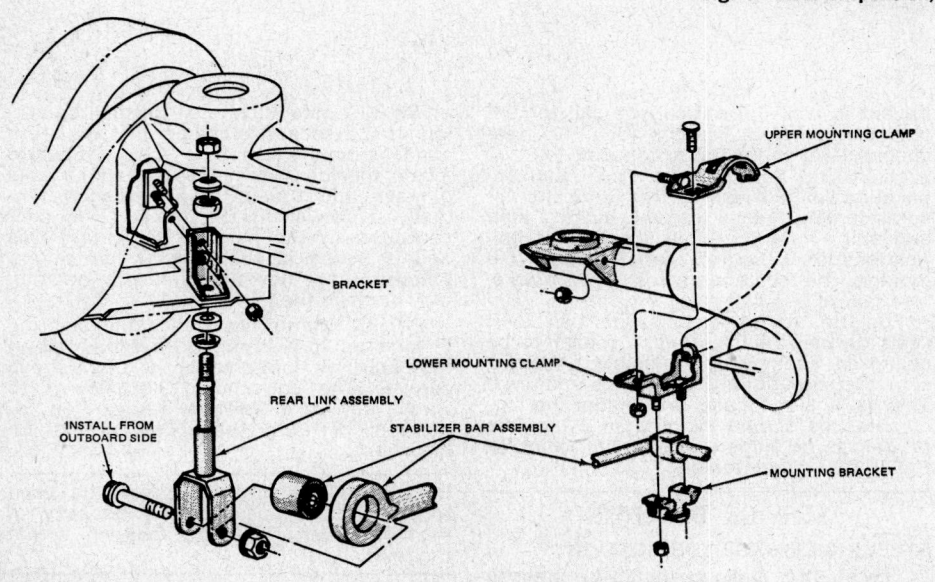

STABILIZER BAR, REPLACE

1972-75 Montego & Torino

1. Remove bolts securing stabilizer bar to rear link assemblies on both sides, Fig. 5.
2. Remove nuts securing mounting bracket to lower mounting clamp and remove bar.
3. Reverse procedure to install.

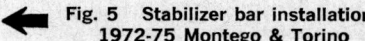 Fig. 5 Stabilizer bar installation. 1972-75 Montego & Torino

Front End & Steering Section

FRONT SUSPENSION

1972-75 Torino, Montego & 1974-75 Cougar

The front suspension, Fig. 1, has been redesigned with the coil spring mounted on the lower arm rather than on the upper arm as previous.

All Except 1972-75 Torino, Montego & 1974-75 Cougar

Referring to Fig. 2, each front wheel rotates on a spindle. The upper and lower ends of the spindle are attached to ball joints that are mounted to an upper and lower control arm. The upper arm pivots on a bushing and shaft assembly that is bolted to the underbody. The lower arm pivots on a bolt that is located in an underbody bracket.

A coil spring seats between the upper arm and the top of the spring housing. A double-acting shock absorber is bolted to the arm and the top of the spring housing.

Struts, which are connected between the lower control arms and the underbody, prevent the arms from moving fore and aft.

LUBRICATION

1969-75

These cars are equipped with an extended chassis lubrication feature which is made possible by a new type of special lubricant combined with special seals and bearing materials which extends the lubrication period to 36,000 miles.

SERVICE BULLETIN

Some uninformed service people recommended that conventional grease fittings be installed and that the car be lubricated every 1000 miles. This is completely unnecessary and, in fact, may cause damage to the special seals used in the lubrication points.

The use of conventional lubricants not only can do damage to the special seals but is incompatible with the special lubricant. Moreover, after the special sealing plugs have been replaced by conventional grease fittings, dirt and water can enter and cause excessive wear, rendering the units unfit for further service.

SERVICE BULLETIN

BALL JOINT LUBRICATION: The ball joint seals have been redesigned to provide improved sealing and longer life. The new seals can be damaged and sealing characteristics destroyed if excessive lu-

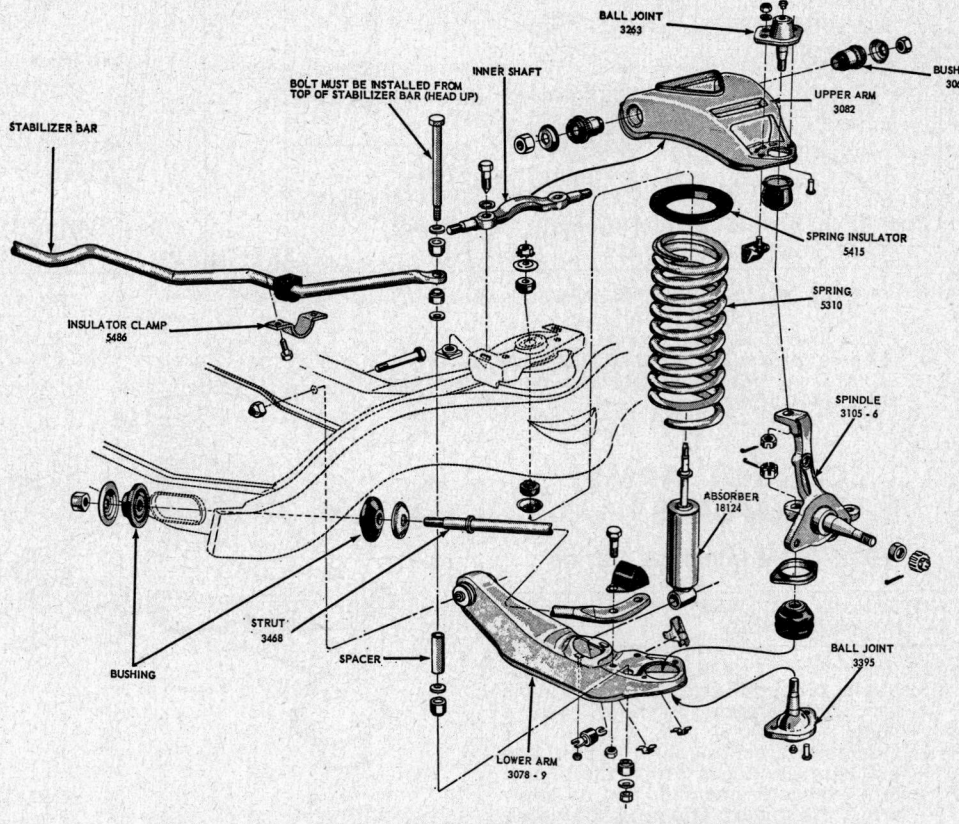

Fig. 1   Front suspension. 1972-75 Montego, Torino & 1974-75 Cougar

bricant is used. Specifications call for the addition of only 10 grams (one level teaspoonful) of lubricant to the ball joint at each 36,000 mile interval. The initial application of 10 grams of lubricant insures forcing grease into the bearing area and still allows for three subsequent lubrications of 10 grams each without ballooning the seals and resultant premature failure.

For the above reasons the ball joint seals on new vehicles might appear to be collapsed and give the mistaken impression that additional lubricant is required. This is not the case and under no circumstances should more than 10 grams of grease be added to the ball joint at the 36,000 mile intervals.

SERVICE BULLETIN

STEERING LINKAGE LUBRICATION:

The steering linkage should be greased

at 36,000 mile intervals. Normal breathing of the socket joints permits moisture condensation within the joint. Moisture inside the joint will cause no appreciable damage and the joint will function normally. However, if the moisture is concentrated in the bearing grease grooves and is frozen at the time of lubrication, grease cannot flow and pressure greasing may damage the joint.

Do not attempt to grease the steering linkage on these models if it has set in temperatures lower than 20 deg. above zero F. The car should be allowed to warm up in a heated garage for 30 minutes or until the joints accept lubrication.

IMPORTANT: A torch must not be used to heat joints because this quantity of heat will melt the nylon bearing within the joint.

WHEEL ALIGNMENT
All Except 1972-75 Torino, Montego & 1974-75 Cougar

As shown in Fig. 3, caster is controlled by the front suspension strut. To obtain positive caster, loosen the strut rear nut and tighten the strut front nut against the bushing. To obtain negative caster, loosen the strut front nut and tighten the strut rear nut against the bushing.

Camber is controlled by the eccentric cam located at the lower arm attachment to the side rail. To adjust camber, loosen the camber adjustment bolt nut at the rear of the body bracket. Spread the body bracket at the camber adjustment bolt area just enough to permit lateral travel of the arm when the adjustment bolt is turned. Rotate the bolt and eccentric clockwise from the high position to increase camber or counterclockwise to decrease it.

1972-75 Torino, Montego & 1974-75 Cougar

Caster and camber can be adjusted by loosening the bolts that attach the upper suspension arm to the shaft at the frame side rail, and moving the arm assembly in or out in the elongated bolt holes, Fig. 4. Since any movement of the arm affects both caster and camber, both factors should be balanced against one another when making the adjustment.

Install the tool with the pins in the frame holes and the hooks over the upper arm inner shaft. Tighten the hook nuts snug before loosening the upper arm inner shaft attaching bolts, Fig. 4.

Caster, Adjust
1. Tighten the tool front hook nut or loosen the rear hook nut as required to increase caster to the desired angle.
2. To decrease caster, tighten the rear hook nut or loosen the front hook nut as required.

> NOTE: The caster angle can be checked without tightening the inner shaft retaining bolts.

3. Check the camber angle to be sure it did not change during the caster adjustment and adjust if necessary.
4. Tighten the upper arm inner shaft retaining bolts and remove tool.

Camber, Adjust
1. Install as previously outlined.
2. Loosen both inner shaft retaining bolts.
3. Tighten or loosen the hook nuts as necessary to increase or decrease camber.
4. Recheck caster angle.

TOE-IN, ADJUST

Check the steering wheel spoke position when the front wheels are in the straight-ahead position. If the spokes are not in the normal position, they can be adjusted while toe-in is being adjusted.
1. Loosen clamp bolts on each tie rod end sleeve.

2. Adjust toe-in. If steering wheel spokes are in their normal position, lengthen or shorten both rods equally to obtain correct toe-in. If spokes are not in normal position, make necessary rod adjustments to obtain correct toe-in and steering wheel spoke alignment.

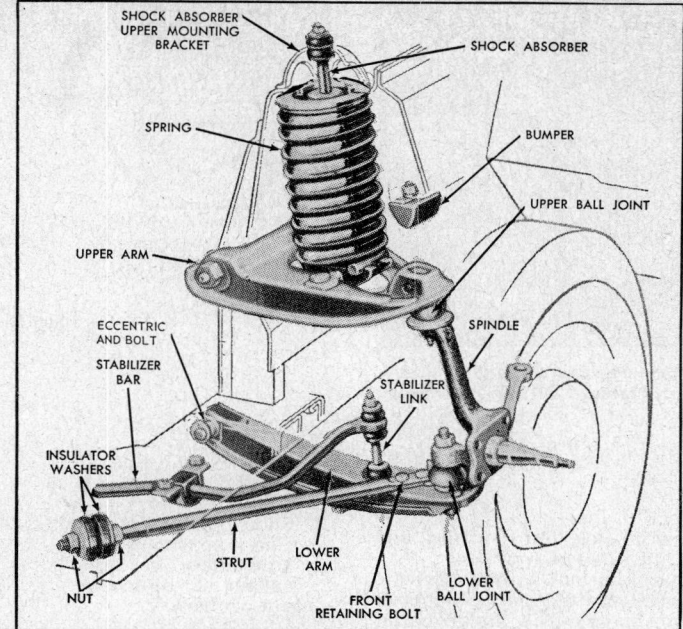

Fig. 2 Front suspension. All except 1972-75 Montego, Torino & 1974-75 Cougar

WHEEL BEARINGS, ADJUST

1969-75

1. With wheel rotating, tighten adjusting

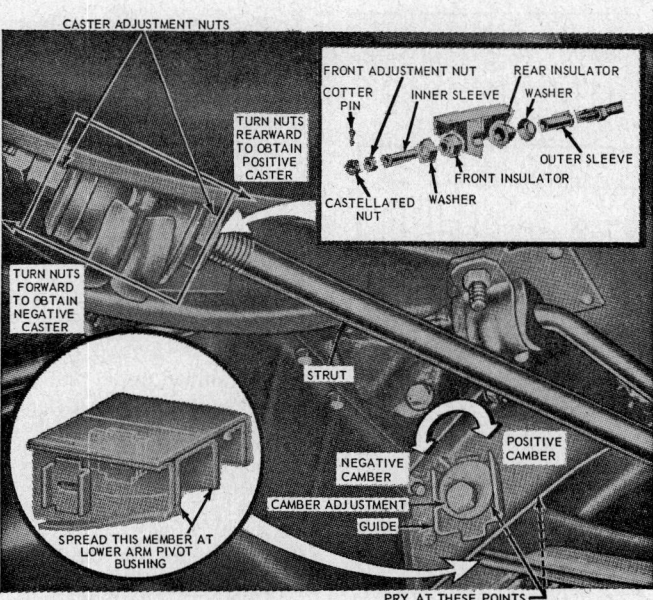

Fig. 3 Caster and camber adjustments. All except 1972-75 Torino and Montego & 1974-75 Cougar

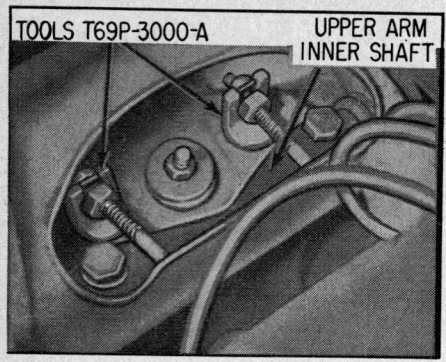

Fig. 4 Caster and Camber adjustment. 1972-75 Torino, Montego & 1974-75 Cougar

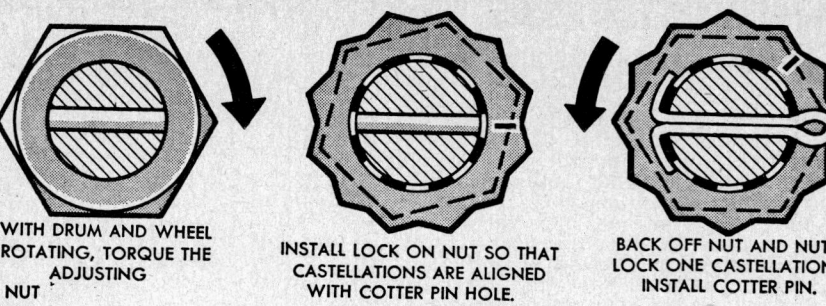

WITH DRUM AND WHEEL ROTATING, TORQUE THE ADJUSTING NUT

INSTALL LOCK ON NUT SO THAT CASTELLATIONS ARE ALIGNED WITH COTTER PIN HOLE.

BACK OFF NUT AND NUT LOCK ONE CASTELLATION INSTALL COTTER PIN.

Fig. 5 Front wheel bearing adjustment

nut to 17-25 ft. lbs.

2. Back off adjusting nut ½ turn and retighten nut to 10-15 inch lbs.
3. Place nut lock on nut so that castellations on lock are aligned with cotter pin hole in spindle and install cotter pin, Fig. 5.
4. Check front wheel rotation, if it rotates noisily or rough, clean, inspect or replace wheel bearings as necessary.

WHEEL BEARINGS, REPLACE

(Disc Brakes)

1. Raise car and remove front wheels.
2. Remove caliper mounting bolts.

NOTE: It is not necessary to disconnect the brake lines for this operation.

3. Slide caliper off of disc, inserting a clean spacer between the shoes to hold them in their bores after the caliper is removed. Position caliper out of the way.

NOTE: Do not allow caliper to hang by brake hose.

4. Remove hub and disc assembly. Grease retainer and inner bearing can now be removed.

CHECKING BALL JOINTS FOR WEAR

Upper Ball Joint

1972-75 Montego, Torino & 1974-75 Cougar

1. Raise vehicle and place floor jacks beneath lower control arms.
2. Grasp the lower edge of tire and move the wheel in and out.
3. While the wheel is being moved observe any movement between the upper end of the spindle and upper arm. If any movement is observed replace the ball joint.

Exc. 1972-75 Torino, Montego & 1974-75 Cougar

1. Raise car on frame contact hoist or by floor jacks placed beneath underbody until wheel falls to full down position as shown in Fig. 6. This will unload upper ball joint.
2. With front wheel bearings properly adjusted, attach a dial indicator to the upper control arm and position the indicator so that its plunger rests against the inner side of the wheel rim adjacent to the upper arm ball joint.
3. Grasp tire at top and bottom and slowly move it in and out, Fig. 6. Reading on dial will indicate the amount of radial play. If reading exceeds ¼", replace the upper ball joint.

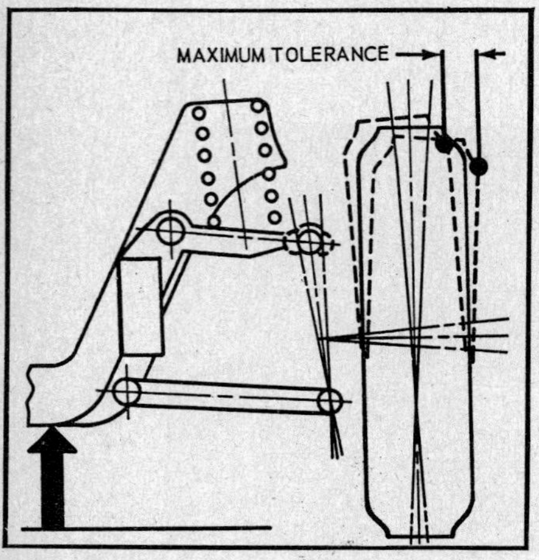

Lower Ball Joint

1972-75 Montego, Torino & 1974-75 Cougar

1. Raise vehicle and place floor jacks under the lower control arms, Fig. 7.
2. Adjust wheel bearings and place a dial indicator to the lower arm and position the indicator so that the plunger rests against the inner side of the wheel rim adjacent to the lower ball joint.
3. Grasp tire at top and bottom and move it slowly in and out. Reading on dial will indicate the amount of radial play. If reading exceeds ¼ inch replace the ball joint.

Exc. 1972-75 Torino, Montego & 1974-75 Cougar

1. With car jacked up as directed above, grasp the lower edge of the tire and move it in and out.
2. As wheel is being moved in and out, observe lower end of spindle and lower arm.
3. Any movement between lower end of spindle and lower arm indicates ball joint wear and loss of preload. If such movement is observed, replace lower arm and/or ball joint.

Fig. 6 Measuring upper ball joint for radial play. All except 1972-75 Montego, Torino & 1974-75 Cougar

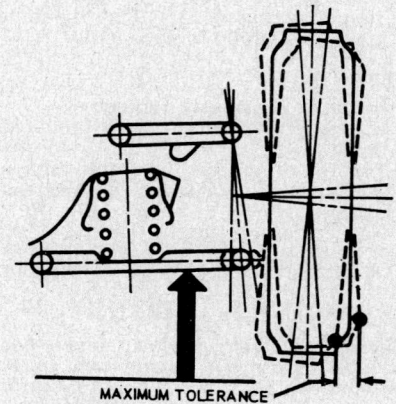

Fig. 7 Measuring lower ball joint for radial play. 1972-75 Montego, Torino & 1974-75 Cougar

NOTE: During the foregoing check, the ball joints will be unloaded and may move. Therefore disregard any movement of the upper ball joint when checking the lower ball joint and any movement of the lower ball joint when checking the upper ball joint. Also, do not mistake loose wheel bearings for a worn ball joint.

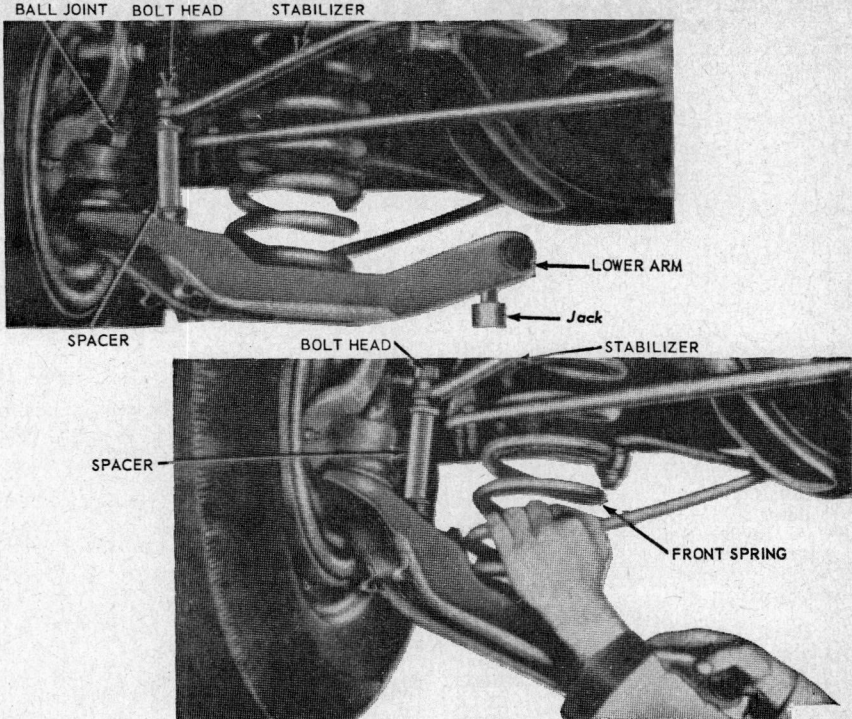

Fig. 8   Removing or installing front spring. 1972-75 Montego, Torino & 1974-75 Cougar

BALL JOINT, REPLACE

The ball joints are riveted to the upper and lower control arms. The upper ball joint can be replaced by removing the rivets and retaining the new ball joint to the upper control arm with bolts, nuts and washers furnished with the ball joint repair kit. The lower ball joints are furnished as an assembly with the lower control arm. When removing an upper ball joint, use a suitable pressing tool to loosen the ball joint from the spindle.

SHOCK ABSORBER, REPLACE

Exc. 1972-75 Torino, Montego & 1974-75 Cougar
1. Raise hood and remove upper mounting bracket-to-spring tower retaining nuts.
2. Raise front of car and place safety stands under lower control arms.
3. Remove shock absorber lower retaining nuts and washers.
4. Lift shock absorber from spring tower.
5. Reverse procedure to install.

1972-74 Torino, Montego & 1974 Cougar
1. Remove upper mounting nut, washer and bushing from shock absorber.
2. Raise vehicle and install safety stands.
3. Remove the shock absorber lower retaining screws and remove shock absorber.

COIL SPRING, REPLACE

All Except 1972-75 Montego, Torino & 1974-75 Cougar
1. Remove shock absorber and upper mounting bracket as an assembly.
2. Raise car on hoist and install safety stands.
3. Remove wheel, hub and drum.
4. Install a suitable spring compressor and compress spring.
5. Remove two upper-arm-to-spring tower retaining nuts and swing upper arm outward from spring.
6. Release spring compressor. Then remove spring.
7. Reverse procedure to install.

1972-75 Montego, Torino & 1974-75 Cougar
1. Raise vehicle and support front end of frame with jack stands.

2. Disconnect shock absorber from lower arm and place a jack under the lower arm for support, Fig. 8.
3. Remove strut and rebound bumper bolts and disconnect lower end of sway bar stud from lower arm.
4. Remove the nut and bolt that retains the inner end of the lower arm to the crossmember.
5. Carefully lower jack relieving spring pressure on the lower arm, then remove the spring.

STEERING GEAR, REPLACE

1969-75 Integral Power Steering Gear

These models use an integral power steering gear which replaces the linkage power steering used previously. Remove the gear assembly as follows:
1. Disconnect pressure and return lines from gear and plug openings to prevent entry of dirt.
2. Remove two bolts that secure flex coupling to the gear and to the column.
3. Raise vehicle and remove pitman arm with suitable puller.
4. If vehicle is equipped with snychromesh transmission, remove clutch release lever retracting spring to provide clearance to remove gear.
5. Support gear and remove three gear attaching bolts.

1969-75 Manual Steering Gear
1. Remove flex coupling bolts.
2. Remove pitman arm nut and remove pitman arm from sector shaft using a puller.
3. On vehicles with manual transmission it may be necessary to disconnect the clutch linkage and on V8 models it may be necessary to lower the exhaust system.
4. Unfasten and remove steering gear.

POWER STEERING
Pump Pressure

The normal oil pressure against either steering stop with engine idling is 750 to 900 psi.

Control Valve Removal
1. Disconnect fluid fittings at control valve and drain fluid from lines by turning wheels to left and right several times.
2. Loosen clamp at right-hand end of sleeve. Remove roll pin from steering arm-to-idler arm rod through slot in sleeve.
3. Remove ball stud from sector shaft.
4. Turn wheels fully to left and unthread control valve from idler arm rod.

FORD MUSTANG II & PINTO

NOTE: 1969-73 Mustang Models are covered elsewhere in this manual.

OLD CAR SPECIFICATIONS: For 1946-68 Tune Up and Wheel Alignment Specifications see main index.

INDEX OF SERVICE OPERATIONS

PAGE NO.

ACCESSORIES

Air Conditioning 2-20
Automatic Level Controls 2-39
Blower Motor, Remove 1-475
Clock Troubles 2-11
Heater Core, Replace 1-474
Power Top Troubles 2-18
Power Window Troubles 2-18
Radio, Replace 1-473

BRAKES

Anti-Skid Brakes 2-162
Brake Troubles, Mechanical 2-17
Disc Brake Service 2-133
Hydraulic System Service 2-123
Master Cylinder, Replace 1-499
Parking Brake, Adjust 1-498
Service Brakes, Adjust 1-498

CLUTCH

Clutch Pedal, Adjust 1-494
Clutch, Replace 1-495
Clutch Troubles 2-12

COOLING SYSTEM

Cooling System Troubles 2-6
Variable Speed Fans 2-38
Water Pump, Replace:
 1600 cc 1-481
 2000 cc 1-481
 2300 cc 1-488
 2800 cc 1-492

ELECTRICAL

Alternator Service 2-69
Blower Motor, Remove 1-475
Dash Gauge Service 2-50
Distributor, Replace 1-470
Distributor Service:
 Standard 2-525
 Transistorized 2-535
Electrical Troubles 2-8
Headlamps, Concealed Type 2-46
Headlight Aiming 2-45
Ignition Coils and Resistors 2-521
Ignition Lock, Replace 1-470
Ignition Switch, Replace 1-471
Ignition Timing 2-518
Instrument Cluster Removal 1-472
Light Switch, Replace 1-471
Neutral Safety Switch, Replace 1-472
Seat Belt Interlock Systems 2-311
Starter Service 2-54
Starter, Replace 1-470
Starter Switch Service 2-67
Stop Light Switch, Replace 1-472
Turn Signal Switch, Replace 1-472
Turn Signal Troubles 2-11

PAGE NO.

Windshield Wiper Motor, Replace 1-473
Windshield Wiper Troubles 2-19

ENGINE

Engine Identification 1-493
Engine Service:
 1600 cc 1-476
 2000 cc 1-476
 2300 cc 1-482
 2800 cc 1-489
 V8-302 1-493
Engine Troubles 2-1

ENGINE LUBRICATION

Emission Control Systems 2-545
Oil Pan, Replace & Oil Pump Repairs:
 1600 cc 1-480
 2000 cc 1-480
 2300 cc 1-486
 2800 cc 1-492

FUEL SYSTEM

Carburetor Adjustments and Specs. .. 2-372
1975 Carburetors 1-716
Emission Control Systems 2-545
Fuel Pump:
 1600 cc 1-481
 2000 cc 1-481
 2300 cc 1-488
 2800 cc 1-493
Fuel Pump Service 2-369
Fuel System Troubles 2-2

PROPELLER SHAFT & U JOINTS

Propeller Shaft 1-498
Universal Joint Service 2-117

REAR AXLE & SUSPENSION

Axle Shaft, Bearing and Seal 1-496
Leaf Springs & Bushings, Replace .. 1-499
Rear Axle Description 1-496
Rear Axle Troubles 2-16
Shock Absorber, Replace 1-499

SPECIFICATIONS

Alternator 1-467
Belt Tension:
 1600 cc 1-481
 2000 cc 1-481
 2300 cc 1-488
 2800 cc 1-492
Brakes 1-467
Capacities 1-469
Carburetors 2-372
Cooling System 1-469
Crankshaft and Bearings 1-468
Distributors 1-466
Engine Tightening Torque 1-468
Fuel Pump Pressure:
 1600 cc 1-481

PAGE NO.

 2000 cc 1-481
 2300 cc 1-488
 2800 cc 1-492
General Engine Specs. 1-463
Ignition Coils and Resistors 2-521
Pistons, Rings and Pins 1-468
Rear Axle 1-470
Starting Motors 1-467
Tune Up 1-464
Valve Lift:
 1600 cc 1-477
 2000 cc 1-477
 2300 cc 1-482
 2800 cc 1-490
Valve Timing:
 1600 cc 1-477
 2000 cc 1-477
 2300 cc 1-482
 2800 cc 1-490
Valves 1-465
Wheel Alignment 1-469

STEERING GEAR

Horn Sounder, Removal 1-472
Mechanical Gear, Replace 1-503
Mechanical Gear Service 2-170
Mechanical Gear Troubles 2-17

SUSPENSION, FRONT

Ball Joints, Replace 1-502
Ball Joints, Check for Wear 1-502
Coil Spring, Replace 1-502
Shock Absorber, Replace 1-502
Suspension, Description of 1-500
Toe-In, Adjust 1-500
Wheel Alignment, Adjust 1-500
Wheel Bearings, Adjust 1-501
Wheel Bearings, Replace 1-501

TRANSMISSIONS

Four Speed Manual:
 Replace 1-495
 Repairs 2-199
Automatic Units 2-231
 1975 Linkage 1-495

TUNE UP

Service 2-517
Specifications 1-464

WINDSHIELD WIPER

Wiper Arms 1-473
Wiper Blades 1-472
Wiper Linkage, Replace 1-473
Wiper Motor, Replace 1-473
Wiper Switch, Replace 1-473
Wiper Troubles 2-19

FORD MUSTANG II & PINTO

ENGINE & SERIAL NUMBER LOCATION: Vehicle warranty plate on rear face of left front door.

ENGINE IDENTIFICATION: Engine code is last letter in serial number on vehicle warranty plate.

Year	Engine	Engine Code
1971–73	4-98①	W
1971–74	4-122②	X
1974-75	4-140③	Y
1974-75	V6-171④	Z
1975	V8-302	F

①—1600 cc engine. ③—2300 cc engine.
②—2000 cc engine. ④—2800 cc engine.

GRILLE IDENTIFICATION

1971-73 Pinto

1974-75 Pinto

1974 Mustang II

1975 Mustang II

GENERAL ENGINE SPECIFICATIONS

Year	Engine	Carburetor	Bore and Stroke	Piston Displacement, Cubic Inches	Compression Ratio	Maximum Brake H.P. @ R.P.M.	Maximum Torque Lbs. Ft. @ R.P.M.	Normal Oil Pressure Pounds
1971	4-98①	1 Barrel	3.188 x 3.056	98①	8.4	75 @ 5000	96 @ 3000	35
	4-122②	2 Barrel	3.57 x 3.03	122②	9.0	100 @ 5600	120 @ 3600	50
1972	4-98①③	1 Barrel	3.188 x 3.056	98①	8.0	54 @ 4600	80 @ 2400	35–60
	4-122②③	2 Barrel	3.57 x 3.03	122②	8.2	86 @ 5400	103 @ 3200	35–60
1973	4-98①③	1 Barrel	3.188 x 3.056	98①	8.1	54 @ 4600	81 @ 2400	35
	4-122②③	2 Barrel	3.57 x 3.03	122②	8.2	④	98 @ 3800	50
1974	4-122②③	2 Barrel	3.575 x 3.029	122②	8.2	80 @ 5400	98 @ 3000	45–65
	4-140③⑤	2 Barrel	3.781 x 3.126	140⑤	8.4	82 @ 4600	113 @ 2600	40–60
	4-140③⑤	2 Barrel	3.781 x 3.126	140⑤	8.4	88 @ 5000	116 @ 2600	40–60
	V6-171③⑥	2 Barrel	3.66 x 2.70	171⑥	8.2	105 @ 4600	140 @ 3200	40–55
1975	4-140③⑤	2 Barrel	3.781 x 3.126	140⑤	8.4	85.5 @ 4800	113 @ 2600	50
	V6-171③⑥	2 Barrel	3.66 x 2.70	171⑥	8.2	110 @ 5000	135 @ 3200	40–55
	V8-302③⑦	2 Barrel	4.00 x 3.00	302	8.0	140 @ 3800	228 @ 2600	40–60

①—1600 cc engine.
②—2000 cc engine.
③—Net Rating—as installed in vehicle.
④—Exc. station wagon, 85 @ 5600; station wagon, 83 @5200.
⑤—2300 cc engine.
⑥—2800 cc engine.
⑦—Refer to the Ford & Mercury—Compact & Intermediate Chapter for Service procedures on this engine.

TUNE UP SPECIFICATIONS

OLD CAR SPECIFICATIONS: For 1946-68 Tune Up Specifications see main index.

★When using a timing light, disconnect vacuum hose or tube at distributor and plug opening in hose or tube so idle speed will not be affected.

●When checking compression, lowest cylinder must be within 75 percent of highest.

▲Before removing wires from distributor cap, determine location of the No. 1 wire in cap, as distributor position may have been altered from that shown at the end of this chart.

Year	Spark Plug		Distributor		Ignition Timing★			Carb. Adjustments					
	Type	Gap Inch	Point Gap Inch	Dwell Angle Deg.	Firing Order Fig. ▲	Timing BTDC ①	Mark Fig.	Hot Idle Speed③		Air Fuel Ratio		Idle "CO" %	
								Std. Trans.	Auto. Trans.②	Std. Trans.	Auto. Trans.	Std. Trans.	Auto. Trans.
1971													
4-98, 1600 cc	AGR-22	.030	.025	38–42	A	12°	C	800/500	—	—	—	1.2	—
4-122, 2000 cc	BRF-32	.025	.025	38–42	B	6°	D	750	650D	—	—	1.2	1.2
1972													
4-98, 1600 cc	AGR-22	.030	.025	36–40	A	12°	C	900/600	—	—	—	1.2	—
4-122, 2000 cc	BRF-42	.034	.025	36–40	B	6°④	D	750/500	650/500	—	—	1.2	1.2
1973													
4-98, 1600 cc	AGR-32	.034	.025	36–40	A	12°	C	900	—	11 to 1	—	1.5	—
4-122, 2000 cc	BRF-42	.030	.025	37–41	B	⑤	D	750	650	11 to 1	11 to 1	1.5	1.5
1974													
4-122, 2000 cc	BRF-42	.034	.025	35–41	B	6	D	750	650	⑥	⑥	—	—
4-140, 2300 cc	AGRF-52	.034	.027	35–41	G	6	E	850	750	11 to 1	11 to 1	.15	.15
V6-171, 2800 cc	AGR-42	.034	.027	35–41	H	12	F	750	650	12.7 to 1	12.7 to 1	.7	.4
1975													
4-140, 2300 cc	AGRF-52	.034	—	—	G	⑦	E	850	750D	—	—	—	—
V6-171, 2800 cc	AGR-42	.034	—	—	H	⑧	F	850	700D	—	—	—	—
V8-302⑨	ARF-42	.044	—	—	I	6°	J	—	700D	—	—	—	—

①—BTDC: Before top dead center.
②—D: Drive.
③—Headlamps on Hi Beam—Air Conditioner OFF. Where two speeds are listed, lower speed indicates solenoid disconnected.
④—California vehicles with Auto. Trans. 9°.
⑤—Auto. trans., 9°; man. trans., 6°.
⑥—11.7:1 Except Calif.; 10:1 Calif.
⑦—Exc. Calif. Auto. Trans., 6° BTDC; Calif. Auto. Trans., 10° BTDC.
⑧—Manual Trans., 6° BTDC; Exc. Calif. Auto. Trans., 10° BTDC; Calif. Auto. Trans., 8° BTDC.
⑨—Refer to the Ford & Mercury—Compact & Intermediate Chapter for service procedures on this engine.

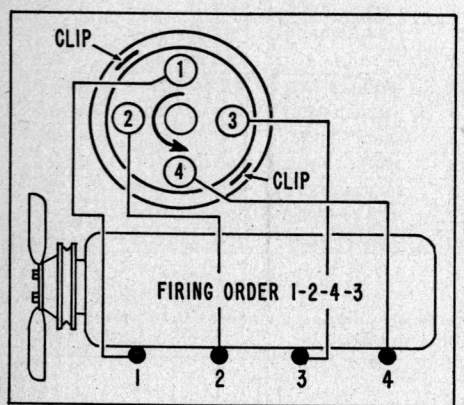

Fig. A

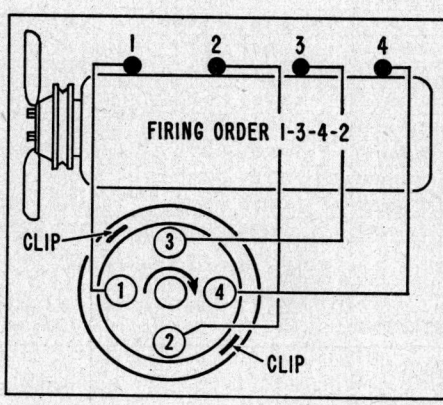

Fig. B

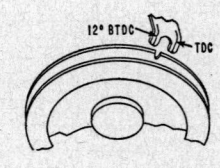

Fig. C

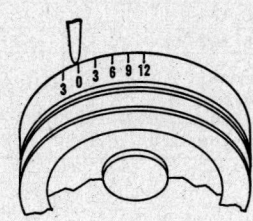

Fig. D

Continued

TUNE UP NOTES—Continued

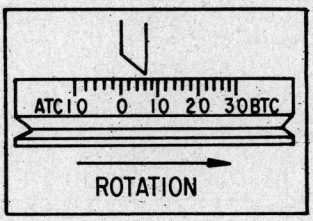

Fig. E

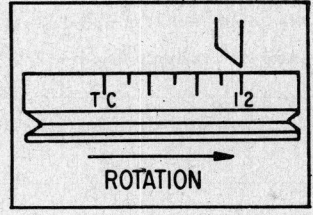

Fig. F

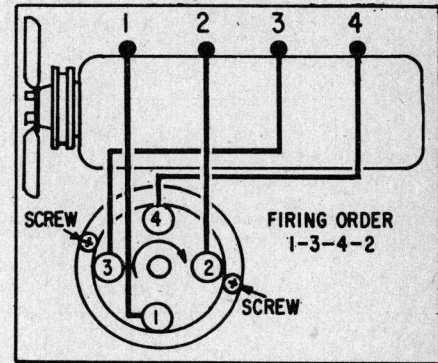

FIRING ORDER 1-3-4-2

Fig. G

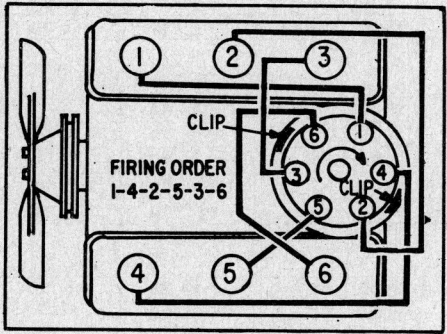

FIRING ORDER 1-4-2-5-3-6

Fig. H

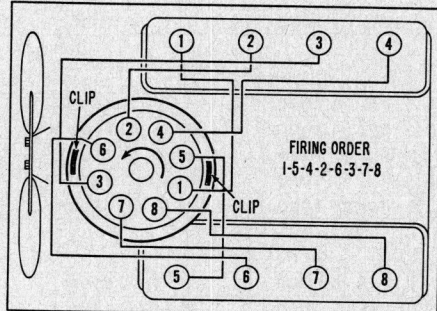

FIRING ORDER 1-5-4-2-6-3-7-8

Fig. I

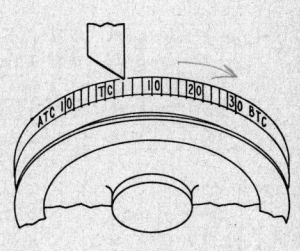

Fig. J

VALVE SPECIFICATIONS

Year	Engine	Valve Lash		Valve Angles		Valve Spring Installed Height	Valve Spring Pressure Lbs. @ In.	Stem Clearance		Stem Diameter, Standard	
		Int.	Exh.	Seat	Face			Intake	Exhaust	Intake	Exhaust
1971	4-98	.010H	.017H	45	45	1.263	118 @ .957	.0008–.0030	.0017–.0039	.3100	.3100
	4-122	.008①	.010①	45	45	1.417	144 @ 1.059	.0015–.0025	.0015–.0025	.3149	.3149
1972	4-98	.010H	.017H	44	45	1.263	122 @ .953	.0008–.0027	.0017–.0036	.3102	.3093
	4-122	.008①	.010①	44	45	1.418	176 @ 1.02	.0008–.0025	.0018–.0035	.3162	.3152
1973	4-98	.010H	.017H	45	44	1.266	118 @ .957	.0008–.0027	.0017–.0036	.3102	.3093
	4-122	.008①	.010①	45	44	1.418	176 @ 1.02	.0008–.0025	.0018–.0035	.3162	.3152
1974	4-122	.008①	.010①	45	44	1.406	176 @ 1.02	.0008–.0025	.0018–.0035	.3159–.3167	.3149–.3156
	4-140	.008C②	.010C②	45	44	1.56	210 @ 1.16	.0010–.0027	.0015–.0022	.3416–.3423	.3418–.3411
	6-171	.014H	.016H	45	44	1.593	144 @ 1.222	.0008–.0025	.0018–.0035	.3167–.3159	.3156–.3149
1975	4-140	—	—	45	45	1.56	189 @ 1.16	.0006–.0023	.0015–.0032	.3420–.3427	.3411–.3418
	V6-171	.014H	.016H	45	45	1.585	144 @ 1.222	.0008–.0025	.0018–.0035	.3157–.3167	.3149–.3156
	V8-302⑤	.090	.190	45	45	③	④	.0017–.0027	.0015–.0032	.3416–.3423	.3411–.3418

①—Set Hot or Cold.
②—With hydraulic valve lash adjuster completely collapsed.
③—Intake 1.69; Exhaust 1.60.

④—Intake 200 @ 1.31; Exhaust 200 @ 1.22.
⑤—Refer to the Ford & Mercury—Compact & Intermediate Chapter for service procedures on this engine.

DISTRIBUTOR SPECIFICATIONS

★If unit is checked on vehicle double the RPM and degrees to get crankshaft figures.

Breaker arm spring tension—17–21.

Distributor Part No.①	Centrifugal Advance Degrees @ RPM of Distributor				Vacuum Advance		Distributor Retard
	Advance Starts	Intermediate Advance		Full Advance	Inches of Vacuum To Start Plunger	Max. Adv. Dist. Deg. @ Vacuum	Max. Ret. Dist. Deg. @ Vacuum
1971							
D1FZ-A	0–½ @ 350	3¾–5¾ @ 750	6¼–8¼ @ 1000	7½–9½ @ 1500	11¾ @ 2500	5	7½ @ 25	4 @ 20
D1FZ-B	0–½ @ 400	1½–3½ @ 750	5½–7½ @ 1000	7¾–9¾ @ 1500	14 @ 2500	5	8 @ 25	7 @ 20
D1FZ-C	0–½ @ 350	3–5 @ 1000	8½–10½ @ 1500	10½–12½ @ 2000	12½ @ 2500	5	10 @ 25	4 @ 20
1972							
72HF-DC	½–2½ @ 500	5½–7½ @ 750	6½–8½ @ 1000	9½–11½ @ 1500	14 @ 2000	5	7½ @ 20	—
72HF-FA	½–2½ @ 500	5½–7½ @ 750	6½–8½ @ 1000	9½–11½ @ 1500	14 @ 2000	5	7½ @ 20	4 @ 20
72HF-SC	0–½ @ 500	0–1 @ 750	3–5 @ 1000	8½–10½ @ 1500	15½ @ 2000	5	7½ @ 20	—
72IF-TA	0–½ @ 500	1½–3½ @ 750	5½–7½ @ 1000	7½–9½ @ 1500	12 @ 2000	5	8 @ 20	7 @ 20
72IF-YA	0–½ @ 500	1½–3½ @ 750	5½–7½ @ 1000	7½–9½ @ 1500	12 @ 2000	5	8 @ 20	7 @ 20
1973							
72IF-AHA	0–½ @ 500	1–3 @ 750	5–7 @ 1000	7–9 @ 1500	11½ @ 2000	5	7 @ 20	7 @ 20
73HF-AA	½–2½ @ 500	5–7 @ 750	8½ @ 1000	9–11 @ 1500	14 @ 2000	5	7½ @ 20	—
73HF-BA	0–1 @ 500	1–3 @ 750	3–5 @ 1000	7½–9½ @ 1500	14 @ 2000	5	7½ @ 20	—
73HF-GA	0–½ @ 500	½–2½ @ 750	2½–4½ @ 1000	5½–7½ @ 1500	11 @ 2000	5	7½ @ 20	—
1974							
74HF-EA	1–3 @ 500	5–7 @ 750	6½–8½ @ 1000	9½–11½ @ 1500	12–14 @ 2000	5	6 @ 20	—
74HF-LA	0–1 @ 500	1–3 @ 750	4–6 @ 1000	7–9 @ 1500	9½–11½ @ 2000	5	6 @ 20	—
D4ZE-AA	0–1 @ 500	4–6 @ 750	4–6 @ 1000	9½–11½ @ 1500	11½–14 @ 2000	5	7½ @ 20	—
D4ZE-BA	0–1 @ 500	4–6 @ 750	7–9 @ 1000	9¼–11½ @ 1500	11½–14 @ 2000	5	7½ @ 20	—
D4ZF-DA	0–1 @ 500	1½–3½ @ 750	6–8 @ 1000	9½–11½ @ 1500	11½–14 @ 2000	5	4½ @ 20	—
74TF-LA	0–½ @ 500	1–3 @ 750	3½–5½ @ 1000	7½–9½ @ 1500	8–10 @ 2000	5	4 @ 20	7 @ 20
74TF-MA	0–½ @ 500	1–3 @ 750	3½–5½ @ 1000	7½–9½ @ 1500	8–10 @ 2000	5	4 @ 20	4 @ 20
D4ZE-KA	0–1 @ 500	4–6½ @ 750	7–9 @ 1000	9¼–11½ @ 1500	12¾ @ 2000	5	6 @ 20	—
74TF-SA	0–½ @ 500	1–3 @ 750	3½–5½ @ 1000	7½–9½ @ 1500	9 @ 2000	5	3 @ 20	—
1975							
D5DE-KA	0–2 @ 775	2¾–4¾ @ 950	4¾–7 @ 1500	6¾–9¼ @ 2000	9½ @ 2350	4	10 @ 14½	3 @ 7
D5DE-NA	0–2 @ 550	2½–4½ @ 675	3¾–6 @ 1100	7–9½ @ 2000	10⅛ @ 2500	4	10 @ 14½	—
D5ZE-AA	0–2 @ 600	1–3 @ 650	2¾–5 @ 1000	5¼–7½ @ 1500	11⅝ @ 2500	4.8	4 @ 7½	—
D52E-EA	0–2 @ 675	5¼–7¼ @ 1025	7½–9¾ @ 1500	10–12½ @ 2000	12¾ @ 2250	4	4 @ 7	—
D52E-FA	0–2 @ 725	5½–7½ @ 1125	7¾–10 @ 1500	10¾–13¼ @ 2000	12¾ @ 2150	4	4 @ 7½	3 @ 7½
75TF-EA②	0–2 @ 650	2–4 @ 800	5–7 @ 1200	8–10 @ 1600	9 @ 2000	4¼	2½ @ 6¾	6 @ 10

①—Basic part No. 12127.

ALTERNATOR & REGULATOR SPECIFICATIONS

| Year | Make or Model | Current Rating | | Field Current @ 75°F. | | Voltage Regulator | | | | Field Relay | |
		Amperes	Volts	Amperes	Volts	Make or Model	Voltage @ 75°F.	Contact Gap	Armature Air Gap	Armature Air Gap	Closing Voltage @ 75°F.
1971–72	D0ZF-B	38	15	2.4	12	D0AF-A	13.5–15.3	—	—	—	2.0–4.2
	D0AF-G	42	15	2.9	12	D0AF-A	13.5–15.3	—	—	—	2.0–4.2
1973	Orange①	42	15	2.9	12	D3TZ-A	13.5–15.3	—	—	—	2.5–4.0
	Purple①	38	15	2.4	12	D3TZ-A	13.5–15.3	—	—	—	2.5–4.0
	Green①	61	15	2.9	12	D3TZ-A	13.5–15.3	—	—	—	2.5–4.0
	All	70	15	2.9	12	D3TZ-A	13.5–15.3	—	—	—	2.5–4.0
1974–75	Purple①	38	15	2.9	12	D4AF-AA	13.5–15.3	—	—	—	2.5–4.0
	Green①	61	15	2.9	12	D4TF-AA	13.5–15.3	—	—	—	2.5–4.0
	All	70	15	2.9	12	D4TF-AA	13.5–15.3	—	—	—	2.5–4.0
1975	Orange①	42	15	2.9	12	D4AF-AA	13.5–15.3	—	—	—	2.5–4.0
	Red①	55	15	2.9	12	D4AF-AA	13.5–15.3	—	—	—	2.5–4.0

①—Color of identification tag.

STARTING MOTOR SPECIFICATIONS

| Year | Engine Model | Ident. No. | Brush Spring Tension, Ounces | No Load Test | | | Torque Test | | |
				Amperes	Volts	R.P.M.	Amperes	Volts	Torque Lbs. Ft.
1971–72	All	D22F-AA	40 Min.	70	—	—	460	5	9
1973	All	D22F-AB	40 Min.	70	12	8500	460	5	9
1974	4-122, 140	D42F-AA	40 Min.	—	—	—	—	—	—
	6-171	D4ZF-AA	40 Min.	—	—	—	—	—	—
1975	4-140	D42F-AB	40 Min.	—	—	—	—	—	—
	V6-171	D4ZF-AA	40 Min.	—	—	—	—	—	—
	V8-302	D5OF-AA	80 Min.	—	—	—	—	—	—

BRAKE SPECIFICATIONS

| Year | Model | Brake Drum Inside Diameter | Wheel Cylinder Bore Diameter | | | Master Cylinder Bore Diameter | | |
			Front Disc Brakes	Front Drum Brakes	Rear Brakes	With Disc Brakes	With Drum Brakes	With Power Brakes
1971–72	Pinto	9.0	2.125	1.00	.7187	.9375	.9375	—
1973	Pinto	9.0	2.127	1.00	.7187①	.9375	.9375	—
1974	Mustang II & Pinto	9.0	2.60	—	.875	.9375	—	.9375
1975	Mustang II & Pinto	9.0	2.60	—	8.70	.9375	—	.9375

①—Sta. Wagon .875.

FORD MUSTANG II & PINTO

ENGINE TIGHTENING SPECIFICATIONS

★Torque specifications are for clean and lightly lubricated threads only. Dry or dirty threads produce increased friction which prevents accurate measurement of tightness.

Year	Engine	Spark Plugs Ft. Lbs.	Cylinder Head Bolts Ft. Lbs.	Intake Manifold Ft. Lbs.	Exhaust Manifold Ft. Lbs.	Rocker Arm Shaft Bracket Ft. Lbs.	Rocker Arm Cover Ft. Lbs.	Connecting Rod Cap Bolts Ft. Lbs.	Main Bearing Cap Bolts Ft. Lbs.	Flywheel to Crankshaft Ft. Lbs.	Vibration Damper or Pulley Ft. Lbs.
1971–73	4-98	22–28	65–70	①	②	25–30	2½–3½	30–35	65–70	50–55	24–28
	4-122	14–20	65–80	12–15	15–18	③	4–6	29–34	65–75	47–51	39–43
1974–75	4-122	14–20	65–80	12–15	15–18	③	4–6	29–34	65–75	47–51	39–43
	4-140	10–15	80–90	14–21	16–23	—	4–7	30–36	80–90	54–64	80–114
	6-171	14–22	65–80	15–18	14–18	9–25④	3–5	21–25	65–75	47–51	92–103
1975	8-302⑤	15–20	65–72	17–25	12–16	17–23④	3–5	19–24	60–70	75–85	70–90

①—Studs 9-12 ft.-lbs., nuts 12-15 ft.-lbs., bolts 12-15 ft.-lbs.
②—Studs 9-12 ft.-lbs., nuts 15-18 ft.-lbs.
③—Rocker arm ball stud nut 32-36 ft.-lbs.
④—Rocker arm stud nut.
⑤—Refer to the Ford & Mercury—Compact & Intermediate Chapter for service procedures on this engine.

PISTONS, PINS, RINGS, CRANKSHAFT & BEARINGS

Year	Engine	Piston Clearance	Ring End Gap①		Wrist-pin Diameter	Rod Bearings		Main Bearings		Thrust on Bear. No.	Shaft End Play
			Comp.	Oil		Shaft Diameter	Bearing Clearance	Shaft Diameter	Bearing Clearance		
1971–72	4-98	②	.009	.009	.8119	1.9372	.0004–.0024	2.1257	.0004–.0024	3	.003–.011
	4-122	.001–.002	.0189	.016	.9475	2.0468	.0006–.0026	2.2441	.0006–.0019	3	.004–.008
1973	4-98	②	.009	.009	.8119	1.9372	.0004–.0024	2.1257	.0005–.0016	3	.003–.011
	4-122	0.001–0.002	.015	.016	.9448	2.0468	.0006–.0026	2.2436	.0006–.0016	3	.003–.011
1974	4-122	.0010–.0020	.015	.016	.9448	2.0468	.0006–.0026	2.2446	.0006–.0016	3	.003–.011
	4-140	.0013–.0021	.010	.015	.9120	2.0468	.0009–.0027	2.3996	.0008–.0015	3	.004–.008
	6-171	.0010–.0020	.015	.015	.9447	2.1268	.0006–.0022	2.2437	.0006–.0019	3	.003–.011
1975	4-140	.0023–.0039	.010	.015	.9120	2.0472	.0008–.0024	2.3990	.0008–.0026	3	.004–.008
	V6-171	.0020–.0036	.015	.016	.9456	2.1256	.0006–.0021	2.2437	.0006–.0019	3	.004–.008
	V8-302③	.0018–.0026	.010	.010	.9122	2.1236	.0008–.0026	2.2486	.0005–.0024	3	.004–.008

①—Fit rings in tapered bores for clearance listed in tightest portion of ring travel.
②—1971, .0016–.0022; 1972–73, No. 1, 2 & 3 bore, .0016–.0022, No. 4 bore, .0019–.0025.
③—Refer to the Ford & Mercury—Compact & Intermediate chapter for service procedures on this engine.

COOLING SYSTEM & CAPACITY DATA

Year	Model or Engine	Cooling Capacity, Qts.			Radiator Cap Relief Pressure, Lbs.		Thermo. Opening Temp.	Fuel Tank Gals.	Engine Oil Refill Qts. ①	Transmission Oil			Rear Axle Oil Pints
		No Heater	With Heater	With A/C	With A/C	No A/C				3 Speed Pints	4 Speed Pints	Auto. Trans. Qts.	
1971	4-98	6	6¾	—	—	12-15	186	11	3½②	—	2½	—	2.2
	4-122	6¾	7½	7½	12-15	12-15	186	11	5	—	2½	8	2.2
1972-73	4-98	6¾	7¾	—	—	12-15	186	11	3½②	—	2½	—	2¼
	4-122	7½	8½	8½	12-15	12-15	186	11	5	—	2½	8	2¼
1974	4-122	7½	8½	8½	12-16	12-16	186	③	5	—	2.8	8	3
	4-140	7½	8½	9½	12-16	12-16	186	③	5	—	⑤	8	3
	6-171	11½	12½	12½	12-16	12-16	186	13	5②	—	4.5	8	3
1975	4-140	—	8¾	9	12-16	12-16	191	④	4½②	—	⑤	⑥	⑧
	V6-171	—	12½	13¼	12-16	12-16	186	④	5②	—	⑤	⑦	4
	V8-302	—	16½	16½	12-16	12-16	191	16½	4②	—	—	—	—

①—Includes 1 qt. for filter.
②—Includes ½ qt. for filter.
③—Pinto: sedan, 13; wagon, 12.
④—Exc. Sta. Wag., 13 gals.; Sta. Wag. 14 gals. Add 3½ gals. with auxiliary fuel tank.
⑤—Pinto, 2.8 pts.; Mustang II, 3½ pts.
⑥—Pinto, 6.7 qts.; Mustang II, 8 qts.
⑦—Pinto, 7 qts.; Mustang II, 7½ qts.
⑧—Pinto, 2.2 pts.; Mustang II, 3 pts.; units with 8 inch ring gear, 4 pts.

WHEEL ALIGNMENT SPECIFICATIONS

OLD CAR SPECIFICATIONS: For 1946-68 Wheel Alignment Specifications see main index.

Year	Model	Caster Angle, Degrees		Camber Angle, Degrees				Toe-In Inch	Toe-Out on Turns, Deg.	
				Limits		Desired				
		Limits	Desired	Left	Right	Left	Right		Outer Wheel	Inner Wheel
1971-72	Exc. Wagon	+1 to +2	+1½	0 to +1½	0 to +1½	+¾	+¾	3/16	18.95	20
	Wagon	−½ to +3½	+1½	−¼ to +1¾	−¼ to +1¾	+¾	+¾	3/16	18.95	20
1973	Exc. Wagon	−1 to +3	+1	−¼ to +1¾	−¼ to +1¾	+¾	+¾	1/8	—	—
	Wagon	−1½ to +2½	+½	−¼ to +1¾	−¼ to +1¾	+¾	+¾	1/8	—	—
1974	Mustang II	−¼ to +1¾	+¾	−½ to +1½	−½ to +1½	+½	+½	1/8	18.84	20
	Pinto	−¾ to +3¼	+1¼	−¼ to +1¾	−¼ to +1¾	+¾	+¾	¼	18.84	20
1975	Pinto Exc. Wag.	−¾ to 3¼	+1¼	−¼ to +1¾	−¼ to +1¾	+¾	+¾	¼	18.84	20
	Mustang II	−⅛ to +1⅞	+⅞	−½ to +1½	−½ to +1½	+½	+½	1/8	18.84	20
	Wagon	−½ to 3½	+1½	−¼ to +1¾	−¼ to +1¾	+¾	+¾	¼	18.84	20

REAR AXLE SPECIFICATIONS

Year	Model	Carrier Type	Ring Gear & Pinion Backlash Inch	Nominal Pinion Locating Shim, Inch	Pinion Bearing Preload				Differential Bearing Preload	Pinion Nut Torque Ft.-Lbs.
					New Bearings With Seal Inch-Lbs.	Used Bearings With Seal Inch-Lbs.	New Bearings Less Seal Inch-Lbs.	Used Bearings Less Seal Inch-Lbs.		
1971	All	Integral	.008–.012	.030	17–32	6–12	—	—	.008–.012①	140
1972	All	Integral	.008–.012	.030	15–30	6–12	—	—	.004–.008①	140
1973	All	Integral	.008–.012	.030	19–27	6–12	—	—	.004–.008①	140
1974–75	All	Integral	.008–.012	.030	17–27	6–12	—	—	.008–.012①	140
	All	Removable	.008–.012	—	17–27	6–12	—	—	.004–.008①	140

①—Case spread with new bearings; with used bearings, .003–.005".

Electrical Section

DISTRIBUTOR, REPLACE

1600 cc Engine

1. Remove distributor cap and disconnect vacuum lines from distributor.
2. Scribe a mark on distributor body and the engine block indicating the position of the body in the block, and scribe another mark on the distributor body showing position of rotor.
3. Remove hold down bolt and remove distributor.

Exc. 1600 cc Engine

NOTE: On some 1974 2000 cc engines, it may be necessary to position Thermactor pump aside to gain access to distributor.

1. Remove distributor cap and disconnect vacuum lines from distributor.
2. Rotate the engine until the timing notch in the pulley is at the specified BTC mark. Check that No. 1 cylinder is on compression stroke by removing oil filler cap. The cam lobe should be visible through the opening. The distributor rotor should now be pointing at the No. 1 cylinder mark on the distributor body.
3. Remove hold down bolt and remove distributor.

NOTE: *The hex shaft that drives the oil pump may stick in the distributor and be withdrawn from the pump.*

STARTER, REPLACE

1. Raise vehicle on hoist.
2. Disconnect starter cable from starter terminal.
3. Remove starter attaching bolts. Then move starter forward over the steering linkage and remove starter.

IGNITION LOCK

1971

1. Disconnect the battery ground cable.
2. Remove the steering wheel horn button or trim pad and steering wheel. Insert a wire pin in the lock cylinder hole located inside the column halfway down the housing, Fig. 1.

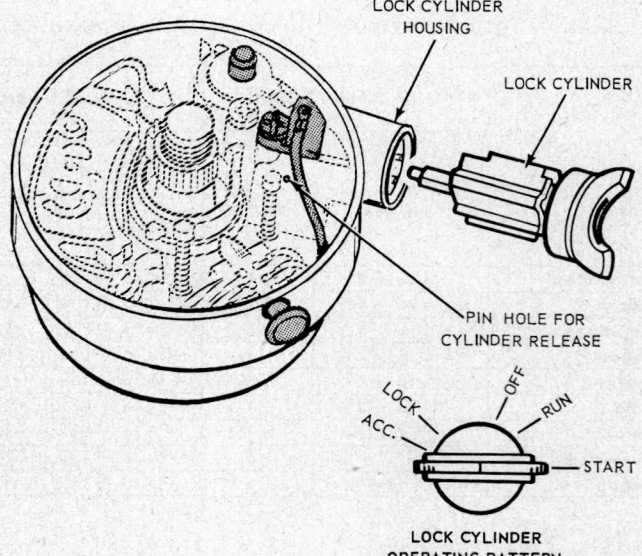

Fig. 1 Ignition lock

3. With the ignition key, turn the lock cylinder to the *ON* position.
4. Remove the lock cylinder by depressing the wire pin and pulling up on the cylinder; then, remove the wire pin.
5. To install insert the lock cylinder into the cylinder housing in the flange casting and turn the key to the *OFF* position. This action will extend the lock cylinder retaining pin into the flange.
6. With the key in the lock, rotate the cylinder to insure correct operation in

all positions.
7. Replace the steering wheel and trim pad or horn button. Reconnect the battery cable.

1972-75

1. Disconnect the battery ground cable.
2. Remove the steering wheel trim pad and the steering wheel. Insert a wire pin in the hole located inside the column halfway down the lock cylinder housing, Fig. 1.
3. Place the gear shift lever in *PARK* (with auto. trans) or *REVERSE* (with manual trans) turn the lock cylinder with the ignition key to *RUN* position.
4. Depress the wire while pulling up on the lock cylinder to remove. Remove the wire pin.
5. To install insert the lock cylinder into the housing in the flange casting, and turn the key to *OFF* position. This action will extend the cylinder retaining pin into the cylinder housing.
6. Turn the key to check for correct operation in all positions.
7. Install the steering wheel and trim pad. Reconnect the battery ground cable.

IGNITION SWITCH, REPLACE

1. Remove shrouding from steering column and detach and lower steering column from brake support bracket.
2. Disconnect battery ground cable.
3. Disconnect switch wiring at plug, Fig. 1A.
4. Remove two nuts that retain switch to column.
5. Remove the pin that connects switch plunger directly to actuator and remove the switch.
6. To install switch, both the locking mechanism at top of column and the switch must be in LOCK position for correct adjustment.
7. Move shift lever into Park (with automatic transmission) or Reverse (with manual transmission), turn the

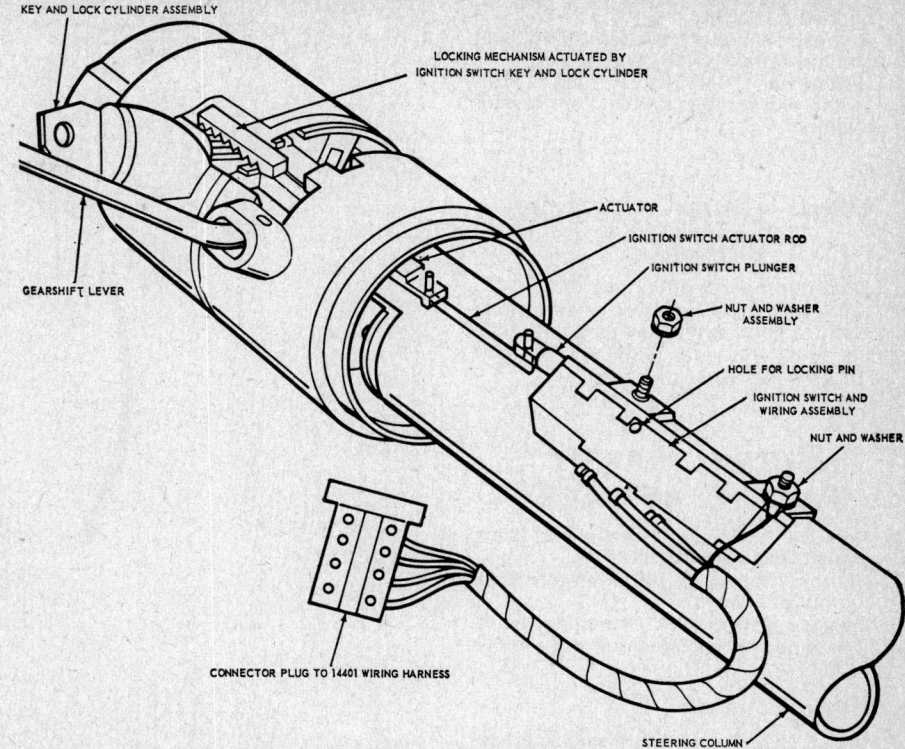

Fig. 1A Ignition switch installation. 1971-75 Pinto & 1974 Mustang II

key to LOCK position and remove the key.

NOTE: *New switches, when received, are already pinned in LOCK position by a plastic shipping pin inserted in a locking hole on top of switch.*

8. Position the hole in the end of switch plunger to the hole in the actuator and install the connecting pin.
9. Position switch on column and install retaining nuts, but do not tighten them.
10. Move switch up and down along column to locate the mid-position of rod lash and then tighten nuts.
11. Remove the plastic or substitute locking pin, connect battery and check switch for proper start in PARK or NEUTRAL.

LIGHT SWITCH, REPLACE

1974-75 Mustang II

1. Disconnect battery ground cable.
2. Depress shaft release button by inserting a screwdriver through hole in underside of instrument panel, then remove knob and shaft.
3. Remove bezel nut, lower switch, disconnect electrical connector and remove switch.

1971-75 Pinto

1. Disconnect battery ground cable.
2. Remove instrument cluster as de-

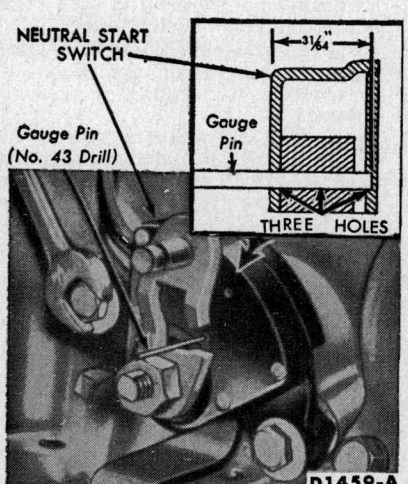

Fig. 3 Neutral safety switch adjustment

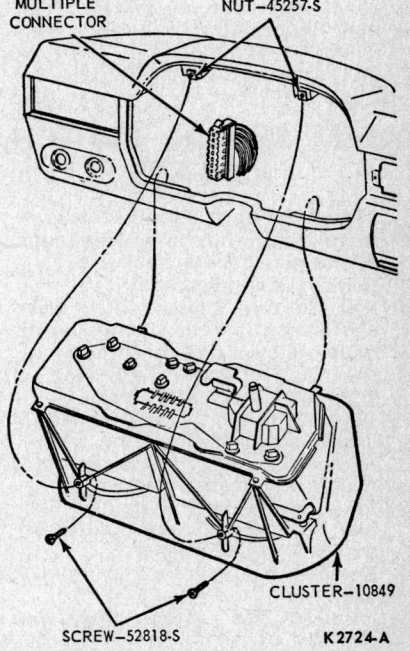

Fig. 4 Instrument cluster removal. 1971-75 Pinto

3. Remove headlight switch knob and shaft assembly and retaining nut.
4. Disconnect connector plug from switch and remove switch from cluster opening.

STOP LIGHT SWITCH REPLACE

1. Disconnect wires at connector.
2. Remove hairpin retainer, slide switch, push rod and nylon washers and bushing away from the pedal and remove the switch, Fig. 2.

NEUTRAL SAFETY SWITCH, REPLACE

1. Remove downshift linkage rod from transmission downshift lever.
2. Remove downshift outer lever retaining nut and lever.
3. Remove two switch attaching bolts.
4. Disconnect wire connector and remove switch.

Installation

1. Install switch on transmission and replace attaching bolts.
2. With transmission manual lever in neutral, rotate switch and install gauge pin (No. 43 drill) into gauge pin hole, Fig. 3.
3. Tighten switch attaching bolts and remove gauge pin.
4. Install outer downshift lever and attaching nut.
5. Install downshift linkage rod to downshift lever.
6. Install switch wire connector and check operation of switch. The engine should start only with lever in Neutral or Park.

TURN SIGNAL SWITCH, REPLACE

1. Disconnect battery ground cable.
2. Remove horn button by pressing down and turning counterclockwise.
3. Remove steering wheel.
4. Remove turn signal switch lever by unscrewing it from column.
5. Snap off lower column shroud.
6. Remove two screws attaching upper column shroud and remove.
7. Disconnect main wiring harness from steering column connector.
8. Remove steering column wiring connector from metal retainer.
9. Remove plastic clip holding ignition and turn signal wire harnesses together to metal retainer.
10. Remove buzzer terminal from hard shell connector.
11. Remove one screw from buzzer terminal at column and three screws holding signal switch to casting.
12. Pull switch and wiring up out of column.

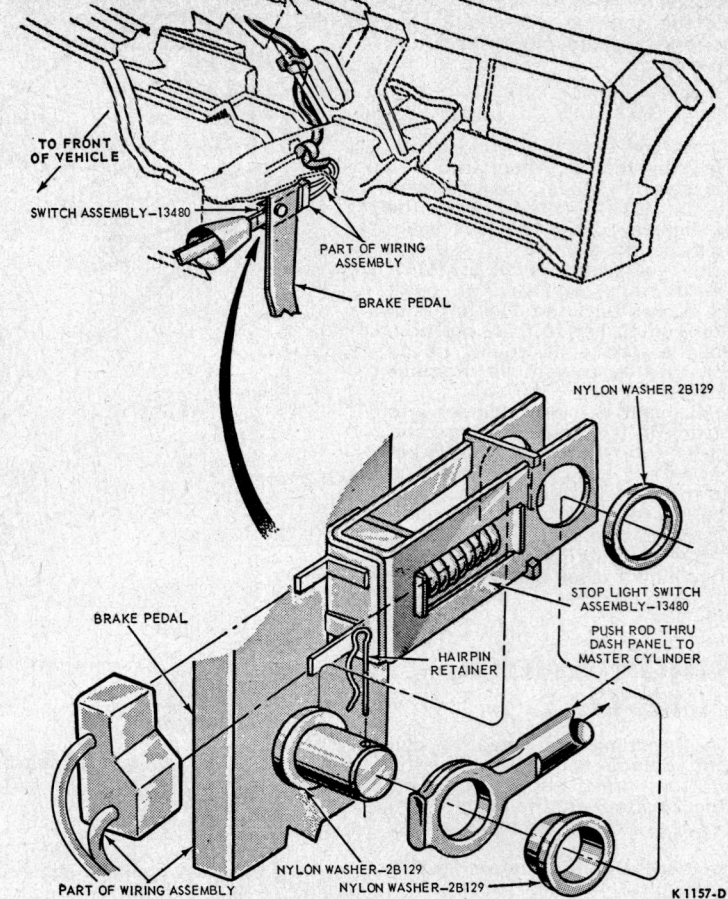

Fig. 2 Stoplight switch installation

HORN SOUNDER

The horn button can be removed by depressing it and turning it counterclockwise.

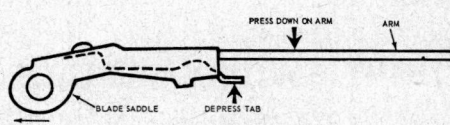

Fig. 5 Trico bayonet type blade

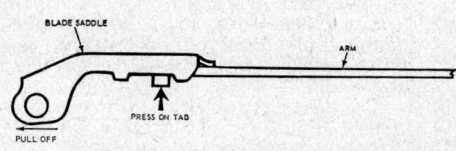

Fig. 6 Anco bayonet type blade

INSTRUMENT CLUSTER

1974-75 Mustang II

1. Disconnect battery ground cable.
2. Remove wiper switch and light switch knobs, then light switch bezel.
3. Remove instrument cluster trim cover.
4. Disconnect speedometer cable by pressing on flat section of quick disconnect.
5. Remove cluster retaining screws, pull cluster from instrument panel, disconnect electrical connectors, then remove cluster.

1971-75 Pinto

1. Disconnect battery ground cable.
2. From under instrument panel, disconnect speedometer cable.
3. Remove two retaining screws at top of cluster and swing cluster down away from panel, Fig. 4.

W/S WIPER BLADES

NOTE: Trico and Anco Blades are used and both come in two types Bayonet type and

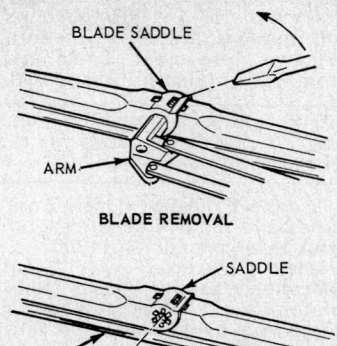

BLADE REMOVAL

BLADE INSTALLATION

Fig. 7 Pin type blade

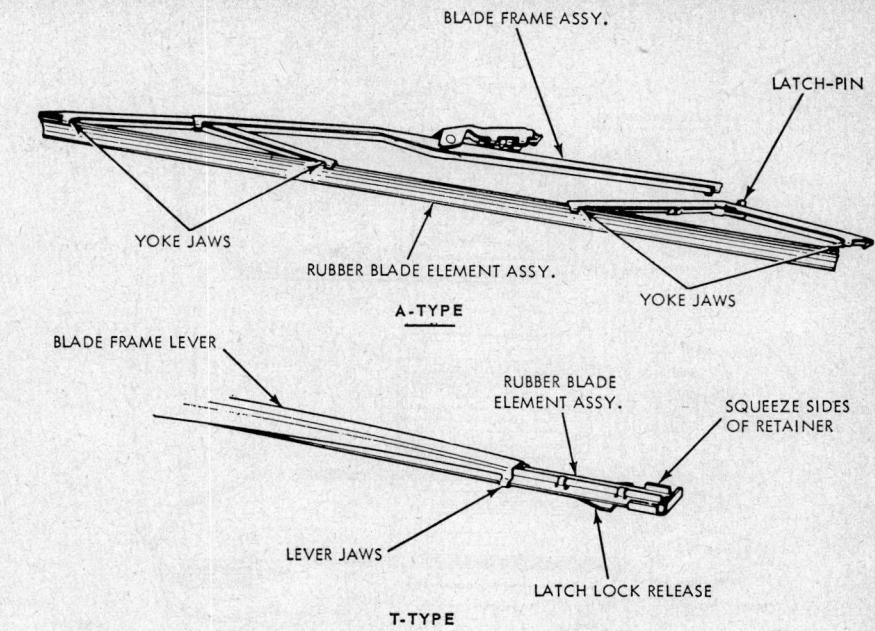

A-TYPE

T-TYPE

Fig. 8 Wiper blade element

Side Saddle Pin type.

Bayonet Type: To remove the *Trico* type press down on the arm to unlock the top stud. Depress the tab on the saddle, Fig. 5, and pull the blade from the arm. To remove the *Anco* type press inward on the tab, Fig. 6, and pull the blade from the arm. To install a new blade assembly slide the blade saddle over the end of the wiper arm so that the locking stud snaps into place.

Side Saddle Pin Type: To remove the pin type (Trico or Anco) insert an appropriate tool into the spring release opening of the blade saddle, depress the spring clip and pull the blade from the arm, Fig. 7. To install, push the blade saddle on to the pin so that the spring clip engages the pin. To replace the rubber element in a *Trico* blade squeeze the latch lock release and pull the element out of the lever jaws, Fig. 8. Remove *Anco* element by depressing the latch pin, Fig. 8, and sliding the element out of the yoke jaws. To install insert the element through the yoke or lever jaws. Be sure the element is engaged at all points.

W/S WIPER ARMS

Swing the arm and blade assembly away from the windshield. While holding the assembly in this position pull the arm off the pivot shaft using an appropriate tool, Fig. 9. To install, hold the arm and blade in the swing out position and push the arm on to the pivot shaft.

W/S WIPER MOTOR

1. Loosen two nuts and disconnect wiper pivot shaft and link from the motor drive arm ball.
2. Remove three motor attaching screws and lower motor away from under the left side of the instrument panel.
3. Disconnect wiper motor wires and remove motor.

W/S WIPER TRANSMISSION

NOTE: On 1973-75 Pinto equipped with air conditioning, remove blower motor to gain access to wiper transmission as described further on in this chapter.

1. Remove wiper arms and blades from pivot shafts.
2. Loosen two nuts retaining wiper pivot shaft and link assembly to the motor drive arm ball.
3. Remove three screws attaching each pivot shaft and remove assembly from under left side of instrument panel.

W/S WIPER SWITCH

1974-75 Mustang II

1. Disconnect battery ground cable.

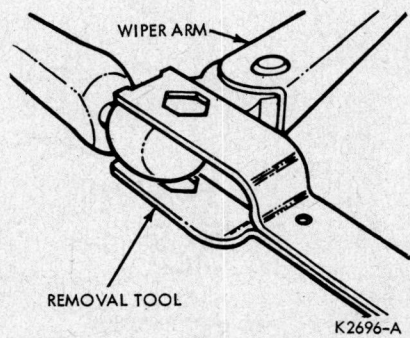

Fig. 9 Wiper arm

2. Remove switch knob and bezel nut, pull switch from panel, disconnect electrical connector and remove switch.

1971-75 Pinto

1. Remove instrument cluster as outlined previously.
2. Insert a thin bladed screwdriver into the slot in the switch knob and depress the spring. Then pull the knob from the switch shaft.
3. Remove wiper switch bezel nut. Then unplug wires and remove switch.

RADIO, REPLACE

NOTE: When installing radio, be sure to adjust antenna trimmer for peak performance.

1974-75 Mustang II

1. Disconnect battery ground cable.
2. Remove radio knobs, discs, shaft nuts and washers.
3. Remove radio rear support to instrument panel nut.
4. Lower radio, disconnect wiring and remove radio.

1971-75 Pinto

1. Disconnect battery ground cable.
2. On 1973-75 models remove instrument panel trim brace cover.
3. On all models, remove rear support to radio attaching bolt.
4. Remove four screws attaching the bezel to the instrument panel opening.
5. Pull radio out from instrument panel

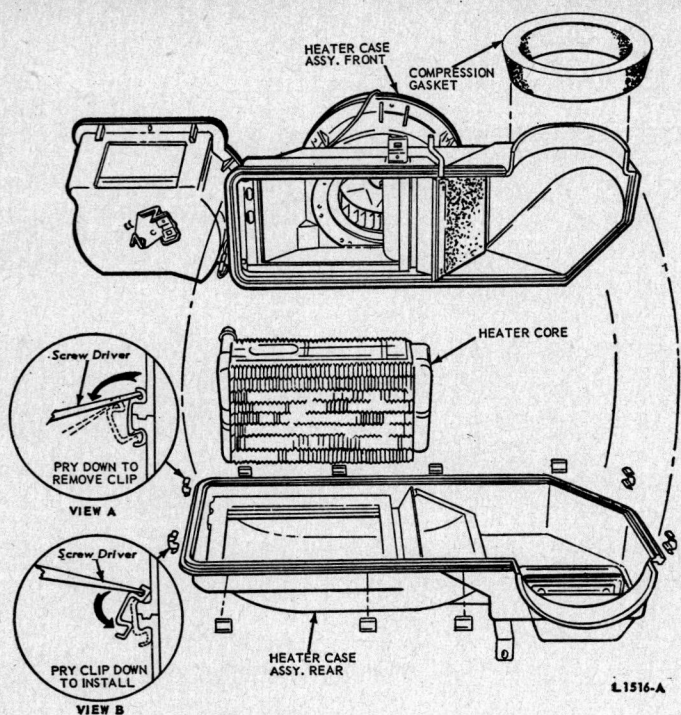

Fig. 10 Heater core removal

and disconnect speaker, power and antenna wires and remove radio.

HEATER CORE REMOVAL

Less Air Conditioning
1. Drain coolant and disconnect battery.
2. Disconnect blower motor wire at engine side of dash.
3. Disconnect heater hoses at engine block.
4. Remove four heater assembly-to-dash mounting nuts from the engine side of the dash.
5. Remove the glove box.
6. Disconnect control cables from heater. Remove mounting bracket clips and disconnect cables from door crank arms.
7. Remove radio as outlined previously.
8. Working inside car, remove snap rivet that attaches the forward side of the defroster air duct to the plenum chamber. Move the air duct back into the defroster nozzle to disengage it from the tabs on the plenum chamber. Now, tilt the forward edge of the duct up and forward to disengage it from the nozzle and remove it from the left side of the heater assembly.
9. Remove heater case-to-instrument panel support bracket mounting screw and remove the heater case. At the same time, pull the two heater hoses in through the dash panel. Then disconnect the hoses from the heater core in the case.
10. Remove compression gasket from cowl air inlet.

11. Remove eleven clips from around the front and rear case flanges and separate the front and rear halves of the case, Fig. 10.
12. Lift heater core from front half of case.

With Air Conditioning, 1974-75 All
1. Disconnect battery ground cable,
drain radiator and discharge refrigerant from A/C system.
2. Remove refrigerant lines and the front half of refrigerant manifold.

NOTE: Remove manifold mounting stud to ensure clearance for removal of evaporator case.

3. Disconnect heater hoses from core tubes and remove condensation drain hose in engine compartment.
4. Remove glove box.
5. Disconnect vacuum hoses from evaporator case and temperature control cable from blend door crank arm.
6. Remove heat distribution duct.

NOTE: On Mustang II, remove mode door vacuum motor.

7. On Mustang II, remove lower section of the air conditioning defrost plenum.
8. On Pinto, remove staples retaining fold down door on plenum, Fig. 11. Bend fold down door from locating tabs on plenum and remove adapter duct.

NOTE: During installation, position fold down door between locating tabs and tape in place with two pieces of black tape, Fig. 11.

9. On all models, remove blower motor and wheel from blower scroll.
10. Install a 1/4-20 hex washer head screw in mounting tab of inlet duct to upper cowl bracket, holding inlet duct in place.

NOTE: Leave screw in position during installation of case assembly.

11. Remove inlet duct to evaporator case screws.

NOTE: One upper case to inlet duct screw is located under outside-recirc. motor mounting bracket.

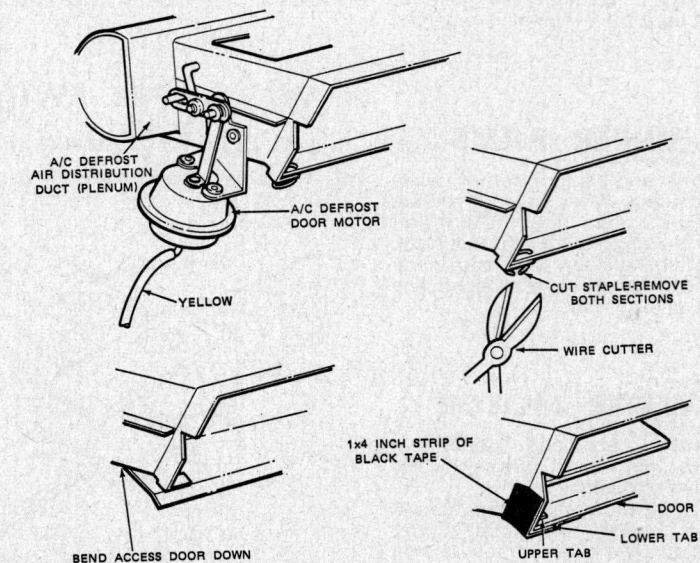

Fig. 11 A/C defrost air distribution duct fold down door. 1974-75 Pinto

12. Remove evaporator to cowl bracket screws and the evaporator to dash panel nuts in engine compartment. Rotate evaporator down and away from instrument panel and remove from under panel.
13. Remove upper to lower case screws and rubber seal from heater core tubes.
14. Remove upper half of evaporator case and move rubber seal on evaporator core forward and pull evaporator core from lower case.
15. Remove heater core upper straps, air deflector mounting screw, then remove air deflector and heater core.

With Air Conditioning, 1971-73 Pinto
1. Drain engine coolant, discharge refrigerant from A/C system and disconnect battery.
2. Disconnect heater hoses from heater core tubes.
3. Disconnect expansion valve from evaporator core tubes and apply tape over each core tube to keep out foreign material.
4. Remove three evaporator housing-to-dash panel mounting stud nuts.
5. Remove glove box and right air duct.
6. Disconnect blue vacuum hose from door motor and remove A/C defrost plenum chamber.
7. Disconnect red and yellow vacuum hoses from left door motor and the white hose from the right door motor.
8. Disconnect vacuum harness multiple connector from vacuum selector valve on the control assembly.
9. Disconnect temperature control cable from door crank arm on the evaporator housing, and disconnect purple and green vacuum hoses from the adjacent water valve vacuum switch.
10. Remove screw that retains evaporator housing to cowl upper support and remove the A/C assembly rearward and away from dash panel in order to clear mounting studs.
11. Remove tape from red and yellow vacuum hoses on top of blower housing. Disengage the green, white and purple vacuum hoses from clip on top of evaporator housing.
12. Disconnect wire connectors from A/C thermostat switch on evaporator housing and from resistor on blower housing. Disconnect blower ground wire.
13. Lower evaporator and blower housing and remove from vehicle.
14. Remove rubber dash panel seal from evaporator housing.
15. Remove eleven clips that hold two halves of housing together.

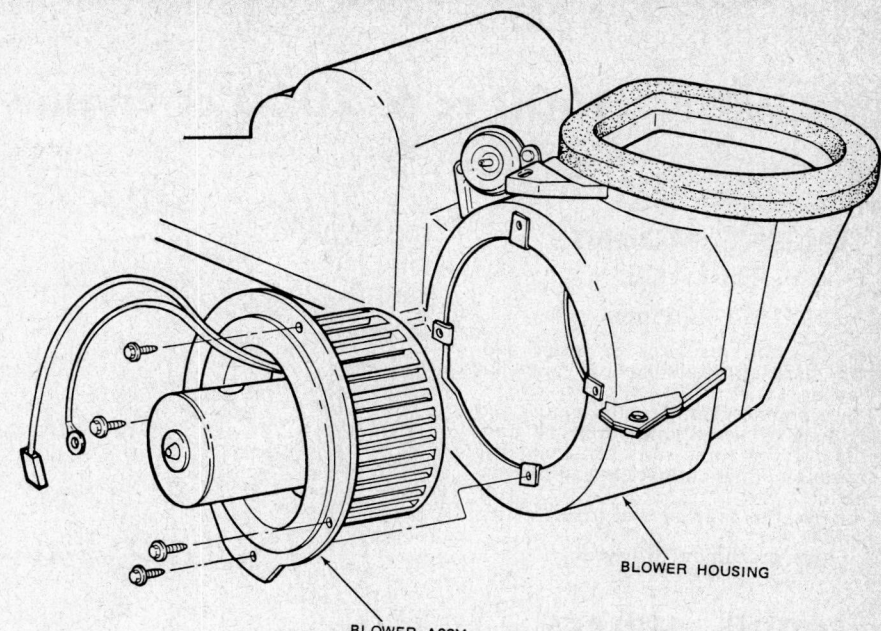

Fig. 12 Blower motor. 1971-75 All (Typical)

BLOWER HOUSING

BLOWER ASSY.

16. Remove A/C thermostat switch from upper housing.
17. Remove evaporator core from upper housing.
18. Remove temperature blend door upper frame.
19. Remove retaining clip from temperature door crank arm, slide crank arm out of door and lower housing and remove the door.
20. Remove temperature blend door lower frame.
21. Remove heater core from lower housing.

BLOWER MOTOR REMOVE

Less Air Conditioning
1. Follow procedure to remove the heater core as described previously.
2. Disconnect the blower motor lead wire (orange) from the resistor.
3. Remove the four blower mounting plate nuts and remove the motor and wheel assembly, Fig. 12.
4. Reverse procedure to install.

With Air Conditioning, 1974-75 All
   To remove the blower motor on these models, refer to "Heater Core, Removal," under 1974-75 with air conditioning procedure and follow steps 1 through 9.

With Air Conditioning, 1971-73 Pinto
1. Remove the lower cover plate from the A/C De-Frost plenum by removing the two retaining screws.
2. Remove the air distribution duct from the blower housing.
3. Remove the blower housing mounting stud nut and lock plate.
4. Turn the blower housing clockwise to unlock the slotted tabs on the blower housing from their lock pins on the evaporator housing. There are two tabs and pins. Remove the blower housing.
5. Cut the gaskets around the A/C outlets at the break line.
6. Remove seven clips, and separate both halves of the blower housing.
7. Remove three blower motor mounting plate retaining nuts, and remove the motor and wheel assembly from the housing.
8. When installing, make sure that the A/C-Heat door is positioned properly before clipping the right and left housings together.

1600 cc & 2000 cc Engine Section

ENGINE MOUNTS REPLACE

1971-74 Pinto

1. Remove the insulator to lower support bracket attaching nut and flat washer, Fig. 1.
2. Raise engine slightly using a jack and a block of wood under the oil pan. Remove the three nuts attaching the insulator upper-support bracket to the engine.
3. Remove the bracket and insulator assembly.
4. Reverse procedure to install.

ENGINE, REPLACE

1600 cc Engine

1. Remove hood and disconnect battery lead and ground wire.
2. Drain coolant, disconnect radiator hoses at the engine and remove the radiator.
3. Disconnect hot air pipe at air cleaner and remove air cleaner.
4. Disconnect heater hoses from water pump and intake manifold.
5. Disconnect accelerator linkage from carburetor.
6. Disconnect temperature gauge and oil pressure gauge sender unit leads and alternator leads.
7. Disconnect exhaust pipe from manifold and remove hot air pipes from manifold, where applicable.
8. Disconnect fuel intake pipe from pump.
9. Disconnect distributor leads from coil, leads from spark plugs and remove distributor cap.
10. Jack up front of car and support with stands.
11. Remove starter motor, clutch housing lower bolts and remove the cover.
12. Remove stands and jack from under car.
13. Remove clutch housing to engine bolts.
14. Install suitable lifting bracket to engine and support engine with hoist.
15. Disconnect engine mounts from crossmember.
16. Support transmission and pull engine forward off main drive gear and lift from engine compartment.

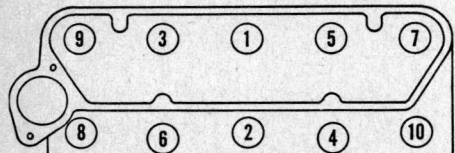

Fig. 2 Cylinder head tightening sequence. 1600 cc engine

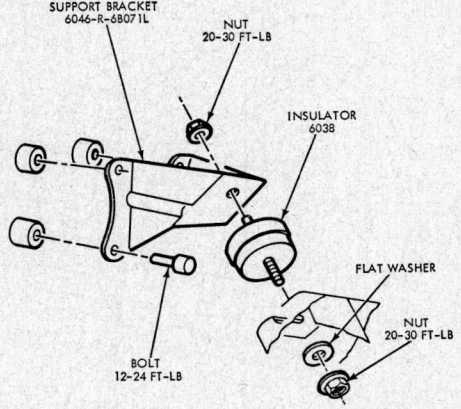

Fig. 1 Engine mount

2000 cc Engine

1. Drain coolant from radiator and oil from crankcase.
2. Raise hood and secure in vertical position.
3. Remove air cleaner and exhaust manifold shroud.
4. Disconnect battery ground cable.
5. Remove radiator hoses and remove radiator and fan.
6. Disconnect heater hoses from water pump and carburetor choke fitting.
7. Disconnect wires from alternator and starter and disconnect accelerator cable from carburetor. On A/C vehicles, remove compressor from bracket and position it out of way with lines attached.
8. Disconnect flex fuel line from tank line and plug tank line.
9. Disconnect primary wire at coil and disconnect oil pressure and temperature sending unit wires at sending units.
10. Remove starter and raise vehicle to remove the flywheel or converter housing upper attaching bolts.
11. Disconnect inlet pipe at exhaust manifold. Disconnect engine mounts at underbody bracket and remove flywheel or converter housing cover.
12. On vehicle with manual shift, remove flywheel housing lower attaching bolts.
13. On vehicle with automatic transmission, disconnect converter from flywheel and remove converter housing lower attaching bolts.
14. Lower vehicle and support transmission and flywheel or converter housing with a jack.
15. Attach engine lifting hooks to brackets and carefully lift engine out of engine compartment.

CYLINDER HEAD, REPLACE

1600 cc Engine

1. Disconnect hoses at air cleaner and remove air cleaner.
2. Disconnect fuel lines at pump and carburetor.
3. Drain coolant and disconnect spark plug leads.
4. Disconnect heater and vacuum hoses at intake manifold and at choke housing.
5. Disconnect lead from temperature gauge sender unit.
6. Detach exhaust pipe and move clear of cylinder head.
7. Disconnect throttle linkage and distributor vacuum pipe from carburetor.
8. Remove thermostat housing, pull to one side and remove thermostat.
9. Remove rocker cover and gasket.
10. Remove rocker arm shaft bolts evenly and lift off rocker shaft assembly.
11. Lift out push rods and keep them in their correct order for installation.
12. Remove cylinder head bolts and lift off cylinder head.
13. Reverse procedure to install and tighten bolts in sequence shown in Fig. 2.

2000 cc Engine

1. Drain cooling system and remove air cleaner and rocker arm cover.
2. Remove exhaust manifold and remove intake manifold, carburetor and decel valve as an assembly.
3. Remove camshaft drive belt cover.
4. Loosen drive belt tensioner and remove drive belt.
5. Remove water outlet elbow from head.
6. Remove cylinder head attaching bolts.

NOTE: The cylinder head retaining bolts have 12 point heads.

7. Lift head and camshaft assembly from engine.
8. Reverse procedure to install and tighten bolts in sequence shown in Fig. 2A.

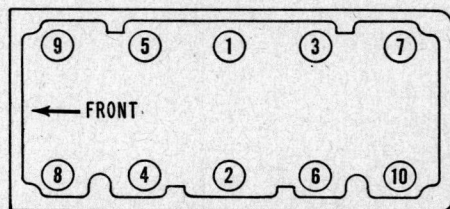

Fig. 2A Cylinder head tightening sequence. 2000 cc engine

1600 cc Engine — Set Hot

Valve Depressed	Valves to Adjust to .010	.017
no. 1	no. 3	no. 8
no. 2	no. 7	no. 5
no. 3	no. 6	no. 1
no. 5	no. 2	no. 4

Fig. 3 Valve adjustment table. 1600 cc engine

NOTE: Do not overtighten the valve cover retaining screws, also make certain the valve cover gasket is aligned properly. It is possible to block the oil return hole on the right side of the front camshaft bearing support if the above cautions are not adhered to. If the oil return hole becomes blocked, sufficient oil pressure can build up in the front camshaft bearing area and push the oil seal out of position.

VALVE ARRANGEMENT

Front to Rear

1600 cc Engine	E-I-I-E-E-I-I-E
2000 cc Engine	E-I-E-I-E-I-E-I

VALVE LIFT SPECS.

Engine	Year	Intake	Exhaust
1600 cc	1971	.2967	.3199
	1972-73	.3247	.3351
2000 cc	1971-74	.3993	.3993

VALVE TIMING

Intake Opens Before TDC

Engine	Year	Degrees
1600 cc	1971-73	17
2000 cc	1971	18
	1972-74	24

VALVES, ADJUST

1600 cc Engine

1. Start engine and allow it to idle for 20 minutes.

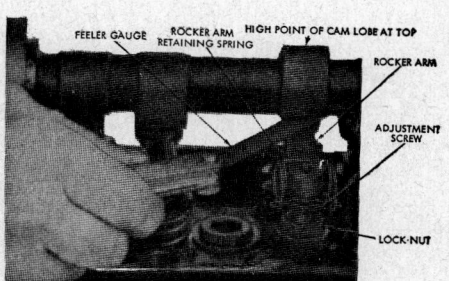

Fig. 4A Checking valve clearance. 1971 2000 cc engine

2. Turn engine off and remove air cleaner and wires from spark plugs.
3. Pull rubber grommet from bracket on rocker cover and lay wires over heater hose.
4. Remove screw retaining throttle cable to rocker cover.
5. Disconnect throttle cable link from ball stud and move cable out of way.
6. Pry linkage out of carburetor arm.
7. Unfasten and remove rocker cover being careful not to lose throttle rod retaining spring.
8. Rotate crankshaft clockwise by hand until number 1 valve is completely depressed and adjust valves 3 and 8. Valves are numbered from 1 to 8 (front to rear). Consult Fig. 3 and continue through the sequence shown until all valves are adjusted.

2000 cc Engine

1. If there is a clamp between heat shroud pipe and air cleaner duct and valve assembly, loosen the clamp.
2. Disconnect crankcase ventilation hose and carbon cannister hose at air cleaner.
3. Remove wing nuts and unsnap wire clips on air cleaner cover and lift air cleaner off carburetor.
4. Remove screws (11 mm) from rocker cover.
5. Remove spark plug wires from retainer and move out of way.
6. Remove rocker cover.
7. Rotate the crankshaft clockwise by hand until the high point of the number 1 cam lobe is pointing down. Check clearances on valves 6 and 7. Consult Fig. 4 and continue on through sequence until all valves are adjusted, Figs. 4A and 4B.

VALVE GUIDES

Valve guides consist of holes bored in the cylinder head. For service, the guides can be reamed oversize to accommodate valves with oversize stems. Valves with oversize stems are available in .003", .015" and .030" oversizes on all engines except the 1974 2000 cc engine. Valves with oversize stems for the 1974 2000 cc engine are available in oversizes of .008", .016" and .032".

ROCKER ARM SERVICE

1600 cc Engine

1. Remove rocker arm cover.
2. Remove rocker shaft attaching bolts and lift off rocker shaft assembly.
3. Remove cotter pin from one end of shaft and slip flat washer, crimped washer and second flat washer off the shaft. The rocker arm shaft supports, rocker arms and springs can now be removed.
4. Remove plugs from shaft ends by drilling a hole in one plug. Insert a long rod through the drill plug and knock the opposite plug out of the shaft. Remove drilled plug in same manner.

2000 cc Engine — Set at Any Temperature

Valve Depressed	Valves to Adjust to .008	.010
no. 1	no. 6	no. 7
no. 2	no. 8	no. 3
no. 3	no. 2	no. 5
no. 6	no. 4	no. 1

Fig. 4 Valve adjustment table. 2000 cc engine

5. To assemble, refit new plugs in ends of shaft. The bolt hole in the rocker arm shaft support must be on the same side as the adjusting screw in the rocker arm. The rocker arms are right and left handed, the rocker pads being inclined towards the supports. Install cotter pins with heads upwards and bend over the legs to secure.

2000 cc Engine

1. Remove air cleaner.
2. Remove rocker arm cover.
3. Rotate crankshaft as required to place the low side of the camshaft lobe next to the rocker arm that is being replaced.
4. Remove the rocker arm retaining spring.
5. Depress the valve spring with Tool T71P6565-A just enough to remove the rocker arm.

NOTE: Refer to "NOTE" under "Cylinder Head, Replace" before installing valve cover.

VALVES, GRIND

NOTE: The intake valves on the 1600 cc engine have aluminized faces. Under no conditions should the faces of aluminized valves be ground or lapped in as this will remove the coating and reduce the valves' wear and heat resistant properties. If valve

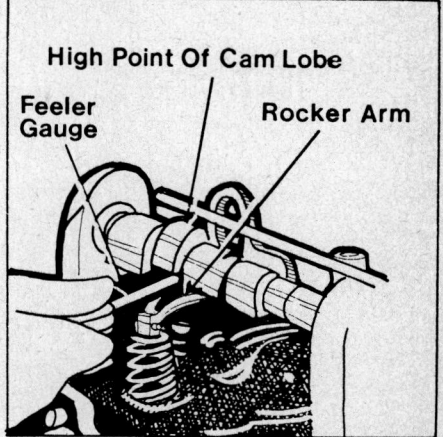

Fig. 4B Checking valve clearance. 1972-74 2000 cc engine

FORD MUSTANG II & PINTO

SEAL
Tool T71P-6150-A
A3423-A

Fig. 5 Removing crankshaft oil seal. 2000 cc engine

faces are worn or pitted it will be necessary to install new valves and to resurface the valve seats or alternatively lap the seats using dummy valves. The exhaust valves may be lapped in or the faces ground as required.

VALVE LIFTERS, REPLACE

1600 cc Engine—The chilled cast iron tappets can only be removed from the engine after the camshaft has been removed. See "Camshaft, Replace" further on in this section.

TIMING CASE COVER

1600 cc Engine
1. Drain coolant and disconnect radiator hoses at engine.
2. Remove radiator assembly.
3. Remove fan belt and then remove fan and water pump pulley.
4. Remove water pump.
5. Remove crankshaft pulley with suitable puller.
6. Remove the front cover. When replacing cover, install a new oil seal as this seal can only be replaced with the cover removed.

2000 cc Engine
It is not necessary to remove the front cover to replace the crankshaft oil seal. Proceed as follows:
1. Remove alternator belt.
2. Remove crankshaft pulley bolt and slide pulley off shaft.
3. Remove camshaft drive belt and slide sprocket and belt guide off the crankshaft. If sprocket cannot be slid off shaft use a puller.
4. Install tool T71P-6150A over end of crankshaft and remove seal, Fig. 5.
5. Install a new seal with tool T71P-6150B, Fig. 6.

TIMING CHAIN/BELT

1600 cc Engine
The timing chain can be replaced after removing the front cover as follows:
1. Remove the crankshaft oil slinger.
2. Remove the camshaft sprocket and

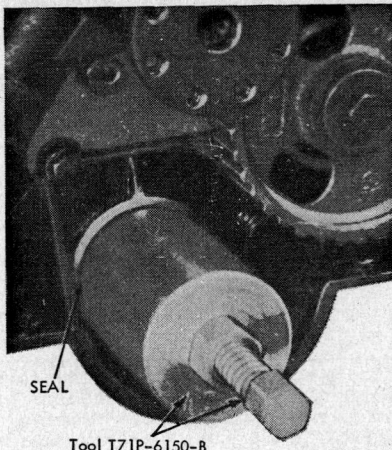

SEAL
Tool T71P-6150-B
A3422-A

Fig. 6 Installing crankshaft oil seal. 2000 cc engine

disconnect timing chain. When replacing chain, be sure to align marks when the sprocket is fitted, Fig. 7.

2000 cc Engine
1. Place crankshaft on TDC.
2. Remove the three camshaft drive belt cover screws and remove cover.
3. Loosen camshaft drive belt tensioner adjustment bolt, Fig. 8 and force the tensioner toward the exhaust manifold side of engine to relax belt tension, then tighten the bolt.
4. Lift the belt off the sprockets.

NOTE: Do not rotate the crankshaft

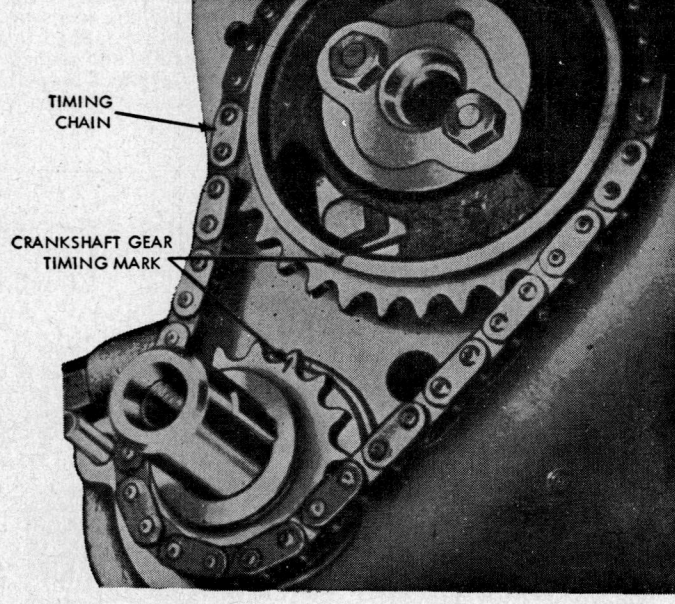

Fig. 7 Valve timing marks. 1600 cc engine

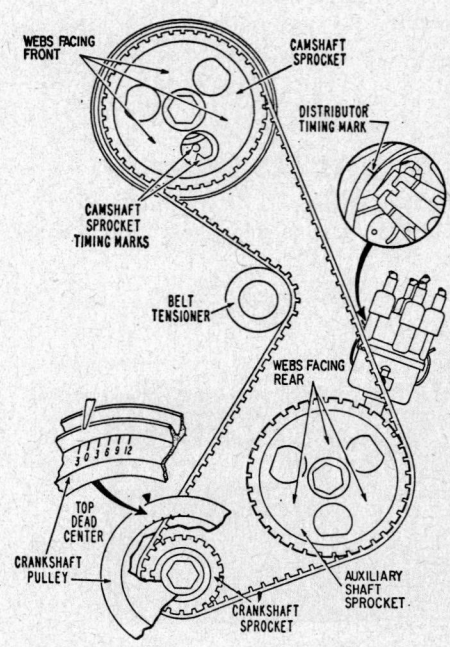

Fig. 8 Timing marks. 2000 cc engine

1–478

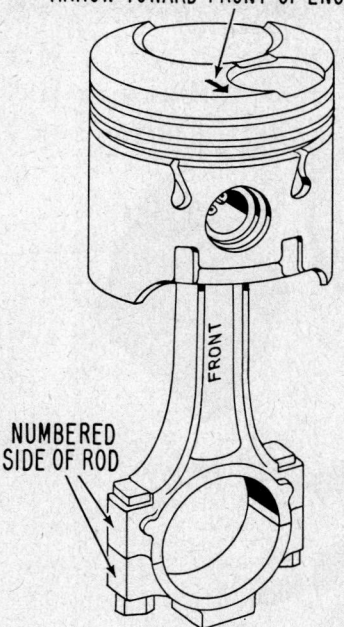

ARROW TOWARD FRONT OF ENGINE

NUMBERED SIDE OF ROD

FRONT

Fig. 9 Piston and rod. 1600 cc engine

or the camshaft after the belt is removed. Rotating either one will impair valve timing.

5. To install, make sure timing marks are aligned as in Fig. 8 and place the belt over the sprockets.
6. Loosen the tensioner adjustment bolt to place tension on the belt.
7. Rotate the crankshaft two complete turns to place the timing marks in the proper position and to remove all slack from the belt. Torque the adjustment bolt and the pivot bolt.
8. Position camshaft drive belt cover and install screws.
9. Start engine and check ignition timing and adjust as required.

CAMSHAFT, REPLACE

1600 cc Engine

1. Remove engine as previously described.
2. With engine mounted on a stand, disconnect fuel line at pump.
3. Loosen alternator belt and remove belt.
4. Remove fan and water pump pulley.
5. Remove oil and fuel pumps from cylinder block.
6. Remove distributor.
7. Remove rocker arm cover and remove rocker arm shaft assembly.
8. Withdraw push rods from block and keep them in order for installation.
9. Invert engine on stand and remove the oil pan.
10. Remove dipstick, crankshaft pulley, front cover and oil slinger.
11. Remove timing chain tensioner and remove camshaft sprocket and chain.
12. With engine inverted, remove camshaft thrust plate and withdraw camshaft.

2000 cc Engine

After removal of cylinder head, proceed as follows:

1. Remove rocker arms.
2. Remove camshaft gear bolt and washer, and slide the gear and the belt guide plate off the shaft.
3. Remove camshaft thrust plate from rear of head and carefully slide camshaft from the rear of the head.

PISTON & ROD, ASSEMBLE

1600 cc Engine

Assemble the rod to the piston with the Front mark on the rod on the same side of the assembly as the arrow in the piston crown, Fig. 9.

2000 cc Engine

Assemble the piston to the rod with the oil squirt hole in the rod positioned to

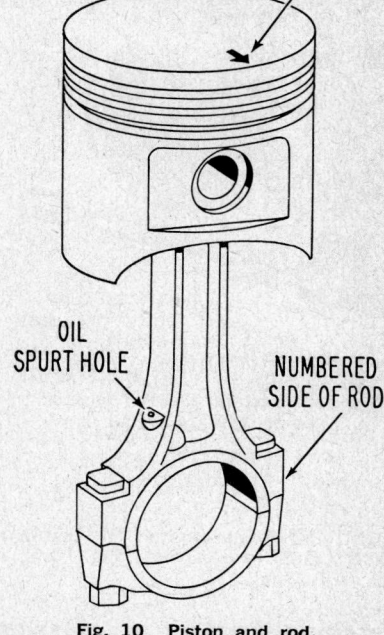

ARROW TOWARD FRONT OF ENGINE

OIL SPURT HOLE

NUMBERED SIDE OF ROD

Fig. 10 Piston and rod. 2000 cc engine

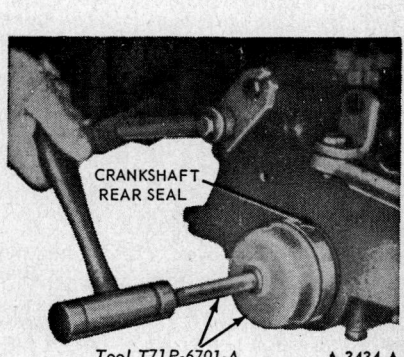

CRANKSHAFT

CRANKSHAFT REAR SEAL

Fig. 12 Removing crankshaft rear oil seal. 2000 cc engine

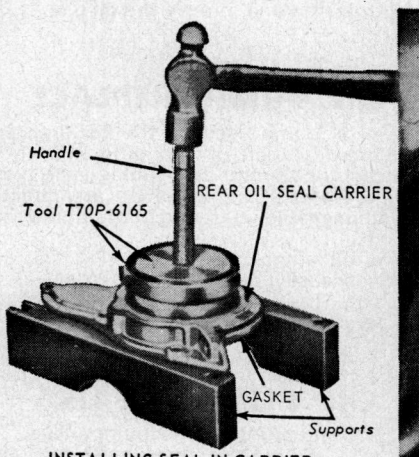

Handle

Tool T70P-6165

REAR OIL SEAL CARRIER

GASKET

Supports

INSTALLING SEAL IN CARRIER

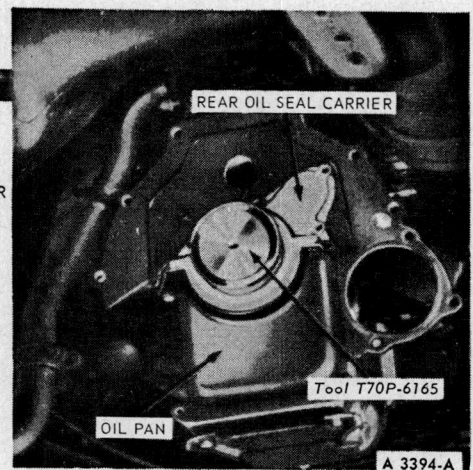

REAR OIL SEAL CARRIER

Tool T70P-6165

OIL PAN

A 3394-A

Fig. 11 Installing crankshaft rear oil seal. 1600 cc engine

CRANKSHAFT REAR SEAL

Tool T71P-6701-A

A 3434-A

Fig. 13 Installing crankshaft rear oil seal. 2000 cc engine

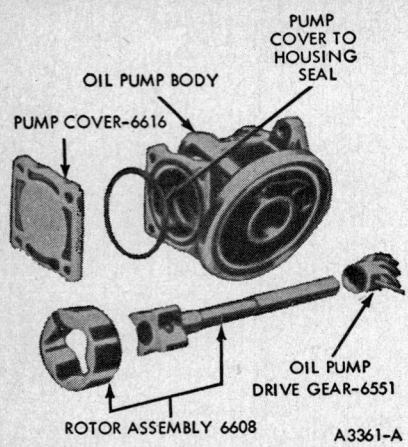

Fig. 14 Eccentric Bi-Rotor type oil pump. 1600 cc engine

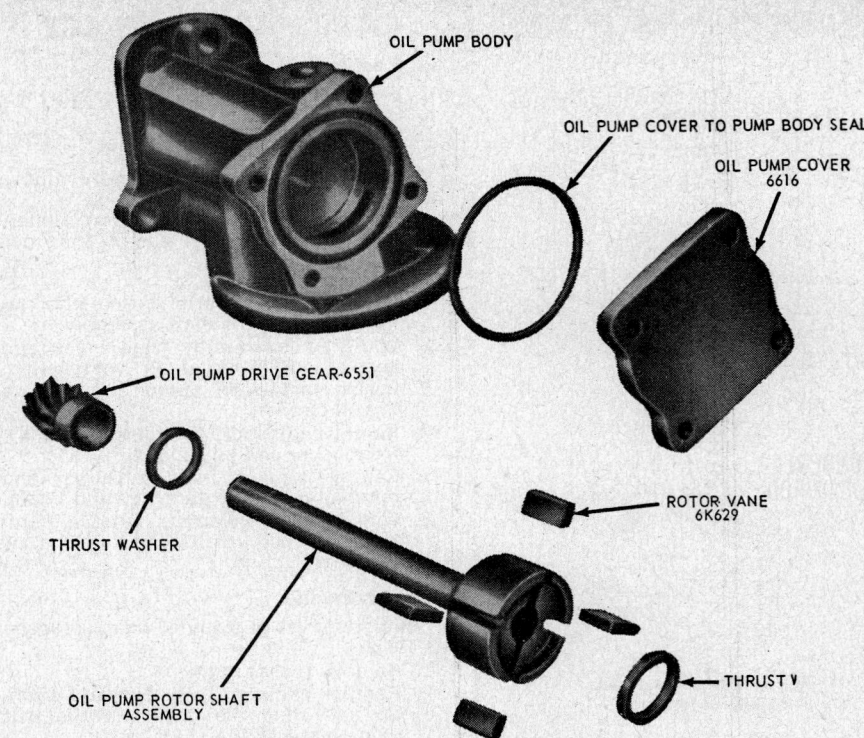

Fig. 15 Sliding vane type oil pump. 1600 cc engine

the right side of the engine. The arrow on the piston must face forward, Fig. 10.

PISTONS, PINS & RINGS

1600 cc Engine

Oversize pistons and rings are available in .0015, .0025 and .0030". Oversize pins are not available.

2000 cc Engine

Oversize pistons and rings are available in .0020 and .0040". Oversize pins are not available.

MAIN & ROD BEARINGS

Undersize main bearings are available in .010, .020 and .030". Rod bearing undersizes are available in .010, .020, .030 and .040" on the 1600 cc engine. Only .010 and .020" undersizes are available on the 2000 cc engine.

CRANKSHAFT OIL SEAL

1600 cc Engine

With the engine removed and mounted on a work stand, proceed as follows:
1. Remove the pressure plate bolts evenly and remove the pressure plate and clutch disc.
2. Remove the flywheel.
3. Remove the oil pan and gaskets.
4. Remove the rear oil seal carrier and use tool T70P-6165 to remove and install a new seal, Fig. 11.

2000 cc Engine

1. Remove transmission, clutch and flywheel or the automatic transmission, converter and flywheel.
2. Remove crankshaft rear seal with a sheet metal screw as shown in Fig. 12.
3. Install new seal with tool T71P-6701A as shown in Fig. 13.

OIL PAN, REPLACE

1600 cc Engine

1. Drain crankcase and remove oil dipstick.
2. Disconnect battery ground cable.
3. Disconnect throttle linkage from carburetor.
4. Disconnect steering cable from rack and pinion.
5. Disconnect rack and pinion from crossmember and move it forward to provide clearance for oil pan.

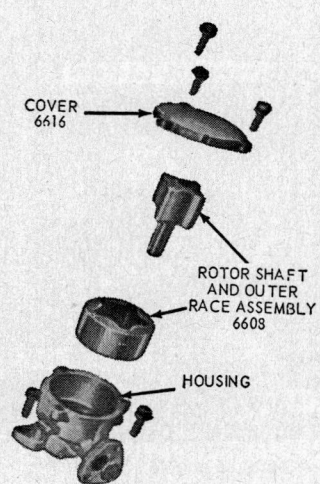

Fig. 16 Oil pump assembly. 2000 cc engine

6. Remove three bolts and remove starter motor.
7. Remove left bottom bolt from lower rear cover and remove cover.
8. Unfasten and remove the oil pan.

2000 cc Engine

1. Drain crankcase and remove oil dipstick and flywheel inspection cover.
2. Disconnect steering cable from rack and pinion.
3. Disconnect rack and pinion from crossmember and move it forward to provide clearance.
4. Unfasten and remove the oil pan.

OIL PUMP, REPLACE

The oil pump used on the 1600 cc engine may be one of two different types, an eccentric bi-rotor or a sliding vane type, Figs. 14 and 15. The pumps are directly interchangeable, differing only in internal design.

The oil pump on 2000 cc, Fig. 16, engines is easily removed after removal of the pan. It is not necessary to remove the pan on 1600 cc engines.

OIL PUMP REPAIRS

1. On the bi-rotor type pump, Figs. 14 and 16, remove filter body and element and extract sealing ring from the groove.
2. Remove end plate and withdraw O ring from groove in body.
3. Check clearance between lobes of

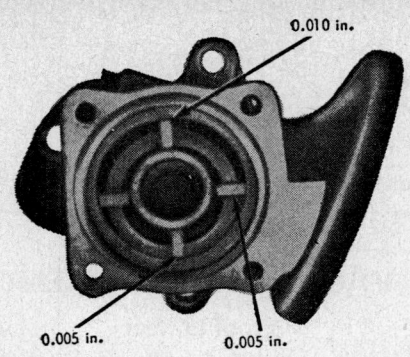

Fig. 17 Checking vane and rotor clearances. 1600 cc engine vane pump

inner and outer rotors. This should not exceed .006". Rotors are supplied only in a matched pair.

4. Check clearance between outer rotor and the housing. This should not exceed .010".
5. Place a straightedge across face of pump body. Clearance between face of rotors and straightedge should not exceed .005".
6. If necessary to replace rotor or drive shaft, remove outer rotor and then drive out retaining pin securing the skew gear to drive shaft and pull off the gear.
7. Withdraw inner rotor and drive shaft.

On the sliding vane type pump, Fig. 15, if clearances exceed those shown in Figs. 17 and 18, it will be necessary to rebuild or replace the pump.

BELT TENSION DATA

	New	Used
1971-74 All	140	110

WATER PUMP, REPLACE

1. Drain cooling system and disconnect heater hose and radiator lower hose from the pump.
2. Loosen alternator and remove the belt.
3. Remove the fan, spacer and pulley.
4. On 2000 cc engine, remove the camshaft drive belt cover.
5. Unfasten and remove the pump.

FUEL PUMP PRESSURE

Year	Engine	Pressure, Lbs.
1971-74	4 cyl	3½-4½

FUEL PUMP, REPLACE

1. Disconnect inlet and outlet lines at pump.

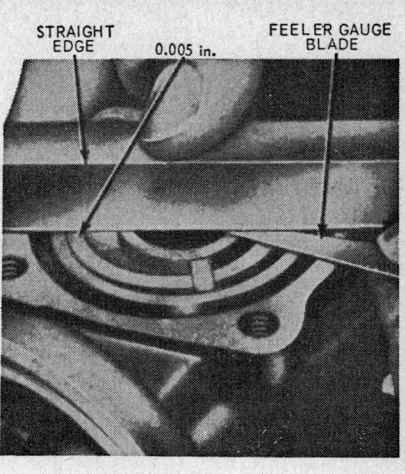

Fig. 18 Checking vane and rotor end-float. 1600 cc engine vane pump

2. Unfasten and remove the fuel pump.
3. On 2000 cc engine, remove the actuator rod.

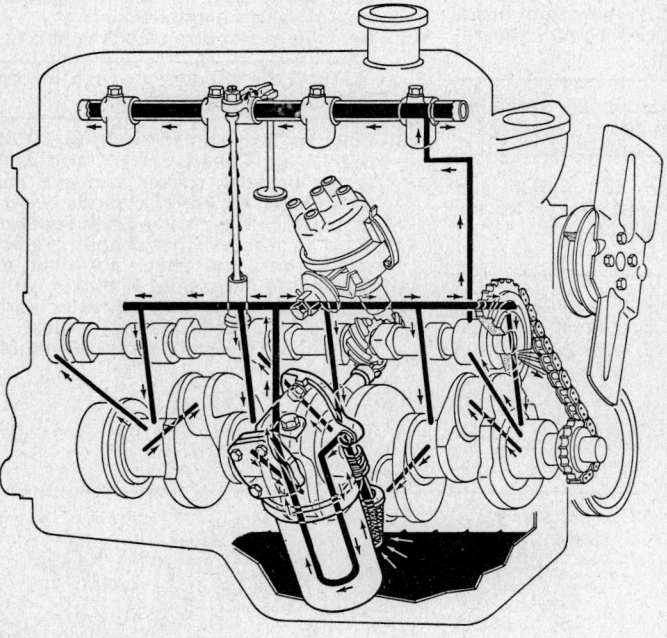

Engine oiling system. 1600 cc engine

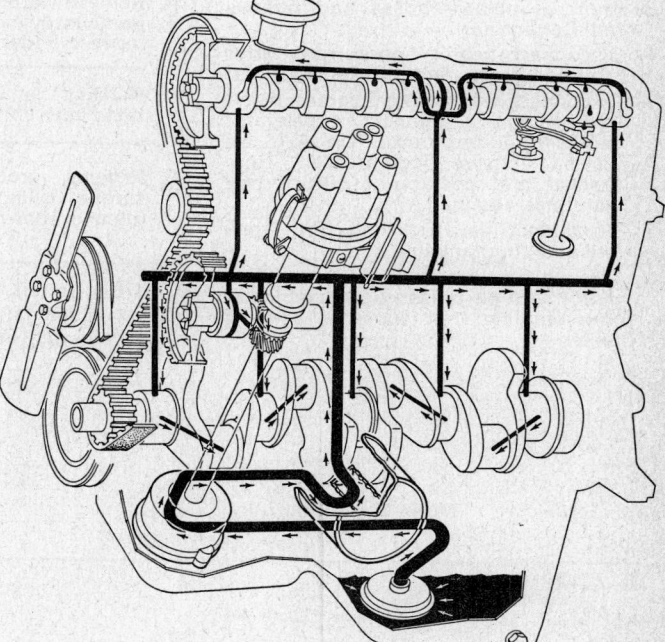

Engine oiling system. 2000 cc engine

2300 cc Engine Section

NOTE: This U.S. built engine is designed to metric specifications and therefore metric tooling will be required.

ENGINE MOUNTS, REPLACE

1974-75 Mustang II & Pinto

1. Remove fan shroud screws and support engine with a suitable jack and place a piece of wood under oil pan.
2. Remove insulator to support bracket through bolt, Figs. 1 and 2.
3. Remove support bracket mounting bolts, raise engine slightly, then remove support bracket.
4. Remove insulator to engine block bolts and insulator.
5. Reverse procedure to install.

ENGINE, REPLACE

1. Drain coolant from radiator and oil from crankcase.
2. Raise hood and secure in vertical position.
3. Remove air cleaner and exhaust manifold shroud.
4. Disconnect battery ground cable.
5. Remove radiator hoses and remove radiator and fan.
6. Disconnect heater hoses from water pump and carburetor choke fitting.
7. Disconnect wires from alternator and starter and disconnect accelerator cable from carburetor. On A/C vehicles, remove compressor from bracket and position it out of way with lines attached.
8. Disconnect flex fuel line from tank line and plug tank line.
9. Disconnect primary wire at coil and disconnect oil pressure and temperature sending unit wires at sending units.

10. Remove starter and raise vehicle to remove the flywheel or converter housing upper attaching bolts.
11. Disconnect inlet pipe at exhaust manifold. Disconnect engine mounts at underbody bracket and remove flywheel or converter housing cover.
12. On vehicle with manual shift, remove flywheel housing lower attaching bolts.
13. On vehicle with automatic transmission, disconnect converter from flywheel and remove converter housing lower attaching bolts.
14. Lower vehicle and support transmission and flywheel or converter housing with a jack.
15. Attach engine lifting hooks to brackets and carefully lift engine out of engine compartment.

CYLINDER HEAD, REPLACE

1. Drain cooling system and remove air cleaner and rocker arm cover.
2. Remove intake and exhaust manifolds and carburetor.
3. Remove timing case cover and drive belt.
4. Remove water outlet elbow from head.
5. Remove cylinder head bolts, then remove cylinder head.

NOTE: The cylinder head retaining bolts have 12 point heads.

6. Reverse procedure to install and torque cylinder head bolts in sequence shown in, Fig. 3.

CAUTION: When installing cylinder head, position camshaft at 5 o'clock position, Fig. 3, allowing minimal protrusion of the valves from the cylinder head.

VALVE ARRANGEMENT

Front to Rear

2300 cc Engine . . . . E-I-E-I-E-I-E-I

VALVE LIFT SPECS.

Engine	Year	Intake	Exhaust
2300 cc	1974-75	.400	.400

VALVE TIMING

Intake Opens Before TDC

Engine	Year	Degrees
2300 cc	1974-75	22

VALVES, ADJUST

The valve lash on this engine cannot be adjusted due to the use of hydraulic valve lash adjusters, Fig. 4. However, the valve train can be checked for wear as follows:

1. Crank engine to position camshaft with flat section of lobe facing rocker arm of valve being checked.
2. Remove rocker arm retaining spring.

NOTE: Late models do not incorporate the retaining spring.

3. Collapse lash adjuster with tool T74P-6565B and insert correct size feeler gauge between rocker arm and camshaft lobe, Fig. 5. If clearance is not as listed in the "Valve Specifications" chart in front of this chapter, remove rocker arm and check for wear and replace as necessary. If rocker arm is found satisfactory, check valve spring assembled height and adjust as needed. If valve spring assembled

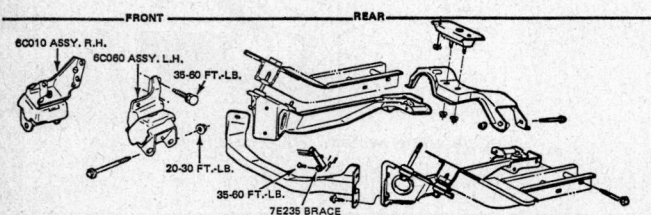

Fig. 1 Engine mount installation. 1974-75 Mustang II

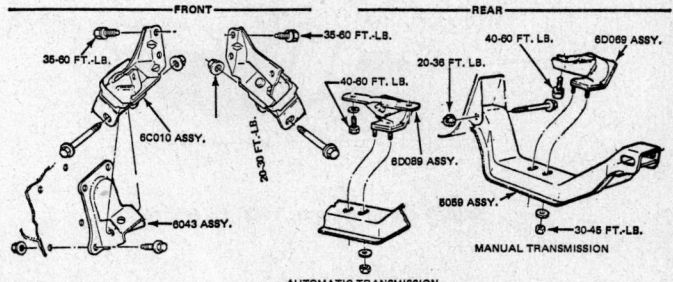

Fig. 2 Engine mount installation. 1974-75 Pinto

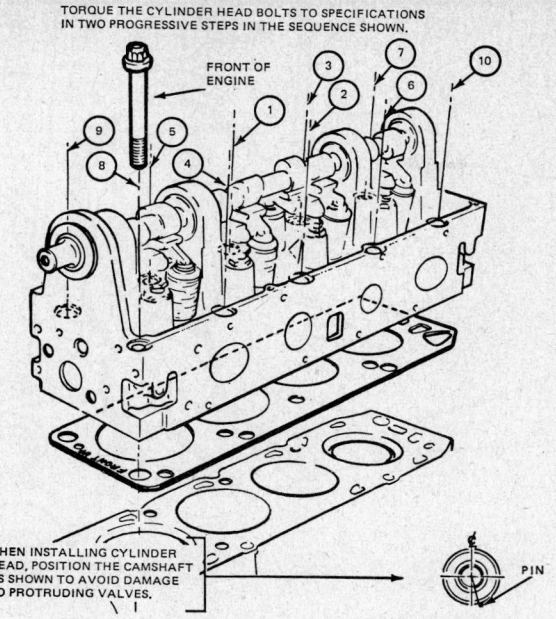

TORQUE THE CYLINDER HEAD BOLTS TO SPECIFICATIONS IN TWO PROGRESSIVE STEPS IN THE SEQUENCE SHOWN.

FRONT OF ENGINE

WHEN INSTALLING CYLINDER HEAD, POSITION THE CAMSHAFT AS SHOWN TO AVOID DAMAGE TO PROTRUDING VALVES.

PIN

Fig. 3   Cylinder head installation. 2300 cc engine

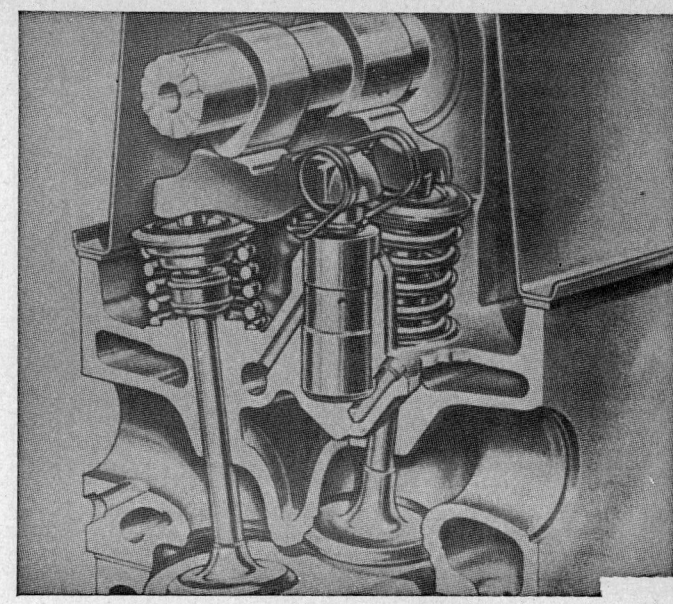

Fig. 4   Valve train installation. 2300 cc engine

height is within specifications listed in the front of this chapter, remove lash adjuster and clean or replace as necessary.

VALVE GUIDES

Valve guides consist of holes bored in the cylinder head. For service the guides can be reamed oversize to accommodate valves with oversize stems of .008, .016 and .032".

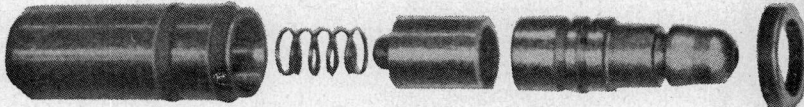

Fig. 6   Valve lash adjuster, Type I. 2300 cc engine

Fig. 7   Valve lash adjuster, Type II. 2300 cc engine

CAM ON BASE CIRCLE

FEELER GAUGE

T74P-6565-B

Fig. 5   Checking valve clearance. 2300 cc engine

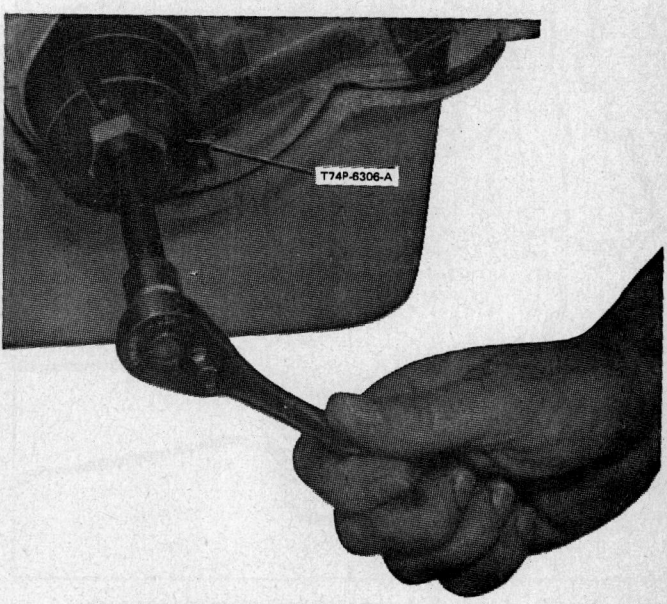

T74P-6306-A

Fig. 8   Crankshaft sprocket removal. 2300 cc engine

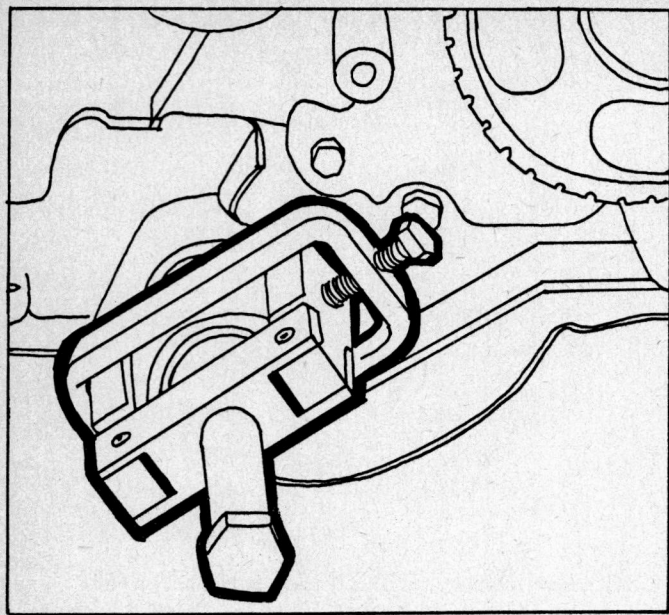

Fig. 9   Crankshaft front oil seal removal. 2300 cc engine

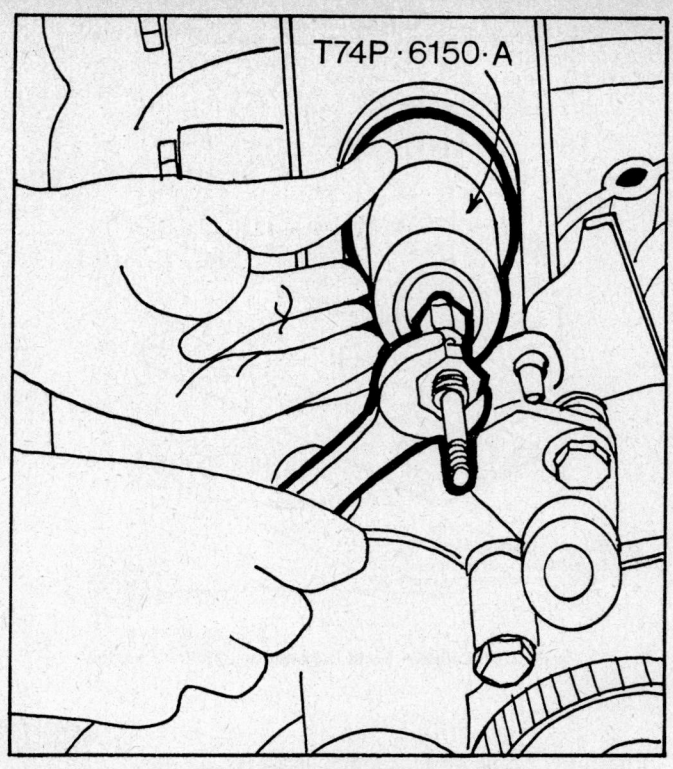

T74P·6150·A

Fig. 10   Engine front seals installation. 2300 cc engine

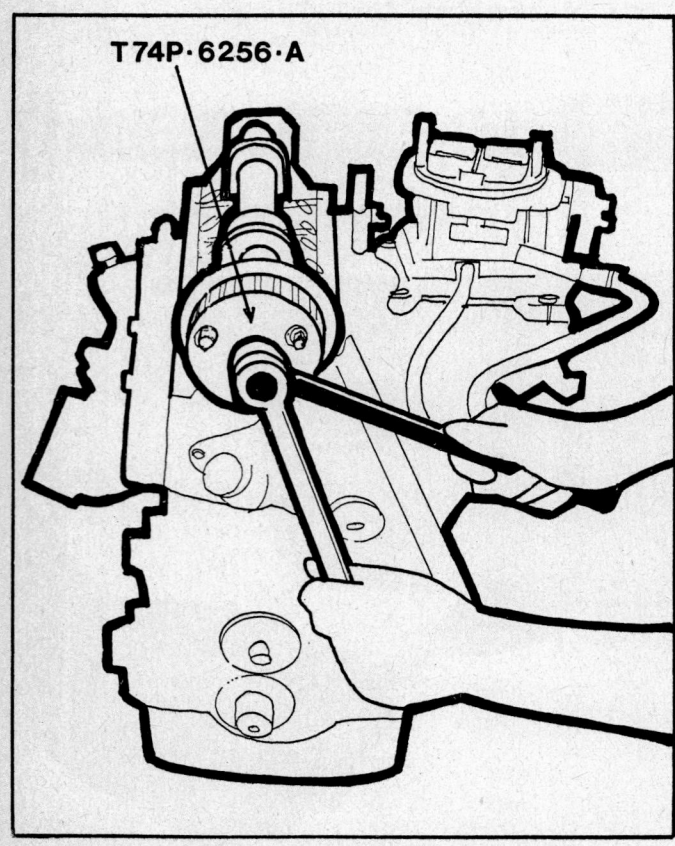

T74P·6256·A

Fig. 12   Camshaft & auxiliary shaft sprockets removal.
2300 cc engine

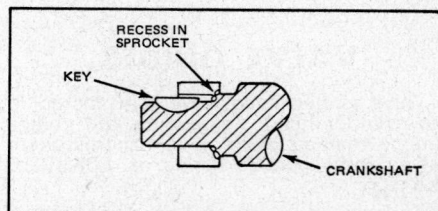

RECESS IN
SPROCKET

KEY

CRANKSHAFT

Fig. 11   Crankshaft sprocket installation.
2300 cc engine

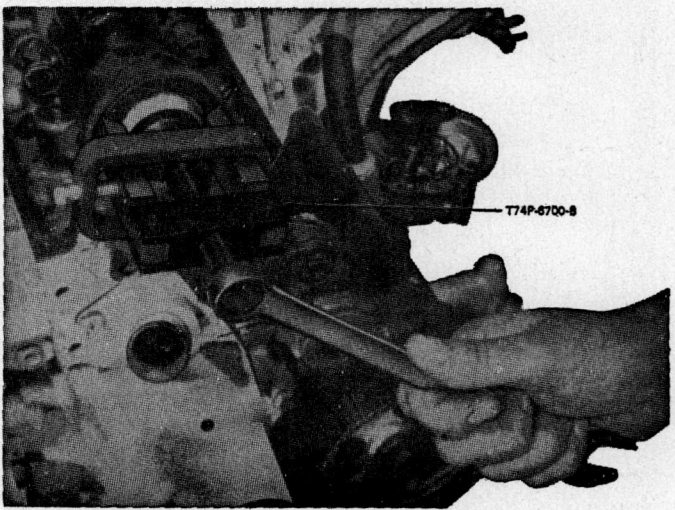

T74P-6700-B

Fig. 13   Camshaft & auxiliary shaft seals removal.
2300 cc engine

ROCKER ARM SERVICE

1. Remove rocker arm cover.
2. Rotate camshaft until flat section of lobe faces rocker arm being removed.
3. With tool T74P-6565B, collapse lash adjuster and, if necessary, valve spring and slide rocker arm over lash adjuster.
4. Reverse procedure to install.

NOTE: Before rotating camshaft, ensure that lash adjuster is collapsed to prevent valve train damage.

LASH ADJUSTER, REPLACE

The hydraulic valve lash adjusters can be removed after rocker arm removal. There are two types of lash adjusters available, Type I, being the standard lash adjuster, Fig. 6, and Type II, having a .020 inch oversize outside diameter, Fig. 7.

FRONT ENGINE SEALS, REPLACE

To gain access to the front engine seals, remove the timing belt cover and proceed as follows:

Crankshaft Oil Seal

1. Without removing cylinder front cover, remove crankshaft sprocket with tool T74P-6306A, Fig. 8.
2. Remove crankshaft oil seal with tool T74P-6700B, Fig. 9.
3. Install a new crankshaft oil seal with tool T74P-6150A, Fig. 10.
4. Install crankshaft sprocket with recess facing engine block, Fig. 11.

Camshaft & Auxiliary Shaft Oil Seals

1. Remove camshaft or auxiliary shaft sprocket with tool T74P-6256A, Fig. 12.
2. Remove oil seal with tool T74P-6700B, Fig. 13.
3. Install a new oil seal with tool T74P-6150A, Fig. 10.
4. Install camshaft or auxiliary shaft sprocket with tool T74P-6256A with center arbor removed.

TIMING BELT

1. Position crankshaft at TDC, No. 1 cylinder compression stroke.
2. Remove timing belt cover, loosen belt tensioner, and remove belt from sprockets, Fig. 14. Tighten tensioner bolt, holding tensioner in position.

NOTE: Do not rotate crankshaft or camshaft after belt is removed. Rotating either component will result in improper valve timing.

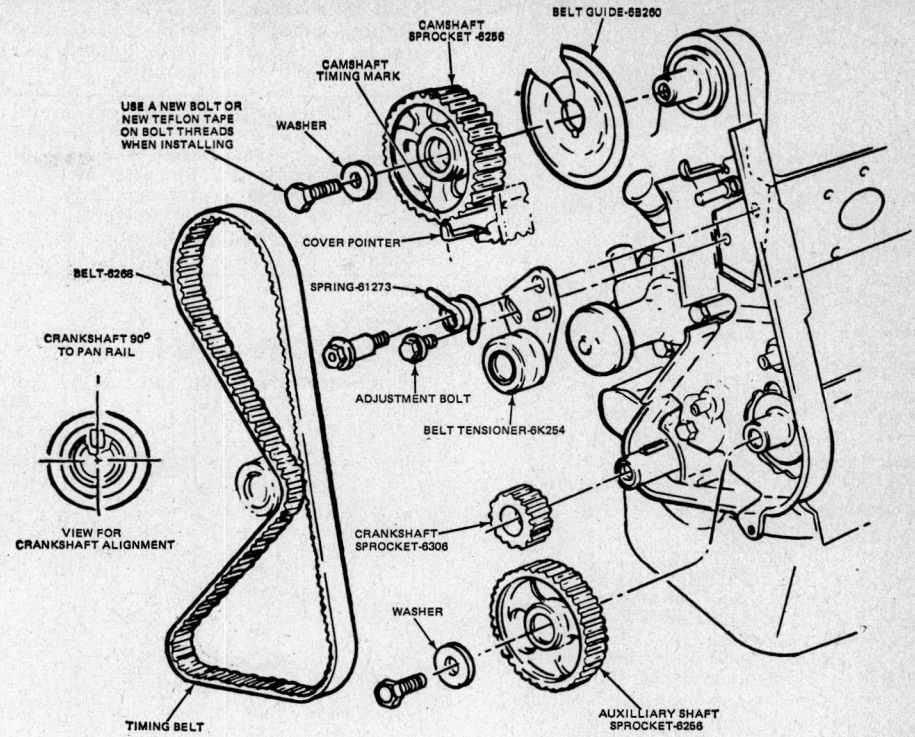

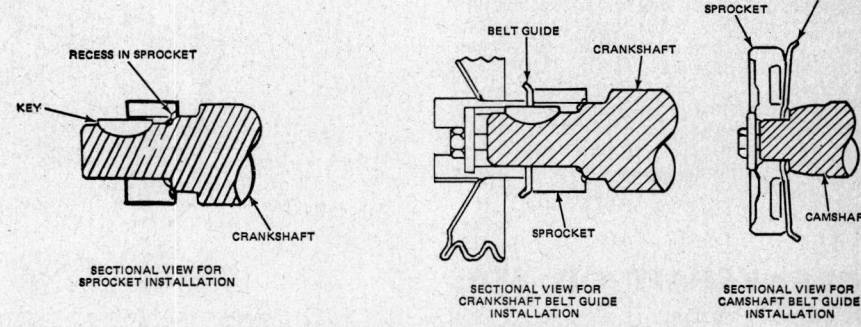

Fig. 14   Drive belt & sprockets installation. 2300 cc engine

3. To install belt, ensure timing marks are aligned, Fig. 15, and place belt over sprockets.
4. Loosen tensioner bolt, allowing tensioner to move against belt.
5. Rotate crankshaft two complete turns, removing slack from belt. Torque tensioner adjustment and pivot bolts and check alignment of timing marks, Fig. 15.
6. Install timing belt cover.

CAMSHAFT, REPLACE

1. Remove rocker arm cover and rocker arms.
2. Remove timing belt cover, camshaft sprocket bolt and washer, then slide sprocket and belt guide off camshaft.
3. Remove camshaft retaining plate from rear of head, then remove camshaft from front of head.

PISTON & ROD, ASSEMBLE

Assemble the rod to the piston with the arrow on top of piston facing front of engine, Fig. 16.

PISTONS, PINS & RINGS

Oversize pistons are available in oversizes of .003", .020", .030" and .040". Oversize rings are available in .020", .030" and .040" oversizes. Oversize pins are not available.

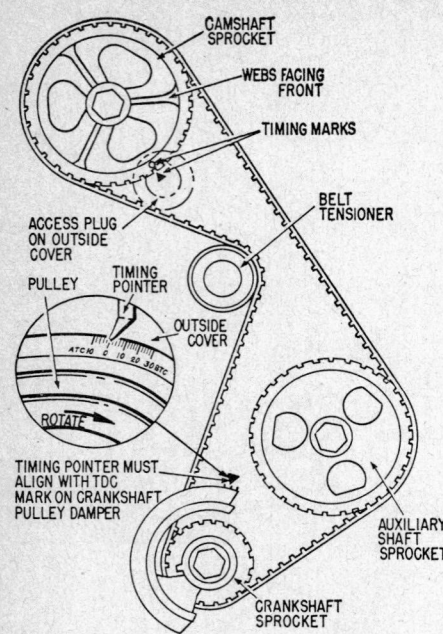

Fig. 15   Valve timing marks.
2300 cc engine

MAIN & ROD BEARINGS

Undersize main bearings are available in .002″, .020″, .030″ and .040″ undersizes. Undersize rod bearings are available in undersizes of .002″, .010″, .020″, .030″ and .040″.

The crankshaft and main bearings are installed with arrows on main bearing caps facing front of engine, Fig. 17. Install PCV baffle between bearing journals No. 3 and 4.

CRANKSHAFT OIL SEAL

1. Remove oil pan.
2. Remove rear main bearing cap.
3. Loosen remaining bearing caps, allowing crankshaft to drop down about 1/32″.
4. Install a sheet metal screw into seal and pull screw to remove seal.
5. Carefully clean seal groove in block with a brush and solvent. Also clean seal groove in bearing cap.
6. Dip seal halves in clean engine oil.
7. Carefully install upper seal half in its groove with locating tab toward rear of engine, Fig. 18, by rotating it on shaft journal of crankshaft until approximately 3/8″ protrudes below the parting surface. *Be sure no rubber has been shaved from outside diameter of seal by bottom edge of groove.*
8. Retighten main bearing caps and torque to specifications.
9. Install lower seal in main bearing cap with undercut side of seal toward front of engine, and allow seal to protrude about 3/8″ above parting surface to mate with upper seal upon

cap installation.
10. Apply suitable sealer to parting faces of cap and block. Install cap and torque to specifications.

NOTE: If difficulty is encountered in installing the upper half of the seal in position, lightly lap (sandpaper) the side of the seal opposite the lip side using a medium grit paper. After sanding, the seal must be washed in solvent, then dipped in clean engine oil prior to installation.

OIL PAN

1. Drain crankcase and remove oil dip-

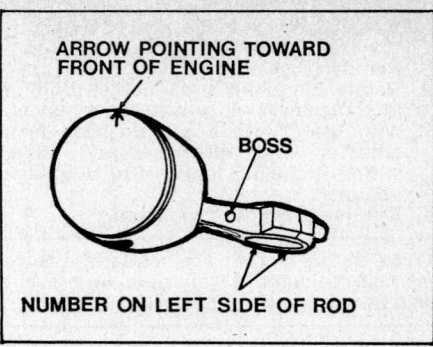

Fig. 16   Piston & rod. 2300 cc engine

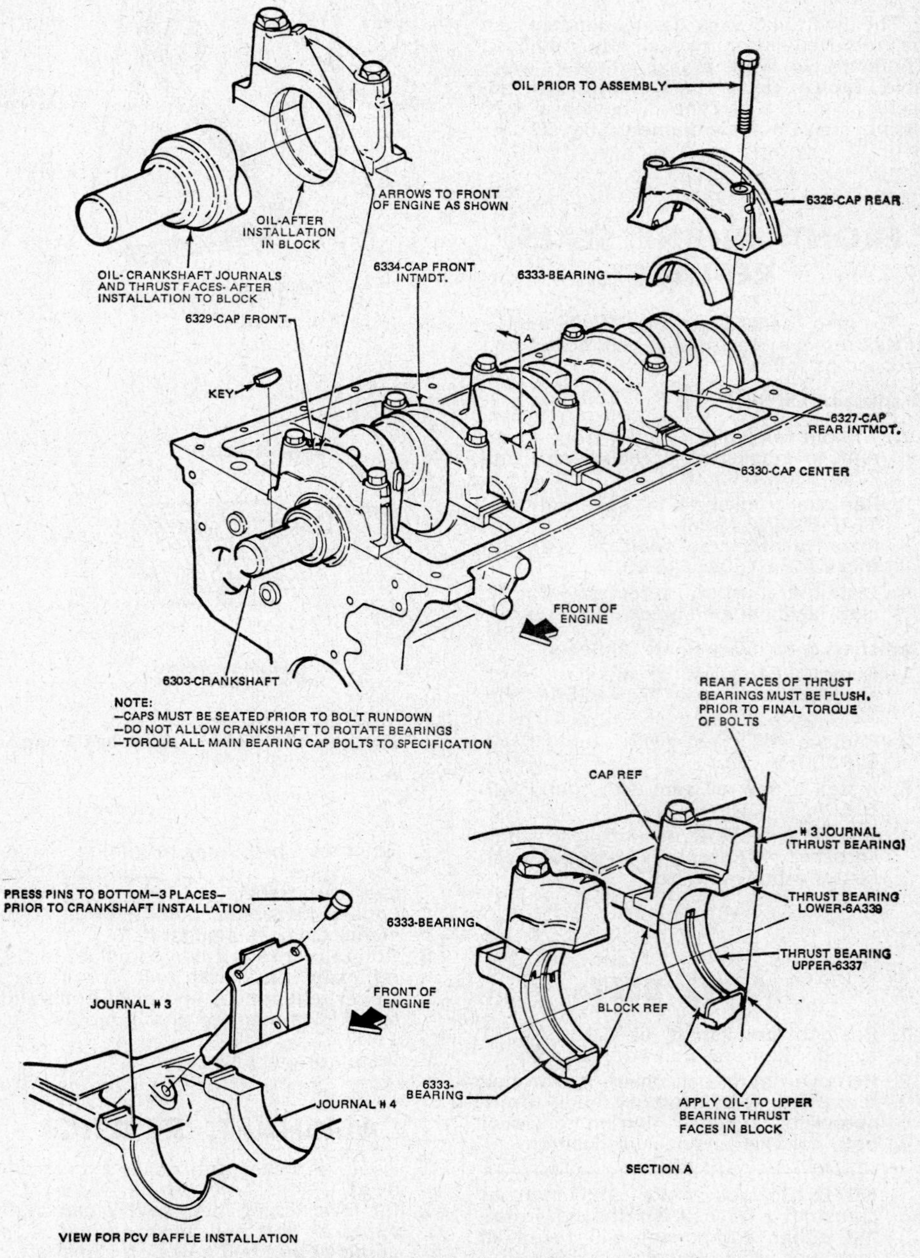

NOTE:
—CAPS MUST BE SEATED PRIOR TO BOLT RUNDOWN
—DO NOT ALLOW CRANKSHAFT TO ROTATE BEARINGS
—TORQUE ALL MAIN BEARING CAP BOLTS TO SPECIFICATION

Fig. 17   Crankshaft & main bearing installation. 2300 cc engine

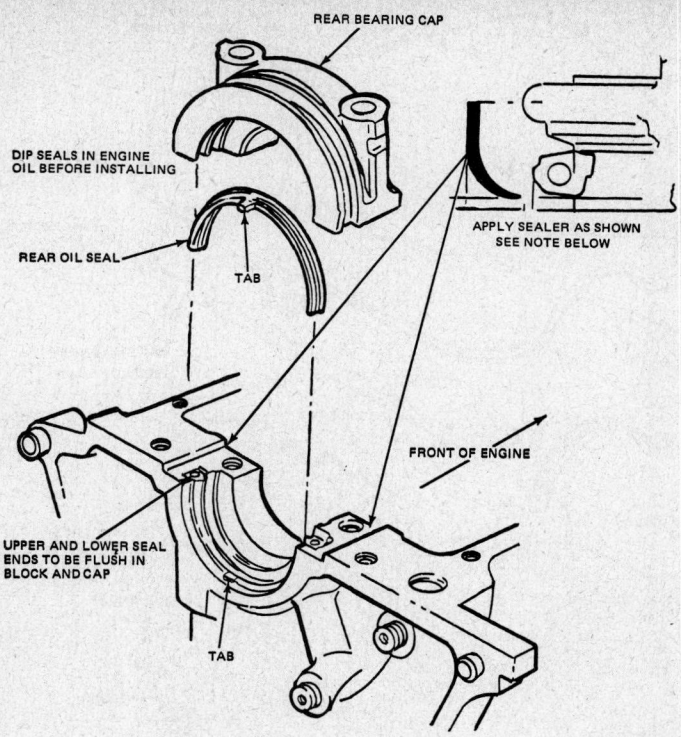

REAR BEARING CAP

DIP SEALS IN ENGINE
OIL BEFORE INSTALLING

REAR OIL SEAL

TAB

APPLY SEALER AS SHOWN
SEE NOTE BELOW

FRONT OF ENGINE

UPPER AND LOWER SEAL
ENDS TO BE FLUSH IN
BLOCK AND CAP

TAB

SEALER NOTE: CLEAN THE AREA WHERE SEALER
IS TO BE APPLIED BEFORE INSTALLING THE SEALS.
USE FORD SPOT REMOVER B7A-19521-A OR EQUIVALENT.
AFTER THE SEALS ARE IN PLACE, APPLY A 1/16 INCH
BEAD OF C3AZ-19562-A OR -B SEALER AS SHOWN.
SEALER MUST NOT CONTACT SEALS.

Fig. 18   Crankshaft rear oil seal installation. 2300 cc engine

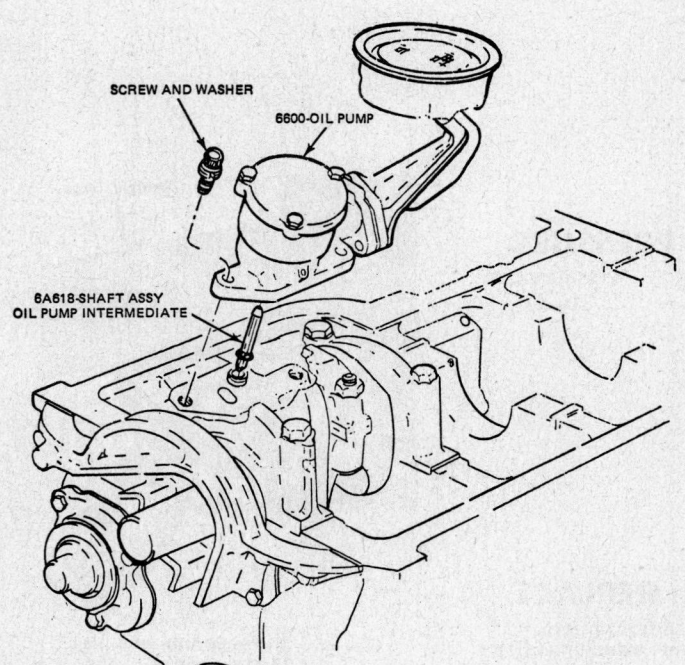

SCREW AND WASHER

6600-OIL PUMP

6A618-SHAFT ASSY
OIL PUMP INTERMEDIATE

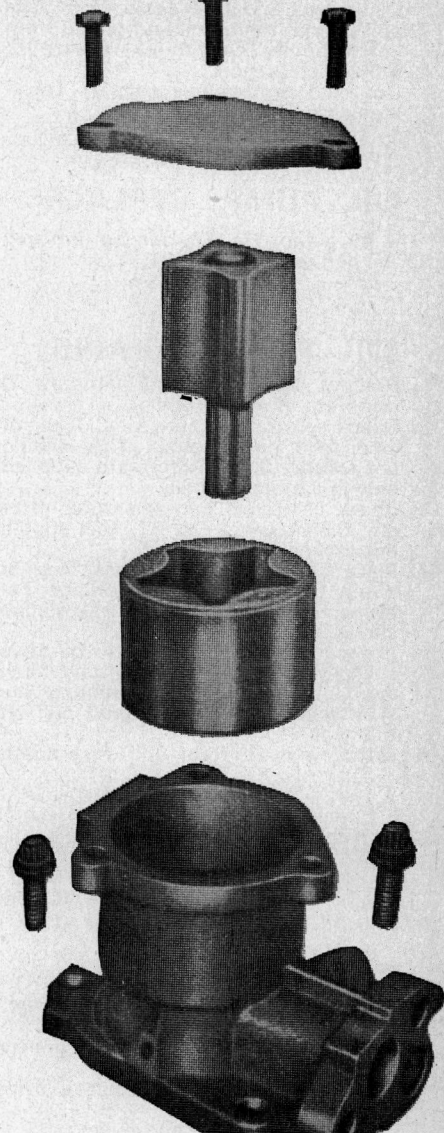

Fig. 20   Oil pump. 2300 cc engine

**Fig. 21   Oil pump installation.
2300 cc engine**

stick and flywheel inspection cover.
2. Disconnect steering cable from rack and pinion, then rack and pinion from crossmember and move forward to provide clearance.
3. Unfasten and remove oil pan. To install oil pan, refer to Fig. 19.

OIL PUMP, REPLACE

The oil pump, Fig. 20, can be removed after oil pan removal, Fig. 21.

OIL PUMP REPAIRS

1. Remove end plate and withdraw O ring from groove in body.
2. Check clearance between lobes of inner and outer rotors. This should not exceed .006". Rotors are supplied only in a matched pair.
3. Check clearance between outer rotor and the housing, Fig. 22. This should not exceed .010".
4. Place a straightedge across face of pump body, Fig. 23. Clearance between face of rotors and straightedge should not exceed .005".
5. If necessary to replace rotor or drive shaft, remove outer rotor and then drive out retaining pin securing the skew gear to drive shaft and pull off the gear.
6. Withdraw inner rotor and drive shaft.

BELT TENSION DATA

	New Ft. Lbs.	Used Ft. Lbs.
1974-75 All	140	110

WATER PUMP, REPLACE

1. Drain cooling system and disconnect hoses from pump.
2. Loosen alternator and remove drive belt.
3. Remove fan, spacer and pulley.
4. Remove water pump attaching bolts and water pump.

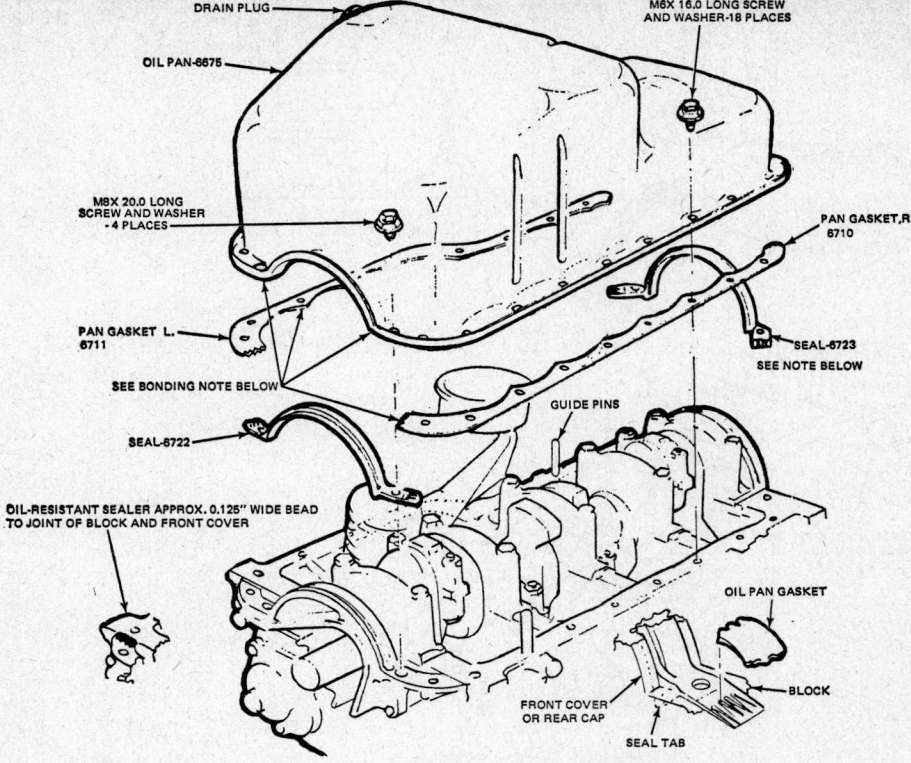

Fig. 19   Oil pan installation. 2300 cc engine

FUEL PUMP PRESSURE

Year	Engine	Pressure Lbs.
1974-75	2300 cc	3½-4½

FUEL PUMP, REPLACE

1. Disconnect fuel lines from pump.
2. Remove fuel pump attaching bolts and fuel pump.

Fig. 22   Checking outer rotor to housing clearance. 2300 cc engine

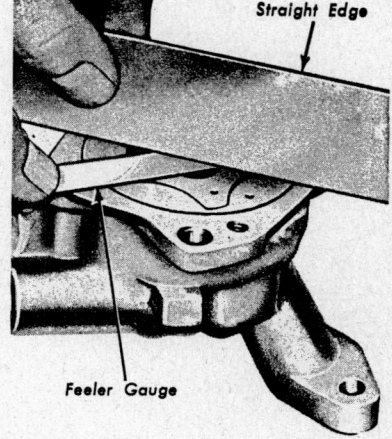

Fig. 23   Checking rotor end play. 2300 cc engine

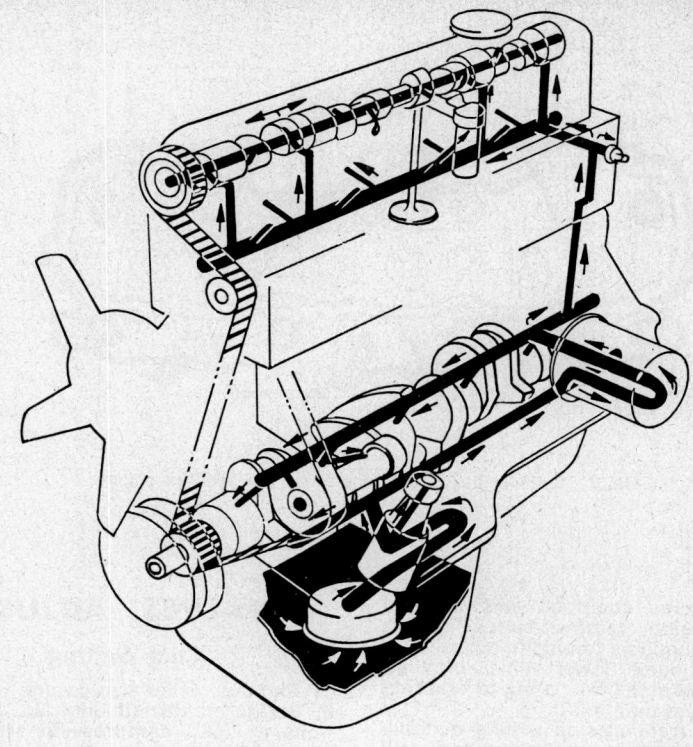

Engine oiling system. 2300 cc engine

2800 cc V6 Engine Section

ENGINE MOUNTS, REPLACE

1975 Pinto & 1974-75 Mustang II

1. Remove fan shroud screws and support engine with a suitable jack and a block of wood under the oil pan.
2. Remove insulator to insulator support bracket through bolt, support bracket to frame bolts, raise engine slightly, then remove support bracket, Fig. 1.
3. Remove insulator assembly to engine block bolts, then remove insulator and heat shield.

ENGINE, REPLACE

1975 Pinto & 1974-75 Mustang II

1. Disconnect battery cables and remove hood.
2. Remove air cleaner and intake duct.
3. Drain cooling system, disconnect radiator hoses from radiator, then remove radiator. Disconnect heater hoses from engine block and water pump.

NOTE: Remove fan shroud and position shroud over fan before removing radiator.

4. Remove alternator and bracket.

5. Disconnect ground wires from engine block.
6. Disconnect fuel tank line from fuel pump and plug line.
7. Disconnect all linkage from engine and wires from ignition coil.

NOTE: If equipped with Thermactor system, remove or disconnect system components interfering with engine removal.

8. Raise vehicle and place on jack stands.
9. Disconnect exhaust pipes from exhaust manifold and remove starter.
10. Remove engine front support through bolts.
11. On vehicles equipped with automatic transmission, disconnect converter from flywheel, remove downshift rod, then remove converter housing to engine bolts and adapter plate to converter housing bolt.

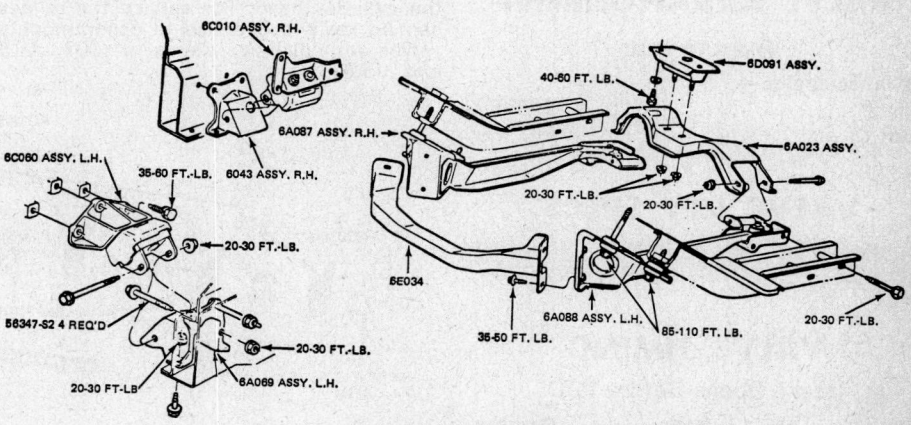

Fig. 1 Engine mounts. 1974-75 Mustang II

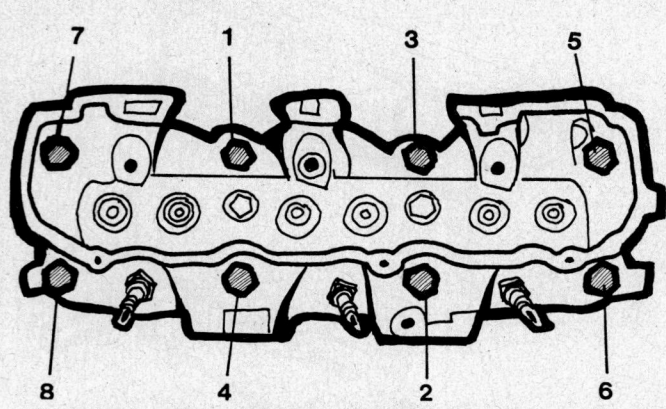

Fig. 2 Cylinder head tightening sequence. 2800 cc engine

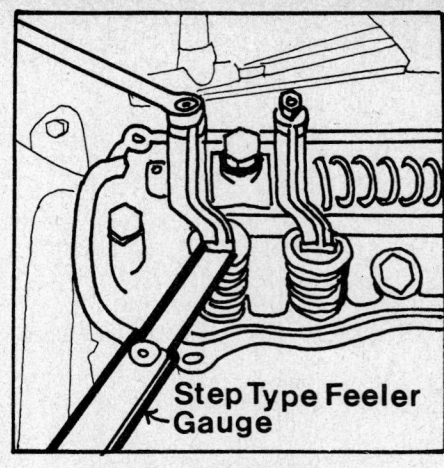

Fig. 3   Adjusting valve lash.
2800 cc engine

12. On vehicles equipped with manual transmission, remove clutch linkage and bell housing to engine bolts.
13. On all models, lower vehicle and attach a suitable lifting sling to brackets on exhaust manifold.
14. Support transmission with a suitable jack, raise engine slightly and pull from transmission, then lift engine from engine compartment.

CYLINDER HEAD, REPLACE

1. Disconnect battery ground cable, disconnect linkage and drain coolant.
2. Remove distributor, coolant hoses, rocker arm covers, fuel line and filter, carburetor and intake manifold.
3. Remove rocker arm shaft, oil baffles and push rods.
4. Remove exhaust manifold.
5. Remove cylinder head bolts and cylinder head.
6. Reverse procedure to install and torque bolts in sequence shown in, Fig. 2.

VALVE ARRANGEMENT

Front to Rear

2800 cc engine—
Right . . . . I-E-I-E-E-I
Left . . . . I-E-E-I-E-I

VALVE LIFT SPECS.

Engine	Year	Intake	Exhaust
2800 cc	1974-75	.3730	.3730

VALVE TIMING

Intake Opens Before TDC

Engine	Year	Degrees
2800 cc	1974-75	20

VALVES, ADJUST

Cold Setting

1. Remove rocker arm covers.
2. Rotate crankshaft until No. 1 cylinder is at TDC, compression stroke, and set valve lash on No. 1 cylinder to specifications as listed in the "Valve Specifications" table.
3. Rotate crankshaft 120 degrees and set valve lash on No. 4 cylinder.
4. Rotate crankshaft an additional 120 degrees and set valve lash on No. 2 cylinder. The remaining valves are adjusted in the same manner as above, following the firing order found in the front of this chapter.

Hot Setting

With engine at operating temperature and idling, set valve lash with a step type feeler gauge, Fig. 3, to specifications as listed in the "Valve Specifications" table.

VALVE GUIDES

Valve guides consist of holes bored in the cylinder head. For service the guides can be reamed oversize to accommodate valves with oversize stems of .003, .015 and .030".

Fig. 4   Rocker arm replacement.
2800 cc engine

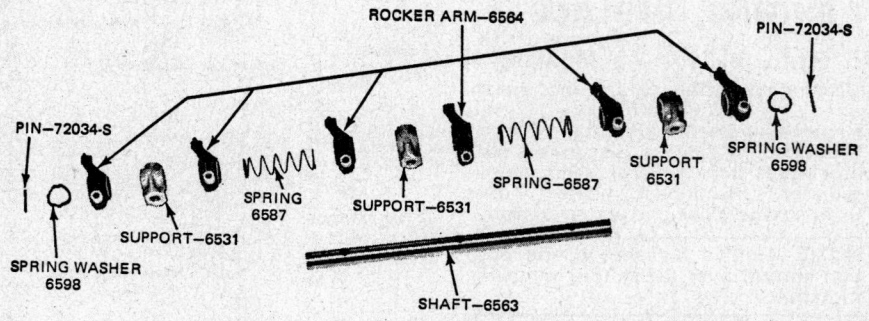

Fig. 5   Rocker arm shaft assembly. 2800 cc engine

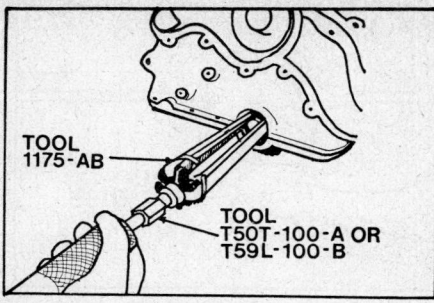

Fig. 6 Removing crankshaft oil seal. 2800 cc engine

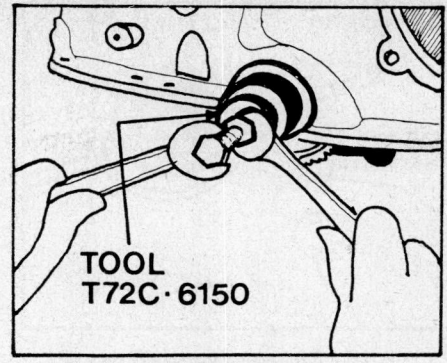

Fig. 7 Installing crankshaft oil seal. 2800 cc engine

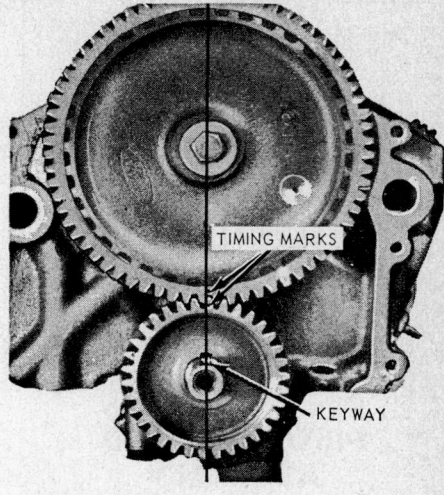

Fig. 8 Valve timing marks. 2800 cc engine

ROCKER ARM SERVICE

1. Disconnect throttle rod from carburetor and remove rocker arm cover.
2. Remove rocker arm shaft stand bolts, rocker arm shaft assembly and oil baffle, Fig. 4.
3. Remove cotter pin and spring washer from ends of rocker shaft and slide rocker arms, springs and shaft supports off shaft, marking components for proper reassembly, Fig. 5.
4. Remove plugs from shaft ends by drilling a hole in one plug, insert a long rod through drilled plug and knock the opposite plug from shaft. Remove the drilled plug in same manner.
5. With a blunt tool, install plugs in end of rocker shafts with cup side out.
6. Install spring washer and cotter pin on one end of shaft and install components in proper sequence as marked during disassembly.

NOTE: Oil holes in rocker shaft must face downward during installation.

VALVE LIFTERS, REPLACE

Remove cylinder head as outlined previously and using a magnet, remove lifters from their bores.

TIMING CASE COVER

The crankshaft front oil seal may be serviced without removing the cylinder front cover as follows:
1. Drain coolant and remove radiator, crankshaft pulley and water pump drive belt.
2. Pull oil seal from front cover, Fig. 6.
3. Install new oil seal with tool T72C-6150, Fig. 7.
4. Install crankshaft pulley, water pump drive belt, radiator, then refill cooling system.

TIMING GEARS

1. Drain, then remove radiator and oil pan.
2. Remove cylinder front cover and water pump.
3. Align timing marks, Fig. 8.
4. Using a suitable gear puller, remove crankshaft gear and key.
5. Remove camshaft gear with a suitable gear puller.

NOTE: Do not rotate crankshaft or camshaft with gears removed as rotation of either component can result in improper valve timing.

6. Install key in camshaft, then press camshaft gear onto camshaft.
7. Install key in crankshaft, then press crankshaft gear onto crankshaft with tool T72C-6150, Fig. 9, and make sure timing marks are aligned, Fig. 8.
8. Install cylinder front cover, water pump, radiator and oil pan.
9. Refill cooling system and oil pan. Start engine and adjust ignition timing, if necessary.

CAMSHAFT, REPLACE

1. Remove cylinder heads as outlined under "Cylinder Head, Replace" procedure.
2. Remove radiator and oil pan.
3. Remove crankshaft pulley, cylinder front cover and water pump.
4. Remove camshaft gear with a suitable puller, then camshaft thrust plate, Fig. 10.
5. Pull camshaft from engine block using care to avoid damaging camshaft bearings.

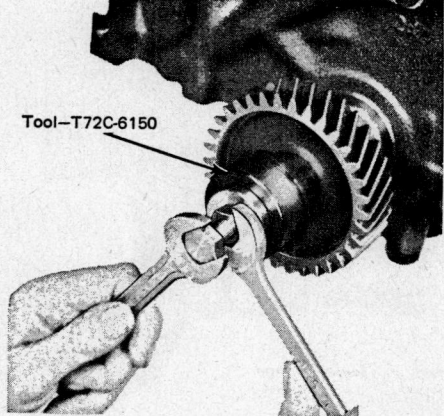

Fig. 9 Crankshaft gear installation. 2800 cc engine

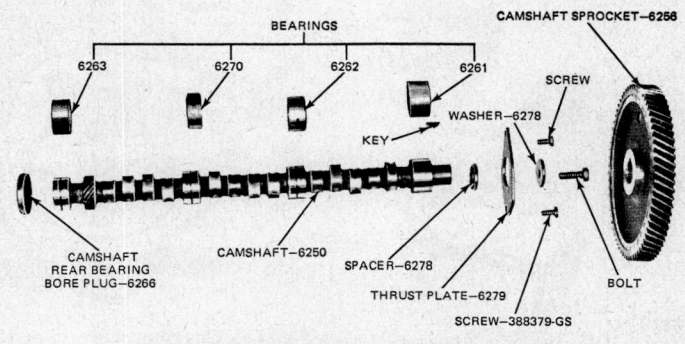

Fig. 10 Camshaft components. 2800 cc engine

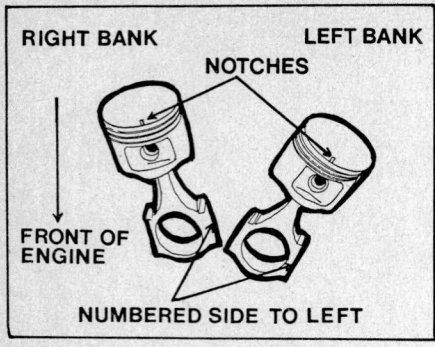

Fig. 11   Piston & rod. 2800 cc engine

Fig. 12   Removing crankshaft rear oil seal. 2800 cc engine

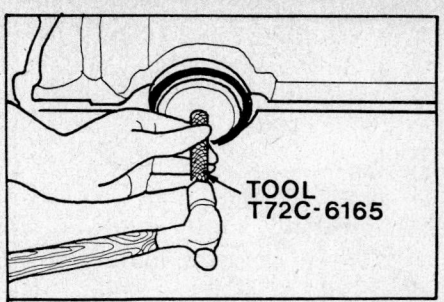

Fig. 13   Installing crankshaft rear oil seal. 2800 cc engine

PISTON & ROD ASSEMBLY

Assemble the piston to the rod with the notches facing front of engine and the numbered side of the rod toward left side of engine, Fig. 11.

PISTONS, PINS & RINGS

Oversize pistons and rings are available in .020″ and .040″ oversizes. Oversize pins are not available.

CRANKSHAFT OIL SEAL

1. Remove transmission, clutch or converter, and flywheel.
2. Remove crankshaft rear oil seal with a sheet metal screw, Fig. 12.
3. Install new seal with tool T72C-6165, Fig. 13.

OIL PAN, REPLACE

1. Disconnect battery ground cable, remove fan shroud attaching bolts and place shroud over fan.
2. Loosen alternator bracket and adjusting bolts.

3. Raise vehicle and drain oil pan.
4. Remove splash shield and starter.
5. Remove engine insulator to support bracket through bolts, raise engine and place wood blocks between insulator and support brackets.
6. Remove clutch or converter housing cover.
7. Remove oil pan bolts and oil pan.

OIL PUMP, REPLACE

The oil pump, Fig. 14, can be removed after oil pan removal.

OIL PUMP REPAIRS

1. Remove end plate and withdraw O ring from groove in body.
2. Check clearance between lobes of inner and outer rotors. This should not exceed .006″. Rotors are supplied only in a matched pair.
3. Check clearance between outer rotor and the housing, Fig. 15. This should not exceed .010″.
4. Place a straightedge across face of pump body, Fig. 16. Clearance between face of rotors and straightedge should not exceed .005″.
5. If necessary to replace rotor or drive shaft, remove outer rotor and then drive out retaining pin securing the skew gear to drive shaft and pull off the gear.
6. Withdraw inner rotor and drive shaft.

BELT TENSION DATA

	New Ft. Lbs.	Used Ft. Lbs.
1974-75 All	140	110

WATER PUMP, REPLACE

1. Drain coolant and disconnect heater hose and lower radiator hose from pump.
2. Loosen alternator and remove drive belt.
3. Remove fan and pulley.
4. Remove water pump mounting bolts, water pump, water inlet housing and thermostat.

FUEL PUMP PRESSURE

Year	Engine	Pressure Lbs.
1974-75	2800 cc	3½-4½

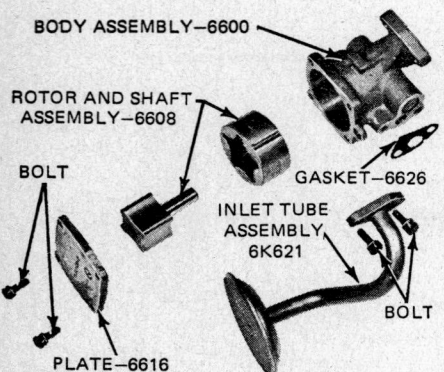

Fig. 14   Oil pump. 2800 cc engine

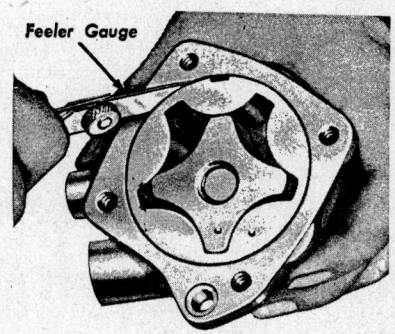

Fig. 15   Checking outer rotor to housing clearance. 2800 cc engine

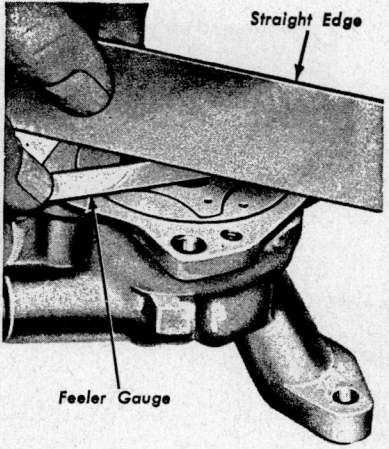

Fig. 16   Checking rotor end play. 2800 cc engine

FUEL PUMP, REPLACE

1. Disconnect fuel lines from pump.
2. Remove fuel pump attaching bolts and fuel pump.

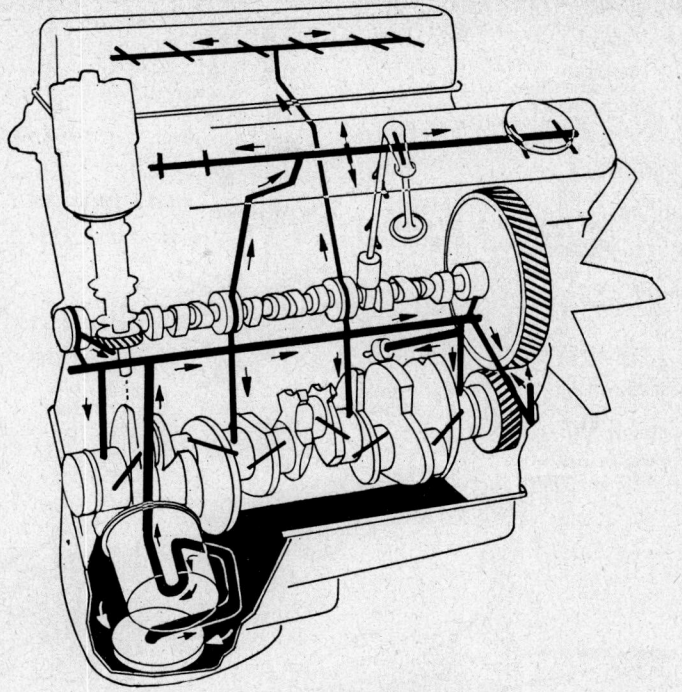

Engine oiling system. 2800 cc engine

V8 Engine Section

NOTE: Refer to the Ford & Mercury—Compact & Intermediate chapter for detailed service on this engine.

ENGINE MOUNTS REPLACE

1975 Mustang II

1. Remove fan shroud screws and support engine with a suitable jack and a block of wood under the oil pan.
2. Remove insulator to frame through bolt, Fig. 1.
3. Remove insulator to engine block attaching bolts.
4. Raise engine slightly, then remove insulator and heat shield, if equipped.
5. Reverse procedure to install.

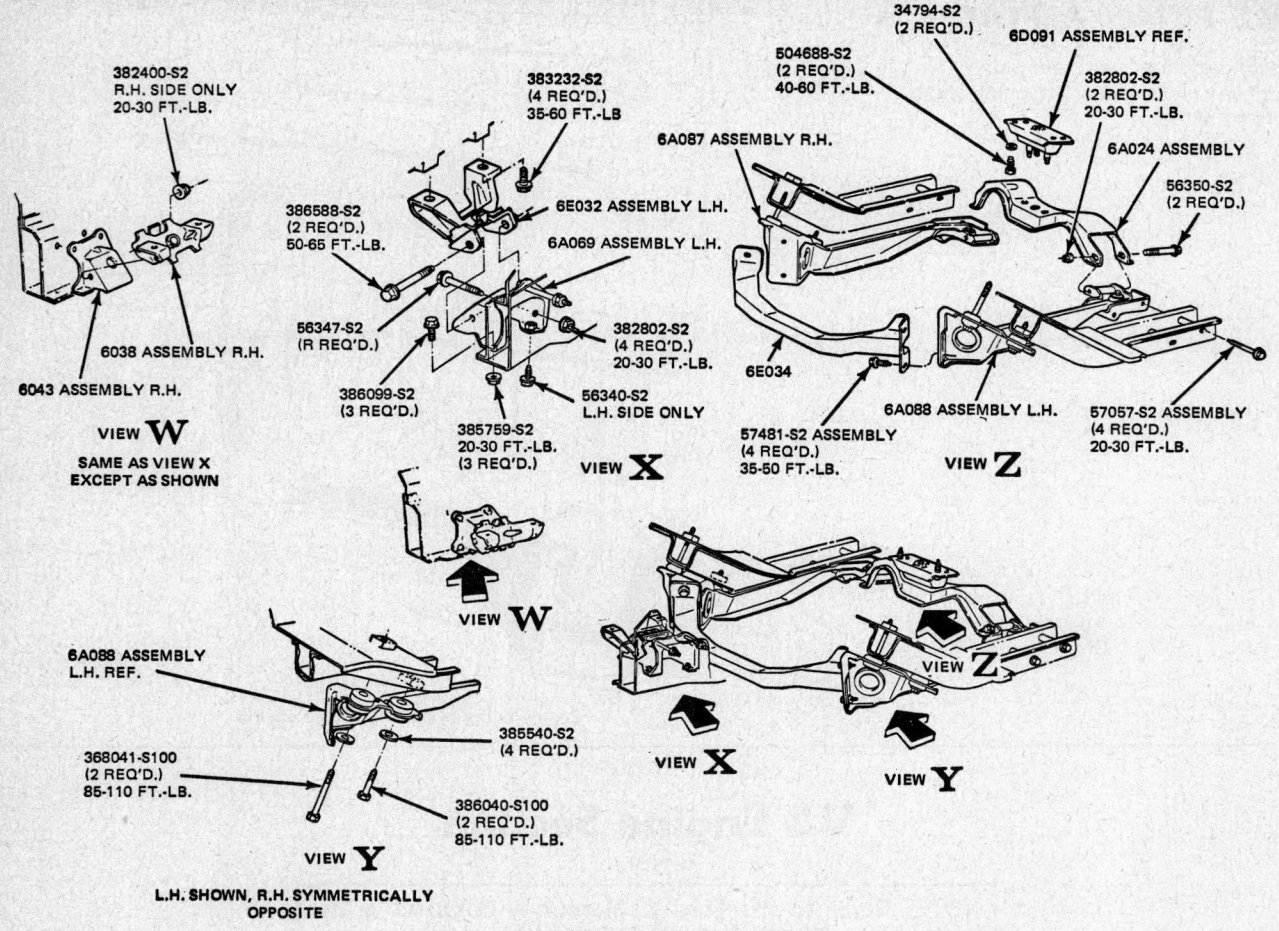

382400-S2
R.H. SIDE ONLY
20-30 FT.-LB.

386588-S2
(2 REQ'D.)
50-65 FT.-LB.

383232-S2
(4 REQ'D.)
35-60 FT-LB

6E032 ASSEMBLY L.H.

6A069 ASSEMBLY L.H.

6A087 ASSEMBLY R.H.

34794-S2
(2 REQ'D.)

6D091 ASSEMBLY REF.

504688-S2
(2 REQ'D.)
40-60 FT.-LB.

382802-S2
(2 REQ'D.)
20-30 FT.-LB.

6A024 ASSEMBLY

56350-S2
(2 REQ'D.)

6038 ASSEMBLY R.H.

6043 ASSEMBLY R.H.

56347-S2
(R REQ'D.)

382802-S2
(4 REQ'D.)
20-30 FT.-LB.

386099-S2
(3 REQ'D.)

56340-S2
L.H. SIDE ONLY

385759-S2
20-30 FT.-LB.
(3 REQ'D.)

6E034

57481-S2 ASSEMBLY
(4 REQ'D.)
35-50 FT.-LB.

6A088 ASSEMBLY L.H.

57057-S2 ASSEMBLY
(4 REQ'D.)
20-30 FT.-LB.

VIEW W
SAME AS VIEW X
EXCEPT AS SHOWN

VIEW X

VIEW Z

VIEW W

6A088 ASSEMBLY
L.H. REF.

368041-S100
(2 REQ'D.)
85-110 FT.-LB.

385540-S2
(4 REQ'D.)

386040-S100
(2 REQ'D.)
85-110 FT.-LB.

VIEW Y

L.H. SHOWN, R.H. SYMMETRICALLY
OPPOSITE

VIEW Z

VIEW X

VIEW Y

Fig. 1   Engine mounts. 1975 Mustang II

Clutch & Transmission Section

CLUTCH PEDAL, ADJUST
Early 1971

1. From under car, pull the flexible cable toward front of car until "C" clip can be removed from cable. Remove the clip.
2. Continue to pull cable toward front of car until all free movement of the release bearing is eliminated.
3. While holding cable in zero free movement position, place a .135" spacer against flywheel boss on the engine side and install the "C" clip into closest possible groove next to the spacer, Fig. 1.
4. Remove the spacer and release the cable.

Late 1971; 1972-74 Pinto

The C clip has been eliminated from the cable and is replaced by a locknut. To adjust, proceed as follows:

1. From under car, loosen cable locknuts and adjusting nut at flywheel housing.
2. Pull cable toward front of car until all free movement of the release lever is eliminated.
3. Holding cable in this position, place a ¼" spacer block against the flywheel housing boss (on engine side). Run adjusting nut against the spacer finger tight.
4. Tighten the front locknut against the adjusting nut, being careful not to disturb the adjustment. Torque locknut to 40-60 ft. lbs.
5. With spacer still in place, tighten the rear locknut against the flywheel housing boss. Remove the spacer.

1974-75 Mustang II

1. Remove cable retaining clip at dash panel and remove cable retaining screw from fender apron.
2. Pull cable toward front of vehicle until nut can be rotated. Rotate nut from adjustment sleeve about ¼ inch.
3. Release cable to neutralize the linkage and pull cable until free movement of release lever is eliminated.
4. Rotate adjusting nut toward adjustment sleeve until contact is made, then index into the next notch.
5. Install cable retaining clip, cable retaining bracket and retaining screw.

1975 Pinto

1. Loosen clutch cable lock nut at flywheel housing.
2. Pull cable toward front of vehicle so the nylon adjuster nut tabs are clear of the housing boss, then rotate nut

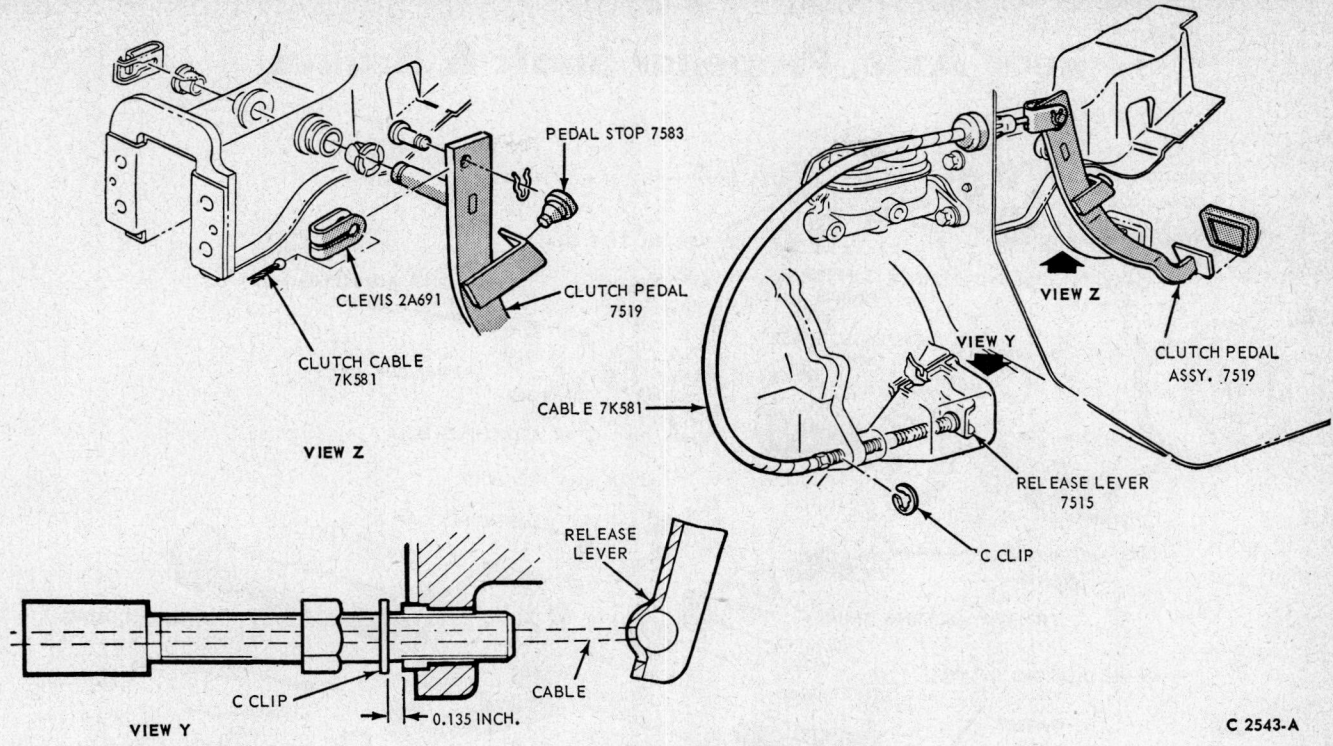

PEDAL STOP 7583

CLEVIS 2A691

CLUTCH PEDAL 7519

CLUTCH CABLE 7K581

VIEW Z

CABLE 7K581

VIEW Z

CLUTCH PEDAL ASSY. 7519

RELEASE LEVER 7515

C CLIP

RELEASE LEVER

C CLIP

CABLE

0.135 INCH.

VIEW Y

C 2543-A

Fig. 1   Clutch linkage. Early 1971

toward vehicle front approximately ¼ inch.

3. Release the cable, neutralizing the system, and pull cable forward again so release lever free movement is eliminated.

4. Rotate the adjusting nut until contact is made between index tab face and the housing, then index the tabs to engage the nearest housing groove.

5. Torque lock nut to 15 ft. lbs.

CLUTCH, REPLACE

1. From inside the car, remove shift lever by bending the locking tabs, removing the ''C'' clip and unscrewing the lever from transmission housing.

2. Raise vehicle on a hoist.

3. Disconnect drive shaft from U joint

flange and slide drive shaft off transmission output shaft. Insert tool over output shaft to prevent loss of lubricant.

4. Disconnect speedometer cable from extension housing.

5. Disconnect lower end of clutch cable at release lever.

6. Remove starter motor.

7. Remove bolts securing engine rear plate to front lower part of flywheel housing.

8. Remove bolt attaching engine rear support. Also remove crossmember attaching bolts and remove the crossmember.

9. Remove bolts attaching flywheel housing to engine block.

10. Move transmission and flywheel assembly rearward until housing clears the clutch pressure plate. Lower trans-

mission and remove.

11. Unfasten and remove the pressure plate, marking same to assure correct assembly.

FOUR SPEED TRANS., REPLACE

The transmission is removed as described under ''Clutch Replace''.

1975 AUTO. TRANS. LINKAGE, ADJUST

Linkage adjustment procedures for 1975 models are the same as those for 1974 models as outlined elsewhere in this manual.

Rear Axle, Propeller Shaft & Brakes

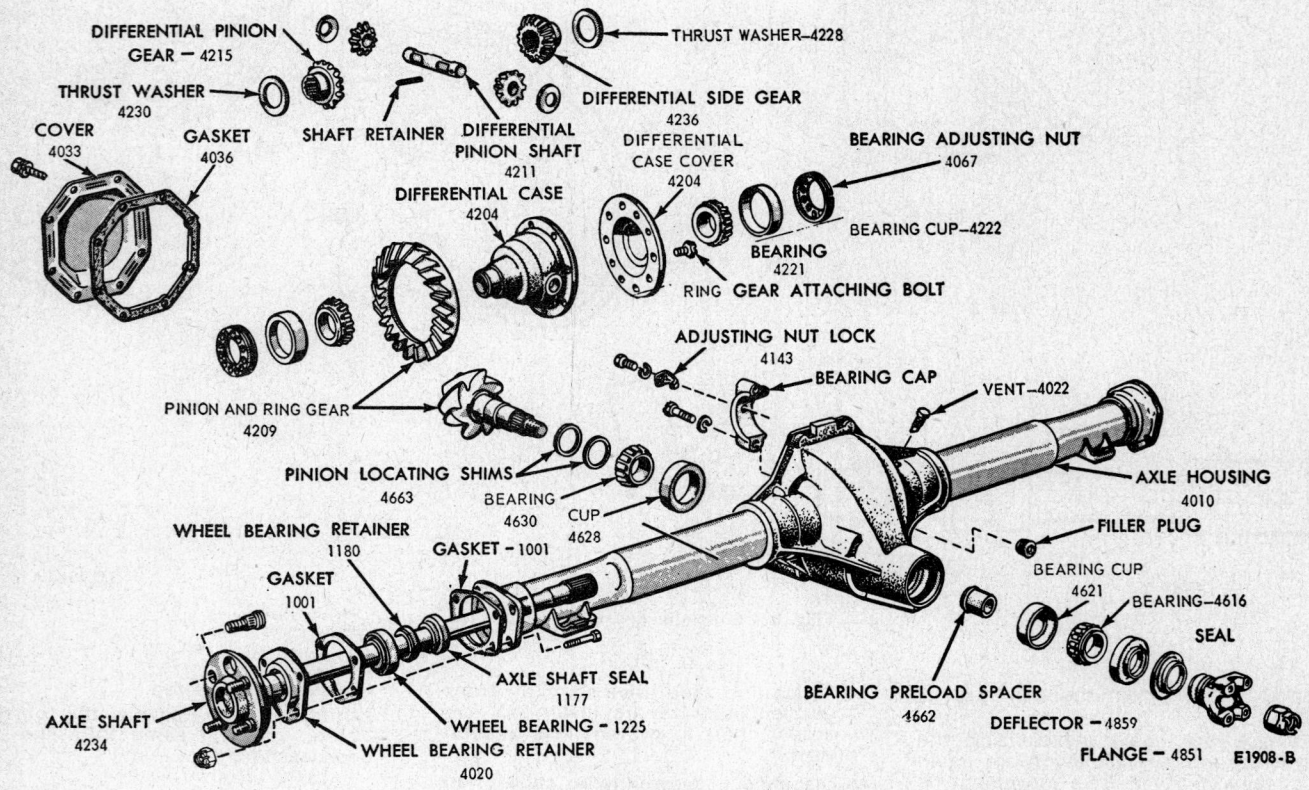

Fig. 1 Disassembled integral rear axle

REAR AXLE

Integral Type

This rear axle, Fig. 1, is an integral design hypoid with the centerline of the pinion set below the centerline of the ring gear. The semi-floating axle shafts are retained in the housing by ball bearings and bearing retainers at axle ends.

The differential is mounted on two opposed tapered roller bearings which are retained in the housing by removable caps. Differential bearing preload and drive gear backlash is adjusted by nuts located behind each differential bearing cup.

The drive pinion assembly is mounted on two opposed tapered roller bearings. Pinion bearing preload is adjusted by a collapsible spacer on the pinion shaft. Pinion and ring gear tooth contact is adjusted by shims between the rear bearing cone and pinion gear.

Axle Shaft, Bearing & Oil Seal

1. Remove wheel and tire from brake drum.
2. Remove Tinnerman nuts that secure brake drum to axle flange and remove brake drum.

3. Working through hole in each axle flange, remove nuts that secure wheel bearing retainer plate. Then pull the axle shaft assembly out of the housing being careful not to cut or rough up the seal.

NOTE: *The brake backing plate must not be dislodged. Replace one nut to hold the plate in place after shaft is removed.*

4. If wheel bearing is to be replaced, loosen inner retainer ring by nicking it deeply with a chisel in several places. It will then slide off.
5. Remove bearing from shaft.

Removable Carrier Type

In these axles, Fig. 2, the drive pinion is straddle-mounted by two opposed tapered roller bearings which support the pinion shaft in front of the drive pinion gear, and a straight roller bearing that supports the pinion shaft at the rear of the pinion gear. The drive pinion is assembled in a pinion retainer that is bolted to the differential carrier. The tapered roller bearings are preloaded by a collapsible

spacer between the bearings. The pinion is positioned by a shim or shims located between the drive pinion retainer and the differential carrier.

The differential is supported in the carrier by two tapered roller side bearings. These bearings are preloaded by two threaded ring nuts or sleeves between the bearings and the pedestals. The differential assembly is positioned for proper ring gear and pinion backlash by varying the adjustment of these ring nuts. The differential case houses two side gears in mesh with two pinions mounted on a pinion shaft which held in place by a pin. The side gears and pinions are backed by thrust washers.

The axle shafts are of unequal length, the left shaft being shorter than the right. The axle shafts are mounted in sealed ball bearings which are pressed on the shafts.

Axle Shaft, Replace

1. Remove wheel assembly.
2. Remove brake drum from flange.
3. Working through hole provided in axle shaft flange, remove nuts that secure wheel bearing retainer.

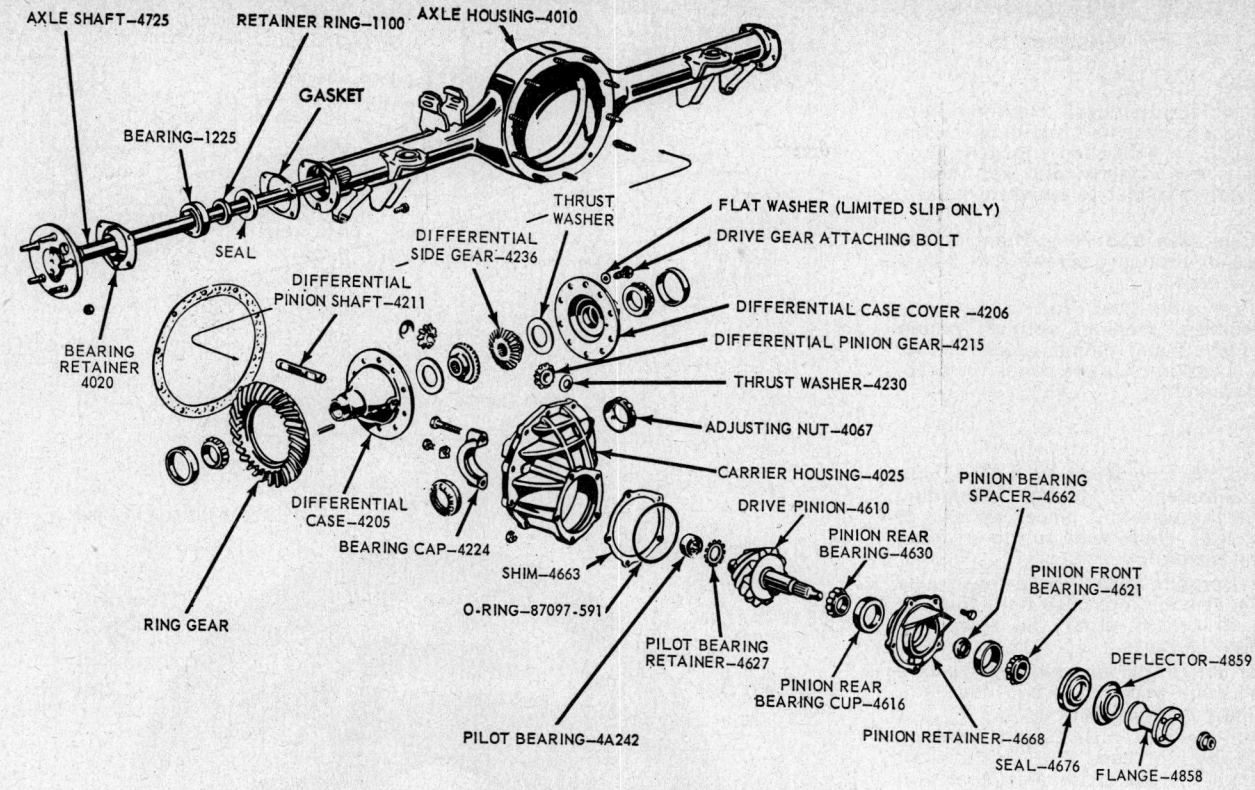

Fig. 2 Disassembled rear axle with removable carrier

4. Pull axle shaft out of housing. If bearing is a tight fit in axle housing use a slide hammer-type puller. *Brake carrier plate must not be dislodged. Install one nut to hold the plate in place after axle shaft is removed.*

NOTE: On 1974-75 models, remove brake backing plate.

5. If the axle shaft bearing is to be replaced, loosen the inner retainer by nicking it deeply with a chisel in several places. The bearing will then slide off easily.

6. Press bearing from axle shaft.
7. Inspect machined surface of axle shaft and housing for rough spots that would affect sealing action of the oil seal. Carefully remove any burrs or rough spots.
8. Press new inner bearing retainer on shaft until it seats firmly against shoulder on shaft.
9. Press inner bearing retainer on shaft until it seats firmly against bearing.
10. If oil seal is to be replaced, use a hook-type tool to pull it out of housing. Wipe a small amount of oil resistant sealer on outer edge of seal before it is installed.

Installation

1. Place a new gasket on each side of brake carrier plate and slide axle shaft into housing. Start the splines into the differential side gear and push the shaft in until bearing bottoms in housing.
2. Install retainer and tighten nuts to 30-40 ft. lbs.
3. Install brake drum and wheel.

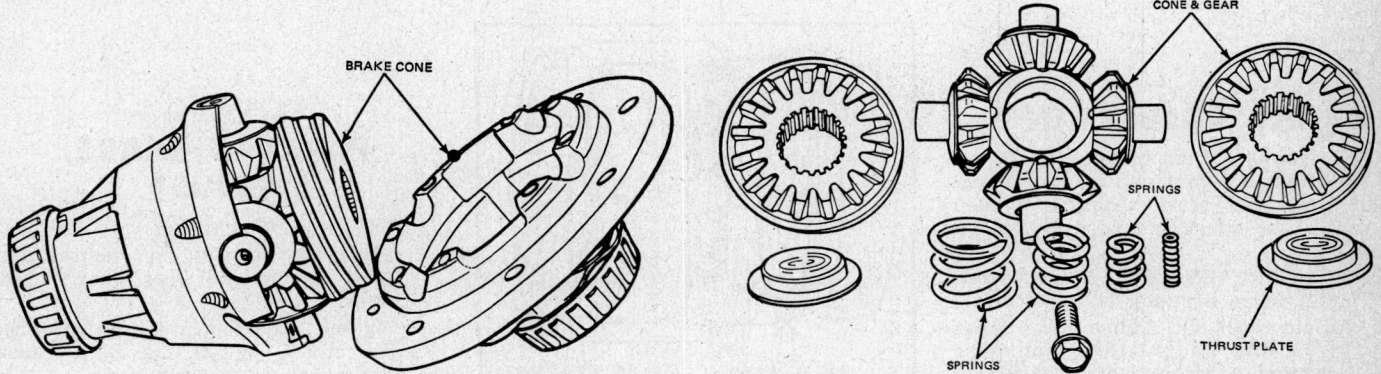

Fig. 3 Borg Warner locking differential. 1974-75 Mustang II

Fig. 4 Borg Warner locking differential disassembled. 1974-75 Mustang II

Locking Differential
1974-75 Mustang II

Disassembly

1. With differential case clamped in a vise, loosen case half retaining screws, leaving 3 to 4 threads engaged. Then loosen vise slightly and tap flange half with a mallet to separate halves, Fig. 3.
2. Remove case from vise, then remove case half retaining screws and flange half of case.
3. Remove side gear and brake cone assemblies, pre-load springs, pinion cross shaft and pinion gears, Fig. 4. Note location of brake cones for proper reassembly.

Assembly

1. Clamp an axle shaft in a vise with approximately 3 inches extending above the vise and place cap half of case over shaft with inside of case facing upward.
2. Place proper brake cone over axle and seat cone into case half, then install in proper order the remaining differential parts.
3. Place flange half of case over second brake cone and install two case half retaining screws finger tight.
4. Install second axle shaft through flange half of case and rotate shaft to align splines. With axle shafts in position, install and tighten case half retaining screws, then remove axle shafts.

PROPELLER SHAFT

1. To maintain balance, mark relationship of rear drive shaft yoke and the drive pinion flange of the axle if alignment marks are not visible.
2. Disconnect rear U-joint from companion flange, Fig. 5. Wrap tape around loose bearing caps to prevent them from falling off spider. Pull drive shaft toward rear of car until slip yoke clears transmission extension housing and the seal. Install tool in extension housing to prevent lubricant leakage.

BRAKE ADJUSTMENTS

The hydraulic drum brakes, Fig. 6, are self-adjusting and require a manual adjustment only after brake shoes have been replaced. The adjustment is made as follows:

1. Using tool HRE 8650, Fig. 7, determine inside diameter of brake drum.
2. Reverse tool and adjust brake shoes to fit the gauge. Hold automatic adjusting lever out of engagement while rotating adjusting screw, to prevent burring slots in screw.

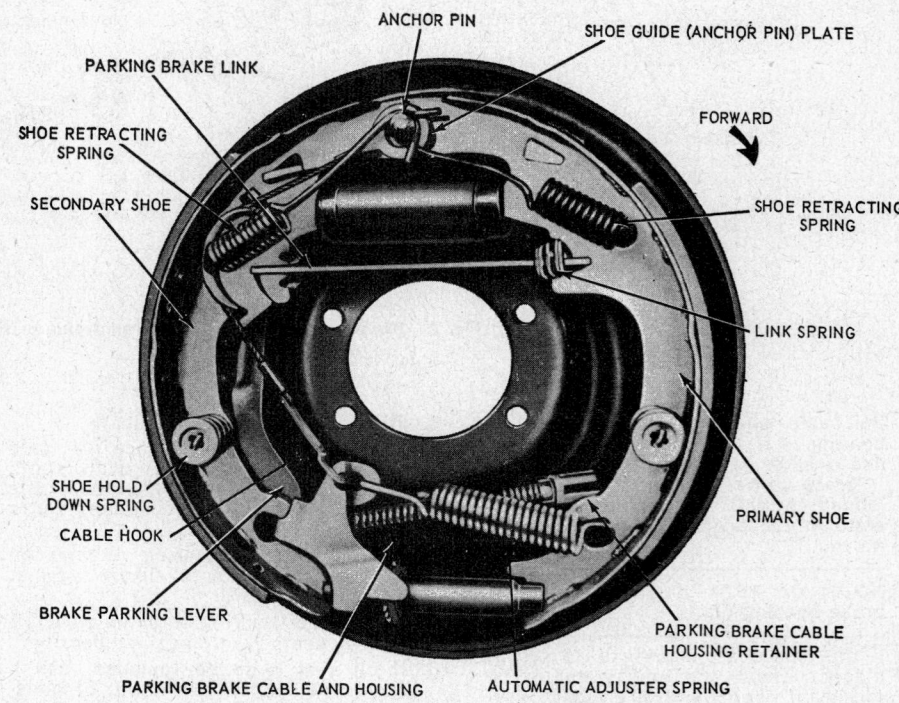

Fig. 5 Drive shaft and universal joints disassembled

Fig. 6 Self-adjusting brake assembly. Rear shown

Fig. 7 Brake adjustment

JUST SET TO DRUM DIAMETER HERE . . .

FIND CORRECT BRAKE SHOE DIAMETER HERE

PARKING BRAKE, ADJUST

1. Release parking brake.
2. Place transmission in Neutral and raise vehicle until rear wheels clear floor.
3. Tighten adjusting nut on equalizer rod at the control, Fig. 8, to cause the rear wheel brakes to drag.
4. Loosen adjusting nut until rear brakes are just free.

MASTER CYLINDER, REPLACE

1. Disconnect stoplight switch wires at connector. Remove spring retainer and slide stop light switch off brake pedal pin just far enough to clear end of pin, then lift switch straight upward from the pin.
2. Slide master cylinder push rod and nylon washers and bushings off brake pedal pin.
3. Remove brake tube from master cylinder ports.
4. Unfasten and remove master cylinder forward and upward from vehicle.

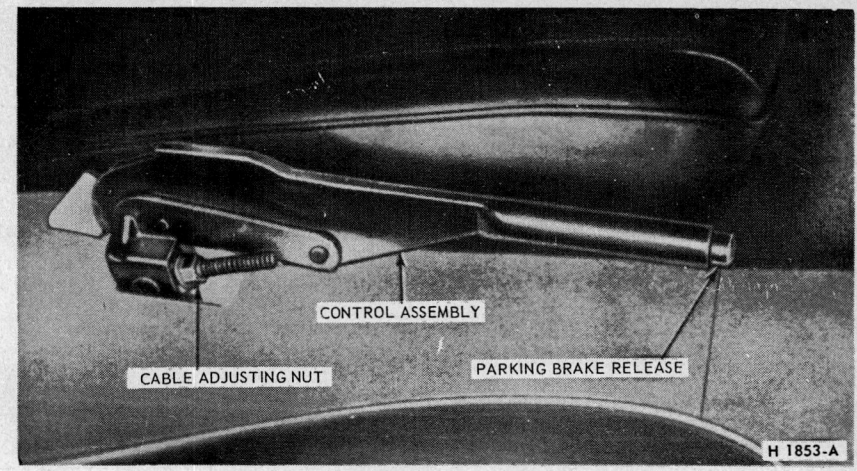

Fig. 8 Parking brake adjustment

Rear Suspension

SHOCK ABSORBER, REPLACE

1. With rear axle supported properly disconnect shock absorber from lower mounting.
2. Remove bolts securing upper mounting bracket to underbody.
3. Remove bracket from shock absorber.
4. Reverse procedure to install.

LEAF SPRINGS & BUSHINGS, REPLACE

1. Raise rear of vehicle and support at frame. Support axle with a suitable jack.
2. Disconnect shock absorbers from lower mountings.
3. Lower jack and remove spring plate "U" bolts and spring plate, Fig. 1.
4. Raise axle to remove weight from spring and disassemble rear shackle.
5. Remove spring front mount bolt.
6. Replace spring front eye bushing as necessary, Figs. 2 and 3.
7. Reverse procedure to install.

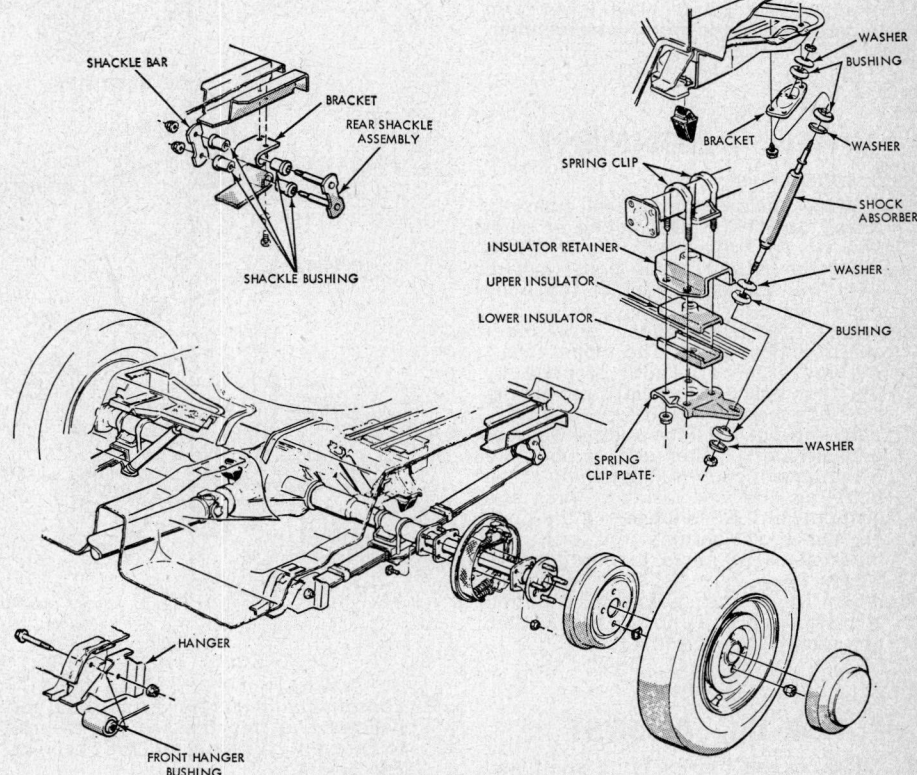

Fig. 1 Mustang II & Pinto rear suspension

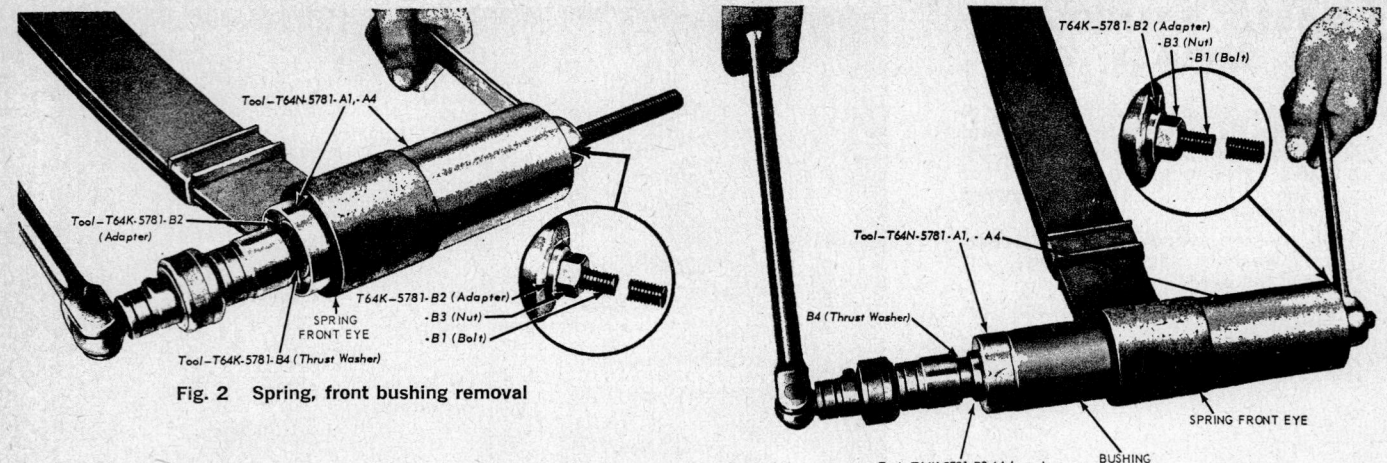

Fig. 2   Spring, front bushing removal

Fig. 3   Spring, front bushing installation

Front End & Steering Section

FRONT SUSPENSION

The upper and lower ends of the spindle are attached to upper and lower ball joints which are mounted in upper and lower arms. The upper arm pivots on a bushing and shaft assembly which is bolted to the frame. The lower arm pivots on a bolt in the front crossmember, Fig. 1.

WHEEL ALIGNMENT

Caster and Camber

1. Working inside front wheel housing, install tool T71P-3000A, one at each end of the upper arm inner shaft. Turn the special tool bolts inward until the bolt ends contact the body metal, Fig. 2.
2. Loosen the two upper arm inner shaft-to-body bolts. The upper shaft will move inboard until stopped by the tool bolt ends solidly contacting the body metal.
3. Turn the special tool bolts inward or outward until caster and camber are within specifications. Tightening these bolts on the special tool force the arm outward; while loosening the bolts on the tools permits the arm and inner shaft to move inboard due to weight force.
4. When properly adjusted, tighten shaft-to-body bolts to 75-105 ft. lbs. and remove the special tools.

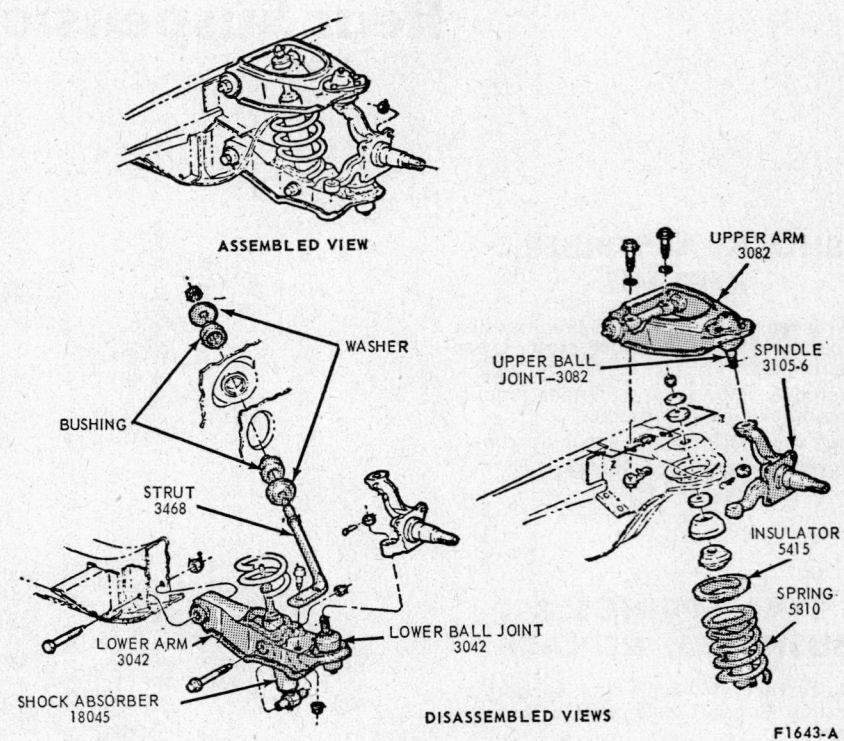

ASSEMBLED VIEW

DISASSEMBLED VIEWS

F1643-A

Fig. 1   Front suspension assembly. Typical

TOE-IN, ADJUST

1. Check to see that steering shaft and steering wheel marks are in alignment and in the top position.
2. Loosen clamp screw on the tie rod bellows and free the seal on the rod to prevent twisting of the bellows, Fig. 3.
3. Loosen tie rod jam nut.
4. Use suitable pliers to turn the tie rod inner end to correct the adjustment to specifications. Do not use pliers on tie rod threads. Turning to reduce number of threads showing will increase toe-in. Turning in the opposite direction will reduce toe-in.

WHEEL BEARINGS, ADJUST

1. Raise vehicle until wheel and tire clear floor.
2. Remove wheel cover and dust cap from hub.
3. Remove cotter pin and lock nut.
4. While rotating wheel assembly, torque the adjusting nut to 17-25 ft. lbs. to seat the bearings.
5. Using a 1⅛" box wrench, back off the adjusting nut one half turn. Retighten the nut to 10-15 in. lbs. with a torque wrench or finger tight.
6. Locate the nut lock on the adjusting nut so the castellations on the lock are aligned with the cotter pin hole in the spindle.
7. Install new cotter pin and replace dust cap and wheel cover.

WHEEL BEARINGS, REPLACE

(Disc Brakes)

1. Raise car and remove front wheels.
2. Use a ¾" wrench to loosen the large bolt at top of caliper assembly and washer at the front of the caliper. Loosen it until it can be turned with the fingers.
3. Remove the smaller bolt at bottom of caliper with a ⅝" wrench.
4. Insert a strong piece of wire carefully through the upper opening in the caliper and fasten it. Position the free end of the wire over the suspension upper arm.
5. When removing caliper from disc the brake pads must be held apart. Do this by inserting a piece of wood or cardboard. While holding the caliper, remove the large bolt in front. Now carefully slide the caliper back and slightly upward to remove it. While doing this, insert the wood or cardboard between the brake pads.
6. Carefully move caliper back to sus-

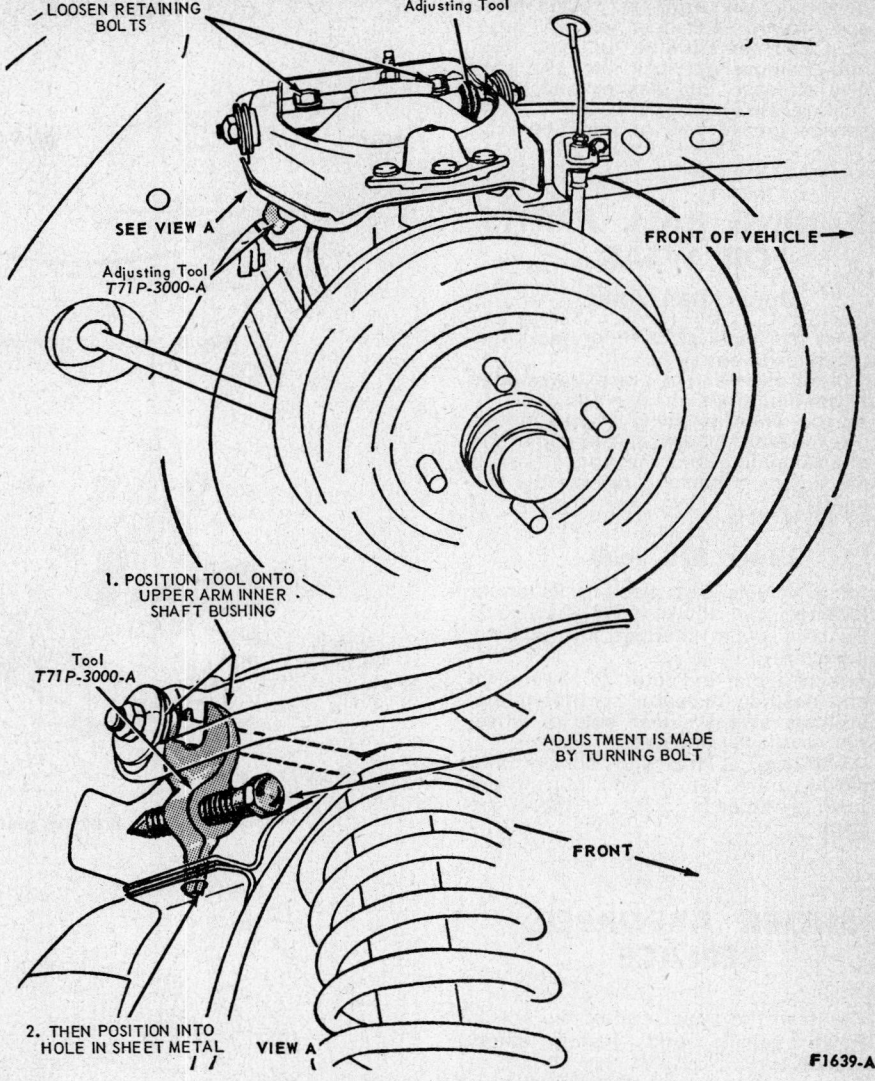

Fig. 2 Caster and camber adjustment

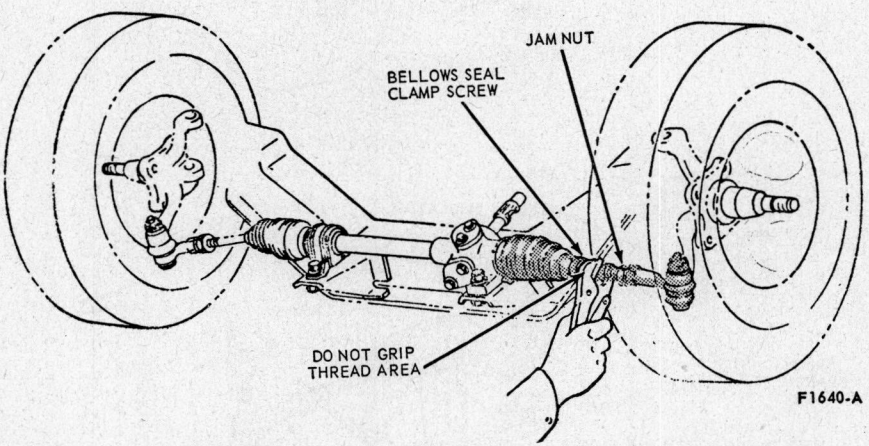

Fig. 3 Toe-in adjustment

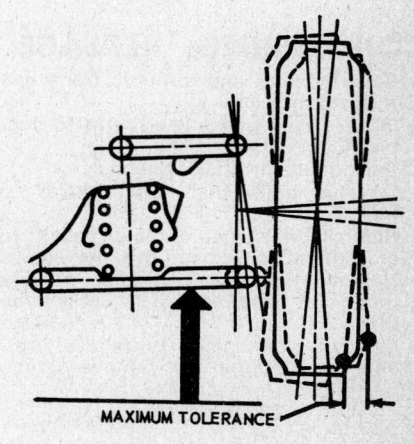

Fig. 4 Measuring lower ball joint play

pension upper arm and fasten loose end of wire so caliper will not drop.

7. Dust cap can now be removed from hub. Remove nut lock, etc. and rock disc to ease out washer and outer bearing. Disc can now be removed to service grease seal or inner bearing.

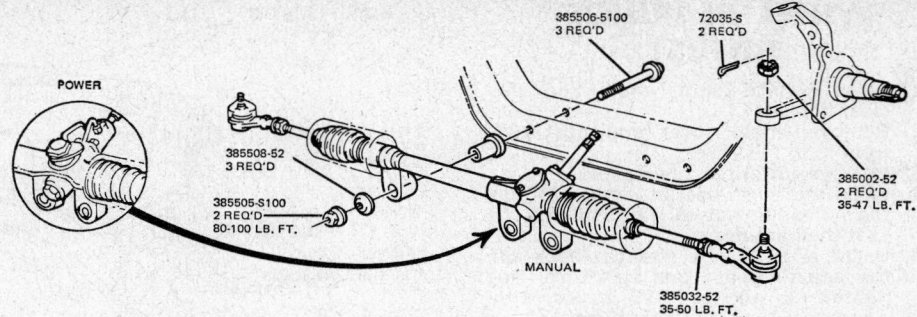

Fig. 5   Steering gear installation. 1974-75 Mustang II

CHECKING BALL JOINTS FOR WEAR

Upper Ball Joint

1. Raise car and place floor jacks beneath lower arms.
2. Ask an assistant to grasp lower edge of tire and move wheel in and out.
3. As the wheel is being moved, notice any movement between the upper end of the spindle and the upper arm. If movement is present, replace the ball joint.

Lower Ball Joint

1. Raise vehicle and place jacks under lower arms as shown in Fig. 4.
2. Be sure wheel bearings are properly adjusted.
3. Attach a dial indicator to lower arm and position indicator so that plunger rests against inner side of wheel rim near lower ball joint.
4. Grasp tire at top and bottom and slowly move tire in and out. If the reading exceeds .250", replace the joint.

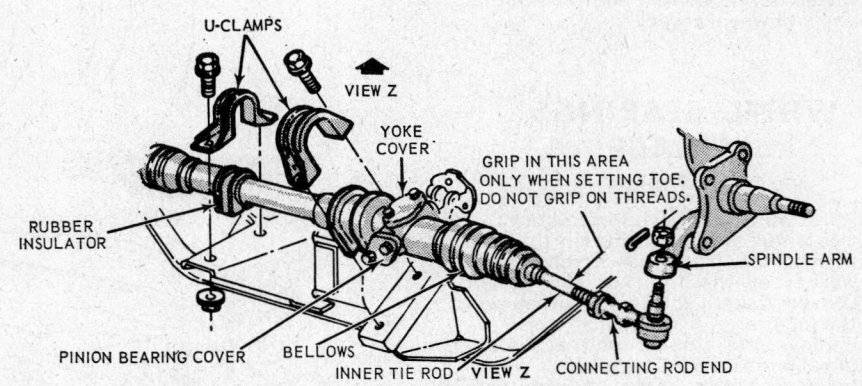

Fig. 6   Steering gear installation. 1973-75 Pinto

SHOCK ABSORBER, REPLACE

1. Unfasten the upper end of the shock.
2. Raise vehicle and install safety stands.
3. Unfasten lower end of shock. It may be necessary to use a pry bar to free "T" shaped end of the shock from the lower end.

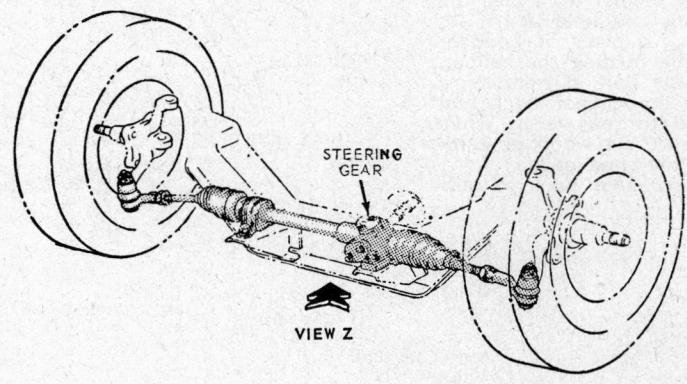

COIL SPRING, REPLACE

1. Raise vehicle and support front end with safety stands.
2. Place a jack under lower arm to support it.
3. Disconnect lower end of shock.
4. Remove bolts that attach strut to lower arm.
5. Remove nut that retains shock to crossmember and remove the shock.
6. Remove nut and bolt that secures inner end of lower arm to crossmember.
7. Carefully lower jack to relieve pressure from spring and remove spring.

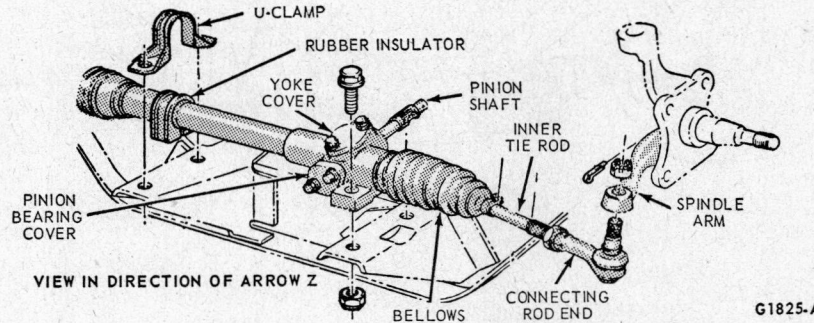

Fig. 7   Steering gear installation. 1971-72 Pinto

BALL JOINTS, REPLACE

The ball joints are riveted to the control arms. The ball joints can be replaced on the car by removing the rivets and replacing them with new attaching bolts, nuts and washers furnished with the kit.

When removing a ball joint, use a suitable pressing tool to force the ball joint out of the spindle.

STEERING GEAR, REPLACE

1973-75 Pinto & 1974-75 Mustang II

1. Disconnect battery ground cable, turn ignition "On" and raise vehicle.

2. Remove tie rod end retaining nuts and using ball joint separator (tool 3290C), separate tie rod ends from spindle arms, Figs. 5 and 6.
3. Remove pinion shaft to flexible coupling bolt and the bolts securing steering gear to crossmember.
4. Turn front wheels, then remove steering gear from left side of vehicle.

1971-72 Pinto

1. Position steering wheel in straight ahead position and raise vehicle on a hoist.

2. Remove bolts retaining the flexible coupling to the pinion shaft, Fig. 7.
3. Remove four nuts and bolts securing the steering gear to the mounting pads on the crossmember.
4. Remove the U-clamp.
5. Remove cotterpins and loosen nuts securing connecting rod ends to the spindle arms.
6. Use ball joint separator (tool 3290C) to separate the connecting rod ends from the spindle arms.
7. Remove nuts from connecting rods and remove gear from vehicle left side.

FORD THUNDERBIRD

OLD CAR SPECIFICATIONS: For 1946-68 Tune Up and Wheel Alignment Specifications see main index.

Service procedures on the V8-400 are covered in the Ford & Mercury car chapters.

INDEX OF SERVICE OPERATIONS

PAGE NO.

ACCESSORIES

Air Conditioning 2-20
Automatic Level Controls 2-39
Blower Motor, Remove 1-517
Clock Troubles 2-11
Heater Core, Replace 1-517
Power Top Troubles 2-18
Power Window Troubles 2-18
Radio, Replace 1-516
Speed Controls, Adjust 1-517

BRAKES

Anti-Skid Brakes 2-162
Brake Troubles, Mechanical 2-17
Disc Brake Service 2-133
Hydraulic System Service 2-123
Parking Brake, Adjust 1-527
Power Brake Unit, Replace 1-527
Service Brakes, Adjust 1-526

COOLING SYSTEM

Cooling System Troubles 2-6
Variable Speed Fans 2-38
Water Pump, Replace 1-523

ELECTRICAL

Alternator Service 2-69
Blower Motor, Remove 1-517
Dash Gauge Service 2-50
Distributor, Replace 1-511
Distributor Service:
  Standard 2-525
  Transistorized 2-535
Electrical Troubles 2-8
Headlamps, Concealed Type 2-46
Headlight Aiming 2-45
Horn Sounder, Remove 1-513
Ignition Coils and Resistors 2-521
Ignition Lock, Replace 1-511
Ignition Switch, Replace 1-512
Ignition Timing 2-518
Instrument Cluster Removal 1-514
Light Switch, Replace 1-512
Neutral Safety Switch, Replace .. 1-513
Seat Belt Interlock Systems 2-311
Starter Service 2-54
Starter, Replace 1-511
Starter Switch Service 2-67
Stop Light Switch, Replace 1-513
Turn Signal Switch, Replace 1-513
Turn Signal Troubles 2-11
Windshield Wiper Motor, Replace . 1-515
Windshield Wiper Troubles 2-19

PAGE NO.

ENGINE

Camshaft, Replace 1-523
Camshaft Bearings 1-523
Cylinder Head, Replace 1-521
Engine Identification 1-505
Engine Mounts 1-521
Engine, Replace 1-521
Engine Troubles 2-1
Main Bearings 1-523
Piston Pins 1-523
Piston Rings 1-523
Piston and Rod, Assemble 1-523
Pistons 1-523
Rocker Arm Stud 1-522
Rod Bearings 1-523
Timing Case Cover, Replace 1-522
Timing Chain, Replace 1-523
Valves, Adjust 1-522
Valve Arrangement 1-522
Valve Guides 1-522
Valve Lifters 1-522

ENGINE LUBRICATION

Emission Control Systems 2-545
Oil Pan, Replace 1-523
Oil Pump Repairs 1-523

FUEL SYSTEM

Carburetor Adjustments and Specs. 2-372
1975 Carburetors 1-716
Emission Control Systems 2-545
Fuel Pump, Replace 1-524
Fuel Pump Service 2-369
Fuel System Troubles 2-2

PROPELLER SHAFT & U JOINTS

Propeller Shaft 1-526
Universal Joint Service 2-117

REAR AXLE & SUSPENSION

Axle Shaft, Bearing and Seal 1-525
Coil Springs, Replace 1-528
Control Arms, Replace 1-529
Rear Axle Description 1-524
Rear Axle Troubles 2-16
Shock Absorber, Replace 1-528
Stabilizer Bar, Replace 1-529
Track Bar & Bushing, Replace 1-529

SPECIFICATIONS

Alternator 1-509
Belt Tension 1-523

PAGE NO.

Brakes 1-510
Capacities 1-510
Carburetors 2-372
Cooling System 1-510
Crankshaft and Bearings 1-508
Distributors 1-507
Engine Tightening Torque 1-507
Fuel Pump Pressure 1-524
General Engine Specs. 1-505
Ignition Coils and Resistors 2-521
Pistons, Rings and Pins 1-508
Rear Axle 1-508
Starting Motors 1-509
Tune Up 1-506
Valve Lift 1-522
Valve Timing 1-522
Valves 1-508
Wheel Alignment 1-509

STEERING GEAR

Horn Sounder Removal 1-513
Power Gear, Replace 1-531

SUSPENSION, FRONT

Ball Joints, Replace 1-530
Ball Joints, Check for Wear 1-530
Coil Spring, Replace 1-531
Lubrication 1-530
Shock Absorber, Replace 1-530
Suspension, Description of 1-530
Toe-In, Adjust 1-530
Wheel Alignment, Adjust 1-530
Wheel Bearings, Adjust 1-530
Wheel Bearings, Replace 1-530

TRANSMISSIONS 2-231

1975 Linkage 1-524

TUNE UP

Service 2-517
Specifications 1-506

WINDSHIELD WIPER

Wiper Arms 1-515
Wiper Blades 1-514
Wiper Motor, Replace 1-515
Wiper Linkage, Replace 1-516
Wiper Switch, Replace 1-516
Wiper Troubles 2-19

ENGINE & SERIAL NUMBER LOCATION

Vehicle Warranty Plate On Left Front Door Pillar.

1969

1970

1971

ENGINE IDENTIFICATION

*Serial number on vehicle Warranty Plate.

Year	Engine	Engine Code
1969–73	V8-429	N
1972	V8-400	S
1973–75	V8-460	A

1972

1973

1974

1975

GENERAL ENGINE SPECIFICATIONS

Year	Engine	Car-buretor	Bore and Stroke	Piston Dis-place-ment, Cubic Inches	Com-pres-sion Ratio	Maximum Brake H.P. @ R.P.M.	Maximum Torque Lbs. Ft. @ R.P.M.	Normal Oil Pressure Pounds
1969–70	360 Horsepower.............V8-429	4 Barrel	4.36 x 3.59	429	11.00	360 @ 4600	476 @ 2800	35–60
1971	360 Horsepower.............V8-429	4 Barrel	4.36 x 3.59	429	10.30	360 @ 4600	480 @ 2800	35–75
1972	212 Horsepower①...........V8-400	2 Barrel	4.00 x 4.00	400	8.4	172 @ 4000	298 @ 2200	35–75
	212 Horsepower①...........V8-429	4 Barrel	4.36 x 3.59	429	8.50	212 @ 4400	327 @ 2600	35–75
	224 Horsepower①...........V8-460	4 Barrel	4.3600 x 3.850	460	8.50	224 @ 4400	357 @ 2800	35–60
1973	208 Horsepower.............V8-429	4 Barrel	4.36 x 3.59	429	8.0	208 @ 4400	327 @ 2600	35–65
	208 Horsepower.............V8-460	4 Barrel	4.36 x 3.85	460	8.0	208 @ 4400	338 @ 2800	35–65
1974	220 Horsepower.............V8-460	4 Barrel	4.36 x 3.85	460	8.0	220 @ 4000	355 @ 2600	35–65
1975	253 Horsepower①...........V8-460	4 Barrel	4.36 x 3.85	460	8.0	253 @ 4400	386 @ 2600	35–65

①—Ratings are NET—as installed in the vehicle.

TUNE UP SPECIFICATIONS

OLD CAR SPECIFICATIONS: For 1946-68 Tune Up Specifications see main index.

★When using a timing light, disconnect vacuum hose or tube at distributor and plug opening in hose or tube so idle speed will not be affected.

●When checking compression, lowest cylinder must be within 75 percent of highest.

▲Before removing wires from distributor cap, determine location of the No. 1 wire in cap, as distributor position may have been altered from that shown at the end of this chart.

Year	Spark Plug		Distributor		Ignition Timing★			Carb. Adjustments					
	Type	Gap Inch	Point Gap Inch	Dwell Angle Deg.	Firing Order Fig. ▲	Timing BTDC ①	Mark Fig.	Hot Idle Speed		Air Fuel Ratio		Idle "CO" %	
								Std. Trans.	Auto. Trans.②	Std. Trans.	Auto. Trans.	Std. Trans.	Auto. Trans.
1969													
8-429	BF-42	.034	.017	26–31	A	6°⑤	B	—	550D④	—	14.3 to 1	—	1.2
1970													
8-429	BRF-42	.034	.017	26–31	A	⑬	B	—	600D⑩	—	14.5 to 1	—	0.75
1971													
8-429	BRF-42	.034	.017	26–31	A	⑬	D	—	600D	—	14.5 to 1	—	.075
1972													
8-400	ARF-42	.034	.017	26–30	C	⑦	D	—	625D⑩	—	—	—	0.10
8-429	BRF-42	.034	.017	26–30	A	10°⑧	D	—	600D⑩	—	—	—	0.3
8-460	BRF-42	.034	.017	26–30	A	⑪	D	—	600D⑩	—	—	—	0.3
1973													
8-429	ARF-42	.034	.017	26–30	A	10°	D	—	600D⑩	—	—	—	0.5⑫
8-460	ARF-42	.034	.017	26–30	A	14°	D	—	600D⑩	—	—	—	0.4⑫
1974													
8-460	ARF-52	③	⑨	—	A	14°	D	—	650D⑥	—	—	—	—
1975													
8-460	ARF-52	③	⑨	—	A	14°	D	—	650D	—	—	—	—

① —BTDC: Before top dead center.
② —D: Drive. N: Neutral.
③ —Exc. Calif., .054 inch; Calif. .044 inch.
④ —With headlights and A/C on.
⑤ —Whenever idle speed or ignition timing is adjusted, vacuum line to brake release mechanism must be disconnected and plugged to prevent parking brake from releasing when selector is moved to Drive.
⑥ —With lights and A/C off.
⑦ —Exc. Calif. 8° BTC, Calif. 6° BTC.
⑧ —Built after Dec. 31, 1971, 14°.
⑨ —Breakerless distributor.
⑩ —With headlamp on Hi Beam—Air Conditioning OFF.
⑪ —Exc. Calif. 10° BTC, Calif 6° BTC.
⑫ —For Calif. 0.2.
⑬ —Single diaphragm 14°, Dual diaphragm 4°.

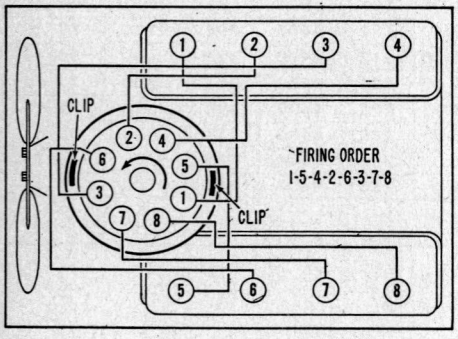

Fig. A

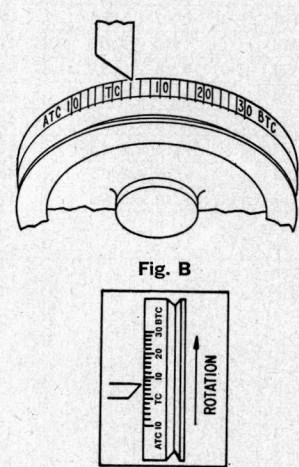

Fig. B

Fig. D

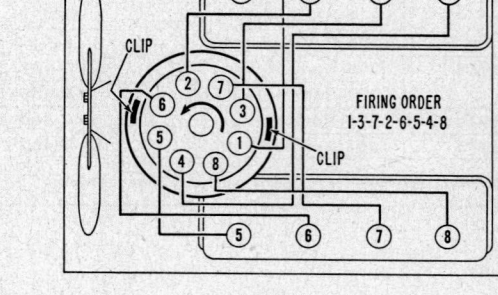

Fig. C

DISTRIBUTOR SPECIFICATIONS

★If unit is checked on vehicle, double the RPM and degrees to get crankshaft figures.
Breaker arm spring tension—17–21.

| Distributor Part No.① | Centrifugal Advance Degrees @ RPM of Distributor | | | | Vacuum Advance | | Distributor Retard |
	Advance Starts	Intermediate Advance		Full Advance	Inches of Vacuum to Start Plunger	Max. Adv. Dist. Deg. @ Vacuum	Max. Retard Dist. Deg. @ Vacuum
1969							
C8VF-A	0–½ @ 350	2½–4½ @ 750	6½–8½ @ 1000	8–10¼ @ 1500	14 @ 2975	5	12 @ 25	—
1970-71							
D0AF-Z	0–½ @ 350	2¼–4¼ @ 750	6½–8½ @ 1000	8–10¼ @ 1500	14 @ 2950	5	11 @ 25	—
1972							
D2AF-RA	½–2½ @ 500	2–4 @ 750	3½–5½ @ 1000	6½–9 @ 1500	12 @ 2000	5	13½ @ 20	4 @ 20
D2AF-SA	½–2½ @ 500	2–4 @ 750	3½–5½ @ 1000	6½–9 @ 1500	12 @ 2000	5	13½ @ 20	4 @ 20
D2MF-EA	0–1 @ 500	2–4 @ 750	4½–6½ @ 1000	6–8 @ 1500	9½ @ 2000	5	11½ @ 20	4 @ 20
D2MF-FA	0–1 @ 500	2–4 @ 750	4½–6½ @ 1000	6–8 @ 1500	9½ @ 2000	5	11½ @ 20	4 @ 20
D2SF-EA	0–1 @ 500	0–1½ @ 750	2½–4½ @ 1000	4½–6½ @ 1500	8½ @ 2000	5	—	—
D2VF-BA	0–2 @ 700	6–8 @ 1000	7½–10 @ 1500	—	12½ @ 2000	5	11½ @ 20	—
1973							
D3VF-AA	0–1 @ 500	0–1½ @ 750	3–5 @ 1000	4–6 @ 1500	7½ @ 2000	5	11½ @ 20	—
D3MF-DA	0–1 @ 500	1½–4 @ 750	5½–7½ @ 1000	7½–9 @ 1500	10½ @ 2000	5	11 @ 20	—
D3SF-BA	0–1 @ 500	½–2½ @ 750	5½–8 @ 1000	10–12 @ 1500	13½ @ 2000	5	11 @ 20	—
D3VF-CA	0–1 @ 500	0–1½ @ 750	4–6 @ 1000	6–8 @ 1500	10 @ 2000	5	11 @ 20	—
D3MF-BA	0–1 @ 500	0–1½ @ 750	3½–5½ @ 1000	7½–10 @ 1500	11 @ 2000	5	7 @ 20	—
D3VF-BA	0–1 @ 500	0–2½ @ 750	5–7 @ 1000	7½–10 @ 1500	12 @ 2000	5	7 @ 20	—
1974-75							
D4VE-CA	0–½ @ 500	0–½ @ 750	3–5 @ 1000	7–9 @ 1500	10½ @ 2000	5	11¼ @ 20	—

①—Basic part No. 12127

ENGINE TIGHTENING SPECIFICATIONS

★Torque specifications are for clean and lightly lubricated threads only. Dry or dirty threads produce increased friction which prevents accurate measurement of tightness.

Year	Engine	Spark Plugs Ft. Lbs.	Cylinder Head Bolts Ft. Lbs.	Intake Manifold Ft. Lbs.	Exhaust Manifold Ft. Lbs.	Rocker Arm Shaft Bracket Ft. Lbs.	Rocker Arm Cover Ft. Lbs.	Connecting Rod Cap Bolts Ft. Lbs.	Main Bearing Cap Bolts Ft. Lbs.	Flywheel to Crankshaft Ft. Lbs.	Vibration Damper or Pulley Ft. Lbs.
1969–70	V8-429	15–20	130–140	25–30	28–33	65–75①	5–6	40–45	95–105	75–85	75–90
1971	V8-429	15–20	130–140	25–30	28–33	75–85①	5–6	40–45	95–105	75–85	70–90
1972	V8-400	10–15	95–105	②	12–16	18–25①	3–5	40–45	95–105	—	70–90
1972–73	V8-429, 460	15–20	130–140	25–30	28–33	18–25①	5–6	40–45	95–105	75–85	70–90
1974–75	V8-460	—	130–140	22–32	28–33	18–25①	5–6	40–45	95–105	75–85	70–90

①—Rocker arm stud to cylinder head. ②—¼" bolt 6–9; 5/16" bolt 21–25; 3/8" bolt 27–33.

FORD THUNDERBIRD

VALVE SPECIFICATIONS

Year	Engine Model	Valve Lash Int.	Valve Lash Exh.	Valve Angles Seat	Valve Angles Face	Valve Spring Installed Height	Valve Spring Pressure Lbs. @ In.	Stem Clearance Intake	Stem Clearance Exhaust	Stem Diameter Intake	Stem Diameter Exhaust
1969–70	8-429	.075–.125①		45	44	1¹³⁄₁₆	253 @ 1.33	.0010–.0027	.0010–.0027	.3416–.3423	.3416–.3423
1971	8-429	.105–.155①		45	45	1¹³⁄₁₆	229 @ 1.33	.0010–.0027	.0010–.0027	.3416–.3423	.3416–.3423
1972	8-400	.100–.150①		45	45	1¹³⁄₁₆	229 @ 1.33	.0010–.0027	.0015–.0032	.3416–.3423	.3411–.3418
	8-429	.075–.125①		45	45	1¹³⁄₁₆	229 @ 1.33	.0010–.0027	.0010–.0027	.3416–.3423	.3416–.3423
	8-460	.105–.155①		44.5	45.5	1¹³⁄₁₆	229 @ 1.33	.0010–.0027	.0010–.0027	.3416–.3423	.3416–.3423
1973	8-429	.075–.125①		45	44	1¹³⁄₁₆	169 @ 1.39	.0010–.0027	.0010–.0027	.3416–.3423	.3416–.3423
	8-460	.105–.155①		45	44	1¹³⁄₁₆	169 @ 1.39	.0010–.0027	.0010–.0027	.3416–.3423	.3416–.3423
1974	8-460	.075–.125①		45	44	1¹³⁄₁₆	252 @ 1.33	.0010–.0027	.0010–.0027	.3416–.3423	.3416–.3423
1975	8-460	.075–.175①		45	44	1¹³⁄₁₆	229 @ 1.33	.0010–.0027	.0010–.0027	.3416–.3423	.3416–.3423

①—Clearance specified is obtained at valve stem with lifter collapsed. See "Valves, Adjust" text.

PISTONS, PINS, RINGS, CRANKSHAFT & BEARINGS

Year	Engine Model	Piston Clearance	Ring End Gap① Comp.	Ring End Gap① Oil	Wrist-pin Diameter	Rod Bearings Shaft Diameter	Rod Bearings Bearing Clearance	Main Bearings Shaft Diameter	Main Bearings Bearing Clearance	Thrust on Bear. No.	Shaft End Play
1969–73	8-429	.0014–.0022	.010	.015	1.0400	2.4992–.25000	.0008–.0028	2.9994–3.0002	.0005–.0015	3	.004–.008
1972	8-400	.0014–.0022	.010	.015	.9752	2.3103–2.3111	.0008–.0026	2.9994–3.0002	.0009–.0026	3	.004–.010
1972–73	8-460	.0014–.0022	.010	.015	1.0400	2.4992–2.5000	.0008–.0028	2.9994–3.0002	.0005–.0025	3	.004–.008
1974	8-460	.0014–.0022	.010	.015	1.0400	2.4992–2.5000	.0008–.0028	2.9994–3.0002	②	3	.004–.008
1975	8-460	.0014–.0022	.010	.015	1.0400	2.4992–2.5000	.0008–.0026	2.9998	②	3	.004–.008

①—Fit rings in tapered boxes for clearance listed in tightest portion of ring travel.
②—#1, .0004–.0020, others .0012–.0028.

REAR AXLE SPECIFICATIONS

Year	Model	Carrier Type	Ring Gear & Pinion Backlash Inch	Nominal Pinion Locating Shim, Inch	Pinion Bearing Preload New Bearings With Seal Inch-Lbs.	Pinion Bearing Preload Used Bearings With Seal Inch-Lbs.	Pinion Bearing Preload New Bearings Less Seal Inch-Lbs.	Pinion Bearing Preload Used Bearings Less Seal Inch-Lbs.	Differential Bearing Preload	Pinion Nut Torque Ft.-Lbs.
1969–72	All	Removable	.008–.012	.015	22–32③	8–14⑥	—	—	.008–.012④	②⑤
1973	All	Removable	.008–.012	.015	17–27③	8–14③	—	—	.008–.012④	②⑤
1974–75	All	Removable	.008–.012	.015	17–27③	8–14③	—	—	.008–.012④	②⑦

②—If torque is not possible, install new spacer.
③—With collapsible spacer. With solid spacer 13–33 inch-lbs.
④—Case spread with new bearings. With used beaings .005–.008".
⑤—With 9" ring gear 175 ft.-lbs. With 9⅜" ring gear 200 ft.-lbs.
⑥—With collapsible spacer. With solid spacer 15–35 inch-lbs. with seal in place.
⑦—With collapsible spacer 170 ft.-lbs., with solid spacer 200 ft.-lbs.

STARTING MOTOR SPECIFICATIONS

Year and Model	Ident.	Rotation ①	Brush Spring Tension, Ounces	No Load Test			Torque Test		
				Amperes	Volts	R.P.M.	Amperes	Volts	Torque Ft. Lbs.
1969 V8-429	C9AF-A	C	40	70	12	10000	700	5	15.5
1970–73 V8-429	D0VF-A	C	40	70	12	10000	700	5	15.5
1972–73 V8-460	D2VF-AA	C	40	70	12	10000	700	5	15.5
1974 V8-460	D4VF-AA	C	80	90	12	—	—	—	—
1974 V8-460	D5AF-AB	C	80	90	12	—	—	—	—

①—As viewed from the drive end.   C—Clockwise.

ALTERNATOR & REGULATOR SPECIFICATIONS

Year	Model No. (10300)	Current Rating①		Field Current @ 75°F.		Voltage Regulator②				Field Relay	
		Amperes	Volts	Amperes	Volts	Part No. (10316)	Voltage @ 75°F.	Contact Gap	Armature Air Gap	Armature Air Gap	Closing Voltage @75°F.
1969	C9SF-B	65	15	2.9	12	C3SZ-B	13.5–15.3	⑧	⑧	⑧	2.0–4.2
1969–70	C8LF-B	55	15	2.9	12	C8SZ-A④	13.3–15.3	⑧	⑧	⑧	⑧
1970	D0AF-H	65	15	2.9	12	C3SZ-B	13.5–15.3	⑧	⑧	⑧	2.0–4.2
1971	D0SF-A	55	15	2.9	12	C3SZ-B	13.3–15.3	⑧	⑧	⑧	—
	D1AF-BA	65	15	2.9	12	C3SZ-B	13.5–15.3	⑧	⑧	⑧	2.0–4.2
1972	D2OF-EA	55	15	2.9	12	C3SZ-B	⑧	⑧	⑧	⑧	—
	D2AF-CA	65	15	2.9	12	D2TF-AA	13.5–15.3	⑧	⑧	⑧	2.5–4.0
	D2OF-AA	70	15	2.9	12	D3TF-AA	13.5–15.3	⑧	⑧	⑧	2.5–4.0
1973	All (Green)	61	15	2.9	12	D3TZ-A	13.5–15.3	⑧	⑧	⑧	2.5–4.0
	All	70	15	2.9	12	D3TZ-A	13.5–15.3	⑧	⑧	⑧	2.5–4.0
1974–75	All (Green)	61	15	2.9	12	D4AF-AA	13.5–15.3	⑧	⑧	⑧	2.5–4.0
	All	70	15	2.9	12	D4TF-AA	13.5–15.3	⑧	⑧	⑧	2.5–4.0
	All	90	15	2.9	12	—	13.5–15.3	⑧	⑧	⑧	2.5–4.0

①—Stamped on housing.   ⑧—Not adjustable.   ④—Integral regulator solid state.
②—Stamped on cover.

WHEEL ALIGNMENT SPECIFICATIONS

OLD CAR SPECIFICATIONS: For 1955-68 Wheel Alignment Specifications see main index.

Year	Model	Caster Angle, Degrees		Camber Angle, Degrees				Toe-In. Inch	Toe-Out on Turns, Deg.	
		Limits	Desired	Limits Left	Limits Right	Desired Left	Desired Right		Outer Wheel	Inner Wheel
1969	All	0 to +2	+1	−¼ to +1¼	−¼ to +1¼	+½	+½	3/16	18¼	20
1970	All	0 to +2	+1	−¼ to +1¼	−¼ to +1¼	+½	+½	3/16	19¼	20
1971	All	−1 to +3	+1	−½ to +1½	−½ to +1½	+½	+½	3/16	19¼	20
1972	All	−1 to +3	+1	+¼ to +1¾	−¼ to +1¾	+¾	+¾	3/16	17.74	20
1973	All	−½ to +3½	+1½	−¼ to +1¾	−¼ to +1¾	+¾	+¾	3/16	17.74	20
1974	All	+½ to +3½	+2	0 to +2	−½ to +1½	+1	+½	3/16	18.07	20
1975	All	+2½ to +5½	+4	0 to +2	−½ to +1½	+1	+½	3/16	18.09	20

FORD THUNDERBIRD

BRAKE SPECIFICATIONS

Year	Model	Brake Drum Inside Diameter	Wheel Cylinder Bore Diameter			Master Cylinder Bore Diameter		
			Front Disc Brakes	Front Drum Brakes	Rear Brakes	With Disc Brakes	With Drum Brakes	With Power Brakes
1969–71	All	11.03	2¾	—	¹⁵⁄₁₆	1.00	1.00	1.00
1972–75	All	11.03	3.100	—	1.00	1.00	—	1.00

COOLING SYSTEM & CAPACITY DATA

Year	Model or Engine	Cooling Capacity, Qts.			Radiator Cap Relief Pressure, Lbs.		Thermo. Opening Temp. ①	Fuel Tank Gals.	Engine Oil Refill Qts. ②	Transmission Oil			Rear Axle Oil Pints
		No Heater	With Heater	With A/C	With A/C	No A/C				3 Speed Pints	4 Speed Pints	Auto. Trans. Qts. ③	
1969	V8-429	19½	20½	20½	12-15	12-15	195	24	4	—	—	12¾	5
1970	V8-429	17½	18½	18½	12-15	12-15	188	④	4	—	—	12¾	5
1971	V8-429	18½	19½	16½	12-15	12-15	188	23	4	—	—	12¾	5
1972	V8-400	16¾	17¾	18½	12-15	12-15	188	22½	4	—	—	12¾	5
	V8-429	17¾	18¾	19½	12-15	12-15	188	22½	4	—	—	12¾	5
	V8-460	19	20	20	12-15	12-15	188	22½	4	—	—	12½	5
1973	All	18½	19½	19½	12-15	12-15	188	22½	4	—	—	12½	5
1974	V8-460	—	19½	19½	12-16	12-16	191	26½	4	—	—	12½	5
1975	V8-460	—	—	19.3	12-16	12-16	191	26½	4	—	—	12½	5

①—For permanant type anti-freeze.　　②—Add one quart with filter change.　　③—Approximate. Make final check with dipstick.
④—California vehicles 22½; all others 24.

Electrical Section

DISTRIBUTOR, REPLACE
Removal

1. To remove the distributor, disconnect the primary wire and vacuum control pipe. On some models the work may be made easier if the accelerator pull back spring is disconnected.
2. Remove distributor cap.
3. Scribe a mark on the distributor body indicating the position of the rotor, and scribe another mark on the body and engine block indicating position of distributor body in block. These marks can be used as guides when installing distributor in a correctly timed engine.
4. Remove hold down screw and screws and lift distributor out of block. *Do not crank engine while distributor is removed or the initial timing operation will have to be performed.*

Installation

If the crankshaft has not been disturbed, install the distributor, using the scribed marks previously made on the distributor body and engine block as guides.

If the crankshaft has been rotated while the distributor was removed from the engine, it will be necessary to retime the engine. Crank the engine to bring No. 1 piston on top dead center of its compression stroke. Align the timing mark on the vibration damper or pulley with the timing pointer (see *Tune Up* chart). Install the distributor so that the rotor points to the No. 1 spark plug wire terminal in the distributor cap.

NOTE: Make sure the oil pump intermediate shaft properly engages the distributor shaft. It may be necessary to crank the engine with the starter, after the distributor drive gear is properly engaged, in order to engage the oil pump intermediate shaft.

STARTER, REPLACE
1970-75

The starter does not use an auxiliary starter relay as did previous models therefore when replacing starter be sure to disconnect battery ground cable. Removal is otherwise the same as previous models.

1969

To provide working clearance, it may be necessary to turn wheels fully to the right and to disconnect the steering idler arm from the frame.

When installing the starter, be sure all mating surfaces are clean to insure a good electrical ground. To maintain proper alignment, hold the starter squarely against the mounting plate and fully inserted into the mounting hole while tightening the mounting bolts.

IGNITION LOCK, REPLACE
1970-75

1. Disconnect the battery ground cable.
2. **Units With Fixed Steering Columns:** Remove the steering wheel and trim pad. Insert a wire pin in the hole located inside the column halfway down the lock cylinder housing, Fig. 1. **Units With Tilt Steering Columns:** Insert wire pin in the hole located on the outside of the flange casting next to the emergency flasher button, Fig. 1.
3. Place the gear shift lever in *PARK* position, and turn the lock cylinder with the ignition key to *RUN* position.
4. Depress the wire pin while pulling up on the lock cylinder to remove. Remove the wire pin.
5. To install insert the lock cylinder into the housing in the flange casting, and turn the key to *OFF* position. Be certain that the cylinder is fully inserted before turning to the *OFF* position. This action will extend the cylinder retaining pin into the cylinder housing.
6. Turn the key to check for correct operation in all positions.
7. Install the steering wheel and trim pad on fixed column units.
8. Connect the battery ground cable.

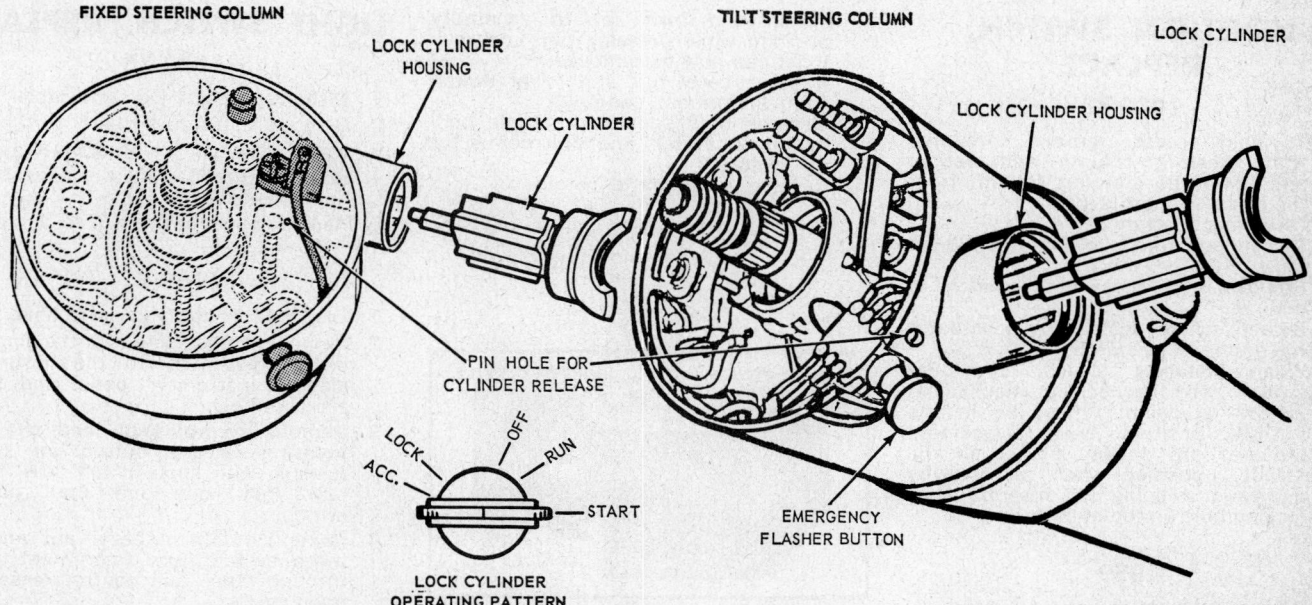

FIXED STEERING COLUMN

LOCK CYLINDER HOUSING

LOCK CYLINDER

PIN HOLE FOR CYLINDER RELEASE

LOCK ACC. OFF RUN START

LOCK CYLINDER OPERATING PATTERN

TILT STEERING COLUMN

LOCK CYLINDER

LOCK CYLINDER HOUSING

EMERGENCY FLASHER BUTTON

Fig. 1 Ignition lock, 1970-75

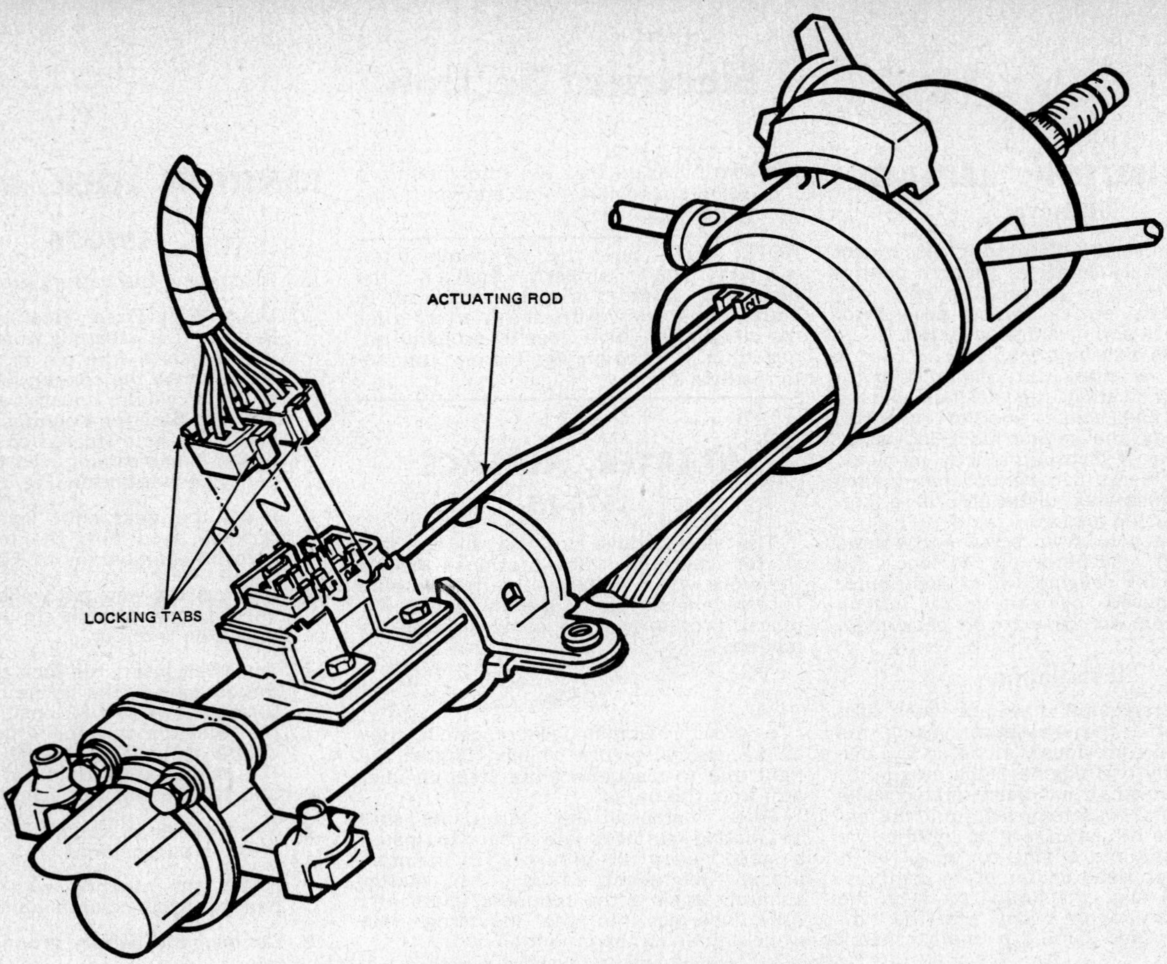

ACTUATING ROD

LOCKING TABS

Fig. 2   Ignition switch installation. 1970-75 (typical)

IGNITION SWITCH, REPLACE

1970-75

1. To gain access, remove shrouding from steering column and detach and lower the steering column from the brake support bracket.
2. Disconnect battery cable.
3. Disconnect switch wiring at multiple plug.
4. Remove nuts that retain switch to column.
5. Detach switch plunger from actuator rod and remove switch.
6. When installing switch, both the switch and the locking mechanism at top of column must be in the "LOCK" position. New replacement switches are already pinned in the "LOCK" position when received by a plastic shipping pin inserted in a locking hole on top of switch.

1969

1. Disconnect battery ground cable.
2. Insert wire pin in hole in ignition switch and turn key to accessory position while pressing pin. Lock cylinder can now be removed.
3. Remove bezel nut and lower switch from instrument panel.
4. Depress tabs securing multiple connector to switch and pull connector off switch.
5. Reverse procedure to install.

KNOB RELEASE BUTTON

Fig. 3   Light switch (typical)

LIGHT SWITCH, REPLACE

1972-75

1. Disconnect battery ground cable.
2. Remove instrument cluster trim panel.
3. Remove switch mounting plate.
4. Remove bezel nut and disconnect multiple connector.
5. Remove vacuum lines, if so equipped.

1969-71

1. Disconnect battery ground cable.
2. Remove three screws attaching air control assembly to the lower left side of instrument panel and lower the assembly.
3. Remove control knob and shaft by pressing release button on switch housing with knob in full "ON" position. Pull knob and shaft out of switch.
4. Remove retaining bezel nut and remove switch from instrument panel through the air control assembly opening.
5. Reverse procedure to install.

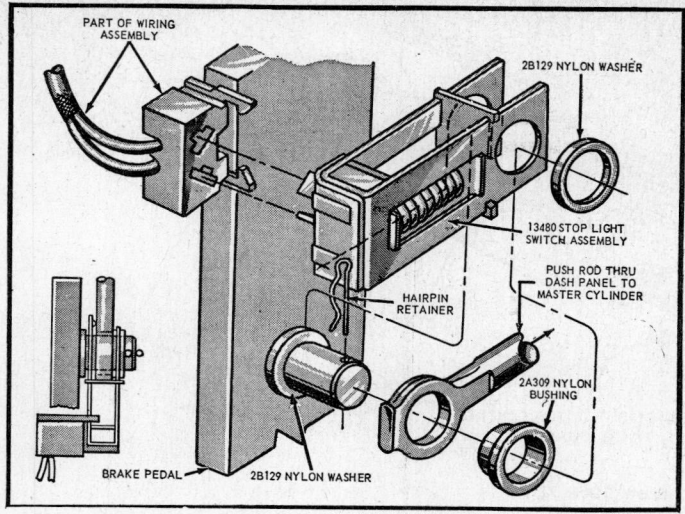

Fig. 4   Mechanical stop light switch. 1969-75

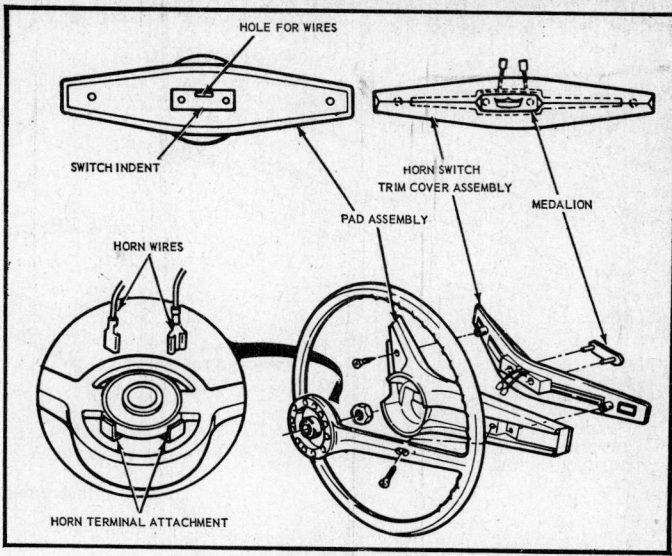

Fig. 5   Steering wheel and horn switch. 1970-71

STOP LIGHT SWITCH, REPLACE

1969-75

1. Disconnect wires at connector.
2. Remove hairpin retainer. Slide stop light switch, push rod and nylon washers and bushing away from pedal, and remove switch, Fig. 4.
3. Position switch, push rod, bushing and washers on brake pedal pin in the order shown, and install hairpin retainer.
4. Connect wires and install wires in clip.

NEUTRAL SAFETY SWITCH

1970-75

The neutral start switch has been eliminated from all column shift vehicles. A series of steps have been designed into the steering column selector lever hub casting which eliminates the need for a switch.

1969

Adjustment Procedure

1. Loosen retaining screws and with selector lever held lightly against the Neutral stop, rotate switch until a start is obtained. Tighten attaching screws to 20 in-lbs.
2. With the switch properly adjusted, place selector lever in the "1" position and push the Park reset button to the left until it stops. *The Park reset must be performed whenever the switch has been adjusted.*

HORN SOUNDER

1970-75

A two spoke steering wheel with a pressure sensitive horn switch built into the trim cover is used, Fig. 5. If the switch needs to be replaced, the entire horn switch/trim cover assembly will have to be replaced.

1969 Rim-Blow Type

The rubber insert and copper strip is not replaceable. If a new insert assembly is required, the entire steering wheel will have to be replaced.

1. Remove pad from steering wheel.
2. Remove medallion from pad.
3. After removing the retaining nut, the steering wheel can be removed with a suitable puller.

1969 Except Rim-Blow Type

1. Disconnect battery ground cable.
2. Remove center medallion from wheel.
3. Remove three screws from center of wheel and remove horn buttons.
4. Reverse procedure to install.

TURN SIGNAL SWITCH, REPLACE

1971-75

1. Remove retaining screw from underside of steering wheel spoke and lift off the pad horn switch/trim cover and medallion as an assembly. Disconnect horn switch wires from terminals.
2. Remove steering wheel retaining nut and steering wheel.
3. Remove turn signal switch lever by

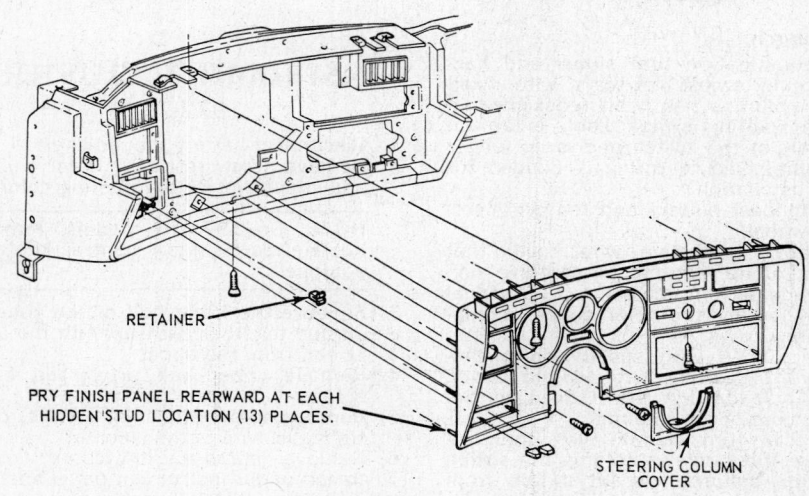

Fig. 6   Instrument cluster panel. 1972-75

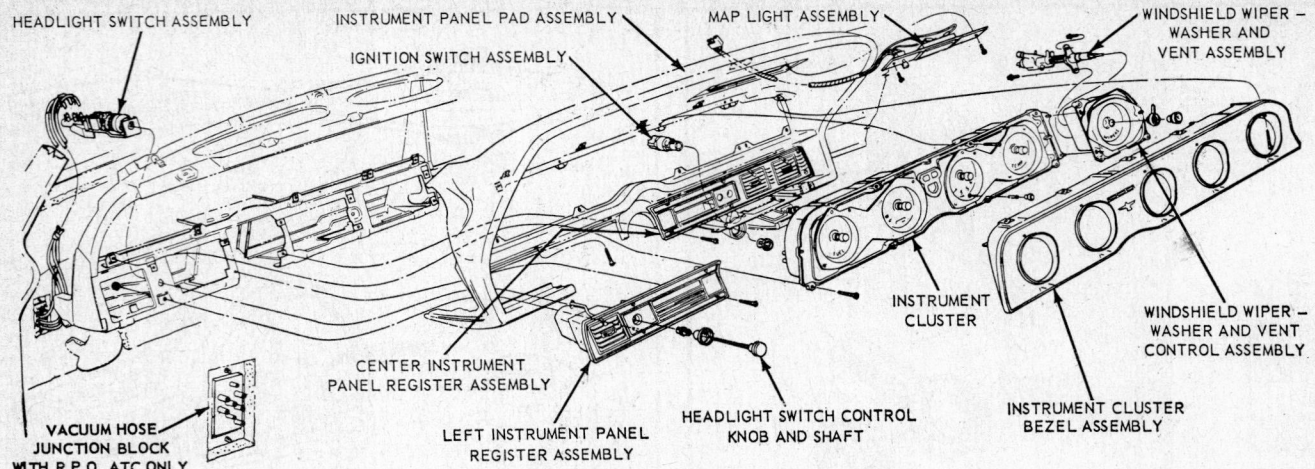

HEADLIGHT SWITCH ASSEMBLY — INSTRUMENT PANEL PAD ASSEMBLY — MAP LIGHT ASSEMBLY — WINDSHIELD WIPER – WASHER AND VENT ASSEMBLY

IGNITION SWITCH ASSEMBLY

INSTRUMENT CLUSTER

WINDSHIELD WIPER – WASHER AND VENT CONTROL ASSEMBLY

INSTRUMENT CLUSTER BEZEL ASSEMBLY

CENTER INSTRUMENT PANEL REGISTER ASSEMBLY

LEFT INSTRUMENT PANEL REGISTER ASSEMBLY

HEADLIGHT SWITCH CONTROL KNOB AND SHAFT

VACUUM HOSE JUNCTION BLOCK WITH R.P.O. ATC ONLY

Fig. 7   Instrument cluster. 1969-71

unscrewing it from column.
4. Remove shroud from under steering column.
5. Disconnect steering column wiring connector plugs and remove screws that secure switch assembly to column.
6. On vehicles with tilt column, remove wires and terminals from steering column connector plug.

NOTE: *Record the color code and location of each wire before removing it from connector. A hole provided in the flange casting on fixed columns makes it unnecessary to separate the wires from the connector. The plug with wires installed can be guided through the hole.*

7. Remove plastic cover sleeve from wiring harness and remove the switch and wires from top of column.
8. Reverse procedure to install.

1969-70

Fixed Column

The combination turn signal and hazard warning switch for cars with fixed steering columns has been redesigned in that the warning switch knob is an integral part of the switch and is no longer replaceable. Electric wiring is bonded for ease of installation.
1. Disconnect battery and remove steering wheel.
2. Remove protective wire cover that runs along bottom of steering column tube and disconnect electrical plug, noting the color codes and location.
3. If equipped with speed control, remove the sleeve around the wiring and pull the first three speed control wires out of the column.
4. Remove turn signal lever, then remove three screws holding the switch to the column and lift switch from column.
5. Reverse procedure to install.

1969-70

Tilt Column

1. Disconnect ground cable at battery.
2. Remove steering wheel.
3. Unscrew turn indicator lever.
4. Remove emergency flasher control knob.
5. Remove upper tilt mechanism cover (2 screws).
6. Remove five screws from lower finish panel under steering column and remove plate.
7. Disconnect multiple connector beneath instrument panel and at base of steering column.
8. Disconnect connector block from bullet connectors by depressing tabs one at a time and remove plastic cover over wires.
9. Position lower collar down and remove plastic clip from side of steering column.
10. Remove two screws from switch and remove switch and wires from column.
11. Reverse procedure to install.

INSTRUMENT CLUSTER
1972-75

1. Disconnect battery ground cable.
2. Remove screw retaining lower cluster applique cover below steering column.

NOTE: On 1974-75 models, remove heated rear window control knob, if equipped.

3. Squeeze the lower half of the column shroud together and separate the lower half from the upper.
4. Remove upper half of shroud from column.
5. Remove screw attaching PRNDL control cable wire to the column.
6. Remove heated backlite control knob.
7. Reach under instrument panel and depress the button on side of headlight switch while withdrawing switch con-

trol knob and shaft assembly.
8. Reach under panel and disconnect speedo cable.
9. Remove threaded headlight switch bezel.
10. Remove windshield wiper/washer control knob and bezel.
11. Remove cigar lighter from its receptacle.
12. Remove four screws retaining cluster front cover.
13. Insert a right angle standard tip screwdriver along edges of the finish panel withdrawing studs in sequence gradually around the periphery of the panel, Fig. 6.
14. Remove four screws retaining cluster to panel.
15. Pull cluster away from panel; disconnect cluster feed plug from its receptacle in the printed circuit.
16. Tilt cluster out, top first, and move the cluster toward center of car.

1969-71

1. Disconnect battery ground cable.
2. Remove instrument panel bezel, Fig. 7.
3. Remove clock adjusting knob, then push button retainers, mask and lens from instrument cluster.
4. Remove speedometer attaching screws and speedometer from cluster, then disconnect speedometer cable.
5. Remove cluster to instrument panel retaining screws.
6. Remove rear vent and wiper control assembly to instrument panel attaching screws.
7. Pull cluster from panel, disconnect electrical connectors from cluster and remove cluster.
8. Reverse procedure to install.

W/S WIPER BLADES

NOTE: Trico and Anco blades are used and both come in two types; Bayonet type and Side Saddle Pin type.

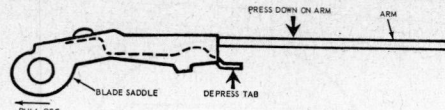

Fig. 8   Trico bayonet type blade

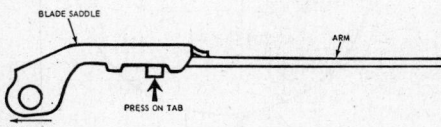

Fig. 8A   Anco bayonet type blade

Bayonet Type: To remove the *Trico* type press down on the arm to unlock the top stud. Depress the tab on the saddle, Fig. 8, and pull the blade from the arm. To remove the *Anco* type press inward on the tab, Fig. 8A, and pull the blade from the arm. To install a new blade assembly slide the blade saddle over the end of the wiper arm so that the locking stud snaps into place.

Side Saddle Pin Type: To remove the pin type insert an appropriate tool into the spring release opening of the blade saddle, depress the spring clip and pull the blade from the arm, Fig. 9. To install, push the blade saddle on to the pin so that the spring clip engages the pin. To replace the rubber element in a *Trico* blade squeeze the latch lock release and pull the element out of the lever jaws, Fig. 10. Remove the *Anco* element by depressing the latch pin, Fig. 10, and sliding the element out of the yoke jaws. To install insert the element through the yoke or lever jaws. Be sure the element is engaged at all points.

W/S WIPER ARMS
1969-71

Swing the arm and blade assembly away from the windshield and insert a 3/32 inch pin through the pin hole as shown in Fig. 11. Swinging the assembly away from the windshield will release the spring loaded attaching clip in the arm from the pivot shaft. Inserting the pin will hold it in the released position. The arm can now be pulled off the pivot shaft. *Do not* pry off with a screwdriver. Leave the pin in the arm until after installation. A new arm comes with a pin already installed to hold it in the released position. Make sure the pivot shaft is in parked position when installing new assembly. Push the arm onto the pivot shaft. Lock the arm to the pivot shaft by removing the pin.

1972-75

Raise the blade end of the arm off the windshield and move the slide latch, Fig. 12, away from the pivot shaft. This action will unlock the wiper arm from the pivot shaft and hold the blade end of the arm off the glass at the same time. The wiper arm can now be pulled off the pivot shaft without the aid of any tools.

W/S WIPER MOTOR, REPLACE
1972-75

1. Disconnect battery ground cable.
2. Remove wiper arm and blade assemblies.
3. Remove left cowl screen for access

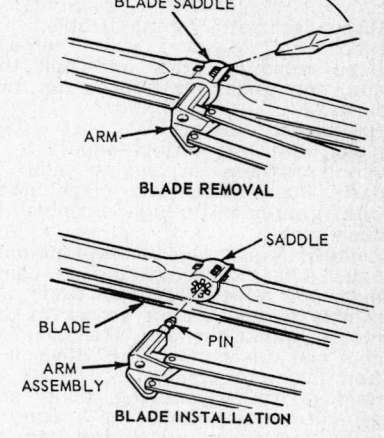

Fig. 9   Pin type blade

through cowl opening.
4. Disconnect linkage drive arm from motor output arm crankpin by removing the retaining clip.
5. From engine side of dash, disconnect wire connectors from motor.
6. Remove bolts that retain motor to dash and remove motor. If output arm catches on dash during removal, handturn the arm clockwise so it will clear.

1971

1. Remove wiper arm and blade assemblies.
2. Remove air cleaner.
3. Remove retaining screws and remove cowl top panel. Disconnect washer hose.
4. Remove the clip retaining the left wiper link to the motor and disconnect the link.
5. Disconnect both hydraulic lines from motor. Be careful not to burn hands with hot hydraulic fluid.
6. Remove the three bolts retaining motor to cowl. Disconnect wiper control cable and remove motor through left cowl opening.

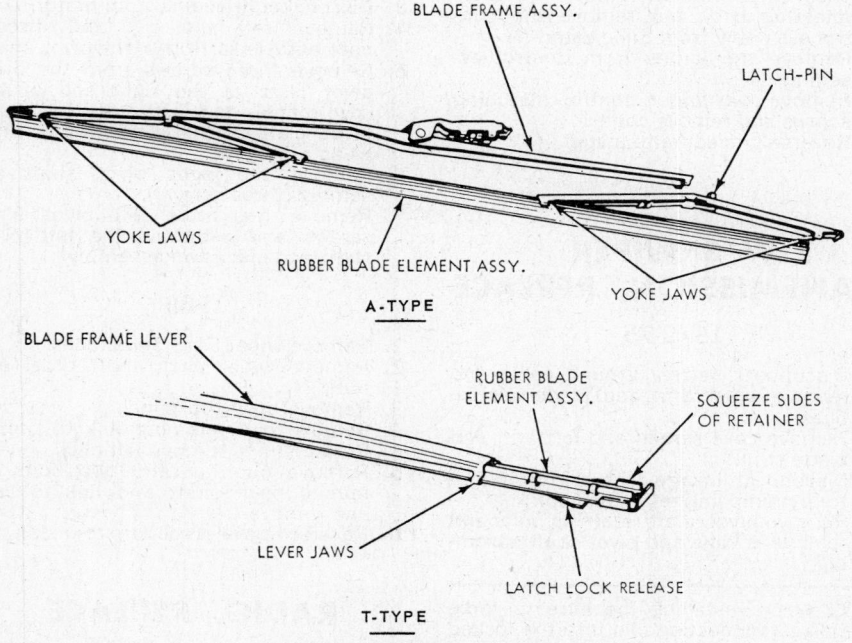

Fig. 10   Wiper blade element

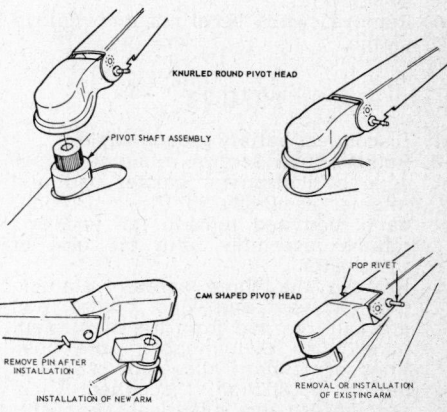

Fig. 11   Wiper arm. 1969-71

1970

1. Disconnect battery ground cable.
2. Disconnect washer hose, remove three retaining bolts and pull the cowl top grille out from under two slips.
3. Disconnect connector plug (two plugs with intermittent wiper) from wiring harness at engine side of dash. Push wiring and plugs along with grommet through opening in dash panel.
4. Remove four motor-to-cowl retaining bolts. Lift motor out and at same time pull wiper arm and blade assembly to the left for access to the motor crank pin clip. Remove the clip and disconnect the drive link from the motor crank pin.
5. Remove three retaining bolts and separate motor from the mounting plate and cover and wiring harness assembly.

1969

The cowl top panel is retained with eight screws and the two rear hood panel bumpers instead of 14 retaining screws. The wiper motor is attached to the upper cowl panel with three screws instead of two.
1. Remove wiper arm and blades.
2. Remove pivot shaft bezel.
3. Remove air cleaner.
4. Remove cowl top panel.
5. Remove seal plate from dash panel (2 screws).
6. Remove two clips retaining wiper links to motor. Rotate link to remove left clip.
7. Disconnect hydraulic line under hood.
8. Disconnect hydraulic line in cowl from motor.
9. Unfasten motor from mounting bracket (2 bolts). Disconnect control cable and remove motor.

W/S WIPER SWITCH, REPLACE

1972-75

1. Remove instrument cluster finish panel.
2. Remove wiper switch mounting plate.
3. Disconnect cigar lighter and wiper switch wires.
4. Remove switch bezel nut and remove switch.

1970-71

1. Disconnect battery ground cable.
2. Remove five screws retaining upper edge of instrument cluster pad and retainer assembly to the instrument panel pad and retainer assembly from the face of the cluster.
3. Remove the three screws retaining the rear vent and wiper control pod and pull the pod from the instrument panel. On 1971 models, note positions of vacuum hoses for reference during installation. Disconnect vacuum hoses and electrical connector and remove illumination bulbs.

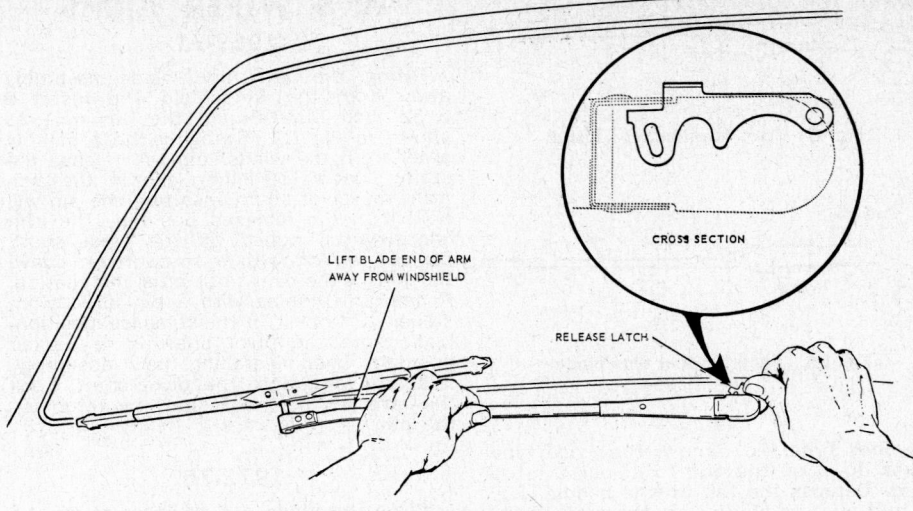

Fig. 12 Wiper arm. 1972-75

4. On 1971 models, remove clip retaining the control cable to the control and remove the control assembly.
5. Remove control knobs and remove the two screws retaining switch and remove the switch.

1969

1. Disconnect battery ground cable.
2. Remove five screws attaching the top of the cluster bezel to the instrument panel. Loosen five screws attaching bottom of the bezel to the instrument panel pad retainer and remove the bezel.
3. Remove three screws attaching the wiper and rear vent control to the instrument panel.
4. Disconnect vacuum hoses, lights and push on connector; remove the cable retaining clip; and remove the control assembly from the cluster.
5. Remove the knobs from control assembly.
6. Remove two wiper control attaching screws and remove control.
7. Reverse procedure to install.

W/S WIPER TRANSMISSION, REPLACE

1972-75

1. Disconnect battery ground cable and remove wiper arm and blade assemblies.
2. Remove cowl screen and left arm and blade stop.
3. Disconnect linkage drive arm from motor by removing retaining clip.
4. Remove pivot shaft retaining bolts and remove linkage and pivot shaft assemblies.

NOTE: When installing, be sure to force the linkage connecting clip into the locked position.

1971

1. Remove wiper arm and blade assemblies. Be sure to release tension arm retaining clip from the tension arm retaining stud on the left pivot assembly.
2. Remove retaining screws and remove the cowl vent grille. Disconnect windshield washer hoses.
3. Remove clip retaining the link assembly to the motor. Remove screws retaining pivot shaft and link assembly to the cowl and remove the pivot shaft and link assembly.

1970

1. Disconnect battery ground cable.
2. Disconnect washer hose and remove cowl vent top panel.
3. Disconnect drive link from motor.
4. Remove retaining clip and disconnect both links from right pivot shaft.
5. Remove three screws from the drive pivot plate at the right end of the cowl panel and withdraw the drive pivot plate and the two drive links as an assembly.
6. Remove the right pivot shaft assembly (three screws).
7. Remove the three left pivot shaft screws and withdraw the left pivot shaft and link as an assembly.

1969

1. Remove wiper arms and blades.
2. Remove wiper pivot shaft bezel and nuts.
3. Remove cowl top panel.
4. Remove clip retaining link to motor. Rotate link to remove left clips.
5. Remove one nut and two bolts retaining pivot shaft and link to cowl and remove.
6. Reverse above procedure to install.

RADIO, REPLACE

NOTE: When installing radio, be sure to

adjust antenna trimmer for peak performance.

1974-75

1. Disconnect battery ground cable.
2. Pull radio knobs and discs from shafts.
3. Remove twilight sentinental amplifier.
4. Remove air conditioning duct located under radio.
5. Remove radio rear support to panel screw and disconnect radio electrical leads, then remove radio.

1972-73

1. Disconnect battery ground cable.
2. Pull radio knobs off shafts.
3. Remove nut from radio control shafts.
4. Remove radio rear support attaching screw at instrument panel.
5. Disconnect power and speaker wires at connectors.
6. Disconnect antenna lead and remove radio.

1970-71

1. Disconnect battery ground cable.
2. Pull knobs off radio control shafts and remove cover plate located below steering column.
3. Remove the nut from the right radio control shaft.
4. Remove six screws and remove the trim applique from in front of radio.
5. Remove nut and washer from right radio control shaft.
6. Remove the screw attaching front left side of radio to instrument panel.
7. Remove radio rear support attaching screw.
8. Disconnect radio power wires at connectors.
9. Disconnect antenna lead-in cable and remove radio.

1969

1. Disconnect battery ground cable.
2. Pull knobs off radio control shafts.
3. Remove cover plate located below steering column.
4. Remove six screws and remove trim applique from in front of radio.
5. Remove nut and washer from right radio control shaft.
6. Remove screw attaching the front left side of radio to instrument panel.
7. Remove radio rear support attaching screw.
8. Disconnect radio power wires and speaker leads at connectors.
9. Disconnect antenna lead in cable and remove radio.
10. Reverse procedure to install.

BLOWER MOTOR REMOVE

1969-71

1. Disconnect the battery ground cable.
2. On **Air Cond Models:** Remove the courtesy light from the lower edge of the instrument panel. Remove the glove box liner.
3. Remove the right cowl side trim panel.

4. Remove the six duct mounting flange screws. Reach through the recirculating door opening and remove the vacuum motor hose from the vacuum motor and remove the duct assembly.
5. Disconnect the lead wire to the blower motor.
6. Remove one screw on the motor mounting plate. Rotate the motor mounting plate counterclockwise to un-lock the mounting plate from the case. Remove the motor and wheel assembly through the opening in the cowl side panel.
7. Reverse above to install.

1972-75

1. Disconnect the battery ground cable.
2. Remove the glove box for access.
3. Remove the recirc air register and duct assembly from the blower lower housing to the dash panel.
4. Disconnect the white hose from the outside-recirc air door vacuum motor and remove the vacuum motor from the blower lower housing. Leave the motor actuator connected to the door crank arm, Fig. 13.
5. Disconnect the blower lead wire (orange) from the harness connector, disconnect the motor ground wire (black).
6. Remove the six upper to lower blower housing flange screws.
7. Separate the blower lower housing and motor assembly from the upper housing and remove it from under the instrument panel.
8. Remove the blower motor and wheel assembly from the lower housing.
9. Reverse the above to install.

HEATER CORE REMOVAL

1972-75

1. Drain coolant and disconnect heater hoses from core.
2. Remove glove box.
3. Remove heater air outlet register from plenum assembly (2 snap clips).
4. Remove temperature control cable assembly mounting screw and disconnect end of cable from blend door crank arm (1 spring nut).
5. Remove the blue and red vacuum hoses from the high-low door vacuum motor; the yellow hose from the panel-defrost door motor, and the brown hose at the inline tee connector to the temperature by-pass door motor, Fig. 14.
6. Disconnect wiring connector from resistor.
7. Remove ten screws from around flange of plenum case and remove the rear case half of the plenum.
8. Remove mounting nut from heater core tube support bracket.
9. Remove core.

NOTE: When installing, apply body sealer between front and rear case halves and make sure core mounting gasket is properly installed.

1970-71

1. Remove hood and air cleaner and drain engine coolant.
2. Disconnect wiper hydraulic lines.
3. Disconnect heater hoses at heater core.
4. Disconnect vacuum hose at top of housing and remove oil pressure sender unit from back of engine.
5. Remove transmission dip stick and tube assembly.
6. Disconnect multiple connector leading to icing switch.
7. Remove evaporator housing front cover.
8. Remove heater core housing cover.
9. Remove heater core retaining bracket and remove the core.
10. Reverse the procedure to install.

1969

1. Remove hood and carburetor air cleaner.
2. Disconnect vacuum supply hose on top of heater case and pull it away from case mounting studs and disconnect hydraulic lines at wiper motor.
3. Remove transmission dipstick and tube.
4. Disconnect multiple connector leading to thermostat switch inside heater case cover and to resistor on front of cover.
5. Remove five nuts and two screws from heater core case cover and take off cover.
6. Slide heater core from case.

SPEED CONTROLS

1972-75

Adjust the bead chain to obtain .06-.25″ actuator arm free travel when the engine is at hot idle, Fig. 15. The adjustment should be made to take as much slack as possible out of the chain without restricting the carburetor lever from returning to idle. On vehicles with a solenoid anti-diesel valve, perform this adjustment with the ignition switch in the ON position.

1970-71

Linkage Adjustment

Adjust the bead chain to obtain .06-.25″ actuator arm free travel when the engine is at hot idle, Fig. 16.

1969

Bead Chain Adjustment

This is the only adjustment required for proper functioning of the system and assure a normal engine idle.

Adjust the chain to maintain ½″ to 1″ ball slack with engine at hot idle, Fig. 17.

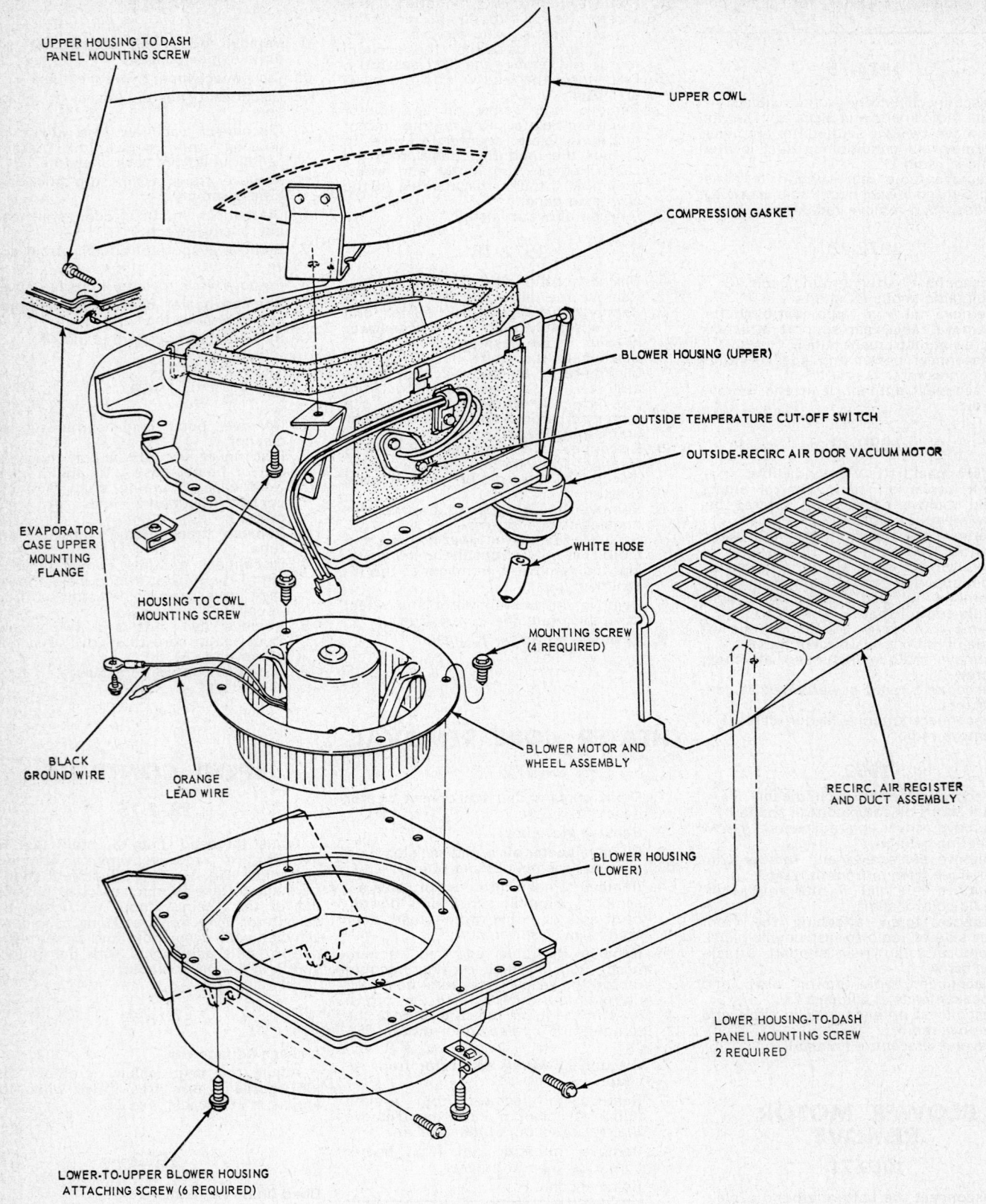

UPPER HOUSING TO DASH PANEL MOUNTING SCREW

UPPER COWL

COMPRESSION GASKET

BLOWER HOUSING (UPPER)

OUTSIDE TEMPERATURE CUT-OFF SWITCH

OUTSIDE-RECIRC AIR DOOR VACUUM MOTOR

EVAPORATOR CASE UPPER MOUNTING FLANGE

HOUSING TO COWL MOUNTING SCREW

WHITE HOSE

MOUNTING SCREW (4 REQUIRED)

BLACK GROUND WIRE

ORANGE LEAD WIRE

BLOWER MOTOR AND WHEEL ASSEMBLY

RECIRC. AIR REGISTER AND DUCT ASSEMBLY

BLOWER HOUSING (LOWER)

LOWER HOUSING-TO-DASH PANEL MOUNTING SCREW 2 REQUIRED

LOWER-TO-UPPER BLOWER HOUSING ATTACHING SCREW (6 REQUIRED)

Fig. 13 Blower motor. 1972-75

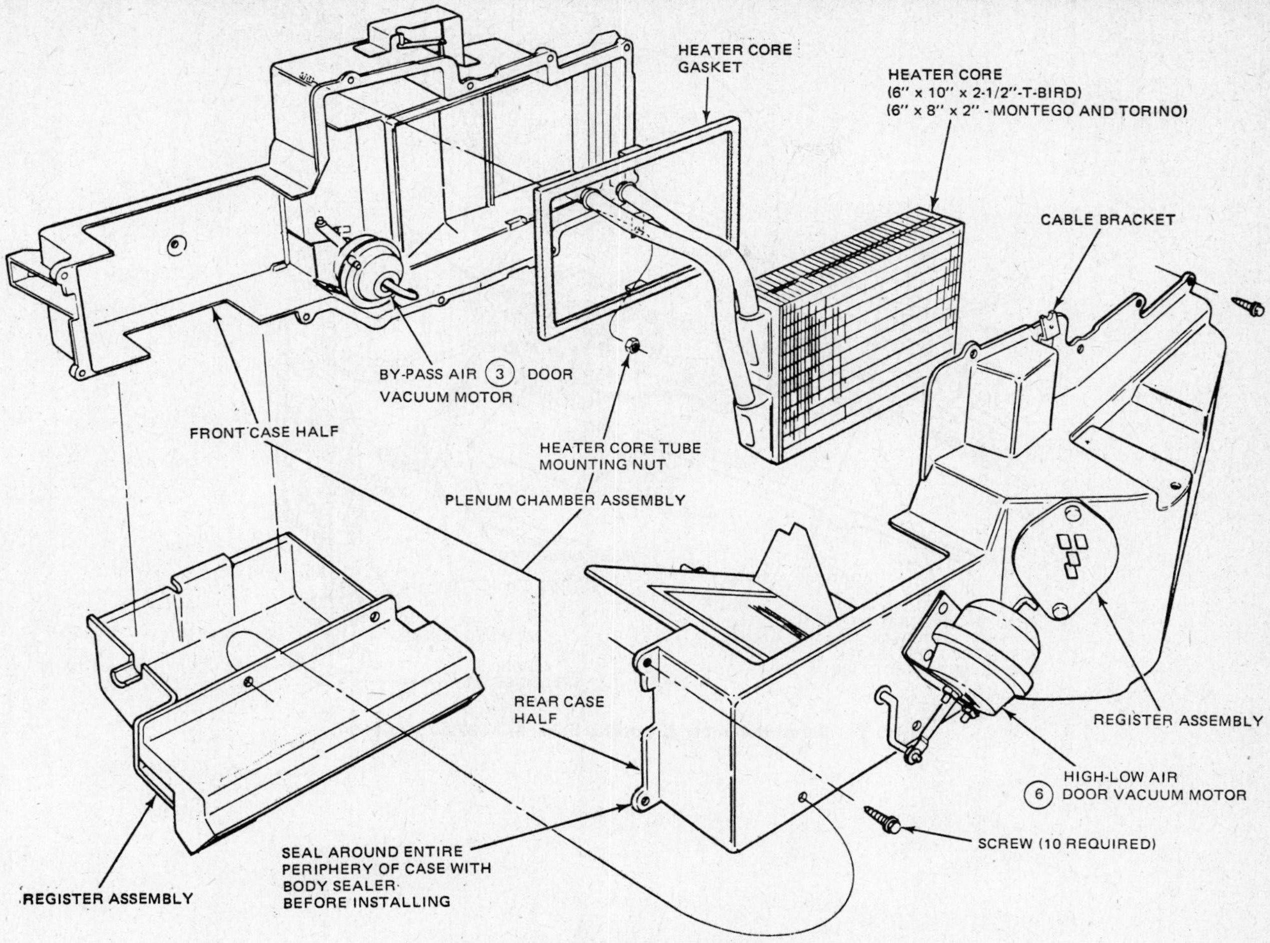

HEATER CORE
GASKET

HEATER CORE
(6" x 10" x 2-1/2"-T-BIRD)
(6" x 8" x 2" - MONTEGO AND TORINO)

CABLE BRACKET

BY-PASS AIR ③ DOOR
VACUUM MOTOR

FRONT CASE HALF

HEATER CORE TUBE
MOUNTING NUT

PLENUM CHAMBER ASSEMBLY

REGISTER ASSEMBLY

HIGH-LOW AIR
⑥ DOOR VACUUM MOTOR

REAR CASE
HALF

SCREW (10 REQUIRED)

REGISTER ASSEMBLY

SEAL AROUND ENTIRE
PERIPHERY OF CASE WITH
BODY SEALER
BEFORE INSTALLING

Fig. 14   Heater core. 1972-75

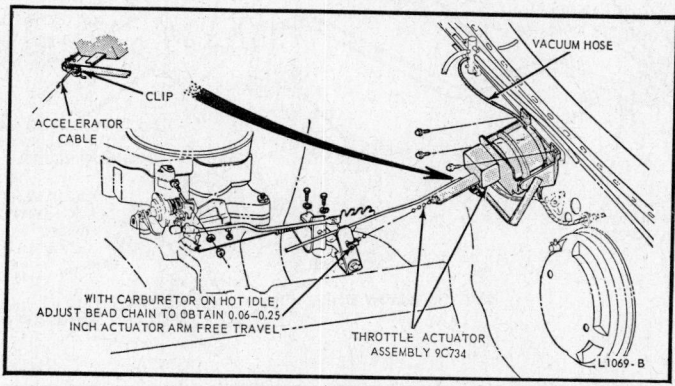

VACUUM HOSE

CLIP

ACCELERATOR
CABLE

WITH CARBURETOR ON HOT IDLE,
ADJUST BEAD CHAIN TO OBTAIN 0.06-0.25
INCH ACTUATOR ARM FREE TRAVEL

THROTTLE ACTUATOR
ASSEMBLY 9C734

L1069-B

Fig. 16   Throttle actuator assembly. 1970-71

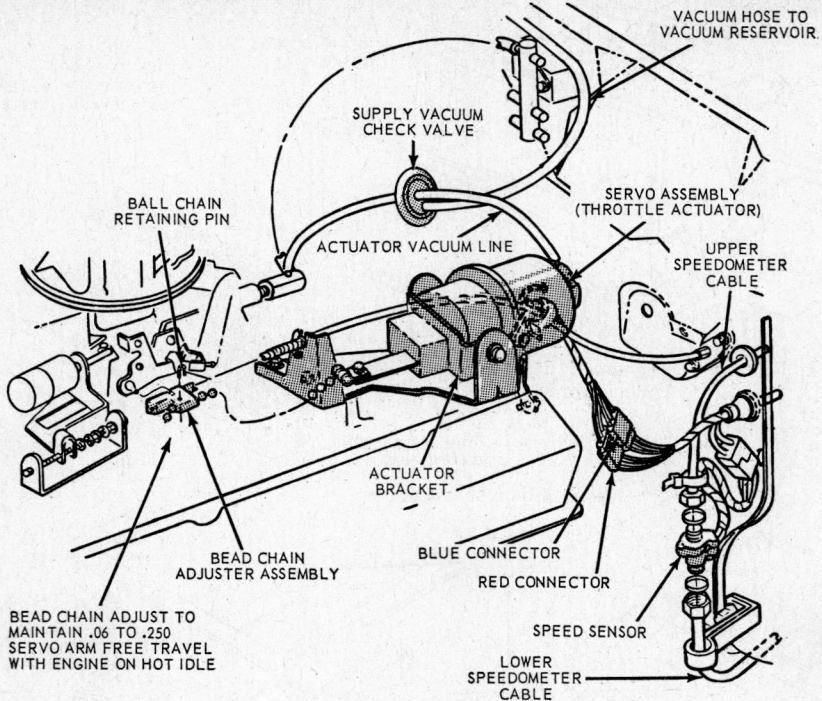

Fig. 15   Servo assembly & throttle linkages. 1972-75 (typical)

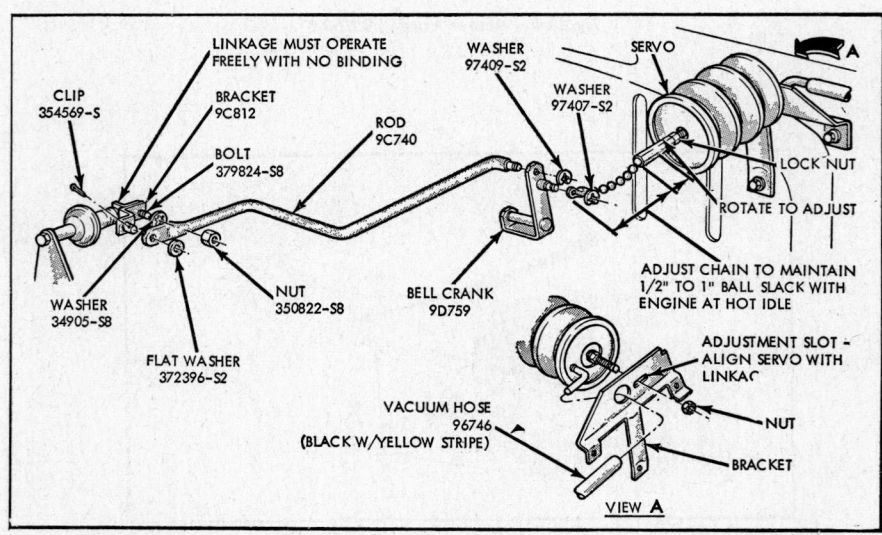

Fig. 17   Servo assembly and accelerator linkage. 1969

Engine Section

Service procedures on the V8-400 are covered in the Ford & Mercury car chapters

ENGINE MOUNTS REPLACE

1969-71

1. Disconnect battery and raise vehicle on hoist. Remove starter.
2. Remove the long bolt and nut that attaches the insulator to support bracket, Fig. 1.
3. Place jack and wood under the engine oil pan and raise engine about one inch.
4. Remove insulator to engine bolts and lock washers, and remove insulator.
5. Reverse above to install.

1972-75

1. Remove the fan shroud attaching screws and support the engine with a jack and a block of wood placed under the leading edge of the oil pan.
2. Remove the through bolt and nut attaching the insulator to the frame crossmember, Figs. 2 and 3.
3. Remove the insulator to upper bracket attaching nuts.
4. Raise the engine enough to remove the insulator and heat shield if so equipped.
5. Reverse above to install.

ENGINE, REPLACE

Because of engine compartment tolerances, the engine should not be removed and installed with the transmission attached.

1. Drain cooling system and crankcase.
2. Remove radiator and air cleaner.

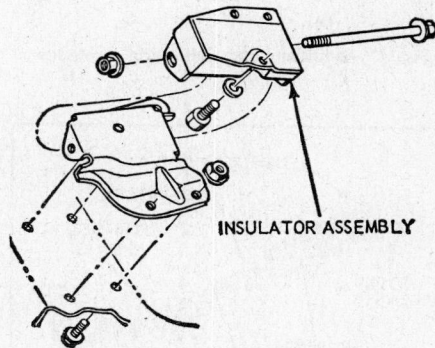

Fig. 1   Engine mount. 1969-71

3. Remove hood.
4. Remove fuel and vacuum lines and all hoses, wires and linkage attached to engine.
5. Disconnect exhaust pipe from manifolds.
6. Remove starter and automatic transmission filler tube.
7. Remove converter or flywheel housing lower cover.
8. Support transmission with jack.
9. Unfasten converter or flywheel housing from engine.
10. Remove engine mounting bolts and lift engine out of chassis.

CYLINDER HEAD REPLACE

NOTES

Before installing cylinder head, wipe off engine block gasket surface and be certain no foreign material has fallen into cylinder bores, bolt holes or in the valve lifter area. It is good practice to clean out bolt holes with compressed air.

Some cylinder head gaskets are coated with a special lacquer to provide a good seal once the parts have warmed up. Do not use any additional sealer on such gaskets. If the gasket does not have this lacquer coating, apply suitable sealer to both sides.

Tighten cylinder head bolts at little at a time in three steps in the sequence shown in the illustrations. Final tightening should be to the torque specifications listed in the *Engine Tightening* table. After the bolts have been torqued to specifications, *they should not be disturbed.*

In instances where cylinder head gasket leakage is hard to control, aluminum paint can be applied to the gasket as a sealer.

Spray one coat of the aluminum paint on both sides of the gasket and allow the paint to dry. Then spray a second coat on both sides and, while the paint is still wet, install the gasket. Torque the head and manifold bolts to specifications to complete the job.

1969-75

1. Remove intake manifold, carburetor and radiator supply tank as a unit.
2. Disconnect exhaust pipes from manifolds. It may also be necessary to unbolt and lay aside the power steering pump, air conditioning compressor and mounting bracket. Remove air conditioning evaporator housing and capillary tube as an assembly from dash panel.
3. Remove bolts and lift off head.
4. Install cylinder heads in reverse order of removal and tighten bolts in the sequence shown in Fig. 4.

NOTE

The cylinder head gaskets are marked "Top" or "Front" stamped near the front end of the gasket. The gasket is properly installed when the word is at the forward end of the engine and water passage holes line up. This results in the sealing beads on the right head gasket being inverted with respect to the left head gasket.

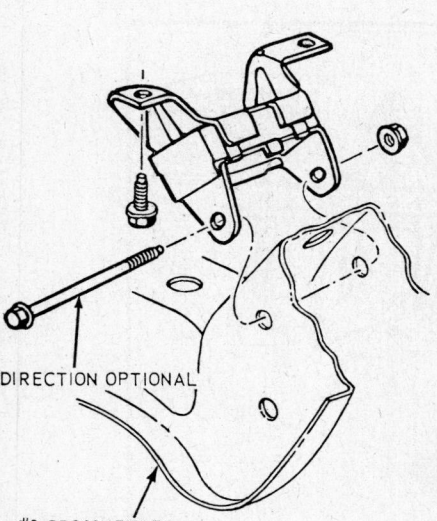

DIRECTION OPTIONAL

#2 CROSSMEMBER

Fig. 2   Engine mount. 1972 V8-400

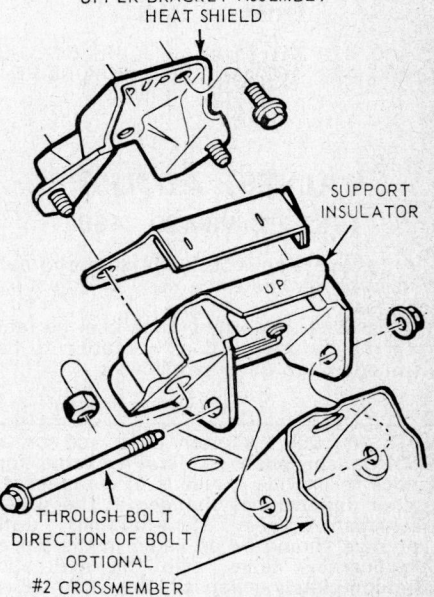

UPPER BRACKET ASSEMBLY
HEAT SHIELD

SUPPORT INSULATOR

UP

THROUGH BOLT
DIRECTION OF BOLT OPTIONAL
#2 CROSSMEMBER

Fig. 3   Engine mount. 1972-75 V8-429, 460

ROCKER ARM STUDS

1969-71 V8-429, 460

Rocker arm studs are screwed into threaded bores in the cylinder head bosses. To install, apply water resistant sealer to stud threads that screw into cylinder head. Install stud and torque to 65-75 ft-lbs. Apply Lubriplate to top of valve stem and at push rod guide in cylinder head. Install rocker arm, fulcrum and stud nut.

1972-75 V8-429, 460

The rocker arm is supported by a fulcrum bolt which fits through the fulcrum seat and threads into the cylinder head. To disassemble, remove the bolt, oil deflector, fulcrum seat and rocker arm.

VALVE LIFT SPECS.

Engine	Year	Intake	Exhaust
8-400	1972	.422	.427
8-429	1969-73	.443	.486
8-460	1972-73	.443	.486
	1974-75	.442	.486

VALVE TIMING

Intake Opens Before TDC

Engine	Year	Degrees
8-400	1972	17
8-429	1969-71	16
	1972-73	8
8-460	1972-75	8

VALVE ARRANGEMENT

Front to Rear

V8-400, 429, 460 Right . . . . . I-E-I-E-I-E-I-E
V8-400, 429, 460 Left . . . . . . E-I-E-I-E-I-E-I

VALVES, ADJUST

1969-75, V8-429, 460

A positive stop rocker arm stud and nut is used to eliminate the need of adjusting valve lash.

It is very important that the correct push rod be used and all components be installed and torqued as follows.

NOTE: A .060" shorter push rod or a .060" longer push rod are available for service to provide a means of compensating for dimensional changes in the valve mechanism. Valve stem-to-rocker arm clearance should be as listed in the Valve Specifications table, with the hydraulic lifter completely collapsed. Repeated valve grind jobs will decrease this clearance to the point that if not compensated for the

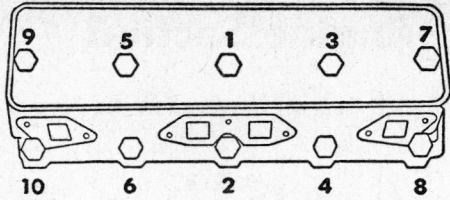

Fig. 4 Cylinder head tightening sequence

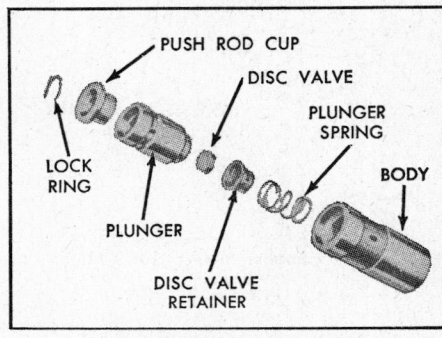

Fig. 5 Hydraulic valve lifter (typical)

lifters will cease to function.

To check the clearance, bring the piston of the cylinder being checked on top dead center of the compression stroke. Then with hydraulic lifter collapsed, check the clearance between valve stem and rocker arm. If the clearance is less than the minimum, the .060" shorter push rod should be used. If clearance is more than the maximum, the .060" longer push rod should be used. (See Valve Specifications table).

1. Position the piston of the cylinder being worked on at TDC of its compression stroke.
2. Install rocker arm stud and torque to 65-75 ft-lbs.
3. Lubricate and install rocker arm and fulcrum.
4. Thread nut onto stud until it contacts stud shoulder. Torque to 18-22 in-lbs.

VALVE GUIDES

Valve guides in these engines are an integral part of the head and, therefore, cannot be removed. For service, guides can be reamed oversize to accommodate one of three service valves with oversize stems (.003", .015" and .030").

Check the valve stem clearance of each valve (after cleaning) in its respective valve guide. If the clearance exceeds the service limits of .004" on the intake or .005" on the exhaust, ream the valve guides to accommodate the next oversize diameter valve.

HYDRAULIC VALVE LIFTERS

The internal parts of each hydraulic valve lifter assembly are a matched set. If these are mixed, improper valve operation may result. Therefore, disassemble, inspect and test each assembly separately to prevent mixing the parts, Fig. 5.

1. Remove the intake manifold.
2. Remove the rocker arms and shafts.
3. Remove the push rods, keeping them in a rack in sequence so that they may be installed in their original location.
4. Remove the valve lifters with a magnet rod and place them in a rack in sequence so that they may be installed in their original location.
5. Reverse procedure to install.

TIMING CASE COVER

NOTE: If it becomes necessary to replace the oil seal in the timing case cover the cover must be removed.

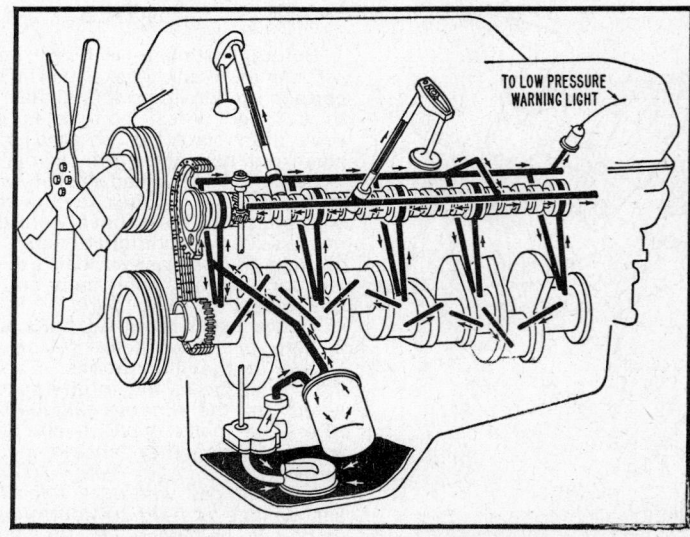

Engine lubrication system. V8-429, 460

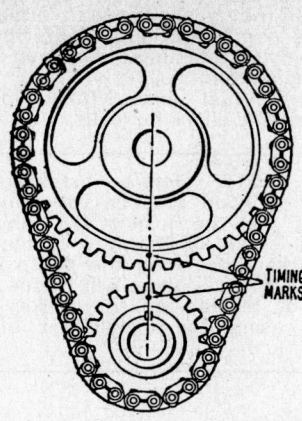

Fig. 6 Valve timing marks, V8-429, 460

1969-75, V8-429, 460

1. Drain cooling system and crankcase.
2. Remove fan and shroud.
3. Remove radiator.
4. Remove drive belts and water pump pulley. Remove compressor support if so equipped.
5. Remove bolt and washer attaching crankshaft damper. Remove damper with suitable puller. Remove Woodruff key from crankshaft.
6. Remove power steering pump.
7. Remove fuel pump.
8. Remove front cover to cylinder block bolts. Cut the oil pan seal flush with cylinder block face prior to separating cover from cylinder block. Remove front cover and water pump as a unit.

TIMING CHAIN

1969-75

1. To remove the chain, first take off the front cover as outlined previously.
2. Crank engine until timing mark on camshaft sprocket is adjacent to timing mark on crankshaft sprocket, Fig. 6.
3. Remove camshaft sprocket cap screw and fuel pump eccentric.
4. Slide both sprockets and chain forward and remove as an assembly.
5. Reverse foregoing procedure to install the chain, being sure to align the timing marks as shown.

CAMSHAFT, REPLACE

1969-74, V8-429, 460

1. Remove timing cover, chain and sprockets as outlined previously.
2. Remove intake manifold and carburetor as an assembly.
3. Remove rocker arm covers. Back off

rocker arm stud nuts, turn rocker arms sideways and remove push rods in sequence.
4. Remove valve lifters.
5. If air conditioned, discharge refrigeration system. Disconnect line to evaporator at receiver dryer. Unfasten condenser from radiator support and position out of way.
6. Remove camshaft thrust plate retaining bolts and carefully remove camshaft from engine.
7. Reverse above procedure to install.

CAMSHAFT BEARINGS

When necessary to replace camshaft bearings, the engine will have to be removed from the vehicle and the plug at the rear of the cylinder block will have to be removed in order to utilize the special camshaft bearing removing and installing tools required to do this job. If properly installed, camshaft bearings require no reaming—nor should this type bearing be reamed or altered in any manner in an attempt to fit bearings.

PISTON & ROD, ASSEMBLE

All V8's

Assemble the pistons to the rods as shown in Fig. 7.

PISTONS, PINS & RINGS

Pistons are available in oversizes of .003, .020, .030, .040 and .060".
Piston pins are available in oversizes of .001 and .002".
Rings are available in oversizes of .002, .010, .020, .030 and .040".

MAIN & ROD BEARINGS

Main and rod bearings are available in undersizes of .002, .010, .020 and .030".

OIL PAN, REPLACE

1969-75, V8-429, 460

1. Disconnect radiator shroud from radiator if so equipped and position over fan.
2. Raise car on a hoist and drain crankcase.
3. Disconnect engine front support insulators from underbody crossmember. Place floor jack under front edge of oil pan, with block of wood between jack and oil pan. Raise engine just enough to insert $1\frac{1}{4}$" blocks of wood between insulators and underbody side members. Remove floor jack.
4. Disconnect starter cable, unfasten and remove starter.
5. Remove end attachments of stabilizer bar and rotate ends of bar down to raise center of bar. Remove oil filter.
6. Unbolt and remove oil pan ahead of

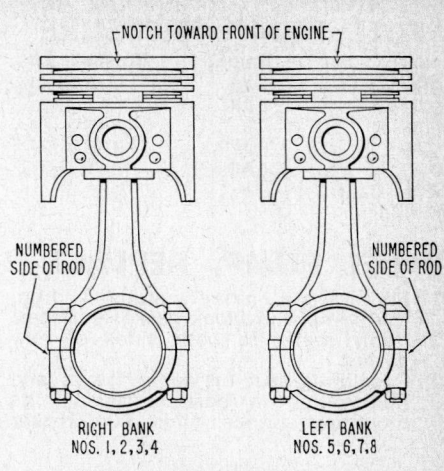

Fig. 7 Piston and rod assembly

underbody crossmember.
7. Reverse above procedure to install.

OIL PUMP REPAIRS

Rotor Type Pump, Fig. 8

1. With all parts clean and dry, check the inside of the pump housing and the outer race and rotor for damage or excessive wear.
2. Check the mating surface of the pump cover for wear. If this surface is worn, scored or grooved, replace the cover.
3. Measure the clearance between the outer race and housing. This clearance should be .006-.009".
4. With the rotor assembly installed in the housing, place a straight edge over the rotor assembly and housing. Measure the clearance between the straight edge and the rotor and outer race. Recommended limits are .001-.0035". The outer race, shaft and rotor are furnished only as an assembly.
5. Check the drive shaft-to-housing bearing clearance by measuring the O.D. of the shaft and the I.D. of the housing bearing. The recommended clearance limits are .0015-.0029".
6. Inspect the relief valve spring for a collapsed or worn condition.
7. Check the relief valve piston for scores and free operation in the bore. The specified piston clearance is .0015-.0029".

BELT TENSION DATA

	New	Used
1969-75 All	140	110

WATER PUMP, REPLACE

1969-75, V8-429, 460

Refer to procedure for removing timing cover mentioned previously.

FUEL PUMP PRESSURE

Year	Engine	Pressure Lbs.
1969	All	4½-6½
1970-73	All	5-7
1974	①	5½-6½
1974	②	6½-7½
1975	All	5.7-7.7

①Exc. Calif.
②Calif.

FUEL PUMP, REPLACE

1. Remove all gasket material from the pump and block gasket surfaces. Apply sealer to both sides of new gasket.
2. Position gasket on pump flange and hold pump in position against its mounting surface. Make sure rocker

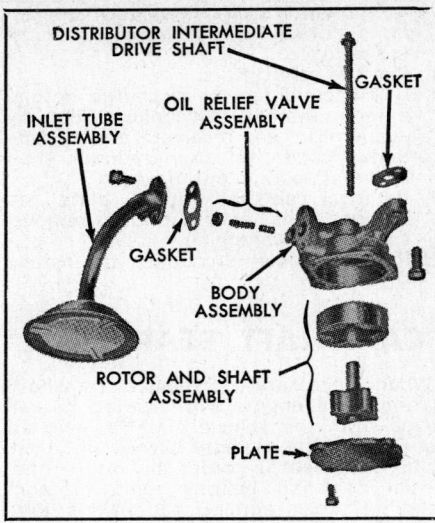

Fig. 8   Rotor type oil pump

arm is riding on camshaft eccentric.
3. Press pump tight against its mounting. Install retaining screws and tighten them alternately.
4. Connect fuel lines. Then operate engine and check for leaks.

SERVICE NOTE: Before installing the pump, it is good practice to crank the engine so that the nose of the camshaft eccentric is out of the way of the fuel pump rocker arm when the pump is installed. In this way there will be the least amount of tension on the rocker arm, thereby easing the installation of the pump.

Transmission Section

NOTE: 1975 linkage adjustment information is in this section. Repair procedures on both automatic and manual shift transmissions are covered elsewhere in this manual. Procedures for removing automatic transmissions as well as linkage adjustments on 1969-74 models are included in the automatic transmission chapters. See Chapter Index.

1975 AUTO TRANS.
LINKAGE, ADJUST

Linkage adjustment procedures for 1975 models are the same as those for 1974 models as outlined elsewhere in this manual.

Rear Axle, Propeller Shaft & Brakes

REAR AXLES

Fig. 1 illustrates the rear axle assembly used on these cars. When necessary to overhaul the unit, refer to the *Rear Axle Specifications* table in this chapter.

Description

In these axles, Fig. 1, the drive pinion is straddle-mounted by two opposed tapered roller bearings which support the pinion shaft in front of the drive pinion gear, and straight roller bearing that supports the pinion shaft at the rear of the pinion gear. The drive pinion is assembled in a pinion retainer that is bolted to

the differential carrier. The tapered roller bearings are preloaded by a collapsible spacer between the bearings. The pinion is positioned by a shim or shims located between the drive pinion retainer and the differential carrier.

The differential is supported in the carrier by two tapered roller side bearings. These bearings are preloaded by two threaded ring nuts or sleeves between the bearings and pedestals. The differential assembly is positioned for proper ring gear and pinion backlash by varying the adjustment of these ring nuts. The differential case houses two side gears in mesh with two pinions mounted on a pinion shaft which is held in place by a pin.

The side gears and pinions are backed by thrust washers. With high performance engines, an optional rear axle having a four-pinion differential is also used.

The axle shafts are of unequal length, the left shaft being shorter than the right. The axle shafts are mounted in sealed ball bearings that are pressed on the shafts.

Diff. Carrier Assy.

Service Bulletin

All Ford Built Rear Axles: Recent manufacturing changes have eliminated the need for marking rear axle drive pinions for individual variations from nominal shim thicknesses. In the past, these pinion markings, with the aid of a shim selection table, were used as a guide to select correct shim thicknesses when a gear set or carrier assembly replacement was performed.

With the elimination of pinion markings, use of the shim selection table is no longer possible and the methods outlined below must be used.

1. Measure the thickness of the original pinion depth shim removed from the axle. Use the same thickness upon installation of the replacement carrier or drive pinion. If any further shim change is necessary, it will be indicated in the tooth pattern check.
2. If the original shim is lost, substitute a nominal shim for the original and use the tooth pattern check to determine if further shim changes are required.

Remove & Replace

In servicing the rear axles it is not necessary to remove the rear axle assembly for any normal repairs. The axle shafts and carrier assembly can easily be removed from the vehicle, leaving the axle housing in place.

1. Place a drain pan under the carrier and housing to catch the old grease when the carrier is separated from the housing.
2. Use a wire brush to clean dirt from the area around the carrier and housing mating surfaces. Then wipe the area clean with a cloth dampened in solvent.

3. Remove axle shafts and drive shaft as explained below.
4. Unfasten carrier from housing and lift out carrier.
5. Reverse removal procedure to install, using a new gasket between the carrier and housing.

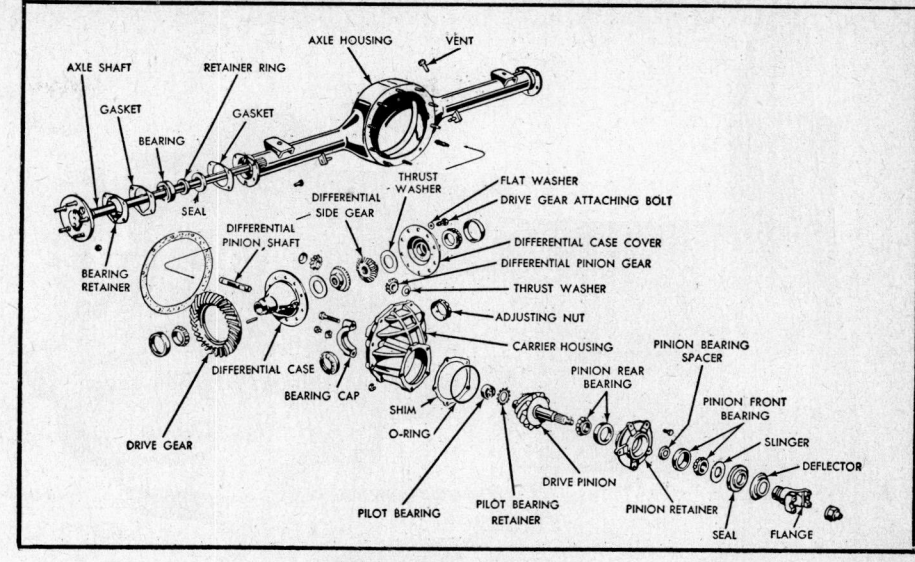

Fig. 1   Rear axle disassembled

AXLE SHAFTS
Removal

1. Remove wheel assembly.
2. Remove brake drum or caliper.
3. Working through hole provided in axle shaft flange, remove nuts that secure bearing retainer.
4. Pull axle shaft out of housing. If bearing is a tight fit in axle housing, use a slide hammer-type puller. *Brake carrier plate must not be dislodged. Install one nut to hold plate in place after axle shaft is removed.*
5. Loosen inner bearing retainer by nicking it deeply with a cold chisel in several places. On 1969-73 units with ball bearing axle bearings and 1974-75 units with tapered roller axle bearings, drill a $\frac{1}{4}$ inch hole not more than $\frac{5}{16}$ inch deep in retainer ring surface before using cold chisel. The bearing retainer will then slide off shaft easily.

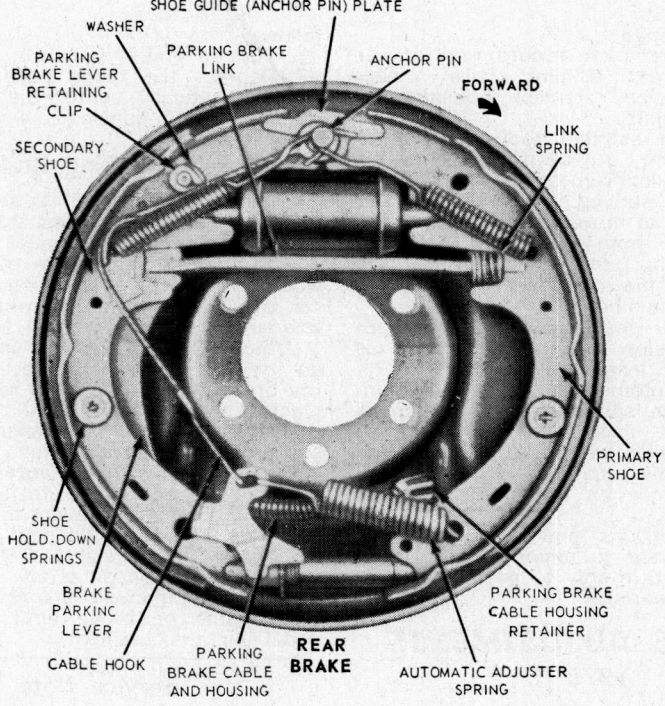

Fig. 2   Rear brake on 1969-75

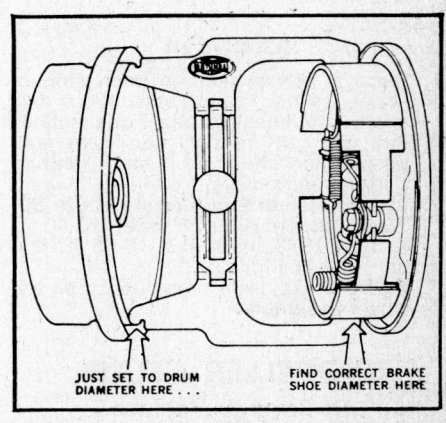

Fig. 3   Brake adjustment with gauge

Fig. 4 Caliper assembly. 1975 rear wheel disc brakes

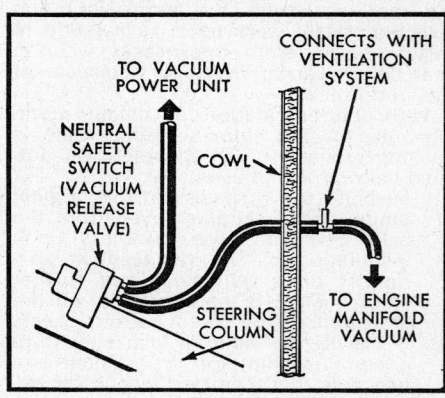

Fig. 5 Vacuum connections for automatic parking brake release. (typical)

6. Press bearing from axle shaft.
7. Inspect machined surfaces of axle shaft and housing for rough spots that would affect the sealing action of the oil seal. Carefully remove any burrs or rough spots.
8. Press new bearing on shaft until it seats firmly against shoulder on shaft.
9. Press inner bearing retainer on shaft until it seats firmly against bearing.
10. If oil seal is to be replaced, use a hook-type tool to pull it out of the housing. Wipe a small amount of oil resistant sealer on outer edge of seal before it is installed.

Installation

1. Place a new gasket on each side of brake carrier plate and slide axle shaft into housing. Start the splines into the differential side gear and push the shaft in until bearing bottoms in housing.
2. Install retainer and torque nuts to 50-75 ft. lbs. on 1969-72 units, 20-40 ft. lbs. on 1973 units and 35-55 ft. lbs. on 1974-75 units.
3. Install brake drum or caliper, then the wheel assembly.

PROPELLER SHAFT
Remove & Replace

1. Disconnect rear U-joint from drive

pinion flange.
2. Pull drive shaft toward rear of car until front U-joint yoke clears transmission extension housing and output shaft.
3. Install a suitable tool, such as a seal driver, in seal to prevent lube from leaking from transmission.
4. Before installing, check U-joints for freedom of movement. If a bind has resulted from misalignment after overhauling the U-joints, tap the ears of the drive shaft sharply to relieve the bind.
5. If rubber seal installed on end of transmission extension housing is damaged, install a new seal.
6. On an automatic transmission, lubricate yoke spline with special spline lubricant. *This spline is sealed so that transmission fluid does not "wash" away spline lubricant.*
7. Install yoke on transmission output shaft.
8. Install U-bolts and nuts which attach U-joint to pinion flange. Tighten U-bolts evenly to prevent binding U-joint bearings.

BRAKE ADJUSTMENTS
1970-75

A new self centering pressure differential valve is used which no longer requires bleeding at the opposite end of the car to cause the brake warning light to go out. This is now accomplished as

follows:
1. Turn on ignition switch.
2. Depress the brake pedal. This will automatically center the plunger in the switch causing the light to go out.

Self-Adjusting Brakes

These brakes, Fig. 2, have self-adjusting shoe mechanisms that assure correct lining-to-drum clearances at all times. The automatic adjusters operate only when the brakes are applied when the car is moving rearward or when it comes to an uphill stop.

Although the brakes are self-adjusting, an initial adjustment is necessary when the brake shoes have been relined or replaced, or when the length of the star wheel adjuster has been changed during some other service operation.

Frequent usage of an automatic transmission forward range to halt reverse vehicle motion may prevent the automatic adjusters from functioning, thereby inducing low pedal heights. Should low pedal heights be encountered, it is recommended that numerous forward and reverse stops be made until satisfactory pedal height is obtained.

Service Note

If a low pedal height condition cannot be corrected by making numerous reverse stops (provided the hydraulic system is free of air) it indicates that the self-adjusting mechanism is not functioning. Therefore, it will be necessary to remove the brake drum, clean, free up and lubricate the adjusting mechanism. Then adjust the brakes as follows, being sure the parking brake is fully released.

Adjustment

1. Remove adjusting hole cover from brake backing plate and, from the backing plate side, turn the adjusting screw upward with a screwdriver or other suitable tool to expand the shoes until a slight drag is felt when the drum is rotated.
2. Remove the drum.
3. While holding the adjusting lever out of engagement with the adjusting screw, back off the adjusting screw $3/4$ turn with the fingers.

NOTE—If finger movement will not turn the screw, free it up. If this is not done, the adjusting lever will not turn the screw during subsequent vehicle operation. Lubricate the screw with oil and coat with wheel bearing grease. Any other adjustment procedure may cause damage to the adjusting screw with consequent self-adjuster problems.

4. Install wheel and drum, and adjusting hole cover. Adjust brakes on remaining wheels in the same manner.
5. If pedal height is not satisfactory, drive the vehicle and make sufficient reverse stops until proper pedal height is obtained.

Revised Brake Adjustment

The adjustment is made with the drums removed, using the brake gauge shown in Fig. 3. With the gauge, determine the inside diameter of the drum braking surface. Reverse the tool as shown and adjust the brake shoe diameter to fit the gauge. Hold the automatic adjusting lever out of engagement while rotating the adjusting screw to prevent burring the screw slots. Rotate the gauge around the brake shoes to be sure of the setting. After the brake drums and wheels have been installed, complete the adjustment by applying the brakes several times while backing the vehicle.

REAR WHEEL DISC BRAKE & PARKING BRAKE SERVICE

Sliding caliper rear disc brakes are used on some 1975 models. The caliper is basically the same as the larger front wheel caliper, however, a parking brake mechanism and a larger inner brake shoe anti-rattle spring has been added, Fig. 4. A hydraulically powered brake booster (Hydroboost) provides the power assist for this four wheel disc brake system.

The parking brake lever, located at the rear of the caliper, is actuated by a cable system similar to rear drum brake applications. When the parking brake is applied, the cable rotates the lever and operating shaft. Three steel balls, placed in pockets

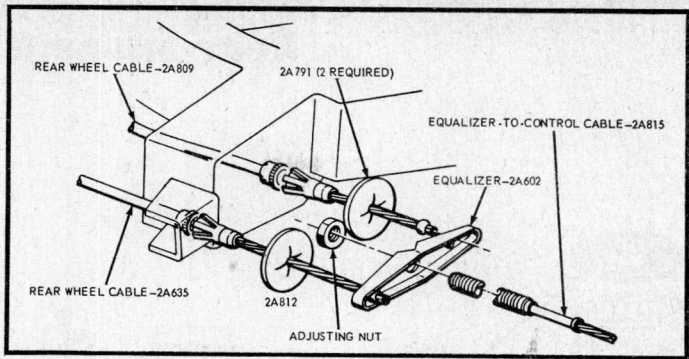

Fig. 6 Parking brake linkage. 1969-71

between the opposing heads of the operating shaft and thrust screw, roll between ramps formed in the pockets and force the thrust screw away from the operating shaft, in turn, driving the capiler piston and brake shoe assembly against the rotor. An automatic adjuster in the assembly compensates for lining wear and maintains proper clearance in the parking brake mechanism.

The cast iron rotors are ventilated by curved fins located between the braking surfaces and are designed to cause the rotor to act as an air pump when the vehicle is traveling forward. The rotors are not interchangeable and are identified by a Right or Left marking cast inside the hat section of the rotor. The rotor is secured to the axle flange in the same manner as a rear brake drum. A splash shield is bolted to a forged axle adapter to protect the inboard rotor surface.

NOTE: Refer to the "Lincoln Continental" chapter, "Transmission, Rear Axle, Propeller Shaft and Brake" section for service procedures.

PARKING BRAKE, ADJUST

1969-75 Vacuum Release Unit

The vacuum power unit, Fig. 5, will release the parking brake automatically when the transmission selector lever is moved into any driving position with the engine running. The brakes will not release automatically, however, when the selector lever is in neutral or park position with the engine running, or in any other position with the engine off.

The lower end of the release handle extends out for alternate manual release in the event of vacuum power failure or for optional manual release at any time.

1970-75

1. Make sure parking brake is released.
2. Place transmission in neutral and raise the vehicle.
3. Tighten the adjusting nut against the cable equalizer to cause rear brakes to drag.
4. Then loosen the adjusting nut until the rear wheels are fully released. There should be no drag.
5. Lower vehicle and check operation.

1969

1. Check the parking cables when the

brakes are fully released. If the cables are loose, adjust as follows:
2. Fully release parking brake pedal by pushing down the manual release lever.
3. Depress the parking brake pedal approximately $1 1/4"$.
4. Raise the vehicle. With the transmission in neutral, turn the adjusting nut forward against the equalizer, Fig. 6, until a moderate drag is felt when turning the rear wheels (approximately 100 lbs. of force at the outside diameter of the tire is required to turn the rear wheels).
5. Release the parking brake and check to be sure the brake shoes return to the fully released position.
6. Depress the parking brake pedal until it is fully engaged.
7. Release the parking brake again and check as in step 5.
8. If the rear brakes do not fully release, check the cables for kinks or binds and free as required.
9. Depress parking brake pedal $2"$. Under normal conditions this will satisfactorily hold the car.
10. Release pedal again, then depress pedal $1/2"$; the brakes should not drag.

POWER BRAKE UNIT, REPLACE

1. Disconnect vacuum hose at booster.
2. Remove three bolts and loosen one to allow brace between cowl and spring tower to be positioned inboard to obtain clearance.
3. Remove master cylinder from booster. It is not necessary to disconnect brake lines.
4. Working under instrument panel, disconnect booster push rod link from brake pedal as follows: 1) disconnect stop light switch wires at connector and remove hairpin clip, 2) slide stop light switch off pedal just far enough for switch outer hole to clear pin, then tilt switch straight upward from pin, 3) slide master cylinder push rod and nylon washer and bushing from brake pedal pin.
5. Unfasten and remove booster from dash panel, sliding push rod link out from engine side of dash panel.
6. Remove dust seal from push rod link and place it in slot of dash panel for installation.
7. Reverse procedure to install.

Rear Suspension

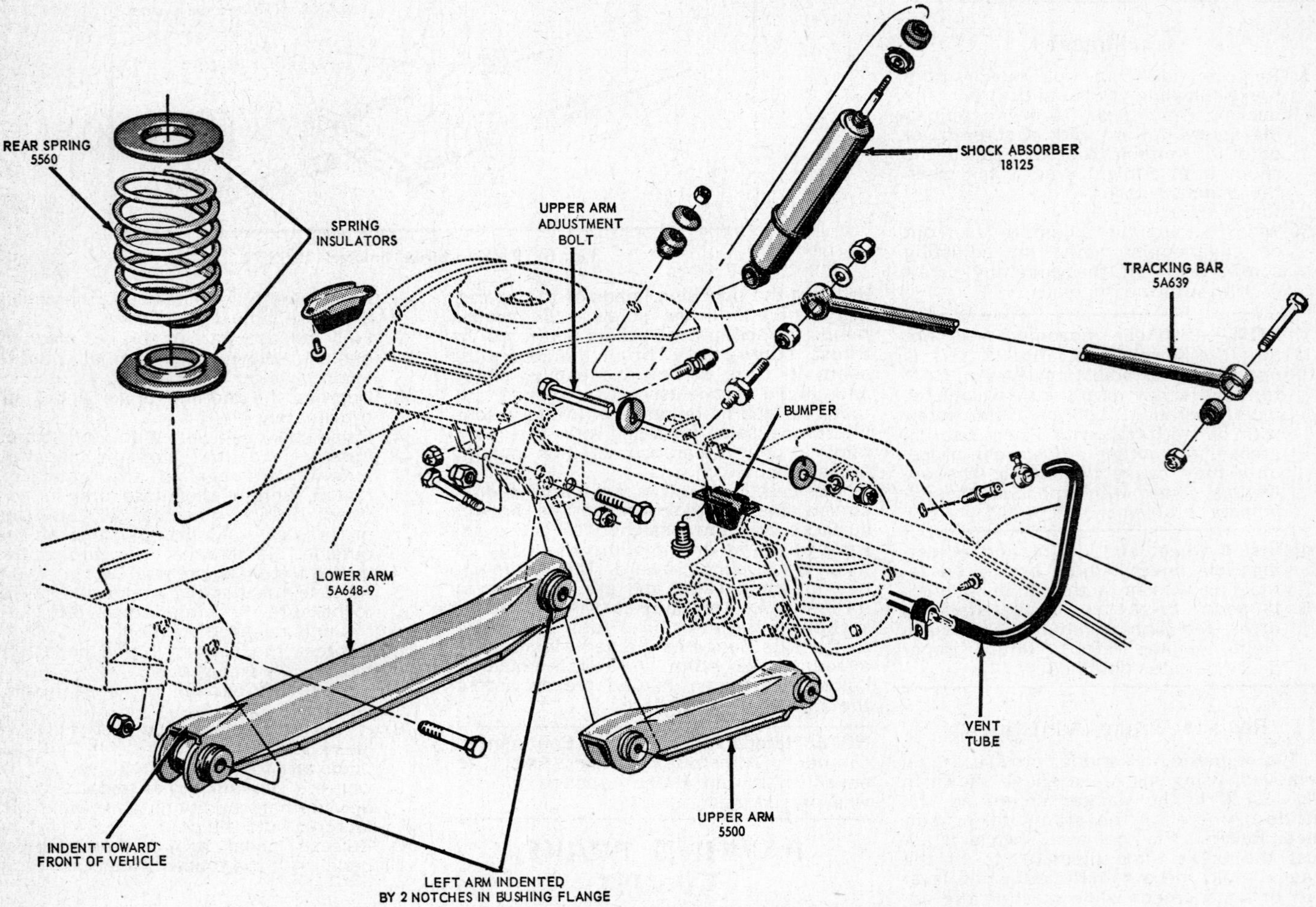

REAR SPRING
5560

SPRING
INSULATORS

UPPER ARM
ADJUSTMENT
BOLT

SHOCK ABSORBER
18125

TRACKING BAR
5A639

BUMPER

LOWER ARM
5A648-9

VENT
TUBE

INDENT TOWARD
FRONT OF VEHICLE

UPPER ARM
5500

LEFT ARM INDENTED
BY 2 NOTCHES IN BUSHING FLANGE

Fig. 1   Rear suspension, 1969-71 models (typical)

SHOCK ABSORBER, REPLACE

1. With rear axle supported properly disconnect shock absorber at upper mounting and compress it to clear hole in spring seat.
2. Disconnect shock absorber from stud on axle bracket.
3. Reverse procedure to install.

COIL SPRINGS, REPLACE

1. Raise rear of vehicle and support at frame. Support rear axle with a suitable jack.
2. Disconnect shock absorbers at lower mountings.
3. On 1973 models, disconnect brake line from rear brake hose and remove hose to bracket clip.
4. Lower axle to remove springs.
5. Reverse procedure to install. On 1969-71, install an insulator between upper

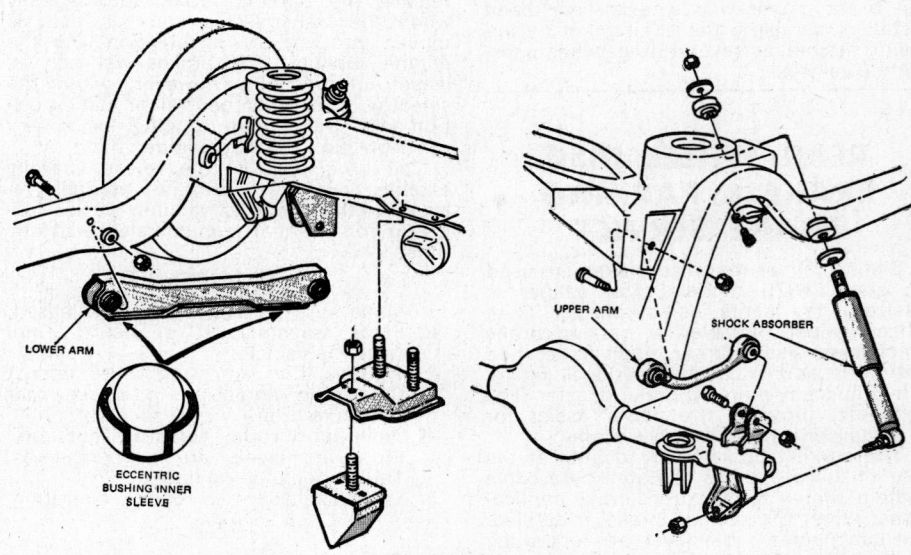

LOWER ARM

ECCENTRIC
BUSHING INNER
SLEEVE

UPPER ARM

SHOCK ABSORBER

Fig. 2   Rear suspension, 1972-75 models

and lower seats and the spring, Fig. 1. On 1972-75, an insulator is installed only between upper seat and the spring, Fig. 2.

CONTROL ARMS, REPLACE

NOTE: On 1972-75 models, upper and lower control arms must be replaced in pairs.

1. Raise rear of vehicle and support at frame. Support axle with a suitable jack.
2. On 1969-71 models, disconnect track bar from frame mounting bracket, Fig. 1.
3. On all models lower axle and install a second jack under differential pinion nose.
4. Disconnect control arm from axle bracket. On upper arms, disconnect arm from crossmember and on lower arms, disconnect arm from frame attachment bracket.
5. Reverse procedure to install.

STABILIZER BAR, REPLACE

1972-75

1. Remove bolts securing stabilizer bar to rear link assemblies on both sides, Fig. 3.
2. Remove nuts securing mounting bracket to lower mounting clamp and remove bar.
3. Reverse procedure to install.

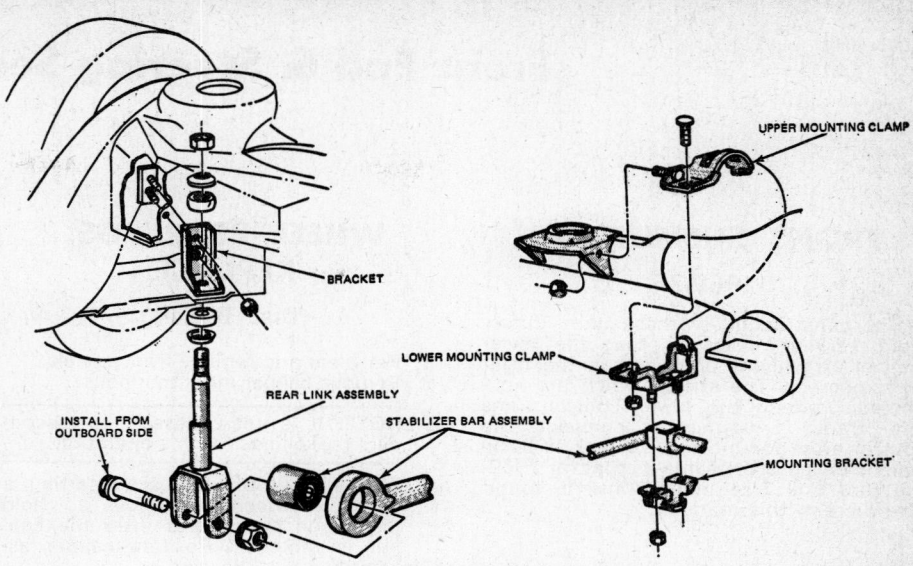

Fig. 3   Stabilizer bar installation, 1972-75 models

TRACK BAR & BUSHING, REPLACE

1969-71

1. Remove cover from track bar axle attachment, then disconnect track bar from mounting stud.
2. Disconnect track bar from frame side rail.
3. On 1970-71 models, replace frame bracket bushing, by collapsing the .030 inch ferrule and driving from bushing. Install bushing and new inner ferrule and compress bushing and washer to 2.16 inch and place inner ferrule over edge of inner washer.
4. Reverse procedure to install.

Front End & Steering Section

FRONT SUSPENSION

1969-75

The construction of these units differs from earlier models in that the lower control arm pivots on a bolt in the front crossmember. The struts, which are connected between the lower control arms and frame crossmember, prevent the control arms for moving forward or backward. Service is the same as that for 1969-75 Ford Full Size models and is found elsewhere in this manual.

LUBRICATION

Lubrication should be performed at 36,000-mile intervals at which time the special plugs should be removed and specially formulated grease applied with a hand-operated gun. This extended lubrication interval is made possible by a special type chassis lubricant combined with special seals and bearing materials. Under no circumstances should the special plugs be removed and fittings installed to accommodate conventional type grease as damage to the special seals may result.

WHEEL ALIGNMENT

1969-75

Wheel alignment is adjusted in the same manner as described for 1969-75 Ford Full Size models and is found elsewhere in this manual.

TOE-IN, ADJUST

Turn both tie rod adjusting sleeves an equal amount until toe-in is correct.

WHEEL BEARINGS, ADJUST

1969-75

1. With wheel rotating, tighten adjusting nut to 17-25 ft. lbs.
2. Back off adjusting nut ½ turn and retighten nut to 10-15 inch lbs.
3. Place nut lock on nut so that castellations on lock are aligned with cotter pin hole in spindle and install cotter pin.
4. Check front wheel rotation, if it rotates noisily or rough, clean, inspect or replace wheel bearings as necessary.

WHEEL BEARINGS, REPLACE

(Disc Brakes)

1. Raise car and remove front wheels.
2. Remove caliper mounting bolts.

NOTE: It is not necessary to disconnect brake lines for this operation.

3. Slide caliper off of disc, inserting a spacer between the shoes to hold pistons in their bores after the caliper is removed. Position caliper assembly out of the way.

NOTE: Do not allow caliper to hang by the brake line.

4. Remove hub and disc assembly. Grease retainer and inner bearing can now be removed.

CHECKING BALL JOINTS FOR WEAR

If loose ball joints are suspected, first be sure the front wheel bearings are properly adjusted and that the control arms are tight.

On 1969-75 models, the upper ball joint should be replaced if there is any noticeable looseness at the joint. Lower ball joint should be replaced if radial play exceeds .250″, and if there is any noticeable axial play at the joint.

BALL JOINTS, REPLACE

The upper and lower ball joints are riveted to the control arms. On later models, the upper ball joint is pressed into the upper control arm whereas the lower ball joint is riveted to the lower control arm.

When replacing a riveted ball joint, remove the rivets and retain the ball joint to its control arm with the bolts, nuts and washers furnished with the ball joint kit. Also, use a suitable pressing tool to force the ball joint studs out of the spindle.

SHOCK ABSORBER, REPLACE

1969-75

To remove a shock absorber, unfasten

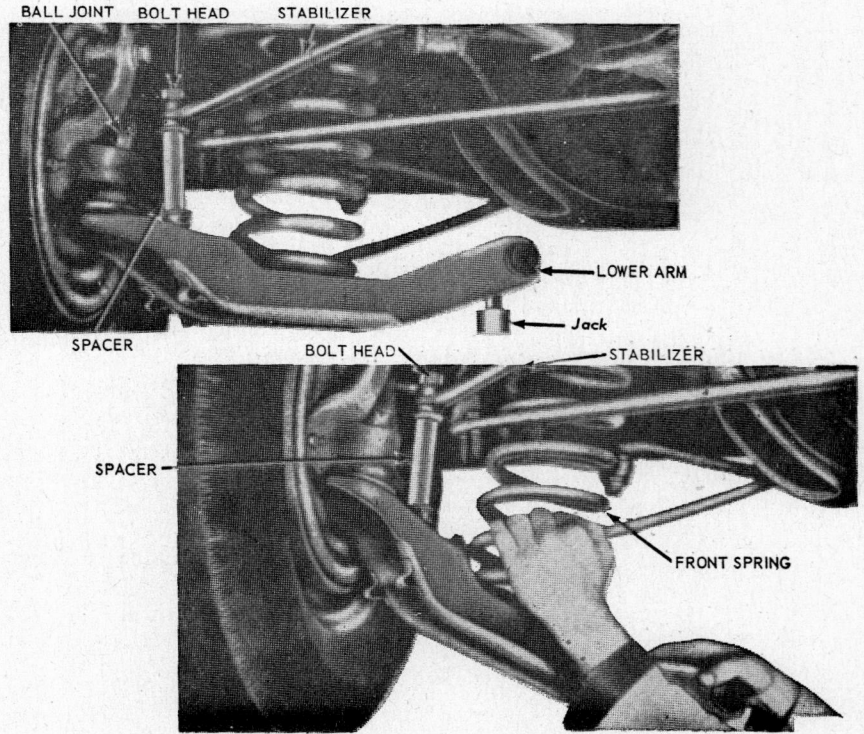

Fig. 1 Coil spring removal & installation

it from the frame at its upper end. Remove the two cap screws that retain the shock absorber mounting plate to the lower control arm and lower the shock absorber unit.

To install, reverse the removal procedure and tighten the two lower cap screws to 13-18 lbs. ft. torque.

COIL SPRING, REPLACE
1969-75

1. Raise vehicle and support front end of frame with jack stands.
2. Disconnect shock absorber from lower arm and place a jack under the lower arm for support, Fig. 1.
3. Remove strut and rebound bumper bolts and disconnect lower end of sway bar stud from lower arm.
4. Remove the nut and bolt that retains the inner end of the lower arm to the crossmember.
5. Carefully lower jack to relieve the spring pressure on the lower arm, then remove the spring.

POWER STEERING, REPLACE
1969-75

1. Disconnect pressure and return lines from steering gear. Cap each line and plug each port to prevent entry of dirt.
2. Remove bolt that secures flex joint to steering gear.
3. Raise the vehicle and remove sector shaft nut and pitman arm.

NOTE: Do not damage seals.

4. Support steering gear and remove three retaining bolts. Remove flex coupling clamp bolt and work steering gear free of coupling and remove from vehicle.

LINCOLN CONTINENTAL

OLD CAR SPECIFICATIONS: For 1946-68 Tune Up and Wheel Alignment Specifications see main index.

INDEX OF SERVICE OPERATIONS

ACCESSORIES   PAGE NO.

Air conditioning 2-20
Automatic Level Controls 2-39
Blower Motor, Remove 1-547
Clock Troubles 2-11
Heater Core, Replace 1-547
Power Top Troubles 2-18
Power Window Troubles 2-18
Radio, Replace 1-545
Speed Controls, Adjust 1-546

BRAKES

Anti-Skid Brakes 2-162
Brake Troubles, Mechanical 2-17
Disc Brake Service:
    Front 2-133
    Rear 1-555
Hydraulic System Service 2-123
Parking Brake, Adjust 1-559
Power Brake Unit, Replace 1-559
Service Brakes, Adjust 1-554
Vacuum Release Parking Brake Unit 1-559

COOLING SYSTEM

Cooling System Troubles 2-6
Variable Speed Fans 2-38
Water Pump, Replace 1-551

ELECTRICAL

Alternator Service 2-69
Blower Motor, Remove 1-547
Dash Gauge Service 2-50
Distributor, Replace 2-538
Distributor Service:
    Standard 2-525
    Transistorized 2-535
Electrical Troubles 2-8
Headlamps, Concealed Type 2-46
Headlight Aiming 2-45
Horn Sounder, Remove 1-541
Ignition Coils and Resistors 2-521
Ignition Lock, Replace 1-538
Ignition Switch, Replace 1-538
Ignition Timing 2-518
Instrument Cluster Removal 1-541
Light Switch, Replace 1-538
Neutral Safety Switch, Replace 1-540
Starter Service 2-54
Starter, Replace 1-538
Starter Switch Service 2-67
Stop Light Switch, Replace 1-540
Turn Signal Switch, Replace 1-541
Turn Signal Troubles 2-11
Windshield Wiper Motor, Replace 1-543
Windshield Wiper Troubles 2-19

ENGINE   PAGE NO.

Camshaft, Replace 1-550
Cylinder Head, Replace 1-548
Engine Identification 1-533
Engine Mounts 1-548
Engine, Replace 1-548
Engine Troubles 2-1
Main Bearings 1-550
Piston Pins 1-550
Piston Rings 1-550
Piston and Rod, Assemble 1-550
Pistons 1-550
Rocker Arm Stud 1-549
Rod Bearings 1-550
Timing Case Cover, Replace 1-549
Timing Chain, Replace 1-549
Valves, Adjust 1-548
Valve Arrangement 1-549
Valve Guides 1-549
Valve Lifters 1-549

ENGINE LUBRICATION

Emission Control Systems 2-545
Oil Pan, Replace 1-551
Oil Pump, Repairs 1-551

FUEL SYSTEM

Carburetor Adjustment and Specs. 2-372
1975 Carburetors 1-716
Emission Control Systems 2-545
Fuel Pump, Replace 1-552
Fuel Pump Service 2-369
Fuel System Troubles 2-2

PROPELLER SHAFT & U JOINTS

Propeller Shaft 1-553
Universal Joint Service 2-117

REAR AXLE & SUSPENSION

Axle Shaft, Bearing and Seal 1-553
Coil Springs, Replace 1-559
Control Arms, Replace 1-559
Rear Axle Description 1-552
Rear Axle Troubles 2-16
Shock Absorber, Replace 1-559
Stabilizer Bar, Replace 1-560
Track Bar & Bushings, Replace 1-561

SPECIFICATIONS

Alternator 1-537
Belt Tension 1-551
Brakes 1-536

PAGE NO.

Capacities 1-537
Carburetors 2-372
Cooling System 1-537
Crankshaft and Bearings 1-536
Distributors 1-535
Engine Tightening Torque 1-537
Fuel Pump Pressure 1-551
General Engine Spec. 1-533
Ignition Coils and Resistors 2-521
Pistons, Rings and Pins 1-536
Rear Axle 1-536
Starting Motors 1-536
Tune Up 1-534
Valve Lift 1-549
Valve Timing 1-549
Valves 1-535
Wheel Alignment 1-538

STEERING GEAR

Horn Sounder, Removal 1-541
Power Gear, Replace 1-564
Steering Wheel, Replace 1-541

SUSPENSION, FRONT

Ball Joints, Check for Wear 1-563
Ball Joints, Replace 1-563
Coil Spring, Replace 1-563
Lubrication 1-561
Shock Absorber, Replace 1-563
Suspension, Description of 1-561
Toe-In, Adjust 1-562
Wheel Alignment, Adjust 1-561
Wheel Bearings, Adjust 1-563
Wheel Bearings, Replace 1-563

AUTOMATIC TRANSMISSIONS 2-231

    1975 Linkage 1-552

TUNE UP

Service 2-517
Specifications 1-534

WINDSHIELD WIPER

Wiper Arms 1-543
Wiper Blades 1-543
Wiper Linkage, Replace 1-544
Wiper Motor, Replace 1-543
Wiper Switch, Replace 1-545
Wiper Troubles 2-19

SERIAL & ENGINE NUMBER LOCATION
Vehicle Warranty Plate on Left Front Door Pillar

1969 Continental

1969-71 Mark III

1970 Continental

1971 Continental

ENGINE IDENTIFICATION
*Serial number on vehicle Warranty Plate.

Engine code for 1969–75 is the last letter in the serial number.

Year	Engine	Engine Code*
1969–75	V8-460	A

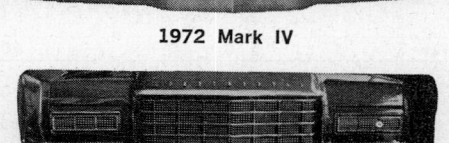

1972 Mark IV

1973 Continental

1974 Lincoln

1974 Mark IV

1975 Mark IV

1975 Continental

1972 Continental

1973 Mark IV

1975 Continental

GENERAL ENGINE SPECIFICATIONS

Year	Engine	Car-buretor	Bore and Stroke	Piston Dis-place-ment, Cubic Inches	Com-pres-sion Ratio	Maximum Brake H.P. @ R.P.M.	Maximum Torque Lbs. Ft. @ R.P.M.	Normal Oil Pressure Pounds
1969–70	365 Horsepower.............V8-460	4 Barrel	4.3600 x 3.850	460	10.5	365 @ 4600	500 @ 2800	35–60
1971	365 Horsepower.............V8-460	4 Barrel	4.3600 x 3.850	460	10.2	365 @ 4600	500 @ 2800	35–60
1972	212 Horsepower①..........V8-460	4 Barrel	4.3600 x 3.850	460	8.50	212 @ 4400	342 @ 2800	35–60
	224 Horsepower①..........V8-460	4 Barrel	4.3600 x 3.850	460	8.50	224 @ 4400	357 @ 2800	35–60
1973	208 Horsepower①..........V8-460	4 Barrel	4.3600 x 3.850	460	8.0	208 @ 4400	338 @ 2800	35–70
	219 Horsepower①..........V8-460	4 Barrel	4.3600 x 3.850	460	8.0	219 @ 4400	360 @ 2800	35–70
1974	215 Horsepower①..........V8-460	4 Barrel	4.362 x 3.850	460	8.0	215 @ 4000	350 @ 2600	35–65
	220 Horsepower①..........V8-460	4 Barrel	4.362 x 3.85	460	8.0	220 @ 4000	355 @ 2600	35–65
1975	253 Horsepower.............V8-460	4 Barrel	4.362 x 3.85	460	8.0	253 @ 4400	386 @ 2600	35–62

①—Ratings are NET—as installed in the vehicle.

TUNE UP SPECIFICATIONS

OLD CAR SPECIFICATIONS: For 1946-68 Wheel Alignment Specifications see main index.

★When using a timing light, disconnect vacuum hose or tube at distributor and plug opening in hose or tube so idle speed will not be affected.

●When checking compression, lowest cylinder must be within 75 percent of highest.

▲Before removing wires from distributor cap, determine location of No. 1 wire in cap, as distributor position may have been altered from that shown at the end of this chart.

Year	Spark Plug		Distributor		Ignition Timing ★			Carb. Adjustments					
								Hot Idle Speed		Air Fuel Ratio		Idle CO %	
	Type	Gap Inch	Point Gap Inch	Dwell Angle Deg.	Firing Order Fig. ▲	Timing BTDC ①	Mark Fig.	Std. Trans.	Auto. Trans.②	Std. Trans.	Auto. Trans.	Std. Trans.	Auto. Trans.
1969													
V8-460③	BRF-42	.034	.017	26–31	C	10°⑥	B	—	550D⑤	—	14.3 to 1	—	1.2
1970													
V8-460	BRF-42	.034	.017	26–31	C	10°⑥	A	—	600D⑦	—	14.4 to 1	—	1.0
1971													
V8-460	BRF-42	.034	.017	26–31	C	5°⑥	D	—	600D⑦	—	14.2 to 1	—	0.9
1972													
V8-460 Exc. Calif.	BF-42	.034	.017	26–30	C	10°⑥	D	—	625D⑦	—	—	—	0.3
V8-460 Calif.	BF-42	.034	.017	26–30	C	6°⑥	D	—	625D⑦	—	—	—	0.3
1973													
V8-460	ARF-42	.034	.017	24–30	C	14°	D	—	600D	—	—	—	0.4⑩
1974													
V8-460	ARF-52	.054	⑪	—	C	14°	D	—	650D	—	—	—	—
1975													
V8-460	ARF-52	.044	⑪	—	C	14°	D	—	650D	—	—	—	—

①—BTDC-Before top dead center.
②—D-Drive. N-Neutral.
③—With IMCO system.
⑥—With headlights on and A/C "Full On".

⑥—Whenever idle speed or ignition timing is adjusted, vacuum line to brake release mechanism must be disconnected and plugged to prevent parking brake from releasing when selector is moved to Drive.

⑦—Headlamps on Hi Beam—Air Conditioner OFF.
⑩—For California 0.2.
⑪—Breakerless distributor.

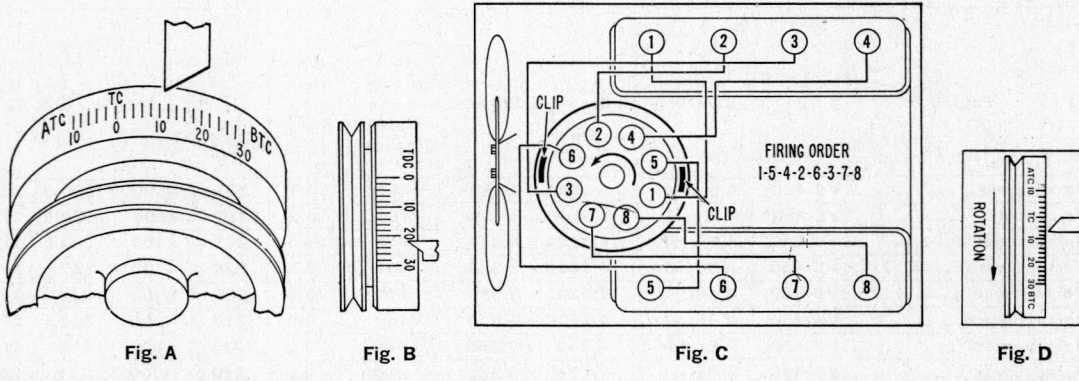

Fig. A   Fig. B   Fig. C   Fig. D

FIRING ORDER 1-5-4-2-6-3-7-8

DISTRIBUTOR SPECIFICATIONS

★Note: If unit is checked on vehicle, double the RPM and degrees to get crankshaft figures.

Breaker arm spring tension—17–21.

| Distributor Part No.① | Centrifugal Advance Degrees @ RPM of Distributor | | | | | Vacuum Advance | | Distributor Retard |
	Advance Starts	Intermediate Advance			Full Advance	Inches of Vacuum to Start Plunger	Max. Adv. Dist. Deg. @ Vacuum	Max. Retard Dist. Deg. @ Vacuum
1969								
C8VF-G	0–½ @ 350	¾–2¾ @ 750	4½–6½ @ 1000	6–8¼ @ 1500	11 @ 2575	5	12 @ 25	—
1970								
D0VF-B	0–½ @ 350	¾–2¾ @ 750	4½–6½ @ 1000	6–8¼ @ 1500	11 @ 2575	5	12 @ 25	—
1971								
D1VF-AA	0–½ @ 350	¾–2¾ @ 750	4½–6½ @ 1000	6–8¼ @ 1500	13 @ 2500	5	8½ @ 25	—
1972								
D2VF-AA	0–1 @ 500	1½–3½ @ 750	5½–7½ @ 1000	7–9 @ 1500	10½ @ 2000	5	11½ @ 20	—
D2VF-BA	0–1 @ 500	1–3 @ 750	6½–8½ @ 1000	7½–10 @ 1500	11½ @ 2000	5	12 @ 20	—
1973								
D3VF-AA	0–1 @ 500	0–1½ @ 750	3–5 @ 1000	4–6 @ 1500	7½ @ 2000	5	11 @ 20	—
D3VF-BA	0–1 @ 500	0–2½ @ 750	5–7 @ 1000	7½–10 @ 1500	12 @ 2000	5	7 @ 20	—
D3VF-AA	0–1 @ 500	0–1½ @ 750	4–6 @ 1000	6–8 @ 1500	10 @ 2000	5	11 @ 20	—
1974-75								
D4VE-CA	0–½ @ 500	0–½ @ 750	3–5 @ 1000	7–9 @ 1500	9½ @ 2000	5	11¼ @ 20	—

①—Basic part No. 12127.

VALVE SPECIFICATIONS

| Year | Engine Model | Valve Lash | | Valve Angles | | Valve Spring Installed Height | Valve Spring Pressure Lbs. @ In. | Stem Clearance | | Stem Diameter | |
		Int.	Exh.	Seat	Face			Intake	Exhaust	Intake	Exhaust
1968–74	V8-460	②④		45	44	1¹³⁄₁₆	⑧	.0010–.0027	.0010–.0027	.3416–.3423	..3416–.3423
1975	V8-460	.075–.175		45	45	1¹³⁄₁₆	248 @ 1.33	.0010–.0027	.0010–.0027	.3416–.3423	.3416–.3423

②—Valve lifter adjustment is 1 turn down after contact. Check as in note①.
⑧—1969-72 and 1974 80 @ 1.810; 1973 75 @ 1.78.
④—1969-70, .075–.125; 1971–73; .105–.155; 1974, .075–.125.

LINCOLN CONTINENTAL

STARTING MOTOR SPECIFICATIONS

Year	Car Model	Ident. No.	Brush Spring Tension Ounces	No Load Test			Torque Test		
				Amperes	Volts	R.P.M.	Amperes	Volts	Torque Lbs. Ft.
1969	All	C9AF-A	40	70	12	10000	700	5.0	15½
1970–71	All	D0VF-A	40	70	12	10000	700	5.0	15½
1972–73	All	D2VF-AA	40	70	12	10000	700	5.0	15½
1974	All	D4VF-AB	—	—	—	—	—	—	—
1975	All	D5AF-AB	80	—	—	—	—	—	—

PISTONS, PINS, RINGS, CRANKSHAFT & BEARINGS

Year	Model	Piston Clearance	Ring End Gap①		Wrist-pin Diameter	Rod Bearings		Main Bearings			
			Comp.	Oil		Shaft Diameter	Bearing Clearance	Shaft Diameter	Bearing Clearance	Thrust on Bear. No.	Shaft End Play
1969–73	V8-460	.0014–.0022	.010	.015	1.040	2.4992–2.5000	.0008–.0015	2.9994–3.0002	.0005–.0015	3	.004–.008
1974	V8-460	.0022–.0030	.010	.015	1.040	2.4992–2.5000	.0008–.0028	2.9994–3.0002	②	3	.004–.008
1975	V8-460	.0013–.0023	.010	.015	1.040	2.4992–2.500	.0008–.0028	2.9998	②	3	.004–.008

①—Fit rings in tapered bores for clearance listed in tightest portion of ring travel.
②—#1 .0004–.002; others .0012–.0028.

BRAKE SPECIFICATIONS

Year	Model	Brake Drum Inside Diameter	Wheel Cylinder Bore Diameter			Master Cylinder Bore Diameter		
			Front Disc Brakes	Front Drum Brakes	Rear Brakes	With Disc Brakes	With Drum Brakes	With Power Brakes
1969	Lincoln	11.090	1.938	—	15⁄16	1	1	1
1969–70	Mark III	11.030	2.755	—	15⁄16	1		1
1970	Lincoln	11.090	2.755	—	15⁄16	1		1
1971	All	11.030	2.755	—	15⁄16	1		1
1972–74	Lincoln	11.030	3.100	—	1.000①	1		1
	Mark IV	11.030	3.100	—	1.000	1		1
1975	Lincoln	11.03	3.1	—	1②	1⅛	—	1⅛
	Mark IV	③	3.1	—	2.6	1⅛	—	1⅛

①—1972 Lincoln .938.
②—On models with 4 wheel disc brakes, 2.6".
③—4 wheel disc brakes.

REAR AXLE SPECIFICATIONS

Year	Model	Carrier Type	Ring Gear & Pinion Backlash Inch	Nominal Pinion Locating Shim, Inch	Pinion Bearing Preload				Differential Bearing Preload	Pinion Nut Torque Ft.-Lbs.
					New Bearings With Seal Inch-Lbs.	Used Bearings With Seal Inch-Lbs.	New Bearings Less Seal Inch-Lbs.	Used Bearings Less Seal Inch-Lbs.		
1969	All	Removable	.008–.012	.015	15–35	—	12½–32½	—	.008–.012②	200①
1970–72	All	Removable	.008–.012	.015	8–14③	20–30③	—	—	.008–.012②	④
1973–74	All	Removable	.008–.012	.015	17–27③	8–14③	—	—	.008–.012②	④

①—If torque cannot be obtained, install new spacer.
②—Case spread with new bearings; with used bearings .005–.008".
③—Bearing set with collapsible spacer; with solid spacer 13–33 inch-lbs.
④—With collapsible spacer 170 ft. lbs., with solid spacer 200 ft. lbs.

ALTERNATOR & REGULATOR SPECIFICATIONS

Year	Make or Model①	Current Rating② Amperes	Current Rating② Volts	Field Current @ 75°F. Amperes	Field Current @ 75°F. Volts	Voltage Regulator③ Make or Model⑥	Voltage Regulator③ Voltage @ 75°F.	Voltage Regulator③ Contact Gap	Voltage Regulator③ Armature Air Gap	Field Relay Armature Air Gap	Field Relay Closing Voltage @ 75°F.
1969–72	D0AZ-F	55	15	2.8–3.3	12	C3SZ-B⑤	—	—	—	—	—
1973	All	61	15	2.9	12	D3TZ-A	13.5–15.3	—	—	—	2.5–4.0
	All	70	15	2.9	12	D3TZ-A	13.5–15.3	—	—	—	2.5–4.0
	All	90	15	2.9	12	D3TZ-A	13.5–15.3	—	—	—	2.5–4.0
1974	All Red	55	15	2.9	12	D4TZ-A	—	—	—	—	—
	All Green	61	15	2.9	12	D4TZ-A	—	—	—	—	—
	All	70	15	2.9	12	D4TZ-A	—	—	—	—	—
	All	90	15	2.9	12	D4TZ-A	—	—	—	—	—
1975	Green	61	—	—	—	D4TF-AA	13.5–15.3	—	—	—	2.5–4.0
	All	70	—	—	—	D4TF-AA	13.5–15.3	—	—	—	2.5–4.0
	All	90	—	—	—	D3VF-AB	13.5–15.3	—	—	—	2.5–4.0

①—Basic No. 10300.
②—Stamped on housing.
③—Stamped on cover.
⑤—Integral regulator solid state.
⑥—Basic No. 10316.

ENGINE TIGHTENING SPECIFICATIONS*

★Torque specifications are for clean and lightly lubricated threads only. Dry or dirty threads produce increased friction which prevents accurate measurement of tightness.

Year	Spark Plugs Ft. Lbs.	Cylinder Head Bolts Ft. Lbs.	Intake Manifold Ft. Lbs.	Exhaust Manifold Ft. Lbs.	Rocker Arm Shaft Bracket Ft. Lbs.	Rocker Arm Cover Ft. Lbs.	Connecting Rod Cap Bolts Ft. Lbs.	Main Bearing Cap Bolts Ft. Lbs.	Flywheel to Crankshaft Ft. Lbs.	Vibration Damper or Pulley Ft. Lbs.
1969–73 V8-460	15–20	130–140	25–30	28–33	65–75①	5–6	40–45	95–105	75–85	75–90
1974–75 V8-460	15–20	130–140	22–32	28–33	18–25①	5–6	40–45	95–105	75–85	70–90

①—Rocker arm stud.

COOLING SYSTEM & CAPACITY DATA

Year	Model or Engine	Cooling Capacity, Qts. No Heater	Cooling Capacity, Qts. With Heater	Cooling Capacity, Qts. With A/C	Radiator Cap Relief Pressure, Lbs. With A/C	Radiator Cap Relief Pressure, Lbs. No A/C	Thermo. Opening Temp.①	Fuel Tank Gals.	Engine Oil Refill Qts.②	Transmission Oil 3 Speed Pints	Transmission Oil 4 Speed Pints	Transmission Oil Auto. Trans. Qts.③	Rear Axle Oil Pints
1969	V8-462	22½	23½	23½	12–15	12–15	185	25½	4	—	—	13½	5
	V8-460	—	22	22	12–15	12–15	185	25½	4	—	—	13½	5
1970	Lincoln	—	20½	—	12–15	12–15	188	24④	4	—	—	13	5
	Mark III	—	20½	—	12–15	12–15	188	24④	4	—	—	12¾	5
1971	Lincoln	—	19½	19½	12–15	12–15	188	23	4	—	—	13	5
	Mark III	—	19½	19½	12–15	12–15	188	23	4	—	—	12¾	5
1972–73	Lincoln	—	19½	19½	12–15	12–15	188	22	4	—	—	13⑤	5
	Mark IV	—	19½	19½	12–15	12–15	188	22½	4	—	—	12¾⑤	5
1974	Lincoln	—	20½	20½	12–16	12–16	191	22	4	—	—	12½	5
	Mark IV	—	20½	20½	12–16	12–16	191	26½	4	—	—	12½	5
1975	Lincoln	—	—	19¾	12–16	12–16	191	24¼	4	—	—	12½	5
	Mark IV	—	—	20	12–16	12–16	191	26½	4	—	—	12½	5

①—With alcohol type anti-freeze, use a 160° unit.
②—Add one quart with filter change.
③—Approximate. Make final check with dipstick.
④—California vehicles 22½.
⑤—1973 Models 12½ quarts.

WHEEL ALIGNMENT SPECIFICATIONS

OLD CAR SPECIFICATIONS: For 1946-68 Wheel Alignment Specifications see main index.

Year	Model	Caster Angle, Degrees		Camber Angle, Degrees				Toe-In. Inch	Toe-Out on Turns, Deg.①	
		Limits	Desired	Limits		Desired			Outer Wheel	Inner Wheel
				Left	Right	Left	Right			
1969	Lincoln	−½ to −2½	−1½	−¼ to +1¼	−¼ to +1¼	+½	+½	⅛	17¾	20
1969–70	Mark III	0 to +2	+1	−¼ to +1¼	−¼ to +1¼	+½	+½	3/16	19¼	20
1971–74	Lincoln	−½ to +3½	+1½	−½ to +1½	−½ to +1½	+½	+½	⅛	②	20
1971	Mark III	−1 to +3	+1	−½ to +1½	−½ to +1½	+½	+½	3/16	19.28	20
1972	Mark IV	−1 to +3	+1	−¼ to +1¾	−¼ to +1¾	+¾	+¾	3/16	17.74	20
1973	Mark IV	−½ to +3½	+1½	−¼ to +1¾	−¼ to +1¾	+¾	+¾	3/16	17.74	20
1974	Mark IV	+¼ to +3¼	+1¾	−¼ to +1¾	−¾ to +1¼	+¾	+¼	3/16	18.07	20
1975	Lincoln	−½ to +3½	+1½	−½ to +1½	−½ to +1½	+½	+½	⅛	18.16	20
	Mark IV	+2¼ to +5¼	+3¾	−¼ to +1¾	−¾ to +1¼	+¾	+¼	3/16	18.09	20

①—Incorrect toe-out, when other adjustments are correct, indicates bent steering arms.

②—1971 18.70; 1972 18.43; 1973-74 18.16.

Electrical Section

DISTRIBUTOR, REPLACE

1. On vehicles with conventional ignition systems, disconnect primary wire from ignition coil. On vehicles with breakerless ignition systems, disconnect distributor wiring from connector from main wiring harness.
2. Disconnect vacuum advance lines and remove distributor cap.
3. Scibe a mark on distributor body and engine block indicating position of rotor in distributor and distributor in engine.
4. Remove distributor hold-down clamp and bolt and lift distributor from engine. Do not crank engine after distributor is removed, otherwise the distributor will have to be initially timed to the engine.
5. Install distributor in reverse order of removal. Then start engine and adjust timing.

STARTER, REPLACE

1969-75

1. Disconnect battery ground cable and support vehicle on hoist.
2. Disconnect cable and wires from solenoid.
3. On 1973-75 Mark IV models, loosen the two front brace retaining bolts, then remove all other brace retaining bolts and allow brace to hang.
4. Turn wheels fully to the right and remove the two bolts attaching the steering idler arm to the frame.
5. Remove starter attaching bolts and remove starter.

IGNITION LOCK REPLACE

1970-75

1. Disconnect the battery ground cable.
2. **Units With Fixed Steering Columns:** Remove the steering wheel trim pad. Insert a wire pin in the hole located inside the column halfway down the lock cylinder housing, Fig. 1. **Units With Tilt Steering Columns:** Insert wire pin in the hole located on the outside of the flange casting next to the emergency flasher button, Fig. 1.
3. Place the gear shift lever in *Park* position, and turn the lock cylinder with the ignition key to the *Run* position.
4. Depress the wire pin while pulling up on the lock cylinder to remove. Remove the wire pin.
5. To install insert the lock cylinder into the housing in the flange casting, and turn the key to the *Off* position. Be certain that the cylinder is fully inserted before turning to the *Off* position. This action will extend the cylinder retaining pin into the cylinder housing.
6. Turn the key to check for correct operation in all positions.
7. Install the steering wheel and trim pad on fixed column units.
8. Connect the battery ground cable.

IGNITION SWITCH, REPLACE

1970-75 All

1. Remove shrouding from steering column and detach and lower steering column from brake support bracket.
2. Disconnect battery cable.
3. Disconnect switch wiring at multiple plug, Figs. 2 and 2A.
4. Remove two nuts that retain switch to column.
5. Detach switch plunger from actuator rod and remove the switch.
6. When installing switch, both the locking mechanism at the top of the column and the switch must be in the "LOCK" position for correct adjustment. New replacement switches are already pinned in "LOCK" position by a plastic pin inserted in a locking hole.

1969 All

1. Disconnect battery ground cable.
2. Insert wire pin in hole in ignition switch and turn key to accessory position while pressing pin. Lock cylinder can now be removed, Fig. 3.
3. Remove bezel nut and lower switch from instrument panel.
4. Depress tabs securing multiple connector to switch and pull connector off switch.
5. Reverse procedure to install.

LIGHT SWITCH, REPLACE

1972-75 Mark IV

1. Disconnect battery ground cable.
2. Remove instrument cluster trim panel.
3. Remove the headlight switch mount-

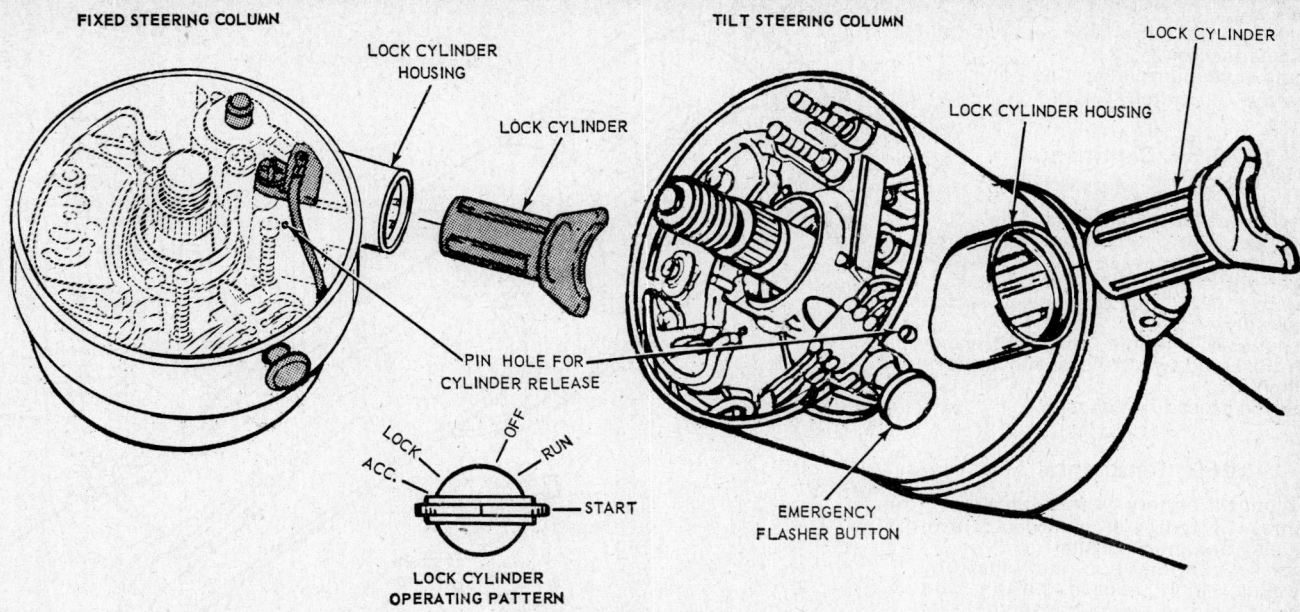

FIXED STEERING COLUMN

LOCK CYLINDER HOUSING

LOCK CYLINDER

TILT STEERING COLUMN

LOCK CYLINDER HOUSING

LOCK CYLINDER

PIN HOLE FOR CYLINDER RELEASE

LOCK ACC. OFF RUN START

LOCK CYLINDER OPERATING PATTERN

EMERGENCY FLASHER BUTTON

Fig. 1   Ignition lock cylinder

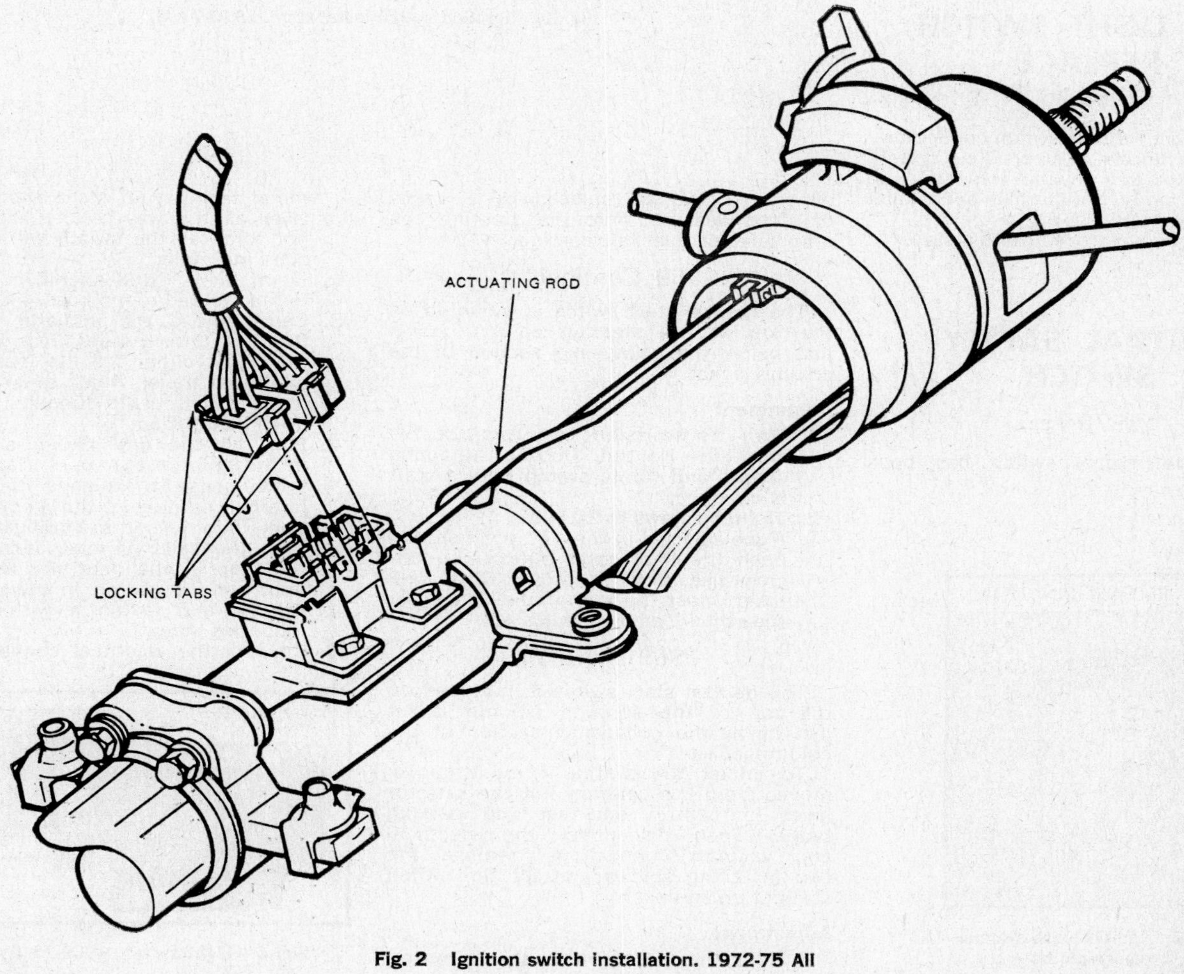

ACTUATING ROD

LOCKING TABS

Fig. 2   Ignition switch installation. 1972-75 All

ing plate.
4. Remove bezel nut and disconnect multiple connector.
5. Remove vacuum lines, if so equipped.
6. Remove the switch.

1970-75 Continental
1969-71 Mark III

1. Disconnect battery ground cable.
2. Remove control knob and shaft by pressing knob release button and pulling it out of switch housing, Fig. 4.
3. Remove bezel nut and lower switch assembly.
4. Disconnect multiple plug and vacuum hoses at switch body and remove switch.
5. Reverse procedure to install.

1969 Continental

1. Disconnect battery ground cable.
2. Remove 8 screws from lower control housing and drop housing.
3. Remove control knob and shaft by pressing knob release button and pulling it out of switch housing, Fig. 4.
4. Disconnect wiring connector to switch.
5. Remove bezel nut and remove switch.
6. Reverse procedure to install.

STOP LIGHT SWITCH, REPLACE
1969-75

1. Disconnect wires at switch connector.
2. Remove hairpin retainer, slide switch, push rod and nylon washers and bushing away from brake pedal, and remove switch, Fig. 5.
3. Reverse above procedure to install.

NEUTRAL SAFETY SWITCH
1970-75

The neutral safety switch has been

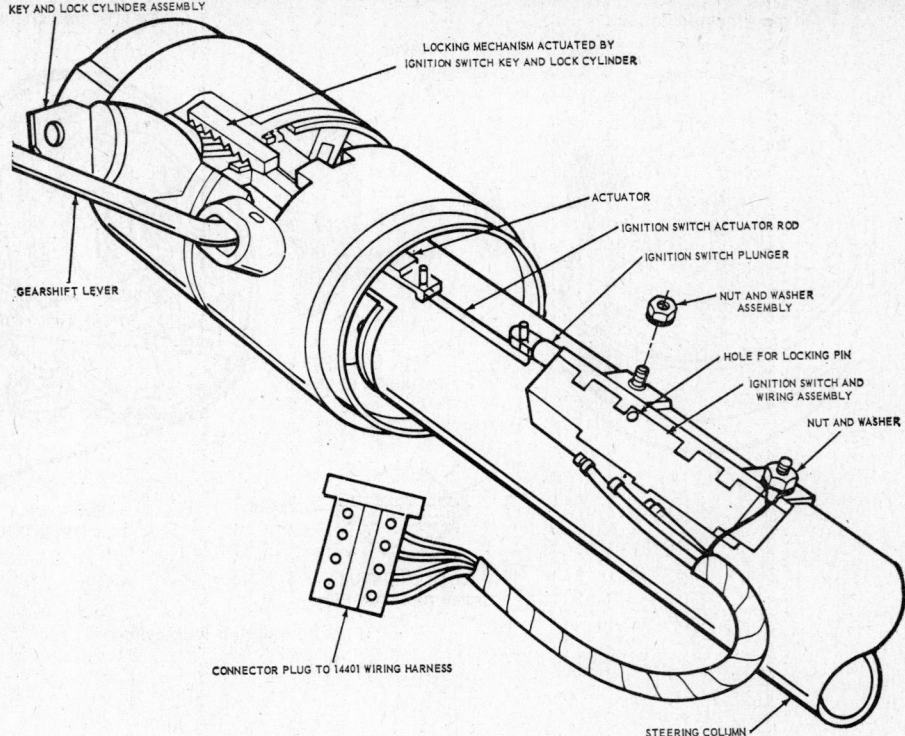

Fig. 2A   Ignition switch installation. 1970-71 All

eliminated and is replaced by a series of steps designed into the steering column selector lever hub casting.

1969 Continental

The neutral start switch is mounted on the top of the steering column jacket just below the collapsible section of the column jacket.

Adjustment

1. With transmission lever against the stop in Neutral, loosen retaining screws and rotate switch until a start is obtained.
2. Tighten screws to 20 in-lbs.
3. Place selector in the "1" position and push the Park reset button counterclockwise until it stops. *The Park reset must be performed whenever the switch has been adjusted.*

1969 Mark III

The neutral start switch is mounted on the top of the steering column jacket just below the collapsible section of the column jacket.

To adjust the switch it must be removed from the column. Put the selector lever in neutral and set the parking brake. Then disconnect the electrical and vacuum connections, remove the two fastening screws and lift the switch straight up and out.

Adjustment

1. Hold the switch with the wire ter-

minal facing you. Move the actuator lever all the way to the left but do not force as the switch will be damaged internally.
2. Insert a $3/32''$ drill shank in the hole in the tapered round boss.
3. Gently move the actuator lever to the right until it stops. This will move the Park circuit to its position of minimum travel, which must be done if the switch is to function properly upon installation.
4. Pull out the drill gauge and fit it in the hole on the top surface of the switch case to engage the switch internal carrier in the neutral position. Then reinsert the drill gauge.
5. With the selector lever held against the stop in the neutral detent position, set the switch in place on the column and fasten it with the two mounting screws.
6. Connect the electrical connector and

Fig. 3   Ignition lock cylinder release pin hole

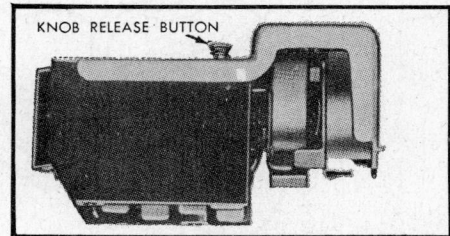

Fig. 4   Light switch. 1969-75 (typical)

any vacuum hose, and be sure to remove the drill gauge before operating the selector lever.

TURN SIGNAL SWITCH, REPLACE
1971-75

1. Remove retaining screw from underside of steering wheel spoke and lift off the pad horn switch/trim cover and medallion as an assembly.
2. Disconnect horn switch wires from terminals.
3. Remove steering wheel retaining nut and remove steering wheel using suitable puller.
4. Remove turn signal switch lever by unscrewing it from steering column.
5. Remove shroud from under steering column.
6. Disconnect steering column wiring connector plugs and remove the screws that secure switch assembly to the column.
7. On vehicles with tilt column, remove wires and terminals from steering column wiring connector plug.

NOTE: *Record the color code and location of each wire before removing it from connector. A hole provided in the flange on fixed columns makes it unnecessary to separate the wires from the connector plug. The plug with wires installed can be guided through the hole.*

8. Remove the plastic cover sleeve from the wiring harness and remove the switch and wires from the top of the column.

1969-70

1. Disconnect battery and remove steering wheel.
2. Remove protective wire cover that runs along bottom of steering column tube and disconnect electrical plug, noting color codes and location. If equipped with tilt steering column, tape wire ends together and attach a piece of heavy cord to the wires to help pull them through the column during installation.
3. If equipped with speed control, remove the sleeve around the wiring and pull the first three speed control wires out of the column.
4. Unscrew turn signal lever. If equipped with speed control, first separate the wire to the set-speed switch.
5. If equipped with tilt column, remove upper collar and push lower collar down. Remove wiring retaining clip.
6. Remove switch retaining screws and remove switch.
7. Reverse procedure to install.

HORN SOUNDER & STEERING WHEEL
1972-75 All

1. Disconnect battery ground cable.

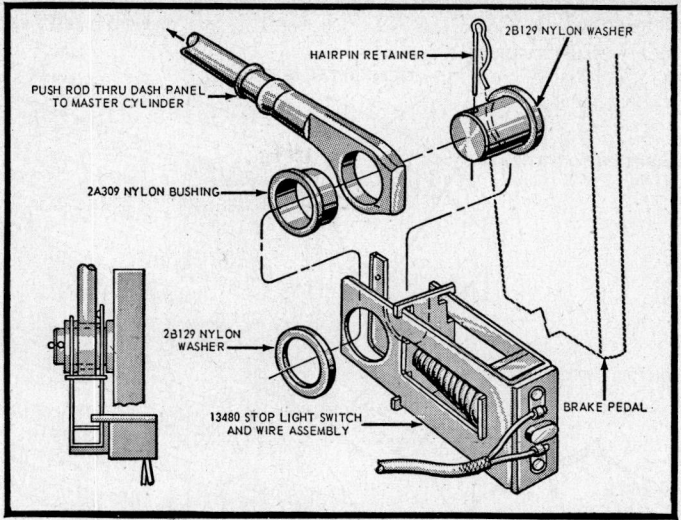

Fig. 5   Stop light switch. 1969-75

2. Remove screws from behind wheel spoke holding crash pad to wheel. Lift pad and disconnect horn wires. Disconnect speed control wires if used and remove pad.
3. Remove steering wheel nut. Install a suitable puller and remove steering wheel.

1969-71 Mark III

1. Disconnect battery ground cable.
2. Remove the medallion from steering wheel spoke pad by gently prying out with a knife blade. Working from the underside of the spoke, remove the two screws that secure the crash pad. Remove pad.
3. Disconnect two horn wires at horn switch assembly. Remove steering wheel nut and, using a suitable puller, remove steering wheel.

NOTE: *Do not use hammer or knock-off type puller. Striking the puller or shaft may cause damage to the bearings or collapsible column.*

1969-71 Continental

1. Turn hub cap counterclockwise and lift it from steering wheel.
2. Remove hub mounting plate from top of wheel.
3. Remove nut and pull off wheel.

INSTRUMENT CLUSTER
1974-75 Continental

1. Disconnect battery ground cable.
2. Remove steering column trim shroud and instrument panel lower pad.
3. Disconnect lower instrument cluster electrical connector from printed circuit.
4. Remove PRND21 control cable to steering column screw.
5. Remove instrument cluster retaining screws, pull cluster from panel and disconnect electrical connector.

6. Remove instrument cluster.

1972-75 Mark IV

1. Disconnect battery ground cable.
2. Remove three screws attaching upper access cover to instrument panel pad.
3. Remove one screw retaining lower cluster applique cover below steering column.
4. Squeeze lower half of steering column shroud together and separate lower half from upper.
5. Remove upper half of shroud from column.
6. Remove one screw attaching PRNDL control cable to steering column.
7. Remove headed backlite control knob.
8. Reach under panel and depress the button on side of headlight switch while withdrawing switch control knob and shaft. Remove headlight switch bezel.
9. Reach under panel and disconnect speedo cable.
10. Remove wiper/washer control knob.
11. Remove threaded wiper/washer bezel.
12. Remove cigar lighter from its receptacle.
13. Remove four screws retaining cluster front cover.
14. Insert a right angle standard tip screwdriver along edges of finish panel withdrawing studs in sequence gradually around periphery of panel.
15. Remove two screws from cluster light baffle at cluster top.
16. Remove four screws retaining cluster to instrument panel.
17. Pull cluster away from panel and disconnect printed circuit feed plug.
18. Tilt cluster out, bottom first, and move cluster toward center of vehicle.

1970-73 Continental

1. Remove the instrument panel pad. The cluster trim cover does not have to be removed if only the cluster is being removed.
2. Reach under instrument panel and

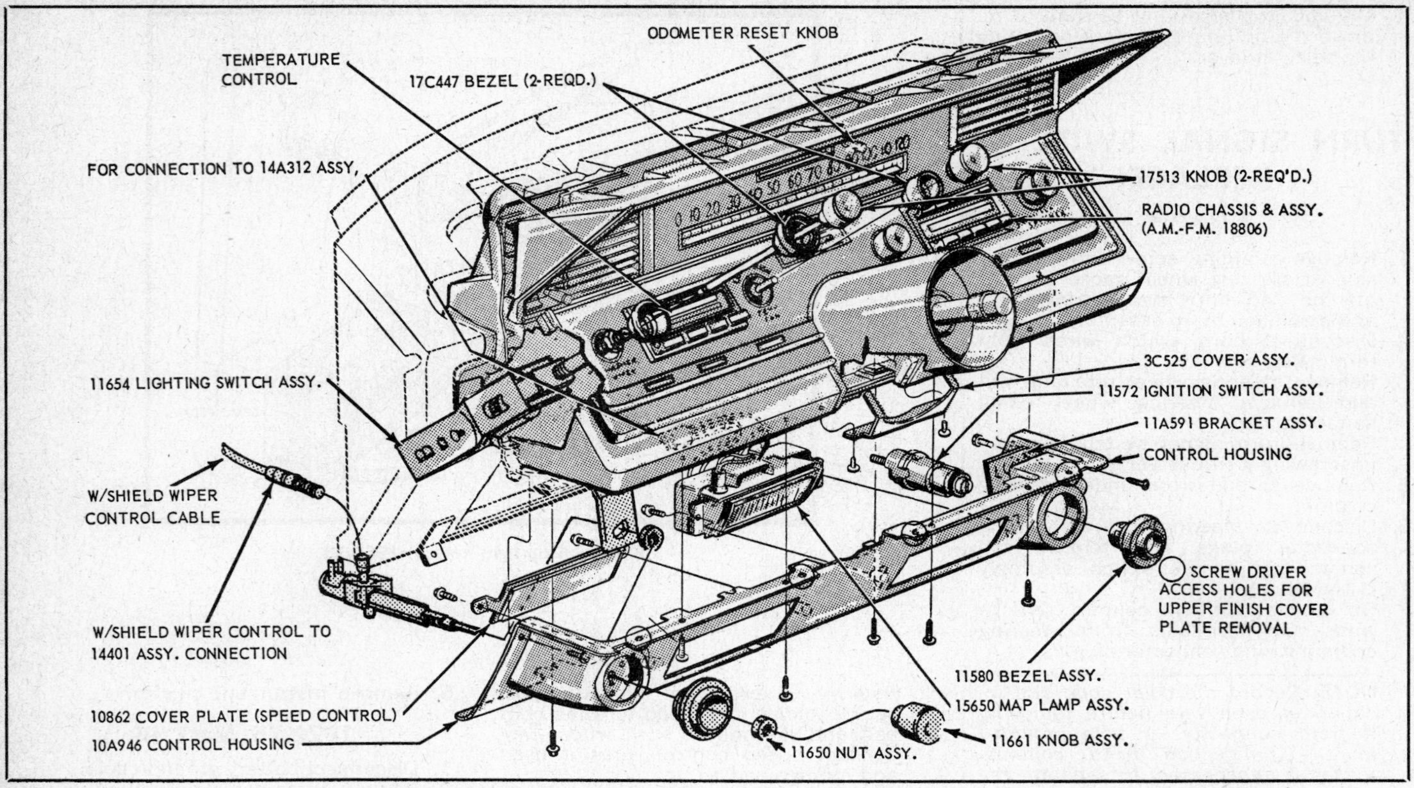

ODOMETER RESET KNOB
TEMPERATURE CONTROL
17C447 BEZEL (2-REQD.)
FOR CONNECTION TO 14A312 ASSY.
17513 KNOB (2-REQ'D.)
RADIO CHASSIS & ASSY. (A.M.-F.M. 18806)
11654 LIGHTING SWITCH ASSY.
3C525 COVER ASSY.
11572 IGNITION SWITCH ASSY.
11A591 BRACKET ASSY.
CONTROL HOUSING
W/SHIELD WIPER CONTROL CABLE
SCREW DRIVER ACCESS HOLES FOR UPPER FINISH COVER PLATE REMOVAL
W/SHIELD WIPER CONTROL TO 14401 ASSY. CONNECTION
11580 BEZEL ASSY.
15650 MAP LAMP ASSY.
10862 COVER PLATE (SPEED CONTROL)
11661 KNOB ASSY.
10A946 CONTROL HOUSING
11650 NUT ASSY.

Fig. 6 Instrument cluster and controls. 1969 Continental

disconnect cluster printed circuit plug.

3. From the passenger side, remove the cluster-to-cluster housing retaining screws and swing the cluster away from housing.
4. From the underside of the cluster, unhook the pointer control cable from the PRND21 pointer lever.
5. Remove the cable retaining clip from cluster and remove the cluster.

NOTE: When replacing the cluster be sure to connect the control wire to the PRNDL pointer and attach the cable to the cluster with the retainer.

1969-71 Mark III

1. Disconnect battery ground cable.
2. Remove screws retaining upper edge of instrument cluster pad and retainer assembly to panel pad. Remove pad and retainer from face of cluster.
3. Remove clock knob and instrument cluster mask retainers and remove mask.
4. Remove three speedometer to cluster screws and pull speedometer from cluster. Disconnect two speedometer cable to cluster screws and clamps, release the tab of the plastic retainer and remove it from the cable. If equipped with speed control, the speedometer cable may be disconnected at the speed control unit instead.
5. Remove eight cluster to panel retaining screws and three screws retaining rear vent and wiper control pod. Pull cluster and pod out of the panel.
6. Disconnect the multiple connector and the low fuel warning and dual brake warning lights at the printed circuit and remove the cluster.

PRESS DOWN ON ARM
ARM
BLADE SADDLE
DEPRESS TAB
PULL OFF

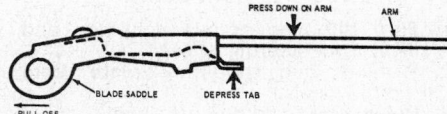

Fig. 7 Trico Bayonet wiper blade

BLADE SADDLE
ARM
PRESS ON TAB
PULL OFF

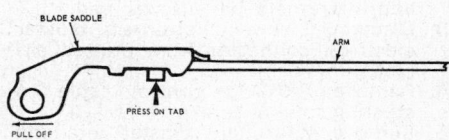

Fig. 8 Anco Bayonet wiper blade

1969 Continental

Speedometer

1. Disconnect battery ground cable.
2. Remove air conditioning register casting screws, pull unit rearward and support on the ducts.
3. Remove cluster hood to crash pad screws, windshield molding screws and windshield molding.
4. Remove crash pad forward edge screws and nuts, disconnect speaker wire, then remove crash pad.
5. Remove radio knobs and bezels, heater, air conditioning and windshield wiper control knobs, then remove nuts and retainers from the control shafts.
6. Remove screws from lower control housing and lower the housing.
7. Remove screws securing finish cover to underside of instrument panel.
8. Remove odometer reset knob and screws securing upper cluster finish cover, then remove cover.
9. Remove right hand cluster air conditioning register screws and remove air hose.
10. Disconnect speedometer cable and speedometer retaining screws. Remove speedometer.

Fuel Gauge

1. Perform steps 1, 5, 6 and 7 outlined in the above procedure.
2. Remove fuel gauge retaining screws and electrical connectors, then remove fuel gauge.

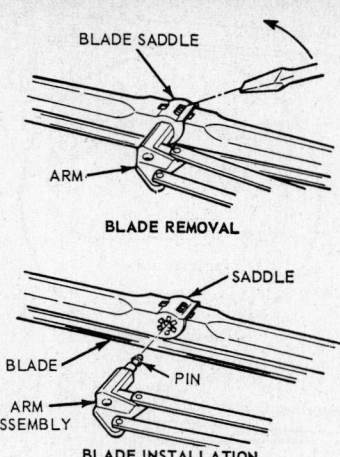

BLADE REMOVAL

BLADE INSTALLATION

Fig. 9 Pin type wiper blade

W/S WIPER BLADES

NOTE: Trico and Anco blades are used and come in two types; Bayonet type and Side Saddle Pin type.

Bayonet Type: To remove the *Trico* type press down on the arm to unlock the top stud. Depress the tab on the saddle, Fig. 7, and pull the blade from the arm. To remove the *Anco* type press inward on the tab, Fig. 8, and pull the blade from the arm. To install a new blade assembly slide the blade saddle over the arm so that the locking stud snaps into place.

Side Saddle Pin Type: To remove the pin type insert an appropriate tool into the spring release opening of the blade saddle, depress the spring clip and pull the blade from the arm, Fig. 9. To install, push the blade saddle onto the pin so that the spring clip engages the pin. To replace the rubber element in a *Trico* blade squeeze the latch lock release and pull the element out of the lever jaws, Fig. 10. Remove the *Anco* element by depressing the latch pin, Fig. 10, and sliding the element out of the yoke jaws. To install, insert the element through the yoke or lever jaws. Be sure the element is engaged at all points.

W/S WIPER ARMS
1969-72 (Exc. Mark IV)

Swing the arm and blade assembly away from the windshield and insert a 3/32″ inch pin through the pin hole as shown in Fig. 11. Swinging the assembly away from the windshield will release the spring loaded attaching clip in the arm from the pivot shaft. Inserting the pin will hold it in the released position. The arm can now be pulled off the pivot shaft. *Do not* pry off with a screwdriver. Leave the pin in the arm until after installation. A new arm comes with a pin already installed to hold it in the released position. Make sure the pivot shaft is in parked position when installing new assembly. Push the arm onto the pivot shaft. Lock the arm to the pivot shaft by removing the pin.

1972 Mark IV & 1973-75 All

NOTE: On 1973-75 Continental and 1974-75 Mark IV, disconnect the windshield washer hose from wiper arm before attempting to remove the arm.

Raise the blade end of the arm off the windshield and move the slide latch, Fig. 12, away from the pivot shaft. This action will unlock the wiper arm from the pivot shaft and hold the blade end of the arm off the glass at the same time. The wiper arm can now be pulled off the pivot shaft without the aid of any tools.

W/S WIPER MOTOR, REPLACE

1971 Continental; 1972-75 All

1. Disconnect battery ground cable.
2. Remove wiper arm and blade assemblies.
3. Remove left cowl screen for access through cowl opening.
4. Disconnect linkage drive arm from motor output arm crankpin by removing the retaining clip.
5. From engine side of dash, disconnect wire connectors from motor.
6. Remove bolts that retain motor to dash and remove the motor. If the output arm catches on dash during removal, handturn the arm clockwise so it will clear the opening in dash.

NOTE: *Before installing motor be sure the output arm is in the Park position.*

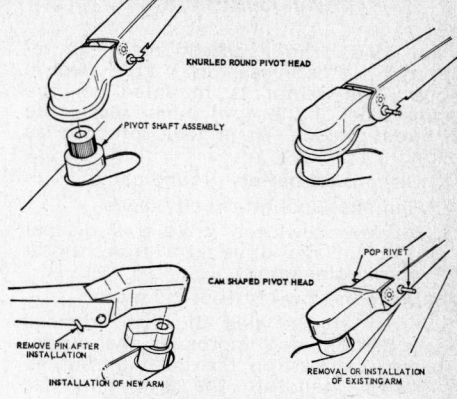

Fig. 11 Wiper arm. 1969-72 except Mark IV

1971 Mark III

1. Remove wiper arm and blade assemblies.
2. Remove the air cleaner.
3. Remove retaining screws and remove the cowl top panel. Disconnect washer hose.
4. Remove clip retaining left wiper link to motor and disconnect the link.
5. Disconnect hydraulic lines from motor being careful not to burn hands with hot hydraulic fluid.
6. Remove three bolts retaining motor to cowl and disconnect wiper control cable and remove through left cowl opening.

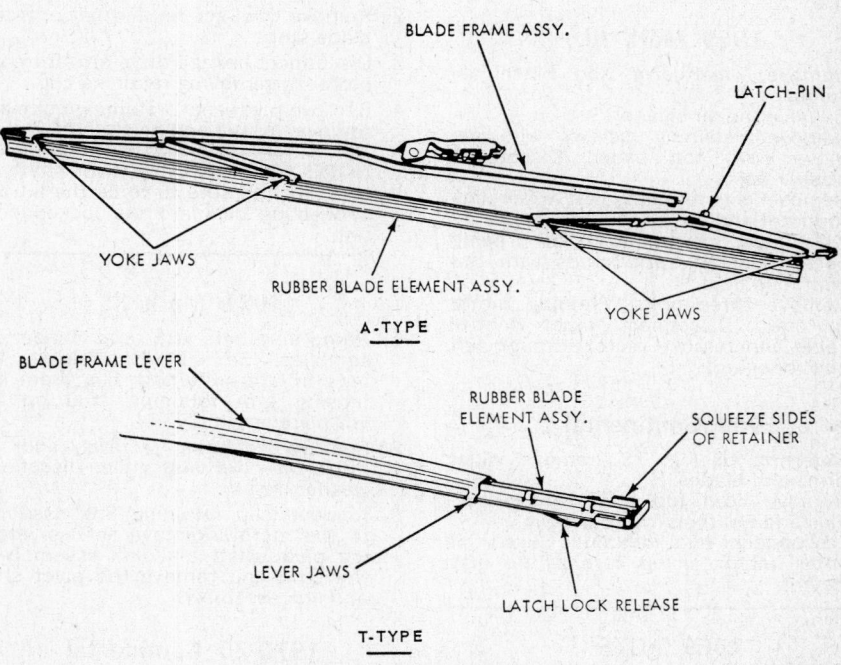

Fig. 10 Wiper blade element

1970 Continental

For 1970, the hydraulic motor is replaced by a depressed park type electric motor. The motor is mounted on the engine side of the cowl panel under the left front fender. To remove, proceed as follows:

1. Disconnect battery ground cable.
2. Remove wiper arms and blades.
3. Remove cowl top grille and disconnect linkage drive arm from motor output crankpin.
4. Disconnect wires from the motor.
5. From engine side of dash, remove bolts retaining motor. If the output arm catches on the dash during removal, handturn the arm clockwise so it will clear the opening in the dash.

Late 1970 Mark III

All vehicles built after 9-22-69 will again use the hydraulic wiper system which was used on previous models. The major difference is the elimination of the surge chamber. Service is similar to 1969 models.

Early 1970 Mark III

The hydraulic motor used previously is replaced by an oscillating type, two speed electric motor. Removal is as follows:

1. Disconnect battery ground cable and washer hose.
2. Remove the cowl vent top panel.
3. Remove four bolts that retain the plastic cover and motor to the cowl panel.
4. Remove the plastic cover.
5. Disconnect the drive link from the motor arm.
6. Disconnect motor wiring at connector and remove the motor.

1969 Mark III

1. Remove wiper arm and blade assemblies.
2. Remove the air cleaner.
3. Remove retaining screws and remove cowl top panel. Disconnect washer hose.
4. Remove clip retaining left wiper link to motor and disconnect the link.
5. Disconnect hydraulic lines being careful not to burn hands with hot hydraulic fluid.
6. Remove three bolts retaining motor to cowl. Disconnect wiper control cable and remove motor through left cowl opening.

1969 Continental

1. Referring to Fig. 13, remove wiper arms and blades.
2. Remove cowl top grille, wiper nozzles and weatherstrip (6 screws).
3. Disconnect two hydraulic lines at wiper motor, *using care as oil may be hot.*

1969 NOTE

The windshield wiper is hydraulically

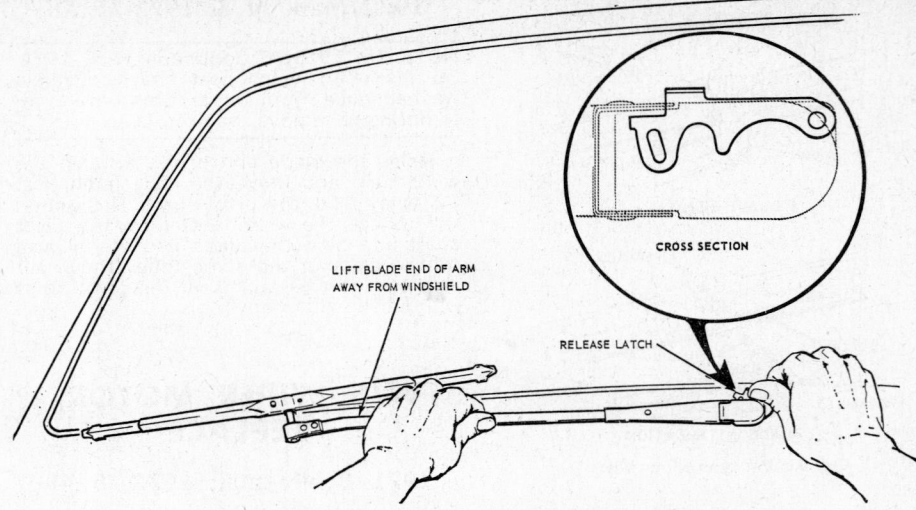

Fig. 12   Wiper arm. 1972 Mark IV & 1973-75 All

LIFT BLADE END OF ARM AWAY FROM WINDSHIELD

CROSS SECTION

RELEASE LATCH

operated. Hydraulic power for the motor is obtained from the power steering unit. Hydraulic fluid flows from the pump, through the steering gear to the wiper motor, and then to the fluid reservoir. During wiper operation, a part of the fluid is by-passed through the motor by a valve on the motor.

W/S WIPER TRANSMISSION

1972-75 Mark IV

1. Disconnect battery ground cable and remove wiper arm and blades.
2. Remove cowl screen and left arm and blade stop.
3. Disconnect linkage drive arm from the motor by removing retaining clip.
4. Remove pivot shaft retaining bolts and remove linkage and pivot shaft.

NOTE: When installing pivot shaft assemblies, be sure to force the linkage connecting clip into the locked position.

1971 Mark III

1. Remove wiper arm and blade assemblies. Be sure to release the tension arm retaining clip from the tension arm retaining stud on the left pivot assembly.
2. Remove retaining screws and remove the cowl vent grille. Disconnect washer hoses.
3. Remove clip retaining link assembly to the motor. Remove screws retaining pivot shaft and link assembly to the cowl and remove the pivot shaft and link assembly.

1970-75 Continental

1. Disconnect battery ground cable.

2. Remove wiper arm and blade assemblies.
3. Remove cowl screens for access to linkage.
4. Disconnect left linkage arm from the drive arm by removing the clip.
5. Remove three bolts retaining left pivot shaft assembly to the cowl and remove the left arm and pivot shaft assembly through cowl opening.
6. Disconnect linkage drive arm from motor crankpin by removing the clip.
7. Remove three bolts that connect the drive arm pivot assembly to the cowl and remove the pivot shaft drive arm and right arm as an assembly.

1970 Mark III

1. Disconnect battery ground cable.
2. Disconnect washer hose and remove cowl vent top panel.
3. Disconnect drive link from motor arm and disconnect both links from the right pivot shaft assembly.
4. Remove three screws from the drive pivot plate at the right end of the cowl panel and withdraw the drive pivot plate and the two drive links as an assembly.
5. Remove the right pivot shaft (three screws).
6. Remove the three left pivot shaft screws and withdraw the left pivot shaft and link as an assembly.

1969 Mark III

1. Remove wiper arm and blade assemblies, being sure to release the tension arm retaining clip from the stud on the left pivot assembly.
2. Remove cowl top panel and disconnect washer hose.
3. Remove link retaining clip and pivot shaft assembly to cowl screws. Remove pivot shaft and link assembly.
4. Reverse procedure to install.

1969 Continental

1. Remove wiper arms and blades.

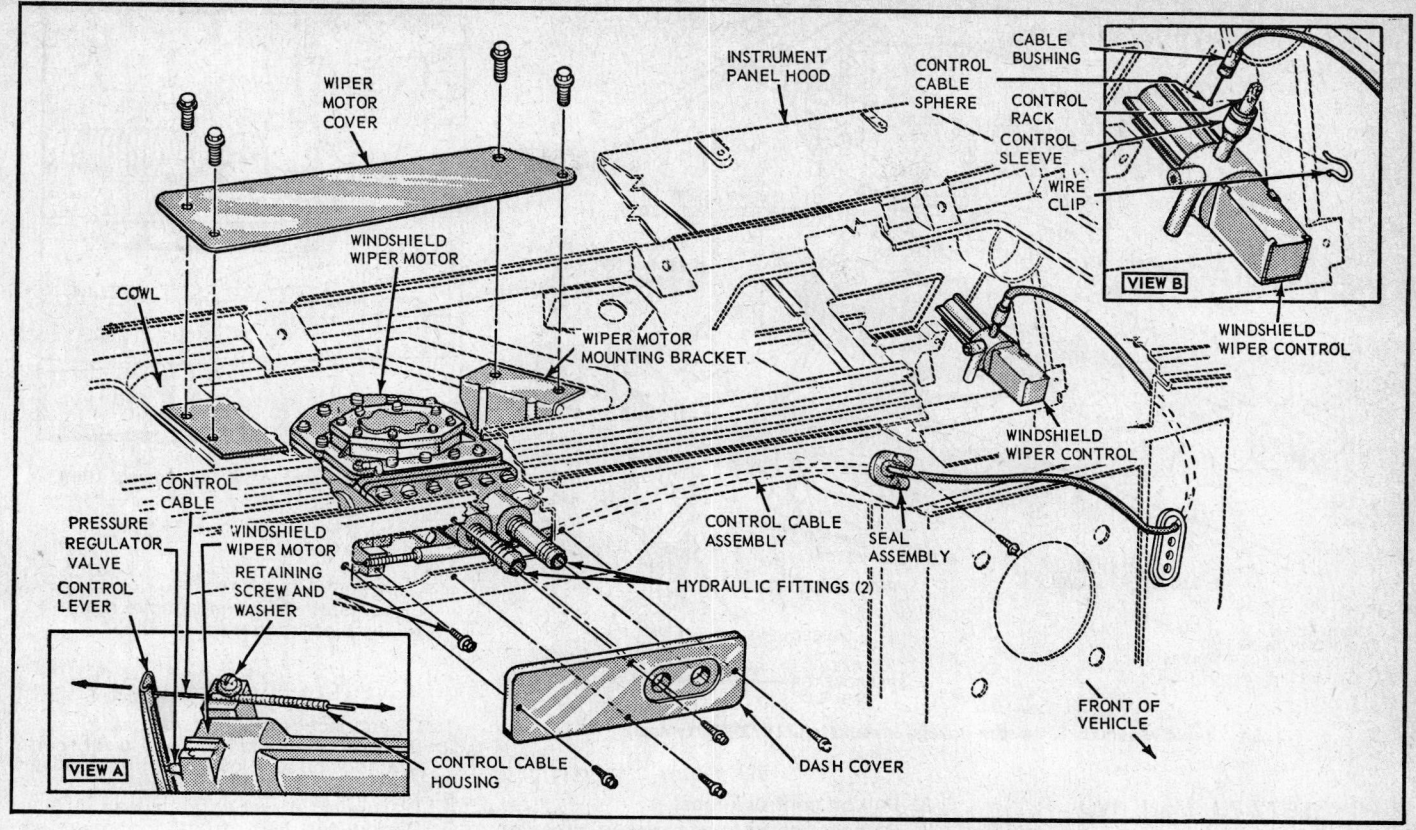

Fig. 13 Windshield wiper control and motor installation. 1969

2. Remove cowl grille (6 screws) and disconnect w a s h e r hoses and weatherstrip.
3. Remove drive arm clip.
4. Remove three bolts at each pivot.
5. Remove pivots from connecting linkage and lift assembly out through left side of cowl.
6. Reverse procedure to install.

W/S WIPER SWITCH

1972-75 Mark IV

1. Disconnect battery ground cable.
2. Remove instrument cluster finish panel.
3. Remove switch mounting plate and disconnect cigar lighter and wiper switch wires.
4. Remove switch bezel nut and remove switch.

1970-75 Continental

1. Disconnect battery ground cable.
2. Pull the knob and remove retaining nut and gasket from switch shaft.
3. Lower switch from behind instrument panel and disconnect the multiple connector.

1969-71 Mark III

1. Disconnect battery ground cable.

2. Remove five retaining screws and remove instrument cluster pad and retainer from face of cluster.
3. Remove three retaining screws and pull wiper control pod from panel. Disconnect vacuum hoses and electrical connector and remove bulbs. Remove control cable retaining clip and remove control assembly.
4. Remove control knobs, two retaining screws and remove control unit.

1969 Continental

1. Disconnect battery ground cable.
2. Remove eight screws from lower control housing and drop housing.
3. Remove knob and bezel.
4. Remove nut on control shaft and lower the control.
5. Turn wiper control knob counterclockwise to the stop.
6. Remove wire clip, Fig. 13. Slide cable bushing up and out of control sleeve (view B). Remove control cable sphere from control rack.
7. Disconnect plug connector from wiring harness. Disconnect two vacuum hoses and remove wiper control.
8. Reverse procedure to install.

RADIO REMOVAL

NOTE: When installing radio, be sure to

adjust antenna trimmer for peak performance.

1974-75 Mark IV

1. Disconnect battery ground cable.
2. Pull radio knobs and discs from shafts.
3. Remove twilight sentinel amplifier.
4. Remove air conditioning duct located under radio.
5. Remove radio rear support to panel screw, disconnect radio electrical leads and remove radio.

1973-75 Continental

1. Disconnect battery ground cable.
2. Remove radio knobs and discs, then map light assembly.
3. Remove steering column shroud, ash tray door pad and instrument cluster panel pad.
4. Remove center register applique, then disconnect cigar lighter and glove box light switch electrical connectors.
5. Remove radio bracket to instrument panel tab nut and radio mounting bracket to instrument panel screws.
6. Pull radio out, disconnect wiring and remove radio.

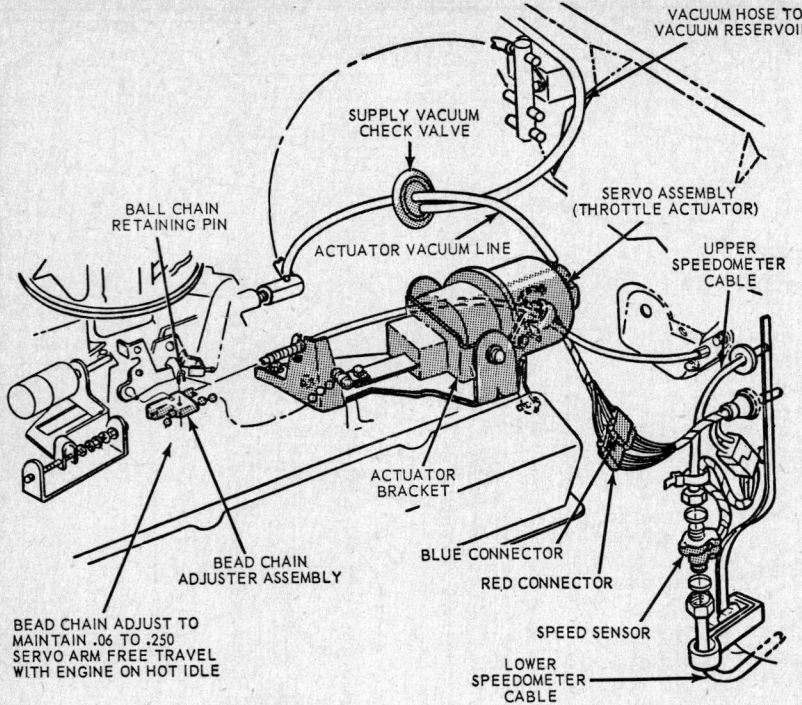

Fig. 14 Servo assembly & throttle linkage installation. 1972-75 (typical)

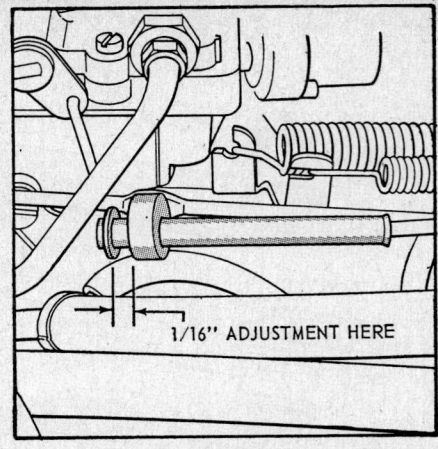

Fig. 15 Control cable adjustment. 1969

1972-73 Mark IV

1. Disconnect battery ground cable.
2. Pull radio control knobs off shafts.
3. Remove nut from both radio shafts.
4. Remove radio rear support attaching screw at instrument panel.
5. Disconnect radio power and speaker wires at connectors.
6. Disconnect antenna and remove radio.

1970-72 Continental

1. Disconnect battery ground cable.
2. Remove map light assembly.
3. Remove right and left inspection covers.
4. Remove lower instrument panel pad.
5. Remove the glove box. Open ash tray and let it hang open.
6. Remove glove box switch.
7. Through glove box opening remove two nuts retaining radio finish panel to the instrument panel.
8. Remove radio knobs.
9. Remove two screws at top of finish panel. Position panel out and disconnect cigar lighter and light from the right panel.
10. Through the glove box opening remove the nut from the lower right corner of the center finish panel.
11. Remove radio top support nut and the three mounting screws. Pull radio out, disconnect power leads and antenna cable and remove radio.

1969-71 Mark III

1. Disconnect battery ground cable.

2. Pull off control knobs.
3. Remove cover plate below steering column, and the nut from right radio control shaft.
4. Remove six screws and remove trim from front of radio.
5. Remove nut and washer from right control shaft, and screw attaching front left side of radio to instrument panel.
6. Remove rear support attaching screw,

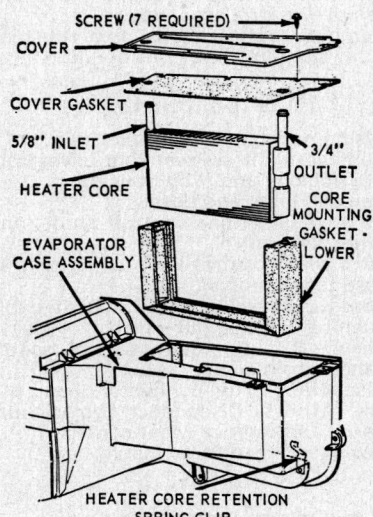

Fig. 16 Heater core removal. 1973-75 Continental

disconnect wires and remove radio.
7. Reverse procedure to install.

1969 Continental

1. Disconnect battery ground cable.
2. Remove eight screws in lower control housing and lower the housing.
3. Disconnect lead from speakers.
4. Disconnect power antenna lead.
5. Disconnect lead from foot-operated switch for AM/FM radios (if equipped).
6. Disconnect one two-way disconnect for pilot light and radio power.
7. Remove two knobs and bezels on selector shafts.
8. Remove two nuts and retainers on selector shafts.
9. Remove two screws attaching radio bracket to lower reinforcement on instrument panel.
10. Remove two nuts from selector shafts.
11. Disconnect antenna lead and remove radio.

SPEED CONTROLS

1972-75

Adjust the bead chain to obtain .06-.25" actuator arm free travel when engine is at hot idle, Fig. 14. The adjustment should be made to take as much slack as possible out of the bead chain without restricting the carburetor lever from returning to idle. On vehicles with solenoid anti-diesel valve, perform the adjustment with the ignition switch in the ON position.

1970-71

A mercury cut-off switch has been mounted in the speed control regulator. The cut-off switch makes certain that the speed control is shut off when the vehicle is suddenly stopped. When installing a regulator, use a level to make certain the mercury will operate properly. It may be necessary to place washers under one of the mounting studs to make it level.

Linkage Adjustment

Adjust the servo chain to obtain a ½ to 1 ball slack when the engine is at hot idle.

1969 Mark III

Linkage Adjustment

Adjust the servo chain to obtain a ½ to 1 ball link slack when the engine is at hot idle.

1969 Continental

Control Cable, Adjust

With the carburetor set at hot idle, adjust the Bowden cable to provide a 1/16" clearance between the Bowden cable end "C" washer and the accelerator linkage sleeve, Fig. 15.

HEATER CORE REMOVAL

1973-75 Continental

1. Drain radiator and disconnect heater hoses from core.
2. Remove heater core cover and gasket, then lift heater core and lower mounting gasket from evaporator housing, Fig. 16.

1972-75 Mark IV

1. Drain radiator and disconnect heater hoses from core.
2. Remove glove box, then heater air outlet register from plenum assembly by disengaging the snap clips.
3. Disconnect temperature control cable from blend door crank arm.
4. Remove vacuum hoses from high-low door motor, panel-defrost door motor and the in-line tee connector to temperature by-pass door motor.
5. Disconnect resistor wiring and remove plenum case flange screws, then remove plenum case rear half.
6. Remove heater core tube support bracket nut and heater core.

1970-72 Continental

1. Drain the engine coolant.
2. Disconnect vacuum junction valve from dash panel and move valve and hoses away from case.
3. Disconnect speed control from dash, if so equipped, and move it away.
4. Disconnect multiple connector from blower resistor and the harness from the clip on the case.
5. Disconnect heater hoses from the case and the hose support clamp from the case. Move the hoses and the water valve away from the case.
6. Remove case cover-to-case flange screws and the wire harness clip.
7. Remove six case cover-to-back plate stud nuts.
8. Remove one upper case-to-dash panel mounting screw.
9. Remove two case-to-dash panel mounting stud nuts, one on the inboard mounting flange and one below the case on the lower flange.
10. Carefully move the heater core cover assembly forward to clear the mounting studs and lift it up and out of the car.
11. Remove the spring clips from the core tubes on the front of the core cover.
12. Remove three core end plate mounting screws and remove the plate. The heater core and gasket can now be removed from the cover.

1969-71 Mark III

1. Remove hood and air cleaner and drain radiator.
2. Disconnect wiper motor hydraulic lines, vacuum supply hose, icing switch multiple connector and heater hoses.
3. Remove oil pressure sending unit and transmission dip stick and tube.
4. Remove evaporator housing front cover and heater core housing cover.
5. Remove heater core retaining bracket and heater core.

1969 Continental

1. Remove air cleaner and harness clamp on top evaporator-heater case in engine compartment.
2. Take off actuator for temperature blending door, adjacent to evaporator-heater case.
3. Remove retaining screws and heater core cover plate and lift out core.

BLOWER MOTOR REMOVE

1972-75 Mark IV

1. Remove glove box, recirculating air register and duct assembly.
2. Remove blower lower housing to dash screws.
3. Disconnect vacuum hose from outside-recirculating air door motor and remove motor from blower lower housing, leaving motor actuator connected to door crank arm.
4. Disconnect blower motor wiring and remove blower motor housing flange screws.
5. Separate upper and lower blower housing and remove lower housing and motor from under instrument panel.
6. Remove blower motor from lower housing.

1971 Mark III

1. Disconnect battery ground cable.
2. Remove glove box and right cowl side trim panel.
3. Remove fuse panel mounting screws and position panel out of way.
4. Remove duct mounting screws and disconnect vacuum hose from vacuum motor, then remove duct.
5. Remove screw from blower motor mounting plate and rotate mounting plate counter-clockwise, disengaging plate from case.
6. Disconnect blower motor wiring and remove motor through cowl side panel opening.

1970 All & 1971-75 Continental

1. Remove the hood.
2. Remove the right hood hinge and right fender inner support brace as an assembly.
3. Disconnect the blower motor air cooling tube from the motor.
4. Disconnect the motor lead wire from the harness and the ground wire from the dash panel.
5. Disconnect the rear section of the right front fender apron from the fender around the wheel opening (7 screws) and remove the two lower fender-to-cowl mounting screws.
6. Separate the fender apron from the fender wheel opening so that the apron can be pushed downward away from the blower motor.
7. Remove the four blower motor mounting plate screws. Move the motor and wheel forward out of the blower scroll and remove the assembly through the opening while applying pressure to the fender apron to enlarge the opening at the hinge area.

1969

NOTE: The blower motor is located in the right front fender well.

1. Remove the right front fender splash shield which is held by six bolts.
2. Remove the four screws retaining the blower motor to the housing. Disconnect the electrical leads and remove the motor.
3. Reverse above to install.

Engine Section

ENGINE MOUNTS REPLACE

CAUTION: Whenever self-locking mounting bolts and nuts are removed, they must be replaced with new self-locking bolts and nuts.

1969 Lincoln; 1970-71 Mark III

1. Block the rear wheels and set the parking brake. Raise the front of the vehicle with a floor jack and install safety stands.
2. Remove the nuts and washers which secure the engine front support insulators to the underbody crossmember, Fig. 2.
3. Place a block of wood between a jack and the front edge of the oil pan. Raise the front of the engine about 2 inches to allow clearance for removal of the insulators.
4. Remove the bolts securing the support insulator to the cylinder block.

1970-75 Lincoln

1. Block the rear wheels and set the parking brake. Raise front of vehicle and install safety stands.
2. Remove the bolts that attach the support bracket to the cylinder block, Fig. 3.
3. Place a block of wood between a jack and the front edge of the oil pan. Raise the engine high enough to provide clearance to remove the support and not damage the radiator.
4. Remove the through bolts from the support insulator. Lift the insulator from the number 2 crossmember.
5. Remove the bracket-to-insulator attaching bolt and separate the units.

1972-75 Mark IV

1. Remove the fan shroud attaching screws and support the engine using a jack and a block of wood under the oil pan.
2. Remove the through bolt and nut attaching the insulator to the frame crossmember, Fig. 4.
3. Remove the insulator to upper bracket attaching nuts.
4. Raise the engine enough to remove the insulator and heat shield if so equipped.
5. If required, the upper bracket can now be removed by removal of the three screws holding the bracket to the cylinder block.

ENGINE, REPLACE

In addition to the usual items such as fuel lines, linkage and radiator hoses, the following operations must be performed:

1. Remove hood, radiator and air cleaner.
2. Remove power steering pump and starter.
3. Disconnect exhaust pipes from manifolds. On Mark III, disconnect idler arm at frame bracket.
4. Support transmission with a suitable jack.
5. Unfasten engine mountings and attach lifting rig to engine.
6. Remove bell housing to engine attaching bolts and carefully lift engine out of chassis. *Be sure to support transmission with front end tilted up to prevent converter from falling out.*

CYLINDER HEADS
1969-75 V8-460

1. Remove intake manifold and carburetor as an assembly.
2. Disconnect resonator inlet pipe at exhaust manifold.
3. Loosen air conditioner compressor belt if so equipped.
4. Loosen alternator retaining bolts and remove bolt retaining alternator bracket to right head.
5. If air conditioned, isolate compressor at service valves and hoses from compressor. Remove nuts retaining compressor bracket to water pump. Remove bolts retaining compressor to upper mounting bracket and lay compressor out of way. Remove compressor upper bracket from head.
6. If not air conditioned, remove bolts retaining power steering reservoir bracket to left head and position reservoir out of way.
7. Remove rocker arm covers. Loosen rocker arm stud nuts and turn rocker arms to side. Remove push rods in sequence so they can be installed in their positions.
8. Remove head retaining bolts and lift head with exhaust manifold.
9. Reverse procedure to install.

VALVE CLEARANCE
1969-75 V8-460

A positive stop rocker arm stud and nut eliminates the need of adjusting the valve lash. It is very important that the correct push rod be used and all com-

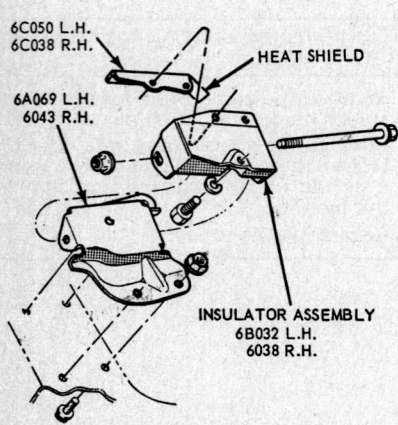

Fig. 2 Engine mount. 1969; 1970-71 Mark III

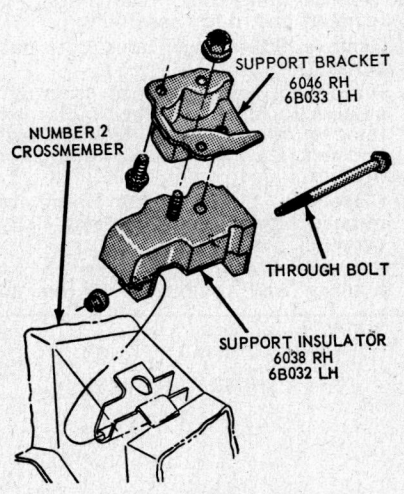

Fig. 3 Engine Mount. 1970-75 Lincoln

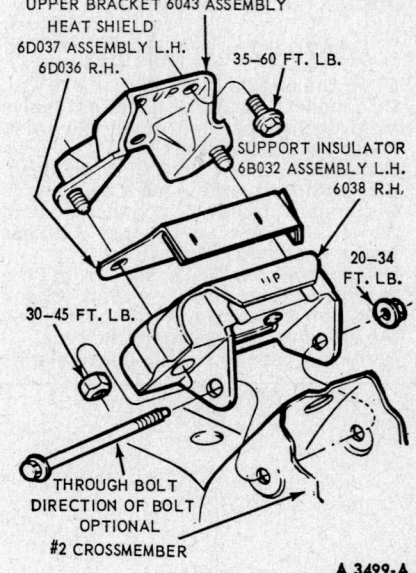

Fig. 4 Engine Mount. 1972-75 Mark IV

ponents be installed and torqued as follows:

1. Position the piston of the cylinder being worked on at TDC of the compression stroke.
2. Install positive stop stud and torque to 65-75 ft.-lbs.
3. Lubricate and install the rocker arm and fulcrum on the stud. Thread nut onto stud until it contacts the shoulder then tighten it to 18-22 ft-lbs.

NOTE: A .060" shorter push rod or a .060" longer push rod are available for service to provide a means of compensating for dimensional changes in the valve mechanism. Valve stem-to-rocker arm clearance should be as listed in the *Valve Specifications* table, with the hydraulic lifter completely collapsed. Repeated valve grind jobs will decrease this clearance to the point that if not compensated for the lifters will cease to function.

To check the clearance, bring the piston of the cylinder being checked on top dead center of the compression stroke. Then with hydraulic lifter collapsed, check the clearance between valve stem and rocker arm. If the clearance is less than the minimum, the .060" shorter push rod should be used. If clearance is more than the maximum, the .060" longer push rod should be used. (See *Valve Specifications* table).

VALVE ARRANGEMENT
Front to Rear

Right Bank . . . . I-E-I-E-I-E-I-E
Left Bank . . . . E-I-E-I-E-I-E-I

VALVE LIFT SPECS.

Engine	Year	Intake	Exhaust
V8-460	1969-73	.443	.486
	1974	.442	.486
	1975	.436	.481

VALVE TIMING
Intake Opens Before TDC

Engine	Year	Degrees
V8-460	1969-71	16
	1972-75	8

ROCKER ARM STUDS
1972-75 V8-460

The rocker arm is supported by a fulcrum bolt which fits through the fulcrum seat and threads into the cylinder head. To disassemble, remove the bolt, oil deflector, fulcrum seat and rocker arm.

1969-71 V8-460

Rocker arm studs are screwed into threaded bores in the cylinder head bosses. To install, apply water resistant sealer to stud threads that screw into cylinder head. Install stud and torque to 65-75 ft-lbs. Apply Lubriplate to top of

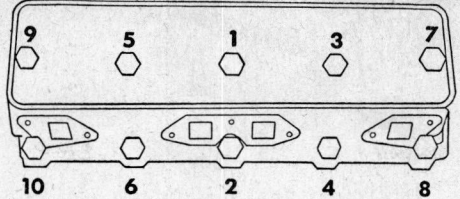

Fig. 6 Cylinder head tightening

valve stem and at push rod guide in cylinder head. Install rocker arm, fulcrum and stud nut.

VALVE GUIDES

Valve guides in these engines are an integral part of the head and, therefore, cannot be removed. For service, guides can be reamed oversize to accommodate one of three service valves with oversize stems (.003", .015" and .030").

Check the valve stem clearance of each valve (after cleaning) in its respective valve guide. If the clearance exceeds the service limits of .004" on the intake or .005" on the exhaust, ream the valve guides to accommodate the next oversize diameter valve.

HYDRAULIC VALVE LIFTERS

The internal parts of each hydraulic valve lifter assembly are a matched set. If these are mixed, improper valve operation may result. Therefore, disassemble, inspect and test each assembly separately to prevent mixing the parts.

Fig. 9, illustrates the type of hydraulic lifter used. See the *Trouble Shooting Chapter* under the heading *Engine Noises* for causes of hydraulic valve lifter noise.

TIMING CASE COVER

NOTE: If necessary to replace the cover oil seal the cover must first be removed.

V8-460

1. Drain cooling system and crankcase.
2. Remove fan and radiator.
3. Remove drive belts and water pump pulley. Remove compressor support if so equipped.
4. Remove bolt and washer retaining crankshaft damper and, using a suitable puller, remove damper. Remove Woodruff key from crankshaft.
5. Remove power steering pump.
6. Loosen by-pass hose and remove heater return tube at water pump.
7. Remove fuel pump.
8. Remove front cover to cylinder block bolts. Cut oil pan seal flush with cylinder block face prior to separating cover from the cylinder block. Remove front cover and water pump as a unit.

TIMING CHAIN

1. To remove the chain, first take off the timing chain cover as outlined previously.
2. Crank the engine until the timing mark on the camshaft sprocket is adjacent to the timing mark on the crankshaft sprocket, Fig. 10.
3. Remove cap screws, lock plate and fuel pump eccentric from front of camshaft.
4. Place a screwdriver behind the camshaft sprocket and carefully pry the sprocket and chain off the camshaft.
5. Reverse the foregoing procedure to install the chain, being sure to align the timing marks as shown in Fig. 10.

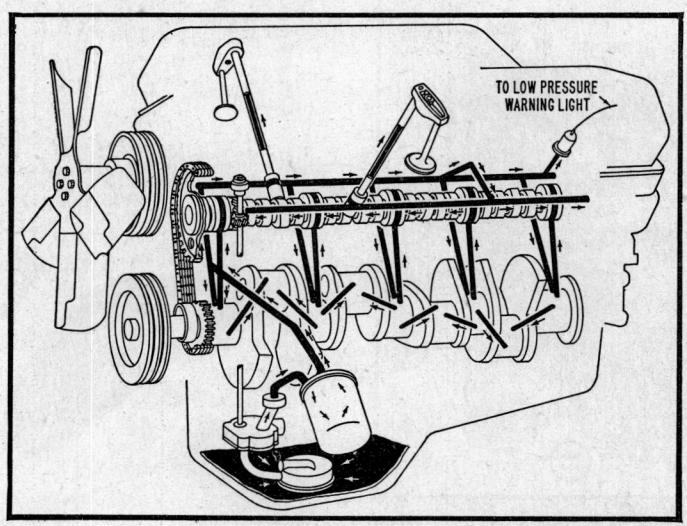

Engine lubrication. V8-460

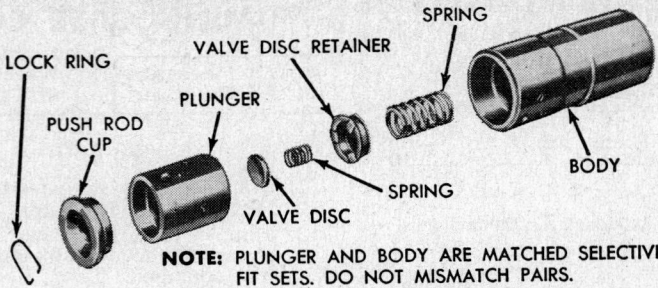

NOTE: PLUNGER AND BODY ARE MATCHED SELECTIVE FIT SETS. DO NOT MISMATCH PAIRS.

Fig. 9 Hydraulic valve lifter disassembled (typical)

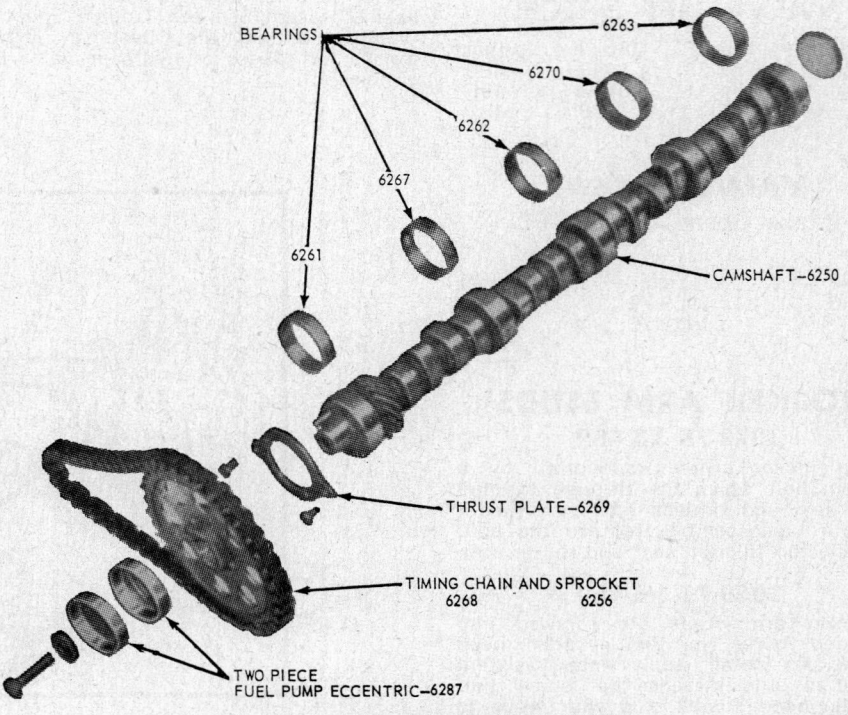

Fig. 10 Valve timing marks

CAMSHAFT, REPLACE

If it is necessary to replace the camshaft only it may be accomplished without removing the engine from the chassis. But if the camshaft bearings are to be replaced the engine will have to be removed. To remove the camshaft, proceed as follows:

V8-460

1. Drain crankcase and remove oil pan.
2. Remove timing cover, chain and sprockets as outlined previously.
3. Remove intake manifold and carburetor as an assembly.
4. Remove rocker arm covers. Back off all rocker arm stud nuts, turn rocker arms sideways and remove push rods in sequence.
5. Remove valve lifters.
6. If air conditioned, unbolt and lay condenser on left fender. Secure in this position.
7. Remove grille center support.
8. Remove camshaft thrust plate bolts and carefully remove camshaft from front of engine, Fig. 11.
9. Reverse above procedure to install.

PISTON & ROD, ASSEMBLE

If the old pistons are serviceable, make certain that they are installed on the rods from which they were removed. The assembly must be made as shown in Fig. 12.

PISTONS, RINGS & PINS

Pistons are available in standard size and oversizes .020 and .030".

Rings are available in standard size and oversizes of .020, .030 and .040".

Pins are available in standard size only.

MAIN & ROD BEARINGS

Main and rod bearings are available in standard size and undersizes of .002, .010, .020 and .030".

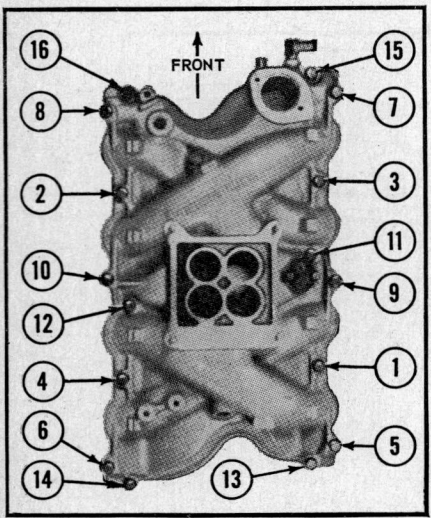

Intake manifold tightening sequence. V8-460

Fig. 11 Camshaft and related parts. V8-460

OIL PAN, REPLACE
V8-460

1. Disconnect radiator shroud from radiator.
2. Raise vehicle on hoist and drain crankcase.
3. Disconnect idler arm from underbody.
4. Loosen starter retaining bolts.
5. Remove cylinder block to converter housing supports.
6. Disconnect engine front support insulators from underbody crossmember. Place floor jack under front of oil pan, with block of wood between jack and oil pan. Raise engine just enough to insert 1" blocks of wood between insulators and underbody side members. Remove floor jack.
7. Remove end attachments of front stabilizer and rotate ends of bar down to raise center of bar. Remove oil filter.
8. Remove oil pan bolts and lower pan to underbody crossmember. Remove splash shield from right side of pan.
9. Disconnect pressure line at power steering pump. Remove bolts retaining pump to front cover and rotate pump to clear oil pan. Remove oil pan.
10. Reverse procedure to install oil pan.

OIL PUMP

To remove the pump, drop the oil pan as outlined above. Then remove the two bolts that attach the pump to the crankcase and remove pump, gasket and the intermediate shaft.

To disassemble, remove the pump cover plate, Fig. 14, and lift out the rotor

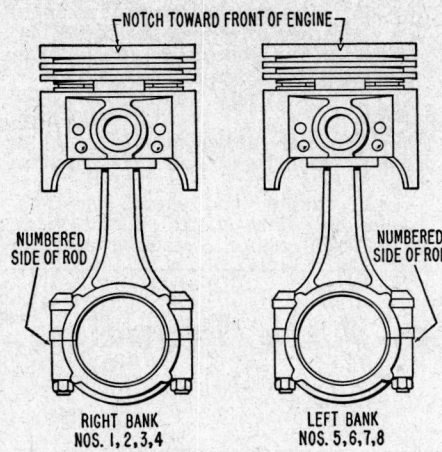

NOTCH TOWARD FRONT OF ENGINE

NUMBERED SIDE OF ROD

RIGHT BANK NOS. 1,2,3,4

NUMBERED SIDE OF ROD

LEFT BANK NOS. 5,6,7,8

Fig. 12   Piston and rod assembly

and shaft. Scrape the stake marks that hold the relief valve in the pump housing until the retainer can be removed. Then remove the retainer, spring and relief valve from the pump housing. Inspect the pump as follows:

1. With all parts clean and dry, check the inside of the pump housing and the outer race and rotor for damage or excessive wear.
2. Check the mating surface of the pump cover for wear. If this surface is worn, scored or grooved, replace the cover.
3. Measure the clearance between the outer race and housing. This clearance should be .006-.012".
4. With the rotor assembly installed in the housing, place a straight edge over the rotor assembly and housing.

Measure the clearance between the straight edge and the rotor and outer race. Recommended limits are .0015-.004".
5. Check the drive shaft-to-housing bearing clearance by measuring the O.D. of the shaft and the I.D. of the housing bearing. The recommended clearance limits are .0015-.0029".
6. Inspect the relief valve spring for a collapsed or worn condition.
7. Check the relief valve piston for scores and free operation in the bore.

BELT TENSION DATA

	New	Used
1969-75 All	140	110

WATER PUMP, REPLACE
V8-460

1. Drain cooling system.
2. Remove shroud and fan.
3. Remove drive belts and water pump pulley.
4. Remove bolts attaching compressor bracket to water pump if so equipped.
5. Loosen alternator bracket and remove bolts attaching bracket to water pump.
6. Disconnect lower radiator hose, heater return tube and bypass hose at water pump.
7. Remove remaining water pump bolts and remove water pump.

FUEL PUMP PRESSURE

Year	Engine	Pressure, Lbs.
1969	V8-460	4½-6½
1970-73	V8-460	5-7
1974-75	V8-460 ①	5½-6½
1974-75	V8-460 ②	6.2-7.2

① Exc. Calif.
② Calif.

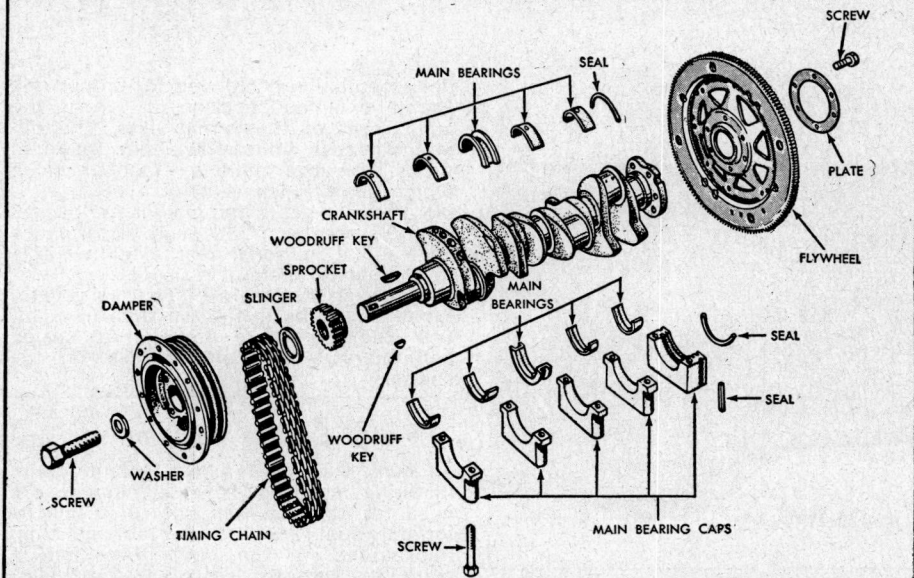

Fig. 13   Crankshaft and related parts

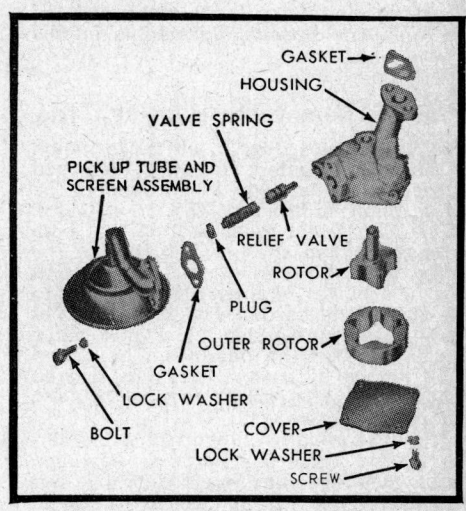

Fig. 14   Oil pump assembly

FUEL PUMP, REPLACE

Removal

1. Remove hose clamps and fuel line hoses from pump inlet and vapor discharge connections. Disconnect fuel filter from fuel line.
2. Loosen but do not remove pump attaching capscrews. Crank engine until fuel pump eccentric on camshaft is in a position which applies the least tension on fuel pump rocker arm. Then remove capscrews and pump.
3. If replacement of fuel pump push rod is required, remove access cover from cylinder front cover and remove push rod.

Installation

1. Remove old gasket material from pump mounting pad and pump flange.
2. Install adapter and vapor discharge valve in new pump. Install heat shield and tighten retaining nuts. If pump push rod was removed, install it on eccentric sleeve and install access cover to cylinder front cover.
3. Apply sealer to both sides of new gasket. Position gasket on pump flange and hold pump in position on cylinder front cover. Make sure rocker arm is riding on push rod.
4. Press pump tight against cylinder front cover. Install and tighten retaining screws.
5. Connect fuel lines. Then operate engine and check for leaks.

Transmission, Rear Axle, Propeller Shaft & Brakes

1974-75 AUTO. TRANS. LINKAGE ADJUST

1974-75 Mark IV

1. Place selector lever in D position tight against the stop.
2. Remove nut from transmission end of cable and remove cable from lever stud.
3. Shift manual lever at transmission into D position, second detent from back.
4. Place cable end on transmission manual lever stud, using care to align flats on the stud with the flats on the cable. Start attaching nut.
5. Make sure selector lever has not moved from D stop; then tighten nut to 10-15 ft. lbs.
6. Check operation for all lever positions.

1975 Continental

The control linkage adjustment procedures are the same as described for the 1973-74 models in the rear of this manual.

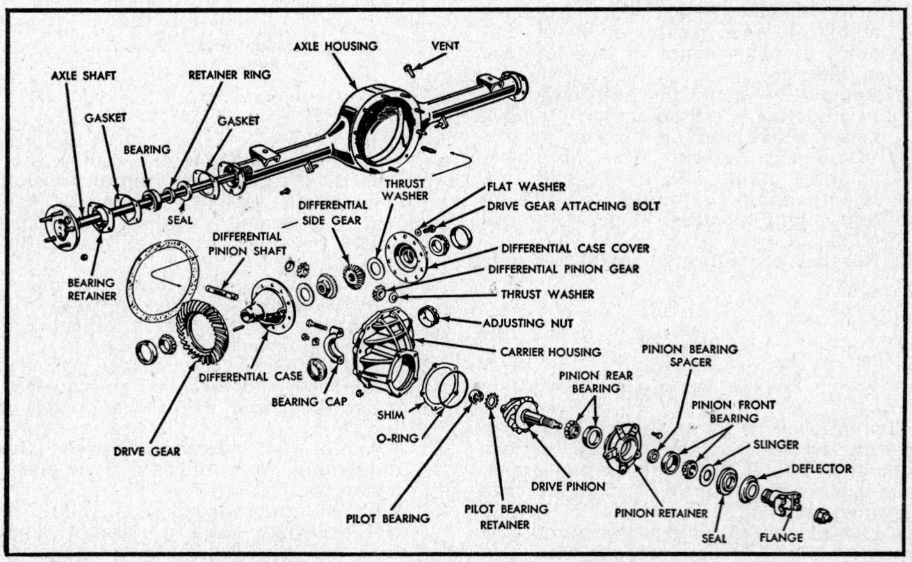

Fig. 1 Rear axle assembly. 1969-75

REAR AXLES

Fig. 1 illustrates the rear axle assemblies used on these cars. When necessary to overhaul either of these units, refer to the *Rear Axle Specifications* table in this chapter.

1969-75 Removable Housing Type

In these axles, Fig. 1, the drive pinion is straddle-mounted by two opposed tapered roller bearings which support the pinion shaft in front of the drive pinion gear, and straight roller bearing that supports the pinion shaft at the rear of the pinion gear. The drive pinion is assembled in a pinion retainer that is bolted to the differential carrier. The tapered roller bearings are preloaded by a collapsible spacer between the bearings. The pinion is positioned by a shim or shims located between the drive pinion retainer and the differential carrier.

The differential is supported in the carrier by two tapered roller side bearings. These bearings are preloaded by two threaded ring nuts or sleeves between the bearings and pedestals. The differen-

Fig. 2 Removing nuts from rear bearing retainer

tial assembly is positioned for proper ring gear and pinion backlash by varying the adjustment of these ring nuts. The differential case houses two side gears in mesh with two pinions mounted on a pinion shaft which is held in place by a pin. The side gears and pinions are backed by thrust washers. With high performance engines, an optional rear axle having a four-pinion differential is also used.

The axle shafts are of unequal length, the left shaft being shorter than the right. The axle shafts are mounted in sealed ball bearings that are pressed on the shafts.

Service Bulletin

All Ford Built Rear Axles: Recent manufacturing changes have eliminated the need for marking rear axle drive pinions for individual variations from nominal shim thicknesses. In the past, these pinion markings, with the aid of a shim selection table, were used as a guide to select correct shim thicknesses when a gear set

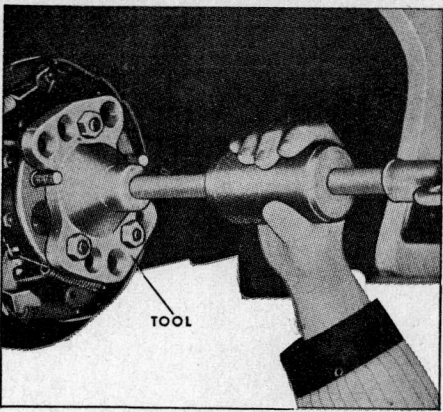

Fig. 3 Removing axle shaft with slide hammer-type puller

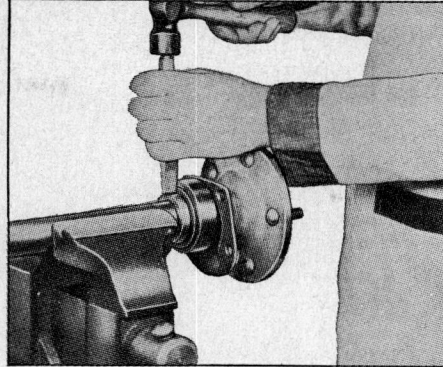

Fig. 4 Splitting bearing inner retainer for bearing removal

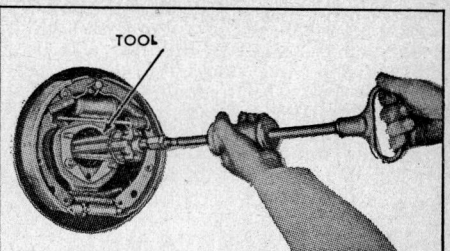

Fig. 5 Using hook-type tool to remove oil seal

or carrier assembly replacement was performed.

With the elimination of pinion markings, use of the shim selection table is no longer possible and the methods outlined below must be used.

1. Measure the thickness of the original pinion depth shim removed from the axle. Use the same thickness upon installation of the replacement carrier or drive pinion. If any further shim change is necessary, it will be indicated in the tooth pattern check.
2. If the original shim is lost, substitute a nominal shim for the original and use the tooth pattern check to determine if further shim changes are required.

DIFFERENTIAL CARRIER, REPLACE

1969-75 Rear Axles

In servicing the rear axles shown in Fig. 1, it is not necessary to remove the rear axle assembly for any normal repairs. The axle shafts and carrier assembly can easily be removed from the ve-

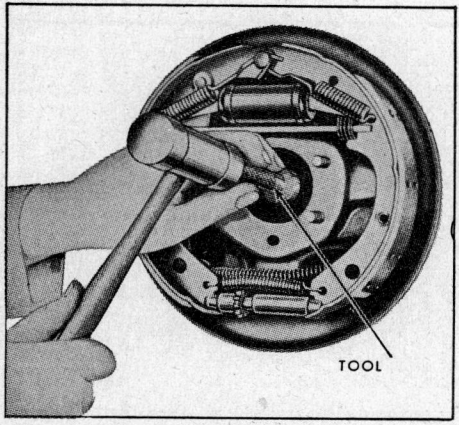

Fig. 6 Using special driver to install oil seal

hicle, leaving the axle housing in place.

1. Place a drain pan under the carrier and housing to catch the old grease when the carrier is separated from the housing.
2. Use a wire brush to clean dirt from the area around the carrier and housing mating surfaces. Then wipe the area clean with a cloth dampened in solvent.
3. Remove axle shafts and drive shaft as explained below.
4. Unfasten carrier from housing and lift out carrier.
5. Reverse removal procedure to install, using a new gasket between the carrier and housing.

AXLE SHAFTS

1. Remove wheel assembly.
2. Remove brake drum from flange.
3. Working through hole provided in axle shaft flange, Fig. 2, remove nuts that secure wheel bearing retainer.
4. Pull axle shaft out of housing with a slide hammer-type puller, Fig. 3. *Brake carrier plate must not be dislodged. Install one nut to hold the plate in place after axle shaft is removed.*
5. If axle shaft bearing is to be replaced, loosen inner retainer by nicking it deeply with a chisel in several places, Fig. 4. The bearing will then slide off easily.
6. Press bearing from axle shaft.
7. Inspect machined surface of axle shaft and housing for rough spots that would affect the sealing action of the oil seal. Carefully remove any burrs or rough spots.
8. Press new bearing on shaft until it seats firmly against shoulder on shaft.
9. Press inner bearing retainer on shaft until it seats firmly against bearing.
10. If oil seal is to be replaced, use a hook-type tool to pull it out of the housing, Fig. 5. Wipe a small amount of oil resistant sealer on outer edge of seal before it is installed, Fig. 6.

Installation

1. Place a new gasket on each side of

brake carrier plate and slide axle shaft into housing. Start splines into differential side gear and push the shaft in until bearing bottoms in housing.
2. Install retainer and tighten nuts to 30-40 ft. lbs.
3. Install brake drum and wheel.

PROPELLER SHAFT

To maintain proper drive line balance, mark the drive shaft, universal joints, slip yoke and companion flange before removing the shaft assembly so it can be reinstalled in its original position.

1. Remove cap-screws attaching slip yoke to front U-joint.
2. Push slip yoke forward on transmission output shaft and lower front of drive shaft.
3. Remove nuts, lockwashers and U-bolts attaching rear U-joint to differential drive pinion flange.
4. Remove shaft assembly.
5. Reverse removal procedure to install the assembly, and torque capscrews and U-bolts to 15-18 ft. lbs.

PROPELLER SHAFT BALANCE

If detailed parts of the drive shaft as-

Fig. 7 Checking pinion nose angle. To make this tool, obtain a common protractor and drill a small hole at the exact center of the base line (0°). Attach a string and weight as shown

sembly have been replaced and shaft vibration is encountered after installation, disconnect the shaft at the slip yoke. Rotate the slip yoke and transmission output shaft 180°; then reconnect the shaft to the yoke. If vibration persists, disconnect the shaft at the rear axle flange and rotate the flange and drive pinion 180° and reconnect shaft to flange.

DRIVE LINE ANGLE CHECK

Vibration or "shudder" which is noticeable either on fast acceleration or when coasting (using engine for a brake) may be caused by rear axle housing being loose on rear springs or by excessive drive line angles. If the rear axle U-bolts are loose, torque the nuts to 50-60 ft. lbs.

Drive line angles may be corrected by tilting the rear axle pinion nose up or down as required. Tapered shims (wedges) are available in three angles: $\frac{1}{2}$, 1 and $1\frac{1}{2}$ degrees with no more than one wedge to be used on a side.

To determine if shimming or a change of shimming is required, check the pinion nose angle as related to the rear riding height of the car. After checking and recording riding height, check the pinion nose angle as follows:
1. Measure pinion nose angle as shown in Fig. 7.
2. Compare riding height measurement and pinion nose angle with those shown in the following chart:

Riding Height	Pinion Nose Angle*
6"	4° Down
7"	$3\frac{1}{2}$° Down
8"	3° Down
9"	$2\frac{1}{2}$° Down

*Plus or minus $\frac{1}{4}$°
3. If nose angle does not compare to related riding height, remove U-bolt nuts and install appropriate wedges between each spring insulator upper retainer and axle housing mounting pad.

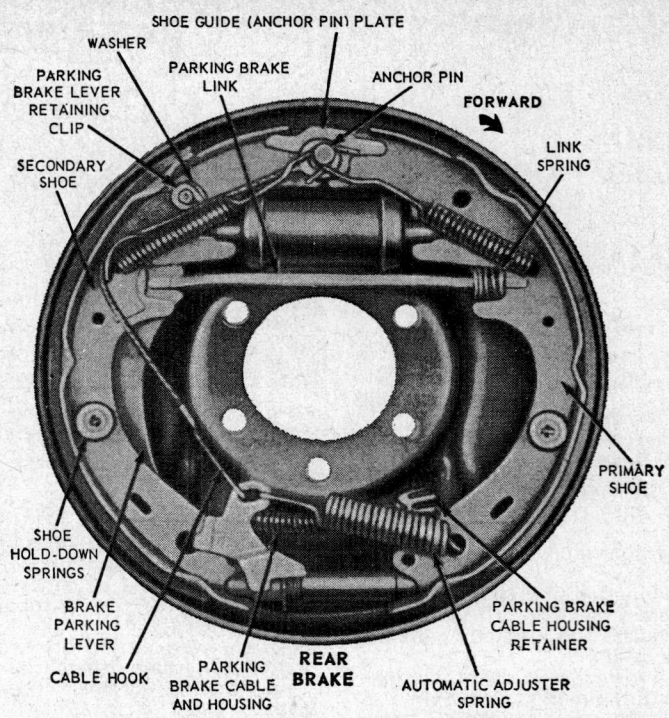

Fig. 8 Rear only on 1969-75

4. Install and torque U-bolt nuts to 50-60 ft. lbs. Make sure lower insulator retainer contacts upper retainer.

BRAKE ADJUSTMENTS

NOTE: For 1970-75 a new self-centering pressure differential valve is used which no longer requires bleeding at the opposite end of the car to cause the brake warning light to go out. To center the new valve, after any brake repair or bleeding, it is only necessary to turn the ignition switch on and depress the brake pedal. This action will center the piston and the light will go out.

These brakes, Fig. 8, have self-adjust-

ing shoe mechanisms that assure correct lining-to-drum clearances at all times. The automatic adjusters operate only when the brakes are applied when the car is moving rearward or when the car comes to an uphill stop.

Although the brakes are self-adjusting, an initial adjustment is necessary when the brake shoes have been relined or replaced, or when the length of the star wheel adjuster has been changed during some other service operation.

Frequent usage of an automatic transmission forward range to halt reverse vehicle motion may prevent the automatic adjusters from functioning, thereby inducing low pedal heights. Should low pedal heights be encountered, it is recommended that numerous forward and re-

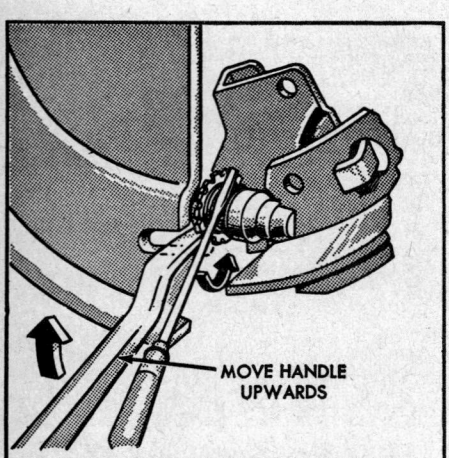

Fig. 9 Backing off brake adjustment by disengaging adjuster lever with screwdriver

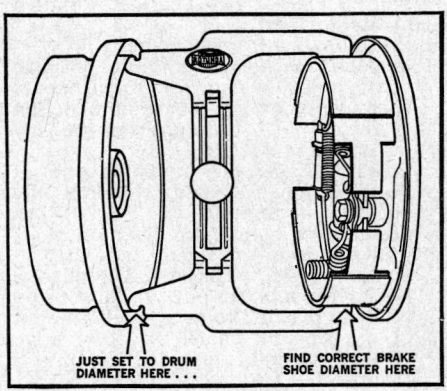

Fig. 10 Brake adjustment with gauge

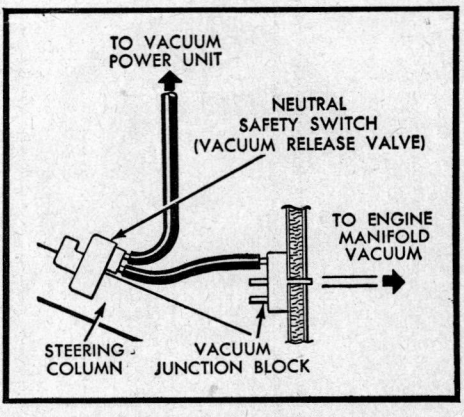

Fig. 11 Vacuum connections for automatic parking brake release. 1969-75

verse stops be made until satisfactory pedal height is obtained.

NOTE

If a low pedal height condition cannot **be** corrected by making numerous reverse stops (provided the hydraulic system is free of air) it indicates that the automatic adjusting mechanism is not functioning. Therefore, it will be necessary to remove the brake drum, clean, free up and lubricate the adjusting mechanism. Then adjust the brakes, being sure the parking brake is fully released.

Adjustment

1. Remove adjusting hole cover from brake backing plate and, from the backing plate side, turn adjusting screw upward with a screwdriver or other suitable tool to expand the shoes until a slight drag is felt when the drum is rotated.
2. Remove the drum.
3. While holding the adjusting lever out of engagement with the adjusting screw, Fig. 9, back off the adjusting screw ¾ turn with the fingers.

NOTE: *If finger movement will not turn the screw, free it up. If this is not done, the adjusting lever will not turn the screw during subsequent vehicle operation. Lubricate the screw with oil and coat with wheel bearing grease. Any other adjustment procedure may cause damage to the adjusting screw with consequent self-adjuster problems.*

4. Install wheel and drum, and adjusting hole cover. Adjust brakes on remaining wheels in the same manner.
5. If pedal height is not satisfactory, drive the vehicle and make sufficient reverse stops until proper pedal height is obtained.

SERVICE BULLETIN

When servicing a vehicle requiring a brake adjustment, the metal knock-out plugs should NOT be removed. Rather the drums should be removed and brakes inspected for a malfunction.

Although the brakes are self-adjusting, an initial adjustment will be necessary after a brake repair, such as relining or replacement. The initial adjustment can be obtained by the new procedure which follows:

1. Use the brake shoe adjustment gauge shown in Fig. 10 to obtain the drum inside diameter as shown. Tighten the adjusting knob on the gauge to hold this setting.
2. Place the opposite side of the gauge over the brake shoes and adjust the shoes by turning the adjuster screw until the gauge just slides over the linings. Rotate the gauge around the lining surface to assure proper lining diameter adjustment and clearance.
3. Install brake drum and wheel. Final

Fig. 12   Sectional view of rear disc brake caliper

adjustment is accomplished by making several firm reverse stops, using the brake pedal.

REAR WHEEL DISC BRAKE & PARKING BRAKE SERVICE

Sliding caliper rear disc brakes are used on some 1975 models. The caliper is basically the same as the larger front wheel caliper, however, a parking brake

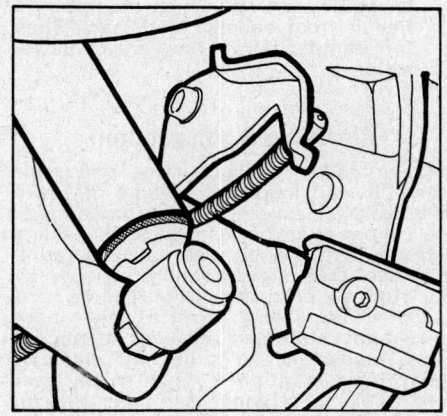

Fig. 13   Parking lever and cable installation

mechanism and a larger inner brake shoe anti-rattle clip has been added, Fig. 12. A hydraulically powered brake booster (Hydroboost) provides the power assist for this four wheel disc brake system.

The parking brake lever, located at the inboard side of the caliper, is actuated by a cable system similar to rear drum brake applications. When the parking brake is applied, the cable rotates the lever and operating shaft. Three steel balls, placed in pockets between the opposing heads of the operating shaft and thrust screw, roll between ramps formed in the pockets and force the thrust screw away from the operating shaft, in turn, driving the caliper piston and brake shoe assembly against the rotor. An automatic adjuster in the assembly compensates for lining wear and maintains proper clearance in the parking brake mechanism.

The cast iron rotors are ventilated by curved fins located between the braking surfaces and are designed to cause the rotor to act as an air pump when the vehicle is traveling forward. The rotors which are not interchangeable, are identified by a Right or Left marking cast inside the hat section of the rotor. The rotors are secured to the axle flange in the same manner as rear brake drums. A splash shield bolted to a forged axle adapter, protects the inboard rotor surface.

Caliper Removal

NOTE: After performing any service work, obtain a firm brake pedal before moving vehicle.

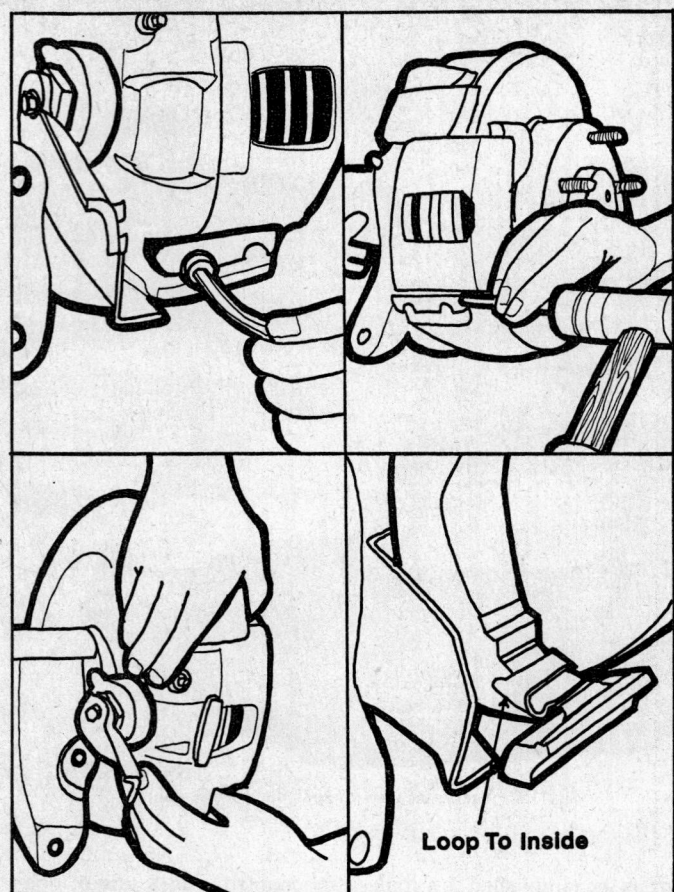

Fig. 14 Removing rear caliper assembly

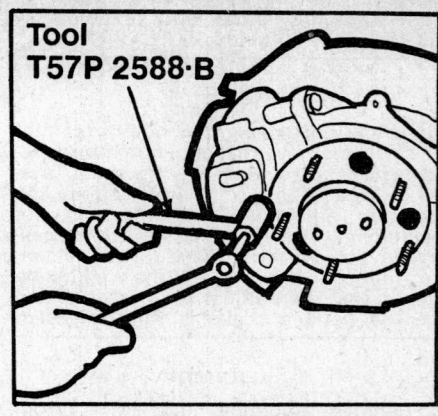

Fig. 15 Adjusting piston depth for lining installation

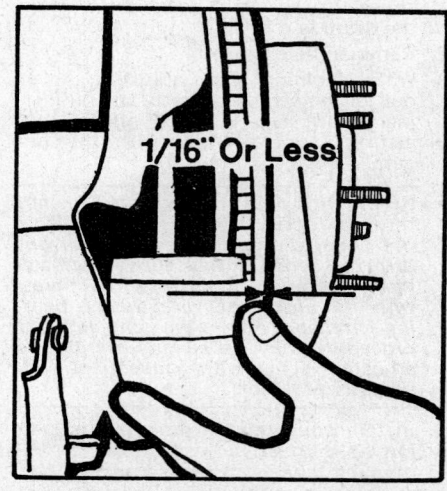

Fig. 16 Checking lining clearance

1. Raise vehicle and support on safety stands, then remove tire and wheel assemblies.
2. Disconnect fitting on rear brake tube from hose end fitting at frame mounted bracket and plug end of brake tube to prevent loss of fluid and entry of dirt. Remove horseshoe retaining clip from hose fitting and disengage hose from bracket.
3. Disconnect parking cable from lever, Fig. 13, using care to avoid kinking or cutting cable or return spring, then remove retaining screw from caliper retaining key, Fig. 14.
4. Slide caliper retaining key and support spring from anchor plate, Fig. 14. If necessary, use a hammer and brass drift, being careful to avoid damaging key on sliding ways or hitting parking brake lever.

NOTE: If caliper cannot be removed due to rust build-up on outer edge of rotor, scrape off loose scale, being careful not to damage braking surfaces. If rotor wear or scoring prevents removal of caliper, it will be necessary to loosen caliper end retainer ½ turn maximum, to allow piston to be forced back into its bore. To loosen end retainer, remove parking brake lever and mark or scribe end retainer and caliper housing to be sure that end retainer is not loosened more than ½ turn, then force

piston back in its bore, Fig. 14, and move caliper back and forth to center rotor and remove caliper. If retainer must be loosened more than ½ turn, use caution, as the seal between the thrust screw and housing may be broken and brake fluid will enter parking brake mechanism chamber. In this case, the end retainer must be removed and the internal parts cleaned and lubricated.

5. Remove inner shoe and lining assembly from anchor plate, then tap lightly on outer shoe and lining assembly to free it from caliper. Mark each shoe for identification if they are to be re-used.

Cleaning & Inspection

Clean caliper, anchor plate and rotor assembly and inspect for signs of brake fluid leakage, excessive wear or damage. The caliper must be inspected for leakage both in piston boot area and operating shaft seal area. Lightly sand or wire brush any rust or corrosion from caliper and anchor plate sliding surfaces and inner brake shoe abutment surfaces in anchor plate. Inspect brake shoes for wear. If either lining is within 1/32 inch of any rivet head, replace both shoe and lining assemblies from both wheels in order to maintain equal brake action.

Caliper Installation

1. If end retainer has been loosened only ½ turn, reinstall caliper in anchor plate using key. Do not install shoe and lining assembly. Torque end retainer to 75-95 ft. lbs. and install parking brake actuating lever on its keyed spline. Lever arm must point down and rearward so that parking brake cable will pass freely under axle. Torque retainer screw to 16-22 ft. lbs.

NOTE: Parking brake lever must rotate freely after torquing retainer screw.

2. Remove caliper from anchor plate. If new shoe and lining assemblies are to be installed, the piston must be bottomed in caliper bore using tool T57P-2588-B to provide clearance. Remove rotor and install caliper without lining and shoe assemblies in anchor plate using key only. Install tool and while holding shaft, rotate tool handle counterclockwise until the tool seats firmly against piston, Fig. 15. Loosen handle about ¼ turn, and while holding handle rotate tool shaft clockwise until piston is fully bot-

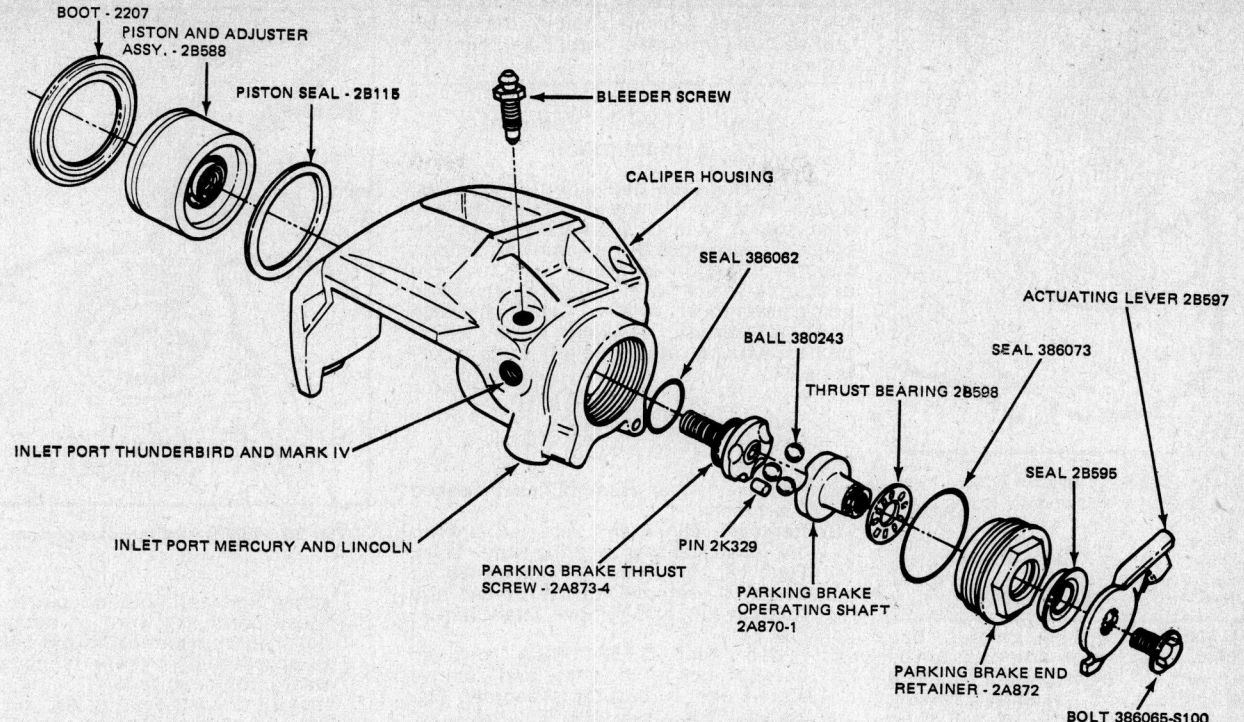

Fig. 17   Rear disc brake caliper assembly

tomed in bore (piston will continue to
turn even after it is bottomed). Turn
tool handle until there is no further
inward movement of piston and there
is a firm seating force, then remove
caliper from mounting plate and reinstall rotor.

3. Making certain that brake shoe anti
rattle clip is in place in lower inner
brake shoe support on anchor plate
with loop of clip toward inside of
anchor plate, Fig. 14, position inner
brake shoe and lining assembly on
anchor plate.

4. Install outer brake shoe with lower
flange ends against caliper abutments
and brake shoe upper flanges over
shoulders on caliper legs. The shoe
upper flanges fit tightly against machined shoulder surfaces.

NOTE: If old brake shoes and lining
assemblies are re-used, be certain the
shoes are installed in their original
positions as marked for identification
during removal.

5. Lubricate caliper and anchor sliding
ways with M1C-167-A (LPS-ESA-100)
grease, using care to prevent lubricant from getting on braking surfaces,
then position caliper housing lower
V-groove on anchor plate lower abutment surfaces.

6. Rotate caliper until it is completely
over rotor, being careful not to damage piston dust boot, then pull caliper outboard until inner shoe and
lining is firmly seated against rotor.
Measure clearance between outer lining and rotor which should be $1/16$ inch
or less, Fig. 16. If it is greater, remove caliper and move piston outward to narrow gap. Follow procedure
in step 2 and note that $1/4$ turn of
the shaft counterclockwise, moves

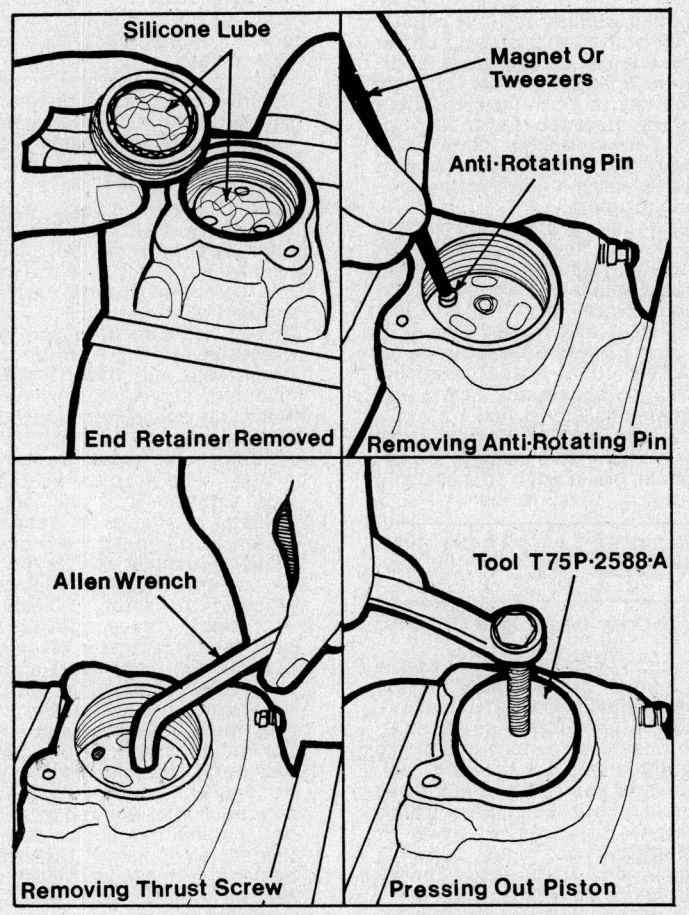

Fig. 18   Disassembling rear disc brake caliper

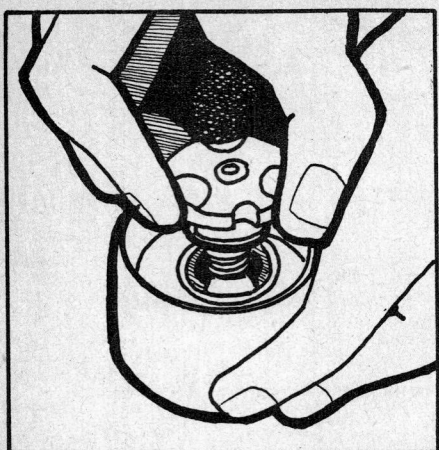

Fig. 19 Checking parking brake adjuster operation

piston about $1/16$ inch.

CAUTION: A clearance greater than $1/16$ turn may allow adjuster to be pulled out of piston when service brake is applied, causing parking brake to fail to adjust. It will then be necessary to replace piston/adjuster assembly.

7. While holding caliper against anchor plate upper abutment surfaces, center caliper over lower anchor plate abutment, then position caliper support spring and key in slot and slide them into opening between lower end of caliper and lower anchor plate abutment until key semi-circular slot is centered over retaining screw threaded hole in anchor plate.
8. Install key retaining screw and torque to 12-16 ft. lbs., then reinstall brake hose on caliper. On Lincoln and Mercury models, place a new gasket on fitting and torque to 20-30 ft. lbs. On Thunderbird and Mark IV models, place a new gasket on each side of fitting outlet, then install attaching bolts through washers and fitting and torque bolts to 17-25 ft. lbs.
9. Position upper end of flexible hose in bracket and install retaining clip, then connect brake tube to hose and torque fitting to 10-15 ft. lbs.

NOTE: Do not twist or coil brake hose, the stripe on the hose must be kept straight.

10. Connect parking brake lever to lever on caliper.
11. Bleed brake system, then with engine running pump brake pedal lightly about 40 times allowing 1 second between pedal applications. An alternate with engine off is to pump brake pedal lightly about 10 times to discharge accumulator, then pump brake pedal firmly about 30 times. Check parking brake for excessive travel or very light effort, if so, repeat pumping brake pedal, and if necessary check parking brake cable tension.
12. Install wheel and torque nuts to 70-115 ft. lbs.

NOTE: Before moving vehicle, make certain that a firm brake pedal has been obtained.

Shoe & Lining Removal & Installation

To remove shoe and lining assemblies, follow "Caliper Removal" procedure and omit step 3 as it is not necessary to disconnect brake hose. After removing caliper, support it with a length of wire to avoid damaging brake hose. To install shoe and lining assemblies, follow "Caliper Installation" procedure, making certain that proper parking brake adjustment is obtained.

Caliper Overhaul

Disassemble

1. Remove caliper assembly as described previously.
2. Remove caliper end retainer, operating shaft, thrust bearing and balls, Fig. 17, then using a magnet or tweezers, remove thrust screw anti rotation pin, and remove thrust screw, Fig. 18.
3. Install tool T75P-2588-A through back of caliper housing and remove piston and carburetor assembly, Fig. 18.

CAUTION: Use care not to damage polished surface in thrust screw bore and do not attempt to remove or press adjuster can, as it is a press fit in piston.

4. Remove and discard piston seal, boot, thrust O-ring seal, end retainer, O-ring and end retainer lip seal.

Cleaning & Inspection

1. Clean all metal parts with alcohol, then using clean, dry compressed air, blow out and dry all grooves and passages making sure the caliper bore and component parts are free of any foreign material.
2. Inspect caliper bore for damage or excessive wear. The thrust screw must be smooth and free of pits. If piston is pitted, scored or chrome plating is worn, replace piston and adjuster assembly.
3. Adjuster can must be bottomed in piston to be properly seated and provide consistent brake operation. If adjuster can is loose, appears high in piston, is damaged, or if brake adjustment is usually too tight, too loose or not functioning, replace piston/adjuster assembly. Check adjuster operation by assembling thrust screw into piston/adjuster assembly, then pull the two parts apart about $1/4$ inch and release them, Fig. 19. When pulling on the two parts, the brass drive ring must remain stationary causing the nut to rotate. When releasing the two parts, the nut must remain stationary and drive ring must rotate. If action does not follow this pattern, replace piston/adjuster assembly.
4. Inspect ball pockets, threads, grooves, bearing surfaces of thrust screw, operating shaft, balls and anti rotation pin for wear, brinnelling or pitting. Replace operating shaft, balls, thrust

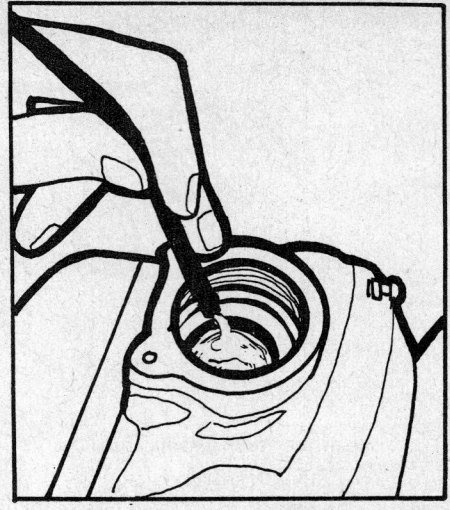

Fig. 20 Filling piston/adjuster assembly

screw and anti rotation pin if any of these parts are worn or damaged. A polished appearance on the ball paths is acceptable if there is no sign of wear into the surface.
5. Inspect thrust bearing for corrosion, pitting or wear and replace as necessary.
6. Inspect end plug bearing surface for wear or brinnelling and replace as necessary. A polished appearance on bearing surface is acceptable if there is no sign of wear into surface.
7. Inspect operating lever for damage and replace as necessary.

Assemble

1. Coat new caliper piston seal with clean brake fluid and install it in caliper making certain that seal is not twisted and is fully seated in groove.
2. Install new dust boot by seating flange squarely in outer groove of caliper bore, then coat piston/adjuster assembly with clean brake fluid and install it in caliper bore. Spread dust boot over piston as it is installed and seat dust boot in piston groove.
3. Install caliper in vise, Fig. 20, and fill piston/adjuster assembly with clean brake fluid.
4. Coat new thrust screw O-ring with clean brake fluid and install it in thrust screw groove, then install thrust screw into piston adjuster assembly until top surface of thrust screw is flush with bottom of threaded bore, being careful to avoid cutting O-ring seal. Index notches on thrust screw and caliper housing and install anti rotation screw.
5. Place a ball in each of three pockets of thrust screw and apply a liberal amount of silicone grease M1C-169-A on parking brake components, then install operating shaft on balls.
6. Coat thrust bearing with silicone grease and install it on operating shaft, then install a new lip seal and O-ring on end retainer.
7. Lightly coat O-ring seal and lip seal with silicone grease and install end retainer in caliper. Firmly hold oper-

ating shaft against internal mechanism while installing end retainer to prevent mislocation of balls. If lip seal moves out of position, reseat seal. Torque end retainer to 75-95 ft. lbs.

NOTE: Parking brake lever must rotate freely after torquing.

8. Install parking brake lever on keyed spline facing down and rearward. Torque retaining screw to 16-22 ft. lbs.
9. Bottom piston using tool T75P-2588-B and install caliper as described previously.

PARKING BRAKES, ADJUST

1970-75

1. Make sure the parking brake is fully released.
2. Place transmission in neutral and raise the vehicle.
3. Tighten the adjusting nut against the cable equalizer to cause rear wheel brake drag. Then loosen the adjusting nut until the rear brakes are fully released. There should be no brake drag.
4. Lower the vehicle and check operation.

1969

1. Fully release parking brake.
2. Loosen adjusting nut on equalizer rod, then turn lock nut in front of equalizer several turns forward.
3. Depress parking brake slowly until initial locking position is obtained.
4. Turn adjusting nut forward against equalizer until about 100 lbs. of force at the outside diameter of the tire is required to turn the rear wheels.
5. Tighten lock nut against equalizer.
6. Release parking brake and check to make sure that there is no drag when rear wheels are turned.

1969-75 Vacuum Release Unit

The vacuum power unit, Fig. 11, will release the parking brake automatically when the transmission selector lever is moved into any driving position with the engine running. The brakes will not release automatically, however, when the selector lever is in neutral or park position with the engine running, or in any other position with the engine off.

The lower end of the release handle extends out for alternate manual release in the event of vacuum power failure or for optional manual release at any time.

POWER BRAKE UNIT, REPLACE

Vacuum Booster

1969-75

1. Disconnect battery ground cable.
2. Disconnect stop light switch wires and remove switch retaining pin. Slide switch off pin so switch outer hole clears pin, then remove switch. Slide booster push rod, nylon washers and bushing off brake pedal pin.
3. Remove master cylinder and position aside without damaging hydraulic lines.
4. Disconnect vacuum hose from booster and remove booster attaching nuts and booster.
5. Reverse procedure to install.

Hydro-Boost

1. Disconnect stoplight switch wires at connector and remove hairpin retainer, then slide stoplight switch off brake pedal pin far enough for switch outer hole to clear pin and remove pin from switch.
2. Slide hydro-boost push rod and nylon washers and bushing off brake pedal pin.
3. Remove master cylinder and position to one side without disturbing hydraulic lines.

NOTE: It is not necessary to disconnect brake lines, but care should be taken not to deform lines.

4. Disconnect pressure, steering gear and return lines from booster, then plug lines and ports in hydro-boost to prevent entry of dirt.
5. Remove hydro-boost retaining nuts, and remove assembly sliding push rod link from engine side of dash panel.

Rear Suspension

SHOCK ABSORBER, REPLACE

1. With the rear axle supported properly disconnect shock absorber at upper mounting and compress it to clear hole in spring seat.
2. Disconnect shock absorber from stud on axle bracket.
3. Reverse procedure to install.

COIL SPRINGS, REPLACE

1. Raise rear of vehicle and support at frame. Support rear axle with a suitable jack.
2. Disconnect shock absorbers at lower mountings.
3. Lower axle to remove springs.
4. Reverse procedure to install. On all models except 1972-75 Mark IV, install an insulator between upper and lower seats and the spring, Fig. 1. On 1972-75 Mark IV, an insulator is installed only between upper seat and the spring, Fig. 2.

CONTROL ARMS, REPLACE

NOTE: The 1972-75 Mark IV upper and lower control arms are replaced in pairs.

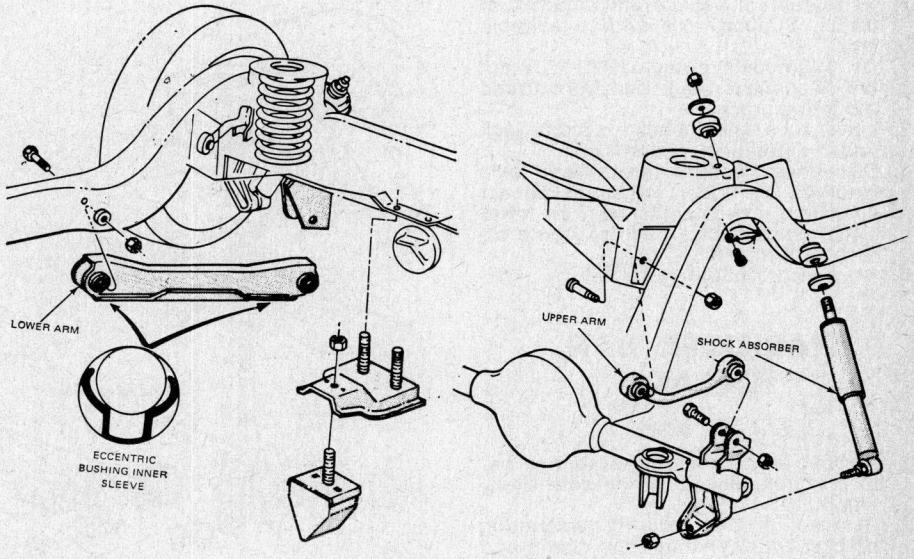

Fig. 2   Rear suspension. 1972-75 Mark IV

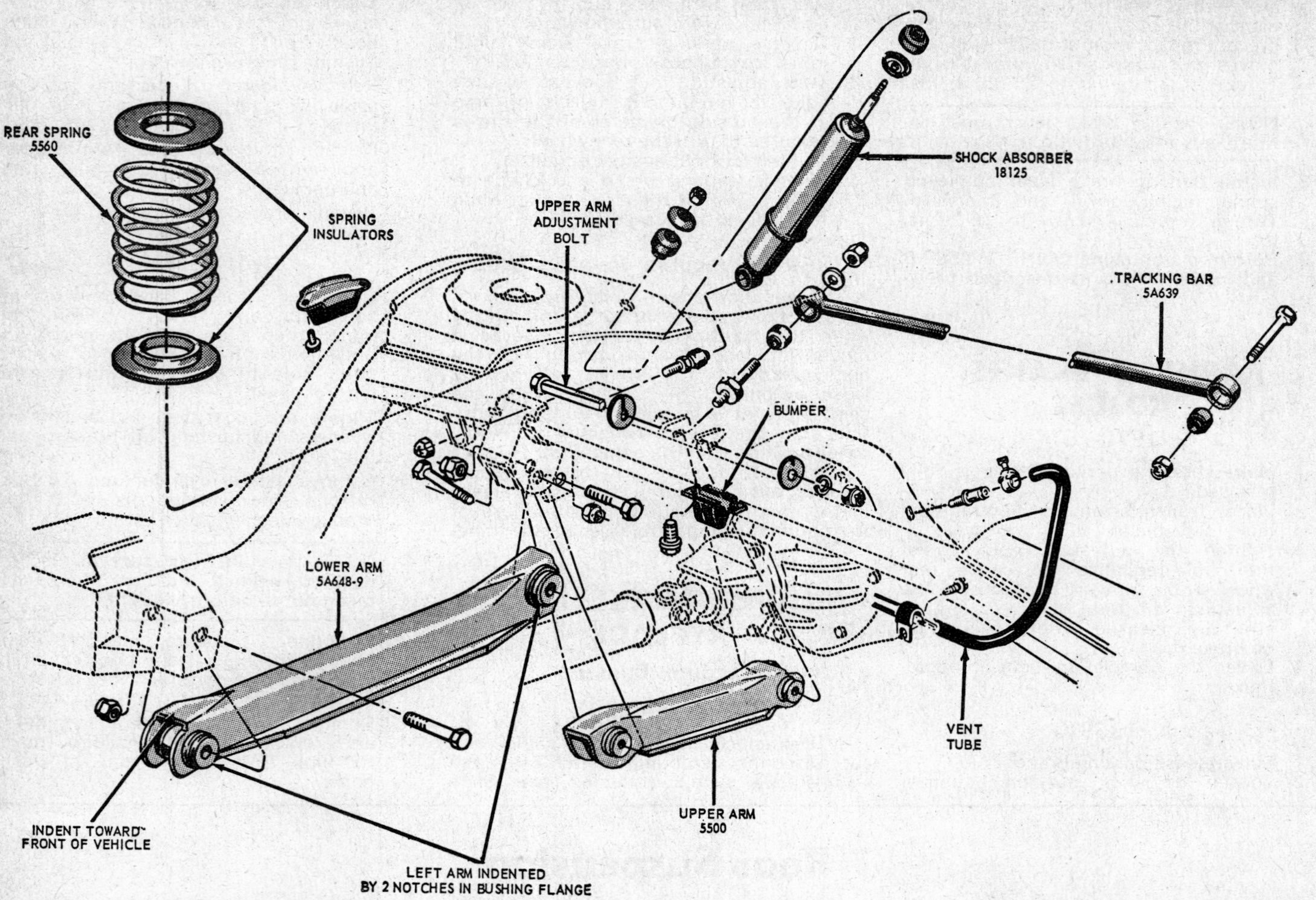

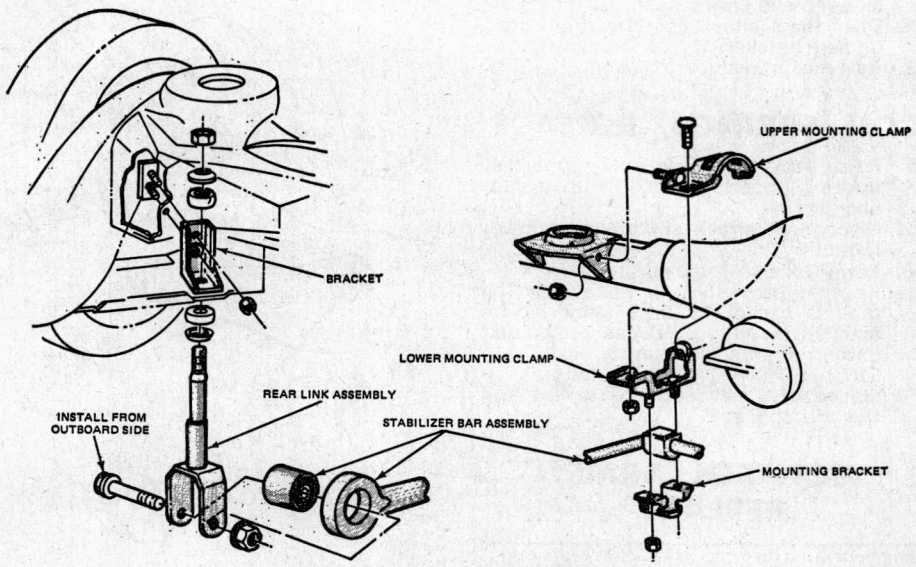

REAR SPRING
.5560

SPRING
INSULATORS

UPPER ARM
ADJUSTMENT
BOLT

SHOCK ABSORBER
18125

TRACKING BAR
5A639

BUMPER

LOWER ARM
5A648-9

VENT
TUBE

INDENT TOWARD
FRONT OF VEHICLE

LEFT ARM INDENTED
BY 2 NOTCHES IN BUSHING FLANGE

UPPER ARM
5500

Fig. 1   Rear suspension, 1969-71 Mark III & 1969-75 Continental

1. Raise rear of vehicle and support at frame. Support axle with a suitable jack.
2. On all models except 1972-75 Mark IV, disconnect track bar from frame mounting bracket.
3. Lower axle and install a second jack under differential pinion nose.
4. Disconnect control arm from axle bracket. On upper arms, disconnect arm from crossmember and on lower arms, disconnect arm from frame attachment bracket.
5. Reverse procedure to install.

STABILIZER BAR, REPLACE

1972-75 Mark IV

1. Remove bolts securing stabilizer bar to rear link assemblies on both sides, Fig. 3.
2. Remove nuts securing mounting bracket to lower mounting clamp and remove bar.
3. Reverse procedure to install.

BRACKET

UPPER MOUNTING CLAMP

REAR LINK ASSEMBLY

LOWER MOUNTING CLAMP

STABILIZER BAR ASSEMBLY

MOUNTING BRACKET

INSTALL FROM
OUTBOARD SIDE

Fig. 3   Stabilizer bar installation. 1972-75 Mark IV

TRACK BAR & BUSHINGS REPLACE

1. Remove cover from track bar axle attachment, then disconnect track bar from mounting stud.
2. Disconnect track bar from frame side rail.
3. On 1970-71 Mark III, replace frame bracket bushing by collapsing the .030 inch ferrule and driving out from bushing. Install bushing and new inner ferrule and compress bushing and washer to 2.16 inch and place inner ferrule over edge of inner washer.
4. Reverse procedure to install.

Front End and Steering Section

FRONT SUSPENSION
1969 Mark III & 1970-75 All

Referring to Fig. 1, each wheel rotates on a spindle. The upper and lower ends of the spindle are attached to upper and lower ball joints that are mounted to an upper and lower control arm. The upper control arm pivots on a shaft assembly that is bolted to the frame. The lower control arm pivots on a bolt in the front crossmember. The struts, which are connected between the lower control arms and frame crossmember, prevent the control arms from moving forward or backward.

1969 Continental

The front wheel suspension is a ball joint type utilizing coil springs and double acting shock absorbers. Fore and aft movement of each front wheel is controlled by a non-adjustable type stabilizing strut connected to the suspension lower control arm and to a point forward on the front crossmember, Fig. 2. A single rubber-cored bushing is used at the inner end of the lower control arm. Caster and camber are adjusted without the use of shims but rather by movement of the serrated upper control arm shaft.

LUBRICATION

1969-75 STEERING LINKAGE: The steering linkage should be lubricated at 36,000 mile intervals. Normal breathing of socket joints permits moisture condensation within the joint. Moisture inside the joint assembly will cause no appreciable damage and the joint will function normally. However, if the moisture is concentrated in the bearing grease grooves and is frozen at the time of attempted lubrication, grease cannot flow and pressure greasing may damage the joint assembly.

Do not attempt to lubricate the steering linkage if it has set in temperatures lower than 20 deg. above zero F. The vehicle should be allowed to warm up in a heated garage for 30 minutes or until the joints accept lubrication.

IMPORTANT: A torch must not be used to heat joints because this quantity of heat will melt the nylon bearing within the joint.

Ball Joint Lubrication

Ball joints should be lubricated with special grease formulated just for this purpose every 36,000 miles on 1969.

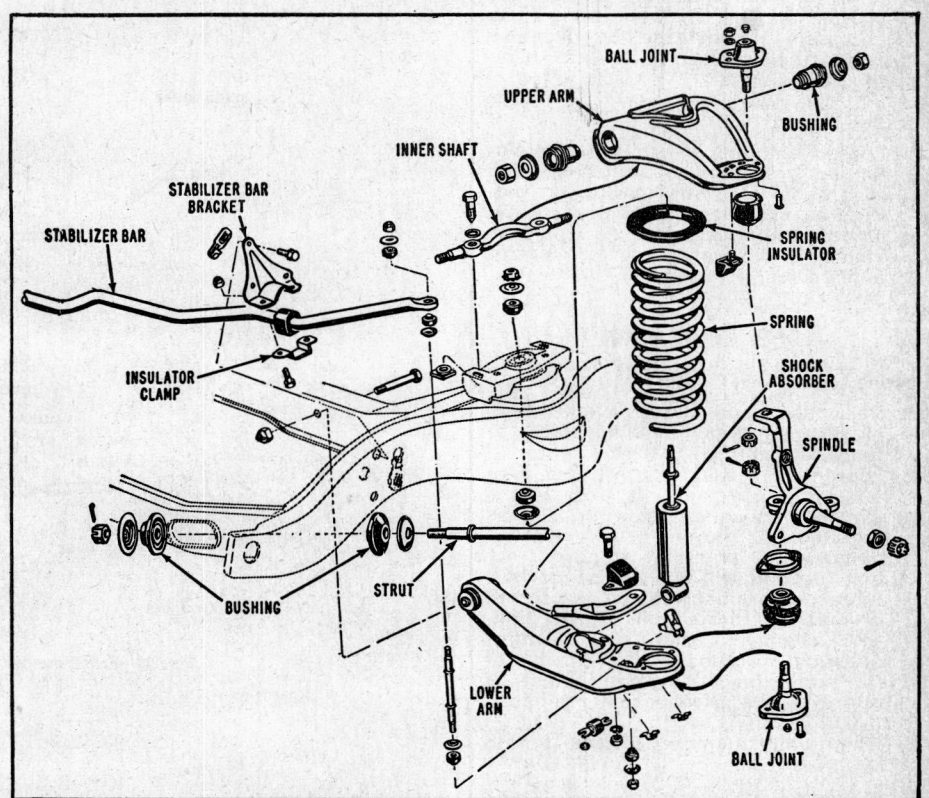

Fig. 1 Front suspension. 1969 Mark III & 1970-75 All

Lubrication points are fitted with screw plugs. The plugs should be removed, grease fittings installed and, after applying the grease, remove the fittings and reinstall the plugs.

WHEEL ALIGNMENT

SERVICE BULLETIN

WHEEL BALANCING DIFFERS: On cars with disc brakes, dynamic balancing of the wheel-and-tire assembly on the car should not be attempted without first pulling back the shoe and lining assemblies from the rotor. If this is not done, brake drag may burn out the motor on the wheel spinner.

The drag can be eliminated by removing the wheel, taking out the two bolts holding the caliper splash shield, and detaching the shield. Then push the pistons into their cylinder bores by applying steady pressure on the shoes on each side of the rotor for at least a minute. If necessary, use waterpump pliers to apply the pressure.

After the pistons have been retracted, reinstall the splash shield and wheel. The wheel-and-tire assembly can then be dynamically balanced in the usual way. After the balancing job has been completed, be sure to pump the brake pedal several times until the shoes are seated and a firm brake pedal is obtained.

LINCOLN CONTINENTAL

1969 Mark III & 1970-75 All

Caster and camber can be adjusted by loosening the bolts that attach the upper suspension arm to the shaft at the frame side rail, and moving the arm assembly in or out in the elongated bolt holes, Fig. 3. Since any movement of the arm affects both caster and camber, both factors should be balanced against one another when making the adjustment.

Caster, Adjust

1. To adjust caster, install the adjusting tool as shown in Fig. 3.
2. Loosen both upper arm inner shaft retaining bolts and move either front or rear of the shaft in or out as necessary to increase or decrease caster angle. Then tighten bolt to retain adjustment.

Camber, Adjust

1. Loosen both upper arm inner retaining bolts and move both front and rear ends of shaft inward or outward as necessary to increase or decrease camber angle.
2. Tighten bolts and recheck caster and readjust if necessary.

1969 Continental

Caster, Adjust

1. Raise hood and unsnap clips retaining top of rubber bushing shield to fender apron.
2. Loosen bolts that secure upper control arm shaft to frame and, with a pry bar, move shaft in or out as required. A movement of approximately $\frac{3}{32}$" at either front or rear bolt location will change caster $\frac{1}{2}$°. Inboard movement of the front bolt, or outboard movement of rear bolt, will change caster in negative direction. Outboard movement of front bolt or inboard movement of rear bolt will change caster in positive direction.
3. When adjustment is correct, torque

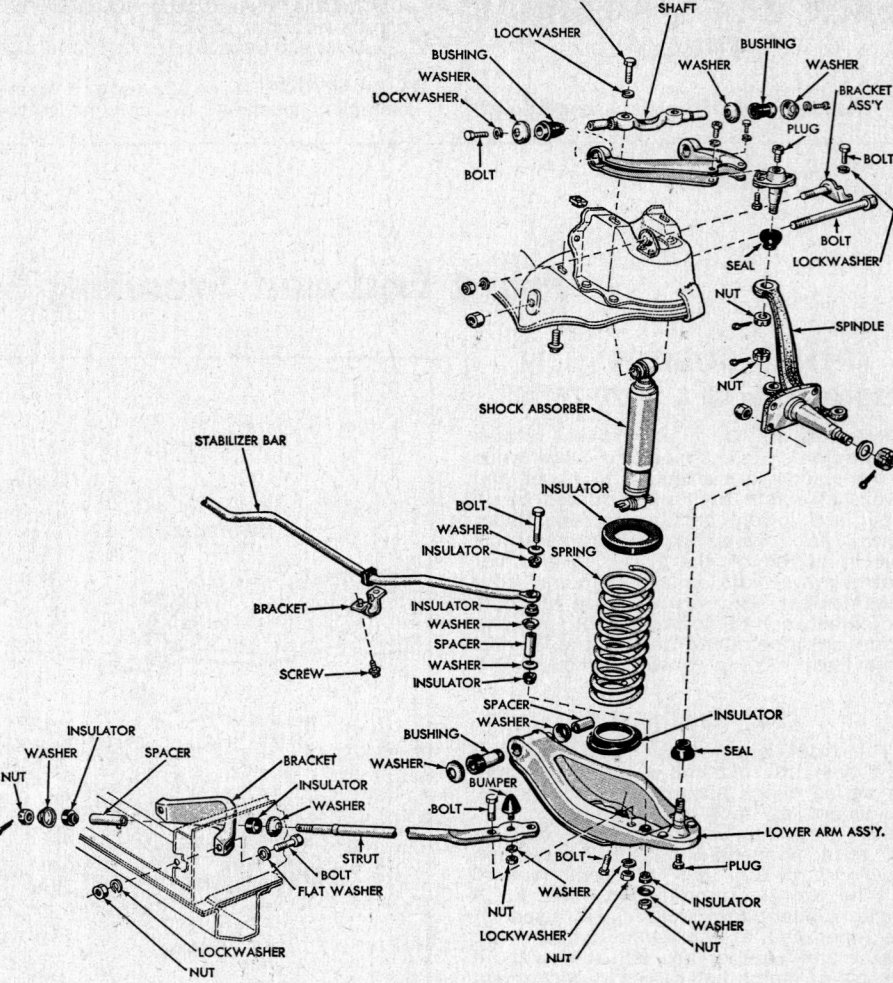

Fig. 2 Front suspension. 1969 Continental

shaft retaining bolts to 100-125 ft. lbs.

Camber, Adjust

1. Raise hood and unsnap clips retaining top of bushing rubber shield to fender apron.
2. Loosen bolts that secure upper control arm shaft to frame and, with a pry bar, move shaft in or out as required. A movement of approximately $\frac{3}{64}$" of the entire shaft will change camber $\frac{1}{4}$°. Inboard movement will change camber in negative direction. Outboard movement will change camber in positive direction.
3. When adjustment is correct, torque shaft retaining bolts to 100-125 ft. lbs.

Toe-In, Adjust

Position the front wheels in their straight-ahead position. Then turn both tie rod adjusting sleeves an equal amount until the desired toe-in setting is obtained.

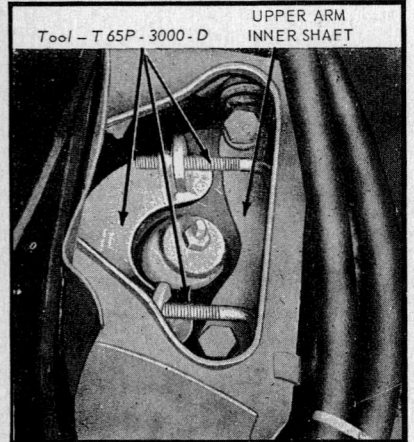

Fig. 3 Caster and camber adjusting tool. 1969 Mark III & 1970-75 All

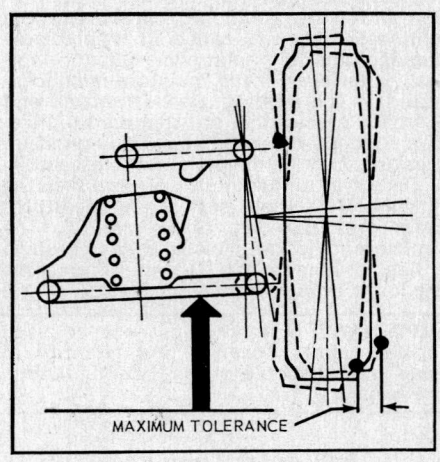

Fig. 4 Checking ball joints for wear

WHEEL BEARINGS, ADJUST

1969-75

1. With wheel rotating, tighten adjusting nut to 17-25 ft. lbs.
2. Back off adjusting nut ½ turn and retighten nut to 10-15 inch lbs.
3. Place nut lock on nut so that castellations on lock are aligned with cotter pin hole in spindle and install cotter pin.
4. Check front wheel rotation, if it rotates noisily or rough, clean, inspect or replace wheel bearings as necessary.

WHEEL BEARINGS, REPLACE

(Disc Brakes)

1. Raise car and remove front wheels.
2. Remove caliper mounting bolts.

   NOTE: It is not necessary to disconnect the brake line for this operation.

3. Slide caliper off of the disc, inserting a spacer between the shoes to hold them in their bores after the caliper is removed. Position caliper assembly out of the way.

   NOTE: Do not allow caliper to hang by brake hose.

4. Remove hub and disc. Grease retainer and inner bearing can now be removed.

CHECKING BALL JOINTS FOR WEAR

Upper Ball Joint

1. Raise car on floor jacks placed beneath lower control arms.
2. Grasp lower edge of tire and move wheel in and out.
3. As wheel is being moved in and out, observe upper end of spindle and upper arm.
4. Any movement between upper end of spindle and upper arm indicates ball joint wear and loss of preload. If such movement is observed, replace upper ball joint.

   NOTE: During the foregoing check, the lower ball joint will be unloaded and may move. Disregard all such movement of the lower joint. Also, do not mistake loose wheel bearings for a worn ball joint.

Lower Ball Joint

1. Raise car on jacks placed under lower control arms as shown in Fig. 4.
2. With a dial indicator attached to the lower arm, position indicator so that the plunger rests against inner side of wheel rim adjacent to lower ball joint.

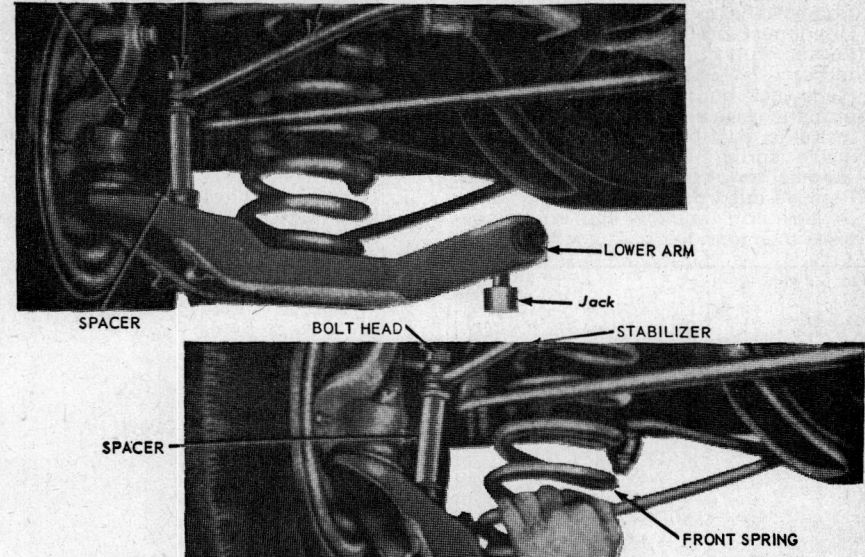

Fig. 5   Front spring replacement. 1969 Mark III & 1970-75 All

3. Grasp tire at top and bottom and slowly move tire in and out. Note reading on dial, which is the radial play. If the reading exceeds ¼", replace lower ball joint.

BALL JOINTS, REPLACE

The upper ball joints on Continental models are bolted to the upper control arm, while on the Mark III, the ball joints are riveted to the arm. The lower ball joints are riveted to the lower control arm on all models.

When replacing a riveted joint, remove the rivets and retain the new joint in its control arm with the bolts, nuts and washers furnished with the ball joint kit.

Use a suitable pressing tool to force the ball joint from the spindle.

SHOCK ABSORBER, REPLACE

1969 Continental

1. Remove stud nut at upper eye of shock absorber. Remove upper eye stud bracket to crossmember bolt and remove stud bracket.
2. Unfasten shock absorber from lower control arm. Then lower and remove shock absorber.
3. Reverse above procedure to install.

1969 Mark III & 1970-75 All

1. Remove nut, washer and bushing from upper end of shock absorber.
2. Raise vehicle and support on stands.
3. Remove screws retaining shock absorber to lower control arm and remove shock absorber.
4. Reverse procedure to install.

COIL SPRING, REPLACE

1969 Mark III & 1970-75 All

1. Raise vehicle and support front end of frame with jack stands.
2. Disconnect shock absorber from lower arm and place a jack under the lower arm to support it, Fig. 5.
3. Remove strut and rebound bumper bolts and disconnect lower end of sway bar stud from lower arm.
4. Remove the nut and bolt retaining inner end of the lower arm to crossmember.
5. Carefully lower jack relieving spring pressure on the lower arm, then remove spring.

1969 Continental

1. Raise and support car as for replacing lower ball joint.
2. Remove brake assembly.

3. Remove shock absorber and drag strut from lower arm.

4. Disconnect stabilizer from lower arm.

5. Loosen nut from ball joint stud two turns.

6. Place jack under outer end of lower arm and raise arm several inches.

7. Install a suitable spring compressor inside spring with jaws of tool toward center of car.

8. Remove nut from ball joint stud. Lower jack until spindle and spring are free, then remove spring and insulators.

9. Reverse above procedure to install.

POWER STEERING UNIT, REPLACE

1969-75

1. Disconnect lines from steering gear and plug lines and ports to prevent entry of dirt.

2. Remove the two bolts securing flex coupling to steering gear and to column.

3. Raise vehicle and remove sector shaft nut and pitman arm.

NOTE: Do not damage the seals.

4. Support steering gear and remove three attaching bolts. Remove flex coupling clamp bolt and work steering gear free of coupling, then remove steering gear from vehicle.

OLDSMOBILE
(Exc. Starfire)

TORONADO: Service procedures that apply to the Toronado only will be found starting on page 1-614.
OLD CAR SPECIFICATIONS: For 1946-68 Tune Up and Wheel Alignment Specifications see main index.

INDEX OF SERVICE OPERATIONS

PAGE NO.

ACCESSORIES
Air Conditioning 2-20
Air Cushion Restraint Systems 2-367
Automatic Level Controls 2-39
Blower Motor, Remove 1-590
Clock Troubles 2-11
Heater Core, Replace 1-589
Power Top Troubles 2-18
Power Window Troubles 2-18
Radio, Replace 1-588
Speed Controls, Adjust 1-591

BRAKES
Anti-Skid Brakes 2-162
Brake Troubles, Mechanical 2-17
Disc Brake Service 2-133
Hydraulic System Service 2-123
Master Cylinder, Replace 1-606
Parking Brake, Adjust 1-605
Power Brake Unit, Replace 1-606
Service Brakes, Adjust 1-605

CLUTCH
Clutch Pedal, Adjust 1-601
Clutch, Replace 1-601
Clutch Troubles 2-12

COOLING SYSTEM
Cooling System Troubles 2-6
Variable Speed Fans 2-38
Water Pump, Replace 1-598

ELECTRICAL
Alternator Service 2-69
Back-Up Light Switch, Replace 1-583
Blower Motor, Remove 1-590
Clutch Start Switch 1-583
Dash Gauge Service 2-50
Distributor, Replace 1-581
Distributor Service:
  Standard 2-525
  Transistorized 2-535
Electrical Troubles 2-8
Headlamps, Concealed Type 2-46
Headlight Aiming 2-45
Horn Sounder, Remove 1-584
Ignition Coils and Resistors 2-521
Ignition Lock, Replace 1-582
Ignition Switch, Replace 1-582
Ignition Timing 2-518
Instrument Cluster Removal 1-585
Light Switch, Replace 1-582
Neutral Start Switch, Replace 1-583
Seat Belt Interlock Systems 2-311
Starter Service 2-54
Starter, Replace 1-582
Starter Switch Service 2-67
Stop Light Switch, Replace 1-583
Turn Signal Switch, Replace 1-583
Turn Signal Troubles 2-11
Windshield Wiper Motor, Replace 1-587
Windshield Wiper Troubles 2-19

ENGINE
Camshaft, Replace 1-595
Cylinder Head, Replace 1-593
Engine Identification 1-566
Engine Mounts 1-593

PAGE NO.

Engine (Conventional), Replace 1-593
Engine (Toronado), Replace 1-614
Engine Troubles 2-1
Main Bearings 1-596
Piston Pins 1-596
Piston Rings 1-596
Piston and Rod, Assemble 1-596
Pistons 1-596
Rocker Arms 1-594
Rod Bearings 1-596
Timing Case Cover (Conventional) 1-595
Timing Case Cover (Toronado) 1-614
Timing Chain, Replace 1-595
Valve Arrangement 1-593
Valve Guides 1-595
Valve Lifters 1-595
Valves, Remove 1-594

ENGINE LUBRICATION
Emission Control Systems 2-545
Oil Pan, Replace 1-597
Oil Pump Repairs 1-598

FUEL SYSTEM
Carburetor Adjustments and Specs. 2-372
Dual Jet Carburetor 1-599
Emission Control Systems 2-545
Fuel Pump, Replace 1-598
Fuel Pump Service 2-369
Fuel System Troubles 2-2

PROPELLER SHAFT & U JOINTS
(Conventional)
Propeller Shaft 1-604
Universal Joint Service 2-117

REAR AXLE & SUSPENSION
Axle Shaft, Bearing & Seal 1-604
Coil Springs, Replace: Std. Cars 1-606
  Toronado 1-624
Control Arms & Bushings: Std. Cars ... 1-608
  Toronado 1-624
Leaf Springs & Bushings: Std. Cars ... 1-606
  Toronado 1-624
Rear Axle Description: Std. Cars 1-603
  Toronado 1-622
Rear Axle Troubles 2-16
Shock Absorber, Replace: Std. Cars ... 1-606
  Toronado 1-624
Stabilizer Bar, Replace 1-609
Wheel Bearings, Adjustment: Toronado . 1-622
Wheel Spindle, Replace: Toronado 1-622

SPECIFICATIONS
Alternator 1-576
Belt Tension 1-598
Brakes 1-581
Capacities 1-577
Carburetors 2-372
Cooling System 1-577
Crankshaft and Bearings 1-579
Distributors 1-574
Engine Tightening Torque 1-573
Fuel Pump Pressure 1-598
General Engine Specs. 1-569
Ignition Coils and Resistors 2-521
Pistons, Rings and Pins 1-579
Rear Axle 1-575

PAGE NO.

Starting Motors 1-579
Tune Up 1-570
Valve Lift 1-594
Valve Timing 1-594
Valves 1-576
Wheel Alignment 1-580

STEERING GEAR
Horn Sounder Removal 1-584
Mechanical Gear, Replace 1-613
Mechanical Gear Service 2-170
Mechanical Gear Troubles 2-17
Power Gear, Replace (Conventional) ... 1-613
Power Gear, Replace (Toronado) 1-628
Steering Wheel, Replace 1-584

SUSPENSION, FRONT
Ball Joint, Replace: Std. Cars 1-611
  Toronado 1-627
Ball Joint Checks: Std. Cars 1-610
  Toronado 1-626
Coil Spring, Replace 1-611
Lubrication: Std. Cars 1-609
  Toronado 1-624
Shock Absorber, Replace: Std. Cars ... 1-611
  Toronado 1-628
Suspension Description: Std. Cars 1-609
  Toronado 1-624
Toe-In, Adjust: Std. Cars 1-610
  Toronado 1-626
Wheel Alignment, Adjust: Std. Cars ... 1-610
  Toronado 1-625
Wheel Bearings, Adjust 1-610
Wheel Bearings, Replace: Std. Cars ... 1-610
  Toronado 1-627

TORONADO FRONT DRIVE
C.V. U-Joint Service 1-618
Drive Axles, Replace 1-617
Final Drive, Description of 1-619
Final Drive, Replace 1-621
Output Shaft & Seals 1-620

TRANSMISSIONS
Three Speed Manual:
  Replace 1-601
  Repairs 2-177
  Linkage, Adjust 1-602
Four Speed Manual:
  Replace 1-602
  Repairs 2-199
  Linkage, Adjust 1-602
Automatic Units 2-231
  1975 Linkage 1-602
Toronado Transmission, Replace 1-615

TUNE UP
Service 2-517
Specifications 1-570

WINDSHIELD WIPER
Wiper Arms 1-587
Wiper Blades 1-587
Wiper Linkage, Replace 1-587
Wiper Motor, Replace 1-587
Wiper Switch, Replace 1-588
Wiper Troubles 2-19

VEHICLE IDENTIFICATION PLATE: 1969-1975 on left upper dash.

ENGINE NUMBER LOCATION

1969-71 & 1973-75 6-250: Right side of engine block directly to rear of distributor.
1969-74 V8s: Stamped on oil fill tube.

1975 Omega V8-350; on left bank cylinder head. V8-260, V8-455 & V8-350 Exc. Omega, stamped on oil filter tube.

ENGINE IDENTIFICATION CODE

YEAR	ENGINE	ENGINE PREFIX
1969	6-250	VA-B-E-F
	V8-350 2 Bar. Carb.	QI-A-B
	V8-350 4 Bar. Carb.	QV-N-P
	V8-350 2 Bar. Carb.	TL-B-D
	V8-350 4 Bar. Carb.	QX
	V8-400 4 Bar. Carb.	QW-R-S
	V8-400 4 Bar. Carb.	QU-T
	V8-455 2 Bar. Carb.	UJ-C-D
	V8-455 4 Bar. Carb.	UN-O
	V8-455 4 Bar. Carb.	UL
	V8-455 4 Bar. Carb.	US-T-V
	V8-455 4 Bar. Carb.	UW
1970	6-250	VB-F
	V8-350 2 Bar. Carb.	QI-A-J
	V8-350 2 Bar. Carb.	TL-D-C
	V8-350 2 Bar. Carb.	QV-N-P
	V8-350 4 Bar. Carb.	QX-D
	V8-455 2 Bar. Carb.	UJ-C-D
	V8-455 2 Bar. Carb.	TY-X
	V8-455 4 Bar. Carb.	TU-W-V
	V8-455 4 Bar. Carb.	TQ-P
	V8-455 4 Bar. Carb.	UN-O
	V8-455 4 Bar. Carb.	TS-T
	V8-455 4 Bar. Carb.	UL
	V8-455 4 Bar. Carb.	US-T-W-V
1971	6-250	VB-F
	V8-350 2 Bar. Carb.	QI-A-J
	V8-350 2 Bar. Carb.	TE-D-C
	V8-350 4 Bar. Carb.	QB-O-N-P
	V8-455 2 Bar. Carb.	UC-D-E

YEAR	ENGINE	ENGINE PREFIX
	V8-455 4 Bar. Carb.	TQ-P
	V8-455 4 Bar. Carb.	TU-N
	V8-455 4 Bar. Carb.	TS-B-T-L
	V8-455 4 Bar. Carb.	TW-V-A
	V8-455 4 Bar. Carb.	UN-O-S-T
1972	V8-350 2 Bar. Carb.	QA-B-C
	V8-350 2 Bar. Carb.	QN-O
	V8-350 4 Bar. Carb.	QD-E
	V8-350 4 Bar. Carb.	QJ-K-P-Q
	V8-455	UA-B-S-T
	V8-455	UL-N-O
	V8-455	UD-E-U-V
1973	6-250 Std. Tr.	CCC, CCD
	6-250 Auto Tr.	CCA, CCB
	V8-350 2 Bar. Carb.	QS, T, P
	V8-350 2 Bar. Carb.	QN, O, P
	V8-350 4 Bar. Carb.	QA, B, J, K
	V8-350 4 Bar. Carb.	QU, V, C
	V8-350 4 Bar. Carb.	QD, E, L
	V8-455	UD, B
	V8-455	UA, S, T
	V8-455	UU, V
1974	6-250 Std. Tr.	CCC, CCD
	6-250 Auto. Tr.	CCA, CCB
	V8-350 2 Bar. Carb.	QS, QT
	V8-350 4 Bar. Carb.	QB, QC, QL
	V8-350 4 Bar. Carb.	QO, QU, QW
	V8-350 4 Bar. Carb.	TB, TC, TL, TO
	V8-455 2 Bar. Carb.	UU, UW
	V8-455 4 Bar. Carb.	UA, UB, UC

YEAR	ENGINE	ENGINE PREFIX
	V8-455 4 Bar. Carb.	UD, UL, UO
	V8-455 4 Bar. Carb.	UP, UN, UR
	V8-455 4 Bar. Carb.	UV, UX, VP
	V8-455 4 Bar. Carb.	VA, VB, VC
	V8-455 4 Bar. Carb.	VD, VL, VO
1975	6-250 Std. Tr. [1]	CJU
	6-250 Auto. Tr. [1]	CJT
	6-250 Auto. Tr. [2]	CJL
	V8-260 Std. Tr. [1]	QA, QK
	V8-260 Std. Tr. a/c [1]	QD, QN
	V8-260 Std. Tr. [2]	TA, TK
	V8-260 Std. Tr. a/c [2]	TD, TN
	V8-260 Auto. Tr. [1]	QE, QP
	V8-260 Auto. Tr. a/c [1]	QJ, QQ
	V8-260 Auto. Tr. [2]	TE, TP
	V8-260 Auto. Tr. a/c [2]	TJ, TQ
	V8-350 Auto. Tr. [1]	RW, QL
	V8-350 Auto. Tr. a/c [1]	RX, QO, QX
	V8-350 Auto. Tr. [2]	RN, TL
	V8-350 Auto. Tr. a/c [2]	RO, TO, TX
	V8-400 Auto. Tr. [1]	YM, YT
	V8-455 Auto. Tr. [1]	UB, UE, UP
	V8-455 Auto. Tr. a/c [1]	UC, UD, UP
	V8-455 Auto. Tr. [2]	VB, VE, VP
	V8-455 Auto. Tr. a/c [2]	VC, VD, VP

[1]—Except California.
[2]—California.

GRILLE IDENTIFICATION

1969 F-85, Cutlass, Vista Cruiser

1969 "4-4-2"

1969 Delta 88, Royale

1969 98

1969 Toronado

1970 F-85, Cutlass, Vista Cruiser

GRILLE IDENTIFICATION—Continued

1970 Cutlass Supreme

1970 "4-4-2"

1970 Delta 88

1970 Delta Royale

1970 98

1970 Toronado

1971 F-85, Cutlass

1971 Cutlass Supreme

1971 Cutlass "S"

1971 "4-4-2"

1971 Delta Royale

1971 98

1971 Toronado

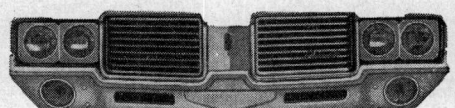

1972 Cutlass "S"

1972 Delta 88 & Royale

1972 98

1972 Toronado

1973 Omega

1973 Cutlass

1973 88

1973 98

GRILLE IDENTIFICATION—Continued

1973 Toronado

1974 Omega

1974 Cutlass, Supreme & Vista Cruiser

1974 88

1974 98

1974 Toronado

1975 Omega

1975 Cutlass Supreme

1975 Cutlass Salon

1975 Cutlass "S"

1975 Delta 88

1975 98

1975 Toronado

GENERAL ENGINE SPECIFICATIONS

Year	Engine	Car-buretor	Bore and Stroke	Piston Dis-place-ment, Cubic Inches	Compres-sion Ratio	Maximum Brake H.P. @ R.P.M.	Maximum Torque Lbs. Ft. @ R.P.M.	Normal Oil Pressure Pounds
1969	155 Horsepower............②6-250	1 Barrel	3.875 x 3.53	250	8.50	155 @ 4200	240 @ 2000	30-45
	250 Horsepower............V8-350	2 Barrel	4.057 x 3.385	350	9.00	250 @ 4400	355 @ 2600	30-45
	310 Horsepower............V8-350	4 Barrel	4.057 x 3.385	350	10.25	310 @ 4800	390 @ 3200	30-45
	310 Horsepower............V8-455	2 Barrel	4.125 x 4.250	455	9.00	310 @ 4200	490 @ 2400	30-45
	325 Horsepower............V8-350	4 Barrel	4.057 x 3.385	350	10.50	325 @ 5400	360 @ 3600	30-45
	325 Horsepower............V8-400	4 Barrel	3.870 x 4.250	400	10.50	325 @ 4600	440 @ 3000	35-50
	350 Horsepower............V8-400	4 Barrel	3.870 x 4.250	400	10.50	350 @ 4800	440 @ 3200	35-50
	360 Horsepower............V8-400	4 Barrel	3.870 x 4.250	400	10.50	360 @ 5400	440 @ 3600	35-50
	365 Horsepower............V8-455	4 Barrel	4.125 x 4.250	455	10.25	365 @ 4600	510 @ 3000	30-45
	375 Horsepower............V8-455	4 Barrel	4.125 x 4.250	455	10.25	375 @ 4600	510 @ 3000	30-45
	390 Horsepower............V8-455	4 Barrel	4.125 x 4.250	455	10.25	390 @ 5000	500 @ 3200	30-45
	400 Horsepower............V8-455	4 Barrel	4.125 x 4.250	455	10.25	400 @ 4800	500 @ 3200	30-45
1970	155 Horsepower............②6-250	1 Barrel	3.875 x 3.53	250	8.50	155 @ 4200	240 @ 2000	30-45
	250 Horsepower............V8-350	2 Barrel	4.057 x 3.385	350	9.00	250 @ 4400	355 @ 2600	30-45
	310 Horsepower............V8-350	4 Barrel	4.057 x 3.385	350	10.25	310 @ 4800	390 @ 3200	30-45
	310 Horsepower............V8-455	2 Barrel	4.125 x 4.250	455	9.00	310 @ 4200	490 @ 2400	30-45
	320 Horsepower............V8-455	2 Barrel	4.125 x 4.250	455	10.25	320 @ 4200	500 @ 2400	30-45
	325 Horsepower............V8-350	4 Barrel	4.057 x 3.385	350	10.50	325 @ 5400	360 @ 3600	30-45
	365 Horsepower............V8-455	4 Barrel	4.125 x 4.250	455	10.50	365 @ 5000	500 @ 3200	30-45
	370 Horsepower............V8-455	4 Barrel	4.125 x 4.250	455	10.50	370 @ 5200	500 @ 3600	30-45
	375 Horsepower............V8-455	4 Barrel	4.125 x 4.250	455	10.25	375 @ 4600	510 @ 3000	30-45
	390 Horsepower............V8-455	4 Barrel	4.125 x 4.250	455	10.25	390 @ 5000	500 @ 3200	30-45
	400 Horsepower............V8-455	4 Barrel	4.125 x 4.250	455	10.25	400 @ 3200	500 @ 3200	30-45
1971	110 Horsepower①............②6-250	1 Barrel	3.875 x 3.53	250	8.10	110 @ 3800	185 @ 1600	30-45
	155 Horsepower①............V8-350	2 Barrel	4.057 x 3.385	350	8.10	155 @ 4000	275 @ 2400	30-45
	180 Horsepower①............V8-350	4 Barrel	4.057 x 3.385	350	8.10	180 @ 4000	275 @ 2400	30-45
	185 Horsepower①............V8-455	2 Barrel	4.125 x 4.250	455	8.10	185 @ 3600	355 @ 2000	30-45
	225 Horsepower①............V8-455	4 Barrel	4.125 x 4.250	455	8.10	225 @ 3600	360 @ 2600	30-45
	260 Horsepower①............V8-455	4 Barrel	4.125 x 4.250	455	8.10	260 @ 4400	370 @ 3200	30-45
	265 Horsepower①............V8-455	4 Barrel	4.125 x 4.250	455	8.10	265 @ 4200	375 @ 2800	30-45
1972	160 Horsepower①............V8-350	2 Barrel	4.057 x 3.385	350	8.50	160 @ 4000	275 @ 2400	30-45
	175 Horsepower①............V8-350	2 Barrel	4.057 x 3.385	350	8.50	175 @ 4000	295 @ 2600	30-45
	180 Horsepower①............V8-350	4 Barrel	4.057 x 3.385	350	8.50	180 @ 4000	275 @ 2800	30-45
	200 Horsepower①............V8-350	4 Barrel	4.057 x 3.385	350	8.50	200 @ 4400	300 @ 3200	30-45
	225 Horsepower①............V8-455	4 Barrel	4.125 x 4.250	455	8.50	225 @ 3600	360 @ 2600	30-45
	250 Horsepower①............V8-455	4 Barrel	4.125 x 4.250	455	8.50	250 @ 4200	370 @ 2800	30-45
	265 Horsepower①............V8-455	4 Barrel	4.125 x 4.250	455	8.50	265 @ 4200	375 @ 2800	30-45
	270 Horsepower①............V8-455	4 Barrel	4.125 x 4.250	455	8.50	270 @ 4400	370 @ 3200	30-45
	300 Horsepower①............V8-455	4 Barrel	4.125 x 4.250	455	8.50	300 @ 4700	410 @ 3200	30-45
1973	100 Horsepower①............②6-250	1 Barrel	3.875 x 3.53	250	8.25	100 @ 3600	175 @ 1600	40
	160 Horsepower①............V8-350	2 Barrel	4.057 x 3.385	350	8.5	160 @ 3800	275 @ 2400	30-45
	180 Horsepower①............V8-350	4 Barrel	4.057 x 3.385	350	8.5	180 @ 3800	275 @ 2800	30-45
	225 Horsepower①............V8-455	4 Barrel	4.125 x 4.250	455	8.5	225 @ 3600	360 @ 2600	30-45
	250 Horsepower①............V8-455	4 Barrel	4.125 x 4.250	455	8.5	250 @ 4000	375 @ 2800	30-45
	270 Horsepower①............V8-455	4 Barrel	4.125 x 4.250	455	8.5	270 @ 4200	370 @ 3200	30-45
1974	100 Horsepower①............②6-250	1 Barrel	3.87 x 3.53	250	8.5	100 @ 3600	175 @ 1800	40
	180 Horsepower①............V8-350	4 Barrel	4.057 x 3.385	350	8.5	180 @ 3800	275 @ 2800	30-45
	200 Horsepower①............V8-350	4 Barrel	4.057 x 3.385	350	8.5	200 @ 4200	300 @ 3200	30-45
	210 Horsepower①............V8-455	4 Barrel	4.126 x 4.250	455	8.5	210 @ 3600	350 @ 2400	30-45
	230 Horsepower①............V8-455	4 Barrel	4.126 x 4.250	455	8.5	230 @ 3800	370 @ 2800	30-45
	275 Horsepower①............V8-455	4 Barrel	4.126 x 4.250	455	8.5	275 @ 4200	395 @ 3200	30-45

Continued

GENERAL ENGINE SPECIFICATIONS—Continued

Year	Engine	Car-buretor	Bore and Stroke	Piston Dis-place-ment, Cubic Inches	Com-pres-sion Ratio	Maximum Brake H.P. @ R.P.M.	Maximum Torque Lbs. Ft. @ R.P.M.	Normal Oil Pressure Pounds
1975	105 Horsepower①...........6-250②	1 Barrel	3.87 x 3.53	250	8.25	105 @ 3800	185 @ 1200	36-41
	110 Horsepower①...........V8-260	2 Barrel	3.50 x 3.385	260	8.5	110 @ 3400	205 @ 1600	30-45
	165 Horsepower①.........V8-350③	4 Barrel	3.80 x 3.85	350	8.0	165 @ 3800	260 @ 2200	37
	170 Horsepower①.........V8-350	4 Barrel	4.057 x 3.385	350	8.5	170 @ 3800	275 @ 2400	30-45
	190 Horsepower①.........V8-400④	4 Barrel	4.1212 x 3.75	400	7.6	190 @ 3400	350 @ 2000	55-60
	190 Horsepower①.........V8-455⑤	4 Barrel	4.126 x 4.25	455	8.5	190 @ 3600	350 @ 2400	30-45
	215 Horsepower①.........V8-455⑥	4 Barrel	4.126 x 4.25	455	8.5	215 @ 3600	370 @ 2400	30-45

①—All horsepower and torque ratings are net.
②—See Chevrolet Chapter for service procedure on this engine.
③—Omega only. See Buick Chapter for service procedures on this engine.
④—See Pontiac Chapter for service procedures on this engine.
⑤—Exc. Toronado.
⑥—Toronado.

TUNE UP SPECIFICATIONS

OLD CAR SPECIFICATIONS: For 1946-68 Tune Up Specifications see main index.

★When using a timing light, disconnect vacuum hose or tube at distributor and plug opening in hose or tube so idle speed will not be affected. Timing should be set at 850 RPM on V8's.

●When checking compression, lowest cylinder must be within 80 percent of highest.

▲Before removing wires from distributor cap, determine location of the No. 1 wire in cap, as distributor position may have been altered from that shown at the end of this chart.

Year	Spark Plug		Distributor		Ignition Timing★			Carb. Adjustments					
	Type	Gap Inch	Point Gap Inch	Dwell Angle Deg.	Firing Order Fig. ▲	Timing BTDC ①	Mark Fig.	Hot Idle Speed		Air Fuel Ratio		Idle "CO" %	
								Std. Trans.	Auto. Trans. ②	Std. Trans.	Auto. Trans.	Std. Trans.	Auto. Trans.
1969													
6-250 Std. Trans.⑭	R46N	.035	③	31-34	N	TDC	B	775⑪	—	—	—	—	—
6-250 Auto. Trans.⑭	R46N	.035	③	31-34	N	4°	B	—	625D⑪	—	—	—	—
8-350, 250 H.P.	R46S	.030	.016	30	F	6°	A	675⑪	600D⑪	—	—	—	—
8-350, 310 H.P.	R45S	.030	.016	30	F	8°	A	675⑪	575D⑪	—	—	—	—
8-350, 325 H.P.	R43S	.030	.016	30	F	12°	A	675⑪	575D⑪	—	—	—	—
8-400, 325 H.P.	R44S	.030	.016	30	F	8°⑨⑬	A	—	575D⑪	—	—	—	—
8-400, 350 H.P.	R44S	.030	.016	30	F	2°⑨	A	750⑪	—	—	—	—	—
8-400, 360 H.P.	R43S	.030	.016	30	F	14°⑫	A	750⑪	650D⑪	—	—	—	—
8-455, 310 H.P.	R45S	.030	.016	30	F	6°⑨	A	675⑪	600D⑪	—	—	—	—
8-455, 365 H.P.	R44S	.030	.016	30	F	8°⑨	A	—	575D⑪	—	—	—	—
8-455, 375 H.P.	R44S	.030	.016	30	F	8°⑨	A	—	575D⑪	—	—	—	—
8-455, 400 H.P.	R44S	.030	.016	30	F	10°⑨	A	—	575D⑪	—	—	—	—
1970													
6-250 Std. Trans.⑭	R46T	.035	③	31-34	N	TDC	B	750	—	—	—	—	—
6-250 Auto. Trans.⑭	R46T	.035	③	31-34	N	4°	B	—	600D	—	—	—	—
8-350, 250 H.P.⑤	R46S	.030	.016	30	F	10°⑯	A	750	575D	—	—	—	—
8-350, 250 H.P.⑥	R46S	.030	.016	30	F	8°⑯	A	675	575D	—	—	—	—
8-350, 310 H.P.	R45S	.030	.016	30	F	10°⑯	A	650	575D	—	—	—	—
8-350, 325 H.P.	R43S	.030	.016	30	F	14°⑯	A	750	625D	—	—	—	—

Continued

TUNE UP SPECIFICATIONS—Continued

OLD CAR SPECIFICATIONS: For 1946-68 Tune Up Specifications see main index.

★When using a timing light, disconnect vacuum hose or tube at distributor and plug opening in hose or tube so idle speed will not be affected. Timing should be set at 850 RPM on V8's.

●When checking compression, lowest cylinder must be within 80 percent of highest.

▲Before removing wires from distributor cap, determine location of the No. 1 wire in cap, as distributor position may have been altered from that shown at the end of this chart.

Year	Spark Plug		Distributor		Ignition Timing★			Carb. Adjustments					
	Type	Gap Inch	Point Gap Inch	Dwell Angle Deg.	Firing Order Fig. ▲	Timing BTDC ①	Mark Fig.	Hot Idle Speed		Air Fuel Ratio		Idle "CO" %	
								Std. Trans.	Auto. Trans. ③	Std. Trans.	Auto. Trans.	Std. Trans.	Auto. Trans.
1970—Continued													
8-455, 310 H.P.	R46S	.030	.016	30	F	8° ⑯	A	675	575D	—	—	—	—
8-455, 320 H.P.	R45S	.030	.016	30	F	8° ⑯	A	—	575D	—	—	—	—
8-455, 365 H.P.	R44S	.030	.016	30	F	8° ⑨	A	750	650D	—	—	—	—
8-455, 370 H.P.	R44S	.030	.016	30	F	8° ⑨	A	750	650D	—	—	—	—
8-455, 375 H.P.	R45S	.030	.016	30	F	12° ⑯	A	750	600D	—	—	—	—
8-455, 390 H.P.	R45S	.030	.016	30	F	8° ⑯	A	—	600D	—	—	—	—
8-455, 390 H.P. ④	R44S	.030	.016	30	F	12° ⑯	A	—	600D	—	—	—	—
8-455, 400 H.P.	R44S	.030	.016	30	F	12° ⑯	A	—	600D	—	—	—	—
1971													
6-250⑭	R46TS	.035	③	31-34	N	4°	C	550	500D	—	—	1.0	1.0
8-350, 155 H.P.	R46S	.040	.016	30	F	10° ⑯	A	750	600D	—	—	0.6	0.6
8-350, 180 H.P. S.Tr.	R45S	.040	.016	30	F	10° ⑯	A	750	—	—	—	0.3	—
8-350, 180 H.P. A.Tr.	R46S	.040	.016	30	F	12° ⑯	A	—	600D	—	—	—	0.3
8-350, 260 H.P.	R45S	.040	.016	30	F	10° ⑯	A	750	600D	—	—	0.3	0.3
8-455, 185 H.P.	R46S	.040	.016	30	F	8° ⑯	A	750	600D	—	—	0.6	0.6
8-455, 225 H.P.	R46S	.040	.016	30	F	8° ⑯	A	—	600D	—	—	0.6	0.6
8-455, 260 H.P.④S.Tr.	R45S	.040	.016	30	F	12° ⑯	A	750	—	—	—	0.3	—
8-455, 260 H.P.④A.Tr.	R45S	.040	.016	30	F	10° ⑯	A	—	600D	—	—	—	0.3
8-455, 265 H.P.	R46S	.040	.016	30	F	10° ⑯	A	—	600D	—	—	0.3	0.3
1972													
8-350 2 Bar. Carb.	R46S	.040	.016	30	F	8° ⑯	A	750	650D	—	—	0.3	0.3
8-350 4 B. Carb. St. Tr.	R45S	.040	.016	30	F	8° ⑯	A	750	—	—	—	0.3	—
8-350 4 B. Carb. A. Tr.	R46S	.040	.016	30	F	12° ⑯	A	—	600D	—	—	—	0.3
8-455, 250, 270 H.P.	R46S	.040	.016	30	F	8° ⑯	A	—	600D	—	—	0.3	0.3
8-455, 300 H.P.	R45S	.040	.016	30	F	10°	A	1000	650D	—	—	0.3	0.3
8-455 Others—St. Tr.	R45S	.040	.016	30	F	10° ⑯	A	750	—	—	—	0.3	—
8-455 Others—A. Tr.	R46S	.040	.016	30	F	8° ⑯	A	—	650D	—	—	—	0.3
1973													
6-250⑭	R46TS	.035	③	31-34	N	6°	C	700	600D	—	—	0.3	0.3
8-350 2 Bar.⑤	R46S	.040	.016	30	F	14° ⑯	A	—	700D	—	—	—	0.3
8-350 2 Bar.⑥	R46S	.040	.016	30	F	12° ⑯	A	—	700D	—	—	—	0.3
8-350 4 Bar. Std. Tr.	R45S	.040	.016	30	F	8° ⑯	A	1100	—	—	—	0.3	—
8-350 4 Bar. Auto. Tr.	R46S	.040	.016	30	F	12° ⑯⑮	A	—	650D	—	—	—	0.3
8-455⑤	R45S	.040	.016	30	F	10° ⑯	A	1000	—	—	—	0.3	—
8-455⑥	R46S	.040	.016	30	F	8° ⑯	A	—	650D	—	—	—	0.3

Continued

TUNE UP SPECIFICATIONS—Continued

OLD CAR SPECIFICATIONS: For 1946-68 Tune Up Specifications see main index.

★ When using a timing light, disconnect vacuum hose or tube at distributor and plug opening in hose or tube so idle speed will not be affected. Timing should be set at 750 RPM on V8's.

● When checking compression, lowest cylinder must be within 70 percent of highest.

▲ Before removing wires from distributor cap, determine location of the No. 1 wire in cap, as distributor position may have been altered from that shown at the end of this chart.

Year	Spark Plug		Distributor		Ignition Timing ★			Carb. Adjustments						
								Hot Idle Speed		Air Fuel Ratio		Idle "CO" %	
	Type	Gap Inch	Point Gap Inch	Dwell Angle Deg.	Firing Order Fig. ▲	Timing BTDC ①	Mark Fig.	Std. Trans.	Auto. Trans.②	Std. Trans.	Auto. Trans.	Std. Trans.	Auto. Trans.
1974													
6-250⑭	R46TS	.035	.019	31–34	N	8°⑦	C	850N	600D	—	—	0.3	0.3
8-350 4 Bar.	R46S	.040	.019	30	F	12°⑯	H	—	650D	—	—	0.2	0.2
8-455, 275 H.P.	R45S	.040	.019	30	F	14°⑯	H	—	650D	—	—	0.2	0.2
8-455 4 Bar.	R46S	.040	.019	30	F	8°⑯	H	—	650D	—	—	0.2	0.2
8-455 4 Bar.⑧	R46SX	.080	—	—	F	8°⑯	H	—	650D	—	—	0.2	0.2
8-455 4 Bar.⑬	R46S	.040	.019	30	F	10°⑯	H	—	650D	—	—	0.2	0.2
8-455 4 Bar.⑧⑬	R46SX	.080	—	—	F	10°⑯	H	—	650D	—	—	0.2	0.2
1975													
6-250⑭	R46TX	.060	—	—	—	10°	C	850	⑲	—	—	—	—
V8-260	R46SX	.080	—	—	—	⑰	G	750	650D	—	—	—	—
V8-350⑩	R45TSX	.060	—	—	—	12°	D	—	600D	—	—	—	—
V8-350	R46SX	.080	—	—	—	20°⑯	H	—	650D	—	—	—	—
V8-400⑱	R45TSX	.060	—	—	—	16°⑯	E	—	650D	—	—	—	—
V8-455	R46SX	.080	—	—	—	16°⑯	H	—	650D	—	—	—	—
V8-455⑬	R46SX	.080	—	—	—	12°⑯	H	—	650D	—	—	—	—

① —BTDC: Before top dead center.
② —D: Drive. N: Neutral. Add 50 R.P.M. to slow idle speed for air conditioned cars with A/C off.
③ —New points .019", used points .016".
④ —Air Induction.
⑤ —Intermediate cars.
⑥ —Full size cars.
⑦ —At 600 rpm with auto. trans. and 850 rpm with manual trans.

⑧ —With High Energy Ignition system.
⑨ —At 850 R.P.M.
⑩ —Omega only. See Buick Chapter for service procedures on this engine.
⑪ —With A/C "OFF" and idle compensator held closed.
⑫ —At 1250 R.P.M.
⑬ —Toronado.
⑭ —See Chevrolet Chapter for service procedures on this engine.

⑮ —Vista-Cruiser 10°.
⑯ —At 1100 R.P.M.
⑰ —Exc. Calif., 16° BTDC; Calif., 18° BTDC. At 1100 R.P.M.
⑱ —See Pontiac Chapter for service procedures on this engine.
⑲ —Exc. Calif., 550D; Calif., 600D.

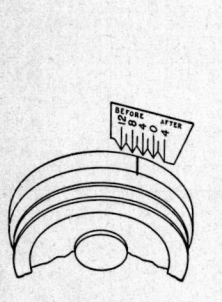

Fig. A

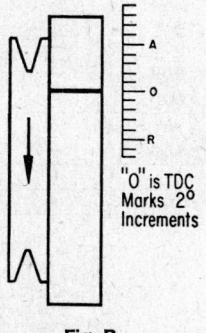

Fig. B

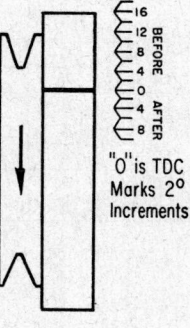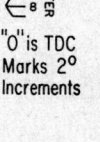

Fig. C

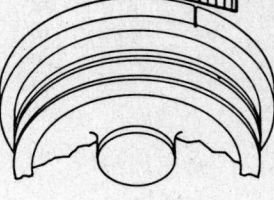

Fig. D

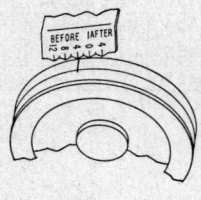

Fig. E

Continued

TUNE UP NOTES—Continued

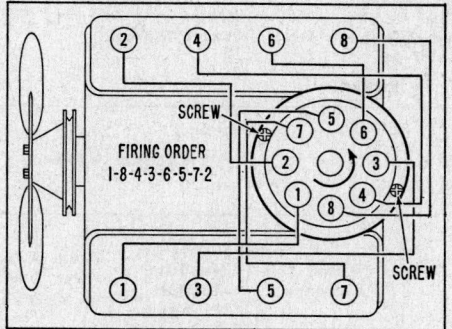

Fig. F

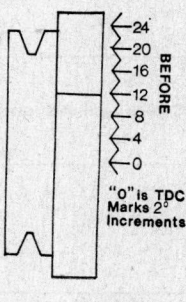

Fig. G

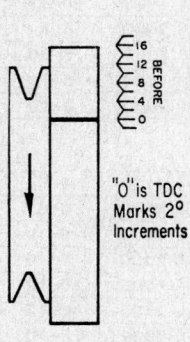

Fig. H

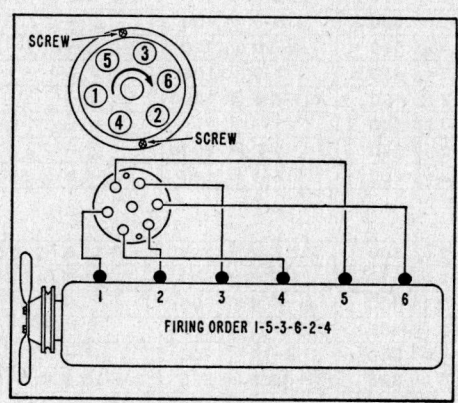

Fig. N

ENGINE TIGHTENING SPECIFICATIONS★

★Torque specifications are for clean and lightly lubricated threads only. Dry or dirty threads produce increased friction which prevents accurate measurement of tightness.

Year	Engine Model	Spark Plugs Ft. Lbs.	Cylinder Head Bolts Ft. Lbs.	Intake Manifold Ft. Lbs.	Exhaust Manifold Ft. Lbs.	Rocker Arm Shaft Bracket Ft. Lbs.	Rocker Arm Cover Ft. Lbs.	Connecting Rod Cap Bolts Ft. Lbs.	Main Bearing Cap Bolts Ft. Lbs.	Flywheel to Crankshaft Ft. Lbs.	Vibration Damper or Pulley Ft. Lbs.
1969–74	6-250④	25①	95	⑧	⑧	—	5	35	65	60	—
	V8-350	35	80⑥	35–40⑦	25	25②	7	42	70–80⑧	⑨	160③
	V8-400	35	80⑥	35–40⑦	25	25②	7	42	100–120	⑨	160③
	V8-455	35	80⑥	35–40⑦	25	25②	7	42	100–120	⑨	160③
1975	6-250④	15	95	35	30	—	45⑬	35	65	60	60
	V8-260	35	85	40	25	25②	7	42	80⑫	60	310
	V8-350⑩	15	80	45	28	30	4	40	115	60	140③
	V8-350	35	85	40	25	25②	7	42	80⑫	60	310
	V8-400⑪	15	95	40	30	—	8	43	100⑫	95	—
	V8-455	35	85	40	25	25②	7	42	120	60	310

①—1973–74, 15 ft. lbs.
②—Rocker arm pivot bolt to head.
③—Minimum.
④—See Chevrolet Chapter for service procedures on this engine.
⑤—Outer clamp 20 ft.-lbs., all others 30 ft.-lbs.
⑥—1972–74, 85 ft. lbs.
⑦—Clean and dip entire bolt in engine oil before tightening.
⑧—Rear 100–120 ft.-lbs.
⑨—Auto. trans. 60, std. trans. 80.
⑩—Omega only. See Buick chapter for service.
⑪—See Pontiac Chapter for service.
⑫—Rear 120 ft.-lbs.
⑬—Inch pounds.

DISTRIBUTOR SPECIFICATIONS

★Note: If unit is checked on vehicle, double the RPM and degrees to get crankshaft figures.
Breaker arm spring tension—19–23.

Distributor Part No.①	Centrifugal Advance Degrees @ RPM of Distributor					Vacuum Advance			Distributor Retard
	Advance Starts	Intermediate Advance			Full Advance	Inches of Vacuum to Start Plunger	Max. Adv. Dist. Deg. @ Vacuum		Max. Retard Dist. Deg. @ Vacuum
1969									
1110463	0–3 @ 500	2.2–5.2 @ 580	9.5–11.5 @ 975	—	17 @ 2100	6–8	13 @ 16		—
1110464	0–2 @ 510	1.5–3.5 @ 600	7.5–9.5 @ 975	—	15 @ 2100	6–8	13 @ 16		—
1111930	0–2 @ 400	6–8 @ 900	—	—	12 @ 2000	8–10	9 @ 18½		—
1111932	.4–2.4 @ 500	8–10 @ 900	—	—	12 @ 2000	8–10	12 @ 20½		—
1111933	.5–2.5 @ 450	7–9 @ 1000	—	—	11 @ 1900	10–12	8 @ 18		—
1111934	0–2 @ 400	6.5–8.5 @ 1200	—	—	15 @ 2000	6–8	12 @ 17½		—
1111935	.4–2.4 @ 700	—	—	—	8 @ 1500	8–10	12 @ 20½		—
1111936	0–2 @ 550	5–7 @ 1000	—	—	11 @ 1800	8–10	12 @ 20½		—
1111961	0–1.8 @ 400	1.7–4 @ 500	2.2–4.2 @ 520	—	16 @ 2000	8–10	12 @ 20½		—
1970									
1110463	0–3 @ 500	2.2–5.2 @ 580	9.5–11.5 @ 975	—	17 @ 2100	6–8	13 @ 15.5		—
1110464	0–2 @ 510	1.5–3.5 @ 600	7.5–9.5 @ 975	—	15 @ 2100	6–8	13 @ 15.5		—
1111975	0–2 @ 400	6–8 @ 900	—	—	12 @ 2000	8–10	10.8 @ 23		—
1111976	0–2 @ 405	7¼–9¾ @ 1025	—	—	16 @ 2000	8–10	13.8 @ 25		—
1111977	0.4–2.4 @ 500	8–10 @ 900	—	—	12 @ 2000	10–13	12.8 @ 25		—
1111979	0–3.5 @ 375	7–10.3 @ 575	8.6–10.6 @ 625	—	16 @ 1500	10–13	12.8 @ 25		—
1111980	0–2 @ 400	6.5–8.5 @ 1200	—	—	15 @ 2000	8–10	13.8 @ 25		—
1111981	0.4–2.4 @ 700	—	—	—	8 @ 1500	10–13	12.8 @ 25		—
1111982	0–2 @ 550	5–7 @ 1000	—	—	11 @ 1800	10–13	12.8 @ 25		—
1971									
1110489	0–2 @ 635	6–8 @ 1150	—	—	13 @ 2050	7–9	10.5 @ 18		—
1112033	0–2 @ 400	6.5–8.5 @ 1200	—	—	15 @ 2000	8–10	12.5 @ 20½		—
1112034	0.8–4 @ 450	4.5–7.8 @ 570	6.2–8.2 @ 620	—	14 @ 1500	6–8	13 @ 17½		—
1112036	0.4–2.4 @ 500	8–10 @ 900	—	—	12 @ 2000	6–8	13 @ 17½		—
1112078	0–2 @ 500	0–3 @ 550	—	—	9 @ 1950	8–10	—		—
1112079	0–2 @ 385	10–12 @ 1000	—	—	18 @ 2050	6–8	13 @ 17½		—
1112085	0.6–2.6 @ 600	6–8 @ 1025	—	—	14 @ 2000	6–8	13 @ 17½		—
1972									
1112033	0–2 @ 540	5–7 @ 1000	—	—	11 @ 1800	8–10	12.5 @ 20½		—
1112034	0.8–4 @ 450	4.5–7.8 @ 570	6.2–8.2 @ 620	—	14 @ 1500	6–8	13 @ 17½		—
1112036	0.4–2.4 @ 500	8–10 @ 900	—	—	12 @ 2000	6–8	13 @ 17½		—
1112085	0–2 @ 400	8–10 @ 1050	—	—	16 @ 2000	6–8	13 @ 17½		—
1112106	0–2 @ 485	8–11 @ 1000	—	—	16 @ 2000	6–8	13 @ 17½		—
1112172	0–2 @ 575	3.5–5.5 @ 1000	—	—	9 @ 1700	8–10	12.5 @ 20½		—
1973									
1112198	0–2 @ 575	3.5–5.5 @ 1000	—	—	9 @ 1700	7–9	9 @ 14		—
1112222	0–2 @ 485	8–11 @ 1000	—	—	16 @ 2000	5–7	8 @ 12		—

Continued

DISTRIBUTOR SPECIFICATIONS—Continued

★Note: If unit is checked on vehicle, double the RPM and degrees to get crankshaft figures.
Breaker arm spring tension—19–23.

Distributor Part No.①	Centrifugal Advance Degrees @ RPM of Distributor					Vacuum Advance		Distributor Retard
	Advance Starts	Intermediate Advance			Full Advance	Inches of Vacuum to Start Plunger	Max. Adv. Dist. Deg. @ Vacuum	Max. Retard Dist. Deg. @ Vacuum
1973-74								
1110499	0 @ 465	1 @ 635	7 @ 1150	—	12 @ 2050	6–8	6 @ 15½	—
1112195	0–2 @ 400	8–10 @ 1050	—	—	16 @ 2000	5–7	8 @ 12	—
1112197	0–2 @ 540	5–7 @ 1000	—	—	11 @ 1800	7–9	9 @ 16.6	—
1112225	0–2 @ 380	5–7 @ 550	11–13 @ 1050	—	19 @ 2000	5–7	8 @ 12	—
1112226	0–2 @ 400	8–10 @ 1050	—	—	16 @ 2000	3½–4½	10 @ 13	—
1974								
1112506	0–2 @ 540	5–7 @ 1000	—	—	11 @ 1800	7–9	9 @ 16.6	—
1112531	0–2 @ 540	5–7 @ 1000	—	—	11 @ 1800	6	9 @ 10	—
1112532	0–2 @ 540	5–7 @ 1000	—	—	11 @ 1800	4	10 @ 13	—
1112550	0 @ 375	7 @ 600	—	—	13 @ 1500	12	8 @ 18	—
1112825	0–2 @ 575	3.5–5.5 @ 1000	—	—	9 @ 1700	6	9 @ 10	—
1112827	0–2 @ 575	3.5–5.5 @ 1000	—	—	9 @ 1700	7	12 @ 17	—
1112828	0–2 @ 400	8–10 @ 1050	—	—	16 @ 2000	3½–4½	10 @ 13	—
1112829	0–2 @ 575	3.5–5.5 @ 1000	—	—	9 @ 1700	4	10 @ 13	—
1112830	0–2 @ 575	3.5–5.5 @ 1000	—	—	9 @ 1700	7	12 @ 17	—
1975								
1110650	0 @ 550	3½ @ 1150	—	—	8 @ 2100	4	7½ @ 12	—
1112863	0 @ 550	3½ @ 1150	—	—	8 @ 2100	4	12 @ 14¼	—
1112896	0 @ 550	3 @ 1150	—	—	6 @ 2250	7	7 @ 11	—
1112928	0 @ 600	2 @ 700	—	—	8 @ 2200	7	12½ @ 12	—
1112936	0 @ 500	—	—	—	9½ @ 2000	6½	12 @ 16	—
1112937	0 @ 500	—	—	—	6½ @ 1800	8	9 @ 13	—
1112951	0 @ 325	9½ @ 1200	—	—	14 @ 2200	4	12 @ 15	—
1112952	0 @ 500	3½ @ 1050	—	—	7 @ 1800	8	9 @ 13	—
1112953	0 @ 500	—	—	—	9½ @ 2000	8	9 @ 16	—

①—Stamped on distributor housing plate.

REAR AXLE SPECIFICATIONS

Year	Model	Carrier Type	Ring Gear & Pinion Backlash		Pinion Bearing Preload			Differential Bearing Preload		
			Method	Adjustment	Method	New Bearings Inch-Lbs.	Used Bearings Inch-Lbs.	Method	New Bearings Inch-Lbs.	Used Bearings Inch-Lbs.
1969–73	Toronado	Removable	Shims	.005–.009	Shims	2–5③	2–3④	Shims	15–20①	5–7①
	All Others	Integral	Shims	.005–.008	②	20–30	5–15	Shims	.010	.010
	Full Size	Integral	Shims	.005–.009	Spacer	24–32	8–12	Shims	20–30	10–20
1974	Toronado	Removable	Shims	.005–.009	Shims	2–15	2–5	Shims	10–15	5–7
	Others	Integral	Shims	.005–.009	Spacer	24–32	8–12	Shims	—	—

①—Over pinion bearing preload.
②—Tighten pinion shaft nut with inch-pound torque wrench.
③—1969–73, 2–15 inch-lbs.
④—1969–73, 2–5 inch-lbs.

VALVE SPECIFICATIONS

Year	Model	Valve Lash Int.	Valve Lash Exh.	Valve Angles Seat	Valve Angles Face	Valve Spring Installed Height	Valve Spring Pressure Lbs. @ In.	Stem Clearance Intake	Stem Clearance Exhaust	Stem Diameter Intake	Stem Diameter Exhaust
1969	6-250(8)	1 Turn(3)		46	45	1.66	186 @ 1.27	.001–.0027	.0015–.0032	.3410–.3417	.3410–.3417
	V8-350	Hydraulic(6)		45	46	1.67	187 @ 1.27	.001–.0027	.0015–.0032	.3425–.3432	.3420–.3427
	V8-400 4 B. C.	Hydraulic(6)		(4)	(5)	1.67	187 @ 1.27	.001–.0027	.0015–.0032	.3425–.3432	.3420–.3427
	V8-400 2 B. C.	Hydraulic(6)		45	46	1.67	187 @ 1.27	.001–.0027	.0015–.0032	.3425–.3432	.3420–.3427
	V8-455	Hydraulic(6)		45	46	1.67	187 @ 1.27	.001–.0027	.0015–.0032	.3425–.3432	.3420–.3427
	Toronado	Hydraulic(6)		(5)		1.67	187 @ 1.27	.001–.0027	.0015–.0032	.3425–.3432	.3420–.3427
1970	6-250(8)	1 Turn(3)		46	45	1.66	186 @ 1.27	.001–.0027	.0015–.0032	.3410–.3417	.3410–.3417
	V8-350	Hydraulic(6)		(4)	(5)	1.67	187 @ 1.27	.001–.0027	.0015–.0032	.3425–.3432	.3420–.3427
	V8-455(9)	Hydraulic(6)		45	46	1.67	187 @ 1.27	.001–.0027	.0015–.0032	.3425–.3432	.3420–.3427
	V8-455(10)	Hydraulic(6)		(4)	(5)	1.67	187 @ 1.27	.001–.0027	.0015–.0032	.3425–.3432	.3420–.3427
	Toronado	Hydraulic(6)		(4)	(5)	1.67	187 @ 1.27	.001–.0027	.0015–.0032	.3425–.3432	.3420–.3427
1971	6-250(8)	1 Turn(3)		46	45	1.66	186 @ 1.27	.001–.0027	.0015–.0032	.3410–.3417	.3410–.3417
	V8-350	Hydraulic(6)		45	46	1.67	187 @ 1.27	.001–.0027	.0015–.0032	.3425–.3432	.3420–.3427
	V8-455(9)	Hydraulic(6)		45	46	1.67	187 @ 1.27	.001–.0027	.0015–.0032	.3425–.3432	.3420–.3427
	V8-455(10)	Hydraulic(6)		(4)	(5)	1.67	187 @ 1.27	.001–.0027	.0015–.0032	.3425–.3432	.3420–.3427
1972	V8-350(1)	Hydraulic(6)		(11)	(12)	1.67	187 @ 1.27	.001–.0027	.0015–.0032	.3425–.3432	.3420–.3427
	V8-350(7)	Hydraulic(6)		45	46	1.67	198 @ 1.23	.001–.0027	.0015–.0032	.3425–.3432	.3420–.3427
	V8-455 "98"	Hydraulic(6)		(11)	(12)	1.67	187 @ 1.27	.001–.0027	.0015–.0032	.3425–.3432	.3420–.3427
	V8-455 Toronado	Hydraulic(6)		45	46	1.67	196 @ 1.23	.001–.0027	.0015–.0032	.3425–.3432	.3420–.3427
	V8-455 Others	Hydraulic(6)		(4)	(5)	1.67	206 (7) 1.19	.001–.0032	.0015–.0027	.3425–.3432	.3420–.3427
1973–74	6-250(8)	1 Turn(3)		46	45	1.66	186 @ 1.27	.001–.0027	.0015–.0032	.3410–.3417	.3410–.3417
	V8-350	Hydraulic(6)		(2)	(13)	1.67	187 @ 1.27	.001–.0027	.0015–.0032	.3425–.3432	.3420–.3427
	V8-455	Hydraulic(6)		(2)	(13)	1.67	187 @ 1.27	.001–.0027	.0015–.0032	.3425–.3432	.3420–.3427
1975	6-250(8)	1 Turn(3)		46	45	1.66	186 @ 1.27	.001–.0027	.0015–.0032	.3410–.3417	.3410–.3417
	V8-260	Hydraulic(6)		(2)	(13)	1.67	187 @ 1.27	.001–.0027	.0015–.0032	.3425–.3432	.3420–.3427
	V8-350(14)	Hydraulic(6)		45	45	1.727	177 @ 1.45	.0015–.0035	.0015–.0032	.3717–.3720	.3723–.3730
	V8-350	Hydraulic(6)		(2)	(13)	1.67	187 @ 1.27	.001–.0027	.0015–.0032	.3425–.3432	.3420–.3427
	V8-400(15)	Hydraulic(6)		(4)	(16)	—	—	.0016–.0033	.0021–.0038	.3712–.3719	.3407–.3414
	V8-455	Hydraulic(6)		(2)	(13)	1.67	187 @ 1.27	.001–.0027	.0015–.0032	.3425–.3432	.3420–.3427

(1)—Except California.
(2)—Intake 45°, exhaust 31°.
(3)—Tighten rocker arm adjusting screw to eliminate all push rod end clearance. Then tighten screw the number of turns listed.
(4)—Intake 30°, exhaust 45°.
(5)—Intake 30°, exhaust 46°.
(6)—No adjustment.
(7)—California.
(8)—See Chevrolet Chapter for service procedures on this engine.
(9)—Except "4-4-2" models.
(10)—"4-4-2" models.
(11)—Intake 45°, exhaust 30°.
(12)—Intake 46°, exhaust 30°.
(13)—Intake 44°, exhaust 30°.
(14)—Omega only. See Buick Chapter for service procedures.
(15)—See Pontiac Chapter for service procedures.
(16)—Intake 29°; Exhaust 44°.

ALTERNATOR & REGULATOR SPECIFICATIONS

Year	Model	Rated Hot Output Amps.	Field Current 12 Volts @ 80° F.	Output @ 14 Volts 2000 R.P.M. Amps.	Output @ 14 Volts 5000 R.P.M. Amps.	Model	Field Relay Air Gap In.	Field Relay Point Gap In.	Field Relay Closing Voltage	Voltage Regulator Air Gap In.	Voltage Regulator Point Gap In.	Voltage Regulator Voltage @ 125° F.
1969	1100734	42	2.2–2.6	28	40	1119515	.015	.030	6.3–8.3	.060	.014	13.5–14.4
	1100767	37	2.2–2.6	25	35	1119515	.015	.030	6.3–8.3	.060	.014	13.5–14.4
	1100777	55	2.2–2.6	32	50	1119515	.015	.030	6.3–8.3	.060	.014	13.5–14.4
	1100853	37	4.0–4.5	—	32	—	—	—	—	—	—	—

Continued

ALTERNATOR & REGULATOR SPECIFICATIONS—Continued

Year	Model	Rated Hot Output Amps.	Field Current 12 Volts @ 80° F.	Output @ 14 Volts 2000 R.P.M. Amps.	Output @ 14 Volts 5000 R.P.M. Amps.	Model	Field Relay Air Gap In.	Field Relay Point Gap In.	Field Relay Closing Voltage	Voltage Regulator Air Gap In.	Voltage Regulator Point Gap In.	Voltage @ 125° F.
1970	1100777	55	2.2–2.6	32	50	1119515	.015	.030	6.3–8.3	.060	.014	13.5–14.4
	1100878	42	2.2–2.6	28	40	1119515	.015	.030	6.3–8.3	.060	.014	13.5–14.4
	1100879	37	2.2–2.6	25	35	1119515	.015	.030	6.3–8.3	.060	.014	13.5–14.4
	1100880	37	4.0–4.5	—	32	—	—	—	—	—	—	—
	1100886	63	2.8–3.2	35	59	1119515	.015	.030	6.3–8.3	.060	.014	13.5–14.4
	1100888	37	2.2–2.6	25	35	1119515	.015	.030	6.3–8.3	.060	.014	13.5–14.4
	1100890	55	4.0–4.5	—	50	—	—	—	—	—	—	—
	1100891	55	2.2–2.6	32	50	1119515	.015	.030	6.3–8.3	.060	.014	13.5–14.4
	1100892	55	2.2–2.6	32	50	1119515	.015	.030	6.3–8.3	.060	.014	13.5–14.4
	1100893	55	2.2–2.6	32	50	1119515	.015	.030	6.3–8.3	.060	.014	13.5–14.4
	1100907	61	2.2–2.6	33	58	1119515	.015	.030	6.3–8.3	.060	.014	13.5–14.4
1971	1100553	63	4.0–4.5	—	—	1119519	—	—	—	—	—	13.5–14.4
	1100566	37	2.2–2.6	—	—	1119515	—	—	—	—	—	13.5–14.4
	1100567	42	2.2–2.6	—	—	1119515	—	—	—	—	—	13.5–14.4
	1100568	55	2.2–2.6	—	—	1119515	—	—	—	—	—	13.5–14.4
	1100569	55	2.2–2.6	—	—	1119515	—	—	—	—	—	13.5–14.4
	1100570	61	2.2–2.6	—	—	1119515	—	—	—	—	—	13.5–14.4
	1100888	37	2.2–2.6	—	—	1119515	—	—	—	—	—	13.5–14.4
	1100934	37	4.0–4.5	—	—	—	—	—	—	—	—	—
	1100935	55	4.0–4.5	—	—	—	—	—	—	—	—	—
1972	1100573	42	4.0–4.5	—	—	—	—	—	—	—	—	—
	1100597	61	4.0–4.5	—	—	—	—	—	—	—	—	—
	1102435	42	2.2–2.6	—	—	1119515	—	—	—	—	—	13.5–14.4
	1102437	55	2.2–2.6	—	—	1119515	—	—	—	—	—	13.5–14.4
	1102439	55	2.2–2.6	—	—	1119515	—	—	—	—	—	13.5–14.4
	1102440	37	2.2–2.6	—	—	1119515	—	—	—	—	—	13.5–14.4
	1102463	61	2.2–2.6	—	—	1119515	—	—	—	—	—	13.5–14.4
1973-74	1100497	37	—	—	—	Integral	—	—	—	—	—	13.8–14.8
	1100573	42	—	—	—	Integral	—	—	—	—	—	—
	1100934	37	—	—	—	Integral	—	—	—	—	—	—
	1102367	55	—	—	—	Integral	—	—	—	—	—	—
	1102368	61	—	—	—	Integral	—	—	—	—	—	—
1975	1102399	37	—	—	—	—	—	—	—	—	—	—
	1102481	37	—	—	—	—	—	—	—	—	—	—
	1102483	37	—	—	—	—	—	—	—	—	—	—
	1102488	57	—	—	—	—	—	—	—	—	—	—
	1102493	42	—	—	—	—	—	—	—	—	—	—
	1102549	61	—	—	—	—	—	—	—	—	—	—
	1102550	63	—	—	—	—	—	—	—	—	—	—

COOLING SYSTEM & CAPACITY DATA

Year	Model or Engine	Cooling Capacity, Qts. No Heater	Cooling Capacity, Qts. With Heater	Cooling Capacity, Qts. With A/C	Radiator Cap Relief Pressure, Lbs. With A/C	Radiator Cap Relief Pressure, Lbs. No A/C	Thermo. Opening Temp. ①	Fuel Tank Gals.	Engine Oil Refill Qts. ②	Transmission Oil 3 Speed Pints	Transmission Oil 4 Speed Pints	Transmission Oil Auto. Trans. Qts. ⑫	Rear Axle Oil Pints
1969	6-250	11.5	12.2	12.2	15	15	195	20	4	3½	—	⑩	3.69
	8-350	14.5	15.2	15.7	15	15	195	20⑬	4	3½	4.90	⑩	3.69
	8-400, 4-4-2	15.5	16.2	17.2	15	15	195	20	4	3½	4.90	⑮	3.69

Continued

COOLING SYSTEM & CAPACITY DATA—Continued

Year	Model or Engine	Cooling Capacity, Qts.			Radiator Cap Relief Pressure, Lbs.		Thermo. Opening Temp. ①	Fuel Tank Gals.	Engine Oil Refill Qts. ②	Transmission Oil			Rear Axle Oil Pints
		No Heater	With Heater	With A/C	With A/C	No A/C				3 Speed Pints	4 Speed Pints	Auto. Trans. Qts. ⑫	
1969	Delta, 98	—	17.5	18	15	15	195	25	4	4.9	—	⑩	5.32③
	Toronado	—	18	18.5	15	15	195	24	5	—	—	⑮	4
1970	6-250	11	12	12.0	15	15	195	20	4	3½	—	③	3¾
	8-350⑯	14	15	15.5	15	15	195	20⑬	4	3½	2¼	③	3¾
	8-350⑰	15.5	16.5	16.5	15	15	195	25	4	3½	2¼	⑩	3¾
	8-455⑯	15	16	16.5	15	15	195	20⑬	4	3½	2¼	⑩	3¾
	8-455⑰	—	17.5	18	15	15	195	25	4	4½	2¼	⑩	5⅓
	Toronado	—	18	18.5	15	15	195	24	5	—	—	⑩	4
1971	6-250	12	13	13	15	15	195	19⑱	4	3½	—	③	4¼
	8-350⑯	15	16	17	15	15	195	19⑱	4	⑲	2¼	⑩	4¼
	8-350⑰	15	16	17	15	15	195	24	4	3½	—	⑩	⑳
	8-455⑯	16	17	18	15	15	195	19	4	⑲	2¼	⑩	4¼
	8-455⑰	—	17	18	15	15	195	24	4	3½	—	⑩	⑳
	Toronado	—	18	19	15	15	195	24	5	—	—	⑩	4
1972	8-350⑯	—	15.2	15.7	15	15	195	19⑬	4	3½	3½	⑩	⑳
	8-350⑰	—	16.2	16.7	15	15	195	24	4	—	—	⑩	4¼
	8-455⑯	—	15.2	15.7	15	15	195	19⑬	4	3½	3½	⑩	4¼
	8-455⑰	—	17	17.5	15	15	195	24	4	—	—	⑩	5½
	Toronado	—	19.5	20	15	15	195	25	5	—	—	⑩	4
1973	6-250	11½	12½	12½	15	15	195	21	4	3½	—	⑩	4¼
	8-350 Omega	—	15½	16½	15	15	195	21	4	3½	—	⑩	4¼
	8-350 Cutlass	—	16	16	15	15	195	22	4	3½	2¼	⑩	4¼
	8-350 "88"	—	16¼	16¼	15	15	195	26	4	—	—	⑩	5½
	8-455 Cutlass	—	17	18	15	15	195	22	4	—	2¼	⑩	4¼
	8-455⑰	—	17	17½	15	15	195	26㉑	4	—	—	⑩	5½
	Toronado	—	19½	20	15	15	195	26	4	—	—	㉒	4
1974	6-250	—	15½	—	15	15	195	21	4	3.5	—	⑩	4¼
	8-350 Omega	—	18½	19½	15	15	195	21	4	3.5	—	⑩	4¼
	8-350 Cutlass	—	20④	20④	15	15	195	22	4	—	—	⑩	4¼
	8-350⑰	—	21⑤	21⑤	15	15	195	26	4	—	—	⑩	4¼
	8-350 Sta. Wagon	—	20④	20④	15	15	195	22	4	—	—	⑩	5½
	8-455 Cutlass	—	21	21½⑥	15	15	195	22	4	—	—	⑩	4¼
	8-455⑰	—	21	21½⑥	15	15	195	26	4	—	—	⑩	5½
	8-455 Sta. Wagon	—	21	21½⑥	15	15	195	22	4	—	—	⑩	5½
	Toronado	—	21	21½	15	15	195	26	5	—	—	㉒	4
1975	6-250 Omega	—	15½	19½	15	15	195	21	4	3½	—	⑩	⑨
	6-250 Cutlass	—	17	17	15	15	195	22	4	3½	—	⑩	⑨
	8-260 Omega	—	18½	19½	15	15	195	21	4	3½	—	⑩	⑨
	8-260 Cutlass	—	23½	23½④	15	15	195	22	4	3½	—	⑩	⑨
	8-350 Omega	—	18½	19½	15	15	195	21	4	—	—	⑩	⑨
	8-350⑦	—	20	20④	15	15	195	26⑧	4	—	—	⑩	⑨
	8-400	—	21½	22⑥	15	15	195	26⑧	4	—	—	⑩	⑨
	8-455	—	21	21½⑥	15	15	195	26⑧	4	—	—	⑩	⑨
	Toronado	—	21	21½	15	15	195	26	5	—	—	⑫	4

①—For alcohol type anti-freeze use a 160° unit.
②—Add one quart with filter change.
③—Oil pan only 2 qts. After overhaul 10 qts.
④—With heavy duty cooling system add 2½ qts.
⑤—With heavy duty cooling system add 1½ qts.
⑥—With heavy duty cooling system add 2 qts.
⑦—Intermediate and full size.
⑧—Intermediate and station wagons 22 gallons.
⑨—8½" ring gear 4¼ pts., 8⅞" ring gear 5½ pts., 9⅜ ring gear 5½ pts.
⑩—Oil pan only 3 qts. After overhaul 10 qts.
⑫—Approximate; make final check with dipstick.
⑬—Vista-Cruiser 23 gallons.
⑭—With Jetaway, 3.69 pts.
⑮—Refill 4 qts.
⑯—Intermediate cars.
⑰—Full size cars.
⑱—Vista-Cruiser 22 gallons.
⑲—Standard unit 3½, heavy duty 4½.
⑳—With 10 bolt cover 4¼; with 12 bolt cover 5½.
㉑—Custom Cruiser 22 gallons.
㉒—Oil pan only 4 qts. after overhaul 12 qts.

PISTONS, PINS, RINGS, CRANKSHAFT & BEARINGS

Year	Model	Piston Clearance	Ring End Gap① Comp.	Oil	Wrist-pin Diameter	Rod Bearings Shaft Diameter	Bearing Clearance	Main Bearings Shaft Diameter	Bearing Clearance	Thrust on Bear. No.	Shaft End Play
1969–70	6-250⑧	.0005–.0016	.010	.015	.9271	1.999–2.000	.0007–.0027	2.2983–2.2988	.0003–.0029	7	.002–.006
	V8-350	.001–.002	.010	.015	.9805	2.1238–2.1248	.0004–.0033	③	.0005–.0021⑤	3	.004–.008
	V8-400 (1969)	.001–.002	.010	.015	.9805	2.4988–2.4998	.0004–.0033	2.9993–3.0003	.0005–.0021⑥	3	.004–.008
	V8-455	.001–.002	.013	.015	.9805	2.4988–2.4998	.0004–.0033	2.9993–3.0003	.0005–.0021⑥	3	.004–.008
1971	6-250⑧	.0005–.0016	.010	.015	.9271	1.999–2.000	.0007–.0027	2.2983–2.2988	.0003–.0029	7	.002–.006
	V8-350	.001–.002	.010	.015	.9805	2.1238–2.1248	.0004–.0033	③	.0005–.0021⑤	3	.004–.008
	V8-455	.001–.002	.013	.015	.9805	2.4988–2.4998	.002–.011	2.9993–3.0003	.0005–.0021⑥	3	.004–.008
1972	V8-350	.001–.002	.010	.015	.9805	2.1238–2.1248	.0004–.0033	③	.0005–.0021⑤	3	.004–.008
	V8-455	.001–.002	.010	.015	.9805	2.4988–2.4998	.002–.011	2.9993–3.0003	.0005–.0021⑥	3	.004–.008
1973-74	6-250⑧	.0005–.0016	.010	.015	.9271	1.999–2.000	.0007–.0027	2.3004	.0003–.0029	7	.002–.006
	V8-350	.001–.002	.010	.015	.9805	2.1238–2.1248	.0004–.0033	③	.0005–.0021⑤	3	.004–.008
	V8-455	.001–.002	.010	.015	.9805	2.4988–2.4998	.0004–.0033	2.9993–3.0003	.0005–.0021⑥	3	.004–.008
1975	6-250⑧	.0005–.0015	.010	.015	.9271	1.9928–2.000	.0007–.0027	2.2983–2.2993	.0003–.0029	7	.002–.006
	V8-260	.001–.002	.010	.015	.9805	2.1238–2.1248	.0004–.0033	③	.0005–.0021⑤	3	.004–.008
	V8-350④	.0008–.0014	.013	.015	.9392	1.991–2.000	.0005–.0026	2.9995	.004–.0015	3	.002–.006
	V8-350	.001–.002	.010	.015	.9805	2.1238–2.1248	.0004–.0033	③	.0005–.0021⑤	3	.004–.008
	V8-400⑦	.0029–.0037	②	.035	.9802	2.25	.0005–.0026	3.00	.0002–.0017	4	.003–.009
	V8-455	.001–.002	.010	.015	.9805	2.4988–2.4998	.0004–.0033	2.9993–3.0003	.0005–.0021⑥	3	.004–.008

①—Fit rings in tapered bores for clearance listed in tightest portion of ring travel.
②—Top—.019, #2—.015.
③—No. 1: 2.4988-2.4998; Nos. 2, 3, 4, 5: 2.4985-2.4995.
④—Omega only. See Buick Chapter for service procedures.
⑤—Rear .0015–.0031.
⑥—Rear .002–.0034.
⑦—See Pontiac Chapter for service procedures.
⑧—See Chevrolet Chapter for service procedures on this engine.

STARTING MOTOR SPECIFICATIONS

Year	Model	Starter Number	Brush Spring Tension Oz.①	Free Speed Test Amps.	Volts	R.P.M.	Resistance Test③ Amps.	Volts
1969	8-455 "98"	1108333	35	70–99②	10.6	7800–12000	—	—
	8-350, 400, 455	1108348	35	70–105②	10.6	3800–6200	480–540②	3.0
	8-350 2 B. Carb.	1108349	35	65–100②	10.6	3600–5100	300–360②	3.5
	Toronado	1108352	35	70–105②	10.6	3800–6200	480–540②	3.0
	6-250	1108365	35	49–87②	10.6	6200–10700	—	—
1970–71	6-250	1108365	35	49–87②	10.6	6200–10700	—	—
	8-350	1108386	35	55–80②	9	3500–6000	—	—
	8-350, 455	1108387	35	45–80②	9	4000–6500	—	—
	8-455	1108389	35	65–95②	9	7500–10500	—	—
	Toronado	1108352	35	70–105②	10.6	3800–6200	480–540②	3.0
1972–73	6-250	1108365	35	49–87②	10.6	6200–10700	—	—
	8-350	1108386	35	55–80②	9	3500–6000	—	—
	8-455	1108387	35	45–80②	9	4000–6500	—	—
	Toronado	1108352	35	70–105②	10.6	3800–6200	480–540②	3.0
1974	6-250	1108365	35	—	—	—	—	—
	8-350	1108516	35	—	—	—	—	—
	8-455	1108517	35	—	—	—	—	—
	Toronado	1108518	35	—	—	—	—	—

Continued

STARTING MOTOR SPECIFICATIONS—Continued

Year	Model	Starter Number	Brush Spring Tension Oz.①	Free Speed Test			Resistance Test③	
				Amps.	Volts	R.P.M.	Amps.	Volts
1975	6-250	1108365	35	50–80	9	5500–10500	—	—
	6-250	1108774⑤	35	50–80	9	5500–10500	—	—
	8-260	1108765	35	55–80	9	3500–6000	—	—
	8-350④	1108762	35	55–80	9	3500–6000	—	—
	8-350	1108765	35	55–80	9	3500–6000	—	—
	8-400	1108758	35	65–95	9	7500–10500	—	—
	8-455	1108766	—	—	—	—	—	—

①—Minimum. ②—Includes solenoid. ④—Omega only. ⑤—Has "R" terminal removed.
⑥—Check capacity of motor by using a 500 ampere meter and a carbon pile rheostat to control voltage. Apply volts listed across motor with armature locked. Current should be as listed.

WHEEL ALIGNMENT SPECIFICATIONS

OLD CAR SPECIFICATIONS: For 1946-68 Wheel Alignment Specifications see main index.

Year	Model	Caster Angle, Degrees		Camber Angle, Degrees				Toe-In. Inch	Toe-Out on Turns, Deg.①	
		Limits	Desired	Limits		Desired			Outer Wheel	Inner Wheel
				Left	Right	Left	Right			
1969	Intermediates	−½ to −2	−1¼	−¼ to +½	−¼ to +½	+⅛	+⅛	⅛–³⁄₁₆	18.6	20
	F.S.C.②③	−½ to −1½	−1¼	−¼ to +½	−¼ to +½	+⅛	+⅛	⅛–³⁄₁₆	18.3	20
	F.S.C.②④	−½ to −1½	−¾	−¼ to +½	−¼ to +½	+⅛	+⅛	⅛–³⁄₁₆	18.7	20
	Toronado	−1½ to −2½	−2	−½ to +¼	−½ to +¼	+⅛	+⅛	0–¹⁄₁₆	18.1	20
1970	Intermediates	−½ to −2	−1¼	−¼ to +½	−¼ to +½	+⅛	+⅛	⅛–³⁄₁₆	18.6	20
	F.S.C.②③	−½ to −1½	−1¼	−¼ to +½	−¼ to +½	+⅛	+⅛	⅛–³⁄₁₆	18.3	20
	F.S.C.②④	−½ to −1½	−¾	−¼ to +½	−¼ to +½	+⅛	+⅛	⅛–³⁄₁₆	17.7	20
	Toronado	−1½ to −2½	−2	−¼ to +½	−½ to +½	+⅛	+⅛	0–¹⁄₁₆	18.2	20
1971–72	Intermediates	−¾ to −2¼	−1¼	−¼ to +¾	−¾ to +¼	+¼	−¼	0	—	—
	F.S.C.②	+½ to +1½	+1	−¼ to +¾	−¾ to +¼	+¼	−¼	0	—	—
	Toronado	−1½ to −2½	−2	−¼ to +¾	−¾ to +¼	+¼	−¼	0	—	—
1973	Omega	0 to +1	+½	−¼ to +¾	−¼ to +¾	+¼	+¼	⅛–¼	—	—
	Cutlass③	−½ to −1½	−1	+½ to +1½	0 to +1	+1	+½	0–⅛	—	—
	Cutlass④	−½ to +½	0	+½ to +1½	0 to +1	+1	+½	0–⅛	—	—
	88, 98	+½ to +1½	+1	+½ to +1½	0 to +1	+1	+½	¹⁄₁₆–³⁄₁₆	—	—
	Toronado	−1½ to −2½	−2	−¼ to +¾	−¾ to +¼	+¼	−¼	0	—	—
1974	Omega	0 to +1	+½	−¼ to +¾	−¼ to +¾	+¼	+¼	⅛–¼	—	—
	Cutlass Exc. Sal.⑥	−½ to +½	0	+½ to +1½	0 to +1	+1	+½	0–⅛	—	—
	Cutlass Salon⑥	+1½ to +2½	+2	+½ to +1½	0 to +1	+1	+½	0–⅛	—	—
	88, 98⑥	+½ to +1½	+1	+½ to +1½	0 to +1	+1	+½	−¹⁄₁₆ to +³⁄₁₆	—	—
	Toronado⑥	−1½ to −2½	−2	−¼ to +¾	−¾ to +¼	+¼	−¼	0	—	—
1975	Omega③	−1½ to −½	−1	+¼ to +1¼	+¼ to +1¼	+¾	+¾	0 to ⅛	—	—
	Omega④	+½ to +1½	+1	+¼ to 1¼	+¼ to 1¼	+¾	+¾	0 to ⅛	—	—
	Cutlass⑥	+1½ to +2½	+2	+½ to +1½	0 to +1	+1	+½	0 to ⅛	—	—
	88, 98⑥	+1 to +2	+1½	+½ to +1½	0 to +1	+1	+½	0 to ⅛	—	—
	Sta. Wagons⑥	+1 to +2	+1½	+½ to +1½	0 to +1	+1	+½	0 to ⅛	—	—
	Toronado⑥	−1 to +1	0	−¼ to +¾	−¾ to +¼	+¼	−¼	0 to ¹⁄₁₆	—	—

①—Incorrect toe-out, when other adjustments are correct, indicates bent steering arms.
②—F.S.C.-Full size car.
③—Manual Steering.
④—Power Steering.
⑥—Left and right side "camber" should be different at least ¼° and no more than ¾° with the left side having the greater (+) reading.

BRAKE SPECIFICATIONS

Year	Model	Brake Drum Inside Diameter	Wheel Cylinder Bore Diameter			Master Cylinder Bore Diameter		
			Disc Brake	Front Drum Brake	Rear Drum Brake	Disc Brakes	Drum Brakes	Power Brakes
1969	Intermediate Cars	9½	2¹⁵⁄₁₆	1⅛	¹⁵⁄₁₆①	1⅛	1	1
	Intermediate Wagons	9½	2¹⁵⁄₁₆	1⅛	¹⁵⁄₁₆①	1⅛	1	1
	Delta, 98	11	2¹⁵⁄₁₆	1³⁄₁₆	1	1	1	1
	Toronado	11	2¹⁵⁄₁₆	1⅛	⅞	1¹⁄₁₆	1	1
1970	Intermediate Cars	9½	2¹⁵⁄₁₆	1⅛	⅞	1⅛	1	②
	Intermediate Wagons	9½	2¹⁵⁄₁₆	1⅝	1	1⅛	1	②
	Delta, 98	11	2¹⁵⁄₁₆	1³⁄₁₆	¹⁵⁄₁₆	1⅛	1	②
	Toronado	11	2¹⁵⁄₁₆	—	¹⁵⁄₁₆	1⅛	—	1⅛
1971–72	Intermediate Cars	9½	2¹⁵⁄₁₆	1⅛	⅞	1⅛	1	1
	Intermediate Wagons	9½	2¹⁵⁄₁₆	—	1	1⅛	—	1
	Delta, 98	11	2¹⁵⁄₁₆	—	¹⁵⁄₁₆	1⅛	—	1
	Custom Cruiser	12	2¹⁵⁄₁₆	—	1	1⅛	—	1
	Toronado	11	2¹⁵⁄₁₆	—	¹⁵⁄₁₆	1⅛	—	1
1973–74	Omega	9½	2¹⁵⁄₁₆	1⅛	⅞	1⅛	1	1
	Cutlass	9½	2¹⁵⁄₁₆	—	⅞	1⅛	—	1⅛
	Vista Cruiser	11	2¹⁵⁄₁₆	—	¹⁵⁄₁₆	1⅛	—	1⅛
	Custom Cruiser	12	2¹⁵⁄₁₆	—	1	1⅛	—	1⅛
	88, 98 & Toronado	11	2¹⁵⁄₁₆	—	¹⁵⁄₁₆	1⅛	—	1⅛
1975	Omega, Cutlass	9½	2¹⁵⁄₁₆	—	⅞	1⅛	—	1⅛
	Cruiser, Vista Cruiser	11	2¹⁵⁄₁₆	—	⅞	1⅛	—	1⅛
	Custom Cruiser	12	2¹⁵⁄₁₆	—	1	1⅛	—	1⅛
	88, 98, Toronado	11	2¹⁵⁄₁₆	—	¹⁵⁄₁₆	1⅛	—	1⅛

①—1³⁄₁₆" with front disc brakes.   ②—With drum brakes 1"; with disc brakes 1⅛".

Electrical Section

1975 HIGH ENERGY IGNITION SYSTEM (H.E.I.)

Refer to the "Tune-Up Service" chapter, Electronic Ignition Systems section for service procedures. However, service procedures for the 6-250 H.E.I. distributor are slightly different since the ignition coil is externally mounted.

DISTRIBUTOR, REPLACE

1. Disconnect primary wire from distributor and disconnect pipe from vacuum control unit.

   NOTE: On H.E.I. systems, disconnect feed and module connectors from distributor cap.

2. Remove distributor cap.
3. Crank engine until distributor rotor is in position to fire No. 1 cylinder and the timing mark (see *Tune Up Chart*) is aligned with the timing indicator.
4. Remove distributor clamp and lift

Fig. 1   Ignition lock remove. 1969-75

the distributor out of the crankcase.

Installation, All Models

1. Check to make sure that the timing mark is aligned with the timing indicator with No. 1 piston on the compression stroke in position to fire.
2. Place a new seal or gasket on distributor housing.
3. Rotate distributor cam until rotor is in position to fire No. 1 cylinder.
4. Rotate oil pump shaft with screwdriver to align slot in shaft with tongue on lower end of distributor shaft.
5. Install distributor in crankcase.
6. Install distributor clamp and bolt with lockwasher, leaving bolt just loose enough to permit movement of distributor.
7. Rotate distributor housing until breaker points just start to open and tighten clamp bolt. This will permit starting engine for setting timing.
8. Connect pipe to vacuum control and primary wire to terminal stud.
9. Install distributor cap. If spark plug

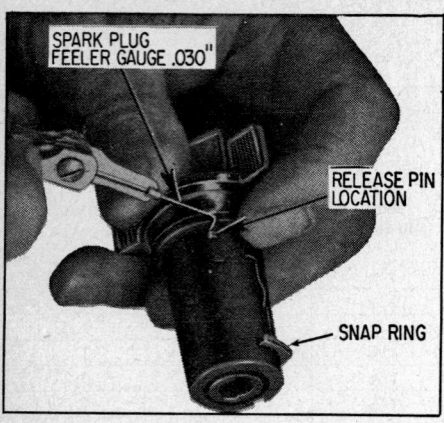

Fig. 2 Ignition lock disassembly. 1969

wires are disconnected from cap make certain that wires are connected in accordance with firing orders.

10. Check and set ignition timing.

NOTE: When using a timing light to adjust ignition timing, the connection should be made at the No. 1 spark plug. Forcing foreign objects through the boot at the No. 1 terminal of the distributor cap will damage the boot and could cause engine misfiring.

IGNITION LOCK REPLACE

1969-75

CAUTION: On vehicles equipped with an Air Cushion Restraint system, turn ignition switch to "Lock," disconnect battery ground cable and tape end, thereby deactivating system.

1. Follow the procedure to remove the turn signal switch as described further on.
2. Position the lock assembly in "ACCESSORY" position for 1969-70 models and in "RUN" position for 1971-75 models. Insert a long thin screwdriver into the slot as shown in Fig. 1 and pull outward on lock assembly to remove.

IGNITION LOCK DISASSEMBLY

1969

1. To separate the lock from the cylinder turn the ignition key to the "ACCESSORY" position, Fig. 2 (fully counterclockwise looking at key).
2. Depress the brass pin down and turn the lock cylinder clockwise; cylinder will pop out but will still be retained about 1/4". Remove the key from the lock.

3. Tap sleeve lightly on bench with snap ring down to move the warning buzzer cam inboard. Cam must be inboard before lock cylinder can be removed.
4. Remove lock cylinder, lock & wave washer from sleeve.

1970-75

The ignition lock assembly is not repairable due to staking of the adapter lock to the lock cylinder. Therefore a new lock assembly service package must be obtained for any failure.

STARTER, REPLACE

1969 V8-400

1. Disconnect battery and hoist car.
2. Disconnect clutch return spring at clutch release yoke.
3. Disconnect exhaust pipe from left exhaust manifold.
4. Loosen upper and remove lower starter-to-engine brace bolt.
5. Remove two starter-to-block bolts.
6. Move starter forward and downward, then disconnect wires from three starter terminals.
7. Rotate starter counterclockwise while pulling forward and downward on front of starter and remove starter. *On 4-4-2 with automatic transmission, adequate clearance can be obtained by removing flywheel housing cover.*

1969-73 Except V8-400

1. Disconnect battery.
2. Noting position of wires, disconnect starter wiring.
3. With manual shift transmission, remove flywheel housing cover (4 screws).
4. Remove upper support attaching bolt.
5. Remove starter (2 bolts).

NOTE: If equipped with dual exhaust, the left-hand exhaust pipe may have to be disconnected to provide clearance.

IGNITION SWITCH, REPLACE

1969-75

CAUTION: On vehicles equipped with an Air Cushion Restraint system, turn ignition switch to "Lock," disconnect battery ground cable and tape end, thereby deactivating system.

1. Disconnect battery ground cable.
2. Turn ignition lock to:
   a. "Lock" for all 1969 models.
   b. "Run" for all 1970 models.
   c. "Off-Unlocked" for all 1971-75 models with fixed steering columns.
   d. "Accessory" for all 1971-75 models with tilt or tilt and telescope

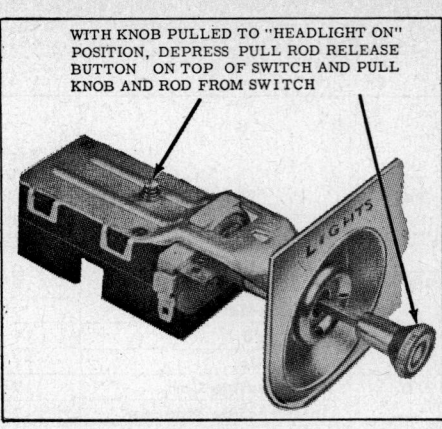

WITH KNOB PULLED TO "HEADLIGHT ON" POSITION, DEPRESS PULL ROD RELEASE BUTTON ON TOP OF SWITCH AND PULL KNOB AND ROD FROM SWITCH

Fig. 3 Light switch with release button (typical)

columns.

3. Remove cover attaching bolts, loosen toe pan clamp bolts and remove trim cap from lower part of panel.
4. Remove bracket retaining nuts and lower steering column to the seat.
5. Disconnect and remove switch.
6. Be sure that lock is in same position as when switch was removed then install switch onto actuator and column. On 1969-71 models, insert a .090 inch pin through positioning hole in switch.
7. Connect wiring and reinstall column.

LIGHT SWITCH, REPLACE

1974-75 Senior Cars

CAUTION: On vehicles equipped with an Air Cushion Restraint system, turn ignition switch to "Lock," disconnect battery ground cable and tape end, thereby deactivating system.

1. Disconnect battery ground cable.
2. Without disconnecting vacuum hoses or electrical connectors, remove heater or air conditioning control.
3. Remove switch escutcheon and pull switch through heater or air conditioning control opening in cluster and disconnect electrical connector.
4. Reverse procedure to install.

1969-73 All & 1974-75 Intermediates

1. On 1969 intermediate models with A/C, remove left-hand outlet duct.
2. Disconnect multiple connector from switch.
3. Pull knob out to headlight ON position, then depress spring-loaded button on switch body and pull knob out of switch assembly, Fig. 3.
4. Remove switch escutcheon.
5. Remove switch from rear of panel.
6. On 1969 Toronado, disconnect vac-

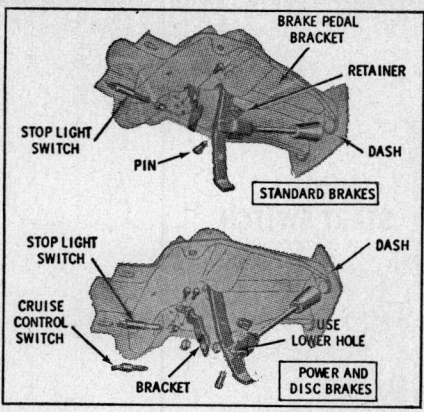

Fig. 4   Brake switch installation. 1969-75

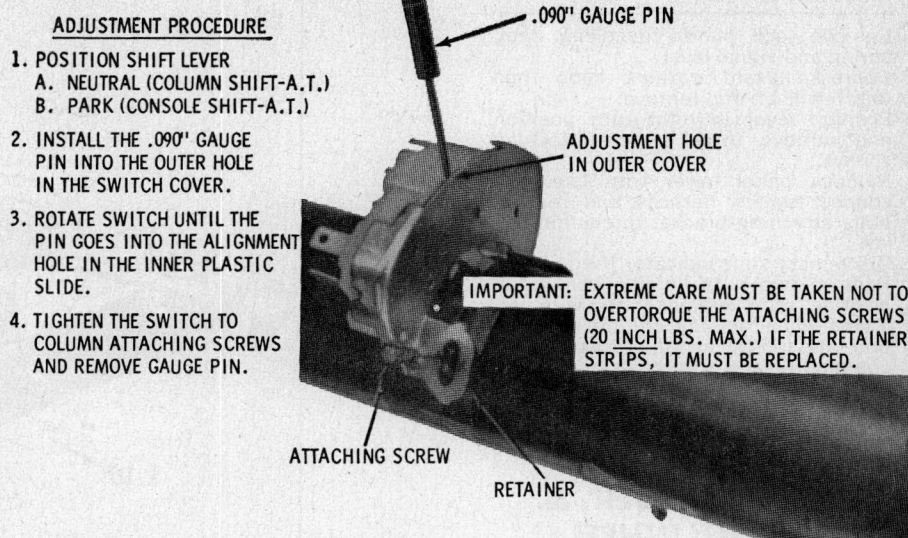

ADJUSTMENT PROCEDURE

1. POSITION SHIFT LEVER
   A. NEUTRAL (COLUMN SHIFT-A.T.)
   B. PARK (CONSOLE SHIFT-A.T.)
2. INSTALL THE .090" GAUGE PIN INTO THE OUTER HOLE IN THE SWITCH COVER.
3. ROTATE SWITCH UNTIL THE PIN GOES INTO THE ALIGNMENT HOLE IN THE INNER PLASTIC SLIDE.
4. TIGHTEN THE SWITCH TO COLUMN ATTACHING SCREWS AND REMOVE GAUGE PIN.

IMPORTANT: EXTREME CARE MUST BE TAKEN NOT TO OVERTORQUE THE ATTACHING SCREWS (20 INCH LBS. MAX.) IF THE RETAINER STRIPS, IT MUST BE REPLACED.

Fig. 5   Neutral safety switch adjustment. 1973-75 Auto. Trans.

uum hoses and note color coding of each.

STOP LIGHT SWITCH
1969-75

The stop light switch is attached to the brake pedal bracket and is actuated by the brake pedal arm, Fig. 4. When installing the switch, insert switch into tubular clip until switch body seats on tube clip. Pull brake pedal rearward until it contacts brake pedal stop. This moves the switch in the tubular clip providing proper adjustment.

CLUTCH START SWITCH
1969-75

All cars equipped with a manual transmission use a clutch start switch which is mounted on the pedal bracket. The switch closes when the clutch is depressed and completes solenoid connection. When installing switch, no adjustment is necessary.

NEUTRAL START & BACK-UP LIGHT SWITCH

The neutral safety switch is mounted on the steering column or inside the console on floor shift models with automatic transmission.

Checking

1. Apply parking brake firmly.
2. Position selector lever into "D" range and turn ignition switch to "Start".
3. While holding switch on "Start", slowly move selector lever toward "N" position until engine cranks and starts.

4. Without moving selector lever after engine starts, depress accelerator pedal slightly to determine whether or not transmission is in gear. If switch is properly adjusted, transmission will not be in gear.

NOTE: If equipped with back-up lights, lights should operate with ignition on and selector lever in reverse.

1971-75

For 1973-75 vehicles equipped with automatic transmission, refer to Fig. 5. For all other models, follow procedure outlined below:
1. Place selector in "Neutral" for column shift or "Park" for console shift vehicles.
2. Install a .090 inch gauge pin into outer hole in switch cover, Fig. 6.
3. On all except 1972-75 manual transmission vehicles, rotate switch until pin fits into alignment hole in inner plastic slide.
4. On all models, tighten switch to column screws and remove gauge pin.

1969-70

Adjustment (Except Console)
1. Place transmission in drive detent with switch installed and drive lug engaged in shift tube.
2. Adjust switch so gauge pin hole will align between contact support and switch bracket permitting insertion of gauge pin, Fig. 6.

Adjustment (Console Type)
1. Remove console.
2. On 1969 units, place shift lever against neutral stop. On 1970, place lever in Park.
3. On 1969 units, adjust switch to dimension shown in Fig. 7. On 1970, dimension is $2^1/_{16}$".

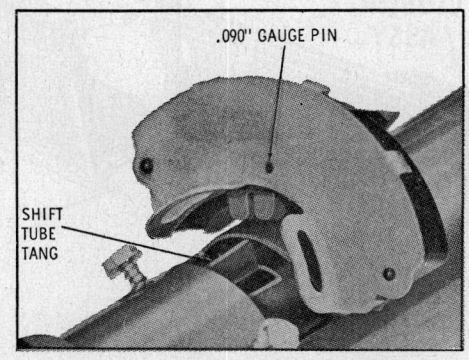

Fig. 6   Neutral safety switch adjustment. 1969-75 exc. 1973-75 auto. trans. (typical)

TURN SIGNAL SWITCH
1969-75

CAUTION: On vehicles equipped with an Air Cushion Restraint system, turn ignition switch to "Lock," disconnect battery ground cable and tape end, thereby deactivating system.

1. Disconnect battery ground cable.
2. Remove steering wheel.
3. Remove cover screws and cover.
4. Using suitable compressor, depress lock plate far enough to remove the "C" ring from shaft.

NOTE: On Tilt & Travel, compressor

must be positioned on large lips of cancelling cam.

5. Remove lock plate, cancelling cam, spring and signal lever.
6. Depress hazard warning knob then unscrew knob and remove.
7. Position lever in right turn position and remove three switch attaching screws.
8. Remove panel lower trim cap, disconnect switch harness and remove bolts attaching bracket to column jacket.
9. Disconnect shift indicator if equipped.
10. Remove two nuts holding column in position, remove bracket and wire protector while holding column in position then loosely install bracket to hold column in place.
11. Tape switch wires at connector keeping wires flat, then carefully remove wires and switch.

HORN SOUNDER & STEERING WHEEL
1969-75 All

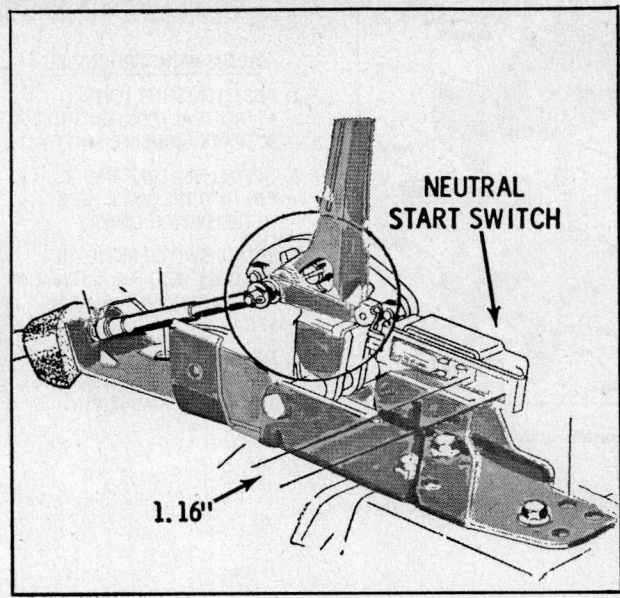

Fig. 7   Neutral start switch (console type). 1969-70

CAUTION: On vehicles equipped with an Air Cushion Restraint System, turn ignition switch to "Lock," disconnect battery ground cable and tape end, thereby deactivating system. Also, on these vehicles, it is necessary to remove the drivers cushion module before removing steering wheel. With tool J-24628-2, remove the module to steering wheel screws, lift module and disconnect horn wire. Then, with tool J-24628-3, disconnect module wire connector from slip ring.

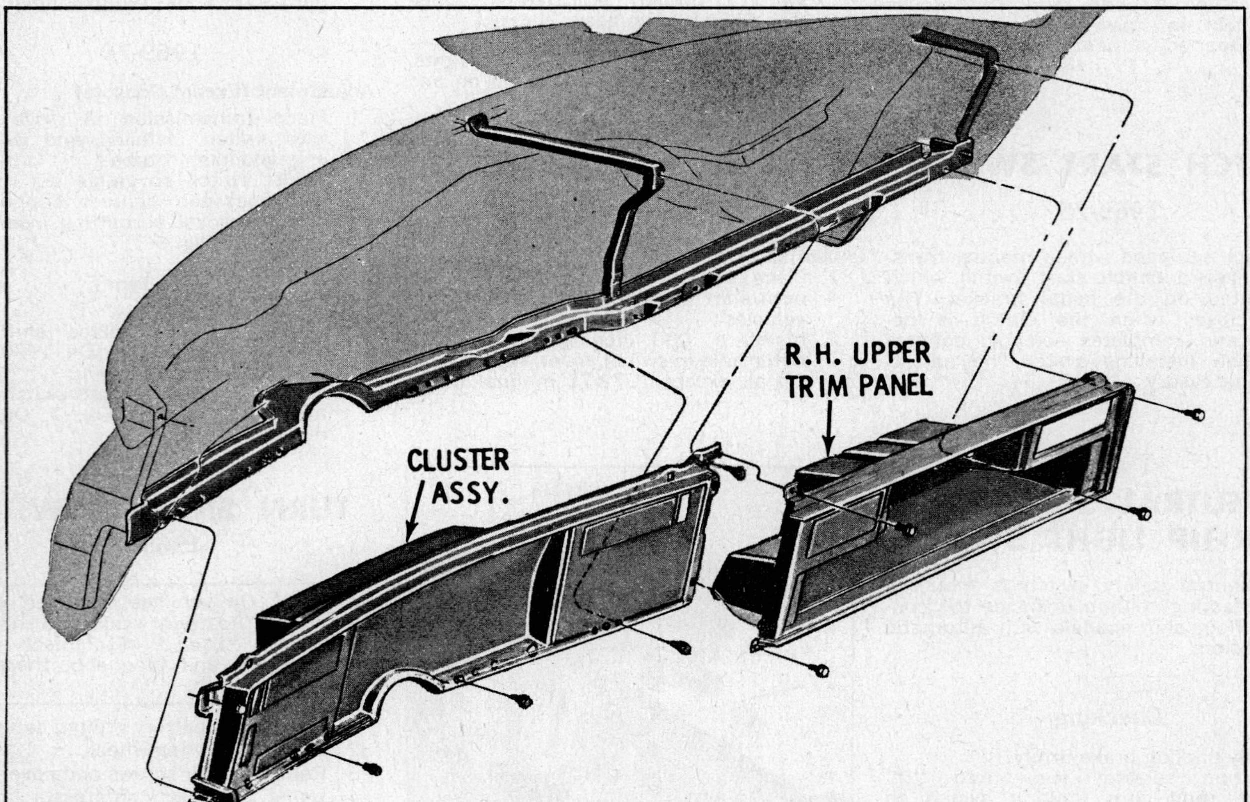

Fig. 8   Instrument cluster. 1974-75 Full Size models

1. Disconnect battery ground cable.
2. For tilt and travel steering column proceed as follows:
   a. On 1969-71 models, pull up to remove pad assembly. On 1972-75 models, remove pad assembly retaining screws, disconnect connector and remove pad assembly.
   b. Move locking lever counterclockwise until full release is obtained. Scribe a mark on the plate assembly where the two screws attach plate assembly to locking lever (for ease of installation) and remove the two screws.
   c. Unscrew and remove plate assembly.
3. For standard wheel, pull up on horn cap retainer assembly and on 1972-75 models, disconnect horn contacts.
4. For Deluxe and Rim Blow wheel, on 1969-71 models, pull down and out on pad assembly to remove. On 1972-75 models, remove three screws from pad assembly and disconnect connectors.
5. On sport wheel, pull up on and remove emblem and horn contact assembly from wheel.
6. On Wood Grain wheel, carefully pry horn cap assembly from wheel.
7. On all models, remove steering wheel nut and using a suitable puller, remove steering wheel.

NOTE: On 1975 models, remove snap ring before steering wheel nut.

8. Reverse procedure to install.

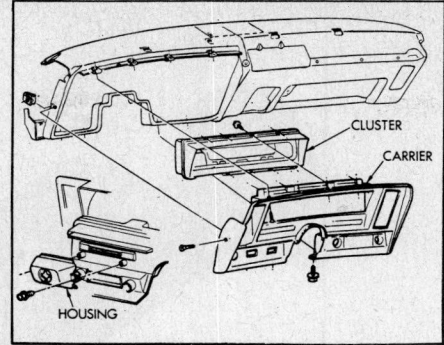

Fig. 9 Instrument cluster. 1973-75 Omega

INSTRUMENT CLUSTER

1974-75 Senior Cars

CAUTION: On vehicles equipped with an Air Cushion Restraint system, turn ignition switch to "Lock," disconnect battery ground cable and tape end, thereby de-activating system.

1. Disconnect battery ground cable.
2. Disconnect electrical connections at flood lamp or map lamp and remove lamp.
3. Carefully pry speakers from clips, disconnect electrical connections and remove speakers.
4. Remove instrument panel pad screws through speaker openings.
5. Remove screws from lower left outside edge of instrument panel pad, instrument cluster above speedometer, lower right hand corner of glove box and glove box top edge.
6. Pull at center edge of instrument panel pad, releasing clips holding instrument panel pad to windshield edge and remove instrument panel pad.
7. Disconnect the right hand instrument panel cover from lower trim panel and remove glove box door.

NOTE: Cover is secured by one screw and five studs pushed through clips mounted in lower panel.

8. If equipped with air conditioning, disconnect upper right hand air hose from duct.
9. On all models, disconnect electrical connectors from clock, trunk release and glove box lamp.
10. Remove the upper trim panel.
11. Disconnect the left hand instrument panel cover, slide steering column cover up the column and pull the left hand instrument panel cover from lower trim panel.

NOTE: Cover is secured by six studs pushed through clips mounted in

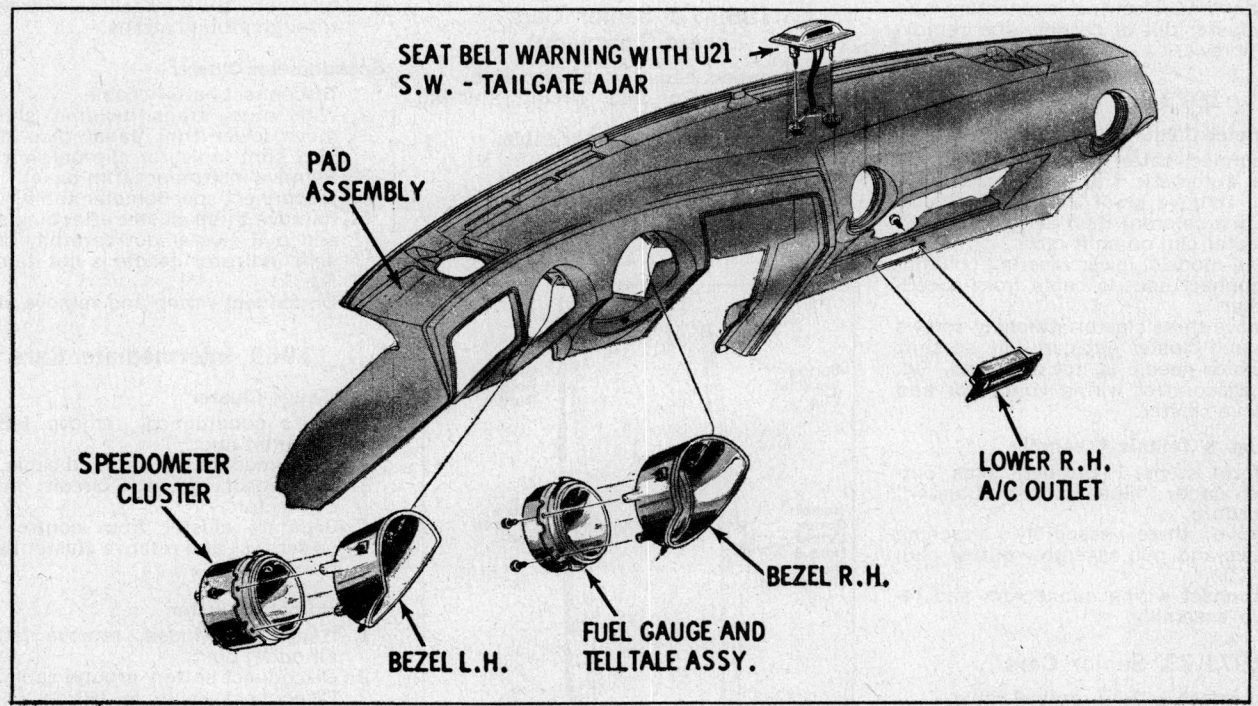

SEAT BELT WARNING WITH U21
S.W. - TAILGATE AJAR

PAD ASSEMBLY

SPEEDOMETER CLUSTER

BEZEL L.H.

FUEL GAUGE AND TELLTALE ASSY.

BEZEL R.H.

LOWER R.H. A/C OUTLET

Fig. 10 Instrument cluster. 1973-75 Cutlass

lower panel.

12. If equipped with air conditioning, disconnect upper left hand air hose from duct.
13. On all models, disconnect temperature and defroster cables from heater case and remove radio to radio support nut.
14. Remove instrument cluster attaching screws, Fig. 8, pull cluster outward and disconnect speedometer cable.
15. Disconnect electrical connectors from instrument cluster and the vacuum harness from air conditioning or heater control.
16. Disconnect radio electrical connectors, pull fiber optic element from washer fluid indicator lens and remove screw from windshield wiper switch ground.
17. Remove three screws securing wiring harness to lower corners of instrument cluster, then disconnect harness from three retaining clips.
18. Remove instrument cluster assembly.

1973-75 Omega

1. Disconnect battery ground cable.
2. Lower steering column.

> NOTE: Apply protective material to mast jacket to prevent damage to painted surfaces.

3. Remove three screws from front of heater control securing it to cluster.
4. Remove radio knobs, washers, bezel nuts and front support at lower edge of instrument cluster. This allows radio to remain in the panel.
5. Remove screws at top, bottom and side of cluster securing it to instrument panel, Fig. 9.
6. Tilt cluster forward and reach behind to disconnect speedo cable, speedminder and electrical connectors and lift cluster out of carrier after removing screws.

1973-75 Cutlass

Speedometer Cluster
1. Disconnect battery ground cable.
2. With automatic transmission column shift, remove lower trim cover (below steering column) then disconnect shift indicator clip on shift bowl.
3. On all models, lower steering column.
4. Disconnect speedo cable from speedometer.
5. Remove three cluster attaching screws and pull cluster out carefully so that shift indicator needle is not damaged, Fig. 10. Disconnect wiring connector and remove cluster.

Fuel Gauge & Telltale Assembly
1. Perform steps 1 through 3 as outlined under "Speedometer Cluster" procedure.
2. Remove three assembly attaching screws and pull assembly out of pad, Fig. 10.
3. Disconnect wiring connectors and remove assembly.

1971-73 Senior Cars

1. Disconnect battery ground cable.
2. Remove steering column trim cover and left trim panel.

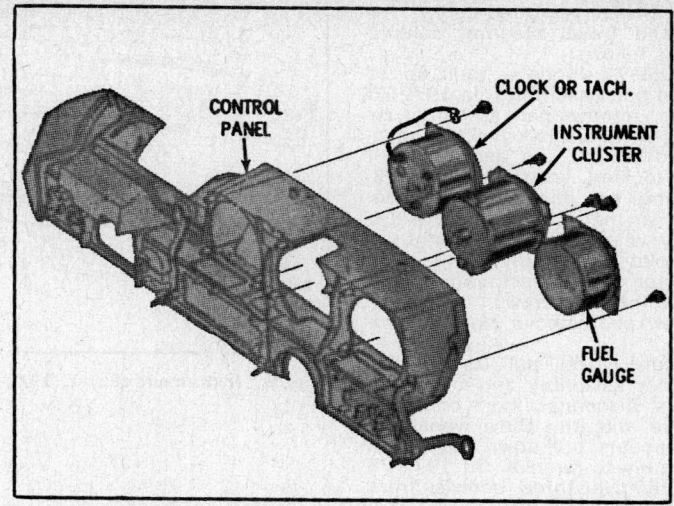

Fig. 11   Instrument cluster. 1970-72 Cutlass

3. Remove shift indicator needle.
4. Disconnect speedo cable at speedo. If equipped with Cruise Control, disconnect cable at regulator and push about 6" of cable through toe pan.
5. Turn ignition to RUN position and place shift lever in Drive.
6. Remove two screws from sides of cluster.
7. Remove two screws (outboard) from top of cluster.
8. Pull out on cluster until wiring connector can be disconnected.
9. Pull cluster from dash.

1969-70 Senior Cars (Except Toronado)

1. Disconnect negative battery cable.
2. Disconnect printed circuit multiple connector.
3. Disconnect speedometer cable.

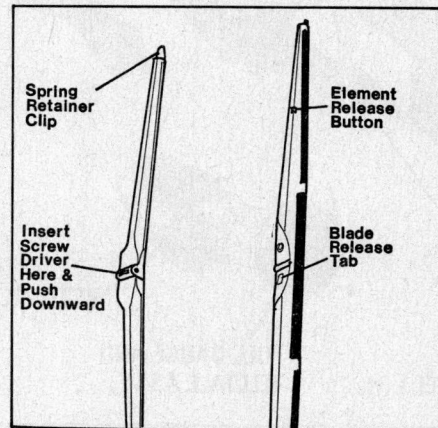

Fig. 12   Wiper blade retainers

4. Remove pad and bezel assembly.
5. Remove three screws attaching cluster housing to instrument panel and remove cluster.

1970-72 Intermediate Cars

Fuel Gauge Cluster
1. Disconnect battery cable.
2. Remove instrument trim panel.
3. Remove three cluster attaching screws, pull cluster out and disconnect wiring, Fig. 11. Remove cluster.
4. When installing cluster, be sure that two of the attaching screws go through ground straps.

Speedometer Cluster
1. Disconnect battery cable.
2. With auto. trans. column shift, remove lower trim panel then disconnect shift indicator clip on shift bowl.
3. Remove instrument trim panel.
4. Disconnect speedometer cable.
5. Remove three cluster attaching screws and pull cluster out carefully so that shift indicator needle is not damaged, Fig. 11.
6. Disconnect wiring and remove cluster.

1969 Intermediate Cars

Fuel Gauge Cluster
1. If air conditioned, remove left-hand air outlet duct.
2. Disconnect battery ground cable.
3. Disconnect printed circuit multiple connector.
4. Separate cluster from control panel (2 screws) and remove cluster through front of pad.

Speedometer Cluster
1. If air conditioned, remove left-hand air outlet duct.
2. Disconnect battery ground cable.
3. Disconnect multiple wiring connector from printed circuit.
4. If column shift with automatic trans-

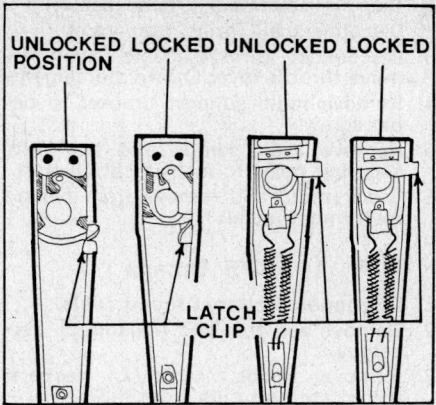

UNLOCKED LOCKED UNLOCKED LOCKED POSITION

LATCH CLIP

Fig. 13 Wiper arms

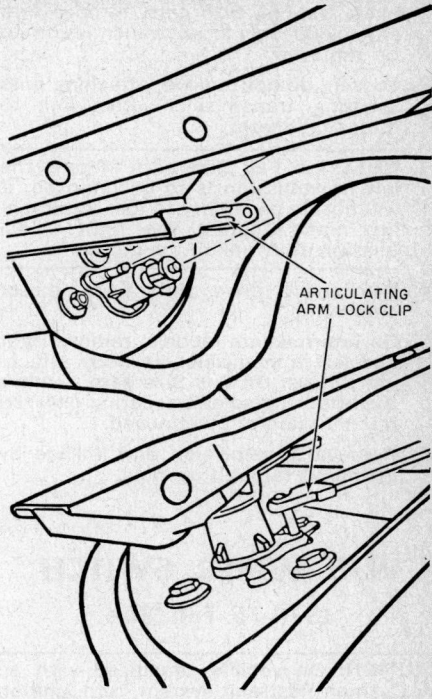

ARTICULATING ARM LOCK CLIP

Fig. 14 Wiper articulating lock clip

off the wiper arm pin. Two methods are also used to retain the blade element in the blade assembly, Fig. 12. One method uses a press type release button. When the button is depressed, the two piece blade assembly can be slid off the blade element. The other method uses a spring type retainer clip in the end of the blade element. When the retainer clip is squeezed together, the blade element can be slid out of the blade assembly.

NOTE: To be sure of correct installation, the element release button, or the spring element retaining clip should be at the end of the wiper blade assembly nearest the wiper transmission.

mission, disconnect shift indicator link.
5. Separate cluster from control panel (2 screws) and remove cluster through front of pad.

1969-70 Toronado

1. Disconnect battery ground cable.
2. Disconnect Cruise Control cable at regulator (if equipped).
3. Disconnect speedometer cable at transmission.
4. Remove screws from right-hand lower pad and filler.
5. Unfasten steering column clamp (2 nuts) and retain wedge for use when installing.
6. If equipped with tilt and travel, tilt down to lowest position and let steering wheel rest on seat cushion. With a standard column, use a 4" x 4" block of wood between steering wheel and seat. This will prevent accidental disconnecting of hoses and wiring when tilting control panel out to perform service repairs.
7. Loosen two control housing bracket bolts about ¼".
8. Disconnect radio lead-in.
9. Remove two control housing upper screws and tilt control panel outward from the top.
10. Disconnect printed circuit connectors.
11. Remove radio if speedometer is to be removed.
12. Separate cover from cluster (8 screws).
13. Cluster components are now accessible for service.

W/S WIPER BLADES

Two methods are used to retain wiper blades to wiper arms, Fig. 12. One method uses a press type release tab. When the release tab is depressed the blade assembly can be slid off the wiper arm pin. The other method uses a coil spring retainer. A screwdriver must be inserted on top of the spring and the spring pushed downward. The blade assembly can then be slid

W/S WIPER ARMS

Models w/Rectangular Motor

1. Wiper motor must be in park position.
2. Use suitable tool to minimize the possibility of windshield or paint finish damage during arm removal.
3. Remove arm by prying up with tool to disengage arm from serrated transmission shaft.
4. To install arm to transmission rotate the required distance and direction so that blades rest in proper position.

Models w/Round Motor

1. Wiper motor must be in park position.
2. Raise hood to gain access to wiper arm.
3. *On Intermediate Models:* Lift arm off transmission shaft. On left arm, slide articulating arm lock clip, Fig. 13, away from transmission pivot pin and lift arm off pin. *On Full Size Models:* Lift arm and slide latch clip, Fig. 14, out from under wiper arm.
4. Release wiper arm and lift arm assembly off transmission shaft.

W/S WIPER MOTOR, REPLACE

1971-75

1. Raise hood and remove cowl screen or grille.
2. Reach through cowl opening and loosen transmission drive link attaching nuts to motor crankarm.
3. Disconnect wiring and washer hoses.
4. Disconnect transmission drive link from motor arm.
5. Remove motor attaching screws.
6. Remove motor while guiding crankarm through opening.

1969-70 Intermediate Cars

1. Disconnect wiring and washer hoses.
2. Remove wiper blade and arm.
3. Remove the motor attaching screws.
4. Lift rear edge of vent screen and loosen nuts attaching transmission to motor crank arm. Loosen bolts only until the crankarm will slide out of transmission socket.

1969-70 Full Size Cars

1. Disconnect wiring and washer hoses.
2. Remove three motor attaching screws.
3. Remove access hole plug.
4. Reaching through access hole, loosen two transmission crank arm nuts.
5. Hold motor with one hand and with the other move wiper arm halfway through its travel to center crank arm in dash hole.
6. Remove motor while guiding crank arm through hole.

W/S WIPER TRANSMISSION, REPLACE

1969-75

Rectangular Motor
1. Remove wiper arms and blades.
2. Raise hood and remove cowl vent screen or grille.
3. Disconnect wiring from motor.
4. Loosen, do not remove, transmission drive link to motor crankarm attaching nuts and disconnect drive link from crankarm.
5. Remove right and left transmission to body attaching screws and guide transmission and linkage out through cowl opening.

Round Motor
1. Raise hood and remove cowl vent screen.
2. On Intermediate models, remove right and left wiper arm and blade assem-

blies. On Full Size cars, remove arm and blade only from transmission to be removed.

3. Loosen, do not remove, attaching nuts securing transmission drive link to motor crankarm.

NOTE: On Full Size cars, if only the left transmission is to be removed, it will not be necessary to lossen attaching nuts securing the right transmission drive link to the motor.

4. Disconnect drive link from motor crankarm.

5. On Intermediate models, remove right and left transmission to body attaching screws. On Full Size cars, remove the attaching screws securing only the transmission to be removed.

6. Remove transmission and linkage by guiding it through opening.

W/S WIPER SWITCH

1974-75 Full Size

CAUTION: On vehicles equipped with an Air Cushion Restraint system, turn ignition switch to "Lock," disconnect battery ground cable and tape end, thereby deactivating system.

1. Disconnect battery ground cable.

2. Remove air conditioning or heater control without disconnecting vacuum harness or electrical connectors.

3. Remove headlamp switch escutcheon and pull headlamp switch through air conditioning or heater control opening without removing electrical connector.

4. Remove windshield wiper switch knob and two switch attaching nuts through air conditioning or heater control opening, then pull switch through opening, disconnect electrical connector and remove switch.

1973 Full Size

1. Disconnect battery ground cable.

2. Remove left hand flood lamp lens and let lamp assembly hang.

3. Remove screws from steering column, left side of trim cap.

4. Remove lower left hand trim panel screws, then disconnect the temperature cable on bottom of air conditioning or heater control.

5. Remove control panel attaching screws and control panel, guiding wiring and hoses through opening.

6. Remove electrical connector from wiper switch, wiper switch knob, switch retaining screws and switch.

1973-74 Cutlass

1. Disconnect battery ground cable.

2. Remove steering column trim cover screws and if equipped with air conditioning, disconnect outlet hose.

3. Disconnect parking brake cable.

4. Remove left hand control panel screws, pull control panel from instrument panel and disconnect wiring.

5. Remove electrical connector from wiper switch, wiper switch knob, switch retaining screws and switch.

1973-75 Omega

1. Disconnect battery ground cable.

2. Remove switch electrical connector, switch retaining screws and switch from behind instrument panel.

1971-72 Full Size Cars

1. Remove control panel.

2. Remove wiring connector from switch.

3. Pull wiper knob from front of switch.

4. Remove switch attaching screws and remove switch.

1971-72 Intermediate Cars

1. Disconnect battery ground cable.

2. Remove instrument trim panel.

3. Remove three fuel gauge cluster attaching screws and pull out cluster so cluster wiring can be disconnected. Remove cluster.

4. Disconnect washer/wiper connector from switch.

5. Remove knob from switch.

6. Remove switch attaching screws and remove switch.

1969-70 Except Toronado

1. On intermediate models with air conditioning, remove left-hand air outlet duct.

2. Pull wiper knob from switch.

3. Remove switch escutcheon.

4. Remove wiper and washer switch from rear of control panel.

5. Disconnect switch wiring.

1969-70 Toronado

1. Disconnect battery ground cable.

2. Disconnect wiring at switch.

3. Unfasten and remove switch from rear of control panel.

RADIO REMOVAL

NOTE: When installing radio, be sure to adjust antenna trimmer for peak performance.

1974-75 Senior Cars

CAUTION: On vehicles equipped with an Air Cushion Restraint system, turn ignition switch to "Lock," disconnect battery ground cable and tape end, thereby deactivating system.

1. Disconnect battery ground cable.

2. Disconnect all wiring from radio.

3. Disconnect throttle cable, then remove throttle lever and reinforcement.

4. Remove radio support bracket to tie-bar screw.

5. Remove radio knobs and two nuts securing radio to instrument cluster.

6. Lower radio and remove from behind instrument panel.

1973-75 Omega

1. Disconnect battery ground cable.

2. Remove ash tray and housing as necessary.

3. Remove knobs, controls, washers, trim plate and nuts from radio.

4. Remove hoses from center A/C distribution duct.

5. Disconnect all leads to radio.

6. Remove screws or nuts from radio rear mounting bracket and remove radio.

1973-74 Cutlass

1. Disconnect battery ground cable.

2. Remove four screws from steering column trim cover and remove cover.

3. Remove knobs from radio by pulling outward on knobs.

4. Remove nuts from front of radio.

5. Remove four screws holding R.H. Control Panel to dash and gently pull panel outward and up.

6. Remove screw from radio support bracket.

7. Remove four screws holding ash tray housing to tie bar and remove housing assembly.

8. Disconnect all leads and remove radio.

1971-73 Senior Cars

1. Loosen ground strap at lower valance panel support.

2. Remove radio support bracket nut at rear of radio.

3. Disconnect three flood lamps from bezel for clearance.

4. Remove four screws that hold bezel in instrument panel.

5. Pull bezel forward as far as possible.

6. Disconnect electrical connectors at rear of radio.

7. Remove radio knobs, attaching nuts and escutcheons.

8. Remove radio from rear of bezel.

1971-72 Intermediate Cars & 1969-70 Except Toronado

1. If Air Conditioned, remove manifold.

2. Disconnect all wiring and antenna.

3. Remove knobs and attaching nuts from front of dash.

4. Remove attaching bolt (bracket to control panel) and remove radio from rear of panel.

1969-70 Toronado

1. Remove control knobs and nuts from front of dash.

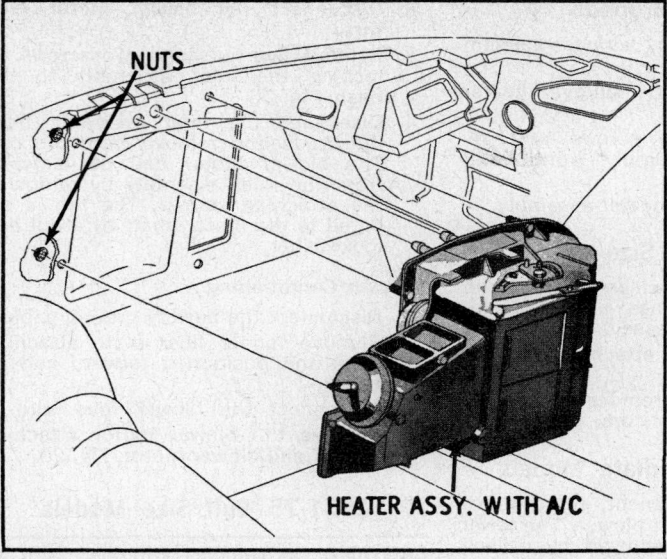

Fig. 15   Heater core. 1971-75 Full Size models & 1973-75 Cutlass (Typical)

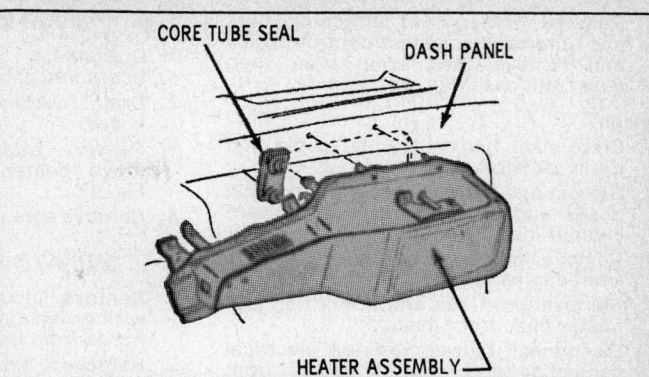

Fig. 16   Heater core. 1973-75 Omega (Typical)

2. Remove control panel.
3. Disconnect radio feed wire.
4. Disconnect dial lamp.
5. Remove attaching nut from support to radio.
6. Remove radio from rear of control panel.

HEATER CORE REMOVAL
1974-75 Full Size Cars

CAUTION: On vehicles equipped with an Air Cushion Restraint system, turn ignition switch to "lock," disconnect battery ground cable and tape end, thereby de- activating system.

1. Disconnect battery ground cable and drain radiator.
2. Disconnect heater hoses and plug hoses and core openings to prevent coolant loss.
3. Remove heater case to dash panel attaching nuts, Fig. 15.
4. Remove instrument panel trim cover and the heater case to cowl bolts.
5. Remove instrument panel pad, then electrical connectors from glovebox light and clock.

6. Remove right hand upper trim panel and on models equipped with A/C, remove manifold from heater case.
7. On all models, remove defroster duct from heater case and disconnect lower dash trim panel.
8. Disconnect temperature and defroster cables, then the vacuum hose from heater case. Remove heater case from dash, then core from case.

1973-75 Intermediate Models
Less Air Conditioning
Cutlass

1. Disconnect battery ground cable and drain radiator.
2. Disconnect heater hoses and plug hoses and core openings to prevent coolant loss.

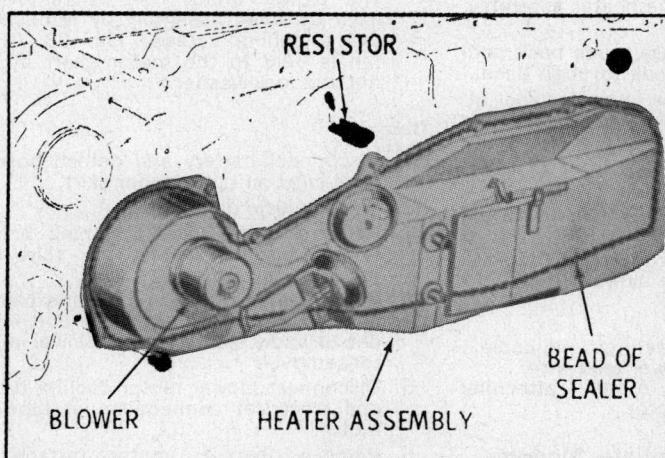

Fig. 17   Heater core & blower motor. 1969-70 Toronado (Typical)

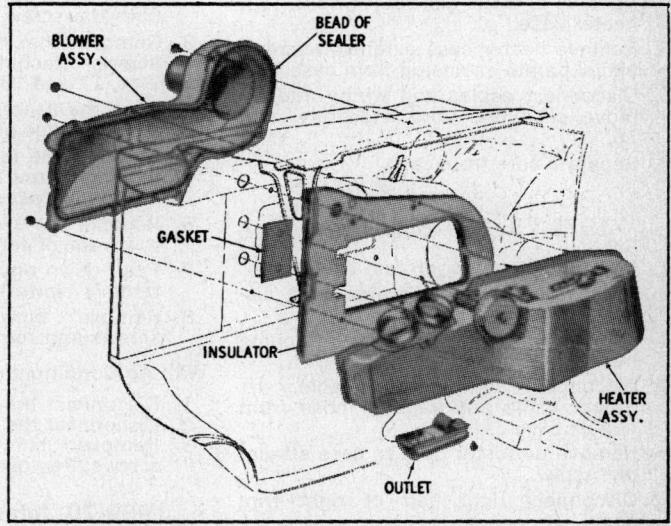

Fig. 18   Heater core & blower motor. 1969-70 Full Size models exc. Toronado (Typical)

3. Remove heater case attaching nuts and screws, disconnect control cables and remove case from dash, then core from case, Fig. 15.

Omega

1. Disconnect battery ground cable and drain radiator.
2. Disconnect heater hoses and plug hoses and core openings to prevent coolant loss.
3. Remove heater case retaining nuts from engine side of dash, Fig. 16.
4. Remove glove box and door, then pull heater case from dash.
5. Disconnect blower resistor electrical connector and control cables from case, then remove heater case from dash and core from case.

With Air Conditioning

Cutlass

1. Disconnect battery ground cable and drain radiator.
2. Remove glove box and the center A/C manifold.
3. Disconnect vacuum hoses and temperature cable from heater case.
4. Disconnect heater hoses and plug hoses and core openings to prevent coolant loss.
5. Remove heater case to dash panel attaching bolts, then heater case from dash and core from case, Fig. 15.

Omega

1. Disconnect battery and drain coolant.
2. Disconnect upper heater hose from core.
3. Remove right front fender skirt bolts and lower skirt to gain access to lower heater hose clamp. Disconnect lower hose and remove lower right hand heater core and case attaching nut.
4. Remove glove box and door.
5. Remove recirculation vacuum diaphragm at right kick panel.
6. Remove heater outlet (at bottom of heater case).
7. Remove cold air distributor duct from heater case.
8. Remove heater case extension screws and separate extension from case.
9. Disconnect cables and wiring and remove case and core assembly, Fig. 16.
10. Separate core from case.

1971-73 Full Size Cars

1. Disconnect battery ground cable.
2. Drain radiator below heater level, disconnect heater hoses.
3. Remove four heater case attaching nuts to dash panel, Fig. 15.
4. Disconnect temperature cable, defroster cable and vacuum hose from heater case.
5. Remove defroster duct to case attaching screw.
6. Disconnect right half of right trim panel.
7. Remove heater case from inside car.
8. Remove heater core from case.

1969-70 Toronado

1. Disconnect blower wiring, vacuum hoses and cables.
2. Drain coolant and remove heater hoses.
3. Remove attaching screws and remove heater assembly from cowl, Fig. 17.
4. Remove core from heater assembly.

1969-70 Full Size Cars

1. Remove glove box and disconnect wiring, vacuum lines and defroster hoses from heater case.
2. Remove blower attaching screws and nuts, Fig. 18.
3. From inside car, remove heater assembly and take out core.

1969-72 Intermediate Models

1. In engine compartment, remove five attaching nuts from blower. The lower outboard nut is removed by drilling a $\frac{3}{4}$" hole through fender filler panel at dimple or, if no dimple is provided, disconnect the right fender at the bottom and block it away from the body. Remove nut through this opening, Fig. 19.
2. Disconnect resistor wiring and three control cables.
3. Remove heater case assembly from under dash. Exposed core can now be removed.

BLOWER MOTOR REMOVE

1969-70 Full Size Models

Less Air Conditioning

1. Disconnect blower feed wire.
2. Remove upper sheet metal screw holding the heater inlet to dash by using approximately three feet of $\frac{3}{8}$" extensions and a $\frac{7}{16}$" socket through the opening between the fender filler plate and the fender forward of the right front wheel. Guide the socket onto the screw and remove.
3. Remove the rest of the nuts and screws attaching the heater assembly, Figs. 17 and 18.
4. Push the heater case studs back until studs do not protrude through dash.
5. Remove one fender to dash panel attaching screw just over the blower assembly case.
6. Remove the two bolts from the bottom rear of fender.
7. Push down on inner fender panel and remove blower assembly.
8. Remove blower motor attaching screws and remove blower motor.

With Air Conditioning

1. Disconnect the battery ground cable.
2. Disconnect the blower feed wire.
3. Remove blower motor attaching screws. Remove motor.

1969-70 Intermediate Models

Less Air Conditioning

1. Remove the right front wheel.

2. Disconnect the blower motor feed wire.
3. Remove five nuts and two screws attaching the inlet assembly to the dash, Fig. 20.
4. Disengage the inlet assembly from the studs and remove from the car. The blower motor can be removed from the inlet assembly by removing the attaching screws. The fan is secured to the motor shaft by a nut and lockwasher.

With Air Conditioning

1. Disconnect the battery ground cable.
2. Remove fender filler plate attaching bolts and position it forward and inboard.
3. Disconnect the blower feed wire.
4. Remove the blower motor attaching screws and blower motor, Fig. 20.

1971-75 Full Size Models

CAUTION: On vehicles equipped with an Air Cushion Restraint system, turn ignition switch to "Lock," disconnect battery ground cable and tape end, thereby deactivating system.

1. Disconnect battery.
2. Remove the right front wheel.
3. Remove canister or battery.
4. Remove the three filler plates to radiator support screws.
5. Remove the filler plate to wheelhouse attaching screws. Remove filler plate.
6. Remove the blower motor attaching screws and connector, Fig. 20.
7. Remove the blower motor.

1971-74 Intermediate Models

Less Air Conditioning

Cutlass

1. Remove the right front fender filler panel.
2. Disconnect the blower motor wiring.
3. Remove the five nuts and two screws securing the inlet assembly to dash.
4. Disengage the inlet assembly from the studs and remove from the car. The blower motor can be removed from the inlet assembly by removing the attaching screws, Fig. 20. The fan is held to the motor shaft by a nut and lock-washer.

Omega

1. Disconnect battery and detach hoses from clips on right fender skirt.
2. Raise vehicle on hoist.
3. Remove fender skirt attaching bolts except those retaining the skirt to radiator support.
4. Pull out then down on skirt and place block of wood between skirt and fender to allow clearance for blower motor removal.
5. Disconnect blower motor cooling tube and electrical connections at blower motor.
6. Remove blower motor attaching screws and remove blower motor, Fig. 21. Gently pry motor flange if sealer acts as an adhesive.

With Air Conditioning

1973-75 Cutlass

1. Disconnect battery ground cable and blower motor feed wire.
2. Remove screws securing blower motor to dash, then the blower motor, Fig. 20.
3. Reverse procedure to install.

Exc. 1973-75 Cutlass

1. Disconnect the battery cable.
2. Remove the fender filler plate attaching bolts and position it forward and inboard.
3. Disconnect the blower feed wire.
4. Remove the blower motor attaching screws and blower motor, Fig. 21.

SPEED CONTROLS

1971-75

Vacuum Brake Release Switch, Adjust

The vacuum valve should be pushed all the way into the retaining clip. Pulling the brake pedal up to the stop will automatically adjust the valve.

Servo Rod, Adjust

Adjust servo rod length so that bell-crank clearance is .020-.040" when carburetor is at slow idle.

1969-70

Brake Release Switch, Adjust

1. Disconnect multiple connector at regulator.
2. Turn ignition switch to accessory position.
3. Using a test lamp, ground one test lamp lead and touch the other to terminal No. 2 in harness connector.
4. Adjust switch so that lamp will light when brake pedal is fully re-

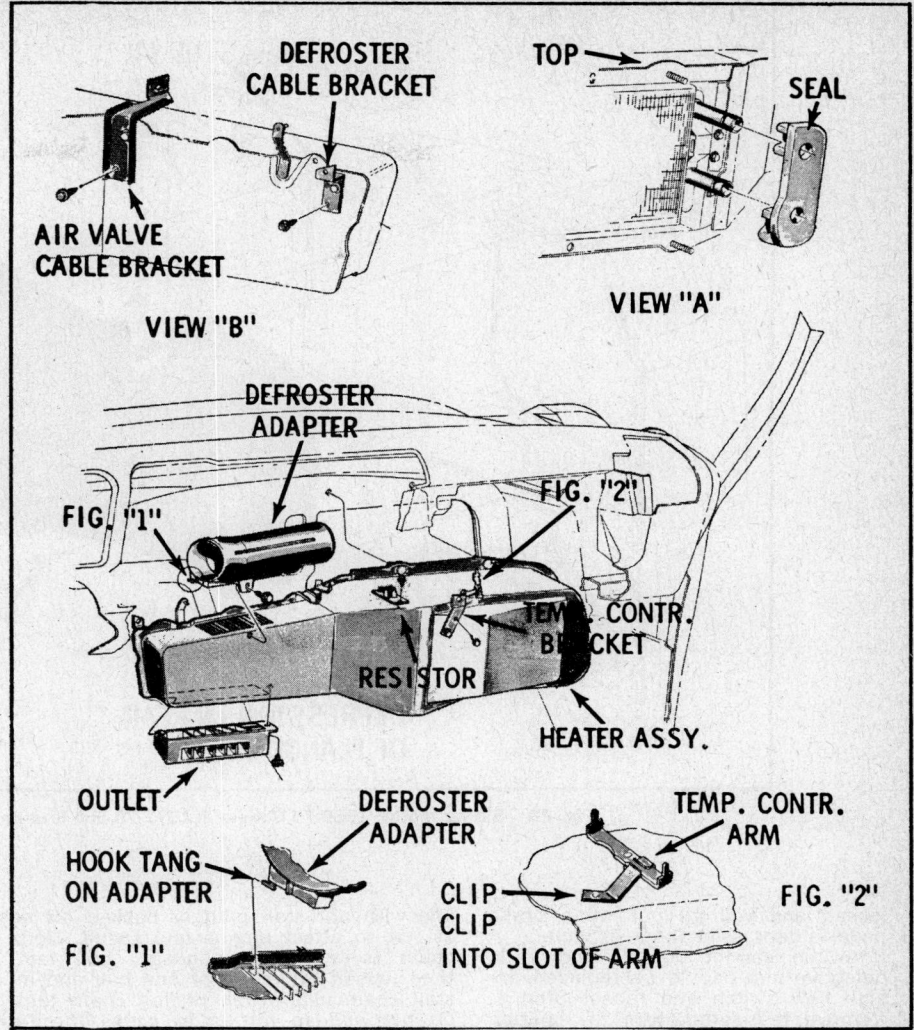

Fig. 19 Heater core. 1969-72 Cutlass (Typical)

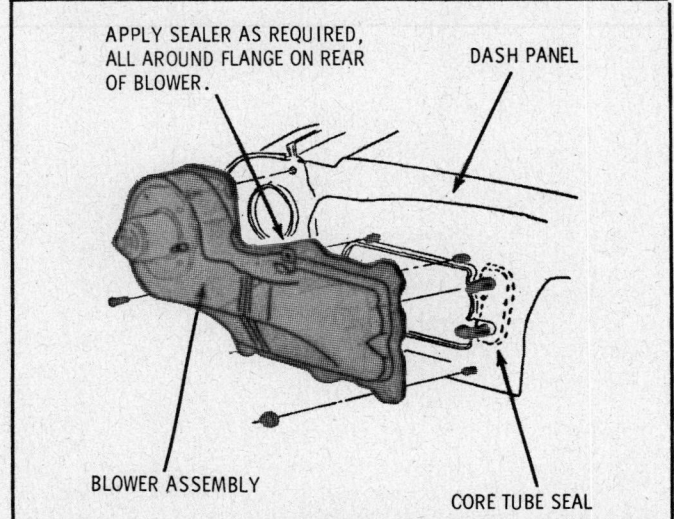

Fig. 21 Blower motor. 1973-75 Omega (Typical)

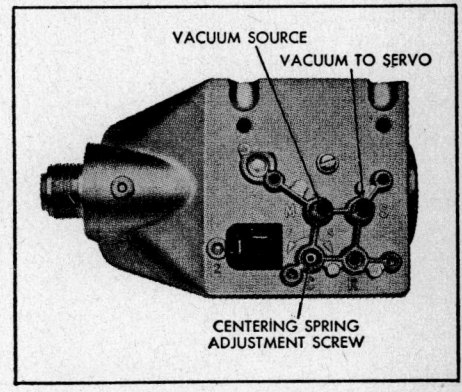

Fig. 22 Centering spring adjustment. 1969-70

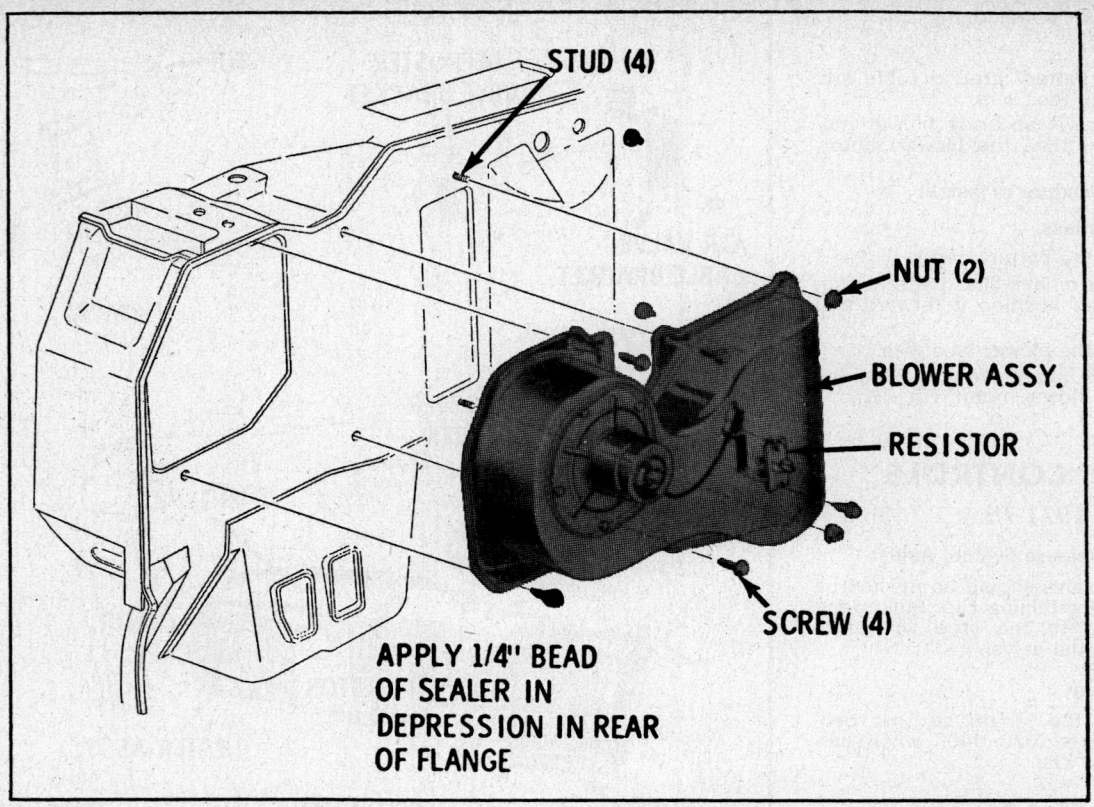

STUD (4)

NUT (2)

BLOWER ASSY.

RESISTOR

SCREW (4)

APPLY 1/4" BEAD
OF SEALER IN
DEPRESSION IN REAR
OF FLANGE

Fig. 20   Blower motor. 1969-75 Cutlass & 1971-75 Full Size models (Typical)

leased and will go out when brake pedal is depressed about 1/4 inch.
5. If switch cannot be adjusted, it is defective and should be replaced. Install new switch and repeat Step 4.
6. Remove test lamp, turn off ignition key and plug connector to regulator.

Chain Linkage, Adjust

Chain linkage should never be taut. To adjust, start engine set carburetor at hot idle with anti-stall plunger backed off so as not to affect engine idle speed. Hook chain to accelerator linkage, pull taut, then loosen by length of one ball and install chain clip. *When pulling chain taut, do not pull so far as to cause throttle to open.*

Centering Spring, Adjust

1. If speed control system holds speed three or more mph higher than selected speed, turn centering spring adjusting screw (C) toward (S) 1/32" or less, Fig. 22.

2. If speed control system holds speed three or more mph below selected speed, turn centering spring adjusting screw (C) toward (F) 1/32" or less. Do *not move adjustment screw (R).*

Engine Section

IMPORTANT: See the Toronado supplement for procedures on removing the engine and transmission, and method of servicing the front suspension, drive axles and final drive (differential) immediately following this chapter.

See Chevrolet Chapter for Service Procedures on 6-250 Engine.
See Buick Chapter for Service Procedures on 1975 Omega V8-350 Engine.
See Pontiac Chapter for Service Procedures on 1975 V8-400 Engine.

NOTE: Material marked "F.S.C." means Olds Full Size Car or Senior Models

ENGINE MOUNTS

1973-75 Six

1. Remove engine mount nut and through bolt.
2. Raise engine and remove mount from frame.
3. Install new mount on frame, lower engine and install through bolt.

1969-71 Six

1. Remove nut, washer, spacer then engine mount through bolt, Fig. 1.
2. Raise engine to release weight from mount.
3. Remove mount, stop bracket and frame bracket assembly from crossmember, then remove stop bracket and mount from frame bracket.
4. Install stop bracket and new mount on frame bracket, then install assembly on crossmember.
5. Lower engine, install through bolt and tighten mount bolts.

1969-75 V8

Removal or replacement of a motor mount can be accomplished by supporting the weight of the engine at the area of the mount to be replaced.

RAISING ENGINE

1969-75 V8s

1. Mark hood hinge before removing to aid in proper alignment upon reassembly.
2. Drain radiator and disconnect battery.
3. Disconnect radiator hoses, heater hoses, vacuum hoses, power steering pump hoses (if necessary), starter cable at junction block, engine-to-body ground strap, fuel hose from fuel line, wiring and accelerator linkage.
4. Remove fan blade and pulley, coil and upper radiator support.
5. Raise car.
6. Disconnect exhaust pipes at manifolds.

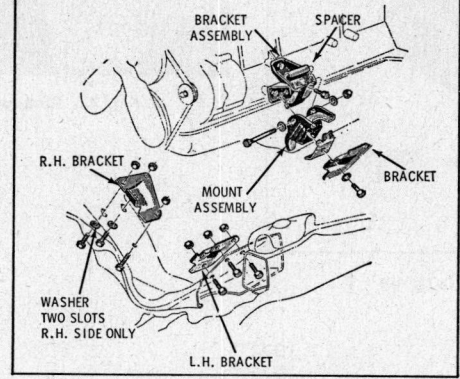

Fig. 1   Engine mounts. 1969-71 Six

7. Remove torque converter cover and install a suitable holding tool to keep converter from falling out when engine is removed.
8. Remove engine mounting bolts and support engine.
9. Lift engine and secure transmission chain support to frame or support transmission with a jack.
10. Unfasten converter from flywheel (3 bolts) and transmission from engine (6 bolts).
11. Lower car and remove engine.
12. Reverse procedure to install.

NOTE

On V8 engines, whenever installation of a front engine mounting becomes necessary, the cap screws fastening the mounting to the frame or bracket should first be screwed finger tight, then tightened alternately, one at a time. *Do not tighten one cap screw in position independently of the other.* This is extremely important since the lower portion of the assembly would not seat evenly in the upper portion. The front mounting must be properly positioned and tightened, otherwise the mounting will not properly function as an insulator.

CYLINDER HEAD, REPLACE

Some cylinder head gaskets are coated with a special lacquer to provide a good seal once the parts have warmed up. Do not use any additional sealer on such gaskets. If the gasket does not have this lacquer coating, apply suitable sealer to both sides.

Tighten cylinder head bolts a little at a time in three steps in the sequence shown in the illustrations. Final tightening should be to the torque specifications listed in the *Engine Tightening* table.

V8-260, 350, 400, 455

1. Drain radiator and cylinder block.
2. Disconnect spark plug wires and remove intake manifold.
3. Disconnect exhaust crossover pipe for left side and/or crossover pipe and exhaust pipe for right side.
4. Remove valve cover (loosen or remove any accessory brackets that interfere).
5. Remove ground strap from right cylinder head.
6. Remove exhaust manifold, rocker arms and push rods from head to be removed.
7. Reverse removal procedure to install head, and tighten bolts in the sequence shown in Fig. 2.

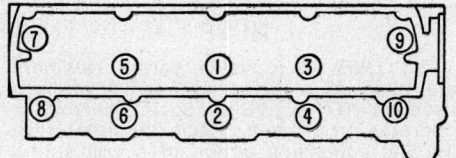

Fig. 2   Cylinder head tightening sequence. V8-260, 350, 400, 455

VALVE ARRANGEMENT

Front to Rear

6-250 . . . . E-I-I-E-E-I-I-E-E-I-I-E
V8-260, 350, 400, 455 . . . . I-E-I-E-E-I-E-I

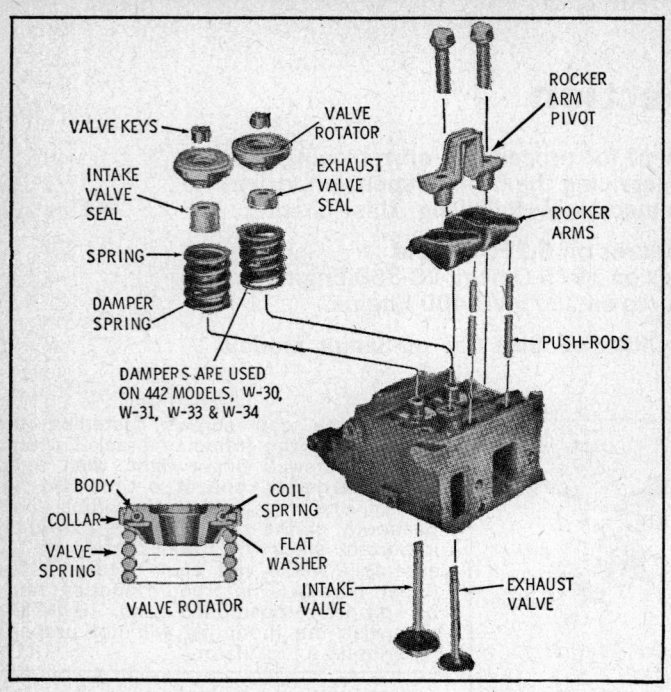

Fig. 3   Cylinder head exploded. 1970-75 V8

HOLD ROCKER ARM STUD WITH WRENCH WHEN REMOVING ROCKER ARM NUT

Fig. 4   Removing rocker arm. V8-260, 350, 400, 455

VALVE LIFT SPECS.

Engine	Year	Intake	Exhaust
6-250	1969-75	.388	.388
V8-260	1975	.395	.395
V8-350	1969-70	.435	.435
	1971-72[2][5]	.400	.400
	1971-72[4]	.472	.472
	1972[10]	.440	.440
	1973-74[1]	.440	.440
	1973-75[2]	.400	.400
V8-350[11]	1975	.382	.382
V8-400	1969[4]	.472	.472
	1969[5]	.430	.432
V8-400[12]	1975	.410	.410
V8-455	1969-70[5]	.435	.435
	1971[1]	.435	.435
	1971[9]	.472	.472
	1972	.435	.435
	1973-74[3]	.474	.472
	1973-75	.435	.435

[1]—4 bar. carb. [2]—2 bar. carb.
[3]—Cutlass
[4]—4 bar. carb., std. trans.
[5]—4 bar. carb., auto. trans.
[6]—310, 365 H.P. [7]—375 H.P.
[8]—385 H.P.
[9]—"4-4-2".
[10]—California
[11]—Omega only. See Buick Chapter for service procedures.
[12]—See Pontiac Chapter for service procedures.

VALVE TIMING

Intake Opens Before TDC

Engine	Year	Degrees
6-250	1969-75	16
V8-260	1975	14
V8-350	1969-70	16
	1971[5][6]	14
	1971[7]	30
	1972[5][7]	16
	1972[6]	30
	1972[8]	22
	1973-74	22
	1973-74[5]	16
V8-350[9]	1975	19
V8-400	1969[1]	30
	1969[2]	21
V8-400[10]	1975	30
V8-455	1969-70[4]	20
	1971-75	20
	1971 Toronado	22
	1971 "4-4-2"[1]	30
	1971 "4-4-2"[2]	24
	1973-74[3]	28

[1]—Std. trans. [2]—Auto. trans.
[3]—Cutlass
[4]—GT & 400 H.P.—24.
[5]—2 bar. carb.
[6]—4 bar. carb., std. trans.
[7]—4 bar. carb., auto. trans.
[8]—California
[9]—Omega only. See Buick Chapter for service procedures.
[10]—See Pontiac Chapter for service procedures.

ROCKER ARMS

NOTE

On 1969 V8's, valve spring retainers are used in place of the valve rotators used on 1970-75 V8's, Fig. 3. The rotator operates on a sprag clutch principle utilizing the collapsing action of a coil spring to give rotation to the rotor body which turns the valve.

V8-260, 350, 400, 455

1. To remove rocker arm assemblies, first remove valve cover.
2. Hold stud to prevent it from turning and remove rocker arm stud nuts, washer, lock plates, pivots and rocker arms, Fig. 4.

NOTE: Remove each set (one set per cylinder) as a unit.

Installation

1. Torque studs to 35 ft-lbs. Later engines use pivots and the pivot bolts are torqued to 25 ft-lbs.
2. Position a set of rocker arms (for one cylinder) on proper studs.
3. Install pivots and lock plates, being sure tangs on lock plates seat properly in the pivots. Coat wear points with lubricant.
4. Install flat washers and nuts, being sure both valve lifters are in closed valve position when nuts are tightened.

CAUTION: Never exceed specified torque of 25 ft-lbs on nuts. Check to be sure clearance exists between push rod and push rod hole in cylinder head. If no clearance exists, lock plate must be replaced.

5. Reverse removal procedure to install cover, noting data in Fig. 9.

VALVES, REMOVE

NOTE

Whenever a new valve is installed or after grinding valves, it will be necessary to measure valve stem height using the Special Tool shown in Figs. 5 and 6.

On V8-260, 350 engines, there should be a minimum clearance of .035 inch between gauge surface and the valve

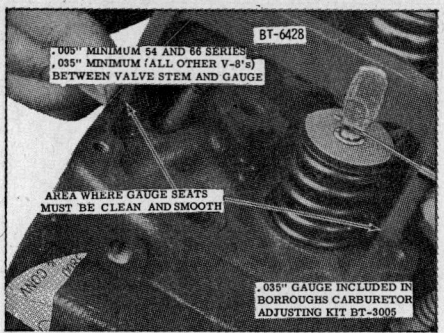

Fig. 5 Measuring valve stem height. V8-260, 350, 400, 455

stem, Fig. 5. On V8-400, 455 engines, the minimum clearance is .005 inch.

On 1970-75 engines, check valve rotator height, Fig. 6. If valve stem tip extends less than .005 inch above rotator, replace the valve. On 1969 engines, check the valve retainer height, Fig. 6. If valve stem tip extends less than .030 inch above retainer, replace the valve.

Lacking this tool the only alternative is to lay flat feeler gauges on the retainer and check the distance between the retainer and valve stem tip.

VALVE GUIDES

V8-260, 350, 400, 455

Valve stem guides are not replaceable, due to being cast in place. If valve guide bores are worn excessively, they can be reamed oversize.

If a standard valve guide bore is being reamed, use a .003" or .005" oversize reamer. For the .010" oversize valve guide bore, use a .013" oversize reamer. If too large a reamer is used and the spiraling is removed, it is possible that the valve will not receive the proper lubrication.

NOTE: Occasionally a valve guide will be oversize as manufactured. These are marked on the cylinder head as shown in Fig. 7. If no markings are present, the guide bores are standard. If oversize markings are present, any valve replacement will require an oversize valve. Service valves are available in standard diameters as well as .003", .005", .010" and .013" oversize.

VALVE LIFTERS

Valve lifters in production engines may be one of four sizes: standard, .001, .002 or .003 in. oversize. It is important when replacing one or more lifters that the proper size lifter be ordered. An identification numeral is etched on all lifter bodies except standard. The cylinder block is marked for lifter size on the rail under the push rod cover. Valve lifters .005 in. oversize are available for service replacement.

Plungers are not interchangeable because they are selectively fitted to the bodies at the factory.

If plunger and body appear satisfactory blow off with air to remove all particles of dirt. Install the plunger in the body without other parts and check for free movement. A simple test is to be sure that the plunger will drop of its own weight in the body, Fig. 8.

TIMING CASE COVER

NOTE: When it becomes necessary to replace the cover oil seal, the cover need not be removed.

V8-260, 350, 400, 455

1. Drain cooling system and disconnect heater hose, by-pass hose and both radiator hoses.
2. Remove all belts, fan and pulley, crankshaft pulley and pulley hub.
3. Remove oil pan.
4. Unfasten and remove cover, timing pointer and water pump assembly.

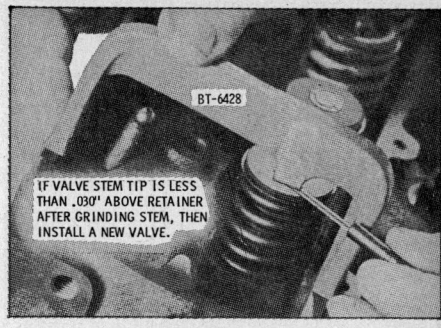

Fig. 6 Measuring valve retaining or valve rotor height. V8-260, 350, 400, 455

TIMING CHAIN

V8-260, 350, 400, 455

1. After removing front cover, remove fuel pump eccentric, oil slinger, crankshaft sprocket, chain and camshaft sprocket.
2. Install camshaft sprocket, crankshaft sprocket and timing chain together, aligning timing marks as shown in Fig. 10.
3. Install fuel pump eccentric with flat side rearward, Fig. 11. Then install oil slinger and replace front cover.

CAMSHAFT, REPLACE

V8-260, 350, 400, 455

1. Remove grille and radiator.
2. If air conditioned it will be necessary to remove condenser.
3. Remove fuel pump and front cover.
4. Remove oil slinger, timing chain and sprockets.

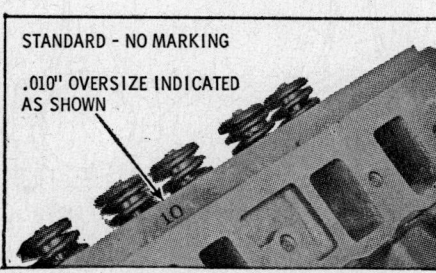

Fig. 7 Valve guide bore marking. V8-260, 350, 400, 455

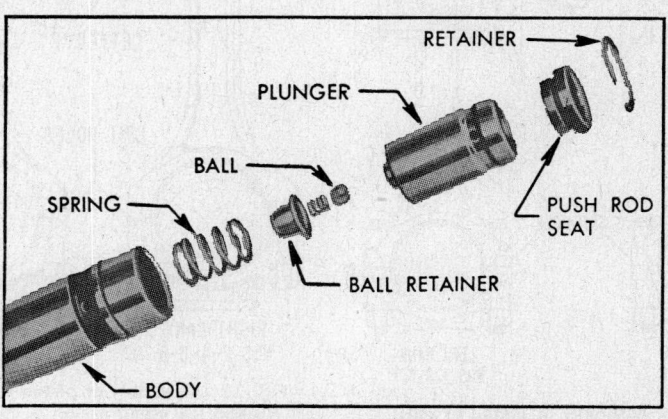

Fig. 8 Hydraulic valve lifter (typical)

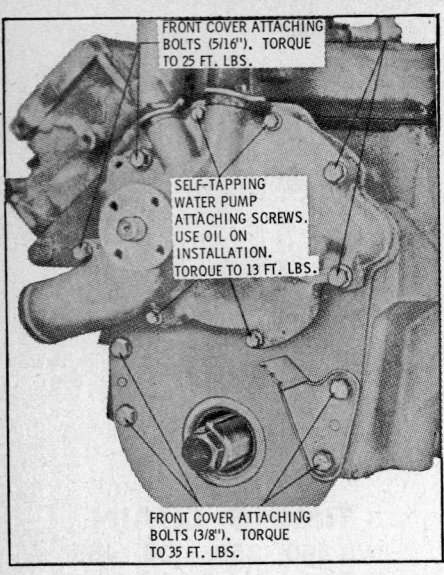

Fig. 9   Engine front cover bolts.
V8-350, 400, 455

Fig. 10   Timing chain position.
V8-350, 400, 455

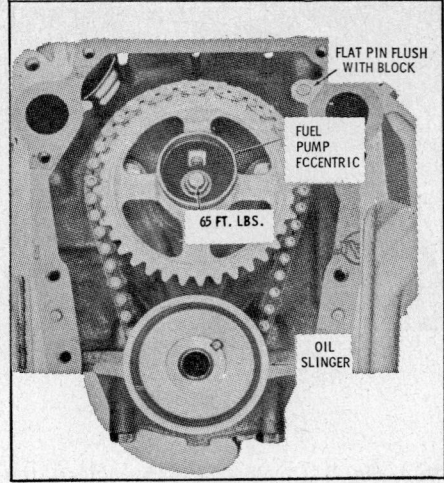

Fig. 11   Fuel pump eccentric.
V8-350, 400, 455

5. Remove distributor, intake manifold, rocker arm assemblies, push rods and valve lifters.
6. Slide camshaft out of engine.

NOTE: *To insure proper camshaft installation, and to provide initial lubrication, it is extremely important that the camshaft be coated with GM Concentrate (Part No. 582099).*

PISTON & ROD, ASSEMBLE

Lubricate the piston pin hole and piston pin to facilitate installation of pin,

then position the connecting rod with its respective piston as shown in Figs. 12 through 17.

PISTONS, RINGS & PINS

Pistons are available in standard sizes and oversizes of .010 and .030".
Rings are available in standard sizes and oversizes of .010 and .030".

MAIN & ROD BEARINGS

Main bearings are available in standard sizes and undersizes of .0005, .001, .0015, .002, .010 and .020".
Rod bearings are available in standard sizes and undersizes of .001, .002, .005, .010, .012 and .020 inch.

NOTE

Main bearing clearances not within specifications must be corrected by the use of selective upper and lower shells. Fig. 18 illustrates the undersize identification marking on the bearing tang.

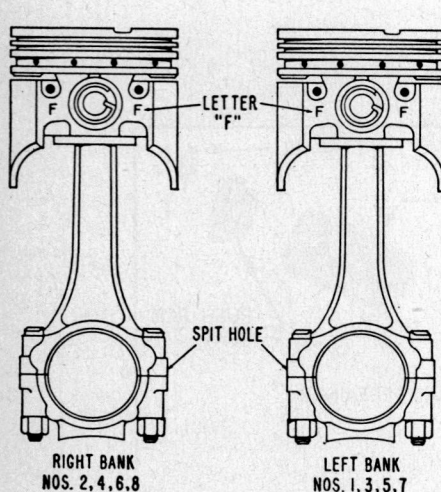

Fig. 12   Assembly of piston to rod.
1973-75 V8-260, 350

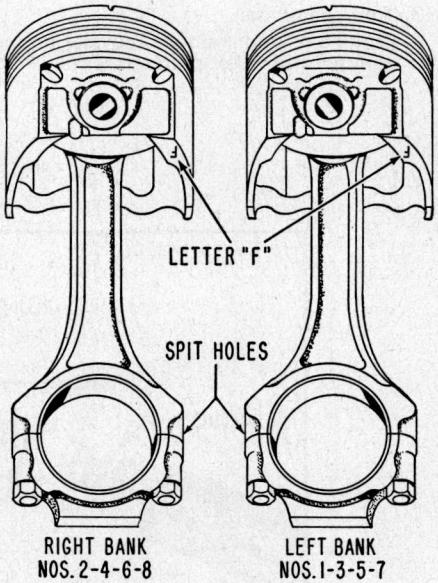

Fig. 13   Assembly of piston to rod. 1969
V8-455 low compression & 1970 V8-455
high compression

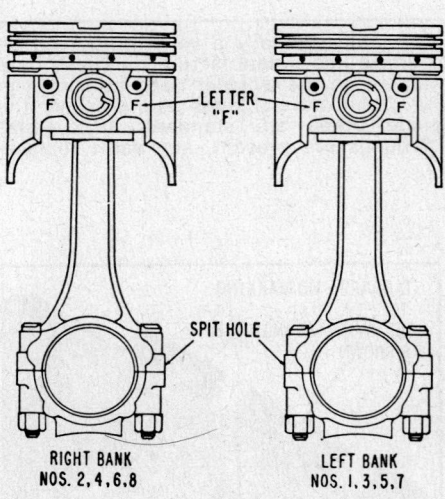

Fig. 14   Assembly of piston to rod.
1969-72 V8-350 exc. 1969-70
high performance

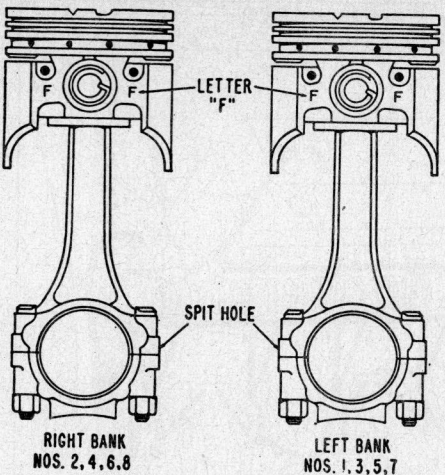

Fig. 15 Assembly of piston to rod. 1969-70 V8-350 high performance

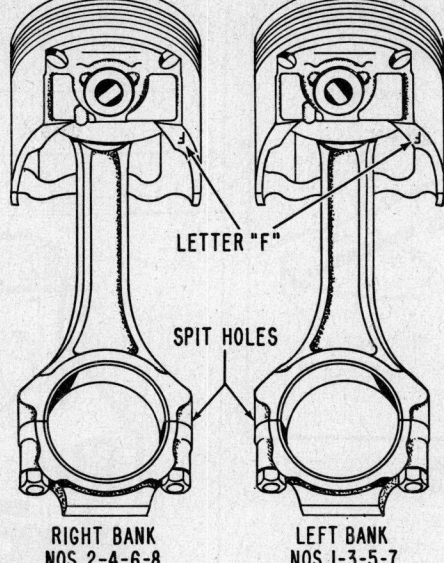

Fig. 16 Assembly of piston to rod. 1969 V8-400

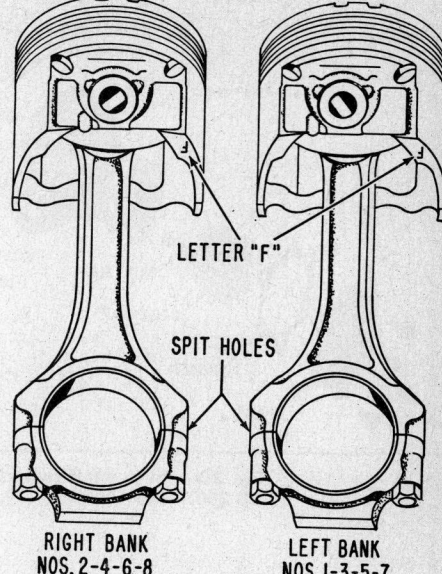

Fig. 17 Assembly of piston to rod. 1969 V8-455 high compression & all 1971-75 V8-455

OIL PAN

1973-75 V8

1. Remove distributor cap and align rotor with No. 1 firing position.
2. Disconnect ground cable, remove dip stick and drain oil pan.
3. Remove upper radiator support and on 88 and 98, remove fan shroud attaching screws.
4. Remove flywheel cover and starter.
5. Disconnect exhaust pipes and crossover pipe on single exhaust models.
6. Disconnect engine mounts and raise engine.
7. Remove oil pan bolts and oil pan.

1969-72 V8 (Except F-85 V8-400 & 455)

1. Remove oil level dipstick.
2. Raise car and drain oil.
3. On F-85 models, disconnect exhaust pipe from right exhaust manifold.

4. On Olds F.S.C models, lower steering relay rod by disconnecting idler arm or pitman arm.
5. Disconnect engine mounts and raise front of engine as far as possible.

CAUTION: Be sure distributor does not contact cowl and fan blades do not contact fan shroud.

6. Bring No. 1 piston up on top center.
7. Remove crossover pipe and starter.
8. Unfasten and remove oil pan.

F-85 V8-400

1. Disconnect battery ground cable.

2. Remove upper radiator baffle.
3. Remove drive shaft, transmission crossmember, transmission and flywheel.
4. Disconnect left exhaust pipe and starter.
5. Disconnect right-hand engine mount.

NOTE: It is necessary to raise both the front and rear of engine and tilt it to the left, using the left engine mount as a pivot.

6. Use a suitable support bar and insert a 1" block between tool and right rear corner of oil pan to obtain additional lift on right side.

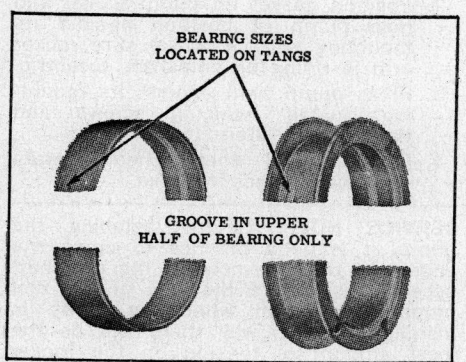

Fig. 18 Main bearing size location. V8-260, 350, 400, 455

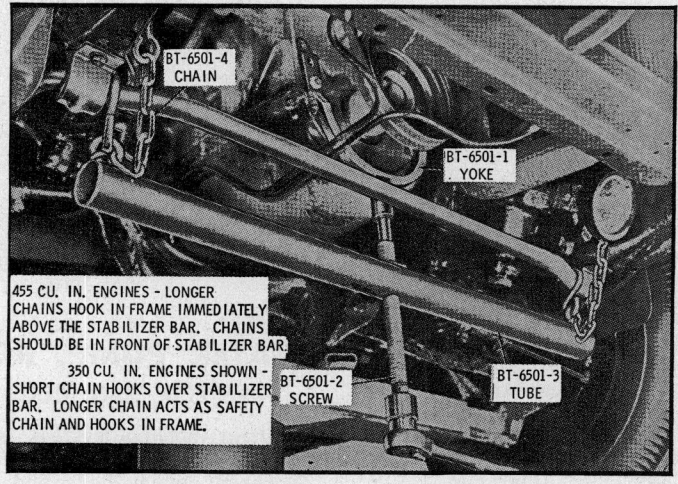

Fig. 19 Engine support bar. F-85 V8-455

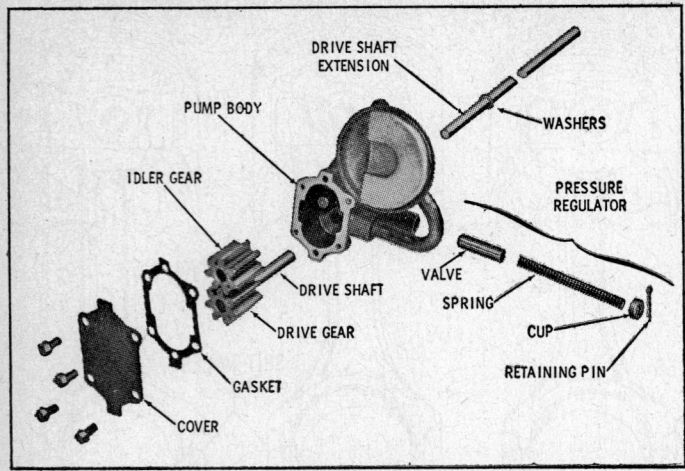

Fig. 20 Oil pump disassembled.
V8-260, 350, 400, 455 (Typical)

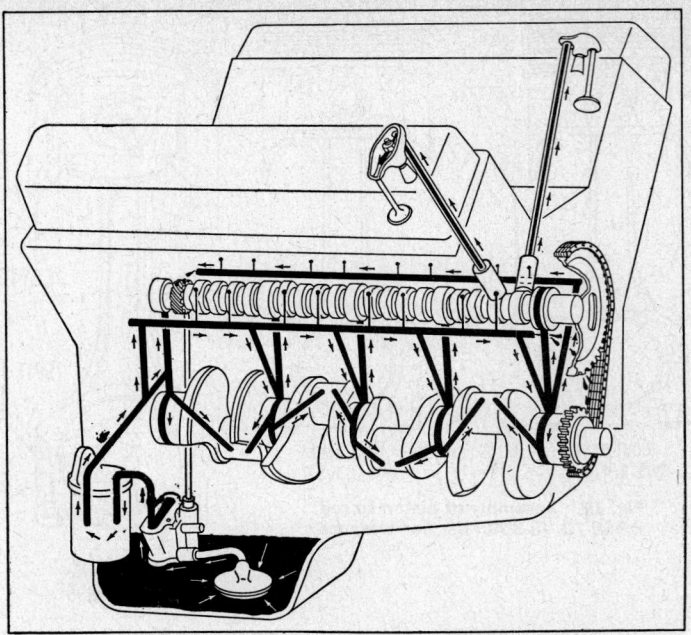

Engine lubrication. V8-260, 350, 400, 455

7. Raise front of engine.

NOTE: Remove lower two right-hand engine cover bolts to permit the lifting tool to clear water pump outlet. Do not bolt tool to block since engine must rock when being raised. Tool No. BT-6501-3 is available for this operation. Position fork of tool to lift pulley hub.

8. Raise right side of engine about 2½" and insert a block between upper and lower right-hand mounts.
9. Remove support bar tool from rear of engine.
10. Unfasten and remove pan.

NOTE: Before removing pan, have No. 1 and 2 connecting rod journals at the 4 or 7 o'clock position as viewed from front of engine.

11. Reverse procedure to install.

F-85 V8-455

1. Disconnect battery ground cable.
2. Disconnect fan shroud.
3. Raise car and drain oil.
4. Remove drive shaft and disconnect exhaust pipe and starter.
5. Install engine support bar, Fig. 19, and remove inspection cover. Disconnect modulator line, speedometer cable, oil cooler lines, solenoid wire and linkage.
6. Remove transmission crossmember, transmission and flywheel.
7. Remove right engine mount, raise engine 2" and install wedge block.
8. Loosen left engine mount-to-block bolts enough to permit removal of oil pan bolts.
9. Remove oil pan.

OIL PUMP REPAIRS
V8-260, 350, 400, 455

1. Remove oil pan and pump baffle. Remove attaching screws and remove pump and drive shaft extension.
2. To service the pump, refer to Fig. 20.
3. To install, insert the drive shaft extension through the opening in the block until the shaft mates into the distributor drive gear. Position pump onto rear main bearing cap and torque the attaching bolts to 35 ft-lbs.
4. Install oil pump baffle and pan.

BELT TENSION DATA

	New Lbs.	Used Lbs.
1969-75—		
V8 All	110-140	70
6 Cyl—		
Air Condition	135-145	95
Air Pump—		
1969	70-80	55
1970-75	120-130	75
Fan and Power Steering	120-130	75

WATER PUMP, REPLACE
V8-260, 350, 400, 455

1. Drain cooling system and remove heater and lower hoses from pump.
2. Loosen pulley belts and remove fan and pulley. On air conditioned cars,

remove clutch fan assembly and pulley.
3. Unfasten and remove pump from front cover.

FUEL PUMP PRESSURE

Year	Engine	Pressure, Lbs.
1970-75	Six	4-5
1969	Six	3-5
1971-75	V8	5½-6½
1970	V8	5-6
1969	V8	5-7

FUEL PUMP, REPLACE

1. Remove all gasket material from the pump and block gasket surfaces. Apply sealer to both sides of new gasket.
2. Position gasket on pump flange and hold pump in position against its mounting surface. Make sure rocker arm is riding on camshaft eccentric.
3. Press pump tight against its mounting. Install retaining screws and tighten them alternately.
4. Connect fuel lines. Then operate engine and check for leaks.

SERVICE NOTE: Before installing the pump, it is good practice to crank the engine so that the nose of the camshaft eccentric is out of the way of the fuel pump rocker arm when the pump is installed. In this way there will be the least amount of tension on the rocker arm, thereby easing the installation of the pump.

DUAL-JET 2MC ADJUSTMENT SPECIFICATIONS

See Tune Up Chart in car chapters for hot idle speeds.

Year	Carb. Model	Float Level	Pump Rod		Idle Vent	Air Valve	Fast Idle (Bench)	Choke Rod	Vacuum Break	Air Valve Dash-pot	Choke Unloader	Air Valve Lockout	Secondary Metering Rods	Air-Valve Valve Spring Wind-Up
			Hole	Adj.										
1975	7045156	5/32	Inner	9/32	—	—	—	.130	.150①	—	.275	—	—	—
	7045297	3/16	Inner	9/32	—	—	—	.130	.180②	—	.275	—	—	—
	7045298	5/32	Inner	9/32	—	—	—	.130	.150②	—	.275	—	—	—
	7045356	5/32	Inner	9/32	—	—	—	.160	.180②	—	.275	—	—	—
	7045598	5/32	Inner	9/32	—	—	—	.160	.150①	—	.275	—	—	—

①—Rich; Lean .230.
②—Rich; Lean .275.

DUAL-JET 2MC ADJUSTMENTS

The Rochester 2MC carburetor (Dual-Jet) is a two barrel, single stage unit, incorporating the design features of the primary side of the Quadrajet (four Barrel) carburetor. The Dual-Jet unit is similar in appearance to the Quadrajet carburetor, however, there are no secondary throttle valves or secondary metering system. The power piston controls fuel metering during all phases of operation.

Float Level Adjustment

Fig. 1—With adjustable T-scale, measure from top of float bowl gasket surface (gasket removed) to top of float at toe (locate gauging point 3/16" back from toe). Adjust as directed in the illustration to the dimension listed in the *2MC Specifications Chart*. Make sure retaining pin is held firmly in place and tang of float is seated on float needle.

Pump Rod Adjustment

Fig. 2—With throttle valves completely closed and pump rod in specified hole in pump lever, measure from top of choke valve wall (next to vent stack) to top of pump stem. Dimension should be as listed in the *2MC Specifications Chart*. To adjust, bend pump lever as required.

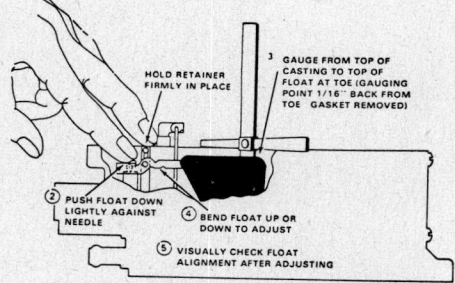

Fig. 1   Float level adjustment

Choke Coil Lever Adjustment

Fig. 3—With thermostatic coil assembly removed, push upward on coil tang until choke valve closes. Insert gauge specified in the 2MC Specifications Chart into choke housing hole. The lower edge of choke coil lever should just contact gauge. To adjust, bend choke rod as required.

Choke Rod Adjustment

Fig. 4—With fast idle adjustment made, and cam follower on second step of fast idle cam and against the high step, push upward on choke coil lever until choke valve closes. Dimension between upper edge of choke valve and air horn wall should be as specified in the 2MC Specifications Chart. Adjust by bending tang on intermediate choke lever.

Vacuum Break Adjustment

Fig. 5—With vacuum break diaphragm stem against its seat and choke valve held toward the closed position, the dimension between lower edge of choke valve and air horn, at choke lever end, should be as specified. To adjust, bend tang on vacuum break plunger stem.

Choke Unloader Adjustment

Fig. 6—With choke valve held closed by means of a rubber band on vacuum break lever, open throttle valves fully. With valves in this position, dimension between lower edge of choke valve and air horn wall should be as specified. To adjust, bend tang on fast idle lever.

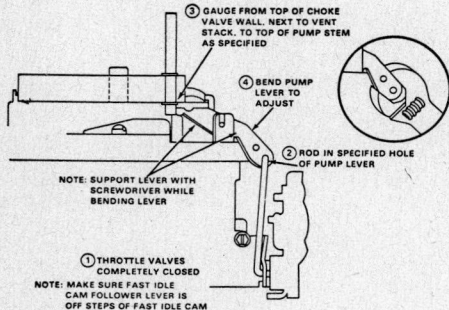

Fig. 2   Pump rod adjustment

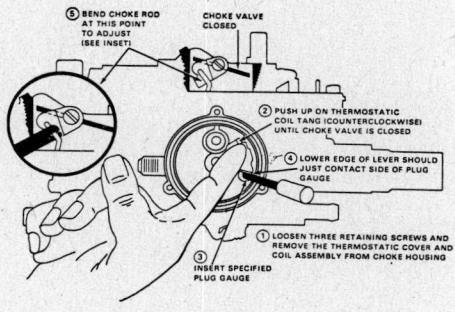

Fig. 3   Choke coil lever adjustment

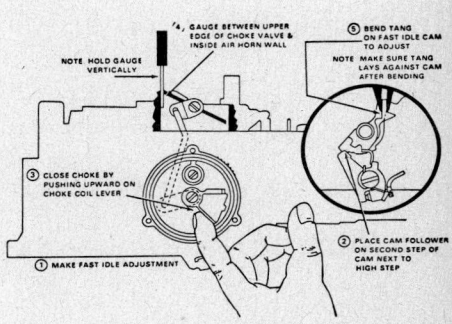

Fig. 4   Choke rod adjustment

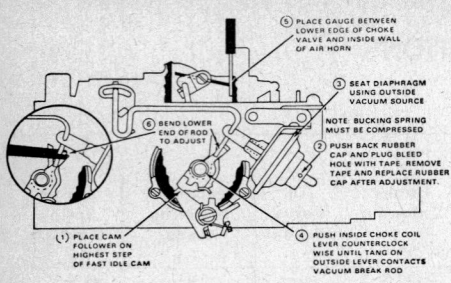

Fig. 5   Vacuum break adjustment

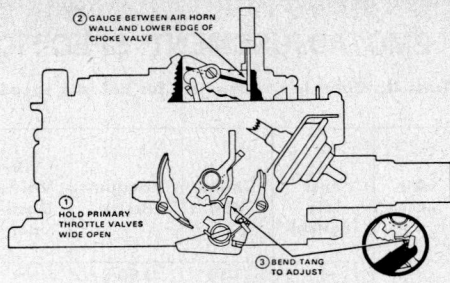

Fig. 6   Choke unloader adjustment

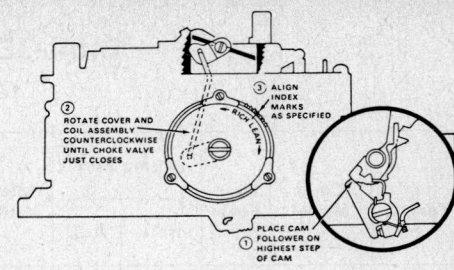

Fig. 7   Choke coil adjustment

Choke Coil Adjustment

Fig. 7—Place the fast idle cam follower on the highest step of the fast idle cam. Rotate choke cover and coil assembly counter-clockwise until the choke valve just closes and the index point on cover aligns with the specified index point on the choke housing.

Clutch and Transmission Section

NOTE: 1975 linkage adjustment information is in this section. Repair procedures on both automatic and manual shift transmissions are covered elsewhere in this manual. Procedures for removing automatic transmission as well as linkage adjustments on 1969-74 models are included in the automatic transmission chapters. See Chapter Index.

CLUTCH PEDAL, ADJUST
1969-75

1. To adjust clutch pedal free travel, loosen lock nut on adjusting rod and remove swivel retainer.
2. Adjust swivel to obtain a free pedal play of ¾" to 1" for all models except 1973 Cutlass and 1973-75 Omega. Free pedal play on 1973 Cutlass should be ¾" to 1¼" and on 1973-75 Omega ⅞" to 1½".
3. Install swivel retainer, tighten lock nut and recheck adjustment.

CLUTCH, REPLACE
1971-72 Two Plate Clutch

1. Support engine and remove transmission.
2. Remove flywheel housing leaving starter attached to engine. Release yoke and ball stud will remain with housing.

NOTE: Before removing clutch assembly, note location of "O" marks on edges of clutch cover, front pressure plate and flywheel. If marks are not visible, scribe or prick punch the parts so they can be reassembled in same position.

3. Remove clutch cover to flywheel attaching bolts and remove the cover assembly with the front pressure plate attached, Fig. 1. The front driven plate can now be removed. Observe the driven plate before removing to be sure which side of the driven plate is the flywheel side.
4. With the clutch assembly on the bench, pressure plate side up, remove the three cover straps to front pressure plate attaching bolts and remove the front pressure plate and the driven plate.

NOTE: Before lifting the front pressure plate and driven plate from the cover, observe which side of the pressure plate goes towards the flywheel. It is possible to assemble both parts reversed. A washer or shim (.027") is used between each strap and the front pressure plate.

5. Reverse removal procedure to install referring to Fig. 2.

1969-75 Exc. Two Plate Clutch

1. Remove transmission.
2. Disconnect clutch release spring and clutch rod.
3. Remove clutch release bearing.
4. Remove flywheel housing, leaving starter attached to engine. Release yoke and ball stud will remain in housing.
5. Scribe mark on clutch cover to flywheel for correct assembly.
6. Unfasten and remove clutch cover and disc.
7. Reverse removal procedure to install clutch and adjust clutch pedal free play.

THREE SPEED MANUAL TRANS., REPLACE
1969-75

1. Disconnect throttle linkage from cowl bracket to prevent damage.
2. Raise car and remove drive shaft.
3. Disconnect shift rods from shift levers and the TCS switch wiring, if equipped.
4. Support rear of engine.
5. Remove cross support bar-to-rear transmission mount attaching bolts.
6. Disconnect parking brake cables from cross support and remove cross support bar.
7. If equipped with dual exhaust it may be necessary to disconnect left-hand exhaust pipe at exhaust manifold to provide clearance.
8. Disconnect speedometer cable.
9. Remove transmission upper attaching bolts and install aligning studs in the bolt holes.
10. Remove lower bolts and remove transmission.
11. Reverse procedure to install.

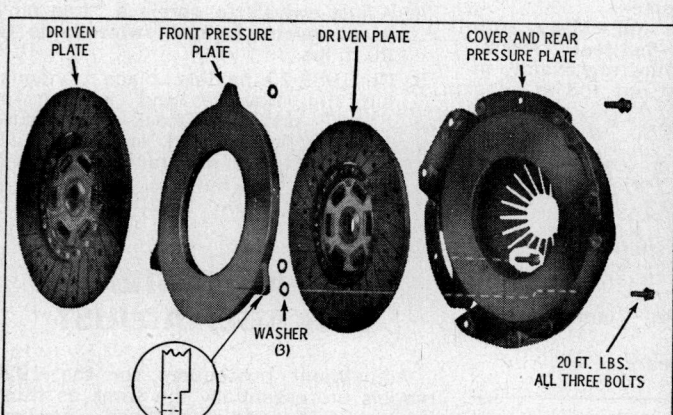

Fig. 1   Exploded view of two-plate clutch

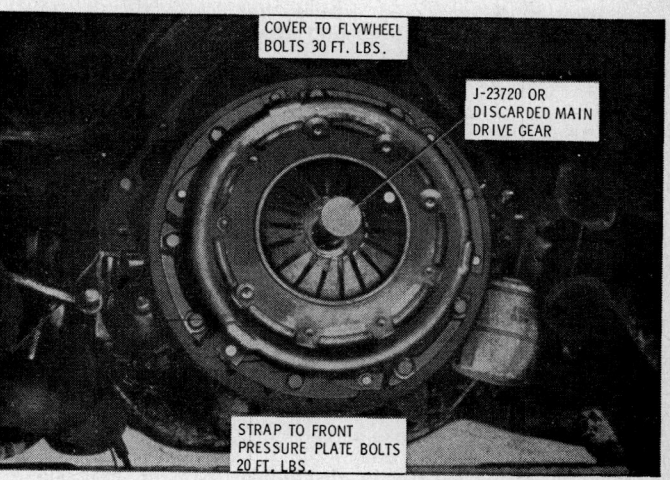

Fig. 2   Two-plate clutch installation

3 SPEED SHIFT LINKAGE, ADJUST

1969-75 Column Shift

On 1969-75 models, detent must be adjusted as follows. Place transmission in Reverse, loosen shift rods at transmission. Push up on reverse rod until detent in column is felt and tighten bolt for 1st-Reverse rod to 20 ft. lbs. Continue adjustment as follows:

1. Place transmission in Neutral.
2. Loosen swivel nuts on shift rods at transmission.
3. Use a suitable rod as an aligning tool and position it in the slot provided in mast jacket so alignment rod enters holes in low-reverse lever and the interlock pawl.
4. With transmission levers in neutral, tighten swivel nuts to 23 ft-lbs.
5. Remove aligning rod. Make sure neutral positions between low-reverse and second-third are exactly in line. If not, readjust one rod to bring them in line.
6. Check shift operation with engine stopped. Start engine and recheck.
7. On 1969-75 models, place transmission in Reverse and ignition in "Lock" position. Check to be sure key can be removed, steering wheel will not turn and transmission will not shift out of Reverse.

1973-75 Floor Shift

1. Place shift lever in Neutral and raise vehicle.
2. Loosen shift rod swivel nuts and disconnect rods from shifter, then insert a ¼ inch pin into shifter, Fig. 3.
3. Adjust swivel to obtain free pin length, tighten swivel nuts and connect shift rods to shifter.
4. With shift lever in Reverse and ignition key in Lock, loosen equalizer clamp and lightly pull back drive rod against stop. Torque equalizer clamp screw to 23 ft. lbs.
5. To check for proper operation:
   a. Place ignition key in Lock and shift lever in Reverse and ensure that key can be removed and steering wheel is locked.
   b. Place ignition key in Off and shift lever in Neutral and ensure that key cannot be removed and steering wheel is unlocked.

1969-71 3 SPEED HEAVY DUTY TRANS., REPLACE

1. Disconnect throttle linkage from cowl bracket to prevent damage.
2. Raise car and remove drive shaft.
3. Disconnect shift rods from shift levers (column shift).
4. With floor shift, remove shift lever knob and disconnect back-up lamp wiring (if equipped).
5. Disconnect equalizer shaft at side of transmission.
6. Support rear of engine.
7. Disconnect parking brake cable.
8. Remove cross support bar.
9. It may be necessary to disconnect

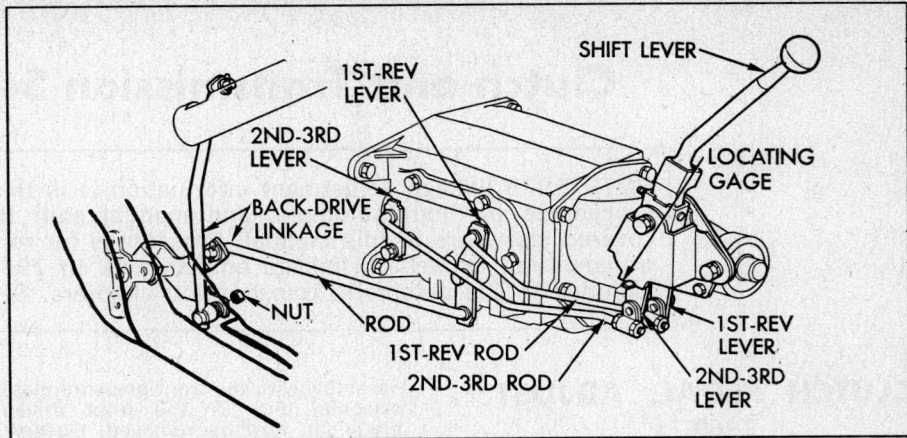

Fig. 3   Shift linkage. 1973-75 Omega floor shift

left exhaust pipe from exhaust manifold to provide clearance if equipped with dual exhaust.
10. Remove transmission upper bolts and install aligning studs in the bolt holes.
11. Remove lower bolts and slide transmission out of car.
12. Reverse procedure to install.

Shift Linkage, Adjust

On 1969-71 models, detent must be adjusted as follows: Place transmission in Reverse and loosen swivel bolt on back drive rod at equalizer. Push up lightly on back drive rod until stop is felt and tighten bolt to 20 ft. lbs. Continue adjustment.

1. Position transmission in neutral.
2. Loosen clamp screws on shift rods.
3. Use a suitable aligning rod and position it in slot provided in mast jacket so that it enters holes in low-reverse lever and the interlock pawl.
4. With floor shift, a ¼" diameter pin is inserted through shift lever bracket and levers.
5. With transmission levers in neutral, tighten clamp screws to 23 ft-lbs. On 1969-71 models, place transmission in Reverse and ignition in "Lock" position. Check to be sure key can be removed, steering wheel will not turn and transmission will not shift out of Reverse.
6. Remove alignment rod. Make sure neutral positions between low-reverse and second-third are exactly in line. If not, readjust one rod to bring them in line.

4 SPEED TRANS., REPLACE

1969-73

1. Remove propeller shaft and disconnect shift rods from shift levers at transmission.
2. Disconnect back-up lamp switch wires (if equipped).
3. Support engine at rear.

NOTE: On models with dual exhaust it may be necessary to disconnect

left-hand exhaust pipe from manifold to provide clearance.

4. Disconnect speedometer cable.
5. Disconnect parking brake cables from crossmember, then remove crossmember.
6. Remove three bolts that retain shift lever assembly to extension housing. If shift lever assembly removal is not required, it may be left hanging in floor seal.
7. Unfasten transmission and remove from car.

4 SPEED SHIFT LINKAGE, ADJUST

1969-73

1. On 1969-73, place transmission in Reverse and loosen swivel bolt on back drive rod at equalizer. Push up lightly on back drive rod until stop is felt and tighten bolt to 20 ft. lbs.
2. All models: Place transmission in Neutral and loosen shift rods.
3. Using a suitable rod, align levers in Neutral.
4. Adjust swivels to obtain a "free pin" fit at levers. Tighten swivel bolts to 20 ft. lbs.
5. On 1969-73 models, place transmission in Reverse and ignition in "Lock" position. Check to be sure key can be removed, steering wheel will not turn and transmission will not shift out of Reverse.

1975 AUTO. TRANS. LINKAGE, ADJUST

Adjustment procedures for the 1975 models are essentially the same as those for the 1974 units as outlined elsewhere in this manual.

Rear Axle, Propeller Shaft & Brakes

NOTE: Material marked F.S.C. means Full Size Car or Senior Models

REAR AXLE

Figs. 1 and 2 illustrate the rear axle assemblies used on conventional models. When necessary to overhaul any of these units, refer to the *Rear Axle Specifications* table in this chapter.

Integral Carrier
1969-75 Type "O"

As shown in Fig. 1, the drive pinion is mounted on two tapered roller bearings that are preloaded by two selected spacers. The drive pinion is positioned by shims located between a shoulder on the pinion and the rear bearing. The front bearing is held in place by a large nut.

The differential is supported in the carrier by two tapered roller side bearings. These are preloaded by inserting shims between the bearings and the pedestals. The differential assembly is positioned for ring gear and pinion backlash by varying these shims.

Major service work on the differential carrier assembly may be performed with the unit in the car provided a drive-on or twin-post hoist is available. If neither of these hoists are available, the rear axle assembly should be removed from the vehicle. The reason for this is that the axle tubes are pressed into the differential carrier housing and welded.

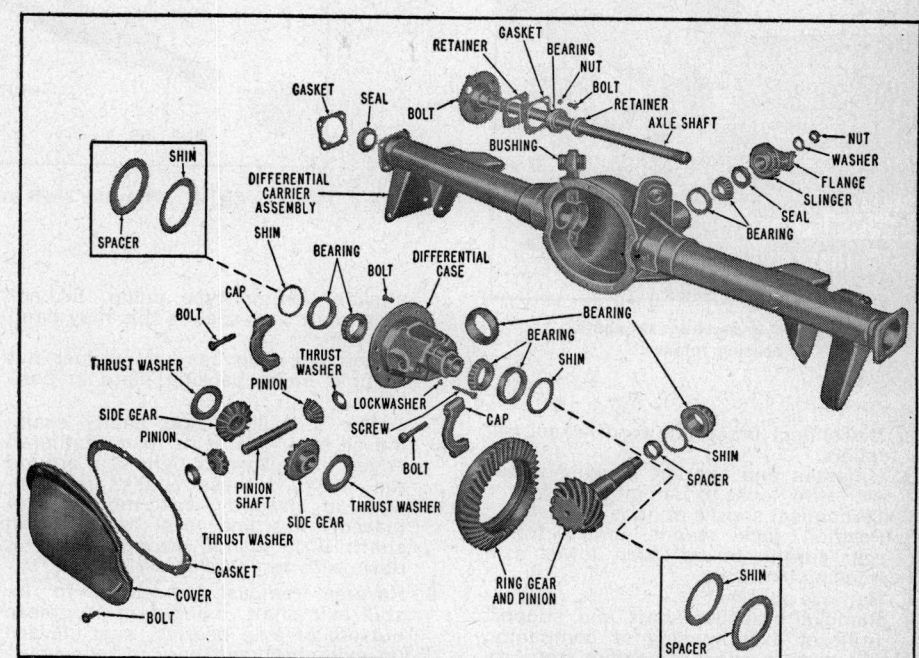

Fig. 1   Integral carrier type rear axle. 1969-75 Type "O" axle

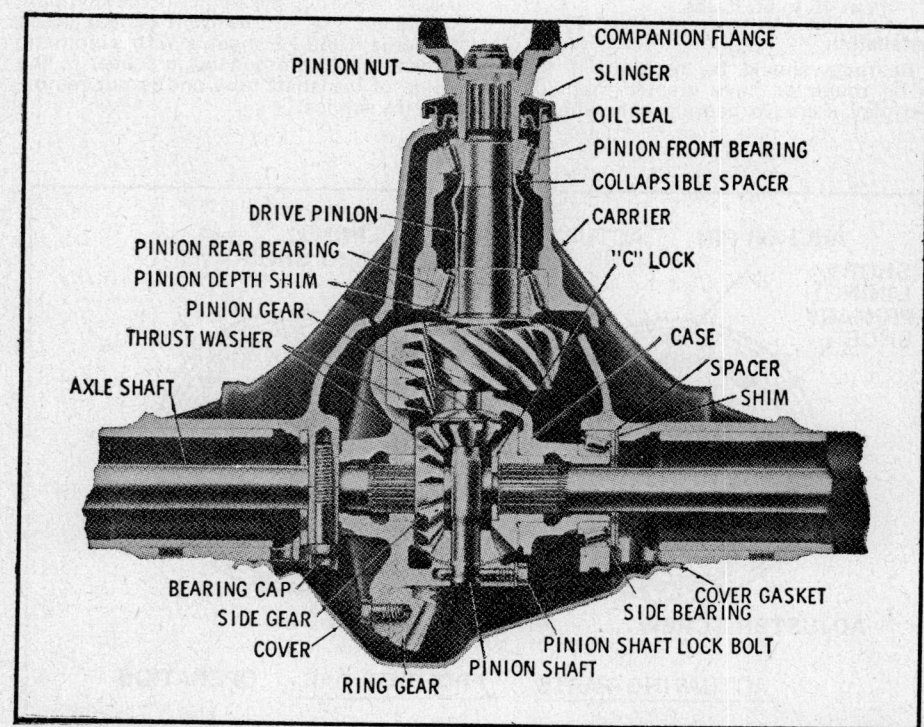

Fig. 2   Integral carrier type differential. 1969-75 Type "C" axle

1969-75 Type "C"

In these rear axles, Fig. 2, the rear axle housing and differential carrier are cast into an integral assembly. The drive pinion assembly is mounted in two opposed tapered roller bearings. The pinion bearings are preloaded by a spacer behind the front bearing. The pinion is positioned by a washer between the head of the pinion and the rear bearing.

The differential is supported in the carrier by two tapered roller side bearings. These bearings are preloaded by spacers located between the bearings and carrier housing. The differential assembly is positioned for proper ring gear and pinion backlash by varying these spacers. The differential case houses two side gears in mesh with two pinions mounted on a pinion shaft which is held in place by a lock pin. The side gears and pinions are backed by thrust washers.

Remove & Replace

Construction of the axle assembly is such that service operations may be performed with the housing installed in the vehicle or with the housing removed and installed in a holding fixture. The following procedure is necessary only when the housing requires replacement.

1. Hoist car and remove rear wheels, drums and axle shafts.

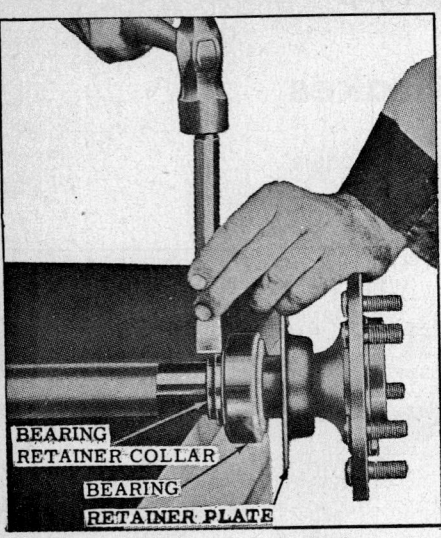

Fig. 3 Removing axle shaft bearing retainer

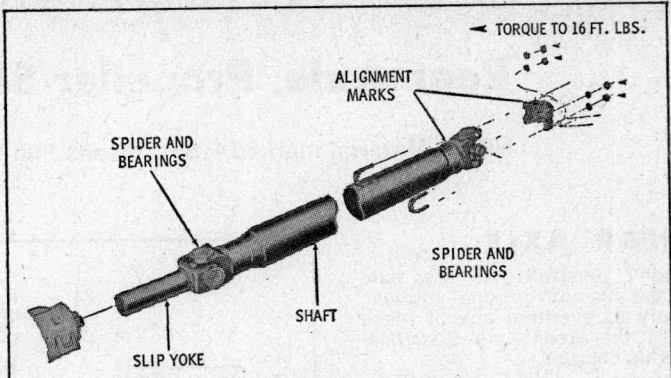

Fig. 4. Propeller shaft installation. 1969-75 (typical)

2. Disconnect brake line from wheel cylinders.
3. Unfasten and support backing plates with wire hooks to frame kickup.
4. Disconnect shocks at housing.
5. Position jack stands under frame rear torque boxes, then lower axle housing to stands.
6. Remove springs.
7. Remove propeller shaft and support front of axle housing at companion flange to prevent assembly from rotating when the control arms are disconnected.
8. Remove control arm bolts at axle housing.
9. Remove support at companion flange and lower axle housing.
10. Remove assembly to bench and transfer parts to new axle housing.
11. Reverse procedure to install.

AXLE SHAFT, REPLACE

1969-75 Type "C"

1. Raise vehicle and remove wheel and brake drum.
2. Clean all dirt from area of carrier cover.
3. Drain lubricant from carrier by removing cover.
4. Remove differential pinion shaft lock screw and shaft.
5. Push flanged end of axle shaft toward center of vehicle and remove "C" lock from button end of shaft.
6. Remove axle shaft from housing, being careful not to damage oil seal.
7. Reverse procedure to install.

1969-75 Type "O"

Removal
1. Remove wheel and brake drum.
2. Remove axle bearing retainer (4 nuts).
3. Pull axle shaft from housing. If bearing is a tight fit in housing, use

a slide hammer-type puller. Do not drag shaft over seal as this may damage seal.
4. Attach one axle bearing retainer nut to hold brake backing plate in position.
5. Before installing axle shaft, examine oil seal. The seals have feathered edges which form a tight seal around the shaft. If these edges are damaged in any way, seal must be replaced. Examine seal surface on shaft; if it is not smooth, dress it down with very fine emery cloth.
6. Reverse removal procedure to install axle shaft, being sure to grease outside of axle bearing, seal surface on axle shaft and bore of axle housing with differential lubricant. Place new gasket and bearing retainer over studs, install nuts and tighten them 45 to 60 ft. lbs.

Installation

Bearings should be replaced if found to be rough or have greater than .020" end play. Remove bearing only when new

bearing is to be installed; once removed it must not be reused.
1. With axle shaft removed from housing, split bearing retainer with a chisel, Fig. 3.
2. Press bearing off shaft.
3. Press new bearing on shaft up against shoulder on shaft.
4. Press retainer on shaft up against bearing.
5. Reverse removal procedure to install axle shaft.

PROPELLER SHAFT
1969-75

The propeller shaft is of one or two piece construction with a single or double U-joint securing the shaft to the companion flange, Fig. 4. The front or rear yokes on some 1969-72 models with automatic transmissions are bonded in rubber to the inside of the shaft tube and is not removable for service.

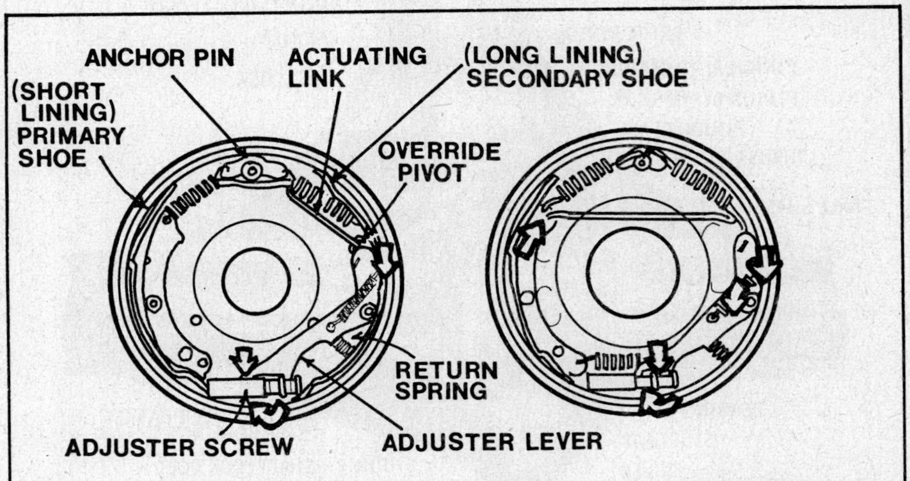

Fig. 5 Typical self-adjusting brake

1. To remove, remove nuts holding U-bolts at differential companion flange.
2. If U-joint bearings are not retained by a metal retaining strap, use a piece of wire or tape to hold bearings on U-joint cross.
3. Lower rear of shaft and slide rearward.
4. Reverse removal procedure to install the shaft. First, however, apply one ounce of seal lubricant to the splines of the slip yoke.

BRAKE ADJUSTMENTS
1969-75

These brakes, Fig. 5, have self adjusting shoe mechanisms that assure correct lining-to-drum clearances at all times. The automatic adjusters operate only when the brakes are applied as the car is moving rearward or when the car comes to an uphill stop.

Although the brakes are self-adjusting, an initial adjustment is necessary after the brake shoes have been relined or replaced, or when the length of the star wheel adjuster has been changed during some other service operation.

Frequent usage of an automatic transmission forward range to halt reverse vehicle motion may prevent the automatic adjusters from functioning, thereby inducing low pedal heights. Should low pedal heights be encountered, it is recommended that numerous forward and reverse stops be made until satisfactory pedal height is obtained.

NOTE

If a low pedal height condition cannot be corrected by making numerous reverse stops (provided the hydraulic system is free of air) it indicates that the self-adjusting mechanism is not functioning. Therefore, it will be necessary to

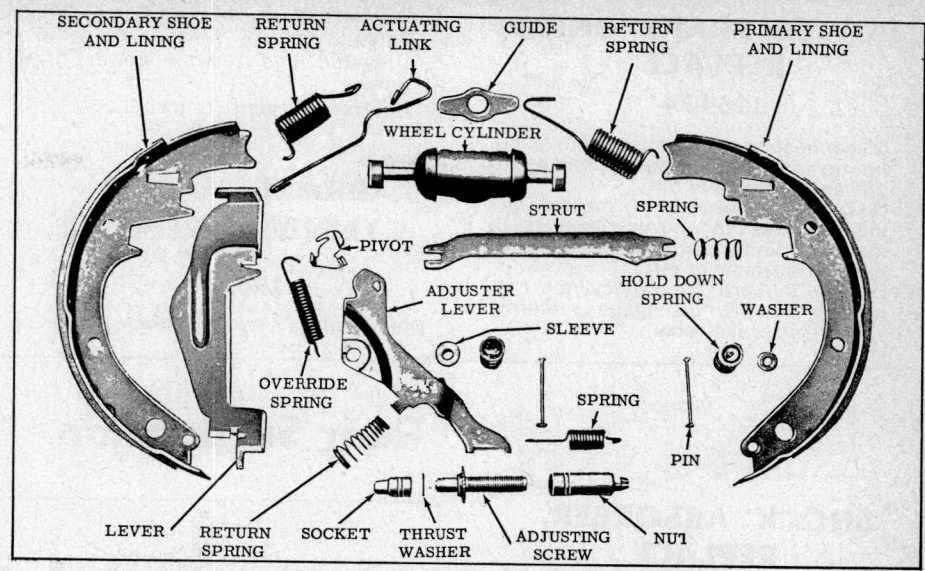

Fig. 5A   Drum brake assembly exploded

remove the brake drum, clean, free up and lubricate the adjusting mechanism. Then adjust the brakes as follows, being sure the parking brake is fully released.

Adjustment

NOTE: Inasmuch as there is no way to adjust these brakes with the drums installed, the following procedure is mandatory after new linings are installed or if it becomes necessary to change the length of the brake shoe adjusting screw.

1. With brake drums removed, position the caliper shown in Fig. 6 to the inside diameter of the drum and tighten the clamp screw.
2. Next position brake shoe end of the caliper tool over the brake shoes as shown in Fig. 7.

3. Rotate the gauge slightly around the shoes to insure that the gauge contacts the linings at the largest diameter.
4. Adjust brake shoes until the gauge is a snug fit on the linings at the point of largest lining diameter.

NOTE: If it is necessary to back off the brake shoe adjustment, it will be necessary to hold the adjuster lever away from the adjuster screw, Fig. 8.

PARKING BRAKE, ADJUST
1969-75

With parking brake fully released, adjust rear cables by first tightening the brake equalizer adjusting nut until a heavy resistance is felt when rotating rear wheels forward. Then loosen equalizer adjusting nut 7 full turns.

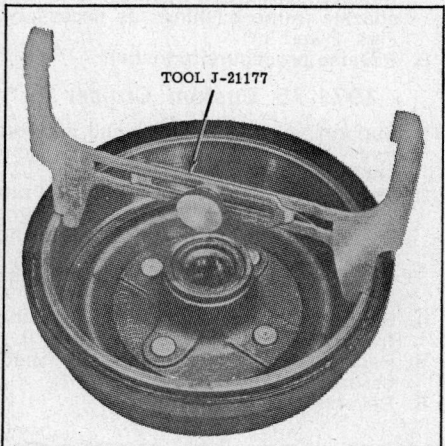

Fig. 6   Brake shoe gauge measuring inside diameter of brake drum. 1969-75

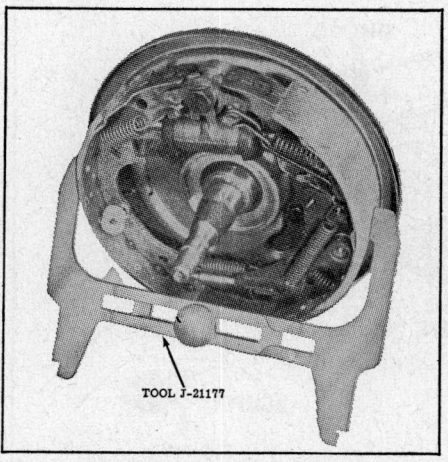

Fig. 7   Brake shoe gauge measuring outside diameter of brake shoes. 1969-75

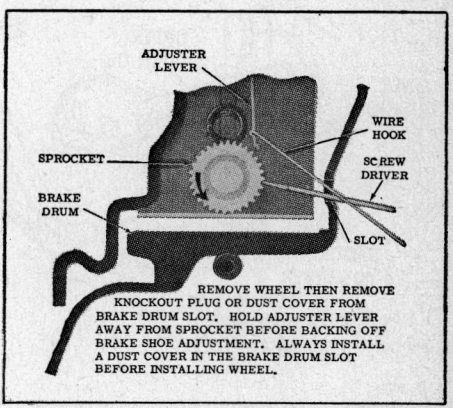

Fig. 8   Backing off brake shoe adjustment

POWER BRAKE UNIT, REPLACE

1969-74

1. Disconnect vacuum hose from vacuum cylinder and cover openings to prevent entrance of dirt.
2. Disconnect pipes from master cylinder outlets and cover openings in master cylinder and end of pipes to prevent entrance of dirt.
3. Loosen inboard master cylinder attaching nut to disengage metering valve (disc brakes only).

4. Disconnect air valve rod from brake pedal.
5. Unfasten and remove power brake unit.
6. Reverse procedure to install.

BRAKE MASTER CYLINDER, REPLACE

1969-75

The standard brake master cylinder on Olds F.S.C. can be removed without disconnecting the push rod and clevis. On all cars equipped with power brakes, the master cylinder can be removed without removing the vacuum cylinder from the car.

1. Be sure area around master cylinder is clean, then disconnect the hydraulic lines at master cylinder. Plug or tape end of line to prevent entrance of dirt or loss of brake fluid.
2. On F-85 and Omega models, remove push rod-to-brake pedal clevis pin.
3. On all models, unfasten (4 bolts) and remove master cylinder.

Rear Suspension

SHOCK ABSORBER, REPLACE

With rear axle properly supported, disconnect shock absorber from upper and lower mountings.

LEAF SPRINGS & BUSHINGS, REPLACE

1973-75 Omega

1. Support vehicle at frame and support rear axle, relieving tension from spring.
2. Disconnect shock absorbers from lower mountings and loosen spring front mounting bolt.
3. Remove spring retainer bracket to underbody screws, lower rear axle and remove retainer bracket.
4. Disconnect parking brake cable from spring plate bracket.

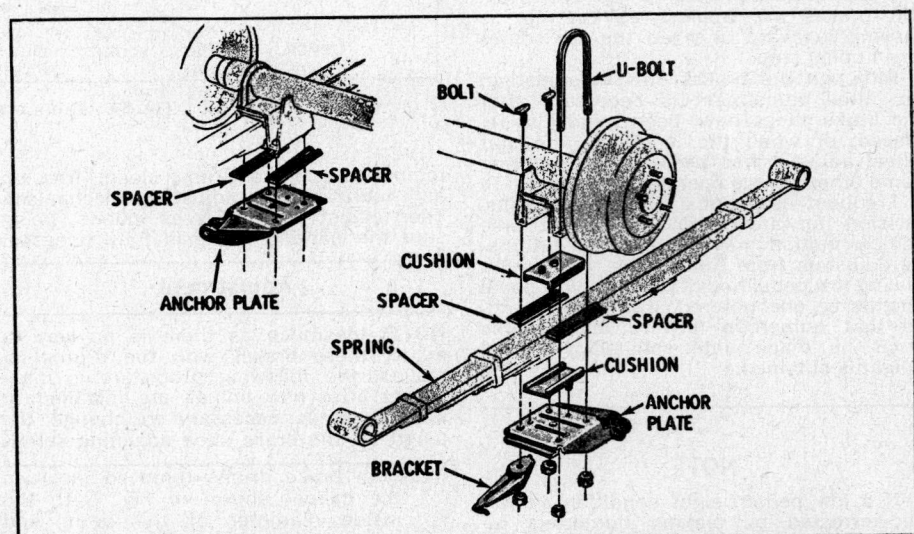

Fig. 1   Rear suspension. 1973-75 Omega

5. Remove "U" bolts and spring plate, Fig. 1.
6. Support spring, remove spring front mounting bolt and rear shackle bolts.
7. Replace spring eye bushings and rear shackle frame bushings as necessary, Figs. 2 and 3.
8. Reverse procedure to install.

1971-75 Custom Cruiser

1. Support vehicle at frame and support rear axle, relieving tension from spring.
2. Disconnect shock absorbers from lower mountings and if removing right hand leaf spring, loosen tailpipe and resonator assembly.
3. Remove rear shackle bolts, "U" bolts and spring plate, Fig. 4.
4. Support spring and remove spring front mount bolt.
5. Replace spring front bushing as necessary, Figs. 5, 6 and 7.
6. Reverse procedure to install.

COIL SPRING, REPLACE

1. Support vehicle at frame and support

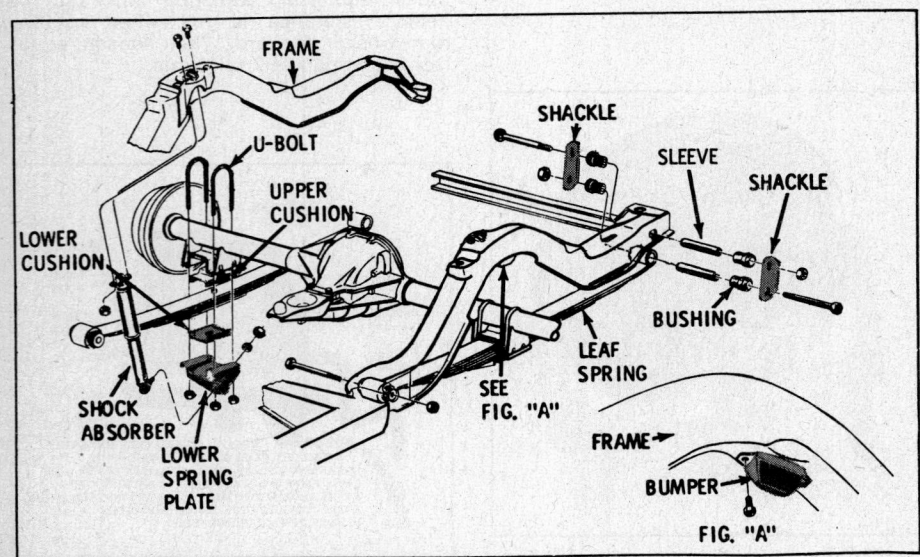

Fig. 4   Rear suspension. 1971-75 Custom Cruiser

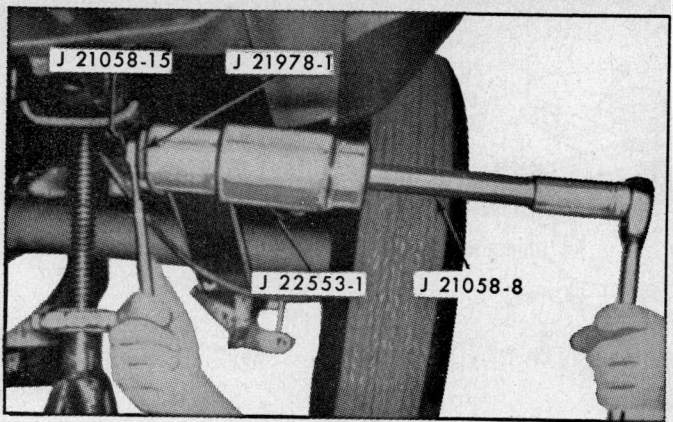

Fig. 2   Leaf spring bushings removal. 1973-75 Omega

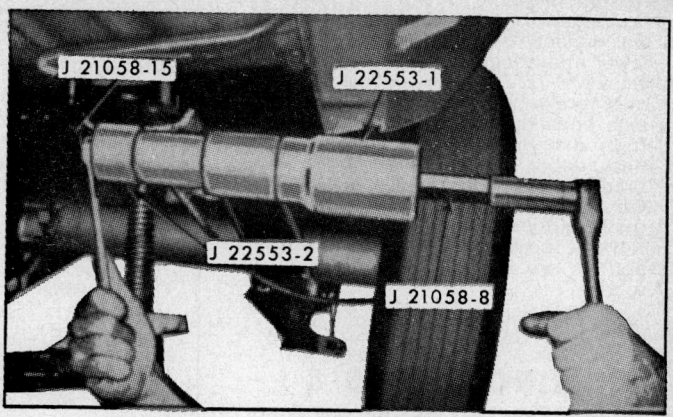

Fig. 3   Leaf spring bushings installation. 1973-75 Omega

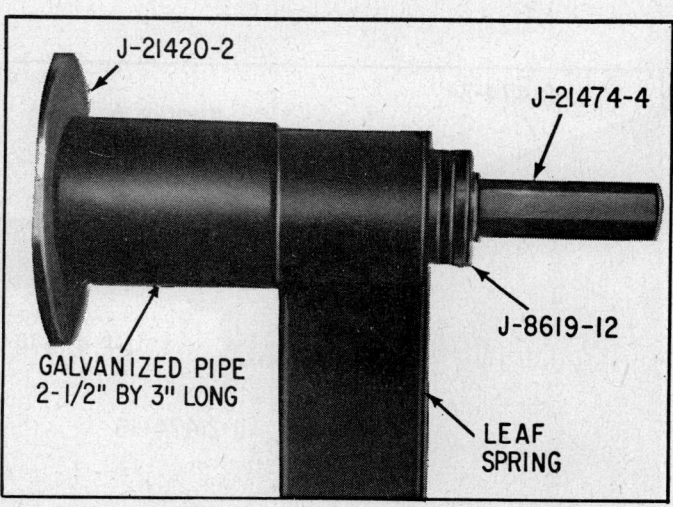

Fig. 5   Spring front bushing removal. 1971-75 Custom Cruiser

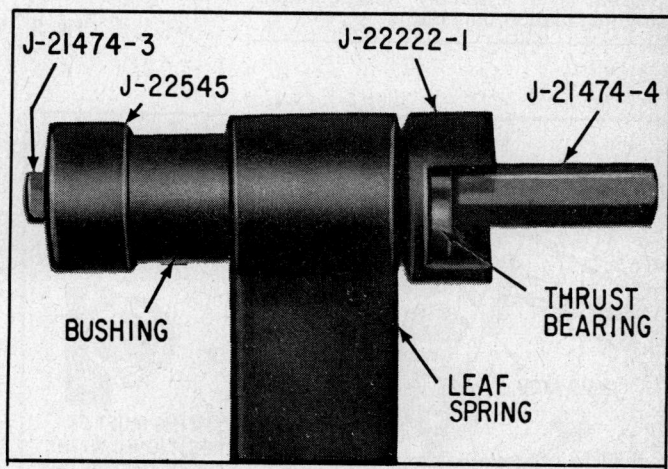

Fig. 6   Spring front bushing partial installation.
1971-75 Custom Cruiser

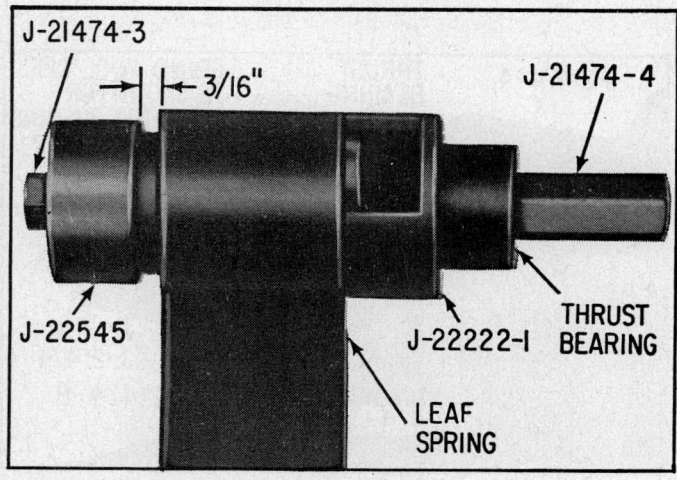

Fig. 7   Spring front bushing complete installation.
1971-75 Custom Cruiser

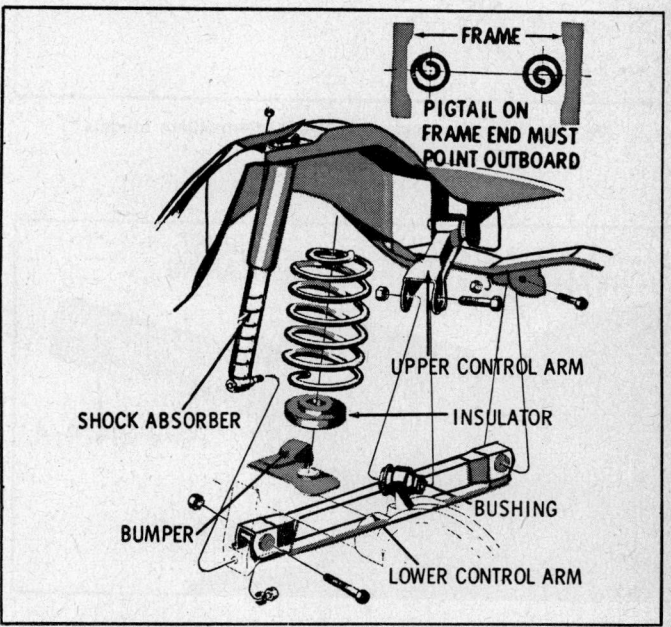

Fig. 8   Rear suspension. 1969-70 full size models

rear axle with a suitable jack.
2. Disconnect shock absorbers from lower mountings.
3. On 1972-75 full size models, disconnect brake line junction block from axle housing and remove brake lines from axle housing retainers. Disconnect upper control arms from axle brackets.
4. On all models lower rear axle to remove springs.
5. Reverse procedure to install insuring springs are indexed properly, Figs. 8 to 10.

CONTROL ARMS & BUSHINGS, REPLACE

NOTE: Replace control arms one at a time to prevent axle assembly misalignment, making installation difficult.

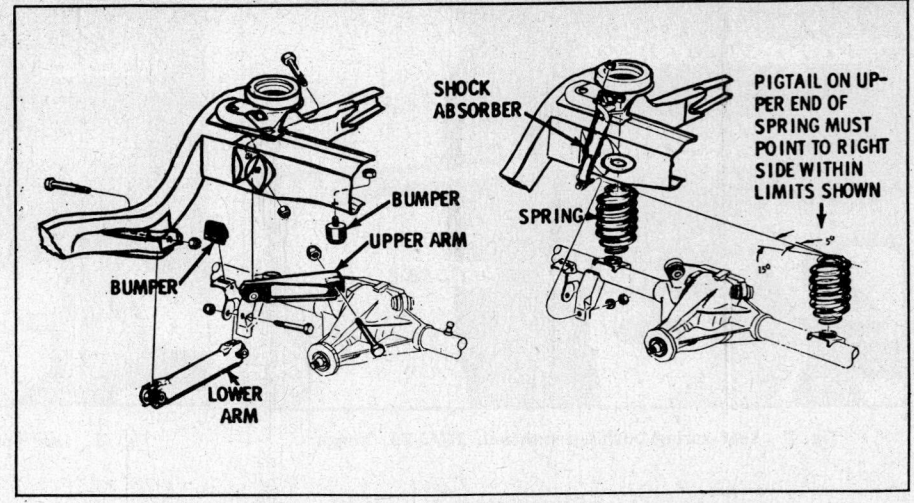

Fig. 9   Rear suspension. 1971-75 full size models & 1973-75 Cutlass

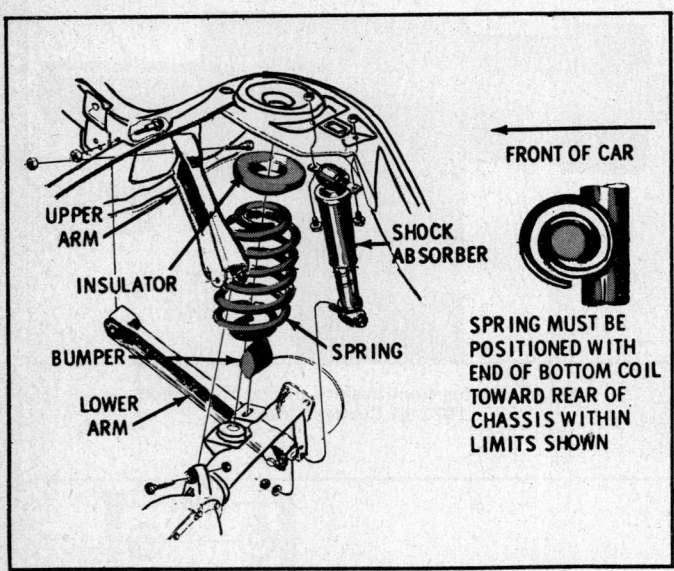

Fig. 10   Rear suspension. 1969-72 intermediate models

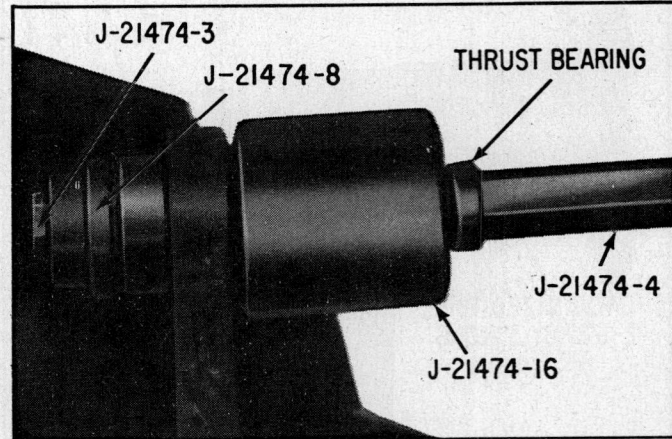

Fig. 11   Upper control arm axle bracket bushing removal. 1969 models with type "C" axle

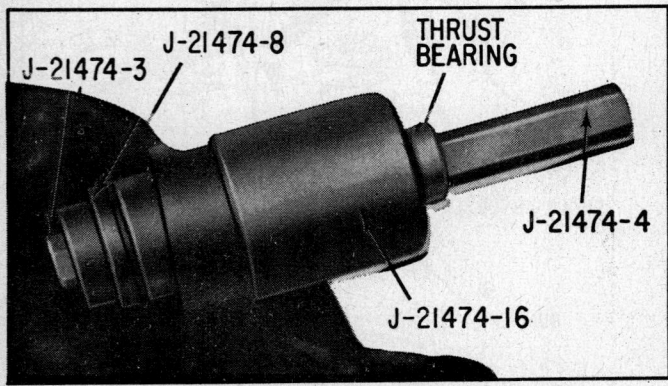

Fig. 13   Upper control arm axle bracket bushing removal. 1969 models with type "O" axle & all 1970-75 models

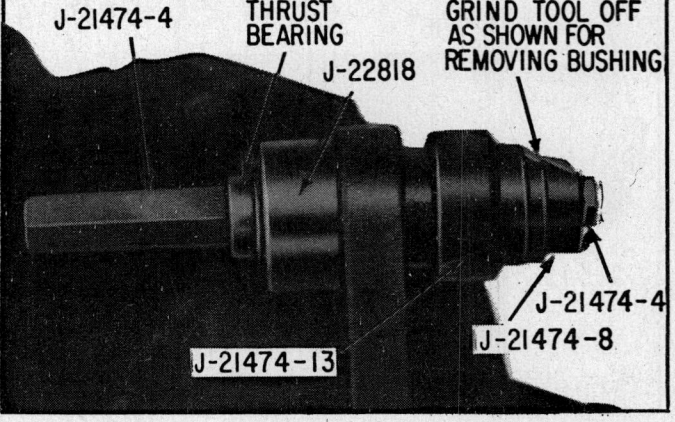

Fig. 12   Upper control arm axle bracket bushing installation. 1969 models with type "C" axle

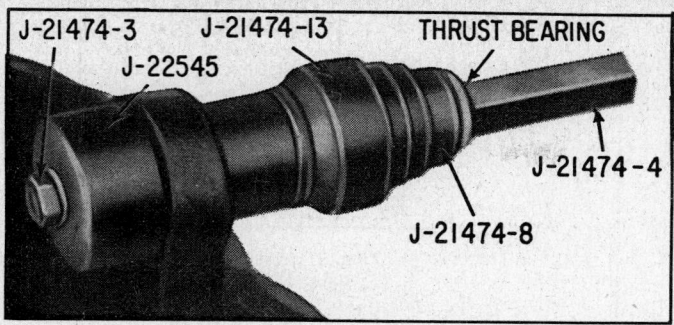

Fig. 14 Upper control arm axle bracket bushing installation. 1969 models with type "O" axle & all 1970-75 models

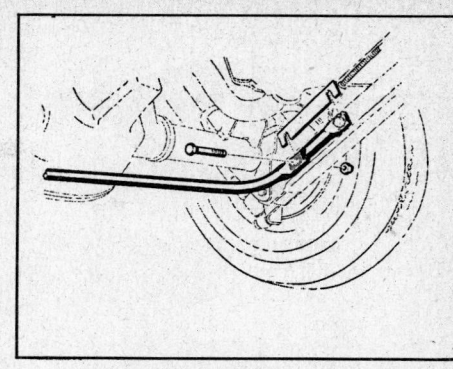

Fig. 15 Stabilizer bar installation (typical)

Upper Control Arms

1. Support vehicle at frame and rear axle.
2. Remove control arm front and rear mount bolts.
3. Replace axle housing bushing as necessary, Figs. 11 thru 14.
4. Reverse procedure to install. Tighten control arm bolts with vehicle at curb height.

Lower Control Arms

Follow "Upper Control Arms" procedure for replacement of lower control arms.

NOTE: Lower control arm bushings are not serviceable.

STABILIZER BAR, REPLACE

1. Support vehicle at rear axle.
2. Remove bolts attaching stabilizer bar to the lower control arms, Fig. 15.
3. Reverse procedure to install.

Front End and Steering Section

NOTE: Material marked F.S.C. means Full Size Car or Senior Models

FRONT SUSPENSION

As shown in Figs. 1 and 2, the front suspension is of the conventional "A" frame design with ball joints. Double acting shock absorbers are mounted within the coil springs. Caster and camber are controlled by shims.

LUBRICATION

An extended lubrication period of every six months or 12,000 miles for 1969-70 vehicles and four months or 6,000 miles for 1971-74 vehicles is prescribed, whichever occurs first. The ball joints are fitted with plugs which must be removed and grease fittings installed. After applying the approved type of grease, remove the fittings and reinstall the plugs.

IMPORTANT: On Intermediates, if ball joints are noisy, the plugs must be removed and approximately one teaspoonful of specified grease applied directly to the plug hole with a hand-operated, ball type nozzle grease gun. Do not install grease fittings or attempt to fill with a pressure gun. Either method will result in overfill or mixing of greases which may harm the part.

Before using a new grease gun of this type, first count the number of turns or pumps required to obtain approximately one teaspoonful of grease.

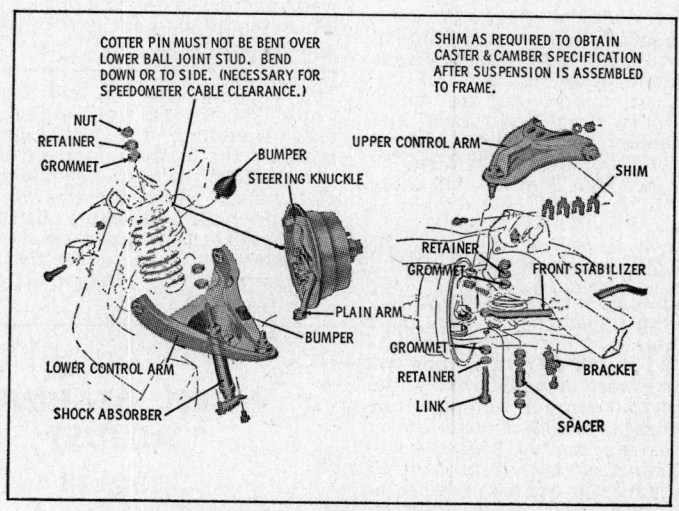

Fig. 1 Front suspension. 1969-75 Full Size Car

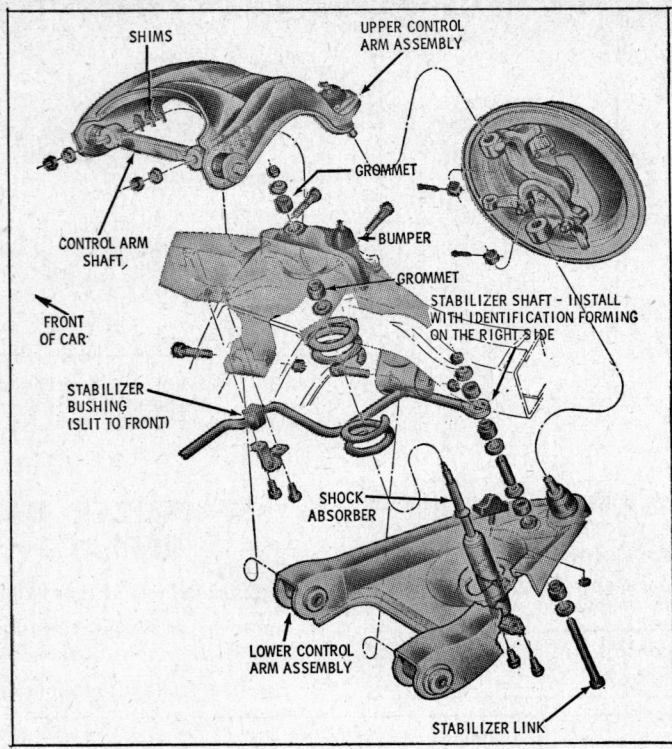

SHIMS
UPPER CONTROL ARM ASSEMBLY
GROMMET
CONTROL ARM SHAFT
BUMPER
GROMMET
FRONT OF CAR
STABILIZER SHAFT - INSTALL WITH IDENTIFICATION FORMING ON THE RIGHT SIDE
STABILIZER BUSHING (SLIT TO FRONT)
SHOCK ABSORBER
LOWER CONTROL ARM ASSEMBLY
STABILIZER LINK

Fig. 2   Front suspension. 1969-74 Intermediate Models

Shim Thickness	One shim added to or subtracted from BOTH BOLTS will change camber	One shim added to or subtracted from FRONT BOLT ONLY will change caster
.030"	1/8°	1/8°
.060"	5/16°	7/16°
.120"	5/8°	7/8°

Fig. 3   Wheel alignment shim data. 1969-72 Olds F.S.C.

Shim Thickness	One shim added to or subtracted from BOTH BOLTS will change CAMBER	One shim added to or subtracted from FRONT BOLT ONLY will change CASTER
.020"	1/8°	3/16°
.030"	3/16°	1/4°
.060"	3/8°	1/2°
120"	3/4°	1°

Fig. 4   Wheel alignment shim data. 1969-72 Inter.

WHEEL ALIGNMENT

1969-75 Full Size Cars

Camber and caster are adjusted by shims placed between the upper pivot shafts and the frame. In order to remove or install shims, *do not remove weight from front wheels.* Loosen pivot shaft-to-frame bolts. To gain access to these bolts, loosen top and rear fasteners on fender filler plate aprons.

To decrease positive caster, add shim at the front bolt. To increase positive caster, remove shim at the front bolt. To increase camber, remove shims at both front and rear bolt. To decrease camber, add shims at both bolts.

By adding or subtracting an equal amount of shims from both front and rear bolts, camber will change without affecting caster adjustment. On 1969-72 models, refer to Fig. 3 when changing shims.

1969-75 Intermediates

Caster and camber is adjusted by shimming at the upper control arm shaft attaching points.

Adding shims at the front locations will change caster toward negative with practically no change in camber. Adding shims at the rear locations will change caster toward positive and camber toward negative. Adding equal shims at both front and rear locations will not change caster but will change camber toward negative.

To adjust, loosen both front and rear bolts to free shims for removal or addition. On 1969-72 models, refer to Fig. 4 when changing shims.

TOE-IN, ADJUST

To adjust the toe-in, loosen the clamps at both ends of the adjustable tubes at each tie rod. Then turn the tubes an equal amount until the toe-in is correct. Turning the tubes in the direction the wheels revolve when the car moves forward decreases the toe-in and vice-versa. When the adjustment is complete, tighten all clamp screws.

The steering knuckle and steering arm "rock" or tilt as front wheel rises and falls. Therefore, it is vitally important to position the bottom face of the tie rod end parallel with the machined surface at the outer end of the steering arm when tie rod length is adjusted. Severe damage and possible failure can result unless this precaution is taken. The tie rod sleeve clamps must be straight down to provide clearance.

WHEEL BEARINGS, ADJUST

1969-75

1. While rotating hub and drum assem-
bly, tighten nut to 30 ft-lbs to insure all parts are properly seated.
2. Back off nut 1/2 turn.
3. Retighten nut finger tight and install retaining ring or cotter key if possible. If unable to install retaining ring or cotter key, back off nut (not to exceed 1/24 of a turn) until tabs on clip align with serrations in nut.

WHEEL BEARINGS, REPLACE

(Disc Brakes) 1969-75

1. Raise car and remove front wheels.
2. Remove brake pads and caliper assembly but do not disconnect brake line. Suspend caliper from a wire loop or hook to avoid strain on the brake hose.
3. Remove grease cap, cotter pin and nut. Pull off hub and disc assembly. Grease retainer and inner bearing can now be removed.

CHECKING BALL JOINTS FOR WEAR

If loose ball joints are suspected, first

be sure the front wheel bearings are properly adjusted and that the control arms are tight. Then check ball joints for wear as follows:

Referring to Fig. 5, raise wheel with a jack placed under the lower control arm as shown. Then test by moving the wheel up and down to check axial play, and rocking it at the top and bottom to measure radial play.

1973-75 Omega

1. Upper ball joint should be replaced if looseness exceeds .125".
2. Lower ball joint should be replaced if looseness exceeds 1/16".

NOTE: Beginning with 1975 models, a wear indicator is built into the lower ball joint, Fig. 6.

1969-75 Cutlass

1. Upper ball joint should be replaced if looseness exceeds .125".
2. Lower ball joint should be replaced if looseness exceeds .025" on 1973 models or .125" on previous models.

NOTE: Beginning with 1974 models, a wear indicator is built into the lower ball joint, Fig. 6.

1969-75 Full Size Cars

1. Upper ball joint should be replaced if looseness exceeds .125".
2. Lower ball joint should be replaced if looseness exceeds .125" on 1969-72 models.

NOTE: Beginning with 1973 models, a wear indicator is built into the lower ball joint. Refer to Fig. 6.

BALL JOINTS, REPLACE

On some models the ball joints are riveted to the control arms. All service ball joints, however, are provided with bolt, nut and washer assemblies for replacement purposes.

Some ball joints are pressed into the control arms, in which case they may be pressed out and new ones installed.

SHOCK ABSORBER REPLACE

Senior Models

1. Remove upper pivot bolt from shock absorber.
2. Remove two capscrews and washers attaching shock absorber to lower control arm and remove shock absorber.
3. Reverse above procedure to install.

Intermediate Models

1. Remove upper attaching nut, retainer and grommet from shock absorber.
2. Remove two bolts and washers attaching shock absorber to lower con-

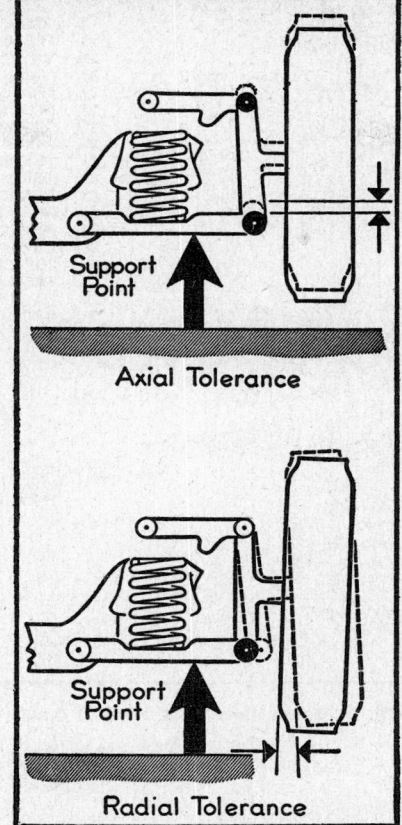

Fig. 5 Checking ball joints for wear

trol arm and remove shock absorber.
3. To install, position grommet and retainer over shock and slide shock up through spring and frame. Install and tighten attaching nut and lower capscrews.

COIL SPRING, REPLACE

1970-75 Intermediate Models

1. Raise front of car and support frame with floor stands.
2. Remove wheel and disconnect speedometer cable from steering knuckle (if equipped).
3. Disconnect stabilizer link and speedometer cable clamp from lower control arm.
4. Loosen lower control arm shaft bushing bolts.
5. Remove shock absorber.
6. Position floor jack under lower control arm between spring seat and ball joint. Raise jack until it supports lower control arm.
7. Using suitable compressor, compress spring slightly and disconnect lower ball joint from steering knuckle.
8. Slowly lower floor jack until spring is fully extended and remove spring.

IMPORTANT: Left and right coil springs should not be interchanged. Spring part number is stamped on outer side of end coil.

INSTALLATION: Reverse removal procedure to install spring. However, first tape

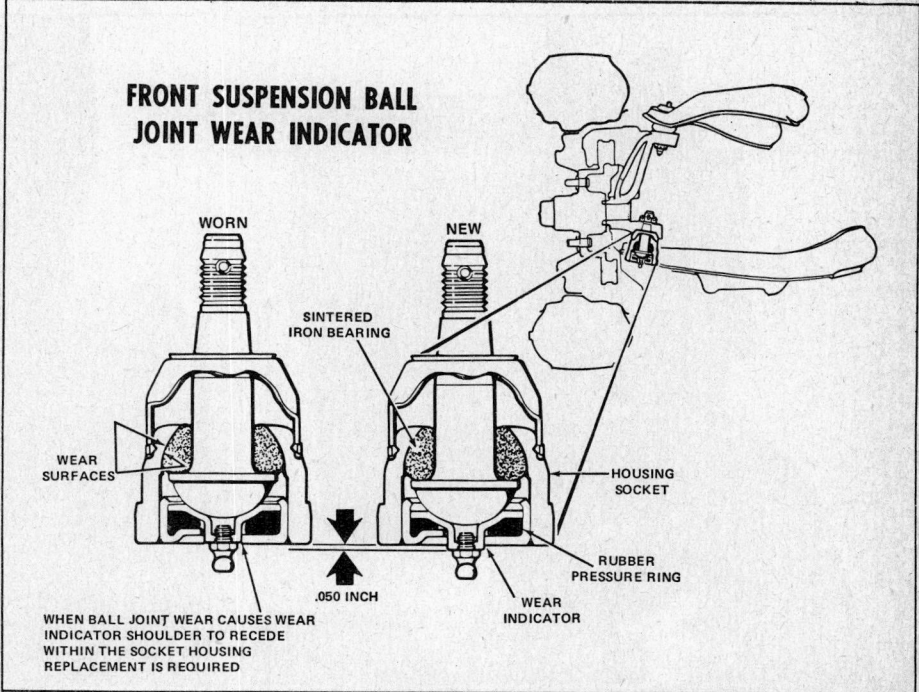

FRONT SUSPENSION BALL JOINT WEAR INDICATOR

WORN

NEW

SINTERED IRON BEARING

WEAR SURFACES

HOUSING SOCKET

RUBBER PRESSURE RING

WEAR INDICATOR

.050 INCH

WHEN BALL JOINT WEAR CAUSES WEAR INDICATOR SHOULDER TO RECEDE WITHIN THE SOCKET HOUSING REPLACEMENT IS REQUIRED

Fig. 6 Ball joint wear indicator. 1973 full size cars & 1974 Exc. Omega & 1975 All

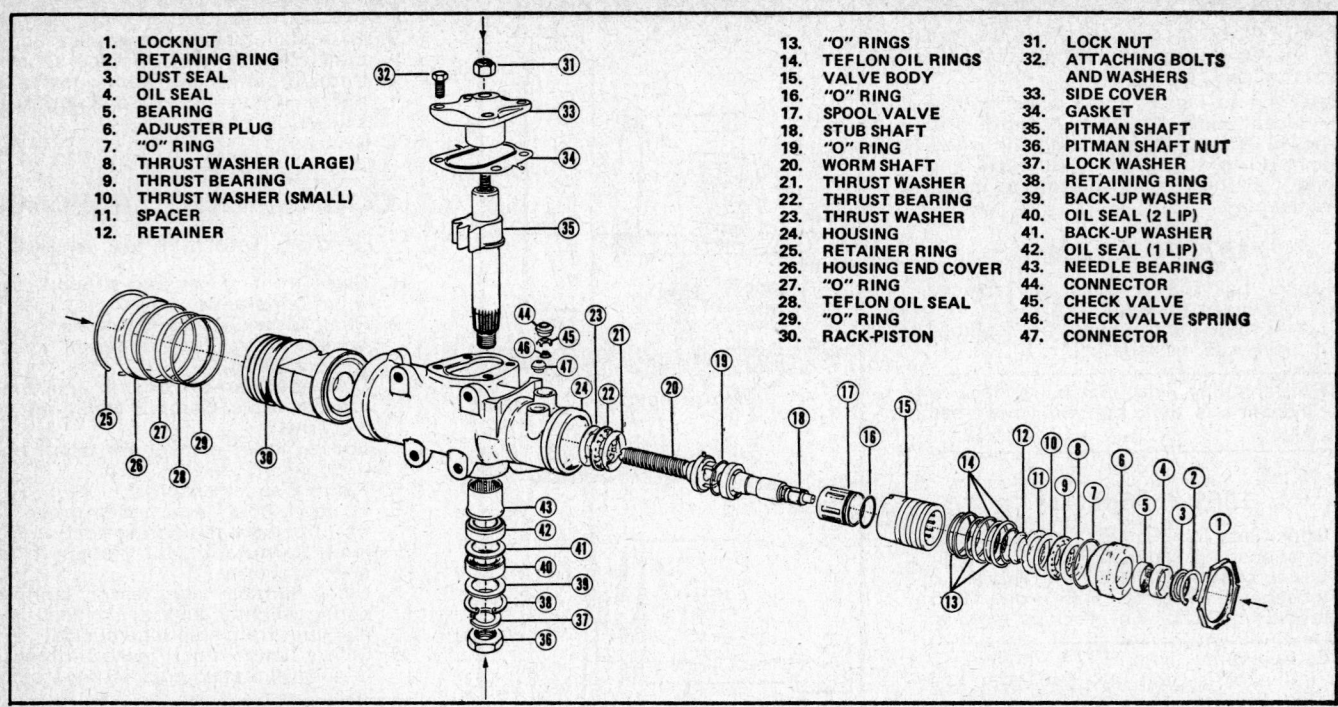

1. LOCKNUT
2. RETAINING RING
3. DUST SEAL
4. OIL SEAL
5. BEARING
6. ADJUSTER PLUG
7. "O" RING
8. THRUST WASHER (LARGE)
9. THRUST BEARING
10. THRUST WASHER (SMALL)
11. SPACER
12. RETAINER
13. "O" RINGS
14. TEFLON OIL RINGS
15. VALVE BODY
16. "O" RING
17. SPOOL VALVE
18. STUB SHAFT
19. "O" RING
20. WORM SHAFT
21. THRUST WASHER
22. THRUST BEARING
23. THRUST WASHER
24. HOUSING
25. RETAINER RING
26. HOUSING END COVER
27. "O" RING
28. TEFLON OIL SEAL
29. "O" RING
30. RACK-PISTON
31. LOCK NUT
32. ATTACHING BOLTS AND WASHERS
33. SIDE COVER
34. GASKET
35. PITMAN SHAFT
36. PITMAN SHAFT NUT
37. LOCK WASHER
38. RETAINING RING
39. BACK-UP WASHER
40. OIL SEAL (2 LIP)
41. BACK-UP WASHER
42. OIL SEAL (1 LIP)
43. NEEDLE BEARING
44. CONNECTOR
45. CHECK VALVE
46. CHECK VALVE SPRING
47. CONNECTOR

Fig. 7   Power steering gear. 1975 Omega

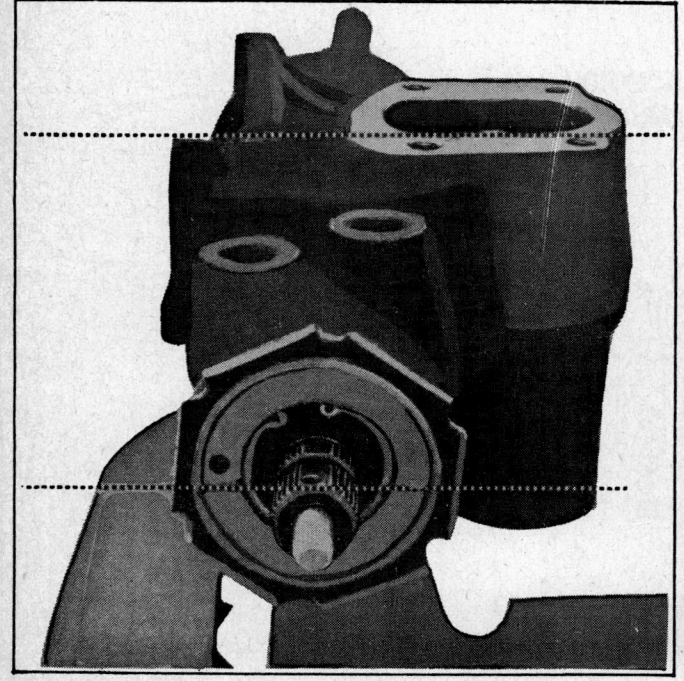

Fig. 8   Aligning stub shaft

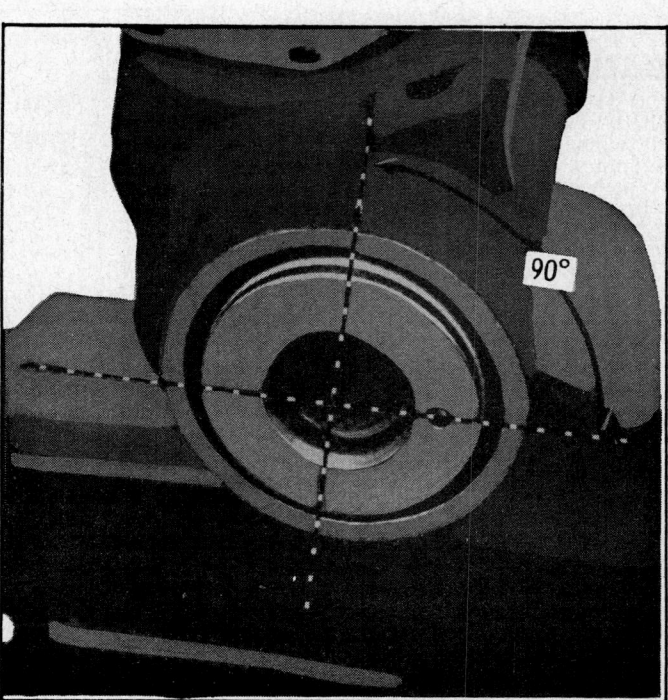

Fig. 9   Aligning rack piston

spring insulator to top of spring at least six places. Top of spring may be identified by flat coil which will allow insulator to seat squarely on top coil.

While holding spring and insulator against pilot in frame crossmember, tilt spring so it will pivot in lower control arm. Rotate spring so end of bottom coil will index with edge of hole in control arm spring seat. Coil should not cover any portion of hole.

1969 All & 1970-75 Senior Models

1. Raise car and support frame with floor stands.
2. Remove wheel and tire and disconnect stabilizer link.
3. Remove shock absorber.
4. Using a suitable compressor, compress spring slightly to permit removal of lower control arm bushing bolts. Leave ball joints connected to control arm.
5. Control arm can now be lowered at the inner end to permit removal of spring.
6. Reverse procedure to install taking care to torque the control arm bushing bolts only with the weight of the car on the wheels.

MANUAL STEERING GEAR, REPLACE

1. Remove two flex coupling flange nuts.

NOTE: On 1975 models, remove coupling shield.

2. Hoist and support car with stands under outer ends of lower control arms.
3. Remove nut and use a puller to remove pitman arm.
4. Remove gear-to frame bolts.
5. Position steering linkage and speedometer cable (if equipped) out of the way and withdraw gear assembly from under car.
6. Reverse procedure to install unit.

POWER STEERING GEAR, REPLACE

1. Remove coupling flange hub bolt.

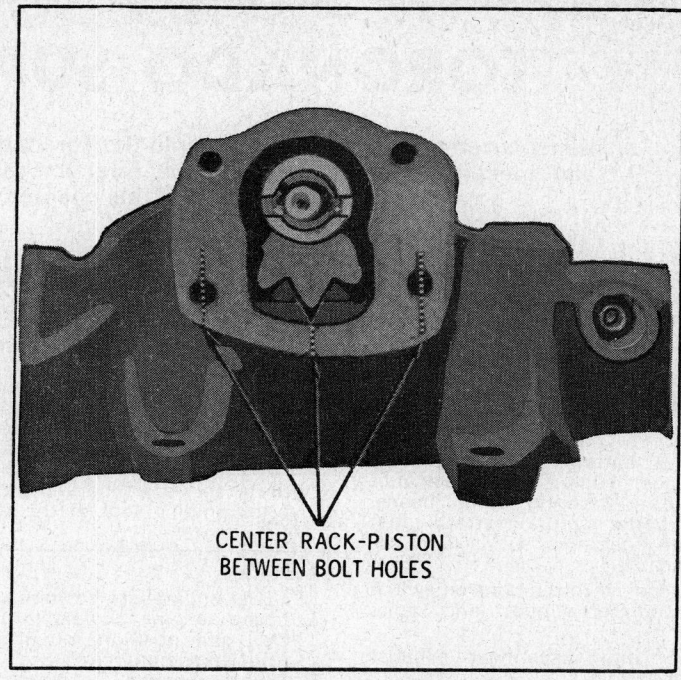

Fig. 10 Centering rack piston

CENTER RACK-PISTON BETWEEN BOLT HOLES

2. Disconnect hoses from pump and cap pump and hose fittings.
3. Remove pitman arm nut and, using a suitable puller, remove pitman arm.
4. Remove gear-to-frame bolts. Permit lower shaft to slide free of coupling flange, then remove gear with hoses attached.

1975 OMEGA POWER STEERING GEAR

Some 1975 Omega steering gears incorporate a worm gear and rack piston assembly in place of the recirculating ball nut and worm used on other models. The service procedures for this steering gear is the same as those found in the "Power Steering" chapter, Saginaw Rotary Valve section. However, assembly of the rack piston onto the worm is different since the worm may be started into the rack piston in six different positions and only one position is correct. Assemble rack piston onto the worm as follows:

1. Rotate stub shaft until stub shaft flat is parallel with side cover surface, Fig. 8.
2. Lubricate rack piston teflon seal with power steering fluid and install rack piston into housing with small index hole 90° clockwise from retainer ring knockout hole, Fig. 9.
3. With rack piston held firmly against worm gear end rotate stub shaft counter-clockwise until an audible click is heard, then rotate stub shaft clockwise, engaging rack piston to worm.
4. Center rack piston "V" groove in side cover opening between the two inner bolt holes, then install pitman shaft to align rack piston, Fig. 10. The stub shaft flat should be parallel with side cover surface.

TORONADO SUPPLEMENT

Items covered in this section apply to the Toronado only. For service procedures and specifications not covered here, refer to the conventional Oldsmobile section of this chapter.

Engine & Transmission Section

ENGINE, REPLACE

1. Drain radiator and remove hood, marking hinge as a guide for reassembly.
2. Disconnect battery, radiator hoses, cooler lines, heater hoses, vacuum hoses, power steering pump hoses, engine-to-body ground strap, fuel hose from fuel line, wiring and accelerator cable.
3. Remove coil, throttle control switch bracket, radiator support and radiator.
4. Raise car and disconnect exhaust pipes at manifold.
5. Remove starter.
6. Remove torque converter cover and three bolts securing converter to flywheel.
7. Attach a tool of the type shown in Fig. 1 to support final drive assembly.
8. Remove two bolts from right output shaft support bracket and one through bolt attaching final drive to engine block on left side.
9. Remove engine mount-to-crossmember nuts.
10. Lower car and support engine with a fixture of the type shown in Fig. 2.
11. Remove six transmission-to-engine bolts and lift engine from car.

NOTE: If car is to be moved, install a converter holding tool of the type shown in Fig. 1.

Installation

1. Lower engine into position.
2. Locate engine dowels into transmission and position mount studs into front crossmember.
3. Secure engine to transmission (6 bolts).
4. Remove engine lifting rig and raise car.
5. Secure torque converter to flywheel.
6. Install engine mount nuts.
7. Install torque converter cover and starter.
8. Install two bolts attaching right output shaft support bracket and one through bolt attaching final drive to engine block on left side.
9. Remove final drive supporting tool.
10. Connect exhaust pipes and lower car.
11. Install remaining parts removed in reverse order of removal.

ENGINE FRONT COVER

With Engine & Oil Pan Removed

1. Disconnect by-pass hose from water pump.
2. Remove cover-to-block bolts and remove cover, timing pointer and water pump.
3. Install cover and torque as shown in Fig. 2.

Oil Pan

1. Remove engine as outlined.
2. Remove dipstick, drain oil and remove mount from front cover.
3. Unfasten and remove oil pan.
4. Apply sealer to both sides of pan gaskets (cork) and install on block.
5. Install front and rear rubber seals.

NOTE: REVISE CONVERTER HOLDING TOOL J-21654. DRILL A 3/8" HOLE 15-5/8" FROM ONE EXISTING HOLE.

FINAL DRIVE SUPPORT BT-6322

Fig. 1   Final drive supporting tool

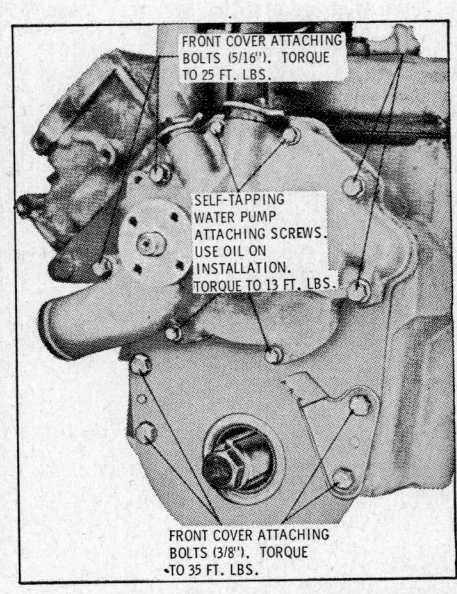

FRONT COVER ATTACHING BOLTS (5/16"). TORQUE TO 25 FT. LBS.

SELF-TAPPING WATER PUMP ATTACHING SCREWS. USE OIL ON INSTALLATION. TORQUE TO 13 FT. LBS.

FRONT COVER ATTACHING BOLTS (3/8"). TORQUE TO 35 FT. LBS.

Fig. 2   Engine front cover bolts

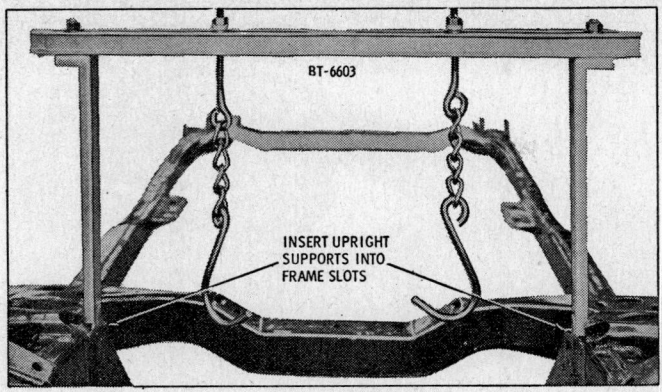

Fig. 3   Installing support bars

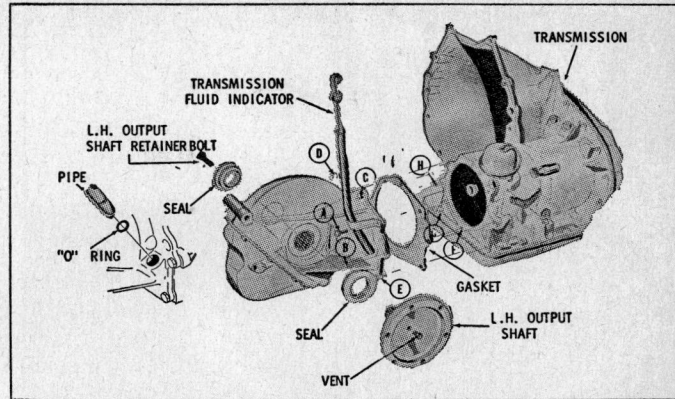

Fig. 4   Transmission attachment

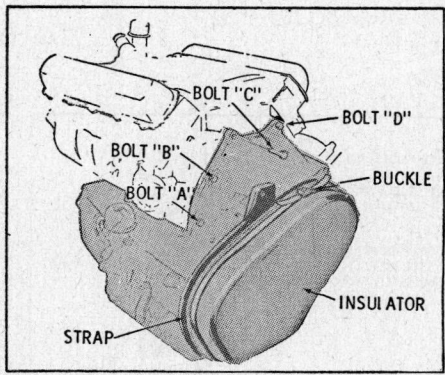

Fig. 5   Transmission-to-engine attachment

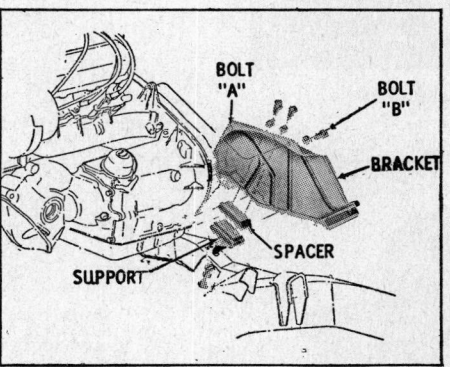

Fig. 6   Transmission-to-engine attachment

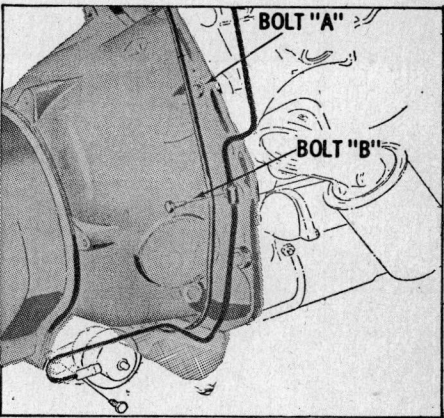

Fig. 7   Engine mount attachment

6. Wipe lube on seal area and install pan. Torque $5/16$" bolts to 15 ft-lbs and $1/4$" bolts to 10 ft-lbs.
7. Install mount on front cover and install engine.

TRANSMISSION
Less Final Drive

Removal

1. Disconnect battery, oil cooler lines at transmission and speedometer cable at governor.
2. Install engine support rig of the type shown in Fig. 3.
3. Remove nut "D" and bolts "A", "B" and "C", Fig. 4. A special wrench must be used on nut "D".
4. Remove bolts indicated in Fig. 5.
5. Remove flywheel cover plate bolts.
6. Hoist car and remove starter.
7. Rotate flywheel until all bolts are removed.
8. Disconnect vacuum modulator line and stator wiring.
9. Install transmission lift.
10. Remove shift linkage.

11. Remove bolts "E", "F" and "G" and nut "H", Fig. 4.

NOTE: When last three transmission-to-final drive bolts are removed a quantity of oil will be lost.

12. Remove bolts indicated in Fig. 6.
13. Remove bolts indicated in Fig. 7. Then remove the four bracket-to-engine mount bolts.
14. Slide transmission rearward and down. Engine mount bracket will follow transmission down. Install converter holding tool, Fig. 1.
15. After transmission is removed from car, the link belt assembly or cover insulator can be replaced.

Link Belt or Sprockets

Removal

1. Remove sprocket housing cover attaching bolts and cover.
2. Remove sprocket bearing retaining snap rings from retaining grooves in support housing located under drive and driven sprockets, Fig. 8.

NOTE: Do not remove the snap rings from beneath the sprockets, leave

them in a loose position between the sprockets and the bearing assemblies.

3. Remove drive and driven sprockets, link belt, bearings and shafts simultaneously by alternately pulling upwards and driven support housing, Fig. 9.

NOTE: If sprockets and link belt are difficult to remove, place a small piece of masonite, or similar material between the sprocket and a short pry bar. Alternately pry upward under each sprocket. Do not pry on links or aluminum case, Fig. 10.

4. Remove link belt from drive and driven sprockets.

Installation

1. Place link belt around the drive and driven sprockets so that the links engage the teeth of the sprockets, colored guide link which has etched numerals facing link cover.
2. Simultaneously place link belt, drive and driven sprockets into support housing, Fig. 8. Using a plastic mallet, gently seat the sprocket bearing assemblies into the

Fig. 8   Removing or installing retaining rings

DRIVEN SPROCKET

DRIVE SPROCKET

LINK BELT

Fig. 9   Removing or installing sprockets and link assembly

1/8 INCH FIBER BOARD

Fig. 10   Removing tight sprockets

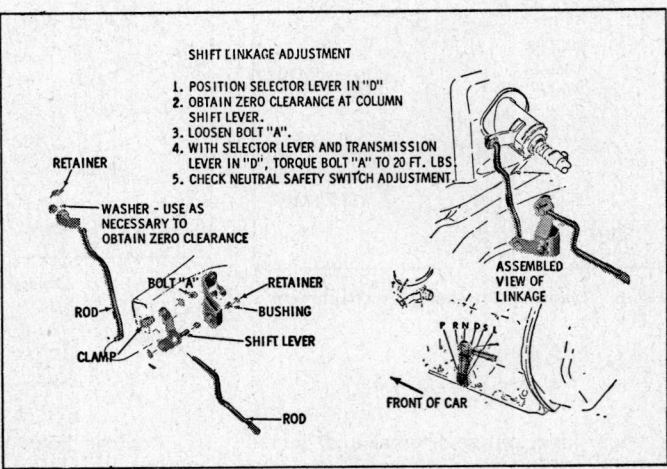

SHIFT LINKAGE ADJUSTMENT

1. POSITION SELECTOR LEVER IN "D"
2. OBTAIN ZERO CLEARANCE AT COLUMN SHIFT LEVER.
3. LOOSEN BOLT "A".
4. WITH SELECTOR LEVER AND TRANSMISSION LEVER IN "D", TORQUE BOLT "A" TO 20 FT. LBS.
5. CHECK NEUTRAL SAFETY SWITCH ADJUSTMENT.

RETAINER

WASHER - USE AS NECESSARY TO OBTAIN ZERO CLEARANCE

ROD

CLAMP

BOLT "A"

RETAINER

BUSHING

SHIFT LEVER

ROD

ASSEMBLED VIEW OF LINKAGE

P R N D S L

FRONT OF CAR

Fig. 11   Shift linkage adjustment

support housings.

4. Install sprocket assembly to support housing snap rings, Fig. 9.

5. Install new case to cover and plate assembly sprocket housing gasket.

NOTE: Important: One sprocket cover housing attaching bolt is ¼ inch longer. This bolt must be installed in the tapped hole located directly over

the cooler fittings on the transmission case.

6. Install sprocket housing cover and plate assembly and eighteen attaching bolts. Torque bolts to 8 ft. lbs.

Installation of Transmission

When installing the transmission, the motor mount bracket must be positioned loosely on the link assembly cover until the transmission is in place; then reverse

removal procedure. Torque bolts to ft-lbs as follows:

Engine-to-converter housing 30
Engine bracket-to-transmission 55
Engine bracket-to-rubber mount 55
Oil cooler lines to transmission—
   1969-72 30
   1974-75 20
Final drive-to-transmission 25
Converter-to-flywheel 35
Adjust shift linkage as directed in Fig. 11.

Drive Axles & Final Drive Section

DRIVE AXLES
Description

Drive axles are a complete flexible assembly and consist of an axle shaft and an inner and outer constant velocity joint, Fig. 1. The right axle shaft has a torsional damper mounted in the center. The inner constant velocity joint has complete flexibility plus inward and outward movement. The outer constant velocity joint has complete flexibility only.

NOTE: Whenever any operations call for disconnecting, connecting, removal or installation of the drive axles, care must be used to prevent damage to constant velocity joint seals. Seals may be wrapped with floor mat rubber or old inner tube, etc. Make sure rubber protective covers that are used are removed before car is started or driven.

DRIVE AXLE, REPLACE
Right Side Unit
Removal
1. Hoist car under lower control arms.
2. Remove axle nut, Fig. 3.
3. Remove oil filter element.
4. Remove inner constant velocity (C.V.) joint attaching bolts.
5. Push inner C.V. joint outward enough to disengage from R.H. final drive output shaft and move rearward.
6. Remove R.H. output shaft bracket bolts to engine and final drive.
7. Remove R.H. final drive output shaft.
8. Remove drive axle assembly.

NOTE: Care must be used to see that C.V. joints do not turn to full extremes and that seals are not damaged against shock absorber or stabilizer bar.

Installation
1. Place R.H. drive axle into lower control arm and enter outer race splines into knuckle.
2. Lubricate final drive output shaft seal with approved seal grease.
3. Install R.H. output shaft into final drive and attach support bolts to engine and brace. Torque to 50 ft-lbs.
4. Move R.H. drive axle toward front of car and align with R.H. output shaft. Install attaching bolts and torque to 65 ft-lbs.
5. Install oil filter element.
6. Install washer and nut on drive axle. Torque to 60 ft-lbs and insert cotter pin.

Left Side Unit
Removal
1. Hoist car under lower control arms.
2. Remove wheel and drum.

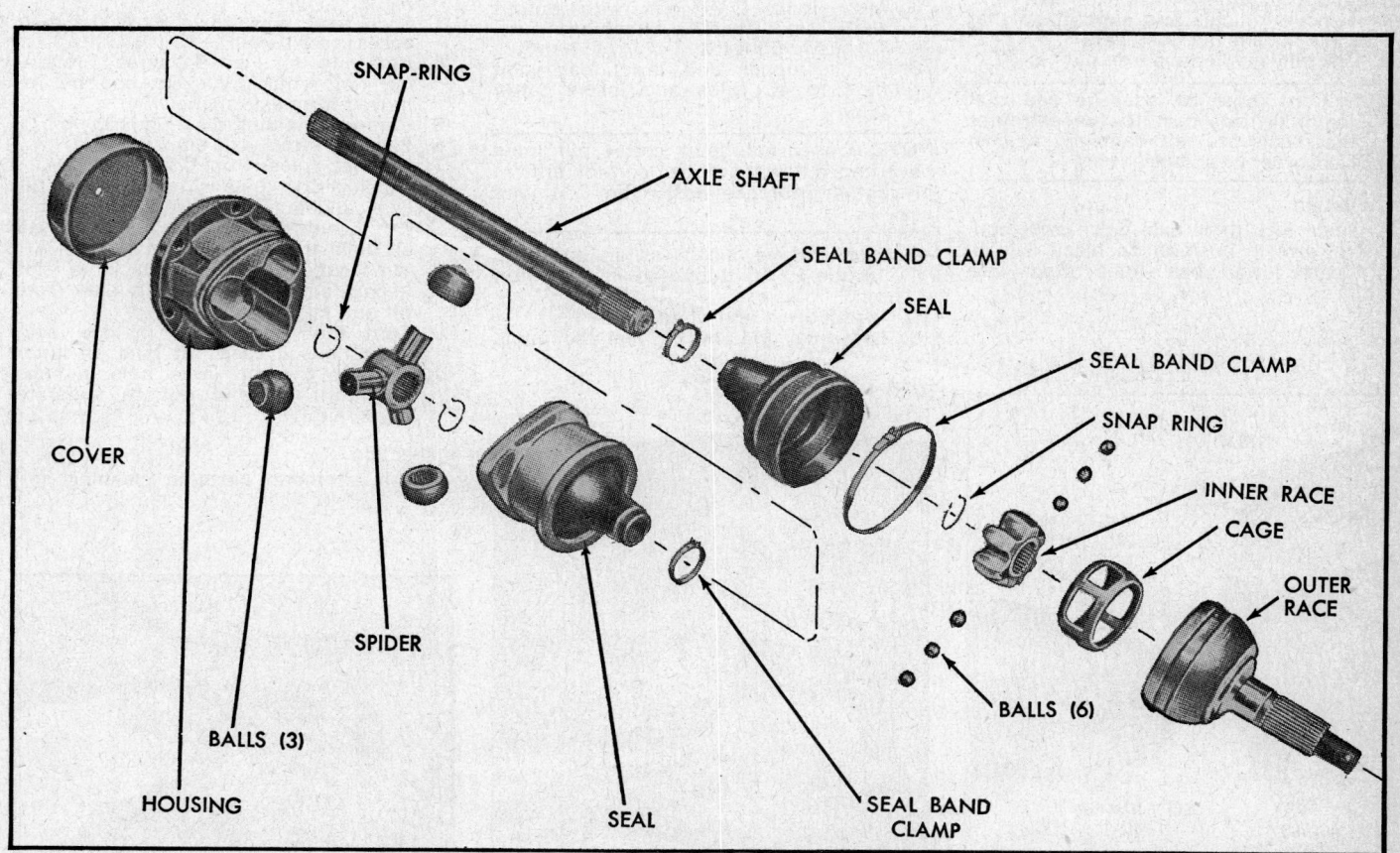

Fig. 1 Drive axle assembly. 1969-75

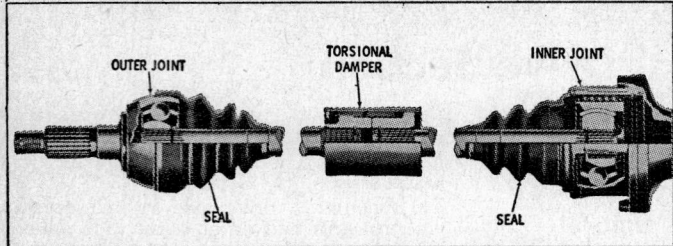

Fig. 2   Drive axle disassembled (right side)

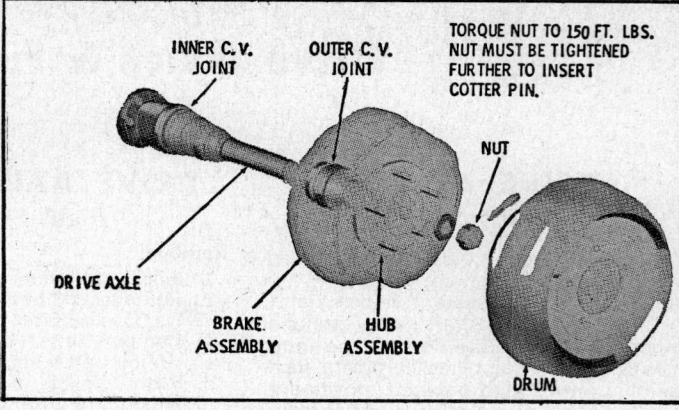

Fig. 3   Drive axle installed

3. Remove drive axle nut.
4. Position access slot in hub so that each attaching bolt (4) can be removed, Fig. 4. It will be necessary to push aside adjuster lever to remove one of the bolts.
5. Remove hub assembly, Fig. 4. It will be neceseary to push aside adjuster lever for clearance.
6. Remove tie-rod end nut.
7. Using a hammer and brass drift, drive on knuckle until tie-rod end stud is free.
8. Remove bolts from drive axle and L.H. output shaft, Fig. 5.
9. Remove upper control arm ball joint nut. Using hammer and brass drift, drive on knuckle until upper ball joint stud is free, Fig. 6.
10. Remove ball joint, Fig. 7, being careful not to damage drive axle seal.
11. Remove knuckle and support so that brake hose is not damaged.
12. Carefully guide drive axle out.

NOTE: Care must be used to see that C.V. joints do not turn to full extremes and that seals are not damaged against shock absorber or stabilizer bar.

Installation

1. Guide L.H. drive axle onto lower control arm in position on block, Fig. 5.
2. Insert lower ball joint stud into knuckle and attach nut (do not tighten).
3. Center L.H. drive axle in opening of knuckle and insert upper ball joint stud.
4. Place brake hose clip over upper ball joint stud and install nut (do not tighten).
5. Insert tie-rod end stud into knuckle and attach nut. Torque to 45 ft-lbs and insert cotter pin.
6. Lubricate hub bearing OD with E.P. grease and install. Torque to 65 ft-lbs.
7. Align inner C.V. joint with output shaft and install attaching nuts. Torque to 65 ft-lbs.
8. Torque upper and lower ball joint nuts to 40 ft-lbs and insert cotter pins.

NOTE: Upper ball joint cotter pin must be crimped toward upper control arm to prevent interference with outer C.V. joint seal.

9. Install drive axle washer and nut. Torque to 60 ft-lbs and install cotter pin.
10. Install drum and wheel.
11. Lower car and check wheel alignment.

C.V. JOINT SERVICE

NOTE: The C.V. joints are to be replaced as a unit and are only disassembled for repacking and replacement of seals.

Outer C.V. Joint 1969-75

Disassemble

1. Insert axle in vise, clamping on mid-portion only.
2. Remove inner and outer seal clamps, Fig. 8.
3. Slide seal down axle shaft to gain access to C.V. joint.
4. Referring to Fig. 9, spread retaining ring until C.V. joint can be removed from axle spline.
5. Remove retaining ring, Fig. 10.
6. Slide seal from axle shaft.
7. Remove grease from C.V. joint.
8. Holding C.V. joint with one hand, tilt cage and inner race so that one ball can be removed. Continue until all six balls are removed, Fig. 11.
9. Turn cage 90° and with large slot in cage aligned with land in inner race, lift out, Fig. 12.
10. Turn inner race 90° in line with large hole in case, lift land on inner race up through large hole in cage and turn up and out to separate parts, Fig. 13.

Inspection

Wash all metal parts in cleaning sol-

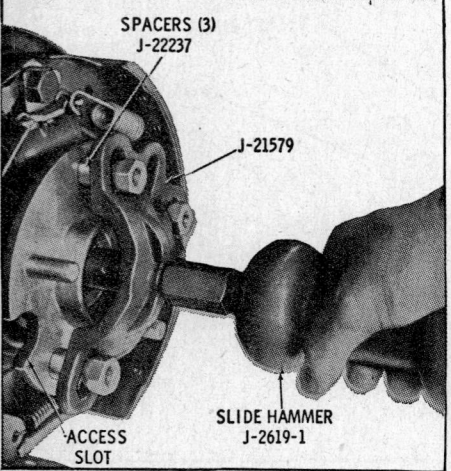

Fig. 4   Removing hub

Fig. 5   Installing support block

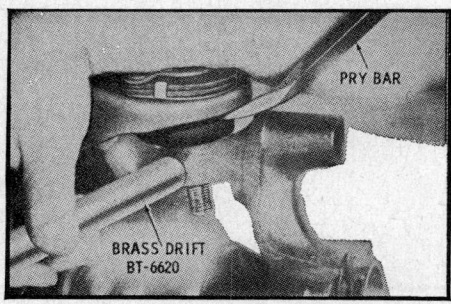

Fig. 6   Removing upper ball joint

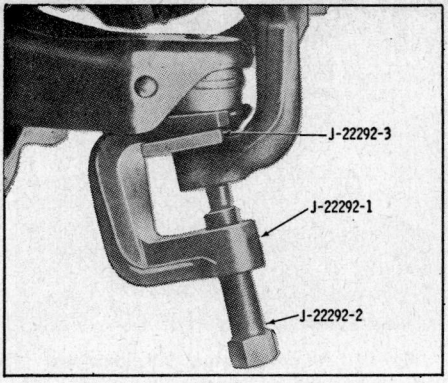

Fig. 7   Removing lower ball joint

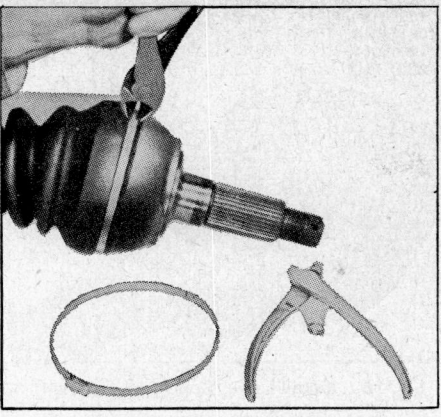

Fig. 8   Cutting seal clip

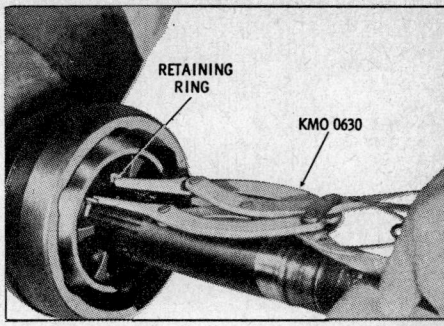

Fig. 9   Removing retaining ring

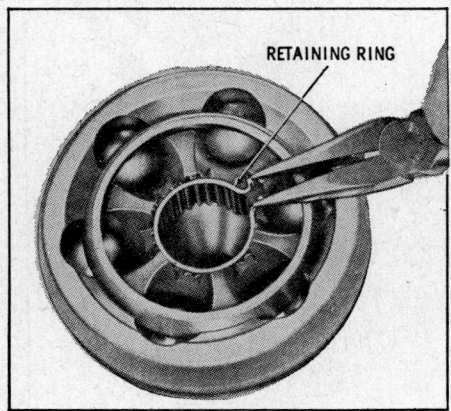

Fig. 10   Removing or installing retaining ring

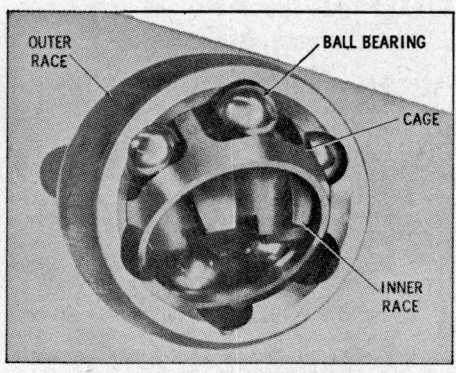

Fig. 11   Removing balls from outer race

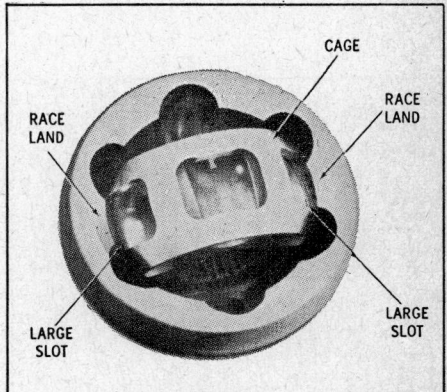

Fig. 12   Positioning cage for removal

vent and dry with compressed air. Rubber seal should be replaced whenever joint is disassembled for service. Inspect all metal parts for nicks, cracks, breaks or scores. If any defects are found the joint assembly will have to be replaced as a unit.

Reassemble

1. Insert land of inner race into large hole in cage and pivot to install in cage, Fig. 13.
2. Align inner race as shown in Fig. 12 and pivot inner race 90° to align in outer race as shown in Fig. 14.
3. Insert balls one at a time until all six are installed. Inner race and cage will have to be tilted as shown in Fig. 14 so that each ball can be inserted.
4. Pack joint full of approved lubricant. Pack inside of seal with approved lubricant until folds of seal are full.
5. Place small keystone clamp on axle shaft.
6. Install seal on axle shaft.
7. Install retaining ring into inner race, Fig. 10.
8. Insert axle shaft into splines of

outer C.V. joint until retaining ring secures shaft.
9. Position seal in slot of outer race.
10. Install large keystone clamp over seal and secure, Fig. 15. Then install small keystone clamp over seal and secure, Fig. 16.

Inner C.V. Joint 1969-75

1. Clamp mid portion of axle shaft in vise and remove small seal clamp.
2. Remove large end of seal from C.V. joint by prying out peened spots and driving off with hammer and chisel, Fig. 17.
3. Carefully slide seal down axle shaft.
4. Carefully lift housing from spider assembly and remove "O" ring from housing outer surface.

NOTE: Place a rubber band over ends of spider to retain the three balls and needle bearings.

5. Remove retaining ring from end of axle.
6. Remove spider assembly from axle.
7. Remove inner retaining ring, seal and cover, Fig. 18.
8. Remove balls from spider, being care-

ful not to lose any needles.
9. Reverse procedure to assemble, being sure to stake housing in six evenly spaced places after reassembly.

FINAL DRIVE, 1969-75

Description, Fig. 19

The final drive assembly, mounted and splined directly to the automatic transmission, consists of a pinion drive gear, a ring gear (bolted to the case), case assembly with two side gears and two pinion gears that are retained to the case with a pinion shaft. A lock pin is used instead of a bolt to lock the pinion shaft to the case. There are thrust washers used behind the side gears and shims behind the pinion gears the same as in a conventional differential. The left side gear is different than the right side gear in that it has a threaded retainer plate to which the left output shaft bolts. The two side bearings are the same and the preload shims are identical for the right and left side. The carrier is identical in external appearance and mounts to the transmission the same as in the past models.

The output shafts remain identical in external appearance as in the past. The left output shaft has the retainer bolt going through the shaft to the side gear.

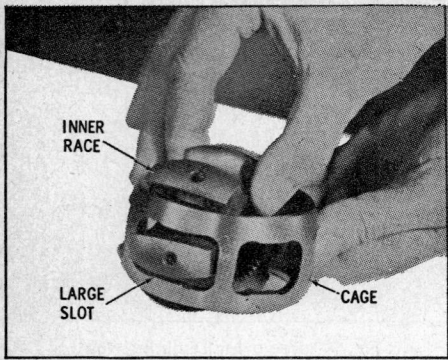

Fig. 13   Removing inner race from ball cage

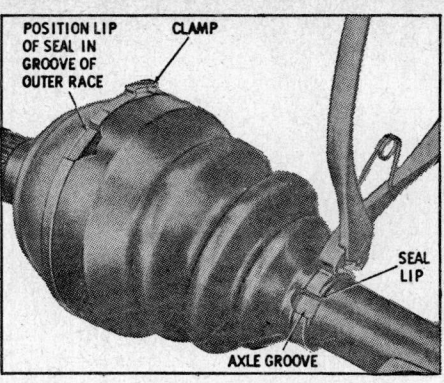

Fig. 16   Installing keystone clamp (small)

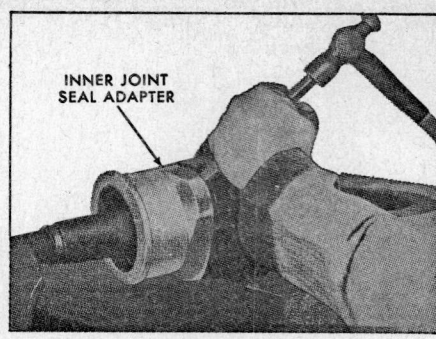

Fig. 17   Removing inner C.V. joint seal

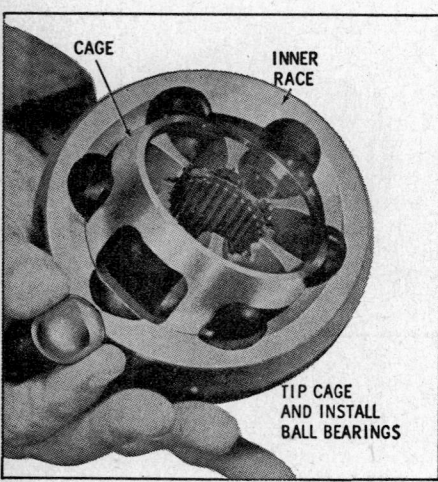

Fig. 14   Installing balls in outer race

OUTPUT SHAFT & SEALS
R.H. Shaft, Bearing & Seal

Removal

1. Disconnect battery. Hoist car.
2. Remove engine oil filter element.
3. Disconnect R.H. drive axle.
4. Disconnect support from engine and brace.
5. Remove output shaft assembly.

Installation Figs. 21 and 22

1. If removed, assemble bearing and related parts. Position assembly in a press and install bearing until seated against shoulder on shaft. Pack area between bearing and retainer with wheel bearing grease, then install slinger. Install seal if removed.
2. Install remaining parts removed in reverse order of removal.

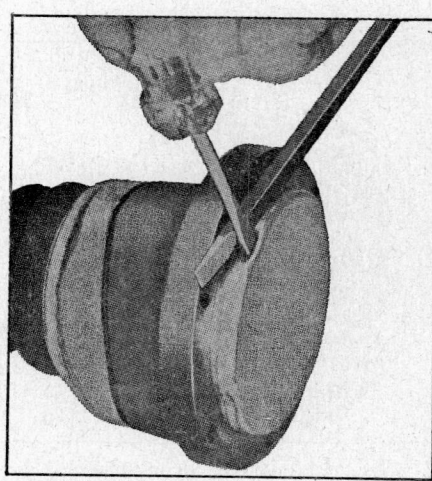

Fig. 18   Removing housing cover

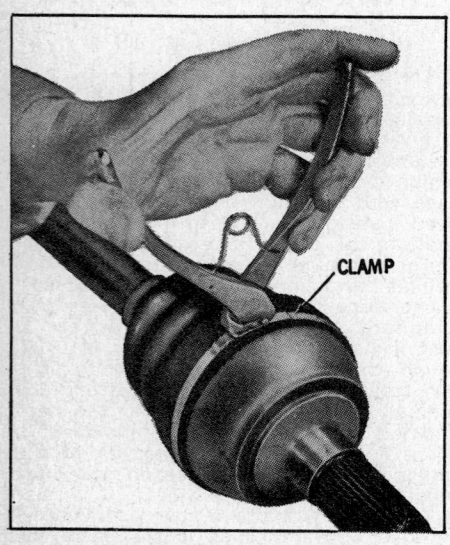

Fig. 15   Installing keystone clamp (large)

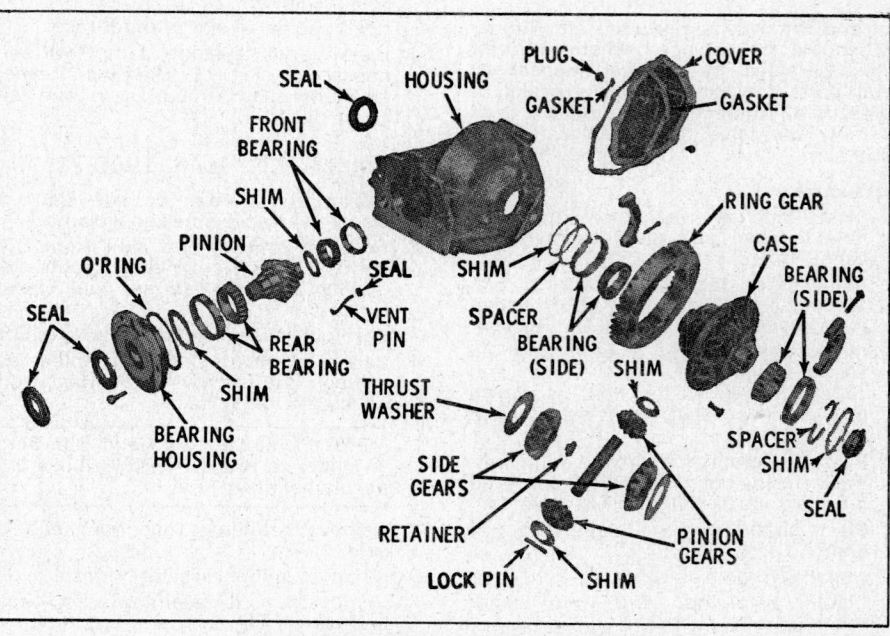

Fig. 19   Final drive disassembled. 1969-75

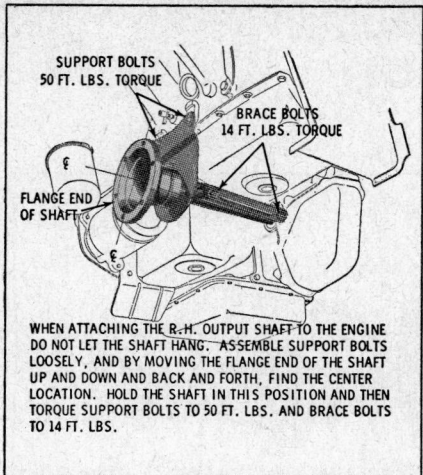

WHEN ATTACHING THE R.H. OUTPUT SHAFT TO THE ENGINE DO NOT LET THE SHAFT HANG. ASSEMBLE SUPPORT BOLTS LOOSELY, AND BY MOVING THE FLANGE END OF THE SHAFT UP AND DOWN AND BACK AND FORTH, FIND THE CENTER LOCATION. HOLD THE SHAFT IN THIS POSITION AND THEN TORQUE SUPPORT BOLTS TO 50 FT. LBS. AND BRACE BOLTS TO 14 FT. LBS.

Fig. 21 Aligning right
output shaft

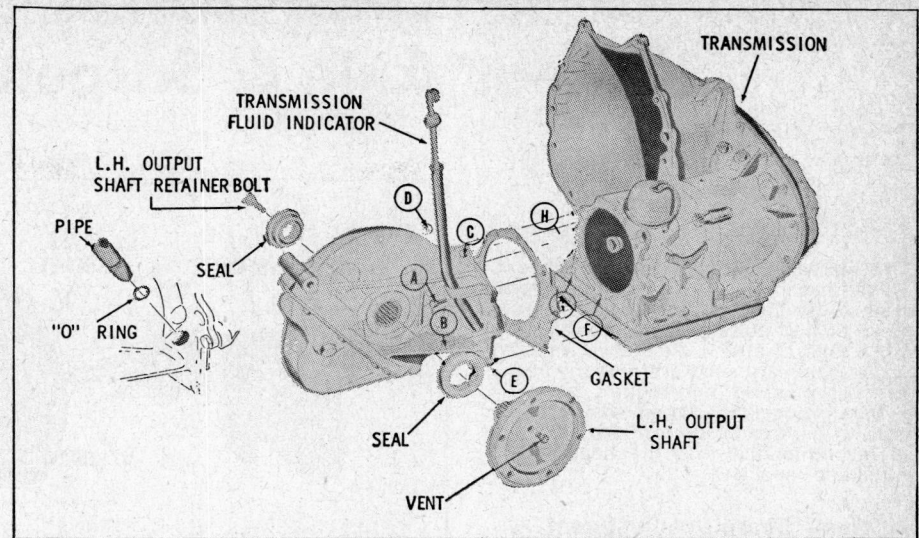

Fig. 23 Final drive attachment. 1969-75

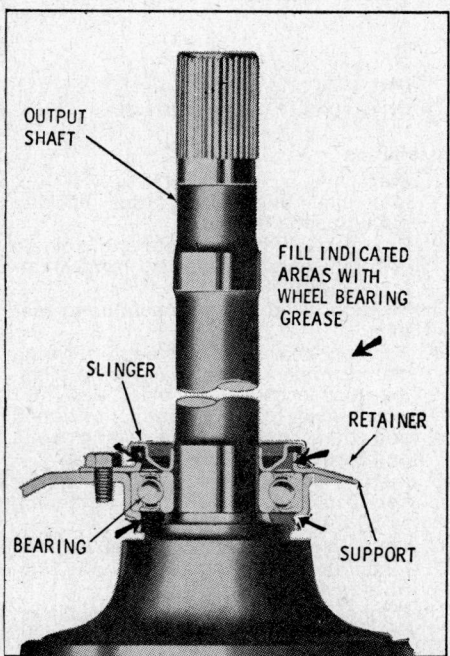

Fig. 22 Output shaft assembled
(right side)

L.H. Output Shaft, Bearing & Seal

NOTE: The L.H. output shaft can normally be removed only after removing the final drive assembly from the car. However, if the L.H. drive axle has been removed for any reason, the output shaft and seal can be removed as follows:

1. Remove R.H. output shaft as outlined above.
2. Remove L.H. output shaft retaining bolt and remove shaft.
3. Apply approved lubricant to the seal, then insert output shaft into final drive, indexing splines of shaft with splines on final drive.
4. Install and torque L.H. output shaft retaining bolt to 45 ft-lbs.
5. Install R.H. output shaft in reverse order of removal.

FINAL DRIVE, REPLACE

1. Disconnect battery and raise hood.
2. Remove bolts "A", "B", "C" and nut "D", Fig. 23. Nut "D" must be removed with a special wrench. It may be necessary to remove transmission filler tube to obtain clearance.
3. Hoist car. If a two-post lift is used the car must be supported with floor stands at the front frame rails and the front post lowered.
4. Disconnect both drive axles from output shafts.
5. Remove engine oil filter element.
6. Disconnect brace from final drive, then disconnect R.H. output shaft from engine. Remove output shaft from final drive.
7. Referring to Fig. 24, remove bolt "X" and loosen bolts "Y" and "Z".
8. Remove final drive cover and allow lubricant to drain.
9. Position transmission lift with

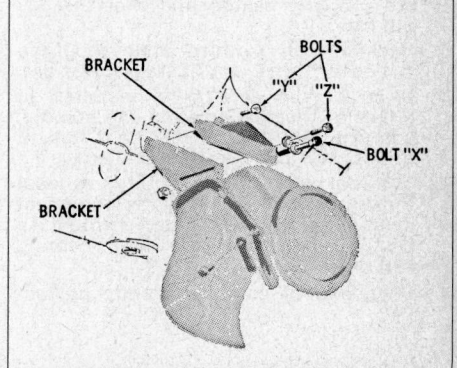

Fig. 24 Disconnecting final
drive from engine

adapter for final drive. Install an anchor bolt through final drive housing and lift pad.
10. Referring to Fig. 23, remove bolts "E", "F", "G" and nut "H".
11. Move transmission lift toward front of car to disengage final drive splines from transmission. Provide a container to catch transmission fluid.
12. Lower transmission lift and remove final drive from lift.
13. Using a $^9/_{16}$" socket, remove L.H. output shaft retaining bolt and pull shaft from final drive.
14. Reverse procedure to install.

Rear Axle & Suspension

REAR AXLE

The rear axle used on these models is a welded assembly of the beam type with a drop center. The rear wheel spindles are a press fit and bolted to the rear axle assembly, Figs. 1 and 2. As shown, tapered roller bearings are used in the rear wheels. These bearings do not require regularly scheduled repacking. When major brake service work is to be performed, however, it is recommended that the bearings be cleaned and repacked.

Wheel Bearing Adjustment

Adjustment of the rear wheel bearings should be made while revolving the wheel at least three times the speed of the nut rotation when taking torque readings.

1. Check to make sure that hub is completely seated on wheel spindle.
2. While rotating wheel, tighten spindle nut to 30 ft-lbs. Make certain all parts are properly seated and that threads are free.
3. Back nut off ½ turn, then retighten nut to 2 ft. lbs. and install cotter pin.
4. If cotter pin cannot be installed in either of the two holes in the spindle, with the nut at 2 ft. lbs., back nut off until cotter pin can be installed.
5. The rear hub must be rotated at least three revolutions during tightening of spindle nut. The final adjustment to be 2 ft. lbs. to provide .004" bearing end play.
6. Peen end of cotter pin snug against

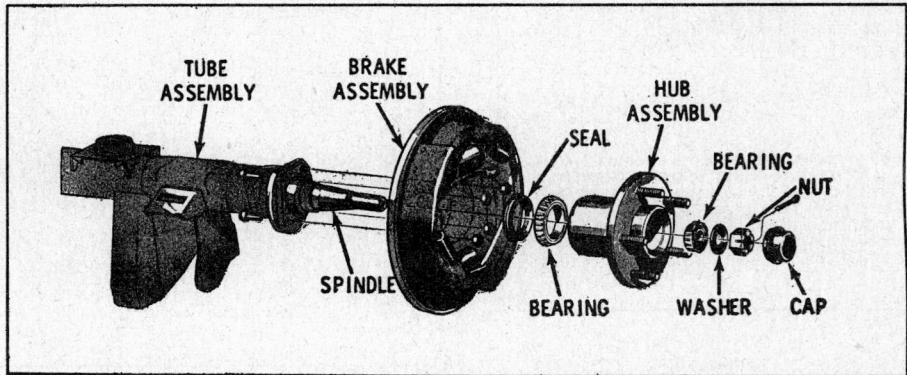

Fig. 1   Rear wheel hub & spindle less True-Track brake

side of nut. If it can be moved with a finger, vibration may cause it to wear and break.

Wheel Spindle, Replace

1. Raise and support rear of car and remove hub.
2. Disconnect brake line at wheel cylinder.
3. Unfasten and remove brake backing plate and position out of the way.
4. Place jack under rear axle.
5. Remove four nuts from center spring clamp and lower rear axle until spindle is accessible, Figs. 1 and 2.
6. Remove lower spring insulator from

rear axle.
7. Drive spindle out of rear axle.

Installation

1. Start new spindle, with keyway up, into axle and install four backing plate to spindle nuts.
2. Progressively tighten nuts until spindle is fully seated and then remove attaching nuts and bolts.
3. Position lower spring insulator to rear axle.
4. Position rear axle to center spring clamp, making sure that spring aligning pin locates into axle. See that lower insulator is properly positioned and that center spring clamp bolts engage rear axle mounting holes.
5. Install four nuts securing center spring clamp to rear axle, tightening to 30 ft-lbs.
6. Install new gasket on wheel spindle.
7. Install brake backing plate and tighten nuts to 40 ft-lbs.
8. Connect brake line to wheel cylinder, tightening fitting to 14 ft-lbs.
9. Install rear hub.

Rear Axle, Replace

1. Raise and support rear of car with jack stands at rear frame pads ahead of rear wheel opening.
2. Remove rear wheels and hubs.
3. Disconnect brake lines at wheel cylinders.
4. Disconnect parking brake cable at equalizer.
5. Disconnect rubber brake hose at underbody connector.
6. Disconnect overtravel lever link from bracket on rear axle.
7. Remove spring guides retaining parking brake cable to center spring clamp.
8. If rear axle is being replaced, remove brake backing plates.
9. Supporting rear axle at center with a

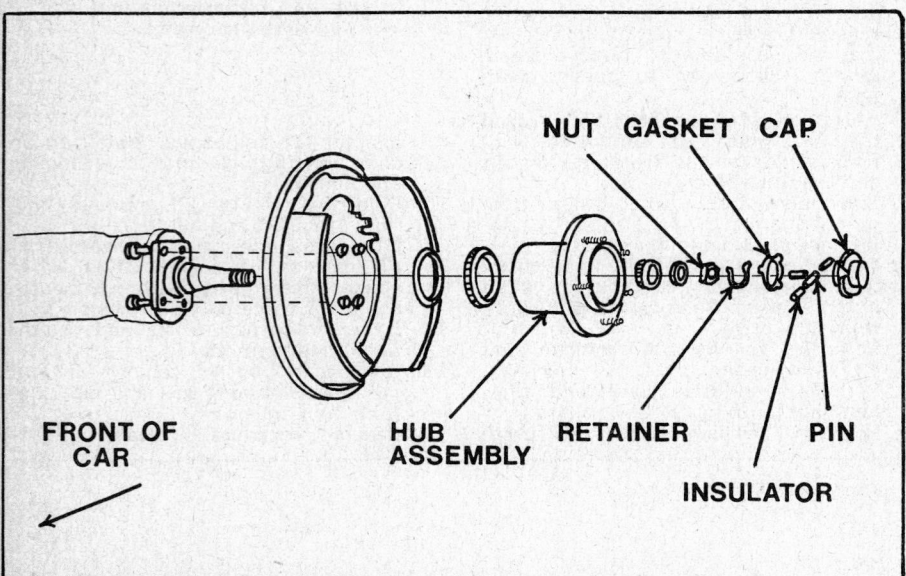

Fig. 2   Rear wheel hub & spindle with True-Track brake

Fig. 3   Rear suspension. 1969-70

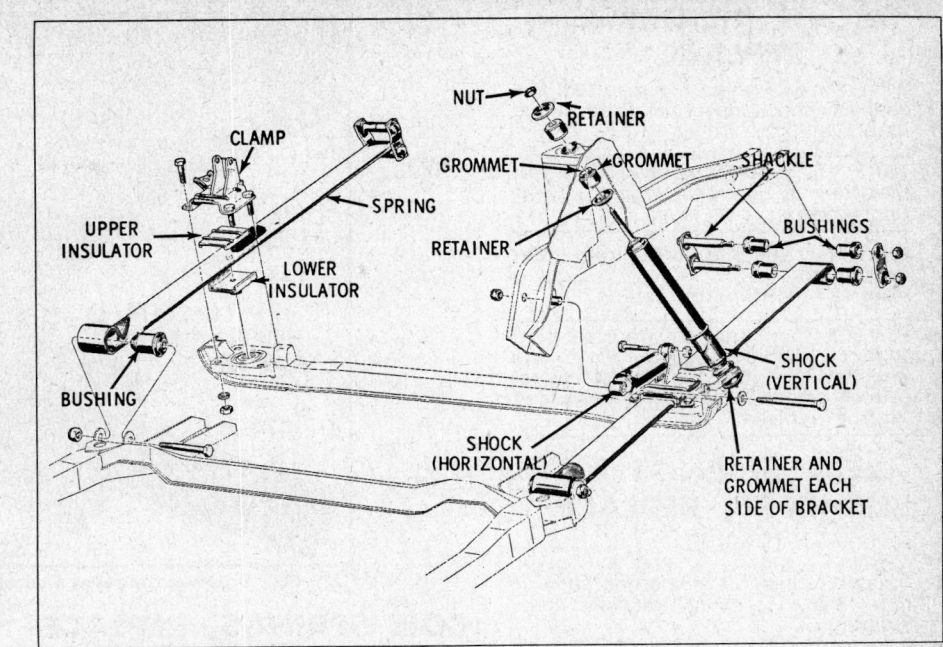

jack, remove eight nuts (4 each side) from center spring clamp assemblies.

10. Lower rear axle with jack and remove from car.

11. Remove lower spring insulators from rear axle.

12. If rear axle is being replaced, remove bolt securing brake line junction fitting to axle. Remove brake line, overtravel lever link bracket, and drive spindles from axle.

13. Reverse procedure to install.

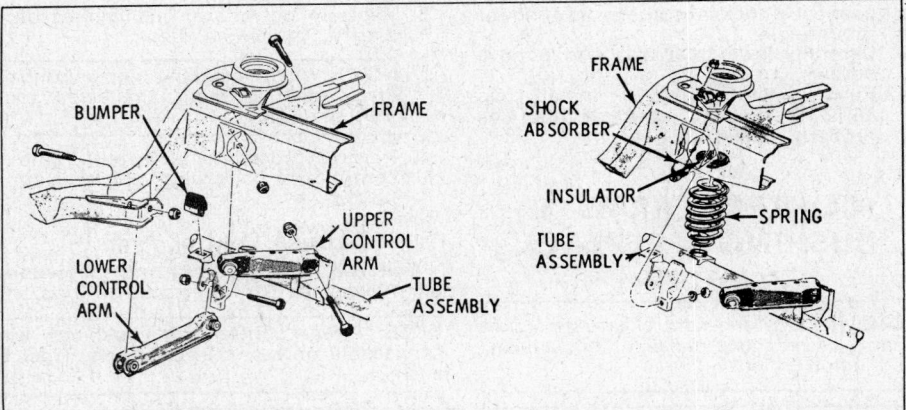

Fig. 4   Rear suspension. 1971-74

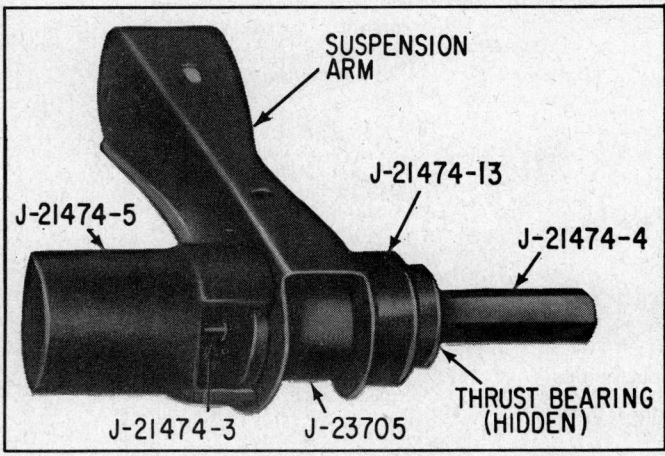

Fig. 5   All front bushings & lower control arm rear bushing removal. 1971 models

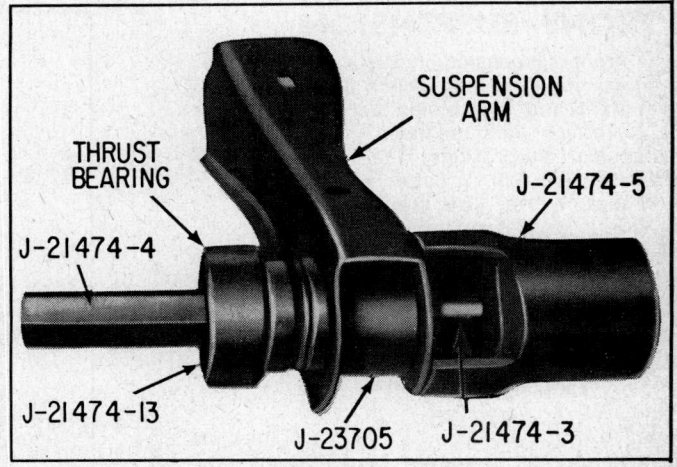

Fig. 6   All front bushings & lower control arm rear bushing installation. 1971 models

SHOCK ABSORBER, REPLACE

1. With rear axle properly supported, disconnect shock absorber from upper mounting.

   NOTE: On 1969-70 models, the upper mounting is accessible from trunk by removing an access plug.

2. Disconnect shock absorber from lower mounting.
3. Reverse procedure to install.

NOTE: 1969-70 models incorporate horizontal shock absorbers in addition to the conventional type, Fig. 3. To replace, remove front and rear attaching bolts and lift unit from vehicle.

LEAF SPRINGS & BUSHINGS, REPLACE
1969-70

1. Support vehicle at frame and support rear axle, relieving tension from spring.
2. Remove nut from spring front mounting bolt.
3. Remove rear shackle nuts and shackle outer link.
4. Remove spring center clamp attaching bolts and lift clamp assembly up, shock absorber will hold clamp in position.
5. Disconnect resonator bracket from frame and allow resonator to hang free.
6. Lower rear axle until it clears spring, support spring, remove rear shackle bolts and spring front mounting bolt.
7. Replace spring eye bushing or rear shackle bushings as necessary. To replace eye bushing, wedge a small screwdriver or chisel between edge of spring and end of eye, expanding the eye. Drive bushing from eye with a hammer, with eye still expanded drive new bushing into eye.
8. Reverse procedure to install.

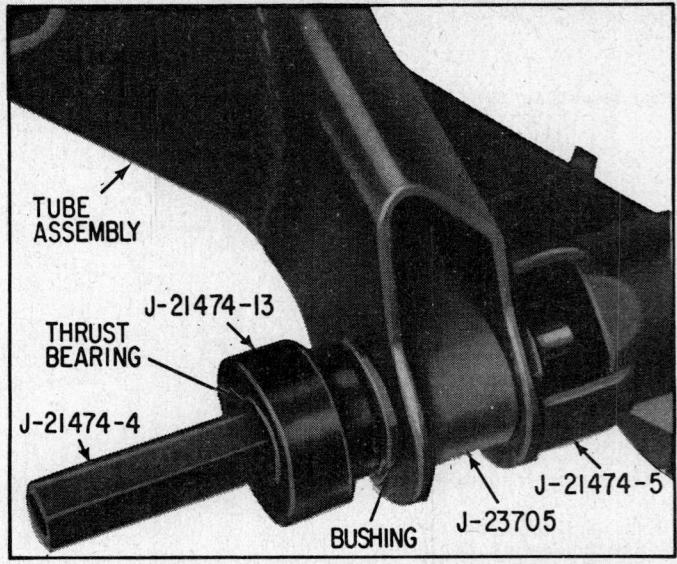

Fig. 7 Upper control arm bushing removal. 1971-75 models

COIL SPRINGS, REPLACE
1971-75

1. Support vehicle at frame.
2. With rear axle properly supported, disconnect shock absorbers from lower mountings.
3. Carefully lower rear axle and remove springs.
4. Reverse procedure to install. On 1972-73 models, springs must be properly indexed, Fig. 4.

CONTROL ARMS & BUSHINGS, REPLACE
1971-75

NOTE: Replace one control arm at a time to prevent rear axle misalignment, making installation difficult.

Upper Control Arms

1. Support vehicle at frame and rear axle.
2. Remove control arm front and rear mounting bolts.
3. Replace control arm bushings as necessary, Figs. 5, 6 and 7.

   NOTE: When installing upper control arm rear bushing, reverse tool # J-21474-13.

4. Reverse procedure to install. Tighten control arm bolts with vehicle at curb height.

Lower Control Arms

Follow "Upper Control Arms" procedure for replacement of lower control arms.

NOTE: Lower control arm bushings are serviceable only on 1971 models, Figs. 5 and 6.

Front Suspension & Steering Section

FRONT SUSPENSION

The front suspension consists of control arms, stabilizer bar, shock absorbers and a right and left torsion bar, Figs. 1 and 2. Torsion bars are used instead of conventional coil springs. The front end of the torsion bar is attached to the lower control arm. The rear of the torsion bar is mounted into an adjustable arm at the torsion bar cross member. The riding height of the car is controlled by this adjustment.

LUBRICATION
1971-75

Lubrication is required every four months or 6,000 miles with an approved lubricant.

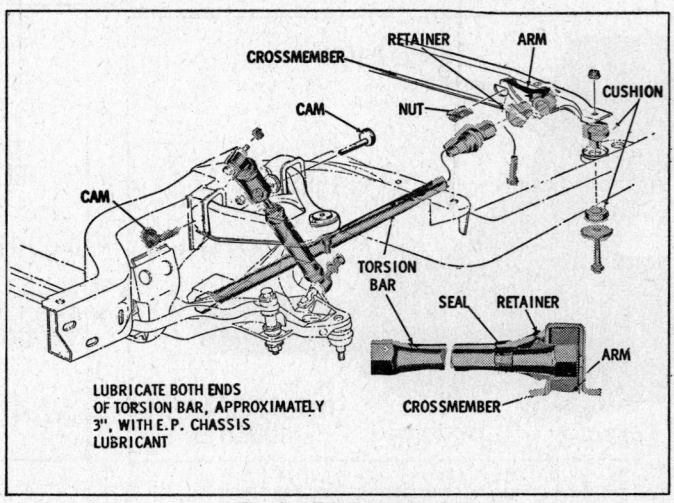

Fig. 1 Front suspension

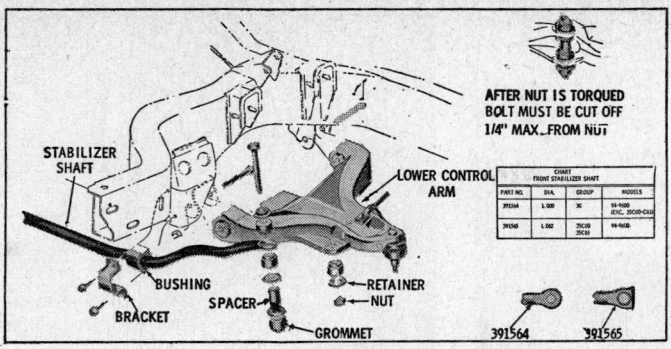

Fig. 2   Front suspension

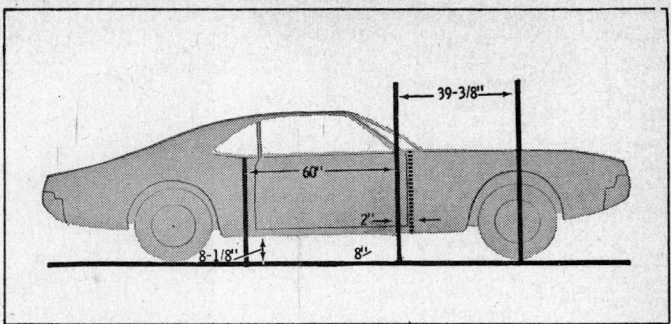

Fig. 3   Riding heights

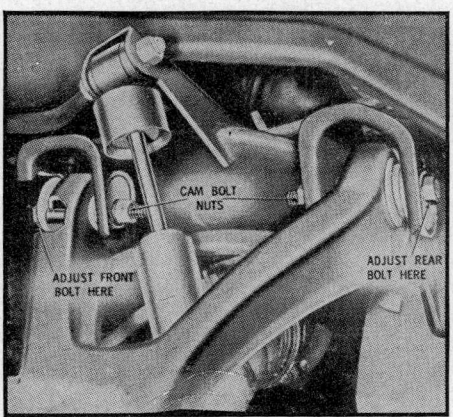

Fig. 4   Front wheel alignment cams

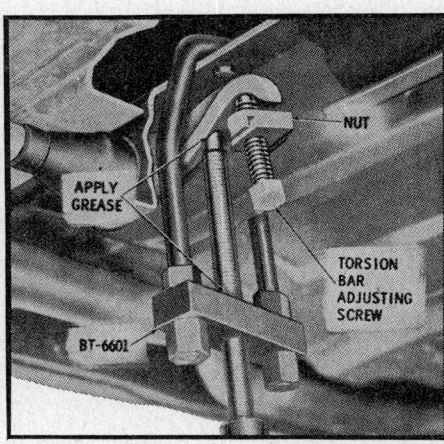

Fig. 5   Removing torsion bar

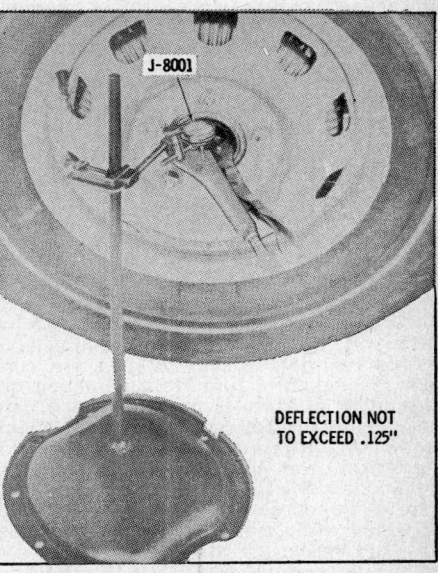

Fig. 6   Ball joint vertical check

1969-70

The steering linkage should be lubricated every 12 months or 12,000 miles, whichever occurs first, using a commercially available multi-purpose grease.

Ball joints should be lubricated and inspected at 36,000 miles (no time limit) and every 12 months or 12,000 miles thereafter, using a commercially available multi-purpose lubricant.

WHEEL ALIGNMENT

NOTE: When checking wheel alignment the car must be on a level surface, gas tank full or a compensating weight added, front seat all the way to the rear, and tires (front and rear) inflated to 24 psi. All doors must be closed and no passengers or additional weight should be in the car or trunk.

1. Check rocker panel to ground dimensions, Fig. 3. Front to rear must be within 1″ and side-to-side within ⅝″ of the dimensions shown.
2. Raise car and check wheel runout. Set in center of runout and lower car.
3. Loosen nuts on inboard side of upper control arm cam bolts, Fig. 4.
4. Check camber and adjust if necessary with the rear cam bolt. Camber reading on the right and left wheel should be within ½° of each other.

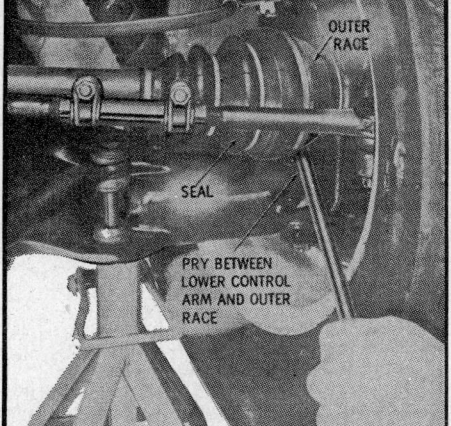

Fig. 7   Pry bar installation

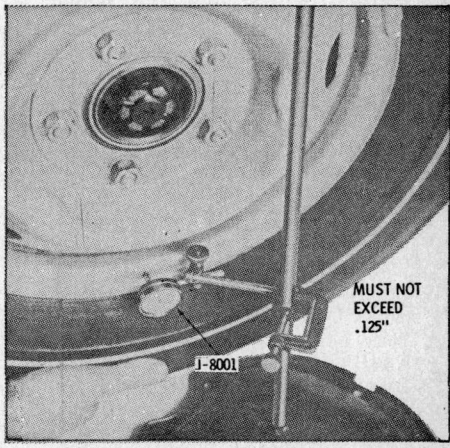

Fig. 8   Ball joint horizontal check

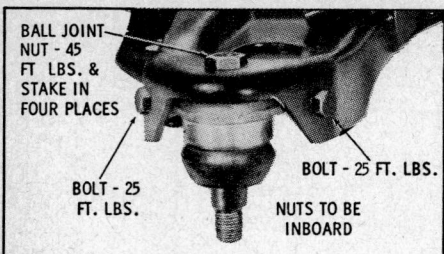

BALL JOINT NUT - 45 FT LBS. & STAKE IN FOUR PLACES

BOLT - 25 FT. LBS.

BOLT - 25 FT. LBS.

NUTS TO BE INBOARD

Fig. 9 Installing service ball joint

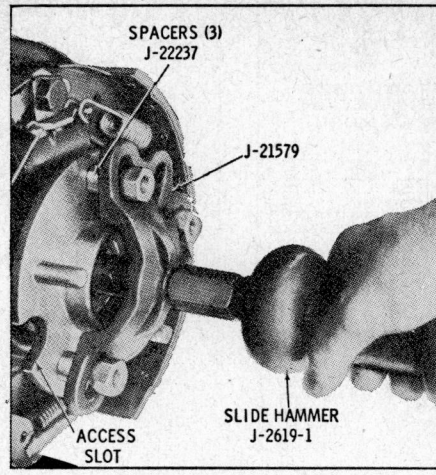

SPACERS (3) J-22237

J-21579

SLIDE HAMMER J-2619-1

ACCESS SLOT

Fig. 10 Removing hub assembly

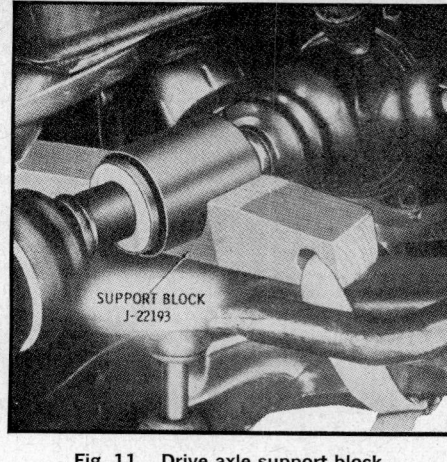

SUPPORT BLOCK J-22193

Fig. 11 Drive axle support block

5. Take a caster reading. If necessary to adjust, turn wheel to straight ahead position. Use camber reading scale for making this adjustment.
   a. Turn rear bolt so camber reading is ¼° more than the original setting for every one degree of caster change needed for a correct reading. Turn to plus side of camber if caster is negative and to negative camber if caster is positive.
   b. Turn front cam bolt so camber will return to its original proper setting that was made on the camber adjustment.
   c. Recheck caster reading.

NOTE: If a problem exists where you should run out of cam to gain the correct reading, first turn front cam bolt so high part of cam is pointing up. Then turn rear cam bolt so high part of cam is pointing down. This is a location to start from and a correct setting can be obtained with the foregoing procedure. Torque upper control arm cam nuts to 75 ft-lbs. Hold head of bolt securely as any movement of the cam will affect your final setting, which will necessitate a recheck of the camber and caster adjustment.

TOE-IN, ADJUST

1. Center steering wheel.
2. Loosen tie-rod nuts and adjust to proper setting.
3. Tighten tie-rod nuts to 20 ft.-lbs. Position tie-rod clamps so opening of clamp is facing up. This is necessary as interference and a possible tie up of front end linkage could occur if clamps snag anything while turning.

TORSION BAR
Removal

1. Hoist car and place floor stands under front frame horns.
2. Slide seat at rear of torsion bar forward.
3. Use a tool of the type shown in Fig. 5.
4. Turn torsion bar adjusting bolt counterclockwise, counting the number of turns necessary to remove.

Record this number for installing.
5. Remove adjusting bolt and nut.
6. Turn center screw of tool until torsion bar is completely relaxed.
7. Place block of wood on hoist (6"x6"x8") and raise under lower control arm until drive axle is horizontal.
8. Remove stabilizer bolt and related parts. Discard bolt.
9. Place a daub of paint on bottom side of torsion bar.
10. Slide torsion bar forward until it bottoms in lower control arm (adjusting arm will drop out). *Do not mar, scratch or in any way damage torsion bar as replacement will be necessary if such conditions exist.*
11. Remove crossmember bolt from side torsion bar is being replaced.
12. Remove center bolt from tool.
13. Raise crossmember and twist rearward until torsion bar clears member.
14. Slowly raise lower control arm until maximum height is attained.
15. Raise center crossmember until contact is made with floor pan.
16. Pull rearward on torsion bar with HANDS ONLY until bar is out of lower control arm. *It may be necessary to use air blowing into nut of lower control arm to relieve vacuum caused by grease.*

Installation

NOTE: Check rubber seal for damage; replace if necessary. Check retainer for excessive wear and replace if necessary. A new retainer is required on replacement of torsion bar. Stake as shown in Fig. 1.

1. Grease both ends of torsion bar for about 3" with E.P. chassis lube.
2. With daub of paint in same location as when removed, insert bar into lower control arm nut and push forward until bar bottoms.
3. Pry crossmember back and align bar with hole in crossmember.

4. Lower crossmember and install center bolt in tool, Fig. 5.
5. Lower front lower control arm until drive axle is horizontal.
6. Install torsion bar arm and pull bar rearward until fully seated in arm.
7. Install crossmember bolt through rubber mounting and torque to 40 ft-lbs.
8. Lower front lower control arm and remove wood block.
9. Install new bolt in stabilizer bar to lower control arm. Torque to 14 ft-lbs. *Cut off bottom of bolt so that ¼" is remaining below nut.*
10. Using the tool shown in Fig. 5 or its equivalent, tighten torsion bar arm to install lock plate under arm and through crossmember.
11. Grease threads of torsion bar adjuster with chassis lube and turn into nut the same number of turns required to remove.
12. Remove tool. Lower car to floor.
13. Check riding height, Fig. 3. Correct by turning torsion bar adjusting bolt as required.

BALL JOINT CHECKS
Vertical Check

1. Raise car and place jack stands under both lower control arms as near as possible to lower ball joints.
2. Install dial indicator, Fig. 6.
3. Place a pry bar as shown in Fig. 7 and push down on bar. Use care to see that drive axle seal is not damaged. Reading must not exceed .125".

Horizontal Check

1. With car placed on floor stands, install dial indicator, Fig. 8.
2. Grasp front wheel and rock top and bottom of tire. Read dial gauge, then reverse the push-pull procedure.
3. Horizontal deflection on dial gauge should not exceed .125" at wheel

rim. This procedure checks both upper and lower ball joints.

BALL JOINTS, REPLACE

Lower Ball Joint

1. Remove knuckle.
2. Hacksaw three rivet heads off.
3. Using a 7/32" drill, drill side rivets 3/16" deep.
4. Drive center rivet until joint is out of control arm.
5. Install service ball joint into control arm and torque bolts and nuts as shown in Fig. 9.
6. Replace knuckle.

Upper Ball Joint

1. Raise car and support on floor stands.
2. Remove wheel and drum.
3. Remove hub assembly, Fig. 10.
4. Remove upper ball joint nut and brake line hose clip from ball joint.
5. Remove anchor bolt.
6. Lift brake plate outward over end of axle shaft and support so brake hose is not damaged.
7. Place support block as shown, Fig. 11.
8. Using a brass drift and hammer loosen and remove ball joint.
9. Install new ball joint and replace parts in reverse order of removal.

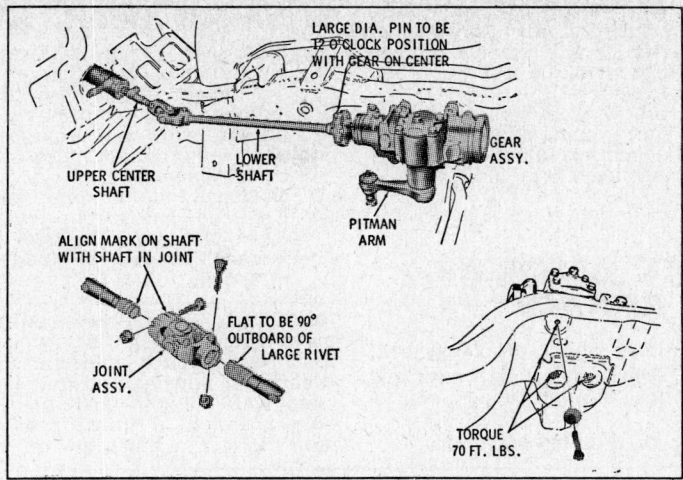

Fig. 12   Steering gear and shaft

WHEEL BEARING & STEERING KNUCKLE, REPLACE

1. Raise and support vehicle under lower control arms.
2. Remove drive axle nut and washer and remove wheel and tire assembly.
3. Remove brake hose clip from ball joint and replace nut, then remove brake caliper off disc, and using a length of wire support caliper on suspension.

NOTE: Do not allow caliper to hang from brake hose as this could cause damage and premature failure of hose.

4. Mark hub and disc assembly for alignment during assembly and remove disc, then strike steering knuckle in area of upper ball joint until upper ball joint is loose.

CAUTION: Use extreme care to prevent striking and damaging brake hose or ball joint seal.

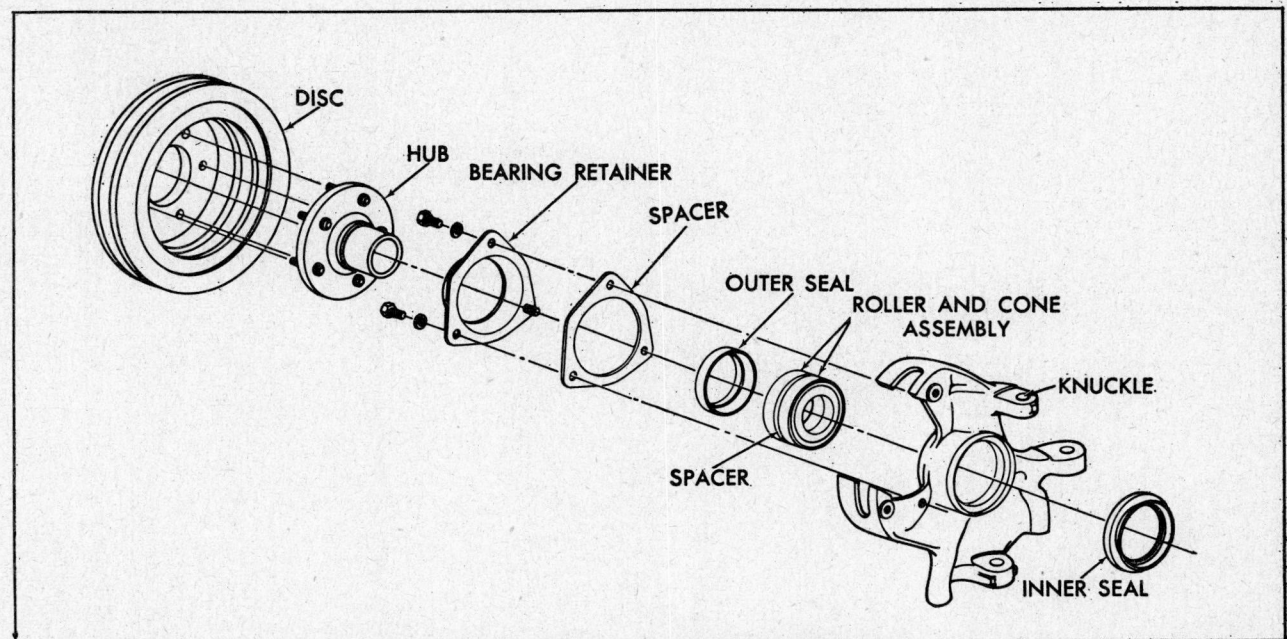

Fig. 13   Wheel bearing & steering knuckle assembly

5. Place a short length of rubber hose over lower control arm torsion bar connector to avoid damage to inboard tri-pot joint seal when hub and knuckle are removed.
6. Using appropriate puller, disconnect tie rod end, upper and lower ball joints and remove steering knuckle and hub assembly, Fig. 12.

SHOCK ABSORBER, REPLACE

1. Remove upper shock attaching bolt.
2. Remove lower attaching nut and guide shock through upper control arm.
3. Reverse procedure to install.

STEERING GEAR, REPLACE

1. Referring to Fig. 12, remove coupling flange hub bolt.
2. Disconnect hoses from power steering pump and cap pump and hose fittings. On cars equipped with a cooler disconnect return hose from cooler inlet pipe.
3. Hoist car and pull off pitman arm.
4. Unfasten gear from frame, permit lower shaft to slide free of coupling flange, then remove gear with hoses attached.

NOTE: Before installing steering gear, apply a sodium soap fibre grease to gear mounting pads to prevent squeaks between gear housing and frame. Make sure alignment pin on gear housing enters hole provided in frame side rail. Make sure there is a minimum of .040" clearance between coupling hub and steering gear upper seal.

Install coupling hub bolt and torque to 18 ft-lbs. Before tightening steering gear attaching bolts, shift gear as necessary to place it in the same plane as the steering shaft so that the flexible coupling is not distorted. Tighten gear-to-frame bolts to 70 ft-lbs. and pitman shaft nut to 220 ft-lbs.

5. After hoses are connected to pump, add power steering fluid as necessary to bring the fluid level to the full mark. Run engine at idle for 30 seconds, then run at a fast idle for a minute before turning steering wheel. With engine running, turn steering wheel through its full travel two or three times to bleed air from system. Recheck oil level and add oil if necessary.

PONTIAC

All Intermediate & Full Size Models

OLD CAR SPECIFICATIONS: For 1946-68 Tune Up and Wheel Alignment Specifications see main index.

INDEX OF SERVICE OPERATIONS

PAGE NO.

ACCESSORIES

Air Conditioning 2-20
Automatic Level Controls 2-39
Blower Motor, Remove 1-655
Clock Troubles 2-11
Heater Core, Replace 1-654
Power Top Troubles 2-18
Power Window Troubles 2-18
Radio, Replace 1-654
Speed Controls, Adjust 1-655

BRAKES

Anti-Skid Brakes 2-162
Brake Troubles, Mechanical 2-17
Disc Brake Service 2-133
Hydraulic System Service 2-123
Master Cylinder, Replace 1-672
Parking Brake, Adjust 1-672
Power Brake Unit, Replace 1-672
Service Brakes, Adjust 1-672

CLUTCH

Clutch Pedal, Adjust 1-668
Clutch, Replace 1-668
Clutch Troubles 2-12

COOLING SYSTEM

Cooling System Troubles 2-6
Variable Speed Fans 2-38
Water Pump, Replace 1-662

ELECTRICAL

Alternator Service 2-69
Blower Motor, Remove 1-655
Clutch Start Switch 1-651
Dash Gauge Service 2-50
Distributor, Replace 1-650
Distributor Service:
  Standard 2-525
  Transistorized 2-535
Electrical Troubles 2-8
Headlamps, Concealed Type 2-46
Headlight Aiming 2-45
Horn Sounder, Remove 1-651
Ignition Coils and Resistors 2-521
Ignition Lock, Replace 1-650
Ignition Switch, Replace 1-650
Ignition Timing 2-518
Instrument Cluster, Removal 1-651
Light Switch, Replace 1-650
Neutral Safety Switch, Replace .. 1-651
Seat Belt Interlock Systems 2-311
Starter Service 2-54
Starter, Replace 1-650
Starter Switch Service 2-67
Stop Light Switch, Replace 1-651
Turn Signal Switch, Replace 1-651
Turn Signal Troubles 2-11
Windshield Wiper Motor, Replace . 1-653
Windshield Wiper Troubles 2-19

ENGINE, OVERHEAD CAMSHAFT 1-663

PAGE NO.

ENGINE, Conventional

Camshaft, Replace 1-659
Crankshaft Oil Seal 1-660
Cylinder Head, Replace 1-657
Engine Identification 1-630
Engine Mounts 1-656
Engine, Replace 1-656
Engine Troubles 2-1
Main Bearings 1-660
Piston Pins 1-660
Piston Rings 1-660
Piston and Rod, Assemble 1-660
Pistons 1-660
Rocker Arm Studs 1-658
Rod Bearings 1-660
Timing Case Cover, Replace 1-659
Timing Chain, Replace 1-659
Valve Arrangement 1-658
Valve Guides 1-659
Valve Lifters 1-659

ENGINE LUBRICATION

Emission Control Systems 2-545
Oil Pan, Replace 1-660
Oil Pump, Replace 1-662

FUEL SYSTEM

Carburetor Adjustments and Specs. 2-372
Emission Control Systems 2-545
Fuel Pump, Replace 1-662
Fuel Pump Service 2-369
Fuel System Troubles 2-2

PROPELLER SHAFT & U JOINTS

Propeller Shaft 1-671
Universal Joint Service 2-117

REAR AXLE & SUSPENSION

Axle Shaft, Bearing and Seal 1-671
Coil Spring, Replace 1-675
Control Arms & Bushings, Replace .. 1-675
Leaf Spring & Bushings, Replace .. 1-673
Rear Axle Description 1-670
Rear Axle Troubles 2-16
Shock Absorber, Replace 1-673
Stabilizer Bar & Bushings, Replace . 1-675

SPECIFICATIONS

Alternator 1-645
Belt Tension 1-662
Brakes 1-644
Capacities 1-647
Carburetors 2-372
Cooling System 1-647
Crankshaft and Bearings 1-644
Distributors 1-639

PAGE NO.

Engine Tightening Torque 1-646
Fuel Pump Pressure 1-662
General Engine Specs. 1-634
Ignition Coils and Resistors ... 2-521
Pistons, Rings and Pins 1-644
Rear Axle 1-646
Starting Motors 1-642
Tune Up 1-636
Valve Lift 1-658
Valve Timing 1-658
Valves 1-642
Wheel Alignment 1-647

STEERING GEAR

Horn Sounder Removal 1-651
Mechanical Gear, Replace 1-678
Mechanical Gear Service 2-170
Mechanical Gear Troubles 2-17
Power Gear, Replace 1-678
Steering Wheel, Replace 1-651

SUSPENSION, FRONT

Ball Joints, Replace 1-677
Ball Joints, Check for Wear 1-677
Coil Spring, Replace 1-678
Lubrication 1-676
Shock Absorber, Replace 1-678
Suspension, Description of 1-676
Toe-In, Adjust 1-676
Wheel Alignment, Adjust 1-676
Wheel Bearings, Adjust 1-677
Wheel Bearings, Replace 1-677

TRANSMISSIONS

Three Speed Manual:
  Replace 1-668
  Repairs 2-177
  Linkage, Adjust 1-668
Four Speed Manual:
  Replace 1-669
  Repairs 2-199
  Linkage, Adjust 1-669
Automatic Units 2-231
  1975 Linkage 1-669

TUNE UP

Service 2-517
Specifications 1-636

WINDSHIELD WIPER

Wiper Arms 1-653
Wiper Blades 1-653
Wiper Linkage, Replace 1-653
Wiper Motor, Replace 1-653
Wiper Switch, Replace 1-654
Wiper Troubles 2-19

SERIAL NUMBER LOCATION
1969-75: On plate fastened to upper left instrument panel area, visible through windshield.

ENGINE IDENTIFICATION

The V8 engine code is located beneath the production engine number on a machined pad on the right-hand bank of the engine block.

The 6-cylinder engine code for 1969 vehicles is stamped on the cylinder head-to-block contact surface behind oil filler tube and on pad at front right-hand side of cylinder block at rear of distributor for 1970-75 vehicles.

1969

CODE	TRANS.	ENGINE
ZC	④	6-250⑨
ZF	⑥	6-250⑨
ZH	④	6-250②
ZL	⑥	6-250②
WM	④	V8-350①
WN	④	V8-350②
WU	④	V8-350①
WV	④	V8-350②
XB	⑥	V8-350①
XC	⑥	V8-350②
XS	⑥	V8-350①
XU	⑥	V8-350②
WC	④	V8-350①
WP	④	V8-350②
XL	⑥	V8-350①
XR	⑥	V8-350②
YE	⑥	V8-350①
YN	⑥	V8-350②
YJ	⑥	V8-350②
WH	④	V8-400②
WQ	④	V8-400②
WS	④	V8-400②
WT	④	V8-400③
WZ	④	V8-400③
WW	④	V8-400②
XM	⑥	V8-400②
XN	⑥	V8-400②
XP	⑥	V8-400②
XX	⑥	V8-400①
YS	⑥	V8-400②
YT	⑥	V8-400②
YW	⑥	V8-400②
YZ	⑥	V8-400②
WD	④	V8-400①
WA	④	V8-400①
WB	④	V8-400①
WE	④	V8-400①
YA	⑥	V8-400①
YB	⑥	V8-400①
YC	⑥	V8-400①
YD	⑥	V8-400①
WX	④	V8-400②
XH	⑥	V8-400②
XZ	⑥	V8-400②
YF	⑥	V8-400②
WG	④	V8-428②
WJ	④	V8-428②
WF	④	V8-428②
WL	④	V8-428②
XE	⑥	V8-428③
XK	⑥	V8-428②
XJ	⑥	V8-428②
XF	⑥	V8-428②
XG	⑥	V8-428②
YL	⑥	V8-428②
YH	⑥	V8-428②
YK	⑥	V8-428②

1970

CODE	TRANS.	ENGINE
CG	⑥	6-250
RF	④	6-250
ZB	④	6-250
ZG	⑥	6-250
W7	④	V8-350①
X7	⑥	V8-350①
WU	④	V8-350①
YU	⑥	V8-350①
WE	④	V8-400①
YB	⑥	V8-400①
YD	⑥	V8-400①
XZ	⑥	V8-400②
XV	⑥	V8-400②
YZ	⑥	V8-400②
XX	⑥	V8-400①
XP	⑥	V8-400②
WS	④	V8-400②
WW	④	V8-400②
WT	④	V8-400②
WS	⑤	V8-400②
XH	⑥	V8-400②
YB	④	V8-400①
WX	④	V8-400②
YS	⑥	V8-400②
WH	⑧	V8-400⑧
XN	⑥	V8-400⑧
WG	④	V8-455②
YH	⑥	V8-455③
XF	⑥	V8-455②
WA	④	V8-455②
YA	⑥	V8-455②

1971

CODE	TRANS.	ENGINE
ZB	④	6-250
ZG	⑥	6-250
CAA	④	6-250
CAB	⑥	6-250
CCA	④	V8-307①
CCC	⑥	V8-307①
WN	④	V8-350①
YP	⑤	V8-350①
WP	⑥	V8-350①
YN	⑥	V8-350①
WR	④	V8-350①
WU	⑤	V8-350①
YU	⑥	V8-350①
YX	⑥	V8-400①
WX	④	V8-400①
XR	⑥	V8-350①
WT	④	V8-400②
WK	④	V8-400①
WS	④	V8-400①
XX	⑥	V8-400①
YS	⑥	V8-400②
WL	④	V8-455③

1972

CODE	TRANS.	ENGINE
WC	⑤	V8-455③
WJ	④	V8-455③
YC	⑥	V8-455③
WG	④	V8-455①
YG	⑥	V8-455③
YE	⑥	V8-455③
YA	⑥	V8-455②

1972

CODE	TRANS.	ENGINE
W6	④	6-250
Y6	⑥	6-250
CBG	④	6-250
CBJ	⑥	6-250
CBA	④	6-250
CBC	⑥	6-250
CKG	④	V8-307
CKH	⑥	V8-307
CAY	④	V8-307
CAZ	⑥	V8-307
YV	⑥	V8-350
YR	④	V8-350
WR	⑥	V8-350
YX	⑥	V8-400①
WS	④	V8-400③
WK	⑥	V8-400③
YS	⑥	V8-400③
ZX	⑥	V8-400①
YH	⑥	V8-455①
YC	⑥	V8-455③
YA	⑥	V8-455③
WM	④	V8-455③
YB	⑥	V8-455③
ZH	⑥	V8-455①

1973

CODE	TRANS.	ENGINE
CCC	④	6-250
CCD	④	6-250
CCA	⑥	6-250
CCB	⑥	6-250
XR	④	V8-350
Y2	④	V8-350
YR	⑥	V8-350
Y7	⑥	V8-350
YV	⑥	V8-350
XV	⑥	V8-350
ZR	⑥	V8-350
ZV	⑥	V8-350
YL	⑥	V8-350
WA	⑥	V8-350①
WC	⑥	V8-350①
WD	⑥	V8-350①
WF	⑥	V8-350①
WL	⑥	V8-350①

Continued

ENGINE IDENTIFICATION—Continued

CODE	TRANS.	ENGINE	CODE	TRANS.	ENGINE	CODE	TRANS.	ENGINE
WN	⑤	V8-350①	WT	⑤	V8-455②	YP	⑥	V8-350②
XC	⑥	V8-350①	W8	⑤	V8-455⑧	YN	⑥	V8-350②
XF	⑥	V8-350①	Y8	⑥	V8-455⑧	ZP	⑥	V8-350②
X2	⑤	V8-350①	ZC	⑥	V8-455②	AH	⑥	V8-400①⑩
YW	⑥	V8-350①	ZA	⑥	V8-455②	AT	⑥	V8-400②⑩
ZB	④	V8-350①	YK	⑥	V8-455②	A3	⑥	V8-400①
ZD	④	V8-350①	YD	⑥	V8-455②	YH	⑥	V8-400①
W5	⑥	V8-400①	XA	⑥	V8-455③	YJ	⑥	V8-400①
XH	⑥	V8-400①	XD	⑥	V8-455②	ZH	⑥	V8-400①
XI	⑤	V8-400①	XE	⑥	V8-455③	WR	④	V8-400②⑩
XK	⑥	V8-400②	XJ	⑥	V8-455③	WT	④	V8-040②
XN	⑤	V8-400②	XL	⑥	V8-455③	YF	⑥	V8-400①⑩
XX	⑥	V8-400②	XM	⑥	V8-455③	YK	⑥	V8-400②⑩
XZ	⑥	V8-400②	XO	⑥	V8-455③	YL	⑥	V8-400②⑩
X3	⑤	V8-400①	XT	⑥	V8-455③	YM	⑥	V8-400②⑩
X4	⑤	V8-400②	XY	⑥	V8-455③	YZ	⑥	V8-400②⑩
X5	⑥	V8-400②	X7	⑥	V8-455③	Y3	⑥	V8-400②⑩
YF	④	V8-400②	ZE	④	V8-455③	YT	⑥	V8-400②
YG	④	V8-400②	ZJ	④	V8-455③	ZD	⑥	V8-400①⑩
Y6	④	V8-400②	ZZ	④	V8-455③	ZJ	⑥	V8-400①⑩
YP	⑥	V8-400①				ZK	⑥	V8-400①⑩
Y4	⑥	V8-400①		**1974**		ZS	⑥	V8-400②⑩
YX	⑥	V8-400①				ZT	⑥	V8-400②
Y1	④	V8-400①	CCR	④	6-250⑨	AW	⑥	V8-455②⑩
WK	⑤	V8-400②	CCX	⑥	6-250⑨	A4	⑥	V8-455②⑩
YS	⑥	V8-400②	CCW	⑤	6-250⑨	YR	⑥	V8-455②⑩
WS	⑤	V8-400②	AA	⑥	V8-350①⑩	YW	⑥	V8-455③⑩
WP	⑤	V8-400②	WB	④	V8-350①	YX	⑥	V8-455③⑩
Y3	⑥	V8-400②	WA	④	V8-350①	YY	⑥	V8-455②⑩
YN	⑥	V8-400②	YB	⑥	V8-350①	Y4	⑥	V8-455②⑩
ZS	⑥	V8-400②	YA	⑥	V8-350①	Y6	⑥	V8-455②⑩
YY	⑥	V8-400②	YC	⑥	V8-350①	Y9	⑥	V8-455③⑩
ZX	⑥	V8-400①	YS	⑥	V8-350②⑩	YU	⑥	V8-455②
ZN	⑥	V8-400②	AD	⑥	V8-400①	ZU	⑥	V8-455②
ZK	⑥	V8-400①	ZB	⑥	V8-350①	ZW	⑥	V8-455②⑩
YZ	⑥	V8-400②	ZA	⑥	V8-350①	ZX	⑥	V8-455②⑩
YT	⑥	V8-400②	WP	④	V8-350②	Z4	⑥	V8-455②⑩
WW	⑤	V8-455②	WN	④	V8-350②	Z6	⑥	V8-455③⑩
YC	⑥	V8-455②				W8	④	V8-455⑧
YA	⑥	V8-455②				Y8	⑥	V8-455⑧

①—Two barrel carburetor.
②—Four barrel carburetor.
③—High output engine.
④—Manual trans.
⑤—Four speed manual trans.
⑥—Automatic trans.
⑧—Super Duty engine.
⑨—One barrel carburetor.
⑩—High Energy Ignition System (H.E.I.).

GRILLE IDENTIFICATION

1969 Tempest, Custom and LeMans

1969 GTO

1969 Firebird

1969 Catalina, Executive, Ventura

1969 Bonneville

1969 Grand Prix

GRILLE IDENTIFICATION—Continued

1970 GTO

1970 Tempest and LeMans

1970-71 Firebird

1970 Catalina, Executive

1970 Bonneville

1970 Grand Prix

1971 T-37 and LeMans

1971 GTO

1971 Catalina

1971 Grand Prix

1971 Bonneville

1971 Grand Ville

1971-72 Ventura II

1972 LeMans

1972 Catalina

1972 Grand Ville

1972 Bonneville

1972 Grand Prix

1973 Ventura

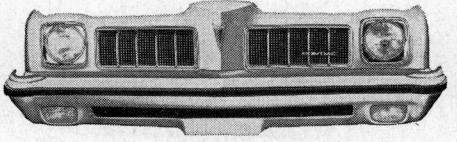

1973 Luxury LeMans

1973 GTO

GRILLE IDENTIFICATION—Continued

1973 Firebird

1973 Grand Am

1973 Catalina

1973 Grand Ville

1973 Grand Prix

1974 Ventura Custom

1974 GTO

1974 LeMans Sport

1974 Luxury LeMans

1974 Firebird

1974 Grand Am

1974 Catalina

1974 Bonneville

1974 Grand Prix

1974 Grand Ville

1975 Ventura

1975 LeMans

1975 Grand LeMans

1975 Firebird

1975 Grand Am

1975 Catalina

GRILLE IDENTIFICATION—Continued

| 1975 Bonneville | 1975 Grand Prix | 1975 Grand Ville & Grand Safari |

GENERAL ENGINE SPECIFICATIONS

Year	Engine	Car-buretor	Bore and Stroke	Piston Dis-place-ment, Cubic Inches	Com-pres-sion Ratio	Maximum Brake H.P. @ R.P.M.	Maximum Torque Lbs. Ft. @ R.P.M.	Normal Oil Pressure Pounds
1969	175 Horsepower..............6-250	1 Barrel	3.8750 x 3.52	250	9.00	175 @ 4800	240 @ 2600	26–36
	215 Horsepower..............6-250	4 Barrel	3.8750 x 3.52	250	10.50	215 @ 5200	255 @ 3800	26–36
	230 Horsepower..............6-250	4 Barrel	3.8750 x 3.52	250	10.50	230 @ 5400	260 @ 3600	26–36
	265 Horsepower............V8-350	2 Barrel	3.8750 x 3.75	350	9.20	265 @ 4600	355 @ 2800	30–40
	325 Horsepower............V8-350	4 Barrel	3.8750 x 3.75	350	10.50	325 @ 5100	380 @ 3200	55–60
	330 Horsepower............V8-350	4 Barrel	3.8750 x 3.75	350	10.50	330 @ 5100	380 @ 3200	55–60
	265 Horsepower............V8-400	2 Barrel	4.1200 x 3.75	400	8.60	265 @ 4600	397 @ 2400	30–40
	290 Horsepower............V8-400	2 Barrel	4.1200 x 3.75	400	10.50	290 @ 4600	428 @ 2500	30–40
	330 Horsepower............V8-400	4 Barrel	4.1200 x 3.75	400	10.75	330 @ 4800	430 @ 3300	30–40
	335 Horsepower............V8-400	4 Barrel	4.1200 x 3.75	400	10.75	335 @ 5000	430 @ 3400	30–40
	345 Horsepower............V8-400	4 Barrel	4.1200 x 3.75	400	10.75	345 @ 5400	430 @ 3700	30–40
	350 Horsepower............V8-400	4 Barrel	4.1200 x 3.75	400	10.50	350 @ 5000	445 @ 3000	55–60
	350 Horsepower............V8-400	4 Barrel	4.1200 x 3.75	400	10.75	350 @ 5000	445 @ 3000	55–60
	366 Horsepower............V8-400	4 Barrel	4.1200 x 3.75	400	10.75	366 @ 5100	445 @ 3600	30–40
	370 Horsepower............V8-400	4 Barrel	4.1200 x 3.75	400	10.75	370 @ 5500	445 @ 3900	30–40
	360 Horsepower............V8-428	4 Barrel	4.1200 x 4.00	428	10.50	360 @ 4600	472 @ 3200	30–40
	370 Horsepower............V8-428	4 Barrel	4.1200 x 4.00	428	10.50	370 @ 4800	472 @ 3200	55–60
	390 Horsepower............V8-428	4 Barrel	4.1200 x 4.00	428	10.75	390 @ 5200	465 @ 3400	55–60
1970	155 Horsepower..............①6-250	1 Barrel	3.875 x 3.53	250	8.50	155 @ 4200	235 @ 1600	30–45
	255 Horsepower............V8-350	2 Barrel	3.8750 x 3.75	350	8.80	255 @ 4600	355 @ 2800	30–40
	265 Horsepower............V8-400	2 Barrel	4.1200 x 3.75	400	8.80	265 @ 4600	397 @ 2400	30–40
	290 Horsepower............V8-400	2 Barrel	4.1200 x 3.75	400	10.00	290 @ 4600	428 @ 2500	30–40
	330 Horsepower............V8-400	4 Barrel	4.1200 x 3.75	400	10.00	330 @ 4800	445 @ 2900	30–40
	350 Horsepower............V8-400	4 Barrel	4.1200 x 3.75	400	10.25	350 @ 5000	445 @ 3000	55–60
	366 Horsepower............V8-400	4 Barrel	4.1200 x 3.75	400	10.50	366 @ 5100	445 @ 3600	30–40
	370 Horsepower............V8-400	4 Barrel	4.1200 x 3.75	400	10.50	370 @ 5500	445 @ 3900	30–40
	360 Horsepower............V8-455	4 Barrel	4.1510 x 4.21	455	10.00	360 @ 4300	500 @ 2700	30–40
	370 Horsepower............V8-455	4 Barrel	4.1510 x 4.21	455	10.25	370 @ 4600	500 @ 3100	30–40
1971	145 Horsepower..............①6-250	1 Barrel	3.875 x 3.53	250	8.50	145 @ 4200	230 @ 1600	30–45
	200 Horsepower............②V8-307	2 Barrel	3.875 x 3.25	307	8.50	200 @ 4600	300 @ 2400	30–45
	250 Horsepower............8-350	2 Barrel	3.8750 x 3.75	350	8.0	250 @ 4400	350 @ 2400	30–40
	265 Horsepower............8-400	2 Barrel	4.1200 x 3.75	400	8.2	265 @ 4400	400 @ 2400	30–40
	300 Horsepower............8-400	4 Barrel	4.1200 x 3.75	400	8.2	300 @ 4800	400 @ 3600	30–40
	280 Horsepower............8-455	2 Barrel	4.1510 x 4.21	455	8.2	280 @ 4400	455 @ 2000	30–40
	325 Horsepower............8-455	4 Barrel	4.1510 x 4.21	455	8.2	325 @ 4400	455 @ 3200	30–40
	335 Horsepower............8-455	4 Barrel	4.1510 x 4.21	455	8.4	335 @ 4800	480 @ 3600	30–40
1972	110 Horsepower③..............①6-250	1 Barrel	3.875 x 3.53	250	8.50	110 @ 3800	185 @ 1600	30–45
	130 Horsepower③..............②8-307	2 Barrel	3.875 x 3.25	307	8.50	130 @ 4400	230 @ 2400	30–45
	160 Horsepower③............8-350	2 Barrel	3.875 x 3.75	350	8.00	160 @ 4400	270 @ 2000	30–40
	175 Horsepower③............8-350	2 Barrel	3.875 x 3.75	350	8.00	175 @ 4400	275 @ 2000	30–40
	175 Horsepower③............8-400	2 Barrel	4.1200 x 3.75	400	8.2	175 @ 4000	310 @ 2400	30–40

Continued

GENERAL ENGINE SPECIFICATIONS—Continued

Year	Engine	Car-buretor	Bore and Stroke	Piston Dis-place-ment, Cubic Inches	Com-pres-sion Ratio	Maximum Brake H.P. @ R.P.M.	Maximum Torque Lbs. Ft. @ R.P.M.	Normal Oil Pressure Pounds
1972	200 Horsepower③............8-400	2 Barrel	4.1200 x 3.75	400	8.2	200 @ 4000	325 @ 2400	30–40
	200 Horsepower③............8-400	4 Barrel	4.1200 x 3.75	400	8.2	200 @ 4000	295 @ 2800	30–40
	250 Horsepower③............8-400	4 Barrel	4.1200 x 3.75	400	8.2	250 @ 4400	325 @ 3200	30–40
	185 Horsepower③............8-455	2 Barrel	4.1510 x 4.21	455	8.2	185 @ 4000	350 @ 2000	30–40
	200 Horsepower③............8-455	2 Barrel	4.1510 x 4.21	455	8.2	200 @ 4000	370 @ 2000	30–40
	220 Horsepower③............8-455	4 Barrel	4.1510 x 4.21	455	8.2	220 @ 3600	350 @ 2400	30–40
	230 Horsepower③............8-455	4 Barrel	4.1510 x 4.21	455	8.2	230 @ 4400	360 @ 2800	30–40
	250 Horsepower③............8-455	4 Barrel	4.1510 x 4.21	455	8.2	250 @ 3600	370 @ 2400	30–40
	250 Horsepower③............8-455	4 Barrel	4.1510 x 4.21	455	8.2	250 @ 3600	375 @ 2400	30–40
	300 Horsepower③............8-455	4 Barrel	4.1510 x 4.21	455	8.4	300 @ 4000	415 @ 3200	30–40
1973	100 Horsepower③............①6-250	1 Barrel	3.87 x 3.53	250	8.2	100 @ 3600	175 @ 1600	30–45
	150 Horsepower③............8-350	2 Barrel	3.88 x 3.75	350	7.6	150 @ 4000	270 @ 2000	55–60
	175 Horsepower③............④8-350	2 Barrel	3.88 x 3.75	350	7.6	175 @ 4400	280 @ 2400	55–60
	170 Horsepower③............8-400	2 Barrel	4.12 x 3.75	400	8.0	170 @ 3600	320 @ 2000	55–60
	185 Horsepower③............④8-400	2 Barrel	4.12 x 3.75	400	8.0	185 @ 4000	320 @ 2400	55–60
	200 Horsepower③............8-400	4 Barrel	4.12 x 3.75	400	8.0	200 @ 4000	310 @ 2400	55–60
	230 Horsepower③............④8-400	4 Barrel	4.12 x 3.75	400	8.0	230 @ 4400	325 @ 3200	55–60
	215 Horsepower③............8-455	4 Barrel	4.1510 x 4.21	455	8.0	215 @ 3600	350 @ 2400	55–60
	250 Horsepower③............④8-455	4 Barrel	4.1510 x 4.21	455	8.0	250 @ 4000	370 @ 2800	55–60
	290 Horsepower③............8-455	4 Barrel	4.1510 x 4.21	455	8.4	290 @ 4000	395 @ 3200	75–80
	310 Horsepower③............④8-455	4 Barrel	4,1510 x 4.21	455	8.4	310 @ 4000	390 @ 3600	75–80
1974	100 Horsepower③............①6-250	1 Barrel	3.88 x 3.53	250	8.2	100 @ 3600	175 @ 1600	30–45
	155 Horsepower③............8-350	2 Barrel	3.88 x 3.75	350	7.6	155 @ 3600	275 @ 2400	55–60
	170 Horsepower③............④8-350	2 Barrel	3.88 x 3.75	350	7.6	170 @ 4000	290 @ 2400	55–60
	170 Horsepower③............8-350	4 Barrel	3.88 x 3.75	350	7.6	170 @ 4000	280 @ 2000	55–60
	200 Horsepower③............④8-350	4 Barrel	3.88 x 3.75	350	7.6	200 @ 4400	295 @ 2800	55–60
	175 Horsepower③............8-400	2 Barrel	4.12 x 3.75	400	8.0	175 @ 3600	315 @ 2000	55–60
	190 Horsepower③............④8-400	2 Barrel	4.12 x 3.75	400	8.0	190 @ 4000	330 @ 2400	55–60
	200 Horsepower③............8-400	4 Barrel	4.12 x 3.75	400	8.0	200 @ 4000	320 @ 2400	55–60
	225 Horsepower③............④8-400	4 Barrel	4.12 x 3.75	400	8.0	225 @ 4000	330 @ 2800	55–60
	215 Horsepower③............8-455	4 Barrel	4.15 x 4.21	455	8.0	215 @ 3600	355 @ 2400	55–60
	250 Horsepower③............④8-455	4 Barrel	4.15 x 4.21	455	8.0	250 @ 4000	380 @ 2800	55–60
	290 Horsepower③............④8-455	4 Barrel	4.15 x 4.21	455	8.4	290 @ 4000	395 @ 3200	75–80
1975	105 Horsepower③............6-250①	1 Barrel	3.87 x 3.53	250	8.25	105 @ 3800	—	36–41
	110 Horsepower③..........V8-260⑤	2 Barrel	3.50 x 3.385	260	8.5	110 @ 3400	205 @ 1600	30–45
	155 Horsepower③..........V8-350	2 Barrel	3.8762 x 3.75	350	7.6	155 @ 4000	—	55–60
	175 Horsepower③..........V8-350	4 Barrel	3.8762 x 3.75	350	7.6	175 @ 4000	—	55–60
	145 Horsepower③..........V8-350	2 Barrel	3.80 x 3.85	350	8.0	145 @ 3200	—	37
	165 Horsepower③..........V8-350⑥	4 Barrel	3.80 x 3.85	350	8.0	165 @ 3800	260 @ 2200	37
	170 Horsepower③..........V8-400	2 Barrel	4.1212 x 3.75	400	7.6	170 @ 4000	—	55–60
	185 Horsepower③..........V8-400	4 Barrel	4.1212 x 3.75	400	7.6	185 @ 3600	—	55–60
	200 Horsepower③..........V8-455	4 Barrel	4.1522 x 4.21	455	7.6	200 @ 3500	—	55–60

①—For service on this engine, see Six Cylinder in Chevrolet Chapter.
②—For service on this engine, see Eight Cylinder in Chevrolet Chapter.
③—Ratings are NET—as installed in the vehicle.
④—With dual exhausts.
⑤—See Oldsmobile Chapter for service procedures.
⑥—Ventura only. See Buick Chapter for service procedures.

TUNE UP SPECIFICATIONS

OLD CAR SPECIFICATIONS: For 1946-68 Tune Up Specifications see main index.

★When using a timing light, disconnect vacuum hose or tube at distributor and plug opening in hose or tube so idle speed will not be affected.

●When checking compression, lowest cylinder must be within 80% of the highest.

▲Before removing wires from distributor cap, determine location of the No. 1 wire in cap, as distributor position may have been altered from that shown at the end of this chart.

Year	Spark Plug		Distributor		Ignition Timing★			Carb. Adjustments					
								Hot Idle Speed③		Air Fuel Ratio		Idle CO %	
	Type	Gap Inch	Point Gap Inch	Dwell Angle Deg.	Firing Order Fig. ▲	Timing BTDC ①	Mark Fig.	Std. Trans.	Auto. Trans.②	Std. Trans.	Auto. Trans.	Std. Trans.	Auto. Trans.
1969													
6-250 1 Bar. Carb.	R44NS	.035	.016	31–34	A	TDC	F	700/500	600/500D⑦	—	—	—	—
6-250 4 Bar. Carb.	R44NS	.035	.016	31–34	A	5°	F	850/600	600/500D⑦	—	—	—	—
8-350 2 Bar. Carb.	R45S	.035	.016	30	D	9°	C	850	650D⑦	—	—	—	—
8-350 4 Bar. Carb.	R45S	.035	.016	30	D	9°	C	1000	650D⑦	—	—	—	—
8-400 2 Bar. Carb.	R45S	.035	.016	30	D	9°	C	850	650D⑦	—	—	—	—
8-400 4 Bar. Carb.	⑪	.035	.016	30	D	9°	C	1000	650D⑦	—	—	—	—
8-400 Ram Air	⑪	.035	.016	30	D	15°	C	1000/650	650/500D⑦	—	—	—	—
8-428	R44S	.035	.016	30	D	9°	C	1000	650D⑦	—	—	—	—
1970													
6-250⑩ Std. Tr.	R46T	.035	.019	31–34	E	TDC	G	750/400	—	—	—	—	—
6-250⑩ Auto. Tr.	R46T	.035	.019	31–34	E	4°	G	—	600/400D	—	—	—	—
8-350 2 Bar. Carb.	R46S	.035	.016	30	D	9°	C	800	650D	—	—	—	—
8-400 2 Bar. Carb.	R46S	.035	.016	30	D	9°	C	800	650D	—	—	—	—
8-400 4 Bar. Carb.	R45S	.035	.016	30	D	9°	C	950	650D	—	—	—	—
8-400 Ram Air	R44S	.035	.016	30	D	15°	C	1000/650	750/500D	—	—	—	—
8-455	R45S⑫	.035	.016	30	D	9°	C	950	650D	—	—	—	—
1971													
6-250⑩	R46TS	.035	.019	32½	E	4°	H	850/550	650/500D	—	—	1.0	1.0
8-307⑭ Std. Tr.	R45TS	.035	.019	30	B	4°	H	550	—	—	—	1.0	—
8-307⑭ Auto. Tr.	R45TS	.035	.019	30	B	8°	H	—	550D	—	—	—	1.0
8-350 2 Bar. Carb.	R47S	.035	.016	30	D	12°	I	800	600D	—	—	1.0	1.0
8-400 2 Bar. Carb.	R47S	.035	.016	30	D	8°	I	—	600D	—	—	1.0	1.0
8-400 4 Bar. Carb.	R46S	.035	.016	30	D	12°	I	1000/600	700D	—	—	1.0	1.0
8-455	R46S	.035	.016	30	D	12°	I	—	650D	—	—	1.0	1.0
8-455 H.O.	R46S	.035	.016	30	D	12°	I	1000/600	700D	—	—	1.0	—
1972													
6-250⑩	R46T	.035	.019	32½	E	4°	H	850/450	650/450D	—	—	—	—
8-307⑭ Std. Tr.	R44T	.035	.016	30	B	4°	H	900/450	—	—	—	—	—
8-307⑭ Auto. Tr.	R44T	.035	.016	30	B	8°	H	—	600/450D	—	—	—	—
8-350	R46TS	.035	.016	30	D	8°	I	800	—	—	—	—	—
8-350	R46TS	.035	.016	30	D	10°	I	—	625D	—	—	—	—
8-400 2 Bar. Carb.	R46TS	.035	.016	30	D	10°	I	—	625D	—	—	—	—
8-400 4 Bar. Carb.	R45TS	.035	.016	30	D	10°	I	1000/600	700/500D	—	—	—	—
8-455 2 Bar. Carb.	R45TS	.035	.016	30	D	10°	I	—	625D	—	—	—	—
8-455 4 Bar. Carb.	R45TS	.035	.016	30	D	10°	I	—	650/500D	—	—	—	—
8-455 H.O. Std. Tr.	R45TS	.035	.016	30	D	8°	I	1000/600	—	—	—	—	—
8-455 H.O. Auto. Tr.	R45TS	.035	.016	30	D	10°	I	—	700/500D	—	—	—	—

Continued

TUNE UP SPECIFICATIONS—Continued

OLD CAR SPECIFICATIONS: For 1946-68 Tune Up Specifications see main index.

★When using a timing light, disconnect vacuum hose or tube at distributor and plug opening in hose or tube so idle speed will not be affected.

●When checking compression, lowest cylinder must be within 80% of the highest.

▲Before removing wires from distributor cap, determine location of the No. 1 wire in cap, as distributor position may have been altered from that shown at the end of this chart.

Year	Spark Plug		Distributor		Ignition Timing ★			Carb. Adjustments					
								Hot Idle Speed③		Air Fuel Ratio		Idle CO %	
	Type	Gap Inch	Point Gap Inch	Dwell Angle Deg.	Firing Order Fig. ▲	Timing BTDC ①	Mark Fig.	Std. Trans.	Auto. Trans.②	Std. Trans.	Auto. Trans.	Std. Trans.	Auto. Trans.
1973													
6-250	R46T	.035	⑮	32½	E	6°	H	700/450	600D	—	—	—	—
V8-350 Std. Tra.	R46TS	.040	.016	30	D	10°	I	900/600	—	—	—	0.2	—
V8-350 Auto. Tra.	R46TS	.040	.016	30	D	12°	I	—	650D	—	—	—	0.2
V8-400 2 Bar. Carb.	R46TS	.040	.016	30	D	⑯	I	—	650D	—	—	0.2	0.2
V8-400 4 Bar. Carb.	R45TS	.040	.016	30	D	⑯	I	1000/600	650D	—	—	0.2	0.2
V8-455	R45TS	.040	.016	30	D	⑯	I	1000	650D	—	—	0.2	0.2
V8-455 S.D.	R44TS	.040	.016	30	D	⑯	I	1000/600	750/500D	—	—	0.2	0.2
1974													
6-250	R46T	.035	⑮	32½	E	6°	H	850	600D	—	—	0.2	0.2
V8-350 2 Bar. Carb.	R46TS	.040	⑮	30	D	⑯	I	900	650D	—	—	0.2	0.2
V8-350 2 Bar. Carb.④	R46TS	.040	⑮	30	D	10°	I	—	625D	—	—	—	0.2
V8-350 4 Bar. Carb.	R46TS	.040	⑱	30	D	⑯	I	1000	650D	—	—	0.2	0.2
V8-350 4 Bar. Carb.④	R46TS	.040	⑬	30	D	10°	I	—	625D	—	—	—	0.2
V8-400 2 Bar. Carb.	R46TS	.040	⑮	30	D	⑯	I	—	650D	—	—	—	0.2
V8-400 2 Bar. Carb.④	R46TS	.040	⑮	30	D	10°	I	—	625D	—	—	—	0.2
V8-400 4 Bar. Carb.	R45TS	.040	⑮	30	D	⑯	I	1000	650D	—	—	0.2	0.2
V8-400 4 Bar. Carb.④	R45TS	.040	⑮	30	D	10°	I	—	625D	—	—	—	0.2
V8-455	R45TS	.040	⑯	30	D	⑯	I	—	650D	—	—	—	0.2
V8-455④	R45TS	.040	⑮	30	D	10°	I	—	625D	—	—	—	0.2
V8-455 S.D.	R44TS	.040	⑮	30	D	12°	I	1000	750D	—	—	0.2	0.2
1975													
6-250⑩	R46TX	.060	—	—	⑨	10°	H	800	650D	—	—	—	—
V8-260⑤	R46SX	.080	—	—	⑳	16°	J	750	650D	—	—	—	—
V8-260④⑤	R46SX	.080	—	—	⑳	18°	J	750	650D	—	—	—	—
V8-350	R46TSX	.060	—	—	⑳	⑧	I	800	⑲	—	—	—	—
V8-350⑥	R45TSX	.060	—	—	⑳	12°	K	800	600D	—	—	—	—
V8-400 2 Bar. Carb.	R46TSX	.060	—	—	⑳	16°	I	800	650D	—	—	—	—
V8-400 4 Bar. Carb.⑬	R45TSX	.060	—	—	⑳	16°	I	800	650D	—	—	—	—
V8-400 4 Bar. Carb.⑰	R45TSX	.060	—	—	⑳	⑱	I	800	650D	—	—	—	—
V8-400 4 Bar. Carb.④	R45TSX	.060	—	—	⑳	12°	I	800	650D	—	—	—	—
V8-455	R45TSX	.060	—	—	⑳	16°	I	800	650D	—	—	—	—
V8-455④	R45TSX	.060	—	—	⑳	10°	I	800	625D	—	—	—	—

①—BTDC: Before top dead center.
②—D: Drive. N: Neutral.
③—Where two figures are given, the higher is with solenoid active.
④—California.
⑤—See Oldsmobile Chapter for service procedure.
⑥—Ventura only. See Buick Chapter for service procedures.

⑦—With A/C off.
⑧—Std. Trans. 12°, Auto. Trans. 16°.
⑨—From front to rear 1-2-3-4-5-6, firing order 1-5-3-6-2-4.
⑩—For service on this engine, see Six Cylinder in Chevrolet Chapter.
⑪—GTO uses R44S; all others use R45S.
⑫—Use R44S on Ram Air option.
⑬—All except Firebird, Gran Prix and California.

⑭—For service on this engine, see Chevrolet Chapter.
⑮—New points .019", used points .016".
⑯—Std. trans. 10° BTDC. Auto trans. 12° BTDC.
⑰—Firebird and Grand Prix except California.
⑱—Std. Trans. 12°, Auto. Trans. 10°.
⑲—2 BBI. Carb. 600 RPM, 4 BBI. Carb. 650 RPM.
⑳—Left bank 1-3-5-7, right bank 2-4-6-8, firing order 1-8-4-3-6-5-7-2.

Continued

TUNE UP SPECIFICATIONS—Continued

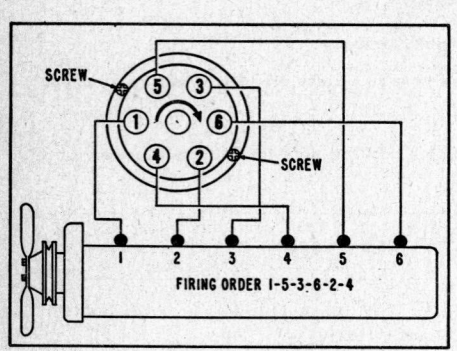

Fig. A

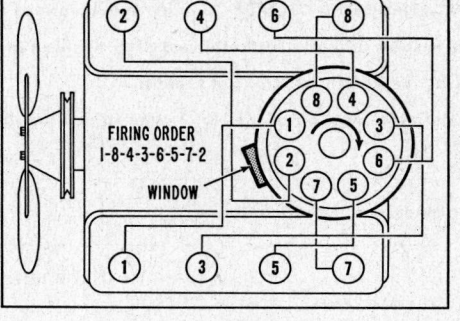

Fig. B

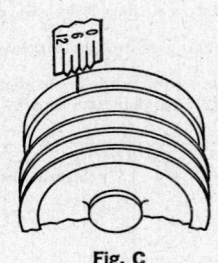

Fig. C

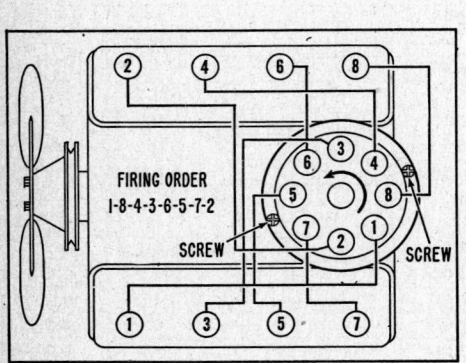

Fig. D

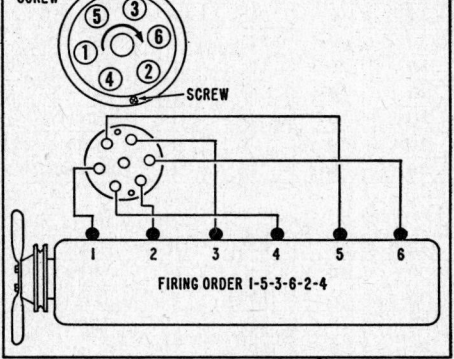

Fig. E

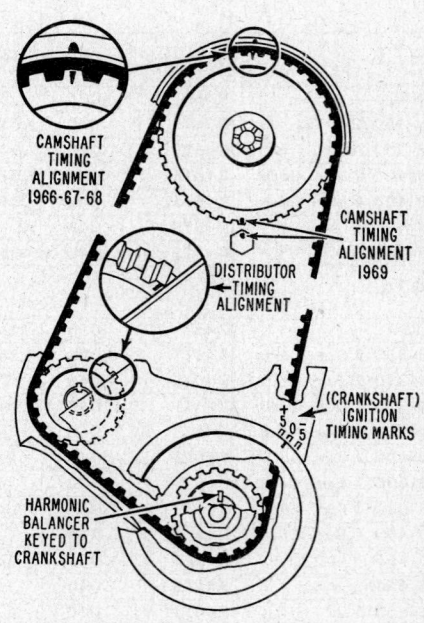

Fig. F

Fig. I

Fig. G

Fig. H

Fig. J

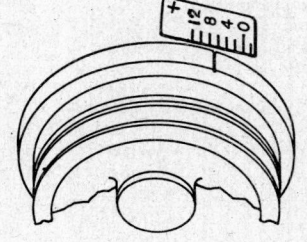

Fig. K

DISTRIBUTOR SPECIFICATIONS

★Note: If unit is checked on vehicle, double the RPM and degrees to get crankshaft figures.

Distributor Part No.①	Centrifugal Advance Degrees @ RPM of Distributor					Vacuum Advance		Distributor Retard
	Advance Starts	Intermediate Advance			Full Advance	Inches of Vacuum to Start Plunger	Max. Adv. Dist. Deg. @ Vacuum	Max. Retard Dist. Deg. @ Vacuum
1969								
1110474④	0–2 @ 550	6–8 @ 875	—	—	13.5 @ 2375	5–7	7.5 @ 11.5	—
1110475④	0–4.5 @ 500	9–11 @ 1050	—	—	15 @ 2200	5–7	7.5 @ 11.5	—
1111253④	0–2 @ 500	5–7 @ 1000	—	—	11 @ 2300	10–12	10 @ 18.8	—
1111940④	0.5–2.5 @ 500	7.5–9.5 @ 950	—	—	17 @ 2275	8–10	10 @ 17	—
1111941⑤	0–2 @ 660	5–7 @ 1100	—	—	12 @ 2300	8–10	10 @ 17	—
1111942④	1–3 @ 550	6.5–8.5 @ 975	—	—	13 @ 2400	6–8	10 @ 14¾	—
1111946⑤	0–2 @ 500	5–7 @ 1000	—	—	11 @ 2300	8–10	10 @ 17	—
1111952⑤	1–3 @ 700	5–7 @ 1000	—	—	11 @ 2300	10–12	10 @ 18.8	—
1111959④	0–2.2 @ 550	4.5–6.5 @ 1200	—	—	12 @ 2300	8–10	10 @ 17	—
1111960④	1–3.3 @ 700	6–8 @ 1000	—	—	12 @ 2300	8–10	10 @ 17	—
1970								
1110463④	0–2 @ 450	11.5 @ 975	—	—	16 @ 2100	6–8	11½ @ 17	—
1110464④	0–2 @ 450	8.5 @ 975	—	—	14 @ 2100	6–8	11½ @ 17	—
1111105⑥	0–2 @ 800	—	—	—	8 @ 2200	8–10	10 @ 17	—
1111148⑥	0–2 @ 400	6 @ 950	—	—	13 @ 2300	8–10	10 @ 17	—
1111176⑥	0–2 @ 550	6 @ 950	—	—	13 @ 2350	8–10	10 @ 17	—
1112007④	0–2 @ 400	6 @ 950	—	—	13 @ 2300	8–10	10 @ 17	—
1112008④	0–2 @ 550	6 @ 950	—	—	13 @ 2350	6–8	10 @ 14¾	—
1112009⑥	0–2 @ 400	5.5 @ 2200	—	—	11 @ 2300	8–10	10 @ 17	—
1112010⑥	0–2 @ 550	5.5 @ 1100	—	—	11 @ 2300	8–10	10 @ 17	—
1112011⑥	0–2 @ 600	6 @ 1050	—	—	14 @ 3050	8–10	10 @ 17	—
1112012⑥	0–2 @ 400	—	—	—	8 @ 2200	8–10	10 @ 17	—
1112013⑥	0–2 @ 600	6 @ 1050	—	—	14 @ 3050	8–10	10 @ 17	—
1112024⑥	0–2 @ 550	5.5 @ 1150	—	—	11 @ 2300	8–10	10 @ 17	—
1971								
1110489④	0–2 @ 550	7 @ 1150	—	—	12 @ 2050	7–9	11½ @ 17	—
1112068	0–2 @ 800	6 @ 1000	—	—	14 @ 2300	6–8	10 @ 14¾	—
1112069	0–2 @ 800	5½ @ 1000	—	—	11 @ 2300	6–8	10 @ 14¾	—
1112070	0–2 @ 575	3 @ 825	—	—	11 @ 2300	6–8	10 @ 14¾	—
1112071	0–2 @ 800	—	—	—	12 @ 2300	8–10	10 @ 17	—
1112072	0–2 @ 825	3 @ 825	—	—	11 @ 2300	8–10	10 @ 17	—
1112073	0–2 @ 500	4 @ 750	—	—	13 @ 2225	6–8	10 @ 14¾	—
1112083	0–2 @ 600	6 @ 1050	—	—	11 @ 2300	6–8	10 @ 14¾	—
1972								
1110489④	0–2 @ 650	7 @ 1150	—	—	12 @ 2050	7–9	11½ @ 17	—
1112005	0–2 @ 600	6 @ 1100	—	—	12 @ 2250	7–9	10.3 @ 17.8	—
1112039	0–2 @ 650	—	—	—	11 @ 2100	7–9	10½ @ 18	—
1112118	0–1 @ 800	2.5–4.5 @ 1000	—	—	10 @ 2300	6–8	10 @ 15	—
1112119	0–1 @ 800	3.5 @ 1000	—	—	13 @ 2300	8–10	10 @ 17	—
1112121	0–1 @ 700	4–6 @ 1200	—	—	13 @ 2300	6–8	10 @ 15	—
1112122	0–1 @ 800	—	—	—	13 @ 2300	8–10	10 @ 17	—
1112127	0–1 @ 700	3–5 @ 1000	—	—	11 @ 2300	8–10	10 @ 17	—
1112133	0–1 @ 575	4.5–6.5 @ 1000	—	—	15 @ 2300	6–8	10 @ 15	—
1112140	0–1 @ 800	4.5–6.5 @ 1000	—	—	12 @ 2300	6–8	10 @ 15	—
1112145	0–1 @ 700	3.5 @ 1000	—	—	11 @ 2300	8–10	10 @ 17	—

Continued

DISTRIBUTOR SPECIFICATIONS—Continued

★Note: If unit is checked on vehicle, double the RPM and degrees to get crankshaft figures.

Distributor Part No.①	Centrifugal Advance Degrees @ RPM of Distributor					Vacuum Advance		Distributor Retard
	Advance Starts	Intermediate Advance			Full Advance	Inches of Vacuum to Start Plunger	Max. Adv. Dist. Deg. @ Vacuum	Max. Retard Dist. Deg. @ Vacuum
1973								
1110499	0 @ 650	7 @ 1150	—	—	12 @ 2050	7	11½ @ 15	—
1112191	0 @ 575	3.8 @ 850	—	—	9 @ 1950	10	12½ @ 16	—
1112199	0 @ 615	4 @ 790	—	—	12 @ 1875	8	12½ @ 15	—
1112201	0 @ 600	6.5 @ 1050	—	—	12 @ 1790	7	12½ @ 12	—
1112202	0 @ 700	8 @ 1050	—	—	13 @ 1725	7	12½ @ 12	—
1112203②	0 @ 600	4 @ 750	—	—	9 @ 2000	10	12½ @ 16	—
1112216	0 @ 600	6½ @ 1050	—	—	12 @ 1790	3	10 @ 9.6	—
1112218	0 @ 600	8.5 @ 950	—	—	10 @ 1650	6	10 @ 12	—
1112220	0 @ 575	3.8 @ 850	—	—	9 @ 1950	5	12.5 @ 11	—
1112224	0 @ 610	4 @ 790	—	—	12 @ 1875	5	12.5 @ 11	—
1112232	0 @ 600	5 @ 850	—	—	11 @ 2300	5	12.5 @ 11	—
1112233②	0 @ 600	5 @ 850	—	—	11 @ 2300	9	12.5 @ 14	—
1112507②	0 @ 600	4 @ 750	—	—	9 @ 2000	5	12.5 @ 11	—
1112510	0 @ 500	4 @ 700	—	—	12 @ 1900	7	12.5 @ 12	—
1112511	0 @ 500	4 @ 700	—	—	12 @ 1900	8	12.5 @ 15	—
1112810②	0 @ 600	4 @ 750	—	—	9 @ 2000	9	10 @ 16	—
1112811	0 @ 575	3.8 @ 850	—	—	9 @ 1950	7	12.5 @ 12	—
1973-74								
1112205	0 @ 600	5 @ 850	—	—	11 @ 2300	9	12.5 @ 14	—
1112231	0 @ 600	5 @ 850	—	—	11 @ 2300	9	12.5 @ 13.5	—
1112804	0 @ 600	6.5 @ 1065	—	—	12 @ 1790	7	10 @ 14	—
1112805	0 @ 600	4 @ 775	—	—	12 @ 1875	9	10 @ 16	—
1112806	0 @ 650	8 @ 1050	—	—	13 @ 1725	7	10 @ 14	—
1112807	0 @ 575	4.5 @ 850	—	—	9 @ 1950	9	10 @ 16	—
1112808	0 @ 600	6.5 @ 1075	—	—	12 @ 1790	5	12.5 @ 11	—
1112809	0 @ 600	4 @ 790	—	—	12 @ 1875	7	12.5 @ 12	—
1112812②	0 @ 600	5 @ 850	—	—	11 @ 2300	9	10 @ 16	—
1112813	0 @ 600	5 @ 850	—	—	11 @ 2300	9	10 @ 16	—
1112814	0 @ 600	5 @ 850	—	—	11 @ 2300	7	12.5 @ 11.5	—
1974								
1110499	0 @ 550	7 @ 1150	—	—	12 @ 2050	7	12 @ 15	—
1112210	0 @ 600	4 @ 850	—	—	9 @ 1950	9	10 @ 16	—
1112212	0 @ 600	5 @ 850	—	—	11 @ 2300	9	10 @ 16	—
1112213	0 @ 600	5 @ 850	—	—	11 @ 2300	7	12½ @ 12	—
1122341③	0 @ 600	6.5 @ 1065	—	—	12 @ 1790	7	10 @ 14	—
1112235③	0 @ 600	6.5 @ 1075	—	—	13 @ 1725	5	12½ @ 11	—
1112236③	0 @ 650	8 @ 1050	—	—	13 @ 1725	7	10 @ 14	—
1112237③	0 @ 600	4 @ 775	—	—	12 @ 1875	9	10 @ 16	—
1112238③	0 @ 600	4 @ 790	—	—	12 @ 1875	7	12 @ 12	—
1112239③	0 @ 600	5 @ 850	—	—	11 @ 2300	9	12½ @ 14	—
1112240③	0 @ 600	5 @ 850	—	—	11 @ 2300	7	12½ @ 11½	—
1112243③	0 @ 600	5 @ 850	—	—	11 @ 2300	9	12½ @ 13½	—
1112512③	0 @ 600	5 @ 850	—	—	11 @ 2300	9	10 @ 16	—
1112513③	0 @ 575	4.5 @ 850	—	—	9 @ 1950	9	10 @ 16	—
1112546	0 @ 600	4 @ 800	—	—	12 @ 1800	9	10 @ 16	—
1112547	0 @ 600	4 @ 800	—	—	12 @ 1800	7	12½ @ 12	—
1112810②	0 @ 600	4 @ 800	—	—	9 @ 2000	9	10 @ 16	—

Continued

DISTRIBUTOR SPECIFICATIONS—Continued

★Note: If unit is checked on vehicle double the RPM and degrees to get crankshaft figures.

Distributor Part. No.①	Centrifugal Advance Degrees @ RPM of Distributor				Vacuum Advance		Distributor Retard
	Advance Starts	Intermediate Advance		Full Advance	Inches of Vacuum to Start Plunger	Max. Adv. Dist. Deg. @ Vacuum	Max. Retard Dist. Deg. @ Vacuum
1974—Continued							
1112821	0 @ 500	4 @ 700	—	—	12 @ 1900	7	10 @ 14	—
1112822③	0 @ 500	4 @ 700	—	—	12 @ 1900	7	10 @ 14	—
1112833	0 @ 600	3 @ 825	—	—	12 @ 2000	9	10 @ 16	—
1112834③	0 @ 600	3 @ 825	—	—	12 @ 2000	9	10 @ 16	—
1112856③	0 @ 610	5 @ 800	—	—	12 @ 1900	—	10 @ 14	—
1112857	0 @ 610	5 @ 800	—	—	12 @ 1900	—	10 @ 14	—
1112859	0 @ 575	4 @ 850	—	—	9 @ 1950	7	10 @ 14.5	—
1112860③	0 @ 575	4 @ 850	—	—	9 @ 1950	7	10 @ 14.5	—
1112871	0 @ 600	5 @ 875	—	—	11 @ 2300	9	12½ @ 16	—
1112876	0 @ 600	3 @ 775	—	—	12 @ 900	9	10 @ 16	—
1112878	0 @ 600	4 @ 800	—	—	9 @ 1950	7	10 @ 14	—
1975							
1110650	0 @ 600	—	—	—	7 @ 2100	4	8 @ 15	—
1112495	0 @ 550	7 @ 1100	—	—	9 @ 2200	7	12½ @ 12	—
1112498	0 @ 600	2 @ 700	—	—	8½ @ 1800	6	12 @ 13	—
1112500	0 @ 600	3 @ 800	—	—	10 @ 2200	7	12½ @ 12	—
1112863	0 @ 550	5½ @ 1150	—	—	10 @ 2100	4	8 @ 15	—
1112896	0 @ 550	3 @ 1050	—	—	6 @ 2250	7½	7 @ 12	—
1112918	0 @ 500	5½ @ 1000	—	—	7 @ 2200	7	10 @ 11	—
1112928	0 @ 600	2 @ 700	—	—	8 @ 2200	7	12½ @ 12	—
1112929	0 @ 500	4 @ 700	—	—	10 @ 2200	7	10 @ 14	—
1112930	0 @ 700	3½ @ 1000	—	—	5 @ 2200	7	10 @ 11	—
1112946	0 @ 500	4 @ 700	—	—	10½ @ 1800	7	12 @ 15	—
1112947	0 @ 600	2 @ 700	—	—	10 @ 1900	8	10 @ 15	—
1112948	0 @ 500	4 @ 700	—	—	10 @ 2200	8	10 @ 15	—
1112500	0 @ 600	3 @ 800	—	—	10 @ 2200	7	12½ @ 12	—

①—Stamped on distributor housing plate.   ②—Transistorized Unitized distributor.   ③—Uni-Set ignition points.
④—Breaker arm spring tension—19–23.   ⑤—Breaker arm spring tension—28–31.   ⑥—Breaker arm spring tension—28–32.

STARTING MOTOR SPECIFICATIONS

Year	Model	Starter Number	Brush Spring Tension Oz①	Free Speed Test			Resistance Test③	
				Amps.①	Volts	R.P.M.①	Amps.①	Volts
1969	6-230, 6-250	1107499	35	49–76②	10.6	6200–9600	270–310	4.3
	V8s	1107293	—	—	—	—	—	—
	V8s	1107355	35	70–99②	10.6	6800–9400	410–480②	3.0
	6-250 Auto. Trans.	1107594	—	50②	9	5500–10500	—	—
	6-250 Firebird	1108329	—	50②	9	5500–10500	—	—
	V8-400 Firebird	1108335	—	65②	9	7500–10500	—	—
	V8-400 Ram Air Eng.	1108353	—	65②	9	7500–10500	—	—
	V8-350 Firebird	1108328	—	55②	9	3500–6000	—	—
1970	6-250	1108439	—	50②	9	5500–10500	—	—
	V8-350	1108434	—	55②	9	3500–6000	—	—
	V8-400, 455	1108435	—	65②	9	7500–10500	—	—
1971–72	6-250	1108365	35	50②	9	5500–10500	—	—
	V8-307	1108367	35	50–80②	9	5500–10500	—	—
	V8-350	1108445	—	55②	9	3500–6000	—	—
	V8-400, 455	1108446	—	65②	9	7500–10500	—	—
	V8-455	1108436	—	65②	9	7500–10500	—	—
1973–74	6-250	1108365	35	50②	9	5500–10500	—	—
	V8-350	1108224	—	—	—	—	—	—
	V8-400, 455	1108225	—	—	—	—	—	—
	V8-455④	1108226	—	65②	9	7500–10500	—	—
1975	6-250	1108365	—	—	—	—	—	—
	V8-260⑥	1108745	—	—	—	—	—	—
	V8-350⑤	1108762	—	—	—	—	—	—
	V8-350	1108758	—	—	—	—	—	—
	V8-400, 455	1108759	—	—	—	—	—	—

①—Minimum.   ②—Includes solenoid.
③—Check capacity of motor by using a 500 ampere meter and a carbon pile rheostat to control voltage. Apply volts listed across motor with armature locked. Current should be as listed.
④—With super-duty engine.
⑤—Ventura models only. See Buick Chapter for services procedures.
⑥—See Oldsmobile Chapter for service procedures.

VALVE SPECIFICATIONS

Year	Model	Valve Lash		Valve Angles		Valve Spring Installed Height	Valve Spring Pressure Lbs. @ In.	Stem Clearance		Stem Diameter	
		Int.	Exh.	Seat	Face			Intake	Exhaust	Intake	Exhaust
1969	6-250, 1 B.C.	Hydraulic⑦		46	45	1.629	170 @ 1.23	.0016–.0033	.0021–.0038	.3407–.3414	.3407–.3414
	6-250, 4 B.C.	Hydraulic⑦		46	45	1.629	122 @ 1.10	.0016–.0033	.0021–.0038	.3407–.3414	.3407–.3414
	8-350, 2 B.C.	Hydraulic⑦		45	⑧	1.582④	140 @ 1.13	.0016–.0033	.0021–.0038	.3407–.3414	.3407–.3414
	8-350, 4 B.C.	Hydraulic⑦		45	⑧	1.591④	140 @ 1.13	.0016–.0033	.0021–.0038	.3407–.3414	.3407–.3414
	8-400, 2 B.C.	Hydraulic⑦		⑨	⑩	1.582④	140 @ 1.13	.0016–.0033	.0021–.0038	.3407–.3414	.3407–.3414
	8-400, 4 B.C.	Hydraulic⑦		⑨	⑩	1.561④	185 @ 1.29	.0016–.0033	.0021–.0038	.3407–.3414	.3407–.3414
	8-400 Ram Air	Hydraulic⑦		⑨	⑩	1.591④	185 @ 1.29	.0016–.0033	.0021–.0038	.3407–.3414	.3407–.3414
	8-428	Hydraulic⑦		⑨	⑩	1.582④	140 @ 1.13	.0016–.0033	.0021–.0038	.3407–.3414	.3407–.3414
1970	6-250⑤	1 Turn②		46	45	1.66	186 @ 1.27	.0010–.0027	.0010–.0027	.3410–.3417	.3410–.3417
	8-350	Hydraulic⑦		45	44	1.582④	130 @ 1.70	.0016–.0033	.0021–.0038	.3412–.3419	.3412–.3419
	8-400, 265 H.P.	Hydraulic⑦		45	44	1.582④	④⑥	.0016–.0033	.0021–.0038	.3412–.3419	.3407–.3414
	8-400, 290 H.P.	Hydraulic⑦		45	44	1.582④	④⑥	.0016–.0033	.0021–.0038	.3412–.3419	.3407–.3414
	8-400, 330 H.P.	Hydraulic⑦		45	44	1.582④	④⑪	.0016–.0033	.0021–.0038	.3412–.3419	.3407–.3414
	8-400, 350 H.P.	Hydraulic⑦		⑨	⑬	1.591④	132 @ 1.181	.0016–.0033	.0021–.0038	.3412–.3419	.3407–.3414
	8-400 Ram Air	Hydraulic⑦		⑨	⑬	1.591④	132 @ 1.178	.0016–.0033	.0021–.0038	.3412–.3419	.3407–.3414
	8-400 Ram Air IV	Hydraulic⑦		⑨	⑬	1.818④	222 @ 1.291	.0016–.0033	.0021–.0038	.3412–.3419	.3407–.3414
	8-455	Hydraulic⑦		⑨	⑬	1.561④	④⑫	.0016–.0033	.0021–.0038	.3412–.3419	.3407–.3414

Continued

VALVE SPECIFICATIONS—Continued

Year	Model	Valve Lash Int.	Valve Lash Exh.	Valve Angles Seat	Valve Angles Face	Valve Spring Installed Height	Valve Spring Pressure Lbs. @ In.	Stem Clearance Intake	Stem Clearance Exhaust	Stem Diameter Intake	Stem Diameter Exhaust
1971	6-250⑤	1 Turn②	1 Turn②	46	45	1.66	186 @ 1.27	.0010–.0027	.0015–.0032	.3410–.3417	.3410–.3417
	8-307①	1 Turn②	1 Turn②	46	45	1.70	200 @ 1.25	.0010–.0027	.0010–.0027	.3410–.3417	.3410–.3417
	8-350	Hydraulic⑦	Hydraulic⑦	⑨	⑬	—	—	.0016–.0033	.0021–.0038	.3412–.3419	.3410–.3417
	8-400	Hydraulic⑦	Hydraulic⑦	⑨	⑬	—	—	.0016–.0033	.0021–.0038	.3412–.3419	.3407–.3414
	8-400 Ram Air	Hydraulic⑦	Hydraulic⑦	⑨	⑬	—	—	.0016–.0033	.0021–.0038	.3412–.3419	.3407–.3414
	8-455	Hydraulic⑦	Hydraulic⑦	⑨	⑬	—	—	.0016–.0033	.0021–.0038	.3412–.3419	.3407–.3414
1972	6-250⑤	1 Turn②	1 Turn②	46	45	1.66	186 @ 1.27	.0010–.0027	.0015–.0032	.3410–.3417	.3410–.3417
	8-307①	1 Turn②	1 Turn②	46	45	1.70	200 @ 1.25	.0010–.0027	.0010–.0027	.3410–.3417	.3410–.3417
	8-350	Hydraulic⑦	Hydraulic⑦	⑭	⑮	1.66	186 @ 1.27	.0010–.0027	.0010–.0027	.3410–.3417	.3410–.3417
	8-400 2 Bar. Carb.	Hydraulic⑦	Hydraulic⑦	45	44	1.59④	126 @ 1.21④	.0016–.0033	.0021–.0038	.3412–.3419	.3407–.3414
	8-400 4 Bar. Carb.	Hydraulic⑦	Hydraulic⑦	③	⑧	1.56④	135 @ 1.15④	.0016–.0033	.0021–.0038	.3412–.3419	.3407–.3414
	8-455	Hydraulic⑦	Hydraulic⑦	③	⑧	1.56④	137 @ 1.14④	.0016–.0033	.0021–.0038	.3412–.3419	.3412–.3419
1973-74	6-250	1 Turn②	1 Turn②	46	45	1.66	186 @ 1.27	.0010–.0027	.0015–.0032	.3410–.3417	.3410–.3417
	8-350	Hydraulic⑦	Hydraulic⑦	⑯	⑬	—	—	.0016–.0033	.0021–.0038	.3400	.3400
	8-400 2 Bar. Carb.	Hydraulic⑦	Hydraulic⑦	⑯	⑬	—	—	.0016–.0033	.0021–.0038	.3400	.3400
	8-400 4 Bar. Carb.	Hydraulic⑦	Hydraulic⑦	⑯	⑬	—	—	.0016–.0033	.0021–.0038	.3400	.3400
	8-455	Hydraulic⑦	Hydraulic⑦	⑯	⑬	—	—	.0016–.0033	.0021–.0038	.3400	.3400
1975	6-250⑤	1 Turn	1 Turn	46	45	1.66	186 @ 1.27	.0010–.0027	.0010–.0027	.3410–.3417	.3410–.3417
	V8-260⑰	Hydraulic㉑	Hydraulic㉑	⑱	⑲	1.67	187 @ 1.27	.0010–.0027	.0015–.0032	.3425–.3432	.3420–.3427
	V8-350⑳	Hydraulic㉑	Hydraulic㉑	45	45	1.727	180 @ 1.34	.0015–.0035	.0015–.0032	.3720–.3730	.3723–.3730
	V8-350	Hydraulic⑦	Hydraulic⑦	③	⑧	1.727	180 @ 1.34	.0016–.0033	.0021–.0038	.3412–.3419	.3407–.3414
	V8-400	Hydraulic⑦	Hydraulic⑦	③	⑧	1.54	135 @ 1.13	.0016–.0033	.0021–.0038	.3412–.3419	.3407–.3414
	V8-455	Hydraulic⑦	Hydraulic⑦	③	⑧	1.57	135 @ 1.16	.0016–.0033	.0021–.0038	.3412–.3419	.3407–.3414

①—For service on this engine, see Chevrolet Chapter.

②—With valve fully closed, turn rocker arm nut down until all play in push rod is eliminated, then tighten nut one additional turn.

③—Intake 30°, exhaust 45°.

④—Outer spring.

⑤—For service on this engine, see Six Cylinder in Chevrolet Chapter.

⑥—Intake 126 @ 1.206, exhaust 134 @ 1.170.

⑦—No adjustment. On V8's, rocker arms are correctly positioned when ball retainer nuts are tightened to 20 ft.-lbs.

⑧—Intake 29°, exhaust 44°.

⑨—Small valve engines, intake and exhaust 45°. Large valve engines intake 30° and exhaust 45°.

⑩—Small valve engines, intake 46° and exhaust 44°. Large valve engines, intake 29° and exhaust 44°.

⑪—Intake 133 @ 1.172, exhaust 134 @ 1.168.

⑫—Intake 137 @ 1.151, exhaust 137 @ 1.148.

⑬—Small valve engines, intake 44° and exhaust 44°. Large valve engines, intake 29° and exhaust 44°.

⑭—Small valve engines, 46°. Large valve engines, 45°.

⑮—Small valve engines, intake 46° and exhaust 45°. Large valve engines, intake and exhaust 45°.

⑯—Small valve engines, intake 45° and exhaust 45°. Large valve engines, intake 30° and exhaust 45°.

⑰—See Oldsmobile Chapter for service procedures.

⑱—Intake 45°, exhaust 59°.

⑲—Intake 46°, exhaust 60°.

⑳—Ventura only. See Buick Chapter for service procedures.

㉑—No adjustment.

PISTONS, PINS, RINGS, CRANKSHAFT & BEARINGS

Year	Model	Piston Skirt Clearance	Ring End Gap①		Wrist-pin Diameter	Rod Bearings		Main Bearings			
			Comp.	Oil		Shaft Diameter	Bearing Clearance	Shaft Diameter	Bearing Clearance	Thrust on Bear. No.	Shaft End Play
1969	6-250	.0022–.0038	.015	.035	.9272	2.00	.0005–.0028	2.30	.0003–.0020	7	.002–.006
	V8-350	.0025–.0031	.020	.035	.9802	2.25	.0005–.0025	3.00	.0002–.0020	4	.003–.009
	V8-400	.0025–.0031⑤	.020	.035	.9802	2.25	.0005–.0025	3.00	.0002–.0020	4	.003–.009
	V8-428	.0030–.0036	.020	.035	.9802	2.25	.0005–.0025	3.25	.0002–.0020	4	.003–.009
1970–72	6-250④	.0005–.0015	.010	.015	.9272	2.00	.0007–.0027	2.30	.0003–.0029	7	.002–.006
	V8-307⑧	.0005–.0011	.010	.015	.927	2.099–2.100	.0013–.0035	⑨	②	5	.002–.006
	V8-350	.0025–.0033	.019	.035	.9802	2.25	.0005–.0025	3.00	.0002–.0017	4	.0035–.0085
	V8-400	.0025–.0033	⑥	.035	.9802	2.25	.0005–.0025	3.00	.0002–.0017	4	.0035–.0085
	V8-455	.0025–.0033	⑦	.035	.9802	2.25	.0005–.0026	3.25	.0005–.0021	4	.0035–.0085
1973-74	6-250	.0005–.0015	.010	.015	.9272	2.00	.0007–.0027	2.30	.0003–.0029	7	.002–.006
	V8-350	.0029–.0037	⑥	.035	.9802	2.25	.0005–.0025	3.00	.0002–.0017	4	.003–.009
	V8-400	.0029–.0037	⑧	.035	.9802	2.25	.0005–.0025	3.00	.0002–.0017	4	.003–.009
	V8-455	⑩	⑦	.035	.9802	2.25	⑪	3.25	⑫	4	.003–.009
1975	6-250⑧	.0005–.0015	.010	.015	.9272	2.000	.0007–.0027	2.30	.0003–.0029	7	.002–.006
	V8-260⑬	—	.010	.015	.9805	2.124	.0005–.0026	⑮	⑯	3	.004–.008
	V8-350⑭	.0008–.0014	.013	.015	.9396	2.000	.0005–.0026	2.9995	.0004–.0015	3	.003–.009
	V8-350	.0029–.0037	.019	.035	.9802	2.25	.0005–.0025	3.00	.0002–.0017	4	.0035–.0085
	V8-400	.0029–.0037	⑥	.035	.9802	2.25	.0005–.0026	3.00	.0002–.0017	4	.0035–.0085
	V8-455	.0021–.0029	⑦	.035	.9802	2.25	.0010–.0031	3.25	.0005–.0021	4	.0035–.0085

①—Fit rings in tapered bores for clearance listed in tightest portion of ring travel.
②—No. 1: .0008–.002; No. 2, 3, 4, .0011–.0023; No. 5: .0017–.0033.
④—For service on this engine, see Six Cylinder in Chevrolet Chapter.
⑤—V8-400 Ram Air IV use .0055–.0061.
⑥—Top ring .019″, second ring .015″.
⑦—Top ring .021″, second ring .015″.
⑧—For service on this engine, see Chevrolet Chapter.
⑨—Front: 2.4502, Rear: 2.4507, others: 2.4505.

⑩—1973 exc. super-duty .0025″–.0033″, super-duty .0064″–.0072″; 1974 exc. super-duty .0021″–.0029″, super-duty .0064″–.0072″.
⑪—Exc. super-duty .0005″–.0025″, super-duty .0015″–.0031″.
⑫—Exc. super-duty .0005″–.0021″, super-duty .0010″–.0026″.
⑬—See Oldsmobile Chapter for service procedures.
⑭—Ventura only. See Buick Chapter for service procedures.
⑮—No. 1—2.4998; No. 2, 3, 4, 5; 2.4985–2.4995.
⑯—No. 1, 2, 3, 4 .0005–.0021; No. 5—.0015–.0031.

BRAKE SPECIFICATIONS

Year	Model	Brake Drum Inside Diameter	Wheel Cylinder Bore Diameter			Master Cylinder Bore Diameter		
			Disc Brake	Front Drum Brake	Rear Drum Brake	Disc Brakes	Drum Brakes	Power Brakes
1969–73	①	9½	2¹⁵⁄₁₆	1⅛	⅞	1⅛	1	1
	Pontiac	11②	2¹⁵⁄₁₆	1⅛	¹⁵⁄₁₆	1⅛	1	1
1974	①	9½③	2¹⁵⁄₁₆	1⅛	1⅛④	1⅛	1	1
	Pontiac	11⑤	2¹⁵⁄₁₆	—	¹⁵⁄₁₆	1⅛	1	1
1975	Ventura	9½	2¹⁵⁄₁₆	—	⅞	1	—	1⅛
	⑥	9½③	2¹⁵⁄₁₆	—	⅞⑦	1	—	1⅛
	Grand Prix	11	2¹⁵⁄₁₆	—	¹⁵⁄₁₆	—	—	1⅛
	Pontiac	11⑧	2¹⁵⁄₁₆	—	¹⁵⁄₁₆⑧	—	—	1⅛

①—Intermediates, Ventura II, Firebird and Grand Prix.
②—1971-73 Wagon, 12″.
③—Wagon, 11″.
④—Wagon, ¹⁵⁄₁₆″.
⑤—Wagon 12″.
⑥—Firebird and intermediates.
⑦—Wagon ¹⁵⁄₁₆″.
⑧—Wagon 1″.

ALTERNATOR & REGULATOR SPECIFICATIONS

Year	Alternator					Regulator						
				Output @ 14 Volts			Field Relay			Voltage Regulator		
	Model	Rated Hot Output Amps.	Field Current 12 Volts @ 80° F.	2000 R.P.M. Amps.	5000 R.P.M. Amps.	Model	Air Gap In.	Point Gap In.	Closing Voltage	Air Gap In.	Point Gap In.	Voltage @ 125° F.
1969–70	1100699	42	2.2–2.6	28	40	1119515	.015	.030	1.5–3.2	.067	.014	13.5–14.4
	1100700	55	2.2–2.6	32	50	1119515	.015	.030	1.5–3.2	.067	.014	13.5–14.4
	1100702	60	4.0–4.5	36	58	1116368	—	—	—	—	—	13.4–14.1
	1100703	60	4.0–4.5	36	58	1116368	—	—	—	—	—	13.4–14.1
	1100704	37	2.2–2.6	25	35	1119515	.015	.030	1.5–3.2	.067	.014	13.5–14.4
	1100736	37	2.2–2.6	25	35	1119515	.015	.030	1.5–3.2	.067	.014	13.5–14.4
	1100737	55	2.2–2.6	32	50	1119511	—	—	—	.067	.015	13.5–14.4
	1100738	55	2.2–2.6	32	50	1119511	—	—	—	.067	.015	13.5–14.4
	1100739	42	2.2–2.6	28	40	1119511	—	—	—	.067	.015	13.5–14.4
	1100740	60	4.0–4.5	36	58	1116370	—	—	—	—	—	13.7–14.3
	1100745	55	2.2–2.6	32	50	1119515	.015	.030	1.5–3.2	.067	.014	13.5–14.4
	1100747	55	2.2–2.6	32	50	1116370	—	—	—	—	—	13.7–14.3
	1100758	66	4.1–4.5	38	62	1116370	—	—	—	—	—	13.7–14.3
	1100760	55	2.2–2.6	32	50	1119515	.015	.030	1.5–3.2	.067	.014	13.5–14.4
	1100761	37	2.2–2.6	25	35	1119515	.015	.030	1.5–3.2	.067	.014	13.5–14.4
	1100762	37	2.2–2.6	25	35	1119515	.015	.030	1.5–3.2	.067	.014	13.5–14.4
	1100763	66	4.1–4.5	38	62	1116370	—	—	—	—	—	13.7–14.3
	1100800	55	2.2–2.6	—	—	—	—	—	—	—	—	—
	1100801	42	—	—	—	—	—	—	—	—	—	—
	1100830	55	2.2–2.6	32	50	1119515	.015	.030	1.5–3.2	.067	.014	13.5–14.4
	1100832	37	2.2–2.6	25	35	1119515	.015	.030	1.5–3.2	.067	.014	13.5–14.4
	1100905	37	2.2–2.6	25	35	1119515	.015	.030	1.5–3.2	.067	.014	13.5–14.4
1971	1100550	37	4.0–4.5	—	32	—	—	—	—	—	—	—
	1100920	55	4.0–4.5	—	50	—	—	—	—	—	—	—
	1100927	37	4.0–4.5	—	32	—	—	—	—	—	—	—
	1100928	55	4.0–4.5	—	50	—	—	—	—	—	—	—
	1101015	80	4.0–4.5	—	74	—	—	—	—	—	—	—
	1100566	37	2.2–2.6	25	35	1119515	.015	.030	1.5–3.2	.067	.014	13.8–14.8
	1100836	37	2.2–2.6	25	35	1119515	.015	.030	1.5–3.2	.067	.014	13.8–14.8
	1100843	61	2.2–2.6	33	58	1119515	.015	.030	1.5–3.2	.067	.014	13.8–14.8
1972	1100927	37	4.0–4.5	—	32	—	—	—	—	—	—	—
	1100928	55	4.0–4.5	—	50	—	—	—	—	—	—	—
	1101015	80	4.0–4.5	—	74	—	—	—	—	—	—	—
	1100566	37	—	—	35	1119515	.015	.030	1.5–3.2	.067	.014	13.8–14.8
	1102440	37	—	—	32	1119515	.015	.030	1.5–3.2	.067	.014	13.8–14.8
	1102463	61	—	—	55	1119515	.015	.030	1.5–3.2	.067	.014	13.8–14.8
1973–74	1100497	37	4.0–4.9	—	36①	Integral	—	—	—	—	—	—
	1100927	37	4.0–4.5	—	32	Integral	—	—	—	—	—	—
	1100928	55	4.0–4.5	—	50	Integral	—	—	—	—	—	—
	1101015	80	4.0–4.5	—	74	Integral	—	—	—	—	—	—
1975	1100497	37	—	—	—	—	—	—	—	—	—	—
	1101027	80	—	—	—	—	—	—	—	—	—	—
	1102347	61	—	—	—	—	—	—	—	—	—	—
	1102399	37	—	—	—	—	—	—	—	—	—	—
	1102457	55	—	—	—	—	—	—	—	—	—	—
	1102481	37	—	—	—	—	—	—	—	—	—	—
	1102482	55	—	—	—	—	—	—	—	—	—	—

①—At 7000 R.P.M.

PONTIAC—Exc. Astre

ENGINE TIGHTENING SPECIFICATIONS*

★Torque specifications are for clean and lightly lubricated threads only. Dry or dirty threads produce increased friction which prevents accurate measurement of tightness.

Year	Model	Spark Plugs Ft. Lbs.	Cylinder Head Bolts Ft. Lbs.	Intake Manifold Ft. Lbs.	Exhaust Manifold Ft. Lbs.	Rocker Arm Ft. Lbs.	Rocker Arm Cover Ft. Lbs.	Connecting Rod Cap Bolts Ft. Lbs.	Main Bearing Cap Bolts Ft. Lbs.	Flywheel to Crank-shaft Ft. Lbs.	Vibration Damper or Pulley Ft. Lbs.
1969	6 Cyl.	20	95	30	30	—	15	33	100	60	160
	V8's	20	95	40	30	20	5	43	100③	95	160
1970–72	6 Cyl.④	15	95	②	25	—	55⑤	35	65	60	—
	V8-307⑦	15	65	30	20⑥	—	45⑤	45	75	60	60
	V8's	25	95	40	30	20	8	43	100③	95	160
1973–74	6 Cyl.④	15	95	②	25	—	55⑤	35	65	60	—
	V8's	15	95	40	30	20	8	①	100③	95	160

①—Exc. V8-455 Super Duty 43 ft. lbs. On V8-455 Super Duty torque in 10 ft. lbs. steps until 60 lbs. measure for .006″–.008″ bolt elongation from original length, if less then .006″ proceed with 5 ft. lb. steps as necessary to obtain proper elongation.
②—Outer 20, all others 30.
③—Rear 120.
④—For service on this engine, see Six Cylinder in Chevrolet Chapter.
⑤—Inch pounds.
⑥—Inside bolts 30 ft. lbs.
⑦—For service on this engine, see Chevrolet Chapter.

REAR AXLE SPECIFICATIONS

Year	Model	Carrier Type	Ring Gear & Pinion Backlash		Pinion Bearing Preload			Differential Bearing Preload		
			Method	Adjustment	Method	New Bearings Inch-Lbs.	Used Bearings Inch-Lbs.	Method	New Bearings Inch-Lbs.	Used Bearings Inch-Lbs.
1969–72	All	Integral	Shims	.005–.009	③	20–30	14–20	Shims	②	②
1970–72	—	Integral①	Shims	.005–.008	Spacer	20–25	10–15	Shims	②	②
1971–72	Ventura II	Integral①	Shims	.005–.008	Spacer	25	10	Shims	②	②
1973	All	Integral	Shims	.005–.009	③	20–25	10–15	Shims	②	②
1974	All	Integral	Shims	.005–.009	③	24–32	8–12	Shims	②	②

①—Type C differential (use "C" washers to retain axle shafts).
③—Tighten pinion shaft nut with inch-pound torque wrench.
②—Slip fit plus .008″ tight.

WHEEL ALIGNMENT SPECIFICATIONS

OLD CAR SPECIFICATIONS: For 1946-68 Wheel Alignment Specifications see main index.

| Year | Model | Caster Angle, Degrees | | Camber Angle, Degrees | | | | Toe-In. Inch | Toe-Out on Turns, Deg. | |
| | | Limits | Desired | Limits | | Desired | | | Outer Wheel | Inner Wheel |
				Left	Right	Left	Right			
1969–70	Firebird (1969)	0 to +1	+½	0 to +½	0 to +½	+¼	+¼	⅛−¼	18	20
	Firebird (1970)	−½ to +½	Zero	+½ to +1½	+½ to +1½	+1	+1	⅛−³⁄₁₆	18	20
	Intermediates	−1 to −2	−1½①	0 to +½	0 to +½	+¼	+¼	0−⅛	18	20
	Full Size Models	−1 to −2	−1½	0 to +½	0 to +½	+¼	+¼	0−⅛ .	18	20
1971-72	Firebird	−½ to +½	Zero	+½ to +1½	+½ to +1½	+1	+1	⅛−¼	18	20
	Ventura II	0 to +1	+½	−¼ to +¾	−¼ to +¾	+½	+½	⅛ to ¼	—	20
	②	−1 to −2	−1½	−½ to +½	−½ to +½	Zero	Zero	¹⁄₁₆−³⁄₁₆	18	20
	③	+½ to +1½	+1	+¼ to +1¼	+¼ to +1¼	+¾	+¾	⅛−¼	18	20
1973–74	Firebird	−½ to +½	Zero	+½ to +1½	+½ to +1½	+1	+1	⅛−¼	—	—
	Ventura	0 to +1	+½	−¼ to +¾	−¼ to +¾	+¼	+¼	⅛−¼	—	—
	Grand Prix	+2½ to +3½	+3	+½ to +1½	0 to +1	+1	+½	0−⅛	—	—
	Intermediates	④	⑤	+½ to +1½	0 to +1	+1	+½	0−⅛	—	—
	③	+½ to +1½	+1	+½ to +1½	0 to +1	+1	+½	0−⅛	—	—
1975	Ventura	−½ to +1½	+½	−½ to +1	−½ to +1	+¼	+¼	0−³⁄₁₆	—	—
	Firebird	−1 to +1	Zero	+¼ to +1¾	+¼ to +1¾	+1	+1	¹⁄₁₆−⁵⁄₁₆	—	—
	Intermediate⑥	+½ to +1½	+1	+½ to +1½	0 to +1	+1	+½	0−⅛	—	—
	Intermediate⑦	+1¼ to +2¼	+1¾	+½ to +1½	0 to +1	+1	+½	0−⅛	—	—
	Grand Prix	+2½ to +3½	+3	+½ to +1½	0 to +1	+1	+½	0−⅛	—	—
	Pontiac	+1 to +2	+1½	+½ to +1½	0 to +1	+1	+½	0−⅛	—	—

①—Station Wagons, −2°.
②—Intermediates and Grand Prix.
③—Catalina, Grandville and Bonneville.
④—Manual steering −1½ to −½, Power steering −½ to +½.
⑤—Manual steering −1°, Power steering 0°.
⑥—Manual Steering.
⑦—Power steering.

COOLING SYSTEM & CAPACITY DATA

| Year | Model or Engine | Cooling Capacity, Qts. | | | Radiator Cap Relief Pressure, Lbs. | | Thermo. Opening Temp. ① | Fuel Tank Gals. | Engine Oil Refill Qts. ② | Transmission Oil | | | Rear Axle Oil Pints |
		No Heater	With Heater	With A/C	With A/C	No A/C				3 Speed Pints	4 Speed Pints	Auto. Trans. Qts. ⑫	
1969	6-250	—	12	12¼	14-17	14-17	190	21½⑮	4½⑯	3½	3½	⑰	3
	8-350 Tempest	—	20	21¼	14-17	14-17	190	21½⑮	5	3½	3½	⑰	3
	8-400 Tempest	—	18¼	19¾	14-17	14-17	190	21½⑮	5	3½	3½	⑰	3
	8-350 Firebird	—	19½	20¼	14-17	14-17	190	18½	5	3½	3½	⑰	3
	8-400 Firebird	—	18½	18¾	14-17	14-17	190	18½	5	3½	3½	⑰	3
	8-400 Pontiac	—	18	18	14-17	14-17	190	26½⑦	5	2.8	—	⑰	4½
	8-428 Pontiac	—	17¼	17¼	14-17	14-17	190	26½⑦	5	2.8	—	⑰	4½
	8-400 Grand Prix	—	18¾	21	14-17	14-17	190	21½	5	2.8	2.5	⑰	3
	8-428 Grand Prix	—	17½	17½	14-17	14-17	190	21½	5	2.8	2.5	⑰	3
1970	6-250	—	11.3	13	14-17	14-17	195	21.5	4	3.5	2½	3¼⑲	3
	V8-350 Tempest	—	19.6	19.6	14-17	14-17	190	21.5	5	⑱	2½	3¼⑲	3
	V8-350 Pontiac	—	19.6	19.6	14-17	14-17	190	26⑦	5	⑱	—	3¼⑲	4½
	V8-400 G.T.O.	—	18.3	18.3	14-17	14-17	190	21.5	5	2.8	2½	3¼⑲	3⑳
	V8-350 Firebird	—	19½	20¼	14-17	14-17	190	19½③	5	④	2½	⑤	3¾
	V8-400 Firebird	—	18½	18¾	14-17	14-17	190	19½③	5	④	2½	⑤	3¾

Continued

COOLING SYSTEM & CAPACITY DATA—Continued

Year	Model or Engine	Cooling Capacity, Qts.			Radiator Cap Relief Pressure, Lbs.		Thermo. Opening Temp. ①	Fuel Tank Gals.	Engine Oil Refill Qts. ②	Transmission Oil			Rear Axle Oil Pints
		No Heater	With Heater	With A/C	With A/C	No A/C				3 Speed Pints	4 Speed Pints	Auto. Trans. Qts. ⑫	
1970	V8-400 Pontiac	—	18	18	14–17	14–17	190	26[7]	5	2.8	—	3¼[19]	4½
	V8-400 Gr'd Prix	—	18.7	21.1	14–17	14–17	190	21.5	5	2.8	2½	3¼[19]	3[20]
	V8-455 Gr'd Prix	—	17.5	19.9	14–17	14–17	190	21.5	5	2.8	2½	3¼[19]	3[20]
	V8-455 Pontiac	—	17.2	17.2	14–17	14–17	190	26[7]	5	2.8	—	3¼[19]	4½
1971	6-250 Firebird	—	12	—	14–17	14–17	195	17	4	3.5	3.5	3[19]	4¼
	6-250 Tempest	—	13	12.4	14–17	14–17	195	19[6]	4	3.5	—	3[19]	3
	6-250 Ventura II	—	12.4	—	14–17	14–17	195	16	4	3.5	—	3[19]	3¾
	8-307 Ventura II	14.5	15.5	16.5	14–17	14–17	195	16	4	3.5	—	3[19]	3¾
	8-350 Firebird	—	19.4	20.3	14–17	14–17	195	19	5	3.5	3.5	3[19]	4¼
	8-350 Tempest	—	20.2	20.9	14–17	14–17	195	19[6]	5	3.5[21]	2.5	3[19]	3
	8-350 Pontiac	—	20.2	21	14–17	14–17	195	23.6[22]	5	2.8	—	3[19]	3
	8-400 Firebird	—	18.6	18.7	14–17	14–17	195	17	5	2.8	2.5	3¾[19]	4¼
	8-400 Tempest	—	18.6	20.8	14–17	14–17	195	19[6]	5	2.8	2.5	3¾[19]	3
	8-400 Pontiac	—	18.6	19.6	14–17	14–17	195	23.6[22]	5	2.8	2.5	3¾[19]	3
	8-400 Gr'd Prix	—	18.7	19.7	14–17	14–17	195	23.5	5	2.8	2.5	3¾[19]	3[20]
	8-455 Firebird	—	17.9	18.7	14–17	14–17	195	17	5	2.8	2.5	3¾[19]	4¼
	8-455 Tempest	—	18.6	20.8	14–17	14–17	195	19[6]	5	2.8	2.5	3¾[19]	3
	8-455 Pontiac	—	17.9	19	14–17	14–17	195	23.6[22]	5	—	2.5	3¾[19]	3
	8-455 Gr'd Prix	—	18.7	19.7	14–17	14–17	195	23.5	5	—	—	3¾[19]	3[20]
1972	6-250 Ventura II	—	12	16	14–17	14–17	195	16	4	3½	—	⑤	3¾
	6-250 Firebird	—	12	—	14–17	14–17	195	17	4	3½	—	⑤	4¼
	6-250 Le Mans	—	13	12.4	14–17	14–17	195	20[23]	4	3½	—	⑤	5[20]
	8-307 Ventura II	—	15	16	14–17	14–17	195	16	4	3	—	⑤	3¾
	8-350 Ventura II	—	19.4	20.3	14–17	14–17	195	16	5	—	—	⑤	3¾
	8-350 Firebird	—	19.4	20.3	14–17	14–17	195	17	5	2.8	2.5	6	4¼
	8-350 LeMans	—	20.2	20.9	14–17	14–17	195	20[23]	5	3½	2.5	6	3[20]
	8-400 Pontiac	—	18.6	19.6	14–17	14–17	195	25[23]	5	—	—	7½	5½
	8-400 Firebird	—	18.6	18.7	14–17	14–17	195	17	5	—	2.5	7½	4¼
	8-400 LeMans	—	18.6	20.8	14–17	14–17	196	20[23]	5	2.8	2.5	7½	3[20]
	8-400 Gr'd Prix	—	18.7	19.7	14–17	14–17	195	26	5	—	—	7½	3[20]
	8-455 Pontiac	—	17.9	19.0	14–17	14–17	195	25[23]	5	—	—	7½	5½
	8-455 Firebird	—	17.9	18.9	14–17	14–17	195	17	5	—	2.5	7½	4¼
	8-455 LeMans	—	17.9	18.9	14–17	14–17	195	20[23]	5	—	2.5	7½	3[20]
1973	6-250 Ventura II	—	12	—	14–17	14–17	195	21.5	4	3½	—	1½[8]	3¾
	6-250 Firebird	—	12.4	—	14–17	14–17	195	18	4	3½	—	4[8]	4¼
	6-250 Le Mans	—	12.4	13.4	14–17	14–17	195	22	4	3½	—	4[8]	3[28]
	8-350 Ventura II	—	19.5	20.5	14–17	14–17	195	21.5	4	3½	3½	4[27]	3¾
	8-350 Firebird	—	19.5	20.5	14–17	14–17	195	18	5	3½	3½	4[27]	4¼
	8-350 Le Mans	—	20.2	21.4	14–17	14–17	195	22	5	3½[28]	3½	4[27]	3[28]
	8-400 Pontiac	—	18.6	19.4	14–17	14–17	195	26[14]	5	—	—	3¾[8]	5½[29]
	8-400 Firebird	—	18.6	19.2	14–17	14–17	195	18	5	—	2½	3¾[8]	4¼
	8-400 Le Mans	—	18.6	19.8	14–17	14–17	195	22[24]	5	2¾	2½	3¾[8]	3[28]
	8-400 Grand Prix	—	18.6	19.2	14–17	14–17	195	25	5	—	—	3¾[8]	3[28]
	8-455 Pontiac	—	18.0	18.4	14–17	14–17	195	26[14]	5	—	—	3¾[8]	5½[29]
	8-455 Firebird	—	18.0	19.0	14–17	14–17	195	18	5	—	2½	3¾[8]	4¼
	8-455 Le Mans	—	18.0	19.0	14–17	14–17	195	22[24]	5	—	2½	3¾[8]	3[28]
1974	6-250 Ventura	—	13.1	—	14–17	14–17	195	21.5	4	3½	—	4½[26]	3¾
	6-250 Firebird	—	13.5	—	14–17	14–17	195	21.5	4	3½	—	4½[26]	4¼
	6-250 Le Mans	—	14.7	—	14–17	14–17	195	22	4	3½	—	4½[26]	3[28]
	8-350 Ventura	—	20.0	20.0	14–17	14–17	195	21.5	5	3½	2½	4½[26]	3¾
	8-350 Firebird	—	22.0	22.9	14–17	14–17	195	21.5	5	3½	2½	4½[26]	4¼
	8-350 Le Mans	—	21.3	23.6	14–17	14–17	195	22	5	3½[28]	2½	4½[26]	3[28]
	8-350 Pontiac	—	21.6	22.4	14–17	14–17	195	25.8	5	—	—	4½[11]	4¼[29]

Continued

COOLING SYSTEM & CAPACITY DATA—Continued

Year	Model or Engine	Cooling Capacity, Qts.			Radiator Cap Relief Pressure, Lbs.		Thermo. Opening Temp. ①	Fuel Tank Gals.	Engine Oil Refill Qts. ②	Transmission Oil			Rear Axle Oil Pints
		No Heater	With Heater	With A/C	With A/C	No A/C				3 Speed Pints	4 Speed Pints	Auto. Trans. Qts. ⑫	
1974	8-400 Firebird	—	21.9	22.9	14–17	14–17	195	21.5	5	—	2½	4½⑪	4¼
	8-400 Le Mans	—	21.3	22.8	14–17	14–17	195	22㉔	5	—	2½	4½⑪	3㉘
	8-400 Grand Prix	—	21.6	24.0	14–17	14–17	195	25	5	—	—	4½⑪	3㉚
	8-400 Pontiac	—	21.6	22.4	14–17	14–17	195	25.8	5	—	—	4½⑪	4¼㉙
	8-455 Firebird	—	20.3	21.3	14–17	14–17	195	21.5	5	—	2½	4½⑪	4¼
	8-455 Le Mans	—	21.1	21.6	14–17	14–17	195	22㉔	5	—	—	4½⑪	3㉘
	8-455 Grand Prix	—	20.2	22.2	14–17	14–17	195	25	5	—	—	4½⑪	3㉚
	8-455 Pontiac	—	19.8	22.3	14–17	14–17	195	25.8	5	—	—	4½⑪	4¼㉙
1975	6-250 Ventura	—	12.1	—	14–17	14–17	195	20.5	4	3½	—	3¾	4¼
	6-250 Firebird	—	12.5	—	14–17	14–17	195	20.2	4	3½	—	3¾	4¼
	6-250 Le Mans	—	13.3	—	14–17	14–17	195	21.8	4	3½	—	3¾	4¼
	V8-260 Ventura	—	—	—	14–17	14–17	195	20.5	4	3½	—	3¾	4¼
	V8-350 Ventura	—	16.9	17.2	14–17	14–17	190	20.5	4	—	—	3¾	4¼
	V8-350 Firebird	—	22	22.8	14–17	14–17	195	20.2	5	3½	2½	3¾	4¼
	V8-350 Le Mans	—	21.3	23.2	14–17	14–17	195	21.8	5	—	—	3¾	4¼
	V8-400 Firebird	—	22	⑨	14–17	14–17	195	20.2	5	—	2½	3¾	4¼
	V8-400 Le Mans	—	21.3	⑩	14–17	14–17	195	21.8⑬	5	—	—	3¾	4¼㉛
	V8-400 Grand Prix	—	21.6	24	14–17	14–17	195	25	5	—	—	3¾	5.31
	V8-400 Pontiac	—	21.6	22.4	14–17	14–17	195	25.8⑭	5	—	—	3¾	5.31㉜
	V8-455 Le Mans	—	22.3	22.2	14–17	14–17	195	21.8⑬	5	—	—	3¾	4¼㉛
	V8-455 Grand Prix	—	20.2	21.6	14–17	14–17	195	25	5	—	—	3¾	5.31
	V8-455 Pontiac	—	19.8	22.3	14–17	14–17	195	25.8⑭	5	—	—	3¾	5.31

①—With alcohol-type anti-freeze use a 160° unit.
②—Add one quart with filter change.
③—With Evaporative Control System 17.
④—Saginaw 3.5, Muncie 4.
⑤—Two speed unit; oil pan 1½ qts., complete refill 9½ qts. Turbo Hydra Matic 350; oil pan 2½ qts., complete refill 5 qts. Turbo Hydra Matic 400; oil pan 3¾ qts., complete refill 9½ qts.
⑥—Station Wagons 21.5.
⑦—Station Wagons 24 gals.
⑧—Oil pan only. After overhaul 9½ qts.
⑨—2 BBI. Carb. 22.8 qts., 4 BBI. Carb. 23.6 qts.
⑩—2 BBI. Carb. 23.2 qts., 4 BBI. Carb. 23.6 qts.

⑪—Oil pan only. After overhaul 12 qts.
⑫—Approximate. Make final check with dipstick.
⑬—Grand Am 25 gals., Sta. Wagon 22 gals.
⑭—Station Wagons 22 gals.
⑮—Station Wagons 20 gals.
⑯—Add ½ qt. with filter change.
⑰—Two speed unit; oil pan 2½ qts. and complete refill 7½ qts. Three speed unit ("J" Prefix); oil pan 3 qts. and complete refill 10 qts. Three speed unit ("P" Prefix); oil pan 3.7 qts. and complete refill 9½ qts.
⑱—Standard unit 3.5 pints, heavy duty 2.8 pints.
⑲—Oil pan only.

⑳—5 pts. with 8¾" ring gear.
㉑—Heavy duty 2.8.
㉒—Station Wagons 22.5.
㉓—Station Wagon 23.
㉔—Grand Am 25 gals.
㉕—Muncie 2¾ pints.
㉖—Oil pan only. After overhaul 11 qts.
㉗—Oil pan only. After overhaul 10½ qts.
㉘—"C" Type 4.9 pints.
㉙—"C" Type 4¼ pints.
㉚—"C" Type 3.9 pints.
㉛—Station Wagon 5.31 pts.
㉜—8½" ring gear 4¼ pts.

Electrical Section

1975 HIGH ENERGY IGNITION SYSTEM (H.E.I.)

Service procedures for the V8 H.E.I. distributors are found in the "Electronic Ignition System" section of the "Tune Up Service" chapter. Service procedures for the H.E.I. distributor used on the 6-250 engine differ slightly since the ignition coil is mounted externally.

On all 1975 H.E.I. distributors, a special RFI rotor is used to further reduce radio interference.

DISTRIBUTOR, REPLACE

1. Disconnect distributor-to-coil primary wire.

   NOTE: On H.E.I. systems, disconnect feed and module connectors from distributor cap.

2. Remove distributor cap.
3. Crank engine so rotor is in position to fire No. 1 cylinder and timing mark on vibration damper is indexed with pointer.
4. Remove vacuum line from distributor.
5. Remove distributor clamp.
6. Lift distributor from engine.

Installation

1. Check to see that engine is at firing position for No. 1 cylinder.
2. Install new gasket on block.
3. Install distributor so vacuum unit faces right side of engine and rotor points toward contact in cap for No. 1 cylinder.
4. Install distributor clamp, leaving screw loose enough to allow distributor to be turned for adjustment.
5. Attach vacuum line to distributor.
6. Install wires in distributor cap.
7. Attach distributor primary wire.
8. Adjust point gap, replace cap and set ignition timing.

NOTE: When using a timing light to adjust ignition timing, the connection should be made at the No. 1 spark plug. Forcing foreign objects through the boot at the No. 1 terminal of the distributor cap will damage the boot and could cause engine misfiring.

STARTER, REPLACE

1969-75 Six-Cyl.

1. Disconnect ground cable at battery.
2. Disconnect cable and wiring harness leads from starter solenoid.
3. Unfasten and remove starter.

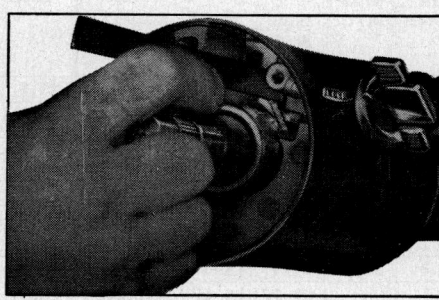

Fig. 1   Ignition lock replace: 1969-75

1969-75 V8s

1. Disconnect cable from battery.
2. Raise front of car and pull battery cable and solenoid wire loom down so they hang free of surrounding parts.
3. Unfasten and remove starter with cable and solenoid wire loom.
4. Remove wires from solenoid and cable from clamp or solenoid bracket.
5. Reverse procedure to install.

IGNITION LOCK REPLACE

1969-75

1. Follow the procedure to remove the turn signal switch as described further on.
2. Remove the lock cylinder in "RUN" position by inserting a thin tool (screwdriver or knife blade), Fig. 1, into the slot next to the switch mounting screw boss (right hand slot) and depress spring latch at bottom of slot, which releases lock. Remove lock by pulling out of housing.

NOTE: If this is the first time the lock cylinder is being removed, the slot will be covered by a thin casting "flash" which is easily broken when inserting thin tool.

Fig. 2   Ignition switch. 1969-75 (typical)

IGNITION SWITCH, REPLACE

1969-75

1. Disconnect battery and loosen toe pan screws.
2. Lower steering column from instrument panel.

   NOTE: On some models it may be necessary to remove the upper column mounting bracket if it hinders the servicing of switch.

3. Disconnect switch wires and remove switch.
4. To replace switch move key lock to OFF-LOCK position.
5. Move actuator rod hole in switch to OFF-LOCK position, Fig. 2.
6. Install switch with rod in hole.

Switch Lock Cylinder

1. Place ignition key in lock and depress lock plunger by inserting a small pin through hole in lock cap.
2. While holding plunger in, turn key about 20-deg. counterclockwise to release lock cylinder and remove cylinder from switch.
3. To install, insert key in cylinder. Then with key and cylinder turned about 20-deg. counterclockwise, insert cylinder in lock and rotate clockwise to lock in place.

FREE UP LOCK: Occasionally an ignition lock may stick, making it difficult to insert key and turn lock. If this occurs, blow a small quantity of powdered graphite into the lock key hole and operate key several times until lock operates freely.

If ignition switch will not free up by the use of the graphite, it must be replaced. To remove a stuck lock use a ⅜" drill and drill out the center of the cylinder. The lock tumblers must be destroyed before the cylinder can be removed.

LIGHT SWITCH, REPLACE

1969-75

1. Remove battery cable, pull knob to "On" position, depress latch button and remove knob and shaft.
2. Remove retaining nut.
3. Remove wire connector and remove switch.
4. On vacuum-operated headlight models, remove vacuum connector.
5. Reverse procedure to install.

STOP LIGHT SWITCH, REPLACE

1969-75

The stop light switch has a slip fit in the mounting sleeve which permits positive adjustment by pulling the brake pedal up firmly against the stop. The pedal arm forces the switch body to slip in the mounting sleeve bushing to position the switch properly.

1. Disconnect wires from switch and remove switch from bracket.
2. Position switch in bracket and push in to maximum distance. Brake pedal arm moves switch to correct distance on rebound. Check if pedal is in full return position by lifting slightly by hand.
3. Connect switch wires by inserting plug on switch.

NEUTRAL SAFETY SWITCH

1974-75

1. Loosen switch retaining screws and place selector lever in "Reverse" on manual transmission models or "Neutral" on automatic transmission models.
2. Rotate switch until alignment hole in outer cover aligns with hole in inner contact carrier. Insert a .089 inch gauge pin into alignment hole on manual transmission models or a .096 inch gauge pin into alignment hole on top of switch on automatic transmission models. On all models, gauge pin is inserted approximately $\frac{3}{8}$ inch.
3. Tighten switch retaining screws and remove gauge pin.

1971 Column & 1972-73 All

1. Loosen switch retaining screws and place selector lever in "Drive" for 1971 column shift and 1972 console shift models, or "Neutral" for 1972 column shift and all 1973 models.
2. Rotate switch until alignment hole in outer cover aligns with hole in inner contact carrier and insert a .092 inch gauge pin into alignment hole approximately $\frac{3}{8}$ inch.

NOTE: On 1973 automatic transmission models, alignment hole is located on top of switch.

3. Tighten switch retaining screws and remove gauge pin.

1971 Console & 1969-70 All

1. To replace switch, position shift tube in drive position.
2. Insert switch drive tang in shifter tube slot and assemble switch to column jacket.
3. To adjust switch, position and hold shift lever in low range while inserting blade of reset gauge J23056-2 into the RESET slot of switch. Be sure the tool is inserted about $\frac{9}{16}$".

4. Insert blade of gauge J22701-5 into ADJUST slot of switch and move shift lever to park position and remove gauge.
5. Check starter in all ranges.

CLUTCH START SWITCH

1969-75

All cars equipped with a manual transmission use a clutch start switch which is mounted on the pedal bracket. The switch closes when the clutch is depressed and completes solenoid connection. When installing switch, no adjustment is necessary.

TURN SIGNAL SWITCH

1969-75

NOTE: On tilt column, the column must first be lowered from panel.

1. Remove steering wheel using puller.

CAUTION: Do not hammer on end of shaft as hammering could collapse shaft or loosen plastic injections which maintain column rigidity.

2. Remove three cover screws and lift cover off shaft.

NOTE: Screw retainers will be lost if screws are removed completely from cover.

3. Depress lock plate and pry round wire lock ring out of shaft groove.
4. Slide upper bearing preload spring and turn signal cancelling cam off shaft.
5. Slide thrust washer off shaft and remove turn signal lever.
6. Push hazard warning switch in and unscrew knob.
7. Pull turn signal wiring connector out of bracket on jacket and disconnect.
8. Remove three turn signal switch screws and pull switch straight up.

HORN SOUNDER & STEERING WHEEL

1969-75

1. Lift ornament out of wheel hub.
2. Remove nut and washer from shaft.
3. Remove horn bar (deluxe wheel) or extension and switch assembly (standard wheel).
4. Use a suitable puller to remove wheel.
5. Reverse procedure to install, making sure wheel is in straight ahead position.

INSTRUMENT CLUSTER

1975 All Exc. GTO & Ventura

1. Disconnect battery ground cable.

2. Remove upper and lower instrument panel trim plates.
3. Remove shift indicator cable.
4. On Firebird, loosen steering column nuts and lower column approximately $\frac{1}{2}$ inch.
5. On all models, remove cluster retaining screws, pull cluster outward and disconnect speedometer cable and printed circuit connector, then remove cluster.

1973 GTO & LeMans

1. Disconnect battery ground cable.
2. Remove ash tray and lower instrument panel trimplate.
3. Remove radio knobs and upper trim panel plate.
4. Lower steering column.
5. Remove cluster screws, disconnect speedometer cable circuit connector.
6. Remove cluster.

1973 Grand Prix & Grand Am

1. Disconnect battery ground cable.
2. Remove upper and lower trim panel plates.
3. Lower steering column.
4. Remove cluster screws, disconnect speedometer cable and remove cluster.

1971-75 Ventura & 1974 GTO

1. Disconnect battery and remove steering column cover trim.
2. Remove three screws retaining heater or A/C control panel to instrument panel carrier.
3. Remove radio control knobs, bezels and nuts.
4. Remove screws at top, bottom and side of carrier securing it to instrument panel pad.
5. Disconnect shift quadrant indicator cable at shaft bowl (if automatic), remove two steering column to panel nuts.
6. Remove toe plate cover and five toe plate to cowl screws, lower column from panel and protect it with shop towels or tape.
7. Remove ground wire screw from under left side of panel pad above kick pad and disconnect speedo cable from under dash.
8. Tilt carrier and cluster rearward, disconnect printed circuit and cluster ground connectors and rest assembly on top of column.
9. Remove screws from cluster to carrier assembly and remove cluster.

1971-73 Catalina, Grandville, Bonneville

1. Disconnect battery and remove upper instrument panel trim plate.
2. Remove transmission shift indicator (if automatic) and speedometer cluster bezel.
3. Remove cluster retaining screws, pull rearward, disconnect speedometer cable and printed circuit connector.

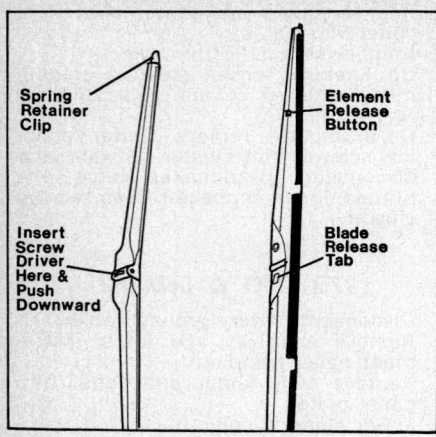

Fig. 3   W/S wiper blades

1971-72 T-37, LeMans & GTO

1. Disconnect battery and remove lower A/C duct if equipped.
2. Remove lower instrument panel trim and glove box.
3. Lower steering column.
4. Disconnect speedometer cable and heater cable at heater case.
5. Remove three instrument panel screws at gauges.
6. Remove three right upper instrument panel nuts.
7. Remove lower instrument panel bolts at right and left ends and at steering column.
8. Position crash pad outward on column.
9. Disconnect printed circuit.
10. Remove instrument panel harness retaining screws.
11. Remove cluster retaining screws and remove cluster.

1971-72 Grand Prix

1. Disconnect battery and remove lower A/C duct if equipped.
2. Remove pillar post mouldings and filler plate at windshield.
3. Remove lower instrument panel trim at steering column.
4. Disconnect speedometer cable and radio antenna lead.
5. Lower steering column.
6. Remove upper air outlet vents and instrument panel attaching screws at steering column, console, ends and upper center.
7. Remove lower defroster duct screw at heater case.
8. Position instrument panel pad outward on column.
9. Disconnect printed circuit.
10. Remove wire harness retaining screws and cluster ground screw.
11. Remove cluster mounting screws and cluster.

1970-73 Firebird

1. Disconnect battery cable and upper

instrument panel trim plate.
2. Remove lower instrument panel trim and bracket at steering column.
3. Loosen two steering column nuts to lower column.
4. Remove cluster screws, pull rearward, disconnect speedometer cable and printed circuit connector.

1969-70 Grand Prix

1. Disconnect battery and remove glove box.
2. Disconnect speedo cable and wire connectors at headlight switch, wipers, turn signal, ignition switch, printed circuit, heater and air conditioner panel.
3. Remove lower column trim and disconnect air control cable at heater case.
4. Remove screws at instrument locations and instrument panel to column support.
5. Remove screws at outboard lower ends of panel.
6. Remove screws retaining right and left side of instrument panel to body. To do this, remove upper vent nozzles by inserting two thin blade screwdrivers on right and left side of nozzle to disengage retaining clips.
7. Remove upper instrument panel cover plate. Studs are pushed into retainers, pry up carefully to remove.
8. Remove two upper panel retaining screws and upper speaker support bracket screw.
9. Remove console to instrument panel screws.
10. Loosen toe plate screws.
11. Remove column to lower panel retaining nuts and lower column.
12. Pull entire instrument panel rearward on left far enough to gain access to cluster.
13. Remove ground strap screws and panel harness retaining screws.
14. Remove cluster retaining screws and remove cluster.

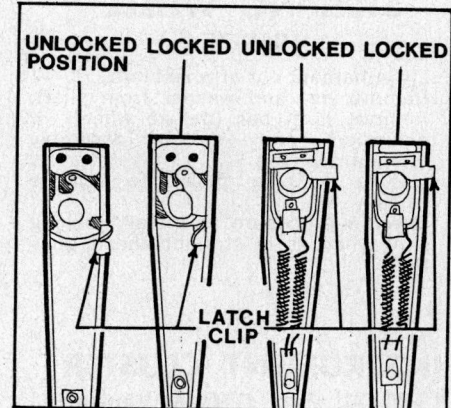

Fig. 5   W/S wiper arms

UNLOCKED LOCKED UNLOCKED LOCKED
POSITION

LATCH CLIP

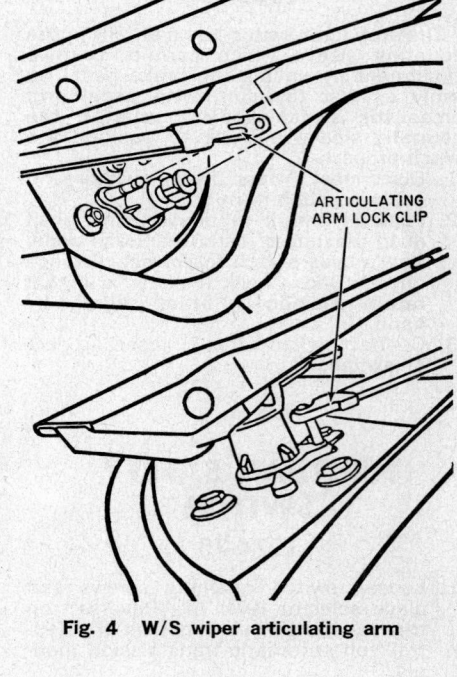

Fig. 4   W/S wiper articulating arm

ARTICULATING ARM LOCK CLIP

1969-70 Pontiac

1. Disconnect battery.
2. Remove lower instrument panel cover and remove radio.
3. Remove heater or air conditioning control panel.
4. Disconnect speedometer, printed circuit connector, cigar lighter and instrument panel harness from rear of cluster.
5. Remove four cluster retaining screws.
6. Position ground straps so that cluster may be pulled from studs and removed towards center of car.

1969-70 Tempest

1. Disconnect battery and remove glove box.
2. Disconnect speed cable and wire connectors at light switch, wiper, turn signal, ignition switch, printed circuit, heater and air conditioning control panel.
3. Remove lower column trim and disconnect air control cable at heater case.
4. Remove three screws at instrument locations.
5. Remove two screws at instrument panel to column support, one screw at each outboard lower end of panel and three nuts above glove box (inner).
6. Loosen two right hand toe plate screws and two screws clamping right toe plate to left toe plate.
7. Remove column to instrument panel bracket nuts and lower column.
8. Pull entire instrument panel rearward far enough to gain access to cluster.

9. Remove ground strap screws and two panel harness retaining screws.
10. Remove cluster retaining screws and remove cluster.

1969 Firebird

1. Disconnect battery and remove lower instrument panel cover.
2. Remove ash tray bracket screws and radio retaining nuts and glove box.
3. Disconnect heater control cables and wire connectors.
4. Disconnect speedo cable and remove upper L. H. vent duct connector.
5. Disconnect headlamp switch shaft.
6. Remove screws across top and bottom of instrument plate and nut on right side (stud through steel portion of dash).
7. Drop steering column by loosening toe plate screws and removing lower column support nuts.
8. Protect top of column and pull panel rearward to rest on column.
9. Disconnect printed circuit accessory, wiper and cigar lighter.
10. Remove ground strap, cluster retaining screws and carefully remove cluster.

W/S WIPER BLADES

Two methods are used to retain wiper blades to wiper arms, Fig. 3. One method uses a press type release tab. When the release tab is depressed the blade assembly can be slid off the wiper arm pin. The other method uses a coil spring retainer. A screwdriver must be inserted on top of the spring and the spring pushed downward. The blade assembly can then be slid off the wiper arm pin. Two methods are also used to retain the blade element in the blade assembly, Fig. 3. One method uses a press type release button. When the button is depressed, the two piece blade assembly can be slid off the blade element. The other method uses a spring type retainer clip in the end of the blade element. When the retainer clip is squeezed together, the blade element can be slid out of the blade assembly.

NOTE: To be sure of correct installation, the element release button, or the spring element retaining clip should be at the end of the wiper blade assembly nearest the wiper transmission.

W/S WIPER ARMS

With Rectangular Motor

1. Wiper motor must be in park position.
2. Use suitable tool to minimize the possibility of windshield or paint finish damage during arm removal.
3. Remove arm by prying up with tool to disengage arm from serrated transmission shaft.
4. To install arm to transmission rotate the required distance and direction so that blades rest in proper position.

With Round Motor

1. Wiper motor must be in park position.
2. Raise hood to gain access to wiper arm.
3. **On Intermediate Models:** Lift arm off transmission shaft. On left arm, slide articulating arm lock clip, Fig. 4, away from transmission pivot pin and lift arm off pin. **On Full Size Models:** Lift arm and slide latch clip, Fig. 5, out from under wiper arm.
4. Release wiper arm and lift arm assembly off transmission shaft.

W/S WIPER MOTOR, REPLACE

1971-75

1. Raise hood and remove cowl screen or grille.
2. Disconnect wiring and washer hoses.
3. Reaching through opening, loosen transmission drive link to crankarm attaching nuts.
4. Remove drive link from motor crankarm.
5. Remove three motor attaching screws and remove motor while guiding crankarm through opening.

1970 Firebird

1. Remove two cowl screen attaching screws from center of cowl screen.
2. Pry cowl screen up at eight integral clips and remove.

NOTE: Install screw as an alternate method of retention in hole provided in screen adjacent to clips.

3. Reaching through cowl opening, loosen two transmission crankarm attaching nuts.
4. Remove transmission crankarm.
5. Disconnect wiring and washer hoses.
6. Remove three motor attaching screws and remove motor while guiding crankarm through hole.

1969 All; 1970 Exc. Firebird

1. Remove hoses and wires connected to wiper.
2. On Pontiac, remove retainer securing wiper crank to transmission linkage. This can be done by removing plastic plug from left side of upper shroud, above wiper motor.
3. On Tempest and Grand Prix, remove screen and loosen clamp securing wiper crank to linkage.
4. Remove screws securing wiper assembly to dash.
5. On Firebird, carefully pull wiper assembly away from firewall until retainer securing wiper crank to transmission can be removed.
6. Remove wiper motor.

W/S WIPER TRANSMISSION, REPLACE

1971-75

With Rectangular Motor

1. Remove wiper arms and blades.
2. Raise hood and remove cowl vent screen or grille.
3. Disconnect wiring from motor.
4. Loosen, do not remove, transmission drive link to motor crankarm attaching nuts and disconnect drive link from crankarm.
5. Remove right and left transmission to body attaching screws and guide transmission and linkage assembly out through opening.

NOTE: When installing, motor must be in Park position.

With Round Motor

1. Raise hood and remove cowl vent screen.
2. On Intermediates, remove right and left wiper arm and blade assemblies. On Full Size cars, remove the arm and blade only from the transmission to be removed.
3. Loosen, do not remove, attaching nuts securing transmission drive link to motor crankarm.

NOTE: On Full Size cars, if only the left transmission is to be removed, it will not be necessary to loosen nuts securing the right assembly.

4. Disconnect transmission drive link from motor crankarm.
5. On Intermediate models, remove right and left transmission to body attaching screws. On Full Size cars, remove the attaching screw securing the transmission to be removed.
6. Remove transmission and linkage assembly by guiding it through opening.

NOTE: When installing, motor must be in Park position.

1969-70

1. Remove wiper arms and blades.
2. Remove fresh air intake screen or grille.
3. Remove wiper transmission screws.
4. On Pontiac models, remove center support screws.
5. On Depressed Park Optional System models, remove retainer securing linkage that attaches to wiper motor crank. On Pontiac models, this can be done by removing plastic plug from left side of upper shroud, directly above wiper motor.
6. On Tempest models, remove retainer securing right wiper transmission to linkage that attaches to wiper motor crank.
7. Remove transmission and linkage.
8. Reverse procedure to install.

W/S WIPER SWITCH

1973-75 Exc. Ventura & 1974 GTO

1. Disconnect battery ground cable. Remove upper and lower instrument panel trimplates.
2. Remove switch mounting plate and disconnect connector.
3. Remove switch retaining screws and remove switch.

1971-72 Catalina, Grandville & Bonneville

1. Disconnect battery and remove upper and lower instrument panel trim plates.
2. Remove speedometer bezel and cluster.
3. Disconnect headlamp, windshield wiper and accessory switch connectors.
4. Remove instrument panel bezel assembly screws, pull rearward and disconnect vent control cable if equipped.
5. Remove wiper switch from backside of bezel assembly.

1971-72 T-37, LeMans, GTO & Grand Prix

1. Disconnect battery and remove lower A/C duct if equipped.
2. Disconnect wire connector.
3. Remove ground strap screw.
4. Unfasten and remove switch.

1971-75 Ventura & 1974 GTO

1. Disconnect battery ground cable.
2. From under dash, disconnect wiring from switch.
3. Remove three screws retaining switch to lower instrument panel and remove switch from panel.

1970-72 Firebird

1. Remove upper and lower instrument panel trim plates.
2. Disconnect wire and unfasten and remove switch.

1969-70 Pontiac, Tempest & Grand Prix

1. Disconnect battery and wire from switch.
2. Remove retaining nuts.
3. Position ground straps and remove switch.

1969 Firebird

1. Disconnect battery.
2. Remove upper vent duct.
3. Remove switch retaining screws and reposition ground straps.
4. Remove switch.

RADIO, REPLACE

NOTE: When installing radio, be sure to adjust antenna trimmer for peak performance.

1973-75 LeMans Grand Am & 1973 GTO

1. Disconnect battery and remove radio knobs and bezels.
2. Remove upper and lower trimplates.
3. Remove radio retaining screws.
4. Remove radio from opening, disconnect connections and antenna lead-in while radio is being pulled out.
5. If new unit is being installed, remove bushing from old unit and install on replacement unit.

1971-75 Catalina, Grandville & Bonneville

1. Disconnect battery and remove radio knobs and hex nuts.
2. Remove upper and lower instrument panel trim plates and front lower radio bracket.
3. Remove glove box and disconnect all connections to radio.
4. Loosen screw holding radio brace to side of radio and slide radio toward front seat.

1971-72 T-37, LeMans, GTO & Grand Prix

1. Disconnect battery and remove lower A/C duct if equipped.
2. Remove radio control knobs and hex nuts.
3. Remove radio support bracket bolt.
4. Disconnect all leads to radio and remove radio.

1971-75 Ventura & 1974 GTO

1. Disconnect battery ground cable.
2. Remove radio knobs, bezels, nuts and side braces screw and disconnect wiring and antenna.
3. Remove radio from under dash.

1970-75 Firebird

1. Disconnect battery.
2. Remove glove box and door and right lower A/C duct if equipped.
3. Remove radio knobs and hex nuts and trim plate.
4. Disconnect all leads to radio.
5. Remove radio bracket and radio from passenger side of instrument panel.

1969 All; 1970 Exc. Firebird

1. Disconnect antenna and wires from radio.
2. Remove knobs, springs, nuts and bezels from control shafts.
3. Remove screws securing radio to dash or to brace and carefully remove radio.

HEATER CORE REMOVAL

1971-75 Without Air Cond.

All except Ventura & 1974 GTO
1. Drain radiator and disconnect heater hoses from core.
2. Remove retaining nuts from core case studs on engine side of dash.
3. Inside car, remove glove box and door on Firebird and heater outlet from case on Firebird.
4. Remove defroster duct retaining screw from heater case and pull entire heater assembly from firewall.
5. Disconnect control cables and wiring and remove assembly. On 1969-72 Grand Prix, disconnect vacuum hoses.
6. Remove core tube seal and core retaining strips and remove core.

Ventura & 1974 GTO
1. Drain radiator and disconnect heater hoses from core.
2. Disconnect battery ground cable.
3. Remove retaining nuts from core case studs on engine side of dash.
4. On 1974-75 models, remove glove box and door.
5. On all models, drill out lower right hand heater case stud with 1/4 inch drill from inside vehicle.
6. Pull entire heater core and case assembly from firewall.
7. Disconnect cables and wiring and remove assembly from car.
8. Remove core tube seal and core retaining strips and remove core.

1971-75 With Air Cond.

Catalina, Grand Ville & Bonneville
1. Drain radiator and disconnect heater hoses from core.
2. Remove three nuts and one screw retaining core and case to dash.
3. Remove glove box and upper and lower instrument panel trim plates.
4. Remove radio.
5. Remove cold air duct and heater outlet duct.
6. Remove defroster duct to heater case screw.
7. Disconnect A/C temperature cable at heater case.
8. Disconnect vacuum hoses from diaphragms on heater case and remove core and case assembly.
9. Remove core from case (three screws).

1973-75 LeMans, Grand Am, Grand Prix & 1973 GTO
1. Drain radiator and disconnect heater hoses from core.
2. Remove glove box, cold air duct and heater outlet and defroster duct screw.
3. Disconnect heater core case from dash. Remove blower motor resistor to gain access to case upper retaining nut.
4. Move case assembly rearward, freeing case studs from cowl and remove assembly.
5. Disconnect temperature cable and vacuum hoses from case and remove screws securing core inside of case.

1971-72 LeMans, Grand Ville, Grand Prix & GTO

1. Drain radiator and disconnect heater hoses from core.
2. Remove lower duct and outlet assembly.
3. Remove glove box.
4. Remove defroster duct attaching screw.
5. Remove screws retaining case to dash.
6. Move core and case assembly rearward to free attaching studs from cowl and remove assembly.
7. Disconnect cables and wiring.
8. Mark heater cam and bracket assembly in three places to insure proper installation.
9. Remove heater cam and bracket assembly.
10. Remove front case to rear case attaching screws.
11. Separate front and rear case.
12. Remove screws retaining core attaching bands and remove core.

Firebird

1. Drain radiator.
2. Remove glove box and door.
3. Remove cold air duct (lower right hand duct) and remove left and center lower A/C ducts.
4. Jack right front area of car and place on safety stand.
5. Remove rocker panel trim on right side and remove screws holding forward portion of rocker panel trim attaching bracket.
6. Remove three lower fender bolts at rear of fender.
7. Remove four fender to skirt bolts at rear of wheel opening.
8. Remove two fender skirt bolts near blower motor area.
9. Pry rear portion of fender out at bottom to gain access to hose clamp on lower core hose and disconnect hose.
10. Disconnect water pump to core hose at core.
11. Remove heater case retaining nuts under hood at dash.
12. Remove two heater case retaining bolts (inside car).
13. Remove console, if equipped. If equipped with tape player, remove console with tape player intact. If equipped with tape player and no console, remove tape player.
14. Disconnect temperature cable at heater case.
15. Remove heater outlet duct.
16. Remove lower defroster duct screw at heater case.
17. Remove right kick panel.
18. Remove heater core and case.
19. Disconnect vacuum hoses from heater case.
20. Remove core from case.

Ventura & 1974 GTO

1. Disconnect battery and drain coolant.
2. Disconnect upper heater hose from core.
3. Remove right front fender skirt bolts and lower skirt to gain access to lower heater hose clamp. Disconnect lower hose and remove lower right hand heater core and case attaching nut.

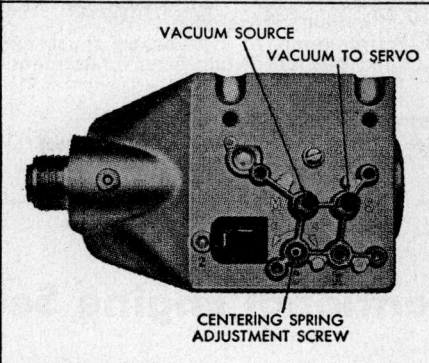

Fig. 6 Centering spring adjustment. 1969-75 Cruise Control

4. Remove glove box and door.
5. Remove recirculation vacuum diaphragm at right kick panel.
6. Remove heater outlet (at bottom of heater case).
7. Remove cold air distributor duct from heater case.
8. Remove heater case extension screws and separate extension from case.
9. Disconnect cables and wiring and remove case and core assembly.
10. Separate core from case.

1970

1. Drain radiator and remove heater hoses at their connections beside the air inlet assembly.
2. Remove retaining nuts from core case studs on engine side of dash.
3. On Firebird, remove the glove box and door and the heater outlet from the heater case.
4. Remove defroster duct retaining screw from heater case and pull entire heater assembly from firewall.
5. Remove all cables, wiring and vacuum hoses if used from heater and remove assembly.
6. Remove core tube seal and core assembly retaining strips and remove core.

1969

1. Drain radiator and remove heater hoses at their connections beside air inlet assembly.
2. Remove five nuts from core case studs on engine side of dash.
3. Inside the car, pull entire heater assembly from firewall.
4. Remove cables and all electrical connectors from heater and remove heater. On Grand Prix, remove vacuum hoses.
5. Remove core tube seal and core retaining strips and remove core.

BLOWER MOTOR REMOVE

1970-75

Catalina, Bonneville, Firebird & Grand Ville

1. Raise car and remove right front

wheel.
2. Cut access hole approx. ¾ of the way along the outline stamped on the right hand fender skirt. Bend cut section of skirt outward for access to blower motor.
3. Disconnect blower motor feed wire.

LeMans, Grand Am, Grand Prix & 1970-73 GTO

1. Disconnect blower motor feed wire.
2. Remove blower motor retaining screws.
3. Remove blower motor.

Ventura & 1974 GTO

1. Disconnect battery and detach hoses from clips on right fender skirt.
2. Raise vehicle on hoist.
3. Remove fender skirt attaching bolts except those retaining the skirt to radiator support.
4. Pull out then down on skirt and place block of wood between skirt and fender to allow clearance for blower motor removal.
5. Disconnect blower motor cooling tube and electrical connections at blower motor.
6. Remove blower motor attaching screws and remove blower motor. Gently pry motor flange if sealer acts as an adhesive.

1969

Less Air Conditioning

1. On all models except Grand Prix, remove battery and tray and on Firebird, unclip hoses.
2. On all models except Grand Prix, remove fender skirt.
3. On all models, disconnect blower motor feed wire.
4. Remove blower motor retaining screws. Remove blower motor.

With Air Conditioning

1. Unclip hoses from fender skirt.
2. Remove rocker moulding.
3. Loosen lower rear fender retaining screws to allow bottom of fender to move.
4. Remove fender skirt. On Firebird first remove battery and tray then remove fender and skirt as an assembly.
5. Remove blower motor retaining screws. Remove motor feed wire and cooling tube.
6. Remove blower motor.

SPEED CONTROLS

1969-75 Cruise Control

Brake Release Switch, Adjust

Apply brake pedal and push both switches forward as far as possible. Pull pedal forcibly rearward to adjust switches.

Chain Linkage, Adjust 1970-75

This adjustment is no longer necessary because of the use of cable-connection to the carburetor.

PONTIAC—Exc. Astre

Chain Linkage, Adjust 1969

1. Start engine and set carburetor to hot idle position.
2. Thread bead chain through hole in carburetor lever extension.
3. Adjust bead chain at extension to provide minimum slack and assemble clip to extension by straddling extension.
4. A minimum of two beads must extend outside of clip after adjustment. Cut off excess chain.

Centering Spring, Adjust

If speed control holds speed three or more mph higher than selected speed, turn centering screw (C) clockwise 1/8 turn or less, Fig. 6.

If speed control holds speed three or more mph below selected speed, turn centering adjustment screw (C) counterclockwise 1/8 turn or less. *Do not move adjustment screw (R).*

Conventional Engine Section

For service on V8-350 Ventura see Buick Chapter
See page 1-663 for the Overhead Camshaft Engine
For service on 6-250 & V8-307 see Chevrolet Chapter
For service on V8-260 see Oldsmobile Chapter

ENGINE MOUNTS REPLACE

1970-75 Six

1. Raise engine to release weight from mount to be replaced.
2. Remove insulator to engine bracket through bolt(s), Figs. 1 and 2.
3. Raise engine approximately 1" above front insulators.
4. Remove front insulator by unscrewing frame bracket to insulator bolt and lifting insulator from bolt.

1969-70 V8

1. Disconnect battery ground cable.
2. Raise engine to release weight off front mounts.
3. Remove bolts fastening engine insulators to engine.
4. Raise engine just clear of insulator.
5. Remove insulator.

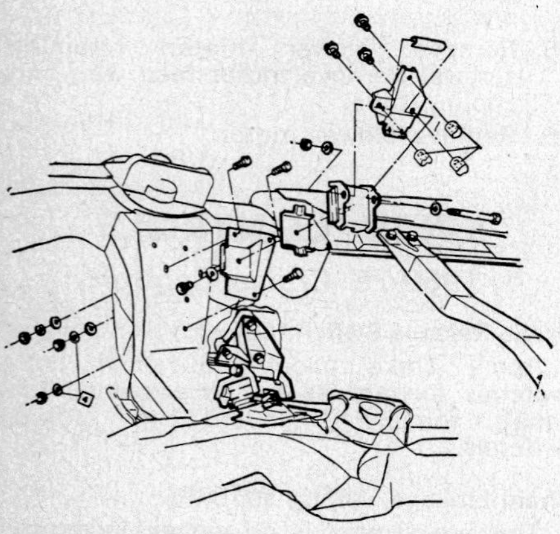

1971-75 V8

1. Disconnect battery ground cable.
2. Raise engine to release weight off front mounts.
3. On **Intermediate Models** remove stabilizer bracket to frame bolts. **On Grand Prix Models** remove the idler arm to frame bolts and disconnect pitman arm from shaft.
4. Remove bolts securing insulators to frame and engine.
5. Remove insulators.

ENGINE, REPLACE

1970-75

1. Disconnect battery cables at battery and drain cooling system.
2. Scribe alignment marks on hood and remove hood from hinges.
3. Disconnect all wiring, ground straps, fuel lines and vacuum hoses from engine.

NOTE: On 1973-74 V8's, remove thermal feed switch, located on rear of left cylinder head on all models except Ventura. On Ventura models, switch is located on the right cylinder head.

4. Remove air cleaner and upper radiator shield assembly.
5. Disconnect radiator hoses and heater hoses at engine.
6. Remove fan and disconnect accelerator linkage.
7. If equipped with power steering or air conditioning, remove pump and/or compressor from mountings and set aside. Do not disconnect hoses.
8. On V8, disconnect transmission vacuum modulator line and power brake vacuum line at carburetor and fold back out of way.
9. Raise vehicle on hoist and drain crankcase.
10. Disconnect exhaust pipe from manifold and remove starter.
11. If equipped with automatic transmission, remove converter cover and three converter retaining bolts and slide converter to rear.
12. With manual transmission, disconnect clutch linkage and remove clutch cross shaft.
13. Remove four lower bell housing bolts.
14. Disconnect transmission filler tube support and starter wire harness shield from cylinder head.
15. Remove two front motor mount to frame bracket bolts.
16. Lower vehicle and using a jack and block of wood, support transmission.
17. Support weight of engine with suitable lifting device.

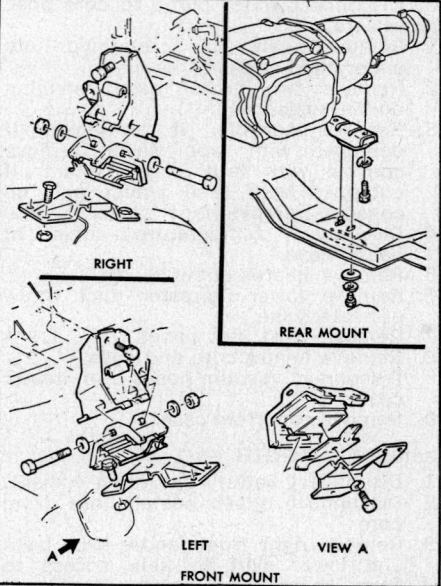

Fig. 2   Engine mounts. 1971-72 Ventura 6 cyl.

Fig. 1   1970-72 Tempest & Firebird 6 cyl.

1-656

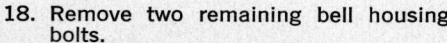

Fig. 3 Installing rocker arm stud without removing cylinder head. Engines with push rod oiling

Fig. 4 Slots filed in rocker arm stud

18. Remove two remaining bell housing bolts.
19. Raise transmission slightly.
20. Position engine forward to free it from transmission and remove from car by tilting front of engine up.

1969 Pontiac & 1969 Tempest & Firebird V8

1. Scribe alignment marks around hood and remove hood.
2. Disconnect engine wiring harness and engine-to-body ground straps.
3. Remove air cleaner and fan shield.
4. If equipped with manual transmission, remove radiator.
5. With power steering or air conditioning, remove pump and compressor from mounting brackets and set aside. Do not disconnect hoses.
6. Remove engine fan and pulley.
7. Disconnect accelerator control linkage and linkage support bracket.
8. If equipped, disconnect automatic transmission vacuum modulator line and power brake vacuum line at car-

buretor and fold back out of the way.

NOTE: On Firebird with A/C, remove wiper motor.

9. Raise vehicle and drain crankcase.
10. Disconnect fuel lines and exhaust pipes.
11. Disconnect starter wires.
12. With automatic transmission, remove converter cover, converter retaining bolts and slide converter to rear.
13. With manual transmission, disconnect clutch linkage, remove clutch cross shaft, starter and lower flywheel cover.
14. Remove lower bell housing bolts.
15. Remove front engine mounts at frame.
16. Lower vehicle.
17. Using jack and block of wood, support transmission.
18. Remove remaining bell housing bolts.
19. Raise transmission slightly. Then, using suitable lifting equipment, remove engine.
20. Reverse procedure to install.

CYLINDER HEAD

NOTE: Pontiac recommends no numerical sequence for tightening cylinder heads. However, they may be tightened by starting at the center bolts and then working alternately from side to side and outward toward the ends.

V8 Engines

1. Remove intake manifold, push rod cover and rocker arm cover.
2. Loosen all rocker arm nuts and move rocker arms off push rods.
3. Remove push rods, keeping them in order so they may be installed in their original locations.
4. Detach exhaust crossover pipe from manifolds.
5. Remove battery ground strap and engine ground strap on left head or engine ground strap.
6. Unfasten and remove head with exhaust manifold attached.

NOTE: To remove left cylinder head on 1972-74 V8-455 HO, SD engines, it is necessary to remove the exhaust manifold and the inner panel of the carburetor heat stove from the cylinder head.

CAUTION: Use extreme care when handling heads as the rocker arm studs are hardened and may crack if struck.

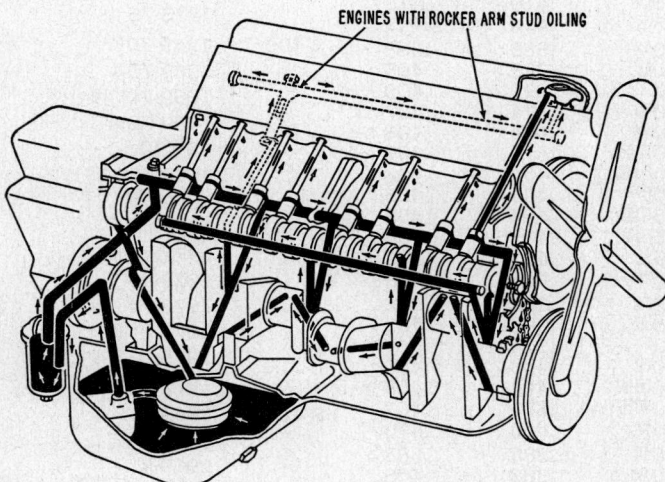

Engine oiling system. V8s (except V8-307)

Fig. 5 Tools positioned to remove rocker arm stud

NOTE: *If left head is being removed, it will be necessary to raise head off dowel pins, move it forward and "jockey" it in order to clear power steering and power brake equipment if so equipped.*

7. Reverse removal procedure to install the heads.

ROCKER ARM STUDS

1969-75 V8 With Screw in Stud

1. Remove rocker arm cover.
2. Remove rocker arm and nut.
3. Using a deep socket, remove rocker stud.
4. Install new stud and tighten to 50 ft. lbs.
5. Install rocker arm and tighten nut to 20 ft. lbs.
6. Install rocker cover using new gasket.

1969-73 V8 With Push Rod Oiling - Pressed in Stud

NOTE: Engines with push rod oiling are: 1969-73 all, and all 389 Tri-Power engines. On these engines, rocker arm studs can now be replaced without removing the cylinder head. This is accomplished by the use of a new .005" oversize stud and a new reamer (J-22126), which is available from the Service Tool Division of Kent-Moore Organization, Inc., 28635 Mound Road, Warren, Michigan 48092.

1. Disconnect battery cable and drain radiator.
2. Pack oily rags around stud and over engine openings before removing stud.
3. After removing stud as outlined for earlier models, carefully ream stud hole, using the new reamer. This reamer is made with a removable pilot shaft. Stud hole must first be reamed with pilot shaft attached to reamer. Pilot shaft should then be removed and stud hole must be reamed again.
4. Clean stud hole and surrounding area. *If reamer did not clean up completely, it will be necessary to replace cylinder head.*
5. Remove intake manifold and valley cover.
6. Position rocker arm on new .005" stud and place rocker arm installer J-8927 on stud in place of rocker arm ball, Fig. 3.
7. Coat rocker arm stud with white lead and oil and drive stud into cylinder head about half way ($7/16$").
8. Clamp straight-edge on cylinder head as shown in Fig. 3, and position valve train gauge J-8928 in push rod hole so that it seats properly in rocker arm. *When working on right cylinder head, heater hose connector will have to be removed before straight-edge can be positioned correctly.*
9. With valve seated, drive rocker arm stud into cylinder head until the result outlined in Fig. 3 is obtained.
10. Remove tools and rocker arm. Then install push rod, rocker arm, ball, and tighten rocker arm ball retaining nut. Finally, install parts removed and fill radiator.

VALVE ARRANGEMENT

Front to Rear

Six Cyl. . . . . E-I-I-E-E-I-I-E-E-I-I-E

V8s . . . . E-I-I-E-E-I-I-E

VALVE LIFT SPECS.

Year	Engine	Intake	Exhaust
1969	6-250[7]	.400	.400
	6-250[2]	.438	.438
	8-350[1]	.376	.412
	8-350[2][5]	.414	.413
	8-350[2][6]	.410	.413
	8-400[1][3]	.375	.410
	8-400[1][4][5]	.410	.414
	8-400[1][4][6]	.376	.412
	8-400[2][5]	.413	.413
	8-400[2][6]	.410	.413
	8-400[5]	.413	.413
	8-400[6]	.414	.413
	8-400[8]	.516	.516
	8-428[5]	.410	.413
	8-428[6]	.410	.414
	8-428[9][5]	.414	.413
	8-428[9][6]	.410	.413
1970	6-250	.388	.388
	8-350	.376	.412
	8-400[1]	.376	.412
	8-400[2]	.410	.414
	8-400[12]	.527	.527
	8-455[5]	.414	.413
	8-455[6]	.410	.413
1971	6-250	.388	.388
	8-350[5]	.376	.412
	8-350[6]	.410	.414
	8-400[1]	.376	.412
	8-400[2]	.410	.413
	8-455[1]	.376	.412
	8-455[2]	.410	.413
	8-455[9]	.414	.413
1972	6-250[13]	.388	.388
	6-250[14]	.388	.405
	8-307	.390	.409
	8-350[15]	.374	.407
	8-350[16]	.404	.408
	8-400[1][15]	.374	.407
	8-400[1][16]	.404	.408
	8-400[2]	.403	.406
	8-455[1][15]	.404	.408
	8-455[1][16]	.403	.406
	8-455[2]	.403	.406
	8-455[9]	.408	.406
1973	6-250[15]	.388	.388
	6-250[16]	.388	.405
	8-350	.374	.407
	8-400[5]	.403	.406
	8-400[6][2]	.404	.408
	8-400[6][1]	.374	.407
	8-455[11]	.470	.470
1974	6-250[15]	.388	.388
	6-250[16]	.388	.405
	8-350	.374	.407
	8-350[5]	.403	.406
	8-400[6][2]	.404	.408
	8-400[6][1]	.374	.407
	8-455[10]	.403	.406
	8-455[11]	.406	.406
1975	6-250	.388	.405
	8-350	.377	.413
	8-400[1]	.377	.415
	8-400[2]	.410	.415
	8-455	.410	.414

[1]—2 bar. carb.   [2]—4 bar. carb.
[3]—Reg. fuel.   [4]—Premium fuel.
[5]—Std. trans.   [6]—Auto. trans.
[7]—One bar. carb.   [8]—Ram air eng.
[9]—Hi perf. eng.
[10]—Except Super Duty.
[11]—Super Duty Engine.
[12]—Ram Air IV engine.
[13]—Without Air Injector Pump.
[14]—With Air Injector Pump.
[15]—Exc. California cars.
[16]—California cars.

VALVE TIMING

Intake Opens Before TDC

Engine	Year	Degrees
6-250	1969[7]	14
	1969[2][5]	22
	1969[2][6]	14
	1970-75	16
8-307	1971-72	28
8-350	1969[1]	22
	1969[2][5]	31
	1969[2][6]	23
	1970	22
	1971[5]	26
	1971[6]	30
	1972[1][12]	26
	1972[1][13]	30
	1973-75	26
8-400	1969-70[4]	23
	1969-70[4]	30
	1969-70[1][3]	22
	1969-70[8]	42
	1971[1]	26
	1971[2]	23
	1972[1][12]	26
	1972[1][13]	30
	1972[2]	23
	1973[2][5]	23
	1973-74[2][6]	30
	1973-74[1][6]	38
	1975[1]	26
	1975[2]	30
8-428	1969[5]	23
	1969[5]	23
	1969[6]	30
	1969[9][5]	31
	1969[9][6]	23

8-455	1970[5]	31
	1970[6]	23
	1970[9]	23
	1971[1]	30
	1971[2]	23
	1971[9]	31
	1972[1][12]	30
	1972[1][13]	23
	1972[2]	23
	1972[9]	31
	1973[6][1]	26
	1973-74[10]	23
	1973-74[6][2]	30
	1974[11]	38
	1975	23

[1]—2 bar. carb. [2]—4 bar. carb.
[3]—Regular fuel. [4]—Prem. fuel.
[5]—Std. trans. [6]—Auto. trans.
[7]—1 bar. Carb.
[8]—Ram Air IV engine.
[9]—Hi perf. eng.
[10]—Except Super Duty.
[11]—Super Duty Engine.
[12]—Except California cars.
[13]—California cars.

VALVE GUIDES

Valve guides are cast integral with the cylinder head. Valves with oversize stems are available in .001", .003" and .005" larger than standard.

Oversize reamers are required to enlarge valve guide holes to fit the oversize stems. For best results when installing .005" oversize valve stem use a .003" oversize reamer first and then ream to .005" oversize. Always reface the valve and valve seat after reaming valve guide. Valves are marked .001, .003 or .005 with colored ink.

VALVE LIFTERS

Remove intake manifold, push rod cover and rocker arm cover. Loosen rocker arm ball nut and move rocker

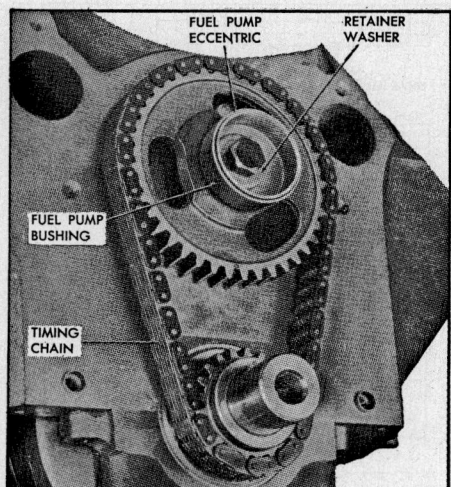

Fig. 7 Front of engine with timing case cover removed. V8 engines

arm off push rod. Remove push rod.

Remove lifter or lifters. If more than one lifter is to be replaced, be sure to identify them (push rods as well) so they will be installed in the same position, Fig. 6.

TIMING COVER

NOTE: If necessary to replace the cover oil seal it can be accomplished without removing the timing chain cover.

1969-75 V8s

1. Drain cooling system.
2. Loosen alternator adjusting bolts.
3. Remove fan and accessory drive belts.
4. Remove fan and pulley.
5. Disconnect radiator hoses.
6. Remove fuel pump.
7. Remove vibration damper.
8. Remove front four oil pan-to-timing chain cover screws, Fig. 14.
9. Remove cover attaching screws.
10. Pull cover forward to clear studs and remove.

TIMING CHAIN
V8 Engines

1. Remove timing chain cover, making certain O-ring seal and hollow dowels are retained for installation at assembly.
2. Remove fuel pump eccentric, bushing and timing chain cover oil seal, Fig. 7.
3. Align timing marks to simplify proper positioning of sprockets during assembly, Fig. 8.

NOTE: The valve timing marks, Fig. 8, does not indicate TDC, compression stroke for No. 1 cylinder for use during distributor installation. When installing the distributor, rotate engine until No. 1 cylinder is on compression stroke and the camshaft timing mark is 180° from the valve timing position shown in Fig. 8.

4. Slide off chain and sprockets.
5. Install new chain and sprockets, making sure timing marks are

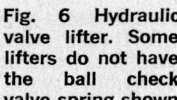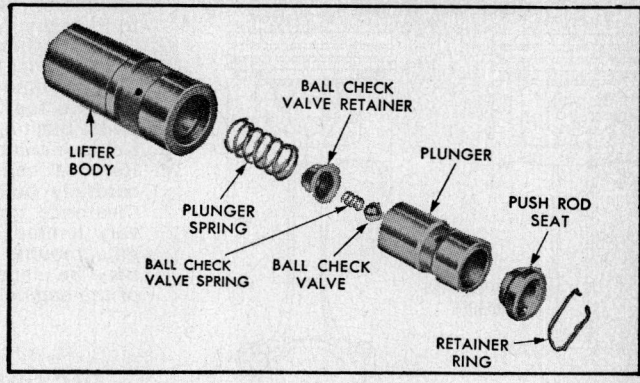

Fig. 6 Hydraulic valve lifter. Some lifters do not have the ball check valve spring shown

aligned exactly on a straight line passing through the shaft centers, Fig. 8. Camshaft should extend through sprocket so that hole in fuel pump eccentric will locate on shaft.
6. Install fuel pump eccentric and bushing, indexing tab on eccentric with keyway cutout in sprocket. Install retainer bolt with washer and tighten securely.
7. Making sure hollow dowels are in place in block, place timing chain cover gasket over studs and dowels.
8. Install cover, making sure O-ring seal is in place.

CAMSHAFT
All V8s

The camshaft and camshaft bearings can be replaced with the engine installed in the car or with engine removed and disassembled for overhaul. However, to replace the rear camshaft bearing without removing and completely disassembling the engine, the propeller shaft, transmission and clutch housing must first be removed. The procedure for removing the camshaft is as follows:
1. Remove radiator, fan and pulleys.
2. On air conditioned cars, remove al-

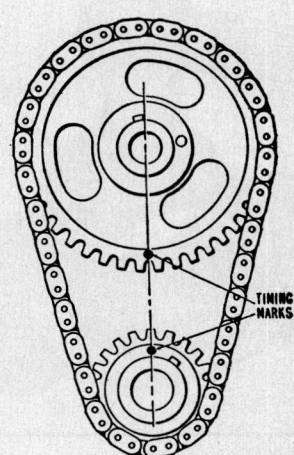

Fig. 8 Valve timing marks. V8 engines

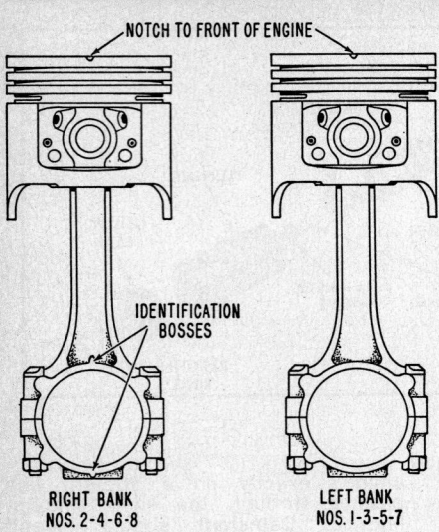

NOTCH TO FRONT OF ENGINE

IDENTIFICATION BOSSES

RIGHT BANK NOS. 2-4-6-8 LEFT BANK NOS. 1-3-5-7

Fig. 9 Piston and rod assembly. 1969-75 V8s (Oil spurt hole toward camshaft)

ternator and its mounting bracket.
3. Remove crankcase ventilator hose or outlet pipe.
4. Remove rocker arm covers.
5. Remove intake manifold. *Make certain "O" ring seal between intake manifold and timing chain cover is retained and installed during assembly.*
6. Remove push rod cover.
7. Loosen rocker arm ball retaining nuts so that rocker arms can be disengaged from push rods and turned sideways.
8. Remove push rods and hydraulic lifters, keeping them in proper se-

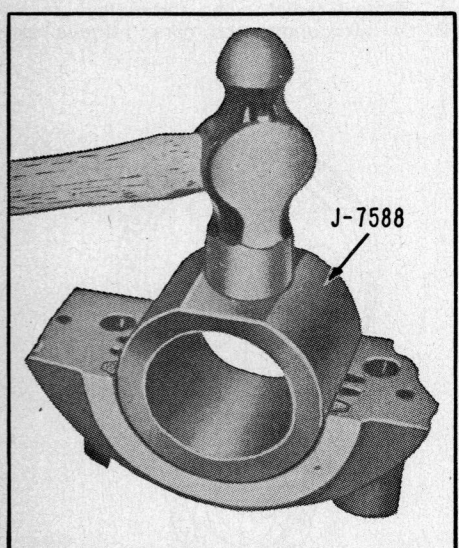

J-7588

Fig. 11 Installing rear main bearing oil seal. V8-350, 400, 455 engines

quence so that they may be returned to their original locations.
9. Remove vibration damper.
10. Remove fuel pump.
11. Remove timing chain cover.
12. Remove fuel pump eccentric and fuel pump bushing.
13. Remove chain and sprockets.
14. Remove camshaft thrust plate and carefully pull camshaft from engine. *Clearance for camshaft removal is very limited and, in cases where engine mounts are worn excessively, it may be necessary to raise the front of the engine to permit removal.*

PISTON & ROD, ASSEMBLE

Assemble pistons and rods as indicated in Fig. 9.

NOTE: The connecting rod squirt hole has been eliminated from all early production 1973 engines. The early and late connecting rods are completely interchangeable without any complications starting with the 1971 production engines.

PISTONS, PINS & RINGS

Pistons and rings are available in standard sizes and oversizes of .001, .002, .005, .010, .020 and .030 inch.

Piston pins are available in oversizes of .001 and .003" on four cylinder engines and 1969-74 V8s. No oversizes are supplied on 6 cylinder engines.

MAIN & ROD BEARINGS

Main bearings are available in standard sizes and undersizes of .001 and .002".

Rod bearings are available in standard sizes and undersizes of .001 and .002".

CRANKSHAFT OIL SEAL
1969-75 V8

1. Remove oil pan, oil pump and pump drive shaft.
2. Remove oil baffle and cylinder block-to-oil baffle tube.
3. Remove rear main bearing cap.
4. Use tool shown in Fig. 12 made from brass bar stock to pack upper seal as follows:
   a. Insert tool against one end of oil seal in cylinder block and drive seal gently into groove until tool bottoms.
   b. Remove tool and repeat at other end of seal in cylinder block.
5. Clean block and bearing cap parting line thoroughly.
6. Form a new seal in cap.
7. Remove newly formed seal from cap and cut four pieces about ⅜" long from this seal.
8. Work two ⅜" pieces into each end of

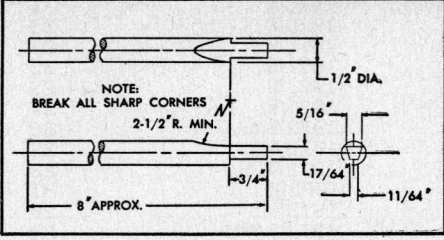

Fig. 10 Rear main bearing oil seal tool. V8-350, 400

the gaps which have been made at the end of seal in cylinder block. Without cutting off the ends, work these seal pieces in until flush with parting line, being sure that no fibers are protruding over the metal adjacent to the groove.
9. Form another new seal in the cap.
10. Assemble the cap to the block and torque to specifications.
11. Remove cap and inspect parting line to insure that no seal material has been compressed between the block and cap.
12. Apply a 1/16" bead of sealer from the center of the seal to the external cork groove.
13. Reassemble the cap and torque to specifications.

OIL PAN
1971-75 Ventura

1. Disconnect battery ground cable.
2. If equipped with power steering, remove drive belt and tilt pump upward.
3. Remove two fan shroud screws and position shroud so it will swing up with engine.
4. Raise car and drain oil.
5. Disconnect exhaust pipe to manifold

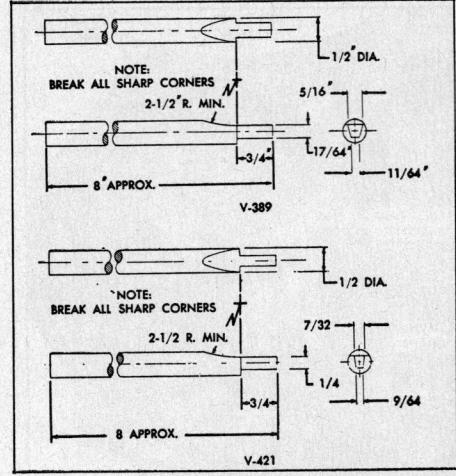

V-389

V-421

Fig. 12 Rear main bearing seal tool dimensions. Make from brass bar stock. Pontiac V8s

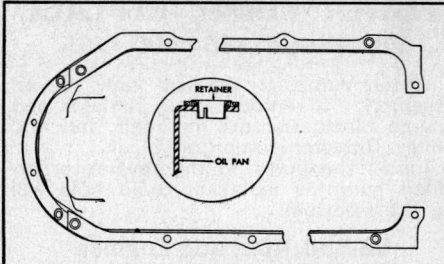

Fig. 13 Installing oil pan gasket retainers. V8-350, 400, 455 engines

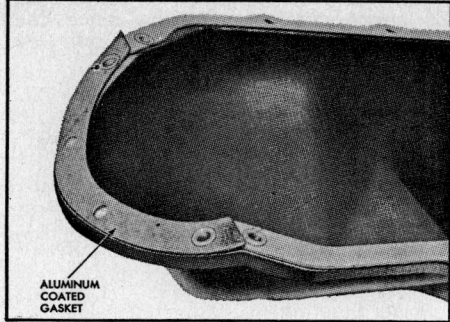

Fig. 14 Front oil pan gasket overlapping side gaskets. V8-350, 400, 455 engines

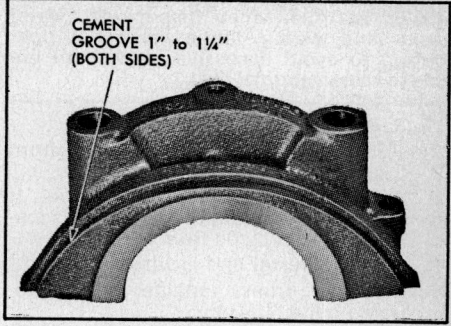

Fig. 15 Rear oil pan gasket positioned in bearing cap. V8-350, 400, 455 engines

bolts and let exhaust pipes hang down.
6. Remove flywheel dust cover.
7. Remove starter with wiring attached and position out of way.
8. Remove both frame bracket to engine mount thru bolts.
9. Attach a suitable engine lifting tool to engine.
10. Remove oil pan bolts.
11. Raise engine until pan can be removed.

1970-75 Except Ventura

NOTE: On 1970 Tempest, T-37 and LeMans models with manual transmission, it will be necessary to remove the engine before removing the oil pan. On all other models, proceed as follows:

1. Disconnect battery cable at battery and remove fan.
2. Make sure all hoses and wiring are routed properly to avoid bind when engine is raised.
3. Raise vehicle and drain crankcase.
4. On 1971-75 Firebird and Grand Prix, disconnect steering idler arm at frame and pitman arm from shaft. On 1970 full size Pontiac, disconnect steering idler arm support from frame.
5. Disconnect exhaust pipes from manifolds.
6. Remove starter assembly (set to one side with wires attached), starter motor bracket and flywheel inspection cover.
7. On 1971-75 T-37, LeMans and Grand Am and 1971-73 GTO, remove stabilizer shaft to frame bracket attaching bolts to insure free movement of lifting device. It may also be necessary to loosen the fuel pump to timing cover bolts for clearance.
8. On all models, attach lifting tool, loosen oil pan bolts and raise engine until oil pan can be removed.

1969 Tempest V8

1. Disconnect battery positive cable.
2. Remove fan blade assembly.
3. Inspect all hoses and wiring for proper routing to avoid excessive binding when engine is raised 4½".
4. Raise car and drain crankcase.
5. Disconnect idler arm from frame and drop steering linkage.
6. Disconnect exhaust crossover pipe on single exhaust models.

7. Remove starter motor and flywheel cover.
8. Position lifting tool J22603 in place with J22603-8 crossbar in position on lifting tool. Bolt tool to timing cover.
9. Using frame jack, support engine at J22603 and remove motor mount to frame bolts.
10. Raise engine about 4½" and remove oil pan.

1969 Firebird V8

1. Disconnect positive battery cable.
2. Disconnect fan shroud from radiator.
3. Remove air cleaner and distributor cap.
4. Make sure all hoses and wiring are free so as not to bind when engine is raised 4½" and moved forward 1½".
5. Raise car and drain crankcase.
6. Disconnect idler arm from frame.
7. Disconnect crossover pipe. If equip-

ped with dual exhausts, disconnect exhaust pipes from manifolds.
8. Remove starter and flywheel cover.
9. Attach lifting tool J22603 to engine and place crossbar J22603-8 in position on tool.
10. Using frame jack or transmission jack, support engine at tool J22603 and remove motor mounts from engine.
11. Remove rear transmission to crossmember bolts.
12. Raise engine 4½" and at the same time move engine forward 1½".
13. Remove oil pan.

1969 Pontiac

1. Disconnect battery ground cable.
2. Remove fan shield.
3. On A/C cars, remove fan and pulley.
4. Disconnect engine ground cables.
5. On A/C cars, remove compressor from mounting brackets and position to one side.

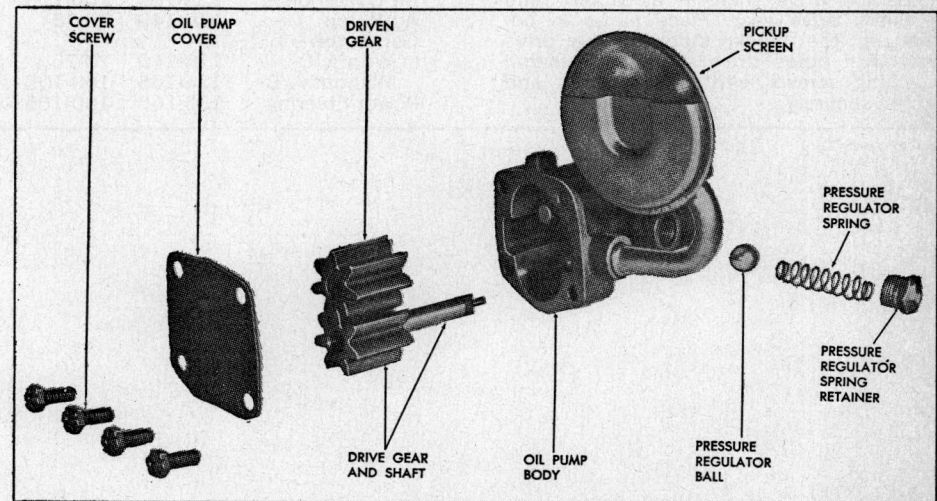

Fig. 16 Oil pump disassembled. V8 Pontiac engines

NOTE: At this time, inspect all water hoses and wiring harnesses for proper routing to avoid excessive bind when engine is raised about 4½".

6. Raise car and drain crankcase.
7. Disconnect steering idler arm from frame.
8. Remove exhaust crossover pipe. If equipped with dual exhausts disconnect exhaust pipes from manifolds.
9. Remove starter and flywheel cover.
10. Remove front engine mount-to-frame bolts.

On 1969 models, special Engine Lifting Tool (J-22603) is available. Bolt tool to timing chain cover with bolts provided with tool. Using frame jack or automatic transmission jack, support engine at Tool J-22603 and remove engine mounts. Loosen rear transmission mount. It may be necessary to remove this mount and rest rear of transmission on cross-member to obtain necessary clearance. Remove oil pan bolts and raise engine *straight up* until transmission is against floor pan. Remove pan by first rotating clockwise (facing forward) to clear oil pump.

NOTE: If work other than oil pan gasket replacement is to be performed, support engine with suitable blocks of wood and remove engine support.

OIL PUMP

V8 Engines

Remove oil pan. While holding pump in place, remove attaching screws. Lower the pump away from the block with one hand while removing the oil pump drive shaft with the other.

Remove oil screen and pressure regulator parts. Detach cover from pump body and take out gears, Fig. 16.

Examine all parts for damage and assemble. Do not attempt to change oil pressure by varying length of pressure regulator spring.

Position drive shaft in distributor and oil pump drive gear. Place pump in position in the block, indexing the drive shaft with pump drive gear shaft. Install attaching screws with lock washers and tighten securely.

Removal and installation of pump does not affect distributor timing since the oil pump and distributor drive gear are mounted on the distributor shaft.

BELT TENSION DATA

	New Lbs.	Used Lbs.
1969—		
Air Condition	145	105
Generator to Power Steering	60	50
Power Steering Pump	145	105
Water Pump to Generator	120	75
1970—		
Six Cylinder—		
Air Condition	130-150	90-110
Power Steering	100-125	60-85
Water Pump to Generator	100-125	60-85
V8-Models—		
Air Condition	135-150	100-105
Power Steering	135-150	100-105
Water Pump to Generator	110-125	70-75
1971-72—		
Six Cylinder—		
Air Condition	135-145	85-95
Generator	120-130	70-80
Power Steering	120-130	70-80
V8-Models—		
Air Condition	135-150	100-105
Generator—		
With A/C	135-150	100-105
Without A/C	110-125	70-75
Power Steering	120-130	70-80
1973—		
V8 Models—		
Air Condition	135-150	100-105
Generator—		
With A/C	135-150	100-105
Without A/C	110-125	70-75
Power Steering	135-150	100-105
1973-74—		
Six Cylinder—		
Air Pump	100-125	70-90
Alternator	100-125	70-90
Power Steering	100-130	70-90
1974—		
V8 Models—		
Air Condition	135-165	100-105
Air Pump	110-140	70-75
Generator—		
With A/C	110-140	70-75
Without A/C	135-165	100-105
Power Steering	135-165	100-105

WATER PUMP, REPLACE

V8s Except 350, 400, 455

Water pump is serviced only as an assembly. To remove, drain radiator and engine block. Remove fan belt, fan and pulley. Unfasten pump from block.

Install the pump in the reverse order. When pump is installed, drain hole will be at the bottom.

V8-350, 400, 455 Engines

To remove water pump, which is *serviced only as an assembly*, drain cooling system. Remove fan belt, fan and pulley. Unfasten and remove pump from engine.

When pump is installed on engine, drain hole will be at bottom. Tighten pump attaching nuts to 15 ft. lbs.

FUEL PUMP PRESSURE

Year	Engine	Pressure Lbs.
1969	Six	4-5½
1969	V8	5-6½
1970-71	Six	4-5
1970-71	V8	5-6½ ①
1972-74	Six	3-5
1972-74	V8	3-6½
1975	Six	4-5
1975	V8	5-6½

①With A/C and all 4 Bar. Carbs. 6½-8

FUEL PUMP, REPLACE

1. Remove all gasket material from the pump and block gasket surfaces. Apply sealer on both sides of new gasket.
2. Position gasket on pump flange and hold pump in position against its mounting surface. Make sure rocker arm is riding on camshaft eccentric.
3. Press pump tight against its mounting. Install retaining screws and tighten them alternately.
4. Connect fuel lines. Then operate engine and check for leaks.

SERVICE NOTE: Before installing the pump, it is good practice to crank the engine so that the nose of the camshaft eccentric is out of the way of the fuel pump rocker arm when the pump is installed. In this way there will be the least amount of tension on the rocker arm, thereby easing the installation of the pump.

Overhead Camshaft Engine Section

INDEX OF SERVICE OPERATIONS

Accessory Drive Housing 1-667	Engine Mounts 1-663	Oil Pump 1-667
Camshaft 1-664	Engine, Replace 1-663	Pistons, Rings & Pins 1-668
Camshaft Sprocket or Seal 1-663	Fuel Pump Drive 1-667	Rear Main Bearing Oil Seal 1-668
Crankcase Cover, Front 1-667	Housing, Accessory Drive 1-667	Rocker Arms 1-665
Crankcase Cover Seal 1-666	Hydraulic Valve Lash Adjusters 1-665	Rocker Arm Cover 1-664
Crankshaft Bearings 1-668	Oil Pan 1-667	Timing Belt, Adjust 1-663
Cylinder Head 1-665	Oil Pressure Regulator 1-667	Valve Service 1-666
Distributor Drive 1-667		Valve Springs & Seals 1-665

ENGINE MOUNTS REPLACE

1969 Six

1. Support engine using suitable engine lifting tool.
2. Remove insulator to engine bracket through bolts, Figs. 1 and 2.
3. Raise engine approximately 1″ above front insulators.
4. Remove front insulator by removing insulator to block bolt.
5. Remove insulator.

ENGINE, REPLACE

1. Disconnect cables at battery.
2. Drain cooling system.
3. Scribe alignment marks on hood around hood hinges and remove hood.
4. Disconnect engine wiring harness and engine ground straps.
5. Remove air cleaner and fan shield.
6. Disconnect all hoses at engine.
7. With manual transmission, remove radiator.
8. If equipped with power steering or air conditioning, remove pump and compressor from mounting brackets and set aside (do not disconnect hoses).
9. Remove engine fan and pulley.
10. Disconnect accelerator linkage.
11. Disconnect transmission vacuum modulator line and power brake vacuum line at carburetor and fold back out of the way.
12. Raise vehicle and drain crankcase.
13. Disconnect fuel lines at fuel pump, exhaust pipes from manifold and starter wires.
14. If equipped with automatic transmission, remove converter cover and 3 converter retaining bolts and slide converter to rear.
15. If equipped with manual transmission, disconnect clutch linkage and remove clutch shaft. Remove four lower bell housing bolts (two each side).
16. Disconnect transmission filler tube support and starter wire harness shield from cylinder head.
17. Remove two front engine mounts to-frame thru bolts.
18. Lower vehicle.
19. Support transmission with a jack and block of wood.

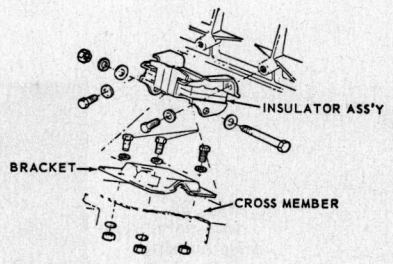

Fig. 1 Engine mounts. 1969 Tempest

20. Remove two remaining bell housing bolts, raise transmission slightly and remove engine.
21. Reverse procedure to install. Do not lower engine completely while jack is supporting transmission.

TIMING BELT, ADJUST

1. Remove 3 screws on front of top cover. Lift up cover to disengage side clips. Remove retaining clips

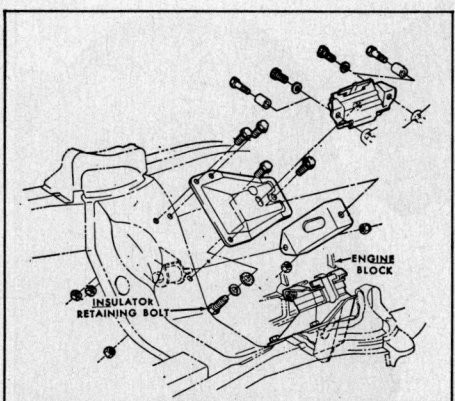

Fig. 2 Engine mounts. 1969 Firebird

from cover.
2. Using the equipment shown in Fig. 3, set the pointer of the fixture on the zero mark. *This calibration must be performed prior to each use of the fixture to insure an accurate belt adjustment.*
3. Remove camshaft sprocket-to-camshaft bolt and install the fixture on the belt with the rollers on the outside (smooth) surface of belt. Thread the fixture mounting bolt into camshaft sprocket bolt location finger tight.
4. Squeeze indicator end (upper) of fixture and quickly release so that fixture assumes released or relaxed position.
5. With the tool installed as directed, adjust accessory drive housing, Fig. 3A, up or down as required to obtain a tension adjuster indicator centered in the green range with drive housing mounting bolts torqued to 15 ft-lbs.
6. Remove tension fixture and install sprocket retaining bolt, making sure bolt threads and washer are free of dirt. Install cover.

CAMSHAFT SPROCKET OR SEAL

CAUTION: Do not use tools of any type, other than hands, to pry on timing belt during belt removal or replacement or during other service operations.

1. Remove timing belt top front cover. *For ease on reassembly, index three timing marks as shown in Fig. 3B.*
2. Loosen accessory drive housing bolts, Fig. 3A.
3. Remove belt from camshaft sprocket.
4. Remove sprocket.

NOTE: If necessary to replace camshaft seal, reinstall sprocket bolt. Thread a tool of the type shown, Fig. 4, into camshaft seal. Tighten center bolt on tool until seal is extracted. Install a suitable seal protector and pilot, Fig. 5, on end of camshaft. Slide seal over on tool, then drive it in place, Fig. 6.

5. Install sprocket, indexing pin on sprocket with hole in camshaft.
6. Install sprocket bolt finger tight.
7. Align timing marks and install belt.
8. Adjust timing and belt tension.

9. Torque sprocket bolt to 40 ft-lbs and install top cover.

ROCKER ARM COVER

1. Drain cooling system and disconnect radiator hose at fitting on cover.
2. Remove timing belt top cover.
3. Align timing marks and remove belt from camshaft sprocket.
4. Disconnect necessary fuel and vacuum lines.
5. Unfasten and remove rocker arm cover.
6. Reverse procedure to install.

CAMSHAFT

1. Remove camshaft sprocket and seal.
2. Remove rocker arm cover.
3. Using tools of the type shown in Fig. 7, drive camshaft from rocker cover.

CAUTION: *Do not allow camshaft to damage bearing surfaces of rocker cover.*

4. Remove parts shown from rear of camshaft, Fig. 8.
5. Remove water outlet fitting and thermostat from rocker cover.
6. Clean all parts and inspect for wear or damage. Minor nicks or scratches on edge of bearing surface can be corrected with a suitable scraper or file.

Installation

1. Install camshaft into rocker cover.

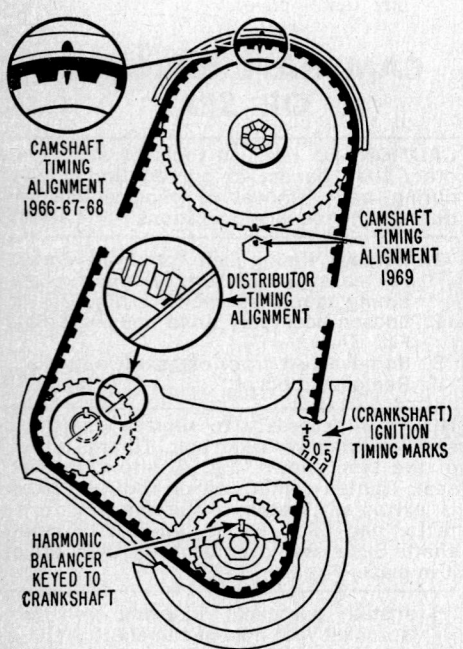

Fig. 3B Valve timing marks

2. Install thrust washer, Fig. 9.
3. Install retaining bolt and washer and torque to 40 ft-lbs.
4. Using a tool of the type shown in Fig. 10, drive plug in so it is fully seated.

IMPORTANT: A camshaft bore plug not fully seated could result in excessive camshaft end play which is .003" to .009" when read at the sprocket end with a dial indicator.

5. Replace water outlet fitting and thermostat.

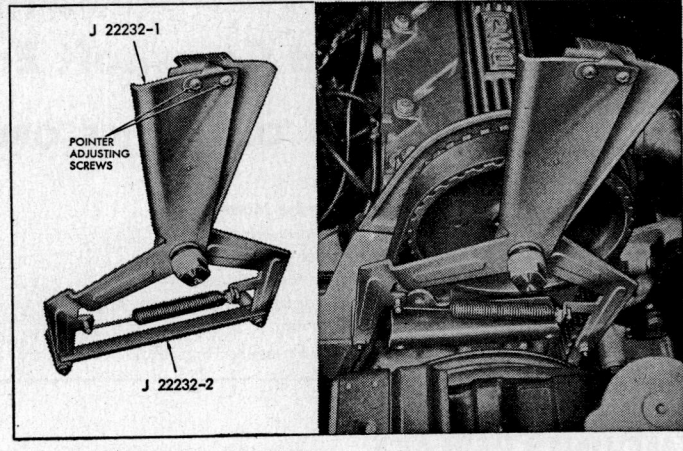

Fig. 3 Adjusting timing belt with tension fixture shown

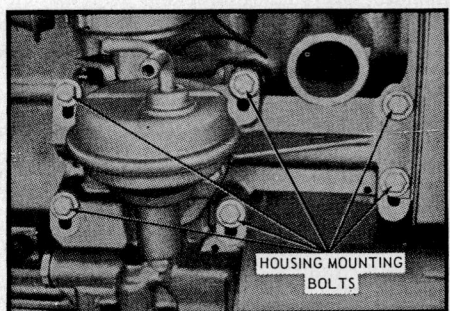

Fig. 3A Accessory drive housing mounting bolts

Fig. 4 Removing camshaft seal

Fig. 5 Seal and protector tool installed

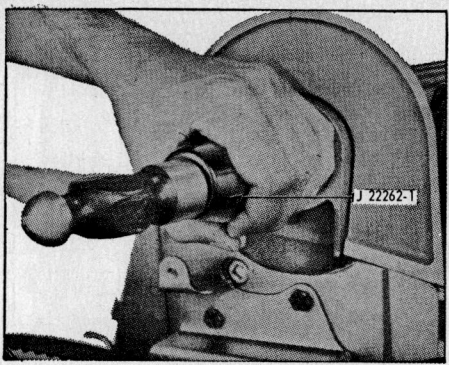

Fig. 6   Installing camshaft seal

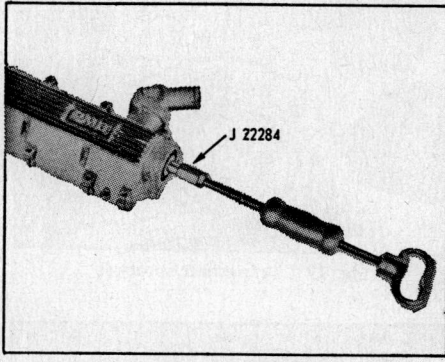

Fig. 7   Removing camshaft

ROCKER ARM OR VALVE LASH ADJUSTER

1. Remove rocker arm cover.
2. Remove rocker arm and hydraulic lash adjuster assembly and store so that each assembly can be installed in its original location.

NOTE: If a new lash adjuster is to be installed, it will be necessary to check the leak-down rate and prime the adjuster before installation.

3. Install retainer clip, Fig. 11.
4. Place each lash adjuster in its ori-

ginal location, and install rocker cover.

Lash Adjuster Service

NOTE: Because of the important part hydraulic lash adjusters play in the operation of the engine, and the close tolerances to which they are manufactured, proper handling and, above all, cleanliness, cannot be overstressed when servicing these parts.

New adjusters are serviced as individual units, packaged with a plastic coating. Leave the coating on until ready to check leak-down rate. It is necessary to remove the oil from the new adjusters prior to checking leak-down rate since special oil is in new adjusters. Fill adjusters with SAE 10 oil before checking leak-down rate. If leak-down test equipment is not available, the supplier should check lash adjusters for you.

Removing Stuck Lash Adjuster

After removing the rocker arm, fill the vent hole adjacent to the stuck lifter with engine oil. Using a length of 3/16″ diameter rod approximately 4″ in length, insert it into the top of the vent hole and strike the end of the rod with a hammer. The hydraulic effect of the oil on the base of the lash adjuster will then break the adjuster free from the boss in the cylinder head. The use of pliers for this operation is not recommended since lifter damage will result.

VALVE SPRINGS & SEALS

Valve springs and seals can be replaced without removing the cylinder head if tools of the type shown in Fig. 14 are available.

1. Remove rocker arm cover.
2. Remove rocker arm of valve being serviced.
3. Remove spark plug from cylinder of valves to be serviced and install an air hose with an adapter that will screw into the spark plug hole.

CAUTION: When applying compressed air into the spark plug hole to hold the valve up, be sure the piston is all the way down in the cylinder, otherwise the fan will turn.

4. Install the hook end of the tool into

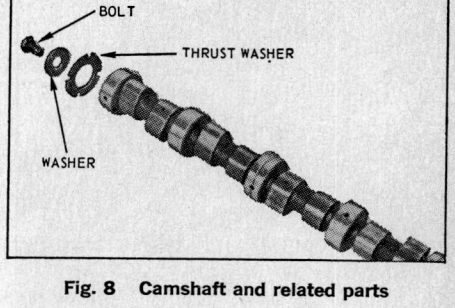

Fig. 8   Camshaft and related parts

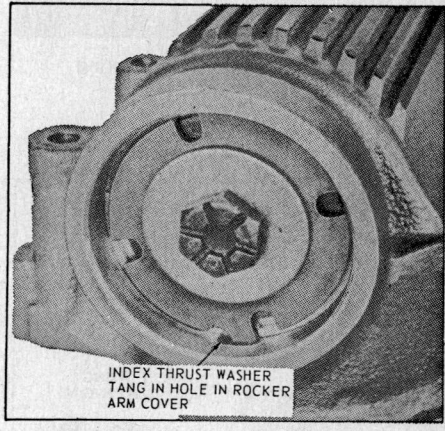

Fig. 9   Thrust washer installation

the oil feed hole in lash adjuster bore. Hold in place and install fork end of valve spring compressor as shown. Compress valve spring, remove valve cup locks. Then remove tool, valve spring, cup shield and valve stem seal.

CYLINDER HEAD
Removal

1. Drain cooling system and remove air cleaner.

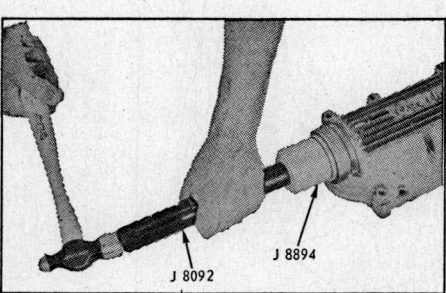

Fig. 10   Installing camshaft bore plug

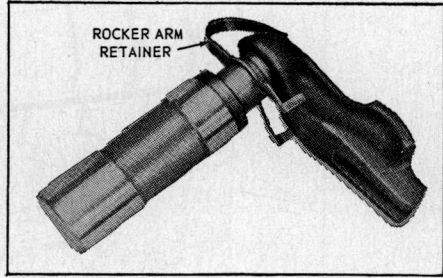

Fig. 11   Rocker arm retainer and lash adjuster

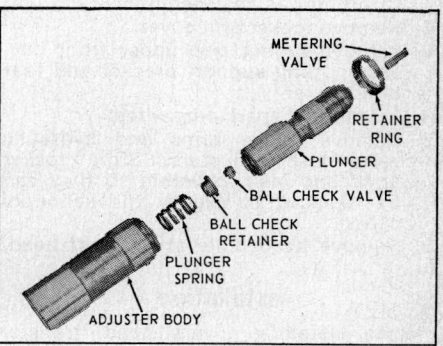

Fig. 12   Hydraulic lash adjuster disassembled

Fig. 14 Depressing valve spring

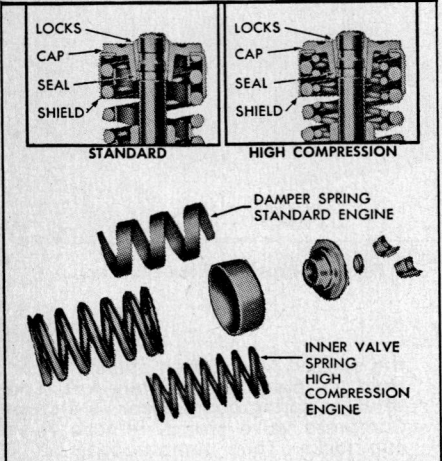

Fig. 15 Valves and related parts

Head bolts are of two different lengths. When inserted in proper holes, all bolts will project an equal distance from head. Do not use sealer of any kind on threads. Pontiac recommends no numerical sequence for tightening cylinder head bolts. Tighten them a little at a time, starting at the center bolts and working alternately from side to side outward to the end bolts.

VALVE SERVICE

Fig. 15 shows the valves and related parts.

Valves with oversize stems are available in .001", .003" and .005" larger than standard. The same valve stem-to-guide clearance listed in the *Valve Specifications* table applies for oversize stems.

Carefully ream the valve guide. For best results when installing a .005" oversize valve stem, use a .003" oversize reamer first, then ream the .005" oversize. Always reface the valve seat after reaming valve guide.

When installing valve springs, place the closed coil end toward the cylinder head.

CRANKCASE COVER SEAL

1. Remove upper timing cover.
2. Align timing marks, Fig. 3B.
3. Remove fan and water pump pulley.
4. Remove vibration damper.
5. Remove timing belt lower cover, Fig. 16.
6. Loosen accessory drive mounting bolts to provide slack in timing belt, Fig. 3A.
7. Remove timing belt.
8. Remove crankshaft timing belt flange and sprocket, Fig. 17.
9. Pry seal from front of crankcase.
10. Install new seal with lip of seal inward, using a suitable seal driver.
11. Reverse procedure to install, being sure to align the belt timing marks and adjust belt tension, Fig. 3.

Fig. 16 Lower front timing belt cover bolts

Fig. 17 Crankshaft sprocket

Fig. 18 Front crankcase with cover removed

2. Disconnect accelerator pedal cable at bellcrank on manifold and fuel and vacuum lines at carburetor.
3. Disconnect exhaust pipe at manifold flange, then remove manifold bolts and clamps. Remove manifolds and carburetor as an assembly.
4. Remove rocker arm cover.
5. Remove timing belt upper front cover mounting support bracket and rear lower cover.
6. Disconnect spark plug wires.
7. Remove rocker arms and hydraulic valve lash adjusters. *Store rocker arms and lash adjusters so they can be replaced in exactly the same location.*
8. Remove head bolts and lift off head.

Installation

When installing a new head, transfer all serviceable parts to new head using new seals on intake and exhaust valve stems and new manifold gaskets.

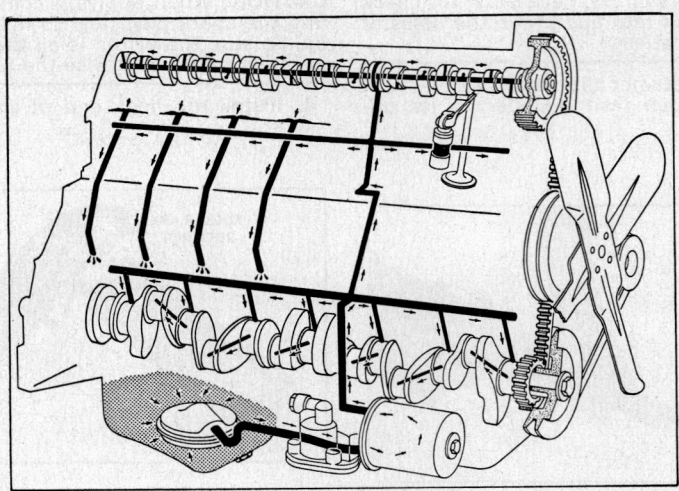

Engine oiling system. OHC Six

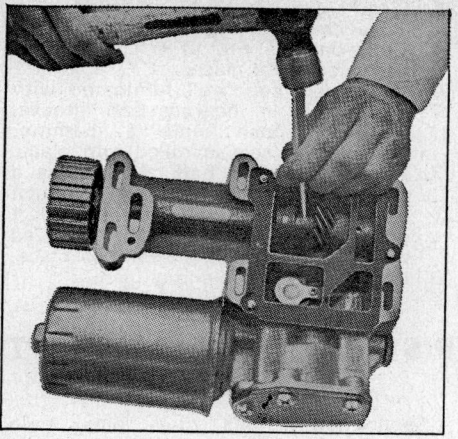

Fig. 20 Removing eccentric and distributor drive gear retaining pin

OIL FILTER
BY-PASS VALVE

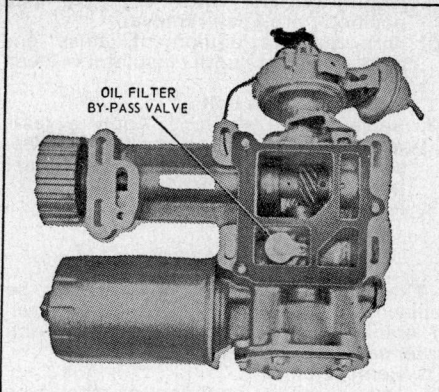

Fig. 19 Oil filter by-pass valve

UPPER
LOWER

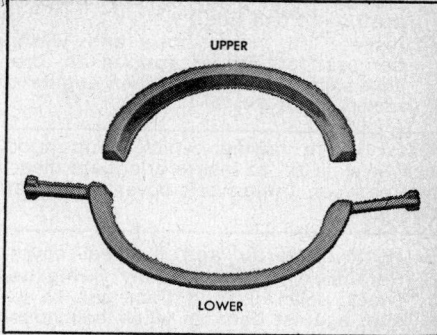

Fig. 22 Rear main bearing oil seal

J 22264

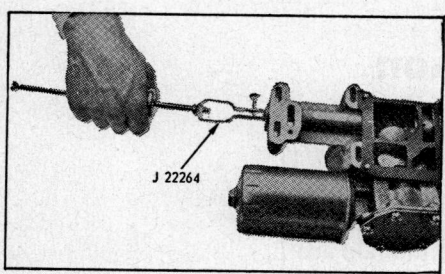

Fig. 21 Removing bearing and seal

J 22325-2
J 22325

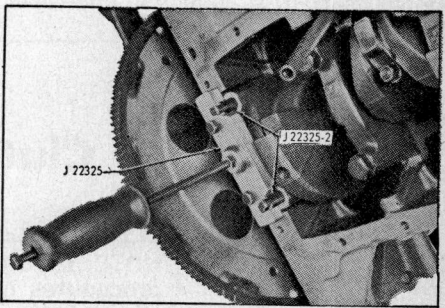

Fig. 23 Removing rear main bearing cap

FRONT CRANKCASE COVER

1. Remove crankshaft sprocket.
2. Remove 4 front oil pan-to-crankcase cover bolts.
3. Loosen remaining oil pan bolts as necessary to provide clearance between cover and pan. *It may be necessary to jar oil pan to gain necessary clearance.*
4. Remove 5 cover bolts.
5. Remove cover and gasket. Clean gasket surface, using care to see that gasket particles do not fall into oil pan.
6. Reverse procedure to install, Fig. 18.

ACCESSORY DRIVE HOUSING

Oil Pressure Regulator Valve

1. Remove cap, washer and spring from housing.
2. Using a magnet, remove valve from housing.
3. Reverse procedure to install.

Oil Pump

1. Remove pump cover and gasket.
2. Remove two gears.
3. Replace worn parts, install cover with new gasket and torque bolts to 20 ft-lbs.

Housing Assembly

1. Remove timing belt top cover.
2. Align timing marks, Fig. 3B.
3. Loosen 6 housing-to-cylinder block bolts, Fig. 3A.
4. Remove timing belt from camshaft sprocket and distributor drive.
5. Disconnect fuel lines from fuel pump.
6. Remove distributor cap, vacuum lines and wires from distributor.
7. Remove housing assembly.
8. Reverse procedure to install, using new housing gasket. Be sure to align timing marks and adjust timing belt tension.

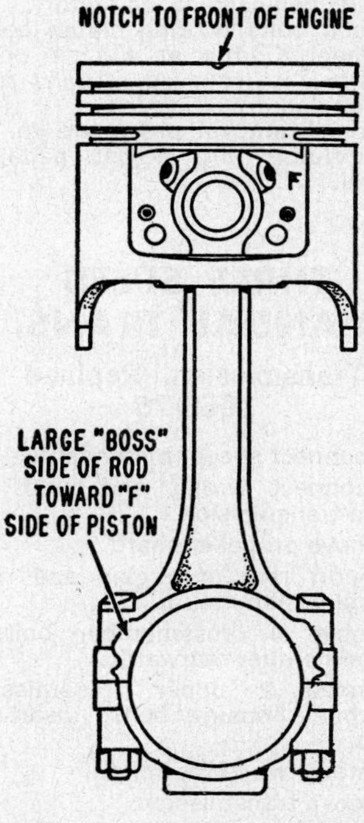

NOTCH TO FRONT OF ENGINE
F
LARGE "BOSS"
SIDE OF ROD
TOWARD "F"
SIDE OF PISTON

Fig. 24 Piston and rod assembly

Oil Filter By-Pass Valve

1. Remove housing assembly.
2. Remove valve retaining screw, Fig. 19.
3. Remove by-pass valve.
4. Reverse procedure to install.

Sprocket, Seal, Fuel Pump, Distributor Drive

1. Remove housing assembly.
2. Look for and write down location of sprocket timing mark and direction of distributor rotor, then remove distributor.
3. Remove drive gear retaining pin, Fig. 20. Position shaft to allow adequate clearance in housing body for pin removal.
4. Remove shaft and sprocket.
5. If necessary to replace bearing or seal use a slide hammer and tool of the type shown in Fig. 21 to remove seal or bearing and seal together.
6. Reverse procedure to install.

OIL PAN

1. Disconnect battery cable.
2. Remove air cleaner.
3. On air conditioned cars, remove com-

pressor from mounting brackets and position to one side.

4. Inspect all water hose and wiring harness for proper routing to prevent excessive binding when engine is raised about 4½".

NOTE: Before raising vehicle prop hood open at least 6" to insure adequate clearance between timing belt cover and inner hood panel.

5. Remove starter and flywheel cover.
6. Reroute or disconnect any wiring between bellcrank and floor pan to insure against damage when bell housing contacts floor pan.
7. Loosen transmission insulator-to-crossmember bolts.
8. Remove right and left engine insulator-to-frame bracket thru bolts.
9. Rotate vibration damper until timing mark is at bottom so crankshaft

counterweights will be in proper position for oil pan removal.
10. With suitable equipment, raise engine at front until insulators clear frame brackets.
11. Remove oil pan bolts.
12. Raise engine at front. Apply a rearward force on engine-transmission assembly until oil pan clears flywheel housing and remove pan.
13. Reverse procedure to install.

Rear Main Bearing Seal

The rear main bearing oil seal can be replaced (both halves) without removal of crankshaft. Always replace upper and lower seal as a unit, Fig. 22.
1. Remove oil pan.
2. Use a slide hammer of the type shown in Fig. 23 to remove bearing cap.
3. Pry seal from groove and bearing cap side seals.

4. Clean crankshaft surface.
5. Place new side seals in position and place bearing cap in vise and compress seals into place.
6. Insert new seal well lubricated with engine oil in bearing cap groove. Gradually push with a hammer handle until seal is rolled into place.
7. To replace upper half of seal, use a small hammer and brass pin punch to tap one end of oil seal until it protrudes far enough to be removed with pliers. Push new seal into place.
8. Install bearing cap and oil pan.

PISTONS & CRANKSHAFT BEARINGS

Service on pistons, rings, pins, main and rod bearings are conventional.
Assemble pistons to rods as shown in Fig. 24.

Clutch & Transmission Section

NOTE: 1975 linkage adjustment information is in this section. Repair procedures on both automatic and manual shift transmissions are covered elsewhere in this manual. Procedures for removing automatic transmissions as well as linkage adjustments on 1969-74 models are included in the automatic transmission chapters. See Chapter Index

CLUTCH PEDAL, ADJUST

1969-75 All Models

1. Unhook linkage return spring.
2. With clutch pedal against stop, loosen lock nut enough to allow adjusting rod to be turned out of swivel (V8) or push rod (6-cyl.) and rearward against clutch fork until clutch release bearing contacts pressure plate fingers lightly.
3. Rotate adjustable rod into swivel or push rod 3½ turns and tighten lock nut.
4. Install return spring and check for 1 to 1½ inch free pedal travel.

CLUTCH, REPLACE

1969-75 All

1. Disconnect battery-to-starter cable.
2. Remove transmission as outlined below.
3. Remove release bearing through rear opening in clutch housing.
4. Remove pedal return spring, starter, front flywheel housing shield and flywheel housing.

5. Mark clutch cover and flywheel to insure reassembly in the same position as balanced at the factory.
6. Loosen bolts holding clutch cover to flywheel a little at a time until all tension is relieved. Then remove clutch and driven disc.
7. Reverse removal procedure to install the clutch and adjust pedal free travel.

THREE SPEED MANUAL TRANS.

Transmission, Replace 1969-75

1. Disconnect speedometer cable.
2. Disconnect wiring and shift levers from transmission.
3. Remove propeller shaft.
4. Support rear of engine and remove transmission mount.
5. Remove 4 crossmember bolts and slide member rearward.
6. Remove 2 upper transmission-to-flywheel housing bolts, insert guide pins.
7. Remove two lower bolts.
8. Remove transmission.
9. Reverse procedure to install.

SHIFT LINKAGE 3 SPEED TRANS.

1972-75

Column Shift

1. Set gearshift lever in Reverse and lock ignition.
2. Loosen swivel clamp screw at 1st & Rev. transmission shifter lever (both levers on Ventura) and loosen screw to swivel clamp at cross shaft assembly.
3. Position 2nd & 3rd transmission shifter levers in Neutral and 1st & Rev. shifter lever in Reverse.
4. Tighten swivel clamp screw at 1st & Rev. shifter level to 20 ft. lbs, unlock steering column and shift into Neutral. *On Ventura models, pull down slightly on 1st & Rev. gearshift control rod to remove any slack in column mechanism before tightening clamp screw.*
5. Align steering column lower levers in Neutral (unlock steering column on Ventura) and insert a .186" dia. pin through hole in steering column lower levers.
6. Tighten swivel clamp screw at cross shaft to 20 ft. lbs. *On Ventura models position 2 & 3 shifter lever in Neutral*

and tighten swivel clamp nut at 2nd & 3rd shifter lever to 20 ft. lbs.

7. Remove gauge pin and check complete shift pattern.

Floor Shift (Exc. 1973-75 Muncie)

Follow procedure outlined for 1970-71 floor shift.

Floor Shift (1973-75 Muncie)

1. Place shift control lever in Neutral and insert a .250" pin into shifter assembly alignment holes. Be sure pin engages notch in far side of shifter housing.
2. Loosen swivel clamp screw to upper rod, loosen jam nuts at shifter assembly control rod trunnions, and disconnect 2nd & 3rd and 1st & Rev. trunnion and pin assemblies from both shifter levers.
3. With control rods disconnected, manually move shifter levers to check that transmission gears are in Neutral.
4. With gears and shifter assemblies in Neutral, adjust pin assemblies on their control rods so they align with and enter freely into their holes in shifter levers. Retain each with a plain washer and retainer clip and tighten jam nuts to 20 ft. lbs.
5. Remove gauge pin and check complete pattern for smooth operation.
6. Position shaft lever in Reverse, set steering column upper rod in Lock position and lock ignition. With transmission in Reverse, the ignition key must turn freely to its lock position.
7. Push up on upper rod to take up clearance in steering column lock mechanism and torque screw of adjusting swivel clamp to 20 ft. lbs.

1970-71

Column Shift

1. Set gearshift lever in Reverse position and lock ignition.
2. Loosen swivel clamp screws at transmission shifter lever (1st & Rev) and at cross shaft assembly.
3. Position front transmission shifter lever (2nd & 3rd) in Neutral position and rear transmission shifter lever (1st & Rev) in Reverse position.
4. Tighten swivel clamp screw at transmission 1st & Rev lever, unlock steering column and shift into Neutral.
5. Align gearshift lower control levers on column in Neutral position and insert a .185" pin through hole in levers.
6. Tighten swivel clamp screw at cross shaft to 20 ft. lbs., remove gauge and check operation.
7. Shift transmission into third speed (high gear) and adjust the T.C.S. switch so that the plunger is fully depressed against the 2nd & 3rd shifter lever.

Floor Shift

1. With steering column unlocked, position the shaft control lever into Neutral.
2. Loosen swivel clamp nut retaining the gearshift control rod to the idler lever.
3. Loosen trunnion jam nuts on 1st & Rev control rod, loosen jam nuts on 2nd & 3rd control rod and insert a .250" gauge pin into shifter assembly.
4. Manually position both transmission shifter levers in Neutral and torque jam nuts to 25 ft. lbs.
5. Remove gauge pin from shifter assembly and check operation.
6. Adjust backdrive by shifting into Reverse gear, set gearshift control rod in Lock position and lock the steering column.
7. Push up on gearshift control rod to take up clearance in column lock mechanism and torque adjusting swivel clamp nut to 20 ft. lbs.

1969 All

Column Shift

1. Align upper and lower gearshift levers on steering column in neutral position. Where provision has been made, insert a 3/16" gauge pin through holes in levers.
2. Loosen clamp screws at transmission control rods.
3. Position levers on transmission in neutral.

4. Tighten clamp screws to 20 ft-lbs.

Floor Shift

1. Position selector lever in neutral.
2. Loosen trunnion jam nut on transmission control rods.
3. Place transmission lever and bracket assembly in neutral. Where provision has been made, install a 1/4" gauge pin through hole in bracket.
4. Position transmission lever in neutral.
5. Tighten jam nuts to 30 ft-lbs.
6. Remove gauge pin.

4 SP. TRANS., REPLACE
1969-75

Follow procedure outlined for 1969-75 three-speed model.

SHIFT LINKAGE 4 SPEED TRANS.

1. Place selector lever in neutral.
2. Loosen trunnion nuts on transmission control rod.
3. Place transmission lever and bracket assembly in neutral and install a gauge pin through hole and slot provided in bracket.
4. Position lever on transmission in neutral.
5. Tighten trunnion nuts and remove gauge pin.
6. On 1969-75 units, position shift lever in Reverse, set steering column lever in Lock position and lock ignition. Push up on control rod to remove clearance and tighten nut of adjusting swivel to 20 ft.-lbs.

1975 AUTO. TRANS. LINKAGE, ADJUST

Adjustment procedures for the 1975 linkages are essentially the same as those for 1974 units which are outlined elsewhere in this manual.

Rear Axle, Propeller Shaft & Brake Section

REAR AXLES

Figs. 1 and 2 illustrate the rear axle assemblies used on 1969-75 conventional models. When necessary to overhaul either of these units, refer to the *Rear Axle Specifications* table in this chapter.

All 1969 & 1970-75 Except Type "C"

In this rear axle, Fig. 1, the rear axle housing and differential carrier are cast into an integral assembly. The drive pinion assembly is mounted in two opposed tapered roller bearings. The pinion bearings are preloaded by a spacer behind the front bearing. The pinion is positioned by a washer between the head of the pinion and the rear bearing.

The differential is supported in the carrier by two tapered roller side bearings. These bearings are preloaded by shims located between the bearings and carrier housing. The differential assembly is positioned for proper ring gear and pinion backlash by varying these shims. The differential case houses two side gears in mesh with two pinions mounted on a pinion shaft which is held in place by a lock screw. The side gears and pinions are backed by thrust washers.

Diff. Carrier Assy

All 1969 & 1970-75 except Type "C"

Construction of the axle assembly is such that service operations may be performed with the housing installed in the vehicle or with the housing removed and installed in a holding fixture. The following procedure is necessary only when the housing requires replacement.

1. Raise car and place a floor jack under

center of axle housing so it starts to raise rear axle assembly. Place car stands solidly under body members on both sides.
2. Disconnect rear U-joint from drive pinion flange and support propeller shaft out of the way.

3. Remove both axle shafts.
4. Support both brake backing plates out of the way.
5. Disconnect rear brake hose bracket by removing top cover bolt. Remove brake line from housing by bending back tabs.
6. Loosen remaining cover bolts, break loose cover about ⅛" and allow lube to drain.
7. Disconnect shock absorbers at axle housing. Lower jack under housing until rear springs can be removed.
8. Disconnect upper control arms at axle housing.
9. Disconnect lower control arms at axle housing and remove rear axle assembly from vehicle.
10. Reverse removal procedure to install the unit.

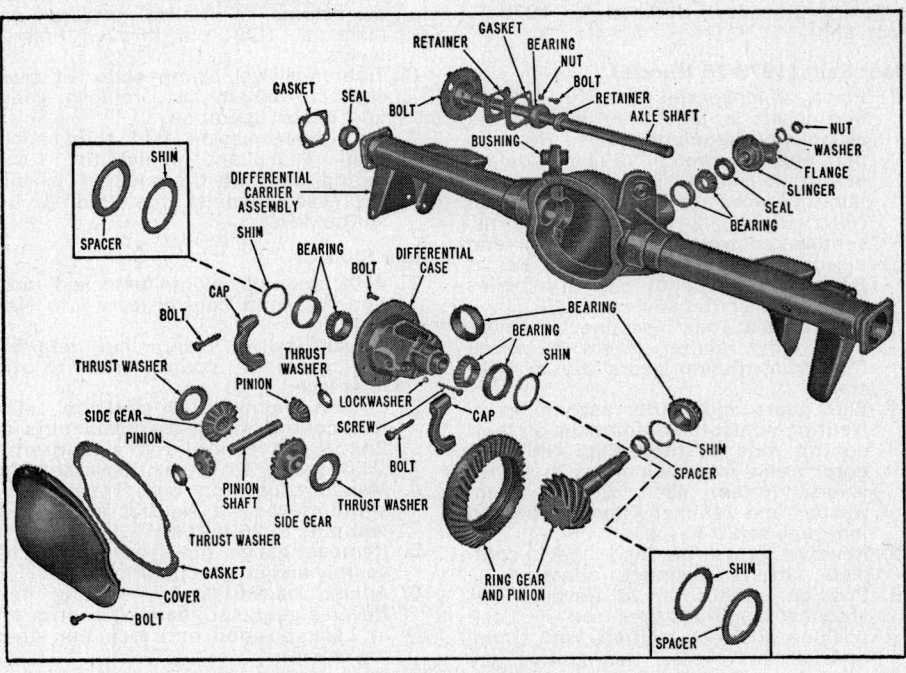

Fig. 1   Rear axle assembly exploded. All 1969 and 1970-75 except type "C"

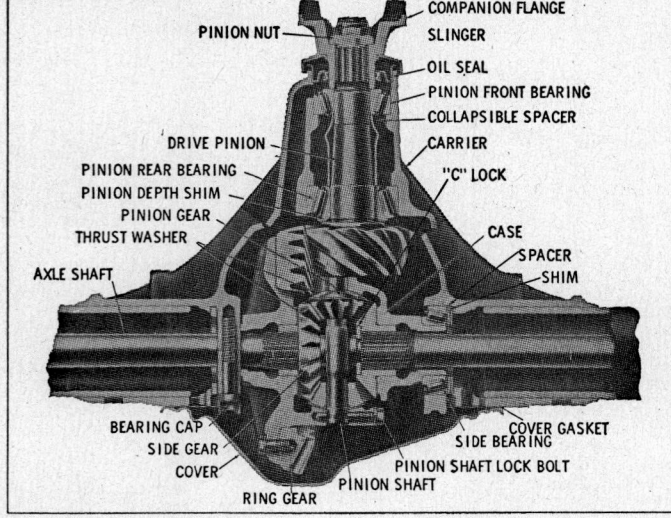

Fig. 2   1970-75 type "C" differential case

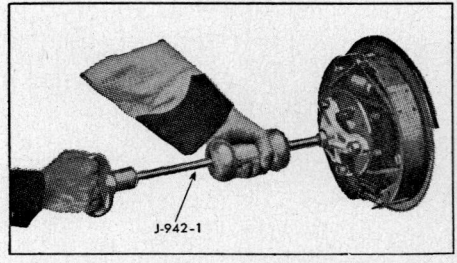

Fig. 3   Removing axle shaft with slide hammer-type propeller

Axle Shaft, Replace

NOTE: Design allows for axle shaft end play of .032" on 1969-73 models and 1974-75 "P" axles, .018" on 1974 "B" and "O" axles and .022" on 1974 "C", "G" and "K" axles. This end play can be checked with the wheel and brake drum removed by measuring the difference between the end of the housing and the axle shaft flange while moving the axle shaft in and out by hand.

On 1973-75 "C" axles, excessive end play can be compensated for by using selective thickness "C" locks. On all other 1969-75 axles, excessive end play cannot be compensated for by inserting a shim inboard of the bearing in the housing since it ignores the end play of the bearing itself, and may result in improper seating of the gasket or backing plate against the housing. If end play is excessive, the axle shaft and bearing should be removed and the cause of the excessive end play corrected.

All 1969 & 1970-75 except Type "C"

1. To remove, take off wheels and brake drums.
2. Remove nuts holding retainer plates and brake backing plates. Pull retainers clear of bolts and reinstall two lower nuts finger tight to hold backing plate in position.
3. Use a slide hammer-type puller to remove axle shaft, Fig. 3.

Axle Shaft Bearing

1. Press axle shaft bearing off shaft.
2. Press new bearing against shoulder on shaft.

CAUTION: Outer retainer plate which retains bearing in housing must be on axle shaft before bearing is installed. A new outer retainer gasket can be installed after bearing. Use care not to wedge outer retainer between bearing and shoulder of shaft. Do not press bearing and inner retainer on in one operation.

3. Press new inner retainer ring against bearing.

Axle Shaft Seal

1. Insert suitable tongs behind seal and pull straight out to remove seal.
2. Apply sealer to outside diameter of new seal.
3. Position seal over a suitable installer and drive straight into axle housing until tool bottoms on bearing shoulder in housing.

Axle Shaft, Install

1. Apply a coat of wheel bearing grease in bearing recess of housing. Also lightly lubricate the axle shaft with rear axle lube from the sealing surface to about 6" inboard.
2. Install *new* axle housing-to-brake backing plate gasket.
3. Install brake assembly with backing plate in proper position.
4. With a *new* outer retainer gasket in proper position, insert axle shaft until splines engage differential. *Do not*

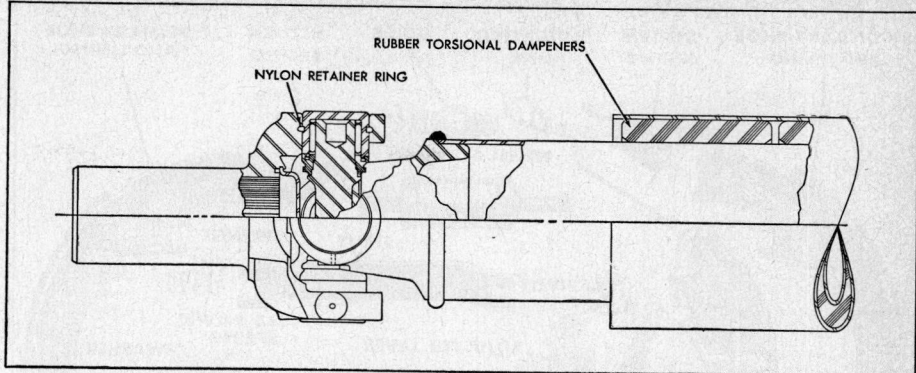

Fig. 4   Insulated propeller shaft. 1969 (typical)

allow shaft to drag on seal.
5. Drive axle shaft into position.
6. Place new outer retainer gasket and retainer over studs and install nuts, torqueing them to 45-55 ft-lbs.
7. Install brake drums and wheels.

1970-75 Type "C" axle

1. Raise and support car leaving the rear wheels and differential suspended.
2. Remove rear wheels and brake drums.
3. Remove differential cover and drain lubricant.
4. Remove pinion shaft lock bolt and pinion shaft.
5. Push axle shaft inward to permit removal of "C" locks then remove axle shaft.
6. Install axle shaft bearing and seal remover and remove the bearing and seal.

PROPELLER SHAFT
1969-75

Two designs of propeller shaft are used, a solid type which is of one piece tubular steel construction, and a "rubber" type which incorporates rubber torsional dampers between two concentric tubes of steel.

Two methods are used to retain the U-joint bearings to the yoke: conventional snap rings are used at the companion flange of the differential: the remaining six U-joint bearings are held in place with nylon rings.

SERVICE NOTE: Because of the elastic properties of the nylon retainers, Fig. 4, it is not possible to drive the bearings out in the conventional manner. They must be pressed out, which shears the nylon retainers in half, rendering the bearings and journal unsuitable for further use. Therefore, when reassembling, a new bearing and journal assembly employing the conventional snap ring retainers must be used.

CAUTION: Do not attempt to replace the U-joints of propeller shafts from cars equipped with axles of 3.42 ratio and over. They are high speed balanced assemblies and replacement of composite U-joint will destroy this balance.

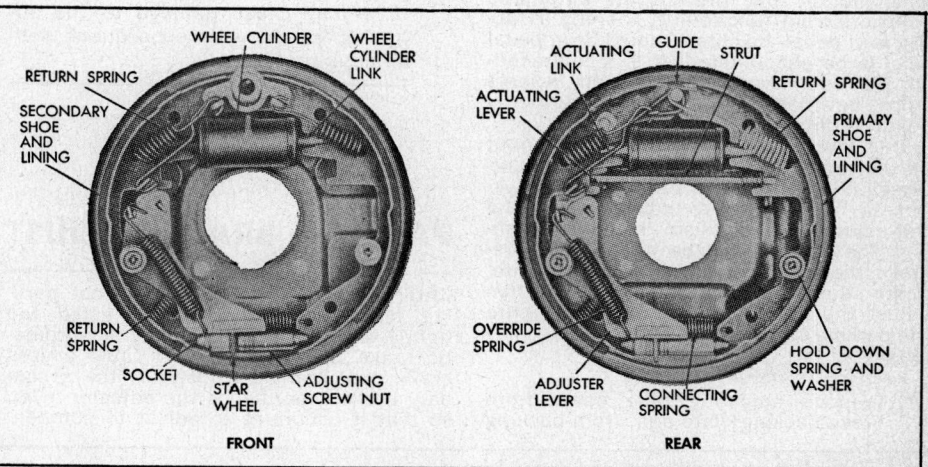

Fig. 5   Right front and rear brake. 1969-75 (typical)

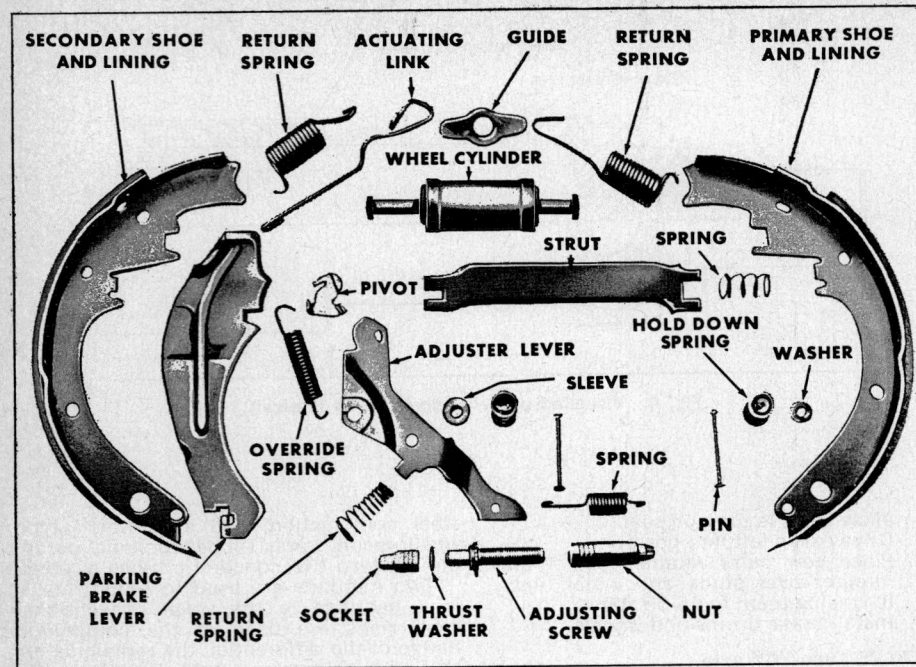

SECONDARY SHOE AND LINING — RETURN SPRING — ACTUATING LINK — GUIDE — RETURN SPRING — PRIMARY SHOE AND LINING

WHEEL CYLINDER

STRUT — SPRING

PIVOT — HOLD DOWN SPRING — WASHER

ADJUSTER LEVER — SLEEVE

OVERRIDE SPRING — SPRING — PIN

PARKING BRAKE LEVER — RETURN SPRING — SOCKET — THRUST WASHER — ADJUSTING SCREW — NUT

Fig. 5A   Typical right rear self adjusting brake

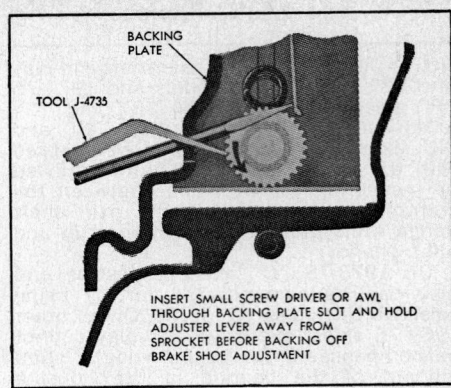

BACKING PLATE

TOOL J-4735

INSERT SMALL SCREW DRIVER OR AWL THROUGH BACKING PLATE SLOT AND HOLD ADJUSTER LEVER AWAY FROM SPROCKET BEFORE BACKING OFF BRAKE SHOE ADJUSTMENT

Fig. 6   Backing off adjusting screw. 1969-73

BRAKE ADJUSTMENTS
1969-75 Self-Adjusting Brakes

These brakes, Figs. 5, 5A have self-adjusting shoe mechanisms that assure correct lining-to-drum clearances at all times. The automatic adjusters operate only when the brakes are applied as the car is moving rearward or when the car comes to an uphill stop.

Although the brakes are self-adjusting, an initial adjustment is necessary after the brake shoes have been relined or replaced, or when the length of the star wheel adjuster has been changed during some other service operation.

Frequent usage of an automatic transmission forward range to halt reverse vehicle motion may prevent the automatic adjusters from functioning, thereby inducing low pedal heights. Should low pedal heights be encountered, it is recommended that numerous forward and reverse stops be made until satisfactory pedal height is obtained.

If a low pedal height condition cannot be corrected by making numerous reverse stops (provided the hydraulic system is free of air) it indicates that the self-adjusting mechanism is not functioning. Therefore, it will be necessary to remove the drum, clean, free up and lubricate the adjusting mechanism. Then adjust the brakes as follows, being sure the parking brake is fully released.

Adjustment

1. Remove adjusting hole cover from brake backing plate and, from backing plate side, turn adjusting screw upward with a screwdriver or other suitable tool to expand the shoes until a slight drag is felt when the drum is rotated.
2. Remove brake drum.
3. While holding adjusting lever out of engagement with the adjusting screw, Fig. 6, back off the adjusting screw one full turn with the fingers.

NOTE: *If finger movement will not turn the screw, free it up. If this is not done, the adjusting lever will not turn the screw during subsequent vehicle operation. Lubricate the screw with oil and coat with wheel bearing grease. Any other adjustment procedure may cause damage to the adjusting screw with consequent self-adjuster problems.*

PARKING BRAKE, ADJUST

CAUTION: It is very important that parking brake cables are not adjusted too tightly causing brake drag. With automatic brake adjusters, a tight cable causes brake drag and also positions the secondary brake shoe, hence the adjuster lever, so that it continues to adjust to compensate for wear caused by the drag. The result is a cycle of wear and adjustment that can wear out linings very rapidly.

1969-75

1. Jack up both rear wheels.
2. Pull parking brake pedal five to seven notches from fully released position.
3. Loosen equalizer rear lock nut. Adjust forward nut until a light to moderate drag is felt when rear wheels are rotated.
4. Tighten lock nut. Fully released parking brake and rotate rear wheels to be sure there is no drag.

POWER BRAKE UNIT, REPLACE
1969-75 All Models

1. Disconnect vacuum hose at vacuum check valve. Plug hose and cover valve opening to exclude dust.
2. Disconnect pipe(s) from master cylinder hydraulic port and cover opening and pipe end to exclude dirt.
3. Remove clevis pin from brake pedal inside car.
4. Remove nuts from rear half housing and remove power cylinder assembly.
5. Reverse removal procedure to install.

BRAKE MASTER CYLINDER, REPLACE
1969-75

1. Disconnect brake lines from two outlets on master cylinder and tape end of lines to prevent entrance of dirt.
2. Disconnect master cylinder push rod from brake pedal.
3. Remove master cylinder from dash.

Rear Suspension

SHOCK ABSORBER, REPLACE

NOTE: If vehicle is equipped with Super-lift shock absorbers, bleed system air pressure through service valve before disconnecting lines at shock absorber fittings.

1. With rear axle supported properly, disconnect shock absorber from lower mounting stud. Use a wrench to prevent mounting stud rotation.
2. Disconnect shock absorber from upper mounting.
3. Reverse procedure to install.

LEAF SPRING & BUSHINGS, REPLACE

1970-75 Firebird, 1971-75 Station Wagons, Ventura & 1974 GTO

1. Support vehicle at frame and support rear axle, removing tension from spring.
2. Disconnect shock absorbers at lower mountings.
3. Remove "U" bolts, spring plate and upper cushion pad.
4. Loosen rear shackle nuts and spring front mounting bolt, Fig. 1.
5. On all except station wagons, disconnect spring front mounting bracket from underbody, drop spring and remove bracket from spring. On station wagons, remove spring front mount bolt.
6. Support spring and remove lower rear shackle bolt.
7. To replace bushings, refer to Figs. 2 and 3.
8. Reverse procedure to install.

1969 Firebird

1. Perform steps 1 and 2 as outlined in above procedure.
2. Loosen spring front mount bolt.

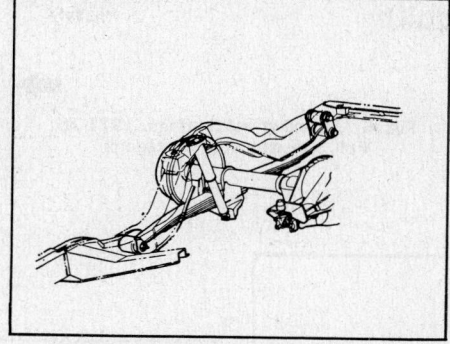

Fig. 1   Leaf spring suspension. 1969-75 Firebird, 1971-75 Station Wagons, Ventura & 1974 GTO (typical)

3. Remove spring retainer bracket to underbody screws, lower axle and remove bracket.
4. Disconnect parking brake cable from spring plate bracket and remove "U" bolts and spring plate.
5. Support spring, remove spring front mount bolt and rear shackle bolt from spring.
6. To replace bushings, refer to Figs. 2 and 3.
7. Reverse procedure to install.

Leaf Spring Service

NOTE: The main leaf may be serviced separately, however, if any of the smaller leaves require replacement, the entire assembly must be replaced.

1. Clamp spring in a vise, remove spring clips and center bolt, then carefully

Fig. 3   Leaf spring front bushing installation

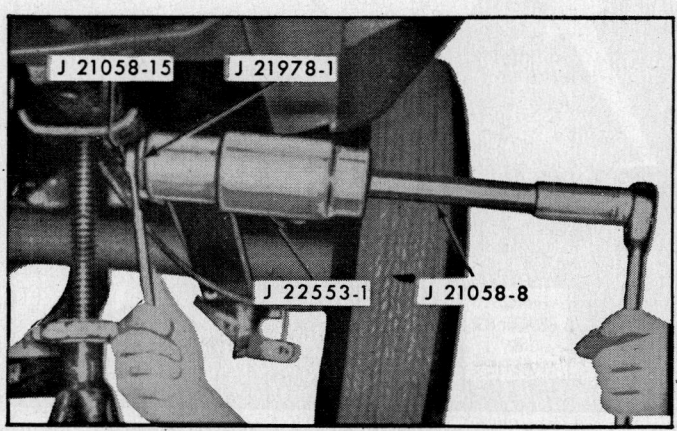

Fig. 2   Leaf spring front bushing removal

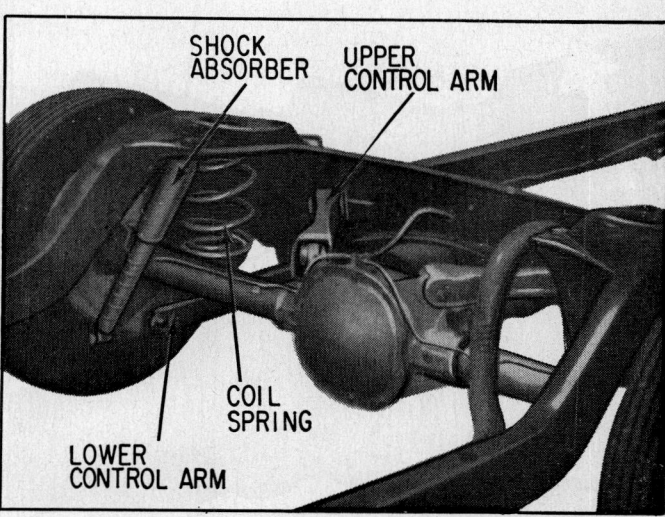

Fig. 4   Coil spring suspension (typical)

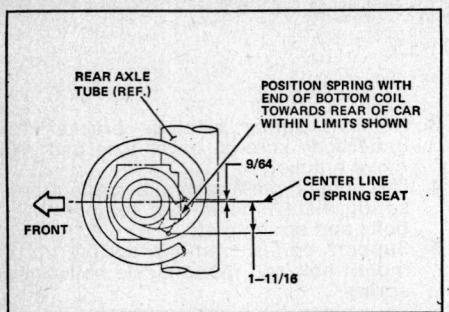

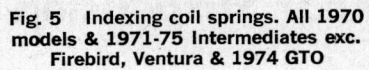

Fig. 5   Indexing coil springs. All 1970 models & 1971-75 Intermediates exc. Firebird, Ventura & 1974 GTO

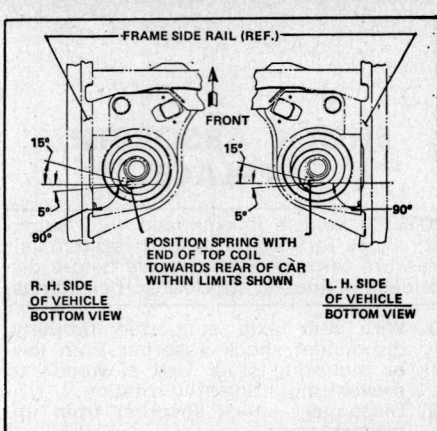

Fig. 6   Indexing coil springs. 1971-75 Full Size exc. station wagons

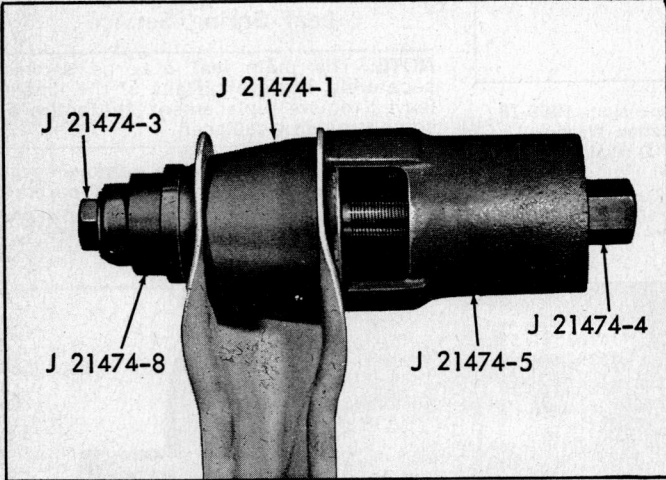

Fig. 7   All front bushings & lower control arm rear bushing removal

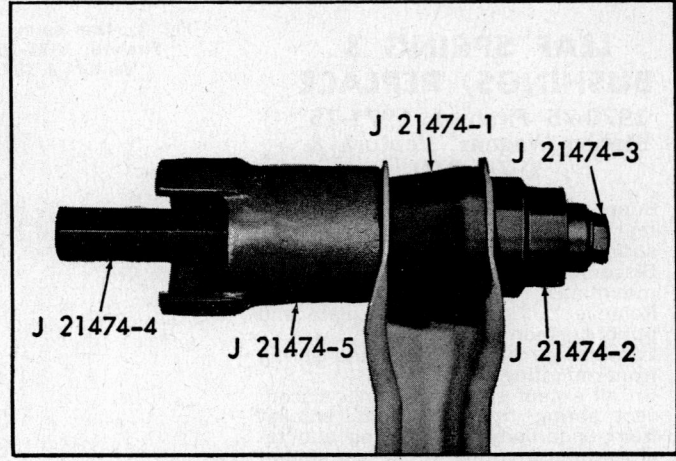

Fig. 8   All front bushings & lower control arm rear bushing installation

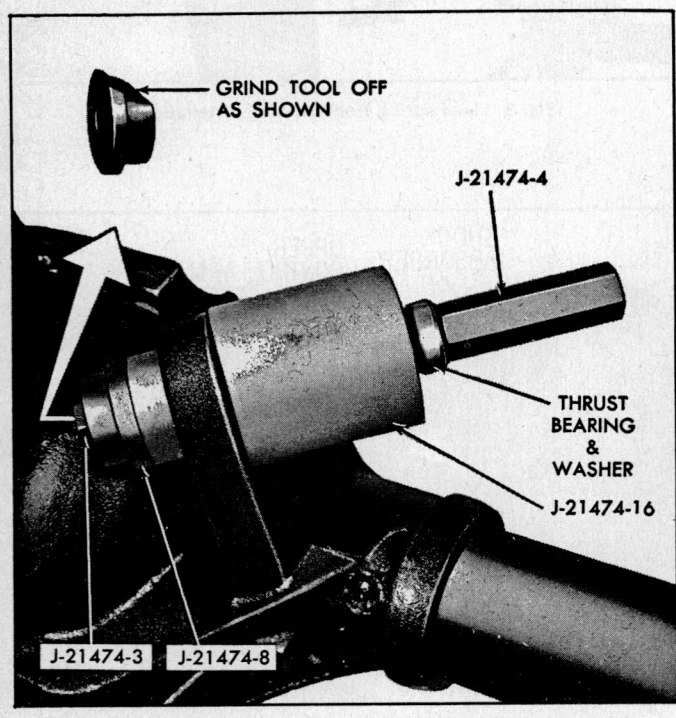

Fig. 9   Upper control arm rear bushing removal. 1970-75 models

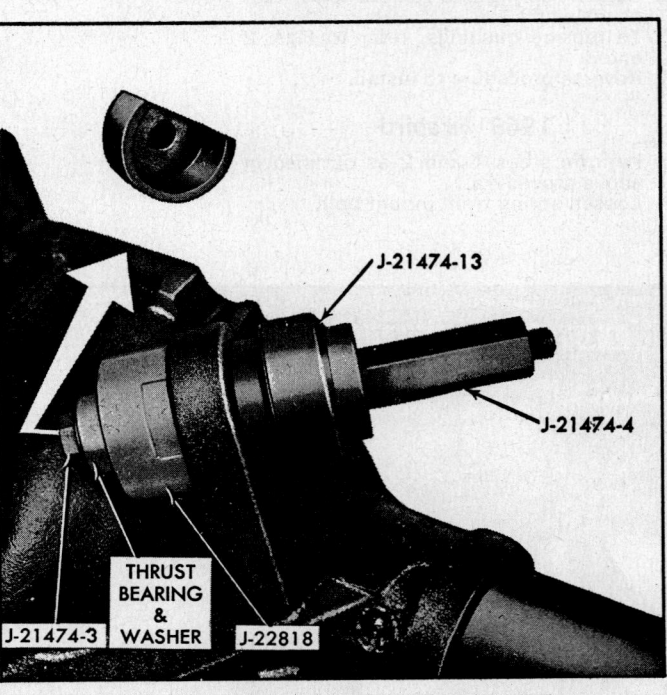

Fig. 10   Upper control arm rear bushing installation. 1970-75 models

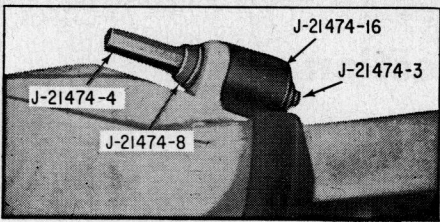

Fig. 11   Upper control arm rear bushing removal. 1969 models

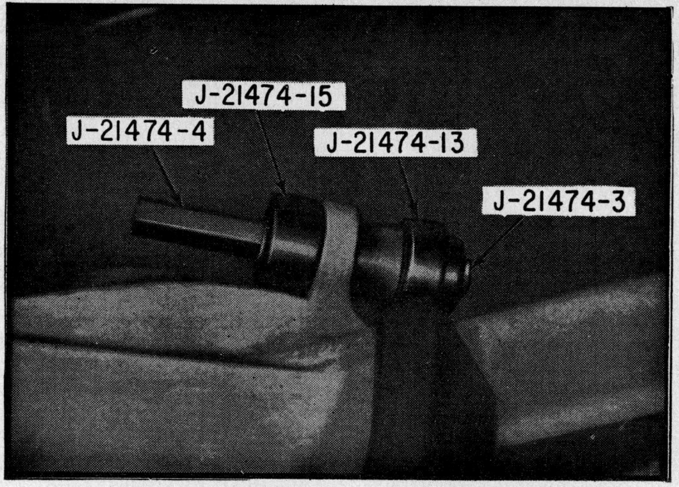

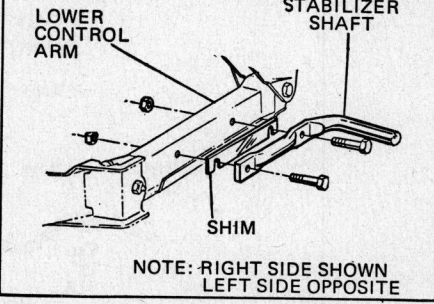

Fig. 12   Upper control arm rear bushing installation. 1969 models

open vise, allowing spring to expand.
2. Replace main leaf and use a drift to align center bolt holes, compress spring in a vise, remove drift and install new center bolt.
3. Align spring leaves and bend spring clips into position.

NOTE: Over tightening spring clips will bind spring action.

COIL SPRING, REPLACE

1. Support vehicle at frame and support rear axle with a suitable jack.
2. Disconnect brake line and axle housing connector from axle housing.
3. Disconnect shock absorbers from lower mountings, lower axle and remove springs, Fig. 4.
4. Replace upper spring seat insulator, if necessary.
5. Reverse procedure to install and properly index springs, Figs. 5 and 6.

CONTROL ARMS & BUSHINGS, REPLACE

NOTE: Replace control arms one at a time to prevent axle misalignment, making installation difficult.

Upper Control Arms

1. Support vehicle at frame and rear axle.
2. Remove control arm front and rear mounting bolts.
3. Replace bushings as necessary, Figs. 7 thru 12.
4. Reverse procedure to install. Tighten control arm bolts with vehicle at curb height.

Lower Control Arms

Follow "Upper Control Arms" procedure for replacement of lower control arms. Lower control arm bushings are serviceable, Figs. 7 and 8.

NOTE: On 1970-73 GTO, remove stabilizer bar, outlined under "Stabilizer Bar, Re-

Fig. 13   Stabilizer bar installation. 1970-73 GTO

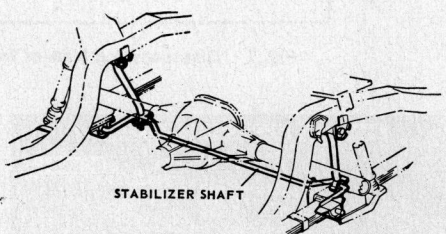

Fig. 14   Stabilizer bar installation. 1970-74 Firebird Formula, Trans Am, 1972-75 Ventura & 1974 GTO

place" 1970-73 GTO procedure, before removing lower control arm mounting bolts.

STABILIZER BAR & BUSHINGS, REPLACE

1970-73 GTO

1. With vehicle supported at rear axle, remove bolts attaching stabilizer bar to lower control arms, Fig. 13.
2. Replace bushings as necessary.
3. Reverse procedure to install. Install shims, Fig. 13, if needed, equally on each side of stabilizer bar and tighten attaching bolts with vehicle at curb height.

1974 GTO, 1972-74 Ventura, 1970-74 Firebird Formula & Trans Am

1. With vehicle supported at rear axle, disconnect stabilizer bar from spring plate attachments, Fig. 14.
2. Disconnect stabilizer bar from upper support links and remove support links from frame brackets.
3. Replace bushings as necessary.
4. Reverse procedure to install. Tighten attaching bolts with vehicle at curb height.

Front Suspension & Steering Section

FRONT SUSPENSION
1969-75

The front suspension is of the conventional "A" frame design with coil springs and ball joints. The ball joints have a "fixed boot" grease seal for protection against the entry of dirt and water. The steering knuckles and spindles are of integral design and brake cylinders are rigidly attached to the knuckles with the backing plates serving principally as a support for brake shoes and as a protective cover.

On most 1971-75 models, an integral steering knuckle which is a combination steering knuckle, brake caliper support and steering arm is used. On other models, the steering knuckle is of the conventional type with a separate steering arm.

Rubber bushings at the inner ends of the upper control arms pivot on shafts attached to the car frame. Caster and camber adjustments are made with shims at this point, Fig. 1. Direct acting shock absorbers operate within the coil springs.

LUBRICATION

These cars are completely lubricated at the factory with a special long-lasting chassis grease and under normal conditions chassis lubrication will not be required for 12,000 miles or one year whichever comes first. For subsequent lubrications, the specially formulated grease is recommended and is available at Pontiac dealers.

NOTE: If conventional chassis lubrication is used, relubrication at four months or 6000 miles, whichever occurs first, is necessary.

WHEEL ALIGNMENT
1969-75 All Models

Caster and camber adjustments are made by placing shims between the upper pivot shafts and frame, Fig. 2. Both adjustments can be made at the same time. In order to remove or install shims, raise car to remove weight from front wheel, then loosen control arm shaft-to-frame bolts.
1. To decrease positive caster add shims to front bolt.
2. To increase positive caster remove shims from front bolt.
3. To increase camber remove shims from both front and rear bolts.
4. To decrease camber add shims to both front and rear bolts.
5. Compensate for drift to right due to road camber by setting left angle ¼° greater than right.

NOTE: By adding or subtracting an equal amount of shims from front and rear bolts, camber will be changed without affecting caster.

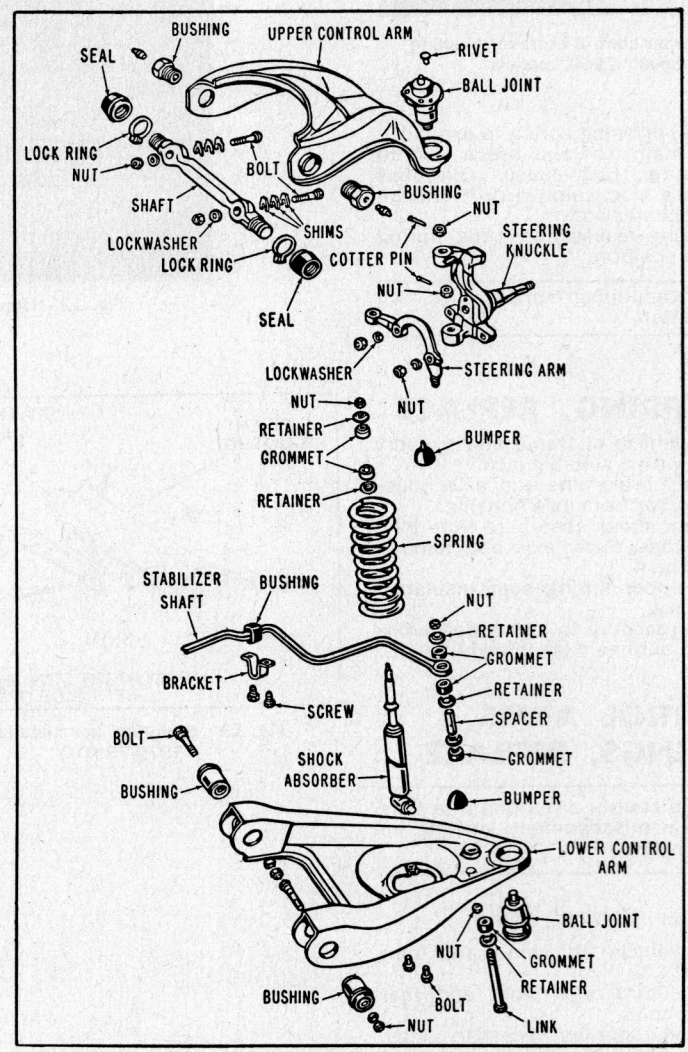

Fig. 1   Disassembled view of front suspension. 1969-74 (typical)

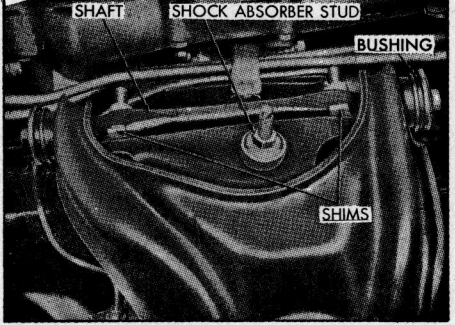

Fig. 2   Caster and camber shim location

6. After the correct number of shims have been installed, torque pivot shaft mounting bolts to 55-75 ft-lbs.

TOE-IN, ADJUST

1. With wheels in straight ahead position, loosen tie rod clamp bolts and turn tubes an equal amount until toe-in is according to specifications. Turn right tie rod in direction of forward rotation of wheels to increase toe-in. Turn left tie rod in opposite direction to increase toe-in.
2. Tighten tie rod adjuster sleeve bolts to 14-20 ft-lbs, making sure bolts are to lower rear side of tie rod.

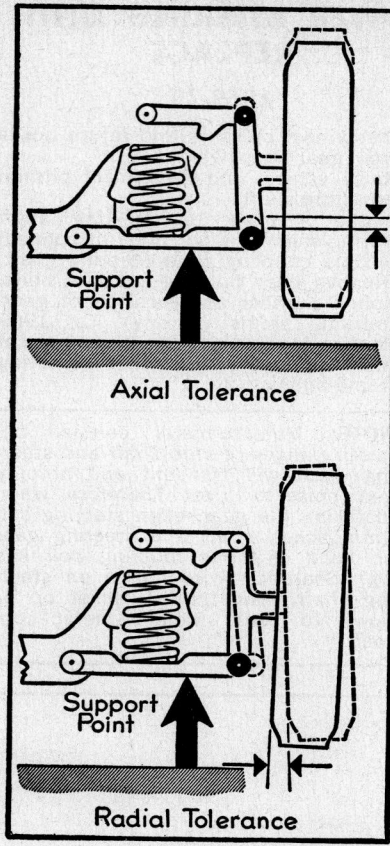

Fig. 3 Checking ball joints for wear

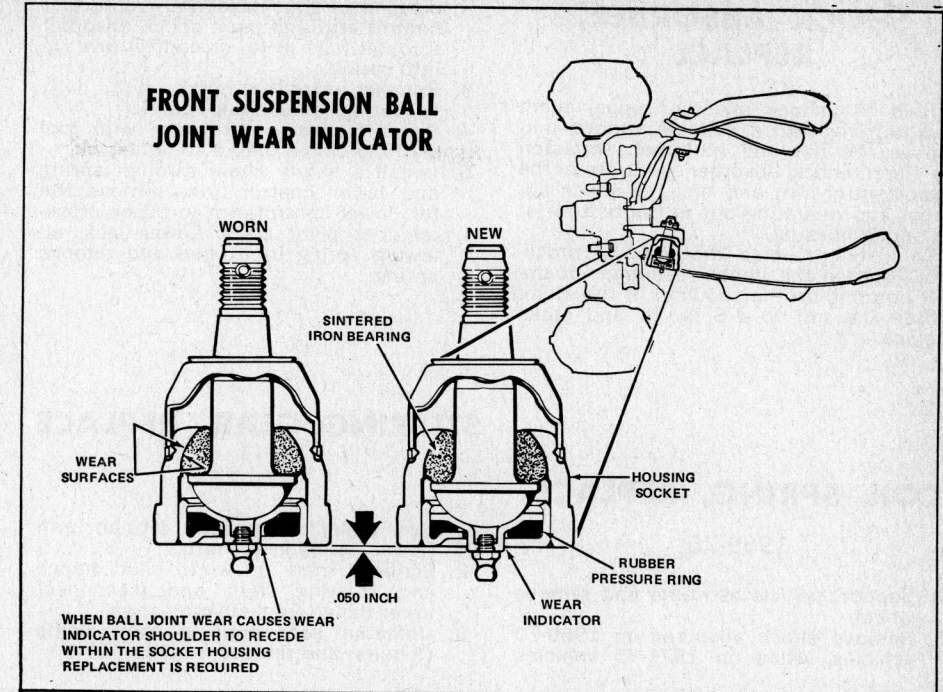

FRONT SUSPENSION BALL JOINT WEAR INDICATOR

WORN

NEW

SINTERED IRON BEARING

WEAR SURFACES

HOUSING SOCKET

RUBBER PRESSURE RING

.050 INCH

WEAR INDICATOR

WHEN BALL JOINT WEAR CAUSES WEAR INDICATOR SHOULDER TO RECEDE WITHIN THE SOCKET HOUSING REPLACEMENT IS REQUIRED

Fig. 4 Ball joint wear indicator. 1973 Catalina, Bonneville, Grandville & 1974 models exc. GTO & Ventura & all 1975

WHEEL BEARINGS, ADJUST

1974-75

1. While rotating wheel, torque spindle nut to 12 ft. lbs.
2. Back off spindle nut until just loose, then retighten by hand.
3. Loosen spindle nut until cotter pin can be inserted, however, do not loosen spindle nut more than ½ flat.
4. With bearing properly adjusted, there should be .001-.005 inch end play.

1969-73

1. While rotating wheel, snug-up spindle nut.
2. Back off spindle nut, then retighten by hand.
3. Loosen spindle nut until cotter pin can be inserted.

NOTE: Spindle nut must not be even finger tight.

4. With bearing properly adjusted, there should be .001-.005 inch end play on 1969-71 models and .001-.008 inch end play on 1972-73 models.

WHEEL BEARINGS, REPLACE

(Disc Brakes)

1. Raise car and remove front wheels.
2. Remove brake hose support to caliper mounting bracket screw.
3. Remove caliper to mounting bracket bolts.

NOTE: Do not place strain on brake hose.

4. Remove spindle nut, and disc and hub assembly. Grease retainer and inner bearing can now be removed.

CHECKING BALL JOINTS FOR WEAR

Before checking ball joints for wear, make sure the front wheel bearings are properly adjusted and that the control arms are tight.

Referring to Fig. 3, raise wheel with a jack placed under the lower control at the point shown. Then test by moving the wheel up and down to check axial play, and rocking it at the top and bottom to measure radial play.

1. Upper ball joint should be replaced if there is any noticeable looseness at this joint.
   If the ball joint is the type using a built in rubber pre-load cushion it will be necessary to remove the ball stud from the knuckle. Then replace the ball joint retaining nut on the ball stud. Using a socket and torque wrench, measure amount of torque required to turn the ball stud in its socket. If any torque is required, the ball joint is satisfactory. If no torque is required, the ball joint must be replaced.
2. Lower ball joint should be replaced if radial play exceeds .250".
3. Lower ball joint should be replaced if axial play between lower control arm and spindle exceeds the following:
   1969-75 .... .050"

NOTE: A visual wear indicator is built into the lower ball joint on the 1973 Bonneville, Catalina and Grand Ville and 1974 models except GTO and Ventura and all 1975 models, Fig. 4.

If the ball joint is the type using a built-in rubber pre-load cushion it will be necessary to remove the ball stud from the knuckle. Then replace the ball joint retaining nut on the ball stud. Using a socket and torque wrench, measure the amount of torque required to turn the ball stud in its socket. If any torque is required, the ball joint is satisfactory. If no torque is required, the ball joint must be replaced.

BALL JOINTS, REPLACE

On all models the upper ball joint is riveted to the control arm. All service ball joints, however, are provided with bolt, nut and washer assemblies for replacement purposes.

The lower ball joint is pressed into the control arm. They may be pressed out and new joints pressed in.

SHOCK ABSORBER, REPLACE

Hold the shock absorber upper stem from turning with a suitable wrench and remove the nut and grommet. Unfasten the lower shock absorber pivot from the lower control arm and pull the shock absorber and mounting out at the bottom of the spring housing.

To install, reverse the removal procedure. Tighten the upper retaining nut until it bottoms on the shoulder of the stem. Torque the nut to 4-6 lb. ft. and stake in place.

COIL SPRING, REPLACE

1969-75

1. Support vehicle at frame and remove wheel.
2. Remove shock absorber on 1969-70 vehicles, while on 1971-75 vehicles disconnect shock absorber from lower control arm and push shock absorber through hole in lower control arm up into spring.
3. Remove stabilizer link nut, link, spacer, grommets and retainer.
4. Support lower control arm with tool J-23028 bolted onto a suitable jack.
5. Install a safety chain through spring and lower control arm, remove the two lower control arm to frame crossmember pivot bolts. Lower jack, allowing spring to expand and remove spring.

STEERING GEAR, REPLACE

1969-75

1. Use puller to remove pitman arm from steering gear shaft.
2. Scribe a mark on worm shaft flange and steering shaft and disconnect lower flange from steering shaft
3. Unfasten gear housing from frame (3 bolts) and remove from car.

POWER STEERING UNIT, REPLACE

1969-75

1. Disconnect pressure and return hoses from gear housing.
2. Raise vehicle and disconnect pitman arm from shaft.
3. Scribe a mark on steering shaft worm shaft flange and disconnect flexible coupling from steering shaft.
4. Remove gear housing-to-frame bolts, noting number and location of gear-to-frame shims (if any). On 1969 Pontiac models a brake hose bracket must be removed prior to removing frame bolts.

NOTE: *Metal-to-metal contact between flanges of stub shaft and steering shaft will transmit and amplify gear noise to driver. Therefore, when installing the gear, align steering column jacket, shaft and steering gear so head of lower coupling bolt has 1/4" clearance from flange on steering shaft. Adjust mast jacket up or down to avoid metal-to-metal contact.*

Year	Engine or Car Model	Spark Plug Gap	Distributor Point Gap	Distributor Dwell Angle	Firing Order	Ignition Timing BTDC or Mark	Ignition Timing Mark Location	Valve Lash Intake	Valve Lash Exhaust	Wheel Alignment Caster Degrees	Wheel Alignment Camber Degrees	Wheel Alignment Toe-In Inch
AMERICAN MOTORS												
1958	Six L-Head	.035	.016	28–35	153624	3°	Damper	.016H	.018C	Zero	+¼	1/16–3/16
	Six O-Head	.035	.016	28–33	153624	5°	Damper	.012H	.016H	Zero	+¼	1/16–3/16
	V8-250	.035	.016	28–32	18436572[1]	5°	Damper	.012H	.014H	+½[4]	Zero	1/16–3/16
	V8-327	.035	.016	28–32	18436572[1]	5°	Damper	Zero	Zero	+½[4]	Zero	1/16–3/16
1959	Flat Head Six	.035	.016	28–35	153624	3°	Damper	.016C	.018C	+¼[4]	Zero	1/16–3/16
	OHV Six	.035	.016	28–35	153624	5°	Damper	.012H	.016H	+¼[4]	Zero	1/16–3/16
	V8-250	.035	.016	28–32	18436572[1]	TDC	Damper	.012H	.014H	+½[4]	Zero	1/16–3/16
	V8-327	.035	.016	28–32	18436572[1]	5°	Damper	Zero	Zero	+½[4]	Zero	1/16–3/16
1960	American[5]	.035	.020	37–41	153624	3°	Damper	.016C	.018C	+¼[8]	Zero	1/16–3/16
	American Custom[6]	.035	.016	28–35	153624	8°	Damper	.012H	.016H	+¼[8]	Zero	1/16–3/16
	American Custom[7]	.035	.016	28–35	153624	10°	Damper	.012H	.016H	+¼[8]	Zero	1/16–3/16
	Rambler 6	.035	.016	28–35	153624	5°	Damper	.012H	.016H	+¼[8]	Zero	1/16–3/16
	V8-250	.035	.016	28–32	18436572[1]	TDC	Damper	.012H	.014H	+½[2]	Zero	1/16–3/16
	V8-327-250 H.P.	.035	.016	28–32	18436572[1]	TDC	Damper	Zero	Zero	+½[2]	Zero	1/16–3/16
	V8-327-270 H.P.	.035	.016	28–32	18436572[1]	5°	Damper	Zero	Zero	+½[2]	Zero	1/16–3/16
1961	American[5]	.035	.020	37–41	153624	3°	Damper	.016C	.018C	+½[8]	Zero	1/16–3/16
	American Custom[6]	.035	.016	28–35	153624	8°	Damper	.012H	.016H	+½[8]	Zero	1/16–3/16
	American Custom[7]	.035	.016	28–35	153624	10°	Damper	.012H	.016H	+½[8]	Zero	1/16–3/16
	Rambler 6	.035	.016	28–35	153624	8°	Damper	.012H	.016H	+½[4]	Zero	1/16–3/16
	V8-250 Std. Trans.	.035	.016	28–32	18436572[1]	TDC	Damper	.012H	.014H	+½[4]	Zero	1/16–3/16
	V8-250 Auto. Trans.	.035	.016	28–32	18436572[1]	5°	Damper	.012H	.014H	+½[4]	Zero	1/16–3/16
	V8-327	.035	.016	28–32	18436572[1]	5°	Damper	Zero	Zero	+½[4]	Zero	1/16–3/16
1962	American L-Head 6	.035	.020	36–42	153624	3°	Damper	.016C	.018C	Zero[7]	[10]	1/8
	American OHV-6[5]	.035	.016	28–35	153624	8°	Damper	.012H[8]	.016H[8]	Zero[7]	[10]	1/8
	American OHV-6[6]	.035	.016	28–35	153624	10°	Damper	Zero[9]	Zero[9]	Zero[7]	[10]	1/8
	Rambler 6	.035	.016	28–35	153624	5°	Damper	.012H	.016H	Zero[7]	[10]	1/8
	V8-327 Std. Tr.	.035	.020	28–32	18436572[1]	5°	Damper	Zero	Zero	Zero[3]	[10]	1/8
	V8-327 Auto. Tr.	.035	.020	28–32	18436572[1]	3°	Damper	Zero	Zero	Zero[3]	[10]	1/8
1963	American L-Head 6	.035	.016	31–34	153624	3°	Damper	.016C	.018C	Zero[7]	[10]	1/8
	American OHV-6[5]	.035	.016	31–34	153624	8°	Damper	.012H[12]	.016H[12]	Zero[7]	[10]	1/8
	American OHV-6[6]	.035	.016	31–34	153624	10°	Damper	.012H[12]	.016H[12]	Zero[7]	[10]	1/8
	Rambler 6	.035	.016	31–34	153624	[11]	Damper	.012H[12]	.016H[12]	Zero[3]	[10]	1/8
	6-232	.035	.016	31–34	153624	5°	Damper	Zero	Zero	Zero[3]	[10]	1/8
	V8 Std. Trans.	.035	.016	28–32	18436572[1]	TDC	Damper	Zero	Zero	Zero[3]	[10]	1/8
	V8 Auto. Trans.	.035	.016	28–32	18436572[1]	5°	Damper	Zero	Zero	Zero[3]	[10]	1/8
1964	American L-Head 6	.035	.016	31–34	153624	3°	Damper	.016C	.018C	+¼[13]	Zero	1/16–3/16
	American OHV-6[5]	.035	.016	31–34	153624	8°	Damper	.012H[12]	.016H[12]	+¼[13]	Zero	1/16–3/16
	American OHV-6[6]	.035	.016	31–34	153624	10°	Damper	.012H[12]	.016H[12]	+¼[13]	Zero	1/16–3/16
	Rambler 6	.035	.016	31–34	153624	5°	Damper	.012H	.016H	+¼[13]	Zero	1/16–3/16
	6-232	.035	.016	31–34	153624	5°	Damper	Zero	Zero	+¼[13]	Zero	1/16–3/16
	V8-Std. Trans.	.035	.016	28–32	18436572[1]	TDC	Damper	Zero	Zero	+¼[13]	Zero	1/16–3/16
	V8-Auto. Trans.	.035	.016	28–32	18436572[1]	5°	Damper	Zero	Zero	+¼[13]	Zero	1/16–3/16
1965	American L-Head 6	.035	.016	31–34	153624	3°	Damper	.016C	.018C	+¼[13]	Zero	1/16–3/16
	American OHV-6[5]	.035	.016	31–34	153624	8°	Damper	.012H	.016H	+¼[13]	Zero	1/16–3/16
	American OHV-6[6]	.035	.016	31–34	153624	10°	Damper	.012H	.016H	+¼[13]	Zero	1/16–3/16
	6-199, 232	.035	.016	31–34	153624	5°	Damper	Zero	Zero	+¼[13]	Zero	1/16–3/16
	V8-287, 327	.035	.016	28–32	18436572[1]	5°	Damper	Zero	Zero	+¼[13]	Zero	1/16–3/16
1966	6-199	.035	.016	31–34	153624	10°[14]	Damper	Zero	Zero	+¼[13]	Zero	1/16–3/16
	6-232	.035	.016	31–34	153624	5°	Damper	Zero	Zero	+¼[13]	Zero	1/16–3/16
	V8-287, 327	.035	.016	28–32	18436572[1]	5°[14]	Damper	Zero	Zero	+¼[13]	Zero	1/16–3/16
	V8-290	.035	.016	29–31	18436572[1]	TDC	Damper	Zero	Zero	+¼[13]	Zero	1/16–3/16
1967	6-199 Delco-Remy	.035	.016	31–34	153624	3°[14]	Damper	Hydraulic[15]		Zero[3]	Zero	1/8
	6-199 Prestolite	.035	.019	36–42	153624	3°[14]	Damper	Hydraulic[16]		Zero[3]	Zero	1/8
	6-232 Delco-Remy	.035	.016	31–34	153624	5°	Damper	Hydraulic[15]		Zero[3]	Zero	1/8
	6-232 Prestolite	.035	.020	36–42	153624	5°	Damper	Hydraulic[16]		Zero[3]	Zero	1/8
	V8's Delco-Remy	.035	.016	29–31	18436572[1]	TDC	Damper	Hydraulic[16]		Zero[3]	Zero	1/8
	V8's Prestolite	.035	.016	27–32	18436572[1]	TDC	Damper	Hydraulic[16]		Zero[3]	Zero	1/8

Continued

Year	Engine or Car Model	Spark Plug Gap	Distributor		Firing Order	Ignition Timing		Valve Lash		Wheel Alignment		
			Point Gap	Dwell Angle		BTDC or Mark	Mark Location	Intake	Exhaust	Caster Degrees	Camber Degrees	Toe-In Inch

AMERICAN MOTORS—Continued

Year	Engine or Car Model	Spark Plug Gap	Point Gap	Dwell Angle	Firing Order	BTDC or Mark	Mark Location	Intake	Exhaust	Caster Degrees	Camber Degrees	Toe-In Inch
1968	6-199, 232 Std. Tr.	.035	.016	31–34	153624	TDC	Damper	Hydraulic(15)		(16)	Zero	1/8
	6-199, 232 Auto. Tr.	.035	.016	31–34	153624	5°	Damper	Hydraulic(15)		(16)	Zero	1/8
	V8-290, 343, 390	.035	.016	29–31	18436572	TDC	Damper	Hydraulic(15)		(16)	Zero	1/8

(1)—Cylinder numbering (front to rear): Left bank 1-3-5-7, right bank 2-4-6-8.
(2)—With power steering +3/4°.
(3)—With power steering +1°.
(4)—Deluxe and Super.
(5)—Standard transmission.
(6)—Automatic transmission.
(7)—Power steering +2.°
(8)—Cast iron block.
(9)—Aluminum block.
(10)—Left +1/4°, right 0.
(11)—Early 5°, late 8°.
(12)—With aluminum block hydraulic lifters are used and clearance is "Zero".
(13)—With power steering +1 1/2.
(14)—California vehicle set at TDC.
(15)—No adjustment.
(16)—Rebel & Ambassador; −1/2, American, AMX & Javelin; w/Power Steering +3/4; w/Manual Steering; Zero.

BUICK

Year	Engine or Car Model	Spark Plug Gap	Point Gap	Dwell Angle	Firing Order	BTDC or Mark	Mark Location	Intake	Exhaust	Caster Degrees	Camber Degrees	Toe-In Inch
1946–49	All Models	.025	.016	21–30	16258374	"ADV"	Flywheel	.015H(1)	.015H(1)	+3/8	+3/8	1/32
1950–52	All Models	.025	.016	21–30	16258374	"ADV"	Flywheel	.015H(1)	.015H(1)	+3/4	+3/8	3/32
1953	Series 40	.025	.016	21–30	16258374	"ADV"	Flywheel	.015H	.015H	Zero	+3/8	3/32
	All Others	.032	.016	21–30	12784563(2)	"ADV"	Flywheel	Zero	Zero	Zero	+3/8	3/32
1954	All	.032	.016	21–30	12784563(2)	5°	Damper	Zero	Zero	−1/4	+3/8	1/32
1955	All Models	.032	.016	26–33	12784563(2)	5°	Damper	Zero	Zero	−1/8	+3/8	0–1/16
1956	All Models	.032	.016	26–33	12784563(2)	5°	Damper	Zero	Zero	−1/2	+3/8	1/16–1/8
1957	All Models	.032	(3)	30	12784563(2)	5°	Damper	Zero	Zero	−1 3/4	+1/2	1/16–1/8
1958	All Models	.032	(3)	30	12784563(2)	(4)	Damper	Zero	Zero	−1/2	+1/2	1/16–1/8
1959	364, 401, Std. Tr.	.032	.016(3)	30	12784563(2)	5°	Damper	Zero	Zero	−1 1/2	+1/2	1/16–5/32
	364, 401 Auto. Tr.	.032	.016(3)	30	12784563(2)	12°	Damper	Zero	Zero	−1 1/2	+1/2	1/16–5/32
1960	364, 401 Std. Tr.	.032	.016(3)	30	12784563(2)	5°	Damper	Zero	Zero	−2	+1/2	1/16–5/32
	364, 401 Auto. Tr.	.032	.016(3)	30	12784563(2)	12°	Damper	Zero	Zero	−2	+1/2	1/16–5/32
1961–62	364, 401	.032	.016(3)	30	12784563(2)	12°	Damper	Zero	Zero	−2	+1/3	3/16–5/32
	V6-198	.035	.016(3)	30	165432(5)	5°	Damper	Zero	Zero	−2	−5/8	7/32–5/16
	V8-215	.035	.016(3)	30	18436572(6)	5°	Damper	Zero	Zero	−2	−5/8	7/32–5/16
1963	401, 425 Std. Tr.	.035	.016(3)	30	12784563(2)	5°	Damper	Zero	Zero	−1/2	+1/3	7/32–5/16
	401, 425 Auto. Tr.	.035	.016(3)	30	12784563(2)	12°	Damper	Zero	Zero	−1/2	+1/3	7/32–5/16
	V6-198	.035	.016(3)	30	165432(5)	5°	Damper	Zero	Zero	−2	−5/8	7/32–5/16
	V8-215	.035	.016(3)	30	18436572(6)	5°	Damper	Zero	Zero	−2	−5/8	7/32–5/16
1964	V6-225	.035	.016(3)	30	165432(5)	5°	Damper	Zero	Zero	−1/2	+1/2	7/32–5/16
	V8-300 Special	.035	.016(3)	30	18436572(6)	2 1/2°	Damper	Zero	Zero	−1/2	+1/2	7/32–5/16
	V8-300 LeSabre	.035	.016(3)	30	18436572(6)	2 1/2°	Damper	Zero	Zero	−1/2	+1/4	7/32–5/16
	V8-401, 425	.035	.016(3)	30	12784563(2)	2 1/2°(7)	Damper	Zero	Zero	−1/2	+1/4	7/32–5/16
1965	V6-225	.035	.016(3)	30	165432(5)	5°	Damper	Zero	Zero	−1/2	+1/2	1/8–1/4
	V8-300 Special	.035	.016(3)	30	18436572(6)	2 1/2°	Damper	Zero	Zero	−1/2	+1/2	1/8–1/4
	V8-300 Le Sabre	.035	.016(3)	30	18436572(6)	2 1/2°	Damper	Zero	Zero	+1	+1/2	7/32–5/16
	V8-401, 425	.035	.016(3)	30	12784563(2)	2 1/2(7)	Damper	Zero	Zero	+1	+1/2	7/32–5/16
1966	V6-225	.035	.016(3)	30	165432(5)	5°	Damper	Zero	Zero	−1/2	+1/2	1/8–1/4
	V8-300, 340	.035	.016(3)	30	18436572(6)	2 1/2°	Damper	Zero	Zero	(8)	+1/2	(9)
	V8-401, 425	.035	.016(3)	30	12784563(2)	2 1/2(7)	Damper	Zero	Zero	(8)	+1/2	(9)
1967	V6-225 Exc. Cal.	.035	.016(3)	30	165432(5)	5°	Damper	Hydraulic(11)		(8)	(12)	(9)
	V6-225 Cal.(10)	.035	.016(3)	30	165432(5)	5°	Damper	Hydraulic(11)		(8)	(12)	(9)
	V8's Exc. Cal.	.035	.016(3)	30	18436572(6)	2 1/2°	Damper	Hydraulic(11)		(8)	(12)	(9)
	V8's Cal.(10)	.035	.016(3)	30	18436572(6)	2 1/2°	Damper	Hydraulic(11)		(8)	(12)	(9)
1968	6-250 Std. Tr.	.030	.019	32	153624	TDC	Damper	1 Turn(13)		−1/2	+1/2	1/8–1/4
	6-250 Auto. Tr.	.030	.019	32	153624	4°	Damper	1 Turn(13)		−1/2	+1/2	1/8–1/4
	V8-350	.030	.016	30	18436572(6)	TDC	Damper	Hydraulic(11)		(8)	(12)	(9)
	V8-400	.030	.016	30	18436572(6)	TDC	Damper	Hydraulic(11)		(8)	(12)	(9)
	V8-430	.030	.016	30	18436572(6)	TDC	Damper	Hydraulic(11)		(8)	(12)	(9)

(1)—With mechanical valve lifters. Zero lash with hydraulic lifters.
(2)—Cylinders numbering (front to rear): Right bank 1-3-5-7, left bank 2-4-6-8.
(3)—Turn adjusting screw clockwise until engine begins to misfire, then back off screw 1/2 turn.
(4)—Std. Trans. 5°, Auto. Trans. 12°.
(5)—Cylinders numbering (Front to rear): Right bank 2-4-6, Left bank 1-3-5.
(6)—Cylinders numbering (Front to rear): Right bank 2-4-6-8, Left bank 1-3-5-7.
(7)—12° for V8-425 with 2 carbs. and automatic transmission.
(8)—Full size cars +1; others −1/2.
(9)—Full size cars 7/32–5/16; others 1/8–1/4.
(10)—Air Injection Reactor (A.I.R.).
(11)—No adjustment.
(12)—Full size cars +1/4; others +1/2.
(13)—Turn rocker arm adjusting screw down until all lash is removed. Then turn screw down the additional number of turns specified.

Year	Engine or Car Model	Spark Plug Gap	Point Gap	Dwell Angle	Firing Order	BTDC or Mark	Mark Location	Intake	Exhaust	Caster Degrees	Camber Degrees	Toe-In Inch
CADILLAC												
1946–47	All Models	.030	.016	21–30	18736542①	②	Damper	Zero	Zero	−2⅛	Zero	1/16
1948–51	All Models	.035	.016	21–30	18436572①	③	Damper	Zero	Zero	Zero	Zero	3/32
1952–53	All Models	.035	.0125	31	18436572①	③	Damper	Zero	Zero	Zero	Zero	3/32
1954	All Models	.035	.016	31	18436572①	③	Damper	Zero	Zero	Zero	Zero	3/32
1955	All Models	.035	.016	26–33	18436572①	"A"	Damper	Zero	Zero	−½	Zero	3/16–¼
1956–57	All Models	.035	④	30	18436572①	"A"	Damper	Zero	Zero	−½	Zero	3/16–¼
1958	All Models	.035	④	30	18436572①	5°	Damper	.025"Min.⑤	.025"Min.⑤	−½	Zero	3/16–¼⑥
1959–62	All Models	.035	④	30	18436572①	5°	Damper	.025"Min.⑤	.025"Min.⑤	⑦	⑧	3/16–¼⑥
1963–66	All Models	.035	④	30	18726543①	5°	Damper	Zero	Zero	−1	⑨	3/16–¼
1967	Eldorado	.035	④	30	18726543①	5°	Damper	Hydraulic⑩		Zero	Zero	0–⅛
	All Others	.035	④	30	18726543①	5°	Damper	Hydraulic⑩		−1	⑨	3/16–¼
1968	Eldorado	.035	④	30	15634278⑪	5°	Damper	Hydraulic⑩		Zero	Zero	0–⅛
	All others	.035	④	30	15634278⑪	5°	Damper	Hydraulic⑩		−1	⑨	3/16–¼

①—Cylinder numbering (front to rear): Left bank 1-3-5-7, right bank 2-4-6-8.
②—"IGA" or "IGN" mark.
③—"A" mark for premium fuel, "C" mark for regular fuel.
④—Turn adjusting screw clockwise until engine begins to misfire, then back out screw ½ turn.
⑤—Clearance between valve stem and rocker arm with hydraulic lifters collapsed and lifters on heel of cam.
⑥—Air suspension cars 1/16".
⑦—1959-60 Ser. 60, 62 −½, Ser. 75 −1¼, 1961-62 All −1.
⑧—1959-60 Zero, 1961-62 −¼.
⑨—Left side Zero; right side −¼.
⑩—No adjustment.
⑪—Cylinder numbering (front to rear): Left bank 2-4-6-8, right bank 1-3-5-7.

Year	Engine or Car Model	Spark Plug Gap	Point Gap	Dwell Angle	Firing Order	BTDC or Mark	Mark Location	Intake	Exhaust	Caster Degrees	Camber Degrees	Toe-In Inch
CHECKER MOTORS												
1968	6-230 Std. Tr.	.035	①	31–34	153624	TDC	Damper	Hydraulic②		+2	+1③	1/16–⅛
	6-230 Auto. Tr.	.035	①	31–34	153624	4°	Damper	Hydraulic②		+2	+1③	1/16–⅛
	V8-307	.035	①	28–32	18436572	2°	Damper	Hydraulic②		+2	+1③	1/16–⅛
	V8-327	.035	①	28–32	18436572	4°	Damper	Hydraulic②		+2	+1③	1/16–⅛
	V8-327 ⑧	.035	①	28–32	18436572	8°	Damper	Hydraulic②		+2	+1③	1/16–⅛④

①—New points, .019", used, .016". On V8's, turn adjusting screw in (clockwise) until engine misfires, then back off ½ turn.
②—No adjustment.
③—Aerobus +1½.
④—Aerobus ⅛–3/16.
⑧—Aerobus.

Year	Engine or Car Model	Spark Plug Gap	Point Gap	Dwell Angle	Firing Order	BTDC or Mark	Mark Location	Intake	Exhaust	Caster Degrees	Camber Degrees	Toe-In Inch
CAMARO												
1967	6-230	.035	②	31–34	153624	4°	Damper	1 Turn④		+½	+¼	⅛–¼
	6-230①	.035	②	31–34	153624	4°	Damper	1 Turn④		+½	+¼	⅛–¼
	6-250	.035	②	31–34	153624	4°	Damper	1 Turn④		+½	+¼	⅛–¼
	6-250①	.035	②	31–34	153624	4°	Damper	1 Turn④		+½	+¼	⅛–¼
	8-302	.035	②	28–32	18436572③	6°	Damper	.030H	.030H	+½	+¼	⅛–¼
	8-327, 210 H.P.	.035	②	28–32	18436572③	2°	Damper	1 Turn④		+½	+¼	⅛–¼
	8-327, 210 H.P.①	.035	②	28–32	18436572③	2°	Damper	1 Turn④		+½	+¼	⅛–¼
	8-327, 275 H.P.	.035	②	28–32	18436572③	8°	Damper	1 Turn④		+½	+¼	⅛–¼
	8-327, 275 H.P.①	.035	②	28–32	18436572③	6°	Damper	1 Turn④		+½	+¼	⅛–¼
	8-327, 350 H.P.	.035	②	28–32	18436572③	10°	Damper	1 Turn④		+½	+¼	⅛–¼
	8-327, 350 H.P.①	.035	②	28–32	18436572③	10°	Damper	1 Turn④		+½	+¼	⅛–¼
	8-396, 375 H.P.	.035	②	28–32	18436572③	6°	Damper	.020H	.024H	+½	+¼	⅛–¼
	8-350	.035	②	28–32	18436572③	4°	Damper	1 Turn④		+½	+¼	⅛–¼
	8-350①	.035	②	28–32	18436572③	4°	Damper	1 Turn④		+½	+¼	⅛–¼
1968	6-230, 250 Std. Tr.	.035	②	31–34	153624	TDC	Damper	1 Turn④		+½	+½	⅛–¼
	6-230, 250 Auto. Tr.	.035	②	31–34	153624	4°	Damper	1 Turn④		+½	+½	⅛–¼
	8-302	.035	②	28–32	18436572③	4°	Damper	.030H	.030H	+½	+½	⅛–¼
	8-327, 210 H.P.⑤	.035	②	28–32	18436572③	2°ATC	Damper	1 Turn④		+½	+½	⅛–¼
	8-327, 210 H.P.⑥	.035	②	28–32	18436572③	2°	Damper	1 Turn④		+½	+½	⅛–¼
	8-327, 275 H.P.⑤	.035	②	28–32	18436572③	TDC	Damper	1 Turn④		+½	+½	⅛–¼
	8-327, 275 H.P.⑥	.035	②	28–32	18436572③	4°	Damper	1 Turn④		+½	+½	⅛–¼

Continued

Year	Engine or Car Model	Spark Plug Gap	Distributor		Firing Order	Ignition Timing		Valve Lash		Wheel Alignment		
			Point Gap	Dwell Angle		BTDC or Mark	Mark Location	Intake	Exhaust	Caster Degrees	Camber Degrees	Toe-In Inch

CAMARO—Continued

Year	Engine or Car Model	Spark Plug Gap	Point Gap	Dwell Angle	Firing Order	BTDC or Mark	Mark Location	Intake	Exhaust	Caster Degrees	Camber Degrees	Toe-In Inch
1968	8-350, 295 H.P.⑤	.035	②	28–32	18436572③	TDC	Damper	1 Turn④		+½	+½	⅛–¼
	8-350, 295 H.P.⑥	.035	②	28–32	18436572③	4°	Damper	1 Turn④		+½	+½	⅛–¼
	8-396, 325 H.P.	.035	②	28–32	18436572③	4°	Damper	1 Turn④		+½	+½	⅛–¼
	8-396, 375 H.P.	.035	②	28–32	18436572③	10°	Damper	.024H	.028H	+½	+½	⅛–¼

①—With air injection reactor system.
②—New points .019″, used .016″. On V-8s, turn adjusting screw in (clockwise) until engine misfires; then back off ½ turn.
③—From front to rear, left bank 1-3-5-7, right bank 2-4-6-8.
④—Turn rocker arm stud until all lash is eliminated, then tighten nut the additional turn listed.
⑤—With standard transmission.
⑥—With automatic transmission.

CHEVELLE

Year	Engine or Car Model	Spark Plug Gap	Point Gap	Dwell Angle	Firing Order	BTDC or Mark	Mark Location	Intake	Exhaust	Caster Degrees	Camber Degrees	Toe-In Inch
1964	6-194	.035	①	31–34	153624	8°	Damper	1 Turn③		−1	+¾	1/16–3/16
	6-230	.035	①	31–34	153624	4°	Damper	1 Turn③		−1	+¾	1/16–3/16
	V8-283	.035	①	28–32	18436572②	4°	Damper	1 Turn③		−1	+¾	1/16–3/16
	V8-327, 250 H.P.	.035	①	28–32	18436572②	4°	Damper	1 Turn③		−1	+¾	1/16–3/16
	V8-327, 300 H.P.	.035	①	28–32	18436572②	8°	Damper	1 Turn③		−1	+¾	1/16–3/16
1965	6-194	.035	①	31–34	153624	8°	Damper	1 Turn③		④	+½	⅛–¼
	6-230	.035	①	31–34	153624	4°	Damper	1 Turn③		④	+½	⅛–¼
	V8-283, 195 H.P.	.035	①	28–32	18436572②	4°	Damper	1 Turn③		④	+½	⅛–¼
	V8-283, 220 H.P.	.035	①	28–32	18436572②	6°	Damper	1 Turn③		④	+½	⅛–¼
	V8-327, 250 H.P.	.035	①	28–32	18436572②	4°	Damper	1 Turn③		④	+½	⅛–¼
	V8-327, 300 H.P.	.035	①	28–32	18436572②	8°	Damper	1 Turn③		④	+½	⅛–¼
	V8-327, 350 H.P.	.035	①	28–32	18436572②	8°	Damper	1 Turn③		④	+½	⅛–¼
1966	6-194	.035	①	31–34	153624	⑥	Damper	1 Turn③		④	+½	⅛–¼
	6-230	.035	①	31–34	153624	4°	Damper	1 Turn③		④	+½	⅛–¼
	V8-283	.035	①	28–32	18436572②	4°	Damper	1 Turn③		④	+½	⅛–¼
	V8-327	.035	①	28–32	18436572②	⑦	Damper	1 Turn③		④	+½	⅛–¼
	V8-396	.035	①	28–32	18436572③	4°	Damper	1 Turn③		④	+½	⅛–¼
1967	6-230, 250	.035	⑧	31–34	153624	4°	Damper	1 Turn③		④	+½	⅛–¼
	6-230, 250⑥	.035	⑧	31–34	153624	4°	Damper	1 Turn③		④	+½	⅛–¼
	8-283	.035	⑧	28–32	18436572②	4°	Damper	1 Turn③		④	+½	⅛–¼
	8-283 Std. Tr.⑤	.035	⑧	28–32	18436572②	TDC	Damper	1 Turn③		④	+½	⅛–¼
	8-283 Auto. Tr.⑥	.035	⑧	28–32	18436572②	4°	Damper	1 Turn③		④	+½	⅛–¼
	8-327, 275 H.P.	.035	⑧	28–32	18436572②	8°	Damper	1 Turn③		④	+½	⅛–¼
	8-327, 275 H.P.⑤	.035	⑧	28–32	18436572②	6°	Damper	1 Turn③		④	+½	⅛–¼
	8-327, 325 H.P.	.035	⑧	28–32	18436572②	10°	Damper	1 Turn③		④	+½	⅛–¼
	8-327, 325 H.P.⑤	.035	⑧	28–32	18436572②	10°	Damper	1 Turn③		④	+½	⅛–¼
	8-396	.035	⑧	28–32	18436572③	4°	Damper	1 Turn③		④	+½	⅛–¼
	8-396⑥	.035	⑧	28–32	18436572③	4°	Damper	1 Turn③		④	+½	⅛–¼
1968	6-230, 250 Std. Tr.	.035	⑧	31–34	153624	TDC	Damper	1 Turn③		④	+½	⅛–¼
	6-230, 250 Auto. Tr.	.035	⑧	31–34	153624	4°	Damper	1 Turn③		④	+½	⅛–¼
	8-307	.035	⑧	28–32	18436572②	2°	Damper	1 Turn③		④	+½	⅛–¼
	8-327, 275 H.P.⑨	.035	⑧	28–32	18436572②	TDC	Damper	1 Turn③		④	+½	⅛–¼
	8-327, 275 H.P.⑩	.035	⑧	28–32	18436572②	4°	Damper	1 Turn③		④	+½	⅛–¼
	8-327, 325 H.P.	.035	⑧	28–32	18436572③	4°	Damper	1 Turn③		④	+½	⅛–¼
	8-396, 350 H.P.⑨	.035	⑧	28–32	18436572③	TDC	Damper	1 Turn③		④	+½	⅛–¼
	8-396, 350 H.P.⑩	.035	⑧	28–32	18436572③	4°	Damper	1 Turn③		④	+½	⅛–¼

①—New points .019″, used .016″.
②—Cylinder numbering (front to rear): Left bank 1-3-5-7, right bank 2-4-6-8.
③—Turn rocker arm adjusting screw down until all lash is removed. Then turn screw down the additional number of turns specified.
④—Super Sport −½; all others −1.
⑤—With Air Injection Reactor system (A.I.R.).
⑥—With manual transmission and Air Injection Reactor 3°; all others 8°.
⑦—With automatic transmission and Air Injection Reactor 2° ATDC; all others 8° BTDC.
⑧—New points, .019″, used .016″. On V8s, turn adjusting screw in (clockwise) until engine misfires; then back off ½ turn.
⑨—With standard transmission.
⑩—With automatic transmission.

Year	Engine or Car Model	Spark Plug Gap	Distributor Point Gap	Distributor Dwell Angle	Firing Order	Ignition Timing BTDC or Mark	Ignition Timing Mark Location	Valve Lash Intake	Valve Lash Exhaust	Wheel Alignment Caster Degrees	Wheel Alignment Camber Degrees	Wheel Alignment Toe-In Inch
CHEVROLET												
1946–48	All Models	.040	.022	31–37	153624	Ball	Flywheel	.006H	.013H	Zero	−¼	1/32
1949–52	Std. Trans.	.035	.022	31–37	153624	Ball	Flywheel	.006H	.013H	+½	+½	1/16
1950–52	Powerglide	.035	.022	31–37	153624	Ball	Flywheel	1½ Turns②		+½	+½	1/16
1953	Std. Trans.	.035	.016	38–45	153624	①	Flywheel	.006H	.013H	+½	+½	1/8
	Powerglide	.035	.016	38–45	153624	①	Flywheel	1½ Turns②		+½	+½	1/8
1954	Std. Trans.	.035	.016	38–45	153624	Ball	Flywheel	.006H	.016H	+½	+½	1/8
	Powerglide	.035	.016	38–45	153624	Ball	Flywheel	1½ Turns②		+½	+½	1/8
1955	6 Std. Trans.	.035	③	28–35	153624	Ball	Flywheel	.006H	.013H	Zero	+½	1/8–3/16
	6 Powerglide	.035	③	28–35	153624	Ball	Flywheel	1½ Turns②		Zero	+½	1/8–3/16
	V8 Std. Trans.	.035	③	26–33	18436572④	4°	Damper	.008H	.016H	Zero	+½	1/8–3/16
	V8 Powerglide	.035	③	26–33	18436572④	4°	Damper	1 Turn②		Zero	+½	1/8–3/16
1956–57	Six	.035	③	28–35	153624	Ball	Flywheel	1½ Turns②		+1	+½	1/8–3/16
	V8	.035	③	26–33	18436572④	4°	Damper	1 Turn②		+1	+½	1/8–3/16
1958	Six	.035	③	28–35	153624	Ball	Flywheel	1½ Turns		Zero	+½	1/16–3/16
	V8	.035	③	30	18436572④	4°	Damper	1 Turn		Zero	+½	1/16–3/16
1959	6-235	.035	②	28–35	153624	Ball	Flywheel	1½ Turns		Zero	+½	1/16–3/16
	8-283	.035	③	30	18436572④	4°	Damper	1 Turn		Zero	+½	1/16–3/16
	8-283 Special Cam	.035	③	30	18436572④	4°	Damper	.012H	.018H	Zero	+½	1/16–3/16
	8-348	.035	③	30	18436572④	8°	Damper	1 Turn		Zero	+½	1/16–3/16
1960–61	6-235 Hydraulic	.035	③	28–35	153624	Ball	Flywheel	1½ Turns		Zero	+½	1/16–3/16
	6-235 Mechanical	.035	③	28–35	153624	Ball	Flywheel	.008H	.015H	Zero	+½	1/16–3/16
	8-283 170 H.P.	.035	③	30	18436572④	4°	Damper	1 Turn⑦		Zero	+½	1/16–3/16
	8-283 230 H.P.	.035	③	30	18436572④	4°	Damper	1 Turn⑦		Zero	+½	1/16–3/16
	8-283 Special Cam	.035	③	30	18436572④	4°	Damper	.012H	.018H	Zero	+½	1/16–3/16
	8-348 250 H.P.	.035	③	30	18436572④	8°	Damper	1 Turn⑦		Zero	+½	1/16–3/16
	8-348 280 H.P.	.035	⑤	⑥	18436572④	8°	Damper	1 Turn⑦		Zero	+½	1/16–3/16
	8-348 305 H.P.	.035	③	30	18436572④	8°	Damper	1 Turn⑦		Zero	+½	1/16–3/16
	8-348 320 H.P.	.035	③	30	18436572④	8°	Damper	.008H	.018H	Zero	+½	1/16–3/16
	8-348 335 H.P.	.035	⑤	⑥	18436572④	12°	Damper	.008H	.018H	Zero	+½	1/16–3/16
	8-348 340 H.P. (1961)	.035	③	30	18436572④	8°	Damper	.008H	.018H	Zero	+½	1/16–3/16
	8-348 350 H.P. (1961)	.035	⑤	⑥	18436572④	8°	Damper	.008H	.018H	Zero	+½	1/16–3/16
	8-409 360 H.P. (1961)	.035	③	30	18436572④	12°	Damper	.008H	.018H	Zero	+½	1/16–3/16
1962	6-235	.035	③	28–35	153624	⑧	Flywheel	1 Turn⑦		Zero	+½	1/8
	V8-283	.035	③	30	18436572④	4°	Damper	1 Turn⑦		Zero	+½	1/8
	V8-327	.035	③	30	18436572④	4°	Damper	1 Turn⑦		Zero	+½	1/8
	V8-327 Special Cam	.035	③	30	18436572④	8°	Damper	.008H	.018H	Zero	+½	1/8
	V8-409	.035	⑤	⑥	18436572④	12°	Damper	.008H	.018H	Zero	+½	1/8
1963	6-230	.035	③	31–34	153624	4°	Damper	1 Turn②		Zero	+½	1/16–3/16
	V8-283	.035	③	30	18436572④	4°	Damper	1 Turn②		Zero	+½	1/16–3/16
	V8-327 250 H.P.	.035	③	30	18436572④	4°	Damper	1 Turn②		Zero	+½	1/16–3/16
	V8-327 300 H.P.	.035	③	30	18436572④	8°	Damper	1 Turn②		Zero	+½	1/16–3/16
	V8-409 340 H.P.	.035	③	30	18436572④	6°	Damper	1 Turn②		Zero	+½	1/16–3/16
	V8-409 400 H.P.	.035	③	30	18436572④	12°	Damper	⑨		Zero	+½	1/16–3/16
	V8-409 425 H.P.	.035	③	30	18436572④	12°	Damper	⑨		Zero	+½	1/16–3/16
1964	6-230	.035	③	31–34	153624	4°	Damper	1 Turn②		Zero	+½	1/32–3/32
	V8-283	.035	③	30	18436572④	4°	Damper	1 Turn②		Zero	+½	1/32–3/32
	V8-327, 250 H.P.	.035	③	30	18436572④	4°	Damper	1 Turn②		Zero	+½	1/32–3/32
	V8-327, 300 H.P.	.035	③	30	18436572④	8°	Damper	1 Turn②		Zero	+½	1/32–3/32
	V8-409, 340 H.P.	.035	③	30	18436572④	6°	Damper	1 Turn②		Zero	+½	1/32–3/32
	V8-409, 400 H.P.	.035	③	30	18436572④	12°	Damper	⑨		Zero	+½	1/32–3/32
	V8-409, 425 H.P.	.035	③	30	18436572④	12°	Damper	⑨		Zero	+½	1/32–3/32
1965	6-230	.035	③	31–34	153624	4°	Damper	1 Turn②		+¾	+¼	1/8–¼
	V8-283	.035	③	30	18436572④	4°	Damper	1 Turn②		+¾	+¼	1/8–¼
	V8-327, 250 H.P.	.035	③	30	18436572④	4°	Damper	1 Turn②		+¾	+¼	1/8–¼
	V8-327, 300 H.P.	.035	③	30	18436572④	8°	Damper	1 Turn②		+¾	+¼	1/8–¼
	V8-396, 325 H.P.	.035	③	30	18436572④	4°⑩	Damper	1 Turn②		+¾	+¼	1/8–¼
	V8-396, 425 H.P.	.035	③	30	18436572④	10°	Damper	.020H	.024H	+¾	+¼	1/8–¼
	V8-409, 340 H.P.	.035	③	30	18436572④	6°	Damper	1 Turn②		+¾	+¼	1/8–¼
	V8-409, 400 H.P.	.035	③	30	18436572④	12°	Damper	.018H	.030H	+¾	+¼	1/8–¼

Continued

Year	Engine or Car Model	Spark Plug Gap	Distributor Point Gap	Distributor Dwell Angle	Firing Order	Ignition Timing BTDC or Mark	Ignition Timing Mark Location	Valve Lash Intake	Valve Lash Exhaust	Caster Degrees	Camber Degrees	Toe-In Inch

CHEVROLET—Continued

Year	Engine or Car Model	Spark Plug Gap	Point Gap	Dwell Angle	Firing Order	BTDC or Mark	Mark Location	Intake	Exhaust	Caster Degrees	Camber Degrees	Toe-In Inch
1966	6-250	.035	③	31-34	153624	6°	Damper	1 Turn②		+¾	+¼	⅛-¼
	V8-283	.035	③	30	18436572④	4°	Damper	1 Turn②		+¾	+¼	⅛-¼
	V8-327	.035	③	30	18436572④	8°	Damper	1 Turn②		+¾	+¼	⅛-¼
	V8-327⑪	.035	③	30	18436572④	2°⑫	Damper	1 Turn②		+¾	+¼	⅛-¼
	V8-396	.035	③	30	18436572④	4°	Damper	1 Turn②		+¾	+¼	⅛-¼
	V8-427, 390 H.P.	.035	—	—	18436572④	4°	Damper	1 Turn②		+¾	+¼	⅛-¼
	V8-427, 425 H.P.	.035	—	—	18436572④	10°	Damper	.020H	.024H	+¾	+¼	⅛-¼
1967	6-250	.035	⑬	31-34	153624	4°	Damper	1 Turn③		+¾	+¼	⅛-¼
	6-250⑪	.035	⑬	31-34	153624	4°	Damper	1 Turn③		+¾	+¼	⅛-¼
	8-283	.035	⑬	28-32	18436572④	4°	Damper	1 Turn③		+¾	+¼	⅛-¼
	8-283 Std. Tr.⑪	.035	⑬	28-32	18436572④	TDC	Damper	1 Turn③		+¾	+¼	⅛-¼
	8-283 Auto. Tr.⑪	.035	⑬	28-32	18436572④	4°	Damper	1 Turn③		+¾	+¼	⅛-¼
	8-327, 275 H.P.	.035	⑬	28-32	18436572④	8°	Damper	1 Turn③		+¾	+¼	⅛-¼
	8-327, 275 H.P.⑪	.035	⑬	28-32	18436572④	6°	Damper	1 Turn③		+¾	+¼	⅛-¼
	8-396, 325 H.P.	.035	⑬	28-32	18436572④	4°	Damper	1 Turn③		+¾	+¼	⅛-¼
	8-396, 325 H.P.⑪	.035	⑬	28-32	18436572④	4°	Damper	1 Turn③		+¾	+¼	⅛-¼
	8-427, 385 H.P.	.035	⑬	28-32	18436572④	4°	Damper	1 Turn③		+¾	+¼	⅛-¼
	8-427, 385 H.P.⑪	.035	⑬	28-32	18436572④	4°	Damper	1 Turn③		+¾	+¼	⅛-¼
1968	6-250 Std. Tr.	.035	⑬	31-34	153624	TDC	Damper	1 Turn②		+¾	+¼	⅛-¼
	6-250 Auto. Tr.	.035	⑬	31-34	153624	4°	Damper	1 Turn②		+¾	+¼	⅛-¼
	8-307	.035	⑬	28-32	18436572④	2°	Damper	1 Turn②		+¾	+¼	⅛-¼
	8-327, 250 H.P.	.035	⑬	28-32	18436572④	4°	Damper	1 Turn②		+¾	+¼	⅛-¼
	8-327, 275 H.P.⑭	.035	⑬	28-32	18436572④	TDC	Damper	1 Turn②		+¾	+¼	⅛-¼
	8-327, 275 H.P.⑮	.035	⑬	28-32	18436572④	4°	Damper	1 Turn②		+¾	+¼	⅛-¼
	8-396, 325 H.P.	.035	⑬	28-32	18436572④	4°	Damper	1 Turn②		+¾	+¼	⅛-¼
	8-396, 375 H.P.	.035	⑬	28-32	18436572④	4°	Damper	.024H	.028H	+¾	+¼	⅛-¼
	8-427, 385 H.P.	.035	⑬	28-32	18436572④	4°	Damper	1 Turn②		+¾	+¼	⅛-¼

①—Before Engine No. LAA-283230 and LAQ-117209, set timing 7/32″ after timing ball. Starting with these engine numbers, set timing at the ball.
②—Turn rocker arm adjusting screw down until all lash is removed. Then turn screw down the additional number of turns specified.
③—New points .019″, used points .016″.
④—Cylinder numbering (front to rear): Left bank 1-3-5-7, right bank 2-4-6-8.
⑤—New Points .018″, used .015″.
⑥—Each set of points 28-30° total both sets 33-35°.
⑦—For long travel lifters 2 turns.
⑧—First short vertical line clockwise from ball in flywheel.
⑨—Early production: intake .012H, exhaust .020H. Engines date stamped TO-1118QA or QB: intake .018H, exhaust .030H.
⑩—Transistorized ignition 6° BTDC.
⑪—Automatic transmission and Air Injection Reactor system (A.I.R.).
⑫—After top dead center.
⑬—New points, .019″, used .016″. On V8s, turn adjusting screw in (clockwise) until engine misfires; then back off ½ turn.
⑭—With standard transmission.
⑮—With automatic transmission.

CHEVY II & NOVA

Year	Engine or Car Model	Spark Plug Gap	Point Gap	Dwell Angle	Firing Order	BTDC or Mark	Mark Location	Intake	Exhaust	Caster Degrees	Camber Degrees	Toe-In Inch
1962-63	4-153	.035	②	31-34	1342	4°	Damper	1 Turn④		+1	+½	¼
	6-194	.035	②	31-34	153624	8°	Damper	1 Turn④		+1	+½	¼
1964	4-153	.035	②	31-34	1342	4°	Damper	1 Turn④		+1	+½	3/16-5/16
	6-194	.035	②	31-34	153624	8°	Damper	1 Turn④		+1	+½	3/16-5/16
	6-230	.035	②	31-34	153624	4°	Damper	1 Turn④		+1	+½	3/16-5/16
	V8-283, 195 H.P.	.035	②	30	18436572③	4°	Damper	1 Turn④		+1	+½	3/16-5/16
	V8-283, 220 H.P.	.035	②	30	18436572③	8°	Damper	1 Turn④		+1	+½	3/16-5/16
1965	4-153	.035	②	31-34	1342	4°	Damper	1 Turn④		+1	+½	¼-⅜
	6-194	.035	②	31-34	153624	8°	Damper	1 Turn④		+1	+½	¼-⅜
	6-230	.035	②	31-34	153624	4°	Damper	1 Turn④		+1	+½	¼-⅜
	V8-283, 195 H.P.	.035	②	30	18436572③	4°	Damper	1 Turn④		+1	+½	¼-⅜
	V8-283, 220 H.P.	.035	②	30	18436572③	6°	Damper	1 Turn④		+1	+½	¼-⅜
	V8-327, 250 H.P.	.035	②	30	18436572③	4°	Damper	1 Turn④		+1	+½	¼-⅜
	V8-327, 300 H.P.	.035	②	30	18436572③	8°	Damper	1 Turn④		+1	+½	¼-⅜
1966	4-153	.035	②	31-34	1342	4°	Damper	1 Turn④		+1	+½	¼-⅜
	6-194	.035	②	31-34	153624	8°	Damper	1 Turn④		+1	+½	¼-⅜
	6-194⑤	.035	②	31-34	153624	3°	Damper	1 Turn④		+1	+½	¼-⅜

Continued

Year	Engine or Car Model	Spark Plug Gap	Distributor Point Gap	Distributor Dwell Angle	Firing Order	Ignition Timing BTDC or Mark	Ignition Timing Mark Location	Valve Lash Intake	Valve Lash Exhaust	Caster Degrees	Camber Degrees	Toe-In Inch
CHEVY II & NOVA—Continued												
1966	6-230	.035	[2]	31-34	153624	4°	Damper	1 Turn[4]		+1	+1/2	1/4-3/8
	V8-283	.035	[2]	30	18436572[3]	4°	Damper	1 Turn[4]		+1	+1/2	1/4-3/8
	V8-327, 275 H.P.	.035	[2]	30	18436572[3]	8°	Damper	1 Turn[4]		+1	+1/2	1/4-3/8
	V8-327, 275 H.P.[6]	.035	[2]	30	18436572[3]	2°[7]	Damper	1 Turn[4]		+1	+1/2	1/4-3/8
	V8-327, 350 H.P.	.035	[2]	30	18436572[3]	10°	Damper	1 Turn[4]		+1	+1/2	1/4-3/8
	V8-396	.035	[2]	30	18436572[3]	4°	Damper	1 Turn[4]		+1	+1/2	1/4-3/8
1967	4-153	.035	[9]	31-34	1342	4°	Damper	1 Turn[4]		+1	+1/2	1/4-3/8
	6-194	.035	[9]	31-34	153624	4°	Damper	1 Turn[4]		+1	+1/2	1/4-3/8
	6-194 Std. Tr.[8]	.035	[9]	31-34	153624	2°	Damper	1 Turn[4]		+1	+1/2	1/4-3/8
	6-194 Auto. Tr.[8]	.035	[9]	31-34	153624	4°	Damper	1 Turn[4]		+1	+1/2	1/4-3/8
	6-250	.035	[9]	31-34	153624	4°	Damper	1 Turn[4]		+1	+1/2	1/4-3/8
	6-250[8]	.035	[9]	31-34	153624	4°	Damper	1 Turn[4]		+1	+1/2	1/4-3/8
	8-283	.035	[9]	28-32	18436572[3]	4°	Damper	1 Turn[4]		+1	+1/2	1/4-3/8
	8-283 Std. Tr.[8]	.035	[9]	28-32	18436572[3]	TDC	Damper	1 Turn[4]		+1	+1/2	1/4-3/8
	8-283 Auto. Tr.[8]	.035	[9]	28-32	18436572[3]	4°	Damper	1 Turn[4]		+1	+1/2	1/4-3/8
	8-327, 275 H.P.	.035	[9]	28-32	18436572[3]	8°	Damper	1 Turn[4]		+1	+1/2	1/4-3/8
	8-327, 275 H.P.[8]	.035	[9]	28-32	18436572[3]	6°	Damper	1 Turn[4]		+1	+1/2	1/4-3/8
1968	4-153 Std. Tr.	.035	[9]	31-34	1342	TDC	Damper	1 Turn[4]		+1/2	+1/2	1/8-1/4
	4-153 Auto. Tr.	.035	[9]	31-34	1342	4°	Damper	1 Turn[4]		+1/2	+1/2	1/8-1/4
	6-230, 250 Std. Tr.	.035	[9]	31-34	153624	TDC	Damper	1 Turn[4]		+1/2	+1/2	1/8-1/4
	6-230, 250 Auto. Tr.	.035	[9]	31-34	153624	4°	Damper	1 Turn[4]		+1/2	+1/2	1/8-1/4
	8-307	.035	[9]	28-32	18436572[3]	2°	Damper	1 Turn[4]		+1/2	+1/2	1/8-1/4
	8-327, 275 H.P.[10]	.035	[9]	28-32	18436572[3]	TDC	Damper	1 Turn[4]		+1/2	+1/2	1/8-1/4
	8-327, 275 H.P.[11]	.035	[9]	28-32	18436572[3]	4°	Damper	1 Turn[4]		+1/2	+1/2	1/8-1/4
	8-350, Std. Tr.	.035	[9]	28-32	18436572[3]	TDC	Damper	1 Turn[4]		+1/2	+1/2	1/8-1/4
	8-350, Auto. Tr.	.035	[9]	28-32	18436572[3]	4°	Damper	1 Turn[4]		+1/2	+1/2	1/8-1/4

[1]—For long travel lifters 2 turns.
[2]—New points .019″, used points .016″.
[3]—Cylinder numbering (front to rear): Left bank 1-3-5-7, right bank 2-4-6-8.
[4]—Turn rocker arm adjusting screw down until all lash is removed. Then turn screw down the additional number of turns specified.
[5]—Manual transmission and Air Injection Reactor system (A.I.R.).
[6]—Automatic transmission and Air Injection Reactor system (A.I.R.).
[7]—After top dead center.
[8]—With Air Injection Reactor (A.I.R.).
[9]—New points, .019″, used points .016″. On V8s, turn adjusting screw in (clockwise) until engine misfires; then back off 1/2 turn.
[10]—With standard transmission.
[11]—With automatic transmission.

Year	Engine or Car Model	Spark Plug Gap	Distributor Point Gap	Distributor Dwell Angle	Firing Order	Ignition Timing BTDC or Mark	Ignition Timing Mark Location	Valve Lash Intake	Valve Lash Exhaust	Caster Degrees	Camber Degrees	Toe-In Inch
CHRYSLER												
1946-48	Six	.025	.020	35-38	153624	[2]	Damper	.008H	.010H	Zero	+3/8	1/32
	Eight	.025	.017	37-30	16258374	[2]	Damper	.008H[3]	.010H[3]	Zero	+3/8	1/32
1949-50	Six	.035	.020	35-38	153624	"0"	Damper	.008H	.010H	-2	+3/8	1/32
	Eight	.035	.017	27-30	16258374	"0"	Damper	.008H[3]	.010H[3]	-2	+3/8	1/32
1951-52	Six	.035	.020	35-38	153624	[2]	Damper	.008H	.010H	-2	Zero	Zero
	V8	.035	.017	[4]	18436572[5]	"0"	Damper	Zero	Zero	-2	Zero	Zero
1953-54	Six	.035	.020	35-38	153624	"0"	Damper	.008H	.010H	-2	Zero	Zero
	V8	.035	.017	[4]	18436572[5]	[6]	Damper	Zero	Zero	-2	Zero	Zero
1955	300	.035	.017	[4]	18436572[5]	10°	Damper	.015H	.024H	[9]	[10]	0-1/16
	Others	.035	.017	[4]	18436572[5]	6°	Damper	Zero	Zero	[9]	[10]	0-1/16
1956	Windsor	.035	.017	31	18436572[5]	2°	Damper	Zero	Zero	[9]	[10]	1/8
	New Yorker	.035	.017	[7]	18436572[5]	4°	Damper	Zero	Zero	[9]	[10]	1/8
	300B	.035	.017	31	18436572[5]	8°	Damper	.015H	.024H	[9]	[10]	1/8
1957	300C	.035	.017	[8]	18436572[5]	4°	Damper	.015H	.024H	[11]	[12]	3/32-5/32
	New Yorker	.035	.017	[8]	18436572[5]	6°	Damper	Zero	Zero	[11]	[12]	3/32-5/32
	Others	.035	.017	29	18436572[5]	6°	Damper	Zero	Zero	[11]	[12]	3/32-5/32
1958	V8-354	.035	.017	27-32	18436572[5]	[13]	Damper	.060-.210[14]		[15]	[12]	3/32-5/32
	V8-392 New Yorker	.035	.017	[8]	18436572[5]	6°	Damper	.060-.210[14]		[15]	[12]	3/32-5/32
	V8-392 "300D"	.035	.017	[8]	18436572[5]	6°	Damper	.015H	.024H	[15]	[12]	3/32-5/32
1959	V8-383	.035	.017	27-32	18436572[5]	10°	Damper	.060-.210[14]		-3/4	[13]	1/8
	V8-413	.035	.017	[7]	18436572[5]	10°	Damper	.060-.210[14]		-3/4	[12]	1/8

Continued

CHRYSLER—Continued

Year	Engine or Car Model	Spark Plug Gap	Distributor		Firing Order	Ignition Timing		Valve Lash		Wheel Alignment		
			Point Gap	Dwell Angle		BTDC or Mark	Mark Location	Intake	Exhaust	Caster Degrees	Camber Degrees	Toe-In Inch
1960	V8-383	.035	.017	27-32	18436572⑤	10°	Damper	.060-.210⑭		⑪	⑯	⅛
	V8-413 New Yorker	.035	.017	27-32	18436572⑤	10°	Damper	.060-.210⑭		⑪	⑯	⅛
	V8-413 "300F" S.T.	.035	.017	⑦	18436572⑤	10°	Damper	.060-.210⑭		⑪	⑯	⅛
	V8-413 "300F" A.T.	.035	.017	⑦	18436572⑤	5°	Damper	.060-.210⑭		⑰	⑯	⅛
1961	V8-361 Newport	.035	.017	27-32	18436572⑤	10°	Damper	.060-.210⑭		⑰	⑱	⅛
	V8-383 Windsor	.035	.017	27-32	18436572⑤	10°	Damper	.060-.210⑭		⑰	⑱	⅛
	V8-413 New Yorker	.035	.017	27-32	18436572⑤	10°	Damper	.060-.210⑭		⑰	⑱	⅛
	V8-413 "300G" S.T.	.035	.017	⑦	18436572⑤	10°	Damper	.060-.210⑭		⑰	⑱	⅛
	V8-413 "300G" A.T.	.035	.017	⑦	18436572⑧	5°	Damper	.060-.210⑭		⑰	⑱	⅛
1962	V8-361 Newport	.035	.017	27-32	18436572⑤	10°	Damper	.060-.210⑭		⑰	⑱	⅛
	V8-383 "300"	.035	.017	27-32	18436572⑤	10°	Damper	.060-.210⑭		⑰	⑱	⅛
	V8-413 New Yorker	.035	.017	27-32	18436572⑤	10°	Damper	.060-.210⑭		⑰	⑱	⅛
	V8-413 "300H"	.035	.017	⑦	18436572⑤	10°	Damper	.015H	.024H	⑰	⑱	⅛
1963	V8-361 Newport	.035	.017	27-32	18436572⑤	10°	Damper	.060-.210⑭		⑰	⑱	⅛
	V8-383 "300"	.035	.017	27-32	18436572⑤	10°	Damper	.060-.210⑭		⑰	⑱	⅛
	V8-413 "300"	.035	.017	⑦	18436572⑤	10°	Damper	.060-.210⑭		⑰	⑱	⅛
	V8-413 New Yorker	.035	.017	28-33	18436572⑤	10°	Damper	.060-.210⑭		⑰	⑱	⅛
	V8-413 "300J"	.035	.017	⑦	18436572⑤	12½°	Damper	.015H	.024H	⑰	⑱	⅛
1964	V8-361 Newport	.035	.017	28-33	18436572⑤	10°	Damper	.060-.210⑭		⑰	⑱	⅛
	V8-383 "300"	.035	.017	28-33	18436572⑤	10°	Damper	.060-.210⑭		⑰	⑱	⅛
	V8-413 "300"	.035	.017	⑦	18436572⑤	10°	Damper	.060-.210⑭		⑰	⑱	⅛
	V8-413 New Yorker	.035	.017	28-33	18436572⑤	10°	Damper	.060-.210⑭		⑰	⑱	⅛
	"300K" 1 Carb.	.035	.017	⑦	18436572⑤	10°	Damper	.060-.210⑭		⑰	⑱	⅛
	"300K" 2 Carbs.	.035	.017	⑦	18436572⑤	12½°	Damper	.017H	.028H	⑰	⑱	⅛
1965	V8-383	.035	.017	28-32	18436572⑤	10°	Damper	.060-.210⑭		⑰	⑱	⅛
	V8-413, 340 H.P.	.035	.017	28-32	18436572⑤	12½°	Damper	.060-.210⑭		⑰	⑱	⅛
	V8-413, 360 H.P.	.035	.017	①	18436572⑤	12½°	Damper	.060-.210⑭		⑰	⑱	⅛
1966	V8-383, 440	.035	.017	28-32	18436572⑤	12½°	Damper	.060-.210⑭		⑰	⑱	⅛
	V8-383, 440⑲	.035	.017	28-32	18436572⑤	5°	Damper	.060-.210⑭		⑰	⑱	⅛
1967	V8-383, 440⑳	.035	.017	28-32	18436572⑤	12½°	Damper	Hydraulic㉓		⑰	⑱	⅛
	V8-383, 440㉑	.035	.017	28-32	18436572⑧	5°	Damper	Hydraulic㉓		⑰	⑱	⅛
	V8-383, 440㉒	.035	.017	28-32	18436572⑤	TDC	Damper	Hydraulic㉓		⑰	⑱	⅛
1968	V8-383 Std. Tr.㉔	.035	.017	28-33	18436572⑤	TDC	Damper	Hydraulic㉓		⑰	⑱	⅛
	V8-383 Auto. Tr.㉔	.035	.017	28-33	18436572⑧	7½°	Damper	Hydraulic㉓		⑰	⑱	⅛
	V8-383 Std. Tr.㉕	.035	.017	28-33	18436572⑤	TDC	Damper	Hydraulic㉓		⑰	⑱	⅛
	V8-383 Auto. Tr.㉕	.035	.017	28-33	18436572⑤	5°	Damper	Hydraulic㉓		⑰	⑱	⅛
	V8-440 Std. Tr.	.035	.017	28-33	18436572⑤	TDC	Damper	Hydraulic㉓		⑰	⑱	⅛
	V8-440 Auto. Tr.	.035	.017	28-33	18436572⑤	7½°	Damper	Hydraulic㉓		⑰	⑱	⅛
	V8-440 Std. Tr.㉖	.035	.017	28-33	18436572⑤	5°	Damper	Hydraulic㉓		⑰	⑱	⅛
	V8-440 Auto. Tr.㉖	.035	.017	28-33	18436572⑤	TDC	Damper	Hydraulic㉓		⑰	⑱	⅛

①—Each set of points 27-31°; total dwell both sets 36-40°.
②—Second line after "0" mark.
③—Zero lash for hydraulic valve lifter jobs.
④—Each set of points 26-28°, total dwell both sets 32-36°.
⑤—Engine numbering (front to rear): Left bank 1-3-5-7, right bank 2-4-6-8.
⑥—Fourth line after "0" mark.
⑦—Each set of points 27-32°, total dwell both sets 34-40°.

⑧—Each set of points 29-32°, total dwell both sets 36-39°.
⑨—Manual steering —2°, power steering 0°.
⑩—Left side +½°, right side 0°.
⑪—Manual steering —¾°, power steering +¾°.
⑫—Left side +⅜°, right side 0°.
⑬—Windsor 8°, Saratoga 6°.
⑭—With lifter collapsed.
⑮—Manual steering —¾°, Power steering 0°.
⑯—Left side +⅜°, Right side +⅛°.
⑰—Manual Steering —½°, Power Steering +¾°.

⑱—Left side +½°, right side +¼°.
⑲—With CAP (Cleaner Air Package). Timing set after top dead center.
⑳—Without CAP (cleaner air package).
㉑—With CAP (cleaner air package) and Torqueflite.
㉒—With CAP (cleaner air package) and manual transmission.
㉓—No adjustment.
㉔—Two barrel carburetor.
㉕—Four barrel carburetor.
㉖—High performance engine.

Year	Engine or Car Model	Spark Plug Gap	Distributor Point Gap	Distributor Dwell Angle	Firing Order	Ignition Timing BTDC or Mark	Ignition Timing Mark Location	Valve Lash Intake	Valve Lash Exhaust	Wheel Alignment Caster Degrees	Wheel Alignment Camber Degrees	Wheel Alignment Toe-In Inch
CORVAIR												
1960-61	All	.035	(1)	31-34	145236(6)	(2)	Pulley	1 Turn(3)		(4)	+1	(5)
1962-63	Turbo-Air, Std. Tr.	.035	(1)	31-34	145236(6)	4°	Damper	1 Turn(3)		+1¾	+½	¼-⅜
	Turbo-Air, Auto. Tr.	.035	(1)	31-34	145236(6)	13°	Damper	1 Turn(3)		+1¾	+½	¼-⅜
	Monza, Powerglide	.030	(1)	31-34	145236(6)	13°	Damper	1 Turn(3)		+1¾	+½	¼-⅜
	Super Turbo-Air	.030	(1)	31-34	145236(6)	13°	Damper	1 Turn(3)		+1¾	+½	¼-⅜
	Turbocharged Eng.	.030	(1)	31-34	145236(6)	24°	Damper	1 Turn(3)		+1¾	+½	¼-⅜
1964	95 H.P.-Std. Trans.	.035	(1)	31-34	145236(6)	6°	Damper	1 Turn(3)		+1¾	Zero	¼-⅜
	95 H.P.-Auto. Trans.	.035	(1)	31-34	145236(6)	14°	Damper	1 Turn(3)		+1¾	Zero	¼-⅜
	110 Horsepower	.030	(1)	31-34	145236(6)	14°	Damper	1 Turn(3)		+1¾	Zero	¼-⅜
	150 Horsepower	.030	(1)	31-34	145236(6)	24°	Damper	1 Turn(3)		+1¾	Zero	¼-⅜
1965-66	95 H.P.-Std. Trans.	.035	(1)	31-34	145236(6)	6°	Damper	1 Turn(3)		+3	+1	¼
	95 H.P.-Auto. Trans.	.035	(1)	31-34	145236(6)	14°	Damper	1 Turn(3)		+3	+1	¼
	110 Horsepower	.030	(1)	31-34	145236(6)	14°(8)	Damper	1 Turn(3)		+3	+1	¼
	4 Carb. Engine	.030	(1)	31-34	145236(6)	18°(7)	Damper	1 Turn(3)		+3	+1	¼
	Turbocharged Eng.	.030	(1)	31-34	145236(6)	24°	Damper	1 Turn(3)		+3	+1	¼
1967	95 H.P. Std. Tr.	.035	(1)	31-34	145236(6)	6°	Damper	1 Turn(3)		+1⅞	+1	3/16-5/16
	95 H.P. Auto. Tr.	.035	(1)	31-34	145236(6)	14°	Damper	1 Turn(3)		+1⅞	+1	3/16-5/16
	95 H.P.(9)	.035	(1)	31-34	145236(6)	TDC	Damper	1 Turn(3)		+1⅞	+1	3/16-5/16
	110 H.P.	.030	(1)	31-34	145236(6)	14°	Damper	1 Turn(3)		+1⅞	+1	3/16-5/16
	110 H.P. w P/G, A/C	.030	(1)	31-34	145236(6)	24°	Damper	1 Turn(3)		+1⅞	+1	3/16-5/16
	110 H.P.(9)	.030	(1)	31-34	145236(6)	4°	Damper	1 Turn(3)		+1⅞	+1	3/16-5/16
1968	95 H.P.	.035	(1)	31-34	145236(6)	(10)	Damper	1 Turn(3)		(12)	(13)	3/16-5/16
	110 H.P.	.030	(1)	31-34	145236(6)	(11)	Damper	1 Turn(3)		(12)	(13)	3/16-5/16
	140 H.P.	.030	(1)	31-34	145236(6)	4°	Damper	1 Turn(3)		(12)	(13)	3/16-5/16
1969	95 H.P. Std. Tr.	.035	(1)	31-34	145236(6)	6°	Damper	1 Turn(3)		(12)	(13)	3/16-5/16
	95 H.P. Auto. Tr.	.035	(1)	31-34	145236(6)	14°	Damper	1 Turn(3)		(12)	(13)	3/16-5/16
	110 H.P. Std. Tr.	.035	(1)	31-34	145236(6)	4°	Damper	1 Turn(3)		(12)	(13)	3/16-5/16
	110 H.P. Auto. Tr.	.035	(1)	31-34	145236(6)	12°	Damper	1 Turn(3)		(12)	(13)	3/16-5/16
	140 H.P.	.035	(1)	31-34	145236(6)	4°	Damper	1 Turn(3)		(12)	(13)	3/16-5/16

(1)—New points .019″, used .016″.
(2)—For Dist. No.'s (1110259, 260) 13°. Dist No.'s (1110256-7) 16°. All others 4°.
(3)—Tighten adjusting screw until all clearance between valve stem and rocker arm has been eliminated. Then tighten screw the additional number of turns listed to center the lifter plunger.
(4)—1960 +3, 1961 +2.
(5)—1960 ⅛-3/16, 1961 ¼-⅜.
(6)—Engine numbering (rear to front): Right bank 1-3-5, left bank 2-4-6.
(7)—With head gasket (Part No. 3891552) set at 14°.
(8)—1966 with A/C 24°.
(9)—With A.I.R. system.
(10)—Manual trans. 6°, automatic trans. 14°.
(11)—Manual trans. 4°, automatic trans. 12°.
(12)—+1½° to +2¼°.
(13)—+½ to +1½.

Year	Engine or Car Model	Spark Plug Gap	Distributor Point Gap	Distributor Dwell Angle	Firing Order	Ignition Timing BTDC or Mark	Ignition Timing Mark Location	Valve Lash Intake	Valve Lash Exhaust	Wheel Alignment Caster Degrees	Wheel Alignment Camber Degrees	Wheel Alignment Toe-In Inch
CORVETTE												
1953-54	All Models	.035	.015	41-47	153624	Ball	Flywheel	.010H	.020H	+½	+½	⅛
1955	Six	.035	.015	41-47	153624	Ball	Flywheel	.006H	.013H	+½	+½	0-⅛
	V8	.035	.019	(1)	18436572(2)	4°	Damper	.008H	.018H	+½	+½	0-⅛
1956	All Models	.035	.019	(1)	18436572(2)	4°	Damper	.008H	.018H	+½	+½	0-⅛
1957	220 Horsepower	.035	.019	(1)	18436572(2)	4°	Damper	1 Turn(3)		+½	+½	0-⅛
	245 Horsepower	.035	.019	(1)	18436572(2)	12°	Damper	1 Turn(3)		+½	+½	0-⅛
	250 Horsepower	.035	.019	(1)	18436572(2)	13°	Pulley	1 Turn(3)		+½	+½	0-⅛
	270 Horsepower	.035	.019	(1)	18436572(2)	12°	Damper	1 Turn(3)		+½	+½	0-⅛
	283 Horsepower	.035	.019	(1)	18436572(2)	6°	Damper	.012H	.018H	+½	+½	0-⅛
1958-59	230 Horsepower	.035	(4)	30	18436572(2)	4°	Damper	1 Turn(3)		(6)	(7)	0-⅛
	245 Horsepower	.035	(4)	30	18436572(2)	4°	Damper	1 Turn(3)		(6)	(7)	0-⅛
	250 Horsepower	.035	(5)	(1)	18436572(2)	4°	Damper	1 Turn(3)		(6)	(7)	0-⅛
	270 Horsepower	.035	(5)	(1)	18436572(2)	7°	Damper	.012H	.018H	(6)	(7)	0-⅛
	290 Horsepower	.035	(5)	(1)	18436572(2)	14°	Damper	.012H	.018H	(6)	(7)	0-⅛

Continued

CORVETTE—Continued

Year	Engine or Car Model	Spark Plug Gap	Distributor Point Gap	Distributor Dwell Angle	Firing Order	Ignition Timing BTDC or Mark	Ignition Timing Mark Location	Valve Lash Intake	Valve Lash Exhaust	Wheel Alignment Caster Degrees	Wheel Alignment Camber Degrees	Wheel Alignment Toe-In Inch
1960-61	230 Horsepower	.035	[4]	30	18436572[2]	4°	Damper	1 Turn[3]		+2	Zero	[8]
	245 Horsepower	.035	[4]	30	18436572[2]	12°	Damper	1 Turn[3]		+2	Zero	[8]
	270 Horsepower	.035	[5]	[1]	18436572[2]	12°	Damper	.012H	.018H	+2	Zero	[8]
	275 Horsepower	.035	[5]	[1]	18436572[2]	8°	Damper	.012H	.018H	+2	Zero	[8]
	315 Horsepower	.035	[5]	[1]	18436572[2]	18°	Damper	.012H	.018H	+2	Zero	[8]
1962	250 Horsepower	.035	[4]	30	18436572[2]	4°	Damper	1 Turn[3]		+2	Zero	¼
	300 Horsepower	.035	[4]	30	18436572[2]	8°	Damper	1 Turn[3]		+2	Zero	¼
	340 Horsepower	.035	[5]	[1]	18436572[2]	10°	Damper	.008H	.018H	+2	Zero	¼
	360 Horsepower	.035	[5]	[1]	18436572[2]	10°	Damper	.008H	.018H	+2	Zero	¼
1963	250 Horsepower	.035	[5]	30	18436572[2]	4°	Damper	1 Turn[3]		+½	+2½	¼
	300 Horsepower	.035	[5]	30	18436572[2]	8°	Damper	1 Turn[3]		+½	+2½	¼
	340 Horsepower	.035	[5]	30	18436572[2]	10°	Damper	.008H	.018H	+½	+2½	¼
	360 Horsepower	.035	[5]	30	18436572[2]	10°	Damper	.008H	.018H	+½	+2½	¼
1964	250 Horsepower	.035	[5]	30	18436572[2]	4°	Damper	1 Turn[3]		+½	+2½	3/16-5/16
	300 Horsepower	.035	[6]	30	18436572[2]	8°	Damper	1 Turn[3]		+½	+2½	3/16-5/16
	365 Horsepower	.035	[5]	30	18436572[2]	10°	Damper	.030H	.030H	+½	+2½	3/16-5/16
	375 Horsepower	.035	[5]	30	18436572[2]	10°	Damper	.030H	.030H	+½	+2½	3/16-5/16
1965	250 Horsepower	.035	[5]	30	18436572[2]	4°	Damper	1 Turn[3]		+1½	+¾	7/32-11/32
	300 Horsepower	.035	[5]	30	18436572[2]	8°	Damper	1 Turn[3]		+1½	+¾	7/32-11/32
	350 Horsepower	.035	[5]	30	18436572[2]	8°	Damper	1 Turn[3]		+1½	+¾	7/32-11/32
	365 Horsepower	.035	[5]	30	18436572[2]	12°	Damper	.030H	.030H	+1½	+¾	7/32-11/32
	375 Horsepower	.035	[5]	30	18436572[2]	12°	Damper	.030H	.030H	+1½	+¾	7/32-11/32
	425 Horsepower	.035	[5]	30	18436572[2]	10°	Damper	.020H	.024H	+1½	+¾	7/32-11/32
1966	300 Horsepower	.035	[5]	30	18436572[2]	6°	Damper	1 Turn[3]		+1	+¾	3/16-5/16
	300 Horsepower[9]	.035	[5]	30	18436572[2]	4°[10]	Damper	1 Turn[3]		+1	+¾	3/16-5/16
	350 Horsepower	.035	[5]	30	18436572[2]	10°	Damper	1 Turn[3]		+1	+¾	3/16-5/16
	390 Horsepower	.035	—	—	18436572[2]	4°	Damper	1 Turn[3]		+1	+¾	3/16-5/16
	425 Horsepower	.035	—	—	18436572[2]	8°	Damper	.020H	.024H	+1	+¾	3/16-5/16
1967	8-327, 300 H.P.	.035	[13]	28-32	18436572[2]	6°	Damper	1 Turn[3]		+1	+¾	3/16-5/16
	8-327, 300 H.P.[9][11]	.035	[13]	28-32	18436572[2]	4° ATC	Damper	1 Turn[3]		+1	+¾	3/16-5/16
	8-327, 300 H.P.[9][12]	.035	[13]	28-32	18436572[2]	4° ATC	Damper	1 Turn[3]		+1	+¾	3/16-5/16
	8-427	.035	[13]	28-32	18436572[2]	4°	Damper	1 Turn[3]		+1	+¾	3/16-5/16
	8-427[9]	.035	[13]	28-32	18436572[2]	4°	Damper	1 Turn[3]		+1	+¾	3/16-5/16
	8-427, 425 H.P.	.035	[13]	28-32	18436572[2]	12°[14]	Damper	.022H	.024H	+1	+¾	3/16-5/16
	8-427, 435 H.P.	.035	[13]	28-32	18436572[2]	5°	Damper	.024H	.028H	+1	+¾	3/16-5/16
	8-427, 435 H.P.[9]	.035	[13]	28-32	18436572[2]	5°	Damper	.024H	.028H	+1	+¾	3/16-5/16
1968	8-327, 300 H.P.	.035	[13]	28-32	18436572[2]	4°	Damper	1 Turn[3]		[15]	[16]	[17]
	8-327, 350 H.P.	.035	[13]	28-32	18436572[2]	4°	Damper	1 Turn[3]		[15]	[16]	[17]
	8-427, 390 H.P.	.035	[13]	28-32	18436572[2]	4°	Damper	1 Turn[3]		[15]	[16]	[17]
	8-427, 400 H.P.	.035	[13]	28-32	18436572[2]	4°	Damper	1 Turn[3]		[15]	[16]	[17]
	8-427, 425 H.P.	.035	[13]	28-32	18436572[2]	4°	Damper	.024H	.028H	[15]	[16]	[17]
	8-427, 430 H.P.	.035	[13]	28-32	18436572[2]	12°	Damper	.022H	.024H	[15]	[16]	[17]
	8-427, 435 H.P.	.035	[13]	28-32	18436572[2]	4°	Damper	.024H	.028H	[15]	[16]	[17]

[1]—Each set of points 28-30°, total dwell both sets 33-35°.
[2]—Engine numbering (front to rear): Left bank 1-3-5-7, right bank 2-4-6-8.
[3]—Turn rocker arm adjusting screw clockwise until all lash is eliminated, then turn screw the additional number of turns specified.
[4]—New points .018", used .015".
[5]—New points .019", used .016".
[6]—1958 +2¼°, 1959 +2°.
[7]—1958 +½°, 1959 Zero.
[8]—1960 0—⅛, 1961 ⅛ +⅜°.
[9]—With Air Injection Reactor system (A.I.R.).
[10]—After top dead center.
[11]—Manual transmission.
[12]—Automatic transmission.
[13]—New points, .019", used .016". On V8s, turn adjusting screw in (clockwise) until engine misfires; then back off ½ turn.
[14]—At 800 R.P.M.
[15]—Manual steer. +1°, Power steer. +2¼°.
[16]—Manual steer., +¾°, Power steer. +¾°, Rear wheel align. —¾°.
[17]—Manual steer., 3/16 to 5/16, Power steer. 3/16 to 5/16, Rear wheel align. 1/32 to 3/32.

Year	Engine or Car Model	Spark Plug Gap	Distributor		Firing Order	Ignition Timing		Valve Lash		Wheel Alignment		
			Point Gap	Dwell Angle		BTDC or Mark	Mark Location	Intake	Exhaust	Caster Degrees	Camber Degrees	Toe-In Inch
CROSLEY												
1946-52	All Models	.025	.020	46	1-3-4-2	12°	Flywheel	.005C	.007C	10°	2°	3/64-1/16
DE SOTO												
1946-48	All Models	.030	.020	35-38	153624	"O"	Damper	.008H	.010H	Zero	+3/8	1/32
1949-50	All Models	.035	.020	35-38	153624	①	Damper	.008H	.010H	−2	+3/8	1/32
1951	All Models	.035	.020	35-38	153624	①	Damper	.008H	.010H	−2	Zero	Zero
1952-53	Six	.035	.020	35-38	153624	①	Damper	.008H	.010H	−2	Zero	Zero
	V8	.035	.018	②	18436572③	④	Damper	Zero	Zero	−2	Zero	Zero
1954	Six	.035	.020	39	153624	⑤	Damper	.008H	.010H	−2	Zero	Zero
	V8	.035	.018	②	18436572③	④	Damper	Zero	Zero	−2	Zero	Zero
1955	2 Bar. Carb.	.035	.017	②	18436572③	4°	Damper	Zero	Zero	⑥	⑦	0-1/16
	4 Bar. Carb.	.035	.017	34	18436572③	10°	Damper	Zero	Zero	⑥	⑦	0-1/16
1956	V8-330 2 Bar. Carb.	.035	.017	27-32	18436572③	8°	Damper	Zero	Zero	⑥	⑦	3/32-5/32
	V8-330 4 Bar. Carb.	.035	.017	27-32	18436572③	4°	Damper	Zero	Zero	⑥	⑦	3/32-5/32
	V8-341	.035	.017	27-32	18436572③	6°	Damper	Zero	Zero	⑥	⑦	3/32-5/32
1957	V8-325	.035	.017	27-32	18436572③	6°	Damper	Zero	Zero	⑧	⑨	3/32-5/32
	V8-341	.035	.017	27-32	18436572③	6°	Damper	Zero	Zero	⑧	⑨	3/32-5/32
1958	V8-350, 361 1 Carb.	.035	.017	27-32	18436572③	6°	Damper	.060-.210⑪		⑫	⑨	3/32-5/32
	V8-361 2 Carbs.	.035	.017	⑩	18436572③	8°	Damper	.060-.210⑪		⑫	⑨	3/32-5/32
1959	V8-361, 383 1 Carb.	.035	.017	27-32	18436572③	10°	Damper	.060-.210⑪		⑧	⑨	1/8
	V8-383 Two Carbs.	.035	.017	⑬	18436572③	10°	Damper	.060-.210⑪		⑧	⑨	1/8
1960	V8-361, 383	.035	.017	27-32	18436572③	10°	Damper	.060-.210⑪		⑧	⑦	1/8
1961	V8-361	.035	.017	27-32	18436572③	10°	Damper	.060-.210⑪		⑭	⑮	1/8

①—Third line after "O" mark.
②—Each set of points 26-28°, total dwell both sets 32-36°.
③—Cylinder numbering (front to rear): Left bank 1-3-5-7, right bank 2-4-6-8.
④—Fourth line after "O" mark.
⑤—Second line after "O" mark.
⑥—Manual steering −2°, power steering 0°.
⑦—Left side +3/8°, right side +1/8°.
⑧—Manual steering −3/4°, power steering +3/4°.
⑨—Left side +3/8°, right side 0°.
⑩—Each set of points 29-32°; total dwell both sets 36-39°.
⑪—With lifter collapsed.
⑫—Manual steering −3/4°, power steering 0°.
⑬—Each set of points 27-32°; total dwell both sets 34-40°.
⑭—Manual steering −1/2°, power steering +3/4°.
⑮—Left side +1/2°, right side +1/4.°

Year	Engine or Car Model	Spark Plug Gap	Point Gap	Dwell Angle	Firing Order	BTDC or Mark	Mark Location	Intake	Exhaust	Caster	Camber	Toe-In
DODGE												
1946-48	All Models	.025	.020	35-38	153624	①	Damper	.008H	.010H	Zero	+3/8	1/16
1949	All Models	.025	.020	35-38	153624	①	Damper	.008H	.010H	Zero	+3/8	1/32
1950	All Models	.035	.020	35-38	153624	①	Damper	.008H	.010H	Zero	+3/8	1/32
1951-52	All Models	.035	.020	35-38	153624	①	Damper	.008H	.010H	Zero	Zero	Zero
1953-54	Six	.035	.020	36-42	153624	①	Damper	.010H	.010H	Zero	Zero	Zero
	V8	.035	.017	②	18436572③	4°	Pulley	Zero	Zero	Zero	Zero	Zero
1955	Six	.035	.020	39	153624	2°	Damper	.010H	.010H	⑤	⑥	0-1/16
	V8	.035	.017	②	18436572③	4°	Damper	Zero	Zero	⑤	⑥	0-1/16
1956	Six	.035	.020	39	153624	2°	Damper	.010H	.010H	⑤	⑥	3/32-5/32
	V8-270	.035	.017	29-32	18436572③	4°	Damper	Zero	Zero	⑤	⑥	3/32-5/32
	V8-315 2 Bar. Carb.	.035	.017	29-32	18436572③	6°	Damper	Zero	Zero	⑤	⑥	3/32-5/32
	V8-315 4 Bar. Carb.	.035	.017	29-32	18436572③	6°	Damper	.012H	.022H	⑤	⑥	3/32-5/32
1957	Six	.035	.020	39	153624	0°	Damper	.010H	.010H	⑦	⑧	3/32-5/32
	V8-325	.035	.017	29-32	18436572③	6°	Damper	Zero	Zero	⑦	⑧	3/32-5/32
	V8-354 One Carb.	.035	.017	29-32	18436572③	6°	Damper	Zero	Zero	⑦	⑧	3/32-5/32
	V8-354 Two Carbs.	.035	.017	④	18436572③	2°	Damper	.015H	.024H	⑦	⑧	3/32-5/32
1958	Six	.035	.020	39	153624	2°	Damper	.010H	.010H	⑩	⑧	3/32-5/32
	V8's	.035	.017	29-32	18436572③	6°	Damper	.060-.210⑨		⑩	⑧	3/32-5/32
1959	Six	.035	.020	39	153624	2½°	Damper	.010H	.010H	⑦	⑧	1/8
	V8	.035	.017	29-32	18436572③	10°	Damper	.060-.210⑨		⑦	⑧	1/8
1960	Six	.035	.020	36-42	153624	5°	Pulley	.010H	.020H	⑦	⑪	1/8
	V8	.035	.017	27-32	18436572③	⑫	Damper	⑬	⑭	⑦	⑪	1/8

Continued

Year	Engine or Car Model	Spark Plug Gap	Distributor Point Gap	Distributor Dwell Angle	Firing Order	Ignition Timing BTDC or Mark	Ignition Timing Mark Location	Valve Lash Intake	Valve Lash Exhaust	Wheel Alignment Caster Degrees	Wheel Alignment Camber Degrees	Wheel Alignment Toe-In Inch

DODGE—Continued

Year	Engine or Car Model	Spark Plug Gap	Point Gap	Dwell Angle	Firing Order	BTDC or Mark	Mark Location	Intake	Exhaust	Caster	Camber	Toe-In
1961	6-170, 225	.035	.020	40-45	153624	2½°	Pulley	.010H	.020H	(15)	(16)	⅛
	6-225 4 Bar. Carb.	.028	.020	40-45	153624	10°	Pulley	.010H	.020H	(15)	(16)	⅛
	V8-318 Std. Tr.	.035	.017	27-32	18436572(3)	5°	Damper	.010H	.018H	(15)	(16)	⅛
	V8-318 Auto. Tr.	.035	.017	27-32	18436572(3)	10°	Damper	.010H	.018H	(15)	(16)	⅛
	V8-361 2 Bar. Carb.	.035	.017	27-32	18436572(3)	10°	Damper	.060-.210(9)		(15)	(16)	⅛
	V8-361 4 Bar. Carb.	.035	.017	27-32	18436572(3)	10°	Damper	.016C	.028C	(15)	(16)	⅛
	V8-383	.035	.017	(17)	18436572(3)	7½°	Damper	.016C	.028C	(15)	(16)	⅛
1962	6 Cyl.	.035	.020	40-45	153624	2½°	Pulley	.010H	.020H	(15)	(16)	⅛
	8-318 Std. Tr.	.035	.017	27-32	18436572(3)	5°	Damper	.013H	.021H	(15)	(16)	⅛
	8-318 Auto. Tr.	.035	.017	27-32	18436572(3)	10°	Damper	.013H	.021H	(15)	(16)	⅛
	8-361 "880"	.035	.017	27-32	18436572(3)	10°	Damper	.060-.210(9)		(15)	(16)	⅛
	8-361 Dart, Polara	.035	.017	27-32	18436572(3)	10°	Damper	.060-.210(9)		(15)	(16)	⅛
	8-361 Hi-Perf.	.035	.017	(17)	18436572(3)	10°	Damper	.060-.210(9)		(15)	(15)	⅛
	8-383, 413 Hi-Perf.	.035	.017	(17)	18436572(3)	10°	Damper	.060-.210(9)		(15)	(16)	⅛
	8-413 Ram, Man.	.035	.017	(17)	18436572(3)	10°	Damper	.060-.210(9)		(15)	(16)	⅛
1963	6 Cyl.	.035	.020	40-45	153624	2½°	Damper	.010H	.020H	(15)	(16)	⅛
	8-318 Std. Trans.	.035	.017	28-33	18436572(3)	5°	Damper	.013H	.021H	(15)	(16)	⅛
	8-318 Auto. Trans.	.035	.017	28-33	18436572(3)	10°	Damper	.013H	.021H	(15)	(16)	⅛
	8-361, 383 2 B. Carb.	.035	.017	28-33	18436572(3)	10°	Damper	.060-.210(9)		(15)	(16)	⅛
	8-383 4 B. Carb.	.035	.017	(17)	18436572(3)	10°	Damper	.060-.210(9)		(15)	(16)	⅛
	8-426	.035	.017	(17)	18436572(3)	10°	Damper	.028C	.032C	(15)	(16)	⅛
1964	6 Cyl.	.035	.020	40-45	153624	2½°	Damper	.010H	.020H	(15)	(16)	⅛
	8-273 Std. Trans.	.035	.017	28-33	18436572(3)	5°	Damper	.013H	.021H	(16)	(16)	⅛
	8-273 Auto. Trans.	.035	.017	28-33	18436572(3)	10°	Damper	.013H	.021H	(16)	(16)	⅛
	8-318 Std. Trans.	.035	.017	28-33	18436572(3)	5°	Damper	.013H	.021H	(15)	(16)	⅛
	8-318 Auto. Trans.	.035	.017	28-33	18436572(3)	10°	Damper	.013H	.021H	(15)	(16)	⅛
	8-361, 383 2 B. Carb.	.035	.017	28-33	18436572(3)	10°	Damper	.060-.210(9)		(15)	(16)	⅛
	8-413	.035	.017	28-33	18436572(3)	10°	Damper	.060-.210(9)		(15)	(16)	⅛
	8-383, 426 4 B. Carb.	.035	.017	(17)	18436572(3)	10°	Damper	.060-.210(9)		(15)	(16)	⅛
	8-426 Hemi Charg.	.020	.017	(18)	18436572(3)	(19)	Damper	.028C	.032C	(15)	(16)	⅛
1965	6 Cyl.	.035	.020	40-45	153624	2½°	Damper	.010H	.020H	(15)	(16)	⅛
	8-273 Std. Trans.	.035	.017	28-33	18436572(3)	5°	Damper	.013H	.021H	(15)	(16)	⅛
	8-273 Auto. Trans.	.035	.017	28-33	18436572(3)	10°	Damper	.013H	.021H	(16)	(16)	⅛
	8-273 4 Bar. Carb.	.035	.017	28-33	18436572(3)	10°	Damper	.013H	.021H	(15)	(16)	⅛
	8-318 Std. Trans.	.035	.017	28-33	18436572(3)	5°	Damper	.013H	.021H	(15)	(16)	⅛
	8-318 Auto. Trans.	.035	.017	28-33	18436572(3)	10°	Damper	.013H	.021H	(15)	(16)	⅛
	8-361, 383 2 Bar. Carb.	.035	.017	28-32	18436572(3)	10°	Damper	.060-.210(9)		(15)	(16)	⅛
	8-383 4 Bar. Carb.	.035	.017	(20)	18436572(3)	10°	Damper	.060-.210(9)		(15)	(16)	⅛
	8-413	.035	.017	(20)	18436572(3)	12½°	Damper	.060-.210(9)		(15)	(16)	⅛
	8-426	.035	.017	(20)	18436572(3)	10°	Damper	.060-.210(9)		(15)	(16)	⅛
1966	6-170	.035	.020	40-45	153624	5°	Damper	.010H	.020H	(15)	(16)	⅛
	6-170(21)	.035	.020	40-45	153624	5°(22)	Damper	.010H	.020H	(15)	(16)	⅛
	6-225	.035	.020	40-45	153624	2½°	Damper	.010H	.020H	(15)	(16)	⅛
	6-225(21)	.035	.020	40-45	153624	5°(22)	Damper	.010H	.020H	(15)	(16)	⅛
	8-273 Std. Tr.	.035	.017	28-32	18436572(3)	5°	Pulley	.013H	.021H	(15)	(16)	⅛
	8-273 Auto. Tr.	.035	.017	28-32	18436572(3)	10°	Pulley	.013H	.021H	(15)	(16)	⅛
	8-273 2 Bar. Carb.(21)	.035	.017	28-32	18436572(3)	5°(22)	Damper	.013H	.021H	(15)	(16)	⅛
	8-273 4 Bar. Carb.	.035	.017	(20)	18436572(3)	10°	Damper	.013H	.021H	(15)	(16)	⅛
	8-273 4 Bar. Carb.(21)	.035	.017	(20)	18436572(3)	5°(22)	Damper	.013H	.021H	(15)	(16)	⅛
	8-318 Std. Tr.	.035	.017	28-32	18436572(3)	5°	Damper	.013H	.021H	(15)	(16)	⅛
	8-318 Auto. Tr.	.035	.017	28-32	18436572(3)	10°	Damper	.013H	.021H	(15)	(16)	⅛
	8-318 2 Bar. Carb.(21)	.035	.017	28-32	18436572(3)	4°(22)	Damper	.013H	.021H	(15)	(16)	⅛
	8-361, 383 2 B. C.	.035	.017	28-32	18436572(3)	12½°	Damper	.060-.210(9)		(15)	(16)	⅛
	8-361, 383 2 B. C.(21)	.035	.017	28-32	18436572(3)	5°(22)	Damper	.060-.210(9)		(15)	(16)	⅛
	8-383, 426, 440 4B.C.	.035	.017	28-32	18436572(3)	12½°	Damper	.060-.210(9)		(15)	(16)	⅛
	8-383,426,440 4B.C.(21)	.035	.017	28-32	18436572(3)	5°(22)	Damper	.060-.210(9)		(15)	(16)	⅛

Continued

Year	Engine or Car Model	Spark Plug Gap	Distributor Point Gap	Distributor Dwell Angle	Firing Order	Ignition Timing BTDC or Mark	Ignition Timing Mark Location	Valve Lash Intake	Valve Lash Exhaust	Caster Degrees	Camber Degrees	Toe-In Inch
DODGE—Continued												
1967	6-170, 225 [23]	.035	.020	40–45	153624	5°	Damper	.010H	.020H	[15]	[16]	⅛
	6-170 [21]	.035	.020	40–45	153624	5° [22]	Damper	.010H	.020H	[15]	[16]	⅛
	6-225 [21]	.035	.020	40–45	153624	TDC	Damper	.010H	.020H	[15]	[16]	⅛
	8-273 Std. Tr. [23]	.035	.017	28–32	18436572 [3]	5°	Damper	.013H	.021H	[15]	[16]	⅛
	8-273 Auto. Tr. [23]	.035	.017	28–32	18436572 [3]	10°	Damper	.013H	.021H	[15]	[16]	⅛
	8-273 [21]	.035	.017	28–32	18436572 [3]	5° [22]	Damper	.013H	.021H	[15]	[16]	⅛
	8-273, 4 B.C. [23]	.035	.017	[20]	18436572 [3]	10°	Damper	.013H	.021H	[15]	[16]	⅛
	8-273, 4 B.C. [21]	.035	.017	[20]	18436572 [3]	5° [22]	Damper	.013H	.021H	[15]	[16]	⅛
	8-318 Std. Tr. [23]	.035	.017	28–32	18436572 [3]	5°	Damper	Hydraulic [27]		[15]	[16]	⅛
	8-318 Auto. Tr. [21]	.035	.017	28–32	18436572 [3]	10°	Damper	Hydraulic [27]		[15]	[16]	⅛
	8-318 [21]	.035	.017	28–32	18436572 [3]	5° [22]	Damper	Hydraulic [27]		[15]	[16]	⅛
	8-383 [23]	.035	.017	28–32	18436572 [3]	12½°	Damper	Hydraulic [27]		[15]	[16]	⅛
	8-383 [21] [24]	.035	.017	28–32	18436572 [3]	5°	Damper	Hydraulic [27]		[15]	[16]	⅛
	8-383 [21] [25]	.035	.017	28–32	18436572 [3]	TDC	Damper	Hydraulic [27]		[15]	[16]	⅛
	8-440, 440 Hi Perf. [23]	.035	.017	28–32	18436572 [3]	12½°	Damper	Hydraulic [27]		[15]	[16]	⅛
	8-440, 440 Hi Perf. [21] [24]	.035	.017	28–32	18436572 [3]	5°	Damper	Hydraulic [27]		[15]	[16]	⅛
	8-440, 440 Hi Perf. [21] [25]	.035	.017	28–32	18436572 [3]	TDC	Damper	Hydraulic [27]		[15]	[16]	⅛
	8-426 Hemi [23]	.035	.017	[26]	18436572 [3]	12½°	Damper	.028C	.032C	[15]	[16]	⅛
	8-426 Hemi [21]	.035	.017	[26]	18436572 [3]	TDC	Damper	.028C	.032C	[15]	[16]	⅛
1968	6-170 Std. Trans.	.035	.020	40–45	153624	5° ATC	Damper	.010H	.020H	[15]	[16]	⅛
	6-170 Auto. Tr.	.035	.020	40–45	153624	2½° ATC	Damper	.010H	.020H	[15]	[16]	⅛
	6-225	.035	.020	40–45	153624	TDC	Damper	.010H	.020H	[15]	[16]	⅛
	V8-273 Std. Trans.	.035	.017	28–33	18436572 [3]	5° ATC	Damper	Hydraulic [27]		[15]	[16]	⅛
	V8-273 Auto. Tr.	.035	.017	28–33	18436572 [3]	2½° ATC	Damper	Hydraulic [27]		[15]	[16]	⅛
	V8-318 Std. Trans.	.035	.017	28–33	18436572 [3]	5° ATC	Damper	Hydraulic [27]		[15]	[16]	⅛
	V8-318 Auto. Tr.	.035	.017	28–33	18436572 [3]	2½° ATC	Damper	Hydraulic [27]		[15]	[16]	⅛
	V8-340 Std. Trans.	.035	.017	[20]	18436572 [3]	TDC	Damper	Hydraulic [27]		[15]	[16]	⅛
	V8-340 Auto. Tr.	.035	.017	[20]	18436572 [3]	5°	Damper	Hydraulic [27]		[15]	[16]	⅛
	V8-383 Std. Tr. [28]	.035	.017	28–33	18436572 [3]	TDC	Damper	Hydraulic [27]		[15]	[16]	⅛
	V8-383 Auto. Tr. [28]	.035	.017	28–33	18436572 [3]	5°	Damper	Hydraulic [27]		[15]	[16]	⅛
	V8-383 Std. Tr. [29]	.035	.017	28–33	18436572 [3]	TDC	Damper	Hydraulic [27]		[15]	[16]	⅛
	V8-383 Auto. Tr. [29]	.035	.017	28–33	18436572 [3]	7½°	Damper	Hydraulic [27]		[15]	[16]	⅛
	V8-440 Std. Tr. [30]	.035	.017	[26]	18436572 [3]	TDC	Damper	Hydraulic [27]		[15]	[16]	⅛
	V8-440 Auto. Tr. [30]	.035	.017	28–33	18436572 [3]	5°	Damper	Hydraulic [27]		[15]	[16]	⅛
	V8-440 Std. Trans.	.035	.017	28–33	18436572 [3]	TDC	Damper	Hydraulic [27]		[15]	[16]	⅛
	V8-440 Auto. Trans.	.035	.017	28–33	18436572 [3]	7½°	Damper	Hydraulic [27]		[15]	[16]	⅛
	V8-426	.035	.017	[26]	18436572 [3]	TDC	Damper	.028C	.032C	[15]	[16]	⅛

[1]—With Fluid Drive "O", others 2°.
[2]—Each set of points 26–28°, total dwell both sets 32–36°.
[3]—Cylinder numbering (front to rear): Left bank 1-3-5-7, right bank 2-4-6-8.
[4]—Each set of points 29–32°, total dwell both sets 36–39°.
[5]—Manual steering −2°, power steering 0°.
[6]—Left side +½°, right side 0°.
[7]—Manual steering −¾°, power steering +¾°.
[8]—Left side +⅜°, right side 0°.
[9]—With lifters collapsed.
[10]—Manual steering +¼, power steering +¾.

[11]—Left side +⅜°, right side +⅛°.
[12]—V8-383 Ram manifold 7½°, others 10°.
[13]—V8-318 .010H, V8-361, 383 .060–.210 w/lifters collapsed, V8-361, 383 Ram .016C.
[14]—V8-318 .018H, V8-361, 383 .060–.210 w/lifters collapsed, V8-361, 383 Ram .018C.
[15]—Manual steering −½, power steering +¾.
[16]—Left side +½°, right side +¼°.
[17]—Each set of points 27–32°. Total dwell both sets 34–40°.
[18]—Each set 27–31°, total dwell both sets 34–38°.
[19]—With N61Y plugs, 31° at 3000 R.P.M.; with N58R plugs, 34° at 3000 R.P.M.

[20]—Each set of points 27–31°; total dwell both sets 36–40°.
[21]—With Cleaner Air Package (CAP).
[22]—After top dead center.
[23]—Without CAP (cleaner air package).
[24]—Torqueflite.
[25]—Manual transmission.
[26]—Each set of points 27–32°; total dwell both sets 37–42°.
[27]—No adjustment.
[28]—Four barrel carb.
[29]—Two barrel carb.
[30]—High performance engine.

Year	Engine or Car Model	Spark Plug Gap	Distributor Point Gap	Distributor Dwell Angle	Firing Order	Ignition Timing BTDC or Mark	Ignition Timing Mark Location	Valve Lash Intake	Valve Lash Exhaust	Wheel Alignment Caster Degrees	Wheel Alignment Camber Degrees	Wheel Alignment Toe-In Inch

EDSEL

Year	Engine or Car Model	Spark Plug Gap	Point Gap	Dwell Angle	Firing Order	BTDC or Mark	Mark Location	Intake	Exhaust	Caster Degrees	Camber Degrees	Toe-In Inch
1958	Std. Trans.	.034	.015	26–28	15426378[1]	3°	Damper	Hydraulic		+1[2]	+1[3]	1/8
	Auto. Trans.	.034	.015	26–28	15426378[1]	6°	Damper	Hydraulic		+1[2]	+1[3]	1/8
1959–60	6 Cyl. Std. Tr.	.034	.025	35–38	153624	4°	Damper	.019H	.019H	+1/2	+1 1/4	1/8
	6 Cyl. Auto. Tr.	.034	.025	35–38	153624	6°	Damper	.019H	.019H	+1/2	+1 1/4	1/8
	V8-292 Std. Tr.	.034	.015	26–28	15486372[1]	3°	Damper	.019H	.019H	+1/2	+1 1/4	1/8
	V8-292 Auto. Tr.	.034	.015	26–28	15486372[1]	6°	Damper	.019H	.019H	+1/2	+1 1/4	1/8
	Other V8s Std. Tr.	.034	.015	26–28	15426378[1]	3°	Damper	Hydraulic		+1/2	+1 1/4	1/8
	Other V8s Auto. Tr.	.034	.015	26–28	15426378[1]	6°	Damper	Hydraulic		+1/2	+1 1/4	1/8

[1]—Cylinder numbering (front to rear): Right bank 1-2-3-4, left bank 5-6-7-8.
[2]—Corsair and Citation — 3/4°.
[3]—Corsair and Citation + 3/8°.

FORD & MERCURY—Compact & Intermediate Models

Year	Engine or Car Model	Spark Plug Gap	Point Gap	Dwell Angle	Firing Order	BTDC or Mark	Mark Location	Intake	Exhaust	Caster Degrees	Camber Degrees	Toe-In Inch
1960–61	6 Cyl. Std. Tr.	.034	.025	37–42	153624	4°	Pulley	.016H	.016H	+1/2	+1/2	1/4–5/16
	6 Cyl. Auto. Tr.	.034	.025	37–42	153624	10°	Pulley	.016H	.016H	+1/2	+1/2	1/4–5/16
1962	6 Cyl. Std. Tr.	.034	.025	37–42	153624	4°	Damper	.016H	.016H	[1]	+1/2	[3]
	6 Cyl. Auto. Tr.	.034	.025	37–42	153624	10°	Damper	.016H	.016H	[1]	+1/2	[3]
	V8-Std. Tr.	.034	.017	26–31	15426378[3]	4°	Damper	3/4 Turn[4]		Zero	+1/2	1/8
	V8-Auto Tr.	.034	.017	26–31	15426378[3]	12°	Damper	3/4 Turn[4]		Zero	+1/2	1/8
1963	6-144 Std. Tr.	.034	.025	37–42	153624	8°	Damper	.066–.216[5]		[1]	[6]	[7]
	6-144 Auto. Tr.	.034	.025	37–42	153624	12°	Damper	.066–.216[5]		[1]	[6]	[7]
	6-170 Std. Tr.	.034	.025	37–42	153624	6°	Damper	.066–.216[5]		[1]	[6]	[7]
	6-170 Auto. Tr.	.034	.025	37–42	153624	12°	Damper	.066–.216[5]		[1]	[6]	[7]
	V8-Std. Tr.	.034	.017	26–31	15426378[3]	6°	Damper	3/4 Turn[4]		[1]	[6]	[7]
	V8-Auto. Tr.	.034	.017	26–31	15426378[3]	10°	Damper	3/4 Turn[4]		[1]	[6]	[7]
1964	6-144 Std. Tr.	.034	.025	37–42	153624	8°	Damper	.066–.216[5]		+1/2	+1/2	[8]
	6-144 Auto. Tr.	.034	.025	37–42	153624	12°	Damper	.066–.216[5]		+1/2	+1/2	[8]
	6-170 Std. Tr.	.034	.025	37–42	153624	6°	Damper	.066–.216[5]		+1/2	+1/2	[8]
	6-170 Auto. Tr.	.034	.025	37–42	153624	12°	Damper	.066–.216[5]		+1/2	+1/2	[8]
	6-200 Std. Tr.	.034	.025	37–42	153624	6°	Damper	.066–.216[5]		+1/2	+1/2	[8]
	6-200 Auto. Tr.	.034	.025	37–42	153624	12°	Damper	.066–.216[5]		+1/2	+1/2	[8]
	V8-260 Std. Tr.	.034	.017	26–31	15426378[3]	6°	Damper	3/4 Turn[4]		+1/2	+1/2	[8]
	V8-260 Auto. Tr.	.034	.017	26–31	15426378[3]	10°	Damper	3/4 Turn[4]		+1/2	+1/2	[8]
	V8-289 Std. Tr.[23]	.034	.017	26–31	15426378[3]	6°	Damper	3/4 Turn[4]		+1/2	+1/2	[8]
	V8-289 Auto. Tr.[23]	.034	.017	26–31	15426378[3]	10°	Damper	3/4 Turn[4]		+1/2	+1/2	[8]
	V8-289 Hi. Perf.	.034	.020	33–36	15426378[3]	10°	Damper	.020H	.020H	+1/2	+1/2	[8]
1965	6-170 Std. Tr.	.034	.025	37–42	153624	6°	Damper	.066–.216[5]		[10]	[11]	[12]
	6-170 Auto. Tr.	.034	.025	37–42	153624	12°	Damper	.066–.216[5]		[10]	[11]	[12]
	6-200 Std. Tr.	.034	.025	37–42	153624	6°	Damper	.066–.216[5]		[10]	[11]	[12]
	6-200 Auto. Tr.	.034	.025	37–42	153624	12°	Damper	.066–.216[5][9]		[10]	[11]	[12]
	V8-260 Std. Tr.	.034	.017	26–31	15426378[3]	6°	Damper	3/4 Turn[4]		[10]	[11]	[12]
	V8-260 Auto. Tr.	.034	.017	26–31	15426378[3]	10°	Damper	3/4 Turn[4]		[10]	[11]	[12]
	V8-289[23]	.034	.017	26–31	15426378[3]	6°	Damper	3/4 Turn[4]		[10]	[11]	[12]
	V8-289 Hi. Perf.	.030	.020	30–33	15426378[3]	12°	Damper	.018H	.018H	[10]	[11]	[12]
1966	6-170, 200 Std. Tr.	.034	.025	37–42	153624	6°	Damper	.067–.200[5]		[13]	[14]	1/4
	6-170, 200 Auto. Tr.	.034	.025	37–42	153624	12°	Damper	.067–.200[5]		[13]	[14]	1/4
	6-170, 200[15]	.034	.025	37–42	153624	TDC	Damper	.067–.200[5]		[13]	[14]	1/4
	V8-289[23]	.034	.017	26–31	15426378[3]	6°	Damper	.067–.200[5]		Zero	[14]	1/4
	V8-289[15][23]	.034	.017	26–31	15426378[3]	TDC	Damper	.067–.200[5]		Zero	[14]	1/4
	V8-289 Hi. Perf.	.030	.020	30–33	15426378[3]	12°	Damper	.018H	.018H	Zero	[14]	1/4
	V8-390	.034	.017	26–31	15426378[3]	10°	Damper	.050–.150[16]		Zero	1/4	1/4
	V8-390[15]	.034	.017	26–31	15426378[3]	6°	Damper	.050–.150[16]		Zero	1/4	1/4
1967	6-170, 200 Std. Tr.	.034	.025	37–42	153624	6°	Damper	.066–.216[5]		[17]	[18]	[19]
	6-170, 200 Auto. Tr.	.034	.025	37–42	153624	12°	Damper	.066–.216[5]		[17]	[18]	[19]

Continued

Year	Engine or Car Model	Spark Plug Gap	Distributor		Firing Order	Ignition Timing		Valve Lash		Wheel Alignment		
			Point Gap	Dwell Angle		BTDC or Mark	Mark Location	Intake	Exhaust	Caster Degrees	Camber Degrees	Toe-In Inch

FORD & MERCURY—Compact & Intermediate Models—Continued

Year	Engine or Car Model	Spark Plug Gap	Point Gap	Dwell Angle	Firing Order	BTDC or Mark	Mark Location	Intake	Exhaust	Caster Degrees	Camber Degrees	Toe-In Inch
1967	6-170⑮	.034	.025	37–42	153624	TDC	Damper	.066–.216⑤		⑰	⑱	⑲
	6-200⑮	.034	.025	37–42	153624	5°	Damper	.066–.216⑤		⑰	⑱	⑲
	V8-289㉓	.034	.017	26–31	15426378③	6°	Damper	¾ Turn④		⑰	⑱	⑲
	V8-289⑮㉓	.034	.017	26–31	15426378③	TDC	Damper	¾ Turn④		⑰	⑱	⑲
	V8-289 Hi. Perf.	.030	.020	30–33	15426378③	12°	Damper	.018H	.018H	⑰	⑱	⑲
	V8-289 Hi. Perf.⑮	.030	.020	30–33	15426378③	6°	Damper	.018H	.018H	⑰	⑱	⑲
	V8-390	.034	.017	26–31	15426378③	10°	Damper	.100–.200⑤		⑰	⑱	⑲
	V8-390⑮	.034	.017	26–31	15426378③	6°	Damper	.100–.200⑤		⑰	⑱	⑲
1968	6-170	.034	.027	37–42	153624	6°	Damper	.066–.166⑤		⑰	㉑	⑲
	6-200	.034	.027	37–42	153624	6°	Damper	.066–.166⑤		⑰	㉑	⑲
	8-289 2 B. Carb.	.034	.021	24–29	15426378③	6°	Damper	¾ Turn④		⑰	㉑	⑲
	8-289 4 B. Carb.㉒	.034	.020	30–33	15426378③	6°	Damper	.018H	.018H	⑰	㉑	⑲
	8-302 2 B. Carb.	.034	.021	24–29	15426378③	6°	Damper	¾ Turn④		⑰	㉑	⑲
	8-302 4 B. Carb.⑮	.034	.021	30–33	15426378③	6°	Damper	¾ Turn④		⑰	㉑	⑲
	8-302 4 B. Carb.⑳	.034	.017	26–31	15426378③	6°	Damper	¾ Turn④		⑰	㉑	⑲
	8-390 2 B. Carb.⑮	.034	.021	30–33	15426378③	6°	Damper	.100–.200⑤		⑰	㉑	⑲
	8-390 2 B. Carb.⑳	.034	.017	26–31	15426378③	6°	Damper	.100–.200⑤		⑰	㉑	⑲
	8-390 4 B. Carb.⑮	.034	.021	30–33	15426378③	6°	Damper	.100–.200⑤		⑰	㉑	⑲
	8-390 4 B. Carb.⑳	.034	.017	26–31	15426378③	6°	Damper	.100–.200⑤		⑰	㉑	⑲
	8-390 "GT"	.034	.016	26–31	15426378③	6°	Damper	.100–.200⑤		⑰	㉑	⑲
	8-427	.034	.017	26–31	15426378③	6°	Damper	.100–.200⑤		⑰	㉑	⑲
	8-428 Cobra Jet	.034	.017	26–31	15426378③	6°	Damper	.100–.200⑤		⑰	㉑	⑲

①—Comet and Falcon +½°, Fairlane and Meteor zero.
②—Comet and Falcon ¼″–5⁄16″, Fairlane and Meteor ⅛″.
③—Cylinder numbering (front to rear): right bank 1-2-3-4, left bank 5-6-7-8.
④—Tighten rocker arm adjusting screw to eliminate all push rod end clearance, then tighten screw the number of turns listed.
⑤—Clearance is obtained at valve stem tip with hydraulic lifter collapsed. If clearance is less than the minimum install an undersize push rod; if greater than the maximum install an oversize push rod.
⑥—Comet and Falcon +⅜°, Fairlane zero, Meteor +½°.
⑦—Comet and Falcon ¼″–5⁄16″, Fairlane ¼″, Meteor ⅛″.
⑧—Comet and Falcon ¼″–5⁄16″, Fairlane 3⁄16″–5⁄16″.
⑨—Engines built after 3-29-65 clearance should be .067–.200″.
⑩—Comet and Falcon +¾°, Fairlane zero, Mustang (6 cyl. +1°, V8 zero).
⑪—Fairlane +¼°, all others +½°.
⑫—Comet ¼″, Falcon 9⁄32″, Fairlane and Mustang 7⁄32″.
⑬—Mustang +1°, all others zero.
⑭—Mustang +½°, all others +¼°.
⑮—With Thermactor Emission System.
⑯—Engines built after 12-20-65, .050″–.200″.
⑰—Cougar and Mustang +¼°, all others −½°.
⑱—Cougar and Mustang +1°, Falcon and Comet +¼°, Fairlane +½°.
⑲—Cougar and Mustang 3⁄16″, all others ¼″.
⑳—With I.M.C.O. system.
㉑—Cougar and Mustang +1°, all others +¼°.
㉒—High performance.
㉓—All except high performance.

Year	Engine or Car Model	Spark Plug Gap	Point Gap	Dwell Angle	Firing Order	BTDC or Mark	Mark Location	Intake	Exhaust	Caster Degrees	Camber Degrees	Toe-In Inch
			Distributor			Ignition Timing		Valve Lash		Wheel Alignment		

FORD & MERCURY—Full Size Models

Year	Engine or Car Model	Spark Plug Gap	Point Gap	Dwell Angle	Firing Order	BTDC or Mark	Mark Location	Intake	Exhaust	Caster Degrees	Camber Degrees	Toe-In Inch
1946–47	Six	.030	.015	36	153624	[1]	[1]	.014C	.014C	+6¾°	+⅝	1/16
	V8	.030	.015	36[2]	15486372[3]	[1]	[1]	.012C	.014C	+6¾°	+⅝	1/16
1948	Six	.030	.025	35	153624	Groove	Pulley	.014C	.014C	+6¾	+⅝	1/16
	V8	.030	.015	36[2]	15486372[3]	[1]	[1]	.012C	.014C	+6¾	+⅝	1/16
1949	Six	.030	.025	36	153624	Groove	Pulley	.010C	.014C	-¼	+½	1/8
	V8	.030	.015	28	15486372[3]	Groove	Pulley	[4]	[4]	-¼	+½	1/8
	V8[5]	.030	.015	28	15486372[3]	Groove	Pulley	.012C	.014C	Zero	+⅜	1/8
1950	Six	.030	.025	36	153624	Groove	Pulley	.010C	.014C	-¼	+½	3/16
	V8	.030	.015	28	15486372[3]	Groove	Pulley	.014C	.018C	-¼	+½	3/16
	V8[5]	.030	.015	28	15486372[3]	Groove	Pulley	.012C	.014C	Zero	+⅜	1/8
1951	Six	.030	.025	36	153624	Groove	Pulley	.010C	.014C	-¼	+½	3/16
	V8	.030	.025	28	15486372[3]	Groove	Pulley	.014C	.018C	[17]	[18]	[19]
1952–53	Six	.035	.025	36	153624	Groove	Damper	.015H	.015H	-½	+½	3/32
	V8	.030	.015	28	15486372[3]	Groove	Pulley	.014C	.018C	[20]	[21]	[22]
1954	Six	.035	.025	36	153624	3°	Damper	.015H	.015H	+½	+¾	3/32
	V8 Std. Trans.	.035	.015	28	15486372[3]	3°	Pulley	.019H	.019H	+½	+¾	3/32
	V8 Fordmatic	.035	.015	28	15486372[3]	6°	Pulley	.019H	.019H	+½	+¾	3/32
	V8[5]	.030	.015	28	15486372[3]	3°	Pulley	.018C	.018C	-¾	+⅜	1/8
1955	Six	.034	.025	35–38	153624	3°	Damper	.015H	.019H	+1	+¾	1/16-1/8
	V8 Std. Trans.	.034	.015	26–28	15486372[3]	3°	Damper	.019H	.019H	[23]	[24]	[25]
	V8 Fordmatic	.034	.015	26–28	15486372[3]	6°	Damper	.019H	.019H	[23]	[24]	[25]
1956	Six Std. Trans.	.034	.025	35–38	153624	4°	Damper	.019H	.019H	+1	+¾	1/16-1/8
	Six Fordmatic	.034	.025	35–38	153624	6°	Damper	.019H	.019H	+1	+¾	1/16-1/8
	V8 Std. Trans.	.034	.015	26–28	15486372[3]	3°	Damper	.019H	.019H	[23]	[24]	[25]
	V8 Fordmatic	.034	.015	26–28	15486372[3]	6°	Damper	.019H	.019H	[23]	[24]	[25]
1957	Six Std. Trans.	.034	.025	35–38	153624	4°	Damper	.019H	.019H	+1	+1	1/16-1/8
	Six Fordmatic	.034	.025	35–38	153624	6°	Damper	.019H	.019H	+1	+1	1/16-1/8
	V8 Std. Trans.	.034	.015	26–28	15486372[3]	3°	Damper	.019H	.019H	+1	+1	1/16-1/8
	V8 Fordmatic	.034	.015	26–28	15486372[3]	6°	Damper	.019H	.019H	+1	+1	1/16-1/8
	V8-312[5]	.034	.015	26–28	15486372[3]	6°	Damper	.019H	.019H	-¾	+⅜	3/16-5/16
	V8-368[5]	.034	.015	26–28	15486372[3]	8°	Damper	Zero	Zero	-¾	+⅜	3/16-5/16
1958	6-223 Std. Trans.	.034	.025	35–38	153624	4°	Damper	.019H	.019H	+½	+1	1/16-1/8
	6-223 Auto. Trans.	.034	.025	35–38	153624	6°	Damper	.019H	.019H	+½	+1	1/16-1/8
	V8-292 Std. Trans.	.034	.015	26–28	15486372[3]	3°	Damper	.019H	.019H	+½	+1	1/16-1/8
	V8-292 Auto. Trans.	.034	.015	26–28	15486372[3]	6°	Damper	.019H	.019H	+½	+1	1/16-1/8
	V8-332 Std. Trans.	.034	.015	26–28	15426378[3]	3°	Damper	.026H	.026H	+½	+1	1/16-1/8
	V8-332 Auto Trans.	.034	.015	26–28	15426378[3]	6°	Damper	.026H	.026H	+½	+1	1/16-1/8
	V8-312[5]	.034	.015	26–28	15486372[3]	[26]	Pulley	.019H	.019H	-¾	+⅜	3/16-5/16
	V8-383, 430[5]	.034	.015	26–28	15426378[3]	[27]	Damper	.078-.218[10]		-¾	+⅜	3/16-5/16
1959	6-223 Std. Trans.	.034	.025	37–42	153624	6°	Damper	.019H	.019H	+½	+1	1/32-1/8
	6-223 Auto. Trans.	.034	.025	37–42	153624	12°	Damper	.019H	.019H	+½	+1	1/32-1/8
	V8-292 Std. Trans.	.034	.017	26–31	15486372[3]	5°	Damper	.019H	.019H	+½	+1	1/32-1/8
	V8-292 Auto. Trans.	.034	.017	26–31	15486372[3]	12°	Damper	.019H	.019H	+½	+1	1/32-1/8
	V8-332 Std. Trans.	.034	.017	26–31	15426378[3]	5°	Damper	.062-.1875[10]		+½	+1	1/32-1/8
	V8-332 Auto. Trans.	.034	.017	26–31	15426378[3]	8°	Damper	.062-.1875[10]		+½	+1	1/32-1/8
	V8-352 Std. Trans.	.034	.017	26–31	15426378[3]	5°	Damper	.062-.1875[10]		+½	+1	1/32-1/8
	V8-352 Auto. Trans.	.034	.017	26–31	15426378[3]	8°	Damper	.062-.1875[10]		+½	+1	1/32-1/8
	V8-312[5]	.034	.017	26–31	15486372[3]	[26]	Damper	.019H	.019H	-¾	+⅜	1/16-3/16
	V8-383, 430[5]	.034	.017	26–31	15426378[3]	8°	Damper	.078-.218[10]		-¾	+⅜	1/16-3/16
1960	6-233 Std. Trans.	.034	.025	37–42	153624	6°	Damper	.019H	.019H	+⅝	+¾	1/8-1/4
	6-233 Auto. Trans.	.034	.025	37–42	153624	10°	Damper	.019H	.019H	+⅝	+¾	1/8-1/4
	V8-292 Std. Trans.	.034	.017	26–31	15486372[3]	5°	Damper	.019H	.019H	+⅝	+¾	1/8-1/4
	V8-292 Auto. Trans.	.034	.017	26–31	15486372[3]	12°	Damper	.019H	.019H	+⅝	+¾	1/8-1/4
	V8-352 Std. Trans.	.034	.017	26–31	15426378[3]	5°	Damper	.078-.218[10]		+⅝	+¾	1/8-1/4
	V8-352 Auto. Trans.	.034	.017	26–31	15426378[3]	8°	Damper	.078-.218[10]		+⅝	+¾	1/8-1/4

Continued

FORD & MERCURY—Full Size Models—Continued

Year	Engine or Car Model	Spark Plug Gap	Distributor Point Gap	Distributor Dwell Angle	Firing Order	Ignition Timing BTDC or Mark	Ignition Timing Mark Location	Valve Lash Intake	Valve Lash Exhaust	Wheel Alignment Caster Degrees	Wheel Alignment Camber Degrees	Wheel Alignment Toe-In Inch
1960	V8-312⑤	.034	.017	26-31	15486372③	㉖	Damper	.019H	.019H	-¾	+⅜	1/16-3/16
	V8-383, 430⑧	.034	.017	26-31	15426378③	8°	Damper	.078-.218⑩		-¾	+⅜	1/16-3/16
1961	6-233 Std. Trans.	.034	.025	37-42	153624	6°	Damper	.019H	.019H	Zero	+⅜	⅛-¼
	6-233 Auto. Trans.	.034	.025	37-42	153624	12°	Damper	.019H	.019H	Zero	+⅜	⅛-¼
	V8-292 Std. Trans.	.034	.017	26-31	15486372③	5°	Damper	.019H	.019H	Zero	+⅜	⅛-¼
	V8-292 Auto. Trans.	.034	.017	26-31	15486372③	12°	Damper	.019H	.019H	Zero	+⅜	⅛-¼
	V8-352, 390 Std. Tr.	.034	.017	26-31	15426378③	5°	Damper	.078-.218⑩		Zero	+⅜	⅛-¼
	V8-352, 390 Auto. Tr.	.034	.017	26-31	15426378③	8°	Damper	.078-.218⑩		Zero	+⅜	⅛-¼
	V8-390, 375 H.P.	.034	.020	26-31	15426378③	14°	Damper	.020H	.020H	Zero	+⅜	⅛-¼
	V8-390, 401 H.P.	.034	.020	26-31	15426378③	14°	Damper	.020H	.020H	Zero	+⅜	⅛-¼
1962	6-223 Std. Trans.	.034	.025	37-42	153624	6°	Damper	.025H	.025H	Zero	+⅜	⅛-¼
	6-223 Auto. Trans.	.034	.025	37-42	153624	12°	Damper	.025H	.025H	Zero	+⅜	⅛-¼
	V8-292 Std. Trans.	.034	.017	26-31	15486372③	5°	Damper	.019H	.019H	Zero	+⅜	⅛-¼
	V8-292 Auto. Trans.	.034	.017	26-31	15486372③	12°	Damper	.019H	.019H	Zero	+⅜	⅛-¼
	V8-352, 390 Std. Tr.	.034	.017	26-31	15426378③	5°	Damper	.078-.218⑩		Zero	+⅜	⅛-¼
	V8-352, 390 Auto. Tr.	.034	.017	26-31	15426378③	8°	Damper	.078-.218⑩		Zero	+⅜	⅛-¼
	V8-390, 375 H.P.	.034	.020	26-31	15426378③	5°	Damper	.025H	.025H	Zero	+⅜	⅛-¼
	V8-390, 401 H.P.	.034	.020	26-31	15426378③	5°	Damper	.025H	.025H	Zero	+⅜	⅛-¼
	V8-406, 385 H.P.	.034	.020	26-31	15426378③	8°	Damper	.025H	.025H	Zero	+⅜	⅛-¼
	V8-406, 405 H.P.	.034	.020	26-31	15426378③	8°	Damper	.025H	.025H	Zero	+⅜	⅛-¼
1963	6-223 Std. Trans.	.034	.025	37-42	153624	4°	Damper	.025H⑧	.025H⑧	Zero	+⅜	⅛-¼
	6-223 Auto. Trans.	.034	.025	37-42	153624	10°	Damper	.025H⑧	.025H⑧	Zero	+⅜	⅛-¼
	V8-260 Std. Trans.	.034	.017	26-31	15426378③	6°	Damper	¾ Turn⑨		Zero	+⅜	⅛-¼
	V8-260 Auto. Trans.	.034	.017	26-31	15426378③	10°	Damper	¾ Turn⑨		Zero	+⅜	⅛-¼
	V8-289 Std. Trans.	.034	.017	26-31	15426378③	6°	Damper	¾ Turn⑨		Zero	+⅜	⅛-¼
	V8-289 Auto. Trans.	.034	.017	26-31	15426378③	10°	Damper	¾ Turn⑨		Zero	+⅜	⅛-¼
	V8-352 Std. Trans.	.034	.017	26-31	15426378③	5°	Damper	.083-.183⑩		Zero	+⅜	⅛-¼
	V8-352 Auto. Trans.	.034	.017	26-31	15426378③	8°	Damper	.083-.183⑩		Zero	+⅜	⅛-¼
	V8-390, Std. Trans.⑥	.034	.017	26-31	15426378③	5°	Damper	.083-.183⑩		Zero	+⅜	⅛-¼
	V8-390 Auto. Trans.⑥	.034	.017	26-31	15426378③	8°	Damper	.083-.183⑩		Zero	+⅜	⅛-¼
	V8-390⑦	.034	.017	26-31	15426378③	6°	Damper	.083-.183⑩		Zero	+⅜	⅛-¼
	V8-390, 330 H.P.	.034	.017	26-31	15426378③	10°	Damper	.025H	.025H	Zero	+⅜	⅛-¼
	V8-406, 427	.035	.017	26-31	15426378③	5°	Damper	.025H	.025H	Zero	+⅜	⅛-¼
	V8-406, 427 2 Carbs.	.034	.017	26-31	15426378③	8°	Damper	.025H	.025H	Zero	+⅜	⅛-¼
1964	6-223 Std. Trans.	.034	.025	37-42	153624	4°	Damper	.025H⑧	.025H⑧	Zero	+⅝	⅛-¼
	6-223 Auto. Trans.	.034	.025	37-42	153624	10°	Damper	.025H⑧	.025H⑧	Zero	+⅝	⅛-¼
	V8-289 Std. Trans.	.034	.017	26-31	15426378③	6°	Damper	¾ Turn⑨		Zero	+⅝	⅛-¼
	V8-289 Auto. Trans.	.034	.017	26-31	15426378③	10°	Damper	¾ Turn⑨		Zero	+⅝	⅛-¼
	V8-352 Std. Trans.	.034	.017	26-31	15426378③	6°	Damper	⑪		Zero	+⅝	⅛-¼
	V8-352 Auto. Trans.	.034	.017	26-31	15426378③	10°	Damper	⑪		Zero	+⅝	⅛-¼
	V8-390 Std. Trans.	.034	.017	26-31	15426378③	4°	Damper	⑪		Zero	+⅝	⅛-¼
	V8-390 Auto. Trans.	.034	.017	26-31	15426378③	6°	Damper	⑪		Zero	+⅝	⅛-¼
	V8-390 Std. Trans.⑫	.034	.017	26-31	15426378③	4°	Damper	.025H	.025H	Zero	+⅝	⅛-¼
	V8-390 Auto. Trans.⑫	.034	.017	26-31	15426378③	6°	Damper	.025H	.025H	Zero	+⅝	⅛-¼
	V8-427	.034	.017	26-31	15426378③	8°	Damper	.025H	.025H	Zero	+⅝	⅛-¼
1965	6-240 Std. Trans.	.034	.025	37-42	153624	6°	Damper	¾ Turn⑨		+1	+½	5/32
	6-240 Auto. Trans.	.034	.025	37-42	153624	8°	Damper	¾ Turn⑨		+1	+½	5/32
	V8-289	.034	.017	26-31	15426378③	6°	Damper	¾ Turn⑨		+1	+½	5/32
	V8-352	.034	.017	26-31	15426378③	6°	Damper	.050-.150⑩		+1	+½	5/32
	V8-390⑦⑥	.034	.017	26-31	15426378③	6°⑩	Damper	.050-.150⑩		+1	+½	3/16
	V8-390 Std. Trans.	.034	.017	26-31	15426378③	4°	Damper	.050-.150⑩		+1	+½	㉘
	V8-390 Auto. Trans.	.034	.017	26-31	15426378③	6°⑩	Damper	.050-.150⑩		+1	+½	㉘
	V8-390 Std. Trans.⑫	.034	.017	26-31	15426378③	4°	Damper	.025H	.025H	+1	+½	㉘
	V8-390 Auto. Trans.⑫	.034	.017	26-31	15426378③	6°⑩	Damper	.025H	.025H	+1	+½	㉘
	V8-427	.030	.020	⑬	15426378③	8°	Damper	.025H	.025H	+1	+½	㉘

Continued

FORD & MERCURY—Full Size Models—Continued

Year	Engine or Car Model	Spark Plug Gap	Distributor		Firing Order	Ignition Timing		Valve Lash		Wheel Alignment		
			Point Gap	Dwell Angle		BTDC or Mark	Mark Location	Intake	Exhaust	Caster Degrees	Camber Degrees	Toe-In Inch
1966	6-240 Std. Trans.	.034	.025	37-42	153624	6°	Damper	¾ Turn⑨		+½	+¼	³⁄₁₆
	6-240 Auto Trans.	.034	.025	37-42	153624	12°	Damper	¾ Turn⑨		+½	+¼	³⁄₁₆
	6-240 Std. Trans.⑭	.034	.025	37-42	153624	TDC	Damper	¾ Turn⑨		+½	+¼	³⁄₁₆
	6-240 Auto. Trans.⑭	.034	.025	37-42	153624	4°	Damper	¾ Turn⑨		+½	+¼	³⁄₁₆
	V8-289	.034	.017	26-31	15426378③	6°	Damper	¾ Turn⑨		+½	+¼	³⁄₁₆
	V8-289⑭	.034	.017	26-31	15426378③	TDC	Damper	¾ Turn⑨		+½	+¼	³⁄₁₆
	V8-352, 390, 428	.034	.017	26-31	15426378③	10°⑯	Damper	.050-.150⑩⑮		+½	+¼	³⁄₁₆
	V8-352, 390, 428⑭	.034	.017	26-31	15426378③	6°⑯	Damper	.050-.150⑩⑮		+½	+¼	³⁄₁₆
	V8-410⑤	.034	.017	26-31	15426378③	10°⑯	Damper	.050-.150⑩⑮		+½	+¼	³⁄₁₆
	V8-410⑤⑭	.034	.017	26-31	15426378③	6°⑯	Damper	.050-.150⑩⑮		+½	+¼	³⁄₁₆
	V8-427	.030	.020	22-24	15426378③	10°	Damper	.025H	.025H	+½	+¼	³⁄₁₆
1967	6-240 Std. Trans.	.034	.025	37-42	153624	6°	Damper	¾ Turn⑨		+1	+½	³⁄₁₆
	6-240 Auto. Trans.	.034	.025	37-42	153624	10°	Damper	¾ Turn⑨		+1	+½	³⁄₁₆
	6-240 Std. Trans.⑭	.034	.025	37-42	153624	TDC	Damper	¾ Turn⑨		+1	+½	³⁄₁₆
	6-240 Auto. Trans.⑭	.034	.025	37-42	153624	4°	Damper	¾ Turn⑨		+1	+½	³⁄₁₆
	V8-289	.034	.017	26-31	15426378③	6°	Damper	¾ Turn⑨		+1	+½	³⁄₁₆
	V8-289⑭	.034	.017	26-31	15426378③	TDC	Damper	¾ Turn⑨		+1	+½	³⁄₁₆
	V8-390,410, 428	.034	.017	26-31	15426378③	10°⑯	Damper	.100-.200⑩		+1	+½	³⁄₁₆
	V8-390, 410, 428⑭	.034	.017	26-31	15426378③	6°⑯	Damper	.100-.200⑩		+1	+½	³⁄₁₆
	V8-427	.030	.020	22-24	15426378③	8°	Damper	.025H	.025H	+1	+½	³⁄₁₆
1968	6-240	.034	.027	35-40	153624	6°	Damper	¾ Turn⑨		+1	+½	³⁄₁₆
	V8-302	.034	.021	24-29	15426378③	6°	Damper	¾ Turn⑨		+1	+½	³⁄₁₆
	V8-390 Std. Trans.⑭	.034	.017	26-31	15426378③	6°	Damper	.100-.200⑩		+1	+½	³⁄₁₆
	V8-390 Auto. Trans.㉖	.034	.021	26-31	15426378③	6°	Damper	.100-.200⑩		+1	+½	³⁄₁₆
	V8-428 Std. Trans.⑭	.034	.017	26-31	15426378③	6°	Damper	.100-.200⑩		+1	+½	³⁄₁₆
	V8-428 Auto. Trans.㉖	.034	.021	24-29	15426378③	6°	Damper	.100-.200⑩		+1	+½	³⁄₁₆
	V8-427	.034	.017	26-31	15426378③	6°	Damper	.100-.200⑩		+1	+½	³⁄₁₆

①—There are no timing marks. Spark can be advanced or retarded by adjusting the vacuum brake set screw on distributor housing.

②—Total dwell for both breakers.

③—Cylinder numbering (front to rear): Right bank 1-2-3-4, left bank 5-6-7-8.

④—Up to Serial No. 8BA-622468: intake .012C, exhaust .014C. Later cars, intake .014C, exhaust .018C.

⑤—Used on Mercury models.

⑥—Four barrel carburetor.

⑦—Two barrel carburetor.

⑧—"Silent Lash"—Clearance specified is obtained at valve stem tip with eccentric spring compressed.

⑨—Tighten rocker arm adjusting screw to eliminate all push rod end clearance, then tighten screw the number of turns listed.

⑩—Clearance specified is obtained at valve stem tip with hydraulic lifter collapsed.

⑪—Before 11-18-63 .083-.183", from 11-18-63 .050-.150" (see note ⑩).

⑫—High performance.

⑬—Conventional ignition 30-33°, transistor ignition 22-24°.

⑭—With Thermactor Emission System.

⑮—Engines built after 12-20-65, .050-.200".

⑯—Whenever idle speed or ignition timing is adjusted, vacuum line to brake release mechanism (if equipped) must be disconnected and vacuum hole plugged to prevent parking brake from releasing when selector lever is moved to Drive.

⑰—Ford —¼°, Mercury zero.

⑱—Ford +½°, Mercury +⅜°.

⑲—Ford ³⁄₁₆", Mercury ⅛".

⑳—Ford —½°, Mercury —¾°.

㉑—Ford +½°, Mercury +⅜°.

㉒—Ford ³⁄₃₂", Mercury ⅛".

㉓—Ford +1°, Mercury —¾°.

㉔—Ford +¾°, Mercury +⅜°.

㉕—Ford ¹⁄₁₆" to ⅛", Mercury ³⁄₃₂" to ⁵⁄₃₂".

㉖—Standard transmission 3°, automatic transmission 6°.

㉗—V8-383-4°, V8-430-7°.

㉘—Ford ⁵⁄₃₂", Mercury ³⁄₁₆".

㉙—With I.M.C.O.

Year	Engine or Car Model	Spark Plug Gap	Distributor Point Gap	Distributor Dwell Angle	Firing Order	Ignition Timing BTDC or Mark	Ignition Timing Mark Location	Valve Lash Intake	Valve Lash Exhaust	Wheel Alignment Caster Degrees	Wheel Alignment Camber Degrees	Wheel Alignment Toe-In Inch

FORD THUNDERBIRD

Year	Engine or Car Model	Spark Plug Gap	Point Gap	Dwell Angle	Firing Order	BTDC or Mark	Mark Location	Intake	Exhaust	Caster Degrees	Camber Degrees	Toe-In Inch
1955–56	All Models	.034	.015	26–28	15486372(1)	(2)	Damper	.019H	.019H	+1	+3/4	1/16–1/8
1957	All Models	.034	.015	26–28	15486372(1)	(2)	Damper	.019H	.019H	+1	+1	1/16–1/8
1958	All Models	.034	.015	26–28	15426378(1)	(2)	Damper	.062–.1875(3)		+1	+1	1/16–1/8
1959	All Models	.034	.017	26–31	15426378(1)	(4)	Damper	(5)		+1	+1	1/16–1/8
1960	All Models	.034	.017	26–31	15426378(1)	(4)	Damper	.078–.218(3)		+1	+1	1/16–1/8
1961	All Models	.034	.017	26–31	15426378(1)	8°	Damper	.078–.218(3)		+1/2	+1/2	1/16–1/8
1962	V8-390	.034	.017	26–31	15426378(1)	6°	Damper	.100–.200(3)		−1/2	+1/2	1/16–1/8
	V8-429	.035	.017	26–31	15426378(1)	6°	Damper	.075–.175(3)		−1/2	+1/2	1/16–1/8
1963	V8-390	.034	.017	26–31	15426378(1)	6°	Damper	.083–.183(3)		−1 1/2	+3/8	1/8–1/4
1964	V8-390	.034	.017(6)	26–31(7)	15426378(1)	6°	Damper	(8)		−1 1/2	+3/8	1/8–1/4
1965	V8-390	.034	.017(6)	26–31(7)	15426378(1)	6°(9)	Damper	.050–.150(3)		−1 1/2	+1/2	1/32–9/32
1966	L/Thermactor	.034	.017(6)	26–31(7)	15426378(1)	10°(9)	Damper	.050–.150(3)		−1 1/2	+1/2	3/16
	W/Thermactor	.034	.016(6)	26–31(7)	15426378(1)	6°(9)	Damper	.050–.150(3)		−1 1/2	+1/2	3/16
1967	L/Thermactor	.034	.017	26–31	15426378(1)	10°(9)	Damper	.100–.200(3)		+1/2	+1	3/16
	W/Thermactor	.034	.017	26–31	15426378(1)	6°(9)	Damper	.100–.200(3)		+1/2	+1	3/16
1968	8-390	.034	.017	26–31	15426378(1)	6°(5)	Damper	.100–.200(3)		+1	+1/2	3/16
	8-429	.034	.017	26–31	15426378(1)	6°(5)	Damper	.075–.125(10)		+1	+1/2	3/16

(1)—Cylinder numbering (front to rear): Right bank 1-2-3-4, left bank 5-6-7-8.
(2)—Standard transmission 3°, Fordomatic 6°.
(3)—Clearance specified is obtained at valve stem with lifter collapsed.
(4)—Standard transmission 5°, automatic transmission 8°.
(5)—V8-352 (.078–.218(3)), V8-430 (.126–.226(3)).
(6)—With transistor ignition .020″.
(7)—With transistor ignition 22–24°.
(8)—Engines built prior to Nov. 18, 1963 .083–.183″(3); engines built from Nov. 18, 1963 .050–.150″(3).
(9)—Whenever idle speed or ignition timing is adjusted, vacuum line to brake release mechanism must be disconnected and plugged to prevent parking brake from releasing when selector is moved to Drive.
(10)—One turn down after contact.

HENRY J

Year	Engine or Car Model	Spark Plug Gap	Point Gap	Dwell Angle	Firing Order	BTDC or Mark	Mark Location	Intake	Exhaust	Caster Degrees	Camber Degrees	Toe-In Inch
1951–54	Four Cyl.	.030	.020	44–47	1342	5°	Flywheel	.014C	.014C	Zero	+1/2	1/4
	Six Cyl.	.030	.020	35–38	153624	TDC	Damper	.014C	.014C	Zero	+1/2	1/4

HUDSON

Year	Engine or Car Model	Spark Plug Gap	Point Gap	Dwell Angle	Firing Order	BTDC or Mark	Mark Location	Intake	Exhaust	Caster Degrees	Camber Degrees	Toe-In Inch
1946–47	Six Cyl.	.032	.020	35–38	153624	(1)	Flywheel	.010H	.012H	+1	+1	1/32
	Eight Cyl.	.032	.017	27–30	16258374	TDC	Flywheel	.006H	.008H	+1	+1	1/32
1948–49	Six Cyl.	.032	.020	35–38	153624	UDC 1-6	Flywheel	.010H	.012H	+1	+1	1/32
	Eight Cyl.	.032	.017	27–30	16258374	UDC 1-8	Flywheel	.006H	.008H	+1	+1	1/32
1950–52	Six Cyl.	.032	.020	35–38	153624	UDC 1-6	Flywheel	.008H	.010H	+1	+1	1/32
	Eight Cyl.	.032	.017	27–30	16258374	UDC 1-8	Flywheel	.008H	.010H	+1	+1	1/32
1953–54	Jets	.032	.020	39	153624	(2)	Damper	.010H	.012H	+1	+3/4	1/32
	Wasps, Hornet	.032	.020	39	153624	UDC 1-6	Flywheel	.008H	.010H	+1	+3/4	1/32
1955	Wasp	.032	.020	39	153624	Line	Damper	.010C	.014C	(5)	Zero	1/16–3/16
	Hornet 6	.032	.020	39	153624	UDC 1-6	Flywheel	.010C	.014C	(5)	Zero	1/16–3/16
	Hornet V8	.035	.017	38	18436572(4)	5°	Damper	Zero	Zero	(5)	Zero	1/16–3/16
1956	Wasp	.032	.020	39	153624	Line	Damper	.010C	.014C	(5)	Zero	1/16–3/16
	Hornet 6	.030	.020	39	153624	UDC 1-6	Flywheel	Zero	Zero	(5)	Zero	1/16–3/16
	Hornet V8	.035	.017	(6)	18436572(4)	5°	Damper	Zero	Zero	(5)	Zero	1/16–3/16
	Special	.035	.016	26–33	18436572(4)	5°	Damper	Zero	Zero	(5)	Zero	1/16–3/16
1957	All Models	.035	.016	28–32	18436572(4)	5°	Damper	Zero	Zero	(5)	Zero	1/16–3/16

(1)—1/2″ before DC mark.
(2)—Long line before "1 UDC" mark.
(4)—Cylinder numbering (front to rear): Left bank 1-3-5-7, right bank 2-4-6-8.
(5)—Manual steering +1/2°, power steering +1°.
(6)—Dual breaker units 38°, single breaker 31°.

IMPERIAL

Year	Engine or Car Model	Spark Plug Gap	Distributor Point Gap	Distributor Dwell Angle	Firing Order	Ignition Timing BTDC or Mark	Ignition Timing Mark Location	Valve Lash Intake	Valve Lash Exhaust	Wheel Alignment Caster Degrees	Wheel Alignment Camber Degrees	Wheel Alignment Toe-In Inch
1946-48	All Models	.025	.017	27-30	16258374	2°	Damper	.008H	.010H	Zero	+3/8	1/32
1949-50	All Models	.035	.017	27-30	16258374	"O"	Damper	.008H(3)	.010H(3)	-2	+3/8	1/32
1951-54	All Models	.035	.017	(1)	18436572(2)	"O"	Damper	Zero	Zero	-2	Zero	Zero
1955	All Models	.035	.017	(1)	18436572(2)	6°	Damper	Zero	Zero	(6)	(7)	0-1/16
1956	All Models	.035	.017	(4)	18436572(2)	4°	Damper	Zero	Zero	(6)	(7)	1/8
1957	All Models	.035	.017	(5)	18436572(2)	6°	Damper	Zero	Zero	(8)	(9)	3/32-5/32
1958	All Models	.035	.017	(5)	18436572(2)	6°	Damper	.060-.210(10)		(11)	(9)	3/32-5/32
1959	All Models	.035	.017	(12)	18436572(2)	10°	Damper	.060-.210(10)		-3/4	(9)	1/8
1960	All Models	.035	.017	27-32	18436572(2)	10°	Damper	.060-.210(10)		(8)	(7)	1/8
1961-63	All Models	.035	.017	27-32	18436572(2)	10°(15)	Damper	.060-.210(10)		(13)	(14)	1/8
1964	All Models	.035	.017	28-33	18436572(2)	10°(15)	Damper	.060-.210(10)		(13)	(14)	1/8
1965	All Models	.035	.017	28-32	18436572(2)	10°(15)	Damper	.060-.210(10)		(13)	(14)	1/8
1966	All Models	.035	.017	28-32	18436572(2)	12 1/2°(15)	Damper	.060-.210(10)		(13)	(14)	1/8
	All Models(16)	.035	.017	28-32	18436572(2)	5°(17)(15)	Damper	.060-.210(10)		(13)	(14)	1/8
1967	V8-383(18)	.035	.017	28-32	18436572(2)	12 1/2°	Damper	Hydraulic(21)		(13)	(14)	1/8
	V8-383(16)(19)	.035	.017	28-32	18436572(2)	5°	Damper	Hydraulic(21)		(13)	(14)	1/8
	V8-383(16)(20)	.035	.017	28-32	18436572(2)	TDC	Damper	Hydraulic(21)		(13)	(14)	1/8
	V8-440(18)	.035	.017	28-32	18436572(2)	12 1/2°(15)	Damper	Hydraulic(21)		(13)	(14)	1/8
	V8-440(16)(17)	.035	.017	28-32	18436572(2)	5°(15)	Damper	Hydraulic(21)		(13)	(14)	1/8
1968	V8-440 Auto. Trans.	.035	.017	28-33	18436572(2)	7 1/2°	Damper	Hydraulic(21)		(13)	(14)	1/8

①—Each set of points 26-28°, total dwell both sets 32-36°.
②—Cylinder numbering (front to rear): Left bank 1-3-5-7, right bank 2-4-6-8.
③—Zero lash with hydraulic valve lifters.
④—Each set of points 29-32°, total dwell both sets 32-36°.
⑤—Each set of points 29-32°, total dwell both sets 36-39°.
⑥—Manual steering -2°, power steering 0°.
⑦—Left side +3/8°, right side +1/8°.
⑧—Manual steering -3/4°, power steering +3/4°.
⑨—Left side +3/8°, right side 0°.
⑩—With lifter collapsed.
⑪—Manual steering -3/4°, power steering 0°.
⑫—Each set of points 27-32°. Total dwell both sets 34-40°.
⑬—Manual steering -1/2°, power steering +3/4°.
⑭—Left side +1/2°, right side +1/4°.
⑮—Whenever idle speed or ignition timing is adjusted, vacuum line to brake release mechanism must be disconnected and plugged to prevent parking brake from releasing when selector lever is moved to Drive. Set idle speed with A/C compressor operating.
⑯—With Cleaner Air Package (CAP).
⑰—After top dead center.
⑱—Without CAP (cleaner air package).
⑲—Torqueflite.
⑳—Manual transmission.
㉑—No adjustment.

KAISER-FRAZER

Year	Engine or Car Model	Spark Plug Gap	Distributor Point Gap	Distributor Dwell Angle	Firing Order	Ignition Timing BTDC or Mark	Ignition Timing Mark Location	Valve Lash Intake	Valve Lash Exhaust	Wheel Alignment Caster Degrees	Wheel Alignment Camber Degrees	Wheel Alignment Toe-In Inch
1947-48	All Models	.032	.020	35-38	153624	"O"(1)	Damper(1)	.014C(2)	.014C	Zero	+3/8	1/16
1949-50	All Models	.032	.020	35-38	153624	4°	Damper	.014C	.014C	Zero	+3/8	1/16
1951-53	All Models	.032	.020	35-38	153624	4°	Damper	.014C	.014C	Zero	+1/2	1/8
1954	All Models	.030	.016	38-45	153624	4°	Damper	.014C	.014C	Zero	+1/2	1/8

①—Early models TDC mark on flywheel. ②—Up to Eng. No. 10769, .010H.

LINCOLN CONTINENTAL

Year	Engine or Car Model	Spark Plug Gap	Distributor Point Gap	Distributor Dwell Angle	Firing Order	Ignition Timing BTDC or Mark	Ignition Timing Mark Location	Valve Lash Intake	Valve Lash Exhaust	Wheel Alignment Caster Degrees	Wheel Alignment Camber Degrees	Wheel Alignment Toe-In Inch
1946-48	All Models	.028	.015	36	(1)	(3)	(3)	Zero	Zero	+4	+7/8	3/32
1949-51	All Models	.030	.015	28	15486372(2)	Mark	Damper	Zero	Zero	Zero	+3/8	1/8
1952-54	All Models	.030	.015	28	15486372(2)	3°	Damper	Zero	Zero	-3/4	+3/8	1/8
1955	All Models	.034	.015	26-28	15486372(2)	5°	Damper	Zero	Zero	-3/4	+3/8	3/32-5/32
1956-57	All Models	.034	.015	26-28	15486372(2)	5°	Damper	Zero	Zero	-3/4	+3/8	1/8-3/16
1958	All Models	.034	.015	26-28	15426378(2)	6°	Damper	.078-.218(4)		-3/4	+3/8	1/8-3/16
1959-62	All Models	.034	.017	26-31	15426378(2)	(5)	Damper	.078-.218(4)		-3/4	+3/8	(6)
1963	All Models	.034	.017	26-31	15426378(2)	8°	Damper	.078-.178(4)		-1 1/2	+1/2	1/8-1/4
1964	All Models	(7)	(8)	(9)	15426378(2)	8°	Damper	.078-.178(4)		-1 1/2	+1/2	1/8-1/4
1965	All Models	(7)	(8)	(9)	15426378(2)	6°(10)	Damper	.050-.150(4)		-1 1/2	+3/4	1/32-9/32
1966	All Models	(7)	(8)	(9)	15426378(2)	10°(10)	Damper	.050-.150(4)		-1 1/2	+1/2	1/8
	All Models(11)	.034	.017	26-31	15426378(2)	10°(10)	Damper	.050-.150(4)		-1 1/2	+1/2	1/8
1967	All Models	.034	.017	26-31	15426378(2)	10°(10)	Damper	.083-.183(4)		-1 1/2	+1/2	1/8
	All Models(11)	.034	.017	26-31	15426378(2)	10°(10)	Damper	.083-.183(4)		-1 1/2	+1/2	1/8

Continued

Year	Engine or Car Model	Spark Plug Gap	Point Gap	Dwell Angle	Firing Order	BTDC or Mark	Mark Location	Intake	Exhaust	Caster Degrees	Camber Degrees	Toe-In Inch

LINCOLN CONTINENTAL—Continued

Year	Engine or Car Model	Spark Plug Gap	Point Gap	Dwell Angle	Firing Order	BTDC or Mark	Mark Location	Intake	Exhaust	Caster Degrees	Camber Degrees	Toe-In Inch
1968	V8-460⑫	.034	.017	26–31	15426378②	10°⑩	Damper	.083–.183④		−1½	+½	⅛
	V8-462⑫	.034	.017	26–31	15426378②	10°⑩	Damper	.075–.175⑬		−1½	+½	⅛

①—Cylinder numbering (front to rear): Left bank 1-3-5-7-9-11, right bank 2-4-6-8-10-12. Firing order 1-4-9-8-5-2-11-10-3-6-7-12.
②—Cylinder numbering (front to rear): Right bank 1-2-3-4, left bank 5-6-7-8.
③—There are no timing marks. Spark may be advanced or retarded by adjusting vacuum brake set screw on distributor housing.
④—With rocker arm rotated to collapse lifter, the clearance listed should exist between end of valve stem and rocker arm.
⑤—1959 6°, 1960-62 8°.
⑥—1959-60 ⅛-³⁄₁₆, 1961-62 ¹⁄₁₆-³⁄₁₆.
⑦—Conventional ignition .034", Transistor ignition .030".
⑧—Conventional ignition .017", Transistor ignition .020".
⑨—Conventional ignition 26–31°, Transistor ignition 22–24°.
⑩—Whenever idle speed or ignition timing is adjusted, vacuum line to brake release mechanism must be disconnected and plugged to prevent parking brake from releasing when selector is moved to Drive.
⑪—With Thermactor Emission System.
⑫—With I.M.C.O.
⑬—Valve lifter adjustment is 1 turn down after contact. Check as described in note④.

NASH

Year	Engine or Car Model	Spark Plug Gap	Point Gap	Dwell Angle	Firing Order	BTDC or Mark	Mark Location	Intake	Exhaust	Caster Degrees	Camber Degrees	Toe-In Inch
1946-48	"600" 6	.025	.020	35–38	153624	IGN	Damper	.015H	.015H	+½	+½	⁵⁄₃₂
	Ambassador	.025	.020	35–38	153624	IGN	Damper	.015H	.015H	−¼	+½	¹⁄₁₆
1949	"600" 6	.030	.022	31–37	153624	IGN	Damper	.015H	.015H	+¼	Zero	⅛
	Ambassador	.025	.022	31–37	153624	IGN	Damper	.015H	.015H	+¼	Zero	⅛
1950	Rambler	.030	.022	31–37	153624	TDC	Damper	.016C	.018C	+1	+½	¼
	Statesman	.030	.022	31–37	153624	TDC	Damper	.016C	.018C	+¼	Zero	⅛
	Ambassador	.030	.022	31–37	153624	TDC	Damper	.012H	.016H	+¼	Zero	⅛
1951	Rambler	.030	.022	31–37	153624	TDC	Damper	.016C	.018C	+1	+½	¼
	Statesman	.030	.022	31–37	153624	TDC	Damper	.016C	.018C	Zero	Zero	⅛
	Ambassador	.030	.022	31–37	153624	TDC	Damper	.012H	.016H	Zero	Zero	⅛
1952-54	Rambler	.030	.022	31–37	153624	4°③	Damper	.016C	.018C	+1	+½	¼
	Statesman	.030	.022	31–37	153624	4°③	Damper	.016C	.018C	+¼	Zero	⅛
	Ambassador	.030	.022	31–37	153624	TDC	Damper	.012H	.016H	+¼	Zero	⅛
1955	Statesman	.030	.022	31	153624	4°③	Damper	.016C	.018C	+½②	Zero	¹⁄₁₆-³⁄₁₆
	Ambassador 6	.030	.016	38–45	153624	4°③	Damper	.012H	.016H	+½②	Zero	¹⁄₁₆-³⁄₁₆
	Ambassador V8	.035	.017	38	18436572①	5°	Damper	Zero	Zero	+½②	Zero	¹⁄₁₆-³⁄₁₆
1956	Statesman 6	.030	.016	28–35	153624	4°③	Damper	.012H	.016H	+½②	Zero	¹⁄₁₆-³⁄₁₆
	Amb. Spec. V8	.035	.016	26–33	18436572①	5°	Damper	Zero	Zero	+½②	Zero	¹⁄₁₆-³⁄₁₆
	Ambassador 6	.030	.020	39	153624	4°③	Damper	.012H	.016H	+½②	Zero	¹⁄₁₆-³⁄₁₆
	Ambassador V8	.035	.017	31	18436572①	5°	Damper	Zero	Zero	+½②	Zero	¹⁄₁₆-³⁄₁₆
1957	Ambassador V8	.035	.016	30	18436572①	5°	Damper	Zero	Zero	+½②	Zero	¹⁄₁₆-³⁄₁₆

①—Cylinder numbering (front to rear): Left bank 1-3-5-7, right bank 2-4-6-8.
②—With power steering +¾°.
③—After top dead center.

OLDSMOBILE—All Intermediate & Full Size Models

Year	Engine or Car Model	Spark Plug Gap	Point Gap	Dwell Angle	Firing Order	BTDC or Mark	Mark Location	Intake	Exhaust	Caster Degrees	Camber Degrees	Toe-In Inch
1946-48	Six Cyl.	.040	.022	31–37	153624	TDC	Flywheel	.008H	.011H	−⅜	+¼	³⁄₃₂
	Eight Cyl.	.030	.016	21–30	16258374	Ball	Flywheel	.008H	.011H	−⅜	+¼	³⁄₃₂
1949-50	Six Cyl.	.040	.022	31–37	153624	TDC	Flywheel	.008H	.011H	−⅜	Zero	³⁄₃₂
	V8	.030	.016	26–33	18736542①	②	Pulley	Zero	Zero	−⅜	Zero	³⁄₃₂
1951	All Models	.030	.016	26–33	18736542①	Slot	Pulley	Zero	Zero	−⅜	Zero	³⁄₃₂
1952-54	All Models	.030	.016	26–33	18736542①	Slot	Pulley	Zero	Zero	−⅜	+¼	³⁄₃₂
1955-56	All Models	.030	.016	26–33	18736542①	④	Damper	Zero	Zero	−⅜	Zero	¹⁄₁₆-⅛
1957	All Models	.030	⑧	30	18736542①	④	Damper	Zero	Zero	+⅜	Zero	¹⁄₁₆-⅛
1958	All Models	.030	⑧	30	18736542①	5°	Damper	Zero	Zero	−½	+⅛	0-⅛
1959	V8-371, 394	.030	⑧	30	18736542①	5°	Damper	Zero	Zero	−½	+⅛	0-⅛
1960	With 2 Bar. Carb.	.030	⑧	30	18736542①	5°	Damper	Zero	Zero	−½	+⅛	0-⅛
	With 4 Bar. Carb.	.030	⑧	30	18736542①	5°	Damper	Zero	Zero	−½	+⅛	0-⅛
1961	F85 Std. Tr.-155 H.P.	.040	⑧	30	18436572①	5°	Damper	Zero	Zero	−1	+⅜	0-⅛
	F85 Auto. Tr.-155 H.P.	.040	⑧	30	18436572①	7½°	Damper	Zero	Zero	−1	+⅜	0-⅛
	F85 Std. Tr.-185 H.P.	.040	⑧	30	18436572①	5°	Damper	Zero	Zero	−1	+⅜	0-⅛
	F85 Auto. Tr.-185 H.P.	.040	⑧	30	18436572①	7½°	Damper	Zero	Zero	−1	+⅜	0-⅛
	F85-215 H.P.	.025	⑧	30	18436572①	10°	Damper	Zero	Zero	−1	+⅜	0-⅛

Continued

OLDSMOBILE—All Intermediate & Full Size Models—Continued

Year	Engine or Car Model	Spark Plug Gap	Distributor Point Gap	Distributor Dwell Angle	Firing Order	Ignition Timing BTDC or Mark	Ignition Timing Mark Location	Valve Lash Intake	Valve Lash Exhaust	Wheel Alignment Caster Degrees	Wheel Alignment Camber Degrees	Wheel Alignment Toe-In Inch
1961	Olds. with 2 Bar. Carb.	.030	③	30	18736542①	5°	Damper	Zero	Zero	−½	+⅛	0−⅛
	Olds. with 4 Bar. Carb.	.030	③	30	18736542①	5°	Damper	Zero	Zero	−½	+⅛	0−⅛
1962	F85, 155 H.P. Std. Tr.	.030	③	30	18436572①	5°	Damper	Zero	Zero	−1¼	Zero	0−⅛
	F85, 155 H.P. Auto. Tr.	.030	③	30	18436572①	7½°	Damper	Zero	Zero	−1¼	Zero	0−⅛
	F85, 185 H.P. Std. Tr.	.030	③	30	18436572①	5°	Damper	Zero	Zero	−1¼	Zero	0−⅛
	F85, 185 H.P. Auto. Tr.	.030	③	30	18436572①	7½°	Damper	Zero	Zero	−1¼	Zero	0−⅛
	F85, 215 H.P.	.025	③	30	18436572①	10°	Damper	Zero	Zero	−1¼	Zero	0−⅛
	Olds 260 H.P.	.030	③	30	18736542①	2½°	Damper	Zero	Zero	−½	+⅛	0−⅛
	Olds All Others	.030	③	30	18736542①	5°	Damper	Zero	Zero	−½	+⅛	0−⅛
1963	F85, 155 H.P. Std. Tr.	.030	③	30	18436572①	5°	Damper	Zero	Zero	−1¼	Zero	0−⅛
	F85, 155 H.P. Auto. Tr.	.030	③	30	18436572①	7½°	Damper	Zero	Zero	−1¼	Zero	0−⅛
	F85, 185 H.P.	.025	③	30	18436572①	7½°	Damper	Zero	Zero	−1¼	Zero	0−⅛
	F85, 195 H.P.	.030	③	30	18436572①	7½°	Damper	Zero	Zero	−1¼	Zero	0−⅛
	F85, 215 H.P.	.025	③	30	18436572①	10°	Damper	Zero	Zero	−1¼	Zero	0−⅛
	Olds-260 H.P.	.030	③	30	18736542①	2½°	Damper	Zero	Zero	−½	+¼	0−⅛
	Olds-All Others	.030	③	30	18736542①	5°	Damper	Zero	Zero	−½	+¼	0−⅛
1964	F85, V6-225	.030	③	30	165432⑤	5°	Damper	Zero	Zero	−1	+⅛	1/16−⅛
	F85, V8-330	.030	③	30	18436572①	7½°	Damper	Zero	Zero	−1	+⅛	1/16−⅛
	Olds, V8-330	.030	③	30	18436572①	7½°	Damper	Zero	Zero	−½	+⅛	0−1/16
	V8-394 Std. Tr.	.030	③	30	18736542①	2½°	Damper	Zero	Zero	−½	+⅛	0−1/16
	V8-394 Auto. Tr.	.030	③	30	18736542①	5°	Damper	Zero	Zero	−½	+⅛	0−1/16
1965	V6-225	.030	③	30	165432⑤	5°	Damper	Zero	Zero	−1¼	+⅛	⅛−3/16
	V8-330	.030	③	30	18436572①	7½°	Damper	Zero	Zero	⑥	+⅛	⅛−3/16
	V8-400	.030	③	30	18436572①	7½°	Damper	Zero	Zero	⑥	+⅛	⅛−3/16
	V8-425, 2 Bar. Carb.	.030	③	30	18436572①	⑦	Damper	Zero	Zero	−1	+⅛	⅛−3/16
	V8-425, 4 Bar. Carb.	.030	③	30	18436572①	5°	Damper	Zero	Zero	−1	+⅛	⅛−3/16
1966	6-250	.035	.019	31−34	153624	6°	Damper	1 Turn⑧		−1¼	+⅛	⅛−3/16
	V8-330, 400	.030	③	30	18436572①	7½°	Damper	Zero	Zero	⑥	+⅛	⅛−3/16
	V8-425, 2 B.C.	.030	③	30	18436572①	⑦	Damper	Zero	Zero	⑥	+⅛	⅛−3/16
	V8-425, 4 B.C.	.030	③	30	18436572①	7½°	Damper	Zero	Zero	⑥	+⅛	⑨
1967	6-250	.035	⑩	31−34	153624	4°	Damper	1 Turn⑧		−1¼	+⅛	⅛−3/16
	V8-330, 400	.030	③	30	18436572①	7½°⑪	Damper	Hydraulic⑫		⑥	+⅛	⅛−3/16
	V8-425 2 B.C.	.030	③	30	18436572①	5°⑪	Damper	Hydraulic⑫		⑥	+⅛	⅛−3/16
	V8-425 4 B.C.	.030	③	30	18436572①	7½°⑪	Damper	Hydraulic⑫		⑥	+⅛	⑨
1968	6-250 Std. Trans.	.035	⑩	31−34	153624	TDC	Damper	1 Turn⑧		⑯	+⅛	⅛−3/16
	6-250 Auto. Trans.	.035	⑩	31−34	153624	4°	Damper	1 Turn⑧		⑯	+⅛	⅛−3/16
	8-350, 250 H.P.	.030	.016	30	18436572①	5°⑭	Damper	Hydraulic⑫		⑯	+⅛	⅛−3/16
	8-350, 300 H.P.	.030	.016	30	18436572①	7½°⑪	Damper	Hydraulic⑫		⑯	+⅛	⅛−3/16
	8-350, 310 H.P.	.030	.016	30	18436572①	7½°⑪	Damper	Hydraulic⑫		⑯	+⅛	⅛−3/16
	8-400, 290 H.P.	.030	.016	30	18436572①	5°⑪	Damper	Hydraulic⑫		⑯	+⅛	⅛−3/16
	8-400, 350 H.P.	.030	.016	30	18436572①	7½°⑪	Damper	Hydraulic⑫		⑯	+⅛	⅛−3/16
	8-400	.030	.016	30	18436572①	2½°⑪	Damper	Hydraulic⑫		⑯	+⅛	⅛−3/16
	8-400, 442⑬	.030	.016	30	18436572①	10°⑪	Damper	Hydraulic⑫		−1¼°	+⅛	⅛−3/16
	8-455, 310 H.P.	.030	.016	30	18436572①	5°⑪	Damper	Hydraulic⑫		⑯	+⅛	⅛−3/16
	8-455, 320 H.P.	.030	.016	30	18436572①	7½°⑪	Damper	Hydraulic⑫		⑯	+⅛	⅛−3/16
	8-455, 4 B. Carb.	.030	.016	30	18436572①	7½°⑪	Damper	Hydraulic⑫		⑯	+⅛	⅛−3/16
	Toronado⑬	.030	.016	30	18436572①	10°⑮	Damper	Hydraulic⑫		−2°	+⅛	0−1/16

①—Cylinder numbering (front to rear): Left bank 1-3-5-7, right bank 2-4-6-8.
②—Between two steel balls.
③—Turn adjusting screw in (clockwise) until engine begins to misfire, then back off screw ½ turn.
④—Cars with one notch, set at leading edge of notch. Cars with three notches, set at center one.
⑤—Cylinder numbering (front to rear): Left bank 1-3-5, right bank 2-4-6.
⑥—Intermediates set at −1¼, Full size car set at −1, Toronado set at −2.
⑦—Low compression engine set at 7½°; high compression engine set at 5°.
⑧—Tighten rocker arm adjusting screw to eliminate all pushrod end clearance. Then tighten screw the number of turns listed.
⑨—Toronado set at 0−1/16, all others set at ⅛−3/16.
⑩—New points .019″, used points .016″.
⑪—At 850 R.P.M.
⑫—No adjustment.
⑬—With A.I.R. system.
⑭—With a/c "off" and idle compensator held closed.
⑮—At 1250 rpms.
⑯—Intermediates, −1¼°, full size car manual steer, −1¼°. Full size car power steer, −¾°.

Year	Engine or Car Model	Spark Plug Gap	Distributor		Firing Order	Ignition Timing		Valve Lash		Wheel Alignment		
			Point Gap	Dwell Angle		BTDC or Mark	Mark Location	Intake	Exhaust	Caster Degrees	Camber Degrees	Toe-In Inch
PACKARD												
1946	Six Cyl.	.030	.020	35	153624	4°	Damper	.007H	.010H	−1	Zero	1/32
	Eight Cyl.	.030	.017	27–30	16258374	5°	Damper	.007H	.010H	−1	Zero	1/32
	Super Eight	.030	.017	27–30	16258374	4°	Damper	Zero	Zero	−2	Zero	1/32
1947	Six Cyl.	.030	.020	35	153624	6°	Damper	.007H	.010H	−1	Zero	1/32
	Eight Cyl.	.030	.017	27–30	16258374	7°	Damper	.007H	.010H	−1	Zero	1/32
	Super Eight	.030	.017	27–30	16258374	6°	Damper	Zero	Zero	−2	Zero	1/32
1948–50	Eight	.030	.017	27–30	16258374	6°	Damper	.007H	.010H	−1	Zero	1/32
	Super Eight	.030	.017	27–30	16258374	6°	Damper	.007H	.010H	−1	Zero	1/32
	Custom Eight	.030	.017	27–30	16258374	6°	Damper	Zero	Zero	−2	Zero	1/32
1951–53	200	.030	.017	27–30	16258374	6°	Damper	.007H	.010H	−1	Zero	1/32
	Others	.028	.017	26–33	16258374	6°	Damper	Zero	Zero	−1	Zero	1/32
1954	5400-1-2-11	.025	.017	27–30	16258374	6°	Damper	.007H	.010H	−1	Zero	1/32
	Others	.025	.016	26–33	16258374	TDC	Damper	Zero	Zero	−1	Zero	1/32
PLYMOUTH												
1946–50	All Models	.025	.020	35–38	153624	DC	Damper	.010H	.010H	0	+3/8	1/32
1951–53	All Models	.035	.020	35–38	153624	DC	Damper	.010H	.010H	0	0	0
1954	All Models	.035	.020	36–42	153624	2°	Pulley	.010H	.010H	0	0	0
1955	Six Cyl.	.035	.020	39	153624	2°	Damper	.010H	.010H	−1	④	1/8
	V8	.035	.017	①	18436572②	4°	Pulley	Zero	Zero	−1	④	1/8
1956	Six Cyl.	.035	.020	39	153624	2°	Damper	.010H	.012H	−1	④	1/8
	V8-270	.035	.017	31	18436572②	4°	Pulley	Zero	Zero	−1	④	1/8
	V8-277	.035	.017	31	18436572②	4°③	Damper	.012H	.020H	−1	④	1/8
	V8-318	.035	.017	31	18436572②	4°	Damper	.010H	.018H	−1	④	1/8
1957	Six Cyl.	.035	.020	39	153624	2°	Damper	.010H	.010H	⑧	⑨	1/8
	V8-277	.035	.017	29	18436572②	⑥	Pulley	.008H	.018H	⑧	⑨	1/8
	V8-301	.035	.017	29	18436572②	⑦	Pulley	.008H	.018H	⑧	⑨	1/8
	V8-318	.035	.017	⑤	18436572②	8°	Damper	.008H	.018H	⑧	⑨	1/8
1958	6-230	.035	.020	39	153624	2°	Damper	.010H	.010H	⑧	⑨	3/32–5/32
	V8-318 D't IBP-4003F	.035	.017	27–32	18436572②	10°	Damper	.010H	.018H	⑧	⑨	3/32–5/32
	V8-318 D't IBP-4003D	.035	.017	27–32	18436572②	10°	Damper	.010H	.018H	⑧	⑨	3/32–5/32
	V8-318 D't IBS-4003	.035	.017	⑤	18436572②	8°	Damper	.010H	.018H	⑧	⑨	3/32–5/32
	V8-350	.035	.017	⑤	18436572②	8°	Damper	.060–.210⑩		⑧	⑨	3/32–5/32
1959	6-230	.035	.020	39	153624	2½°	Damper	.010H	.010H	⑧	⑨	1/8
	8-318	.035	.017	27–32	18436572②	10°	Damper	.010H	.018H	⑧	⑨	1/8
	8-361	.035	.017	⑪	18436572②	7½°	Damper	.060–.210⑩		⑧	⑨	1/8
1960	6-170, 225 Valiant	.035	.020	40–45	153624	2½°	Pulley	.010H	.020H	⑬	⑭	1/8
	6-Cyl. 4 Bar. Carb.	.028	.020	40–45	153624	10°	Pulley	.010H	.020H	⑬	⑭	1/8
	6-225 Std. Tr. Ply.	.035	.020	36–42	153624	2½°	Pulley	.010H	.020H	⑬	⑭	1/8
	6-225 Auto. Tr. Ply.	.035	.020	36–42	153624	5°	Pulley	.010H	.020H	⑬	⑭	1/8
	8-318 Std. Trans.	.035	.017	27–32	18436572②	5°	Damper	.010H	.018	⑬	⑭	1/8
	8-318 Auto. Trans.	.035	.017	27–32	18436572②	10°	Damper	.010H	.018	⑬	⑭	1/8
	8-361, 383	.035	.017	27–32	18436572②	10°	Damper	.060–.210⑩		⑬	⑭	1/8
	8-383 Ram Manifold	.035	.017	27–32	18436572②	7½°	Damper	.016C	.028C	⑬	⑭	1/8
1961	6-170, 225	.035	.020	36–42	153624	2½°	Pulley	.010H	.020H	⑬	⑮	1/8
	8-318 Std. Trans.	.035	.017	27–32	18436572②	5°	Damper	.010H	.018H	⑬	⑮	1/8
	8-318 Auto. Trans.	.035	.017	27–32	18436572②	10°	Damper	.010H	.018H	⑬	⑮	1/8
	8-361	.035	.017	⑪	18436572②	10°	Damper	⑫	②	⑬	⑮	1/8
	8-383	.035	.017	⑪	18436572②	7½°	Damper	.016C	.028C	⑬	⑮	1/8
1962	6-170, 225	.035	.020	40–45	153624	2½°	Pulley	.010H	.020H	⑬	⑮	1/8
	8-318 Std. Tr.	.035	.017	27–32	18436572②	5°	Damper	.013H	.021H	⑬	⑮	1/8
	8-318 Auto. Tr.	.035	.017	27–32	18436572②	10°	Damper	.013H	.021H	⑬	⑮	1/8
	8-361	.035	.017	⑪	18436572②	10°	Damper	.060–.210⑩		⑬	⑮	1/8
1963	6-170, 225	.035	.020	40–45	153624	2½°	Pulley	.010H	.020H	⑬	⑮	1/8
	8-318 Std. Tr.	.035	.017	28–33	18436572②	5°	Damper	.013H	.021H	⑬	⑮	1/8
	8-318 Auto. Tr.	.035	.017	28–33	18436572②	10°	Damper	.013H	.021H	⑬	⑮	1/8

Continued

PLYMOUTH—Continued

Year	Engine or Car Model	Spark Plug Gap	Point Gap	Dwell Angle	Firing Order	BTDC or Mark	Mark Location	Intake	Exhaust	Caster Degrees	Camber Degrees	Toe-In Inch
1963	8-361, 383	.035	.017	28–33	18436572[2]	10°	Damper	.060–.210[10]		[13]	[15]	⅛
	8-383, 426 Hi-Perf.	.035	.017	[11]	18436572[2]	10°	Damper	.060–.210[10]		[13]	[15]	⅛
1964	6-170, 225	.035	.020	40–45	153624	2½°	Damper	.010H	.020H	[13]	[15]	⅛
	8-273 Std. Tr.	.035	.017	28–33	18436572[2]	5°	Damper	.013H	.021H	[13]	[15]	⅛
	8-273 Auto. Tr.	.035	.017	28–33	18436572[2]	10°	Damper	.013H	.021H	[13]	[16]	⅛
	8-318 Std. Tr.	.035	.017	28–33	18436572[2]	5°	Damper	.013H	.021H	[13]	[15]	⅛
	8-318 Auto. Tr.	.035	.017	28–33	18436572[2]	10°	Damper	.013H	.021H	[13]	[16]	⅛
	8-361	.035	.017	28–33	18436572[2]	10°	Damper	.060–.210[10]		[13]	[15]	⅛
	8-383, 426	.035	.017	[11]	18436572[2]	10°	Damper	.060–.210[10]		[13]	[15]	⅛
	8-426 Hemi-Charg.	.020	.017	[16]	18436572[2]	[17]	Damper	.028C	.032C	[13]	[15]	⅛
1965	6-170, 225	.035	.020	40–45	153624	2½°	Damper	.010H	.020H	[13]	[15]	⅛
	8-273 Std. Tr.	.035	.017	28–33	18436572[2]	5°	Damper	.013H	.021H	[13]	[15]	⅛
	8-273 Auto. Tr.	.035	.017	28–33	18436572[2]	10°	Damper	.013H	.021H	[13]	[15]	⅛
	8-273 4 Bar. Carb.	.035	.017	[18]	18436572[2]	10°	Damper	.013H	.021H	[13]	[15]	⅛
	8-318 Std. Tr.	.035	.017	28–33	18436572[2]	5°	Damper	.013H	.021H	[13]	[15]	⅛
	8-318 Auto. Tr.	.035	.017	28–33	18436572[2]	10°	Damper	.013H	.021H	[13]	[15]	⅛
	8-361, 383	.035	.017	28–32	18436572[2]	10°	Damper	.060–.210[10]		[13]	[19]	⅛
	8-426	.035	.017	[18]	18436572[2]	10°	Damper	.060–.210[10]		[13]	[15]	⅛
1966	6-170	.035	.020	40–45	153624	5°	Damper	.010H	.020H	[13]	[15]	⅛
	6-170[19]	.035	.020	40–45	153624	5°[21]	Damper	.010H	.020H	[13]	[15]	⅛
	6-225	.035	.020	40–45	153624	2½°	Damper	.010H	.020H	[13]	[15]	⅛
	6-225[19]	.035	.020	40–45	153624	5°[21]	Damper	.010H	.020H	[13]	[16]	⅛
	8-273 Std. Tr.	.035	.017	28–32	18436572[2]	5°	Damper	.013H	.021H	[13]	[15]	⅛
	8-273 Auto. Tr.	.035	.017	28–32	18436572[2]	10°	Damper	.013H	.021H	[13]	[15]	⅛
	8-273, 4 B.C.	.035	.017	28–32	18436572[2]	10°	Damper	.013H	.021H	[13]	[15]	⅛
	8-273[19]	.035	.017	28–32	18436572[2]	5°[21]	Damper	.013H	.021H	[13]	[18]	⅛
	8-318 Std. Tr.	.035	.017	28–32	18436572[2]	5°	Damper	.013H	.021H	[13]	[15]	⅛
	8-318 Auto. Tr.	.035	.017	28–32	18436572[2]	10°	Damper	.013H	.021H	[13]	[16]	⅛
	8-318[19]	.035	.017	28–32	18436572[2]	4°[21]	Damper	.013H	.021H	[13]	[15]	⅛
	8-361, 383 2 B.C.	.035	.017	28–32	18436572[2]	12½°	Damper	.060–.210[10]		[13]	[15]	⅛
	8-361, 383 2 B.C.[19]	.035	.017	28–32	18436572[2]	5°[21]	Damper	.060–.210[10]		[13]	[19]	⅛
	8-383, 440 4 B.C.	.035	.017	28–32	18436572[2]	12½°	Damper	.060–.210[10]		[13]	[15]	⅛
	8-383, 440 4 B.C.[19]	.035	.017	28–32	18436572[2]	5°[21]	Damper	.060–.210[10]		[13]	[15]	⅛
	8-426	.035	.017	[20]	18436572[2]	12½°	Damper	.060–.210[10][22]		[13]	[15]	⅛
1967	6-170, 225[27]	.035	.020	40–45	153624	5°	Damper	.010H	.020H	[13]	[15]	⅛
	6-170[19]	.035	.020	40–45	153624	5°[21]	Damper	.010H	.020H	[13]	[15]	⅛
	6-225[19]	.035	.020	40–45	153624	TDC	Damper	.010H	.020H	[13]	[15]	⅛
	8-273, 318 Std. Tr.[27]	.035	.017	28–32	18436572[2]	5°	Damper	[25]		[13]	[15]	⅛
	8-273, 318 Auto. Tr.[19]	.035	.017	28–32	18436572[2]	10°	Damper	[25]		[13]	[15]	⅛
	8-273[19]	.035	.017	28–32	18436572[2]	5°[21]	Damper	.013H	.021H	[13]	[15]	⅛
	8-273, 4 B.C.[27]	.035	.017	[18]	18436572[2]	10°	Damper	.013H	.021H	[13]	[15]	⅛
	8-273, 4 B.C.[19]	.035	.017	[18]	18436572[2]	5°[21]	Damper	.013H	.021H	[13]	[15]	⅛
	8-318[19]	.035	.017	28–32	18436572[2]	5°[21]	Damper	Hydraulic[26]		[13]	[15]	⅛
	8-383, 440[27]	.035	.017	28–32	18436572[2]	12½°	Damper	Hydraulic[26]		[13]	[15]	⅛
	8-383, 440[19][24]	.035	.017	28–32	18436572[2]	5°	Damper	Hydraulic[26]		[13]	[15]	⅛
	8-383, 440[19][24]	.035	.017	28–32	18436572[2]	TDC	Damper	Hydraulic[26]		[13]	[15]	⅛
	8-426 Hemi[27]	.035	.017	[20]	18436572[2]	12½°	Damper	.028C	.032C	[13]	[15]	⅛
	8-426 Hemi[19]	.035	.017	[20]	18436572[2]	TDC	Damper	.028C	.032C	[13]	[15]	⅛
1968	6-170 Std. Trans.	.035	.020	40–45	153624	5° ATC	Damper	.010H	.020H	[13]	[15]	⅛
	6-170 Auto. Trans.	.035	.020	40–45	153624	2½° ATC	Damper	.010H	.020H	[13]	[15]	⅛
	6-225	.035	.020	40–45	153624	TDC	Damper	.010H	.020H	[13]	[15]	⅛
	V8-273 Std. Trans.	.035	.017	28–33	18436572[2]	5° ATC	Damper	Hydraulic[26]		[13]	[15]	⅛
	V8-273 Auto. Trans.	.035	.017	28–33	18436572[2]	2½° ATC	Damper	Hydraulic[26]		[13]	[15]	⅛
	V8-318 Std. Trans.	.035	.017	28–33	18436572[2]	5° ATC	Damper	Hydraulic[26]		[13]	[16]	⅛
	V8-318 Auto. Trans.	.035	.017	28–33	18436572[2]	2½° ATC	Damper	Hydraulic[26]		[13]	[15]	⅛
	V8-340 Std. Trans.	.035	.017	[20]	18436572[2]	TDC	Damper	Hydraulic[26]		[13]	[15]	⅛

Continued

PLYMOUTH—Continued

Year	Engine or Car Model	Spark Plug Gap	Distributor: Point Gap	Distributor: Dwell Angle	Firing Order	Ignition Timing: BTDC or Mark	Ignition Timing: Mark Location	Valve Lash: Intake	Valve Lash: Exhaust	Wheel Alignment: Caster Degrees	Wheel Alignment: Camber Degrees	Wheel Alignment: Toe-In Inch
1968	V8-340 Auto. Trans.	.035	.017	(20)	18436572 (2)	5°	Damper	Hydraulic (26)		(13)	(15)	1/8
	V8-383 Std. Trans. (28)	.035	.017	28–33	18436572 (2)	TDC	Damper	Hydraulic (26)		(13)	(15)	1/8
	V8-383 Auto. Trans. (28)	.035	.017	28–33	18436572 (2)	5°	Damper	Hydraulic (26)		(13)	(15)	1/8
	V8-383 Std. Trans. (29)	.035	.017	28–33	18436572 (2)	TDC	Damper	Hydraulic (26)		(13)	(15)	1/8
	V8-383 Auto. Trans. (29)	.035	.017	28–33	18436572 (2)	7½°	Damper	Hydraulic (26)		(13)	(15)	1/8
	V8-440 Std. Trans. (30)	.035	.017	(20)	18436572 (2)	TDC	Damper	Hydraulic (26)		(13)	(15)	1/8
	V8-440 Auto. Trans. (30)	.035	.017	28–33	18436572 (2)	5°	Damper	Hydraulic (26)		(13)	(15)	1/8
	V8-440 Std. Trans.	.035	.017	28–33	18436572 (2)	TDC	Damper	Hydraulic (26)		(13)	(15)	1/8
	V8-440 Auto. Trans.	.035	.017	28–33	18436572 (2)	7½°	Damper	Hydraulic (26)		(13)	(15)	1/8
	V8-426 Hemi	.035	.017	(20)	18436572 (2)	TDC	Damper	.028C	.032C	(13)	(15)	1/8

(1)—Each set of points 26–28°. Total dwell both sets 32–36°.

(2)—Cylinder numbering (front to rear): Left bank 1-3-5-7, right bank 2-4-6-8.

(3)—TDC on V8-277 engine with four barrel carburetor.

(4)—Left side +½°, right side 0°.

(5)—Each set of points 29–32°. Total dwell both sets 36–39°.

(6)—With IBJ distributor TDC, with IBP distributor 4°.

(7)—With IBP-4003A distributor 4°, with IBP-4003 10°.

(8)—With manual steering −¾°, power steering +¾°.

(9)—Left side +⅜°, right side 0°.

(10)—With lifter collapsed.

(11)—Each set of points 27–32°; Total dwell both sets 34–40°.

(12)—W/2 Bar. Carb. .060–.210 w/lifter collapsed. W-4 Bar. Carb. Intake .016C Exhaust .028C.

(13)—Manual steering −½°, power steering +¾°.

(14)—Left side +⅜°, right side +⅛°.

(15)—Left side +½°, right side +¼°.

(16)—Each set 27–31°. Total dwell both sets 34–38°.

(17)—With N61Y plugs, 31° at 3000 R.P.M. (with N58R plugs, 34° at 3000 R.P.M.).

(18)—Each set of points 27–31°; total dwell both sets 36–40°.

(19)—With Cleaner Air Package (CAP).

(20)—Each set of points 27–32°; total dwell both sets 37–42°.

(21)—After top dead center.

(22)—With mechanical lifters; intake .028C, exhaust .032C.

(23)—Torqueflite.

(24)—Manual transmission.

(25)—8-273 Valve Lash, intake .013H, exhaust .021H; 8-318, Hydraulic no adjustment.

(26)—No adjustment.

(27)—Without Cleaner Air Package (CAP).

(28)—With 4 bbl. carb.

(29)—With 2 bbl. carb.

(30)—With high performance engine.

PONTIAC—All Intermediate & Full Size Models

Year	Engine or Car Model	Spark Plug Gap	Distributor: Point Gap	Distributor: Dwell Angle	Firing Order	Ignition Timing: BTDC or Mark	Ignition Timing: Mark Location	Valve Lash: Intake	Valve Lash: Exhaust	Wheel Alignment: Caster Degrees	Wheel Alignment: Camber Degrees	Wheel Alignment: Toe-In Inch
1946–48	Six Cyl.	.025	.022	31–37	153624	IGN	Flywheel	.012H	.012H	−¾	Zero	1/32
	Eight Cyl.	.025	.016	21–30	16258374	IGN	Flywheel	.012H	.012H	−¾	Zero	1/32
1949–52	Six Cyl.	.025	.022	31–37	153624	(1)	Damper	.012H	.012H	−¾	Zero	1/32
	Eight Cyl.	.025	.016	21–30	16258374	(1)	Damper	.012H	.012H	−¾	Zero	1/32
1953	Six Cyl.	.025	.016	31–37	153624	(2)	Damper	.012H	.012H	Zero	+½	1/32
	Eight Cyl.	.025	.016	21–30	16258374	(1)	Damper	.012H	.012H	Zero	+½	1/32
1954	Six Cyl.	.025	.016	38–45	153624	(2)	Damper	.012H	.012H	Zero	+½	1/32
	Eight Cyl.	.025	.016	21–30	16258374	(1)	Damper	.012H	.012H	Zero	+½	1/32
1955	All Models	.035	.016	26–33	18436572 (4)	(5)	Damper	Zero	Zero	−1	+½	0–1/16
1956	V8 One Carb.	.035	.016	26–33	18436572 (4)	(5)	Damper	Zero	Zero	−1	+½	0–1/16
	V8 Two Carbs.	.035	.016	26–33	18436572 (4)	10°	Damper	Zero	Zero	−1	+½	0–1/16
1957	All Models	.035	(3)	30	18436572 (4)	(5)	Damper	Zero	Zero	−1	+½	0–1/16
1958	All Models	.035	(3)	30	18436572 (4)	6°	Damper	Zero	Zero	−1	+½	0–1/16
1959–60	All Models	.035	(3)	30	18436572 (4)	6°	Damper	Hydraulic		−½	+½	0–1/16
1961	4-195	.035	.016	74–76	1342	6°	Damper	Hydraulic		−1½	+¼	0–1/16
	V8-215	.032	016	28–32	18436572 (4)	5°	Damper	Hydraulic		−1⅔	+0° 8′	0–1/8
	V8-389	.035	(3)	30	18436572 (4)	6°	Damper	Hydraulic		−1⅔	+0° 8′	0–1/8
1962	4-195 Dist. 1110282	.035	.016	74–76	1342	6°	Damper	Zero	Zero	−1⅔	+¼	0–1/8
	4-195 Dist. 1110283	.035	.016	74–76	1342	6°	Damper	Zero	Zero	−1⅔	+0° 8′	0–1/8
	4-195 Dist. 1110284	.035	.016	31–34	1342	6°	Damper	Zero	Zero	−1⅔	+0° 8′	0–1/8
	4-195 Dist. 1110285	.035	.016	31–34	1342	6°	Damper	Zero	Zero	−1⅔	+0° 8′	0–1/8
	V8-215	.032	.016	28–32	18436572 (4)	5°	Damper	Zero	Zero	−1⅔	+0° 8′	0–1/8
	V8-389	.035	(3)	30	18436572 (4)	6°	Damper	Zero	Zero	−1½	+¼	0–1/8
1963	4-195	.035	.016	31–34	1342	6°	Damper	Zero	Zero	−1⅔	+0° 8′	0–1/8
	V8-326	.035	(3)	30	18436572 (4)	6°	Damper	Zero	Zero	−1⅔	+0° 8′	0–1/8
	V8-389 One Carb.	.035	(3)	30	18436572 (4)	6°	Damper	Zero	Zero	−1½	+¼	0–1/8
	V8-389 Tri-Carb.	.035	(3)	30	18436572 (4)	6°	Damper	Zero	Zero	−1½	+¼	0–1/8
	V8-421 Tri-Carb.	.035	(3)	30	18436572 (4)	6°	Damper	Zero	Zero	−1½	+¼	0–1/8

Continued

Year	Engine or Car Model	Spark Plug Gap	Distributor Point Gap	Distributor Dwell Angle	Firing Order	Ignition Timing BTDC or Mark	Ignition Timing Mark Location	Valve Lash Intake	Valve Lash Exhaust	Wheel Alignment Caster Degrees	Wheel Alignment Camber Degrees	Wheel Alignment Toe-In Inch

PONTIAC—All Intermediate & Full Size Models—Continued

Year	Engine or Car Model	Spark Plug Gap	Point Gap	Dwell Angle	Firing Order	BTDC or Mark	Mark Location	Intake	Exhaust	Caster Degrees	Camber Degrees	Toe-In Inch
1964–65	6-215	.035	.016	31–34	153624	4°	Damper	1 Turn⑥		⑦	+¼	0–⅛
	V8-326	.035	③	30	18436572④	6°	Damper	Zero	Zero	⑦	+¼	0–⅛
	V8-389, 421	.035	③	30	18436572④	6°	Damper	Zero	Zero	⑦	+¼	0–⅛
1966	6-230	.035	.016	31–34	153624	5°	Damper	Zero	Zero	⑦	+¼	0–⅛
	6-230⑧	.035	.016	31–34	153624	5°⑨	Damper	Zero	Zero	⑦	+¼	0–⅛
	V8	.035	③	30	18436572④	6°	Damper	Zero	Zero	⑦	+¼	0–⅛
	V8⑧	.035	③	30	18436572④	4°	Damper	Zero	Zero	⑦	+¼	0–⅛
	Tri Carb. V8	.035	③	30	18436572④	6°	Damper	Zero	Zero	−1½	+¼	0–⅛
1967	6-230	.035	.016	31–34	153624	5°	Damper	Hydraulic⑩		−1½	⑪	0–1⅛
	6-230⑧	.035	.016	31–34	153624	TDC	Damper	Hydraulic⑩		−1½	⑪	0–1⅛
	V-8's	.035	③	30	18436572④	6°	Damper	Hydraulic⑩		−1½	⑪	0–1⅛
	V-8's⑧	.035	③	30	18436572④	6°	Damper	Hydraulic⑩		−1½	⑪	0–1⅛
1968	6-250 1 Bar. Carb.	.035	.016	31–34	153624	TDC	Damper	Hydraulic⑩		⑫	+¼	⑬
	6-250 4 Bar. Carb.	.035	.016	31–34	153624	5°	Damper	Hydraulic⑩		⑫	+¼	⑬
	8-350	.035	.016	28–32	18436572④	9°	Damper	Hydraulic⑩		⑫	+¼	⑬
	Firebird 400	.035	.016	28–32	18436572④	9°	Damper	Hydraulic⑩		⑫	+¼	⑬
	Firebird 400 H.O.	.035	.016	28–32	18436572④	9°	Damper	Hydraulic⑩		⑫	+¼	⑬
	Firebird Ram Air	.035	.016	28–32	18436572④	9°	Damper	Hydraulic⑩		⑫	+¼	⑬
	Pontiac 400, 2 B.C.	.035	.016	28–32	18436572④	9°	Damper	Hydraulic⑩		⑫	+¼	⑬
	Pontiac 400, 4 B.C.	.035	.016	28–32	18436572④	9°	Damper	Hydraulic⑩		⑫	+¼	⑬
	8-428	.035	.016	28–32	18436572④	9°	Damper	Hydraulic⑩		⑫	+¼	⑬

①—Early 1949, "IGN" mark. Late 1949 and 1950-54, first line to come under pointer is for standard heads, second line for high compression heads, and third line is TDC.
②—Center of three lines.
③—Turn adjusting screw in (clockwise) until engine misfires, then back off screw ½ turn.
④—Cylinder numbering (front to rear): Left bank 1-3-5-7, right bank 2-4-6-8.

⑤—First line to come under pointer while cranking engine.
⑥—With valve fully closed, turn rocker arm nut down until all play in push rod is eliminated, then tighten nut additional turns specified.
⑦—Tempest wagons —2, all other cars —1½.
⑧—With Air Injection Reactor system (A.I.R.).
⑨—After top dead center.

⑩—No adjustment. On V8's, rocker arms ar correctly positioned when ball retainer nuts are tightened to 20 ft. lbs.
⑪—Intermediates +¼, full size +⅜.
⑫—Firebird +½°, Intermediates and full size −1½°.
⑬—Firebird ⅛"–¼", Intermediates and full size 0"–⅛".

STUDEBAKER

Year	Engine or Car Model	Spark Plug Gap	Point Gap	Dwell Angle	Firing Order	BTDC or Mark	Mark Location	Intake	Exhaust	Caster Degrees	Camber Degrees	Toe-In Inch
1946	Champion	.025	.020	35–38	153624	IGN	Damper	.016C	.016C	+1½	+½	3/32
1947–48	Champion	.025	.020	35–38	153624	IGN	Damper	.016C	.016C	+½	+½	3/32
	Commander	.025	.020	35–38	153624	IGN	Damper	.016C	.016C	+½	+½	3/32
1949	Champion	.025	.020	35–38	153624	IGN	Damper	.016C	.016C	+1	+½	3/32
	Commander	.025	.020	35–38	153624	IGN	Damper	.016C	.016C	−2½	+½	3/32
1950	Champion	.025	.020	35–38	153624	IGN	Damper	.016C	.016C	−1½	+½	3/32
	Commander	.025	.022	31–37	153624	IGN	Damper	.016C	.016C	−2	+½	3/32
1951–52	Champion	.025	.020	35–38	153624	IGN	Damper	.016C	.016C	−1¾	+½	3/32
	Commander	.035	.016	21–30	18436572①	IGN	Damper	.015H	.015H	−1¾	+½	3/32
1953–54	Champion	.025	.020	38–40	153624	IGN	Damper	.016C	.016C	−1¾	+½	3/32
	Commander	.035	.016	28–34	18436572①	IGN	Damper	.022H	.022H	−1¾	+½	3/32
1955	Six Cyl.	.030	.020	39	153624	IGN	Damper	.016C	.016C	−1¾	+½	1/16–⅛
	V8	.035	.013	28–34	18436572①	IGN	Damper	.026C	.026C	−1¾	+½	1/16–⅛
1956	Six Cyl.	.030	.020	39	153624	IGN	Damper	.016C	.016C	−1¾	+½	1/16–⅛
	Studebaker V8	.035	.016	26–33	18436572①	IGN	Damper	.026C	.026C	−1¾	+½	1/16–⅛
	Packard V8	.035	.017	31	18436572①	IGN	Damper	Zero	Zero	−1¾	+½	1/16–⅛
1957	Six Cyl.	.030	.020	39	153624	IGN	Damper	.016C	.016C	−1¾	+½	1/16–⅛
	V8	.035	.016	26–33	18436572①	IGN	Damper	.026C	.026C	−1¾	+½	1/16–⅛
	Golden Hawk	.035	.016	26–33	18436572①	IGN	Damper	.026C	.026C	−1¾	+½	1/16–⅛

Continued

STUDEBAKER—Continued

Year	Engine or Car Model	Spark Plug Gap	Distributor		Firing Order	Ignition Timing		Valve Lash		Wheel Alignment		
			Point Gap	Dwell Angle		BTDC or Mark	Mark Location	Intake	Exhaust	Caster Degrees	Camber Degrees	Toe-In Inch
1958	6-186	.030	.020	38–40	153624	2°	Damper	.016C	.016C	−1¾②	+½③	1/16–1/8
	V8-259, 289	.035	.016	28–34	18436572①	4°	Damper	.026C	.026C	−1¾②	+½③	1/16–1/8
1959	Six Cyl.	.030	.020	38–40	153624	2°	Damper	.018C④	.018C④	−2¼②	+½③	1/16–1/8
	V8	.035	.016	28–34	18436572①	4°	Damper	.026C	.026C	−2¼②	+½③	1/16–1/8
1960	Six Cyl.	.030	.020	38–40	153624	2°	Damper	.018C	.018C	−2¼②	+½③	1/16–1/8
	V8	.035	.016	28–34	18436572①	4°	Damper	.026C	.026C	−2¼②	+½③	1/16–1/8
1961–62	Six Cyl.	.035	.020	37–41	153624	2°	Damper	.026C	.026C	−½②	+½③	¼④
	V8	.035	.016	28–32	18436572①	4°	Damper	.026C	.026C	−½②	+½③	¼④
1963–64	Six Cyl.	.035	.020	37–41	153624	2°	Damper	.026C	.026C	−½②	+½③	¼④
	V8 Std. Engine	.035	.017	27–31	18436572①	4°	Damper	.026C	.026C	−½②	+½③	¼④

①—Cylinder numbering (front to rear): Left bank 1-3-5-7, right bank 2-4-6-8. ②—Not more than ½° variation between wheels. ③—−½ more favored on drivers side. ④—With Power Steering ⅛".

Imported Car Data

Year	Model	Spark Plug Gap, In.	Breaker Gap, In.	Dwell Angle Deg.	Firing Order	Timing & Mark Location	Intake	Exhaust	Engine Oil Qts.	Coolant Qts. W/ Heater	Caster	Camber	Toe-in
							Valve Lash		**Capacities**		**Wheel Alignment**		

AUSTIN-HEALEY

Year	Model	Spark Plug Gap	Breaker Gap	Dwell	Firing Order	Timing	Intake	Exhaust	Oil Qts	Coolant	Caster	Camber	Toe-in
1969	Sprite	.024	.014	—	1342	4° BTC①	.012	.012	4	6	3°	3/4°	0—1/8
1969–70	America	.025	.015	—	1342	3° BTC①	.012	.012	5-1/2	4	②	③	④
1971	America	.025	.015	57–63	1342	Flywheel	.012	.012	6	4	5-1/2°	3/4°	④
1973	Marina	.035	.015	60	1342	12° BTDC⑤	.013H	.013H	3.8	5.3	+2°	+1/6°	1/16
1974	Marina	.035	.015	60	1342	12° BTDC⑤	.013H	.013H	3.8	5.3	+1-1/2°	0°	1/16

①—Mark located on pulley. Timed at No. 1 cyl., front of engine.　　④—+1/16" toe-out.
②—+5-1/2° ±1/2°.　　⑤—Timed at No. 1 cyl., front of engine.
③—+3/4 ± 1°.

BMW

Year	Model	Spark Plug Gap	Breaker Gap	Dwell	Firing Order	Timing	Intake	Exhaust	Oil Qts	Coolant	Caster	Camber	Toe-in
1969–72	1600, 2002	.035	.016	60	1342	①	.0069	.0069	4.3②	7.4	+3°	0°	.079
	2000 Ti	.035	.016	60	1342	③	.0069	.0069	4.3②	7.4	+3°	0°	.079
	6 Cyl.	.024	.014	35–41	153624	④	.011	.011	5.3②	12.2	+9-1/2°	0°	.04

①—Timed at No. 1 cyl., front of engine. Disconnect vacuum hose & align ball on flywheel with the pointer at 1400 RPM.
②—Less filter.
③—Timed at No. 1 cyl., front of engine. Disconnect vacuum hose & align ball on flywheel with the pointer at 2300 RPM.
④—Timed at No. 1 cyl., front of engine. Disconnect vacuum hose & align ball on flywheel with the pointer at 1700 RPM.

DATSUN

Year	Model	Spark Plug Gap	Breaker Gap	Dwell	Firing Order	Timing	Intake	Exhaust	Oil Qts	Coolant	Caster	Camber	Toe-in
1969–70	SPL 311	.030	—	50–55	1342	10° BTC①	.017H	.017H	4	9	1°30′	1°26′	1/8
	SRL 311	.030	—	50	1342	10° BTC①	.008H	.012H	7	9	1°30′	1°25′	1/8
1971	PL 510 Sedan	.034	.020	49–55	1342	①②	.010	.012	4.5	6.8	+1-2/3°	+1°	5/16
	PL 510 Sta. Wag.	.034	.020	49–55	1342	①②	.010	.012	4.5	6.8	+2°	+1-1/6°	1/8
	PL 521	.034	.020	49–55	1342	①②	.010	.012	4.5	—	—	—	—
1971–72	LB 110	.034	.020	49–55	1342	5° BTDC①	.014	.014	3.3	5	—	—	—
	240Z Man. Tr.	.034	.020	35–41	153624	5° BTDC①	.010	.012	5	8	—	—	—
	240Z Auto. Tr.	.034	.020	33–39	153624	①③	.010	.012	5	8	—	—	—
1972	PL 510 Sedan	.034	.020	49–55	1342	①④	.010	.012	4.5	—	+1-2/3°	+1°	5/16
	PL 510 Sta. Wag.	.034	.020	49–55	1342	①④	.010	.012	4.5	—	+2°	+1-1/6°	1/8
	PL 521	.034	.020	49–55	1342	①④	.010	.012	4.5	—	—	—	—
1973	LB 110	.034	.020	49–55	1342	5° BTDC①	.014	.014	3.3	5	+1-1/12°	+1-1/12°	13/64
	PL 510 Series	.030	.020	49–55	1342	①⑤	.010	.012	4.5	7	+1-7/12°	+5/12°	11/64
	PL 610	.030	.020	49–55	1342	①⑤	.010	.012	4.5	7	+1-1/2°	+1-3/4°	19/64
	PL 620	.030	.020	49–55	1342	①⑤	.010	.012	4.5	6.5	+1-5/6°	+1-1/4°	3/16
	240Z Man Tr.	.034	.020	35–41	153624	7° BTDC①	.010	.012	5	8	+2-11/12°	+5/6°	9/64
	240Z Auto. Tr.	.034	.020	33–39	153624	①⑤	.010	.012	5	8	+2-11/12°	+5/6°	9/64
1974	B 210	.032	.020	49–55	1342	5° BTDC①	.014	.014	3.3	5.3	+1-3/4°	+1-1/6°	1/8
	PL 610	.030	.020	49–55	1342	12° BTDC①	.010	.012	4.5	7.3	+2°	+2°	1/2
	PL 620	.030	.020	49–55	1342	12° BTDC①	.010	.012	4.5	7	+1-1/2°	+1-1/4°	1/8
	PL 710	.030	.020	49–55	1342	12° BTDC①	.010	.012	4.5	6.9	+1-2/3°	+1-29/32°	1/2
	260Z	.032	.014⑦	—	153624	8° BTDC①	.010	.012	4.5	8.4	+2-11/12°	+3/4°	1/8

①—Mark located on pulley. Timed at No. 1 cyl., front of engine.
②—Primary points, 10° BTDC; secondary points, TDC.
③—Primary points, TDC; secondary points, 10° BTDC.
④—Primary points, 7° BTDC; secondary points, TDC.
⑤—Primary points, 12° BTDC; secondary points, 8° BTDC.
⑥—Primary points, 15° BTDC; secondary points, 5° BTDC.
⑦—Distributor air gap.

DODGE COLT

Year	Model	Spark Plug Gap	Breaker Gap	Dwell	Firing Order	Timing	Intake	Exhaust	Oil Qts	Coolant	Caster	Camber	Toe-in
1971–73	All	.028	.020	52	1342	TDC①	.006H	.010H	3.7	7.2	+1-1/4°	+1°	②
1974	98	.030	.020	49–55	1342	①③	.006H	.010H	4.2	6.6	+7/8°	+7/8°	②
	122	.030	.020	49–55	1342	3° BTDC①	.006H	.010H	4.4	8.3	+7/8°	+7/8°	②

①—Mark located on pulley. Timed at No. 1 cyl., front of engine.
②—.08–.23 inch.
③—Exc. Calif. auto. trans., TDC; Calif. auto. trans., 3° BTDC.

Continued

Year	Model	Spark Plug Gap, In.	Breaker Gap, In.	Dwell Angle Deg.	Firing Order	Timing & Mark Location	Intake	Exhaust	Engine Oil Qts.	Coolant Qts. W/Heater	Caster	Camber	Toe-in
FIAT													
1969	124 Sedan	.026	.018	60	1342	TDC①	.008C	.008C	4	6.3	+2-1/4°	+1/2°	1/4
1969–70	850 Sedan	.026	.018	57	1342	10° BTDC⑧	.006C	.006C	3.5	8	+9°	+2-1/64°	1/4
1970	124 Spider	.024	.017	55	1342	5° BTDC①	.008C	.020C	4.2	8	—	—	—
	850 Spider	.024	.017	55	1342	TDC⑧	.006C	.008C	4.2	8	—	—	—
1971	124 Sedan, Sta. Wag.	.022	.018	60③	1342	TDC①	.008C	.008C	4	8	+3°	+37/64°	5/16
	124 Spider, Sport Coupe	.022	.016	55③	1342	5° BTDC①	.018C	.020C	4.2	8	+3-1/2°	+1/2°	9/32
	850 Sedan	.022	.018	60②	1342	10° BTDC⑧	.006C	.006C	3.5	8	+10°	+1-1/6°	1/2
	850 Sport Coupe	.022	.016	55③	1342	TDC⑧	.006C	.008C	4.2	8	+10°	+2°	1/2
	850 Spider, Racer	.022	.016	55③	1342	TDC⑧	.006C	.008C	4.2	8	+10°	+2-1/6°	19/32
1972	124 Sedan, Sta. Wag.	.022	.017	60	1342	TDC①	.008C	.008C	4	8	+3°	+37/64°	17/64
	124 Cp., Spider	.022	.016	55	1342	TDC①	.018C	.020C	4.2	8	+3-1/2°	+37/64°	⑤
	128 Sedan, Sta. Wag.	.022	.016	55	1342	TDC⑨	.012C	.016C	4.5	7	+1-29/32°	+2°	-3/16
	850 Spider	.022	.016	55	1342	TDC⑧	.006C	.008C	4.2	8	+10°	④	⑥
1973	124 Coupe	.022	.016	55	1342	TDC①	.018C	.020C	4-1/4⑦	8	+3-5/64	+17/64°	9/32
	124 Spider	.022	.016	55	1342	TDC①	.018C	.020C	4-1/4⑦	8	+3-1/4°	+1/6°	15/64
	124 Special	.022	.018	60	1342	TDC①	.008C	.008C	4-1/4⑦	8	+2-2/3°	+1/4°	9/32
	128 Sedan, Cp.	.022	.016	55	1342	TDC⑨	.012C	.016C	4-1/2⑦	6-4/5	+1-2/3°	+1-2/3°	-3/16
	850 Spider	.022	.016	55	1342	TDC⑧	.006C	.008C	4-1/2⑦	8	+9°	+1-5/6°	35/64
1974	124	.022	.016	55	1342	TDC①	.018C	.020C	4⑦	8	—	—	—
	128 Exc. A1 & X1-9	.022	.016	55	1342	TDC⑨	.012C	.016C	4-1/2⑦	7	—	—	—
	128 A1 & X1-9	.022	.016	55	1342	TDC⑨	.012C	.016C	4-1/2⑦	11.6	—	—	—

①—Mark located on pulley. Timed at No. 1 cyl., front of engine.
②—At 700 RPM.
③—At 850 RPM.
④—850 Sedan, +1-1/2°; 850 Sport Coupe, +1-2/3°; 850 Spider, +1-5/6°.
⑤—124 Coupe, 17/64; 124 Spider, 15/64.
⑥—850 Sedan, 35/64; 850 Sport Coupe, 29/64; 850 Spider, 35/64.
⑦—With filter.
⑧—Mark located on pulley. Timed at No. 1 cyl., rear of engine.
⑨—Mark located on pulley. Timed at No. 1 cyl., right side of vehicle.

Year	Model	Spark Plug Gap, In.	Breaker Gap, In.	Dwell Angle Deg.	Firing Order	Timing & Mark Location	Intake	Exhaust	Engine Oil Qts.	Coolant Qts. W/Heater	Caster	Camber	Toe-in
FORD													
1969	Cortina 1600	.023	.025	39	1243	4° BTDC①③	.010H	.017H	4.2	6.9	-5/32°	+1-3/4°	5/32
	Cortina 1600 GT	.023	.025	39	1243	4° BTDC②③	.012H	.022H	4.2	6.9	-5/32°	+1-3/4°	5/32
1970	Cortina 1600	.023	.025	39	1243	12° BTDC①	.010H	.017H	4.2	6.1	-5/32°	+1-3/4°	5/32
	Cortina 1600 GT	.023	.025	39	1243	12° BTDC①	.012H	.022	4.2	6.1	-5/32°	+1-3/4°	5/32
1971	Capri 1600	.025	.025	39	1243	12° BTDC③	.010H	.017H	3.5	6.2	+1/2°	-1/2°	1/8
	Capri 2000	.025	.025	39	1342	6° BTDC③④	.008C	.018C	5	7.5	+1/2°	-1/2°	1/8
1972	Capri 1600	.025	.025	38	1243	③⑤	.010H	.017H	3.5	6.5	+1°	+1/2°	1/8
	Capri 2000	.025	.025	38	1342	6° BTDC③④	.008C	.018C	5	8	+1°	+1/2°	1/8
	Capri 2600	.034	.025	37	142536	12° BTDC③	.014C	.016C	5-1/4	8-1/4	+1°	+1/2°	1/8
	Pantera	.034	.020	28	⑦	6° BTDC⑥	Hydraulic		4-1/2	25-1/2	+3-1/2°	0°	1/8
1973	Capri 2000	.030	.025	39	1342	6° BTDC③	.008H	.010H	4	6-1/2	+1-3/4°	0°	1/8
	Capri 2600	.034	.025	39	142536	12° BTDC③	.014C	.016C	4	8-1/2	+1-3/4°	0°	1/8
1974	Capri 2000	.034	.025	35-41	1342	6° BTDC③	.008C	.010C	3-1/2	8.1	+1/2°	0°	1/8
	Capri 2800	.034	.024	35-41	142536	12° BTDC⑥	.014H	.016H	4-1/2	10.8	+1/2°	0°	1/8
	Pantera	.034	.020	30-33	⑦	16° BTDC⑥	Hydraulic		4	24	+2-3/4°	0°	5/32

①—10° if no emission pump is used.
②—8° if no emission pump is used.
③—Mark located on pulley. Timed at No. 1 cyl., front of engine.
④—Exc. Calif.; Calif. Auto only, 10° BTDC.
⑤—Carburetor No. 701W9510EA, 28mm, 12° BTDC; Carburetor No. 701W9510EB, 25mm, 6° BTDC.
⑥—Mark located on pulley. Timed at No. 1 cyl., right front of engine.
⑦—13726548.

Continued

Year	Model	Spark Plug Gap, In.	Breaker Gap, In.	Dwell Angle Deg.	Firing Order	Timing & Mark Location	Valve Lash Intake	Valve Lash Exhaust	Engine Oil Qts.	Coolant Qts. W/ Heater	Caster	Camber	Toe-In

HONDA

Year	Model	Spark Plug Gap	Breaker Gap	Dwell	Firing Order	Timing	Intake	Exhaust	Oil Qts	Coolant	Caster	Camber	Toe-In
1971–72	600	.030	.014	—	12①	10° BTDC②	.004C	.004C	3.2	—	+1°	+1°	.078
1973–74	Civic	.029	.020	49–55	1342	TDC②	.006C	.006C	3.2	4.2	+1-3/4°	+1/2°	.04③

①—Simultaneous firing.   ②—Located on pulley.   ③—Toe-out.

JAGUAR

Year	Model	Spark Plug Gap	Breaker Gap	Dwell	Firing Order	Timing	Intake	Exhaust	Oil Qts	Coolant	Caster	Camber	Toe-In
1969	E Type	.025	.015	33–37	153624	10° BTDC①	.004	.006	9	16	2° ± 1/2	+1/4° ± 1/2	1/16–1/8
1970	XKE, XJ Sedan	.025	.015	32–38	153624	10° BTDC①	.004	.006	9	16	2° ± 1/2	1/4° ± 1/2	1/16–1/8
1971	XJ6	.025	.015	32–38	153624	10° BTDC①	.013	.013	9	10	2-1/4° ± 1/4	1/2° ± 1/4	1/16
	XKE	.025	.015	31–37	153624	10° BTDC①	.013	.013	9	10-1/4	1-3/4° ± 1/4	1/4°	1/16
1972	XJ6	.025	.015	35–41	153624	8° BTDC①	.004	.006	8-3/4	19-1/4	2°–2-1/2°	1/2° ± 1/4	1/16
	Ser-3 V-12	.025	.022	20–25	②	10° BTDC⑥	.014C	.014C	11-1/2	21.6	2-1/4°– 2-3/4°	③	2°
1973	XJ-6	.025	.015	35	153624	8° BTDC①	.013	.013	8-3/4	19	+2-1/4°	+1/2°	3/32
	Ser-3 V-12	.025	.021④	—	②	10° BTDC⑥	.015	.015	11-1/2	21-1/2	+2-1/2°	0°	3/32
1974	Ser-3 V-12	.025	—	—	②	4° ATDC⑤	.013C	.013C	—	—	+21/2°	0°	1/16

①—Mark located on pulley. Timed at No. 1 cyl., rear of engine.
②—Firing order 1-7-5-11-3-9-6-12-2-8-4-10.
③—Front 0° ± 1/4°. Rear 3/4° + 1/4°.
④—Module gap.
⑤—Mark located on pulley. Timed at No. 1 cyl., right front of engine.

MAZDA

Year	Model	Spark Plug Gap	Breaker Gap	Dwell	Firing Order	Timing	Intake	Exhaust	Oil Qts	Coolant	Caster	Camber	Toe-In
1971–72	1200	.032	.018	58	1342	13° BTDC①	.010	.010	3.1	4.3	+3°	+55/60°	.12
	616, 808	.032	.020	52	1342	8° BTDC①	.012	.012	3.8	7.4	+1-1/20°	−1/4°	−.16 to +.08
	R100	.028	.018	58	12	②	—	—	—	7.5	+2°	+1°	.04 to .12
	RX-2, 3	.033	.018	58	12	②	—	—	4.7	8.5	+1-1/20°	−1/4°	−.16 to +.08
1973	618	.031	.020	49–55	1342	①③	.014H	.016H	4.1	8.0	+3/4°	+3/4°	1/8
	808	.031	.020	49–55	1342	①④	.012H	.012H	3.8	7.4	+1-1/4°	+2/3°	1/8
	RX-2	.024	.018	55–61	12	⑥	—	—	4.8⑦	8.4	+1°	+3/5°	1/8
	RX-3	.024	.018	55–61	12	⑥⑤	—	—	4.8⑦	8.4	⑧	⑨	—
1974	808	.030	.018	49–55	1342	①⑩	.012	.012	3.9	7.4	+1-1/4°	+2/3°	1/8
	RX-2	.026	.018	58–62	12	⑥	—	—	4.8	9.9	+1°	+1/2°	1/8
	RX-3	.026	.018	58–62	12	⑥⑪	—	—	4.8	10.2	+1-1/4°	+2/3°	1/8
	RX-4	.026	.018	58–62	12	⑥⑫	—	—	5.5	10.5	+2-1/30°	+1-1/20°	1/8

①—Mark located at crankshaft pulley. Timed at No. 1 cyl., front of engine.
②—Leading distributor, TDC; trailing distributor, 5° ATDC. Mark located at eccentric shaft pulley.
③—Man. Trans., 5° BTDC; Auto. Trans., 3° BTDC.
④—Exc. Sta. Wag., Auto. Trans., 5° BTDC; Sta. Wag. Auto. Trans., 8° BTDC.
⑤—Leading distributor, TDC; trailing distributor, 10° ATDC.
⑥—Timed at lower front (leading) spark plug. Mark located at eccentric shaft pulley.
⑦—Less filter.
⑧—Exc. Sta. Wag., +1/2°; Sta. Wag., +1-1/6°.
⑨—Exc. Sta. Wag., +11/12°; Sta. Wag., +1°.
⑩—Man. Trans., 5° BTDC; Auto. Trans., 8° BTDC.
⑪—Leading distributor, 5° ATDC; trailing distributor, 10° ATDC.
⑫—Leading distributor, 5° ATDC; trailing distributor, 15° ATDC.

MERCEDES-BENZ

Year	Model	Spark Plug Gap	Breaker Gap	Dwell	Firing Order	Timing	Intake	Exhaust	Oil Qts	Coolant	Caster	Camber	Toe-In
1969	230, 250/8	.024	.014	28–32	153624	TDC④	.003C	.007C	5-3/4	11	+2-1/2②°	0°	13/64
1969–71	220/8	.024	.018	45–49	1342	5° ATDC④	.003C	.008C	4-1/4	11	+2-1/2②°	0°	13/64
	280/8	.021⑤	.014	30–36⑥	153624	⑦④	.003C	⑧	5-3/4	12⑨	⑩	0°	⑪
1970–71	250/8	.024	.014	30–36	153624	4° ATDC④	.003C	.008C⑧	5-3/4	11	+2-1/2②°	0°	13/64
1972	220	.024	.016	47–53	1342	5° ATDC④	.003C	.008C	5.3	11.2	4° ± 15′	⑫	⑬
	220D	—	—	—	1342	24° BTDC⑰	.004C	.016C	5.3	11.2	4° ± 15′	⑬	⑮
	250, 250CP	.024	.016	30–36	153624	4° ATDC④	.003C	.008C	6.8	10.5	4° ± 15′	⑫	⑮
	280 S.E. 2.8	.024	.016	30–36	153624	6° ATDC④	.003C	.008C	6.8	11.5	4° ± 15′	⑫	⑮

Continued

Year	Model	Spark Plug Gap, In.	Breaker Gap, In.	Dwell Angle Deg.	Firing Order	Timing & Mark Location	Intake	Exhaust	Engine Oil Qts.	Coolant Qts. W/ Heater	Caster	Camber	Toe-in
MERCEDES—Continued													
1972	280 SE/SEL 4.5	.024	.016	30–34	①	5° ATDC⑱	.003C	.008C	9.2	14.8	4° ± 15'	⑫	⑬
	300 SEL 4.5	.024	.016	30–34	①	5° ATDC⑱	.003C	.008C	9.2	14.8	4° ± 15'	⑬	⑮
	350 SL	.024	.016	30–34	①	5° ATDC⑱	.003C	.008C	9.2	15.8	3°15' ± 20'	⑭	⑮
	600	.024	.016	34–38	①	5° ATDC⑲	.004C	.010C	7.4	24	2° ± 15'	⑭	⑯
1973	220	.024	—	47–53	1342	10° BTDC④	.003C	.008C	4-1/4	10.2	+3-2/3°	+1/4°	5/12°
	220D	—	—	—	1342	24° BTDC⑰	.004C	.016C	4-1/4	10.9	+3-2/3°	+1/4°	5/12°
	280SE/SEL	.024	—	30–34	①	4° ATDC⑱	.003C	.008C	6.2	11.5	⑳	+1/2°	1/3°
	300SEL	.024	—	30–34	①	5° ATDC⑱	.003C	.008C	8	14.7	+4°	+1/3°	1/3°
	450SE/SEL	.024	—	30–34	①	5° ATDC⑱	.003C	.008C	8	16	+10°	-1/6°	5/12°
	450SL/SLC	.024	—	30–34	①	5° ATDC⑱	.003C	.008C	8	16	+3-2/3°	0°	1/3°
1974	230	.024	—	47–53	1342	10° BTDC④	.004C	.008C	6.7	10.5	+3-2/3°	+1/4°	1/8°
	240D	—	—	—	1342	24° BTDC⑰	.004C	.016C	5.7	10.5	+3-2/3°	+1/4°	1/8°
	280, C	.024	—	34–40	153624	4° ATDC④	.004C	.010C	7	11.5	+3-2/3°	+1/4°	5/64°
	450SE/SEL	.024	—	30–34	①	5° ATDC⑱	.004C	.008C	9	16	+10°	-1/6°	1/8°
	450SL/SLC	.024	—	30–34	①	5° ATDC⑱	.004C	.008C	9	16	+3-2/3°	0°	5/64°

①—Firing order 15486372.
②—With Power steer. +3-1/2.
③—1970 sedan—.007C.
④—Mark located on damper or pulley. Timed at No. 1 cyl., front of engine.
⑤—280 S & SEL .024.
⑥—1969 —28° —32°.
⑦—1969; 280S —@ 4000–4500 RPM, vacuum line disconnected 37° BTDC; 280 SE, SEL, SL 30° BTDC. 1970–71; except 280S, 8° ATDC; 280S, 4° ATDC.
⑧—1969 .007C; 1970–71 .008C.
⑨—280S—11-1/2 qts.
⑩—Except 280 SL—w/p. steer. +3-1/2; w/o p. steer. +2-1/2; 280 SL—w/p. steer. +4; w/o p. steer. +3-1/4.
⑪—Except 280 SL—13/64; 280 SL—5/64.
⑫—0°30'—20'.
⑬—0°20'—20'.
⑭—0° ± 10'.
⑮—0°20' ± 10'.
⑯—0°45' ± 10'.
⑰—Injection timing.
⑱—Mark located on damper or pulley. Timed at No. 1 cyl., right front of engine.
⑲—Mark located on damper or pulley. Timed at No. 5 cyl., left front of engine.
⑳—With power steering, +4°; less power steering, +3-1/2°.

Year	Model	Spark Plug Gap, In.	Breaker Gap, In.	Dwell Angle Deg.	Firing Order	Timing & Mark Location	Intake	Exhaust	Engine Oil Qts.	Coolant Qts. W/ Heater	Caster	Camber	Toe-in
MG													
1969	MGC	.025	.015	—	153624	TDC①	.015	.015	7-1/2	11	5°	0°	0°
	MGC/GT	.025	.015	—	153624	TDC①	.015	.015	7-1/2	11	5°	0°	0°
1969–70	MG Midget	.025	.015	—	1342	4° BTDC①	.012H	.012H	3	6	3°	1°	1/16-1/8
	MGB/GT	.025	.015	—	1342	10° BTDC①	.015C	.015C	4-1/2	6	7-1/2°	1°	1/16-3/32
1971	MG Midget	.025	.015	57–63	1342	①②	.012	.012	4	3-1/2	3°	3/4°	0-1/8
	MGB/MGB. GT	.025	.015	57–63	1342	15° BTDC①	.015	.015	5	6	7°	1°	1/16-3/32
1972	MG Midget	.025	.015	57–63	1342	9° BTDC①	.012H	.012H	3.9	3-1/2	3°	3/4°	1/8
	MGB/MGB. GT	.025	.015	57–63	1342	16° BTDC①	.013H	.013H	4.8	6	7°	1°	1/16-3/32
1973–74	MG Midget	.025	.015	60	1342	9° BTDC①	.012H	.012H	3.9	3-1/2	+3°	+3/4°	1/16
	MGB/GT	.025	.015	60	1342	11° BTDC①	.013H	.013H	4.8	6	+7°	+1°	5/64

①—Mark located on pulley. Timed at No. 1 cyl., front of engine.
②—With emission controls, 10° BTDC; less emission controls, 13° BTDC.
③—Toe-out.

Continued

Year	Model	Spark Plug Gap, In.	Breaker Gap, In.	Dwell Angle Deg.	Firing Order	Timing & Mark Location	Intake	Exhaust	Engine Oil Qts.	Coolant Qts. W/ Heater	Caster	Camber	Toe-in
OPEL													
1969	1.1 Litre	.030	.018	50	1342	6-1/2° BTDC(1)	.006H	.010H	2-1/2	5-1/2	+3/4°(4)	+3/4°(3)	1/16
	1.9 Litre	.030	.018	50	1342	6-1/2° BTDC(2)	.012H	.012H	3	6	+3/4°(4)	+3/4°(3)	1/16
1970	1.1 Litre	.030	.018	50	1342	6-1/2° BTDC(1)	.006H	.010H	2-1/2	5-1/2	+2°	+1°	1/16
	1.9 Litre	.030	.018	50	1342	6-1/2° BTDC(2)	.012H	.012H	3	6	+2°	+1°	1/16
1971	1.1 Litre	.030	.018	50	1342	(1)(5)	.006H	.010H	2-3/4(6)	5	+2°	+1°	1/8
	1.9 Litre	.030	.018	50	1342	TDC(2)(8)	Hydraulic		3(7)	6(9)	(10)	+1°	1/8(11)
1972	1900	.030	.018	50	1342	TDC(2)(8)	Hydraulic		3/14	6	+4-1/2°	+1-1/2°	5/32
	GT	.030	.018	50	1342	TDC(2)(8)	Hydraulic		3-1/4	6	+3°	+1-1/2	1/16
1973	GT	.028	.016	50	1342	TDC(2)(8)	Hydraulic		2.9	5.8	+3°	+1°	1/16
1973–74	1900, Manta	.028	.016	50	1342	TDC(2)	Hydraulic		2.9	5.9	+4-1/2°(4)	−1°	5/32

(1)—Mark located on pulley. Timed at No. 1 cyl., front of engine.
(2)—Mark located on flywheel. Timed at No. 1 cyl., front of engine.
(3)—GT, +1/2°.
(4)—Left and right wheel angles must be within 1° of each other.
(5)—At 950 R.P.M. with Vac. Adv. & Retard units disconnected & plugged.
(6)—W/Filter, 3 Qts.
(7)—W/Filter, 3-1/4 Qts.
(8)—At 900 R.P.M. with Vac. Adv. and Retard units disconnected and plugged.
(9)—1900 Series, Std. Trans., 6 Qts.; Auto. Trans., 6.1 Qts.
(10)—1900 Series, +3-1/2°.; Opel, +2°; GT, +3°.
(11)—1900, 3/16.

Year	Model	Spark Plug Gap, In.	Breaker Gap, In.	Dwell Angle Deg.	Firing Order	Timing & Mark Location	Intake	Exhaust	Engine Oil Qts.	Coolant Qts. W/ Heater	Caster	Camber	Toe-in
PEUGEOT													
1969–70	504	.023	.016	55–59	1342	10° BTDC(2)	.004C	.010C	4.22	8.25	+2-2/3°	+5/8°	11/64
1970	404	.023	.016	55–59	1342	10° BTDC(2)	.004C	.010C	4.22	8.25	+2-2/3°	+5/8°	11/64
1971	304	.023	.016	57	1342	5°BTDC(3)	.004C	.010C	4.22	6.1	+1/2°	+1/2°	5/64
	504	.024	.016	57	1342	TDC(4)	.004C	.010C	4.22	8.5	+2-2/3°	+5/8°	7/64
1972	304	.024	.016	61	1342	5° BTDC(3)	.004C	(1)	4	7	+1/2°	+1/2°	5/64
	504	.025	.017	61	1342	5° BTDC(4)	.004C	.010C	5	8.25	+2-2/3°	+5/8°	5/64
1973–74	504	.024	.016	57	1342	5° BTDC(4)	.006C	.012C	4.2	8.25	+2-2/3°	+5/8°	1/8

(1)—Exc. Sta. Wag., .004C; Sta. Wag., 010C.
(2)—Mark located on flywheel. Timed at No. 1 cyl., rear of engine.
(3)—Mark located on clutch housing. Timed at No. 1 cyl. Left side of vehicle.
(4)—Mark located on pulley. Timed at No. 1 cyl. rear of engine.

Year	Model	Spark Plug Gap, In.	Breaker Gap, In.	Dwell Angle Deg.	Firing Order	Timing & Mark Location	Intake	Exhaust	Engine Oil Qts.	Coolant Qts. W/ Heater	Caster	Camber	Toe-in
PLYMOUTH CRICKET													
1971–72	All	.025	.015	60	1342	7° BTDC(1)	.008	.016	3.4	7.7	+1-1/2°	+1-3/4°	5/64

(1)—Mark located on pulley. Timed at No. 1 cyl., front of engine.

Year	Model	Spark Plug Gap, In.	Breaker Gap, In.	Dwell Angle Deg.	Firing Order	Timing & Mark Location	Intake	Exhaust	Engine Oil Qts.	Coolant Qts. W/ Heater	Caster	Camber	Toe-in
PORSCHE/PORSCHE AUDI													
1969	911 E & S	.014	.014	(2)	162435	(17)(23)	.004	.004	9-1/2	—	+6-3/4° ± 3/4°	(9)	(8)
	911T	.024	.014	(2)	162435	(17)(23)	.004	.004	9-1/2	—	+6-3/4° ± 3/4°	(9)	(8)
	912	.022	.016	47–53	1432	3° BTDC(5)	—	—	4.2	—	+6-3/4° ± 3/4°	(9)	(8)
1970–71	Audi S-90	.024	.016	47–53	1342	(12)(28)	.008	.008	4.2	8	1/6° ± 1/3°	(14)	0 to −.079"
	Audi 100LS	.024	.016	47–53	1342	(12)(28)	.016	.016	4.2	8	1/10° ± 1/3°	(15)	0 to −.08"
	911E, S & T	.024	.016	35–41	162435	(16)(23)	.004	.004	9-1/2	—	+6-3/4° ± 3/4°	(9)	(10)
	914	.028(18)	.016	44–50	1432	(5)(19)	.006	.006	(20)	—	6° ± 1/2°	(21)	(22)
	914/6	.024	.016	37–43	162435	(11)(27)	.004	.004	9-1/2	—	6° ± 1/2°	(21)	(22)
1972	911	.024	(1)	(2)	162435	(17)(23)	.004	.004	9-1/2(3)	—	6-5/6° ± 1/2°	(9)	0
	914	.028	.016	47–50	1432	5° BTDC(6)	.004	.004	3-3/4	—	6-1/2°	(21)	.33"
	Audi S-90	.024	.016	47–53	1342	(11)(28)	.008	.016	4-1/4	8	11/60° ± 1/3°	(14)	0 to −.08"
	Audi 100	.024	.016	47–53	1342	(12)(28)	.008	.016	4-1/4	8	1/10° ± 1/3°	(15)	0 to −.08"

Continued

Year	Model	Spark Plug Gap, In.	Ignition Breaker Gap, In.	Dwell Angle Deg.	Firing Order	Timing & Mark Location	Valve Lash Intake	Exhaust	Capacities Engine Oil Qts.	Coolant Qts. W/ Heater	Wheel Alignment Caster	Camber	Toe-in

PORSCHE/PORSCHE AUDI—Continued

Year	Model	Spark Plug Gap	Breaker Gap	Dwell	Firing Order	Timing & Mark	Intake	Exhaust	Engine Oil Qts.	Coolant	Caster	Camber	Toe-in
1973	911E, S & T	.024	.016	(2)	162435	5° ATDC(23)	.004	.004	(6)	—	6-1/12° ± 1/4°	0° ± 1/6°	(24)
	914	.028	.016	44–50	1432	(5)(19)	.006	.006	3.7	—	6° ± 1/2°	(21)	(22)
	Audi 100	.035	.016	47–53	1342	8° ATDC(28)	.008	.016	4.2	8	1/15° ± 1/3°	(25)	(26)
1974	911, S	.022	.014	34–40	162435	5°ATDC(23)	.004	.004	10-1/2	—	+6-1/12°	+1/12°	0
	914	.028	.016	44–50	1432	(5)(19)	.006	.008	3.7	—	+6°	0°	(4)
	Audi 100LS	.038	.016	50	1342	8° ATDC(28)	.008	.016	4-1/4	8	+1/10°	+1/6°	(7)
	Audi Fox	.028	.016	50	1342	TDC(29)	.008	.016	3.1	6-1/2	+1/3°	+5/12°	(13)

①—Bosch .014. Marelli .016.
②—Bosch 35°–41°. Marelli 37°–43°.
③—Type 911S with oil cooled 10.6.
④—1/3° ±1/6°.
⑤—Mark located on pulley. Timed at No. 1 cyl., right front of engine.
⑥—Man. Trans.—911 E & T, 11 qts.; 911S, 13 qts.; Auto. Trans.—911 E & T, 13 qts.; 911S, 16 qts.
⑦—0.008 inch.
⑧—Front, .25; Rear, 0° ±1/6°.
⑨—Front, 0° ±1/3°; Rear −5/6 ±1/3°.
⑩—Front, 0°; Rear, 0° ±1/6°.
⑪—35° BTDC @ 6000 R.P.M. (Engine free or loaded).
⑫—27° BTDC @ 2500 R.P.M.
⑬—+5/12° ±1/4°.
⑭—Front, 1/4° ±1/3°; Rear, 1/2° ±1/4°.
⑮—Front, 11/60° ±1/3°; Rear, 0° ±1/2°.
⑯—911 E & S, see note ⑰. 911T, see note ⑪.
⑰—30° BTDC @ 6000 R.P.M. (Engine free or loaded).
⑱—For winter .020.
⑲—27° BTC @ 3500 R.P.M.
⑳—3.7 qts.; w/o oil filter 3.2 qts.
㉑—Front, 0° ±1/3°; Rear, −1/2° ±1/3°.
㉒—Front, 1/3° ±1/6°; Rear, 0° ±1/4°.
㉓—Mark located on pulley. Timed at No. 1 cyl., left rear of engine.
㉔—Front, 0°; Rear, 0° ±1/3°.
㉕—Front, 1/3° ±1/3°; Rear, −1/2° ±1/4°.
㉖—Toe out 0° to −1/3°.
㉗—Mark located on flywheel. Timed at No. 1 cyl., left rear of engine.
㉘—Mark located on pulley. Timed at No. 1 cyl., front of engine.
㉙—Mark located on flywheel. Timed at No. 1 cyl., front of engine.

RENAULT

Year	Model	Spark Plug Gap	Breaker Gap	Dwell	Firing Order	Timing & Mark	Intake	Exhaust	Engine Oil Qts.	Coolant	Caster	Camber	Toe-in
1969	Renault 16	.025	.018	56	1342	TDC①	.008C	.010C	4-1/2③	7	+2-1/6°	+3/4°	(12)
	Renault 10	.025	.018	56	1342	TDC①	.006C	.008C	3③	7-1/2	+9°	+1-2/3°	(5)
1970–71	Renault 10	.025	.018	57	1342	3° ATDC⑥①	.006C	.008C	3③⑦	7-1/2	+9°	+1-2/3°	(5)
	Renault 16	.024	.018	57	1342	TDC①⑧	.008C	.010C	4-1/2③	7	+2-2/3°	+3/4°	(9)
1972	Renault 12	.025	.016	57	1342	②⑪	.008C	.010C	4-1/2③	9.5	+4°	+1-1/2°	(12)
	Renault 15	.025	.016	57	1342	TDC②	.008C	.010C	4.2③	6	+4°	+1-1/2°	(12)
	Renault 16	.025	.016	57	1342	TDC③	.008C	.010C	4-1/2③	9.5	+4°	+1-1/2°	(12)
	Renault 17	.025	.016	57	1342	TDC②	.010C	.012C	4.7③	5.8	+4°	+1-1/2°	(12)
1973	Renault 12	.025	.016	57	1342	②⑩	.008C	.010C	4③	9.5	+4°	+1-1/2°	(12)
	Renault 15	.025	.016	57	1342	②⑩	.008C	.010C	4③	6	+4°	+1-1/2°	(12)
	Renault 17	.025	.016	57	1342	TDC②④	.010C	.012C	4.7③	5.8	+4°	+1-1/2°	(12)
1974	Renault 12	.026	.018	55	1342	10° BTDC②	.008C	.010C	4-1/2③	9-1/2	+4°	+1-1/2°	(12)
	Renault 15, 17TL	.026	.018	55	1342	10° BTDC②	.008C	.010C	4-1/2③	6	+4°	+1-1/2°	(12)
	Renault 17	.026	.018	55	1342	10° BTDC②	.010C	.012C	5③	5.8	+4°	+1-1/2°	(12)

①—Mark located at pulley. Timed at No. 1 cyl. toward front of vehicle.
②—Mark located at flywheel or converter. Timed at No. 1 cyl., rear of engine.
③—W/filter.
④—At 1000 R.P.M., vacuum hose off.
⑤—3/64 inch out to 5/64 inch in.
⑥—Notch on pulley 1/8″ past pointer (with hole) on timing chain cover.
⑦—Auto. Trans., 3; Man. Trans., 3-1/2.
⑧—Auto. Trans., with timing light, vacuum hose off, eng. idling below 800 R.P.M.
⑨—Toe-out, 0 to 1/8″ at 37mm (1-15/32″) steer. height.
⑩—Man. Trans., 5° BTDC; Auto. Trans., 3° BTDC.
⑪—Man. Trans., TDC; Auto. Trans., 6° BTDC.
⑫—Toe-out, 0 to 1/8″.

SAAB

Year	Model	Spark Plug Gap	Breaker Gap	Dwell	Firing Order	Timing & Mark	Intake	Exhaust	Engine Oil Qts.	Coolant	Caster	Camber	Toe-in
1969	99	.028	—	(5)	1342	9° BTDC⑥	.009	.017	4②	9	+1-1/4°	+3/4°	0
1969–71	95, 96, 97	.026	—	50	1342	6° BTDC①	.014	.016	3-1/2②	7-1/2	+2°	(3)	(4)
1970–71	99C	.028	—	(5)	1342	9° BTDC⑥	.009	.017	4②	9	+1-1/4°	+3/4°	0
	99E	.028	—	(5)	1342	5° BTDC⑥	.009	.017	4②	9	+1-1/4°	+3/4°	0
1972	99C	.028	—	(5)	1342	9° BTDC⑥	.009	.017	4②	9	+3/4°	+3/4°	0
	99E	.028	—	(5)	1342	5° BTDC⑥	.009	.017	4②	9	+3/4°	+3/4°	0
1972–73	95, 96, 97	.026	—	50	1342	3° BTDC①	.014	.016	3-1/2②	7-1/2	+2°	(3)	(4)
1973	99C	.028	—	(5)	1342	14° BTDC⑥	.009	.017	4②	10	+3/4°	+3/4°	0
	99E	.028	—	(5)	1342	8° BTDC⑥	.009	.017	4②	10	+3/4°	+3/4°	0

Continued

Year	Model	Spark Plug Gap, In.	Breaker Gap, In.	Dwell Angle Deg.	Firing Order	Timing & Mark Location	Intake	Exhaust	Engine Oil Qts.	Coolant Qts. W/ Heater	Caster	Camber	Toe-in
SAAB—Continued													
1974	97	.026	.016	50	1342	3° BTDC①	.014	.016	3-1/2②	7-1/2	+2°	0°	.04
	99	.026	.014	50	1342	4° BTDC⑥	.009	.017	4③	10	+3/4°	+3/4°	0

①—Mark located at pulley & front cover. Timed at No. 1 cyl., located right front.
②—Includes filter.
③—Models 95 & 96, +3/4°; Model 97, 0°.
④—Models 95 & 96, .08 inch; Model 97, .04 inch.
⑤—Carburetor equipped, 40°; fuel injected, 50°.
⑥—Mark located at flywheel. Timed at No. 1 cyl., located nearest firewall.

Year	Model	Spark Plug Gap, In.	Breaker Gap, In.	Dwell Angle Deg.	Firing Order	Timing & Mark Location	Intake	Exhaust	Engine Oil Qts.	Coolant Qts. W/ Heater	Caster	Camber	Toe-in
SIMCA													
1969	All	.024	.013	—	1342	4° BTDC①	.012H	.014H	—	—	+1-1/4	+1/4	1/36②
1970–71	All	.024	.013	—	1342	③	.012H	.014H	—	—	+1-1/4	+1/4	1/36②

①—Mark located at pulley. Timed at No. 1 cyl., front of engine.
②—Toe-out.
③—Std. Trans. TDC; Auto Trans. 4° BTDC.

Year	Model	Spark Plug Gap, In.	Breaker Gap, In.	Dwell Angle Deg.	Firing Order	Timing & Mark Location	Intake	Exhaust	Engine Oil Qts.	Coolant Qts. W/ Heater	Caster	Camber	Toe-in
SUBARU													
1969–71	Exc. 1971 "G"	.029	.019	49–55	1324	TDC①	.009C	.010C	2.8	6.2	+2°	+1-5/6°	.2
1971	"G" Model	.029	.019	49–55	1324	TDC①	.012C	.012C	3.4	6.2	+2°	+1-5/6°	.2
1972	All	.029	.019	49–55	1324	6° BTDC①	.012C	.012C	3.4	6.2	+2°	+1-5/6°	.2
1973–74	All	.032	.019	49–55	1324	6° BTDC①	.012C	.012C	3.5	6.2	+3/4°	+1-1/3°	.08–.32

①—Mark located at flywheel. Timed at No. 1 cyl., right front of engine.

Year	Model	Spark Plug Gap, In.	Breaker Gap, In.	Dwell Angle Deg.	Firing Order	Timing & Mark Location	Intake	Exhaust	Engine Oil Qts.	Coolant Qts. W/ Heater	Caster	Camber	Toe-in
TOYOTA													
1969	Land Cruiser	.032	.018	—	153624	7° BTDC①	.008H	.014H	—	—	+1°	+1°	1/8
	Crown	.032	.018	—	153624	10° BTDC①	.004C	.007C	—	—	+1°	+1°	3/64
	Corolla	.032	.018	—	1432	5° BTDC①	.003C	.007C	4	5	+1/2°	+1/2°	5/64
	Corona Mark II	.030	.018	—	1342	②①	.008H	.014H	4-1/2	7.8	+1/6°	+1-1/4°	5/64
1969–70	Corona 1900③	.030	.018	50–54	1243	5° BTDC①	.008H	.014H	6.0	9.0	+1/12°	+1-1/6°	5/64
1970–71	Corona 1900④	.030	.018	50–54	1342	⑤①	.008H	.014H	5.3	8.3	+1/3°	+2/3°	13/64
	Corona MK II	.030	.018	50–54	1342	⑤①	.008H	.014H	5.3	⑥	+5/12°	+1-1/6°	9/32
	Crown	.030	.018	39–43	153624	TDC①	.007H	.010H	5.9	11.6	+1/2°	+1/2°	1/8
	Pickup	.030	.018	50–54	1342	⑤①	.008H	.014H	5.2	7.8	−1/3°	+1°	7/32
1970–73	Corolla 1200	.030	.018	50–54	1342	5° BTDC①	.008H	.012H	3.7	5.1	⑦	+5/6°	1/8
1970–74	Land Cruiser	.030	.018	39–43	153624	7° BTDC⑧	.008H	.014H	9.0	16.1	+1°	+1°	5/32
1971	Celica ST 1900	.030	.018	50–54	1342	⑤①	.008H	.014H	5.3	8.3	+1°	+1°	7/32
1971–74	Corolla 1600	.030	.018	50–54	1342	5° BTDC①	.008H	.013H	3.9	6.9	+1-2/3°	+1°	1/8
1972	Corona MK II	.030	.018	50–54	1342	7° BTDC①	.008H	.014H	5.3	8.7	+5/12°	+1-1/6°	1/4
	Crown	.030	.018	39–43	153624	5° BTDC①	.008H	.014H	5.9	11.5	+1/2°	⑨	3/64
	Mark II	.030	.018	39–43	153624	TDC①	.007H	.010H	5.5	11.4	⑩	+1-1/12°	5/32
1972–73	Carina 1600	.030	.018	50–54	1342	5° BTDC①	.008H	.013H	3.9	6.9	+1°	+1°	7/32
	Corona 1900	.030	.018	50–54	1342	7° BTDC①	.008H	.014H	5.3	⑪	⑫	⑬	⑭
	Pickup	.030	.018	50–54	1342	7° BTDC①	.008H	.014H	5.2	9.0	−1/3°	+1°	15/64
1972–74	Celica ST 2000	.030	.018	50–54	1342	7° BTDC①	.008H	.014H	5.3	8.3	+1°	+1°	13/64

Continued

IMPORTED CAR DATA—Continued

Year	Model	Spark Plug Gap, In.	Breaker Gap, In.	Dwell Angle Deg.	Firing Order	Timing & Mark Location	Intake	Ex-haust	Engine Oil Qts.	Coolant Qts. W/ Heater	Caster	Camber	Toe-in
					Ignition		Valve Lash		Capacities		Wheel Alignment		

TOYOTA—Continued

Year	Model	Spark Plug Gap, In.	Breaker Gap, In.	Dwell Angle Deg.	Firing Order	Timing & Mark Location	Intake	Ex-haust	Engine Oil Qts.	Coolant Qts. W/ Heater	Caster	Camber	Toe-in
1973–74	Mark II	.030	.018	39–43	153624	5° BTDC①	.007H	.010H	5.5	11.4	⑯	+1/2°	5/32
1974	Corolla 1200	.030	.018	50–54	1342	5° BTDC①	.008H	.014H	3.7	5.1	+2°	+5/6°	1/8
	Pickup	.030	.018	50–54	1342	7° BTDC①	.008H	.014H	5.2	9.0	+1/2°	+1	15/64

①—Mark located at pulley. Timed at No. 1 cyl., front of engine.
②—Std. Trans., TDC; Auto. Trans., 5° BTDC.
③—Models RT 43 & 52.
④—Models RT 83 & 93.
⑤—TDC before 3/71; 10° BTDC after 3/71.
⑥—Model RT 78, 7.8 quarts; all others, 8.3 quarts.
⑦—Models KE 25 & 26, +2°; all others, +1-2/3°.
⑧—Mark located at flywheel. Timed at No. 1 cyl., front of engine.
⑨—Model MS 75, +5/12°; all others, +1/2°.
⑩—Model MX28, +2/3°; all others, +5/12°.
⑪—Models RT 104, 114 & 118, 8.7 quarts; all others, 8.4 quarts.
⑫—Models RT 104, 114 & 118, +5/6°; all others, +1/3°.
⑬—Models RT 104, 114 & 118, +7/12°; all others, +2/3°
⑭—Models RT 104, 114 & 118, 3/64 inch; all others, 11/64 inch.
⑮—Model MX 29, +2/3°; all others, +5/12°.

TRIUMPH

Year	Model	Spark Plug Gap, In.	Breaker Gap, In.	Dwell Angle Deg.	Firing Order	Timing & Mark Location	Intake	Ex-haust	Engine Oil Qts.	Coolant Qts. W/ Heater	Caster	Camber	Toe-in
1969–70	TR6	.025	.015	—	153624	4° ATC①	.010	.010	4.7	6.6	1°	④	1/16-1/8
	GT6+	.025	.020	—	153624	4° ATC①	.010	.010	4.7	6.6	1°	⑤	1/16-1/8
	Spitfire Mk III	.025	.015	—	1342	2° ATC①	.010C	.010C	4.2	4.8	+4°	+2°	0-1/16
1971	TR-6	.025	.015	32–38	153624	①	.010	.010	4.8	6.6	2-3/4°⑥	1/4°⑥	1/16
	GT-6X	.025	.015	40–42	153624	①	.010	.010	4.8	6.6	4°⑥	2°⑥	1/16
	Spitfire	.025	.015	40–42	1342	①	.010	.010	4.8	4.5	4-1/2°⑥	2°⑥	1/16
1972	STAG	.025	.015	30–32	②	4° ATDC⑧	.008C	.010C	4.8	11	1°-3°	1	⑦
1972–73	GT-6 Mk-3	.025	.015	40–42	153624	4° ATDC①	.010C	.010C	4.8	6.6	3-1/2°	2-3/4°	1/32
1972–74	Spitfire	.025	.015	38–40	1342	2° ATDC①	.010C	.010C	4.2	4.8	+4°	+3°	1/16-1/8
	TR6	.025	.015	34–37	153624	4° ATDC①	.010C	.010C	4.8	6.6	+2-3/4°	+1/4°	⑦
1973	STAG	.025	.015	30–32	②	4° ATDC⑧	.009	.017	5.4③	11	+2°	+7/8°	1/16-1/8

①—Mark located at pulley. Timed at No. 1 cyl., front of engine.
②—Firing order—1-2-7-8-4-5-6-3.
③—Includes filter.
④—+1/2° ± 1°.
⑤—2-3/4° ± 1°.
⑥—Plus or minus 1/2°.
⑦—Front 1/16"—1/8 Rear 0" to 1/16.
⑧—Mark located at pulley. Timed at No. 2 cyl., right front of engine.

VOLKSWAGEN

Year	Model	Spark Plug Gap, In.	Breaker Gap, In.	Dwell Angle Deg.	Firing Order	Timing & Mark Location	Intake	Ex-haust	Engine Oil Qts.	Coolant Qts. W/ Heater	Caster	Camber	Toe-in
1969	1500	.026	.016	①	1432	TDC②	.004C	.004C	2-1/3	—	+3	+1/2	1/8
	1600	.026	.016	①	1432	TDC②	③	④	2-1/3	—	+4	+1-1/3°	1/8
1970–73	1600⑤	.028	.016	47–53	1432	TDC②	.004C	.004C	2-1/3	—	+4	+1-1/3°	1/8
1970–74	1600⑥	.024	.018	44–50	1432	②⑦	.006C	.006C	2.6	—	⑧	⑨	1/2°
1971–73	1700⑩	.028	.017	—	1432	27° BTDC②	.004C	.004C	3-7/8	—	+1-1/6	+1-1/6°	1/8
1974	Dasher	.028	.015	47–53	1342	⑪	.008C	.016C	3.7	12.6	+1/6°	+5/12°	1/6°
	Type 4	.024	.016	44–50	1432	27° BTDC②	.006C	.006C	3.7	—	+1-3/4°	+1-1/6°	1/3°

①—Exc. VW-113-905-205-H Dist. 47-53. With VW-113-905-205-H Dist. 48-52.
②—Mark located at pulley. Timed at No. 1 cyl., right front of engine.
③—To 672748 (W/1 Carb.) .008. From 672749 (W/1 Carb.) .004. To 6727697 (w/2 Carbs.) .008. From 672698 (w/2 Carbs.) .004.
④—To 672748 (w/1 Carb.) .012. From 672749 (w/1 Carb.) .004. To 672697 (w/2 Carbs.) .012. From 672698 (w/2 Carbs.)
⑤—Type 3.
⑥—Type 1.
⑦—Engines built through July 1970, TDC; August 1970 to Spring 1973, 5° ATDC; From Spring 1973, 7½° BTDC.
⑧—Exc. Super Beetle, +3-1/3°; Super Beetle, +2°.
⑨—Exc. Super Beetle, +1/2°; Super Beetle, +1°.
⑩—Type 4.
⑪—30° BTDC at 3000 R.P.M. with vacuum hoses off. Timed at No. 1 cylinder, front of engine.

Continued

IMPORTED CAR DATA—Continued

Year	Model	Spark Plug Gap, In.	Ignition				Valve Lash		Capacities		Wheel Alignment		
			Breaker Gap, In.	Dwell Angle Deg.	Firing Order	Timing & Mark Location	Intake	Exhaust	Engine Oil Qts.	Coolant Qts. W/Heater	Caster	Camber	Toe-In

VOLVO

Year	Model	Spark Plug Gap, In.	Breaker Gap, In.	Dwell Angle Deg.	Firing Order	Timing & Mark Location	Intake	Exhaust	Engine Oil Qts.	Coolant Qts. W/Heater	Caster	Camber	Toe-In
1969	180S, B20B	.028	.016	60	1342	10° BTDC①	.021C	.021C	3-1/2②	9-1/2	+1/2°	+1/4°③	1/16
1969–71	140, B20B	.028	.016	60	1342	10° BTDC①	.021C	.021C	3-1/2②	9④	+1/2°	+1/4°③	1/16
	164, B30A	.028	.010	40	153624	10° BTDC①	.017C	.017C	5-1/2②	13	+1/2°	+1/4°③	1/16
1970–71	180E, B20E	.028	.016	60	1342	10° BTDC①	.017C	.017C	3-1/2②	9-1/2	+1/2°	+1/4°③	1/16
1972	140 Series	.028	.016	60	1342	10° BTDC①	⑤	⑤	3-1/2②	10	+1/2°	+1/4°	1/16
	164	.028	.016	40	153624	10° BTDC①	⑤	⑤	5-1/2②	13	+1/2°	+1/4°	1/16
	1800 E/ES	.028	.016	60	1342	10° BTDC①	⑤	⑤	3-1/2②	9-1/2	+1/2°	+1/4°	1/16
1973	140 Series	.030	.018	60	1342	10° BTDC①	.016C	.016C	3.4⑥	10.5	+1/2°	+1/4°	1/8
	164	.030	.010	40	153624	10° BTDC①	.021C	.021C	5.5⑦	13	+1-1/2°	+1/4°	1/8
	1800 ES	.030	.018	60	1342	10° BTDC①	.017C	.017C	3.4⑥	9.0	+2-1/4°	+1/4°	1/32
1974	140 Series	.028	.016	60	1342	10° BTDC①	.017C	.017C	4	10	+1-1/2°	+1/4°	1/8
	164	.028	.010	40	153624	10° BTDC①	.021C	.021C	5-1/2	13	+1-1/2°	+1/4°	1/8

①—Mark located at pulley. Timed at No. 1 cylinder, front of engine with vacuum line disconnected.

②—Add 1/2 qt. w/filter.

③—Models P444, 445, 544, 1100, 2100, +3/8°; all others, +1/4°.

④—100 H.P. B180 eng., add 1/2 qt.

⑤—B20B, B30 A & F engines, .021C; B20F engine, .017C. "F" engines are fuel injected.

⑥—W/filter, 4 qts.

⑦—W/filter, 6.3 qts.

Flasher Locations

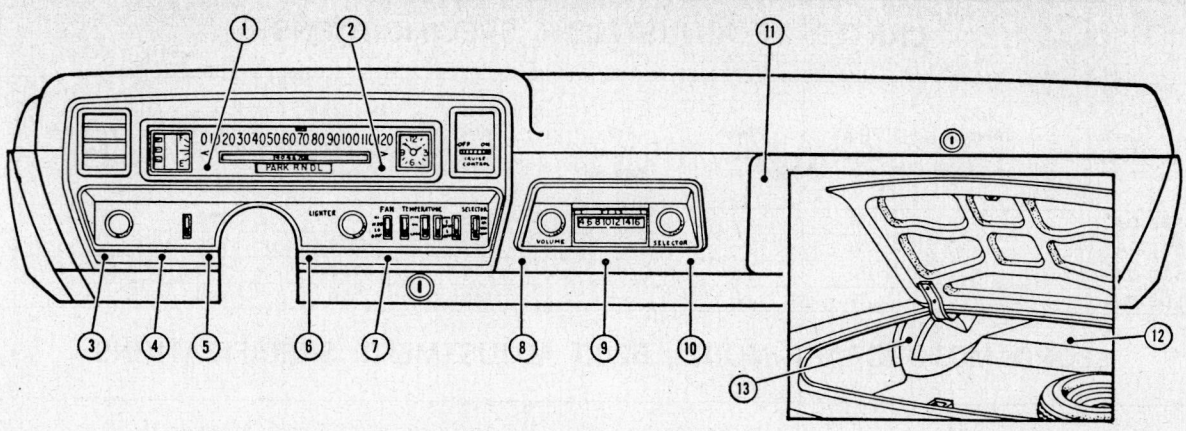

CAR	1969 TSF	1969 HWF	1970 TSF	1970 HWF	1971 TSF	1971 HWF	1972 TSF	1972 HWF	1973 TSF	1973 HWF	1974 TSF	1974 HWF	1975 TSF	1975 HWF
American Motors	2	3	2⑭	3	2⑯	3	3	3	3	3	3	3	3	4
Astre & Vega	—	—	—	—	5	3	5	3	5	3	5	3	5	3
Buick & Special	3	3	3	3	3	3	3	3	3	3	3	3	3	3
Cadillac & Eldorado	5	5	6	8	⑮	3	⑮	3	⑮	3	⑮	3	⑮	3
Camaro	8	3	8	3	8	3	8	3	8	3	8	3	8	3
Chevelle & Monte Carlo	8	3	1	3	7	3	7	3	4	3	4	3	4	3
Chevrolet	8	3	10	3	7	3	7	3	6	3	6	3	6	3
Chevrolet Nova	8	3	10	3	7	3	7	3	10	3	10	3	10	3
Chrysler	5	4	5	4	5	4	5	5	5	5	⑱	⑲	5	5
Comet & Montego	6	5	6	5	5	5	5	5	5	5	5⑳	5⑳	4	3
Cordoba & Charger SE	—	—	—	—	—	—	—	—	—	—	—	—	3	6
Corvette	⑧	3	⑧	3	⑧	3	⑧	3	⑧	3	⑧	3	⑧	3
Cougar	8	10	8	10	11	6	8	10	8	10	5	5	5	5
Dart & Challenger	8	5	8	⑨	8	⑨	10	6	8	③	⑱	⑲	4	5
Dodge	⑤	①	5	6	①	—	①	5	8	6	⑱	⑲	5㉒	5㉓
Fairlane & Torino	6	5	6	5	5	5	5	5	5	5	5	5	3	3
Falcon & Maverick	6	⑩	6	⑩	5	5	5	5	5	5	11	11	11	11
Firebird, Le Mans & Tempest	3	3	3	3	3	3	3	3	3	3	3	3	3	3
Ford	6	5	11	3	8	3	8	3	8	3	3	3	3	3
Ford Pinto	—	—	—	—	10	10	10	10	10	10	11	11	11	11
Granada & Monarch	—	—	—	—	—	—	—	—	—	—	—	—	8	4
Imperial	13	13	5	4	5	4	5	5	5	6	⑱	⑲	5	5
Lincoln	11	11	3⑫	3⑬	6	6	3	3	3	3	7㉑	7㉑	11	3
Mercury	4	6	11	3	8	3	8	3	8	3	3	3	3	3
Monza, Skyhawk & Starfire	—	—	—	—	—	—	—	—	—	—	—	—	3㉔	3㉔
Mustang	1	4	10	8	11	6	8	10	8	10	11	11	7㉔	7㉔
Oldsmobile	3	3	1	3	4	3	4	3	4	3	4	3	4	3
Oldsmobile Cutlass	3	3	3	3	4	3	4	3	4	3	4	3	4	3
Oldsmobile Toronado	3	.3	4	3	4	3	4	3	4	3	4	3	4	3
Plymouth	⑦	⑥	⑦	6	②	—	②	5	8	6	⑱	⑲	5	5
Pontiac & Ventura II	3	3	3	3	3	3	3	3	3	3	3	3	3	3
Thunderbird	13	13	⑪	11	11	6	3	3	3	3	3	3	3	3
Valiant & Barracuda	8	5	8	6	8	6	10	6	8	⑰	⑱	⑲	4	5

TSF: Turn Signal Flasher.   HWF: Hazard Warning Flasher.

①—Location 10 on Coronet & Charger. Location 5 on Polara & Monaco.
②—Location 10 on Belvedere & Satellite. Location 5 on Fury & VIP.
③—Location 6 on Challenger. Location 5 on Dart.
④—Location 4 on Coronet & Charger. Location 8 on Polara & Monaco.
⑤—Location 6 on Belvedere & Satellite. Location 4 on Fury & VIP.
⑥—Location 4 on Belvedere & Satellite. Location 8 on Fury & VIP.
⑦—Extreme lower right corner of instrument panel.
⑧—Location 6 on Challenger. Location 10 on Dart.
⑨—Location 5 on Falcon. Behind ash tray on Maverick.
⑩—To right of glove box.
⑪—Mark III to right of glove box.
⑫—Mark III to left of glove box.
⑬—Location 3 on Hornet and Gremlin.
⑭—On the underside of steering column lower cover.
⑮—Location 3 on Hornet, Gremlin and Javelin.
⑯—Location 6 on Barracuda. Location 5 on Valiant.
⑰—Behind instrument panel, on right side of ash tray.
⑱—On right side of brake pedal support.
⑲—Location 11 on Comet.
⑳—Location 3 on Mark IV.
㉑—Location 3 on Coronet.
㉒—On right side of brake pedal support on Coronet models.
㉓—One flasher used for both systems.

1975 FORD MOTOR CO. CARBURETORS

CARTER YF ADJUSTMENT SPECIFICATIONS

Year	Carb. Model	Idle Mixture Screw Setting	Float Level	Float Drop	Idle Vent Setting	Fast Idle Cam Setting	Dechoke or Unloader Setting	Pulldown Setting	Vacuum Break Setting	Choke Setting
1975	D5DE-DA	①	⅜	—	—	.140	.250	.290	—	2 Rich
	D5DE-EA	①	⅜	—	—	.140	.250	.290	—	2 Rich
	D5DE-GA	①	⅜	—	—	.140	.250	.290	—	2 Rich
	D5DE-MA	①	⅜	—	—	.140	.250	.290	—	2 Rich

FORD MOTORCRAFT MODEL 5200 ADJUSTMENT SPECIFICATIONS

Year	Carb. Model (9510)	Idle Mixture Turns Open	Float Level	Pump Setting (Hole)	Choke Pulldown	Dechoke Clearance	Fast Idle Speed	Fast Idle Cam Clearance	Dashpot Setting	Choke Setting
1975	D52E-AA	①	.046	2	.197	.256	—	.098	—	1 Lean
	D52E-BA	①	.046	2	.197	.256	—	.098	—	1 Lean
	D52E-CA	①	.046	2	.197	.256	—	.098	—	1 Lean
	D52E-DB	①	.046	2	.197	.256	—	.098	—	1 Lean
	D5ZE-EA	①	.046	2	.197	.256	—	.098	—	1 Lean
	D5ZE-FA	①	.046	2	.197	.256	—	.098	—	1 Lean
	D5ZE-GA	①	.046	2	.197	.256	—	.098	—	1 Lean
	D5ZE-HB	①	.046	2	.197	.256	—	.098	—	1 Lean

FORD MOTORCRAFT MODEL 2150 ADJUSTMENT SPECIFICATIONS

Year	Carb. Model (Code 9510)	Idle Mixture Turns Open	Float Level (Dry)	Fuel Level (Wet)	Pump Setting Hole No.	Choke Plate Clearance (Pull down)	Fast Idle Cam Linkage Clearance	Fast Idle Speed (Hot Engine)	Dechoke Clearance	Dashpot Setting	Choke Setting
1975	D5AE-AA	①	—	—	—	—	—	—	—	—	—
	D5DE-AA	①	—	—	—	—	—	—	—	—	—
	D5DE-BA	①	—	—	—	—	—	—	—	—	—
	D5DE-CA	①	—	—	—	—	—	—	—	—	—
	D5DE-DA	①	—	—	—	—	—	—	—	—	—
	D5DE-HA	①	—	—	—	—	—	—	—	—	—
	D5DE-JA	①	—	—	—	—	—	—	—	—	—
	D5ME-AA	①	—	—	—	—	—	—	—	—	—
	D5ME-BA	①	—	—	—	—	—	—	—	—	—
	D5OE-AA	①	—	—	—	—	—	—	—	—	—
	D5OE-BA	①	—	—	—	—	—	—	—	—	—
	D5OE-CA	①	—	—	—	—	—	—	—	—	—
	D5ZE-AA	①	—	—	—	—	—	—	—	—	—
	D5ZE-BA	①	—	—	—	—	—	—	—	—	—
	D5ZE-CA	①	—	—	—	—	—	—	—	—	—
	D5ZE-JA	①	—	—	—	—	—	—	—	—	—

FORD MOTORCRAFT MODEL 4350-4V ADJUSTMENT SPECIFICATIONS

Year	Carb. Model (Code 9510)	Idle Mixture Turns Open	Float Level (Dry)	Pump Setting (Hole No.)	Choke Plate Clearance (Pulldown)	Fast Idle Cam Linkage Setting	Fast Idle Speed (Hot Engine)	Auxiliary Inlet Valve Setting	Dechoke Clearance	Dashpot Setting	Choke Setting
1975	D5AE-CA	①	—	—	—	—	—	—	—	—	—
	D5AE-DA	①	—	—	—	—	—	—	—	—	—
	D5VE-AD	①	—	—	—	—	—	—	—	—	—
	D5VE-BA	①	—	—	—	—	—	—	—	—	—

①—Air/fuel ratio or idle CO% rating is found in Tune Up Specification tables in car chapters.

Each purchaser of a new car receives a new car warranty certificate from the selling dealer. Before placing this certificate in the glove compartment, where it will often be forgotten, the car owner should carefully read it to the point where he fully understands what is required of him so as not to invalidate the terms of the warranty. Typical samples of the various new car warranties are shown.

It is also possible, a purchaser of a vehicle that has been used as a dealer demonstrator, will be given a warranty valid only for the balance or unused portion of the time or mileage left, whichever shall expire first. A person buying a used car may receive a 30 day guarantee or possibly even for longer periods. This would seem to imply that the selling dealer will guarantee this vehicle unconditionally for that expressed period of time. Or possibly, the guarantee is only a 50/50 guarantee which means the car owner would be asked to pay for one half the cost of the repairs and the selling dealer assumes the remaining one half the cost. Whatever the case, be sure you are fully aware of the terms and conditions of the warranty.

Since the passing of the 5 year or 50,000 mile warranty, whichever shall occur first, there has been a resurgence of the so called extended warranty. At the time of car purchase the dealer will explain that for a sum of say $15.00 or $25.00 you can have your warranty extended from the original 12 months or 12,000 miles to 5 years or 50,000 miles, whichever shall occur first. The provision that must be met usually states you must use a certain brand of lubricants and you must have prescribed maintenance servicing, for which you pay the usual charge. It might be necessary for you to return the car to the selling dealer for this servicing although it is generally permissable for the work to be done at another location providing you hold all invoices necessary for you to prove to the selling dealer that the prescribed work had been performed. It is advisable for you to have these conditions clearly defined so there will be no misunderstanding later when the car might be returned for service under this warranty.

Remember, there are many and varied kinds of warranties generally being offered. Know your warranty. But, at such time as a problem should occur and you feel it should be covered by your warranty, discuss this problem with a representative of the selling dealer first. Your next course of action would be to contact the vehicle manufacturers' Zone Office. If you still feel you haven't been satisfied you should then write to the vehicle manufacturers' Customer Relations Department outlining a full history of the problem. This process usually results in a better understanding and avoids the head to head battling which accomplishes very little in the way of straightening out the difficulty.

Warranty Facts Booklet

1974 New Car and Light Truck Warranty

(except Capri, Comet, Courier, Maverick, Mustang II and Pinto)

Ford* and the Selling Dealer jointly warrant for each 1974 model passenger car or light truck (P400 or lower series) sold by Ford that for the earliest of 12 months or 12,000 miles from either first use or retail delivery, the Selling Dealer will repair or replace free of charge any part except tires that is found to be defective in factory materials or workmanship under normal use in the United States or Canada.

All Ford and the Selling Dealer require is that you properly operate, maintain and care for your vehicle, and that you return for warranty service to your Selling Dealer's place of business or to any authorized Ford or Lincoln-Mercury dealer if you are traveling, have moved a long distance or need emergency repairs. Warranty repairs will be made with Ford Authorized Service or Remanufactured Parts.

To the extent allowed by law, THIS WARRANTY IS IN PLACE OF all other warranties, express or implied, including ANY IMPLIED WARRANTY OF MERCHANTABILITY OR FITNESS. Under this warranty, repair or replacement of parts is the only remedy.

* Ford Motor Company except in Canada where it is Ford Motor Company of Canada, Limited.

Please retain this Booklet in your vehicle.

Ford Customer Service Division

Fig. 1   A typical Ford Motor Co. warranty for 1974 models

CHRYSLER CORPORATION'S WARRANTY AND LIMITATION OF LIABILITY - FOR NEW 1974 MODEL PASSENGER CARS

WARRANTY PERIOD: Chrysler Corporation warrants this vehicle for 12 months or 12,000 miles, whichever occurs first, according to the following terms:

WHAT IS COVERED BY THE WARRANTY: Any part of this vehicle manufactured or supplied by Chrysler Corporation (except tires) found defective in material or workmanship.

WHO IS ELIGIBLE: All owners of this vehicle during the warranty period are covered by this warranty.

WARRANT START DATE: The warranty starts on the date of sale to the original retail purchaser or on the date this vehicle is originally placed in service, whichever occurs first.

OBTAINING WARRANTY SERVICE: Warranty service will be provided by the Selling Dealer at his place of business. The Selling Dealer will repair or replace, at Chrysler's option, the defective part without charge for parts or labor.

In the event the owner cannot return to the Seling Dealer (the Selling Dealer has ceased to do business as an authorized dealer or the owner is travelling, has moved or is living in a different locality and cannot return to the Selling Dealer), the owner may obtain warranty service at any authorized Chrysler Motors Corporation dealership.

WHAT IS NOT COVERED BY THE WARRANTY: This warranty will not apply to:

- Any vehicle on which the odometer mileage is altered;
- Normal maintenance services (as outlined in the Operator's Manual supplied with this vehicle) and the parts used in connection with such services;
- Repairs necessitated by accident, abuse, negligence or racing;
- Loss of use of the vehicle, loss of time, inconvenience or other consequential damages.

THIS WARRANTY IS IN LIEU OF ANY OTHER WARRANTIES OR CONDITIONS, INCLUDING MERCHANTABILITY OR FITNESS FOR A PARTICULAR PURPOSE. THE REMEDIES UNDER THIS WARRANTY ARE EXCLUSIVE AND NEITHER CHRYSLER CORPORATION NOR CHRYSLER MOTORS CORPORATION ASSUMES NOR AUTHORIZES ANYONE TO ASSUME FOR THEM ANY OTHER OBLIGATION.

• • •

TIRES—Tires originally installed on new passenger cars are warranted separately by the tire manufacturer and not by Chrysler.

Although the specific terms of these warranties will differ, generally tire manufacturers guarantee their tires for the life of the original tread against defects in material and workmanship and failure caused by normal road hazards such as blow-outs, fabric breaks, cuts, bruises and snags. These guarantees do not cover damage or failure caused by punctures, running flat, fire, wrecks, chain cuts, irregular wears, abuse, etc. Generally these guarantees provide that any tire determined to be defective or damaged within the terms of such guarantee will be repaired or replaced at the tire manufacturer's option. If replacement is made, the owner must pay the tire manufacturer's current adjustment base price plus transportation charges and taxes for such tire less a pro rata allowance based on the amount of the original tread remaining on the tire replaced. In some instances, the owner must also pay a service charge.

Warranty services pertaining to tires may be obtained from an authorized service station of the tire manufacturer or an authorized Chrysler Motors Corporation dealer providing such services. If necessary, an authorized Chrysler Motors Corporation dealer will assist an owner in requesting an adjustment.

The foregoing guarantees specifically provide that they do not cover consequential damage and that they are the only guarantees issued by the tire manufacturers.

BATTERIES—Original equipment batteries will be replaced for up to 36 months on the following basis. Should a battery prove defective during the first 12 months or 12,000 miles, whichever occurs first, it will be replaced without charge under the terms and conditions of the new vehicle warranty. Thereafter, and for up to 36 months from the date of original retail sale or original use of the vehicle, whichever occurred first, a defective battery will be replaced on a pro rata adjustment basis. The pro rata adjustment provides the owner credit towards the purchase of a new battery of equal or greater capacity. The number of months remaining between the time of failure and 36 months will determine the amount of credit. For additional information on the pro rata adjustment period, contact an authorized Chrysler Motors Corporation dealer.

Notice: A battery which is merely discharged is not considered defective.

Fig. 2 A typical Chrysler Corporation warranty for 1974 models

1974 PONTIAC NEW VEHICLE WARRANTY

WHAT IS WARRANTED AND FOR HOW LONG

Pontiac* (Pontiac Motor Division, General Motors Corporation) warrants to the owner of each 1974 model Pontiac passenger car that for a period of 12 months or 12,000 miles, whichever first occurs, it will repair any defective or malfunctioning part of the car —except tires which are warranted separately by the tire manufacturer. This warranty covers only repairs made necessary due to defects in material or workmanship, and needed service adjustments during the first 90 days of the warranty period.

The 12 month/12,000 mile warranty period shall begin on the date the car is delivered to the first retail purchaser or, if the car is first placed in service as a demonstrator or company car prior to sale at retail, on the date the car is first placed in such service.

WHAT IS NOT COVERED BY THE WARRANTY

This warranty does not cover:

1. Conditions resulting from misuse, negligence, alteration, accident, or lack of performance of required maintenance services;
2. The replacement of maintenance items (such as spark plugs, ignition points, positive crankcase ventilation valve, filters, brake and clutch linings) made in connection with normal maintenance services;
3. Loss of time, inconvenience, loss of use of the car or other consequential damages;
4. Any car on which the odometer mileage has been altered and the car's actual mileage cannot be readily determined; or
5. Any car registered and normally operated outside the United States or Canada. The warranty for these cars shall be that authorized for the country in which the car is registered and normally operated.

PONTIAC'S OBLIGATIONS

1. Repairs qualifying under this warranty will be performed by any authorized Pontiac dealer within a reasonable time following delivery of the car to the dealer's place of business.
2. During the first 90 days of the warranty period,

* For vehicles sold in Canada, substitute the name General Motors of Canada Limited wherever the name Pontiac Motor Division appears in this folder.

any authorized Pontiac dealer will make any needed service adjustments.
3. Pontiac will pay the authorized Pontiac dealer for any repairs or 90-day service adjustments under the warranty.

OWNER'S OBLIGATIONS

1. After the first 90 days of the warranty period, needed service adjustments referred to in item 2 of "Pontiac's Obligations" are considered to be items of normal maintenance resulting from use and are to be paid for by the owner.
2. The car must be delivered to an authorized Pontiac dealer's place of business during regular business hours for the performance of warranty repairs or service adjustments.
3. The owner is responsible for maintenance services which may be performed at the owner's option by any repair outlet regularly performing such services.

● ● ● ● ●

This is the only express warranty applicable to 1974 model Pontiac passenger cars and Pontiac neither assumes nor authorizes anyone to assume for it any other obligation or liability in connection with such cars.

WHAT TO DO IF THERE IS A QUESTION REGARDING WARRANTY

The satisfaction and goodwill of owners of Pontiac products are of primary concern to Pontiac dealers and Pontiac Motor Division. In the event a warranty matter is not handled to your satisfaction, the following steps are suggested:

1. Discuss the problem with your Pontiac dealership management.
2. Contact the Pontiac Zone Office (General Motors Zone Office in Canada) closest to you as listed in the Pontiac General Information Owner's Manual.
3. Contact the Customer Services Manager* at the address below.

**PONTIAC MOTOR DIVISION
GENERAL MOTORS CORPORATION
Pontiac, Michigan 48053**

* In Canada contact the Owner Relations Manager at General Motors of Canada Limited, Oshawa, Ontario.

Fig. 3   A typical General Motors warranty for 1974 models

CAR WARRANTIES

1975 BUICK NEW CAR WARRANTY

WHAT IS COVERED

Buick Motor Division, General Motors Corporation,* warrants to owners of 1975 Buick passenger cars which are registered and normally operated in the United States or Canada:

- The Buick dealer of the owner's choice will make any repairs on any part of the car, except tires, made necessary because of defects in material or workmanship for 12 months or 12,000 miles of use, whichever first occurs, from the date the car is delivered to the first retail purchaser or first placed in service as a demonstrator or company car, whichever is earlier, and will make any needed service adjustments during the first 90 days of use.

- Warranty repairs and needed service adjustments will be performed without charge to the owner by the Buick dealer at its place of business within a reasonable time after delivery of the car to the dealer.

WHAT IS NOT COVERED

- Repairs and service adjustments required because of misuse, negligence, alteration, accident or lack of reasonable and proper maintenance are not covered, nor are the replacement of maintenance items (such as spark plugs, positive crankcase ventilation valves, filters, brake and clutch linings) made in connection with normal maintenance services.

- Loss of time, inconvenience, loss of use of the car or other matters not specifically included are not covered.

- Any car registered and normally operated outside the United States or Canada. The warranty for these cars shall be that authorized for the country in which the car is registered and normally operated.

Buick Motor Division, General Motors Corporation, does not authorize any person to create for it any other obligation or liability in connection with these cars.

* For vehicles sold in Canada, substitute the name General Motors of Canada, Limited, wherever the name Buick Motor Division, General Motors Corporation, appears in this folder.

1975 BUICK EMISSION CONTROL SYSTEMS WARRANTY

Buick Motor Division, General Motors Corporation,* warrants to owners of 1975 Buick cars that the car (1) was designed, built, and equipped so as to conform at the time of sale with applicable regulations of the U.S. Federal Environmental Protection Agency, and (2) is free from defects in materials and workmanship at the time of sale which cause the car to fail to conform with applicable Federal Environmental Protection Agency regulations for a period of use of 50,000 miles or 5 years, whichever occurs first.

The 5-year/50,000-mile warranty period shall begin on the date the car is delivered to the first retail purchaser or, if the car is first placed in service as a demonstrator or company car prior to sale at retail, on the date the car is first placed in such service.

OWNER'S OBLIGATION

1. Perform emission system maintenance as required in Maintenance Schedule folder.
2. Use only unleaded gasoline.
3. Receipts covering the performance of regular maintenance should be retained in the event questions arise concerning maintenance. These receipts should be transferred to each subsequent owner of this car.

WHAT IS NOT COVERED BY THE WARRANTY

This warranty does not cover:

1. Conditions resulting from misuse, alteration, accident, failure to use unleaded gasoline or not performing maintenance services;
2. The replacement of maintenance parts (such as spark plugs, PCV valve, and filters) used in regular maintenance services;
3. Loss of time, inconvenience, loss of use of the car or other consequential damages;
4. Any car on which odometer mileage has been changed so that mileage cannot be readily determined.

Buick Motor Division, General Motors Corporation, does not authorize any person to create for it any other obligations or liability in connection with these systems. This warranty is in addition to the 1975 Buick New Car Warranty.

* For vehicles sold in Canada, substitute the name General Motors of Canada, Limited, wherever the name Buick Motor Division, General Motors Corporation, appears in this folder.

Fig. 4 A typical General Motors warranty for 1975 models

1-720

TROUBLE SHOOTING

Index of Symptoms

ENGINE

Starting a stalled engine 2-1
Closed crankcase ventilation 2-2
Engine won't start 2-2
Hard starting 2-3
Engine stalls 2-3
Engine starts but won't drive car 2-4
Engine misfires 2-4
Lack of power 2-4
Poor high speed performance 2-4
Rough engine idle 2-4
Spark knock 2-5
Pre-ignition 2-5
Engine kickback 2-5
Backfire 2-5
Muffler explosion 2-5
After-burning 2-5
Flat spot 2-5
Fails to reach operating temperature ... 2-5
Engine continues to run after ignition is
   turned off 2-5
Engine overheats 2-6
Engine oil leakage 2-6
High oil consumption 2-7
Oil pressure relief valve leaks 2-7
Engine oil dilution 2-7
No oil pressure 2-7

Low oil pressure 2-7
High oil pressure 2-7
Engine noises 2-7
Fuel pump noise 2-8

ELECTRICAL

Battery requires frequent recharging ... 2-8
Starter won't rotate or rotates slowly .. 2-9
Starter spins but won't engage flywheel . 2-9
Starter pinion jammed into flywheel gear 2-9
Starter pinion disengages slowly 2-9
Starter pinion won't release 2-10
Starter noise 2-10
Alternator troubles 2-10
Locating shorts with test lamp 2-10
Fusible links 2-10
Lights flicker 2-10
Lamps fail to burn 2-11
Lights flare up when engine is
   speeded up 2-11
Stop light troubles 2-11
Turn signal troubles 2-11
Clock troubles 2-11
Hazard warning flashers 2-11

AUTOMATIC TRANSMISSIONS   1
CLUTCH 2-12
MANUAL TRANSMISSIONS
   THREE SPEED 2-13
   FOUR SPEED 2-14
OVERDRIVES 2-15
REAR AXLES 2-16
DISC BRAKES 1
DRUM BRAKES 2-17
FRONT SUSPENSION 2-17
STEERING GEARS 2-17
POWER TOPS 2-18
POWER WINDOWS 2-18
POWER SEATS 2-18
WINDSHIELD WIPERS 2-19

1—See Service Chapter.

Engine Troubles

STARTING A STALLED ENGINE

When an engine fails to start the chances are that 90 per cent of the cases will involve the ignition system and seldom the fuel system or other miscellaneous reasons. If a systematic procedure is followed the trouble can almost always be found without the use of special equipment.

To begin with, turn on the ignition switch and if the ammeter shows a slight discharge (or if the telltale lamp lights) it indicates that current is flowing. A glance at the gas gauge will indicate whether or not there is fuel in the tank.

Operate the starter and if the engine turns over freely, both the battery and starter are functioning properly. On the other hand, if the starter action is sluggish it may be due to a discharged or defective battery, loose, corroded or dirty battery terminals, mechanical failure in the starter, starter switch or starter drive. If the starter circuit is okay, skip this phase of the discussion and proceed to ignition.

Starter Circuit Checkout

To determine which part of the starter circuit is at fault, turn on the light switch and again operate the starter. Should the lights go out or become dim, the trouble is either in the battery, its connections or cables. A hydrometer test of the battery should indicate better than 1.250 specific gravity, while a voltmeter, placed across the positive and negative posts, should indicate about 12 volts. If either of these tests prove okay, clean and tighten the battery connections and cable terminals or replace any cable which seems doubtful.

If the lights remain bright when the starter is operated, the trouble is between the battery and the starter, or the starter switch is at fault, since it is evident that there is no electrical connection between these points. If these connections are clean and tight, it is safe to assume that the starter or starter switch is defective.

Neutral Safety Switch

If the ammeter shows a slight discharge (or if the telltale lamp lights) when the ignition is turned on, but the system goes dead when the starting circuit is closed, the neutral safety switch may be at fault. To check, bypass the switch with a suitable jumper. If the engine now starts, adjust or replace the switch.

CAUTION: With the safety switch bypassed, the car can be started in any gear. *Be sure the transmission is in neutral or park and the parking brake is applied.*

Primary Ignition Checkout

Let's assume that the battery and starter are doing their job, and that fuel is reaching the carburetor, but the car does not start, then the trouble must be somewhere in the ignition circuit. But first, before starting your diagnosis, it is advisable to give the whole system a visual inspection which might uncover obvious things such as broken or disconnected wires etc.

The best way to start tracking down ignition troubles is to begin with the primary circuit since this is where troubles show up most frequently. First remove the distributor cap and block the points open with a piece of cardboard, then turn on the ignition and with a test bulb or voltmeter check to see if there is current at the terminal on the distributor. If you do not get a reading at this point, the current is cut off somewhere in the connections leading back to the ignition switch or it may be that the condenser has an internal short to the ground. The latter possibility can be eliminated if you can restore current at the distributor terminal by disconnecting the condenser from the distributor plate so that its outside shell is not grounded. With the possibility of a bad condenser out of the way, work toward the ignition switch and test for current at each connection until you get to one where you get a reading. Between this connection and the distributor lies the trouble.

The foregoing steps in checking the primary circuit should include checking the ignition coil resistor for defects or loose connections. As this is done, bear in mind that while the starter cranks the engine, the resistor is by-passed by the starter switch on Ford and Delco-Remy systems (see Tune Up Chapter for details). This means that while the circuit through the resistor may be satisfactory, a broken connection or high resistance between the starter switch by-pass terminal and the coil would prevent starting. On the other hand, a satisfactory by-pass circuit might start the engine while the engine would stall immediately upon releasing the starter switch if there was a defect in the coil resistance circuit.

If, to begin with, the test equipment shows a current reading at the distributor terminal, it is safe to assume that the trouble is in the unit itself, most likely burned or dirty breaker points. A final positive test for defective breaker points can be made very simply by removing the cardboard from between the points, and positioning the distributor cam by turning the engine to where the points are closed. With the points closed there should be no current at the distributor terminal. If there is current, replace the points.

In an emergency, the points can be cleaned by using the sanded side of a match box, a knife blade, or the sharp edge of a screwdriver to scrape the scale from the contact faces. After cleaning the points, if a gauge is not available to set the gap, a quick adjustment can be made by using four layers of a piece of newspaper. The thickness of the paper is equivalent to about .020", which is the approximate gap setting for most distributors. Of course, at the earliest opportunity, a precise point adjustment should be made.

If the procedure outlined under "Primary Ignition Checkout" does not uncover the trouble then it will be necessary to continue the tests into the secondary ignition circuit.

Secondary Ignition Checkout

First of all, remove the wire from one of the spark plugs, turn on the ignition and operate the starter. While the engine is cranking, hold the terminal of the spark plug wire about 1/4" away from the engine or spark plug base. If the spark is strong and jumps the gap, the trouble is confined to either the spark plugs or lack of fuel. Before going any further, wipe the outside of the plugs to remove any dirt or dampness which would create an easy path for the current to flow, then try to start the engine again. If it still fails to start, remove one of the spark plugs and if it is wet around the base, it indicates that the fuel system is okay, so it naturally follows that the spark plugs are at fault. Remove all the plugs, clean them and set the gaps. An emergency adjustment of spark plug gaps can be made by folding a piece of newspaper into 6 or 7 layers. When changing the gap, always bend the side (ground) electrode and never the center one as there is danger of breaking the insulation.

Fuel System Checkout

If the spark plug that was removed showed no indication of dampness on its base, check the fuel system. A quick check can be made by simply removing the carburetor air cleaner and looking down into the carburetor. Open and close the throttle manually and if fuel is present in the carburetor, the throttle will operate the accelerating pump, causing it to push gasoline through the pump jet. If it does, check the choke valve. If the engine is cold, the choke valve should be closed. If the choke won't close, the engine can be started by covering the carburetor throat while the engine is cranking, provided, of course, that fuel is reaching the carburetor.

Check the operation of the fuel pump by disconnecting the fuel lines from the pump to the carburetor. Crank the engine and if the pump is working, fuel will pulsate out of the line. If not, either the pump isn't working or the line from the tank to the pump is clogged. Before blaming the pump, however, disconnect the line at the inlet side of the pump which leads to the tank and, while a companion listens at the tank, blow through the line. If a gurgling sound is heard back in the tank, the line is open and the trouble is in the pump. Remove the sediment bowl, if so equipped and clean the screen, then replace the bowl and screen, being sure that you have an air-tight fit. If the pump still refuses to function, it should be removed and repaired.

The foregoing discussion will, in most cases, uncover the cause of why an engine won't start. However, if further diagnosis is necessary, the following list will undoubtedly provide the answer.

CLOSED CRANKCASE VENTILATION

If the control valve becomes clogged with carbon or other foreign matter, the ventilation system will not operate and a slight pressure will build up in the crankcase which may cause oil leakage at the rear main bearing or by the piston rings. And should the valve fail to seat it will be impossible to make the engine idle satisfactorily.

SERVICE NOTE: If idle speed is slow, unstable, rolling, frequent stalling, breather backflow and oily engine compartment the ventilator valve may be completely plugged, or the valve may be stuck in the open position. A valve stuck in the closed position is indicated by breather backflow at heavy throttle and oily engine compartment. If the valve is stuck in the intermediate position it will be indicated by rough, fast idle and stalling.

The ventilation valve assembly should be cleaned every six months or 6000 miles (whichever comes first) and more frequently in service such as extensive engine idling during cold weather.

When the valve assembly is removed for cleaning, place a finger over the open end of the ventilator hose or tube and have the engine started. If the ventilator hose or tube and carburetor passages are open and operating normally, a strong suction will be felt and there will be a large change in engine idle quality when the end of the hose is uncovered. If these conditions are not observed, the carburetor passages and/or ventilator hose are plugged and must be cleaned. The carburetor should be removed from the engine and the ventilation passages cleaned by dipping the lower part of the carburetor in the cleaner. A pipe cleaner can be used to aid in cleaning passages.

ENGINE WON'T START

IMPORTANT—Alternator equipped cars cannot be push-started when the battery is completely dead because, unlike a generator, there is no residual magnetism in the rotor.

If the engine fires when the ignition switch is turned on but quits when the switch is released to its running position, it indicates that the ignition coil resistor has lost its continuity or there is a bad connection at the resistor terminals.

Due to Open Primary Ignition Circuit

1. Burned or oxidized ignition points.
2. Ignition coil resistance unit burned out or open.
3. Starting switch ignition coil resistance by-pass circuit open.
4. Ignition points not closing.
5. Breaker arm binding on pivot post, preventing closing of points.
6. Breaker arm spring weak or broken.
7. Breaker arm distorted or bent.
8. Dirty ignition points.
9. Primary lead connection loose at distributor or coil.
10. Primary windings in coil broken.
11. Open ignition switch circuit.

Due to Grounded Primary Ignition Circuit

A grounded coil primary winding, a grounded ignition switch, or a grounded switch-to-coil primary lead will cause excessive current flow and will usually cause wires to burn.

1. Ignition points not opening or closing due to improper adjustment.
2. Ignition points not opening due to worn rubbing block on breaker arm.
3. Faulty bushing in breaker arm.
4. Cracked or faulty insulator at distributor primary terminal.
5. Grounded condenser.
6. Distributor-to-coil lead grounded.
7. Primary coil winding grounded.

Due to Faulty Secondary Ignition Circuit

1. Corroded spark plug cable terminals.
2. Chafed or cracked cable insulation.
3. Ignition coil weak or inoperative.
4. Moisture on ignition coil, terminals, distributor cover, spark plug porcelains, or in distributor.
5. Improper type of spark plugs.
6. Cracked distributor cap or a burned carbon track from distributor cap center terminal to housing.
7. Improper installation of spark plug cables (not correct for firing order).
8. Spark plugs damaged, dirty or wet,

porcelains cracked, or gaps improperly spaced.
9. Rotor contact spring bent or broken.
10. Distributor rotor grounded.
11. Distributor cap center terminal (inner) broken or missing.
12. Broken or burned out radio suppressor in distributor cap.

Due to Battery

1. Battery run down.
2. Terminals loose or badly corroded.
3. Improper ground.
4. Battery cables frayed or undersize.

Due to Starter Motor

1. Not operating properly.
2. Congealed engine oil due to use of too heavy a grade of oil or to the formation of sludge.
3. Starter gear binding in flywheel gear.
4. Defective starter switch.
5. Faulty neutral safety switch on cars with automatic transmission.

Due to Excessive Fuel Supply (Flooding)

The engine is said to be flooded with fuel when a quantity of liquid fuel collects in the intake manifold, and perhaps also in the cylinders. This condition gives a mixture that is much too rich to ignite.
If the carburetor has a provision for opening the choke valve when the throttle is fully open, crank the engine with the throttle open until engine starts. It will start as soon as the extra fuel is pumped out.
If the choke valve is not designed to open when the throttle is fully opened, tie or block the choke valve open and crank the engine until it starts.
Flooding may also occur on the road. If the carburetor supplies too rich a mixture at full throttle, the intake manifold may be flooded with liquid fuel, with the result that when the engine is stopped, heat evaporates the fuel and thus provides an over-rich incombustible mixture. The engine won't start until the rich mixture is pumped out by cranking.
1. Choke not operating property.
2. Automatic choke not properly set.
3. Carburetor unloaded linkage (if equipped) not properly set.
4. Float level set too high.
5. Dirty, worn or faulty needle valve and seat.
6. Float sticking or rubbing against side of fuel bowl.
7. Leak in float, allowing fuel to get inside.
8. Fuel pump pressure too great.

Due to Insufficient Fuel Supply

1. Carburetor inlet needle stuck in its seat, due to gum in fuel.
2. Float level too low.
3. Clogged inlet screen at carburetor.
4. Faulty fuel pump or one of insufficient capacity.
5. Fuel pump strainer clogged.
6. Faulty fuel pump bowl gasket.
7. Flexible line (if used) twisted, deteriorated or restricted.
8. Fuel line to tank clogged, kinked, restricted or leaking.
9. Vent in fuel tank filler cap clogged or restricted.
10. Worn fuel pump camshaft lobe.

HARD STARTING
When Engine is Hot

This condition is usually caused by an over-supply of fuel due to any of the items listed under *Engine Won't Start Due to Excessive Fuel Supply*. In rare cases, an ignition coil may lose its efficiency when it is hot and cause ignition failure.

When Engine is Cold

Many of the conditions enumerated under *Engine Won't Start* also may cause hard starting in cold weather. Of particular importance, however, are the following:
1. Choke setting too lean.
2. Fuel may have kerosene in it or water, or ice in bottom of tank.
3. Ice in fuel filter bowl.
4. Ice in fuel lines.
5. Engine is cranked too slowly or won't turn over because: (a) engine oil is too thick in sub-zero weather; (b) battery weak due to extremely low temperature.
6. Another possibility, although remote, is that the water pump is jammed with ice, which will interfere with cranking engine if fan belt is tight.

Due to Vapor Lock

The term vapor lock means the flow of fuel to the mixing chamber in the carburetor has been stopped (locked) by the formation of vaporized fuel pockets or bubbles caused by overheating the fuel by hot fuel pump, hot fuel lines or hot carburetor.
The more volatile the fuel the greater the tendency for it to vapor lock. Vapor lock is encouraged by high atmospheric temperature, hard driving, defective engine cooling and high altitude.
A mild case of vapor lock will cause missing and hard starting when engine is warm. Somewhat more severe vapor lock will stop the engine which cannot be started again until it has cooled off enough so that any vaporized fuel has condensed to a liquid.

SERVICE NOTE: Some cars equipped with air conditioning have a vapor bypass system. These cars have a special fuel filter which has a metering outlet in the top. Any vapor which forms is bled off and returned to the fuel tank through a separate line alongside the fuel supply line. This system greatly reduces the possibility of vapor lock. However, if vapor lock is suspected examine the bypass valve to see if it is functioning.

Due to Percolation

Percolation means simply that gasoline in the carburetor bowl is boiling over into the intake manifold. This condition is most apt to occur immediately after a hot engine is shut off. Most carburetors have a provision for relieving the vapor pressure of overheated fuel in the carburetor bowl by means of ports. If, however, percolation should take place, the engine may be started by allowing it to cool slightly and then holding the throttle wide open while cranking to clear the intake manifold of excess fuel.

After Long Storage

1. The more volatile components in the fuel have evaporated and those remaining are not sufficiently volatile to provide a combustible mixture.
2. Low or run-down battery.
3. Corrosion of engine parts may result in so much friction that starter cannot crank engine at proper speed, if at all.
4. Pistons, etc. may be struck fast by gummy oil.
5. Engine valves may stick open due to gummy deposits.
6. There is the possibility that any small part essential to the running of the engine may be stuck due to gummy film or to corrosion.
7. Some of these troubles are most likely to occur in hot, humid climate and near salt water.

ENGINE STALLS

Many troubles which prevent smooth running at idle may cause stalling. The list includes almost everything that may cause hard starting or missing. Some of the more common causes are:
1. Engine idle speed set too low.
2. Large air leaks in intake manifold such as a disconnected windshield wiper vacuum line.
3. Ignition points need attention.
4. Engine valves leaking.
5. Vapor lock.
6. Over-supply of fuel (flooding).
7. Valves set too tight.
If carburetor is equipped with a fast idle cam, which increases engine speed when the choke is in operation during the warm-up period, the engine may stall if the fast idle device fails to open the throttle due to sticking or need for adjustment.
On some cars equipped with a fluid coupling or torque converter, if the throttle is closed quickly the engine stalls. To avoid this trouble, most cars have a device which retards the speed of the throttle closing; this is called a throttle return check or dashpot and is usually mounted on the carburetor. It consists of a piston or diaphragm and a spring-closed check valve. If the linkage is out of adjustment or the check valve leaks, the engine will stall.
If the engine quits smoothly when car is in operation, the trouble is often caused by sudden lack of fuel due to:
1. Fuel tank empty.
2. Vapor lock.
3. Flooding.
4. Water in fuel.
5. Frozen fuel line.

Carburetor Icing

The carburetor discharges liquid fuel into the air stream in the form of an atomized spray which evaporates readily. The heat required to evaporate the gasoline is drawn from the entering air, thereby lowering its temperature. The cooler air chills the interior of the carburetor and may cause the moisture in the air to condense into droplets.
Under certain conditions of atmospheric temperature and humidity, the liberated moisture actually collects and freezes on the chilled carburetor surfaces, especially on the throttle plate and surrounding throttle body. When the throttle is almost

completely closed for idling, this ice tends to bridge the gap between the throttle plate and throttle body, thereby cutting off the air supply and causing the engine to stall. Opening the throttle for restarting breaks the ice bridge but does not eliminate the possibility of further stalling until the engine and carburetor has warmed up.

For carburetor icing to occur, the outside air must be cool enough so that the refrigerating effect of fuel evaporation in the carburetor will lower the temperatures of the throttle plate and body below both the dew point of moist air and the freezing point of water. The air must also contain sufficient moisture for appreciable condensation of water to occur when it is chilled in the carburetor.

Generally speaking, carburetor icing occurs when winter grade gasoline (more volatile than summer grade) is used and when the atmospheric temperature ranges from 30° to 50° F. at relative humidities in excess of 65%.

Carburetor icing problems can be reduced by the use of anti-icing additives, such as alcohols, in the fuel. Some fuel refiners use anti-stalling additives in their gasolines which have proved effective in combating carburetor icing.

Another form of carburetor icing has been observed in some engines during high-speed driving on cool, moist days. When certain cars are driven steadily at 60 to 80 mph, the large quantities of cool air passing through the carburetor may result in gradual ice formation within the carburetor's venturi. Since this ice restricts the venturi passage, the resultant increased vacuum in the venturi tends to increase the rate of fuel flow. The fuel-air mixture thus becomes excessively rich, causing loss of power and high fuel consumption.

ENGINE STARTS BUT WON'T DRIVE CAR

1. Broken part in the drive line anywhere from clutch to rear axle shaft.
2. No oil or not enough oil in fluid coupling or torque converter.
3. Some defect in automatic transmission causes binding or dragging of clutches or slipping bands.
4. Engine develops only enough power to run itself due to: (a) extremely lean or rich mixture; (b) excessive engine friction; (c) throttle does not open; (d) very dirty air cleaner; (e) clogged exhaust system.
5. Oil in fluid coupling or torque converter is semi-solid due to zero temperature. This trouble is unlikely if the recommended oil is used.

ENGINE MISFIRES
At All Speeds

1. Fouled spark plug or broken porcelain.
2. Faulty spark plug cables.
3. Low battery voltage.
4. Low generator voltage.
5. Burned or pitted ignition points.
6. Incorrect ignition point gap.
7. Faulty condenser or coil.
8. Weak spark or no spark in one or more cylinders.
9. Faulty distributor cap or rotor.

10. Primary circuit restricted or open intermittently.
11. Primary circuit detoured by short intermittently.
12. Secondary circuit restricted or open intermittently.
13. Secondary circuit detoured by short intermittently.
14. Blown clyinder head gasket between cylinders. This can be noted when missing occurs in two adjacent cylinders.
15. Sticking valves.
16. Hydraulic tappet holds valve open slightly.
17. Broken valve spring.
18. Leak at intake manifold gaskets.
19. Mixture too rich or too lean.

At High Speed

1. Hot spark plugs. Change to colder type but note that a hot plug may be due to loose installation or lack of a plug gasket (if gasket is called for).
2. Ignition point gap much too wide.
3. Breaker arm binding or sticking.
4. Breaker arm spring weak.
5. Sticking engine valves.
6. Valve springs too weak to close valves promptly.
7. Valve springs broken.
8. Valve springs shimmy.
9. Intermittent delivery of fuel to carburetor so that momentarily the mixture is too weak for combustion.
10. Mild vapor lock.
11. Weak spark.
12. Exhaust manifold clogged with carbon.
13. Exhaust manifold, muffler or tail pipe restricted.
14. Improper ignition timing.
15. Centrifugal advance not functioning properly.
16. Manifold heater valve held closed.
17. Dirty carburetor air cleaner.
18. Choke valve not completely open.
19. Carburetor throttle lever loose on shaft.
20. Improper fuel pump operation.
21. Preignition.
22. Incorrect valve timing.

At Low or Idle Speeds

1. Faulty spark plugs.
2. Spark plugs gaps too narrow.
3. Dirty or corroded secondary circuit connections or faulty ignition cables.
4. Cracked or faulty distributor cap. Radial contacts in cap burned or worn.
5. Dirty air cleaner.
6. Leaky valves.
7. Ignition point gap too narrow.
8. Faulty carburetion due to: (a) float level too high or too low; (b) float valve leaking; (c) incorrect or loose jets; (d) restricted or partially clogged idle air passage or jet; (e) air leak occurring between upper and lower carburetor body; (f) air leak occurring around carburetor throttle shaft.
9. Air leaks in intake manifold or carburetor resulting from: (a) loose manifold connections or leaks occurring in vacuum lines; (b) loose manifold nuts or capscrews; (c) broken or damaged intake manifold or carburetor gaskets; (d) cracked manifold; (e) warped or damaged manifold contacting surface.

10. Slight leaks occurring at fuel pump check valves.
11. Air leak occurring around intake valve stem because of excessive valve stem-to-guide clearance.

When Car is Accelerated

If the engine misses when car is accelerated but does not miss when idling the reason is that the spark plugs stop firing because of increased compression pressure caused by:
1. Weak spark.
2. Plug gaps too wide.
3. Plug fouled or damp.
4. Plug porcelain below par.
Also see *Flat Spot*.

LACK OF POWER OR HIGH SPEED PERFORMANCE

It should be noted that the altitude at which the car is operated has a decided effect on performance. A car adjusted for normal altitudes will lack performance at high altitudes, whereas a car which operates normally at high altitudes may have a lean carburetor adjustment and show signs of preignition when operated at sea level.
1. Ignition timing incorrect.
2. Centrifugal governor advance not operating properly.
3. Vacuum advance not operating properly.
4. Ignition points burned, pitted, sticking or bouncing (due to weak breaker arm spring).
5. Faulty spark plugs.
6. Faulty ignition cables.
7. Faulty ignition coil.
8. Faulty carburetion.
9. Lack of engine compression.
10. Preignition.
11. Inoperative manifold heater valve (stuck closed).
12. Restricted carburetor inlet resulting from dirty air cleaner or choke valve not fully open.
13. Carburetor throttle lever loose on shaft.
14. Throttle linkage not properly adjusted.
15. Carburetor throttle valve not completely open.
16. Carburetor accelerating pump not functioning properly.
17. Improper fuel pump operation.
18. Partially restricted exhaust pipe, muffler or tail pipe.
19. Clutch slippage.
20. Excessive rolling resistance resulting from (a) dragging brakes, (b) tight wheel bearings, (c) misalignment of power transmitting units, (d) misalignment of rear axle, (e) underinflated tires.
21. Incorrect rear axle gear ratio.
22. Oversize tires.
23. Incorrect valve timing.
24. Inaccurate speedometer (gives impression of lack of performance).

ROUGH IDLE

The term "rough idle" means that the engine does not run smoothly when idling. The most likely cause is an over-rich mixture but any defect which pro-

duces uneven explosions or missing will cause a rough idle. The most common causes are:
1. Dirty idle jets and passages.
2. Improper idle mixture.
3. Dirty air cleaner.
4. Improper float level.
5. Choke set too rich.
6. Air leak into intake manifold.
7. Clogged idle jets.
8. Improper ignition point gap.
9. Improper spark plug gap.
10. Weak spark.
11. Leaky engine valve.
12. Sticking valve or rocker arm.
13. Broken valve spring.
14. Insufficient tappet clearance.
15. Improper fuel pump pressure.
16. Sticking breaker arm.
17. Hydraulic tappet holds valve open.
18. Fuel volatility too high or too low.

SPARK, KNOCK, PING, DETONATION

All three expressions mean the same thing. It is a sharp metallic knock caused by vibration of the cylinder head and block. The vibration is due to split-second high-pressure waves resulting from almost instantaneous abnormal combustion instead of the slower normal combustion.

The ping may be mild or loud. A mild ping does no harm but a severe ping will reduce power. A very severe ping may shatter spark plugs, break valves or crack pistons.

Pinging is most likely to occur on open throttle at low or moderate engine speed. Pinging is encouraged by:
1. Overheated engine.
2. Low octane fuel.
3. Too high compression.
4. Spark advanced too far.
5. Hot mixture due to hot engine or hot weather.
6. Heavy carbon deposit which increases the compression pressure.

Tendency to ping increases with mixture temperature including high atmospheric temperature; intake manifold heater valve "on" when engine is warm; hot cooling water; hot interior engine surfaces due to sluggish water circulation or water jackets clogged with rust or dirt especially around exhaust valves. Some of these troubles may be confined to one or two cylinders.

If an engine pings objectionably because of too low octane fuel, retard the spark setting but first be sure that the cooling system is in good condition, the mixture not too lean and the combustion chambers free of carbon deposit.

PRE-IGNITION

Pre-ignition means that the mixture is set on fire before the spark occurs, being ignited by a red hot spot in the combustion chamber such as an incandescent particle of carbon; a thin piece of protruding metal; an overheated spark plug, or a bright red hot exhaust valve. The result is reduction of power and overheating accompanied by pinging. The bright red hot exhaust valve may be due to a leak, to lack of tappet clearance, to valve sticking, or a weak or broken spring.

Pre-ignition may not be noticed if not severe. Severe pre-ignition results in severe pinging. The most common cause of pre-ignition is a badly overheated engine.

When the engine won't stop when the ignition is shut off, the cause is often due to red hot carbon particles resting on heavy carbon deposit in a very hot engine.

ENGINE KICKBACK

If ignition is set too far advanced, spark may occur too early when engine is cranked. The first (and only) explosion runs the engine backward. A kickback may jam the starter or break the starter drive housing.

BACKFIRE

Backfiring is a subdued explosion in the intake manifold. Causes are:
1. Lean mixture (often due to dirt or water in fuel).
2. Engine cold and choke too lean.
3. Leaky or sticking intake valve or weak or broken intake valve spring.
4. Leakage of current across distributor cap may cause backfire by enabling spark to occur in a cylinder which is on its intake stroke. Two mixed-up spark plug wires may also cause this trouble.
5. Popping back is synonymous with backfire.

MUFFLER EXPLOSION

1. Late ignition timing.
2. Late valve timing.
3. Burnt exhaust valve(s).
4. Weak or broken exhaust valve spring(s).
5. Tight exhaust valve(s).
6. Intermittent open circuit in primary (ammeter needle swings further away from zero when generator is charging).
7. Intermittent short in primary (ammeter swings toward zero when generator is charging).
8. Short in coil or secondary coil wire.
9. If just a couple of explosions are heard and then no more for a time (even for days) the trouble may be due to a gradually failing condenser.

AFTER-BURNING

A subdued put-putting at the exhaust tail pipe may be due to leaky exhaust valves which permit the mixture to finish combustion in the muffler. If exhaust pipe or muffler is red hot, better let it cool, as there is some danger of setting the car on fire. Most likely to occur when mixture is lean.

FLAT SPOT

If an engine does not respond promptly when the throttle is open quickly it (or the carburetor) is said to have a flat spot. This is usually caused by any of the following:
1. Accelerator pump piston (or diaphragm) leaks.
2. Accelerator pump valves leak.
3. Accelerator pump stroke too short.
4. Accelerator pump passages restricted.
5. Fuel volatility too low or too high.
6. Float level too low.
7. Fuel pump pressure too low.
8. The anti-percolating valve (on some carburetors) may open too soon when throttle is closed. If so, carburetor may have flat spot next time throttle is opened when engine is hot.
9. Fuel too hot due to hot engine and hot weather (see Vapor Lock).
10. If carburetor has a metering pin operated by throttle linkage and also a vacuum piston linked to the throttle to give a rich mixture at part throttle and moderate engine speed, a flat spot will be noted if the device fails to function properly because of stuck piston, vacuum leakage or restricted vacuum passages.
11. If carburetor has vacuum piston which provides richer mixture at part throttle and moderate engine speed by opening an additional passage or jet within carburetor, a flat spot will occur if fuel valves fail to work, or fuel passages are restricted, or if piston does not function because it is sticking, vacuum leakage or restricted vacuum passages.
12. Late ignition timing.

ENGINE FAILS TO REACH OPERATING TEMPERATURE

1. Defective thermostat.
2. Thermostat stuck open.
3. Thermostat removed from vehicle (during flushing cooling system and not replaced).
4. Defective temperature sending unit or dash unit.

ENGINE CONTINUES TO RUN AFTER IGNITION IS TURNED OFF

This condition, known as "dieseling," "run on," or "after running," is caused by improper idle speed and/or high temperature. Idle speed and engine temperature are affected by:

Carburetor Adjustment: High idle speed will increase the tendency to diesel because of the inertia of the engine crankshaft and flywheel. Too low an idle speed, particularly with a lean mixture, will result in an increase in engine temperature, especially if the engine is allowed to idle for long periods of time.

Ignition Timing: Because advanced ignition timing causes a corresponding increase in idle speed and retarded timing reduces idle speed, ignition timing influences the tendency to diesel in the same manner as Carburetor Adjustment.

Fuel Mixture: Enriching the idle fuel mixture decreases the tendency to diesel by causing the engine to run cooler.

Fuel Content: High octane fuels tend to reduce dieseling. Increased fuel content of lead alkyl increases the tendency to diesel. Phosphates and nickel fuel ad-

TROUBLE SHOOTING

ditives help prevent dieseling.

Spark Plugs: Plugs of too high a heat range for the engine in question can cause dieseling.

Throttle Plates: If the throttle plates are not properly aligned in the carburetor bore, a resulting leanness in fuel mixture occurs, contributing to dieseling.

Electrical System: Normally, during dieseling, ignition is self-supplied by a "hot spot," self-igniting fuel, etc. However, there is a possibility of the vehicle's electrical system supplying the necessary ignition. When the ignition switch is turned off, a small amount of current can flow from the generator into the primary of the ignition coil through the generator tell-tale light. This is particularly true when the warning light bulb has been changed for one of increased wattage.

NOTE: "Run on" is more prevalent in an engine when the ignition is turned off before the engine is allowed to return to idle. Therefore, it can be reduced by letting the engine return to idle before shutting off the ignition. "Run on" incidence can be reduced on automatic transmission units by turning off the engine when in gear.

A certain amount of "run on" can be expected from any gasoline engine regardless of make, size or configuration. (Diesel engines operate on this principle.) However, if the above suggestions are correctly employed, "run on" will be reduced to an unnoticeable level.

ENGINE OVERHEATS: WATER COOLED

Water is used to cool the engine and air is used to cool the water. Anything which prevents this water-air system from working properly will cause overheating. Oil or grease in the water will reduce the ability of the water to absorb heat from the block and to transfer heat in the water to the radiator. There are seven basic causes of overheating:
1. Water does not cool engine.
2. Air does not cool water.
3. Slow combustion.
4. Pre-ignition.
5. Detonation.
6. Excessive friction in engine or elsewhere in power transmitting units.
7. Excessive back pressure in exhaust system.

Water Too Hot
1. Slipping fan belt.
2. Not enough water in system.
3. Carburetor mixture too lean.
4. Clogged exhaust system.
5. Late ignition timing.
6. Centrifugal advance fails to advance spark as engine speed increases because weights stick or because of sticking elsewhere in mechanism.
7. Pre-ignition.
8. Detonation.
9. Water circulation impeded by installation of wrong head gasket.
10. Cylinder head gasket installed incorrectly, blocking off water holes.
11. Leaky cylinder head gasket permits exhaust gas to enter water. The gas

bubbles interfere with the ability of the water to cool the engine.
12. Water circulation slowed down by rust, scale or dirt in water jackets.
13. Water distributing tube (when used) within cylinder block rusted out, dented or improperly installed so that not enough water reaches some cylinders, thus causing local overheating.
14. Local overheating at one cylinder (or more) due to heavy deposit of rust, scale or dirt in water jacket around cylinder or exhaust valve port.
15. Water circulation impeded by thermostat which fails to open fully or sticks closed.
16. Water temperature increased by thermostat which fails to open at correct temperature. Or the installation of a thermostat which opens at too high a temperature.
17. Any water hose which has rotted on inside, allowing loosened strips of rubber to impede water circulation.
18. The baffle in top tank may be bent in such a way as to interfere with free discharge of water from the hose.
19. Water passages in radiator are partially clogged with dirt, rust, corrosion or scale (mineral salts).
20. Exterior of radiator clogged with dirt, leaves or insects.
21. Rotting of water hose may weaken it so that pump suction causes it to collapse when engine is running fast, thus throttling the water flow.
22. If water pump seal leaks, air may be drawn into the water. Air bubbles in cooling water reduce the cooling ability of the water.
23. Water pump impeller loose on its shaft or impeller blades corroded.
24. Overheats due to alcohol type antifreeze during mild weather.

Water Leakage

Cylinder Head
1. Loose attaching bolts.
2. Dirty, corroded or burred surface prevents tight fit.
3. Warped surface does not fit tight against gasket.
4. Cracked due to freezing or excessive heat.
5. On overhead valve head, exhaust valve seats may be cracked, allowing water to leak into cylinders and crankcase.

Cylinder Block
1. Dirty, corroded or burred surface prevents tight fit.
2. Warped surface does not fit tight against gasket.
3. Cracked due to freezing or excessive heat.
4. If L-head design, excessive heat may crack exhaust valve seats, allowing water to leak into crankcase.
5. Block cracked due to use of cylinder head bolt which is too long.
6. Leaky expansion plugs or pipe plugs in water jacket.

Cylinder Head Gasket
1. Dirty, corroded or broken.
2. Loose because cylinder head bolts are loose.
3. Leaks because it cannot make tight contact between head and block.

Water Pump
1. Loose pump.
2. Faulty gasket.
3. Improper installation.
4. Warped pump body or dirty metal surfaces.
5. Hole or crack in pump body.
6. Worn seal.
7. Seal improperly installed.
8. Bent pump shaft.
9. Loose bearings or bushings or worn pump shaft.

Radiator
1. Leaks due to freezing or corrosion.
2. Strain due to improper attachment to car.
3. Fan striking radiator.
4. Drain plug or petcock leaks.
5. Radiator baffle bent so that water is directed into overflow pipe.
6. Clogged radiator causing water to pile up in upper tank which causes coolant to flow out overflow pipe.

Hose
1. Hose clamps loose.
2. Hose improperly installed.
3. Hose rotted through.

Heater: See that all heater connections are tight and that its radiator does not leak.

ENGINE OVERHEATS: AIR COOLED

These engines run at a higher operating temperature and depend on circulation of air across the cooling fins to keep temperature at a safe level. Overheating can be caused by:
1. Broken fan belt.
2. Seized blower bearing.
3. Jammed or misadjusted damper doors.
4. Defective damper door thermostats.
5. Engine cooling fins clogged with leaves, dirt, etc.
6. Oil cooler fins clogged.
7. Lean carburetor mixture.
8. Incorrect ignition timing.
9. Preignition.
10. Detonation.

ENGINE OIL LEAKAGE

NOTE: If engine is equipped with a positive crankcase vent valve, check the valve for proper operation before checking cause of leak. A clogged crankcase vent valve can build up pressure in the crankcase which will cause seals and gaskets to leak.

1. Oil pan drain plug loose or gasket missing.
2. Crack or hole in oil pan.
3. Oil pan gasket leaks due to: (a) loose screws; (b) damaged gasket; (c) improperly installed gasket; (d) bent oil pan flange.
4. Timing case cover gasket leaks due to: (a) loose screws; (b) damaged gasket; (c) improperly installed gasket; (d) bent cover flange; (e) leakage at engine support plate.
5. Front crankshaft oil seal leaks due to: (a) worn oil seal; (b) seal not properly installed; (c) rough surface on crankshaft, or fan pulley or

2–6

TROUBLE SHOOTING

damper; (d) damper or pulley loose; (e) seal or cover not centered on crankshaft; (f) oil return passage to crankcase clogged up.
6. Rear main bearing oil seal leaks due to: (a) worn oil seal; (b) improper oil seal installation; (c) worn rear main bearing; (d) rough crankshaft.
7. Oil return passage to crankcase clogged.
8. Expansion plug in block at rear of camshaft leaks due to poor fit, careless installation, or corrosion.
9. Leakage at any external piping.
10. Plugs at ends of oil passages in cylinder block leak.
11. Oil filter leaks.
12. Leakage at distributor housing.
13. Valve cover leaks due to loose screws, defective gasket, improperly installed gasket or bent cover flange.
14. Rocker arm cover or push rod cover leaks because of loose screws, defective gasket, improper gasket installation or bent cover flange.
15. Pipe connections loose on oil gauge or oil filter lines.
16. Loose oil pump or faulty gasket (if pump is on outside of block).
17. Clogged breather and/or crankcase ventilating discharge pipe, permits increase in pressure within engine, thus causing oil to be forced out past any oil seals or gaskets.
18. If oil pressure relief valve is mounted on outside of block, leakage may occur if unit is loose or its gasket defective.

HIGH OIL CONSUMPTION

1. External oil leaks.
2. Leaky piston rings due to wear.
3. Leaky piston rings due to sticking caused by gummy deposit. Try to free up with suitable solvent poured in fuel tank. Blue smoke at tail pipe indicates badly leaking rings.
4. Worn pistons and cylinders.
5. Cylinder block distorted by tightening cylinder head bolts unevenly.
6. Excessive clearance between intake valve stems and guides allows oil mist to be sucked into cylinders.
7. Punctured vacuum pump diaphragm permits oil from crankcase to be sucked into intake manifold.
8. Worn main or rod bearings allow excessive leakage from bearings. Result is cylinder walls are flooded with oil.
9. Oil pressure too high due to faulty action of oil pressure relief valve, or clogged relief passage.
10. If pressure lubricated, loose piston pins may permit excessive leakage to cylinder walls.
11. Grade of oil used is too light. A poor quality oil may become far too thin when engine is hot. Hard driving on hot days will also consume more oil.
12. Clogged crankcase ventilator system.

OIL PRESSURE RELIEF VALVE LEAKS

1. Relief valve needs tighter adjustment.

2. Relief valve spring weak or broken.
3. Valve seat worn or distorted.
4. Plunger type valve face worn.
5. Plunger type valve stuck open.
6. Ball type valve damaged.
7. Pump discharge pipe or passages leak.

ENGINE OIL DILUTION

1. Oil contains foam caused by presence of water in oil. Water may be due to condensation within crankcase or to a leaky cylinder head gasket.
2. Extreme dilution of oil by fuel may add enough liquid to oil to mislead. In extreme cases, oil level may increase. Dilution is greatest when frequent stops are made in cold weather.

NO OIL PRESSURE

1. Oil pressure gauge defective.
2. Pipe to oil pressure gauge stopped up.
3. Not enough oil in crankcase.
4. Oil pump inoperative.
5. Oil pressure relief valve stuck open.
6. Oil passages on discharge side of pump stopped up.
7. Oil screen or passages on intake side of pump stopped up.

LOW OIL PRESSURE

1. Oil pressure gauge inaccurate.
2. Pipe to pressure gauge restricted.
3. Oil too thin due to dilution, poor quality, or too light a grade used.
4. Oil pressure relief valve adjustment too light.
5. Relief valve spring weak.
6. Oil pump gears worn.
7. Oil pump cover worn.
8. Oil pump body or cover loose.
9. Oil pump gasket damaged, improperly installed or too thick.
10. Air leak in oil intake pipe (if oil level is low).
11. Air leak in top of floating screen (if used).
12. Oil intake pipe or screen clogged with water, sludge, gummy oil, dirt or ice.
13. Oil leak in discharge pipe.
14. Loose connections in oil lines.
15. Worn main, rod or camshaft bearings.

HIGH OIL PRESSURE

1. Oil pressure gauge defective.
2. Oil too heavy.
3. Oil pressure relief valve adjustment too heavy.
4. Relief valve spring too stiff.
5. Oil pressure relief passage clogged.
6. Plunger type relief valve stuck by gummy oil or plunger is too tight a fit.
7. Main oil passages on pressure side of pump clogged.

ENGINE NOISES
Loose Main Bearing

A loose main bearing is indicated by a powerful but dull thud or knock when

the engine is pulling. If all main bearings are loose a noticeable clatter will be audible.

The thud occurs regularly every other revolution. The knock can be confirmed by shorting spark plugs on cylinders adjacent to the bearing. Knock will disappear or be less when plugs are shorted. This test should be made at a fast idle equivalent to 15 mph in high gear. If bearing is not quite loose enough to produce a knock by itself, the bearing may knock if oil is too thin or if there is no oil at the bearing.

Loose Flywheel

A thud or click which is usually irregular. To test, idle the engine at about 20 mph and shut off the ignition. If thud is heard, the flywheel may be loose.

Loose Rod Bearing

A metallic knock which is usually loudest at about 30 mph with throttle closed. Knock can be reduced or even eliminated by shorting spark plug. If bearing is not loose enough to produce a knock by itself, the bearing may knock if oil is too thin or if there is no oil at the bearing.

Piston Pin

Piston pin, piston and connecting rod noises are difficult to tell apart.

A loose piston pin causes a sharp double knock which is usually heard when engine is idling. Severity of knock should increase when spark plug to this cylinder is short-circuited. However, on some engines the knock becomes more noticable at 25 to 35 mph on the road.

Piston pin rubs against cylinder wall, caused by lock screw being loose or snap ring broken.

Piston & Rings

1. Excessive clearance between pistons and cylinders (piston slap).
2. Out-of-round or tapered bores.
3. Top piston ring strikes ridge at top of cylinder bore.
4. Carbon deposit on top of piston strikes cylinder head.
5. Piston rubs against cylinder head gasket.
6. Broken piston ring.
7. Excessive side clearance of ring in groove.
8. Worn or broken piston ring lands.
9. Broken piston.

Valves

1. Valve click due to too much tappet clearance, hydraulic tappet not working properly, warped valve, sticking valve, binding rocker arm.
2. Insufficient oil to valve mechanism, especially overhead valves.
3. Worn or scored parts anywhere in valve mechanism.
4. Broken valve springs.
5. Weak valve springs.
6. Cocked valve springs.
7. Excessive tappet guide clearance.
8. Lower end of tappet scored, chipped, rough, worn or broken.
9. Very rough surface on cams.
10. Excessive valve stem-to-guide clearance.

2–7

11. Valve face not concentric with valve stem.
12. Valve seat face not concentric with valve stem.
13. Valve covers on overhead valve engines tightened excessively will amplify normal noise.

Hydraulic Lifters

The malfunctioning of a hydraulic valve lifter is amost always accompanied by a clicking or tapping noise. More or less hydraulic lifter noise may be expected when the engine is cold but if lifters are functioning properly the noise should disappear when the engine warms up.

If all or nearly all lifters are noisy, they may be stuck because of dirty or gummy oil.

If all lifters are noisy, oil pressure to them may be inadequate. Foaming oil may also cause this trouble. If oil foams there will be bubbles on the oil level dipstick. Foaming may be caused by water in the oil or by too high an oil level or by a very low oil level.

If the hydraulic plungers require an initial adjustment, they will be noisy if this adjustment is incorrect.

If one lifter is noisy the cause may be:
1. Plunger too tight in lifter body.
2. Weak or broken plunger spring.
3. Ball valve leaks.
4. Plunger worn.
5. Lock ring (if any) improperly installed or missing.
6. Lack of oil pressure to this plunger.

If ball valve leaks, clean plunger in special solvent such as acetone and reinstall. Too often, plungers are condemned as faulty when all they need is a thorough cleaning.

Gum and dirty oil are the most common causes of hydraulic valve lifter trouble. Engine oil must be free of dirt. Select a standard brand of engine oil and use no other. Mixing up one standard brand with another may cause gummy oil and sticking plungers. Do not use any special oils unless recommended by the car manufacturer and change oil filter or element as recommended intervals.

Timing Gears

1. Gears loose on hubs or shafts.

2. Gears misaligned.
3. Excessive gear backlash.
4. Eccentric gear, usually due to high key.
5. Teeth meshed too tight (new oversize gear).
6. Too much end play in camshaft or crankshaft.
7. Front crankshaft bearing clearance excessive.
8. Chipped tooth usually on camshaft gear.

Timing Chain

1. Chain loose due to wear.
2. Sprocket teeth worn.
3. Sprockets loose on hubs or shafts.
4. Sprockets misaligned.
5. Front camshaft bearing clearance excessive.
6. Front main bearing clearance excessive.
7. Loose vibration damper or drive pulley.

Loose Engine Mountings

Occasional thud with car in operation. Most likely to be noticed at the moment the throttle is opened or closed.

Excessive Crankshaft End Play

A rather sharp rap which occurs at idling speed but may be heard at higher speeds also. The noise should disappear when clutch is disengaged.

Water Pump

1. Water pump shaft pulley loose.
2. Impeller loose on shaft.
3. Too much end play in pump shaft.
4. Too much clearance between shaft and bearings.
5. Impeller blades rubbing against pump housing.
6. Impeller pin sheared off or impeller broken.
7. Rough bearing.
8. Pump seal too hard.

Fan Belt

1. Belt worn or burned.
2. Wrong belt. Does not fit pulley grooves properly.

3. Belt too tight. Squeaks.
4. Belt or pulley dirty or sticky with gummy oil.
5. Pulley bent, cracked or broken.
6. Belt pulleys misaligned.
7. Belt loose; squeaks when engine is accelerated.

Fan

1. Fan blades bent.
2. Fan blades loose on hub.
3. Fan out of balance when made.
4. Fan blades strike radiator.
5. Fan shaft end play excessive.
6. Fan shaft loose on its bearings.
7. Defective fan bearings.
8. Bearings need lubrication.

Engine Vibration

1. Unequal compression in cylinders.
2. Missing at high speed.
3. Unbalanced fan or loose fan blade.
4. Incorrect adjustment of engine mount or damaged mounts.
5. Loose engine mounts.
6. Engine support loose on frame or cylinder block.
7. Unbalanced or sprung crankshaft.
8. Excessive engine friction due to tight pistons, etc.
9. Defective vibration damper.

Fuel Pump Noise

Diagnosis of fuel pumps suspected as noisy requires that some form of sounding device be used. Judgment by ear alone is not sufficient, otherwise a fuel pump may be needlessly replaced in attempting to correct noise contributed by some other component. Use of a stethoscope, a long screwdriver, or a sounding rod is recommended to locate the area or component causing the noise. The sounding rod can easily be made from a length of copper tubing $1/4$ to $3/8$ inch in diameter.

If the noise has been isolated to the fuel pump, remove the pump and run the engine with the fuel remaining in the carburetor bowl. If the noise level does not change, the source of the noise is elsewhere and the original fuel pump should be reinstalled. On models using a fuel pump push rod, check for excessive wear and/or galling of the push rod.

Electrical Troubles

NOTE—Ignition troubles are included in the *Engine Troubles* section under the various operating difficulties these troubles could cause.

BATTERY REQUIRES FREQUENT RECHARGING

Insufficient Current Flow to Battery
1. Defective generator or alternator.

2. Incorrect voltage regulator setting.
3. Regulator contacts oxidized or burned.
4. Sulphated battery.
5. Corroded battery terminals.
6. Regulator not grounded.
7. Loose connections or grounds in lighting or ignition circuits.
8. Slipping fan belt.
9. Blown regulator fuse.
10. Wrong size generator drive pulley.

11. Shortened or open alternator rectifiers.
12. Grounded stator windings in alternator.

Excessive Starting Load Causing Abnormal Current Flow From Battery
1. Frequent use of starting motor.
2. Excessive use of starting motor due to difficulty in starting.
3. Faulty starting motor.
4. Excessive engine friction due to tight pistons, etc., or heavy engine oil.

Excessive Lighting Load
1. Car operation confined largely to night driving.
2. Tail and stop light wires reversed.
3. Stop light switch inoperative (closed at all times).
4. Unnecessary use of head lamps while parking.
5. Ground or short in lighting circuit.

Abnormal Accessory Load
1. Radio.
2. Heater.
3. Windshield defroster.
4. Cigar lighter.
5. Spotlights.

Internal Discharge of Battery
1. Plates badly sulphated.
2. Cell leak due to cracked jar or sealing compound.
3. Water level not maintained at proper height.
4. Plate separators ineffective.
5. Exterior of battery covered with corrosion and acid-soaked dirt which forms a path to ground for current.

Miscellaneous
Radio suppressor connected to generator or regulator field terminal.

STARTER WON'T ROTATE OR ROTATES SLOWLY

If lights become dim or go out when the starter switch is closed, the battery may be too weak to operate the starter. In this case, the engine may be started by pushing the car.

NOTE—Some cars cannot be started by pushing because their automatic transmissions have no rear oil pump to drive the engine through the transmission. In such cases, a fully charged battery should be installed or a "jumper" circuit should be used from another charged battery.
Cars equipped with alternators cannot be push started if the battery is completely dead because alternators retain no residual magnetism.

Due to Starter Circuit
1. Low battery. Lights grow very dim or go out when starter switch is closed.
2. Connections loose, dirty, corroded or broken at battery terminals, starter switch terminal, battery ground strap.
3. Short circuit across starter terminal.

Due to Starter Switch
1. Starter pedal (if any) stuck.
2. Starter switch stuck.
3. Pedal linkage fails to close starter switch (older cars).
4. Defective solenoid.
5. Neutral safety switch on cars with automatic transmissions out of adjustment or defective.
6. Starter switch makes poor contact due to dirt, corrosion, bent parts, weak contact spring.

7. Starter switch fails to close circuit because of sticking or broken contact parts.

Due to Armature & Field Circuits
1. Armature windings burned out, shorted, grounded or open-circuited.
2. Short circuit in armature winding or brush pigtail lead.
3. Broken wire in armature winding or brush pigtail lead.
4. Loose, dirty or corroded connections in armature circuit, including ground.
5. Field coils burned out, shorted or grounded.
6. Broken wire in field winding or broken lead.
7. Loose, dirty or corroded connections in field circuit.

Due to Commutator & Brushes
1. Brush pigtail leads loose or broken.
2. Starter brushes cracked crosswise (prevents flow of current).
3. Arm type brush holder sticks.
4. Brush sticks in sliding brush holder.
5. Bent brush holder misaligns brush and causes poor contact.
6. Starter brushes badly worn.
7. Brush leads shorted or have loose, dirty, corroded or broken connections.
8. Poor brush contact due to weak or broken springs.
9. Brushes coated with oil.
10. High mica between commutator segments prevents brush contact.
11. Commutator bars loose and/or solder melted.
12. Commutator dirty, corroded or burned.

Due to Engine Resistance
1. Piston sticking to cylinders in overheated engine.
2. Pistons struck to cylinders because of gummy oil.
3. Pistons binding in cylinders because of corrosion after long lay-up.
4. Jammed generator armature.
5. Combustion chamber full of water.
6. Solid ice in water pump.
7. Broken part in engine causes jamming.
8. Excessive engine friction, due to cold weather and too heavy oil.

Due to Improper Engine Repairs
1. New rings too tight.
2. New pistons too tight.
3. Main or rod bearings too tight.
4. New camshaft bearings too tight.

Due to Armature Binding
1. Loose field poles.
2. Armature shaft frozen in bearings.
3. Loose end plates.
4. Windings thrown out of armature slots.
5. Armature locked magnetically to field poles because of loose bearings or worn or bent armature shaft.
6. Bendix spring retaining screws loose (jammed against housing).

7. Cracked or distorted drive housing.
8. Starter misaligned.
9. Starter jams because of burred teeth on drive pinion or flywheel gear.
10. Starter pinion (sliding gear type) jams because of incorrect endwise clearance.

STARTER SPINS BUT WON'T ENGAGE FLYWHEEL GEAR
Bendix Type
1. Bendix pinion stuck on shaft due to dirty or gummy shaft or bent shaft.
2. Bendix spring broken.
3. Bendix spring bolt broken.
4. Pinion housing cracked.
5. Drive key sheared.
6. Pinion teeth broken off.
7. Starter ring gear has several teeth missing.
8. Armature shaft broken.

Sliding Gear Type
1. Weak or broken meshing spring.
2. Fault in sliding gear linkage.
3. Fault in solenoid.
4. Over-running clutch worn out or lubricant caked or gummy.
5. Drive key sheared.
6. Pinion teeth broken off.
7. Flywheel ring gear has several teeth missing.
8. Armature shaft broken, dirty or dry.
9. Wrong starter pinion clearance.

STARTER PINION JAMMED INTO FLYWHEEL GEAR
1. Burred teeth on pinion or ring gear.
2. Misalignment of starter or armature shaft.
3. If engine kicks back when being started, Bendix pinion may jam. Loosen starter to free pinion.

STARTER PINION DISENGAGES SLOWLY
Bendix Type
The most probable cause is a dirty Bendix drive shaft. Or the pinion may bind on its shaft due to a bent shaft or too tight a fit between pinion and splines.
When a Bendix Folo-Thru starter drive stays in mesh too long it is probably due to a sticking release pin which is designed to be released by centrifugal force at a certain engine rpm. In such an instance the drive should be replaced.

Sliding Gear Type
1. Pinion binds on its shaft due to too tight a fit or due to bent or burred shaft.
2. Pinion shaft sticky or dirty.
3. Sliding gear operating linkage sticking or binding.
4. Solenoid does not operate properly.

STARTER PINION WON'T RELEASE

Bendix Folo-Thru Drive

Failure to disengage would most probably be caused by a stuck release pin which is designed to be released by centrifugal force at a given engine rpm. If such is the case, replace the drive unit.

Sliding Gear Type

If solenoid operated, the solenoid may be defective. If pedal operated, the shift linkage may be binding or sticking. May also be caused by a defective starting switch on cars with key-starter switch or by improper starter pinion clearance.

STARTER NOISE

1. Loose pole pieces rubbing against armature.
2. Gear noise due to defective teeth.
3. Flywheel ring gear untrue.
4. Starter drive housing loose on flywheel housing.
5. Starter loose on drive housing.
6. Commutator end plate loose.
7. Armature shaft bent.
8. Worn armature shaft, bearings or bushings.
9. Drive pinion shaft bent.
10. Worn drive pinion shaft, bearings or bushings.
11. Misalignment caused by dirt or burrs on mating surfaces.

ALTERNATORS

Alternator Fails to Charge

1. Drive belt loose.
2. Brushes sticking.
3. Open charging circuit.
4. Open in stator winding circuit.
5. Faulty soldered connections at output terminal stud.
6. Rectifiers open circuited.

Low Unsteady Charging Rate

1. Drive belt loose.
2. High resistance at battery terminal posts.
3. Loose connections.
4. Poor ground between engine and body ground wire.
5. Resistance in charging circuit.
6. Open stator windings.

Low Output

1. Grounded stator.
2. Shorted rectifier.
3. Voltage regulator faulty.

Excessive Charging Rate

1. Voltage regulator faulty.
2. Open circuited rectifier.

Noisy Alternator

1. Misaligned belt or pulley, or loose pulley.
2. Shorted rectifier.

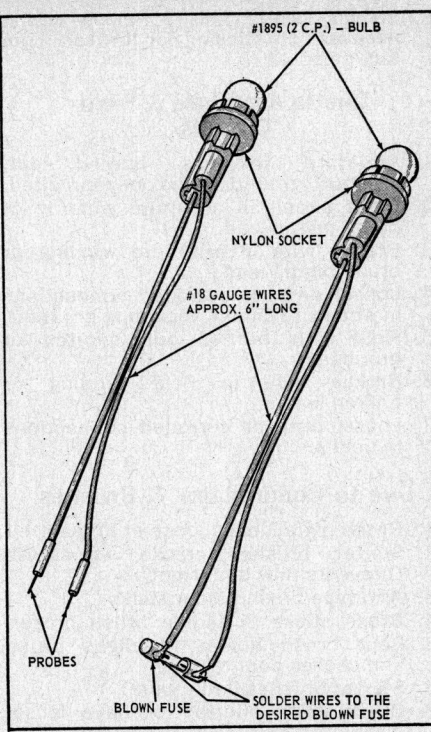

Test lamp for locating shorts

3. Worn bearings.
4. Rotor shaft sprung.

Regulator Points Oxidized

1. Poor ground connections.
2. Improper voltage regulator air gap setting.
3. Shorted field in alternator.
4. Voltage regulator setting too high.

Burned Points or Coil Windings in Regulator

1. Voltage regulator setting too high.

Voltage Regulator Points Stuck

1. Poor ground connections between alternator and regulator.

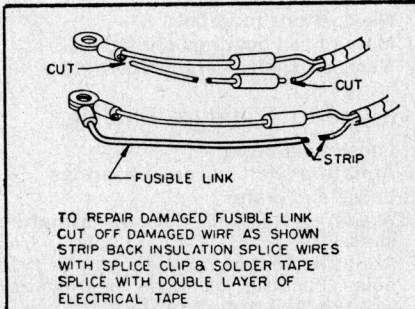

TO REPAIR DAMAGED FUSIBLE LINK CUT OFF DAMAGED WIRE AS SHOWN STRIP BACK INSULATION SPLICE WIRES WITH SPLICE CLIP & SOLDER TAPE SPLICE WITH DOUBLE LAYER OF ELECTRICAL TAPE

Repairing fusible links

LOCATING ELECTRICAL SHORTS WITH TEST LAMP

Due to the complexity of locating electrical short circuits where several circuits are protected by the same fuse, fabricate a test lamp from the material shown in the accompanying illustration. By substituting the test lamp for the blown fuse the short circuit can be isolated.

When the test lamp is inserted into the fuse panel, the bulb will light and continue to glow until the short circuit is removed. Determining which circuit is at fault can be accomplished by disconnecting the affected circuits one at a time until the test lamp goes out. Then trace the circuit to find the cause of the short (wire contacting sharp sheet metal edges, wire pinched between two metal objects, etc.).

For circuits that are not connected to the fuse panel but are protected by an in-line fuse cartridge, use a test lamp having two needle point probes in place of the blown fuse. Insert one probe through the insulation and into the wire on each side of the blown in-line fuse and follow the same testing procedure outlined above.

FUSIBLE LINKS

Some cars starting with 1965 models have fusible links located between the battery and the lower ends of the main supply wires. These links are the weakest point in the electrical supply system for the entire car and, as such, will act as a fuse for every wire harness in the car. Every electrical accessory is still protected by a fuse or circuit breaker, of course, but fusible links have been added to protect the wiring harnesses *before* the fuses.

In the past, if a wire became grounded in the portion between the battery and the fuse block, a long section of the wire would burn out, making replacement of a complete wiring harness necessary. Now, with the fusible links, a short or ground in any unfused wire will cause only a short link to burn out. Because of its location, possibility of a fire, such as was sometimes caused by a burned-out wiring harness, is very remote.

A fusible link is simply a short section of wire that is several sizes smaller in gauge than the wire in the circuit which it protects. If a short or ground occurs the fusible link will melt before the insulation is damaged elsewhere in the circuit. Replace burned-out fusible link as directed in the illustration.

LIGHTS FLICKER
Circuit Breaker Vibrates

When the circuit breaker vibrates and causes lights to flicker it indicates a short in one of the lighting circuits, which may be traced as follows:

1. Pull switch successively to each lighting position. If circuit breaker vibrates in all positions except "off" the trouble should be found in the tail lamp and license lamp circuit, or instrument, map light, or clock light

circuits.

2. If circuit breaker vibrates in parking lamp position only, look for a short in the parking lamp circuit.
3. If circuit breaker vibrates in headlamp position only, inspect headlamp wiring circuit and lamp assemblies. If both filaments in headlamps burn at the same time, check dimmer switch.

LAMPS FAIL TO BURN

1. Burned out bulb.
2. An open circuit in wiring.
3. A defective switch.
4. Burned out fuse.

LIGHTS FLARE UP WHEN ENGINE IS SPEEDED UP

This condition is caused by high voltage in the electrical system due to one or more of the following:

1. Electrolyte in battery low or weak.
2. High resistance in circuit between generator and battery due to loose or dirty connections.
3. Poor ground between generator and engine.
4. Voltage regulator adjusted too high.
5. Voltage regulator inoperative.
6. Ground or short in generator field circuit.

STOP LIGHT TROUBLES

1. If only one stop light fails to burn, check lamp bulb, socket and wiring.
2. If both stop lights fail to burn also check stop light switch and fuse.
3. If stop light burns when brake pedal is released, check stop light switch, brake pedal clearance and for dragging brakes.
4. If compensating port in brake master cylinder is plugged by foreign material, or is covered by the piston primary cut when brake pedal is released, high pressure will be maintained in hydraulic system and stop light switch will remain closed.

TURN SIGNAL TROUBLES

1. If signals are inoperative on both turns, look for a blown fuse or a defective flasher.
2. If stop lights burn, the fuse and rear signal lamp bulbs are okay.
3. An inoperative right signal light may be caused by a burned out bulb at the right indicator or a right signal lamp. The opposite applies for an inoperative left signal light.
4. If bulbs are okay, look for an open circuit or defective switch.
5. If indicator light on dash burns steady when lever is placed in a turn position, check for burned out bulb in park or stop light. If park and stop light bulbs are okay, check for faulty flasher.
6. If indicator light on dash does not burn when lever is in a turn position, check for burned out bulb or a faulty flasher.
7. If switch fails to cancel after completion of turn, remove steering wheel and check for worn or broken mechanism.

ELECTRIC CLOCKS

If clock does not run, check for blown "clock" fuse. If fuse is blown check for short in wiring. If fuse is not blown check for open circuit.

With an electric clock, the most frequent cause of clock fuse blowing is low voltage at the clock which will prevent a complete wind and allow clock contacts to remain closed. This may be caused by any of the following: discharged battery, corrosion on contact surface of battery terminals, loose connections at battery terminals, at junction block, at fuse clips, or at terminal connection of clock. Therefore, if in reconnecting battery or clock it is noted that the clock is not ticking, always check for blown fuse, or examine the circuits at the points indicated above to determine and correct the cause. See *Dash Gauge* chapter for Electric Clock data.

HAZARD WARNING FLASHER TROUBLES

To make a quick check of the system pull Hazard Warning switch to ON position. The rear turn signal bulbs should flash as well as the front turn signal bulbs, turn signal indicator bulbs and pilot bulb. All lights will burn continuously when the brake pedal is depressed; this is normal.

Pilot Bulb Fails to Flash

Check for burned out bulb and loose or defective ground wire. Replace bulb, repair ground wire or tighten ground wire screw. If this does not correct the condition, replace flasher switch and harness assembly. Then repeat quick check procedure.

All Bulbs Fail to Flash

1. Check for loose harness connections at Hazard Warning connectors and secure connectors if necessary.
2. Check for a burned out tail and stop light fuse and replace if necessary.
3. Check for a defective Hazard Warning flasher or switch. This may be done by removing the flasher and installing a known good flasher.
4. Pull switch to ON position. If flasher does not operate properly, replace flasher switch and harness assembly, installing old flasher. If system still does not operate properly, install new flasher along with new switch.

Some Bulbs Fail to Flash While Others are Operative

1. Turn ON ignition switch and turn OFF Hazard Warning switch.
2. Place turn signal lever first to right and then to left turn position. If turn signal circuits operate properly, the Hazard Warning switch and harness assembly should be replaced.
3. If the same bulbs fail to flash, the cause is most likely a burned-out bulb. In the case of turn signal indicator bulbs, a loose or defective ground wire can also cause this condition. Repair as necessary.

NOTE: If any turn signal bulb fails to flash when the turn signal circuit is actuated, the reduced current in the circuit will cause the remaining signals on the side of the car to burn steadily. If the Hazard Warning flasher is energized, however, all turn signal bulbs and indicator bulbs will flash except those that have a circuit defect. They will flash at a constant rate unless the battery is completely run down. This is because the Hazard Warning Flasher overrides the turn signal circuit flasher.

4. If the condition is still not resolved, disconnect the Hazard Warning connectors and again check the operation of the turn signal circuits. If the affected bulbs now flash, replace flasher switch and harness assembly.
5. If the condition is still not resolved, look for defects in the connectors to the affected bulb.
6. Repeat quick check test.

Clutch Troubles

CLUTCH DRAGS

Clutch drag means that when the clutch pedal is depressed fully the clutch disc is not completely released. In consequence it does not come to rest but continues to rotate, being dragged around by the rotation of the engine. Clutch dragging causes clashing of gears, especially when shifting from neutral to low or reverse.

1. Pedal cannot disengage clutch because of excessive free pedal travel. Pedal linkage should be adjusted so that the pedal shank is about 1" from the under side of the toe-board.
2. Worn clutch linkage.
3. Release levers need adjustment.
4. Clutch disc warped out of true.
5. High spots on clutch facing.
6. Broken or loose facings.
7. Loose rivet in facing.
8. Clutch disc hub binds on splined clutch shaft due to bent shaft, tight fit, burred splines or splines covered with gummy oil or dirt.
9. Clutch disc wobbles because of broken springs in hub.
10. Clutch disc hub out of true.
11. Clutch shaft bent.
12. Clutch shaft out of true because of worn bearings.
13. Transmission is not in alignment with flywheel housing.
14. Clutch pressure plate warped, thus throwing release levers out of adjustment.
15. Flange of clutch cover not in alignment with flywheel because of loose attaching screws, bent flange, dirt between flange and flywheel.
16. Grease on clutch facings.
17. Engine misaligned due to deteriorated or broken engine mounts.
18. Loose flywheel housing-to-engine attaching bolts.
19. Release fork pivot worn.

CLUTCH SLIPS

The clutch disc slips whenever the clutch pressure plate fails to hold it tight against the face of the flywheel. If clutch slippage is severe, the engine speed will rise above normal on full throttle in high gear. Slight but continuous slippage may go unnoticed until the clutch facings are ruined by excessive temperature caused by friction.

In a very high percentage of cases, clutch slippage is due to less than zero clearance between the shank of the pedal and the toe-board because of failure to have the pedal adjusted in time. The consequence is worn and burned clutch facings. Before the clutch starts slipping, the normal wear of the facings causes a gradual reduction in clutch pedal free play. When there is no free play of the pedal the clutch starts slipping.

Other causes of clutch slippage are:
1. Driving with foot resting on pedal.
2. Binding or sticking of pedal or its linkage.
3. Binding or sticking of clutch disc hub on clutch shaft.
4. Binding of release levers.
5. Release bearing sleeve sticks.
6. Weak or broken clutch pressure springs.
7. Worn clutch facings.
8. Facings covered with grease or oil.
9. Facings burned.
10. Release levers improperly adjusted.
11. Pressure plate sticks.

CLUTCH GRABS

A clutch is said to grab when it engages too abruptly. The usual causes are:
1. Loss of tension in cushioning plates in the rim of the steel clutch disc. These plates cause the clutch facings to bulge outward slightly. The resulting springy action of the facings aids in producing a smooth, gentle clutch engagement.
2. Use of wrong type of clutch facing.
3. Grease or oil on facings.
4. Clutch springs too stiff.
5. Momentary binding in clutch linkage while clutch is being engaged.
6. Exposed rivet heads due to excessively worn facings or loose rivets.

CLUTCH CHATTERS

If a clutch chatters while it is being engaged, the trouble is caused by rapid gripping and slipping. The usual causes are:
1. Somewhat sticky clutch friction surfaces due to engine or transmission oil leaking from defective seal.
2. Clutch friction surfaces damp or wet.
3. Weak clutch springs.
4. Slight binding in clutch linkage during engagement.
5. Slight binding of pressure plate during engagement.
6. Loose engine mounts.

CLUTCH PEDAL PULSATES

Clutch pedal pulsation has often been termed a nervous pedal. When a slight pressure is applied on the pedal, with the engine running, the pedal will vibrate or bounce with every revolution of the engine. As the pressure on the pedal is increased, the pulsation will cease.
1. Loose or improperly adjusted engine mounts.
2. Collar on clutch release sleeve does not run true due to a bent clutch

shaft, or the clutch shaft misaligned because of misalignment between crankshaft and transmission.
3. Clutch release levers not adjusted to uniform height.

CLUTCH RATTLES

This condition will occur when the engine is idling with transmission in neutral.
1. Excessive clearance at pressure plate driving lugs.
2. Anti-rattle springs or retractor springs on release levers (or release bearing) weak, broken or disconnected.
3. Looseness in clutch pedal operating linkage.
4. Loose flywheel.

NOISE WHEN PEDAL IS DEPRESSED

1. Clutch release bearing worn, dirty, damaged, broken or inadequately lubricated.
2. Clutch shaft bearing or bushing in crankshaft worn, damaged, broken or inadequately lubricated.
3. Clutch shaft rear bearing at front end of transmission, worn, dirty or lacks lubricant.

NOISE WHEN PEDAL IS RELEASED

1. Misalignment of transmission with engine causing slight wobble of clutch disc hub—noticeable with engine idling or at low road speed.
2. Disc hub loose fit on splined clutch shaft.
3. Disc damper springs weak or broken.
4. No pedal play.
5. Weak or broken pedal return spring.
6. Weak or broken release sleeve spring.
7. Clutch linkage sticks.
8. Clutch pedal sticks.
9. Clutch release sleeve sticks.
10. Clutch release fork binds.
11. Bad clutch release bearing.
12. Loose flywheel.

BEARING NOISE

Clutch Release Bearing:—With engine idling, there is a high-pitched rubbing noise when foot rests on clutch pedal.

Clutch Pilot Bearing:—Fairly high-pitched noise when clutch pedal is fully depressed with engine idling.

Three Speed Transmission Troubles
Fully Synchronized Transmission
Car Application Listed in Three Speed Manual Shift Transmission Chapter

STICKING IN GEAR
1. Clutch not releasing completely.
2. Low lubricant level.
3. Corroded transmission levers.
4. Tight main drive gear pilot bushing.
5. Defective synchronizer sleeve or blocking ring.

FORWARD GEARS CLASH
1. Clutch not releasing completely.
2. Weak or broken springs in synchronizer assembly.
3. Worn blocking rings and/or cone surfaces.
4. Broken blocking ring.

NOISY IN FORWARD SPEEDS
1. Insufficient or incorrect lubricant.
2. Transmission misaligned or loose.
3. Main drive gear or bearings worn or damaged.
4. Countergear bearings worn or damaged.
5. Synchronizers worn or damaged.

NOISY IN REVERSE
1. Reverse idler gear or shaft worn or broken.
2. Reverse gear worn or broken.

HARD SHIFTING
1. Improper clutch or adjustment.
2. Worn or damaged shift linkage.
3. Incorrect lubricant.
4. Synchronizers worn or broken.

JUMPING OUT OF GEAR
1. Misadjusted, worn or loose shift linkage.
2. Transmission loose or misaligned.
3. Worn pilot bearing.
4. Excessive end play in main drive gear.
5. Weak detent cam spring.
6. Detent cam notches worn.
7. Worn clutch teeth on main drive gear or synchronizer sleeve.
8. Worn or broken synchronizer.
9. Bent output shaft.

Three Speed Transmission Troubles
General Motors Transmission with Second Speed Gear Located at Rear of Mainshaft
Car Application Listed in Three Speed Manual Shift Transmission Chapter

SLIPS OUT OF HIGH AND/OR 2ND GEAR
1. Transmission mounting bolts loose.
2. Control rods interfere with engine mounts or clutch release lever.
3. Control linkage does not work freely.
4. Gear does not fully engage.
5. Damaged mainshaft pilot bearing.
6. Clutch gear bearing retainer broken or loose.
7. Dirt between transmission case and clutch housing (front mounted), or between transmission case and differential carrier (rear mounted).
8. Misalignment of transmission.
9. Worn or broken synchronizer assembly.
10. Weak springs in transmission cover.

SLIPS OUT OF LOW AND/OR REVERSE
1. First and/or reverse gears damaged from operating at part engagement.
2. Improperly mated splines on inside of first and reverse gear and/or external spline on 2nd and 3rd synchronizer sleeve.
3. Improperly adjusted linkage.
4. Weak springs in transmission cover.

NOISY IN ALL GEARS
1. Not enough lubricant.
2. Worn countergear bearings.
3. Worn or damaged clutch gear and countershaft drive gear.

4. Damaged clutch gear or mainshaft ball bearings.
5. Damaged speedometer gears.

NOISY IN HIGH GEAR
1. Damaged clutch gear bearing.
2. Damaged mainshaft bearing.
3. Damaged speedometer gears.

NOISY IN NEUTRAL WITH ENGINE RUNNING
1. Damaged clutch gear bearing.
2. Damaged mainshaft pilot bearing roller.

NOISY IN ALL REDUCTION GEARS
1. Not enough lubricant.
2. Worn or damaged clutch gear or countershaft drive gear.

NOISY IN SECOND ONLY
1. Damaged or worn 2nd speed gears.
2. Worn or damaged countergear rear bearings.

NOISY IN LOW AND REVERSE ONLY
1. Worn or damaged 1st and reverse sliding gear.

2. Damaged or worn low and reverse countergear.

NOISY IN REVERSE ONLY
1. Worn or damaged reverse idler.
2. Worn reverse idler bushings.
3. Damaged or worn reverse countergear.

EXCESSIVE BACKLASH IN SECOND ONLY
1. Second gear thrust washer worn.
2. Mainshaft rear bearing improperly installed in case.
3. Worn countergear rear bearing.

EXCESSIVE BACKLASH IN REDUCTION GEARS
1. Worn countergear bushings.
2. Excessive end play in countergear.

LEAKS LUBRICANT
1. Too much lube in transmission.
2. Loose or broken clutch gear bearing retainer.
3. Clutch gear bearing retainer damaged.
4. Cover loose or gasket damaged.
5. Operating shaft seal leaks.
6. Idler shaft expansion plugs loose.
7. Countershaft loose in case.
8. Lack of sealant on bolts.

TROUBLE SHOOTING

Three Speed Transmission Troubles

All Transmissions with Low-Reverse Gear Located at Rear of Mainshaft
Car Application Listed in Three Speed Manual Shift Transmission Chapter

NOISES

When diagnosing transmission noise note the gear position in which the noise occurs. Noise present in all gear positions may be due to worn or damaged constant mesh gears or bearings. Noise present in only one gear can usually be traced to the particular gear involved. Other causes of noise are as follows:

1. Misalignment due to loose mounting bolts.
2. Clutch housing misalignment.
3. Dirt or metal chips in lubricant.
4. Not enough lube in transmission.
5. Improper lubricant.

HARD SHIFTING

1. Clutch linkage out of adjustment.
2. Linkage improperly adjusted.
3. Linkage binding due to bent, worn or broken parts.
4. Gearshift tube binding due to misaligned steering gear housing.
5. Improper lube in transmission.
6. Damaged synchronizer assembly.

JUMPS OUT OF GEAR

1. Improper shift procedure.
2. Linkage parts worn, bent, broken or out of adjustment.
3. Excessive end play caused by wear in shift forks, sliding gear fork grooves, thrust washers, mainshaft and countershaft bearings, or clutch pilot bushing.
4. Misalignment or excessive clearance between sliding gear and mainshaft.
5. Damaged synchronizer.
6. Weak springs in transmission cover.

LEAKAGE

1. Overfilled transmission or using a lube that foams or expands while car is in operation.
2. Loose gearshift housing capscrews.
3. Damaged gaskets.
4. Transmission vent plugged.
5. Extension housing rear seal leaks.

Corvair 4-Speed Trans. Troubles

SLIPS OUT OF GEAR

1. Transmission loose on differential carrier.
2. Control linkage binds or does not fully engage.
3. Damaged or missing mainshaft pilot bearings.
4. Clutch gear bearing retainer loose or broken.
5. Dirt between transmission case and differential carrier.
6. Worn or damaged synchronizer.
7. Weak detent spring (s).

NOISY IN ALL GEARS

1. Insufficient lubricant.
2. Worn countergear bearings.
3. Worn or damaged clutch gear and countergear.
4. Damaged clutch gear bearing or mainshaft rear bearing.

NOISY IN HIGH GEAR

1. Damaged clutch gear bearing.
2. Damaged mainshaft bearing.

NOISY IN NEUTRAL

1. Damaged clutch gear bearing.
2. Damaged mainshaft pilot roller bearings.

NOISY IN ALL REDUCTION GEARS

1. Insufficient lubricant.
2. Worn or damaged clutch gear or countergear.

NOISY IN 2nd ONLY

1. Damaged or worn 2nd speed gears.
2. Worn or damaged countergear bearings.

NOISY IN LOW & REVERSE

1. Worn or damaged low and reverse sliding gear.
2. Damaged or worn low and reverse countergear.

NOISY IN REVERSE ONLY

1. Worn or damaged reverse idler gear.
2. Worn reverse idler gear bushings.
3. Worn or damaged countergear reverse teeth.

EXCESSIVE BACKLASH IN ALL REDUCTION GEARS

1. Worn countergear bushings.
2. Excessive end play in countergear.

LEAKS LUBRICANT

1. Excessive amount of lubricant in transmission.
2. Loose or broken clutch gear bearing cover.
3. Clutch gear bearing retainer gasket damaged.
4. Cover loose or gasket damaged.
5. Shifter shall seal leaks.
6. Countershaft loose in case.

Four Speed Transmission Troubles

All Cars Other Than Corvair

NOISY IN ALL SPEEDS

1. Incorrect lubricant level.
2. Incorrect type lubricant.
3. Countergear bearings worn or damaged.
4. Countergear worn or damaged.
5. Clutch gear bearing worn or damaged.
6. Mainshaft bearing worn or damaged.
7. Clutch gear worn or damaged.
8. Transmission misaligned or loose.

NOISY IN 1st SPEED

1. First gear worn or damaged.
2. Countergear worn or damaged.
3. Countergear bearings worn or damaged.
4. Synchronizers worn or broken.
5. Countershaft worn or damaged.

NOISY IN 2nd SPEED

1. Second gear worn or damaged.
2. Countergear worn or damaged.
3. Countergear bearings worn or damaged.
4. Synchronizers worn or broken.
5. Countershaft worn or damaged.

NOISY IN 3rd SPEED

1. Third gear worn or damaged.
2. Countergear worn or damaged.
3. Countergear bearings worn or damaged.
4. Synchronizers worn or broken.
5. Countershaft worn or damaged.

NOISY IN 4th SPEED

1. Clutch shaft bearing worn or damaged.
2. Mainshaft bearing worn or damaged.
3. Synchronizers worn or broken.

NOISY IN REVERSE

1. Reverse idler gear or shaft worn or damaged.
2. Reverse sliding gear worn or damaged.
3. Shift linkage out of adjustment.
4. Shift linkage bent or damaged.
5. Shift linkage parts loose.
6. Shift levers, shafts or forks worn.

SHIFTS HARD

1. Clutch pedal free travel incorrect.
2. Clutch parts worn or damaged.
3. Shift linkage out of adjustment.
4. Shift linkage bent or damaged.
5. Shift linkage parts loose.
6. Shift levers, shafts or forks worn.
7. Lubricant type incorrect.
8. Lubricant level incorrect.

JUMPS OUT OF GEAR

1. Shift linkage out of adjustment.
2. Shift linkage bent or damaged.
3. Shift linkage parts loose.
4. Shift levers, shafts or forks worn.
5. Shift cover loose or gasket damaged.
6. Transmission misaligned or loose.
7. Synchronizers worn or broken.
8. Clutch gear bearing retainer broken.
9. Clutch gear bearing worn or damaged.
10. Clutch pilot bearing worn or broken.
11. Mainshaft and/or pilot worn or damaged.
12. Mainshaft bearing worn or damaged.

LEAKS LUBRICANT

1. Lubricant level incorrect.
2. Lubricant type incorrect.
3. Vent plugged.
4. Clutch gear bearing retainer or gasket loose.
5. Clutch gear bearing retainer broken.
6. Shift cover loose or gasket damaged.
7. Shifter shaft seals leaking.
8. Shift cover bolts not sealed.
9. Countershaft loose in case bore.

Overdrive Troubles

DIAGNOSIS

Figs. 1 and 2 illustrate the overdrive circuit diagrams in use. Since overdrive troubles may originate not only in the mechanical operation of the unit but also in the electrical circuit which controls that unit, always check the control system before disassembling the overdrive. If the trouble is not found after a thorough inspection of the control system, then the transmission and overdrive should be removed for examination. If the overdrive operation is unsatisfactory, look for:

1. Blown fuse in governor-solenoid circuit.
2. Loose terminals on any of the connecting wires.
3. Incorrect terminal locations of connecting wires.
4. Circuits grounded by water, dirt or deformation.
5. Defective solenoid points.
6. Insufficient travel or unsatisfactory contacts in kickdown switch.
7. Excessive end play in governor shaft.
8. Improper adjustment of governor control springs.
9. Burned governor contact points.
10. Damage to governor cap and contacts.
11. Absence of rubber cover to exclude water and dirt.
12. Insufficient travel of shift rod (adjust control cable).

MECHANICAL TROUBLES

Overdrive Won't Drive Unless Locked Up Manually

1. Occasionally the unit may not drive the car forward in direct drive unless locked up by pulling the dash control. This may be caused by one or more broken rollers in the roller clutch, the remedy for which is to replace the entire set of rollers.
2. This condition may also be caused by sticking of the roller retainer upon the cam. This retainer must move freely to push the rollers into engaging position under the pressure of the two actuating springs.
3. Sometimes this condition is due to slight indentations, worn in the cam faces by the rollers spinning, remedied by replacing the cam.

Overdrive Does Not Engage or Lock-Up Does Not Release

1. Dash control improperly connected.
2. Transmission and overdrive improperly aligned.

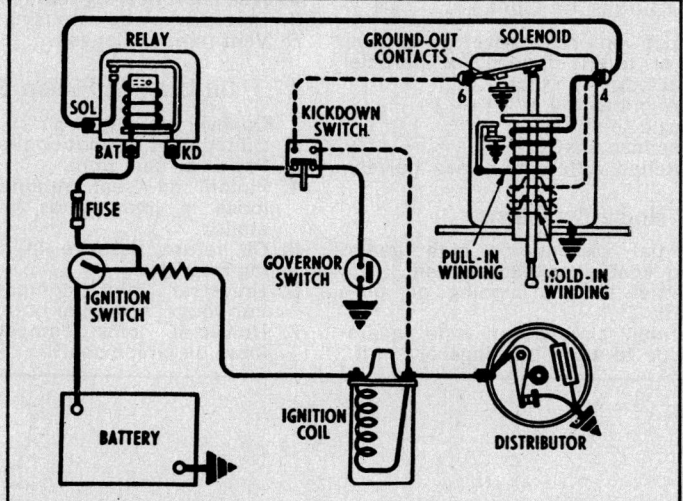

Fig. 1 Overdrive circuit diagram with relay

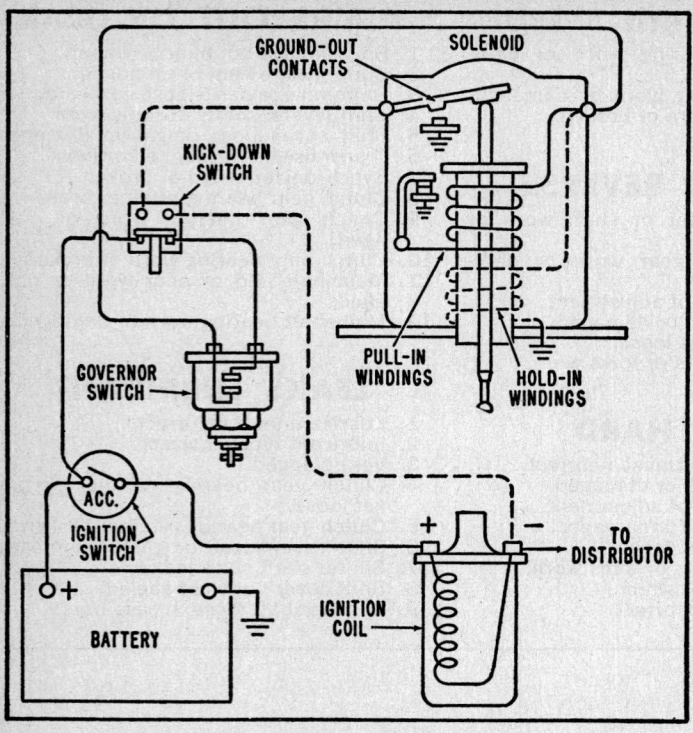

Fig. 2 Overdrive circuit diagram without relay.

3. Kickdown switch improperly adjusted.
4. Improper installation of solenoid.
5. Improper positioning of blocker ring.
6. Broken or slipping governor drive pinion.
7. Too much end play in mainshaft.

Overdrive Engages with Severe Jolt or Noise

Insufficient blocker ring friction may cause the ring to lose its grip on the hub of the sun gear control plate.

Free-Wheels At Speeds Over 30 MPH

If cam roller retainer spring tension is weak the unit will free-wheel at all times.

Rear Axle Troubles

Noise When Pulling Straight Ahead

1. Not enough oil.
2. Wrong grade of oil.
3. Poor quality oil.
4. Ring gear and pinion have excessive backlash.
5. Ring gear and pinion worn.
6. Pinion shaft bearings worn or loose.
7. Pinion shaft end play excessive.
8. Ring gear and pinion misaligned because of bent axle housing or distorted differential case.
9. Ring gear warped.
10. Differential bearings worn or loose.
11. Ring gear rivets or screws loose.
12. Ring gear and pinion not matched set.

Noise When Coasting In Gear

Any axle noise which is heard when the engine is pulling the car is likely to be heard when coasting although not as loud as when pulling.

If ring gear and pinion are meshed too tight, the noise will be greater when decelerating. The noise will disappear when the engine is pulling unless the gears are very tight.

Excessive end play of pinion shaft due to loose pinion nut or incorrect adjustment.

Intermittent Noise

1. Warped ring gear.
2. Loose ring gear rivets or screws.
3. Ring gear improperly installed on differential case due to dirt or burrs between the two.

Knocks or Clicks

1. Flat spot on ring gear or pinion tooth, or tooth chipped, or particle of metal lodged on tooth.
2. Flat spot in bearing.
3. Loose axle shaft key.
4. Loose splined shafts.
5. Mis-matched differential case halves.

Noise On Turns

1. Differential pinions or side gears chipped, scuffed or teeth broken.
2. Differential pinions binding on pinion shaft.
3. Differential pinions or side gears loose due to worn bushings or shaft.

4. Excessive backlash between pinions and side gears.
5. Excessive axle shaft end play.
6. Contacting surfaces between side gear and differential case burred, scored or otherwise damaged.

Oil Leak At Axle Ends

1. Oil level too high.
2. Oil too light or poor quality.
3. Axle shaft oil seals worn.
4. Axle shaft bearing retainer loose.
5. Cracked rear axle housing.
6. Vent (if any) clogged.

Oil Leak At Pinion Shaft

1. Oil level too high.
2. Oil too light or poor quality.
3. Pinion oil seal worn.
4. Pinion oil seal retainer distorted, loose in housing or improperly installed.
5. Oil return passage in carrier housing restricted.
6. Universal joint companion flange hub rough, scored or out of round.
7. Universal joint companion flange loose on pinion shaft.

Drum Brake Troubles

One Brake Drags

1. Brake line restricted.
2. Improperly adjusted or worn wheel bearing.
3. Distorted or improperly adjusted brake shoe.
4. Faulty retracting spring.
5. Drum out of round.
6. Loose backing plate.
7. Faulty wheel cylinder.
8. Dirty brake fluid.
9. Air in hydraulic system.
10. Insufficient shoe-to-backing plate lubrication.

All Brakes Drag

1. Mechanical resistance at pedal or shoes; damaged linkage.
2. Brake line restricted.
3. Distorted or improperly adjusted brake shoes.
4. Dirty brake fluid.
5. Faulty master cylinder.
6. Sticking booster control valve.

Hard Pedal

1. Mechanical resistance at pedal or shoes; damaged linkage.
2. Brake line restricted.
3. Distorted or improperly adjusted brake shoes.
4. Linings glazed or worn.
5. Oil or grease in lining.

Spongy Pedal

1. Leaks or insufficient fluid.
2. Air in hydraulic system.

Car Pulls to One Side

1. Brake line restricted.
2. Improper tire pressure.
3. Improperly adjusted or worn wheel bearing.
4. Distorted or improperly adjusted brake shoes.
5. Faulty retracting spring.
6. Drum out of round.
7. Linings glazed or worn.
8. Oil or grease in lining.
9. Loose lining.
10. Faulty wheel cylinder.
11. Self-adjusters not operating.
12. Worn or binding front suspension parts.

One Wheel Locks

1. Distorted or improperly adjusted brake shoes.
2. Linings glazed or worn.
3. Oil or grease in lining.
4. Loose backing plate.
5. Faulty wheel cylinder.
6. Tire tread worn.

Brakes Chatter

1. Drum out of round.
2. Linings glazed or worn.
3. Oil or grease in lining.
4. Loose backing plate.
5. Loose lining.
6. Poor lining-to-drum contact.
7. Loose front suspension.

Excessive Pedal Travel

1. Leaks or insufficient fluid.
2. Distorted or improperly adjusted brake shoes.

3. Linings glazed or worn.
4. Faulty master cylinder.
5. Air in hydraulic system.
6. Self-adjusters not operating.
7. Cracked drum.

Pedal Gradually Goes to Floor

1. Leaks or insufficient fluid.
2. Faulty master cylinder.

Brakes Uneven

1. Improper tire pressure.
2. Oil or grease in lining.
3. Scored drum.
4. Dirty brake fluid.

Shoe Click Release

1. Self-adjusters not operating.
2. Insufficient shoe-to-backing plate lubrication.
3. "Threads" left by drum turning tool pull shoes sideways.

Noisy or Grabbing Brakes

1. Distorted or improperly adjusted brake shoes.
2. Linings glazed or worn.
3. Oil or grease in lining.
4. Scored drum.
5. Dirty on drum-lining surface.
6. Faulty wheel cylinder.
7. Sticking booster control valve.

Brakes Do Not Apply

1. Leaks or insufficient fluid.
2. Linings glazed or worn.
3. Oil or grease in lining.
4. Dirty brake fluid.
5. Faulty master cylinder.
6. Air in hydraulic system.

Front End & Steering Troubles

Hard Steering

1. Low or uneven tire pressure.
2. Steering gear or connections adjusted too tight.
3. Insufficient or incorrect lubricant used.
4. Excessive caster.
5. Suspension arms bent or twisted.
6. Front spring sagged.
7. Frame bent or broken.
8. Steering knuckle bent.
9. Kingpin galled or frozen in bushing.
10. Excessive steering shaft coupling misalignment.

Excessive Play or Looseness In Steering

1. Steering gear connections adjusted too loose or worn.
2. Steering knuckle bushings worn.
3. Front wheel bearings incorrectly adjusted or worn.
4. Worn ball joints.
5. Worn or loose worm steering shaft bearings.
6. Worn control arm bushings.

Rattle or Chuckle in Steering Gear

1. Insufficient or improper lubricant in steering gear.
2. Excessive backlash in steering gear.
3. Worn or loose worm steering shaft bearings.
4. Pitman arm loose on shaft.

Erratic Steering On Application of Brakes

1. Oil or brake fluid on lining.
2. Brakes improperly adjusted.
3. Front spring weak.
4. Low or uneven tire pressure.
5. Insufficient or uneven caster.
6. Steering knuckle bent.

Car Pulls to One Side

1. Low or uneven tire pressure.
2. Incorrected or uneven caster or camber.

3. Wheel bearings adjusted too tight.
4. Uneven front car height.
5. Toe-in incorrect.
6. Oil or brake fluid on brake lining.
7. Brakes incorrectly or unevenly adjusted.
8. Steering knuckle or knuckle support bent.
9. Frame bent or broken.
10. Shock absorbers inoperative.
11. Rear wheels not tracking with front wheels.
12. Rear axle shifted (spring U bolts loose or center bolt sheared).
13. Broken or weak rear springs.

Scuffed Tires

1. Tire improperly inflated.
2. Toe-in incorrect.
3. Excessive wheel or tire run-out.
4. Steering knuckle bushings worn.
5. Uneven camber.
6. Incorrect toe-out on turns.
7. Suspension arm bent or twisted.
8. Steering knuckle bent.
9. Excessive speed on turns.

TROUBLE SHOOTING

Cupped Tires

1. Improper toe-in.
2. Tires improperly inflated.
3. Wheels, tires or brake drums out of balance.
4. Dragging brakes.
5. Worn steering knuckle bushings.
6. Wheel bearings incorrectly adjusted or worn.
7. Uneven camber.
8. Steering knuckle bent.
9. Excessive mileage without rotating tires.

Front Wheel Shimmy

1. Low or uneven tire pressure.
2. Wheels, tires or brake drums out of balance.
3. Excessive wheel or tire run-out.
4. Shock absorbers inoperative.
5. Steering connections incorrectly adjusted or worn.
6. Steering gear incorrectly adjusted.

7. Front wheel bearings incorrectly adjusted or worn.
8. Incorrect or uneven caster.
9. Steering knuckle bushings worn.
10. Toe-in incorrect.
11. Steering knuckle bent.
12. Eccentric or bulged tires.
13. Stabilizer inoperative.
14. Worn ball joints.
15. Worn control arm bushings.

Front Wheel Tramp

1. Wheels, tires or brake drums out of balance.
2. Wheel or tire not concentric.
3. Shock absorbers inoperative.
4. Stabilizer inoperative.

Car Wanders

1. Low or uneven tire pressure.
2. Steering gear or connections adjusted too loose or worn.
3. Steering gear or connections adjusted too tight.

4. Steering knuckle bushings worn.
5. Improper toe-in.
6. Incorrect or uneven caster or camber.
7. Steering knuckle bent.
8. Kingpin bent.
9. Rear axle shifted (spring U bolts loose or center bolt sheared).
10. Stabilizer inoperative.
11. Kingpins or bushings tight.
12. Bind in lower or upper control arm shaft.
13. Bind in rear spring shackles or dry rear springs.
14. Excessive backlash in steering gear.

Road Shocks

1. High air pressure in tires.
2. Steering gear or connections incorrectly adjusted.
3. Excessive caster.
4. Shock absorbers inoperative.
5. Front springs weak or sagged.
6. Wrong type or size of tires used.
7. Steering knuckle bent.

Power Top, Window & Seat Troubles

Top Will Not Operate

1. Mechanical interference due to luggage or other objects.
2. Hold down strap not removed.
3. Top not free from windshield header studs.
4. Electrical shorts or loose connections in control switch circuit.
5. Dirty control switch contacts.
6. Inoperative power unit motor.
7. Hydraulic fluid low.
8. Power unit pump inoperative.
9. Stoppage in fluid pipes.
10. Faulty hydraulic control valve.
11. Broken port plate in hydraulic pump.

Top Operates in One Direction Only

1. Mechanical interference due to luggage or other objects.
2. Hold down strap not removed.
3. Top not free from windshield header studs.
4. Electrical shorts or loose connections in control switch circuit.
5. Dirty control switch contact.
6. Improperly adjusted control rod.
7. Hydraulic power cylinder faulty.
8. Stoppage in fluid pipes.
9. Faulty hydraulic control valve.

Window Won't Operate from Main Switch Only

1. Broken wire between relay and remote switch.
2. Defective switch in master switch group.

3. Break in wire where it enters door opening.

Window Won't Operate from Main or Door Switch

1. Burned out motor or relay.
2. Defective circuit breaker.
3. Break in battery feed wire from starter solenoid to circuit breaker.

Window Operates In One Direction Only from Main or Door Switch

1. Defective relay.
2. Defective switch.
3. Broken ground wires.
4. Burned out motor.
5. Broken control wire.

Circuit Breaker in Door Clicks On and Off Continuously and Window Won't Operate

1. Control wire grounded.
2. Defective switch.
3. Relay points stuck.

Main Or Door Switch Operates Window In Wrong Direction

1. Lead wires are not connected to proper terminals.

Window Operates Sluggishly

1. Binding window regulator.
2. Broken wires or loose connections.

3. Worn motor brushes.

All Windows Do Not Operate

1. Circuit breaker open in control circuit.
2. Circuit breaker open in power circuit.

Seat Regulators Inoperative

1. Circuit breaker open in control circuit.
2. Circuit breaker open in power circuit.

One Seat Regulator Inoperative

1. Defective wiring between relay and circuit breaker.
2. Defective motor.
3. Defective wiring between switch and circuit breaker.
4. Defective relay.

Seat Regulator Operates in One Direction Only

1. Defective wiring between switch and relay that applies to direction of travel desired.
2. Defective toggle switch.

Seat Regulator Operates Sluggishly

1. Binding mechanism.
2. Defective wiring.
3. Loose connectors or poor ground.
4. Worn or dirty brushes in motor.

Windshield Wiper Troubles

GENERAL INSPECTION

Before deciding that a windshield wiper needs servicing it might be well to consider some of the external factors which affect their operation.

It must be remembered that windshield wipers will operate more slowly when they do their work on dry glass. This is specially true on cars with curved windshields. You will also find that wiper blades may chatter or fail to travel a complete arc on dry glass. It is therefore obvious that any testing of windshield wiper operation should be done after the windshield has been sprayed with water.

Windshield wipers that chatter or do not wipe the glass clean under normal operating conditions (wet windshield) may need only replacement of the wiper arms or blades instead of more extensive service. This can be determined by visual inspection and most replacements can be made simply without the aid of any special tools.

Uneven movement of the wiper arms with respect to one another is usually caused by cables, pivots or cranks that are out of adjustment in the windshield wiper transmission system.

ELECTRIC TYPE

All passenger car electric windshield wiper circuits, regardless of manufacturer, include a control switch, a small shunt wound motor, and the wiring connecting these units to the battery. A circuit breaker or fuse may be mounted as a separate unit or incorporated in the control switch itself. A worm gear on the motor armature shaft drives one or two gears mounted on crankshafts for wiper operation.

A parking switch is mounted on the motor and actuated by a cam on one of the cranks. The parking switch, connected to the battery through a control switch, keeps the motor in operation for a brief period after the control switch has been shut off, allowing the wiper blades to return to the parked position. Both single and two speed motors are used, the latter incorporating one or several resistors in the field circuit. The resistors may be located either in the parking switch housing or in the control switch.

In the following text you will find a list of the conditions you are likely to encounter when faced with a repair job on electric wipers. By consulting these possibilities you will simplify the job of locating the source of trouble. But before going further a few words of caution are in order: After you have made your diagnosis and are ready to make repairs, disconnect the battery to avoid damage under the dash or possible personal injury from accidental shorts. Also, on models which use off-glass parking windshield wipers, never remove or disassemble the motor while in "park" position.

Wipers Won't Operate

1. Discharged battery.
2. Blown fuse or faulty circuit breaker.
3. No power to control switch.
4. Faulty control switch.
5. Faulty parking switch.
6. Binding pivots, cranks or linkages.
7. Poor connection at switch.
8. No ground at motor.
9. Faulty motor.

Wipers Won't Park

1. Incorrect adjustment of parking switch lever.
2. Open circuit in lead feeding parking switch.
3. Faulty parking switch.
4. Faulty control switch.
5. No ground at control switch (variable speed wipers).
6. Motor crank and parking switch improperly assembled.
7. Cams in linkage reversed or binding (variable speed wipers).

Wipers Operate Slowly

1. Discharged battery.
2. Binding pivots, cranks or linkages.
3. Faulty motor windings.
4. High resistance connections or wiring.
5. High resistance in control switch contacts.
6. No ground at control switch (variable speed wipers).
7. Faulty resistance unit (if only high speed in affected).
8. Dirty commutator or sticking brushes.
9. Worn or damaged motor.

Multiple Speed Wipers Operate Only at Single Speed

1. Short or open in motor wiring harness.
2. Incorrect connections at control switch.
3. Faulty control switch.
4. Faulty resistance unit.
5. No ground at control switch.
6. Open shunt field in motor.

VACUUM TYPE

For satisfactory windshield wiper operation, it is necessary to have an adequate supply of vacuum. On some cars the vacuum is made available by tapping directly into the intake manifold. With this type of arrangement it is considered normal for the wipers to slow down or stop entirely while going up a hill or during acceleration, since under those conditions the manifold vacuum would drop below the 8"-10" needed to operate the wipers. These conditions are almost completely eliminated on cars equipped with a vacuum booster pump. The purpose of this pump is to maintain enough vacuum to work the wipers under any driving condition.

Some of the conditions which prevent satisfactory windshield wiper operation are listed in the following text and may be used as a guide to help you locate the source of trouble. Always disconnect the battery when working under the dash.

Wipers Won't Operate

1. No vacuum supply to motor due to pinch, restriction or leak in the windshield wiper hose. A vacuum leak or a disconnected hose can easily be located because a hissing sound will be heard whenever the engine is running.
2. Faulty vacuum booster pump.
3. Wiper control switch inoperative or disconnected at motor.
4. Faulty wiper motor.
5. Frozen or binding pivots and linkages.
6. Linkages or cables improperly installed.

Wipers Operate Slowly

1. Low vacuum due to pinch or partial restriction in the wiper hose.
2. Loss of vacuum due to leaks at joints, fittings or in the wiper hose itself.
3. Faulty vacuum booster pump.
4. Faulty wiper motor.
5. Wiper control switch does not move operating valve on the motor to full "ON" position due to improper adjustment.
6. Air intake on motor (breather port) clogged.
7. Binding pivots, cranks, linkages or binding or frozen idler pulleys on cable tensioners.
8. Cables adjusted too tight.

Wipers Won't Park

1. Faulty parking valve on motor.
2. Wiper control switch out of adjustment.
3. Wiper arms not positioned properly on pivots.

PRESSURE WIPER

The windshield wiper is hydraulically operated. The hydraulic power for the motor is obtained from the power steering unit. Hydraulic fluid flows from the pump, through the steering gear to the wiper motor, and then to the fluid reservoir. During wiper operation, a part of the fluid is by-passed through the motor by a valve on the motor.

Checks and Adjustments: The only adjustment required is the control cable adjustment. To adjust, remove the seal plate mounting screws and position the plate and seal out of the way. Adjust the cable so that the control knob on instrument panel moves the valve control lever on the motor from off to full on.

If the motor operates sluggishly, check the cable adjustment. If this is not the fault, check the hydraulic fluid pressure. If the power steering gear operates satisfactorily, it may be assumed that the fluid pressure is adequate. Check for binding wiper pivot shafts and arms. Repair or replace wiper motor and valves if necessary.

AIR CONDITIONING

NOTE: This chapter deals only with fundamentals and basic system tests. For complete air conditioning service details, Motor's Air Conditioner Service Manual is available. The current edition is an 536 page book that includes after-market units and truck refrigeration as well as system vacuum and wiring diagrams.

CONTENTS

Fundamentals of Refrigeration 2-20

Exercise System 2-20

Trouble Diagnosis 2-22

Trouble Shooting Guide 2-22

Oil Level, Check 2-23

Thermostatic Control Switch 2-24

Chrysler ETR Control 2-25

Suction Throttling Regulators:
   Chrysler EPR Valve 2-25
   Frigidaire POA Valve 2-26

Expansion Valves 2-27

VIR Control 2-27

Compressor Clutches 2-29

A/C Specifications 2-32

Charging Valve Locations 2-37

A/C System Testing

Performance Test 2-29

Purging the System 2-31

Charging the System 2-31

Leak Testing System 2-32

Isolate Compressor for System 2-32

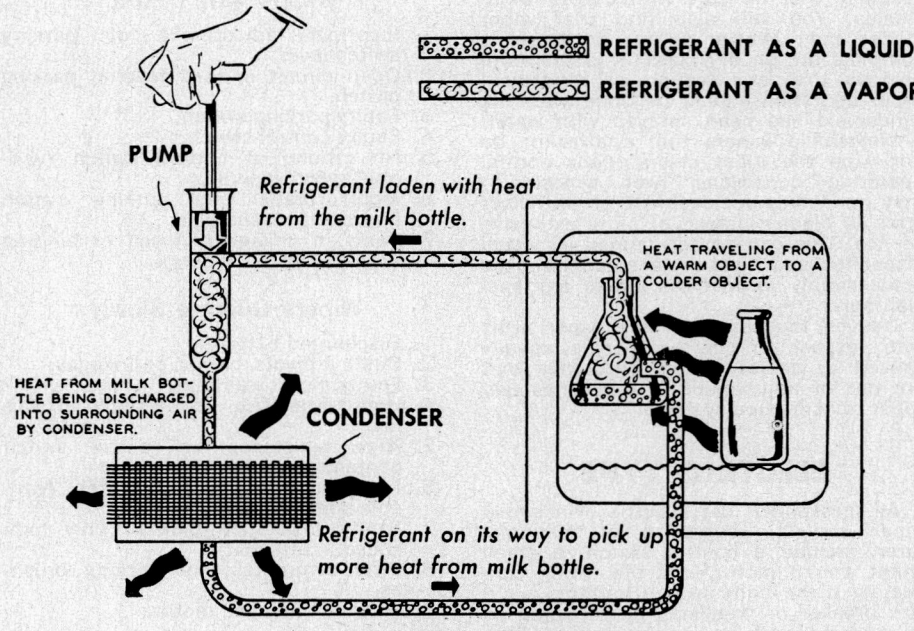

REFRIGERANT AS A LIQUID

REFRIGERANT AS A VAPOR

PUMP

Refrigerant laden with heat from the milk bottle.

HEAT TRAVELING FROM A WARM OBJECT TO A COLDER OBJECT.

HEAT FROM MILK BOTTLE BEING DISCHARGED INTO SURROUNDING AIR BY CONDENSER.

CONDENSER

Refrigerant on its way to pick up more heat from milk bottle.

Diagram showing refrigerant cycle

FUNDAMENTALS OF REFRIGERATION

In order to understand how an air conditioning system works, we must have a knowledge of the fundamentals of refrigeration. And since refrigeration is the process of removing heat from things, an air conditioner removes heat from the surrounding air. In both cases, the process is simplified by one of Nature's laws—heat always moves from a warm object to a cold object.

When we put milk or vegetables into an ice box, they are warmer than the ice. Since heat always travels from warmer to cooler objects, the heat in the milk and vegetables naturally travels to the cold ice. Then, of course, as heat is removed from these articles, they begin to grow cooler—they have less heat than before.

Therefore, if refrigeration is the removal of heat, then anything can be made cooler by finding a method of absorbing heat from it.

In order to maintain cold temperatures, we have to have continuous refrigeration. This is accomplished in modern refrigerators and cooling systems (1) by using a refrigerant that will readily absorb heat and (2) by using the same refrigerant over and over.

Ice can refrigerate effectively *only when it is changing from a solid to a liquid.* A liquid can refrigerate *only when it is changing from a liquid to a vapor.* A vapor cannot refrigerate since the absorption of heat will not change it to any other state. The only thing to do with a vapor is to change it back to a liquid—by removing heat from it.

In other words, if the ice didn't melt, it could absorb a little heat from the objects and the air around it but not enough to do an effective job of cooling. But when it begins to change to a liquid (water), then the ice is absorbing heat rapidly and effectively.

The same applies to a liquid refrigerant. No matter how cold the liquid is, it won't actually "refrigerate" until it is absorbing heat fast enough to change its form into a vapor.

Operating Cycle of Car Air Conditioning System

1. The compressor compresses heat-laden, low-pressure vaporous refrigerant and discharges it into the condenser.

2. In the condenser, the vapor changes into a liquid as the heat is dissipated into the surrounding air.

3. From the condenser, the liquid is forced into the reservoir or receiver, which is simply a storage container the function of which is to ensure a supply of *liquid* Freon to the expansion valve. (The expansion valve functions in much the same manner as a hose nozzle).

4. From the reservoir, the liquid Freon passes through a combination strainer-drier, then through the expansion valve into the evaporator.

5. Being connected to the suction line of the compressor, the evaporator is a low-pressure region in which the refrigerant boils and reverts to a vapor, absorbing heat in the process and thereby cooling the evaporator coil and the air passing over it.

6. Upon leaving the evaporator, the vaporous refrigerant returns to the compressor inlet and completes the refrigeration cycle.

EXERCISE SYSTEM

An important fact most car owners ig-

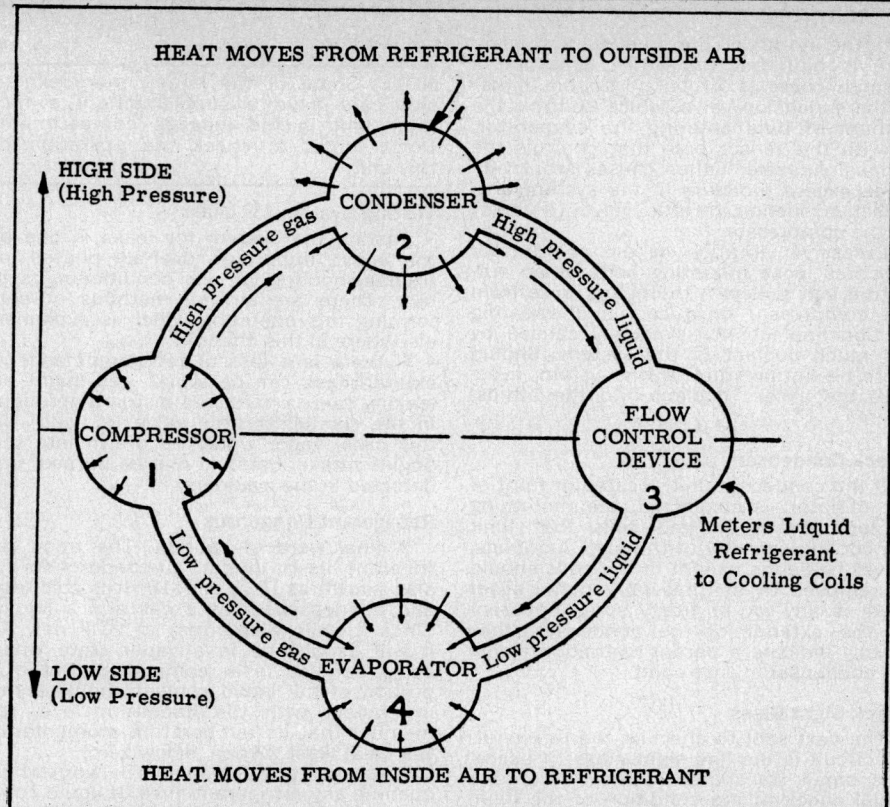

HEAT MOVES FROM REFRIGERANT TO OUTSIDE AIR

HIGH SIDE
(High Pressure)

CONDENSER
2

High pressure gas

High pressure liquid

COMPRESSOR
1

FLOW
CONTROL
DEVICE
3

Meters Liquid
Refrigerant
to Cooling Coils

Low pressure gas

Low pressure liquid

LOW SIDE
(Low Pressure)

EVAPORATOR
4

HEAT MOVES FROM INSIDE AIR TO REFRIGERANT

◄ Air conditioning cycle of operation

▼ How air conditioner works

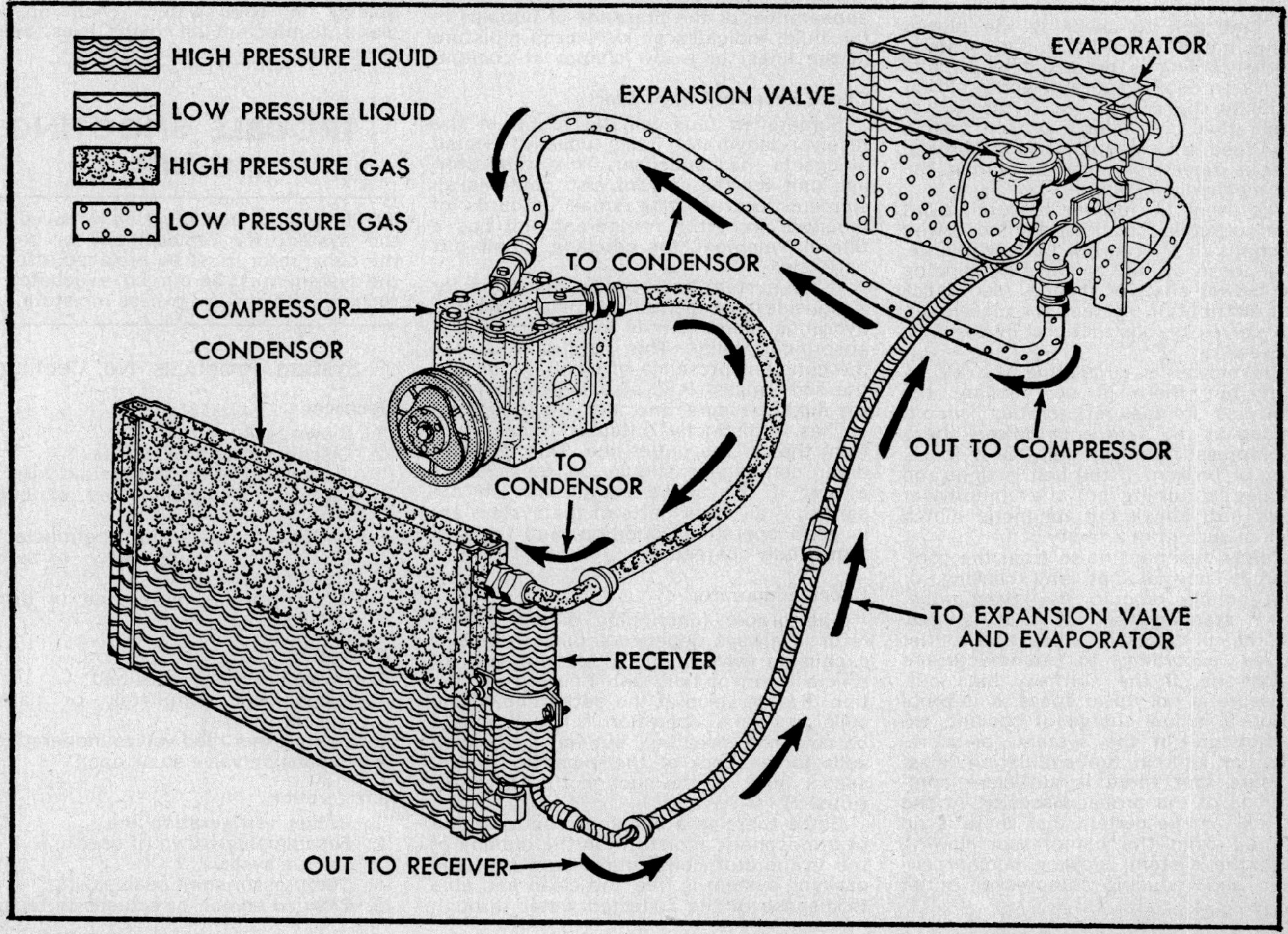

HIGH PRESSURE LIQUID

LOW PRESSURE LIQUID

HIGH PRESSURE GAS

LOW PRESSURE GAS

EVAPORATOR

EXPANSION VALVE

TO CONDENSOR

COMPRESSOR

CONDENSOR

TO
CONDENSOR

OUT TO COMPRESSOR

TO EXPANSION VALVE
AND EVAPORATOR

RECEIVER

OUT TO RECEIVER

AIR CONDITIONING

nore is that car coolers must be used periodically or they will go sour. Car manufacturers are emphatic on this point. They caution that, when the air conditioner is not used regularly, particularly during cold months, it should be turned on for a few minutes once every two or three weeks while the engine is running. This keeps the system in good operating condition.

Checking out the system for the effects of disuse before the onset of summer is one of the most important aspects of car cooler servicing.

First on the list is to clean out the condenser core, mounted in all cases at the front of the car's radiator. All obstructions, such as leaves, bugs, dirt, and the like, must be removed, as these will reduce heat transfer and impair the efficiency of the system. Make sure the space between the condenser and the radiator also is free of foreign matter.

Make certain the evaporator water drain is open. Certain systems have two evaporators, one in the engine compartment and one in the trunk. The evaporator is the device which cools and dehumidifies the air before it enters the car, and the place where refrigerant is changed from a liquid to a vapor. As the core cools the air, moisture condenses on it but the moisture is prevented from collecting in the evaporator by means of the water drain.

TROUBLE DIAGNOSIS
Insufficient or No Cooling

The first unit to check is the blower mechanism and its air-distribution system, since the cooling is produced by a combination of a cool evaporator and a blower to circulate the cooled air. If the blower is inoperative, check for a broken switch, a blown fuse, a loose connection, a broken wire or a defective motor activating the blower mechanism.

In the event the blower is working but the air output is low, look for loose wire connections or shorts, low battery charge, dirty or loose switch contacts or binding of the blower shaft or blades. Also check the air-distribution system for closed air-output valves or obstructions in the flexible hoses.

If the blower is circulating the air efficiently but there is no cooling, the trouble lies in the refrigerating circuit. Beginning at the source of power, check the compressor driving belt. Is it loose, slipping or broken? If the belt is tight and the pulley is turning but the compressor shaft is not, check the magnetic clutch for lack of current or a faulty coil.

A steady, resonant noise from the compressor is normal but any clicking or rattling sounds should be investigated. Using a standard set of twin gauges, check the compressor inlet and outlet pressures according to manufacturer's specifications. If the normally high outlet pressure is not up to specs, it is probably due to a low charge of coolant, excess moisture in the system, or a restriction or kink in the circulation lines.

Be sure that there is sufficient compressor oil of the proper viscosity. At the same time, make certain that there is no excess oil from the compressor flowing through the system, slowing coolant circulation and reducing compressor outlet pressure.

If the normally but inlet-suction pressure is high but the outlet pressure is normal, there is probably trouble either at the expansion valve, which controls the amount of fluid entering the evaporator, or with the sensor bulb that controls the expansion valve. Other causes would include excess moisture in the system or a defective suction throttle valve (if used) on the compressor.

Excessive vibration of the compressor indicates loose mounting bolts or an out-of-true belt pulley. A thumping noise from the compressor or a cool and sweating suction line into it, is usually caused by too much coolant in the system. Should there be no moisture in the system, evacuate the excess coolant into the atmosphere.

Check Condenser

If the condenser unit, located in front of the radiator, is suspected, the first thing to look for is clogged coils that limit the cooling capacity of the unit. Any bugs, leaves or debris caught in the coils should be removed by air pressure. In the event there is any icy or frosty spots apparent on the exterior of the condenser, they usually indicate a partial restriction inside the condenser at that point.

Check Sight Glass

The next spot to check in the refrigerating circuit is the line sight glass (if used). This small transparent device permits a visual check of the condition of the high-pressure liquid coolant. A cloudy, foamy appearance, or the presence of bubbles in the fluid, indicates air or excess moisture in the lines, or a low charge of coolant.

Check Receiver-Dehydrator

Sometimes fault will be found in the receiver-dehydrator unit, usually located alongside the condenser. This small storage unit for the coolant also contains an element for removing small amounts of moisture from the refrigerant and has a filtering element for catching small dirt particles.

If the system has been in operation for a considerable period of time, this dehydrating element may lose its moisture-absorbing ability. This condition causes the constant presence of small bubbles in the sight glass. It is also indicated when the high-pressure line into the dehydrator has a distinctly different temperature from that of the outlet line. This receiver-dryer component should be replaced as a unit if the above symptoms are observed, if all other parts of the system are in good operating condition, and the system is fully charged.

Check Evaporator

The proper functioning of the evaporator is always dependent on an efficient expansion valve at the intake end and an efficient sensor bulb and (if used) a suction throttle valve at the outlet end of the coils. In normal operation, this unit should be cold and sweating, but not iced. Icing calls for a check of the expansion valve, sensor bulb, or the suction throttle valve (if used).

Since there is a constant condensation of atmospheric moisture on the outside of the evaporator coils, make sure that the draining system is free and clean and able to dispose of the collected water through

the car floor.

NOTE: Some of the larger, more expensive cars have a supplementary evaporator unit in the luggage compartment. Don't forget to check the operation of this unit.

Testing System for Leaks

Testing the system for leaks is one of the most important over-all phases of trouble-shooting an air conditioning system. There are several methods of performing this operation which is explained elsewhere in this chapter.

If there is a loss of refrigerant and no external leak can be found, gas might be leaking from a damaged piston diaphragm in the suction throttle valve (if used). In this case, vapor would be drawn into the engine intake manifold and be burned, undetected in the cylinders.

Refrigerant Dangerous

A final word of caution. The freon refrigerant used in car air-conditioners is also known as R-12 or F-12. It is colorless and odorless both as a gas and a liquid. Since it boils (vaporizes) at 21.7 def. F., it will usually be in a vapor state when being handled in a repair shop. But if a portion of the liquid coolant should come in contact with the hands or face, remember that its temperature momentarily will be at least 22 deg. below zero!

Protective goggles should be worn when opening any refrigerant lines. If liquid coolant does touch the eyes, bathe the eyes quickly in cold water. Then apply a bland disinfectant oil to the eyes. See an eye doctor.

TROUBLE SHOOTING GUIDE

NOTE: When a unit must be removed from the system for replacement or repairs, the dehydrator must be replaced also, and the system must be purged, evacuated and recharged to remove excess moisture.

System Produces No Cooling

Electrical
1. Blown fuse.
2. Disconnect or broken wire.
3. Disconnect or broken ground wire.
4. Clutch coil disconnected or burned out.
5. Switch contacts in thermostat (if used) burned excessively, or sensing element defective.
6. Blower motor burned out or disconnected.

Mechanical
1. Loose or broken drive belt.
2. Compressor completely or partially frozen.
3. Compressor reed valves inoperative.
4. Expansion valve stuck open.

Refrigeration
1. Broken refrigeration line.
2. Fusable plug blown (if used).
3. Leak in system.
4. Compressor shaft seal leaking.
5. Clogged screen or screens in receiver-

2–22

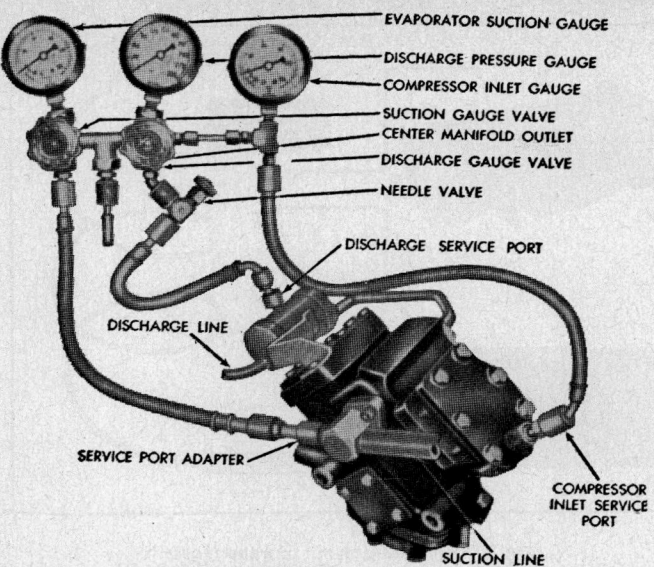

Fig. 1 Chrysler Air-Temp gauge set manifold connections (Typical)

Fig. 2 Manifold gauge set for Frigidaire, Tecumseh and York compressors

dehydrator or expansion valve.
6. Plugged coil or hose.

Insufficient Cooling

Electrical
1. Blower motor operates sluggishly.

Mechanical
1. Compressor clutch slipping.
2. Obstructed blower discharge passage.
3. Clogged air intake filter.
4. Outside air vents open.
5. Insufficient air circulation over condenser coils; fins clogged with dirt, leaves or insects.
6. Evaporator clogged.
7. Evaporator regulator defective or improperly adjusted.

NOTE: The evaporator regulator includes the suction throttling valve (STV) used on General Motors cars, the Pilot-Operated Absolute (POA) valve used on General Motors cars, and the Chrysler Evaporator Pressure Regulator (EPR) or Evaporator Temperature Regulator (ETR) valve. When any of these devices is used in a system, it can be assumed that the system contains no thermostat control.

Refrigeration
1. Insufficient refrigerant in system.
2. Clogged screen in expansion valve.
3. Expansion valve thermal bulb has lost its charge.
4. Clogged screen in receiver.
5. Excessive moisture in system.
6. Air in system.
7. Thermostat defective or improperly adjusted (if used).

System Cools Intermittently

Electrical
1. Defective circuit breaker, blower switch or blower motor.
2. Partial open, improper ground or loose connection in compressor clutch coil.

Mechanical
1. Compressor clutch slipping.

Refrigeration
1. Unit icing up; may be caused by excessive moisture in system, incorrect super-heat adjustment in expansion valve, or thermostat adjusted too low (if used).
2. Thermostat defective (if used).
3. Stuck hot gas by-pass valve, STV, POA or EPR valve.

OIL LEVEL CHECK
Air-Temp, Tecumseh & York Compressors

NOTE: The oil level of these compressors should be checked whenever refrigerant has been lost due to leakage or through normal system servicing.

1. Connect gauges into system, Figs. 1 and 2. Operate system for approximately 10 to 15 minutes with controls set for maximum cooling.

NOTE: On 1974 Chrysler, Fury, Imperial and Monaco models, disconnect and plug the water valve vacuum hose.

2. On all 1969-72 units and 1973 Tecumseh and York systems with manual service valves, isolate the compressor from system. On 1973 Tecumseh and York systems with Schrader type service valves, 1973 Air Temp units and all 1974 units, discharge the refrigerant system.
3. With proper eye protection, remove oil check plug slowly to bleed a small refrigerant charge which may be left in the compressor. Then check oil level, which should be within the limits found in the A/C Specification Table.

Frigidaire Compressors

NOTE: These compressors have no pro-

vision accurately to check oil level on the car. Periodic inspection of oil level has, therefore, been eliminated from installations using this compressor. Oil level check performed with the compressor removed from the car is to be made only under conditions of severe oil loss caused by a compressor oil leak, broken refrigerant hose, or a rupture from crash damage. The system is designed to hold the quantity of refrigeration oil listed in the A/C Data Table. The affinity of Freon 12 and refrigeration oil and the design of the compressor will prevent a full oil charge being contained in the compressor.

1. Purge refrigerant from compressor.
2. Remove compressor from car.
3. Remove oil from compressor.
4. Remove plug on pump.
5. Pour oil from compressor into a clean container calibrated in ounces.
6. Measure oil removed from compressor.
7. Install new oil into compressor. Install plug and tighten.
8. Install compressor on car. Repair damage to system as required to eliminate leaks. Evacuate system, using a suitable vacuum pump. Then charge system with new Freon 12.

Oil Distribution

Whenever a component of the A/C system is replaced, measured quantities of refrigeration oil should be added to the component to assure that the total oil charge in the system is correct before the unit is placed into operation.

The oil is poured directly into the replacement component. If an evaporator is installed, pour oil into the inlet pipe with the pipe held vertically so the oil will drain into the evaporator core. No additional oil is required if valves and hoses are replaced.

1. If the oil drained from the compressor is more than 4 fluid ounces, add to the new compressor the same amount of oil as drained from the replaced unit.

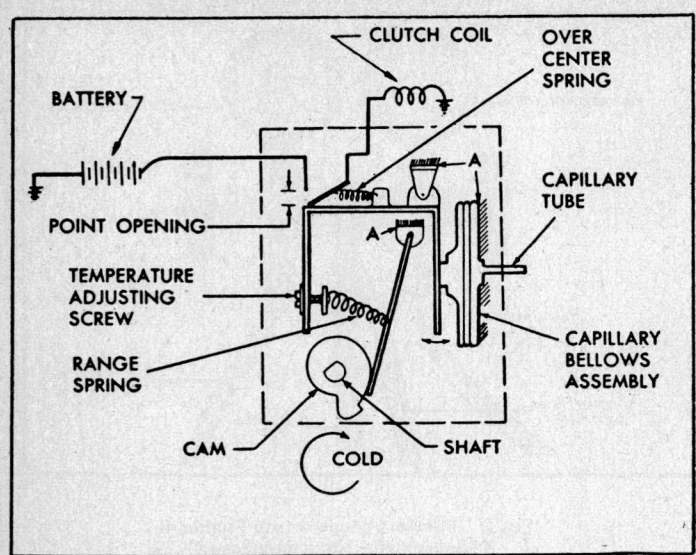

Fig. 3   Wiring diagram of a typical adjustable thermostatic switch

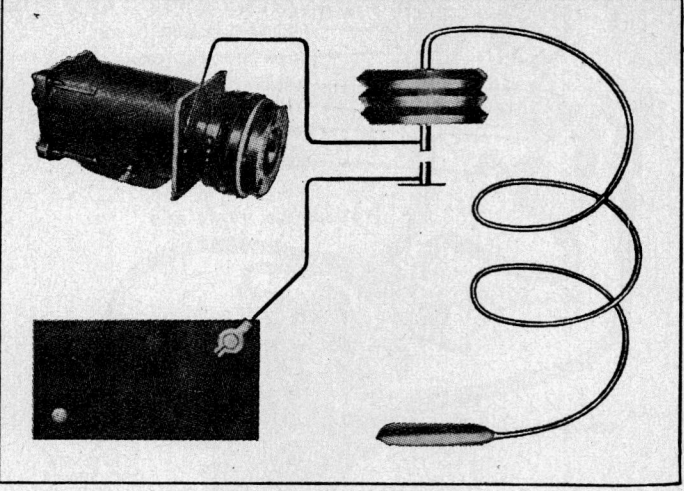

Fig. 4   Schematic layout of a thermostatic-controlled clutch circuit

2. If oil drained from the compressor is less than 4 fluid ounces, add 6 ounces of oil to the new compressor.

3. Oil should be added to replacement components as follows:
Evaporator (front or rear) . . add 3 oz.
Condenser . . . . add 1 oz.
Receiver or VIR . . . . add 1 oz.
Condenser-receiver assembly
add 2 oz.

NOTE: If the system is flushed with sufficient quantity of a flushing agent that would remove oil from the system, install the full amount specified in the A/C Data Table. On a newly installed system, install the full capacity of oil prior to operation. On systems containing metal particles in the oil, replace or overhaul the compressor, replace the receiver-dehydrator and install a high capacity, low pressure drop filter in the liquid line to the filter to protect the expansion valve and new compressor from damage due to foreign particles.

THERMOSTAT CONTROL SWITCH

When an A/C system is not provided with a hot gas by-pass valve or a suction throttling valve (STV, POA or EPR), the pumping action of the compressor is stopped by a thermostatically-controlled switch, Figs. 3 and 4.

The opening and closing of the electrical contacts are controlled by a movement of a temperature sensitive diaphragm or bellows. The bellows has a capillary tube connected to it which is filled with Freon or CO_2. The capillary tube is positioned so that it may have either the cold air from the evaporator pass over it or it may be connected to the tail pipe of the evaporator. In either position, evaporator temperature will affect the temperature-sensitive compound in the capillary

tube by causing it to contract as the evaporator becomes colder. The contraction of the gas will cause the bellows to contract. This action separates the electrical contacts and breaks the electrical circuit to the compressor clutch, which stops compressor operation.

The evaporator begins to warm which, in turn, causes the gas in the capillary tube to expand. The bellows will also begin to expand, moving the electrical contacts closer to each other. At a predetermined point, the expansion of the bellows will bring the contacts together, closing the circuit to the compressor clutch, energizing it and bringing the compressor into operation again. This cycling action will be repeated as long as air conditioning operation is required.

Thermostat, Adjust

Visual inspection must be made to determine if a thermostat is adjustable. All thermostats have a provision for regulating the range between opening and closing the contacts. Some models may have a removable fiber cover under which will be located the adjusting screw. If a set screw is not found here, it may be assumed that the thermostat is not adjustable.

All types, whether or not they have an internal adjustment, have a provision whereby the spring tension and contact spacing may be varied by the driver to regulate evaporator cooling. Temperature control is accomplished by rotating a cam which will increase or decrease spring tension on a pivoting contact hanger. Rotation is accomplished either by movement of a stem on which a knob is fastened or it may be accomplished by a cable arrangement. On thermostats that are adjustable, the procedure is as follows:
1. Connect gauges into the system and adjust A/C controls for maximum cooling.
2. Operate engine for 10 to 15 minutes to stabilize at 1500-1750 rpm.

3. Read high side gauge for full refrigerant charge, which will read high side pressure approximating the temperature-pressure relationship shown in Fig. 5.
4. Check sight glass for absence of bubbles.
5. Read low side gauge for thermostat operation. It should read from 26 psi to 14 psi after system has been stabilized for 10 to 15 minutes.

NOTE: The thermostat should disconnect the compressor clutch for evaporator defrost between high and low readings. If the thermostat will not recycle the clutch, move the temperature control toward the warmer position to check for thermostat contact opening.

6. Count number of psi required for warm-up until contacts close, which should indicate 26 to 32 psi rise between contact opening and reclosing. Check the thermostat at least 3 times for consistent operation.

NOTE: Thermostats are generally but not always located in the evaporator case. A certain amount of diligence will be required to locate the thermostat, especially with some models of luggage compartment units.

7. Remove parts as required to gain access to the thermostat. Open access door to the adjusting screw. Rotate adjusting screw counter-clockwise to lower contact opening, and clockwise to raise point opening pressure.

NOTE: Localities having high mean humidity will require higher contact opening pressure than localities with low mean humidity. Coastal areas with contact opening adjustment lower than 24-26 psi will result in evaporator freeze-up. So-called desert areas

Evaporator Pressure Gauge Reading	Evaporator Temperature F°	High Pressure Gauge Reading	Ambient Temperature
0	-21°	45	20°
0.6	-20°	55	30°
2.4	-15°	72	40°
4.5	-10°	86	50°
6.8	-5°	105	60°
9.2	0°	126	70°
11.8	5°	140	75°
14.7	10°	160	80°
17.1	15°	185	90°
21.1	20°	195	95°
22.5	22°	220	100°
23.9	24°	240	105°
25.4	26°	260	110°
26.9	28°	275	115°
28.5	30°	290	120°
37.0	40°	305	125°
46.7	50°	325	130°
57.7	60°		
70.1	70°		
84.1	80°		
99.6	90°		
116.9	100°		
136.0	110°		
157.1	120°		
179.0	130°		

Fig. 5   Pressure-temperature relationship. Conditions equivalent to 30 mph or 1750 engine rpm

Year	PSI
1969	21-25
1970	21-27
1971-72	21-25
1973-74	22-29

Fig. 7   Evaporator suction pressure EPR test

pipe of the evaporator and the compressor in the low side or suction line, as it is called.

Sometimes it may be difficult to determine exactly what type of control system is used on a particular installation. However, if under-hood inspection of the compressor and lines does not show a control device, it is safe to assume that a thermostat-controlled recycling clutch is used. Generally, then, all suction throttling regulator controls will be located under the hood. The thermostat will not be used, and the clutch will be energized during total operation of this type system.

Constant heat load, ram air, and compressor speed will allow the expansion valve to meter an even flow of refrigerant into the evaporator. Change any of these conditions, however, and the refrigerant flow through the expansion valve will change. Without some means provided to regulate refrigerant flow, the evaporator cooling will become excessive and freeze the moisture condensing on the coils. This results in evaporator icing or freeze-up and requires that the ice on the evaporator be melted before it can resume cooling action.

Installation of a suction throttling control device will compensate for these varying conditions. As the pressure and temperature within the evaporator drop, spring pressure forces a valve within the regulating device toward its seat, retarding the flow of refrigerant. This action increases the pressure back into the evaporator, raising both pressure and temperature. The temperature will not be allowed to drop low enough to freeze over the evaporator coils. A point of balance will soon be reached whereby the refrigerant flow past the valve in the regulator will reach a degree of pressure and temperature sufficient to maintain efficient cooling without evaporator freezing.

Chrysler Air-Temp EPR & EPR-2 Valve

The EPR valve (Evaporator Pressure Regulator) is calibrated to produce maximum cooling without causing frost or ice on the evaporator fins and tubing. If for

with very low humidity can easily tolerate contact opening adjustment of 14-16 psi without evaporator freeze-up.

8. Check operation of thermostat for newly adjusted cycle of operation. Replace thermostat if operating cycle is inconsistent or will not respond to adjustment.

CHRYSLER ETR CONTROL

The ETR System (Evaporator Temperature Regulator), used on 1969-73 Chrysler Corp. Auto Temp A/C systems, consists of an ETR solenoid valve and an ETR switch. The ETR system permits the evaporator to maintain a minimum air temperature without evaporator coil icing at low ambient temperatures. This control system replaces the EPR valve used in standard Chrysler Corp. A/C systems.

The ETR solenoid valve is actuated by the ETR switch which senses evaporator coil temperature through a sensing capillary placed on the evaporator coil fins. The ETR solenoid valve closes when energized, stopping the refrigerant flow to the compressor.

System Testing
1. Connect gauges into system, Fig. 1, with suction and discharge valves closed, then connect a test lamp in series with the ETR switch feed wire at the compressor.
2. Set thumbwheel temperature selector to 65, close windows and run engine at 1000 RPM, then depress Auto button.
3. After approximately five minutes, compare gauge readings and test lamp as indicated in Fig. 6. Discharge pressure may vary, however, a 25 to 30 pound pressure differential indicates actuation of the ETR switch.

SUCTION THROTTLING REGULATORS

Suction throttling regulated systems include any type control used to regulate the flow of refrigerant from the evaporator to the compressor. This control will be located at some point between the tail

Year	Test Lamp	Evap. Suction P.S.I.	Discharge Press. P.S.I.	Compressor Inlet P.S.I.
1969-70	Off	22	180	30
	On	30	150	0 or Below
1971-73	Off	25	180	24
	On	30	150	0 or Below

Fig. 6   Chrysler ETR Control test pressure chart

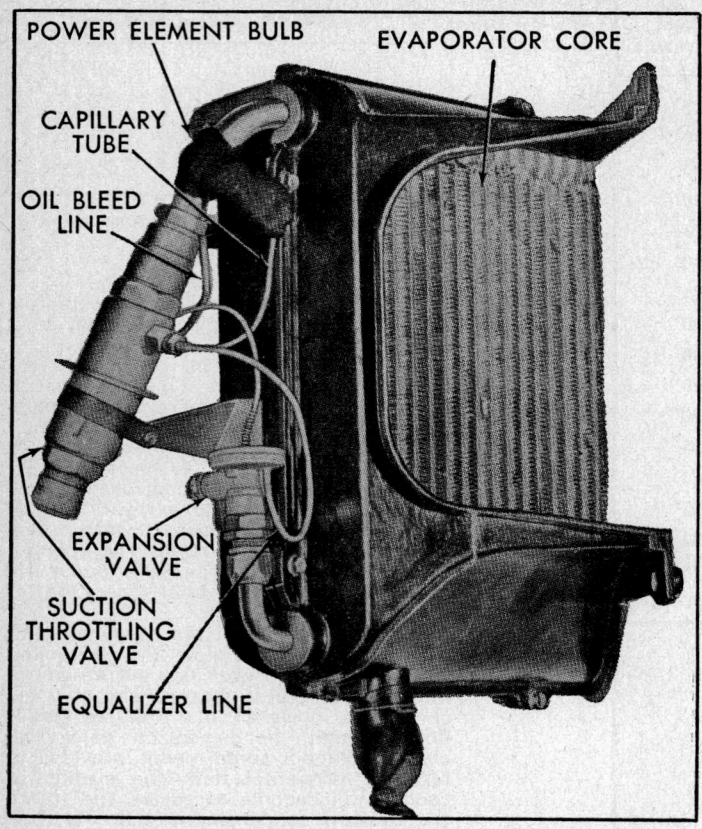

POWER ELEMENT BULB

EVAPORATOR CORE

CAPILLARY TUBE

OIL BLEED LINE

EXPANSION VALVE

SUCTION THROTTLING VALVE

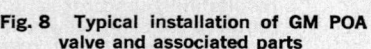

EQUALIZER LINE

Fig. 8   Typical installation of GM POA valve and associated parts

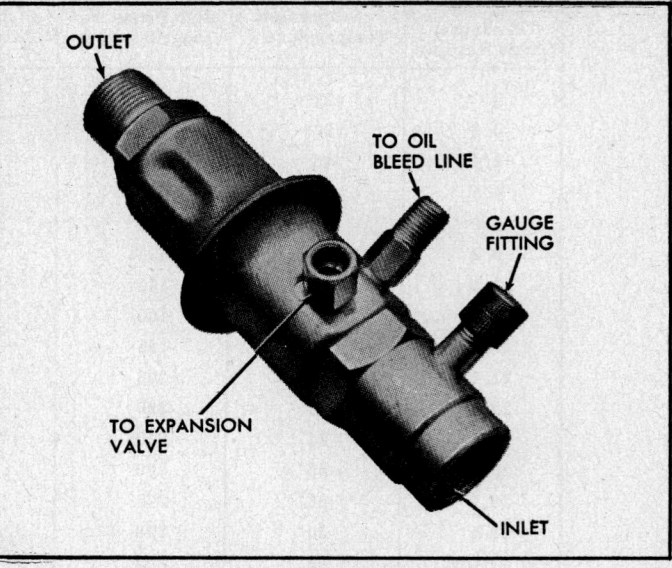

OUTLET

TO OIL BLEED LINE

GAUGE FITTING

TO EXPANSION VALVE

INLET

Fig. 9   Exterior view of POA valve

any reason the factory calibration has been disturbed, the EPR valve may restrict the flow of refrigerant at an evaporator pressure which is either too high for maximum performance or too low to prevent coil freeze-up. The following test determines whether or not the valve is functioning properly.

All 1974 units incorporate an EPR-2 valve which performs the same functions as the EPR valve described above. Servicing and testing procedures remain the same for the EPR-2 valve except unless noted otherwise.

EPR Valve Test

1969-74 (Exc. 1974 Full Size)

1. Close windows and set A/C controls for "Max A/C", high blower and temperature control to full reheat position.
2. Run V8 engines at 800 RPM and 6 cylinder engines at 900 RPM.
3. Operate for a minimum of five minutes to obtain partial stabilization and sufficient reheat to load system.
4. Pressure at the discharge port should be 140 to 210 PSI at this time. If not, check pressure drop across the EPR valve which should be 1 to 4 PSI on 1969-72 units or 1 to 6 PSI on 1973-74 units. If pressure drop is greater than the above limits, the EPR valve and nylon filter suction screen should be replaced.
5. If the EPR valve was found satisfactory, remove the expansion valve

thermo bulb from suction line and immerse bulb into a container filled with ice and water. The compressor inlet pressure should now be 17 PSI or less on 1969-73 units and 15 PSI or less on 1974 units with the evaporator suction pressure as specified in Fig. 7. If the compressor inlet pressure is more than specified, the EPR valve and nylon filter suction screen is faulty and must be replaced.

1974 Full Size

NOTE: This test procedure cannot be used on these vehicles if equipped with the Auto Temp II A/C system since a special tester must be used to trouble-shoot this system.

1. Close windows and set A/C controls for "Max A/C", high blower and the temperature control to full reheat position.
2. Disconnect and plug water valve vacuum hose.
3. Run engine at 800 RPM and operate system for a minimum of five minutes to obtain partial stabilization and sufficient reheat to load system.
4. Pressure at the discharge port should now be 140-240 PSI. If not, check system for proper refrigerant charge. If system charge is satisfactory, check pressure drop across EPR-2 valve which should be 1 to 6 PSI. If pressure drop is greater than specified, replace the EPR-2 valve.

5. If system charge and EPR-2 valve were found satisfactory, place crushed dry ice on H-valve control head for a minimum of 30 seconds and observe evaporator suction pressure which drop below 15 inches Hg. Remove dry ice and evaporator suction pressure should now rise to a minimum of 38 PSI and finally stabilize to 30 PSI. If system does not respond as described above, replace the H-Valve.
6. The EPR-2 valve should now be fully open with a 1 to 6 PSI pressure drop across the valve. If pressure drop is greater than specified, the EPR-2 valve is faulty or a restriction is present in the system.
7. If the EPR-2 valve was found satisfactory in Step 6, reconnect the water valve vacuum hose, open windows and operate system for 15 minutes. Then, set blower at low speed and run engine at 1100 RPM for five minutes to obtain stabilization. The compressor inlet pressure should be 15 PSI or less with the evaporator pressure at 22 to 29 PSI. If compressor inlet pressure is greater than specified, replace the EPR-2 valve.

Frigidaire POA Valve

The POA valve (Pilot Operated Absolute), Figs. 8, 9, 10, differs from the STV in that it has no vacuum diaphragm. The POA valve will not change calibration when the system is operated at a higher altitude due to the atmospheric pressure to which the STV was subjected because of its vacuum diaphragm.

NOTE: When it is found necessary to replace a POA valve, check the interior of the defective valve for corrosion or crystalization of salts. This should indicate moisture in the system. If this condition exists, the receiver-dehydrator should be replaced and the system evacuated for one hour.

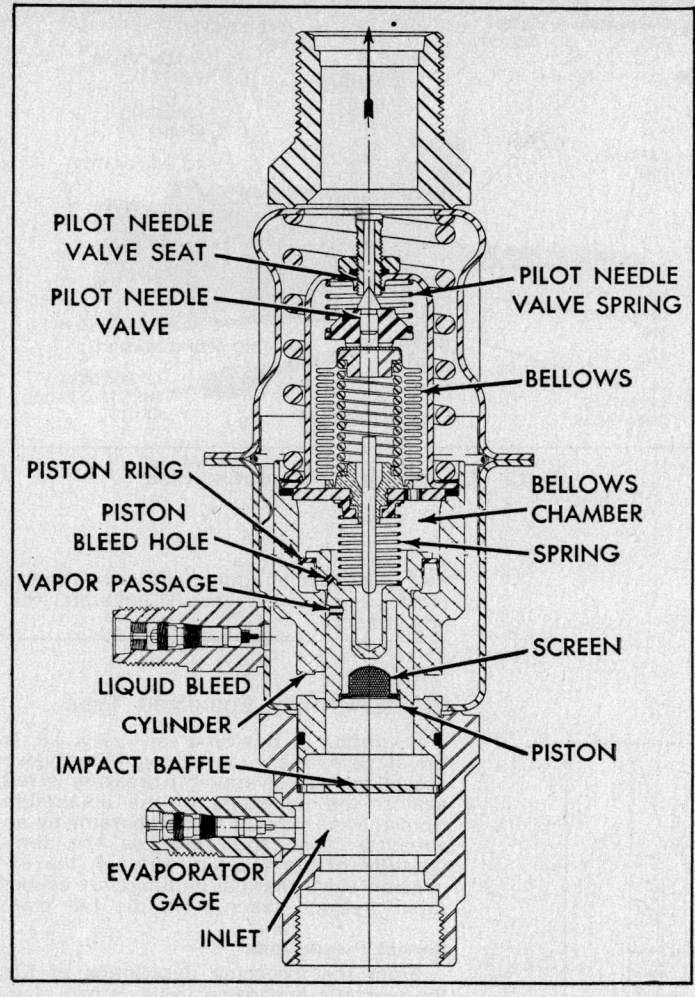

Fig. 10   Sectional view of POA valve

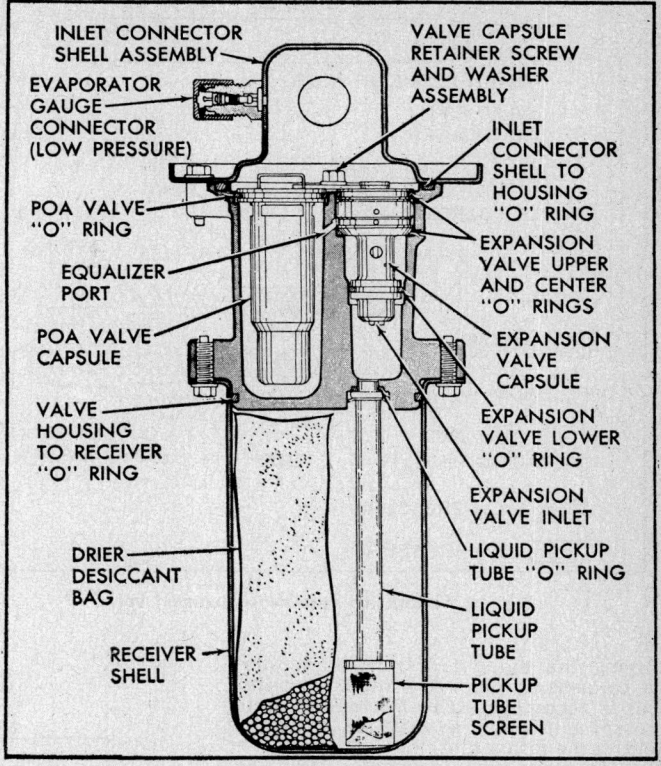

Fig. 11   Sectional view of VIR control

evaporator load conditions. The valve closes when the pressure differential is below 10 PSI to prevent loss of capacity.

NOTE: The filter screen, drier desiccant, thermostatic expansion valve and POA suction throttling valve are serviceable.

When leak-testing the POA valve, it is necessary to check only the hose coupling ends. When using a Propane Torch Leak Detector, no evidence of refrigerant should be present at the POA valve.

The POA valve will provide different gauge readings based on the altitude where the readings are being taken. Correct gauge reading at sea level is 29.5 psi. Gauge readings will be one-half psi higher for each additional 1000 feet of elevation.

The only test for POA valve operation is to check the suction pressure at the valve when making a performance test. If the valve gives improper gauge readings, it must be replaced since it is not repairable or adjustable.

VIR CONTROL
Valves-In Receiver

The VIR assembly, shown in Fig. 11, incorporates the thermostatic expansion valve, POA suction throttling valve, receiver-dehydrator and sight glass. The construction of this unit eliminates the need for an external equalizer line between the thermostatic expansion valve and POA suction throttling valve. Also, the thermobulb and capillary line has been eliminated.

The equalizer function is affected by a port in the wall separating the POA suction throttling valve and thermostatic expansion valve cavities in the VIR unit. The functions of the thermobulb and capillary line is now accomplished directly by the thermostatic expansion valve. The diaphragm end of the thermostatic expansion valve is exposed to refrigerant vapor entering the VIR from the outlet of the evaporator.

The sight glass is located at the inlet of the thermostatic expansion valve and the evaporator gage fitting is located in the inlet connector shell. The VIR unit is mounted adjacent to the evaporator.

The liquid bleed valve, located in the VIR valve housing, opens when a pressure differential greater than 10-20 PSI occurs between evaporator and suction pressures. The valve opening returns oil to the compressor under low refrigerant charge or low

EXPANSION VALVES
Internally Equalized Type

Referring to Fig. 12, the refrigerant enters the inlet and screen as a high pressure liquid. The refrigerant flow is restricted by a metered orifice through which it must pass. As the refrigerant passes through this metered orifice, it changes from a high pressure liquid to a low pressure liquid or from the high side to the low side.

The refrigerant flow through the metered orifice is of the utmost importance. Anything that interferes with this flow seriously affects operation of the entire system.

A sufficient drop in temperature of the area cooled by the evaporator changes the heat transfer requirement of the evaporator. To continue the same flow of refrigerant into the evaporator will result in extreme cooling of the evaporator fins and coils to such an extent that they will freeze over with ice and stop air flow over them.

The flow of refrigerant is controlled by

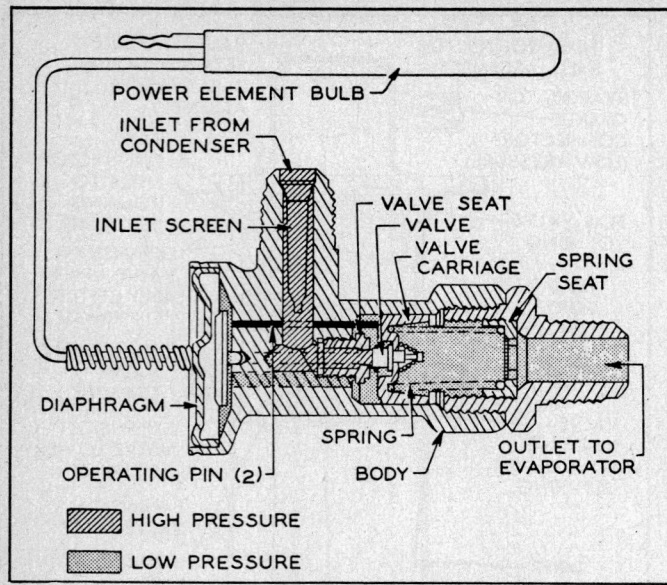

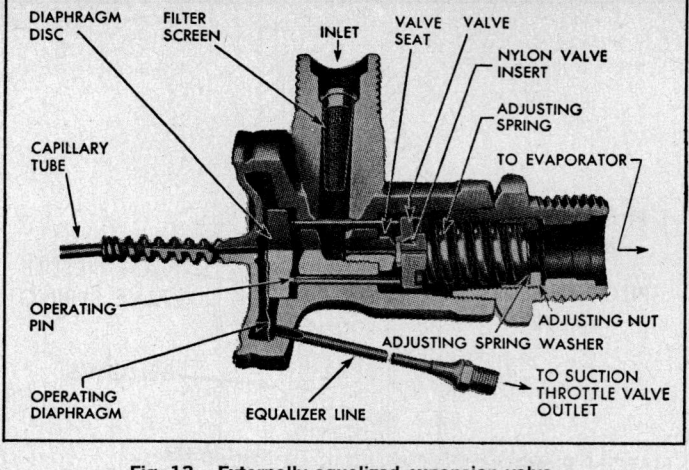

Fig. 13   Externally equalized expansion valve

Fig. 12   Internally equalized expansion valve

varying the amount of refrigerant allowed to pass through the metered orifice. This is accomplished by internal balancing pressures moving a valve or a seat to control the refrigerant flow.

A thermal bulb connected to a diaphragm by a small line and filled with refrigerant gas such as Freon is secured firmly by a clamp to be evaporated tail pipe. The thermal bulb is sensitive to tail pipe temperatures. If the tail pipe becomes warm, the gas inside the bulb will begin to expand, exerting pressure against the diaphragm on the top plate that is connected to the seat or valve by a pin or pins (whichever construction is used). This expansion will then move the seat away from the orifice, allowing an increased refrigerant flow. As the tail pipe temperature drops, the pressure in the thermal bulb also drops, allowing the valve to restrict flow as required by the evaporator.

The pressure of the refrigerant entering the evaporator is fed back to the underside of the diaphragm through the internal equalizing passage. Expansion of the gas in the thermal bulb must overcome the internal balancing pressure before the valve will open to increase refrigerant flow.

A spring is installed against the valve and adjusted to a pre-determined setting at the time of manufacture. This is the super-heat spring, the purpose of which is to prevent slugging of the evaporator with excessive liquid. The adjusted tension of this spring is the determining factor in the opening and closing of the expansion valve. During opening or closing, the super-heat spring tension will retard or assist valve operation as required.

NOTE: For all practical purposes we should not be concerned with the adjustment of this spring. Tension is adjusted from 4 to 16 pounds as required for the unit on which it is to be installed. This original setting is sufficient for the life of the valve, and tampering with the adjustment will only lead to an unsatisfactory opera-

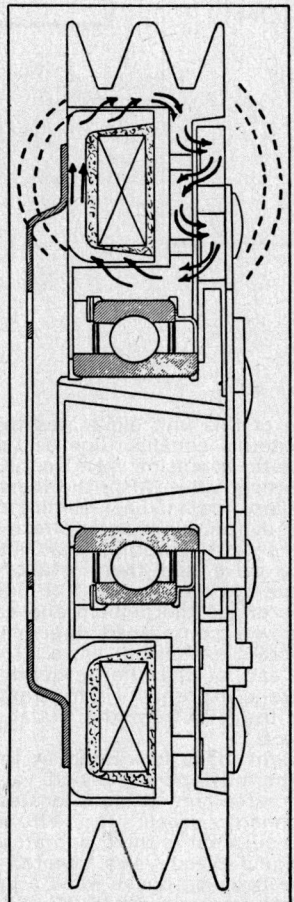

Fig. 14   Path of magnetic flow through compressor clutch

ting unit. Special equipment is required in most cases to accurately calibrate this adjustment.

Externally Equalized Type

Operation of this type valve, Fig. 13, is the same as the internally equalized valve except that the evaporator pressure is fed against the underside of the diaphragm from the tail pipe of the evaporator by an equalizer line. This balances the temperature of the tail pipe through the expansion valve thermal bulb against evaporator pressure taken from the tail pipe.

Service Precautions

From the foregoing description of the thermostatic expansion valve, it can readily be seen that the valve is more sensitive to foreign materials than any other unit in the A/C system. Therefore, the following points should be observed to protect the valve while in service and while servicing the system.

1. The A/C system should be operated at least for short periods throughout the winter season to prevent the internal moving parts from corroding and sticking, which will result in the valve becoming inoperative and necessitating replacement. Periodic operation will also lubricate the entire system and especially the compressor seal, keeping it soft and in condition properly to seal the refrigerant.
2. Clean and replace all accessible screens when servicing.
3. Install a filter if system has excessive foreign materials present.
4. Follow correct evacuation procedure to remove all possible moisture from system.
5. Cap or cover any lines opened for service to prevent entrance of moisture or dirt.
6. Replace dehydrator as soon as excess moisture content is evident. Any system should have the dehydrator replaced at least upon opening the system the third time for service. Also, any time the system has been opened

for a prolonged period from accident or rupture, replace the dehydrator.

7. Handle the thermal bulb and line with extreme care, as excessive bending and rough handling can cause a break that will release the gas, rendering the valve inoperative.

8. Use a back-up wrench when removing any connection to prevent twisting of a line, which may result in weakening or breaking it.

9. Replace expansion valve only with a comparable valve. A numbering system is used to designate the orifice size. Replacing the valve with one with either too small or too large an orifice can seriously affect system operation.

10. Maintain corrosion-free positive contact between thermal bulb and tail pipe. Over a period of time corrosion will form between the two contact surfaces and insulate the two surfaces to such an extent that the operation of the expansion valve will be affected. The clamp may also work loose, preventing positive contact between the two and again affect operation of the expansion valve.

COMPRESSOR CLUTCHES

The clutch units found on automotive A/C systems are of two general types. The first type developed had the magnetic coil installed inside the pulley and rotated with it. This type is called the rotating coil type. The electrical current is carried to the coil by the use of brushes mounted to the compressor frame and contacting a slip ring mounted to the inside of the rotating pulley.

The second type has the magnetic coil mounted to the frame of the compressor and does not rotate. This is called the stationary coil type. This coil being sta-

tionary, correct spacing becomes important to prevent the rotating pulley from contacting the coil and still bring the hub and armature into position to obtain the maximum attraction of the magnetic force.

Each clutch manufacturer furnishes units to fit all models of compressors according to the required specifications for different applications. Therefore, when replacing either the clutch unit or the coil, note carefully that the replacement unit is correct for the vehicle on which it is to be installed.

All clutches operate on the same principle of magnetic attraction. The operation is the same whether the magnetic coil is so mounted that it rotates with the pulley or is solidly mounted to the compressor. Each has a wound core located within a metal cup acting in a manner similar to a horseshoe magnet when the coil is energized magnetically, Fig. 14.

Testing Clutch Coil

To determine if a clutch coil is defective, the following general procedure is enough to meet all requirements regardless of variations of installation. Meter connections given are for negative ground systems; reverse connections for positive ground systems.

Determine Voltage to Coil

1. With ignition switch on and clutch energized, battery voltage should be delivered to the coil. To prepare for the test, expose the connection between the coil and evaporator for electrical checks. *Do not allow exposed wire to contact body of car while switches are ON.*

2. Connect RED lead of a conventional Volt-Ammeter Tester to the exposed wire connection between evaporator and clutch coil.

3. Connect BLACK lead of voltmeter to compressor body.

4. Voltmeter should register battery voltage. If there is no voltage indication, check line fuse, voltage into evaporator, and to the "OFF-ON" switch to locate and repair voltage loss.

Determine Current Draw of Coil

1. Separate wires at connection between evaporator and coil.

2. Connect RED ammeter lead to exposed wire of evaporator.

3. Connect BLACK lead of ammeter to clutch coil wire.

4. Turn switches ON to energize clutch coil.

5. Ammeter should indicate 3 amperes for 12-volt systems; 5 amperes for 6-volt systems.

6. A zero ampere draw indicates an open circuit inside coil; excessive current draw indicates a short-circuit within the coil.

Determine Ground Circuit Resistance

Performance of the resistance test requires that the current draw of the coil be within specifications given above.

1. Connect evaporator and clutch coil wire.

2. Connect RED lead of voltmeter to compressor body.

3. Connect BLACK lead of voltmeter to battery post.

4. Turn switches ON to energize clutch coil.

5. Total resistance from compressor body to battery post cannot exceed .3 of a volt.

6. If resistance is excessive, clean all connections and metal-to-metal contacts, including engine-to-body and compressor-to-engine, to reduce resistance.

A/C System Testing

PERFORMANCE TEST

The system should be operated for at least 15 minutes to allow sufficient time for all parts to become completely stabilized. Determine if the system is fully charged by the use of test gauges and sight glass if one is installed on system. Head pressure will read from 180 psi to 220 psi or higher, depending upon ambient temperature and the type unit being tested. The sight glass should be free of bubbles if a glass is used in the system. Low side pressures should read approximately 15 psi to 30 psi, again depending on the ambient temperature and the unit being tested. It is not feasible to give a definite reading for all types of systems used, as the type control and component installation used on a particular system will directly influence the pressure readings on the high and low sides (see Fig. 5).

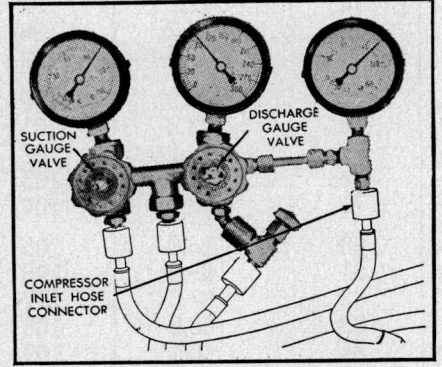

Fig. 15 Purge gauge hoses for Air-Temp compressors

The high side pressure will definitely be affected by the ambient or outside air temperature. A system that is operating normally will indicate a high side gauge reading between 150-170 psi with an 80° F ambient temperature. The same system will register 210-230 psi with an ambient temperature of 100°F. No two systems will register exactly the same, which requires that allowance for variations in head pressures must be considered. Following are the most important normal readings likely to be encountered during the season.

Ambient Temp.	High Side Pressure
80	150-170
90	175-195
95	185-205
100	210-230
105	230-250
110	250-270

Relative Temperature of High and Low Sides

The high side of the system should be uniformly hot to the touch throughout. A difference in temperature will indicate a partial blockage of liquid or gas at this point.

The low side of the system should be uniformly cool to the touch with no excessive sweating of the suction line or low side service valve. Excessive sweating or frosting of the low side service valve usually indicates an expansion valve is allowing an excessive amount of refrigerant into the evaporator. This condition will not necessarily be applicable to those units installed on General Motors vehicles that use the Suction Throttling valve. On these systems the line from the valve to the compressor will normally drop to a much lower reading than the evaporator pressure as the Suction Throttling Valve closes, resulting in the presence of moisture or frosting on this line. This is a normal reaction in this type system and is the result of the construction and operation of the STV or POA and the compressor, having approximately 35% more capacity than previous models of these vehicles that used the hot gas by-pass valve. These factors often cause the line from the STV or POA to the compressor to drop into a partial vacuum under normal operation.

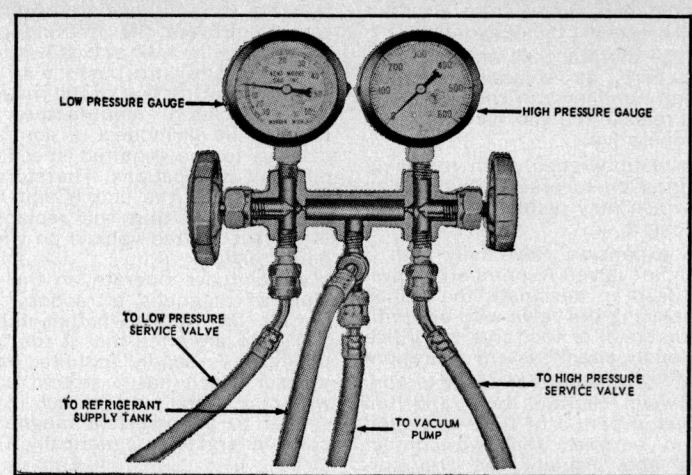

Fig. 16 Purge gauge hoses for Frigidaire, Tecumseh and York compressors

Evaporator Output

At this point, provided all other inspection tests have been performed, and components have been found to operate as they should, a rapid cooling down of the interior of the vehicle should result. The use of a thermometer is not necessary to determine evaporator output. Bringing all units to the correct operating specifications will insure that the evaporator performs as intended.

Temp. F.	Press. PSI	Temp. F.	Press. PSI	Temp. F.	Press. PSI	Temp. F.	Press. PSI	Temp. F.	Press. PSI
0	9.1	35	32.5	60	57.7	85	91.7	110	136.0
2	10.1	36	33.4	61	58.9	86	93.2	111	138.0
4	11.2	37	34.3	62	60.0	87	94.8	112	140.1
6	12.3	38	35.1	63	61.3	88	96.4	113	142.1
8	13.4	39	36.0	64	62.5	89	98.0	114	144.2
10	14.6	40	36.9	65	63.7	90	99.6	115	146.3
12	15.8	41	37.9	66	64.9	91	101.3	116	148.4
14	17.1	42	38.8	67	66.2	92	103.0	117	151.2
16	18.3	43	39.7	68	67.5	93	104.6	118	152.7
18	19.7	44	40.7	69	68.8	94	106.3	119	154.9
20	21.0	45	41.7	70	70.1	95	108.1	120	157.1
21	21.7	46	42.6	71	71.4	96	109.8	121	159.3
22	22.4	47	43.6	72	72.8	97	111.5	122	161.5
23	23.1	48	44.6	73	74.2	98	113.3	123	163.8
24	23.8	49	45.6	74	75.5	99	115.1	124	166.1
25	24.6	50	46.6	75	76.9	100	116.9	125	168.4
26	25.3	51	47.8	76	78.3	101	118.8	126	170.7
27	26.1	52	48.7	77	79.2	102	120.6	127	173.1
28	26.8	53	49.8	78	81.1	103	122.4	128	175.4
29	27.6	54	50.9	79	82.5	104	124.3	129	177.8
30	28.4	55	52.0	80	84.0	105	126.2	130	182.2
31	29.2	56	53.1	81	85.5	106	128.1	131	182.6
32	30.0	57	55.4	82	87.0	107	130.0	132	185.1
33	30.9	58	56.6	83	88.5	108	132.1	133	187.6
34	31.7	59	57.1	84	90.1	109	135.1	134	190.1

Fig. 17   Temperature-pressure relationship for F12 or R12 refrigerant

PURGING SYSTEM

1. Connect gauges into system, Figs. 15, 16, and adjust controls for maximum cooling. *This is necessary when the system has not been operating to return excess oil to the compressor.*
2. Operate engine for 10 to 15 minutes to stabilize the system at 1500-1750 rpm.
3. Shut off engine and controls. Adjust engine speed to slow idle to prevent "dieseling".
4. Open low side hand manifold valve slightly, using a rag or container to catch refrigerant. *Do not discharge the refrigerant near an open flame as a toxic gas (phosgene) can result.*
5. Open high side manifold hand valve. *Open hand valves only enough to bleed refrigerant from system. Too rapid purging will draw excessive oil from compressor and system.*
6. Close gauge manifold shut-off valves when refrigerant ceases to bleed from hose. Both gauges will read zero psi.

Evacuate System with Vacuum Pump

Vacuum pumps suitable for removing air and moisture from A/C systems are commercially available. A specification for system pump-down used here is 28 to 29½" vacuum. This reading can be attained at or near sea level only. For each 1000 feet of altitude this operation is being performed, the reading will be 1" vacuum higher. As an example, at 5000 feet elevation, only 23-24½" of vacuum can be obtained.

1. Connect vacuum pump to gauge manifold. With gauges connected into system, remove cap from vacuum hose connector. Install center hose from gauge manifold to vacuum pump connector. Mid-position high and low side compressor service valves (if used). Open high and low side gauge manifold hand valves.
2. Operate vacuum pump a minimum of 30 minutes for air and moisture removal. Watch compound gauge that system pumps down into a vacuum. System will reach 28-29½" vacuum in not over 5 minutes. If system does not pump down, check all connections and leak-test if necessary.
3. Close gauge manifold hand valves and shut off vacuum pump.
4. Check ability of system to hold vacuum. Watch compound gauge to see that gauge does not rise at a faster rate than 1" vacuum every 4 or 5 minutes. If compound gauge rises at too rapid a rate, install partial charge and leak-test. Then purge system as outlined above.
5. If system holds vacuum, charge system with refrigerant.

Evacuate System Using Charging Station

A vacuum pump is built into the charging station and is constructed to withstand repeated and prolonged use without damage. Complete moisture removal from the system is possible only with a vacuum pump constructed for the purpose.

1. Operate vacuum pump. Connect hose to vacuum pump if system was purged through charging station.
2. Open high and low side gauge valves of charging station.
3. Connect station into 110-volt current.
4. Engage "Off-On" switch to vacuum pump according to directions of specific station being used.
5. System should pump down into a 28-29½" vacuum in not more than 5 minutes. If system fails to meet this specification, repair as necessary.
6. Operate pump a minimum of 30 minutes to remove all air and moisture.
7. Close high and low side gauge valves. Open switch to turn off pump.
8. Check ability of system to hold vacuum by watching compound gauge to see that it does not rise at a rate higher than 1" of vacuum every 4 or 5 minutes: If rise rate is not within specifications, repair system as necessary. If rise rate is within specifications, charge system with refrigerant.

Evacuate System Using Car Engine as a Pump

This procedure is recommended to be used only in an emergency. If a vacuum pump is not available, the compressor should be operated no longer than necessary to remove air from the system. *A vacuum pump must be used for complete moisture removal. The practice of using the car's engine to operate the compressor as a vacuum pump will prove detrimental to the compressor. No compressor manufacturer recommends this procedure.*

1. With gauges connected into system, mid-position high and low side compressor service valves (if used). Open high side gauge manifold hand valve. Operate engine at slow idle speed.
2. Close high side gauge manifold hand valve when compound gauge reaches 20-25" of vacuum.

NOTE: When using the car engine for pump-down, the compound gauge will seldom if ever drop after 25" of vacuum. Continued operation after 25" of vacuum has been reached will increase wear and cause possible damage to the compressor as it is operating without sufficient lubrication.

3. Shut off car engine. Then check ability of system to hold a vacuum by watching the compound gauge to see that gauge does not rise at a faster rate than 1" vacuum every 4 or 5 minutes. If compound gauge rises at too rapid a rate, install a partial charge and leak-test the system. Then purge system and repeat above procedure. If gauge rise is satisfactory, charge system with refrigerant.

CHARGING THE SYSTEM
Using 15-Ounce Containers

To prevent waste and to aid in more accurate charging, refrigerant manufacturers package refrigerant in 15-ounce cans. The small containers are advantageous to small shops doing only a limited amount of A/C service work. The small containers are handled in the same manner as the larger drums except care must be taken not to overheat the cans because of the danger of explosion.

1. Install "Fitz-All" valve to container(s). The Fitz-All valve is available for single cans or three cans. Whichever is used, preliminary installation to the can(s) is the same.
2. Close shut-off valve of Fitz-All valve. Pierce can with mechanism which is part of Fitz-All valve.
3. With the system pumped-down, install charging hose to Fitz-All valve. Loosen charging hose at center connector on gauge manifold.
4. Crack Fitz-All shut-off valve to purge air from charging hose. Tighten charging hose connection on gauge manifold and close shut-off valve.
5. Partially charge system by opening high side gauge manifold hand valve. Open shut-off valve on Fitz-All valve. Invert container(s) to allow liquid Freon to enter high side of system.
6. Complete charge of system. Do not overfill. Use A/C Data table to determine capacity of system being serviced. Close high side gauge manifold hand valve. Start engine and adjust throttle to 1500-1750 rpm. Adjust A/C controls for maximum cooling. Open low side gauge manifold hand valve to allow Freon to be drawn into system. If single containers are used, it will be necessary to replace each as it becomes empty. Watch sight glass until bubbles disappear.
7. To check charge in system, watch for bubbles in sight glass (if used). Read high pressure gauge indication. *Excessive head pressure with a normal low side pressure indicates an overcharge of Freon or air in system. Compressor may or may not be noisy.*
8. Listen for hissing noise in expansion valve as many systems have a hissing in the expansion valve until the system is fully charged.
9. Continue testing system and adjust controls for maximum efficiency.

Using Charging Station

Most stations contain a charging cylinder into which the exact amount of refrigerant required for the system being serviced may be placed while system pump-down is being performed. The refrigerant charging cylinder contained in the station is heated to the correct temperature to insure proper refrigerant flow to all parts of the system as a gas during the charging operation. Fig. 17. Following correct evacuation procedure as to length of time for complete moisture removal, the vacuum pump will so efficiently pump-down the system that opening the correct valves will completely charge the system from the high side, and the use of the compressor in the charging operation will not be required.

1. Prepare charging cylinder for filling: Open storage drum valve. Close all valves on station. Read storage tank gauge pressure. Rotate dial shroud on

charging cylinder to correlate with pressure on gauge. Open cylinder fill valve.

2. Fill charging cylinder: Determine system capacity from A/C Data table. Intermittently open and close pressure relief valve. *When pressure relief valve opens, Freon will enter cylinder and boil. Closing the valve will increase pressure on the Freon, changing it to a liquid to stabilize the refrigerant in the sight glass. Fill to specified level in sight glass and close pressure relief valve.*

3. Charge system: With gauges connected into system, open refrigerant control valve. Open high pressure valve. Remove vacuum hose from pump and crack (barely open) low pressure valve. Allow refrigerant to escape through vacuum hose for approximately 3 seconds. Close high and low pressure valves, and close refrigerant control valve.

4. Continue testing system and adjust controls for maximum efficiency.

LEAK TEST SYSTEM

The propane torch Halide Leak Detector is the most widely used of the detection devices. Therefore, only the procedure for this device will be given. The procedure is the same for any electronic detector, except that the pick-up device registers the presence of refrigerant by a flashing light or high pitched squeal instead of changing the color of the flame. All other steps in preparing the system and leak testing are the same and can be followed as outlined below.

1. Stabilize system at 1500-1750 rpm.

If system is empty of refrigerant, it will be necessary to install a partial charge before continuing. With gauges connected into system, adjust A/C controls for maximum cooling. Operate for 10 to 15 minutes, then shut off car engine.

2. Light leak detector. Open valve to a low flame that will not blow itself out. Warm up until copper element turns cherry red. Lower flame until flame tip is even or slightly below center of element. (For electronic tester, follow preparation procedure as given in operating instructions.)

3. Move leak detector pick-up under hoses, joints, seals, and any possible place for a leak to occur.

NOTE: Freon 12 refrigerant is heavier than air and will move downward. If concentration of refrigerant is located, move pick-up upward to locate leak. Do not inhale fumes produced by burning refrigerant.

4. Watch for color change of flame: Pale blue, no refrigerant; yellow, small amount of refrigerant; purplish-blue, large amount of refrigerant. Repair system as necessary if leaks are located.

5. Check sensitivity of reaction plate: Pass pick-up hose over empty can or crack open refrigerant container; flam should show violent reaction. If no color change, replace reaction plate, following instructions accompanying leak detector. *Too high a flame will result in short life to reaction plate and poor reaction and will soon burn out element.*

6. Charge system if repairs were necessary.

ISOLATE COMPRESSOR FROM SYSTEM

On systems having both a high side and low side service valve, the compressor may be isolated and refrigerant retained in the system while service work is being performed on the compressor or in the engine compartment of the car.

1. Stabilize system at 1500-1750 rpm: With gauges connected into system, adjust A/C controls for maximum cooling. Operate system for 10 to 15 minutes.

2. Isolate compressor: Slowly close low side service valve until low side gauge reads zero psi. Then shut off car engine.

3. Return car engine to idle speed to prevent "dieseling". Completely close low side service valve. Close high side service valve. Purge refrigerant from compressor by cracking low side hand manifold until both gauges read zero psi. *Purge refrigerant slowly to prevent pulling oil from compressor.*

4. Remove gauges from service valves and service valves from compressor. Then perform service work as required.

5. Place compressor in system: Install service valves to compressor, using new gaskets or O-ring seals, whichever are required. Purge air from compressor by cracking high side service valve for 3 seconds with high side hose connector capped and low side hose connector open.

6. Install gauges to service valve connectors and purge air from hoses.

7. Mid-position service valves, continue testing system and adjust controls for maximum performance.

Each make and model of A/C system has its own type of construction. To cover service work on components of all models is beyond the scope of this manual.

AIR CONDITIONING SPECIFICATIONS

Year	Model	Refrigerant Capacity, Lbs.		Refrigeration Oil				Temperature Control Device	Comp. Pulley to Clutch Plate Clearance
					Capacity, Ounces		Oil Level Inches		
		With One Evaporator	With Two Evaporators	Viscosity	With One Evaporator	With Two Evaporators			

AMERICAN MOTORS

Year	Model	With One Evaporator	With Two Evaporators	Viscosity	With One Evaporator	With Two Evaporators	Oil Level Inches	Temperature Control Device	Comp. Pulley to Clutch Plate Clearance
1969–73	Ambassador, Rebel	2¾	—	300	7	—	⅞–1⅛ ②	Thermo. Switch	—
	Matador	2¾	—	300	7	—	⅞–1⅛ ②	Thermo. Switch	—
	Others	2¼	—	300	7	—	⅞–1⅛ ②	Thermo. Switch	—
1974	Ambassador, Matador	3¼	—	300	7	—	⅞–1⅛ ②	Thermo. Switch	—
	Others	2	—	300	7	—	⅞–1⅛ ②	Thermo. Switch	—

BUICK—FULL SIZE CARS

Year	Model	With One Evaporator	With Two Evaporators	Viscosity	With One Evaporator	With Two Evaporators	Oil Level Inches	Temperature Control Device	Comp. Pulley to Clutch Plate Clearance
1969–70	All	4¼	—	525	10½	—	①	POA Valve	.022–.057
1971–72	All	4½	—	525	10½	—	①	POA Valve	.022–.057
1973	All	4	—	525	10½	—	①	POA Valve	.022–.057
1974	All	3¾	—	525	10½	—	①	POA Valve	.022–.057

AIR CONDITIONING SPECIFICATIONS—Continued

| Year | Model | Refrigerant Capacity, Lbs. | | Refrigeration Oil | | | | Temperature Control Device | Comp. Pulley to Clutch Plate Clearance |
| | | With One Evaporator | With Two Evaporators | Viscosity | Capacity, Ounces | | Oil Level Inches | | |
					With One Evaporator	With Two Evaporators			
BUICK—INTERMEDIATE CARS									
1969–72	All	3¾	—	525	10½	—	①	POA Valve	.022–.057
1973	All	4½	—	525	10½	—	①	POA Valve	.022–.057
1974	All	3¾	—	525	10½	—	①	POA Valve	.022–.057
CADILLAC									
1969–73	All	4	5¼	525	10½	13½	①	POA Valve	.031–.057
1974	All	3¾	5	525	10½	13½	①	POA Valve	.031–.057
CAMARO, CHEVROLET, CHEVELLE, NOVA & MONTE CARLO									
1969–74	Four Season	3¾	—	525	11	—	①	POA Valve	.022–.057
	Comfortron	3¾	—	525	11	—	①	POA Valve	.022–.057
	Universal	3	—	525	11	—	①	Thermo. Switch	.022–.057
	All Weather	2½	—	525	11	—	①	Thermo. Switch	.022–.057
CHEVROLET VEGA									
1971–72	All	2¾	—	525	11	—	①	POA Valve	.022–.057
1973–74	All	2¾	—	525	11	—	①	Thermo. Switch	.022–.057
CHEVROLET CORVETTE									
1969–73	All	3¼	—	525	11	—	①	POA Valve	.022–.057
1974	All	3	—	525	11	—	①	POA Valve	.022–.057
CHECKER MOTORS									
1969–74	All	2¾	4½	525	10½	13½	①	Thermo. Switch	.022–.057
CHRYSLER & IMPERIAL									
1969–70	All	3¼	4¼	300	10–11	10–11	1⁹⁄₁₆–2⅜②	EPR Valve⑤	—
1971	All	3¼	4¼	300	10–11	10–11	1⅝–2⅜②	EPR Valve⑤	—
1972	All	3⅓	4⅓	300	10–11	10–11	1⅝–2⅜②	EPR Valve⑤	—
1973	All	3⅓	4⅓	300	10–12	10–12	1⅝–2⅜②	EPR Valve⑥	—
1974	All	5	—	300	10–12	—	1⅝–2⅜②	EPR-2 Valve	
DODGE—FULL SIZE CARS									
1969–70	All	3¼	4¼	300	10–11	10–11	1⁹⁄₁₆–2⅜②	EPR Valve⑤	—
1971	All	3¼	4¼	300	10–11	10–11	1⅝–2⅜②	EPR Valve⑤	—
1972	All	3⅓	4⅓	300	10–11	10–11	1⅝–2⅜	EPR Valve⑤	—
1973	All	3⅓	4⅓	300	10–12	10–12	1⅝–2⅜	EPR Valve⑥	—
1974	All	5	—	300	10–12	10–12	1⅝–2⅜②	EPR-2 Valve	—
DODGE—COMPACT & INTERMEDIATE CARS									
1969–70	Dart 6	2¾	—	300	10–11	—	1⅝–2⅛②	EPR Valve	—
	Coronet, Charger 6	3¼	—	300	10–11	—	2⅛–2¾②	EPR Valve	—
	All V-8	3¼	—	300	10–11	—	1⁹⁄₁₆–2⅜②	EPR Valve	—

AIR CONDITIONING SPECIFICATIONS—Continued

Year	Model	Refrigerant Capacity, Lbs.		Refrigeration Oil				Temperature Control Device	Comp. Pulley to Clutch Plate Clearance
					Capacity, Ounces				
		With One Evaporator	With Two Evaporators	Viscosity	With One Evaporator	With Two Evaporators	Oil Level Inches		
DODGE—COMPACT & INTERMEDIATE CARS—Continued									
1971	6 Cylinder	2¾	—	300	10–11	—	1⅝–2⅛②	EPR Valve	—
	V8	3¼	—	300	10–11	—	1⅝–2⅜②	EPR Valve	—
1972	All	2⅞	—	300	10–11	—	⑥	EPR Valve	—
1973	All	2⅞	—	300	10–12	—	⑦	EPR Valve	—
1974	Exc. Dart	2¾	—	300	10–12	—	⑦	EPR-2 Valve	—
	Dart	3¼	—	300	10–12	—	⑦	EPR-2 Valve	—
FORD—FULL SIZE CARS									
1969	York Comp.	3	—	③	10	—	⅞–1 3/16②	Thermo. Switch	—
	Tecumseh Comp.	3	—	③	11	—	⅞–1⅝②	Thermo. Switch	—
1970	York Comp.	3	—	③	10	—	⑧	Thermo. Switch	—
	Tecumseh Comp.	3	—	③	11	—	⑧	Thermo. Switch	—
1971–72	York Comp.	3¼	—	③	10	—	⑧	Thermo. Switch	—
	Tecumseh Comp.	3¼	—	③	11	—	⑧	Thermo. Switch	—
1973–74	York Comp.	4¼	—	③	10	—	⑧	STV Valve	—
	Tecumseh Comp.	4¼	—	③	11	—	⑧	STV Valve	—
FORD—COMPACT & INTERMEDIATE CARS (EXC. MUSTANG II)									
1969	Falcon, Fairlane	1⅞	—	③	10④	—	⅞–1⅝②④	Thermo. Switch	—
	Mustang	1¾	—	③	10④	—	⅞–1⅜②④	Thermo. Switch	—
1970–71	Exc. Mustang	1⅞	—	③	⑨	—	⑧	Thermo. Switch	—
	Mustang	1¾	—	③	⑨	—	⑧	Thermo. Switch	—
1972–74	York Comp.	⑩	—	③	10	—	⑧	⑪	—
	Tecumseh Comp.	⑩	—	③	11	—	⑧	⑪	—
FORD MUSTANG II									
1974	York Comp.	3¼	—	③	10	—	⑧	STV Valve	—
	Tecumseh Comp.	3¼	—	③	11	—	⑧	STV Valve	—
FORD PINTO									
1971–73	York Comp.	1⅞	—	③	10	—	②⑧	Thermo. Switch	—
	Tecumseh Comp.	1⅞	—	③	11	—	②⑧	Thermo. Switch	—
1974	York Comp.	2¼	—	③	10	—	⑧	STV Valve	—
	Tecumseh Comp.	2¼	—	③	11	—	⑧	STV Valve	—

AIR CONDITIONING SPECIFICATIONS—Continued

LINCOLN

Year	Model	Refrigerant Capacity, Lbs. With One Evaporator	Refrigerant Capacity, Lbs. With Two Evaporators	Refrigeration Oil Viscosity	Refrigeration Oil Capacity, Ounces With One Evaporator	Refrigeration Oil Capacity, Ounces With Two Evaporators	Oil Level Inches	Temperature Control Device	Comp. Pulley to Clutch Plate Clearance
1969	Lincoln	3½	—	③	10④	—	7/8–1 3/16②④	Thermo. Switch	—
	Mark III	2¼	—	③	10④	—	7/8–1 3/16②④	Thermo. Switch	—
1970	Lincoln	4¼	—	③	⑨	—	⑧	Thermo. Switch	—
	Mark III	2¼	—	③	⑨	—	⑧	Thermo. Switch	—
1971	Lincoln	4¼	—	③	10④	—	⑧	Thermo. Switch	—
	Mark III	2¼	—	③	10	—	⑧	Thermo. Switch	—
	Six Cyl. Comp.	—	—	525	10½	—	—	STV Valve	.022–.057
1972–74	Lincoln	4½	—	525	10½	—	—	STV Valve	.022–.057
	Mark IV	4½	—	525	10½	—	—	STV Valve	.022–.057

MERCURY—FULL SIZE CARS

Year	Model	Refrigerant Capacity, Lbs. With One Evaporator	Refrigerant Capacity, Lbs. With Two Evaporators	Refrigeration Oil Viscosity	Refrigeration Oil Capacity, Ounces With One Evaporator	Refrigeration Oil Capacity, Ounces With Two Evaporators	Oil Level Inches	Temperature Control Device	Comp. Pulley to Clutch Plate Clearance
1969	York Comp.	3	—	③	10	—	7/8–1 3/16②	Thermo. Switch	—
	Tecumseh Comp.	3	—	③	11	—	7/8–1 5/8②	Thermo. Switch	—
1970	York Comp.	3	—	③	10	—	⑧	Thermo. Switch	—
	Tecumseh Comp.	3	—	③	11	—	⑧	Thermo. Switch	—
1971–72	York Comp.	3¼	—	③	10	—	⑧	Thermo. Switch	—
	Tecumseh Comp.	3¼	—	③	11	—	⑧	Thermo. Switch	—
1973–74	York Comp.	4¼	—	③	10	—	⑧	STV Valve	—
	Tecumseh Comp.	4¼	—	③	11	—	⑧	STV Valve	—

MERCURY—COMPACT & INTERMEDIATE CARS

Year	Model	Refrigerant Capacity, Lbs. With One Evaporator	Refrigerant Capacity, Lbs. With Two Evaporators	Refrigeration Oil Viscosity	Refrigeration Oil Capacity, Ounces With One Evaporator	Refrigeration Oil Capacity, Ounces With Two Evaporators	Oil Level Inches	Temperature Control Device	Comp. Pulley to Clutch Plate Clearance
1969	Montego	1⅞	—	③	10④	—	7/8–1 3/16②④	Thermo. Switch	—
	Cougar	1¾	—	③	10④	—	7/8–1 3/16②④	Thermo. Switch	—
1970	Montego	1⅞	—	③	⑨	—	⑧	Thermo. Switch	—
	Cougar	1¾	—	③	⑨	—	⑧	Thermo. Switch	—
1971–74	York Comp.	⑫	—	③	10	—	⑧	Thermo. Switch⑬	—
	Tecumseh Comp.	⑫	—	③	11	—	⑧	Thermo. Switch⑬	—

OLDSMOBILE—FULL SIZE CARS

Year	Model	Refrigerant Capacity, Lbs. With One Evaporator	Refrigerant Capacity, Lbs. With Two Evaporators	Refrigeration Oil Viscosity	Refrigeration Oil Capacity, Ounces With One Evaporator	Refrigeration Oil Capacity, Ounces With Two Evaporators	Oil Level Inches	Temperature Control Device	Comp. Pulley to Clutch Plate Clearance
1969–72	All	4½	—	525	10½	—	①	POA Valve	.022–.057
1973–74	All	4	—	525	10½	—	①	POA Valve	.022–.057

OLDSMOBILE—INTERMEDIATE CARS

Year	Model	Refrigerant Capacity, Lbs. With One Evaporator	Refrigerant Capacity, Lbs. With Two Evaporators	Refrigeration Oil Viscosity	Refrigeration Oil Capacity, Ounces With One Evaporator	Refrigeration Oil Capacity, Ounces With Two Evaporators	Oil Level Inches	Temperature Control Device	Comp. Pulley to Clutch Plate Clearance
1969–74	All	4	—	525	10½	—	①	POA Valve	.022–.057

PLYMOUTH—FULL SIZE CARS

Year	Model	Refrigerant Capacity, Lbs. With One Evaporator	Refrigerant Capacity, Lbs. With Two Evaporators	Refrigeration Oil Viscosity	Refrigeration Oil Capacity, Ounces With One Evaporator	Refrigeration Oil Capacity, Ounces With Two Evaporators	Oil Level Inches	Temperature Control Device	Comp. Pulley to Clutch Plate Clearance
1969	Six Cylinder	3¼	4¼	300	10–11	10–11	2⅛–2¾②	EPR Valve⑤	—
	V8	3¼	4¼	300	10–11	10–11	1 9/16–2⅜②	EPR Valve⑤	—
1970–71	Six Cylinder	3¼	4¼	300	10–11	10–11	1⅝–2⅛②	EPR Valve⑤	—
	V8	3¼	4¼	300	10–11	10–11	1⅝–2⅜②	EPR Valve⑤	—
1972	Six Cylinder	3¼	4¼	300	10–11	10–11	1¾–2⅜	EPR Valve⑤	—
	V8	3¼	4¼	300	10–11	10–11	1⅝–2⅜	EPR Valve⑤	—
1973	Six Cylinder	3¼	4¼	300	10–12	10–12	1¾–2⅜	EPR Valve⑤	—
	V8	3¼	4¼	300	10–12	10–12	1⅝–2⅜	EPR Valve⑤	—
1974	All	5	—	300	10–12	—	1¾–2⅜	EPR-2	—

AIR CONDITIONING SPECIFICATIONS—Continued

Year	Model	Refrigerant Capacity, Lbs.		Refrigeration Oil				Temperature Control Device	Comp. Pulley to Clutch Plate Clearance
		With One Evaporator	With Two Evaporators	Viscosity	Capacity, Ounces		Oil Level Inches		
					With One Evaporator	With Two Evaporators			

PLYMOUTH—COMPACT & INTERMEDIATE CARS

Year	Model	With One Evaporator	With Two Evaporators	Viscosity	With One Evaporator	With Two Evaporators	Oil Level Inches	Temp. Control Device	Clearance
1969	Valiant, Barracuda 6	$2\frac{3}{4}$	—	300	10–11	—	$1\frac{5}{8}–2\frac{1}{8}$ ②	EPR Valve	—
	Belvedere, Satellite 6	$3\frac{1}{4}$	—	300	10–11	—	$2\frac{1}{8}–2\frac{3}{4}$ ②	EPR Valve	—
	All V8	$3\frac{1}{4}$	—	300	10–11	—	$1\frac{9}{16}–2\frac{3}{8}$ ②	EPR Valve	—
1970–71	Barracuda, Satellite 6	$3\frac{1}{4}$	$4\frac{1}{4}$	300	10–11	—	$1\frac{5}{8}–2\frac{1}{8}$	EPR Valve⑤	—
	Valiant 6	$2\frac{3}{4}$	—	300	10–11	—	$1\frac{5}{8}–2\frac{1}{8}$	EPR Valve⑤	—
	All V8	$3\frac{1}{4}$	$4\frac{1}{4}$	300	10–11	—	$1\frac{5}{8}–2\frac{3}{8}$	EPR Valve⑤	—
1972	Six Cylinder	$2\frac{3}{4}$	—	300	10–11	—	$1\frac{3}{4}–2\frac{3}{8}$	EPR Valve⑤	—
	V8	$2\frac{3}{4}$	—	300	10–11	—	$1\frac{5}{8}–2\frac{3}{8}$	EPR Valve⑧	—
1973	All	$2\frac{7}{8}$	—	300	10–12	—	⑦	EPR Valve⑤	—
1974	Exc. Valiant	$2\frac{3}{4}$	—	300	10–12	—	⑦	EPR-2 Valve	—
	Valiant	$3\frac{1}{4}$	—	300	10–12	—	⑦	EPR-2 Valve	—

PONTIAC—FULL SIZE CARS

Year	Model	With One Evaporator	With Two Evaporators	Viscosity	With One Evaporator	With Two Evaporators	Oil Level Inches	Temp. Control Device	Clearance
1969–74	All	$4\frac{1}{8}$⑭	—	525	11	—	①	POA Valve	.022–.057

PONTIAC—INTERMEDIATE CARS

Year	Model	With One Evaporator	With Two Evaporators	Viscosity	With One Evaporator	With Two Evaporators	Oil Level Inches	Temp. Control Device	Clearance
1969	Firebird	$3\frac{3}{4}$	—	525	11	—	①	POA Valve	.022–.057
	All Others	$4\frac{1}{8}$	—	525	11	—	①	POA Valve	.022–.057
1970–74	All	$4\frac{1}{8}$⑭	—	525	11	—	①	POA Valve	.022–.057

THUNDERBIRD

Year	Model	With One Evaporator	With Two Evaporators	Viscosity	With One Evaporator	With Two Evaporators	Oil Level Inches	Temp. Control Device	Clearance
1969	All	$2\frac{1}{4}$	—	③	10④	—	$\frac{7}{8}–1\frac{3}{16}$ ②④	Thermo. Switch	—
1970	All	$2\frac{1}{4}$	—	③	11④	—	$\frac{7}{8}–1\frac{1}{16}$④	Thermo. Switch	—
1971	All	$2\frac{1}{4}$	—	③	10④	—	$\frac{7}{8}–1\frac{3}{8}$ ②	Thermo. Switch	—
1972–74	All	$4\frac{1}{2}$	—	525	$10\frac{1}{2}$	—	$\frac{7}{8}–1\frac{1}{16}$ ②	STV Valve	.022–.057

①—See text for procedure.
②—Dipstick reading with compressor installed.
③—Suniso 5G or Capella E.
④—For Tecumseh Comp., oil level is $\frac{7}{8}–1\frac{5}{8}$. Capacity 11 oz.
⑤—Auto Temp uses ETR valve.
⑥—Six cylinder engines, $1\frac{5}{8}–2\frac{1}{8}$; V8 engines, $1\frac{5}{8}–2\frac{3}{8}$.
⑦—Six cylinder engines, $1\frac{3}{4}–2\frac{3}{8}$; V8 engines, $1\frac{5}{8}–2\frac{3}{8}$.
⑧—York Comp.—Vertical mount., $\frac{7}{8}–1\frac{1}{8}$; horizontal mount., $1\frac{3}{16}–1\frac{3}{16}$.
 Tecumseh Comp.—Vertical mount., $\frac{7}{8}–1\frac{3}{8}$; horizontal mount., $\frac{7}{8}–1\frac{5}{8}$.
⑨—York Comp., 10 oz., Tecumseh Comp., 11 oz.
⑩—Maverick, $1\frac{7}{8}$; Torino, $4\frac{1}{2}$; 1972–73 Mustang, $1\frac{3}{4}$.
⑪—Exc. Torino, thermo. switch; Torino, STV valve.
⑫—Comet & 1971 Montego, $1\frac{7}{8}$; 1971–72 Cougar, $1\frac{3}{4}$; 1972–74 Montego & 1973–74 Cougar, $4\frac{1}{2}$.
⑬—1972–74 Montego & 1974 Cougar, STV valve.
⑭—Refer to compressor decal when servicing these systems.

CHARGING VALVE LOCATIONS

Year & Model	High Press.	Low Press.	Year & Model	High Press.	Low Press.	Year & Model	High Press.	Low Press.
AMERICAN MOTORS			**CHEVROLET VEGA**			**FORD (ALL)**		
1969–74	Compressor	Compressor	1971	Exp. Valve	STV(POA)①	1969–74	Compressor	Compressor
BUICK-FULL SIZE			1972	Dis. Pres. Sw.	POA①	**LINCOLN**		
1969–72	Compressor	STV(POA)①	1973–74	Dis. Pres. Sw.	Accumulator	1969–71	Compressor	Compressor
1973–74	Compressor	VIR	**CHEVY NOVA**			1972–74	Compressor	STV
BUICK INTERMEDIATE			1969–71—			**MERCURY (ALL)**		
1969–73	Compressor	STV(POA)	Exc. Below	Compressor	Compressor	1969–74	Compressor	Compressor
1974—			Four Season	Exp. Valve	STV(POA)①	**OLDSMOBILE (ALL)**		
Exc. Apollo	Compressor	VIR	1972–73	Exp. Valve	POA①	1969–74②	Compressor	STV(POA)①
Apollo	Compressor	POA	1974	VIR	VIR	1973–74③	Compressor	VIR
CADILLAC			**CHECKER MOTORS**			**PLYMOUTH (ALL)**		
1969–73②	Vapor Line	STV(POA)①	1969–74	Exp. Valve	POA	1969–74	Compressor	Compressor
1973–74③	Vapor Line	VIR	**CHRYSLER & IMP.**			**PONTIAC (ALL)**		
CAMARO, CHEVELLE, CHEVROLET &			1969–74	Compressor	Compressor	1969–74②	Compressor	STV(POA)①
MONTE CARLO			**CORVETTE**			1973–74③	Compressor	VIR
1969–71—			1969–71	Compressor	STV(POA)①	**T-BIRD**		
Exc. Below	Compressor	Compressor	1972	Compressor	Compressor	1969–71	Compressor	Compressor
Four Season	Exp. Valve	STV(POA)①	1973	Compressor	VIR	1972–74	Compressor	STV
Comfortron	Exp. Valve	STV(POA)①	1974	VIR	VIR			
1972–73	Exp. Valve	POA①	**DODGE (ALL)**					
1974	VIR	VIR	1969–74	Compressor	Compressor			

①—Located at cowl, right side of engine.
②—Except VIR system.
③—With VIR.

VARIABLE SPEED FANS

The fan drive clutch, Fig. 1, is a fluid coupling containing silicone oil. Fan speed is regulated by the torque-carrying capacity of the silicone oil. The more silicone oil in the coupling the greater the fan speed, and the less silicone oil the slower the fan speed.

Two types of fan drive clutches are in use. On one, Fig. 2, a bi-metallic strip and control piston on the front of the fluid coupling regulates the amount of silicone oil entering the coupling. The bi-metallic strip bows outward with a decrease in surrounding temperature and allows a piston to move outward. Th piston opens a valve regulating the flow of silicone oil into the coupling from a reserve chamber. The silicone oil is returned to the reserve chamber through a bleed hole when the valve is closed.

On the other type of fan drive clutch, Fig. 3, a heat-sensitive, bi-metal spring connected to an opening plate brings about a similar result. Both units cause the fan speed to increase with a rise in temperature and to decrease as the temperature goes down.

In some cases a Flex-Fan is used instead of a Fan Drive Clutch. Flexible blades vary the volume of air being drawn through the radiator, automatically increasing the pitch at low engine speeds.

Fig. 1   Typical variable-speed fan installed

Fan Drive Clutch Test

Run the engine at a fast idle speed (1000 rpm) until normal operating temperature is reached. This process can be speeded up by blocking off the front of the radiator with cardboard. Regardless of temperatures, the unit must be operated for at least five minutes immediately before being tested.

Stop the engine and, using a glove or a cloth to protect the hand, immediately check the effort required to turn the fan. If considerable effort is required, it can be assumed that the coupling is operating satisfactorily. If very little effort is required to turn the fan, it is an indication that the coupling is not operating properly and should be replaced.

Service Procedure

CAUTION: When it becomes necessary to remove a fan clutch of the silicone fluid type, Fig. 2, the assembly must be supported in the vertical (on car) position to prevent leaks of silicone fluid from the clutch mechanism. This loss of fluid will render the fan clutch inoperative.

The removal procedure for either type of fan clutch assembly is generally the same for all cars. Merely unfasten the unit from the water pump and remove the assembly from the car.

The type of unit shown in Fig. 2 may by partially disassembled for inspection and cleaning. Take off the capscrews that hold the assembly together and separate the fan from the drive clutch. Next remove the metal strip on the front by pushing one end of it toward the fan clutch body so it clears the retaining bracket. Then push the strip to the side so that its opposite end will spring out of place. Now remove the small control piston underneath it.

Check the piston for free movement of the coupling device. If the piston sticks, clean it with emery cloth. If the bi-metal strip is damaged, replace the entire unit. These strips are not interchangeable.

When reassembling, install the control piston so that the projection on the end of it will contact the metal strip. Then install the metal strip with any identification numerals or letters facing the clutch. After reassembly, clean the clutch drive with a cloth soaked in solvent. Avoid dipping the clutch assembly in any type of liquid. Install the assembly in the reverse order of removal.

The coil spring type of fan clutch cannot be disassembled, serviced or repaired. If it does not function properly it must be replaced with a new unit.

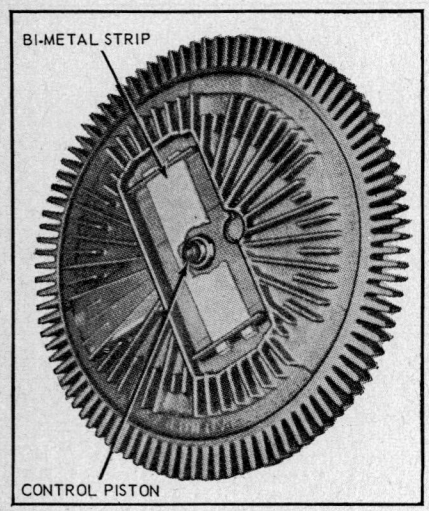

Fig. 2   Variable-speed fan with flat bi-metal thermostatic spring

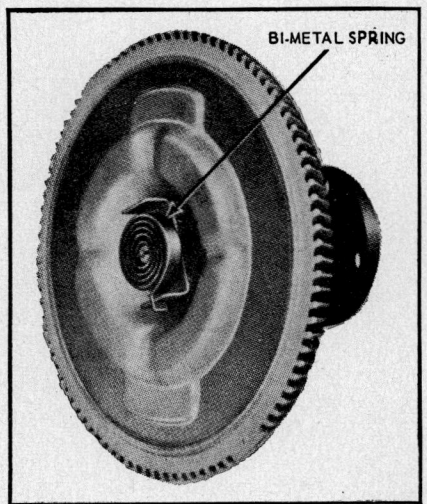

Fig. 3   Variable-speed fan with coiled bi-metal thermostatic spring

AUTOMATIC LEVEL CONTROL

SUPERLIFT SYSTEM

This system, Fig. 1, combines the Superlift shock absorber option with an air compressor and a height control valve. When the Superlift option is used alone, the shocks are filled with (or deflated of) compressed air at any gas station through a fill valve. When used in this system, however, the air pressure is supplied by the compressor and the amount of pressure added or removed is controlled by a sensing valve.

The compressor, a two stage type requiring no lubrication, is designed to operate off engine vacuum to replenish air used from the reservoir which is part of the compressor. As the compressor cycles, the reservoir air pressure gradually increases, causing a back pressure on the secondary stage piston, until it equals the engine vacuum pull against the diaphragm and the unit stops operating until reservoir pressure drops again.

A pressure regulator is attached to the output side of the compressor to limit reservoir outlet pressure to 125 psi. The rear standing height is controlled by a valve which is mounted to the frame, and senses changes in vehicle loading through a link attached to the suspension upper control arm. Changes in the position of the link cause the control valve to either admit or exhaust air from the shocks to return the link to "neutral" position. A 4 to 18 second time delay mechanism inside the control valve prevents transfer of air during normal ride conditions. In this way the system only responds to actual changes in vehicle loading.

Some later systems incorporate a vacuum regulator valve which consists of a relay valve and a deceleration valve. The relay valve is connected to the compressor and the P.C.V. line by rubber hose. The spark advance port of the regulator is connected into the distributor advance vacuum line and the intake manifold port is tapped into the rear of the intake manifold.

When the engine is at slow idle, the compressor will not operate due to insufficient vacuum, Fig. 3. As engine speed increases to fast idle or cruising speed, the increased vacuum is applied through a .020-.025" orifice to the vacuum relay, overcoming valve spring tension and opening the relay valve. Vacuum from the P.C.V. line now acts upon the compressor and allows it to operate, Fig. 4.

During deceleration, vacuum at the rear of the intake manifold exceeds 17" and vacuum at the spark advance port is negligible. Manifold vacuum overcomes deceleration valve spring tension, opening the valve and permitting vacuum to overcome the relay valve spring and open the relay valve to admit P.C.V. vacuum and operate the compressor, Fig. 5.

The Superlift, Fig. 6, is essentially a conventional shock absorber enclosed in an air chamber. A pliable nylon reinforced boot seals the dust tube (air dome) to the reservoir tube (air piston). The unit will extend when inflated and retract when deflated by the control valve. An 8 to 15 psi air pressure is maintained in the unit to minimize boot friction. This is accomplished by a check

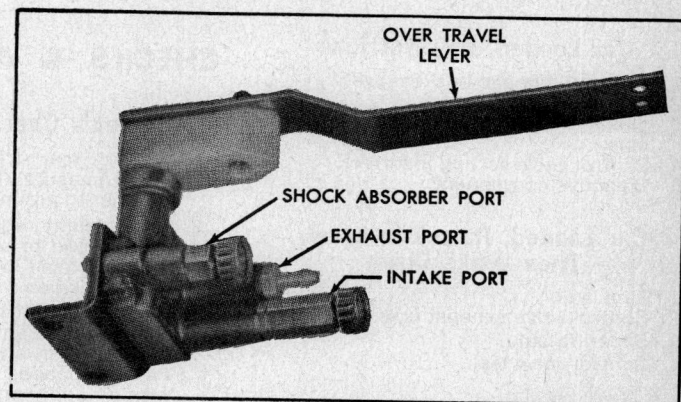

Fig. 2   Height control valve

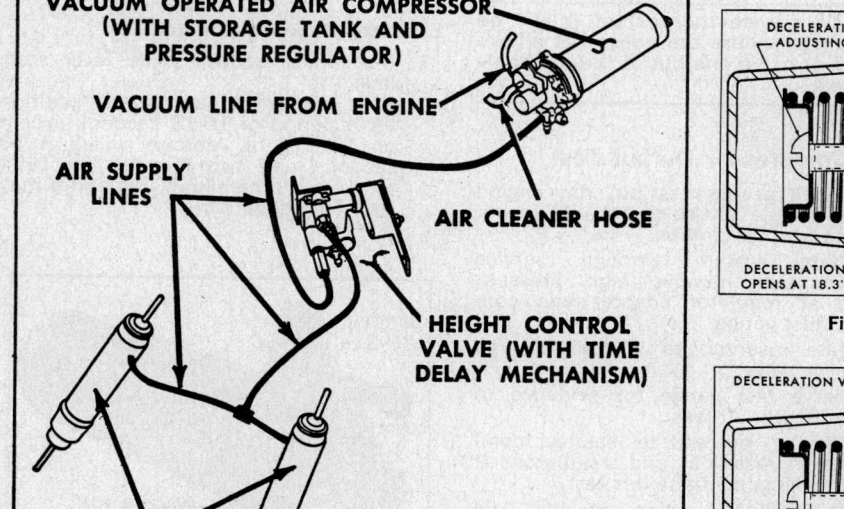

Fig. 1   Schematic diagram of Superlift Automatic Level Control System

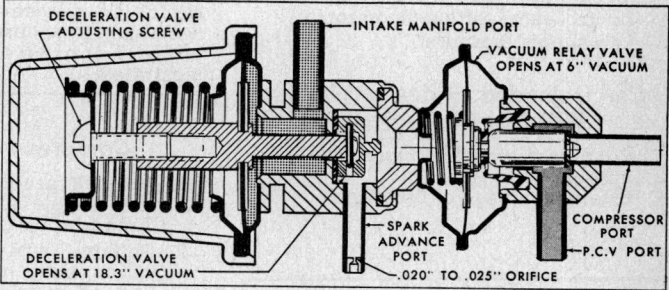

Fig. 3   Vacuum regulator valve in slow idle position

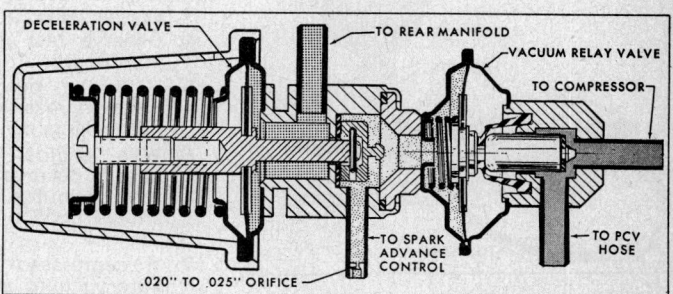

Fig. 4   Vacuum regulator valve in fast idle position

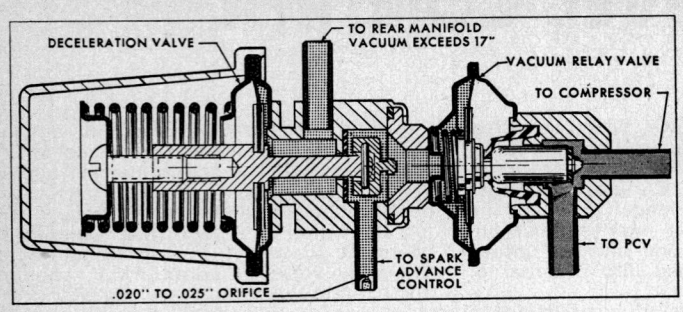

Fig. 5 Vacuum regulator valve in deceleration position

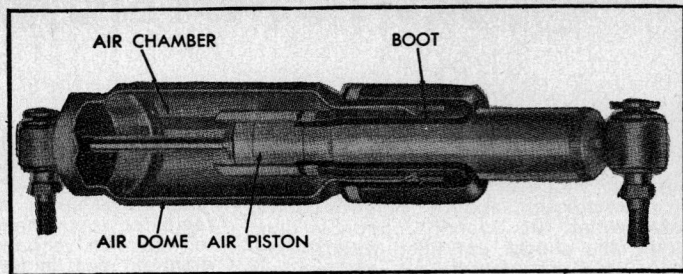

Fig. 6 Superlift shock absorber

valve in the exhaust fitting of the control valve.

TROUBLE SHOOTING GUIDE

Car Loaded, Will Not Rise

1. External damage or breakage.
2. Line leak.
3. Linkage to overtravel lever in wrong hole.
4. Control valve setting incorrect.
5. Defective component.

Car Loaded, Raises to Level, Then Leaks Down

1. Line leak.
2. Control valve exhaust leak.
3. Superlift leak.
4. Control valve leak.

Car Loaded, Raises Partially

1. Load excessive (over 500 lbs at axle) on cars with special springs.
2. Control valve setting incorrect.
3. Low supply pressure.

Car Unloaded, Rides too High, Will Not Come Down

1. Control valve setting incorrect.
2. Improper springs.
3. External damage or breakage.

4. Linkage to overtravel in wrong hole.
5. Defective control valve.

Car Rises When Loaded but Leaks Down While Driving

1. Time delay mechanism not functioning properly.

CHECKS & ADJUSTMENTS

Quick Check of System

1. Record rear trim height of empty car (measure from center of rear bumper to ground).
2. Add weight equivalent to two-passenger load to rear of car. Car should begin to level in 4 to 15 seconds, and final position should be (plus or minus) ½" of measured dimension.
3. Remove weight. After 4 to 18 seconds car should begin to settle. Final unloaded position should be within approximately (plus or minus) ½" of the original measured dimension.

NOTE: To service the system it will be necessary to secure the gauge set shown in Fig. 7 or make one out of the materials illustrated.

Compressor Output Test

1. With all accessories off, run engine until engine settles to hot idle speed. Then turn off ignition.
2. Deflate system through service valve, then remove high pressure line at regulator adapter and connect test gauge.
3. Inflate reservoir to 70 psi through service valve.
4. Observe test gauge for evidence of compressor air leak.
5. If leaking, proceed to leak-test compressor reservoir and regulator. If not leaking, continue this test.
6. With engine running at hot idle speed, observe reservoir build-up for five minutes. Reservoir pressure should build up to a minimum of 90 psi.
7. If compressor fails to cycle, make sure vacuum and air intake lines are open and unobstructed before removing compressor for repair.

8. If build-up is too slow, repair compressor.
9. Satisfactory build-up indicates system problems to be in the control section. However, again observe the test gauge for evidence of an air leak and proceed accordingly.

Regulator Test & Adjustment General Motors

1. Performance test the regulator with a known good compressor on the car.
2. Deflate system through service valve, remove line at regulator and connect test gauge at regulator adapter.
3. Inflate reservoir through service valve to maximum pressure available. If less than 140 psi, start engine to build-up pressure.
4. Regulated pressure on test gauge should build up to 100-130 psi and hold steady within this range.
5. Recheck regulated pressure by momentarily depressing valve core on test gauge and observe reading.
6. If regulated pressure exceeds 130 psi, replace regulator as a unit.

Control Valve Test

Exhaust—Superlifts Inflated

1. Disconnect control valve lever from link.
2. Hold lever down in exhaust position for a period of 15-18 seconds except on 1973 Ford, Mercury which is 30 seconds and two minutes on 1974 models. If time allows, Superlifts may be totally deflated.

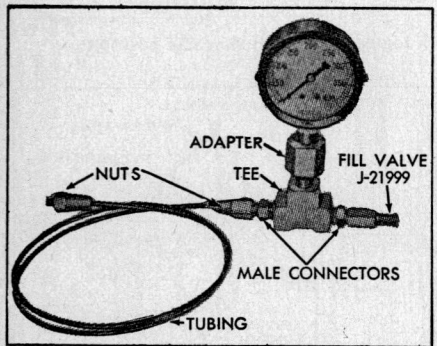

Fig. 7 Test gauge set (Kent-Moore No. J-22124)

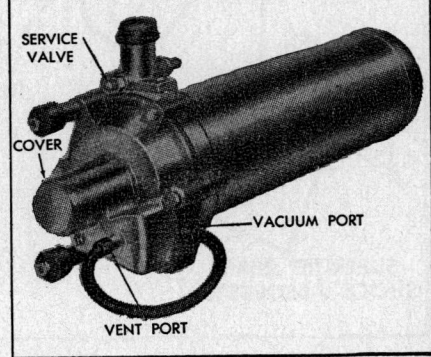

Fig. 8 Assembly leak test preparation

3. If Superlifts deflate, perform Intake Check.

4. If Superlifts do not deflate, remove exhaust adapter from control valve and hold lever down as in Step 2. Replace adapter, O-ring and filter if this deflates Superlifts.

5. Replace control valve if none of the above steps solve problem.

Intake Check—Reservoir Pressure, 125 psi Minimum (Ford, 90 psi Min.)

1. Disconnect overtravel lever from link.

2. Hold lever up in intake position for a period of 15-18 seconds except on 1973-74 Ford, Mercury which is a period of two minutes. If time allows, Superlifts may be totally inflated.

3. If Superlifts inflate and hold, proceed to Time Delay Test.

4. If Superlifts inflate and then leak down, perform leak test on lines and fittings and then on Superlifts and control valve. Repair or replace as required.

Time Delay Test Ford & GM Reservoir Pressure 125 PSI Minimum

1. Disconnect overtravel lever from link.

2. Disconnect lines at Superlift and intake ports.

3. Connect test gauge to intake valve port and apply air pressure (95 lbs.).

4. Move overtravel lever down approximately one inch from neutral position then quickly move lever up two inches. Air should begin to escape from the Superlift port in 4 to 30 seconds. Repeat test.

5. Remove test gauge and plug intake port with fill valve (female end).

6. Connect test gauge to the Superlift port and apply air pressure (95 lbs.).

7. Repeat Step 4. If either test is not within specifications, valve is defective or there has been a loss of silicone fluid.

Trim Adjustment On Car

Trim adjustment should be performed with a full gas tank or the equivalent in load at rate of 6 lbs. per gallon.

All Exc. 1972-74 Ford & Mercury

Preparation

1. Raise car with rear axle supported.

2. Remove Superlift line at control valve, Fig. 2.

3. Connect a Fill Valve Assembly (see Fig. 7).

4. Inflate Superlifts to 8 to 15 psi. Jounce car to neutralize suspension.

5. Connect test gauge to Superlift adapter on control valve and attach air pressure source (80 to 110 psi).

Adjustment

1. Loosen overtravel lever adjusting nut.

2. Hold overtravel body down in exhaust position until air escapes from exhaust valve port.

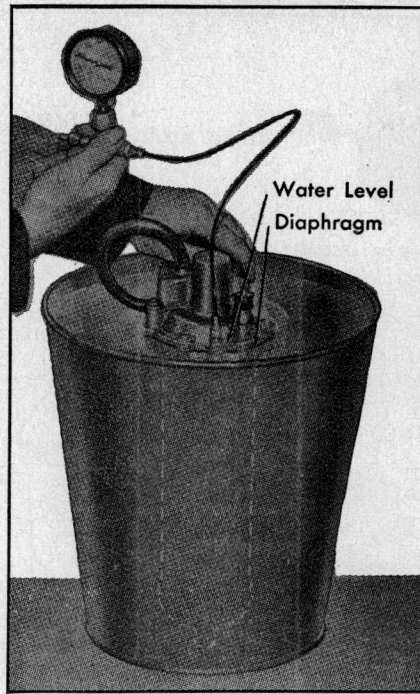

Fig. 9   Checking compressor, reservoir and regulator for leaks

Water Level Diaphragm

3. Slowly move overtravel body and tighten nut at the point of minimum air bleed. With nut tight, a slight continuous air bleed should be noticeable.

Restore System

1. Remove test gauge and air pressure source from Superlift adapter.

2. Remove Fill Valve Assembly from Superlift line and reconnect line to control valve.

3. Lower car and inflate reservoir through service valve.

1972-74 Ford & Mercury

1. Support vehicle by the front and rear suspensions.

2. Disconnect control valve link from rear upper control arm and manually exhaust air from Superlifts.

3. Loosen control valve lever adjusting nut.

4. On 1972 models, place sufficient weight in rear of vehicle to allow for a trim height of 4.96 inches.

5. On all models, adjust lever arm until link enters control arm hole. Or if a downward movement of lever arm of $1/16$ inch on 1972 models and $1/4$ inch on 1973-74 models is required for a fit into the control arm hole.

6. Tighten adjusting nut and connect link to upper control arm.

Leak Tests

Compressor, Reservoir & Regulator

1. Remove assembly intact.

2. Connect test gauge to regulator. Inflate reservoir through service valve to 80-100 psi.

3. Route an 8" rubber hose between vacuum and vent ports, Fig. 8.

4. Submerge in water, Fig. 9, and observe for air leaks at: a) Reservoir weld seam. b) Reservoir-to-compressor O-ring. c) Regulator-to-compressor O-ring. d) Regulator boot defective. e) Boot internal O-ring defective. f) Diaphragm between 1st and 2nd stage housing. g) Tightening thru bolts may correct leak. h) Cover gasket and retainer screw. A few bubbles here is not a leak. A continuous stream indicates defective compressor check valves. i) Service valve. j) Test gauge connections.

5. Correct any leaks detected by either tightening screws or replacing parts.

Control Valve

1. Remove control valve from car.

2. Clean exterior of valve thoroughly.

3. Connect test gauge and air pressure source to intake adapter and open air pressure (80-110 psi).

4. Submerge unit in water. No air should escape if overtravel lever is in "neutral" position. If bubbles escape from Superlift port, replace control valve.

5. Shut off air pressure and detach test gauge from air intake port. Plug intake port with Fill Valve Assembly.

6. Connect test gauge to Superlift port and open air pressure.

7. With overtravel lever in "neutral" position, no air should escape. If bubbles escape from exhaust port, replace control valve.

8. If air escapes around edge of cover plate, tighten screws or replace gasket.

9. Remove control valve from water. Actuate overtravel lever to expel any water from unit.

10. Shut off air pressure and remove line from Superlift port.

Lines and Fittings

1. Disconnect overtravel lever from link.

2. Hold lever up in intake position for maximum Superlift inflation and release.

3. Leak check all connections with a soap and water solution.

Superlifts

1. Disconnect lines and remove unit from car.

2. Inflate individually to 50-60 psi, utilizing Fill Valve (see Fig. 7). Submerge in water and observe unit for leaks.

3. Install Superlifts.

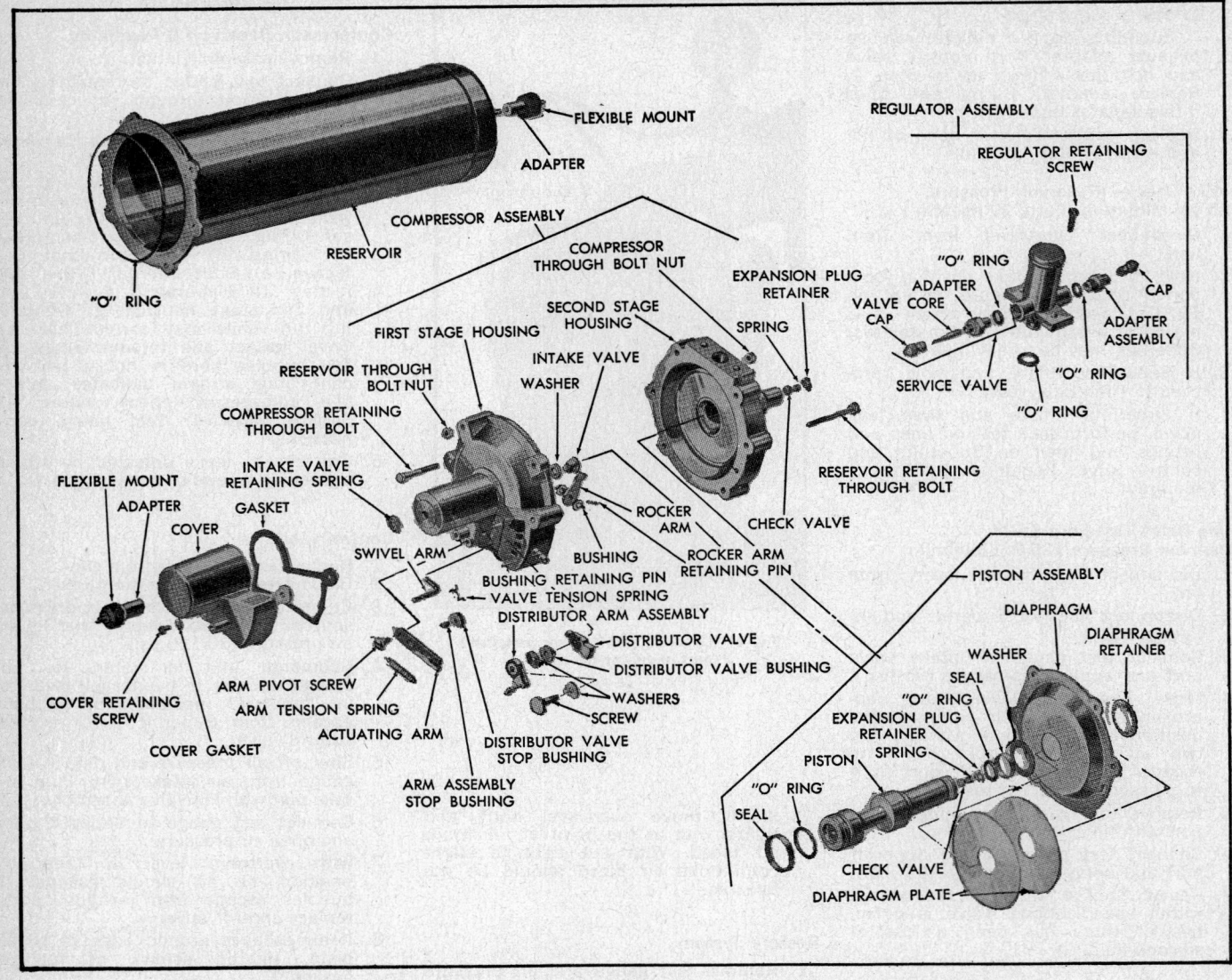

Fig. 10   Exploded view of General Motors compressor, reservoir and regulator

COMPRESSOR SERVICE

Removal

1. On 1969 Lincoln, raise front of vehicle and place on jackstands.
2. On all models, disconnect vacuum and air intake hoses.
3. Remove air intake and vacuum hoses.
4. Unfasten compressor brackets from mounting points.
5. Remove compressor with brackets attached.

6. Deflate system, using service valve, and remove high pressure fitting at pressure regulator.
7. Remove brackets from compressor.

NOTE: The compressor is a precision-built mechanism, Fig. 10. If an overhaul is contemplated, all parts should be handled carefully. Take care to prevent entrance of dirt or foreign matter. Do not lubricate as unit is designed to run dry.

Installation

1. Attach brackets to compressor.
2. Install compressor to its mounting.
3. Attach air intake and vacuum hoses.
4. Secure air line to compressor pressure regulator.
5. Lower car.
6. Inflate reservoir to 140 psi through compressor service valve.
7. Be sure that vacuum and air intake lines are not rubbing against adjacent parts to prevent chafing.

AIR CYLINDER SYSTEM

This system, Fig. 1, consists of a vacuum-operated compressor, control valve, air cylinders and the connecting lines and fittings. In the event of accidental air loss, the conventional coil springs will support the vehicle.

The compressor is operated off engine vacuum and will supply a maximum pressure of 20 psi through the control valve to the air cylinders. The control valve is mounted on the cross member and senses rear riding height through a link attached to the rear suspension upper arm, Fig. 2.

The control valve is actuated by changes in the riding height, which moves the link, opening the proper valve to raise or lower the vehicle by adding or removing air from the air cylinders at the rear.

A dampening piston incorporated in the height control valve acts as a time delay within the valve to prevent rapid air transfer to and from the air cylinders under normal operation while the vehicle is in motion.

A check valve is also provided in the exhaust port of the height control valve to retain 2 to 4 psi residual pressure in the air cylinders when there is little or no load to prevent the coil springs from scuffing them.

The air cylinders are made of $\frac{1}{4}''$ thick butyl rubber and are encased in the rear coil springs.

CHECKING SYSTEM

Quick Check

1. Fill fuel tank or simulate the load at the rate of 6 lbs for each gallon of fuel, otherwise the vehicle should be empty.
2. Add a two-passenger load to the rear bumper or tailgate. Vehicle should lower when weight is added.
3. Start engine and observe rear of vehicle while maintaining load at rear bumper or tailgate.
4. If vehicle does not raise when engine is started or within two minutes, the system is not operating properly.

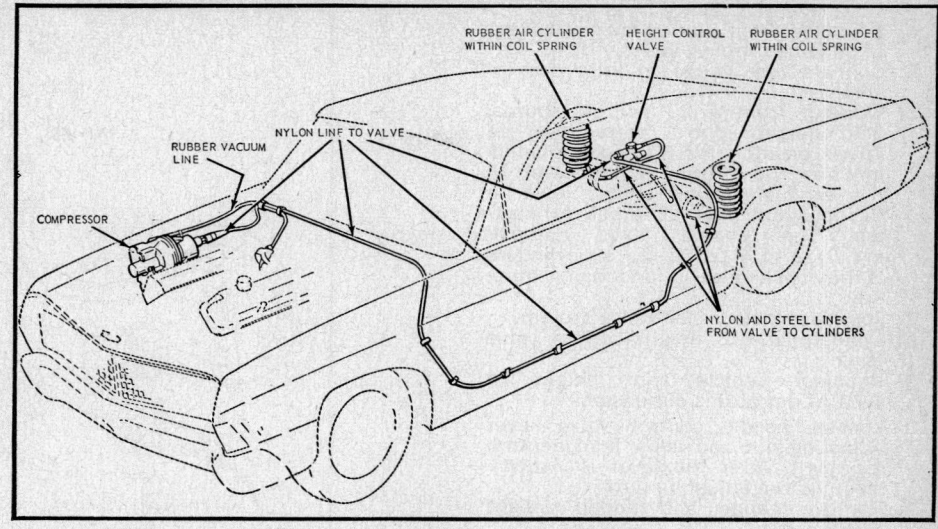

Fig. 1   Air cylinder leveling system

5. If the vehicle raises, remove the load and observe the rear of the vehicle. Air should then exhaust through the height control valve to lower the vehicle.

Compressor Output Check

1. Disconnect output line from compressor.
2. Connect pressure gauge to compressor.
3. Close one valve and open the other.
4. Start engine and note compressor output on gauge. If it is 12 to 20 psi, with a minimum engine vacuum of 15 inches, it can be considered normal.
5. Remove gauge and connect line.

Compressor-to-Control Valve Line Leak Check

1. Disconnect inlet fitting from height control valve.

2. Disconnect air inlet line from height control valve.
3. Connect pressure gauge to line.
4. Start engine and note pressure reading, which should be 12 to 20 psi.
5. Stop engine and observe reading on gauge. It should hold the maximum reading if line is not leaking.
6. Repair line as required to stop leak.

Trim Adjustment

1. Trim height is the distance between top of rear axle to bottom surface of frame side rail, Fig. 3. Raise vehicle on a hoist or jack that will support rear axle.
2. Load rear of vehicle as required to obtain the trim height, Fig. 3.
3. Disconnect link from height control

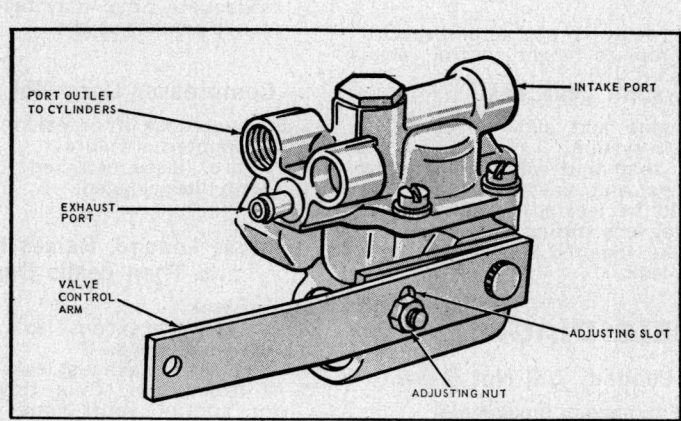

Fig. 2   Height control valve

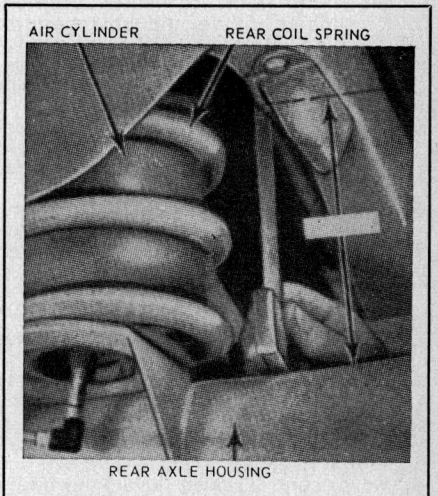

Fig. 3   Measuring trim adjustment; dimension should be 6.70".
Ford and Mercury

valve lever, Fig. 4.

4. Disconnect air line from inlet port of height control valve.
5. Connect test gauge to inlet port of height control valve.
6. Working from a 20 psi air source, hold height control valve lever in raised position for 60 seconds while inflating the system. Lower lever to the exhaust position. Hold lever in this position until air stops exhausting. This should leave approximately 2 to 4 psi in the air cylinders if the check valve is functioning properly.
7. Jounce vehicle to neutralize system.
8. Connect link to height control valve lever.
9. Readjust vehicle trim height to 6.70" if not at this dimension.
10. Loosen height control valve lever adjusting nut and allow it to neutralize itself. After the lever is neutralized, tighten adjusting nut.
11. Remove gauge and added weight from vehicle.
12. Connect air line to height control valve and check for leaks.

Control Valve Check

Exhaust Check, Air Cylinders Inflated

1. Disconnect link from height control valve lever.
2. Hold lever down (exhaust position) until air cylinders deflate, or for a minimum of 30 seconds. Release arm and allow it to return to neutral position.
3. If cylinders deflate perform a trim adjustment.
4. If cylinders do not deflate, disconnect air cylinder line at height control valve to make sure that there is no restriction in line.
5. Connect air cylinder line to control valve and link to lever.

Intake Check, Compressor at Engine Idle

1. Disconnect link from height control valve lever.
2. Hold lever up (intake position) until cylinders inflate or for a minimum of 60 seconds, then release lever and allow it to return to neutral position.
3. If cylinders inflate and hold perform a trim adjustment.
4. If cylinders inflate then leak down, perform a leak test on lines or fittings then check air cylinders.
5. If cylinders do not inflate, disconnect compressor output line at the height control valve and check it for restrictions.
6. If lines and fittings are satisfactory, check height control valve for leaks.
7. Connect link to control valve lever.

Time Delay Check

1. Disconnect link from control valve lever.
2. Disconnect both air lines from height control valve, Fig. 4.
3. Connect test gauge to intake port of control valve. Attach a 20 psi air source to gauge.
4. Move control valve lever downward approximately one inch from the neutral position. One inch distance is measured at end of lever.

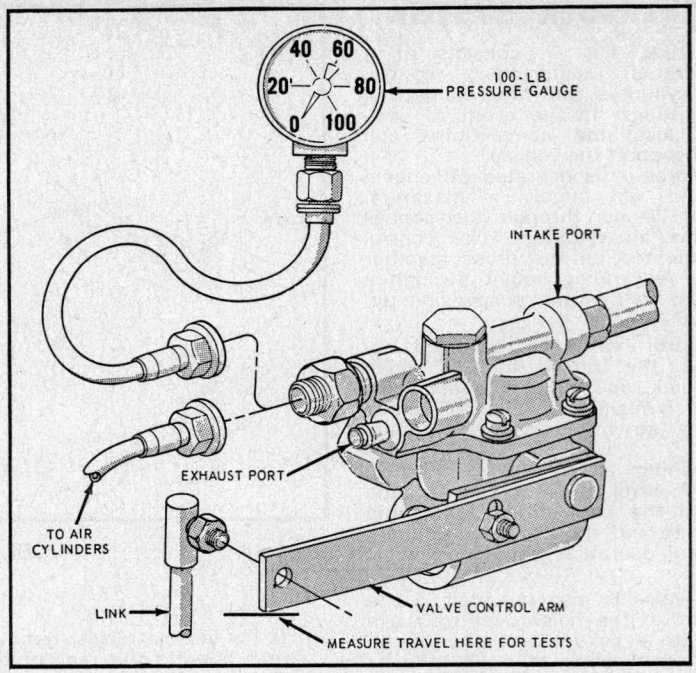

Fig. 4 Test gauge installation

5. Move lever upward two inches, at the same time start timing the number of seconds before air is expelled from air cylinder port. The time delay should be from 1 to 6 seconds. Repeat check to obtain an accurate reading. This operation is for air intake time only.
6. Connect air cylinder line to control valve outlet port.
7. Hold control valve lever in raised position and charge air cylinders with 15 to 20 psi air pressure from intake port of control valve.
8. Move lever to neutral position.
9. Move control valve lever upward approximately one inch from neutral position. One inch dimension is measured from end of lever. Quickly move lever downward two inches, at the same time start timing the number of seconds before air is expelled from exhaust port. The time delay should be from 1 to 6 seconds. Repeat check to obtain accurate reading.
10. If either delay is not within specifications, replace height control valve.

System Leak Test

1. Start engine and allow pressure to build up in system.
2. Apply a soap and water solution to all fittings and lines that are suspected to be leaking. If air bubbles appear at any fitting or section of line, make required repairs to eliminate the leak.

TROUBLE DIAGNOSIS

Vehicle Loaded, Will Not Raise

1. External damage or breakage.
2. Line or cylinder leak.

3. Pump inoperative or output inadequate.
4. Control valve setting incorrect.
5. Inadequate time delay.

Vehicle Loaded, Raises Partially

1. Load excessive (over 250 lbs) at axle.
2. Height control valve setting incorrect.
3. Low supply pressure.

Vehicle Unloaded, Rides too High, Won't Come Down

1. Control valve setting incorrect.
2. External damage or breakage.
3. Defective control valve.

Compressor Cycles Continuously

1. Line leak.
2. Air cylinder ruptured.
3. Inadequate time; may take five minutes to balance at idle.

Compressor Does Not Cycle

1. Vacuum hose off or leaking.
2. Pump internal failure.
3. Lines or hoses restricted.
4. Pump filter clogged.

Vehicle Loaded, Raises to Level and Then Leaks Down

1. Line leak.
2. Control valve exhaust leak.
3. Air cylinder leak.
4. Control valve exhaust leak.
5. If leak down while driving, check for control valve time delay less than one second.

HEADLIGHT AIMING

All headlight adjustments should be made with a half-full tank plus or minus one gallon, with a person seated in the driver's seat and a person seated in the passenger seat, the car unloaded and the trunk empty except for the spare tire and jacking equipment, and recommended pressure in all tires. If necessary, compensate for unspecified gas capacity by adding or removing weight at the tank area at the rate of six pounds per gallon. Before each adjustment, bounce the car by pushing on the center of both the front and rear bumpers, then rock car side-to-side, to level the vehicle.

Headlights can be aimed mechanically or by means of a wall screen. When using a mechanical aimer, follow manufacturer's instructions. To align the No. 1 headlights by means of a wall screen, select a level portion of the shop floor. Lay out the floor and wall as shown in Fig. 1.

Establish the headlight horizontal centerline by subtracting 20 inches from the actual measured height of the headlight lens center from the floor and adding this difference to the 20-inch reference line obtained by sighting over the uprights to obtain dimension B (upper diagram Fig. 2). Draw a horizontal line 2 inches below, and parallel to the headlight horizontal centerline on the screen as measured on the vehicle (dimension A, upper diagram Fig. 2).

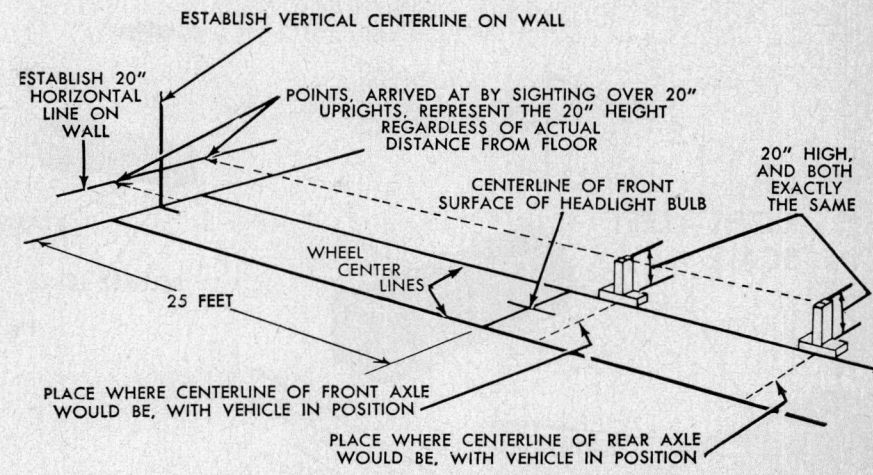

Fig. 1 Floor and wall layout

NO. 1 HEADLIGHT HIGH BEAM ADJUSTMENT
(Four Bulb Cars)

Adjust each No. 1 headlight beam as shown in Fig. 2 upper diagram. **Cover the No. 2 lights when making this adjustment.**

Some states may not approve of the 2-inch dimension for the No. 1 headlights. Check the applicable state law, as a 3-inch dimension may be required.

NO. 2 HEADLIGHT LOW BEAM ADJUSTMENT
(Four Bulb And All Two Bulb Cars)

To align the No. 2 headlights on four bulb cars or the headlights on two bulb cars, a different wall chart is used (lower diagram of Fig. 2). Dimension B for the No. 2 lights will be different than B for the No. 1 lights, but dimension A which is measured on the car will be the same as for the No. 1 lights. **Note that the line of adjustment of the No. 2 lights is the horizontal centerline of the No. 2 lights.** Turn the headlights to low beam and adjust each No. 2 light as shown in Fig. 2.

Each headlight can be adjusted by means of two screws located on the headlight adjusting ring. Always bring each beam into final position by turning the adjusting screws clockwise so that the headlights will be held against the tension springs when the operation is completed.

MECHANICAL AIMERS

There are many different types of mechanical aiming equipment available one of which is shown in Figs. 3 and 4. Some may require a level floor whereas others have levelling devices which compensate for floor level variations.

When using this type of equipment, consult the equipment manufacturers instructions for its proper use.

NO. 1 LIGHT HIGH BEAM DIAGRAM

NO. 2 LIGHT LOW BEAM DIAGRAM

Fig. 2 Headlight wall screens

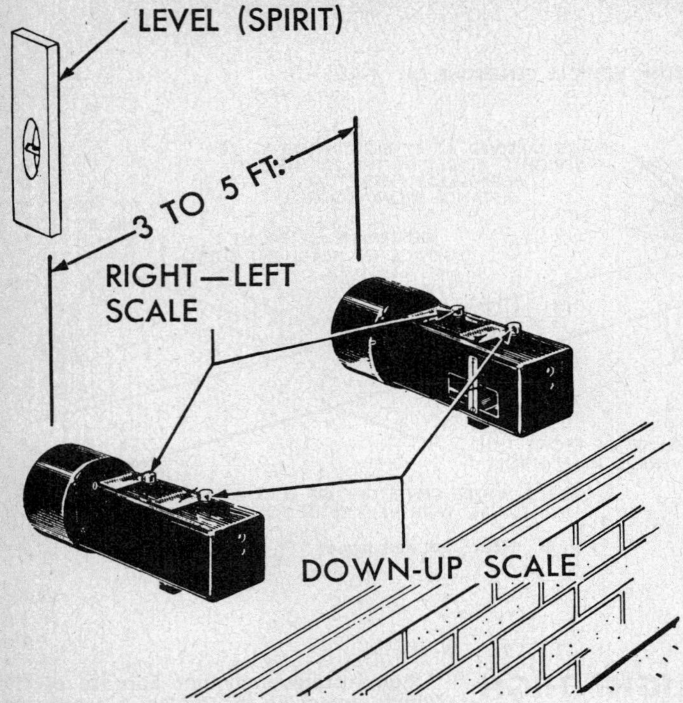

LEVEL (SPIRIT)

3 TO 5 FT.

RIGHT—LEFT SCALE

DOWN-UP SCALE

Fig. 3 Checking calibration of aimer

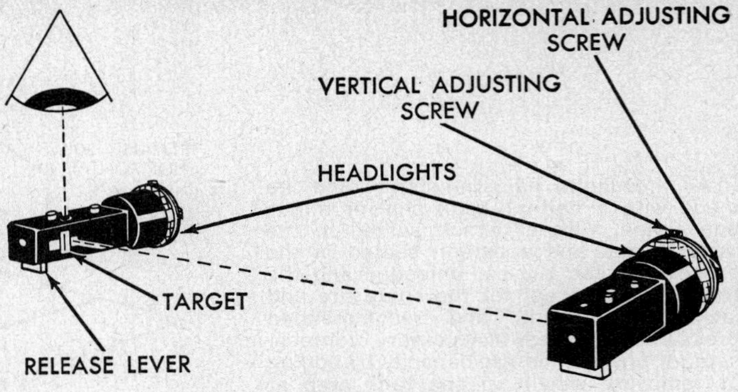

HORIZONTAL ADJUSTING SCREW

VERTICAL ADJUSTING SCREW

HEADLIGHTS

TARGET

RELEASE LEVER

Fig. 4 Mounting and adjusting aimers

CONCEALED HEADLAMPS

BUICK RIVIERA
1969

These headlamps are vacuum controlled through a pair of vacuum actuators, one for each pair of headlamps, Fig. 1. Vacuum is taken at the intake manifold and vacuum storage tank and routed through the headlight switch to one side or the other of the actuator, depending on whether the lights are on or off.

When the lights are off, vacuum is supplied to the lower end of each actuator and the headlamp assemblies are rotated upward and held in this position by the actuators. When the lights are turned on, vacuum is supplied to the upper end of the actuators, causing the assemblies to rotate to the forward position as the electrical connection at the switch is closed to turn on the lights.

Also connected in the vacuum system is a vacuum relay. When the light switch is off, vacuum is applied to the diaphragm in the relay, moving the relay valve to connect the vacuum tank to the lower end of the actuators.

When the light switch is turned on, vacuum flow is cut off and normal air pressure acts on the relay to move the valve to connect the tank to the upper ends of the actuators. Thus, the headlights will remain in the forward position in case of a failure in the vacuum system.

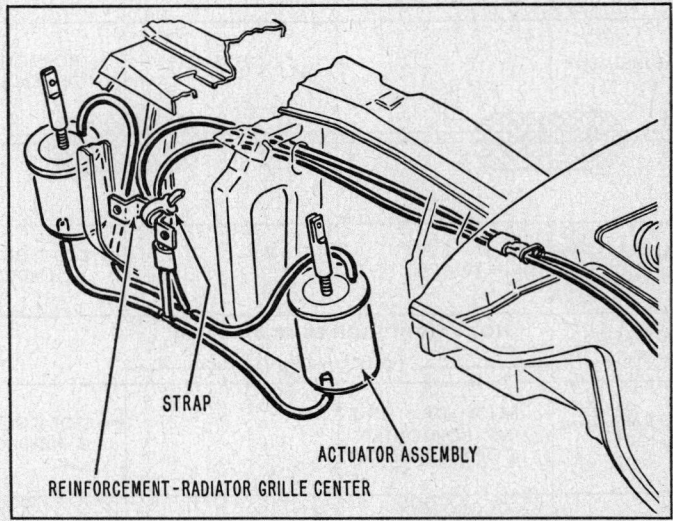

STRAP

ACTUATOR ASSEMBLY

REINFORCEMENT-RADIATOR GRILLE CENTER

Fig. 1 Headlight details. 1969 Buick Riviera

CAMARO RALLY SPORT
1969

The headlamps are fixed and sections of the grille cover them when not in use. Each grille section, or door, is controlled by a vacuum actuator located behind it and connected to the door mechanically, Fig. 2.

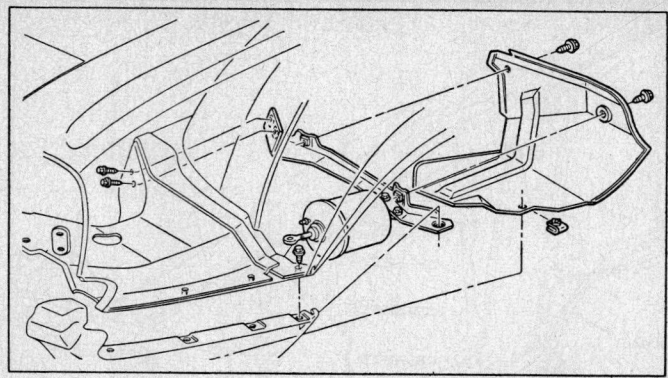

Fig. 2   Headlight details. 1969 Camaro

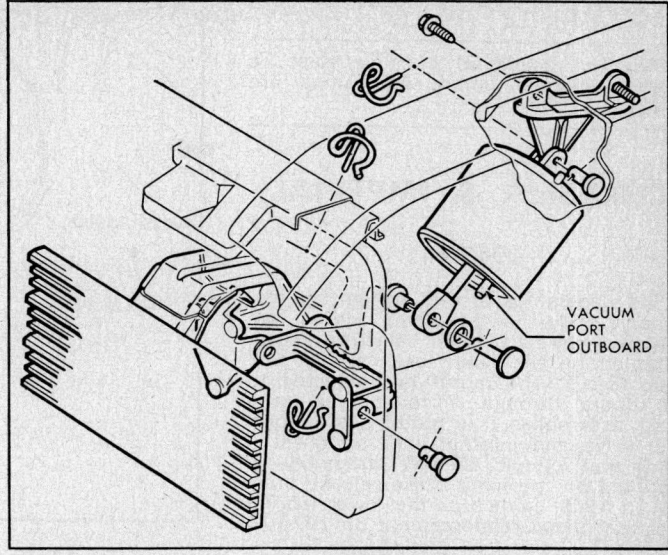

Fig. 3   Headlight details. 1969 Chevrolet

Vacuum from the vacuum storage tank is routed through a vacuum valve which is part of the headlight switch to the actuators to control the position of the doors.

A vacuum relay is also incorporated in the system so that the headlight doors will remain open in case of a failure in the vacuum system.

CHEVROLET
1969

This system uses fixed headlights with moveable, vacuum actuator operated headlight covers, Fig. 3, similar to the 1969 Camaro system.

CORVETTE
1969-74

These units are vacuum operated through separate actuators for each headlamp assembly, Fig. 4. The operation is the same as that for the 1969 Camaro Rally Sport except that the Corvette uses movable headlamp assemblies while the Camaro's lights are fixed. The vacuum actuators cause the headlamp "pods" to be raised up when in the on position and to be lowered flush with hood when turned off. Unlike the earlier Corvette system, the headlamps are lighted and brought into position by the same control switch. A vacuum valve on the headlamp switch routes vacuum to the proper side of the actuators according to the position of the light switch.

ALIGNMENT

1. "In-out", loosen screws fastening slotted bracket to underside of headlamp housing.

2. "Down", lamp cover top to opening; by turning hex head screw fastened to top of pivot link.
3. "Open," fully extended actuator with rod.
   a. Remove spring from actuator rod pin.
   b. Remove cotter pin from rod pin.
   c. Turn actuator rod until bushing hole aligns to forward end of slot in connecting link extended position, with engine idling for vacuum.
   d. Shut off engine, retract actuator rod and unscrew rod ½ turn to preload actuator rod in link.
4. "Up", (bezel to opening alignment). Loosen jam nut and turning bumper covered screw up or down to touch then up 1½ turns more. Micro switch on linkage must shut off

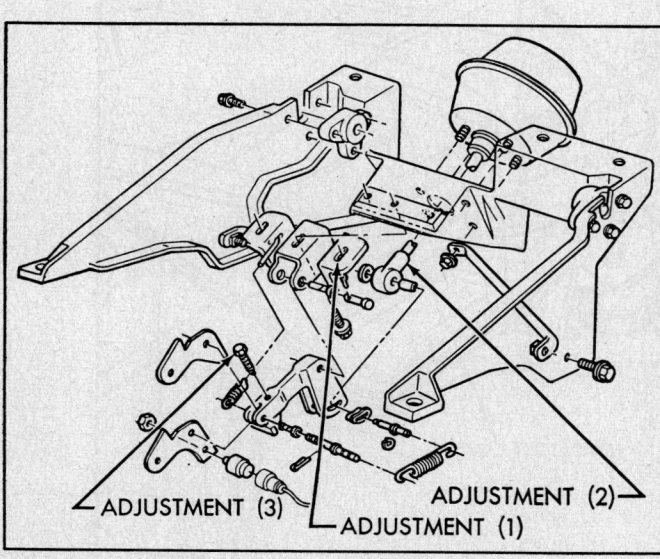

Fig. 4   Headlight details. 1969-74 Corvette

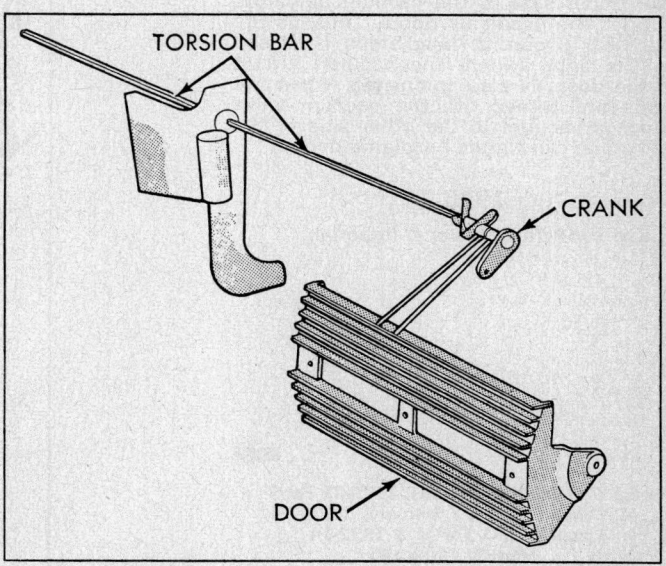

Fig. 5   Headlight details. 1969-74 Chrysler & Imperial (Typical)

CONCEALED HEADLAMPS

warning lamp when lights are fully extended.

NOTE: The headlamp housing must be properly aligned before headlamps are aimed.

CHRYSLER & IMPERIAL

1969-74

The headlamps in this system are stationary and the headlamp doors are operated by a single electric motor mounted on the hood lock vertical support, Fig. 5. The motor is connected to the doors through a torsion bar and crank assemblies. The motor has a worm gear drive and internal limit switches. A relay and circuit breaker assembly is mounted on the hand brake release bracket on 1969 models or the lower left instrument panel reinforcement on 1970-74 models.

To manually open the headlamp doors, disconnect the electrical connectors from motor and rotate the hand wheel located at the lower end of the motor.

CAUTION: Rotating the wheel after the doors reach the end of travel will permanently damage the motor. Also, do not operate motor with headlamp doors disconnected as operating the motor without load will damage motor.

DODGE

1969

This system uses stationary headlamps and moveable headlamp doors. Each door is controlled by a separate vacuum actuator.

Vacuum is supplied from a vacuum tank to a vacuum control valve which is part of the ignition switch. When the headlamps are turned on, the vacuum valve routes vacuum through hoses to the proper side of the vacuum actuators to open the headlamp doors. Thus, as the electrical circuit to headlamps is closed by the light switch, the vacuum circuit to the doors is also completed. When the lights are turned off, the vacuum valve supplies vacuum to the other side of the actuators, closing the headlamp doors.

1970-73

See 1969-74 Chrysler & Imperial.

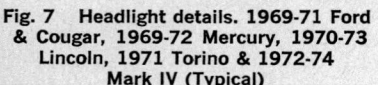

Fig. 7 Headlight details. 1969-71 Ford & Cougar, 1969-72 Mercury, 1970-73 Lincoln, 1971 Torino & 1972-74 Mark IV (Typical)

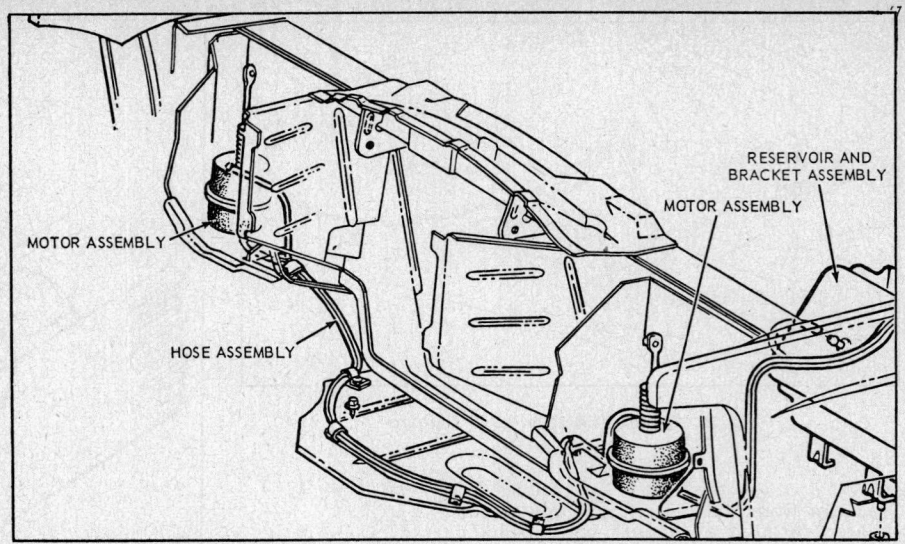

Fig. 6 Headlight details. 1969-71 Lincoln Mk III, 1969 Thunderbird, 1973-74 Mercury, 1974 Lincoln (Typical)

FORD MOTOR CO. CARS

On 1969 Thunderbird, 1969-71 Mark III, 1973-74 Mercury and 1974 Lincoln, the headlamp covers are actuated by two vacuum motors, Fig. 6. On 1969-71 Ford and Cougar, 1969-72 Mercury, 1970-73 Lincoln, 1971 Torino and 1972-74 Mark IV, the headlamp covers are actuated by a single vacuum motor which is connected to them through a torsion bar, Fig. 7.

Vacuum is supplied to one side of the actuator from a vacuum storage tank through the vacuum control valve mounted on the back of the headlamp switch. When the headlamps are turned on, the vacuum valve routes vacuum to the "open" side of the actuator and vents the "close" side to atmospheric pressure. The reverse applies when the lights are turned off.

The covers are equipped with over

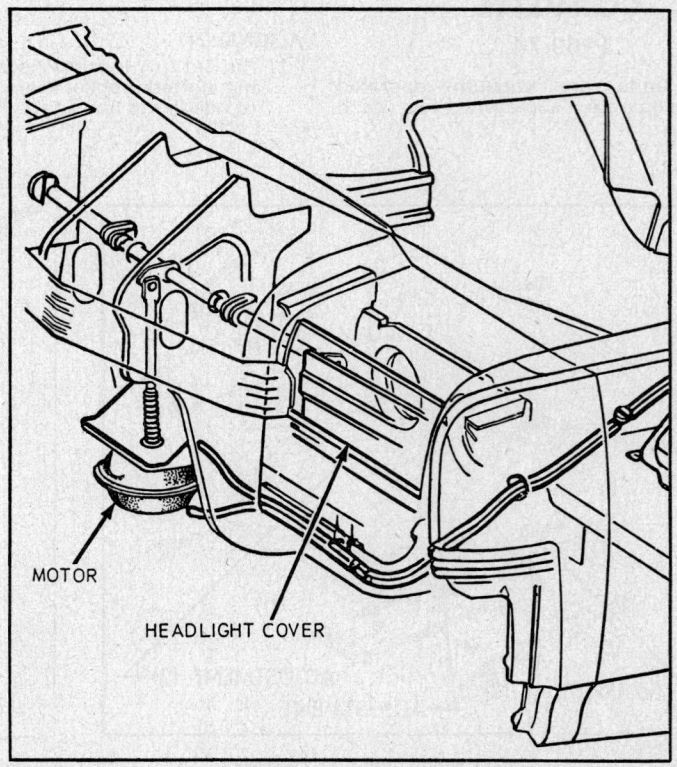

center springs which aid the actuators in holding the doors in position.

OLDSMOBILE TORONADO
1969

Headlamps are fixed and covers are moved by a single, centrally mounted vacuum actuator, Fig. 8. When the headlights are turned on, the vacuum valve on the light switch routes vacuum to the remote control valve which, in turn, routes it to the open side of the actuator and causes the headlamp covers to open. When the lights are turned off, vacuum is routed to the close side of the actuator.

A thermostatic vacuum switch is incorporated in the Outside Air Induction option so that if engine coolant temperature exceeds 220 degrees, vacuum is routed to the actuator and the headlamp covers open to provide more air flow to cool the engine.

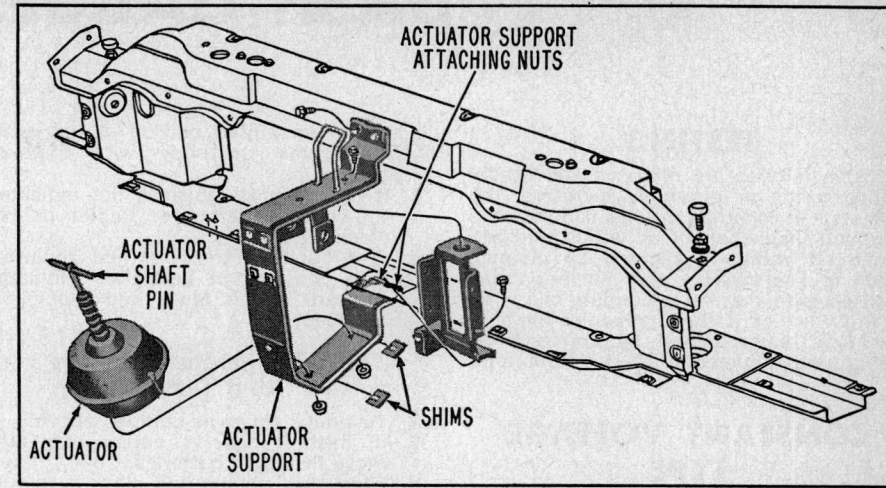

Fig. 8   Headlight details. 1969 Oldsmobile Toronado

PLYMOUTH
1970-72

See 1969-74 Chrysler & Imperial.

PONTIAC GTO
1969

This system uses fixed headlamps and moveable, vacuum controlled headlamp covers, Fig. 9. Each cover is controlled by a separate vacuum actuator which receives vacuum from a vacuum tank through a vacuum valve attached to the light switch. The covers are held in either the open or closed position by overcenter springs.

TROUBLE SHOOTING

Vacuum Type

Examine all hoses for splits, which occur most often around connections. Also, look for kinked or pinched hoses, a condition which often occurs when retaining clips are too tight, thus blocking off vacuum flow.

If inspection reveals that all the hoses are satisfactory, check each vacuum actuator by disconnecting the actuator hoses one at a time and hooking a vacuum gauge to the hose (s). With engine running, if the gauge indicates at least 14 inches of vacuum, the problem is either in the actuator, which must be replaced, or because of jammed covers or linkage.

If the gauge shows less than 14 inches of vacuum, check vacuum at the storage tank, distribution valve, check valve vacuum relay, if used, and at each hose connection.

Electrical Type

Connect a jumper wire directly from the battery to the motor (s). If the system operates, check the headlight or motor control switch. If the switch is eliminated as the cause of trouble, check the wiring; look for loose connections, broken wires or terminals.

If the system fails to operate with the jumper wire, remove the motor for repair or install a new or rebuilt unit.

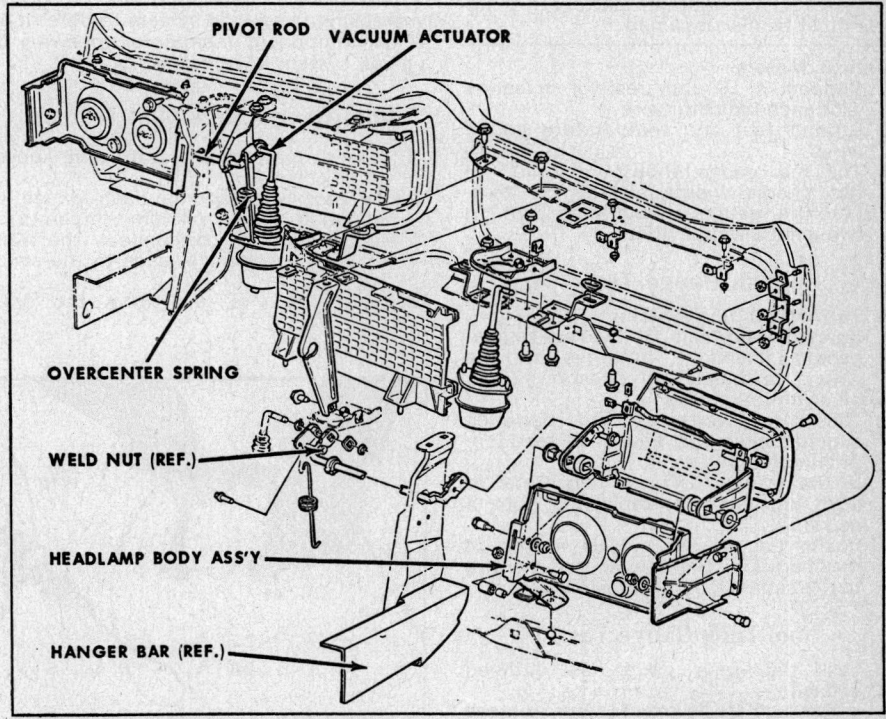

Fig. 9   Headlight details. 1969 GTO

DASH GAUGES

TESTING

Gauge failures are often caused by defective wiring or grounds. Therefore, the first step in locating trouble should be a thorough inspection of all wiring and terminals. If wiring is secured by clamps, check to see whether the insulation has been severed thereby grounding the wire. In the case of a fuel gauge installation, rust may cause failure by corrosion at the ground connection of the tank unit.

CONSTANT VOLTAGE TYPE

Voltage Regulator Test

Except American Motors
1. Turn on ignition switch.
2. Connect one lead of a test light or positive lead of a voltmeter to the feed terminal of one of the gauges without disconnecting wire.
3. If regulator is okay, voltage will oscillate.
4. If it does not, voltage regulator is defective or there is a short or ground between regulator and gauges.

CAUTION: Applying 12 volts to any part of the system except the regulator input terminal or grounding the regulator or system in any way except to connect test equipment may burn out one or more components. When replacing any part of the system, battery ground cable must be disconnected.

American Motors
1. Connect a 10 ohm resistor in series with each indicator wire.
2. Ground fuel and temperature gauge wires.
3. The fuel gauge should read Full to two needle widths above. The temperature gauge should read Hot to two needle widths above.

Dash Gauge Test

1. Turn off ignition switch.
2. Connect terminals of two series-connected flashlight batteries to the gauge terminals in question (fuel, oil or temperature).
3. The three volts of the batteries should cause the gauge to read approximately full scale.
4. If the gauge unit is inaccurate or does not indicate, replace it with a new unit.
5. If the gauge unit still is erratic in its operation, the sender unit or wire to the sender unit is defective.

Fuel Tank Gauge Test

1. Test the dash gauge as outlined above.
2. If dash gauge is satisfactory, remove flashlight batteries.
3. Then disconnect wire at tank unit and ground it momentarily to a clean, unpainted portion of the vehicle frame or body *with ignition switch on.*
4. If the dash gauge does not indicate, the wire is defective. Repair or replace the wire.
5. If grounding the new or repaired wire causes the gauge to indicate, the tank unit is faulty and should be replaced.

Oil & Temperature Sending Unit Tests

1. Test dash gauge as outlined above.
2. If dash gauge is satisfactory, remove flashlight batteries.
3. Then start engine and allow it to run to warm up to normal temperature.
4. If no reading is indicated on the gauge, check the sending unit-to-gauge wire by removing the wire from the sending unit and momentarily ground this wire to a clean, unpainted portion of the engine.
5. If the gauge still does not indicate, the wire is defective. Repair or replace the wire.
6. If grounding the new or repaired wire causes the dash gauge to indicate, the sending unit is faulty.

VARIABLE VOLTAGE TYPE

The procedure given herewith applies to AC, Auto-Lite and Stewart-Warner systems. Following is the method of quickly checking the gauge system to determine which component (sender or receiver) of a given system is defective.

Fuel Gauge Tank Unit Method

1. Use a spare gauge tank unit known to be correct.
2. To test whether the dash gauge in question (fuel, oil or temperature) is functioning, disconnect the wire at the gauge which leads to the sending unit.
3. Attach a wire lead from the dash gauge terminal to the terminal of the "test" tank gauge, Fig. 1.
4. Ground the test tank unit to an unpainted portion of the dash panel and move the float arm.
5. If the gauge operates correctly, the sending unit is defective and should be replaced.
6. If the gauge does not operate during this test, the dash gauge is defective and should be replaced.

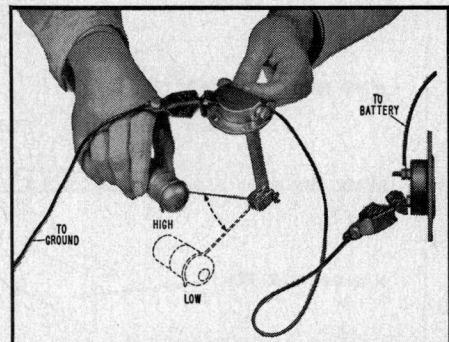

Fig. 1 Hook-up for testing dash gauge with a spare tank unit

AMMETERS

This instrument shows whether the battery is being charged by the generator or alternator or is being discharged by lights, radio, engine, etc. If a constant discharge is indicated on the ammeter, it is a signal that the battery is being run down. It is often a signal that the generator is out of order. Since both a charged battery and a working generator are very necessary—especially with vehicles equipped with many electricity-consuming devices such as heater, defroster, fog lights, radio, etc.—an inoperative ammeter should be given prompt attention.

The typical ammeter, Fig. 2, consists of a frame to which a permanent magnet is attached. The frame also supports an armature and pointer assembly.

When no current flows through the ammeter, the magnet holds the pointer armature so that the pointer stands at the center of the dial. When current passes in either direction through the ammeter, the resulting magnetic field attracts the armature away from the effect of the permanent magnet, thus giving a reading proportional to the strength of the current flowing.

Trouble Shooting

When the ammeter apparently fails to register correctly, there may be trouble in the wiring which connects the ammeter to the generator and battery or in the generator or battery themselves.

To check the connections, first tighten the two terminal posts on the back of the ammeter. Then, following each wire from the ammeter, tighten all connections on the ignition switch, battery and generator. Chafed, burned or broken insulation can be found by following each ammeter wire from end to end.

All wires with chafed, burned or broken insulation should be repaired or replaced. After this is done, and all connections are tightened, connect the battery cable and turn on the ignition switch. The needle should point slightly to the discharge (−) side.

Start the engine and speed it up a little above idling speed. The needle should then move to the charge side (+), and its movement should be smooth.

If the pointer does not behave correctly, the ammeter itself is out of order and a new one should be installed.

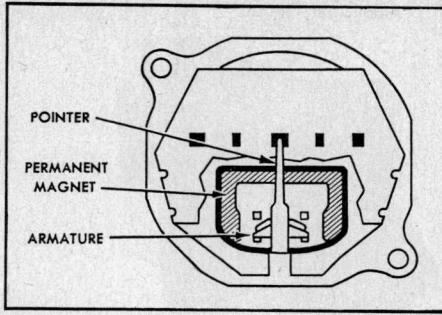

Fig. 2 Drawing of a typical automobile ammeter

OIL PRESSURE INDICATOR LIGHT

Many cars utilize a warning light on the instrument panel in place of the conventional dash indicating gauge to warn the driver when the oil pressure is dangerously low. The warning light is wired in series with the ignition switch and the engine unit—which is an oil pressure switch.

The oil pressure switch contains a diaphragm and a set of contacts. When the ignition switch is turned on, the warning light circuit is energized and the circuit is completed through the closed contacts in the pressure switch. When the engine is started, build-up of oil pressure compresses the diaphragm, opening the contacts, thereby breaking the circuit and putting out the light.

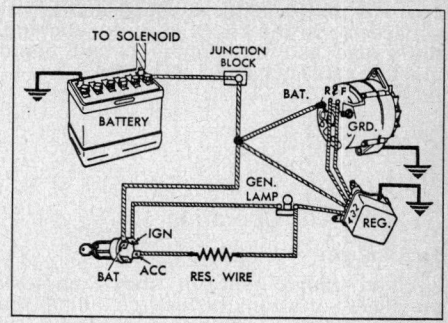

Fig. 3 Wiring diagram of a typical charge indicator light circuit

ALTERNATOR INDICATOR LIGHT

A red alternator "no charge" light is used on many cars in lieu of an ammeter. This light flashes on if the battery is discharging and the alternator is not supplying current.

The light should glow when the ignition is turned on and before the engine is started. If the bulb does not light, either the bulb is burned out or the indicator light wiring has an open circuit. After the engine is started, the light should be out at all times.

If the light fails to go out when the engine is running, the drive belt may be loose or missing or the alternator or voltage regulator may be defective.

Light Circuit

A double contact voltage regulator together with a field relay is used on Delco-Remy and Ford alternators when used with the indicator light. The circuit is as follows:

With the ignition switch turned on (engine not running), current flow is through the ignition switch through the indicator light on the dash panel. From there it goes to a terminal of the regulator (marked "4" or "L" on Delco-Remy or "I" on Ford). The circuit continues through the lower contacts of the voltage regulator (held closed by a spring), out the "F" terminal of the regulator, in the "F" terminal of the alternator, through a brush and slip ring, through another brush and slip ring to ground.

After the engine is started, the voltage output of the alternator immediately closes the field relay. This causes battery voltage from the battery terminal of the regulator (marked "3" or "V" on Delco-Remy or "B" on Ford) to be present at the "4", "L" or "I" terminal. Since battery voltage is present on both sides of the indicator light, the light goes out.

If the generator light comes on with the engine running, the charging circuit should be tested as soon as possible to determine the cause of the trouble.

A typical light circuit is shown in Fig. 3.

Trouble Shooting

The oil pressure warning light should go on when the ignition is turned on. If it does not light, disconnect the wire from the engine unit and ground the wire to the frame or cylinder block. Then if the warning light still does not go on with the ignition switch on, replace the bulb.

If the warning light goes on when the wire is grounded to the frame or cylinder block, the engine unit should be checked for being loose or poorly grounded. If the unit is found to be tight and properly grounded, it should be removed and a new one installed. (The presence of sealing compound on the threads of the engine unit will cause a poor ground).

If the warning light remains lit when it normally should be out, replace the engine unit before proceeding further to determine the cause for a low pressure indication.

The warning light sometimes will light up or will flicker when the engine is idling, even though the oil pressure is adequate. However, the light should go out when the engine is speeded up. There is no cause for alarm in such cases; it simply means that the pressure switch is not calibrated precisely correct.

TEMPERATURE INDICATOR LIGHTS

A temperature (bimetal) switch, located in cylinder head, controls the operation of a "Cold" temperature indicator light with a green lens and a "Hot" temperature indicator light with a red lens. When the cooling system water temperature is below approximately 110 defrees F., the temperature switch grounds the "Cold" indicator circuit and the green light goes on. When the green light goes out, the water temperature is high enough so that the heater can be turned on and be effective. *Note: The car should never be subjected to full throttle accelerations or high speeds until after the green light has gone out.*

If the engine cooling system is not functioning properly and the water temperature should reach a point where the engine approaches an overheated condition, the red light will be turned on by the temperature switch.

NOTE: *As a test circuit to check whether the red bulb is functioning properly, a wire which is connected to the ground terminal of the ignition switch is tapped into its circuit. When the ignition is in the "Start" (engine cranking) position, the ground terminal is grounded inside the switch and the red bulb will be lit. When the engine is started and the ignition switch is in the "On" position, the test circuit is opened and the bulb is then controlled by the temperature switch.*

Trouble Shooting

If the red light is not lit when the engine is being cranked, check for a burned out bulb, an open in the light circuit, or a defective ignition switch.

If the red light is lit when the engine is running, check the wiring between light and switch for a ground, temperature switch defective, or overheated cooling system.

If the "Cold" light is not lit when ignition is on and engine cold, check for a burned out bulb, an open in the light circuit, or a defective temperature switch.

If the "Cold" light stays on after normal engine warm-up period, check for a ground between light and switch, defective temperature switch, or a defective cooling thermostat.

CHRYSLER GAUGE ALERT SYSTEM
L.E.D. (Light Emitting Diode)

The fuel, temperature and ammeter gauges are equipped with a L.E.D. (Light Emitting Diode) mounted in each of the gauge dials, Fig. 4. This diode will illuminate and alert the driver that the system the gauge is monitoring is malfunctioning. The electronic sensor circuit is mounted on the gauge housing. The printed circuit board is permanently attached and is not serviceable. If the L.E.D. is malfunctioning, the gauge and the printed circuit board must be replaced as an assembly.

Operation

Fuel Gauge

When gauge indicator shows approximately $\frac{1}{8}$ of a tank of fuel remaining, the L.E.D. will light alerting the driver of a low fuel situation.

Temperature Gauge

When gauge indicator shows engine temperature approximately 240 to 250 degrees F. the L.E.D. will light alerting the driver of an overheat condition.

Ammeter Gauge

This L.E.D. operates independently of the gauge indicator and monitors system voltage. The L.E.D. will alert the driver of three charging system potential malfunctions.

1. A discharging condition, caused by excessive electrical demand on charging system, (engine at idle rpm).
2. A weak or defective battery with ignition switch in the "ON" position, (before the ignition switch is moved to the "START" position).
3. A weak or defective battery with minimum demand on charging system, while vehicle is being used in stop and go driving (intermittent L.E.D. illumination occurring).

Testing

Fuel And Temperature L.E.D.

Use testor C-3826 for diagnosing systems.

Ammeter L.E.D.

NOTE: Only if battery and charging system are functioning properly can the following test be performed.

Turn ignition switch to the "ON" position and turn on headlights, windshield wipers and stoplights. This will cause excessive demand on charging system activating the L.E.D. immediately or within approximately one minute, if the L.E.D. does not light there is a malfunction in the system. If L.E.D. lights, run engine at approximately 2000 rpm, L.E.D. should stop emitting light, if the L.E.D. continues to emit light there is a malfunction in the system.

NOTE: In all cases of system malfunctions the complete gauge must be replaced.

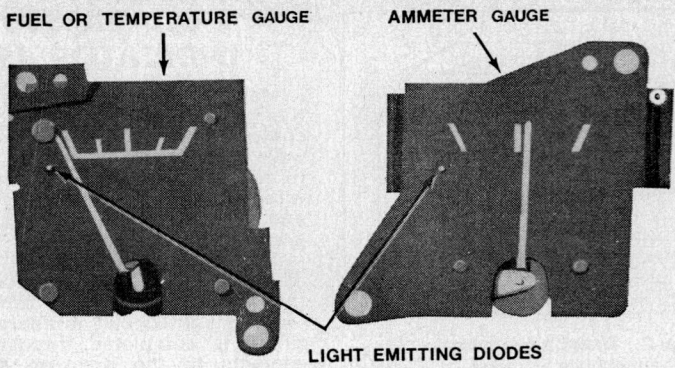

FUEL OR TEMPERATURE GAUGE **AMMETER GAUGE**

LIGHT EMITTING DIODES

Fig. 4   Gauges incorporating the L.E.D. system

SPEEDOMETERS

The following material covers only that service on speedometers which is feasible to perform by the average service man. Repairs on the units themselves are not included as they require special tools and extreme care when making repairs and adjustments and only an experienced speedometer mechanic should attempt such servicing.

The speedometer has two main parts —the indicating head and the speedometer drive cable. When the speedometer fails to indicate speed or mileage, the cable or housing is probably broken.

Speedometer Cable

Most cables are broken due to lack of lubrication or a sharp bend or kink in the housing.

A cable might break because the speedometer head mechanism binds. If such is the case, the speedometer head should be repaired or replaced before a new cable or housing is installed.

A "jumpy" pointer condition, together with a sort of scraping noise, is due, in most instances, to a dry or kinked speedometer cable. The kinked cable rubs on the housing and winds up, slowing down the pointer. The cable then unwinds and the pointer "jumps".

To check for kinks, remove the cable, lay it on a flat surface and twist one end with the fingers. If it turns over smoothly the cable is not kinked. But if part of the cable flops over as it is twisted, the cable is kinked and should be replaced.

Lubrication

The speedometer cable should be lubricated with special cable lubricant every 10,000 miles.

Fill the ferrule on the upper end of the housing with the cable lubricant. Insert the cable in the housing, starting at the upper end. Turn the cable around carefully while feeding it into the housing. Repeat filling the ferrule except for the last six inches of cable. Too much

lubricant at this point may cause the lubricant to work into the indicating hand.

Installing Cable

During installation, if the cable sticks when inserted in the housing and will not go through, the housing is damaged inside or kinked. Be sure to check the housing from one end to the other. Straighten any sharp bends by relocating clamps or elbows. Replace housing if it is badly kinked or broken. Position the cable and housing so that they lead into the head as straight as possible.

Check the new cable for kinks before installing it. Use wide, sweeping, gradual curves where the cable comes out of the transmission and connects to the head so the cable will not be damaged during its installation.

If inspection indicates that the cable and housing are in good condition, yet pointer action is erratic, check the speedometer head for possible binding. The speedometer drive pinion should also be checked. If the pinion is dry or its teeth are stripped, the speedometer may not register properly.

The transmission mainshaft nut must be tight or the speedometer drive gear may slip on the mainshaft and cause slow speed readings.

ELECTRIC CLOCKS

Regulation of electric clocks used on automobiles is accomplished automatically by merely resetting the time. If the clock is running fast, the action of turning the hands back to correct the time will automatically cause the clock to run slightly slower. If the clock is running slow, the action of turning the hands forward to correct the time will automatically cause the clock to run slightly faster (10 to 15 seconds a day).

Winding Clock When Connecting Battery or Clock Wiring

The clock requires special attention when reconnecting a battery that has been disconnected for any reason, a clock that has been disconnected, or when replacing a blown clock fuse. *It is very important that the initial wind be fully made.* The procedure is as follows:

1. Make sure that all other instruments and lights are turned off.
2. Connect positive cable to battery.
3. Before connecting the negative cable, press the terminal to its post on the battery. Immediately afterward strike the terminal against the battery post to see if there is a spark. If there is a spark, allow the clock to run down until it stops ticking, and repeat as above until there is no spark. Then immediately make the permanent connection before the clock can again run down. The clock will run down in approximately two minutes.
4. Reset clock after all connections have been made. *The foregoing procedure should also be followed when reconnecting the clock after it has been disconnected, or if it has stopped because of a blown fuse. Be sure to disconnect battery before installing a new fuse.*

Trouble Shooting

If clock does not run, check for blown "clock" fuse. If fuse is blown check for short in wiring. If fuse is not blown check for open circuit.

With an electric clock, the most frequent cause of clock fuse blowing is low voltage at the clock which will prevent a complete wind and allow clock contacts to remain closed. This may be caused by any of the following: discharged battery, corrosion on contact surface of battery terminals, loose connections at battery terminals, at junction block, at fuse clips, or at terminal connection of clock. Therefore, if in reconnecting battery or clock it is noted that the clock is not ticking, always check for blown fuse, or examine the circuits at the points indicated above to determine and correct the cause.

FIBER OPTIC MONITORING SYSTEM

Fiber optics are non-electric light conductors made up of coated strands which, when exposed to a light source at one end, will reflect the light through their entire length, thereby illuminating a monitoring lens on the instrument panel or fender without the use of a bulb when the exterior lights are turned on.

LOW FUEL WARNING SYSTEM

There are two types of low fuel warning systems, the thermistor and switch types. The thermistor type incorporates an indicator light, low fuel relay and a thermocouple assembly which is attached to the fuel sender outlet tube in the fuel tank. The thermistor temperature is low when submerged in fuel and, in turn, high electrical resistance is evident. When the fuel level drops and the thermistor is exposed to the air, the thermistor heat will increase thus decreasing its resistance allowing current to energize the low fuel

POWER RANGE   DRIVING RANGE

ECONOMY

Fig. 5   Typical vacuum gauge

relay and activate the indicator light. The switch type consists of an indicator light and a low fuel warning switch located on the instrument panel.

The warning switch contacts are closed by the difference in voltage potential between the fuel gauge terminals. This voltage differential will activate the warning switch when the fuel tank is less than $\frac{1}{4}$ full and, in turn, cause the indicator to light.

Trouble Shooting

Both systems incorporate an indicator light which may be checked in the same manner. With ignition switch turned to "ON", the indicator should light. If not, check bulb and all electrical connections. On General Motors switch type, replace warning switch if bulb and connections prove satisfactory. On Ford thermistor and switch type systems, perform additional tests outlined below.

On Ford thermistor system, using an ohmmeter and thermistor assembly out of the fuel, connect one lead to metal housing of sending unit and the other lead to thermistor terminal of sending unit. The ohmmeter should then indicate a resistance of 450 to 600 ohms. If resistance is not within above limits, replace fuel sender.

Improper operation of the warning switch will be indicated when the light remains "ON" when tank is more than $\frac{1}{4}$ full. To test system, disconnect connector on warning switch and turn ignition "ON". Starting with the terminal on the end opposite the blank position, connect a jumper wire between the battery positive terminal and connector terminal. The indicator on instrument panel should light. If not, replace warning switch. Skip the next connector terminal and connect a test lamp between the battery positive terminal and connector terminal. The test lamp should light. If not, trace wire from ignition switch for an open circuit. Test the remaining connector terminals with the test lamp making connections between ground and terminal connectors. If lamp fails to light, trace particular wire for an incomplete circuit.

LOW WASHER FLUID INDICATOR

There are two types of low washer fluid indicating systems used on GM cars. They are the mechanical type and electrically controlled type. The mechanical type of a float and rod assembly, sending unit and a fiber optic. The electrically controlled type consists of a float, magnet, contact points and a resistor.

On the mechanical type, the upper end of the rod extends into the sending unit and has colored red and green portions. When the windshield wipers are activated, a lamp bulb in the sending unit lights either the red or green sections of the rod. The colored light is then picked up by the fiber optic and is transmitted through it to the tell tale lens. The lens will show red or green depending upon washer fluid level.

The electrically controlled indicator is activated when the windshield wipers are engaged. A slight amount of current flows from the wiper motor to the washer bottle float unit. This current will either pass through the contact points or the resistor which is in parallel with the points. When the washer fluid level is high, the magnet holds the contact points open. The current will now flow through the resistor where it is reduced so the indicator will not light. When the washer fluid level is low, the float drops and the magnet will separate from the cap assembly allowing the current to pass through the contact points and activate the indicator light.

Trouble Shooting

On the mechanical indicating system, if the tell tale lens fails to glow when the windshield wipers are activated, check lamp bulb in sending unit and see that fiber optic is not broken.

On the electrically controlled system, the first item to check is the indicator bulb. With the windshield wipers "ON", connect a jumper wire between the two terminals on the washer bottle cap. The indicator should then light. If not, replace bulb. If the bulb is found to be satisfactory, remove cap and float assembly from washer bottle. Float should be able to move to the bottom of the stem and the magnet should separate from the cap. If not, replace float and cap assembly.

VACUUM GAUGE

This gauge, Fig. 5, measures intake manifold vacuum. The intake manifold vacuum varies with engine operating conditions, carburetor adjustments, valve timing, ignition timing and general engine condition.

Since the optimum fuel economy is directly proportional to a properly functioning engine, a high vacuum reading on the gauge relates to fuel economy. For this reason some manufacturers call the vacuum gauge a "Fuel Economy Indicator." Most gauges have colored sectors the green sector being the "Economy" range and the red the "Power" range. Therefore, the vehicle should be operated with gauge registering in the green sector or a high numerical number, Fig. 5, for maximum economy.

STARTING MOTORS

CONTENTS

Starter Trouble Check-Out 2-54
Starter Service 2-55
Prestolite Starters 2-56
Chrysler Direct Drive Starter 2-56
Chrysler Reduction Gear Starter 2-57
Delco-Remy Starters 2-61
Ford Starter With Integral Positive
    Engagement Drive 2-63
Ford Solenoid Actuated Starter 2-65
Starter Drive Troubles 2-66

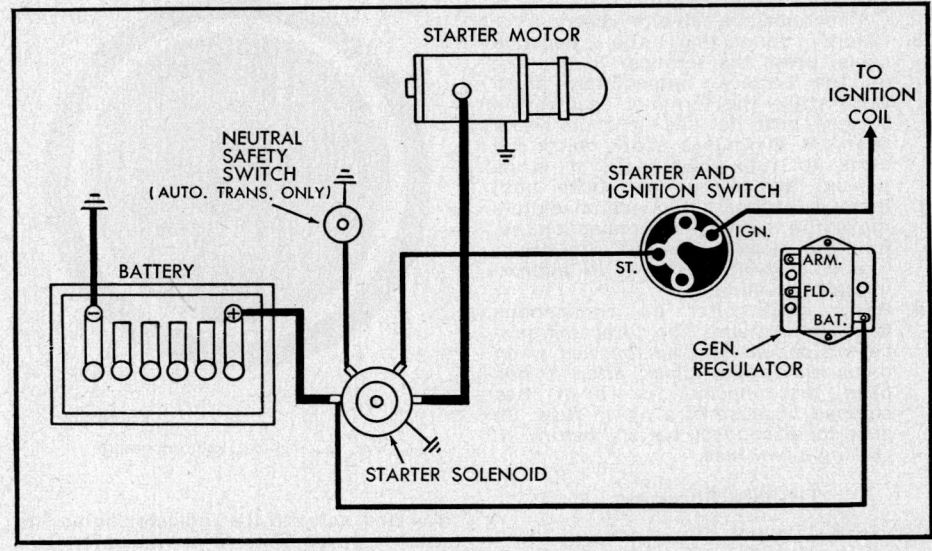

Fig. 1   Wiring diagram of a typical starting circuit

STARTER TROUBLE CHECK-OUT

When trouble develops in the starting motor circuit, and the starter cranks the engine slowly or not at all, several preliminary checks can be made to determine whether the trouble lies in the battery, in the starter, in the wiring between them, or elsewhere. Many conditions besides defects in the starter itself can result in poor cranking performance.

To make a quick check of the starter system, turn on the headlights. They should burn with normal brilliance. If they do not, the battery may be run down and it should be checked with a hydrometer.

If the battery is in a charged condition so that the lights burn brightly, operate the starting motor. Any one of three things will happen to the lights: (1) They will go out, (2) dim considerably or (3) stay bright without any cranking action taking place.

If Lights Go Out

If the lights go out as the starter switch is closed, it indicates that there is a poor connection between the battery and starting motor. This poor connection will most often be found at the battery terminals. Correction is made by removing the cable clamps from the terminals, cleaning the terminals and clamps, replacing the clamps and tightening them securely. A coating of corrosion inhibitor (vaseline will do) may be applied to the clamps and terminals to retard the formation of corrosion.

If Lights Dim

If the lights dim considerably as the starter switch is closed and the starter operates slowly or not at all, the battery may be run down, or there may be some mechanical condition in the engine or starting motor that is throwing a heavy burden on the starting motor. This imposes a high discharge rate on the battery which causes noticeable dimming of the lights.

Check the battery with a hydrometer. If it is charged, the trouble probably lies in either the engine or starting motor itself. In the engine, tight bearings or pistons or heavy oil place an added burden on the starting motor. Low temperatures also hamper starting motor performance since it thickens engine oil and makes the engine considerably harder to crank and start. Also, a battery is less efficient at low temperatures.

In the starting motor, a bent armature, loose pole shoe screws or worn bearings, any of which may allow the armature to drag, will reduce cranking performance and increase current draw.

In addition, more serious internal damage is sometimes found. Thrown armature windings or commutator bars, which sometimes occur on over-running clutch drive starting motors, are usually caused by excessive over-running after starting. This is the result of such conditions as the driver keeping the starting switch closed too long after the engine has started, the driver opening the throttle too wide in starting, or improper carburetor fast idle adjustment. Any of these subject the over-running clutch to extra strain so it tends to seize, spinning the armature at high speed with resulting armature damage.

Another cause may be engine backfire during cranking which may result, among other things, from ignition timing being too far advanced.

To avoid such failures, the driver should pause a few seconds after a false start to make sure the engine has come

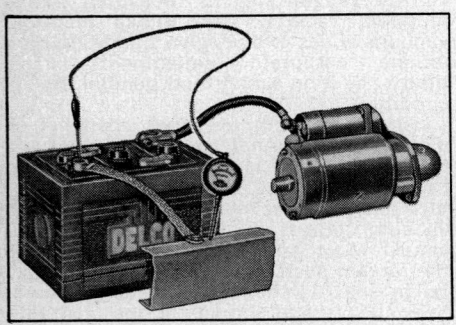

Fig. 2   Checking voltage drop between vehicle frame and grounded battery terminal post

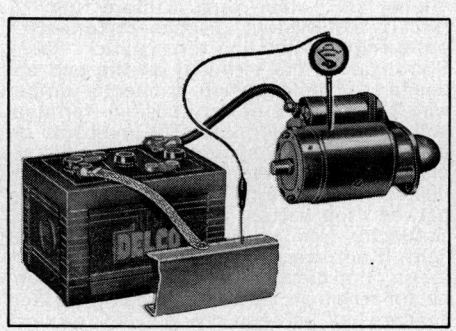

Fig. 3   Checking voltage drop between vehicle frame and starter field frame

Fig. 4   Checking voltage drop between ungrounded battery terminal post and battery terminal on solenoid

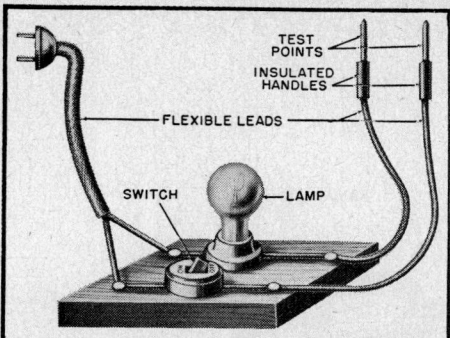

Fig. 5 A simple tester for use in making continuity and ground tests on armature and field windings

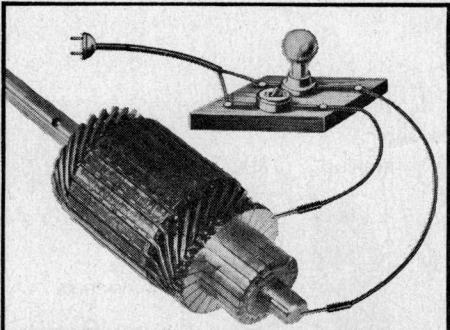

Fig. 6 Checking armature for grounds. If lamp lights armature is grounded and should be replaced

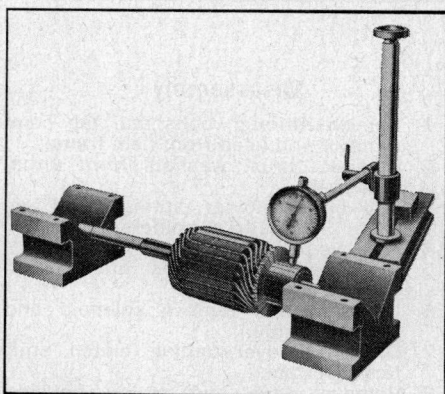

Fig. 7 Measuring commutator runout with dial indicator. Mount shaft in V blocks and rotate commutator. If runout exceeds .003″, commutator should be turned in a lathe to make it concentric

completely to rest before another start is attempted. In addition, the ignition timing should be reset if engine backfiring has caused the trouble.

Lights Stay Bright, No Cranking Action

This condition indicates an open circuit at some point, either in the starter itself, the starter switch or control circuit. The solenoid control circuit can be eliminated momentarily by placing a

heavy jumper lead across the solenoid main terminals to see if the starter will operate. This connects the starter directly to the battery and, if it operates, it indicates that the control circuit is not functioning normally. The wiring and control units must be checked to locate the trouble, Fig. 1.

If the starter does not operate with the jumper attached, it will probably have to be removed from the engine so it can be examined in detail.

Checking Circuit With Voltmeter

Excessive resistance in the circuit between the battery and starter will reduce cranking performance. The resistance can be checked by using a voltmeter to measure voltage drop in the circuits while the starter is operated. There are three checks to be made:

1. Voltage drop between car frame and grounded battery terminal post (not cable clamp), Fig. 2.
2. Voltage drop between car frame and starting motor field frame, Fig. 3.
3. Voltage drop between insulated battery terminal post and starting motor terminal stud (or the battery terminal stud of the solenoid), Fig. 4.

Each of these should show no more than one-tenth (0.1) volt drop when the starting motor is cranking the engine. Do not use the starter for more than 30 seconds at a time to avoid overheating it.

If excessive voltage drop is found in any of these circuits, make correction by disconnecting the cables, cleaning the connections carefully, and then reconnecting the cables firmly in place. A coating of vaseline on the battery cables and terminal clamps will retard corrosion.

NOTE—On some cars, extra long battery cables may be required due to the location of the battery and starter. This may result in somewhat higher voltage drop than the above recommended 0.1 volt. The only means of determining the normal voltage drop in such cases is to check several of these vehicles. Then when the voltage drop is well above the normal figure for all cars checked, abnormal resistance will be indicated and correction can be made as already explained.

STARTING MOTOR SERVICE

To obtain full performance data on a starting motor or to determine the cause of abnormal operation, the starting motor should be submitted to a no-load and torque test. These tests are best performed on a starter bench tester with the starter mounted on it.

From a practical standpoint, however, a simple torque test may be made quickly with the starter in the car. Make sure the battery is fully charged and that the starter circuit wires and terminals are in good condition. Then operate the starter to see if the engine turns over normally. If it does not, the torque developed is below standard and the

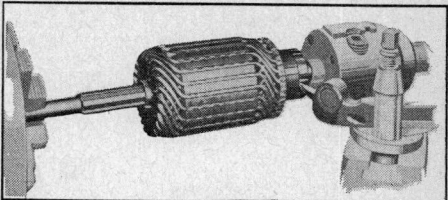

Fig. 8 Turning commutator in a lathe. Take light cuts until worn or bad spots are removed. Then remove burrs with No. 00 sandpaper

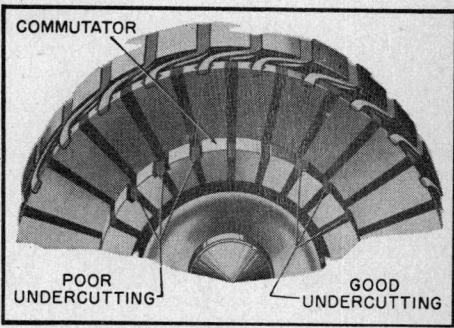

Fig. 9 Good undercutting should be .002″ wider than mica insulation, 1/64″ deep and exactly centered so that there are no burrs on the mica. Do not undercut molded commutators

Fig. 10 Checking armature for short circuit. As armature is rotated by hand, steel strip (hacksaw blade) will vibrate if short circuit exists

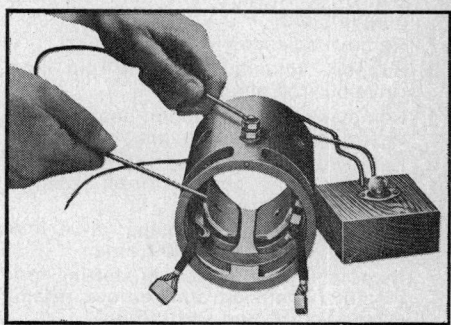

Fig. 11 Testing field coils for grounds. If a ground is present, lamp will light

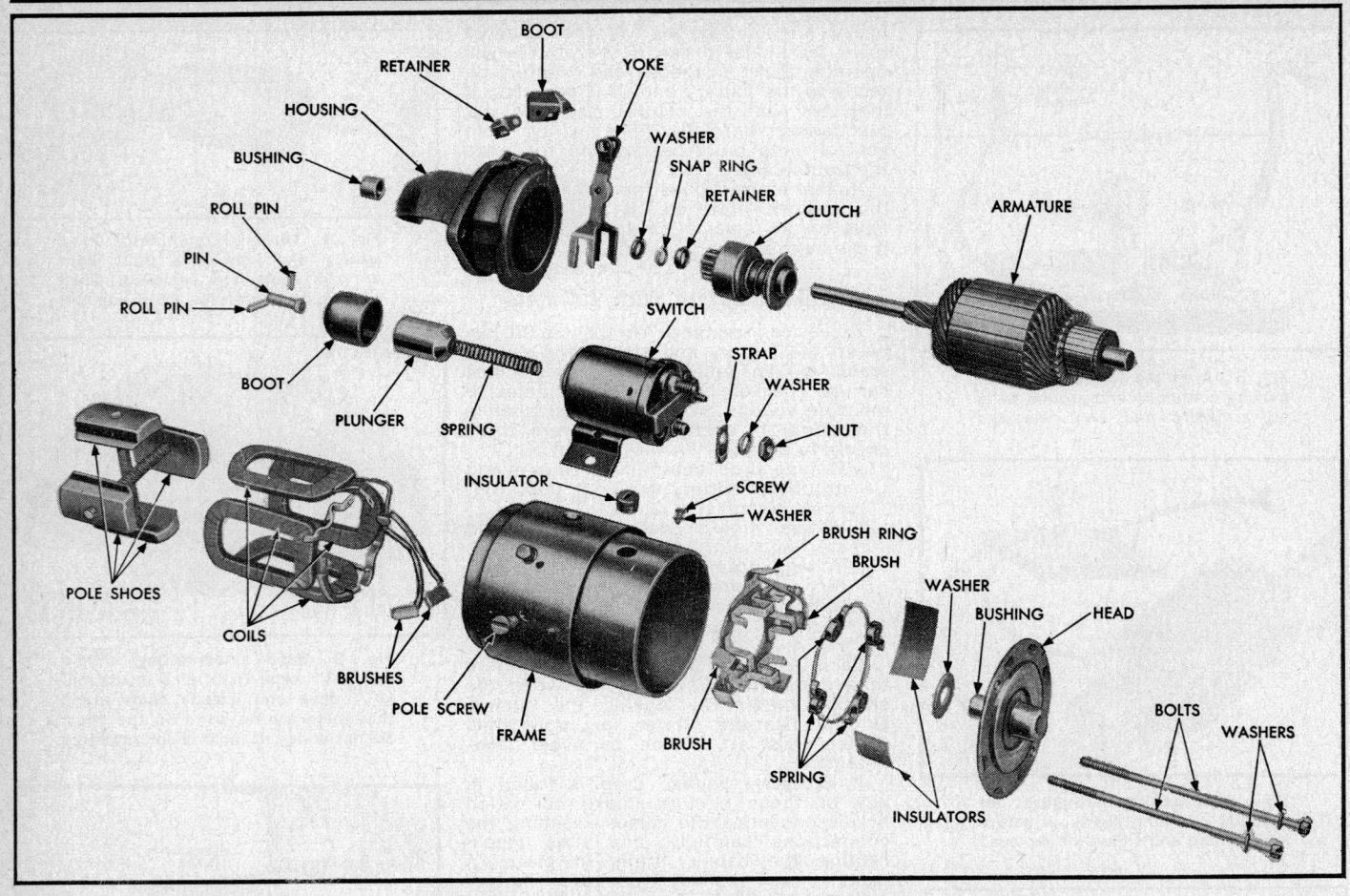

Fig. 12 Prestolite starter with over-running clutch drive

starter should be removed for further checking.

Remove the starter from the engine as outlined in the vehicle chapters, disassemble it as outlined further on and make the tests as suggested in Figs. 6 through 11.

PRESTOLITE STARTERS

Disassembling Overrunning Clutch Motor

1. Referring to Fig. 12, remove roll pin from shifting fork and solenoid coupling pin.
2. Remove solenoid.
3. Support solenoid coupling pin and drive out roll pin.
4. Remove solenoid rubber boot, plunger spring and coupling pin.
5. Remove thru bolts and take out commutator and cover, thrust washer and insulators.
6. Remove drive end housing, drive fork and armature from field frame.
7. Remove roll pin attaching shifting fork to pinion housing and remove retainer, dust cover and shifting fork.
8. Remove spacer and slide pinion gear toward commutator end of armature; then drive stop collar toward

pinion and remove lock ring.
9. Slide starter drive from armature.
10. Remove brush holder ring from field frame (3 screws).
11. Disconnect field lead wire at brush holder ring, disengage the brushes from the holders and carefully slide brush holder ring from field frame.

Overrunning Clutch

Place drive unit on shaft and, while holding armature, rotate pinion. The drive pinion should rotate smoothly in one direction (not necessarily easily), but should not rotate in the opposite direction. If drive unit does not function properly or pinion is worn or burred, replace drive unit.

CHRYSLER DIRECT DRIVE STARTER

This Chrysler built starting motor, Fig. 15, is a four coil assembly with an overrunning clutch type drive and a solenoid shift-type switch mounted on the motor. The brush holders are riveted to a separate brush plate and are not serviced individually. Brush replacement can be made by removing the commutator bearing end head.

Disassembly

1. Remove through bolts and tap commutator end head from field frame.
2. Remove thrust washers from armature shaft.
3. Lift brush holder springs and remove brushes from holders.
4. Remove brush plate.
5. Disconnect field leads at solenoid connector.
6. Unfasten and remove solenoid and boot assembly.
7. Drive out over-running clutch shift fork pivot pin.
8. Remove drive end pinion housing and spacer washer.
9. Note position of shifter fork on starter and remove fork.
10. Slide over-running clutch pinion gear toward commutator end of armature. Drive stop retainer toward clutch pinion gear to expose snap ring and remove snap ring.
11. Slide clutch drive from armature shaft.
12. If necessary to replace the field coils, remove screw that holds ground brushes and raise brushes with the terminal and shunt wire up and away from field frame. Remove pole shoe screws and take out field coils.

Reassembly

1. Lubricate armature shaft and

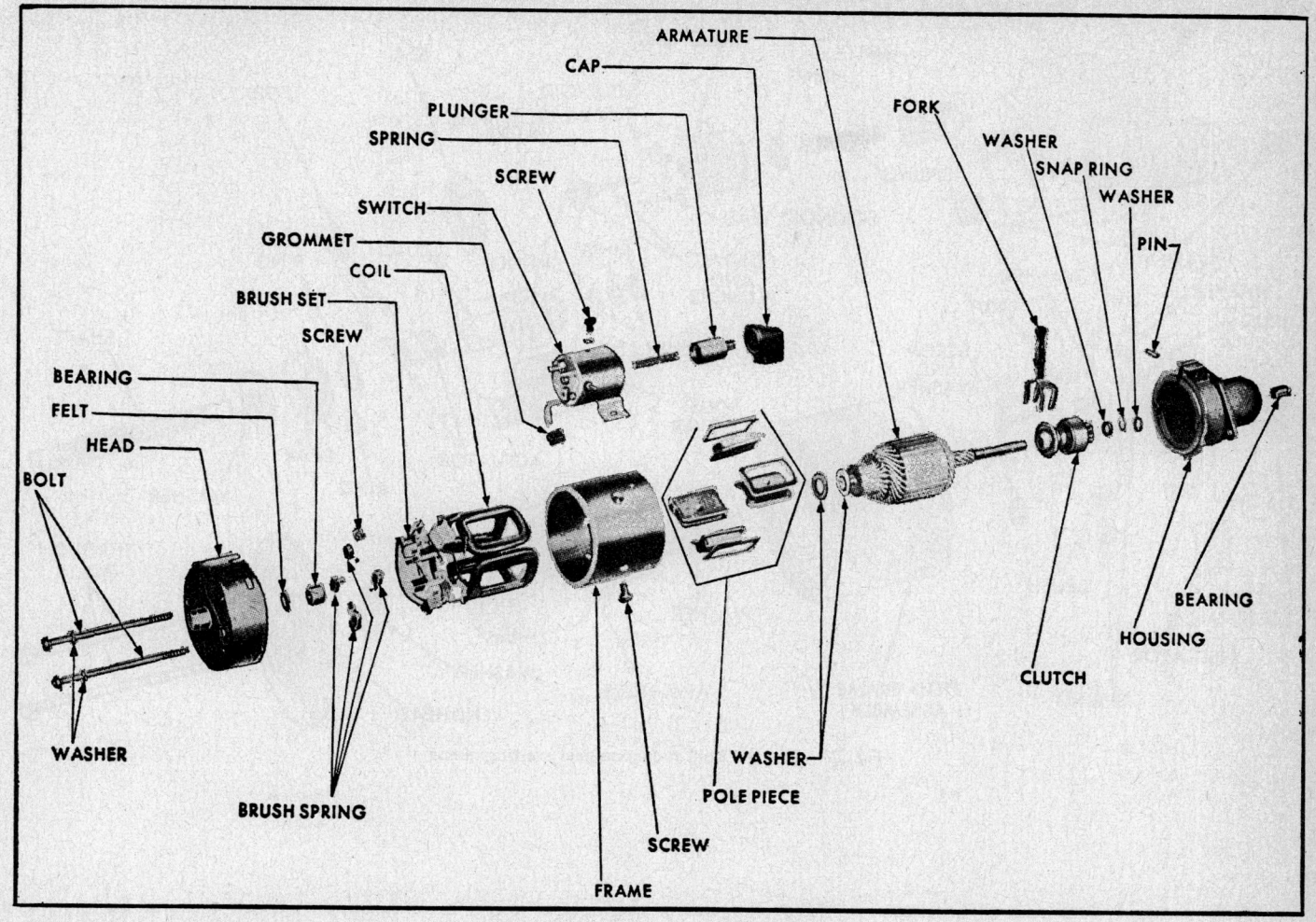

Fig. 15 Chrysler built direct drive starter

splines with SAE 10W or 30W rust preventive oil.

2. Install starter drive, stop collar (retainer), lock ring and spacer washer.
3. Install shifter fork over starter drive spring retainer washer with narrow leg of fork toward commutator. *If fork is not positioned properly, starter gear travel will be restricted, causing a lockup in the clutch mechanism.*
4. Install drive end (pinion) housing on armature shaft, indexing the shift fork with slot in drive end of housing.
5. Install shift fork pivot pin.
6. Install armature with clutch drive, shifter fork and pinion housing. Slide armature into field frame until pinion housing indexes with slot in field frame.
7. Install solenoid and boot assembly and tighten bolts securely.
8. Install ground brushes.
9. Connect field coil leads at solenoid connector.
10. Install brush holder ring, indexing tang of ring in hole of field frame.
11. Position brushes in brush holders. Be

sure field coil lead wires are properly enclosed behind brush holder ring and that they do not interfere with brush operation.

12. Install thrust washer on commutator end of armature shaft to obtain .010" minimum end play.
13. Install commutator end head.
14. Install through bolts and tighten securely.

Adjusting Pinion Clearance

1. Place starter in vise with soft jaws and tighten vise enough to hold starter. *Place a wedge or screwdriver between bottom of solenoid and starter frame to eliminate all deflection in solenoid when making pinion clearance check.*
2. Push in on solenoid plunger link, Fig. 16 (not fork lever) until plunger bottoms.
3. Measure clearance between end of pinion and pin stop with plunger seated and pinion pushed toward commutator end. Clearance should be ⅛". Adjust by loosening solenoid attaching screws and move solenoid

fore and aft as required.

4. Test starter operation for free running and install on engine.

CHRYSLER REDUCTION GEAR STARTER

This reduction gear starting motor, Fig. 17, has an armature-to-engine crankshaft ratio of 45 to 1; a 3½ to 1 reduction gear set is built into the motor assembly. The starter utilizes a solenoid shift. The housing of the solenoid is integral with the starter drive end housing.

Disassembly

1. Place gear housing of starter in a vise with soft jaws. *Use vise as a support fixture only; do not clamp.*
2. Remove through bolts and starter end head assembly.
3. Carefully pull armature up and out of gear housing, and starter frame and field assembly. Remove steel and fiber thrust washer. *The wire of the shunt field coil is soldered to the*

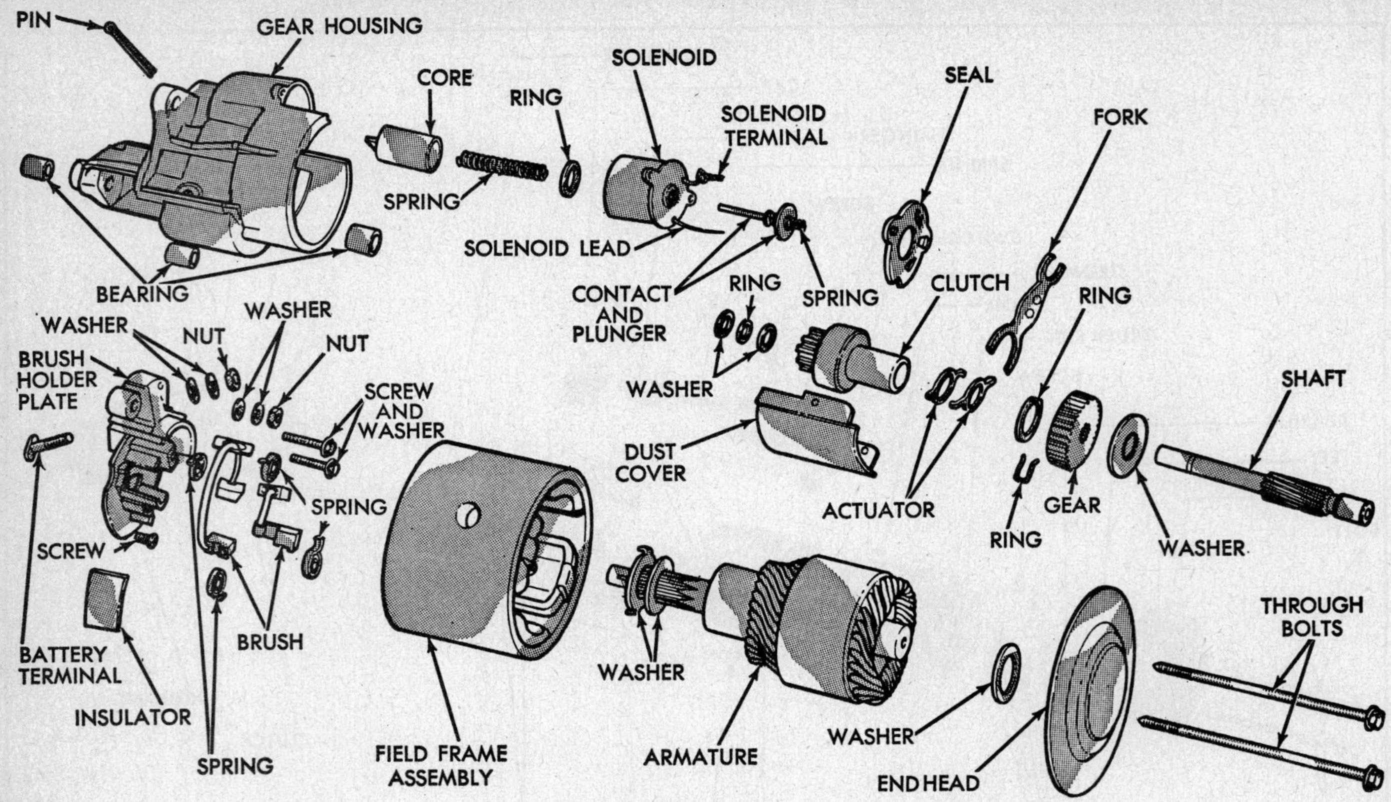

PIN
GEAR HOUSING
CORE
RING
SOLENOID
SOLENOID TERMINAL
SEAL
FORK
SPRING
SOLENOID LEAD
BEARING
CONTACT AND PLUNGER
RING
SPRING
CLUTCH
RING
WASHER
NUT
WASHER
NUT
BRUSH HOLDER PLATE
SCREW AND WASHER
WASHER
SHAFT
DUST COVER
SPRING
ACTUATOR
GEAR
RING
WASHER
SCREW
BRUSH
THROUGH BOLTS
BATTERY TERMINAL
WASHER
INSULATOR
WASHER
FIELD FRAME ASSEMBLY
ARMATURE
SPRING
END HEAD

Fig. 17 Chrysler built reduction gear starting motor

brush terminal. One pair of brushes are connected to this terminal. The other pair of brushes is attached to the series field coils by means of a terminal screw. Carefully pull the frame and field assembly up just enough to expose the terminal screw and the solder connection of the shunt field at the brush terminal. Place two wood blocks between starter frame and gear housing, Fig. 18, to facilitate removal of terminal screw and unsoldering of shunt field wire at brush terminal.

4. Support brush terminal by placing a finger behind terminal and remove screw, Fig. 18.
5. Complete the disassembly procedure by referring to Figs. 19 through 33.

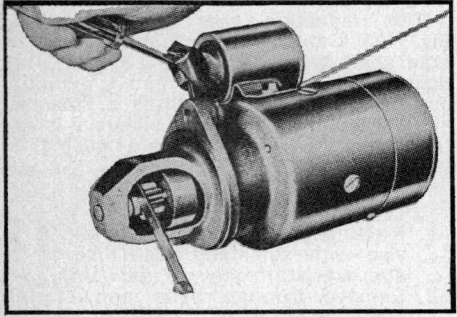

Fig. 16 Clearance between end of pinion and pin stop should be 1/8″ with plunger seated and pinion pushed toward commutator end

FIELD & FRAME ASSEMBLY
TOOL
BRUSH TERMINAL

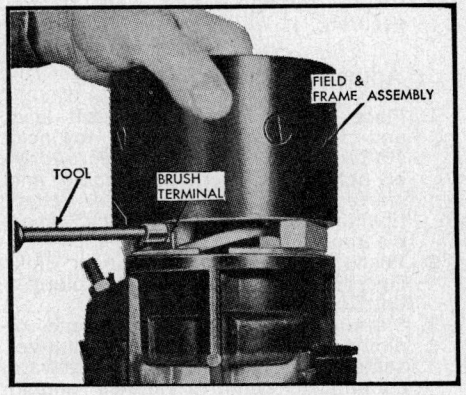

Fig. 18 Removing brush terminal screw

STARTER FRAME
SHUNT FIELD COIL LEAD
STARTER BRUSH TERMINAL POST

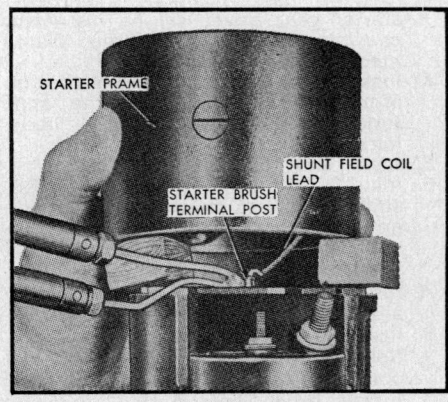

Fig. 19 Unsoldering shunt field coil lead from starter brush terminal

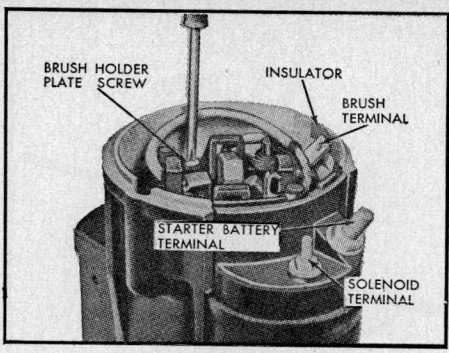

Fig. 20 Remove brush insulator which prevents contact between brush terminal and gear housing. Remove screw attaching brush holder plate to gear housing

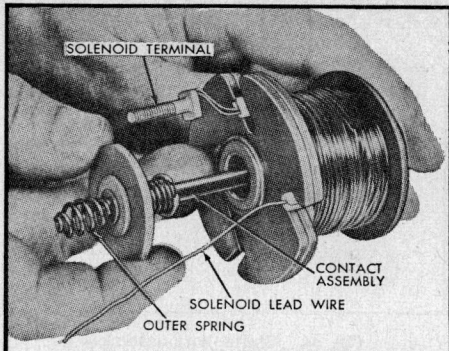

Fig. 24 Remove nut, steel washer and nylon washer from starter battery terminal. Remove terminal from holder plate. Then remove solenoid contact assembly

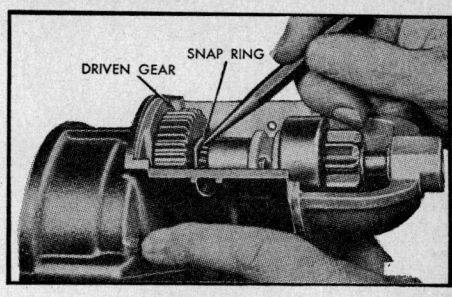

Fig. 28 Release snap ring that positions driven gear on pinion shaft. This ring is under tension and a cloth should be placed over ring to prevent it from springing away after removal

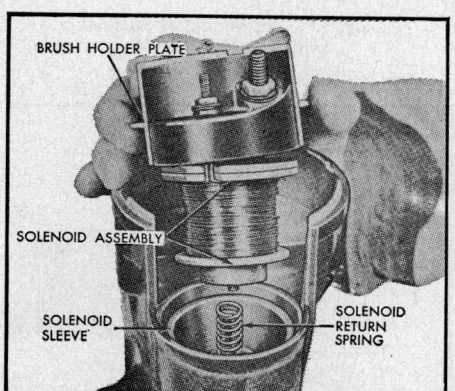

Fig. 21 Remove brush holder plate with brushes and solenoid as a unit

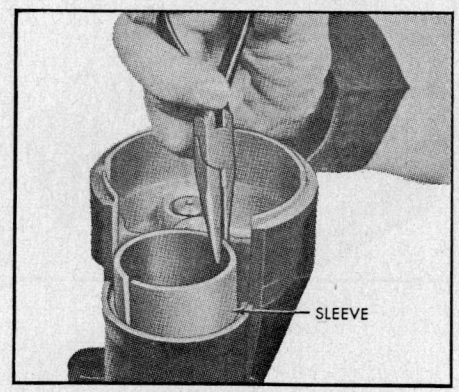

Fig. 25 Remove solenoid coil sleeve

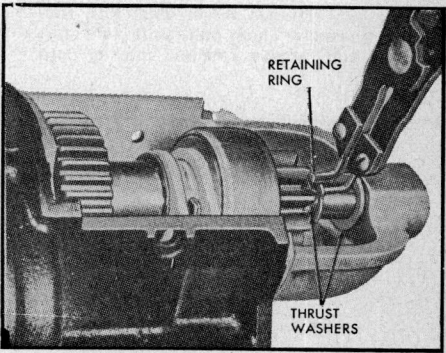

Fig. 29 Release retainer ring at front of pinion shaft. Do not spread ring any greater than the outside diameter of pinion shaft otherwise ring can be damaged

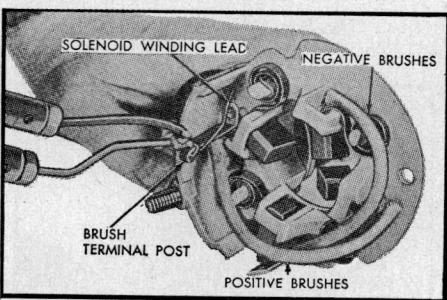

Fig. 22 Unsolder solenoid winding from brush terminal

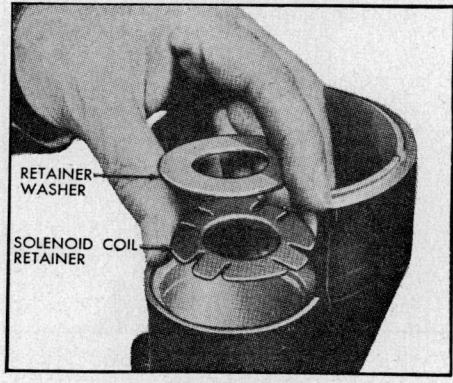

Fig. 26 Remove solenoid return spring (Fig. 21). Then remove solenoid coil retainer washer and retainer from solenoid housing

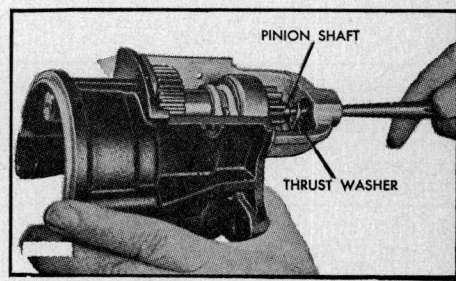

Fig. 30 Push pinion shaft toward rear of housing and remove snap ring and thrust washers

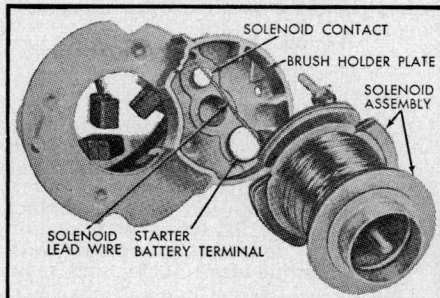

Fig. 23 Remove nut, steel washer and nylon washer from solenoid terminal. Separate brush holder plate from solenoid

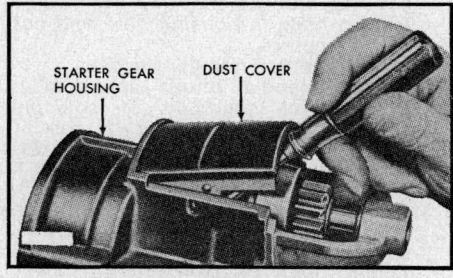

Fig. 27 Remove dust cover from gear housing

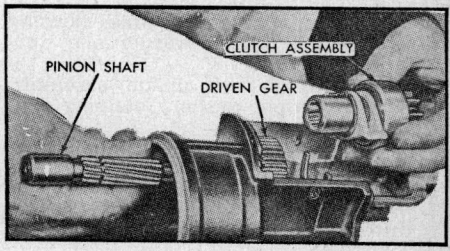

Fig. 31 Lift out clutch and pinion assembly with the two shifter fork nylon actuators

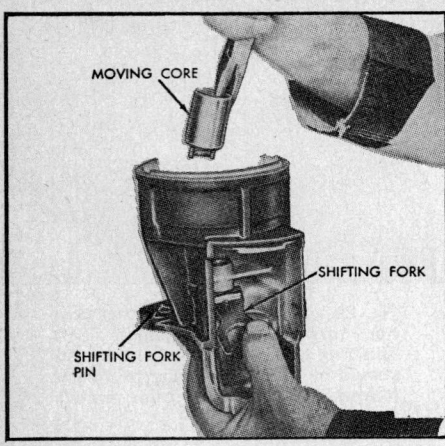

Fig. 32 Remove driven gear and friction washer. Then pull shift fork forward and remove solenoid moving core

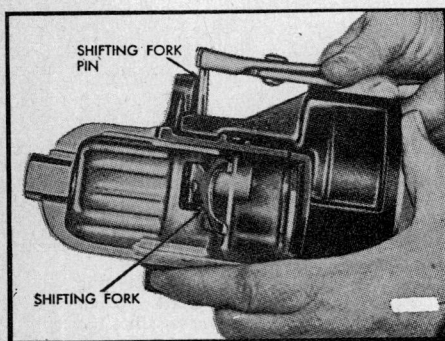

Fig. 33 Remove shift fork retainer pin and take out shift fork

Reassembly

The shifter fork consists of two spring steel plates assembled with two rivets, Fig. 34. There should be about 1/16″ side movement to insure proper pinion gear engagement. Lubricate between plates sparingly with SAE 10 engine oil.

1. Position shift fork in drive housing and install fork retaining pin, Fig. 33. *One tip of pin should be straight, the other tip should be bent at a 15 degree angle away from housing. Fork and pin should operate freely after bending tip of pin.*
2. Install solenoid moving core and engage shifting fork, Fig. 32.
3. Enter pinion shaft in drive housing and install friction washer and driven gear.
4. Install clutch and pinion assembly, Fig. 31, thrust washer, retaining ring, and thrust washer.
5. Complete installation of pinion shaft, engaging fork with clutch actuators, Fig. 35. *Friction washer must be positioned on shoulder of splines of pinion shaft before driven gear is positioned.*
6. Install driven gear snap ring, Fig. 29. Install pinion shaft retaining ring, making sure ring fits tightly in shaft groove.

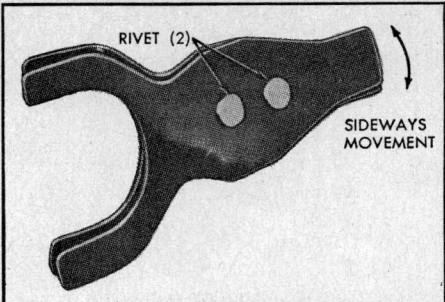

Fig. 34 Shifter fork assembly

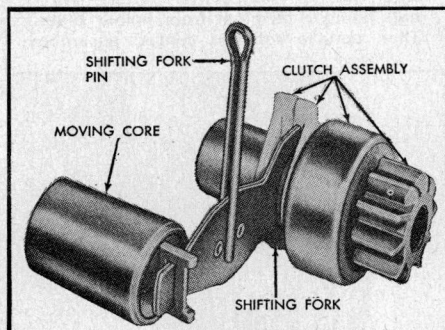

Fig. 35 Shifter fork and clutch arrangement

Fig. 36 Installing solenoid coil and sleeve

7. Install solenoid coil retainer, Fig. 26, with tangs down. *Space retainer in housing bore so that the four tangs rest on ridge in housing bore and not in the recesses.*
8. Install solenoid retainer washer.
9. Install solenoid return spring, Fig. 21. *Inspect condition of solenoid switch contacting washer. If top of washer is burned from arcing, disassemble switch and reverse washer.*
10. Install solenoid contact into solenoid, Fig. 24. Make sure contact spring is positioned in solenoid contact. *Inspect condition of contacts in brush holder plate. If contacts are badly burned, replace brush holder with brushes and contacts as an assembly.*

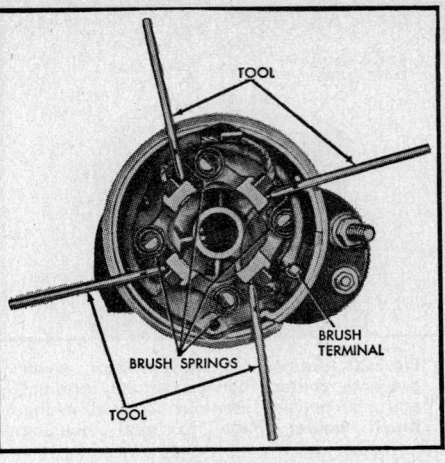

Fig. 37 Positioning of brushes with Tool Set C-3855

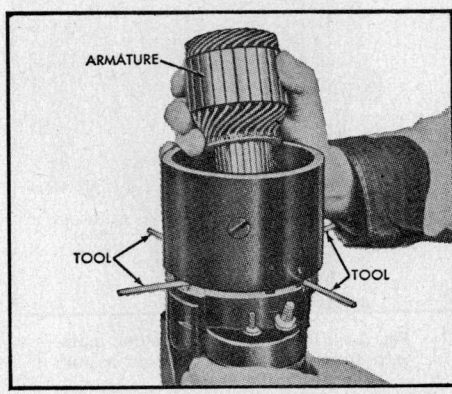

Fig. 38 Installing armature

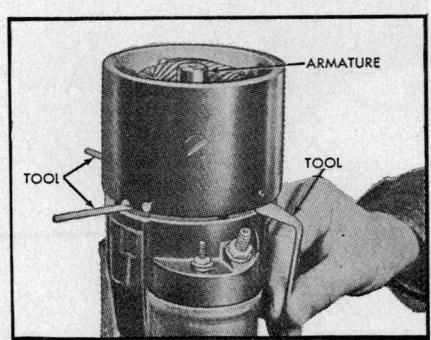

Fig. 39 Removing brush positioning tools

11. Enter solenoid lead wire through hole in brush holder, Fig. 23, and solenoid stud, insulating washer, flat washer and nut.
12. Solder solenoid lead wire to contact terminal, Fig. 22. Wrap wire securely around terminal and solder with a high temperature solder and resin flux.
13. Carefully enter solenoid coil and coil sleeve into bore of gear housing and position brush plate assembly into gear housing, Fig. 36. Align tongue

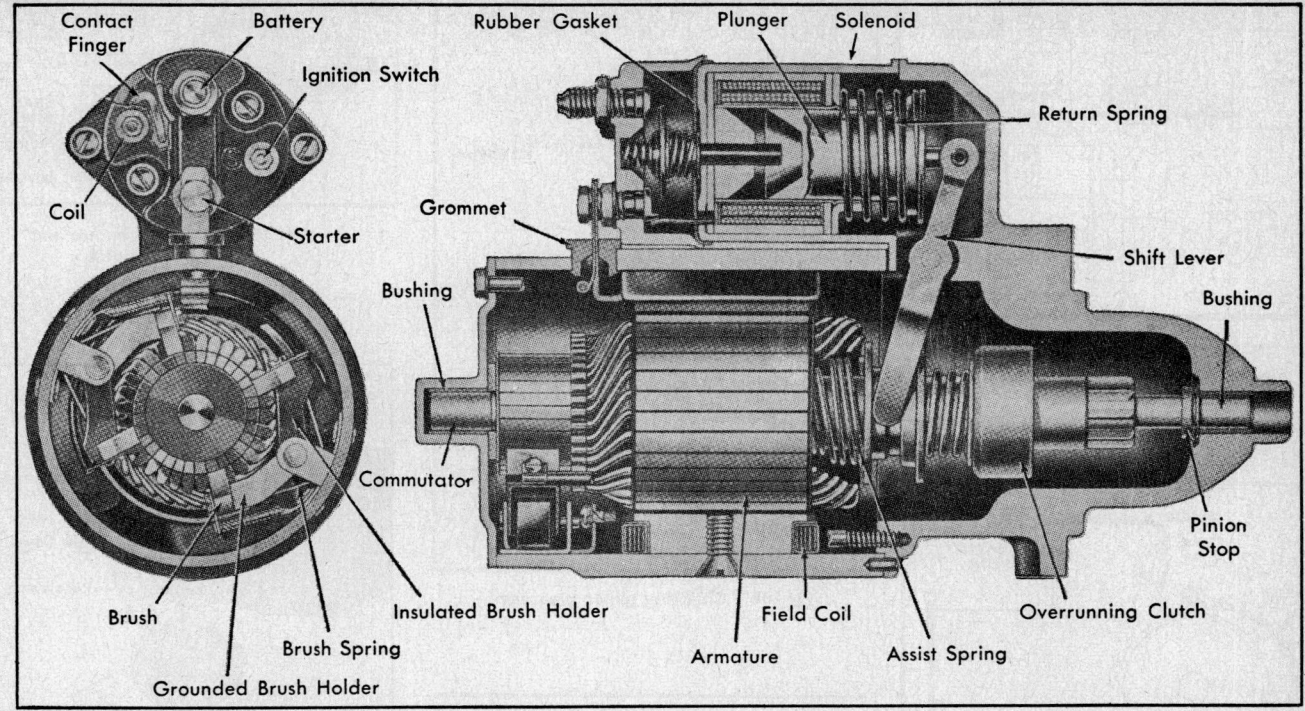

Fig. 40   Delco-Remy starter with enclosed shift lever

of ground terminal with notch in brush holder.

14. After brush holder is bottomed in housing, install attaching screw, Fig. 20. Tighten screw and install flat insulating washer and hold in place with friction tape.
15. Position brushes with tools shown in Fig. 37 or equivalent.
16. Position field frame to exact position and resolder field coil lead, Fig. 19.
17. Install brush terminal screw, Fig. 18.
18. Install armature thrust washer on brush holder plate and enter armature into field frame and gear housing, Fig. 38. Carefully engage splines of shaft with reduction gear.
19. Remove brush positioning tools, Fig. 39. Install fiber and steel thrust washers on armature shaft.
20. Position starter end head, install screws and tighten securely.
21. Install gear housing dust cover. *Make sure dimples on cover are securely engaged in holes provided in gear housing.* Test starter for free running and install on engine.

DELCO-REMY STARTERS

This type starting motor, Fig. 40, has the solenoid shift lever mechanism and the solenoid plunger enclosed in the drive housing, thus protecting them from exposure to road dirt, icing conditions and splash. They have an extruded field frame and an overrunning clutch type of drive. The overrunning clutch is operated by a solenoid switch mounted to a flange on the drive housing.

Solenoid

The solenoid is attached to the drive end housing by two screws. The angle of the nose of the plunger provides a greater bearing area between the plunger and core tube. A molded push rod, Fig. 41, is assembled in the contact assembly. A shoulder molded on the push rod and a cup that can easily be assembled to the rod and locked into position over two molded bosses holds the contact assembly in place.

To disassemble the cup from the push rod, push in on the metal cup and rotate ¼ turn so the molded bosses on the rod are in line with openings in the cup; then slide the metal cup off the rod.

To assemble the metal cup on the rod, locate the parts on the rod as shown and align the large openings in the cup with the molded bosses on the rod; then push in on the cup and rotate it ¼ turn so the small bosses on the rod fall into the keyways of the cup.

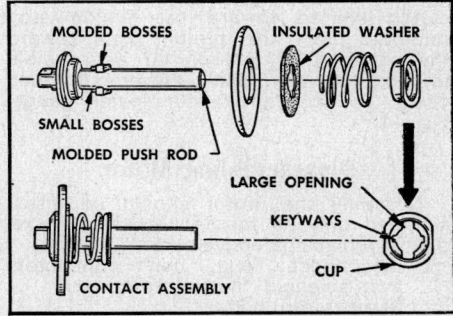

Fig. 41   Solenoid contact assembly

Solenoid Terminals

The terminals of the solenoid are assembled in a molded cover. Some solenoids have an additional small terminal which is identified with the letter "R". To this terminal is attached a small metal finger which makes contact with a disc inside the solenoid when it is energized. On the vehicle, this terminal is connected to the battery side of the ignition coil. The purpose of this is to short out the ignition resistor during cranking and thereby provide high ignition coil output for starting the engine.

Maintenance

Most motors of this type have graphite and oil impregnated bronze bearings which ordinarily require no added lubrication except at times of overhaul when a few drops of light engine oil should be placed on each bearing before reassembly.

Motors provided with hinge cap oilers should have 8-10 drops of light engine oil every 5000 miles, or every 300 hours of operation. Since the motor and brushes cannot be inspected without disassembling the unit, there is no service that can be performed with the unit assembled on the vehicle.

Free Speed Test

With the circuit connected as shown in Fig. 42, use a tachometer to measure armature revolutions per minute. Failure of the motor to perform to specifications may be due to tight or dry bearings, or high resistance connections.

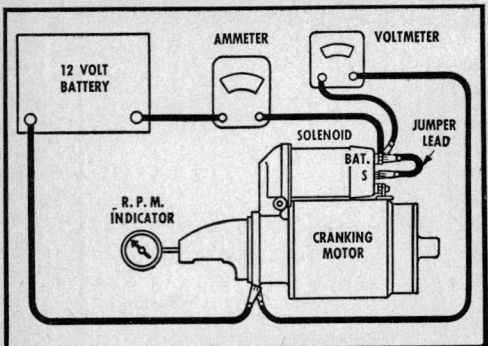

Fig. 42 Connections for checking free speed of motor

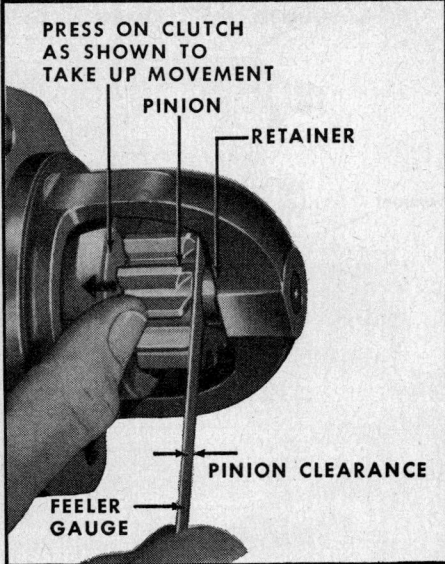

PRESS ON CLUTCH AS SHOWN TO TAKE UP MOVEMENT

PINION

RETAINER

PINION CLEARANCE

FEELER GAUGE

Fig. 44 Checking pinion clearance

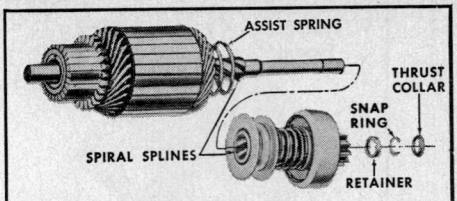

Fig. 46 View of armature and over-running clutch

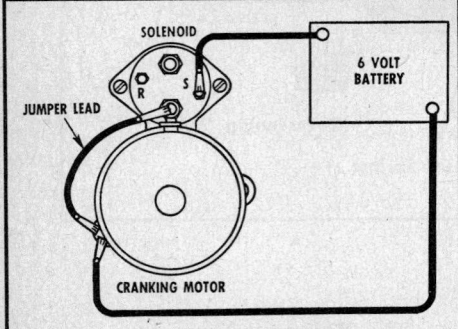

Fig. 43 Connections for checking pinion clearance

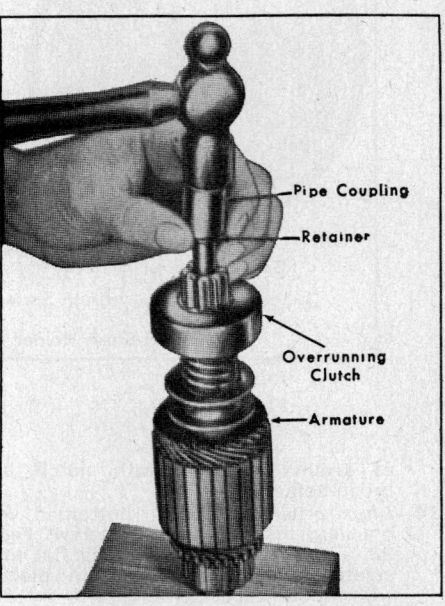

Fig. 47 Removing over-running clutch snap ring retainer

Pinion Clearance

There is no provision for adjusting pinion clearance on this type motor. When the shift lever mechanism is correctly assembled, the pinion clearance should fall within the limits of .010 to .140". When the clearance is not within these limits, it may indicate excessive wear of the solenoid linkage or shift lever yoke buttons.

Pinion clearance should be checked after the motor has been disassembled and reassembled. To check, make connections as shown in Fig. 43. *Caution: Do not connect the voltage source to the ignition coil terminal "R" of the solenoid. Do not use a 12-volt battery*

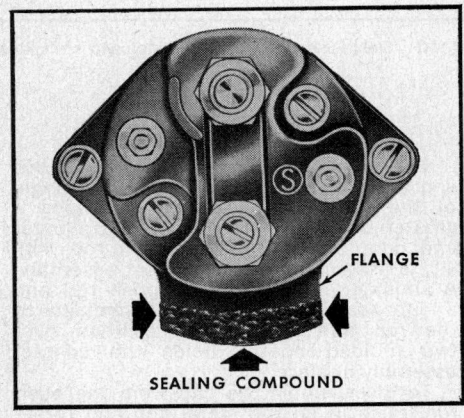

Fig. 45 Sealing solenoid housing to frame

instead of the 6 volts specified as this will cause the motor to operate. As a further precaution to prevent motoring, connect a heavy jumper lead from the solenoid motor terminal to ground.

After energizing the solenoid with the clutch shifted toward the pinion stop retainer, push the pinion back toward the commutator end as far as possible to take up any slack movement; then check the clearance with feeler gauge, Fig. 44.

Disassembling Motor

Normally the motor should be disassembled only so far as necessary to repair or replace defective parts.
1. Disconnect field coil connectors from solenoid "motor" terminal.
2. Remove thru bolts.
3. Remove commutator end frame and field frame assembly.

4. Remove armature assembly from drive housing. On some models it may be necessary to remove solenoid and shift lever assembly from the drive housing before removing the armature assembly. *Important: When solenoid is installed, apply*

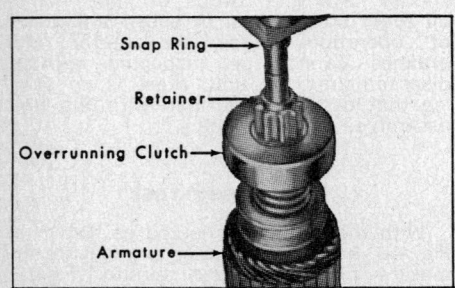

Fig. 49 Installing snap ring onto armature shaft

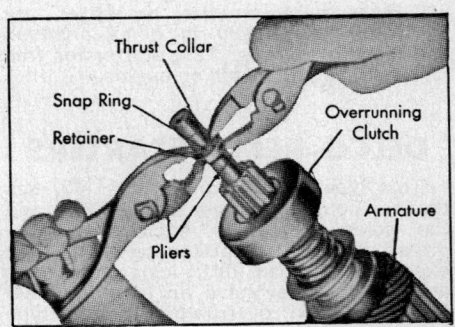

Fig. 50 Installing snap ring into retainer

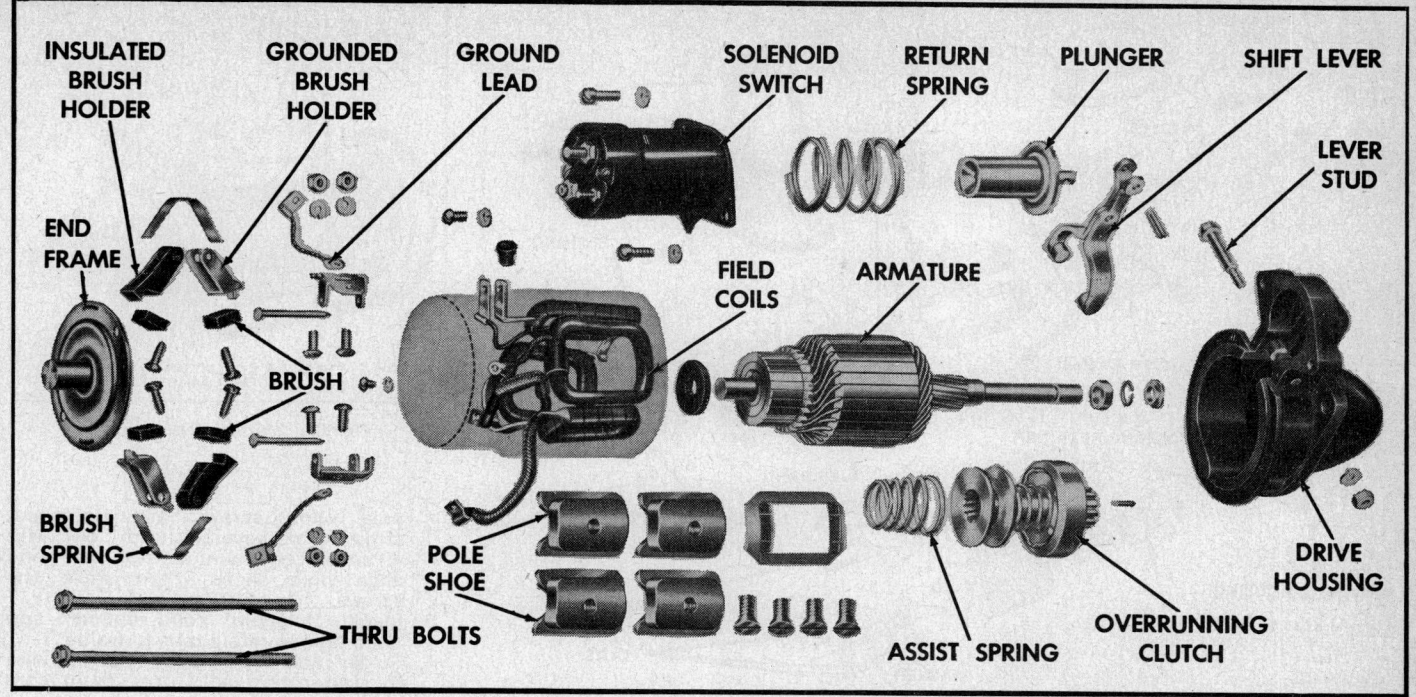

Fig. 48   Disassembled view of Delco-Remy starting motor

sealing compound between field frame and solenoid flange, Fig. 45.
5. Remove overrunning clutch from armature shaft as follows:
   a) Slide thrust collar off end of armature shaft, Fig. 46.
   b) Slide a standard ½" pipe coupling, a ⅝" deep socket or other metal cylinder of suitable size onto shaft so end of coupling or cylinder butts against edge of retainer. Tap end of coupling with hammer, driving retainer toward armature and off snap ring, Fig. 47.
   c) Remove snap ring from groove in shaft. If snap ring is too badly distorted during removal, use a new one when reassembling the clutch.
   d) Slide retainer, clutch and assist spring from armature shaft.

Reassembling Motor, Fig. 48

1. Lubricate drive end and splines of armature shaft with SAE 10 oil. *If heavier oil is used it may cause failure to mesh at low temperatures.*
2. Place "assist" spring on drive end of shaft next to armature, with small end against lamination stack.
3. Slide clutch assembly onto armature shaft with pinion outward.
4. Slide retainer onto shaft with cupped surface facing end of shaft.
5. Stand armature on end on wood surface with commutator down. Position snap ring on upper end of shaft and hold in place with a block of wood. Hit wood block with a hammer forcing snap ring over end of shaft, Fig. 49. Slide snap ring into

groove, squeezing it to ensure a good fit in groove.
6. Assemble thrust collar on shaft with shoulder next to snap ring.
7. Position retainer and thrust collar next to snap ring. With clutch pressed against assist spring, for clearance next to retainer, use two pairs of pliers at the same time (one pair on either side of shaft) to grip retainer and thrust collar. Then squeeze until snap ring is forced into retainer, Fig. 50.
8. Place 4 or 5 drops of SAE 10 oil in drive housing bushing. Make sure thrust collar is in place against snap ring and retainer; then slide armature and clutch assembly into place in drive housing.
9. Attach solenoid and shift lever assembly to drive housing. Be sure lever buttons are located between sides of clutch collar.
10. Position field frame over armature, *applying sealing compound between frame and solenoid flange* (Fig. 45). Position frame against drive housing, using care to prevent damage to brushes.
11. Place 4 or 5 drops of SAE 10 oil in bushing in commutator end frame. Make sure leather brake washer is on armature shaft; then slide commutator end frame onto shaft.
12. Install thru bolts and tighten securely.
13. Reconnect field coil connectors to solenoid "motor" terminal.

FORD AUTO-LITE STARTER WITH INTEGRAL POSITIVE ENGAGEMENT DRIVE

This type starting motor, Fig. 51, is a four pole, series parallel unit with a positive engagement drive built into the starter. The drive mechanism is engaged with the flywheel by lever action before the motor is energized.

When the ignition switch is turned on to the start position, the starter relay is energized and supplies current to the motor. The current flows through one field coil and a set of contact points to ground. The magnetic field given off by the field coil pulls the movable pole, which is part of the lever, downward to its seat. When the pole is pulled down, the lever moves the drive assembly into the engine flywheel, Fig. 52.

When the movable pole is seated, it functions as a normal field pole and opens the contact points. With the points open, current flows through the starter field coils, energizing the starter. At the same time, current also flows through a holding coil to hold the movable pole in its seated position.

When the ignition switch is released from the start position, the starter relay opens the circuit to the starting motor. This allows the return spring to force the lever back, disengaging the drive from the flywheel and returning the movable pole to its normal position, Fig. 53.

Disassembly

It may not be necessary to disassemble

STARTING MOTORS

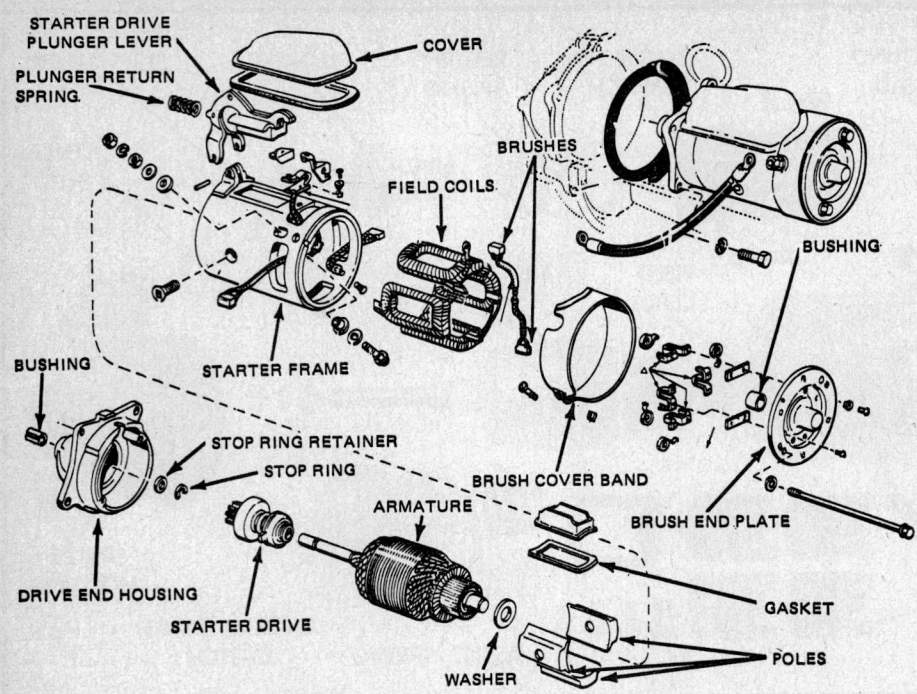

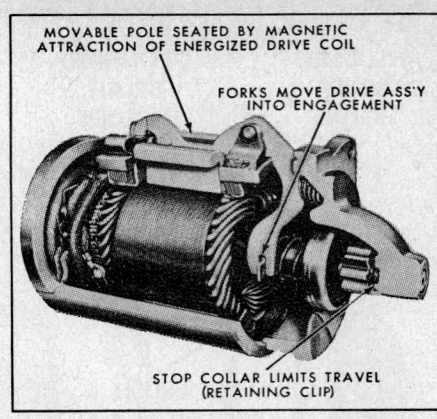

Fig. 52 Starter drive engaged

Fig. 51 Ford Auto-Lite starter with an integral positive engagement drive

the starter completely to accomplish repair or replacement of certain parts. Thus, before disassembling the motor, remove the cover band and starter drive actuating lever cover. Examine brushes to make sure they are free in their holders. Replace brushes if defective or worn beyond their useful limit. Check the tension of each brush spring with a pull scale. Spring Tension should not be less than 45 ounces. If disassembly is necessary, proceed as follows:

1. Remove cover band and starter drive actuating lever cover.
2. Remove through bolts, starter drive

gear housing, drive gear retaining clip cup and starter drive actuating lever return spring. Some 1969-70 units incorporate needle bearings at the drive end. If needle bearings need not be replaced, insert a dummy shaft into the housing while removing the armature, Fig. 54. This will prevent loss of bearings.
3. Remove pivot pin retaining starter gear actuating lever and remove lever and armature.
4. Remove and discard spring clip retaining starter drive gear to end of armature shaft, and remove starter drive gear.
5. Remove commutator brushes from brush holders and remove brush end plate.
6. Remove two screws retaining ground brushes to frame.
7. On the field coil that operates the drive gear actuating lever, bend tab up on field retainer and remove retainer.
8. Remove field coil retainer screws, Fig. 55. Unsolder field coil leads from terminal screw, and remove pole shoes and coils from frame.
9. Remove starter terminal nut and related parts. Remove any excess solder from terminal slot.

Reassembly

1. Install starter terminal, insulator, washers and retaining nut in frame, Fig. 56. Be sure to position slot in screw perpendicular to frame end surface.
2. Install field coils and pole pieces. As

pole shoe screws are tightened, strike frame several sharp blows with a soft-faced hammer to seat and align pole shoes, then stake the screws.
3. Install solenoid coil retainer and bend tabs to retain tabs to frame.
4. Solder field coils and solenoid wire to starter terminal, using rosin core solder.
5. Check for continuity and grounds in the assembled coils.
6. Position solenoid coil ground terminal over ground screw hole nearest starter terminal.
7. Position ground brushes to starter frame and install retaining screws, Fig. 56.
8. Position starter brush end plate to frame with end plate boss in frame slot.
9. Install drive gear to armature shaft and install a new retaining spring clip.
10. Position fiber thrust washer on commutator end of armature shaft and install armature in frame.
11. Install starter drive actuating lever to frame and starter drive, and install pivot pin.
12. Position actuating lever return

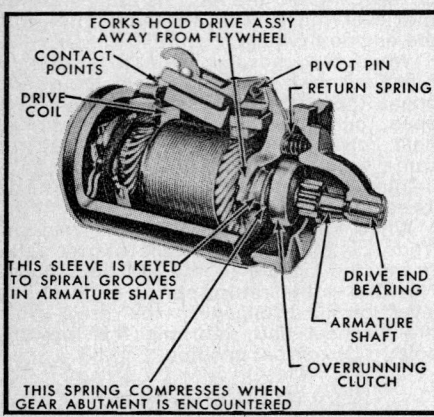

Fig. 53 Starter drive disengaged

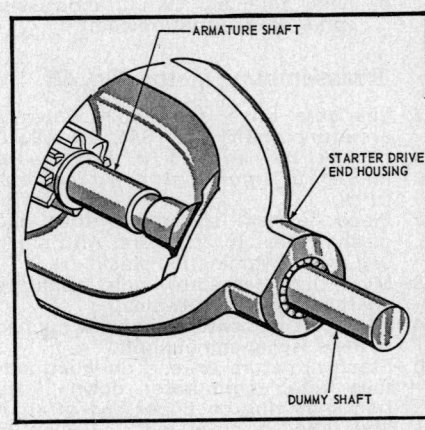

Fig. 54 Using dummy shaft to hold needle bearings in place while servicing 1969-70 starter motor

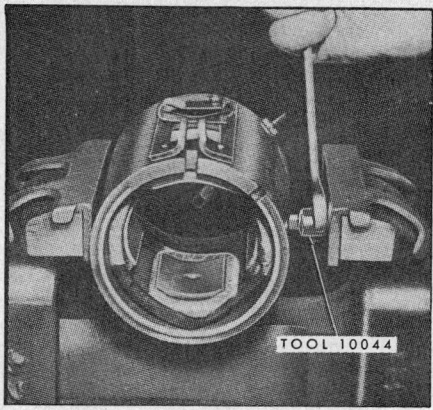

Fig. 55 Removing field coil pole shoe screws

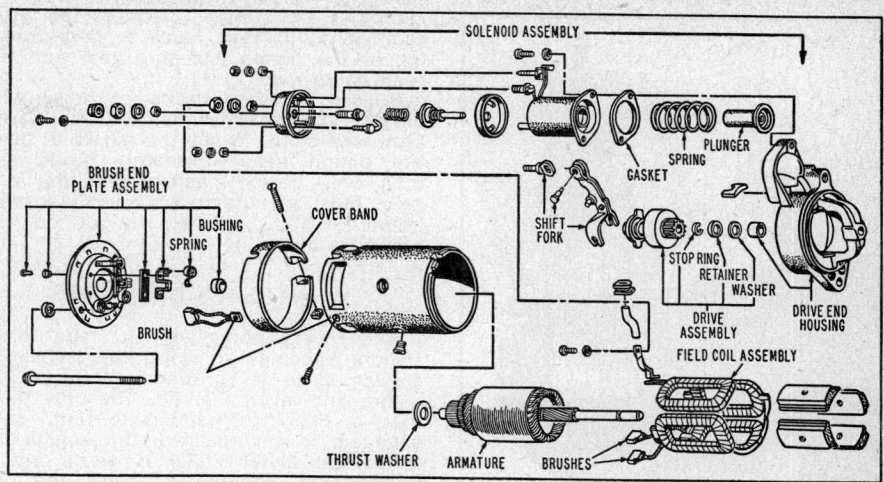

Fig. 57 Ford Auto-Lite solenoid actuated starter, exploded

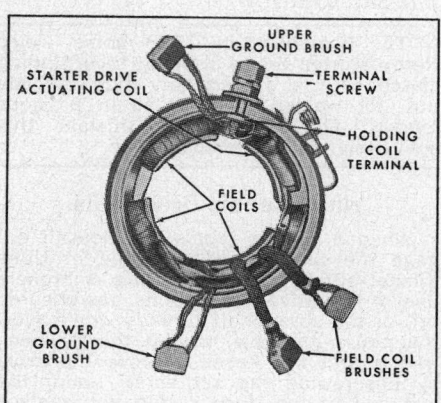

Fig. 56 Field coil assembly

spring and drive gear housing to frame and install through bolts. Do not pinch brush leads between brush plate and frame.

13. Install brushes in holders, being sure to center brush springs on brushes.
14. Position drive gear actuating lever cover on starter and install brush cover band.

FORD AUTO-LITE SOLENOID ACTUATED STARTER

Description

The solenoid assembly, in this unit, is mounted to a flange on the starter drive housing which encloses the entire shift lever and solenoid plunger mechanism. The solenoid incorporates a pull-in winding and a hold-in winding.

Operation

As the solenoid is energized, it shifts the starting motor pinion into mesh with

the engine flywheel ring gear.

At the same time, the solenoid contacts are closed and battery current flows to the motor, turning it and the engine.

After the engine starts, the starter drive is disengaged when the ignition switch is returned from the start position to the run position and the solenoid spring pushes the shift lever back, disengaging the starter drive from the flywheel ring gear.

The starting motor is protected by an overrunning clutch built into the starter drive.

Disassembly, Fig. 57

1. Disconnect the copper strap from the starter terminal of the solenoid, remove the retaining screws and remove solenoid.
2. Loosen retaining screw and slide brush cover band back on frame.
3. Remove commutator brushes from holders. Hold each spring away from the brush with a hook while sliding brush from holder.
4. Remove through bolts and separate end plates and frame.
5. Remove solenoid plunger and shift fork assembly.
6. Remove armature and drive assembly from frame. Remove drive stop ring and slide drive assembly from shaft. Remove fiber thrust washer from commutator end of shaft.
7. Remove drive stop ring retainer from shaft.

Reassembly

1. Install drive assembly on shaft and install new stop ring.
2. Install solenoid plunger and shift fork.
3. Place new retainer in drive housing and install armature and drive in housing. Be sure shift lever tangs properly engage drive assembly.
4. Install fiber washer on commutator end of shaft and position frame to drive housing, being sure to index frame and drive housing correctly.

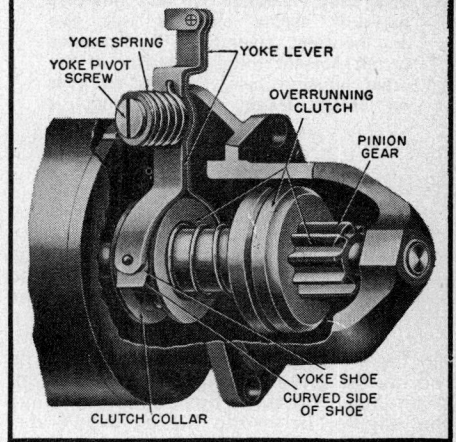

Fig. 58 Overrunning clutch drive. When assembling, make sure curved sides of yoke shoes are toward gear end of clutch. Reversed yoke shoes can cause improper meshing of pinion

5. Install brush plate assembly being sure to index it properly, install through bolts and tighten to 55-75 in lbs.
6. Install brushes by pulling each spring away from holder with a hook to allow entry of the brush. Center the brush springs on the brushes. Press insulated brush leads away from all other components to prevent possible shorts.
7. Install rubber gasket and solenoid.
8. Connect copper strap to starter terminal of solenoid.
9. Position cover band and tighten retaining screw.
10. Connect starter to battery and check operation.

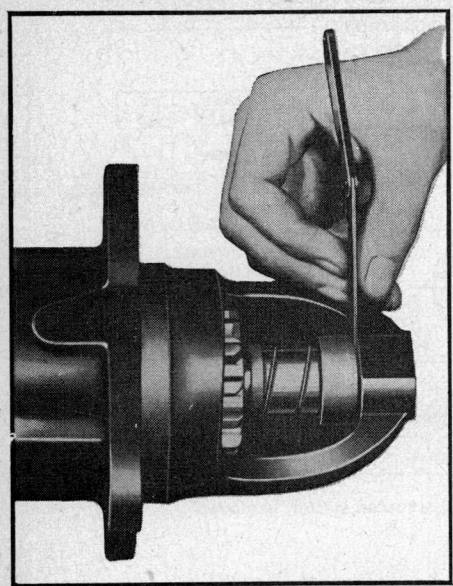

Fig. 59 Measuring overrunning clutch drive stop clearance. Do not compress anti-drift spring as this will give an incorrect clearance. If clearance is not present there is danger of the drive housing being broken as gear or collar slams back against it

STARTER DRIVE TROUBLES

Starter drive troubles are easy to diagnose and they usually cannot be confused with ordinary starter difficulties. If the starter does not turn over at all or if it drags, look for trouble in the starter or electrical supply system. Concentrate on the starter drive or ring gear if the starter is noisy, if it turns but does not engage the engine, or if the starter won't disengage after the engine is started. After the starter is removed, the trouble can usually be located quickly.

Worn or chipped ring gear or starter pinion are the usual causes of noisy operation. Before replacing either or both of these parts try to find out what caused the damage. With the Bendix type drive, incomplete engagement of the pinion with the ring gear is a common cause of tooth damage. The wrong pinion clearance on starter drives of the over-running clutch type leads to poor meshing of the pinion and ring gear and too rapid tooth wear.

A less common cause of noise with either type of drive is a bent starter armature shaft. When this shaft is bent, the pinion gear alternately binds and then only partly meshes with the ring gear. Most manufacturers specify a maximum of .003" radial run-out on the armature shaft.

When Clutch Drive Fails

The over-running clutch type drive seldom becomes so worn that it fails to engage since it is directly activated by a fork and lever, Fig. 58. The only thing that is likely to happen is that, once engaged, it will not turn the engine because the clutch itself is worn out. A much more frequent difficulty and one that rapidly wears ring gear and teeth is partial engagement. Proper meshing of the pinion is controlled by the end clearance between the pinion gear and the starter housing or pinion stop, if used.

The clearance is set with the starter off the car and with the drive in the engaged position. To check the clearance, supply current to the starter solenoid with the electrical connection between starter and solenoid removed. Supplying current to the solenoid but not the starter will prevent the starter from rotating during the test. Take out all slack by pushing lightly on the starter drive clutch housing while inserting a feeler gauge between pinion and housing or pinion stop, Fig. 59.

On late model cars, the solenoids are completely enclosed in the starter housing and the pinion clearance is not adjustable. If the clearance is not correct, the starter must be disassembled and checked for excessive wear of solenoid linkage, shift lever mechanism, or improper assembly of parts.

Failure of the over-running clutch drive to disengage is usually caused by binding between the armature shaft and the drive. If the drive, particularly the clutch, shows signs of overheating it indicates that it is not disengaging immediately after the engine starts. If the clutch is forced to over-run too long, it overheats and turns a bluish color. For the cause of the binding, look for rust or gum between the armature shaft and the drive, or for burred splines. Excess oil on the drive will lead to gumming, and inadequate

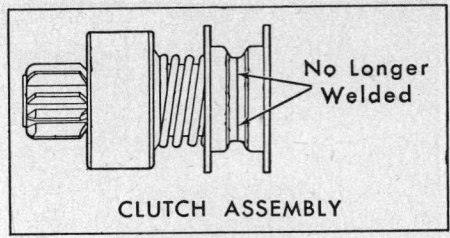

Fig. 60 New design over-running clutch collar

air circulation in the flywheel housing will cause rust.

Over-running clutch drives cannot be overhauled in the field so they must be replaced. In cleaning, never soak them in a solvent because the solvent may enter the clutch and dissolve the sealed-in lubricant. Wipe them off lightly with kerosene and lubricate them sparingly with SAE 10 or 10W oil.

NOTE: Beginning in 1968 some Delco Remy starter drives used an overrunning clutch with a split collar. Side by side but not welded together as in previous models, Fig. 60. Do not mistake this split design as a defective collar.

When Bendix Drive Fails

When a Bendix type drive doesn't engage the cause usually is one of three things: either the drive spring is broken, one of the drive spring bolts has sheared off, or the screwshaft threads won't allow the pinion to travel toward the flywheel. In the first two cases, remove the drive by unscrewing the set screw under the last coil of the drive spring and replace the broken parts. Gummed or rusty screwshaft threads are fairly common causes of Bendix drive failure and are easily cleaned with a little kerosene or steel wool, depending on the trouble. Here again, as in the case of over-running clutch drives, use light oil sparingly, and be sure the flywheel housing has adequate ventilation. There is usually a breather hole in the bottom of the flywheel housing which should be open.

The failure of a Bendix drive to disengage or to mesh properly is most often caused by gummed or rusty screwshaft threads. When this is not true, look for mechanical failure within the drive itself.

STARTING SWITCHES

MAGNETIC and SOLENOID SWITCHES are designed to perform mechanical jobs electromagnetically such as closing a heavy circuit or shifting the starter drive pinion with the engine flywheel ring gear for cranking. Switches of this type consist basically of contacts and a winding (or windings) around a hollow cylinder containing a movable core or plunger. When the winding (or windings) is energized by the battery through an external control circuit the plunger is pulled inward, producing the necessary mechanical movement.

MAGNETIC SWITCHES

The switch shown in Fig. 1 is not designed for disassembly and must be replaced if defective.

In the Delco-Remy switch shown in Fig. 1 the terminals are assembled into a molded terminal ring which is held in place on the switch case by the cover and screws. Gaskets on both sides of the ring seals the contact compartment as a protection against moisture and dirt. The winding assembly is not removable from the case on this unit although the contact disk, plunger and plunger return spring can be removed after the cover is taken off.

NOTE

On vehicles with overrunning clutch starting motors, a magnetic switch is normally used to shift the drive pinion into mesh and to close the starter circuit. There are two variations of three-terminal switches and also one type with four terminals. Any of these switches may be manufactured with either a grounded or insulated base. When installing a switch that is not marked "grounded base" or "insulated base", it must be checked out as follows, using a battery and test lamp in series.

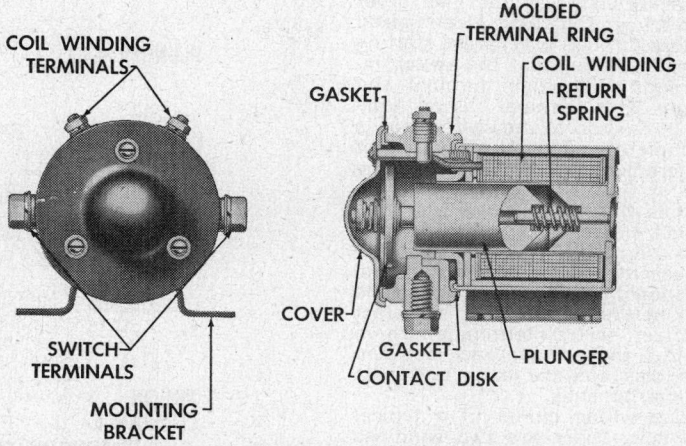

Fig. 1   End and sectional views of a sealed type magnetic switch which uses gaskets to seal the contact compartment

Three Terminal Switches

1. If the switch has a grounded base the test lamp will light when connected between the starter ("S") terminal or ignition ("I") terminal and switch mounting bracket.
2. If the switch has an insulated base the test lamp will light when connected between the "S" and "I" terminals and either one of the 5/16" threaded studs.
3. If the test lamp fails to light when connected between the "S" and "I" terminals and any external part of the switch, disassemble the switch to determine whether the base is grounded or insulated.

Four Terminal Switches

1. If the switch has a grounded base the test lamp will light when connected between the "S" terminal and switch mounting bracket.
2. If the switch has an insulated base the test lamp will light when connected between the "S" and "I" terminals.
3. If the test lamp fails to light when connected between the "S" terminal and any other external part of the switch, disassemble the switch to determine whether it has an insulated or grounded base.

SOLENOID SWITCHES

The solenoid switch on a cranking motor not only closes the circuit between the battery and the cranking motor but also shifts the drive pinion into mesh with the engine flywheel ring gear. This

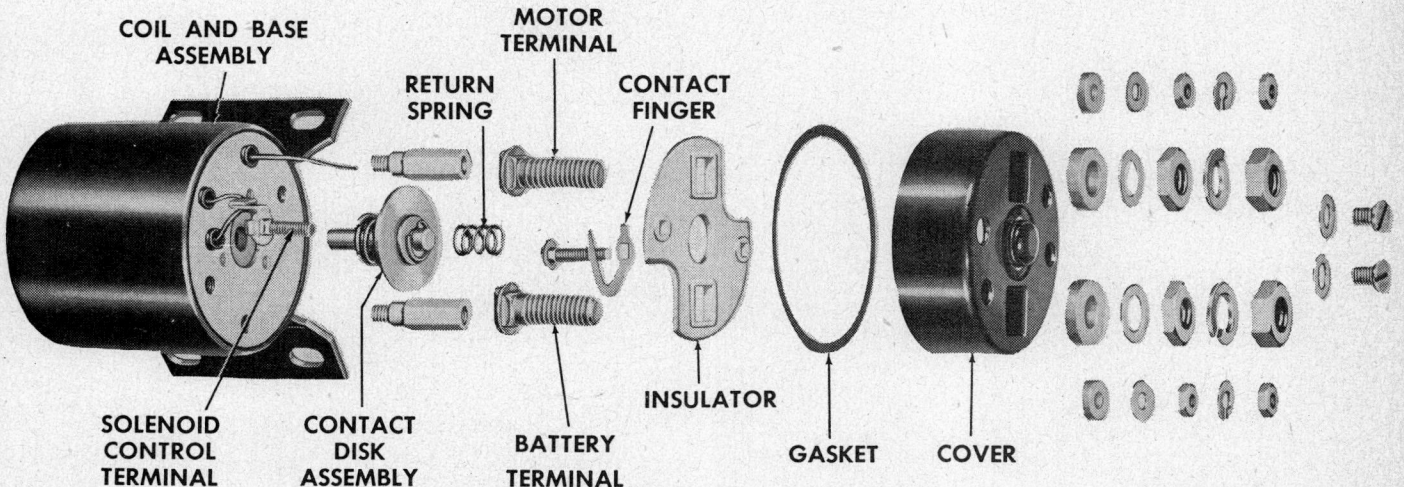

Fig. 2   Exploded view of a typical solenoid switch

2—67

STARTING SWITCHES

is done by means of a linkage between the solenoid switch plunger and the shift lever on the cranking motor (see *Starting Motors* chapter).

Fig. 2 shows a solenoid switch used on vehicles with 12-volt systems. Like other solenoid switches, this type is energized by the battery through a separate starting switch. Note, however, that the switch includes an additional small terminal and contact finger. This terminal has no functional duty in relation to the switch, but is used to complete a special ignition circuit during the cranking cycle only. When the solenoid is in the cranking position, the finger touches the contact disk and provides a direct circuit between the battery and ignition coil.

When reassembling the switch the contact finger should be adjusted to touch the contact disk before the disk makes contact with the main switch terminals. There should be 1/16" to 3/32" clearance between the contact disk and the main terminals when the finger touches.

Fig. 3 is a wiring circuit of a typical solenoid switch. There are two windings in the solenoid; a pull-in winding (shown as dashes) and a hold-in winding (shown dotted). Both windings are energized when the external control switch is closed. They produce a magnetic field which pulls the plunger in so that the drive pinion is shifted into mesh, and the main contacts in the solenoid switch are closed to connect the battery directly to the cranking motor. Closing the main switch contacts shorts out the pull-in winding since this winding is connected across the main contacts. The magnetism produced by the hold-in winding is sufficient to hold the plunger in, and shorting out the pull-in winding reduces drain on the battery. When the control switch

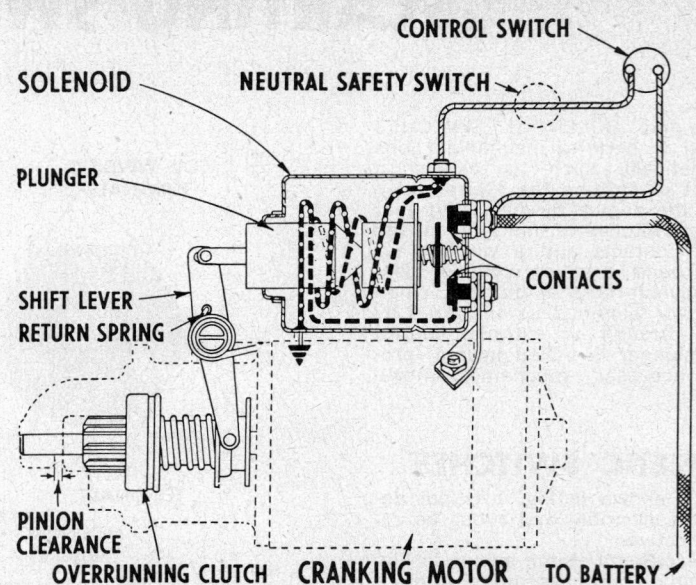

Fig. 3   Wiring circuit of a typical solenoid switch

is opened, it disconnects the hold-in winding from the battery. When the hold-in winding is disconnected from the battery, the shift lever spring withdraws the plunger from the solenoid, opening the solenoid switch contacts and at the same time withdrawing the drive pinion from mesh. Proper operation of the switch depends on maintaining a definite balance between the magnetic strength of the pull-in and hold-in windings.

This balance is established in the design by the size of the wire and the number of turns specified. *An open circuit in the hold-in winding or attempts to crank with a discharged battery will cause the switch to chatter.*

To disassemble the solenoid, remove nuts, washers and insulators from the switch terminal and battery terminal. Remove cover and take out the contact disk assembly.

ALTERNATOR SYSTEMS

CONTENTS

Introduction 2-69
Service Precautions 2-69
American Motors System 2-114
Chrysler System 2-69
Delco-Remy System 2-80
   w/Integral Regulator 2-86
Ford Autolite/Motorcraft System 2-87
   w/Integral Regulator 2-103
High Voltage System 2-105
Leece-Neville System 2-107
Motorola System 2-108
Prestolite System 2-114

INTRODUCTION

Alternators are composed of the same functional parts as the conventional D.C. generator but they operate differently: The field is called a rotor and is the turning portion of the unit. A generating part, called a stator, is the stationary member, comparable to the armature in a D.C. generator. The regulator, similar to those used in a D.C. system, regulates the output of the alternator-rectifier system.

The power source of the system is the alternator. Current is transmitted from the field terminal of the regulator through a slip ring to the field coil and back to ground through another slip ring. The strength of the field regulates the output of the alternating current. This alternating current is then transmitted from the alternator to the rectifier where it is converted to direct current.

These alternators employ a three-phase stator winding in which the phase windings are electrically 120 degrees apart. The rotor consists of a field coil encased between interleaved sections producing a magnetic field with alternate north and south poles. By rotating the rotor inside the stator the alternating current is induced in the stator windings. This alternating current is rectified (changed to D.C.) by silicon diodes and brought out to the output terminal of the alternator.

Diode Rectifiers

Six silicon diode rectifiers are used and act as electrical one-way-valves. Three of the diodes have ground polarity and are pressed or screwed into a heat sink which is grounded. The other three diodes (ungrounded) are pressed or screwed into and insulated from the end head; these diodes are connected to the alternator output terminal.

Since the diodes have a high resistance to the flow of current in one direction and a low resistance in the opposite direction, they may be connected in a manner which allows current to flow from the alternator to the battery in the low resistance direction. The high resistance in the opposite direction prevents the flow of current from the battery to the alternator. Because of this feature no circuit breaker is required between the alternator and battery.

SERVICE PRECAUTIONS

1. Be certain that battery polarity is correct when servicing units. Reversed battery polarity will damage rectifiers and regulators.
2. If booster battery is used for starting, be sure to use correct polarity in hook up.
3. When a fast charger is used to charge a vehicle battery, the vehicle battery cables should be disconnected *unless the fast charger is* equipped with a special Alternator Protector, in which case the vehicle battery cables need not be disconnected. Also the fast charger should never be used to start a vehicle as damage to rectifiers will result.
4. Lead connections to the grounded rectifiers (negative) on Prestolite and Chrysler units should never be soldered as the excessive heat may damage the rectifiers.
5. Unless the system includes a load relay or field relay, grounding the alternator output terminal will damage the alternator and/or circuits. This is true even when the system is not in operation since no circuit breaker is used and the battery is applied to the alternator output terminal at all times. The field or load relay acts as a circuit breaker in that it is controlled by the ignition switch.
6. When adjusting the voltage regulator, do not short the adjusting tool to the regulator base as the regulator may be damaged. The tool should be insulated by taping or by installing a plastic sleeve.
7. Before making any "on vehicle" tests of the alternator or regulator, the battery should be checked and the circuit inspected for faulty wiring or insulation, loose or corroded connections and poor ground circuits.
8. Check alternator belt tension to be sure the belt is tight enough to prevent slipping under load.
9. The ignition switch should be off and the battery ground cable disconnected before making any test connections to prevent damage to the system.
10. The vehicle battery must be fully charged or a fully charged battery may be installed for test purposes.

Chrysler Alternators

Three types of alternators are available on Chrysler Corp. cars; one with an electro-mechanical voltage regulator, Figs. C1 and C2, the insulated brush unit, Figs. C3 and C4 optional on some 1969 cars and the isolated field unit which is standard on later cars, Figs. C5, C5A, C6 and C6A.

The difference between these units is in the area of the brushes. The electro-mechanical unit uses a ground brush, the insulated brush unit has a positive insulated brush with the system grounded through the regulator and the isolated field unit has two separate, insulated, field brushes.

Both the insulated brush and the isolated field units use a fully electronic voltage regulator which is a sealed, non-adjustable unit.

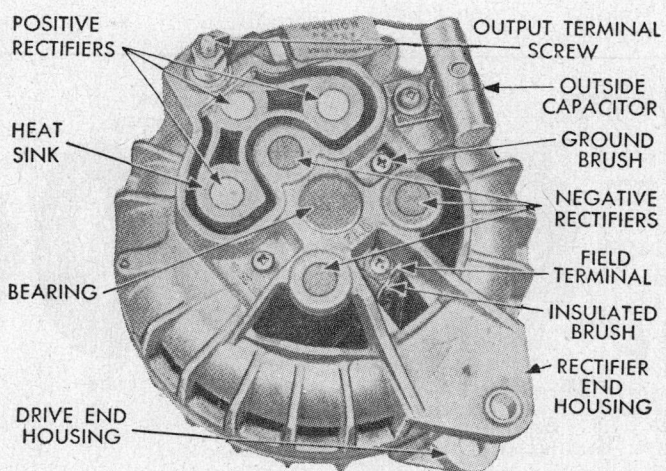

Fig. C1 Chrysler alternator, electro-mechanically regulated unit

TESTING SYSTEM ON VEHICLE

ELECTRO-MECHANICAL UNIT

Field Circuit Resistance Test

1. Referring to Fig. C7, disconnect ignition wire at coil side of ballast resistor and connect a test ammeter and voltmeter in the circuit as shown. All lights and accessories should be turned off.

2. Turn ignition switch on and turn voltmeter selector switch to the low voltage scale and read the meter. The voltage should not exceed .55 volt. A reading in excess of .55 volt indicates high resistance in field circuit between battery and voltage regulator field terminal.

3. If high resistance is indicated, move negative voltmeter lead to each connection along the circuit to the battery. A sudden drop in voltage indicates a loose or corroded connection between that point and the last point tested. To test the terminals for tightness, attempt to move the terminal while observing the voltmeter. Any movement of the meter pointer indicates looseness.

NOTE: *Excessive resistance in the regulator wiring circuit will cause fluctuation in the ammeter.*

---

4. Turn ignition switch off, disconnect test instrument and reconnect ignition primary wire at the coil side of the ballast resistor.

Charging Circuit Resistance Test

With battery in good condition and fully charged, first disconnect the battery ground cable to avoid accidental shorting of the charging or field circuit when making the test connections shown in Fig. C8.

1. With the test instruments connected as shown and with battery ground cable re-connected, start and operate engine at a speed to obtain 10 amperes flowing in the circuit.

2. The voltmeter should not exceed .3 volt. If a higher voltage drop is indicated, inspect, clean and tighten all connections in the charging circuit. A voltage drop test may be performed at each connection to locate the connection with excessive resistance.

3. Turn ignition switch off. Disconnect ground cable at battery to avoid accidental shorting of the charging or field circuit when disconnecting the test instruments. Connect battery lead to alternator "BAT" terminal and tighten securely. Connect ignition lead to regulator ignition terminal and re-connect ground cable at battery.

Current Output Test

1. With test instruments connected in circuit as shown in Fig. C9, connect an engine tachometer.

2. Start and operate at 1250 rpm.

3. Adjust carbon pile rheostat to obtain a reading of 15 volts on the test voltmeter.

4. Observe reading on test ammeter.

5. If the output is slightly less (5 to 7 amperes) than the rated output of the alternator, it may be an indication of an open-circuited diode or other internal alternator problem.

6. If the output is considerably lower than the rated output of the alternator, it may be an indication of a short-circuited diode or other internal alternator problem. In either case the alternator should be removed and tested.

NOTE: *Turn off the carbon pile rheostat immediately after observing reading on test ammeter.*

---

7. If the alternator current output test-

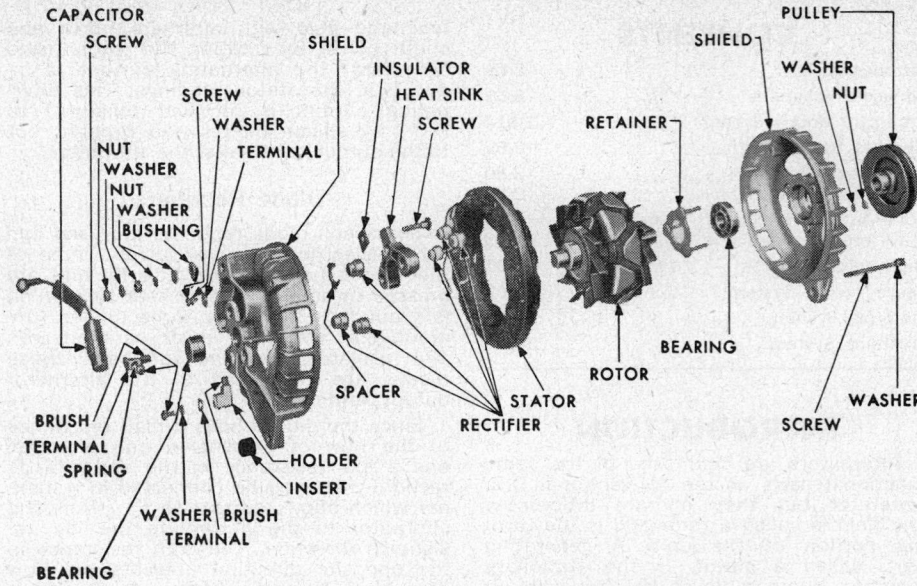

Fig. C2   Electro-mechanically regulated alternator disassembled

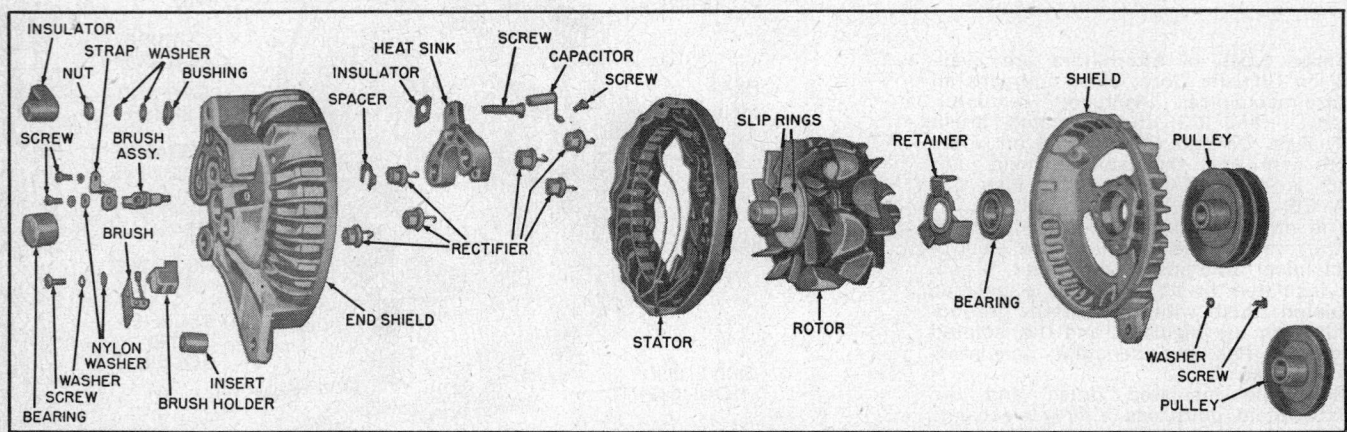

Fig. C3   Insulated brush alternator disassembled

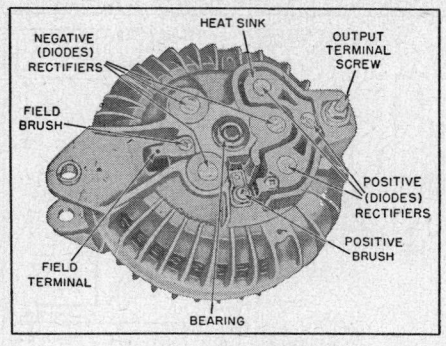

Fig. C4 Insulated brush alternator assembly

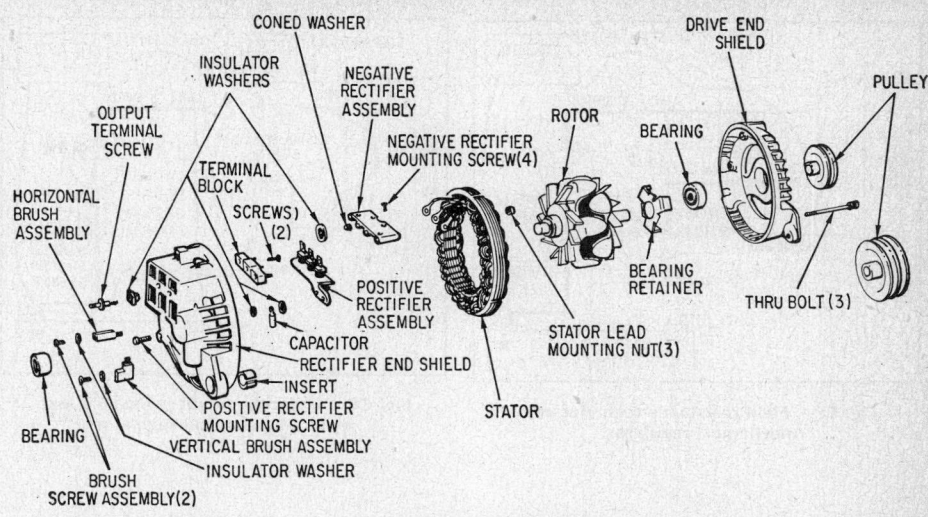

Fig. C5A Isolated field alternator disassembled. 1972-74

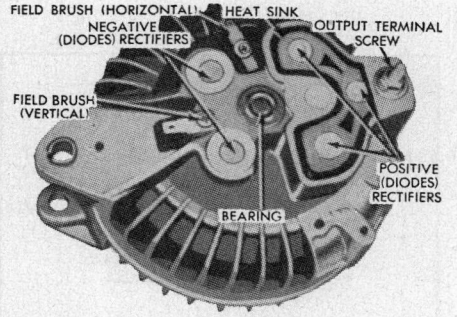

Fig. C6 Isolated field alternator assembly, 1969-71

ed satisfactorily, turn off the ignition switch and remove the jumper lead from the alternator field terminal and output terminal.

Voltage Regulator Test

UPPER CONTACT TEST

1. With engine at normal operating temperature and test instruments connected as shown in Fig. C10, start and operate the engine at 1250 rpm.

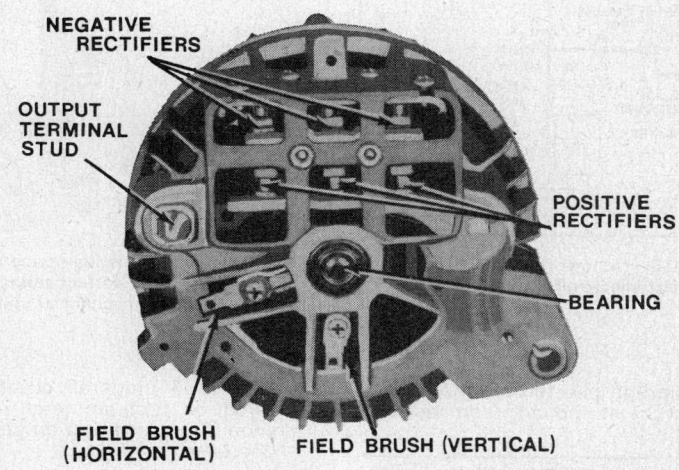

Fig. C6A Isolated field alternator assembly, 1972-74

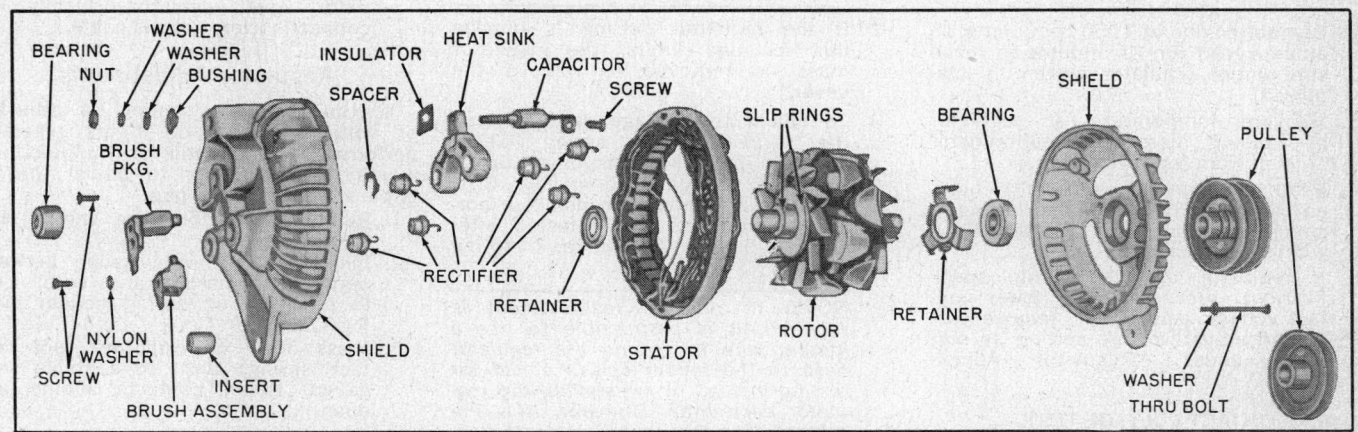

Fig. C5 Isolated field generator disassembled. 1969-71

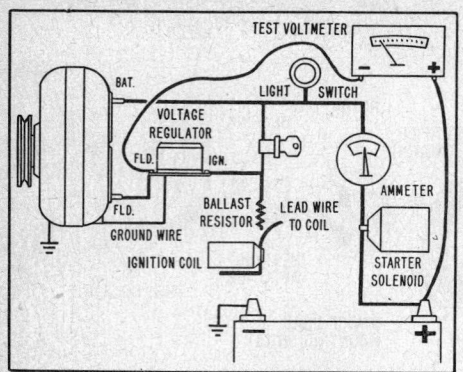

Fig. C7 Field resistance test, electro-mechanical regulator

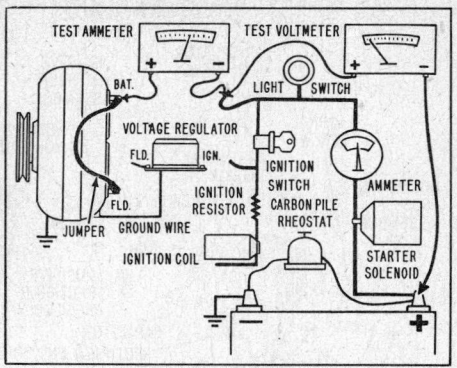

Fig. C8 Charging circuit resistance test, electro-mechanical regulator

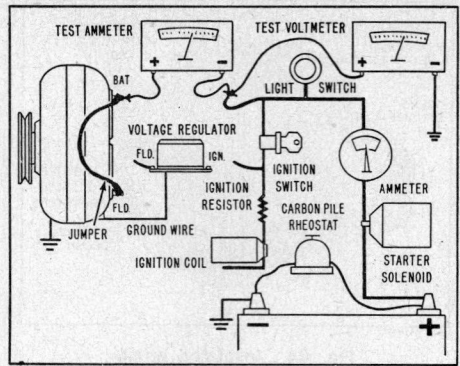

Fig. C9 Current output test, electro-mechanical regulator

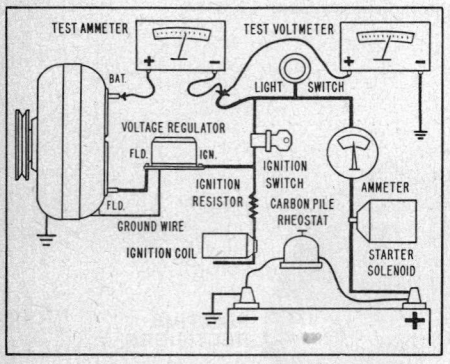

Fig. C10 Voltage regulator test, electro-mechanical regulator

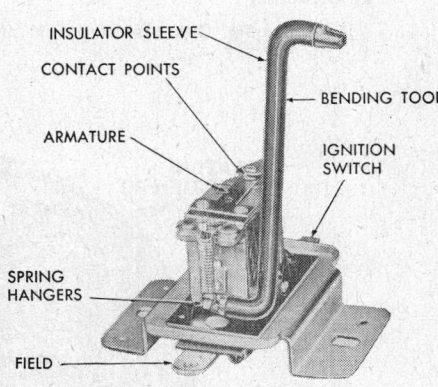

Fig. C11 Adjusting spring tension to obtain correct voltage, electro-mechanical units

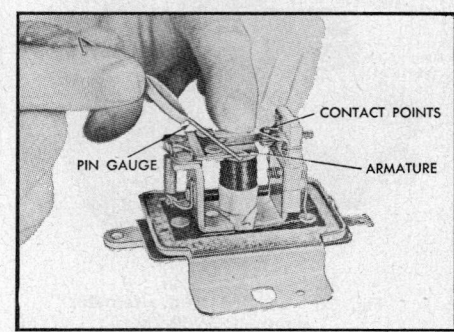

Fig. C12 Measuring armature air gap, electro-mechanical unit

Adjust carbon pile to obtain a 15 ampere output as indicated on test ammeter.

NOTE: *No current reading on the ammeter would indicate either a low regulator setting or a blown fuse wire inside the voltage regulator between upper stationary contact and "IGN" terminal. Correct the cause and replace the fusible wire.*

2. Operate engine at 1250 rpm and a 15 ampere load for 15 minutes to make sure entire regulator system is stabilized.
3. Measure temperature at regulator by holding a reliable thermometer 1/4 inch from regulator cover.
4. Read test ammeter. With fully charged battery and 15 amperes flowing in circuit, voltmeter readings should be within specifications.
5. If regulator operates within specifications, proceed to the lower contact voltage test. If not, remove cover and adjust voltage setting as outlined under "Regulator Adjustments".

LOWER CONTACT VOLTAGE TEST

1. Increase engine speed to 2200 rpm. Vary carbon pile to decrease current

load to 7 amperes output as registered on test ammeter. The voltage should *increase* and amperage should decrease.

NOTE: *There will be a slightly higher voltage at higher engine speeds above 2200 rpm. However, this increased voltage must not exceed the voltage specified by more than .7 volt at any temperature range.*

2. If the regulator setting is outside the specified limits, the regulator must be removed to remove the cover.
3. To adjust the voltage setting, bend *the regulator lower spring hanger down to increase voltage, or up to decrease voltage setting,* Fig. C11. The regulator must be installed, correctly connected, and retested after each adjustment of the lower spring hanger.

NOTE: *If repeated readjustment is required, it is permissible to use a jumper wire to ground the regulator base to the fender splash shield for testing instead of reinstalling the regulator each time. However, it is important that the cover be reinstalled, the regulator connections correctly connected, and the regulator insu-*

lated to prevent grounding the regulator terminals or resistances. When testing, the regulator must be at the same attitude (or angle) as when installed on the vehicle.

4. If the alternator and regulator tested satisfactorily, turn the ignition switch off. Disconnect battery ground cable, then the test instruments. Connect the leads to alternator and regulator. Finally reconnect battery ground cable.

Regulator Adjustments

If the regulator cannot be adjusted or voltage control, or if the regulator performance is erratic or malfunctions, it may be necessary to adjust the air gap and contact point gap.

1. Remove regulator from vehicle and take off cover.
2. Insert a .048" wire gauge between regulator armature and core, next to stop pin on spring hanger side, Fig. C12.
3. Press down on armature (not contact spring) until it contacts wire gauge. Upper contacts should just open.

NOTE: *A battery and test light connected in series to the "IGN" and*

"FLD" terminals may be used to determine accurately the contact opening. When the contacts open, the test light will do dim.

4. Insert a .052" wire gauge between armature and core, next to stop pin on spring hanger side.
5. Press down on armature until it contacts wire gauge. The contacts should remain closed and test light should remain bright.
6. If adjustment is required, adjust air gap by loosening the screw and moving the stationary contact bracket. Make sure air gap is measured with attaching screw fully tightened. Re-measure the gap as directed above.
7. Remove wire gauge. Measure lower contact gap with feeler gauge. which should be .012 to .016". Adjust lower contact gap by bending lower stationary contact bracket.
8. Install regulator cover and then the regulator. Finally, make electrical adjustments as outlined above.

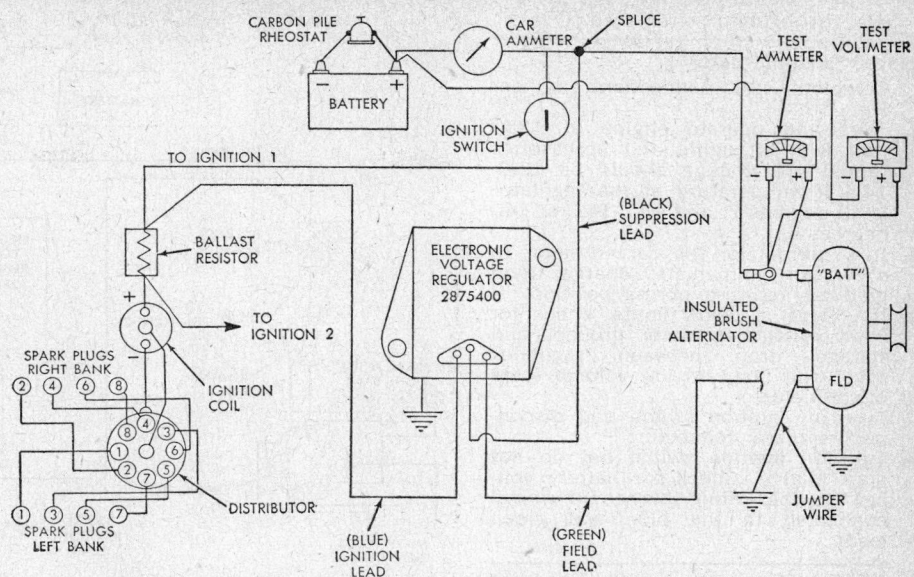

Fig. C13   Charging circuit resistance test, insulated brush units

INSULATED BRUSH & ISOLATED FIELD ALTERNATORS

Charging Circuit Resistance Test

1. Disconnect battery ground cable. Disconnect "Batt" lead at the alternator.
2. Complete test connections as per Figs. C13 and C14.
3. Connect battery ground cable, start engine and operate at idle.
4. Adjust engine speed and carbon pile to obtain 20 amps in the circuit and check voltmeter reading. Reading should not exceed .7 volts. If a voltage drop is indicated, inspect, clean and tighten all connections in the circuit. A voltage drop test at each connection can be performed to isolate the trouble.

Current Output Test

1. Disconnect battery ground cable, complete test connections as per Figs. C15 and C16 and start engine and operate at idle. *Immediately after starting, reduce engine speed to idle.*
2. Adjust the carbon pile and engine speed in increments until a speed of 1250 rpm and 15 volts are obtained.

CAUTION: While increasing speed, do not allow voltage to exceed 16 volts.

3. Check ammeter reading. Output current should be within specifications.

Voltage Regulator Test

NOTE: Battery must be fully charged for test to be accurate.

Insulated Brush Alternator

1. Make test connections as shown in Fig. C17.
2. Start and operate engine at 1250 rpm with all lights and accessories turned off.
3. As the engine starts, the instrument panel ammeter will deflect to the right. If it deflects less than 1/4 scale, turn on high beams and heater blower. If deflection is greater than 1/4 scale, turn on heater blower on high.
4. Voltage should be 13.8-14.4 if temperature at the regulator is 80 degrees F. and 13.3-14.0 at 140 degrees F.
5. If voltage is not correct, and the alternator is satisfactory, turn off ignition and disconnect regulator connector. Check for battery voltage at black and green leads. Turn on ignition without starting engine and check for battery voltage at blue lead. If voltage is not present at these connections, wiring is at fault.
6. Check regulator for good ground.
7. If regulator voltage is .5 volt away from specification, it must be replaced.

NOTE: The field circuit is grounded through the regulator. A good ground is established through the use of cup shaped washers on the regulator mounting screws which cut through body paint. These washers must be reinstalled when-

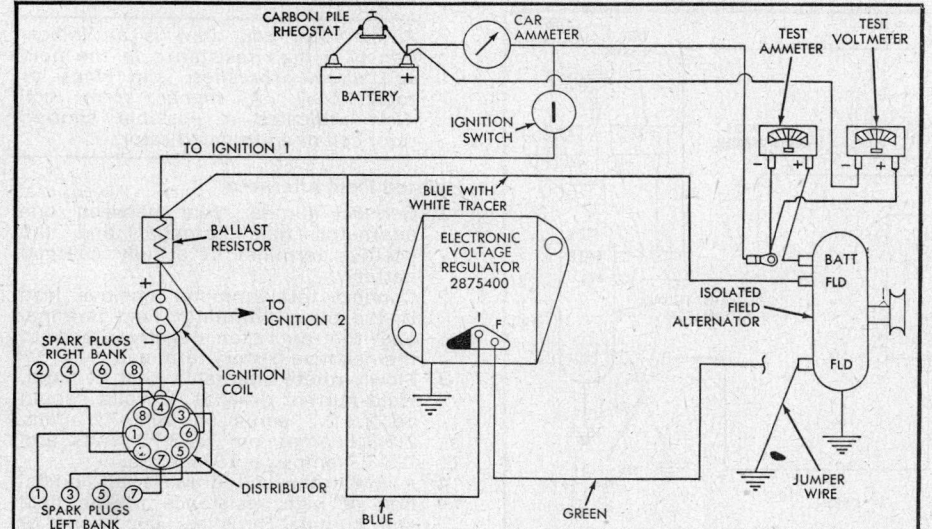

Fig. C14   Charging circuit resistance test, isolated field units

ever the regulator is removed.

Isolated Field Alternator

1. Complete test connections as per Fig. C18.
2. Start and operate engine at 1250 rpm with all lights and accessories turned off. Voltage should be 13.8-14.4 if temperature at the regulator is 80 degrees F. and 13.3-14.0 at 140 degrees F.
3. It is normal for the car ammeter to show an immediate charge then gradually return to normal position.
4. If voltage is below limits, check for good voltage regulator ground, and voltage drop between regulator cover and body on low voltage scale of voltmeter.
5. Turn off ignition switch and disconnect regulator connector.
6. Turn on ingition switch but do not start engine. Check for battery voltage at the wiring harness terminal connected to the blue and green leads.

NOTE: Disconnect wiring harness from regulator when checking the leads.

7. Turn off ignition switch. If voltage is not present at either lead, the problem is in the vehicle wiring or alternator field circuit. *Use care to avoid bending the terminals with voltmeter probe.*
8. If Steps 4-7 tested satisfactorily, change voltage regulator and repeat Step 2. If voltage is slightly above limits, or is fluctuating, proceed as follows:
9. Check voltage regulator ground, check ground between vehicle body and engine.
10. Check ignition switch circuit between battery terminal of ignition switch and voltage regulator. If voltage is more than ½ volt above limits, replace the regulator.

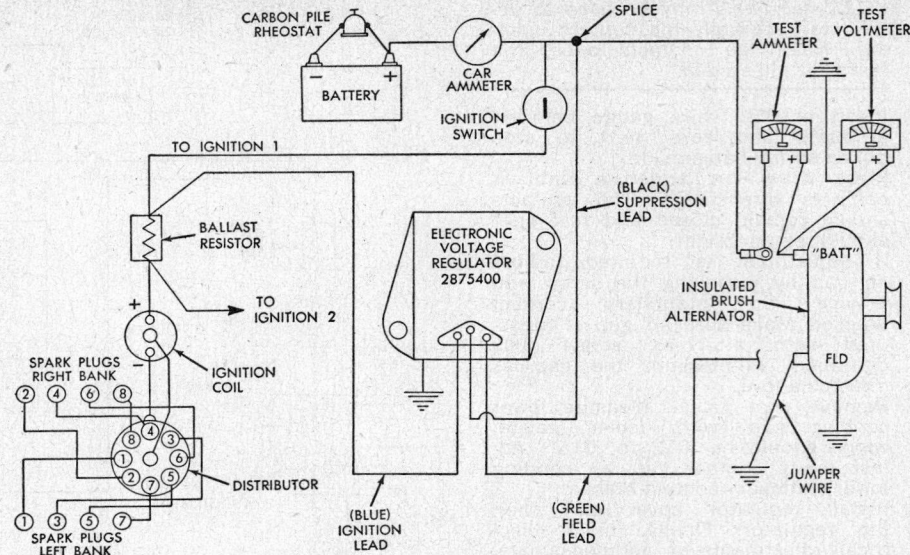

Fig. C15   Current output test, insulated brush unit

BENCH TESTS

If the alternator performance does not meet current output specification limits, it will have to be disassembled for further tests and servicing.

To remove the alternator, disconnect the battery ground cable and the leads at the alternator. Then unfasten and remove the alternator from the vehicle.

Field Coil Draw

Electro-Mechanical Unit

1. Connect a test ammeter positive lead to the battery positive terminal of a fully charged battery.

2. Connect ammeter negative lead to the field terminal of the alternator.
3. Connect a jumper wire to negative terminal of battery, and ground it to the alternator end shield.
4. Slowly rotate alternator rotor by hand. Observe ammeter reading. The field coil draw should be 2.3 to 2.7 amperes at 12 volts.

Insulated Brush Alternator

1. Connect jumper wire between alternator "Batt" terminal and the positive terminal of a fully charged battery. Connect test ammeter positive lead to the alternator field terminal and negative lead to negative battery terminal.
2. Slowly rotate alternator rotor by hand and observe ammeter reading. Field coil draw should be 2.3 to 2.7 amperes at 12 volts.

A low rotor coil draw is an indication of a high resistance in the field coil circuit (brushes, slip rings or rotor coil). A higher rotor coil draw indicates a possible shorted rotor coil or a grounded rotor.

Isolated Field Alternator

1. Connect jumper wire between one alternator field terminal and the positive terminal of a fully charged battery.
2. Connect test ammeter positive lead to the other alternator field terminal and the ammeter negative lead to the negative battery terminal.
3. Slowly rotate alternator rotor by hand. Field current draw at 12 volts should be 2.3-2.7 amps on 1969-71 units, 2.5-3.1 amps on 1972-73 units and 2.5-3.7 amps on 1974 units.
4. A low rotor coil draw is an indication of high resistance in the field coil circuit, (brushes, slip rings or rotor coil). A high rotor coil draw indicates shorted rotor coil or grounded rotor.

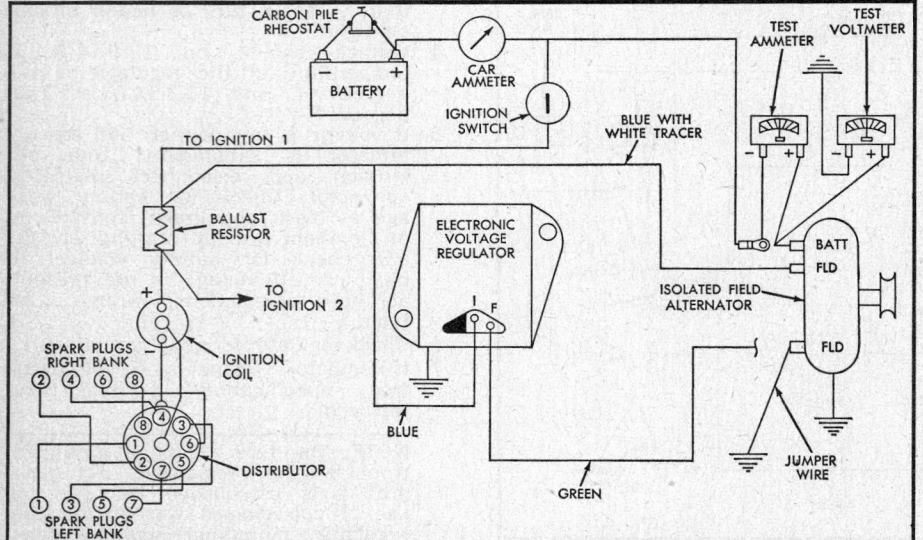

Fig. C16   Current output test, isolated field units

Testing Alternator Internal Field Circuit

Except Isolated Field Alternator

1. Remove ground brush (positive brush on insulated brush alternators). Touch one test prod from a 110 volt test lamp to the alternator insulated brush (field brush on insulated brush units) and the remaining test prod to the end shield. If rotor or insulated brush (field brush on insulated brush units) is not grounded, lamp will not light.

2. If lamp lights, remove insulated brush (field brush on insulated brush units) remove through bolts and separate end shields.

3. Touch one test prod to a slip ring and remaining prod to end shield. If lamp lights, rotor is grounded and must be replaced. If lamp does not brush (field brush on insulated brush units), the insulated brush is grounded.

Isolated Field Alternator, 1969-72

1. Touch one probe of a 110 volt test

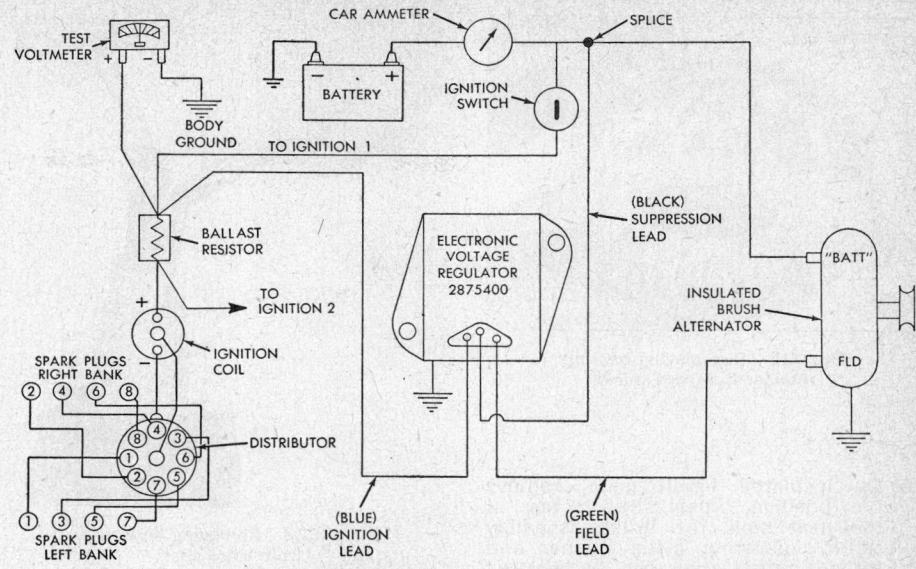

Fig. C17   Voltage regulator test, insulated brush unit

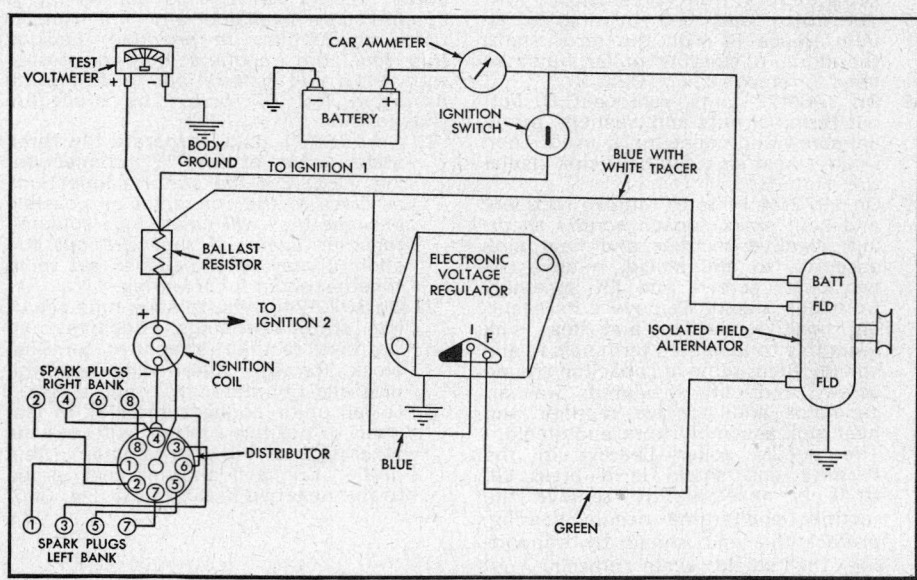

Fig. C18   Voltage regulator test, isolated field units

ALTERNATOR REPAIRS

Disassembly

To prevent possible damage to the brush assemblies, they should be removed before disassembling the alternator. The insulated (field) brush is mounted in a plastic holder which positions the brush against one of the slip rings. In the isolated field type alternator, both brushes are insulated and mounted in plastic holders. Disassembled views of all four types are shown in Figs. C2, C3, C5 and C5A.

1. On 1969-71 units, remove retaining screw lockwasher, insulated washer and field terminal. Carefully lift plastic holder containing the spring and brush from the end housing.

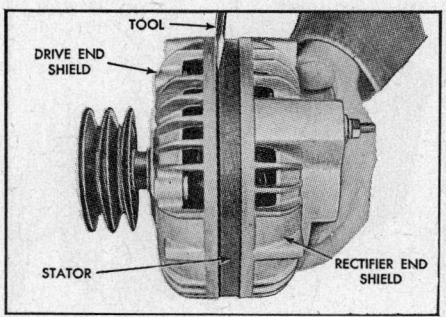

Fig. C19   Separating drive end shield from stator

lamp to one of the alternator field brush terminals and the other to the end shield. If lamp lights, rotor assembly or a field brush is grounded.

2. If lamp lights, remove field brush assemblies, remove through bolts and separate end shields.

3. Touch one test probe to a slip ring and the remaining probe to the end frame. If the lamp lights, rotor is grounded and must be replaced. If lamp does not light, cause is a grounded brush.

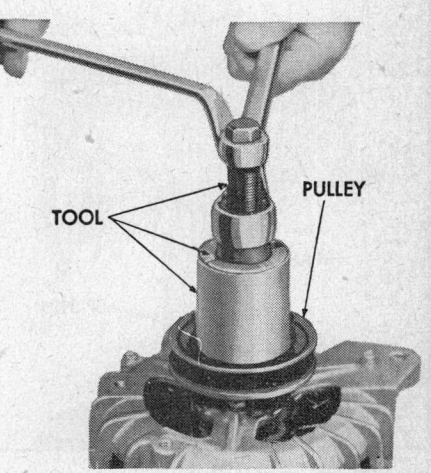

Fig. C20   Removing pulley

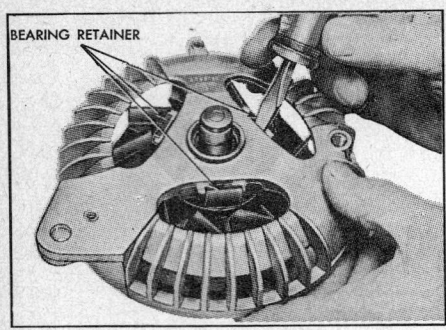

Fig. C21 Disengaging bearing retainer from end shield

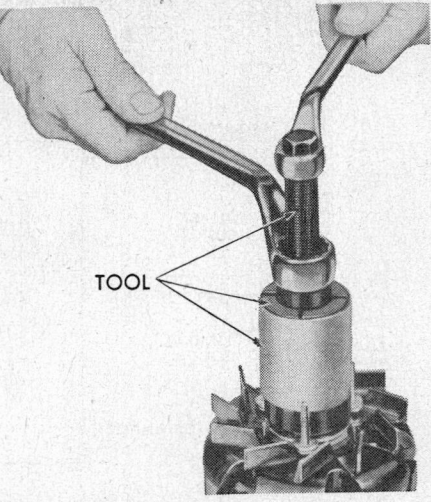

Fig. C22 Removing bearing from rotor shaft

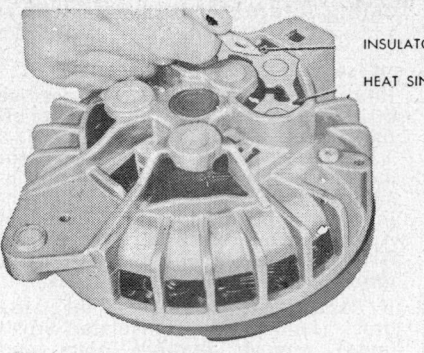

Fig. C23 Removing or installing heat sink insulator

2. On insulated brush units, remove the positive brush strap screw at the heat sink, the brush assembly screw, insulating nylon washer and lift out brush assembly. On isolated field units, remove both brush screws, insulating nylon washers and remove brush assemblies. On electro-mechanical units, remove the ground brush retaining screw and lift the clip, spring and brush from end shield.

NOTE: The stator is laminated; do not burr it or the end shield.

3. Remove through bolts and pry between stator and drive end shield with a screwdriver. Carefully separate drive end shield, pulley and rotor from stator and diode rectifier shield, Fig. C19.
4. The pulley is an interference fit on the rotor shaft; therefore, a suitable puller must be used to remove it, Fig. C20.
5. Pry drive end bearing spring retainer from end shield with a screwdriver, Fig. C21.
6. Support end shield and tap rotor shaft with a plastic hammer to

separate rotor from end shield.
7. The drive end ball bearing is an interference fit with the rotor shaft; therefore, a suitable puller must be used to remove it, Fig. C22.
8. On 1969-71 units, remove D.C. output terminal nuts and washers, terminal screw and capacitor, if used. Then remove heat sink and heat sink insulator, Fig. 23.
9. On 1972-74 units to remove rectifiers and heat sinks, loosen screws securing negative rectifier and heat sink assembly to end shield, remove the two outer screws and lift assembly from end shield. Remove nuts securing positive rectifier and heat sink assembly to insulated terminals in end shield. Then, remove capacitor ground screw and lift insulated washer, capacitor and positive rectifier and heat sink assembly from end shield.
10. The needle roller bearing in the rectifier end shield is a press fit. If it is necessary to remove the rectifier end frame needle bearing, protect the end shield by supporting the shield when pressing out the bearing as shown in Fig. C24.

Testing Diode Rectifiers

A special Rectifier Tester Tool C-3829 provides a quick, simple and accurate method to test the rectifiers without the necessity of disconnecting the soldered rectifier leads. This instrument is commercially available and full instructions for its use is provided. Lacking this tool, the rectifiers may be tested with a 12 volt battery and a test lamp having a No. 67 bulb. The procedure is as follows:

1. On 1969-71 units, separate the three stator leads at the "Y" connection, Fig. C25. Cut the stator connections as close to the connector as possible because they will have to be soldered together again. If they are cut too short it may be difficult to get them together again for soldering.
2. On 1972-74 units, remove nuts securing stator windings, positive and negative rectifier straps to terminal block. Remove stator winding terminals and pry stator from end shield.
3. On all units, connect one side of test lamp to positive battery post and the other side of the test lamp to a test probe. Connect another test probe to the negative battery post, Fig. C26.

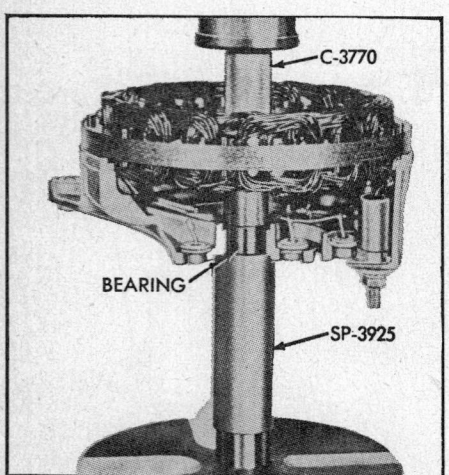

Fig. C24 Removing diode end shield bearing

Fig. C25 Separating the three stator leads

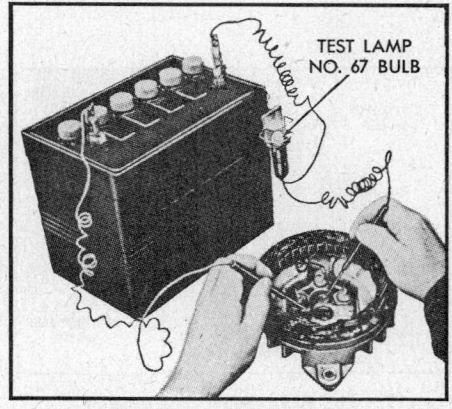

Fig. C26 Testing diodes with a test lamp

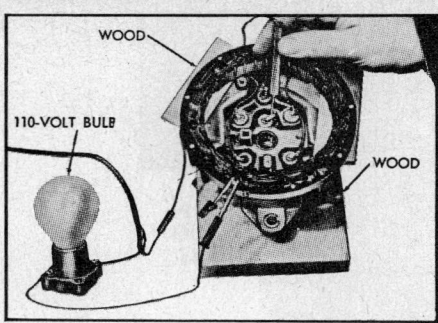

Fig. C27   Testing stator for grounds, 1969-71 units

4. On 1969-71 units, contact outer case of rectifier with one probe and other probe to rectifier center wire. On 1972-74 units, contact heat sink with one probe and strap on top of rectifier with the other probe.
5. On all units, reverse position of probes. If test lamp lights in one direction only, the rectifier is satisfactory. If test lamp lights in both directions, the rectifier is shorted. If test lamp lights in neither direction, the rectifier is open.

NOTE: *Possible cause of an open or a blown rectifier is a faulty capacitor or a battery that has been installed on reverse polarity. If the battery is installed properly and the rectifiers are open, test the capacitor capacity, which should be .50 microfarad plus or minus 20%.*

Testing Stator

1. On 1969-71 units, unsolder rectifiers from stator leads. On 1972-74 units, separate stator from end shields.
2. On 1969-71 units, insulate stator from rectifier shield with wood slats and using a 110 volt test lamp, Fig. C27, test stator for grounds by contacting one test probe to stator pole frame and the other to each stator lead. If test lamp lights, stator is grounded.
3. On 1972-74 units, using a 12 volt test lamp, Fig. C27A, test stator for grounds. Contact one test probe to

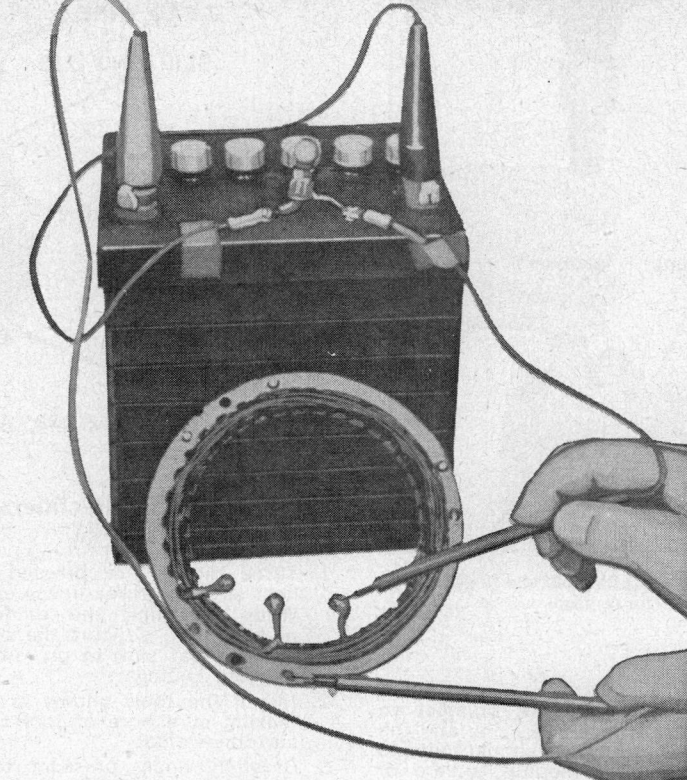

Fig. C27A   Testing stator for grounds, 1972-74 units

any pin on stator frame and the other to each stator lead. If lamp lights, stator is grounded.

NOTE: Remove varnish from stator frame pin to ensure proper electrical connection.

4. On all units, use a 12 volt test lamp to test stator for continuity. On 1969-71 units, connect one probe to all three stator leads at the "Y" connection and contact each of the three stator leads (disconnect from diodes), Fig. C28. On 1972-74 units, contact one stator lead with one probe and the remaining two leads with the other

probe. On all units, if test lamp does not light, the stator has an open circuit.
5. Install new stator if one tested is defective.

Testing Rotor
1972-74

The rotor may be tested electrically for grounded, open or shorted field coils as follows:

Fig. C28   Testing stator windings for continuity (typical)

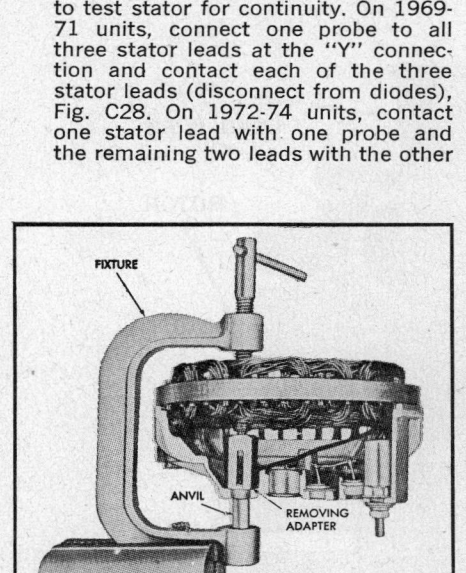

Fig. C29   Removing a diode, 1969-71

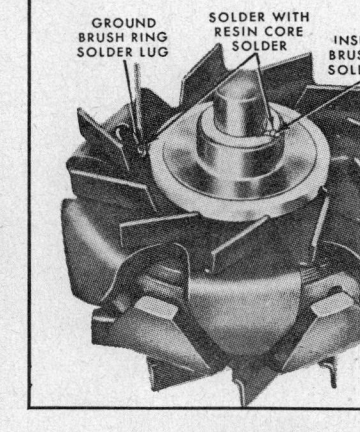

Fig. C30   Soldering points with slip ring installed

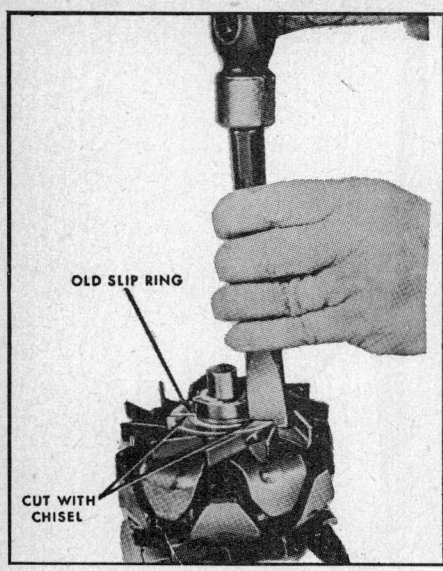

Fig. C31 Cutting old slip rings
for removal

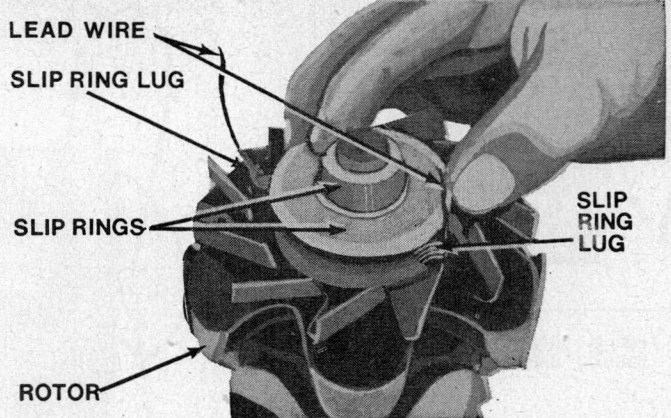

Fig. C32 Aligning slip ring with field lead wires

Grounded Field Coil Test: Connect an ohmmeter between each slip ring and the rotor shaft. The ohmmeter should indicate infinite resistance. If reading is zero or higher, rotor is grounded.

Open or Shorted Field Coil Test: Connect an ohmmeter between the slip rings. If reading is below 3 ohms, field coil is shorted. A resistance of 3 to 4 ohms at room temperature indicates rotor is satisfactory. A reading of 4 to 6 ohms indicates the alternator was operated at a high underhood temperature, however, rotor is still satisfactory. Resistances above 6.5 ohms indicates a high resistance in the field coils and further testing or rotor replacement is required.

Removing Rectifiers 1969-71

1. Three diodes are pressed into the heat sink and three in the end shield. When removing the diodes, it is necessary to support the end shield and/or heat sink to prevent damage to these castings.
2. Install the tools shown in Fig. C29, making sure bore of tool completely surrounds diode.
3. Carefully apply pressure to remove diode from end shield.

Replacing Slip Rings

1. Cut through rotor grease retainer with a chisel and remove retainer and insulator.
2. Unsolder field coil leads at solder lugs, Fig. C30.
3. Cut through copper of both slip rings at opposite points with a chisel, Fig. C31.

4. Break insulator and remove old ring.
5. Clean away dirt and particles of old slip ring from rotor.
6. Scrape ends of field coil lead wires clean for good electrical contact.
7. Position field coil wires aside and place new slip ring on rotor shaft so slip ring lugs are properly positioned for field coil wire connections, Fig. C32.
8. Place installing tool over rotor shaft and with a suitable press, press slip ring onto shaft, Fig. C33.

NOTE: With slip ring bottomed against fan, the field lead wire should clear the access hole, fan and pole piece.

9. Tin field coil lead wires, then coil each lead wire around slip ring lug with first wrap against lug shoulder and winding outward. Solder leads with resin core solder.
10. Test slip rings for ground with a 110 volt test lamp by touching one test lead prod to rotor pole shoe and remaining prod to slip rings. The lamp

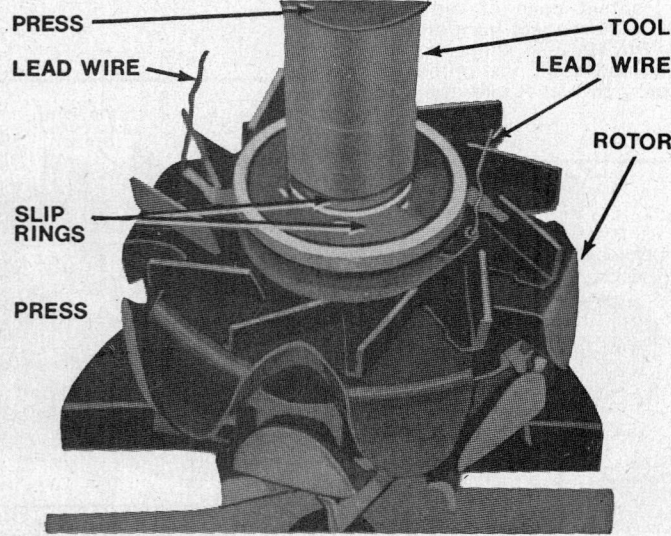

Fig. C33 Installing slip ring

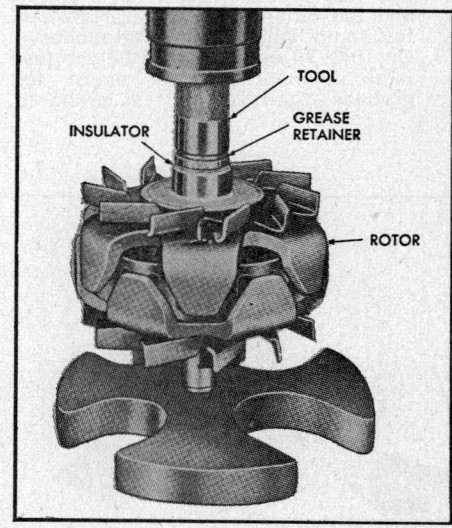

Fig. C34 Installing bearing grease retainer

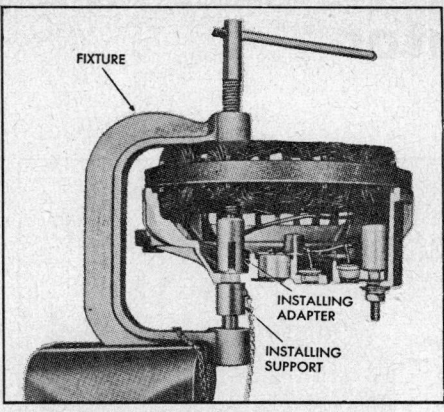

Fig. C35   Installing a diode, 1969-71 units

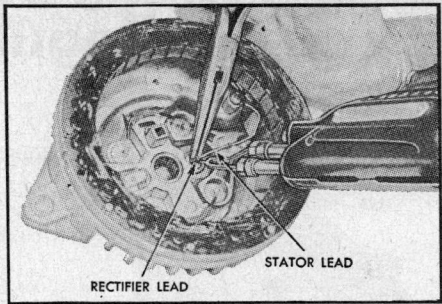

Fig. C36   Soldering diode and stator leads

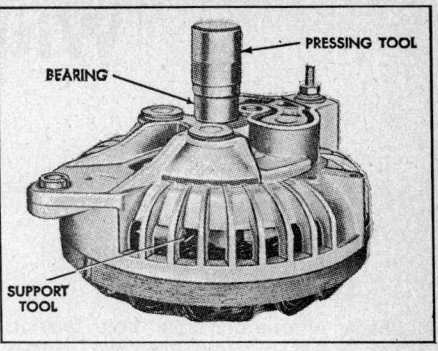

Fig. C37   Installing diode end shield bearing

should not light. If lamp lights, slip rings are shorted to ground, possibly due to a grounded insulated field lead when installing slip ring.

11. If rotor is not grounded, lightly clean slip ring surfaces with No. 00 sandpaper and assemble to alternator.
12. Position grease retainer gasket and retainer on rotor shaft and press retainer on shaft, Fig. C34. Retainer is properly positioned when inner bore of installer tool bottoms on rotor shaft.

Alternator Assemble

1. On 1969-71 units:
   a. Install diodes, Fig. C35.

   NOTE: Do not hammer diode in any manner since this will fracture the thin silicon wafer in the diode, causing complete diode failure.

   b. Clean leads and mate stator lead with diode wire loop, then bend loop snugly around stator lead to provide a good electrical and mechanical connection. Solder wires with resin core solder, holding diode lead wire with pliers just below joint, Fig. C31. Pliers will act as a heat sink and protect diode.

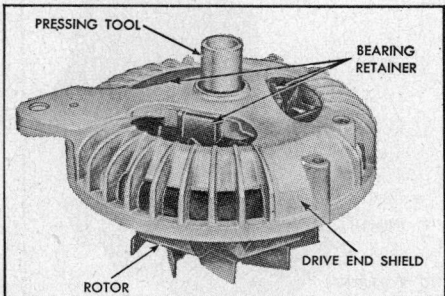

Fig. C38   Installing drive end shield and bearing

NOTE: After soldering, quickly cool soldered connection by touching a damp cloth against it. Also, this will aid in forming a solid joint.

   c. Push stator leads into slots in end shield and cement them to protect leads against possible interference with rotor fan (Cement is Mopar part No. 2299314). Test each diode to ensure proper installation.
2. On all units, install diode end shield bearing, Fig. C37.
3. Install drive end bearing in end shield with bearing retainer plate to hold bearing in position. Place assembly on rotor shaft and press into position, Fig. C38.
4. Press pulley onto rotor shaft until it contacts inner race of bearing, Fig. C39.

NOTE: Do not exceed 6800 lbs.

5. On 1969-71 units:
   a. Ensure heat sink insulator is properly positioned, then install capacitor stud through heat sink and end shield.
   b. Install insulating washers, lockwashers and lock nuts.
   c. Ensure heat sink and insulator are properly positioned, then tighten lock nut.
6. On 1972-74 units:
   a. Install output terminal stud and insulator through end shield. Then place positive heat sink assembly over studs, guiding rectifier straps over studs.
   b. Place capacitor terminal over capacitor end stud and install capacitor shoulder insulator. Ground the capacitor bracket to end shield with a metal screw. Install and tighten positive heat sink lockwashers and nuts.
   c. Slide negative rectifier and heat sink assembly into place, position straps on terminal block studs, then install and tighten attaching screws.
7. Position stator on diode end shield.

8. Position rotor end shield on stator and diode end shield.
9. Align through bolt holes in stator, diode end shield and drive end shield.
10. Compress stator and both end shields by hand and install through bolts, washers and nuts.
11. On 1969 units, install insulated (field) brush in diode end shield. Place bronze terminal on plastic holder with tab of terminal in recess of holder. Then place nylon washer on bronze terminal and install lockwasher and attaching screws.
12. On 1970-74 units, install field brushes into vertical and horizontal holders. Place an insulating washer on each field brush terminal and install lockwashers and attaching screws.

NOTE: Ensure brushes are not grounded.

13. Rotate pulley slowly by hand to be sure rotor fans do not touch diodes, capacitor lead and stator connections.
14. Install alternator and adjust drive belt.
15. Connect leads to alternator.
16. Connect battery ground cable.
17. Start and operate engine and observe alternator operation.
18. If necessary, test current output and regulator voltage setting.

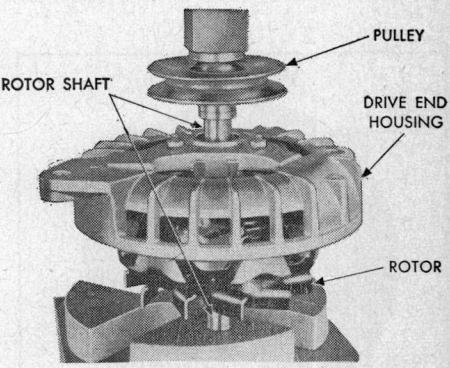

Fig. C39   Installing pulley

Delco-Remy "Delcotron" Alternator With External Regulator

TESTING SYSTEM IN VEHICLE

System Condition Test

1. Check alternator drive belt tension and adjust if necessary. Also, check charging system for proper electrical connections.
2. Connect a voltmeter between junction block relay and the ground at regulator base.

   NOTE: Ensure that voltmeter clip does not contact a resistor or the terminal extension under regulator.

3. On models equipped with an indicator lamp, turn ignition switch to the "ON" position. Lamp should light. If not, check condition of bulb and wiring.
4. On models equipped with an ammeter, turn ignition switch to the "ACC" position with any one accessory turned on, such as the blower motor or radio. Ammeter should indicate a discharge condition. If not, check ammeter circuit.
5. On all models, start engine and observe indicator lamp or ammeter. The indicator lamp should go out or ammeter should move toward charge. If not, check respective circuit.
6. Turn headlamps to high beam and blower motor to high speed and set engine at 1500 RPM. If voltage is 12½ volts or more, proceed to next step. If voltage is less than 12½ volts, perform "Alternator Output Test" to follow. If output test is satisfactory, remove regulator cover and turn voltage adjusting screw to raise voltage to 12½ volts, Fig. D5. If 12½ volts cannot be obtained, replace regulator.
7. Connect a ¼ ohm, 25 watt resistor into charging circuit, Fig. D6.
8. Run engine at 1500 RPM or above for

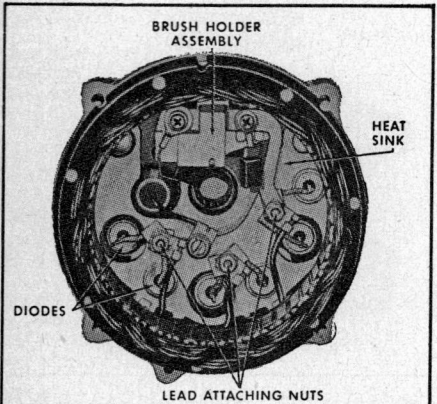

Fig. D2 Alternator internal lead connections, 1969-71

approximately 15 minutes. Cycle the regulator voltage control by disconnecting and reconnecting regulator connector. Note voltage.
9. If voltage reading is between 13.5 and 15.2 volts, regulator is satisfactory.
10. If voltage is not within above limits, remove regulator cover and adjust voltage to 14.2-14.6 volts. Replace regulator cover and run engine for approximately 10 minutes to obtain regulator internal operating temperature. Cycle the regulator and note voltage which should be between 13.5 and 15.2 volts. If not, replace regulator.

Alternator Output Test

1. Disconnect battery ground cable.
2. Connect an ammeter between alternator battery terminal and battery wire and a voltmeter between alternator battery terminal and a proper ground on the alternator, Fig. D7.
3. Disconnect the "F-R" terminal connector and connect a jumper wire between the "F" and alternator battery terminals, Fig. D7.
4. Reconnect the battery ground cable and connect a carbon pile rheostat across the battery terminals.
5. Start engine and slowly bring speed to 1500 RPM with carbon pile adjusted to hold 14 volts. Observe ammeter which should indicate alternator rated amperage. If not, service alternator.

Field Relay Test & Adjustment

1. Connect a voltmeter between regulator No. 2 terminal and the ground, Fig. D8.
2. Run engine at fast idle RPM and note voltage.
3. If zero voltage is indicated at regulator, check circuit between regulator No. 2 terminal and the alternator "R" terminal.

4. If closing voltage exceeds specifications as found in "Alternator & Regulator Specifications" in individual car chapters, adjust as follows:
   a. Connect a voltmeter and a 50 ohm variable resistor into circuit, Fig. D9.
   b. Turn resistor to "Open" position with ignition switch in the "Off" position.
   c. Adjust closing voltage by bending heel iron, Fig. D10.

Tailoring Voltage Regulator

It is important to remember that the voltage setting for one type of operating condition may not be satisfactory for a different type of operating condition. Vehicle under-hood temperatures, operating speeds, and night-time service all are factors which help determine the proper voltage setting. The proper setting is attained when the battery re-

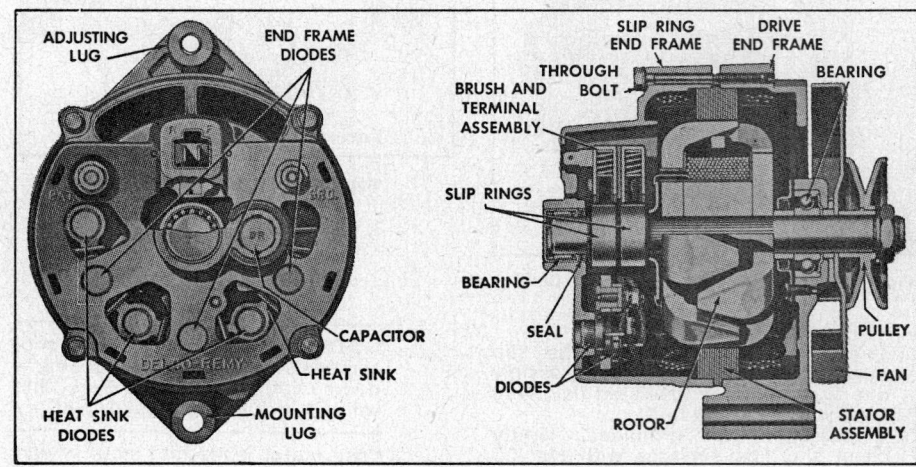

Fig. D1 Sectional end and side views of "Delcotron" alternator (typical)

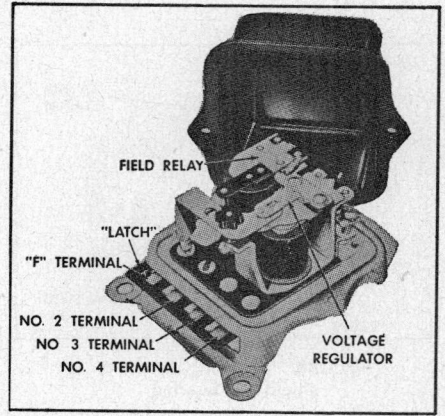

Fig. D3 Voltage regulator. The field relay is used only on vehicles having a charge indicator light instead of an ammeter

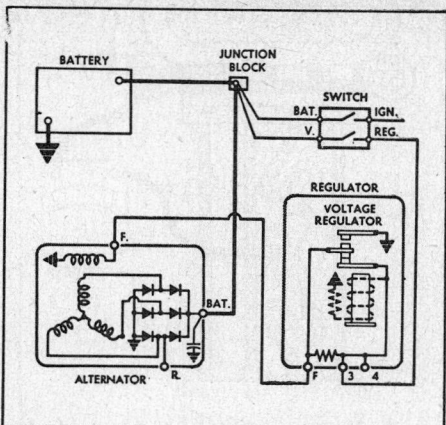

Fig. D4   Wiring diagram of the alternator charging circuit

mains fully charged with a minimum use of water.

If no circuit defects are found, yet the battery remains undercharged, raise the setting by .3 volt, and then check for an improved battery condition over a service period of reasonable length. If the battery remains overcharged, lower the setting by .3 volt, and then check for an improved battery condition. However, never adjust the voltage setting out of the limits specified in car chapters.

ALTERNATOR SERVICE

Alternator Removal

1. Disconnect battery negative cable.
2. Remove two leads at alternator.
3. Loosen adjusting bolts and remove drive belt.
4. Remove alternator retaining bolts and take off alternator.

Alternator Disassembly

1. Remove through bolts and loosen end frames by prying at bolt hole locations.

2. Scribe a reference mark across end frames to aid reassembly. Then, separate slip-ring end frame and stator assembly from drive end frame and rotor assembly.

NOTE: Brushes may drop onto rotor shaft when separating end frames, becoming contaminated with bearing lubricant. Clean brushes prior to installation.

3. Place a piece of tape over slip-ring end frame bearing to prevent entry of foreign material. Also, place tape on rotor shaft at slip-ring end.
4. Remove stator lead attaching nut and separate stator from end frame.
5. On 1972 units:
   a. Remove brush holder and terminal assemblies. Note that one of the three brush holder retaining screws is insulated.
   b. Remove rectifier bridge attaching screw, "Bat" terminal nut, capacitor lead and rectifier bridge from end frame.
   c. Remove capacitor from end frame.
6. On 1969-71 units:
   a. Remove screws, brushes and holder assembly.
   b. Remove "Bat" and "Grd" terminals, heat sink attaching screw and heat sink from end frame.
7. On all models, remove pulley retaining nut, slide washer, pulley and fan from rotor shaft.

NOTE: Use a ⁵⁄₁₆-inch Allen wrench inserted into shaft to hold shaft stationary while removing retaining nut.

8. Remove rotor, spacers, drive end bearing retainer plate and bearing from end frame.

Rotor Checks

1. To check for grounds, connect a 110 volt test lamp for either slip ring to the rotor shaft, Fig. D11. If the lamp lights the field winding is grounded.

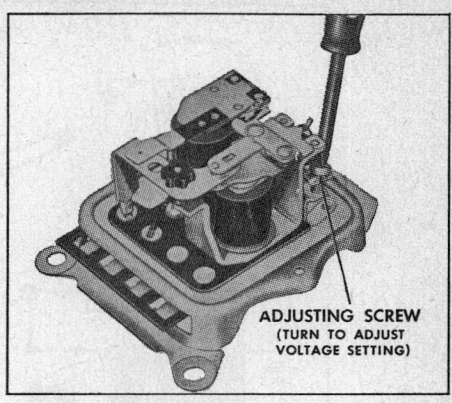

Fig. D5   Adjusting voltage regulator setting

2. To check for opens, connect the test lamp to each slip ring. If the lamp fails to light the winding is open.
3. To check for short circuits, connect a battery and ammeter in series with the two slip rings. The ammeter should indicate field current as specified in the Alternator and Regulator Specifications found in the car chapters.
4. An ammeter reading above the values given indicates shorted windings, and the rotor assembly should be replaced.

Stator Checks

1. To check the stator windings, remove all three stator lead attaching nuts and separate the stator from the end frame.
2. The stator winding may be checked with a 110 volt test lamp. If the lamp lights when connected from any stator lead to the frame, the windings are grounded. If the lamp fails to light when successively connected between each pair of stator leads, the windings are open, Fig. D12.
3. A short circuit in the stator windings is difficult to locate without laboratory test equipment due to the low resistance of the windings. However, if all other electrical checks are normal and the alternator fails to supply rated output, shorted stator windings are indicated.

Rectifier Bridge Check

Caution: Do not use a high voltage for this check, such as 110 volt test lamp.

1. Connect an ohmmeter to the grounded heat sink and one of the terminals. Then, reverse the probes, Fig. D13.
2. If readings in both directions are the same, replace the rectifier bridge assembly following procedure under "Alternator Disassembly", since diodes are not replaced individually.
3. Repeat check between grounded heat sink and other two terminals and between insulated heat sink and the three terminals.

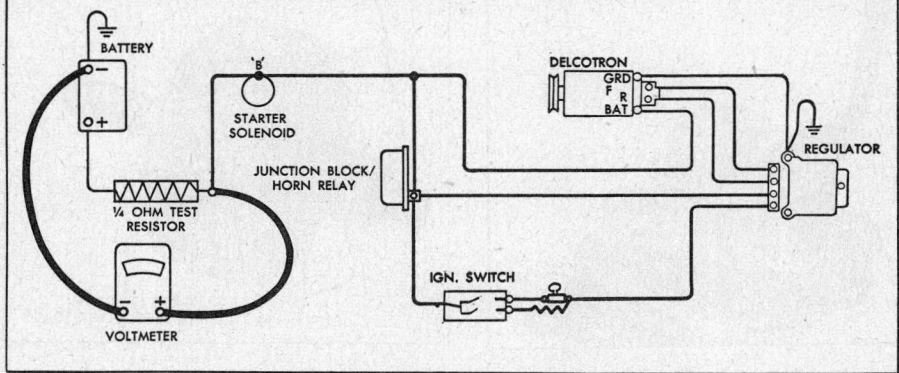

Fig. D6   Voltage setting test connections

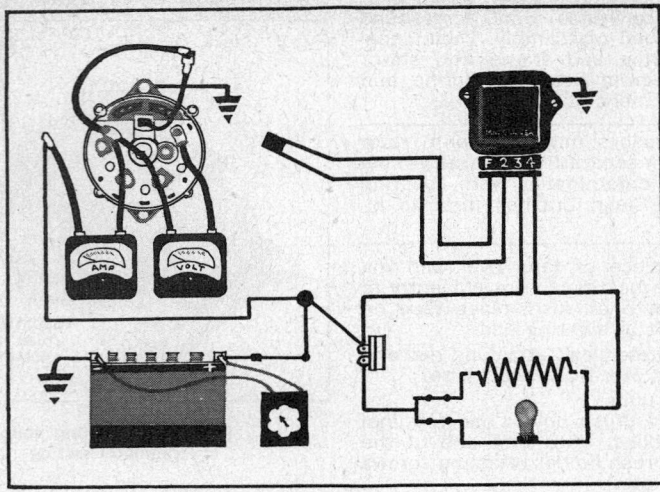

Fig. D7   Alternator output test connections

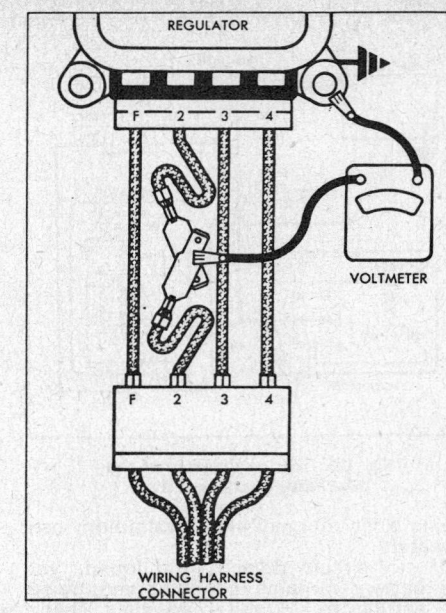

Fig. D8   Field relay test connections

1969-71 Diode Checks

1. Each diode should be checked electrically for a shorted or open condition using a test *lamp of not more than 12 volts*, Fig. D14.
2. With the stator disconnected, connect the test lamp leads across each diode, first in one direction and then in the other.
3. If the lamp lights in both checks, or fails to light in both checks, the diode is defective.
4. When checking a good diode, the lamp will light in only one of the two directions.

1969-71 Diode Replacement

1. To remove a diode, place slip ring

end frame in a vise with the remover equipment mounted as shown in Fig. D15. Tighten the vise to remove the defective diode.
2. To install a diode, place the new diode in the installer, Fig. D16. With the tools installed in the vise as shown, tighten the vise to install the new diode.

CAUTION: *Never attempt to remove or install a diode by striking it as the shock may damage the other diodes.*

Slip Ring Service

If the slip rings are dirty they may be cleaned with No. 400 silicon carbide paper and finish polished with crocus cloth. Spin the rotor in a lathe, or otherwise spin the rotor, and hold the polishing cloth against the slip rings until they are clean.

CAUTION: The rotor must be rotated in

order that the slip rings will be cleaned evenly. Cleaning the slip rings by hand without spinning the rotor may result in flat spots on the slip rings, causing brush noise.

Slip rings that are rough or out-of-round should be trued in a lathe to .002" maximum runout as indicated on a dial gauge. Remove only enough material to make the rings smooth and round. Finish polish with crocus cloth and blow away all dust.

Bearing Replacement

1. The bearing in the drive end frame can be removed by detaching the retainer plate screws and then pres-

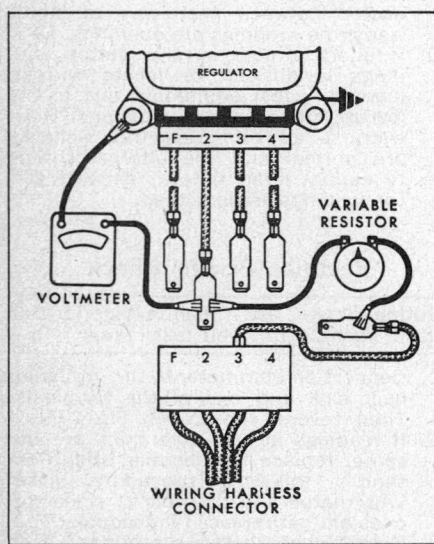

Fig. D9   Field relay closing voltage
test connections

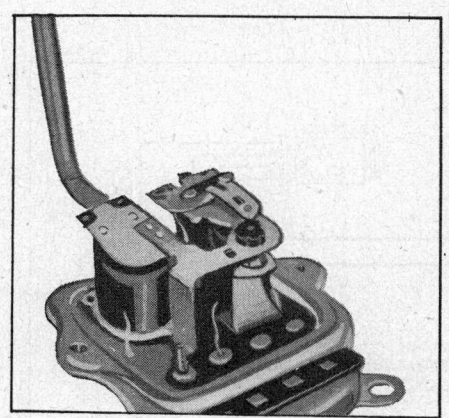

Fig. D10   Adjusting field relay
closing voltage

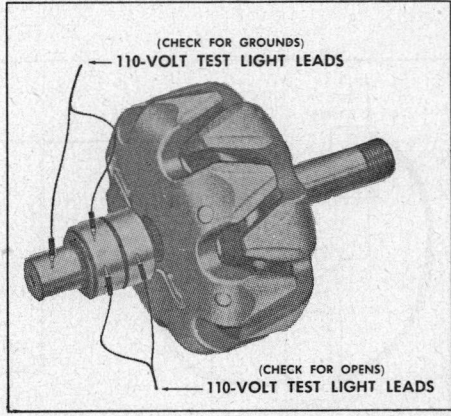

Fig. D11   Checking rotor for
opens or grounds

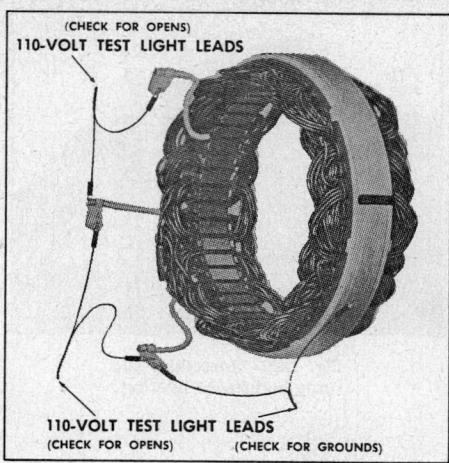

Fig. D12 Checking stator for opens or grounds

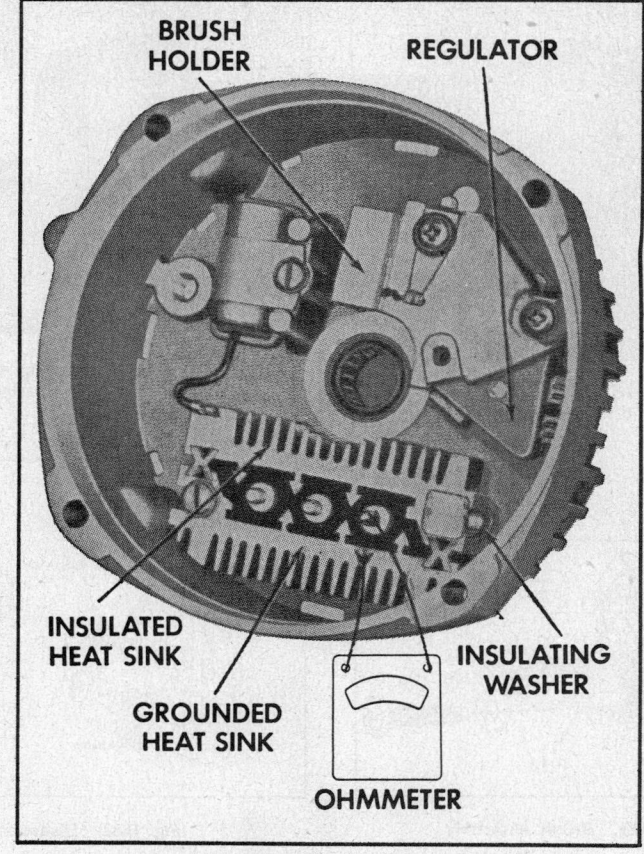

Fig. D13 Rectifier bridge check

Fig. D14 Checking diodes for opens or shorts, 1969-71

sing the bearing from the end frame as shown in Fig. D17.

2. Press in new bearing with a tube or collar that just fits the outer race, Fig. D18. Install a new retainer plate if the felt seal in the existing plate is hardened or worn.

3. The bearing in the slip ring end frame can be removed by pressing with a tube or collar that just fits inside the end frame housing. Press from the outside of the housing towards the inside as shown in Fig. D19.

4. To install the new bearing, place a flat plate over the bearing and press in from the outside towards the inside of the frame until the bearing is flush with the outside of the end frame. Support the inside of the frame with the pipe shown to prevent breakage of the end frame, Fig. D20.

5. Saturate the felt seal with S.A.E. 20 oil and reassemble the felt seal and steel retainer.

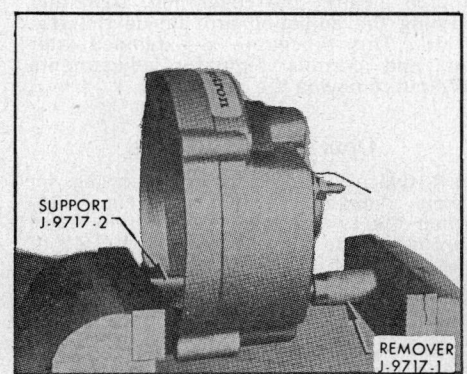

Fig. D15 Removing a diode, 1969-71

Fig. D16 Installing a diode, 1969-71

Fig. D17 Removing drive end frame bearing

DELCOTRON with External Regulator

Fig. D18   Installing drive end frame bearing

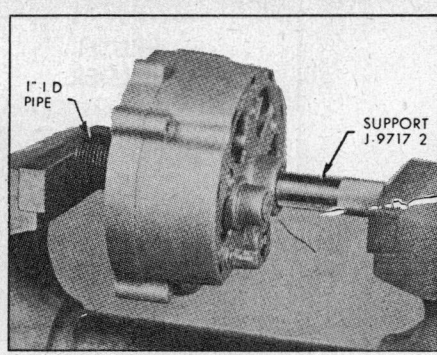

Fig. D19   Removing slip ring end frame bearing

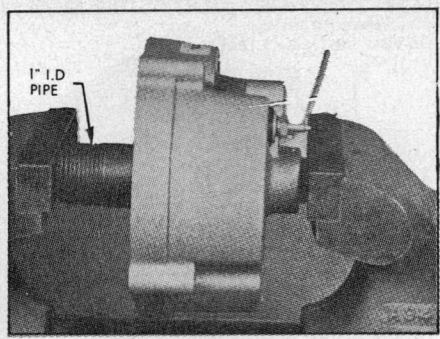

Fig. D20   Installing slip ring end frame bearing

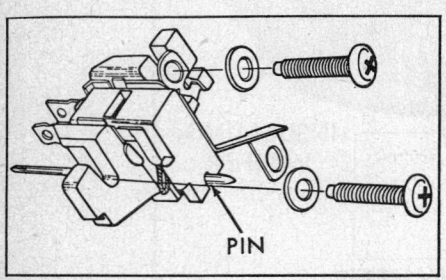

Fig. D21   Brush assembly

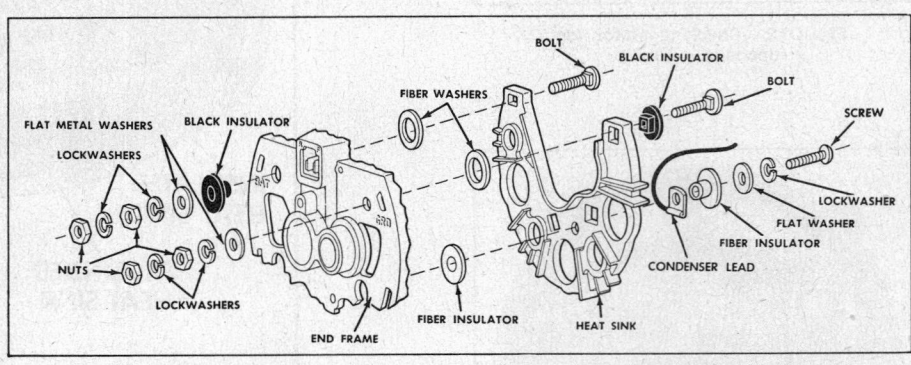

Fig. D22   Disassembled view of heat sink and related parts, 1969-71

Brush Replacement

1. When the slip ring end frame assembly is separated from the rotor and drive end frame, the brushes will fall down onto the shaft and come in contact with the lubricant. If the brushes are to be re-used, they must be thoroughly cleaned with a soft dry cloth immediately. Also, the shaft must be thoroughly cleaned before reassembly.
2. Inspect the brush springs for damage or corrosion. If there is any doubt as to the condition of the springs, they should be replaced.
3. To install new brushes, remove the brush holder assembly from the end frame by detaching the two screws.
4. Install the springs and brushes into the brush holder, and insert a straight wire or pin into the holes at the bottom of the holder to retain the brushes, Fig. D21.
5. Attach the brush holder assembly to the end frame, noting carefully the proper stack-up of the parts as shown. Allow the straight wire to protrude through the hole in the end frame.

1969-71 Heat Sink Replacement

1. Remove the "BAT" and "GRD" terminals from the end frame and the screw attaching the condenser lead to the heat sink.

2. During reassembly, note carefully the proper stack-up of parts as shown in Fig. D22.

Alternator Reassembly

1. Reassembly is the reverse of disassembly. Refer to Fig. D2 for connection of internal leads.
2. When installing the pulley, secure the rotor in a vise only tight enough to permit tightening the shaft nut to a torque of 40-50 ft. lbs. If excessive pressure is applied to the rotor, the assembly may become distorted.
3. To install the slip ring end frame to the rotor and drive end frame, remove the tape over the bearing and shaft (if used for protection) upon disassembly, and make sure the shaft is perfectly clean.
4. Insert a straight wire as previously mentioned through the holes in the brush holder and end frame to retain the brushes in the holder. Then withdraw the wire after the alternator has been completely assembled. The brushes will then drop onto the slip rings.

TRANSISTOR REGULATOR

The transistor regulator, Fig. D23, is an assembly composed principally of transistors, diodes, resistors, a capacitor, and a thermistor to form a completely static unit containing no moving parts.

The transistor is an electrical devise which limits the alternator voltage to a preset value by controlling the alternator field current. The diodes, capacitor and resistors act together to aid the transistor in controlling the voltage, which is the only function that the regulator performs in the charging circuit. The thermistor provides a temperature-compensated voltage setting.

The voltage at which the alternator operates is determined by the regulator adjustment. The regulator voltage setting can be adjusted externally by removing a pipe plug in the cover, Fig. D23, and turning the adjusting arm inside the regulator. This procedure is explained later on, and permits regulator adjustments without removing the cover.

Operating Principles

A typical wiring diagram showing internal circuits is shown in Fig. D24. When the switch is closed, current flows through diode D1 and transistor TR1 in the regulator to the alternator "F" terminal, and then through the alternator field winding to ground.

When alternator voltage reaches a preset value, the other components of the regulator cause transistor TR1 alternately to "turn-off" and "turn-on" the alternator field current. The regulator thus

2-84

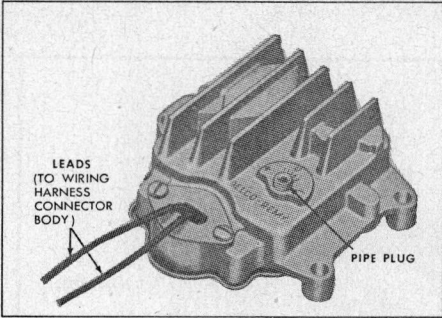

Fig. D23 Transistor regulator

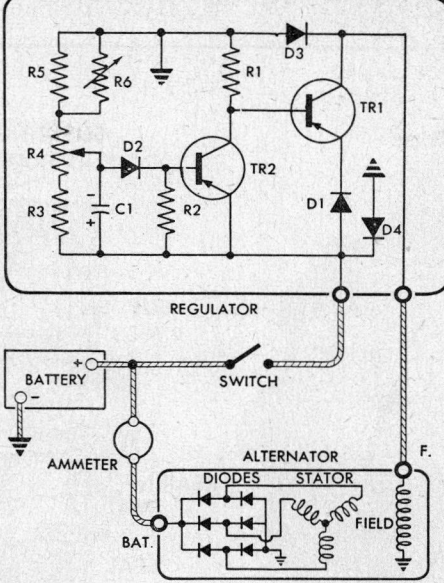

Fig. D24 Wiring diagram of transistor regulator in charging circuit

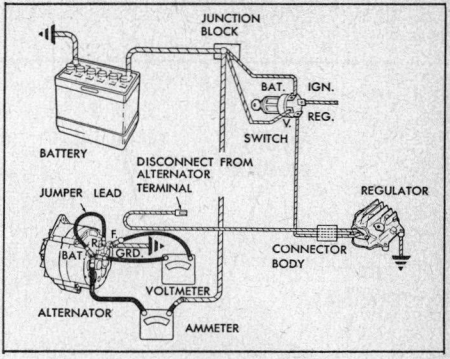

Fig. D25 Checking charging circuit for undercharged battery condition

operates automatically to limit the alternator voltage to a preset value.

Checking Circuit

1. Connect test ammeter and voltmeter in circuit as shown in Fig. D25, and connect a jumper wire from alternator "F" terminal to alternator "BAT" terminal.
2. Operate alternator at specified speed, turn on accessories as required to obtain specified voltage and observe output.
3. If current output is low, remove and check the alternator as outlined previously.
4. If the alternator failure was caused by a defective stator or diodes, the repaired alternator may be installed back on the vehicle and no further checks are needed.
5. If the alternator failure was caused by a defective field winding, the repaired alternator may be installed back on the vehicle and the following checks must be made to locate possible damage to regulator.
6. Referring to Fig. D25, remove jum-

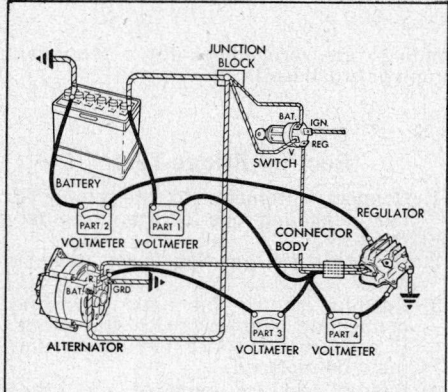

Fig. D26 Checking charging circuit for overcharged battery condition

per lead and reconnect wiring harness connector to alternator "F" terminal.

7. Turn on ignition switch but do not start engine.
8. Connect voltmeter positive lead to battery positive terminal and negative lead into regulator black lead connector body to make connection to regulator (Part 1, Fig. D26). Record voltage drop.
9. Connect voltmeter to negative terminal of battery and ground on regulator (Part 2, Fig. D26). Record voltage drop.
10. If addition of voltage readings is greater than .3 volt, check ignition switch for poor contacts and system wiring for high resistance. If voltage difference is less than .3 volt, proceed as follows, referring to Part 3, Fig. D26.
11. Connect voltmeter positive lead to regulator positive terminal and voltmeter negative lead to alternator "F" terminal. Slide voltmeter positive lead into regulator connector body (black lead terminal) to make connection. Record voltage.
12. If the voltage is .9 volt or less, replace regulator, as transistor is shorted. If voltage is 2.0 volts or greater, replace regulator as transistor is open. If voltage is between .9 and 2.0 volts, proceed as follows:
13. Operate engine at approximately 1500 rpm for 10 minutes with low beam headlights on. Referring to Part 4, Fig. D26, with engine running at 1500 rpm, record voltage reading from regulator positive ter-

minal to ground by sliding voltmeter lead into regulator connector body black lead terminal to make connection.

14. Compare with Fig. D27. Ambient temperature is temperature of air measured $\frac{1}{4}$" from regulator cover.
15. If voltage reading is within specifications, charging system is satisfactory but voltage setting may need to be changed to a different value to meet the requirements of driving conditions.
16. To do this, remove the pipe plug on regulator and insert a small screwdriver in adjustment slot. Turn counterclockwise for an undercharged battery one or two notches to increase setting.
17. For an overcharged battery, as evidenced by excessive water usage, turn clockwise one or two notches to decrease setting. For each notch moved, voltage setting will change by approximately .3 volt. Then check for an improved battery condition over a service period of reasonable length.
18. If voltage is not within specifications, check to see if the adjustment arm is in the center position. If the voltage reads out of specifications in the center position, replace the regulator.

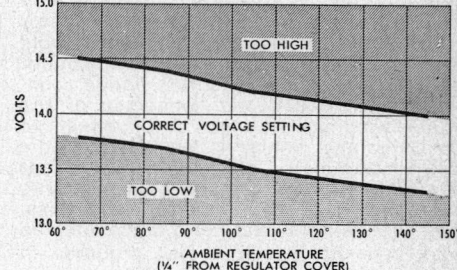

Fig. D27 Temperature correction chart

Delcotron Type SI Integral Charging System

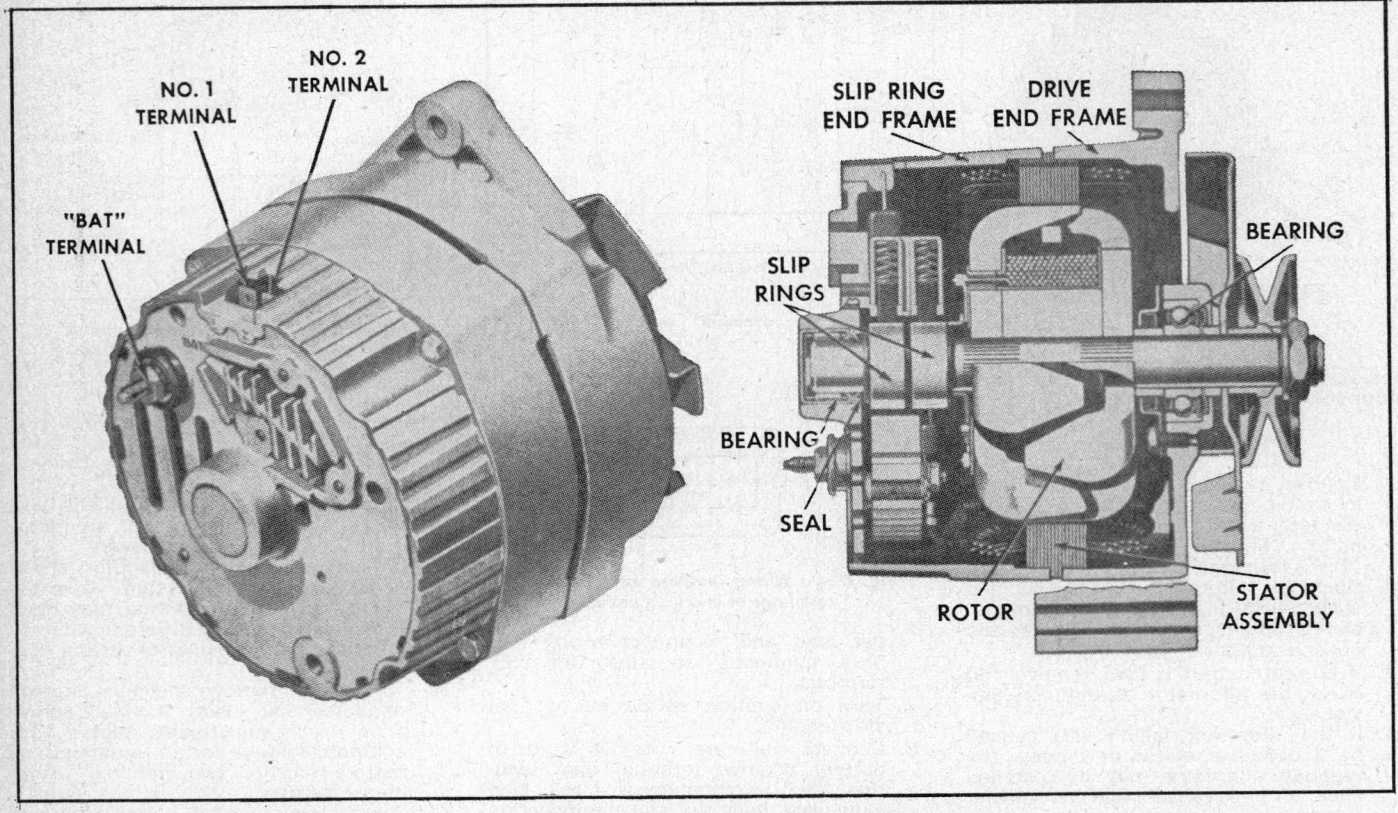

Fig. 1   Delcotron Type SI Integral Charging System

DESCRIPTION

This unit, Fig. 1, features a solid state regulator mounted inside the alternator slip ring end frame, Fig. 2, along with the brush holder assembly. All regulator components are enclosed in a solid mold with no need or provision for adjustment of the regulator. A rectifier bridge, containing six diodes and connected to the stator windings, changes A.C. voltage to D. C. voltage which is available at the output terminal. Generator field current is supplied through a diode trio which is also connected to the stator windings. The diodes and rectifiers are protected by a capacitor which is also mounted in the end frame.

No maintenance or adjustments of any kind are required on this unit.

SYSTEM TESTS

Alternator

The procedures for testing the al-ternator proper are similar to the standard Delcotron.

Diode Trio

1. With diode unit removed, connect an ohmmeter to the single connector and to one of the three connectors.
2. Observe the reading. Reverse ohmmeter leads.
3. Reading should be high with one connection and low with the other. If both readings are the same, unit must be replaced.
4. Repeat between the single connector and each of the three connectors.

NOTE: There are two diode units differing in appearance. These are completely interchangeable.

The diode unit can be checked for a grounded brush lead while still installed in the end frame by connecting an ohmmeter from the brush lead clip to the end frame as in Steps 1 and 2 above. If both readings are zero, check for a grounded brush or brush lead.

Rectifer Bridge Test

1. Connect ohmmeter to the grounded heat sink and one of the three terminals.
2. Observe the reading then reverse leads.
3. Reading should be high with one connection and low with the other. If both readings are the same, unit must be replaced.
4. Repeat test for each of the other terminals.

Voltage Regulator/Brush Lead Test

Connect an ohmmeter from the brush lead clip to the end frame, note reading, then reverse connections. If both readings are zero, either the brush lead clip is grounded or the regulator is defective.

Fig. 2 Slip ring end frame. SI Delcotron

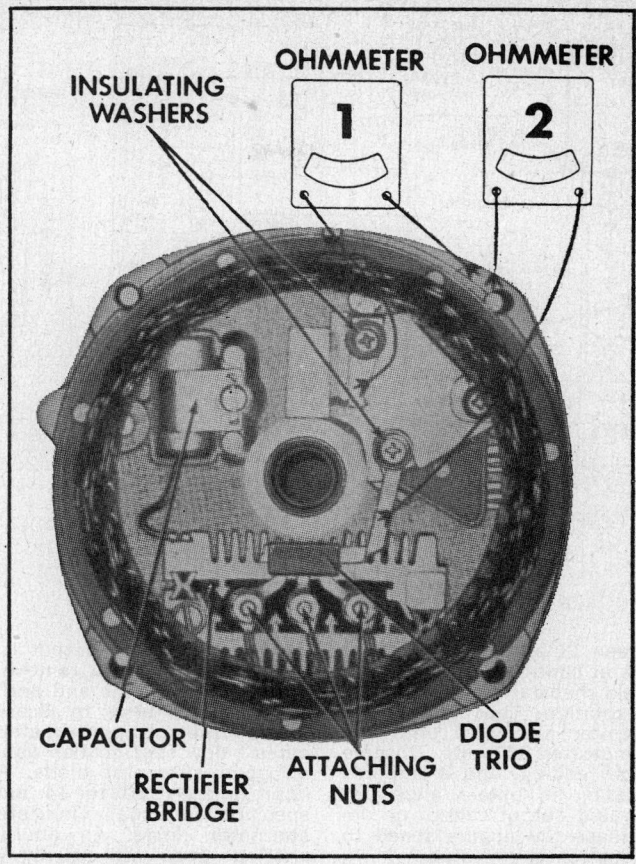

INSULATING WASHERS

OHMMETER 1

OHMMETER 2

CAPACITOR

RECTIFIER BRIDGE

ATTACHING NUTS

DIODE TRIO

Ford Autolite/Motorcraft Alternator

CONTENTS

In Vehicle Tests 2-87
Bench Tests 2-90
Voltmeter Test 2-93
Regulator Test 2-92
Regulator Adjust 2-93
Alternator Repairs 2-95, 96, 100
Brush Replacement 2-99, 101
Cleaning & Inspection Procedures 2-102

GENERAL

A charge indicator lamp or ammeter can be used in charging system.

If a charge indicator lamp is used in the charging system, Figs. 1, 3, 6, the system operation is as follows: when the ignition switch is turned ON, a small electrical current flows through the lamp filament (turning the lamp on) and through the alternator regulator to the alternator field. When the engine is started, the alternator field rotates and produces a voltage in the stator winding. When the voltage at the alternator stator terminal reaches about 3 volts, the regulator field relay closes. This puts the same voltage potential on both sides of the charge indicator lamp causing it to go out. When the field relay has closed, current passes through the regula-

tor A terminal and is metered to the alternator field.

If an ammeter is used in the charging system, Figs. 2, 4, 5, the regulator I terminal and the alternator stator terminal are not used. When the ignition switch is turned ON, the field relay closes and electrical current passes through the regulator A terminal and is metered to the alternator field. When the engine is started, the alternator field rotates causing the alternator to operate.

NOTE: The ammeter indicates current flow into (charge) or out of (discharge) the vehicle battery.

SYSTEM TESTING

NOTE: The operations and on vehicle test procedures are same as for the side terminal alternator. However, the internal wiring, Figs. 3, 4, 5 and 6 and bench test procedures differ.

Alternator in Vehicle Tests
Alternator Output Test

When the alternator output test is con-

ducted off the car, a test bench must be used. Follow the procedure given by the test bench equipment manufacturer.

NOTE: When the alternator is removed from the vehicle for this purpose, always disconnect the battery ground cable as the alternator output connector is connected to the battery at all times.

Test Procedure

1. Make the connections and tester knob adjustments, Figs. 7 and 8 (Output Test). Be sure that the field rheostat knob is at the OFF position at the start of this test.

2. Close the battery adapter switch. Start the engine, then open the battery adapter switch.

3. Increase the engine speed to approximately 2000 rpm (use a tachometer following the manufacturers instructions). Turn off all lights and electrical accessories.

4. Turn the field rheostat clockwise until 15 volts is indicated on the voltmeter upper scale. Turn the master control clockwise until the voltmeter indi-

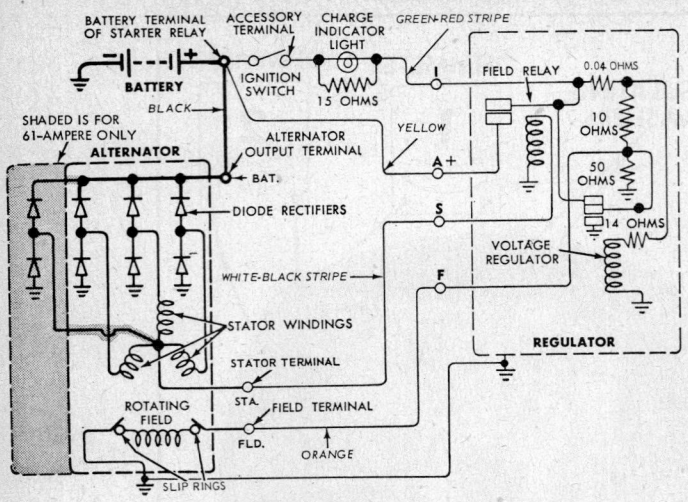

Fig. 1 Indicator light rear terminal alternator charging system

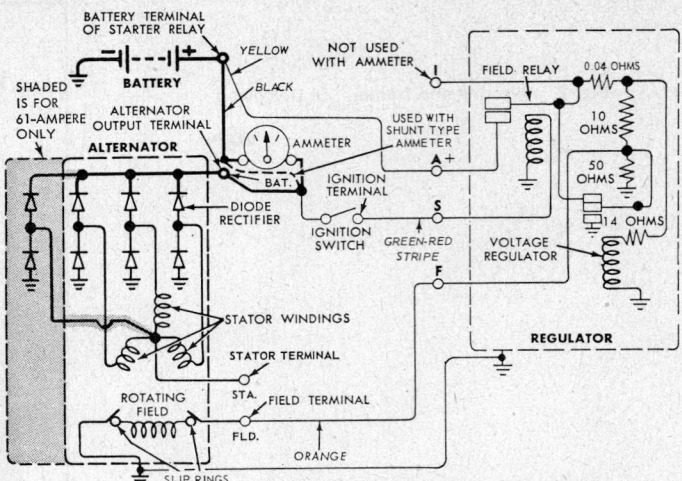

Fig. 2 Ammeter rear terminal alternator charging system

cates between 11 and 12 volts. Holding the master control in this position, turn the field rheostat clockwise to its maximum rotation. Turn the master control counter clockwise until the voltmeter indicates 15 volts. Observe the ammeter reading. Add 2 amperes to this reading to obtain alternator output. If rated output cannot be obtained, increase the engine speed to 2900 rpm and repeat this step.

5. Return the field rheostat knob to OFF, release the master control knob, and stop the engine. Disconnect the test equipment, if no further tests are to be made.

If the alternator output is not O.K., it will be necessary to remove the alternator from the vehicle and perform the necessary bench tests to locate the defect.

An output of approximately 2 to 5 amperes below specification usually indicates an open alternator diode. An output of approximately 10 to 14 amperes below specification usually indicates a shorted alternator diode. An alternator with a shorted diode will usually whine, which will be most noticeable at idle speeds.

Stator Neutral Voltage Test

The alternator STA terminal is connect-

ed to the stator coil neutral or center point of the alternator windings, Figs. 1 thru 6. The voltage generated at this point is used to close the field relay in the charge indicator light system.

To test for the stator neutral voltage, disconnect the regulator connector plug from the regulator. Make the connections and tester knob adjustments, Fig. 9. Start the engine and run it at 1000 rpm (use a tachometer). Turn off all lights and accessories. Rotate the field rheostat clockwise until at least 6 volts is indicated on the voltmeter upper scale. If 6 volts or more is not obtained, remove the alternator and perform the diode and sta-

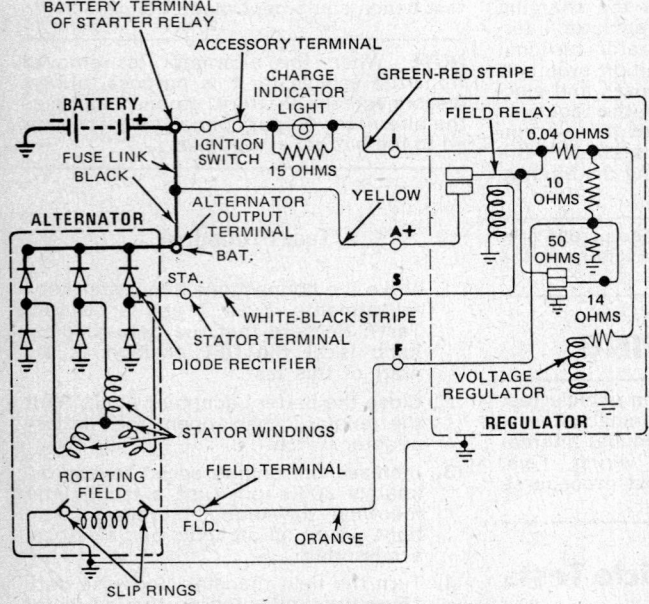

Fig. 3 Indicator light side terminal alternator charging system. 65 & 70 amp systems

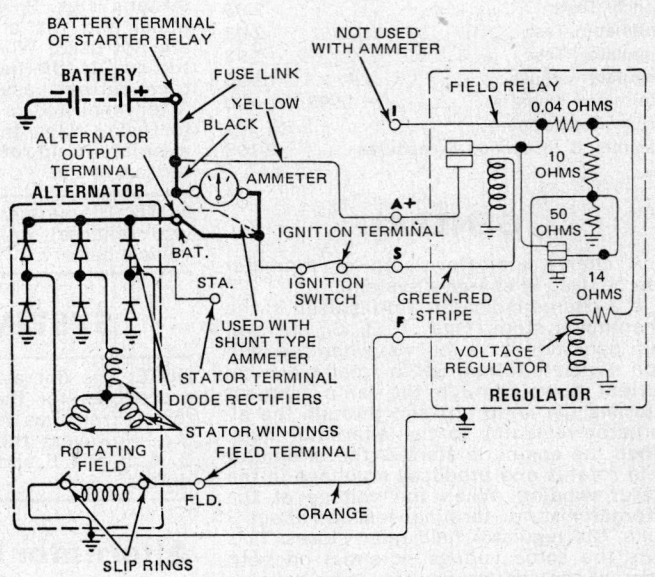

Fig. 4 Ammeter side terminal alternator charging system. 65 & 70 amp systems

FORD AUTOLITE/MOTORCRAFT ALTERNATOR

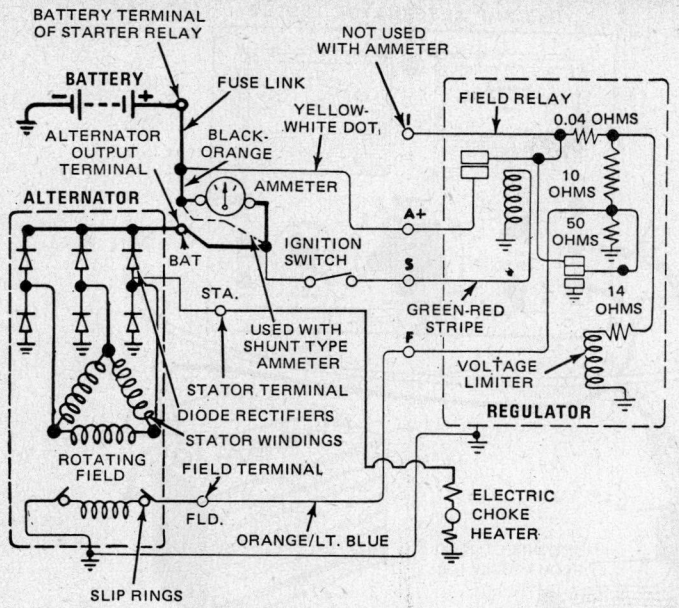

Fig. 5 Ammeter side terminal alternator. 90 amp system

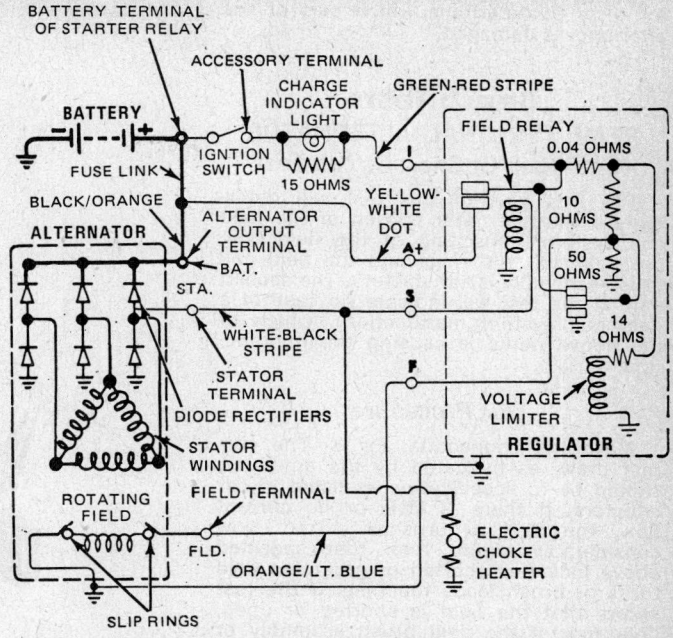

Fig. 6 Indicator light side terminal alternator. 90 amp system

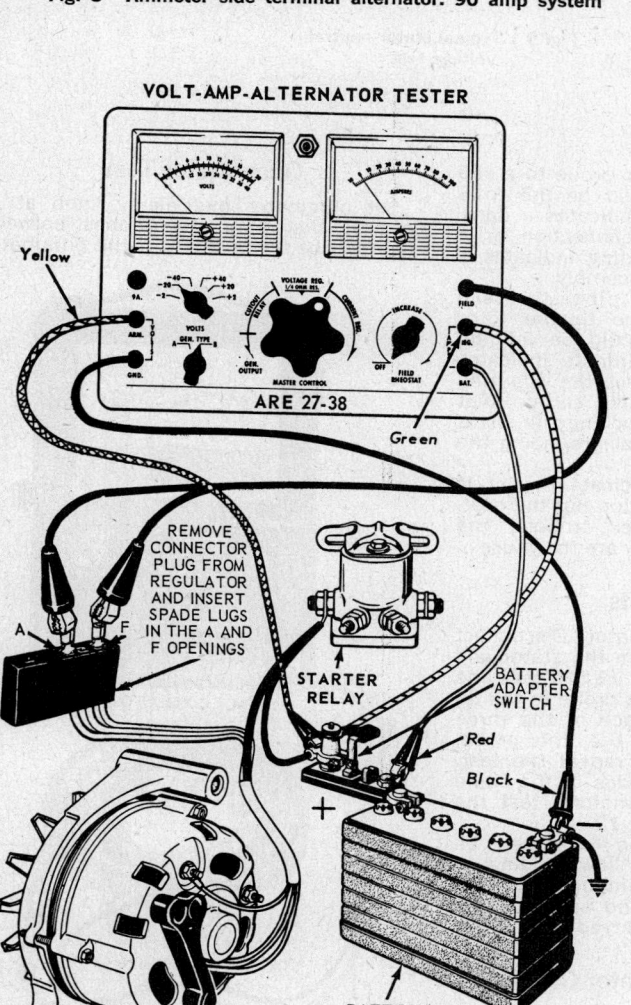

Fig. 7 Alternator output test

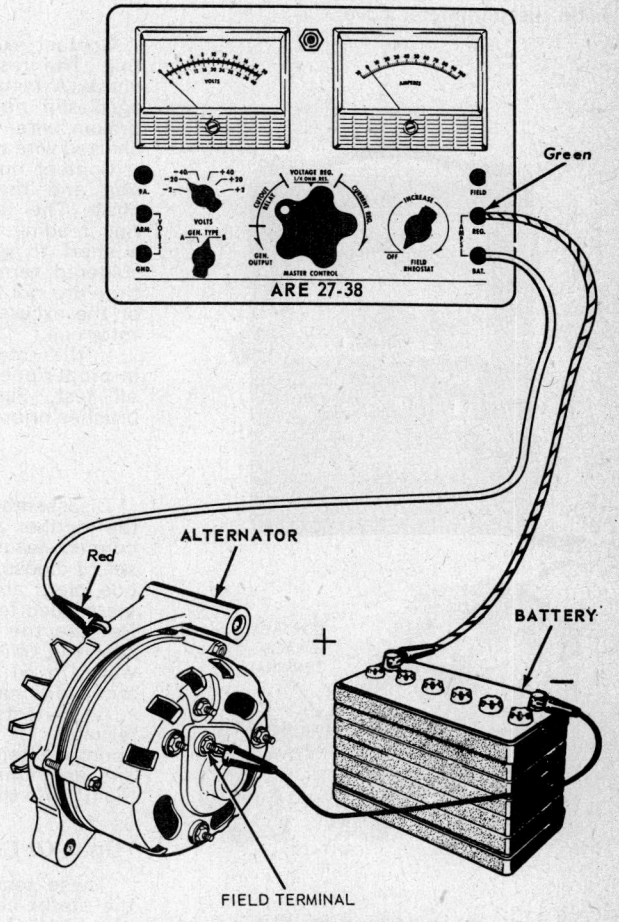

Fig. 8 Alternator field open or short circuit test

tor tests to determine which part of the alternator is damaged.

Bench Tests
REAR TERMINAL ALTERNATOR
Field Open Or Short Circuit Test

The first part of this test will determine if the alternator portion of the field coil system, consisting of the field coil, the field coil slip rings and the field coil brush assembly is satisfactory. The second part of the test will indicate (in case of a field coil system malfunction), which of the above items is causing the malfunction.

Test Procedure

Make the connection, Fig 8. The current draw, as indicated by the ammeter, should be to specification as listed in car chapters. If there is little or no current flow, the field or brushes current flow considerably higher than that specified above indicates shorted or grounded field turns or brush leads touching. If the test shows that the field is shorted or open, determine if the field brush assembly or slip rings are at fault.

Disassemble front housing and rotor from the rear housing and stator, check the resistance of the rotor with ohmmeter. Set the ohmmeter multiply-by knob at 1 and calibrate the ohmmeter as indicated inside the ohmmeter cover.

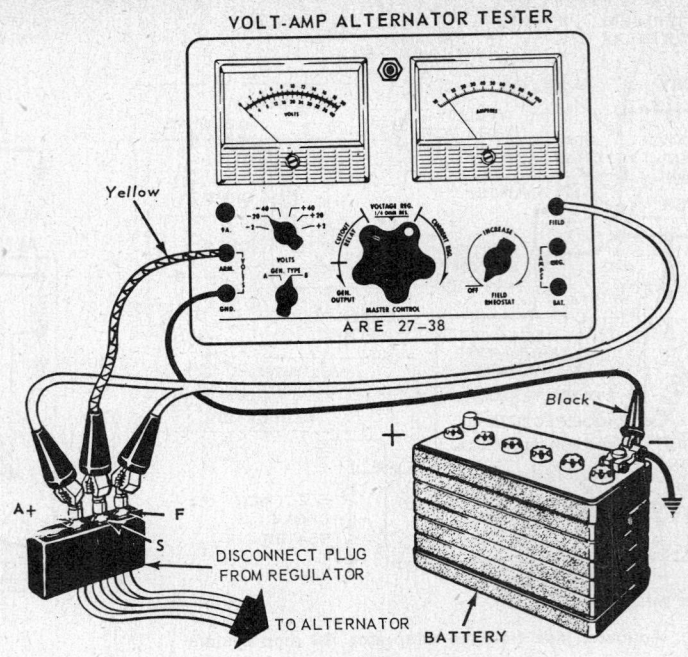

Fig. 9   Typical stator neutral voltage test

Contact each ohmmeter probe to a slip ring. The resistance should be 3.5 to 5 ohms. A higher reading indicates a damaged slip ring soldered connection or a broken wire. A lower reading indicates a shorted wire or slip ring assembly.

Contact one ohmmeter probe to a slip ring and the other probe to the rotor shaft. The resistance should be infinite. Any reading other than infinite indicates a short to ground. Inspect the slip ring soldered terminals to make certain that they are not bent and touching the shaft, or the excess solder is not grounding the rotor coil.

If the rotor checks indicate that it is in proper operating condition but the overall test, Fig. 8 indicates trouble, the brushes or brush assembly are the cause.

Diode Tests

Disassemble the alternator. Disconnect the rectifier assembly from the stator and connect leads, Fig. 10 or 11. To test one set of diodes, contact one probe to the diode plate and contact each of the three stator lead terminals with the other probe. Reverse the probes and repeat the test. Test the other set of diodes in the same way. On 61-ampere alternators, test the two additional diodes, Fig. 12.

All 6 tests (8 tests on 61-ampere alternator) should show a low reading of approximately 60 ohms in one direction and an infinite reading (no needle movement) with the probes reserved.

Open Or Grounded Stator Coil Tests

These tests are made to determine if the stator coil is operating properly. Disassemble the stator from the alternator and rectifier assembly.

Open Stator Test

Set ohmmeter multiple-by knob at 1. Connect the ohmmeter probes between each pair of stator leads. If the ohmmeter

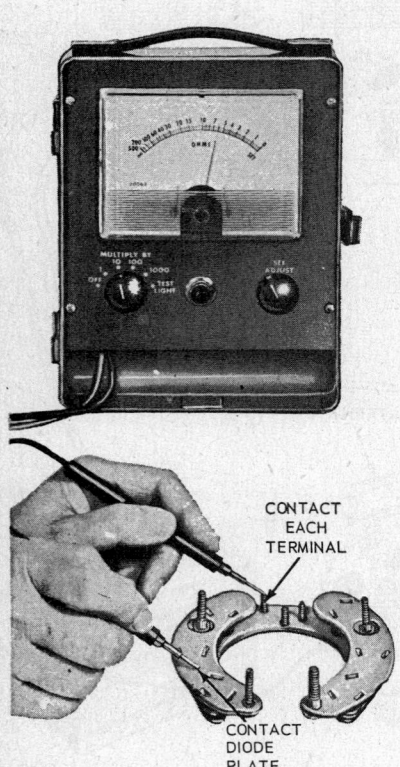

Fig. 10   Diode test. 38, 42 & 55 amp alternators

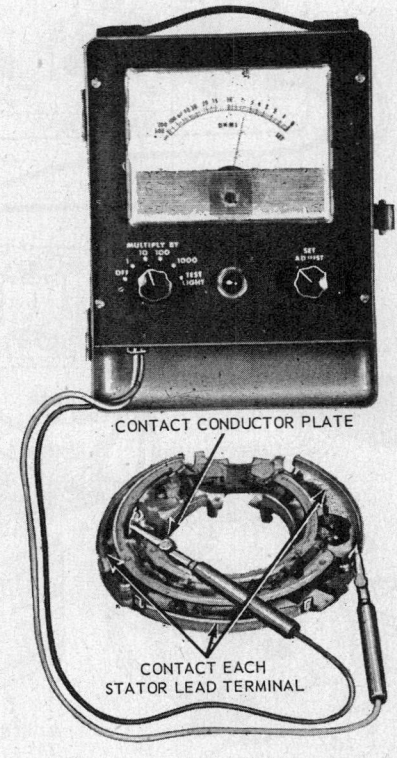

Fig. 11   Diode test. 65-amp rear terminal alternator

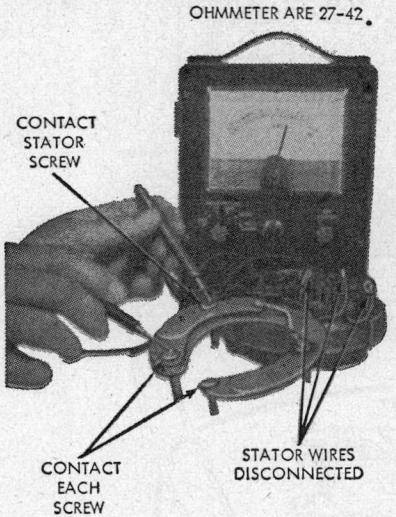

OHMMETER ARE 27-42

CONTACT STATOR SCREW

CONTACT EACH SCREW

STATOR WIRES DISCONNECTED

Fig. 12   Booster plate diode test. 61-amp alternator

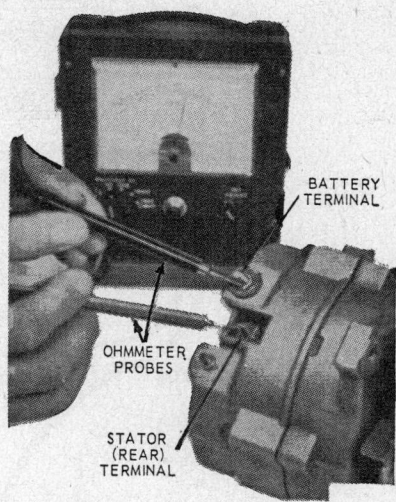

BATTERY TERMINAL

OHMMETER PROBES

STATOR (REAR) TERMINAL

Fig. 13   Rectifier short or grounded and stator grounded test

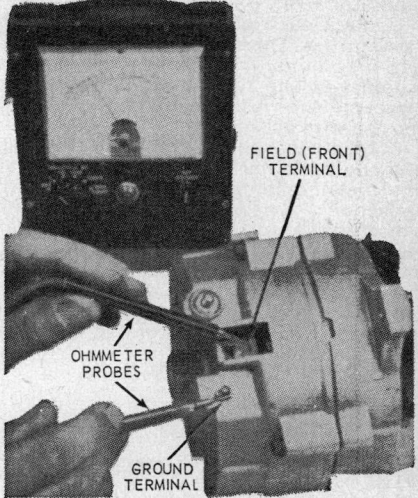

FIELD (FRONT) TERMINAL

OHMMETER PROBES

GROUND TERMINAL

Fig. 14   Field open or short circuit test

does not show equal readings between each pair of stator leads, the stator is open and must be replaced.

Grounded Stator Test

Connect the ohmmeter probes to one of the stator leads and to the stator laminated core. Be sure that the probe makes a good electrical connection with the stator core. The metal should show an infinite reading (no meter movement). If the meter does not indicate an infinite reading (needle moves), the stator winding is shorted to the core and must be replaced. Repeat this test for each of the stator leads.

SIDE TERMINAL ALTERNATOR
Rectifier Short or Grounded and Stator Grounded Test

Set ohmmeter Multiply By knob at 10, and calibrate meter.

Contact one ohmmeter probe to the alternator BAT terminal, Fig. 13, the other probe to the STA terminal (rear blade terminal). Then, reverse the ohmmeter probes and repeat the test. A reading of about 60 ohms should be obtained in one direction and no needle movement with the probes reversed. A reading in both directions indicates a bad positive diode, a grounded positive diode plate or a grounded BAT terminal.

Perform the same test using the STA and GND (ground) terminals of the alternator. A reading in both directions indicates either a bad negative diode, a grounded stator winding, a grounded stator terminal, a grounded positive diode plate, or a grounded BAT terminal.

Infinite readings (no needle movement) in all four probe positions in the preceeding tests indicates an open STA terminal lead connection inside the alternator.

Field Open or Short Circuit Test

Set the ohmmeter Multiply By knob at 1 and calibrate meter.

Contact the alternator field terminal with one probe and the ground terminal with the other probe, Fig. 14. Then, spin the alternator pulley. The ohmmeter reading should be between 4 and 200 ohms, and should fluctuate while the pulley is turning. An infinite reading (no meter movement) indicates an open brush lead, worn or stuck brushes, or a bad rotor assembly. An ohmmeter reading less than

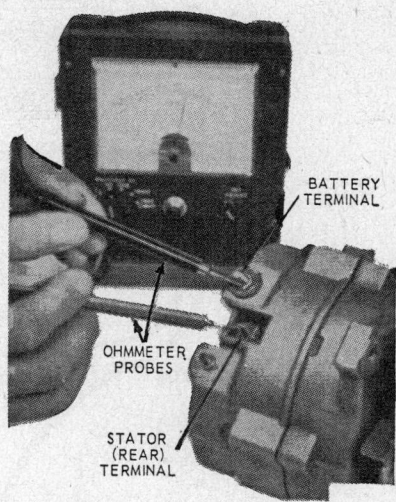

OHMMETER ARE 27-42

CONTACT EACH TERMINAL

CONTACT DIODE PLATE

CONTACT TERMINAL SCREW

Fig. 15   Side terminal alternator diode test

4 ohms indicates a grounded brush assembly, a grounded field terminal or a bad rotor.

Diode Test

Remove the rectifier assembly from the alternator. Set the ohmmeter Multiply By knob at 10 and calibrate meter.

To test one set of diodes-contact one probe to the terminal bolt, Fig. 15 and contact each of the three stator lead terminals with the other probe. Reverse the probes and repeat the test. All diodes should show a low reading of about 60 ohms in one direction, and an infinite reading (no needle movement) with the probes reversed. Repeat the preceding tests for the other set of diodes except that the other terminal screw is used.

If the meter readings are not as specified, replace the rectifier assembly.

Stator Coil Open or Grounded Test

Disassemble the stator from the alternator.

Set ohmmeter Multiply By knob at 1, and calibrate meter. Connect the ohmmeter probes between each pair of stator leads (3 different ways). The ohmmeter must show equal readings for each pair or stator leads. Replace the stator if the readings are not the same.

Set ohmmeter Multiply By Knob at 1000. Connect the ohmmeter probes to one of the stator leads and to the stator laminated core. Be sure that the probe makes a good electrical connection with the stator core. The meter should show an infinite reading (no meter movement). If the meter does not indicate an infinite reading (needle moves), the stator winding is shorted to the core and must be replaced. Repeat this test for each stator lead.

Rotor Open or Short Circuit Test

Disassemble the front housing and rotor from the rear housing and stator. Set the ohmmeter. Multiply By knob at 1 and calibrate meter.

Contact each ohmmeter probe to a rotor slip ring. The meter reading should be 3 to 5½ ohms. A higher reading indicates a damaged slip ring solder connection or a broken wire. A lower reading indicates a shorted wire or slip ring.

Contact one ohmmeter probe to a slip ring and the other probe to the rotor shaft. The meter reading should be infinite (no deflection). A reading other than infinite indicates the rotor is shorted to the shaft. Inspect the slip ring soldered terminals to be sure they are not bent and touching the rotor shaft, or that excess solder is grounding the rotor coil connections to the shaft. Replace the rotor if it is shorted and cannot be repaired.

REGULATOR TESTS
1969-71 UNITS
Voltage Limiter Test

Voltage limiter calibration tests must be made with the regulator cover in place and the regulator at normal operating temperature (equivalent to the temperature after 20 minutes of operation on the car with the hood down).

For accurate voltage limiter testing, the battery specific gravity must be at least 1.230. If the battery is low in charge, either charge it to 1.230 specific gravity or substitute a fully charged battery, before making a voltage limiter test.

To test the voltage regulator on the car, make the test connections to the battery, Fig. 16. Turn all accessories off, including door operated dome lights. Close the battery adapter switch, start the engine, then open the adapter switch. Attach a voltage regulator thermometer to the regulator cover. Operate the engine at approximately 2000 rpm for an additional 5 minutes. (Use a tachometer).

When the battery is charged, and the voltage regulator has been temperature stabliized, the ammeter should indicate less than 10 amperes with the master control set at the ¼—OHM position.

Cycle the regulator as follows (mechanical regulators only): turn the ignition key to OFF to stop the engine, close the adapter switch, start the engine, and open the adapter switch. Increase the engine speed to 2000 rpm. Allow the battery to normalize for about one minute, then read the voltmeter. Read the thermometer, and compare the voltmeter reading with the voltage, Fig. 17, for the ambient temperature indicated on the thermometer. After each adjustment, be sure to cycle the regulator before each reading (mechanical regulator only).

NOTE. The readings must be made with the cover in place (mechanical regulator only).

If the regulator voltage is not within specifications replace voltage regulator.

Field Relay Test Electro-Mechanical Regulator

Remove the regulator from the car, and remove the regulator cover. Make the connections Fig. 18. Slowly rotate the field

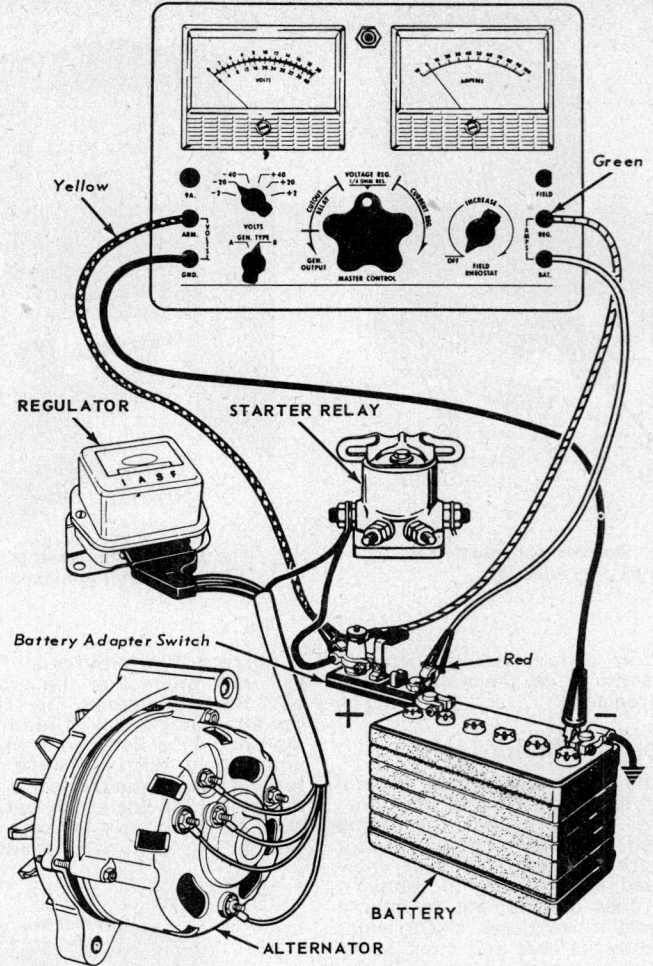

Fig. 16   Typical voltage limiter tests

rheostat control clockwise from the maximum counterclockwise position until the field relay contacts close. Observe the voltmeter reading at the moment that the relay contacts close. This is the relay closing voltage. If the relay closes immediately, even with the field rheostat close to the maximum counterclockwise position, push the red button between the two meters, and repeat the test. If the closing voltage is not within specification, unit must be replaced.

Ambient Air Temperature °F	Voltage Limiter Setting (Volts)
50	14.1—15.1
75	13.9—14.9
100	13.7—14.7
125	13.6—14.6

Fig. 17   Voltage limiter setting vs ambient air temperature. Mechanical or transistor regulator

Field Relay Test-Transistor Regulator

Disconnect the relay connector plug. Make the connections, Fig. 18. Slowly rotate the field rheostat control clockwise from the maximum counterclockwise position until the test light comes on. Observe the voltmeter reading at the moment that the light comes on. This is the relay closing voltage. If the relay closes immediately, even with the field rheostat close to the maximum counterclockwise position, push the red button between the two meters, and repeat the test. If the closing voltage is not to specification as listed in car chapters, replace the relay.

1972-74 UNITS

The alternator must be adjusted within specification, and the charging system electrical connections must be clean and tight before testing the regulator.

Test Procedure

Connect the voltmeter positive lead to the battery positive terminal, and the negative lead to the battery negative terminal. Turn off all electrical loads. Then, check and record the voltmeter reading. Connect the red lead of a tachometer to the dis-

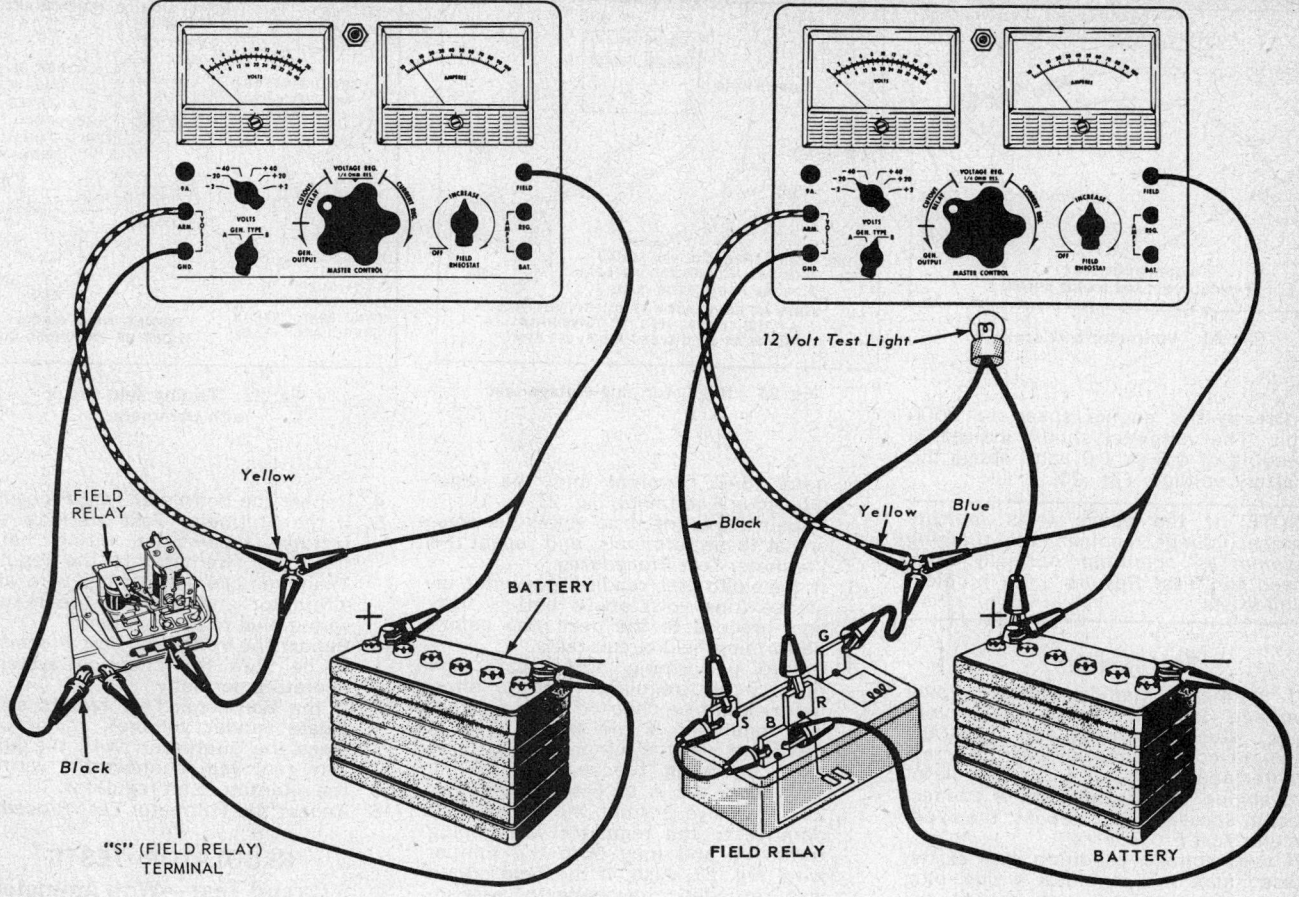

MECHANICAL REGULATOR   TRANSISTOR REGULATOR

Fig. 18 Autolite regulators field relay test

tributor terminal of the coil and the block tachometer lead to a good ground.

Place the transmission shift lever in the neutral or park position and start the engine. Increase the engine speed to 1800-2200 rpm for 2 or 3 minutes. Check and record the voltmeter reading., it should be 1 to 2 volts higher than the first reading. If the reading is less than 1 volt or greater than 2½ volts, replace the voltage regulator. If the reading is between 1 and 2 volts, turn on the headlights and heater blower. The voltage should not decrease more than ½ volt. Replace the regulator if the voltage drop is greater than ½ volt.

REGULATOR ADJUSTMENTS

1974 Transistorized Regulator

The only adjustment of this regulator is the voltage limiter adjustment. This adjustment is made with regulator at normal operating temperature. Remove the regulator cover and using a fiber rod, turn voltage adjusting screw clockwise to raise voltage setting or counter-clockwise to lower voltage setting. Refer to the "Alternator & Regulator Specifications" as listed in the individual car chapters for proper voltage setting.

1969-74 UNITS ELECTRO-MECHANICAL REGULATOR

The Autolite electro-mechanical regulator is factory calibrated and sealed and is not to be adjusted. If the regulator is not calibrated within the specified limits as listed in car chapters, it must be replaced.

VOLTMETER TEST

NOTE: *Additional simplified procedure for testing the charging system (using a voltmeter) has been developed and is highly recommended. However preceding test procedures should not be disregarded.*

NOTE: *All lights and electrical systems in the off position, parking brake applied, transmission in neutral and a charged battery (at least 1200 specific gravity).*

1. Connect the negative lead of the voltmeter to the negative battery cable clamp (not bolt or nut).
2. Connect the positive lead of the voltmeter to the positive battery cable clamp (not bolt or nut).
3. Record the battery voltage reading shown on the voltmeter scale.
4. Connect the red lead of a tachometer to the distributor terminal of the coil and the black tachometer lead to a good ground.
5. Then, start and operate the engine at approximately 1500 rpm. With no other electrical load (foot off brake pedal and car doors closed), the voltmeter reading should increase (1 volt) and not exceed (2 volts) above the first recorded battery voltage reading. The reading should be taken when the voltmeter needles stops moving.
6. With the engine running, turn on the heater and/or air conditioner blower motor to (high speed) and headlights to (high beam).

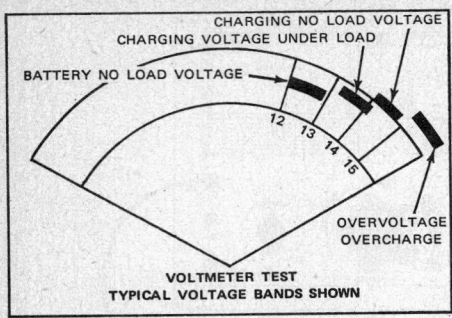

Fig. 20   Voltmeter test scale

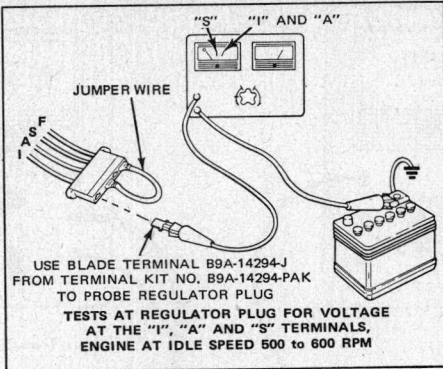

Fig. 21   Regulator plug voltage test

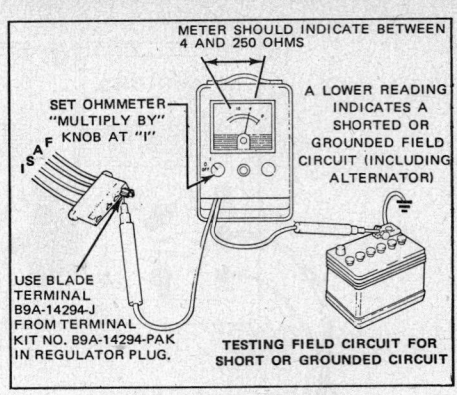

Fig. 22   Testing field circuit with Ohmmeter

7. Increase the engine speed to 2000 rpm. The voltmeter should indicate a reading of 0.5 to 1.0 volts above the battery voltage, Fig. 20.

NOTE: *If the above tests indicate proper voltage readings, the charging system is operating normally. Proceed to "Test Results" if a problem still exists.*

Test Results

1. If voltmeter reading indicates *over voltage* (2.0 volts above battery voltage), stop the engine and check the ground connections between the regulator and alternator and/or regulator to engine. Clean and tighten connections securely and repeat the *Voltmeter Test Procedures.*
2. If *over voltage* condition still exists, disconnect the regulator wiring plug from the regulator and repeat the *Voltmeter Test Procedures.*
3. If *over voltage* still exists with the regulator wiring plug disconnected, repair the short in the wiring harness between the alternator and regulator. Then, replace the regulator and connect the regulator wiring plug to the regulator and repeat the *Voltmeter Test Procedures.*
4. If the voltmeter reading does not increase (one volt), check for the presence of battery voltage at the *alter-*

nator BAT terminal and the *regulator plug A* terminal, Fig. 21.
Repair the wiring if no voltage is present at these terminals, and repeat the *Voltmeter Test Procedures.*
5. If the voltmeter·reading does *not* increase (one volt) above battery voltage, proceed to the next step *before* performing field circuit tests.
6. Before performing other tests, the field circuit (regulator plug to alternator) must be checked for a grounding condition. If the field circuit is grounded and the jumper wire is used as a check at the regulator wiring plug from the A to F terminals, Fig. 21, excessive current will cause heat damage to the regulator wiring plug terminals and may burn the jumper wire, Fig. 21. Also, if the field circuit was grounded, the connector wire inside the regulator will be burned open and an under voltage condition will result.
7. The field circuit should be checked with the regulator wiring plug disconnected and an ohmmeter connected from the *F* terminal of the regulator wiring plug to the battery ground. The ohmmeter should indicate between 4 and 250 ohms, Fig. 22.
8. A check for the regulator burned-open wire is made by connecting an ohmmeter from the *I* to *F* terminals of the regulator, Fig. 23. The reading should indicate *O* (no resistance). If the reading indicates approximately *10 ohms*, the connector wire inside the regulator is burned open. *The field circuit grounded condition must be found and repaired before installing a new regulator.*

Field Circuit and Alternator Tests

1. If the field circuit is satisfactory, disconnect the regulator wiring plug at the regulator and connect the jumper wire from the *A* to the *F* terminals on the regulator wiring plug, Fig. 24.
2. Repeat the *Voltmeter Test Procedures.*
3. If the *Voltmeter Test Procedures* still indicate a problem of (under voltage), remove the jumper wire at the regulator plug and leave the plug disconnected from the regulator, Figs. 25 and 26. Connect a jumper wire to the *FLD* and *BAT* terminals on the alternator, Figs. 25 and 26.

4. Repeat the *Voltmeter Test Procedures.*
5. If the *Voltmeter Test* are now satisfactory, repair the wiring harness from the alternator to the regulator. Then, remove the jumper wire at the alternator and connect the regulator wiring plug to the regulator.
6. Repeat the *Voltmeter Test Procedures,* to be sure the charging system is operating normally.
7. If the *Voltmeter Test* results still indicate (under voltage), repair or replace the alternator. With the jumper wire removed, connect the wiring to the alternator and regulator.
8. Repeat the *Voltmeter Test Procedures.*

REGULATOR TESTS
S Circuit Test—With Ammeter

1. Connect the positive lead of the voltmeter to the S terminal of the regulator wiring plug Fig. 21. Turn the ignition switch to the ON position. *Do not start the engine.*
2. The voltmeter reading should indicate battery voltage.
3. If there is *no* voltage reading, disconnect the positive voltmeter lead from the positive battery clamp and repair the S wire lead from the ignition switch to the regulator wiring plug.
4. Connect the positive voltmeter lead to the positive battery cable terminal

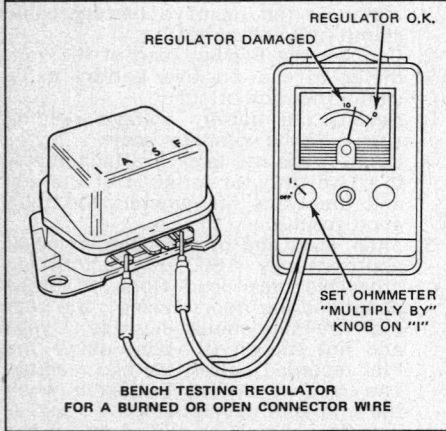

Fig. 23   Testing regulator for a burned or open connector wire

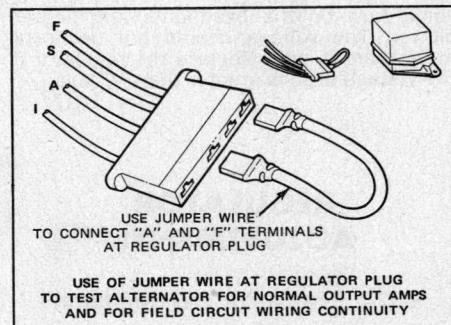

Fig. 24   Regulator plug. Jumper wire connection

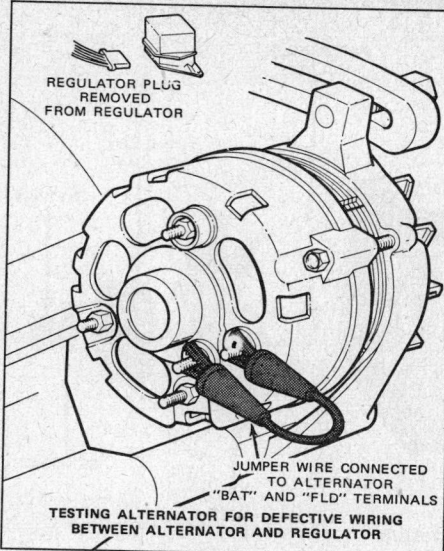

REGULATOR PLUG REMOVED FROM REGULATOR

JUMPER WIRE CONNECTED TO ALTERNATOR "BAT" AND "FLD" TERMINALS

TESTING ALTERNATOR FOR DEFECTIVE WIRING BETWEEN ALTERNATOR AND REGULATOR

Fig. 25   Rear terminal alternator. Jumper wire connection

and repeat the *Voltmeter Test Procedures.*

S and I Circuit Test—With Indicator Light

1. With the engine idling, connect the positive lead of the voltmeter to the S terminal and then to the I terminal of the regulator wiring plug, Fig. 21. The voltage of the S circuit should read approximately 1/2 of the I circuit.
2. If no voltage is present, repair the alternator or the wiring circuit at fault. Reconnect the positive voltmeter lead to the positive battery cable terminal and repeat the *Voltmeter Test Procedures.*
3. If the above tests are satisfactory, install a new regulator.
4. Then, remove the jumper wire from the regulator wiring plug and connect the wiring plug to the regulator. Repeat the *Voltmeter Test Procedures.*

ALTERNATOR REPAIRS
Rear Terminal Alternator Except 65-Ampere Unit

NOTE: Use a 100 watt soldering iron.

Disassembly

1. Mark both end housings and the stator with a scribe mark for assembly, Fig. 27.
2. Remove the three housing through bolts.
3. Separate the front housing and rotor from the stator and rear housing.
4. Remove all the nuts and insulators from the rear housing and remove the rear housing from the stator and rectifier assembly.
5. Remove the brush holder mounting

screws and remove the holder, brushes, brush springs, insulator and terminal.

6. If replacement is necessary, press the bearing from the rear housing, supporting the housing on the inner boss.
7. If the rectifier assembly is being replaced, unsolder the stator leads from the printed-circuit board terminals, and separate the stator from the rectifier assembly.
8. Original production alternators will have one of three types of rectifier assembly circuit boards, Fig. 28; one has the circuit board spaced away from the diode plates with the diodes exposed. Another type is a single circuit board with built-in diodes. The third type circuit board has built-in diodes with an additional booster diode plate containing two diodes. This circuit board is used only in the 61-ampere alternator.

   If the alternator rectifier has an exposed diode circuit board, remove the screws from the rectifier by rotating the bolt heads 1/4 turn clockwise to unlock them and then remove the screws, Fig. 28. Push the stator terminal screw straight out on a rectifier with the diodes built into the circuit board, Fig. 28. Avoid turning the screw while removing to make certain that the straight knurl will engage the insulators when installing. Do not remove the grounded screw, Fig. 29.

   On 61-ampere alternator rectifier, press the stator terminal screw from the circuit board, Fig. 30. When the terminal screw has moved about 1/4 inch, remove the nut from the end of the screw and lift the screw from the circuit board.

NOTE: Do not twist the screw in the circuit board.

9. Remove the drive pulley nut, Fig. 31. Then, pull the lockwasher, pulley, fan, fan spacer, front housing and rotor stop from the rotor shaft.
10. Remove the three screws that hold the front end bearing retainer, and remove the retainer. If the bearing is damaged or has lost its lubricant, support the housing close to the bearing boss and press out the old bearing from the housing.
11. Perform a diode test and a field open or short circuit test.

Assembly

NOTE: Refer to "Cleaning and Inspection" procedures before reassembly.

1. The rotor, stator and bearings must not be cleaned with solvent. Wipe these parts off with a clean cloth.
2. Press the front bearing in the front housing bearing boss (put pressure on the outer race only), and install the bearing retainer, Fig. 27.
3. If the stop-ring on the rotor drive shaft was damaged, install a new stop-ring. Push the new ring on the shaft and into the groove.

NOTE: *Do not open the ring with snap*

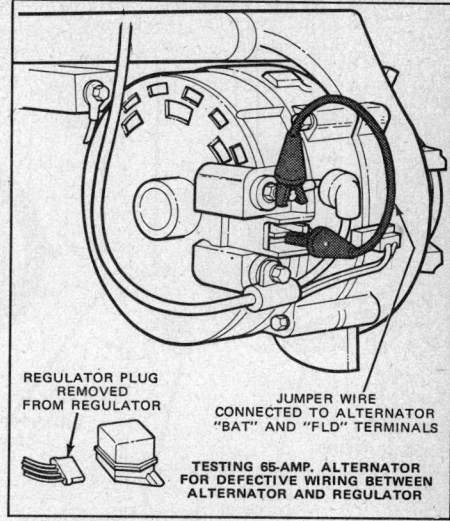

REGULATOR PLUG REMOVED FROM REGULATOR

JUMPER WIRE CONNECTED TO ALTERNATOR "BAT" AND "FLD" TERMINALS

TESTING 65-AMP. ALTERNATOR FOR DEFECTIVE WIRING BETWEEN ALTERNATOR AND REGULATOR

Fig. 26   Side terminal 65-amp alternator. Jumper wire connection

ring pliers as permanent damage will result.

4. Position the rotor stop on the drive shaft with the recessed side against the stop-ring.
5. Position the front housing, fan spacer, fan, pulley and lock washer on the drive shaft and install the retaining nut. Torque the retaining nut, Fig. 31, to 60-100 ft lbs.
6. If the rear housing bearing was removed, support the housing on the inner boss and press in a new bearing flush with the outer end surface.
7. Place the brush springs, brushes, brush terminal and terminal insulator in the brush holder and hold the brushes in position by inserting a piece of stiff wire in the brush holder, Fig. 32.
8. Position the brush holder assembly in the rear housing and install the mounting screws. Position the brush leads in the brush holder, Fig. 33.
9. Wrap the three stator winding leads around the circuit board terminals and solder them. Position the stator neutral lead eyelet on the stator terminal screw and install the screw in the rectifier assembly, Fig. 34.
10. For a rectifier with the diodes exposed insert the special screws through the wire lug, dished washers and circuit board, Fig. 28. Turn them 1/4 turn counterclockwise to lock them. For single circuit boards with built in diodes, insert the screws straight through the wire lug, insulating washer and rectifier into the insulator, Fig. 29.

NOTE: The dished washers are to be used only on the circuit board with exposed diodes, Fig. 28. If they are used on the single circuit board, a short circuit will occur. A flat insulating washer is to be used between the stator terminal and the board when a single circuit board is used, Fig. 29.

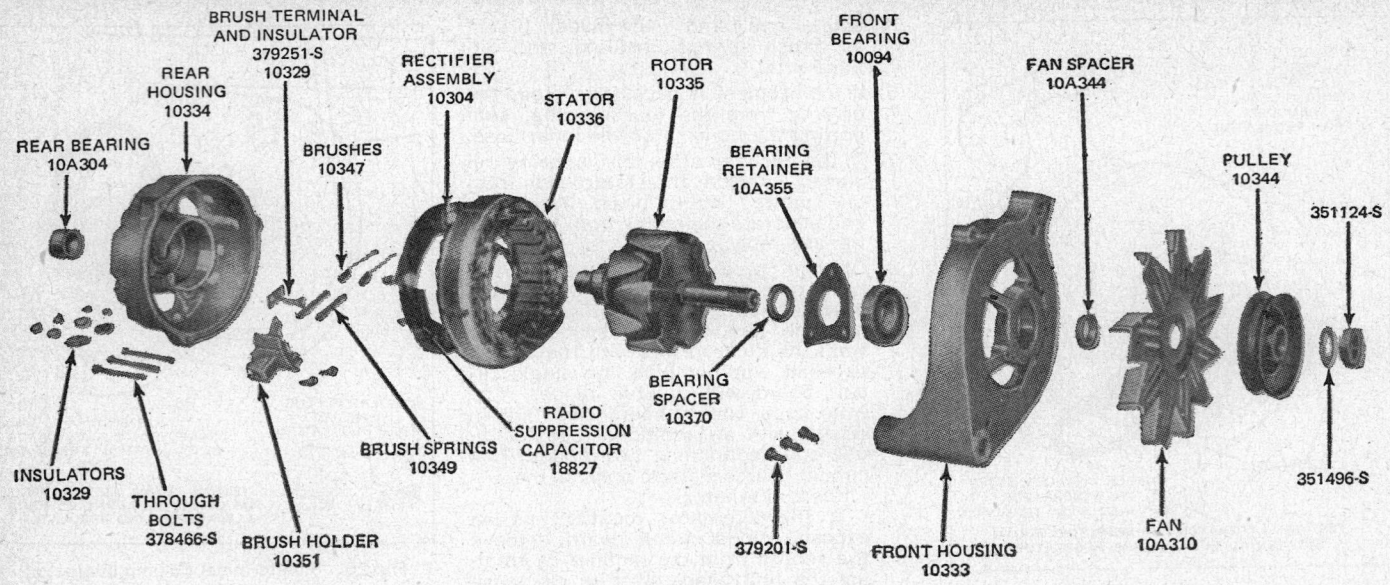

Fig. 27   Disassembled alternator

11. For a rectifier with a booster diode plate (61-Ampere Alternator only), proceed as follows:
    a. Position the stator wire terminal on the stator terminal screw and position the screw into the rectifier. Position the square insulator over the screw and into the square hole in the rectifier, Fig. 35.
    b. Rotate the terminal screw until it locks in position. Then, press the screw in finger tight.
    c. Position the stator wire, Fig. 36. Press the terminal screw into the rectifier and insulator, Fig. 37.
12. Position the radio noise suppression capacitor on the rectifier terminals. On the circuit board with exposed diodes, install the STA and DAT terminal insulators, Fig. 34. On the single circuit board, position the square stator-terminal insulator in the square hole in the rectifier assembly, Fig. 29. Position the BAT terminal insulator, Fig. 38.
    Position the stator and rectifier assembly in the rear housing. Make certain that all terminal insulators are seated properly in the recesses, Fig. 34. Position the STA (black), BAT (red) and FLD (orange) insulators on the terminal bolts, and install the retaining nuts, Fig. 39.
13. Wipe the rear end bearing surface of the rotor shaft with a clean lint-free rag.
14. Position the rear housing and stator assembly over the rotor and align the scribe marks made during disassembly. Seat the machined portion of the stator core into the step in both end housings. Install the housing through bolts. Remove the brush retracting wire, and put a daub of water-proof cement over the hole to seal it.

Rear Terminal 65-Ampere Alternator

NOTE: Use a 200 watt soldering iron.

Disassembly

1. Remove the brush holder and cover assembly from the rear end housing, Fig. 40.
2. Mark both end housings and the stator with a scribe mark for assembly.
3. Remove the three housing through bolts.
4. Separate the front housing and rotor from the stator and rear housing.
5. Remove the drive pulley nut, lockwasher, flat washer, pulley, fan, fan spacer and rotor from the front housing, Fig. 31.
6. Remove the three screws that hold the front bearing retainer, and remove

the retainer. If the bearing is damaged or has lost its lubricant, support the housing close to the bearing boss and press out the bearing from the housing.
7. Remove all the nut and washer assemblies and insulators from the rear housing and remove the rear housing from the stator and rectifier assembly.
8. If replacement is necessary, press the bearing from the rear housing, supporting the housing on the inner boss.
9. Unsolder the three stator leads from the rectifier assembly, and separate the stator from the assembly.
10. Perform a diode test and an open and grounded stator coil test.

Assembly

NOTE: Refer to "Cleaning and Inspection" procedures before reassembly.

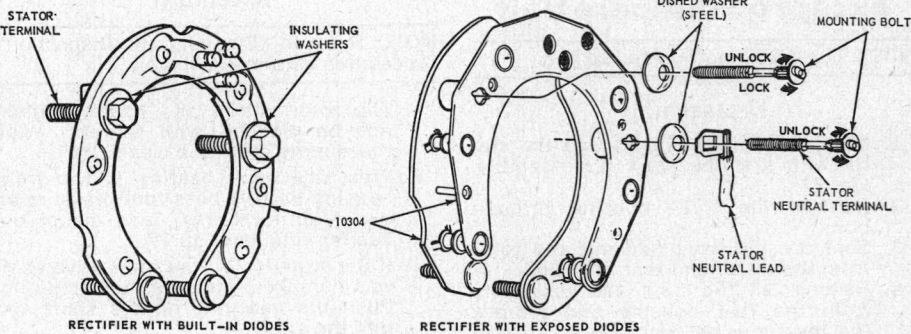

Fig. 28   Rectifier assembly

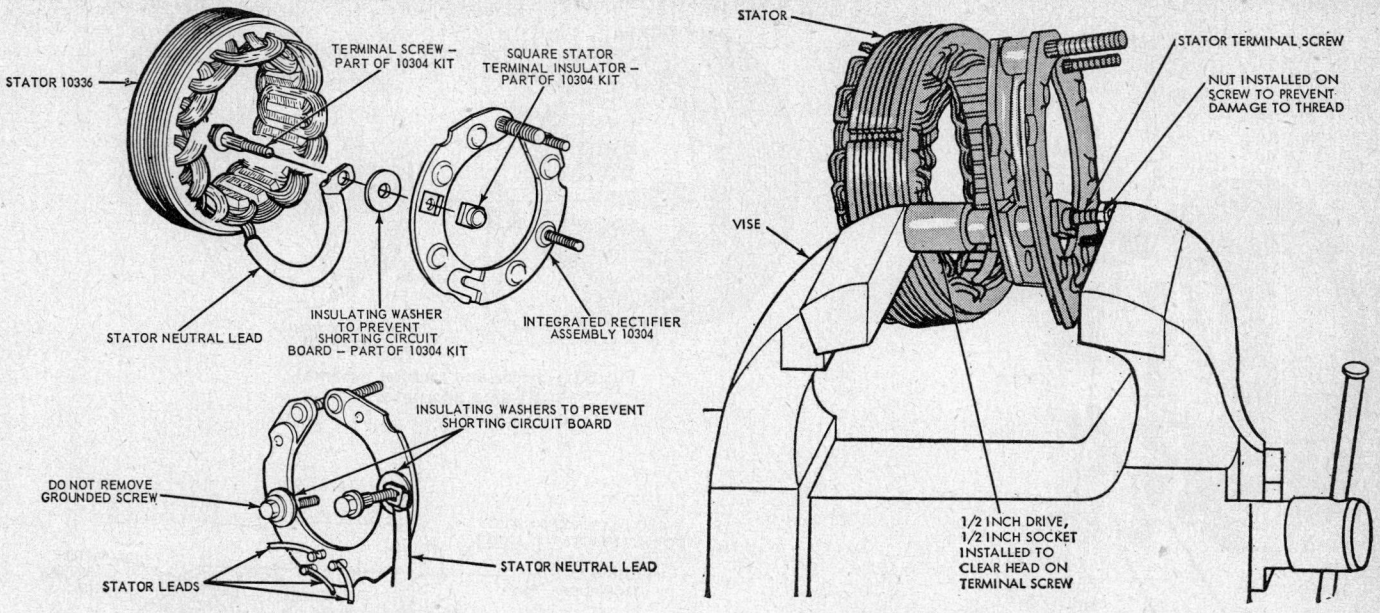

Fig. 29 Stator terminal installation. Integral rectifier circuit board

Fig. 30 Stator terminal screw removal. 61-amp alternator

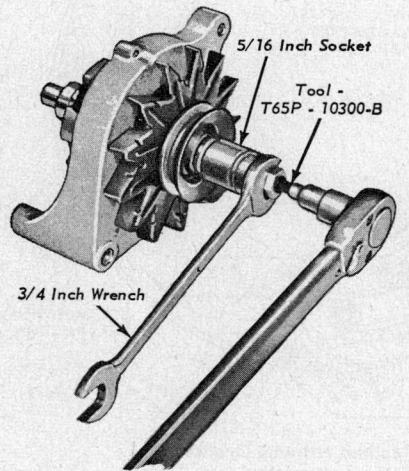

Fig. 31 Typical pulley removal

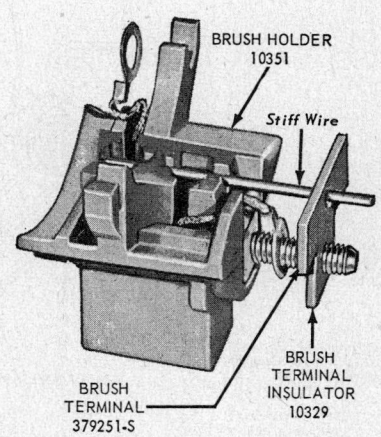

Fig. 32 Brush holder assembly

PRESS FIRMLY AGAINST HOUSING

Fig. 33 Typical brush lead positions

1. If the front bearing is being replaced, press the new bearing in the bearing boss putting pressure on the outer race only. Then, install the bearing retainer, and tighten the retainer screws until the tips of the retainer screws touch the housing.

2. Position the rectifier assembly to the stator, wrap the three stator leads around the diode plate terminals and solder them, Fig. 41.

3. If the rear housing bearing was removed, press in a new bearing from the inside of the housing until the bearing is flush with the outer end surface. Put pressure on the bearing outer race only.

4. Install the BAT-GRD insulator, Fig. 41, and position the stator and rectifier assembly in the rear housing.

5. Install the STA (purple) and BAT (red) terminal insulators on the terminal bolts and install the nut and washer assemblies.

NOTE: Make certain that the shoulders on all insulators both inside and outside of the housing are seated properly before tightening the nuts.

6. Position the front housing over the rotor and install the fan spacer, fan, pulley, flat and lock washers and nut on the rotor shaft, Fig. 31.

7. Wipe the rear bearing surface of the rotor shaft with a clean lint free rag.

8. Position the rotor with the front housing into the stator and rear housing assembly, and align the scribe marks made during disassembly. Seat the machined portion of the stator core into the step in both housing, and install the through bolts.

9. On 1970-72 units hold the brushes in position by inserting a stiff wire in the brush holder, Fig. 42.

10. Position the brush holder assembly into the rear housing and install the three mounting screws. On 1970-73 units remove the brush retracting wire and put a daub of water-proof cement over the hole to seal hole.

NOTE: On 1969 units the brush holders rotate on a plastic rod. This rod must be properly seated in the recess in the rear housing.

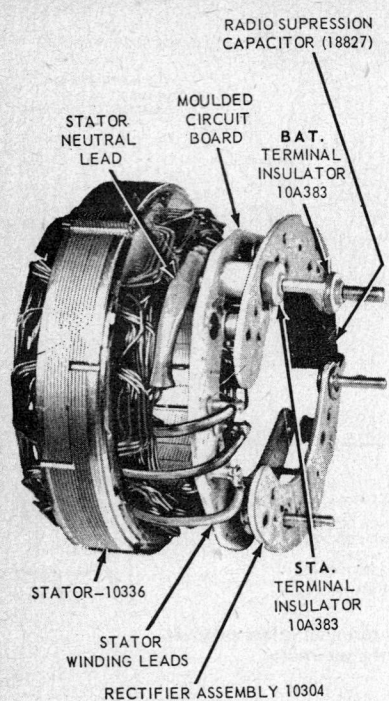

Fig. 34 Stator lead connections.
Except 61-amp alternator

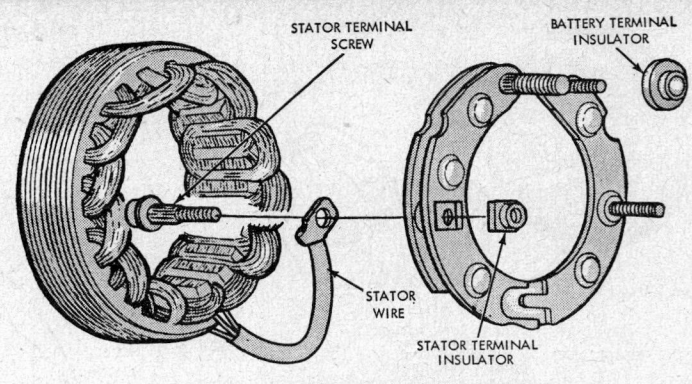

Fig. 35 Stator and rectifier assembly.
61-amp alternator

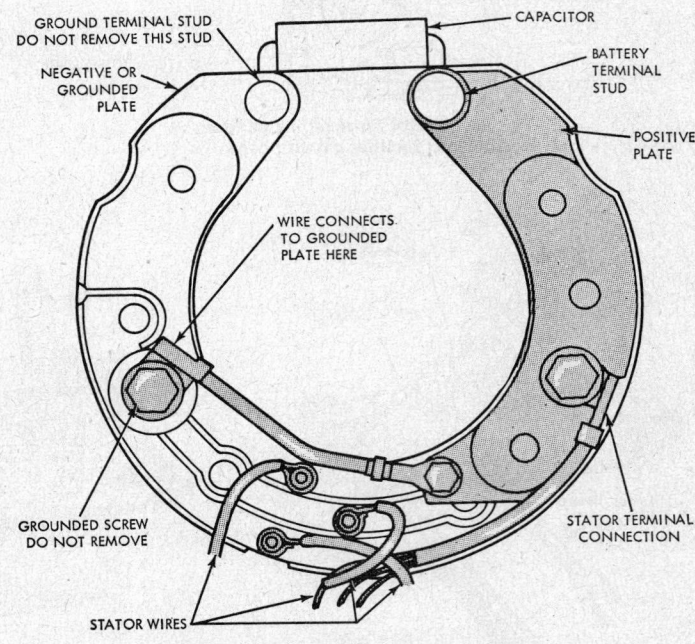

Fig. 36 Rectifier terminal locations.
61-amp alternator

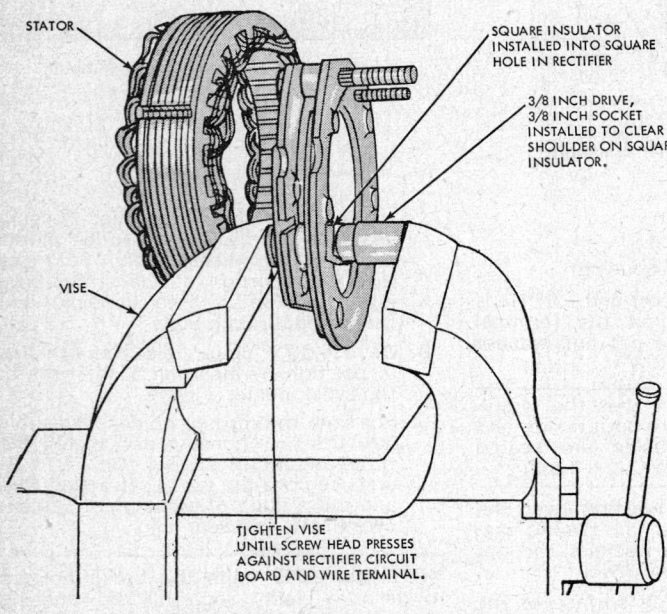

Fig. 37 Stator terminal screw installation.
61-amp alternator

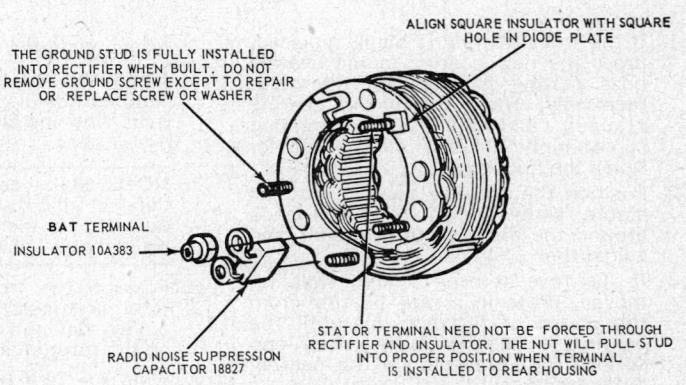

Fig. 38 Fiber-glass circuit board
terminal insulators

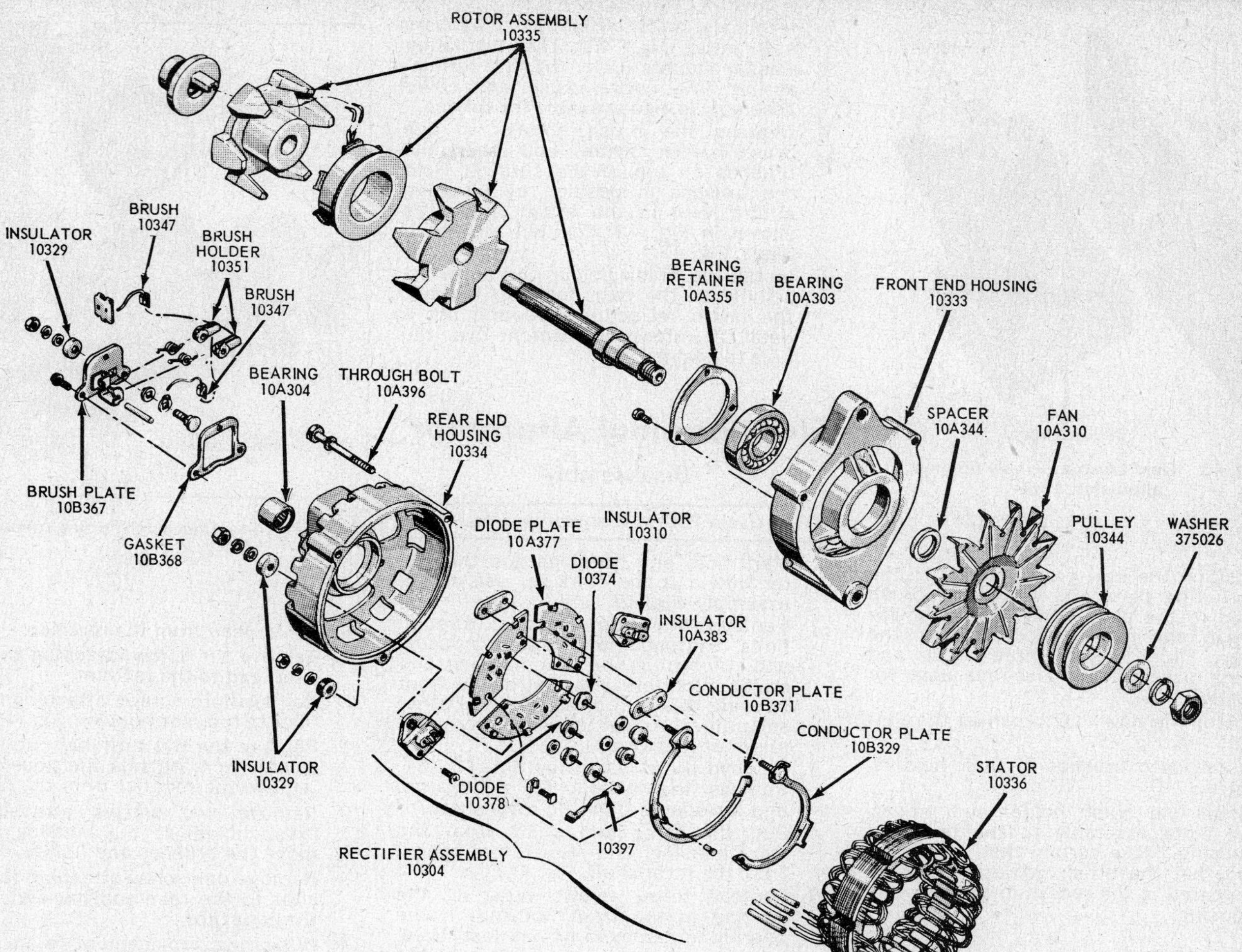

ROTOR ASSEMBLY
10335

INSULATOR
10329

BRUSH
10347

BRUSH
HOLDER
10351

BRUSH
10347

BEARING
10A304

THROUGH BOLT
10A396

REAR END
HOUSING
10334

BRUSH PLATE
10B367

GASKET
10B368

BEARING
RETAINER
10A355

BEARING
10A303

FRONT END HOUSING
10333

SPACER
10A344

FAN
10A310

PULLEY
10344

WASHER
375026

DIODE PLATE
10A377

INSULATOR
10310

DIODE
10374

INSULATOR
10A383

CONDUCTOR PLATE
10B371

CONDUCTOR PLATE
10B329

STATOR
10336

INSULATOR
10329

DIODE
10378

10397

RECTIFIER ASSEMBLY
10304

Fig. 40   Disassembled 65-amp alternator

Brush Replacement
1969 ALTERNATOR

1. Remove the brush holder and mounting plate assembly from the rear end housing.

2. Slide the FLD brush out of its holder and unsolder the brush lead from the terminal lug.
3. Slide the ground brush out of its holder. Unsolder the brush lead from the plate, and remove the brush.

BAT-GRD INSULATOR

FLD TERMINAL

BRUSH RETRACTING WIRE

Fig. 39   Alternator terminal locations

STATOR LEADS

Fig. 41   Stator lead connections

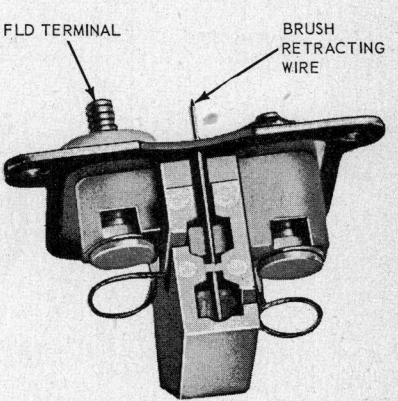

Fig. 42   Field brush assembly 65-amp alternator. 1970-72

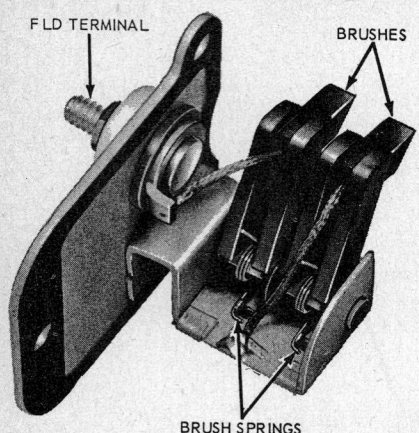

Fig. 43 Field brush assembly 65-amp alternator. 1969

terminals, bolts, brush holder washers and nuts, Fig. 42. The insulating washer mounts under the FLD terminal nut. The entire brush and cover assembly is also available for service.

4. Depress the brush springs in the brush holder cavities and insert the brushes on top of the springs. Hold the brushes in position by inserting a stiff wire in the brush holder as shown in Fig. 42. Position the brush leads, Fig. 42.

5. Install the brush holder and cover assembly to the rear housing. Remove the brush retracting wire and put a daub of water-proof cement over the hole to seal it.

Side Terminal Alternator

Disassembly

NOTE: Use a 200 watt soldering iron.

1. Mark both end housings and the stator with a scribe mark for use during assembly, Fig. 45.
2. Remove the four housing through bolts, and separate the front housing and rotor from the rear housing and stator. Slots are provided in the front housing to aid in disassembly. *Do not separate the rear housing from the stator at this time.*
3. Remove the drive pulley nut, Fig. 31. Remove the lockwasher, pulley, fan and fan spacer from the rotor shaft.
4. Pull the rotor and shaft from the front housing, and remove the spacer from the rotor shaft, Fig. 45.
5. Remove three screws retaining the bearing to the front housing. If the bearing is damaged or has lost its lubricant, remove the bearing from the housing. To remove the bearing, support the housing close to the bearing boss and press the bearing from the housing.
6. Unsolder and disengage the three stator leads from the rectifier, Fig. 46.
7. Lift the stator from the rear housing.
8. Unsolder and disengage the brush

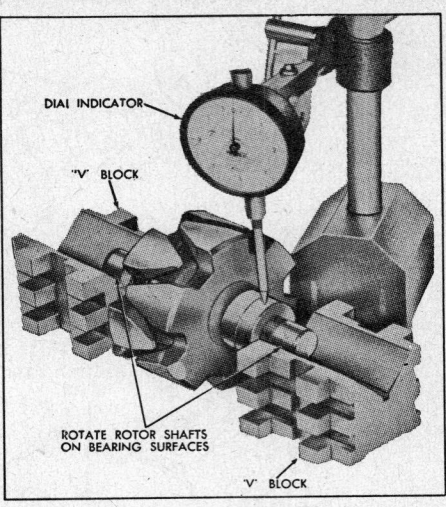

Fig. 44 Checking slip ring runout

holder lead from the rectifier.

9. Remove the screw attaching the capacitor lead to the rectifier.
10. Remove four screws attaching the rectifier to the rear housing, Fig. 46.
11. Remove the two terminal nuts and insulator from outside the housing, and remove the rectifier from the housing.
12. Remove two screws attaching the brush holder to the housing and remove the brushes and holder.
13. Remove one screw attaching the capacitor to the rear housing and remove the capacitor.
14. If bearing replacement is necessary, support the rear housing close to the bearing boss and press the bearing out of the housing from the inside.

Assembly

NOTE: Refer to "Cleaning and Inspection"

4. Position the new ground brush to the mounting plate and solder the brush lead to the plate. Make sure that the brush springs are hooked over the lugs, Fig. 43. The entire brush and plate assembly is also available for service.
5. Solder the new FLD brush to the FLD stud lug, Fig. 43.
6. Install both brushes in their holders, Fig. 43.
7. Install the brush holder and mounting plate assembly to the rear end housing. Make certain that the plastic rod that the brush holders rotate on is seated in the recess in the rear end housing.

1970-72 ALTERNATOR

1. Remove the brush holder and cover assembly from the rear housing.
2. Remove the terminal bolts from the brush holder and cover assembly, and remove the brush assemblies.
3. Position the new brush terminals on the terminal bolts and assemble the

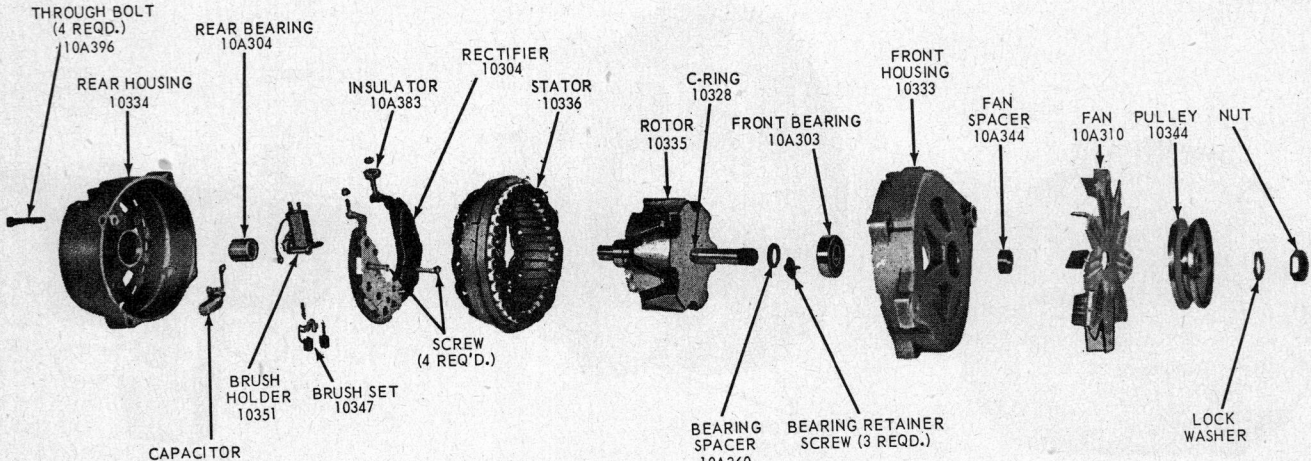

Fig. 45 Disassembled 65-amp side terminal alternator

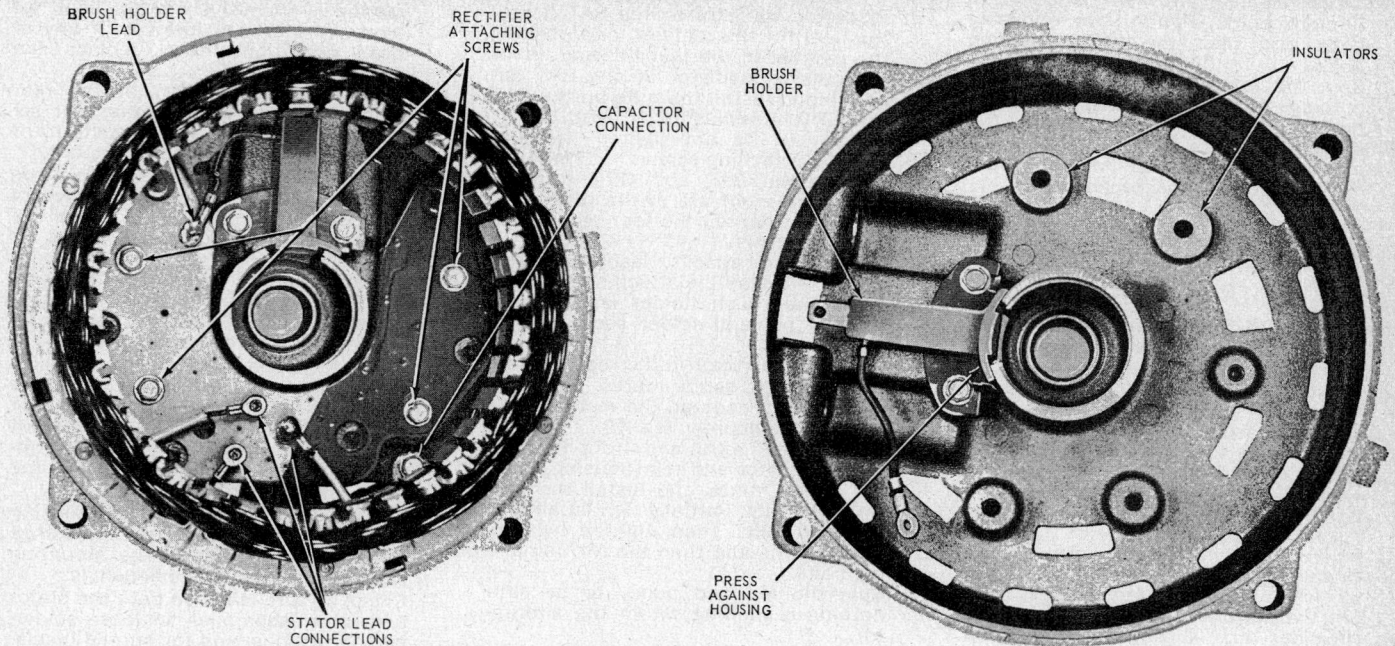

Fig. 46   Stator lead connections

Fig. 48   Brush holder and rectifier insulators installed

procedures before reassembly.

1. If the front housing bearing is being replaced, press the new bearing in the housing.

   NOTE: *Put pressure on the bearing outer race only.* Then, install the bearing retaining screws.

2. Place the inner spacer on the rotor shaft and insert the rotor shaft into the front housing and bearing.

3. Install the fan spacer, fan, pulley, lockwasher and nut on the rotor shaft, Fig. 31. Torque nut to 60-100 ft. lbs.

4. If the rear bearing is being replaced, press a new bearing in from inside the housing until it is flush with the boss outer surface.

5. Position the brush terminal on the brush holder, Fig. 47. Install the springs and brushes in the brush holder, and insert a piece of stiff wire to hold the brushes in place, Fig. 47.

6. Position the brush holder in the rear housing and install the attaching screws. Push the brush holder toward the rotor shaft opening and tighten the brush holder attaching screws.

7. Position the capacitor to the rear housing and install the attaching screw.

8. Place the two cup shaped (rectifier) insulators on the bosses inside the housing, Fig. 48.

9. Place the insulator on the BAT (large) terminal of the rectifier, and position the rectifier in the rear housing. Place the outside insulator on the BAT terminal, and install the nuts on the BAT and GRD terminals *finger tight.*

10. Install but do not tighten the four rectifier attaching screws.

11. Tighten the BAT and GRD terminal nuts on the outside of the rear housing. Then, tighten the four rectifier

attaching screws.

12. Position the capacitor lead to the rectifier and install the attaching screw.

13. Press the brush holder lead on the rectifier pin and solder securely, Fig. 46.

14. Position the stator in the rear housing and align the scribe marks. Press the three stator leads on the rectifier pins and solder securely, Fig. 46.

15. Position the rotor and front housing into the stator and rear housing. Align the scribe marks and install the four through bolts. Tighten two opposing bolts and then the two remaining bolts.

16. Spin the fan and pulley to be sure nothing is binding within the alternator.

17. Remove the wire retracting the brushes, and place a daub of waterproof cement over the hole to seal it.

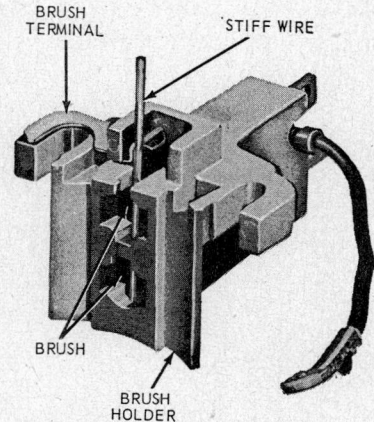

Fig. 47   Brush holder assembly

Brush Replacement
Removal

1. Mark both end housings and the stator with a scribe mark for use during assembly.

2. Remove the four housing through bolts, and separate the front housing and rotor from the rear housing and stator. Slots are provided in the front housing to aid in disassembly.

   NOTE: Do not separate the rear housing and stator.

3. Unsolder and disengage the brush holder lead from the rectifier.

4. Remove the two brush holder attaching screws and lift the brush holder from the rear housing.

5. Remove the brushes from the brush holder.

Installation

1. Insert the brushes into the brush holder and position the terminal on the brush holder.

2. Depress the brushes and insert a 1½ inch piece of stiff wire, Fig. 47, to hold the brushes in the retracted position.

3. Position the brush holder to the rear housing, inserting the wire used to retract the brushes through the hole in the rear housing.

4. Install the brush holder attaching screws. Push the brush holder toward the rotor shaft opening and tighten the attaching screws.

5. Press the brush holder lead on the rectifier pin and solder securely.

6. Position the rotor and front housing into the stator and rear housing. Align the scribe marks and install the four

through bolts. Tighten two opposing bolts and then the two remaining bolts.

7. Spin the fan and pulley to be sure nothing is binding within the alternator.

8. Remove the wire retracting the brushes, and place a daub of waterproof cement over the hole to seal it.

Rectifier Replacement
Removal

1. Mark both end housings and the stator with a scribe mark for use during assembly, Fig. 45.

2. Remove the four housing through bolts, and separate the front housing and rotor from the rear housing and stator. Slots are provided in the front housing to aid in disassembly.

NOTE: *Do not separate the rear housing and stator at this time.*

3. Unsolder and disengage the three stator leads from the rectifier, Fig. 46. Lift the stator from the rear housing.

4. Unsolder and disengage the brush holder lead from the rectifier.

5. Remove the screw attaching the capacitor lead to the rectifier.

6. Remove four screws attaching the rectifier to the rear housing, Fig. 46.

7. Remove two terminal nuts and insulator from outside the housing, and remove the rectifier from the housing.

Installation

1. Insert a piece of wire through the hole in the rear housing to hold the brushes in the retracted position.

2. Place the two cup shaped (rectifier) insulators on the bosses inside the housing, Fig. 48.

3. Place the insulator on the BAT (large) terminal) of the rectifier, and position the rectifier in the rear housing. Place the outside insulator on the BAT terminal, and install the nuts on the BAT and GRD terminals finger tight.

4. Install but do not tighten the four rectifier attaching screws.

5. Tighten the BAT and GRD terminal nuts on the outside of the rear housing. Then, tighten the four rectifier attaching screws.

6. Position the capacitor lead to the rectifier and install the attaching screw.

7. Press the brush holder lead on the rectifier pin and solder securely, Fig. 46.

8. Position the stator in the rear housing and align the scribe marks. Press the three stator leads on the rectifier pins and solder securely, Fig. 46.

9. Position the rotor and front housing into the stator and rear housing. Align the scribe marks and install the four through bolts. Partially tighten all four through bolts. Then, tighten two opposing bolts and then the two remaining bolts.

10. Spin the fan and pulley to be sure nothing is binding within the alternator.

11. Remove the wire retracting the brushes in the brush holder, and place a daub of waterproof cement over the hole in the rear housing to seal it.

Cleaning and Inspection Procedures

1. The rotor, stator, and bearings must not be cleaned with solvent. Wipe these parts off with a clean cloth.

2. Rotate the front bearing on the drive end of the rotor drive shaft. Check for any scraping noise, looseness or roughness that will indicate that the bearing is excessively worn. Look for excessive lubricant leakage. If any of these conditions exist, replace the bearing.

3. Inspect the rotor shaft at the rear bearing surface for roughness or severe chatter marks. Replace the rotor assembly if the shaft is not smooth.

4. Place the rear end bearing on the slip-ring end of the shaft and rotate the bearing on the shaft. Make the same check for noise, looseness or roughness as was made for the front bearing. Inspect the rollers and cage for damage. Replace the bearing if these conditions exist, or if the lubricant is lost or contaminated.

5. Check the pulley and fan for excessive looseness on the rotor shaft. Replace any pulley or fan that is loose or bent out of shape. Check the rotor shaft for stripped or damaged threads. Inspect the hex hole in the end of the shaft for damage.

6. Check both the front and rear housing for cracks. Check the front housings for stripped threads in the mounting gear. Replace defective housings.

7. Check all wire leads on both the stator and rotor assemblies for loose soldered connections, and for burned insulation. Resolder poor connections. Replace parts that show burned insulation.

8. Check the slip rings for nicks and surface roughness. Check the slip rings for runout, Fig. 44. Nicks, scratches and slight slip ring runout may be removed by turning down the slip rings. Do not go beyond the minimum diameter limit. If the slip rings are badly damaged, the entire rotor will have to be replaced, as it is serviced as a complete assembly.

9. Replace any parts that are burned or cracked. Replace brushes and brush springs that are not to specification.

Ford Autolite/Motorcraft Alternator With Integral Regulator

DESCRIPTION

Alternator

The alternator used with this unit is basically the same as the standard Ford Autolite unit. Modifications have been made in the brush holder assembly, rear end frame and the stator assembly to accommodate the integral regulator. Except for tests outlined here, refer to preceding chapter for service procedures.

Integral Regulator

The integral regulator, Fig. 1, consists of an integrated, solid state circuit, made up of transistors, diodes and resistors, all connected by aluminum conductors and fabricated within a 1/8" square silicon crystal. This is a one piece, non-adjustable unit which must be replaced if it malfunctions, or if it is not calibrated within specified limits of 13.5 to 15.3 volts between 50 and 125 degrees F.

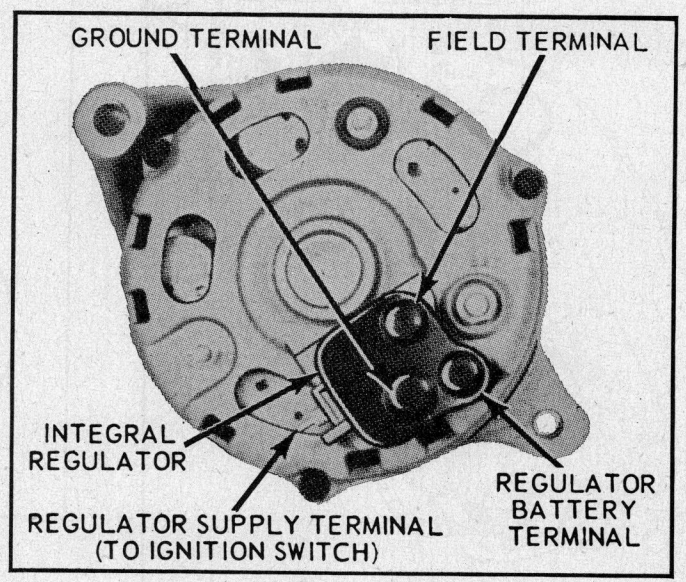

Fig. 1 Alternator with integral regulator

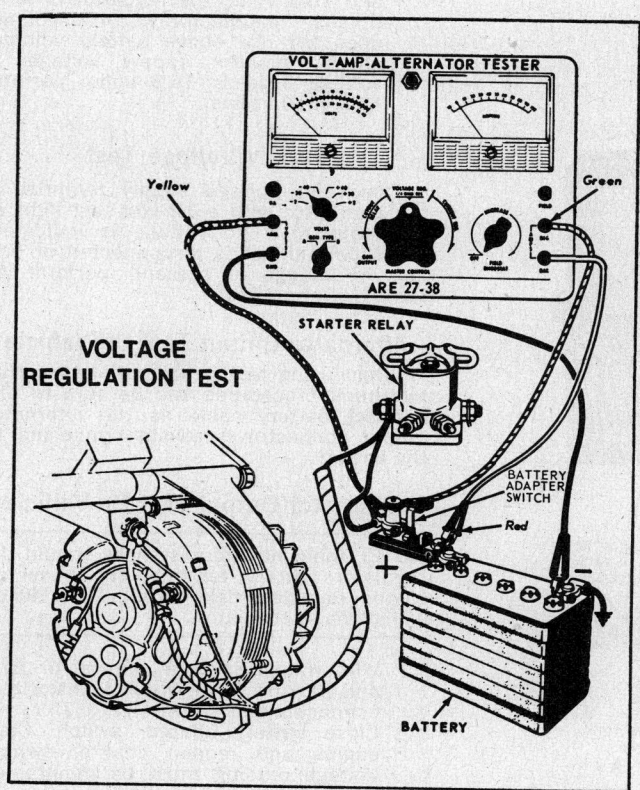

Fig. 2 Voltage regulator test

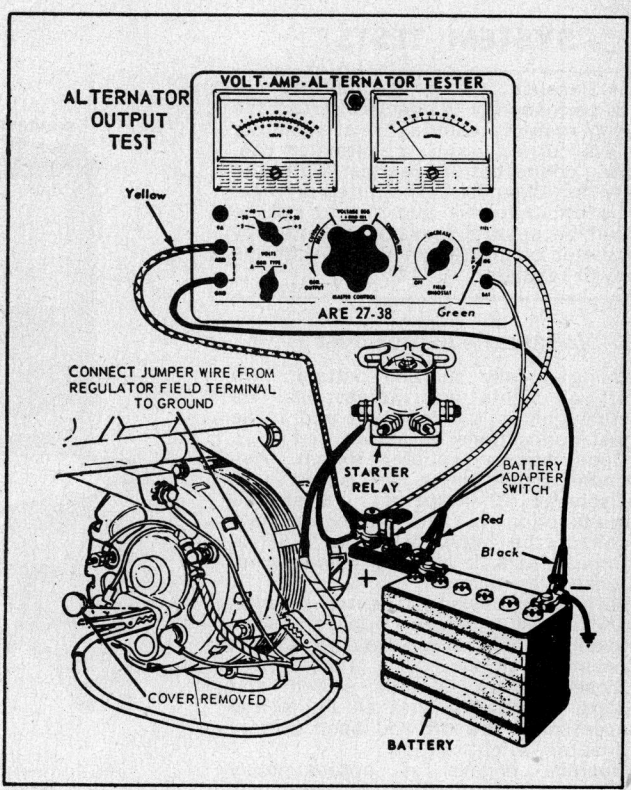

Fig. 3 Alternator output test

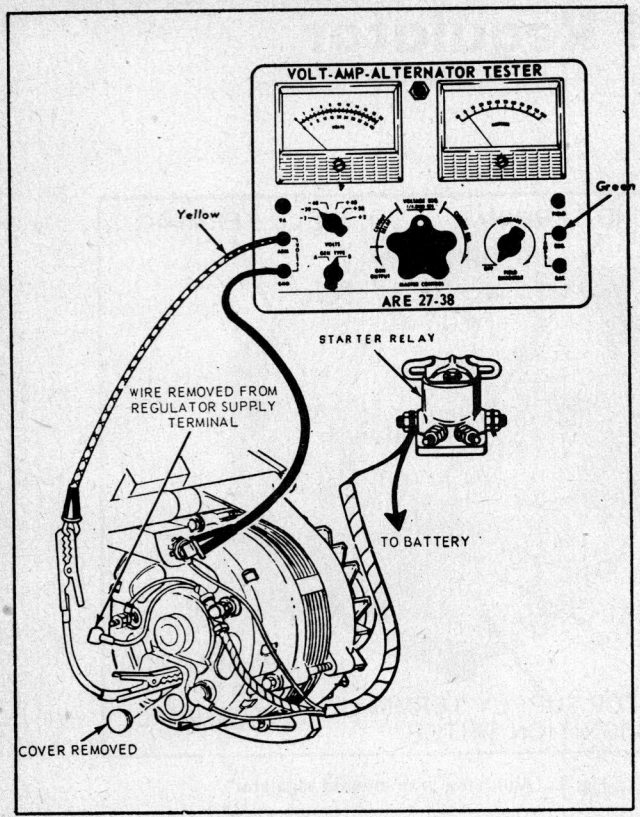

Fig. 4   Field voltmeter test

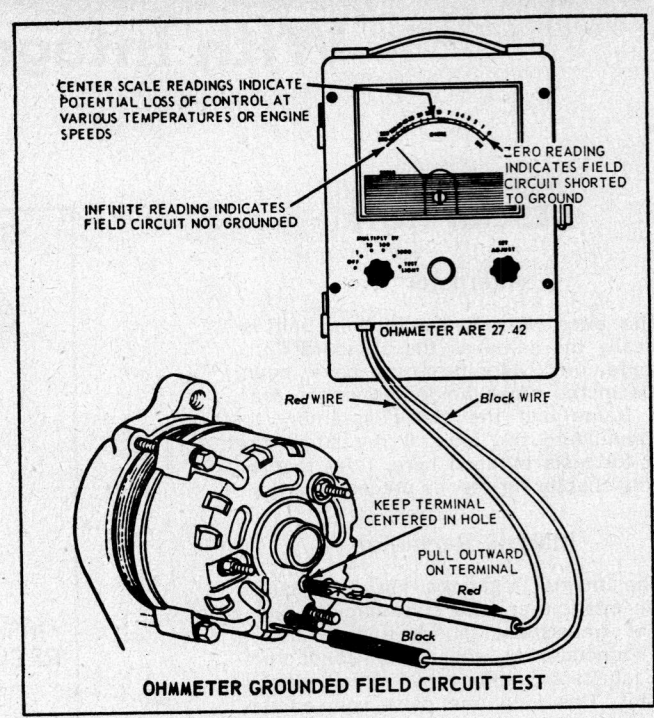

Fig. 5   Ohmmeter field circuit test

SYSTEM TESTS

NOTE: Because the voltage sensing circuit is permanently connected across the charging system, resulting in a small but harmless current drain, a voltmeter cannot be connected in series with the battery for diagnosis. The integral regulator is not defective and should not be replaced because of leakage indicated by a voltmeter connected in series with the battery or regulator.

Voltage Regulator Test

1. Using a fully charged battery, turn off all lights and accessories. Be sure ignition switch is off and make test connections as shown in Fig. 2.
2. Open battery adapter switch. Ammeter should show zero amperes. A discharge (2 amperes) indicates a malfunction in the alternator field coil or the regulator. Refer to Field Circuit Tests. If ammeter shows zero, proceed as follows:
3. With transmission in neutral or park and parking brake applied, place tester master control at the ¼ ohm resistor position.
4. Close battery adapter switch and start engine. Be sure all lights and accessories are off and open battery adapter switch.
5. Operate engine at approximately 2000 rpm for 5 minutes, and check

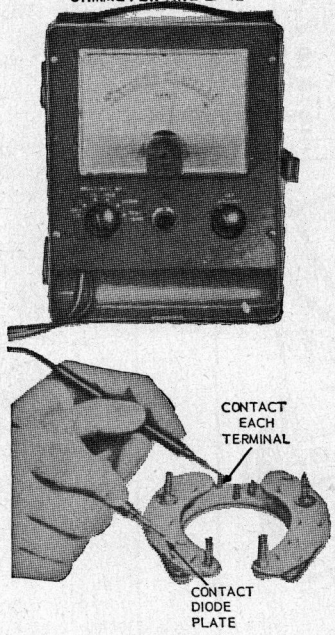

OHMMETER ARE 27-42

CONTACT EACH TERMINAL

CONTACT DIODE PLATE

Fig. 6   Diode test

voltage. If voltage is between 13.3 and 15.3 volts, the regulator is functioning satisfactorily. If voltage does not rise above battery voltage, check regulator supply voltage. If voltage exceeds 15.3 volts, perform field circuit tests.

Supply Voltage Test

Check for voltage supply terminal of the alternator with a 12 volt test light or a voltmeter. If no voltage is indicated, the supply circuit is disconnected or broken. If voltage is present, perform Alternator Output Test.

Alternator Output Test Off Vehicle

When using test bench, refer to manufacturer's procedures and be sure to disconnect battery cable as the alternator output connector is always connected to the battery.

Alternator Output Test On Vehicle

NOTE: Under no circumstances should the regulator battery terminal be connected to the regulator field terminal. To do so will damage regulator.

1. With transmission in neutral or park and parking brake applied, make test connections as shown in Fig. 3.
2. Close battery adapter switch. Start engine and reopen adapter switch. Voltage reading must be maintained between 10 and 15 volts.

3. Increase engine speed to 2000 rpm. Turn off all lights and accessories.
4. Turn master control clockwise until voltmeter shows 15 volts. At 15 volts, ammeter should register 50 to 57 amperes. If alternator is working properly, regulator must be replaced.
5. Return engine speed to idle before releasing master control knob.
6. An alternator output of 2 to 8 amperes below minimum specification usually indicates an open diode rectifier. An alternator with a shorted diode will usually whine, most noticeably at idle speed.

Field Voltmeter Test

1. Turn off ignition switch and remove wire from regulator supply terminal.
2. Make test connections as shown in Fig. 4. Open battery adapter switch.

NOTE: if there was an ammeter drain that stopped when supply terminal was disconnected, an ignition switch or wiring problem is indicated. If discharge continues (2 or more amperes), proceed as follows:

3. Voltmeter should read 12 volts. If there is no voltage reading, the field circuit is open or grounded. Perform Alternator Field Ohmmeter Test. If ohmmeter tests show alternator field is okay, the regulator is shorted and must be replaced.
4. If voltmeter reading in Step 3 is more than one volt but less than battery voltage, a partial ground in the alternator field circuit is indicated. Perform Field Ohmmeter Test to isolate trouble between alternator and regulator.

Field Ohmmeter Test

1. Disconnect battery ground cable and remove regulator from alternator.
2. Make ohmmeter connections as shown in Fig. 5.
3. If any of the conditions shown in Fig. 5 are found, remove and repair alternator. If alternator is okay, replace the regulator.

Diode Bench Test

1. Disassemble alternator and disconnect diode assembly from stator.

Make test connections as shown in Fig. 6.
2. Touch one ohmmeter lead to diode plate and the other to each of the three stator lead terminals. Reverse probes and repeat test. Test the other set of diodes the same way.
3. All tests should show a low reading of approximately 60 ohms in one direction and an infinite reading with the probes reversed.

Open Stator Test

Connect ohmmeter probes between each pair of stator leads. If ohmmeter does not show equal readings between each pair of stator leads, the stator is open and must be replaced.

Grounded Stator Test

Connect ohmmeter probes between one of the stator leads and the stator core. If the ohmmeter shows any reading, stator is grounded and must be replaced.

Ford Sierracin
High Voltage Alternator

DESCRIPTION

This alternator, used with the Ford Sierracin system, Fig. 1, delivers approximately 120 volts to heat the front and rear windows on some Ford Co. vehicles. This system is completely isolated from the main vehicle system to prevent high voltage feed into the main system. Plastic shielded wiring is used between the alternator output terminals and the window heating elements, Fig. 2. Note that a high voltage warning tag is attached to the wiring at each junction.

ALTERNATOR TESTING

CAUTION: Since this is a 120 volt system and danger of electrical shock is present, all testing must be done with the field lead disconnected, using an ohmmeter and the engine stopped. Do not attempt to check alternator output voltage at the output terminal.

Field Coil Test

Connect an ohmmeter to the field terminal stud and the rear housing, avoiding contact with epoxy on housing since this will act as an insulator, Fig. 3. Field coil resistance is 2.8 ohms, however, reading will vary with brush contact resistance. A resistance between 3 and 250 ohms indicates the field circuit is satisfactory.

Stator Coil Tests

Check stator coil resistance by connecting an ohmmeter between two of the three output terminals in the connector, Fig. 4. Resistance should be approximately one ohm.

Check stator coils for grounds by connecting an ohmmeter to one output terminal and the rear housing. Hands should not contact probes or terminals during this test. A reading of infinity indicates coil is satisfactory. Check all three coils in this manner.

Field Circuit Voltage Test

Remove field terminal connector and connect a voltmeter between metal termination and rear housing. A voltage of 12 to 13 volts should be noted with the system control switch in the "On" position and zero volts in the "Off" position.

ALTERNATOR REPAIRS

Disassembly

1. Scribe reference marks between end

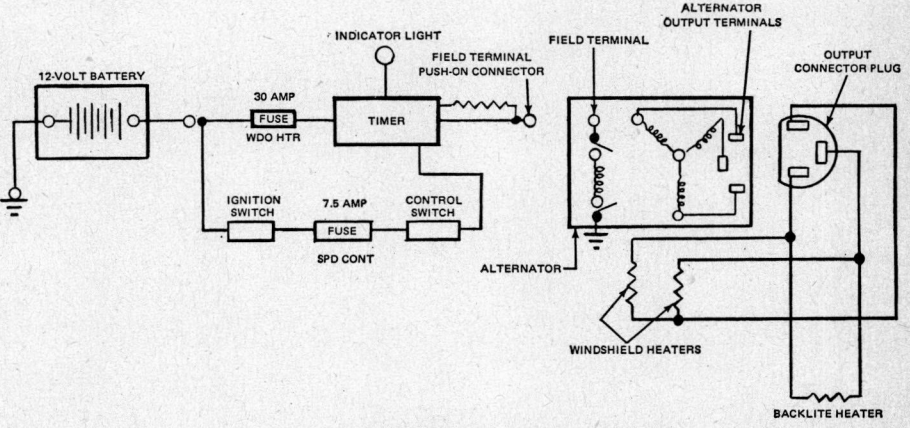

Fig. 1   High voltage alternator system circuit

FORD SIERRACIN HIGH VOLTAGE ALTERNATOR

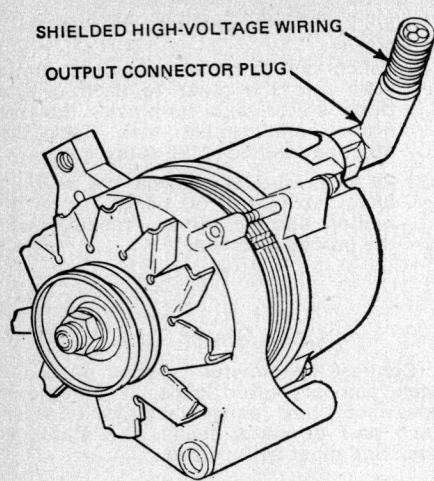

SHIELDED HIGH-VOLTAGE WIRING

OUTPUT CONNECTOR PLUG

Fig. 2 High voltage alternator assembly

housings to aid reassembly.
2. Remove through bolts and separate front end housing and rotor assembly from rear housing.
3. Remove outlet plug retaining nuts, then separate stator from rear end housing.
4. Remove brush holder attaching screws, brush holder, insulator and terminal.
5. If necessary, press out rear housing bearing while supporting housing on inner boss.
6. Remove drive pulley nut, lockwasher, pulley fan, fan spacer, front housing and rotor stop from rotor shaft.
7. If necessary, remove front bearing retainer and press bearing from housing while supporting housing on the bearing boss.

Assembly

1. If removed, press front bearing into housing putting pressure on outer race. Install bearing retainer.
2. To replace stop ring, if damaged, push new stop ring into groove in rotor shaft.

NOTE: Do not spread stop ring with snap ring pliers since permanent damage will result.

3. Position rotor stop on shaft with recessed side against stop ring, then install front housing, fan spacer, fan, pulley, lockwasher and retaining nut.
4. If removed, press rear housing bearing into bearing while supporting housing on inner boss. Bearing is properly installed when bearing is

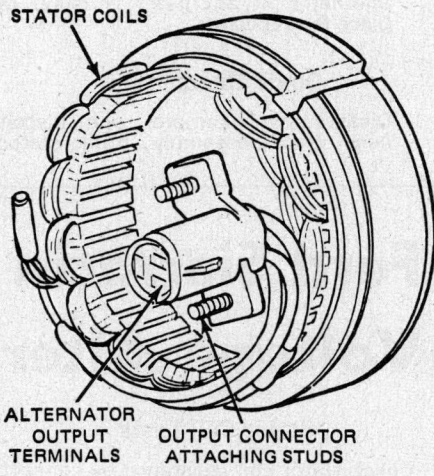

STATOR COILS

ALTERNATOR OUTPUT TERMINALS

OUTPUT CONNECTOR ATTACHING STUDS

Fig. 4 Stator assembly

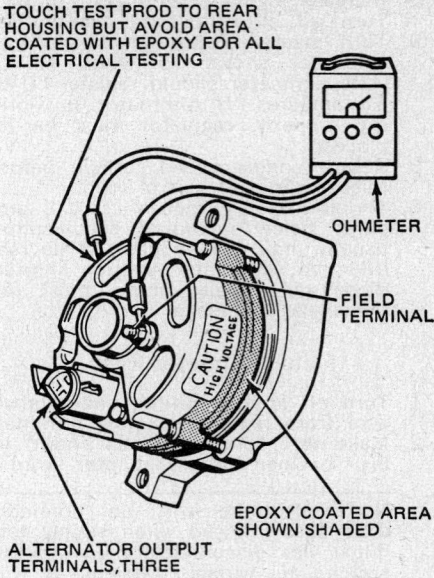

TOUCH TEST PROD TO REAR HOUSING BUT AVOID AREA COATED WITH EPOXY FOR ALL ELECTRICAL TESTING

OHMETER

FIELD TERMINAL

CAUTION HIGH VOLTAGE

EPOXY COATED AREA SHOWN SHADED

ALTERNATOR OUTPUT TERMINALS, THREE

Fig. 3 Field coil test

flush with outer end surface.
5. Assemble brush holder and insert a stiff wire to hold brushes in position. Place assembly in rear housing and install brush holder mounting screws and the output connector retaining nuts.
6. Place rear housing and stator assembly over front housing and rotor assembly, aligning reference marks, and seat the machined portion of stator core into the step in both end housings. Remove brush retracting wire.
7. Install alternator into vehicle and check for proper operation.

Leece-Neville Alternators

65 AMP. ALTERNATORS

System Testing

Testing procedures for these alternators are same as the procedures outlined in the "Ford Alternator" section of this chapter.

ALTERNATOR REPAIRS

Disassembly

1. Remove pulley nut, pulley, fan, shaft key and spacer.
2. Remove brushes and terminal insulator, then brush holder assembly from housing, Fig. LN1.
3. Remove through bolts and separate brush end housing and stator from alternator.
4. Remove AC terminal nuts and stator from end housing.
5. Remove rotor from drive end housing with a gear puller or a suitable press, then front bearing retainer and bearing from housing.
6. Unsolder field leads from slip rings and remove slip rings and bearing from rotor shaft.
7. Remove rectifier assembly bolts, terminals and insulators, then the rectifier assembly and stator terminal insulator.

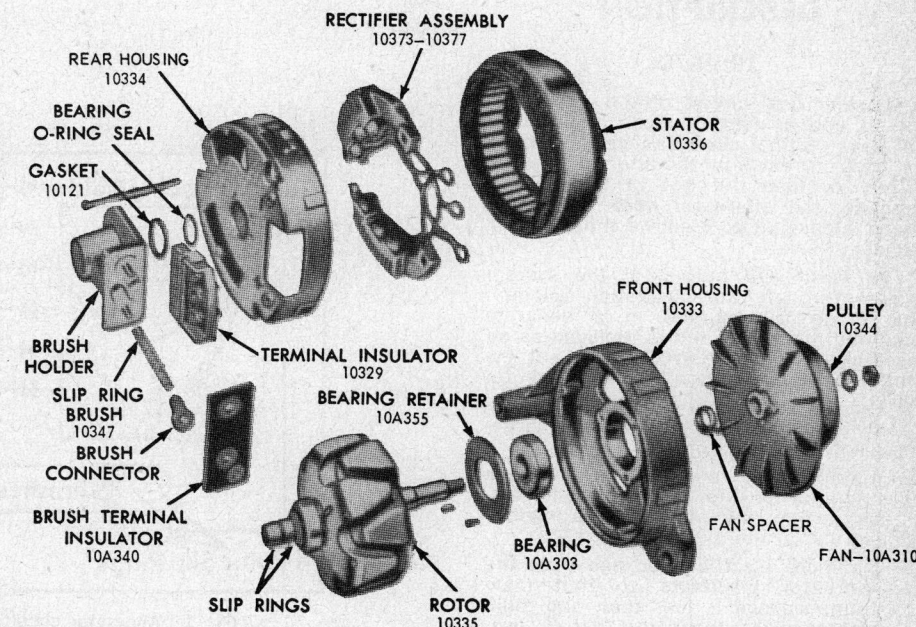

Fig. LN1   65 Amp alternator disassembled

Assembly

1. Press bearing onto slip ring end of rotor shaft, putting pressure on bearing inner race. Heat slip rings, then carefully press slip rings onto rotor shaft and solder field leads to slip rings.
2. Press bearing into drive end housing, putting pressure on bearing outer race.
3. Press drive end housing and bearing onto rotor shaft, putting pressure on bearing inner race.
4. Install stator insulator and rectifier insulators. Place rectifier assemblies into housing and install mounting screws and terminals, ensuring rectifiers are insulated from end frame and wires are under tabs extending from heat sinks therefore preventing interference with rotor, Fig. LN2.
5. Install stator and align through bolt holes with end housing. Place stator terminals over rectifier terminals and install nuts, Fig. LN2.
6. Place brush end housing and stator assembly over rotor and install and tighten through bolts.
7. Install brush holder with "O" ring between holder and frame, place brushes and springs into holder with extruded portion of brush connectors against terminal screw shoulders. Hold brush connectors in position and install terminal insulator.
8. Install spacer, shaft key, fan, puller and nut.

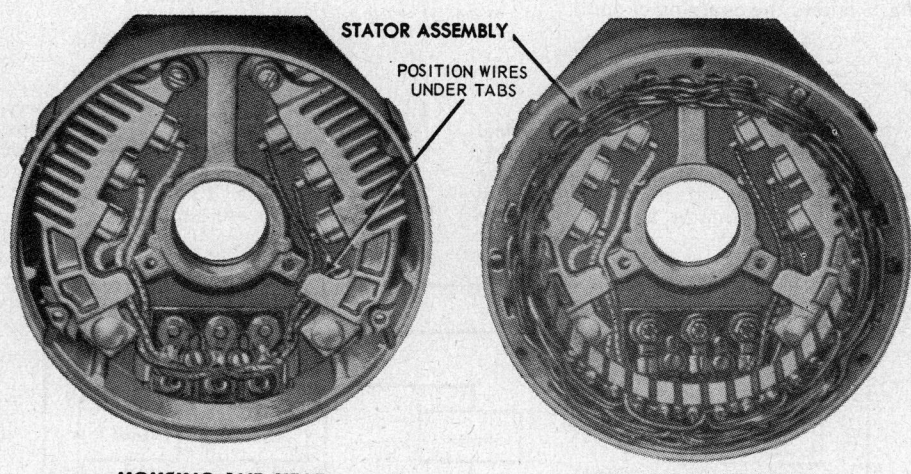

Fig. LN2   Slip ring end housing, rectifier & stator assembly, 65 amp alternator

Motorola Alternator

DESCRIPTION

1969-70

The electrical circuit of the alternator, Figs. 1 and 2, uses 6 silicon diodes in a full wave rectifier circuit. Since the diodes will pass current from the alternator to the battery or load but not in the reverse direction, the alternator does not use a circuit breaker. Fig. 3 shows the charging circuit.

The entire DC output of the system passes through the "Isolation Diode". This diode is mounted in a separate aluminum heat sink and is replaced as an assembly. The isolation diode is not essential for rectification. It is used to:

1. Provide an automatic solid state switch for illuminating the charge-discharge indicator light.
2. Automatically connect the voltage regulator to the alternator and battery when the alternator is operating.
3. Eliminate electrical leakage over the alternator insulators so that maximum leakage is less than one milliampere when the car is not in use.

1971-74

The electrical circuit, Fig. 4, of these units differ from previous units in that a field diode assembly is used. Also, on alternators used in 1973-74 American Motors cars equipped with a four barrel carburetor, an extra terminal is used on the rear housing which provides about seven volts of alternating current to the heating element of the electric assisted choke.

The field diode (diode trio) assembly incorporates three diodes mounted on a circuit board or on some 1974 units, a potted type diode trio is used, Fig. 4A. The input leads are connected to the stator windings in parallel with the positive diodes. The diode output leads are connected to a metal grommet in the circuit board and is secured to the insulated regulator terminal.

A portion of the alternating current and voltage developed in the stator windings is rectified by the field diode assembly. This voltage is sensed by the voltage regulator to provide current to the field windings. Fig. 5 shows the charging circuit.

Voltage Regulator

The voltage regulator is an electrical switching device sealed at the factory, requiring no adjustments. It senses the voltage appearing at the regulator terminal of the alternator and supplies the necessary field current for maintaining the system voltage at the output terminal.

TESTING SYSTEM IN VEHICLE

Alternator Output Test
1974

1. Connect a voltmeter to the battery, start engine and turn on headlamps.
2. Run engine for two minutes at 1000 RPM and observe voltmeter. If voltage remains above 13 volts, alternator and regulator are satisfactory.

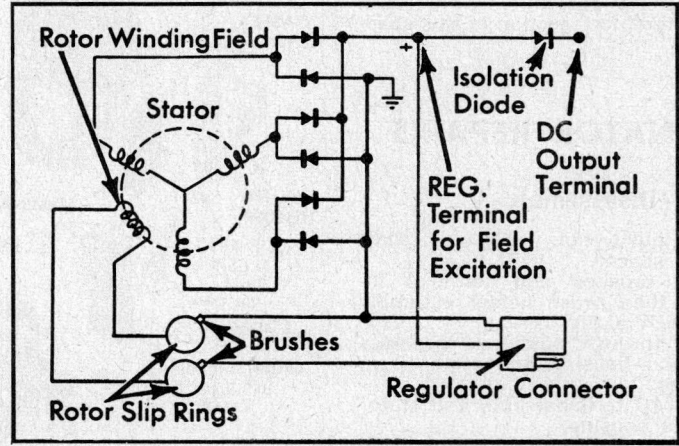

Fig. 1   Alternator circuit diagram. 1969-70 35 amp

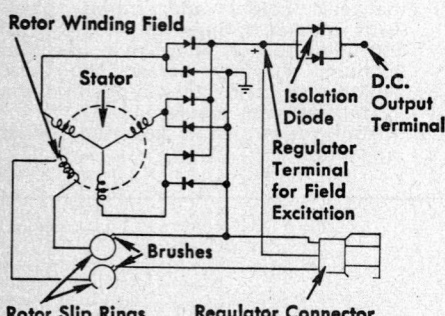

Fig. 2   Alternator circuit. 1969-70 55 amp

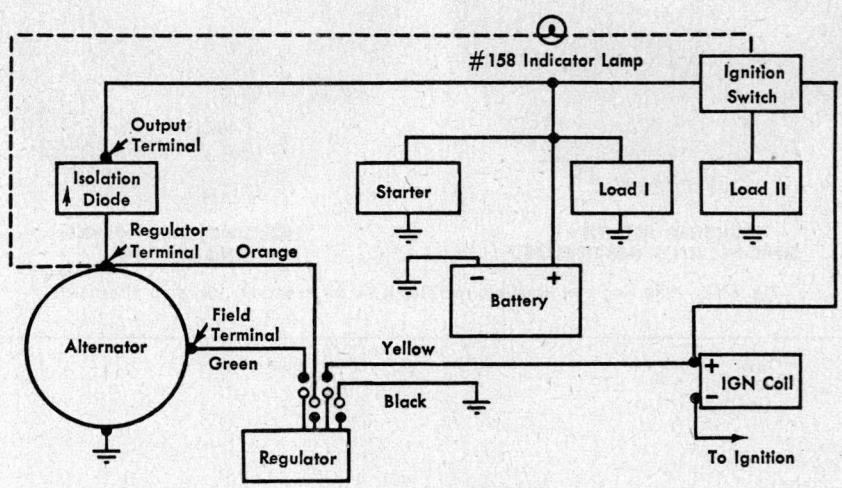

Fig. 3   Charging circuit diagram. 1969-70

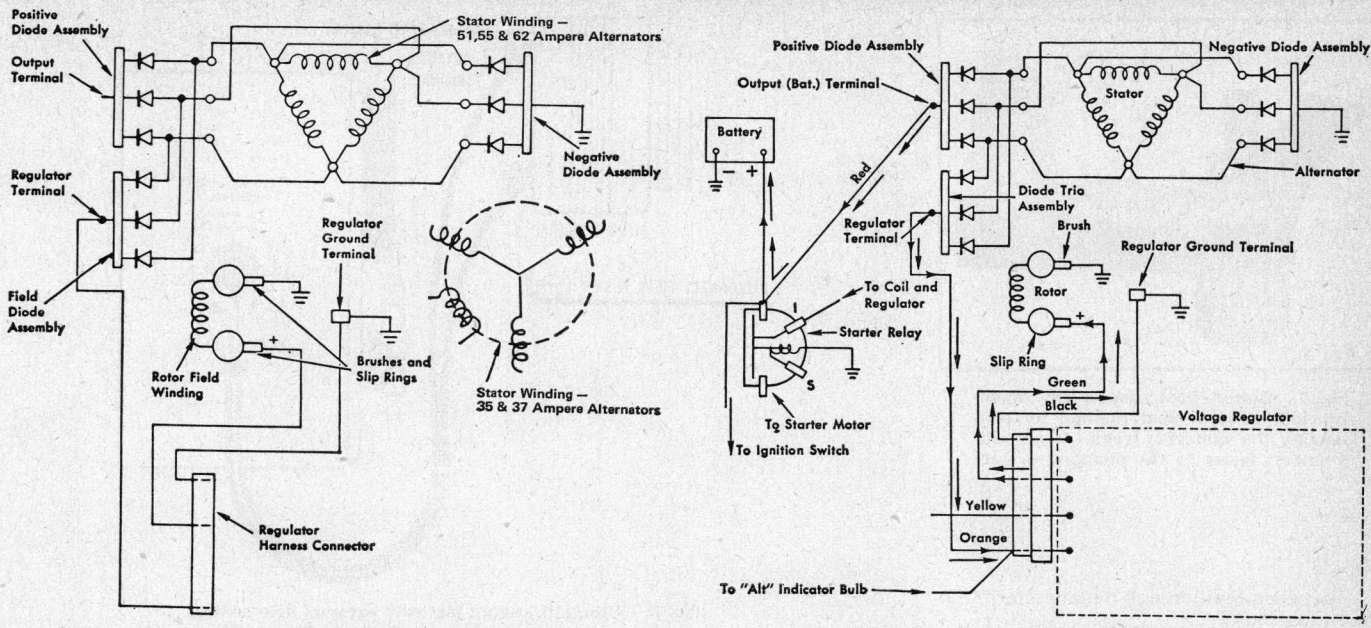

Fig. 4   Alternator circuit. 1971-74 35, 37, 51, 55 & 62 amp

Fig. 5   Charging circuit diagram. 1971-74 (typical)

1969-73

1. Connect test leads as shown in Fig. 6.
2. Turn ground polarity switch to Negative and voltage selector to 16 volt position. Place load control knob in Direct position.
3. Close battery post adapter switch, Fig. 7, and start engine. Run engine at 2000 RPM and allow to warm up.
4. Turn load control knob until highest reading is noted on ammeter. This reading should be within 10 amps of the alternator rated output. If not, further proceed with this test as outlined below.
5. Disconnect field and ground wire connector at alternator.
6. Connect a jumper wire (J-21053) to field terminal and connect one test lead to jumper and the other to output terminal, Fig. 8.
7. Close battery post adapter switch and start engine. Open adapter switch and run engine at 2000 RPM.
8. Slowly rotate field control knob clockwise and note highest ammeter reading. Do not allow voltage to exceed 16 volts.
9. Stop engine and install a jumper wire

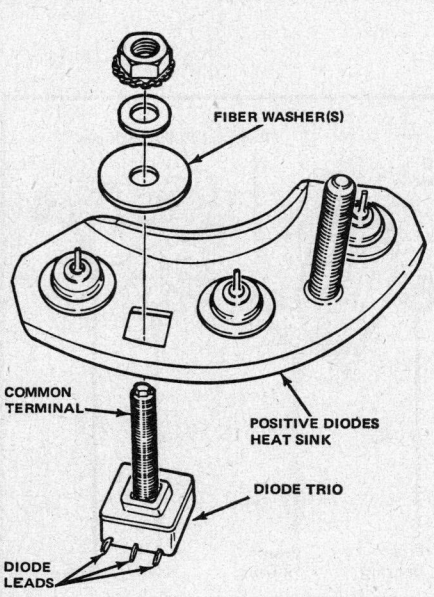

Fig. 4A   Potted type diode trio. 1974

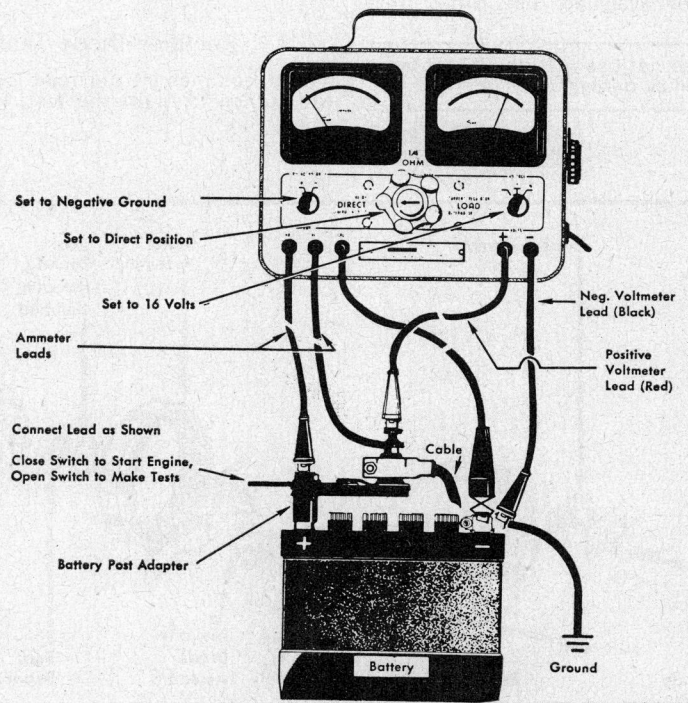

Fig. 6   Alternator test connections

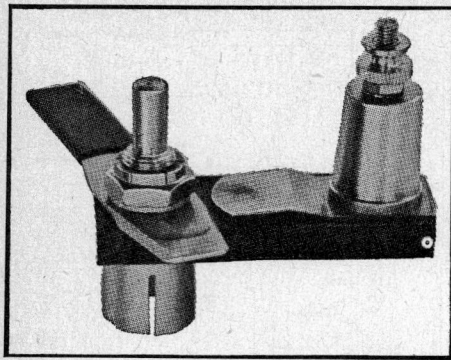

Fig. 7 Battery post adapter tool which provides a convenient method for connecting the ammeter leads of the volt-ammeter tester to the charging system

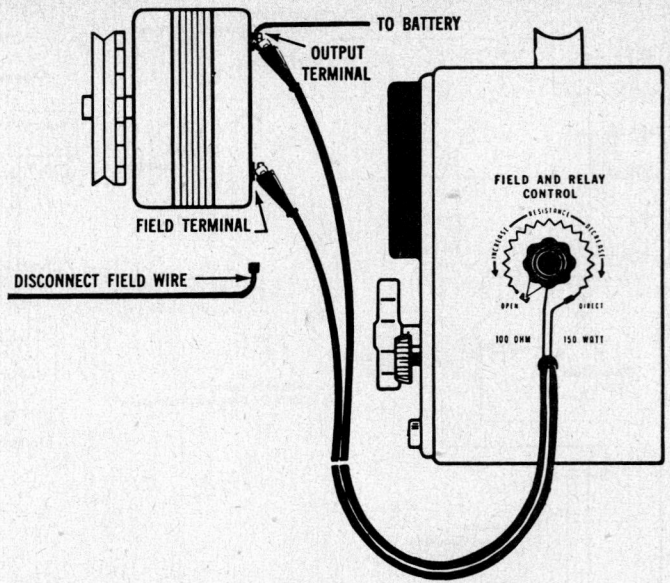

Fig. 8 Alternator output test with external field control

between ignition coil negative terminal and ground.

10. Turn ground polarity switch to Positive and ignition switch ON. Note ammeter reading, which should not exceed 5 amps, and add this reading to reading taken in Step 8. Total reading should be approximately the same as alternator rated output. If not, alternator must be repaired.

Isolation Diode Test

1969-70

If a commercial diode tester is used, follow the Test Equipment Manufacturer's instructions. If a commercial tester is not available, use a DC Test Lamp.

CAUTION: *Do not use a 120 volt test lamp as diodes will be damaged.*

---

1. Connect test lamp to output terminal and regulator terminal of isolation diode.
2. Reverse test probes.
3. The test lamp should light in one direction but should not light in the other direction.
4. If the test lamp lights in both directions the isolation diode is shorted.
5. If the test lamp does not light in either direction, isolation diode is open.

Rectifier Diode Tests

Any commercial in-circuit diode tester will suffice to make the test. Follow Test

Equipment Manufacturer's instructions.

Check diodes individually after the diodes have been disconnected from the stator. A shorted stator coil or shorted insulating washers or sleeves on positive diodes would make diodes appear to be shorted.

A test lamp will not indicate an open condition unless all three diodes of either assembly are open. However, a shorted diode can be detected. This test is not 100% effective but can be used if so desired when an in-circuit diode tester is not available.

The test lamp should light in one direction but not in the other direction. If the test lamp lights in both directions, one or more of the diodes of the assembly being tested is shorted. If the test lamp does not light in either direction,

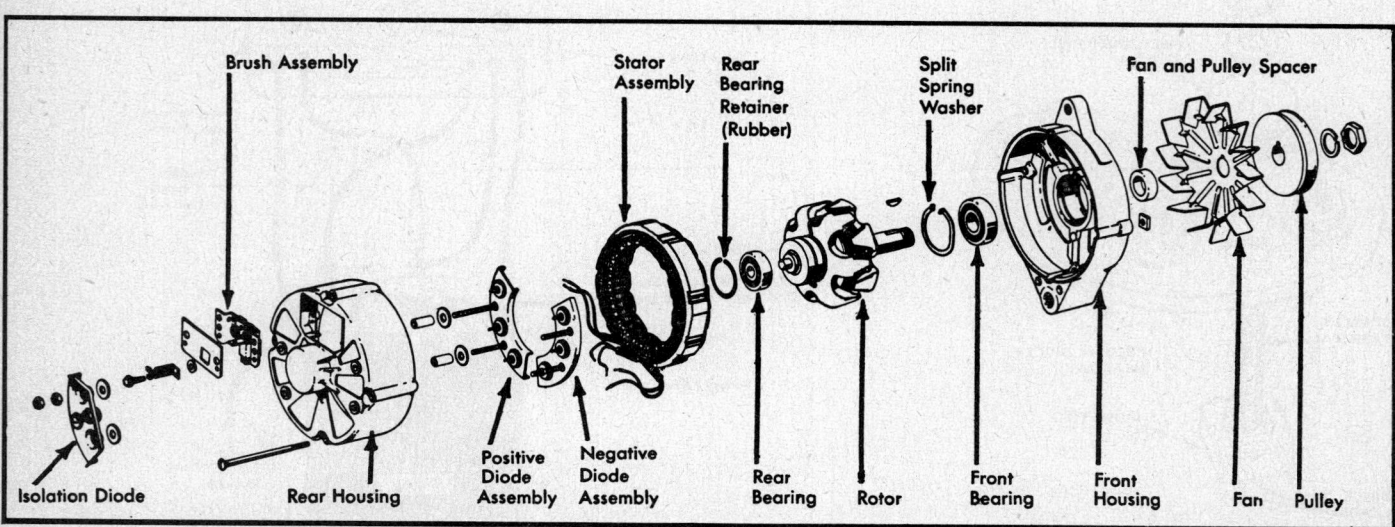

Fig. 9 Alternator disassembled. 1969-70

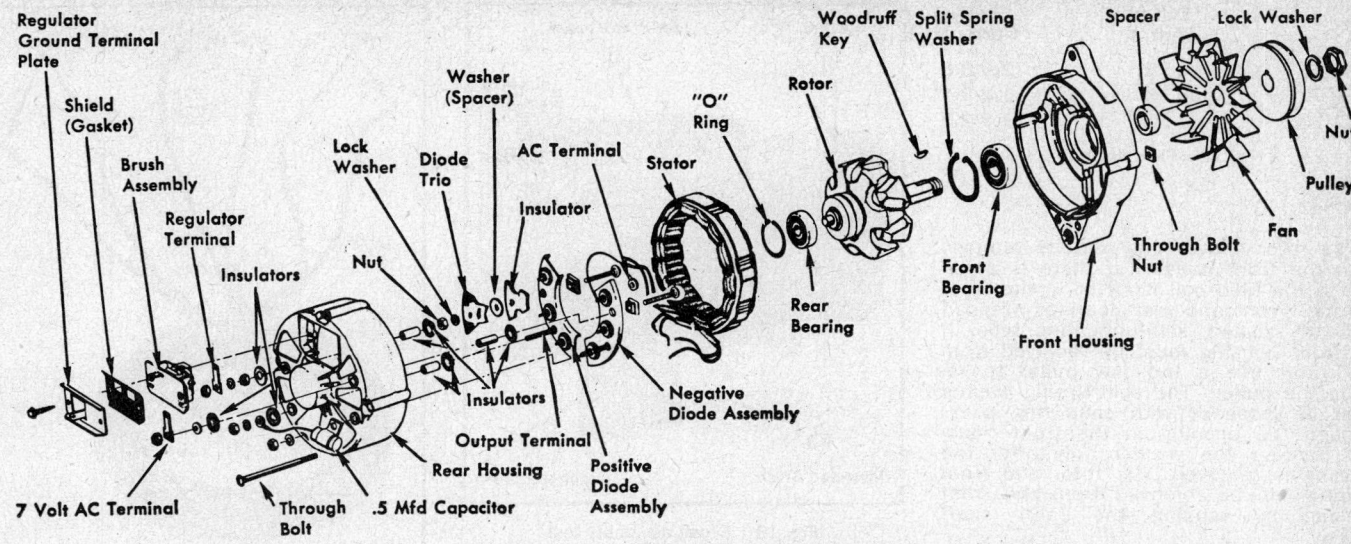

Fig. 10   Alternator disassembled. 1971-74 NOTE: model shown has AC terminal for 1973-74 electric choke

all three diodes in the assembly are open. Check diodes individually after disassembly to ascertain findings.

NOTE: *A shorted stator coil would appear as a shorted negative diode. Also check stator for shorts after disassembly.*

Field Diode (Diode Trio) Test

1. Using a voltmeter, connect positive lead to alternator output terminal and negative lead to regulator terminal.
2. Start and run engine at idle speed. The voltmeter should then read .6 volt or less. If reading is over .6 volt, replace field diode assembly.

Voltage Regulator Test

1974

1. Connect a voltmeter to the battery, start engine and turn on headlamps.
2. Run engine at 1000 RPM for several minutes to establish voltage regulator operating temperature.
3. Voltage should be within 13.1 to 14.3 volts when regulator temperature is between 100°F and 150°F.

1969-73

1. With test equipment connected, Fig. 6, run engine at 2000 RPM and open battery post adapter switch.
2. Place load control knob in the 1/4 ohm position. Voltmeter reading should be 14.0 to 14.8 volts for 1968-70 units or 13.8 to 14.2 for 1971-73 units. The reading is taken when the unit is at 80°F. If voltage is not within above limits, replace voltage regulator.

ALTERNATOR REPAIRS

Disassembly, Figs. 9 and 10

Brush Assembly

The brush assembly can be removed in most cases with the alternator on the vehicle. The spring clip is bent back so that the field terminal plug can be removed. Remove the two self-tapping screws, field plug retainer spring and cover. Pull brush assembly straight out far enough to clear locating pins, then lift brush assembly out. The complete brush assembly is available for replacement.

Isolation Diode, 1969-70

Remove the 2 lock nuts securing the isolation diode to the rear housing and

Fig. 11   Field coil test

slide it off the studs. The diode is replaced as an assembly.

Rear Housing

Remove the 4 through bolts and nuts. Carefully separate the rear housing and stator from the front housing by using 2 small screwdrivers and prying the stator from the front housing at 2 opposing slots where the "through bolts" are removed. Do not burr the stator core which would make assembly difficult.

Caution: *Do not insert screwdriver blade deeper than 1/16" to avoid damaging stator winding.*

Stator and Diode Assembly

Do not unsolder stator-to-diode wire junction. Remove stator and diode as an assembly. Avoid bending stator wire at junction holding positive and negative diode assembly from housing.

Remove 4 lock nuts and insulating washers. The insulating washers and nylon sleeves are used to insulate the positive plate studs from the housing. With the 4 nuts removed, the stator can be separated from rear housing by hand.

Diode Replacement

To replace field diode assembly, remove nylon sleeve, insulating washer and hold-down nut from regulator stud. Unsolder field diode wires from positive diodes. *When replacing positive or negative diodes, make note of diode assembly to stator connections, and make sure replacement diode assembly connections are the same. The positive diode assembly has red markings, the negative black markings.*

In soldering and unsoldering leads from diodes, grasp the diode lead with pliers between the diode and stator lead to be removed. This will give better heat dissipation and protect the diode. Do not exert excessive stress on diode lead.

Year	Output Amps	Field Current
1969-71	35	2.0-2.6
1969-71	55	1.8-2.4
1972-74	All	1.8-2.5

Fig. 12   Field current

ROTOR

The rotor should only require removal from the front housing if there is a defect in the field coil itself or in the front bearing. Front and rear bearings are permanently sealed, self-lubricating type. If the front housing must be removed from the rotor, use a two jaw puller to remove the pulley. The split spring washer must be loosened with snap ring pliers through the opening in the front housing. Remove the washer only after the housing is removed. The rotor and front bearing can be removed from the front housing by tapping the rotor shaft slightly.

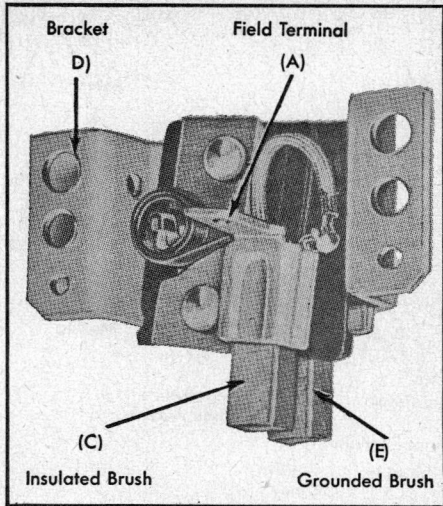

Fig. 13   Brush assembly test

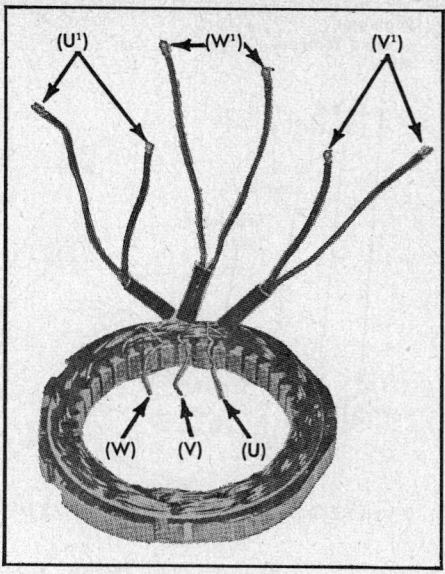

Fig. 16   Stator coil shorts and continuity tests

NOTE: Make certain that the split spring washer has been removed from its groove before attempting to remove the front housing from the bearing.

Alternator Bench Tests

Field Coil Test

The rotor should be tested for grounds

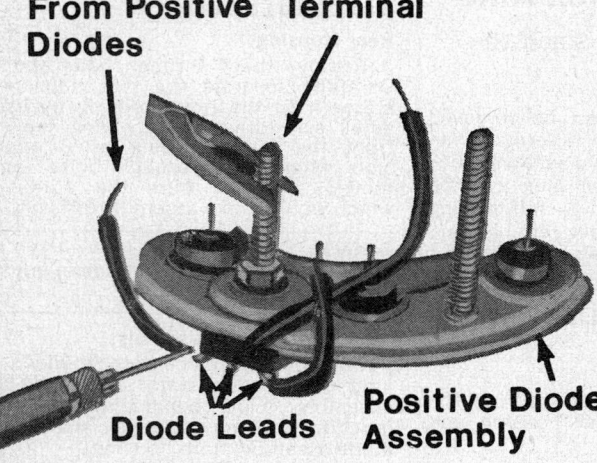

Unsolder All Diode Trio Wires From Positive Diodes

Diode Trio Common Terminal

Diode Leads

Positive Diode Assembly

Potted Type

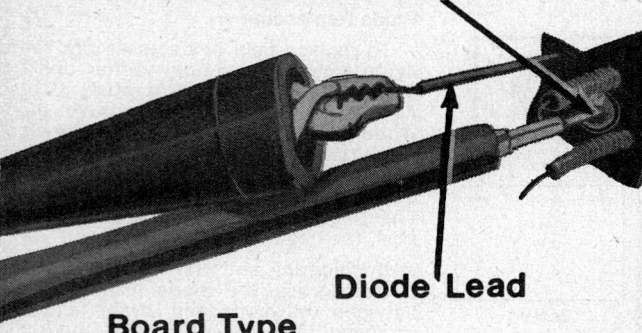

Center Mount Eyelet (Common Diode Connection)

Diode Lead

Board Type

Fig. 14   Diode trio bench test. 1974 alternators

CONNECT TO HEAT SINK

CONNECT TO DIODE LEAD

Fig. 15   Rectifier diodes bench test. 1974 alternators

and for shorted turns in the winding. The ground test is made with test probes connected in series with a 110 volt test lamp. Place one test probe on the slip ring and the other probe on the rotor core. If the bulb lights the rotor is grounded.

To test for shorted turns, check rotor field current draw as shown in Fig. 11. Slowly reduce resistance of rheostat to zero. With full battery voltage applied to the field coil, field current should be as shown in Fig. 12. Excessive current draw indicates shorted turn in field winding.

Brush Insulation Test

Connect an ohmmeter or a test lamp to the field terminal and bracket. Resistance should be high (infinite) or test lamp should not light. If resistance is low or if test lamp lights, brush assembly is shorted and must be replaced.

Continuity Test

Connect an ohmmeter to field terminal and brush. Use an alligator clip to assure good contact to brush, test points "A" and "C" in Fig. 13.

CAUTION: *Do not chip brush.*

Resistance reading should be zero. Move brush and brush lead wire to make certain that brush lead wire connections are not intermittent. Resistance reading should not vary when brush and lead wire are being moved around. Connect ohmmeter to bracket and grounded brush, test points "E" and "D", Fig. 13. Resistance reading should be zero.

1974 Diode Tests

Diode Trio: Unsolder diode trio leads and using a 12 volt meter which draws a one amp maximum load, connect test leads providing current path, Fig. 14. Hold this connection for at least two minutes, then reverse test leads immediately. Test each diode in this manner. If current flows in both directions, neither direction or flows intermittently, the diode trio must be replaced.

Rectifier Diodes: The same method of testing is used for the rectifier diodes as for the diode trio, Fig. 15. However, a 20 amp load is used when testing the rectifier diodes.

NOTE: A diode can be tested for opens or shorts using an ohmmeter. Reason for applying an electrical load to the diodes, in turn generating heat, is to detect intermittent diode failures.

Stator In-Circuit Test

When making the in-circuit stator leakage test, some consideration must be given to the rectifier diodes that are connected to the stator winding. The negative diode assembly will conduct in one direction when properly polarized. A shorted diode in the negative diode assembly would make the stator appear to be shorted. For this reason, the rectifier diode plate assembly and stator must be checked individually after alternator has been disassembled if the problem is localized to the stator.

CAUTION: *Use a special diode continuity light or a DC test lamp. Do not use a 120 volt test lamp as diodes will be damaged.*

1. Connect the test lamp to a diode terminal of the negative assembly and ground terminal.
2. Reverse test probes. The lamp should light in one direction but not in the other.
3. If the test lamp does not light in either direction, this indicates that all three rectifiers in the negative diode assembly are open.
4. If the test lamp lights in both directions, the stator winding is shorted to stator or one of the negative diodes is shorted.
5. Check stator again when it is disassembled from diode assemblies.
6. With alternator disassembled, connect an ohmmeter or test lamp probes to one of the diode terminals and to stator.
7. Resistance reading should be infinite or test lamp should not light.
8. If resistance reading is not infinite or test lamp lights, high leakage or a short exists between stator winding and stator. In either case, stator should be replaced.

Stator Coil Shorts Test

1. This test checks for shorts between stator coil windings. The winding junctions must be separated as shown in Fig. 16. An ohmmeter or test lamp may be used.
2. Connect one of the test probes to test point "U" and the other to test point "V" and then to test point "W". Resistance should be infinite or test lamp should not light.
3. Connect test probes to test V and W. Resistance should be infinite or test lamp should not light. In either test, if resistance reading is not infinite or test lamp lights, high leakage or a short exists between stator windings. Stator should be replaced.

Continuity Test

1. Measure resistance of each winding in stator between test points U and U1, V and V1, W and W1, Fig. 16. Resistance should be a fraction of an ohm (approximately .1 Ohm). An extremely accurate instrument would be necessary to ascertain shorted turns. Only an open condition can be detected with a commercial type ohmmeter.
2. If the alternator has been disassembled because of an electrical malfunction, replace stator only after all other components have been checked and found to be satisfactory.

Assemble Alternator

1. Clean bearing and inside of bearing hub of front housing. Support front housing and, using a suitable driver, apply sufficient pressure to outside race of bearing to seat bearing.
2. Insert split spring washer hub of front housing, seating washer into groove of hub.

NOTE: *Do not use a screwdriver or any small object to compress washer that can slip off and damage bearing seal. Make certain that split spring washer has been installed prior to assembling front housing and rotor.*

3. Use sufficient pressure to seat front bearing against shoulder on rotor shaft. The bearing drive tool must fit the inner race of bearing.
4. Install fan and pulley.
5. Use a 7/16" socket to fit inside race of rear bearing and apply sufficient pressure to drive bearing against shoulder of rotor shaft.
6. Assemble front and rear housings.
7. Make certain that rear bearing is properly seated in rear housing hub and that diode wires are properly dressed so that rotor will not contact diode wires.
8. Align stator slots with rear housing through bolt holes, then align front housing through bolt holes with respect to rear housing.

NOTE: *The position of the brush and belt adjusting screw boss must be in the same relative position to each other.*

9. Spin rotor to make certain that rotor is not contacting diode wires. Install bolts and tighten evenly.
10. Before mounting isolation diode, make certain that positive rectifier diode plate has been properly insulated from housing.
11. Install brush assembly, cover and field plug retainer spring.

Prestolite & American Motors Alternators

Alternator Output Test

1. Disconnect battery positive terminal.
2. Install battery post "knife switch" then complete test connections as per Fig. P1.
3. Close knife switch and start engine. Set engine speed at approximately 2000 rpm.
4. Open knife switch and adjust control knob clockwise to Load position until maximum ammeter reading is obtained. Add 5 amps to reading. Total reading should be the rated output of the alternator.

Regulator Test

1. Make test connections as per Fig. P1.
2. With engine speed at 2000 rpm, set control knob to ¼ ohm position.
3. Read voltmeter. The reading should be not less than 13 volts and not more than 15 volts.

NOTE: Voltage readings vary due to underhood temperatures.

4. Return engine to idle, stop engine. Ammeter should read zero, indicating that isolation diode is functioning properly.
5. If a current draw exists, the isolation diode must be tested for leakage.

Isolation Diode Test

1. Close knife switch. Disconnect auxiliary or regulator lead from alternator.
2. Connect the positive voltmeter lead to the auxiliary or regulator terminal of the alternator and negative lead to the case of the alternator.
3. Set voltmeter to the 2 volt scale.
4. With regulator connected to the alternator and the ignition switch and all accessories off, measure voltage at the auxiliary or regulator terminal.
5. Voltage should not exceed .1 volt. Voltage in excess of .1 volt indicates that the isolation diode is leaking and must be replaced.

External Field Control Test

1. With the engine stopped and all test connections completed as per Fig. P1, disconnect field terminal from alternator and connect field rheostat as per Fig. P2.
2. With knife switch open, rotate rheostat to full clockwise (direct) position. Ammeter should read approximately minus 2 amps. If not, alternator brushes or rotor field windings are defective. Rotate rheostat back to full counterclockwise (open) position.
3. Close knife switch and set engine

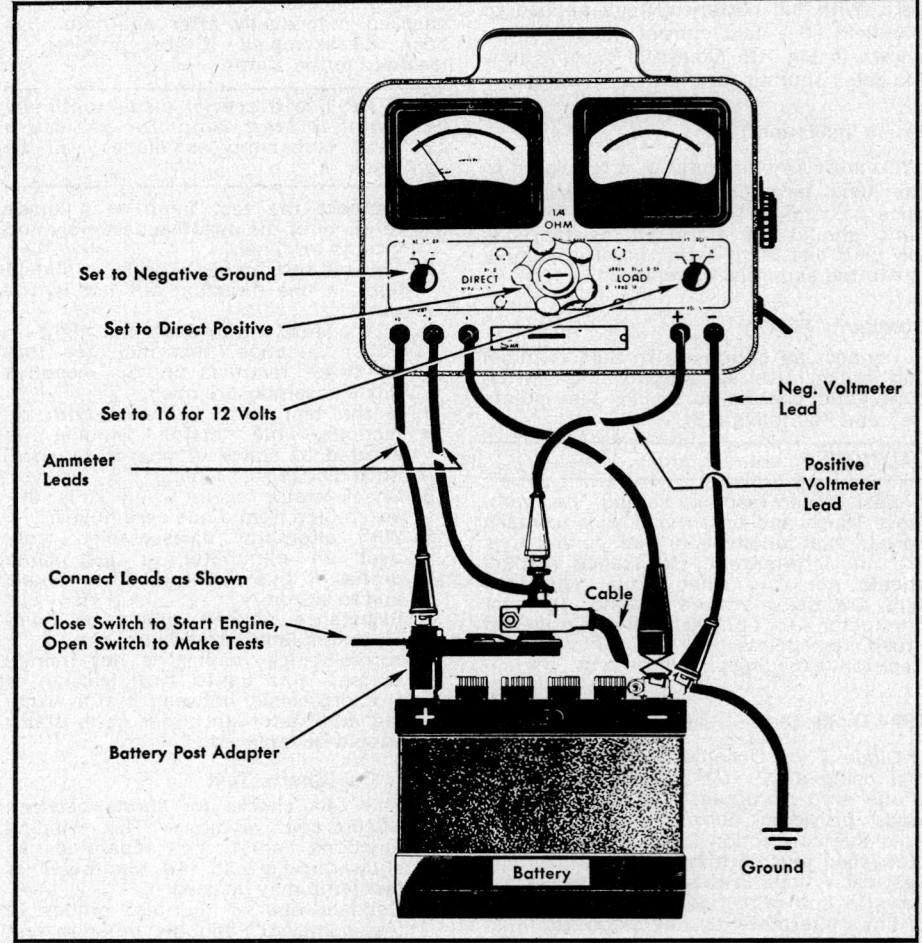

Fig. P1   Charging circuit test connections

Set to Negative Ground

Set to Direct Positive

Set to 16 for 12 Volts

Ammeter Leads

Neg. Voltmeter Lead

Positive Voltmeter Lead

Connect Leads as Shown

Cable

Close Switch to Start Engine, Open Switch to Make Tests

Battery Post Adapter

Battery

Ground

speed at 2000 rpm. Open knife switch.
4. Rotate rheostat control until alternator specified output less 5 amps is obtained.
5. If output is low, alternator is defective. If output is satisfactory, regulator is at fault.

ALTERNATOR REPAIRS

Disassembly, Fig. P3

Brush Assembly

The brush assembly can be removed with the alternator on the car. Remove the two mounting screws and the cover. Tip the brush holder away from the alternator and remove. The brushes can be replaced by removing the retaining screws.

Rear Housing and Stator

The rear housing and stator must be removed as a unit. Mark housing and stator before disassembling to insure correct assembly.

Remove four retaining screws and tap lightly on stator and rear housing with a plastic mallet to separate from front drive housing.

Diode Replacement

To replace negative or positive rectifier diodes or the isolation diode, the stator leads must be unsoldered. When soldering or unsoldering any diodes, use a pair of pliers and a small piece of water soaked cotton for heat dissipation to protect the diode.

With stator removed, remove mounting nuts from "Aux" and "Output" terminals and remove the heat sink. Use a suitable press type tool to remove and

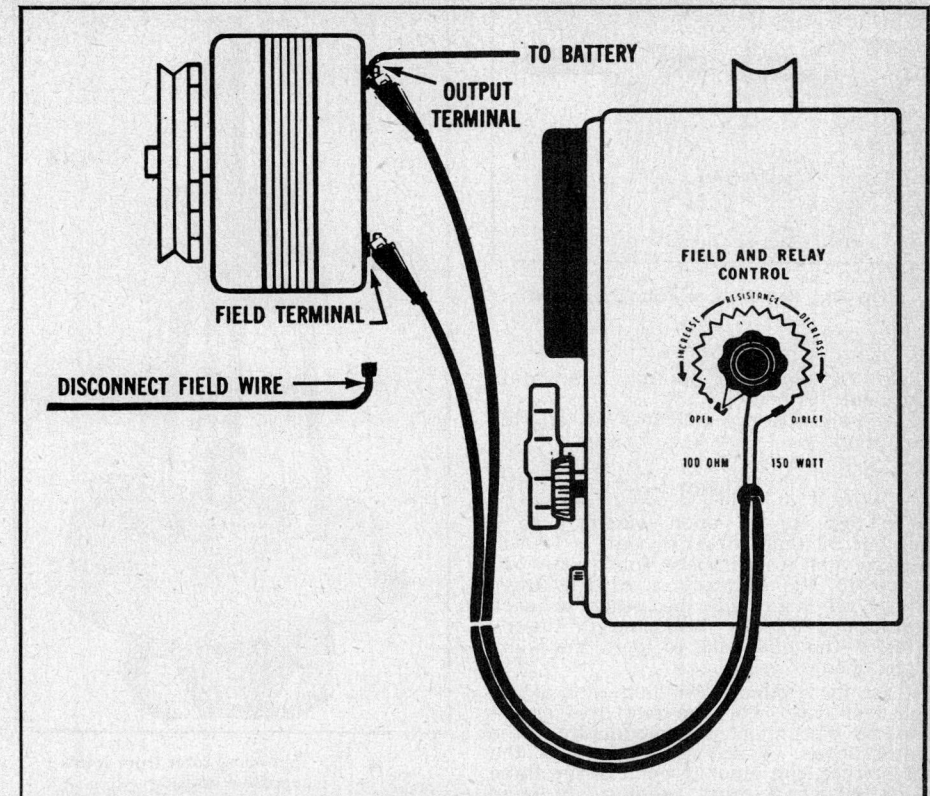

Fig. P2 Alternator test with external field control

install diodes, Fig. P4. *Do not drive diodes in or out as damage will result.*

Positive diodes are installed in the heat sink; negative diodes are installed in the rear housing.

With diodes correctly installed, resolder stator leads.

Rotor Replacement

Remove retaining nut and, using a suitable puller, remove pulley. Remove fan, woodruff key and spacer. Remove rotor from front housing with puller, Fig. P5.

BENCH TESTS
Rotor

Test the rotor for grounds by touching one probe of a 110 volt test lamp to a slip ring and the other to the rotor core. If bulb lights the rotor winding is grounded.

To test for shorts, check rotor field current draw as shown in Fig. P6. Use rheostat to adjust the voltage to 10.0 volts. Field current should be 2.4-2.5

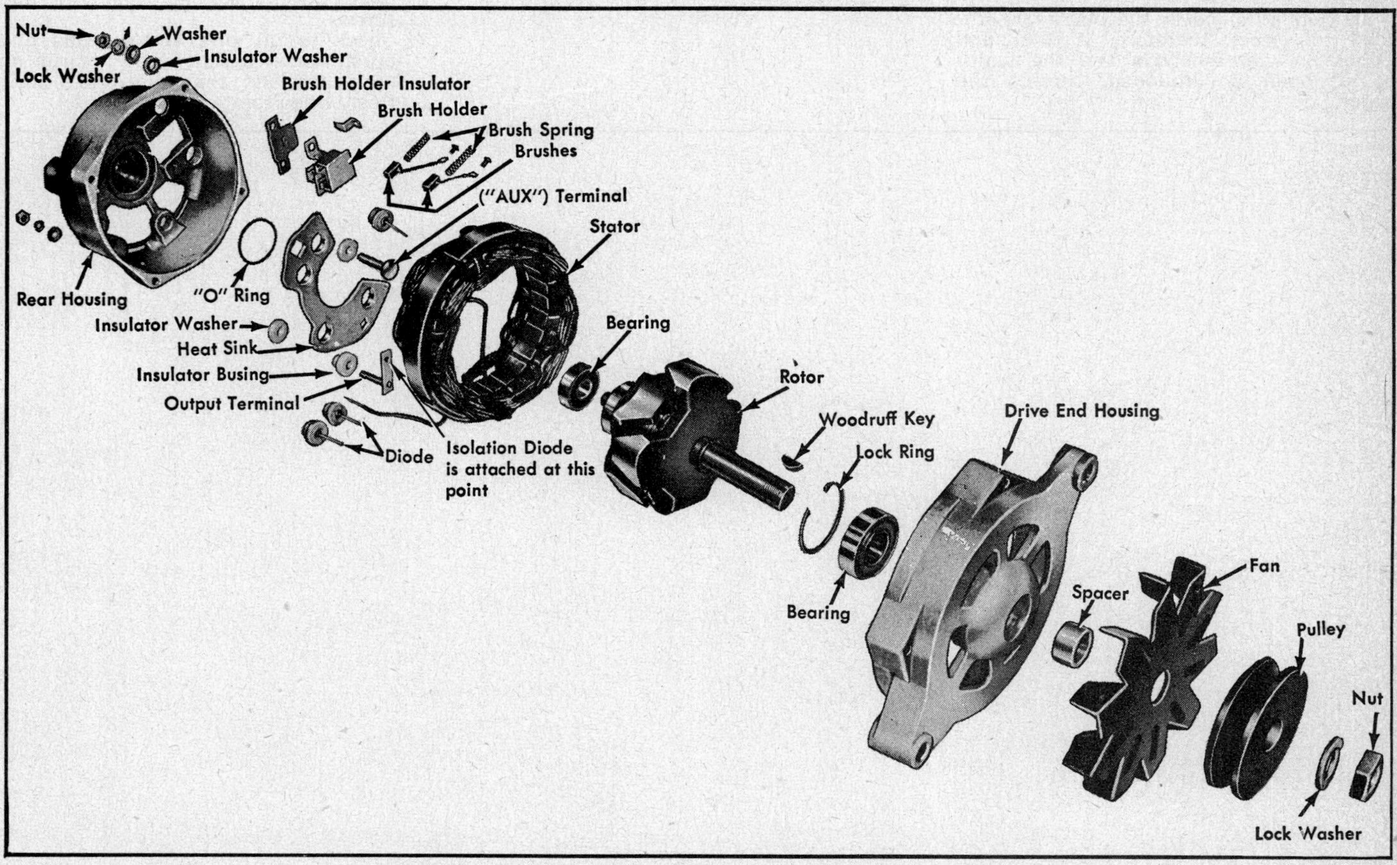

Fig. P3 Exploded view of Prestolite and American Motors alternator

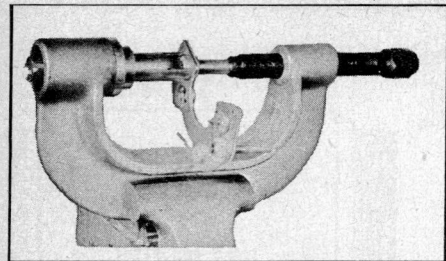

Fig. P4   Removing or installing diodes

Fig. P5   Removing rotor from front end drive housing

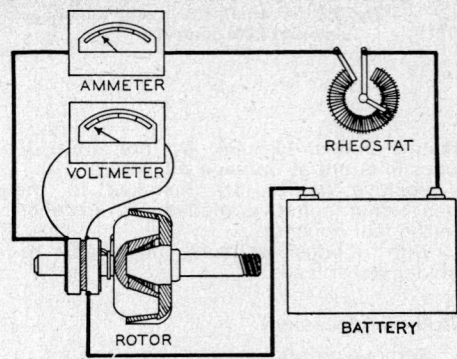

Fig. P6   Meter connections for testing rotor field current draw

amps. Battery must be fully charged to carry out this test.

Excessive draw indicates a shorted field winding.

Stator

To test for an open winding use a number 57 bulb in series with a 12 volt battery and test probes. Touch one test probe to the connection of the three stator windings and the other to each stator lead that is connected to the diodes. If the bulb fails to light, the winding is open.

Test for grounded winding with a 110 volt test lamp. For this test it is necessary to disconnect the diodes from the stator leads. Touch one lead to the stator core, the other to each of the three leads of the stator winding. If lamp lights, winding is grounded.

Shorted windings in the stator are difficult to detect, therefore, if rotor and diodes are not defective and the stator is not open or grounded, replace the stator.

Alternator, Assemble

1. Press front bearing into the front end drive housing, making sure the dust seal faces the rotor. Install bearing retainer stop ring.
2. Install spacer, fan and pulley. Install lockwasher and nut and tighten securely.
3. Install heat sink, negative diodes and stator. Solder all stator-to-diode connections that were previously disconnected.
4. Install rotor and front end drive housing to stator and rear housing.
5. Align marks made during disassembly on housings and install four retaining screws.
6. Install brush holder assembly and screws.
7. Check to be sure stator leads and brush holder assembly do not rub on the rotor and that the rotor turns freely when rotated by hand.

UNIVERSAL JOINTS

SERVICE NOTES

Before disassembling any universal joint, examine the assembly carefully and note the position of the grease fitting (if used). Also, be sure to mark the yokes with relation to the propeller shaft so they may be reassembled in the same relative position. Failure to observe these precautions may produce rough car operation which results in rapid wear and failure of parts, and place an unbalanced load on transmission, engine and real axle.

When universal joints are disassembled for lubrication or inspection, and the old parts are to be reinstalled, special care must be exercised to avoid damage to universal joint spider or cross and bearing cups.

NOTE: Some late model cars use an injected nylon retainer on the universal joint bearings. When service is necessary, pressing the bearings out will sheer the nylon retainer. Replacement with the conventional steel snap ring type is then necessary.

CROSS & ROLLER TYPE

Figs. 1, 2 and 3 illustrate typical examples of universal joints of this type. They all operate on the same principle and similar service and replacement procedures may be applied to all.

Disassembly

1. Remove snap rings (or retainer plates) that retain bearings in yoke and drive shaft.
2. Place U-joint in a vise.
3. Select a wrench socket with an outside diameter slightly smaller than the U-joint bearings. Select another wrench socket with an inside diameter slightly larger than the U-joint bearings.
4. Place the sockets at opposite bearings in the yoke so that the smaller socket becomes a bearing pusher and the larger socket becomes a bearing receiver when the vise jaws come together, Fig. 4. Close vise jaws until both bearings are free of yoke and remove bearings from the cross or spider.
5. If bearings will not come all the way out, close vise until bearing in receiver socket protrudes from yoke as much as possible without using excessive force. Then remove from vise and place that portion of bearing which protrudes from yoke between vise jaws. Tighten vise to hold bearing and drive yoke off with a soft hammer.
6. To remove opposite bearing from yoke, replace in vise with pusher socket on exposed cross journal with receiver socket over bearing cup. Then tighten vise jaws to press bearing back through yoke into receiving socket.
7. Remove yoke from drive shaft and again place protruding portion of bearing between vise jaws. Then tighten vise to hold bearing while driving yoke off bearing with soft hammer.
8. Turn spider or cross ¼ turn and use the same procedure to press bearings out of drive shaft.

Reassembly

1. If old parts are to be reassembled, pack bearing cups with universal joint grease. *Do not fill cups completely or use excessive amounts as over-lubrication may damage seals during reassembly.* Use new seals.
2. If new parts are being installed, check new bearings for adequate grease before assembling.
3. With the pusher (smaller) socket, press one bearing part way into drive shaft. Position spider into the partially installed bearing. Place second bearing into drive shaft. Fasten drive shaft in vise so that bearings are in contact with faces of vise jaws, Fig. 5. *Some spiders are provided with locating lugs which must face toward drive shaft when installed,* Fig. 6.
4. Press bearings all the way into position and install snap rings or retainer plates.

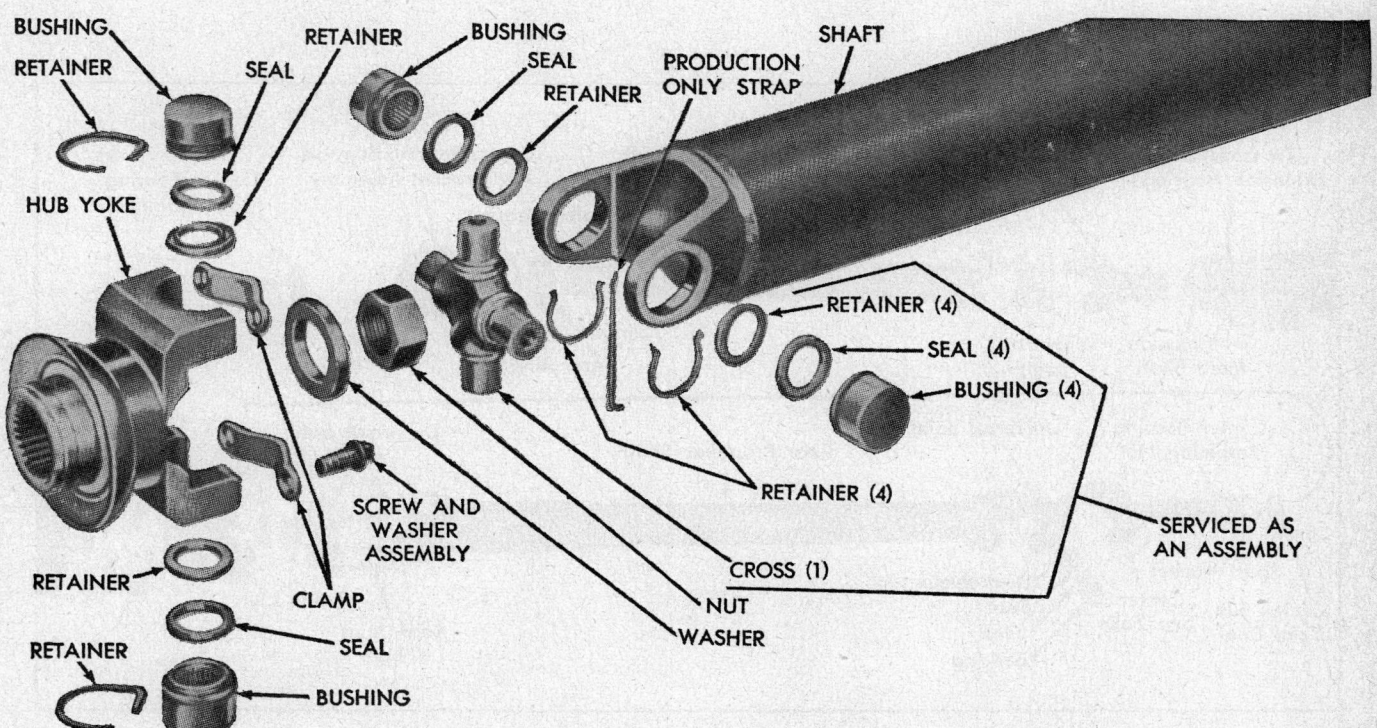

Fig. 1   Cross and roller type universal joint. Chrysler-built cars

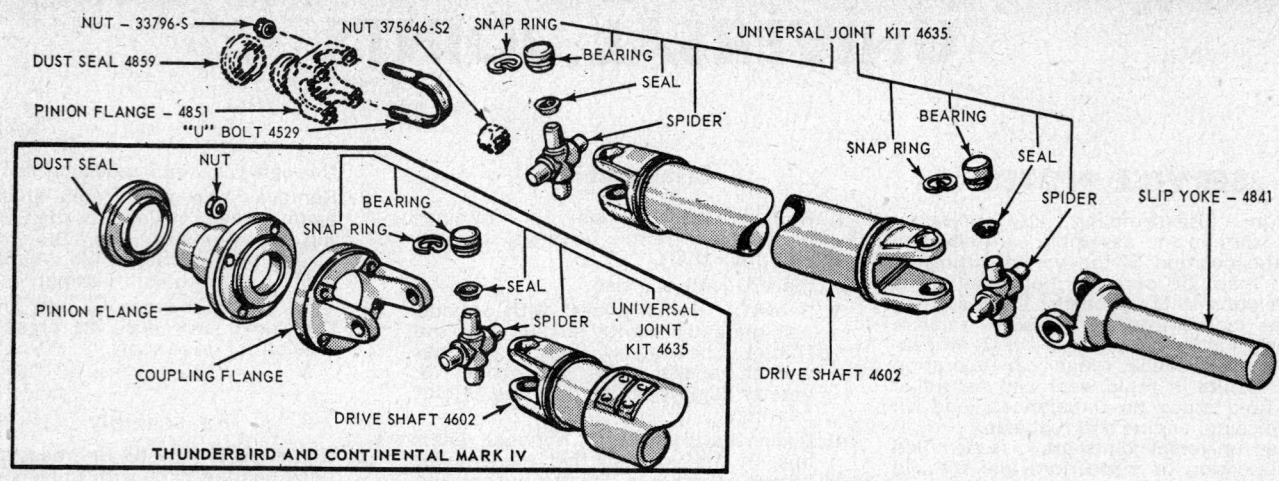

Fig. 2 Cross and roller universal joints and propeller shaft. Ford-built cars

5. Install bearings in yoke in same manner. When installation is completed, check U-joint for binding or roughness If free movement is impeded, correct the condition before installation in vehicle.

CONSTANT VELOCITY TYPE

This type of U-joint, Fig. 7, is composed of two conventional cross and roller joints connected with a special link yoke. Because the two joint angles are the same,

even though the usual U-joint fluctuation is present within the unit, the acceleration of the front joint (within the yoke) is always neutralized by the deceleration of the rear joint (within the yoke) and vice versa. The end result is the front and rear propeller shafts always turn at a constant velocity.

General Motors

NOTE: Not all General Motors CV joints are serviceable. CV joints which are serviceable are 74 Chevrolet, 1969-74 Buick, 1972-74 Cadillac and 1973-74 Oldsmobile

and Pontiac. 1971-73 Chevrolet CV joints are not serviceable and require a complete propeller shaft replacement if the CV joints fail. However, beginning in September, 1972, the Chevrolet replacement propeller shaft is serviceable, Fig. 8.

For ease of handling and to prevent damage to the constant velocity U-joints, the front and rear propeller shafts must be separated at the slip joint before any service is attempted.

Disassemble Slip Joint
1. Pry lockwasher from flats on bearing locknut.

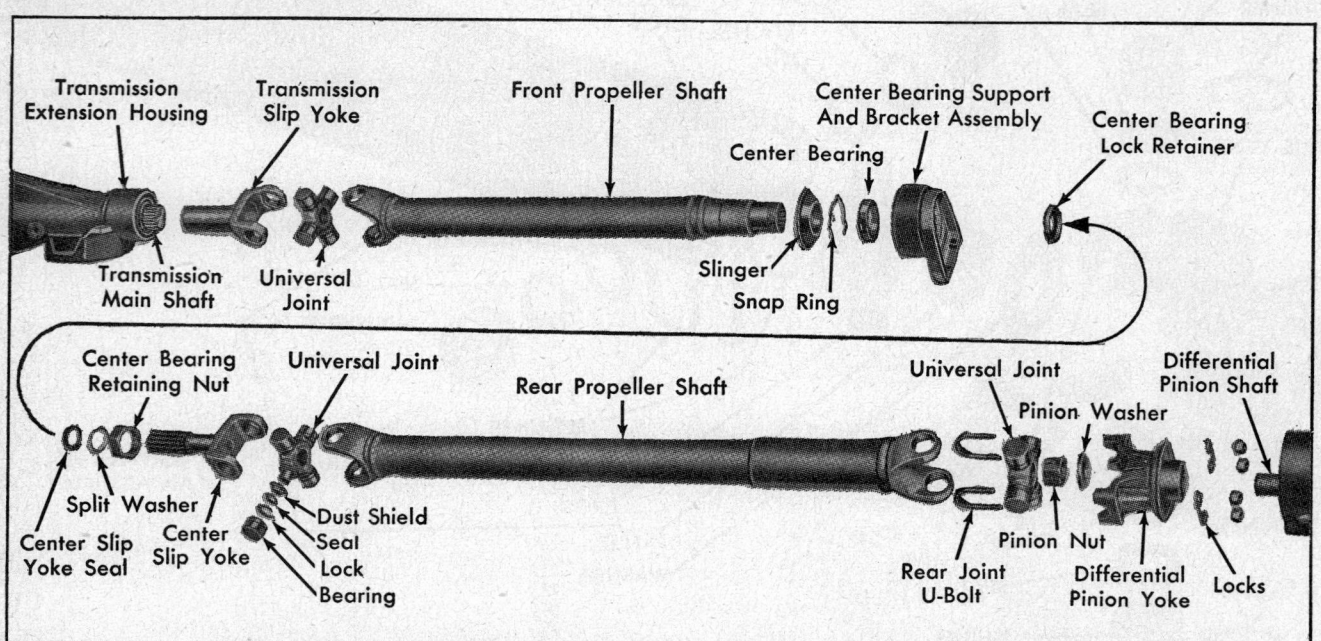

Fig. 3 Example of a two-piece propeller shaft with three cross and roller universal joints and center bearing support assembly. Cadillac

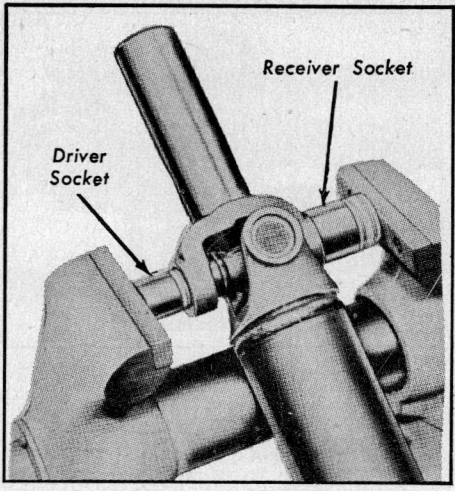

Fig. 4 Removing bearings from yoke using small and large wrench sockets as pusher and receiver tools, respectively

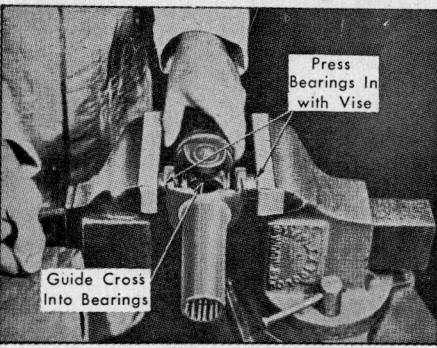

Fig. 5 Installing bearings into drive shaft yoke

Fig. 6 Some units have locating lugs which must face propeller shaft when installed

2. Loosen locknut until free of threads and slide locknut and seal against constant velocity joint.
3. Slide rear propeller shaft from front propeller shaft, making sure that index spring wire in splines is not lost.

Disassemble Constant Velocity U-Joint

1. Mark yokes before disassembly to be sure reassembly is made in same relative position of components, Fig. 9.
2. Disassemble rear section of constant velocity U-joint first as follows:
3. Remove snap rings from bearings using a punch.
4. Place rear propeller shaft yoke in a vise. Shaft must be supported horizontally and link yoke must be free to move vertically, Fig. 10.
5. Using a pipe coupling or a wrench socket with the inside diameter slight-

ly larger than outside diameter of bearing, Fig. 10, drive link yoke downward until about a ¼" of bearing projects from yoke. *Do not attempt to drive yoke down farther than ball socket will allow easily.*
6. Rotate shaft 180 degrees and repeat Steps 3, 4 and 5.
7. Clamp ¼" projecting portion of either bearing in vise and remove bearing by driving link yoke upward. Remove other bearing in same manner, Fig. 11.
8. Separate spider, shaft yoke and shaft from link yoke.
9. To remove bearings from shaft yoke, clamp spider in vise with its jaws bearing against ends of spider journals. Yoke must be free to move vertically between jaws of vise.
10. Using the same bearing remover tool as in Step 5, apply force on shaft yoke around bearing. Drive yoke downward until bearing is free of yoke.

Centering Ball Replacement

The centering ball is only serviceable on 1973 models. Fig. 12 identifies Oldsmobile and Pontiac. Replacement pro-

cedure is as follows:
1. With CV joint disassembled, position inner part of tool J-23677 on centering ball, Fig. 13.
2. Install outer cylinder of tool J-23677 over inner part, thread nut onto tool and pull centering ball off stud.
3. Place replacement ball on stud and using a suitable tool, drive ball onto stud until it seats firmly against

Fig. 8 Chevrolet serviceable and non-serviceable propeller shaft

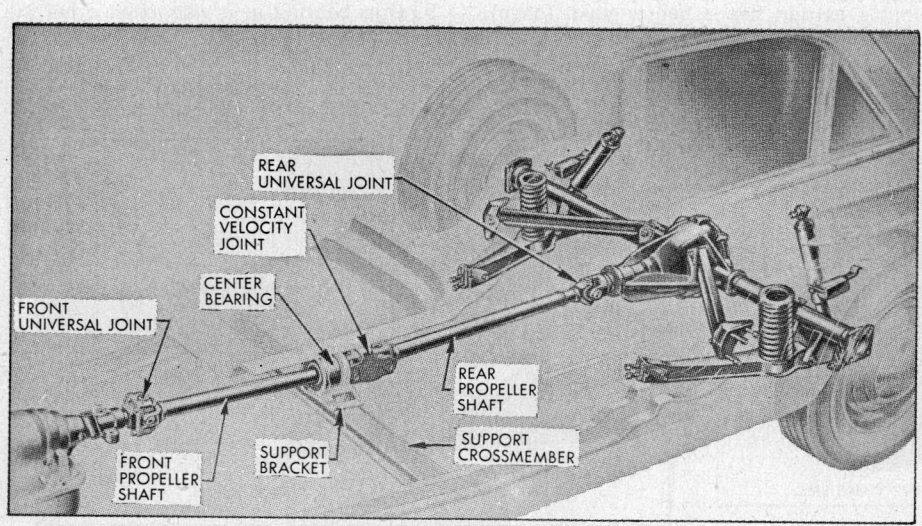

Fig. 7 Two piece propeller shaft with constant velocity universal joint. General Motors

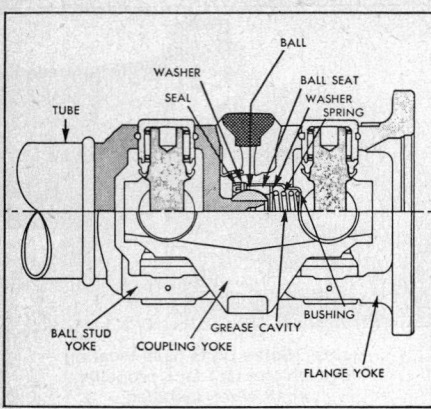

Fig. 9   Cross-section of typical GM constant velocity U-joint

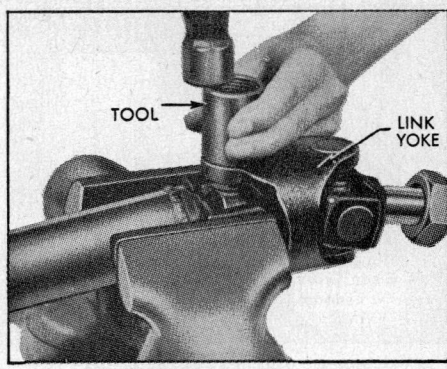

Fig. 10   Driving bearing from link yoke

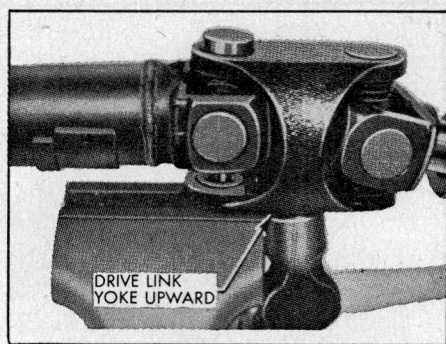

Fig. 11   Removing bearing

shoulder at base of stud.

4. Assemble ball seats and related parts into ball cavity as shown in Fig. 14. All parts must be adequately lubricated with lubricant provided with kit.
5. Lubricate centering ball seal with approved lubricant and install with sealing lip tipping inward. Fill ball cavity with lubricant.

Reassemble Constant Velocity U-Joint—

All yokes must be carefully assembled using the marks made before disassembly for reference. Assemble front section of constant velocity joint first.

1. Position spider inside splined yoke. Install bearings by pressing between vise jaws. Make sure that spider journals enter bearings squarely to avoid damage, Fig. 15.
2. Fully install bearings and install snap rings.
3. Position splined yoke and spider inside link yoke and install bearings into link yoke in same manner as for splined yoke.
4. Position spider inside rear propeller shaft yoke and install bearings.
5. Lubricate ball and socket with a high

grade of extreme pressure grease.
6. Position spider of rear propeller shaft assembly in link yoke.
7. Engage socket with ball of splined yoke assembly. *Make sure that all reference marks are properly aligned.*
8. Install bearings into link yoke in same manner as above while holding spring loaded ball and socket assembly together to make sure that spider journals enter bearings squarely.

Reassemble Slip Joint

1. Make sure locknut, seal and split washer are in place on smooth part of spline shaft. Also make sure that index spring wire is in place in splines and that spacer washer and large lockwasher are in place on rear end of front propeller shaft.
2. Align index spring with missing internal spline in rear end of propeller shaft and slide slip joint together, Fig. 16.
3. Install locknut and tighten securely. Bend in rim of lockwasher to engage flat of locknut firmly.

1969-71 Mark III, Thunderbird & 1969-74 Lincoln

These vehicles incorporate a double cardan type constant velocity joint at each end of the drive shaft, Fig. 17. Each double cardan has a center yoke (cage),

a centering socket yoke and a stud yoke which is welded to each end of the tube assembly. The splines on the yoke and transmission output shaft permit drive shaft to move in and out as the axle moves up and down. All drive shaft assemblies are balanced and should be kept free of under coating.

Disassembly

1. Mark location of spiders, center yoke and centering socket yoke as related to stud yoke.

NOTE: The spiders must be assembled with bosses in their original position to provide proper clearance.

2. Remove snap rings that secure bearings in front of center yoke, then position tool, Fig. 18, and thread clockwise until bearing protrudes about ⅜-inch out of yoke.
3. Remove drive shaft from vise and tighten bearing in vise then tap the center yoke, Fig. 19, to free it from bearing.
4. Remove the two bearings from the spider, Fig. 20, then reposition the tool on the yoke and move the remaining bearing in the opposite direction so that it protrudes about ⅜ inch out the yoke.
5. Grip bearing in a vise, then drive the

Fig. 12   Oldsmobile and Pontiac serviceable and non-serviceable centering balls

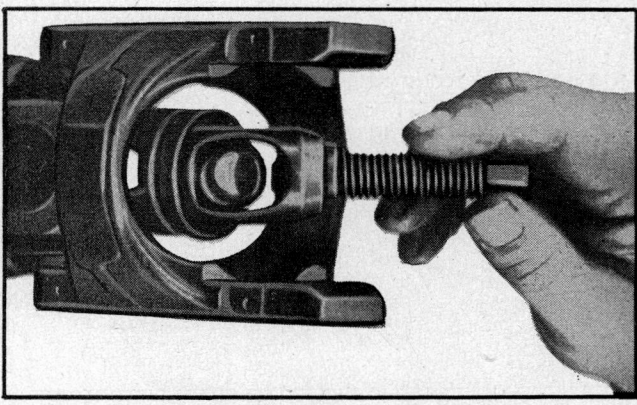

Fig. 13   Removing centering ball with tool J-23677

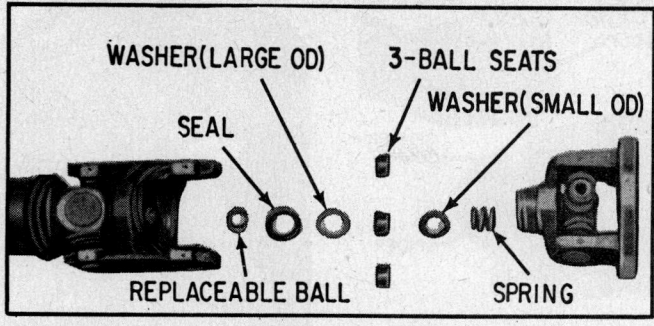

Fig. 14 Centering ball assembly

Fig. 15 Installing bearings

center yoke freeing it from bearing, Fig. 19, and remove spider from center yoke.

6. Pull centering socket yoke off center stud, Fig. 21, then remove rubber seal from centering ball stud.

7. Remove the snap rings from center and drive shaft yokes, then position tool on drive shaft yoke, Fig. 22, and press bearing outward until inside of center yoke almost contacts the slinger ring at the front of the drive shaft yoke.

NOTE: Pressing beyond this point can distort the slinger ring. Fig. 23 shows the interference point.

8. Clamp exposed end of bearing in a

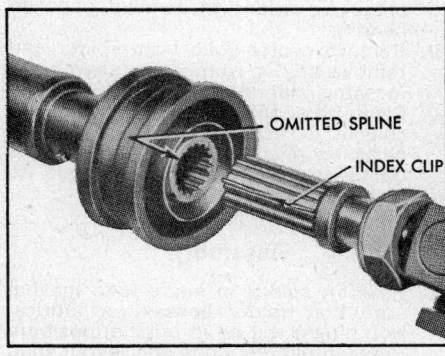

Fig. 16 Aligning index spring with missing internal spline on propeller shaft

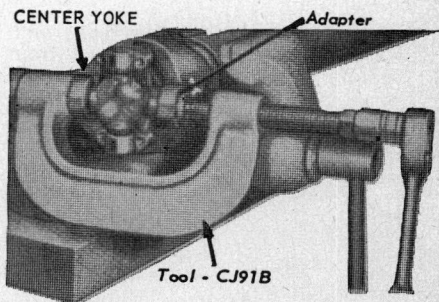

Fig. 18 Partially pressing bearing from center yoke

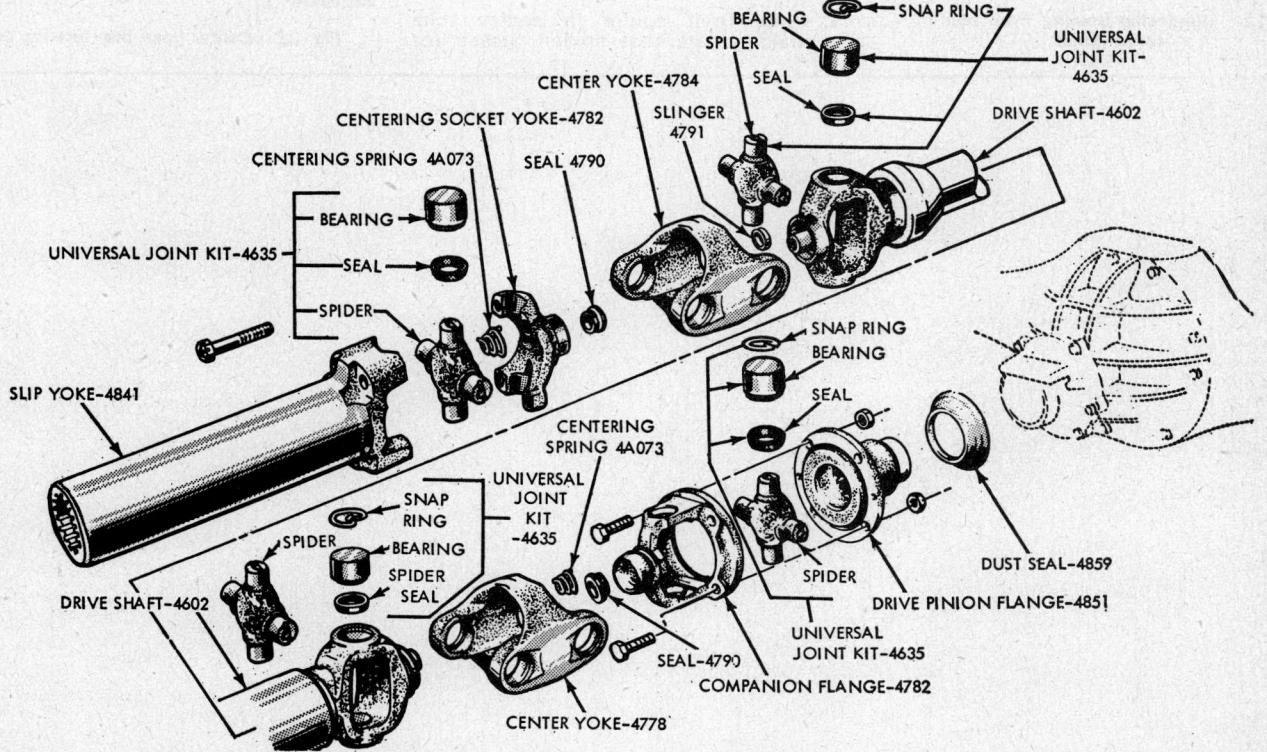

Fig. 17 Constant velocity type universal joint

UNIVERSAL JOINTS

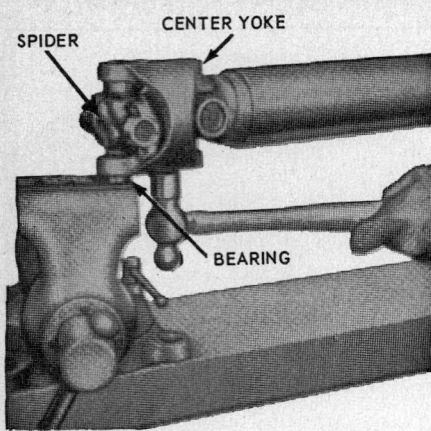

Fig. 19   Removing bearing from center yoke

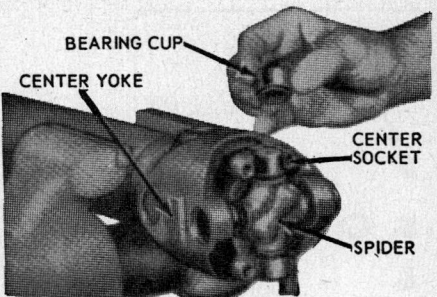

Fig. 20   Removing bearing cup from centering yoke

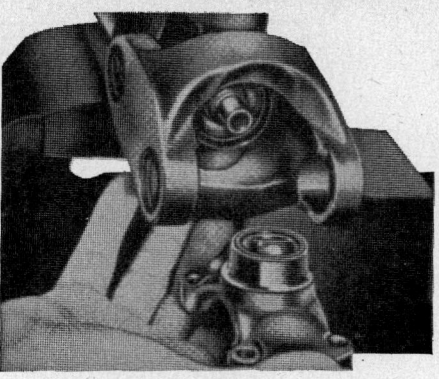

Fig. 21   Removing center socket yoke

vise and drive the center yoke with a soft face hammer freeing it from bearing, then reposition tool and

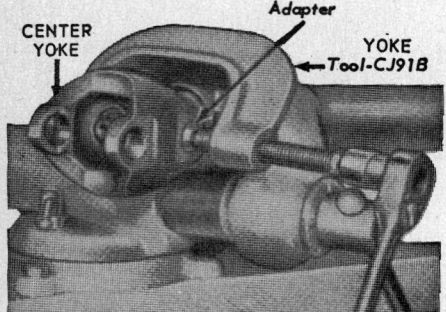

Fig. 22   Removing bearing from rear of center yoke

press on spider to remove opposite bearing.
9. Remove center yoke from spider and remove spider from drive shaft yoke in same manner.
10. Clean all serviceable parts in cleaning solvent. If using a repair kit, use all parts supplied in kit. If driveshaft is damaged, it should be replaced to insure a balanced assembly.

Assembly

1. Position spider in shaft yoke making sure that spider bosses (or lubrication plugs) will be in original position. Press in bearing cups and install snap rings.
2. Position center yoke over spider ends then press in bearing cups and install snap rings.
3. Install new seal on centering stud and position centering socket yoke on stud.
4. Place front spider in center yoke making sure that spider bosses (or

lubrication plugs) are properly positioned. Press in bearing cups and install snap rings.
5. Applying pressure on centering socket, install remaining bearing cup.
6. If using a repair kit, remove plug from each spider and lubricate universal joints. Reinstall plug.

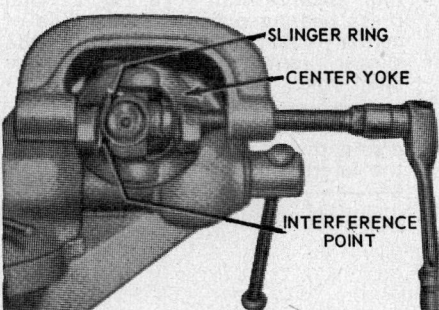

Fig. 23   Center yoke interference point

HYDRAULIC BRAKE SYSTEM

For Brake Adjustments, see Car Chapters

DUAL MASTER CYLINDER SYSTEM

When the brake pedal is depressed, both the primary (front brake) and the secondary (rear brake) master cylinder pistons are moved simultaneously to exert hydraulic fluid pressure on their respective independent hydraulic system. The fluid displacement of the two master cylinders is proportioned to fulfill the requirements of each of the two independent hydraulic brake systems, Figs. 2 and 3.

If a failure of a rear (secondary) brake system should occur, initial brake pedal movement causes the unrestricted secondary piston to bottom in the master cylinder bore. Primary piston movement displaces hydraulic fluid in the primary section of the dual master cylinder to actuate the front brake system.

Should the front (primary) brake system fail, initial brake pedal movement causes the unrestricted primary piston to bottom out against the secondary piston. Continued downward movement of the brake pedal moves the secondary piston to displace hydraulic fluid in the rear brake system to actuate the rear brakes.

The increased pedal travel and the increased pedal effort required to compensate for the loss of the failed portion of the brake system provides a warning that a partial brake system failure has occurred When the ignition switch is turned on, a brake warning light on the instrument panel provides a visual indication that one of the dual brake systems has become inoperative.

Should a failure of either the front or rear brake hydraulic system occur, the hydraulic fluid pressure differential resulting from pressure loss of the failed brake system forces the valve toward the low pressure area to light the brake warning lamp.

Brake Warning Light Switches

There are three basic types of brake

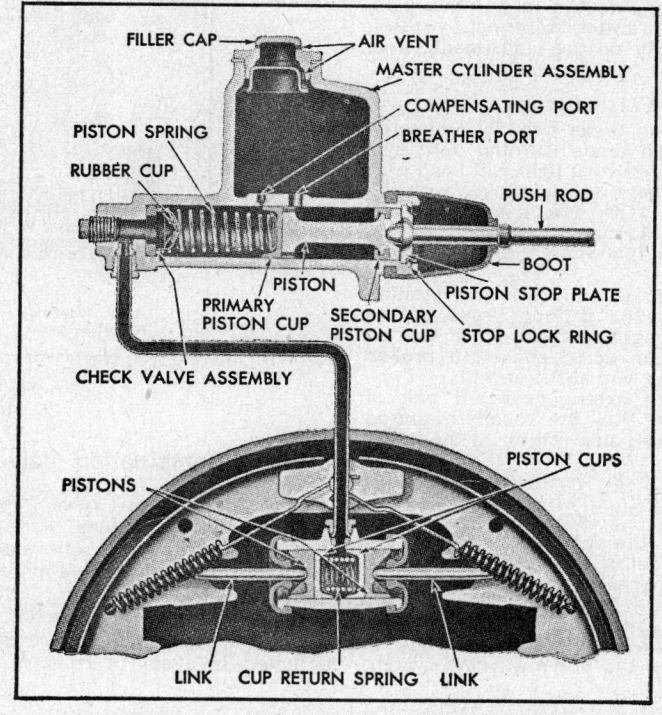

Fig. 1 Schematic diagram of a typical hydraulic brake system

warning light switches as shown in Figs. 5, 6 and 7, and usually they form a common electrical circuit with the brake warning light.

When a pressure differential occurs between the front and rear brake systems, the valves will shuttle toward the side with the low pressure.

As shown in Fig. 5, movement of the differential valve forces the switch plunger upward over the tapered shoulder of the valve to close the switch contacts and light the dual brake warning lamp, signaling a brake system failure.

In Fig. 6 the valve assembly consists of two valves in a common bore that are spring loaded toward the centered position. The spring-loaded switch contact plunger rests on top of the valves in the centered position (right view). When a pressure differential occurs between the front and rear brake systems, the valves

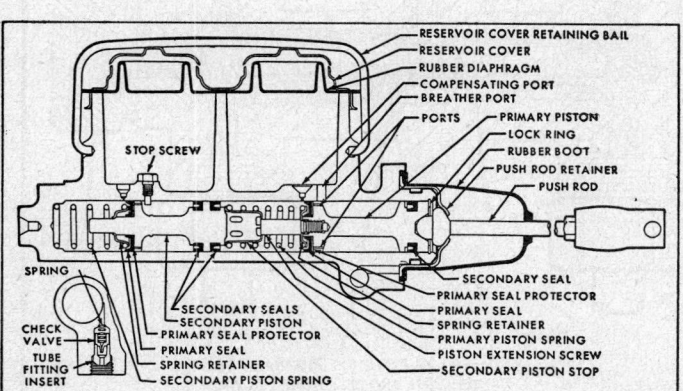

Fig. 2 Delco-Moraine dual master cylinder used with drum brakes (typical)

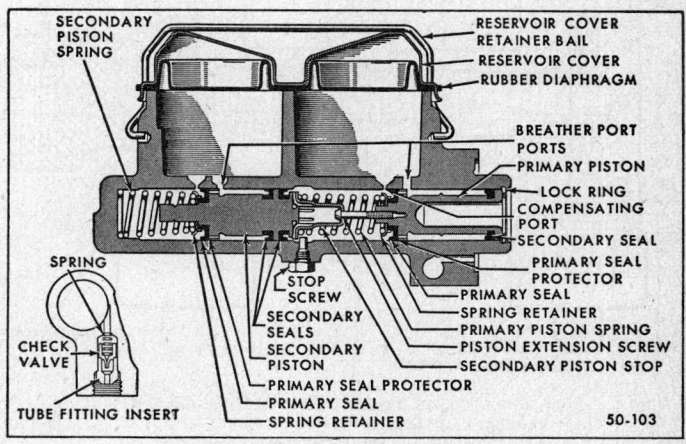

Fig. 3 Bendix dual master cylinder used with drum brakes (typical)

will shuttle toward the side with the low pressure. The spring-loaded switch plunger is "triggered" and the ground circuit for the warning light is completed, lighting the lamp (left view).

In Fig. 7, as pressure falls in one system, the other system's normal pressure forces the piston to the inoperative side, contacting the switch terminal, causing the warning light on the instrument panel to glow.

Testing Warning Light System

If the parking brake light is connected into the service brake warning light system, the brake warning light will flash only when the parking brake is applied with the ignition turned ON. The same light will also glow should one of the two service brake systems fail when the brake pedal is applied.

To test the system, turn the ignition ON and apply the parking brake. If the lamp fails to light, inspect for a burned out bulb, disconnected socket, a broken or disconnected wire at the switch.

Fig. 8 is an exterior view of one of these switches. They are usually mounted on the left frame side rail or on the brake pedal bracket.

To test the brake warning system, raise the car and open a wheel bleeder valve while a helper depresses the brake pedal and observes the warning light on the instrument panel. If the bulb fails to light, inspect for a burned out bulb, disconnected socket, or a broken or disconnected wire at the switch. If the bulb is not burned out, and the wire continuity is proven, replace the brake warning switch.

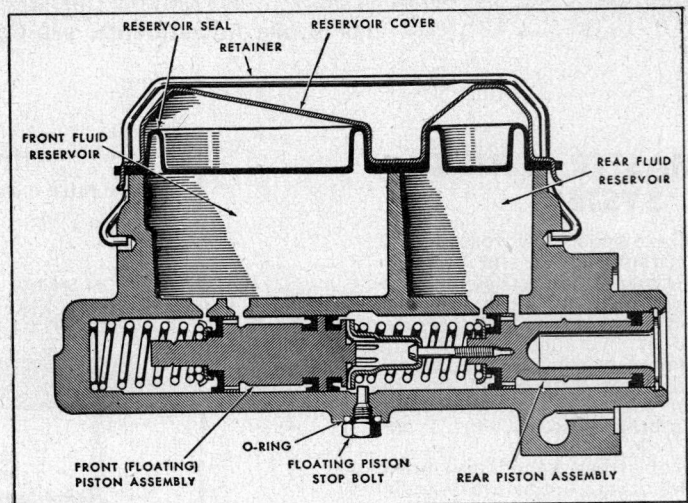

Fig. 4   Bendix dual master cylinder used with disc brakes (typical)

Combination Valve

The combination valve, Fig. 9 is a metering valve, failure warning switch, and a proportioner in one assembly and is used on disc brake applications. The metering valve delays front disc braking until the rear drum brake shoes contact the drum. The failure warning switch is actuated in event of front or rear brake system failure, in turn activating a dash warning lamp. The proportioner balances front to rear braking action during rapid deceleration.

Metering Valve

When the brakes are not applied, the metering valve permits the brake fluid to flow through the valve, thus allowing the fluid to expand and contract with temperature changes.

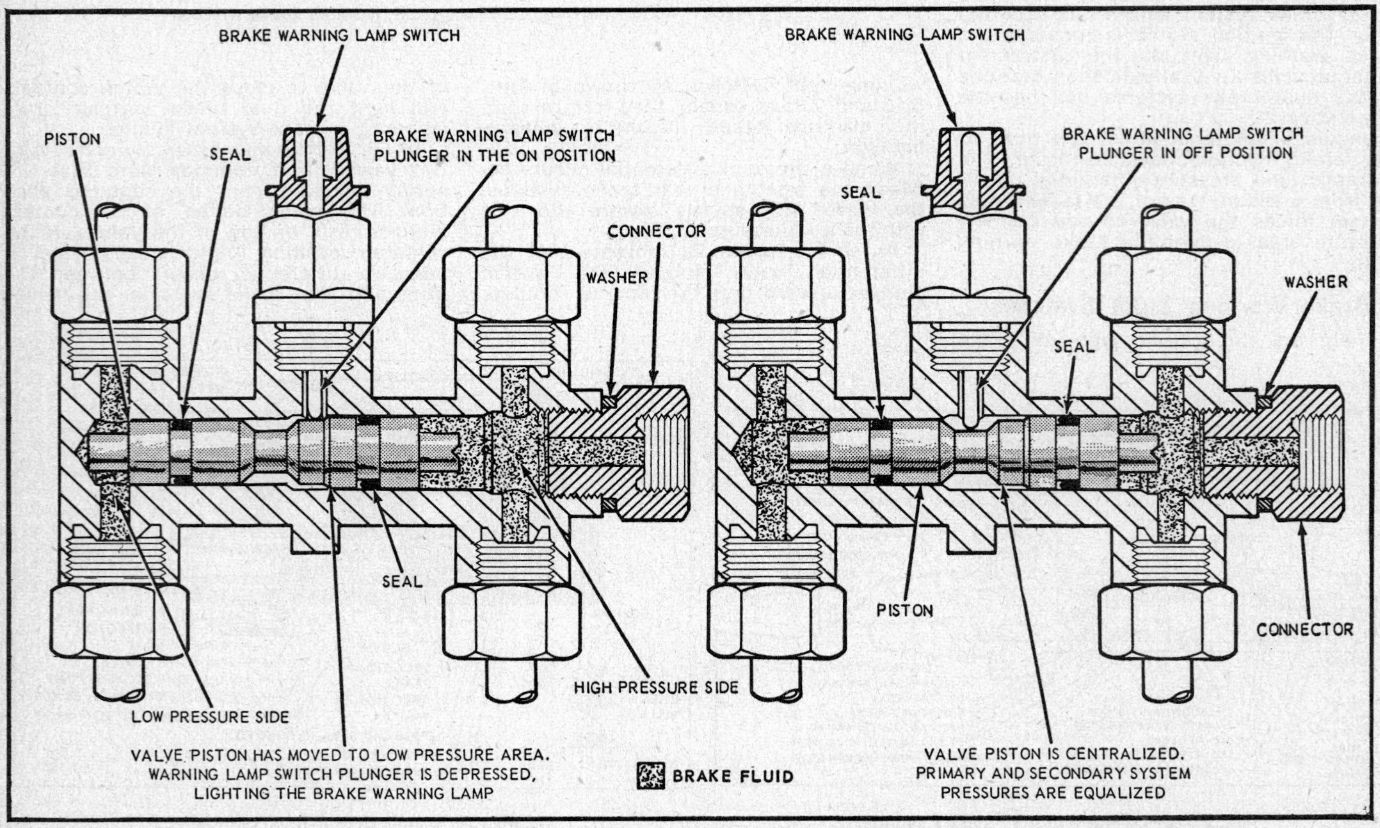

Fig. 5   Pressure differential valve and brake warning light switch

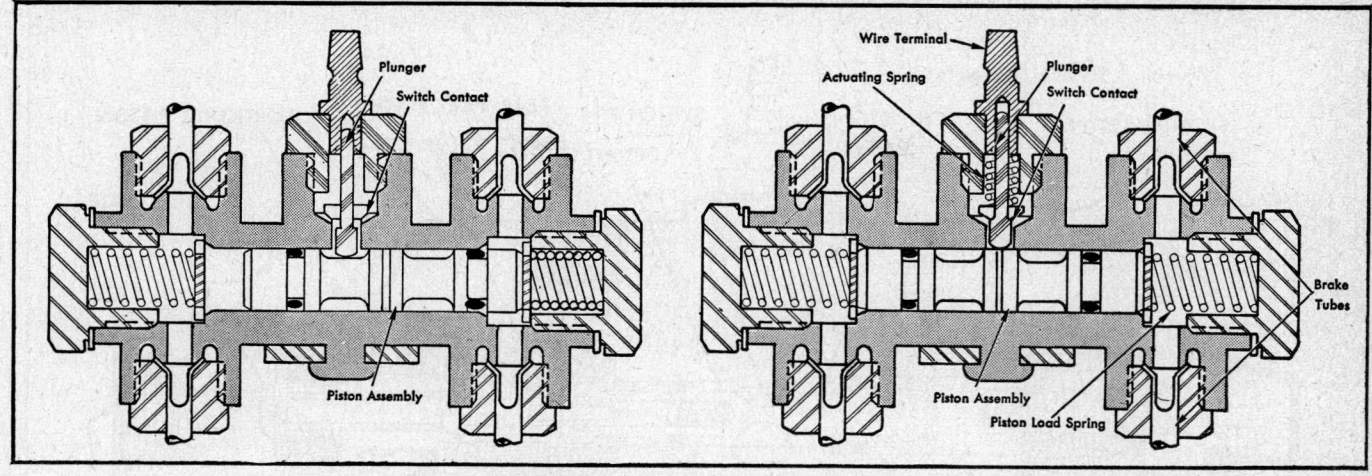

Fig. 6 Pressure differential valve and brake warning light switch

When the brakes are initially applied, the metering valve stem moves to the left, preventing fluid to flow through the valve to the front disc brakes. This is accomplished by the smooth end of the metering valve stem contacting the metering valve seal lip at 4 to 30 PSI, Fig. 10. The metering valve spring holds the retainer against the seal until a predetermined pressure is produced at the valve inlet port which overcomes the spring pressure and permits hydraulic pressure to actuate the front disc brakes, Fig. 11. The increased pressure into the valve is metered through the valve seal, to the front disc brakes, producing an increased force on the diaphragm. The diaphragm then pulls the pin, in turn pulling the retainer and reduces the spring pressure on the metering valve seal. Eventually, the pressure reaches a point at which the spring is pulled away by the diaphragm pin and retainer, leaving the metering valve unrestricted, permitting full pressure to pass through the metering valve.

Failure Warning Switch

If the rear brake system fails, the front system pressure forces the switch piston to the right, Fig. 12. The switch pin is then forced up into the switch, completing the electrical circuit and activates the dash warning lamp.

When repairs are made and pressure returns to the system, the piston moves to the left, resetting the switch. The detent on the piston requires approximately 100 to 450 PSI to permit full reset of the piston. In event of front brake system failure, the piston moves to the left and the same sequence of events are followed as for rear system failure except the piston resets to the right.

Proportioner

During rapid deceleration, a portion of the vehicle's weight is transferred to the front wheels. This resultant loss of weight at the rear wheels must be compensated for to avoid early rear wheel skid. The proportioner reduces the rear brake system pressure, delaying rear wheel skid. The pressure developed within the valve acts against the large end of the piston, overcoming the spring pressure and moves the piston to the left, Fig. 13. Ths piston then contacts the stem seat and proportions (restricts) line pressure through the valve.

During normal braking action, the proportioner is not functional. Brake fluid flows into the proportioner between the piston center hole and the valve stem, through the stop plate and to the rear brakes. Spring pressure loads the piston, during normal braking, causing it to rest against the stop plate, Fig. 14.

Brake Distribution Valve & Switch

This switch assembly which is used on front drum brake systems and Corvette four wheel disc brake systems, is connected to the outlet ports of the master cylinder and also to the brake warning light that warns the driver if either the front or rear brake system has failed.

When hydraulic pressure is equal in both front and rear brake systems, the switch remains centered, Fig. 15. If pressure fails in one of the systems, hydraulic pressure moves the piston toward the inoperative side, Fig. 16. The shoulder of the piston contacts the switch terminal, providing a ground and lighting the warning lamp.

Master Cylinder Service

Figs. 17 to 21 show an array of dual master cylinders. With cylinder removed from vehicle, and from brake booster if so equipped, remove the covers and disassemble the unit as suggested by the illustration of the unit being serviced.

When disassembled, wash all parts in alcohol *only*. Use an air hose to blow out all passages, orifices and valve holes. Air dry and place parts on clean paper or lint-free cloth. Inspect master cylinder bore for scoring, rust, pitting or etching. Any of these conditions will require replacement of the housing. Inspect master cylinder pistons for scoring, pitting or distortion. Replace piston if any of these conditions exist.

If either master cylinder housing or piston is replaced, clean new parts with alcohol and blow out all passages with air hose.

Examine reservoirs for foreign matter

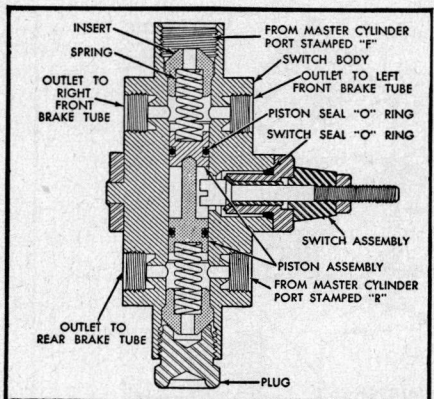

Fig. 7 Pressure differential valve and brake warning light switch

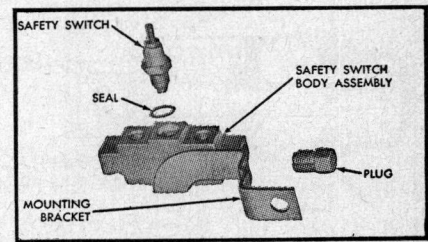

Fig. 8 Typical pressure valve and brake warning light switch. These switches are usually mounted on the left frame side rail

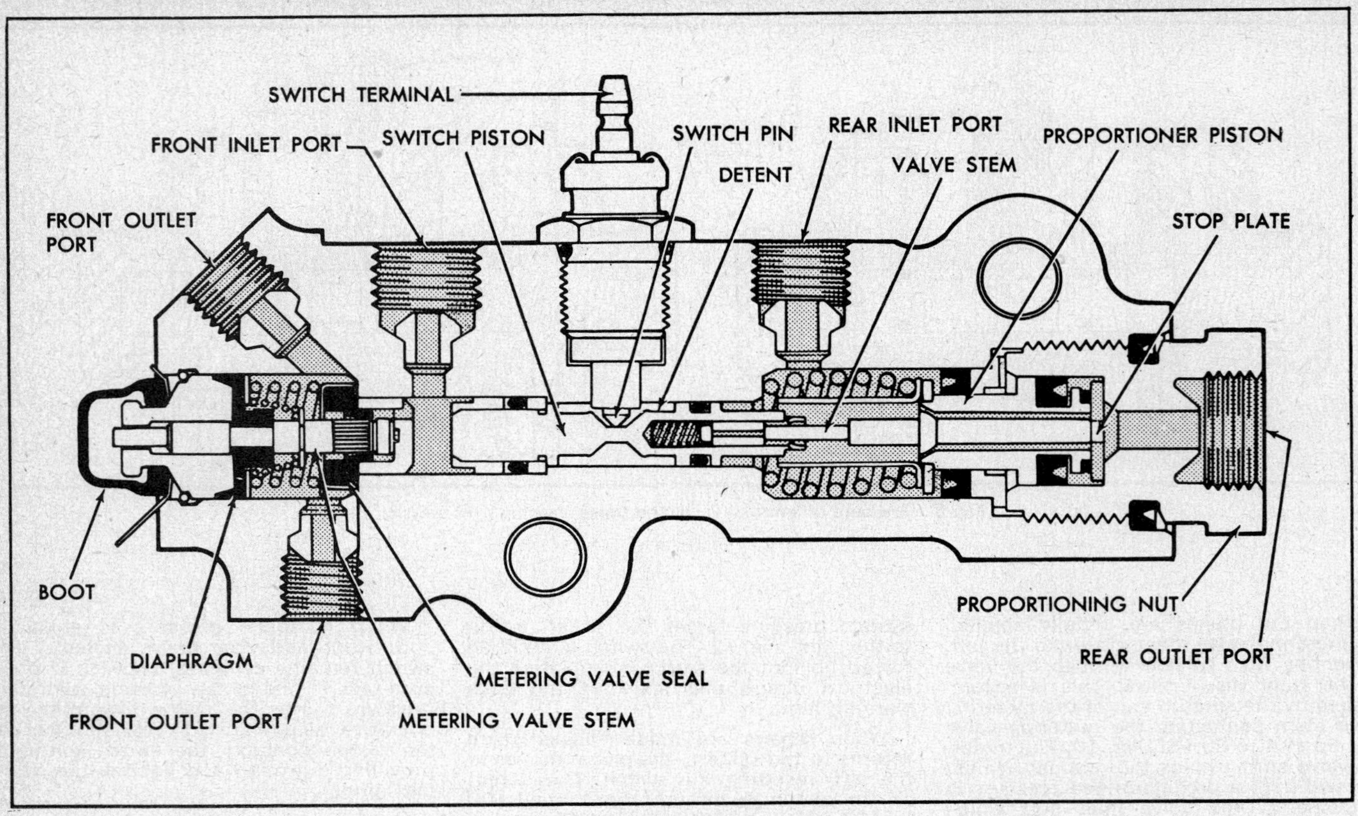

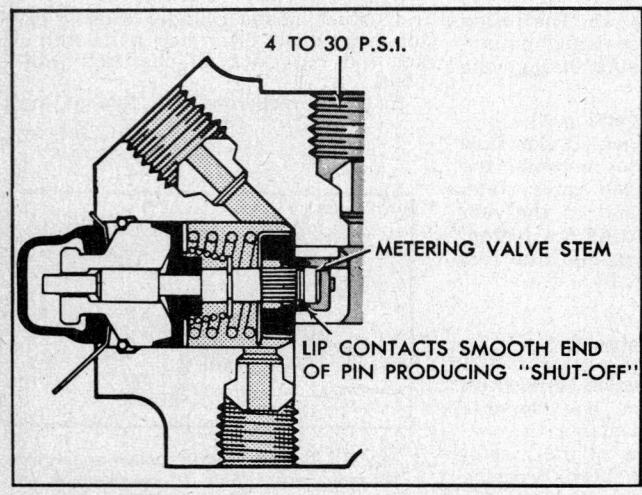

Fig. 9 Combination valve

and check all passages for restrictions. If there is any suspicion of contamination or evidence of corrosion, completely flush hydraulic system as outlined below.

When overhauling a master cylinder, use all parts contained in repair kit. Before starting reassembly, dip all cups, seals, pistons, springs, check valves and retainers in alcohol and place in a clean pan or on clean paper. *Wash hands with soap and water only to prevent contamination of rubber parts from oil, kerosene or gasoline.* During assembly, dip all parts in clean, heavy duty brake fluid.

Inspect through side outlet of dual master cylinder housing to make certain cup lips do not hand up on edge of hole or turn back, which would result in faulty operation. A piece of $3/16$" rod with an end rounded off will be helpful in guiding cups past hole.

BLEEDING BRAKES

NOTE: Chrysler Corp. recommends only pressure bleeding for all 1969-74 models, while Ford Motor Co. recommends that 1969-71 Lincoln Continental, 1970-71

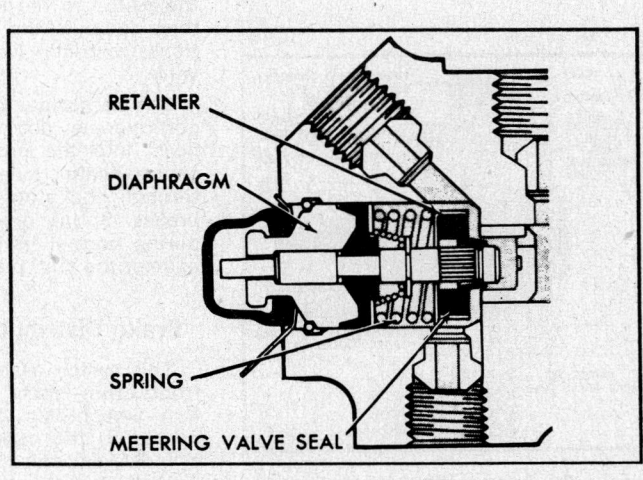

Fig. 10 Metering valve, initial braking

Fig. 11 Metering valve, continued braking

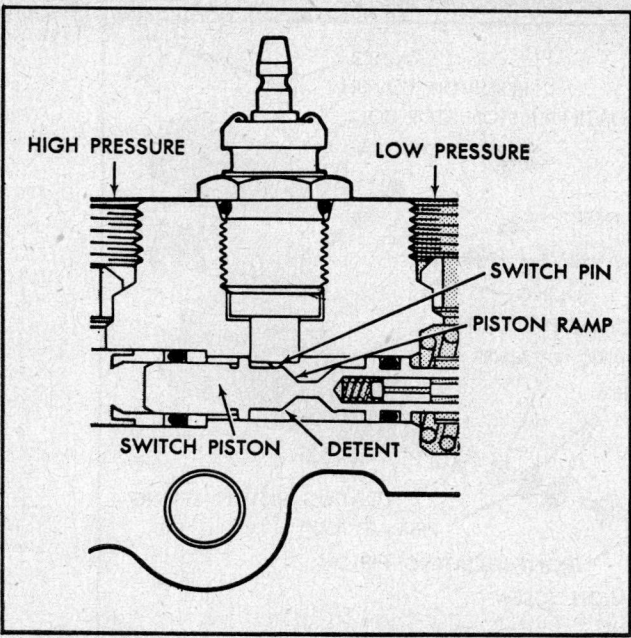

Fig. 12 Failure warning switch, rear system failure

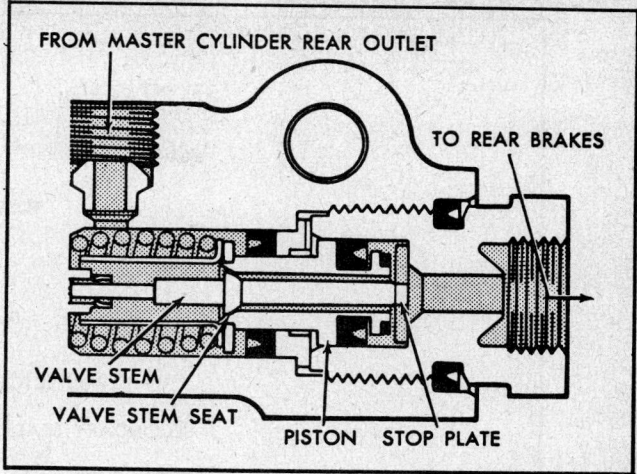

Fig. 13 Proportioner, rapid deceleration

Ford, Mercury, Mark III and Thunderbird and all 1972 models, must be pressure bled.

The bleeding operation itself is fairly well standardized. First step in all cases is cleaning the dirt from the filler cap before removing it from the master cylinder. This should be done thoroughly.

Pressure bleeding is fastest because the master cylinder doesn't have to be re-filled several times, and the job can be done by one man. To prevent air from the pressure tank getting into the lines, do not shake the tank while air is being added to the tank or after it has been pres-surized. Set the tank in the required loca-tion, bring the air hose to the tank, and

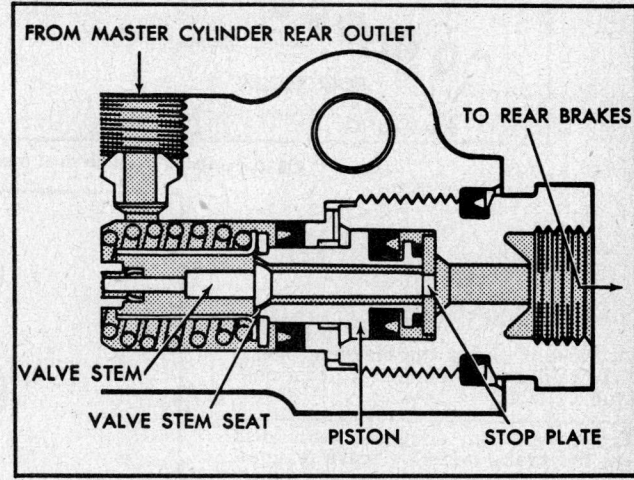

Fig. 14 Proportioner, normal braking

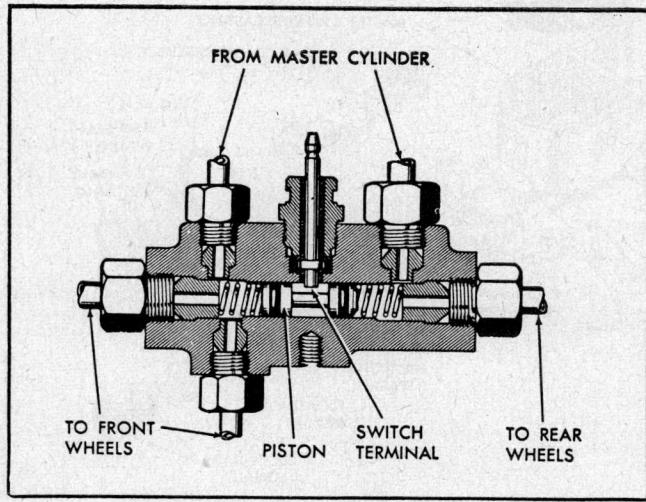

Fig. 15 Brake distribution switch (normal)

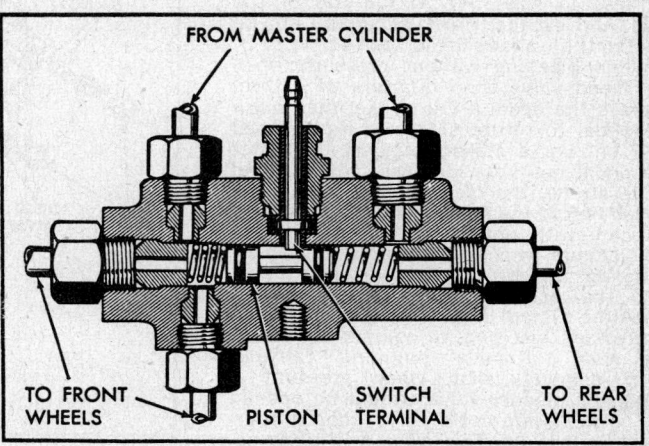

Fig. 16 Brake distribution switch (failed)

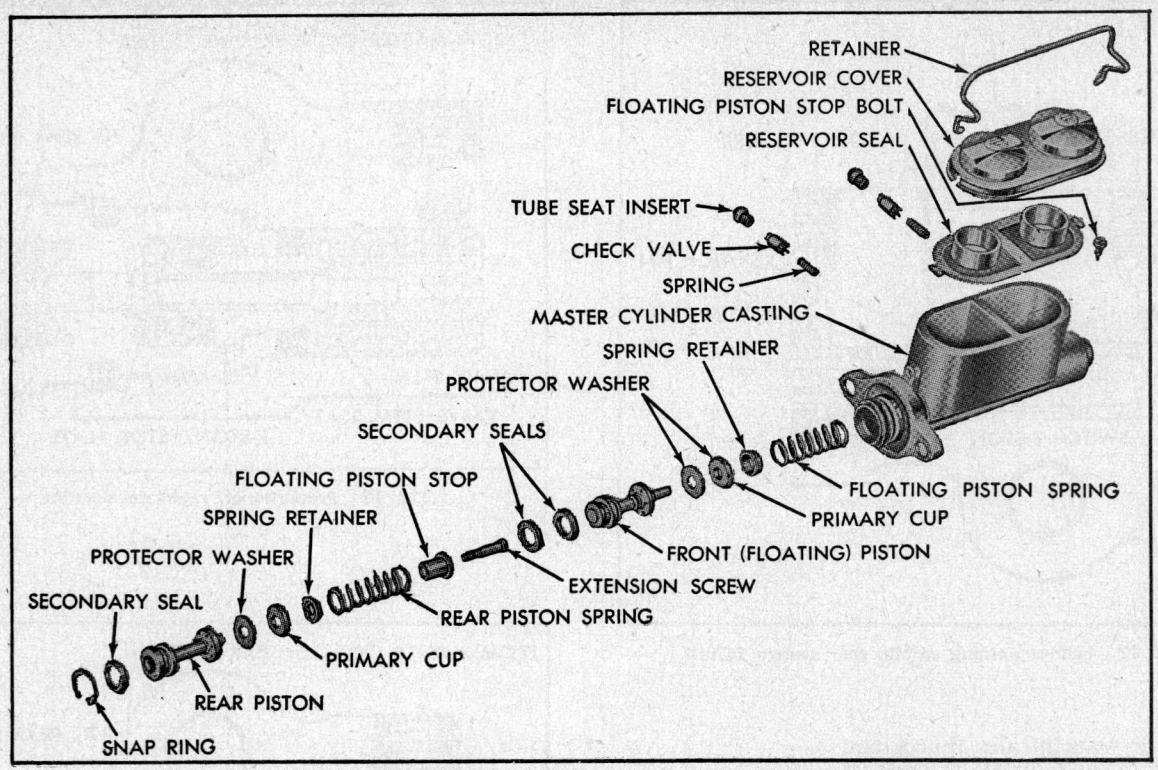

Fig. 17 Delco-Moraine dual master cylinder disassembled (GM cars)

Labels (Fig. 17):
RETAINER
RESERVOIR COVER
FLOATING PISTON STOP BOLT
RESERVOIR SEAL
TUBE SEAT INSERT
CHECK VALVE
SPRING
MASTER CYLINDER CASTING
SPRING RETAINER
PROTECTOR WASHER
SECONDARY SEALS
FLOATING PISTON STOP
SPRING RETAINER
PROTECTOR WASHER
SECONDARY SEAL
SNAP RING
REAR PISTON
PRIMARY CUP
REAR PISTON SPRING
EXTENSION SCREW
FRONT (FLOATING) PISTON
PRIMARY CUP
FLOATING PISTON SPRING

do not move it during the bleeding operation. The tank should be kept at least one-third full.

NOTE: On vehicles equipped with disc brakes, the brake metering valve or combination valve must be held in its position, using the recommended tool, (C-4121 for Chrysler Corp., J-22742 for Ford Motor Co. and J-23709 for General Motors).

If air does get into the fluid, releasing the pressure will cause the bubbles to increase in size, rise to the top of the fluid, and escape. Pressure should not be greater than about 35 lb. per sq. in.

When bleeding without pressure, open the bleed valve three-quarters of a turn, depress the pedal a full stroke, then allow the pedal to return slowly to its released position. Some makers suggest that after the pedal has been depressed to the end of its stroke, the bleeder valve should be closed before the start of the return stroke. On cars with power brakes, first reduce the vacuum in the power unit to zero by pumping the brake pedal several times with the engine off before starting to bleed the system.

Pressure bleeding, of course, eliminates the need for pedal pumping. Chrysler Corp. suggests that, when pressure is used, the bleeder valve should be opened and closed intermittently at about four-second intervals. This gives a whirling action to the fluid in the wheel cylinder, and helps expel the air.

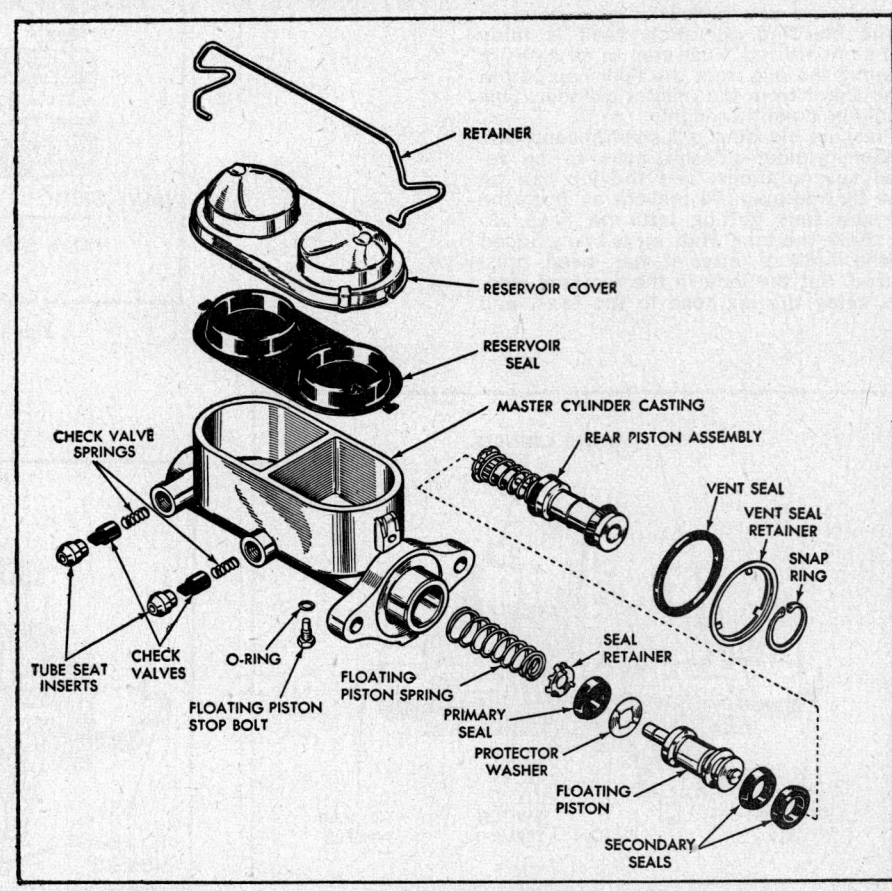

Fig. 18 Bendix dual master cylinder disassembled used with drum brakes (GM and American Motors)

Labels (Fig. 18):
RETAINER
RESERVOIR COVER
RESERVOIR SEAL
MASTER CYLINDER CASTING
REAR PISTON ASSEMBLY
VENT SEAL
VENT SEAL RETAINER
SNAP RING
CHECK VALVE SPRINGS
TUBE SEAT INSERTS
CHECK VALVES
O-RING
FLOATING PISTON STOP BOLT
FLOATING PISTON SPRING
PRIMARY SEAL
PROTECTOR WASHER
SEAL RETAINER
FLOATING PISTON
SECONDARY SEALS

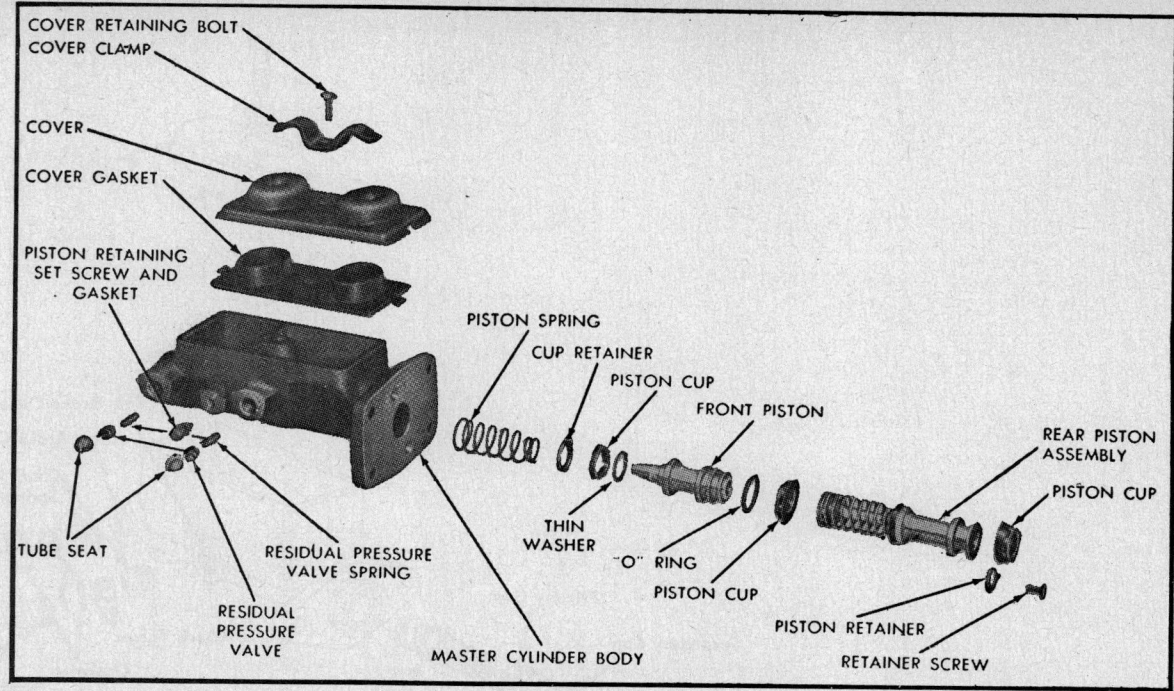

Fig. 19 Bendix dual master cylinder disassembled used with drum brakes (Chrysler line)

At one time, some car makers recommended that a clean container be used for the drained fluid, so that the fluid could be reused. All now agree that drained fluid should be discarded. Care should be taken not to spill brake fluid, since this can damage the finish of the car.

Flushing is essential if there is water, mineral oil or other contaminants in the lines, and whenever new parts are installed in the hydraulic system. Fluid contamination is usually indicated by swollen and deteriorated cups and other rubber parts.

Wheel cylinders on disc brakes are equipped with bleeder valves, and are bled in the same manner as wheel cylinders for drum brakes.

Bleeding is necessary on all four wheels if air has entered the system because of low fluid level, or the line or lines have been disconnected. If a line is disconnected at any one wheel cylinder, that cylinder only need be bled. Of course, on brake reline jobs, bleeding is advisable to remove any air or contaminants.

Master cylinders equipped with bleeder valves should be bled first before the wheel cylinders are bled. In all cases where a master cylinder has been overhauled, it must be bled. Where there is no bleeder valve, this can be done by leaving the line (or lines) loose, actuating the brake pedal to expel the air and then tightening the line (or lines).

NOTE: After overhauling a dual master cylinder used in conjunction with disc brakes, it is advisable to bleed the cylinder before installing it on the car. The reason for this recommendation is that air may be trapped between the master cylinder pistons because there is only one

residual pressure valve (check valve) used in these units.

The recommended precedure for Chrysler Line cars is as follows:
1. Clamp master cylinder in a vise and attach the special Bleeding Tubes (Tool No. C-4029) Fig. 15. *Be sure that the residual pressure valve is on the end of the tube in the large capacity reservoir as shown. This keeps the brake fluid from being syphoned out of the reservoir while bleeding.*
2. Fill both reservoirs with approved brake fluid.
3. Using a wooden stick or dowel (cars with power brakes) depress push rod slowly and allow the pistons to return under pressure of the springs. Do this several times until all air bubbles are expelled.
4. Remove bleeding tubes from cylinder and install cover and gasket.
5. Install master cylinder on car and bleed wheel cylinders, preferably with a pressure bleeder.

Alternate Method
1. Support assembly in a vise and fill both reservoirs with brake fluid.
2. Loosely install a plug in each outlet port of the cylinder. Depress push rod several times until air bubbles cease to appear in the brake fluid.
3. Tighten plugs and attempt to depress the piston. Piston travel should be restricted after all air is expelled.
4. Install master cylinder on car and bleed wheel cylinders, preferably with a pressure bleeder.

Testing Dual Master Cylinders

Be sure that the master cylinder com-

pensates in both ports. This can be done by applying the brake pedal lightly (engine running with power brakes), and observing for brake fluid squirting up in the reservoirs. This may only occur in the front chamber. To determine if the rear compensating port is open, pump up the brakes rapidly and hold the pedal down. Have an observer watch the fluid in the rear reservoir while the pedal is raised. A disturbance in the fluid indicates that the compensating port is open.

Wheel Bleeding Sequence

Difference of opinion as to whether the longest or shortest line should be bled first still exists. To be safe, use the sequence given below, recommended by the car manufacturers.

Chrysler Corp. cars . . . . RR-LR-RF-LF
Ford Company cars . . . . RR-LR-RF-LF
General Motors cars:
  All except Chevrolet . . . . LF-RF-LR-RR
  Chevrolet Division . . . . . LR-RR-LF-RF
American Motors . . . . RR-LR-RF-LF

Dual Master Cylinder Bleeding Notes

Ford Motor Co. Cars

After the normal bleeding operation has been completed, note that the brake warning light will be ON because the pressure differential valve has moved off center, and must be returned to the central position. To do this, loosen the valve's inlet tube on the side opposite the wheel cylinder that was bled last. Apply the brake pedal slowly until the warning light goes out, and tighten fitting. Replace any

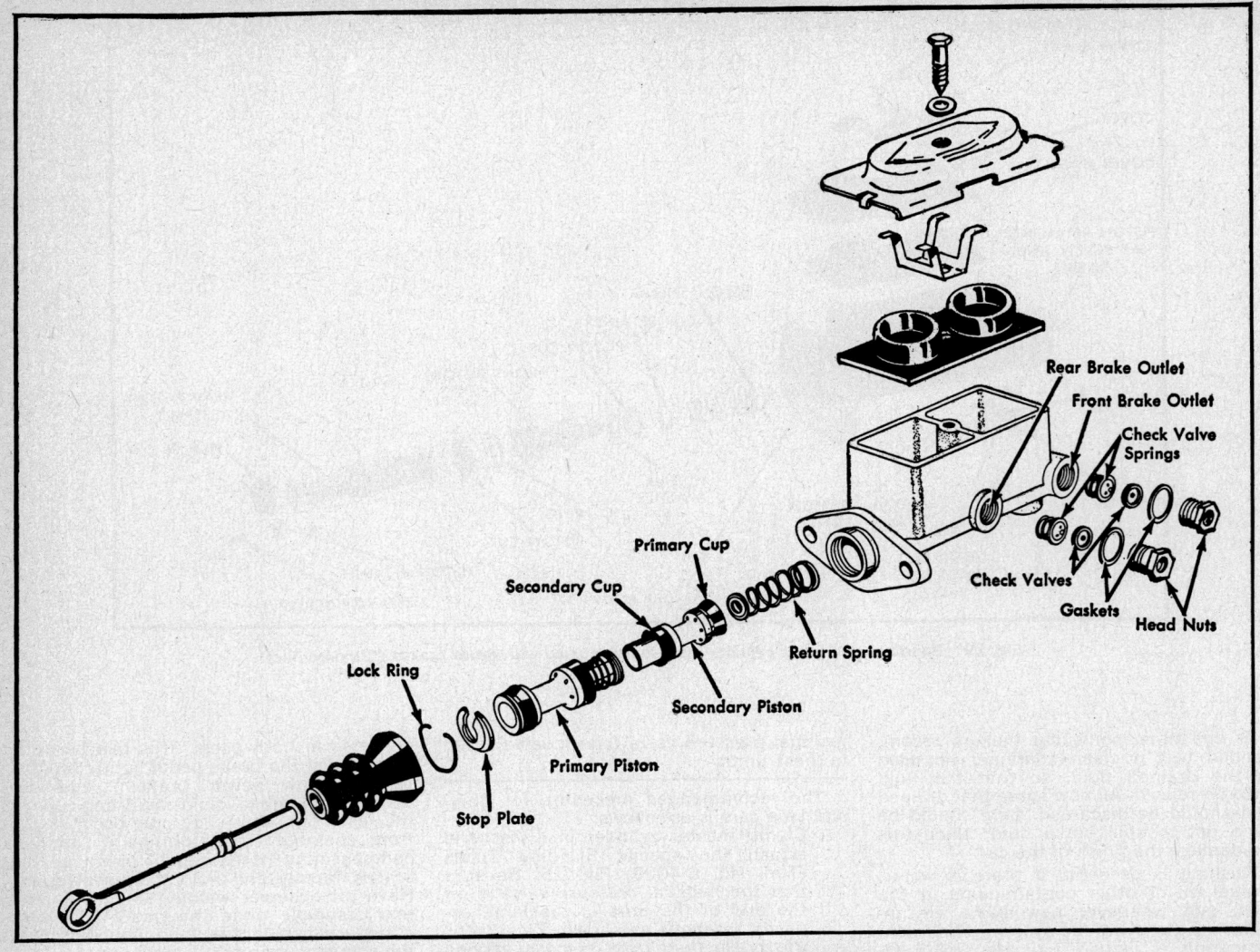

Fig. 20 Wagner dual master cylinder disassembled (Rambler American)

fluid that has leaked out during the operation.

NOTE: 1970-74 cars use a self-centering valve. After any bleeding operation, turn ignition switch to ACC or ON position and depress brake pedal. Valve will center itself.

General Motors Cars

On vehicles equipped with combined drum and disc brakes, the pressure differential valve must be held in its open position while bleeding the brakes using a pressure type bleeder. This is done by depressing the plunger and holding it in place using a special tool. When using pressure bleeding equipment follow the recommendations of the manufacturer.

Corvette

On Corvette models with disc brakes on all four wheels, there are two bleeder valves on each rear wheel disc brake. Remove the rear wheels to bleed. A single valve is used on front disc brakes.

American Motors

Before bleeding brakes, disconnect the switch terminal wire and remove nylon switch terminal, contact plunger actuating spring, and nylon plunger with contact.

In the event the valve has "triggered", the valve centering spring pressure may hold the switch plunger. If this happens, apply a slight amount of brake pedal pressure while releasing the plunger from the valve body.

After the bleeding operation, assemble the plunger spring and install valve with contact down. Install the nylon terminal and connect warning light wire to valve terminal. In the event brake fluid leaks from the center terminal body opening when the terminal is removed, replace the valve assembly.

Chrysler Corp.

Some Chrysler built cars with disc brakes are equipped with front disc brake pressure metering valve which is located on the left frame rail directly under the battery.

The purpose of the metering valve is to provide a better match of the front disc brakes with the rear drum brakes, resulting in improved braking balance *in light pedal applications.*

Gravity bleed and pedal methods are not affected by the presence of the metering valve. However, pressure bleeding is influenced by the metering valve.

Bleed pressure, which is normally about 35 psi, is high enough to cause the metering valve to close, which stops the flow of fluid to the front brakes. However, the valve can be held open manually by depressing the pressure release plunger (located at the bottom of the valve) in its uppermost position by hand or secured with masking tape while bleeding the brakes.

CAUTION: Under no conditions should a rigid clamp, wedge or block be used to se-

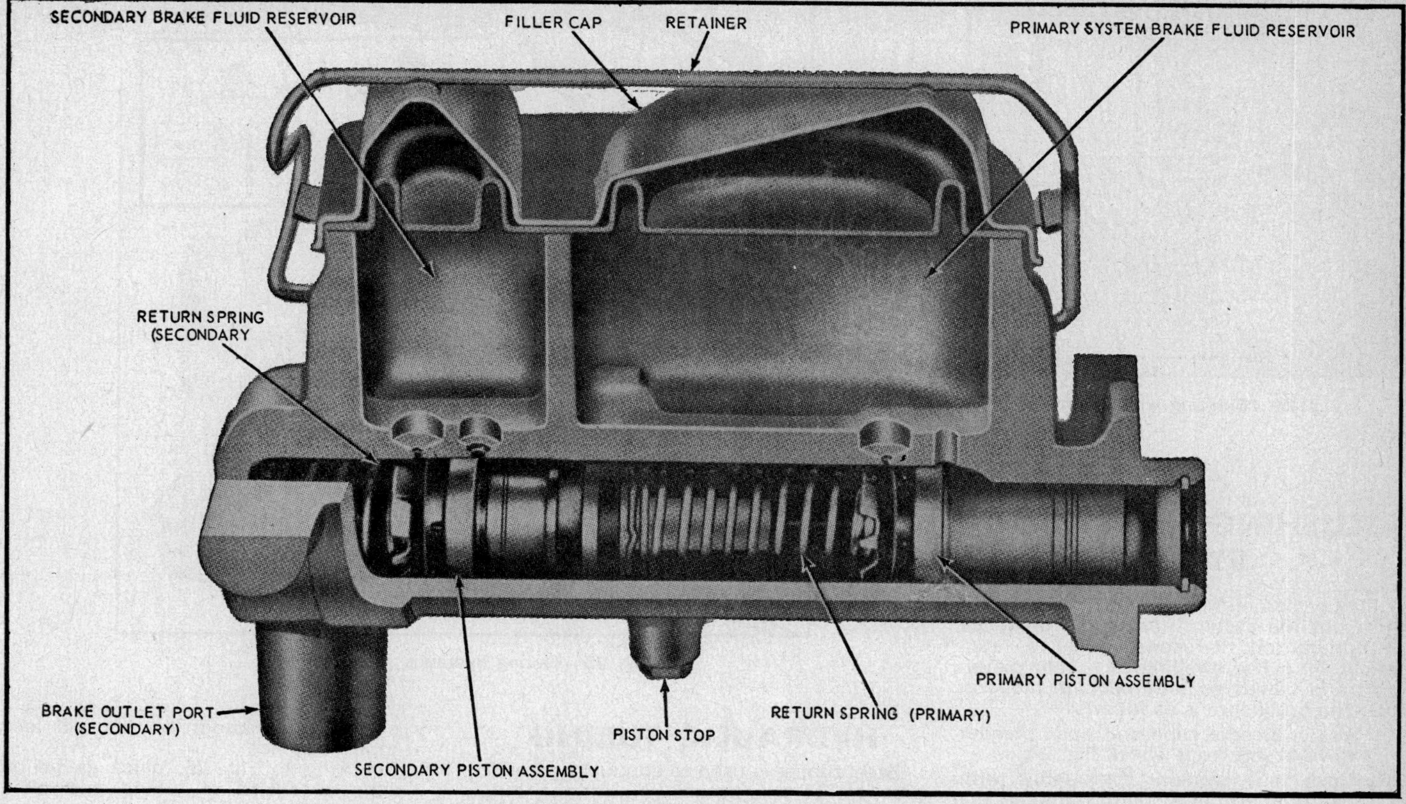

SECONDARY BRAKE FLUID RESERVOIR — FILLER CAP — RETAINER — PRIMARY SYSTEM BRAKE FLUID RESERVOIR

RETURN SPRING (SECONDARY)

BRAKE OUTLET PORT (SECONDARY)

PRIMARY PISTON ASSEMBLY

PISTON STOP — RETURN SPRING (PRIMARY)

SECONDARY PISTON ASSEMBLY

Fig. 21 Cutaway view of Bendix dual master cylinder used with disc brakes (typical)

cure the plunger as this can cause an internal failure in the valve. It should be noted that the pressure release plunger of the valve is already in its uppermost position when there is no pressure present.

WHEEL CYLINDERS

1. Remove wheel, drum and brake shoes.
2. Disconnect hydraulic line at wheel cylinder. *Do not pull metal line away from cylinder as the cylinder connection will bend metal line and make installation difficult. Line will separate from cylinder when cylinder*

is moved away from brake backing plate.
3. Remove screws holding cylinder to brake plate and remove cylinder.

Overhaul

1. Referring to Fig. 22 as a guide, remove boots, pistons, springs and cups from cylinder.
2. Place all parts, except cylinder casting in alcohol. Wipe cylinder walls with alcohol.
3. Examine cylinder bore. A scored bore may be honed providing the diameter is not increased more than .005". Replace worn or damaged parts from the repair kit.

4. Before assembling, wash hands with soap and water only as oil, kerosene or gasoline will contaminate rubber parts.
5. Lubricate cylinder wall and rubber cups with brake fluid.
6. Install springs, cups, pistons and boots in housing.
7. Wipe end of hydraulic line to remove any foreign matter.
8. Place hydraulic cylinder in position. Enter tubing into cylinder and start connecting fitting.
9. Secure cylinder to backing plate and then complete tightening of tubing fitting.
10. Install brake shoes, drum and wheel.
11. Bleed system as outlined previously, and adjust brakes.

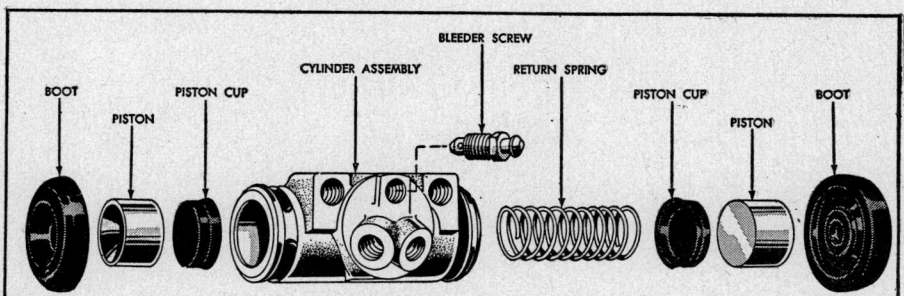

BOOT — PISTON — PISTON CUP — CYLINDER ASSEMBLY — BLEEDER SCREW — RETURN SPRING — PISTON CUP — PISTON — BOOT

Fig. 22   Disassembled view of typical wheel cylinder

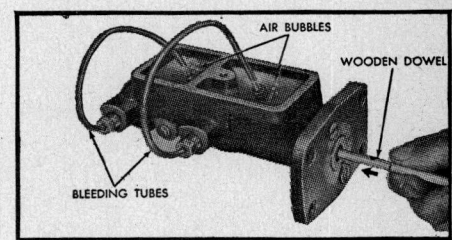

AIR BUBBLES — WOODEN DOWEL

BLEEDING TUBES

Fig. 23   Bleeding master cylinder used in conjunction with disc brakes

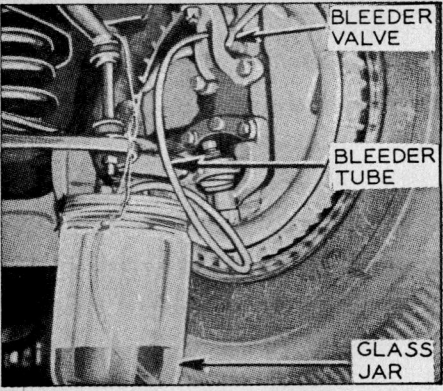

Fig. 24   Bleeding wheel cylinder

FLUSHING HYDRAULIC SYSTEM

It may sometime become necessary to flush out the system due to the presence of mineral oil, kerosene, gasoline, etc., which will cause swelling of rubber piston cups and valves so they become inoperative. The procedure is as follows:

1. Attach bleeder tube and open bleeder valve at left front wheel, Fig. 24.
2. Flush out system thoroughly with clean denatured alcohol, pumping the fluid from the master cylinder reservoir and out of the wheel cylinder bleeder valve.
3. Repeat Steps 1 and 2 at remaining wheel cylinders. To ensure thorough flushing, about ½ pint of alcohol should be bled through each wheel cylinder.
4. Replace all rubber parts in master and wheel cylinders. Thoroughly clean cylinders and pistons in alcohol before installing new parts.
5. After installing parts, fill system with recommended brake fluid and flush system of cleaning solution and then bleed brakes. In doing this, pump brake fluid from wheel cylinder bleeder valves until clear fluid flows from bleeder tube and then, if necessary, continue until no air bubbles emerge from bleeder tube.

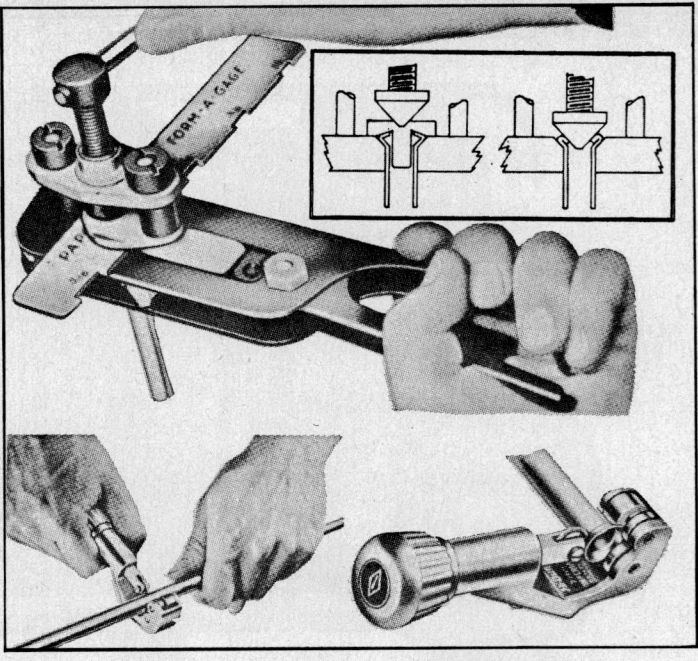

Fig. 25   Flaring hydraulic brake tubing

HYDRAULIC TUBING

Steel tubing is used to conduct hydraulic pressure to the brakes. All fittings, tubing and hose should be inspected for rusted, damaged or defective flared seats. The tubing is equipped with a double flare or inverted seat to insure more positive seating in the fitting. To repair or reflare tubing, proceed as follows:

1. Using the tool shown in Fig. 25 or its equivalent, cut off the damaged seat or damaged tubing.
2. Ream out any burrs or rough edges showing on inside edges of tubing. This will make the ends of the tubing square and insure better seating of the flared end. *Before flaring tubing, place a compression nut on tubing.*
3. Open handles of flaring tool and rotate jaws of tool until mating jaws of tubing size are centered in the area between vertical posts.
4. Slowly close handles with tubing inserted in jaws but do not apply heavy pressure to handle as this will lock tubing in place.
5. Referring to Fig. 25, place gauge on edge over end of tubing and push tubing through jaws until end of tubing contacts recessed notch of gauge matching size of tubing.
6. Squeeze handles of flaring tool and lock tubing in place.
7. Place proper size plug of gauge down in end of tubing. Swing compression disc over gauge and center tapered flaring screw in recess in disc.
8. Lubricate taper of flaring or screw and screw in until plug gauge has seated in jaws of flaring tool. This action has started to invert the extended end of tubing.
9. Remove gauge and apply lubricant to tapered end of flaring screw and continue to screw down until tool is firmly seated in tubing.
10. Remove tubing from flaring tool and inspect the seat. If seat is cracked, cut off cracked end and repeat flaring operation.

DISC BRAKES

CONTENTS

BENDIX Opposed Pistons......2-136

American Motors, 1969-70
Buick Senior Cars, 1969
Dodge Coronet, 1969
Plymouth Belvedere, 1969

BUDD Opposed Pistons........2-139

Imperial, 1969

DELCO-MORAINE Single Piston
2-148

Buick Intermediate Cars, 1969-74
Buick Senior Cars, 1970-74
Cadillac, 1969-73
Checker Motors, 1969-74
Chevrolet Line (except Camaro 4-Wheel
   Disc Option & Corvette), 1969-74
Eldorado, 1969-74
Oldsmobile, F-85 & Toronado, 1969-74
Pontiac Line, 1969-74

DELCO-MORAINE Opposed Pistons
2-140

Camaro Four Wheel Disc Option, 1969
Corvette, 1969-74

FORD Center Abutment.......2-152

Pinto, 1971-73

FORD Sliding Caliper...........2-155

Comet, 1974
Cougar, 1974
Ford Full Size, 1973-74
Lincoln Continental, 1973-74
Mark IV, 1972-74
Maverick, 1974
Mercury, 1973-74
Montego, 1972-74
Mustang II, 1974
Pinto, 1974
Torino, 1972-74
Thunderbird, 1972-74

KELSEY-HAYES Sliding Caliper.2-156

Chrysler, 1974
Dodge Dart, 1973-74
Dodge Monaco, 1974
Imperial, Four Wheel Disc Brake, 1974
Imperial Parking Brake, 1974
Plymouth Fury, 1974
Plymouth Valiant, 1973-74

KELSEY-HAYES Opposed Pistons
2-143

Dodge Dart, 1969-72
Plymouth Barracuda, 1969
Plymouth Valiant, 1969-72

KELSEY-HAYES Single Piston..2-146

American Motors, 1971-74
Chrysler, 1969-73
Cougar 1969-73
Dodge Challenger & Coronet, 1970-74
Dodge Charger, 1969-74
Dodge Polara & Monaco, 1969-73
Fairlane, 1969-71
Falcon, 1969
Ford Full Size, 1969-72
Imperial, 1970-73
Lincoln Continental, 1970-72
Mark III, 1969
Mark IV, 1970-71
Mercury, 1969-72
Montego, 1969-71
Mustang, 1969-73
Plymouth Barracuda, 1970-74
Plymouth Fury, 1969-73
Plymouth Satellite, 1969-74
Thunderbird, 1970-71
Torino, 1969-71

Rotor Specifications...........2-161

TROUBLE SHOOTING

Excessive Pedal Travel

1. Shoe and lining knock back after violent cornering or rough road travel.
2. Piston and shoe and lining assembly not properly seated or positioned.
3. Air leak or insufficient fluid in system or caliper.
4. Loose wheel bearing adjustment.
5. Damaged or worn caliper piston seal.
6. Improper booster push rod adjustment.
7. Shoe out of flat more than .005".
8. Rear brake automatic adjusters inoperative.
9. Improperly ground rear brake shoe and lining assemblies.

Brake Roughness or Chatter; Pedal Pumping

1. Excessive lateral run-out of rotor.
2. Rotor excessively out of parallel.
3. Wheel bearings incorrectly adjusted.
4. Rear drums out of round.
5. Brake pad reversed.

Excessive Pedal Effort

1. Frozen or seized pistons.
2. Brake fluid, oil or grease on linings.
3. Shoe and lining worn below specifications.
4. Proportioning valve malfunction.
5. Booster inoperative.
6. Leaking booster vacuum check valve.
7. Restricted, dented, kinked or collapsed brake lines or hoses.

8. Partial system failure.
9. Fading due to incorrect brake lining.

Pull, Uneven or Grabbing Brakes

1. Frozen or seized pistons.
2. Brake fluid, oil or grease on linings.
3. Caliper out of alignment with rotor.
4. Loose caliper attachment.
5. Unequalized front tire pressure.
6. Unmatched tires on same axle.
7. Incorrect front end alignment.
8. Loose front end parts.
9. Lining protruding beyond end of shoe.
10. Restricted brake tubes or hoses.
11. Malfunctioning caliper assembly.
12. Inoperative combination valve.
13. Power brake unit malfunctioning.

Brake Rattle

1. Excessive clearance between shoe and caliper or between shoe and splash shield.
2. Shoe hold-down clips missing or improperly positioned.

Heavy Brake Drag

1. Frozen or seized pistons.
2. Operator riding brake pedal.
3. Incomplete brake pedal return due to linkage interference.
4. Faulty booster check valve holding pressure in hydraulic system.
5. Residual pressure in front brake hydraulic system.
6. Stuck master cylinder piston.
7. Restricted brake lines or hoses.
8. Incorrect parking brake adjustment.
9. Check valve in lines to front wheels.

Caliper Brake Fluid Leak

1. Damaged or worn caliper piston seal.
2. Scores in cylinder bore.
3. Corrosion build-up in cylinder bore or on piston surface.
4. Metal clip in seal groove.

No Braking Effect When Pedal is Depressed

1. Piston and shoe and lining assembly not properly seated or positioned.
2. Air leak or insufficient fluid in system or caliper.
3. Damaged or worn caliper piston seal.
4. Bleeder screw open.
5. Air in hydraulic system or improper bleeding.
6. Hydraulic leaks.
7. Master cylinder primary cup worn or damaged.
8. Master cylinder bore corroded, worn or scored.
9. Caliper cylinder bore corroded, worn or scored.

Rear Brakes Locking On Application

On brake systems equipped with a proportioning or rear pressure regulator valve, should the valve malfunction rear brakes may receive excess pressure, resulting in wheel lock-up.

SERVICE PRECAUTIONS

Brake Lines & Linings

Remove one of the front wheels and in-

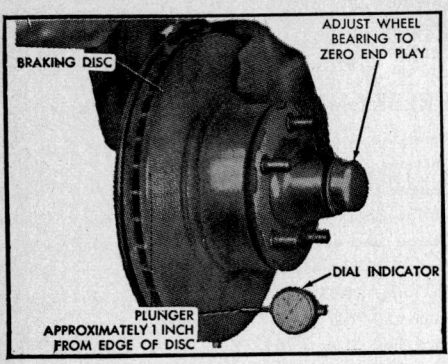

Fig. 1   Checking brake disc for runout

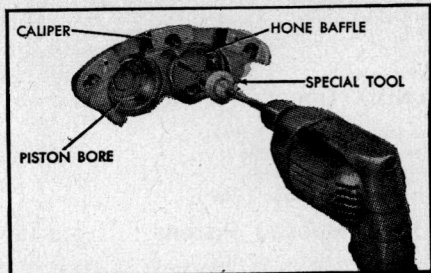

Fig. 2   Honing caliper piston bore

spect the brake disc, caliper and linings. (The wheel bearings should be inspected at this time and repacked if necessary).

Do not get any oil or grease on the linings. If the linings are worn to within .030" of the surface of the shoe, replace both sets of shoe and lining assemblies. It is recommended that both front wheel sets be replaced whenever a respective shoe and lining is worn or damaged. Inspect and, if necessary, replace rear brake linings also.

If the caliper is cracked or fluid leakage through the casting is evident, it must be replaced as a unit.

Shoe & Lining Wear

If visual inspection does not adequately determine the condition of the lining, a physical check will be necessary.

To check the amount of lining wear, remove a wheel from the car, the caliper from the steering knuckle, and the shoe and lining assemblies. Three thickness measurements should be taken (with a micrometer) across the middle section of the shoe and lining; one reading at each side and one reading in the center.

When a shoe and lining assembly has worn to a thickness of .180", it should be replaced. If shoes do not require replacement, reinstall them in their original inner and outer positions.

Brake Roughness

The most common cause of brake chatter on disc brakes is a variation in thickness of the disc. If roughness or vibration is encountered during highway operation or if pedal pumping is experienced at low speeds, the disc may have excessive thickness variation. To check for this condition, measure the disc at 12 points with a micrometer at a radius approximately one inch from edge of disc. If thickness measurements vary by more than .0005", the disc should be replaced with a new one.

Excessive lateral runout of braking disc may cause a "knocking back" of the pistons, possibly creating increased pedal travel and vibration when brakes are applied.

Before checking the runout, wheel bearings should be adjusted. The readjustment is very important and will be required at the completion of the test to prevent bearing failure. Be sure to make the adjustment according to the recommendations

given under *Front Wheel Bearings, Adjust* in the car chapters.

Brake Disc Service

Servicing of disc brakes is extremely critical due to the close tolerances required in machining the brake disc to insure proper brake operation. In manufacturing brake discs, tolerances of the rubbing surfaces for flatness is .001" and usually for parallelism .0005". Lateral runout of the faces should not exceed .004 to .005" in most cases although the limit on Ford Company cars is only .002".

The maintenance of these close controls of the shape of the rubbing surfaces is necessary to prevent brake roughness. In addition, the surface finish must be non-directional and maintained at a micro inch finish. This close control of the rubbing surface finish is necessary to avoid pulls and erratic performance and promote long lining life and equal lining wear of both left and right brakes.

In light of the foregoing remarks, refinishing of the rubbing surfaces should not be attempted unless precision equipment, capable of measuring in micro inches (millionths of an inch) is available.

To check runout of a disc, mount a dial indicator on a convenient part (steering knuckle, tie rod, disc brake caliper housing) so that the plunger of the dial indicator contacts the disc at a point one inch from the outer edge, Fig. 1. If the total indicated runout exceeds specifications, install a new disc.

General Precautions

1. Grease or any other foreign material

must be kept off the caliper, surfaces of the disc and external surfaces of the hub, during service procedures. Handling the brake disc and caliper should be done in a way to avoid deformation of the disc and nicking or scratching brake linings.

2. If inspection reveals rubber piston seals are worn or damaged, they should be replaced immediately.

3. During removal and installation of a wheel assembly, exercise care so as not to interfere with or damage the caliper splash shield, the bleeder screw or the transfer tube.

4. Front wheel bearings should be adjusted to specifications.

5. Be sure vehicle is centered on hoist before servicing any of the front end components to avoid bending or damaging the disc splash shield on full right or left wheel turns.

6. Before the vehicle is moved after any brake service work, be sure to obtain a firm brake pedal.

7. The assembly bolts of the two caliper housings should not be disturbed unless the caliper requires service.

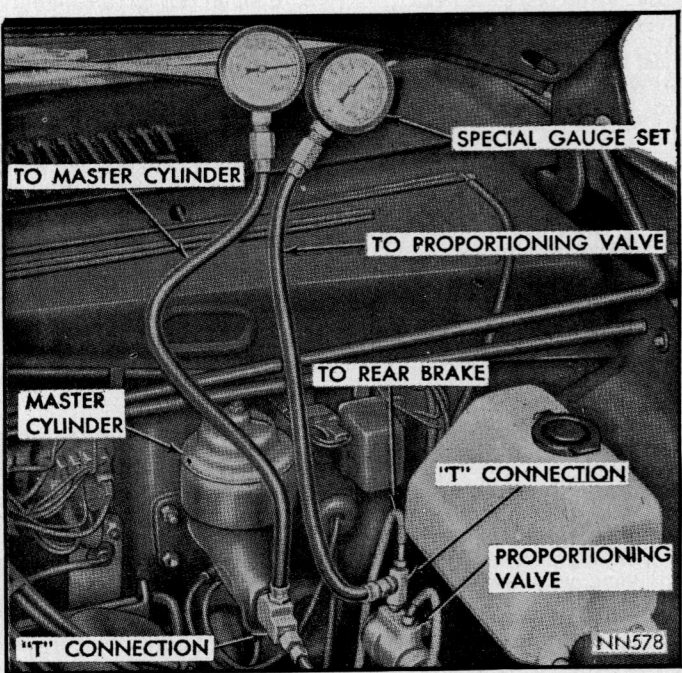

Fig. 3   Gauge hook-up for testing proportioning valve (typical)

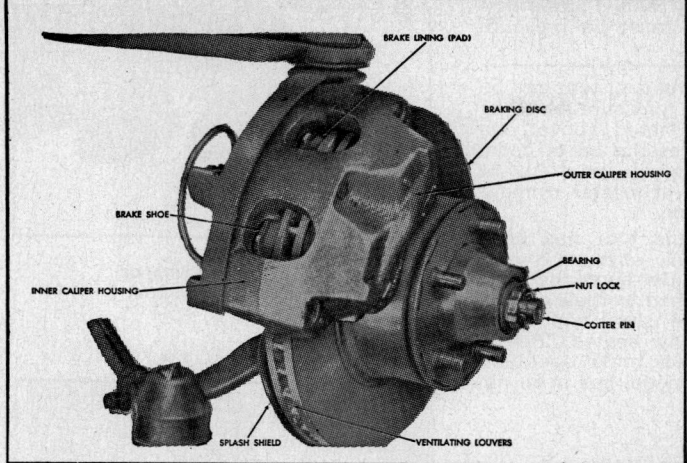

Fig. 4   Bendix opposed piston disc brake

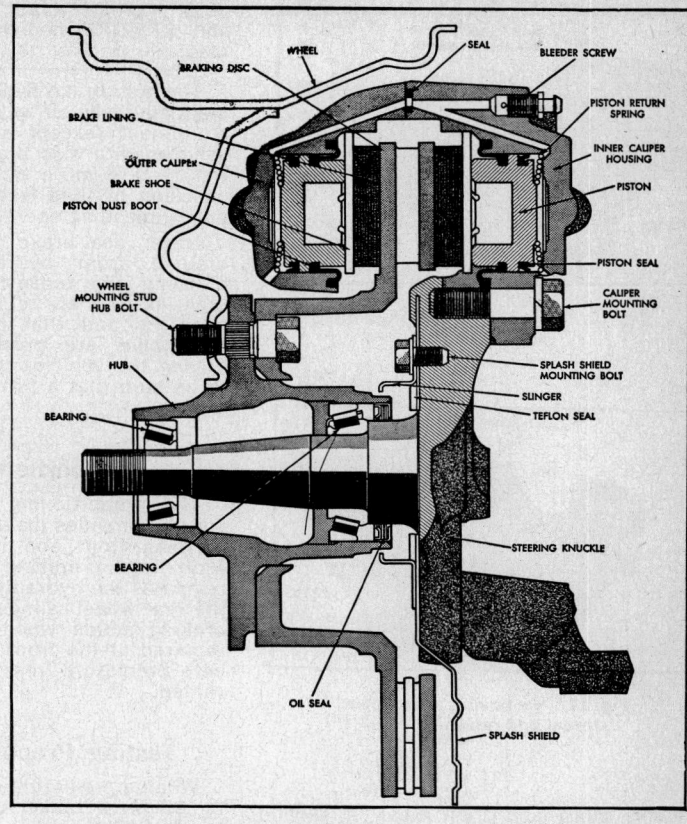

Fig. 5   Sectional view of Bendix opposed piston disc brake

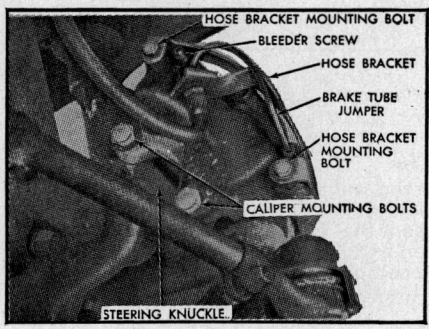

Fig. 6   Caliper mounting

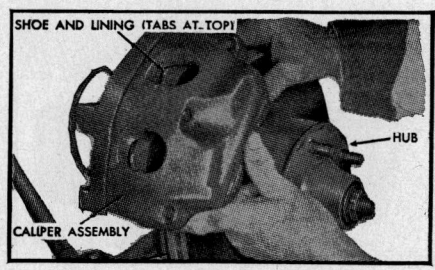

Fig. 7   Removing or installing caliper

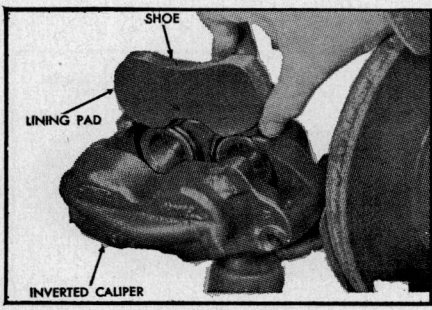

Fig. 8   Removing or installing
brake shoe and lining

Inspection of Caliper

Should it become necessary to remove the caliper for installation of new parts, clean all parts in alcohol, wipe dry using lint-free cloths. Using an air hose, blow out drilled passages and bores. Check dust boots for punctures or tears. If punctures or tears are evident, new boots should be installed upon reassembly.

Inspect piston bores in both housings for scoring or pitting. Bores that show light scratches or corrosion can usually be cleaned with crocus cloth. However, bores that have deep scratches or scoring may be honed, provided the diameter of the bore is not increased more than .002". If the bore does not clean up within this specification, a new caliper housing should be installed (black stains on the bore walls are caused by piston seals and will do no harm).

When using a hone, Fig. 2, be sure to install the hone baffle before honing bore. The baffle is used to protect the hone stones from damage. Use extreme care in cleaning the caliper after honing. Remove all dust and grit by flushing the caliper with alcohol. Wipe dry with clean

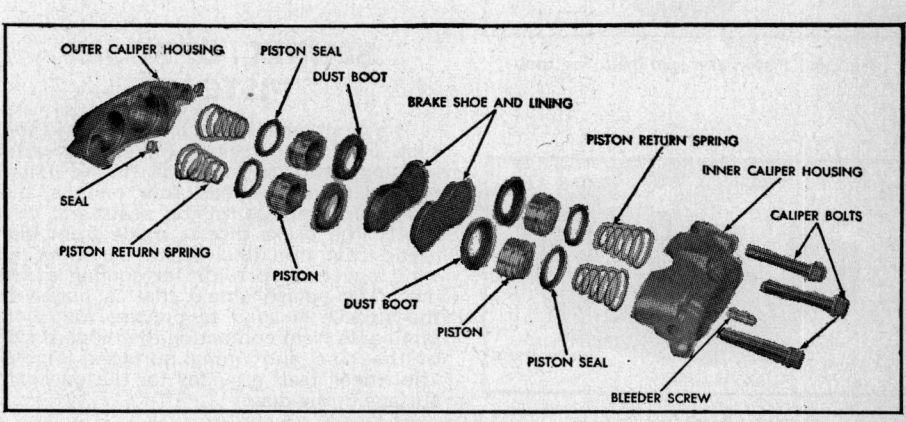

Fig. 9   Exploded view of caliper assembly

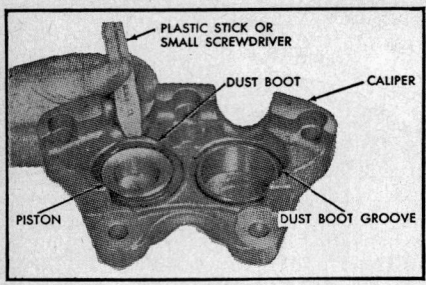

Fig. 10   Removing piston dust boot

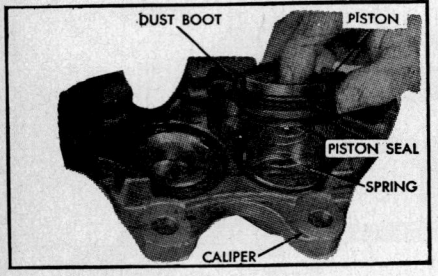

Fig. 11   Removing piston boot, seal and return spring

lint-less cloth and then clean a second time in the same manner.

Bleeding Disc Brakes

NOTE: Chrysler Corp. recommends only pressure bleeding for all 1969-74 models, while Ford Motor Co. recommends that 1969-71 Lincoln Continental, 1970-71

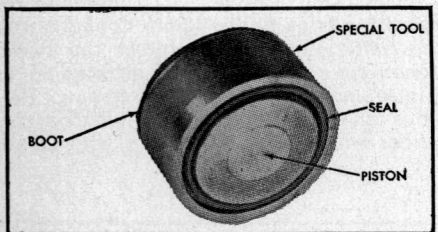

Fig. 14   Piston and seal installing tool

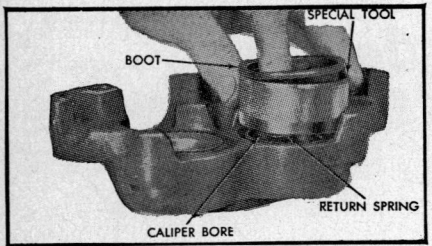

Fig. 15   Installing piston, seal and dust boot

Ford, Mercury, Mark III and Thunderbird and all 1972 models, must be pressure bled.

The disc brake hydraulic system can be bled manually or with pressure bleeding equipment (except as noted above). On vehicles with disc brakes the brake pedal will require more pumping and frequent checking of fluid level in master cylinder during bleeding operation.

Never use brake fluid that has been drained from hydraulic system when bleeding the brakes. Be sure the disc brake pistons are returned to their normal positions and that the shoe and lining assemblies are properly seated. Before driving the vehicle, check brake operation to be sure that a firm pedal has been obtained.

Proportioning Valve

The proportioning valve (when used), Fig. 3, provides balanced braking action between front and rear brakes under a wide range of braking conditions. The valve regulates the hydraulic pressure applied to the rear wheel cylinders, thus limiting rear braking action when high pressures are required at the front brakes. In this manner, premature rear wheel skid is prevented.

Testing Proportioning Valve

When a premature rear wheel slide is obtained on a brake application, it usually is an indication that the fluid pressure to the rear wheels is above the 50% reduction ratio for the rear line pressure and that a malfunction has occured within the proportioning valve.

To test the valve, install gauge set shown in Fig. 3 in brake line between master cylinder and proportioning valve, and at output end of proportioning valve and brake line as shown. Be sure all joints are fluid tight.

Have a helper exert pressure on brake pedal (holding pressure). Obtain a reading on master cylinder output of approximately 700 psi. While pressure is being held as above, reading on valve outlet should be 550-610 psi. If the pressure readings do not meet these specifications, the valve should be removed and a new valve installed.

BENDIX OPPOSED PISTONS

The front wheel disc brake, Fig. 4, consists of a fixed caliper (inner and outer housing), two friction pads (brake lining) molded to steel shoes, four pistons, piston return springs, piston seals and dust boots. The brake disc is made from high grade cast iron and has a series of air vent louvers to provide for cooling of the disc. The splash shield that is bolted to the spindle is used to prevent road contaminants from contacting the inboard side of the disc and lining surfaces, Fig. 5. The wheel itself provides for the outboard surface of the disc.

The brake disc is mounted on the front wheel hub by five bolts, and is straddled

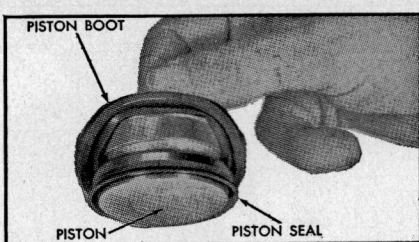

Fig. 12   Removing or installing piston boot

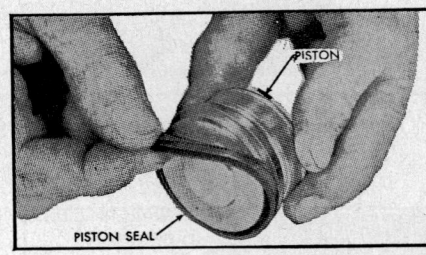

Fig. 13   Removing or installing piston seal

by the caliper which is attached to the steering knuckle by two bolts. Inserted between the pistons and the disc are the shoe and lining assemblies, which are held in position by parallel machined abutments within the caliper.

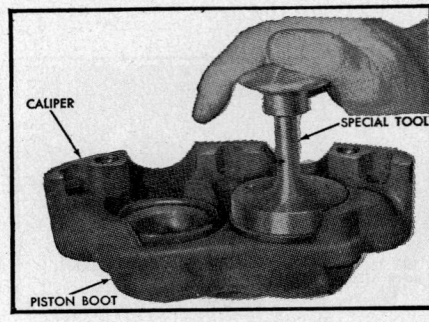

Fig. 16   Installing piston dust boot in caliper groove

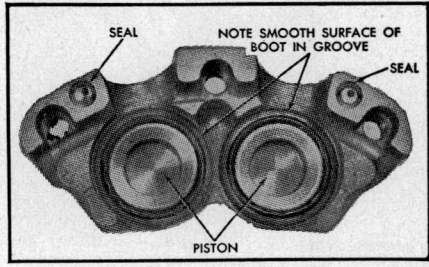

Fig. 17   Pistons and boots installed in caliper

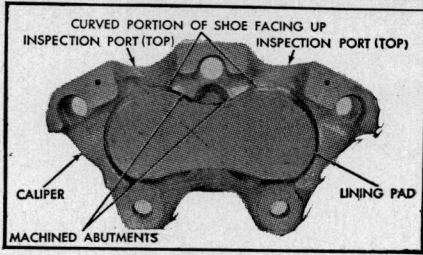

Fig. 18 Shoes and linings correctly positioned in caliper

Brake Shoe Removal

1969-70 American Motors & 1969 Buick

1. Remove wheel assembly and disconnect hydraulic tubing from mounting bracket.
2. On 1969 Buick models:
   a. Remove upper and loosen lower caliper mounting bolt, then rotate upper end of caliper rearward.
   b. Connect one end of drain hose to bleeder screw and submerge other end in a container partially filled with brake fluid, then open bleed screw and bottom pistons. Tighten bleeder screw after pistons are bottomed.

NOTE: This step is necessary to prevent overflow of reservoir when installing new disc brake pads.

3. On 1969-70 American Motors:
   a. Loosen caliper mounting bolts then hold lower edge of caliper and remove lower bolt. Shake caliper until all shims fall out and mark these as "Lower".
   b. Press in on upper edge of caliper to hold shims on upper mounting bolt. Remove bolt and mark these shims as "Upper".

NOTE: Original shim thickness must be replaced in same locations when caliper is installed.

   c. Support caliper assembly using a length of wire.
4. Using two screwdrivers between shoe and pistons, press pistons into bottom of their cylinders and remove pad assembly from calipers.

1969 Belvedere & Coronet

1. Remove wheel assemblies.
2. Remove caliper-to-steering knuckle bolts, Fig. 6.
3. Remove caliper from disc by sliding it up and away from disc, Fig. 7.
4. Remove brake shoes and lining assemblies one at a time through bottom opening, Fig. 8.

Brake Shoe Installation

All Models

1. Referring to Fig. 8, slide shoe and lining assemblies into position in caliper, one at a time, with curved portion (with tabs) entering first and

metal shoe against open ends of pistons. Using fingers, spread linings apart until pistons are seated in their bores.
2. Slide caliper into position over brake disc and align mounting holes. As caliper is being installed, be sure that lining slides easily along brake disc.
3. Install caliper mounting bolts and torque to 85 ft. lbs for American Motors, Belvedere and Coronet and to 70 ft. lbs for Buick models.

NOTE: On American Motors, the original shim thickness must be installed in the same location between the caliper mounting lugs and bracket. If exact shim thickness is unknown, the caliper must be adjusted as outlined under "Caliper Adjustment."

4. Make sure disc rotates freely and with minimum drag.
5. Install wheel assembly.

CAUTION: Road test vehicle and make several heavy 40 mph stops to wear off any foreign material on the brakes and to seat the linings. The vehicle may pull to one side if this is not done.

Removing Caliper

1. Remove wheels.
2. Disconnect brake line at caliper housing and install a pipe plug in the tube opening.
3. Remove bolts that attach hose bracket to caliper.
4. Remove caliper mounting bolts.
5. Remove caliper from brake disc by slowly sliding it up and away from disc.

Disassembling Caliper

1. Referring to Fig. 9, drain caliper, then place it in a vise.
2. Separate caliper halves and remove two crossover seals.

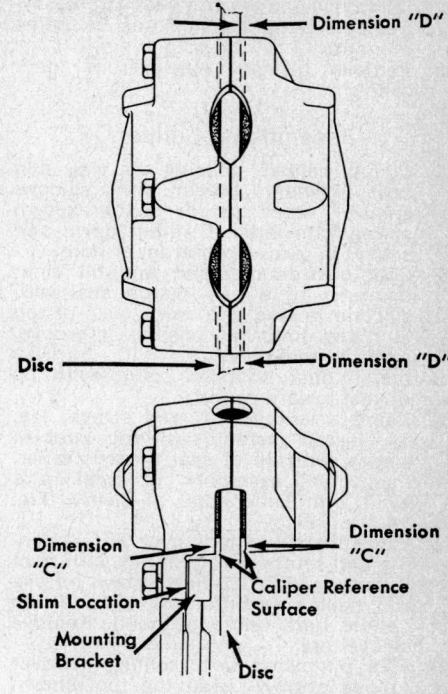

Fig. 19 Disc to caliper clearance checking points

3. Using a screwdriver, pry exposed dust boot out of groove, Fig. 10. Be sure to hold piston compressed during this operation.
4. Remove piston, seal and dust boot from caliper, Fig. 11. Remove piston return spring.
5. Remove piston dust boot by grasping edge and pulling out of its groove, Fig. 12.
6. Remove fingers, roll piston seal out of

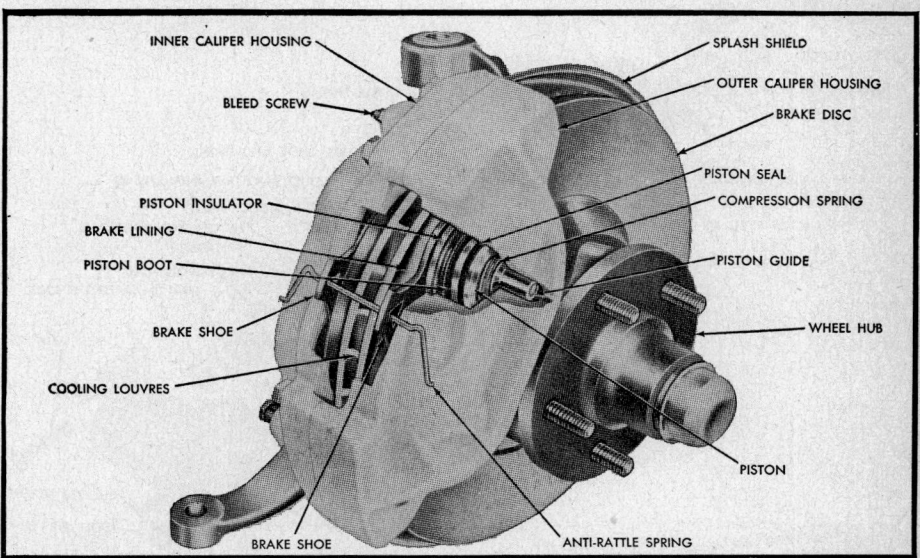

Fig. 20 Budd opposed piston disc brake assembly

its groove and discard seal, Fig. 13.

7. Remove remaining pistons in same manner.
8. Remove bleeder screw from inner caliper.

Assembling Caliper

1. Clamp caliper housing in vise and coat cylinder bores with silicone grease, then install piston return spring with large diameter down and seated in recess at bottom of bore.
2. Coat outside diameter and fill inner diameter of a new piston seal with silicone grease and work over piston land and down into position in groove, using fingers only.
3. Install dust boot on piston with lip of seat toward piston.
4. Using a suitable tapered sleeve, Fig. 14, install piston, seal and boot in sleeve, with lip of seal towards taper. Push in on assembly until seal lip is even with knife edge of sleeve, Fig. 14.
5. Place installing tool over bore opening and return spring. Index with boot in caliper, Fig. 15. Press down on piston, sliding piston out of tool and into caliper bore until bottomed. Remove sleeve tool.
6. Position piston boot sealing lip over groove evenly. Using the tool shown in Fig. 16 or its equivalent, press down on tool, forcing boot sealing lip into caliper groove. Remove tool and install remaining pistons in same manner, Fig. 17.
7. Test pistons for smooth operation in their bores by depressing with fingers.
8. Lightly clamp outer caliper half in vise and install new crossover passage seals in position in recess of caliper mating surface, Fig. 17.

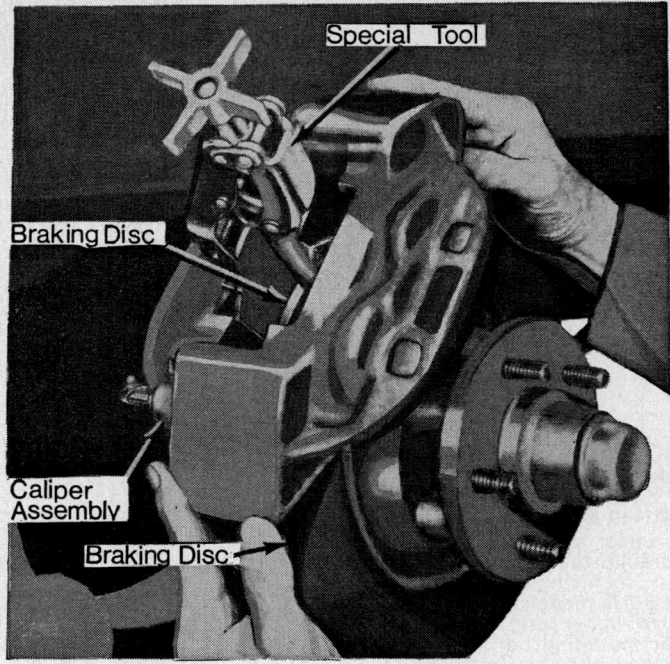

Fig. 21 Piston compression tool installed

9. Place mating caliper half over one clamped in vise, install attaching bolts and torque to 120-140 ft-lbs.
10. Install brake shoes in caliper with curved portion (with tabs) entering first and metal shoe against open ends of pistons. Using fingers, spread linings apart until pistons are seated in their bores, Fig. 18.
11. Install bleeder screw and tighten lightly.

Installing Caliper

1. Check runout of brake disc with dial indicator as outlined previously.

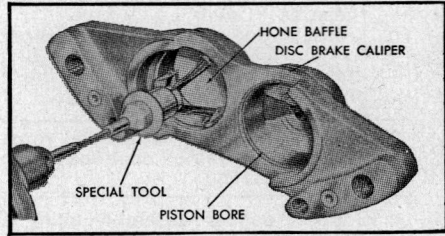

Fig. 23 Honing piston bore

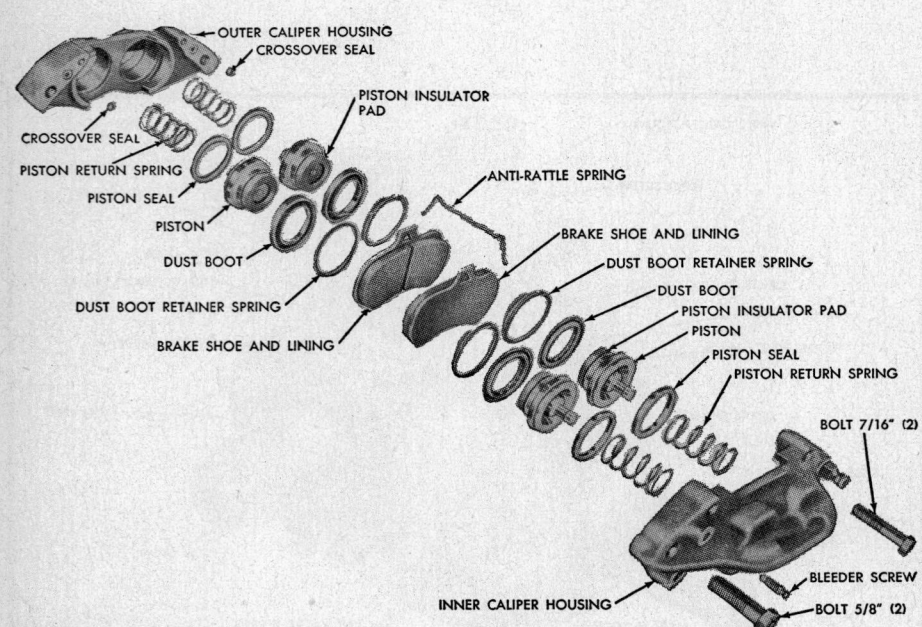

Fig. 22 Budd disc brake caliper disassembled

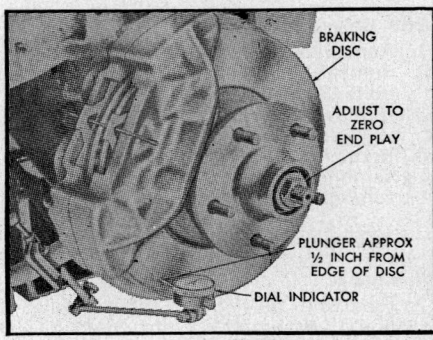

Fig. 24 Checking brake disc for runout

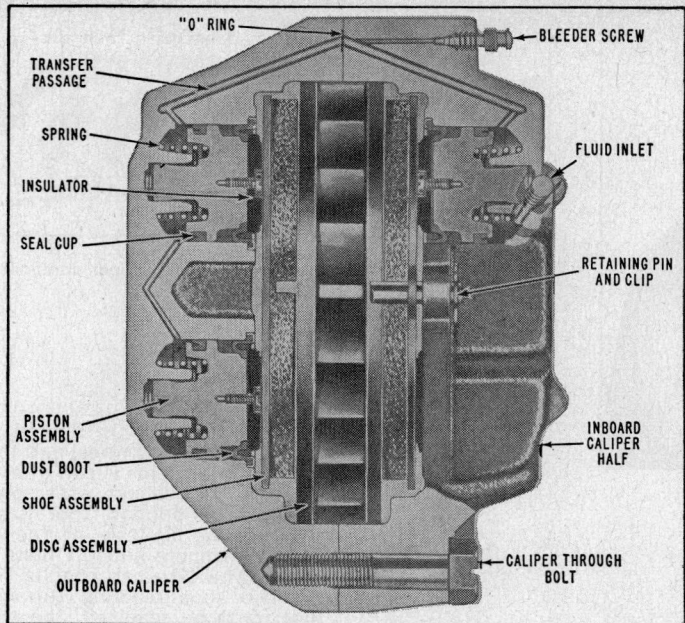

Fig. 25 Delco-Moraine disc brake assembly

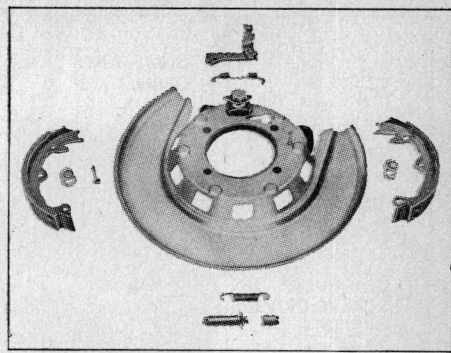

Fig. 26 Delco-Moraine parking brake components

2. Install caliper over disc and align mounting holes. Install mounting bolts and torque to 85 ft. lbs for American Motors and Plymouth Belvedere models and 70 ft. lbs for Buick models.

NOTE: As caliper is being lowered into place, be sure that linings ride freely over disc.

3. Connect brake line at caliper housing, then position brake hose bracket. Install bracket and attaching bolts and tighten securely.
4. Follow normal bleeding procedure, being sure all air bubbles have escaped.
5. Replenish brake fluid in master cylinder.
6. Install wheels and road test as suggested previously.

Caliper Adjustment 1969-70 American Motors

The caliper reference surfaces and friction faces of the disc must be within .010 inch on both sides of the disc, Fig. 19 (Dimension C). Use feeler gauges to check to see if both ends of the caliper are centered relative to the rubbing surfaces of the disc. If clearance is not within specifications, loosen the caliper mounting bolts and add or remove shims as necessary between the caliper mounting lugs and mounting bracket.

The caliper and disc must also be parallel so that dimension "D" Fig. 19, is equal within .005 inch at each end of the caliper. If clearance is not within specifications, add or remove shims as required on one or the other mounting lug bolt. After proper clearance has been obtained, torque mounting bolts to 85 ft. lbs.

BUDD OPPOSED PISTONS

The Budd Disc brake, Fig. 20, consists of a fixed caliper (inner and outer housing) two friction pads (brake lining) bonded to steel shoes, four pistons, piston return springs, piston seals, dust boots and retainers. The brake disc is made from high grade cast iron and has a series of air vent louvers to provide cooling for the brake aseembly. The splash shield has a series of stamped vents so designed as to supply additional air for cooling.

Removing Lining

1. Remove wheels.
2. Remove brake shoe anti-rattle spring.
3. Remove bolts that attach caliper assembly to steering knuckle and knuckle arm.
4. Slowly slide caliper up and away from brake shoe.
5. Carefully invert caliper and remove brake shoe assembly (one at a time).
6. Insert piston compressing tool C-3992 between piston insulator pads and turn knob on tool until pistons are fully compressed, Fig. 21.

Installing Lining

1. Slide brake disc shoe and lining assembly into position in caliper (one at a time).
2. Position shoes, then install tool C-3992 between shoes. Adjust tool so that it holds shoes apart and that it will slip out easily when contacted by disc.
3. Install caliper mounting bolts and torque to 80-90 ft. lbs.

CAUTION: Road test vehicle and apply several heavy 40 mph stops to wear off any foreign material on brakes and to seat units. The vehicle may pull to one side or the other if this is not done. This condition will be more noticeable if only one wheel was worked on.

Removing Caliper

1. Remove wheels.
2. Remove anti-rattle clips, then disconnect brake line from caliper and install a plug.
3. Remove caliper mounting bolts, then slowly slide caliper assembly up and away from disc.
4. Remove lining pads, then install compressing tool C-3992 and turn knob until pistons are fully compressed, Fig. 21.

Disassembling Caliper

1. Referring to Fig. 22, remove piston compression tool and four bolts that hold two halves of caliper together.
2. Separate halves and remove two crossover seals.
3. Using a small screwdriver, pry out exposed end of piston dust boot retainer spring and uncoil from its groove to release dust boot.
4. Using same screwdriver, work dust boot out of groove. Be sure to hold piston compressed during this operation.
5. Remove piston, seal and dust boot from caliper. Remove piston return spring.
6. Remove piston dust boot by grasping edge and pulling out of its groove.
7. Pry piston seal out of its groove and discard.
8. Remove remaining three pistons in same manner.
9. Remove bleeder screw from inner caliper housing.

Cleaning & Inspection

1. Clean all parts in brake fluid and wipe dry. Using an air hose, blow out drilled passages and bores.

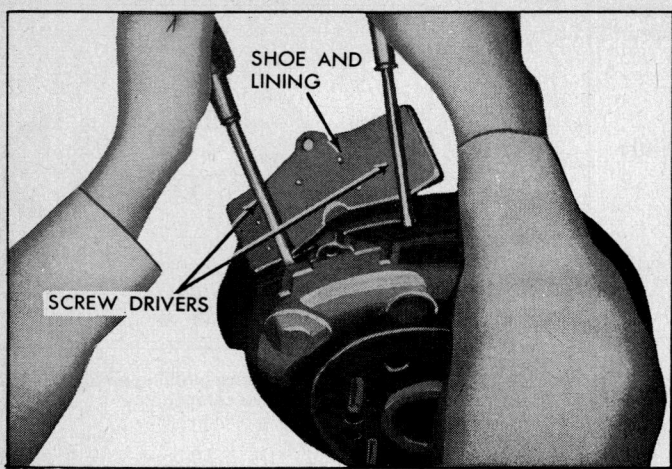

Fig. 27 Installing Delco Moraine disc brake shoes

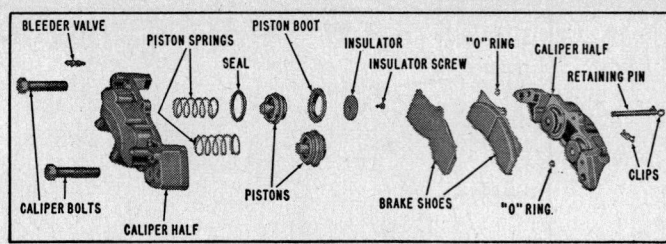

Fig. 28 Delco-Moraine disc brake caliper components

2. Check dust boots for punctures and tears. If punctures or tears are evident, new boots should be installed.
3. Inspect piston bores in both housings for scoring or pitting. Bores that show light scratches or corrosion can usually be cleaned with crocus cloth. However, bores that have deep scratches or scoring may be honed, Fig. 23, providing the diameter of bore is not increased more than .002". If the bore does not clean up within this specification, a new caliper housing must be installed. Black stains on bore walls are caused by the piston seals and will do no harm.
4. When honing, Fig. 23, be sure to install the hone baffle before honing bore. The baffle is used to protect hone stones from damage.
5. Use extreme care in cleaning the caliper after honing. Remove all dust and grit by flushing caliper with brake fluid. Wipe dry with clean, lintless cloth and then clean a second time in like manner.

Assembling Caliper

1. Referring to Fig. 22, clamp caliper in a vise, then install piston return spring. Be sure spring is seated in recess in bottom of bore.
2. Coat outside diameter and fill inner diameter of a new piston seal with silicone grease and work over piston land and down into position in groove, using fingers only.
3. Install dust boot on piston with lip of boot toward piston pad.
4. Install piston over return spring and press down until piston bottoms in bore.
5. Using a small, blunt screwdriver, work lip of boot into groove, around diameter of bore. Use care so as not to puncture boot during this operation, or a new boot will have to be installed.
6. Install retainer spring by inserting one end in position in groove and continue to install around diameter of bore until retainer is fully seated. Be sure boot is completely locked in position

by retainer and that retainer is fully seated in groove.
7. Install remaining pistons in same manner, then test pistons for smooth operation in their bores by depressing with fingers.
8. Lightly clamp outer caliper half in vise and install new crossover seals, then place mating caliper half over one installed in vise.
9. Install attaching bolts and torque $7/16$ inch bolts to 55 ft. lbs and $5/8$ inch bolts to 150 ft. lbs.
10. Install bleeder screw.

Installing Caliper

1. Before installing caliper over disc, check disc for runout with a dial gauge as shown in Fig. 24. Lateral runout should not exceed .005"; if runout is excessive, remove disc and check its mounting surface on wheel hub. Runout of hub should not exceed .004".
2. Install caliper assembly over disc and align mounting holes. Install mounting bolts and torque to 80-90 ft. lbs.
3. Connect brake line at caliper housing and allow caliper to fill with brake fluid then close bleeder screw. Be sure all air bubbles have escaped when bleeding the caliper. Replenish brake fluid in master cylinder.
4. Install wheels and road test vehicle as outlined previously.

DELCO-MORAINE OPPOSED PISTONS

These brakes are used on all four wheels. The components of the disc brake system are shown in Fig. 25. The caliper assemblies replace the conventional wheel cylinder, brake shoes and linings, and the disc replaces the brake drum.
The caliper assembly contains four pistons, two acting on each shoe with one shoe on each side of the disc.

The brake disc is riveted to the hub flange at the front wheel and to the spindle flange at the rear wheel. The disc rotates through the caliper assembly, which is bolted to a support that is attached to the steering knuckle at the front wheel and the spindle support bolts at the rear wheel. The disc has cooling fins between the two shoe reacting surfaces. When a disc must be replaced, the rivets can be drilled out and then the wheel studs will be used for disc retension purposes.
A miniature set of brake shoes, mounted on a flange plate and shield assembly attached to the rear wheel spindle support bolts, are used for vehicle parking, Fig. 26.

Removing Lining

1. To prevent overflow, remove two thirds of brake fluid from master cylinder.
2. Support vehicle on hoist and remove wheel.
3. Remove cotter pin from inboard end of retaining pin. On 1969-70 models with heavy duty brakes, two retaining pins must be removed, one from each end of caliper.
4. Remove inboard and outboard shoe by pulling up.

Installing Lining

1. Install inboard and outboard shoe one at a time. Use two screwdrivers to push pistons back as shoes are inserted, Fig. 27.
2. Install retaining pin through outboard caliper half, outboard shoe, inboard shoe and inboard caliper half. Insert a new $3/32$ x $5/8$ inch plated cotter pin through retaining pin. On 1969-70 models with heavy duty brakes, install two retaining pins, one at each end of caliper.
3. Repeat above procedure at each wheel where shoes are to be replaced.
4. Refill master cylinder, then install wheel and lower vehicle.

CAUTION: Do not move vehicle until a firm brake pedal has been obtained.

Calipers

The caliper assembly, Fig. 28 comes in two halves assembled by strong bolts at the flange end. The two halves contain fluid crossover passages from one to the

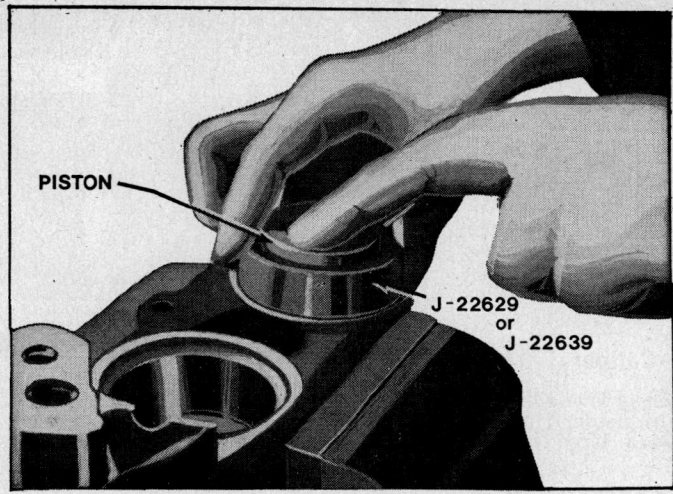

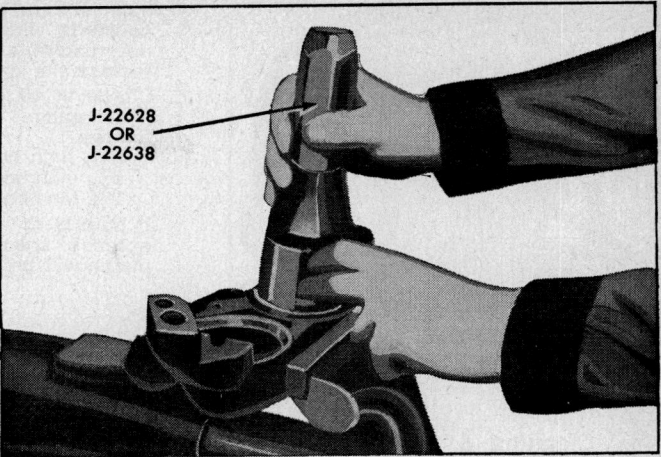

Fig. 29 Installing piston in caliper

Fig. 30 Installing boot seal in caliper

other, sealed with "O" rings.

The bleeder screw is threaded into a passage drilled to intersect the fluid cross-over passage. The bleeder screws are located at the front of each caliper. There are two bleeder screws, one inboard, one outboard at the rear wheels, and one bleeder screw at the inboard side at the front wheel. It is necessary, therefore, to remove the rear wheel when bleeding the rear caliper.

Removing Caliper

1. Support vehicle on hoist and remove wheel.
2. On front caliper, disconnect brake hose from support bracket. On rear caliper, disconnect tubing from inboard caliper. Tape open tube or line

end to prevent entry of dirt.
3. Remove caliper mounting bolts and remove caliper.

Disassembling Caliper

1. Remove brake hose from front caliper.
2. Remove cotter pin from retaining pin, then remove pin and shoe assembly from caliper.

NOTE: On 1969-70 models with heavy duty brakes, two retaining pins must be removed.

3. Remove caliper retaining bolts and separate caliper halves, then remove the two O-rings from fluid transfer cavities in ends of caliper halves.

4. Push piston into caliper as far as it will move, then insert a screwdriver under inner edge of steel ring in boot and using piston as a fulcrum, pry piston boot from its seat in caliper half.

CAUTION: Use care not to puncture seal when removing pistons from caliper.

5. Remove pistons and springs from caliper half, then remove boot and seal from piston.

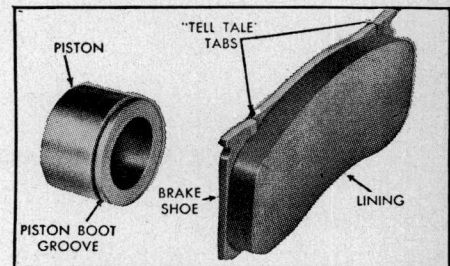

Fig. 32 Brake piston, shoe and lining assembly

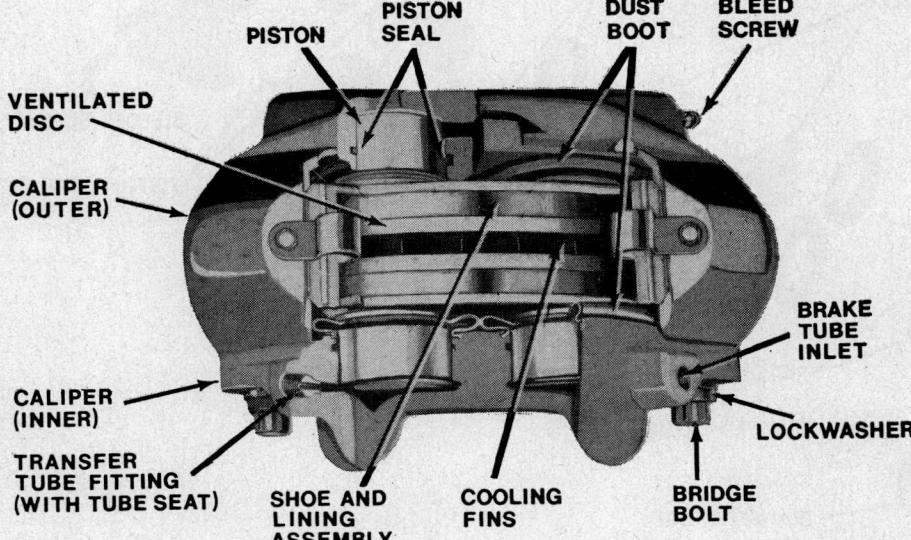

Fig. 31 Kelsey-Hayes opposed piston disc brake

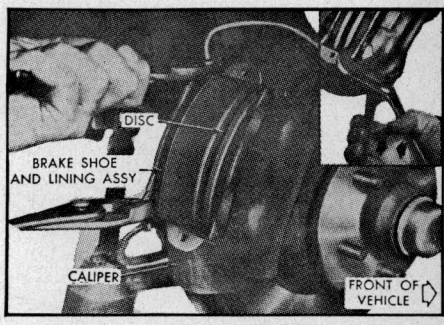

Fig. 33 Removing brake shoe and lining

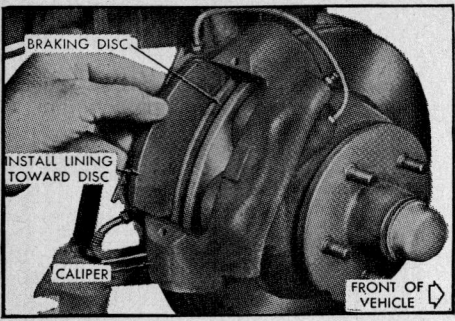

Fig. 34 Installing brake shoe and lining

Cleaning & Inspection

1. Clean all metal parts using clean brake fluid, removing all traces of dirt and grease.

CAUTION: Never use mineral base cleaning solvents as they can cause deterioration of rubber parts or make them soft and swollen.

2. Using air pressure, blow out all fluid passages in caliper halves, making sure that these passages are not obstructed.
3. Discard all rubber parts and replace with new service kit parts.
4. Inspect piston bores. They must be free of scores and pits. A damaged bore will cause leaks and unsatisfactory brake operation. If either caliper

half is damaged to the extent that polishing with fine crocus cloth will not restore to satisfactory condition, replace the caliper half.

5. Check fit of piston in bore using a feeler gauge. Clearance should be as follows:

2 1/16 inch bore	.0045-.010
1 7/8 inch bore	.0045-.010
1 3/8 inch bore	.0035-.009

If bore is not damaged and clearance exceeds specifications, only a new piston will be required.

Assembling Caliper

1. Install seal in piston groove which is closest to flat end of piston. The seal lip must face toward large end of piston.

NOTE: Make certain seal lips are in piston groove and do not extend over step in end of groove.

2. Place spring in piston bore, then lubricate seal with brake fluid.
3. Install piston assembly in bore using tool J-22591, 22629 or 22639, Fig. 29. Use care not to damage seal lip as piston is pressed past edge of bore.
4. Install piston boot in groove closest to concave end of piston with fold in boot facing toward end of piston with seal attached.
5. Make certain that piston slides smoothly into bore until end of piston is flush with end of bore. If not, re-

check piston assembly and position of piston spring and seal.

6. Using boot seal installer tool J-22592, J-22628 or J-22638, Fig. 30, over piston, seat steel boot retaining ring evenly into counterbore.

NOTE: Boot retaining ring must be flush or below machined face of caliper. Any distortion or uneven seating could allow corrosive elements to enter bore.

7. Install O-rings in cavities around brake fluid transfer holes at both ends of outboard caliper halves. Lubricate caliper bolts with Delco Brake Lube #540032 (or equivalent) or clean

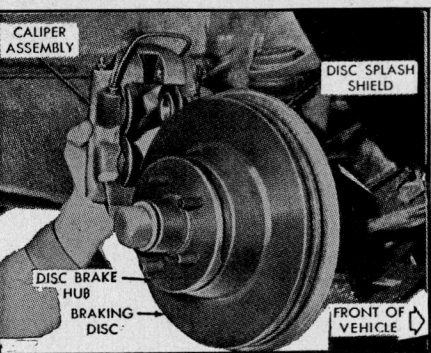

Fig. 35 Replacing brake disc caliper

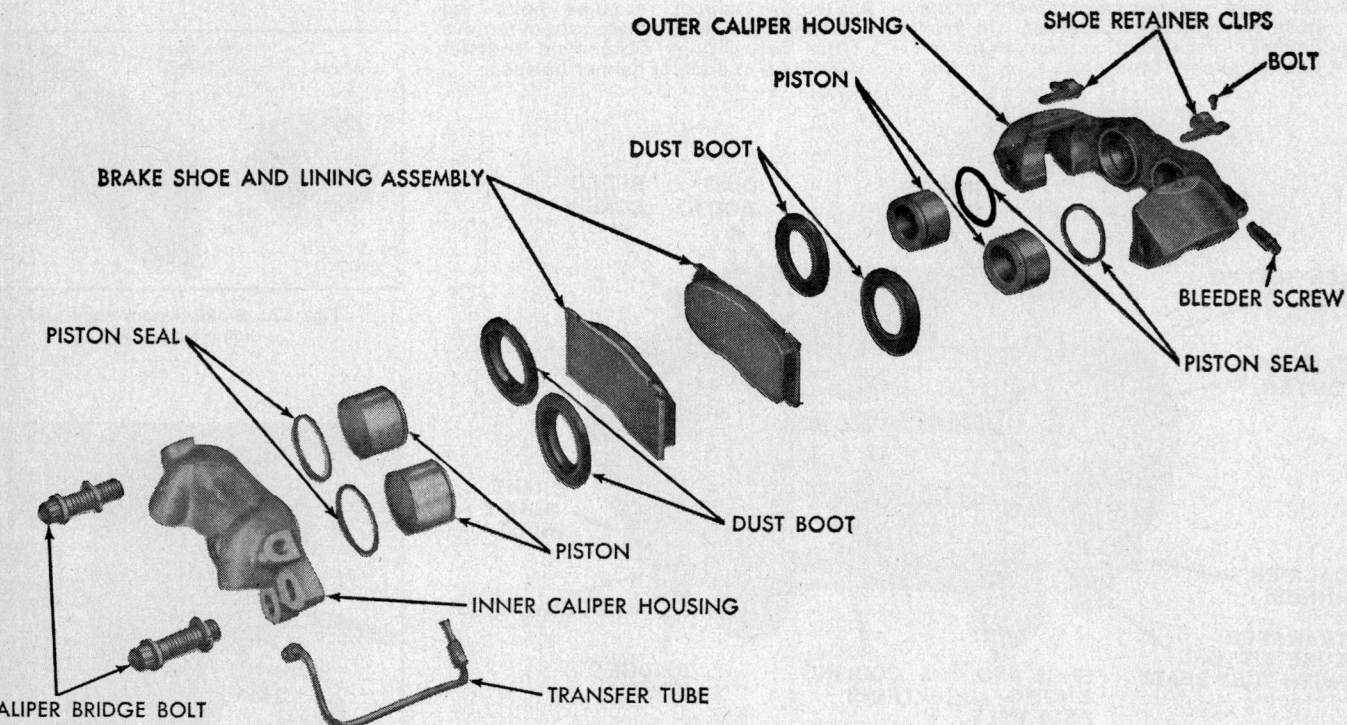

Fig. 36 Caliper disassembled

brake fluid, then secure caliper halves together and torque caliper bolts to 130 ft. lbs.

Installing Caliper

1. Mount caliper over disc, then using two screwdrivers, depress pistons so that caliper can be lowered into place.

NOTE: Use care not to damage boots on edge of disc as caliper is installed.

2. Install mounting bolts and torque to 70 ft. lbs.

CAUTION: If reusing old shoe assemblies, be sure to install shoes in same location from which removed.

3. Install disc pads as outlined previously.
4. Place a new copper gasket on male end of front wheel brake hose and install brake hose in calipers. With wheels straight ahead, pass female end of hose through support bracket, then making certain that tube seat is clean, connect brake line tube nut to caliper and tighten securely.
5. Allowing hose to seek a normal position, without twist, insert hose fitting in support bracket and secure with "U" shaped retainer, then while turning steering geometry from stop to stop, check that hose does not contact other parts at anytime. If contact does occur, remove "U" shaped retainer and twist hose in a direction that will eliminate hose contact. Re-install retainer and recheck for hose contact. If satisfactory, place steel tube connecter in hose fitting and tighten securely.
6. If rear caliper is being serviced, connect brake line to caliper.
7. Bleed brakes and install wheels.

CAUTION: Do not move vehicle until a firm pedal has been obtained.

Service Summary

1. There is no brake shoe adjustment on the disc brakes.
2. The groove in the brake shoe is an indicator of brake wear. When the groove is just about gone it is time for shoe replacement.
3. When replacing shoes it is necessary to siphon fluid from master cylinder reservoir to make room for fluid return to the reservoir when pushing the caliper pistons back into their bores to make room for the thickness of the new shoes.
4. The shoes have a directional arrow on the back of the shoe plate. This arrow points to the forward rotation of the disc, and the purpose is for aligning the grain of the lining material in relation to the disc.
5. When bleeding the calipers, the rear wheel must be removed to reach the outboard bleeder screw.
6. A retaining clip of thin metal is used to hold the pistons into the bores while installing the new brake shoes.
7. The caliper assembly is removable, after disconnecting the brake line, by removing the two mounting bolts and lifting the assembly off the disc.

8. The disc is riveted to the spindle flange in production. However, the rivets may be drilled out and the wheel studs and nuts are sufficient to hold the new disc in place when replacing the disc.
9. The rear wheel spindle must be removed to gain access to the parking brake shoes. It is necessary then to remove the caliper, the axle drive shaft, the spindle drive shaft yoke and remove the spindle and disc as an assembly from the wheel support. You now have access to the parking brake shoes the same as any other conventional bendix type brake shoe, Fig. 26.
10. If the car is equipped with the special optional knock-off hub assemblies, the adapters must be removed to gain access to the parking brake adjustment.

KELSEY-HAYES OPPOSED PISTON TYPE BRAKE

This type brake, Fig. 31, is a fixed caliper, opposed piston, non-energized, ventilated type, actuated by the hydraulic system. There is no lateral movement of either the disc or the caliper. The caliper assembly consists of two caliper housings bolted together. Each half contains two cylinder bores. Each cylinder contains a seal, piston and externally attached molded rubber dust boot to seal the cylinder bore from contamination. The pistons are sealed by rubber piston seals positioned in grooves machined in the cylinder bores which provide hydraulic sealing between pistons and cylinder bores.

An additional feature of this brake system is a "tell-tale" tab sounding device which indicates when replacement of the shoe and lining assemblies are required, Fig. 32. The tabs on the shoes create an audible metallic scraping noise from the brake by metal-to-metal contact on the braking disc. This warns the driver that the lining has worn to a minimum thickness, at which time it should be replaced.

Checking Running Clearance

To check the lining-to-disc running clearance, remove wheel and caliper splash shield. Insert a feeler gauge between lining and disc. Clearance ordinarily should be .003-.006". However, if the vehicle was stopped by a brake application just prior to checking the clearance, it is considered normal for the brakes to drag slightly.

Brake Shoe Replace

1. Raise vehicle on hoist or stands.
2. Remove wheel assembly.
3. Remove shoe retainer spring assemblies.
4. Using two pairs of pliers, grasp tabs on outer ends of shoes and remove shoe and lining by pulling outward, Fig. 33.

NOTE: Due to a ridge of rust that may have formed on the disc surface outside of lining contact area, it may be necessary to force the piston back slightly into its bore.

This is done by forcing the shoe back with water pump pliers placed on corner of shoe and caliper housing as shown, Fig. 33.

Installation

1. Push all pistons back into their bores until bottomed to allow for installation of new shoes. This can be done by placing a flat-sided metal bar against piston and exerting a steady force until bottomed.
2. Slide new shoe and lining into caliper with ears of shoe resting on bridges of caliper, Fig. 34. Be sure shoe is fully seated and lining is facing disc.
3. Slide remaining shoe and lining into caliper, using same procedure as above.
4. Install shoe retainer spring in place on caliper.
5. Pump brake pedal several times until a firm pedal has been obtained and shoe and linings have been properly seated.
6. Install wheel. Replenish master cylinder fluid as required.

CAUTION: Road test vehicle and make several heavy 40 m.p.h. stops to wear off any foreign material on the brakes and to seat the units. The vehicle may pull to one side or the other if this is not done. It should not be necessary to bleed the system after replacing linings.

Servicing Caliper

Removal

1. Raise car on hoist or stands.
2. Remove wheel assembly.
3. Disconnect front brake flexible hose from brake tube at frame mounting bracket. Plug tube to prevent loss of fluid.
4. Remove bolts that attach caliper to steering knuckle.

NOTE: Should it become necessary to install a new flexible brake hose, scribe a mark on hose bracket on side where hose enters, and position of hose retaining clip underneath. When reassembling, be sure open end of retaining clip is facing out and away from caliper.

5. Slowly slide caliper up and away from brake disc, Fig. 35.

Disassembly

1. Referring to Fig. 36, remove shoe retainer clips and transfer tube from caliper.
2. Mount caliper in a vise with soft jaws and remove transfer tube.
3. Remove shoe and lining units.
4. Remove bridge bolts and separate caliper halves.
5. Peel dust boot out and away from caliper housing retainer and out of piston groove, Fig. 37. Remove remaining boots in same manner.
6. Using Tool C-3999, remove each piston, Fig. 38.

CAUTION: Care must be used so as not to scratch, burr or otherwise damage piston on outside diameter. To do so effects sealing qualities of piston. Draw piston straight out of its bore. If a piston be-

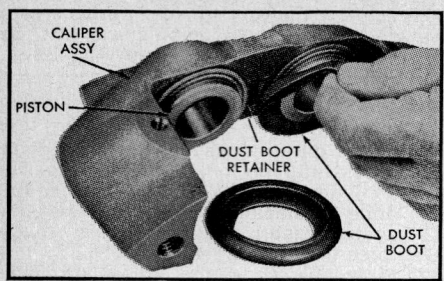

Fig. 37   Removing dust boot from piston and caliper

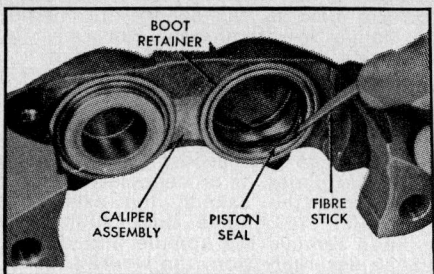

Fig. 39   Removing piston seals from caliper

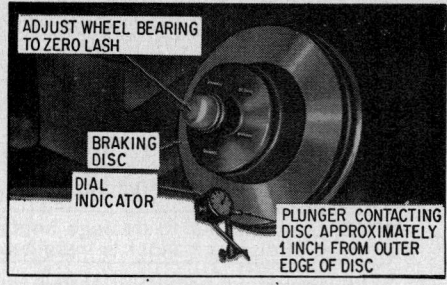

Fig. 41   Checking brake disc runout

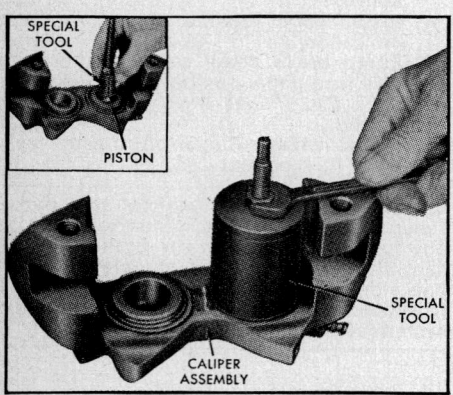

Fig. 38   Removing piston from caliper

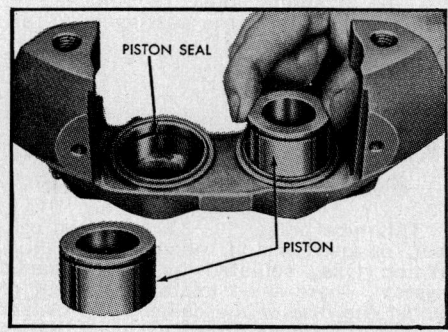

Fig. 40   Installing piston in caliper

Fig. 42   Single piston disc brake (typical)

comes cocked, removal is more difficult and piston or bore may be damaged.

7. Using a small pointed wooden or plastic tool, remove piston seals from grooves in cylinder bore, Fig. 39. Discard old seals.

Cleaning & Inspection

Refer to "BUDD OPPOSED PISTONS" section for cleaning and inspection.

Assembling Caliper

1. Clamp inner caliper half in a vise (with protector jaws) by mounting lugs.
2. If it was necessary to install a new dust boot retainer ring, contact area on housing should be cleaned and Loctite Sealant Grade H (or equivalent) applied to retainer ring on surface where it seats in housing, then install retainer ring.
3. Dip new piston seals in brake fluid and install in caliper grooves. Seal should be positioned at one area in groove and gently worked around cylinder bore with a finger until properly seated. *Be sure seals are not twisted or rolled.*
4. Coat outside diameter of pistons with brake fluid and install them in cylinder bores, Fig. 40, with open end of piston and boot retaining groove facing out of cylinder.

5. Position piston squarely in bore and apply slow steady pressure. *If piston will not position itself, remove it and check seal for proper position in groove.*
6. Install new dust boot over caliper retaining ring and in piston groove. Install remaining boots in same manner.
7. Install caliper half on one clamped in vise. Assemble with bridge bolts and torque to 70-80 ft-lbs.

CAUTION: Under no circumstances should

the bridge bolts be substituted or replaced by inferior bolts as this could cause caliper failure, resulting in an accident.

8. Install and tighten transfer tube.
9. Install bleeder screw loosely.

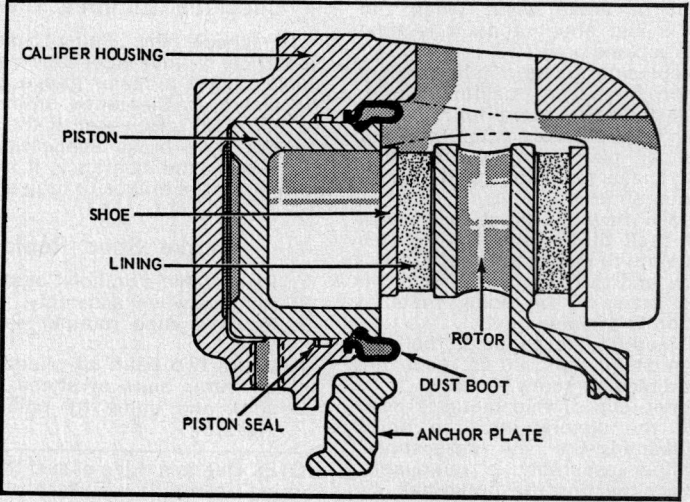

Fig. 43   Single piston disc brake caliper (typical)

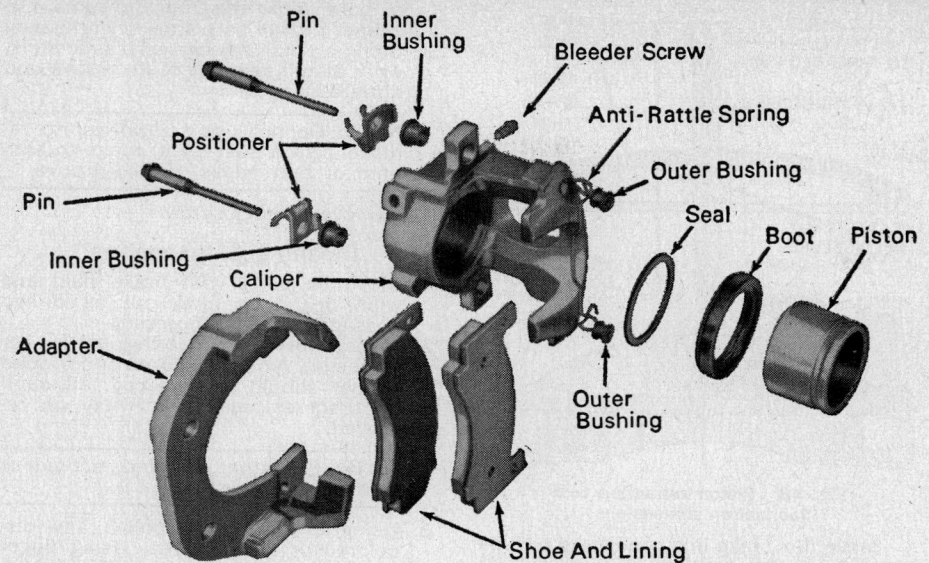

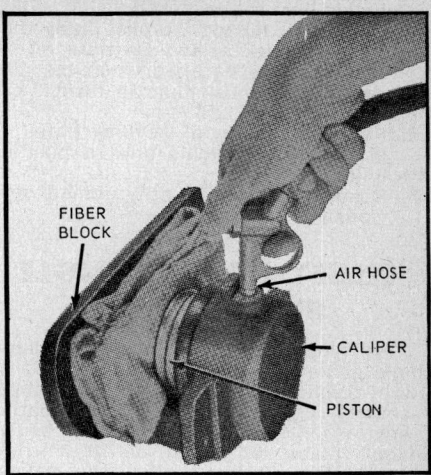

Fig. 45 Removing piston with air pressure

Fig. 44 Single piston disc brake caliper disassembled. (typical of American Motors and Chrysler Corp.)

Installation

1. Before installing caliper, check brake disc for runout. Mount a dial indicator as shown in Fig. 41 and check lateral runout, which should not exceed .0025". If runout is excessive, install a new disc. *Be sure wheel bearings are adjusted to zero end play during this check. Readjust wheel bearings after checking runout.*

Check thickness variation of disc by measuring disc with a micrometer at twelve points at a radius of about 1 inch from edge of disc. If thickness measurements vary more than .0005 inch, the disc should be replaced.

2. Install caliper over disc. Install mounting bolts and torque as indicated:
   Dodge & Plymouth:
   1969-72 . . . . . 50-80 ft.-lbs.
   Lincoln Continental:
   1969 . . . . . . 100-140 ft.-lbs.

NOTE: A check should be made to be sure that brake disc runs squarely and centrally within caliper opening. There should be .090" to .120" clearance between outside diameter of disc and caliper. There should also be a minimum of .050" from either disc face to machined groove in outboard caliper.

3. Install shoe and lining units.
4. Install shoe retainer springs in place on caliper.
5. Open bleeder screw, then connect

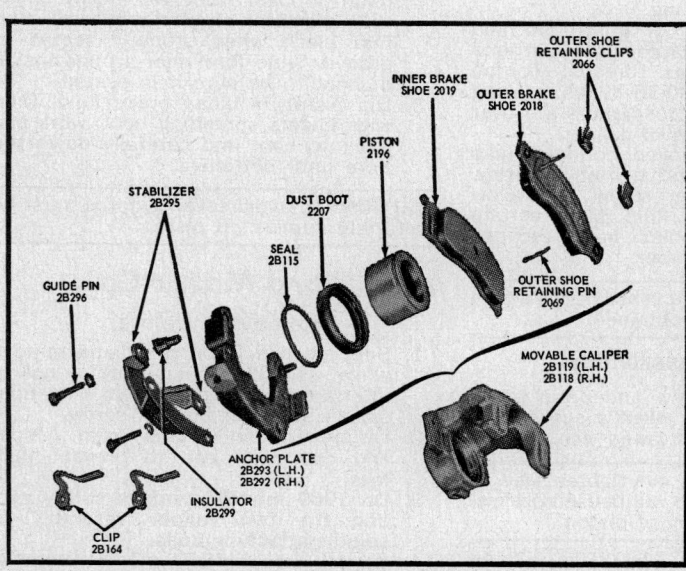

Fig. 46 Single piston disc brake caliper disassembled. (typical of Ford Motor Co.)

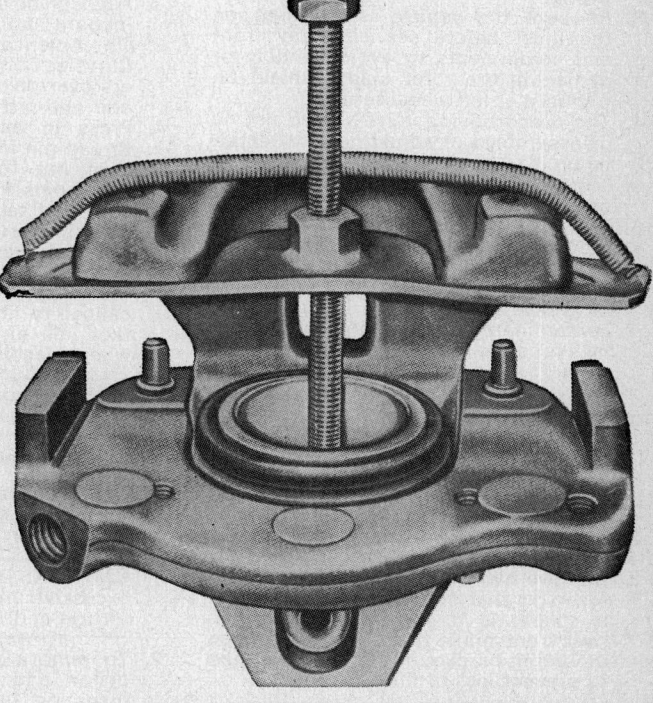

Fig. 47 Installing piston retracting tool

brake line to caliper housing. Allow caliper to fill with brake fluid, then close bleeder screw. Be sure all air bubbles have escaped when bleeding caliper. Replenish fluid in master cylinder.

6. Pump brake pedal several times to actuate piston seals and to position linings.

7. Road test vehicle as outlined previously.

KELSEY-HAYES SINGLE PISTON TYPE

This type brake is a floating caliper, single piston, ventilated unit, actuated by the hydraulic system, Fig. 42. The caliper assembly, Fig. 43, is made up of a floating caliper assembly and an anchor plate. The anchor plate is bolted to the wheel spindle arm by two bolts. The caliper is attached to the anchor plate through two spring steel stabilizers. The caliper slides on two guide pins which also attach to the stabilizers. A single piston is used. The cylinder bore contains a piston with a molded rubber dust boot to seal the cylinder bore from contamination and also to return the piston to the released position when hydraulic pressure is released. Also a rubber piston seal is used to provide sealing between cylinder and piston.

Service Precautions

In addition to the precautions described at the beginning of this chapter, the following must be observed.

1. If the piston is removed for any reason the piston seal must be replaced.
2. During removal and installation of a wheel assembly, use care not to interfere with and damage the caliper splash shield or the bleeder screw fitting.
3. Be sure the vehicle is centered on the hoist before servicing any front end components to avoid bending or damaging the rotor splash shield on full right or left wheel turns.
4. The proportioning valve should not be disassembled or adjustments attempted on it.
5. The wheel and tire must be removed separately from the brake rotor.
6. The caliper assembly must be removed from the spindle prior to removal of shoe and lining assembly.
7. Do not attempt to clean or restore oil or grease soaked brake linings. When contaminated linings are found, linings must be replaced in complete axle sets.

American Motors & Chrysler Corp.

Removing Lining & Caliper

1. Support vehicle on hoist and remove wheel assembly.
2. Remove two thirds of brake fluid from reservoir that serves disc brakes.
3. If caliper is to be removed, disconnect front brake hose from tube from mounting bracket and plug brake tube to prevent loss of fluid.

NOTE: If pistons are to be removed,

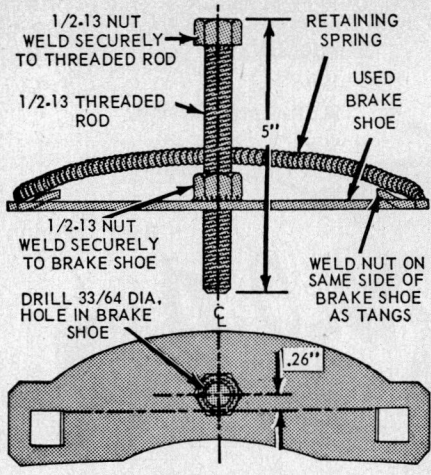

Fig. 48 Piston retracting tool fabrication dimensions

leave flex brake line connected to tube at mounting bracket.

4. Remove caliper guide pins, Fig. 44. On American Motors and 1969-72 Chrysler Corp. models, remove positioners and anti-rattle clips.
5. Slide outboard and inboard shoe assembly out of caliper and adaptor.
6. Remove inner and outer bushings from caliper.

Installing Lining & Caliper

1. Install new inner and outer bushings Fig. 44, then slide shoe and lining assembly into place in caliper and adaptor making certain that metal portion of shoe is fully in recess of caliper and adaptor.
2. Holding inboard shoe assembly in place, carefully slide caliper down into position in adaptor and over rotor. Align guide pin holes of adaptor and inboard and outboard shoes.
3. On American Motors and 1969-72 Chrysler Corp. models, install positioners over guide pins with open ends up and anti-rattle spring.
4. Press in on end of guide pin and thread pin into adaptor using extreme care not to cross threads. Torque guide pins from 30-35 ft. lbs. making sure that tabs of positioners are over machined surfaces of caliper.
5. If caliper was removed, connect brake hose to caliper and tighten securely, then open bleeder screw and allow caliper to fill with fluid. Make certain that all air bubbles have escaped when bleeding caliper.

CAUTION: Do not move vehicle until a firm brake pedal has been obtained.

Caliper Disassembly

1. Open bleeder screw and drain brake fluid from caliper then place caliper assembly in a soft jawed vice.

CAUTION: Do not overtighten vise as excessive pressure will cause bore distortion and binding of piston.

2. To remove piston place a cloth over piston and apply compressed air to fluid port in caliper, Fig. 45. Use extreme care to avoid damage to piston

or bore. Allow dust boot to remain in caliper groove as piston is withdrawn.

3. Using a small wooden or plastic stick, work piston seal out of its groove and discard seal.

NOTE: Do not use screwdriver to remove piston seal as it could scratch bore or burr edges of seal groove.

4. Remove bleeder screw.

Cleaning & Inspection

1. Clean all parts with brake fluid and wipe dry, then blow out all drilled passages using compressor.
2. Inspect bore for scoring, pitting or corrosion. A deeply scored or corroded caliper should be replaced, although light scores and stains may be removed.

NOTE: If piston is pitted, scored or worn, replace piston.

3. Using crocus cloth, polish any discolored or stained area. Using finger pressure rotate crocus cloth in cylinder bore. Do not slide cloth in and out of bore under pressure or use any other form of abrasive or abrasive cloth. Black stains on bore wall are caused by piston seals and will do no harm.
4. Bores that have deep scratches or scores, should be honed providing that the diameter of the bore is not increased more than .002 inch.
5. Using a feeler gauge, check clearance of piston in bore. Clearance should be .002-.006 inch. If clearance exceeds this specification, replace caliper assembly.

Caliper Assembly

1. Dip new piston seal in clean brake fluid and install in bore groove. Seal should be positioned and gently worked around groove until properly seated.
2. Dip new dust boot in clean brake fluid and install in caliper by working into outer groove. Boot will seem larger than diameter of groove but will snap into place when properly seated in groove. Slide forefinger around inside of boot to be sure it is seated.
3. Dip piston in clean brake fluid, then with fingers spreading boot, work piston into boot and carefully down the bore until bottomed.

CAUTION: To avoid cocking, force must be uniformly applied on piston.

Ford Motor Co.

Removing Caliper

1. Support vehicle on hoist and remove wheel assembly being careful not to interfere with or damage caliper splash shield or bleeder screw.
2. Disconnect brake line from caliper and cap open end to prevent fluid loss.
3. On 1969 models, remove safety wire and the two caliper assembly to spindle attaching bolts.
4. On all except 1969 models, remove caliper locating pins and lower stabilizer attaching bolts and discard stabilizers.

5. Lift caliper assembly from rotor.

NOTE: If both caliper assemblies are removed, identify them as left and right as they are not interchangeable.

Installing Caliper

1. Install caliper assembly over rotor.
2. On 1969 models;
   a. Align mounting bolt holes with those in spindle.

NOTE: It may be necessary to push caliper piston into bore to obtain clearance between lining and rotor.

   b. Install caliper to spindle bolts and first torque upper bolt to 110-140 ft. lbs then torque lower bolt to 90-120 ft. lbs. for full size and 55-75 ft. lbs for intermediate models. Install safety wire and push ends against spindle.
3. On 1970-73 models;
   a. Place outer brake shoe against rotor surface during caliper installation, in anchor plate to prevent pinching piston boot between inner brake shoe and piston.
   b. Position new stablizer and install and torque locating pins to 25-35 ft. lbs.

NOTE: Make certain that locating pins are free of oil, grease or dirt.

   c. Install stabilizer to anchor plate screws and torque to 8-11 ft. lbs.
4. Using a new copper gasket on each side of hose fitting, install hose on caliper and torque attaching bolt to 17-25 ft. lbs.
5. Bleed brake system then centralize pressure differential valve as described:
   a. On 1969 models, turn ignition switch to "ON" or "ACC" positions and loosen brake line fitting at outlet port of differential valve on opposite side of brake system that was repaired or bled last, then depress brake pedal until brake warning light goes out and tighten brake line fitting.
   b. On 1970-73 models, turn ignition switch to "ON" or "ACC" and depress brake pedal until brake warning light goes out.
6. Apply brake pedal several times to seat brake linings.

CAUTION: Do not move vehicle until a firm brake pedal has been obtained.

Removing Lining

1969 Models

1. Support vehicle on hoist and remove wheel assembly.
2. Remove caliper assembly as described previously. To aid in caliper removal, apply a steady inward pressure against inner shoe and lining assembly. Maintain pressure for at least a minute until piston is pushed into its bore.
3. Slide the outer two outer shoe retaining clips off retaining pins, Fig.

46, then remove retaining pins and remove shoe from stationary caliper.
4. Slide inner brake shoe outward until it is free of hold down springs, then remove brake shoe.
5. Remove caliper locating pins and stabilizer attaching bolts, then remove and discard stabilizers.
6. Remove locating pin insulators from anchor plate.

1970-72 Full Size Models

1. Remove half of brake fluid capacity from master cylinder.
2. Support vehicle on hoist and remove wheel assembly.
3. Remove inner shoe hold down clips, then place a small screwdriver under outer shoe retaining clip tang and lift away from pin groove and slide clip from shoe retaining pin. Remove outer shoe retaining clip and remove outer shoe.
4. Remove caliper locating pins and upper stabilizer to anchor plate bolt, then remove upper stabilizer to avoid interference with brake hose.
5. Lift caliper assembly from anchor plate and remove outer shoe and retaining pins from caliper assembly.
6. Support caliper from suspension with a wire and remove caliper locating pin insulators.
7. Remove inner shoe and lining assembly and inspect rotor.

1970-73 Intermediate

1. Support vehicle and remove wheel assembly being careful to avoid damage or interference with caliper splash shield or bleeder screw.
2. Remove caliper as described previously.
3. Remove inner brake shoe hold down clips and locating pin insulators from anchor plate and remove inboard shoe and lining assembly.
4. To remove outer brake shoe, place a small screwdriver under outer brake shoe retaining clip tang and lift away from pin groove and slide clip from brake shoe retaining pin. Remove outer brake shoe retaining clip and remove outer brake shoe.

Installing Lining

NOTE: When new shoe and lining assemblies are being installed to replace worn linings it will be necessary to push the piston all the way into the caliper bore. This will displace fluid from the caliper into the master cylinder reservoir. Check the primary (front) brake system reservoir level and remove fluid to approximately half full before replacing brake shoes. This will prevent overflow. Do not reuse the removal fluid.

1969 Models

1. Install new caliper locating pin insulators in anchor plate.
2. Position caliper in anchor plate, then install new stabilizers and loosely install caliper locating pins. Locating pins should be free of oil, grease or dirt.

NOTE: If caliper locating pins are rusted or corroded, they should be replaced.

3. Position outer brake shoe on caliper and install two retaining pins and clips.
4. Install inner brake shoe so that ears of shoe are on top of anchor plate bosses and under shoe hold down springs.
5. Position shoe and lining assemblies so that caliper can be placed over rotor. Rotate a hammer handle between linings to provide proper clearance.
6. Install caliper over rotor on spindle. Install the two caliper attaching bolts and first torque the upper bolt to 110-140 ft. lbs. then torque the lower bolt to 90-120 ft. lbs. for full size and 55-75 ft. lbs for intermediate models. Install safety wire, twist ends at least five turns and push wire ends against spindle.
7. With moderate pressure applied to brake pedal, torque stabilizer attaching screws to 8-11 ft. lbs. and locating pins to 25-35 ft. lbs.

1970-72 Full Size & 1970-73
Intermediate Models

1. Install inner brake shoe in anchor plate and new caliper locating pin insulators.
2. Install inner brake shoe hold down clips and torque retaining screws to 6-10 ft. lbs.
3. Install piston retracting tool in caliper with brake shoe lances positioned in slots in caliper outer legs and retract piston, Fig. 47. The piston retracting tool can be fabricated from a discarded outer brake shoe and threaded rod, Fig. 48. When using piston retracting tool, turn threaded rod one half turn at a time and pause to permit piston to move in seal. As piston nears bottom of travel, reduce time interval to insure bottoming of piston.
4. Install new outer brake shoe and lining assembly on caliper and install retaining pins and clips.
5. Install caliper as described previously.

Caliper Disassembly

1. Remove caliper assembly from vehicle.
2. Remove caliper locating pins from caliper assembly and remove anchor plate from caliper.
3. Slide the two outer shoe retaining clips off retaining pins, then remove retaining pins and outer brake shoe from caliper.
4. Slide inner brake shoe outward until it is free of hold down springs, then remove brake shoe.
5. To remove piston, apply air pressure to fluid port, Fig. 45. Place a cloth over piston before applying pressure to prevent damage to piston. If piston is seized and cannot be removed, tap lightly around piston while applying pressure.

NOTE: If piston is stuck, care should be taken when applying air as piston could develop considerable force.

6. Remove dust boot and piston seal from caliper.

Cleaning & Inspection

Clean all metal parts with alcohol, then

using compressed air, clean out and dry all grooves and passages. Make certain that caliper bore and component parts are completely free of any foreign material.

Check cylinder bore and piston for damage or excessive wear. Replace piston if pitted, scored, or the chrome plating is worn off.

Caliper Assembly

1. Apply clean brake fluid to caliper piston seal and install it in cylinder bore. Be sure seal does not become twisted and that it is fully seated in groove.
2. Install a new dust boot by setting flange squarely in outer groove of caliper bore.
3. Coat piston with clean brake fluid and install it in cylinder bore. Spread dust boot over piston as it is installed, then seat dust boot in piston groove.
4. Position inner brake shoe so that ears of the shoe rest on top of anchor plate bosses and beneath hold down springs.
5. Install new caliper locating pin insulators in anchor plate and position caliper on anchor plate.
6. Apply alcohol to caliper locating pins and install them loosely in anchor plate.

NOTE: Make certain that guide pins are free of oil, grease or dirt.

---

7. Install caliper as previously outlined.

DELCO-MORAINE SINGLE PISTON

This single piston sliding caliper assembly, Fig. 49, incorporates a one piece housing with the inboard side of the housing bored for the piston. A seal within the housing bore provides a hydraulic seal between the piston and housing wall.

A spring steel scraper (wear sensor) is incorporated on each inboard shoe. When the shoe lining has worn to within .030 inch of the shoe, the sensor scrapes the rotor and emits an audible high frequency sound indicating that the linings should be replaced.

The caliper assembly used on all models except Vega, Fig. 49, slides on its mounting bolts whereas the caliper on Vega models, the caliper assembly slides on mounting sleeves which are secured by two mounting pins. Upon brake application, fluid pressure against the piston forces the inboard shoe and lining assembly against the inboard side of the disc. This action causes the caliper assembly to slide until the outboard lining comes into contact with the disc. As pressure builds

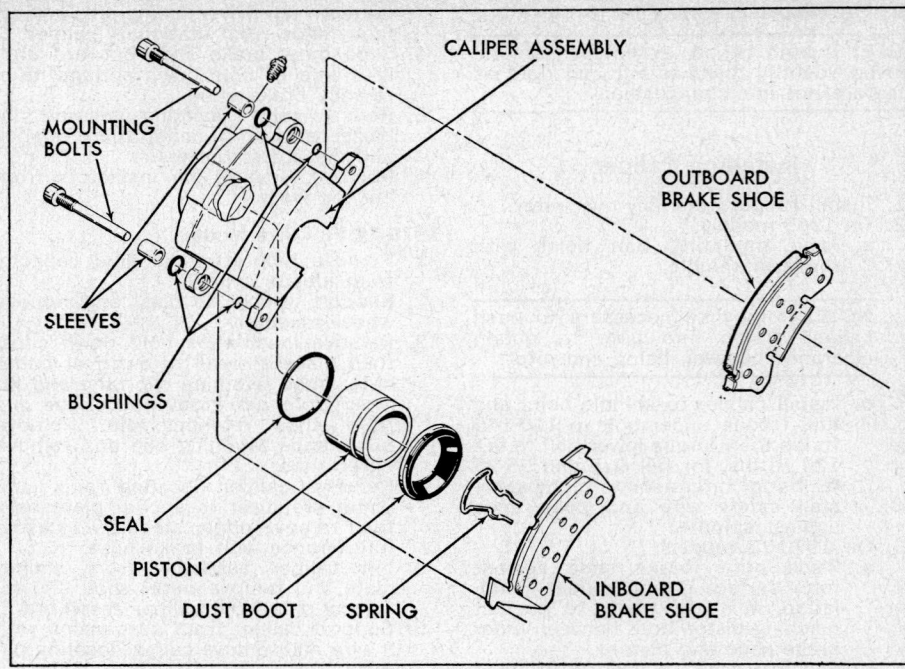

Fig. 49   Single piston caliper. Exploded

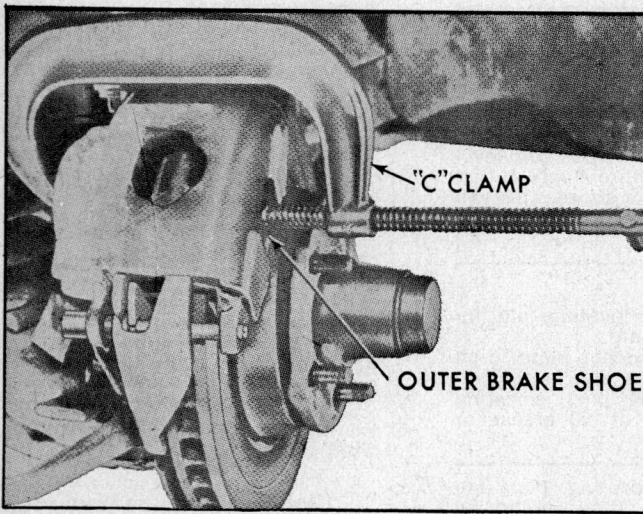

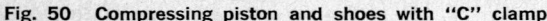

Fig. 50   Compressing piston and shoes with "C" clamp

Fig. 51   Installing support spring

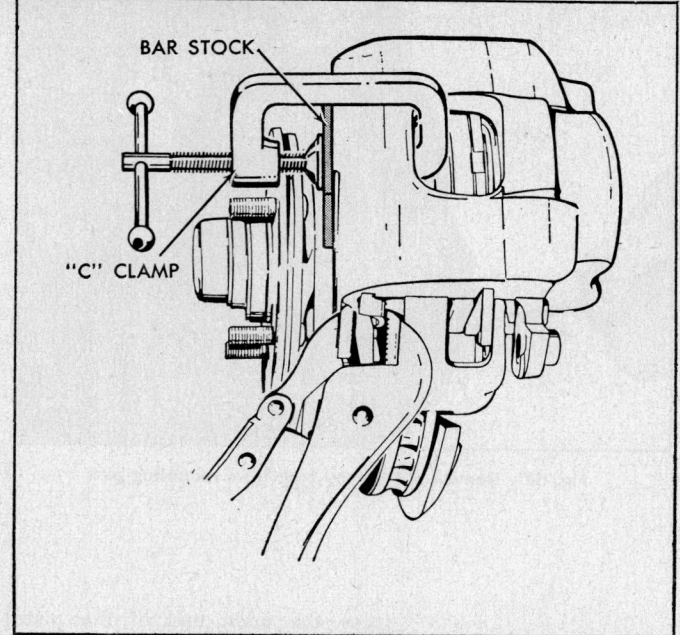

Fig. 52   Fitting shoe to caliper

Fig. 53   Clinching loop eared brake shoe

up, the linings are pressed against the disc with increased force.

All Except Vega

Caliper Removal

1. Siphon enough brake fluid out of the master cylinder to bring fluid level to $1/3$ full to avoid fluid overflow when the caliper piston is pushed back into its bore.

2. Raise vehicle and remove front wheels.
3. Using a "C" clamp, as illustrated in Fig. 50, push piston back into its bore.
4. Remove two mounting bolts and lift caliper away from disc.

Brake Shoe Removal

1. Remove caliper assembly as outlined above.
2. Remove inboard shoe. Dislodge outboard shoe and position caliper on the front suspension so the brake hose

will not support the weight of the caliper.
3. Remove shoe support spring from piston.
4. Remove two sleeves from inboard ears of the caliper.
5. Remove four rubber bushings from the grooves in each of the caliper ears.

Brake Shoe Installation

1. Lubricate new sleeves, rubber bushings, bushing grooves and mounting bolt ends with Delco Silicone Lube or its equivalent.
2. Install new bushings and sleeves in caliper ears.

NOTE: Position the sleeve so that the

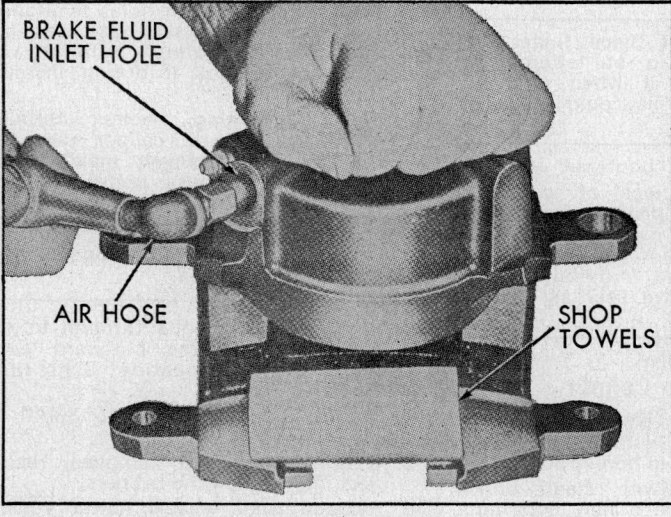

Fig. 54   Removing piston from caliper

Fig. 55   Installing boot to piston

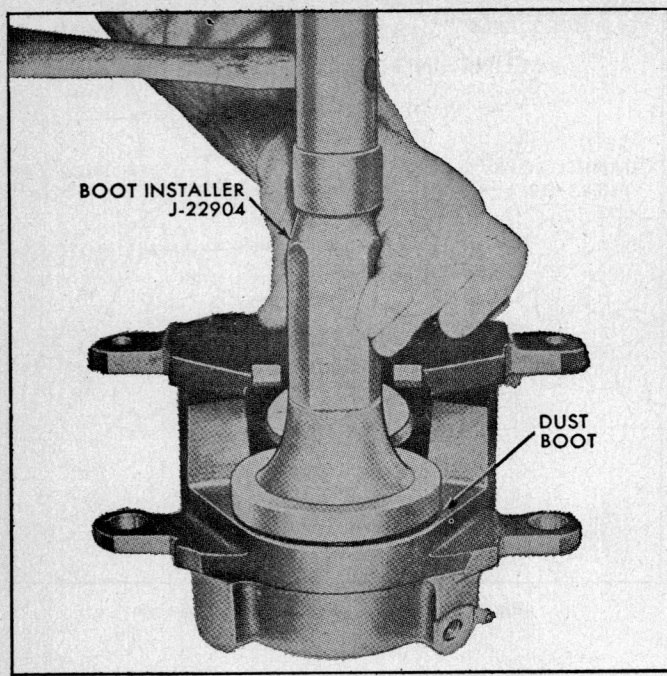

Fig. 56   Installing boot to caliper

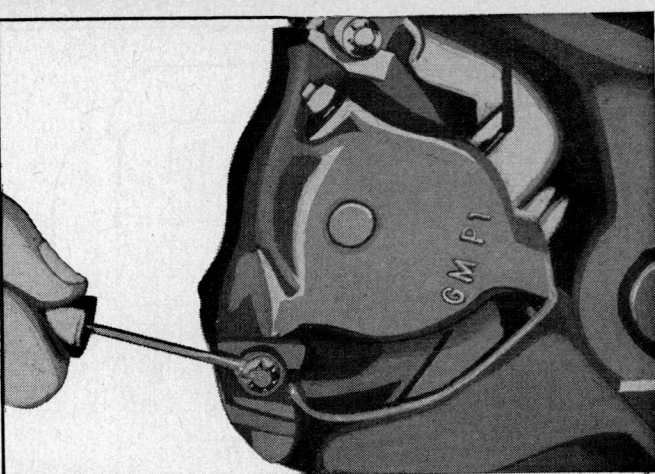

Fig. 57   Removing stamped nuts from mounting pins

end toward the shoe is flush with the machined surface of the ear.

3. Install shoe support spring in piston cavity, Fig. 51.

4. Position inboard shoe in caliper so spring ends centrally contact shoe edge. Initially, this will place the shoe on an angle. Push upper edge of shoe down until shoe is flat against caliper. When properly seated, spring ends will not extend past shoe more than .100".

5. Position outboard shoe in caliper with shoe ears over caliper ears and tab at bottom of shoe engaged in caliper cutout.

6. With shoes installed, lift caliper and rest bottom edge of outboard lining on outer edge of brake disc to be sure there is no clearance between outboard shoe tab and caliper abutment.

7. Using a ¼" x 1" x 2½" metal bar to bridge caliper cutout, clamp outboard shoe to caliper with a "C" clamp. Bend both ears of outboard shoe over caliper until clearance between shoe ear and caliper (measured at both the edge and side of the caliper) is .005" or less, Fig. 52.

8. Remove "C" clamp then install caliper and torque mounting bolts to 30-40 ft. lbs.

9. On 1973-74 vehicles, clinch upper ears of outboard shoe by positioning pliers with one jaw on top of upper ear and one jaw in notch on bottom shoe opposite ear, Fig. 53. Ears are to be flat against caliper housing with no radial clearance. If clearance exists, repeat clinching procedure.

Disassembling Caliper

1. Remove caliper as outlined above.
2. Disconnect hose from steel line, remove U shaped retainer and withdraw hose from frame support bracket.
3. After cleaning outside of caliper, remove brake hose and discard copper gasket.
4. Drain brake fluid from caliper.
5. Pad caliper interior with clean shop towels and use compressed air to remove piston, Fig. 54.

NOTE: Use just enough air pressure to ease piston out of bore. Do not blow piston out of bore.

CAUTION: Do not place fingers in front of piston in an attempt to catch or protect it when applying compressed air. This could result in serious injury.

6. Carefully pry dust boot out of bore.
7. Using a small piece of wood or plastic, remove piston seal from bore.

NOTE: Do not use a metal tool of any kind to remove seal as it may damage bore.

8. Remove bleeder valve.

Assembling Caliper

1. Lubricate caliper piston bore and new piston seal with clean brake fluid. Position seal in bore groove.
2. Lubricate piston with clean brake fluid and assemble a new boot into the groove in the piston so the fold

faces the open end of the piston, Fig. 55.

3. Using care not to unseat the seal, insert piston into bore and force the piston to the bottom of the bore.
4. Position dust boot in caliper counterbore and install, Fig. 56.

NOTE: Check the boot installation to be sure the retaining ring moulded into the boot is not bent and that the boot is installed below the caliper face and evenly all around. If the boot is not fully installed, dirt and moisture may enter the bore and cause corrosion.

5. Install the brake hose in the caliper using a new copper gasket.
6. Install shoes and re-install caliper assembly.

Caliper Installation

1. Position caliper over disc, lining up holes in caliper with holes in mounting bracket. If brake hose was not disconnected during removal, be sure not to kink it during installation.
2. Start mounting bolts through sleeves in inboard caliper ears and the mounting bracket, making sure ends of bolts pass under ears on inboard shoe.

NOTE: Right and left calipers must not be interchanged.

3. Push mounting bolts through to engage holes in the outboard ears. Then thread mounting bolts into bracket.
4. Torque mounting bolts to 30-40 ft. lbs.
5. If brake hose was removed, reconnect it and bleed the calipers.
6. Replace front wheels, lower vehicle and add brake fluid to master

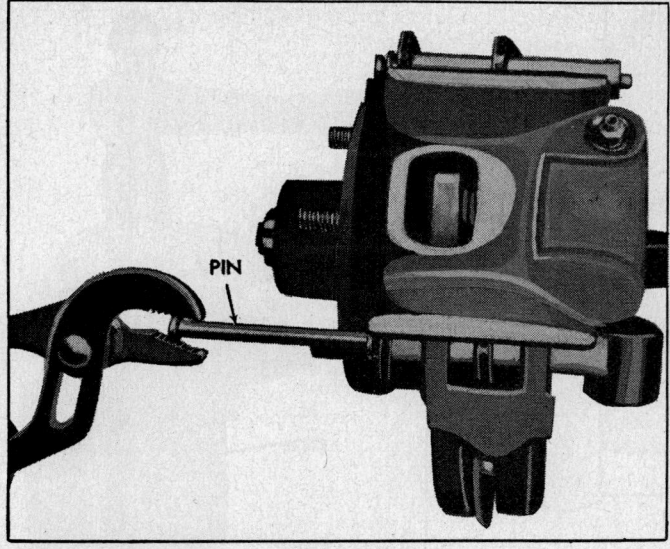

Fig. 58   Removing mounting pins

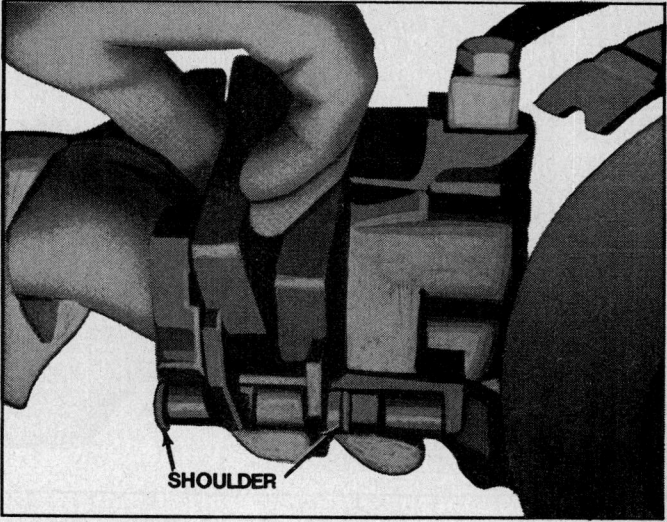

Fig. 59   Mounting sleeves and brake shoe installation

cylinder to bring level to ¼″ from top.

NOTE: Before moving vehicle, pump brake pedal several times to be sure it is firm. Do not move vehicle until a firm pedal is obtained.

VEGA

Lining Removal

1. Support vehicle on hoist and remove wheel assembly.
2. Remove the two mounting pin stamped nuts, Fig. 57, and slide out the mounting pins, Fig. 58.
3. Lift caliper off disc and support caliper

from suspension using wire.
4. Slide inboard and outboard shoes past mounting sleeve openings and remove mounting sleeves and bushing assemblies.
5. If caliper is to be removed, disconnect brake line.

Lining Installation

1. Install new sleeves with bushings on caliper grooves, Fig. 59.

NOTE: The "shouldered end" of sleeve must be installed toward outside.

2. Install inner shoe on caliper and slide shoe ears over sleeve, Fig. 59. Install the outer shoe in the same manner.

CAUTION: If pads are being re-used, they must be installed in same loca-

tion as when removed.

3. Mount caliper on rotor. If brake line was disconnected, reconnect and torque bolt to 22 ft. lbs.

NOTE: To avoid overflow, it may be necessary to remove half of brake fluid capacity from master cylinder.

4. Install mounting pins from outside in and install stamped nuts, Fig. 60. Nuts should be pressed on as far as possible using a suitable size socket that just seats on outer edge of nut.
5. Install wheel assembly and lower vehicle.
6. Add brake fluid to within ¼ inch from top of master cylinder and test brake operation to insure a firm brake pedal before moving vehicle.

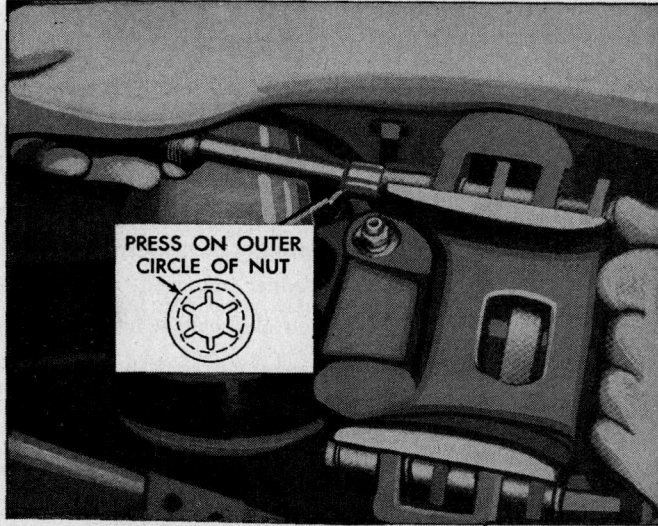

PRESS ON OUTER CIRCLE OF NUT

Fig. 60   Installing stamped nuts on mounting pins

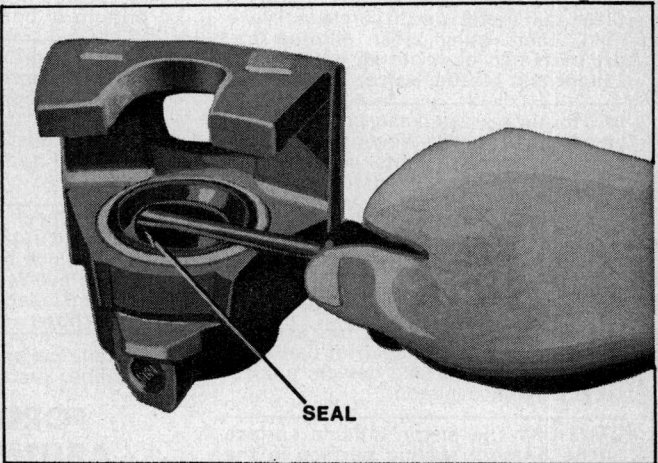

SEAL

Fig. 61   Dust boot seal removal

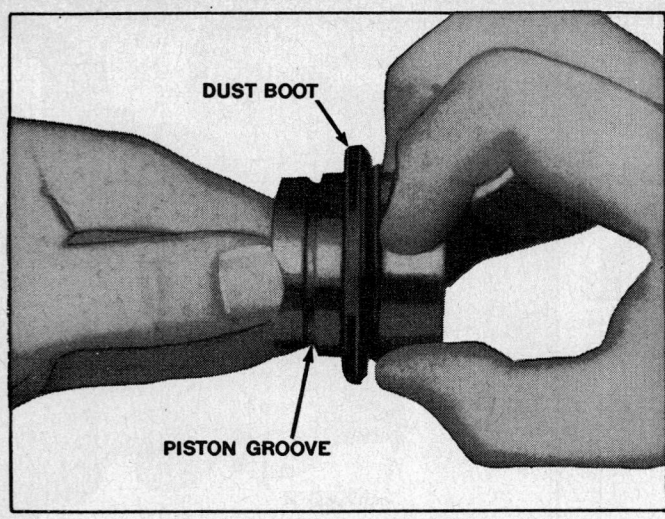

Fig. 62 Installing piston on boot

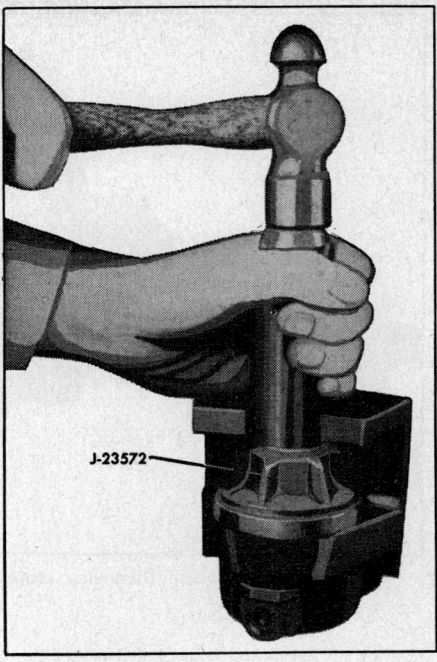

Fig. 63 Seating dust boot in caliper

Caliper Disassembly

1. Remove caliper as described under "Lining Removal".
2. Drain brake fluid from caliper and clean exterior of caliper using clean brake fluid.
3. Using clean towels, pad interior of caliper and remove piston by applying just enough compressed air to fluid inlet port to ease piston out of bore.

CAUTION: Do not place fingers in front of piston in an attempt to catch or protect it when applying compressed air.

4. Carefully using a screwdriver so as not to scratch piston bore, pry dust boot out of piston bore, Fig. 61.
5. Using a piece of wood or plastic so as not to damage bore, remove piston seal from its groove in caliper bore.
6. Remove bleeder screw.

Cleaning & Inspection

1. Clean all metal parts in clean brake fluid, then using clean filtered air, dry parts and blow out all passages in caliper and bleeder valve.

NOTE: Always use clean brake fluid to clean caliper parts. Never use mineral base cleaning solvents as they can cause rubber parts to deteriorate and become soft and swollen, also the use of lubricated compressed air will leave a film of oil on metal parts that may damage rubber parts when they come in after reassembly.

2. Inspect piston surface for scoring, nicks, corrosion and worn or damaged plating. If any surface defects are detected, replace piston.

CAUTION: The piston outside surface is the primary sealing surface in the caliper. It is manufactured and plated to close tolerances, therefore refinishing by any means or the use of any abrasive is not recommended.

3. Check caliper bore for same defects as piston. The piston bore is not plated and stains or minor corrosion may be polished with crocus cloth.

CAUTION: Do not use emery cloth or any other form of abrasive and thoroughly clean caliper after use of crocus cloth. If caliper cannot be cleaned up in this manner, replace caliper.

Caliper Assembly

NOTE: The dust boot and piston seal are to be replaced each time that the caliper is disassembled.

1. Lubricate piston bore and new piston seal with clean brake fluid, then position seal in caliper bore groove.
2. Lubricate piston with clean brake fluid and assemble a new boot into groove in piston, Fig. 62.
3. Install piston into bore using care not to unseat seal, then force piston to bottom of bore.

NOTE: Approximately 50-100 pounds of force are required to push piston to bottom of bore.

4. Position dust boot in caliper counterbore and seat boot using tool shown in Fig. 63.

NOTE: Check boot installation to make sure that retaining ring moulded into boot is not bent and that boot is installed evenly all around. If boot is not fully installed, dirt and moisture may enter bore.

5. Install caliper as described under "Caliper Installation".

FORD CENTER ABUTMENT TYPE

This is a single piston, sliding caliper type brake but instead of the torque being taken by the caliper assembly, it is transmitted directly to the U-shaped anchor plate. The caliper housing performs only the necessary clamping action against the disc, Fig. 64.

Caliper Removal

NOTE: Siphon a portion of the brake fluid from the larger master cylinder reservoir before servicing unit.

1. Remove wheel and tire and remove cotter pins from caliper support key.
2. Using a drift and a light hammer, remove caliper support key, being careful to avoid damaging key or machined surfaces, Fig. 65.
3. Rotate lower end of caliper housing toward the rear and upward and remove caliper from anchor plate. It is not necessary to disconnect hydraulic line for this operation.
4. Suspend caliper housing with wire or lay caliper on support strut. Do not let caliper hang by its own weight from hydraulic line.

Caliper Disassembly

1. With caliper removed as described previously, disconnect brake hose. Cap hose and plug caliper inlet to prevent fluid loss.
2. With caliper on work bench, remove inlet plug and drain fluid from housing.
3. Position caliper as in Fig. 66, and place shop cloths as shown.
4. Apply air pressure slowly to caliper inlet port to remove piston.

NOTE: If high pressure is applied quickly, piston may pop out and cause injury. A cocked or seized piston can be eased out by rapping sharply on piston end with a soft brass hammer.

5. Remove boot from piston and seal from caliper cylinder bore, Fig. 67.

Caliper Overhaul

1. Remove any rust or corrosion from machined surfaces of caliper housing.
2. Clean housing and piston with iso-propyl alcohol. Clean and dry out grooves and passages with compressed air. Make sure cylinder bore is free of all foreign material.
3. Check cylinder bore, seal groove and piston for wear or damage. Replace piston if pitted or worn.
4. Remove any rust or corrosion from machined surfaces of anchor plate still mounted on car and inspect plate for damage.
5. Inspect anti-rattle clips for damage. Clips should have four tabs, Fig. 67, and a looped type spring. Replace any damaged parts.

Brake Shoe and Lining, Replace

1. Remove caliper housing as outlined previously.
2. As shoe and lining assemblies are

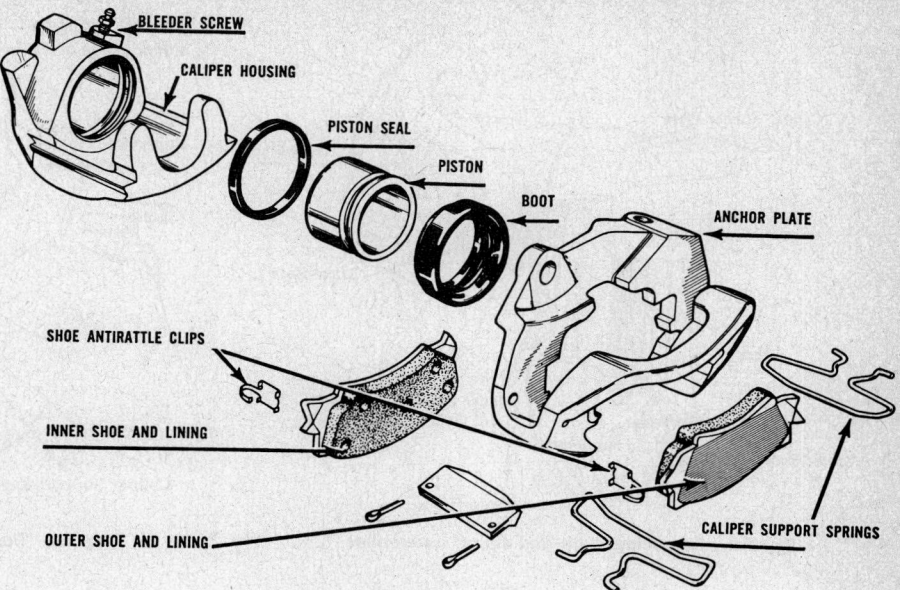

Fig. 64 Center abutment disc brake exploded

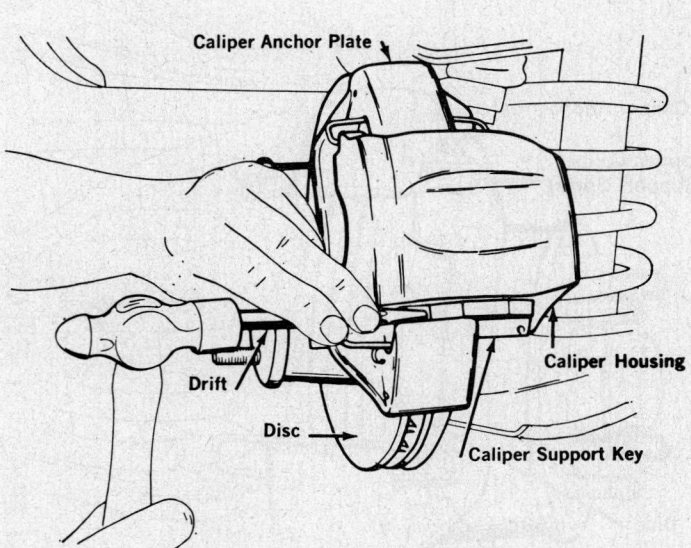

Fig. 65 Removing caliper support key

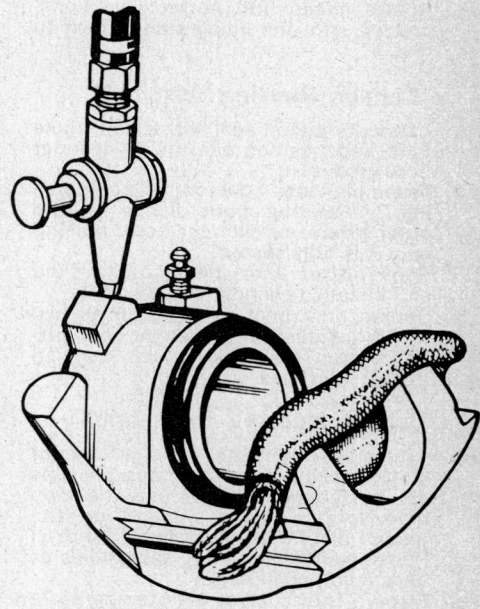

Fig. 66 Removing caliper piston with air pressure

Fig. 67 Caliper piston assembly

now exposed, tilt upper edge of shoes away from disc and then take out shoe and lining assemblies, Fig. 68. Shoes are identical and interchangeable.

3. Take three thickness & measurements of each shoe and lining with a micrometer.
4. If there is less than .030" of lining above rivet heads, replace shoes on both front wheels.
5. Position new shoe and lining assemblies in anchor plate by tilting the

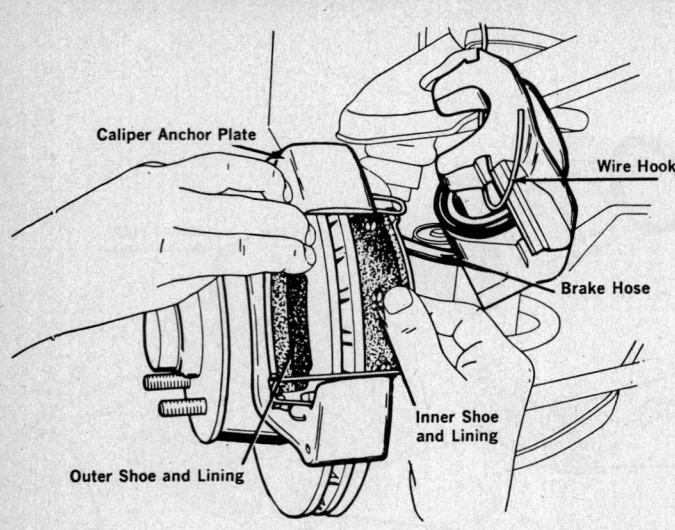

Fig. 68 Removing shoe and lining assemblies

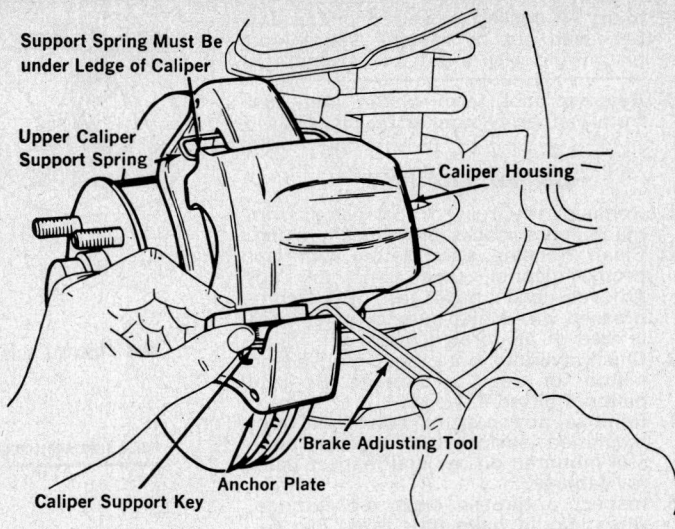

Fig. 69 Positioning caliper housing on anchor plate

shoe and sliding the bottom edge into place.

6. Rotate shoes into correct positions, making sure the lining side is next to disc.

Caliper Housing Assembly

1. Lubricate piston seal with clean brake fluid and position seal in its cylinder bore groove.
2. Assemble dust boot on caliper housing by seating boot flange in the outer groove of cylinder bore, making sure it is fully seated.
3. Coat piston with clean brake fluid and install in cylinder bore.
4. Spread dust boot over piston as piston is installed and then bottom piston in the bore. Seat dust boot in its piston groove.

Caliper Housing Installation

1. Assemble anti-rattle clips in anchor plate, making sure that tabs on clips are positioned properly and the loop type springs are positioned on the anchor plate side, away from the disc.
2. Position shoe and lining assemblies as described previously.
3. Place a thin coat of high-temperature lubricant on anchor plate and caliper surfaces that will be in contact after caliper is installed. Avoid getting lubricant on linings.
4. Position caliper in anchor plate, making sure that the top, trailing edge, of the caliper is properly positioned and the caliper support spring is under the projecting ledge of the caliper.
5. Insert a brake adjusting tool, or wide blade screwdriver, between the bottom, leading edge, of the caliper and adjacent anchor plate surface. Pry downward so that caliper housing is pressed upward and inward toward the spindle, Fig. 69.
6. Insert caliper support key between caliper housing and anchor plate. Be sure key is properly positioned and that caliper support springs are still

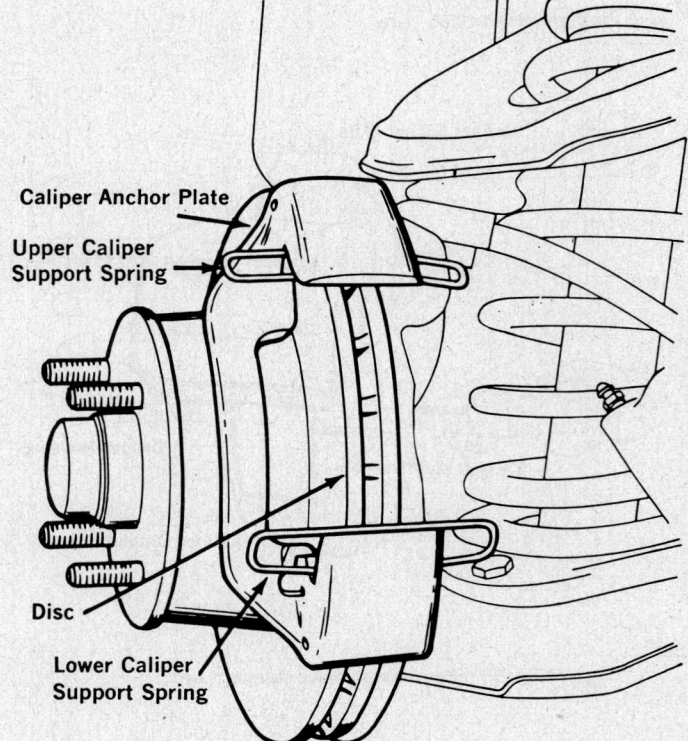

Fig. 70 Position of caliper support springs

in proper position, Fig. 70.

7. Center the support key so that cotter pin holes are on each side of the anchor plate and insert a new cotter pin in each hole.
8. Connect brake hose to caliper inlet port. Bleed system.

Anchor Plate

1. In the event the anchor plate was removed, position it on steering arm and install both mounting bolts finger tight. Tighten upper bolt first to 90-120 ft. lbs. and then tighten lower

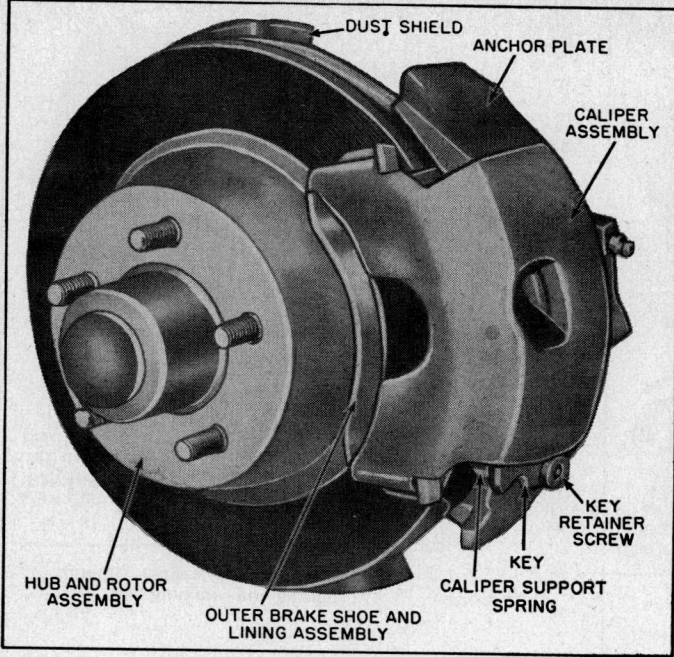

Fig. 71   Sliding caliper disc brake

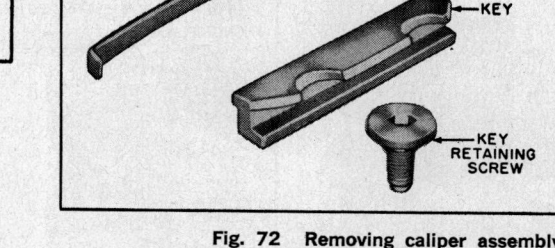

Fig. 72   Removing caliper assembly

bolt to 55-75 ft. lbs.
2. Replace caliper housing as described previously.

FORD SLIDING CALIPER

The caliper assembly is made up of a sliding caliper housing assembly and an anchor plate, Fig. 71.

The anchor plate is bolted to the wheel spindle arm. Two angular machined surfaces on the upper end of the caliper housing contact mating machined surfaces of the anchor plate. A steel, plated key and a caliper support spring is fitted between the angular machined surfaces of the lower end of the caliper and the machined surface of the anchor plate. The key is held in position with a retaining screw. The caliper is held in position against the mating surfaces of the anchor plate by means of the caliper support spring. A brake shoe anti-rattle spring clip is provided on the anchor plate at the lower end of the inner brake shoe and lining assembly. The inner and outer brake shoe assemblies are not interchangeable.

The sliding caliper contains a single cylinder and a piston with a molded dust boot to seal the cylinder bore from contamination. A square section rubber piston seal is positioned in a groove in cylinder bore to provide sealing between cylinder and piston.

Caliper Removal

1. Raise car and support with safety stands. Block both rear wheels if a jack is used.
2. Remove wheel and tire assembly from hub.
3. Disconnect brake hose from caliper.
4. Remove retaining screw from caliper retaining key, Fig. 71.
5. Slide caliper retaining key and support spring either inward or outward from anchor plate. Use hammer and drift, if necessary, to remove the key and caliper support spring. Use care to avoid damaging the key.
6. Lift caliper assembly away from anchor plate by pushing caliper down against anchor plate and rotate upper end upward out of anchor plate, Fig. 72.
7. Remove inner shoe and lining from anchor plate. The brake shoe anti-rattle clip (inner shoe only) may become displaced at this time and if so, reposition it on anchor plate, Fig. 73. Tap lightly on outer shoe and lining to free it from caliper.
8. Clean caliper, anchor plate and rotor

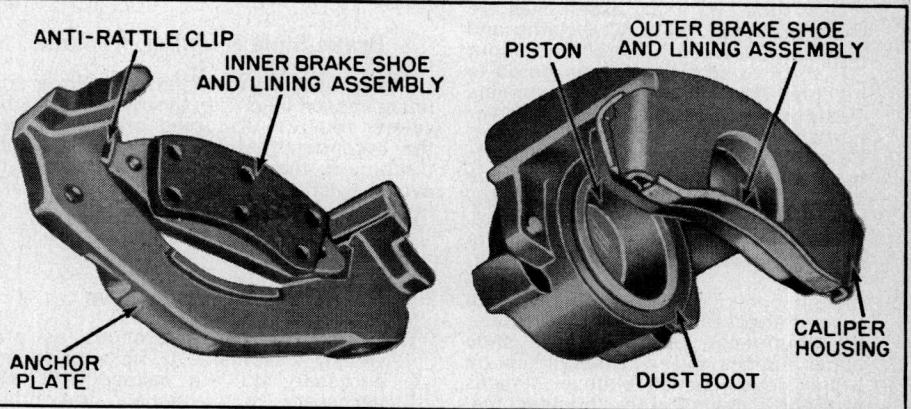

Fig. 73   Caliper and outer shoe removed from anchor plate

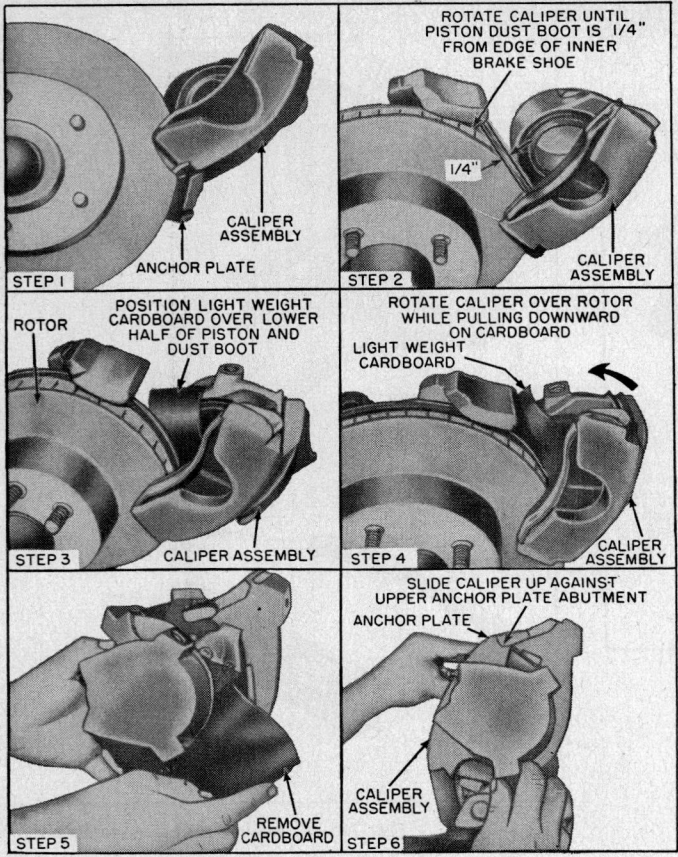

Fig. 74 Installing caliper assembly

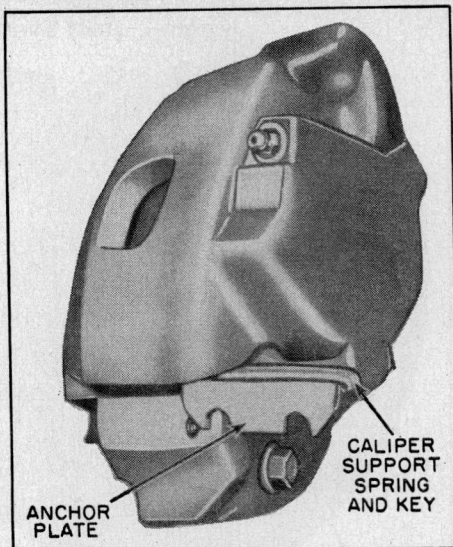

Fig. 75 Installing caliper support spring and retaining key

assemblies and inspect them for signs of fluid leakage, wear or damage. If either lining is worn to within 1/32" of any rivet head, both shoe and lining assemblies must be replaced. Also, if necessary to replace shoes and lining on one wheel, they must be replaced on both wheels to maintain equal brake action.

Caliper Installation

1. If new shoe and lining assemblies are to be installed, use a 4" C-clamp and a block of wood 1¾" x 1" and about ¾" thick to seat the caliper piston in its bore. This must be done to provide clearance for the caliper to fit over new shoes when installed.
2. Be sure brake shoe anti-rattle clip is in place on lower inner brake shoe support on anchor plate with pigtail of clip toward inside of anchor plate. Position inner shoe and lining on anchor plate with lining toward rotor, Fig. 73.
3. Install outer shoe and lining with lower flange ends against the caliper leg abutments and the brake shoe upper flanges over the shoulders on caliper legs. The shoe upper flanges fit tightly against the shoulder machined surfaces. If the same brake shoes and linings are to be used, be

sure they are installed in their original positions.
4. Remove C-clamp if used, from the caliper (the piston will remain seated in its bore).
5. Position caliper housing lower V groove on anchor plate lower abutment surface, Fig. 74. Refer to Figs. 74 and 75 to complete assembly following steps shown. Connect brake hose, bleed brakes and replace wheel.
6. Install key retaining screw and torque to 12-20 ft. lbs.

Brake Shoe & Lining, Replace

The procedure to replace the shoe and lining assemblies is the same as the caliper removal discussed previously with the exception that it is not necessary to disconnect the brake hose. Use care to avoid twisting or stretching the brake hose.

Hub & Rotor Remove

1. Remove caliper and shoes as previously described. If no repairs are necessary on the caliper it is not necessary to disconnect the brake hose. The caliper can be temporarily secured to the upper suspension arm.

Do not remove the anchor plate and be careful not to stretch or twist the brake hose.
2. Remove grease cap from wheel spindle and remove cotter pin and nut lock from wheel bearing adjustment nut.
3. Remove wheel bearing adjusting nut and grasp the hub and rotor and pull it out far enough to loosen the washer and outer wheel bearing. Then push it back in and remove the washer, outer wheel bearing and remove the hub and rotor.

KELSEY-HAYES SLIDING CALIPER

This sliding caliper single piston system uses a one piece hub and is actuated by the hydraulic system and disc assembly, Fig. 76. Alignment and positioning of the caliper is achieved by two machined guides or "ways" on the adaptor, while caliper retaining clips allow lateral movement of the caliper, Fig. 77. Outboard shoe flanges are used to position and locate the shoe on the caliper fingers, Fig. 78, while the inboard shoe is retained by the adaptor, Fig. 65. Braking force applied onto the outboard shoe is transferred to the caliper, while braking force applied onto the inboard shoe is transferred directly to the adaptor.

A square cut piston seal provides a hydraulic seal between the piston and the cylinder bore, Fig. 76. A dust boot with a wiping lip installed in a groove in the cylinder bore and piston, prevents contamination in the piston and cylinder bore area. Adjustment between the disc and the shoe is obtain automatically by the outward relocation of the piston as the inboard lining wears and inward movement of the caliper as the outboard lining wears.

Caliper Removal

1. Raise the vehicle and remove front wheel.
2. Remove caliper retaining clips and anti-rattle springs, Fig. 77.
3. Remove caliper from disc by slowly sliding caliper assembly out and away from disc.

NOTE: Use some means to support caliper. Do not let caliper hang from hydraulic line.

Brake Shoe Removal

1. Remove caliper assembly as outlined above.
2. Remove outboard shoe by prying between the shoe and the caliper fingers, Fig. 80, since flanges on outboard shoe retain caliper firmly.

NOTE: Caliper should be supported to avoid damage to the flexible brake hose.

3. Remove inboard brake shoe from the adaptor, Fig. 79.

Brake Shoe Installation

NOTE: Remove approximately ⅓ of the brake fluid out of the reservoir to prevent overflow when pistons are pushed back into the bore.

1. With care, push piston back into bore until bottomed.
2. Install new outboard shoe in recess of caliper.

NOTE: No free play should exist between brake shoe flanges and caliper fingers, Fig. 81.

If up and down movement of the shoe shows free play, shoe must be removed and flanges bent to provide a slight interference fit, Fig. 78. Reinstall shoe after modification, if shoe can not be finger snapped into place, use light "C" clamp pressure, Fig. 82.
3. Position inboard shoe with flanges inserted in adaptor "ways," Fig. 79.
4. Carefully slide caliper assembly into adaptor and over the disc while aligning caliper on machined "ways" of adaptor.

NOTE: Make sure dust boot is not pulled out from groove when piston and boot slide over the inboard shoe.

5. Install anti-rattle springs and retaining clips and torque retaining screws to 180 inch-pounds.

NOTE: The inboard shoe anti-rattle spring is to be installed on top of the retainer spring plate, Fig. 77.

Caliper Disassembly

1. With caliper and shoes removed as described previously, place caliper onto the upper control arm and slowly depress brake pedal, in turn hydraulically pushing piston out of bore.

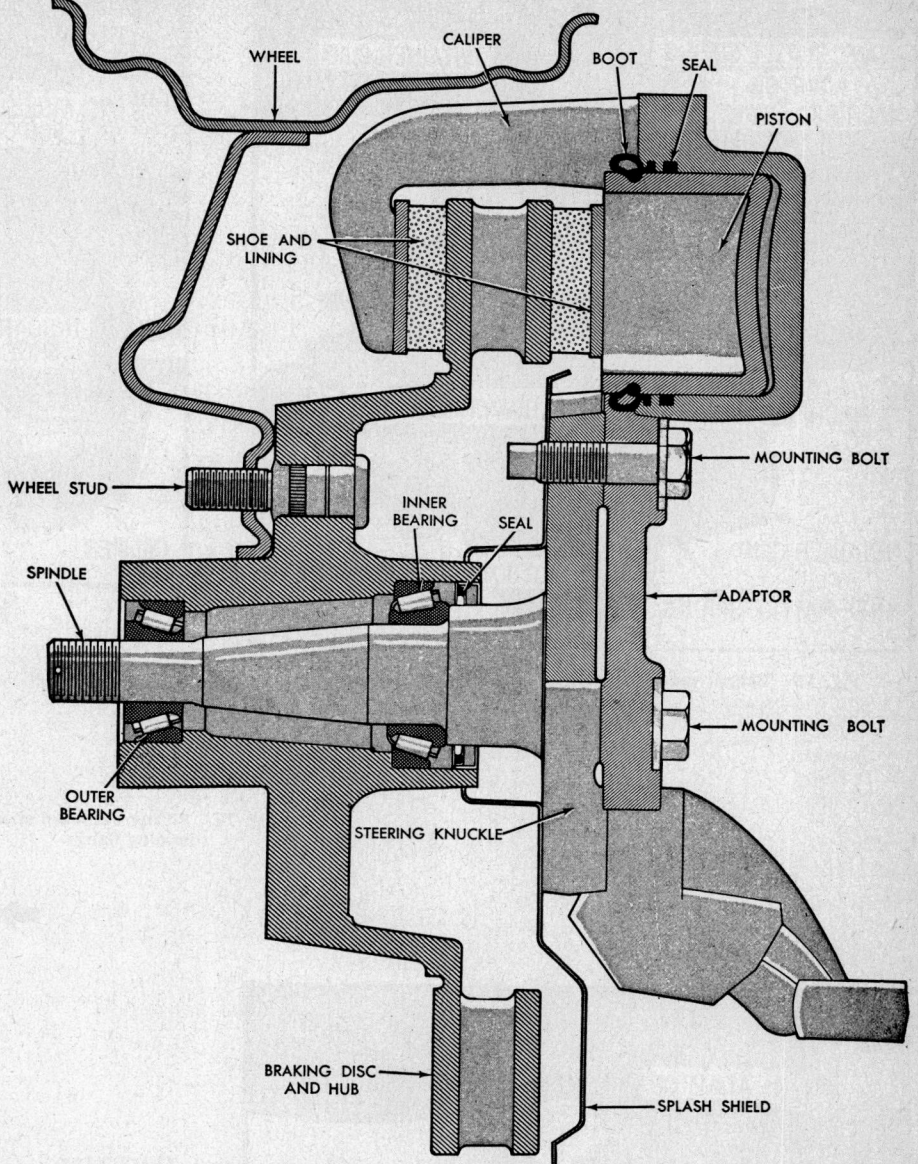

Fig. 76 Sectional view of Kelsey-Hayes sliding caliper front disc brake

NOTE: Pedal will fall when piston passes bore opening.

2. Support pedal below first inch of pedal travel to prevent excessive fluid loss.
3. To remove piston from the opposite caliper, disconnect flexible brake line at frame bracket, from vehicle side where piston has been removed previously and plug tube to prevent pressure loss. By depressing brake pedal this piston can also be hydraulically pushed out.
    Important: Air pressure should never be used to remove piston from bore.
4. Mount caliper in a vise equipped with protector jaws.

NOTE: Excessive vise pressure will distort caliper bore.

5. Remove the dust boot, Fig. 83.
6. Insert a suitable tool such as a small, pointed wooden or plastic object between the cylinder bore and the seal and work seal out of the groove in the piston bore.

NOTE: A metal tool such as a screwdriver should not be used since it can cause damage to the piston bore or burr the edges of the seal groove.

Caliper Assembly

1. Before installing the new piston seal

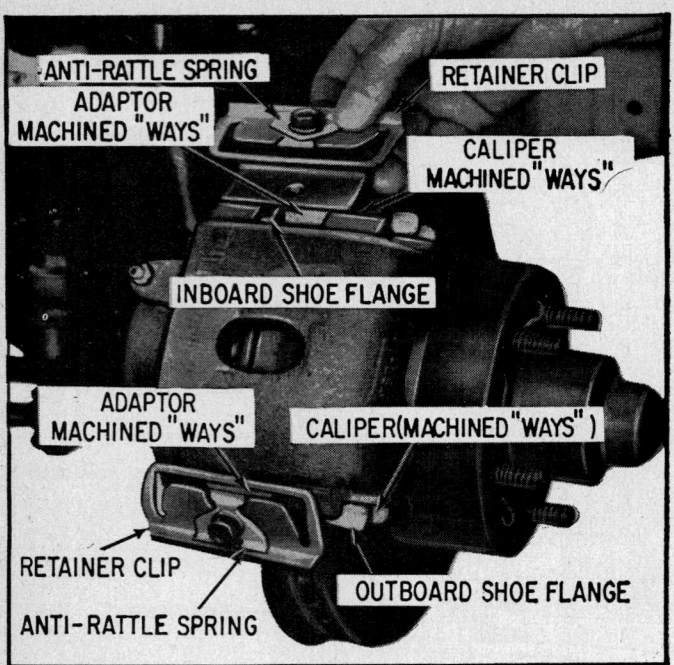

Fig. 77   Caliper machined "ways" and assembly retention

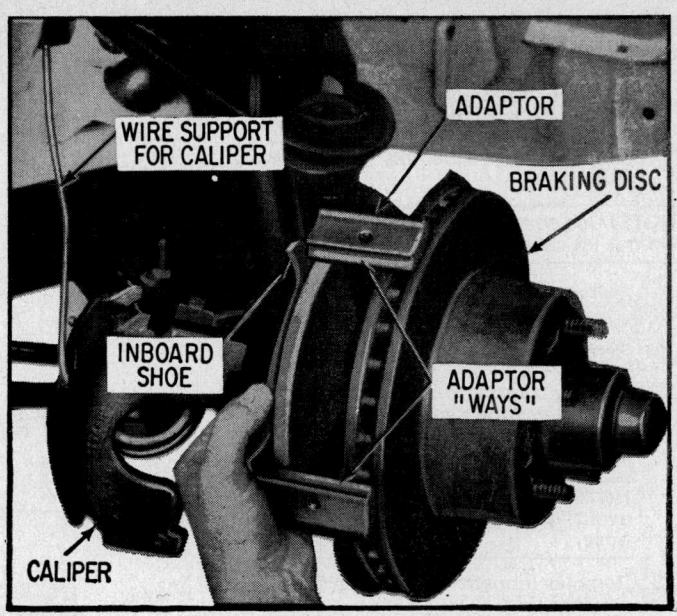

Fig. 79   Replacing inboard shoe

Fig. 78   Fitting outboard shoe retaining flange

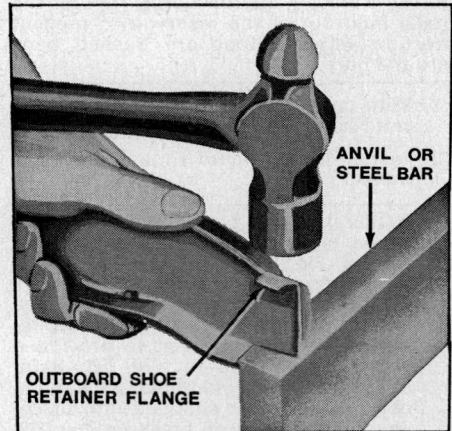

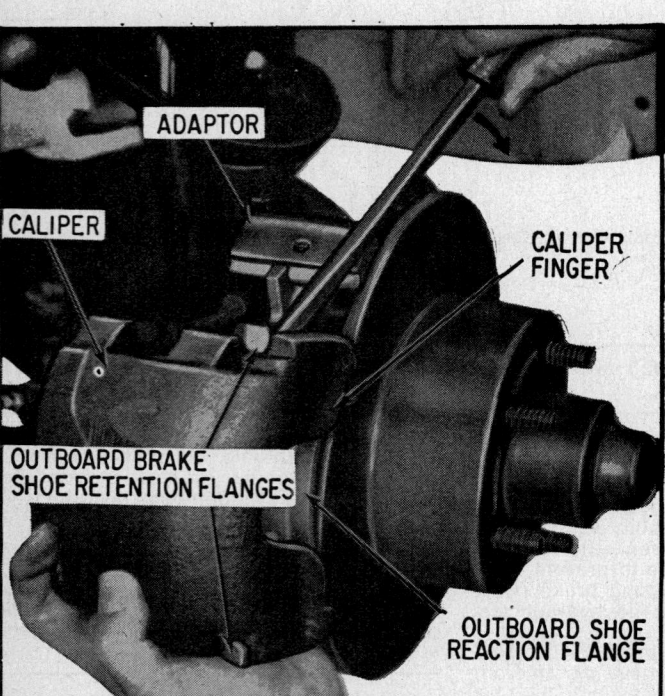

Fig. 80   Removing outboard shoe

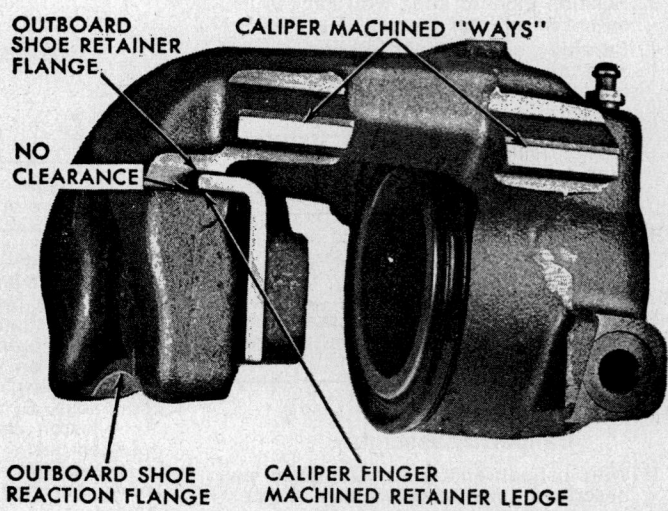

Fig. 81   Positioning outboard shoe onto caliper finger machined retainer ledge

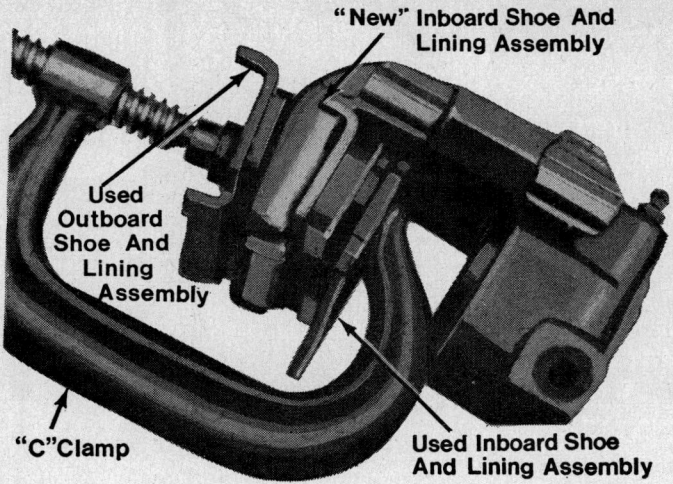

Fig. 82   Installing outboard shoe using "C" clamp

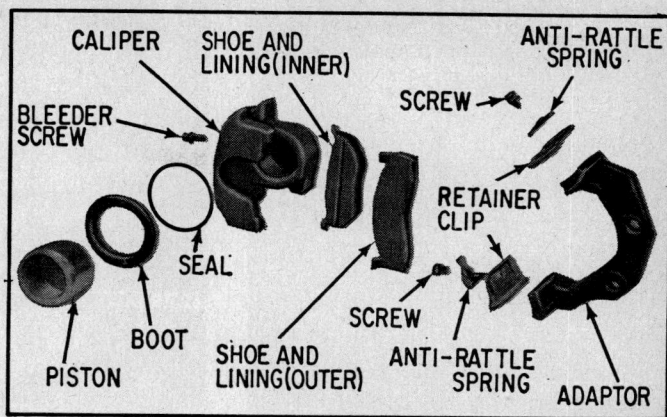

Fig. 83   Exploded view of a Kelsey-Hayes sliding caliper disc brake

in groove of bore, dip seal in Ucon LB1145Y24 lubricant or equivalent. Work seal gently into the groove (using clean fingers) until seal is properly seated, make sure that seal is not twisted or rolled.

NOTE: Old seals should never be re-used.

2. With new piston boot lubricated generously with Ucon LB1145Y24 or equivalent. Using finger pressure, install into caliper by pushing into outer groove of the caliper bore. When properly positioned in groove boot will snap into place. Double check to make sure boot is properly installed and seated by running finger around the inside of the boot.

3. Plug high pressure inlet to caliper and bleeder screw hole and coat piston with a generous amount of lubricant. Spread boot with finger and work piston into boot while pressing down on piston. As piston is depressed, entrapped air below piston will force boot around piston and into its groove.

4. Remove the plug and apply uniform force to the piston (avoid cocking piston) until piston bottoms in bore.

5. Install caliper and shoes as described under "Brake Shoe Installation."

REAR WHEEL DISC BRAKE & PARKING BRAKE SERVICE

1974 Imperial

The parking brake assembly of this system is mounted on the axle flange and intermediate disc brake adaptor. The rotor has an internal 7 inch drum surface for the internal expanding parking brake shoes, Fig. 84. Service to system should be performed as follows:

Disassembly

1. Support vehicle on a stand and remove rear wheel.
2. Remove caliper retaining screws and anti rattle spring assemblies, Fig. 77. Slide caliper from adaptor machined ways and position caliper on leaf spring for support, Fig. 85.
3. Remove inboard shoe from adaptor ways and remove parking brake adjusting access hole plug.
4. Using brake adjusting tool C-4223, release parking brake adjustment and remove disc/drum.
5. Remove lower shoe spring, Fig. 86. Spread brake shoes slightly and remove adjusting star wheel and upper shoe spring, Fig. 87.
6. Move brake shoes off support and remove brake shoe retainers, springs and nails and remove from support, Fig. 88.
7. Disconnect park brake cable from

lever and snap ring retainer from shaft and remove lever, Fig. 89.
8. Remove inner snap ring from shaft and remove cam lever, cam and shaft, Fig. 90.

Cleaning & Inspection

1. Brush or wipe (dry) metal portions of the brake shoes. Inspect lining contact area, the lining should show contact marks across its entire area. Shoes showing contact on one side should be replaced.
2. Using a suitable solvent, clean brake support. Inspect for burrs and remove as necessary.
3. Clean cam lever, cam, shaft and operating lever. Inspect for damaged or distorted parts, including O-rings and replace as necessary. Replace any parts that do not permit freedom of operation. Apply lubricant to threads, sockets and washers.

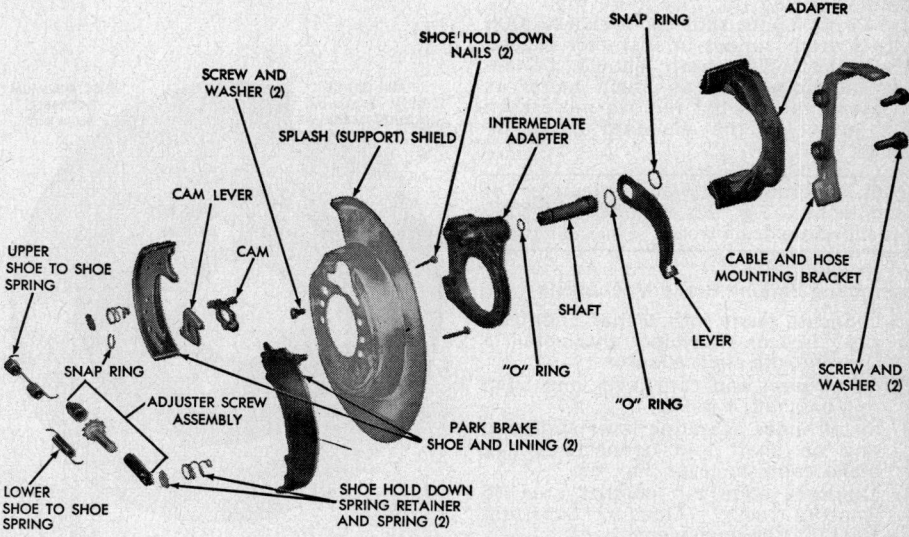

Fig. 84   Rear wheel parking brake assembly

DISC BRAKES

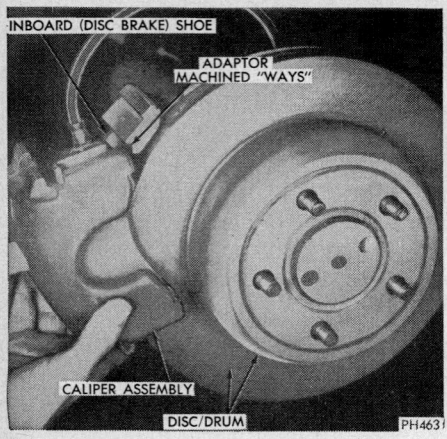

Fig. 85   Replacing caliper assembly

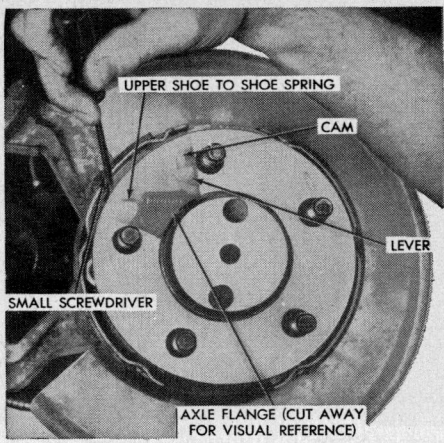

Fig. 87   Replacing upper shoe to shoe spring

Fig. 89   Park brake operating level location

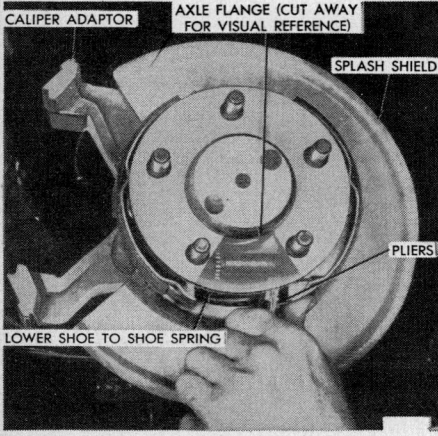

Fig. 86   Replacing lower shoe to shoe spring

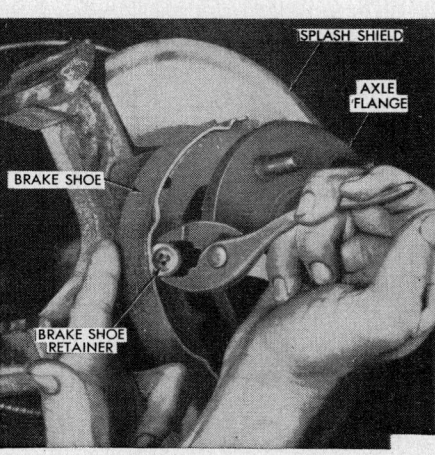

Fig. 88   Replacing brake shoe retainer, springs and nails

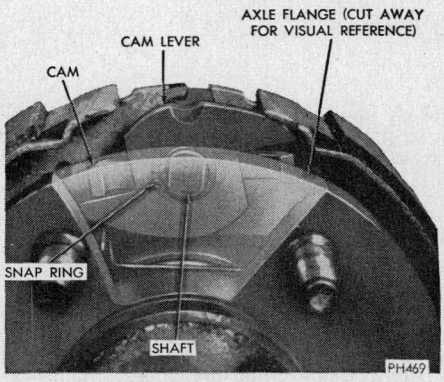

Fig. 90   Outer cam, cam lever, snap ring and shaft location

Drum Refacing

Check drum diameter and runout. Drum diameter should not vary more than .002 inch. Drum runout should not exceed .006 inch. If drum runout or diameter exceed these limits, the drum should be refaced. Remove only as much metal as necessary, but do not remove more than .060 inch over the standard brake diameter.

NOTE: Maximum allowable diameter of 7.090 inches, Fig. 91, includes the .030 inch allowable drum wear.

Assembling Parking Brake Mechanism

1. Lubricate shaft with Mopar Lubricant #2932524 or equivalent and install in intermediate shaft adaptor.
2. Install cam and cam lever and snap ring on shaft, Fig. 90.
3. Install inner operating lever and snap ring on shaft and connect parking brake cable to lever, Fig. 89.
4. Lubricate shoe tab contact area (6 places) with Mopar Lubricant #2932524 or equivalent.
5. Place brake shoes on support and in-

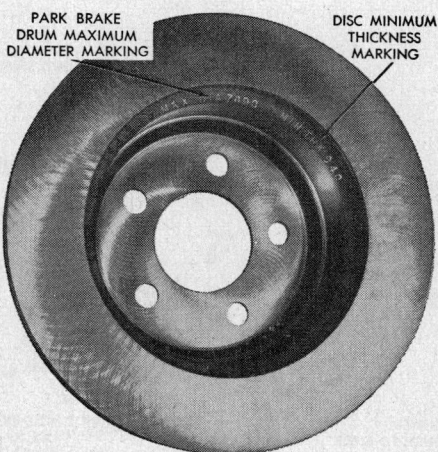

Fig. 91   Maximum drum diameter marking

stall retaining nails, springs and retainers, Fig. 88.
6. Install upper shoe spring and adjuster wheel, Fig. 87.

NOTE: Adjuster star wheel is forward on left side of vehicle and to the rear on right side of vehicle.

7. Install lower shoe spring and install disc drum, Fig. 86.

Assembling Caliper

1. Place inboard shoe on adaptor with shoe flanges in adaptor ways, Fig. 85.
2. Carefully slide caliper assembly into place in adaptor and over disc, Fig. 85. Align caliper on machined ways of adaptor.

NOTE: Be careful not to pull dust boot from its grooves as the piston and boot slide over the inboard shoe.

3. Install anti rattle springs and retaining clips and torque screws, Fig. 77.

NOTE: Inboard shoe anti rattle spring must always be installed on top of retainer spring plate.

DISC BRAKE ROTOR SPECIFICATIONS

CAR	Year	Nominal Thickness	Minimum Thickness	Thickness Variation Parallelism	Run-out (T.I.R.)	Finish (Micro-In.)	CAR	Year	Nominal Thickness	Minimum Thickness	Thickness Variation Parallelism	Run-out (T.I.R.)	Finish (Micro-In.)
American Mtrs.	1969–70	.500	.450	.0005	.005	15–80	Ford & Mercury Full Size	1969	1.185	1.140	.0007	.002	15–80
	1971–74	1.000	.940	.0005	.005	15–80		1970–72	1.180	1.120	.0007	.003	15–80
Belvedere, Charger, Coronet & Satellite	1969	.886	.816	.0005	.005	40		1973–74	1.180	1.120	.0005②	.003	15–80
	1970	1.000	.980	.0005	.002	15–80	Imperial	1969	.877	—	—	.005	30–60
	1971–72	1.000	.940	.0005	.002	15–80		1970	1.250	1.200	.0005	.002	15–80
	1973–74	1.000	.940	.0005	.004	15–80		1971–72	1.250	1.180	.0005	.002	15–80
Buick Full Size	1969	1.000	.965	.0005	.005	30–50		1973–74	③	④	.0005	.004	15–80
	1970	1.000	.965	.0005	.004	30–50	Lincoln	1969	1.245	1.215	.0007	.002	15–80
	1971–72	1.290	1.230	.0005	.005	30–80		1970–72	1.180	1.120	.0007	.003	15–80
	1973–74	1.290	1.215	.0005	.005	30–80		1973	1.180	1.120	.0005	.003	15–80
Buick Intermediate	1969–70	1.000	.965	.0005	.004	30–50		1974	1.180	1.120	.0025	.003	15–80
	1971–72	1.040	.980	.0005	.004	30–80	Mark III, IV	1969	1.185	1.140	.0007	.002	15–80
	1973–74	1.040	.965	.0005	.005	30–80		1970–72	1.180	1.120	.0007	.003	15–80
Cadillac	1969–70	1.250	1.230	.0007	.002	15–80		1973–74	1.180	1.120	.00025	.003	15–80
	1971–72	1.240	1.220	.0007	.002	15–80	Oldsmobile	1969	1.250	1.215	.0005	.004	30–50
	1973	1.240	1.220	.0007	.005	15–80		1970	1.250	1.215	.0007	.002	30–50
	1974	—	1.220	.0005	.005	—		1971–72	1.290	1.215	.0005	.002	30–50
Camaro & Chevelle	1969	1.000	.965	.0005	.004	30–50		1973–74	1.290	1.215	.0005	.005	30–50
	1970	1.000	.965	.0005	.002	30–50	Olds F-85, Cutlass, Omega	1969	1.000	.965	.0005	.004	30–50
	1971–74	1.035	.980	.0005	.005	20–60		1970	1.035	.965	.0005	.004	30–50
Challenger & Barracuda	1969	.810	—	.0005	.002	15–80		1971–74	1.040	.965	.0005	.004	30–50
	1970	1.000	.980	.0005	.002	15–80	Olds Toronado	1969	1.250	1.215	.0005	.004	30–50
	1971–72	1.000	.940	.0005	.002	15–80		1970	1.250	1.215	.0005	.002	30–50
	1973–74	1.000	.940	.0005	.004	15–80		1971–74	1.245	1.170	.0005	.002	30–50
Chevrolet	1969	1.250	1.215	.0005	.004	30–50	Mustang II & Pinto	1971–73	.750	.685	.0007	.003	15–80
	1970	1.250	1.215	.0005	.002	30–50		1974	.870	.810	.0005	.003	15–80
	1971–72	1.250	1.230	.0005	.005	20–60	Pontiac Full Size	1969	1.240	1.195	.0007	.004	20–60
	1973–74	1.285	1.230	.0005	.005	20–60		1970–71	1.250	1.215	.0007	.004	20–60
Chevy Nova	1969	1.000	.965	.0005	.004	30–50		1972–74	1.285	1.215	.0007	.004	20–60
	1970	1.000	.965	.0005	.002	30–50	Pontiac Intermediate Exc. Firebird & Ventura	1969	1.000	.960	.0007	.004	20–60
	1971–74	1.035	.980	.0005	.005	20–60		1970–71	1.085	.965	.0007	.004	20–60
Chrysler	1969–70	1.250	1.200	.0005	.002	15–80		1972–74	1.035	.965	.0007	.004	20–60
	1971–72	1.250	1.180	.0005	.002	15–80	Pontiac Firebird	1969	1.000	.960	.0007	.004	20–60
	1973–74	1.250	1.180	.0005	.004	15–80		1970	1.040	.965	.0005	.005	30–80
Comet & Maverick	1974	.870	.810	.0005	.003	15–80		1971	1.085	.965	.0007	.004	20–60
Corvette	1969–70	1.250	1.215	.0005	.004	30–50		1972–74	1.035	.965	.0007	.004	20–60
	1971–74	1.250	1.230	.0005	.005	20–60	Thunderbird	1969	1.185	1.140	.0007	.002	15–80
Dart & Valiant	1969–72	.810	—	.0005	.002	15–80		1970–72	1.180	1.120	.0007	.003	15–80
	1973–74	1.000	.940	.0005	.004	15–80		1973–74	1.180	1.120	.00025	.003	15–80
Dodge & Plymouth Full Size	1969–70	1.250	1.200	.0005	.002	15–80	Vega	1971–72	.500	.470	.0005	.002	20–60
	1971–72	1.250	1.180	.0005	.002	15–80		1973–74	.500	.455	.0005	.002	20–60
	1973–74	1.250	1.180	.0005	.004	15–80	Ventura	1971–73	1.035	.980	.0005	.004	20–60
Eldorado	1969–73	1.210	1.190	.0005	.008	15–80		1974	1.035	.965	.0007	.004	20–60
	1974	—	1.190	.0005	—	—							
Ford & Mercury Intermediate	1969	.940	.895	.0007	.002	15–80							
	1970–73	.935	.875	.0007	.002	15–80							
	1972①	1.180	1.120	.0007	.003	15–80							
	1973–74①	1.180	1.120	.0005	.003	15–80							

①—Montego, Torino & 1974 Cougar.
②—1974 Mercury, .0004.
③—Front, 1.400; Rear, 1.000.
④—Front, 1.180; Rear, .940.

ANTI-SKID BRAKE SYSTEMS

CHRYSLER SURE BRAKE

This system is designed to prevent any wheel from locking up during brake applications above a speed of about 5mph. The system reduces skid potential of a locked wheel and still maintains brake pressure for maximum stopping effort. The end result is to improve directional control and steerability of the vehicle, and in many cases to reduce the distance required to bring the vehicle to a stop.

The major components of the system are shown in Fig. 1. These include a mechanically driven speed sensor at each wheel, a logic controller located inside the right rear quarter panel and three pressure modulators; one modulator is under each front fender ahead of the wheels and one is in the engine compartment next to the radiator on the right side of the vehicle.

OPERATION

Engine Running—Vehicle Not in Motion

The wheel sensors do not generate any signals for transmission to the logic controller when the vehicle is not in motion. Hence, the logic controller sends no commands to the pressure modulator.

Engine Running—Vehicle in Motion

With the vehicle in motion, alternating current voltage is generated at each wheel sensor and sent to the logic controller. The logic controller processes the signals received from the wheel sensors to sample the speed of each wheel. If the brakes are not applied or if they are applied lightly, the controller does not send any commands to the pressure modulator.

When the brakes are applied with greater force, the controller, based on wheel sensor signals, determines the rate at which each wheel is decelerating. If the rate is great and might produce wheel slippage or lockup, the controller sends a command to the modulator that controls the braking for the wheel or wheels concerned.

Exercise Cycle

If the engine is started with the brake pedal depressed, the pressure modula-

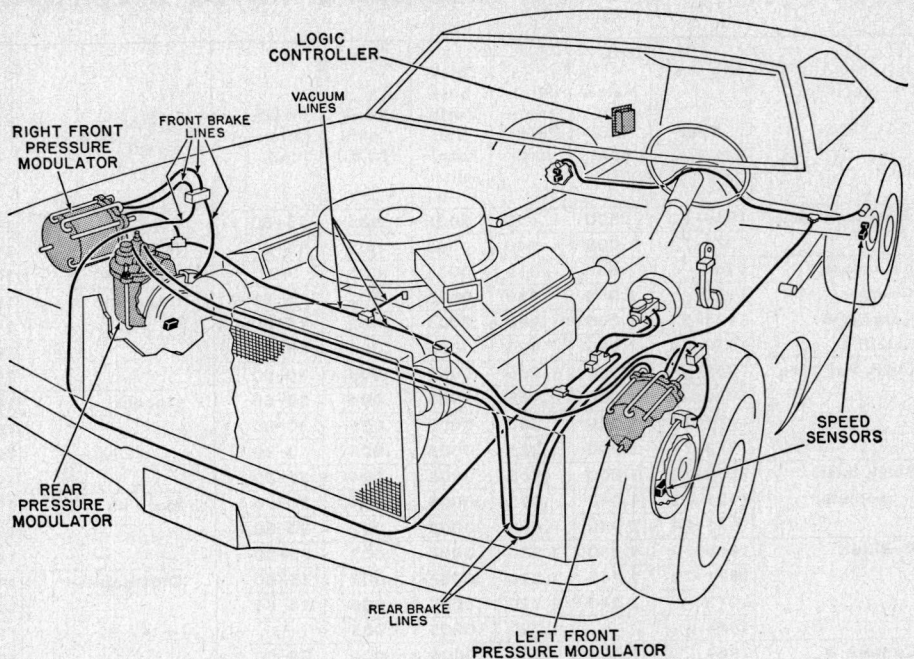

Fig. 1   Chrysler Sure Brake system components

tors go through two exercise cycles. When the ignition switch is turned from OFF to START all three modulators cycle once, and when the switch returns from START to ON the modulators cycle again. These cycles are to insure that the system is working properly. The cycles can be heard under some conditions, but should not be a cause for concern.

Warning System

The Sure Brake System includes a secondary system to warn the driver of certain types of failures in the system. The warning system uses the brake warning light. The warning light will be on under the following conditions:

1. It the pressure modulator is activated in the absence of a brake light signal.

2. If the controller sends a signal to open the air valve on a modulator in the absence of a signal to open the by-pass valve.

3. If the electrical continuity of the air valve lead wire is broken.

4. If all speed sensor signals are not received at the controller, or if the signals are not properly converted in the controller at speeds above 15 mph.

NOTE: Due to the complexities of testing this system and the various voltage charts necessary, it is recommended the unit be returned to a dealer for service. For this reason, a procedure for disabling the Sure Brake System to allow the car to be operated safely, follows.

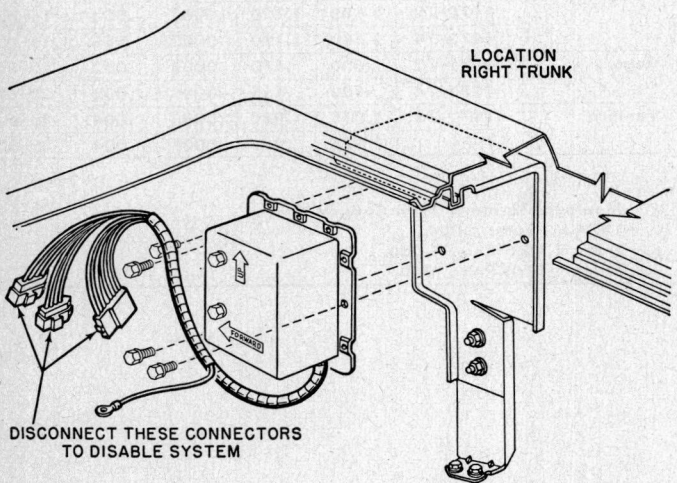

Fig. 2   Disconnecting logic controller

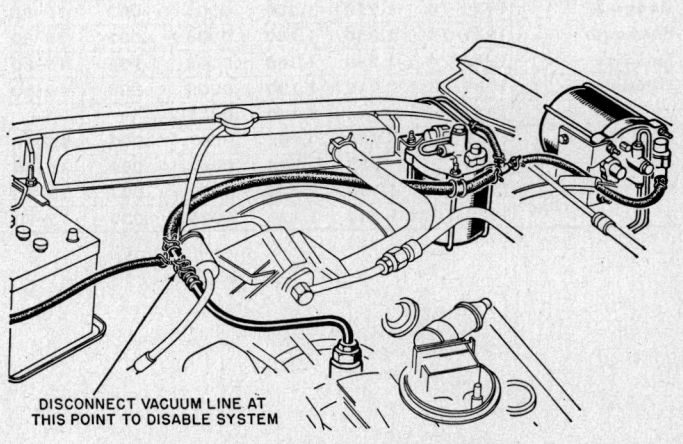

Fig. 3   Disconnect vacuum lines. 1969-73

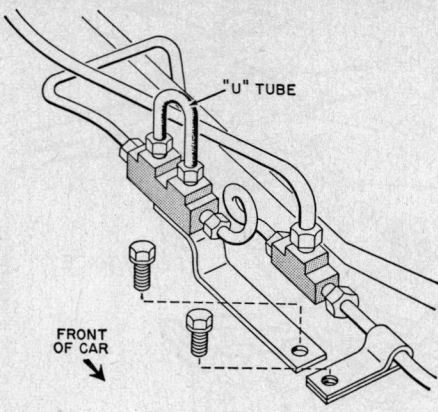

Fig. 4 Placing "U" tube in system to disable front wheel modulators

DISABLING THE SURE BRAKE SYSTEM

If necessary parts or service is not available, the system should be disabled. The brakes will then function the same as those on cars without this system. Proceed as follows:

Disconnect the logic controller (all three connectors), Fig. 2. On 1969-73 units, disconnect the vacuum supply hose at the "T" connection leading to the modulator, Fig. 3, and the line to the intake manifold should be plugged and the line to the modulators should be taped to keep out dirt.

An additional step may be necessary to disable the system. If a pressure modulator diaphragm plate sticks in the retracted or partially retracted position the basic hydraulic brake system will be affected. Test for this by placing car on a hoist and spin wheels by hand to insure they are free. With the brakes applied, attempt to spin wheels, release brakes and spin wheels again. If a wheel spins with the brakes applied or does not rotate with brakes released, the modulator for that wheel must be by-passed. This can be accomplished as follows:

1. On front wheel modulators, a "U" tube should be placed in the system after the modulator tubes have been removed, Fig. 4.

2. On rear wheel modulator, route the brake line from rear wheels directly into the rear of safety tee after modulator line has been disconnected, Fig. 5. Also, both hydraulic tubes should be disconnected at the brake warning switch metering valve. This completely by-passes the modulator for the rear brakes.

FORD "SURE TRACK"

This system is designed to keep the rear end of a vehicle tracking the front end correctly by controlling rear brake lockup during "panic stops." The system consists of sensors, valves, an actuator

and a tiny computer to control the rate of deceleration of the rear wheels. The rate of deceleration of a rotating wheel is measured in terms of "slip" relative to the vehicle speed. If the car is traveling at 50mph and the wheel with the brakes applied is turning at 40mph, there is a 20 percent slip. The 10 to 20 percent slip range is just short of locking the brakes and it is in this range that maximum braking is accomplished. Ideally, the 10 to 20 percent slip should be maintained throughout the speed range as the vehicle slows down, so the relationship between vehicle speed and wheel speed is constantly changing and must be constantly corrected.

In the Sure Track system, this relationship is controlled electrically by automatically pumping the brakes in cycles when the rear wheels begin to lock up under heavy braking. By this rapid application and release of the brakes the locking point is never reached or is reached and released so fast that the wheels do not stop turning.

Sensor 1969 & Early 1970: A mechanically driven electro magnetic sensor is located at each rear wheel. Each sensor consists of a rotor, which is pressed onto the axle shaft outboard of the wheel bearing and a stator which bolts to the brake backing plate, Fig. 6. When the axle turns, teeth of the rotor pass the teeth of the stator, cutting magnetic lines of force and setting up an electrical current, in proportion to the speed of the rear wheels. Two wires from each of the sensors conduct impulses to the control module.

Sensor Late 1970 & 1971-74. A single sensor stator assembly, Figs. 7 and 8, is mounted on the rear axle drive pinion housing with the sensor rotor pressed onto the companion flange outboard of the grease seal. This unit operates in the same manner as the two wheel sensors used on the 1969 units to generate elec-

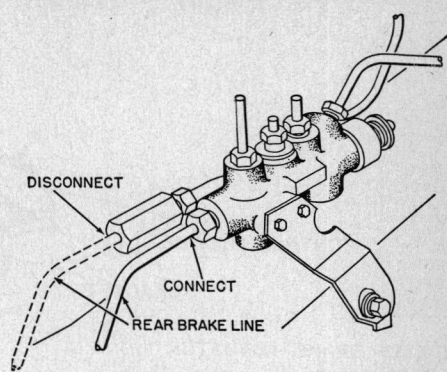

Fig. 5 Connections at safety tee to disable rear wheel modulators

tric current. The AC voltage, generated in proportion to driveshaft speed, is conducted from the sensor to the control module.

Control Module: The control module is mounted under the glove box in the passenger compartment and operates on the sum of the signals from the sensor(s).

When the sum of the signals drops abruptly below a predetermined level due to rapid deceleration, the module sends an electrical signal to the actuator solenoid to release the rear brakes. Then, when rear wheel speed increases again, the module de-energizes the solenoid, allowing the brakes to reapply. This cycle continues until the driver releases the brake pedal past the full pressure point or the vehicle slows to less than 4 mph.

Actuator: The vacuum operated actuator, Fig. 9, is mounted on the vehicle right frame rail under the toe board. The actuator is divided into two chambers by a diaphragm with a spring positioned ahead of the diaphragm.

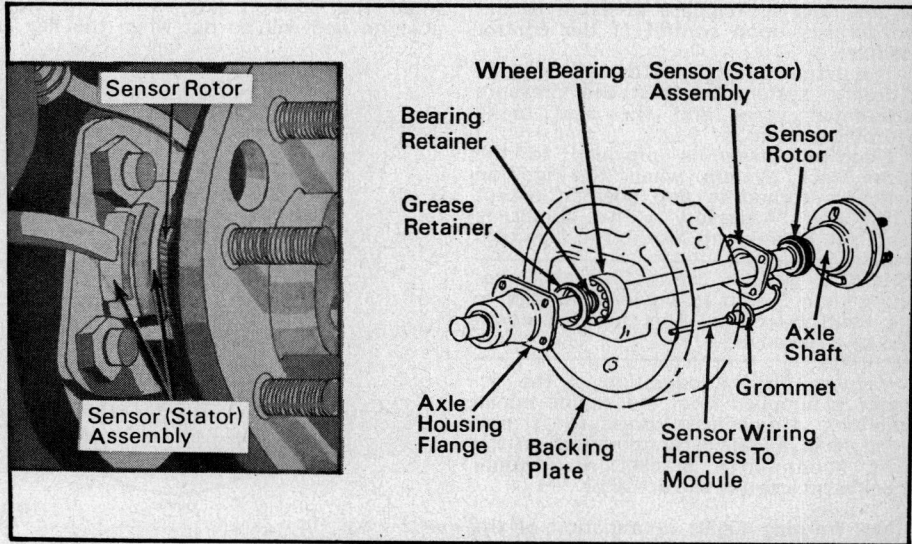

Fig. 6 Sensor components. 1969 & Early 1970 Sure Track

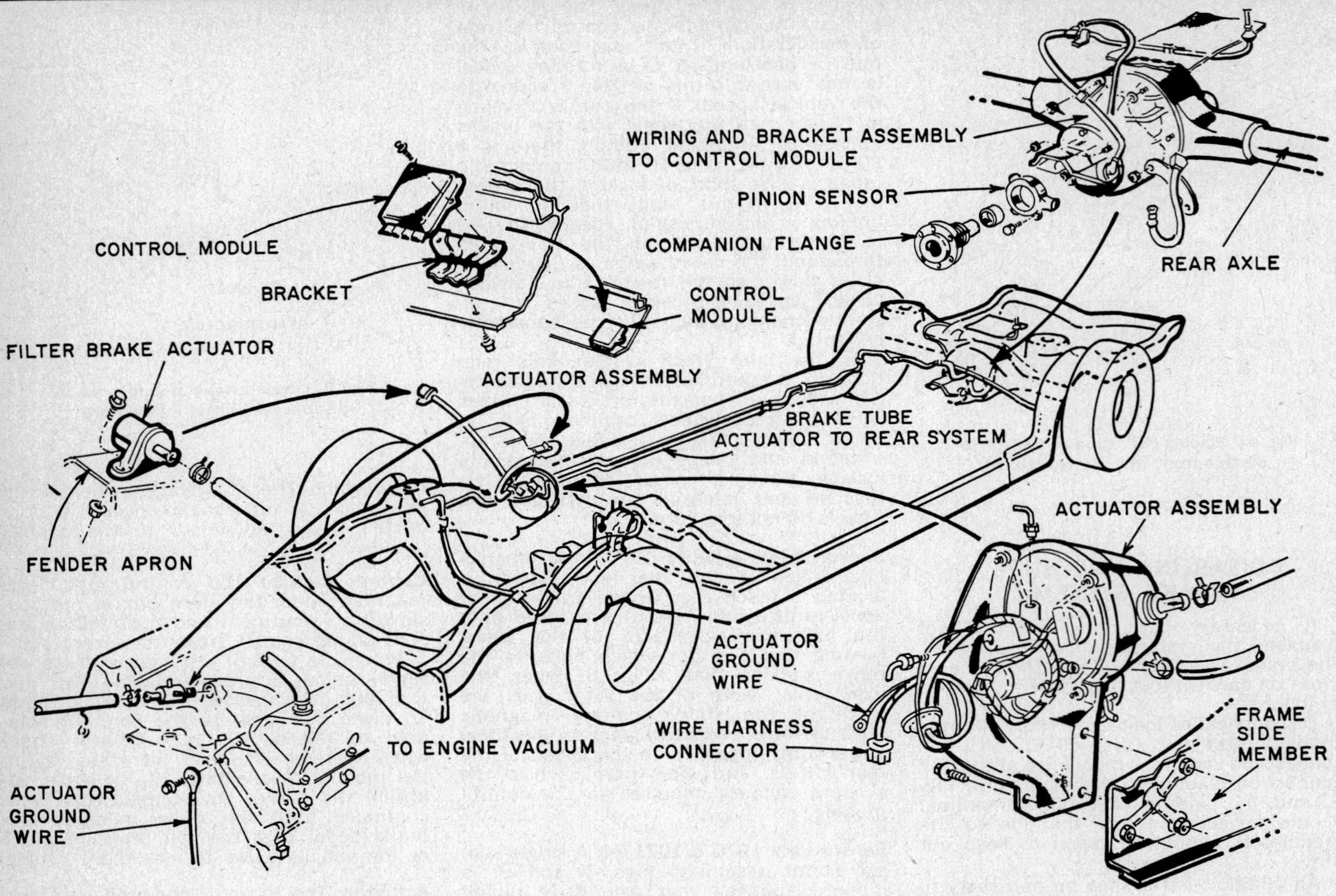

CONTROL MODULE

BRACKET

FILTER BRAKE ACTUATOR

FENDER APRON

ACTUATOR GROUND WIRE

ACTUATOR ASSEMBLY

TO ENGINE VACUUM

ACTUATOR GROUND WIRE

WIRE HARNESS CONNECTOR

WIRING AND BRACKET ASSEMBLY TO CONTROL MODULE

PINION SENSOR

COMPANION FLANGE

CONTROL MODULE

REAR AXLE

BRAKE TUBE ACTUATOR TO REAR SYSTEM

ACTUATOR ASSEMBLY

FRAME SIDE MEMBER

Fig. 7   Ford Sure Track components. Late 1970 & 1971-74 (typical)

In addition, the actuator contains a hydraulic cylinder, a solenoid and a time delay switch (failure switch), all functioning together to regulate pressure to the rear brakes upon control of the control module.

The actuator is connected to the brake hydraulic system between the pressure differential valve and the rear brake hydraulic system.

Electrical power is provided to the Sure Track system when the ignition switch is turned to any position except "Off" and "Accessory". The circuit is protected by a 3-amp fuse in the fuse box.

CAUTION: Do not use a fuse of higher rating than 3-amp to prevent damage to the control module. This fuse is identified by a red cover.

Vacuum for the operation of the actuator is supplied from the engine intake manifold. Atmospheric pressure is provided from an air filter mounted on the right hood hinge bracket. A vacuum check is included in the actuator.

Brake Warning Light: Illumination of the brake warning switch indicates a malfunction in the brake hydraulic system or in the

Sure Track unit and requires immediate service of the brake system.

As a test, the warning light will go on when the ignition key is in the start position and will go out when the key is

returned to the run position.

To determine if the trouble is in the Sure Track system or the brake hydraulic system, disconnect the switch plug from the hydraulic system differential switch.

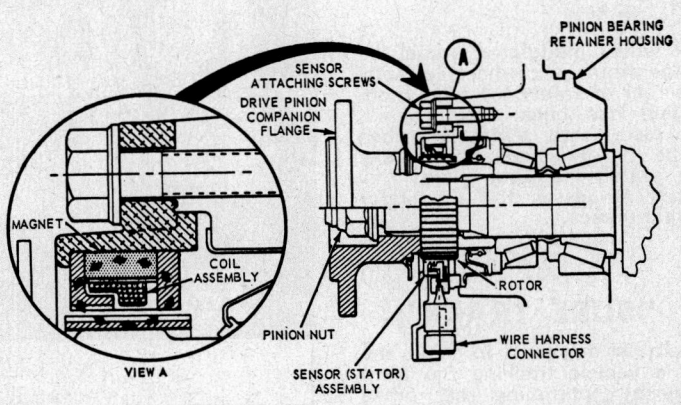

Fig. 8   Crossectional view of Sure Track sensor assembly. Late 1970 & 1971-74

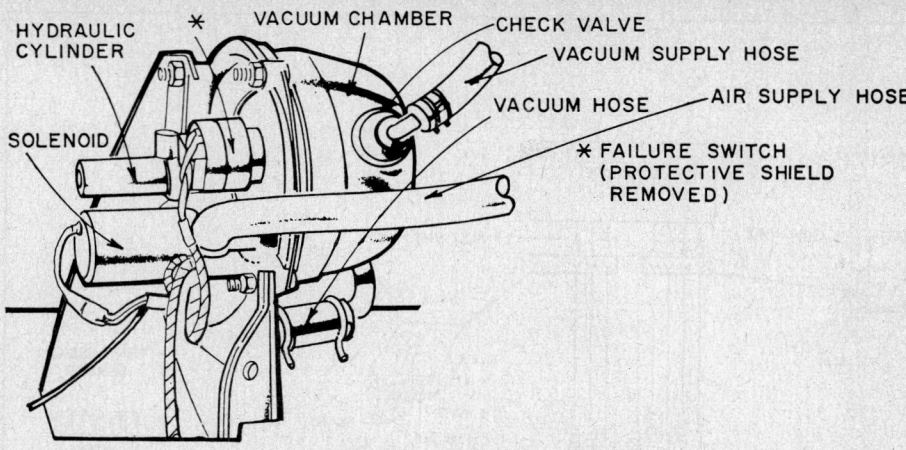

Fig. 9 Actuator assembly. Sure Track

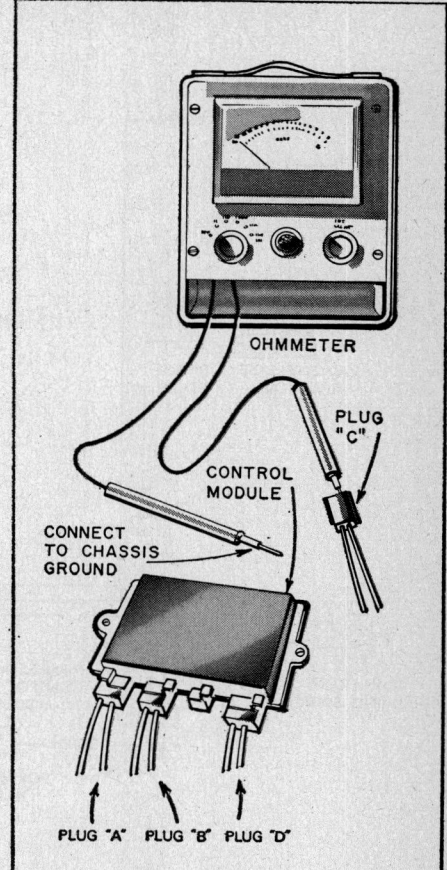

Fig. 10 Checking control module

If the light now goes out the brake hydraulic system is at fault. If the light remains on, check Sure Track system.

Functional Testing

1. Turn ignition key to "On" and listen for solenoid click and actuator cycle.

   NOTE: It may be necessary to run engine prior to performing this check to assure a vacuum supply in the actuator.

2. Raise rear wheels to clear floor.
3. With engine at operating temperature, place transmission in Drive and accelerate to approximately 25 mph. It may be necessary to increase engine speed slightly to obtain sufficient cycling of the Sure Track system for easy observation of its operation.
4. Apply the brakes quickly and firmly. If the Sure Track is functioning properly, it will cycle five or six times or until the brake pedal is released.

NOTE: Both wheels must be turning for this test or the system will not operate.

Sensor Test

1. Remove plug "C" from module and connect an ohmmeter between the two contacts of the sensor lead plug, Fig. 10. Resistance should be as indicated below:

   NOTE: On 1969 & Early 1970 models, a modulator with five plugs is used. When performing this check, disconnect plugs "C" and "E" and check for the specified resistance between the two contacts of either plug.

   1969 & Early 1970 . . 2000 (±500) ohms
   Late 1970 . . . . .1600-3200 ohms
   1971-74 . . . . .2400-3200 ohms

2. With ohmmeter connected between chassis ground and one of the two contacts of sensor lead plug, there should be infinite resistance.
3. If resistance is not within limits on both checks, isolate sensor(s) from other components at rear axle.
4. On 1969 and early 1970 models, check resistance of sensor lead wires from floor pan harness to sensor assembly at rear wheel. Move wires during test to check for internal break. On late 1970 and 1971-74 models, repeat resistance test with sensor leads disconnected from rear axle pinion housing.
5. If resistance is within specifications, problem is in wiring harness between sensor and module.
6. If resistance is not within specifications, replace sensor assembly.

Solenoid Test

1. Remove plug "A" from control module, Fig. 10, then connect an ohmmeter between the two contacts of the solenoid (red) and system ground (black) lead plug. Resistance should be 4-8 ohms.
2. If resistance is lower than 4 ohms, inspect solenoid wiring for a grounded condition. If resistance is higher than 8 ohms, inspect solenoid wiring for an open condition.

   NOTE: Refer to "System Ground Test" for connector check.

3. If wiring is satisfactory, replace actuator assembly.

System Ground Test

1. Remove plug "A" from module, Fig. 10, then connect an ohmmeter between chassis ground and system ground (black lead of plug). Resistance should be less than 1 ohm.
2. If resistance is greater than 1 ohm, check ground system wiring harness for loose or broken wires.
3. With ohmmeter still connected, move ground wires (black) at actuator harness to intermediate harness connector in and out. If meter fluctuates, it indicates a poor connection.
4. To repair a loose connection, separate connector and inspect system ground wiring connector terminals for an oversize condition. If terminal is oversize, use a pointed tool to force it together. Reinstall connectors and retest system for normal operation.
5. On 1969-72 models, connect an ohmmeter between system ground plug sleeve (black) and solenoid high (red), Fig. 10. If resistance is below 1000 ohms, the actuator coil or solenoid high (red) is shorted to ground.

GM TRACK MASTER & TRUE TRACK

Operation

This system Figs. 11, 12 and 13, incorporates a speed sensor mounted on each rear wheel, Fig. 14, on 1971-74 Eldorado and Toronado models and a transmission mounted speed sensor, Fig. 15 on 1972-74 Cadillac models. It combines a controller under the instrument panel and a modulator on the cowl in the engine compartment to prevent rear wheel lock-up.

The sensors produce an electrical signal that is proportional to wheel speed.

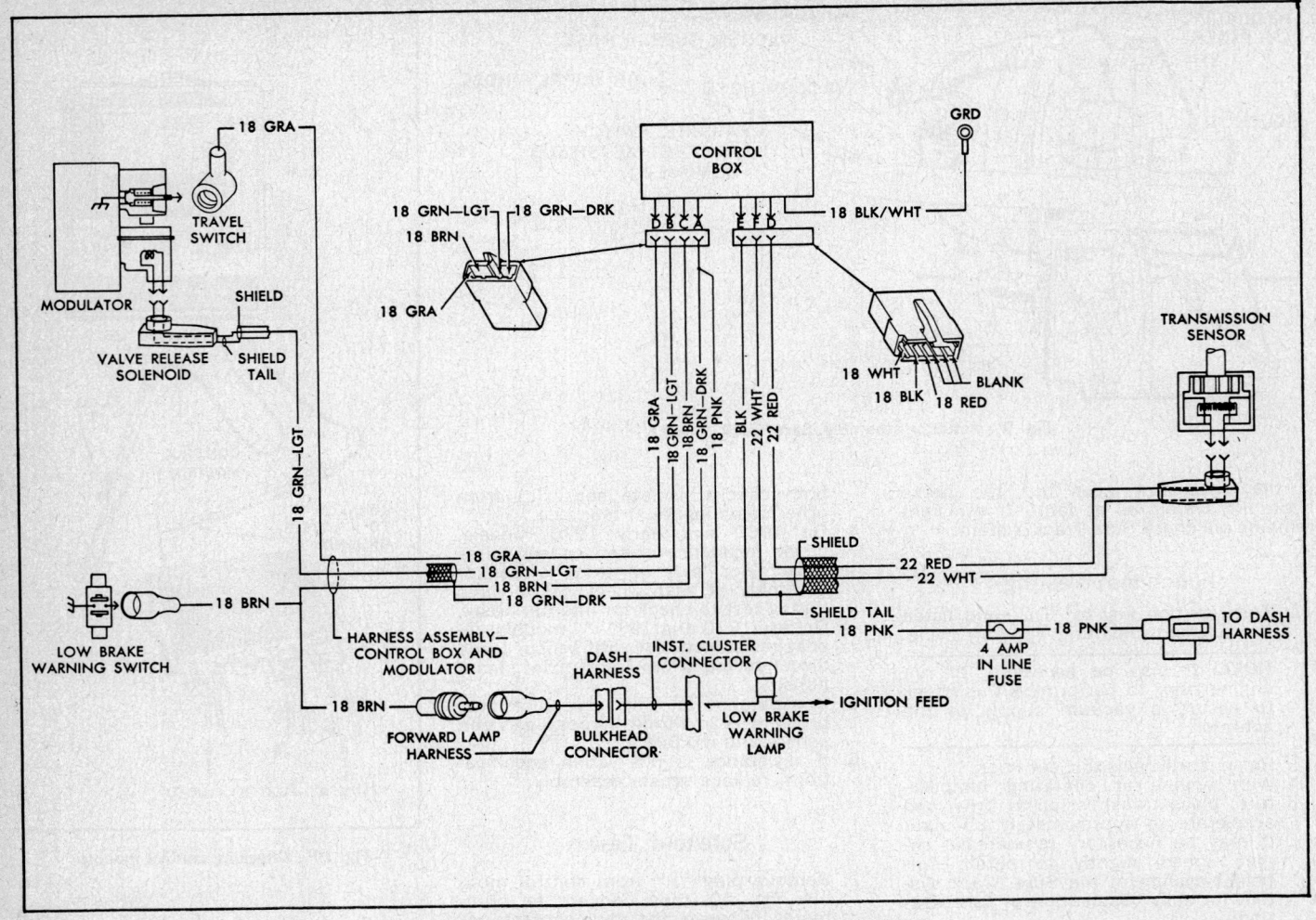

Fig. 11   Track Master wiring circuit. 1972-74 Cadillac

This signal is monitored by the controller. A wheel that is not locking during brake application will gradually decelerate. When a wheel has started to lock, it will decelerate abruptly at a rate much greater than the car's deceleration. When the controller determines that the signal from the sensors changes too rapidly, and the car is approaching a skid, the controller energizes the modulator solenoid.

The modulator, Figs. 16 and 17, contains a diaphragm both sides of which are exposed to intake manifold vacuum as long as the solenoid is not energized. When the solenoid is energized, atmospheric pressure is allowed to reach the top side of the diaphragm, forcing it down against the support spring. The displacement piston is lowered along with the diaphragm. This seals off hydraulic pressure from the master cylinder to the rear wheel cylinders by closing the hydraulic check valve. The lowering of the displacement piston also increases the area in the hydraulic chamber immediately below the check valve. This increased area results in decreased hydrau-

lic pressure and partial brake release.

With the brakes partially released, the wheels accelerate and, as car speed is approached, the controller senses the condition and de-energizes the modulator, allowing full brake application until a locking condition is again sensed.

The entire cycle of brake release and re-application occurs in about 1/3 second. During a stop where brake pressure is sufficient to cause lock-up, the cycling will continue until the car is slowed to approximately 5 mph or until the brakes are released by the driver.

The brake system warning light also operates in conjunction with the modulator travel switch in case of system malfunctions. When the switch is open for more than approximately four seconds, except during a skid controlled stop, the controller turns on the warning light. An exception to this is an open in the feed circuit from the ignition switch, which is indicated without the four second delay. When a malfunction is indicated, the lamp remains lighted until the ignition is turned off.

Wheel Speed Sensor Adjustment Eldorado & Toronado

NOTE: New sensors are furnished with a piece of tape on pick up end. This tape must be left on for adjustment.

1. Install sensor in backing plate so that taped end contacts teeth on hub.

   NOTE: If no tape is present on end of sensor, remove brake drum and a .010 inch feeler gauge between sensor and hub, Fig. 18.

2. While holding sensor against hub, install retaining screw and torque to 75 inch lbs.
3. Coat harness connector with wheel bearing grease and install connector and secure with clamp, Fig. 14.
4. Install brake drum, if removed.

Trouble Shooting

Brake Warning Light Does Not Light (Check When Ignition Switch Is In Start Position):

1. Burned out bulb.

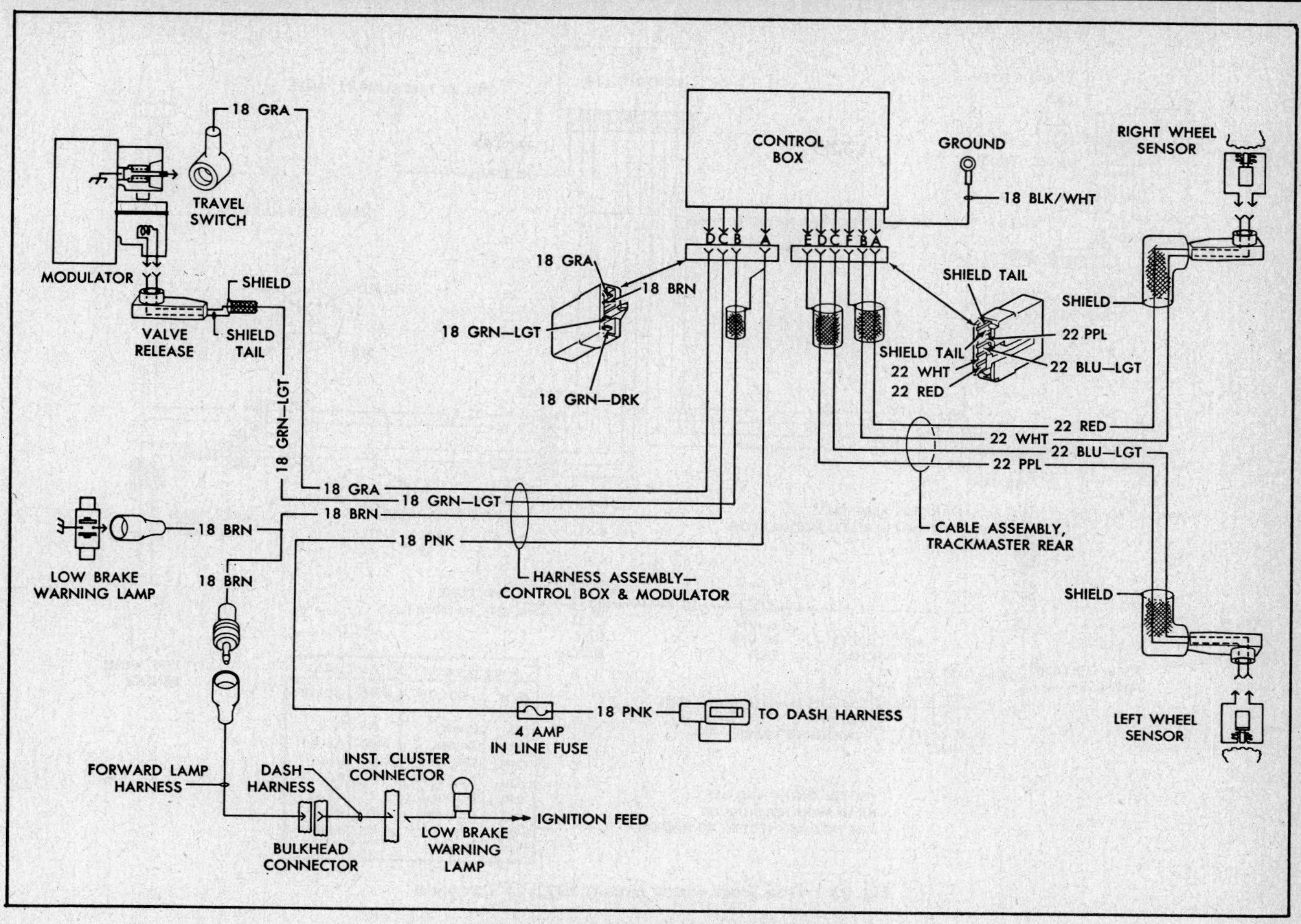

Fig. 12 Track Master wiring circuit. 1971-74 Eldorado

2. Blown instrument fuse.
3. Open in bulb circuit.

Immediate Brake Light When Ignition Is Turned To On Position:
1. Leak in hydraulic system.
2. Blown skid control fuse.
3. Open in controller circuit.
4. Faulty controller.
5. Less than 12 volts at controller due to faulty connections or open in wiring circuit.
6. Shorted parking brake switch.
7. Shorted electrical lead to parking brake switch and or brake lamp.
8. Shorted solenoid or lead to ground blows skid control fuse.
9. Shorted pressure differential switch (System OK).

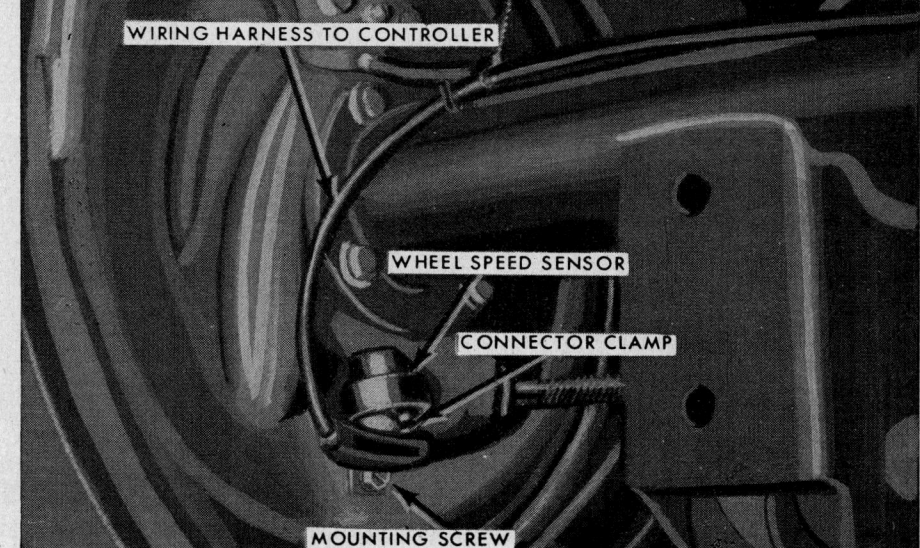

Fig. 14 Rear wheel speed sensor. 1971-74 Eldorado and Toronado

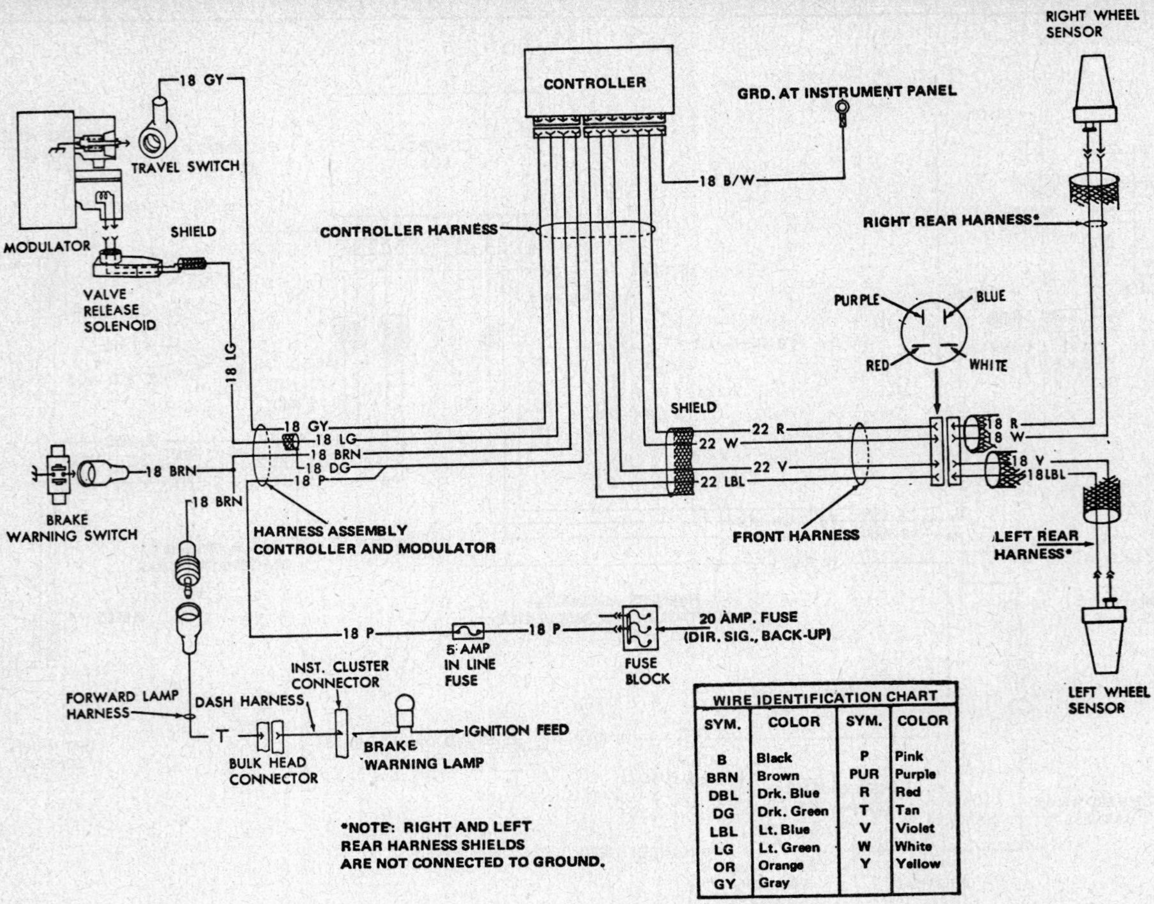

RIGHT WHEEL SENSOR
CONTROLLER
GRD. AT INSTRUMENT PANEL
18 GY
TRAVEL SWITCH
18 B/W
MODULATOR
SHIELD
CONTROLLER HARNESS
RIGHT REAR HARNESS*
VALVE RELEASE SOLENOID
18 LG
PURPLE
BLUE
RED
WHITE
SHIELD
18 GY
18 LG
18 BRN
18 DG
18 P
18 BRN
22 R
22 W
22 V
22 LBL
18 R
18 W
18 V
18 LBL
BRAKE WARNING SWITCH
18 BRN
HARNESS ASSEMBLY CONTROLLER AND MODULATOR
FRONT HARNESS
LEFT REAR HARNESS*
18 P
5 AMP IN LINE FUSE
18 P
20 AMP. FUSE (DIR. SIG., BACK-UP)
FUSE BLOCK
LEFT WHEEL SENSOR
INST. CLUSTER CONNECTOR
FORWARD LAMP HARNESS
DASH HARNESS
T
IGNITION FEED
BRAKE WARNING LAMP
BULK HEAD CONNECTOR
*NOTE: RIGHT AND LEFT REAR HARNESS SHIELDS ARE NOT CONNECTED TO GROUND.

WIRE IDENTIFICATION CHART

SYM.	COLOR	SYM.	COLOR
B	Black	P	Pink
BRN	Brown	PUR	Purple
DBL	Drk. Blue	R	Red
DG	Drk. Green	T	Tan
LBL	Lt. Blue	V	Violet
LG	Lt. Green	W	White
OR	Orange	Y	Yellow
GY	Gray		

Fig. 13 True Track wiring circuit. 1971-74 Toronado

CLAMP
BOLT
SPACER
SPEEDOMETER CABLE
CLAMP
CONNECTOR FROM CONTROLLER

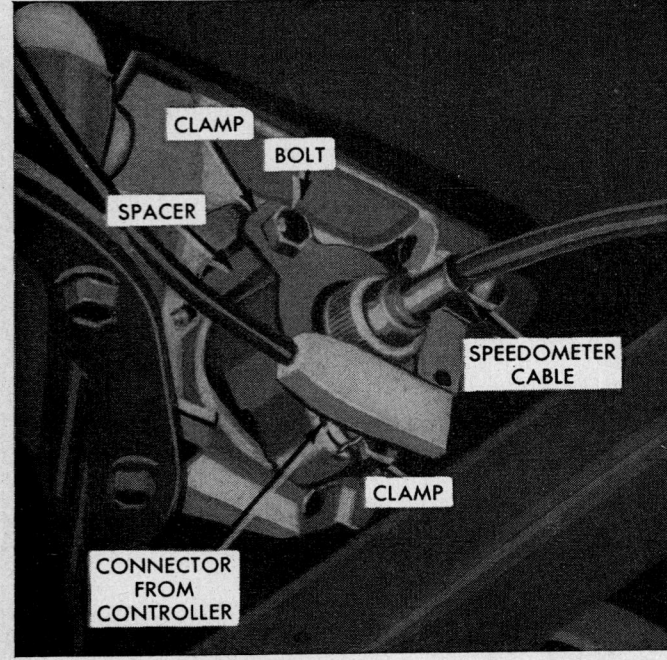

Fig. 15 Transmission mounted speed sensor. 1972-74 Cadillac

WHEEL SENSOR
HUB
FEELER GAGE
WIRING HARNESS CONNECTOR

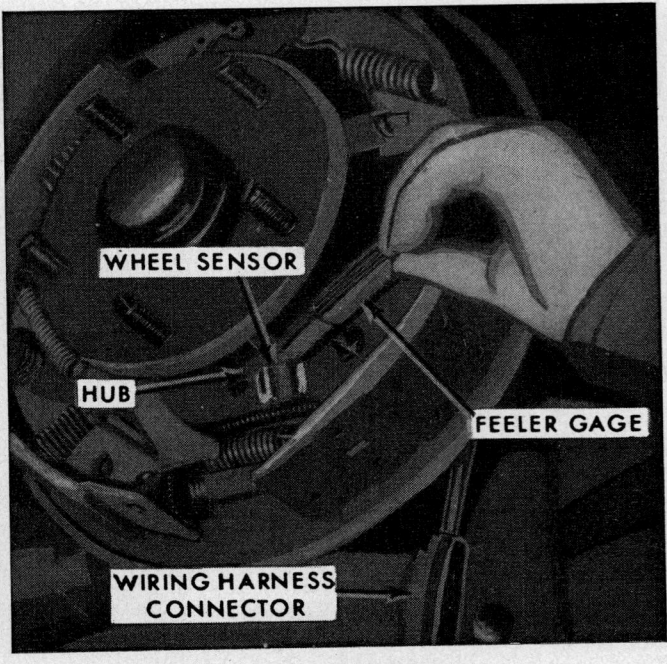

Fig. 18 Adjusting wheel speed sensor. 1971-74 Eldorado and Toronado

NOTE: For the following conditions, it is assumed that the brake lamp circuit operates normally and there are no hydraulic leaks or air trapped in the brake system. All following conditions are with ignition switch ON or engine running.

No Brake Light, System Inoperative, Exercise Cycle OK (Engine Running Or Ignition Switch On):

1. Wheel sensor not being driven due to missing dust cap or sensor quill (Eldorado and Toronado).
2. Transmission sensor seized or not being driven (Cadillac).
3. Incorrect sensor adjustment (Eldorado and Toronado).
4. Both sensor leads shorted to each other (not shorted to ground).
5. Faulty controller.

No Brake Light, System Inoperative, No Exercise Cycle:

1. Loss of ground to controller.
2. Bad connection at controller or modulator.
3. Modulator seized in de-energized position.
4. Solenoid valve seized in de-energized position.
5. Faulty controller.

Brake Light Lights After 2-5 Second Delay, System Inoperative, Exercise Cycle O.K.

1. Speed sensor leads open.
2. Speed sensor leads shorted to ground.
3. Modulator travel switch open.
4. Faulty connection at travel switch.
5. Faulty controller.

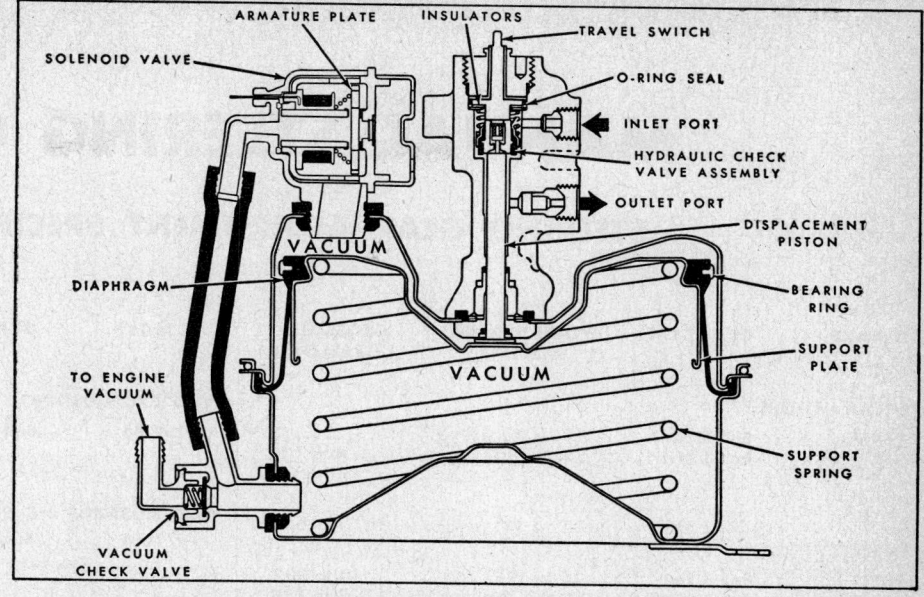

Fig. 16   Modulator assembly during normal braking. G.M. Computerized Skid Control

Brake Light Lights After 2-5 Second Delay, System Inoperative, No Exercise Cycle:

1. Solenoid leads open.
2. Faulty controller.

False Releases While Car Is In Motion:

1. Frayed shield leads causing intermittent short.
2. Sensor drive shaft rubbing in wheel spindle due to improper adjustment (Eldorado and Toronado).

3. Missing or damaged insulators.
4. Sensor damper deteriorated.
5. Bad electrical connections.
6. Faulty controller.

False Releases While Vehicle Is Parked:

1. Bad electrical connections.
2. Faulty controller.

Does Not Cycle Down To 5 MPH During Maximum Braking:

1. Insufficient operating vacuum.
2. Faulty controller.

Brake Light On 2-5 Seconds After High Brake Pressure Is Applied:

1. Defective differential and proportioning valve.

Brake Light Comes On During a Stop, Or When Brake Is Depressed Firmly And Goes Off When Brake Pedal Is Released:

1. Hydraulic fluid leak.
2. Air in brake system.

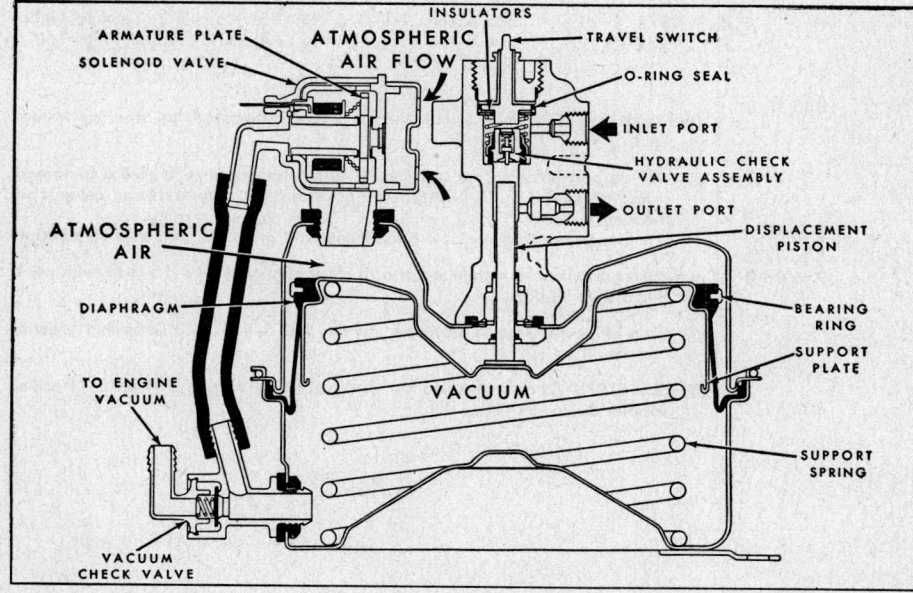

Fig. 17   Modulator assembly during release. G.M. Computerized Skid Control

MANUAL STEERING GEARS

STEERING GEAR ADJUSTMENT SPECIFICATIONS

CAR MAKE	GEAR TYPE	WORM BEARING PRELOAD	CROSS SHAFT PRELOAD
AMERICAN MOTORS			
1969-73	Ball & Nut...........④.....................⑤		
1974	Ball & Nut........5 to 8①.............4 to 10①		
BUICK (EXC. APOLLO)			
1969	Ball & Nut........5 to 9①...........10 to 20①		
1970-72	Ball & Nut........2 to 7①.............7 to 18①		
1973-74	Ball & Nut........5 to 8①.............9 to 16①		
BUICK APOLLO			
1973	Ball & Nut........4 to 6①.............9 to 15①		
1974	Ball & Nut........5 to 8①.............9 to 15①		
CHECKER MOTORS			
1969-71	Ball & Nut........5 to 8①.............9 to 18①		
1972-74	Ball & Nut........4 to 6①.............9 to 15①		
CHEVROLET (EXC. CORVETTE)			
1969-71	Ball & Nut........5 to 8①.............9 to 18①		
1972-74	Ball & Nut........4 to 6①.............9 to 15①		
CHRYSLER			
1969-71	Ball & Nut........1 to 4①.............8 to 11①		
CORVETTE			
1969	Ball & Nut........5 to 8①.............9 to 18①		
1970-71	Ball & Nut........4 to 7①.............8 to 17①		
1972-74	Ball & Nut........4 to 6①.............9 to 15①		
DODGE			
1969-74	Ball & Nut........1 to 4①.............8 to 11①		

CAR MAKE	GEAR TYPE	WORM BEARING PRELOAD	CROSS SHAFT PRELOAD
FORD (EXC. MUSTANG II & PINTO)			
1969-74	Ball & Nut........4 to 5①.............9 to 10①		
FORD MUSTANG II & PINTO			
1971-74	Rack & Pinion...........②.....................③		
MERCURY			
1969-74	Ball & Nut........4 to 5①.............9 to 10①		
OLDSMOBILE			
1969-71	Ball & Nut........4 to 7①.............8 to 17①		
1972-74	Ball & Nut........5 to 8①.............9 to 16①		
PLYMOUTH			
1969-74	Ball & Nut........1 to 4①.............8 to 11①		
PONTIAC			
1969-70	Ball & Nut..........7①.............16①		
1971	Ball & Nut........5 to 8①.............4 to 10①		
1972-74	Ball & Nut........5 to 8①.............9 to 16①		

①—Measured with inch-pound torque wrench attached to steering wheel nut.

②—For support yoke to rack adjustment, add selected shims to give a combined pack thickness of .005-.006 inch greater than gap between cover and housing flange.
For pinion bearing preload adjustment, add one .005 inch shim to pack.

③—Effort required to sustain input shaft rotation should be 7-15 in-lb, with gear filled with lubricant.

④—Exc. 1972-73 Gremlin, Hornet & Javelin, 2 to 6; 1972-73 Gremlin, Hornet & Javelin, 4 to 10.

⑤—Exc. 1972-73 Gremlin, Hornet & Javelin, 12 to 18; 1972-73 Gremlin, Hornet & Javelin, 14 to 18.

Recirculating Ball Worm & Nut Gear

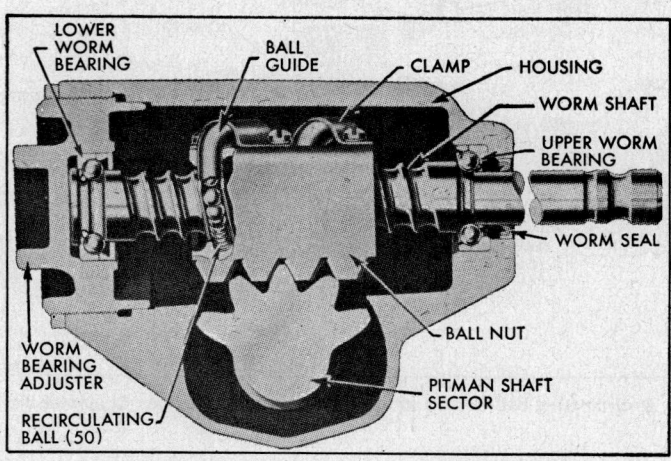

Fig. 1 Recirculating ball-worm and nut steering gear

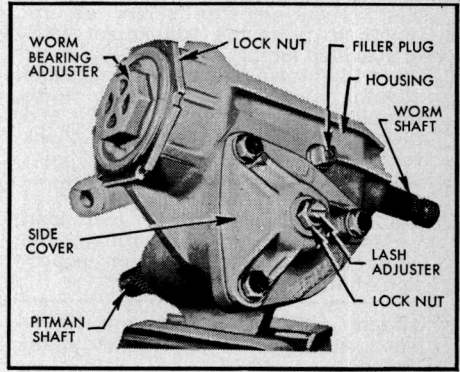

Fig. 2 Steering gear adjustments

DESCRIPTION

As shown in Fig. 1, the worm on the lower end of the steering shaft and the ball nut which is mounted on the worm have mating spiral grooves in which steel balls circulate to provide a low friction drive between worm and nut.

Two sets of balls are used, ranging in number from approximately 20 to 30 to a set, depending upon the size of the steering gear unit. Each set of balls operate independently of the other. The circuit through which each set of balls circulates includes the grooves in the worm and ball nut and a ball return guide attached to the outer surface of the nut.

When the wheel and steering shaft turn to the left, the ball nut is moved downward by the balls which roll between the worm and nut. As the balls reach the outer surface of the nut they enter the return guides which direct them across and down into the ball nut where they enter the circuit again.

When a right turn is made the ball nut moves upward and balls circulate in the reverse direction.

The teeth on the ball nut engage teeth on the sector which is forged integral with the pitman shaft. The teeth on the ball nut are made so that a "high point" or tighter fit exists between the ball nut and pitman shaft sector teeth when the front wheels are in the straight-ahead position. The teeth on the sector are tapered slightly so that a proper lash may be obtained by moving the pitman shaft endwise by means of a lash adjuster screw which extends through the gear housing side cover. The head of the lash adjuster and the selectively fitted shim fit snugly into a T-slot in the end of the pitman shaft so that the screw also controls end play of the shaft. The screw is locked by an external lock nut.

GEAR ADJUSTMENTS

There are two adjustments on the steering gear: worm bearing preload and pitman shaft overcenter preload, Fig. 2. **Important:** Never attempt to adjust the steering gear while it is connected to the steering linkage. The gear must be free of all outside load in order to properly make any steering gear adjustment.

Preliminary

1. Tighten steering gear mounting bolts.
2. Disconnect steering linkage from steering arm or gear.
3. Turn wheel slowly from one extreme to the other.
   Caution: Never turn the wheel hard against the stopping point in the gear as damage to the ball nut assembly may result.
4. Steering wheel should turn freely and smoothly throughout its entire range.
   Note: Roughness indicates faulty internal parts requiring disassembly of gear unit. Hard pull or binding indicates an excessively tight adjustment of the worm bearings, or excessive misalignment of the steering shaft. Any excessive misalignment

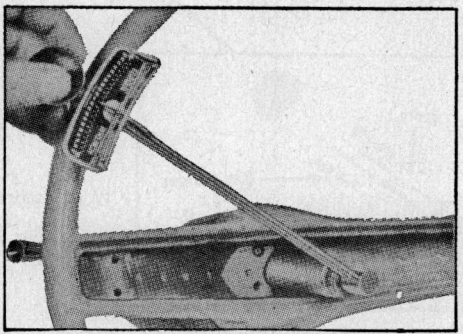

Fig. 3 Checking adjustments with inch-pound torque wrench

must be corrected before the gear can be properly adjusted.

NOTE: Specifications in the Steering Gear Adjustment Specifications chart are given in inch pounds as measured with a torque wrench pulling on steering wheel nut, Fig. 3.

Checking Worm Bearing Preload

1. Turn steering wheel gently in one direction until it stops. This positions gear away from "high point" load.
2. Attach torque wrench and check the torque required to turn the wheel steadily in the range where lash exists between ball nut and pitman shaft sector.
3. If adjustment is not within specified limits, adjust worm bearing preload.

Adjust Worm Bearing Preload

1. Loosen worm bearing adjuster lock nut, using a drift, Fig. 2.
2. Turn bearing adjuster as required to bring the adjustment within specified limits.
3. Tighten lock nut and recheck preload.

Checking Pitman Shaft Over-Center Preload

1. Turn steering wheel from one extreme to the other while counting the total turns, then turn wheel back 1/2 the number of turns. This positions steering gear on "high point" where a preload should exist between ball nut and pitman shaft teeth.
2. Attach torque wrench and check torque or pull required to turn the wheel through the "high point" range.
3. If adjustment is not within the specified limits, adjust as follows:

Adjust Pitman Shaft Overcenter Preload

1. Loosen lock nut and turn pitman shaft lash adjuster screw as required to bring the adjustment within specified limits.
2. After tightening lock nut, rotate steering wheel back and forth through the "high point" and through the entire range to check for tight spots.

NOTE: If lash cannot be removed at the "high point", or if gear load varies greatly and feels rough, the gear should be removed for inspection of internal parts.

3. Attach linkage to steering gear when adjustments have been completed.

STEERING GEAR REPAIRS

Disassembly

1. Clamp steering in a vise with wormshaft in horizontal position.
2. Rotate wormshaft from stop to stop, noting number of turns. Then, turn wormshaft back exactly halfway to center the gear. Loosen wormshaft lock nut.
3. Remove side cover attaching screws, lightly tap end of pitman shaft with a mallet and lift side cover and pitman shaft assembly from housing.

NOTE: If pitman shaft sector does not clear housing opening, rotate wormshaft until sector passes through opening.

4. Remove wormshaft lock nut and adjuster plug assembly, then wormshaft

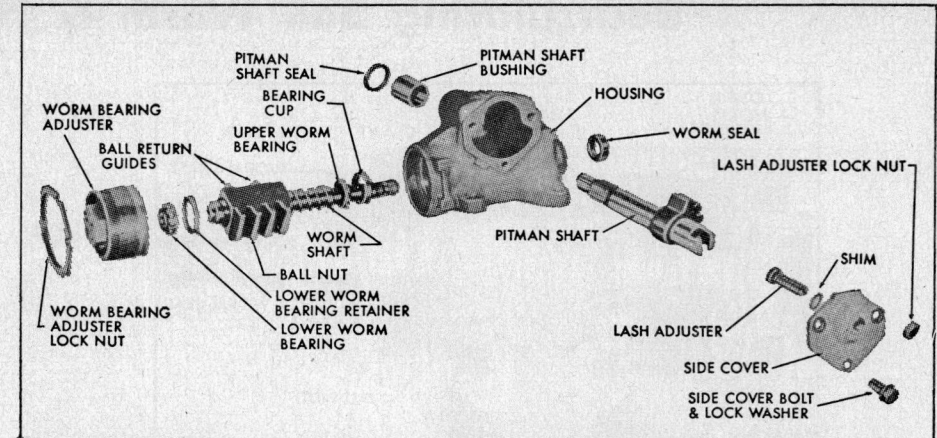

Fig. 4   Recirculating ball-worm and nut gear disassembled, exc. Chevrolet Corvette

and ball nut from housing.
5. On all units except Chevrolet Corvette, remove upper wormshaft bearing from shaft, Fig. 4. Pry lower bearing retainer from adjuster plug and remove bearing.
6. On Chevrolet Corvette, remove lower wormshaft bearing from shaft, Fig. 5.
7. On all units, remove lash adjuster screw lock nut, turn adjuster screw clockwise through side cover, then slide screw and shim from pitman shaft slot.
8. Pry pitman shaft and wormshaft seals from housing.

Inspection of Parts

1. Clean and inspect all ball and roller

bearings and races, including race in housing.
2. Inspect pitman shaft bushings in gear housing and end cover. Replace bushings in housing and replace end cover if bushings are worn excessively.
3. Replace pitman shaft and wormshaft seals to avoid leakage of lubricant.
4. Inspect steering shaft for wear or pits in bearing races, which would require replacement of shaft.
5. Check shaft for straightness.
6. Inspect teeth of ball nut and pitman shaft. If scored or excessively worn it is advisable to replace both parts to insure proper mating of teeth.

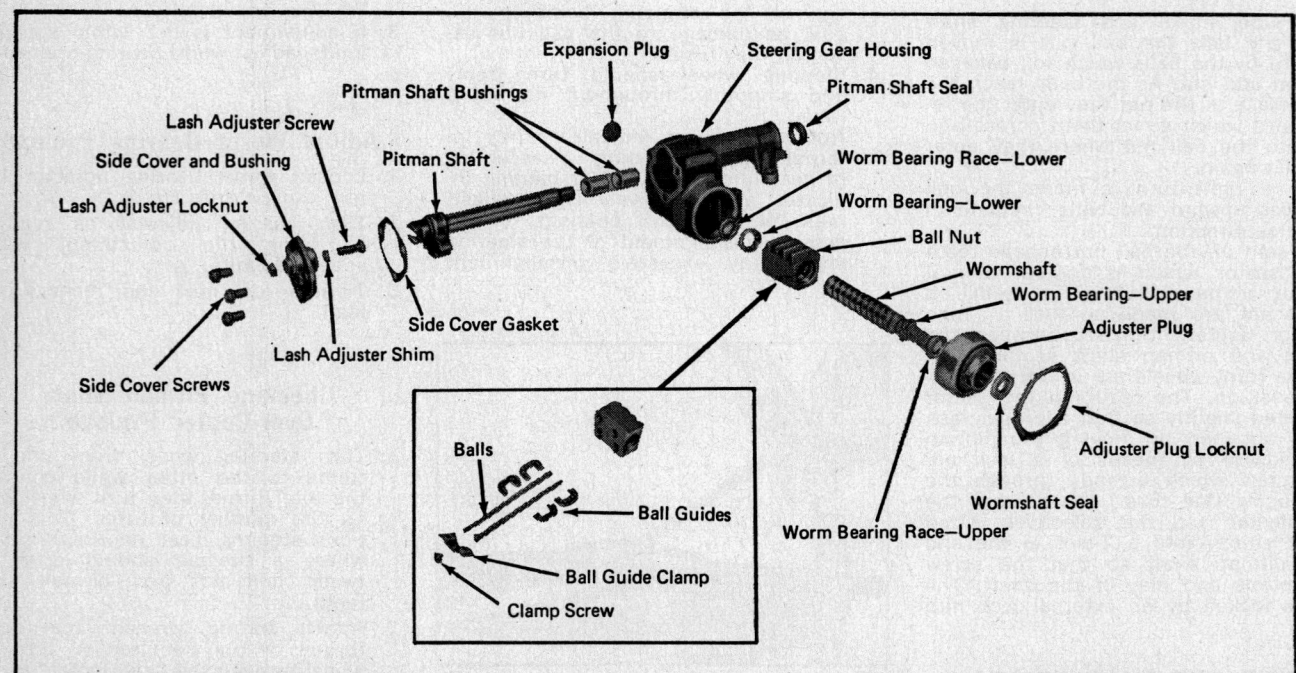

Fig. 5   Recirculating ball-worm and nut gear disassembled. Chevrolet Corvette

7. Check serrations of pitman shaft; if twisted, replace shaft.
8. Check pitman shaft adjuster screw for proper end play with a feeler gauge inserted between screw head and pitman shaft. On all units except Chrysler Corp. models, end play should not exceed .002 inch. On Chrysler Corp. models, end play limit is .004 inch. If end play is greater than specified, selective thickness shims are available in thicknesses of .063, .065, .067 and .069 inch.
9. Inspect steering column jacket for distortion. A ripple or wavy feeling of jacket surface, particularly at lower end, will usually indicate a sprung jacket. Replace jacket if sprung or otherwise damaged.
10. Inspect control shaft bearing in tube of gear housing, and steering shaft upper bearing in control lever housing support. Replace worn or damaged parts.

Ball Nut Servicing

NOTE: Servicing of the ball nut assembly is not necessary provided no binding or tightness is noted when rotated on the wormshaft.

1. Remove ball guide clamp and ball guides.
2. Turn ball nut upside down and rock wormshaft so balls drop from nut, into a clean container.

3. Check balls for signs of pitting or other defects. Inspect ball guides at the ends where the balls are deflected or picked up from the helical path.
4. Place ball nut on wormshaft so shallow end of nut teeth faces toward the left as viewed from wormshaft upper end and ball guide holes facing upward.
5. On all units except Chevrolet Corvette:
   a. Place ball guide halves together and insert guides into upper and lower circuits.
   b. Install exactly one half the total number of balls into one circuit while rotating wormshaft away from circuit. Fill remaining circuit in same manner.
6. On Chevrolet Corvette:
   a. Count out exactly one half total number of balls and place in separate container.
   b. Fill one circuit in ball nut while rotating wormshaft away from hole. With one half of a ball guide with groove facing upward, place remaining balls from circuit in groove. Place ball guide halves together and plug open ends with a suitable grease, then push guides into guide holes. Ball guides may be gently tapped into place, if necessary.
7. On all units, install ball guide clamp. Rotate wormshaft to check proper installation of balls.

Reassembly

NOTE: Lubricate all seals, bushings, bearings and gears with recommended lubricant prior to installation.

1. On all units except Chevrolet Corvette, place upper bearing over wormshaft and insert wormshaft assembly into housing, Fig. 4. Install bearing into wormshaft adjuster race and, guiding bearing onto wormshaft end, install adjuster and tighten until almost all lash is removed from wormshaft, then install lock nut.
2. On Chevrolet Corvette, place wormshaft lower bearing into housing race, Fig. 5. Install upper bearing and adjuster plug assembly onto wormshaft and insert assembly into housing, guiding wormshaft into lower bearing.
3. On all units, install lash adjuster and shim into pitman shaft slotted end.
4. Ensure ball nut is in center of travel and insert pitman shaft into housing with center tooth on sector meshing with center groove on ball nut.
5. Fill gear housing with recommended lubricant. Then, thread side cover onto lash adjuster screw using a screwdriver to turn screw counterclockwise through threaded opening in side cover until screw bottoms. Back off screw one half turn and install lock nut and cover retaining screws.

Rack & Pinion

DESCRIPTION

A pinion gear, machined on the input shaft, engages the rack and rotation of the input shaft pinion causes the rack to move laterally. On 1971 and early 1972 Pinto models, the gear input shaft is connected to the steering shaft by a flexible cable. On late 1972 Pinto, 1973-74 Pinto and 1974 Mustang II models, the gear input shaft is connected to the steering shaft by a U-joint shaft and flexible coupling. Tie rods are attached to each end of the rack joint, allowing the tie rods to move with the action of the front suspension.

The gears is sealed at both ends with rubber bellows and is filled with 5 oz. of lubricant for 1971-73 units or 7 oz. on 1974 units at initial assembly. Checking or refilling is not necessary unless fluid leakage has occurred or repair is necessary.

Couplings connecting tie rods are retained on the rack and pinned and cannot be disassembled. Replacement of inner rods, rack housing or upper pinion bearing, requires installation of a new steering gear assembly.

With the steering gear in proper adjustment and front suspension and linkage in good condition, there should be no more than 3/8 inch free play measured at the rim of the steering wheel.

When front wheels are off the ground, do not turn steering wheel quickly or forcefully from stop to stop as this will build-up

hydraulic pressure within the gear, which in turn could damage or force off the bellows.

When turning steering wheel from stop to stop with vehicle stationary, there should be no knock produced by the steering gear. If a knock is produced, adjustment of rack preload and pinion bearing should be checked. A faint knock produced while driving on an extremely rough road is acceptable.

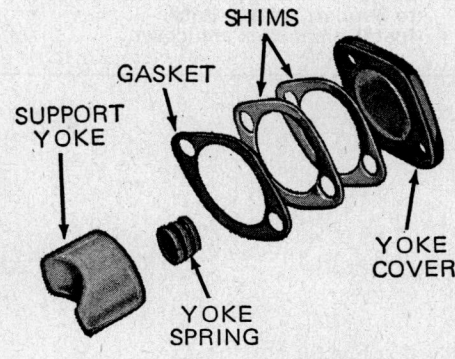

Fig. 6   Support yoke arrangement

GEAR ADJUSTMENTS

There are two adjustments on the steering gear: support yoke to rack fit and pinion bearing preload. The steering gear must be removed from vehicle to perform both adjustments.

Support Yoke To Rack Adjustment

1. Clean exterior of steering gear.
2. Place steering gear in a soft jawed vise with yoke cover up. Use mounting pad to hold gear.
3. Remove yoke cover, gasket, shims and yoke spring, Fig. 6.
4. Clean housing and flange area.
5. Omitting gasket, shims and spring, reinstall yoke and cover.
6. Tighten cover bolts until cover just touches yoke.
7. Measure gap between cover and housing flange. With gasket included add selected shims (3F518) to give a combined pack thickness of .005-.006 inch greater than measured gap.
8. Remove cover and install gasket, selected shims, spring and cover.
9. Apply sealant (ESW-M46-132-A) Permatex No. 3 to cover bolt threads and torque bolts to 15-20 ft-lbs.
10. Check steering gear for smooth operation with no binding or slackness.

Pinion Bearing Preload Adjustment

1. Clean exterior of steering gear.

2. Place steering gear in a soft jawed vise with pinion cover up. Use mounting pads to hold gear.
3. Loosen yoke cover bolts to relieve spring tension on rack.
4. Remove pinion cover and clean flange area.
5. Remove gasket and shims, Fig. 7.
6. Install a new gasket and fit shims until shim pack is flush with gasket. Check with a straight edge using light pressure.
7. Assemble shim pack, with the thinnest selected shim first followed by the .093 inch shim and cover.
8. Install one .005 inch shim to preload bearings. The thickest shim (.093 inch) should be next to cover.
9. Apply sealant (ESW-M46-732-A) Permatex No. 3 to bolt threads and torque pinion bearing cover bolts and support yoke cover bolts to 15-20 ft-lbs.

STEERING GEAR REPAIRS

Bellows Seal (Either Side) Replace

Disassembly

1. Place steering gear in a soft jawed vise. Use mounting pads to hold gear.
2. Loosen both bellows retaining clips and remove bellows.
3. Keep gear body below level of bellows to avoid spilling the lubricant. Empty lubricant into suitable container.
4. With gear in a vertical position, move rack back and forth from stop to stop several times to remove remaining lubricant.

Assembly

1. Install steering gear in a soft jawed vise with end where bellows is to be installed on in an upright position.
2. Move rack so that the upper rod is fully extended.
3. Add 5 ounces of D2AZ-19580-B gear lubricant under bellows at inner tie rod joint into gear housing. Move rack back and forth to distribute the lubricant.

NOTE: Do not add more lubricant than specified, as pressurization of the gear could occur and could cause bellows to burst or be forced loose.

4. Using lubricant D2AZ-19580-B, lubricate tie rod in area of bellows contact.
5. Install bellows clips. To avoid interference with components of the vehicle,

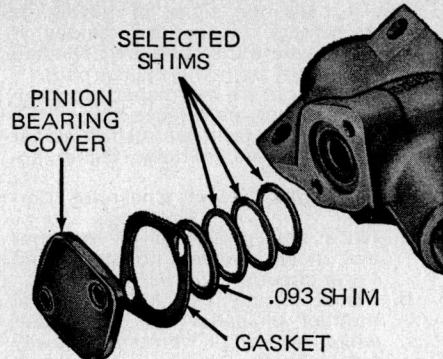

Fig. 7 Pinion bearing cover and shim arrangement

place bellows clips in the same plane as the pinion shaft and screw ends pointing upward.
6. Install screw end caps.

Input Shaft Seal

1. Clean input shaft and seal area. Use care not to scratch or damage pinion shaft.
2. Pry pinion seal from its bore and discard.
3. Using lubricant C1AZ-1959-B, lubricate seal and install seal over shaft.
4. Use a piece of tubing to engage outer flange of seal and press or tap seal into its bore until flange is flush with shoulder of bore.

NOTE: If outer edge of seal is not engaged at assembly, damage to the seal will result.

Rack Support Yoke, Spring, Gasket, Shims and Cover

Disassembly

1. Clean exterior of steering gear.
2. Place steering gear in a soft jawed vise with yoke cover up.
3. Remove yoke cover, shims, gasket and yoke spring.
4. Discard gasket.

Assembly

1. Clean cover and cover flange areas.
2. Assemble yoke and spring.
3. Install a new gasket. If yoke to rack spring tension adjustment is needed or new shims are to be installed, refer to Support Yoke to Rack.
4. Install shim pack and cover.

5. Apply sealant (ESW-M46-132-A) Permatex No. 3 to cover bolt threads and torque bolts to 15-20 ft-lbs.

Pinion Shaft Cover, Gasket, Shims, Lower Bearing, Shaft and Spacer

Disassembly

1. Clean exterior of steering gear.
2. Place gear in a soft jawed vise.
3. Loosen rack support cover bolts to relieve yoke spring tension on rack.
4. Move rack to either lock and note position of flat on input shaft.

NOTE: It is important that the flat be aligned in this position during assembly. If the pinion is not assembled in the same position, the steering wheel will not be in the straight position.

5. Remove pinion cover, shims and gasket. Discard gasket.
6. Remove pinion lower bearing and pinion shaft.
7. Remove spacer.
8. Inspect all parts for damage and replace as required.

Assembly

1. Clean pinion shaft cover flange. Clean all parts to be assembled in a suitable solvent.
2. Using lubricant D2AZ-19580-B, lubricate spacer, pinion shaft and bearing. Lubricate the inside diameter of the pinion seal with chassis lubricant.
3. Place steering gear in a soft jawed vise with pinion shaft cover flange up.
4. Assemble spacer into place against bearing face.
5. Move rack to one lock and assemble pinion. The flat on shaft must be in same position as noted before disassembly.
6. Assemble bearing, aligning shaft with inside diameter of bearing by rotating shaft and applying side pressure. Tap bearing into its bore until it is recessed below shoulder of bore.

NOTE: If bearing preload needs adjustment or a new shim pack is to be installed, refer to "Pinion Bearing Preload Adjustment" procedure.

7. Assemble shim pack with thinnest shim(s) first and the .093 inch next to the cover.
8. Install new gasket.
9. Apply sealant (ESW-M46-132-A) Permatex No. 3 to cover bolt threads and torque pinion bearing cover bolts and support yoke cover bolts to 15-20 ft-lbs.

OVERDRIVE

See Trouble Shooting Chapter For Diagnosis Procedure On These Units

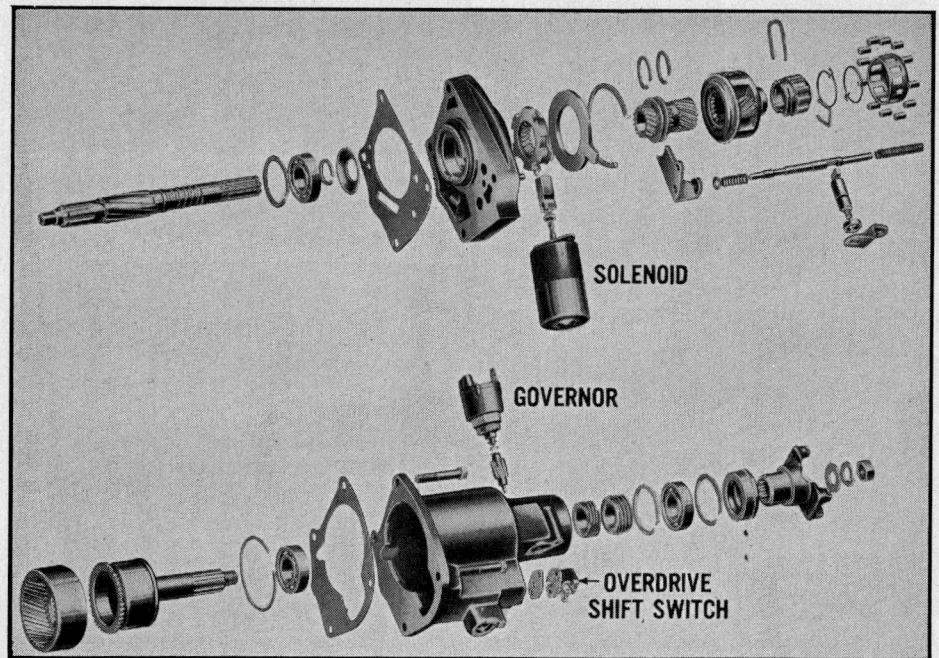

SOLENOID

GOVERNOR

OVERDRIVE SHIFT SWITCH

Fig. 2 Second version of full-electric overdrive with centrifugal governor. This unit is similar to the first version except the design of the second version is more compact. Some models do not use the shift (lockout) switch

Overdrive units are essentially automatic two-speed planetary transmissions attached to the rear of conventional three-speed transmissions. As shown in Fig. 1, the heart of the over-drive is the planetary unit consisting of sun gear, planetary pinions and internal (ring) gear. In overdrive, the pinions are connected to the mainshaft, and revolve around the sun gear which holds against rotation. The internal gear, connected to the tailshaft, is thus forced to rotate at a speed greater than the mainshaft. The engagement of the gearset is controlled by coupling the internal gear to the tail shaft, or holding the sun gear stationary, or by a combination of the two methods.

By following the procedure shown pictorially in Figs. 3 through 12, no difficulty should be experienced in servicing these units.

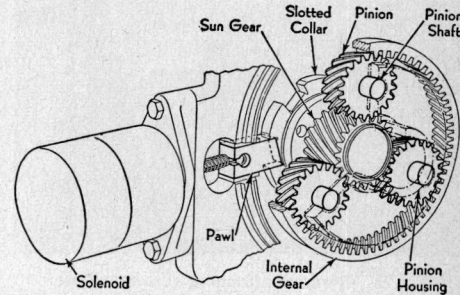

Sun Gear   Slotted Collar   Pinion   Pinion Shaft

Pawl

Solenoid   Internal Gear   Pinion Housing

Fig. 1 Through the planetary unit shown, the overdrive provides a higher gear ratio, and when in operation, engine speed is approximately 30 per cent slower than when operating in conventional high gear

Fig. 3 Remove companion flange and governor. Also lockout switch if so equipped

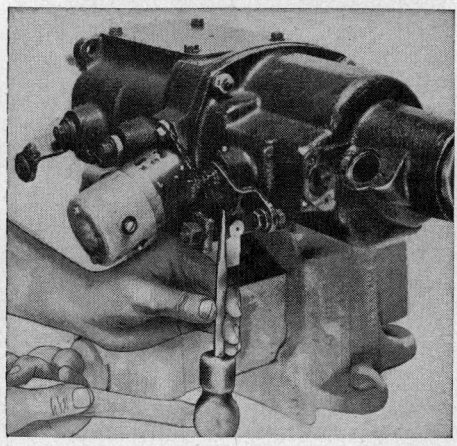

Fig. 4 After driving out locating pin, pull shift shaft as far as possible to disengage operating cam from shift rail. Remove overdrive housing. Tap end of shaft to prevent its coming off with housing and spilling free wheel rollers. Parts inside housing may then be removed.

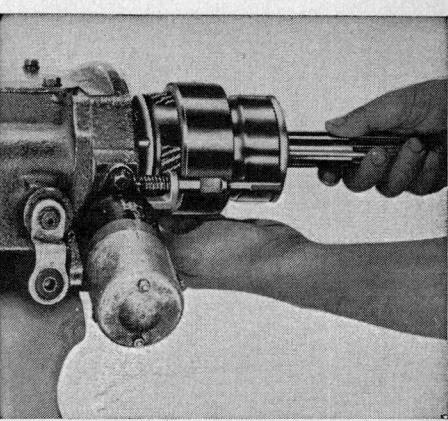

Fig. 5 Hold the adapter plate to the transmission case with one screw and remove the overdrive shaft, catching the free wheel rollers as shown. Removing snap ring permits ring gear to be taken off shaft.

Fig. 6   Remove retaining clip and take off free wheel unit and pinion cage

Fig. 7   Separate pinion cage from free wheel unit by removing retaining clip

Fig. 8   Remove overdrive sun gear and shift rail

Fig. 9   Remove attaching screws, rotate solenoid ¼ turn and take off

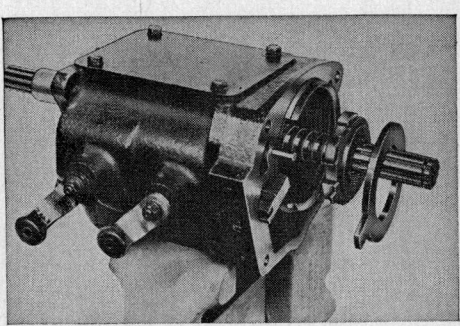

Fig. 10   After releasing snap ring from adapter plate, remove sun gear cover plate, blocker and solenoid pawl

Fig. 11   At this point, if repairs are to be made on the transmission, remove the mainshaft, adapter plate, gears and synchronizer as a unit

Fig. 12   Reverse the order of disassembly to assemble the unit. After inserting the pawl with the notched side up as shown, install blocker assembly and cover plate, being sure blocker ring and pawl are properly positioned. Then install large snap ring in adapter plate

THREE SPEED MANUAL SHIFT TRANSMISSIONS

See Car Chapters for procedures on removing the transmission and adjusting the gearshift linkage

APPLICATION INDEX

	Type No.	Page
AMERICAN MOTORS		
1969-72 Heavy Duty	7	2-190
1969-74 Exc. Heavy Duty	1	2-178
1974 Heavy Duty	6	2-187
BUICK—Seniors		
1969-71 Heavy Duty	6	2-187
1969-71 Exc. Heavy Duty	8	2-192
BUICK—Intermediates		
1969 Floor Shift	6	2-187
1969-74 Exc. Heavy Duty	8	2-192
1970 Heavy Duty	2	2-179
CAMARO		
1969-74 (Exc. Heavy Duty)	8	2-192
1969-74 Heavy Duty	2	2-179
CHEVELLE & MONTE CARLO		
1969-74 (Exc. Heavy Duty)	8	2-192
1969-74 Heavy Duty	2	2-179
CHEVROLET		
1969-73 Exc. Heavy Duty	8	2-192
1969-73 Heavy Duty	2	2-179
CHEVROLET VEGA		
1971-72	9	2-194
1973-74	8	2-192
CHEVY NOVA		
1969-74 Exc. Heavy Duty	8	2-192
1969-74 Heavy Duty	2	2-179

	Type No.	Page
CHRYSLER		
1969	4	2-184
1970-71	3	2-182
COMET & MONTEGO		
1969-74	6	2-187
CORVETTE		
1969 Exc. V8-396	8	2-192
1969 Heavy Duty	2	2-179
COUGAR		
1969-72	6	2-187
DODGE DART		
1969-74 (Exc. Heavy Duty)	5	2-184
1970-74 Heavy Duty	3	2-182
DODGE		
1969-74 (Exc. Heavy Duty)	5	2-184
1969	4	2-184
1970-74 Heavy Duty	3	2-182
FAIRLANE & TORINO		
1969-74	6	2-187
FALCON & MAVERICK		
1969-74	6	2-187
FORD		
1969-72	6	2-187

	Type No.	Page
MERCURY		
1969-71	6	2-187
MUSTANG		
1969-73	6	2-187
OLDSMOBILE—Seniors		
1969-71	6	2-187
OLDS—Intermediates		
1969 Floor Shift	6	2-187
1969-74	8	2-192
1970-72	2	2-179
PLYMOUTH		
1969-74 (Exc. Heavy Duty)	5	2-184
1969 Heavy Duty Unit	4	2-184
1970-74 Heavy Duty	3	2-182
PONTIAC—Seniors		
1969-71	6	2-187
1971 Grand Prix	2	2-179
PONTIAC—Intermediates		
1969-74 Exc. Heavy Duty	8	2-192
1969 Heavy Duty	6	2-187
1970-74 Heavy Duty	2	2-179
VALIANT		
1969-74 (Exc. Heavy Duty)	5	2-184
1970-74 Heavy Duty	3	2-182

Type One

DISASSEMBLE TRANS.

1. Remove transmission cover and shift levers.
2. Remove front retainer and gasket and front bearing snap rings.
3. Align notch in clutch shaft with 3rd speed gear and use suitable puller to remove clutch shaft using care not to lose rollers.
4. Remove front bearing with puller.
5. Remove extension case and remove snap rings that retain speedometer drive gear.
6. Remove speedometer gear using care not to lose drive ball.
7. Remove rear bearing snap rings and remove rear bearing with a puller.
8. Move mainshaft to side and remove shift forks.
9. Place front synchronizer in 2nd speed position and remove mainshaft by tilting front of shaft up and lifting through top of case, Fig. 3.
10. If equipped, remove transmission controlled spark switch assembly.
11. Use a punch to remove roll pins from shift shafts and push shafts into case. Detent assembly may now be removed from case.
12. Using a brass drift drive reverse idler gear shaft out of rear of case and remove idler gear. Do not lose rollers.
13. To retain rollers in countershaft gear, use a dummy shaft to drive countershaft out of rear of case.
14. After disassembling mainshaft carefully inspect all bearings and gear.

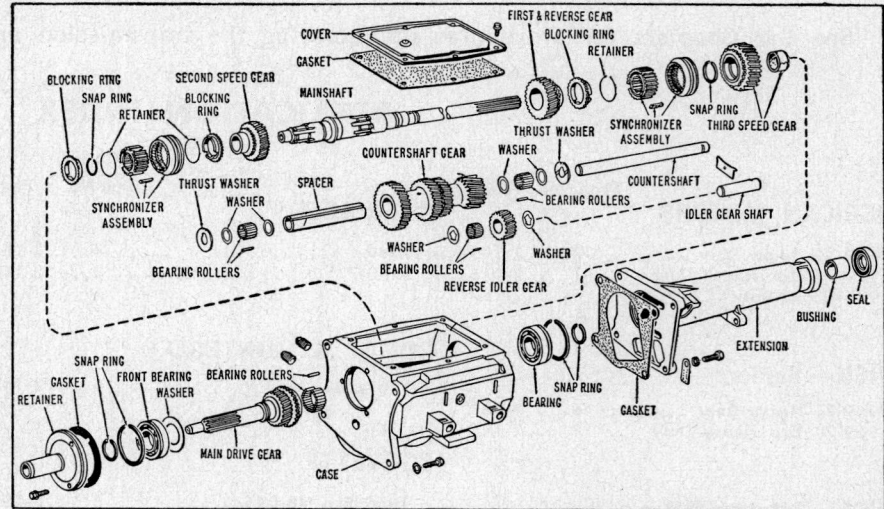

Fig. 1   Type 1 fully synchronized transmission exploded

Fig. 3   Removing mainshaft

REASSEMBLE TRANS.

Mainshaft Assemble

1. Place low speed gear and friction ring on shaft with friction ring hub facing toward rear of shaft.
2. Insert low speed synchro-gear into synchro-collar with deep end of gear facing the low speed gear.

NOTE: Synchro-plates and retainer ring are installed with large end of plates facing toward groove in synchro-hub.

3. Place synchro-clutch assembly on shaft with groove in synchro-collar facing toward low speed gear and

Fig. 2   Removing clutch shaft with puller

Fig. 4   Installing mainshaft with Pilot End Support J-22994

install low speed synchro-clutch snap ring.

NOTE: Snap rings are available in selective thicknesses. Clearance between first gear and collar on mainshaft must be .003-.012 inch.

4. Place second speed gear and friction ring on front of shaft with gear hub and friction ring facing toward front of shaft.
5. Install second speed synchro-gear into synchro-collar with deep end of gear facing toward rear of shaft.
6. Position synchro-clutch assembly with one synchro-plate in 12 o'clock position. Place either tang of retainer ring on synchro-plate at 12 o'clock position and install ring, feeding it in a clockwise direction. Install retainer ring on opposite side of assembly in same manner.
7. Place second speed synchro assembly on shaft with deep end facing toward rear of shaft and install second gear snap ring.

NOTE: Snap rings are available in selective thicknesses. Clearance between second gear and collar must be .003-.018 inch.

8. Install reverse gear onto mainshaft.

Countergear

1. Coat bore at each end of counter gear with grease to hold rollers in place.
2. Install dummy shaft in countergear and install spacer, washers and rollers.
3. Place countergear in transmission case and position thrust washers at each end so tabs align with slots in case.
4. Use a plastic mallet to install countershaft.

Reverse Idler Gear

1. Coat bore of idler gear with grease to retain rollers.
2. Install idler gear in case and position thrust washers.
3. Use plastic mallet to install idler gear shaft.

Shifter Shafts

1. Partially install shifter shafts in transmission case.
2. Align detent assembly with shifter shafts and case stud.
3. Push shift detent assembly and shift shafts into place and install roll pins.
4. If equipped, install transmission controlled spark switch.

Mainshaft Installation

1. Place front synchronizer in 2nd speed position and place mainshaft in case.
2. Move mainshaft to side and install shift forks by pulling detent lever up and placing forks in the shifting assembly.
3. Position mainshaft assembly in center of case and install Pilot End Support J-22994, Fig. 4.
4. Place rear bearing on mainshaft and drive bearing into position and install snap ring.
5. Install speedometer gear and snap ring.

Final Assembly

1. Install rollers in clutch shaft using grease to retain them.
2. Slide clutch shaft into position through front of case.
3. Install front bearing, snap rings, gasket and retainer.
4. Replace seal if necessary and install extension housing, shift levers and case cover.
5. Fill transmission with lubricant and check operation.

Type Two

DISASSEMBLE TRANS.
Case Components

1. Remove side cover assembly, gasket and shift forks.
2. Remove clutch gear retainer and gasket.
3. Remove clutch gear bearing to stem snap ring, then slide bearing off over clutch gear stem. The clutch gear bearing is a slip fit on the gear and into the case bore.
4. Remove rear extension to case bolts.
5. Rotate extension to left until groove in extension housing flange lines up with the reverse idler shaft. Drive reverse idler shaft out of gear and case, Fig. 2.
6. Remove entire clutch gear, mainshaft and extension assembly through case rear opening. Remove reverse idler gear from case.

Mainshaft Disassembly

1. Remove clutch gear from mainshaft, Fig. 3.
2. Expand extension snap ring and tap end of mainshaft to remove extension, Fig. 4.
3. Depress speedometer gear retaining clip and slide gear from mainshaft.
4. Remove rear bearing snap ring, support Reverse gear and press on rear of mainshaft to remove Reverse gear, thrust washer and rear bearing.
5. Remove 1st and Reverse sliding clutch hub snap ring from mainshaft.

6. Support 1st gear and press on rear of mainshaft to remove the clutch assembly, blocker ring and 1st gear.
7. Remove 2nd and 3rd speed sliding clutch hub snap ring.
8. Support 2nd gear and press on front of mainshaft to remove clutch assembly, 2nd speed blocker ring and 2nd speed gear.

Synchronizer Clutch Keys & Springs

NOTE: Clutch hubs and sleeves are a selected assembly and should be kept together as originally assembled, but the keys and springs may be replaced separately.

Before disassembling synchronizers, mark hub and sleeve so they can be matched upon reassembly.

Place the keys and springs in position so all three keys are engaged by both springs. The tanged end of each spring should be installed into different key cavities on either side. Slide sleeve onto hub, aligning marks made before disassembly.

NOTE: A groove around the outside of the hub identifies the end that must be opposite the fork slot in the sleeve.

Mainshaft Reassemble

With front of mainshaft up:

1. Install 2nd speed gear with clutching teeth upward; the rear face of the gear will butt against the shoulder on the shaft.
2. Install blocker ring with teeth downward over gear. All three blocker rings used in this unit are identical.
3. Install 2nd and 3rd synchronizer assembly with fork slot downward and press onto splines until it bottoms. Install snap ring.

NOTE: Be sure the notches of the blocker ring align with the keys of the synchronizer assembly.

With rear of mainshaft up:
4. Install 1st speed gear with clutching teeth upward. Install a blocker ring with teeth downward over synchronizer surface of the gear.
5. Install 1st and Reverse synchronizer assembly with fork slot up.

NOTE: Be sure the notches of the blocker ring align with the keys of the synchronizer assembly and that both synchronizer sleeves face the front of the mainshaft.

6. Install snap ring.
7. Install Reverse gear with clutching teeth downward. Install steel thrust washer.
8. Press rear bearing onto mainshaft with snap ring slot downward. Install snap ring.
9. Install speedometer drive gear and retaining clip.

REASSEMBLE TRANS.

1. Load a double row of roller bearings and a thrust washer at each end of the countergear. Use heavy grease to hold them in place.
2. Place countergear through case rear opening with tanged thrust washer (tang away from gear) at each end and install countergear shaft and woodruff key from rear of case.

   NOTE: Be sure countershaft picks up both thrust washers and that the tangs are aligned with their notches in the case.

3. Position reverse idler gear in case but do not install shaft.
4. Install mainshaft assembly into rear extension housing.
5. Load roller bearings into clutch gear bore, install blocker ring onto clutch gear and install clutch gear assembly onto mainshaft.

   NOTE: Be sure notches in blocker ring align with keys in synchronizer assembly.

6. Using new gasket, install the mainshaft assembly through the rear of the case. Be sure the clutch gear engages the teeth of the countergear anti-lash plate and that the oil slinger is in place on the clutch gear.
7. Rotate extension housing and install reverse idler shaft and woodruff key. Install extension bolts.
8. Install front bearing on clutch gear stem, install snap ring and bearing retainer.
9. With synchronizers in Neutral, install cover assembly. Be sure forks align with their synchronizer sleeve grooves.

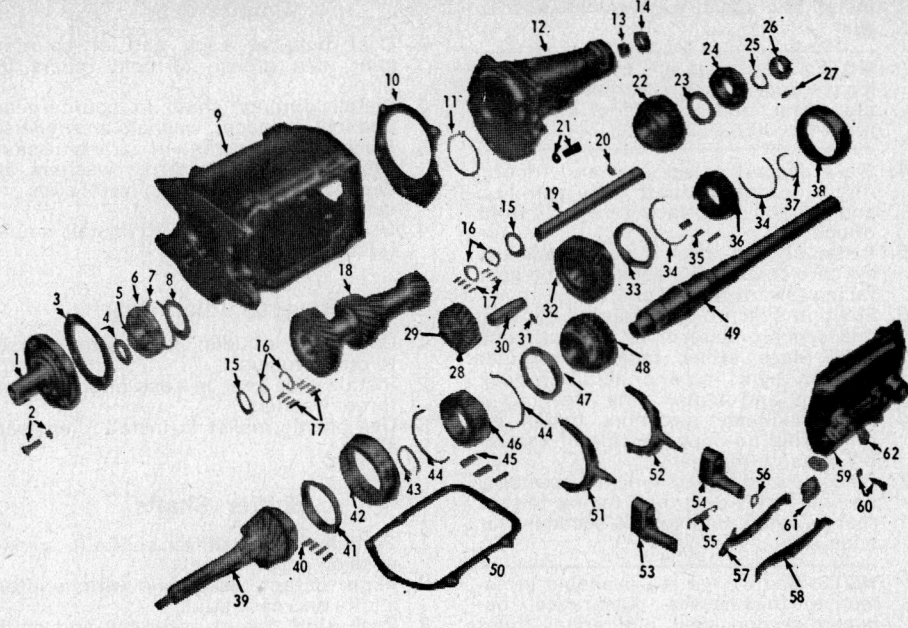

1. Bearing Retainer	18. Countergear	35. Synchronizer Keys
2. Bolt and Lock Washer	19. Countershaft	36. 1st and Reverse Synchronizer Hub Assembly
3. Gasket	20. Woodruff Key	
4. Oil Seal	21. Bolt (Extension-to-Case)	37. Snap Ring
5. Snap Ring (Bearing-to-Main Drive Gear)	22. Reverse Gear	38. 1st and Reverse Synchronizer Collar
	23. Thrust Washer	39. Main Drive Gear
6. Main Drive Gear Bearing	24. Rear Bearing	40. Pilot Bearings
	25. Snap Ring	41. 3rd Speed Blocker Ring
7. Snap Ring Bearing	26. Speedometer Drive Gear	
8. Oil Slinger		42. 2nd and 3rd Synchronizer Collar
9. Case	27. Retainer Clip	
10. Gasket	28. Reverse Idler Gear	43. Snap Ring
11. Snap Ring (Rear Bearing-to-Extension)	29. Reverse Idler Bushing	44. Synchronizer Key Spring
	30. Reverse Idler Shaft	45. Synchronizer Keys
12. Extension	31. Woodruff Key	46. 2nd and 3rd Synchronizer Hub
13. Extension Bushing	32. 1st Speed Gear	
14. Oil Seal	33. 1st Speed Blocker Ring	47. 2nd Speed Blocker Ring
15. Thrust Washer		48. 2nd Speed Gear
16. Bearing Washer	34. Synchronizer Key Spring	49. Mainshaft
17. Needle Bearings		

50. Gasket	
51. 2nd and 3rd Shifter Fork	
52. 1st and Reverse Shifter Fork	
53. 2-3 Shifter Shaft Assembly	
54. 1st and Reverse Shifter Shaft Assembly	
55. Spring	
56. O-Ring Seal	
57. 1st and Reverse Detent Cam	
58. 2nd and 3rd Detent Cam	
59. Side Cover	
60. Bolt and Lock Washer	
61. TCS Switch and Gasket	
62. Lip Seal	

Fig. 1 Type three fully synchronized transmission. Exploded view

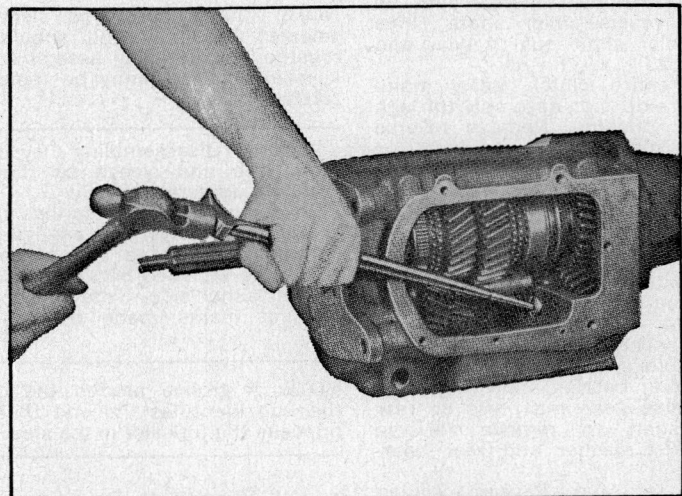

Fig. 2 Removing reverse idler shaft

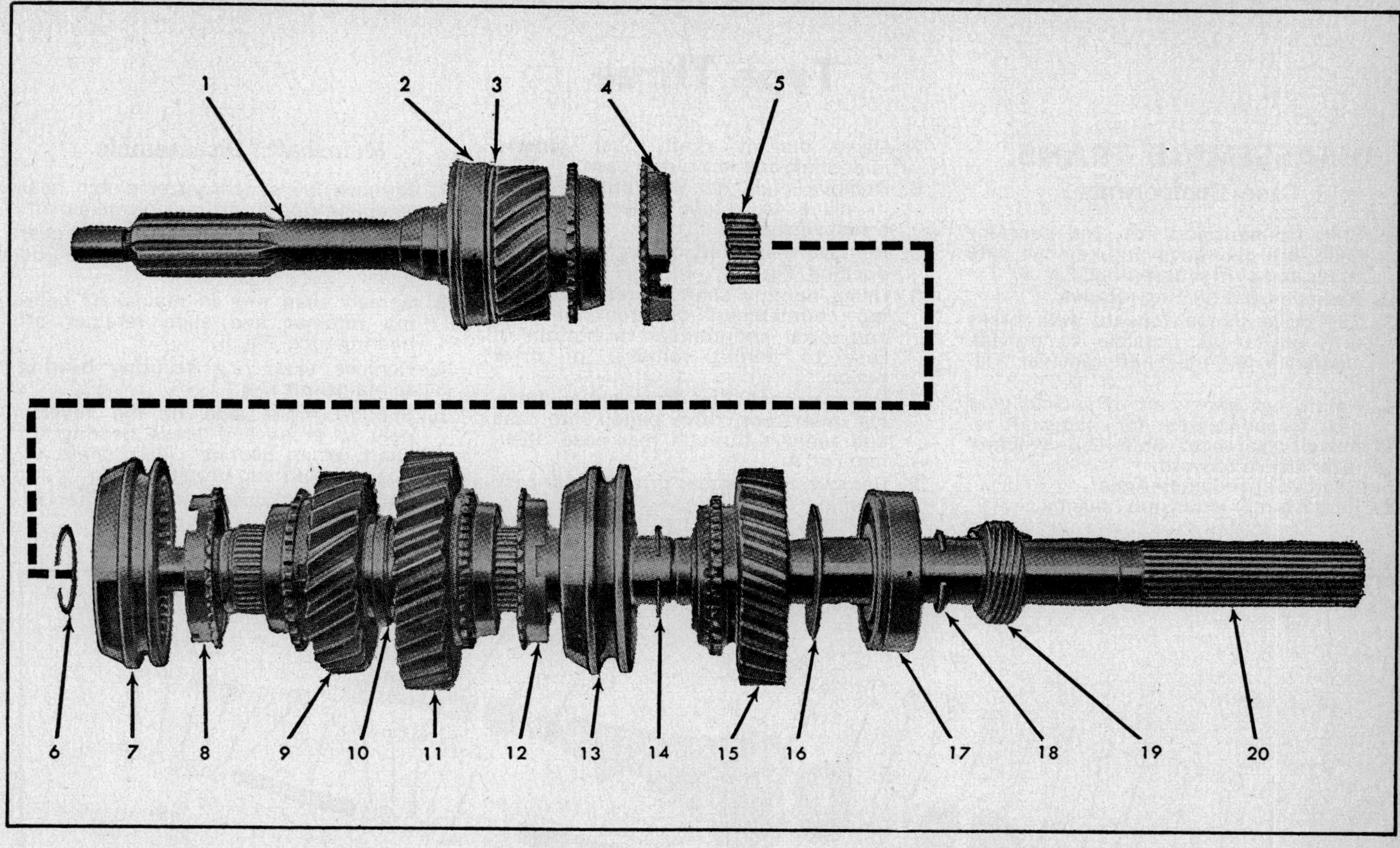

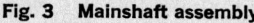

1. Clutch Gear
2. Clutch Gear Bearing
3. Oil Slinger
4. 3rd Speed Blocker Ring
5. Mainshaft Pilot Bearings (16)
6. Snap Ring
7. 2-3 Synchronizer Assembly
8. 2nd Speed Blocker Ring
9. 2nd Speed Gear
10. Shoulder (Part of Mainshaft)
11. 1st Speed Gear
12. 1st Speed Blocker Ring
13. 1st Speed Synchronizer Assembly
14. Snap Ring
15. Reverse Gear
16. Reverse Gear Thrust Washer
17. Rear Bearing
18. Snap Ring
19. Speedo Drive Gear
20. Mainshaft

Fig. 3   Mainshaft assembly

Fig. 4   Removing extension housing snap ring

Type Three

DISASSEMBLE TRANS.
Case Components

1. Shift transmission into 2nd gear for shift fork clearance and remove side cover and shifter assembly, Fig. 1.
2. Remove front bearing retainer.
3. Tap drive pinion forward with brass drift as far as possible to provide clearance for mainshaft removal, Fig. 2.
4. Rotate cut away part of second gear next to countergear for mainshaft removal clearance. Shift 2-3 synchronizer sleeve forward.
5. Remove speedometer gear.
6. Remove rear extension housing.

7. Using dummy shaft, push reverse idler shaft and key out of case.
8. Remove idler gear with dummy shaft in place to retain rollers. Remove thrust washers.
9. Remove mainshaft through rear case opening, Fig. 3.
10. Using dummy shaft to retain rollers, tap countershaft out rear of case and lower countergear to bottom of case to permit removal of drive pinion.
11. Remove snap ring from pinion bearing outer race, drive pinion into case and remove through rear case opening, Fig. 4.
12. Remove countergear through rear case opening.

Mainshaft, Disassemble

1. Remove 2-3 synchronizer clutch gear retaining ring from front of mainshaft.
2. Slide 2-3 synchronizer and 2nd gear stop ring off of shaft. Remove 2nd gear.
3. Spread snap ring in mainshaft bearing retainer and slide retainer off bearing race, Fig. 5.
4. Remove snap ring securing bearing to mainshaft.
5. Support front side of the reverse gear in press and press bearing off shaft. *When bearing clears shaft, do not allow parts to drop through.*
6. Remove 1st-Reverse synchronizer re-

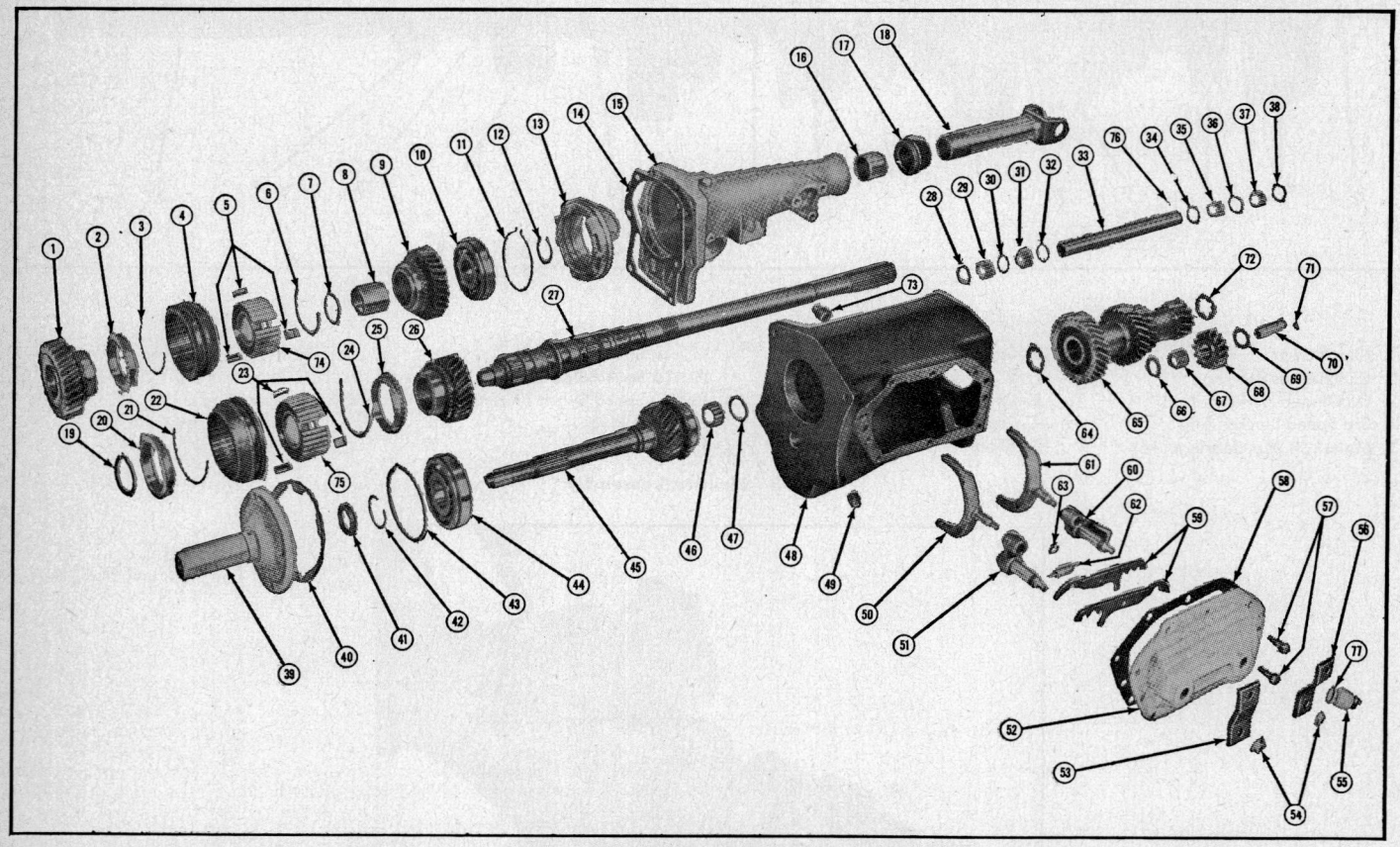

1. Gear, First	14. Gasket	27. Shaft, Output	40. Gasket	53. Lever	66. Washer
2. Ring	15. Extension	28. Washer	41. Seal	54. Nut Locking	67. Roller
3. Spring	16. Bushing	29. Roller	42. Snap Ring	55. Switch	68. Gear, Idler
4. Sleeve	17. Seal	30. Washer	43. Snap Ring	56. Lever	69. Washer
5. Struts (3)	18. Yoke	31. Roller	44. Bearing	57. Bolt	70. Shaft
6. Spring	19. Snap Ring	32. Washer	45. Pinion, Drive	58. Gasket	71. Key
7. Snap Ring	20. Ring	33. Countershaft	46. Roller	59. Lever, Interlock	72. Washer
8. Bushing	21. Spring	34. Washer	47. Snap Ring	60. Lever	73. Plug, Filler
9. Gear, Reverse	22. Sleeve	35. Washer	48. Case	61. Fork	74. Gear, Clutch
10. Bearing	23. Struts (3)	36. Washer	49. Plug, Drain	62. Spring	75. Gear, Clutch
11. Snap Ring	24. Spring	37. Roller	50. Fork	63. Snap Ring	76. Key
12. Snap Ring	25. Ring	38. Washer	51. Lever	64. Washer	77. Gasket
13. Retainer	26. Gear, Second	39. Retainer	52. Housing	65. Gear, Countershaft	

Fig. 1   Type 4 fully synchronized three speed transmission

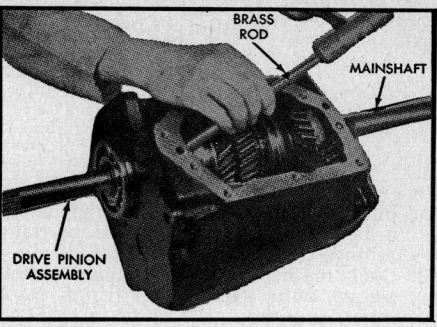

Fig. 2 Tapping drive pinion forward for mainshaft clearance

Fig. 3 Removing mainshaft assembly

Fig. 4 Removing drive pinion

taining ring and remove synchronizer assembly from mainshaft, Fig. 6.
7. Remove 1st gear and stop ring.
8. Reverse procedure to assemble mainshaft.

Mainshaft, Reassemble

1. Slide 1st gear and stop ring onto mainshaft and against flange, Fig. 7.
2. Slide 1st-Reverse synchronizer over mainshaft, indexing hub slots to stop ring lugs.
3. Install clutch gear snap ring on mainshaft.
4. Install reverse gear and mainshaft bearing, support inner race of bearing and press shaft through to shoulder. *Be sure snap ring groove on outer race is forward.* Install bearing retaining ring on mainshaft.
5. Spread snap ring in mainshaft bearing retainer and slide retainer over bearing. Be sure snap ring seats in

groove.
6. Referring to Fig. 1, install 2nd gear, stop ring and 2nd-3rd gear synchronizer. Install snap ring.

Transmission, Assemble

1. Using dummy shaft to hold rollers in place and heavy grease to hold thrust washers, carefully place countergear assembly in bottom of case. *Do not finish installation until drive pinion is installed.*
2. Load rollers and retaining ring in drive pinion bore and install drive pinion through rear case opening and into case bore. Install large snap ring on bearing and install front bearing retainer.
3. Align countergear with its shaft bore and install countershaft through gear, driving dummy shaft out as countershaft is installed. Install countershaft key.

4. Carefully tap drive pinion forward to provide mainshaft installation clearance.
5. With 2-3 synchronizer sleeve fully forward and cut out on 2nd gear turned so it is toward countershaft, insert mainshaft assembly through rear case opening.

NOTE: If installation is correct, the bearing retainer will bottom in the case without force. If not, check for strut, roller or stop ring is out of position.

6. Using dummy shaft to hold rollers, install reverse idler in case and install idler shaft and key.
7. Install rear extension housing, speedometer gear and with transmission shifted in 2nd gear, install cover and shifter assembly.

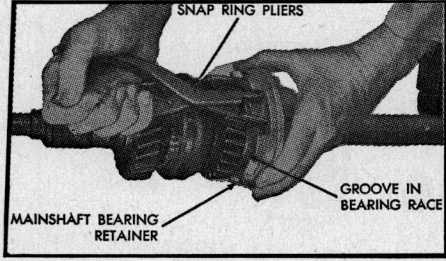

Fig. 5 Removing mainshaft bearing retainer

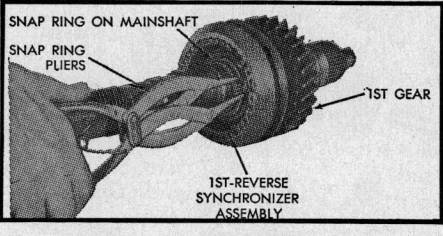

Fig. 6 Removing 1st-Reverse synchronizer snap ring

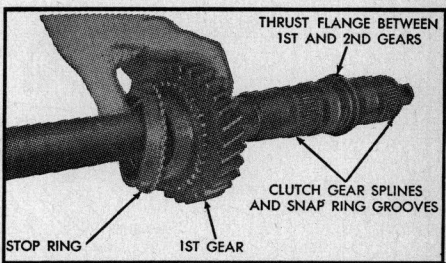

Fig. 7 First gear installation

Types Four & Five

NOTE

These transmissions, Figs. 1 and 2, are quite similar, the chief difference being the cut of the mainshaft splines and the double set of counter gear needle bearings used in the heavy duty unit, Fig. 1. Note that in Fig. 2 there are only one set of needle bearings at each end of the counter gear. The procedure which follows apply to both units unless otherwise indicated.

DISASSEMBLE TRANS.

1. Pull flange from rear of mainshaft.
2. Slide extension housing off mainshaft.
3. Remove transmission cover.

Main Drive Gear

1. Remove drive gear bearing retainer.
2. On H.D. models, Fig. 1, when removing drive gear from transmission, slide front synchronizer inner stop ring from short splines on gear as assembly is being removed from case.
3. On S.D. models, Fig. 2, grasp drive gear shaft and pull assembly out of case. *Be careful not to bind inner synchronizer ring on drive gear clutch teeth.*
4. Remove bearing rollers from drive gear pocket, using a hook or flat blade.

Counter Gear

1. Use a suitable bearing loading tool to drive countershaft toward rear of case until key can be removed from countershaft. Then drive countershaft all the way out, keeping loading tool tight against end of countershaft to keep needle bearings in place.

Mainshaft

1. With transmission in reverse, remove outer center bearing snap ring, using a hook or flat blade, then partially remove mainshaft.
2. Cock mainshaft, then remove clutch sleeve, outer synchronizer rings, front inner ring and 2-3 shift fork, Figs. 3 and 4.
3. Remove clutch gear snap ring. Slide clutch gear off end of mainshaft.
4. Slide 2nd speed gear, stop ring and synchronizer spring off mainshaft.
5. Remove low-reverse sliding gear and shift fork as mainshaft is withdrawn from case.
6. Lift counter gear assembly from case.

Reverse Idler Gear

1. Drive reverse idler shaft towards rear and out of case. Remove key from end of shaft.
2. Lift out idler gear, thrust washers and needle bearings from case.

Gearshift Mechanism
HEAVY DUTY UNIT, Fig. 5

1. Remove both lever shaft seals.

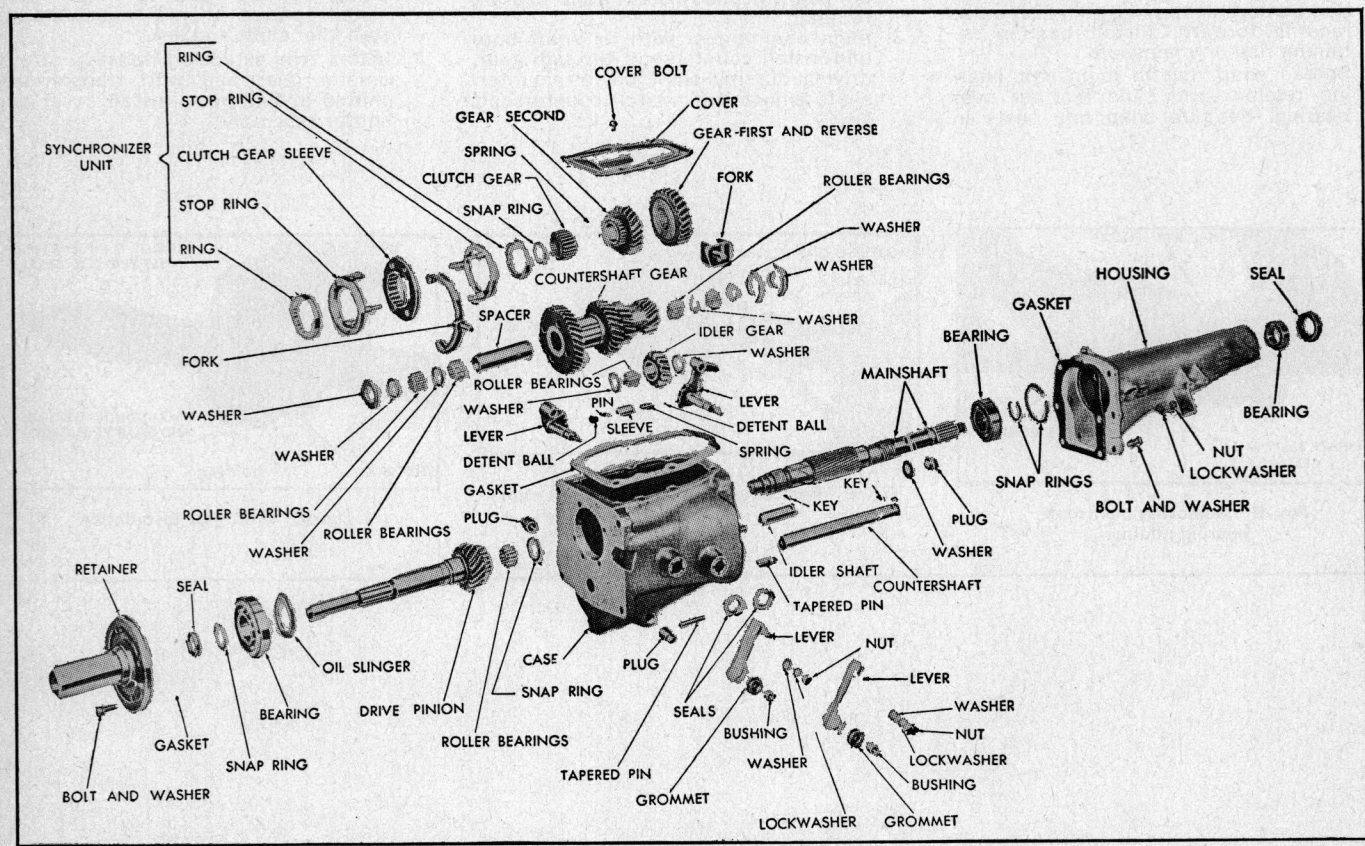

Fig. 1   Type 4 heavy duty transmission disassembled

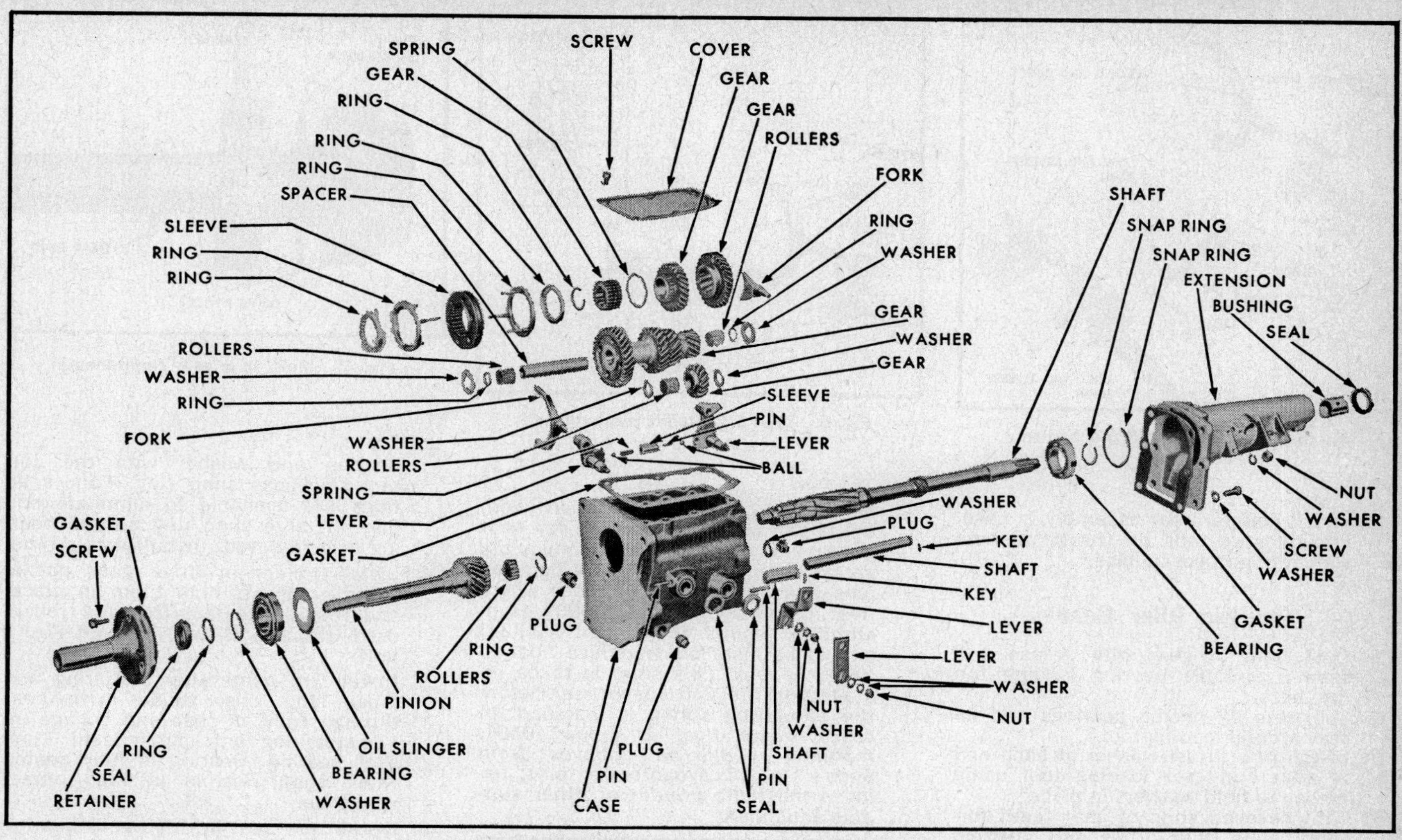

Fig. 2 Type 5 standard duty transmission disassembled. Note that low-reverse mainshaft gear shift fork groove goes to the front

2. Drive tapered lock pins from lever shafts, driving from bottom toward top of transmission.
3. Remove lever shafts from transmission, being careful not to lose spring-loaded detent balls.
4. Remove interlock sleeve, spring, pin and balls.

STANDARD DUTY UNIT, Fig. 6

1. Remove operating levers from shafts.
2. Drive out tapered pin from either of two lever shafts, then withdraw shaft from inside of case. The detent balls are spring-loaded; as the shaft is being withdrawn, ball will drop to bottom of case.

3. Remove interlock sleeve, spring, pin and both balls from case. Then drive out remaining tapered pin and slide shaft out of transmission.
4. Drive out shaft seals and discard.

REASSEMBLE TRANS.
Gearshift Mechanism

1. Center two new seals over holes in case, then drive both seals into case.
2. Slide low-reverse shaft into rear boss of case, through seal and into position. Lock with tapered pin. Turn level until center (neutral) detent is in line with interlock bores. Use sealer on pins.
3. Slide interlock sleeve in its bore, followed by one interlock ball. Install interlock spring and pin.
4. Place remaining interlock ball on top of spring. Depress interlock ball and at the same time install 2-3 lever into fully seated position with center (neutral) detent aligned with detent ball. Secure shaft with tapered pin.

Counter Gear

1. Slide bearing spacer over bearing loading tool. Coat bore of gear with lubricant. Then slide tool and spacer into gear bore.

2. Lubricate needle bearings and install half the total of bearings at each end of gear around loading tool (Type 4 transmission uses a total of 88 bearings, Type 5 uses 44 total).
3. Install bearing retainer rings at each end of gear. Apply grease to hold bearings in place.
4. Thrust washers are available in two sizes, marked A and B. Make a selection to obtain .004-.012" total end play of counter gear.
5. Install thrust washers at each end of assembly and over loading tool, using grease to hold washers in place.

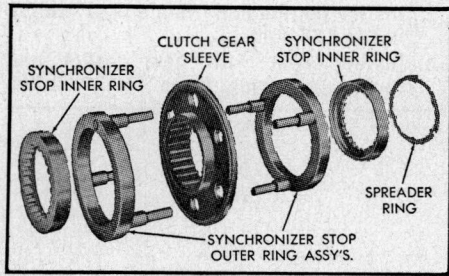

Fig. 3 Type 4 synchronizer unit

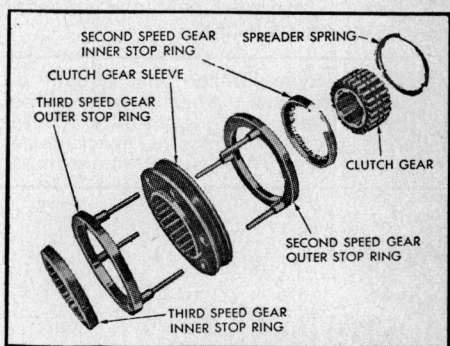

Fig. 4 Type 5 synchronizer unit

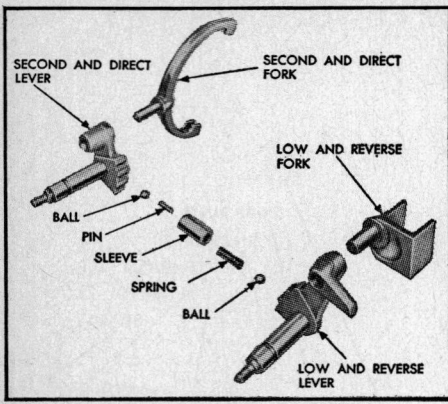

Fig. 5   Type 4 gearshift mechanism

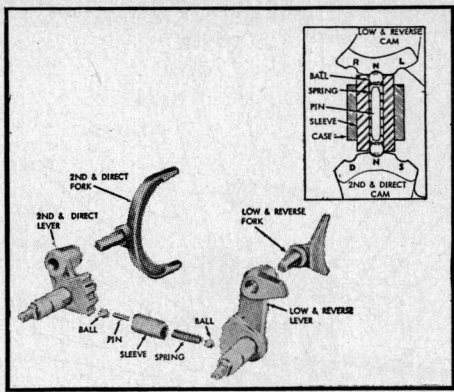

Fig. 6   Type 5 gearshift mechanism

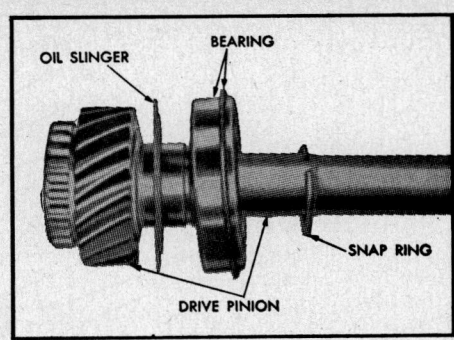

Fig. 7   Main drive gear components

6. Install counter gear assembly in case, making sure tabs on thrust washers slide into grooves in case.

Reverse Idler Gear

1. Coat bore of gear with grease and slide a suitable bearing loading too into bore.
2. Lubricate 22 needle bearings and install around loading tool.
3. Install new thrust washer at each end of gear and over loading tool using grease to hold washers in place.
4. With bevelled ends of gear teeth forward, slide gear down into position in case.
5. Install gear shift in its opening at rear of case.
6. Install key in shaft, and position shaft with keyway.
7. Raise idler gear slightly to align with shaft, then drive shaft into case through thrust washer and gear until end of shaft is about 1/64" below surface of case.

Mainshaft

1. If new bearing is to be installed, press it on mainshaft and install snap ring.
2. Install low-reverse fork with offset to rear. Engage fork in low-reverse sliding gear. Position in case by shifting into reverse.
3. Slide mainshaft into case and through low-reverse gear.
4. Install 2-3 shift fork with offset toward rear.
5. Install 2nd speed gear and spreader spring on mainshaft.

NOTE: *Synchronizer float should be .050" to .090" when measured between end of synchronizer outer ring pin and opposite synchronizer outer ring. This measurement must*

be made 180 degrees apart with equal gap on both pin ends for float determination. To be acceptable, the gauge should be a snug fit between pins and outer rings. In cases where float dimension is over .090", synchronizer shims (part no. 2464724) should be installed to reduce float to .090" or less. This shim is to be installed on the 2nd speed gear before the energizing spring is installed. In cases where float is below .050", material should be removed from ends of all six synchronizer pins, using a magnetic grinder or other suitable equipment.

6. Install 2nd gear inner stop ring and outer stop ring assembly. Engage synchronizer clutch sleeve with 2-3 shift fork.
7. Slide clutch gear over end of mainshaft and down against 2nd speed gear. Select a snap ring of the correct thickness and install. This snap ring eliminates end play and must be a snug fit.
8. Measure clearance between clutch gear and 2nd speed gear. Limits are .002-.011". If clearance is in excess of .011", "gear jump-out" may result.
9. Position mainshaft further in case by tapping on outer bearing race until bearing bottoms. Install a snap ring of the correct thickness in case.

Main Drive Gear

1. Slide oil slinger (if removed) over shaft and down against gear, Fig. 7.
2. Slide bearing over shaft with snap ring groove away from gear end. Seat bearing on shaft with a press. *Be sure slinger does not hang up in snap ring groove during pressing operation.*
3. Install keyed washer. Then secure

bearing and washer with the correct thickness snap ring. Four snap rings are available to eliminate end play. If large snap ring around bearing was removed, install at this time.
4. Install rollers in drive gear pocket using grease to hold them in place, and retain with lock ring (14 rollers used with Fig. 2 unit, 15 with Fig. 1 unit).
5. Install 3rd gear outer stop ring and inner stop ring. Guide drive gear through front of case and engage inner stop ring with clutch teeth. Then seat bearing. Bearing is fully seated when snap ring is in full contact with case.
6. Install new seal in drive gear bearing retainer. Slide bearing retainer (less gasket) down against case.
7. Hold retainer against case and measure clearance between case and retainer, using a feeler gauge. Select a gasket .003" to .004" thicker than the clearance to eliminate all end play in bearing.
8. Install gasket selected and reinstall bearing retainer. Install attaching bolts and tighten to 23 ft-lbs. torque.
9. Install the countershaft, driving the bearing loading tool forward and out of counter gear until key can be inserted in shaft. Continue to drive shaft into case until about 1/64" below surface of case.

Extension Housing & Cover

1. Slide extension housing over mainshaft and down against case, at the same time guiding mainshaft into oil seal. Torque attaching bolts to 50 ft-lbs.
2. Install companion flange and torque nut to 175 ft-lbs.
3. Install cover with new gasket and torque attaching bolts to 12 ft-lbs.

Type Six

DISASSEMBLE TRANS.

1. Remove transmission cover, Fig. 1.
2. Remove extension housing. To prevent mainshaft from following housing (with resultant loss of needle bearings) tap end of mainshaft while withdrawing housing.
3. Remove front bearing retainer.
4. Remove filler plug from right side of case. Then working through plug opening, drive roll pin out of case and countershaft with small punch, Fig. 2.
5. Hold counter gear with a hook and, with a dummy shaft, push countershaft out rear of case until counter gear can be lowered to bottom of case, Fig. 3.
6. Pull main drive gear forward until gear contacts case, then remove large snap ring.

> **NOTE:** On some models, it is necessary to move gear forward to provide clearance when removing mainshaft assembly. On other models, the drive gear is removed from front of case.

7. Remove snap ring and slide speedometer drive gear off mainshaft. Remove lock ball from shaft.
8. Remove snap ring and remove mainshaft rear bearing from shaft and case, Fig. 4.
9. Place both shift levers in neutral (central) position.
10. Remove a set screw that retains detent springs and plugs in case. Remove one spring and plug. Fig. 5.
11. Remove low-reverse set screw and slide shift rail out through rear of case.
12. Rotate low-reverse shift fork upward and lift it from case.
13. Remove 2-3 set screw and rotate 2-3 shift rail 90 degrees with pliers.
14. Lift interlock plug from case with a magnet rod.
15. Tap inner end of 2-3 shift rail to remove expansion plug from front of case. Remove shift rail.
16. Remove 2-3 detent plug and spring from detent bore.
17. Rotate 2-3 shift fork upward and lift from case.
18. Lift mainshaft assembly out through top of case.
19. On some transmissions used on Ford Co. vehicles, push main drive gear into case until bearing is free of bore, then lift gear and bearing through top of case.
20. Working through front bearing opening, drive reverse idler gear shaft out through rear of case with a drift, Fig. 6.
21. Lift reverse idler gear and two thrust washers from case.
22. Lift counter gear and thrust washers from case, Fig. 7. Be careful not to allow dummy shaft and needle bearings to fall out of gear.

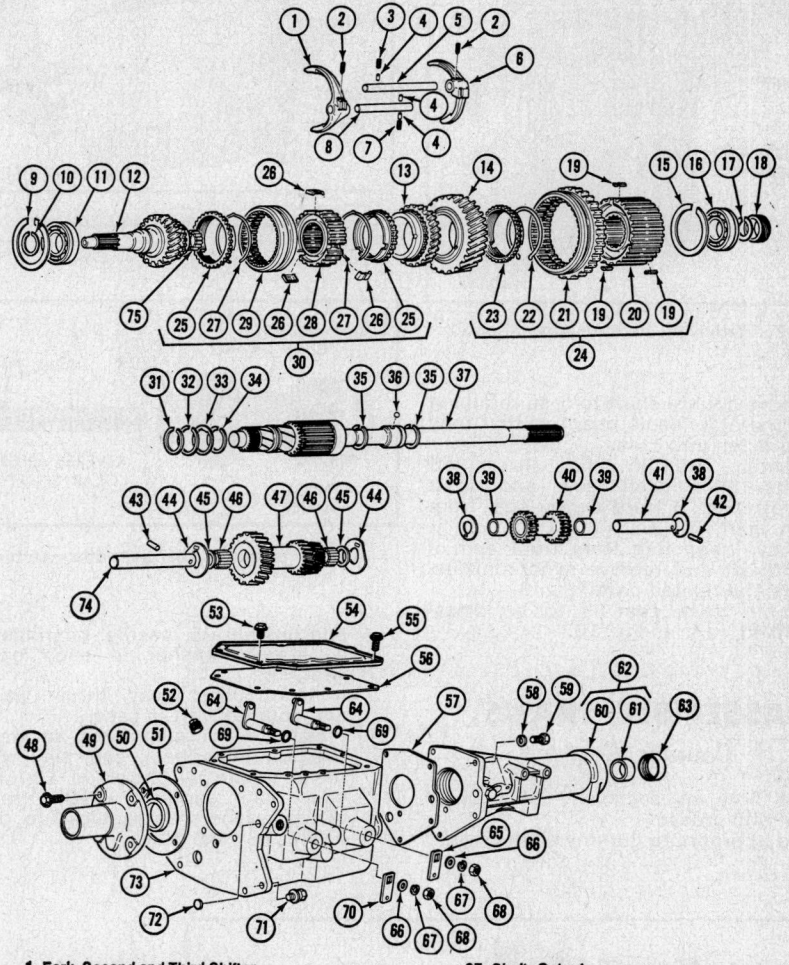

1. Fork, Second and Third Shifter
2. Setscrew, Shifter Fork (2)
3. Spring, Upper Detent (Long)
4. Plugs, Gear Shift Detent and Interlock (3)
5. Shift Rail, First and Reverse
6. Fork, First and Reverse Shifter
7. Spring, Lower Detent (Short)
8. Shift Rail, Second and Third
9. Ring, Locating (Snap) Front Bearing
10. Ring, Retaining (Snap) Front Bearing to Clutch Shaft
11. Bearing, Front
12. Shaft, Clutch
13. Gear, Second
14. Gear, First
15. Ring, Locating (Snap) Rear Bearing
16. Bearing, Rear
17. Ring, Retaining (Snap) Rear Bearing
18. Gear, Speedometer Drive
19. Insert, First and Reverse Synchronizer (3)
20. Hub, First and Reverse
21. Sleeve and Gear, First and Reverse
22. Spring, Insert, First and Reverse Synchronizer
23. Ring, Blocking, First and Reverse Synchronizer
24. Synchronizer Assembly, First and Reverse
25. Ring, Blocking, Second and Third Synchronizer (2)
26. Insert, Second and Third Synchronizer (3)
27. Spring, Insert, Second—Third Synchronizer (2)
28. Hub, Second and Third
29. Sleeve, Second and Third Gear
30. Second—Third Synchronizer Assembly
31. Ring, Retaining (Snap) Output Shaft
32. Ring, Retaining (Snap) First Gear
33. Washer, Thrust (Tabbed) First Gear
34. Ring, Retaining (Snap) First-Reverse Hub
35. Ring, Retaining (Snap) (2) Rear Bearing and Speedometer Gear
36. Lock Ball, 1/4 Diameter—Speedometer Gear
37. Shaft, Output
38. Washer, Thrust, Reverse Idler Gear (2)
39. Bushing, Reverse Idler Gear (2)
40. Gear, Reverse Idler
41. Shaft, Reverse Idler Gear
42. Pin, Roll, Reverse Idler Gear Shaft
43. Pin, Roll, Countershaft
44. Washer, Thrust, Countershaft Gear (2)
45. Retainer, Countershaft Needle Bearing
46. Needle Bearing, Countershaft Gear (50)
47. Gear, Countershaft
48. Bolt, Front Bearing Cap
49. Cap, Front Bearing
50. Oil Seal, Front Bearing Cap
51. Gasket, Front Bearing Cap
52. Plug, Transmission Fill
53. Bolt, Top Cover
54. Top Cover, Case
55. Bolt, Top Cover
56. Gasket, Top Cover
57. Gasket, Extension Housing
58. Lockwasher, Extension Housing Bolt (5)
59. Bolt, Extension Housing
60. Extension Housing
61. Bushing, Extension Housing (Included with Housing)
62. Housing Assembly, Extension
63. Seal, Oil, Extension Housing
64. Shaft, Shifter Fork
65. Lever, First and Reverse Shifter
66. Flatwasher, Shifter Levers (2)
67. Lock, Washer Shifter Levers (2)
68. Nut, Hex, Shifter Levers (2)
69. O-Ring, Shifter Shaft (2)
70. Lever, Second and Third Shifter
71. Bolt, Transmission Mounting (4)
72. Plug, Expansion
73. Case, Transmission
74. Countershaft
75. Bearings, Clutch Shaft Roller

Fig. 1   Type 6 transmission disassembled

THREE SPEED TRANSMISSIONS

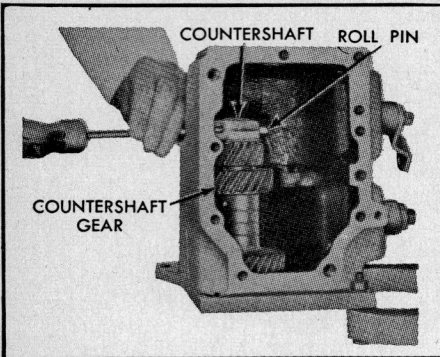

Fig. 2   Removing countershaft roll pin

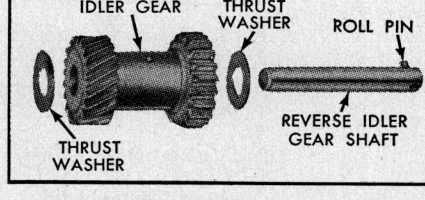

Fig. 3   Removing countershaft

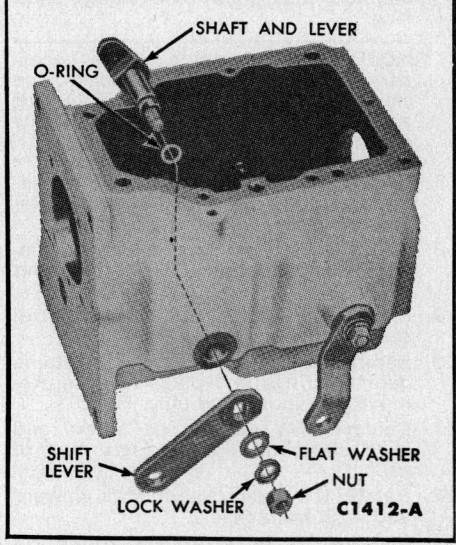

Fig. 6   Reverse idler gear disassembled

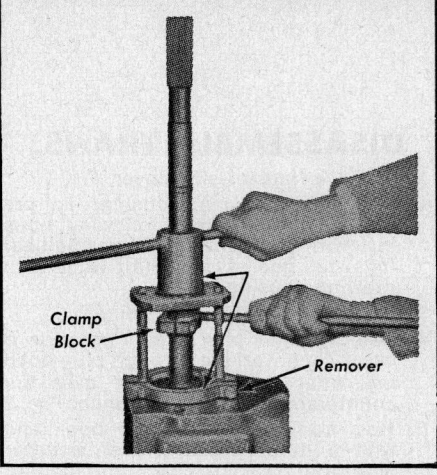

Fig. 4   Removing mainshaft bearing

23. Remove countershaft-to-case retaining pin and any needle bearings that may have fallen into case.
24. Unfasten and lift shift levers off shafts. Slide each lever and shaft out of case. Discard O-ring seal from each shaft, Fig. 8.
25. Remove snap ring from front end of mainshaft and remove synchronizers, gears and related parts, Fig. 9.
26. If main drive gear is to be disassembled, refer to Fig. 10.

REASSEMBLE TRANS.

Counter Gear

1. Coat bore at each end of counter gear with grease.
2. Hold appropriate dummy shaft in gear

and install 25 needle bearings and a retainer washer in each end of gear, Fig. 7.
3. Install counter gear, thrust washers and countershaft in case.
4. Place transmission case in vertical position and check end play with a feeler gauge as shown in Fig. 13. If end play exceeds .018", replace thrust washers as required to obtain .004-.018" end play.

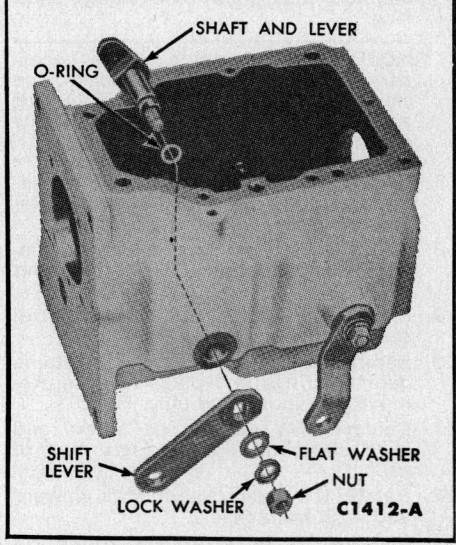

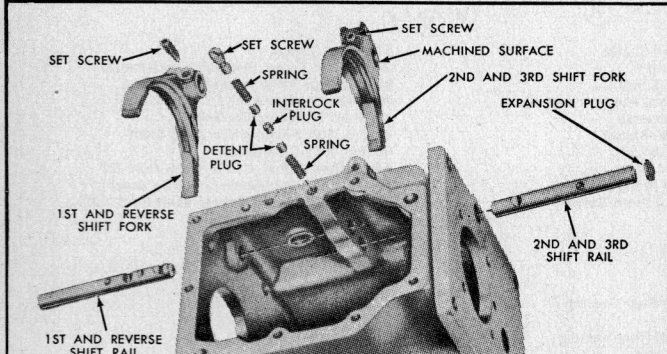

Fig. 5   Shift rails and forks disassembled

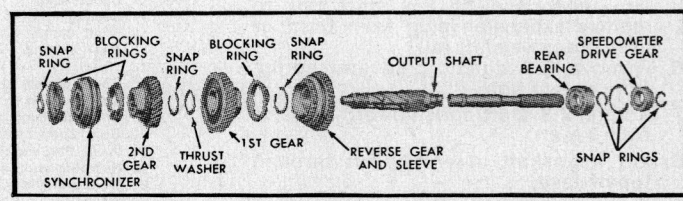

Fig. 8   Shift lever and related parts

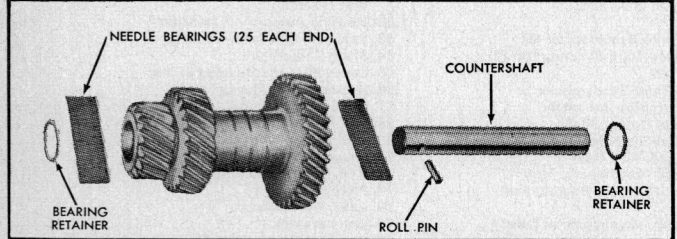

Fig. 7   Counter gear disassembled

Fig. 9   Mainshaft disassembled

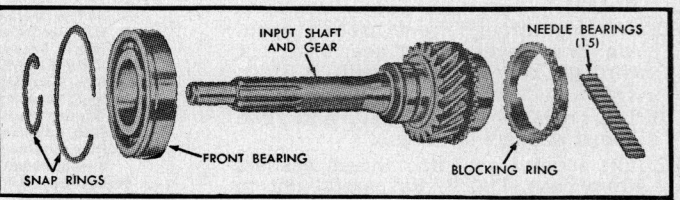

Fig. 10   Main drive gear disassembled

2-188

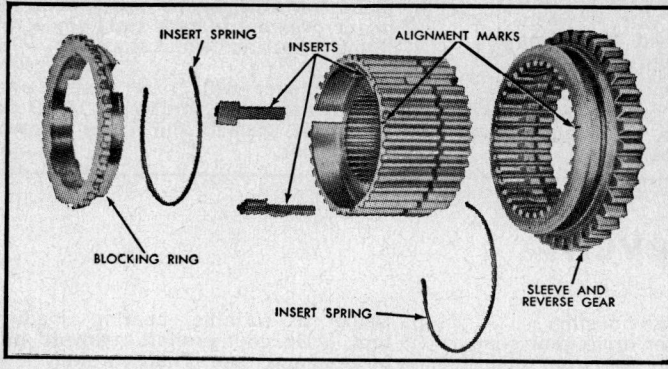

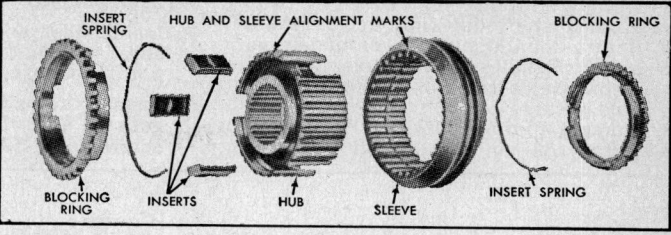

Fig. 12 Second-high synchronizer disassembled

Fig. 11 Low-reverse synchronizer disassembled

5. Once end play has been established, remove countershaft with dummy shaft.
6. Allow counter gear assembly to remain in case.

Reverse Idler Gear

1. Install idler gear, thrust washers and shaft in case.
2. Make sure that thrust washer with flat side is at the web end, and that the spur gear is toward the rear of case, Fig. 6.
3. Check reverse idler gear end play in same manner and to the same clearance as the counter gear. If end play is within limits of .004-.018" leave gear in case.

Low-Reverse Synchronizer

1. Install an insert spring, Fig. 11, in groove of low-reverse synchronizer hub. Make sure spring covers all insert grooves.
2. Start hub in sleeve, making sure that alignment marks are properly indexed.
3. Position three inserts in hub, making sure that small end is over spring and that shoulder is on inside of hub.
4. Slide sleeve and reverse gear onto hub until detent is engaged.
5. Install other insert spring in front of hub to hold inserts against hub.

Second-Third Synchronizer

1. Install one insert spring, Fig. 12, into a groove of synchronizer hub, making sure that all three insert slots are fully covered.
2. With alignment marks on hub and sleeve aligned, start hub into sleeve.
3. Place three inserts on top of retaining spring and push assembly together.
4. Install remaining insert spring so that spring ends cover same slots as do other spring. Do not stagger springs.
5. Place a synchronizer blocking ring in each end of sleeve.

Main Drive Line

1. Lubricate mainshaft splines and machined surfaces with transmission lube.

2. Slide low-reverse synchronizer, Fig. 9, onto mainshaft with teeth end of gear facing toward rear of shaft. Secure in place with snap ring.
3. Coat tapered machined surface of low gear with grease. Place blocking ring on greased surface.
4. Slide low gear onto mainshaft with blocking ring toward rear of shaft. Rotate gear as necessary to engage the three notches in blocking ring with synchronizer inserts. Secure low gear with thrust washer and snap ring.
5. Coat tapered machined surface of 2nd gear with grease and slide blocking ring onto it. Slide 2nd gear with blocking ring and 2-3 synchronizer onto mainshaft. Tapered machined surface of 2nd gear must be toward front of shaft. Make sure that notches in blocking ring engage synchronizer inserts. Secure synchronizer with snap ring.
6. Install new O-ring on each of two shift lever shafts, Fig. 8. Lubricate shafts with transmission lube and install them in case. Secure each lever on its shaft with a flat washer, lock washer and nut.
7. Coat bore of main drive gear shaft with thick coat of grease. Install 15 needle bearings in gear pocket, Fig. 10.

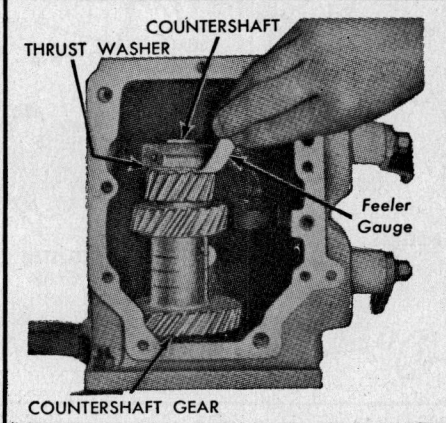

Fig. 13 Checking counter gear end play

8. Position drive gear assembly into case.
9. Place a detent spring and plug in case, Fig. 5. Place 2-3 shift fork in synchronizer groove. Rotate fork into position and install 2-3 shift rail. It will be necessary to depress detent plug to enter rail in bore. Move rail inward until detent plug engages center (neutral) notch. Secure fork to shaft with set screw.
10. Install interlock plug in case. If 2-3 shift rail is in neutral position, top of interlock will be slightly lower than surface of low-reverse shift rail bore.
11. Place low-reverse shift fork in groove of synchronoizer. Rotate fork into position and install low-reverse shift rail. Move rail inward until center (neutral) notch is aligned with detent bore. Secure fork to shaft with set screw.
12. Install remaining detent plug and spring. Secure spring with slotted head set screw. Turn set screw in until head is flush with case.
13. Install new expansion plug in case.
14. Install large snap ring on drive bearing. Work drive gear into case and onto mainshaft until snap ring is seated against case. Make sure that needle bearings do not fall out of place and that notches in blocking ring engage inserts in synchronizer.

NOTE: *The foregoing applies only to transmissions used with V8-352 and 390 engines. On all other models, the drive gear is installed through front of case with bearing in place on shaft.*

15. Position new front bearing retainer gasket on case. Place bearing retainer on case, making sure oil return groove is at the bottom. Install and tighten attaching screws to 19-25 ft-lbs.
16. Install large snap ring on mainshaft rear bearing. Place bearing on mainshaft with snap ring end toward rear of shaft. Press bearing into place and secure with snap ring.
17. Hold speedometer drive gear lock ball in detent and slide gear into place. Secure gear with snap ring.

Final Assembly

1. Place transmission in vertical position. Working through drain hole in bottom of case, align bore of counter gear and thrust washers with bore of case, using a screwdriver.

THREE SPEED TRANSMISSIONS

2. Working through rear of case, push dummy shaft out with countershaft. Before countershaft is completely inserted, make sure the hole that accommodates roll pin is aligned with hole in case.
3. Working through lubricant filler hole, install roll pin (Fig. 2) in case and countershaft.
4. Install filler and drain plugs, making sure magnetic plug is installed in bottom of case.
5. Install extension housing with new gasket and torque attaching cap screws to 42-50 ft-lbs.
6. Place transmission in gear, pour lubricant over entire gear train while rotating input and output shafts.
7. Install cover with new gasket and torque attaching screws to 14-19 ft-lbs. Coat gasket and cover screws with sealer.

Type Seven

DISASSEMBLE TRANS.

1. Referring to Fig. 1, remove cover.
2. Remove extension housing. *To prevent mainshaft from following housing (with resultant loss of needle bearings) tap end of mainshaft while withdrawing extension housing.*
3. Remove speedometer drive gear snap ring, gear and drive ball from mainshaft.
4. Remove idler gear shaft and countershaft retainer. If necessary tap front ends of both shafts to free retainer.
5. Using a suitable bearing loading tool, drive countershaft rearward out of gear and case. Then carefully lower counter gear to bottom of case, Fig. 2.
6. After removing main drive gear bearing retainer, remove drive gear and

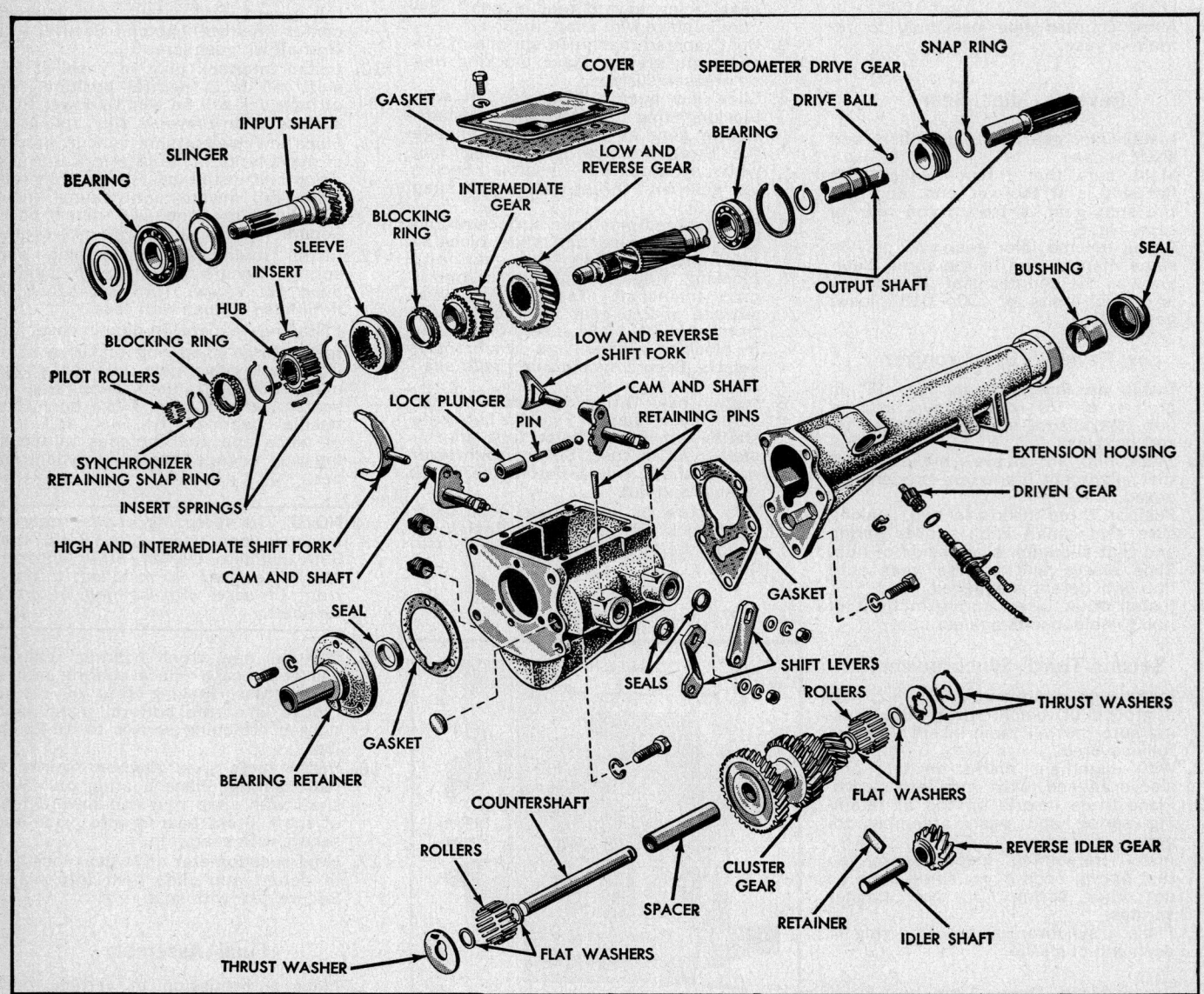

Fig. 1 Type 7 transmission. Note that longer end of synchronizer hub goes to the front. CAUTION: On some models the shift fork groove for low-reverse sliding gear goes to rear as shown; on other models fork goes to front. Check position after cover is removed

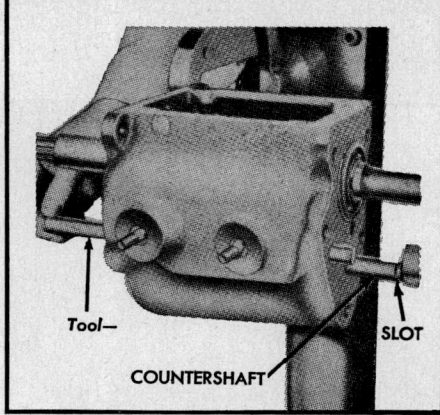

Fig. 2   Countershaft removal and installation

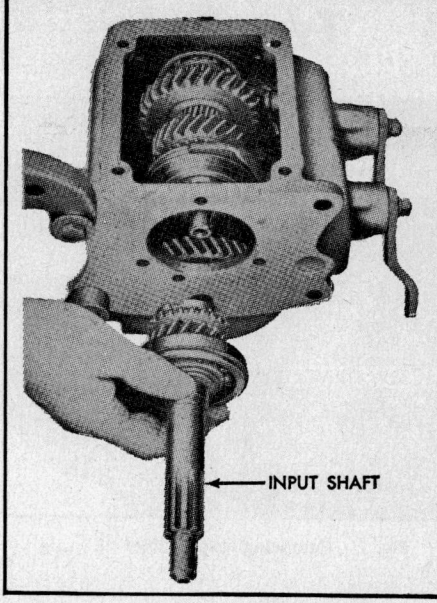

Fig. 3   Removing main drive gear

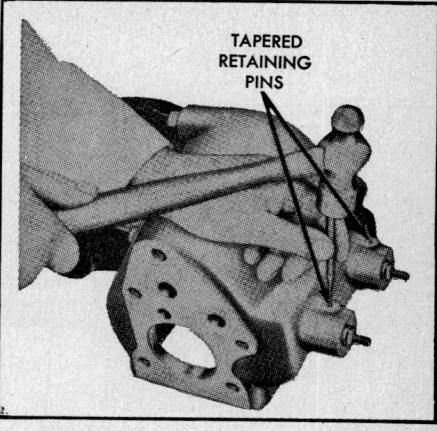

Fig. 4   Removing shift shaft retaining pins. Note that pins are driven out from the bottom

front synchronizer blocking ring from case, Fig. 3.

7. Remove synchronizer retaining snap ring from mainshaft. Then, while holding synchronizer together, pull mainshaft out of case. Lift synchronizer, gears and shift forks from case. *For reference on reassembly, note which end of synchronizer hub faces forward.*

8. Drive reverse idler shaft out of case and lift out idler gear, shaft and counter gear.

9. Remove shift levers.

10. From underside of case, drive out tapered pins, Fig. 4. Using a plastic hammer, drive 2-3 shift cam and shaft toward outside of case and separate balls and springs from plunger. Push out cam and shaft assemblies and remove plunger.

11. If necessary, shift lever oil seals may be removed with a slide hammer type hooked tool.

12. Remove snap ring and press main drive gear out of bearing and oil slinger.

13. Remove snap ring and press bearing from mainshaft.

REASSEMBLE TRANS.

1. Press main drive gear bearing and oil slinger on shaft, securing with snap ring.

2. Press mainshaft bearing on shaft and secure with snap ring.

3. Insert spacer and dummy shaft, Fig. 2, into counter gear. Position one flat washer at each end of spacer. Apply grease to needle bearings and

assemble them around dummy shaft at each end of gear. Apply grease to other two flat washers and thrust washers and assemble at each end of counter gear. Note position of tangs on thrust washers, Fig. 1.

4. Position counter gear assembly in bottom of case with larger gear toward front.

5. Install low-reverse shift cam through case opening. Assemble spacer and spring in plunger. Hold plunger in position and install 2-3 cam and shaft in case opening, allowing balls to register in cam detents.

6. Align cam and shaft grooves with openings in shaft bosses, and install retaining pins, Fig. 4. Check cam action; bent pins may restrict movement.

7. Position reverse idle gear, and insert shaft (from rear) through case just far enough to hold gear.

8. After assembling three inserts in synchronizer hub and securing them with two spring retainers, insert hub into 2-3 synchronizer sleeve. Install one block ring in rear side of hub. Coat blocking rings with grease.

9. Using a coating of grease, assemble needle bearings in drive gear pocket and install front synchronizer blocking ring on drive gear shaft.

10. Install shift forks in shift lever shafts with large fork in 2-3 shaft. Web of low-reverse fork must be to rear of shaft center.

11. Start mainshaft through rear of case. Place low-reverse gear on shaft, followed by 2nd speed gear. Tilt mainshaft enough to allow rear shift fork to engage sliding gear groove.

12. With *longer hub forward*, slide synchronizer onto mainshaft and engage synchronizer sleeve in 2-3 shift fork.

13. Install synchronizer hub and snap ring.

14. Position main drive gear and front synchronizer blocking ring.

15. Place a new gasket on drive gear bearing retainer. If shaft oil seal was removed from retainer, install a new seal. Install bearing retainer, using sealer on bolts. Line up oil drain groove in retainer with oil hole in case.

16. Raise counter gear assembly and align dummy shaft with countershaft opening in case. Start countershaft into case from rear, and carefully drive shaft into position.

17. Install idler gear shaft and retainer.

18. Secure speedometer drive gear and ball with snap ring.

19. Using a new gasket, install extension housing.

20. Start new seal over each cam and shaft and drive in seals.

21. Fill transmission to proper level with lubricant. Then, using a new gasket and sealer on bolts, install transmission cover.

NOTE: *Cover gasket vent holes must be toward rear and cover vent hole must be toward front.*

Type Eight

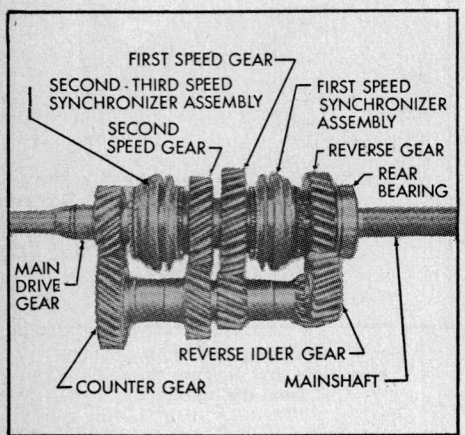

Fig. 1 Type 8 Saginaw three speed transmission

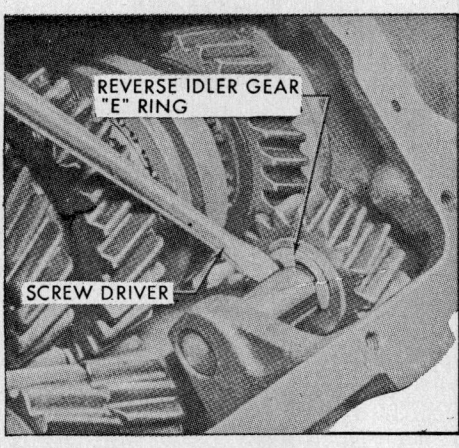

Fig. 2 Removing reverse idler "E" ring

Fig. 3 Removing rear bearing retainer after spreading snap ring as shown

Disassemble

1. Drain lubricant and remove damper assembly on Vega transmissions.
2. Remove side cover and gasket.
3. Remove front bearing retainer.
4. Remove clutch gear bearing-to-stem snap ring then slide bearing off over clutch gear stem. The clutch gear bearing is a slip fit on the gear and into the case bore.
5. Remove extension-to-case bolts.
6. Remove reverse idler shaft-to-gear "E" ring, Fig. 2.
7. Remove clutch gear, mainshaft and extension assembly together through rear case opening.
8. Expand snap ring and remove rear bearing retainer and mainshaft from extension, Fig. 3.
9. Drive countershaft and woodruff key out through the rear of the case. Remove countergear and bearings.
10. Use a long drift and drive reverse

Fig. 4 Removing counter shaft, using aligning arbor to hold needle bearings in place

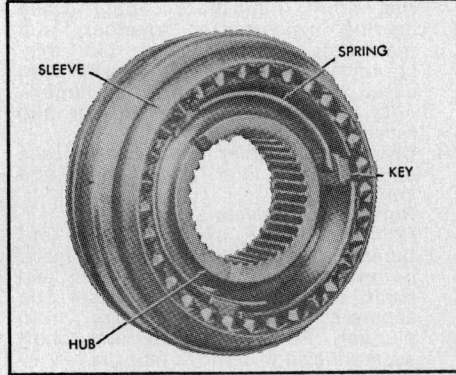

Fig. 6 Synchronizer assembly

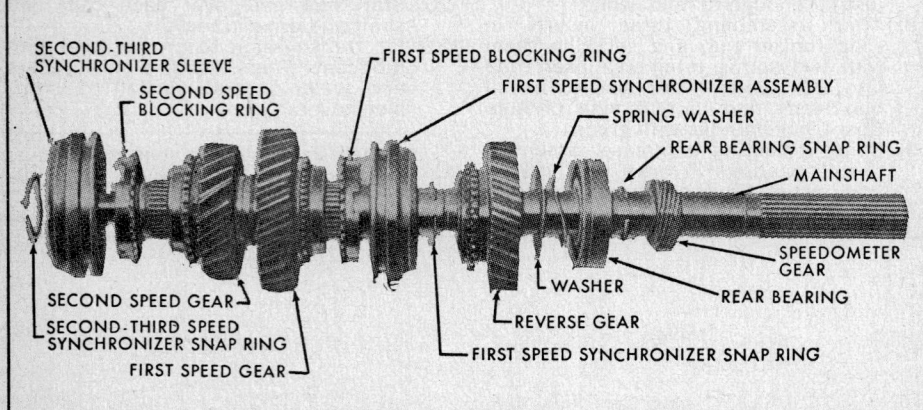

Fig. 5 Mainshaft and related parts assembled loosely to show location of parts

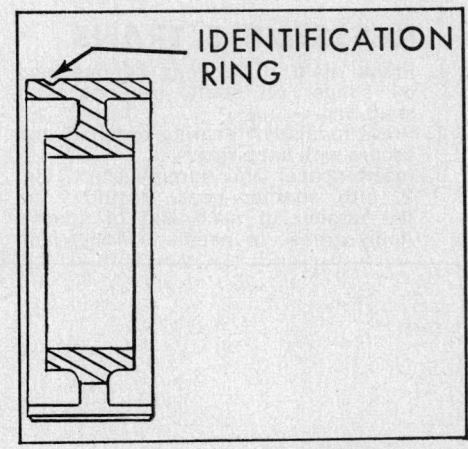

Fig. 7 Identification chamfer around synchronizer hub

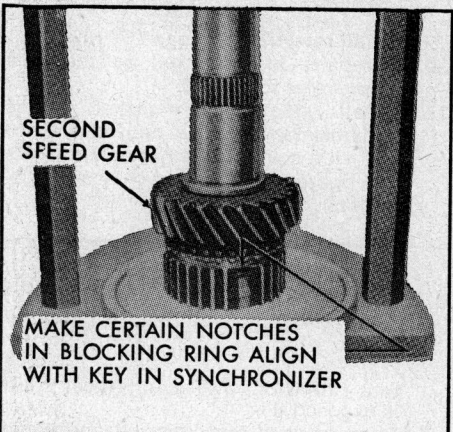

Fig. 8   Installing second speed gear

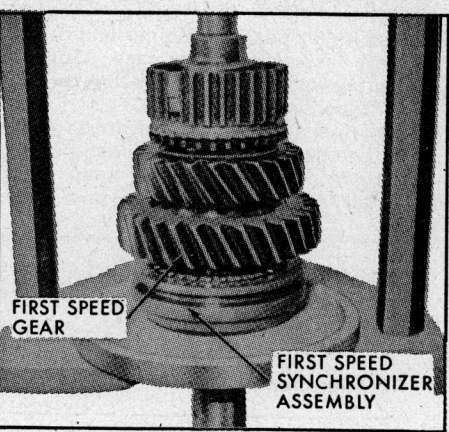

Fig. 9   Installing first speed gear

Fig. 10   Countergear with riveted anti-rattle gear. Except Vega

idler shaft and key through rear of case.
11. Remove reverse idler gear tanged thrust washer.

Disassemble Mainshaft

1. Remove clutch gear, roller bearings and blocking ring from mainshaft. Referring to Fig. 5, remove 2-3 synchronizer sleeve.
2. Remove speedometer gear.
3. Remove rear bearing snap ring, and press off rear bearing, spring washer, thrust washer and Reverse gear.
4. Remove 1st and Reverse sliding clutch hub snap ring and clutch assembly, 1st speed blocker ring and gear.

Synchronizers

NOTE: The synchronizer hubs and sliding sleeves are a selected assembly and should be kept together as originally assembled. The keys and springs may be replaced if worn or broken.

1. Mark hub and sleeve so they can be

Fig. 11   Vega counter-gear

reassembled in same position.
2. Remove sleeve from synchronizer hub.
3. Remove keys and springs from hub.
4. Place three keys and two springs in position (one on each side of hub) so all three keys are engaged by both springs, Fig. 6. The tanged end of each synchronizer spring should be installed in different key cavities on either side of hub. Slide sleeve onto hub, aligning marks made before disassembly.

NOTE: A chamfer or groove around the outside of synchronizer hub identifies the end that must be opposite the fork slot in the sleeve, Fig. 7.

Assemble Mainshaft

With front of mainshaft up:
1. Install second speed gear with clutching teeth upward.
2. Install blocking ring with clutching teeth downward. All blocking rings in this unit are identical.
3. Press 2-3 synchronizer onto mainshaft, Fig. 8. *Be sure notches in blocking ring align with keys in synchronizer.*
With rear of mainshaft up:
4. Install first speed gear with clutching teeth upward.
5. Install blocking ring on gear with teeth downward.
6. Press first and reverse synchronizer onto mainshaft. *Be sure notches in blocking ring align with keys in synchronizer.* Install snap ring.
7. Install reverse gear, thrust washer, spring washer, rear bearing and bearing snap ring.
8. Install speedometer gear.

Assemble Transmission

1. Install countergear-to-case thrust washers. Install countergear into case from rear. Make certain wooruff key is in place. Note that anti rattle gear is riveted to countergear in four

places and is not serviced separately, Fig. 10.

NOTE: Vega transmissions do not use an anti-rattle gear, Fig. 11.

2. Install reverse idler gear tanged steel thrust washer. Install idler gear, shaft and woodruff key. *Reverse idler gear snap ring will be installed after installation of mainshaft.*
3. Install rear bearing retainer. Spread snap ring in retainer to allow snap ring to drop around rear bearing. Press on end of mainshaft until snap ring engages groove in rear bearing.

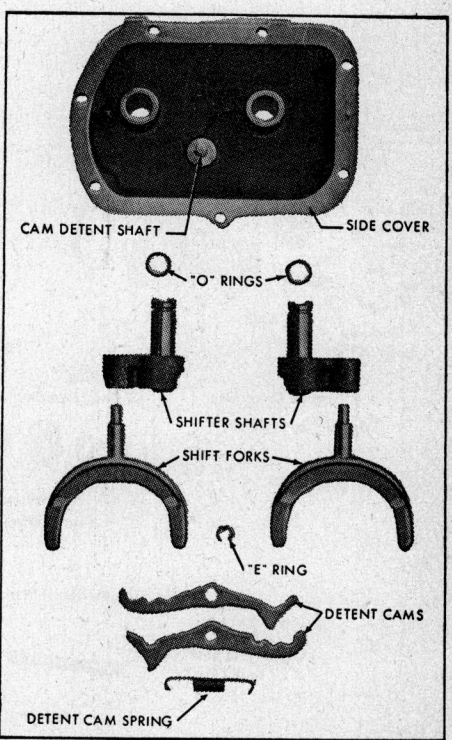

Fig. 12   Disassembled view of side cover

4. Install 14 needle rollers in main drive gear pocket, using grease to hold them in place. Assemble third speed blocking ring on main drive gear. Pilot main drive gear and blocking ring over front of mainshaft. Make certain notches in blocking ring align with keys in 2-3 synchronizer.
5. Install rear bearing retainer-to-case gasket, using heavy grease to hold gasket in place.
6. Install rear bearing retainer and mainshaft assembly into case. Torque bearing retainer-to-case bolts to 35-55 ft-lbs. torque.
7. Install bearing on main drive gear. Outer snap ring groove must be toward front of gear. Install snap ring.
8. Install front bearing retainer and gasket.
9. Install reverse idler gear "E" ring.
10. If repairs are required to the side cover, refer to Fig. 12.
11. Install side cover gasket. Place transmission gears in neutral and install side cover. Install attaching bolts and tighten evenly to avoid cover distortion.

Type Nine

DISASSEMBLE TRANS.

1. Refer to Fig. 1 and proceed as follows: Remove TCS and backup lamp switches and shift lever boot.
2. Remove cotter pins from each end of shift control rod, Fig. 2. Remove washers and control rod.
3. Remove serrated pin retaining selector lever to the boss on rear extension, Fig. 3.
4. Remove retaining rings, wave washer and selector ring from selector ring from selector shaft.

NOTE: Slide selector lever and shift idler lever shaft from intermediate shift lever assembly while simultaneously removing selector ring. Selector lever will just slip off selector ring.

5. Remove transmission case cover and invert transmission to drain oil.
6. Remove rear extension bolts and rotate extension until countergear shaft is exposed, Fig. 4.
7. From front of transmission and using tool J-23562, remove countergear shaft. Be sure that lock ball is not lost, Fig. 5. With special tool inserted lift countergear from case and remove thrust washers.
8. Using a 1/8" pin punch to remove lock pins, engage second gear to prevent 2-3 fork pin binding against case. Drive out lock pins from both shifter forks.

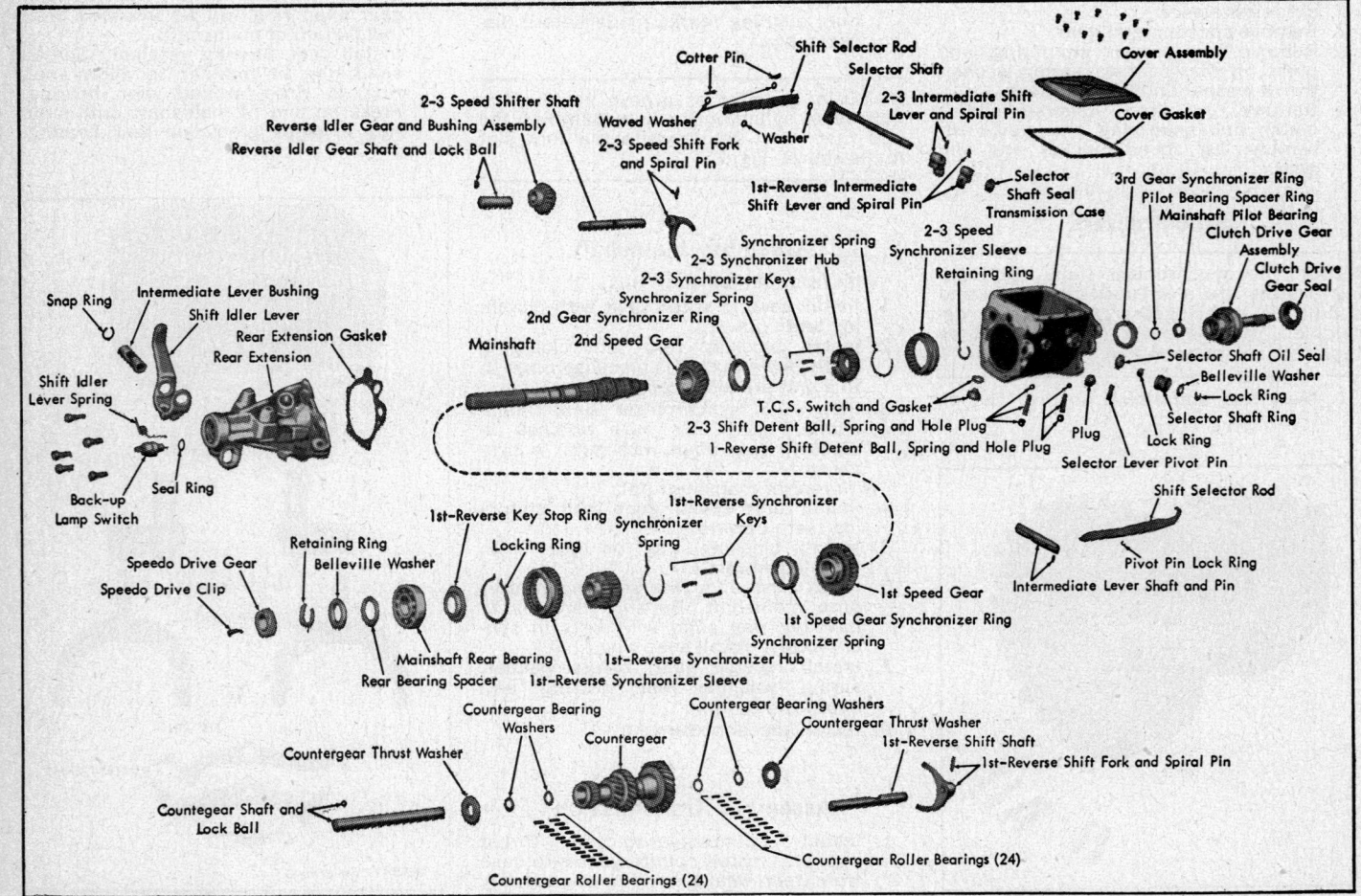

Fig. 1   Exploded view of Type 9 transmission

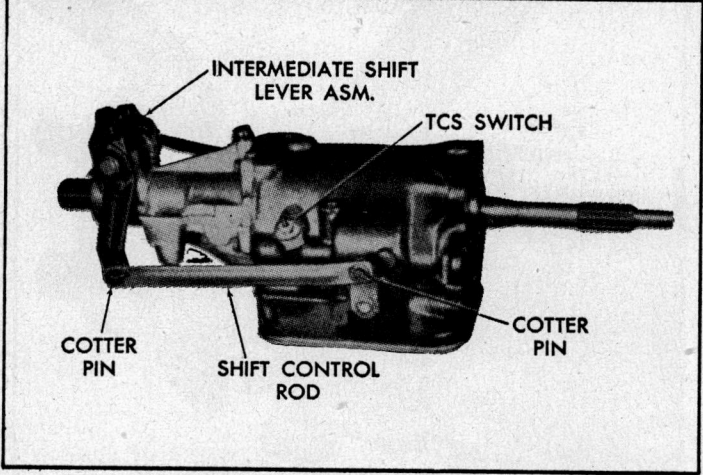

Fig. 2   Cotter pins securing shift control rod

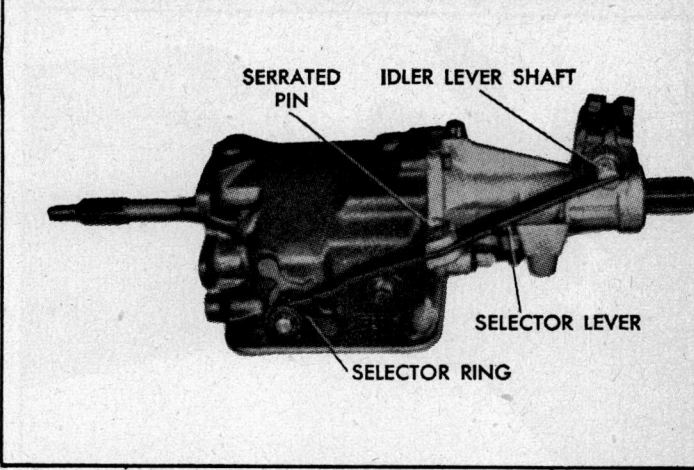

Fig. 3   Pin securing selector lever

NOTE: Before driving shifter shafts, place transmission in 3rd gear and make sure 2nd-3rd intermediate lever engages shifter shaft. This allows selector shaft and intermediate levers to pivot as shifter shaft is driven from case.

9. Insert a long narrow drift through bolt hole at rear of case and drive 2nd-3rd shifter shaft out front of case, Fig. 6. Remove fork from case.
10. Using a suitable drift, drive 1st-Reverse shifter shaft out front of case, Fig. 7 and remove fork.
11. Remove selector shaft intermediate lever lock pins, Fig. 8, and remove shaft and levers from case.
12. Remove snap ring from rear bearing retainer groove and slide rear extension from mainshaft assembly, Fig. 9.
13. Remove clutch drive gear from case. Position 1st-Reverse sliding gear to

rear of hub shaft and remove mainshaft assembly, Fig. 10. Remove lock pins and detent balls from bottom of case.
14. Insert a punch into shaft rail detent holes and drive out hole plugs and springs.
15. Using tool J-22923, remove reverse idler shaft and gear from case, Fig. 11.

Mainshaft Disassembly

1. Remove snap ring in front of clutch hub, Fig. 12.

NOTE: The synchronizer hubs and sliding sleeves are a selected assembly and should be kept together as originally assembled.

2. Depress retaining clamp and slide speedo drive gear from shaft.
3. Remove snap ring, belleville washer

and spacer from shaft, Fig. 13.
4. Support 1st gear and press mainshaft until bearing and synchronizers are free on shaft, Fig. 14. Remove all loose parts.
5. Support 2nd speed gear and press shaft from 2nd-3rd synchronizer and 2nd speed gear, Fig. 15.

Drive Gear Bearing

1. Remove snap ring retaining bearing on shaft.
2. Support outer race of bearing and press drive gear from bearing.
3. Position new bearing on shaft with slinger toward gear and press onto shaft using tool J-5390 or other suitable piece of pipe.
4. Install snap ring on shaft behind bearing, Fig. 16.

Mainshaft Assembly

IMPORTANT: The snychronizer hubs and

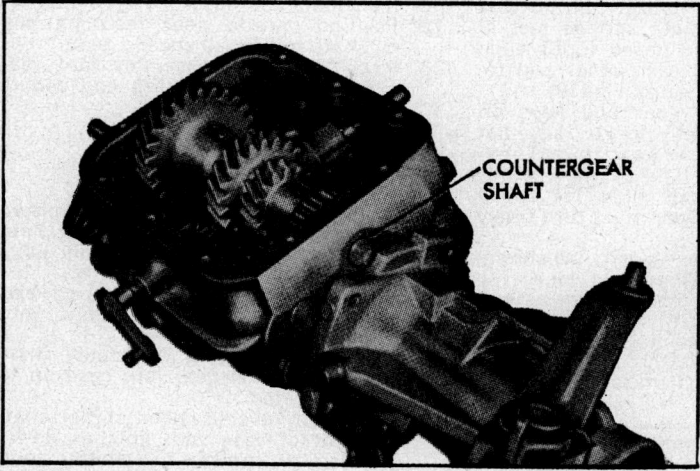

Fig. 4   Countergear shaft exposed for removal

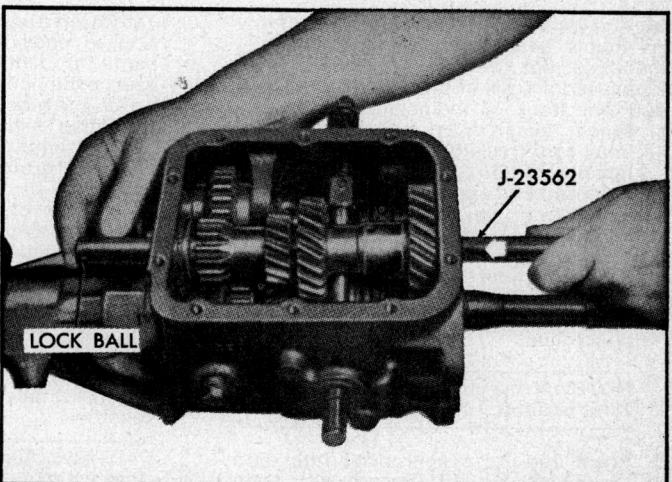

Fig. 5   Removing countergear shaft

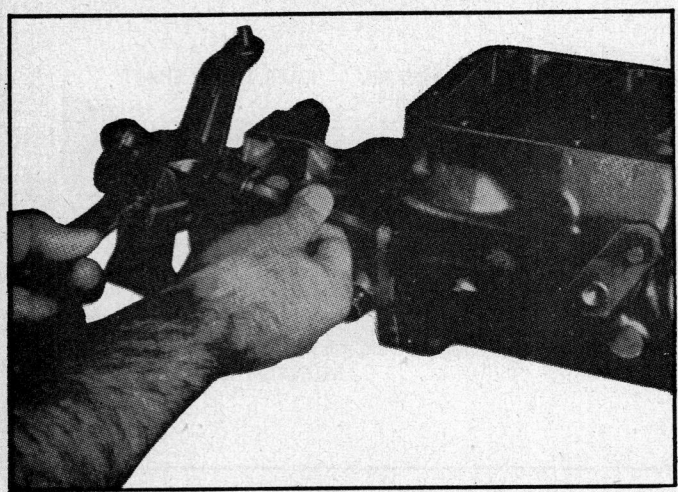

Fig. 6   Removing 2nd-3rd shifter shaft

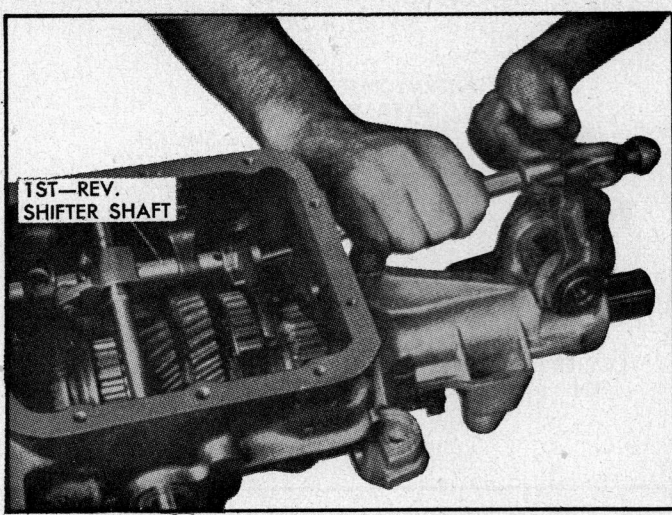

Fig. 7   Removing 1st-Reverse shifter shaft

Fig. 8   Removing selector shaft intermediate lever pins

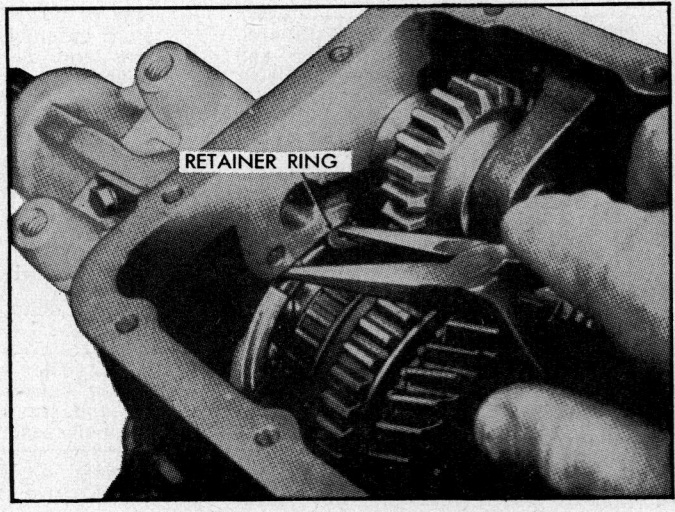

Fig. 9   Releasing rear extension retainer ring

sliding sleeves are a selected assembly and should be kept together as originally assembled, but the keys and springs may be replaced if worn or broken.

1. From front of mainshaft install 2nd speed gear onto mainshaft. Gear must turn freely on shaft.
2. Install 2nd-3rd speed synchronizer ring onto 2nd speed gear cone.
3. Install front and rear synchronizer key springs into 2nd-3rd synchronizer hub so that hooked spring ends rest in the same slot and raised ends are against the blocker rings.
4. Install sliding sleeve and keys on clutch hub.

NOTE: Arrow on keys must point to front of shaft.

5. Press 2nd-3rd synchronizer hub onto mainshaft, Fig. 17. Secure with snap ring.
6. Install both clutch key springs into 1st-Reverse synchronizer hub so that hooked ends of both springs rest in same hub slot and raised spring ends are positioned to each other and towards the blocker rings, Fig. 18.
7. Assemble sliding gear and keys on hub assembly with longer key flat and fork groove on gear toward rear of shaft.
8. From rear of shaft slide 1st speed gear onto shaft. Gear must turn freely on shaft, Fig. 19.
9. Place 1st-Reverse speed synchronizer ring onto 1st speed gear cone.
10. Slide 1st-Reverse synchronizer assembly onto mainshaft. Slide stop ring, rear extension retaining ring and rear bearing onto shaft. Support rear bearing inner race and press components together.

CAUTION: Align slots in synchronizer rings with keys.

11. Place spacer and belleville washer on mainshaft and secure with snap ring.
12. Position speedo gear retaining clip on shaft and install speedo gear.
13. Place mainshaft assembly into rear extension up to its stop and secure with retaining ring.

ASSEMBLE TRANS.

1. Install new gasket onto rear extension and slide mainshaft assembly into case. Install one or two retainer bolts to keep extension from rotating.
2. From the front, slide lock ring and pilot roller bearing assembly onto mainshaft.
3. Install blocker ring on clutch drive gear and install gear into case up to snap ring stop.
4. Insert 1st-Reverse speed shifter shaft at front of case with notches down, pushing it through the shifter fork, positioning fork shoulder toward front of case. Drive lock pin in place allow-

MOVE 1st-REV. SYNCHRONIZER
SLEEVE REARWARD ON SHAFT

Fig. 10   Removing mainshaft assembly

J-22923

Fig. 11   Removing reverse idler gear shaft

SNAP RING

Fig. 12   Removing snap ring in front of clutch hub

SNAP RING
BELLEVILLE WASHER
SPACER

Fig. 13   Removing rear bearing snap ring

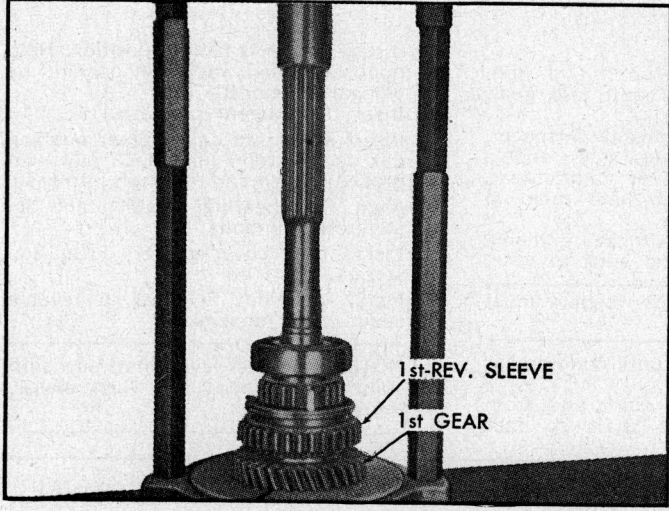

1st-REV. SLEEVE
1st GEAR

Fig. 14   Removing rear bearing from mainshaft

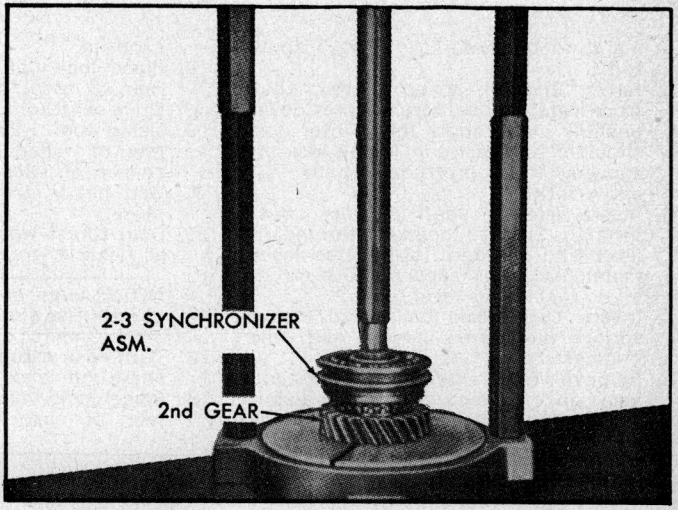

2-3 SYNCHRONIZER ASM.
2nd GEAR

Fig. 15   Removing 2nd-3rd clutch hub from mainshaft

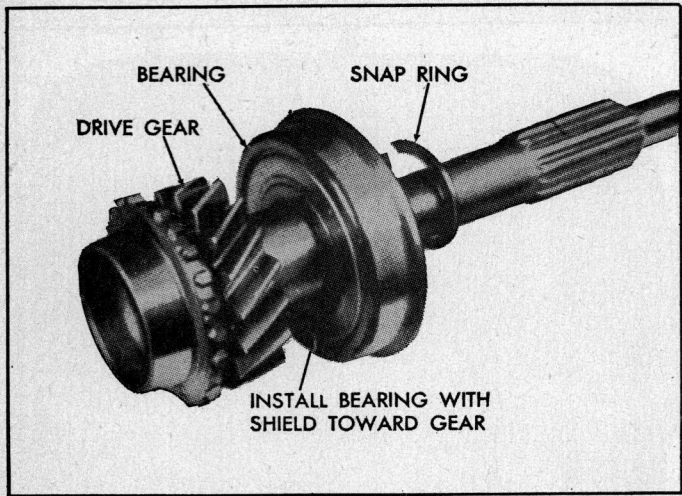

Fig. 16   Drive gear assembly

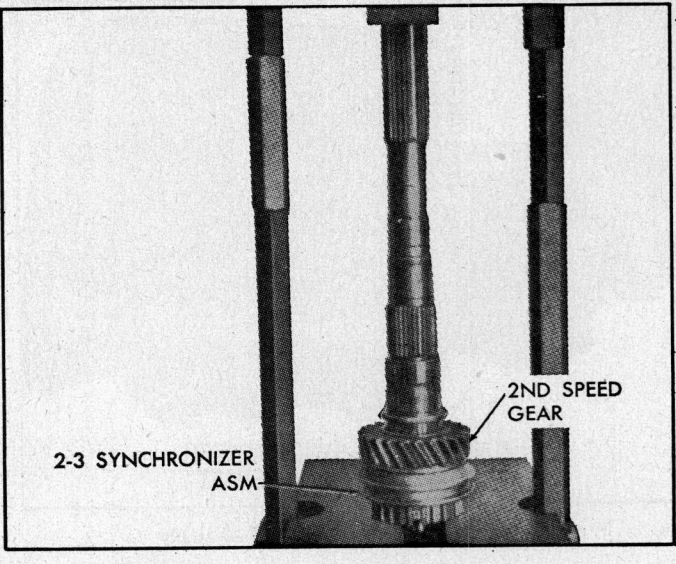

Fig. 17   Pressing 2nd-3rd synchronizer on mainshaft

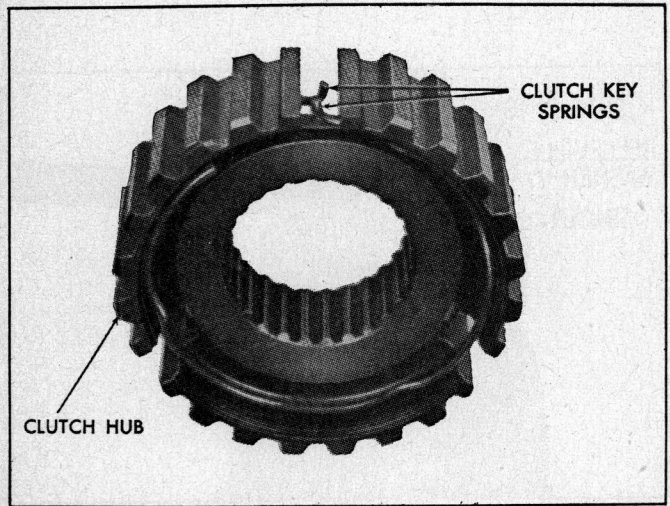

Fig. 18   Both clutch key springs installed

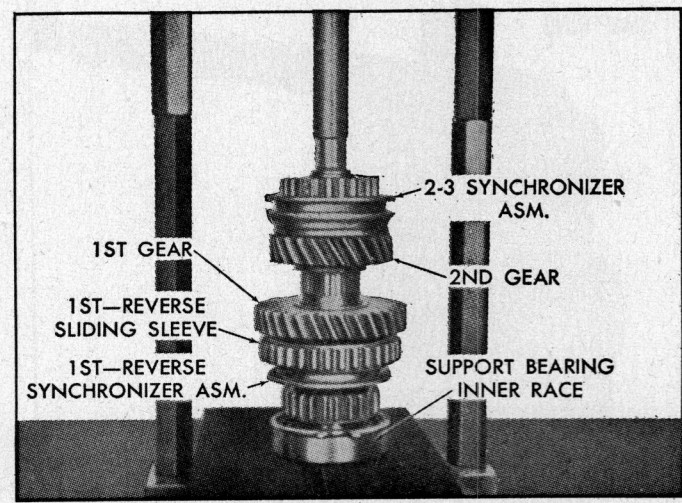

Fig. 19   Pressing mainshaft components together

ing it to protrude $1/16$ to $5/64''$ above fork.

5. Insert 2nd-3rd speed shifter shaft from front of case, with notches down, pushing it through the shifter fork shoulder toward front. Install lock pin allowing it to protrude $1/16$ to $5/64''$ above fork.

6. Insert selector shaft in case, push through 2nd-3rd speed intermediate lever and through 1st-Reverse lever. Install lock pins allowing to protrude $1/16$ to $5/64''$ above lever.

7. Insert both lock balls and thrust springs into bores in case and drive in plugs.

8. Remove rear extension bolts, pull back on extension and rotate extension until bore for reverse idler is exposed.

9. Place lock ball into shaft and from rear of case install shaft into gear. Drive shaft into place.

10. Using tool J-23562 install a spacer, row of roller bearings (24) and a spacer at each end of countergear. Use heavy grease to hold them in place.

11. Coat thrust washer with ball and roller bearing grease and stick to case.

NOTE: Lugs of thrust washers must fit into case slots.

12. Turn case extension until countergear shaft bore is exposed.

13. Place lock ball into shaft and from rear of case insert shaft so that thrust washer is held in position. Hold opposite thrust washer in position by using a short drift.

14. Insert countergear into case.

15. Insert shaft into countergear pushing out special tool. Align lock ball with groove in case and tap shaft into case.

16. Align rear bearing retainer and install retaining bolts.

17. Install case cover gasket, cover and screws.

18. Install gearshift linkages in reverse sequence to removal.

NOTE: Start idler lever shaft into shift control simultaneously when installing selector ring.

FOUR SPEED MANUAL SHIFT TRANSMISSIONS

See Car Chapters for Linkage Adjustments and Removal Procedures

APPLICATION INDEX

Car Make	Transmission Type	Page
AMERICAN MOTORS		
1969-74	1	2-200
BUICK—Intermediates		
1969-73 Muncie	3	2-206
CAMARO		
1969-74 Muncie	3	2-206
1969-74 Saginaw	6	2-215
CHEVELLE & MONTE CARLO		
1969-74 Muncie	3	2-206
1969-74 Saginaw	6	2-215
CHEVROLET		
1969 Muncie	3	2-206
1969 Saginaw	6	2-215
CHEVROLET VEGA		
1971-72	7	2-218
1973-74 Saginaw	6	2-215
CHEVY NOVA		
1969-74 Muncie	3	2-206
1969-74 Saginaw	6	2-215
COMET & MONTEGO		
1969-73 V8 Ford	5	2-212
CORVETTE		
1969-74 Muncie	3	2-206
1974	1	2-200
COUGAR		
1969-73	5	2-212

Car Make	Transmission Type	Page
DODGE		
1969-74	4	2-209
FAIRLANE & TORINO		
1969-73 V8 Ford	5	2-212
FALCON		
1969-70 V8 Ford	5	2-212
FORD		
1969 V8 Ford	5	2-212
FORD PINTO		
1971-73 English	8	2-224
1971-74 German	9	2-227
MUSTANG		
1969-73 V8 Ford	5	2-212
MUSTANG II		
1974	2	2-204
OLDS—Intermediates		
1969-74 Muncie	3	2-206
PLYMOUTH		
1969-74	4	2-209
PONTIAC—Seniors		
1969-71 Muncie	3	2-206
PONTIAC—Intermediates		
1969-74 Saginaw	6	2-215
1969-74 Muncie	3	2-206

FOUR SPEED MANUAL SHIFT TRANSMISSIONS

Type One Warner T-10

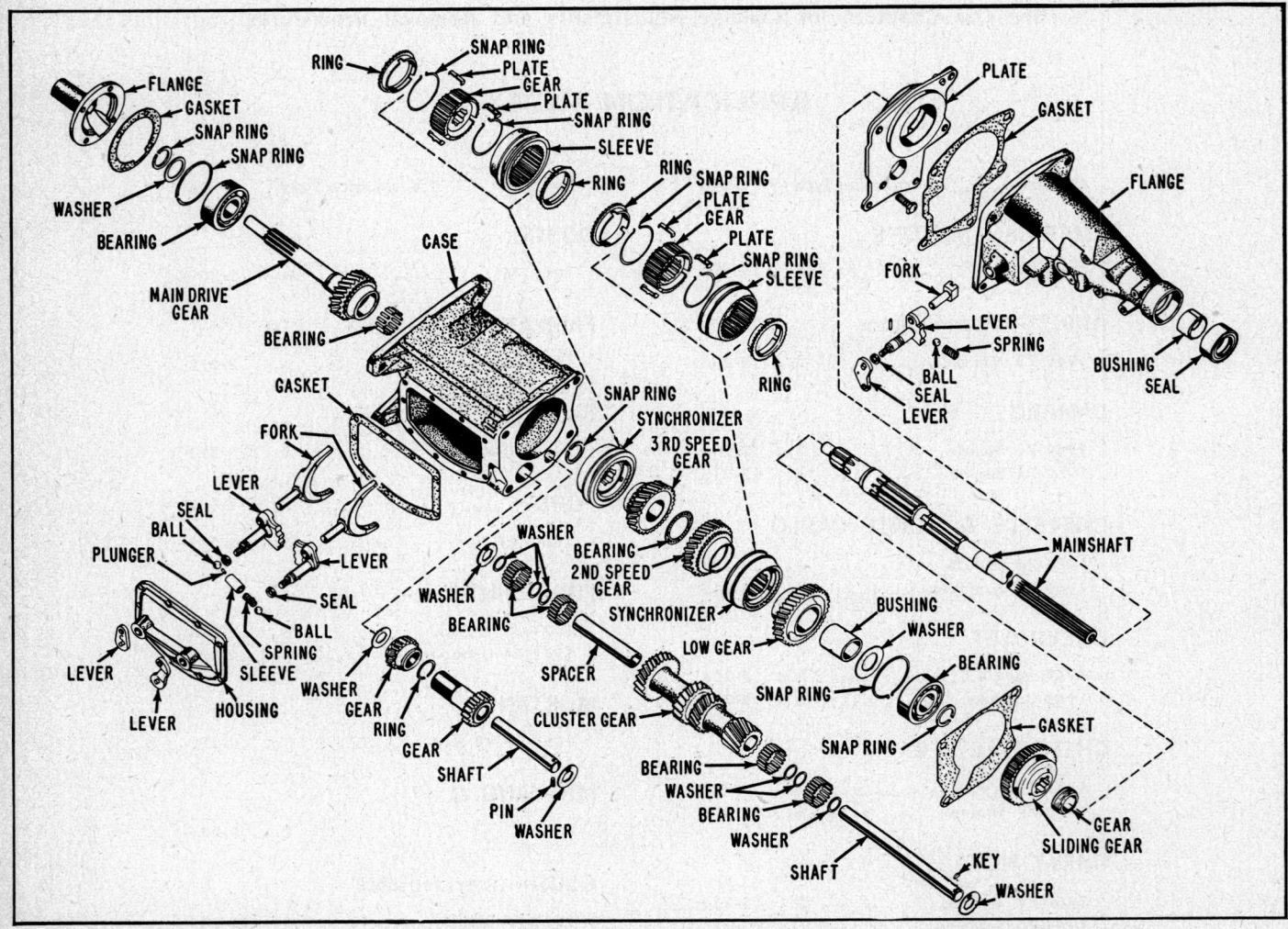

Fig. 1   Type 1 Warner T-10 four speed transmission. Some units do not have the mainshaft low gear bushing shown.

Side Cover, Remove

1. Disconnect control rods from levers.
2. Remove cover assembly from transmission and allow oil to drain.
3. Remove outer shift lever nuts and lockwashers and pull levers from shaft.
4. Carefully push shifter shafts into cover, allowing detent balls to fall free, then remove both shifter shafts.
5. Remove interlock sleeve, pin and poppet spring.

Side Cover, Install

1. Install interlock sleeve and one shifter shaft. Place detent ball into sleeve followed by poppet spring and interlock pin.
2. Start second shifter shaft into posi-

tion and place second detent ball on poppet spring. Compress ball and spring with screwdriver and push shifter shaft fully in.
3. With transmission in neutral and shifter forks and levers in place, lower side cover into place. Install attaching bolts, using sealer on bolts to prevent leakage. Tighten bolts evenly.

Disassemble Transmission

1. Remove side cover as outlined above.
2. Remove front bearing retainer.
3. Drive lock pin from bottom side of reverse shifter lever boss, Fig. 3, and pull shifter out about 1/8". This disengages reverse shift fork from reverse gear.

4. Unfasten extension housing from rear bearing retainer (adapter). Tap extension with soft hammer in rearward direction to start. When reverse idler shaft is out as far as it will go, move extension to left so reverse fork clears reverse gear, and remove extension and gasket.
5. Remove speedometer drive gear with a suitable puller.
6. The rear reverse idler gear, tanged thrust washer and reverse gear may now be removed, Figs. 4 and 5.
7. Remove self-locking bolts attaching rear bearing retainer (adapter) to transmission case. Then carefully remove entire mainshaft assembly.
8. Lift front reverse ider gear and thrust washer from case, Fig. 6.

Fig. 3   Removing reverse shifter lock pin

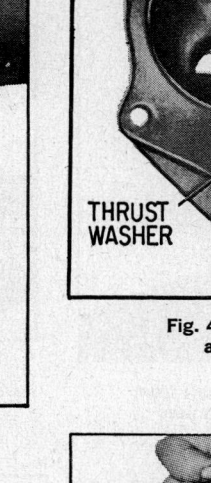

Fig. 4   Reverse idler shaft and reverse shifter

Fig. 5   Reverse gear rear idler removal

Fig. 6   Reverse gear front idler removal

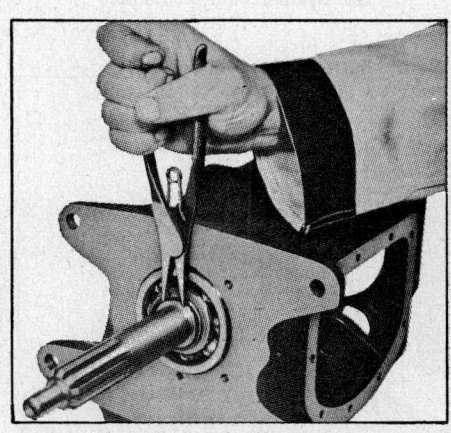

Fig. 7   Removing main drive gear snap ring

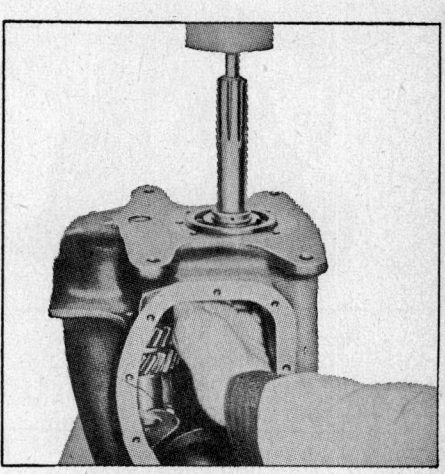

Fig. 8   Removing main drive gear from front bearing

9. Unload bearing rollers from main drive gear and remove 4th speed synchronizing ring.
10. Remove main drive gear snap ring, Fig. 7, and remove spacer washer.
11. With soft hammer, tap main drive gear down from front bearing, Fig. 8.
12. From inside case, tap out front bearing and snap ring.
13. From front of case, tap out countershaft, Fig. 9, using a dummy shaft as shown. Remove countergear and both tanged thrust washers.
14. Remove dummy shaft, all 80 rollers and six spacers from countergear.
15. Remove mainshaft front snap ring, Fig. 10, and slide 3-4 speed synchronizer, 3rd speed gear and synchronizing ring, 2-3 speed gear thrust washer (needle roller bearing), 2nd speed gear and synchronizing ring from front of mainshaft.
16. Spread rear bearing snap ring and

press mainshaft out of retainer, Fig. 11.
17. Remove mainshaft rear snap ring. Support 1-2 speed synchronizer assembly Fig. 12, and press on rear of mainshaft to remove shaft from remaining parts on shaft.

Cleaning & Inspection

1. Wash transmission case inside and out with cleaning solvent and inspect for cracks. Inspect front face of case for burrs and, if present, dress them off with a fine cut mill file.
2. Wash front and rear bearings in cleaning solvent. Blow out bearings with compressed air. *Do not allow bearings to spin; turn them slowly by hand. Spinning bearings will damage race and balls.*
3. Make sure bearings are clean, then lubricate them with light engine oil and check them for roughness. Roughness may be determined by turning outer race by hand.
4. All main drive gear and countergear

bearing rollers should be inspected closely and replaced if they show wear. Inspect countershaft and replace if necessary. Replace all worn spacers.
5. Inspect all gears and first speed gear bushing (or sleeve) and, if necessary, replace all that are worn or damaged.

Synchronizers

Clutch hubs and sliding sleeves are a selected assembly and should be kept together as originally assembled, but the three keys and two springs may be replaced if worn or broken.

Push hub from sliding sleeve. Keys will fall free and springs may be easily removed. To assemble, place the two springs in position (one on each side of hub) so tanged end of each spring falls into same keyway in hub. Place keys in position and, holding them in place, slide hub into sleeve.

Assemble Mainshaft

1. From rear of mainshaft, assemble 1-

Fig. 9   Removing countershaft

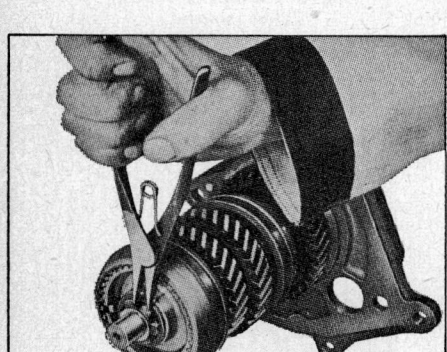

Fig. 10   Removing mainshaft front snap ring

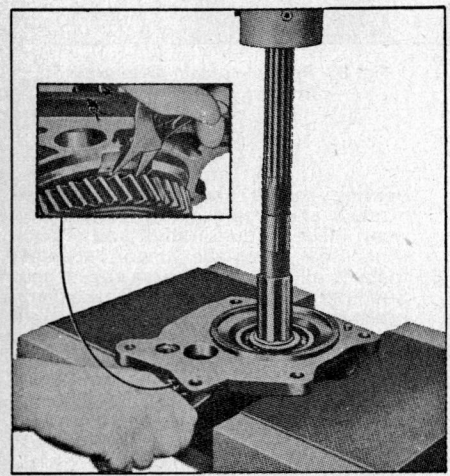

Fig. 11   Removing mainshaft from rear bearing retainer

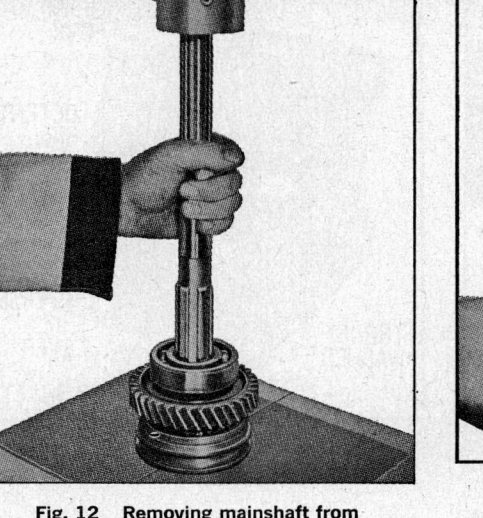

Fig. 12   Removing mainshaft from rear bearing and synchronizer

Fig. 13   Installing first speed gear bushing

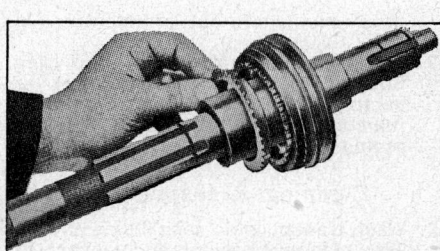

Fig. 14   Installing synchronizer ring

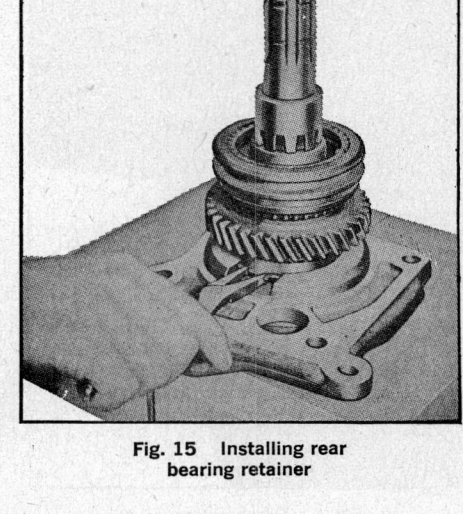

Fig. 15   Installing rear bearing retainer

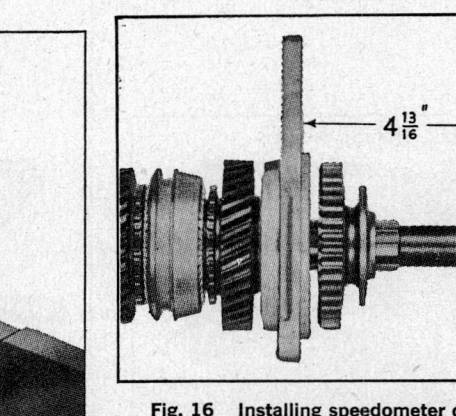

Fig. 16   Installing speedometer drive gear

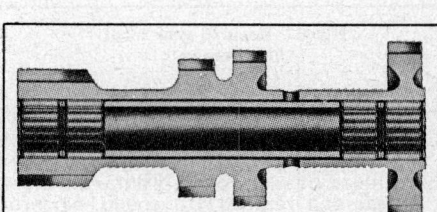

Fig. 17   Cross section of countergear assembly

2 speed synchronizer to mainshaft with sleeve taper toward rear. Press 1st gear bushing on shaft, Fig. 13.

2. Install 1st gear synchronizing ring so that notches in ring correspond to keys in hub, Fig. 14.

3. Install 1st gear with hub toward front, and 1st gear thrust washer. Make certain that grooves in washer are facing 1st gear.

4. Press on rear bearing with snap ring groove toward front of transmission.

5. Choose correct selective fit snap ring and install it in groove in mainshaft behind rear bearing. *Always use new snap ring and do not expand it further than necessary for assembly.*

6. From front of mainshaft, install 2nd gear synchronizing ring so notches in ring correspond to keys in hub.

7. Install 2nd gear with hub of gear toward back of transmission. Install 2-3 speed gear thrust washer (needle roller bearing).

8. Install 3rd gear with hub to front of transmission, and 3rd gear synchronizing ring with notches to front of transmission.

9. Install 3-4 synchronizer with sleeve taper toward front, making sure keys in hub correspond to notches

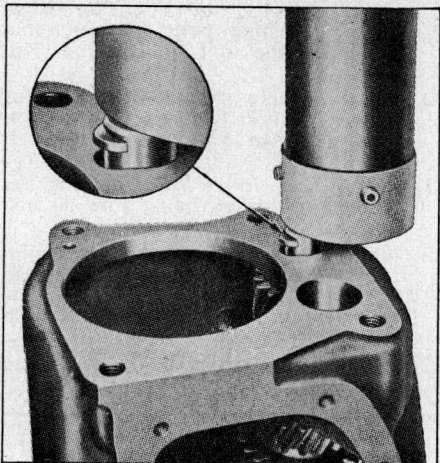

Fig. 18   Installing countershaft

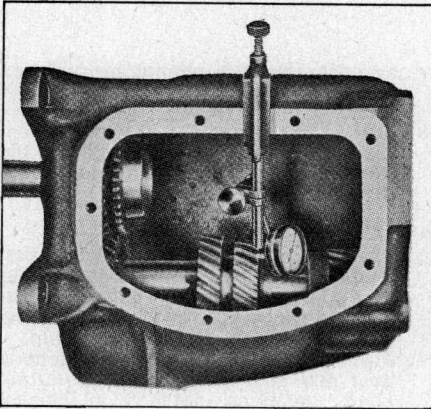

Fig. 19   Checking countershaft end play

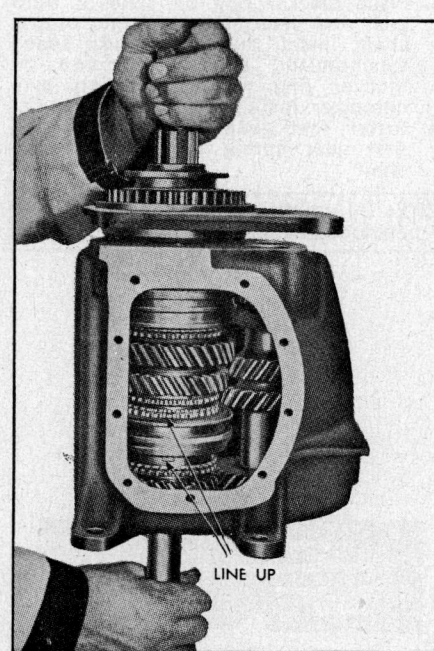

Fig. 20   Installing mainshaft assembly

with 3rd gear synchronizing ring.

10. Install snap ring in groove in mainshaft in front of 3-4 synchronizer. *With the correct size snap ring, 3rd speed gear will have .010-.015" end play with 3-4 synchronizer hub forward against snap ring.*

11. Install rear bearing retainer, Fig. 15. Spread selective fit snap ring in plate to allow snap ring to drop around rear bearing and press end of mainshaft until snap ring engages groove in rear bearing (use largest size snap ring that will fit into groove).

12. Install reverse gear with shift collar to rear.

13. Press speedometer drive gear onto mainshaft. Position speedometer gear as shown in Fig. 16.

Assemble Countergear

1. Install roller spacer in countergear.

2. Using heavy grease to retain rollers, install 20 rollers in either end of countergear, two spacers, 20 more rollers, then one spacer, Fig. 17.

3. Assemble rollers and spacers in the same manner in other end of countergear. Then insert dummy shaft in countergear to retain rollers.

Assemble Transmission

1. Rest case on its side with side cover opening toward you. Place countergear tanged thrust washers in place, retaining them with heavy grease, making sure that tangs are resting in notches in case.

2. Place countergear assembly in bottom of case, making sure that tanged thrust washers are not knocked out of place.

3. Press bearing onto main drive gear with snap ring groove to front.

4. Install spacer washer and selective fit snap ring in groove on gear stem.

5. Install main drive gear assembly through side cover opening and into position in transmission front bore. Tap lightly into place with a soft hammer, if necessary. Place snap ring in groove in front bearing.

6. With transmission resting on its front face, move countergear into mesh with main drive gear, making sure thrust washers remain in place. Install key in end of countershaft and, from front of case, tap or press shaft, Fig. 18, until end of shaft is flush with rear of case and dummy shaft is displaced.

7. Attach dial indicator as shown in Fig. 19 and check end play of countergear. End play must not be more than .025".

8. Install 14 rollers into main drive gear, using heavy grease to hold them in place. Place gasket in position on front face of rear bearing retainer, using heavy grease to hold it in position.

9. Install 4th gear synchronizing ring on main drive gear with clutch key notches toward rear of case.

10. Position reverse idler gear thrust washer (untanged) on machined face

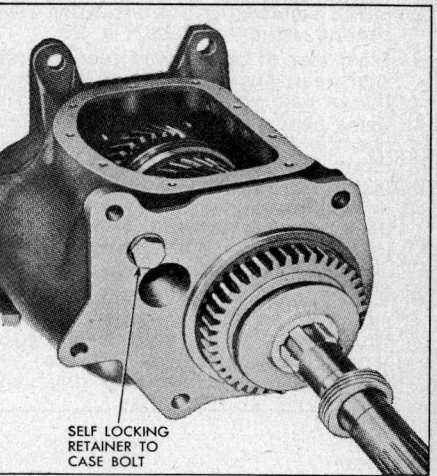

Fig. 21   Self-locking bearing retainer-to-case bolt

Fig. 22   Installing extension housing on transmission case

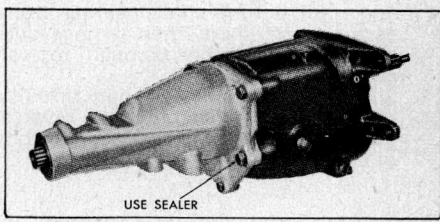

Fig. 23   Sealing lower right attaching bolt

of ear cast in case for reverse idler shaft. Position front reverse idler gear on top of thrust washer, with hub facing toward rear of case.

11. Lower mainshaft assembly into case, making certain that notches on 4th gear synchronizing ring correspond to keys in synchronizer, Fig. 20.

12. Install self-locking bolt attaching rear bearing retainer to case, Fig. 21.

13. From rear of case, insert rear reverse idler gear, engaging splines with portion of gear within case.

14. Using heavy grease, place gasket into position on rear face of rear bearing retainer.

15. Install remaining tanged thrust washer into place on reverse idler shaft, being sure tang on washer is in notch in idler thrust face of extension.

16. Place two synchronizers in neutral position. *If locking-up of gears is encountered, a small amount of petrolatum may be applied to the 1st speed gear synchronizing ring, en-*

abling it to turn freely on 1st speed gear hub.

17. Pull reverse shifter shaft to left side of extension and rotate shaft to bring reverse shift fork to extreme forward position in extension. Line up front and rear reverse idler gears, making sure front thrust washer is in place.

18. Start extension into case. Fig. 22, by carefully inserting reverse idler shaft through reverse idler gears. Slowly push it on shifter shaft until shift fork engages reverse gear shift collar. When fork engages, rotate shifter shaft to move reverse gear rearward, permitting extension to slide onto transmission case.

19. Install extension and retainer to case

attaching bolts, and extension to retainer attaching bolts. Use suitable sealer on the bolt indicated in Fig. 23.

20. Adjust reverse shifter shaft so that groove in shaft lines up with hole in boss and drive in lock pin from top of boss, Fig. 22.

21. Install main drive gear bearing retainer and gasket, being sure oil well lines up with oil outlet hole.

22. Install shift fork in each synchronizer sleeve. With both synchronizers in neutral, install side cover with gasket. Use suitable sealer when installing lower right cover bolt.

23. Install shifter levers, lock washers and nuts.

Type Two

Transmission Disassembly

1. Drain lubricant from transmission by removing the lower extension housing bolt.
2. Drive access plug from rear of extension housing and remove offset lever assembly, Fig. 2-1.
3. Remove extension housing from case.
4. Remove transmission cover, shifter fork and shift rod assembly.
5. Remove front bearing retainer and gasket.
6. Remove spring clip securing reverse lever assembly to pivot bolt, then remove pivot bolt and reverse level assembly.
7. Support countershaft gear with a wire hook. Drive a dummy countershaft through front of case until cluster gear drops to bottom of case, then remove counter shaft through rear of case and lower the cluster gear to bottom of case.
8. Remove input shaft, Fig. 2-2.
9. Remove speedometer drive gear snap ring, slide gear off output shaft and remove lock ball from output shaft.
10. Remove output shaft bearing retaining snap ring. Using the outer snap ring, pull output shaft bearing from case and off shaft, then remove output shaft assembly through top of case.
11. Slide reverse idler gear shaft through rear of case, then remove reverse gear and cluster gear from bottom of case.

Cover Disassembly

1. Remove detent screw, spring and plunger, Fig. 2-1.
2. Pull shifter rod shaft rearward and rotate counter-clockwise. Remove manual selector and interlock to shaft spring pin, shifter shaft, manual selector and the interlock from cover.
3. Remove the first-second shift fork, then the third-fourth shift fork.
4. Reverse procedure for reassembly.

Output Shaft Disassembly

1. Scribe alignment marks on sychronizer and blocker ring for alignment during installation, remove snap ring from front of shaft and slide third and fourth speed synchronizer assembly, blocker rings and third speed gear off shaft, Fig. 2-1.
2. Remove next snap ring, then second speed gear thrust washer, second speed gear and blocker ring from shaft.

NOTE: The first and second speed

synchronizer hub cannot be removed from output shaft.

3. Remove first gear thrust washer from rear of shaft, first gear spring pin retainer and slide first gear and blocker ring off shaft.

Output Shaft Reassembly

1. Place blocker ring on cone of first gear and slide assembly onto output shaft, engaging notches in blocker ring with inserts in synchronizer, Fig. 2-3 and install first gear spring pin.
2. Place blocker ring on cone of second gear and slide assembly onto output shaft, engaging notches in blocker ring with inserts in synchronizer. Install second gear thrust washer and new snap ring.
3. Place blocker ring on cone of third gear and slide assembly onto output shaft, install third and fourth speed synchronizer, engaging notches on blocker ring with inserts on synchronizer. Install new snap ring.
4. Install first gear thrust washer and first gear spring pin retainer onto shaft.

NOTE: Oil grooves in thrust washer must be positioned against gear.

Fig. 2-2   Removing input shaft. RAD four speed transmission

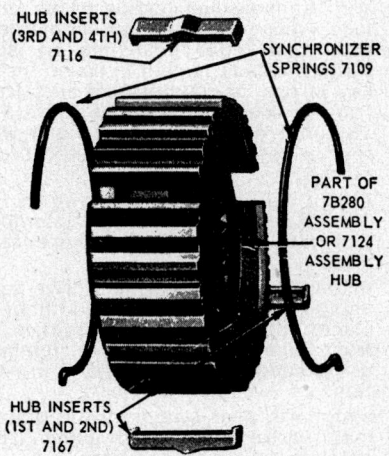

Fig. 2-3   Synchronizer assembly. RAD four speed transmission

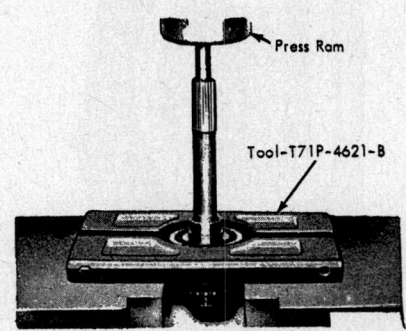

Fig. 2-4   Input shaft bearing removal. RAD four speed transmission

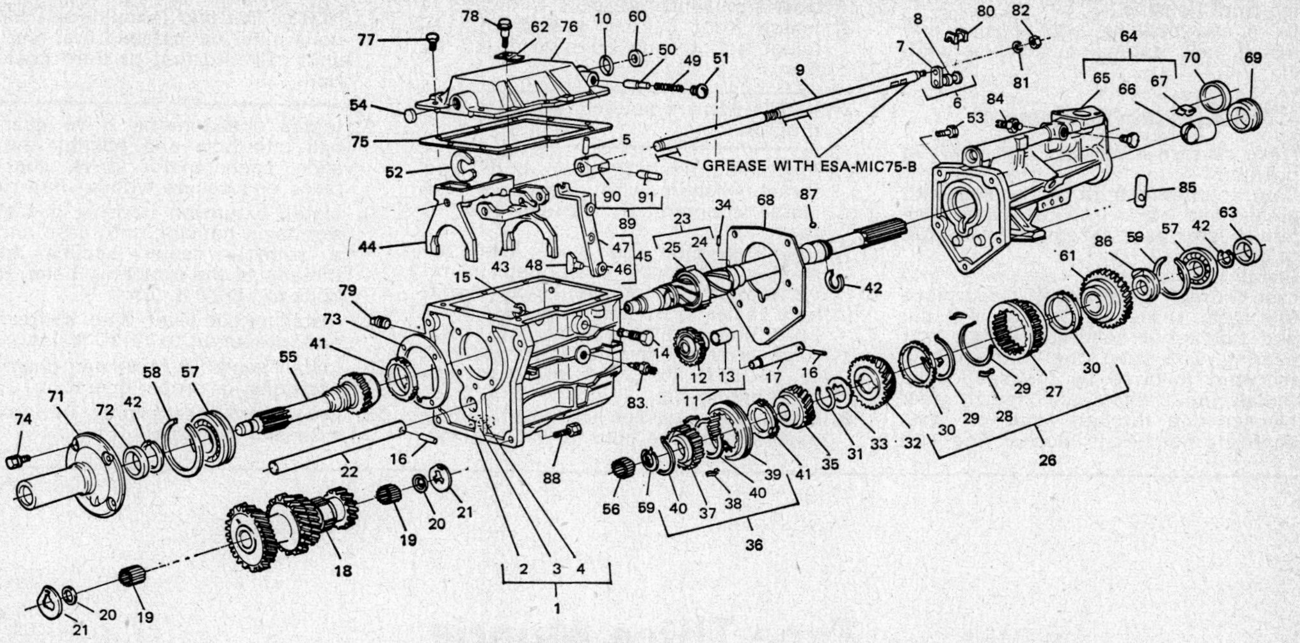

GREASE WITH ESA-MIC75-B

Fig. 2-1 RAD four speed transmission disassembled.

ITEM	PART NAME	ITEM	PART NAME	ITEM	PART NAME
1.	TRANS. CASE ASSY.	31.	2ND SPEED GEAR RETAINING SNAP RING	62.	SPARK CONTROL SWITCH WIRE RETAINING CLIP
2.	CASE	32.	2ND SPEED GEAR	63.	SPEEDOMETER DRIVE GEAR
3.	TRANS. CASE CHIP MAGNET	33.	2ND SPEED GEAR THRUST WASHER	64.	EXTENSION ASSY.
4.	SPRING NUT	34.	PIN	65.	EXTENSION HOUSING
5.	PIN	35.	3RD SPEED GEAR	66.	EXTENSION HOUSING BUSHING
6.	LEVER ASSY.	36.	3RD & 4TH SPEED SYNCHRONIZER ASSY.	67.	SHIFT LEVER REVERSE STOP
7.	OFFSET LEVER	37.	SYNCHRONIZER CLUTCH HUB	68.	EXTENSION HOUSING GASKET
8.	PIN	38.	SYNCHRONIZER HUB INSERTS	69.	EXTENSION HOUSING OIL SEAL
9.	SHIFTER SHAFT	39.	SYNCHRONIZER SLEEVE	70.	EXTENSION HOUSING PLUG
10.	O-RING SEAL	40.	SYNCHRONIZER RETAINING SPRINGS	71.	INPUT SHAFT BEARING RETAINER
11.	REVERSE IDLER ASSY.	41.	SYNCHRONIZER BLOCKING RING	72.	INPUT SHAFT OIL SEAL
12.	REVERSE IDLER GEAR	42.	SNAP RING	73.	INPUT SHAFT BEARING RETAINER GASKET
13.	BUSHING	43.	1ST & 2ND GEAR SHIFT FORK	74.	INPUT SHAFT RETAINING BOLT
14.	REVERSE GEAR SELECTOR FORK PIVOT PIN	44.	3RD & 4TH GEAR SHIFT FORK	75.	CASE COVER GASKET
15.	RETAINING RING	45.	REVERSE GEAR SHIFT RELAY LEVER ASSY.	76.	CASE COVER
16.	PIN	46.	RELAY LEVER RING	77.	CASE COVER RETAINING BOLT
17.	REVERSE IDLER GEAR SHAFT	47.	RELAY LEVER	78.	BOLT
18.	COUNTERSHAFT GEAR	48.	REVERSE GEAR SHIFT FORK	79.	OIL FILLER PLUG
19.	COUNTERSHAFT ROLLER BEARINGS	49.	SHIFTER INTERLOCK SPRING	80.	GEAR SHIFT DAMPER BUSHING
20.	WASHER	50.	MESHLOCK PLUNGER	81.	SPRING LOCK WASHER
21.	COUNTERSHAFT GEAR THRUST WASHERS	51.	SCREW	82.	LEVER RETAINING NUT
22.	COUNTERSHAFT	52.	GEAR SELECTOR INTERLOCK PLATE	83.	BACK-UP LAMP SWITCH
23.	OUTPUT SHAFT ASSY.	53.	EXTENSION HOUSING RETAINING BOLT	84.	SEAT BELT WARNING SENSOR SWITCH
24.	OUTPUT SHAFT	54.	WELSH PLUG	85.	TRANSMISSION IDENTIFICATION TAG
25.	1ST & 2ND GEAR CLUSTER SYNCHRONIZER HUB	55.	INPUT SHAFT	86.	1ST GEAR THRUST WASHER
26.	OUTPUT SHAFT GEAR ASSY.	56.	MAINSHAFT ROLLER BEARINGS	87.	BALL
27.	REVERSE SLIDING GEAR	57.	BALL BEARING	88.	TRANS. RETAINING BOLT
28.	SYNCHRONIZER HUB INSERT	58.	BEARING RETAINING SNAP RING	89.	TRANS. CONTROL SELECTOR ARM ASSY.
29.	SYNCHRONIZER RETAINING SPRING	59.	RETAINING RING	90.	CONTROL SELECTOR ARM
30.	SYNCHRONIZER BLOCKING RING	60.	SHIFT SHAFT SEAL	91.	GEARSHIFT RETAINING PIN
		61.	1ST SPEED GEAR		

Countershaft Gear Bearing, Replace

1. Remove dummy shaft, bearing retainer washers and needle bearings from gear.

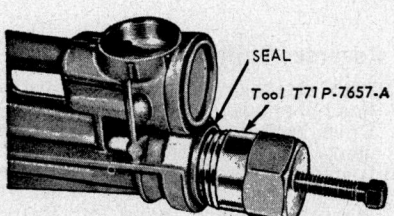

Fig. 2-5 Extension housing seal removal. RAD four speed transmission

2. Coat bore of gear with grease and holding dummy shaft in the gear, install needle bearings and retainer washers at each end of gear.

Input Shaft Bearing, Replace

1. Remove needle bearings from bore of input shaft.
2. Remove input shaft bearing snap ring and press bearing from shaft, Fig. 2-4.
3. Press new bearing onto shaft with snap ring groove facing front of shaft and install new snap ring.
4. Lightly coat bore of input shaft with grease and install needle bearings.

NOTE: A heavy coat of grease will plug bearing lubrication holes.

Extension Housing Bushing and Seal, Replace

1. Remove seal from extension housing, Fig. 2-5.
2. Using a suitable puller, remove bush-

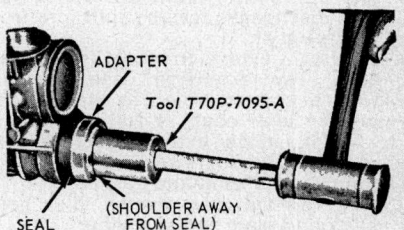

Fig. 2-6 Extension housing seal installation. RAD four speed transmission

3. Drive new bushing into housing and install new extension housing seal, Fig. 2-6.

Transmission Reassembly

1. Place reverse idler gear and shaft in position.
2. Coat countershaft thrust washer with grease and place into case and position cluster gear assembly in bottom of case.
3. Install output shaft assembly into case through cover opening and place first gear thrust washer on roll pin and holding it securely. Install rear bearing, with snap ring groove facing rearward followed by the snap ring.
4. Install input shaft and fourth gear blocker ring through front of case, engaging notches in blocker ring with inserts on synchronizer.
5. Install front bearing gasket and retainer and torque bolts to 11-15 ft. lbs.

NOTE: Apply a suitable sealer to bolt threads.

6. Align countershaft gear bore and thrust washers with case bore and install countershaft through rear of case.
7. Install reverse idle gear lever assembly with fork positioned in reverse idler gear groove. Apply a suitable sealer to threads of reverse lever pivot bolt and install bolt into case. Align lever on pivot bolt, torque bolt to 15-25 ft. lbs., and install reverse lever spring clip.
8. Install cover gasket and cover, wiring clips and torque bolts to 7-10 ft. lbs.

NOTE: The two (shouldered) locating bolts must be installed first and place shift rail into first or third gear position.

9. Install speedometer drive gear lock ball into hole and holding the ball, slide speedometer drive gear into place and secure with a snap ring.
10. Install extension housing gasket and extension housing onto case and with a suitable sealer applied to the threads of the attaching bolts, torque bolts to 18-27 ft. lbs.
11. Install offset lever onto shifter shaft and torque nut to 14-20 ft. lbs.
12. Install gearshift lever and check gear positions for proper operation.
13. Drive new access plug into rear of extension housing.

Type Three Muncie

SIDE COVER, REPLACE

1. Referring to Fig. 3-2 disconnect control rods from levers.
2. Shift transmisson into 2nd speed before removing cover by moving 1-2 shifter lever into forward detent position.
3. Remove cover from case.
4. Reverse procedure to install the cover, being sure first to shift the transmission into 2nd gear. Make sure shift forks are aligned with their respective grooves in synchronizer sliding sleeves.

DISASSEMBLE TRANSMISSION

1. Remove side cover.
2. Remove front bearing retainer.
3. Shift transmission into two gears at once to keep mainshaft from turning, then remove retainer nut from main drive gear.
4. With gears in neutral, drive lock pin from reverse shifter lever boss and pull shifter shaft out about 1/8". This disengages reverse shift fork from reverse gear.
5. Unfasten extension case from main case. Tap extension case rearward with a soft hammer to start. When reverse idler shaft is out as far as it will go, move extension to left so reverse fork clears reverse gear. Then remove extension and gasket.
6. Now remove rear reverse idler gear, shaft and plate thrust washer.
7. Use a suitable puller to remove speedometer gear from mainshaft, after which remove reverse gear.

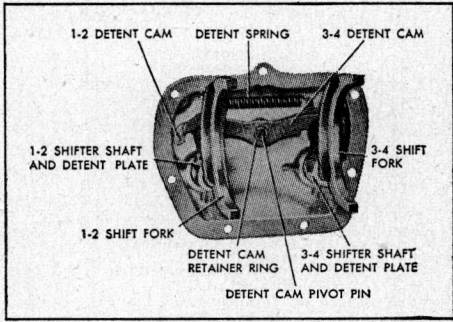

Fig. 3-2 Transmission side cover

8. Slide 3-4 synchronizer clutch sleeve to 4th gear position before trying to remove mainshaft assembly from case.
9. Remove rear bearing retainer and mainshaft assembly from case by tapping retainer with soft hammer.
10. Unload bearing rollers from main drive gear and remove 4th gear synchronizer blocking ring.
11. Lift front half of reverse idler gear and its tanged washer from case.
12. Press main drive gear down into case and remove. From inside of case, tap out front bearing and snap ring.
13. From front of case, press out countershaft. Then remove countergear and both tanged washers.
14. Remove mainshaft front snap ring and strip mainshaft of loose parts.
15. Spread rear bearing retainer snap ring and press mainshaft out of retainer.

NOTE: Early models of this transmission

use a snap ring behind the 1-2 synchronizer hub to retain the hub in position while later units have a sleeve within the 1st speed gear. This sleeve acts as a spacer between the rear bearing and 1-2 synchronizer hub.

16. Remove mainshaft rear snap ring. Support 1st gear in a press and press against rear of shaft to remove it from rear bearing, 1st gear thrust washer, 1st gear and synchronizing ring.
17. Remove 1-2 synchronizer snap ring and remove 1-2 synchronizer unit, 2nd gear synchronizer ring and 2nd gear from shaft, Fig. 3-3.

UNIT REPAIRS
Reverse Idler

Because of the high degree of accuracy to which the reverse idler gear bushings are machined, the bushings are not serviced separately. Check bushings for excessive wear by using a narrow feeler gauge between shaft and bushing. Proper clearance is from .003 to .005".

Reverse Shifter Shaft & Seal

1. With extension case removed as outlined previously, remove shift fork.
2. Drive shifter shaft into case extension, allowing ball detent to drop into case. Remove shaft and ball detent spring.
3. Place ball detent spring into its hole and, from inside extension, install shifter shaft fully into its opening until detent plate is butted against inside

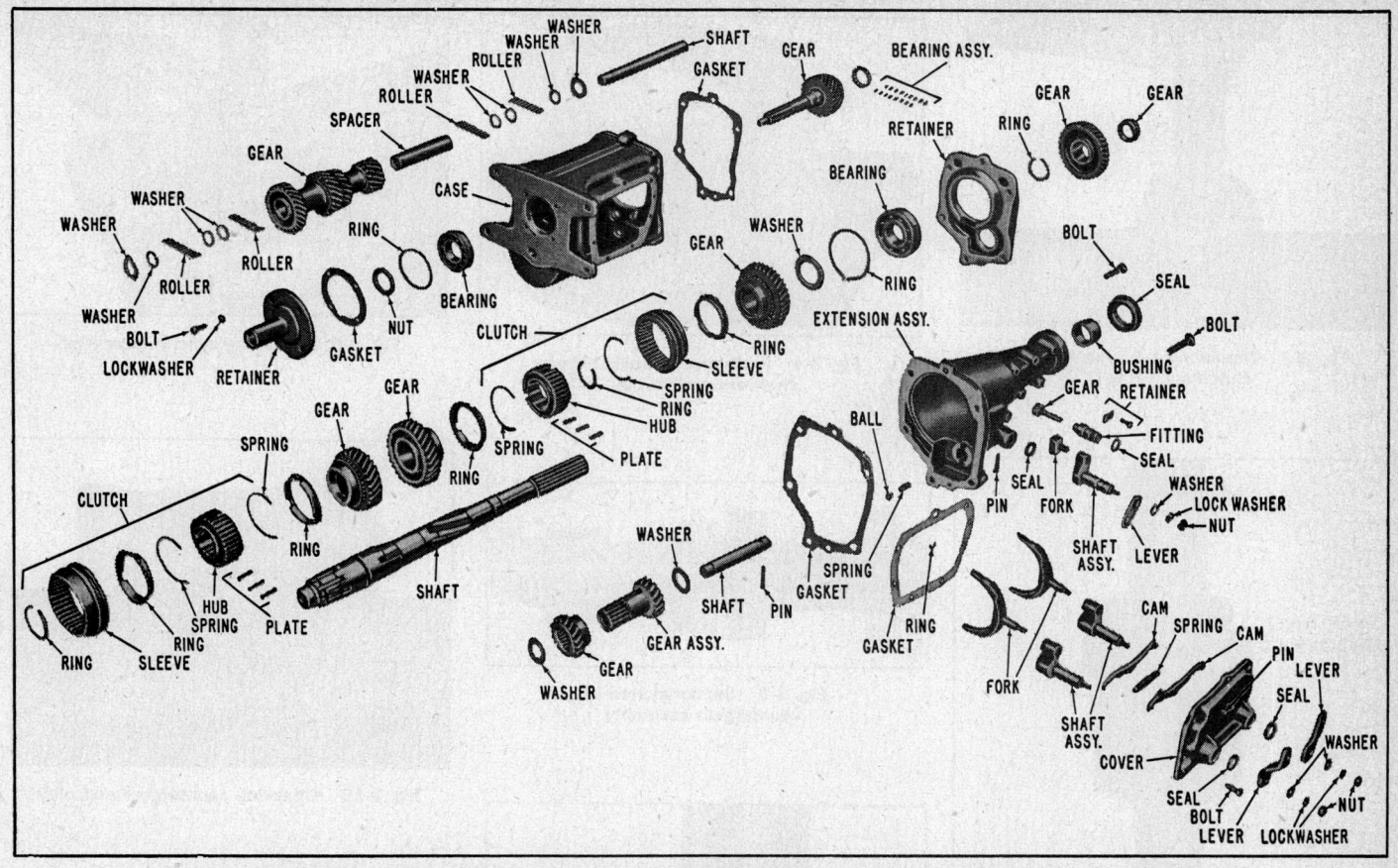

Fig. 3-1 Muncie four speed transmission. Early models use a snap ring (illustrated) behind the 1-2 synchronizer hub to retain the hub in position. Later units have a spacer sleeve within the 1st speed gear, (not illustrated)

of extension housing.

4. Place detent ball on spring, Fig. 3-4, and, holding ball down with thumb or a suitable tool, push shifter shaft back in, away from case until it is directly over ball and turn until ball drops into detent on shaft detent plate.
5. Install shift fork.

NOTE: Do not drive shifter shaft lock pin into place until extension has been installed on transmission case.

Extension Oil Seal or Bushing

If bushing in rear of extension requires replacement, remove oil seal and drive bushing into case extension. Drive new bushing in from the rear. Coat I.D. of bushing with transmission lubricant, then install new oil seal.

Clutch Keys & Springs

NOTE: The clutch hubs and sliding sleeves are a selected assembly and should be kept together as originally assembled. However, the three keys and two springs may be replaced if worn or broken.

1. To replace, push hub from sliding sleeve. Keys will fall free and springs easily removed.
2. Place the two springs in position (one on each side of hub) so all three keys are engaged by both springs. Place keys in position and, holding them in place, slide hub into sleeve.

Assemble Mainshaft

1. From rear of mainshaft, assemble 2nd gear with hub of gear toward rear of shaft.
2. Install 1-2 synchronizer clutch, with clutch sleeve taper to rear, together with a blocker ring on each side so their keyways line up with clutch keys, Fig. 3-5. On early units, install 1-2 synchronizer retainer snap ring (smaller of the two). On later units, install 1st gear spacer sleeve.
3. Install 1st gear (hub toward front) and 1st gear thrust washer.
4. Press rear bearing on mainshaft, Fig. 3-6, being sure to seat bearing firmly.
5. Choose correct selective fit snap ring and install it in groove of mainshaft behind rear bearing. (Snap rings of .084", .087", .090", .093", .096" are available.) With proper snap ring, maximum distance between ring and rear

face of bearing will be from zero to .005".
6. Install 3rd gear (hub to front) and 3rd gear synchronizing ring (notches to front).
7. Install 3-4 clutch assembly with both sleeve taper and hub toward front, making sure keys in hub correspond to notches in 3rd gear synchronizing ring.
8. Install snap ring in mainshaft groove in front of 3-4 synchronizer clutch with ends of snap ring seated behind spline teeth.
9. Install rear bearing retainer. Spread snap ring in plate to allow ring to drop around rear bearing and press on end of mainshaft until snap ring engages groove in rear bearing.
10. Install reverse gear with shift collar to rear.
11. Press speedometer drive gear on mainshaft to distance shown in Fig. 3-7.

Assemble Countergear

1. Install roller spacer in countergear.
2. Using heavy grease to retain rollers, install 28 rollers in either end of countergear, two .050"spacers, 28 more rollers, then one .050" spacer.

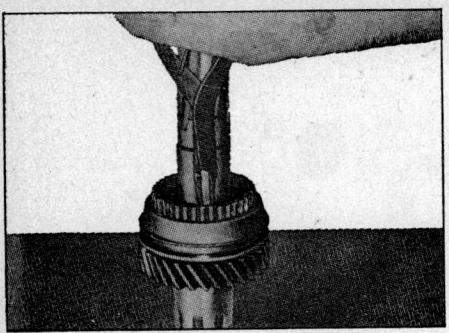

Fig. 3-3   Removing 1-2 synchronizer clutch snap ring

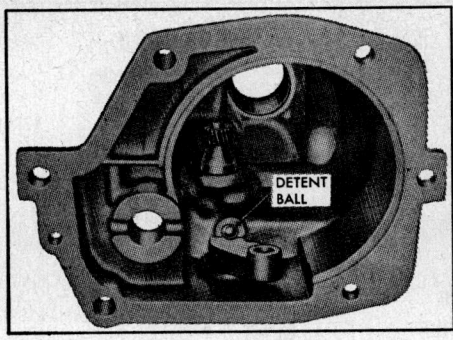

Fig. 3-4   Installing reverse shifter shaft and detent ball

DETENT BALL

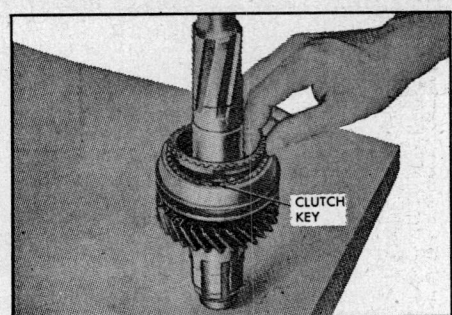

Fig. 3-5   Installing synchronizer ring

CLUTCH KEY

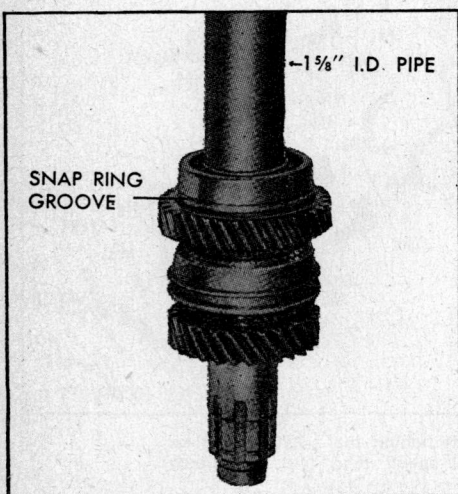

←1⅝" I.D. PIPE

SNAP RING GROOVE

Fig. 3-6   Installing mainshaft rear bearing

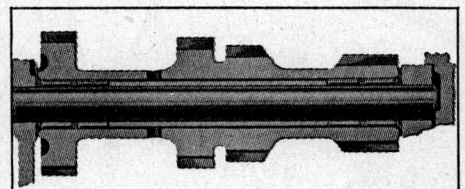

Fig. 3-8   Sectional view of countergear assembly

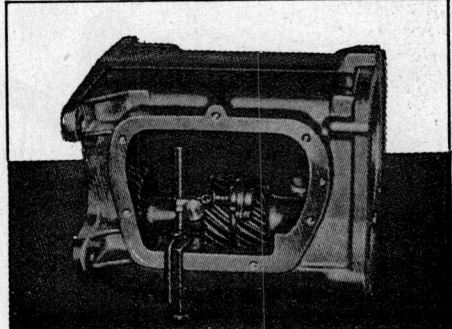

Fig. 3-10   Checking countergear end play

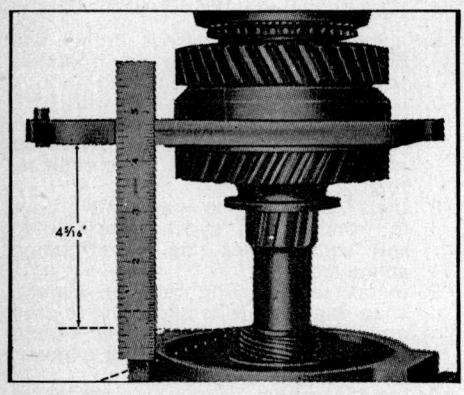

4⁵⁄₁₆"

Fig. 3-7   Installing speedometer drive gear

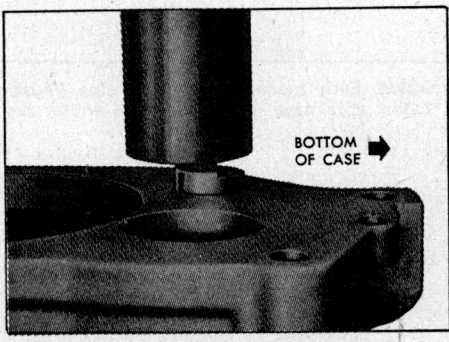

BOTTOM OF CASE →

Fig. 3-9   Installing countershaft

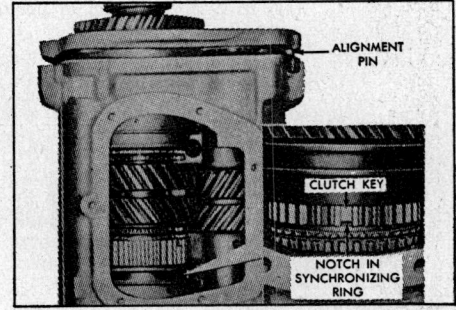

ALIGNMENT PIN

CLUTCH KEY

NOTCH IN SYNCHRONIZING RING

Fig. 3-11   Installing mainshaft assembly

Make same installation at other end of countergear, Fig. 3-8.

ASSEMBLE TRANS.

1. With transmission case on its side, put countergear tanged thrust washers in place, retaining them with heavy grease, and making sure tangs are resting in notches in case.
2. Set countergear in bottom of case.
3. Position transmission so it is resting on its front face.
4. Lubricate and insert countershaft through rear of case. Turn countershaft so flat on end of shaft is horizontal and facing bottom of case.
5. Align countergear with shaft in rear and hole in front of case. Press countershaft into case until flat on shaft is flush with rear of case, Fig. 3-9. Be sure thrust washers remain in place.
6. Attach a dial indicator as shown in Fig. 3-10 and check end play of countergear. If end play is greater than .025", new thrust washers must be installed.
7. Install 17 roller bearings in main drive gear, using heavy grease to hold bearings and cage in place.
8. Install main drive gear and pilot bearings through side cover opening and into transmission front bore.
9. Place gasket in position of front face of rear bearing retainer.
10. Install 4th gear synchronizing ring on main drive gear with notches toward rear.
11. Position tanged reverse idler gear thrust washer on machined face of ear cast in case for reverse idler shaft and hold with heavy grease. Position front reverse idler gear next to thrust washer, with hub facing toward rear.

NOTE: Before attempting to install mainshaft assembly in case, slide 3-4 synchronizer clutch sleeve forward into 4th speed detent position.

12. Lower mainshaft into case making certain notches in 4th speed synchronizing ring correspond to keys in clutch, Fig. 3-11.
13. Tap rear bearing into position.
14. Insert rear reverse idler gear.
15. Install remaining flat thrust washer on reverse idler shaft. If new idler shaft in being used, drive out roll pin and press it into new shaft.
16. Install reverse idler shaft, making sure to pick up rear tanged thrust washer. *Roll pin should be in a vertical position.*
17. Pull reverse shifter shaft to left side of extension and rotate shaft to bring

reverse shift fork forward in extension (reverse detent position). Start extension onto transmission case, while slowly pushing in on shifter shaft to engage shift fork with reverse gear shift collar. Then pilot reverse idler shaft into extension housing, permitting extension to slide into transmission case.
18. Install extension attaching bolts. Torque upper three bolts to 15-25-ft-lbs, and lower three bolts to 25-35 ft-lbs.
19. Push or pull reverse shifter shaft to line up holes and drive in lock pin. Then install shifter lever.
20. Press bearing onto main drive gear (snap ring groove to front) and into case until several main drive gear

retaining nut threads are exposed.
21. Lock transmission by shifting into two gears. Install main drive gear retaining nut. Be sure bearing fully seats against shoulder of gear. Torque nut to 40 ft-lbs and lock it in place by staking securely into shaft hole with center punch.
22. Install main drive gear bearing retainer, using sealer on bolts. Torque to 15-20 ft-lbs.
23. Shift 3-4 sliding sleeve into neutral and 1-2 sliding sleeve into 2nd gear position. Shift side cover 3-4 shift lever into neutral and 1-2 shift lever into 2nd gear.
24. Install side cover with gasket. Torque attaching bolts evenly to avoid cover distortion and torque to 15-20 ft-lbs.

Type Four Chrysler

DISASSEMBLE TRANS.

1. On early models, disconnect shift control rods from shift levers, shift transmission into two gears at once to prevent mainshaft from turning and remove flange from end of mainshaft.
2. All units, unfasten shift housing and with all levers in neutral position,

Fig. 4-2, pull housing out and away from case. Work shift forks out of synchronizer sleeves and remove from case.
3. Remove main drive gear bearing retainer.
4. Unbolt extension housing from transmission case.

5. Slide 3-4 synchronizer slightly forward and slide mainshaft and extension housing out of case, Fig. 4-3.

Disassemble Mainshaft

1. Remove snap ring in front of 3-4

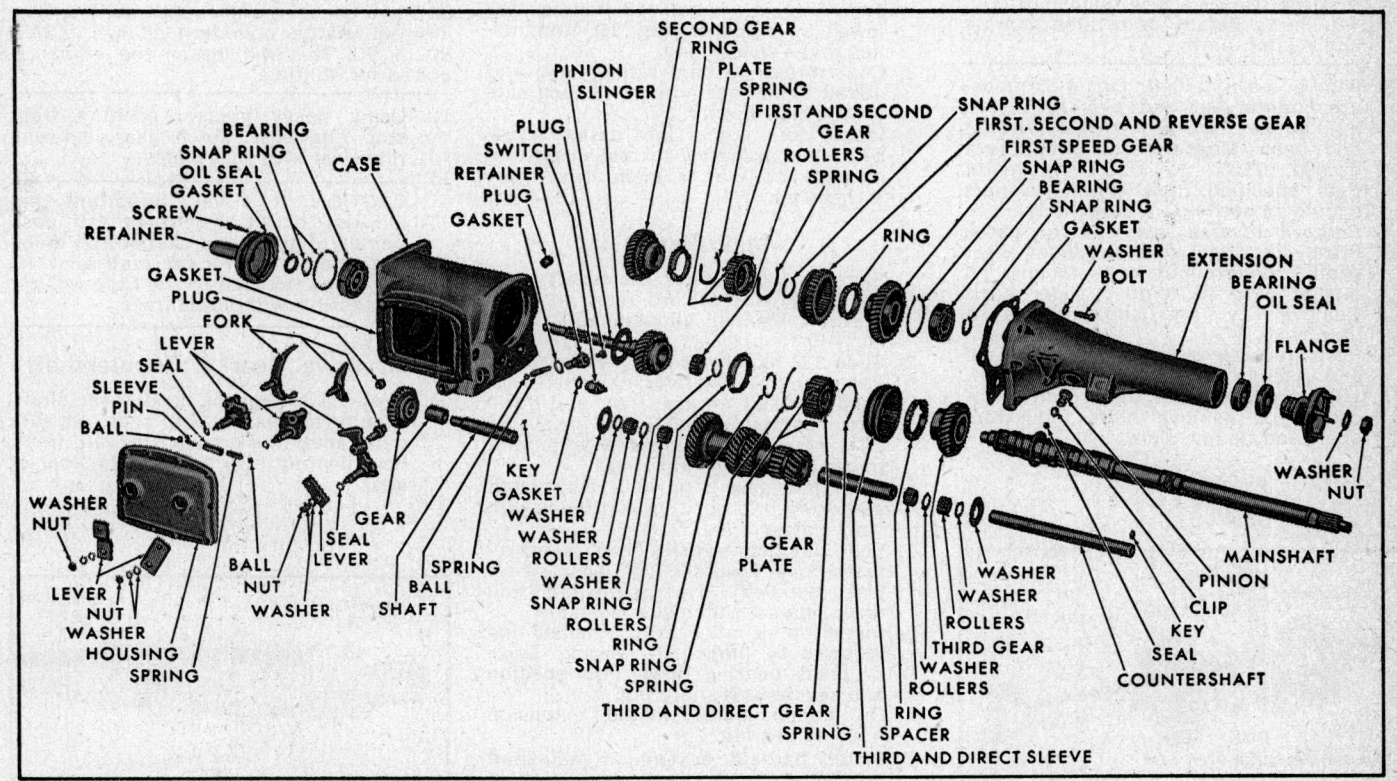

Fig. 4-1 Type Four Chrysler four-speed transmission. NOTE: The drive pinion bearing oil slinger shown has been eliminated with the release of new drive pinions which do not use an oil slinger

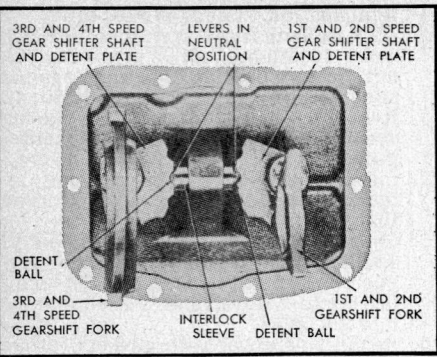

Fig. 4-2 Shift housing assembly

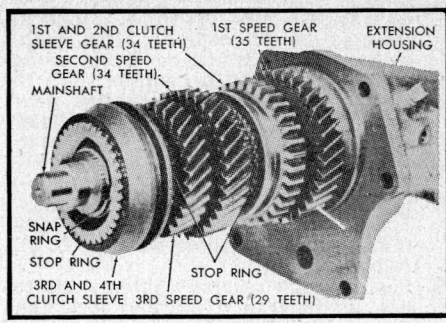

Fig. 4-3 Mainshaft assembly

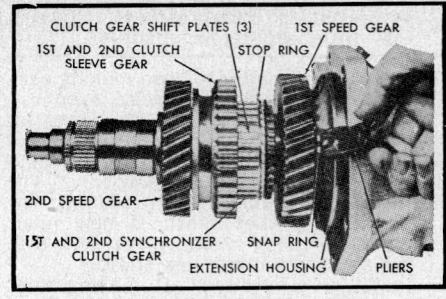

Fig. 4-4 Compressing center bearing snap ring so mainshaft can be pulled from bearing housing

synchronizer and slide off synchronizer.
2. Slide off 3rd gear and stop ring.
3. While holding center bearing snap ring compressed, Fig. 4-4, pull mainshaft assembly and bearing out of extension housing.
4. Remove mainshaft rear bearing snap ring, insert steel plates on front side of 1st speed gear, and press gear and rear bearing from mainshaft. Remove 1st gear stop ring.
5. Remove snap ring and slide 1-2 synchronizer clutch unit from mainshaft.

NOTE: Fig. 4-6 shows mainshaft bearing surfaces. Inspect these surfaces for any condition that would warrant the use of a new mainshaft. Fig. 4-7 shows details of reverse gearing and related parts.

6. With a feeler gauge, Fig. 4-8, measure countergear end play by inserting gauge between thrust washer and gear. Measurement should not exceed .0155" to .028". If greater than specified, new thrust washers should be used upon reassembly.
7. Remove reverse lever detent parts.
8. Press or drive reverse slider gear shaft (from front to rear) far enough out of case to remove slider gear. Remove key from shaft and shaft from case, 4-9.
9. Push reverse lever shaft into case and remove as shown in Fig. 4-10. Lift out detent ball from bottom of case, and remove shift fork from shaft and detent plate.

10. Using a suitable arbor, drive countershaft out of case, allowing cluster gear to rest in bottom of case to permit removal of main drive gear.
11. Remove snap ring and remove main drive gear by driving it into case. Remove snap ring and press bearing from main drive gear.
12. Lift cluster gear from case.

REASSEMBLE TRANS.
Countergear

1. Using heavy grease, coat inside of gear bore at each end, then center bearing spacer. Insert arbor through gear and spacer.
2. Grease needle rollers and, at each end of gear, install 19 rollers, followed by a spacer ring, 19 more rollers and a spacer ring.
3. Coat thrust washers with grease and install them over arbor with tang side toward case boss.
4. Install countergear into case, Fig. 4-11. Allow assembly to rest in bottom of case until after main drive gear is installed.

Mainshaft

1. Slide 2nd gear over mainshaft, synchronizer cone toward rear, and into position against shoulder on shaft, Fig. 4-5.
2. Slide 1-2 clutch sleeve gear including 2nd gear stop ring over mainshaft with shift fork slot toward front, and down into position against 2nd gear. Be sure stop ring is indexed with shift plates and install snap ring.
3. Slide low gear stop ring over shaft and down into position and index with shift plates.
4. Slide 1st gear synchronizer (synchronizer cone toward clutch gear sleeve just installed) over mainshaft and down against clutch sleeve gear.
5. Install mainshaft bearing retainer ring followed by mainshaft bearing. Drive or press bearing down into position and secure with snap ring.
6. On earlier units, install extension housing bearing.
7. Install partially assembled mainshaft into extension housing far enough to engage retaining ring in slot in extension housing. Compress retaining

ring and at same time rest mainshaft in extension housing (see Fig. 4-4). Be sure retaining ring is seated all around slot.
8. Slide 3rd gear on shaft, synchronizer cone toward front, followed by 3rd gear stop ring.
9. Install 3-4 synchronizer clutch assembly with shift fork slot toward rear. Be sure to index rear stop ring with clutch gear shift plates (see Fig. 4-4). Install snap ring.

Service Bulletin

Quiets Gear Rattle: A gear rattle, or neutral noise, having automatic transmission fluid in the case can be quieted by changing the lubricant. Drain the automatic transmission fluid and replace it with SAE-140 multipurpose gear lube. If the SAE-140 causes hard or stiff shifting during cold weather operation, change to SAE-80 or 90. This will lessen the effort required for shifting.

10. Using heavy grease, position front stop ring over clutch gear, indexing ring slots with shift plates.

CAUTION: It is very important that indexing of all stop rings and positioning of gears and clutches on mainshaft be correct, or the mating of the extension housing to the case will not be possible without damage.

Main Drive Gear & Countershaft

1. Slide oil slinger (if used) over shaft, then press bearing onto shaft. Be sure outer snap ring groove is toward front. Seat bearing fully against shoulder of gear.

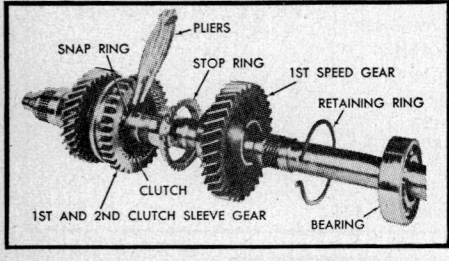

Fig. 4-5 Removing clutch gear snap ring

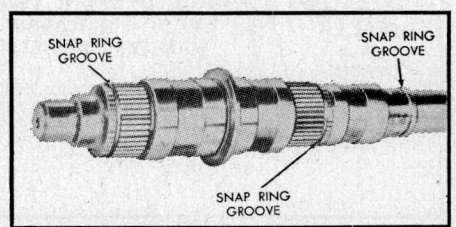

Fig. 4-6 Mainshaft bearing surfaces

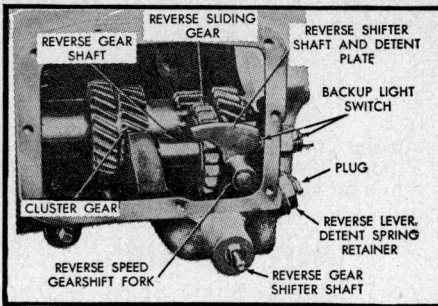

Fig. 4-7   Reverse gearing and countergear

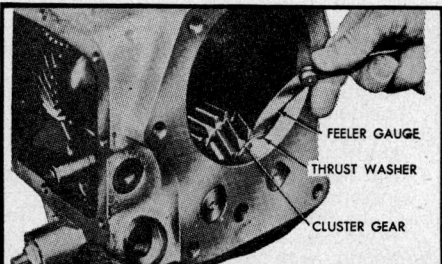

Fig. 4-8   Measuring countergear end play

Fig. 4-9   Removing reverse slider gear

Fig. 4-10   Removing reverse shift fork and lever

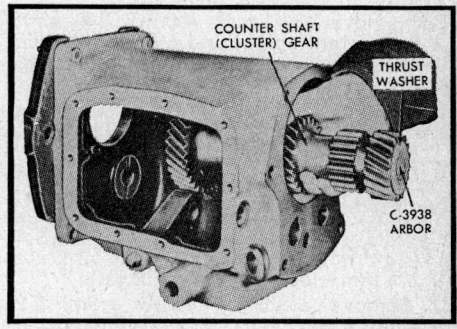

Fig. 4-11   Installing countergear

2. Install new inner snap ring into groove to retain bearing.
3. Install gear and bearing into case and position in front bore. Tap lightly into place. Install outer snap ring in bearing groove.
4. Start countershaft in its bore at rear of case. Raise countergear to mesh with main drive gear. Be sure thrust washer tangs are aligned with slots in case.
5. Drive or press countershaft into gear. Install woodruff key. Continue to press shaft into case until end of shaft is flush with rear face of case.
6. Measure countergear end play (see Fig. 4-8). If end play is greater than .028" install new thrust washers.

Reverse Gearing

1. Install reverse shaft detent and spring. Install spring retainer gasket and retainer (see Fig. 4-7).
2. Position reverse slider gear shaft in end of case and drive it far enough to position slider gear on protruding end of shaft with shift slot toward rear (see Fig. 4-9). At same time engage slot with reverse shift fork.
3. Drive reverse gear shaft into case far enough to permit installation of woodruff key. Drive shaft flush with end of case.

Mainshaft & Extension Housing

1. Grease both sides of extension-housing gasket and stick it on case.
2. Center reverse slider gear on its shaft, then insert mainshaft into case. Be sure 3-4 speed stop ring is indexed with shifter plates.
3. Move 3-4 speed clutch sleeve slightly toward front and at same time align front of mainshaft with main drive gear. Push in on extension housing and bottom against case and housing.
4. Install bolts and tighten securely.
5. Move reverse slider gear ahead to neutral position and install shift housing.

Service Bulletin

Cures Hard Shifting: Hard shifting can result if there is a binding of the shifter shafts in the case or in the cover. This happens when moisture enters between the shaft and bore and causes a build-up of corrosion.

To restore normal shifting, remove the external shift levers from the transmission, leaving the levers attached to the shift rods. It is not necessary to drain oil from the unit.

Place a ¾" diameter hole saw over the shifting shaft protruding from the case and cut a ⅛" deep counterbore in the case. After blowing out the cuttings, apply to the shaft a penetrating oil that will not damage the "O" ring, and work the shaft until it is free. Now apply a liberal amount of multi-purpose grease to the shaft and counterbore, and then insert an "O" ring, available for the purpose, in the counterbore.

Type Five Ford

DISASSEMBLE TRANS.

1. Remove shift linkage and control bracket.
2. Remove transmission cover.
3. Remove extension housing.
4. Remove input shaft bearing retainer.
5. Support countergear with a wire hook. Then working from front of case, push countershaft out rear of case and lower countergear to bottom of case.
6. Place 1-2 shift lever and reverse shift lever in neutral. Place 3-4 shift lever in 3rd speed position.
7. Remove bolt that retains 3-4 shift rail detent spring and plug in left side of case, Fig. 5-2. Remove spring and plug with a magnet.
8. Remove detent mechanism set screw from top of case and take out detent spring and plug with a magnet.
9. Remove attaching screw from 3-4 speed shift fork. Tap on inner end of shift rail to unseat expansion plug from front of case. Then withdraw 3-4 shift rail from front of case. Do not lose interlock pin from shift rail.
10. Remove attaching screw from 1-2 shift fork. Slide 1-2 shift rail out of rear of case.
11. Remove interlock plug and detent plug from top of case with a magnet.
12. On early models, remove snap ring securing speedometer drive gear to output shaft. Slide gear off shaft and remove speedometer drive gear ball. On later units, depress tang on retaining clip and remove gear.
13. Remove snap ring that secures output shaft bearing to shaft and use a suitable puller to remove bearing.
14. Remove input shaft and bearing and blocking ring from front of case.
15. Move output shaft to right side of case to provide clearance for shift forks. Rotate forks as shown in Fig. 5-3 and lift them from case.
16. Support 1st gear to prevent it from sliding off shaft, then lift output shaft assembly from case, Fig. 5-4.

17. Remove reverse gear shift fork attaching screw. Rotate reverse shift rail 90 deg. as shown in Fig. 5-5. Slide shift rail out rear of case and lift fork from case.
18. Remove reverse detent plug and spring from case with a magnet.
19. Remove reverse idler gear shaft from case, Fig. 5-6.
20. Lift reverse idler gear and thrust washers from case.
21. Lift countergear and thrust washers from case.

Disassemble Output Shaft

1. Remove snap ring from front of output shaft. Slide 3-4 synchronizer blocking ring and 3rd gear off shaft, Fig. 5-7.
2. Remove next snap ring and 2nd gear thrust washer. Slide 2nd gear and blocking ring from shaft.
3. Remove next snap ring, thrust washer, 1st speed gear and blocking ring from rear of shaft. On later models, the 1-2 synchronizer hub is a press fit. On

these units, use an arbor press to remove hub. On earlier models, slide hub off output shaft.

UNIT REPAIRS
Cam & Shaft Seals

NOTE: To facilitate reassembly, note position of cams and shafts assemblies and levers before removal from transmission case.

1. Referring to Fig. 5-8, remove three shift levers.
2. Remove three cams and shafts from inside of case.
3. Remove O-ring from each cam and shaft.
4. Dip new O-rings in gear lubricant and install them on cam and shafts.
5. Slide each cam and shaft into its respective bore in case.
6. Secure each shift lever.

Input Shaft Bearing

1. Referring to Fig. 5-9, remove snap ring that secures bearing to shaft.

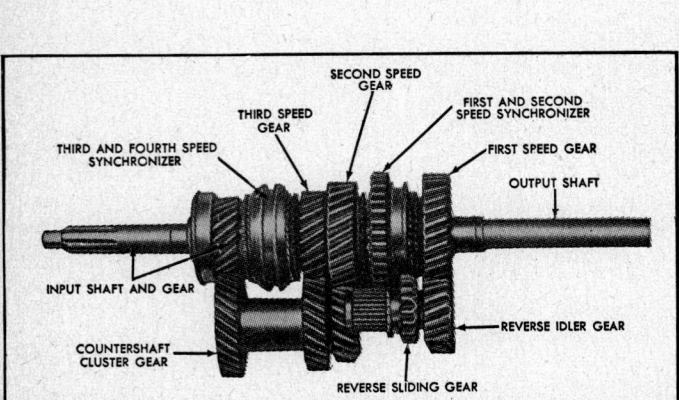

Fig. 5-1   Type Five Ford four speed transmission

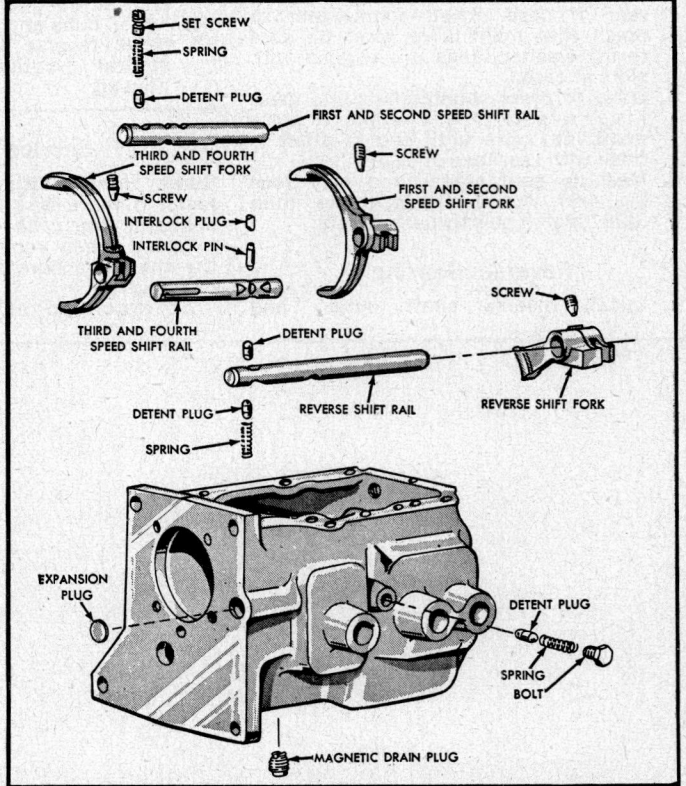

Fig. 5-2   Shift rails and forks disassembled

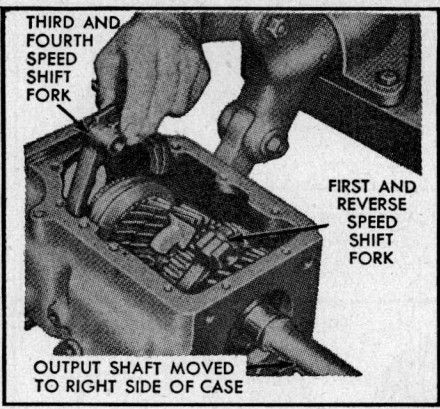

Fig. 5-3 Removing shift forks from case

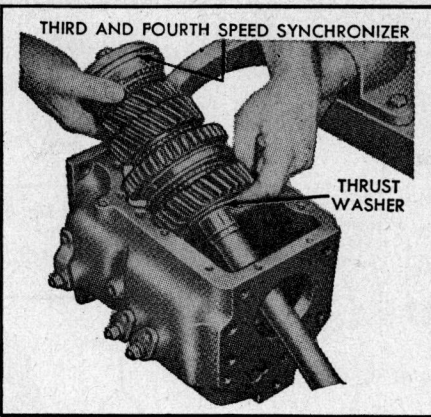

Fig. 5-4 Removing output shaft assembly

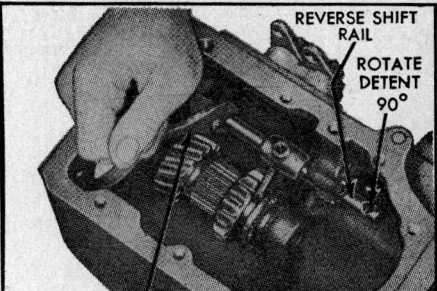

Fig. 5-5 Rotating reverse shift rail

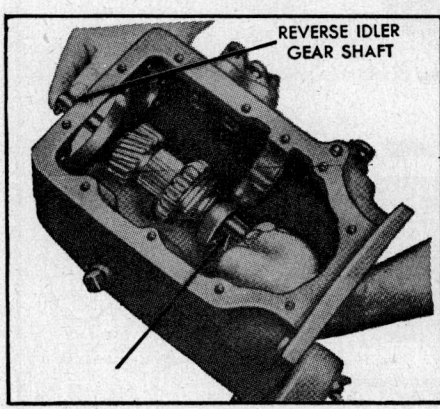

Fig. 5-6 Removing reverse idler gear shaft

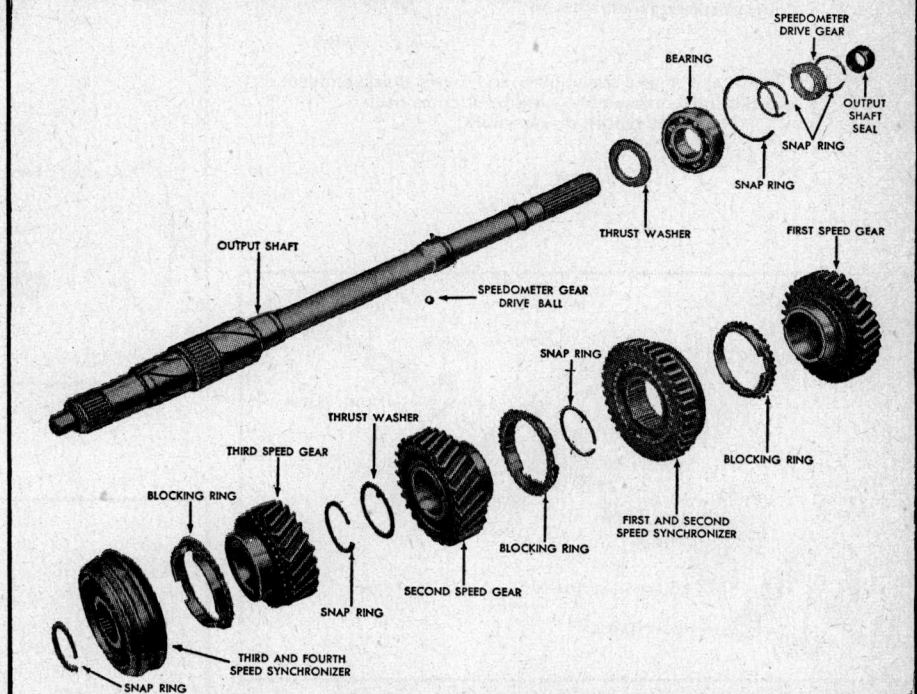

Fig. 5-7 Output shaft disassembled

2. Press input shaft gear out of bearing.
3. Press new bearing onto shaft and secure bearing with snap ring.

Synchronizers

1. Referring to Fig. 5-10, push synchronizer hub from each sleeve.
2. Separate inserts and springs from hubs. Do not mix parts from one synchronizer to another.
3. Position hub in sleeve, being sure that alignment marks are properly indexed.
4. Place three inserts into hub. Install insert springs, making sure that irregular surface (hump) is seated in one of inserts. Do not stagger springs.

Countergear

1. Referring to Fig. 5-11, and with unit disassembled, coat bore in each end of countergear with grease.
2. Hold a suitable dummy shaft in gear and insert 21 rollers and a retainer washer in each end of gear.

Reverse Idler Gear

1. With unit disassembled, Fig. 5-12, coat bore at each end of gear with grease.
2. Hold a suitable dummy shaft in gear and insert 22 rollers and retainer washer at each end of gear.
3. Install sliding gear on reverse idler gear, making sure that shift fork groove is toward front.

REASSEMBLE TRANS.

Countergear

1. Coat countergear thrust surfaces in case with a film of grease and position a thrust washer at each end of case.
2. Place assembled countergear in case.
3. With case in a vertical position, align gear bore and thrust washers with bores in case and install countershaft.
4. With case in horizontal position, check countergear end play with a feeler gauge. If not within limits of .004" to .018", install new thrust washers.
5. After establishing correct end play, install dummy shaft in countergear and allow gear to remain in bottom of case.

Reverse Gearing

1. Coat gear thrust surfaces in case with a film of grease and position two thrust washers in place, Fig. 5-12.
2. Position idler gear, sliding gear,

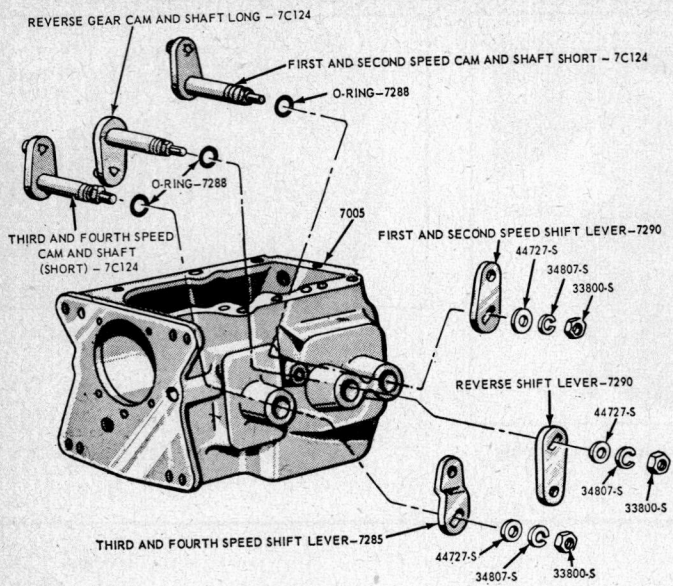

Fig. 5-8 Cams and shafts assemblies and levers disassembled. To facilitate reassembly, note position of each part before disassembly

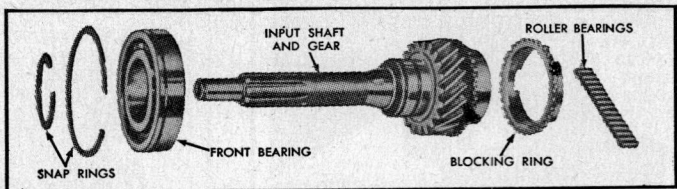

Fig. 5-9 Input shaft gear disassembled

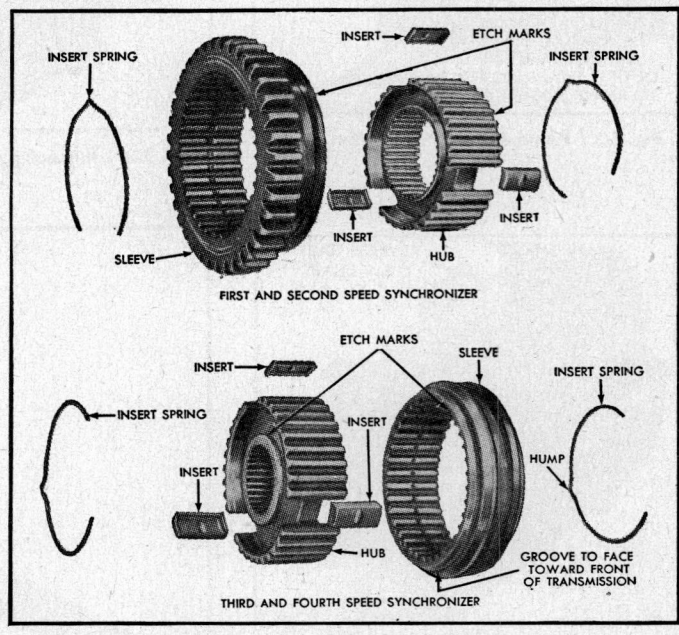

FIRST AND SECOND SPEED SYNCHRONIZER

THIRD AND FOURTH SPEED SYNCHRONIZER

Fig. 5-10 Synchronizers disassembled

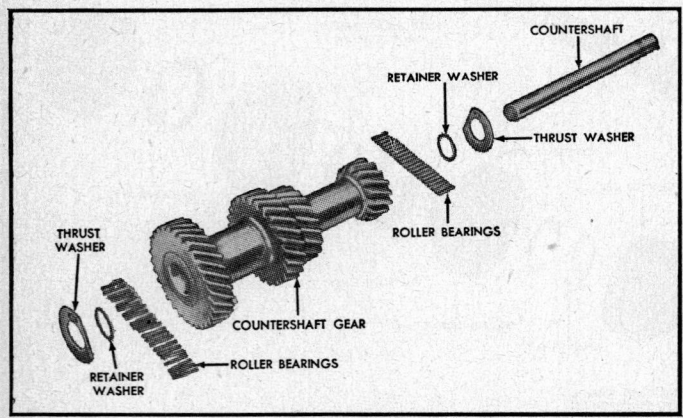

Fig. 5-11 Countergear disassembled

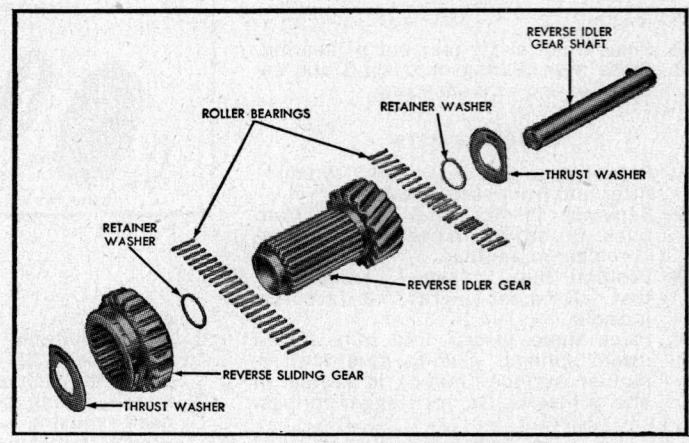

Fig. 5-12 Reverse idler gear disassembled

dummy shaft and roller bearings in place, making sure that shift fork groove in sliding gear is toward front of case.

3. Align gear bore and thrust washers with case bores and install reverse idler shaft.

4. Measure reverse idler gear end play with feeler gauge. If not within the limits of .004" to .018", install new thrust washers.

5. Position reverse gear shift rail detent spring and plug in case. Hold reverse shift fork in place on sliding gear and install shift rail from rear of case. Secure fork to rail with set screw.

Output Shaft

1. Referring to Fig. 5-7, install 1-2 synchronizer on shaft.
2. Slide 2nd gear onto front of shaft with synchronizer coned surface facing to rear.
3. Install 2nd gear thrust washer and snap ring.
4. Slide 3rd gear on shaft with synchronizer coned surface to front.
5. Coat coned surface of 3rd gear with grease and place blocking ring on gear.
6. Slide 3-4 synchronizer onto shaft

making sure inserts in synchronizer engage notches in blocking ring. Install snap ring on front of shaft.

7. Coat coned surface of 2nd gear with grease and place blocking ring on gear.

8. Slide 1-2 synchronizer on rear of shaft, making sure that inserts engage notches in blocking ring and that shift fork groove is toward rear.

9. Coat coned surface of 1st gear with grease and place blocking ring on it.

10. Slide 1st gear onto rear of shaft, making sure notches in blocking ring engage synchronizer inserts.

11. Install thrust washer on rear of shaft and lower output shaft assembly into case, Fig. 5-4.

Shift Rails & Forks

1. Referring to Fig. 5-2, position 1-2 shift fork and 3-4 shift fork in place on their respective gears and rotate them in place.

2. Place detent plug in its bore and place reverse shift rail into neutral position.

3. Coat 3-4 shift rail interlock pin with grease and plate it in shift rail.

4. Align 3-4 shift fork with shift rail bores and slide rail into place, making sure three detents are facing outside of case.

5. Place front synchronizer into 3rd gear position and install set screw in 3-4 shift fork. Move synchronizer to neutral position. Install 3-4 rail detent plug, spring and bolt in left side of case. Place interlock plug (tapered ends) in detent bore.

6. Align 1-2 shift fork with case bores and slide shift rail into place. Secure fork with set screw. Install detent plug and spring in detent bore. Thread set screw into case until its head is flush with case.

Final Assembly

1. Coat input gear bore with just enough grease to hold roller bearings in place, then install 15 roller bearings.

2. Install input gear in case, making sure output shaft pilot enters roller bearings in input gear.

3. Stick a new gasket on input shaft bearing retainer. Dip attaching bolts in sealing compound and install and tighten.

4. Install output shaft bearing and secure with snap ring.

5. On early units, place speedometer gear ball in output shaft, slide gear into place and secure with snap ring. On later units, slip gear onto shaft and secure with retaining clip.

6. With transmission in vertical position, align countergear bore and thrust washers with bore in case and install countershaft.

7. Use a new gasket and secure extension housing to case. Use sealing compound on attaching screws.

8. Pour specified gear lube over entire gear train while rotating output shaft. Then install cover and shift linkage and adjust as outlined in the car chapters.

Type Six Saginaw

DISASSEMBLE TRANSMISSION

1. Remove side cover assembly and shift forks. On Vega transmissions, remove damper assembly which is bolted to extension housing.

2. Remove clutch gear bearing retainer.

3. Remove clutch gear bearing to gear stem snap ring, then remove bearing by pulling clutch gear outward until a screwdriver can be inserted between large snap ring and case to complete removal, Fig. 6-2. Do not remove clutch gear. The bearing is a slip fit on the gear and into the case bore.

4. Remove extension to case bolts and remove clutch gear, mainshaft and extension assembly through rear case opening. Remove clutch gear and blocker ring from mainshaft.

5. Expand extension housing to rear mainshaft bearing snap ring and remove extension, Fig. 6-3.

6. Using a dummy shaft, drive countershaft and woodruff key out through rear of case, Fig. 6-4. Dummy shaft will hold roller bearings in position within countergear bore. Remove countergear.

7. Remove reverse idler gear stop ring and, using a long drift, drive idler shaft and woodruff key out through rear of case.

Disassemble Mainshaft

1. Remove snap ring and press 3-4 syn-

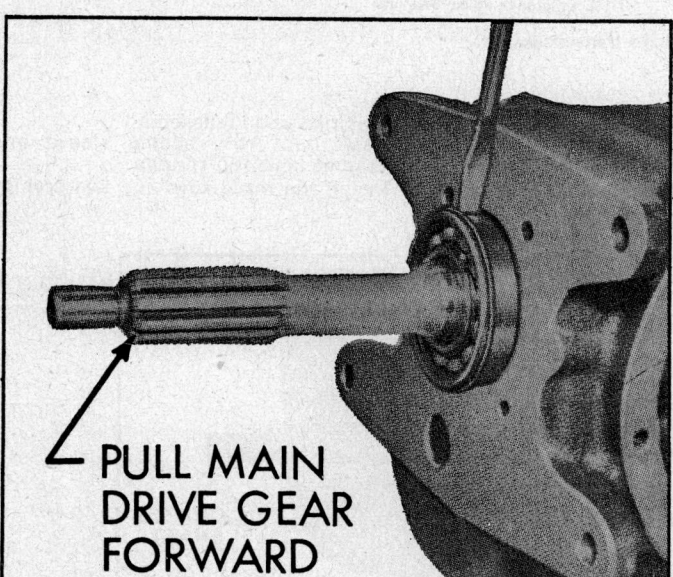

Fig. 6-2 Removing clutch gear bearing

PULL MAIN DRIVE GEAR FORWARD

Fig. 6-3 Removing extension

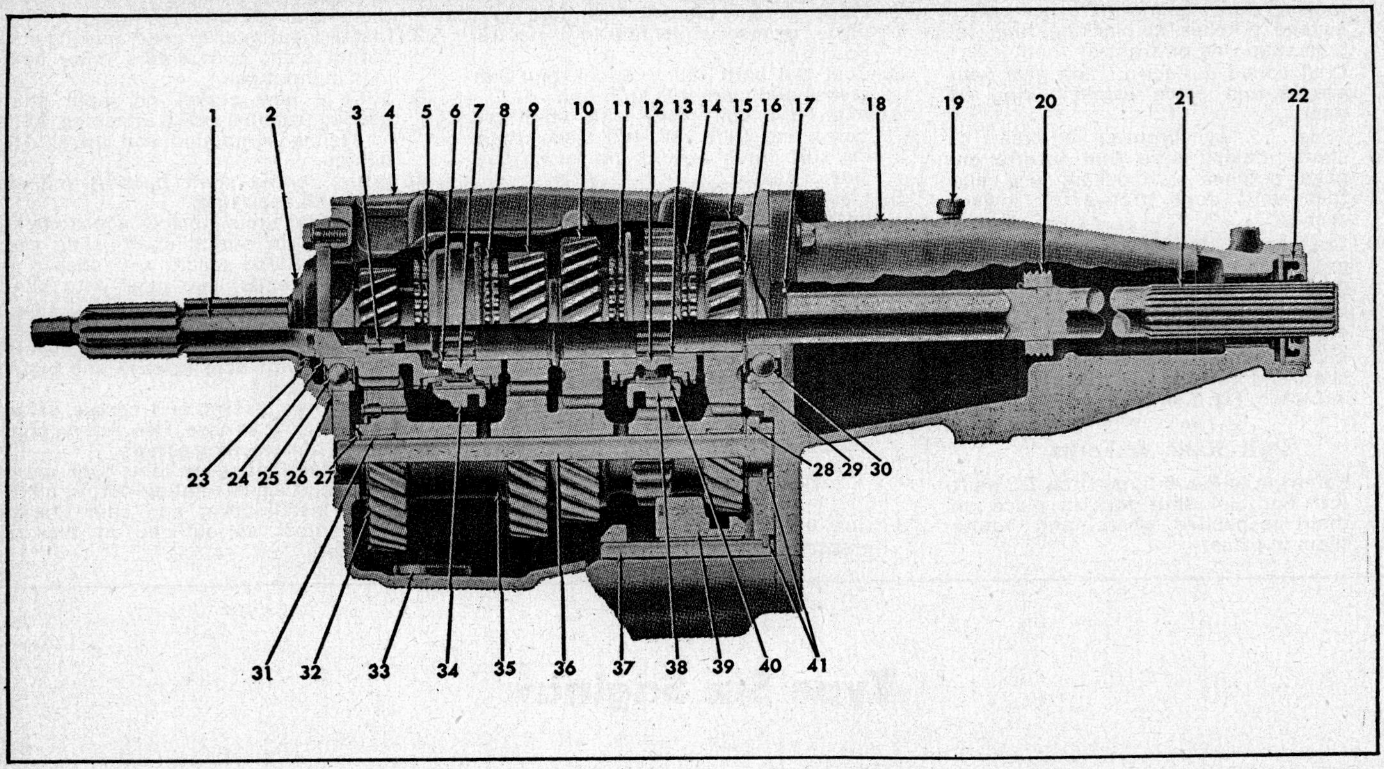

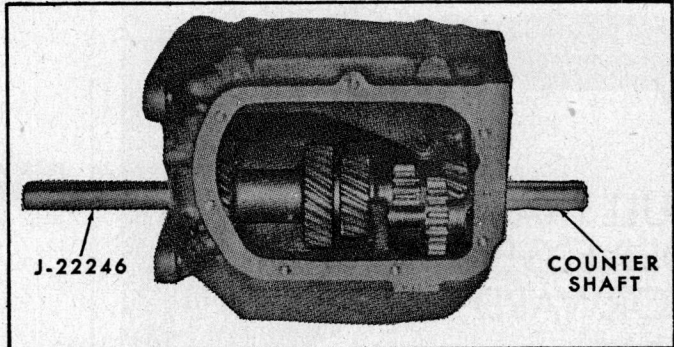

Fig. 6-1 Type six Saginaw transmission

1. Clutch Gear
2. Bearing Retainer
3. Pilot Bearings
4. Case
5. 4th Speed Blocker Ring
6. 4-3 Synch. Snap Ring
7. 4-3 Synch. Hub
8. 3rd Speed Blocker Ring
9. 3rd Speed Gear
10. 2nd Speed Gear
11. 2nd Speed Blocker Ring
12. 1-2 Speed Synch. Hub
13. 1-2 Speed Synch. Snap Ring
14. 1st Speed Blocker Ring
15. First Gear
16. Reverse Gear Thrust and Spring Washers
17. Snap Ring-Bearing to Mainshaft
18. Extension
19. Vent
20. Speedometer Drive Gear and Clip
21. Mainshaft
22. Rear Oil Seal
23. Retainer Oil Seal
24. Snap Ring-Bearing to Gear
25. Clutch Gear Bearing
26. Snap Ring-Bearing to Case
27. Thrust Washer-Front
28. Thrust Washer-Rear
29. Snap Ring-Bearing to Extension
30. Rear Bearing
31. Countergear Roller Bearings
32. Anti-Lash Plate Assembly
33. Magnet
34. 4-3 Synch. Sleeve
35. Countergear Assembly
36. Counter Shaft
37. Reverse Idler Shaft
38. 1-2 Speed Synch. Sleeve and Reverse Gear
39. Reverse Idler Gear (Sliding
40. Clutch Key
41. Woodruff Key

chronizer clutch assembly, 3rd speed blocker ring and 3rd gear off mainshaft, Fig. 6-5.

2. Depress speedometer gear retaining clip and remove gear.

3. Remove rear bearing to mainshaft snap ring, support 1st gear with press plates and press on rear of mainshaft to remove 1st speed gear, thrust washer, spring washer and rear bearing, Fig. 6-6.

4. Remove 1-2 sliding clutch hub snap ring, support 2nd speed gear and press clutch assembly, 2nd speed blocker ring and gear from mainshaft, Fig. 6-7.

Clutch Keys & Springs

NOTE: The clutch hubs and sleeves are a selected assembly and should be kept together as originally assembled, but the

keys and springs may be replaced separately.

1. Mark hub and sleeve so they can be

matched upon reassembly.

2. Push hub from sliding sleeve and remove keys and springs.

3. Install the three keys and two springs

J-22246

COUNTER SHAFT

Fig. 6-4 Removing countershaft

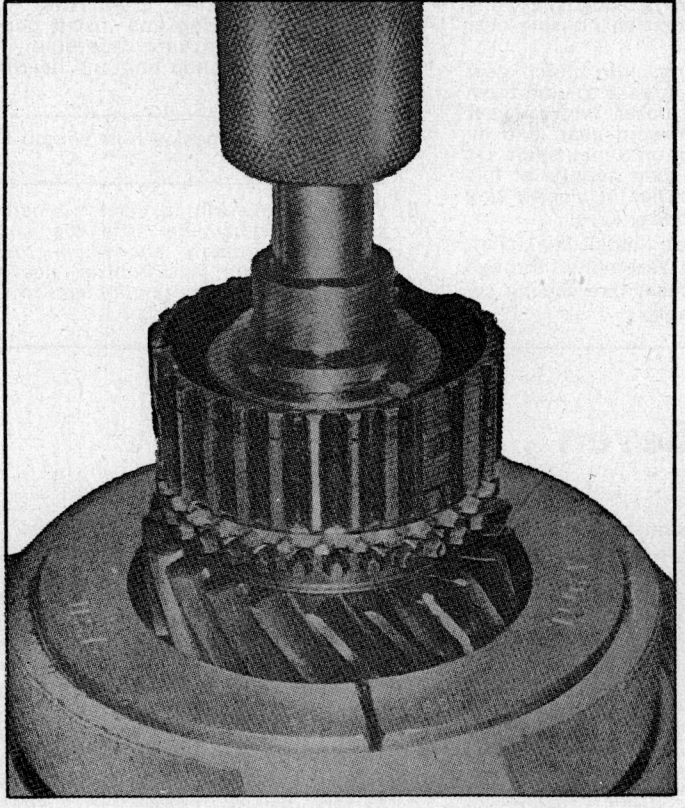

Fig. 6-5   Removing 3-4 synchronizer assembly

Fig. 6-6   Removing 1st gear and rear bearing

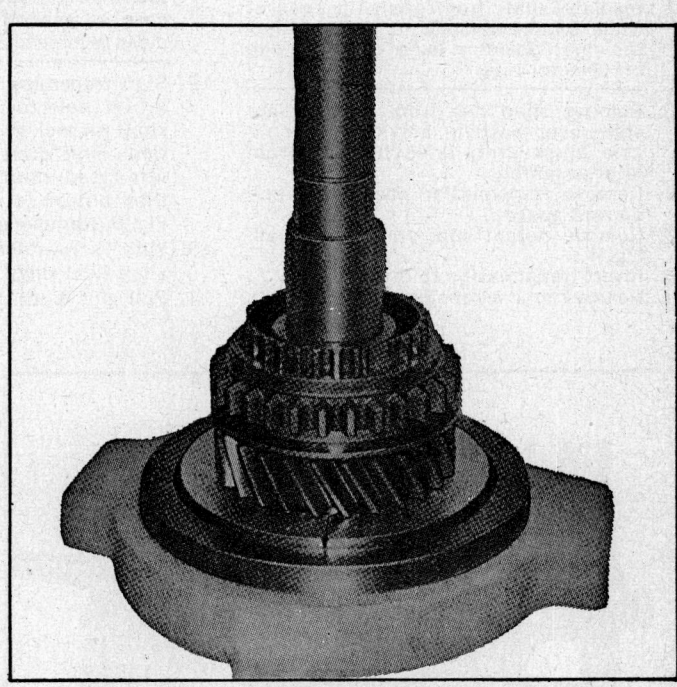

Fig. 6-7   Removing 1-2 synchronizer and 2nd speed gear

so all three keys are engaged by both springs. The tanged end of each spring should be installed into different key cavities on either side. Slide sleeve onto hub, aligning marks made before disassembly.

NOTE: A groove around the outside of the hub identifies the end that must be opposite the fork slot in the sleeve when assembled. This groove indicates the end of the hub with a .070" greater recess depth.

Assemble Mainshaft

With front of mainshaft up:
1. Install 3rd speed gear with clutching teeth upward.
2. Install blocker ring with clutching teeth downward over cone of gear. All blocker rings in this unit are identical.
3. Install 3-4 synchronizer assembly with fork slot downward and press it onto mainshaft until it bottoms. *Be sure the notches of the blocker ring align with the keys of the synchronizer assembly.*
4. Install synchronizer hub to mainshaft snap ring. Both synchronizer snap rings are identical.

With rear of mainshaft upward:
5. Install 2nd speed gear with clutching teeth upward.
6. Install a blocker ring with clutching teeth downward over cone of gear.
7. Press 1-2 synchronizer assembly onto mainshaft with fork slot downward.

Be sure notches in blocker ring align with keys of synchronizer assembly.

8. Install synchronizer hub snap ring.
9. Install a blocker ring with notches downward so they align with the synchronizer keys.

10. Install 1st gear with clutching teeth downward. Install 1st gear thrust washer and spring washer.
11. Press rear bearing onto mainshaft. Install snap ring.
12. Install speedometer drive gear and clip.

ASSEMBLE TRANS.

1. Load a row of roller bearings and a thrust washer at each end of the countergear. Use heavy grease to hold them in place.
2. Install countergear through case rear opening with a tanged thrust washer at each end and install countershaft and woodruff key from rear of case. *Be sure countershaft picks up both thrust washers and that the tangs are aligned with their notches in the case.*
3. Install reverse idler gear, shaft and woodruff key from rear of case.

4. Expand extension housing snap ring and assemble extension housing over mainshaft.
5. Load roller bearings into clutch gear bore, using heavy grease to hold them in place, place blocker ring on gear cone with teeth toward gear, and install gear and ring onto mainshaft. Do not install clutch gear bearing at this time. *Be sure notches in blocker ring align with synchronizer keys.*
6. Using new gasket, install mainshaft and extension assembly through rear opening in case. Use sealing cement on bottom bolt.

7. Install large outer snap ring on clutch gear bearing and install bearing onto gear and into case bore. Install gear stem snap ring and bearing retainer.

NOTE: The retainer oil hole should be at the bottom.

8. With transmission in neutral, install cover assembly. *Be sure the shift forks are properly aligned in their grooves in the synchronizer sleeves before attempting to tighten cover bolts.*

Type Seven

DISASSEMBLE TRANS.

1. Remove TCS and backup lamp switches from case and extension, Fig. 1.
2. Remove cotter pins securing ends of shift control rod and remove rod, Fig. 2.
3. Remove serrated bolt retaining selector lever to boss on rear extension, Fig. 3.
4. Remove lock nut and selector ring.

NOTE: Slide lever and gearshift intermediate shaft from gearshift bracket while simultaneously removing selector ring. Selector lever will just slip off selector ring.

5. Remove snap ring from intermediate shift lever bushing and using a suitable brass drift, drive bushing from lever assembly.
6. Remove transmission case cover and discard gasket.
7. Remove detent cap, spring and ball, Fig. 4.
8. Invert transmission to drain oil.
9. Remove rear extension retaining bolts

and rotate extension to expose countergear shaft, Fig. 5.
10. From front of transmission, using tool J-22911, drive out shaft. Be sure lock ball, Fig. 6, is not lost. With tool J-22911 inserted, take countergear out of case and remove thrust washers from case.
11. Drive out reverse intermediate shift lever pivot pin and remove intermediate lever, Fig. 7.

NOTE: Slide reverse shaft to rear of case so scallop in selector shaft will clear reverse shaft.

12. Shift transmission to neutral and push in on selector shaft. Turn selector shaft so lock pins are in vertical position. First drive lock pin out of 3rd-4th speed intermediate lever cam and then out of 1st-2nd speed lever cam, Fig. 8. Remove selector shaft.
13. With screwdriver, pry out selector shaft seal rings on transmission case.
14. Pull out both lock ball plugs using

tool J-21715 with slide hammer J-7004, Fig. 9. Remove thrust springs and balls.
15. With transmission in 1st gear drive lock pins out of shifter forks and selector levers, Fig. 10. Remove 1st-2nd lever pin first.
16. From rear of transmission, drive out 1st-2nd shifter shaft using a brass drift, Fig. 11. Remove fork from sliding sleeve.
17. Tap 3rd-4th shifter shaft rearward until fork may be removed from shaft. Then drive out 3rd-4th shifter shaft through front of case.
18. Remove clutch drive gear from case.
19. Carefully slide rear extension and mainshaft assembly from case.
20. With tool J-22923 push out reverse idler gear shaft from front towards rear. Be sure lock ball is not lost, Fig. 12. Remove gear and shaft from case.
21. Using a brass drift and from the front of the transmission, drive out reverse

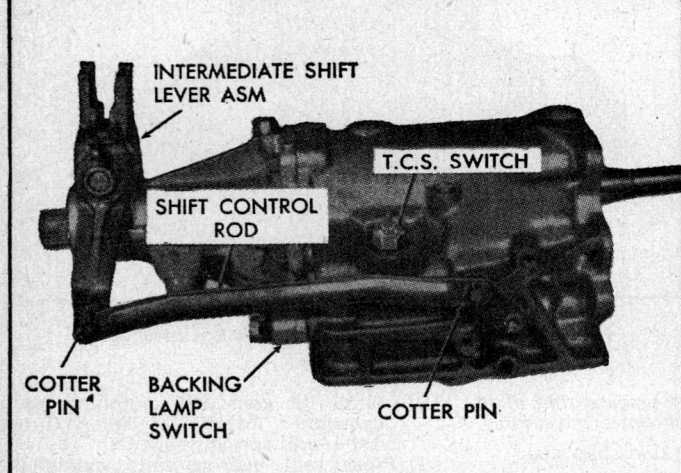

Fig. 2   Cotter pins securing shift control rod

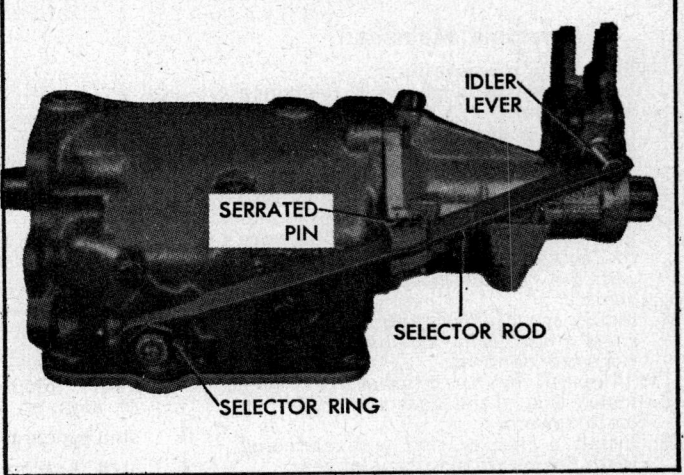

Fig. 3   Serrated pin location

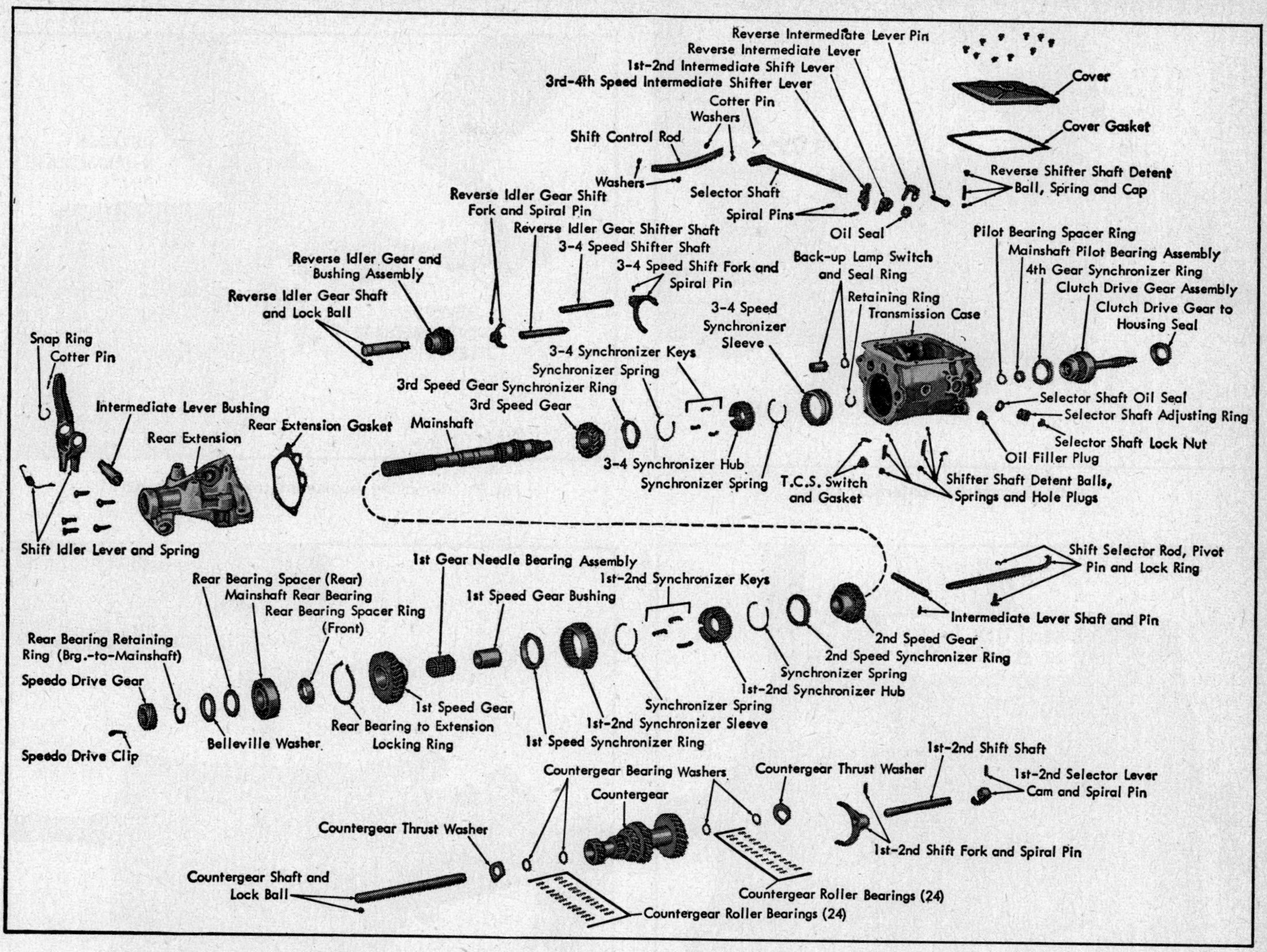

Reverse Intermediate Lever Pin
Reverse Intermediate Lever
1st-2nd Intermediate Shift Lever
3rd-4th Speed Intermediate Shifter Lever
Cotter Pin
Washers
Shift Control Rod
Washers
Selector Shaft
Spiral Pins
Oil Seal
Cover
Cover Gasket
Reverse Shifter Shaft Detent
Ball, Spring and Cap

Reverse Idler Gear Shift
Fork and Spiral Pin
Reverse Idler Gear Shifter Shaft
3-4 Speed Shifter Shaft
3-4 Speed Shift Fork and
Spiral Pin
Back-up Lamp Switch
and Seal Ring
Retaining Ring
Transmission Case
Pilot Bearing Spacer Ring
Mainshaft Pilot Bearing Assembly
4th Gear Synchronizer Ring
Clutch Drive Gear Assembly
Clutch Drive Gear to
Housing Seal

Reverse Idler Gear and
Bushing Assembly
Reverse Idler Gear Shaft
and Lock Ball
3-4 Speed
Synchronizer
Sleeve

Snap Ring
Cotter Pin
3-4 Synchronizer Keys
Synchronizer Spring
3rd Speed Gear Synchronizer Ring
3rd Speed Gear
Selector Shaft Oil Seal
Selector Shaft Adjusting Ring
Selector Shaft Lock Nut
Oil Filler Plug

Intermediate Lever Bushing
Rear Extension Gasket
Mainshaft
3-4 Synchronizer Hub
Synchronizer Spring
T.C.S. Switch
and Gasket
Shifter Shaft Detent Balls,
Springs and Hole Plugs

Rear Extension

Shift Idler Lever and Spring

Shift Selector Rod, Pivot
Pin and Lock Ring
Intermediate Lever Shaft and Pin

1st Gear Needle Bearing Assembly
1st-2nd Synchronizer Keys
Rear Bearing Spacer (Rear)
Mainshaft Rear Bearing
Rear Bearing Spacer Ring
(Front)
1st Speed Gear Bushing
2nd Speed Gear
2nd Speed Synchronizer Ring
Synchronizer Spring
1st-2nd Synchronizer Hub

Rear Bearing Retaining
Ring (Brg.-to-Mainshaft)
Speedo Drive Gear
1st Speed Gear
Rear Bearing to Extension
Locking Ring
Synchronizer Spring
1st-2nd Synchronizer Sleeve
1st Speed Synchronizer Ring
1st Speed Gear
Belleville Washer
Speedo Drive Clip

Countergear Bearing Washers
Countergear
Countergear Thrust Washer
1st-2nd Shift Shaft
1st-2nd Selector Lever
Cam and Spiral Pin

Countergear Thrust Washer
Countergear Shaft and
Lock Ball
Countergear Roller Bearings (24)
Countergear Roller Bearings (24)
1st-2nd Shift Fork and Spiral Pin

Fig. 1 Exploded view of Type 7 transmission

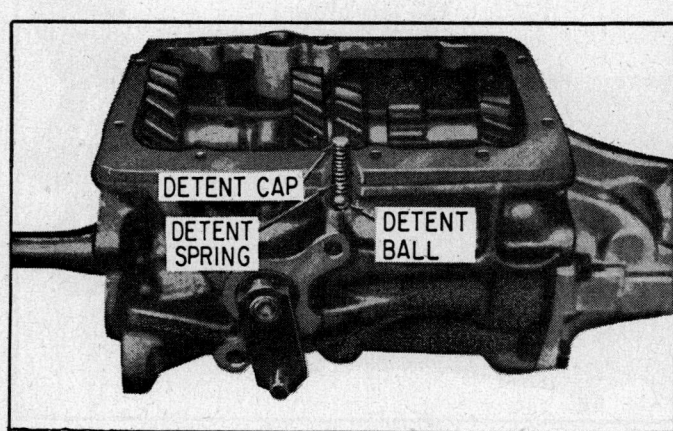

DETENT CAP
DETENT SPRING
DETENT BALL

Fig. 4 Reverse detent cap, spring and ball

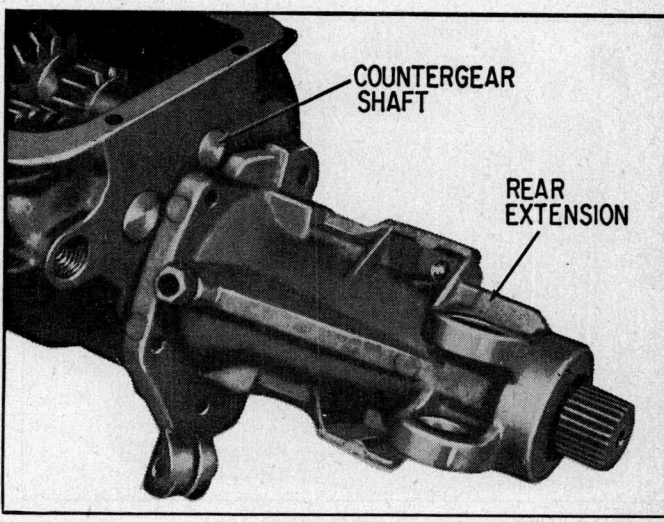

COUNTERGEAR SHAFT
REAR EXTENSION

Fig. 5 Countergear shaft exposed for removal

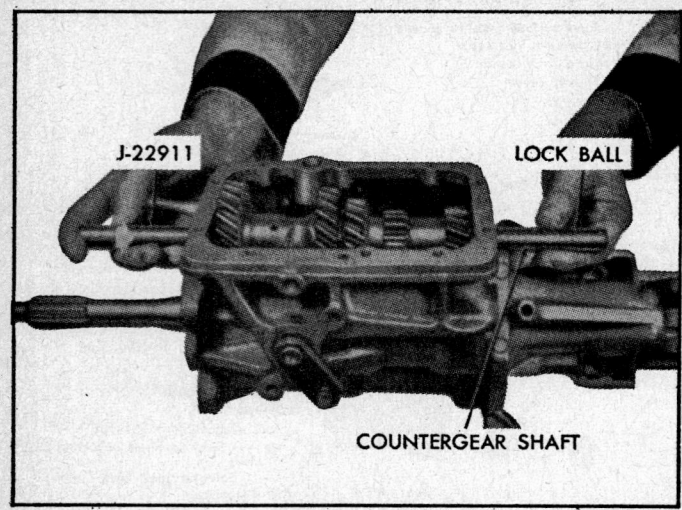

Fig. 6   Removing countergear shaft

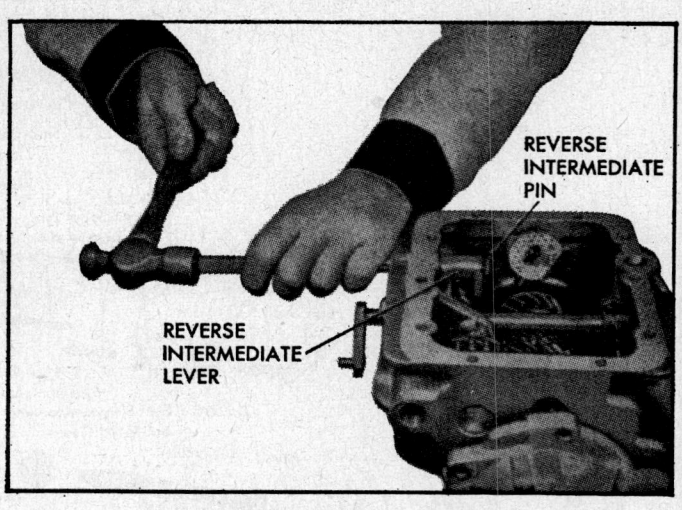

Fig. 7   Removing reverse intermediate lever pin

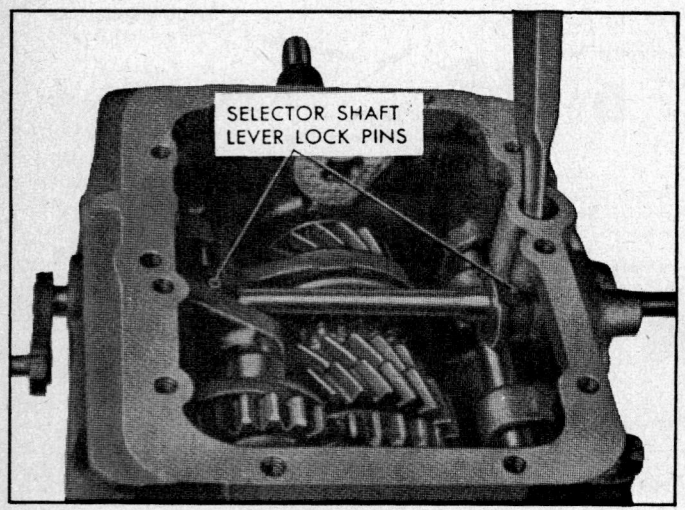

Fig. 8   Removing lock pins from selector shaft levers

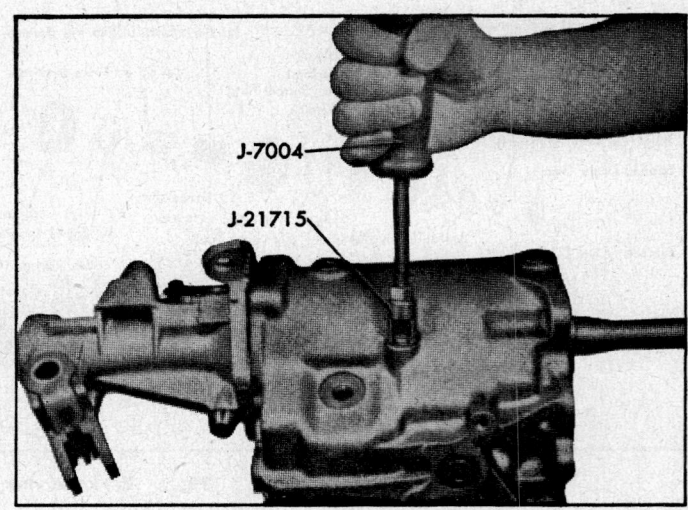

Fig. 9   Removing detent ball lock plugs

Fig. 10   Position of lock pins

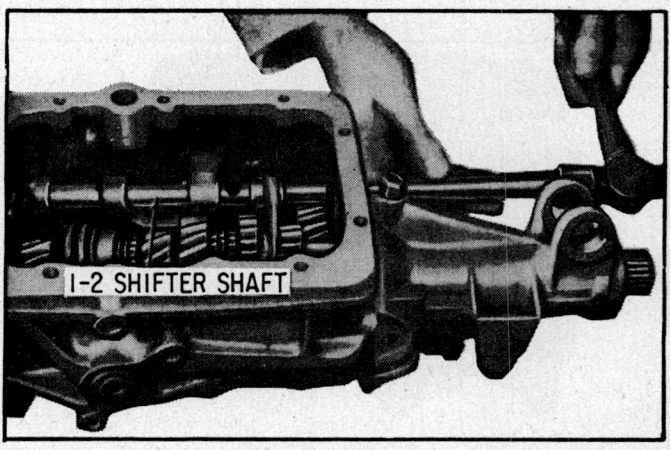

Fig. 11   Removing 1st-2nd shifter shaft

Fig. 12   Removing reverse idler gear shaft

Fig. 13   Removing snap ring from rear extension

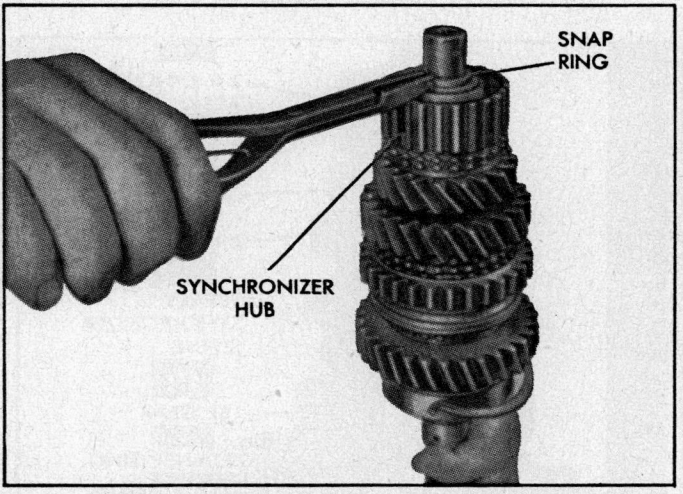

Fig. 14   Removing snap ring in front of synchronizer hub

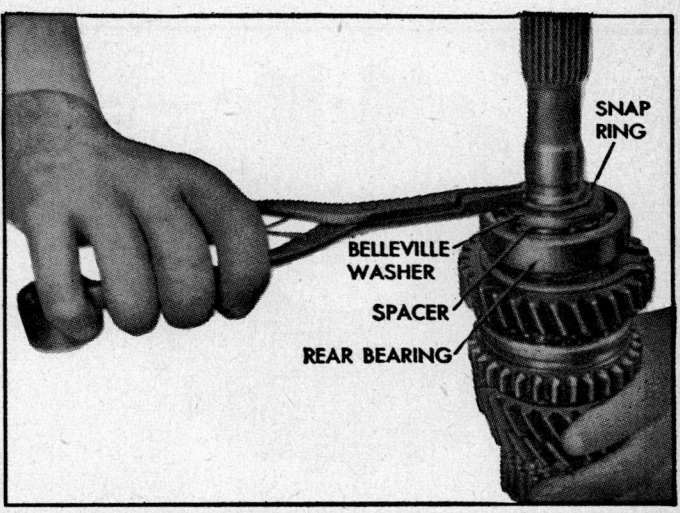

Fig. 15   Removing rear bearing snap ring

Fig. 16   Removing components from mainshaft

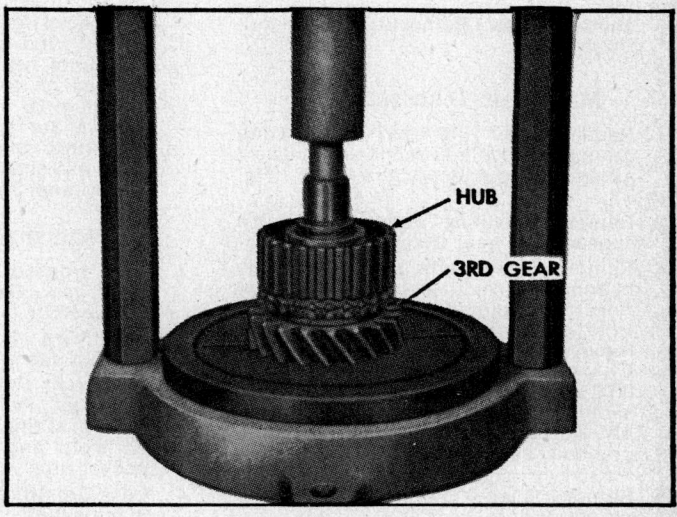

Fig. 17   Removing 3rd speed synchronizer hub

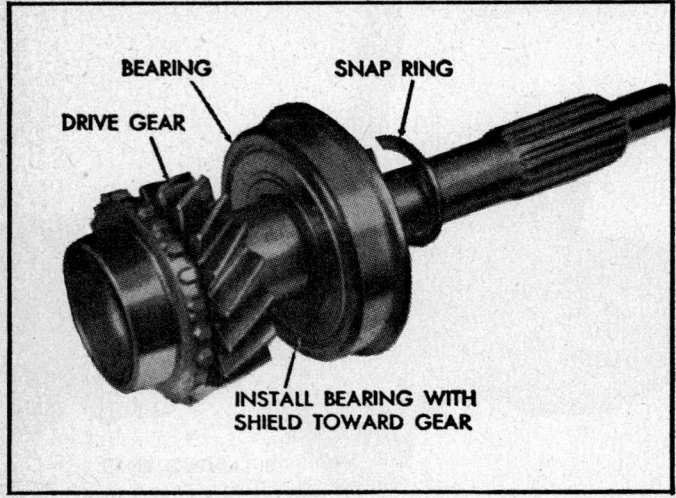

Fig. 18   Drive gear assembly

Fig. 19   Securing 3rd-4th synchronizer hub on mainshaft

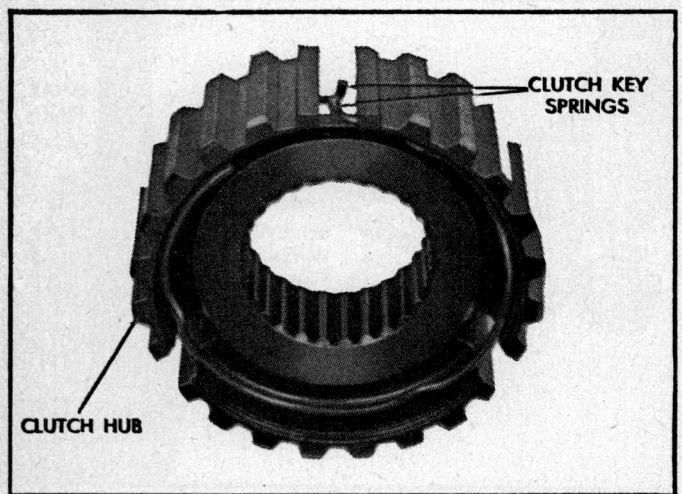

Fig. 20   Both synchronizer key springs installed

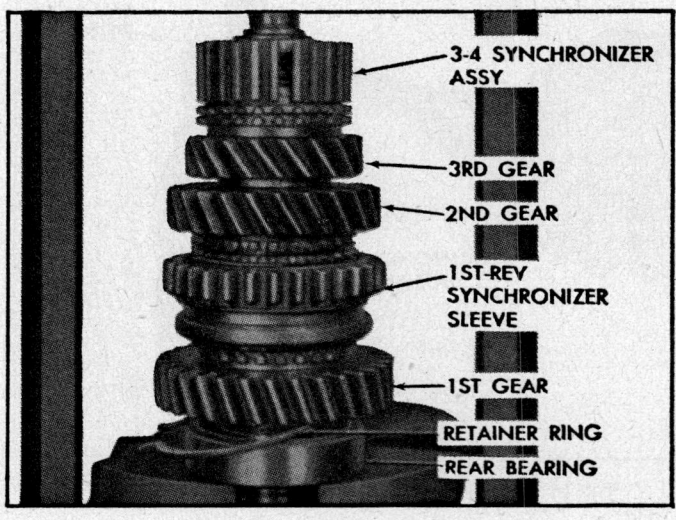

Fig. 21   Pressing mainshaft components

shifter shaft. Remove shifter fork from case.

Mainshaft Disassemble

1. Remove snap ring from rear bearing retainer groove and remove mainshaft assembly from bearing retainer, Fig. 13.
2. Depress retaining clamp and slide speedo drive gear from shaft.
3. Remove loose parts such as needle bearing, spacer ring and synchronizer ring. The sliding sleeve, keys and front clutch key spring may also be removed.

NOTE: The snychronizer hubs and sliding sleeves are a selected assembly and should be kept together as originally assembled.

4. Remove snap ring in front of synchronizer hub, Fig. 14.
5. Remove snap ring, belleville washer and spacer from shaft, Fig. 15.
6. Support 2nd gear and press mainshaft until bearing and synchronizers are free on shaft. Remove all loose parts, Fig. 16.
7. Remove 3rd speed synchronizer hub snap ring. Support 3rd speed gear and press shaft from synchronizer assembly and 3rd speed gear, Fig. 17.

Mainshaft Assemble

1. From front of mainshaft install 3rd speed gear. Gear must turn freely on mainshaft.
2. Install 3rd speed synchronizer ring onto 3rd speed gear cone.
3. Install rear clutch key spring into 3rd-4th speed synchronizer hub so that hooked spring end rests in one of the slots and raised end is toward blocker ring.
4. Press 3rd-4th speed synchronizer hub on mainshaft.
5. Secure 3rd-4th speed synchronizer hub with snap ring, Fig. 19.
6. From rear of mainshaft slide 2nd speed gear onto mainshaft. Gear must turn freely on mainshaft.
7. Place 2nd speed synchronizer ring onto 2nd speed gear cone.
8. Install both synchronizer key springs into 1st-2nd synchronizer hub so that hooks of both springs rest in the same hub slot and other spring ends are positioned opposite to each other and toward blocker rings, Fig. 20. Install sliding gear and keys on hub.
9. Slide 1st-2nd speed synchronizer hub, needle bearing and inner sleeve onto mainshaft. Slide spacer, rear extension retaining ring and rear bearing onto shaft. Support rear bearing inner race and press components together, Fig. 21.

CAUTION: Align slots in synchronizer rings with synchronizer keys.

10. Place spacer and belleville washer on

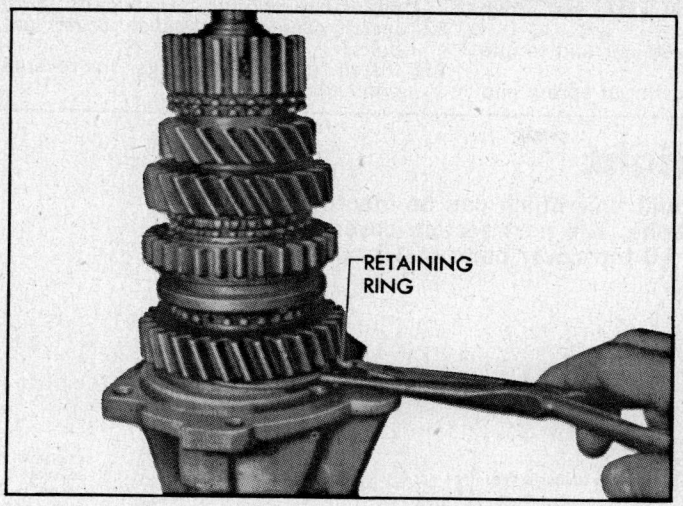

Fig. 22   Installing rear bearing retainer ring

Fig. 23   1st-2nd shifter shaft installed

mainshaft and secure with snap ring.

NOTE: Concave side of belleville washer should face toward bearing.

11. Position speedo gear retaining clip on shaft and install gear.
12. Place mainshaft assembly into rear bearing retainer up to its stop. Secure with snap ring, Fig. 22.
13. Assemble 3rd-4th speed synchronizer on hub with raised end of key springs toward blocker ring.

NOTE: Arrow on keys point towards shifter fork groove (front of shaft).

ASSEMBLE TRANS.

1. With sealer, install new gasket onto rear extension.
2. Slide mainshaft assembly into case.
3. From front, slide spacer ring and needle bearing onto mainshaft.

NOTE: Coat needle bearing with ball and roller bearing grease.

4. Install synchronizer blocker ring on clutch drive gear and install gear into transmission case up to snap ring stop.
5. Insert 1st-2nd shifter shaft at front of case with notches up, pushing it first through "L" shaped selector dog. Dog should be positioned as shown in Fig. 23.
   Then push 1st-2nd selector shaft through shifter fork, positioning shoulder toward front of case. Drive lock pins in place allowing them to protrude 1/16 to 5/64" above fork. Install selector dog pin first.
6. Insert 3rd-4th shifter shaft from front of case with notches down, pushing it through 3rd-4th shifter fork, positioning shouldering toward front, Fig. 24. Install lock pin allowing it to protrude 1/16 to 5/64" above fork.
7. Install reverse shifter shaft from rear

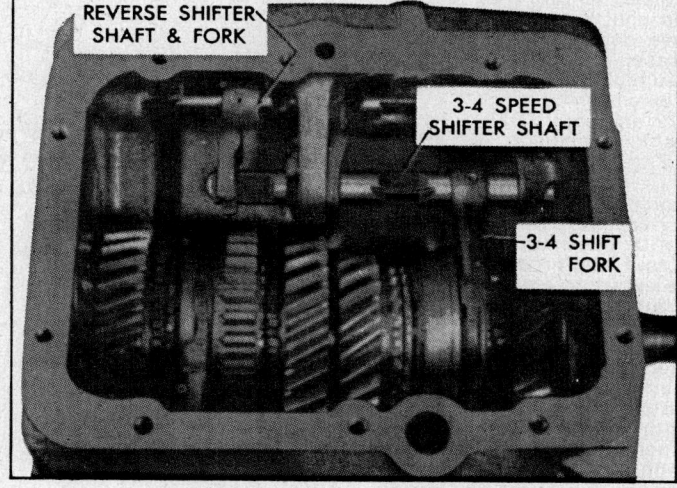

Fig. 24   3rd-4th shifter shaft installed

of case, with notches up, pushing it through reverse shifter fork, Fig. 24. Install lock pin.

NOTE: Position shoulder of shift fork toward front of case.

8. Insert selector shaft in case, push through 3rd-4th speed intermediate lever, then through 1st-2nd speed intermediate lever. Install lock pins.

NOTE: Place transmission in neutral and rotate selector shaft to engage levers with shifter shafts.

9. Engage reverse speed intermediate lever with 3rd-4th speed intermediate lever and install pivot pin. Reverse speed intermediate lever end play on pin should be .004–.012".
10. Insert both lock balls and thrust springs into bores in transmission case and drive in plugs.
11. Turn extension case until bore for reverse idler shaft is exposed.

12. Place lock ball into shaft and from rear of case install shaft into gear.
13. Simultaneously position reverse idler gear and reverse shifter fork.

NOTE: Shifter fork groove of reverse idler gear and shoulder of shifter fork should be toward front of mainshaft.

14. Using tool J-22911, install a spacer, a roll of roller bearings (24) and a spacer at each end of countergear. Use heavy grease to hold them in place.
15. Coat thrust washers with ball and roller bearing grease and stick to case.

NOTE: Lugs of thrust washers must fit into case slots.

16. Turn case extension until countergear shaft bore is exposed.
17. Place lock ball into shaft and from rear of transmission insert shaft so thrust washer is held in position. Hold opposite thrust washer in position by

using a short drift.
18. Insert countergear into case.
19. Insert shaft into countergear and push out special tool J-22911. Align lock

ball with groove in case and drive shaft into case.
20. Align rear bearing retainer and torque bolts to case.
21. Install lock ball and thrust spring and

spring cap into top transmission bore.
22. Install case cover gasket, cover and bolts.
23. Install gearshift linkage in reverse order of removal.

Type Eight

This section covers the English built unit which can be identified by having only 4 top cover bolts. The next section covers the German built unit which has 10 top cover bolts of 10 mm metric size.

DISASSEMBLE TRANS.

1. Remove clutch release bearing and lever from clutch housing.
2. Remove clutch housing to transmission bolts and remove housing.
3. Mount transmission in suitable holding fixture and remove top cover bolts.

NOTE: On late 1973 units, the detent shift spring and ball have been relocated, Fig. 1A. Also note that the fill plug location has been changed.

On 1973 units, remove TRS wire retaining clip and with a suitable magnet, remove detent shift spring and ball from case.
4. Using a suitable tool, pry blanking plug from extension housing.
5. On 1971-72 and early 1973 units, remove meshlock plunger set screw, spring and detent ball from side of case.
6. Using suitable punch, remove roll pin securing shift boss to rail. Be sure the pin can be punched through clear of any output shaft components. It may be necessary to position the synchronizer hub on the output shaft to suit.
7. Withdraw shift rail rearward, taking care not to let the shift boss and C-cam drop into case.
8. To remove shift forks, move 1st-2nd and 3rd-4th synchronizer hubs to their foremost position towards input shaft bearing.
9. Remove spring pin securing 3rd-4th shift fork to relay lever and remove fork.
10. Remove bolts securing extension housing to case.
11. Using a plastic faced mallet, tap the extension housing slightly rearward until it is possible to rotate it so countershaft aligns with cutaway in extension housing flange.
12. Tap countershaft rearward using a drift until it is just clear of front of case. Push countershaft out using a dummy countershaft. The countershaft gear will drop to bottom of case.
13. Remove extension housing and output shaft assembly. It is necessary to push 3rd-4th synchronizer sleeve forward to provide clearance between synchronizer and countershaft gear.

NOTE: Do not move synchronizer sleeve beyond 4th gear position or synchronizer inserts will fall out.

14. Unfasten bearing retainer from front of case and pry the oil seal from the retainer.

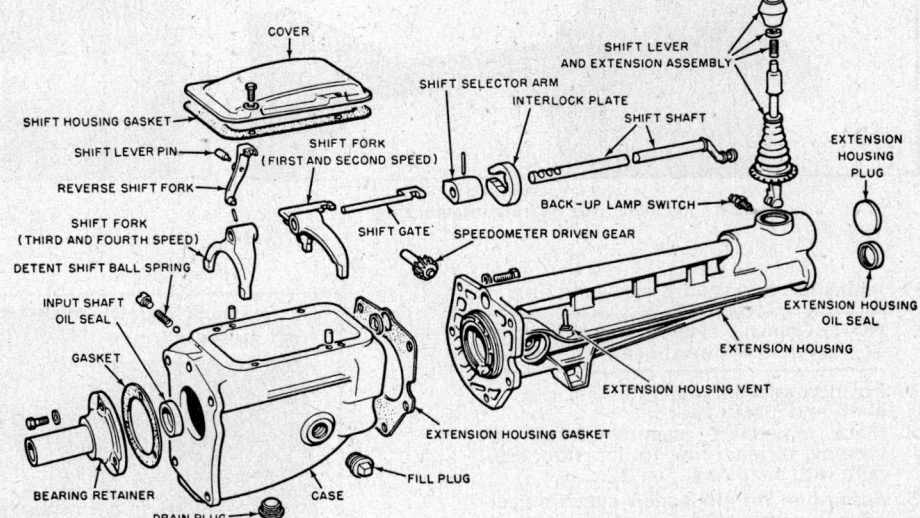
Fig. 1 Type 8 transmission case and related parts

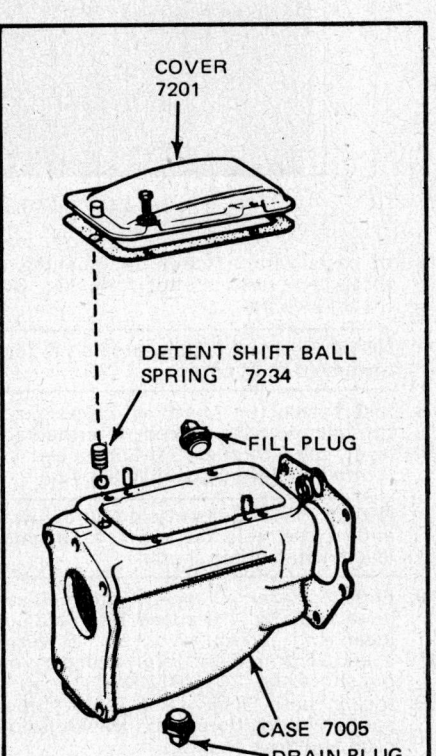

Fig. 1A Late 1973 detent shift ball, spring and fill plug location

15. Remove needle bearing from recess in end of input shaft gear.
16. Remove outer snap ring from around input shaft bearing. Using a suitable drift, tap the outer race inward evenly until bearing is free of case. Lift assembly out of transmission.
17. Remove countershaft gear and two thrust washers from case. In both ends of gear there are 20 needle rollers retained by a washer on each side of each set. Remove the rollers, washers and dummy shaft.
18. Withdraw reverse idler shaft, Fig. 3. Should these tools not be available, locate a nut, flat washer and a sleeve on a 5/16" 24UNF threaded bolt. Screw bolt into reverse idler shaft and tighten nut to withdraw shaft.
19. Slide reverse relay lever from fulcrum pin on case. Do not remove pin.

3rd-4th Synchronizer

1. Lift 4th gear blocking ring from front of 3rd-4th synchronizer.
2. Remove snap ring at forward end of output shaft and discard it. Press output shaft out of 3rd-4th synchronizer and 3rd gear while supporting the shaft so it will not drop.
3. Prior to disassembly of synchronizer

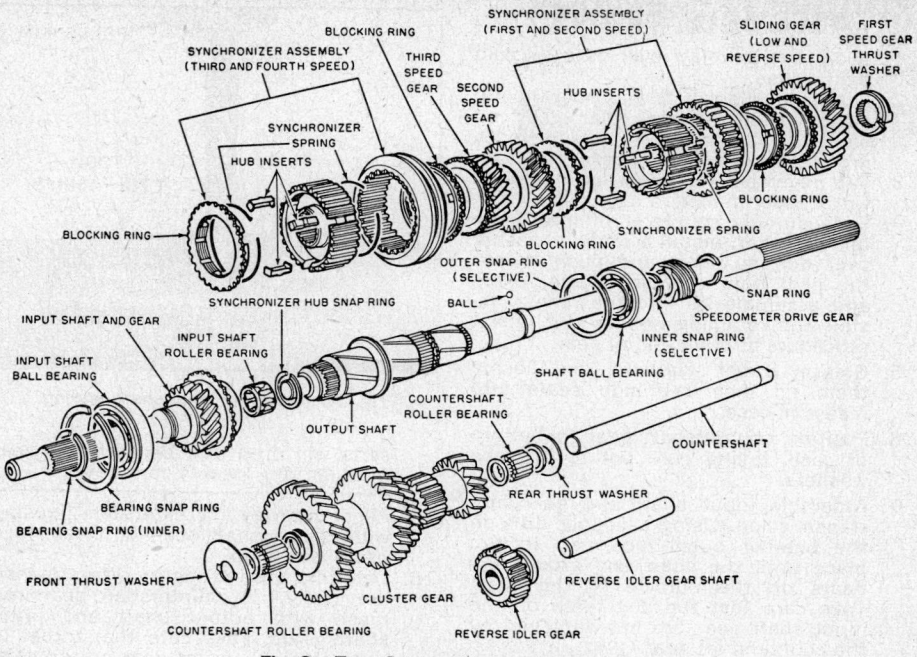

Fig. 2   Type 8 transmission internal parts

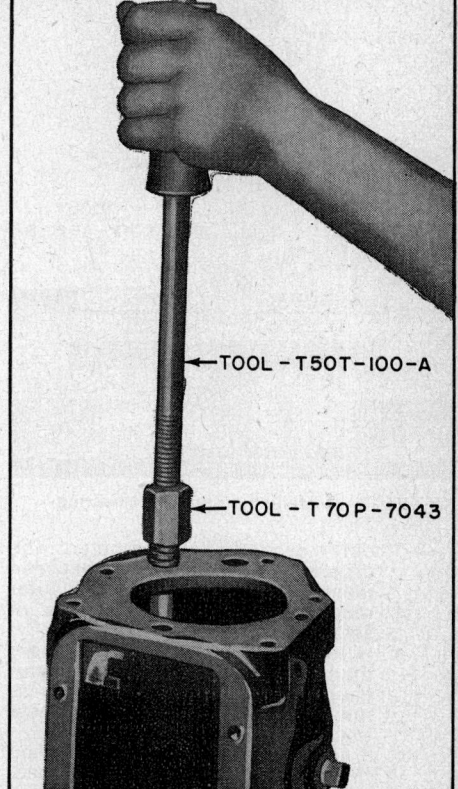

Fig. 3   Removing reverse idler shaft

scribe alignment marks on sleeve and hub so they may be assembled in original positions. Disassemble synchronizer by pulling sleeve off hub and withdrawing inserts and springs.

4. To assemble, reverse procedure and refer to Fig. 4 for proper positioning of synchronizer springs.

1st-2nd Synchronizer

1. Remove snap ring securing output shaft bearing to extension housing. Tap output shaft out of extension using a plastic faced mallet. Remove snap ring retaining speedo gear to out-

put shaft and pull off gear being careful not to lose the drive ball from the shaft. Remove snap ring retaining output shaft bearing.
2. Press low and reverse sliding gear, spacer, snap ring and output shaft bearing from the output shaft.
3. Remove snap ring securing 1st-2nd synchronizer to output shaft.
4. Press 2nd gear and 1st-2nd synchronizer assembly complete with blocking rings off the output shaft.
5. Prior to disassembly of synchronizer, scribe alignment marks on sleeve and hub so they may assembled in original positions. Disassemble unit by pull-

ing sleeve off hub and withdrawing the inserts and springs.
6. To assemble, reverse the procedure and refer to Fig. 4 for proper positioning of synchronizer springs.

Output Shaft

1. When installing output shaft assembly into extension, place master spacer tool T70P-7154 in output shaft bearing bore of extension, Fig. 5.
2. Determine thickness of the snap ring required to remove all end play from the master gauge as follows:
   a. Measure width of shaft bearing

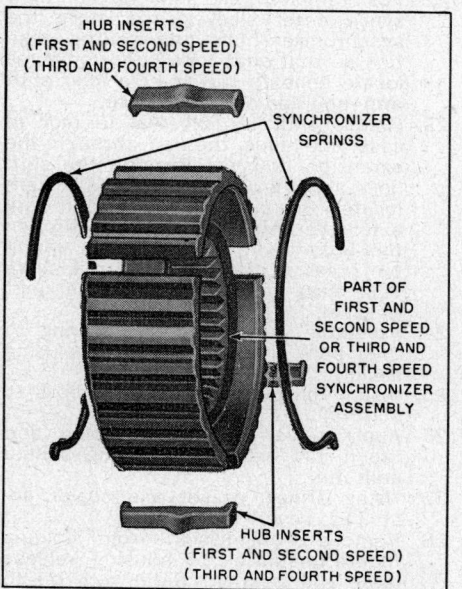

Fig. 4   Synchronizer spring rotation

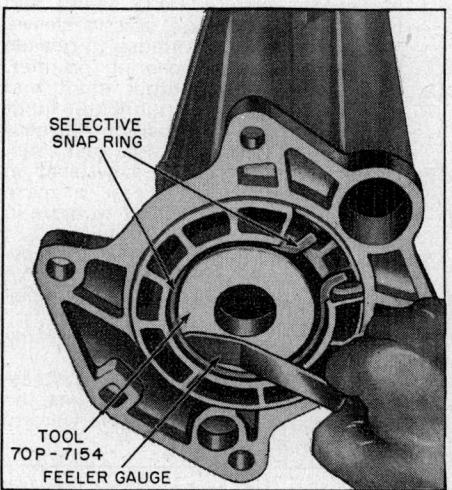

Fig. 5   Determining snap ring thickness

Part Number	Identification	Thickness
DORY-7030-A	Yellow	0.0726–0.0736
DORY-7030-B	Red	0.0715–0.0725
DORY-7030-C	Blue	0.0703–0.0713
DORY-7030-D	Violet	0.0691–0.0701
DORY-7030-E	Green	0.0679–0.0689
DORY-7030-F	Magenta	0.0677–0.0667
DORY-7030-G	Plain	0.0665–0.0655

Fig. 6   Output shaft bearing snap ring thickness chart

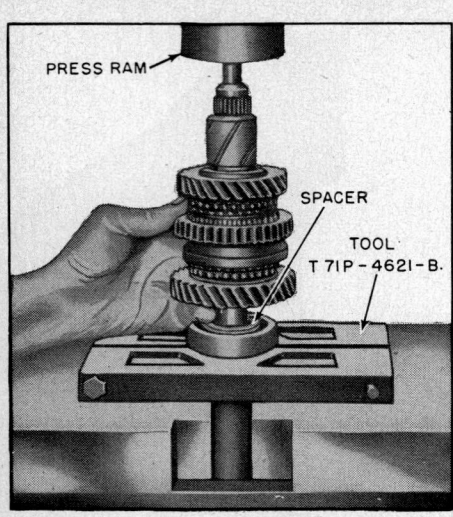

Fig. 7   Installing output shaft bearing

outer race with micrometer. The difference in thickness between master gauge and bearing outer race will determine thickness of selective ring to be used.

b. If bearing race thickness is more than that stamped on master gauge, the snap ring thickness must be decreased by that closest to available ring, Fig. 6.

c. If the thickness is less, the snap ring thickness must be increased.

3. Position the selected snap ring and the bearing on the output shaft.

4. Position tool T71P-4621B on the shaft, then place assembly into press. Press the bearing into place, Fig. 7, and secure with the thickest snap ring that will fit the groove in the output shaft.

5. Locate drive ball in output shaft detent and push speedo gear onto shaft so it just clears the snap ring groove in the shaft. Install a new snap ring to shaft to retain the gear.

6. Heat the front end of the extension housing, using a suitable hot plate or by placing in hot water. This will expand the extension housing so that the shaft can easily be installed.

NOTE: Do not use a welding torch.

7. Secure the output shaft bearing in the extension housing with the snap ring selected previously.

Input Shaft and Gear

1. Remove snap ring from input shaft and discard snap ring.

2. The bearing should not be removed unless it is noisey, rough, spalled or cracked. Position input shaft bearing, Fig. 8, and press bearing off shaft.

3. To assemble, press bearing on input shaft. The bearing must be placed on the shaft with the ring groove facing away from the gear. The tool used to replace the bearing insures that all the load is taken through the bearing inner race so the bearing will not be damaged in the pressing operation.

4. Install the thickest snap ring to secure the bearing to the shaft.

ASSEMBLE TRANS.

1. Slide reverse relay lever onto fulcrum pin on case.

2. Lubricate idler shaft and push it into case. Install reverse idler gear on shaft and locate reverse relay lever in groove in reverse idler gear.

3. Tap reverse idler shaft into position with copper mallet.

4. Slide dummy countershaft into countershaft gear. Install a retainer washer over dummy shaft and push it into the gear bore. Grease needle rollers and assemble 20 into the recess; install 2nd retaining washer and repeat procedure at other end of gear.

5. Grease thrust washers and locate them so their tab side seats into recess in case.

6. Position countershaft gear in bottom of case, taking care not to displace washers.

7. Assemble input shaft and gear into transmission. Using a copper drift on the bearing outer race, tap it into place until the snap ring groove appears on the outside of the case. Take care that the dog teeth on the input shaft gear are not damaged by the countershaft gear.

NOTE: The bearing is an interference fit in the case, it is important that the outer race is tapped. Do not tap on input shaft gear as the bearing will be damaged.

8. Install snap ring to periphery of the bearing.

9. Lubricate input shaft needle bearing and position it in recess of input shaft gear.

10. Place a new oil seal on input shaft retainer and install so lips of seal face transmission. Drive seal into retainer until it bottoms.

11. Lubricate front bearing retainer seal and the seal journal area on input shaft. Place a new gasket on retainer. Fabricate a plastic sleeve and slide it over input shaft splines to prevent damage to seal lip. Be sure that oil groove in retainer is in line with oil passage in case and that gasket does not cover this passage. Coat attaching screws with suitable sealer and install them. Remove plastic sleeve. Apply a light film of grease to release bearing surface on bearing retainer.

12. Prior to installing output shaft and extension assembly, lubricate input shaft gear cone and position 4th gear blocking ring on input shaft gear cone.

13. If necessary, install a new seal in shaft rail aperture in rear of case and use a standard socket to drive in the seal.

14. Thread cord or suitable plastic covered wire under countershaft gear at each end to facilitate lifting into position later.

15. Install new gasket on extension using a sealer.

16. Slide extension and output shaft assembly into position after pulling the 3rd-4th synchronizer sleeve forward to clear countershaft gear.

NOTE: Do not move sleeve beyond 4th gear position as synchronizer in-

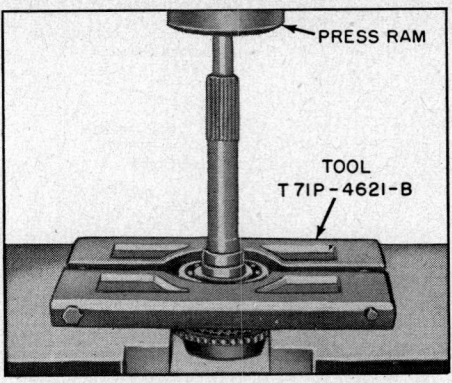

Fig. 8   Removing input shaft bearing

serts will drop out. Be sure 4th gear blocking ring locates correctly.

17. Align cutaway on extension housing with countershaft opening in rear face of transmission.

18. Carefully, with string or wire attached previously, lift countershaft gear into mesh with output shaft and input shaft gears. Take care that thrust in case at each end of gear are not displaced.

19. Check that countershaft gear bore aligns with apertures of countershaft. Push dummy shaft out of gear by inserting countershaft from rear. Finally, tap countershaft into position with suitable mallet. Be sure that lug on rear of countershaft is positioned horizontally so it will install into recess on extension housing flange. The front of the countershaft must be flush with front face of transmission case after installation.

20. Rotate extension so bolts align and push extension fully home onto the transmission. Secure housing to case using sealer on bolts.

21. Replace shift forks on relay lever and secure the 3rd and 4th fork to lever with new roll pin.

22. Position assembled shift forks on their synchronizer sleeves and move the synchronizer hubs into neutral position so that shift fork extension arms locate beneath the reverse idler shift arm mounted on side of case.

23. Grease shift rail oil seal in rear of case and slide the rail through the extension housing. Position the shift boss and the C-cam so that the cam locates the cutouts in the shift fork extension arms. Pass the rail through the boss and forks until the spring pin holes in the boss and rail align. Take care not to damage the shift rail seal.

24. Assemble detent ball and spring to their bore and install set screw using sealer.

25. Install roll pin to retain shift boss to shift rail.

26. Apply sealer to blanking plug and tap it into extension housing behind shift rail.

27. Using a new gasket and sealer, install top cover.

28. Remove transmission from holding fixture, install clutch housing, release lever and bearing. Refill with oil to proper level.

Type Nine

This section covers the German built unit which can be identified by having 10 top cover bolts. The previous section covers the English built unit which has only 4 top cover bolts.

DISASSEMBLE TRANS.

1. Remove clutch release bearing, lever and clutch housing.
2. Remove top cover bolts with 10mm wrench and drain lubricant.
3. Remove threaded plug, spring and shift rail detent plunger from case, Fig. 1.
4. Drive access plug from rear of case, Fig. 2, and drive the interlock plate retaining pin from case, Fig. 3. Lift interlock plate from case.
5. Remove roll pin from selector lever arm, Fig. 2.
6. Tap front end of shaft rail to displace plug at rear of extension housing.
7. Withdraw shift rail from extension and case, Fig. 4.
8. Lift selector arm and shift fork from case.
9. Remove extension housing bolts and tap extension housing with plastic mallet to loosen it from case so it may be rotated.
10. Rotate extension to align countershaft with cutaway in extension flange. Using a brass drift, drive countershaft rearward until it just clears front of case. Install a dummy shaft in the case and gear until the countershaft gear can be lowered to bottom of case, then remove the countershaft.
11. Lift extension housing and mainshaft from case as an assembly, Fig. 5.
12. Remove 10mm input shaft attaching bolts and remove the input shaft and bearing retainer from case as an assembly.
13. Remove reverse idler gear shaft from rear of case, Fig. 6. Remove reverse idler gear and on 74WT transmissions, reverse idler gear spacer, Fig. 6A.
14. Remove countershaft bearing retain-

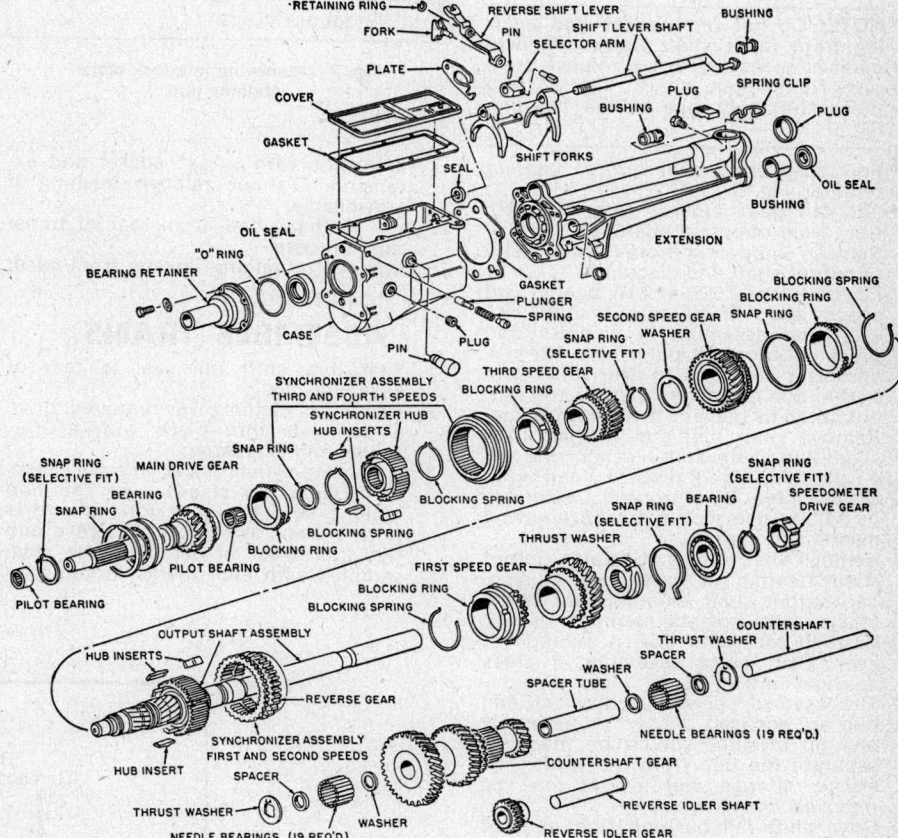

Exploded view of Type 9 transmission

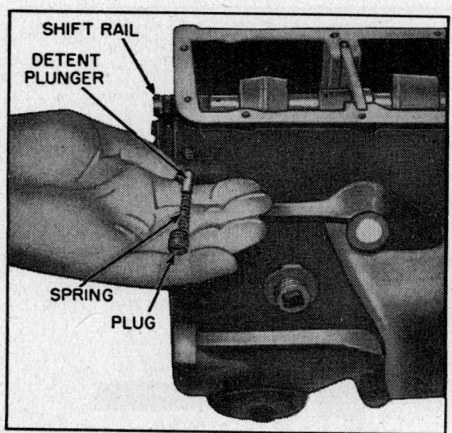

Fig. 1   Shift rail detent plunger

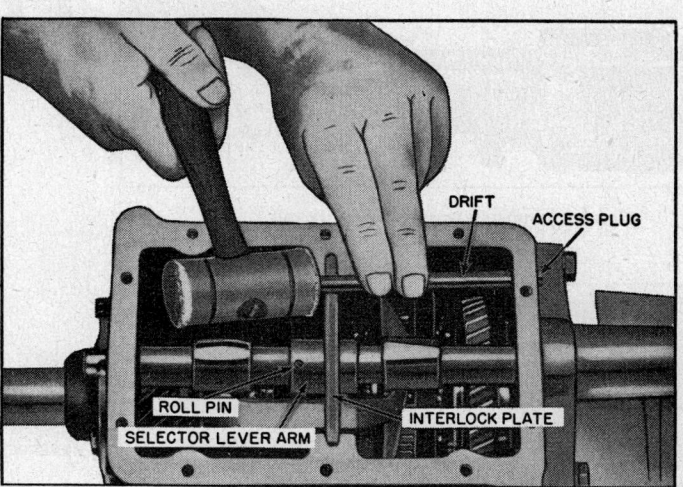

Fig. 2   Removing interlock plate access plug

ing washers, bearings (19 on each end for 74WG transmissions and 21 for 74WT models), dummy shaft and spacer from countershaft gear, Fig. 7.

NOTE: 74WG transmissions have one thrust washer located at each end of the countershaft whereas, the 74WT transmissions have two thrust washers.

15. Remove bearing retainer and pilot bearing from input shaft gear.

NOTE: Do not remove the ball bearing from input shaft unless replacement is necessary. If so, remove snap ring from input shaft, Fig. 8, and press the shaft out of the bearing, Fig. 9.

16. Pry input shaft seal out of bearing retainer, Fig. 8.
17. Lift 4th gear blocker ring, Fig. 10, from front of output shaft.
18. Remove snap ring from forward end of output shaft and discard it.
19. Position tool T69P-4621A behind 3rd speed gear. Place output shaft and extension assembly in a press and press output shaft out of 3rd-4th synchronizer and the 3rd gear while supporting the extension housing and output shaft to prevent it from dropping.
20. Remove snap ring and washer, then slide 2nd gear and blocker ring off output shaft and discard snap ring.
21. Disassemble synchronizer assembly by pulling sleeve off hub and removing inserts and springs.
22. Remove snap ring that retains output shaft bearing in extension housing.
23. Tap output shaft assembly out of extension with a plastic hammer.
24. Position tool T69P-4621A behind 1st gear, then place assembly in press as shown in Fig. 11.
25. The 1st-2nd speed synchronizer and hub are serviced only as an assembly and no attempt should be made to separate the hub from the shaft. The sleeve, springs and inserts may be removed from the hub.
26. Drive shift rail bushing from rear of

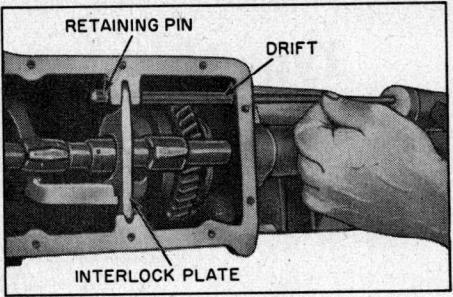

Fig. 3 Removing interlock plate retaining pin

extension with a 9/16" socket and extension. Do not remove bushing if serviceable.
27. Pry shift rail seal from rear of transmission case.
28. Remove remaining linkage from case.

ASSEMBLE TRANS.

1. Seat new shift rail seal in rear of case, Fig. 12.
2. If shift rail bushing was removed, drive a new one into place with a 9/16" socket and extension.
3. If 1st-2nd synchronizer was disassembled, slide the sleeve over the hub making sure the shift fork groove is toward front of shaft. The sleeve and hub are select fit and must be reassembled with etch marks in same lo-

cation. Locate an insert in each of three slots cut in the hub. Install insert spring inside the sleeve beneath the inserts. The tab on end of spring must locate in the section of an insert. Fit the other spring to the opposite face of the synchronizer unit, being sure the spring tab locates in the same insert as the spring just installed and is in the same rotational direction. Looking down at the synchronizer, the tab end of one spring should be in line with the tab of the spring on the opposite side.

NOTE: Oil all parts at time of assembly.

4. Assemble a blocker ring on the 1st gear side of the 1st-2nd synchronizer. Apply grease to the cone surface of the 1st gear. Slide 1st gear onto output shaft so that cone surface engages blocker ring.
5. Position spacer on shaft making certain the large diameter is toward rear of staff.
6. Place master spacer tool T70P-7154 in the output shaft bearing bore of the extension, Fig. 13. Determine thickness of snap ring required to remove all end play from master gauge. Then measure width of the output shaft bearing outer race with a micrometer. The difference in thickness between the master gauge and the bearing outer race will determine thickness of selective snap ring. If the bearing race thickness is more than that stamped on the master gauge, the snap ring thickness must be de-

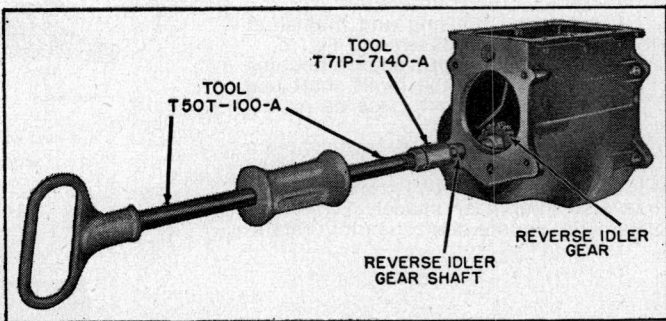

Fig. 6 Removing reverse idler gear shaft

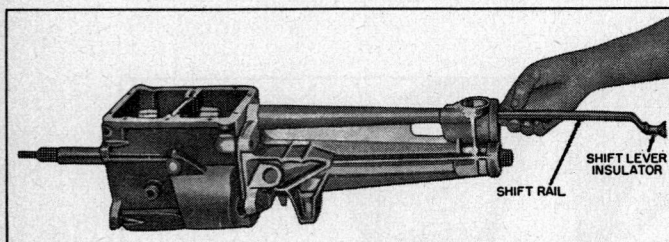

Fig. 4 Removing or installing shift rail

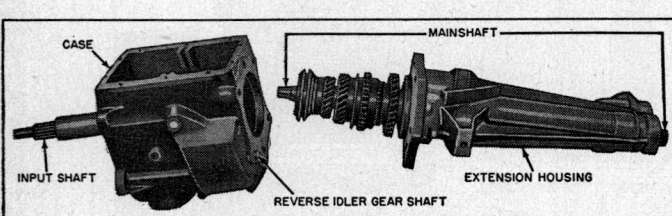

Fig. 5 Removing or installing extension and mainshaft

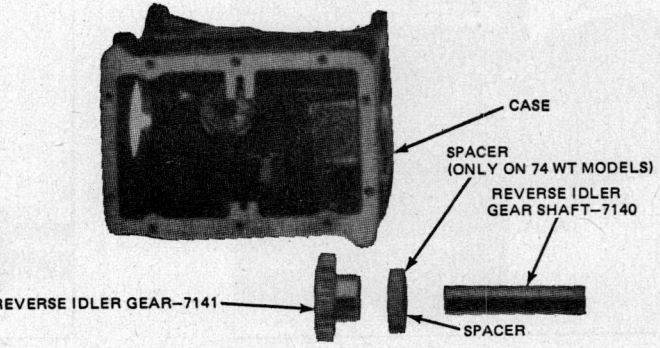

Fig. 6A Reverse idler gear spacer location

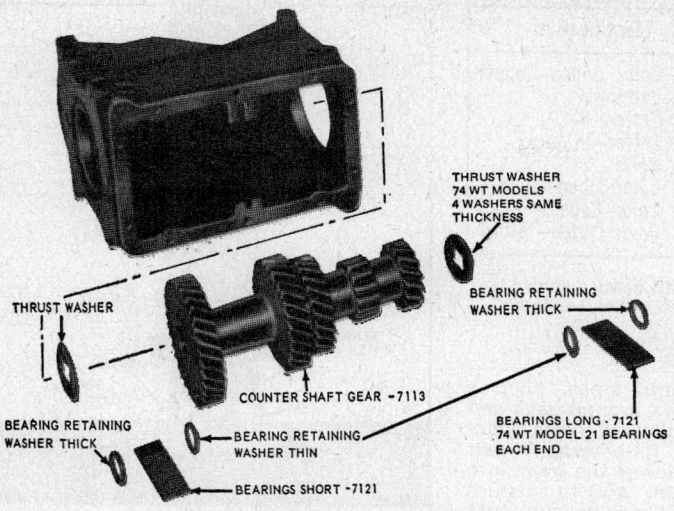

Fig. 7 Countershaft gear disassembled

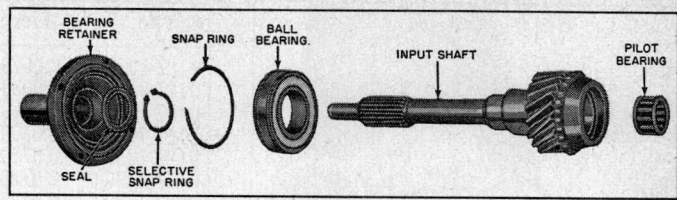

Fig. 8 Input shaft disassembled

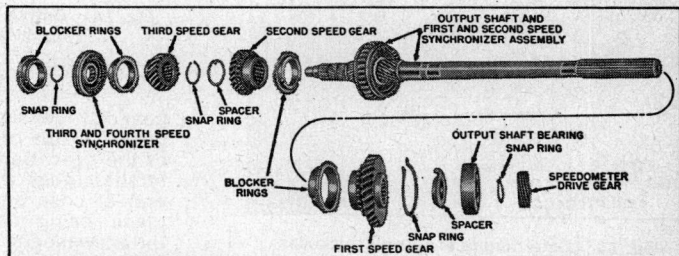

Fig. 10 Output shaft disassembled

creased to the closest available ring, Fig. 14. If the thickness is less, the snap ring thickness must be increased.

7. Position selected snap ring and the bearing on the output shaft. Position tool T69P-4621A on the shaft, then place assembly in a press and press bearing into place. Secure bearing with thickest snap ring that will fit the groove in the output shaft.

8. Slide the synchronizer sleeve over the hub and locate an insert in each of the three slots cut into sleeve. The sleeve and hub are select fit and must be reassembled with etch marks in same relative location.

9. Install an insert spring inside the synchronizer sleeve beneath the inserts. The tab on the end of the spring must locate in the U section of an insert. Fit the other spring to the opposite face of the synchronizer unit, being

sure that the spring tab locates in the same insert as the spring just installed and is in the same rotational direction. Looking down at the unit, the tab end of one spring should be in line with the tab of the spring on the opposite side.

10. Position the 2nd gear and blocker ring on output shaft so that dog teeth face rearward. Install washer and snap ring. Position 3rd gear on output shaft so dog teeth face forward. Apply grease to cones of the gears and assemble the blocker ring on the 3rd gear cone.

11. Position the 3rd-4th synchronizer on output shaft with the hub boss facing forward.

12. Position tool T69P-4621A so that it butts against the boss on the synchronizer hub.

13. Place entire unit, extension end up, in a press and push the synchronizer unit onto the output shaft as far as possible.

14. Retain the 3rd-4th synchronizer to output shaft with snap ring. Pull up on the synchronizer assembly so the snap ring is tight in its groove.

15. Prior to assembling output shaft and extension housing into the case, apply lubricant to the cone of the gear and place the 4th gear blocker ring on the input shaft gear cone.

16. Press the speedo gear onto the shaft with tools shown in Fig. 15, until dowels just contact bearing outer race.

NOTE: The dowels must contact the

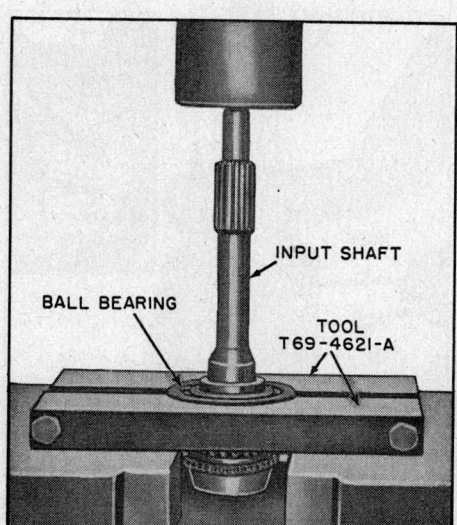

Fig. 9 Removing input shaft bearing

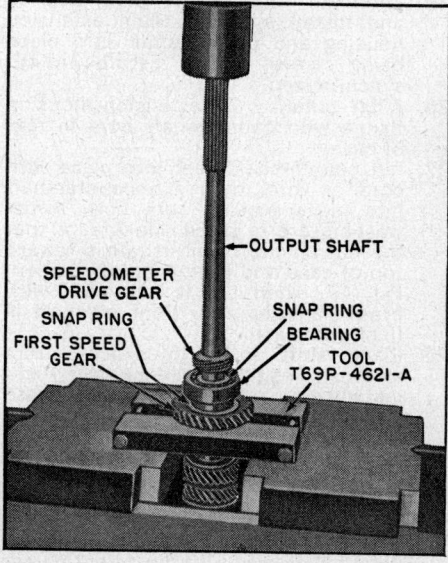

Fig. 11 Removing 1st gear, spacer, output shaft bearing, snap rings and speedo gear from output shaft

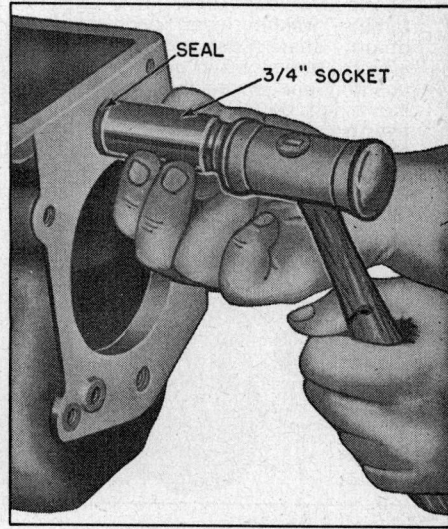

Fig. 12 Installing shift rail seal

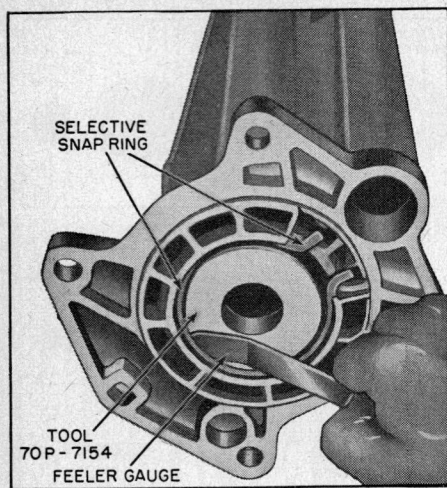

SELECTIVE
SNAP RING

TOOL
70P-7154

FEELER GAUGE

Fig. 13 Determining snap ring thickness

Part No.	Thickness	Identification
D1FZ-7030-A	0.0679-	Color Coded–Copper
D1FZ-7030-B	0.0689-	Letter–W
D1FZ-7030-C	0.0699-	Letter–V
D1FZ-7030-D	0.0709-	Letter–U
D1FZ-7030-E	0.0719-	None
D1FZ-7030-F	0.0728-	Color Coded–Blue
D1FZ-7030-G	0.0738-	Color Coded–Black
D1FZ-7030-H	0.0748-	Color Coded–Brown

Fig. 14 Output shaft bearing snap ring thickness chart

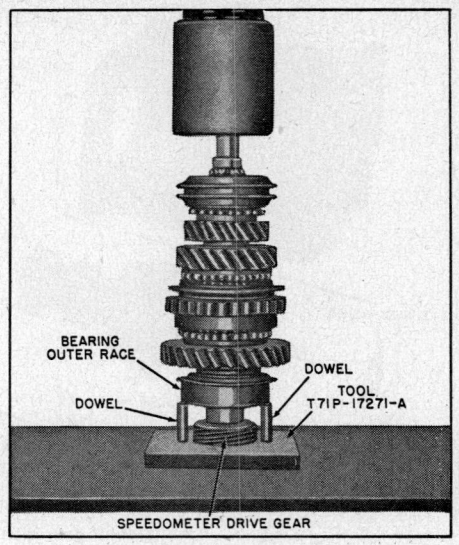

BEARING
OUTER RACE

DOWEL

DOWEL

TOOL
T71P-17271-A

SPEEDOMETER DRIVE GEAR

Fig. 15 Installing speedo drive gear

bearing outer race to properly locate the speedo gear on the shaft.

17. Coat the bearing bore of the extension housing with lubricant and install the output shaft in the housing. It may be necessary to tap the shaft with a plastic hammer while holding the two synchronizer sleeves firmly to prevent sleeve separation from the hubs. Secure it to the extension with the selective snap ring that was previously installed.

18. Press bearing on input shaft with snap ring groove toward front of shaft. Secure bearing to shaft with thickest selective snap ring.

19. Slide spacer and dummy shaft into countershaft gear. Position a thin bearing retaining washer at each end of dummy shaft. Coat the bearings with lubricant. Load long bearings into small end of countershaft gear and the short bearings into large end of gear. Note that the 74WG transmission has 19 bearings at each end and the 74WT transmission has 21 bearings at each end. Fit a thick retaining washer over each end of dummy shaft. Coat each thrust washer with lubricant and on 74WG models position one on each end of dummy shaft and on 74WT models, position two thrust washers on ends of dummy shaft. Make sure the tabs are in the same relative position so they may engage the slots in the case when the

gear is lowered into place. Loop a piece of rope or wire around each end of the gear. Carefully install the countershaft gear with rope through rear end of case and lower the gear into place being careful not to disturb thrust washers and making sure that the tabs engage slots in case.

20. Apply lubricant to reverse idler gear shaft. If selector lever relay was removed, position it on the pivot pin. Secure lever on pin with spring clip. Hold gear in the lever with long hub toward rear of case. Slide reverse idler gear shaft into place and seat the shaft in the case with a copper hammer.

21. Install a new seal in input shaft bearing retainer.

22. Assemble input shaft to case using a new retainer O ring, Fig. 16. If necessary, tap outer race of bearing with copper hammer evenly until outer snap ring is seated against case.

NOTE: Do not tap on input shaft as this may damage the races/or bearings.

23. Carefully slide 3rd-4th speed synchronizer sleeve into 4th speed position (forward to provide clearance).

24. Position new gasket on extension housing.

25. Lubricate input shaft pilot bearing and install in shaft. Slide extension housing and output shaft into place being careful not to disturb 3rd-4th synchronizer.

26. Align cutaway in extension housing flange with countershaft bore in rear of case.

27. Lift countershaft gear into place with cord or wire, then slip countershaft into place making sure both thrust washers are in place. Make sure that the flat on the countershaft is toward top of case and in horizontal position, Fig. 17. Then tap it into case with brass hammer until front of shaft is flush with case.

28. Place shift forks in synchronizers sleeves. Position interlock lever and install new retaining pin. Lubricate shift rail oil seal and slide shift rail through extension housing, transmission case and the 1st and 2nd speed shift fork. Position selector arm on the rail, then slide the rail through the 3rd and 4th speed shift fork, then through the front of case until center detent is aligned with the detent plunger bore. Install new retaining pin in selector arm.

29. Install detent plunger, spring and plug with sealer.

30. Install new access plug in rear of case.

31. Rotate extension to align bolt holes, then install bolts loosely. Before tightening bolts make sure shift rail slides freely in bore.

32. Position new oil seal in input shaft retainer so tension spring and lip face the case. Drive seal into position.

33. Position new O ring in groove in face of case. Install input shaft bearing retainer to case. Be sure that oil passage in case is in line with oil groove in retainer, Fig. 16. Apply sealer to bolts and attach to case.

34. Reinstall clutch release bearing.

35. Apply sealer to new extension housing plug and install it.

36. Install top cover with vent toward rear. Make sure that sealer is applied to bolt over detent plunger bore.

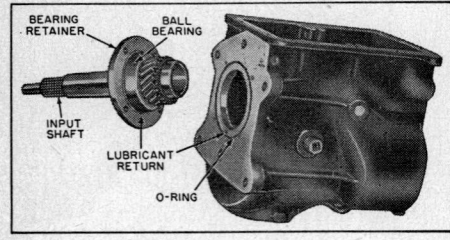

BEARING
RETAINER

BALL
BEARING

INPUT
SHAFT

LUBRICANT
RETURN

O-RING

Fig. 16 Installing input shaft gear

COUNTERSHAFT

FLAT TO BE
PARALLEL TO
TOP OF CASE

FLAT

ROPE

TOOL
T571-500-A

Fig. 17 Installing countershaft

AUTOMATIC TRANSMISSIONS

NOTE:—This chapter deals only with maintenance, adjustments and "in car" repairs. For major service work, Motor's Automatic Transmission Manual is available. Current edition is a 962 page volume that includes 297 pages of oil circuit diagrams mostly in full color.

INDEX

NOTE: For 1975 linkage adjustment information, see car chapters.

CHRYSLER UNITS

Torqueflite with Aluminum Case 2-271

FORD UNITS

C3 Dual Range Automatic 2-281

C4 Dual Range Automatic 2-281

C4 Dual Semi-Automatic 2-290

C6 Dual Range Automatic 2-291

CW Dual Range 2-300

FMX Dual Range 2-300

GENERAL MOTORS UNITS

Buick Super Turbine 300 2-261

Cadillac Eldorado Turbo Hydra-Matic 2-245

Chevrolet Powerglide with Aluminum Case ... 2-265

Chevrolet Torque-Drive 2-252

Oldsmobile Jetaway, 1969 2-261

Olds Toronado Turbo Hydra-Matic 2-245

Pontiac 2-Speed, 1969 2-261

Pontiac 2-Speed, 1970-73 2-265

Turbo Hydra-Matic 400 2-232

Turbo Hydra-Matic 375 2-232

Turbo Hydra-Matic 375B 2-253

Turbo Hydra-Matic 350 2-253

Turbo Hydra-Matic 250 2-253

MISCELLANEOUS

American Motors Shift-Command 2-307

American Motors Torque-Command 2-271

HOW TO PUSH AND TOW AUTOMATIC DRIVE CARS—Inside Back Cover

TURBO HYDRA-MATIC 375, 400

TRANSMISSION IDENTIFICATION

An identification plate is attached to the transmission. The plate indicates year of production, code letters, and serial number.

*Late production 1973 Pontiac transmissions have the number "2" between code letters.

BUICK	CODE
1969 V8-350 LeSabre	BU
V8-400 Sportwagon	BW
V8-400 G.S. 400	BA, BB
V8-430 Wildcat, Electra	BC
V8-430 Riviera	BT
1970 V8-455 G.S. 455	BA
V8-455 G.S. 455 Stage 1	BB
V8-455 Riviera	BT
V8-455 All Others	BC
1971 V8-455 G.S. 455	BS
V8-455 G.S. 455 Stage 1	BB, OW
V8-455 Riviera	BT
V8-455 All Others	BC
1972 V8-455 G. S. 455	BS
V8-455 G. S. 455 Stage 1	BB
V8-455 Centurion Hi Perf.	BU
V8-455 Riviera G. S.; Perf. axles on all models	BT
V8-455 All Others	BC
1973-74 V8-455 Century, Regal less Stage 1	BS
V8-455 Century, Regal Stage 1	BB
All Others—	
Hi Perf.	BT
Exc. Hi. Perf.	BC

CADILLAC	
1969 75 and Commercial Chassis	AB
All Others	AA
1970-74 All Models	AA

CHEVROLET	
1969 V8-350 Chevrolet	CA
V8-396 Chevrolet	CA
V8-427, 390 H.P.	CB
V8-396, 325 H.P.	CC
V8-350, 250 H.P. Chevrolet	CD
V8-327, 235 H.P. Chevrolet	CD
V8-396, 350 H.P. Chevelle, Camaro, Nova	CE
V8-427, 335 H.P.	CF
V8-396, 265 H.P. Chevrolet	CG
V8-427, 390 H.P. Chevrolet	CH
V8-350, 300 H.P. Corvette	CK
V8-427, 400 H.P. Corvette	CL
V8-427, 335 H.P. Chevrolet	CQ
V8-427, 425 H.P. Corvette	CY①
V8-427, 430 H.P. Corvette	CY①
V8-427, 435 H.P. Corvette	CY①
V8-396, 375 H.P. Chevelle, Camaro, Nova	CY①
1970 V8-400 Chevrolet	CA
V8-454 Chevrolet	CB

CHEVROLET—Continued	CODE
V8-400 Chevelle, Monte Carlo	CD
V8-400 Camaro, Chevrolet, Nova	CF
V8-454 Police	CG
V8-350 Corvette	CK
V8-454 Camaro, Chevelle, Nova	CR
V8-454 Chevelle, Monte Carlo, Corvette	CS
V8-400 Camaro, Chevelle, Nova	CW
V8-454 Camaro, Chevelle, Corvette	CY
1971 V8-400 Chevrolet	CA
V8-454 Chevrolet	CB
V8-400 Chevelle	CD
V8-454 Chevelle	CF
V8-350 Corvette	CK
V8-454 Corvette	CS
V8-454 Chevelle, Corvette Hi. Perf.	CY
1972 V8-350, 400 Chevrolet	CA
V8-402 4 Bar. Carb. Chevelle	CD
V8-454 Chevelle	CF
V8-400 Camaro	CK
V8-454 Chevrolet	CR
V8-454 Corvette	CS
V8-350 Camaro, Chevelle, Corvette	CY
1973 V8-400 2 Bar. Carb. Chevrolet	CA
V8-350 2 Bar. Carb. Chevrolet	CF
V8-350 4 Bar. Carb. Chevelle	CG
V8-350 Corvette 190 H.P.	CK
V8-454 Chevrolet	CR
V8-454 Corvette	CS
V8-350 Corvette 250 H.P.	CY
1974 V8-400 Chevrolet	CA
V8-400 2 Bar. Carb. Chevrolet	CB
V8-400 Chevrolet	CG
V8-350 Corvette 190 H.P.	CK
V8-454 Chevrolet	CR
V8-454 Corvette	CS
V8-350 Corvette 250 H.P.	CZ

① High shift point.

OLDSMOBILE	
1969 V8-350 Vista-Cruiser	OA
V8-350 Delta 88 W/Cruise Control	OA
V8-455 4 barrel carb. "98"	OB
V8-455 2 barrel carb. Delta	OC
V8-350 Delta 88	OF
V8-400 4-4-2 Exc. Ram Air	OG
V8-455 4 bar. carb. "98", Delta	OK
V8-400 4 barrel carb. Vista-Cruiser	OP
V8-400 Heavy Duty, Police	OL
V8-455 2 barrel carb. Delta	OR
V8-400 4-4-2 Ram Air	OW
1970 V8-350 Exc. Below	OF
V8-350 W/Cruise Control	OA
V8-455 2 bar. carb. Exc. Below	OC

OLDSMOBILE—Continued	CODE
V8-455 Delta 88, 4 bar. carb.	OB
V8-455 2 bar. carb. Cruise Control	OR
V8-455 Cutlass Exc. SX	OD
V8-455 Cutlass, 442 SX Exc. Ram Air	OG
V8-455 Senior models W/Cruise Control & 4 bar. carb.	OK
V8-455 Vista-Cruiser	OK
V8-455 Police	OL
V8-455 442 Ram Air	OW
1971 V8-455 Supreme 4 Bar. Carb.	OD
V8-455 4-4-2	OG
V8-455 4-4-2 W/Air Induction	OW
V8-455 Vista Cruiser	OA
V8-455 Vista Cruiser 2 Bar. Carb.	OR
V8-455 Vista Cruiser 4 Bar. Carb.	OK
V8-455 Senior Models 2 Bar. Carb.	OR
V8-455 Senior Models Dual Exhaust	OK
V8-455 Delta 88 Single Exhaust	OR
1972 V8-455 Cutlass, 4 Bar. Carb., Dual Exh.	OD
V8-455 Cutlass, 4 Bar. Carb. (W30)	OW
V8-350 Vista Cruiser	OA
V8-350 Senior Models	OA
V8-455 Senior Models	OR
V8-455 Senior Models, Dual Exh.	OK
V8-455 Vista Cruiser, Dual Exh.	OK
1973 V8-455 Cutlass, 4 Bar. Carb.	OD
V8-455 Senior Models, Dual Exh.	OK
V8-455 Senior Models	OR
1974 V8-350 88	OA
V8-455 Cutlass Exc. Calif.	OD
V8-455 Cutlass Calif.	OW
V8-455 Cutlass 275 H.P.	OX
V8-455 88 & 98 Single Exhaust Exc. Calif.	OR
V8-455 88 & 98 Single Exh. Calif.	OL
V8-455 88 & 98 Dual Exhaust	OK
V8-455 Custom Cruiser Exc. Calif.	OK
V8-455 Custom Cruiser Calif.	OE

PONTIAC	
1969 V8-350 2 Barrel carb. (Tempest, Firebird)	PV
V8-350 H.O. (Tempest, Firebird)	PS
V8-400 2 barrel carb.	PB
V8-400 2 barrel carb. (GTO, Grand Prix)	PT
V8-400 4 barrel carb. (Grand Prix)	PW
V8-400 4 barrel carb. (GTO, Firebird)	PX
V8-400 Ram Air (GTO, Firebird)	PQ
V8-428 H.O.	PC
V8-428 Bonneville	PH
V8-428 H.O. (Grand Prix)	PR

Continued

TRANSMISSION IDENTIFICATION—CONTINUED

PONTIAC—Continued	CODE
1970 V8-400 (Pontiac)	PB
V8-400 Ram Air (GTO)	PD
V8-400 (Tempest, Grand Prix)	PT
V8-400 4 bar. carb. (Grand Prix)	PW
V8-400 2 bar. carb. (Firebird)	PF
V8-400 Sports Option	PX
V8-400 Ram Air, HO	PQ
V8-455 Exc. HO (Pontiac)	PA
V8-455 HO (Pontiac)	PC
V8-455 Heavy Duty (Pontiac)	PH
V8-455 HO (Tempest, Grand Prix)	PR
1971 V8-455 (Pontiac)	PA
V8-400 (Pontiac)	PB
V8-400 4 Bar. Carb., W/Dual Exh. (Pontiac)	PC
V8-400 (Pontiac)	PD
V8-455 (Pontiac)	PF
V8-400 2 Bar. Carb. (Police & H.D.)	PH
V8-455 4 Bar. Carb. (Police & H.D.)	PH
V8-455 H.O. (LeMans, GTO, Firebird)	PQ
V8-455 4 Bar. Carb. (LeMans, GTO, Firebird)	PR
V8-400 2 Bar. Carb. (LeMans, GTO, Firebird)	PT
V8-455 4 Bar. Carb. (LeMans, GTO, Firebird, Grand Prix)	PW

PONTIAC—Continued	CODE
V8-400 4 Bar. Carb. (LeMans, GTO, Firebird, Grand Prix)	PX
V8-400 4 Bar. Carb. (LeMans, GTO, Firebird)	PY
1972 V8-400 Wagons	PA
V8-455 2 Bar. Carb. (Pontiac)	PA
V8-400 4 Bar. Carb.	PB
V8-455 4 Bar. Carb. (Pontiac)	PC
V8-400 2 Bar. Carb.	PD
V8-400 4 Bar. Carb. (LeMans, Firebird)	PG
V8-455 HO (LeMans, Firebird)	PQ
V8-455 4 Bar. Carb. (LeMans, Grand Prix)	PR
V8-400 2 Bar. Carb. (LeMans, Firebird)	PT
V8-400 4 Bar. Carb. (Grand Prix)	PX
1973 V8-400 2 Bar. Carb. Wagons	PA
* V8-400 4 Bar. Carb.	PA
V8-400 4 Bar. Carb. (Pontiac)	PB
V8-455 4 Bar. Carb. (Pontiac)	PC
V8-400 2 Bar. Carb. (Exc. Wagon on Pontiac)	PD
V8-350 2 Bar. Carb. (Pontiac)	PF
V8-400 4 Bar. Carb. (Firebird, LeMans, Grand Am)	PT
V8-455 4 Bar. Carb. (Police)	PH

PONTIAC—Continued	CODE
V8-455 SD (Firebird, LeMans, Grand Am)	PQ
V8-455 4 Bar. Carb. (LeMans, Grand Am, Grand Prix)	PR
V8-400 2 Bar. Carb. (Firebird, LeMans, Grand Am)	PT
V8-400 4 Bar. Carb. (Grand Prix)	PX
1974 V8-400 2 Bar. Carb. Sta. Wag.	PA
V8-400 4 Bar. Carb. (Police & H.D.)	PA
V8-400 4 Bar. Carb. (Pontiac)	PB
V8-455 4 Bar. Carb. (Pontiac)	PC
V8-400 2 Bar. Carb. (Pontiac Exc. Calif.)	PD
V8-400 2 Bar. Carb. (Pontiac Calif.)	PF
V8-400 4 Bar. Carb. (LeMans & Firebird, Exc. Calif.)	PG
V8-400 4 Bar. Carb. (LeMans & Firebird, Calif.)	PW
V8-455 4 Bar. Carb. (Police)	PH
V8-455 SD (Firebird)	PQ
V8-455 4 Bar. Carb. (LeMans & Grand Prix)	PR
V8-400 2 Bar. Carb. (LeMans & Firebird, Exc. Calif.)	PT
V8-400 2 Bar. Carb. (LeMans & Firebird, Calif.)	PL
V8-400 4 Bar. Carb. (Grand Prix)	PX
V8-455 4 Bar. Carb. (Firebird)	PZ

GENERAL DESCRIPTION

This transmission, Fig. 1, is a fully automatic unit consisting primarily of a three-element hydraulic torque converter and a compound planetary gear set. Three multiple-disc clutches, two one-way clutches, and two bands provide the friction elements required to obtain the desired functions of the planetary gear set.

The torque converter, the multiple-disc clutches and the one-way clutches couple the engine to the planetary gears through oil pressure, providing three forward speeds and reverse. The torque converter, when required, supplements the gears by multiplying engine torque.

Torque Converter

The torque converter is of welded construction and is serviced as an assembly. The unit is made up of two vaned sections, or halves, that face each other in an oil-filled housing. The pump half of the converter is connected to the engine and the turbine half is connected to the transmission.

When the engine makes the converter pump revolve, it sends oil against the turbine, making it revolve also. The oil then returns in a circular flow back to the converter pump, continuing this flow as long as the engine is running.

Stator

The converter also has a smaller vaned section, called a stator, that funnels the oil back to the converter pump through smaller openings, at increased speed. The speeded up oil directs additional force to the engine-driven converter pump, thereby multiplying engine torque. In other words, without the stator, the unit is nothing more than a fluid coupling.

External Controls

The external control connections to the transmission are:
1. Manual linkage to select the desired operating range.
2. Engine vacuum to operate the vacuum modulator unit.
3. An electrical signal to operate an electric detent solenoid.

Vacuum Modulator

A vacuum modulator is used to sense engine torque input to the transmission automatically. The vacuum modulator transmits this signal to the pressure regulator, which controls line pressure, so that all torque requirements of the transmission are met and proper shift spacing is obtained at all throttle openings.

Detent Solenoid

The detent solenoid is activated by an electric switch at the carburetor. When the throttle is opened sufficiently to close this switch, the solenoid in the transmission is activated, causing a downshift at speeds below 70 mph. At lower speeds, downshifts will occur at lesser throttle openings without use of the electric switch.

TROUBLE SHOOTING GUIDE

Oil Pressure High or Low

1. Vacuum line or fittings clogged or leaking.
2. Vacuum modulator.
3. Modulator valve.
4. Pressure regulator.
5. Oil pump.
6. Governor.

No Drive In Drive Range

1. Low oil level (check for leaks).
2. Manual control linkage not adjusted properly.
3. Low oil pressure. Check for blocked strainer, defective pressure regulator, pump assembly or pump drive gear. See that tangs have not been damaged by converter.
4. Check control valve assembly to see if manual valve has been disconnected from manual lever pin.
5. Forward clutch may be struck or damaged. Check pump feed circuits to forward clutch including clutch drum ball check.
6. Sprag or roller clutch assembled incorrectly.

TURBO HYDRA-MATIC 375, 400

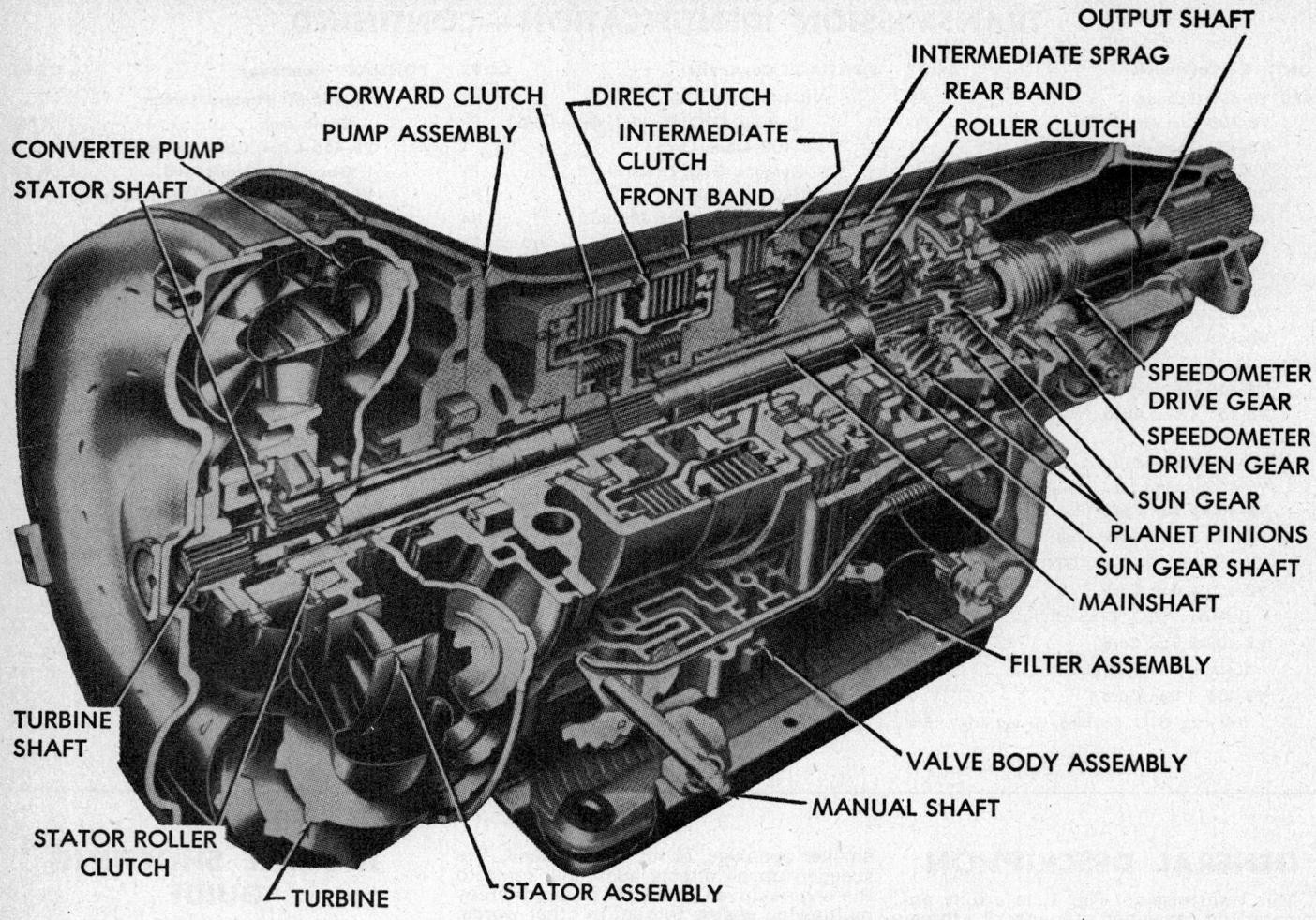

Fig. 1   Cutaway view of transmission assembly

1 - 2 Shift At Full Throttle Only

1. Detent switch may be sticking or defective.
2. Detent solenoid may be stuck open, loose or have leaking gasket.
3. Control valve assembly may be leaking, damaged or incorrectly installed.

1st Speed Only - No 1 - 2 Shift

1. Governor valve may be sticking.
2. Driven gear in governor assembly loose, worn or damaged.
3. The 1-2 shift valve in control valve assembly stuck closed. Check governor feed channels for blocks, leaks, and position. Also check control valve body gaskets for leaks and damage.
4. Intermediate clutch plug in case may be leaking or blown out.
5. Check for porosity between channels and for blocked governor feed channels in case.
6. Check intermediate clutch for proper operation.

No 2 - 3 Shift - 1st & 2nd Only

1. Detent solenoid may be stuck open.

2. Detent switch may not be properly adjusted.
3. Control valve assembly may be stuck, leaking, damaged, or incorrectly installed.
4. Check direct clutch case center support for broken, leaking or missing oil rings.
5. Check clutch piston seals and piston ball check in clutch assembly.

Moves Forward In Neutral

1. Manual control linkage improperly adjusted.
2. Forward clutch does not release.
3. Oil pump.
4. Internal linkage.

No Drive In Reverse or Slips In Reverse

1. Check oil level.
2. Manual control linkage improperly adjusted.
3. Vacuum modulator assembly may be defective.
4. Vacuum modulator valve sticking.
5. Strainer may be restricted or leaking at intake.
6. Regulator or boost valve in pump as-

sembly may be sticking.
7. Control valve assembly may be stuck, leaking or damaged.
8. Rear servo and accumulator may have damaged or missing servo piston seal ring.
9. Reverse band burned out or damaged. Determine that apply pin or anchor pins engage properly.
10. Direct clutch may be damaged or may have stuck ball check in piston.
11. Forward clutch does not release.
12. Low-reverse ball check missing from case.

Slips In All Ranges & On Starts

1. Check oil level.
2. Vacuum modulator defective.
3. Modulator valve sticking.
4. Strainer assembly plugged or leaking at neck.
5. Pump assembly regulator or boost valve sticking.
6. Leaks from damaged gaskets or cross leaks from porosity of case.
7. Forward and direct clutches burned.

Slips 1 - 2 Shift

1. Incorrect oil level.
2. Vacuum modulator valve sticking.
3. Vacuum modulator defective.
4. Pump pressure regulator valve defective.
5. Porosity between channels in case.
6. Control valve assembly.
7. Pump-to-case gasket may be mispositioned.
8. Intermediate clutch plug in case may be missing or leaking excessively.
9. Intermediate clutch piston seal missing or damaged.
10. Intermediate clutch plates burned.
11. Front or rear accumulator oil ring may be damaged.

Slips 2 - 3 Shift

1. Items 1 through 6 under Slips 1-2 Shift will also cause 2-3 shift slips.
2. Direct clutch plates burned.
3. Oil seal rings on direct clutch may be damaged permitting excessive leaking between tower and bushing.

Rough 1 - 2 Shift

1. Modulator valve sticking.
2. Modulator assembly defective.
3. Pump pressure regulator or boost valve stuck or inoperative.
4. Control valve assembly loosened from case, damaged or mounted with wrong gaskets.
5. Intermediate clutch ball missing or not sealing.
6. Porosity between channels in case.
7. Rear servo accumulator assembly may have oil rings damaged, stuck piston, broken or missing spring or damaged bore.

Rough 2 - 3 Shift

1. Items 1, 2 and 3 under Rough 1-2 Shift will also cause rough 2-3 shift.
2. Front servo accumulator spring broken or missing. Accumulator piston may be sticking.

No Engine Braking in Second Speed

1. Front servo or accumulator oil rings may be leaking.
2. Front band may be broken or burned out.
3. Front bank not engaged on anchor pin and/or servo pin.

No Engine Braking In Low Range

1. Low-reverse check ball may be missing from control valve assembly.
2. Rear servo may have damaged oil seal ring, bore or piston; leaking, apply pressure.
3. Rear band broken, burned out or not engaged on anchor pins or servo pin.

No Part Throttle Downshifts

1. Vacuum modulator assembly.
2. Modulator valve.
3. Regulator valve train.
4. Control valve assembly has stuck 3-2 valve or broken spring.

No Detent Downshifts

1. Detent switch needs fuse, connections tightened or adjustment.
2. Detent solenoid may be inoperative.
3. Detent valve train in control valve assembly malfunctioning.

Low or High Shift Points

1. Oil pressure. Check vacuum modulator assembly, vacuum line connections, modulator valve, and pressure regulator valve train.
2. Governor may have sticking valve or feed holes that are leaking, plugged or damaged.
3. Detent solenoid may be stuck open or loose.
4. Control valve assembly. Check detent, 3-2, and 1-2 shift valve trains, and check spacer plate gaskets for positioning.
5. Check case for porosity, missing or leaking intermediate plug.

Won't Hold In Park

1. Manual control linkage improperly adjusted.
2. Internal linkage defective; check for chamfer on actuator rod sleeve.
3. Parking pawl broken or inoperative.

Excessive Creep At Idle

NOTE: Transmissions have the variable pitch stator.

1. High idle speed.
2. Stator switch inoperative or defective.
3. Stator solenoid defective.
4. Pump may have stator valve train stuck.
5. Pump lead wires disconnected or grounded out.
6. Pump feed circuit to stator may be restricted or blocked.
7. Converter out check valve may be broken or stuck.
8. Turbine shaft may have defective oil seal ring.
9. Stator orifice plug in case may be blocked.
10. Converter assembly defective.

Poor Performance - ¾ Throttle

NOTE: Transmissions having the variable pitch stator.

1. Stator and detent switch inoperative.
2. Items 3 through 10 above will also cause poor performance at ¾ throttle.

Noisy Transmission

1. Pump noises caused by high or low oil level.
2. Cavitation due to plugged strainer, porosity in intake circuit or water in oil.
3. Pump gears may be damaged.
4. Gear noise in low gear of Drive Range-transmission grounded to body.
5. Defective planetary gear set.
6. Clutch noises during application can be worn or burned clutch plates.

Forward Clutch Plates Burned

1. Check ball in clutch housing damaged, stuck or missing.
2. Clutch piston cracked, seals damaged or missing.
3. Low line pressure.
4. Manual valve mispositioned.
5. Restricted oil feed to forward clutch.
6. Pump cover oil seal rings missing, broken or undersize; ring groove oversize.
7. Case valve body face not flat or porosity between channels.
8. Manual valve bent and center land not properly ground.

Intermediate Clutch Plates Burned

1. Constant bleed orifice in center support missing.
2. Rear accumulator piston oil ring damaged or missing.
3. 1-2 accumulator valve stuck in control valve assembly.
4. Intermediate clutch piston seal damaged or missing.
5. Center support bolt loose.
6. Low line pressure.
7. Intermediate clutch plug in case missing.
8. Case valve body face not flat or porosity between channels.
9. Manual valve bent and center land not ground properly.

Direct Clutch Plates Burned

1. Restricted orifice in vacuum line to modulator.
2. Check ball in direct clutch piston damaged, stuck or missing.
3. Defective modulator bellows.
4. Center support bolt loose.
5. Center support oil rings or grooves damaged or missing.
6. Clutch piston seals damaged or missing.
7. Front and rear servo pistons and seals damaged.
8. Manual valve bent and center land not cleaned up.
9. Case valve body face not flat or porosity between channels.
10. Intermediate sprag clutch installed backwards.
11. 3-2 valve, 3-2 spring or 3-2 spacer pin installed in wrong location in 3-2 valve bore.

MAINTENANCE
Checking & Adding Fluid

Fluid level should be checked at every engine oil change. The full ("F") and "ADD" marks on the transmission dipstick are one pint apart and determine the correct fluid level at normal operating temperature (170°F.). *Careful attention to transmission oil temperature is necessary as proper fluid level at low operating temperatures will be below the "ADD" mark on the dipstick. Proper fluid level at higher operating temperatures will rise above the "F" mark.*

Fluid level must always be checked with

the car on a level surface, and with the engine running to make certain the converter is full. To determine proper fluid level, proceed as follows:

1. Operate engine at a fast idle for about 1½ minutes with selector lever in park ("P") position.
2. Reduce engine speed to slow idle and check fluid level.
3. With engine running, add Dexron fluid as required to bring it to the proper level.

NOTE: Beginning with 1973 models, Cadillac uses an extended-life Dexron transmission fluid. With this new fluid, strainer replacement and fluid change is now recommended at 100,000 miles under normal operating conditions and 50,000 miles under severe or abnormal service such as trailer towing.

This recommendation applies only to the improved fluid and its availability for service. If the new fluid is not available, the former fluid can be used but then the 24,000 mile maintenance rule will apply.

Beginning with 1973 Chevrolet and late 1973 Buick, Oldsmobile and Pontiac models, a revised type Dexron fluid is used in these transmissions. An early change to a darker color from the usual red color and or a strong odor that is usually associated with overheated fluid is normal, and should not be treated as a positive sign of needed maintenance or unit failure.

The normal maintenance schedule for drain and refill of this type fluid remains unchanged at 24,000 miles under normal service and 12,000 miles under severe operating conditions, such as trailer towing.

CAUTION: *Do not overfill as foaming might occur when the fluid heats up. If fluid level is too low, especially when cold, complete loss of drive may result after quick stops. Extremely low fluid level will result in damage to transmission.*

Draining Bottom Pan Only

1. Disconnect filler tube at bottom pan and allow fluid to drain. Remove and discard filler tube O-ring.
2. Use a new O-ring on filler tube and install tube on pan.
3. Lower car and add three quarts of Dexron transmission fluid through filler tube when replacing intake pipe and strainer assembly. When just draining bottom pan, add only two quarts.
4. Operate engine at a fast idle for about 1½ minutes with selector lever in park ("P") position.
5. Reduce engine speed to slow idle and check fluid level. Then add fluid as required to bring it to the proper level.

Adding Fluid to Fill Dry Transmission and Converter

1. Add seven quarts of fluid through filler tube.
2. Operate engine at a fast idle for about 1½ minutes with selector lever in park ("P") position.
3. Reduce engine speed to slow idle and add three more quarts of fluid.

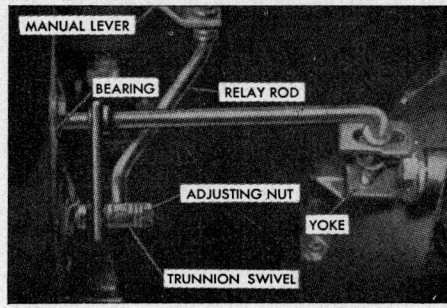

Fig. 2 Manual linkage adjustment. 1969-74 Cadillac (typical)

4. Check fluid level and add as required to bring it to the proper level.

IMPORTANT: Beginning with 1969 General Motors units are equipped with anti-theft systems which lock not only the steering column but the transmission linkage as well. It is essential that this "back drive" linkage also be adjusted when any adjustment to the manual shift linkage is made. This adjustment must be precise as any inaccuracies may result in unit operation without controls in full detent which, in turn, will cause reduced oil pressure and subsequent failure of the transmission.

BACK DRIVE LINKAGE, ADJUST

Adjust back drive at trunnion so that:
1. Transmission is in full detent in each selector position.
2. With key in Run position and transmission in Reverse, key cannot be removed and steering wheel is not locked.
3. With key in Lock position and transmission in Park, key can be removed and steering wheel is locked.

MANUAL LINKAGE, ADJUST

1969-70 Buick Column Shift

1. Loosen shift rod adjusting clamp.
2. Place selector lever against Drive stop.
3. Place transmission in Drive.
4. Tighten clamp bolt to 17-23 ft-lbs.

1969-74 Buick Console Shift

1969-70 All
1. Set transmission shift lever in Drive.
2. Loosen trunnion bolt.
3. Set shift bar assembly in Drive position.
4. Tighten trunnion bolt.
5. Set selector lever in park and set back drive adjustment as described previously.

1971-74 All
1. Loosen trunnion bolt.
2. Set selector lever against Neutral stop.
3. Place transmission in Neutral.
4. Tighten trunnion bolt to 6-9 ft. lbs.
5. Set selector lever in Park and set back drive adjustment as described previously .

1971-74 Buick Column Shift

1. Loosen shift rod adjusting clamp bolts.
2. Place selector lever against Neutral stop.
3. Place transmission in Neutral.
4. Tighten clamp bolt to 17-23 ft. lbs.

1969-74 Cadillac

1. Refer to Fig. 2, loosen nut on steering column manual lever-to-relay rod clamp.
2. Pull relay rod up to position transmission shift valve in PARK; then push rod down to third (neutral) step.
3. Position selector lever in neutral.
4. Tighten clamp nut. Selector lever

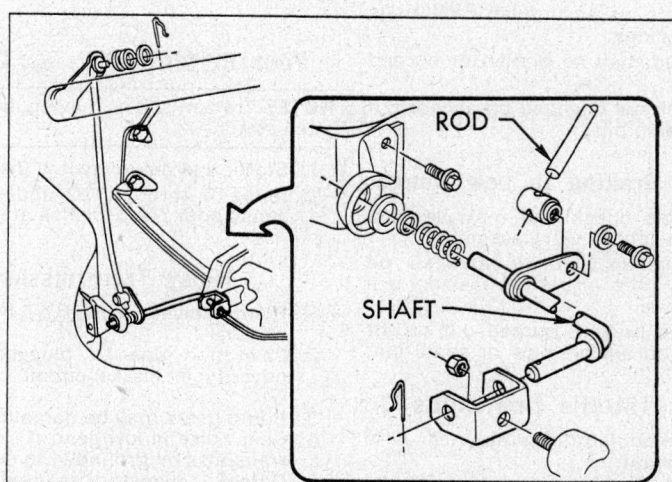

Fig. 3 Manual linkage adjustment. 1969-72 Chevrolet column shift

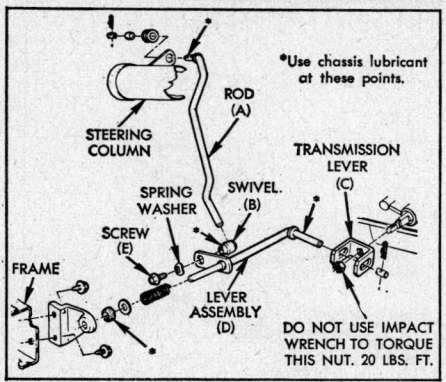

Fig. 4 Column shift linkage. 1973-74 Camaro, Chevrolet

should enter all positions and indicator pointer should index correctly.

Chevrolet Column Shift 1969-72

1. Place selector lever in Drive as determined by transmission detent and loosen adjusting swivel at cross-shaft, Fig. 3.
2. Move the transmission lever so lever contacts mechanical stop on steering column. Tighten swivel and check adjustment for proper operation.
3. Adjust shift indicator needle, if necessary.

1973-74

1. Place transmission lever in Neutral by moving lever counter-clockwise to L1 detent then clockwise three detent positions to Neutral.
2. Place selector lever in Neutral as determined by mechanical stop on steering column. Do not use indicator as reference.
3. Assemble swivel, spring washer and screw to lever assembly then tighten screw to 20 ft. lbs., Figs. 4 and 5.

Chevy Nova 1969-70 Floor Shift

Refer to Fig. 6, and proceed as follows:
1. Loosely assemble nuts (A) and (B) on lower rod (C).
2. Set transmission lever (D) in Drive.
3. Set control pawl rod (E) in the Neutral or Drive notch of detent (F).
4. Apply load in direction of arrow (Y) on actuating lever (G) until pawl rod comes in contact with detent at contact point (Z).
5. Place a .094" spacer (H) between nut (A) and swivel (J), run nut (A) until it touches spacer. Tighten nut (B) against swivel and lock swivel between nuts (A) and (B).
6. Place transmission and shift lever in Park.
7. Install column rod (K) to column lever and cross shaft (L).

NOTE: With shift lever in Park the

ignition key must move freely to Lock position.

Chevelle, Monte Carlo & Camaro 1973-74 Console Shift

1. Place shift lever (J) in Drive and loosen nut (G) so that pin (F) moves freely in slot of transmission lever (C). Fig. 7.
2. Place transmission lever (C) in Drive by moving lever counter-clockwise to L1 detent then clockwise three detent positions to Drive.
3. Tighten nut (G) to 20 ft. lbs.

Camaro, Chevelle and Chevrolet 1970-72 Floor Shift

1. Place shift lever in Drive position, Fig. 8.
2. Raise vehicle. Disconnect cable from transmission lever. Manually place transmission lever in Drive position.
3. Measure distance from rearward face of attachment bracket to center of cable attachment pin. This dimension should be 5½". If not, adjust pin to obtain this dimension.
4. Install cable to transmission lever, lower vehicle and check for proper operation.

Camaro, Chevelle and Chevrolet 1969 Floor Shift

1. Place shift handle in Drive.
2. Raise vehicle. Disconnect cable from transmission lever, Fig. 9. Place transmission in Drive range. Check dimension A and adjust by loosening

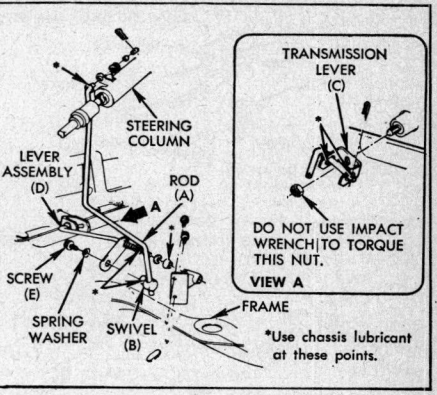

Fig. 5 Column shift linkage. 1973-74 Chevelle & Monte Carlo

stud nut and moving stud to obtain proper setting. Reinstall cable and lock clip.
3. Lower vehicle and remove shift quadrant cover. Raise quadrant plate, disconnect bulbs and remove plate. Remove cable clip and disengage cable from shift lever.
4. Insert a .07" gauge between pawl and detent as shown in view A. Check dimension B. Adjust by loosening bolt A and moving lever to obtain proper adjustment. Tighten bolt.
5. Adjust cable end until it freely enters pin. Install clip.

NOTE: If lift on handle button does not clear detents or detents can be cleared without lifting handle, pawl engagement can be adjusted by raising or lowering of the detent plate after

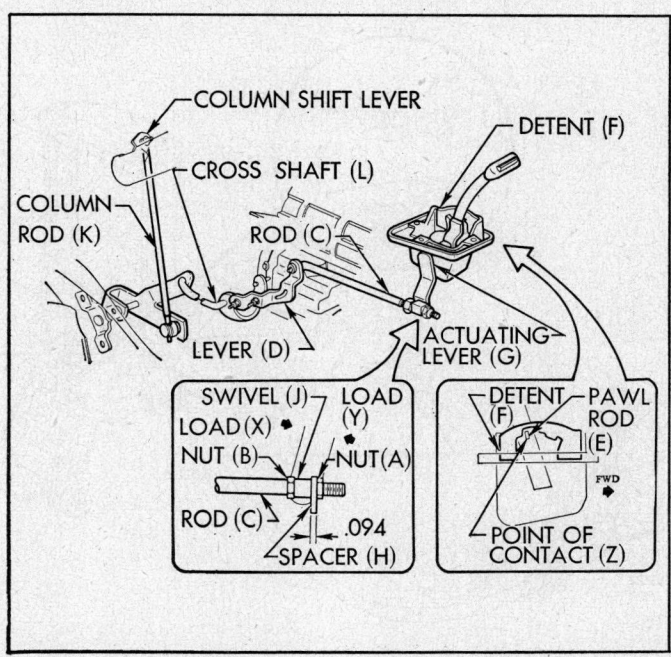

Fig. 6 Manual linkage adjustment. 1969-70 Nova floor shift

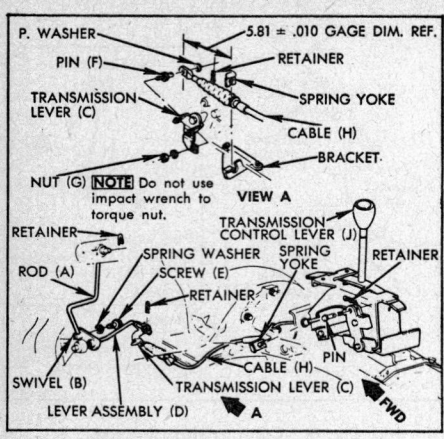

Fig. 7   Console shift adjustment. 1973-74 Camaro, Chevelle & Monte Carlo

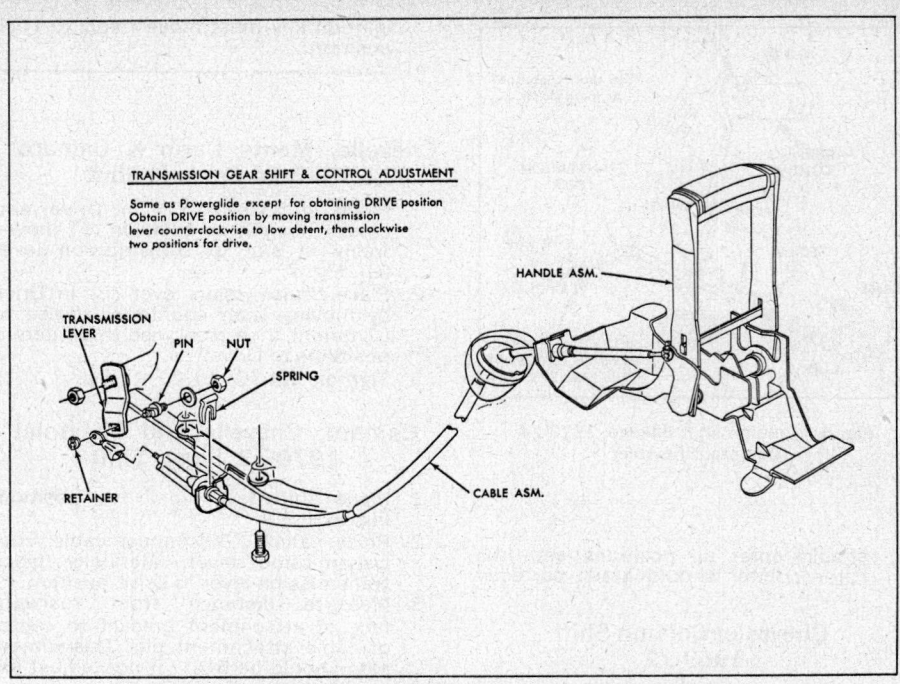

Fig. 8   Console shift linkage. 1970-72 Camaro, Chevelle and Chevrolet

loosening bolt B. If such an adjustment is made, repeat step 4.

6. Remove gauge. Check operation.
7. Reinstall shift plate and cover.

Corvette
1973-74

1. Loosen transmission lever nut.
2. Move transmission lever counterclockwise to its maximum position, then clockwise 5 detent positions to Park.
3. Place shift lever in Park and insert a .040" spacer forward of pawl as shown in Fig. 10 and tighten nut to

20 ft. lbs.

1969-72

1. Place selector lever in Drive, Fig. 12.
2. Place transmission control lever in Drive position by moving lever counterclockwise to low detent, then clockwise two positions for Drive.
3. Install cable and secure with retaining clip and cotter pin.

Oldsmobile

Column Shift, 1971-74

1. Loosen shift rod clamp bolt and place transmission outer lever in Neutral position, Figs. 12 and 13.
2. Push on shift rod until selector lever is against Neutral position stop in upper steering column.
3. Tighten bolt in clamp on lower end of shift rod to 20 ft. lbs.
4. Check for proper operation.

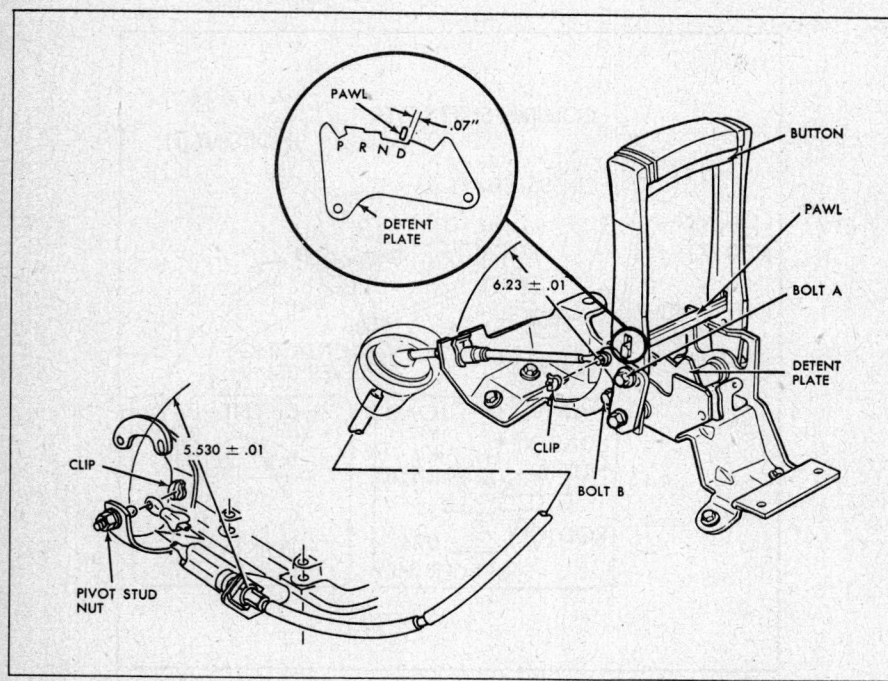

Fig. 9   Console shift linkage adjustment. 1969 Camaro, Chevelle and Chevrolet

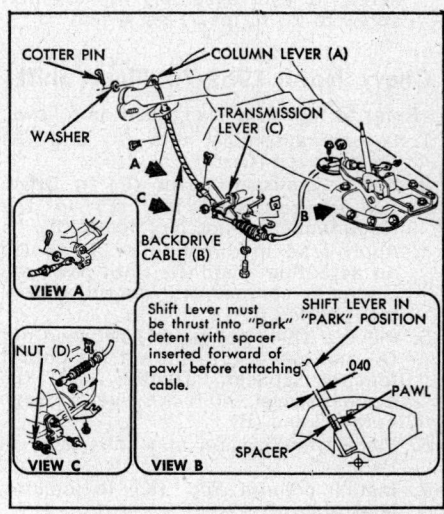

Fig. 10   Floor shift adjustment. 1973-74 Corvette

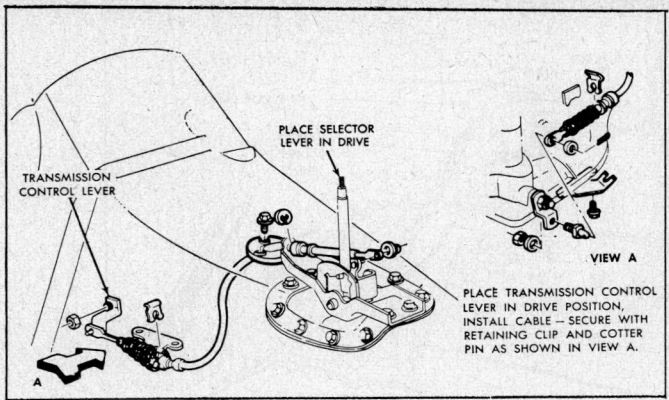

Fig. 11 Shift linkage adjustment. 1969-72 Corvette

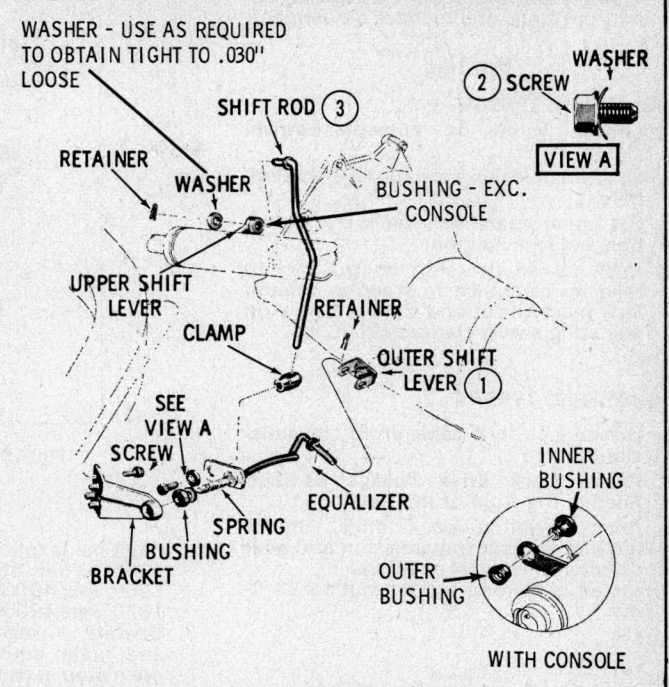

Fig. 12 Shift linkage adjustment. Oldsmobile full size (typical)

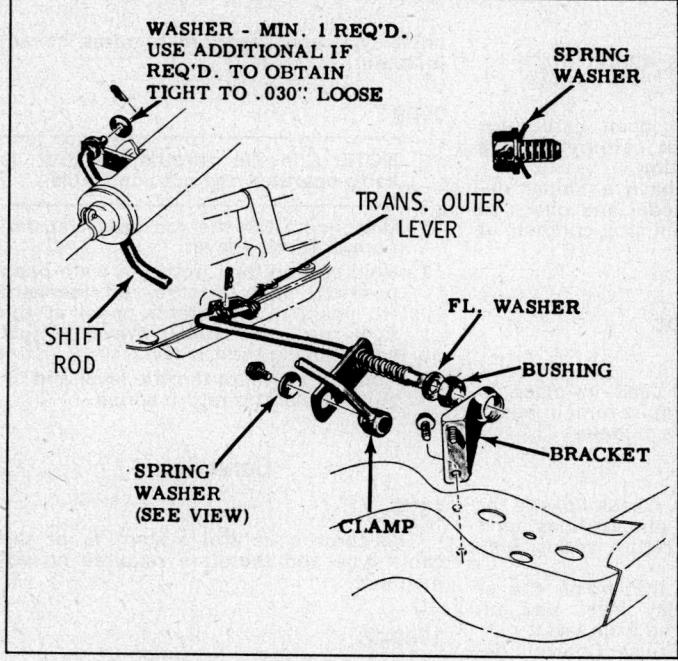

Fig. 13 Shift linkage. Oldsmobile intermediates (typical)

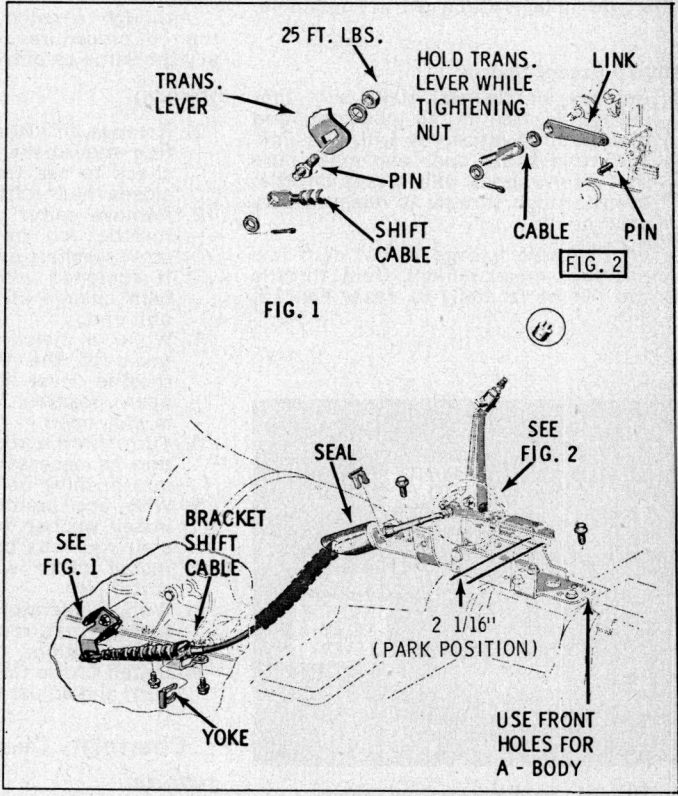

Fig. 14 Console shift adjustment. Oldsmobile

Column Shift, 1969-70

1. Use enough washers to obtain zero clearance at upper shift lever and shift rod, Figs. 12 and 13.
2. Set outer shift lever in "D".
3. Loosen swivel bolt.
4. Push up on shift rod until selector lever is against the "D" position stop in upper steering column.
5. Tighten swivel bolt to 20 ft-lbs.
6. Check neutral switch adjustment.

Console Shift, 1969-74

1. Place shift lever in Park, Fig. 14.
2. Set transmission outer shift lever in Park position.
3. Set pin to just enter hole in shift cable.

4. Tighten nut and check through all detent positions and recheck adjustment.

Pontiac

Column Shift, 1969-74

1. Loosen screw on adjusting swivel clamp.
2. Set transmission selector lever in Park detent.
3. Set upper gearshift lever in Park position and lock ignition.
4. Push up on gearshift control rod to take up clearance in steering column lock mechanism and tighten screw on adjusting swivel clamp to 20 ft. lbs.

Console Shift, 1969-74

1. Disconnect shift cable from transmission.
2. Adjust back drive linkage as outlined at the front of this section.
3. After adjusting back drive, unlock ignition and set transmission and gear selector in Neutral position.
4. Install cable and tighten nut to 30 ft-lbs.

THROTTLE LINKAGE, ADJUST

Buick

1969-70 Special and 1971-74 All

This unit is equipped with a flexible cable type linkage which is not adjustable.

1969-70 Except Special

1. Remove air cleaner. Make sure that linkage is free in all positions and that nothing interferes with the linkage. Hold choke open and make sure that return spring fully closes throttle, even through throttle is released very slowly.
2. With throttle linkage in hot curb idle position, measurement from throttle rod pin horizontally to dash, Fig. 15,

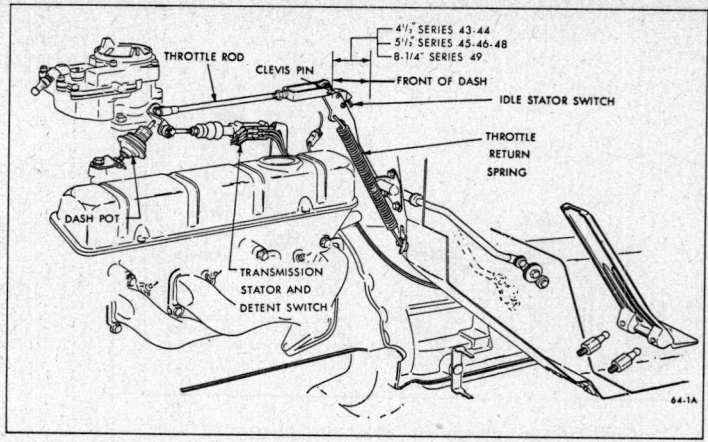

Fig. 15   Throttle linkage adjustment. 1969-70 Buick except Special

must be as follows:
1969-70 Ser. 45, 46, 48000 . 5⅞"
1969 Ser. 49000 . . . . 8¼"
1970 Ser. 49000 . . . . 6⅛"
3. Operate linkage to open carburetor and make sure that carburetor wide open stop is contacting.
4. As a final check, have a helper depress accelerator pedal and check to make sure wide open stop contacts at carburetor.

Cadillac

1971-74

Although a cable is used in place of the rod, procedures to adjust remain basically the same as previous models.

1969-70

1. Remove air cleaner. Check linkage for free movement in all positions, and check to see that return spring fully closes the throttle.
2. Remove cotter pin that holds end of throttle rod in relay lever and remove washers and rod from lever.
3. If equipped with Cruise Control, detach linkage at Cruise Control power unit end.
4. While a helper presses accelerator pedal to the floor, hold carburetor throttle lever in full throttle (wide open) position. Make sure choke valve is wide open.
5. Turn throttle rod end in either direction as necessary to allow free entry into bushing on relay lever Fig. 16.
6. With accelerator pedal released, reinstall washer on throttle rod and install rod into bushing in relay lever.
7. Install other washer and then the cotter pin.
8. With accelerator pedal pressed again to floor mat, recheck throttle for wide open position.
9. Install Cruise Control linkage (if equipped) and adjust if necessary.

Chevrolet, Chevelle & Camaro

1970-74

The throttle control system is of the

cable type and therefore requires no adjustment.

1969

NOTE: Chevelle throttle, control is cable operated and not adjustable.

1. Disconnect throttle rod swivel at carburetor throttle lever.
2. Hold carburetor throttle in wide open position, push throttle rod rearward (to position accelerator pedal at the floor mat) and adjust swivel to just enter hole in throttle lever.
3. Connect swivel to throttle lever and install accelerator return spring.

Corvette

1974

The throttle control system is of the cable type and therefore requires no adjustment.

1969-73

1. Loosen cable clamp bolt and hold accelerator pedal to the floor.

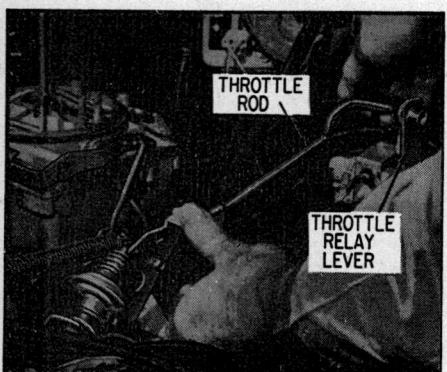

Fig. 16   Throttle linkage adjustment. Cadillac 1969-70

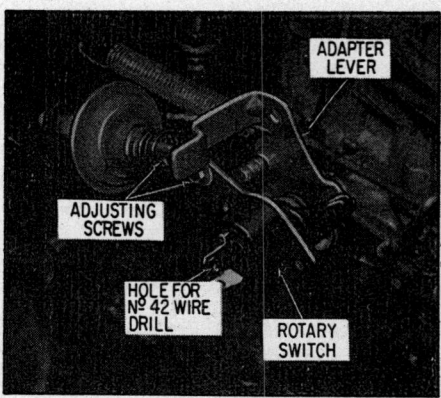

Fig. 17   Detent switch adjustment. 1970-71 Cadillac

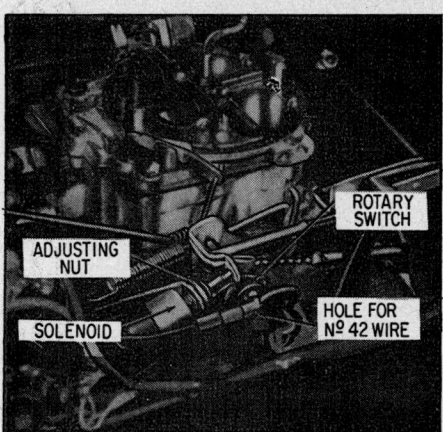

Fig. 18 Detent switch adjustment. 1972-74 Cadillac

2. Move carburetor throttle to wide open position.
3. Tighten cable clamp bolt to 45 in lbs.

Oldsmobile

1970-74

The throttle control system is cable operated and therefore has no adjustment.

Carburetor Rod, 1969

1. With slow idle adjusted and adjusting screw off fast idle cam, disconnect swivel on carburetor rod from auxiliary bellcrank.
2. Push upper lever of auxiliary bellcrank towards cowl until it hits its stop.
3. Pull carburetor rod towards firewall until throttle is wide open.
4. Adjust swivel until swivel pin enters the "2" notch for 2 bbl. carburetor or the "4" notch for 4 bbl. carburetor.
5. Reconnect carburetor rod to auxiliary bellcrank.

Pontiac

1969 Intermediates: 1970-74 All

The throttle control system is of the cable type and requires no adjustment. On 1969-71 models, a reference dimension of $1\frac{9}{16}$ inch between the accelerator pedal and floor pan is used to check for bent bracket assemblies.

1969 Full Size Models

With accelerator rod and throttle return spring disconnected, insert $\frac{1}{4}$" diameter gauge pin through hole in mounting bracket and through holes in throttle control lever. Holding carburetor lever extension at full throttle, adjust rod to line up with carburetor extension stud plus three additional turns toward front of car (counterclockwise). Attach rod, remove gauge pin and connect return spring.

DOWNSHIFT SWITCHES

Buick

Detent Switch, 1972-74

Push switch lever all the way towards dash. Final adjustment is made automatically the first time accelerator pedal is depressed to floor.

Detent Switch, 1971

1. Install cable through throttle lever hole and install retainer (nylon) being sure it is seated.
2. Position retainer on upper end of cable.
3. With throttle cable connected to carburetor and throttle lever, fully depress accelerator pedal to adjust retainer.

Detent Switch, 1969-70

With plunger bottomed in switch, fully depress accelerator pedal and tighten lock screw to 16 ft lbs.

Cadillac

1970-74

1. Remove air cleaner.
2. Make certain carburetor is adjusted to specification and that linkage is at low speed idle setting.
3. Loosen two mounting screws and insert a #42 drill through calibrating hole below lower wire terminal extending through to carburetor side of switch, Figs. 17 and 18. Adjust position of switch so that lever just touches the carburetor adapter plate arm.
4. Tighten mounting screws and remove drill.
5. Install air cleaner.

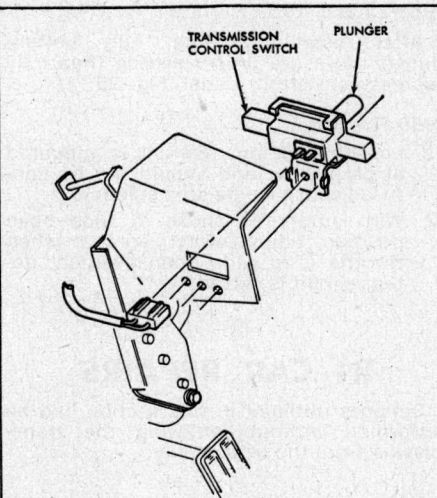

Fig. 20 Detent switch adjustment. 1971-74 Chevrolet Line

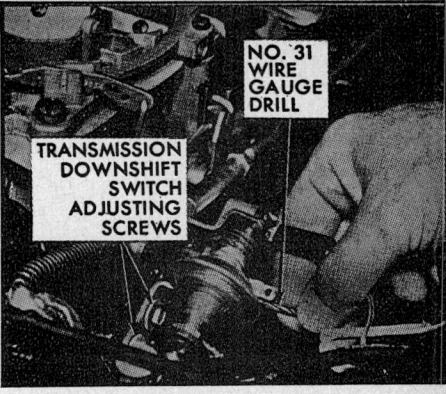

Fig. 19 Downshift adjustment. Cadillac 1969

1969

1. Remove carburetor air cleaner.
2. Make sure that low idle speed is properly adjusted.
3. If downshift switch is properly adjusted, a $\frac{1}{8}$" drill or rod can be inserted through calibrating hole below wire terminal extending through carburetor side of switch, Fig. 19.

NOTE: With this adjustment the stator should break contact $5\frac{1}{2}°$ to $7\frac{1}{2}°$ from closed hot idle throttle and make contact at 40° throttle. The downshift should make contact above 60° throttle.

4. If adjustment is necessary, loosen the two $\frac{7}{16}$" switch mounting screws and position switch for proper alignment as in Step 3.
5. With switch positioned, tighten mounting screws and remove drill or rod from calibrating hole through switch.

Chevrolet Line

1971-74

Install switch as shown in Fig. 20. After installing, press switch plunger as far forward as possible. This switch will then adjust itself the first time the accelerator pedal is pushed to floor.

Camaro, Chevrolet and Nova

1970

1. Refer to Fig. 21 and loosen mounting bolts.
2. With choke in open position, move accelerator to wide open throttle position. Depress detent switch plunger till it bottoms in switch. Move switch towards throttle lever paddle until there is only .23" between lever paddle and plunger.
3. Tighten mounting bolts.

Chevrolet (Except V8-307) & Camaro

1969

1. Loosen mounting bolts.

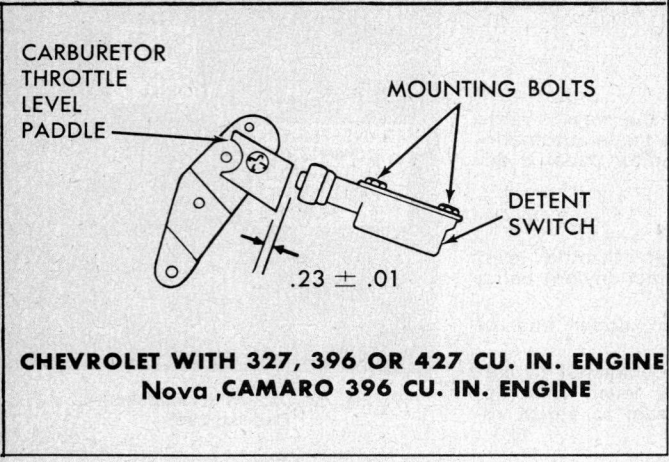

CHEVROLET WITH 327, 396 OR 427 CU. IN. ENGINE
Nova ,CAMARO 396 CU. IN. ENGINE

Fig. 21   Detent switch adjustment. Camaro and Chevrolet except V8-307

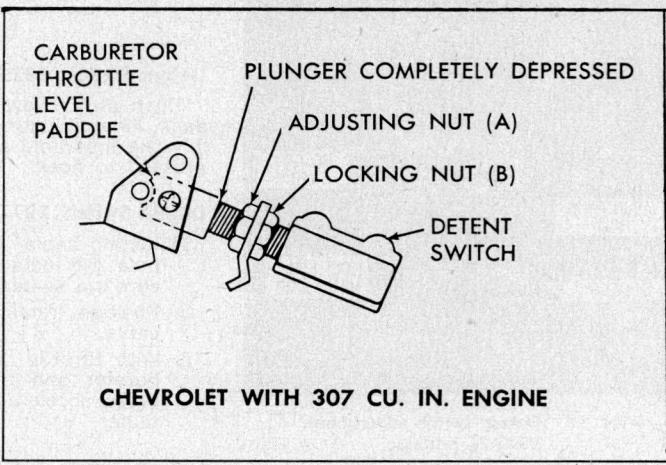

CHEVROLET WITH 307 CU. IN. ENGINE

Fig. 22   Detent switch adjustment. Chevrolet V8-307

2. With automatic choke and accelerator linkage in wide open position, depress detent switch plunger until it bottoms in switch. Move switch toward throttle lever paddle to obtain a clearance of .23″ between lever paddle and plunger, Fig. 21.
3. Tighten mounting bolts.

Chevrolet V8-307

1969
1. Loosen adjusting nut, Fig. 22.
2. With automatic choke in wide open position, turn adjusting nut to bring switch forward until plunger is completely depressed and threaded barrel of switch contacts throttle lever paddle.
3. Tighten lock nut.

Chevelle and Corvette

1969-70
1. Pull detent switch driver rearward until the hole in the switch body aligns with the hole in the driver. Insert a .092″ pin through the aligned holes to a depth of .10″ to hold driver in position, Figs. 23 and 24.
2. Loosen mounting bolt.
3. With accelerator pedal in wide open position, move switch forward until driver contacts accelerator lever.
4. Tighten mounting bolt and remove pin.

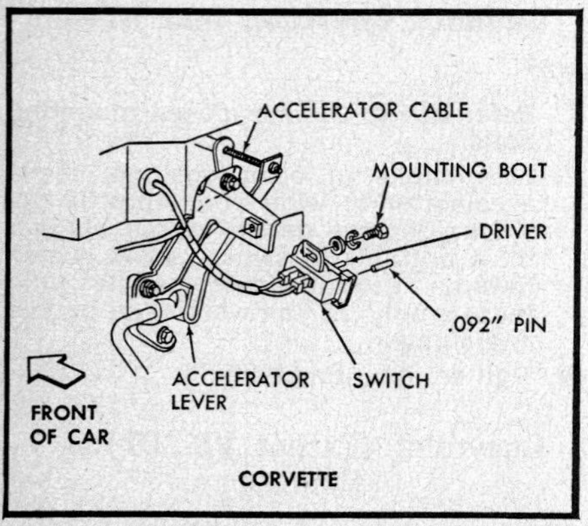

Oldsmobile

1969-74
1. Push plunger of switch forward until flush with switch housing.
2. Push accelerator pedal to wide open position to set switch.
3. Energizing of switch can be checked with a test light.

Pontiac

1969-74 Exc. 1969 Firebird

After installing switch, fully bottom plunger to insure proper setting then fully depress accelerator pedal, Fig. 25.

1969 Firebird
1. Loosen lock nut. Switch is mounted at carburetor and should not be confused with the idle stop solenoid.
2. With automatic choke in wide open position, adjust switch so that when throttle is in wide open position, detent circuit is closed.

IN CAR REPAIRS

Services outlined in this section can be performed without removing the transmission from the vehicle.

Pressure Regulator Valve
1. Remove bottom pan and strainer.
2. Using a screwdriver or steel rod, com-

press regulator boost valve bushing against pressure regulator spring, Fig. 26.

CAUTION: Pressure regulator spring is under extreme pressure and will force valve bushing out of bore when snap ring is removed if valve bushing is not held securely.

3. Continue to exert pressure on valve bushing and remove snap ring. Gradually release pressure on valve bushing until spring force is exhausted.
4. Carefully remove regulator boost valve bushing and valve, and pressure regulator spring. Be careful not to drop parts as they will fall out if they are not held.
5. Remove pressure regulator valve and spring retainer. Remove spacers if present.
6. Reverse procedure to install.

NOTE: A solid type pressure regulator valve must be used only in a pump cover with a "Squared Off" (machined) pressure regulator boss. A pressure regulator valve with oil holes and an orifice cup plug may be used with either type pump.

Fig. 23   Detent switch adjustment. 1969-70 Corvette

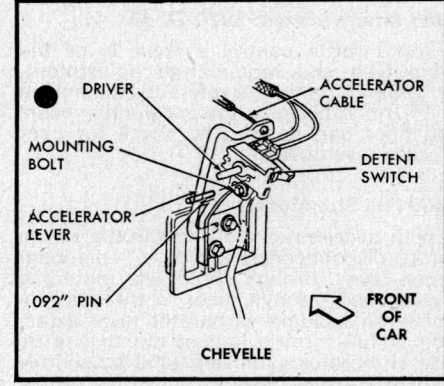

Fig. 24   Detent switch adjustment. 1969-70 Chevelle

Control Valve Body

1. Remove bottom pan and strainer.
2. Disconnect pressure switch lead wire.
3. Remove control valve body attaching screws and detent roller spring assembly. *Do not remove solenoid attaching screws.*
4. Remove control valve body and governor pipes. If care is used in removing control valve body, the six check balls will stay in place above spacer plate.
5. Remove governor pipes and manual valve from control valve body.
6. Reverse procedure to install.

Governor

1. Remove governor cover and discard gasket.
2. Withdraw governor from case.
3. Reverse procedure to install, using a new gasket.

Modulator & Modulator Valve

1. Remove modulator attaching screw and retainer.
2. Remove modulator assembly from case and discard O-ring seal.
3. Remove modulator valve from case.
4. Reverse procedure to install, using a new O-ring seal.

Parking Linkage

1. Remove bottom pan and oil strainer.
2. Unthread jam nut holding detent lever to manual shaft.
3. Remove manual shaft retaining pin from case.
4. Remove manual shaft and jam nut from case.
5. Remove O-ring seal from manual shaft.
6. Remove parking actuator rod and detent lever assembly.
7. Remove parking pawl bracket, pawl return spring and pawl shaft retainer.
8. Remove parking pawl shaft, O-ring seal and parking pawl.
9. Reverse procedure to install, using new seals and gasket.

Rear Seal

1. Remove propeller shaft.
2. Pry out seal with screwdriver.
3. Install new seal with a suitable seal driver.
4. Install propeller shaft.

TRANSMISSION, REPLACE

Buick, 1969-74

1. Raise and support front and rear of car.
2. Disconnect front exhaust crossover pipe if necessary. Remove propeller shaft.
3. Place suitable jack under transmission.
4. Remove vacuum line from vacuum modulator.
5. Separate cooler lines from transmission.
6. Remove transmission crossmember.

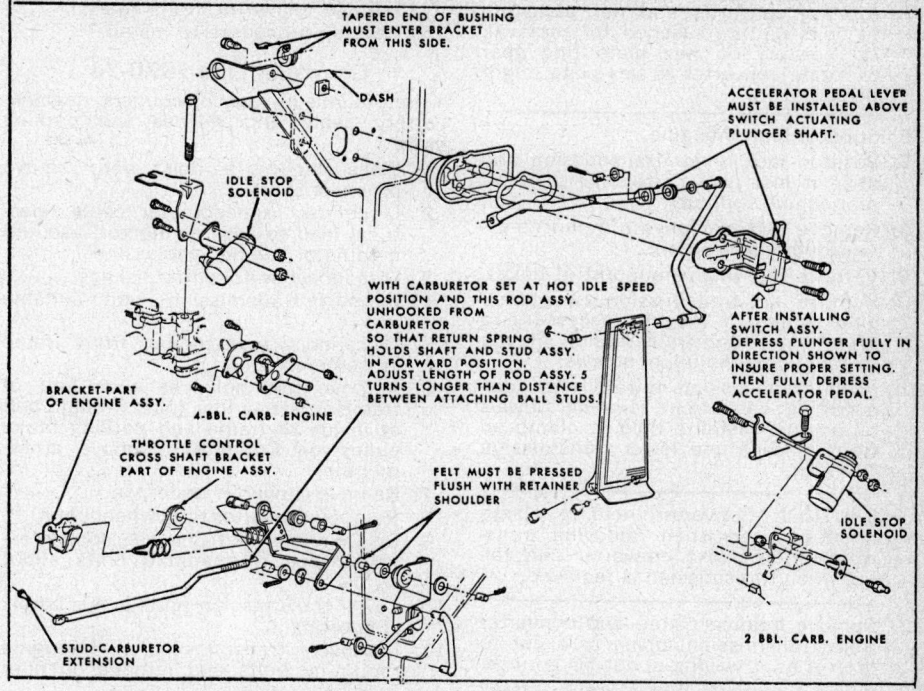

Fig. 25   Detent switch adjustment. 1969-74 Pontiac exc. 1969 Firebird (Typical)

7. Remove detent electrical connector from transmission case.
8. Disconnect speedometer cable.
9. Disconnect shift linkage from transmission.
10. Remove transmission filler pipe.
11. Support engine at oil pan.
12. Remove flywheel cover pan.
13. Mark flywheel and converter pump for reassembly in same position, then remove three converter pump-to-flywheel bolts.
14. Remove transmission-to-engine bolts.
15. Move transmission rearward to provide clearance between converter pump and crankshaft. Install a suitable holding tool to secure converter. Then lower and remove transmission.
16. Reverse above procedure to install.

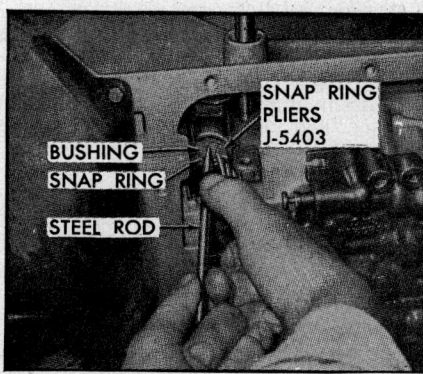

Fig. 26   Removing and installing Pressure regulator valve

Cadillac
1969-72

1. Disconnect negative battery cable.
2. Raise car on hoist or place on jack stands.
3. Disconnect relay rod from trunnion lever and wire relay rod up out of the way to prevent damage while removing transmission.
4. Remove two screws and bearing from frame side rail.
5. Disconnect trunnion from manual yoke on left side of transmission.
6. Remove speedometer drive cable and disconnect detent wires.
7. Remove transmission filler tube bracket screw from right exhaust manifold.
8. Remove filler tube from transmission case and plug hole in case.
9. Disconnect oil cooler pipes at transmission. Cap pipes and plug connector holes in transmission. Position cooler pipes out of the way.
10. Disconnect vacuum pipe hose from vacuum modulator and position pipe out of the way.
11. Remove resonator support bracket from extension housing.
12. Remove propeller shaft.
13. Unfasten and remove two starter motor brackets and slide starter forward.
14. Remove lower flywheel housing cover and two engine-to-transmission struts.
15. Remove three converter-to-flex plate screws.

NOTE: This is done by inserting a heavy screwdriver in open slot under one of weld nuts on converter, and rotating converter and flex plate until bolts can be reached for removal. Do not pry on flex plate ring gear to rotate converter as flex plate might be damaged.

16. Support rear of engine.
17. Position jack under transmission and raise it just enough to take load off rear engine support.
18. Remove two rear engine mount-to-extension housing screws.
19. Remove rear engine support (4 bolts).
20. Remove six transmission case-to-engine screws. It may be necessary to lower engine and transmission slightly to gain access to upper screws.
21. Move transmission toward rear, disengaging case from locating dowels on engine. Install a holding clamp on front of case and lower transmission from car.

CAUTION: Converter holding clamp must be used when removing transmission otherwise converter can fall out when transmission is removed.

22. Remove holding clamp and converter from transmission, using care not to drop it as it weighs about 50 pounds.
23. Reverse removal procedure to install transmission assembly.

1973-74

1. Disconnect negative battery cable and raise vehicle on hoist.
2. Disconnect transmission linkage and remove speedometer drive cable.
3. Disconnect downshift solenoid connector and trackmaster electrical harness, if equipped.
4. Disconnect oil cooler pipes at transmission and cap pipes and plug holes in transmission.
5. Disconnect vacuum modulator hose.
6. Remove starter mount bolts and starter bracket and slide starter forward.
7. Remove propeller shaft.
8. Remove lower flywheel housing cover and three converter to flex plate bolts.

NOTE: This is done by inserting a heavy screwdriver in open slot under one of the welded nuts on converter, and rotating converter and flex plate until bolts can be reached for removal. Do not pry flex plate ring gear to rotate converter as flex plate damage may result.

9. Support rear of engine and remove rear engine mount bolts.
10. Place a jack under transmission and support transmission to remove load from rear engine support.
11. Remove bolts from rear engine support and position out of way.
12. Remove six engine to transmission case bolts. To gain access to upper bolts, lower engine and transmission slightly.
13. Move transmission toward rear of vehicle, disengaging locating dowels and install converter holding tool. Lower transmission from vehicle.
14. Remove converter holding tool and

remove converter from shaft.
15. Reverse procedure to install.

Chevrolet Line 1970-74

Before raising car, disconnect negative battery cable and release the parking brake.

1. Place car on a hoist and remove propeller shaft.
2. Disconnect speedometer cable, electrical lead to case connector, vacuum modulator line and cooler lines.
3. Disconnect shift control linkage.
4. Support transmission with suitable jack.
5. Disconnect rear mount from frame crossmember.
6. Remove two bolts at each end of frame crossmember (plus through bolt at inside of frame and parking brake pulley on Corvette). Remove crossmember.
7. Remove converter underpan.
8. Remove converter to flywheel bolts.
9. On Chevrolet and Chevelle, loosen exhaust pipe to manifold bolts about ¼".
10. Lower transmission until jack is barely supporting it.
11. Remove transmission to engine mounting bolts and remove oil filler tube.
12. Raise transmission to its normal position, support engine with jack and slide transmission rearward from engine and lower it away from car.

NOTE: Use converter holding tool when lowering transmission or keep rear of transmission lower than front so as not to lose converter.

13. Reverse removal procedure to install transmission.

Chevrolet Line 1969

1. Raise car on hoist.
2. On Camaro models, disconnect parking brake cables, and left exhaust pipe from manifold. Remove underbody reinforcement (convertible models only).
3. On Corvette only, remove both exhaust pipes.
4. Remove propeller shaft.
5. Disconnect speedometer cable, electrical leads, vacuum line and oil cooler pipes.
6. Disconnect shift control linkage.
7. Support transmission with suitable jack.
8. Disconnect rear mount from frame crossmember, remove two bolts at each end of crossmember. Remove crossmember.

NOTE: On Corvette models, through bolt at inside of frame and parking brake pulley must also be removed before removing crossmember.

9. Remove converter under pan.
10. Remove converter to flywheel bolts.
11. On Chevrolet and Chevelle, loosen exhaust pipe to manifold bolts to drop

pipes approximately ¼".
12. Lower transmission until jack is barely supporting it, remove engine to transmission bolts, leaving one lower bolt installed. Remove oil filler tube.
13. Raise transmission to its normal position, support engine with jack, remove last attaching bolt and slide transmission rearward and lower it away from vehicle.

CAUTION: Converter holding clamp must be used when removing transmission otherwise converter can fall out when transmission is removed.

14. Remove holding clamp and converter from transmission, using care as it weighs about 50 pounds.
15. Reverse removal procedure to install transmission.

Oldsmobile 1969-74

1. Remove flywheel cover and torque converter attaching bolts.
2. Mark flywheel and converter so they can be installed in same position.
3. Support engine at rear.
4. Disconnect solenoid wires and manual shift linkage at side of transmission.
5. Disconnect oil cooler lines, vacuum modulator line and oil filler pipe.
6. Disconnect parking brake cable.
7. Before removing propeller shaft, scribe marks on drive shaft and companion flange for correct assembly.
8. Disconnect exhaust pipe bracket at rear of crossmember.
9. Support transmission, then remove crossmember.
10. Unfasten transmission from engine.
11. Move transmission away from engine, then, before removing transmission, fasten a suitable piece of strap iron to housing to prevent converter from falling out as transmission is removed.

Pontiac 1969-74

1. Disconnect battery and release parking brake. Then raise car.
2. Remove propeller shaft.
3. Disconnect speedometer cable, electrical lead to case connector, vacuum line at modulator, and oil cooler pipes.
4. Disconnect shift control linkage.
5. Support transmission with jack.
6. Disconnect rear mount from transmission and crossmember.
7. Remove crossmember (2 bolts at each end).
8. Remove converter dust shield.
9. Remove converter-to-flex plate bolts.
10. Loosen exhaust pipe to manifold about ¼", and lower transmission until jack is barely supporting it.
11. Remove transmission-to-engine mount bolts.
12. Raise transmission to its normal position, slide it rearward and lower it away from vehicle.

NOTE: When lowering transmission, keep rear of unit lower than front so as not to drop converter.

13. Reverse procedure to install.

GM FRONT WHEEL DRIVE
TURBO HYDRA-MATIC

TRANSMISSION IDENTIFICATION

CADILLAC ELDORADO

1969-74 . . . . .AJ

OLDSMOBILE TORONADO

1969-70 With High Perf. Eng. . . . . .OM
1969-74 Exc. Below . . . . .OJ
1974 California .OM

DESCRIPTION

This transmission is a fully automatic unit used for front wheel drive applications, Fig. 1. It consists primarily of a three-element hydraulic torque converter, dual sprocket and chain link assembly, compound planetary gear set, three multiple disc clutches, a sprag clutch, a roller clutch, two band assemblies, and a hydraulic control system.

Torque Converter

The torque converter consists of a pump or driving member, a turbine or driven member and a stator or reaction member.

The stator is mounted on a one-way roller clutch which allows it to overrun when not used as a reaction member.

The torque converter couples the engine to the planetary gear set through the use of a drive sprocket, a chain link assembly, and a driven sprocket. Clockwise engine torque turns the drive sprocket clockwise. This, in turn, drives the driven sprocket in a clockwise direction. This in effect is a reverse in the direction of engine torque due to the side mounting of the gear unit.

Planetary Gear Set

The gear set provides three forward ratios and reverse. The approximate gear ratios are: First 2½ to 1, second 1½ to 1, third 1.1 to 1, reverse 2.1 to 1. Second and third are also multiplied by a lesser degree.

Converter stall ratio, first gear (2½ x 2) equals 5 to 1. Converter stall ratio, reverse (2.1 x 2) equals 4.2 to 1.

External Controls

External control connections to the transmission are: a) Engine vacuum, b) 12-volt electrical signals, c) manual linkage control.

Engine vacuum is used to operate the vacuum modulator assembly. The vacuum modulator automatically senses any change in torque input to the transmission that the driver induces through a change in accelerator position.

On all models an electrical signal is used to operate an electrical solenoid. The solenoid is activated by a switch at the carburetor. When the throttle is opened sufficiently to close this switch, the solenoid in the transmission is activated, causing a downshift at speeds below approximately 70 mph. At lower speeds, downshifts will occur at lesser speeds without use of the switch.

TROUBLE SHOOTING GUIDE

NOTE: In many of the following diagnosis procedures, it is recommended that air pressure be applied to help in determining if the seal, rings or pistons are stuck, missing or damaged. Therefore, when air is applied, listen carefully for escaping air and piston action as air is applied to a particular area.

No Drive In "D" Range

1. Low oil level. Check for external leaks or vacuum modulator diaphragm leaking.
2. Manual linkage maladjusted. Correct alignment in manual lever shift quadrant.
3. Low oil pressure.
4. Oil strainer O-ring seal missing or damaged, neck weld leaking, strainer blocked.
5. Oil pump pressure regulator stuck or inoperative. Pump drive gear tangs damaged by converter.
6. Case porosity in intake bore.
7. Control valve. Manual valve disconnected from manual lever pin. (Other shift lever positions would also be affected.)
8. Forward clutch does not apply. Piston cracked; seals missing or damaged. These defects can be checked by removing the valve body and applying air pressure to the drive cavity in the case valve body face. Missing, damaged or worn oil rings on driven support housing can also be checked in this manner at the same time because they can also cause the forward clutch not to apply. Clutch plates burned.
9. Roller clutch inoperative. Rollers worn, damaged springs, or damaged races. May be checked by placing selector lever in "L" range.

No Drive In "R" or Slips In Reverse

1. Low oil level.
2. Manual linkage.
3. Oil pressure. Vacuum modulator defective, modulator valve sticking.
4. Restricted strainer, leak at intake pipe or O-ring seal. Pressure regulator or boost valve sticking.
5. Control valve body gaskets leaking or damaged (other malfunctions may also be indicated). Low-reverse check ball missing from case (this will cause no overrun braking in low range). The 2-3 valve train stuck open (this will also cause 1-3 upshifts in drive range). Reverse feed passage not drilled; also check case passages. Apply air to reverse passage in case valve body face.
6. Rear servo and accumulator. Servo piston seal ring broken or missing. Apply air pressure to drilled hole in intermediate clutch passage of case valve body face to check for piston

operation and excessive leakage. Band apply pin too short (this may also cause no overrun braking or slip in overrun braking in low range).
7. Rear band burned, loose lining, apply pin or anchor pin not engaged; band broken.
8. Direct clutch outer seal damaged or missing. Clutch plates burned (may be caused by stuck ball check in piston).
9. Forward clutch does not release (will also cause drive in neutral range).

Drive In Neutral

1. Manual linkage maladjusted.
2. Forward clutch does not release (this condition will also cause no reverse).

1st Speed Only—No 1-2 Upshift

1. Governor valve sticking; driven gear loose, damaged or worn. If driven gear shows signs of wear or damage, check output flange drive gear for nicks or rough finish.
2. Control valve. The 1-2 shift valve train stuck closed. Dirt, chips or damaged valve in 1-2 shift valve train. Governor feed channels blocked or leaking; pipes out of position. Valve body gaskets leaking or damaged. Case porosity between oil channels. Governor feed passage blocked.
3. Intermediate clutch. Case center support oil rings missing, broken or defective. Clutch piston seals missing, improperly assembled, cut or damaged. Apply air to intermediate clutch passage located in case valve body face to check for these defects.

1-2 Shift Obtained Only At Full Throttle

1. Detent switch sticking or defective.
2. Detent solenoid loose, gasket leaking, sticks open, electrical wire pinched between cover and casting.
3. Control valve body gasket leaking or damaged. Detent valve train stuck.

1st & 2nd Speeds Only No 2-3 Shift

1. Detent solenoid stuck open (the 2-3 shift would occur at very high speeds) may be diagnosed as no 2-3 shift.
2. Detent switch sticking or defective.
3. Control valve body. The 2-3 valve train stuck with dirt or foreign material. Valve body gaskets leaking or damaged.
4. Direct clutch. Case center support oil rings missing or broken. Clutch piston seals missing, improperly assembled, cut or damaged; piston ball check stuck or missing. Apply air to direct clutch passage in case valve body face to check these conditions.

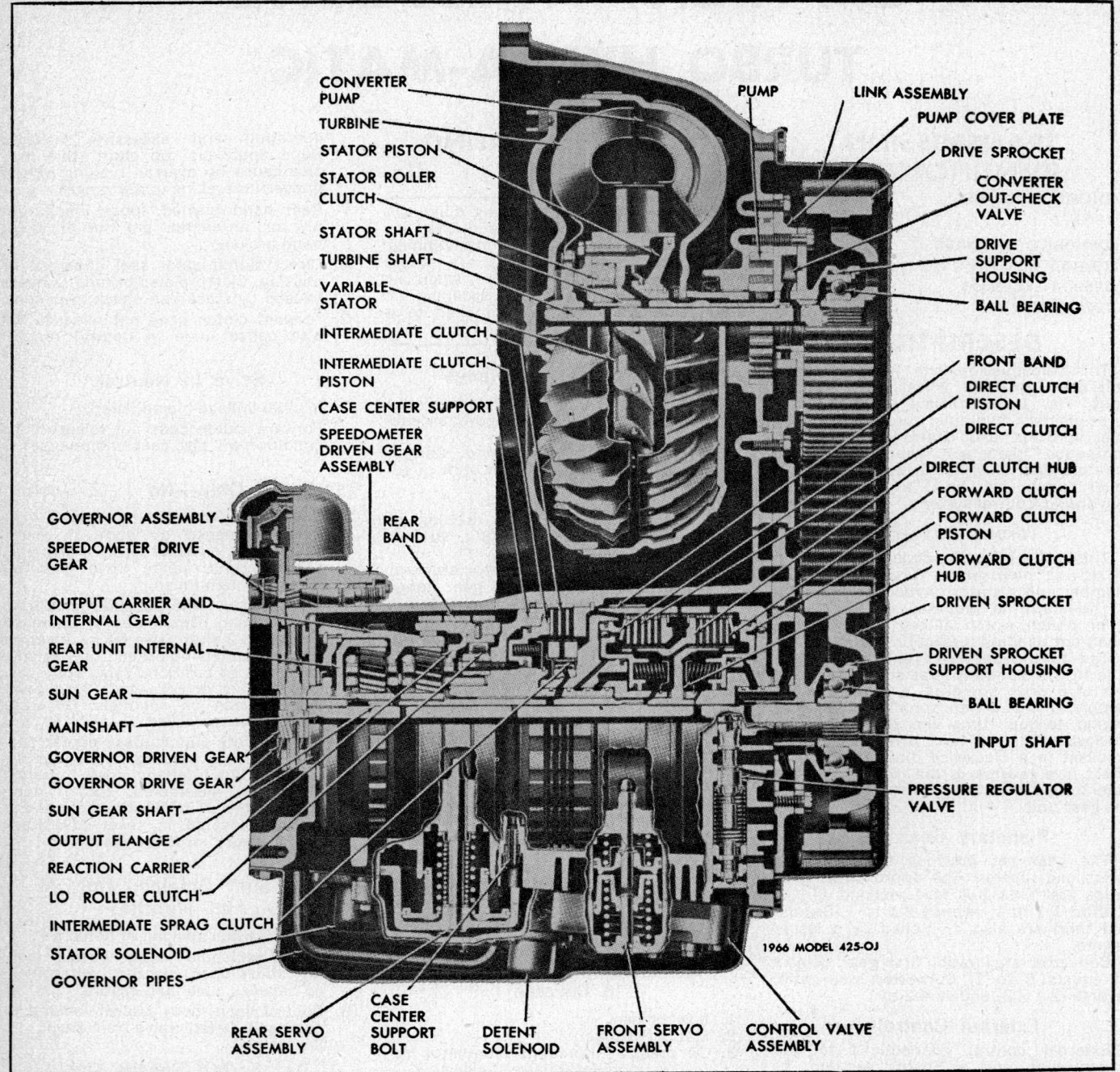

Fig. 1 General Motors Front Wheel Drive Turbo Hydra-Matic

Slips In All Ranges

1. Oil level incorrect.
2. Low oil pressure. Vacuum modulator defective or valve sticking. Oil strainer plugged or leaks at neck; O-ring (case to strainer) missing or damaged. Pressure regulator or boost valve sticking.
3. Case cross channel leaks; porosity.
4. Forward, intermediate and direct clutches slipping. Clutch plates burned. Always look for a primary defect that would cause clutch plates to burn. (Missing feed holes, seals and oil rings, etc., are primary defects).
5. Roller clutch rollers worn; springs or cage damaged, and worn or damaged races (operates normally in low and reverse ranges).

Slips 1 - 2 Shift

1. Oil level incorrect.
2. Low oil pressure. Look for defective vacuum modulator or valve sticking. Pump pressure regulator valve stuck.
3. Front servo accumulator piston cracked or porous, oil ring damaged or missing.
4. Control valve. The 1-2 accumulator valve train (may cause a slip-bump shift). Porous valve body or case valve body face.
5. Rear servo accumulator oil ring missing or damaged; case bore damaged;

piston cracked or damaged.
6. Case porous between oil passages.
7. Intermediate clutch lip seals missing, cut or damaged. Apply air pressure to intermediate clutch passage in case valve body face to check. Clutch plates burned. Case center support leaks in feed circuits (oil rings damaged or grooves damaged) or excessive leak between tower and bushing.

Rough 1 - 2 Shift

1. Oil pressure. Check vacuum modulator for loose fittings, restrictions in line; defective vacuum modulator. Modulator valve stuck. Pressure regulator boost valve stuck.
2. Control valve. 1-2 accumulator valve train; valve body-to-case bolts loose; gaskets inverted, off location, or damaged.
3. Case. Intermediate clutch passage check ball missing or not seating. Case porous between channels.
4. Rear servo accumulator piston stuck. Apply air pressure to 1-2 accumulator passage in case valve body face (you should hear the servo piston move). Broken or missing spring; bore scored or damaged.

Slips 2 - 3 Shift

1. Oil level high or low.
2. Low oil pressure. Modulator defective or valve sticking. Pump pressure regulator valve or boost valve sticking.
3. Control valve. Accumulator piston pin leak at valve body end.
4. Direct clutch piston seals leaking. Case center support oil seal rings damaged or excessive leak between tower and bushing. Apply air to direct clutch passage in case valve body face. If air comes out intermediate passage, center support is defective.

Rough 2 - 3 Shift

1. Oil pressure high. Vacuum modulator defective or valve sticking. Pump pressure regulator valve or boost valve stuck or inoperative.
2. Front servo accumulator spring missing or broken; accumulator piston stuck.

Shifts Occur at too High or too Low Car Speed

1. Oil pressure. Vacuum modulator defective or valve sticking. Leak in vacuum line (engine to transmission). Vacuum modulator line fitting on carburetor blocked. Pump pressure regulator valve or boost valve train stuck.
2. Governor valve stuck or sticking. Feed holes restricted or leaking; pipes damaged or mispositioned.
3. Detent solenoid stuck open or loose on valve body (will cause late shifts).
4. Control valve. Detent valve train sticking; 3-2 valve train sticking; 1-2 shift valve stuck; 1-2 detent valve sticking open (will probably cause early 2-3 shift).

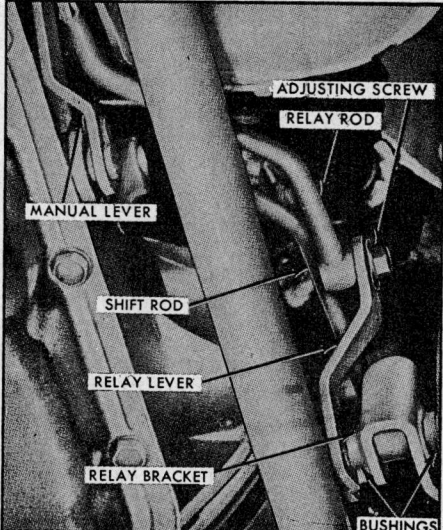

Fig. 2   Manual control linkage adjustment. Cadillac Eldorado (typical)

5. Spacer plate gaskets inverted or mispositioned; orifice holes missing or blocked; check balls missing or mislocated.
6. Case porous in channels or foreign material blocking channels.

No Detent Downshift

1. Detent switch mispositioned or electrical connections loose.
2. Solenoid defective or electrical connections loose.
3. Control valve detent valve train stuck.

No Engine Braking—Super Range 2nd Speed

1. Front servo or accumulator piston rings broken or missing. Case or valve body bores worn oversize, causing excessive leakage.
2. Front band worn or burned (check for cause); band end lugs broken or damaged; band lugs not engaged on anchor pins or servo apply pin (check for cause).

No Engine Braking—Low Range 1st Speed

1. Control valve low-reverse check ball missing from case.
2. Rear servo oil ring damaged or missing; piston damaged or porous, causing a leak in apply pressure.
3. Rear band lining worn or burned (check for cause); band end lugs broken; band ends not engaged on anchor pin or servo apply pin. These items will also cause slip in reverse or no reverse.

Will Not Hold Car In Park Position

1. Manual linkage maladjusted (ex-

ternal).
2. Parking brake lever and actuator rod assembly defective (check for proper actuator spring action). Parking pawl broken or inoperative.

Poor Performance or Rough Idle

1. Stator switch defective or maladjusted.
2. Stator solenoid defective or wire ground to solenoid housing; electrical connection loose; stator valve train stuck (located in valve body); oil feed circuit to stator restricted or blocked (check feed hole in stator shaft); converter-out check valve broken or missing (reed valve located in cover plate under drive support housing).
3. Turbine shaft converter return passage not drilled; oil seal rings broken, worn or missing.
4. Case porous in feed circuit channels or foreign material blocking feed circuit.
5. Converter assembly defective.

Transmission Noise

1. Pump noise. Oil level high or low; water in oil, driving gear assembled upside down; driving or driven gear teeth damaged.
2. Gear noise (1st gear drive range). Check planetary pinions for tooth damage. Check sun gear and front and rear internal gears for tooth finish or damage.
3. Clutch noise during application. Check clutch plates.
4. Sprocket and chain link assembly. Chain link too long (sounds similar to popcorn popping). There will be a rough burr along teeth of drive sprocket if chain link is too long; replace chain link and drive sprocket. Drive or driven sprocket teeth damaged. Engine mounts worn or damaged.

Burned Forward Clutch Plates

1. Check ball in clutch housing damaged, stuck or missing.
2. Clutch piston cracked, seals damaged or missing.
3. Low line pressure.
4. Manual valve mispositioned.
5. Restricted oil feed to forward clutch.
6. Pump cover oil seal rings missing, broken or undersize or ring groove oversize.
7. Case valve body face not flat or porosity between channels.
8. Manual valve bent and center land not ground properly.

Burned Intermediate Clutch Plates

1. Rear accumulator piston oil ring damaged or missing.
2. 1-2 accumulator valve stuck in control valve assembly.
3. Intermediate clutch piston seals damaged or missing.
4. Center support bolt loose.
5. Low line pressure.

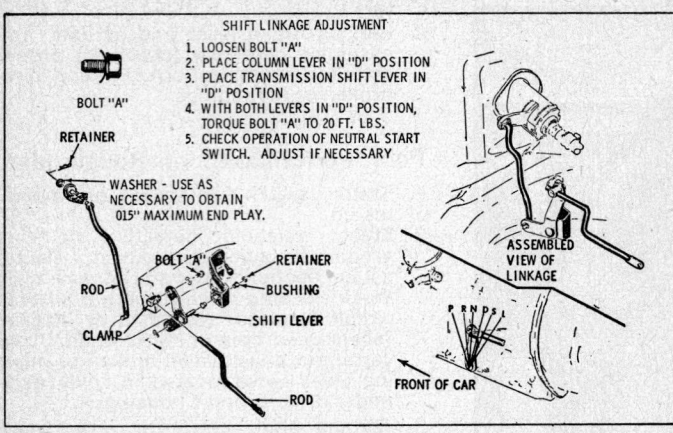

Fig. 3 Shift linkage adjustment. Toronado column shift, 1969-70

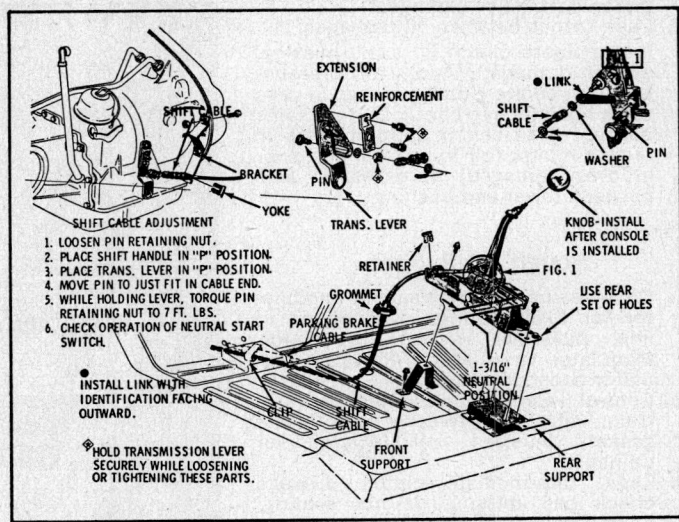

Fig. 4 Shift linkage adjustment. 1969-70 Toronado console shift

6. Intermediate clutch plug in case missing.
7. Case valve body face not flat or porosity between channels.
8. Manual valve bent and center land not ground properly.

Burned Direct Clutch Plates

1. Restricted orifice in vacuum line to modulator.
2. Check ball in direct clutch piston damaged, stuck or missing.
3. Defective modulator bellows.
4. Center support bolt loose.

5. Center support oil rings or grooves damaged or missing.
6. Clutch piston seals damaged or missing.
7. Front and rear servo pistons and seals damaged.
8. Manual valve bent and center land not cleaned up.
9. Case valve body face not flat or porosity between channels.
10. Intermediate sprag clutch installed backwards.

MAINTENANCE
Adding Oil

The fluid level should be checked at every engine oil change interval, and should be changed at 24,000 mile intervals. The fluid level should be checked with the selector lever in PARK position, engine running at idle speed and car on a level surface. The oil indicator and filler tube are located under the hood at the left front corner of the engine. *The filler tube comes out from the final drive housing but it is for the transmission.*

NOTE: If any work is performed on the transmission, it will require the following amounts of oil to bring the oil to the correct level:

1. Pan removed 5½ qts.

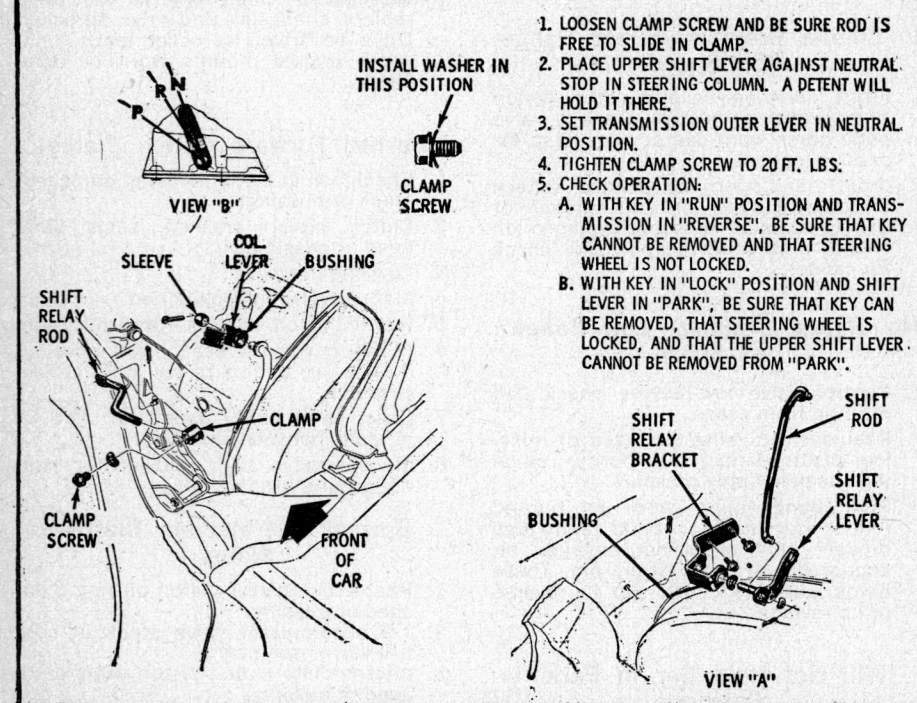

1. LOOSEN CLAMP SCREW AND BE SURE ROD IS FREE TO SLIDE IN CLAMP.
2. PLACE UPPER SHIFT LEVER AGAINST NEUTRAL STOP IN STEERING COLUMN. A DETENT WILL HOLD IT THERE.
3. SET TRANSMISSION OUTER LEVER IN NEUTRAL POSITION.
4. TIGHTEN CLAMP SCREW TO 20 FT. LBS.
5. CHECK OPERATION:
   A. WITH KEY IN "RUN" POSITION AND TRANSMISSION IN "REVERSE", BE SURE THAT KEY CANNOT BE REMOVED AND THAT STEERING WHEEL IS NOT LOCKED.
   B. WITH KEY IN "LOCK" POSITION AND SHIFT LEVER IN "PARK", BE SURE THAT KEY CAN BE REMOVED, THAT STEERING WHEEL IS LOCKED, AND THAT THE UPPER SHIFT LEVER CANNOT BE REMOVED FROM "PARK".

Fig. 4A Shift linkage adjustment. Toronado column shift, 1971-74

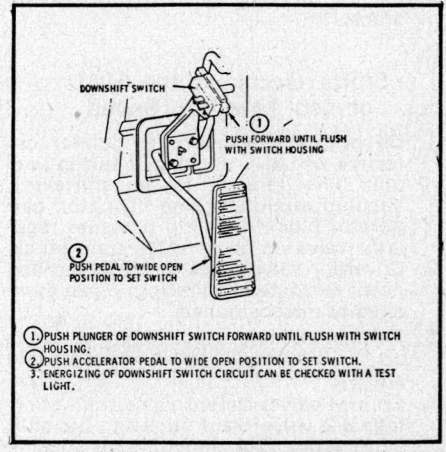

Fig. 4B Downshift switch adjustment. Oldsmobile Toronado

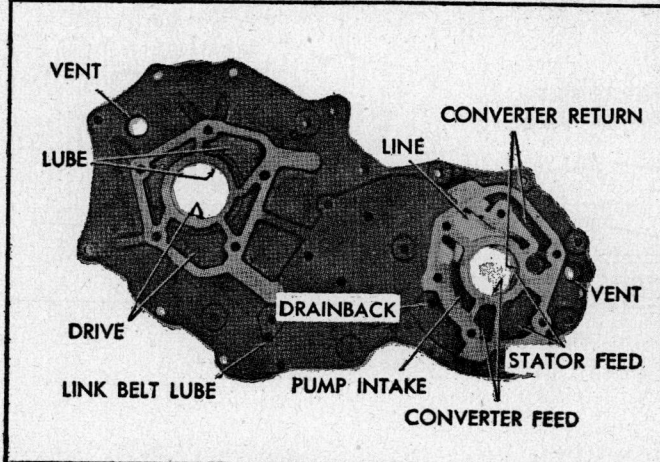

Fig. 5   Location of check balls

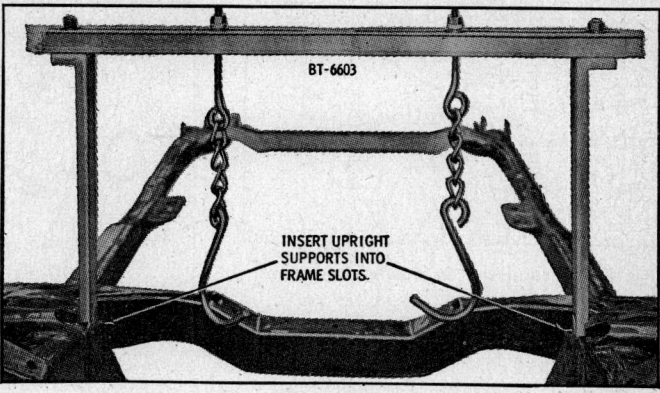

Fig. 6   Installing support bar. Olds Toronado

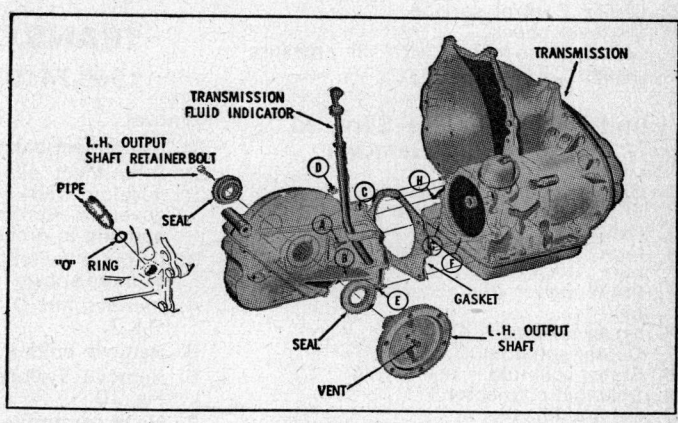

Fig. 7   Transmission attachment

2. Drive cover sprocket housing ½ qt.
3. Converter changed 3½ qts.
4. Total overhaul (total capacity) 13 qts.

Changing Oil

When changing transmission oil, first add 4 quarts, start the engine, and add oil to bring the fluid level to the FULL mark on the dipstick. Use only Dexron automatic transmission oil.

NOTE: Beginning with 1973 models, Cadillac uses an extended-life Dexron transmission fluid. With this new fluid, strainer replacement and fluid change is now recommended at 100,000 miles under normal operating conditions and 50,000 miles under severe or abnormal service such as trailer towing.

This recommendation applies only to the improved fluid and its availability for service. If the new fluid is not available, the former fluid can be used but then the 24,000 mile maintenance rule will apply.

Beginning with late 1973 models, Oldsmobile is using a revised type Dexron fluid. An early change to a darker color from the usual red color and or a strong odor that is usually associated with overheated fluid is normal, and should not be treated as a positive sign of needed maintenance or unit failure.

The normal maintenance schedule for drain and refill of this type fluid remains unchanged at 24,000 miles under normal service and 12,000 miles under severe operating conditions, such as trailer towing.

MANUAL LINKAGE, ADJUST

Cadillac Eldorado

1. Referring to Fig. 2, loosen adjusting screw on relay lever.
2. Pull relay rod up to position transmission shift valve in Park, then push rod down to the third (Neutral) step. Make sure rod is centered in this detent position.
3. Position selector lever in Neutral against quadrant stop in steering column.
4. Tighten relay rod adjusting screw, making sure shift lever is held against Neutral stop while this operation is being performed.

Olds Toronado

Make the adjustment as directed in Figs. 3, 4 and 4A.

DOWNSHIFT SWITCH, ADJUST

Cadillac Eldorado

1. Remove carburetor air cleaner.
2. Make sure that carburetor is properly adjusted and that throttle linkage is at low speed idle setting.
3. On 1969 models, if the downshift switch is properly adjusted, a #31 (wire gauge size) drill can be inserted in the calibrating hole below lower wire terminal extending through to carburetor side of switch. For 1970-74 models use a #42 (wire gauge size).
4. If adjustment is necessary, loosen the two switch mounting screws and position the switch for proper alignment.
5. With switch positioned, tighten mounting screws, remove drill gauge and install air cleaner.

Olds Toronado

Adjust detent downshift switch as described in Fig. 4B.

NOTE: Trailer Hauling Switch (Y-73 option) is bronze colored. When checking the special throttle switches with a test lamp, the test lamp *should light* only when the throttle valves are at idle or at wide open throttle position. The test lamp *will not light* at the 40° throttle opening as it does when checking a regular switch.

IN CAR REPAIRS

Operations Not Requiring Transmission Removal

1. Oil cooler fitting replacement or ad-

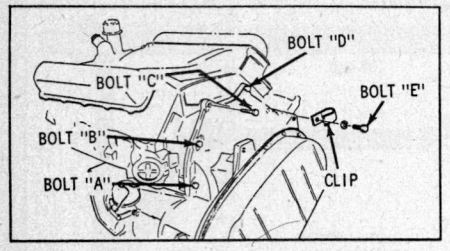

Fig. 8   Transmission to engine attachment

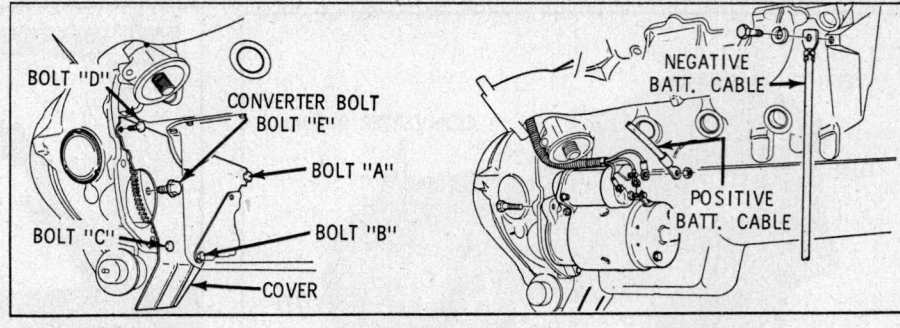

Fig. 9   Converter attachment

justment.
2. Governor assembly service.
3. Vacuum modulator, bushing and valve service.
4. Speedometer drive gear service.
5. Cruise Control service.
6. Oil level check.
7. Oil pressure check with oil pressure gauge.

Units That Can Be Serviced After Oil Pan Removal

1. Oil pan and pan-to-case gasket.
2. Pressure regulator valve assembly.
3. Valve body assembly.
4. Rear servo and accumulator assembly.
5. Front servo and accumulator assembly.
6. Governor pipes.
7. Detent solenoid.
8. Stator solenoid.
9. Solenoid connector.
10. Manual linkage.
11. Parking linkage.
12. Valve body-to-case spacers and gaskets.
13. Check balls for proper location (7 balls), Fig. 5.
14. Detent roller and spring assembly.

TRANS., REPLACE
1969-74 Olds Toronado

Removal

1. Disconnect battery.
2. Disconnect oil cooler lines at transmission and speedometer cable at governor. Remove governor and cover opening to prevent entry of dirt.
3. Install a suitable engine support bar, such as shown in Fig. 6.
4. Remove nut D and bolts A, B and C, Fig. 7.
5. Remove bolts A, B, C, D, Fig. 8.
6. Remove flywheel cover plate bolt, A, Fig. 10.
7. Hoist car and remove starter.
8. Remove bolts B, C and D from flywheel cover plate, Fig. 9.
9. Remove flywheel to converter bolt E, Fig. 9. Rotate flywheel until bolts are removed.

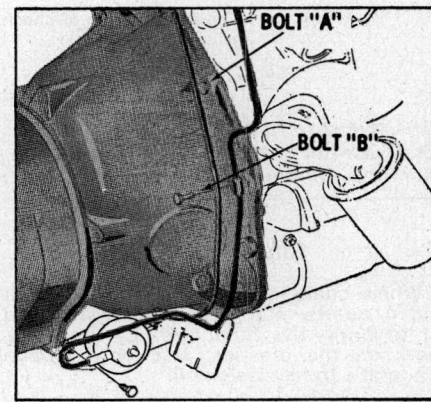

Fig. 10   Transmission to engine attachment

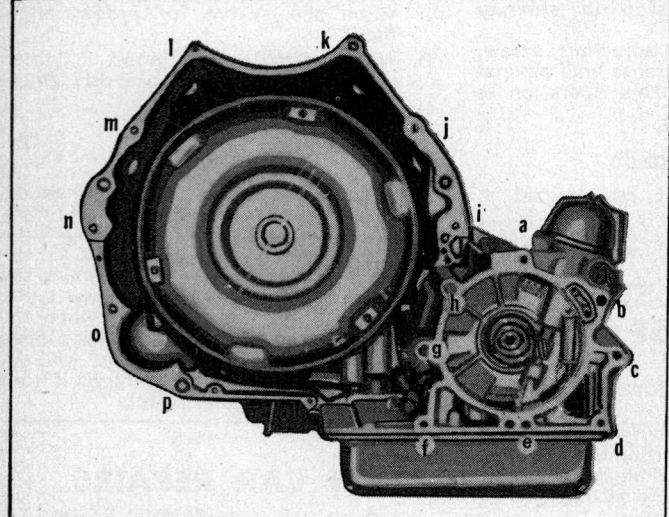

Fig. 11   Transmission attaching bolt locations. Cadillac Eldorado

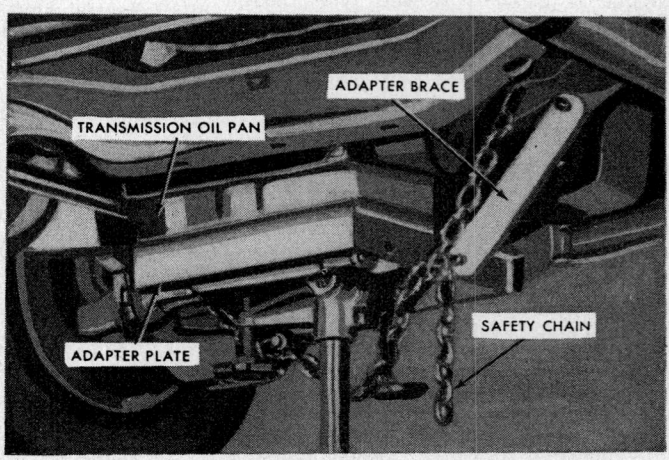

Fig. 12   Positioning transmission jack to transmission. Cadillac Eldorado

10. Disconnect vacuum modulator line and stator wiring.
11. Install transmission lift.
12. Remove shift linkage.
13. Remove bolts E, F, G and nut H, Fig. 7.
14. Remove bolts A and B, Fig. 10.
15. Remove two upper engine mount bracket-to-transmission bolts.
16. Remove four bracket-to-engine mount bolts.
17. Slide transmission rearward and down.
18. Attach converter holding strap to housing to prevent converter from falling out when transmission is being removed.
19. After transmission is removed from vehicle, the link assembly cover insulator can be removed or installed.

Installation

When installing the transmission the engine mount bracket must be positioned loosely on the link assembly cover until the transmission is in place. Then reverse removal procedure and torque bolts to ft-lb values as follows:
Engine to converter housing 30
Engine bracket to transmission 55
Engine bracket to rubber mount 55
Oil cooler lines to transmission—
1969-72 30
1973-74 20
Final drive to transmission 25

1969-73 Cadillac Eldorado

Removal—Figs. 11 and 12
1. Disconnect ground cable at battery.
2. Remove transmission dipstick.
3. Remove filler tube.
4. Remove bolts at locations A, B and C, securing final drive case to transmission.
5. Disconnect speedometer cable from governor and detent solenoid connector from transmission case.
6. Disconnect oil cooler pipes from transmission and on 1969 models also from radiator.
7. Cap pipes and plug connector holes in transmission and radiator.
8. Remove bolt securing cooler pipe bracket to final drive bracket and position pipes away from governor.
9. Remove nut at location H, securing final drive case to transmission.
10. Remove bolts at locations I, J, K and L, securing transmission to engine and adapter plate.
11. Remove upper left bolt securing rear engine mount bracket to transmission.
12. Remove ground strap from cowl.
13. Remove upper left nut securing converter cover plate to transmission.

NOTE: Use a 7/16" universal socket and extension and reach underneath left exhaust manifold. Removal of this screw can be facilitated by having a helper under the car, verbally guiding socket onto nut.

14. On 1969-72 models, position cable with looped ends under engine intake manifold and hook looped ends to chain fall. Take up slack in chain fall and cable, putting engine mounts under tension.

15. On all models, position safety chain over top of transmission.
16. Raise vehicle and place on jack stands. Adjust chain fall on 1969-72 models.
17. Disconnect leads from starter motor.
18. Remove bolt at location O, securing starter motor to transmission case and remove ground strap from bolt.
19. Remove bolt at location P and remove starter.
20. Remove three remaining screws securing converter cover plate to transmission and remove cover plate.
21. Position transmission jack.
22. Disconnect electrical connector from transmission connector.
23. Remove pipe from vacuum modulator.
24. Secure transmission to transmission jack adapter plate with safety chain.
25. Remove three flex plate-to-converter attaching bolts.

NOTE: This can be done by installing a 9/16-18 bolt and washer into end of crankshaft at vibration damper, after removing cork plug, and rotating converter and flex plate until bolts are accessible for removal. Do not pry on flex plate ring gear to rotate flex plate and converter as flex plate may be damaged.

26. Remove bolts at locations M and N securing transmission to engine and adapter plate.
27. On left side of transmission, separate relay rod from manual yoke.
28. Remove bolts at locations D, E and F, and nut at location G, securing final drive to transmission.

NOTE: Position drain pan under point where transmission and final drive meet as approximately 1½ quarts of transmission fluid will be lost when transmission and final drive are separated.

29. Remove five bolts and washers securing rear of acromat (cushion) to front cross bar and frame horns and allow acromat to hang free.
30. Through access holes in bottom of front cross bar, remove left bolt and loosen right bolt securing front engine mount to front cross bar. Turn wheels all the way to the left to provide maximum clearance.
31. Have a helper, using a large pry bar, shift engine forward, while you use a small pry bar to help separate transmission from engine and final drive. *Select pry points with care to avoid damaging any components.*
32. After initial separation has been made, allow transmission oil to drain at final drive junction.
33. Remove two bolts on right side securing rear engine mount bracket to transmission.
34. Through access hole in bottom of transmission support bar, remove two bolts, one each side, securing rear mounts to transmission support bar, and position mounts and bracket rearward to underbody.

35. While a helper pries and holds engine forward, move transmission rearward to disengage transmission case from dowels on engine adapter and to disengage final drive from studs on transmission case. Top of transmission should be tilted slightly rearward.
36. Slowly lower transmission, making certain top of transmission case clears flex plate ring gear and splined input shaft of final drive, until converter is approximately half-way exposed from flex plate.
37. Install a suitable clamp to transmission case at location N to avoid possibility of converter becoming disengaged when transmission is removed.
38. Lower transmission from car.

CAUTION: Rear engine mount bracket will follow transmission from car; to avoid damage or injury, remove bracket as soon as there is sufficient clearance.

39. Remove and discard final drive gasket and clean mounting surface of final drive.

Installation
1. Position transmission, on jack, under car.
2. Install new gasket on final drive, after first soaking gasket with transmission fluid.
3. Position rear engine mount bracket on top of transmission support bar against underbody.
4. Raise transmission in place until converter is approximately half-way covered by flex plate, then remove converter holding clamp.
5. While a helper assists in holding engine forward with pry bar, continue raising transmission, making certain top of transmission case clears splined input shaft of final drive, and position to engine.
6. Position transmission to engine and final drive by aligning following points in the order listed, while a helper assists:
   a. Studs on transmission case to mounting holes in final drive.
   b. Guide holes in transmission case to dowels on adapter.
   c. Internal flange on final drive to transmission.

NOTE: As engagement of splined final drive input shaft to transmission is hidden, extreme care must be taken to avoid damaging transmission and final drive.
   To facilitate engagement of final drive splines, rotate one front wheel while a helper holds the other. When alignment is complete and proper, gap between final drive case and transmission should not exceed ¼".

7. Loosely install bolts (⅜ x 1¼) at locations D and F attaching transmission to final drive and bolt (⅜ x 2½) at location N attaching transmission to engine adapter, alternately tightening bolts to avoid cocking transmission. *Do not torque bolts at this time.*

8. Working in engine compartment, loosely install bolt (⅜ x 1⅜) at location J attaching transmission to adapter. *Do not torque bolt at this time.*

9. Install bolt (⅜ x 1⅜) at location M attaching transmission to adapter plate. *Do not torque bolt at this time.*

10. Position rear engine mount bracket to transmission and loosely install bolts at locations K and L.

11. Position rear engine mounts and bracket to transmission support bar and loosely install bolts through access holes in bottom of bar, attaching mounts to bar.

12. Reposition engine if necessary and install left bolt securing front engine mount to front cross bar. Tighten both front mount bolts to 30-ft.-lbs.

13. Remove transmission jack.

14. Torque rear engine mounts to transmission support bar bolts to 55 ft-lbs. Torque rear engine mounts to transmission bolts (2 on right side) to 55 ft-lbs. Torque transmission to adapter to engine bolts (located N) to 30 ft-lbs. Torque transmission to adapter bolts (location M) to 30 ft-lbs.

NOTE: The procedure for securing the converter to the flex plate outlined in steps 15 through 17 must be strictly followed, otherwise damage to the flex plate and transmission will result from improper installation.

15. Rotate converter until two of the three weld nuts on converter line up with two of the three bolt holes in flex plate. Position converter so that weld nuts are flush with flex plate, making certain converter is not cocked and that pilot in center of converter is properly seated in crankshaft.

16. Loosely install two flex plate to converter bolts through accessible holes in flex plate.

17. Rotate flex plate and converter by rotating bolt previously installed in forward end of crankshaft until third bolt hole is accessible. Install the third flex plate to converter bolt and torque all three bolts to 28-30 foot pounds. Remove bolt from crankshaft and install cork plug.

18. Install hose on vacuum modulator.

19. Install electrical connector to transmission connector.

20. Position converter cover plate to transmission case and install two lower and one upper right bolts securing cover plate to transmission, tightening to 5 ft-lbs.

21. Position starter to transmission case and install bolt at location P.

22. Position ground strap to transmission and install bolt securing ground strap and starter to transmission at location O. Tighten bolts at locations O and P to 25 ft-lbs.

23. Install leads on starter motor.

24. Install bolts at locations C and E and nut at location G, securing transmission to final drive.

25. Torque bolts at locations C through F to 25 foot pounds on 1969-73 models or 35 foot pounds on 1974 models.

26. On 1969-72 models, position acromat (cushion) to front cross bar and frame horns and install five bolts and washers.

27. On all models, connect relay rod to manual yoke with a cotter pin.

28. Check operation of manual linkage and adjust.

29. Lower vehicle.

30. Install bolts at locations A and B and the nut at location H. Torque bolts to 25 foot pounds on 1969-73 models and 35 foot pounds on 1974 models.

31. Install upper left bolt securing converter cover plate to transmission in the manner described for removing it in Step 13.

32. Install bolt at location I and torque bolts at locations I, J, K, and L to 25 foot pounds.

33. Torque oil cooler pipe connectors at transmission case to 28 foot pounds on 1969-72 models and 20 foot pounds on 1973-74 models. Clean cooler pipe ends with a suitable solvent, connect pipes to transmission and torque pipe fittings to 28 foot pounds on 1969-72 models and 20 foot pounds on 1973-74 models.

34. On 1969 models, connect cooler pipes to radiator and torque fittings to 40 foot pounds. Install cooler pipe clamp.

35. On all models, connect speedometer to governor and detent solenoid connector to transmission case.

36. Install new O-ring seal on transmission oil filler tube through hole in final drive case. Fasten filler tube bracket to exhaust manifold.

37. Install body ground strap to firewall.

38. Connect battery cable, fill transmission with fluid and install hood if previously removed.

CHEVROLET TORQUE DRIVE

GENERAL DESCRIPTION

The "Torque-Drive" transmission is basically a modified Powerglide consisting of a torque converter and a two-speed planetary gear set. As the automatic shifting provisions have been removed the transmission can only be shifted manually.

The selector lever positions are PARK-R-N-Hi-1st. 1st speed should be used for speeds up to 20 mph but never exceeding 55 mph. When in Hi position, do not downshift to 1st at speeds above 55 mph.

LUBRICATION & MAINTENANCE

Lubrication, maintenance and service information as it is covered in the Aluminum Case Powerglide section of this manual will also apply to the "Torque-Drive" with the exception of the following operation.

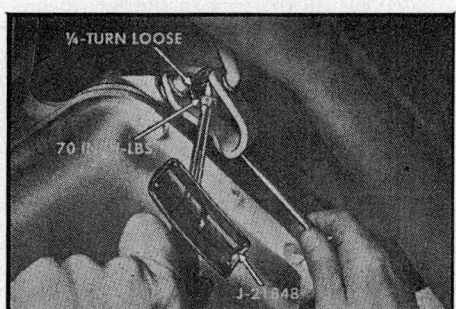

Fig. 1 Low band adjustment (in vehicle)

LOW BAND, ADJUST

Band adjustment should be performed at the first transmission oil change and sooner if slipping is evident.

1. With the selector in Neutral, back off the locknut ¼ turn. Tighten the adjusting screw to 70 in. lbs., Fig. 1.

2. Next, back off the adjusting screw exactly four turns if the band has more than 6,000 miles on it, or three turns if the band has less than 6,000 miles of use.

CAUTION: Be sure to hold the locknut at ¼ turn loose during the adjusting procedure. Then tighten locknut. The amount of back off is not an approximate figure; it must be exact.

TURBO HYDRA-MATIC 250, 350, 375B

TRANSMISSION IDENTIFICATION

A production day and shift built number, transmission model and model year are stamped on the 1-2 accumulator cover, which is located on the middle lower right side of the transmission case.

BUICK   CODE

1969 Except Sportwagon	JH
Sportwagon	JJ
1970 6-250	JE
8-350 2 bar. carb. Exc. LeSabre	JH
8-350 4 bar. carb. Exc. LeSabre	JR
8-350 2 bar. carb. LeSabre	JJ
8-350 4 bar. carb. LeSabre	JS
1971 6-250	JE
V8-350 Exc. Below	LA
V8-350 Gran Sport	MA
V8-350 LeSabre	KL
1972 Skylark & Custom w/Std. Axle	KA
V8-350 LeSabre	KL
V8-350 All Others	KE
1973-74 6-250	JE
V8-350 Century	KA
V8-350 LeSabre	KL

CHEVROLET

1969 V8-350 4 bar. carb. w/3.07 or 3.31 rear axle	FD
With A/C and 3.07, 3.08, 3.31 or 3.36 rear axle	FE
With 3.07, 3.08 or 3.36 and A/C	FG
V8-350 4 bar. carb.	FI
V8-350 2 bar. carb.	FQ
V8-350 2 bar. carb. Chevelle and Nova	FU
Taxi W/3.07 rear axle	IF
V8 Chevy II W/3.36 rear axle	IT
6 cyl. Chevy II W/3.36 rear axle	IS
Chevrolet W/3.07 rear axle	TJ

CHEVROLET—Cont'd   CODE

V8 Chevrolet W/3.08 rear axle and A/C	UX
V8 Police car	YF
V8-350 2 bar. carb. Police car	YL
V8-350 4 bar. carb. Police car	YX
6 cyl. Police car	YY
1970 6 cyl. Taxi W/3.07 rear axle	GQ
V8 Taxi W/3.07 rear axle	GT
Police car	GO, GU
V8-350 4 bar. carb.	GW
V8-400 2 bar. carb. Chevrolet	GY
1971 V8-400 2 bar. carb. Station Wagon	HH
V8-400 2 bar. carb. Chevrolet	HT
V8-350 4 bar. carb. Camaro, Chevelle and Monte Carlo	HW
V8-400 2 bar. carb. Monte Carlo	HY
1972 V8-350 2 or 4 bar. carb. Chevelle	JA
V8-350 2 or 4 bar. carb. Chevelle and Camaro	SA, SB
V8-350 2 bar. carb. Chevrolet	SD, SH
V8-400 2 bar. carb. Chevrolet	SG, SJ
1973 6-250 Camaro, Chevelle and Nova	FA
V8-350 2 or 4 bar. carb. Camaro, Chevelle and Nova	FB
V8-350 2 bar. carb. Chevrolet	FF, FJ
V8-307, V8-350 Taxi, Police or Passenger	FD
V8-400 2 bar. carb. Chevrolet	FH
6-250 Chevelle	JA
6-250 Camaro, Chevelle and Nova	TT
6-250 Camaro and Chevelle	TZ
1974 V8-400 2 Bar. Carb. Chevelle	AW
V8-350 Camaro Exc. Z28, Chevelle & Nova	FB
V8-400 4 Bar. Carb. Chevelle	FB
V8-400 4 Bar. Carb. Chevrolet	FD, FH
V8-350 Police & Taxi	FH
V8-400 2 Bar. Carb. Chevrolet	FH
V8-400 4 Bar. Carb. Chevrolet	FW
V8-350 Police & Taxi	HA
6-250 Camaro, Chevelle & Nova	TT
6-250 Nova	TZ

OLDSMOBILE   CODE

1969 F-85 V8-350 2 bar. carb.	JG
F-85 V8-350 4 bar. carb.	JL
1970 6-250	JE
8-350 2 bar. carb.	JG
8-350 4 bar. carb. Exc. below	JL
8-350 Ram Air	JO
8-350 Vista Cruiser	JM
1971 6-250	JE
V8-350 Exc. Below	LA
V8-350 Delta 88	LL
1972	KA, LA
1973 6-250 Omega	JE
V8-350 Omega & Cutlass 2 bar. carb.	LH
V8-350 Omega & Cutlass 4 bar. carb.	LA
V8-350 Vista Cruiser 4 bar. carb.	LE
1974 6-250 Omega	JE
V8-350 Omega & Cutlass Exc. Calif.	LA
V8-350 Omega & Cutlass Calif.	LC
V8-350 Vista Cruiser Exc. Calif.	LE

PONTIAC

1969 Tempest 6-250 1 bar. carb.	JA
Firebird 6-250 1 bar. carb.	JB
Tempest 6-250 4 bar. carb.	JC
Firebird 6-250 4 bar. carb.	JD
Tempest & Firebird V8-350 2 bar. carb.	JF
1970 Tempest 6-250	JE
Tempest 8-350	JF
Catalina 8-350	JU
1971 6-250	JE
V8-350 Exc. Below	MA
V8-350 Catalina	ML
1972 6-250	JE
V8-307	SB
V8-350	MA
1973 6-250	FA, JE
V8-350 2 bar. carb.	MA
V8-350 W/2.93 rear axle (late)	MC
V8-350 W/3.08 rear axle (late)	ME
1974 6-250 Firebird & LeMans	JE
6-250 Ventura	TZ
V8-350 2 Bar. Carb. w/2.73 or 2.93 rear axle	MA
V8-350 w/3.08 rear axle	ME

DESCRIPTION

The Turbo Hydra-Matic 250, 350, 375B, Figs. 1 and 2, are fully automatic three speed transmissions consisting of a three element torque converter and a compound planetary gear set. The Turbo Hydra-Matic 350, 375B transmission has four multiple-disc clutches, two roller clutches and a band to provide the required friction elements to obtain the desired function of the planetary gear set. The Turbo Hydra-Matic 250 transmission uses an adjustable intermediate band in place of the intermediate clutch found in the Turbo Hydra-Matic 350. Also, the Turbo Hydra-Matic 250 has three multiple-disc clutches and one roller clutch.

The friction elements couple the engine to the planetary gears through oil pressure, providing three forward speeds and one reverse.

The three element torque converter is of welded construction and is serviced as an assembly. The unit consists of a pump or driving member, a turbine or driven member and a stator assembly. When required, the torque converter supplements the gears by multiplying engine torque.

TROUBLE SHOOTING GUIDE

No Drive In Drive Range

1. Low oil level (check for leaks).
2. Manual control linkage improperly adjusted.
3. Low oil pressure due to blocked strainer, defective pressure regulator, pump assembly or pump drive gear. See that tangs have not been damaged by converter. Check case for porosity in intake bore.
4. Check control valve assembly to be sure manual valve has not been disconnected from inner lever.
5. Forward clutch may be stuck or damaged. Check pump feed circuits to forward clutch, including clutch drum ball check.
6. Roller clutch assembly broken or damaged.

Oil Pressure High or Low

High Pressure:
1. Vacuum line or fittings leaking.
2. Vacuum modulator.
3. Modulator valve.
4. Pressure regulator.
5. Oil pump.

Low Pressure:
1. Vacuum line or fittings obstructed.
2. Vacuum modulator.
3. Modulator valve.
4. Pressure regulator.
5. Governor.
6. Oil pump.

1-2 Shift At Full Throttle Only

1. Detent valve may be sticking or link-

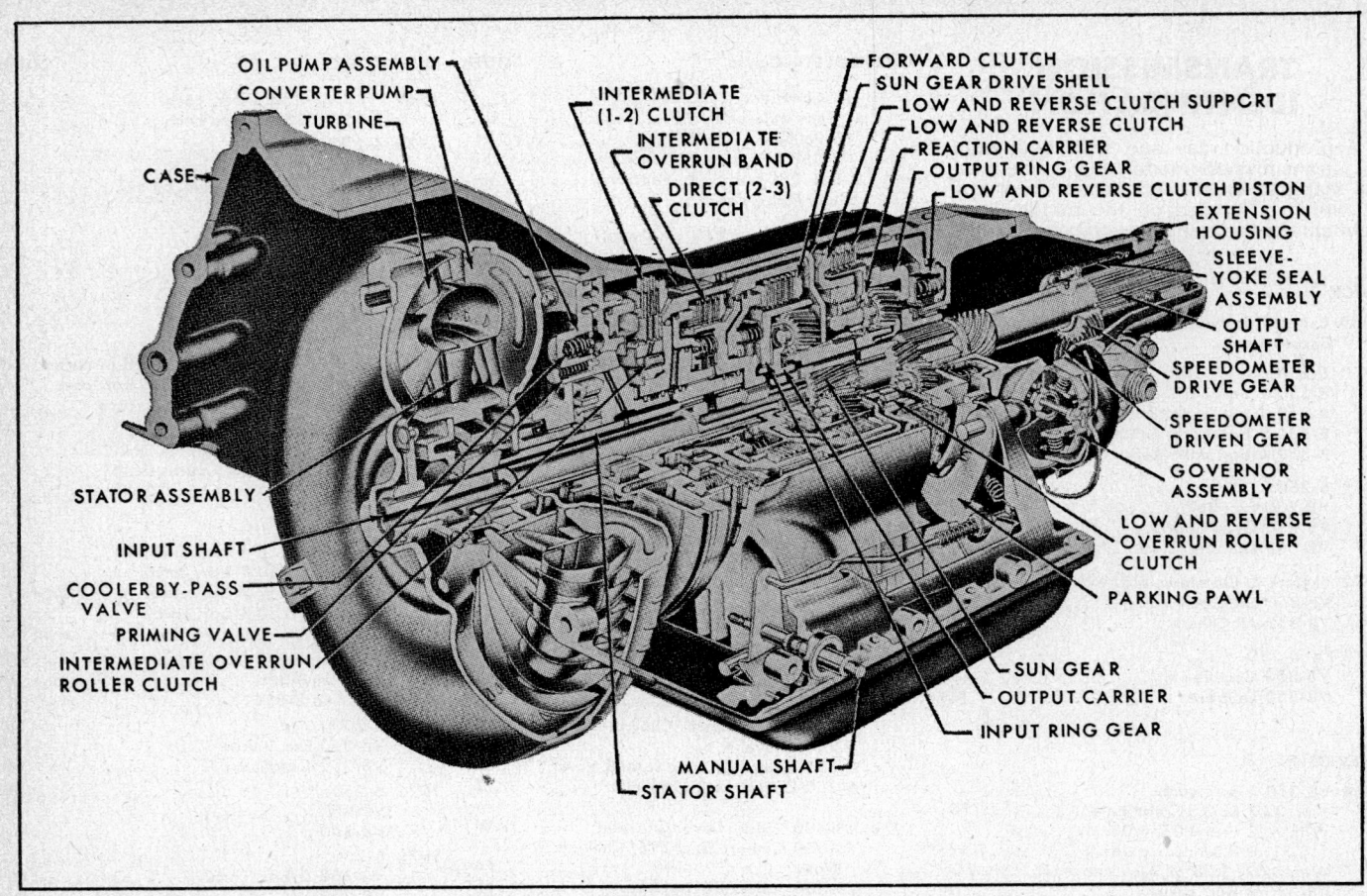

Fig. 1   Cutaway view of Turbo Hydra-Matic 350, 375B transmission

age may be misadjusted.
2. Vacuum line or fittings leaking.
3. Control valve body gaskets leaking, damaged or incorrectly installed. Detent valve train or 1-2 valve stuck.
4. Check case for porosity.

First Speed Only, No 1 - 2 Shift

T.H.M. 250, 350 & 375B
1. Governor valve may be sticking.
2. Driven gear in governor assembly loose, worn or damaged. If driven gear shows damage, check output shaft drive gear for nicks or rough finish.
3. Control valve governor feed channel blocked or gaskets leaking. 1-2 shift valve train stuck closed.
4. Check case for blocked governor feed channels or for scored governor bore which will allow cross pressure leak. Check case for porosity.
5. Intermediate clutch or seals damaged.
6. Intermediate roller clutch damaged.

T.H.M. 250
1. Intermediate servo piston seals damaged, missing or installed improperly.
2. Intermediate band improperly adjusted.
3. Intermediate servo apply rod broken.

1st & 2nd Only, No 2 - 3 Shift
1. Control valve 2-3 shift train stuck. Valve body gaskets leaking, damaged or improperly installed.
2. Pump hub-to-direct clutch oil seal rings broken or missing.
3. Direct clutch piston seals damaged. Piston ball check stuck or missing.

No First Speed

T.H.M. 250
1. Intermediate band adjusted too tightly.
2. 1-2 shift valve stuck in upshift position.

T.H.M. 350, 375B
1. Excessive number of clutch plates in intermediate clutch pack.
2. Incorrect intermediate clutch piston.

Moves Forward In Neutral
1. Manual linkage misadjusted.
2. Forward clutch not releasing.

No Drive In Reverse or Slips In Reverse
1. Low oil level.

2. Manual linkage misadjusted.
3. Modulator valve stuck.
4. Modulator and reverse boost valve stuck.
5. Pump hub-to-direct clutch oil seal rings broken or missing.
6. Direct clutch piston seal cut or missing.
7. Low and reverse clutch piston seal cut or missing.
8. Number 1 check ball missing.
9. Control valve body gaskets leaking or damaged.
10. 2-3 valve train stuck in upshifted position.
11. 1-2 valve train stuck in upshifted position.
12. Intermediate servo piston or pin stuck so intermediate band is applied.
13. Low and reverse clutch piston out or seal damaged.
14. Direct clutch plates burned — may be caused by stuck ball check in piston.
15. Forward clutch not releasing.

Slips In All Ranges
1. Low oil level.
2. Vacuum modulator valve defective or sticking.
3. Filter assembly plugged or leaking.

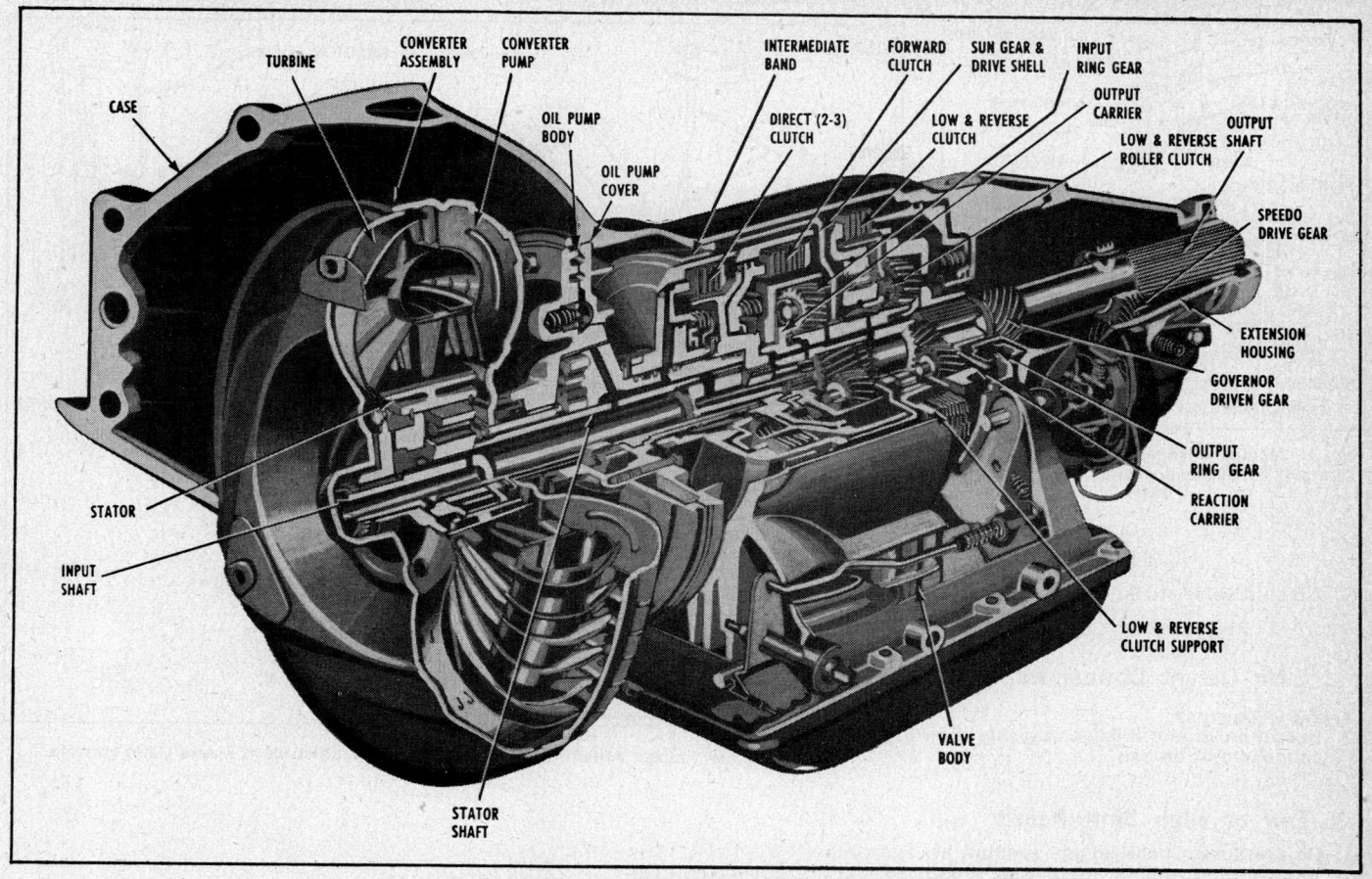

Fig. 2   Cutaway view of Turbo Hydra-Matic 250 transmission

4. Pressure regulator valve stuck.
5. Pump to case gasket damaged.
6. Check case for cross leaks or porosity.
7. Forward clutch slipping.

Slips 1 - 2 Shift

T.H.M. 250, 350 & 375B

1. Low oil level.
2. Vacuum modulator assembly defective.
3. Modulator valve sticking.
4. Pump pressure regulator valve defective.
5. 1-2 accumulator oil ring damaged or missing. Case bore damaged.
6. Pump to case gasket mispositioned or damaged.
7. Check for case porosity.
8. Intermediate clutch piston seals damaged. Clutch plates burned.

T.H.M. 250

1. Intermediate servo piston seals damaged or missing.
2. Burned intermediate band.

T.H.M. 350, 375B

1. 2-3 accumulator oil ring damaged or missing.

Rough 1 - 2 Shift

T.H.M. 250, 350 & 375B

1. Vacuum modulator, check for loose fittings, restrictions in line or defective modulator assembly.
2. Modulator valve stuck.
3. Valve body regulator or boost valve stuck.
4. Pump to case gasket mispositioned or damaged.
5. Check case for porosity.
6. Check 1-2 accumulator assembly for damaged oil rings, stuck piston, broken or missing spring, or damaged case bore.

T.H.M. 250

1. Intermediate band improperly adjusted.
2. Improper or broken servo spring.

T.H.M. 350, 375B

1. Burned intermediate clutch plates.
2. Improper number of intermediate clutch plates.

Slips 2 - 3 Shift

1. Low oil level.
2. Modulator valve or vacuum modulator assembly defective.
3. Pump pressure regulator valve or boost valve; pump to case gasket mispositioned.
4. Check case for porosity.
5. Direct clutch piston seals or ball check leaking.

Rough 2 - 3 Shift

1. High oil pressure. Vacuum leak, modulator valve sticking or pressure regulator or boost valve inoperative.
2. 2-3 accumulator piston stuck, spring broken or missing.

No Engine Braking In Second Speed

1. Intermediate servo or 2-3 accumulator oil rings or bores leaking or accumulator piston stuck.
2. Intermediate band burned or broken.
3. Low oil pressure: Pressure regulator and/or boost valve stuck.

No Engine Braking In 1st Speed

1. Manual low control valve assembly stuck.
2. Low oil pressure: Pressure regulator and/or boost valve stuck.
3. Low and reverse clutch piston inner seal damaged.

No Part Throttle Downshift

1. Oil pressure: Vacuum modulator assembly, modulator valve or pressure regulator valve train malfunctioning.
2. Detent valve and linkage sticking, disconnected or broken.

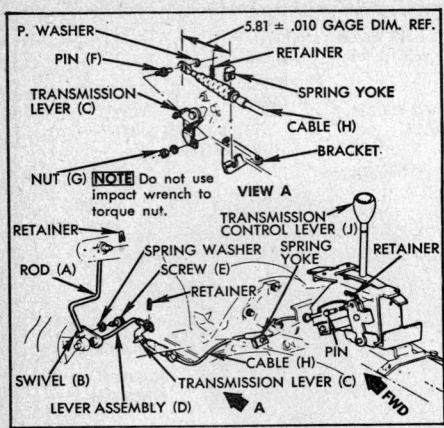

Fig. 3 Manual linkage adjustment. 1973-74 Camaro, Chevelle & Monte Carlo console shift

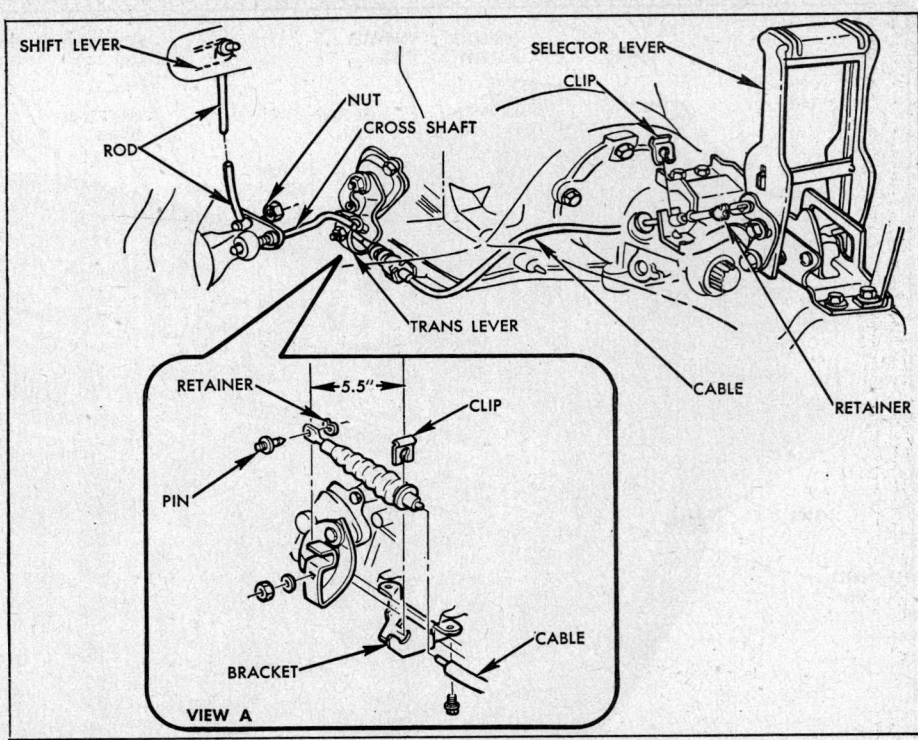

Fig. 4 Manual linkage adjustments. 1969-72 Camaro, Chevelle & Monte Carlo console

3. 2-3 shift valve stuck.

No Detent Downshifts

1. 2-3 valve stuck.
2. Detent valve and linkage sticking, disconnected or broken.

Low or High Shift Points

1. Oil pressure: Check engine vacuum at transmission end of modulator pipe.
2. Vacuum modulator assembly vacuum line connections at engine and transmission, modulator valve, pressure regulator valve train.
3. Check governor for sticking valve, restricted or leaking feed holes, damaged pipes or plugged feed line.
4. Detent valve stuck open.
5. 1-2 or 2-3 valve train sticking.
6. Check case for porosity.

Won't Hold In Park

1. Manual linkage misadjusted.
2. Parking brake lever and actuator assembly defective.
3. Parking pawl broken or inoperative.
4. Defective or improperly installed inner lever and actuating rod assembly.
5. Parking lock bracket loose, burred or rough edges, or improperly installed.
6. Parking pawl disengaging spring missing, broken or installed improperly.

Burned Forward Clutch Plates

1. Check ball in clutch drum damaged, stuck or missing.
2. Clutch piston cracked, seals damaged or missing.
3. Low line pressure.
4. Pump cover oil seal rings missing, broken or undersize; ring groove oversize.
5. Transmission case valve body face not flat or porosity between channels.

Burned Intermediate Clutch Plates

T.H.M. 350, 375B

1. Intermediate clutch piston seals damaged or missing.
2. Low line pressure.
3. Transmission case valve body face not flat or porosity between channels.

Burned Intermediate Band

T.H.M. 250

1. Intermediate servo piston seals damaged or missing.
2. Low line pressure.
3. Transmission case valve body face not flat or porosity between channels.

Burned Direct Clutch Plates

1. Restricted orifice in vacuum line to modulator.
2. Check ball in clutch drum damaged, stuck or missing.
3. Defective modulator.
4. Clutch piston cracked, seals damaged or missing.
5. Transmission case valve body face not flat or porosity between channels.

Noisy Transmission

NOTE: Before checking transmission for noise, ensure noise is not coming from water pump, alternator or any belt driven accessory.

Park, Neutral & All Driving Ranges

1. Low fluid level.
2. Plugged or restricted screen.
3. Damaged screen to valve body gasket.
4. Pososity in valve body intake area.
5. Transmission fluid contaminated with water.
6. Pososity at transmission case intake port.
7. Improperly installed case to pump gasket.
8. Pump gears damaged.
9. Driving gear assembled backwards.
10. Crescent interference in pump.
11. Damaged or worn pump oil seals.
12. Loose converter to flywheel bolts.
13. Damaged converter.

1st, 2nd And/Or Reverse Gear

1. Planetary gears or thrust bearings damaged.
2. Damaged input or output ring gear.

Acceleration In Any Gear

1. Transmission case or transmission oil cooler lines contacting underbody.
2. Broken or loose engine mounts.

Squeal At Low Vehicle Speed

1. Speedometer driven gear shaft seal requires lubrication or replacement.

MAINTENANCE

Fluid should be checked every 6,000 miles with engine idling, selector lever in

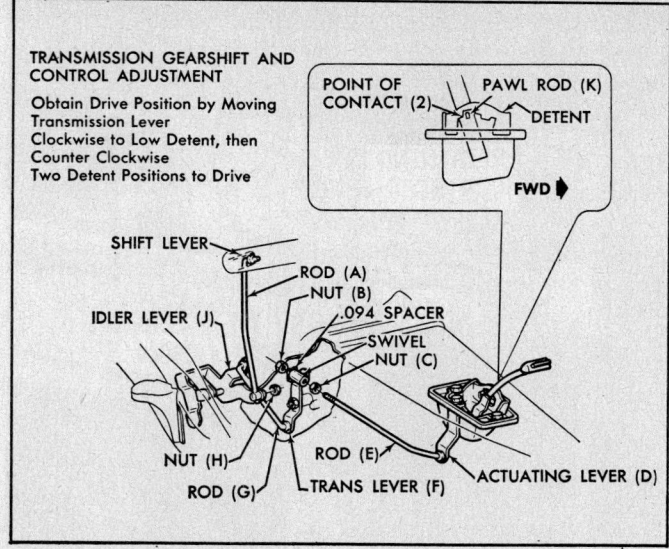

Fig. 5 Manual linkage. Nova console (typical)

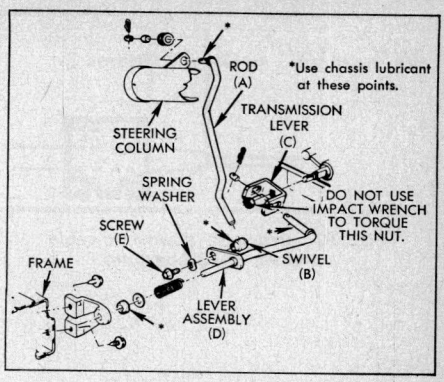

Fig. 6 Column shift linkage.
1973-74 All (Typical)

neutral position, parking brake set and transmssion at operating temperature. Use only General Motors Dexron transmission fluid when adding oil. Do not overfill.

Every 24,000 miles, remove drain plug in transmission oil pan and drain transmission oil sump. Add 1½ quarts after replacing plug, check fluid and add enough fluid to bring level to the Full mark.

NOTE: Beginning with 1973 Chevrolet and late 1973 Buick, Oldsmobile and Pontiac models, a revised type Dexron fluid is used in these transmissions. An early change to a darker color from the usual red color and or a strong odor that is usually associated with overheated fluid is normal, and should not be treated as a positive sign of needed maintenance or unit failure.

The normal maintenance schedule for drain and refill of this type fluid remains unchanged at 24,000 miles under normal service and 12,000 miles under severe operating conditions, such as trailer towing.

MANUAL LINKAGE, ADJUST
Buick

Console Shift
1. Loosen trunnion bolt.
2. Set selector lever against Drive stop.
3. Place transmission in Drive.
4. Tighten trunnion bolt to 6-9 ft-lbs.
5. Set selector lever in Park and set Back Drive Adjustment as outlined below.

Column Shift, 1969-70
1. Loosen adjusting clamp bolt.
2. Place selector lever against Drive stop.
3. Place transmission in Drive.
4. Tighten clamp bolt to 17-23 ft. lbs.

Column Shift, 1971-74
1. Loosen adjusting clamp bolt.
2. Place selector lever against Neutral stop.
3. Place transmission in Neutral.
4. Tighten clamp bolt to 17-23 ft. lbs.

Chevrolet
Camaro, Chevelle & Monte Carlo Console Shift, 1973-74
1. Loosen swivel screw so rod is free to move in swivel, Fig. 3.
2. Place transmission control lever in Drive and loosen pin in transmission lever, so it moves in the slot.
3. Move transmission lever counterclockwise to L1 detent and then three detents clockwise to Drive position. Tighten nut on transmission lever to 20 ft. lbs.
4. Place transmission control lever in Park and ignition switch in the Lock position and pull lightly against lock stop, then tighten swivel screw to 20 ft. lbs. Check for proper operation.

Camaro, Chevelle, Chevrolet & Monte Carlo Console Shift, 1969-72
1. Place shift lever in Drive, Fig. 4.
2. Raise vehicle, disconnect cable from transmission lever and manually place transmission lever in Drive. Measure distance from rearward face of attachment bracket to center of cable attachment stud. This dimension

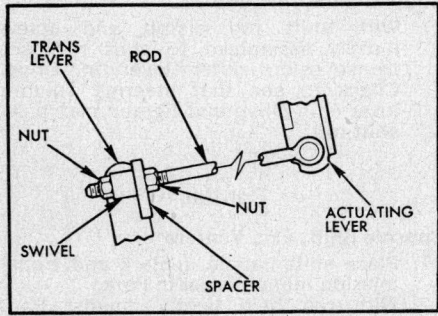

Fig. 7 Manual linkage adjustment. 1972 Vega

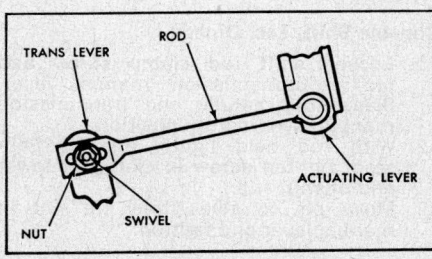

Fig. 8 Manual linkage adjustment. 1973-74 Vega

Fig. 9 Detent cable clip. Buick, Oldsmobile & Pontiac

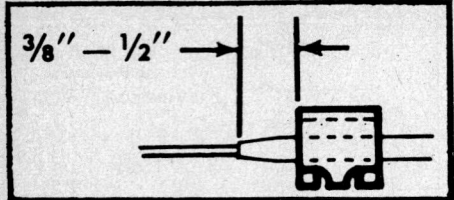

Fig. 10 Rearward downshift cable
retainer. 1972 Chevrolet

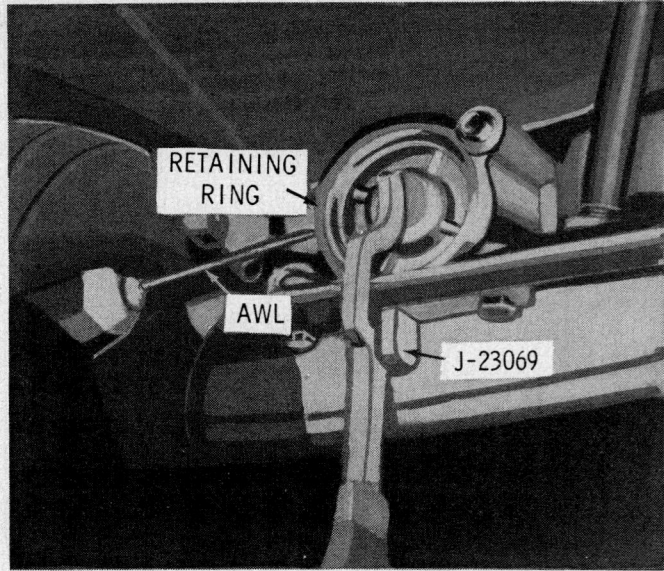

Fig. 11 Intermediate clutch accumulator piston removal

should be 5.5". If not, loosen stud nut and move stud accordingly. Reinstall stud nut and adjust end of cable so that it fits freely on stud. Reinstall clip.

Nova Console Shift, 1969-74

1. Loosen assembly nuts B and C or rod E, Fig. 5.
2. Set transmission lever F in DRIVE.
3. Set pawl rod K in DRIVE notch of detent.
4. Apply load in direction of arrow on actuating lever D until pawl rod K comes in contact with detent at contact point Z.
5. Place a .094" spacer between nut B and swivel, run nut B until it touches spacer. Remove spacer and tighten nut C against swivel and lock swivel between nuts B and C.
6. Set transmission lever F in PARK and turn ignition switch to LOCK.
7. Install rod G to idler lever J and lever F.
8. Install rod A to shift lever and idler lever J. Loosely attach clamp to idler lever.
9. Remove column lash by rotating shift lever in a downward direction and secure with attaching nut H. The foregoing provides .05" overtravel gap in notches of the detent.

Column Shift, 1973-74 All

1. Place transmission lever in Neutral by moving lever counter-clockwise to L1 detent then clockwise three detent positions to Neutral.
2. Place selecter lever in Neutral as determined by the mechanical stop on steering column. Do not use indicator as reference.
3. Assemble swivel, spring washer and screw to lever assembly then tighten screw to 20 ft. lbs., Fig. 6.

Column Shift, 1969-72 All

1. Place selector lever in Drive as determined by the transmission detent.
2. Loosen adjustment swivel at cross shaft and rotate transmission lever so it contacts the Drive stop in the steering column.
3. Tighten swivel and recheck adjustment.
4. Readjust indicator needle if necessary to agree with the transmission detent positions.

5. Readjust neutral safety switch if necessary.
6. Set selector lever in Park and adjust Bakc Drive as outlined below.

Chevrolet Vega
1972

1. Place transmission lever in Neutral by rotating lever clockwise to Park, then two detents counter-clockwise to Neutral.
2. Place shift lever in Neutral.
3. Apply a rearward force on lever until shift lever contacts detent stop. Install a .073 inch spacer between rear nut and swivel and tighten nut finger-tight, Fig. 7.
4. Remove spacer and apply a forward force on lever and tighten rearward nut.

1973-74

1. Loosen nut and perform steps 1 and 2 as outlined in the 1972 Chevrolet Vega adjustment.
2. Insert flats of swivel into slot in rod and tighten nut to 120 pound inches, Fig. 8.

Oldsmobile

Console Shift, Exc. Omega

1. Loosen shift rod clamp screw and pin in transmission manual lever. Place shift handle and transmission manual lever in Park position.
2. With rod held lightly against Park stop, tighten screw in clamp at lower end of shift rod.
3. Move pin to give "free pin" fit in manual lever and tighten.

Console Shift, Omega

1. Transmission manual lever must be free in swivel.
2. Place shift and transmission levers in Neutral.
3. Holding the actuating rod rearward against stop, place a .094" spacer between rear nut and swivel. Tighten nut to contact spacer, remove spacer, hold rear nut and tighten forward nut to lock swivel in place.
4. Loosen shift rod clamp screw and move shift and transmission manual levers to Park position and ignition switch to Lock position.
5. Pull down lightly on shift rod to contact lock stop and tighten clamp screw.
6. Check operation.

NOTE: With ignition key in the Lock position and transmission selector lever in Park, the key can be removed and the steering wheel should be locked.

Column Shift, All 1972-74

1. Loosen shift rod clamp screw and place outer lever in the Neutral position. Hold column shift lever in Neutral position and tighten clamp. Check operation.

Column Shift, All 1969-71

1. With shift rod clamp and screw loosely assembled to shift rod, set transmission outer lever in Drive. Check to see that steering column lever is in Drive and tighten clamp on shift rod.

Pontiac

Console Shift, Exc. Ventura

1. Place shift handle in Park and transmission manual lever in Park.
2. With rod held lightly against Park stop, tighten screw in clamp at lower end of rod.
3. Adjust pin in selector lever to freely

enter the end of the shift cable and tighten pin nut.

Console Shift, Ventura

Refer to the Oldsmobile Omega "Console Shift" adjustment procedure to adjust the console shift linkage.

Column Shift, All

With shift rod clamp and screw loosely assembled to shift rod, set transmission outer lever in Park position. Check to see that steering column lever is in Park position and tighten clamp on shift rod.

BACK DRIVE, ADJUST

1. Disconnect lower rod at transmission lever.
2. Move transmission lever to Park position.
3. Place transmission selector lever in Park position.
4. Attach lower rod to transmission lever and check for proper operation.

NOTE: Any inaccuracies in the above adjustments may result in premature failure of the transmission due to operation without the controls in full detent. Such operation results in reduced oil pressure and in turn partial engagement of the affected clutches.

THROTTLE LINKAGE, ADJUST

Buick

Buick throttle linkage is of the cable type and no provision is made for adjustment.

Chevrolet

Cable Type Exc. 1969-73 Corvette

No provision is made for adjustment of this type throttle linkage.

Rod Type, 1969

1. Disconnect throttle rod swivel at throttle lever on carburetor.
2. Hold carburetor throttle in wide open position, push throttle rod rearward to place accelerator pedal at the floor mat and adjust swivel to just enter hole in throttle lever.
3. Connect swivel to throttle lever and install accelerator return spring.

Corvette, 1969-73

1. Loosen throttle cable clamp bolt.
2. Hold accelerator pedal to floor against stop.
3. Move carburetor throttle lever to wide open position and tighten throttle cable clamp bolt to 45 in-lbs.

Oldsmobile

Cable Type

Cable type controls require no adjustment.

Pontiac

The throttle control system is of the cable type and requires no adjustment. On 1969-71 models, a reference dimension of $1\frac{9}{16}$ inch between the accelerator pedal and floor pan is used to check for bent bracket assemblies.

DETENT CABLE, ADJUST
Buick, Oldsmobile & Pontiac

The detent cable is adjusted from inside the driver's compartment as follows:

1. With engine off, throttle closed and fast idle off, position retainer clip against the insert on the detent cable, Fig. 9.
2. Grasp throttle pedal lever adjacent to the detent cable and pull the carburetor cable to the wide open position. By following this procedure, the detent cable will be adjusted properly.

Chevrolet

On Chevrolet units, the detent cable is adjusted at the carburetor.

1969 All

1. Remove air cleaner.
2. Loosen detent cable screw.
3. With choke off and accelerator linkage properly adjusted, position carburetor lever in the wide open throttle position.
4. Pull detent cable rearward until wide open throttle stop in transmission is felt.

NOTE: Cable must be pulled through detent position to reach wide open throttle stop in transmission.

5. Tighten detent cable screw and check linkage for proper operation.

1970-71 All, 1972 Exc. Chevrolet, 1973-74 Camaro, Nova & Vega

1. Release snap lock.
2. Place carburetor lever in the wide open throttle position, being sure that lever is against the stop, push snap lock down onto cable until the top is flush with the cable.

NOTE: On models equipped with Quadrajet carburetors, be sure that the secondary lock is disengaged before placing lever in wide open throttle position.

1972 Chevrolet

1. Pass detent cable through lower hole in accelerator lever.
2. Place forward retainer on cable and install in hole in lever.
3. Place rearward retainer on cable as shown in Fig. 10.
4. Accelerator cable must be connected at carburetor and accelerator pedal lever, fully depress accelerator pedal to automatically adjust retainer.

1973-74 Chevrolet, Chevelle & Monte Carlo

1. With the accelerator and detent cables connected, depress accelerator pedal to the wide open throttle position. The ball will then slide into the cable sleeve and permanently adjust the cable length.

INTERMEDIATE BAND, ADJUST

Turbo Hydra-matic 250

Since the Turbo Hydra-matic 250 transmission uses an intermediate band instead of a clutch (used in the Turbo Hydra-matic 350 transmission) to control the operation of the planetary gear sets, it is necessary to adjust the intermediate band as follows:

1. Loosen adjusting screw lock nut, located on case right side, $\frac{1}{4}$ turn.
2. Torque adjusting screw to 30 inch pounds, then back off screw 3 turns.
3. Torque adjusting screw lock nut to 15 foot pounds while holding adjusting screw in position.

IN CAR REPAIRS
Valve Body Assembly

1. Remove oil pan and strainer.
2. Remove retaining pin to disconnect downshift actuating lever bracket, remove valve body attaching bolts and detent roller and spring assembly.
3. Remove valve body assembly while disconnecting manual control valve link from range selector inner lever.

CAUTION: Do not drop valve.

4. Remove manual valve and link from valve body assembly.
5. Reverse procedure to install.

Governor

1. On 1969 Oldsmobile to gain access to the governor, remove shift linkage and crossmember bolts. Raise transmission with a suitable jack, remove crossmember and lower transmission.
2. Remove governor cover retainer and cover.
3. Remove governor.

Intermediate Clutch Accumulator Piston Assembly

1. Remove two oil pan bolts adjacent to accumulator piston cover, install compressor on oil pan lip and retain with these two bolts, Fig. 11.
2. Compress intermediate clutch accumulator piston cover and remove retaining ring piston cover and O ring from case.
3. Remove spring and intermediate clutch accumulator piston.

Vacuum Modulator & Modulator Valve Assembly

1. Disconnect vacuum hose from modulator stem and remove vacuum modulator screw and retainer.
2. Remove modulator and its O ring.
3. Remove modulator valve from case.

Extension Housing Oil Seal

1. Remove propeller shaft.
2. Pry out lip seal with screwdriver or small chisel.

Manual Shaft, Range Selector Inner Lever & Parking Linkage Assemblies

1. Remove oil pan and strainer.
2. Remove manual shaft to case retainer and unthread jam nut holding range selector inner lever to manual shaft.
3. Remove jam nut and remove manual shaft from range selector inner lever and case. *Do not remove manual shaft lip seal unless replacement is required.*
4. Disconnect parking pawl actuating rod from range selector inner lever and remove bolt from case.
5. Remove bolts and parking lock bracket.
6. Remove pawl disengaging spring.
7. If necessary to replace pawl or shaft, clean up bore in case and remove shaft retaining plug, shaft and pawl.

TRANSMISSION, REPLACE
BUICK
1969-74

1. Raise car and remove propeller shaft. If necessary, disconnect exhaust crossover pipe.
2. Place suitable jack under transmission and fasten transmission securely to jack.
3. Remove vacuum line from vacuum modulator.
4. Loosen cooler line nuts and separate cooler lines from transmission.
5. Remove detent cable from accelerator lever assembly. *Do not bend cable.* Remove plastic guide from bracket and slide cable out through slot.
6. Remove detent cable from detent valve link.
7. Remove crossmember.
8. Disconnect speedometer cable, shift linkage and filler pipe. Remove filler pipe.
9. Support engine at oil pan.
10. Remove transmission flywheel cover pan.

11. Mark flywheel and converter for reassembly and remove three flywheel to converter bolts.
12. Be sure transmission is supported by transmission jack and remove transmission case to engine block bolts.
13. Move transmission rearward to provide clearance between converter and crankshaft. Install converter holding tool, lower transmission and remove.

CHEVROLET
1969-74

1. Disconnect negative battery cable and raise car.
2. On 1969 Camaro, disconnect parking brake cables, remove underbody reinforcement plate (convertible). Disconnect left exhaust pipe from manifold.
3. On all models, remove propeller shaft, disconnect speedometer cable, detent cable, modulator vacuum line and oil cooler lines.
4. Disconnect shift linkage.
5. Support transmission with suitable jack and remove crossmember.
6. Remove converter under pan.
7. Remove converter to flywheel bolts.
8. On 1969 Chevrolet and Chevelle and all 1970-74 models except Nova, loosen exhaust pipe to manifold bolts approximately $1/4$ inch. Lower transmission until jack is barely supporting transmission.

NOTE: On V8 engines, care must be taken not to lower the rear of the transmission too far as the distributor housing may be forced against firewall causing damage to the distributor.

9. Remove transmission to engine mounting bolts and remove oil filler tube at transmission.
10. Raise transmission to its normal position, support engine with jack and slide transmission rearward from engine and lower it away from vehicle.
11. Reverse procedure to install.

OLDSMOBILE
1969-74

1. From inside the car, slide clip to the end of the detent cable.
2. Remove transmission oil level dipstick.
3. Raise car and remove detent cable from link. Plug hole.
4. Disconnect oil cooler lines at transmission.
5. Remove flywheel cover pan and mark converter and flywheel for reassembly. Remove three flywheel to converter bolts.

6. Disconnect vacuum modulator line. Remove speedometer clip and driven gear. Plug hole.
7. Disconnect shift linkage.
8. Remove propeller shaft.
9. Support transmission with a suitable jack and remove crossmember.
10. Lower transmission slightly and remove transmission to engine bolts.
11. Remove oil level indicator tube and clip holding detent cable to tube.
12. Lower transmission being careful not to damage cooler lines, detent cable, modulator line and shift linkage.
13. Reverse procedure to install.

PONTIAC
1969-74

1. Disconnect battery ground cable and release parking brake.
2. Raise car and remove propeller shaft.
3. Disconnect speedometer cable, vacuum hose at modulator, detent cable at transmission and shift linkage.

NOTE. When removing detent cable, be careful not to bend it.

4. Support transmission with a suitable jack and remove crossmember.
5. On 1969 Firebird L6, remove driveline damper.
6. Remove converter dust pan, mark flywheel and converter for reassembly and remove flywheel to converter bolts. Make sure converter hub is free of converter.
7. Disconnect transmission filler pipe at engine and remove pipe from transmission.
8. Lower transmission and engine to gain access to cooler line fitting nuts and disconnect cooler lines. On some models it may be necessary to loosen the exhaust system.
9. With transmission in lowered position, remove the transmission to engine bolts.
10. Raise transmission to its normal position, support engine and slide transmission rearward and lower it away from car.

NOTE: When lowering transmission, keep rear of transmission lower than the front so as not to lose the converter.

11. Reverse procedure to install.

BUICK SUPER TURBINE 300
OLDS JETAWAY, 1969
PONTIAC TWO SPEED, 1969

TRANSMISSION IDENTIFICATION

The transmissions can be identified by either the metal tag or the stamping on the low servo cover. The data is stamped on the low servo cover. The identification data includes the year of production, code letters or numbers followed by the transmission serial number. The model application is as follows:

BUICK

	CODE
1969 All Sportwagons	MH
All V8-350 engines except Sportwagons	ME
All models with 6-250 engine	LC

OLDSMOBILE MODELS

1969 6-250	LC
V8-350 Except Delta "88"	MM
V8-350 Delta "88"	MS
V8-350 Delta "88" w/Cruise Control	MU

PONTIAC INTERMEDIATE MODELS

1969 Six w/1 bar. carb.—Tempest	LA
Six w/1 bar. carb. & air cond.—Tempest	LD
Six w/1 bar. carb.—Firebird	LF
Six w/1 bar. carb. & air cond.—Firebird	LH
V8-350 w/2 bar. carb.	MA
V8-350 w/2 bar. carb. & air cond.	MC

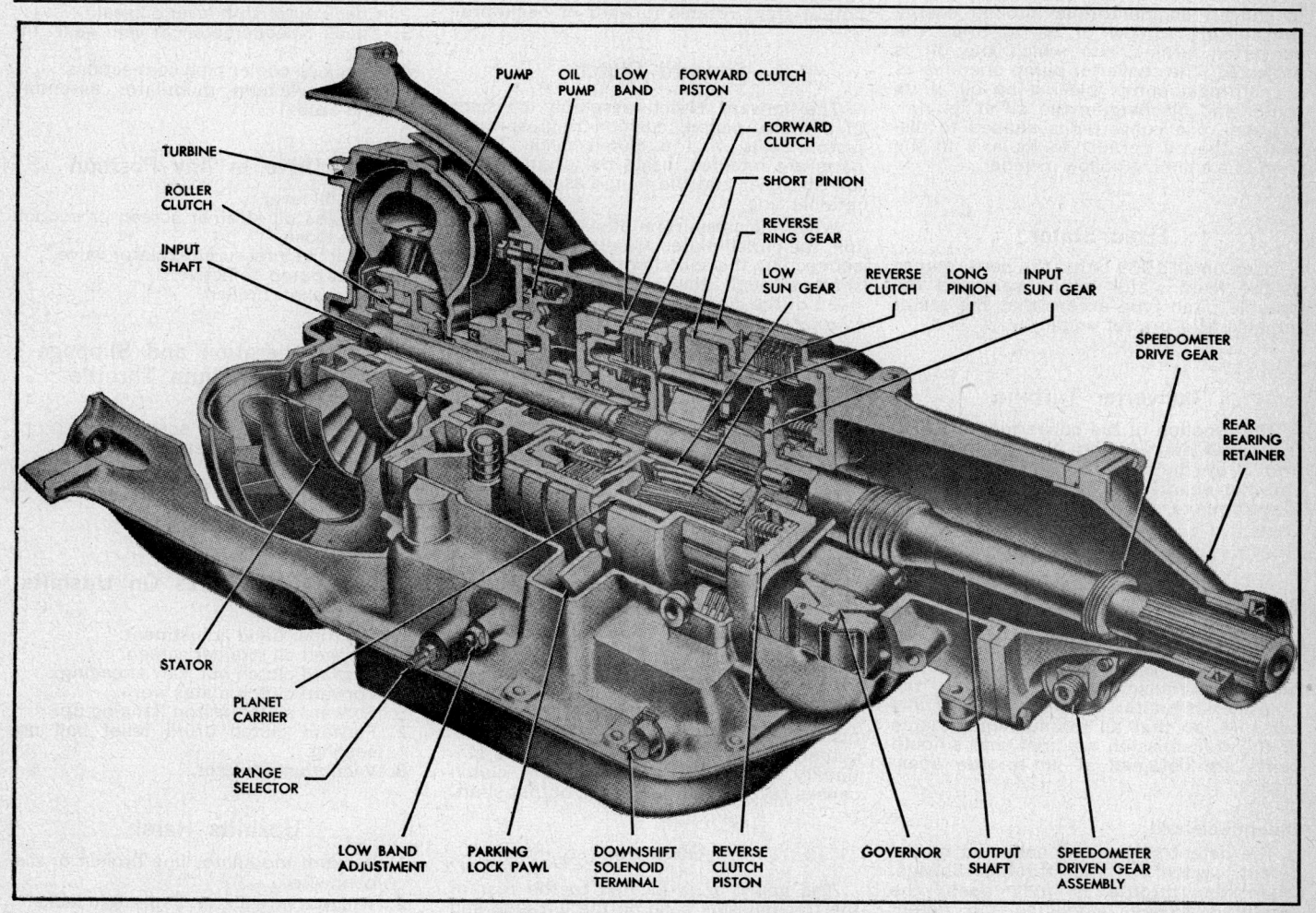

Fig. 1   Cutaway view of transmission

DESCRIPTION

This transmission, Fig. 1, is a combination torque converter and two-speed planetary geared unit. Torque multiplication is obtained hydraulically through the converter and mechanically through the compound planetary gear set. The gear set, in combination with the torque converter, provides a high starting ratio for acceleration from a stop, up steep grades, etc. The torque converter provides torque multiplication for performance and exceptionally smooth operation. It functions as a fluid coupling at normal road load conditions and at higher speeds.

Torque Converter

The torque converter is connected to the engine flywheel and serves as a hydraulic coupling through which engine torque is transmitted to the input shaft. The converter steps up or multiplies engine torque whenever operating conditions demand greater torque than the engine alone can supply.

Converter Pump

The function of the converter pump is to convert engine torque into an energy transmitting a flow of oil to drive the converter turbine into which the oil is projected. The converter pump operates as a centrifugal pump, picking up oil at its center and discharging the oil at its rim. However, the converter is shaped to discharge the oil parallel to its axis in the form of a spinning hollow cylinder.

Fixed Stator

Used on all 1969 units, the performance of the fixed stator is the same as the variable pitch type except that the stator remains at a pre-set angle.

Converter Turbine

The function of the converter turbine is to absorb energy from the oil projected into it by the converter pump and convert the energy into torque and transmit that torque to the input shaft.

External Controls

Vacuum Modulator

The vacuum modulator is used to sense automatically any change in the torque input to the transmission. The vacuum modulator transmits this signal to the pressure regulator, which controls line pressure, so that all torque requirements of the transmission are met and smooth shifts are obtained at all throttle openings.

Detent Solenoid

The detent solenoid is activated by the detent switch in the throttle linkage. When the throttle is fully open, the switch is closed, activating the detent solenoid and causing the transmission to downshift at speeds below approximately 60 mph.

Oil Pump

A positive displacement internal-external gear type oil pump is used to supply oil to fill the converter, for engagement of forward and reverse clutches, for application and release of the low band and to provide oil for lubrication and heat transfer.

Planetary Gear Set

The planetary gear set consists of an input sun gear, low sun gear, long and short pinions, a reverse ring gear and a planet carrier.

The input sun gear is splined to the input shaft. The low sun gear, which is part of the forward clutch assembly, may revolve freely until the low band or high clutch is applied.

The input sun gear is in mesh with three long pinions and the long pinions are in mesh with three short pinions. The short pinions are in mesh with the low sun gear and reverse ring gear.

The input sun gear and short pinions always rotate in the same direction. Application of either the low band or the reverse clutch determines whether the output shaft rotates forward or backward.

Forward Clutch

The forward clutch assembly consists of a drum, piston, cushion ring, springs, piston seals, and a clutch pack. These parts are retained inside the drum by the low sun gear and the flange assembly and retainer ring.

When oil pressure is applied to the piston, the clutch plates are pressed together, connecting the clutch drum to the input shaft through the clutch hub. Engagement of the clutch causes the low sun gear to rotate with the input shaft.

Low Band

The low band is a double-wrap steel band faced with a bonded lining which surrounds the forward clutch drum. The band is hydraulically applied by the low servo piston, and released by spring pressure.

Reverse Clutch

The reverse clutch consists of a piston, cushion ring, inner and outer seal, coil springs, clutch pack, and reaction plate. These parts are retained inside the case by a retaining snap ring.

When oil pressure is applied to the piston, the clutch plates are pressed together, holding the reverse ring gear stationary. This engagement of the clutch causes reverse rotation of the output shaft.

Governor

The governor is located to the rear of the transmission case on the left side and is driven off the output shaft. The purpose of the governor is to generate a speed sensitive modulating oil pressure that increases up to a point with output shaft or car speed.

Valve Body

The valve body assembly is bolted to the bottom of the transmission case and is accessible for service by removing the oil pan. The valve body assembly consists of manual valve, shift valve, modulator limit valve, and high speed downshift timing valve.

TROUBLE SHOOTING GUIDE

Oil Forced Out Of Filler Tube

1. Oil level too high; foaming caused by planet carrier running in oil.
2. Water in oil.
3. Leak in pump suction circuits.

Oil Leaks

1. Check extension oil seal.
2. Check outer shift lever oil seal.
3. Check speedometer driven gear fitting.
4. Check oil cooler pipe connections.
5. Check vacuum modulator assembly and case.

No Drive In Any Position

1. Low oil level.
2. Clogged oil strainer screen or suction pipe loose.
3. Defective pressure regulator valve.
4. Front pump defective.
5. Input shaft broken.

Erratic Operation and Slippage Light to Medium Throttle

1. Low oil level.
2. Clogged oil strainer screen.
3. Servo piston seal leaking.
4. Band facing worn.
5. Low band apply struts disengaged or broken.
6. Vacuum modulator.

Engine Speed Flares On Upshifts

1. Low oil level.
2. Improper band adjustment.
3. Clogged oil strainer screen.
4. Forward clutch not fully engaging.
5. Forward clutch plates worn.
6. Forward clutch piston hanging up.
7. Forward clutch drum relief ball not sealing.
8. Vacuum modulator.

Upshifts Harsh

1. Vacuum modulator line broken or disconnected.
2. Vacuum modulator diaphragm leaks.
3. Vacuum modulator valve stuck.

Closed Throttle (Coast) Downshift Harsh

1. High engine idle speed.
2. Improper low band adjustment.
3. Downshift timing valve malfunction.
4. High main line pressure. Check the following: a) vacuum modulator line broken or disconnected, b) modulator diaphragm ruptured, c) sticking pressure regulator coast valve, pressure regulator valve or vacuum modulator valve.

Car Creeps Excessively In Drive

1. Idle speed too high.

Car Creeps In Neutral

1. Forward clutch not released.
2. Low band not released.

No Drive In Reverse

1. Reverse clutch piston stuck.
2. Reverse clutch plates worn out.
3. Reverse clutch seal leaking excessively.
4. Blocked reverse clutch apply orifice.

MAINTENANCE

Checking Oil Level

The transmission oil level should be checked every 6000 miles. Oil should be added only when the level is near the ADD mark on the dipstick with oil at normal operating temperature.

NOTE: *The difference in oil level between FULL and ADD is one pint.*

To check oil level accurately, the car should be level, the engine should be idled with the transmission oil at normal temperature, and the control lever in Park position.

It is important that the oil level be maintained no higher than the FULL mark. *Do not overfill,* for when the oil level is at the full mark on the dipstick, it is just slightly below the planetary gear unit. If oil is added which brings the level above the full mark, the planetary unit will run in the oil foaming and aerating the oil. This will cause malfunctioning of the transmission assembly due to improper application of the band or clutches and excessive temperature.

If the transmission is found to be consistently low on oil, a thorough inspection should be made to find and correct all external oil leaks. All mating surfaces, such as the oil pan rail, filler tube, governor and modulator should be carefully examined for signs of leakage. The modulator must also be checked to insure that the diaphragm has not ruptured as this would allow transmission oil to be drawn into the intake manifold of the engine. Usually, the exhaust will be excessively smoky if the diaphragm ruptures, due to transmission oil being drawn into the combustion chambers of the engine.

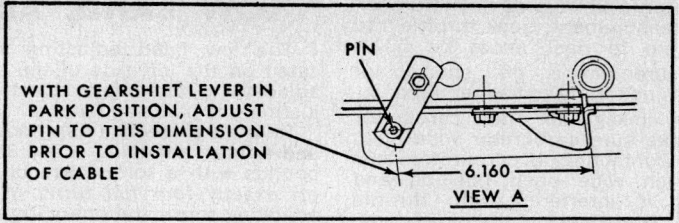

WITH GEARSHIFT LEVER IN PARK POSITION, ADJUST PIN TO THIS DIMENSION PRIOR TO INSTALLATION OF CABLE

PIN

6.160

VIEW A

Fig. 2   Console shift adjustment. Pontiac Tempest & Firebird. Dimension for 1969 is 7.260

Draining & Refilling

Draining the transmission oil at 24,000 mile intervals is recommended. Drain the oil by removing the oil pan (no drain plug is provided). Clean oil strainer.

To refill the transmission, replace the oil pan, using a new gasket, and add five (5) pints of transmission fluid, using filler tube and funnel. Start and allow engine to idle in Park position three to five minutes to warm the oil, then check oil level and add as required to bring the level to the Full mark. Assuming that the converter has not been drained (since it is welded) and allowing for normal spillage or drain-down, approximately six pints will be required for refill.

MANUAL LINKAGE, ADJUST

Buick

1969 Column Shift & Back Drive

1. Loosen swivel clamp bolt.
2. Place selector lever against Drive stop.
3. Place transmission lever in Drive detent (2nd from rear).
4. Torque swivel clamp bolt to 17-23 ft-lbs.

1969 Console Shift & Back Drive

1. Loosen shift rod trunnion nut (1968).
2. Place selector lever against Drive stop.
3. Place transmission in Drive detent (2nd from rear).
4. Tighten adjusting clamp bolt to 17-23 ft-llbs or trunnion nut to 6-9 ft-lbs.
5. Adjust back drive: Place transmission in Park push back drive rod up until column lever hits stop, hold lightly and tighten clamp.

Oldsmobile

1969 Console Shift & Back Drive

1. Place shift handle in Park position, transmission in Park position and ignition key in lock.
2. Loosen shift rod clamp and pull shift rod lightly against lock stop. Tighten shift rod clamp.
3. Move shift cable pin to obtain a free pin fit in transmission lever and tighten nut.
4. Check to be sure that with key in Run position and transmission in Reverse, key cannot be removed and steering wheel is not locked. With key

in Lock position and transmission in Park, be sure that key can be removed and steering wheel is locked.

1969 Column Shift & Back Drive

1. Set transmission shift lever in Drive.
2. Loosen swivel bolt.
3. Hold upper shift lever against Drive stop in upper steering column. Tighten swivel bolt.
4. Check to be sure that with key in Run position, and transmission in Reverse, key cannot be removed and steering wheel is not locked. With key in Lock position and transmission in Park, be sure that key can be removed and steering wheel is locked.

Pontiac Tempest & Firebird

1969 Column Shift & Back Drive

1. Loosen adjusting swivel clamp.
2. Set transmission in Park position.
3. Set upper gearshift lever in Park position and lock ignition.
4. Push up on gearshift control rod to take up clearance in steering column lock mechanism and tighten swivel clamp to 20 ft-lbs. on Tempest and 30 ft-lbs. on Firebird.

1969 Console Shift & Back Drive

1. Disconnect shift cable from transmission range selector lever pin.
2. Set console gearshift lever in Park and lock ignition.
3. Rotate transmission range selector lever clockwise to Park position and adjust pin on selector to 7.260", Fig. 2.
4. Torque pin nut to 30 ft-lbs. and connect shift cable to pin.

THROTTLE LINKAGE

Buick 1969

Intermediate Models

The flexible cable type linkage is used and is not adjustable.

Le Sabre

1. Remove air cleaner.
2. Make sure linkage is free in all positions.
3. Hold choke open and make sure that return spring fully closes throttle, even though throttle is released very slowly.
4. Adjust engine idle speed and mixture.

5. With throttle linkage at hot idle position, measurement from throttle rod clevis pin to dash must be 5⅞".
6. If measurement is off, shorten or lengthen operating rod as required.
7. Operate linkage to open carburetor and make sure carburetor wide open stop is contacting. If carburetor does not reach wide open position and nothing is interfering with throttle linkage, transmission stator and detent switch must be adjusted as outlined below.

Oldsmobile

1969 Models

These units use cable type accelerator controls and no provision is made for adjustment.

Pontiac Tempest & Firebird

1969

Throttle linkage adjustments cannot be made. A reference dimension of 1⁹⁄₁₆" between the bottom of the accelerator pedal roller and floor pan can be used only as a check for bent bracket assemblies.

DOWNSHIFT SWITCH

Buick, Olds, Pontiac 1969

The downshift switch is in the throttle linkage. To adjust, depress the switch plunger fully to insure proper setting, then depress the accelerator pedal fully.

IN CAR REPAIRS

The following operations can be performed without removing the transmission from the car.
1. Oil pan and strainer.
2. Rear bearing retainer.
3. Vacuum modulator.
4. Valve body.
5. Governor.
6. Low servo.
7. Selector and parking mechanism.
8. Pressure regulator valve.

LOW BAND, ADJUST

The low band adjusting screw is located on the left side of the transmission adjacent to the range selector lever. Adjustment is made as follows:

Remove protective cap, loosen lock nut and tighten adjusting screw 35 to 45 inch pounds with a torque wrench. Then back off *exactly four full turns*. While holding adjusting screw stationary, tighten lock nut securely and replace cap.

TRANSMISSION, REPLACE

Buick

1. Raise and support front and rear of car.
2. Disconnect front exhaust crossover pipe if necessary.
3. Remove propeller shaft.
4. Support transmission with suitable jack.
5. Remove line from vacuum modulator.
6. Separate cooler lines from transmission.
7. Remove cross member.
8. Disconnect speedometer cable.
9. Where necessary, disconnect detent solenoid wire.
10. Disconnect shift linkage from transmission.
11. Remove oil filler pipe.
12. Support engine at oil pan.
13. Remove flywheel cover pan.
14. Mark flywheel and converter for reassembly in same position and remove flywheel to converter bolts.
15. Unfasten transmission from engine.
16. Move transmisson rearward to provide clearance between converter pump and crankshaft.
17. Install holding tool to retain converter, then lower transmission from car.
18. Reverse procedure to install.

Oldsmobile

1. Remove transmission oil filler pipe. Hoist car.
2. Disconnect control wires at transmission, and manual rod from transmission lever.
3. Remove propeller shaft.
4. Remove flywheel dust cover.
5. Support engine with a suitable jack or support bar.

6. Remove transmission cross support bar. *On models with dual exhaust, it may be necessary to disconnect the left hand exhaust pipe at exhaust manifold to provide clearance.*
7. Disconnect and cap oil cooler lines.
8. Disconnect speedometer cable (or speed adapter if so equipped) from speedometer driven gear.
9. Remove three flywheel-to-converter attaching bolts. Mark flywheel and converter so they can be assembled in the same relationship.
10. Support transmission with a suitable lift and remove transmission-to-flywheel housing bolts. *It may be necessary to lower engine slightly to permit removal of the upper bolts.*
11. Carefully move transmission rearward and out of car.
12. Reverse removal procedure to install the unit and adjust the shift linkage as outlined below.

Pontiac Tempest & Firebird

1. Disconnect speedometer cable and remove speedometer driven gear to allow oil to drain during removal procedure.
2. Remove propeller shaft.
3. Disconnect vacuum line and downshift switch lead.
4. Disconnect shift linkage from outer shift lever.
5. Support transmission and remove frame crossmember.
6. Remove flywheel housing bottom cover.
7. After removing flywheel-to-converter bolts, make sure converter hub is free of crankshaft.
8. Lower transmission and engine assembly to gain access to cooler line fittings (V8 only). Disconnect cooler lines, using a crowfoot adapter and a suitable extension. *On some cars it may be necessary to loosen exhaust system.*
9. With transmission in lowered position, remove case-to-engine bolts.
10. Move transmission down and to the rear and install a suitable strap across the converter housing to hold the converter in position until transmission is to be disassembled.
11. Reverse removal procedure to install the unit and adjust shift linkage.

CHEVROLET POWERGLIDE
PONTIAC TWO SPEED, 1970-73

TRANSMISSION IDENTIFICATION

On 1969-73 models the unit number is located on the right rear vertical surface of oil pan. There is no particular code with which a transmission may be identified. Therefore, when ordering parts use the transmission serial number. This unit is also used on 1970-73 Pontiac cars.

DESCRIPTION

This Powerglide is essentially a torque converter coupled to a two-speed transmission, Fig. 1. The gear portion of the transmission is a two-speed compound planetary gear set, permitting a gear reduction of 1.82 to 1 on the light duty version and 1.76 to 1 on the heavy duty version. The shift from low gear to direct drive is automatic, and the vehicle speed at which the shifts occur is determined by the interaction of a governor driven by the output shaft and a throttle valve controlled by the accelerator pedal. Thus, the transmission starts with both the torque converter and the gear box multiplying torque. As vehicle speed increases, the gear box section upshifts to direct drive, leaving only the torque converter for any speed-torque changes required. The torque mutliplication ability of the converter multiplied by the planetary gear reduction allows an overall torque multiplication of approximately 4.55 to 1.

Fig. 1 Sectional view of Powerglide with aluminum case

TROUBLE SHOOTING
Oil Forced Out Of Filler Tube

1. Oil level too high; aeration and foaming caused by planet carrier running in oil.
2. Water in oil.
3. Leak in pump suction circuits.

Oil Leaks

1. Transmission case and extension: extension oil seal, shifter shaft oil seal, speedometer driven gear fitting, pressure taps, oil cooler pipe connections, vacuum modulator and case, transmission oil pan gasket.
2. A very smoky exhaust indicates a ruptured vacuum modulator diaphragm.
3. Converter cover pan; front pump attaching bolts, pump seal ring, pump oil seal, plugged oil drain in front pump, porosity in transmission case.

No Drive In Any Position

1. Low oil level.
2. Clogged oil suction screen.
3. Defective pressure regulator valve.
4. Front pump defective.
5. Input shaft broken.
6. Front pump priming valve stuck.

Erratic Operation and Slippage— Light to Medium Throttle

1. Low oil level.
2. Clogged oil suction screen.
3. Improper band adjustment.
4. Band facing worn.
5. Low band apply linkage disengaged or broken.
6. Servo apply passage blocked.
7. Servo piston ring broken or leaking.
8. Converter stator not holding (rare).

Engine Speed Flares On Upshift

1. Low oil level.
2. Improper band adjustment.
3. Clogged oil suction screen.
4. High clutch partially applied—blocked feed orifice.
5. High clutch plates worn.
6. High clutch seals leak.
7. High clutch piston hung up.
8. High clutch drum relief ball not sealing.
9. Vacuum modulator line plugged.
10. Vacuum modulator defective.

Will Not Upshift

1. Maladjusted manual valve lever.
2. Throttle valve stuck or maladjusted.
3. No rear oil pump output caused by stuck priming valve, sheared drive pin or defective pump.
4. Defective governor.
5. Stuck low-drive valve.

Harsh Upshifts

1. Throttle valve linkage improperly adjusted.
2. Vacuum modulator line broken or disconnected.
3. Vacuum modulator diaphragm leaks.

4. Vacuum modulator valve stuck.
5. Hydraulic modulator valve stuck.
6. Improper low band adjustment.

Harsh Closed Throttle (Coast) Downshifts

1. High engine idle speed.
2. Improper band adjustment.
3. Vacuum modulator line broken or disconnected.
4. Modulator diaphragm ruptured.
5. Sticking hydraulic modulator valve, pressure regulator valve or vacuum modulator valve.
6. Downshift timing valve malfunction.

No Downshift (Direct-to-Low) Accelerator Floored

1. Throttle control linkage improperly adjusted.
2. Sticking shifter valve or throttle and detent valve.

Car Creeps In Neutral

1. Manual control linkage improperly adjusted.
2. High clutch or low band not released.

No Drive In Reverse

1. Manual control linkage improperly adjusted.
2. Reverse clutch piston stuck.
3. Reverse clutch plates worn out.
4. Reverse clutch leaking excessively.
5. Blocked reverse clutch apply orifice.

Improper Shift Points

1. Throttle valve linkage improperly adjusted.

2. Incorrectly adjusted throttle velve.
3. Defective governor.
4. Rear pump priming valve stuck.

Burned Clutch Plates

1. Band adjusting screw backed off more than specified.
2. Improper order of clutch plate assembly.
3. Extended operation with low oil level.
4. Stuck relief ball in clutch drum.
5. Abnormally high speed upshift, probably due to:
   a. Improper governor action.
   b. Transmission operated at high speed in manual "Low".

MAINTENANCE
Oil Level

The transmission oil level should be checked every 1000 miles. Oil should be added only when the level is near the "Add" mark on the dipstick with oil hot or at operating temperature.

In order to check oil level accurately, the engine should be idled with the transmission oil hot and the control lever in neutral "N" position.

It is important that the oil level be maintained no higher than the "Full" mark on the oil level gauge. *Do not overfill for when the oil level is at the full mark on the dipstick, it is just slightly below the planetary gear unit. If additional oil is added, bringing the level above the full mark, the planetary unit will run in the oil, foaming and aerating the oil. This aerated oil carried through the various oil pressure passages may cause malfunction of the transmission assembly, resulting in cavitation noise in the converter and improper band or clutch application.*

NOTE: A revised type Dexron fluid is used in 1973 Chevrolet and late 1973 Pontiac transmissions. An early change to a darker color from the usual red color and or a strong odor usually associated with overheated fluid is normal and should not be treated as a positive sign of needed maintenance or unit failure.

The normal maintenance schedule for drain and refill of this type fluid remains unchanged at 24,000 miles under normal service and 12,000 miles under severe operating conditions, such as trailer towing.

Changing Oil

Periodic draining of the oil pan when equipped with a drain plug is recommended every 12,000 miles under normal operating conditions and more frequently under extreme service usage. It is realized that only a portion of the total transmission fluid can be drained at the oil pan. However, the addition of even this volume of fresh fluid will replenish the additives in the remaining fluid sufficiently to increase transmission durability.

After draining the oil pan, pour two quarts of Dexron transmission fluid into the transmission. Then set the parking brake and operate the transmission

through all ranges. With engine idling, transmission selector lever in neutral, and transmission at operating temperature, recheck the fluid level and add fluid as necessary to bring the level to the "Full" mark on the dipstick. Do not overfill as damage to the transmission can result.

Units Without Drain Plug:

When the transmission is to be removed for repairs, drain and refill as follows:

To drain the transmission, carefully loosen the oil pan bolts. Position a receptacle to catch the draining oil. If the transmission is to be removed for repairs, the draining operation may be performed after removal, if desired.

To refill the transmission, remove the dipstick from the filler tube and refill the transmission with Dexron fluid. The engine should then be run at a fast idle speed with the transmission in neutral until the oil warms up. Then add oil as required to raise the fluid level on the dipstick to the "Full" mark. Refill capacity is 1½ quarts.

MANUAL LINKAGE, ADJUST

CAUTION: Shift linkage adjustment must be accurately made. Any inaccuracies may result in premature failure of the transmission due to operation without controls in full detent. Such operation results in reduced oil pressure and in turn partial engagement of the affected clutches. Partial engagement of the clutches with sufficient pressure to cause apparent normal operation of the vehicle will result in failure of the clutches or other internal parts after only a few miles of operation.

1969-73 Chevrolet Column Shift

1. Shift tube and lever assembly must be free in mast jacket.
2. To check for proper adjustment, lift selector lever toward steering wheel. Allow selector lever to be positioned in D by transmission detent.

   NOTE: Do NOT use the indicator pointer as a reference to position the selected lever. When performing linkage adjustment, pointer is adjusted last.

3. Release selector lever. Lever should be inhibited from engaging low range unless the lever is lifted.
4. Lift selector lever towards steering wheel and allow lever to be positioned in N by the transmission detent.
5. Release selector lever. Lever should now be inhibited from engaging reverse range unless lever is lifted.

   NOTE: A properly adjusted linkage will prevent the selector lever from moving from beyond both the neutral detent and the drive detent unless the lever is lifted to pass over the mechanical stop in the steering column.

6. If an adjustment is required, place

the selector lever in D as determined by the transmission detent (see Steps 2 and 3).

7. Loosen adjusting swivel at cross shaft and rotate the transmission lever so that it contacts the drive stop in the steering column.
8. Tighten swivel and recheck adjustment.
9. Readjust indicator needle if required.
10. Adjust back drive linkage as described further on.

1969-73 Nova Console Shift

1. Loosen assembly nuts A and B, Fig. 2, on lower rod.
2. Set transmission lever in Drive position.
3. Set pawl rod in the Neutral or Drive notch of detent.
4. Apply load in direction of arrow on actuating lever until pawl rod comes in contact with detent.
5. Place a .094" spacer between nut and swivel and run nut up until it touches spacer. Tighten nut B against swivel and lock swivel between nuts.
6. Place transmission and shift lever in Park position.
7. Install column rod to column lever, and cross shaft.
8. Set selector lever in Park and adjust Back Drive as described further on.

NOTE: With ignition key in the Lock position and transmission selector lever in Park, the key can be removed and the steering wheel locked.

1973 Vega Console Shift

1. Place transmission lever in Neutral by rotating lever clockwise to Park, then two detents counter-clockwise to Neutral.
2. Place shift lever in Neutral.
3. Insert flats on swivel into slot in rod and tighten nut to 120 pound inches, Fig. 2A.

1971-72 Vega Console Shift

1. Loosen nut and perform steps 1 and 2 as outlined in the 1973 Vega Console Shift adjustment.
2. Apply rearward force on lever until shift lever contacts detent stop. Install a .073 inch spacer between forward nut and swivel and tighten nut against spacer, Fig. 2B.
3. Remove spacer and apply a forward force on lever and tighten rearward nut.

1970-72 Chevelle & Monte Carlo Console Shift

1. Place shift lever in Drive.
2. Raise vehicle. Disconnect cable from transmission lever, Fig. 3.
3. Manually place transmission lever in Drive.
4. Measure distance from rearward face of attachment bracket to center of cable attachment pin. This dimension

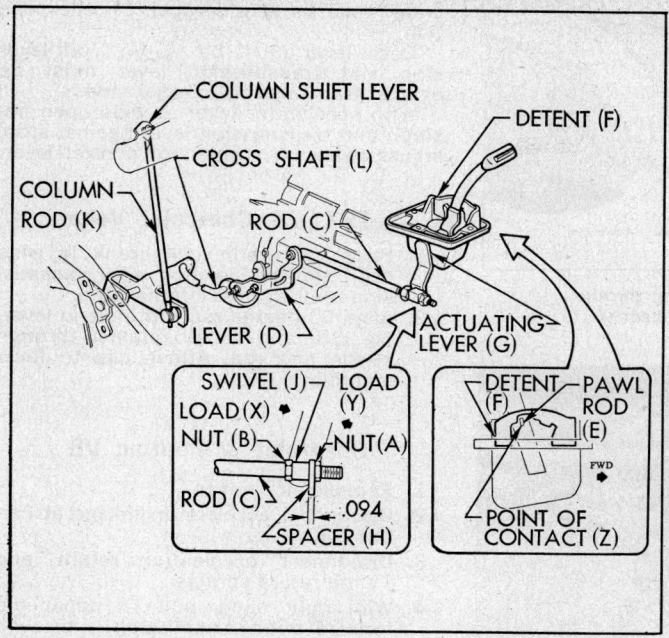

Fig. 2   Manual linkage adjustment. 1969-73
Nova console shift

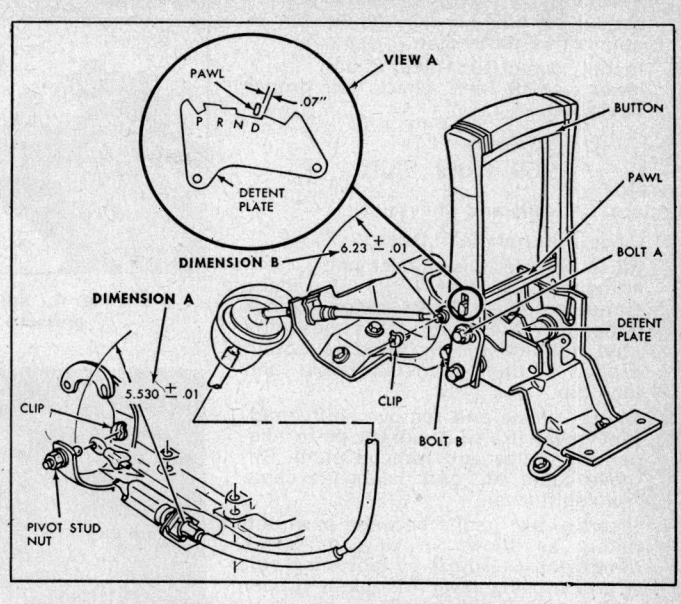

Fig. 3A   Floor shift linkage adjustment. 1969
Camaro, Chevelle & Chevrolet

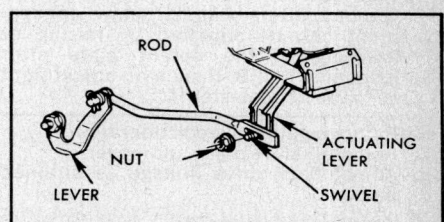

Fig. 2A   Manual linkage adjustment.
1973 Vega console shift

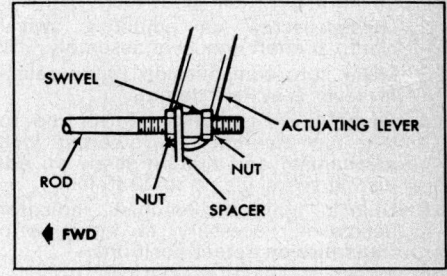

Fig. 2B   Manual linkage adjustment.
1971-72 Vega console shift

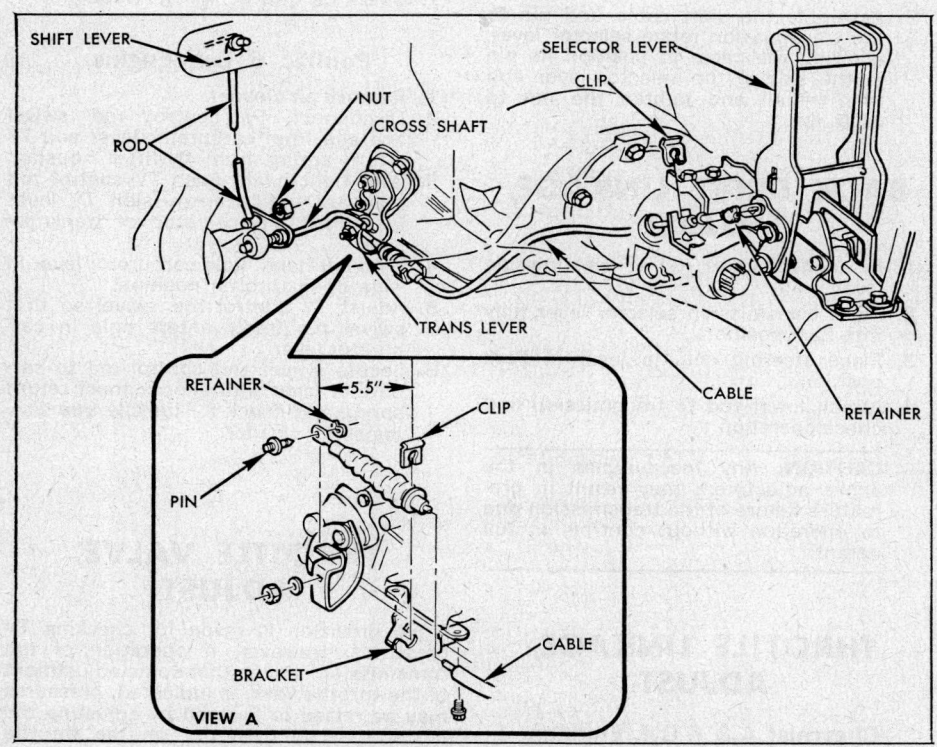

Fig. 3   Floor shift linkage adjustment.
1970-72 Chevelle & Monte Carlo

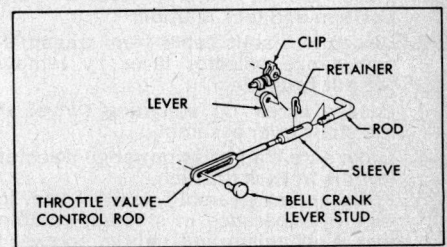

Fig. 3B   Throttle linkage adjustment.
1971-73 Vega

should be 5.5". If not, adjust pin to obtain this dimension.

5. Install cable to transmission lever, lower vehicle and check for proper operation.

1969 Floor Shift

Camaro, Chevelle and Chevrolet

1. Place shift handle in Drive.
2. Raise vehicle. Disconnect cable from transmission lever, Fig. 3A. Place transmission in Drive range. Check dimension A and adjust by loosening stud nut and moving stud to obtain proper setting. Reinstall cable and lock clip.
3. Lower vehicle and remove shift quadrant cover. Raise quadrant plate, disconnect bulbs and remove plate. Remove cable clip and disengage cable from shift lever.
4. Insert a .07" gauge between pawl and detent as shown in view A. Check dimension B. Adjust by loosening bolt A and moving lever to obtain proper adjustment. Tighten bolt.
5. Adjust cable end until it freely enters pin. Install clip.

NOTE: If lift on handle button does not clear detents or detents can be cleared without lifting handle, pawl engagement can be adjusted by raising or lowering of the detent plate after loosening bolt B. If such an adjustment is made repeat step 4.

6. Remove gauge. Check operation.
7. Reinstall shift plate and cover.
8. Adjust back drive linkage as outlined below.

1970-73 Pontiac Column Shift

1. Place steering column selector lever in Park position and lock ignition.
2. Loosen screw on adjusting swivel clamp at shaft and lever assembly.
3. Make sure transmission range selector lever is in Park detent.
4. Push up on gearshift control rod to take up clearance in steering lock mechanism and tighten screw on adjusting swivel clamp to 20 ft. lbs.
5. Unlock ignition, readjust indicator needle if necessary to agree with transmission detent positions.

1970-73 Pontiac Console Shift

1. Place console gearshift lever in Park position and lock ignition.
2. Disconnect shift cable from transmission range selector lever by removing nut from pin.
3. Loosen screw on adjusting swivel at the shaft lever assembly.
4. Make sure transmission range selector lever is in Park position.
5. Push up on gearshift control rod to take up clearance in steering column lock mechanism and tighten screw on adjusting swivel to 20 ft. lbs.
6. Unlock ignition and rotate transmission range selector lever counterclock-

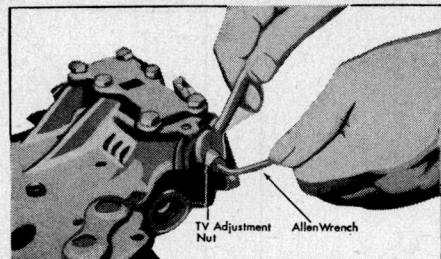

Fig. 4   Adjusting throttle pressure (on bench)

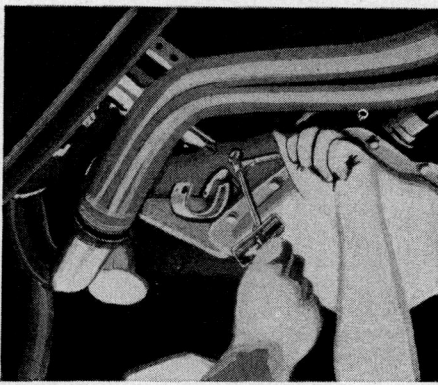

Fig. 4A   Adjusting low band (in vehicle)

wise by two detent positions.

7. Set the console gearshift lever in Neutral range and move it forward against its stop in Neutral.
8. Assemble the shift cable and pin to the transmission range selector lever, allowing the cable to position its pin in the slot of the selector lever and then install and tighten the nut to 20 ft. lbs.

BACK DRIVE LINKAGE, ADJUST

1. Disconnect lower rod at transmission lever.
2. Move transmission selector lever fully into Park position.
3. Place steering column lever in Park position.
4. Attach lower rod to transmission and check operation.

CAUTION: Any inaccuracies in the above adjustment may result in premature failure of the transmission due to operation without controls in full detent.

THROTTLE LINKAGE, ADJUST

Chevrolet 4 & 6 Cyl. Engines Exc. Vega

With accelerator pedal depressed, bell-

crank must be at wide open throttle position.

Dash lever must be $1/64$-$1/16$" off lever stop and transmission lever must be against transmission internal stop.

With accelerator lever in wide open position and transmission lever against stop, adjust swivel to accelerator control lever.

1971-73 Chevrolet Vega

1. Place carburetor bell crank in wide open throttle position and transmission lever against internal stop.
2. Align 90 degree rod with hole in lever, Fig. 3B, and install retainer through sleeve and rod. Attach clip to lever and rod.

Chevrolet & Pontiac V8

1. Remove air cleaner.
2. Disconnect accelerator linkage at carburetor.
3. Disconnect accelerator return and TV rod return springs.
4. With right hand, pull TV upper rod forward until transmission is through detent. With left hand, open carburetor to wide open throttle position. Carburetor must reach wide open throttle position at the same time the ball stud contacts the end of slot in upper TV rod.
5. Adjust swivel on end of upper TV rod to obtain setting described in step 4. Allowable tolerance is about $1/32$".
6. Connect and adjust accelerator linkage.
7. Check for throttle linkage freedom.

Pontiac 6 Cyl. Engine

1. Remove air cleaner.
2. Disconnect TV control rod swivel and clip from carburetor lever and TV return spring from flywheel housing.
3. With right hand, push TV control rod rearward until transmission TV lever is against internal stop of transmission.
4. With left hand, hold carburetor lever in wide open throttle position.
5. Adjust TV control rod swivel so that swivel pin freely enters hole in carburetor lever.
6. Secure swivel and control rod to carburetor lever with clip, connect return spring and check for linkage freeness. Install air cleaner.

THROTTLE VALVE, ADJUST

No provision is made for checking TV pressures. However, if operation of the transmission is such that some adjustment of the throttle valve is indicated, pressures may be raised or lowered by adjusting the position of the jam nut on the throttle valve assembly, Fig. 4.

To raise TV pressure 3 psi, back off the jam nut one full turn. This increases the dimension from the jam nut to the TV valve stop. Conversely, tightening the jam nut one full turn lowers TV pressure 3 psi.

A difference of 3 psi in TV pressure will cause a change of approximately 2 to 3 mph in the wide open throttle upshift point. Smaller pressure adjustments can be made by partial turns of the jam nut. The end of the TV adjusting screw has an allen head so the screw may be held stationary while the jam nut is moved. *Use care when making this adjustment since no pressure tap is provided to check TV pressure.*

LOW BAND, ADJUST

Low band adjustment should be performed at 12,000 mile intervals, or sooner if operating performance indicates low band slippage.

1. Raise vehicle and place selector lever in Neutral.
2. Remove protective cap from transmission adjusting screw.

NOTE: On Chevelle models, to gain clearance between underbody and transmission, it may be necessary to remove rear mount bolts from crossmember and move transmission slightly toward passenger side of vehicle.

Loosen adjusting screw locknut 3/4 turn and hold in this position with a wrench, Fig. 4A.

Using a suitable inch-pound torque wrench as shown, adjust band to 70 inch-lbs and back off four complete turns for a band that has been in operation for 6000 miles or more, or three turns for one in use less than 6000 miles.

CAUTION: Be sure to hold the locknut at 1/4 turn loose during the adjusting procedure. Then tighten locknut. The amount of back off is not an approximate figure; it must be exact.

VACUUM MODULATOR VALVE

1. To remove, disconnect line from vac-

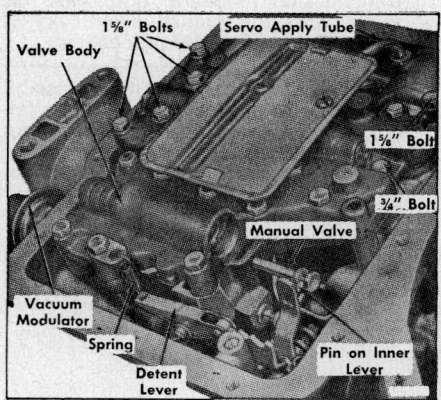

Fig. 7   Control valve assembly installed

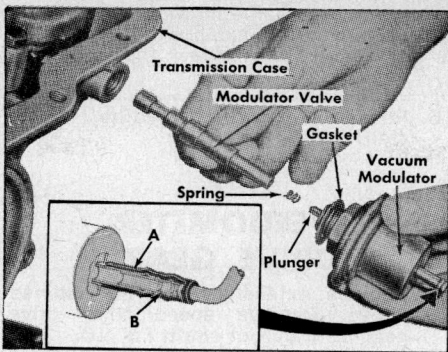

Fig. 5   Vacuum modulator, gasket and valve

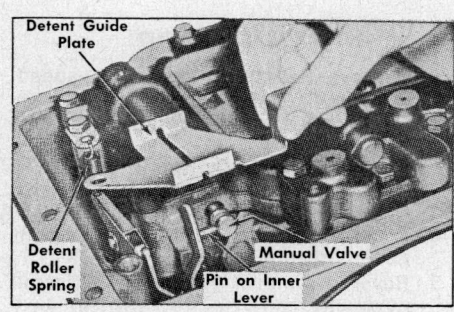

Fig. 6   Detent guide plate installation

uum modulator, Fig. 5.
2. Unscrew vacuum modulator from oil pan.
3. Remove vacuum modulator, gasket and valve.
4. Reverse removal procedure to install.

LOW SERVO

1. Remove servo cover and gasket (3 screws).
2. Remove cover oil seal, servo piston and return spring.
3. Reverse removal procedure to install.

Fig. 8   Inner control levers, parking pawl and bracket

CONTROL VALVE BODY

1. To remove control valve, remove vacuum modulator valve as outlined above.
2. Remove oil pan and gasket.
3. Remove two bolts attaching detent guide plate to valve body and transmission case. Remove guide plate and range selector detent roller spring, Fig. 6.
4. Remove remaining control valve bolts, Fig. 7.
5. Carefully remove valve body and gasket, disengaging servo apply tube from transmission case as valve body is removed.
6. Reverse removal procedure to install valve body, being sure range selector detent lever is in position shown in Fig. 7 and that pin on parking lock and range selector inner lever is engaged in slot in manual valve.

PARKING PAWL

After removing the control valve assembly as outlined above, remove the parking pawl, bracket and inner control levers. To make the installation, proceed as follows:

1. Install parking lock pawl and shaft. Install a new "E" ring on shaft.
2. Install parking lock pawl pull-back spring over its boss to rear of pawl. Short leg of spring should locate in hole in parking pawl, Fig. 8.
3. Install parking lock pawl reaction bracket (2 bolts). Fit actuator assembly between parking lock pawl and bracket.
4. Insert outer shift lever into case, making sure to pick up inner shift lever and parking lock assembly. Tighten Allen head nut.
5. Insert outer TV lever and shaft special washer and O-ring seal into case and pick up inner TV lever. Tighten Allen head nut.
6. Install selector lever detent roller.
7. Install valve body as directed above.

EXTENSION HOUSING SEAL

1. Referring to Fig. 9, disconnect propeller shaft from transmission.
2. Use a suitable puller to remove extension rear oil seal.

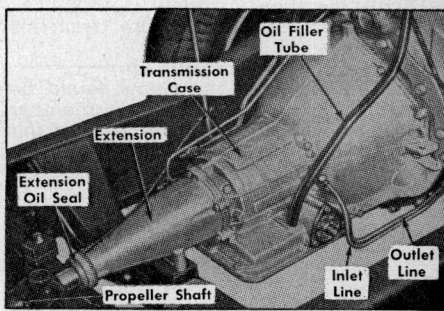

Fig. 9   Exterior of transmission

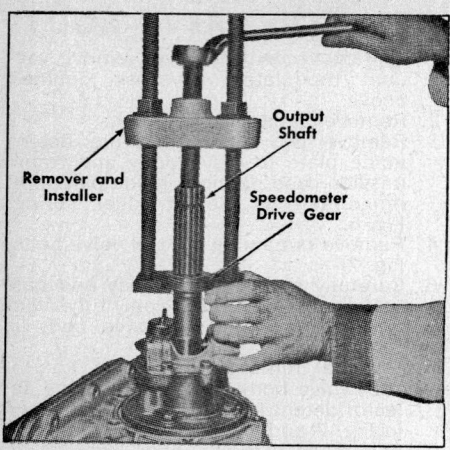

Fig. 10 Removing speedometer drive gear

3. With a suitable installer, drive new seal into bore of extension. Sealing cement should be used at outer diameter of seal to prevent leakage. Wipe off excess cement. Reconnect propeller shaft.

EXTENSION BUSHING

1. Remove extension oil seal as outlined above. Then, using a suitable remover too, pull bushing from rear of extension.
2. Place new bushing in pilot end of a suitable installer and drive bushing into bore of extension. Install rear oil seal.

SPEEDOMETER DRIVEN GEAR

1. Disconnect speedometer drive cable fitting. Remove cap screw and retainer clip holding driven gear in extension and remove gear.
2. Reverse removal procedure to install.

EXTENSION CASE

1. Disconnect propeller shaft from transmission output shaft.
2. Disconnect speedometer cable fitting.
3. Install transmission lift to support transmission and engine.
4. Unfasten extension from support crossmember (2 studs).
5. Unfasten extension from transmission case (5 bolts.)

NOTE: *Remove any shims found between extension and crossmember. Tie shims together as it is vital that*

exactly the same number of shims be used when the extension is reinstalled as these shims affect the drive line angle.

6. Reverse removal procedure to install.

SPEEDOMETER DRIVE GEAR

1. Remove extension case as outlined above. Remove speedometer drive gear from output shaft, Fig. 10.
2. Using a suitable installer, install gear on output shaft and replace extension case.

GOVERNOR

1. Remove extension case and speedometer drive gear as outlined above.
2. Remove "C" clip from governor shaft on weight side of governor.
3. Remove shaft and governor valve from opposite side of governor. Remove two Belleville springs, Fig. 11.
4. Loosen governor drive screw and lift governor from output shaft.
5. Reverse removal procedure to install governor. However, be sure concave side of Belleville springs are against transmission output shaft.

TRANSMISSION, REPLACE
1969-73

1. Disconnect oil cooler lines (external cooled models), vacuum modulator line and speedometer drive cable fitting at transmission. Tie lines out of the way.
2. Disconnect manual and TV rods from transmission.
3. Disconnect propeller shaft from transmission.
4. Attach transmission jack on transmission.
5. Disconnect engine rear mount on transmission extension, then disconnect transmission support crossmember and slide rearward. Remove crossmember on 1969 Camaro.
6. Remove converter underpan. Scribe flywheel-converter relationship for reassembly, then remove flywheel-to-converter bolts.

NOTE: The "light" side of the converter is denoted by a "blue" stripe painted across the ends of the converter cover and housing. This marking should be aligned as closely as possible with the "white" stripe

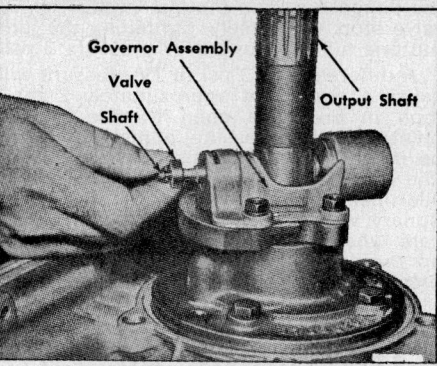

Fig. 11 Removing governor valve and shaft

painted on the engine side of the flywheel outer rim (heavy side of engine) to maintain balance during assembly.

7. Support engine at oil pan rail with a jack or other suitable brace capable of supporting engine when transmission is removed.
8. Lower rear of transmission slightly so that upper transmission housing-to-engine attaching bolts can be reached, using a universal socket and a long extension. Remove upper bolts.

CAUTION: On V8 engines, care must be taken not to lower rear of transmission to far as the distributor housing may be forced against the dash, causing damage to the distributor. It is best to have an assistant observe clearance of all upper engine components while transmission rear end is being lowered.

9. Remove remainder of transmission-to-engine bolts.
10. Remove transmission by moving it slightly to the rear and downward, then remove from under vehicle.

NOTE: Observe converter when moving transmission rearward. If it does not move with the transmission, pry it free of flywheel before proceeding.

CAUTION: Keep front of transmission upward to prevent converter from falling out. Install a suitable holding strap or length of strong wire across the housing to keep the converter in place.

11. Reverse procedure to install.

CHRYSLER TORQUEFLITE &
AMERICAN MOTORS TORQUE-COMMAND

IDENTIFICATION

Transmission identification markings shown in the following application chart are cast in raised letters and numerals on the lower left side of the bell housing. NOTE: There are sufficient variations within each of the main categories listed below to make it necessary to service them by serial number—a stamped 7-digit number appearing on the oil pan side rail.

CHRYSLER CORPORATION

1972-74 6-198, 225 engine................................A-904
        6-225 engine, police & taxi........................A-727
        V8-318 engine.......................................A-904-LA
        V8-318 engine, police & taxi.....................A-727
        V8-340, 360, 400, 440 engines...................A-727

1969-71 6-170, 6-198, 6-225 engines.................A-904-G
        V8-273 engine.......................................A-904-A
        V8-318 engine.......................................A-904-LA

CHRYSLER CORP.—(Continued)

        6-225 police and taxi..............................A-727-RG
        V8-318, V8-340; V8-360 engines................A-727-A
        V8-383, V8-426, V8-440.........................A-727-B

AMERICAN MOTORS

1972-74 6-232, 258 engines............................904
        6-258, V8-304, 360, 401 Heavy Duty..............727
        V8-304 engine.......................................998
        V8-360, 401 engines................................727

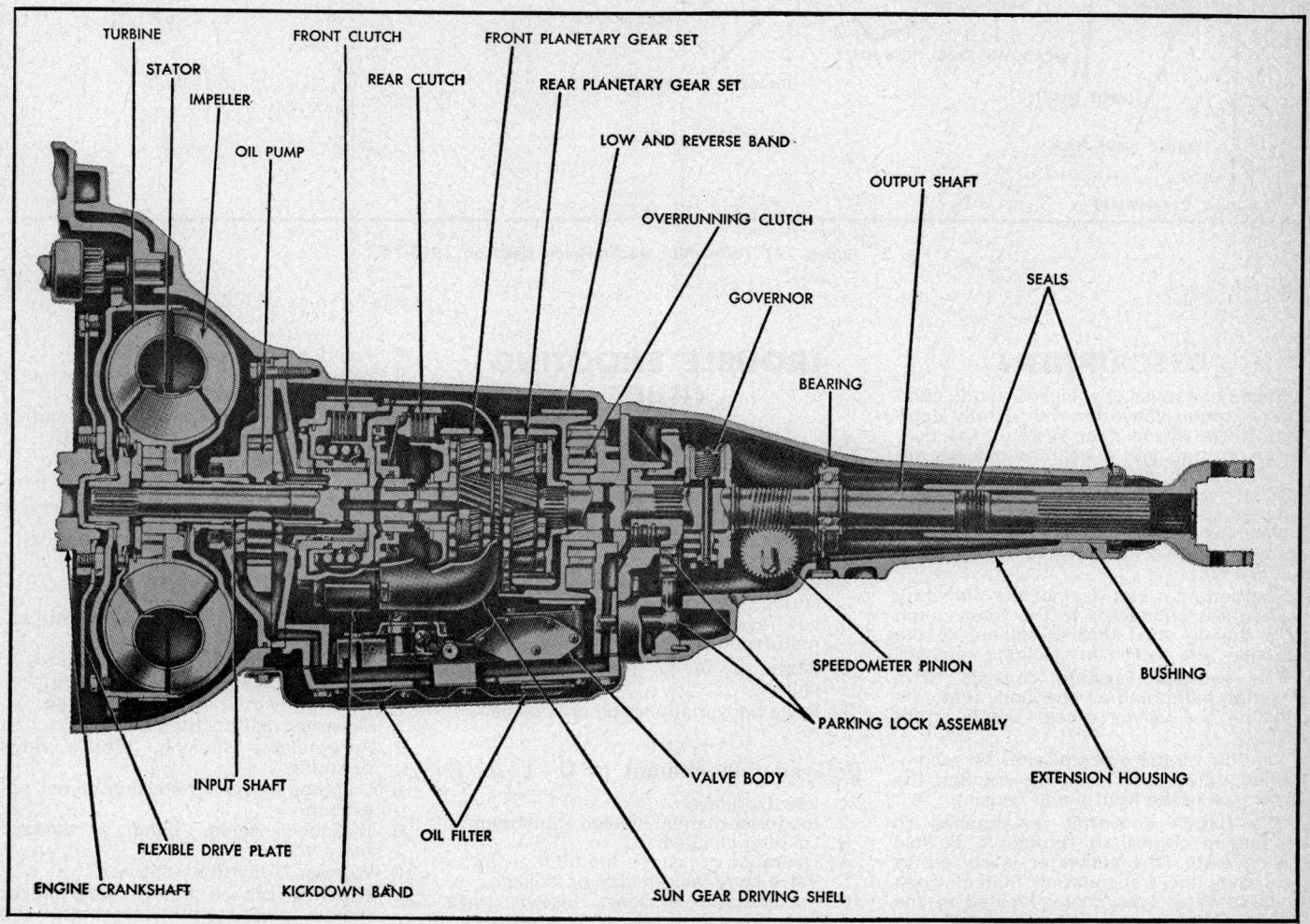

Fig. 1   Series 904 Torqueflite transmission used on 1969-74. 998 model is similar

TORQUEFLITE & TORQUE-COMMAND

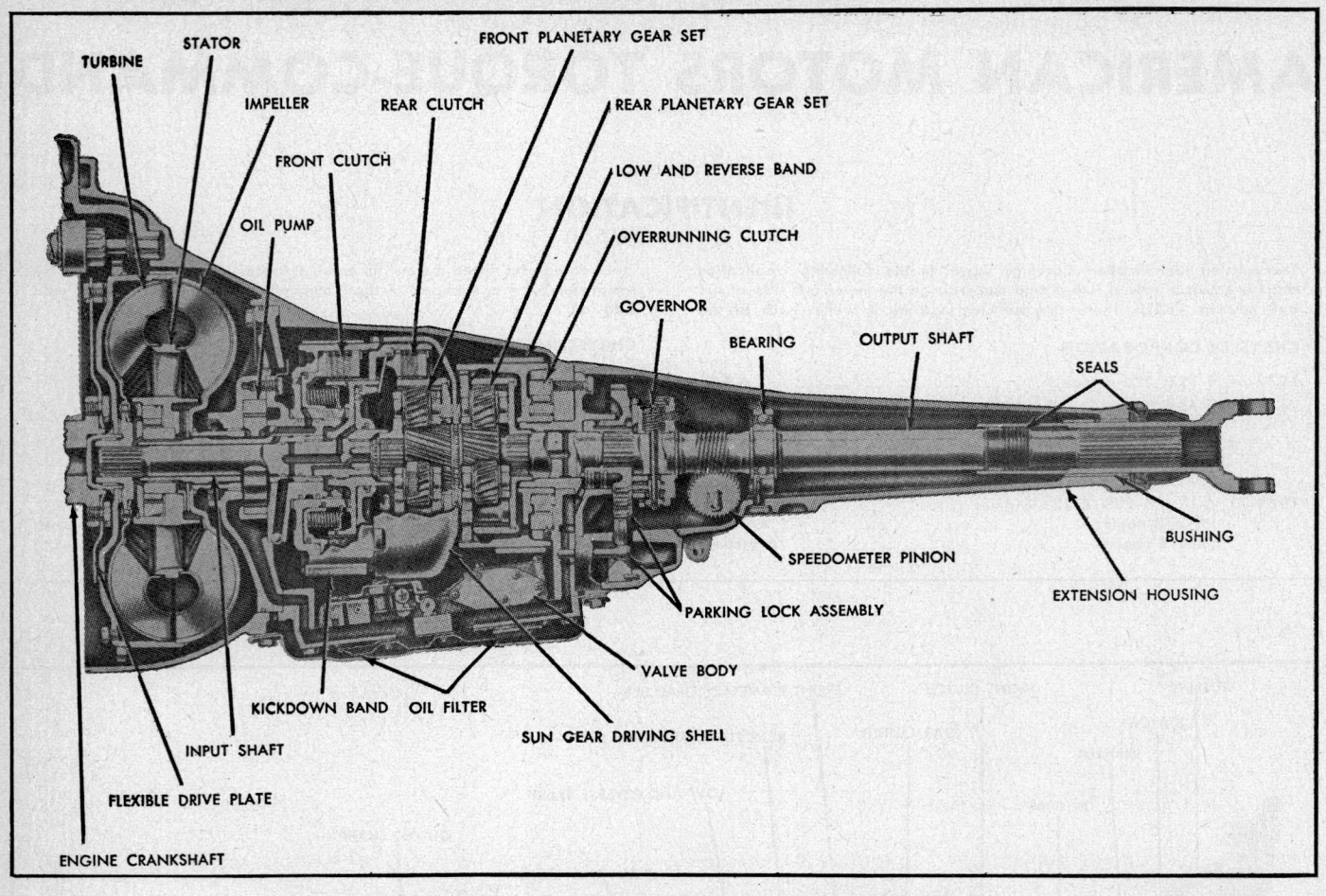

Fig. 2 Series 727 Torqueflite transmission used on 1969-74

DESCRIPTION

These transmissions, Figs. 1 and 2, combine a torque converter with a fully automatic three speed gear system. The converter housing and transmission case are an integral aluminum casting. The transmission consists of two multiple disc clutches, an overrunning (one-way) clutch, two servos and bands and two planetary gear sets to provide three forward speeds and reverse.

The common sun gear of the planetary gear sets is connected to the front clutch by a driving shell that is splined to the sun gear and to the front clutch retainer.

The hydraulic system consists of a single oil pump and a valve body that contains all the valves except the governor valve.

Venting of the transmission is accomplished by a drilled passage through the upper part of the front pump housing.

The torque converter is attached to the engine crankshaft through a flexible driving plate. The converter is cooled by circulating the transmission fluid through an oil-to-water type cooler located in the radiator lower tank. The converter is a sealed assembly that cannot be disassembled.

TROUBLE SHOOTING GUIDE

Harsh Engagement In D - 1 - 2 - R

1. Engine idle speed too high.
2. Hydraulic pressures too high or too low.
3. Low-reverse band out of adjustment.
4. Accumulator sticking, broken rings or spring.
5. Low-reverse servo, band or linkage malfunction.
6. Worn or faulty front and/or rear clutch.
7. Valve body malfunction or leakage.

Delayed Engagement In D - 1 - 2 - R

1. Low fluid level.
2. Incorrect manual linkage adjustment.
3. Oil filter clogged.
4. Hydraulic pressures too high or low.
5. Valve body malfunction or leakage.
6. Accumulator sticking, broken rings or spring.
7. Clutches or servos sticking or not operating.
8. Faulty front oil pump.
9. Worn or faulty front and/or rear clutch.
10. Worn or broken input shaft and/or reaction shaft support seal rings.
11. Aerated fluid.

Runaway or Harsh Upshift and 3 - 2 Kickdown

1. Low fluid level.
2. Incorrect throttle linkage adjustment.
3. Hydraulic pressures too high or low.
4. Kickdown band out of adjustment.
5. Valve body malfunction or leakage.
6. Governor malfunction.
7. Accumulator sticking, broken rings or spring.
8. Clutches or servos sticking or not operating.
9. Kickdown servo, band or linkage malfunction.
10. Worn or faulty front clutch.
11. Worn or broken input shaft and/or reaction shaft support seal rings.
12. Aerated oil.
13. Clogged oil filter.

TORQUEFLITE & TORQUE-COMMAND

No Upshift

1. Low fluid level.
2. Incorrect throttle linkage adjustment.
3. Kickdown band out of adjustment.
4. Hydraulic pressures too high or low.
5. Governor sticking.
6. Valve body malfunction or leakage.
7. Accumulator sticking, broken rings or spring.
8. Clutches or servos sticking or not operating.
9. Faulty oil pump.
10. Kickdown servo, band or linkage malfunction.
11. Worn or faulty front clutch.
12. Worn or broken input shaft and/or reaction shaft support seal rings.
13. Incorrect gearshift linkage adjustment.
14. Governor support seal rings broken or worn.

Delayed Upshift

1. Incorrect throttle linkage adjustment.
2. Kickdown band out of adjustment.
3. Governor support seal rings broken or worn.
4. Worn or broken reaction shaft support seal rings.
5. Governor malfunction.
6. Kickdown servo band or linkage malfunction.
7. Worn or faulty front clutch.

No Kickdown or Normal Downshift

1. Incorrect throttle linkage adjustment.
2. Incorrect gearshift linkage adjustment.
3. Kickdown band out of adjustment.
4. Hydraulic pressure too high or low.
5. Governor sticking.
6. Valve body malfunction or leakage.
7. Accumulator sticking, broken rings or spring.
8. Clutches or servos sticking or not operating.
9. Kickdown servo, band or linkage malfunction.
10. Overrunning clutch not holding.

Erratic Shifts

1. Low fluid level.
2. Aerated fluid.
3. Incorrect throttle linkage adjustment.
4. Incorrect gearshift control linkage adjustment.
5. Hydraulic pressures too high or low.
6. Governor sticking.
7. Oil filter clogged.
8. Valve body malfunction or leakage.
9. Clutches or servos sticking or not operating.
10. Faulty oil pump.
11. Worn or broken input shaft and/or reaction shaft support rings.
12. Governor support seal rings broken or worn.
13. Kickdown servo band or linkage malfunction.
14. Worn or faulty front clutch.

Slips In Forward Drive Positions

1. Low oil level.

2. Aerated fluid.
3. Incorrect throttle linkage adjustment.
4. Incorrect gearshift control linkage adjustment.
5. Hydraulic pressures too low.
6. Valve body malfunction or leakage.
7. Accumulator sticking, broken rings or springs.
8. Clutches or servos sticking or not operating.
9. Worn or faulty front and/or rear clutch.
10. Overrunning clutch not holding.
11. Worn or broken input shaft and/or reaction shaft support seal rings.
12. Clogged oil filter.
13. Faulty oil pump.
14. Overrunning clutch worn, broken or seized.

Slips In Reverse Only

1. Low fluid level.
2. Aerated fluid.
3. Incorrect gearshift control linkage adjustment.
4. Hydraulic pressures too high or low.
5. Low-reverse band out of adjustment.
6. Valve body malfunction or leakage.
7. Front clutch or rear servo sticking or not operating.
8. Low-reverse servo, band or linkage malfunction.
9. Faulty oil pump.
10. Worn or broken reaction shaft support seal rings.
11. Worn or faulty front clutch.

Slips In All Positions

1. Low fluid level.
2. Hydraulic pressures too low.
3. Valve body malfunction or leakage.
4. Faulty oil pump.
5. Clutches or servos sticking or not operating.
6. Worn or broken input shaft and/or reaction shaft support seal rings.
7. Oil filter clogged.
8. Aerated oil.

No Drive In Any Position

1. Low fluid level.
2. Hydraulic pressures too low.
3. Oil filter clogged.
4. Valve body malfunction or leakage.
5. Faulty oil pump.
6. Clutches or servos sticking or not operating.
7. Planetary gear sets broken or seized.

No Drive In Forward Drive Positions

1. Hydraulic pressures too low.
2. Valve body malfunction or leakage.
3. Accumulator sticking, broken rings or spring.
4. Clutches or servos, sticking or not operating.
5. Worn or faulty rear clutch.
6. Overrunning clutch not holding.
7. Worn or broken input shaft and/or reaction shaft support seal rings.
8. Low fluid level.
9. Planetary gear sets broken or seized.
10. Overrunning clutch worn, broken or seized.

No Drive In Reverse

1. Incorrect gearshift control linkage adjustment.
2. Hydraulic pressures too low.
3. Low-reverse band out of adjustment.
4. Valve body malfunction or leakage.
5. Front clutch or rear servo sticking or not operating.
6. Low-reverse servo, band or linkage malfunction.
7. Worn or faulty front and/or rear clutch.
8. Worn or broken reaction shaft support seal rings.
9. Planetary gear sets broken or seized.

Drives In Neutral

1. Incorrect gearshift control linkage adjustment.
2. Valve body malfunction or leakage.
3. Rear clutch worn, faulty, dragging or inoperative.
4. Insufficient clutch plate clearance.

Drags or Locks

1. Kickdown band out of adjustment.
2. Low-reverse band out of adjustment.
3. Kickdown and/or low-reverse servo, band or linkage malfunction.
4. Front and/or rear clutch faulty.
5. Planetary gear sets broken or seized.
6. Overrunning clutch worn, broken or seized.

Grating, Scraping or Growling Noise

1. Kickdown band out of adjustment.
2. Low-reverse band out of adjustment.
3. Output shaft bearing and/or bushing damaged.
4. Governor support binding or broken seal rings.
5. Oil pump scored or binding.
6. Front and/or rear clutch faulty.
7. Planetary gear sets broken or seized.
8. Overrunning clutch worn, broken or seized.

Buzzing Noise

1. Low fluid level.
2. Pump sucking air.
3. Valve body malfunction.
4. Overrunning clutch inner race damaged.
5. Aerated oil.

Hard to Fill, Oil Flows Out Filler Tube

1. High fluid level.
2. Breather clogged.
3. Oil filter clogged.
4. Aerated fluid.

Transmission Overheats

1. Low fluid level.
2. Kickdown band adjustment too tight.
3. Low-reverse band adjustment too tight.

4. Faulty cooling system.
5. Cracked or restricted oil cooler line or fitting.
6. Faulty oil pump.
7. Insufficient clutch plate clearance in front and/or rear clutches.
8. Engine idle too low.
9. Hydraulic pressures too low.
10. Incorrect gearshift linkage adjustment.
11. Kickdown band adjustment too tight.

Starter Will Not Energize in Neutral or Park

1. Incorrect gearshift control linkage adjustment.
2. Faulty or incorrectly adjusted neutral starting switch.
3. Broken lead to neutral switch.

MAINTENANCE

Adding Oil

To check the oil level, apply the parking brake and operate the engine at idle speed with the transmission in Neutral position. Add oil as necessary.

Changing Oil

Fluid and filter changes or band adjustments are not required for average passenger car use. Severe usage such as police, taxi, trailer towing or prolonged operation in city traffic, requires that fluid and filter be changed and bands adjusted every 24,000 miles.

Whenever the factory fill fluid is changed, only fluids of the type labeled DEXRON should be used.

1. Remove drain plug (if equipped) from transmission oil pan and allow oil to drain.

NOTE: *If the oil pan does not have a drain plug, loosen pan bolts and tap pan with a soft mallet to break it loose, permitting fluid to drain.*

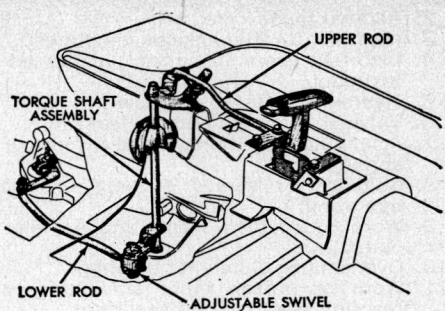

Fig. 3   Console gearshift linkage. 1971-73 Barracuda, Challenger, Charger, Coronet & Satellite

2. Remove flywheel access plate, remove torque converter drain plug and allow to drain. Replace drain plug.
3. Remove transmission oil pan, replace filter or clean intake screen and pan, adjust bands and reinstall.
4. Install initial amount of approved automatic transmission fluid through filler tube (five quarts on Series 904 and 998 units; eight quarts on Series 727 units.
5. Start engine and add approximately one quart while engine is idling.
6. Allow engine to idle for about two minutes. Then with parking brake applied, place transmission in neutral.
7. Add oil as necessary to bring to proper level.

BANDS, ADJUST

Kickdown Band

The kickdown band adjusting screw is located on the left side of the transmission case near the throttle lever shaft.

1. Loosen lock nut and back off approximately five turns. Check adjusting screw for free turning in transmission case.
2. Using an inch-pound torque wrench,

tighten the band adjusting screw to a reading of 72 inch lbs.
3. Back off adjusting screw 2 turns with the following exceptions:

Chrysler Corp.

6-170 engine . . . . 2⅝ turns
V8-426, 1969-71 . . . . . . 1½ turns
V8-440 3 carbs. 1971-72 . 1½ turns
V8-440 dual exhaust,
1971-74 . . . . 2 turns
All other 1971-74 with
A-727 model trans . . . 2½ turns

American Motors

1972
All Exc. V8-360 2
V8-360 . . . . 2½

1973-74
6-232, 258, V8-304, 360①, 401 . . . 2
V8-360 . . . . 2½
6-232①, V8-304① 2½
①Heavy Duty
Hold adjusting screw in this position and tighten locknut.

Low and Reverse Band

1. Raise vehicle, drain transmission and remove oil pan.
2. Inspect fluid for friction material or metal particles which indicate damaged or worn parts.
3. Loosen adjusting screw lock nut and back off nut approximately five turns. Check adjusting screw for free turning in lever.
4. Using an inch pound torque wrench, tighten band adjusting screw to 72 in. lbs. on all except 1974 904 series transmissions. On 1974 904 series transmissions, tighten adjusting screw to 41 in. lbs.
5. Back off adjusting screw the amount of turns indicated:

American Motors

1972-73 904 Series . . . . 3½ turns

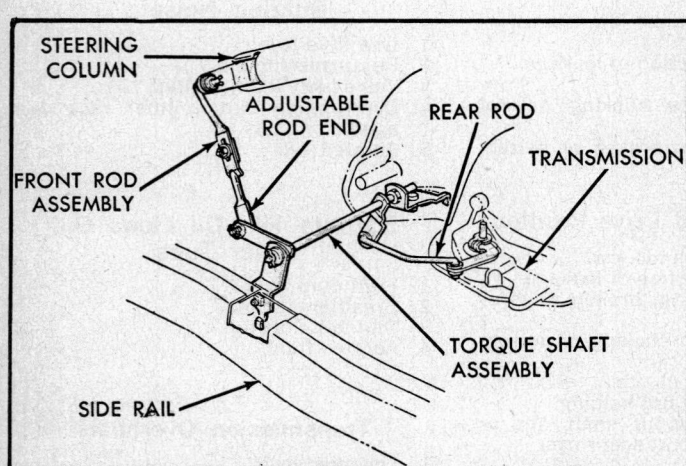

Fig. 4   Column gearshift linkage. 1970-72 Chrysler, Imperial, Fury, Monaco & Polara

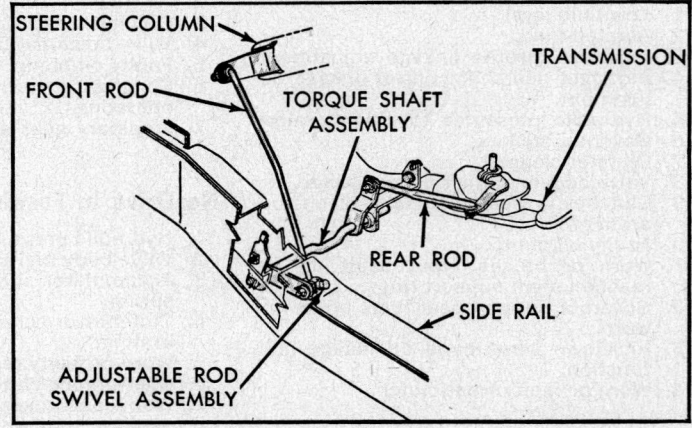

Fig. 5   Column gearshift linkage. 1970-74 Barracuda & Challenger. 1971-74 Coronet, Charger & Satellite. 1974 Chrysler, Imperial, Fury, Polara & Monaco

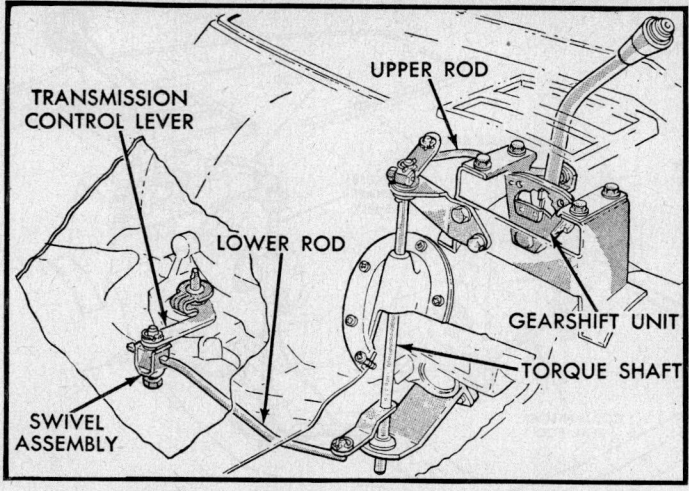

Fig. 6 Console gearshift linkage. 1971-74 Dart & Valiant, 1969 All & 1973 Fury

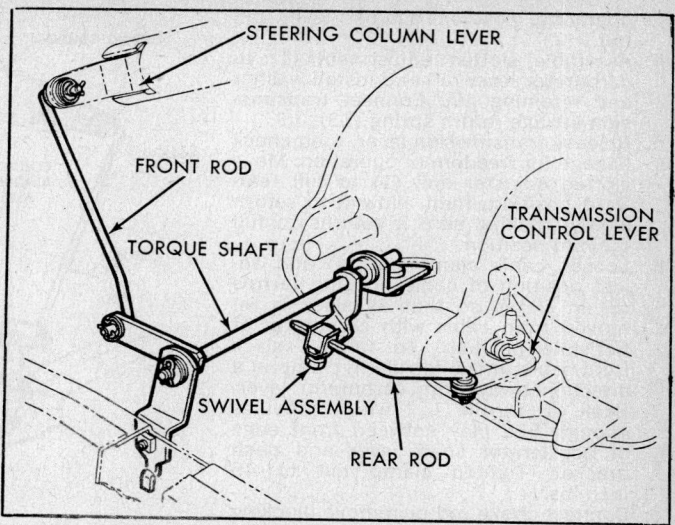

Fig. 7 Column gearshift linkage. 1969 Chrysler, Dodge, Imperial & Plymouth 1970 Belvedere, Charger, Coronet & Satellite; 1970-74 Dart & Valiant

1974 904 Series . . . . 7 turns
998 Series . . . . 4 turns
727 Series . . . . 2 turns

Chrysler Corp.
1969-73 904 Series with
 6 cyl. . . . . 3¼ turns
1974 904 Series with
 6 cyl. . . . . 7 turns
1969-74 904 Series
 with V8-318 . . . . 4 turns
727 Series . . . . 2 turns
6. Hold adjusting screw and tighten to 35 ft. lbs., then install oil pan and refill transmission.

GEARSHIFT CONTROL LINKAGE, ADJUST
1969-74 Chrysler Corp.

1. Referring to Figs. 3 to 9, place selector lever in Park and loosen control rod swivel clamp screw a few turns.

NOTE: On 1972 Chrysler, Fury, Monaco and Polara, the column front lock rod and only the rear rod swivel assembly are adjustable.

2. Move transmission control lever all the way to rear (in Park detent).
3. With both levers still in Park position, tighten swivel clamp screw securely.

1972-74 American Motors

Place the selector lever in the Park position and place the transmission shift lever in the Park detent. Adjust the shift rod to obtain a "free pin" fit. Check steering column lock for ease of operation. Move selector lever to Neutral position and check safety switch operation.

THROTTLE LINKAGE, ADJUST
American Motors
1974

1. Disconnect throttle control spring, then use spring to hold transmission throttle control lever forward against stop, Fig. 10.
2. Block choke open and set throttle off fast idle.

NOTE: On carburetors equipped with a throttle solenoid, energize solenoid and open throttle half way to allow solenoid to lock and return carburetor to idle.

3. Loosen retaining bolt on throttle control adjusting link. On 6 cylinder engines, do not remove spring clip and nylon washer. On V8 engines, remove spring clip and nylon washer from link.
4. On 6 cylinder engines, pull on end of link to eliminate lash and tighten retaining bolt, Fig. 12. On V8 engines, push on end of link to eliminate lash and tighten link retaining bolt, Fig. 11, then install nylon washer and spring clip.
5. Reconnect throttle control rod spring.

1972-73

Before adjusting throttle linkage, set the curb idle speed to specified RPM. Then proceed as follows:
1. Hook a tension spring into hole in transmission throttle lever. Stretch the spring forward and retain it so 8-10 lbs. tension will be applied to the transmission throttle lever, Fig. 10.
2. Remove retainer clip attaching adjustable throttle rod link at the slotted end. Remove tab washer from rod slot and loosen throttle rod slip joint retaining screw.

3. For V8 engines, shorten adjustable rod to remove all slack and tighten slip joint retaining screw, Fig. 11.
4. For six cylinder engines, lengthen adjustable rod to remove all slack and tighten slip joint retaining screw, Fig. 12.
5. Place rod slot over carburetor throttle lever (V8) or bellcrank lever (Six). Install tab washer and retainer clip. The washer tabs must fit into throttle rod slot, Fig. 13.
6. Remove tension spring from transmission throttle lever.

1969-74 Chrysler Corp.

NOTE: Before proceeding with the adjustment, disconnect the choke rod at the carburetor or block the choke valve wide open. Open the throttle slightly to release the fast idle cam, then return carburetor to the hot idle position.
 Hold or fasten the transmission lever firmly forward against the stop while performing the adjustment to insure a proper adjustment.

Models Indicated in Fig. 14
1. With a 3/16" diameter rod (9) placed in the holes provided in the upper bellcrank (6) and lever, adjust length of intermediate transmission rod (10) by means of threaded adjustment (2) at upper end. The ball socket must line up with the ball end with a slight downward effort on rod.
2. Assemble ball socket to ball end and remove 3/16" gauging rod from upper bellcrank and lever.
3. Disconnect return spring (13), then adjust length of carburetor rod (12) by pushing rearward on rod with slight effort and turning threaded adjustment (1). Rear end of slot should contact carburetor lever pin without exerting any forward force when slotted adjuster link (1) is in its normal

operating position against lever pin nut.

4. Assemble slotted adjustment (1) to carburetor lever pin and install washer and retaining pin. Connect transmission linkage return spring (13).

5. Release transmission lever, then check linkage for freedom of operation. Move slotted adjuster link (1) to full rearward position, then allow it to return slowly, making sure it returns to full forward position.

6. Loosen cable clamp nut (4) and adjust position of cable housing ferrule (5) in clamp so that all slack is removed from cable with carburetor at hot idle position. To remove slack from cable, move ferrule in clamp in a direction away from carburetor lever.

7. Back off ferrule ¼" which provides enough free play between front edge of accelerator shaft lever and dash bracket. Tighten clamp nut to 45 inch-lbs.

8. Connect choke rod or remove blocking fixture.

Models Indicated in Fig. 15

1. With a ³/₁₆" diameter rod (9) placed in the holes provided in upper bellcrank and lever, adjust length of intermediate transmission rod (10) by means of threaded adjustment at upper end. The ball socket (2) must line up with the ball end with a slight downward effort on rod.

2. Assemble ball socket (2) to ball end and remove ³/₁₆" rod (9) from upper bellcrank and lever.

3. Disconnect return spring (13), then adjust length of carburetor rod (12) by pushing rearward on rod with a slight effort and turning the threaded adjuster (1). The rear end of slot should contact carburetor lever pin without exerting any forward force on pin when slotted adjuster link (1) is in its normal operating position against lever pin nut.

4. Assemble slotted adjustment (1) to carburetor lever pin and install washer and retaining pin. Assemble transmission linkage return spring (13) in place.

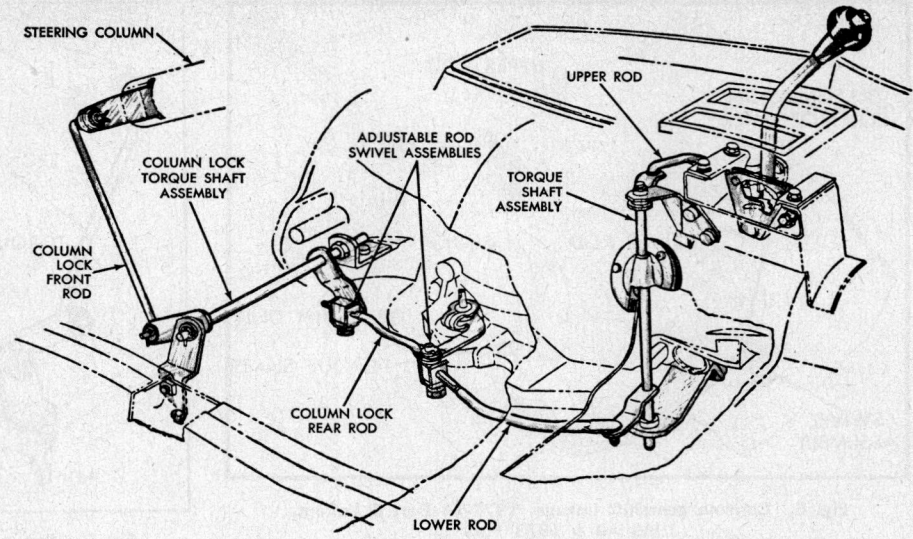

Fig. 8 Console gearshift linkage. 1970 Belvedere, Charger, Coronet, Dart, Satellite & Valiant. 1970-72 Chrysler, Fury, Monaco & Polara

5. Release transmission lever and check linkage for freedom of operation. Move slotted adjuster link (1) to full rearward position and allow it to return slowly, making sure it returns to full forward position.

6. Loosen cable clamp nut (4), adjust position of cable housing ferrule (5) in the clamp so all slack is removed from cable with carburetor at curb idle. To remove slack, move ferrule (5) in the clamp in direction away from carburetor lever.

7. Back off ferrule (5) ¼". This provides ¼" free play between front edge of accelerator shaft lever and dash bracket. Tighten cable clamp nut (4) to 45 inch lbs.

8. Connect choke (8) rod or remove blocking fixture.

Models Indicated in Fig. 16

1. Adjust length of transmission rod by

loosening slotted link lock nut (12). Pull forward on slotted adjuster link (7) so it contacts carburetor lever pin.

2. Tighten transmission rod adjustment lock nut (12) to 95 inch lbs. Check transmission linkage for freedom of operation by moving slotted adjuster link to full rearward position and allow it to return slowly, making sure it returns to full forward position.

3. When carburetor throttle is opened, the transmission lever (9) should begin its travel at the same time with no vertical movement of lever or vertical movement of rod (10) in the lever.

4. Loosen cable clamp nut (5), adjust position of housing ferrule (6) in the clamp so all slack is removed from cable with carburetor at curb idle. To remove slack, move ferrule (6) in the clamp in direction away from carburetor lever.

5. Back off ferrule (6) ¼". This provides ¼" free play between dash mounted accelerator lever and the bracket. Tighten cable clamp nut to 45 inch lbs.

6. Connect choke rod (4) or remove blocking fixture.

Models Indicated in Fig. 17

1. With a ³/₄" diameter rod (9) placed in the holes provided in upper bellcrank and lever, adjust length of transmission rod (10) by means of threaded adjustment at upper end. The ball socket (2) must line up with the ball end with a slight downward effort on rod.

2. Assemble ball socket (2) to ball end and remove ³/₁₆" rod (9) from upper bellcrank and lever.

3. Disconnect return spring (13), washer and retainer pin (14), then adjust length of carburetor rod (12) by pushing rearward on rod with a slight effort and turning the threaded ad-

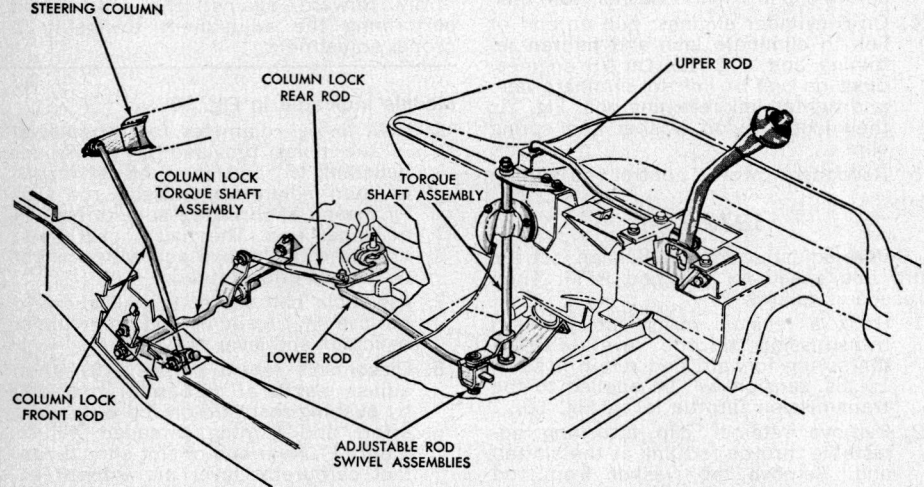

Fig. 9 Console gearshift linkage. 1970 Barracuda & Challenger

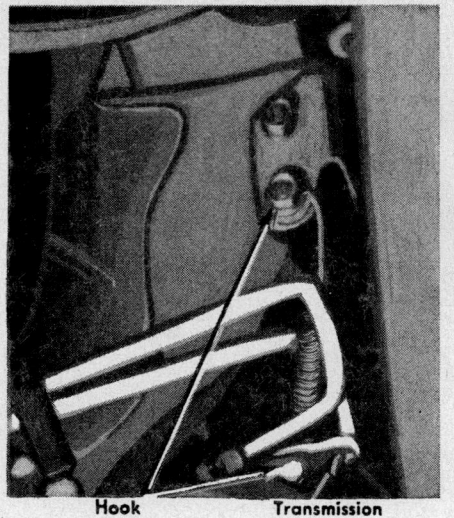

Fig. 10 Install spring on lever.
1972-74 American Motors

Hook Spring   Transmission Throttle Lever

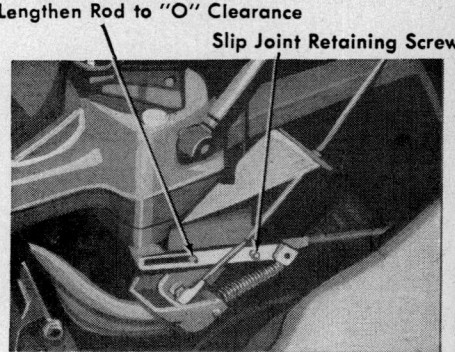

Shorten Rod to "O" Clearance
Slip Joint Retaining Screw

Fig. 11 V8 throttle linkage.
1972-74 American Motors

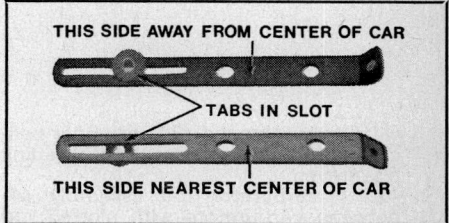

Lengthen Rod to "O" Clearance
Slip Joint Retaining Screw

Fig. 12 Six cylinder throttle linkage.
1972-74 American Motors

justment (1). The rear end of slot should contact carburetor lever pin without exerting any forward force on pin when slotted adjuster link (1) is in its normal operating position against lever pin nut.

4. Assemble slotted adjustment (1) to carburetor lever pin and install washer and retainer pin (14). Assemble transmission linkage return spring (13).

5. Release transmission lever and check linkage for freedom of operation by moving slotted adjuster link (1) to full rearward position, then allow it to return slowly, making sure it returns to the full forward position.

6. Loosen cable clamp nut (4), adjust position of cable housing ferrule (5) in the clamp so that all slack is removed from the cable with carburetor at curb idle. To remove slack, move the ferrule (5) in the clamp in direction away from carburetor lever.

7. Back off ferrule (5) ¼". This provides ¼" free play between front edge of the accelerator shaft lever and the dash bracket. Tighten cable clamp nut (4) to .45 inch lbs.

8. Connect choke rod or remove blocking fixture.

Models Indicated in Fig. 18

1. With a ³⁄₁₆" diameter rod (8) placed in holes provided in upper bellcrank and lever (15), adjust length of transmission rod (9) by means of threaded adjuster at upper end. The ball socket must line up with the ball end with a slight downward effort on rod.

2. Assemble ball socket to ball end and remove ³⁄₁₆" rod (8) from upper bellcrank and lever (15).

3. Disconnect return spring (11), adjust length of rod (20) by pushing rearward on rod with a slight effort and turning threaded adjuster link (2). The rear end of slot should contact carburetor lever stud without exerting any forward force on the stud when slotted adjuster link is in its normal operating position.

4. Assemble slotted adjuster link (2) to carburetor lever stud and install washer and retainer pin. Assemble linkage return spring (11) in place.

5. Release transmission lever and check linkage for freedom of operation by

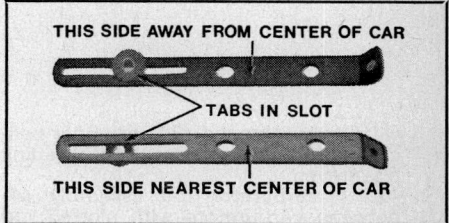

THIS SIDE AWAY FROM CENTER OF CAR
TABS IN SLOT
THIS SIDE NEAREST CENTER OF CAR

Fig. 13 Tab washer in rod slot.
1972-73 American Motors

moving slotted adjuster link (2) to full rearward position, then allow it to return slowly to the full forward position against the stud.

6. Loosen cable clamp nut (12), adjust position of cable housing ferrule. (13) in the clamp (14) so all slack is removed from cable with rear carburetor at curb idle. To remove slack from cable, move ferrule (13) in clamp (14) in direction away from carburetor lever.

7. Back off ferrule (13) ¼". This provides ¼" free play between front edge of accelerator shaft lever and dash bracket. Tighten clamp (14) to 45 inch lbs.

8. Route cable so it does not interfere

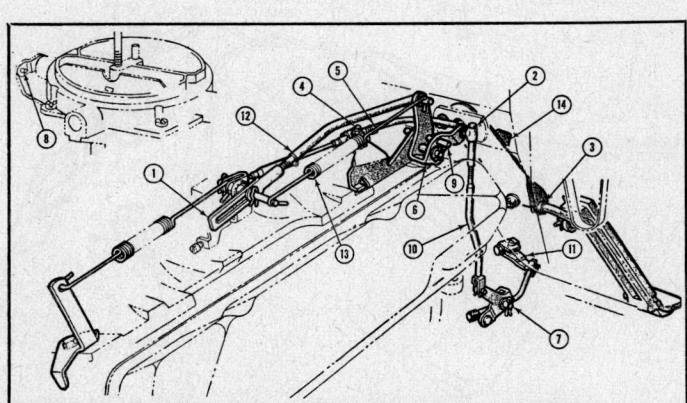

Fig. 14 Throttle linkage adjustment. All 1969 models with 383 and 440 engines. Also 1969 Monaco, Polara & Fury with 318 engine

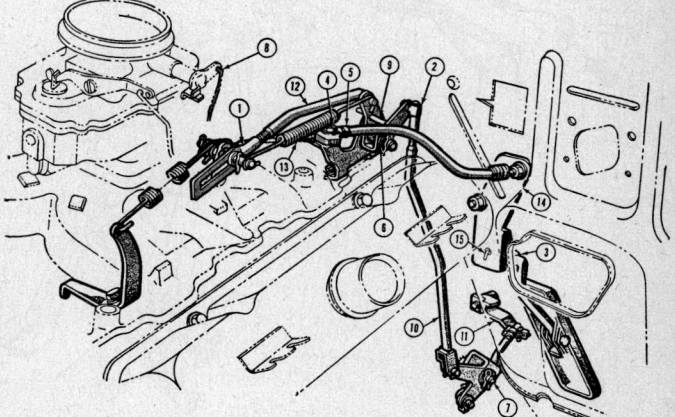

Fig. 15 Throttle linkage adjustment. 1969 Dart, Valiant and Barracuda with 273, 318 or 340 engine. 1970-73 V8 with 3 section rod

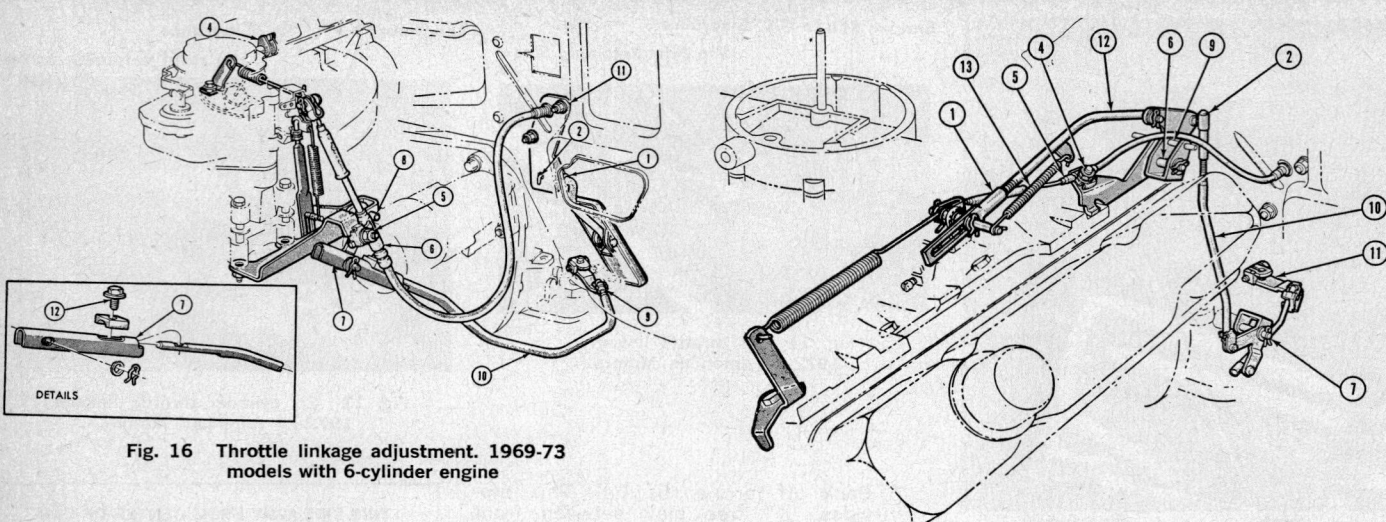

Fig. 16 Throttle linkage adjustment. 1969-73 models with 6-cylinder engine

Fig. 17 Throttle linkage adjustment. 1969 Dart and Barracuda with 383 engine

with carburetor rod (20) or upper bell-crank (15) throughout full throttle linkage travel.

9. Attach carburetor rod assembly (4) between carburetors with slotted rod end (16) attached to outboard side of inboard lever on rear carburetor. With rear carburetor at wide open throttle, adjust length of connector rod (4) so that front carburetor is also at wide open throttle. To lengthen this rod (4) turn adjusting stud (17) clockwise as viewed from front of engine. Tighten lock nut (18).

10. Remove choke valve blocking fixture.

Models Indicated in Fig. 19

1. Disconnect choke at carburetor or block choke valve fully open. Open throttle slightly to release fast idle cam and return carburetor to curb idle position.

2. Loosen transmission throttle rod adjustment lock screw.

3. Hold transmission forward against its stop while adjusting transmission linkage. (On engines with solenoid idle stops, the solenoid plunger must also be in its fully extended position).

4. Adjust the transmission rod by pulling forward on the slotted link with a slight effort so that the rear edge of the slot is against the carburetor lever pin. Tighten transmission rod adjusting lock screw.

NOTE: The slotted link and transmission lever must be held forward while the locking screw is being tightened.

5. To check transmission linkage freedom of operation, move slotted link to the full rearward position, then allow it to return slowly, making sure it returns to the full forward position.

6. Loosen carburetor cable clamp nut. Adjust position of cable housing ferrule in the clamp so that all slack is removed from cable with carburetor at curb idle. To remove slack from cable, move ferrule in the clamp in direction away from carburetor lever.

7. Back off ferrule 1/4". This provides 1/4" free play. Tighten cable clamp nut to 45 inch lbs.

8. Connect choke or remove blocking fixture.

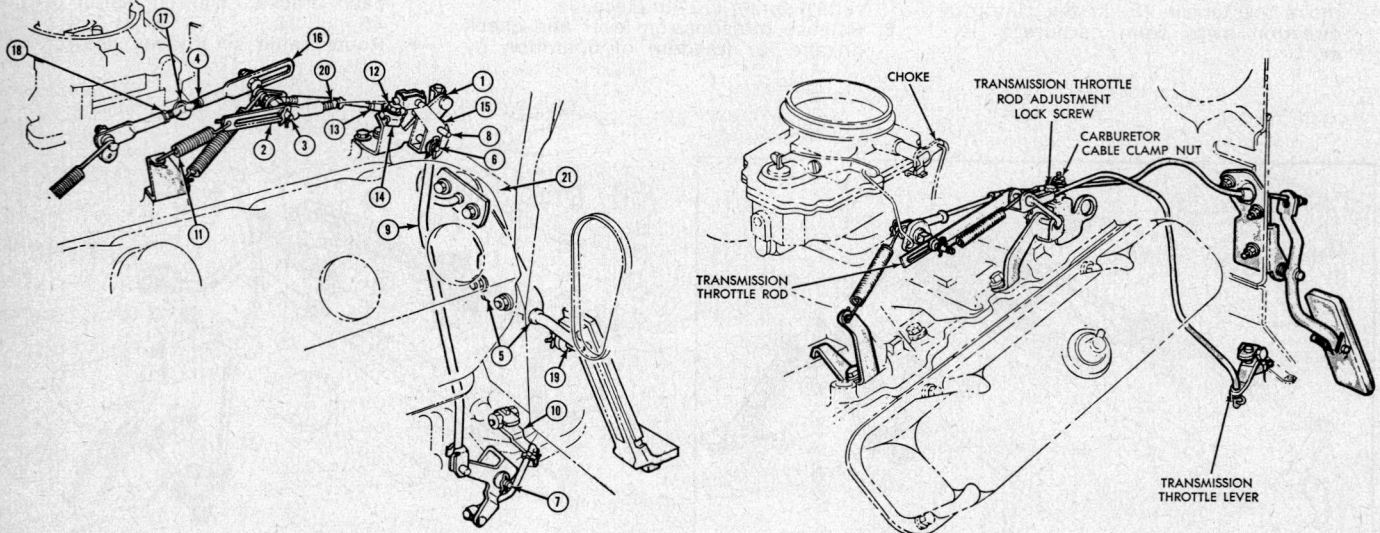

Fig. 18 Throttle linkage adjustment. 1969-71 models with 426 engine

Fig. 19 Throttle linkage adjustment. 1970-73 V8 models with single section throttle rod

Models Indicated in Fig. 20

1. Support vehicle on hoist and loosen swivel lock screw.

   NOTE: To insure correct adjustment, swivel must be free to slide along flat end of throttle rod so that preload spring action is not restricted. If necessary, disassemble and clean or repair parts to assure free action.

2. Hold transmission lever firmly forward against its internal stop and tighten swivel lock screw to 125 inch lbs.

   NOTE: Adjustment is now finished. Linkage backlash was automatically removed by the preload spring.

3. Lower vehicle and test linkage operation by moving throttle rod rearward and slowly releasing it making certain that it returns fully.

EXTENSION HOUSING & PARKING LOCK CONTROL ROD

NOTE: 1973-74 Charger, Coronet, Imperial and Satellite models will require unloading of both torsion bars and dropping on one side torsion bar crossmember for clearance.

1. Mark parts for reassembly and remove propeller shaft.
2. Remove speedometer pinion and adapter assembly, then drain about two quarts of fluid from transmission.
3. Remove extension housing to crossmember bolts, then raise transmission with jack and remove crossmember.
4. Remove extension housing to transmission bolts. On console shift models, remove torque shaft lower bracket to extension housing bolts.

NOTE: In the following step, the gearshift must be in "low" therefore positioning the

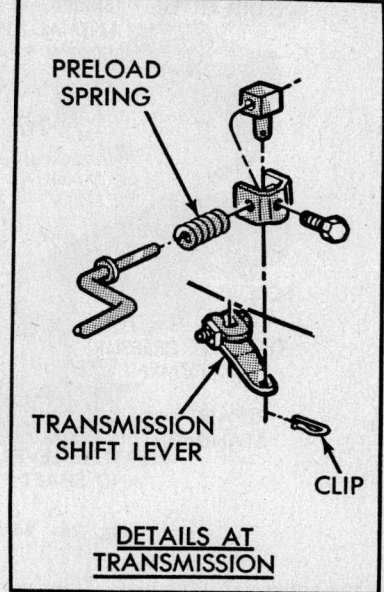

Fig. 20 Throttle linkage adjustment. All 1974 Chrysler Corp. models

parking lock control rod rearward so it can be disengaged or engaged with the parking lock sprag.

5. Remove two screws, plate and gasket from bottom of extension housing mounting pad, then spread snap ring from output shaft bearing, Fig. 21, and carefully tap extension housing off output shaft bearing.
6. Slide extension housing off shaft to remove parking sprag and spring, then remove snap ring and slide reaction plug and pin assembly out of housing, Fig. 22.
7. To replace parking lock control rod, refer to "Valve Body".

OUTPUT SHAFT OIL SEAL

1. Mark propeller shaft to aid in reassembly and remove propeller shaft being careful not to scratch or nick surface on sliding spline yoke.
2. Using a screwdriver and hammer, drive between extension housing and seal and remove seal.
3. Position new seal and drive it into extension housing using tool C-3995 or C-3972.
4. Carefully install yoke into housing, then align marks made at removal and install propeller shaft.

GOVERNOR

1. Remove extension housing, then remove output shaft bearing rear snap ring and remove bearing. On 727 Series, remove remaining snap ring from shaft.
2. Remove snap ring, Fig. 23, from weight end of governor valve shaft and remove valve shaft from governor body.
3. Remove large snap ring from weight end of governor housing, and lift out weight assembly.
4. Remove snap ring from inside governor weight and remove inner weight and spring from outer weight.
5. Remove snap ring from behind governor housing, then slide governor housing and parking brake sprag assembly off input shaft. If necessary, separate governor housing from sprag (4 screws).
6. The primary cause of governor operating failure is due to a sticking governor valve or weights. Rough surfaces may be removed with crocus cloth. Thoroughly clean all parts and check for free movement before assembly.
7. Reverse above operations to assemble and install governor.

VALVE BODY

1. Drain transmission and remove oil pan.
2. Loosen clamp bolts and remove throttle and gear selector levers from manual lever, Fig. 24.
3. Remove neutral safety switch and oil filter.
4. Place a drain pan under transmission and remove the ten valve body to

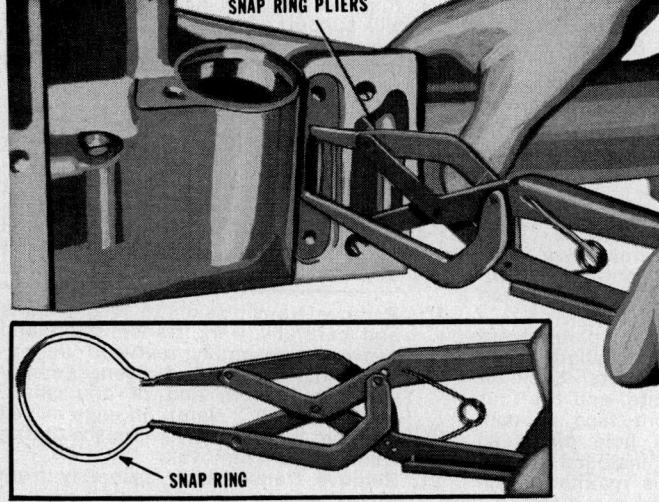

Fig. 21 Removing or installing extension housing snap ring

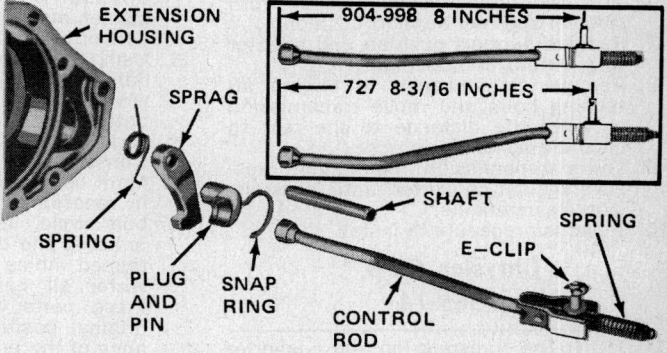

Fig. 22 Parking lock components

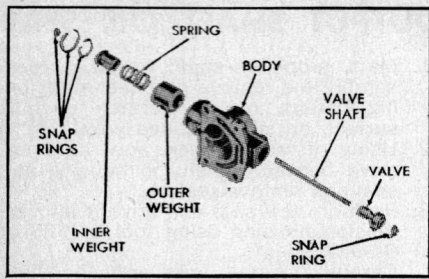

Fig. 23 Governor disassembled

transmission bolts. Hold valve body in place while removing bolts.

5. Carefully lower valve body while pulling it forward to disengage parking control rod.

NOTE: It may be necessary to rotate output shaft to permit parking control rod to clear sprag.

6. Remove accumulator piston and spring from transmission case. Inspect piston for nicks, scores and wear. Inspect spring for distortion. Inspect rings for freedom in piston grooves and wear or breakage. Replace parts as necessary.

TRANSMISSION, REPLACE

American Motors
1972-74

CAUTION: The hood must be open to prevent damage to hood and air cleaner when removing rear crossmember.

1. Remove cover from front of bell housing then turn converter until drain plug is at "6 o'clock" position.
2. Drain converter and transmission. Remove filler tube and starter.
3. Mark rear universal joint and yoke for alignment purposes during installation. Then remove propeller shaft.
4. Disconnect speedometer cable, throttle and shift linkages, neutral safety switch and transmission controlled spark switch wires. Remove transmission oil cooler lines.
5. Mark converter and drive plate for alignment purposes during installation. Remove converter to drive plate bolts.
6. Install a suitable jack under transmission and remove crossmember from side sill and rear support cushion.
7. Remove support cushion and adapter from extension housing.
8. Remove transmission to engine attaching bolts and move transmission an adequate distance to the rear to clear crankshaft.
9. Lower transmission, maintaining pressure against converter, until transmission clears engine.
10. Reverse procedure to install.

Chrysler Corp.
1969-74

CAUTION: The transmission and converter must be removed as an assembly, other-

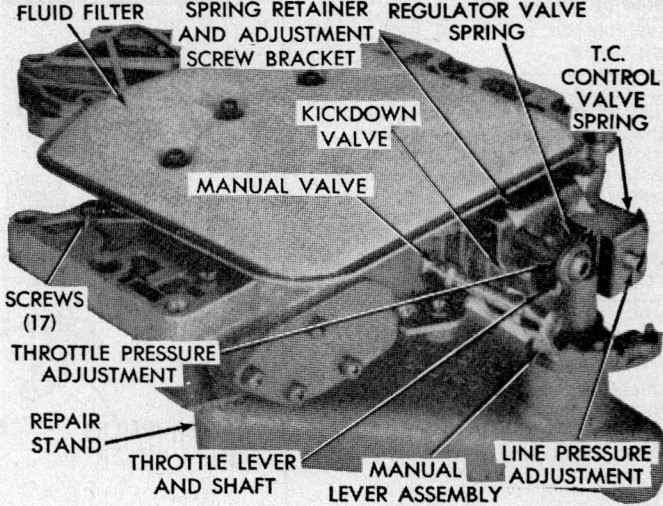

Fig. 24 Valve body external parts

wise, the converter drive plate, front pump bushing and oil seal will be damaged. The drive plate will not support the load; therefore, none of the weight of the transmission should be allowed to rest on the plate during removal.

NOTE: Some 400 CID 2-BBL engines (engine number 4T400-1-03 through 4T400-108) were built with a forged crankshaft requiring a different torque converter and damper than the engines using the cast crankshaft.

This forged crankshaft is normally only used in the 400-4-BBL, HP engine with manual transmission.

If replacement of the crankshaft, torque converter, crankshaft damper or short engine is required, it is important that matching parts are used otherwise severe engine vibration will result, (Consult Chrysler Parts Dept.).

The cast crankshaft engine can be easily identified since it has the letter "E" stamped on the engine numbering pad following the built date.

1. Disconnect battery ground cable.

NOTE: Some models will require that the exhaust system be lowered for clearance.

2. Remove engine to transmission struts (if equipped), then disconnect transmission cooler lines and remove starter motor, cooler line bracket and converter access cover.
3. Using a socket wrench on vibration dampener bolt, rotate engine clockwise until convertor drain plug is at bottom. Remove plug and drain converter, than loosen oil pan and drain transmission.
4. Mark converter and drive plate to aid in reassembly. The crankshaft flange bolt circle, inner and outer circle of holes in the drive plate, and the four tapped holes in front face of converter all have one hole offset so these parts will be installed in the original position. This maintains balance of the engine and converter.
5. Remove converter to drive plate bolts.

Rotate engine clockwise using socket wrench to gain access to all bolts.

CAUTION: Do not rotate converter or drive plate by prying with a screwdriver or similar tool as the drive plate might become distorted. Also, the starter should never be engaged if the drive plate is not attached to the converter with at least one bolt or if the transmission case-to-engine bolts have been loosened.

6. Mark drive shaft to aid in reassembly and remove drive shaft.
7. Disconnect neutral and back-up light switch and gearshift and torque shaft assembly from transmission.

NOTE: When disassembling linkage rods from levers which use plastic grommets as retainers, the grommets should be replaced with new ones.

8. Disconnect throttle rod from lever at left side of transmission, then remove linkage bellcrank from transmission, if so equipped.
9. Install a suitable fixture or jack that will support engine, then raise transmission slightly with a jack to relieve the load on the supports, and remove the crossmember.

NOTE: Some models have a torsion bar anchor crossmember that remains in place and requires a careful downward tilt of front of transmission as it is being lowered. If these models have a vibration dampening weight bolted to rear of extension housing, it must be removed.

10. Remove transmission to engine bolts and carefully work transmission and converter assembly rearward off engine block dowels and disengage converter hub from end of crankshaft. Using a small C-clamp on edge of bell housing, hold converter in place during transmission removal.
11. Remove transmission assembly from under vehicle.
12. Reverse procedure to install.

C3 & C4 DUAL RANGE AUTOMATIC

TRANSMISSION IDENTIFICATION

Each transmission may be identified by the tag attached to the low-reverse servo cover bolt. The tag includes the model prefix and suffix, a service identification number and a build date code. The service identification number indicates changes to service details which affect interchangeability when the transmission model is not changed. For interpretation of this number the Ford Master Parts Catalog should be consulted.

YEAR	CAR MODEL	TRANS. MODEL	ENGINE MODEL
	C3 Transmission		
1974	Mustang II	BKB	4-140
	C4 Transmission		
1969	Fairlane③	PEE-V	V8-302
	Fairlane④	PEE-M	V8-302
	Fairlane③	PEE-AE	6-250
	Fairlane④	PEE-AF	6-250
	Falcon③	PEB-C2	6-170, 200
	Falcon③	PEE-V	V8-302
	Ford③	PEA-A2	6-240
	Ford③	PEA-M1	V8-302
	Ford④	PEA-N1	V8-302
	Montego④	PEE-M	V8-302
	Montego③	PEE-V	V8-302
	Montego③	PEE-AE	6-250
	Montego④	PEE-AF	6-250
	Mustang④	PEB-B2	6-200
	Mustang④	PEE-AC	V8-302
	Mustang④	PEE-AD	6-250
1970	Cougar	PEE-AC2	V8-302
	Fairlane④	PEE-M1	V8-302
	Fairlane③	PEE-V1	V8-302
	Fairlane	PEE-AC1	V8-302
	Fairlane	PEE-AD1	6-250
	Fairlane③	PEE-AE1	6-250
	Fairlane④	PEE-AF1	6-250
	Fairlane	PEF-D	V8-351
	Fairlane	PEF-E	V8-351
	Falcon	PEE-M1	V8-302
	Falcon	PEE-V2	V8-302
	Falcon	PEE-AC1	V8-302
	Falcon	PEE-AD1	6-250
	Falcon	PEE-AE1	6-250
	Falcon	PEE-AF1	6-250
	Falcon	PEB	6-200
	Ford	PEA-M2	6 & V8-302
	Ford	PEA-N2	V8-302
	Ford	PEA-A3	6-240
	Ford③	PEF-A	V8-351
	Ford④	PEF-B	V8-351
	Maverick	PEB-D	6-170, 200
	Maverick	PEB-D1	6-170, 200
	Maverick	PEE-AK	6-250
	Montego④	PEE-M1	V8-302
	Montego③	PEE-V1	V8-302
	Montego③	PEE-AE1	6-250
	Montego④	PEE-AF1	6-250
	Montego③	PEF-D	V8-351
	Montego④	PEF-E	V8-351

YEAR	CAR MODEL	TRANS. MODEL	ENGINE MODEL
	Mustang	PEE-AC1	V8-302
	Mustang	PEE-AD1	6-250
	Mustang	PEB-B3	6-200
1971	Comet③	PEB-D2	6-200
	Comet③	PEB-H	6-200
	Comet③	PEE-AK1	6-250
	Comet④	PEE-AM	6-250
	Comet③	PEE-AH1	V8-302
	Comet④	PEE-AL	V8-302
	Fairlane③	PEE-AE2	6-250
	Fairlane④	PEE-AF2	6-250
	Fairlane③	PEE-M2	V8-302
	Fairlane④	PEE-V2	V8-302
	Fairlane③	PEF-D1	V8-351
	Fairlane④	PEF-E1	V8-351
	Ford	PEA-M3	6-240
	Ford③	PEA-M3	V8-302
	Ford④	PEA-N3	V8-302
	Ford③	PEF-A1	V8-351
	Ford④	PEF-B1	V8-351
	Montego③	PEE-AE2	6-250
	Montego④	PEE-AF2	6-250
	Montego③	PEE-M2	V8-302
	Montego③	PEE-V2	V8-302
	Montego③	PEF-D1	V8-351
	Montego④	PEF-E1	V8-351
	Maverick③	PEB-D2	6-200
	Maverick④	PEB-H	6-200
	Maverick③	PEE-AK1	6-250
	Maverick④	PEE-AM	6-250
	Mustang	PEE-AD2	6-250
	Mustang	PEE-AC2	V8-302
	Pinto	PEJ-B	4-122
1972	Comet③	PEB-D3, 4, 5	6-200
	Comet③	PEB-H1,2, 3, 4	6-200
	Comet③	PEE-AK2, 3	6-250
	Comet④	PEE-AM1, 2, 3	6-250
	Comet③	PEE-AH2, 3	V8-302
	Comet④	PEE-AL1, 2, 3	V8-302
	Ford	PEA-M4, 5	6 & V8-302
	Ford	PEF-A2, 3	V8-351
	Maverick③	PEB-D3, 4, 5	6-200
	Maverick④	PEB-H1, 2, 3, 4	6-200
	Maverick③	PEE-AK2, 3	6-250
	Maverick④	PEE-AM1, 2	6-250
	Maverick③	PEE-AH2, 3	V8-302
	Maverick④	PEE-AL1, 2	V8-302
	Montego③	PEE-AE4, 5	6-250
	Montego④	PEE-AF4, 5	6-250
	Montego③	PEE-V4, 5	V8-302
	Montego④	PEE-M4, 5	V8-302
	Montego③	PEF-D3, 4	V8-351
	Montego④	PEF-E3, 4	V8-351
	Mustang③	PEE-AD3, 4	6-250
	Mustang④	PEE-AC3, 4	V8-302
	Pinto	PEJ-B1, 2	4-122
	Torino③	PEE-AE4, 5	6-250
	Torino④	PEE-AF4, 5	6-250
	Torino③	PEE-V4, 5	V8-302
	Torino④	PEE-M4, 5	V8-302
	Torino③	PEF-D3, 4	V8-351
	Torino④	PEF-E3, 4	V8-351
	Torino④	EDPEF-E4	V8-351

YEAR	CAR MODEL	TRANS. MODEL	ENGINE MODEL
1973	Comet③	PEB-D6	6-200
	Comet④	PEB-H5	6-200
	Comet③	PEE-AK4	6-250
	Comet④	PEE-AM6	6-250
	Comet③	PEE-AH4	V8-302
	Comet④	PEE-AL4	V8-302
	Ford	PEE-M6	V8-302
	Ford	PEF-A4	V8-351
	Maverick③	PEB-D6	6-200
	Maverick④	PEB-H5	6-200
	Maverick③	PEE-AK4	6-250
	Maverick④	PEE-AM4	6-250
	Maverick③	PEE-AH4	V8-302
	Maverick④	PEE-AL4	V8-302
	Montego③	PEE-AE6	6-250
	Montego④	PEE-AF6	6-250
	Montego③	PEE-V6	V8-302
	Montego④	PEE-M6	V8-302
	Montego③	PEF-D5	V8-351
	Montego④	PEF-E5	V8-351
	Mustang④	PEE-AD6	6-250
	Mustang④	PEE-AC6	V8-302
	Pinto	PEJ-B4	4-122
	Torino③	PEE-AE6	6-250
	Torino④	PEE-AF6	6-250
	Torino③	PEE-V6	V8-302
	Torino④	PEE-M6	V8-302
	Torino③	PEF-D5	V8-351
	Torino④	PEF-E5	V8-351
1974	Comet③	PEB-D7	6-200
	Comet④	PEB-H6	6-200
	Comet③	PEE-AK5	6-250
	Comet④	PEE-AM5	6-250
	Comet③	PEE-AH5	V8-302
	Comet④	PEE-AL5	V8-302
	Comet①③	PEE-BH	V8-302
	Comet①④	PEE-BJ	V8-302
	Cougar③	PEF-D6	V8-351
	Cougar④	PEF-E6, 7	V8-351
	Ford	PEF-A5	V8-351
	Maverick③	PEB-D7	6-200
	Maverick④	PEB-H6	6-200
	Maverick③	PEE-AK5	6-250
	Maverick④	PEE-AM5	6-250
	Maverick③	PEE-AH5	V8-302
	Maverick④	PEE-AL5	V8-302
	Maverick①③	PEE-BH	V8-302
	Maverick①④	PEE-BJ	V8-302
	Montego	PEE-V7	V8-302
	Montego	PEF-D6	V8-351
	Mustang II①	PEJ-H	4-140
	Mustang II	PEJ-E	6-171
	Mustang II①	PEJ-J	6-171
	Pinto	PEJ-B6	4-122
	Pinto①	PEJ-G	4-140
	Pinto	PEJ-C	4-140
	Torino	PEE-V7	V8-302
	Torino④	PEE-M7, 8	V8-302
	Torino③	PEF-D6	V8-351
	Torino④	PEF-E6, 7	V8-351

①—California.
③— Column shift.
④—Floor shift.

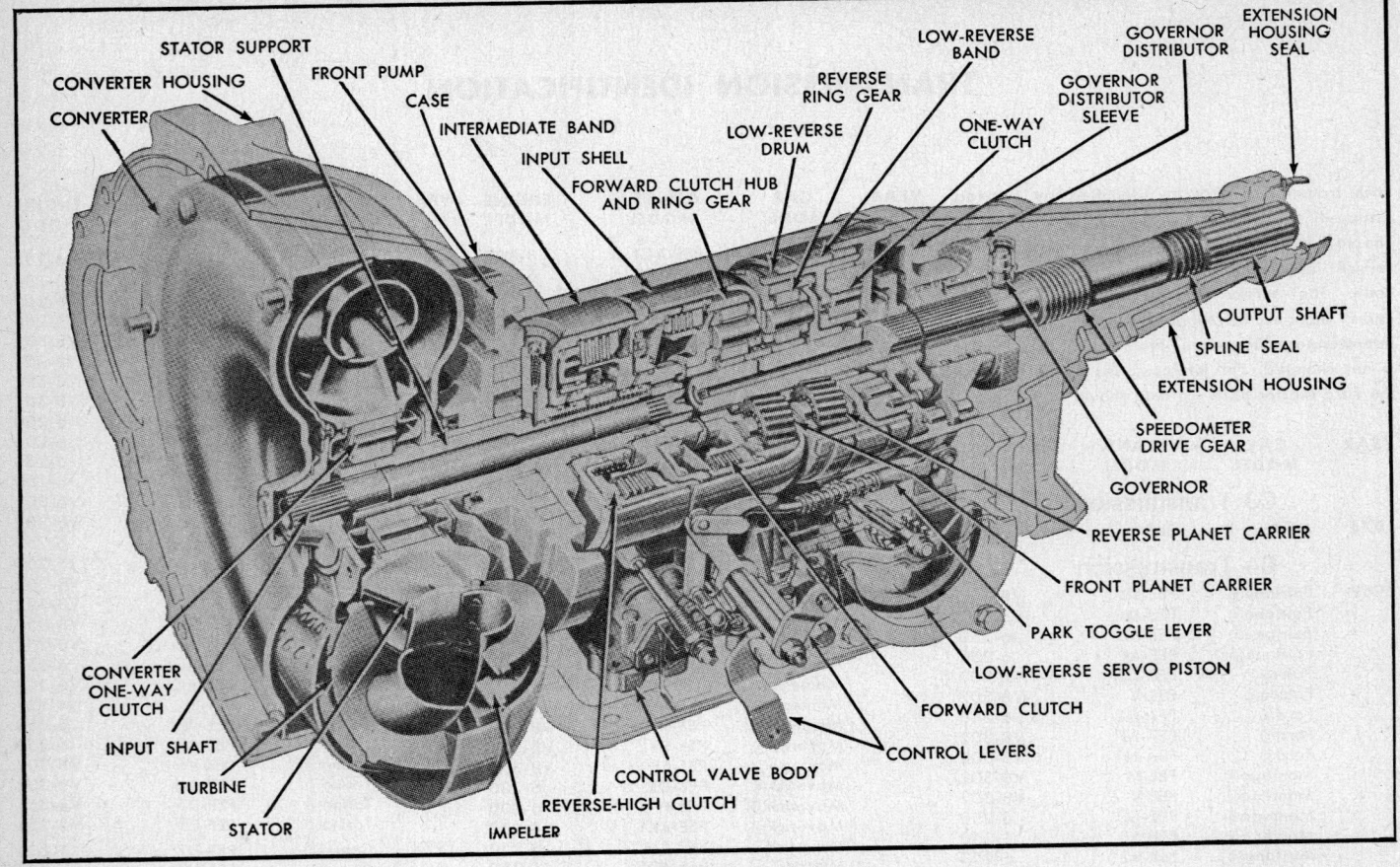

Fig. 1 C4 Dual Range Automatic

DESCRIPTION

The main control assembly incorporates a manually selective first and second gear range. The transmission features a drive range that provides for fully automatic upshifts and downshifts, and manually selected low and second gears.

The transmission consists essentially of a torque converter, a compound planetary gear train, two multiple disc clutches, a one-way clutch and a hydraulic control system, Figs. 1 and 2.

For all normal driving the selector lever is moved to the green dot under "Drive" on the selector quadrant on the steering column or on the floor console. As the throttle is advanced from the idle position, the transmission will upshift automatically to intermediate gear and then to high.

The driver can force downshift the transmission from high to intermediate at speeds up to 65 mph. A detent on the downshift linkage warns the driver when the carburetor is wide open. Accelerator pedal depression through the detent will bring in the downshift.

With the throttle closed the transmission will downshift automatically as the car speed drops to about 10 mph. With the throttle open at any position up to the detent, the downshifts will come in automatically at speeds above 10 mph and in proportion to throttle opening. This pre-

vents engine lugging on steep hill climbing, for example.

When the selector lever is moved to "L" with the transmission in high, the transmission will downshift to intermediate or to low depending on the road speed. At speed above 25 mph, the downshift will be from high to intermediate. At speeds below 25 mph, the downshift will be from high to low. With the selector lever in the "L" position the transmission cannot upshift.

TROUBLE SHOOTING GUIDE

Rough Initial Engagement In D1 or D2

1. Engine idle speed.
2. Vacuum diaphragm unit or tubes restricted, leaking or maladjusted.
3. Check control pressure.
4. Pressure regulator.
5. Valve body.
6. Forward clutch.

1-2 or 2-3 Shift Points Erratic

1. Check fluid level.
2. Vacuum diaphragm unit or tubes restricted, leaking or maladjusted.

3. Intermediate servo.
4. Manual linkage adjustment.
5. Governor.
6. Check control pressure.
7. Valve body.
8. Make air pressure check.

Rough 1-2 Upshifts

1. Vacuum diaphragm unit or tubes restricted, leaking or maladjusted.
2. Intermediate servo.
3. Intermediate band.
4. Check control pressure.
5. Valve body.
6. Pressure regulator.

Rough 2-3 Upshifts

1. Vacuum diaphragm unit or tubes restricted, leaking or maladjusted.
2. Intermediate servo.
3. Check control pressure.
4. Pressure regulator.
5. Intermediate band.
6. Valve body.
7. Make air pressure check.
8. Reverse-high clutch.
9. Reverse-high clutch piston air bleed valve.

Dragged Out 1-2 Shift

1. Check fluid level.

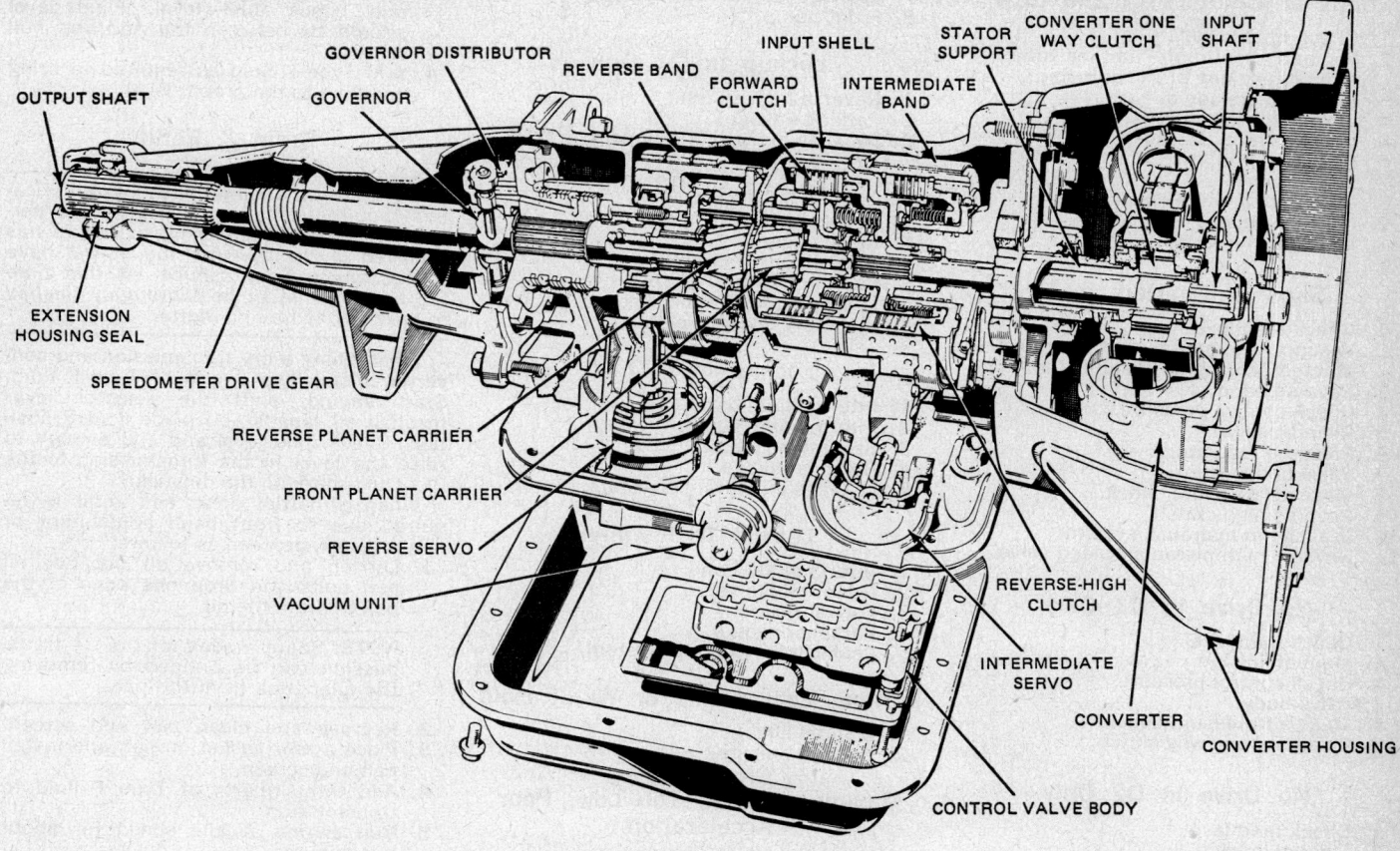

Fig. 2   C3 Dual Range Automatic

2. Vacuum diaphragm unit or tubes restricted, leaking or maladjusted.
3. Intermediate servo.
4. Check control pressure.
5. Intermediate band.
6. Valve body.
7. Pressure regulator.
8. Make air pressure check.
9. Leakage in hydraulic system.

Engine Overspeeds on 2-3 Shift

1. Manual linkage.
2. Check fluid level.
3. Vacuum diaphragm unit or tubes restricted, leaking or maladjusted.
4. Reverse servo.
5. Check control pressure.
6. Valve body.
7. Pressure regulator.
8. Intermediate band.
9. Reverse-high clutch.
10. Reverse-high clutch piston air bleed valve.

No 1-2 or 2-3 Shift

1. Manual linkage.
2. Downshift linkage, including inner lever position.
3. Vacuum diaphragm unit or tubes restricted, leaking or maladjusted.
4. Governor.
5. Check control pressure.
6. Valve body.
7. Intermediate band.

8. Intermediate servo.
9. Reverse-high clutch.
10. Reverse-high clutch piston air bleed valve.

No 3-1 Shift in D1 or 3-2 Shift in D2

1. Governor.
2. Valve body.

No Forced Downshifts

1. Downshift linkage, including inner lever position.
2. Valve body.
3. Vacuum diaphragm unit or tubes restricted, leaking or maladjusted.

Runaway Engine on Forced 3-2 Downshift

1. Check control pressure.
2. Intermediate servo.
3. Intermediate band.
4. Pressure regulator.
5. Valve body.
6. Vacuum diaphragm unit or tubes restricted, leaking or maladjusted.
7. Leakage in hydraulic system.

Rough 3-2 or 3-1 Shift at Closed Throttle

1. Engine idle speed.

2. Vacuum diaphragm unit or tubes restricted, leaking or maladjusted.
3. Intermediate servo.
4. Valve body.
5. Pressure regulator.

Shifts 1-3 in D1 and D2

1. Intermediate band.
2. Intermediate servo.
3. Vacuum diaphragm unit or tubes restricted, leaking or maladjusted.
4. Valve body.
5. Governor.
6. Make air pressure check.

No Engine Braking In 1st Gear —Manual Low

1. Manual linkage.
2. Reverse band.
3. Reverse servo.
4. Valve body.
5. Governor.
6. Make air pressure check.

Slips or Chatters in 1st Gear—D1

1. Check fluid level.
2. Vacuum diaphragm unit or tubes restricted, leaking or maladjusted.
3. Check control pressure.
4. Pressure regulator.
5. Valve body.
6. Forward clutch.
7. Leakage in hydraulic system.
8. Planetary one-way clutch.

Slips or Chatters in 2nd Gear

1. Check fluid level.
2. Vacuum diaphragm unit or tubes restricted, leaking or maladjusted.
3. Intermediate servo.
4. Intermediate band.
5. Check control pressure.
6. Pressure regulator.
7. Valve body.
8. Make air pressure check.
9. Forward clutch.
10. Leakage in hydraulic system.

Slips or Chatters in R

1. Check fluid level.
2. Vacuum diaphragm unit or tubes restricted, leaking or maladjusted.
3. Reverse band.
4. Check control pressure.
5. Reverse servo.
6. Pressure regulator.
7. Valve body.
8. Make air pressure check.
9. Reverse-high clutch.
10. Leakage in hydraulic system.
11. Reverse-high piston air bleed valve.

No Drive In D1 Only

1. Check fluid level.
2. Manual linkage.
3. Check control pressure.
4. Valve body.
5. Make air pressure check.
6. Planetary one-way clutch.

No Drive In D2 Only

1. Check fluid level.
2. Manual linkage.
3. Check control pressure.
4. Intermediate servo.
5. Valve body.
6. Make air pressure check.
7. Leakage in hydraulic system.
8. Planetary one-way clutch.

No Drive in L Only

1. Check fluid level.
2. Manual linkage.
3. Check control pressure.
4. Valve body.
5. Reverse servo.
6. Make air pressure check.
7. Leakage in hydraulic system.
8. Planetary one-way clutch.

No Drive in R Only

1. Check fluid level.
2. Manual linkage.
3. Reverse band.
4. Check control pressure.
5. Reverse servo.
6. Valve body.
7. Make air pressure check.
8. Reverse-high clutch.
9. Leakage in hydraulic system.
10. Reverse-high clutch piston air bleed valve.

No Drive in Any Selector Position

1. Check fluid level.
2. Manual linkage.
3. Check control pressure.
4. Pressure regulator.
5. Valve body.
6. Make air pressure check.

7. Leakage in hydraulic system.
8. Front pump.

Lockup in D1 Only

1. Reverse-high clutch.
2. Parking linkage.
3. Leakage in hydraulic system.

Lockup in D2 Only

1. Reverse band.
2. Reverse servo.
3. Reverse-high clutch.
4. Parking linkage.
5. Leakage in hydraulic system.
6. Planetary one-way clutch.

Lockup in L Only

1. Intermediate band.
2. Intermediate servo.
3. Reverse-high clutch.
4. Parking linkage.
5. Leakage in hydraulic system.

Lockup in R Only

1. Intermediate band.
2. Intermediate servo.
3. Forward clutch
4. Parking linkage.
5. Leakage in hydraulic system.

Parking Lock Binds or Won't Hold

1. Manual linkage.
2. Parking linkage.

Maximum Speed Too Low, Poor Acceleration

1. Engine performance.
2. Brakes bind.
3. Converter one-way clutch.

Noisy in N or P

1. Check fluid level.
2. Pressure regulator.
3. Front pump.
4. Planetary assembly.

Noisy in All Gears

1. Check fluid level.
2. Pressure regulator.
3. Planetary assembly.
4. Forward clutch.
5. Front pump.
6. Planetary one-way clutch.

Car Moves Forward in N

1. Manual linkage.
2. Forward clutch.

MAINTENANCE

Checking Oil Level

1. With transmission at operating temperature, park vehicle on a level surface.
2. Run engine at idle speed with service and parking brakes applied and move selector lever through each range. Return selector lever to Park.

3. With engine idling, remove dipstick and check fluid level. Fluid level should be between the Add and Full marks.
4. Add Type F fluid as required to bring the fluid to the proper level.

Drain & Refill

NOTE: *Normal maintenance and lubrication requirements do not necessitate periodic fluid changes. If a major failure has occurred in the transmission, it will have to be removed for service. At this time the converter must be thoroughly flushed to remove any foreign matter.*

When filling a dry transmission and converter, install five quarts of Type F fluid. Start engine, shift the selector lever through all ranges and place it at P position. Check fluid level and add enough to raise the level in the transmission to the "F" (full) mark on the dipstick.

When a partial drain and refill is required due to front band adjustment or minor repair, proceed as follows:

1. Loosen and remove all but two oil pan bolts and drop one edge of the pan to drain the oil.

NOTE: Some models of the C4 transmission can be drained by removing the filler tube from the pan.

2. Remove and clean pan and screen.
3. Place a new gasket on pan and install pan and screen.
4. Add three quarts of Type F fluid to transmission.
5. Run engine at idle speed for about two minutes.
6. Check oil level and add oil as necessary.
7. Run engine at a fast idle until it reaches normal operating temperature.
8. Shift selector lever through all ranges and then place it in P position.
9. Add fluid as required to bring the level to the full mark.

MANUAL LINKAGE, ADJUST

1969-74

Floor Shift

1. Place transmission selector lever in D position.
2. Raise car and loosen shift rod retaining nut, Fig. 3.
3. Move transmission manual lever to D position (third detent position from rear of transmission).
4. Tighten attaching nut to 10-20 ft. lbs.

NOTE: On some 1970-74 models, after adjusting manual linkage, adjust lock rod as follows:

1. Raise car and loosen rod retaining nut, Fig. 3.
2. Lower car and place shift lever in D position.
3. Align hole in steering column socket casting with column alignment mark and insert a .180" diameter gauge

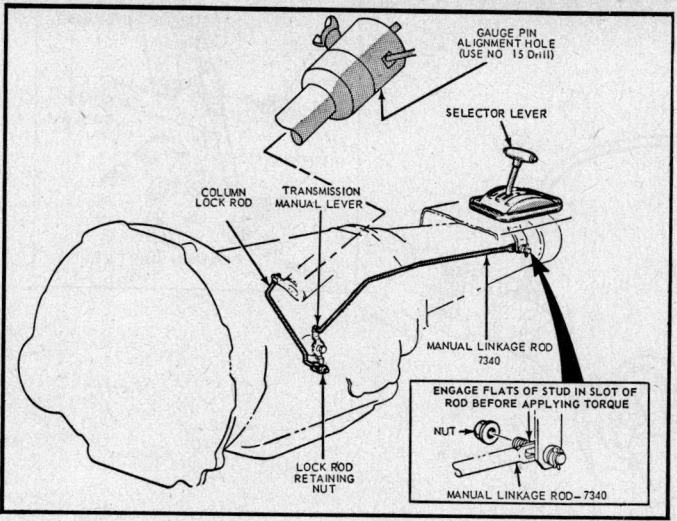

Fig. 3   Manual linkage, floorshift. Typical. Column lock rod is used on some models beginning 1970

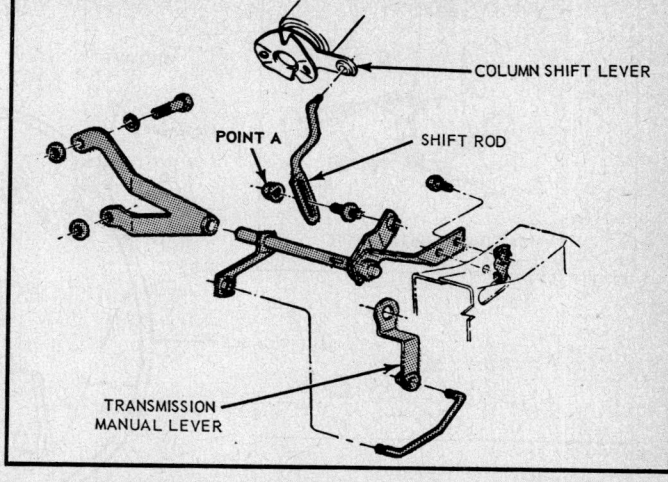

Fig. 4   Manual linkage. 1969-74 Ford column shift. Typical.

pin. Column casting must not rotate with pin in place.
4. Raise car and torque lock rod nut to 10-20 ft. lbs.

Column Shift

1. Place selector lever in D position (HI on Maverick with semi-automatic).
2. Loosen shift rod adjusting nut at point A, Figs. 4 through 8.
3. Shift manual lever at transmission to D or HI position. (Third from rear).
4. Tighten adjusting nut to 10-20 ft. lbs.

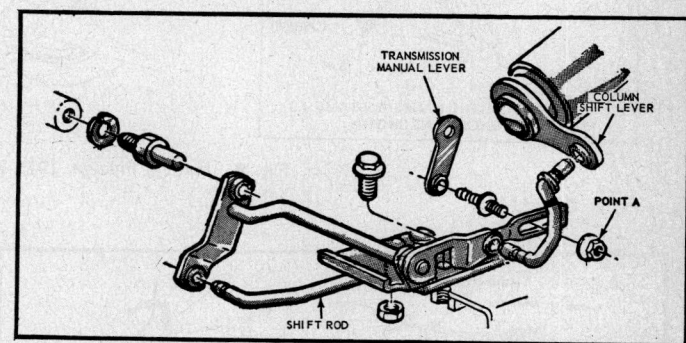

Fig. 5   Manual linkage. 1969-70 Fairlane, Falcon & Montego column shift

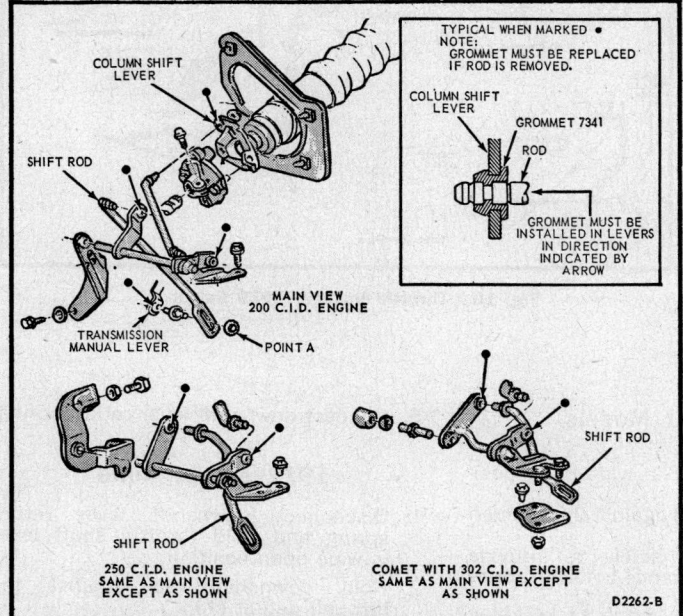

Fig. 6   Manual linkage. 1970-74 Maverick and Comet column shift

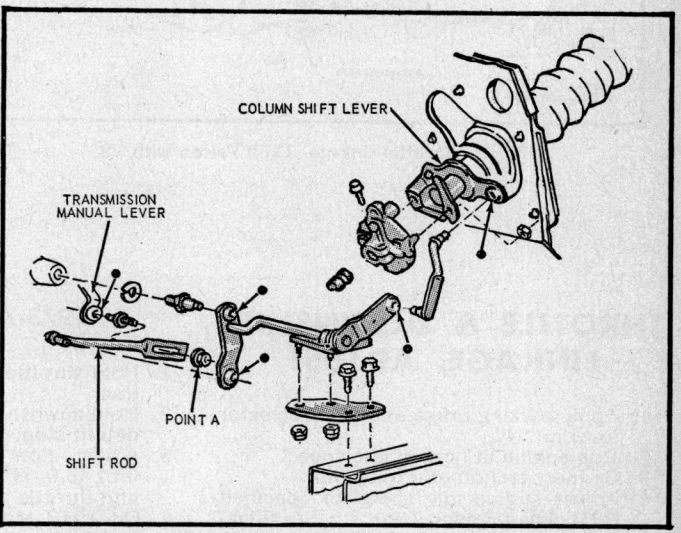

Fig. 7   Manual linkage. 1971 Torino and Montego column shift

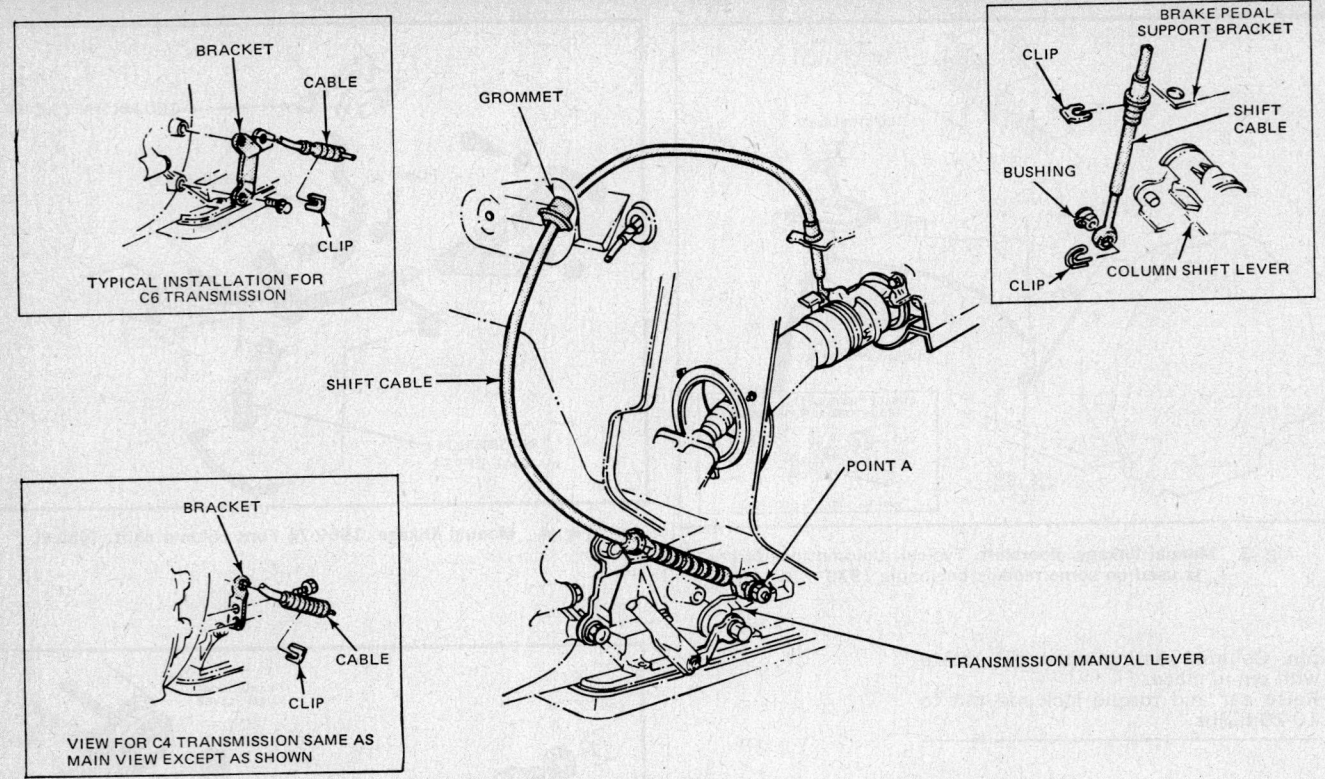

Fig. 8   Manual linkage. 1972-74 Torino & Montego column shift

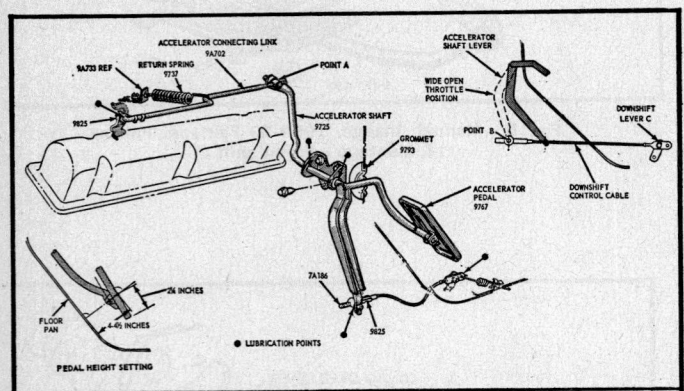

Fig. 9   Throttle linkage. 1969 Falcon with V8

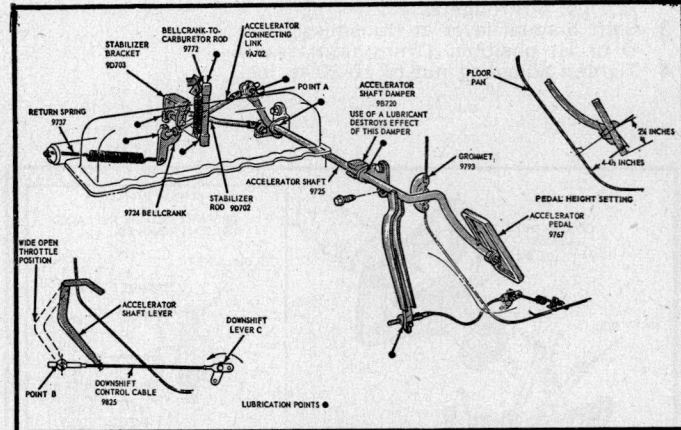

Fig. 10   Throttle linkage. 1969 Falcon 6

THROTTLE & DOWNSHIFT LINKAGE, ADJUST

1. Apply parking brake and place selector lever in "N".
2. Run engine at normal idle speed.
3. Connect tachometer to engine.
4. Adjust engine idle speed to specified RPM listed under Tune Up Specifications in individual car chapters.
5. Proceed with the adjustments as outlined below.

1973-74 All Models

1. Hold throttle lever in wide open position.
2. Hold downshift rod against the through detent stop.
3. Adjust downshift screw to provide 0.01 to 0.08" clearance between screw and throttle arm.
4. On 1973 Mustang, 1973-74 Montego and Torino six cylinder engines, tighten screw lock nut to maintain screw position.

5. Connect downshift lever return spring.

1972 except Pinto

1. Disconnect downshift lever return spring and hold throttle shaft lever in wide open position.
2. Hold downshift rod against the through detent stop.
3. Adjust downshift screw to provide .050-.070" clearance between screw and throttle shaft lever.

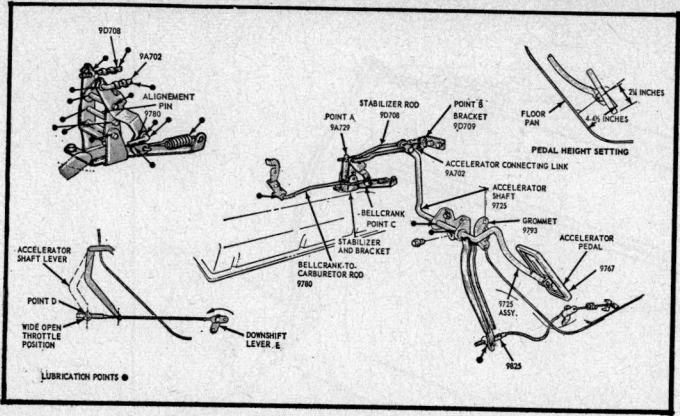

Fig. 11   Throttle linkage. 1969 Comet and Fairlane V8

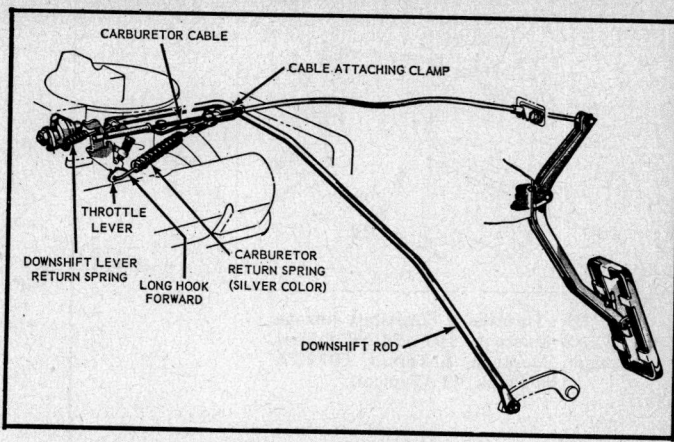

Fig. 12   Throttle linkage. 1969-70 Ford V8

4. On six cylinder engines, tighten lock-nut to maintain screw position.
5. Connect downshift lever return spring.

1971-72 Pinto

1. Disconnect downshift rod return spring. Hold throttle shaft lever in wide open position and hold downshift rod against the through detent stop.
2. Adjust downshift screw to provide .050-.070" clearance between screw tip and throttle shaft lever tab.
3. Connect downshift lever spring.

1969-71 Comet, Fairlane, Falcon, Montego & Mustang & 1969-71 Cougar

NOTE: On Fairlane and Montego V8 units, throttle bellcrank must be adjusted first. Disconnect carburetor rod and accelerator connecting link from bellcrank and stabilizer rod from stabilizer. Insert a ¼" diameter pin through the stabilizer and bracket and adjust the rods so their trunnions freely enter holes. Secure rods and remove pins.

1. On units with rod controlled throttle only, with engine off, check accel-

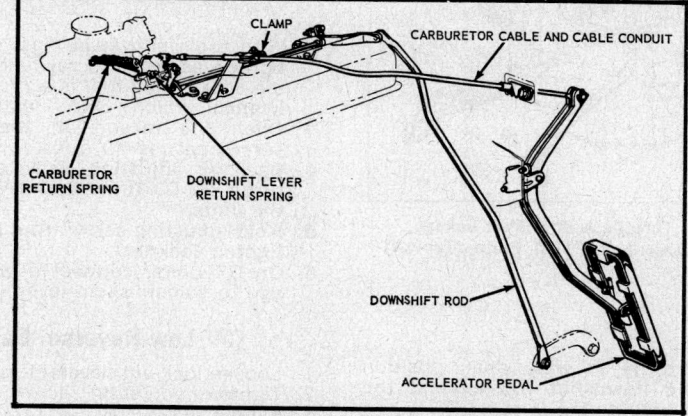

Fig. 13   Throttle linkage. 1969-70 Ford 6

erator pedal for a height of 4½" Figs. 9, 10 and 11. Adjust accelerator connecting link to correct. This step is not required on units with cable controlled throttles.
2. Disconnect downshift control cable from accelerator shaft lever.
3. With carburetor choke in the off posi-

tion, depress the accelerator and block it in the wide open position.
4. Rotate the downshift lever counterclockwise to place it against internal stop.
5. Except 1969 Mustang V8 and all 1970-71: With the lever held in this position and all slack removed from the cable, adjust the trunnion so that it will slide into the lever. Turn it one additional turn to increase length of cable then secure it to the lever with retaining clip.
6. On 1969 Mustang V8 and all 1970-71, turn adjustment screws on carburetor kick down lever to within .040" to .080" gap of contacting pick up surface of carburetor throttle lever.

1969-71 Ford

On all engines, the conduit covering the cable at the carburetor end must be evenly nestled between the clamp and the accelerator shaft bracket. Due to the fixed clamping of the cable conduit, accelerator pedal height adjustment is not required.

1. Disconnect the downshift lever return spring.

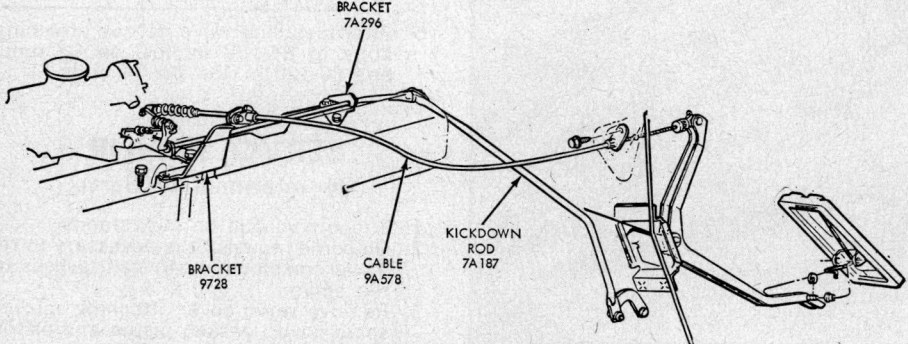

Fig. 14   Throttle & downshift linkage 1971-74 Ford & Mercury (typical)

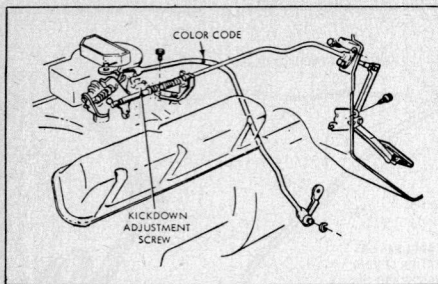

Fig. 15   Throttle & downshift linkage 1971-73 Mustang, 1971-74 V8 Comet, Cougar, Montego, & Torino; 1972-74 Maverick V8 (Typical)

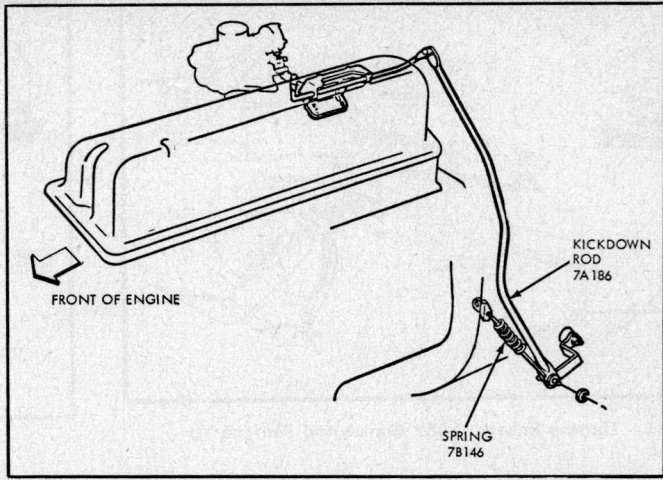

Fig. 16   Downshift linkage 1971-74 6 cyl. Comet, Maverick, Montego, Torino & 1971-73 Mustang

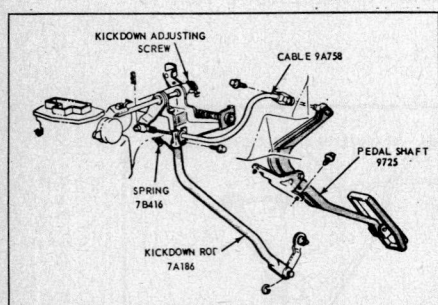

Fig. 17   Throttle & downshift linkage. 1974 Mustang II, 1971-74 Pinto (Typical)

2. Hold throttle in wide open position and hold downshift rod against the through detent stop.
3. Adjust the downshift screw to provide .050"-.070" clearance between the screw and the throttle shaft lever. On 6-240, tighten the lock nut to maintain the screw position. End play adjustments is not required.
4. Connect downshift lever return spring.

1969-70 Ford

1. Apply parking brake and place selector lever at N.
2. With engine idling at normal operating temperature, connect a tachometer.

BANDS, ADJUST

NOTE: The intermediate and low-reverse bands adjusting screw locknut must be discarded and a new one installed each time a band is adjusted.

Intermediate Band

C3 & C4

1. On C3 units, disconnect downshift linkage from transmission lever.
2. On all units, discard adjusting screw locknut and install a new locknut.

3. With tools shown in Figs. 18 and 19, tighten adjusting screw until tool handle clicks. *This tool is a pre-set torque wrench which clicks and overruns when the torque on the adjusting screw reaches 10 ft-lbs.*
4. Back off adjusting screw exactly $1\frac{1}{2}$ turns on C3 units and $1\frac{3}{4}$ turns on C4 units.
5. Hold adjusting screw from turning and tighten locknut.
6. On C3 units, connect downshift linkage to transmission lever.

C4 Low-Reverse Band

1. Loosen lock nut several turns.
2. Tighten adjusting screw until tool handle clicks, Fig. 20. *Tool shown is a pre-set torque wrench which clicks and overruns when the torque on the adjusting screw reaches 10 ft-lbs.*
3. Back off adjusting screw exactly 3 full turns.
4. Hold adjusting screw from turning and tighten lock nut.

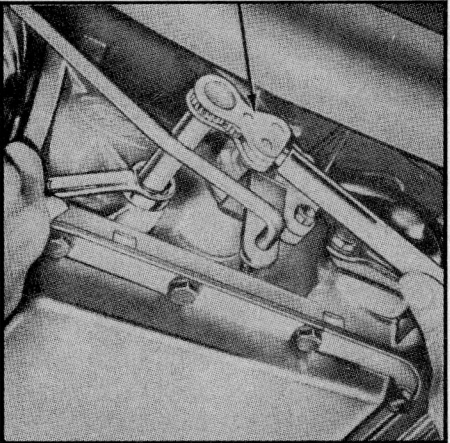

Fig. 18   Intermediate band adjustment. C4

CONTROL VALVE

NOTE: All fasteners used on C3 transmissions are designed to metric specifications.

1. Support vehicle on jack stands.
2. Drain transmission fluid, then remove oil pan, fluid screen, gasket and on early C3 units, remove three spacers.

NOTE: If fluid is to be reused, filter it through a 100 mesh screen.

3. On C3 units:
   a. Remove control valve attaching bolts. Note the different length and location of each bolt.
   b. Carefully remove control valve while unlocking and detaching selector lever connecting rod.
4. On C4 units:
   a. Shift selector lever into PARK and remove the two detent spring to control valve and case bolts.
   b. Remove remaining control valve to case bolts, then while holding manual valve inward, remove control valve.

NOTE: Failure to hold manual valve inward, while removing control valve, could cause manual valve to become damaged.

5. After installing valve, torque attaching bolts to 84-108 in. lbs. on C3 units and 80-120 in. lbs. on C4 units.

SERVO REPAIR
C4 Intermediate Servo

1. Support vehicle on jack stands.
2. On some models, it is necessary to remove crossmember to gain access to the servo.
3. Remove servo cover attaching screws, servo cover, gasket, piston and piston return spring.
4. Replace piston seals. Lubricate new

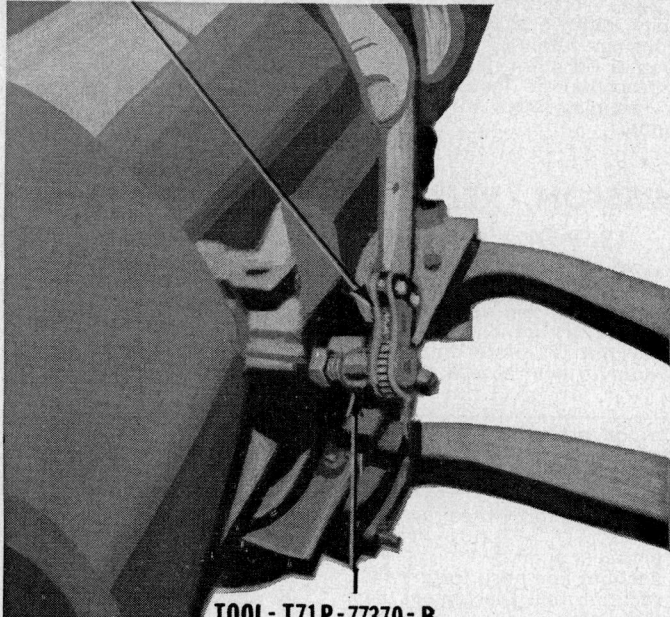

TOOL-T71P-77370-H

TOOL-T71P-77370-B

Fig. 19   Intermediate band adjustment. C3

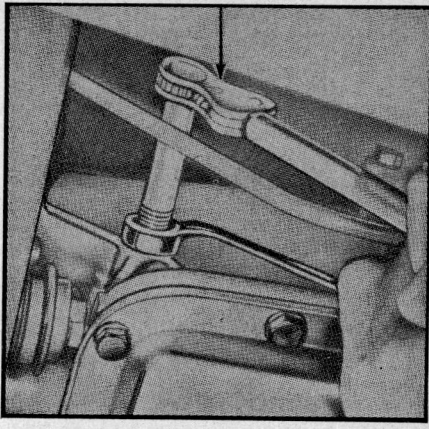

Fig. 20   Low-reverse band adjustment. C4

seals with transmission fluid before installation.

5. Reverse procedure to install.

C4 Low-Reverse Servo

1. Support vehicle on jack stands.
2. Loosen reverse band adjusting screw locknut and torque adjusting screw to 10 foot pounds. With adjusting screw torqued, the band strut is forced against case, preventing the strut from falling out of position when removing servo piston.

3. Remove servo cover retaining bolts, servo cover, seal and servo piston from case.
4. On some models, the piston seal is bonded to the piston, requiring piston replacement. To remove piston from stem, insert a small screwdriver

through hole in stem and remove piston retaining nut, piston, accumulator spring and spacer.

5. On all other models, replace piston seals. Lubricate new seals with transmission fluid before installation.
6. Reverse procedure to install.

C3 Rear Servo

1. Support vehicle on jack stands, then drain transmission.
2. Remove oil filter screws, gasket and on early models, three spacers.
3. Remove servo cover retaining screws, servo cover, piston and spring, Fig. 21.
4. Reverse procedure to intsall.

Fig. 21   Rear servo removal. C3

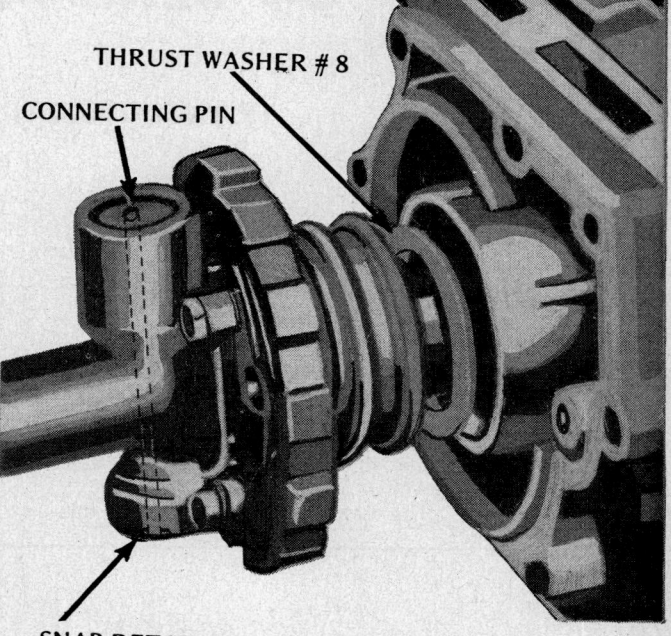

THRUST WASHER # 8

CONNECTING PIN

SNAP RETAINER

Fig. 22   Governor removal. C3

EXTENSION HOUSING

1. Support vehicle on jack stands and remove driveshaft.

   NOTE: Scribe marks on driveshaft yoke and companion flange, to insure proper positioning of driveshaft during assembly.

2. Support transmission with suitable jack and disconnect speedometer cable.

   NOTE: On some models, it will be necessary to disconnect the exhaust system from the exhaust manifolds to perform the following step.

3. Remove engine rear support to crossmember attaching bolts or nuts, then raise transmission slightly and remove rear support from extension housing.

   NOTE: On some models, it will be necessary to remove crossmember in order to remove rear support from extension housing.

4. Loosen extension housing bolts and allow transmission fluid to drain and remove extension housing.

GOVERNOR

1. Remove extension housing as described previously.
2. On C3 units, remove governor retaining pin snap ring, then the retaining pin, Fig. 22.
3. On all units, remove governor to governor housing retaining bolts and slide governor off output shaft.
4. Reverse procedure to install. Torque governor retaining bolts to 7 to 10 foot pounds.

TRANSMISSION, REPLACE

1969-74

1. Support vehicle on jack stands and remove converter housing lower cover.
2. Drain transmission oil pan and the converter. Use a wrench on crankshaft pulley nut to rotate crankshaft and converter to gain access to drain plug.

   NOTE: Do not rotate 2000 cc or 2300 cc engines in opposite direction of normal rotation.

3. Remove converter to flywheel bolts or nuts.
4. Remove propeller shaft.
5. Remove vacuum line hose from transmission vacuum unit. Disconnect vacuum line from clip.
6. If equipped, disconnect TRS switch wire.
7. Remove two extension housing to crossmember bolts.
8. Remove speedometer cable from extension housing.
9. On 1969 models and 1971-74 Comet, Maverick, Mustang and Pinto models, disconnect exhaust pipe from manifold.
10. On 1969 models, disconnect parking brake cable from equalizer lever.
11. On all models, disconnect oil cooler lines from transmission.
12. Remove the manual and kick down linkage rods from transmission shift levers.
13. Where necessary, disconnect the neutral start switch wires.
14. Remove starter.
15. Remove transmission fluid filler tube.
16. On all models except 1971-74 Pinto and 1974 Mustang II:
    a. Support transmission with a suitable jack and remove crossmember.
    b. Remove converter housing to engine bolts and lower transmission from vehicle.
17. On 1971-74 Pinto and 1974 Mustang II:
    a. Raise transmission slightly with a suitable jack and remove engine rear support to crossmember nut.
    b. Remove crossmember attaching bolts and crossmember.
    c. Lower jack, allowing transmission to hang, and raise front of engine with a suitable jack, thereby gaining access to the two upper converter housing to engine bolts.
    d. Secure transmission to jack, remove the lower converter housing to engine bolts, then the two upper bolts, move transmission rearward and lower from vehicle.
18. Reverse procedure to install.

C4 SEMI-AUTOMATIC

TRANSMISSION IDENTIFICATION

Maverick	Code
1970	PEG-A
1971	PEG-A1

GENERAL DESCRIPTION

This unit is essentially the same as the C4 Cruise-O-Matic except that the automatic shifting provisions have been removed.

The major differences between this unit and the C4 are the control valve body and the manual linkage. The manual linkage adjustment procedures are the same as the C4, however, the shift selector position of "Hi" on this unit is the equivalent of "D" on the C4.

For service procedures on this unit, refer to the C4 Dual Range chapter.

TRANSMISSION IDENTIFICATION

An identification tag attached to the servo cover bolt, includes the model prefix and suffix.

YEAR	CAR MODEL	TRANS. MODEL	ENGINE MODEL
1969	Cougar(2)	PGA-AE	V8-390(3)
	Cougar	PGB-AF-1	V8-428(4)
	Fairlane(1)	PGA-AC	V8-390(4)
	Fairlane(2)	PGA-AD	V8-390(4)
	Fairlane(1)	PGB-AG	V8-428(4)
	Fairlane(2)	PGB-AH	V8-428(4)
	Ford(1)	PGA-A3	V8-390(3)
	Ford(2)	PGA-J3	V8-390(3)
	Ford(1)	PGA-Z	V8-429(3)
	Ford(2)	PGA-AA	V8-429(4)
	Ford(2)	PGB-F2	V8-428(4)
	Ford(1)	PBG-G2	V8-390
	Ford(1)	PGB-H2	V8-428(4)
	Ford(1)	PGB-AD	V8-429(4)
	Ford(2)	PGB-AE	V8-429(4)
	Lincoln	PGC-B	V8-460
	Mark III	PGC-C1	V8-460
	Mercury(1)	PGA-A3	V8-390(3)
	Mercury(2)	PGA-J3	V8-390(3)
	Mercury(1)	PGA-Z	V8-429(3)
	Mercury(1)	PGA-AA	V8-429(4)
	Mercury(1)	PGB-F2	V8-428(4)
	Mercury(1)	PGB-G2	V8-390
	Mercury(1)	PGB-H2	V8-428(4)
	Mercury(1)	PGB-AD	V8-429(4)
	Mercury(2)	PGB-AE	V8-429(4)
	Montego(1)	PGA-AC	V8-390(4)
	Montego(2)	PGA-AD	V8-390(4)
	Montego(1)	PGB-AG	V8-428(4)
	Montego(2)	PGB-AH	V8-428(4)
	Mustang(2)	PGA-AE	V8-390(3)
	Mustang(2)	PGB-AF-1	V8-428(4)
	Thunderbird	PGB-J1	V8-429(4)
1970	Cougar	PGB-AF2	V8-428
	Fairlane(2)	PJB-A	V8-429
	Fairlane(1)	PJB-B	V8-429
	Fairlane(1)	PJB-J	V8-429
	Fairlane(1)	PJC-A	V8-429
	Fairlane(1)	PJC-B	V8-429
	Fairlane(1)	PJC-E	V8-429
	Fairlane(2)	PJC-F	V8-429
	Ford(1)	PGA-A4	V8-390
	Ford(2)	PGA-J4	V8-390
	Ford(1)	PGB-F3	V8-428
	Ford(1)	PGB-G3	V8-390
	Ford(1)(3)	PJA-A	V8-429
	Ford(2)(3)	PJA-B	V8-429
	Ford(1)(4)	PJB-C	V8-429
	Ford(2)(4)	PJB-D	V8-429
	Ford(1)(4)	PJB-F	V8-429
	Lincoln	PJD-CF	V8-460
	Mark III	PJD-BE	V8-460
	Mercury(1)	PGA-A4	V8-390
	Mercury(2)	PGA-J4	V8-390
	Mercury(1)	PGB-F3	V8-428
	Mercury(1)	PGB-G3	V8-390
	Mercury(1)(3)	PJA-A	V8-429
	Mercury(2)(3)	PJA-B	V8-429
	Mercury(1)(4)	PJB-C	V8-429
	Mercury(1)	PJB-D	V8-429
	Mercury(1)(4)	PJB-F	V8-429
	Montego(1)	PJB-A	V8-429
	Montego(2)	PJB-B	V8-429
	Montego(1)	PJB-J	V8-429
	Montego(1)	PJC-A	V8-429
	Montego(2)	PJC-B	V8-429
	Montego(1)	PJC-E	V8-429
	Montego(2)	PJC-F	V8-429
	Mustang	PGB-AF2	V8-428
	Thunderbird	PJB-GH	V8-429
1971	Cougar	PGA-AH	V8-351
	Cougar	PJC-G	V8-429
	Fairlane(1)	PGA-AF	V8-351
	Fairlane(1)	PGA-AG	V8-351
	Fairlane(1)	PJC-A	V8-429
	Fairlane(2)	PJC-B	V8-429
	Ford(1)	PGA-A4	V8-390
	Ford(2)	PGA-J4	V8-390
	Ford(1)(5)	PGB-G3	V8-390
	Ford(2)	PJA-A	V8-429
	Ford(2)(3)	PJA-B	V8-429
	Ford(1)	PJA-C	V8-400
	Ford(2)	PJA-D	V8-400
	Ford(4)	PJB-C	V8-429
	Ford(2)(4)	PJB-D	V8-429
	Ford(1)(5)	PJB-F	V8-429
	Ford(1)(5)	PJB-K	V8-400
	Ford(5)	PJC-HI	V8-429
	Lincoln	PJD-F	V8-460
	Mark III	PJD-E	V8-460
	Mercury(1)(3)	PJA-A	V8-429
	Mercury	PJA-C	V8-400
	Mercury(1)(4)	PJB-C	V8-429
	Mercury(1)(5)	PJB-F	V8-429
	Mercury(1)(5)	PJB-K	V8-400
	Mercury(1)(5)	PJC-HI	V8-429
	Montego(1)	PGA-AF	V8-351
	Montego(2)	PGA-AG	V8-351
	Montego(1)	PJC-A	V8-429
	Montego(2)	PJC-B	V8-429
	Mustang	PGA-AH	V8-351
	Mustang	PJC-G	V8-429
	Thunderbird	PJB-H	V8-429
1972	Cougar(3)	PGA-AV1	V8-351
	Cougar(4)	PGA-AU1, 2	V8-351
	Cougar(4)	PGA-AH1, 2	V8-351
	Ford(1)	PJA-C2	V8-400
	Ford(1)	PJA-C2	V8-429
	Ford(1)	PJA-K	V8-400
	Ford(1)	PJB-K1	V8-400
	Ford(1)(5)	PJB-K1	V8-429
	Ford(1)(5)	PJC-H2	V8-429
	Ford(1)(5)	PJC-H4	V8-429
	Lincoln	PJD-F1	V8-460
	Mark IV	PJD-E1	V8-460
	Mercury	PJA-C2	V8-400
	Mercury	PJA-C2	V8-429
	Mercury(5)	PJB-K1	V8-400
	Mercury(5)	PJB-K1	V8-429
	Mercury(5)	PJC-H2	V8-429
	Mercury	PJD-G	V8-460
	Montego(1)	PGA-AF1	V8-351
	Montego(2)	PGA-AG1	V8-351
	Montego(1)	PJA-G	V8-400
	Montego(1)	PJA-G	V8-429
	Montego(1)	PJA-H	V8-400
	Montego(2)	PJA-H	V8-429
	Mustang(3)	PGA-AV1	V8-351
	Mustang	PGA-AU1	V8-351
	Torino(1)(5)	PGA-AW	V8-351
	Torino(2)(3)	AGA-AY	V8-351
	Torino(1)(4)	PGA-AF1	V8-351
	Torino(2)(4)	PGA-AG1	V8-351
	Torino(1)	PJA-G	V8-400
	Torino(1)	PJA-G	V8-429
	Torino(1)(3)	PJA-L	V8-400
	Torino(2)(3)	PJA-M	V8-400
	Torino(2)	PJA-H	V8-400
	Torino(3)	PJA-H	V8-429
	Torino(1)(5)	PJC-J	V8-429
	Thunderbird	PJA-J	V8-400
	Thunderbird	PJA-J	V8-429
	Thunderbird	PJD-E1	V8-460
1973	Cougar(2)(3)	PGA-AV2	V8-351
	Cougar(2)(4)	PGA-AV3	V8-351
	Ford(1)	PJA-C3-4	V8-400
	Ford(1)(5)	PJB-K2-3	V8-400
	Ford(1)(5)	PJB-C1	V8-429
	Ford(1)(5)	PJB-F1	V8-429
	Ford(1)(5)	PJC-H5	V8-460
	Lincoln	PJD-F2	V8-460
	Mark IV	PJD-E2	V8-460
	Mercury(1)	PJB-K2	V8-400
	Mercury(1)	PJA-C3-4	V8-400
	Mercury(1)(5)	PJB-K3	V8-400
	Mercury(1)	PJB-C1	V8-429
	Mercury(1)(5)	PJB-F1	V8-429
	Mercury(1)(5)	PJC-H5	V8-460
	Mercury(1)	PJD-J1	V8-460
	Montego(1)	PGA-AW1	V8-351C
	Montego(2)	PGA-AY1	V8-351C
	Montego(1)	PGA-AZ1	V8-351W
	Montego(2)	PGA-BA1	V8-351W
	Montego(1)(4)	PGA-AF2	V8-351
	Montego(2)(4)	PGA-AG2	V8-351
	Montego(1)	PJA-G1-2	V8-400
	Montego(2)	PJA-H1-2	V8-400
	Montego(1)	PJB-A1-B1	V8-429
	Montego(1)(5)	PJC-J1	V8-460
	Mustang(2)	PGA-AV2	V8-351C
	Mustang(2)	PGA-AV3	V8-351CJ
	Torino(1)	PGA-AW1	V8-351C
	Torino(2)	PGA-AY1	V8-351C
	Torino(2)	PGA-AF2	V8-351CJ
	Torino(2)	PGA-AG2	V8-351CJ
	Torino(1)	PGA-AZ1	V8-351W
	Torino(2)	PGA-BA1	V8-351W
	Torino(1)	PJA-G1-2	V8-400
	Torino(2)	PJA-H1-2	V8-400
	Torino(1)	PJB-A1	V8-429
	Torino(2)	PJB-B1	V8-429
	Torino(1)	PJC-J1	V8-460
	Thunderbird	PJA-J1	V8-429
	Thunderbird	PJD-E2	V8-460
1974	Cougar(1)(3)	PGA-AW	V8-351
	Cougar(1)(4)	PGA-AF3	V8-351
	Cougar(2)(3)	PGA-AY2, 3	V8-351
	Cougar(2)(4)	PGA-AG3, 4	V8-351
	Cougar(1)	PJA-G3	V8-400
	Cougar(2)	PJA-H3, 4	V8-400
	Cougar(1)	PJD-R	V8-460
	Cougar(2)	PJD-S, S1	V8-460
	Ford	PJA-C5	V8-400
	Ford(5)	PJC-H6	V8-460
	Ford	PJD-G3	V8-460
	Lincoln	PJD-F4	V8-460
	Mark IV	PJD-E4	V8-460
	Mercury	PJA-C5	V8-400
	Mercury(5)	PJC-H6	V8-460
	Mercury	PJD-G3	V8-460
	Montego(3)	PGA-AW2	V8-351
	Montego(4)	PGA-AF3	V8-351
	Montego	PJA-C3	V8-400
	Montego(5)	PJC-J2	V8-460

Continued

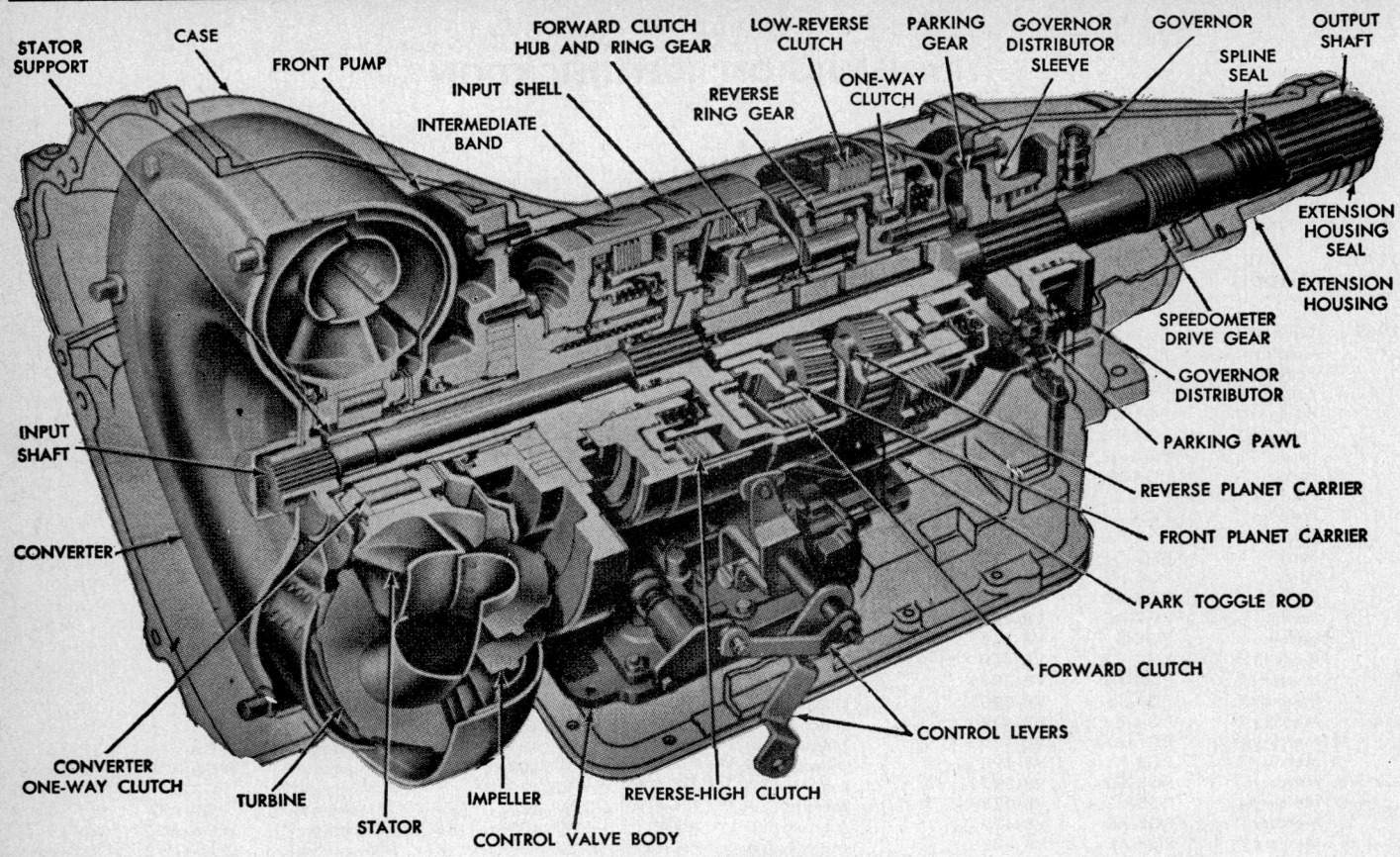

Fig. 1 Sectional view of C6 transmission

TRANSMISSION IDENTIFICATION—Continued

YEAR	CAR MODEL	TRANS. MODEL	ENGINE MODEL	YEAR	CAR MODEL	TRANS. MODEL	ENGINE MODEL	
1974	Montego	PJD-R	V8-460	1974	Torino②④	PJA-H3, 4	V8-400	①—Column shift.
	Torino①③	PGA-AW2	V8-351		Torino①⑤	PJC-J2	V8-460	②—Floor shift.
	Torino②③	PGA-AY2, 3	V8-351		Torino①	PJD-R	V8-460	③—Two barrel carburetor.
	Torino①④	PGA-AF3	V8-351		Torino②	PJD-S, S1	V8-460	④—Four barrel carburetor.
	Torino②④	PGA-AG3, 4	V8-351		Thunderbird	PJD-E4	V8-460	⑤—Police or Fleet.
	Torino①④	PJA-C3	V8-400					

DESCRIPTION

As shown in Fig. 1, the transmission consists essentially of a torque converter, a compound planetary gear train controlled by one band, three disc clutches and a one-way clutch, and a hydraulic control system.

The transmission is made so that a system of manual and automatic shifting is provided.

Automatic & Manual Shifting 1969-74

This unit has a shift pattern which is indicated on the selector as P-R-N-D-2-1. This refers respectively to Park, Reverse, Neutral, Full Automatic, Second Gear (manual), Low Gear (manual).

In this unit an overriding control is provided which enables the driver to exercise his own judgement with regard to the gear ratios to be selected and an understanding of what is possible greatly enhances the pleasure to be derived from driving the car. No automatic mechanism has the power of anticipation, but the driver can see ahead and has the means for over-riding the automatic mechanism.

Automatic Shift

In "D" position the shift sequence is fully automatic in that the transmission starts in low gear and upshifts through second gear to third or high gear.

Manual Shifting

The shift to 2 or 1 is done manually by shifting the lever from neutral to either position. In "1" position, the transmisson starts in 1st (low gear) and is retained. In "2" position it starts in 2nd gear and remains in 2nd gear, regardless of road speed.

Manual Shift To "1"

Manual shifting from "D" to "1" can also be accomplished any time. Here the transmission immediately shifts to second and remains in second until the predetermined governor control speed allows it to shift down to low gear where it remains. The governor speed control at this point eliminates the possibility of a direct down shift to low gear until the road speed is reduced.

Shift Lever Controls

A shift lever button control is used to shift from neutral to reverse or park, also when shifting from "D" to "2" or "1" position. However, the button control function is not required when shifting from neutral to "D", or to shift forward from "1" to "2" position.

Parking Pawl

The transmission gear train is in neutral in both P and N positions. There is no pressure to any clutch and only the transmission input shaft turns. In park, a pawl engages a parking gear which is splined to the transmission output shaft, Fig. 1, to lock the rear wheels to the transmission main case.

A neutral start switch, mounted on the transmission and operated by the selector linkage, completes the engine cranking circuit in P and N only so that the engine cannot be started in any drive gear.

Forced Downshifts

Forced downshifts (kickdown shifts) from high to second gear are possible at speeds as high as 65 mph in D1 or D2. In D1 it is possible to force a downshift to 1st gear up to 30 mph.

The carburetor is at full throttle before the accelerator is floored. Up to full throttle, a "torque demand" downshift to 2nd is possible up to 40 mph. "Kickdown" shifts require depressing the accelerator to the floor to actuate the downshift valve in the transmission.

TROUBLE SHOOTING GUIDE

No Drive In Forward Speeds

1. Manual linkage adjustment.
2. Check control pressure.
3. Valve body.
4. Make air pressure check.
5. Forward clutch.
6. Leakage in hydraulic system.

Rough Initial Engagement in D, D1, D2 or 2

1. Engine idle speed too high.
2. Vacuum diaphragm unit or tubes restricted, leaking or maladjusted.
3. Check control pressure.
4. Valve body.
5. Forward clutch.

1-2 or 2-3 Shift Points Incorrect or Erratic

1. Check fluid level.
2. Vacuum diaphragm unit or tubes restricted, leaking or maladjusted.
3. Downshift linkage, including inner lever position.
4. Manual linkage adjustment.
5. Governor defective.
6. Check control pressure.
7. Valve body.
8. Make air pressure check.

Rough 1-2 Upshifts

1. Vacuum diaphragm unit or tubes restricted, leaking or maladjusted.
2. Intermediate servo.
3. Intermediate band
4. Check control pressure.
5. Valve body.

Rough 2-3 Shifts

1. Vacuum diaphragm or tubes restricted leaking or maladjusted.
2. Intermediate servo.
3. Check control pressure.
4. Intermediate band.
5. Valve body.
6. Make air pressure check.
7. Reverse-high clutch.
8. Reverse-high clutch piston air bleed valve.

Dragged Out 1-2 Shift

1. Check fluid level.
2. Vacuum diaphragm unit or tubes restricted, leaking or maladjusted.
3. Intermediate servo.
4. Check control pressure.
5. Intermediate band.
6. Valve body.
7. Make air pressure check.
8. Leakage in hydraulic system.

Engine Overspeeds on 2-3 Shift

1. Manual linkage adjustment.
2. Check fluid level.
3. Vacuum diaphragm unit or tubes restricted, leaking or maladjusted.
4. Intermediate servo.
5. Check control pressure.
6. Valve body.
7. Intermediate band.
8. Reverse-high clutch.
9. Reverse-high clutch piston air bleed valve.

No 1-2 or 2-3 Shift

1. Manual linkage adjustment.
2. Downshift linkage including inner lever position.
3. Vacuum diaphragm unit or tubes restricted, leaking or malajusted.
4. Governor.
5. Check control pressure.
6. Valve body.
7. Intermediate band.
8. Intermediate servo.
9. Reverse-high clutch.
10. Leakage in hydraulic system.

No 3-1 Shift In D1, 2 or 3-2 Shift In D2 or D

1. Governor.
2. Valve body.

No Forced Downshifts

1. Downshift linkage, including inner lever position.
2. Check control pressure.
3. Valve body.

Runaway Engine on Forced 3-2 Shift

1. Check control pressure.
2. Intermediate servo.
3. Intermediate band.
4. Valve body.
5. Vacuum diaphragm unit or tubes restricted, leaking or maladjusted.
6. Leakage in hydraulic system.

Rough 3-2 Shift or 3-1 Shift at Closed Throttle

1. Engine idle speed.
2. Vacuum diaphragm unit or tubes restricted, leaking or maladjusted.
3. Intermediate servo.
4. Check control pressure.
5. Valve body.

Shifts 1-3 in D, D1, 2, D2

1. Intermediate band.
2. Intermediate servo.
3. Valve body.
4. Governor.
5. Make air pressure check.

No Engine Braking in 1st Gear—Manual Low Range

1. Manual linkage adjustment.
2. Low-reverse clutch.
3. Valve body.
4. Governor.
5. Make air pressure check.
6. Leakage in hydraulic system.

Creeps Excessively

1. Engine idle speed too high.

Slips or Chatters In 1st Gear, D1

1. Check fluid level.
2. Vacuum diaphragm unit or tubes restricted, leaking or maladjusted.
3. Check control peessure.
4. Valve body.
5. Forward clutch.
6. Leakage in hydraulic system.
7. Planetary one-way clutch.

Slips or Chatters In 2nd Gear

1. Check fluid level.
2. Vacuum diaphragm unit or tubes restricted, leaking or maladjusted.
3. Intermediate servo.
4. Intermediate band.
5. Check control pressure.
6. Valve body.
7. Make air pressure check.
8. Forward clutch.
9. Leakage in hydraulic system.

Slips or Chatters In Reverse

1. Check fluid level.
2. Vacuum diaphragm unit or tubes restricted, leaking or maladjusted.
3. Manual linkage adjustment.
4. Low-reverse clutch.
5. Check control pressure.
6. Valve body.
7. Make air pressure check.
8. Reverse-high clutch.
9. Leakage in hydraulic system.
10. Reverse-high clutch piston air bleed valve.

No Drive In D1 or 2

1. Manual linkage adjustment.
2. Check control pressure.
3. Valve body.
4. Planetary one-way clutch.

No Drive In D, D2

1. Check fluid level.
2. Manual linkage adjustment.

3. Check control pressure.
4. Intermediate servo.
5. Valve body.
6. Make air pressure check.
7. Leakage in hydraulic system.

No Drive In L or 1

1. Check fluid level.
2. Check control pressure.
3. Valve body.
4. Make air pressure check.
5. Leakage in hydraulic system.

No Drive In R Only

1. Check fluid level.
2. Manual linkage adjustment.
3. Low-reverse clutch.
4. Check control pressure.
5. Valve body.
6. Make air pressure check.
7. Reverse-high clutch.
8. Leakage in hydraulic system.
9. Reverse-high clutch piston air bleed valve.

No Drive In Any Selector Position

1. Check fluid level.
2. Manual linkage adjustment.
3. Check control pressure.
4. Valve body.
5. Make air pressure check.
6. Leakage in hydraulic system.
7. Front pump.

Lockup In D1 or 2

1. Valve body.
2. Parking linkage.
3. Leakage in hydraulic system.

Lockup In D2 or D

1. Low-reverse clutch.
2. Valve body.
3. Reverse-high clutch.
4. Parking linkage.
5. Leakage in hydraulic system.
6. Planetary one-way clutch.

Lockup In L or 1

1. Valve body.
2. Parking linkage.
3. Leakage in hydraulic system.

Lockup In R Only

1. Valve body.
2. Forward clutch.
3. Parking linkage.
4. Leakage in hydraulic system.

Parking Lock Binds or Does Not Hold

1. Manual linkage adjustment.
2. Parking linkage.

Transmission Overheats

1. Oil cooler and connections.
2. Valve body.
3. Vacuum diaphragm unit or tubes restricted, leaking or maladjusted.
4. Check control pressure.
5. Converter one-way clutch.
6. Converter pressure check valves.

Maximum Speed Too Low, Poor Acceleration

1. Engine performance.
2. Car brakes.
3. Forward clutch.

Transmission Noisy In N and P

1. Check fluid level.
2. Valve body.
3. Front pump.

Noisy In 1st, 2nd, 3rd or Reverse

1. Check fluid level.
2. Valve body.
3. Planetary assembly.
4. Forward clutch.
5. Reverse-high clutch.
6. Planetary one-way clutch.

Car Moves Forward In N

1. Manual linkage adjustment.
2. Forward clutch.

Fluid Leak

1. Check fluid level.
2. Converter drain plugs.
3. Oil pan gasket, filler tube or seal.
4. Oil cooler and connections.
5. Manual or downshift lever shaft seal.
6. 1/8" pipe plugs in case.
7. Extension housing-to-case gasket.
8. Extension housing rear oil seal.
9. Speedometer driven gear adapter seal.
10. Vacuum diaphragm unit or tubes.
11. Intermediate servo.
12. Engine rear oil seal.

MAINTENANCE
Checking Oil Level

1. Make sure car is on a level floor.
2. Apply parking brake firmly.
3. Run engine at normal idle speed. If transmission fluid is cold, run engine at a fast idle until fluid reaches normal operating temperature. When fluid is warm, slow engine to normal idle speed.
4. Shift selector lever through all positions, then place lever at "P". Do not shut down engine during fluid level checks.
5. Clean all dirt from dipstick cap before removing dipstick from filler tube.
6. Pull dipstick out of tube, wipe it clean and push it all the way back in tube.
7. Pull dipstick out of tube again and check fluid level. If necessary, add enough fluid to raise the level to the "F" mark on dipstick. Do not overfill.

Drain & Refill

NOTE: The Ford Motor Company recommends the use of an automatic transmission fluid with Qualification No. M2C-33F (on container) instead of the conventional Type A fluid. The recommended fluid is said to have a greater coefficient of friction and greater ability to handle maximum engine torques without band or clutch slippage.

Normal maintenance and lubrication requirements do not necessitate periodic fluid changes. If a major failure has occurred in the transmission, it will have to be removed for service. At this time the converter must be thoroughly flushed to remove any foreign matter.

1. To drain the fluid, loosen pan attaching bolts and allow fluid to drain.
2. After fluid has drained to the level of the pan flange, remove pan bolts working from rear and both sides of pan to allow it to drop and drain slowly.
3. When fluid has stopped draining, remove and clean pan and screen. Discard pan gasket.
4. Using a new gasket, install pan.
5. Add 3 quarts of recommended fluid to transmission through filler tube.
6. Run engine at idle speed for 2 minutes, and then run it at a fast idle until it reaches normal operating temperature.
7. Shift selector lever through all positions, place it at "P" and check fluid level.
8. If necessary, add enough fluid to transmission to bring it to the "F" mark on the dipstick.

MANUAL LINKAGE, ADJUST
1969-73

Column Shift

1. Place selector lever in D position.
2. Loosen shift rod adjusting nut, point A in Figs. 2 through 8.
3. Shift transmission manual lever to D, third detent from rear of transmission.
4. Make sure selector lever has not moved from D position then tighten adjusting nut to 10-20 ft. lbs.

Floor Shift

1. Place transmission selector lever in D position.
2. Raise car and loosen shift rod retaining nut, Fig. 9.
3. Move transmission manual lever to D position, third detent from rear of transmission.
4. Tighten retaining nut to 10-20 ft. lbs.

NOTE: On some 1970-73 models, after adjusting manual linkage, adjust lock rod as follows:

1. Raise car and loosen lock rod retaining nut, Fig. 9.
2. Lower car and place shift lever in D position.

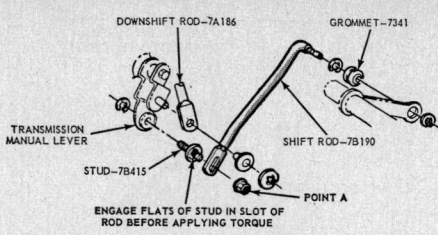

Fig. 2 Column shift linkage. 1969-70 Continental

3. Align hole steering column socket casting with column alignment mark and insert a .180" diameter gauge rod. Column casting must not rotate with rod in place.
4. Raise car and torque lock rod nut to 10-20 ft. lbs.

THROTTLE & DOWNSHIFT LINKAGE

Adjusting the throttle linkage is important to be certain the throttle and kickdown systems are properly adjusted. The kickdown system should come in when the accelerator is pressed through detent, and not before detent. See Figs. 8-15.

1973-74 All Models

1. Hold carburetor lever in the wide open throttle position.
2. Hold downshift rod against through detent stop.
3. Adjust downshift screw to provide .01 to .08 inch clearance between screw and throttle arm.
4. Connect downshift lever return spring.

1969-71 Ford & Mercury, 1970-71 Lincoln, 1972 All

On all engines, the conduit covering the cable at the carburetor end must be evenly nestled between the clamp and the accelerator shaft bracket. Due to the fixed clamping of the cable conduit, accelerator pedal height adjustment is not required.

1. Disconnect downshift lever return spring.
2. Hold throttle in wide open position and hold downshift rod against the through detent stop.
3. Adjust the downshift screw to provide .050"-.070" clearance between the screw and the throttle shaft lever.
4. Connect downshift lever return spring.

1969-71 Mustang & Cougar & 1970-71 Fairlane/Torino & Montego

Because the throttle is cable operated, the transmission kickdown is the only adjustment required.

1. Disconnect the throttle and downshift return springs.
2. Hold the carburetor throttle lever in the wide open position against the stop.
3. Hold the transmission in full downshift position against the internal stop.
4. Turn adjustment screw on the carburetor kickdown lever to within .040"-.080" gap of contacting pickup surface of carburetor throttle lever.
5. Release the transmission and carburetor to the normal free position.
6. Install the throttle and downshift return springs.

1969 Fairlane & Montego

1. With engine off, check and adjust accelerator pedal for a height of 4½", Fig. 10. Adjust connecting link at point "A" to obtain correct dimension.

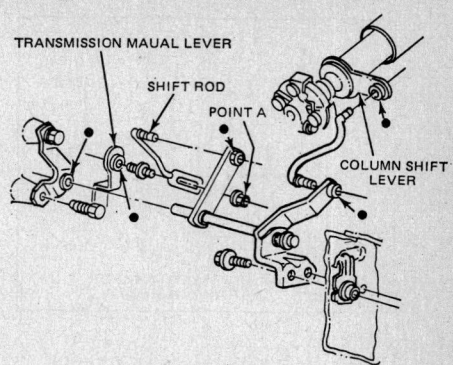

Fig. 3 Column shift linkage. 1971-74 Continental (Typical)

2. Disconnect the downshift control cable or rod at point "B".
3. With the carburetor choke in the off position, depress the accelerator pedal to the floor and block it in the wide open position.
4. Rotate the downshift lever counterclockwise to place it against the internal stop.
5. With the lever held in this position and, if cable is used, all slack is removed from the cable, adjust the trunnion so that it will slide into the accelerator shaft lever. Turn it one additional turn clockwise then secure it to the lever with the retaining clip.
6. Remove the clock and release the accelerator linkage.

1969-71 Mark III, IV & Thunderbird

The conduit covering the accelerator cable at the carburetor end must be evenly nestled between the clamp and the accelerator shaft bracket. Accelerator pedal height adjustment is not required.

1. Disconnect the downshift lever return spring.
2. With the throttle in the wide open position, hold the downshift rod against the through detent stop.
3. Adjust the downshift screw to pro-

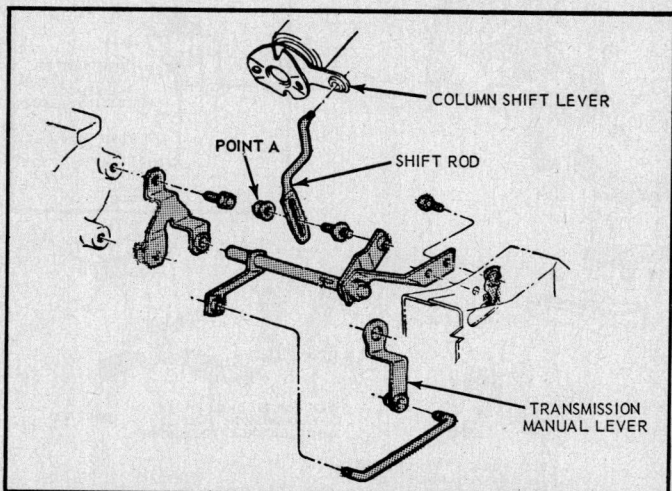

Fig. 4 Column shift linkage. 1969-74 Ford & Mercury (Typical)

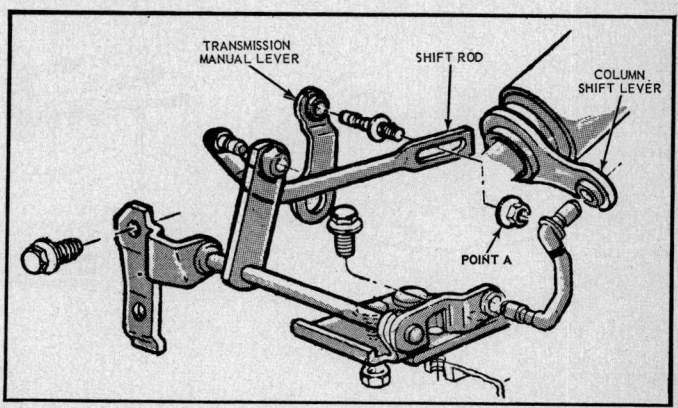

Fig. 5 Column shift linkage. 1969-70 Fairlane & Montego

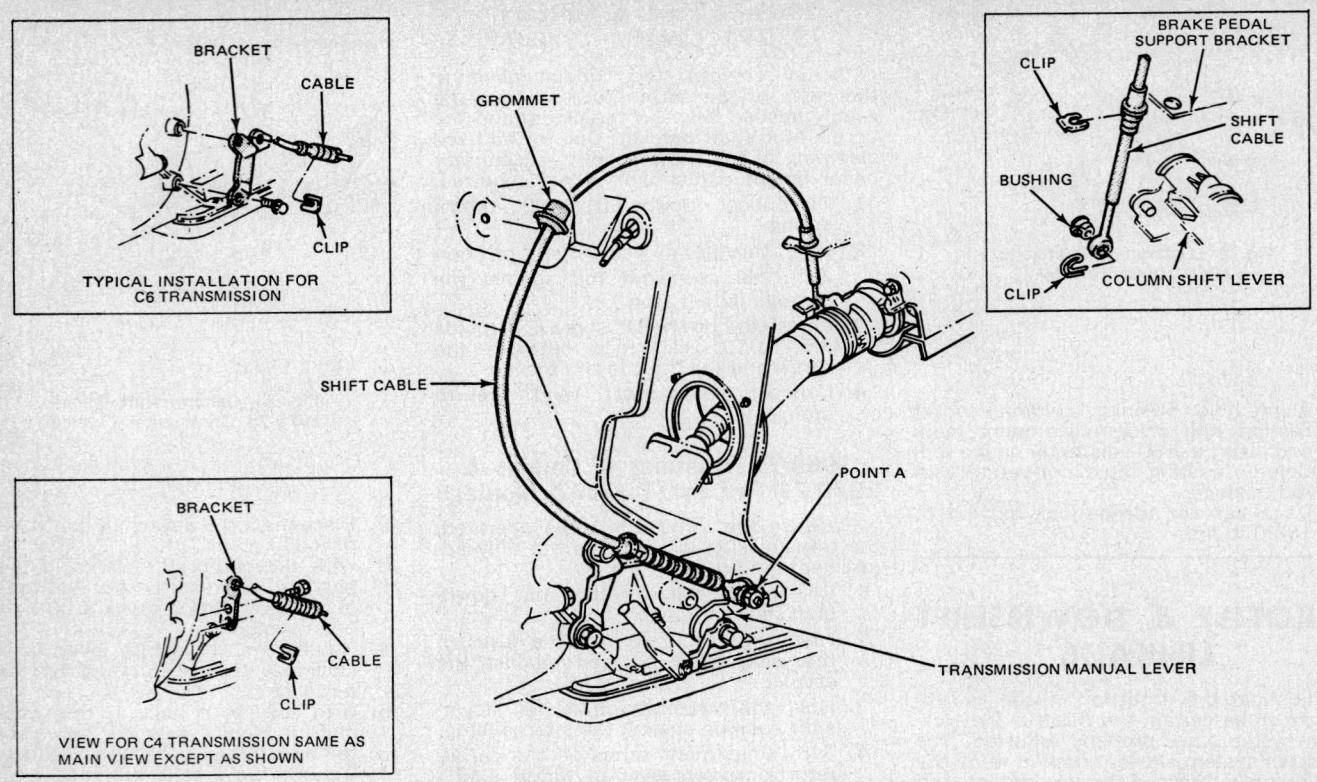

Fig. 6   Column shift linkage. 1972-74 Torino, Montego, Thunderbird & Mark IV

vide .050"-.070" clearance between the screw and the throttle shaft lever. End play adjustment is not required.
4. Connect the downshift return spring.

1969 Lincoln

1. With engine stopped, measure distance from top of accelerator pedal to carpet, Fig. 12. The 3¾" requirement is nominal only. Further adjustment (at accelerator connecting link) after a road test if the kickdown operation is not functioning.
2. Depress accelerator pedal and check

for detent feel and kickdown action of the bellcrank.
3. Disconnect downshift rod from bellcrank. Make sure movable outer bracket on bellcrank is up against stop pin on inner mounting bracket on bellcrank.

4. Pull upward and hold downshift rod against transmission internal stop. Adjust length of rod until hole in rod is aligned with ball stud on bellcrank.
5. Lengthen downshift rod one turn and position it on ball stud. Slide spring clip over end of rod. Tighten lock nut.

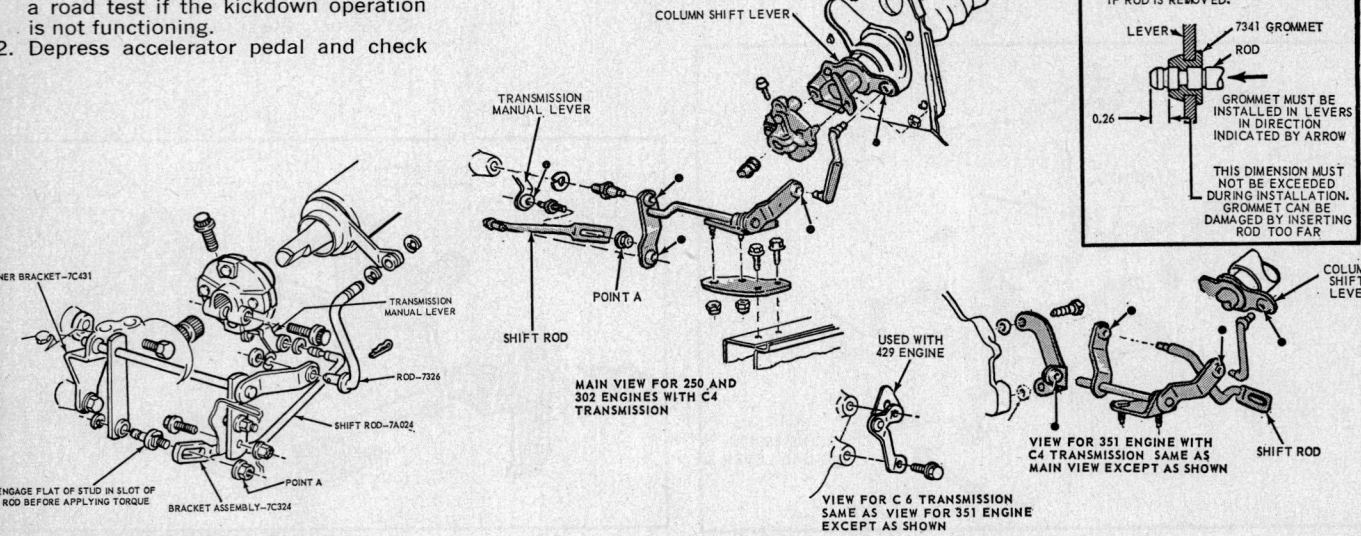

Fig. 7   Column shift linkage.
1969-71 Mark III & Thunderbird

Fig. 8   Column shift linkage. 1971 Montego & Torino

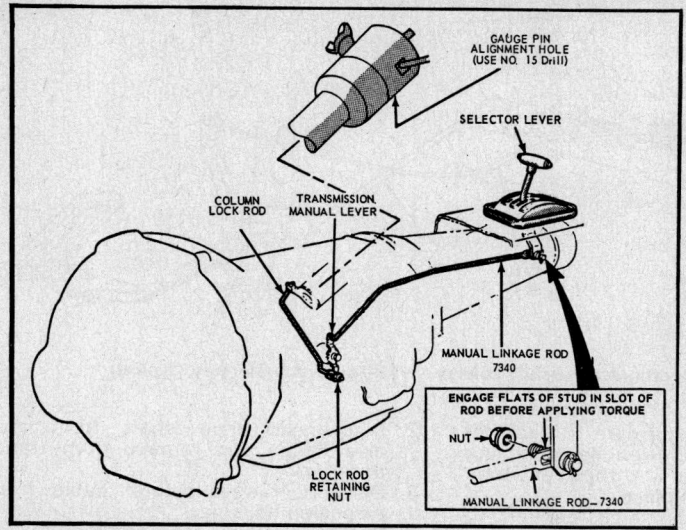

Fig. 9 Manual linkage, floor shift. Typical. Column lock rod is used on some models beginning 1970

Fig. 10 Throttle linkage. 1969 Fairlane & Montego

6. Be sure bellcrank outer bracket remains against stop pin. If it is not against pin, lengthen downshift rod one additional turn. If the downshift rod is adjusted too long the transmission will not upshift because the downshift valve is open to line pressure.

BAND ADJUSTMENT

NOTE: When making the intermediate band adjustment, the lock nut must be discarded and a new one installed each time the band is adjusted.

1. Loosen the locknut on the adjusting screw several turns, Fig. 16.
2. Torque the screw to 10 ft-lbs, or until the adjuster wrench overruns.

3. Back the screw off exactly 1½ turns.
4. Hold the adjustment and torque the locknut to the 35-45 ft-lbs.

OIL PAN & CONTROL VALVE

Removal
1. Raise car on hoist or jack stands.
2. Loosen and remove all but two oil pan bolts from front of case and drop rear edge of pan to drain fluid. Remove and clean pan and screen.
3. Unfasten and remove valve body.

Installation
1. Position valve body to case, making sure that selector and downshift levers are engaged, then install and

torque attaching bolts to specifications.
2. Using a new pan gasket, secure pan to case and torque bolts to specifications.
3. Lower car and fill transmission to the correct level with specified fluid.

INTERMEDIATE SERVO

Removal, Exc. Continental
1. Raise car and remove engine rear support-to-extension housing bolts.
2. Raise transmission high enough to relieve weight from support.
3. Remove support (1 bolt).
4. Lower transmission.
5. Place drain pan beneath servo.
6. Remove servo cover-to-case bolts.
7. Loosen band adjusting screw locknut.
8. Remove servo cover, piston, spring and gasket from case, *screwing band*

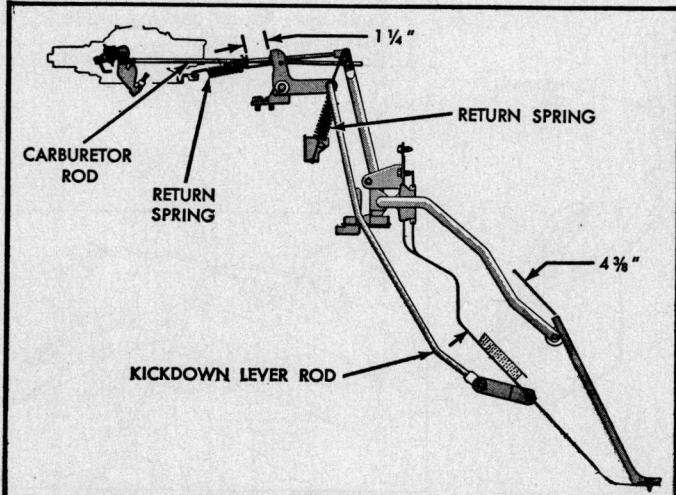

Fig. 11 Thunderbird throttle linkage. 1969 (Typical)

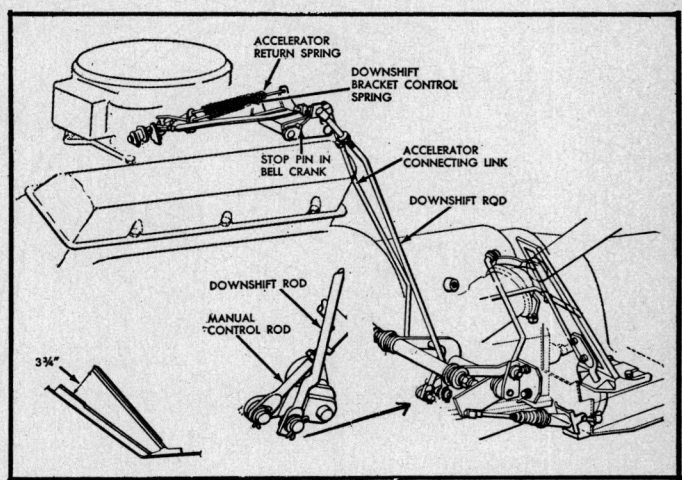

Fig. 12 Lincoln throttle linkage. 1969

adjusting screw inward as piston is re-moved. This insures that there will be enough tension on the band to keep the struts properly engaged in the band end notches while the piston is removed.

Removal, Continental

1. Raise vehicle and remove servo cover retaining bolts.
2. Remove manual and downshift control rod splash shield from frame side rail and reinforcement plate from beneath transmission oil pan.
3. Loosen band adjusting screw locknut.
4. Remove engine rear mount to cross-member nuts and with a suitable jack, raise transmission to remove weight from crossmember.
5. Remove engine rear support to exten-sion housing bolts, then the support.
6. Remove servo cover, piston, spring and gasket from case, turning adjust-ing screw inward as piston is re-moved. This places enough tension on the band to keep struts properly en-gaged in band end notches as piston is withdrawn.

Replacing Seal, Fig. 17

1. Apply air pressure to port in servo cover to remove piston and stem.
2. Remove seals from piston.

NOTE: On Continental, Mark III and Mark IV units, replace complete piston and rod assembly if piston or piston sealing lips are damaged.

3. Remove seal from cover.
4. Dip new seals in transmission fluid.
5. Install seals in piston and cover.
6. Dip piston in transmission fluid and install in cover.

Installation, All

1. Position new gasket on servo cover and spring on piston stem.
2. Insert piston stem in case. Secure cov-

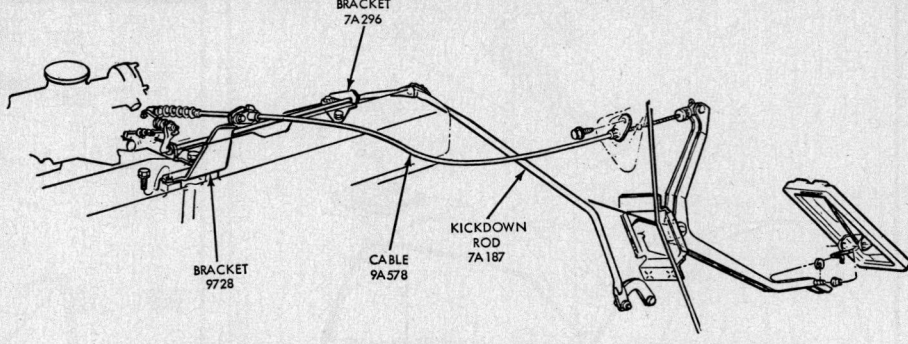

Fig. 13 Throttle & downshift linkage. 1971-74 Ford & Mercury (typical)

er with bolts, taking care to back off band adjusting screw while tightening cover bolts. Make sure that vent tube retaining clip is in place.
3. Raise transmission high enough to install engine rear support. Secure support to extension housing. Lower transmission as required to install support-to-crossmember bolt.
4. On Continental models, secure man-ual and downshift rod splash shield to frame side rail.
5. Remove jack supporting transmission and adjust the band as outlined previously.
6. Lower car and replenish fluid as re-quired.

EXTENSION HOUSING & GOVERNOR

Removal

1. Raise vehicle and disconnect parking brake cable from equalizer and on Continental models, remove the equal-izer.

2. Disconnect drive shaft from rear axle flange and remove from trans-mission.
3. Disconnect speedometer cable from extension housing.
4. Remove engine rear support to ex-tension housing bolts and on Con-tinental models, remove reinforce-ment plate from beneath oil pan.
5. Raise transmission slightly with a suitable jack to remove weight from engine rear support.
6. Remove engine rear support to cross-member bolt and the support.
7. Lower transmission to permit access to extension housing bolts. Remove bolts and slide housing off output shaft.
8. Disconnect governor from distributor (4 bolts) and slide governor off output shaft.

Installation, Fig. 18

1. Secure governor to distributor flange.
2. Position new gasket on transmission.
3. Secure extension housing to case.
4. Raise transmission to position engine rear support on crossmember and install the support attaching bolt.
5. Lower transmission and remove jack. Install engine rear support to exten-sion housing bolts and on Continental models, oil pan reinforcement plate.
6. Install speedometer cable.
7. On Continental models, install parking brake cable equalizer and on all mod-els, connect parking brake cable to equalizer. Adjust parking brake.
8. Install drive shaft.
9. Correct transmission fluid level.

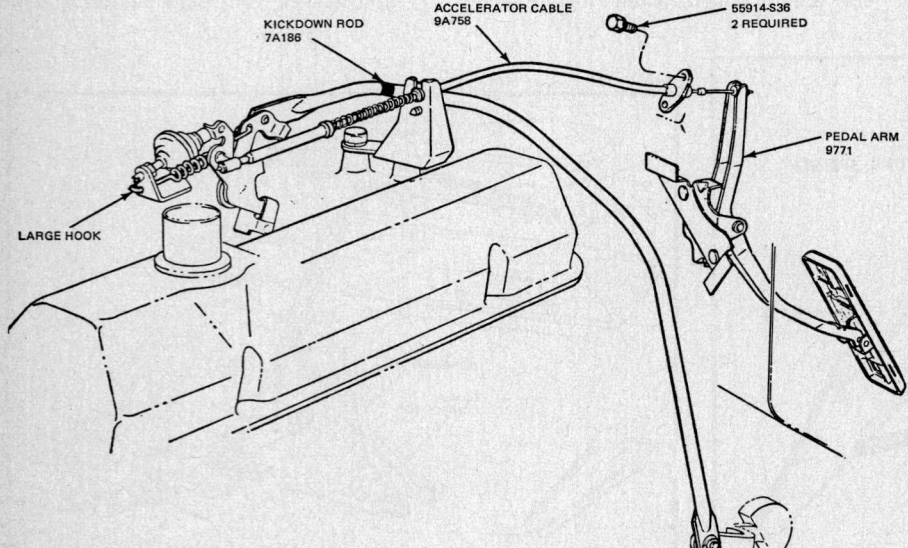

Fig. 14 Throttle & downshift linkage. 1970-74 Mark III, Mark IV & Thunderbird (typical)

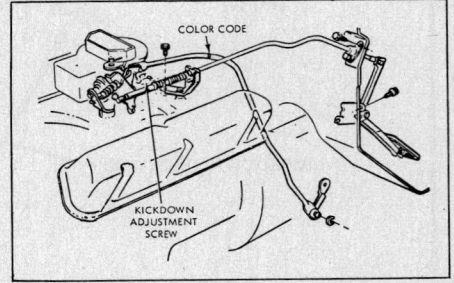

Fig. 15 Throttle & downshift linkage. 1971-73 Cougar, Montego, Mustang & Torino

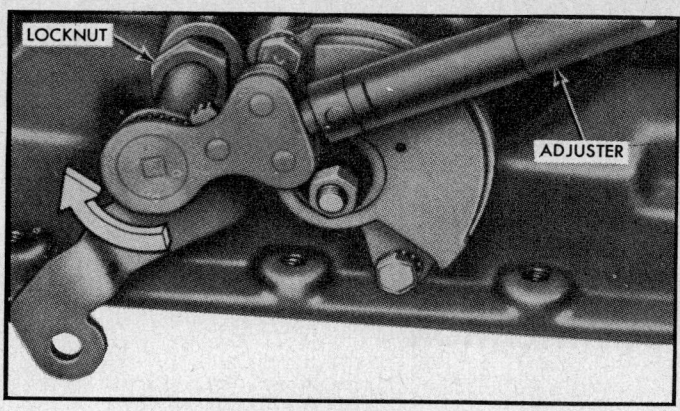

Fig. 16   Band adjustment

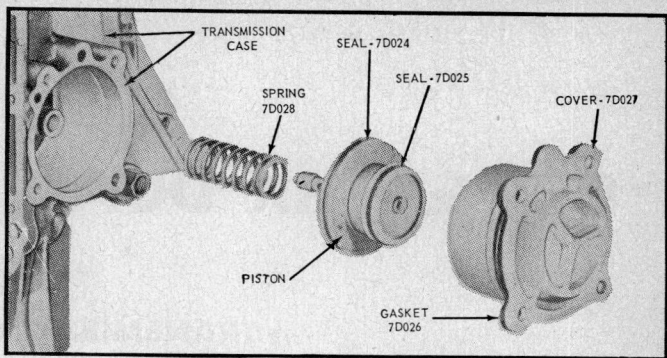

Fig. 17   Intermediate servo disassembled

TRANSMISSION, REPLACE

NOTE: On models with the neutral safety switch wire harness connected at the dash panel, disconnect the harness before raising the vehicle.

1. Raise vehicle and drain transmission and converter.
2. Remove drive shaft and starter.
3. Remove four converter to flywheel attaching bolts.
4. Disconnect parking brake front cable from equalizer.
5. Disconnect speedometer cable and transmission linkage.
6. Disconnect TRS switch wire, if equipped.
7. On 1969-71 Thunderbird, disconnect shift rod bellcrank bracket and allow bracket to hang free.
8. On 1969-74 Continental, remove lower shift rod bellcrank and pry upper shift

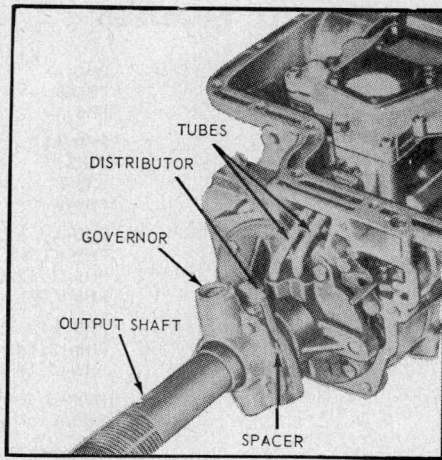

Fig. 18   Governor installed

rod bellcrank from converter housing and allow bellcrank to hang free.
9. Where necessary, disconnect muffler inlet pipes from exhaust manifold.

NOTE: On 1969-73 Mustang and Cougar, disconnect the entire exhaust system and allow it to hang on the rear axle.

10. Support the transmission with a suitable jack, remove parking brake rear cables from the equalizer and remove the crossmember.
11. Lower transmission and remove oil cooler lines, vacuum line and transmission oil filler tube.
12. Secure the transmission to the jack with the chain, remove the converter housing to cylinder block bolts and carefully move the transmission away from the engine, at the same time lowering it to clear the underside of the vehicle.
13. Reverse procedure to install.

CW & FMX DUAL RANGE AUTOMATIC

TRANSMISSION IDENTIFICATION

The identification tag on 1969 FMX units, is attached under the oil pan by a case-to-pan bolt while on 1970-74 FMX units, on the lower right hand extension housing-to-case bolt. On CW units, the identification tag is attached to the transmission case.

CW Transmissions

FORD MODELS

YEAR	ENGINE MODEL	TRANS. MODEL
1973	8-400[3][7]	PHE-A
1974	8-400[3][7]	PHE-A1

FAIRLANE/TORINO & MONTEGO MODELS

YEAR	ENGINE MODEL	TRANS. MODEL
1969	8-351[5][4]	PHB-C
	8-351[3][1]	PHB-D
	8-351[5][4]	PHB-F
	8-351[3][1]	PHB-G
1970	8-351[4]	PHB-R
	8-351[1]	PHB-S
1972	8-351	PHB-C
	8-351	PHB-Z
1973	8-351[4][5][6]	PHB-Z4
	8-351[4][5]	PHB-C3

FMX Transmissions

YEAR	ENGINE MODEL	TRANS. MODEL
1974	V8-302	PHA-J3
	V8-351[3]	PHB-Z5

FORD MODELS

YEAR	ENGINE MODEL	TRANS. MODEL
1969	6-240[4]	PHD-A
	8-302[4]	PHD-B
	8-390[4]	PHB-A
1970	6-240	PHD-A1
	8-302	PHD-B1
	8-351[4]	PHB-L1
	8-351[1]	PHB-V
1971	6-240	PHD-A1, A2
	8-302	PHD-B1, B2
	8-351[4]	PHB-L1, L2
	8-351[1]	PHB-V, V1
1972	6-240	PHD-A4, A5
	8-302	PHB-L3, L4
	8-351	PHB-L3, L4
1973	8-351[5]	PHB-L6, 7
	8-351[6]	PHB-AA
1974	V8-351	PHB-AA1
	V8-351	PHB-L8
	V8-400	PHB-AC1

MERCURY MODELS

YEAR	ENGINE MODEL	TRANS. MODEL
1971	8-351	PHB-L1, L2
1972	8-351	PHB-L3
1973	8-351[5]	PHB-L6
	8-351[6]	PHB-AA
1974	V8-351	PHB-AA1
	V8-400	PHB-AC1

MUSTANG & COUGAR MODELS

YEAR	ENGINE MODEL	TRANS. MODEL
1969	8-351[5][1]	PHB-E
	8-351[5][1]	PHB-H
1970	8-351[5]	PHB-E1
	8-351[5]	PHB-P
1971	8-351[5]	PHB-E2, E3
1972	8-302	PHA-H, H1
	8-351	PHB-E4, E5
1973	8-302	PHB-H3
	8-351[6]	PHB-E7
1974	V8-351[5]	PHB-Z5

[1]—With floor shift.
[2]—With 4 barrel carburetor.
[3]—With 2 barrel carburetor.
[4]—With column shift.
[5]—Windsor engine.
[6]—Cleveland engine.
[7]—Ford sedans with 2.75 rear axle ratio only.

DESCRIPTION

Operation

This transmission features a drive range that provides for fully automatic upshifts and downshifts, and manually selected low and second gears. The six selector lever positions provided are P (park), R (reverse), N (neutral), D (automatic drive range), 2 (second gear hold) and 1 (low gear hold).

D is a fully automatic range providing for a first gear start with automatic upshifts to second and high gear occurring at appropriate intervals.

Second gear (2) is a manually selected second gear hold. When the selector lever is moved to 2, the transmission will engage and remain in second gear, regardless of throttle opening or road speed.

Low gear (1) is a manually selected first gear hold. When the selector lever is moved to this position the transmission will remain in first gear. To provide engine braking, moving the lever to this position will cause the transmission to downshift from 2nd when the car speed reaches about 22 to 39 mph depending on axle ratio and tire size.

D—Drive

The normal automatic driving range is indicated by D. In this range the car starts off in first gear and gives the best combination of automatic gear shifts to provide for economy and full power starts. As the accelerator is depressed and the

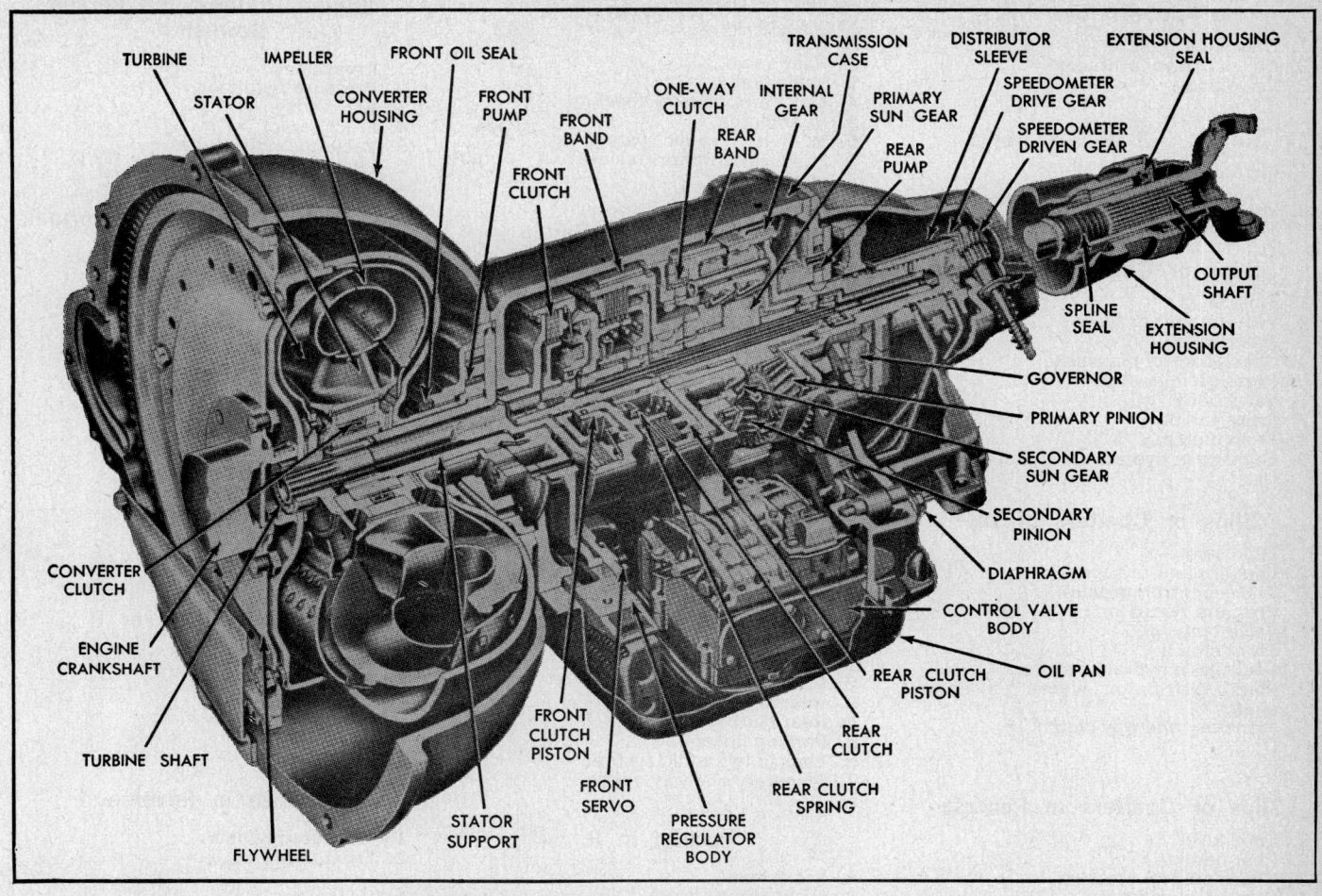

Fig. 1   Cruiseomatic and Mercomatic three speed dual range unit with cast iron case

car picks up speed, automatic shifts to second and high gears will occur. The transmission will automatically downshift as speed decreases. Forced downshifts in D are made by pressing the accelerator pedal all the way to the floor.

2—Second Gear Hold

When the car is started and the shift lever is moved to 2, the car will start off and remain in second gear, regardless of throttle opening or road speed. This range is especially useful for starting the car on icy pavements or other slippery surfaces. Similarly, when engine braking is required and the shift lever is moved from D to 2, the transmission will engage and remain in second gear.

Selector lever position 2 is not a cruising range in the usual sense of the term. While the transmission is capable of limited cruising in second gear, maximum fuel economy and best all-around performance are realized in D range.

1—Low Gear Hold

This range is identical in operation to manual low range except that when the shift lever is moved to 1 to provide engine braking, the automatic shift from second

to low gear will occur between 22 and 39 mph (exact shift point will vary with axle ratio and tire size).

TROUBLE SHOOTING GUIDE

Rough Initial Engagement

1. Idle speed.
2. Vacuum unit or tubes.
3. Front band.
4. Check control pressure.
5. Pressure regulator.
6. Valve body.

Shift Points High, Low or Erratic

1. Fluid level.
2. Vacuum unit or tubes.
3. Manual linkage.
4. Governor.
5. Check control pressure.
6. Valve body.
7. Downshift linkage.

Rough 2-3 Shift

1. Manual linkage.
2. Front band.
3. Vacuum unit or tubes.
4. Pressure regulator.
5. Valve body.
6. Front servo.

Engine Overspeeds, 2-3 Shift

1. Vacuum unit or tubes.
2. Front band.
3. Valve body.
4. Pessure regulator.

No 1-2 or 2-3 Shifts

1. Governor.
2. Valve body.
3. Manual linkage.
4. Rear clutch.
5. Front band.
6. Front servo.
7. Leakage in hydraulic system.
8. Pressure regulator.

CW & FMX DUAL RANGE AUTOMATIC

No Forced Downshifts

1. Downshift linkage.
2. Check control pressure.
3. Valve body.

Rough 3-2 or 3-1 Shifts

1. Engine idle speed.
2. Vacuum unit or tubes.
3. Valve body.

Slips or Chatters in 2nd

1. Fluid level.
2. Vacuum unit or tubes.
3. Front band.
4. Check control pressure.
5. Pressure regulator.
6. Valve body.
7. Front servo.
8. Front clutch.
9. Leakage in hydraulic system.

Slips or Chatters in 1st

1. Fluid level.
2. Vacuum unit or tubes.
3. Check control pressure.
4. Pressure regulator.
5. Valve body.
6. Front clutch.
7. Leakage in hydraulic system.
8. Fluid distributor sleeve in output shaft.
9. Planetary one-way clutch.

Slips or Chatters in Reverse

1. Fluid level.
2. Rear band.
3. Check control pressure.
4. Pressure regulator.
5. Valve body.
6. Rear servo.
7. Rear clutch.
8. Vacuum unit or tubes.
9. Leakage in hydraulic system.
10. Fluid distributor sleeve in output shaft.

No Drive in D or D2

1. Valve body.
2. Make air pressure check.
3. Manual linkage.
4. Front clutch.
5. Leak in hydraulic system.
6. Fluid distributor sleeve in output shaft.

No Drive in D1

1. Manual linkage.
2. Valve body.
3. Planetary one-way clutch.

No Drive in L

1. Manual linkage.
2. Front clutch.
3. Valve body.
4. Make air pressure check.
5. Leak in hydraulic system.
6. Fluid distributor sleeve in output shaft.

No Drive in R

1. Rear band.
2. Rear servo.
3. Valve body.
4. Make air pressure check.
5. Rear clutch.
6. Leak in hydraulic system.
7. Fluid distributor sleeve in output shaft.

No Drive in Any Range

1. Fluid level.
2. Manual linkage.
3. Check control pressure.
4. Pressure regulator.
5. Valve body.
6. Make air pressure check.
7. Leak in hydraulic system.

Lockup in D or D1

1. Manual linkage.
2. Rear servo.
3. Front servo.
4. Rear clutch.
5. Parking linkage.
6. Leak in hydraulic system.

Lockup in D2

1. Manual linkage.
2. Rear band.
3. Rear servo.
4. Rear clutch.
5. Parking linkage.
6. Leak in hydraulic system.
7. Planetary one-way clutch.

Lockup in R

1. Front band.
2. Front servo.
3. Front clutch.
4. Parking linkage.
5. Leak in hydraulic system.

Lockup in L

1. Front band.
2. Pressure regulator.
3. Valve body.
4. Rear clutch.
5. Parking linkage.
6. Leak in hydraulic system.

Parking Lock Binds or Won't Hold

1. Manual linkage.
2. Parking linkage.

Unable to Push Start

1. Fluid level.
2. Manual linkage.
3. Pressure regulator.
4. Valve body.
5. Rear pump.
6. Leak in hydraulic system.

Transmission Overheats

1. Oil cooler and connections.
2. Pressure regulator.
3. Converter one-way clutch.

Engine Runaway on Forced Downshift

1. Front band.
2. Pressure regulator.
3. Valve body.
4. Front servo.
5. Vacuum unit or tubes.
6. Leak in hydraulic system.

Maximum Speed Below Normal, Acceleration Poor

1. Converter one-way clutch.

No 3-1 Downshift

1. Engine idle speed.
2. Vacuum unit or tubes.
3. Valve body.

Noise in Neutral

1. Pressure regulator.
2. Front clutch.
3. Front pump.

Noise in 1-2-3 or R

1. Pressure regulator.
2. Planetary assembly.
3. Front clutch.
4. Rear clutch.
5. Front pump.

Noise in Reverse

1. Pressure regulator.
2. Front pump.

Noise on Coast in Neutral

1. Rear pump.

MAINTENANCE

NOTE: Despite apparent similarities, the CW and FMX transmissions must be serviced as individual units. Although some CW parts are interchangeable with FMX parts, the majority of parts are not interchangeable.

Adding Fluid

The fluid level in the transmission should be checked at 1000-mile intervals Make sure that the car is standing level, and firmly apply the parking brake.

Run the engine at normal idle speed. If the transmission fluid is cold, run the engine at fast idle speed until the fluid reaches normal operating temperature. When the fluid is warm, slow the engine down to normal idle speed, shift the transmission through all ranges and then place the lever or button at P.

Clean all dirt from the transmission fluid dipstick cap before removing the dipstick from the filler tube. Pull the dipstick out of the tube, wipe it clean and

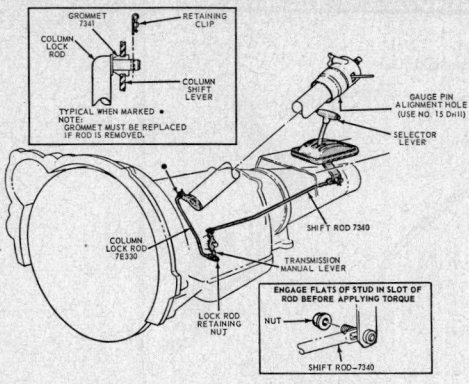

Fig. 2 Manual linkage. 1969-74 floor shift (typical)

push it all the way back into the tube.

Pull the dipstick out again and check the fluid level. If necessary, add enough Type F Automatic Transmission Fluid to the transmission to raise the fluid level to the F (full mark) on the dipstick.

Changing Fluid

NOTE: Normal maintenance and lubrication does not require periodic transmission fluid changes. However, a major transmission repair will require that the fluid be drained and be replaced with type F "lifetime" fluid.

1. Raise and support vehicle on hoist, then place a drain pan under transmission.
2. Loosen pan bolts and drain fluid until it has reached level of pan flange, then remove bolts working from rear and both sides of pan allowing to drop and drain slowly.
3. When fluid has completely drained, remove and thoroughly clean pan and filter.
4. Install filter, then using a new gasket install oil pan and add three quarts of fluid.
5. With transmission at operating temperature and parking brake applied, move shift lever through each range,

allowing time for transmission to engage, then return shift lever to Park.
6. Check fluid level and add fluid as necessary to bring level between ADD and FULL mark.

MANUAL LINKAGE, ADJUST

Cougar, Fairlane/Torino, Ford, Mercury, Montego & Mustang

Floor Shift 1969-74, Fig. 2
1. Place selector lever in D.
2. Raise vehicle and loosen manual shift rod retaining nut.
3. Move transmission manual lever to D position (third detent position from back of transmission).
4. Torque nut to 10-20 ft-lbs.

Column Shift, 1969-74, Figs. 3, 4 and 5
1. Place selector lever in D.
2. Loosen shift rod adjusting nut at point A. On vehicles with a shift cable, remove nut at point A and remove cable from transmission manual lever stud.
3. Shift transmission manual lever into D.
4. On vehicles equipped with a shift cable, place cable end on transmission lever stud, using care to align flats on stud with flats on cable. Install but do not tighten retaining nut.
5. Making certain that selector lever has not moved from D position, torque retaining nut at point A to 10-20 ft. lbs.

NOTE: After adjusting the manual linkage, the steering column lock rod starting with 1970 models, is adjusted as follows:
1. Raise vehicle and loosen lock rod retaining nut.
2. Lower vehicle and place selector lever in D position tight against the D stop.
3. Align the hole in the steering column socket casting with the column alignment mark and insert a .180" diameter gauge pin. The column casting

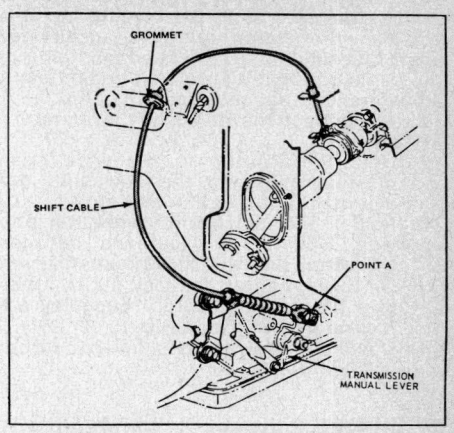

Fig. 3 Manual linkage. 1972-74 Montego & Torino column shift (typical)

must not rotate with gauge pin in position.
4. Raise vehicle and torque lock rod retaining nut to 10-20 ft. lbs.
5. Lower vehicle. Remove gauge pin and check linkage for proper operation.

THROTTLE LINKAGE, ADJUST

1973-74 All

1. Hold throttle lever in wide open position.
2. Hold downshift rod against the through detent stop.
3. Adjust downshift screw to provide .01 to .08 inch clearance between screw and throttle arm.
4. Connect downshift lever return spring.

1969-71 Ford & Mercury 1972 All

The conduit covering the cable at the

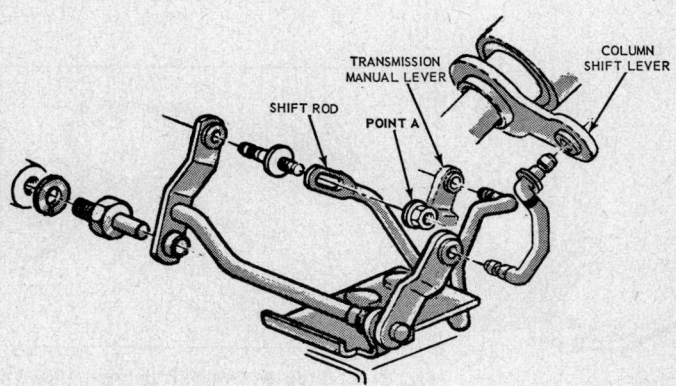

Fig. 4 Manual linkage. 1969-70 Fairlane & Montego, column shift

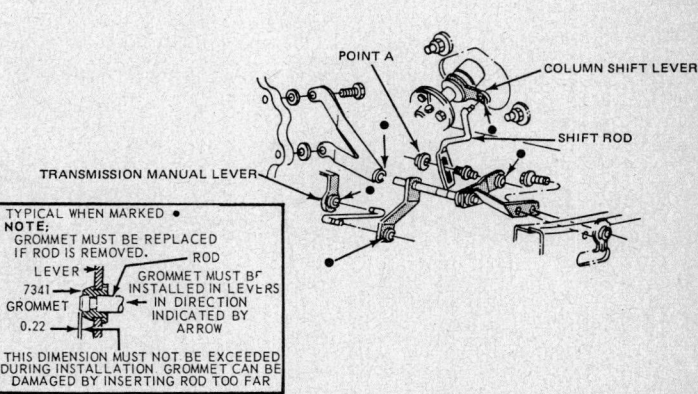

Fig. 5 Manual linkage. 1969-74 Ford & 1971-74 Mercury, column shift

carburetor end must be evenly nestled between the clamp and the accelerator shaft bracket. Due to the fixed clamping of the cable conduit, accelerator pedal height adjustment is not required.

1. Disconnect the downshift lever return spring.
2. Hold the throttle in the wide open position and hold the downshift rod against the through detent stop.
3. Adjust the downshift screw to provide .050"-.070" clearance between the screw and the throttle shaft lever. On Sixes, tighten the lock nut to maintain the screw position. End play adjustment is not required.
4. Connect downshift lever return spring.

1969 Fairlane & Montego

1. With engine off, check accelerator pedal for a height of 4½". Adjust accelerator connecting link to correct.
2. Disconnect downshift control cable from accelerator shaft lever.
3. With carburetor choke in the off position, depress the accelerator and block it in the wide open position.
4. Rotate the downshift lever counter clockwise to place it against the internal stop.
5. With the lever in this position and all slack removed from the cable, adjust the trunnion so that it will slide into the lever. Turn it one additional turn to increase length of cable then secure it to the lever with retaining clip.

1970 Fairlane & Montego
1969-70 Mustang & Cougar

Because the throttle on these models is cable operated, transmission kickdown is the only adjustment required.

1. Disconnect throttle and downshift return springs and disconnect downshift control cable from accelerator shaft lever.
2. With carburetor choke in the off position, depress the accelerator and block it in the wide open position.
3. Rotate the downshift lever counterclockwise to place it against the internal stop.
4. Turn adjustment screws on carburetor kickdown lever to within .040" to .080" gap of contacting pick up surface of carb. throttle lever.

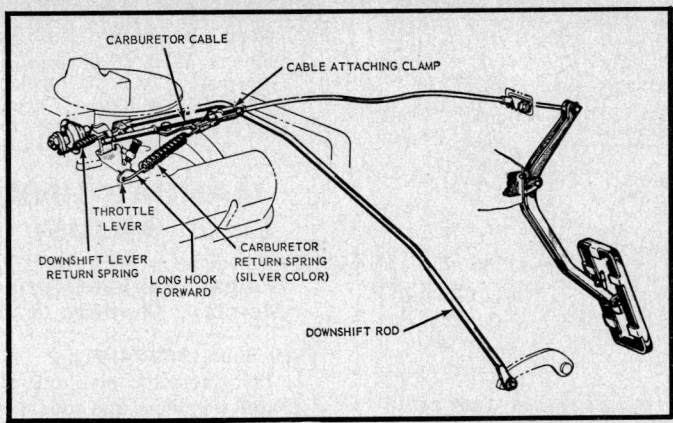

Fig. 6   Throttle linkage. 1969-70 Ford and Mercury

1971 Cougar, Fairlane/Torino, Montego & Mustang

1. Hold transmission in full downshift against stop.
2. Hold carburetor throttle lever in wide open throttle against stop.
3. Turn the adjustment screw on the kickdown lever until a gap of .040-.080 " exists between the carburetor lever and the adjusting screw.
4. Release the transmission and carburetor to the normal free position.
5. Install throttle return spring.

BAND ADJUSTMENTS

NOTE: CW series transmissions incorporate a self-adjusting front band. It is adjusted at time of assembly and requires no further adjustment until unit is overhauled. The rear band should be adjusted at the first 12,000 miles. No further adjustment is required until unit is overhauled.

Front Band

FMX Units

1. Drain fluid from transmission, remove and clean oil pan and screen.
2. Loosen front servo adjusting screw locknut.

3. Pull back on actuating rod and insert a ¼ inch spacer between adjusting screw and servo piston stem, Fig. 9.
4. Tighten adjusting screw to 10 inch-lbs torque. Remove spacer and tighten adjusting screw an additional ¾ turn. Hold adjusting screw stationary and tighten locknut securely.
5. Install oil pan with new gasket and add fluid to transmission.

CW Units

1. Install a .250 inch thick spacer between adjusting screw and servo piston stem, Fig. 10.
2. Using an inch pound torque wrench and an 8 point socket torque adjusting screw to 10 in. lbs. and remove spacer.

NOTE: Adjusting screw has a left hand thread and is self adjusting. After initial adjustment, no further adjustment should be required.

3. Space one way clutch spring .125-.188 inch from lever, otherwise proper automatic adjustments cannot be made.

Rear Band

NOTE: On late 1969 and on all 1970-74 models, there is no access hole in the floor pan to adjust the rear band. With

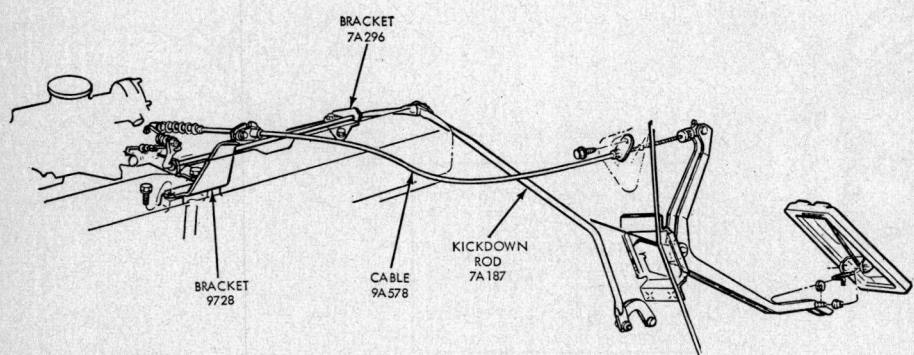

Fig. 7   Throttle & downshift linkage. 1971-74 Ford & Mercury (typical)

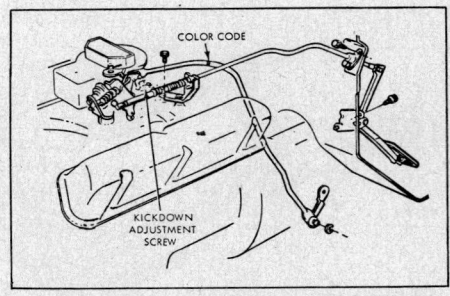

Fig. 8   Throttle & downshift linkage. 1971-74 Cougar, Montego, Torino 1971-73 Mustang (typical)

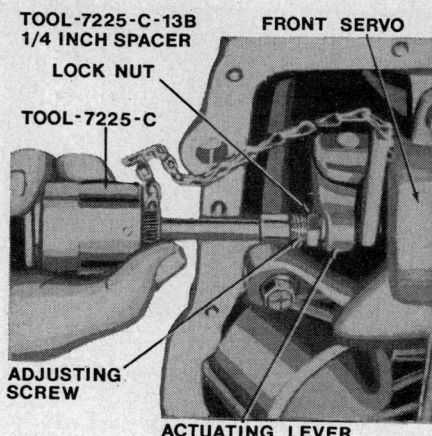

TOOL-7225-C-13B
1/4 INCH SPACER
LOCK NUT
TOOL-7225-C
FRONT SERVO
ADJUSTING SCREW
ACTUATING LEVER

Fig. 9   Front band adjustment. Ford, Mercury and Thunderbird

the use of special tools this band can be adjusted externally as follows, Figs. 11, 12:

1. Loosen rear band adjusting screw lock-nut. A special tool is required to gain access in limited space.
2. Tighten adjusting screw until special tool clicks. It is preset to overrun when torque reaches 10 ft. lbs.

NOTE: If screw is found to be tighter than 10 ft. lbs., loosen screw and tighten until wrench clicks and breaks.

3. Back off adjusting screw 1½ turns on FMX units and 1¼ turns on CW units.

NOTE: Severe damage may result if adjusting screw is not backed off the exact amount of turns indicated.

4. Hold adjusting screw stationary and tighten locknut securely.

1969 Fairlane, Montego, Mustang & Cougar

1. Drain transmission and remove oil pan and filter.
2. Loosen rear servo adjusting screw lock nut.
3. Pull the adjusting screw end of the actuating lever away from the servo body spacer tool between servo ac-

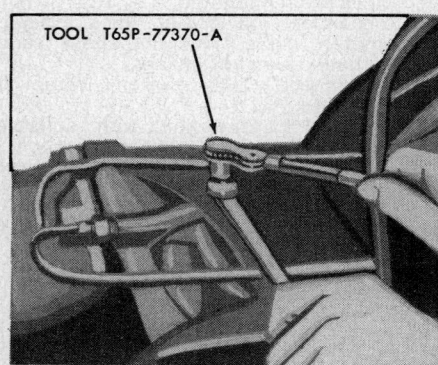

TOOL T65P-77370-A

Fig. 11   Rear band adjustment. 1970-73 Ford, Fairlane, Montego, Torino & 1974 All

cumulator piston and the adjusting screw, Fig. 13.

NOTE: Be sure that flat surfaces of the tool are positioned squarely between the adjusting screw and the accumulator piston. The tool must not touch the servo piston and the tool handle must not touch the servo piston spring retainer.

4. Using a torque wrench with an Allen head socket, tighten the adjusting screw to 24 in-lbs.
5. Back off the adjusting screw 1½ turns. Hold the adjusting screw and tighten the lock nut securely. Remove spacer tool.
6. Replace oil filter and pan and fill transmission.

1969 Ford

The tool shown in Fig. 14 is especially made for this adjustment. However, a satisfactory adjustment may be made by using a conventional torque wrench. Loosen the lock nut and tighten the adjusting screw to a torque of 10 ft-lbs. Then back off the screw exactly 1½ turns and tighten lock nut. *Severe damage may result to the transmission if the adjusting screw is not backed off exactly 1½ turns.*

CONTROL VALVE BODY

1. Support vehicle on hoist, then drain transmission fluid and remove pan.

NOTE: If fluid is to be reused, filter it through a 100-mesh screen before replacing it in transmission.

2. Disconnect hoses from vacuum diaphragm unit, then using Snap-On tool S8696-A, remove vacuum diaphragm and push rod.
3. Remove fluid screen retaining clip and small compensator pressure tube.
4. Remove main pressure oil tube, by gently prying up end that connects to main control valve, then remove other end of tube from pressure regulator.

NOTE: Tube must be removed in this manner. Failure to do so, could kink or bend tube causing excessive internal transmission leakage.

5. Loosen front servo bolts three turns, then remove the three control valve body screws, and lower valve body while pulling it off front servo tubes, being careful not to damage valve body or tubes.
6. Before installing control valve, check for bent manual valve by rolling it on a flat surface.

NOTE: Before torquing control valve attaching bolts, move valve toward center of case until clearance is less than .050 inch between manual valve and actuating pin.

7. After installing control valve, torque control valve attaching bolts to 8-10 ft. lbs., front servo bolts to 30-35 ft. lbs. and vacuum diaphragm to 15-23 ft. lbs.

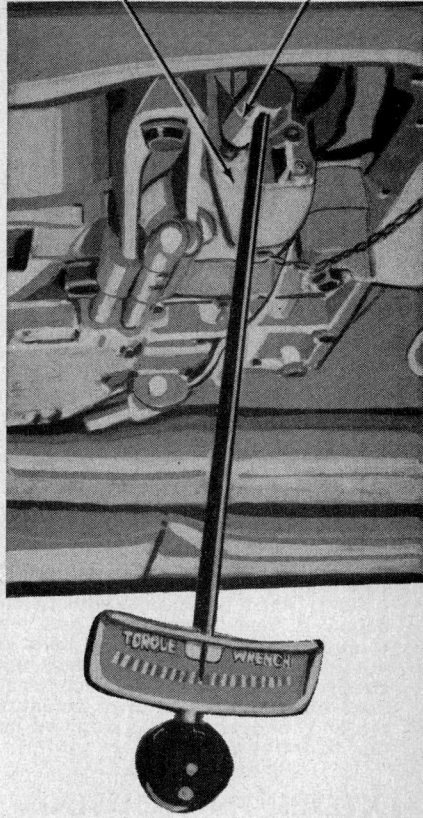

.250" Gauge Block   Ten (10) In.Lb. Torque

Fig. 10   Adjusting front servo band

8. After completing assembly, adjust front and rear bands. If valve body was replaced, adjust control linkage.

FRONT & REAR SERVOS

1. Drain transmission fluid and remove oil pan and screen.
2. Remove vacuum diaphragm, then loosen control valve body attaching bolts.
3. Remove retaining bolts from servo, then hold actuating strut and remove servo. On 1969 PHB units, remove servo dowel.

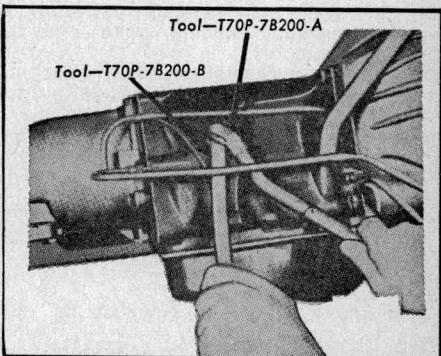

Tool—T70P-7B200-A
Tool—T70P-7B200-B

Fig. 12   Rear band adjustment 1970-74 Cougar & 1970-73 Mustang

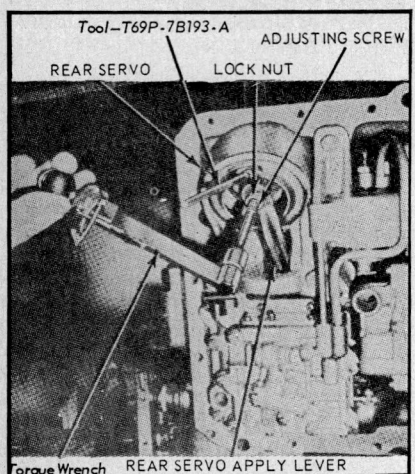

Fig. 13 Adjusting rear band, 1969 Fairlane, Montego, Mustang & Cougar

4. After installation, if front servo was serviced, torque front servo attaching bolts to 30-35 ft. lbs. and adjust front band. If rear servo was serviced, torque rear servo attaching bolts to 40-45 ft. lbs., adjust rear bands and check for less than .050 inch clearance between manual lever actuating pin and manual lever as outlined under "Control Valve."

EXTENSION HOUSING BUSHING & REAR SEAL

Proper removal and installation of extension housing bushing and rear seal will necessitate the use of five specialty tools. When removing bushing and rear seal, the vehicle will have to be raised and driveshaft removed.

EXTENSION HOUSING

1. Drain transmission fluid and remove driveshaft.
2. Disconnect speedometer cable from housing and remove engine rear supports to crossmember nuts.
3. Raise transmission slightly with suitable jack, then remove crossmember to side rail bolts and position the crossmember out of way.
4. Remove the two engine rear support-to-extension housing bolts and remove support.
5. Remove extension housing attaching bolts, then slide housing off output shaft and remove gasket.

NOTE: Hold output shaft and rear support from moving rearward to prevent needle bearing and race from dropping out.

GOVERNOR

1. Remove extension housing as outlined previously.
2. Remove governor to counterweight screws and lift governor from counterweight.

NOTE: When removing governor, hold output shaft and rear support from moving rearward to prevent needle bearing and race from dropping out.

3. When installing governor torque attaching bolts to 50-60 in. lbs.

PRESSURE REGULATON

1. Drain transmission fluid and remove oil pan and fluid screen.
2. Remove small compensator pressure tube from control valve body and pressure regulator.
3. Remove main pressure oil tube by gently prying up end that connects to main control valve assembly, then remove other end of tube from pressure regulator.

NOTE: Tube must be removed in this manner. Failure to do so, could kink or bend tube, causing excessive internal transmission leakage.

4. Remove pressure regulator spring retainer, springs and spacer.

NOTE: Maintain pressure on retainer to prevent springs from falling out.

5. Remove regulator attaching bolts and remove regulator.
6. After installing regulator, torque attaching bolts to 17-22 ft. lbs.

PARKING PAWL

1. Drain transmission fluid and remove driveshaft.
2. Support rear of transmission and remove crossmember, then remove the two engine rear support-to-extension housing bolts and remove support.
3. Disconnect speedometer cable and remove oil pan and screen.
4. Loosen rear band adjusting screw locknut and tighten adjusting screw to 24 in. lbs.

NOTE: This will hold planetary carrier and clutch assemblies in place during parking pawl removal.

5. Remove small compensator pressure tube from pressure regulator and control valve body.
6. Remove main pressure oil tube by gently prying up end that connects to main valve body assembly, then remove other end of tube from pressure regulator.

NOTE: Tube must be removed in this manner. Failure to do so could kink or bend tube, causing excessive internal transmission leakage.

7. Remove vacuum diaphragm and loosen front servo attaching bolts, then remove valve body attaching bolts and lower valve body while pulling it off servo tubes, being careful not to damage valve body or tubes.
8. Remove rear servo bolts and remove servo and struts.
9. Remove extension housing and output shaft rear support.
10. Using a magnet, remove parking pawl pin from case, then working from inside of case, drive on shoulder of toggle lever pin with a small punch

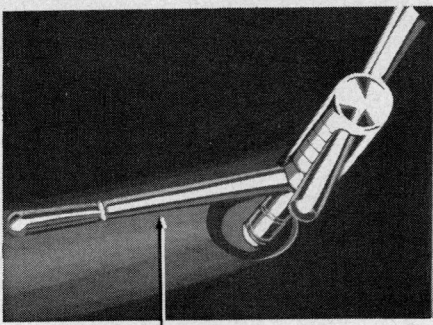

Fig. 14 Rear band adjustment. 1969 Ford

to move retaining plug part way out of case. Using a pair of pliers, remove plug.
11. Slide toggle lever toward front of case. Cock lever to one side to apply pressure on pin, then move toggle to rear of case to move pin outward.
12. Remove pawl and toggle lever as an assembly.
13. During assembly refer to "Control Valve Body" and "Front & Rear Servos" for installation. After assembly, adjust front and rear bands as outlined previously.

TRANSMISSION, REPLACE

NOTE: On some models, it is necessary to remove the two upper converter housing to engine bolts before raising vehicle.

1. Raise vehicle and place on jack stands, then drain transmission oil pan.
2. Remove converter access cover and remove converter drain plug.

NOTE: On 1969 units, two converter drain plugs are used. Remove one plug, rotate converter 180 degrees and remove the other plug. Do not attempt to rotate converter using a wrench on the converter stud nuts.

3. Remove converter to flywheel attaching nuts, reinstall converter drain plugs and converter housing access cover to hold converter in place when transmission is removed.
4. Remove starter and propeller shaft.
5. Where necessary, disconnect exhaust pipes from manifold.
6. Disconnect oil cooler lines, speedometer cable, vacuum hose and manual downshift linkage.
7. Disconnect TRS switch wire, if equipped.
8. Support transmission with suitable jack and remove crossmember.

NOTE: On some models, it is necessary to remove the engine rear support to transmission bolts before crossmember removal.

9. Lower transmission and remove filler tube and dipstick.
10. Remove converter housing-to-engine bolts. Move transmission and jack rearward and lower away from vehicle.
11. Reverse procedure to install.

AMERICAN MOTORS SHIFT-COMMAND

1969-71

TRANSMISSION IDENTIFICATION

An identification plate is attached to the left side of the transmission case. Included on the plate is the transmission model and the serial number of the unit.

DESCRIPTION

Two basic types of this transmission are used, cast iron and aluminum case. Model application is as follows:

Cast Iron:

1969-71 V8 exc. V8-290 w/2 barrel carb and V8-304.

Aluminum Case:

1969-71 Six, V8-290 w/2 barrel carb. and V8-304.

Operation

While valve body and control location vary, gear units and power flow are essentially the same.

These transmissions combine a three-element torque converter and a hydraulically-controlled three speed and reverse planetary gear train. The drive is always through the torque converter and one of the planetary gear ranges.

The torque converter consists of an impeller (pump), a turbine and stator. All these parts operate in a fluid-filled housing which is sealed. The torque converter cannot be serviced and must be replaced as a unit in case of a malfunction.

The planetary gear train in all units transmits power from the torque converter turbine shaft to the transmission output shaft. Hydraulic clutches and servo-operated bands drive or hold certain gears to provide the various output ratios.

When the selector lever is placed in Drive, the transmission starts in 1st, shifts into 2nd, then into Drive. If selector lever is placed in 2nd, the transmission starts and remains in 2nd unless manually shifted into Drive or 1st. Similarly, when selector lever is placed in 1st, transmission starts and remains in 1st unless manually upshifted.

When maximum acceleration is desired in order to pass a slow moving vehicle or to ascend a steep grade, the transmission may be downshifted from 3rd to 2nd by pushing the accelerator to the floor. If pressure is released on the pedal the transmission will automatically upshift to high.

1st is used for going up very steep grades or driving in deep mud, sand or snow. This position is also used for descending steep grades in order to take advantage of engine braking. There is

no automatic upshift in the 1 or 2 position regardless of car speed or throttle position. The selector lever may be moved from 1st to drive at any car speed and the transmission will then accomplish all the automatic upshifts.

TROUBLE SHOOTING GUIDE

Harsh Engagement

1. Front clutch seized or plates distorted.
2. Rear clutch seized or plates distorted.

Delayed Forward Engagement

1. Sealing rings missing or broken.
2. Front clutch piston check valve leaks.

Delayed Reverse Engagement

1. Sealing rings missing or broken.

No Engagement

1. Sealing rings missing or broken.
2. Broken input shaft.
3. Front pump drive tangs or converter hub broken.
4. Front pump worn.
5. Defective converter.

No Forward D-1

1. Sealing rings missing or broken.
2. Front clutch slipping, worn plates or faulty parts.
3. One-way (sprag) clutch slipping or incorrectly installed.
4. Front clutch piston check valve leaks.

No Forward D-2

1. Sealing rings missing or broken.
2. Front clutch slipping, worn plates or faulty parts.
3. Front clutch piston check valve leaks.

No Reverse

1. Sealing rings missing or broken.
2. Rear clutch slipping, worn or faulty parts.
3. Rear band worn or broken.

No Neutral

1. Front clutch seized or distorted plates.

No 1-2 Upshift

1. Sealing rings missing or broken.
2. Output shaft plug missing (6 cyl.).

No 2-3 Upshift

1. Sealing rings missing or broken.
2. Rear clutch slipping, worn or faulty parts.
3. Rear clutch piston ball check leaks.
4. Output shaft plug missing (6 cyl.).

Shift Points Too High

1. Sealing rings missing or broken.

Shift Points Too Low

1. Sealing rings missing or broken.

1-2 Delayed Followed Close By 2-3 Shift

1. Sealing rings missing or broken.
2. Front clutch slipping, worn plates or faulty parts.
3. Front band worn or broken.

2-3 Slips

1. Sealing rings missing or broken.
2. Rear clutch slipping, worn or faulty parts.
3. Front band worn or broken.
4. Rear clutch piston ball check leaks.

Harsh 1-2 Shift

1. Front clutch slipping, worn plates or faulty parts.

Harsh 2-3 Shift

1. Rear clutch seized or plates distorted.

1-2 Ties Up

1. Rear clutch seized or plates distorted.
2. One-way (sprag) clutch seized.

No 2-1 in D-1

1. One-way (sprag) clutch slipping or incorrectly installed.
2. Output shaft plug missing (6 cyl.).

No 2-1 in L Range

1. Rear band worn or broken.
2. Output shaft plug missing (6 cyl.).

No 3-2 Shift

1. Front band worn or broken.
2. Output shaft plug missing (6 cyl.).

Shift Points Too High or Too Low

1. Sealing rings missing or broken.

2-1 Slips

1. Front clutch slipping, worn plates or faulty parts.
2. Front pump drive tangs or converter hub broken.
3. Front clutch piston check valve leaks.

3-2 Slips

1. Sealing rings missing or broken.
2. Rear clutch slipping, worn or faulty parts.
3. Front band worn or broken.
4. Rear clutch piston ball check leaks.

3-1 Shift Above 30 MPH

1. Sealing rings missing or broken.
2. Front band worn or broken.

Harsh 2-1 Shift

1. Sealing rings missing or broken.
2. Front clutch slipping, worn plates or faulty parts.
3. One-way (sprag) clutch slipping or incorrectly installed.

Harsh 3-2 Shift

1. Rear clutch slipping, worn or faulty parts.
2. Rear clutch seized or plates distorted.

Slips or Chatters in Reverse

1. Sealing rings missing or broken.
2. Front clutch seized or plates distorted.
3. Rear clutch slipping, worn or faulty parts.
4. Rear band worn or broken.
5. Rear clutch piston ball check leaks.

Reverse Tie Up

1. Sealing rings missing or broken.
2. Front clutch seized or plates distorted.

Low Idle Pressure

1. Sealing rings missing or broken.
2. Front pump worn.

Low Stall Pressure

1. Sealing rings missing or broken.
2. Front pump worn.
3. Output shaft plug missing (6 cyl.).

Stall Speed Too Low

1. Converter.

Stall Speed Too High D-1

1. Broken output shaft.
2. Broken gears.
3. Sealing rings missing or broken.
4. Front clutch slipping, worn plates or faulty parts.

5. One-way (sprag) clutch slipping or incorrectly installed.
6. Broken input shaft.
7. Converter.
8. Front clutch piston check valve leaks.

Reverse Stall Speed Too High

1. Broken output shaft.
2. Broken gears.
3. Rear band worn or broken.
4. Rear clutch slipping, worn or faulty parts.
5. Broken input shaft.
6. Converter.

Poor Acceleration

1. Output shaft plug missing (6 cyl.).
2. Converter.

Noisy in Neutral

1. Rear clutch seized or plates distorted.
2. Front pump.
3. Front clutch hub thrust washer missing (detectable in N, P, R only).
4. Converter.

Noisy in Park

1. Front pump.
2. Front clutch hub thrust washer missing (detectable in N, P, R only).
3. Converter.

Noisy in All Gears

1. Front pump.
2. Planetary assembly.
3. Converter.

Noisy in 1st & 2nd Gears Only

1. Front pump.
2. Planetary assembly.
3. Forward sun gear thrust washer missing.

Park Brake Does Not Hold

1. Parking linkage.

Oil Out Breather

1. Sealing rings missing or broken.
2. Breather baffle missing.

Oil Out Fill Tube

1. Sealing rings missing or broken.
2. Breather baffle missing.

Ties Up in L or D-1, 1st Gear

1. Rear clutch seized or plates distorted.
2. Sealing rings missing or broken.

Ties Up in D-1 or D-2, 2nd & 3rd Gears

1. Rear clutch seized or plates distorted.
2. Sealing rings missing or broken.
3. One-way (sprag) clutch seized.

Chatters - D-1, D-2 or Low

1. Sealing rings missing or broken.

2. Front clutch slipping, worn plates or faulty parts.
3. Front clutch piston check valve leaks.

MAINTENANCE

The fluid level in the transmission should be checked at 4000-mile intervals. Make sure that the car is standing on a level floor, and firmly apply the parking brake.

With transmission fluid warm, run engine at idle speed. Shift transmission through all ranges and return selector lever to Park.

Clean all dirt from the transmission fluid dipstick cap before removing the dipstick from the filler tube. Pull the dipstick out of the tube, wipe it clean and push it all the way back into the tube.

Pull the dipstick out again and check the fluid level. If necessary, add enough automatic transmission fluid to the transmission to raise the level to the "F" or "Full" mark on the dipstick.

Changing Fluid

The transmission fluid should be changed at 24,000-mile intervals. The procedure is as follows:

1. Raise vehicle and place on jack stands.
2. If filler tube is located in the side of oil pan, remove filler tube to drain oil pan. On other units, loosen oil pan bolts and allow fluid to drain to pan flange level. Then, remove pan attaching bolts from one side to drain remaining fluid.
3. When all oil is drained, remove and clean oil pan and screen. Then, using a new oil pan gasket, install oil pan and screen.
4. Connect filler tube, if removed.
5. Install 3 quarts of approved automatic transmission fluid.
6. Run engine at idle speed for about 2 minutes; then add the additional quantity of oil required for the particular transmission being serviced.
7. Run engine at a fast idle speed until it reaches normal operating temperature.
8. Shift transmission through all ranges; then place it in "P" and check fluid level. If necessary, add enough fluid to bring the level up to the "F" or "Full" mark on the dipstick.

MANUAL LINKAGE, ADJUST

1969 Column & Console Shift

1. Place selector lever in "N" position.
2. Hold selector lever against neutral stop.
3. Adjust linkage to a free fit in transmission outer lever and connect linkage.

1970-71 Column Shift

1. Place selector lever and transmission lever in Neutral.
2. Adjust shift rod trunnion to a free pin fit.
3. Place selector lever in Park and check column lock.

1970-71 Console Shift

1. Loosen park lock-up rod trunnion lock nuts to allow rod movement in trunnion.
2. Place selector lever and transmission lever in Neutral.
3. Adjust linkage for a free pin fit and connect linkage.
4. Place selector lever in Park position and lock steering column. It may be necessary to move lower column lever upward until it is locked. Tighten first lower then upper trunnion nuts while holding trunnion centered in the column lever.

FRONT BAND

Remove transmission oil pan. Loosen locknut on front servo adjusting screw and insert a .250" metal block between end of adjusting screw and servo piston rod, Fig. 1.

With metal block in place, tighten adjusting screw to a torque of 10 inch-pounds and tighten locknut to 23 ft-lbs torque.

NOTE: On cast iron case units, the front servo adjusting screw has a left hand thread.

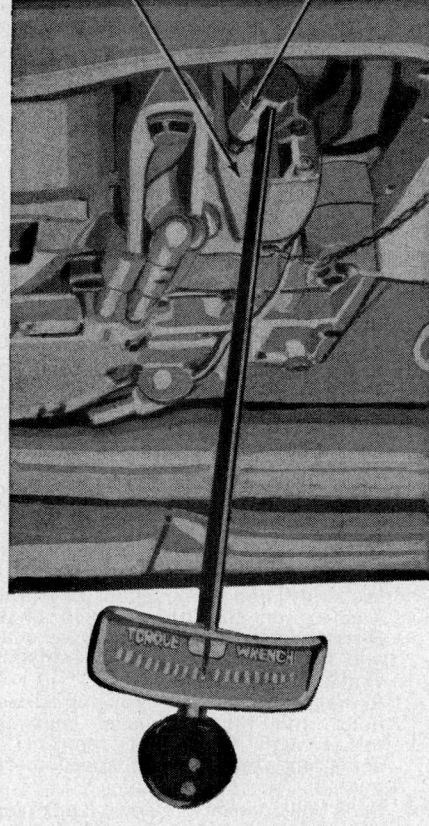

.250" Gauge Block   Ten (10) In. Lb. Torque

Fig. 1   Adjusting front servo band

tubes.

4. Remove front servo apply and release tubes.
5. Disconnect solenoid wire at case connector.
6. Remove control valve attaching screws and remove control valve from transmission.
7. Reverse procedure to install.

Cast Iron Case

1. Drain transmission and remove oil pan.
2. Remove vacuum control unit and rod.
3. Disconnect solenoid wire at case connector.
4. Loosen front servo adjusting screw until arm contacts servo body.

NOTE: On 1969-71 Units, the front servo adjusting screw has left hand threads. Hold bent tang of adjuster wire in counter-clockwise direction, while adjusting screw is turned clockwise to loosen.

5. Some 1969-71 units have two front servo attaching bolts, loosen these bolts.
6. Remove control valve attaching bolts and disconnect front servo pressure tubes from control valve and remove control valve from transmission.

FRONT & REAR SERVOS

It is recommended that these units not be overhauled or replaced to correct a malfunction without first inspecting bands and drums.

REAR BAND, ADJUST

NOTE: To gain access to the rear band adjusting screw, it may be necessary to remove the crossmember bolts and lower the transmission on some models.

Aluminum Case

Loosen locknut and tighten adjusting screw to a torque of 10 ft-lbs. Then back off the adjusting screw ¾ turn and tighten locknut to 28 ft-lbs. torque.

Cast Iron Case

Loosen locknut and tighten adjusting screw to 10 ft-lbs torque. Then back off the adjusting screw 1¼ turns and tighten locknut.

CONTROL VALVE

Aluminum Case

1. Remove filler tube, drain transmission and remove oil pan.
2. Remove vacuum hose from vacuum control unit and remove vacuum unit with push rod attached.
3. Remove rear servo and rear clutch oil

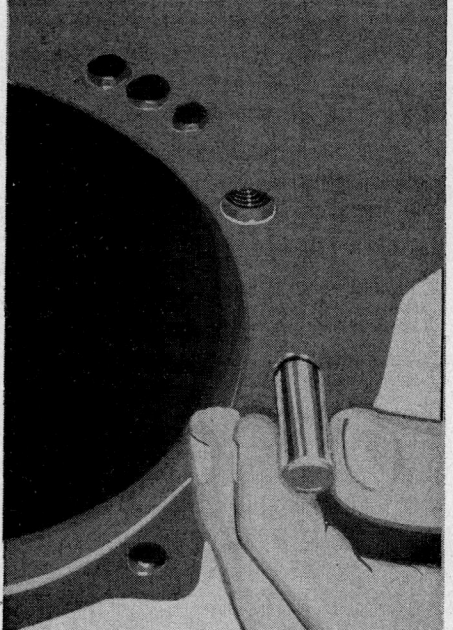

Fig. 2   Removing parking pawl shaft

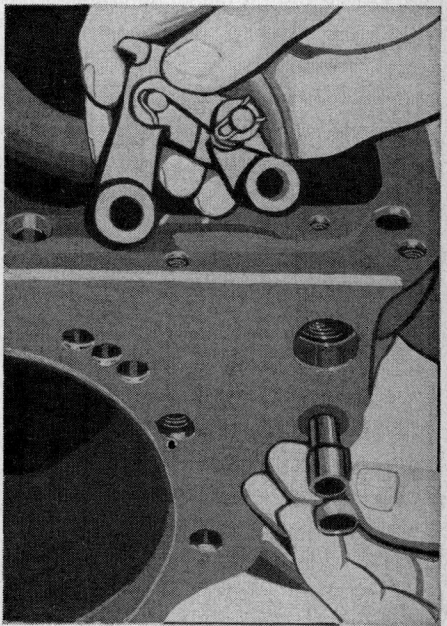

Fig. 3   Removing toggle lever

EXTENSION HOUSING SEAL

Remove propeller shaft or torque tube and propeller shaft from transmission. Pull seal out of extension housing.

Before installing the new seal, inspect the sealing surface of the universal joint yoke for scores. If scores are evident, replace the yoke. Inspect the counterbore in the housing for burrs. Polish all burrs with crocus cloth.

To install the new seal, position it in the bore of the extension housing with the felt side of the seal to the rear. The seal may be driven into the housing with a special tool designed for the purpose.

GOVERNOR

Drain transmission and remove propeller shaft. Support transmission and remove crossmember. Remove speedometer cable from extension housing and on aluminum case units, remove speedometer gear. Remove extension housing using caution not to separate rear case adapter from case as the rear thrust washer may become improperly positioned. Remove two governor body retaining bolts and remove governor from sleeve.

When installing governor into sleeve, be sure side plate faces rearward. Torque retaining bolts to 75 pounds inch.

Remove the governor inspection cover from the extension housing. Rotate the drive shaft to bring the governor body in line with the inspection hole. Remove the two screws which attach the governor body to the counterweight, and remove the body.

Remove the valve from the new governor body. Lubricate the valve with automatic transmission fluid. Install the valve in the body, making sure the valve moves freely in the bore. Install the body in the counterweight. Be sure the fluid passages in the counterweight and body are aligned.

PARKING PAWL, REPLACE

Transmission In Car

Aluminum Case
1. Support engine at rear.
2. Support torque tube with jack.

3. Remove speedometer cable and remove exhaust pipe clamp from lower bracket.
4. Unfasten and remove rear crossmember over exhaust pipe by pulling down on exhaust pipe.
5. Remove oil pan and control valve.
6. Remove parking brake toggle roll pin and remove toggle pin.
7. Unfasten rear extension housing from torque tube adapter and rotate housing clockwise until governor inspection plate is almost level to the bottom. The parking brake anchor pin will then clear extension housing.
8. Remove parking brake anchor pin with a magnet or remove pin from inside of case with needle nose pliers.
9. Remove parking brake toggle link and pawl assembly.
10. Reverse procedure to install.

Cast Iron Case
1. Remove oil pan and screen, pressure regulator and control valve. Disconnect speedometer cable.
2. Completely tighten rear band to prevent movement of planetary assembly and dislocation of thrust washers on the transmission shaft. Disconnect drive shaft or drive shaft and torque tube from the transmission.
3. Remove extension housing-to-case bolts and move housing rearward far enough to permit removal of snap ring which retains speedometer gear.
4. Slide oil delivery sleeve back just far enough so that the oil distributor tubes clear the transmission case.
5. Rotate oil pump housing until parking pawl pin in case is exposed.
6. Disconnect link (parking pawl torsion rod) located between detent lever and torsion lever assembly.
7. Remove hair pin clip retaining torsion lever assembly and remove from shaft.
8. Tap toggle lever pin toward rear of transmission to remove plug and pin, then remove parking pawl pin by working pawl back and forth, Fig. 2.
9. Remove toggle lever and parking pawl assembly from transmission and replace any damaged parts, Fig. 3.
10. Reverse above procedure for reassembly.

TRANSMISSION, REPLACE
1969-71

1. Disconnect battery.
2. Raise car and support with car stands. *Car weight must be on rear springs, therefore, place stands under rear axle tubes.*

NOTE: Before removing the rear crossmember on Javelin and AMX with power steering, it is necessary to open the hood to avoid damage to the hood from the power steering pump wing nut.

3. Disconnect the following:
4. Oil filler tube and drain transmission.
5. Selector linkage at transmission outer manual lever.
6. Speedometer cable at transmission.
7. Vacuum hose and solenoid wire. On 1971 models, disconnect TCS wire, if equipped.
8. Exhaust pipe and remove pipe bracket from converter housing.
9. Position transmission hoist under transmission.
10. Disconnect rear support crossmember from body side sill brackets and transmission.
11. Lower transmission hoist to gain access to upper converter housing to engine bolts and disconnect oil cooler lines.
12. With 199, 232, 258 engines, remove converter housing lower cover.
13. Remove converter access cover (in spacer plate on 290 engine) on V8.
14. Mark converter and drive plate to assure original location upon assembly.
15. Remove converter-to-drive plate capscrews (6-cyl.) stud nuts on V8s.
16. Remove starter mounting bolts and converter housing-to-cylinder block bolts.
17. Push converter housing and converter to rear a sufficient distance to clear crankshaft.

NOTE: Rear of engine tends to raise when transmission weight is removed and may bind the converter in the crankshaft pilot bushing. Blocking the engine up at the front will assist separating converter from crankshaft.

18. Maintain pressure against converter housing and lower assembly until converter housing is clear of engine. Then disconnect propeller shaft and remove transmission from vehicle.
19. Reverse procedure to install.

SEAT BELT INTERLOCK SYSTEMS

INDEX

American Motors 2-311
Chrysler Corporation 2-319
Ford Motor Co. 2-326
General Motors 2-339

AMERICAN MOTORS

Fig. 1 shows the components of the seat belt interlock system. In case of a malfunction in the interlock system, a starter relay is located in the engine compartment to permit starting. The relay is located on the right side next to the starter solenoid and is identified with a decal. Fig. 2 is a system wiring diagram.

NOTE: If a "no start" condition occurs, the fault may be in the seat belt interlock system or in the regular starting system. Manually depress and hold the relay button down while an assistant tries to start the engine. If the engine will not crank while the button is held down, the trouble is not in the interlock system.

CAUTION: Anytime an interlock by-pass start or a solenoid jump start is attempted, be sure the parking brake is applied and the automatic transmission is in Park or manual transmission in Neutral.

Trouble Shooting

Interlock By-Pass Check

Place shift lever in neutral for manual transmissions or park for automatics and apply parking brake with front seat position unoccupied. Turn ignition switch to start position. Engine should crank. If not, refer to chart #1 NO START-FRONT SEATS UNOCCUPIED.

No-Buckle Seat Belt Check

Place shift lever in neutral for manual transmissions and park for automatics and apply parking brake. Activate seat sensor switch, but do not buckle seat belt. Turn ignition switch to start position. Engine should not crank, FASTEN BELTS lamp should light and warning buzzer should sound. If engine starts, refer to Improper Start Chart. Turn ignition switch to the off position.

Repeat above step for center and passenger seat positions.

NOTE: Wait five seconds between each position check.

Warning Buzzer Check

Place shift lever in drive position (release parking brake on manual transmissions). Turn ignition switch to on position and activate seat sensor switch. FASTEN BELTS lamp should come on and buzzer should sound. If not, refer to chart #3 BUZZER AND SAFETY BELT LAMP DIAGNOSIS.

Pre-Buckled, No Start Check

Place shift lever in neutral for manual transmissions and park for automatics and release parking brake. Buckle all front seat belts and while activating each seat sensor switch, turn ignition switch to start position. Engine should not crank. FASTEN BELTS lamp should light and buzzer should sound. If not, refer to chart #4 IMPROPER START.

Proper Start Check

Place shift lever in neutral for manual transmissions or park for automatics with seat belts buckled and apply parking brake. For each front seat position, activate seat sensor switch, buckle and unbuckle seat belt and turn ignition switch to on position. Engine should crank. If not, refer to chart #2 NO START-DRIVER SEATED AND PROPERLY BUCKLED.

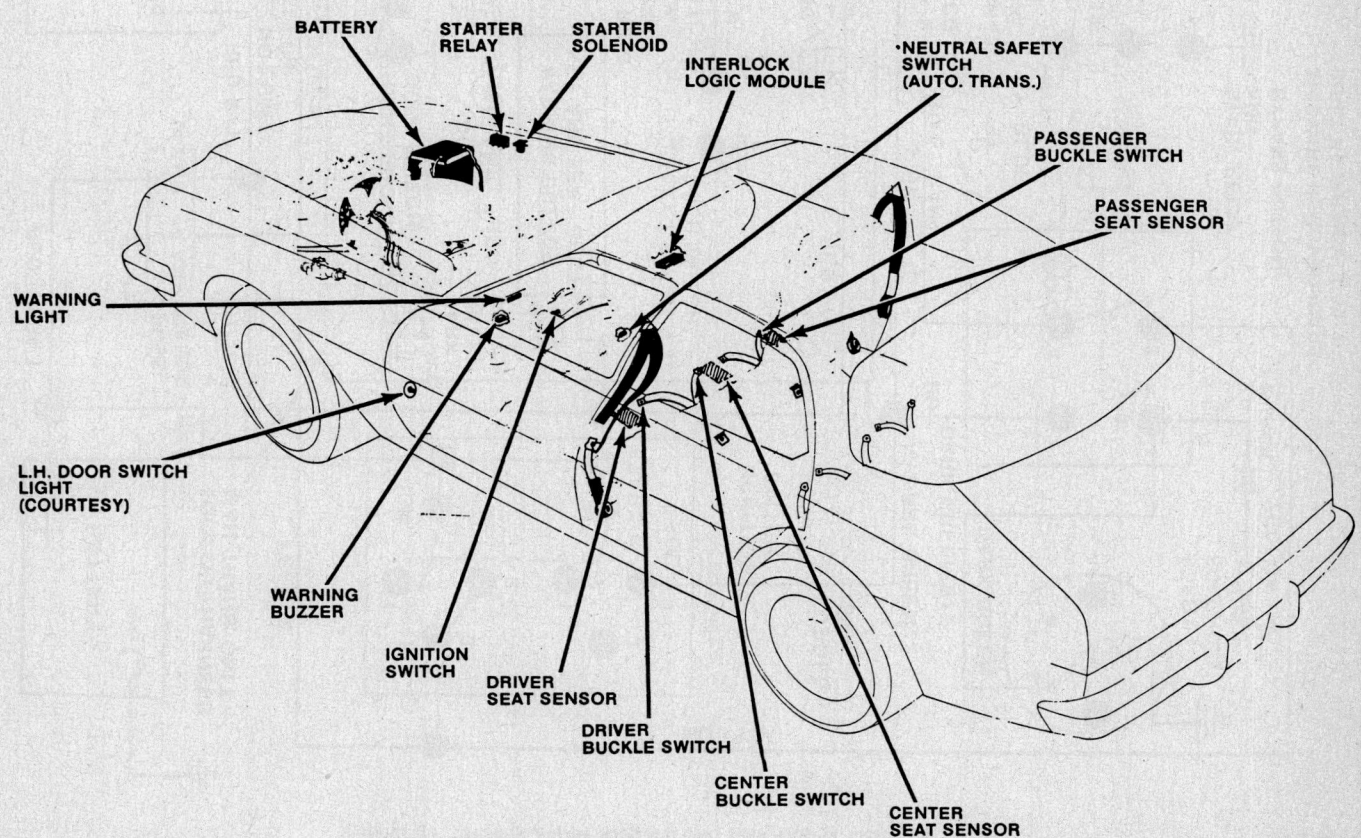

Fig. 1   American Motors seat belt interlock system

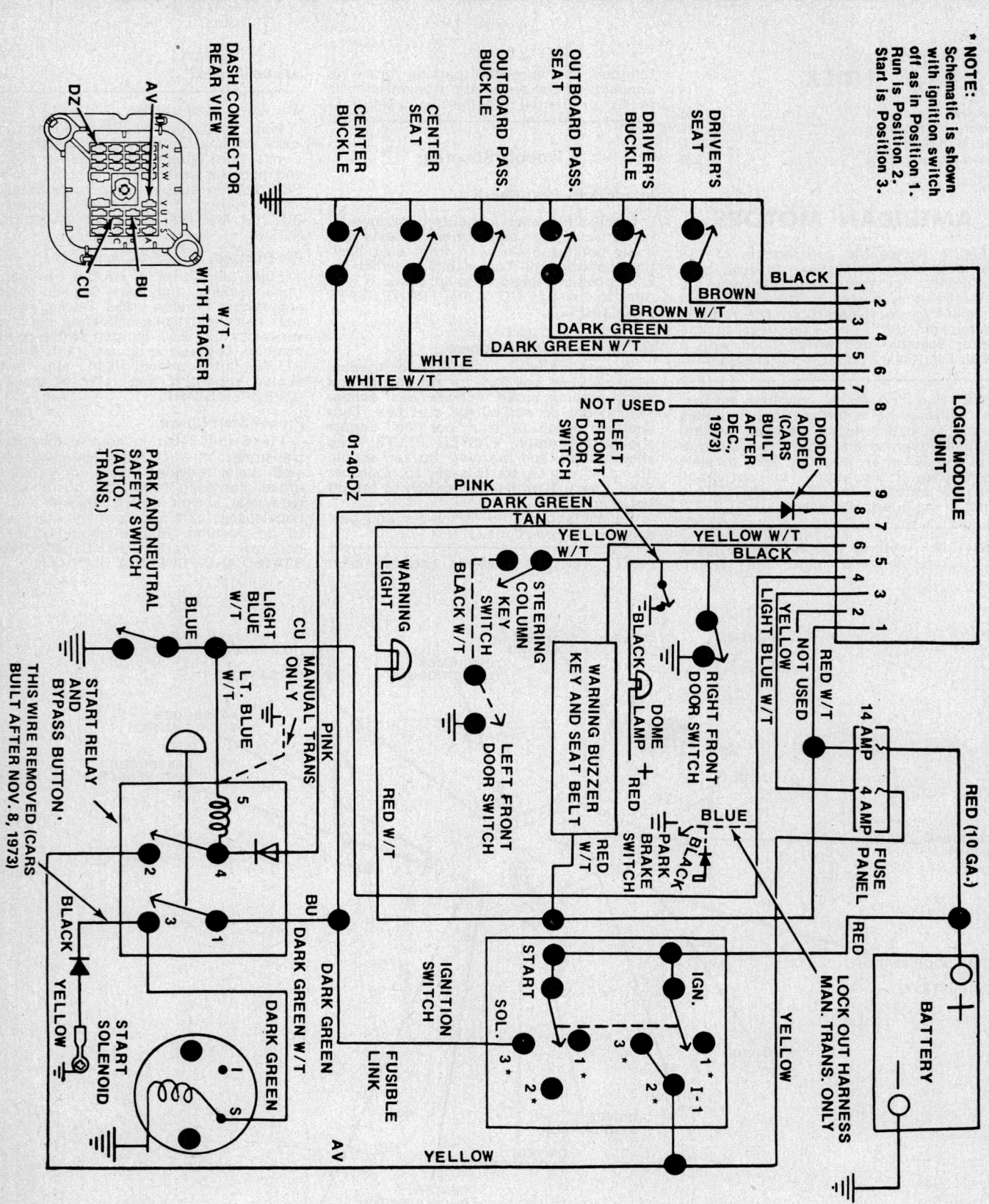

Fig. 2 American Motors seat belt interlock wiring diagram, all models

CHART 1
NO START—FRONT SEATS UNOCCUPIED

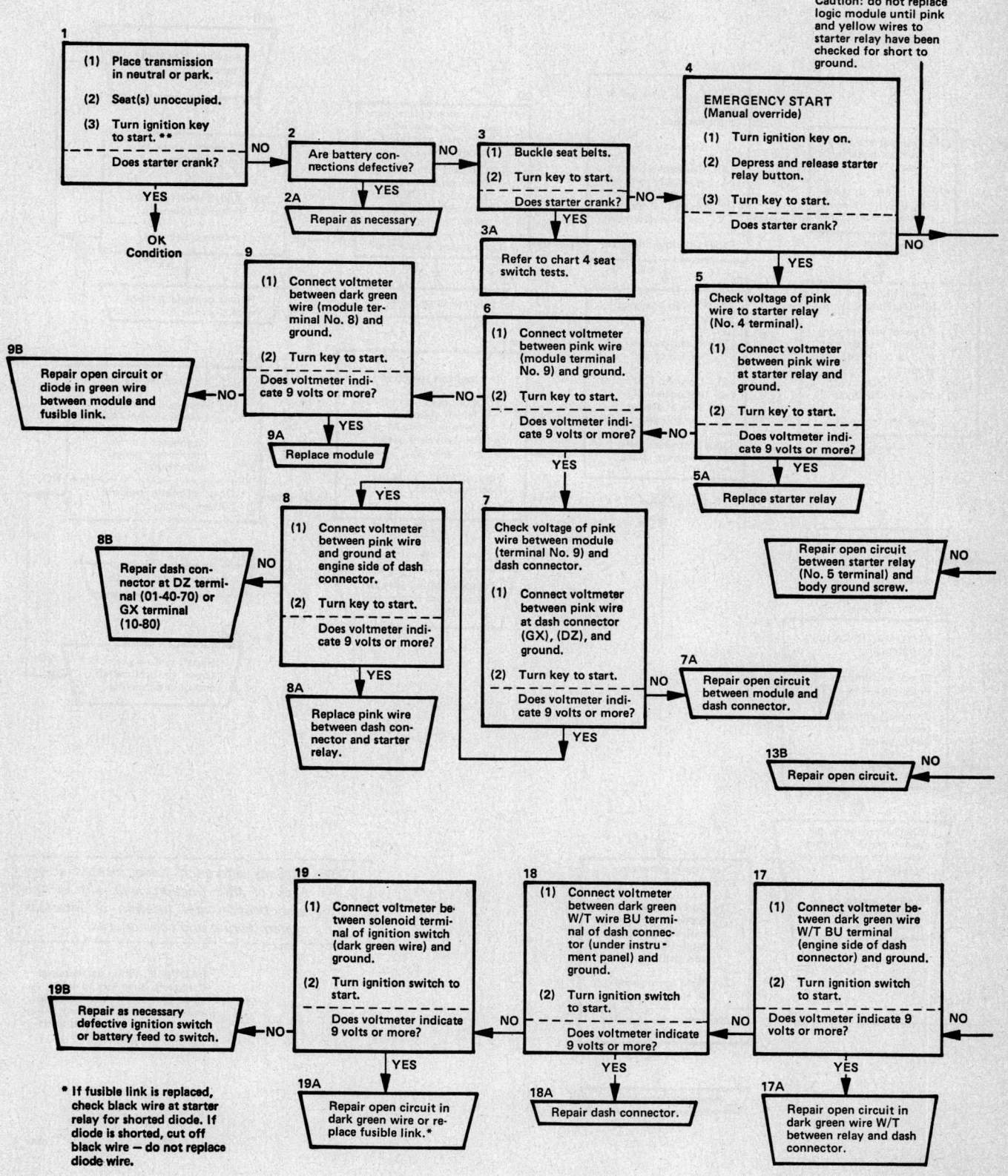

1
(1) Place transmission in neutral or park.
(2) Seat(s) unoccupied.
(3) Turn ignition key to start. **
Does starter crank?

2
Are battery connections defective?

2A
Repair as necessary

3
(1) Buckle seat belts.
(2) Turn key to start.
Does starter crank?

3A
Refer to chart 4 seat switch tests.

Caution: do not replace logic module until pink and yellow wires to starter relay have been checked for short to ground.

4
EMERGENCY START (Manual override)
(1) Turn ignition key on.
(2) Depress and release starter relay button.
(3) Turn key to start.
Does starter crank?

5
Check voltage of pink wire to starter relay (No. 4 terminal).
(1) Connect voltmeter between pink wire at starter relay and ground.
(2) Turn key to start.
Does voltmeter indicate 9 volts or more?

5A
Replace starter relay

OK Condition

9
(1) Connect voltmeter between dark green wire (module terminal No. 8) and ground.
(2) Turn key to start.
Does voltmeter indicate 9 volts or more?

9B
Repair open circuit or diode in green wire between module and fusible link.

9A
Replace module

6
(1) Connect voltmeter between pink wire (module terminal No. 9) and ground.
(2) Turn key to start.
Does voltmeter indicate 9 volts or more?

8
(1) Connect voltmeter between pink wire and ground at engine side of dash connector.
(2) Turn key to start.
Does voltmeter indicate 9 volts or more?

8B
Repair dash connector at DZ terminal (01-40-70) or GX terminal (10-80)

8A
Replace pink wire between dash connector and starter relay.

7
Check voltage of pink wire between module (terminal No. 9) and dash connector.
(1) Connect voltmeter between pink wire at dash connector (GX), (DZ), and ground.
(2) Turn key to start.
Does voltmeter indicate 9 volts or more?

7A
Repair open circuit between module and dash connector.

Repair open circuit between starter relay (No. 5 terminal) and body ground screw.

13B
Repair open circuit.

19
(1) Connect voltmeter between solenoid terminal of ignition switch (dark green wire) and ground.
(2) Turn ignition switch to start.
Does voltmeter indicate 9 volts or more?

19B
Repair as necessary defective ignition switch or battery feed to switch.

19A
Repair open circuit in dark green wire or replace fusible link.*

18
(1) Connect voltmeter between dark green W/T wire BU terminal of dash connector (under instrument panel) and ground.
(2) Turn ignition switch to start.
Does voltmeter indicate 9 volts or more?

18A
Repair dash connector.

17
(1) Connect voltmeter between dark green wire W/T BU terminal (engine side of dash connector) and ground.
(2) Turn ignition switch to start.
Does voltmeter indicate 9 volts or more?

17A
Repair open circuit in dark green wire W/T between relay and dash connector.

* If fusible link is replaced, check black wire at starter relay for shorted diode. If diode is shorted, cut off black wire — do not replace diode wire.

CHART 1
NO START—FRONT SEATS UNOCCUPIED (Continued)

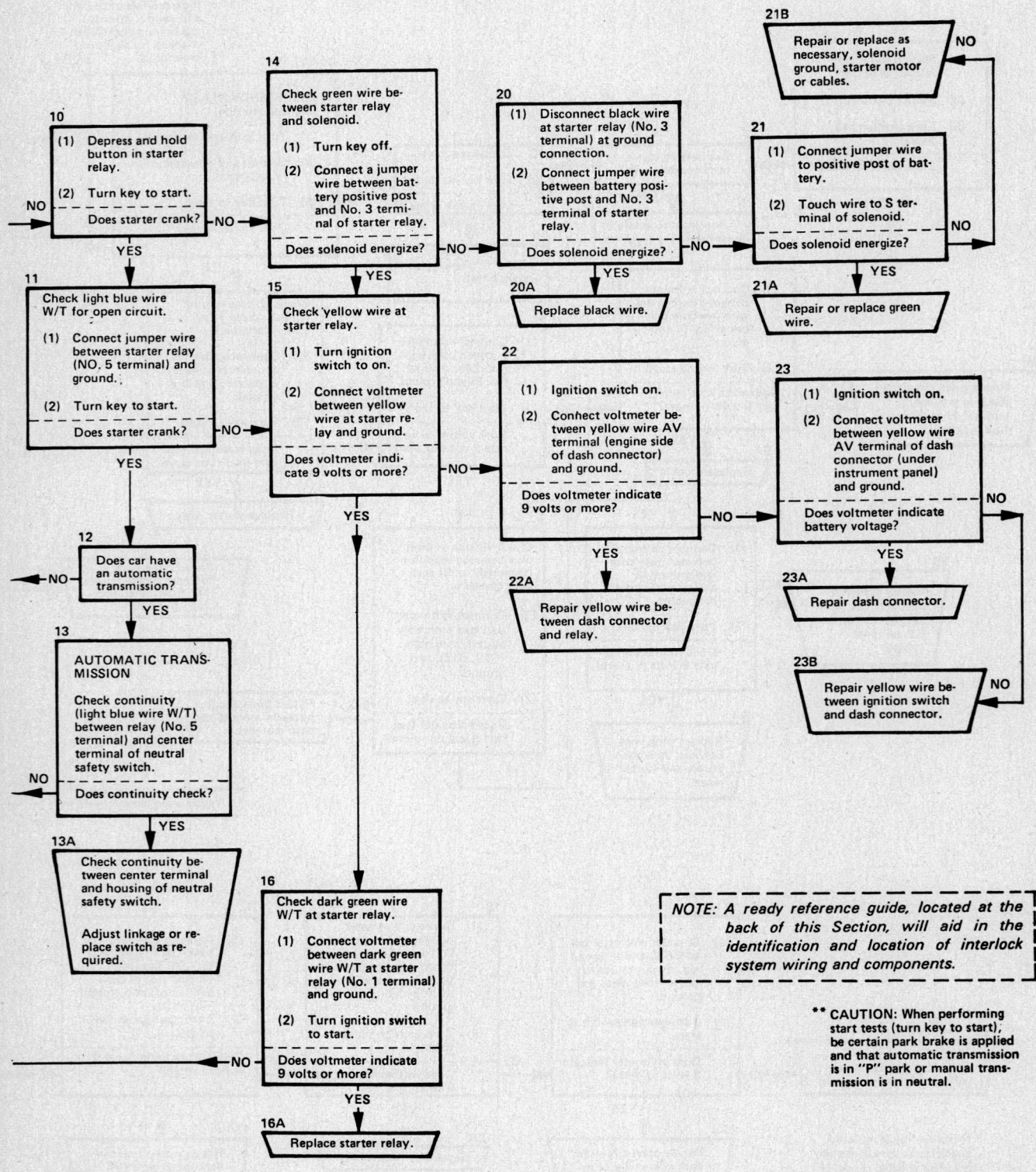

10
(1) Depress and hold button in starter relay.
(2) Turn key to start.

Does starter crank?

11
Check light blue wire W/T for open circuit.
(1) Connect jumper wire between starter relay (NO. 5 terminal) and ground.
(2) Turn key to start.

Does starter crank?

12
Does car have an automatic transmission?

13
AUTOMATIC TRANSMISSION
Check continuity (light blue wire W/T) between relay (No. 5 terminal) and center terminal of neutral safety switch.

Does continuity check?

13A
Check continuity between center terminal and housing of neutral safety switch.
Adjust linkage or replace switch as required.

14
Check green wire between starter relay and solenoid.
(1) Turn key off.
(2) Connect a jumper wire between battery positive post and No. 3 terminal of starter relay.

Does solenoid energize?

15
Check yellow wire at starter relay.
(1) Turn ignition switch to on.
(2) Connect voltmeter between yellow wire at starter relay and ground.

Does voltmeter indicate 9 volts or more?

16
Check dark green wire W/T at starter relay.
(1) Connect voltmeter between dark green wire at starter relay (No. 1 terminal) and ground.
(2) Turn ignition switch to start.

Does voltmeter indicate 9 volts or more?

16A
Replace starter relay.

20
(1) Disconnect black wire at starter relay (No. 3 terminal) at ground connection.
(2) Connect jumper wire between battery positive post and No. 3 terminal of starter relay.

Does solenoid energize?

20A
Replace black wire.

21B
Repair or replace as necessary, solenoid ground, starter motor or cables.

21
(1) Connect jumper wire to positive post of battery.
(2) Touch wire to S terminal of solenoid.

Does solenoid energize?

21A
Repair or replace green wire.

22
(1) Ignition switch on.
(2) Connect voltmeter between yellow wire AV terminal (engine side of dash connector) and ground.

Does voltmeter indicate 9 volts or more?

22A
Repair yellow wire between dash connector and relay.

23
(1) Ignition switch on.
(2) Connect voltmeter between yellow wire AV terminal of dash connector (under instrument panel) and ground.

Does voltmeter indicate battery voltage?

23A
Repair dash connector.

23B
Repair yellow wire between ignition switch and dash connector.

NOTE: A ready reference guide, located at the back of this Section, will aid in the identification and location of interlock system wiring and components.

** CAUTION: When performing start tests (turn key to start), be certain park brake is applied and that automatic transmission is in "P" park or manual transmission is in neutral.

NOTE: W/T = With Tracer

CHART 2
NO START—DRIVER SEATED AND PROPERLY BUCKLED

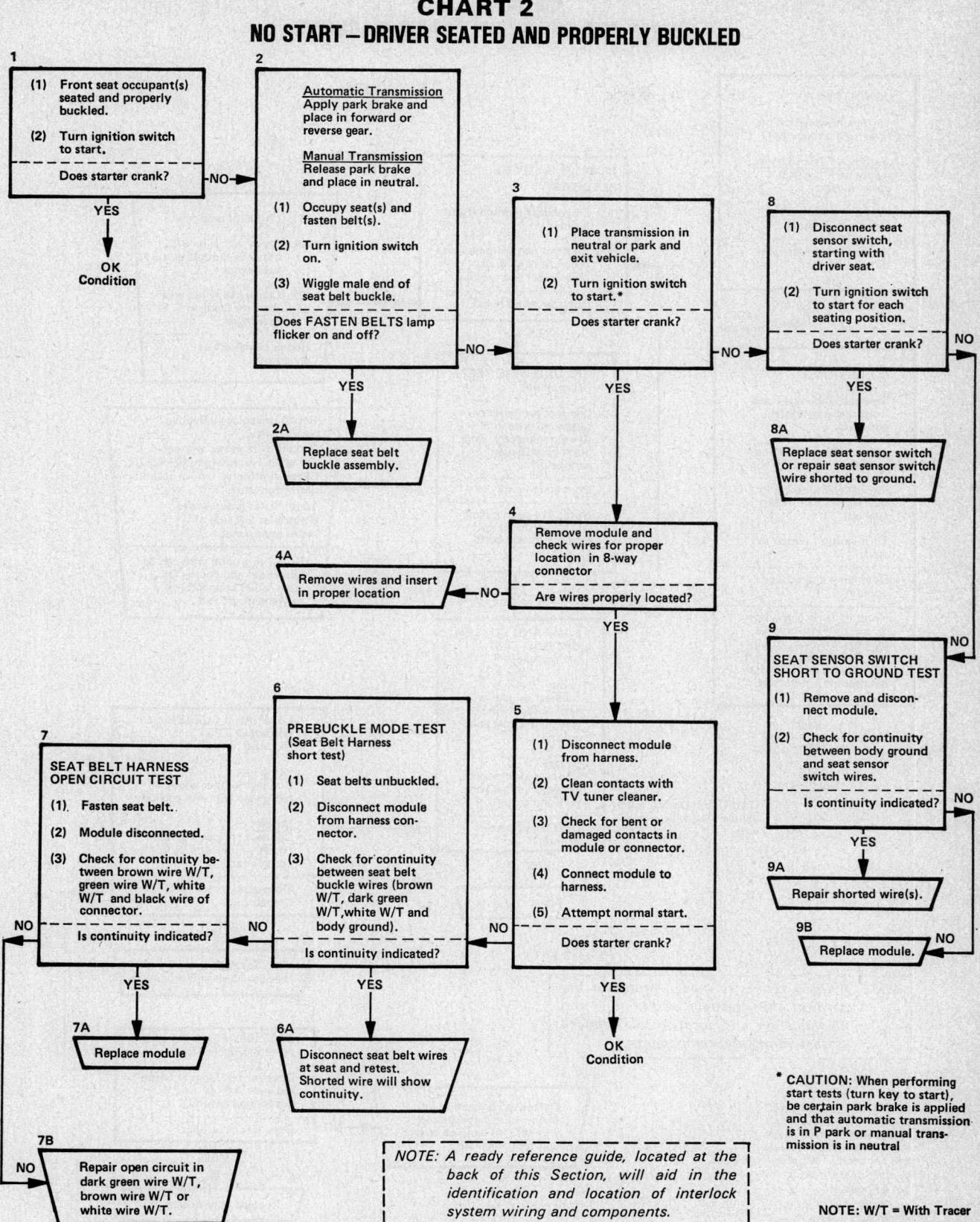

1
(1) Front seat occupant(s) seated and properly buckled.

(2) Turn ignition switch to start.

Does starter crank?

YES → OK Condition

—NO→

2
Automatic Transmission
Apply park brake and place in forward or reverse gear.

Manual Transmission
Release park brake and place in neutral.

(1) Occupy seat(s) and fasten belt(s).

(2) Turn ignition switch on.

(3) Wiggle male end of seat belt buckle.

Does FASTEN BELTS lamp flicker on and off?

—NO→

YES ↓

2A
Replace seat belt buckle assembly.

3
(1) Place transmission in neutral or park and exit vehicle.

(2) Turn ignition switch to start. *

Does starter crank?

—NO→

YES ↓

8
(1) Disconnect seat sensor switch, starting with driver seat.

(2) Turn ignition switch to start for each seating position.

Does starter crank?

NO →

YES ↓

8A
Replace seat sensor switch or repair seat sensor switch wire shorted to ground.

4
Remove module and check wires for proper location in 8-way connector

Are wires properly located?

—NO→

YES ↓

4A
Remove wires and insert in proper location

9
SEAT SENSOR SWITCH SHORT TO GROUND TEST

(1) Remove and disconnect module.

(2) Check for continuity between body ground and seat sensor switch wires.

Is continuity indicated?

NO →

YES ↓

9A
Repair shorted wire(s).

5
(1) Disconnect module from harness.

(2) Clean contacts with TV tuner cleaner.

(3) Check for bent or damaged contacts in module or connector.

(4) Connect module to harness.

(5) Attempt normal start.

Does starter crank?

—NO→

YES ↓

OK Condition

6
PREBUCKLE MODE TEST
(Seat Belt Harness short test)

(1) Seat belts unbuckled.

(2) Disconnect module from harness connector.

(3) Check for continuity between seat belt buckle wires (brown W/T, dark green W/T, white W/T and body ground).

Is continuity indicated?

—NO→

YES ↓

6A
Disconnect seat belt wires at seat and retest. Shorted wire will show continuity.

7
SEAT BELT HARNESS OPEN CIRCUIT TEST

(1) Fasten seat belt.

(2) Module disconnected.

(3) Check for continuity between brown wire W/T, green wire W/T, white W/T and black wire of connector.

Is continuity indicated?

NO →

YES ↓

7A
Replace module

7B
Repair open circuit in dark green wire W/T, brown wire W/T or white wire W/T.

9B
Replace module.

NO →

* CAUTION: When performing start tests (turn key to start), be certain park brake is applied and that automatic transmission is in P park or manual transmission is in neutral

NOTE: A ready reference guide, located at the back of this Section, will aid in the identification and location of interlock system wiring and components.

NOTE: W/T = With Tracer

CHART 3
BUZZER AND SAFETY BELT LAMP DIAGNOSIS

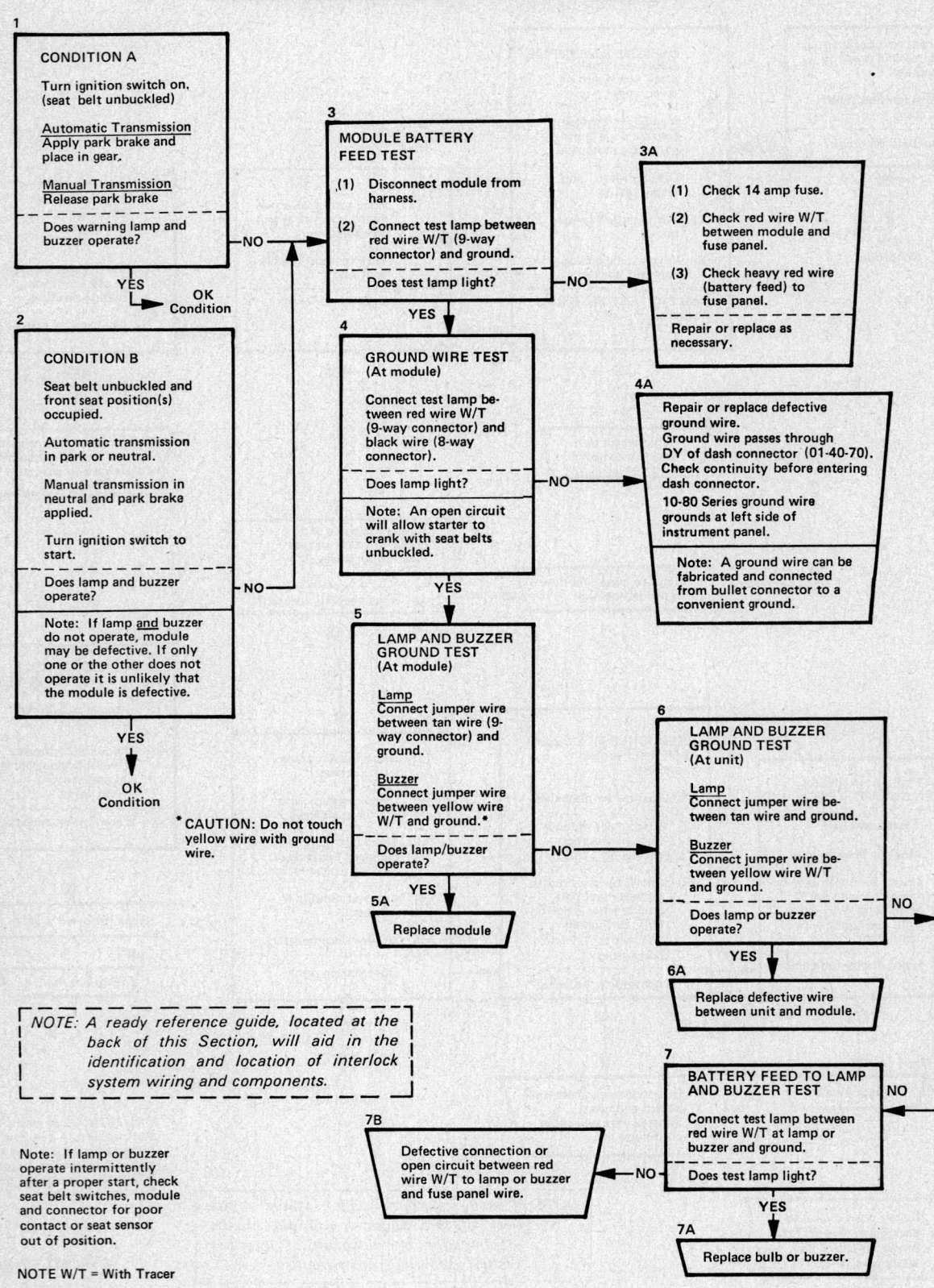

1

CONDITION A

Turn ignition switch on.
(seat belt unbuckled)

Automatic Transmission
Apply park brake and
place in gear.

Manual Transmission
Release park brake

Does warning lamp and
buzzer operate?

→ NO

YES ↓ → OK Condition

2

CONDITION B

Seat belt unbuckled and
front seat position(s)
occupied.

Automatic transmission
in park or neutral.

Manual transmission in
neutral and park brake
applied.

Turn ignition switch to
start.

Does lamp and buzzer
operate?

→ NO

Note: If lamp and buzzer
do not operate, module
may be defective. If only
one or the other does not
operate it is unlikely that
the module is defective.

YES ↓

OK Condition

3

MODULE BATTERY FEED TEST

(1) Disconnect module from
harness.

(2) Connect test lamp between
red wire W/T (9-way
connector) and ground.

Does test lamp light?

→ NO

YES ↓

3A

(1) Check 14 amp fuse.

(2) Check red wire W/T
between module and
fuse panel.

(3) Check heavy red wire
(battery feed) to
fuse panel.

Repair or replace as
necessary.

4

GROUND WIRE TEST
(At module)

Connect test lamp be-
tween red wire W/T
(9-way connector) and
black wire (8-way
connector).

Does lamp light?

→ NO

Note: An open circuit
will allow starter to
crank with seat belts
unbuckled.

YES ↓

4A

Repair or replace defective
ground wire.
Ground wire passes through
DY of dash connector (01-40-70).
Check continuity before entering
dash connector.
10-80 Series ground wire
grounds at left side of
instrument panel.

Note: A ground wire can be
fabricated and connected
from bullet connector to a
convenient ground.

5

LAMP AND BUZZER GROUND TEST
(At module)

Lamp
Connect jumper wire
between tan wire (9-
way connector) and
ground.

Buzzer
Connect jumper wire
between yellow wire
W/T and ground.*

Does lamp/buzzer
operate?

→ NO

YES ↓

5A

Replace module

*CAUTION: Do not touch
yellow wire with ground
wire.

6

LAMP AND BUZZER GROUND TEST
(At unit)

Lamp
Connect jumper wire be-
tween tan wire and ground.

Buzzer
Connect jumper wire be-
tween yellow wire W/T
and ground.

Does lamp or buzzer
operate?

→ NO

YES ↓

6A

Replace defective wire
between unit and module.

7

BATTERY FEED TO LAMP AND BUZZER TEST

Connect test lamp between
red wire W/T at lamp or
buzzer and ground.

Does test lamp light?

→ NO

YES ↓

7A

Replace bulb or buzzer.

7B

Defective connection or
open circuit between red
wire W/T to lamp or buzzer
and fuse panel wire.

NOTE: A ready reference guide, located at the
back of this Section, will aid in the
identification and location of interlock
system wiring and components.

Note: If lamp or buzzer
operate intermittently
after a proper start, check
seat belt switches, module
and connector for poor
contact or seat sensor
out of position.

NOTE W/T = With Tracer

CHART 3
BUZZER AND SAFETY BELT LAMP DIAGNOSIS (Continued)

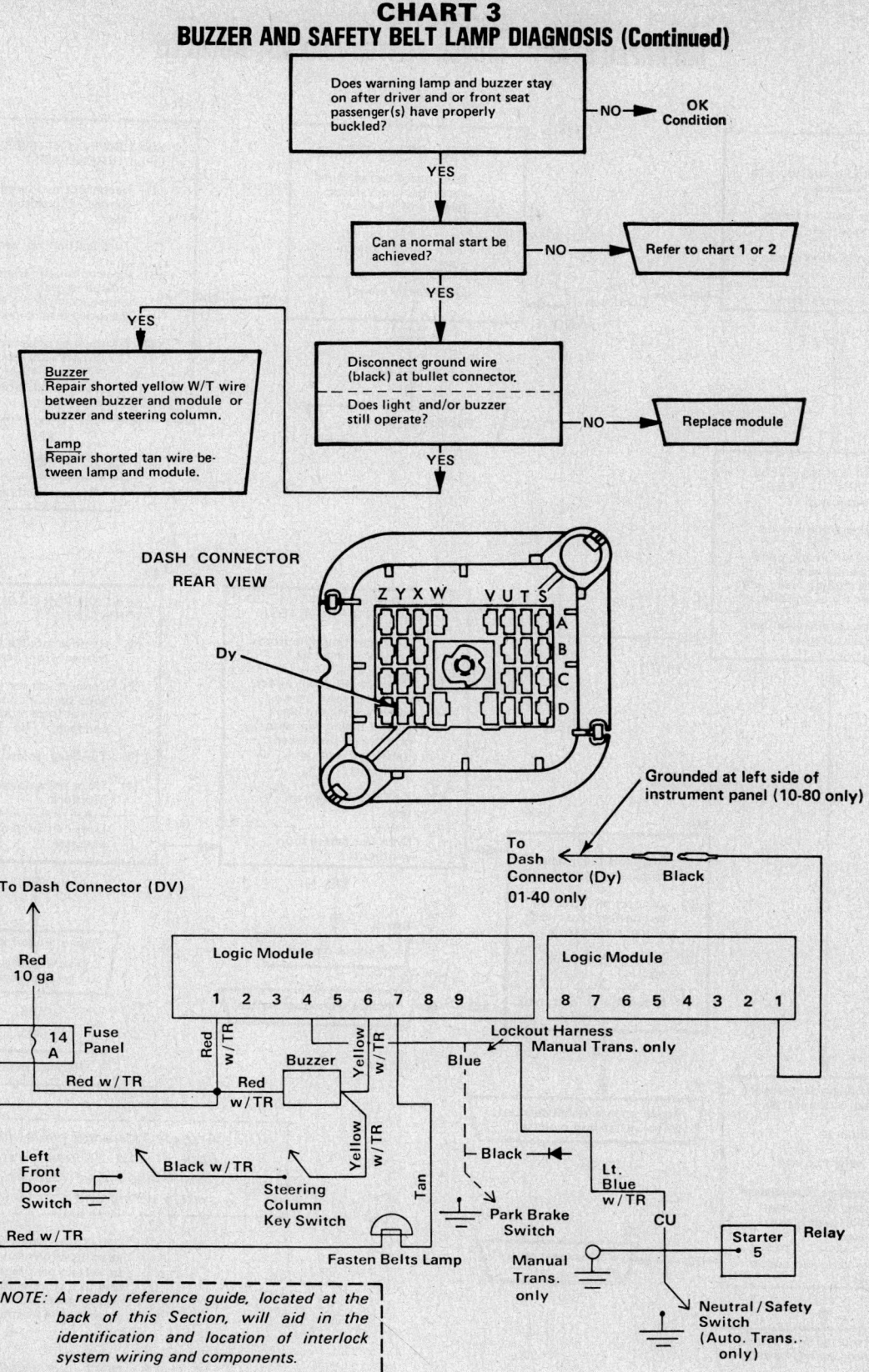

Does warning lamp and buzzer stay on after driver and or front seat passenger(s) have properly buckled?

→ NO → OK Condition

↓ YES

Can a normal start be achieved?

→ NO → Refer to chart 1 or 2

↓ YES

Disconnect ground wire (black) at bullet connector.

Does light and/or buzzer still operate?

→ NO → Replace module

↓ YES

Buzzer
Repair shorted yellow W/T wire between buzzer and module or buzzer and steering column.

Lamp
Repair shorted tan wire between lamp and module.

↑ YES

DASH CONNECTOR
REAR VIEW

Z Y X W   V U T S

A
B
C
D

Dy

Grounded at left side of instrument panel (10-80 only)

To Dash Connector (Dy) 01-40 only   Black

To Dash Connector (DV)

Red 10 ga

14 A   Fuse Panel

Red w/TR

Logic Module

1 2 3 4 5 6 7 8 9

Red w/TR
Buzzer
Yellow w/TR
Blue

Lockout Harness Manual Trans. only

Logic Module

8 7 6 5 4 3 2 1

Left Front Door Switch

Black w/TR

Red w/TR

Steering Column Key Switch

Yellow w/TR

Tan

Black

Park Brake Switch

Fasten Belts Lamp

Lt. Blue w/TR

CU

Starter 5   Relay

Manual Trans. only

Neutral / Safety Switch (Auto. Trans. only)

NOTE: A ready reference guide, located at the back of this Section, will aid in the identification and location of interlock system wiring and components.

CHART 4
IMPROPER START — DRIVER SEATED AND NOT BUCKLED

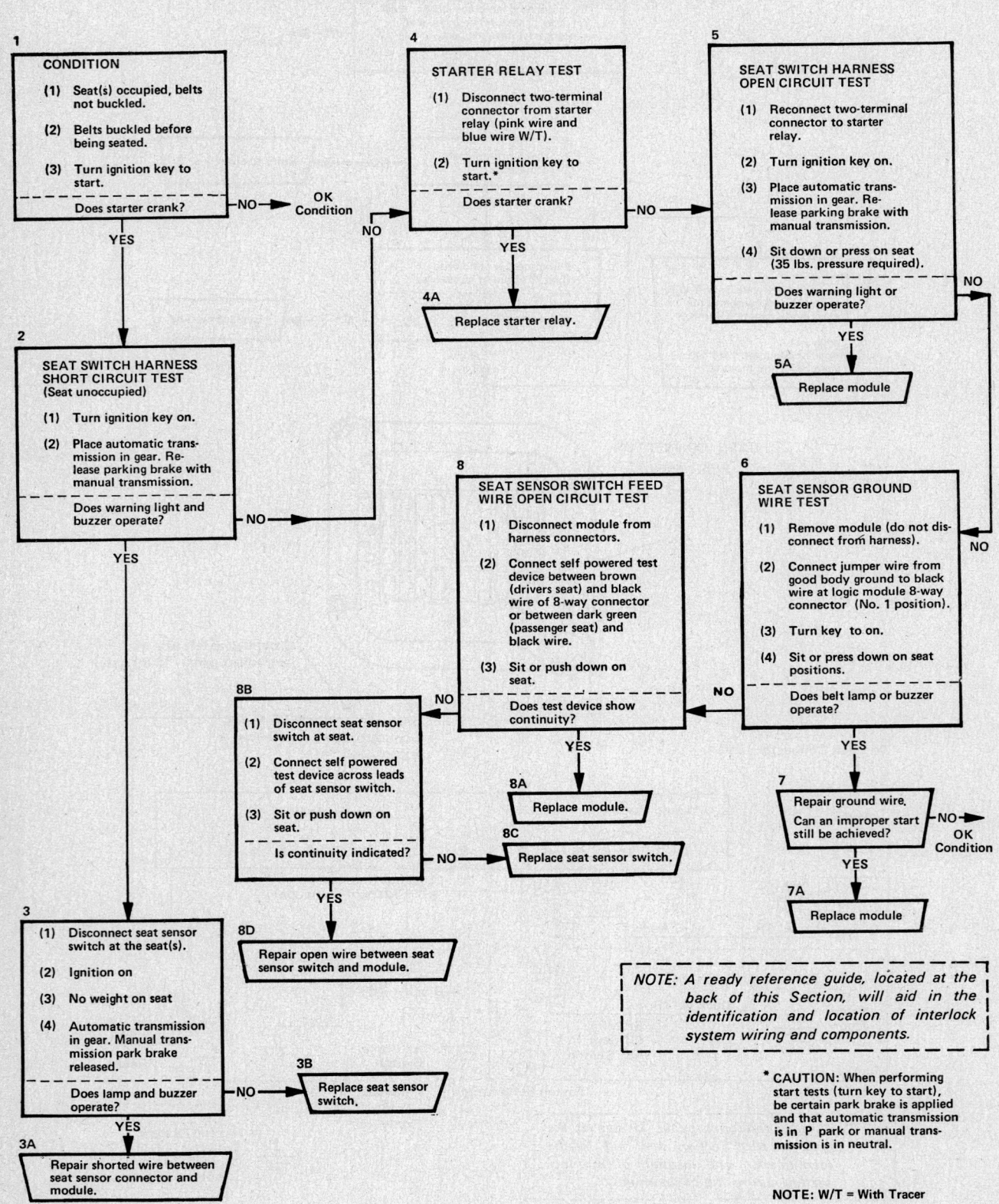

1 CONDITION

(1) Seat(s) occupied, belts not buckled.

(2) Belts buckled before being seated.

(3) Turn ignition key to start.

Does starter crank? — NO → OK Condition

YES ↓

2 SEAT SWITCH HARNESS SHORT CIRCUIT TEST (Seat unoccupied)

(1) Turn ignition key on.

(2) Place automatic transmission in gear. Release parking brake with manual transmission.

Does warning light and buzzer operate? — NO →

YES ↓

3

(1) Disconnect seat sensor switch at the seat(s).

(2) Ignition on

(3) No weight on seat

(4) Automatic transmission in gear. Manual transmission park brake released.

Does lamp and buzzer operate? — NO → **3B** Replace seat sensor switch.

YES ↓

3A Repair shorted wire between seat sensor connector and module.

4 STARTER RELAY TEST

(1) Disconnect two-terminal connector from starter relay (pink wire and blue wire W/T).

(2) Turn ignition key to start.*

Does starter crank? — NO →

YES ↓

4A Replace starter relay.

5 SEAT SWITCH HARNESS OPEN CIRCUIT TEST

(1) Reconnect two-terminal connector to starter relay.

(2) Turn ignition key on.

(3) Place automatic transmission in gear. Release parking brake with manual transmission.

(4) Sit down or press on seat (35 lbs. pressure required).

Does warning light or buzzer operate? — NO →

YES ↓

5A Replace module

8 SEAT SENSOR SWITCH FEED WIRE OPEN CIRCUIT TEST

(1) Disconnect module from harness connectors.

(2) Connect self powered test device between brown (drivers seat) and black wire of 8-way connector or between dark green (passenger seat) and black wire.

(3) Sit or push down on seat.

Does test device show continuity? — NO →

YES ↓

8A Replace module.

8B

(1) Disconnect seat sensor switch at seat.

(2) Connect self powered test device across leads of seat sensor switch.

(3) Sit or push down on seat.

Is continuity indicated? — NO → **8C** Replace seat sensor switch.

YES ↓

8D Repair open wire between seat sensor switch and module.

6 SEAT SENSOR GROUND WIRE TEST

(1) Remove module (do not disconnect from harness).

(2) Connect jumper wire from good body ground to black wire at logic module 8-way connector (No. 1 position).

(3) Turn key to on.

(4) Sit or press down on seat positions.

Does belt lamp or buzzer operate? — NO →

YES ↓

7 Repair ground wire. Can an improper start still be achieved? — NO → OK Condition

YES ↓

7A Replace module

NO → NO

NOTE: A ready reference guide, located at the back of this Section, will aid in the identification and location of interlock system wiring and components.

* CAUTION: When performing start tests (turn key to start), be certain park brake is applied and that automatic transmission is in P park or manual transmission is in neutral.

NOTE: W/T = With Tracer

CHRYSLER CORPORATION

To use the Trouble Shooting procedure, perform each and every Checkout Procedure step beginning with step 1 and continuing until the malfunction occurs. Then proceed to the corresponding Trouble Shooting step and follow the procedure outlined.

Begin the procedure with the car in Neutral on automatic transmission cars or the parking brake applied on manual transmission cars. The ignition key should be in the Off or Lock position.

The seat switches in the driver's seat and the right front passenger seat location must be set by having at least a 150 lb. person or equivalent weight sitting momentarily in that position before tests can proceed. Fig. 3 provides a basic wiring diagram of the system. An interlock component location chart, Fig. 4, is also provided.

Checkout Procedure

An interlock diagnosis chart is supplied to assist in the checkout procedure.

Underhood Switch Operational Check

1. Sit in driver's seat with all doors closed but do not buckle belt. Turn ignition key to Start. Engine should not crank. Light and buzzer should go on while key is in Start. Light and buzzer should go off when key is in Run position.
2. Turn ignition key to Off or Lock. Open hood and depress then release the underhood switch. Sit in driver's seat but do not buckle belt. Turn ignition key to Start. Engine should crank. Light and buzzer should go on while key is in Start.
3. Leave key On for 30 seconds, then turn Off and leave ignition Off for 2½ minutes. Get out of driver's seat and reach in car and buckle driver's seat belt. Sit in driver's seat, close all doors and turn ignition key to Start. Engine should not crank. Light and buzzer should go on while key is in Start.

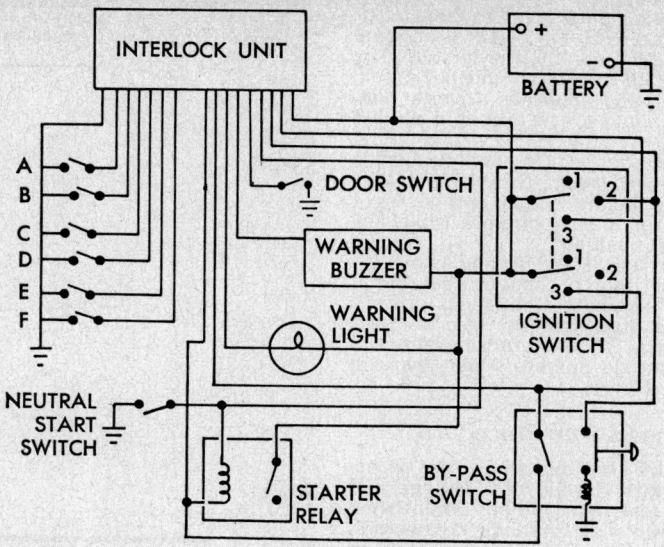

NOTE:
SCHEMATIC IS SHOWN WITH IGNITION SWITCH OFF AS IN POSITION 1. RUN IS POSITION 2. START IS POSITION 3.

Fig. 3   Chrysler Corporation seat belt interlock wiring diagram

Interlock and Sensing Switches

4. With driver in seat and pre-buckled as in step 3 above, leave ignition On and for automatic transmission cars move the gear selector to any forward or reverse gear. For manual transmissions release parking brake. Light and buzzer should go On and stay On.
5. Unbuckle driver's belt and light and buzzer should stay On. Kneel on seat and buckle belt across empty seat. In this way weight is applied to driver's seat before belt is buckled. Light and buzzer should go Off.
6. Get out of car and close door. Go to right side of car and open door. Reach in and buckle right passenger seat belt. Sit on seat and close door and light and buzzer should be On.
7. Unbuckle right passenger belt and light and buzzer should remain On.
8. Buckle right passenger belt and light and buzzer should go Off.
9. Reach over and buckle center passenger belt and move to center seating position. The light and buzzer should go On.
10. Unbuckle the center belt and light and buzzer should remain On.
11. Buckle center seat belt and light and buzzer should turn Off within 5 seconds.
12. Unbuckle center seat belt and move to driver's seat, then place automatic

INTERLOCK COMPONENTS LOCATION CHART

	Buzzer	Buzzer Light Fuse	Interlock Unit	System Fuse	Underhood Switch
Dart & Valiant	Left Side of I/P Above Hand Brake	Fuse #7	Behind Buzzer	Fuse #6	Left Side on Firewall
Charger, Coronet & Satellite	Right Side of I/P Near Side Cowl	Fuse #2	On I/P to Left Of Glove Box	Fuse #1	Right Side on Firewall
Barracuda & Challenger	Rear of I/P and Right of Glove Box	Fuse #4	Left Side of I/P Above A/C Duct	Fuse #1	Left Fender Shield
Chrysler, Fury, Monaco & Imperial	Left Side of Brake Support Bracket	Fuse #3	Mounted Above Buzzer	Fuse #5	Left Hood Hinge

Fig. 4   Chrysler Corporation interlock component location chart

transmission shift lever to Neutral or Park. Depress clutch pedal on manual transmission cars. Turn ignition key to Start and engine should not crank. Unbuckle and rebuckle driver's belt. Engine should crank and light should be Off.

13. Turn ignition to Off and unbuckle driver's belt. Next, turn ignition key to Start. Engine should crank. Light and buzzer should operate while key is in Start position.

14. Turn ignition key Off and move to center or right passenger seat for at least 5 seconds. Return to driver's seat and turn ignition key to Start and engine should crank. Light and buzzer should operate while key is in Start.

Diagnosis Step Procedure

The step by step directions can be accomplished with the aid of a voltage test light and a test light jumper wire. When checking circuits at interlock connectors, test only at wire end of connector as shown in various illustrations.

Step 1—Engine Cranks with Driver Not Buckled

Underhood Switch

1. Remove connector from underhood switch, then return to driver's and turn ignition key to Start. If engine does not crank, replace underhood switch.

Wiring

1. Remove both connectors from interlock unit, then sit in driver's seat and turn ignition to Start. If engine cranks, a wiring short exists. Trace circuits to correct problem.
2. If engine does not crank, check for voltage with test light between red wire in 9-way connector and a good ground, Fig. 5.
3. When connected, test light should turn On. If not, an open circuit exists. Trace circuit and correct.

Driver's Seat Switch

1. Check driver's seat switch by connecting test light to red wire in 9-way connector and to white wire in 8-way connector, Fig. 6.
2. Test light should be On when driver's seat is occupied and Off when the seat is empty. If switch does not operate properly, use a self powered test light to check switch operation across switch connector terminals under seat. If switch does not operate, replace the switch. If switch is OK, check the white wire between the interlock unit and the switch for an open circuit.

Interlock Unit

1. If seat switch, underhood switch and wiring check OK, replace interlock unit.

Step 1A—Warning Light and/or Buzzer do not Turn on when Key is in Start and Off when Key is in Run with Selector in Park or Neutral (Hand Brake Applied for Manual Transmission)

Malfunction of Interlock Unit

A malfunction of the interlock unit will affect both the warning lamp and the

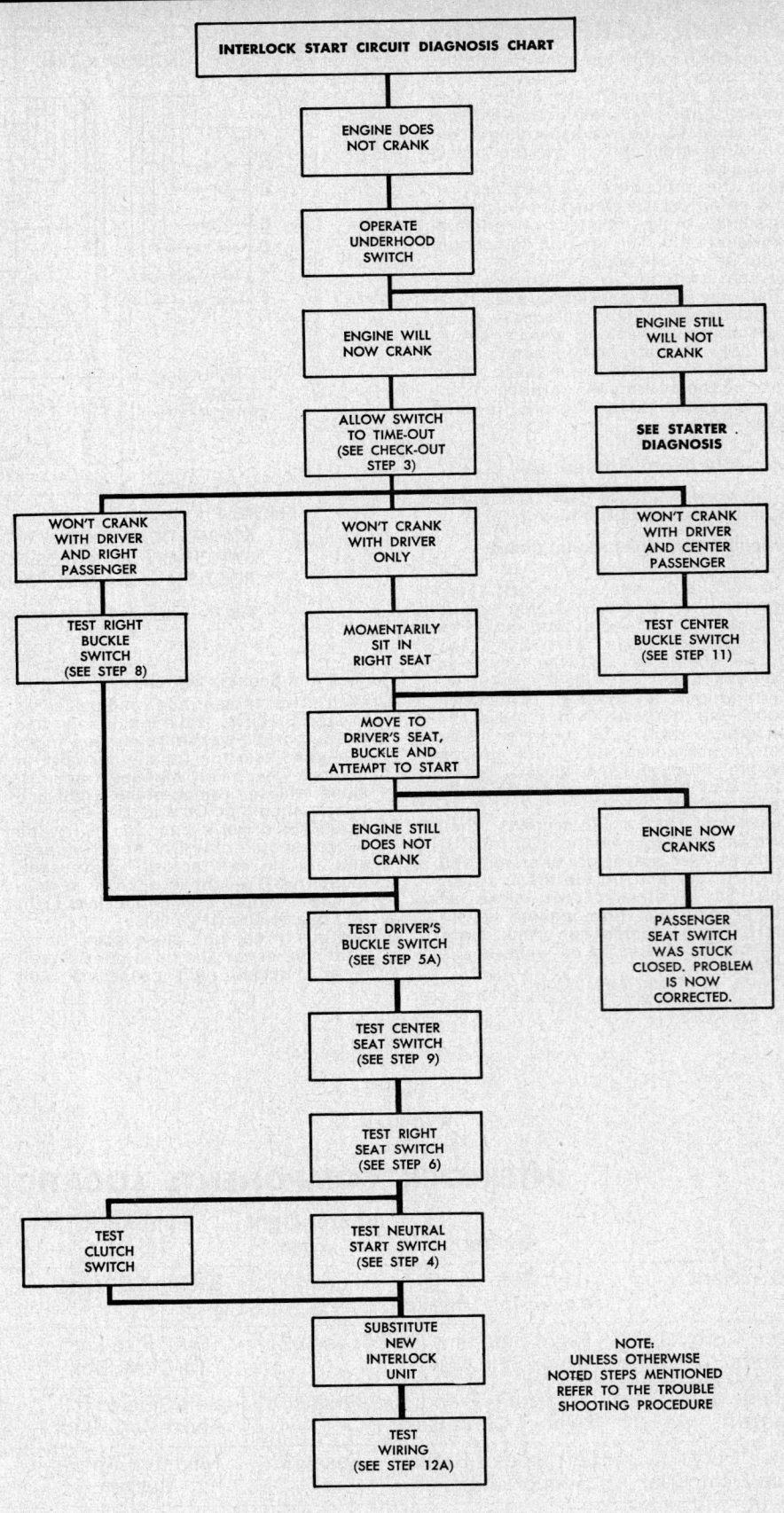

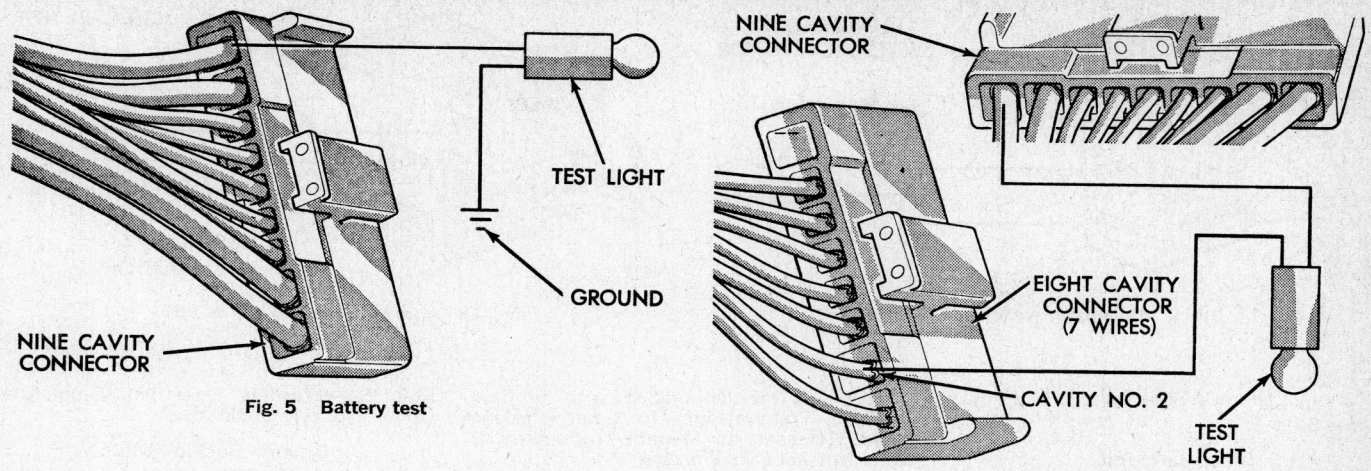

Fig. 5   Battery test

Fig. 6   Driver seat switch test

buzzer. If only one does not function, the interlock unit is not the cause.

1. If both buzzer and warning lamp do not function, check fuse.
2. Remove both connectors with test light from interlock unit. Check for voltage between red wire in 9-way connector and gray wire in 8-way connector, Fig. 7.
3. Test light should turn On. If not, open circuit exists either in red wire or gray wire. Trace circuits and correct.

Light

1. Connect a jumper wire from dark blue with red tracer in 9-way connector to a good ground, Fig. 8.
2. Warning light should turn On. If not, check bulb and wiring.

Buzzer

1. Connect jumper wire from dark blue wire and ground, Fig. 8. Buzzer should come On. If not, check wiring and buzzer.

Interlock Unit

1. If warning lamp, buzzer and wiring check OK, replace interlock.

Step 2—Engine Does Not Crank Following Actuation of Underhood Switch

Underhood Switch

1. Remove connector from underhood switch. Sit in driver's seat and buckle belt. Turn ignition key to Start. If engine does not crank, check neutral switch (step 4). If neutral switch is OK, check starter system. If engine does crank, then with engine not running, turn ignition switch On; test voltage with light between black wire and dark blue wire, Fig. 9. If test lamp does not light, an open circuit exists. Check wiring.
2. Use test lead and momentarily jump between dark blue wire and first one and then the other yellow wire, Fig. 10. The engine should crank. If not, check wiring.
3. Connect test light from yellow wire that did not activate starter to ground. Test lamp should light when key is

turned to Start. If test lamp does not light the problem is in wiring. If no wiring problem is evident, replace underhood switch.

Step 2A—Buzzer And Light Not On
See Step 1A.

Step 3—Engine Cranks When it Should Not. Driver Belt Buckled Before Being Seated

Underhood Switch

1. Remove connector at underhood switch. Return to prebuckled driver's seat and turn key to Start. If engine will not now crank, reconnect underhood switch and repeat checkout steps 2 and 3. Make sure car runs for 30 seconds minimum followed by the ignition Off for at least 2½ minutes. If engine still cranks, replace underhood switch.

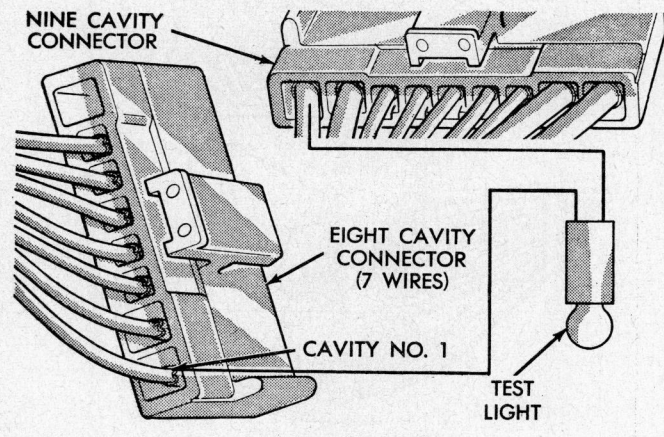

Fig. 7   Ground test

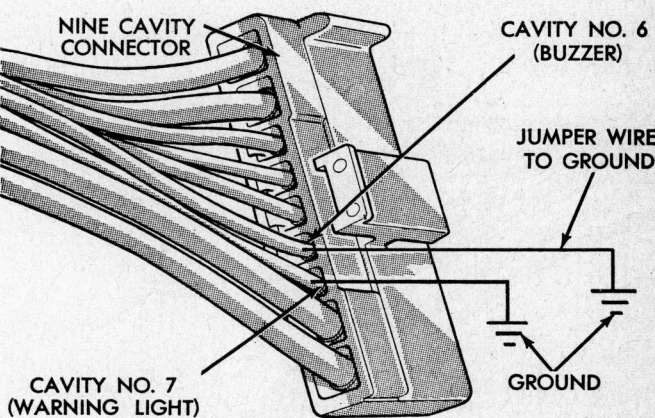

Fig. 8   Buzzer and warning light test

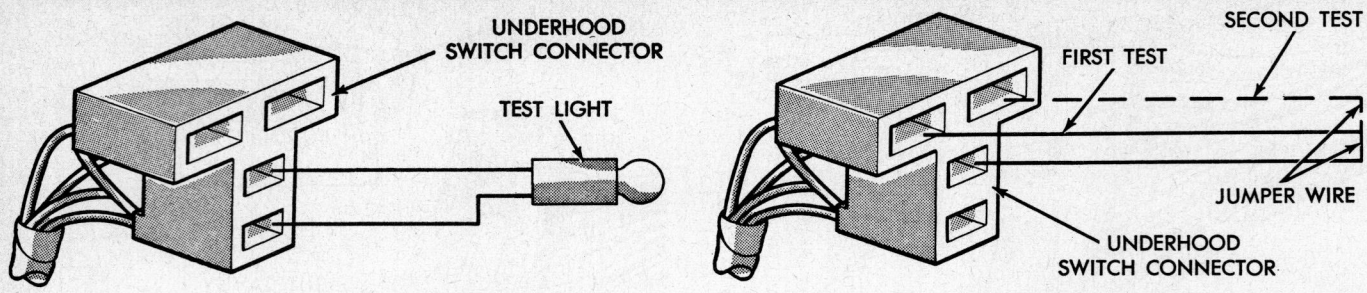

Fig. 9   Underhood switch voltage test

Fig. 10   Underhood switch starter test

Driver's Seat Switch

Use Step 1.

Interlock Unit

Use Step 1.

Step 3A—Buzzer And Warning Light Not On

See Step 1A.

Step 4—Light And Buzzer Do Not Go On When Ignition On, Car Is In Gear, and Driver Belt Buckled Before Being Seated

Ignition Run Input

1. Check system fuse. If OK, remove both connectors from interlock unit. Connect test light to dark blue wire with white tracer in 9-way connector to a good ground, Fig. 11. With ignition On, test light should be On. If not, trace wiring for open circuit.

Neutral Start or Parking Brake Switch

1. Connect test light between dark blue wire with white tracer and brown wire with yellow tracer. Ignition On, Fig. 12.
2. For automatic transmission cars, when selector is in Neutral or Park, test light should turn On and when selector is in gear test light should turn Off. For manual transmission cars, when parking brake is applied test light should turn On. When parking brake is released, test light should turn Off. If not, check wiring and switches.

Interlock Unit

1. Ignition run and neutral start or parking brake switches check OK, replace interlock unit.

Step 5—Driver Unbuckled with Ignition On and Transmission in Gear (Parking Brake Released on Manual Transmission) Does Not Activate Warning

Interlock Unit

1. Replace interlock unit.

Step 5A—Warning Does Not Stop After Driver Properly Buckled

Driver's Buckle Switch

1. Remove both connectors from interlock unit. Connect test light to red wire in 9-way connector and to light

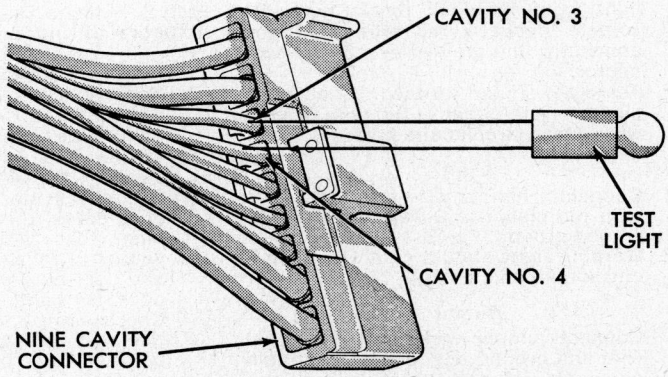

Fig. 12   Neutral start or parking brake test

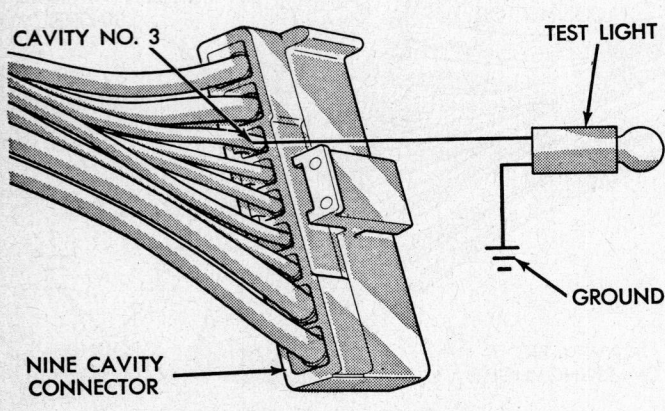

Fig. 11   Ignition run test

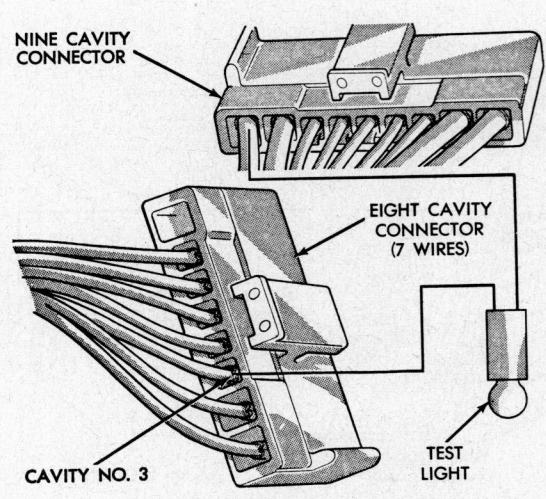

Fig. 13   Driver's buckle switch test

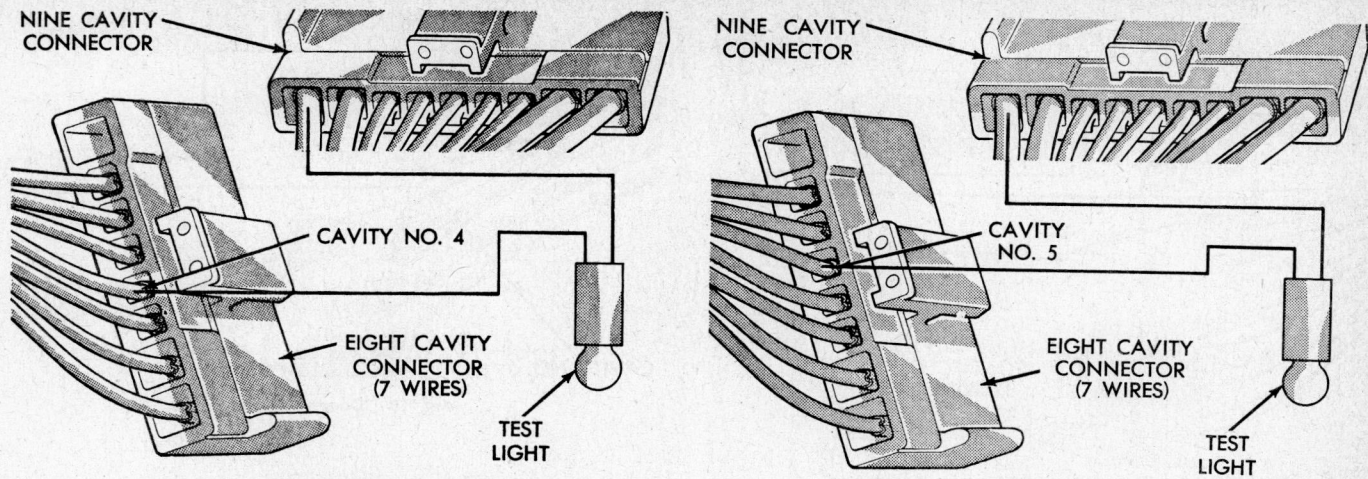

Fig. 14   Right passenger seat switch test

Fig. 15   Right passenger buckle switch test

green wire in 8-way connector, Fig. 13. When belt is unbuckled test light should be Off and when belt is buckled test light should be On. If switch does not operate use a self powered test light to check switch operation at connector attached to switch and located near belt anchor. If switch does not operate properly, replace the buckle webbing and switch assembly. If switch does operate, trouble is in wiring.

Right Passenger Seat Switch
See Step 6.

Control Seat Switch
See Step 9.

Interlock Unit
1. If switch and wiring check OK, replace interlock unit.

Step 6—Right Front Passenger Buckled Before Sitting With Ignition On And Car in Gear Does Not Activate Warning

Right Passenger Seat Switch
1. Remove both connectors from interlock. Connect test light to red wire in 9-way connector and dark green wire in 8-way connector, Fig. 14. Test light should be Off when seat is empty and On when seat is occupied. If switch does not operate use a self powered test light to check switch operation at connector attached to switch and located under seat. If switch still does not operate, replace switch. If switch now checks OK, problem is in wiring.

Interlock Unit
1. If switch and wiring check OK, replace interlock unit.

Step 7—Right Front Passenger Unbuckled With Ignition On and Car In Gear Does Not Activate Warning

Seat Switch
See Step 6.

Interlock Unit
1. Replace interlock unit.

Step 8—Warning Does Not Stop After Right Seat Passenger Properly Buckles

Right Seat Buckle Switch
1. Remove both connectors from interlock unit. Connect test light to red wire in 9-way connector and red wire with white tracer in 8-way connector, Fig. 15.
2. When belt is unbuckled test light should be Off and when belt is buckled test light should be On. If buckle switch does not operate use a self powered test light to check switch operation at switch connector located at rear of seat near belt anchor. If switch still does not operate, replace belt, webbing and switch assembly. If

switch now checks OK, problem is in wiring.

Driver's Seat Switch
See Step 2.

Center Seat Switch
See Step 9.

Interlock Unit
1. If switch and wiring check OK, replace interlock unit.

Step 9—Center Passenger Buckled Before Sitting with Ignition On and Car in Gear Does Not Activate Warning

Center Passenger Seat Switch
1. Remove both connectors from interlock unit. Connect a test light to red wire in 9-way connector and tan wire in 8-way connector, Fig. 16. When

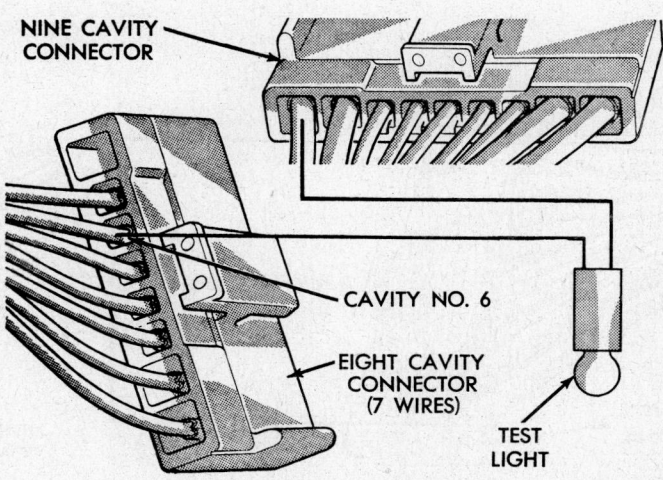

Fig. 16   Center passenger seat switch test

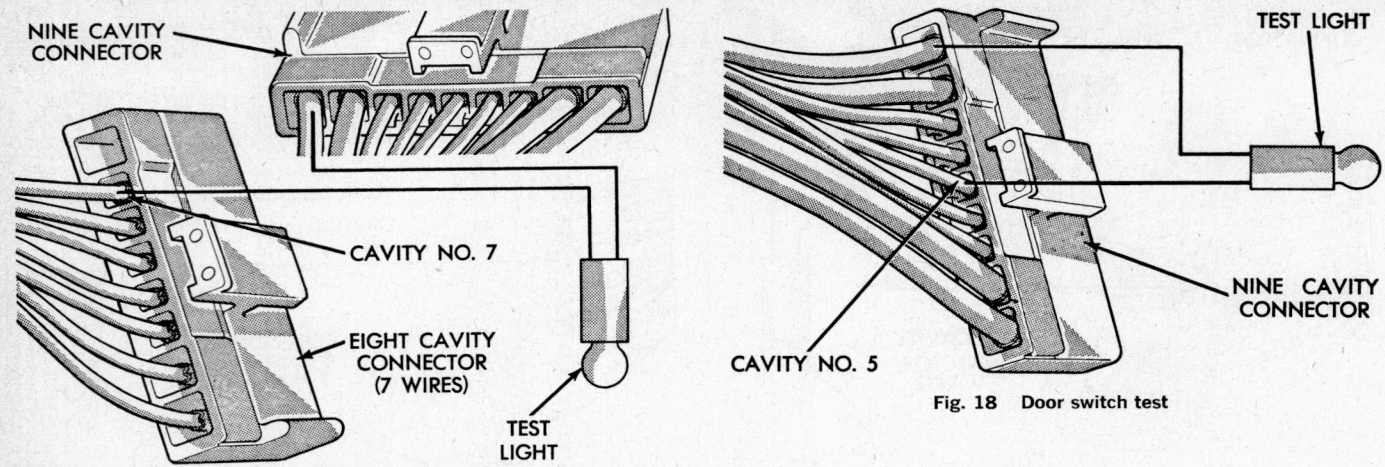

NINE CAVITY CONNECTOR

CAVITY NO. 7

EIGHT CAVITY CONNECTOR (7 WIRES)

TEST LIGHT

Fig. 17   Center passenger buckle switch test

TEST LIGHT

NINE CAVITY CONNECTOR

CAVITY NO. 5

Fig. 18   Door switch test

seat is empty test light should be Off and when seat is occupied test light should be On. If switch does not operate use a self powered test light to check switch operation at connector attached to switch and located under seat. If switch still does not operate properly, replace switch. If switch now checks OK, problem is in wiring.

Interlock Unit

1. If switch and wiring check OK, replace interlock unit.

Step 10—Center Seat Passenger Unbuckled with Ignition On and Car in Gear, Warning Not Activated

Interlock Unit

1. Replace interlock unit.

Step 11—Warning Does Not Stop After Center Passenger Properly Buckles

Center Seat Buckle Switch

1. Remove both connectors from interlock unit. Connect test light to red

wire in 9-way connector and orange wire in 8-way connector, Fig. 17.
2. Test light should be Off only when belt is unbuckled. If switch does not operate use a self powered test light to check operation of switch at connector attached to switch and located at rear of seat near belt anchor. If switch still does not operate properly, replace buckle, webbing and switch assembly. If switch does operate, problem is in wiring.

Driver's Seat Switch

See Step 1.

Right Passenger Seat Switch

See Step 6.

Interlock Unit

1. If switch and wiring check OK, replace interlock unit.

Step 12—Engine Cranks When it Should Not (Driver Prebuckled)

Door Switch

1. Remove both connectors from inter-

lock unit. Connect test light to red wire and the black wire with white tracer, both in the 9-way connector. Test light should be On when door is open and Off when door is closed, Fig. 18.

See Step 1

1. If wiring and door switch are OK, replace interlock unit.

Step 12A—Engine Does Not Crank When Driver Properly Buckled

See Step 1

See Step 5A.

Wiring

1. Remove both connectors from interlock unit. Using jumper wire, momentarily connect red wire to yellow wire with tracer, Fig. 19, and starter should engage.
2. Engine does not crank. Check for voltage with test light between red wire and ground. If no voltage present, check wiring for open circuit.

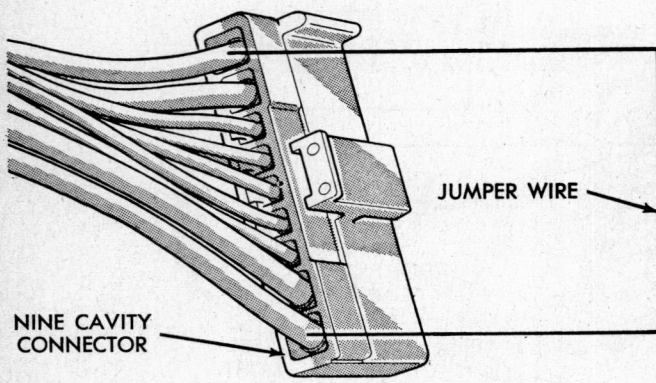

JUMPER WIRE

NINE CAVITY CONNECTOR

Fig. 19   Interlock starter test

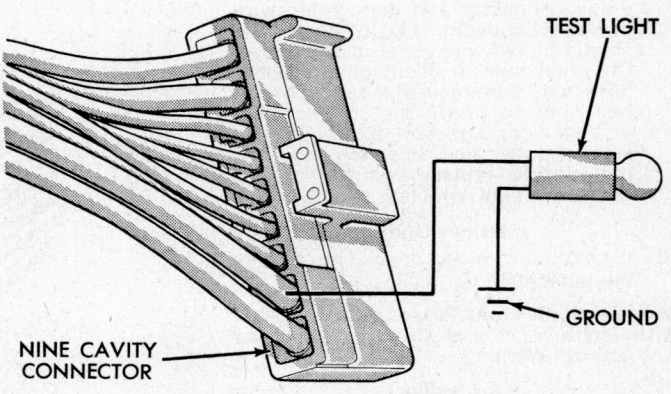

TEST LIGHT

NINE CAVITY CONNECTOR

GROUND

Fig. 20   Starter voltage test

(Red wire is spliced into Battery circuit). If voltage is present, check yellow wire with tracer for an open circuit (wire goes to starter relay). If wiring checks OK, trouble is in starter system.

3. Engine Cranks. Check for voltage with test light between yellow wire and ground, Fig. 20. Light should be On only when key is turned to Start. If not, check circuit to ignition switch. Check for voltage between brown wire and ground, Fig. 21. Light should be On when key is in Start or Run. If not, check circuit to ignition switch.

Step 12B—Warning Occurs When Driver Properly Buckled

Interlock Unit
1. Replace interlock unit.

Step 13—Car Does Not Restart When Driver Unbuckles But Does Not Leave Seat

Interlock Unit
1. Replace interlock unit.

Step 13A—Warning Does Not Occur When

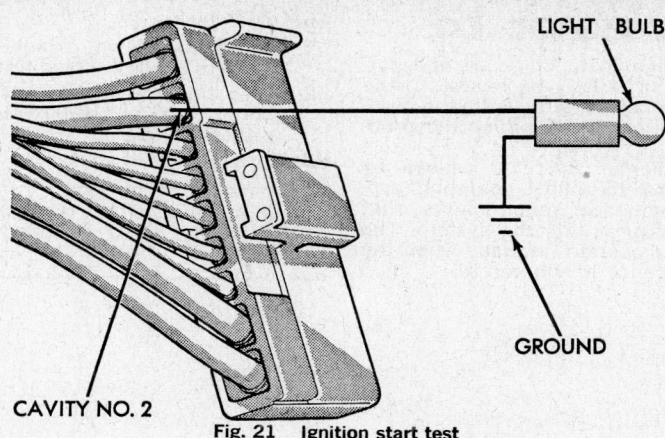

CAVITY NO. 2

Fig. 21   Ignition start test

Driver Unbuckles and Turns Key to Start

Interlock Unit
1. Replace interlock unit.

Step 14—Engine Cranks When it Should Not

Interlock Unit
1. Replace interlock unit.

Step 14A—Warning Does Not Occur

Interlock Unit
1. Replace interlock unit.

FORD MOTOR CO.

Before beginning to diagnose and correct problems that may be related to the Seat Belt Interlock System, verify the problem under the conditions which the problem occured.

Some problems could be caused by operator failing to follow operating procedure or sequence requirements that have been designed into the system. The system should operate normally when the following sequence is adhered to.

Starting Vehicle

1. After sitting down, extend and buckle lap belts at all occupied front seats.
2. Place transmission selector in PARK (automatic) or NEUTRAL (manual) while starting.
3. Turn ignition to start.

NOTE: A seat position is occupied whenever a weight of 47 pounds or more is placed on it.

When the vehicle has stalled after initial start and driver has remained in seat vehicle can be restarted.

After following the vehicle operating procedure if the system does not function properly, refer to the diagnosis guide further on in this chapter.

The seat sensor, connector locations, Fig. 22 and the wiring diagrams, Figs. 23 thru 28 will assist in tracing circuits and identifying accessable test points in order to diagnose symptoms of improper operation.

DIAGNOSTIC SEQUENCE CHARTS

A. Seat belt warning light and buzzer continue to operate when transmission gear selector is placed in PARK (NEUTRAL with manual transmission).

See Chart 1

B. Starter will not operate when lap belts have been extended and buckled in correct sequence.

See Chart 3

C. Starter will not operate after the interlock override switch (under hood) has been pressed.

See Chart 4

D. Warning Light and Buzzer turn on when the car is placed in gear after lap belts have been extended and buckled in the correct sequence and the starter has operated normally.

See Chart 1

E. Warning light and Buzzer do **not** turn on when car is placed in gear, ignition switch positioned at RUN and lap belts for an occupied seat are not extended or buckled.

See Chart 1

F. Starter operates when lap belts for an occupied seat are not extended or buckled or when seat is occupied **after** the belt has been extended or buckled.

See Chart 2

G. Lap belt will not lock.

See Chart 5

H. Lap belt will not extend to connecting position or will not fully retract.

See Chart 6

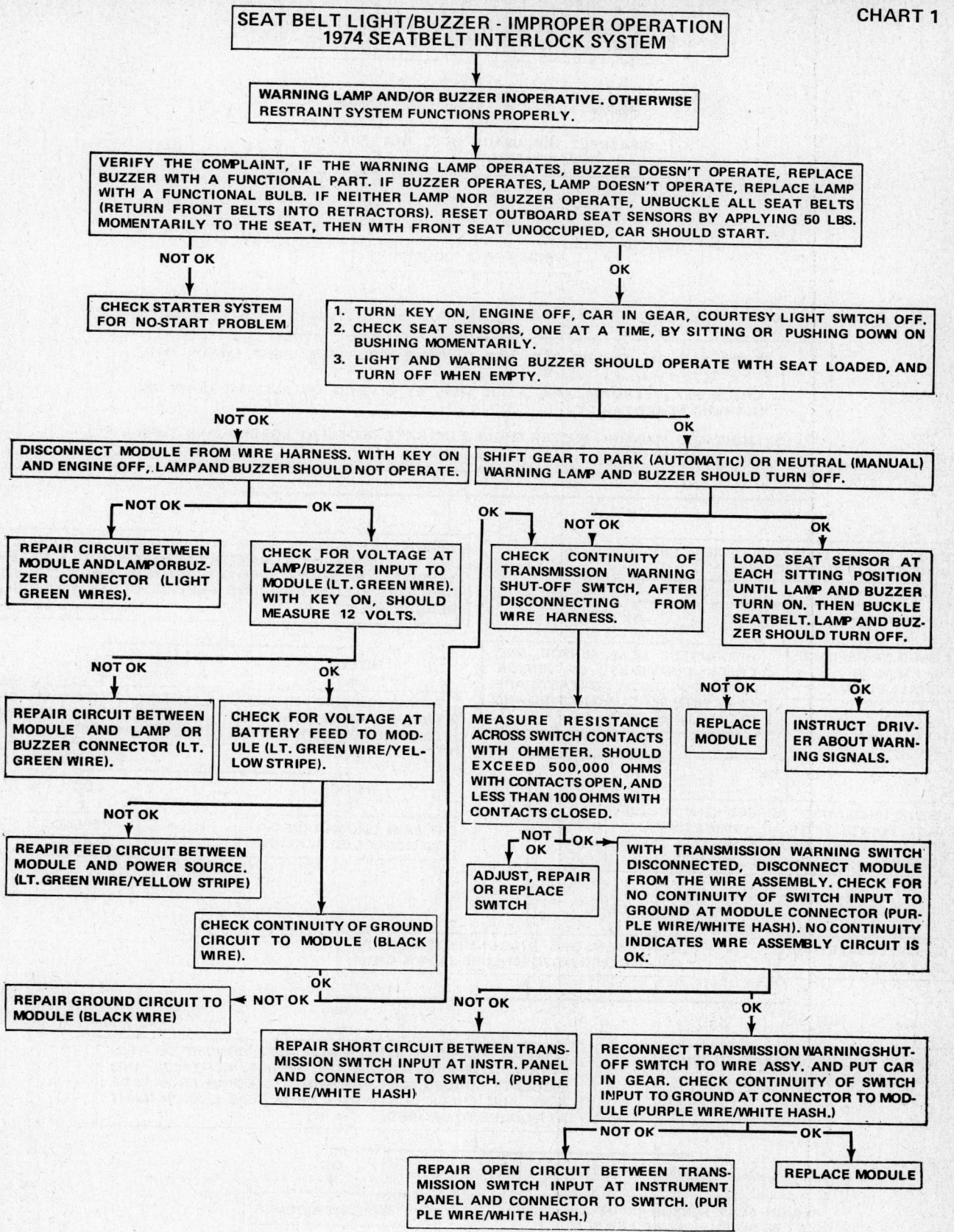

SEAT BELT LIGHT/BUZZER - IMPROPER OPERATION 1974 SEATBELT INTERLOCK SYSTEM

CHART 1

WARNING LAMP AND/OR BUZZER INOPERATIVE. OTHERWISE RESTRAINT SYSTEM FUNCTIONS PROPERLY.

VERIFY THE COMPLAINT, IF THE WARNING LAMP OPERATES, BUZZER DOESN'T OPERATE, REPLACE BUZZER WITH A FUNCTIONAL PART. IF BUZZER OPERATES, LAMP DOESN'T OPERATE, REPLACE LAMP WITH A FUNCTIONAL BULB. IF NEITHER LAMP NOR BUZZER OPERATE, UNBUCKLE ALL SEAT BELTS (RETURN FRONT BELTS INTO RETRACTORS). RESET OUTBOARD SEAT SENSORS BY APPLYING 50 LBS. MOMENTARILY TO THE SEAT, THEN WITH FRONT SEAT UNOCCUPIED, CAR SHOULD START.

NOT OK

CHECK STARTER SYSTEM FOR NO-START PROBLEM

OK

1. TURN KEY ON, ENGINE OFF, CAR IN GEAR, COURTESY LIGHT SWITCH OFF.
2. CHECK SEAT SENSORS, ONE AT A TIME, BY SITTING OR PUSHING DOWN ON BUSHING MOMENTARILY.
3. LIGHT AND WARNING BUZZER SHOULD OPERATE WITH SEAT LOADED, AND TURN OFF WHEN EMPTY.

NOT OK

DISCONNECT MODULE FROM WIRE HARNESS. WITH KEY ON AND ENGINE OFF, LAMP AND BUZZER SHOULD NOT OPERATE.

OK

SHIFT GEAR TO PARK (AUTOMATIC) OR NEUTRAL (MANUAL) WARNING LAMP AND BUZZER SHOULD TURN OFF.

NOT OK

REPAIR CIRCUIT BETWEEN MODULE AND LAMP OR BUZZER CONNECTOR (LIGHT GREEN WIRES).

OK

CHECK FOR VOLTAGE AT LAMP/BUZZER INPUT TO MODULE (LT. GREEN WIRE). WITH KEY ON, SHOULD MEASURE 12 VOLTS.

OK

CHECK CONTINUITY OF TRANSMISSION WARNING SHUT-OFF SWITCH, AFTER DISCONNECTING FROM WIRE HARNESS.

NOT OK

OK

LOAD SEAT SENSOR AT EACH SITTING POSITION UNTIL LAMP AND BUZZER TURN ON. THEN BUCKLE SEATBELT. LAMP AND BUZZER SHOULD TURN OFF.

NOT OK

REPAIR CIRCUIT BETWEEN MODULE AND LAMP OR BUZZER CONNECTOR (LT. GREEN WIRE).

OK

CHECK FOR VOLTAGE AT BATTERY FEED TO MODULE (LT. GREEN WIRE/YELLOW STRIPE).

MEASURE RESISTANCE ACROSS SWITCH CONTACTS WITH OHMETER. SHOULD EXCEED 500,000 OHMS WITH CONTACTS OPEN, AND LESS THAN 100 OHMS WITH CONTACTS CLOSED.

NOT OK

REPLACE MODULE

OK

INSTRUCT DRIVER ABOUT WARNING SIGNALS.

NOT OK

REAPIR FEED CIRCUIT BETWEEN MODULE AND POWER SOURCE. (LT. GREEN WIRE/YELLOW STRIPE)

NOT OK

OK

ADJUST, REPAIR OR REPLACE SWITCH

WITH TRANSMISSION WARNING SWITCH DISCONNECTED, DISCONNECT MODULE FROM THE WIRE ASSEMBLY. CHECK FOR NO CONTINUITY OF SWITCH INPUT TO GROUND AT MODULE CONNECTOR (PURPLE WIRE/WHITE HASH). NO CONTINUITY INDICATES WIRE ASSEMBLY CIRCUIT IS OK.

CHECK CONTINUITY OF GROUND CIRCUIT TO MODULE (BLACK WIRE).

OK **NOT OK**

REPAIR GROUND CIRCUIT TO MODULE (BLACK WIRE)

NOT OK

REPAIR SHORT CIRCUIT BETWEEN TRANSMISSION SWITCH INPUT AT INSTR. PANEL AND CONNECTOR TO SWITCH. (PURPLE WIRE/WHITE HASH)

OK

RECONNECT TRANSMISSION WARNING SHUT-OFF SWITCH TO WIRE ASSY. AND PUT CAR IN GEAR. CHECK CONTINUITY OF SWITCH INPUT TO GROUND AT CONNECTOR TO MODULE (PURPLE WIRE/WHITE HASH.)

NOT OK

REPAIR OPEN CIRCUIT BETWEEN TRANSMISSION SWITCH INPUT AT INSTRUMENT PANEL AND CONNECTOR TO SWITCH. (PURPLE WIRE/WHITE HASH.)

OK

REPLACE MODULE

SEAT BELT INTERLOCK SYSTEMS

CHART 2

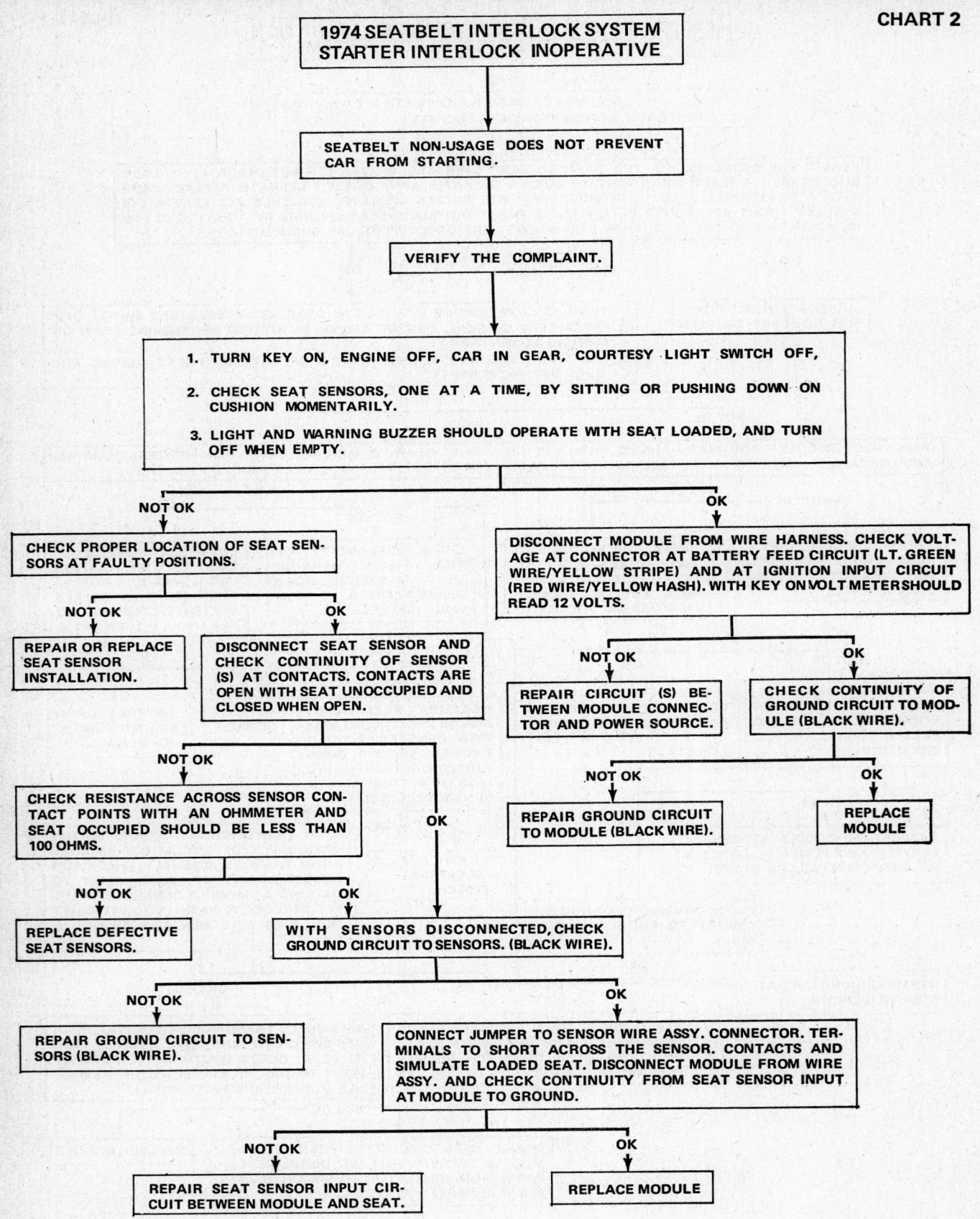

1974 SEATBELT INTERLOCK SYSTEM STARTER INTERLOCK INOPERATIVE

SEATBELT NON-USAGE DOES NOT PREVENT CAR FROM STARTING.

VERIFY THE COMPLAINT.

1. TURN KEY ON, ENGINE OFF, CAR IN GEAR, COURTESY LIGHT SWITCH OFF,

2. CHECK SEAT SENSORS, ONE AT A TIME, BY SITTING OR PUSHING DOWN ON CUSHION MOMENTARILY.

3. LIGHT AND WARNING BUZZER SHOULD OPERATE WITH SEAT LOADED, AND TURN OFF WHEN EMPTY.

NOT OK → CHECK PROPER LOCATION OF SEAT SENSORS AT FAULTY POSITIONS.

   NOT OK → REPAIR OR REPLACE SEAT SENSOR INSTALLATION.

   OK → DISCONNECT SEAT SENSOR AND CHECK CONTINUITY OF SENSOR (S) AT CONTACTS. CONTACTS ARE OPEN WITH SEAT UNOCCUPIED AND CLOSED WHEN OPEN.

      NOT OK → CHECK RESISTANCE ACROSS SENSOR CONTACT POINTS WITH AN OHMMETER AND SEAT OCCUPIED SHOULD BE LESS THAN 100 OHMS.

         NOT OK → REPLACE DEFECTIVE SEAT SENSORS.

         OK → WITH SENSORS DISCONNECTED, CHECK GROUND CIRCUIT TO SENSORS. (BLACK WIRE).

OK → DISCONNECT MODULE FROM WIRE HARNESS. CHECK VOLTAGE AT CONNECTOR AT BATTERY FEED CIRCUIT (LT. GREEN WIRE/YELLOW STRIPE) AND AT IGNITION INPUT CIRCUIT (RED WIRE/YELLOW HASH). WITH KEY ON VOLT METER SHOULD READ 12 VOLTS.

   NOT OK → REPAIR CIRCUIT (S) BETWEEN MODULE CONNECTOR AND POWER SOURCE.

   OK → CHECK CONTINUITY OF GROUND CIRCUIT TO MODULE (BLACK WIRE).

      NOT OK → REPAIR GROUND CIRCUIT TO MODULE (BLACK WIRE).

      OK → REPLACE MODULE

NOT OK → REPAIR GROUND CIRCUIT TO SENSORS (BLACK WIRE).

OK → CONNECT JUMPER TO SENSOR WIRE ASSY. CONNECTOR. TERMINALS TO SHORT ACROSS THE SENSOR. CONTACTS AND SIMULATE LOADED SEAT. DISCONNECT MODULE FROM WIRE ASSY. AND CHECK CONTINUITY FROM SEAT SENSOR INPUT AT MODULE TO GROUND.

   NOT OK → REPAIR SEAT SENSOR INPUT CIRCUIT BETWEEN MODULE AND SEAT.

   OK → REPLACE MODULE

1974
SEATBELT WARNING AND STARTER INTERLOCK SYSTEM
FAULT DIAGNOSIS

CHART 3

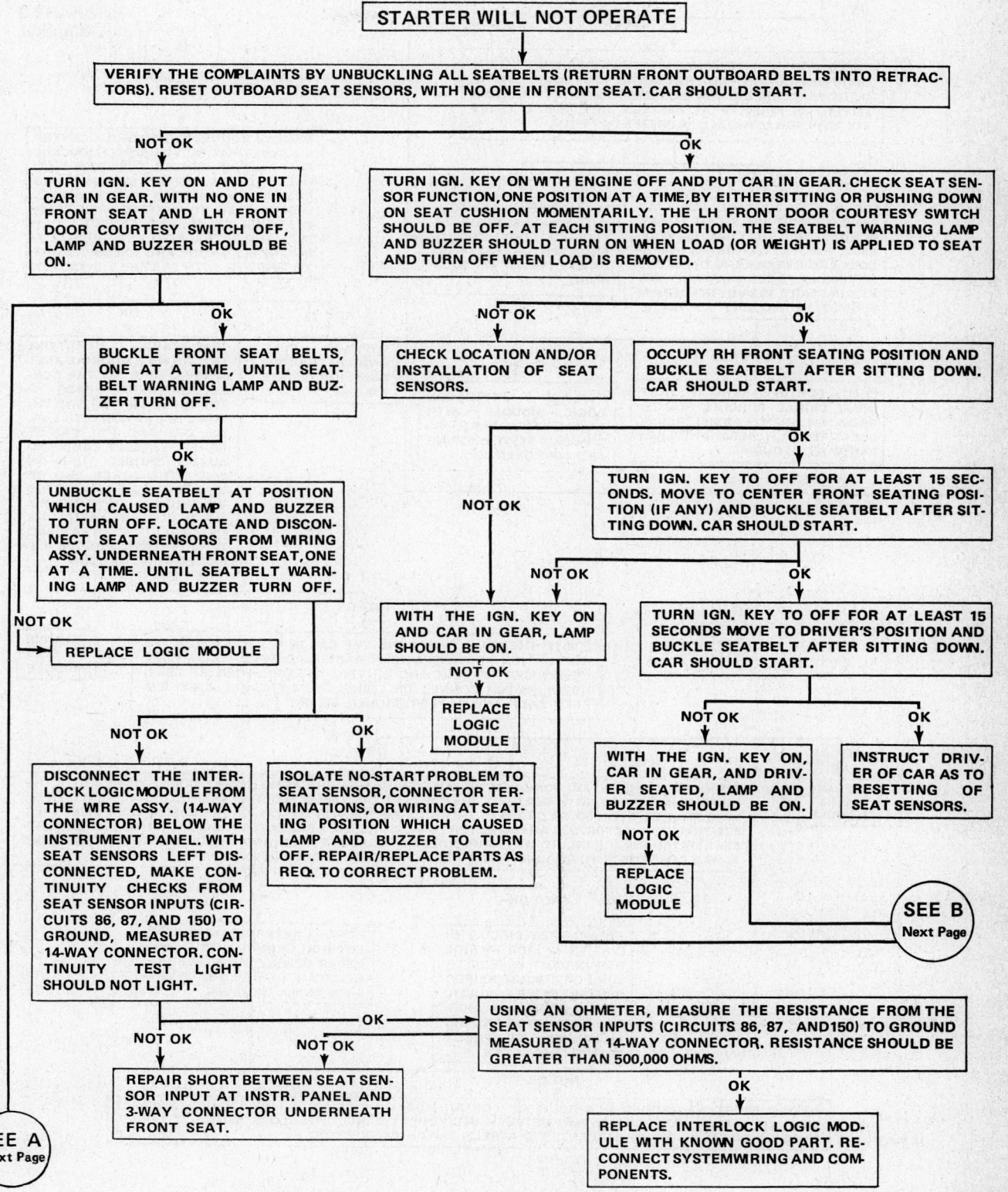

SEAT BELT INTERLOCK SYSTEMS

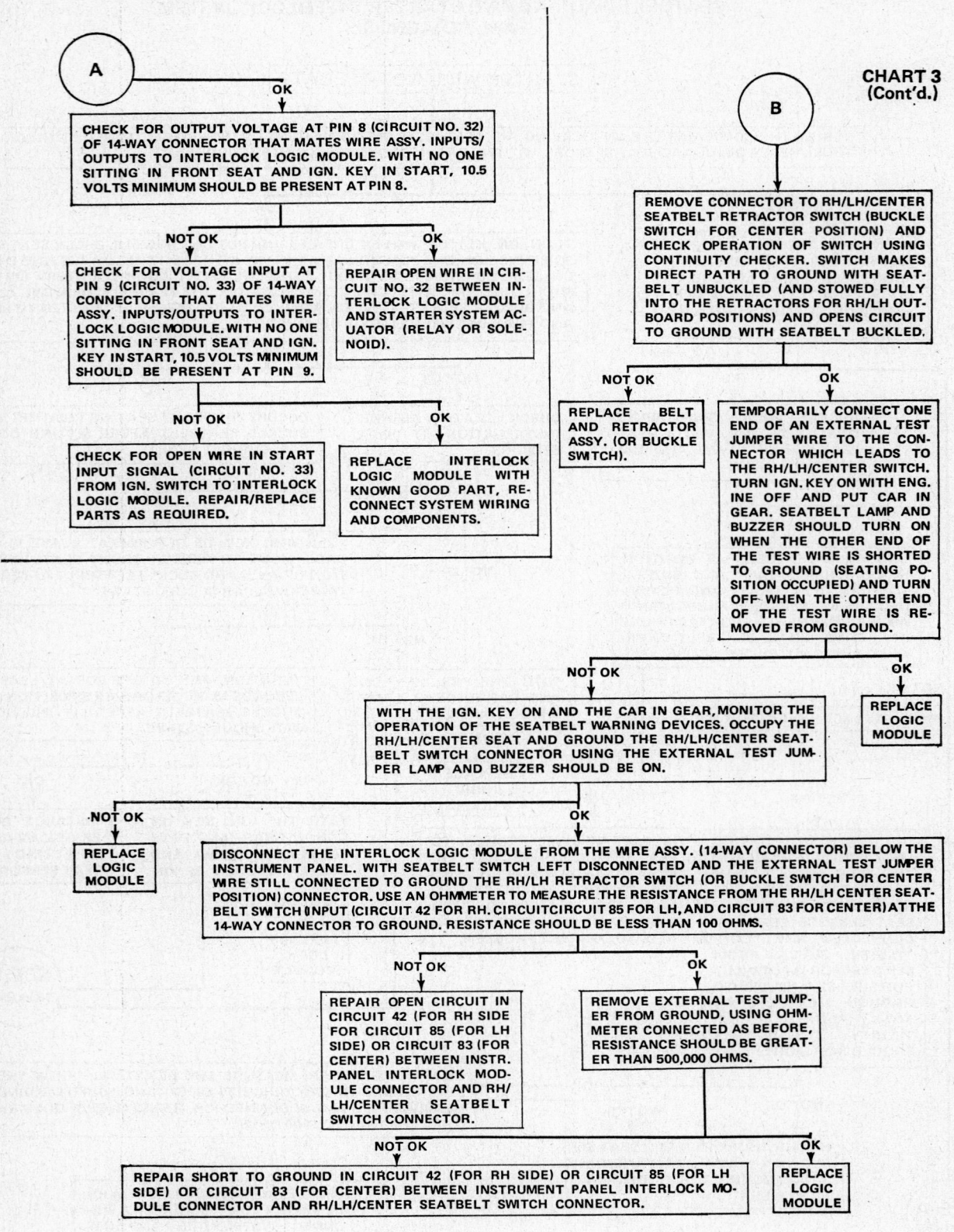

A — OK

CHECK FOR OUTPUT VOLTAGE AT PIN 8 (CIRCUIT NO. 32) OF 14-WAY CONNECTOR THAT MATES WIRE ASSY. INPUTS/OUTPUTS TO INTERLOCK LOGIC MODULE. WITH NO ONE SITTING IN FRONT SEAT AND IGN. KEY IN START, 10.5 VOLTS MINIMUM SHOULD BE PRESENT AT PIN 8.

CHART 3
(Cont'd.)

B

REMOVE CONNECTOR TO RH/LH/CENTER SEATBELT RETRACTOR SWITCH (BUCKLE SWITCH FOR CENTER POSITION) AND CHECK OPERATION OF SWITCH USING CONTINUITY CHECKER. SWITCH MAKES DIRECT PATH TO GROUND WITH SEATBELT UNBUCKLED (AND STOWED FULLY INTO THE RETRACTORS FOR RH/LH OUTBOARD POSITIONS) AND OPENS CIRCUIT TO GROUND WITH SEATBELT BUCKLED.

NOT OK / **OK**

CHECK FOR VOLTAGE INPUT AT PIN 9 (CIRCUIT NO. 33) OF 14-WAY CONNECTOR THAT MATES WIRE ASSY. INPUTS/OUTPUTS TO INTERLOCK LOGIC MODULE. WITH NO ONE SITTING IN FRONT SEAT AND IGN. KEY IN START, 10.5 VOLTS MINIMUM SHOULD BE PRESENT AT PIN 9.

REPAIR OPEN WIRE IN CIRCUIT NO. 32 BETWEEN INTERLOCK LOGIC MODULE AND STARTER SYSTEM ACUATOR (RELAY OR SOLENOID).

NOT OK / **OK**

CHECK FOR OPEN WIRE IN START INPUT SIGNAL (CIRCUIT NO. 33) FROM IGN. SWITCH TO INTERLOCK LOGIC MODULE. REPAIR/REPLACE PARTS AS REQUIRED.

REPLACE INTERLOCK LOGIC MODULE WITH KNOWN GOOD PART, RECONNECT SYSTEM WIRING AND COMPONENTS.

NOT OK / **OK**

REPLACE BELT AND RETRACTOR ASSY. (OR BUCKLE SWITCH).

TEMPORARILY CONNECT ONE END OF AN EXTERNAL TEST JUMPER WIRE TO THE CONNECTOR WHICH LEADS TO THE RH/LH/CENTER SWITCH. TURN IGN. KEY ON WITH ENGINE OFF AND PUT CAR IN GEAR. SEATBELT LAMP AND BUZZER SHOULD TURN ON WHEN THE OTHER END OF THE TEST WIRE IS SHORTED TO GROUND (SEATING POSITION OCCUPIED) AND TURN OFF WHEN THE OTHER END OF THE TEST WIRE IS REMOVED FROM GROUND.

NOT OK / **OK**

WITH THE IGN. KEY ON AND THE CAR IN GEAR, MONITOR THE OPERATION OF THE SEATBELT WARNING DEVICES. OCCUPY THE RH/LH/CENTER SEAT AND GROUND THE RH/LH/CENTER SEATBELT SWITCH CONNECTOR USING THE EXTERNAL TEST JUMPER LAMP AND BUZZER SHOULD BE ON.

REPLACE LOGIC MODULE

NOT OK / **OK**

REPLACE LOGIC MODULE

DISCONNECT THE INTERLOCK LOGIC MODULE FROM THE WIRE ASSY. (14-WAY CONNECTOR) BELOW THE INSTRUMENT PANEL. WITH SEATBELT SWITCH LEFT DISCONNECTED AND THE EXTERNAL TEST JUMPER WIRE STILL CONNECTED TO GROUND THE RH/LH RETRACTOR SWITCH (OR BUCKLE SWITCH FOR CENTER POSITION) CONNECTOR. USE AN OHMMETER TO MEASURE THE RESISTANCE FROM THE RH/LH CENTER SEATBELT SWITCH INPUT (CIRCUIT 42 FOR RH. CIRCUITCIRCUIT 85 FOR LH, AND CIRCUIT 83 FOR CENTER) AT THE 14-WAY CONNECTOR TO GROUND. RESISTANCE SHOULD BE LESS THAN 100 OHMS.

NOT OK / **OK**

REPAIR OPEN CIRCUIT IN CIRCUIT 42 (FOR RH SIDE FOR CIRCUIT 85 (FOR LH SIDE) OR CIRCUIT 83 (FOR CENTER) BETWEEN INSTR. PANEL INTERLOCK MODULE CONNECTOR AND RH/LH/CENTER SEATBELT SWITCH CONNECTOR.

REMOVE EXTERNAL TEST JUMPER FROM GROUND, USING OHMMETER CONNECTED AS BEFORE, RESISTANCE SHOULD BE GREATER THAN 500,000 OHMS.

NOT OK / **OK**

REPAIR SHORT TO GROUND IN CIRCUIT 42 (FOR RH SIDE) OR CIRCUIT 85 (FOR LH SIDE) OR CIRCUIT 83 (FOR CENTER) BETWEEN INSTRUMENT PANEL INTERLOCK MODULE CONNECTOR AND RH/LH/CENTER SEATBELT SWITCH CONNECTOR.

REPLACE LOGIC MODULE

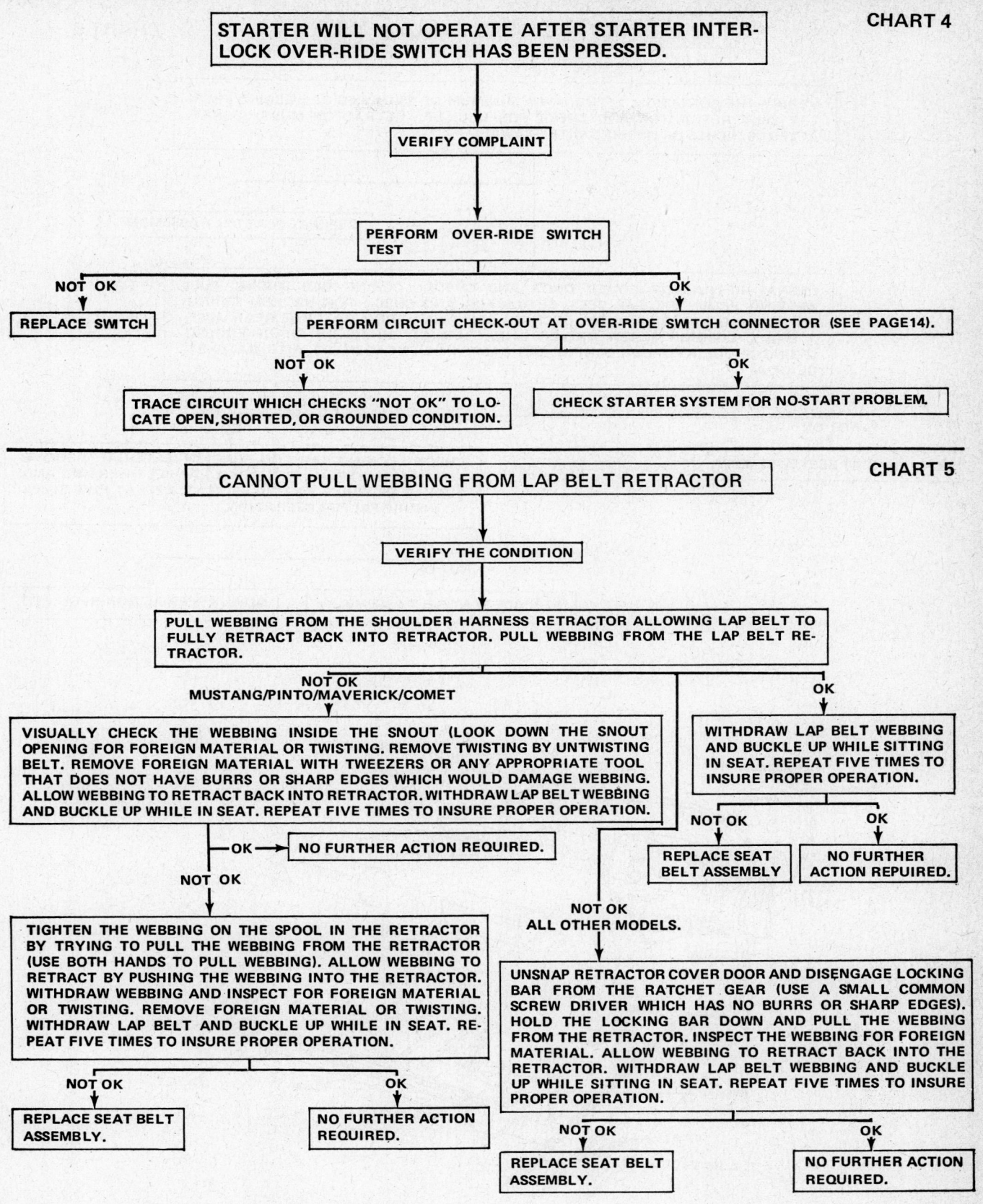

CHART 4

STARTER WILL NOT OPERATE AFTER STARTER INTER-LOCK OVER-RIDE SWITCH HAS BEEN PRESSED.

↓

VERIFY COMPLAINT

↓

PERFORM OVER-RIDE SWITCH TEST

NOT OK → REPLACE SWITCH

OK → PERFORM CIRCUIT CHECK-OUT AT OVER-RIDE SWITCH CONNECTOR (SEE PAGE14).

NOT OK → TRACE CIRCUIT WHICH CHECKS "NOT OK" TO LO-CATE OPEN, SHORTED, OR GROUNDED CONDITION.

OK → CHECK STARTER SYSTEM FOR NO-START PROBLEM.

CHART 5

CANNOT PULL WEBBING FROM LAP BELT RETRACTOR

↓

VERIFY THE CONDITION

↓

PULL WEBBING FROM THE SHOULDER HARNESS RETRACTOR ALLOWING LAP BELT TO FULLY RETRACT BACK INTO RETRACTOR. PULL WEBBING FROM THE LAP BELT RE-TRACTOR.

NOT OK MUSTANG/PINTO/MAVERICK/COMET

VISUALLY CHECK THE WEBBING INSIDE THE SNOUT (LOOK DOWN THE SNOUT OPENING FOR FOREIGN MATERIAL OR TWISTING. REMOVE TWISTING BY UNTWISTING BELT. REMOVE FOREIGN MATERIAL WITH TWEEZERS OR ANY APPROPRIATE TOOL THAT DOES NOT HAVE BURRS OR SHARP EDGES WHICH WOULD DAMAGE WEBBING. ALLOW WEBBING TO RETRACT BACK INTO RETRACTOR. WITHDRAW LAP BELT WEBBING AND BUCKLE UP WHILE IN SEAT. REPEAT FIVE TIMES TO INSURE PROPER OPERATION.

— OK → NO FURTHER ACTION REQUIRED.

NOT OK

TIGHTEN THE WEBBING ON THE SPOOL IN THE RETRACTOR BY TRYING TO PULL THE WEBBING FROM THE RETRACTOR (USE BOTH HANDS TO PULL WEBBING). ALLOW WEBBING TO RETRACT BY PUSHING THE WEBBING INTO THE RETRACTOR. WITHDRAW WEBBING AND INSPECT FOR FOREIGN MATERIAL OR TWISTING. REMOVE FOREIGN MATERIAL OR TWISTING. WITHDRAW LAP BELT AND BUCKLE UP WHILE IN SEAT. RE-PEAT FIVE TIMES TO INSURE PROPER OPERATION.

NOT OK → REPLACE SEAT BELT ASSEMBLY.

OK → NO FURTHER ACTION REQUIRED.

OK

WITHDRAW LAP BELT WEBBING AND BUCKLE UP WHILE SITTING IN SEAT. REPEAT FIVE TIMES TO INSURE PROPER OPERATION.

NOT OK → REPLACE SEAT BELT ASSEMBLY

OK → NO FURTHER ACTION REPUIRED.

NOT OK ALL OTHER MODELS.

UNSNAP RETRACTOR COVER DOOR AND DISENGAGE LOCKING BAR FROM THE RATCHET GEAR (USE A SMALL COMMON SCREW DRIVER WHICH HAS NO BURRS OR SHARP EDGES). HOLD THE LOCKING BAR DOWN AND PULL THE WEBBING FROM THE RETRACTOR. INSPECT THE WEBBING FOR FOREIGN MATERIAL. ALLOW WEBBING TO RETRACT BACK INTO THE RETRACTOR. WITHDRAW LAP BELT WEBBING AND BUCKLE UP WHILE SITTING IN SEAT. REPEAT FIVE TIMES TO INSURE PROPER OPERATION.

NOT OK → REPLACE SEAT BELT ASSEMBLY.

OK → NO FURTHER ACTION REQUIRED.

SEAT BELT INTERLOCK SYSTEMS

LAP BELT RETRACTOR DOES NOT LOCK

CHART 6

VERIFY THE CONDITION. WITHDRAW A MINIMUM OF 18 INCHES OF WEBBING FROM LAP BELT RETRACTOR AND CHECK FOR LOCK-UP. (RETRACTOR MUST LOCK-UP AFTER 18 INCHES OF WEBBING WITHDRAWAL).

REPLACE SEAT BELT ASSEMBLY.

UNSNAP RETRACTOR COVER DOOR AND CHECK LOCKING BAR SPRING. PULL WEBBING FROM THE LAP BELT RETRACTOR AND CHECK FOR BROKEN SPRING ON LOCKING BAR BY MOVING LOCKING BAR AWAY FROM RATCHET GEAR. (USE A SMALL COMMON SCREW DRIVER WHICH HAS NO BURRS OR SHARP EDGES). SPRING SHOULD FORCE LOCKING BAR BACK INTO ENGAGEMENT WITH RATCHET GEAR.

NOT OK

REPLACE SEAT BELT ASSEMBLY.

OK

CHECK LOCKING BAR FOR FOREIGN MATERIAL. REMOVE FOREIGN MATERIAL. WITHDRAW LAP BELT WEBBING AND BUCKLE UP WHILE SITTING IN SEAT. REPEAT FIVE TIMES TO INSURE PROPER OPERATION.

NOT OK

REPLACE SEAT BELT ASSEMBLY.

OK

NO FURTHER ACTION REQUIRED.

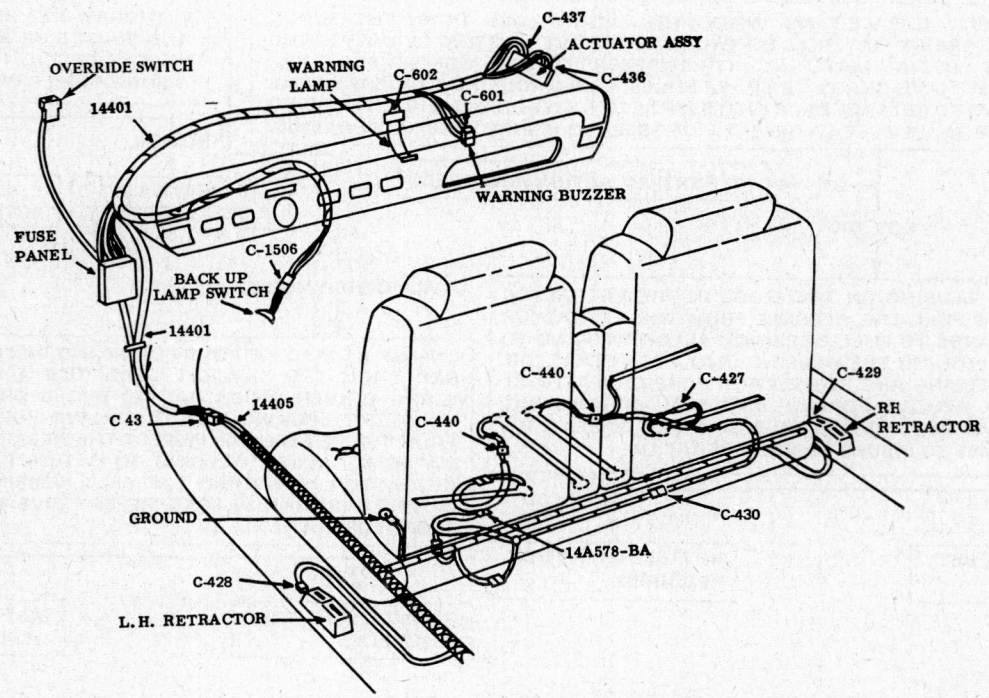

Fig. 22   1974 Ford sensor & connector locations typical

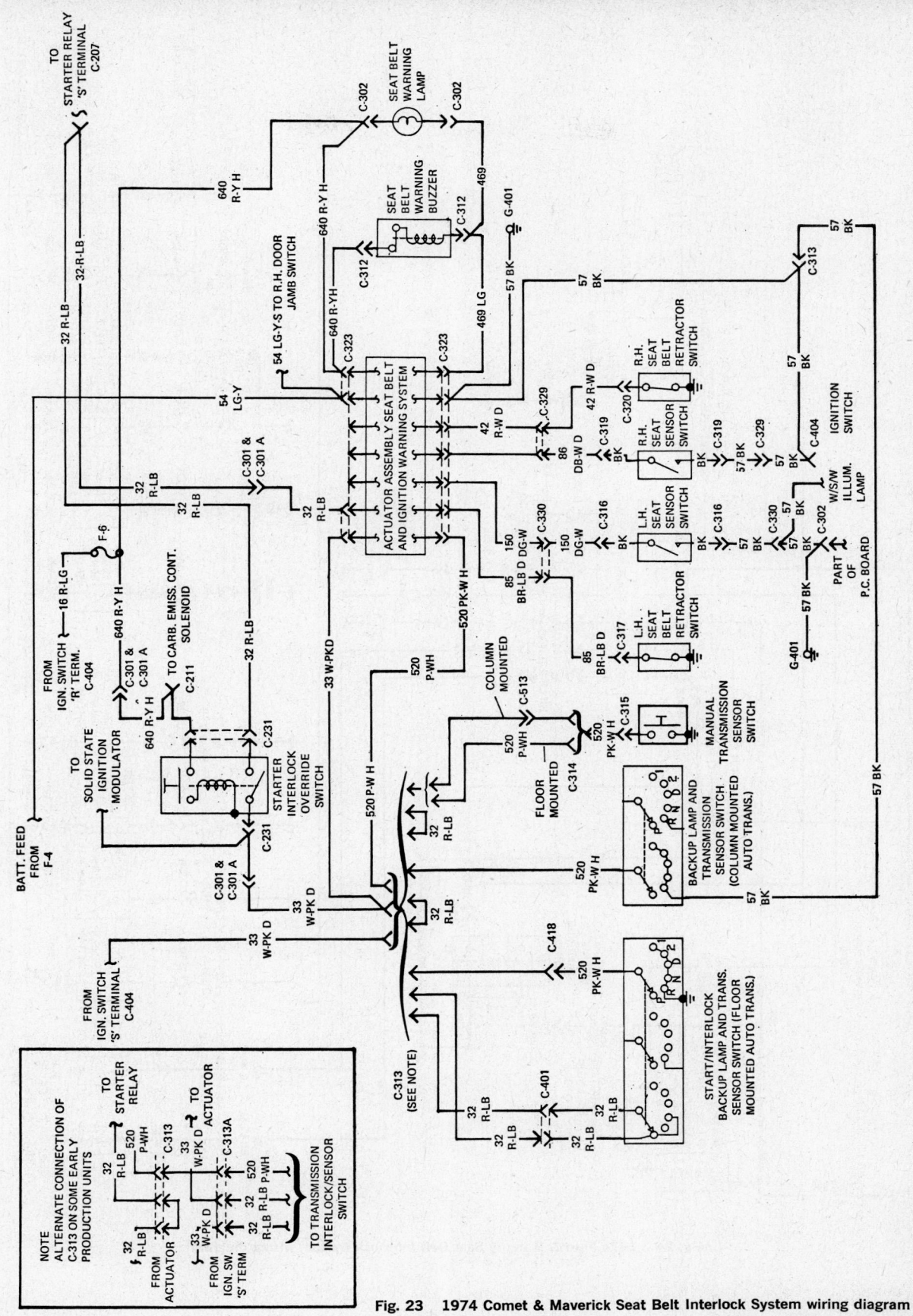

Fig. 23 1974 Comet & Maverick Seat Belt Interlock System wiring diagram

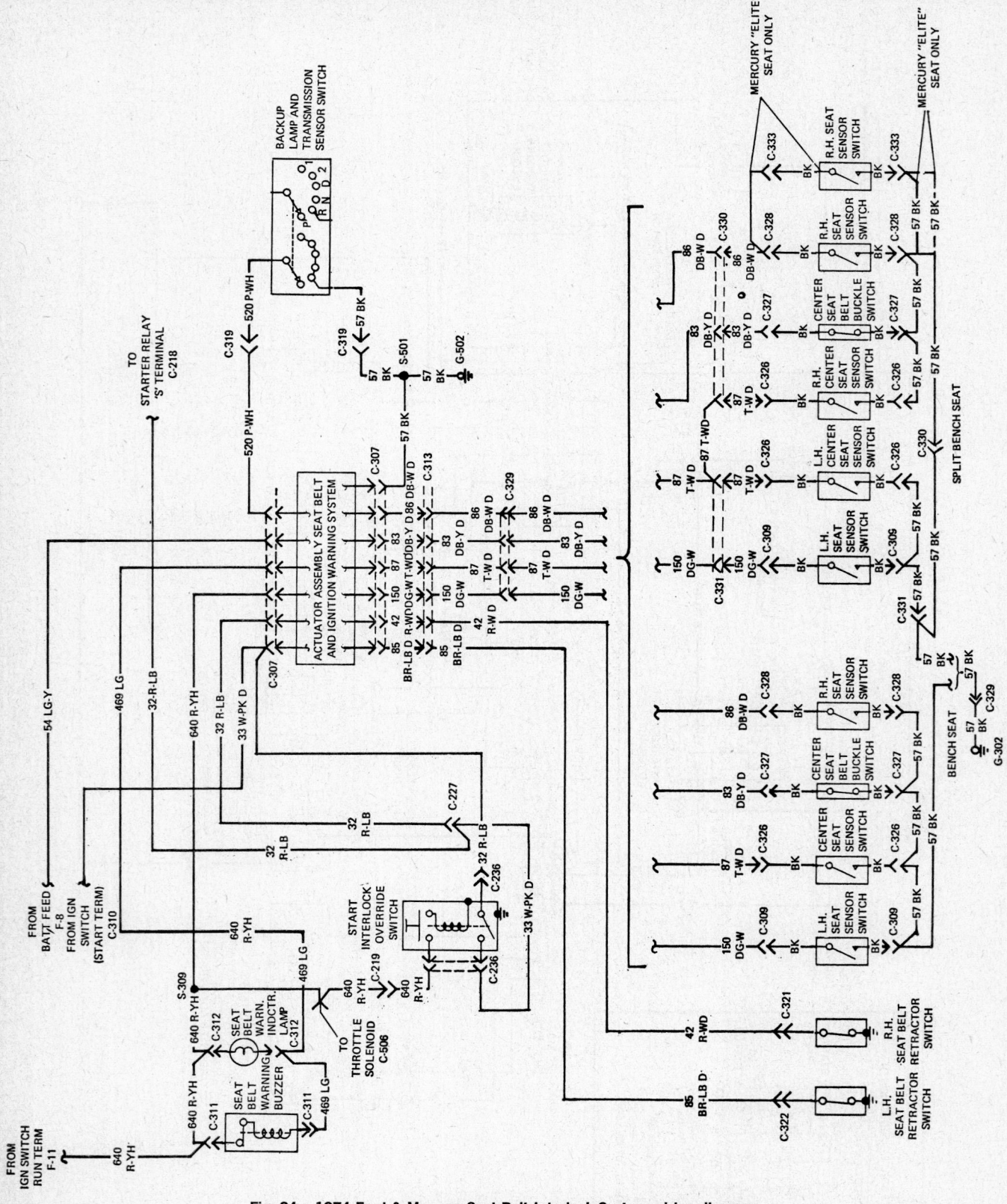

Fig. 24   1974 Ford & Mercury Seat Belt Interlock System wiring diagram

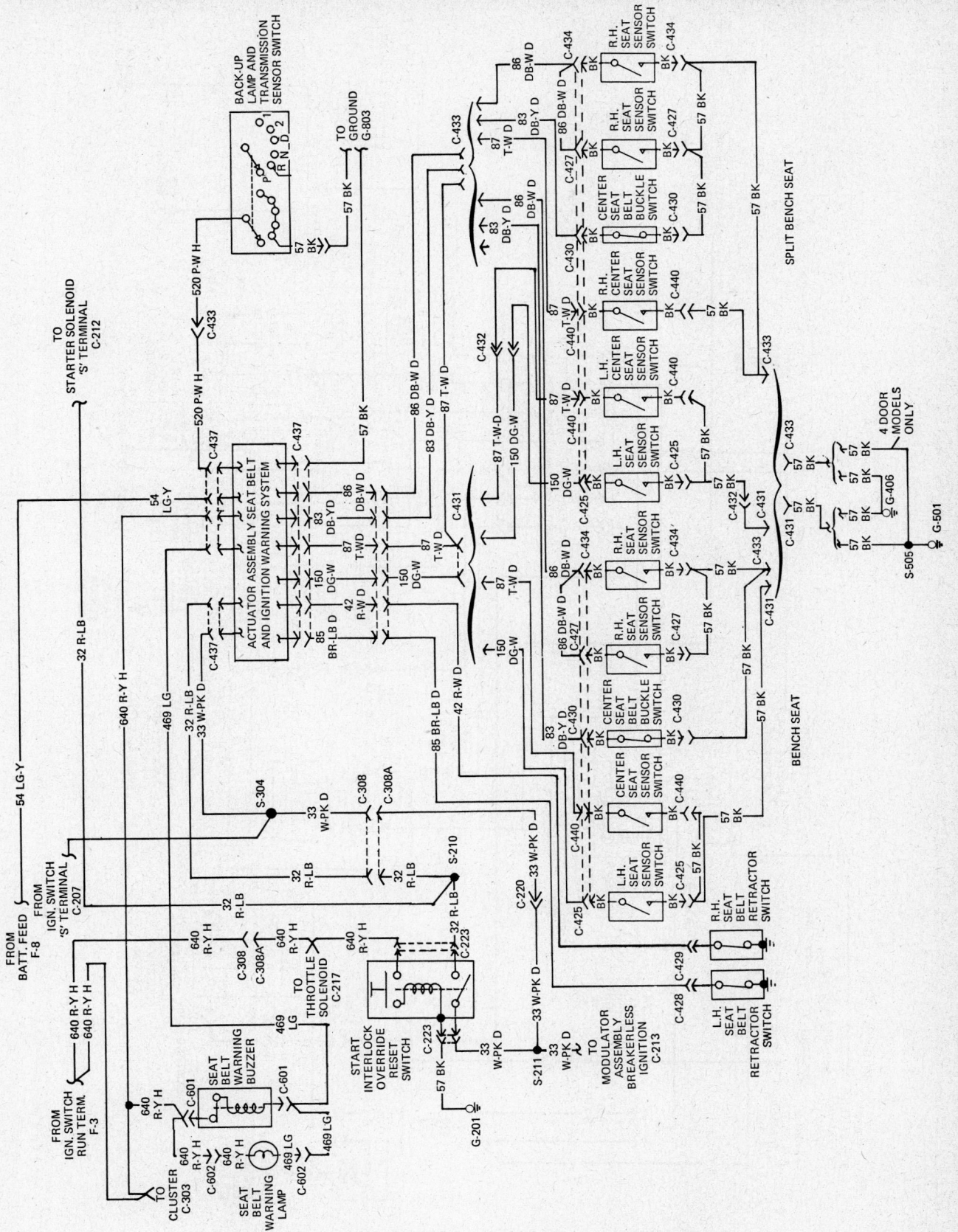

Fig. 25 1974 Lincoln Seat Belt Interlock System wiring diagram

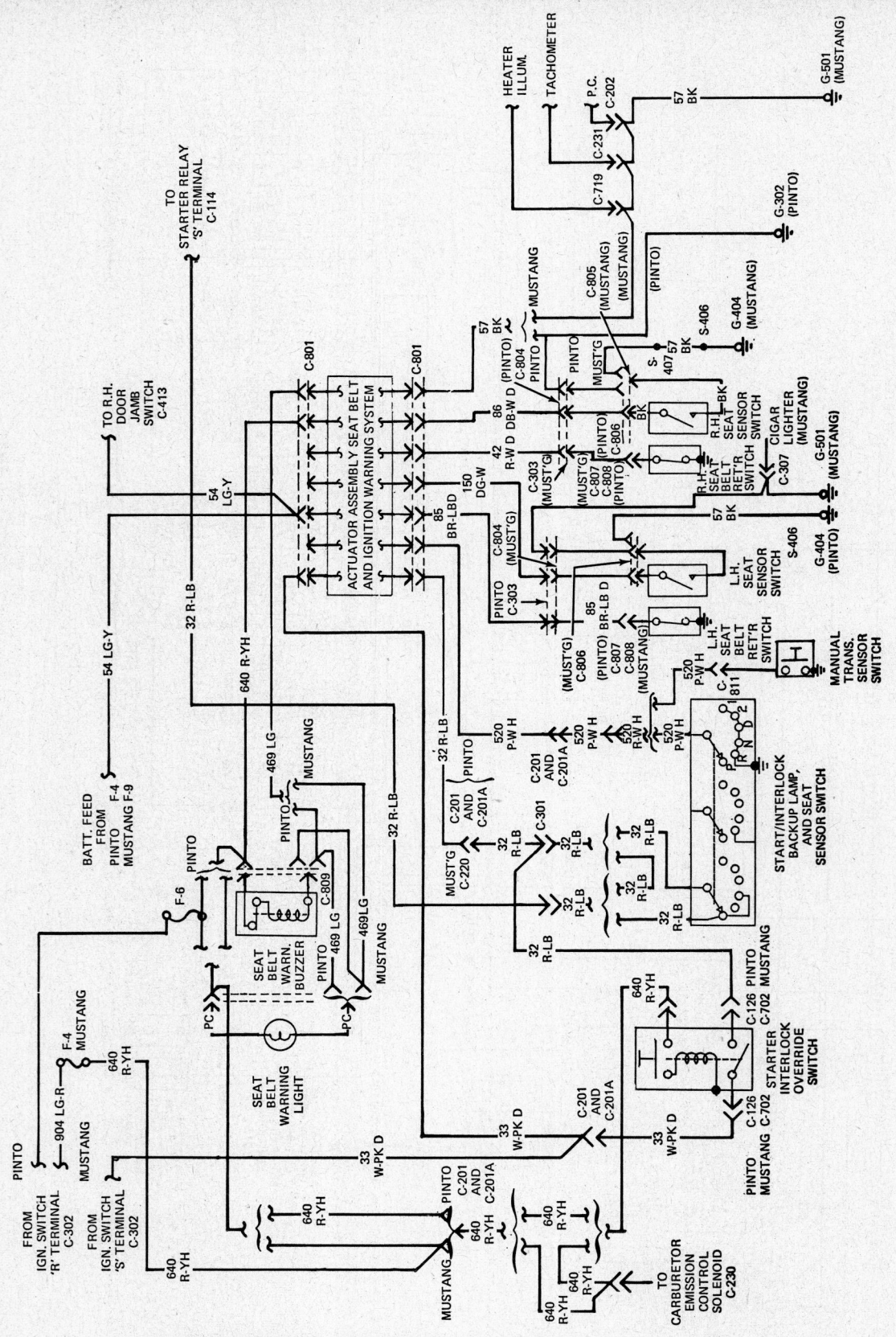

Fig. 26   1974 Mustang II & Pinto Seat Belt Interlock System wiring diagram

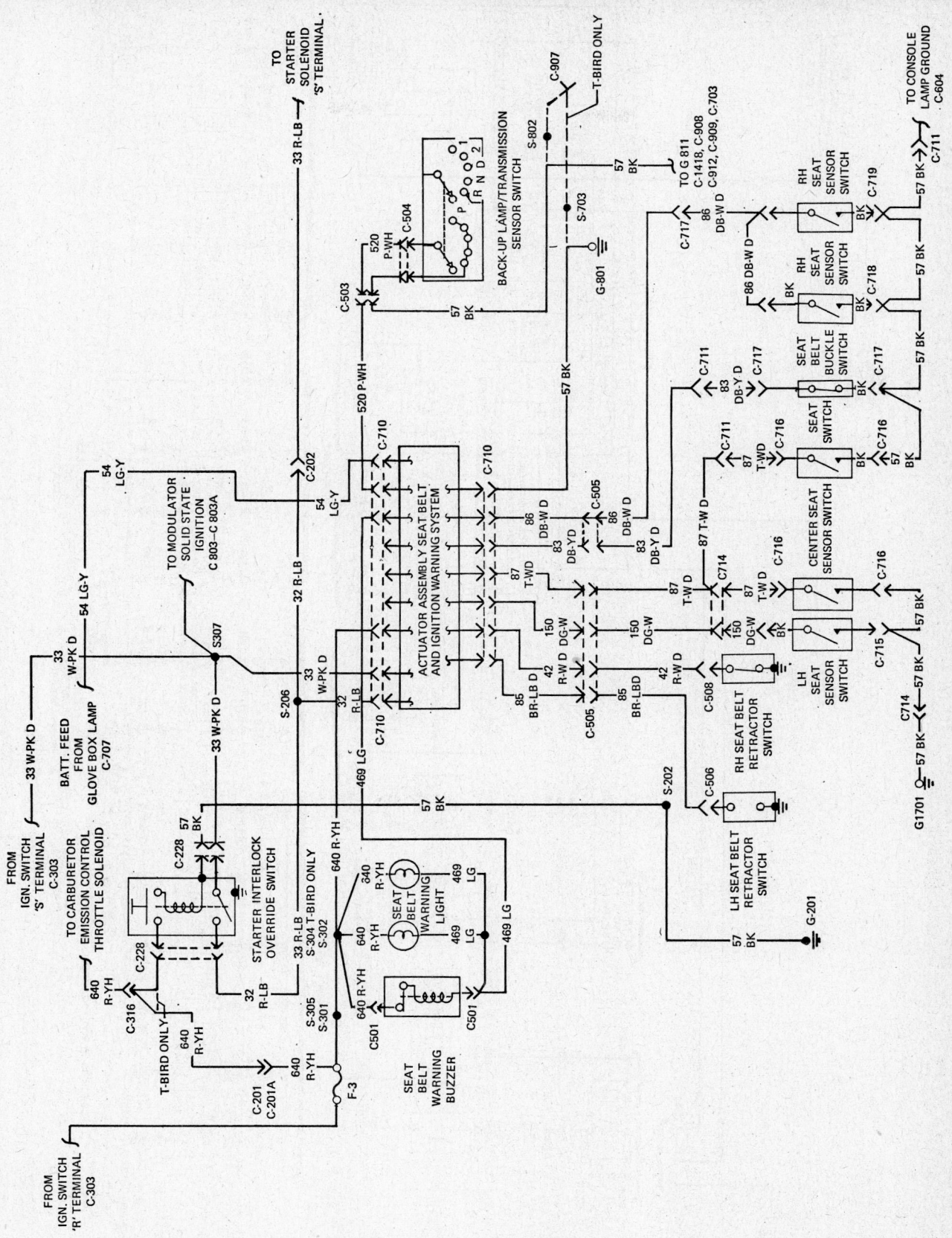

Fig. 27 1974 Mark IV & T-Bird Seat Belt Interlock System wiring diagram

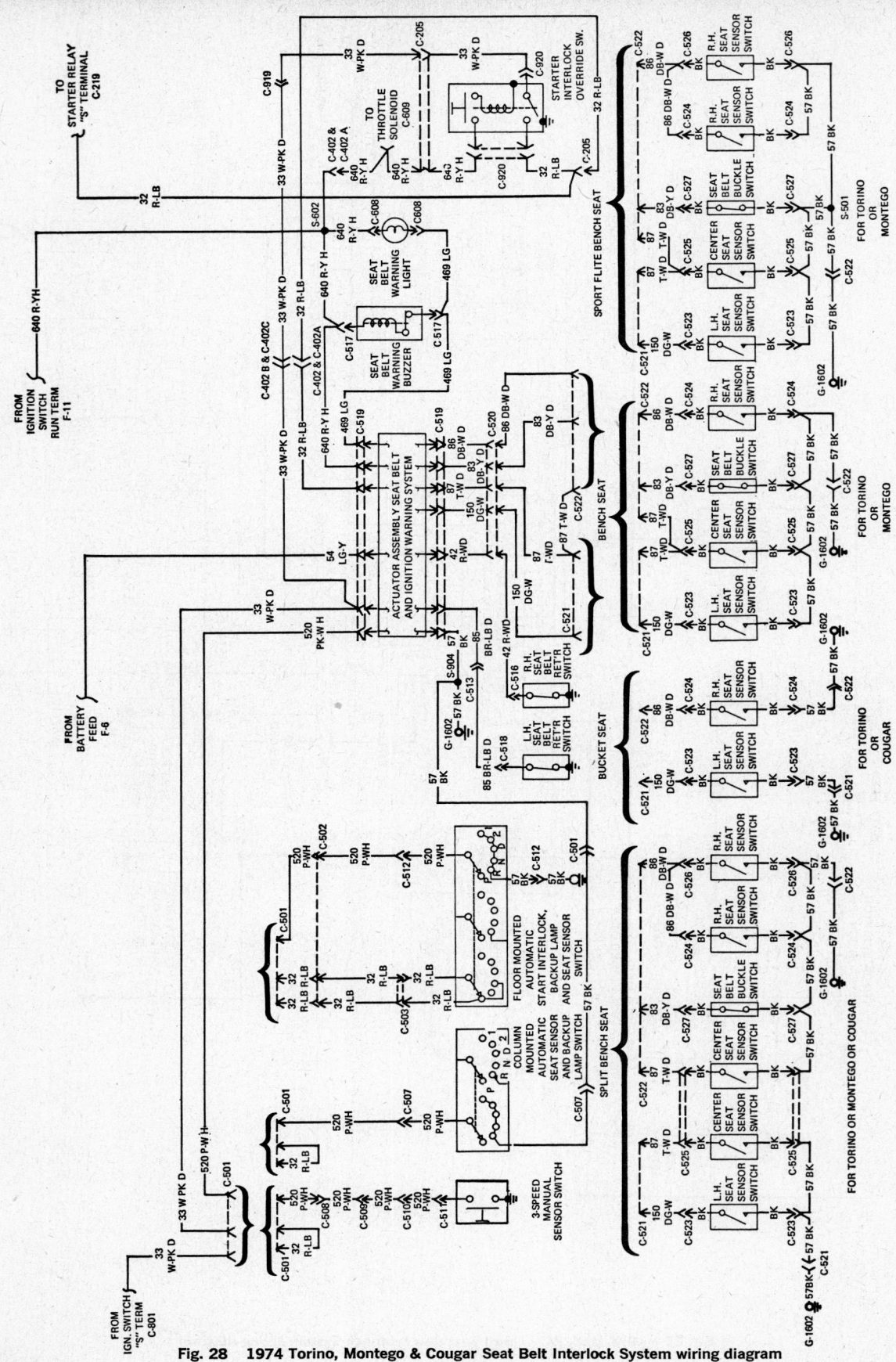

Fig. 28   1974 Torino, Montego & Cougar Seat Belt Interlock System wiring diagram

GENERAL MOTORS CORP.

If the seat belts are not buckled or are buckled before the passengers in the outboard seats are seated, the logic module will activate the interlock relay which will prevent the engine from starting and will activate the warning buzzer and light. The light and buzzer will not come on if the engine is running and a front seat belt is unbuckled if the transmission is in Park or Neutral but will come on if a front seat belt is unbuckled while the engine is running and the transmission in any forward gear.

The logic module incorporates a bounce feature which prevents the interlock system from preventing a start when a buckled in passenger lifts off the seat and deactivates the sensor switch.

If the passenger is off the seat for more than 5-10 seconds the seat belts must be unbuckled and rebuckled before the engine will start.

If the car has been started using the correct starting procedure, it can be restarted with the seat belts unbuckled at front seat occupied positions as long as the driver remains seated. If the driver leaves the car, the interlock relay will activate and the step buckling procedure must be used to start the car.

Mechanic's Start

The vehicle can be started with seat belts in any position if the front seats are unoccupied. To start the engine, reach inside the car and turn the ignition key to "START" without sitting on the seat. The light and buzzer will come on when the front seat is now occupied and the transmission shifted to DRIVE, but will turn off as soon as the seat belts at occupied positions are buckled.

Bypass Relay

A bypass relay on the firewall permits starting the car by bypassing the interlock relay in the event of system failure. To activate the relay, turn the ignition key to "ON." Then, open the hood and press and release the bypass relay button.

NOTE: The override mechanism will be damaged if the button is held in the depressed position.

The engine may then be started by turning the ignition key to "START." The relay will remain engaged until the ignition key is turned to OFF or LOCK.

Electronic Module

Two types of wiring harnesses and electronic modules are used with the seat belt-starter interlock system in 1974. Both wiring harnesses are designed to by-pass the center seat sensor and allow the vehicle to start with an occupant in the center seat position without buckling the seat belt.

The first wiring harness by-passes the center seat sensor through a jumper wire while the other harness by-passes the center seat sensor through the electronic module.

The electronic module with the built-in center seat sensor by-pass can be used with either wiring harness. The module without the built in by-pass can only be used on the wiring harness that incorporates a jumper wire. To determine which wiring harness is being serviced refer to Figs. 29 and 30.

NOTE: All replacement electronic modules will be of the center seat sensor by-pass type.

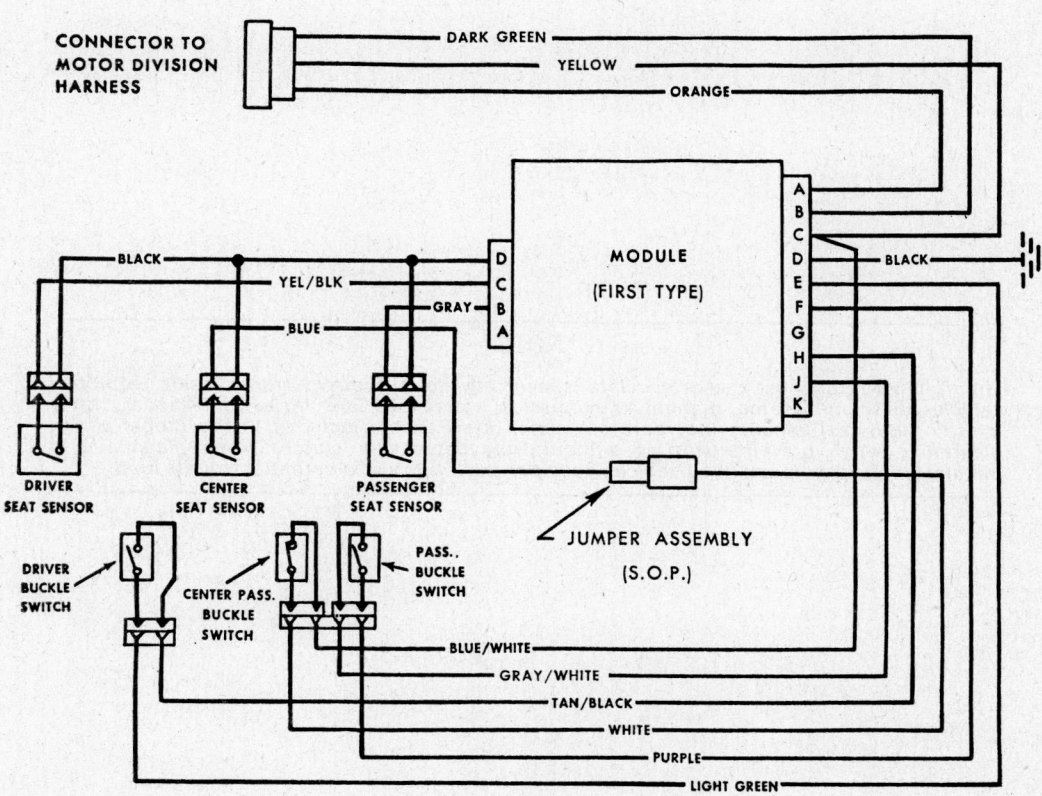

Fig. 29   Electronic module with jumper wire by-pass

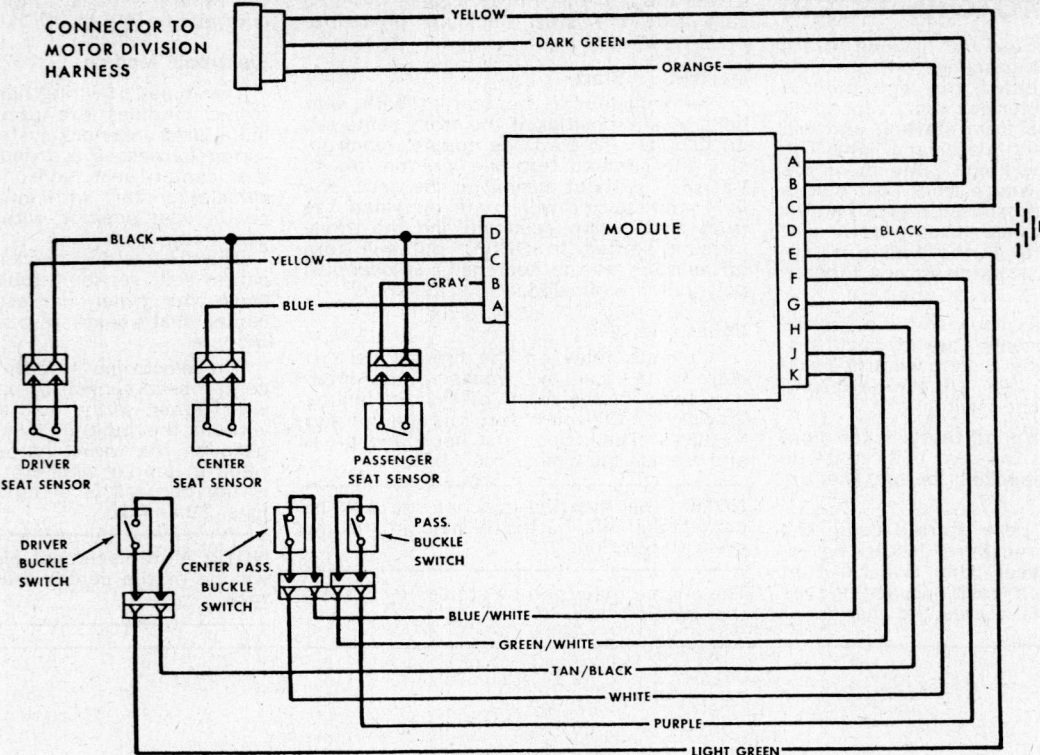

Fig. 30 Electronic module with built in by-pass

NOTE:

The following diagnostic charts relate specifically to automatic transmission equipped vehicles, although some manual transmission references are included. Manual transmission equipped vehicles incorporate a clutch start switch included in the proper wiring diagrams, which prevents starting without fully depressing clutch. When diagnosing a manual transmission equipped vehicle, consider this switch as a potential trouble item.

DIAGNOSIS CHARTS
SEAT BELT / STARTER INTERLOCK SYSTEM

Introduction

This section presents a systematic method of diagnosing and troubleshooting the seat belt/starter interlock system. The charts you will be using are different from the ones you have used before.

They aren't "go — no go" decision trees 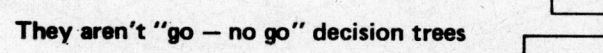 or tables.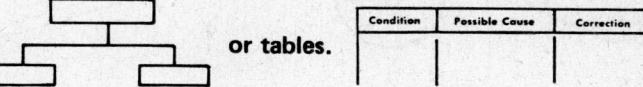

Instead the new diagnosis and troubleshooting charts use pictures plus a few words to help you solve a problem,

and symbols have replaced words.

Using the Charts

The charts are divided into three sections: step, sequence, and result.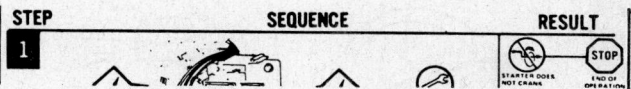

Always start at the first step and go through the complete sequence from left to right.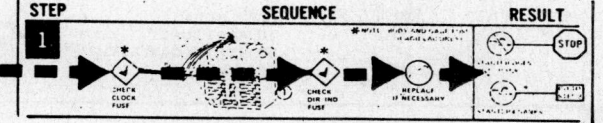

A sequence could be checking the fuses and replacing if necessary. Each sequence ends with a result and tells you the next step to go to.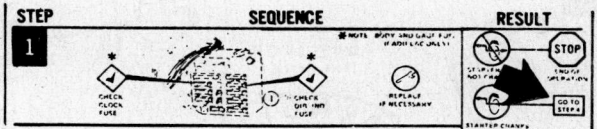

Work through each step of the diagnosis and troubleshooting charts till the system is repaired.

To find where parts are located in the system just look at the parts locator at the top of each chart.

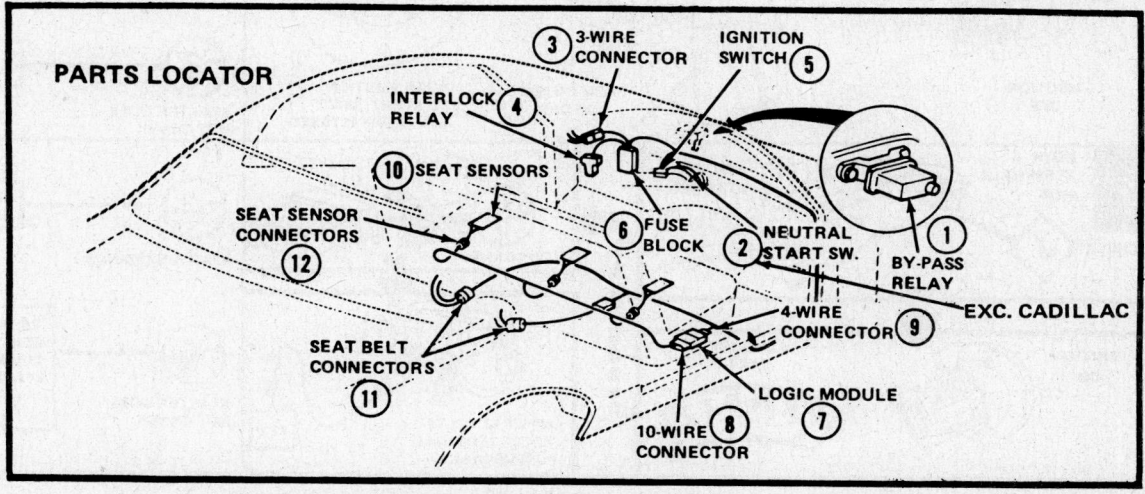

Seat Belt Interlock System. General Motors except Oldsmobile

SEAT BELT INTERLOCK SYSTEMS

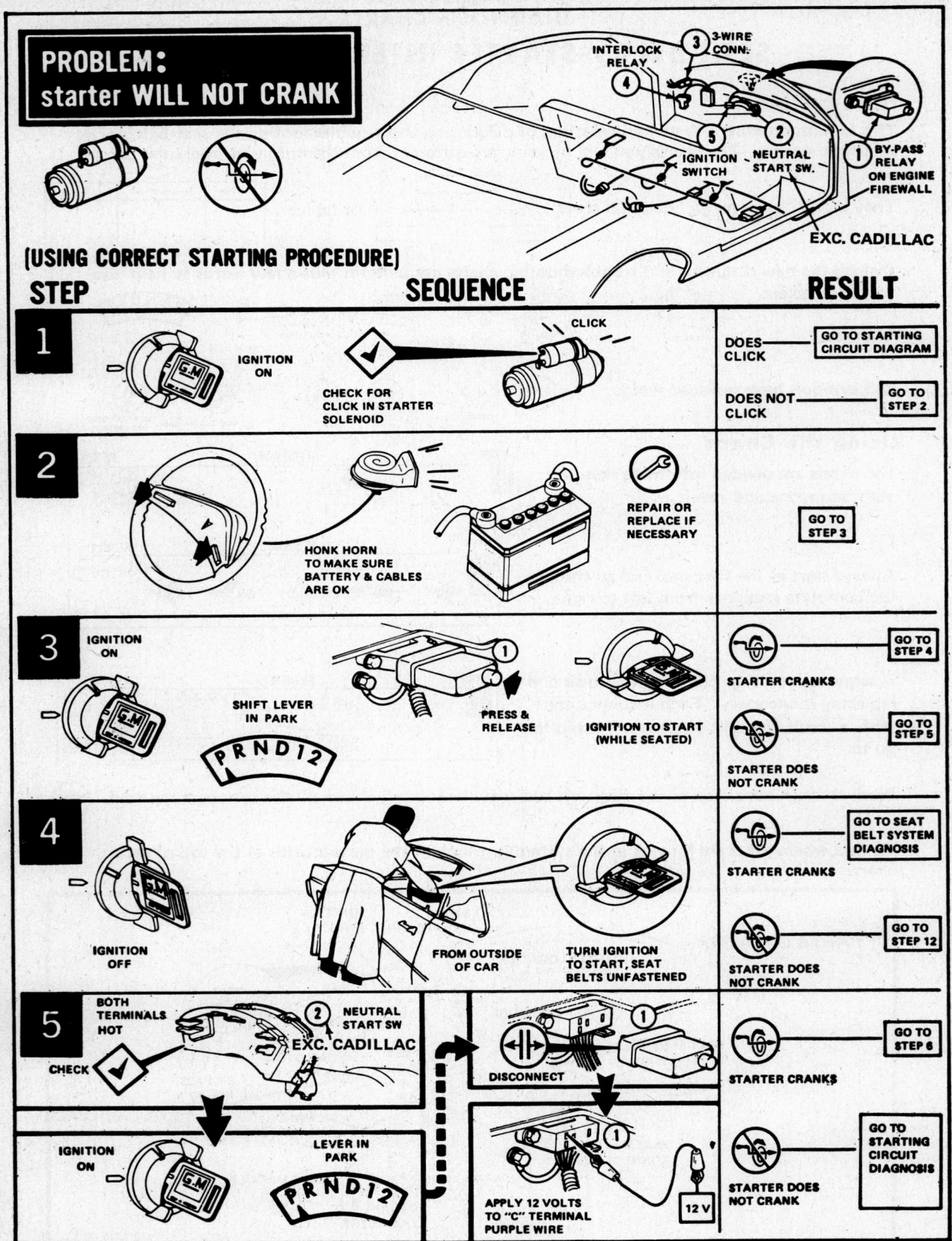

PROBLEM:
starter WILL NOT CRANK

INTERLOCK RELAY

3-WIRE CONN.

4

5 IGNITION SWITCH

2 NEUTRAL START SW.

1 BY-PASS RELAY ON ENGINE FIREWALL

EXC. CADILLAC

(USING CORRECT STARTING PROCEDURE)

STEP	SEQUENCE	RESULT
1	IGNITION ON — CHECK FOR CLICK IN STARTER SOLENOID — CLICK	DOES CLICK → GO TO STARTING CIRCUIT DIAGRAM DOES NOT CLICK → GO TO STEP 2
2	HONK HORN TO MAKE SURE BATTERY & CABLES ARE OK — REPAIR OR REPLACE IF NECESSARY	GO TO STEP 3
3	IGNITION ON — SHIFT LEVER IN PARK — PRND12 — 1 PRESS & RELEASE — IGNITION TO START (WHILE SEATED)	STARTER CRANKS → GO TO STEP 4 STARTER DOES NOT CRANK → GO TO STEP 5
4	IGNITION OFF — FROM OUTSIDE OF CAR — TURN IGNITION TO START, SEAT BELTS UNFASTENED	STARTER CRANKS → GO TO SEAT BELT SYSTEM DIAGNOSIS STARTER DOES NOT CRANK → GO TO STEP 12
5	CHECK — BOTH TERMINALS HOT — 2 NEUTRAL START SW EXC. CADILLAC — IGNITION ON — LEVER IN PARK — PRND12 — 1 DISCONNECT — APPLY 12 VOLTS TO "C" TERMINAL PURPLE WIRE — 12 V	STARTER CRANKS → GO TO STEP 6 STARTER DOES NOT CRANK → GO TO STARTING CIRCUIT DIAGNOSIS

Seat Belt Interlock System. General Motors except Oldsmobile

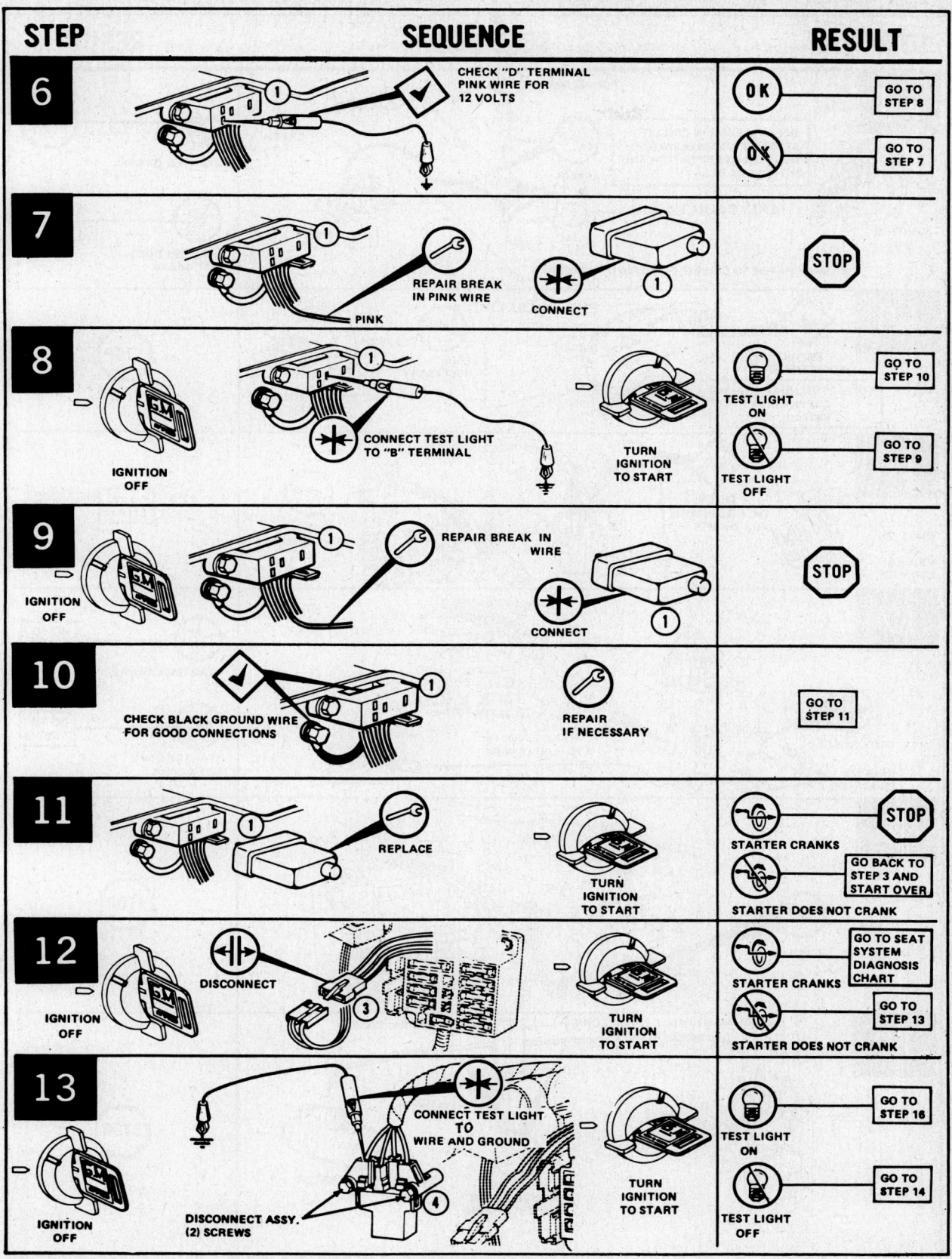

Seat Belt Interlock System. General Motors except Oldsmobile

SEAT BELT INTERLOCK SYSTEMS

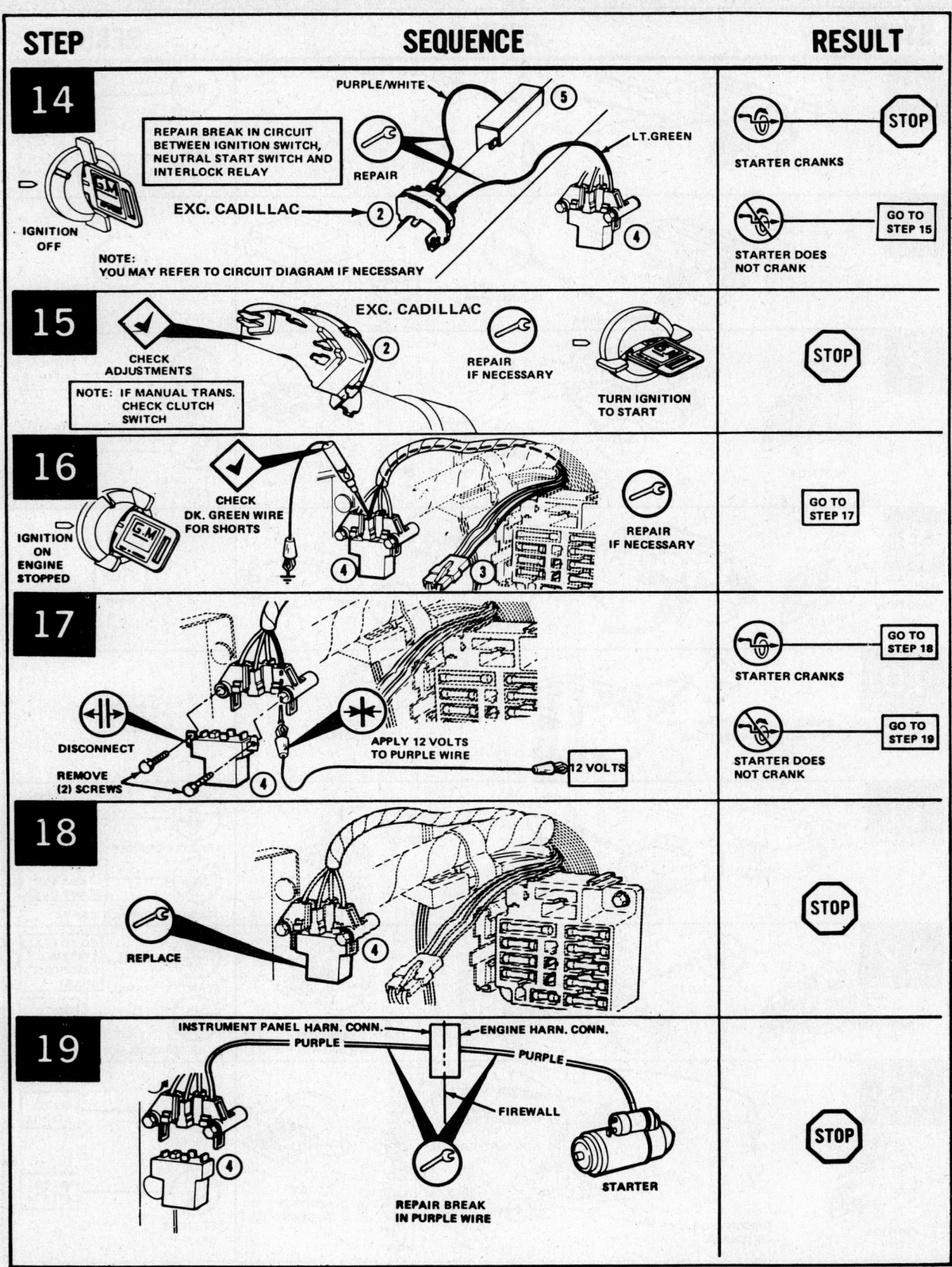

Seat Belt Interlock System. General Motors except Oldsmobile

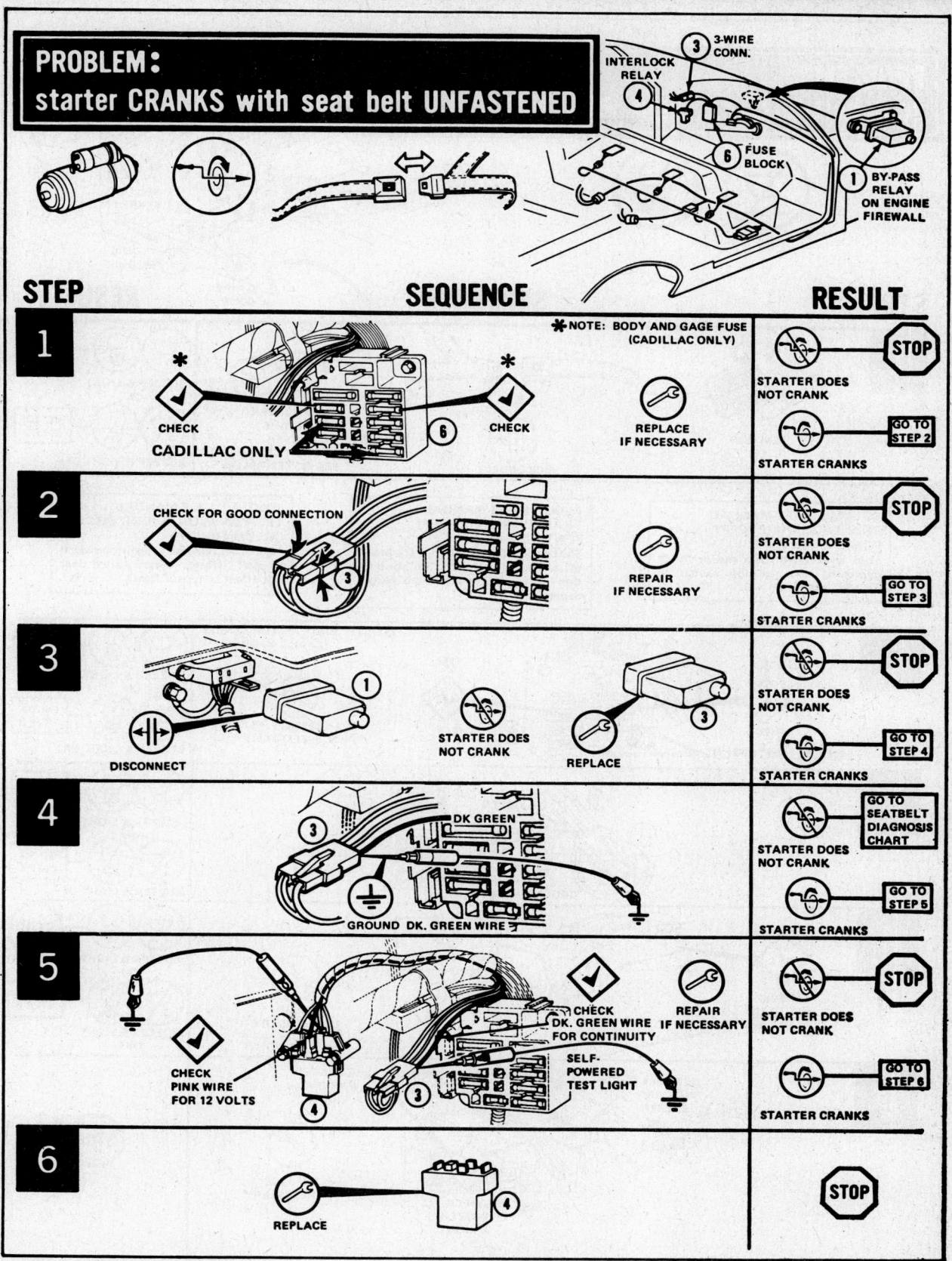

Seat Belt Interlock System. General Motors except Oldsmobile

SEAT BELT INTERLOCK SYSTEMS

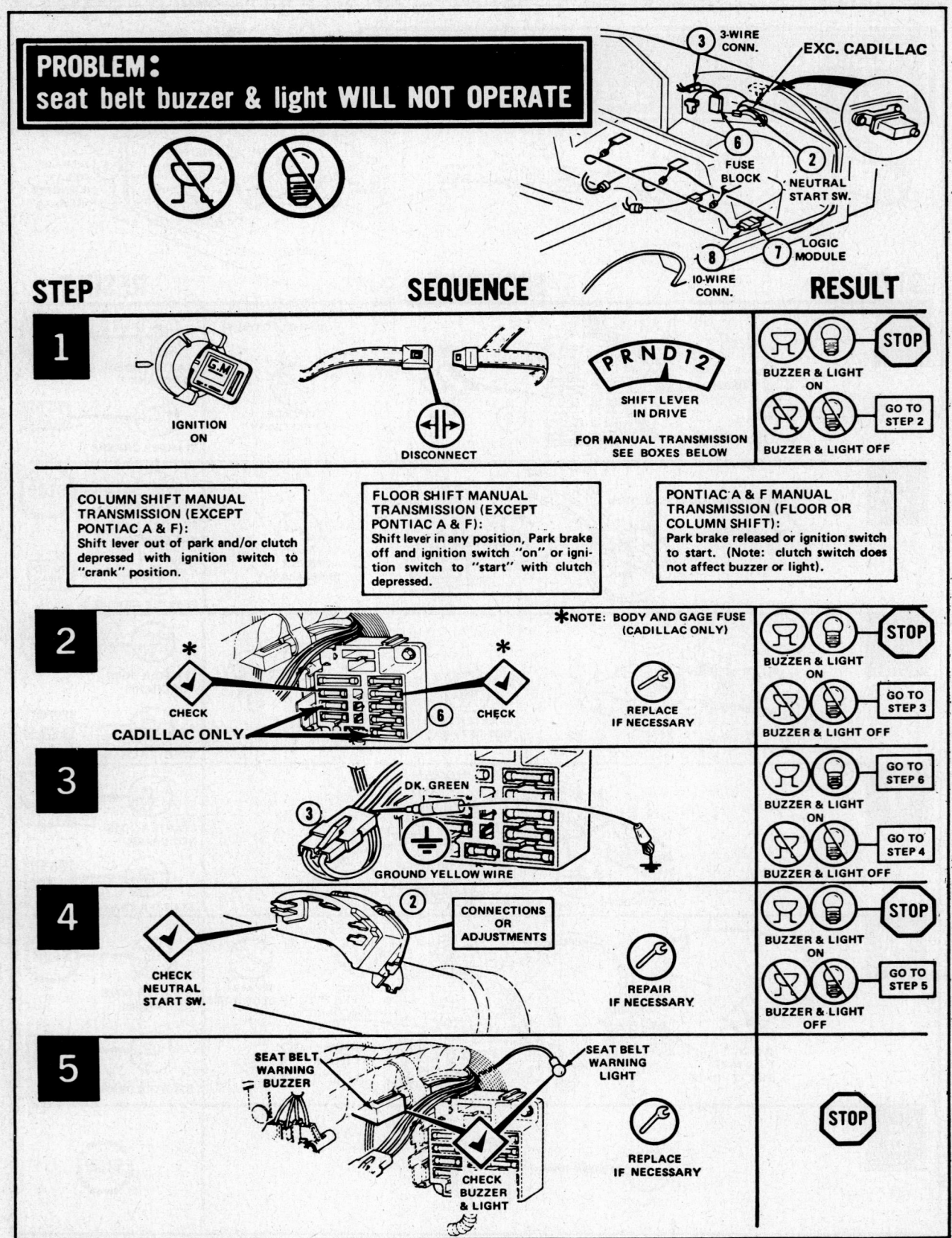

PROBLEM:
seat belt buzzer & light WILL NOT OPERATE

3-WIRE CONN.   EXC. CADILLAC

FUSE BLOCK   NEUTRAL START SW.

LOGIC MODULE

10-WIRE CONN.

STEP	SEQUENCE	RESULT
1	IGNITION ON — DISCONNECT — PRND12 SHIFT LEVER IN DRIVE — FOR MANUAL TRANSMISSION SEE BOXES BELOW	BUZZER & LIGHT ON → STOP / BUZZER & LIGHT OFF → GO TO STEP 2

COLUMN SHIFT MANUAL TRANSMISSION (EXCEPT PONTIAC A & F): Shift lever out of park and/or clutch depressed with ignition switch to "crank" position.

FLOOR SHIFT MANUAL TRANSMISSION (EXCEPT PONTIAC A & F): Shift lever in any position, Park brake off and ignition switch "on" or ignition switch to "start" with clutch depressed.

PONTIAC A & F MANUAL TRANSMISSION (FLOOR OR COLUMN SHIFT): Park brake released or ignition switch to start. (Note: clutch switch does not affect buzzer or light).

STEP	SEQUENCE	RESULT
2	*NOTE: BODY AND GAGE FUSE (CADILLAC ONLY) — CHECK — CADILLAC ONLY — CHECK — REPLACE IF NECESSARY	BUZZER & LIGHT ON → STOP / BUZZER & LIGHT OFF → GO TO STEP 3
3	DK. GREEN — GROUND YELLOW WIRE	BUZZER & LIGHT ON → GO TO STEP 6 / BUZZER & LIGHT OFF → GO TO STEP 4
4	CHECK NEUTRAL START SW. — CONNECTIONS OR ADJUSTMENTS — REPAIR IF NECESSARY	BUZZER & LIGHT ON → STOP / BUZZER & LIGHT OFF → GO TO STEP 5
5	SEAT BELT WARNING BUZZER — SEAT BELT WARNING LIGHT — CHECK BUZZER & LIGHT — REPLACE IF NECESSARY	STOP

Seat Belt Interlock System. General Motors except Oldsmobile

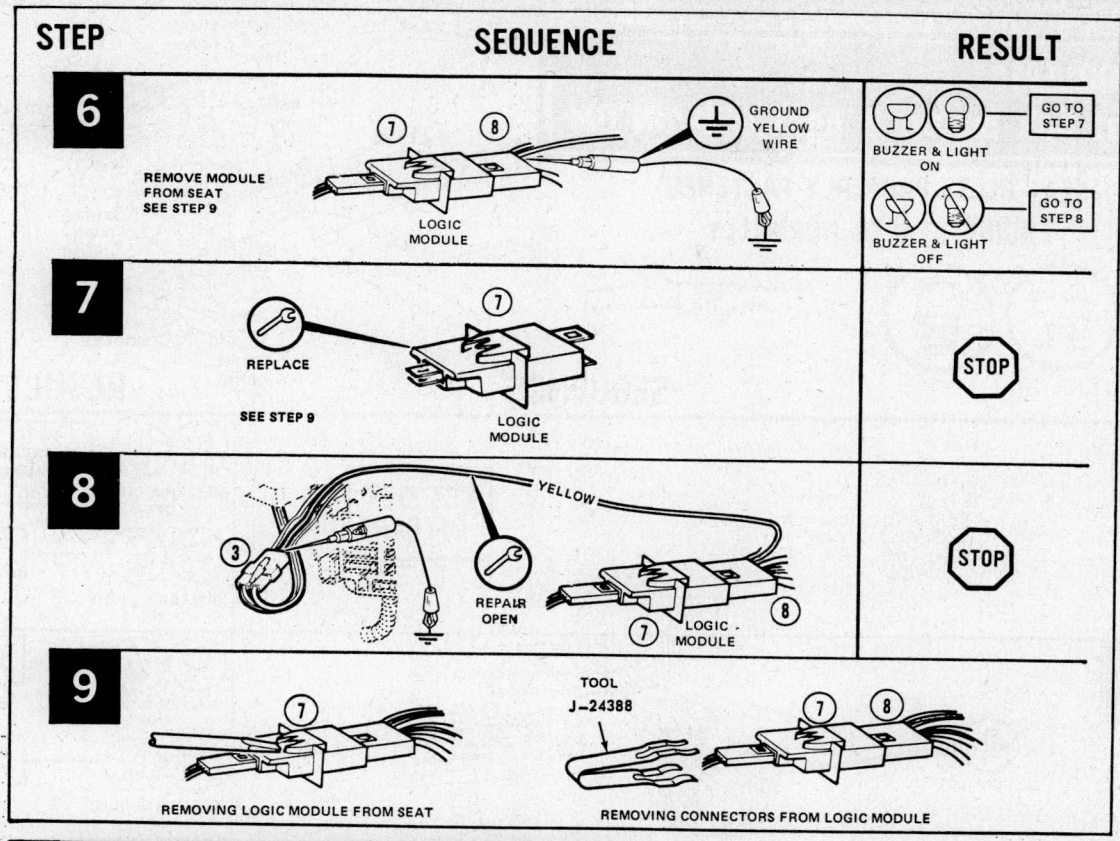

STEP	SEQUENCE	RESULT
6	REMOVE MODULE FROM SEAT SEE STEP 9 — LOGIC MODULE — GROUND YELLOW WIRE	BUZZER & LIGHT ON → GO TO STEP 7 / BUZZER & LIGHT OFF → GO TO STEP 8
7	REPLACE SEE STEP 9 — LOGIC MODULE	STOP
8	YELLOW — REPAIR OPEN — LOGIC MODULE	STOP
9	REMOVING LOGIC MODULE FROM SEAT — TOOL J–24388 — REMOVING CONNECTORS FROM LOGIC MODULE	

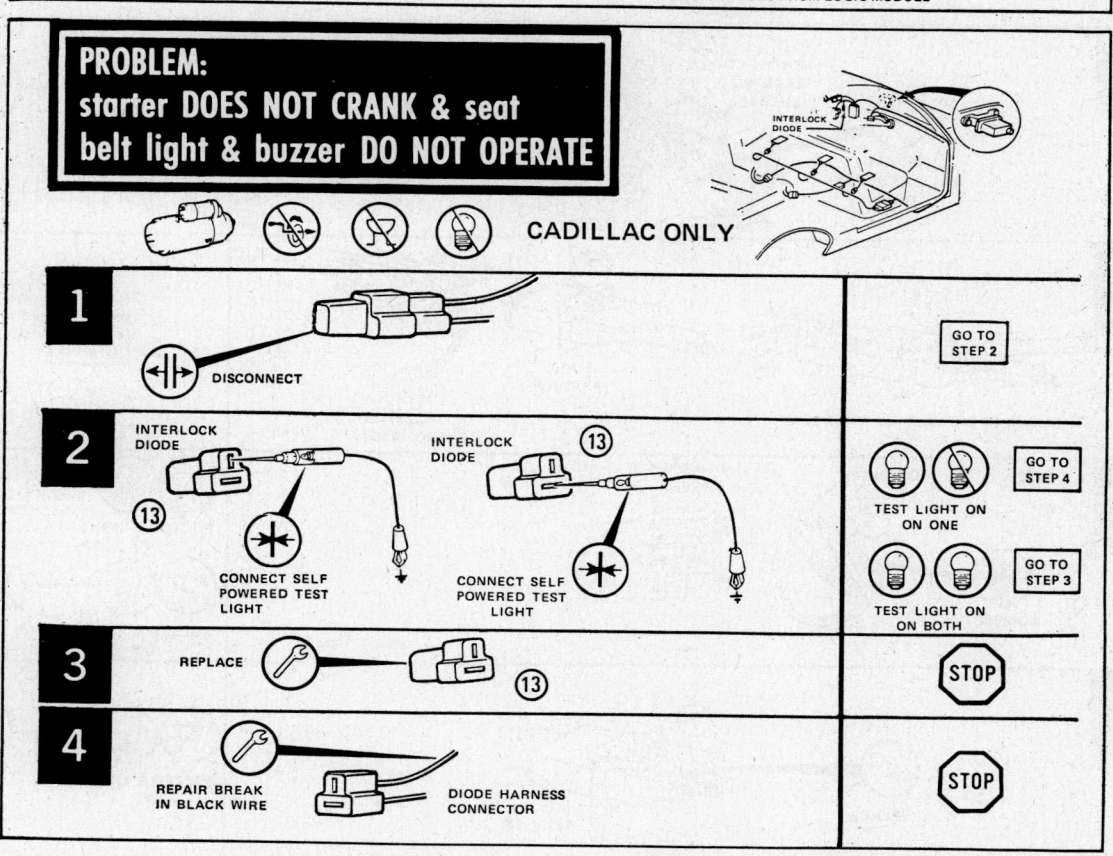

PROBLEM: starter DOES NOT CRANK & seat belt light & buzzer DO NOT OPERATE

CADILLAC ONLY

STEP	SEQUENCE	RESULT
1	DISCONNECT	GO TO STEP 2
2	INTERLOCK DIODE — CONNECT SELF POWERED TEST LIGHT / INTERLOCK DIODE — CONNECT SELF POWERED TEST LIGHT	TEST LIGHT ON ON ONE → GO TO STEP 4 / TEST LIGHT ON ON BOTH → GO TO STEP 3
3	REPLACE	STOP
4	REPAIR BREAK IN BLACK WIRE — DIODE HARNESS CONNECTOR	STOP

Seat Belt Interlock System. General Motors except Oldsmobile

SEAT BELT INTERLOCK SYSTEMS

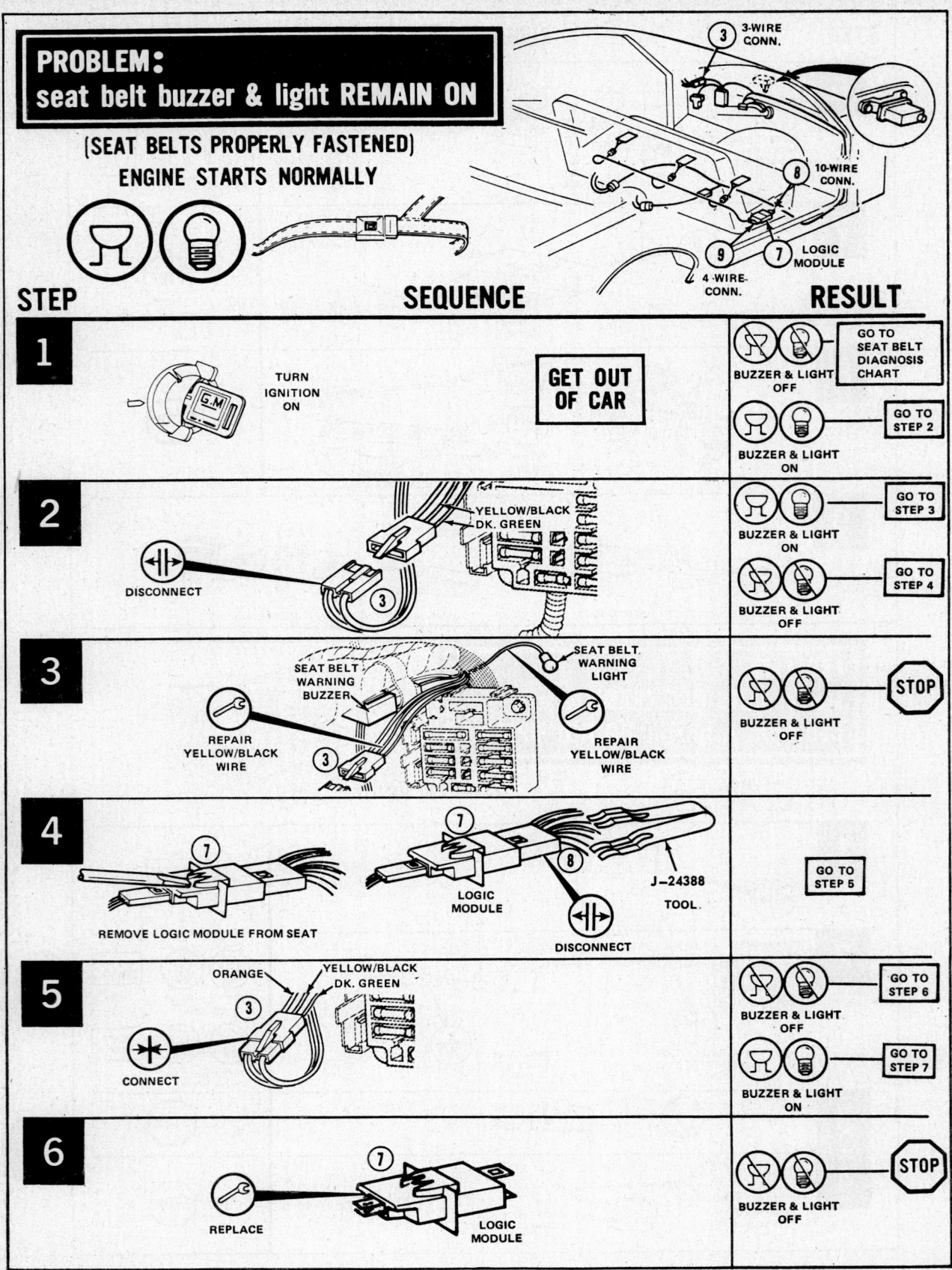

Seat Belt Interlock System. General Motors except Oldsmobile

STEP	SEQUENCE	RESULT
7	③ YELLOW · REPAIR · 10-PIN CONN. ⑧	BUZZER & LIGHT OFF — STOP

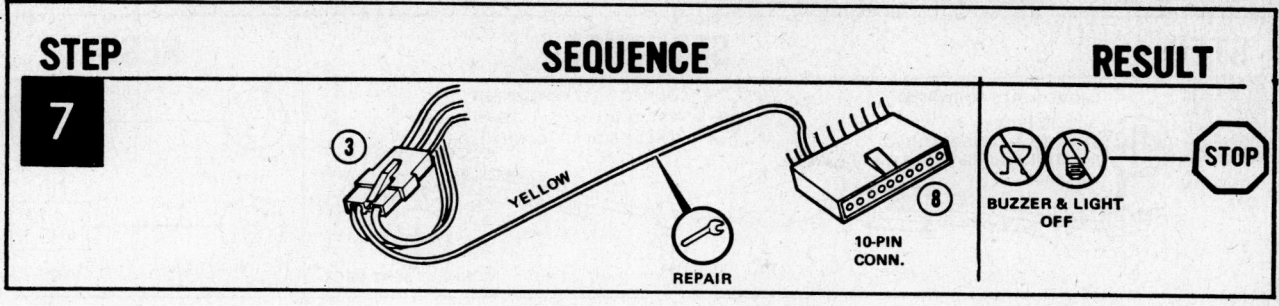

SEAT BELT SYSTEM DIAGNOSIS

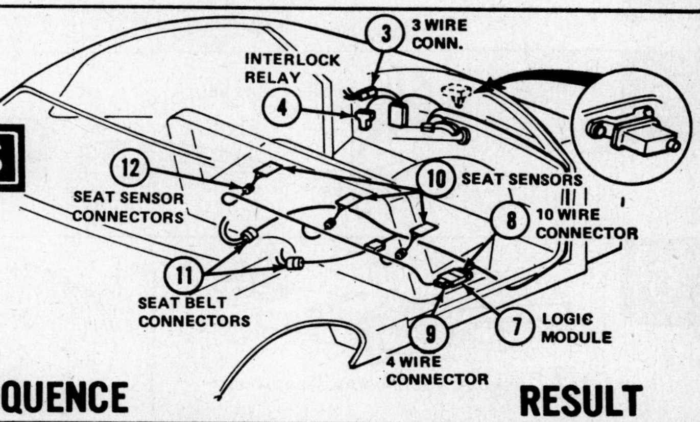

3 WIRE CONN. ③
INTERLOCK RELAY ④
SEAT SENSOR CONNECTORS ⑫
SEAT SENSORS ⑩
10 WIRE CONNECTOR ⑧
SEAT BELT CONNECTORS ⑪
4 WIRE CONNECTOR ⑨
LOGIC MODULE ⑦

STEP	SEQUENCE	RESULT
1	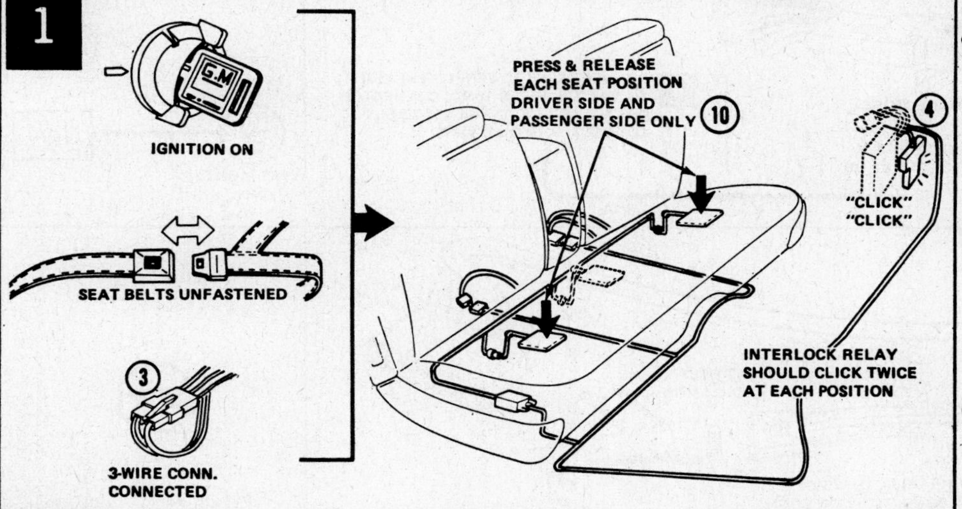 IGNITION ON / SEAT BELTS UNFASTENED / ③ 3-WIRE CONN. CONNECTED — PRESS & RELEASE EACH SEAT POSITION DRIVER SIDE AND PASSENGER SIDE ONLY ⑩ — "CLICK" "CLICK" ④ — INTERLOCK RELAY SHOULD CLICK TWICE AT EACH POSITION	● TWO CLICKS AT BOTH POSITIONS — GO TO STEP - 2 ● TWO CLICKS AT ONE POSITION ONLY — GO TO STEP - 12 ● ONLY ONE CLICK OR NO CLICK AT BOTH POSITIONS — GO TO STEP - 11
2	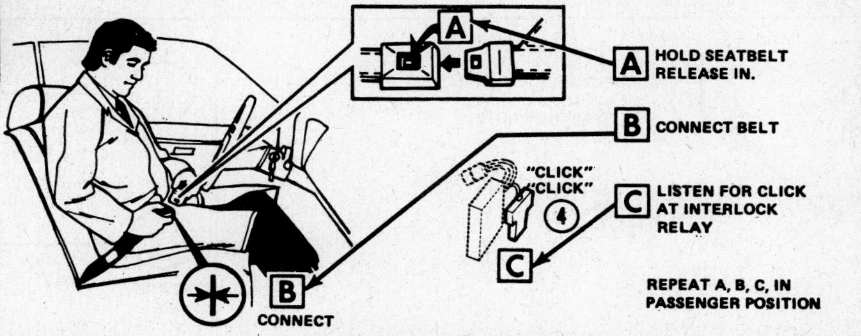 Ⓐ HOLD SEATBELT RELEASE IN. Ⓑ CONNECT BELT Ⓒ LISTEN FOR CLICK AT INTERLOCK RELAY — "CLICK" "CLICK" ④ REPEAT A, B, C, IN PASSENGER POSITION Ⓑ CONNECT	● RELAY DOES NOT CLICK AT EITHER POSITION — GO TO STEP - 6 ● RELAY DOES NOT CLICK AT ONE POSITION — GO TO STEP - 3

Seat Belt Interlock System. General Motors except Oldsmobile.

SEAT BELT INTERLOCK SYSTEMS

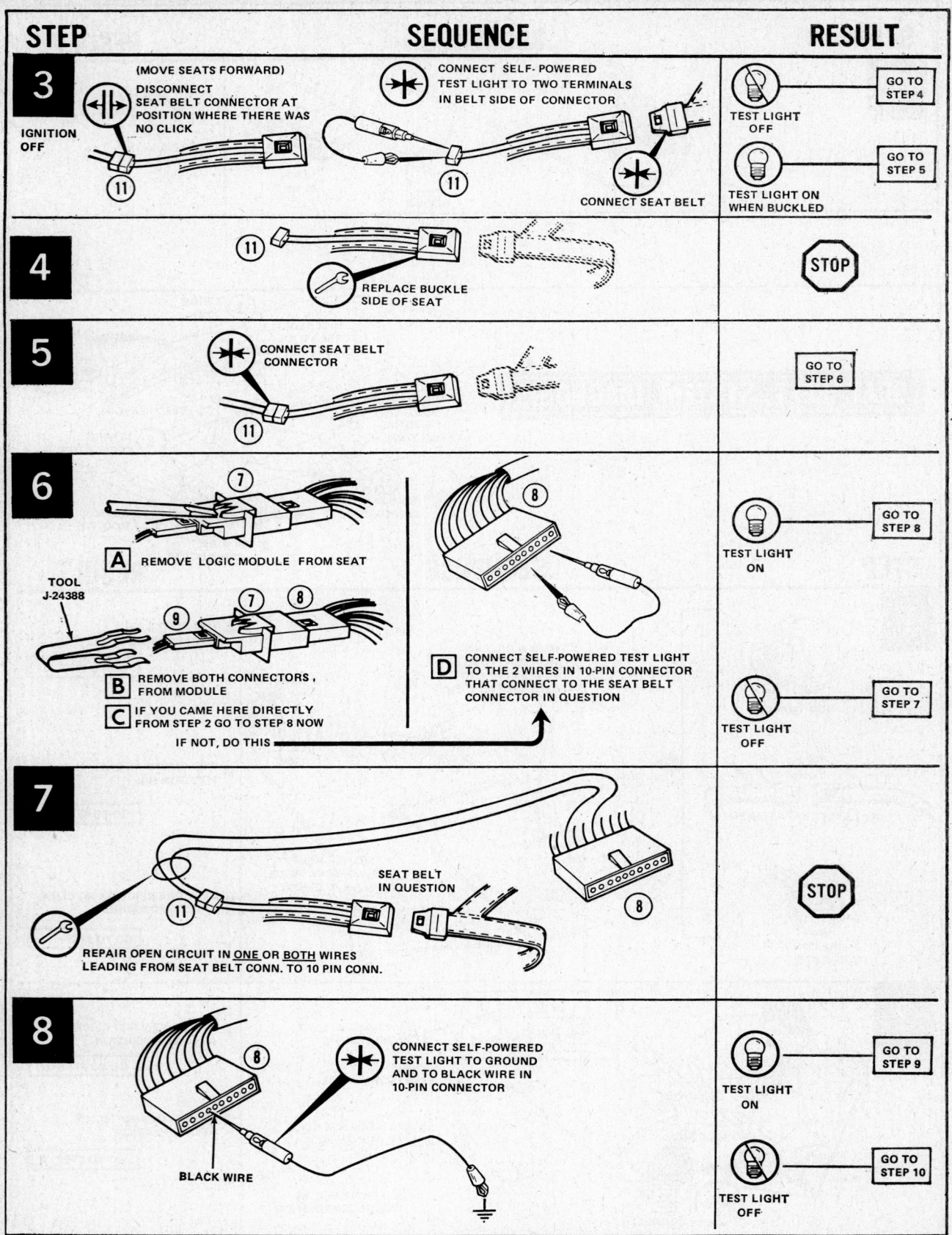

STEP	SEQUENCE	RESULT
3 IGNITION OFF	(MOVE SEATS FORWARD) DISCONNECT SEAT BELT CONNECTOR AT POSITION WHERE THERE WAS NO CLICK (11) — CONNECT SELF-POWERED TEST LIGHT TO TWO TERMINALS IN BELT SIDE OF CONNECTOR (11) — CONNECT SEAT BELT	TEST LIGHT OFF → GO TO STEP 4 — TEST LIGHT ON WHEN BUCKLED → GO TO STEP 5
4	(11) — REPLACE BUCKLE SIDE OF SEAT	STOP
5	CONNECT SEAT BELT CONNECTOR (11)	GO TO STEP 6
6	(7) — ⒶREMOVE LOGIC MODULE FROM SEAT — TOOL J-24388 — (9)(7)(8) — ⒷREMOVE BOTH CONNECTORS FROM MODULE — ⒸIF YOU CAME HERE DIRECTLY FROM STEP 2 GO TO STEP 8 NOW — IF NOT, DO THIS — (8) — ⒹCONNECT SELF-POWERED TEST LIGHT TO THE 2 WIRES IN 10-PIN CONNECTOR THAT CONNECT TO THE SEAT BELT CONNECTOR IN QUESTION	TEST LIGHT ON → GO TO STEP 8 — TEST LIGHT OFF → GO TO STEP 7
7	SEAT BELT IN QUESTION — (11) — (8) — REPAIR OPEN CIRCUIT IN ONE or BOTH WIRES LEADING FROM SEAT BELT CONN. TO 10 PIN CONN.	STOP
8	(8) — CONNECT SELF-POWERED TEST LIGHT TO GROUND AND TO BLACK WIRE IN 10-PIN CONNECTOR — BLACK WIRE	TEST LIGHT ON → GO TO STEP 9 — TEST LIGHT OFF → GO TO STEP 10

Seat Belt Interlock System. General Motors except Oldsmobile

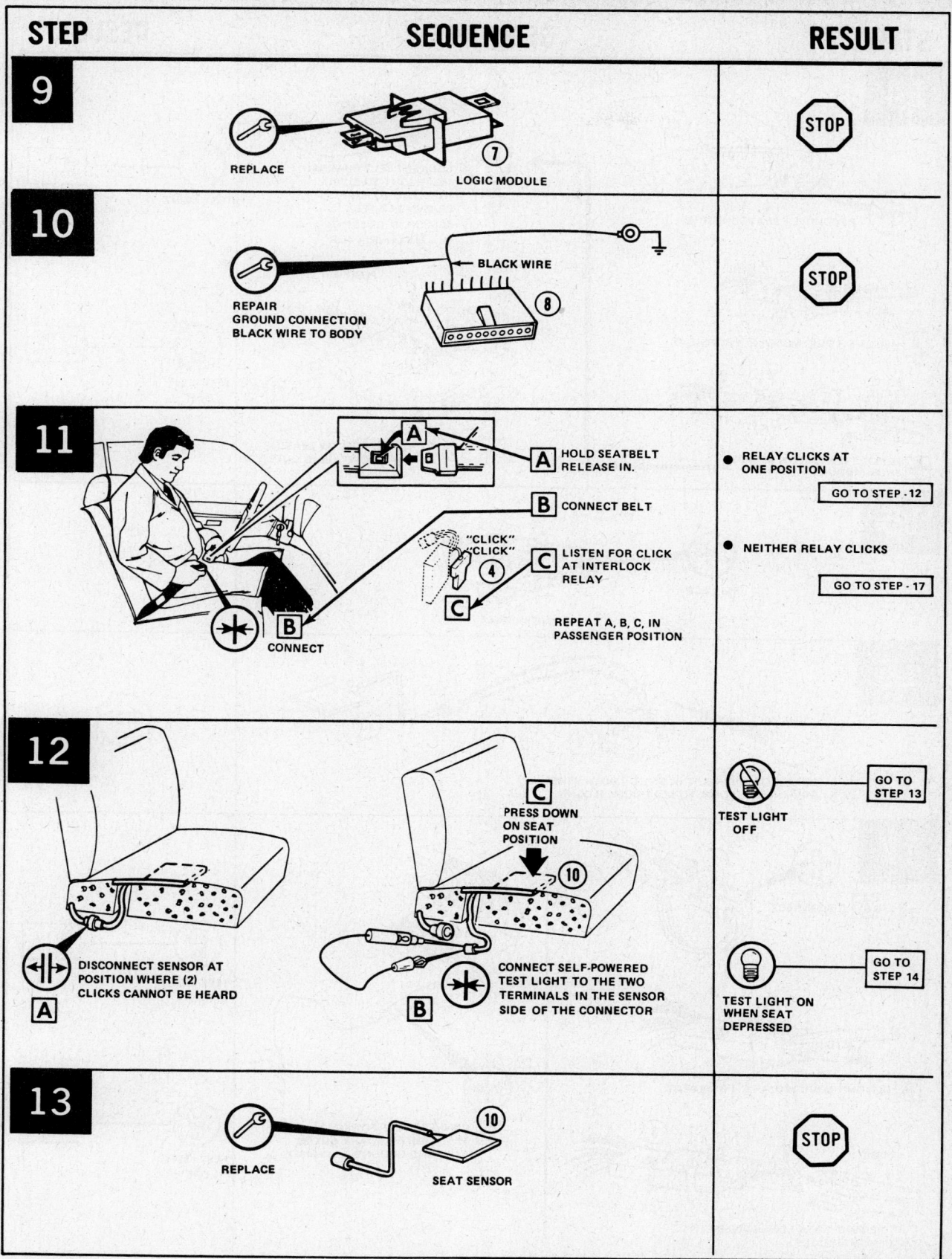

STEP	SEQUENCE	RESULT
9	REPLACE — LOGIC MODULE ⑦	STOP
10	BLACK WIRE — REPAIR GROUND CONNECTION BLACK WIRE TO BODY ⑧	STOP
11	A HOLD SEATBELT RELEASE IN. / B CONNECT BELT / "CLICK" "CLICK" ④ C LISTEN FOR CLICK AT INTERLOCK RELAY / REPEAT A, B, C, IN PASSENGER POSITION / B CONNECT	• RELAY CLICKS AT ONE POSITION — GO TO STEP -12 / • NEITHER RELAY CLICKS — GO TO STEP -17
12	A DISCONNECT SENSOR AT POSITION WHERE (2) CLICKS CANNOT BE HEARD / C PRESS DOWN ON SEAT POSITION ⑩ / B CONNECT SELF-POWERED TEST LIGHT TO THE TWO TERMINALS IN THE SENSOR SIDE OF THE CONNECTOR	TEST LIGHT OFF — GO TO STEP 13 / TEST LIGHT ON WHEN SEAT DEPRESSED — GO TO STEP 14
13	REPLACE — SEAT SENSOR ⑩	STOP

Seat Belt Interlock System. General Motors except Oldsmobile

SEAT BELT INTERLOCK SYSTEMS

STEP	SEQUENCE	RESULT

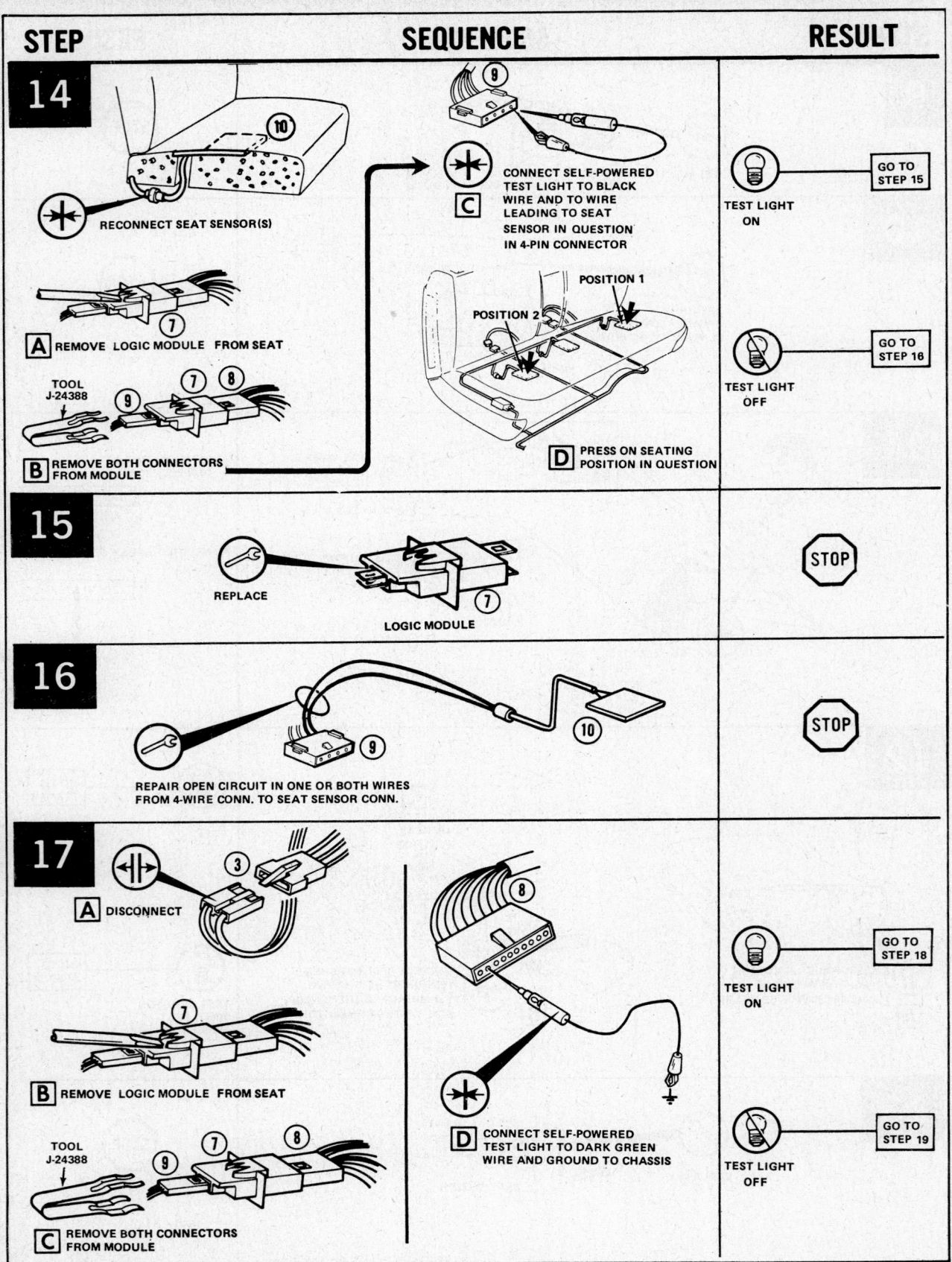

STEP 14

RECONNECT SEAT SENSOR(S)

A. REMOVE LOGIC MODULE FROM SEAT

TOOL J-24388

B. REMOVE BOTH CONNECTORS FROM MODULE

C. CONNECT SELF-POWERED TEST LIGHT TO BLACK WIRE AND TO WIRE LEADING TO SEAT SENSOR IN QUESTION IN 4-PIN CONNECTOR

POSITION 1
POSITION 2

D. PRESS ON SEATING POSITION IN QUESTION

RESULT:
TEST LIGHT ON → GO TO STEP 15
TEST LIGHT OFF → GO TO STEP 16

STEP 15

REPLACE

LOGIC MODULE

RESULT: STOP

STEP 16

REPAIR OPEN CIRCUIT IN ONE OR BOTH WIRES FROM 4-WIRE CONN. TO SEAT SENSOR CONN.

RESULT: STOP

STEP 17

A. DISCONNECT

B. REMOVE LOGIC MODULE FROM SEAT

TOOL J-24388

C. REMOVE BOTH CONNECTORS FROM MODULE

D. CONNECT SELF-POWERED TEST LIGHT TO DARK GREEN WIRE AND GROUND TO CHASSIS

RESULT:
TEST LIGHT ON → GO TO STEP 18
TEST LIGHT OFF → GO TO STEP 19

Seat Belt Interlock System. General Motors except Oldsmobile

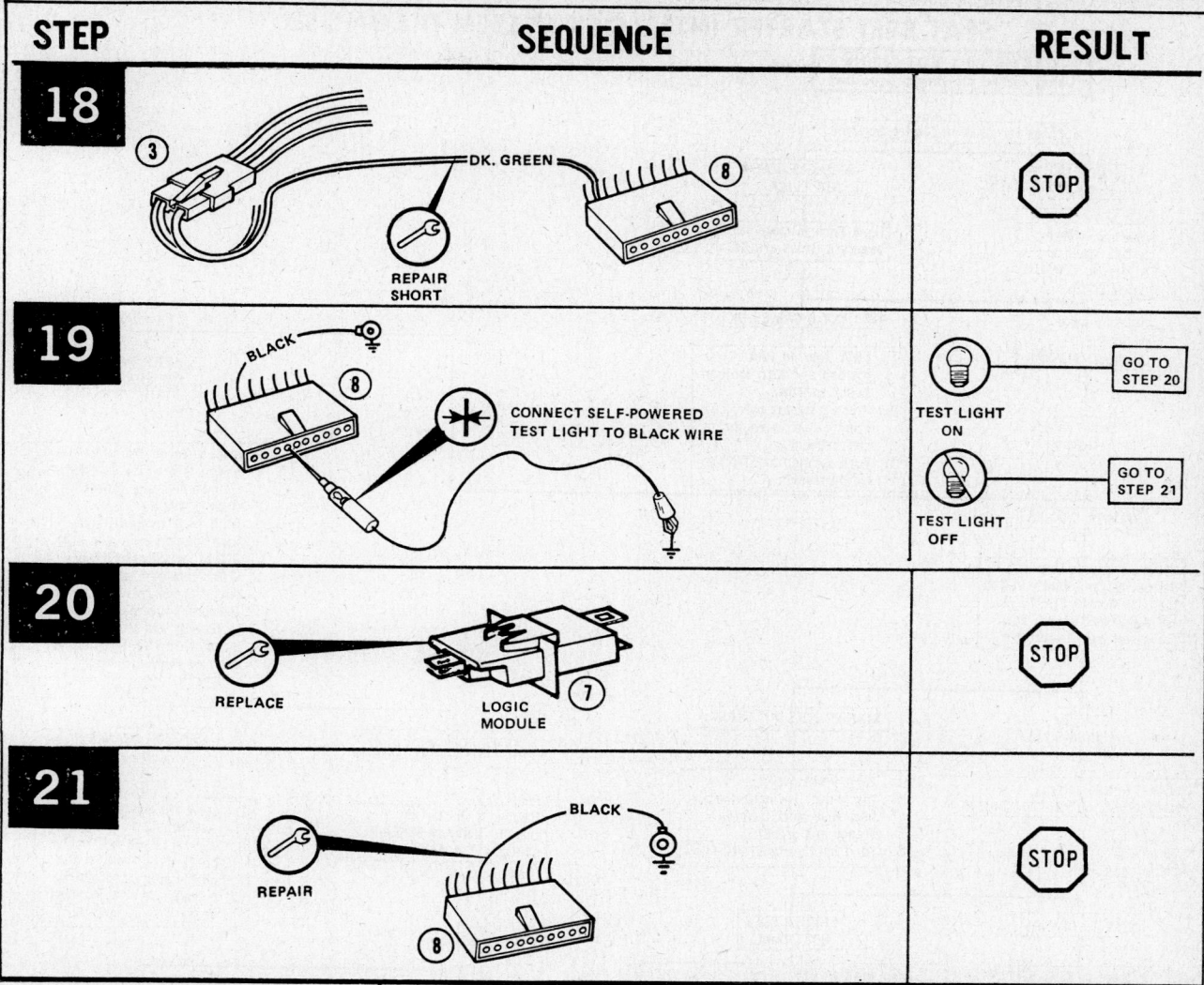

STEP	SEQUENCE	RESULT
18	③ DK. GREEN — REPAIR SHORT — ⑧	STOP
19	BLACK — ⑧ CONNECT SELF-POWERED TEST LIGHT TO BLACK WIRE	TEST LIGHT ON → GO TO STEP 20 / TEST LIGHT OFF → GO TO STEP 21
20	REPLACE — LOGIC MODULE ⑦	STOP
21	REPAIR — BLACK ⑧	STOP

Seat Belt Interlock System. General Motors except Oldsmobile

SEAT BELT INTERLOCK SYSTEMS

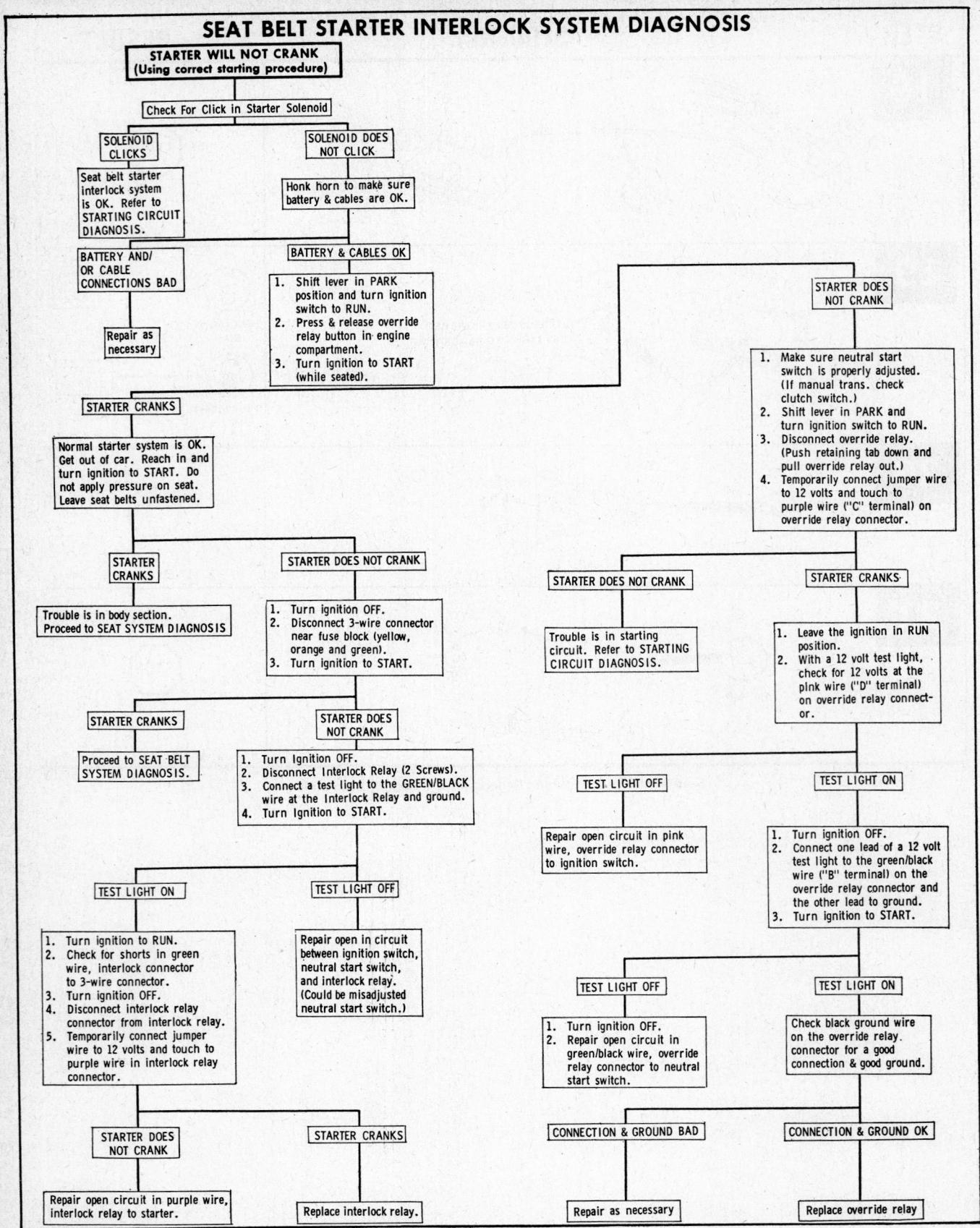

SEAT BELT STARTER INTERLOCK SYSTEM DIAGNOSIS

STARTER WILL NOT CRANK
(Using correct starting procedure)

Check For Click in Starter Solenoid

SOLENOID CLICKS

Seat belt starter interlock system is OK. Refer to STARTING CIRCUIT DIAGNOSIS.

BATTERY AND/ OR CABLE CONNECTIONS BAD

Repair as necessary

SOLENOID DOES NOT CLICK

Honk horn to make sure battery & cables are OK.

BATTERY & CABLES OK

1. Shift lever in PARK position and turn ignition switch to RUN.
2. Press & release override relay button in engine compartment.
3. Turn ignition to START (while seated).

STARTER CRANKS

Normal starter system is OK. Get out of car. Reach in and turn ignition to START. Do not apply pressure on seat. Leave seat belts unfastened.

STARTER CRANKS

Trouble is in body section. Proceed to SEAT SYSTEM DIAGNOSIS

STARTER DOES NOT CRANK

1. Turn ignition OFF.
2. Disconnect 3-wire connector near fuse block (yellow, orange and green).
3. Turn ignition to START.

STARTER CRANKS

Proceed to SEAT BELT SYSTEM DIAGNOSIS.

STARTER DOES NOT CRANK

1. Turn Ignition OFF.
2. Disconnect Interlock Relay (2 Screws).
3. Connect a test light to the GREEN/BLACK wire at the Interlock Relay and ground.
4. Turn Ignition to START.

TEST LIGHT ON

1. Turn ignition to RUN.
2. Check for shorts in green wire, interlock connector to 3-wire connector.
3. Turn ignition OFF.
4. Disconnect interlock relay connector from interlock relay.
5. Temporarily connect jumper wire to 12 volts and touch to purple wire in interlock relay connector.

TEST LIGHT OFF

Repair open in circuit between ignition switch, neutral start switch, and interlock relay. (Could be misadjusted neutral start switch.)

STARTER DOES NOT CRANK

Repair open circuit in purple wire, interlock relay to starter.

STARTER CRANKS

Replace interlock relay.

STARTER DOES NOT CRANK

1. Make sure neutral start switch is properly adjusted. (If manual trans. check clutch switch.)
2. Shift lever in PARK and turn ignition switch to RUN.
3. Disconnect override relay. (Push retaining tab down and pull override relay out.)
4. Temporarily connect jumper wire to 12 volts and touch to purple wire ("C" terminal) on override relay connector.

STARTER DOES NOT CRANK

Trouble is in starting circuit. Refer to STARTING CIRCUIT DIAGNOSIS.

STARTER CRANKS

1. Leave the ignition in RUN position.
2. With a 12 volt test light, check for 12 volts at the pink wire ("D" terminal) on override relay connector.

TEST LIGHT OFF

Repair open circuit in pink wire, override relay connector to ignition switch.

TEST LIGHT ON

1. Turn ignition OFF.
2. Connect one lead of a 12 volt test light to the green/black wire ("B" terminal) on the override relay connector and the other lead to ground.
3. Turn ignition to START.

TEST LIGHT OFF

1. Turn ignition OFF.
2. Repair open circuit in green/black wire, override relay connector to neutral start switch.

TEST LIGHT ON

Check black ground wire on the override relay connector for a good connection & good ground.

CONNECTION & GROUND BAD

Repair as necessary

CONNECTION & GROUND OK

Replace override relay

Oldsmobile Seat Belt Interlock System

SEAT BELT STARTER INTERLOCK SYSTEM DIAGNOSIS (CONTINUED)

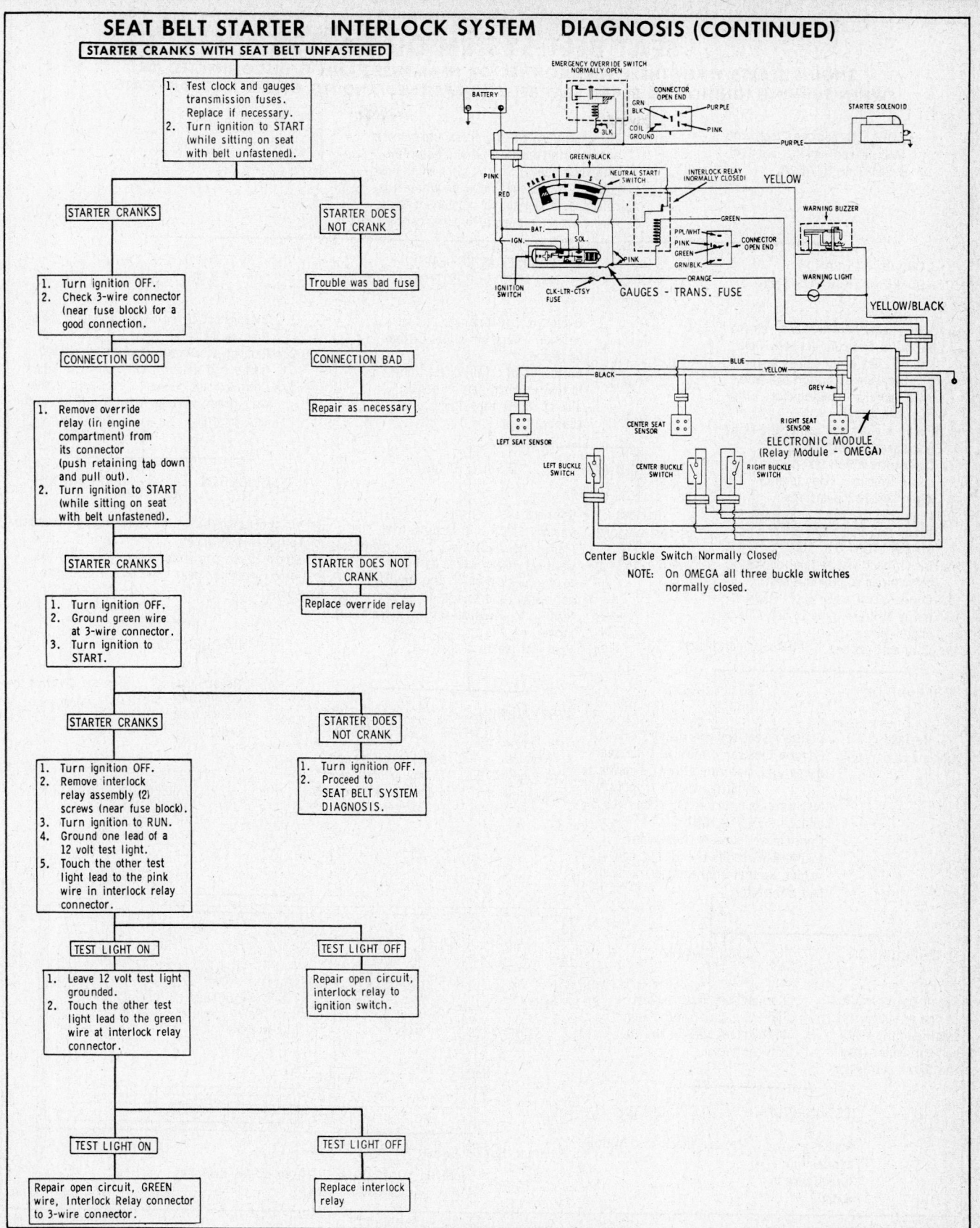

STARTER CRANKS WITH SEAT BELT UNFASTENED

1. Test clock and gauges transmission fuses. Replace if necessary.
2. Turn ignition to START (while sitting on seat with belt unfastened).

STARTER CRANKS

1. Turn ignition OFF.
2. Check 3-wire connector (near fuse block) for a good connection.

STARTER DOES NOT CRANK

Trouble was bad fuse

CONNECTION GOOD

1. Remove override relay (in engine compartment) from its connector (push retaining tab down and pull out).
2. Turn ignition to START (while sitting on seat with belt unfastened).

CONNECTION BAD

Repair as necessary.

STARTER CRANKS

1. Turn ignition OFF.
2. Ground green wire at 3-wire connector.
3. Turn ignition to START.

STARTER DOES NOT CRANK

Replace override relay

STARTER CRANKS

1. Turn ignition OFF.
2. Remove interlock relay assembly (2) screws (near fuse block).
3. Turn ignition to RUN.
4. Ground one lead of a 12 volt test light.
5. Touch the other test light lead to the pink wire in interlock relay connector.

STARTER DOES NOT CRANK

1. Turn ignition OFF.
2. Proceed to SEAT BELT SYSTEM DIAGNOSIS.

TEST LIGHT ON

1. Leave 12 volt test light grounded.
2. Touch the other test light lead to the green wire at interlock relay connector.

TEST LIGHT OFF

Repair open circuit, interlock relay to ignition switch.

TEST LIGHT ON

Repair open circuit, GREEN wire, Interlock Relay connector to 3-wire connector.

TEST LIGHT OFF

Replace interlock relay

Center Buckle Switch Normally Closed

NOTE: On OMEGA all three buckle switches normally closed.

Oldsmobile Seat Belt Interlock System

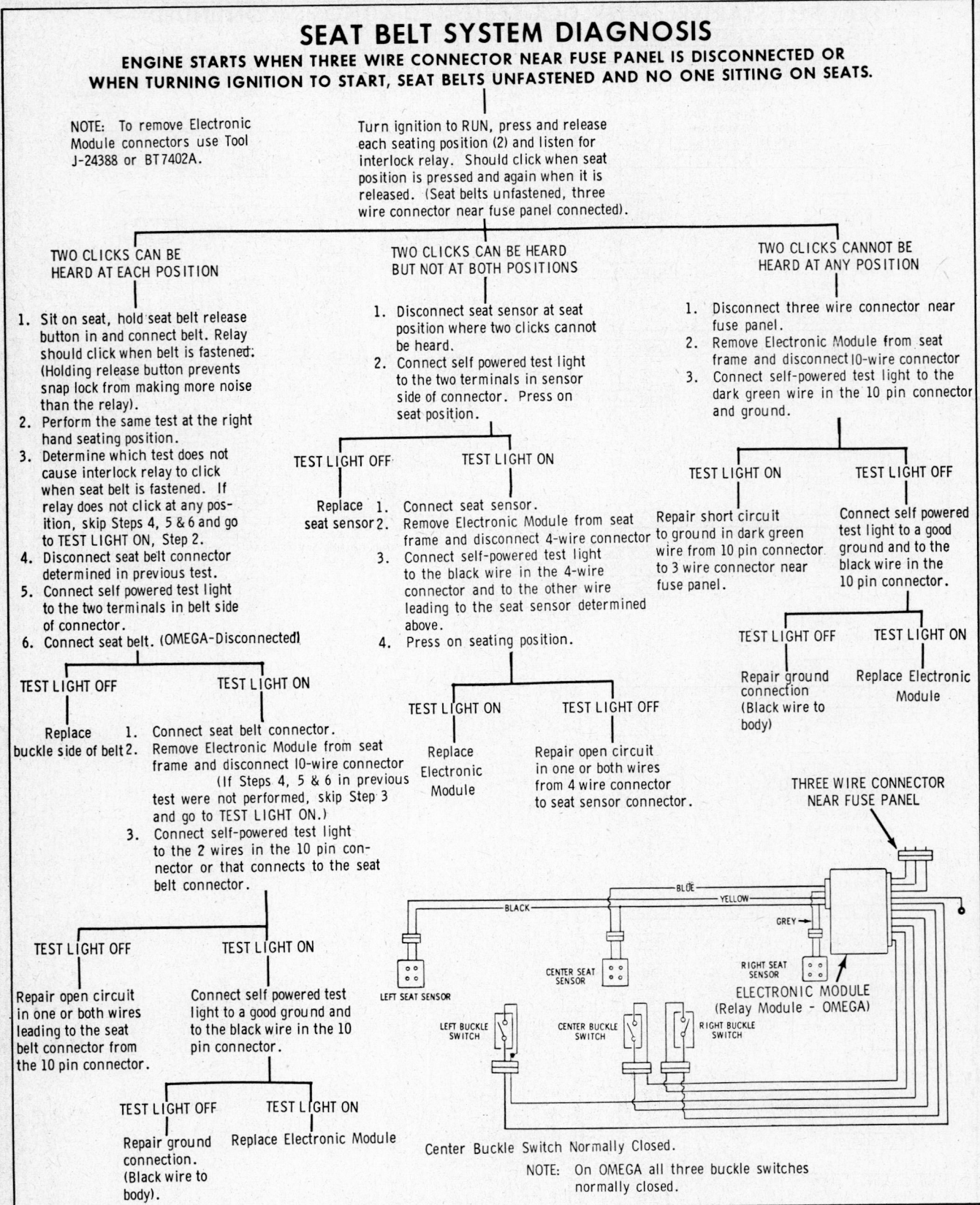

SEAT BELT SYSTEM DIAGNOSIS

ENGINE STARTS WHEN THREE WIRE CONNECTOR NEAR FUSE PANEL IS DISCONNECTED OR WHEN TURNING IGNITION TO START, SEAT BELTS UNFASTENED AND NO ONE SITTING ON SEATS.

NOTE: To remove Electronic Module connectors use Tool J-24388 or BT 7402A.

Turn ignition to RUN, press and release each seating position (2) and listen for interlock relay. Should click when seat position is pressed and again when it is released. (Seat belts unfastened, three wire connector near fuse panel connected).

TWO CLICKS CAN BE HEARD AT EACH POSITION

1. Sit on seat, hold seat belt release button in and connect belt. Relay should click when belt is fastened. (Holding release button prevents snap lock from making more noise than the relay).
2. Perform the same test at the right hand seating position.
3. Determine which test does not cause interlock relay to click when seat belt is fastened. If relay does not click at any position, skip Steps 4, 5 & 6 and go to TEST LIGHT ON, Step 2.
4. Disconnect seat belt connector determined in previous test.
5. Connect self powered test light to the two terminals in belt side of connector.
6. Connect seat belt. (OMEGA-Disconnected)

TEST LIGHT OFF

Replace buckle side of belt

TEST LIGHT ON
1. Connect seat belt connector.
2. Remove Electronic Module from seat frame and disconnect 10-wire connector (If Steps 4, 5 & 6 in previous test were not performed, skip Step 3 and go to TEST LIGHT ON.)
3. Connect self-powered test light to the 2 wires in the 10 pin connector or that connects to the seat belt connector.

TEST LIGHT OFF

Repair open circuit in one or both wires leading to the seat belt connector from the 10 pin connector.

TEST LIGHT ON

Connect self powered test light to a good ground and to the black wire in the 10 pin connector.

TEST LIGHT OFF

Repair ground connection. (Black wire to body).

TEST LIGHT ON

Replace Electronic Module

TWO CLICKS CAN BE HEARD BUT NOT AT BOTH POSITIONS

1. Disconnect seat sensor at seat position where two clicks cannot be heard.
2. Connect self powered test light to the two terminals in sensor side of connector. Press on seat position.

TEST LIGHT OFF

Replace seat sensor

TEST LIGHT ON
1. Connect seat sensor.
2. Remove Electronic Module from seat frame and disconnect 4-wire connector
3. Connect self-powered test light to the black wire in the 4-wire connector and to the other wire leading to the seat sensor determined above.
4. Press on seating position.

TEST LIGHT ON

Replace Electronic Module

TEST LIGHT OFF

Repair open circuit in one or both wires from 4 wire connector to seat sensor connector.

TWO CLICKS CANNOT BE HEARD AT ANY POSITION

1. Disconnect three wire connector near fuse panel.
2. Remove Electronic Module from seat frame and disconnect 10-wire connector
3. Connect self-powered test light to the dark green wire in the 10 pin connector and ground.

TEST LIGHT ON

Repair short circuit to ground in dark green wire from 10 pin connector to 3 wire connector near fuse panel.

TEST LIGHT OFF

Connect self powered test light to a good ground and to the black wire in the 10 pin connector.

TEST LIGHT OFF

Repair ground connection (Black wire to body)

TEST LIGHT ON

Replace Electronic Module

THREE WIRE CONNECTOR NEAR FUSE PANEL

LEFT SEAT SENSOR

CENTER SEAT SENSOR

RIGHT SEAT SENSOR

ELECTRONIC MODULE (Relay Module - OMEGA)

LEFT BUCKLE SWITCH

CENTER BUCKLE SWITCH

RIGHT BUCKLE SWITCH

BLUE   YELLOW

BLACK

GREY

Center Buckle Switch Normally Closed.

NOTE: On OMEGA all three buckle switches normally closed.

Oldsmobile Seat Belt Interlock System

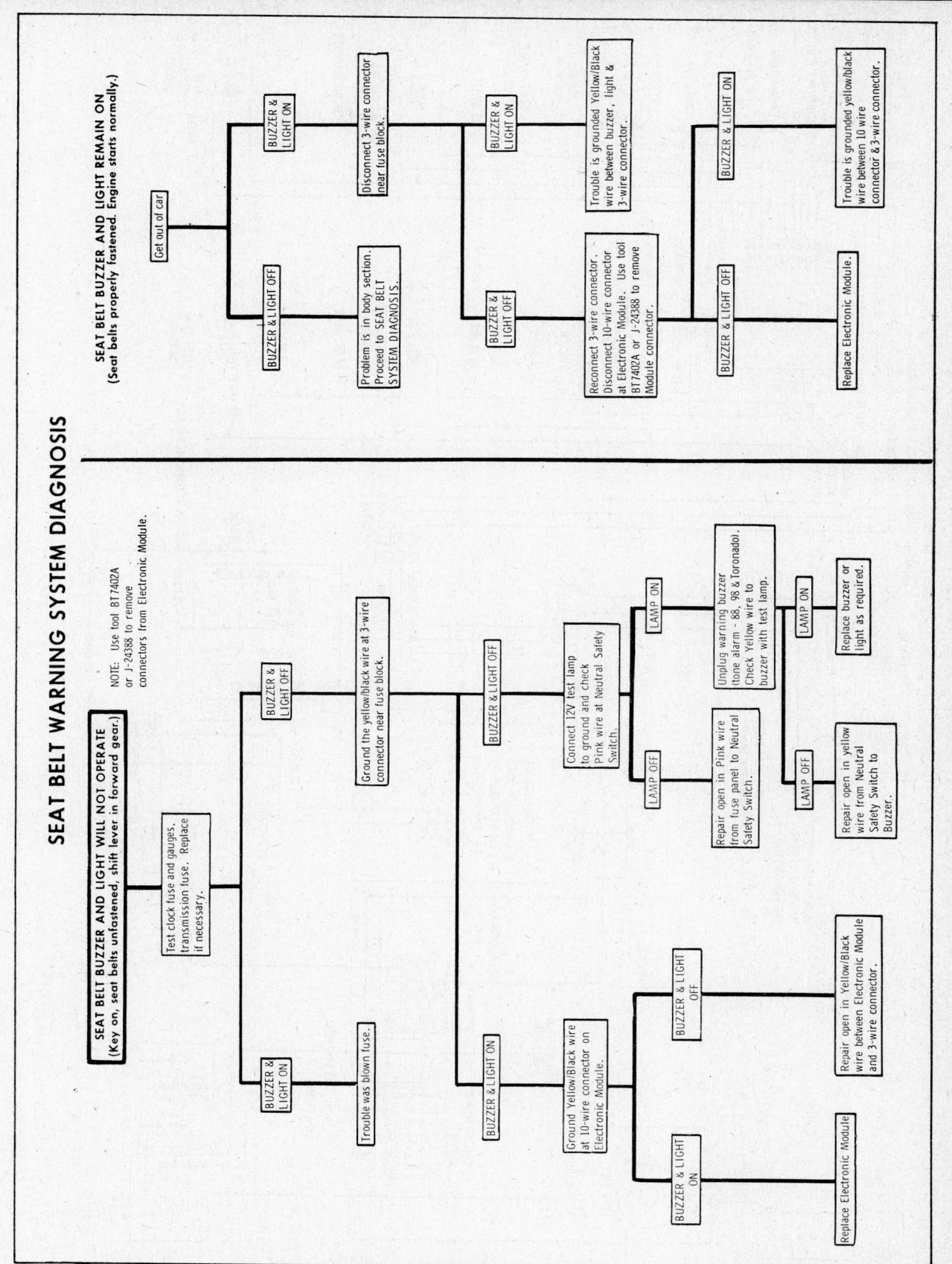

SEAT BELT WARNING SYSTEM DIAGNOSIS

NOTE: Use tool BT7402A or J-24388 to remove connectors from Electronic Module.

SEAT BELT BUZZER AND LIGHT WILL NOT OPERATE
(Key on, seat belts unfastened, shift lever in forward gear.)

- Test clock fuse and gauges, transmission fuse. Replace if necessary.
  - BUZZER & LIGHT OFF
    - Ground the yellow/black wire at 3-wire connector near fuse block.
      - BUZZER & LIGHT OFF
        - Connect 12V test lamp to ground and check Pink wire at Neutral Safety Switch.
          - LAMP ON
            - Unplug warning buzzer (tone alarm - 88, 98 & Toronado). Check Yellow wire to buzzer with test lamp.
              - LAMP ON — Replace buzzer or light as required.
              - LAMP OFF — Repair open in yellow wire from Neutral Safety Switch to Buzzer.
          - LAMP OFF — Repair open in Pink wire from fuse panel to Neutral Safety Switch.
      - BUZZER & LIGHT ON — Ground Yellow/Black wire at 10-wire connector on Electronic Module.
        - BUZZER & LIGHT OFF — Repair open in Yellow/Black wire between Electronic Module and 3-wire connector.
        - BUZZER & LIGHT ON — Replace Electronic Module.
  - BUZZER & LIGHT ON — Trouble was blown fuse.

SEAT BELT BUZZER AND LIGHT REMAIN ON
(Seat belts properly fastened. Engine starts normally.)

- Get out of car
  - BUZZER & LIGHT ON — Disconnect 3-wire connector near fuse block.
    - BUZZER & LIGHT ON — Trouble is grounded Yellow/Black wire between buzzer, light & 3-wire connector.
    - BUZZER & LIGHT OFF — Reconnect 3-wire connector. Disconnect 10-wire connector at Electronic Module. Use tool BT7402A or J-24388 to remove Module connector.
      - BUZZER & LIGHT ON — Trouble is grounded yellow/black wire between 10 wire connector & 3-wire connector.
      - BUZZER & LIGHT OFF — Replace Electronic Module.
  - BUZZER & LIGHT OFF — Problem is in body section. Proceed to SEAT BELT SYSTEM DIAGNOSIS.

Oldsmobile Seat Belt Interlock System

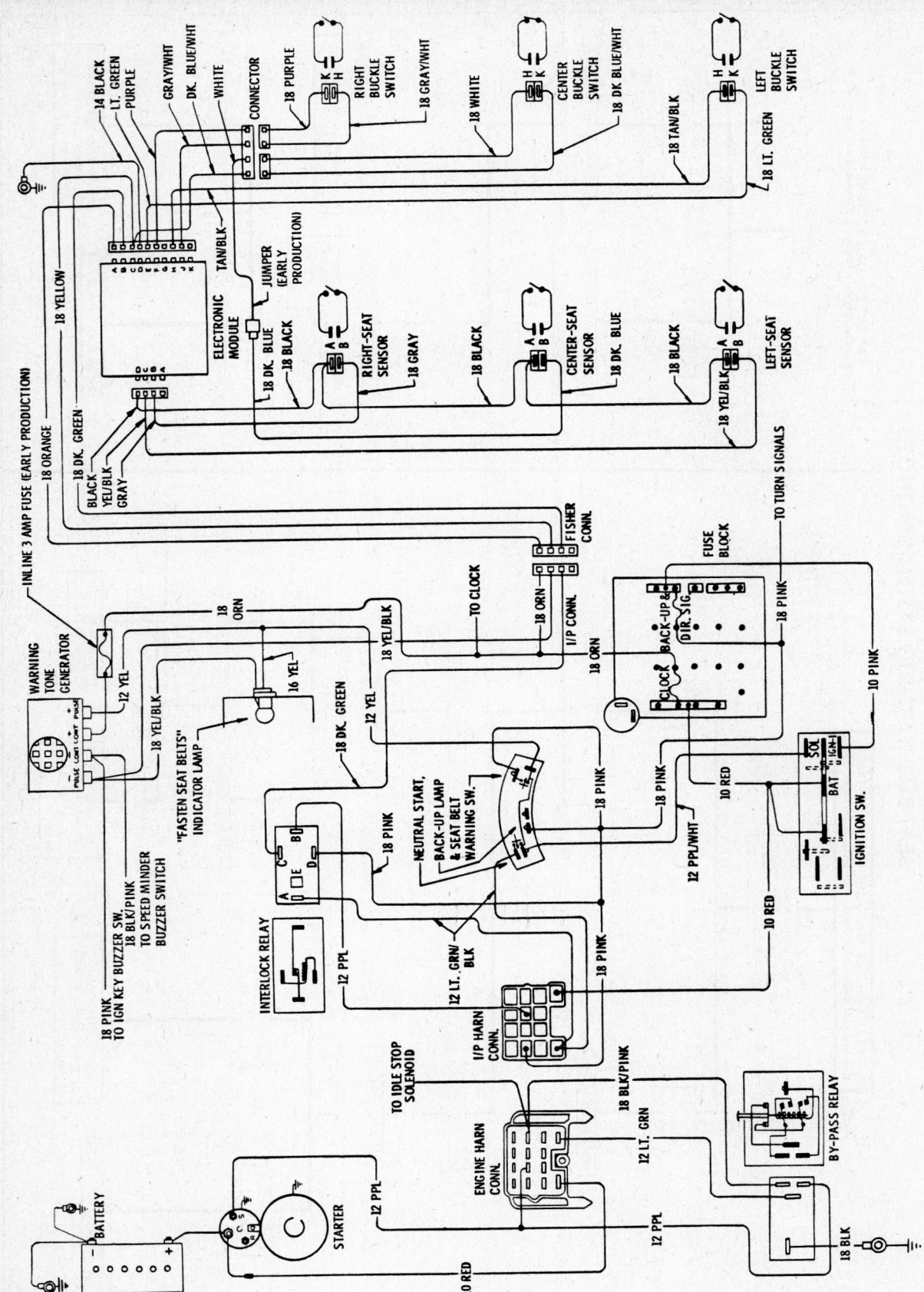

Fig. 31   Interlock system wiring diagram. All Buick exc. Apollo (Early type)

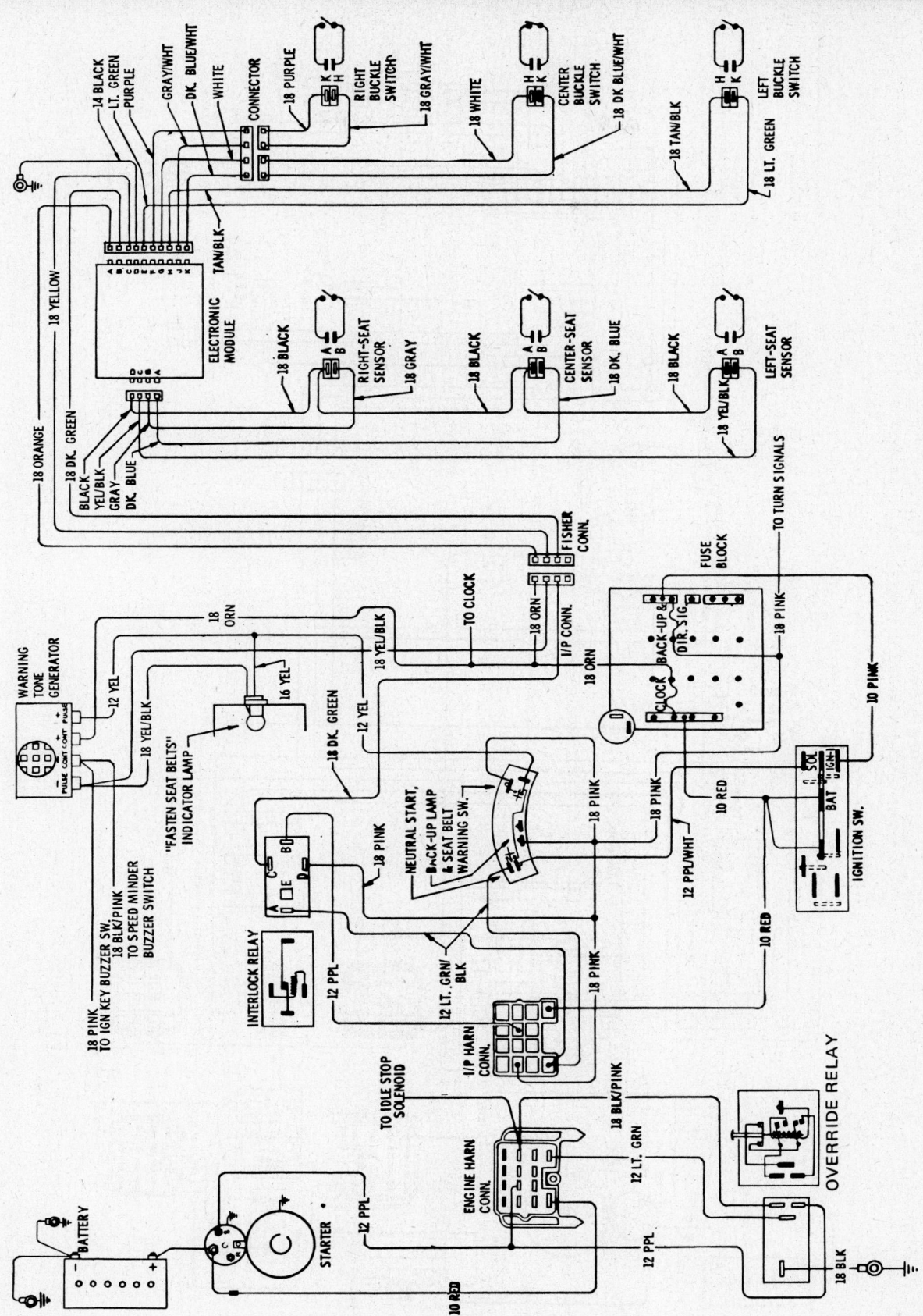

Fig. 32 Interlock system wiring diagram. All Buick exc. Apollo (Late type)

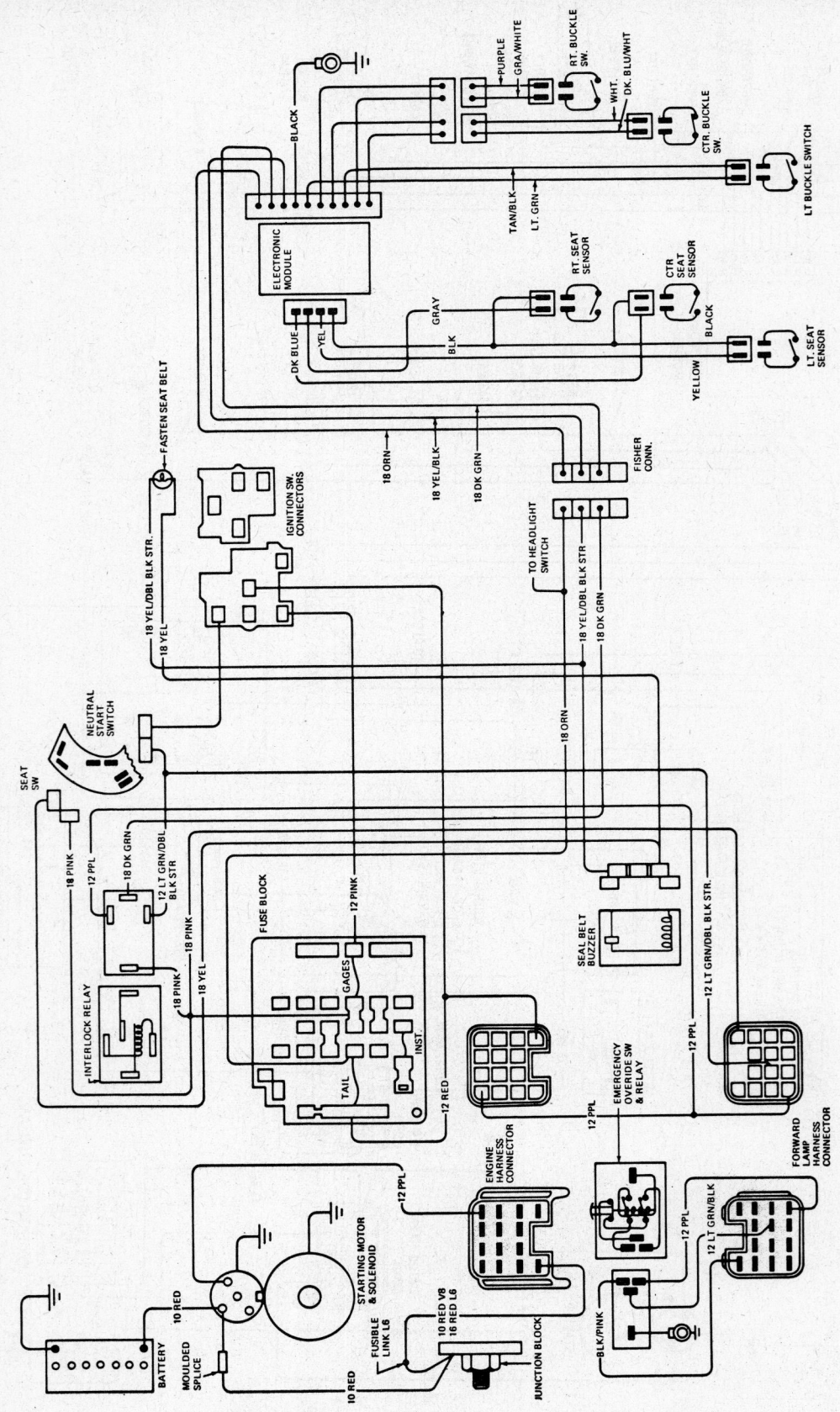

Fig. 33 Interlock system wiring diagram. Apollo with Auto. Trans.

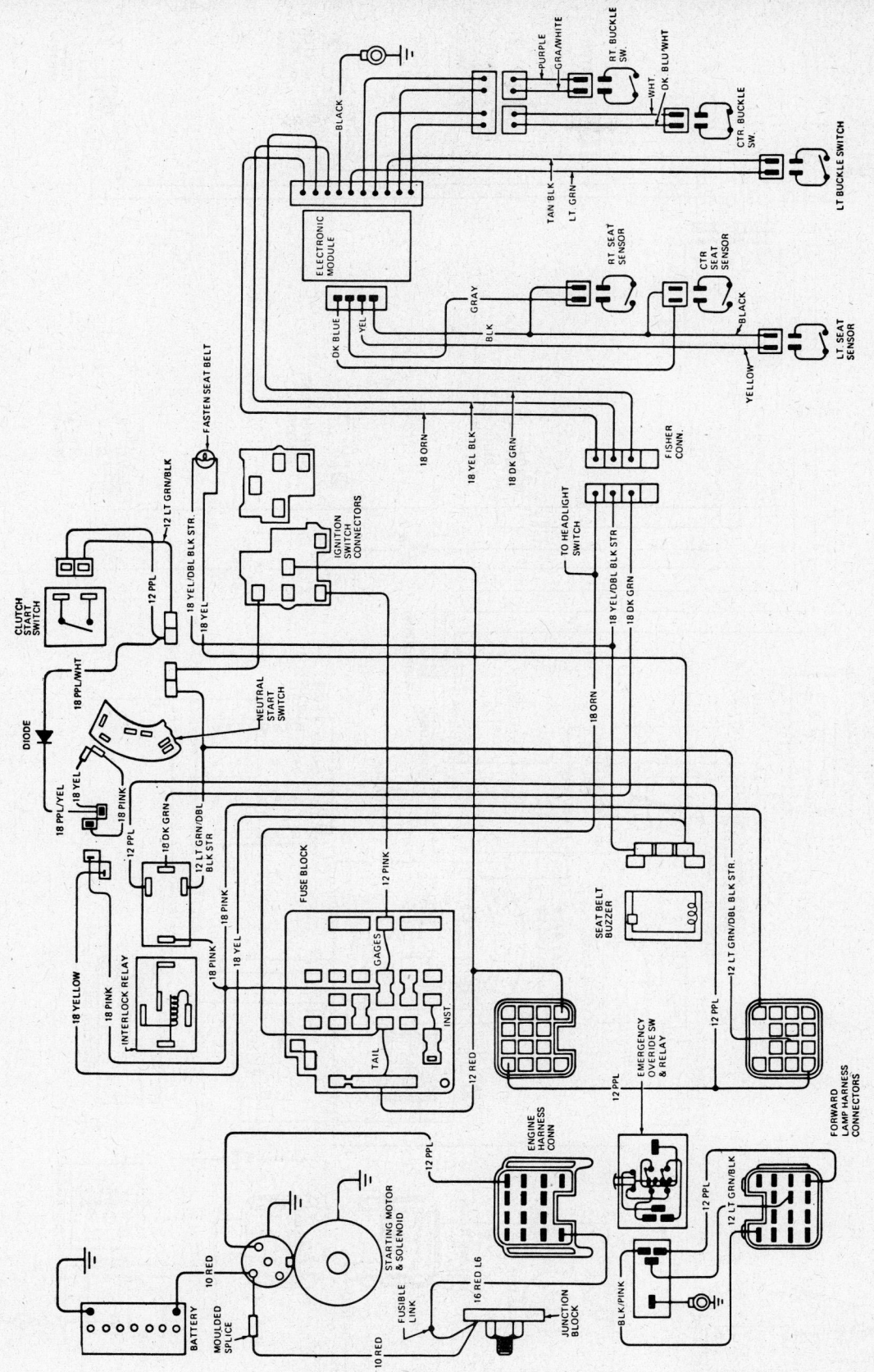

Fig. 34 Interlock system wiring diagram. Apollo with Manual Trans.

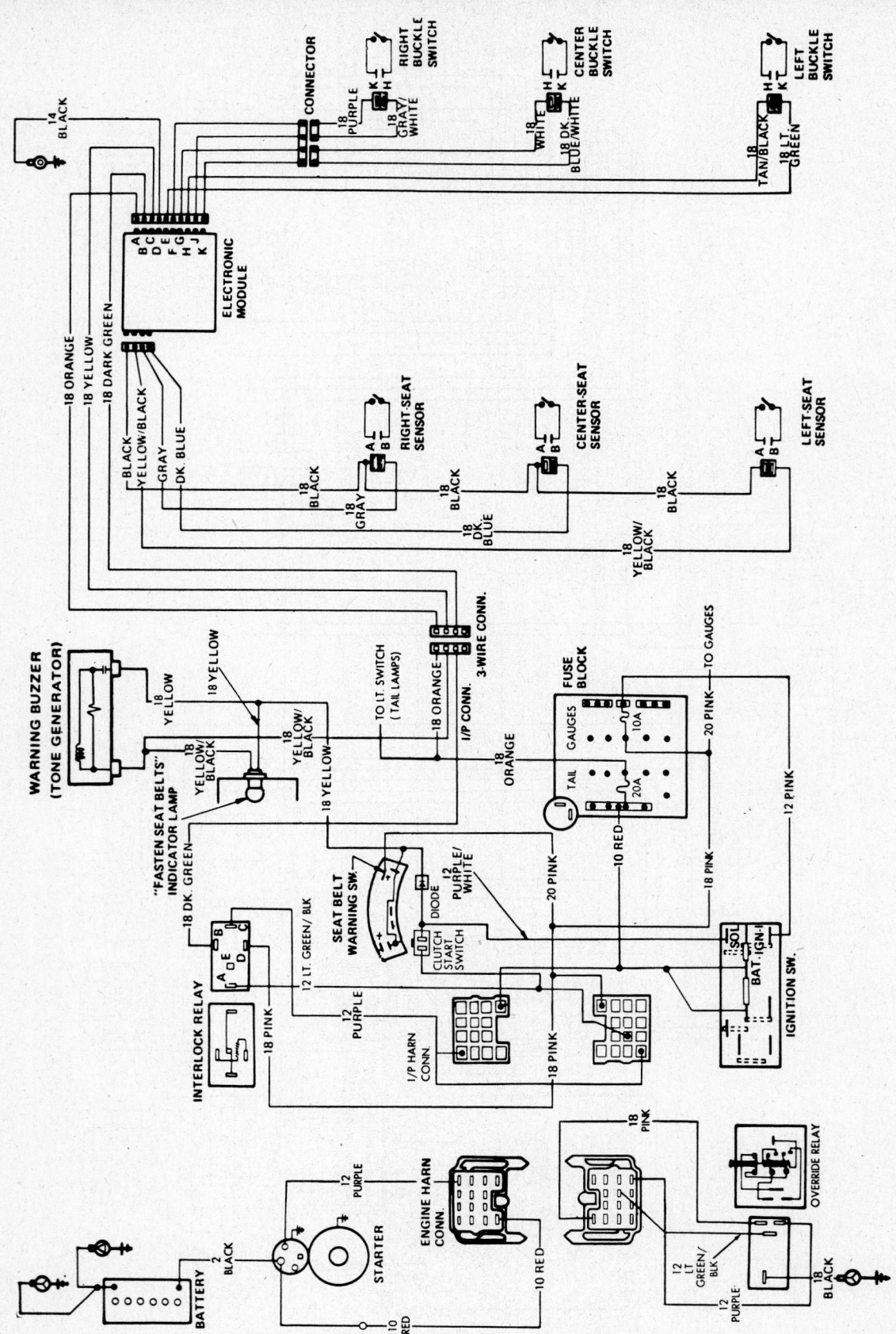

Fig. 35 Interlock system wiring diagram. Chevrolet with Manual Trans.

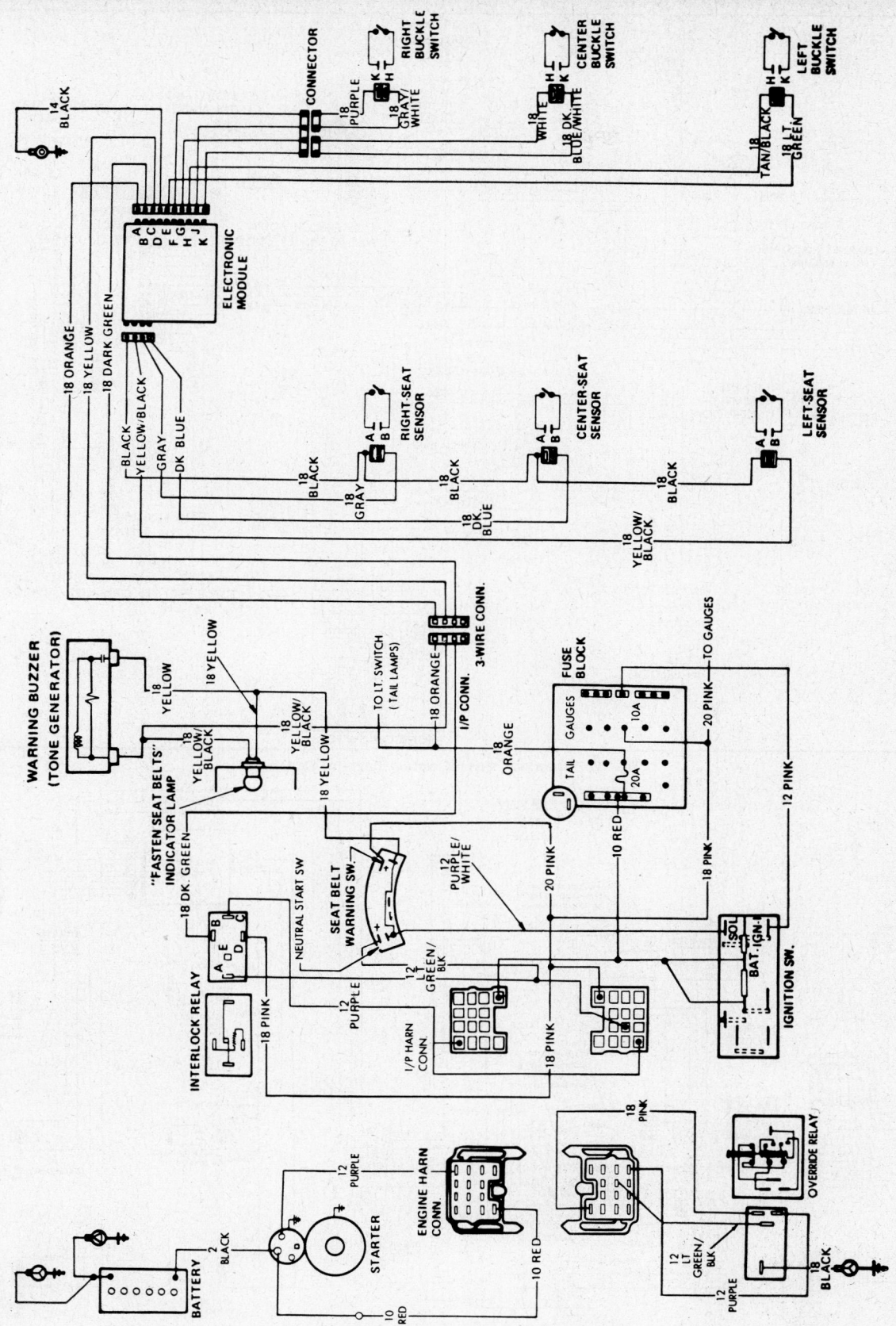

Fig. 36 Interlock system wiring diagram. Chevrolet with Auto. Trans.

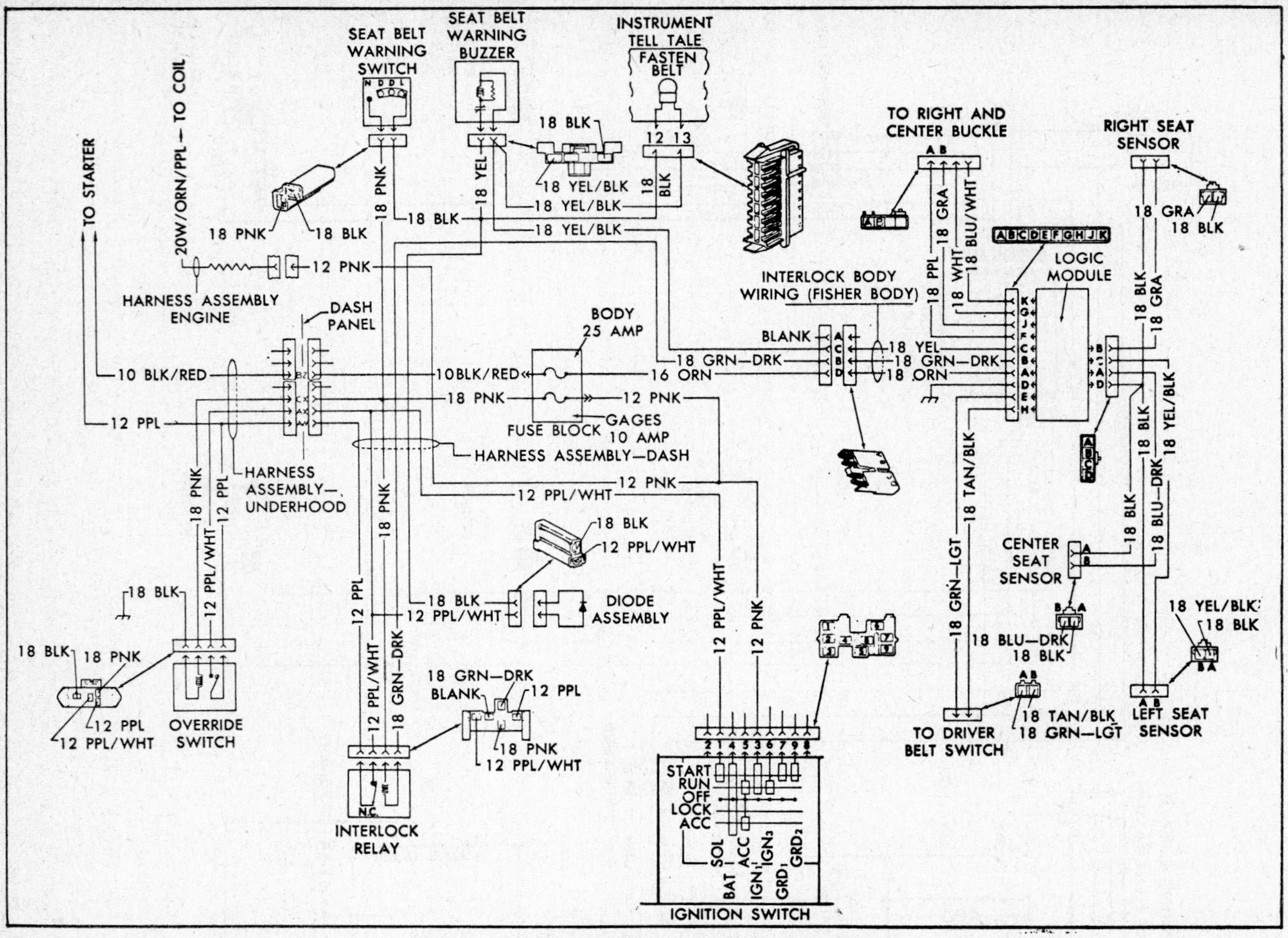

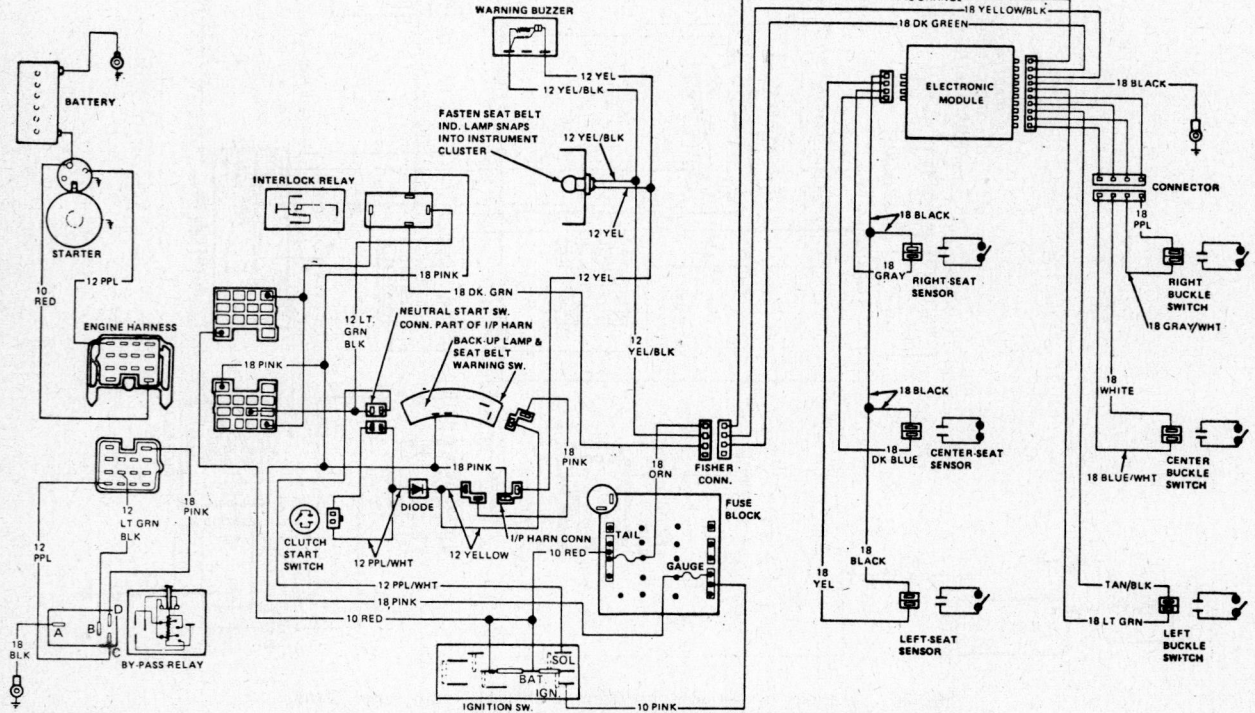

Fig. 37 Interlock system wiring diagram. Cadillac

Fig. 40 Interlock system wiring diagram. Ventura with Auto. Trans.

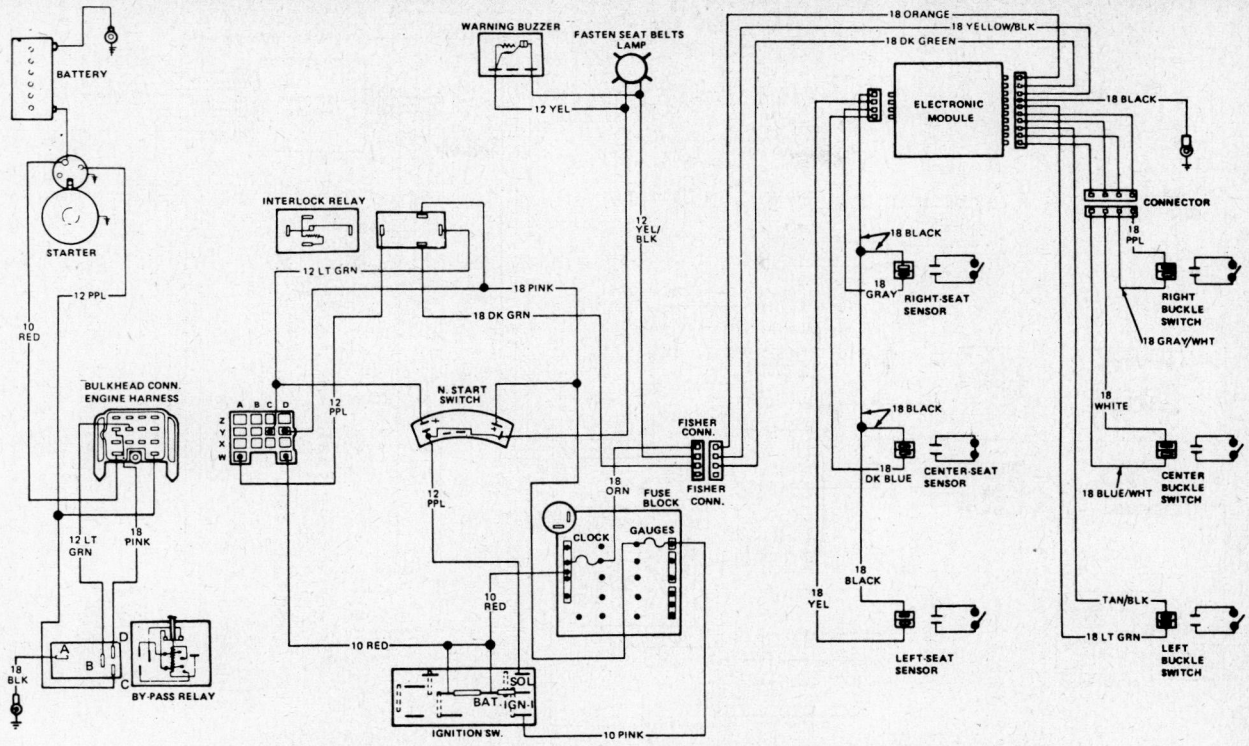

Fig. 38 Interlock system wiring diagram. All Pontiac Auto. Trans. exc. Ventura

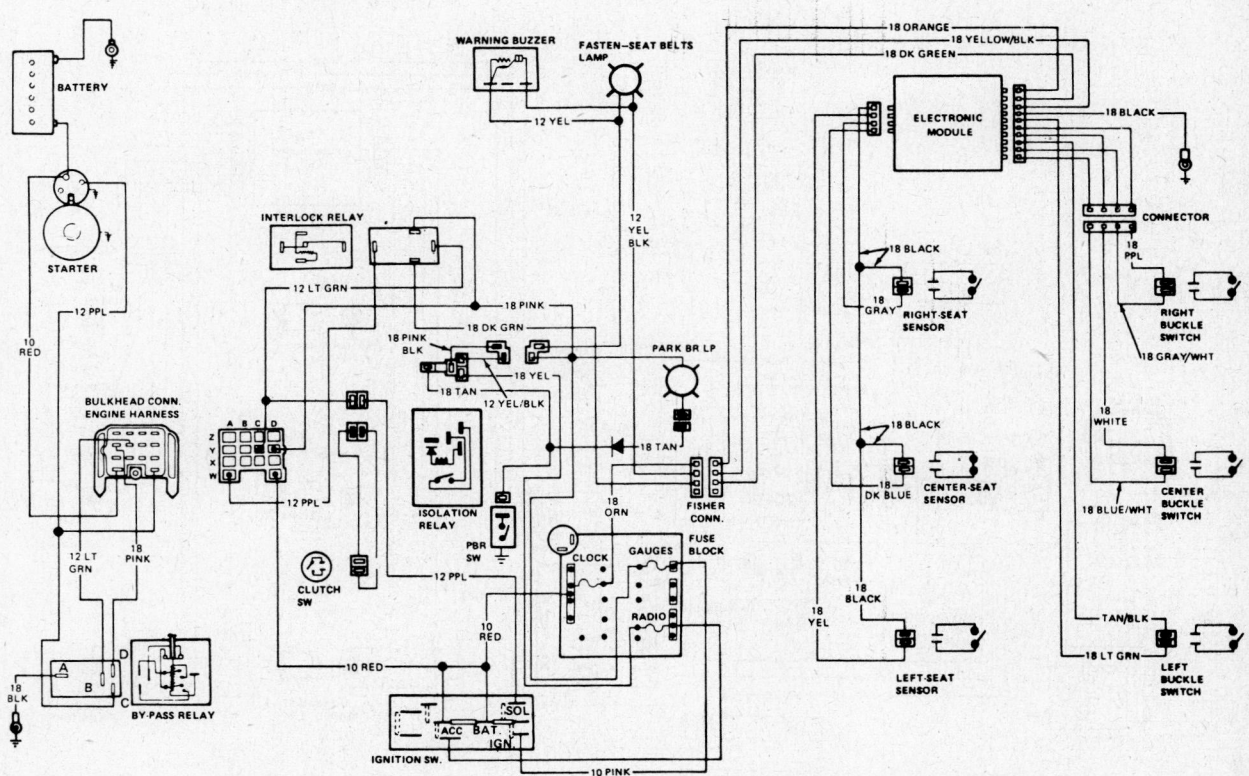

Fig. 39 Interlock system wiring diagram. All Pontiac Manual Trans. exc. Ventura

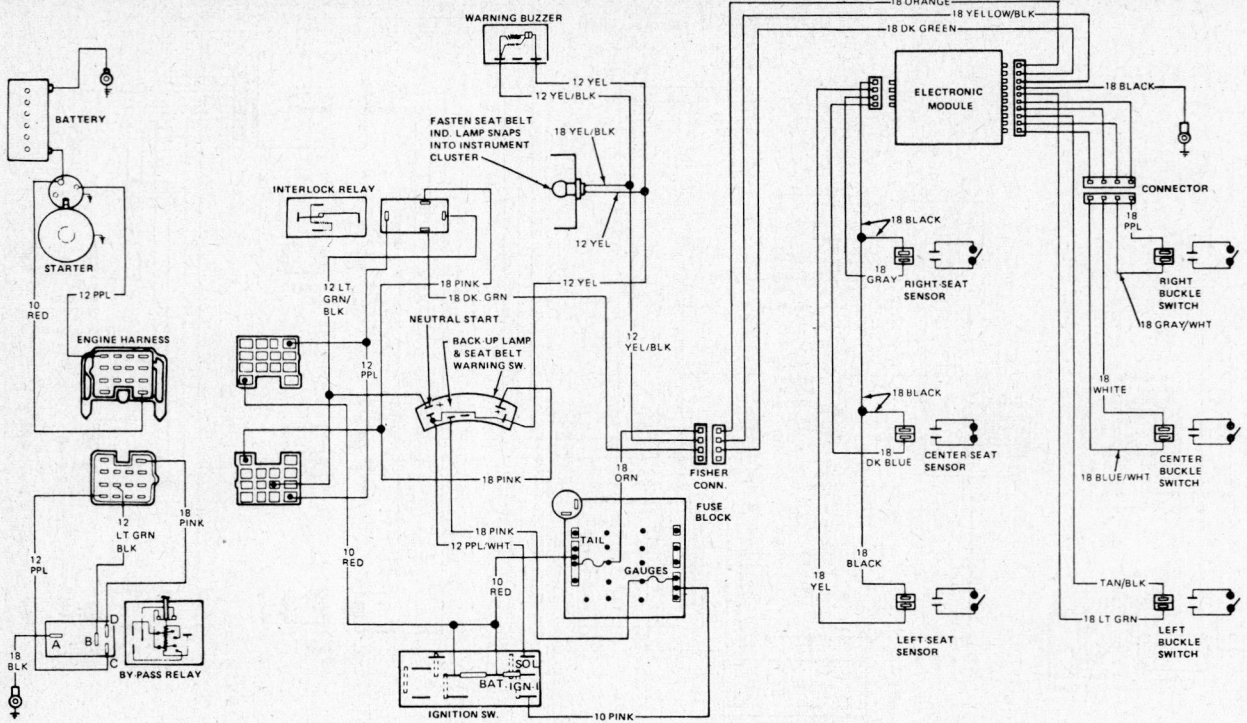

Fig. 41 Interlock system wiring diagram. Ventura with Column Shift & Manual Trans.

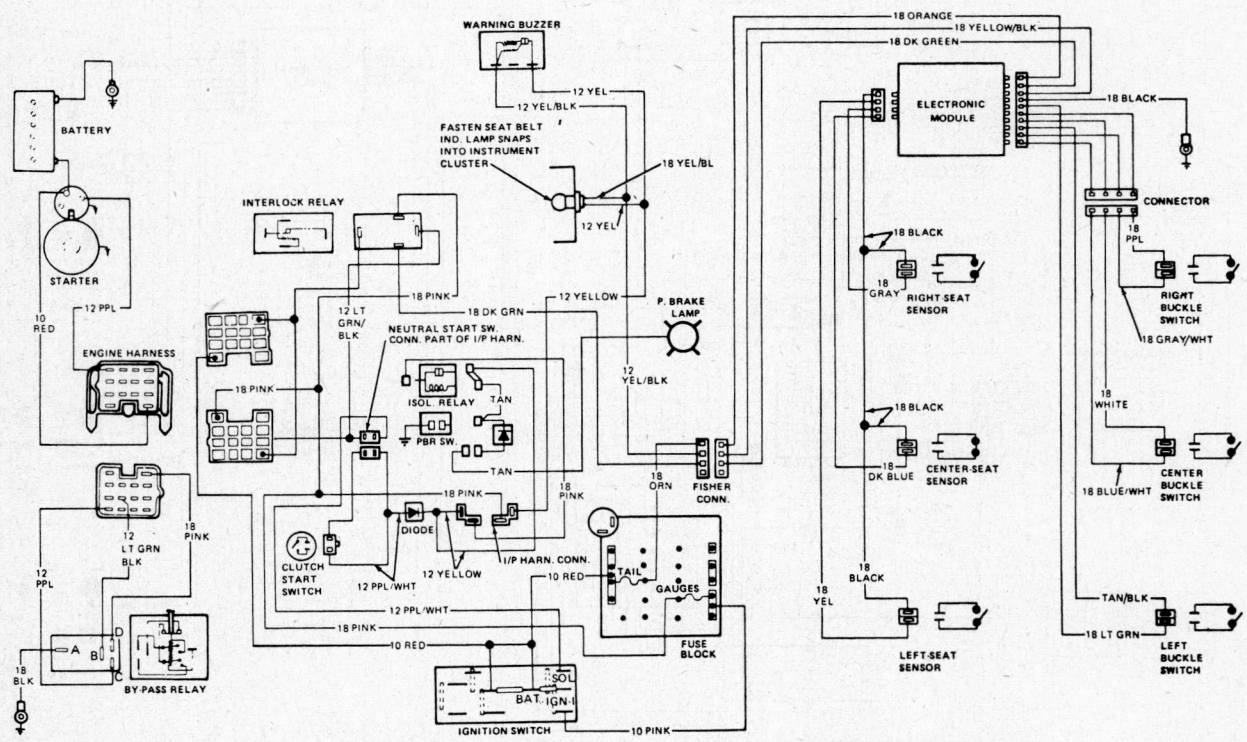

Fig. 42 Interlock system wiring diagram. Ventura with Floor Shift & Manual Trans.

AIR CUSHION RESTRAINT SYSTEMS

GENERAL MOTORS

The Air Cushion Restraint System is designed to deploy for all front seat occupants when the vehicle is involved in a front end accident situation of sufficient force, up to 30° off the center line of the car. Injury reduction is provided through the use of inflatable air cushion assemblies, which are deployed to restrain the occupants, when an accident is sensed by the crash sensing mechanisms.

The complete system, Fig. 1, consists of the following components: The Driver System, Passenger(s) System, Sensing Mechanisms and the Diagnostic System.

Operation

Driver System

The driver system consists of an air cushion and inflator assembly which is stored in the steering wheel hub area and covered by a vinyl trim cover, Fig. 2.

When an accident signal is sensed by the sensing mechanisms, the air cushion is deployed by a gas producing generator that inflates the driver cushion, Fig. 2. The trim cover opens at predetermined rupture seams as the system is deployed.

A knee restraint energy absorbing pad and a telescoping steering column complete the driver protection system.

Passenger(s) System

The passenger(s) system consists of an inflator, air cushions and trim cover. The system is positioned low on the instrument panel and to the right of the centerline of the car. This portion of the system provides protection for the right and center front passengers. It is positioned behind a vinyl-skinned, foam trim cover that opens when the system is deployed.

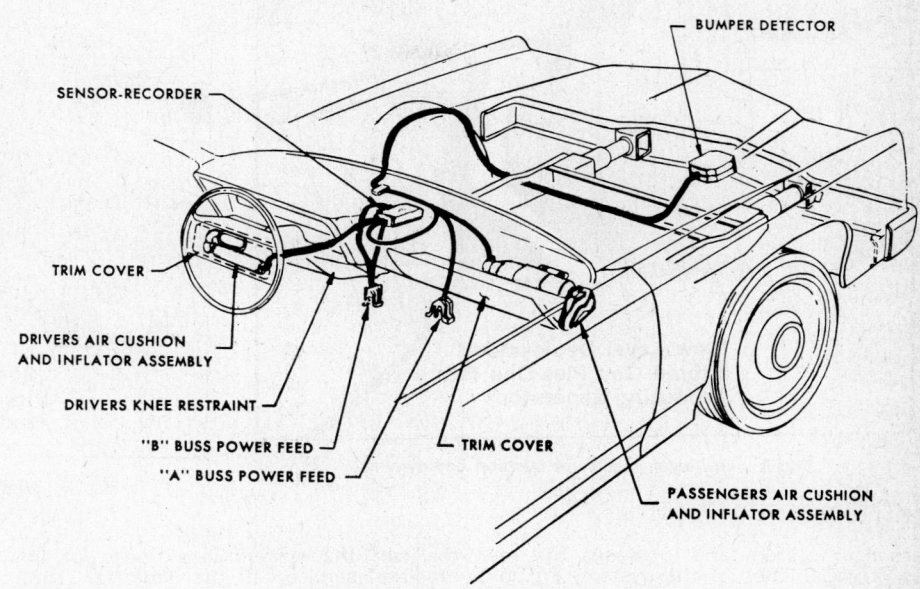

Fig. 1   Air Cushion Restraint System

When a signal is received from the crash sensing mechanisms, stored gas and gas producing generators are used to inflate the air cushion assembly, Fig. 3.

Sensing Mechanisms

The system incorporates two devices to control the deployment of the driver and passenger systems, a bumper impulse detector and a passenger compartment crash sensor.

The bumper impulse detector and/or passenger compartment sensor detects "low-level" front end impacts equal to a 12-18 miles per hour barrier crash early in the accident sequence. When a "low-level" crash signal is received, the driver system is deployed, Fig. 2, and the stored gas in the passenger system inflator assembly is released and one of the two gas producing generators is activated to produce "low-level" deployment of the passenger system, Fig. 4.

The passenger compartment sensor also detects "high-level" front end impacts equivalent to an 18 miles per hour, or greater, barrier crash. It activates a second gas producing generator in the

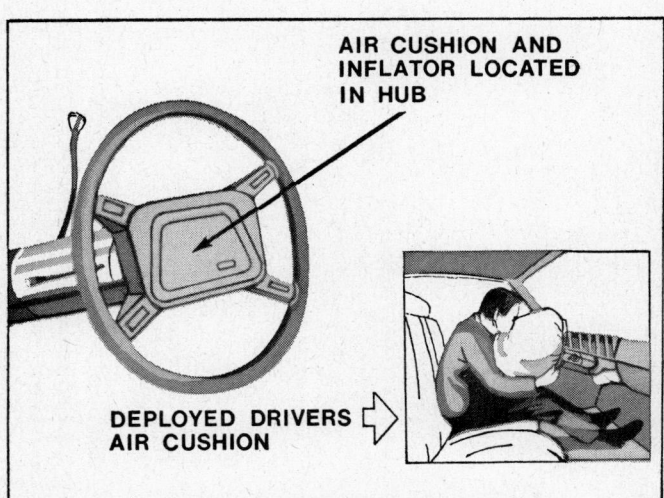

Fig. 2   Driver air cushion deployed

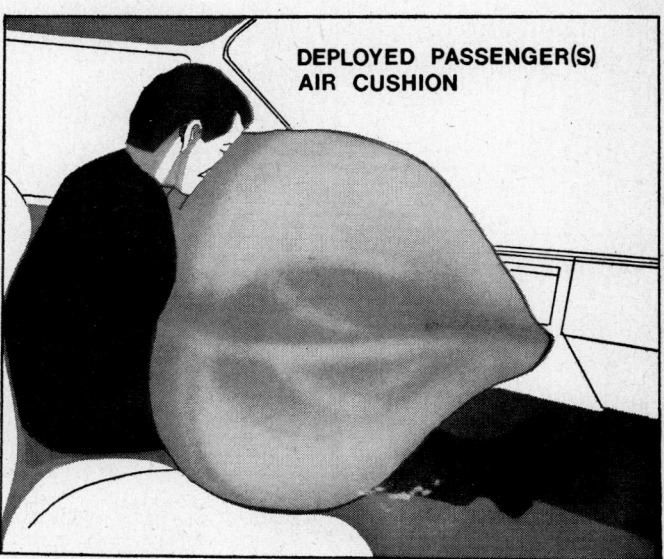

Fig. 3   Passenger air cushion deployed

"Low Level Deployment"
(Stored Gas Plus One Gas
Producing Generator"

Fig. 4   Low-level passenger cushion deployment

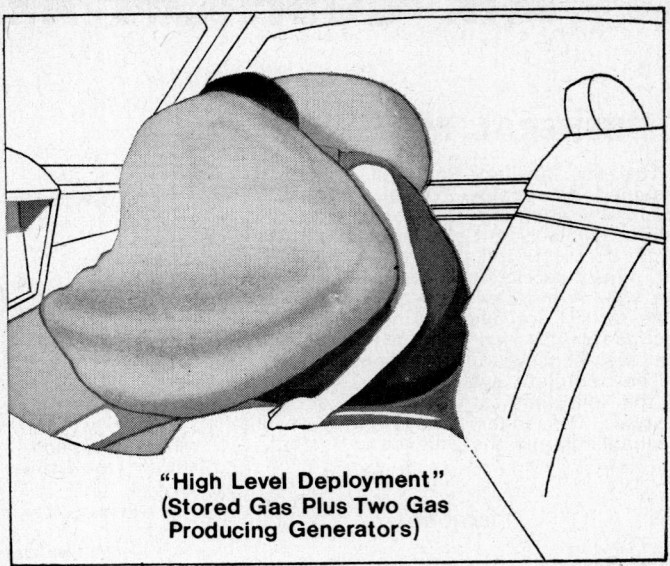

"High Level Deployment"
(Stored Gas Plus Two Gas
Producing Generators)

Fig. 5   High-level passenger cushion deployment

passenger system and increases the restraint capabilities of the system, Fig. 5.

Diagnostic System

The complete Air Cushion Restraint System has an integral electronic diagnostic system, which monitors the systems electrical circuits. It indicates to the driver that the system is either operating properly or is in need of immediate service. This is accomplished by an indicator lamp located on the instrument panel that lights when the ignition switch is first turned "ON".

If the indicator lamp does not light when the ignition switch is first turned "ON," remains lighted after 3-9 seconds, or comes on intermittently when driving the car, the system is in need of immediate service. If the indicator lamp comes on when the ignition switch is first turned "ON," and goes out after 3-9 seconds the system is functioning properly.

Service

WARNING: Do not attempt any servicing or disconnecting of the Air Cushion Restraint System instrument panel, instrument panel components or any other electrical components in the adjacent area, until the negative cable has been disconnected from the battery and the terminal end of the cable taped. This procedure must be followed to prevent accidental deployment of the system which could result in personal injury and/or damage to the system components. In addition, care must be exercised to never strike the sensing mechanisms in a manner which could cause inadvertent deployment or improper operation of the system.

A special tester, J-24628, with substitute loads is used to check the Air Cushion Restraint System to determine whether or not a specific part or the entire system is functioning properly. Therefore, any service by other than properly trained personnel, should not be attempted.

FUEL PUMPS

NOTE: Fuel pump pressures are listed in car chapters.

MECHANICAL FUEL PUMP FIG. 1

Operation

During the suction stroke, the rotation of the camshaft eccentric moves the pump rocker arm which in turn pulls the diaphragm up, causing fuel to be drawn in through the one-way inlet valve. This suction also closes the outlet valve. During the return stroke, the diaphragm is forced down by the diaphragm spring. The resulting fuel pressure opens the outlet valve and closes the inlet valve. Fuel is then forced out through the outlet valve to the carburetor.

Fuel Pump Performance

It is essential that the fuel pump deliver sufficient fuel to supply the requirements of the engine under all operating conditions and that it maintain sufficient pressure in the line between the pump and carburetor to keep the fuel from boiling and to prevent vapor lock.

Excessive fuel pump pressure holds the carburetor float needle valve off its seat, causing high gasoline level in the float chamber which in turn increases gasoline consumption.

The pump usually delivers a minimum of ten gallons of gasoline per hour at top engine speeds, under an operating pressure of from 2 to 6 psi. The highest operating pressure will be attained at idling speed and the lowest at top speed.

Fuel Pump Tests

The fuel pump can be tested on the car with a pressure gauge, a hose and a pint measuring can. With this equipment, it is possible to check the fuel pump to see if it is delivering the proper amount of gasoline at the correct pressure.

Pressure Test

To make the pressure test, disconnect the fuel pipe at the carburetor inlet and attach the pressure gauge and hose between the carburetor inlet and the disconnected fuel pipe, Fig. 3. Take the pressure reading with the engine running. The pressure should be within the limits given in the *Tune Up* chart in each car chapter, depending on the pump model and the car on which it is installed. The pressure should remain constant or return very slowly to zero when the engine is stopped.

Capacity Test

To make this test, connect the hose so the pump will deliver gasoline into the pint measure held at carburetor level. Run the engine at idle speed and note the time it takes to fill the measure. On the average it should take from 20 to

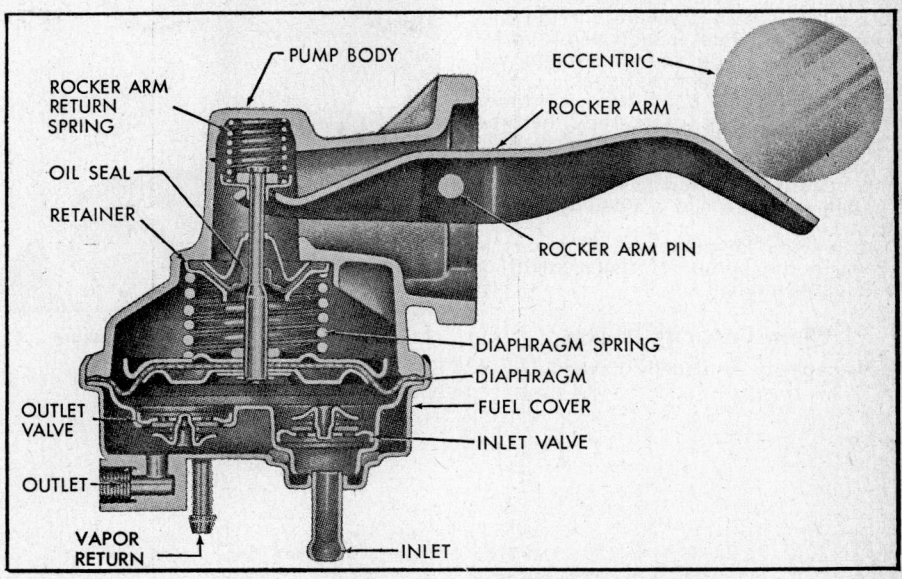

Fig. 1 Single action mechanical fuel pump. Typical

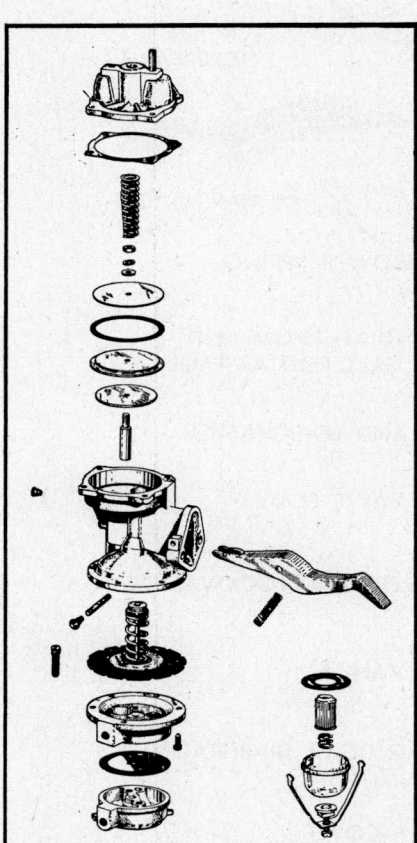

Fig. 2 1969-71 American Motors double action (combination) pump. Exploded

30 seconds, depending on the pump tested.

When Pressure Is Low

Low pressure indicates extreme wear on one part, small wear on all parts, ruptured diaphragm, dirty valve or gummy valve seat.

Wear in the pump usually occurs at the rocker arm pivot pin and on the contacting surfaces of the rocker arm and links. Due to the leverage design, wear at these points is multiplied five times in the movement of the diaphragm. It is apparent therefore, that very little wear will materially reduce the stroke of the diaphragm. The worn parts must be replaced for a satisfactory correction.

The diaphragm pull rod has an oil seal around it which prevents the hot oil vapors from the crankcase coming in contact with the diaphragm. If this seal is damaged, the oil vapors have a tendency to shorten the life of the diaphragm.

The first three conditions—extreme wear on one part, small wear on all parts, and ruptured diaphragm—are brought about by usage, while dirty and/or poor fuel is sually the cause of valve trouble.

When Pressure Is High

High pressure is caused by a tight diaphragm, fuel between diaphragm layers, diaphragm spring too strong, pump link frozen to rocker arm.

A tight diaphragm will stretch slightly on the down stroke. As the pump operates, the diaphragm will rebound on the up stroke beyond its normal position, much as a stretched rubber band when it is suddenly released. This rebound will cause a higher than normal pressure in the pump chamber.

A loose diaphragm retainer nut or poor riveting on the diaphragm assembly may allow fuel to seep between the diaphragm lavers. This will cause a bulge in the diaphragm and have the same effect as a diaphragm that is too tight.

A diaphragm spring that is too strong also causes a high pressure for the diaphragm will operate longer before pressure of the fuel on the diaphragm will overcome the diaphragm spring.

On a combination pump there are times when the operating parts may become badly corroded and the links freeze to the rocker arm. In this condition the pump operates continually, resulting in a very high pressure and a flooding carburetor.

The remedy for all these conditions is to remove the pump for replacement or repair, using a repair kit.

When Capacity Is Low

Low capacity is usually caused by an

Fig. 3   Testing fuel pump pressure

air leak in the intake pipe at these points: fuel pipe fitting at pump, bowl flange or diaphragm flange, fuel bowl. (It is assumed that the conditions of too little fuel have already been checked and the pump is the cause of the difficulty.)

An air leak at fuel pipe fittings indicates either poor installation of pump or a defective fitting. The fitting should be tightened or replaced.

A leak at the diaphragm flange may be caused by a warped cover casting, loose diaphragm cover screws or foreign material between cover casting and diaphragm.

A leak at the bowl flange of the cover casting can usually be corrected by the installation of an extra gasket. A warped top cover indicates that the pump must be replaced.

A chipped glass or bent metal bowl may cause a leak at the bowl flange as may a defective gasket or foreign material between gasket and bowl or cover casting. A chipped glass bowl must be replaced while a dented metal bowl can be straightened.

Fuel Pump Service

NOTE: Most modern fuel pumps are sealed, non-serviceable units. These pumps cannot be repaired and must be replaced as units.

Illustrated are representative fuel pumps among the many serviceable models that have been produced. Before disassembling any pump, scribe a mark across the housings in such a manner that they may be reassembled with inlet and outlet fitting holes in correct location.

When disassembled, clean all parts (except diaphragms) in solvent and blow dry with compressed air. Examine the diaphragm for cracks, torn screws holes or ruptures. If deteriorated, install new diaphragm and pull rod assembly. Check the strainer screen and if found to be corroded or clogged, install a new screen. Check the rocker arm for wear or scoring on that portion that contacts the camshaft eccentric. If arm is scored or worn install a new one.

When reassembling a pump, do not use shellac or other adhesive on a diaphragm.

ELECTRIC FUEL PUMP
1969-70 Buick Riviera

These models have a turbine type electric pump located at the lower end of the fuel pick-up pipe in the bottom of the tank, Fig. 5. This pump is controlled by a switch located near the oil filter and hydraulically connected to the engine oil system so engine oil pressure controls the switch.

Operation

During cranking, current is taken from the starter solenoid and supplied to the pump as long as the starter is energized and oil pressure remains below 3 psi.

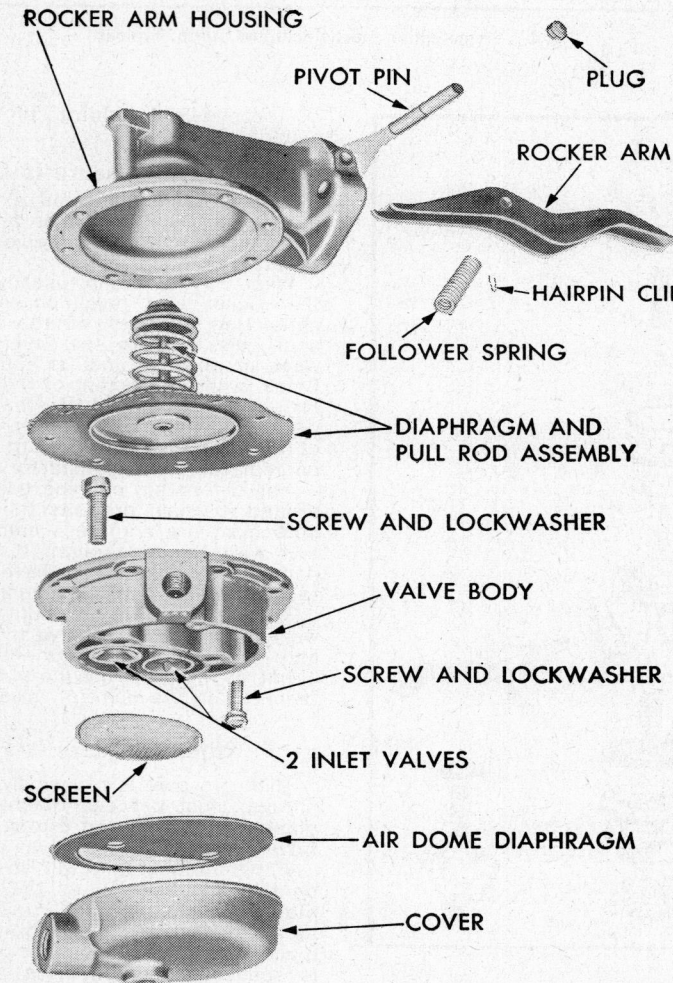

ROCKER ARM HOUSING
PIVOT PIN
PLUG
ROCKER ARM
HAIRPIN CLIP
FOLLOWER SPRING
DIAPHRAGM AND PULL ROD ASSEMBLY
SCREW AND LOCKWASHER
VALVE BODY
SCREW AND LOCKWASHER
2 INLET VALVES
SCREEN
AIR DOME DIAPHRAGM
COVER

Fig. 4   Carter fuel pump 1969-71 Police Interceptor

With the ignition switch in the run position and the engine oil pressure above 3 psi, current is supplied to the pump through another set of contacts in the control switch. If oil pressure drops below 3 psi with the ignition switch in the run position, the control switch opens the current, shutting off the pump.

Fuel Pump Test

1. Turn ignition switch on and be sure oil and generator lights are lit. If not, check fuse.
2. Make sure oil light goes out while cranking engine. If not, remove fuse from in-line holder just above master cylinder and replace with a new 4 amp ⅝" fuse.
3. Disconnect fuel hose from steel pipe and install pressure gauge. With engine idling, minimum pressure is 4½ psi.
4. Insert fuel hose in a suitable container. With engine idling, a pint measure should be filled in 30 seconds.
5. If pressure is low, check voltage at tank connector. If voltage is satisfactory and ground is clean and tight, pump is defective. If only fuel flow is low, check for kinked hoses or lines.
6. If no fuel flow, unplug connector from oil pressure switch and check for current at one of the parallel slots of connector.
7. If current is present at one of the slots, connect a jumper wire between the two slots and again check for flow.
8. If still no fuel flow, raise car and check fuel tank connector for current. If current is present and ground connection is clean and tight, disconnect fuel line at tank and check for fuel flow, check for kinked lines and hoses. If no fuel flow, remove pump.

1971-74 Vega

An electric fuel pump is located in the fuel tank and is an integral part of the tank unit assembly, which includes the fuel gauge metering unit. Since no repairs can be performed on the pump it must be replaced if found faulty.

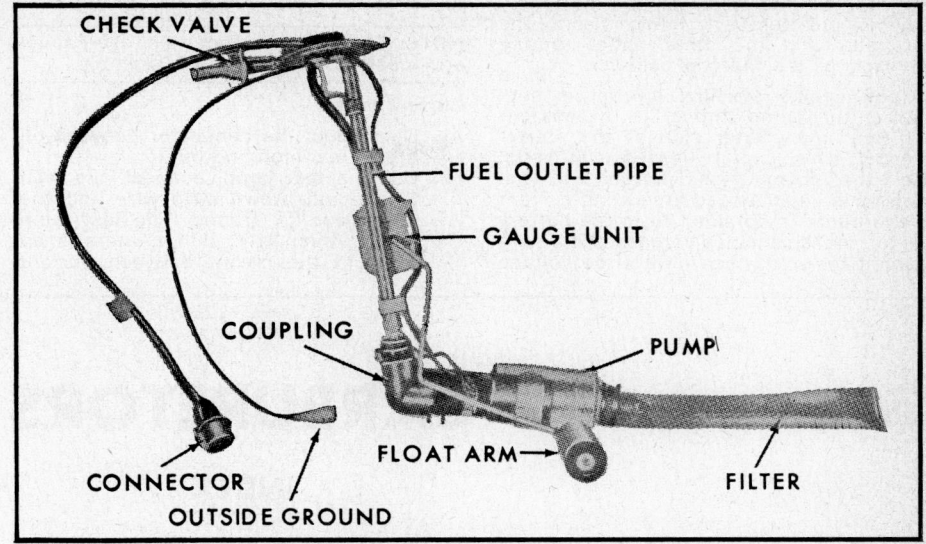

Fig. 5   Electric fuel pump and gauge tank unit assembly. 1969-70 Riviera

Operation

The fuel pump is energized when the ignition switch is in the start position. After the engine starts, the pump receives current through the oil pressure switch as long as there is about 2 pounds of oil pressure. If, for any reason, the oil pressure drops below 2 pounds the contact is broken at the pressure switch and the pump is deactivated.

Fuel Pump Test

NOTE: Operating the pump for more than 30 seconds will seriously damage the motor unless submerged in gasoline.

The following checks should be made:
1. Check fuel flow.
2. Check for proper ground and voltage at the pump.
3. If there is no current at the tank, it will be necessary to check back to the source.

4. If there is fuel flow on the cranking cycle but not when the engine runs, jump the oil pressure switch. If this provides fuel flow, replace the switch.

1972 Imperial w/Air Injection Pump

The pump used on these models is the Bendix solenoid type, Fig. 6. It is mounted in-line and has a variable output feature controlled by engine demand. To prevent the pump from being powered when it is not needed it receives power through the starting relay when the ignition switch is in start position and through the oil pressure switch when the ignition switch is in run position. Therefore the only times the pump runs is during engine start and when the engine is running and has oil pressure.

The bottom of the pump is apparently removable but there is no reason to remove it since this installation has no filter inside it. There is no service to the pump. If it becomes inoperable it is to be replaced.

The pump is located on the left side of the frame in the kick up area about even with the front of the fuel tank. The pump must be mounted so that the outlet is higher than the inlet.

Pump Test

Should the pump fail to produce fuel or produce insufficient fuel, check the following:
1. Vent in tank restricted (this might also cause tank to collapse).
2. Leaks in fuel line or fittings.
3. Dirt or restriction in tank.
4. Restricted fuel filter.
5. Frozen fuel lines.
6. Defective oil pressure switch.
7. Shorted or open wiring.

1972-74 Ford

An electric fuel pump, located in the fuel tank, is used on 1972 429 and 1973-74 460 Police Interceptor vehicles. The fuel is passed through a filter before entering the pump. A dual outlet vapor

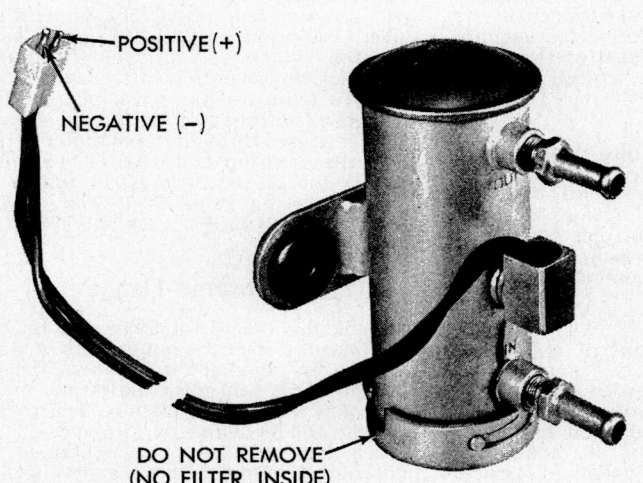

Fig. 6   Electric fuel pump. 1972 Imperial

POSITIVE (+)

NEGATIVE (−)

DO NOT REMOVE
(NO FILTER INSIDE)

separator in the head of the assembly with one outlet routing liquid fuel to the carburetor and the other outlet routing fuel vapor to the charcoal canister.

Upon engine starting. current is supplied to the pump through a by-pass circuit from the starter side of the starter solenoid, this circuit delivers 12 volts. After the engine has started and the solenoid is de-energized, operating current for the pump is obtained from the battery side of the solenoid and passed through a circuit resistor which lowers the voltage

to 8.5 to 10 volts.

NOTE: This pump cannot be overhauled and must be serviced as an assembly.

Current Test

1. Disconnect the connector between oil pressure switch and pump.
2. Using a test lamp, connect one lead to the red/brown strip wire and the other lead to ground. The test lamp should then light, if not, there is an open in the circuit between current

source on either side of starter solenoid and fuel pump.

Pressure & Volume Tests

When performing pressure and volume tests on this pump, it is necessary to provide the pump with the full 12 volts. Connect a jumper wire between the battery side of the starter solenoid and the by-pass circuit pigtail. Pressure for this pump should be 4 PSI minimum and pump should deliver one pint of fuel in 20 seconds.

CARBURETORS

INDEX

PAGE NO.		PAGE NO.		PAGE NO.		PAGE NO.

CARTER MODELS

AFB Adjustments	2-411
Specifications	2-410
AVS Adjustments	2-405
Specifications	2-403
BBD Adjustments	2-393
Specifications	2-391
BBS Adjustments	2-383
Specifications	2-382
Quadra-Jet	see Rochester
RBS Adjustments	2-387
Specifications	2-386
TQ Adjustments	2-416
Specifications	2-415
WCD Adjustments	2-400
Specifications	2-398
WGD Adjustments	2-401
Specifications	2-401
YF Adjustments	2-378
Specifications	2-375

FORD MODELS

1100-1V Adjustments	2-424
Specifications	2-424
1250-1V Adjustments	2-422
Specifications	2-422
1940-1V Adjustments	2-430
Specifications	2-430
2100-2V Adjustments	2-436
Specifications	2-433
4100-4V Adjustments	2-436
Specifications	2-435
4300-4V Adjustments	2-446
Specifications	2-444
5200-2V Adjustments	2-452
Specifications	2-451
6200-2V Adjustments	2-436
Specifications	2-433

HOLLEY MODELS

1920 Adjustments	2-490
Specifications	2-487
1931 Adjustments	2-494
Specifications	2-487
1945 Adjustments	2-495
Specifications	2-488
2210 Adjustments	2-498
Specifications	2-487
2245 Adjustments	2-498
Specifications	2-488
2300 Adjustments	2-501
Specifications	2-487
4150, 4160 Adjustments	2-507
Specifications	2-505
5210 Adjustments	2-515
Specifications	2-515

ROCHESTER MODELS

M, MV Adjustments	2-482
Specifications	2-479
2GC, 2GV Adjustments	2-461
Specifications	2-455
4MC, 4MV Adjustments	2-471
Specifications	2-464

CARBURETION

Since carburetion is dependent in several ways on both compression and ignition, it should always be checked last when tuning an engine. See the car chapter for adjustments for the unit you are interested in.

Before adjusting the carburetor, consider the factors outlined below and which definitely affect engine performance.

Performance Complaints

Flooding, flat spots or other performance complaints are often caused by dirt, or water in the carburetor. To aid in diagnosing the complaint, the carburetor should be carefully removed from the engine without draining the fuel from the bowl. The contents of the fuel bowl can then be examined for contamination as the carburetor is disassembled. A magnet moved through the fuel in the bowl will pick up any iron oxide dust that may have caused needle valve leakage.

Check float setting carefully. Too high a level will cause flooding while too low a level will starve the engine.

Before installing carburetor, fill the

bowl with clean fuel and operate the throttle by hand several times to visually check the discharge from pump jets.

Inspect gasketed surfaces between body and air horn. Small nicks or burrs should be smoothed down to eliminate air or fuel leakage. On carburetors having a vacuum piston, be especially particular when inspecting the top surface of the inner wall of the bowl around the vacuum piston passage. A poor seal at this location may contribute to a "cutting out" on turns complaint.

Dirty or Rusty Choke Housing

In cases where it is found that the interior of the choke housing is dirty, gummed or rusty while the carburetor itself is comparatively clean, look for a punctured or eroded manifold heat tube (if one is used).

Manifold Heat Control Valve

An engine equipped with a manifold heat control valve can operate with the valve stuck in either the open or closed position. Because of this, an inoperative valve is frequently overlooked at vehicle lubrication or tune-up.

A valve stuck in the "heat-off" posi-

tion can result in slow warm up, deposits in combustion chamber, carburetor icing, flat spots during acceleration, low gas mileage and spark plug fouling.

A valve stuck in the "heat-on" position can result in power loss, engine knocking, sticking or burned valves and spark plug burning.

To prevent the possibility of a stuck valve, check and lubricate the valve each time the vehicle is lubricated or tuned-up. Check the operation of the valve manually. To lubricate the valve, place a few drops of penetrating oil on the valve shaft where it passes through the manifold. Then move the valve up and down a few times to work the oil in. *Do not use engine oil to lubricate the valve as it will leave a residue which hampers valve operation.*

Carburetor Flange

Check the flange for looseness on the manifold. If one of the flange nuts is loose as little as one-half turn, a sufficient amount of air will enter the intake manifold below the throttle plate to destroy engine idle and all engine performance.

If a tight fit cannot be obtained by tightening the nuts, install a new gasket but be sure that all the old gasket material has been removed.

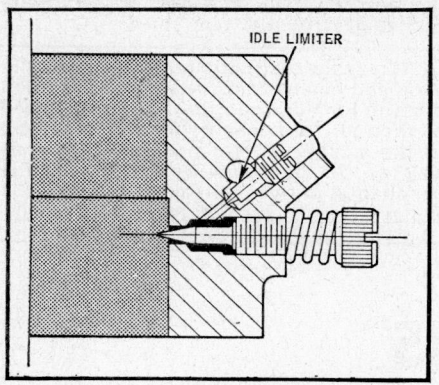

Internal idle mixture limiter

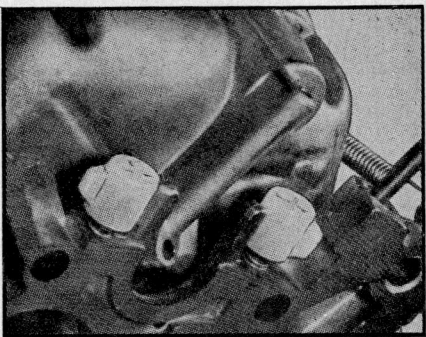

External idle mixture limiter

any accessories which may be connected to the manifold. All such joints should be tested for leaks.

To test the intake manifold for leaks, apply oil from an oil can along the gasket joints with the engine idling. An air leak is indicated when oil is drawn past the gaskets by the suction of the engine. Tighten the nuts or cap screws holding the manifold to the engine and retest for leaks. If tightening fails to stop the leaks, replace the manifold gaskets. If the new gaskets fail to stop the leaks, carefully inspect the manifold for cracks and test any suspicious area with oil.

Throttle Linkage

If the throttle linkage is adjusted so that the accelerator pedal will strike the floor board before the throttle plate is wide open, it will result in low top speed.

Fuel Lines

A restriction of the fuel line will result in an apparent vapor lock action or a definite cut-off of gasoline. This can generally be corrected by blowing out the line with compressed air. In some cases, it may be necessary to replace the line.

Fuel Pump

The pump should be tested to make sure that it will draw an adequate supply of fuel from the tank and deliver it to the carburetor under all conditions of operation. If the pump functions inefficiently, proper adjustment and operation of the carburetor is impossible because the fuel will not be maintained at the prescribed level in the idle passages and main discharge jet (or jets) of the carburetor under all operating conditions.

Fuel Tank

The fuel tank should not be overlooked as a possible source of trouble with carburetion. A shortage of fuel at the fuel pump or carburetor may be caused by pieces of filling station pump hose or other material obstructing the mouth of the feed pipe in the tank, or by a restriction of the air vents in the filler cap and neck.

An unusual amount of dirt, water or gum in the fuel filter indicates that the tank is contaminated with these substances, which should be cleaned out to prevent future failure of the pump or carburetor.

Intake Manifold Leaks

Leakage of air into the intake manifold at any point will affect carburetion and general engine performance. Air may leak into the manifold through the joints at the carburetor or cylinder head, cracks in the manifold, cracks or poor connections in the windshield wiper or windshield washer hose lines, or the connections of

Air Cleaner

An air cleaner with a dirty element, will restrict the air flow through the carburetor and cause a rich mixture at high speeds. In such a condition the air cleaner likewise will not properly remove dirt from the air, and the dirt entering the engine will cause rapid formation of carbon, sticking valves, and wear of piston rings and cylinder bores.

Automatic Choke

The choke mechanism must be inspected and cleaned to make sure it is operating freely. Sluggish action or sticking of the choke will cause excessive fuel consumption, poor performance during warm-up, and possibly hard starting.

The choke thermostat should be set in accordance with the average air temperature as well as the volatility of the fuel being used. It is desirable to have the thermostat set as lean as operating conditions permit in order to avoid an over-rich mixture during engine warm up.

Choke Thermostat

If necessary to adjust the choke more than two marks from the specified setting, either rich or lean, it indicates that the thermostat spring may be bent or has lost its tension.

Carter Float Settings

When replacing a solid float needle and seat with the new type resilient seat, the float setting should be reduced $1/32"$ on AFB, WCFB, WGD and WCD carburetors.

Carburetor Ball Checks

Whenever it becomes necessary to dismantle a carburetor be sure to account for the ball checks that may be found under pump plungers and compensating or power valves.

CARBURETOR IDLE ADJUST

Cars Without Exhaust Emission Controls

There are two basic types of exhaust

emission control systems—air injection type and engine modification type. With both types, the slow idle adjustment method, referred to as "Lean Roll" is to be used. This method insures proper idle, ignition timing and mixture settings for greatest possible exhaust emission reduction and proper engine operation. It should be noted here that smooth idle is extremely sensitive to vacuum leaks. If rough idle is noted, check for vacuum leaks at the carburetor, manifold, etc.

Carburetor Idle Limiters

Some carburetors are equipped with idle adjustment limiters which restrict the maximum idle richness of the air/fuel mixture and prevents overly rich adjustments. There are two types of idle limiters: internal and external (see illustrations). The internal needle limiter is located in the idle channel and is not visible externally. This limiter is set and sealed at the factory and, under no circumstances, during normal service or during overhaul, should the seal be removed and adjustments made to this needle.

The other type of idle limiter is an external idle limiter cap installed on the knurled head of the idle mixture adjusting screw. Any adjustment to the idle fuel mixture on carburetors with this type of limiter must be made within the range of the limiter cap.

Under no circumstances may the limiter cap, the stop boss or the power valve cover, which the limiter caps stop against, be mutilated or deformed in any way to render the limiter inoperative. A satisfactory idle is obtainable within the range of the limiter cap.

The addition of idle limiters does not eliminate the need for adjusting idle speed and mixture. All the limiters do is prevent overly rich mixtures, which increase the amount of hydro-carbons emitted into the atmosphere.

1. With engine at operating temperature, set parking brake and block drive wheels.
2. Make sure choke valve is wide open.
3. On C.C.S. equipped vehicles, see that the air cleaner thermostatic valve is open.
4. On carburetors so equipped, hold hot idle compensator hole closed with eraser on pencil.
5. Turn air conditioner off or on according to directions given in *Tune Up Charts* in car chapters.

6. Set idle mixture screw(s) for maximum idle rpm.
7. Adjust speed screw (or idle stop solenoid screw on C.C.S.) to obtain the specified rpm in Drive or Neutral as specified.
8. Set ignition timing according to specifications with vacuum advance line disconnected and hole in manifold plugged.
9. Adjust mixture screw IN to obtain

10. Adjust mixture screw OUT ¼ turn.
11. Repeat Steps 9 and 10 for second mixture screw (2 and 4 barrel carbs).
12. Readjust speed screw (or solenoid screw) if necessary to obtain specified rpm.
13. On C.C.S. with idle solenoid stop on carburetor, electrically disconnect solenoid and adjust carburetor idle speed screw to obtain 400 rpm in

a 20 rpm drop (lean roll).

neutral, then reconnect wire to solenoid.

NOTE: Exact instructions for each C.C.S. equipped engine-transmission combination is given for this Lean Roll (low idle) speed method on a decal permanently affixed to the vicinity of the radiator support as well as in the *Tune Up Charts* in the car chapter of this manual.

SERVICE BULLETINS

Carter Thermo-Quad

If a stumble or lag is encountered on acceleration on 1973 cars with V8-340, 400, 440 engines with a Carter Thermo-Quad carburetor, it may be caused by an undersize accelerating pump plunger cup. This can be verified by checking the discharge from the accelerating pump discharge jets.

If the condition is considered to be caused by a deficiency in the pump circuit, the plunger should be replaced. A kit #3780111 is available for this purpose and consists of a plunger and check valve seat. The seat must be replaced because it becomes damaged during removal of the plunger.

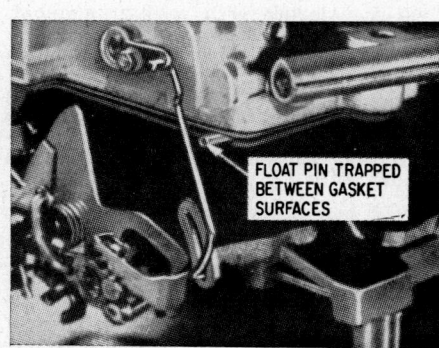

FLOAT PIN TRAPPED BETWEEN GASKET SURFACES

Fig. 1   Carter Thermo-quad float lever pins improperly placed

buretors. When this wrong substitution is made, vacuum leaks occur and cause rough idle due to air bypassing the primary throttle valves through the canister purge passage in he throttle body because the gasket will not seal this passage.

The difference between the throttle body to bowl gaskets is shown in Fig. 2.

Carter Thermo-Quad

When installing the bowl cover on Carter TQ carburetors, it is important that the float lever pins are correctly positioned (centered in their supports). If the pins are not properly placed, they may be trapped between the gasket surfaces. When the bowl cover screws are tightened, the bowl will crack, Fig. 1.

Rochester Quadrajet

Delco/Rochester advises the possibility exists that the wrong throttle body to float bowl gaskets are being used by servicemen on 1970 and later Quadrajet car-

UNSEALED CANISTER PURGE PASSAGE   SEALED CANISTER PURGE PASSAGE

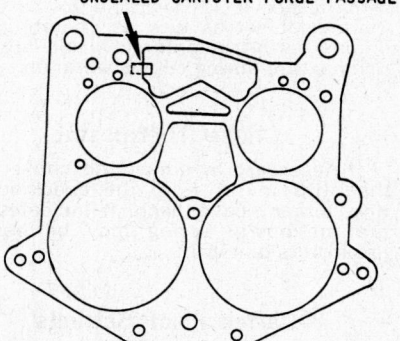 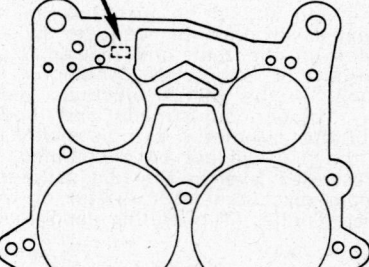

Fig. 2   Delco/Rochester Quadrajet throttle body to float bowl gaskets

Carter Carburetor Section

CARTER YF ADJUSTMENT SPECIFICATIONS

See Tune Up Chart in car chapter for hot idle speed.

Year	Carb. Model	Idle Mixture Screw Setting	Float Level	Float Drop	Idle Vent Setting	Fast Idle Cam Setting	Dechoke or Unloader Setting	Pulldown Setting	Vacuum Break Setting	Choke Setting
AMERICAN MOTORS										
1970	4767S	①	29/64	1¼	.052	2300 RPM	.300	—	—	Index
	4768S	①	29/64	1¼	.052	2300 RPM	.325	—	—	Index
	4769S	①	29/64	1¼	.055	2300 RPM	.300	—	—	Index
	4770S	①	29/64	1¼	.055	2300 RPM	.300	—	—	Index
	4978S	①	29/64	1¼	.055	2300 RPM	.300	—	—	1 Rich
1971	6038S	①	29/64	1¼	—	2300 RPM	.300	—	—	Index
	6093S	①	29/64	1¼	—	2300 RPM	.300	—	—	Index
	6094S	①	29/64	1¼	—	2300 RPM	.300	—	—	1 Rich
	6095S	①	29/64	1¼	—	2300 RPM	.300	—	—	Index
	6096S	①	29/64	1¼	—	2300 RPM	.300	—	—	1 Rich
1972	6199S	①	29/64	1¼	—	1600 RPM	.300	.230	—	Index
	6200S	①	29/64	1¼	—	1600 RPM	.300	.230	—	Index
	6202S	①	29/64	1¼	—	1600 RPM	.300	.230	—	Index
1973	6299S	①	29/64	1¼	—	1600 RPM	.275	.215	—	1 Rich
	6300S	①	29/64	1¼	—	1600 RPM	.275	.215	—	1 Rich
	6400S	①	29/64	1¼	—	1600 RPM	.275	.215	—	1 Rich
	6401S	①	29/64	1¼	—	1600 RPM	.275	.215	—	1 Rich
	6421S	①	29/64	1¼	—	1600 RPM	.275	.215	—	1 Rich
	6422S	①	29/64	1¼	—	1600 RPM	.275	.215	—	1 Rich
	6424	①	15/32	1⅜	—	1600 RPM	.275	.215	—	1 Rich
	6429	①	15/32	1⅜	—	1600 RPM	.275	.215	—	1 Rich
	6430	①	15/32	1⅜	—	1600 RPM	.275	.215	—	1 Rich
	6432	①	15/32	1⅜	—	1600 RPM	.275	.215	—	1 Rich
1973–74	6423	①	15/32	1⅜	—	.190	.275	.215	—	1 Rich
	6431	①	15/32	1⅜	—	.190	.275	.215	—	1 Rich
1974	6510	①	15/32	1⅜	—	.190	.275	.215	—	1 Rich
	5511	①	15/32	1⅜	—	.190	.275	.215	—	1 Rich
	7000	①	15/32	1⅜	—	.190	.275	.215	—	1 Rich
	7001	①	15/32	1⅜	—	.190	.275	.215	—	1 Rich
	7028	①	15/32	1⅜	—	.190	.275	.215	—	1 Rich
	7029	①	15/32	1⅜	—	.190	.275	.215	—	1 Rich
1975	7039	①	15/32	1⅜	—	.180②	.275	.205	—	1 Rich
	7041	①	15/32	1⅜	—	.180②	.275	.205	—	1 Rich
	7061	①	15/32	1⅜	—	.180②	.275	.205	—	1 Rich
	7062	①	15/32	1⅜	—	.180②	.275	.205	—	1 Rich
	7074	①	15/32	1⅜	—	.180②	.275	.205	—	1 Rich

①—Air/fuel ratio or idle CO% rating is found in Tune Up Specification tables in car chapters.
②—1600 RPM hot on 2nd step of cam with TCS solenoid & EGR disconnected.

FORD

Year	Carb. Model	Idle Mixture Screw Setting	Float Level	Float Drop	Idle Vent Setting	Fast Idle Cam Setting	Dechoke or Unloader Setting	Pulldown Setting	Vacuum Break Setting	Choke Setting
1969	C8AF-BF	②	7/32	1¼	—	.035	.280	.265	—	Index
	C8DF-G	②	7/32	1¼	—	.046	.280	.265	—	Index
	C8DF-H	②	7/32	1¼	—	.040	.280	.265	—	1 Lean
1970	D0AF-A	②	3/8	1¼	—	.029	.250	.225	—	Index
	D0AF-B	②	3/8	1¼	—	.025	.250	.225	—	1 Lean
	D0DF-L	②	3/8	1¼	—	.036	.250	.265	—	Index
	D0DF-M	②	3/8	1¼	—	.031	.250	.265	—	Index

Continued

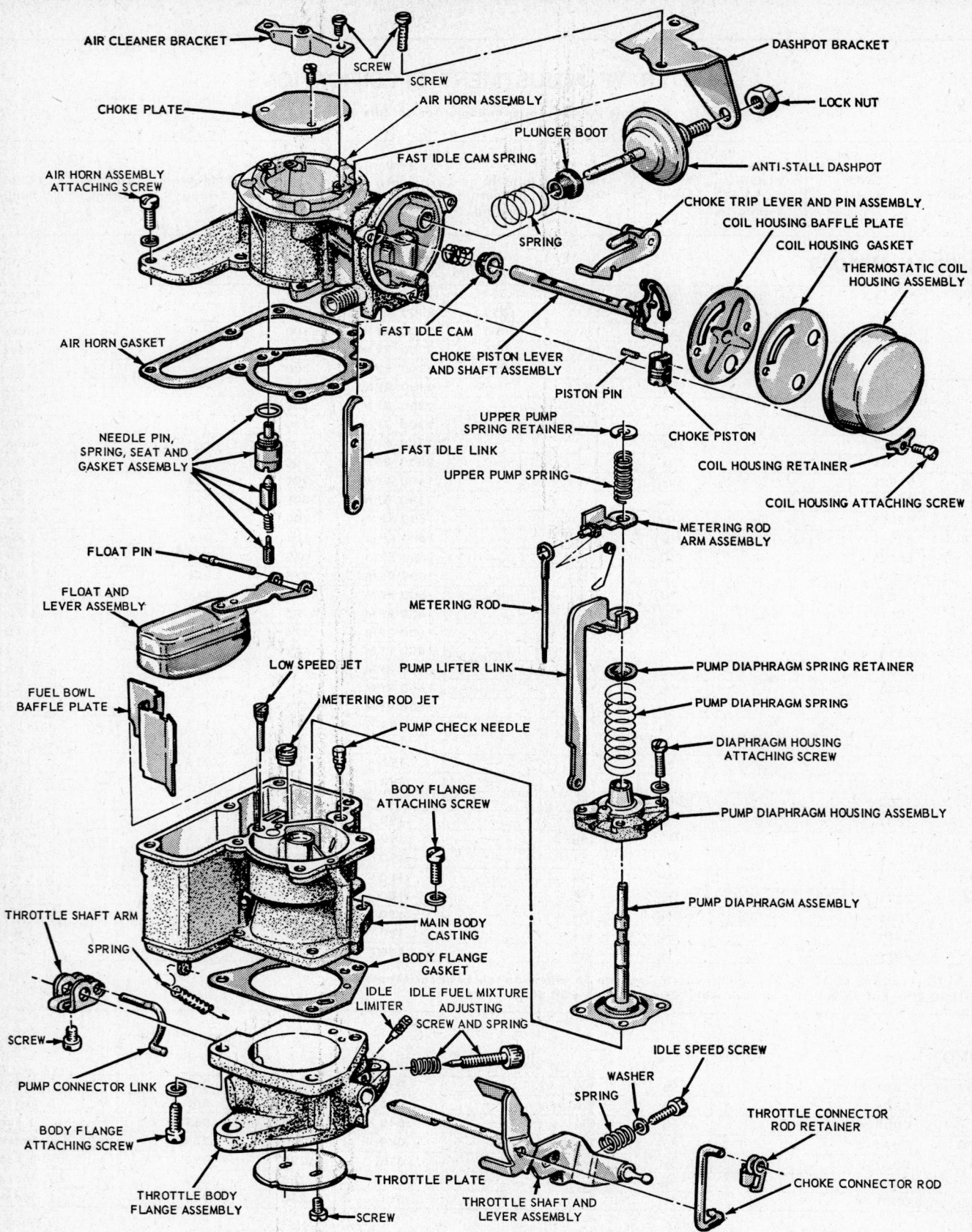

Fig. 1 Carter Model YF carburetor with built-in automatic choke. Note that this unit is provided with an idle limiter screw which is used to prevent an overly rich mixture on cars with exhaust emission control

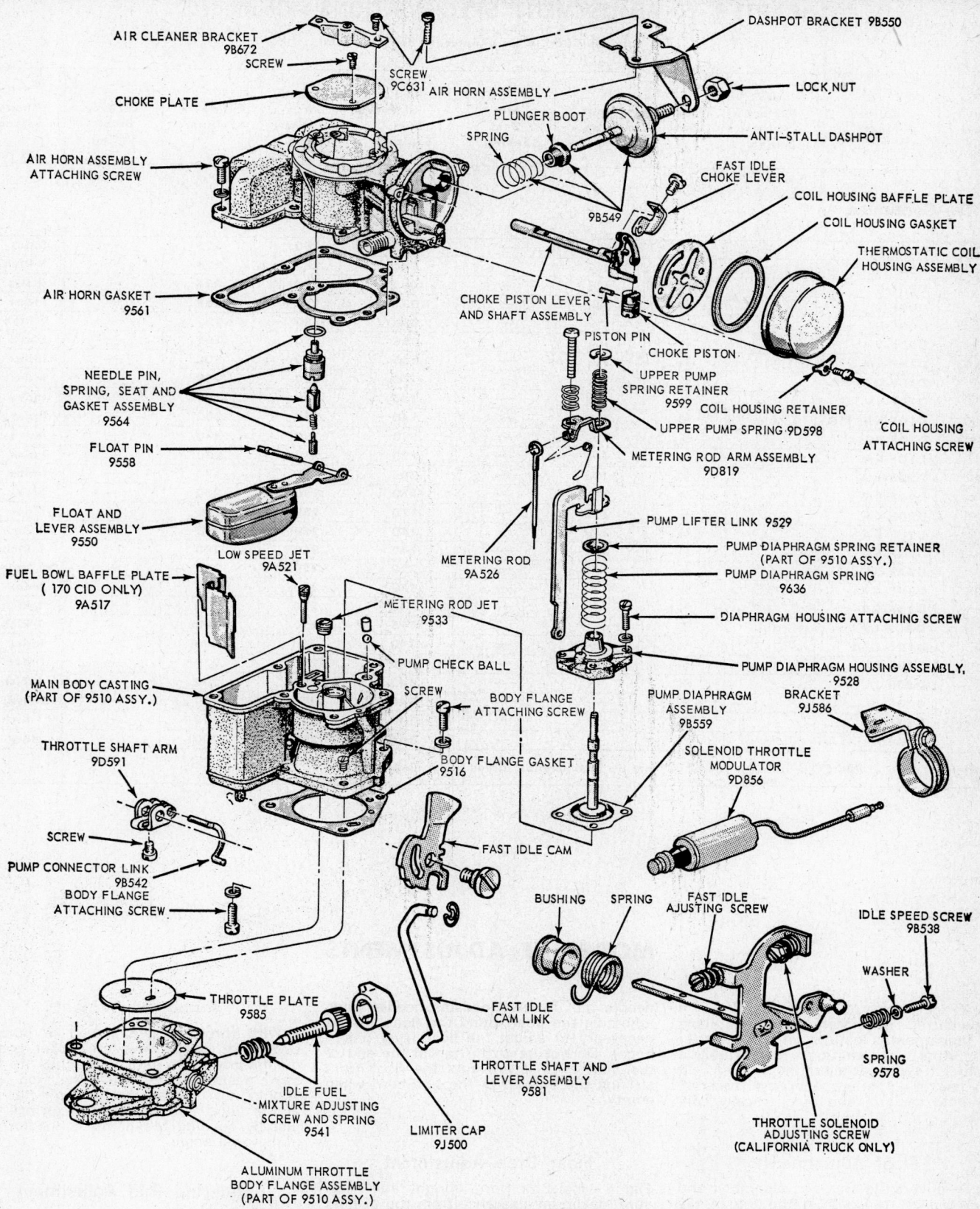

Fig. 1A Carter Model YF carburetor with built-in automatic choke. Note this unit uses an idle limiter cap and throttle positioner solenoid

CARTER CARBURETORS

Year	Carb. Model	Idle Mixture Screw Setting	Float Level	Float Drop	Idle Vent Setting	Fast Idle Cam Setting	Dechoke or Unloader Setting	Pulldown Setting	Vacuum Break Setting	Choke Setting
FORD—Continued										
1970	D0DF-N	②	7/32	1¼	—	.035	.280	.225	—	Index
	D0DF-R	②	7/32	1¼	—	.036	.280	.225	—	1 Rich
	D0DF-S	②	7/32	1¼	—	.035	.280	.225	—	Index
	D0DF-T	②	3/8	1¼	—	.031	.250	.265	—	Index
	D0DF-U	②	7/32	1¼	—	.036	.280	.225	—	1 Rich
	D0DF-V	②	3/8	1¼	—	.036	.250	.265	—	Index
1971	D1DF-EA	②	3/8	1¼	—	.105	.250	.200	—	Index
	D1DF-GA, HA	②	3/8	1¼	—	.170	.250	.230	—	Index
	D1DF-JA, LA	②	3/8	1¼	—	.140	.250	.200	—	Index
	D1DF-KA, MA	②	3/8	1¼	—	.140	.250	.200	—	Index
	D1DF-PA	②	3/8	1¼	—	.190	.250	.200	—	Index
	D1DF-RA	②	3/8	1¼	—	.220	.250	.230	—	Index
1972	D2DF-AA	②	3/8	1¼	—	.105	.280	.170	—	Index
	D2DF-BA	②	3/8	1¼	—	.170	.250	.230	—	Index
	D2DF-CA	②	3/8	1¼	—	.170	.250	.230	—	Index
	D2DF-DA	②	3/8	1¼	—	.140	.250	.200	—	1 Rich
	D2DF-EA	②	3/8	1¼	—	.140	.250	.200	—	1 Rich
	D2AF-JA	②	3/8	1¼	—	.220	.250	.230	—	1 Lean
1973	D3DF-AA	②	3/8	1¼	—	.170	.250	.230	—	Index
	D3DF-CA	②	3/8	1¼	—	.140	.250	.230	—	1 Rich
	D3OF-CA	②	9/16	—	—	.115	.250	.300	—	1 Rich
1974	D4DE-ABA	②	3/8	—	—	.140	.250	.200	—	Index
	D4DE-EA	②	3/8	—	—	.170	.250	.230	—	Index
	D4DE-JA	②	3/8	—	—	.140	.250	.200	—	1 Rich
	D4DE-JB	②	3/8	—	—	.140	.250	.200	—	Index
	D4DE-KA	②	3/8	—	—	.140	.250	.200	—	1 Rich
	D4DE-KB	②	3/8	—	—	.140	.250	.200	—	Index

②—Air/fuel ratio or idle CO% rating is found in Tune Up Specification tables in car chapters.

MODEL YF ADJUSTMENTS

The YF carburetor, Figs. 1 thru 2A, is a single-barrel, downdraft unit combining the fundamental features of other Carter carburetors. In addition, it features a diaphragm-type accelerating pump. It also has a diaphragm-operated metering rod, both vacuum and mechanically controlled.

Float Adjustment

Fig. 3—Invert the air horn assembly, and check the clearance from the top of the float to the bottom of the air horn with the float level gauge. Hold the air horn at eye level when gauging the float level. The float arm (lever) should be resting on the needle pin. Do not load the needle when adjusting the float. Bend the float arm as necessary to adjust the float level (clearance). Do not bend the tab at the end of the float arm. It prevents the float from striking the bottom of the fuel bowl when empty.

Float Drop Adjustment

Fig. 4—Hold air horn upright and measure maximum clearance from top of float to bottom of air horn with float drop gauge. Bend tab at end of float arm to obtain specified setting listed under YF Adjustment Specifications.

Pump Adjustment

With throttle valve seated in bore of carburetor, press down on upper end of diaphragm shaft until it reaches its bottom position. The metering rod arm should now contact the pump lifter link at the outer end nearest the springs. Adjust by bending the pump connector link at its lower angle.

Metering Rod Adjustment

Fig. 5—Back out the idle speed adjusting screw until the throttle plate is closed tight in the throttle bore. Press down on upper end of diaphragm shaft until diaphragm

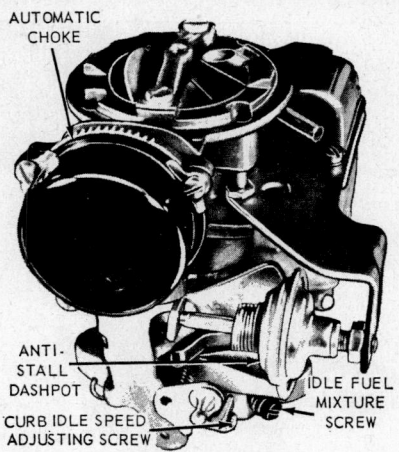

Fig. 2 YF adjustments

Labels: AUTOMATIC CHOKE, ANTI-STALL DASHPOT, CURB IDLE SPEED ADJUSTING SCREW, IDLE FUEL MIXTURE SCREW

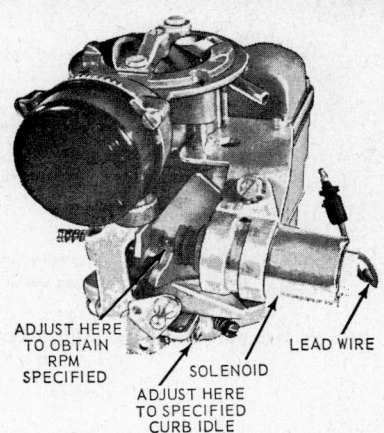

Fig. 2A YF with throttle positioner solenoid

Labels: ADJUST HERE TO OBTAIN RPM SPECIFIED, ADJUST HERE TO SPECIFIED CURB IDLE, SOLENOID, LEAD WIRE

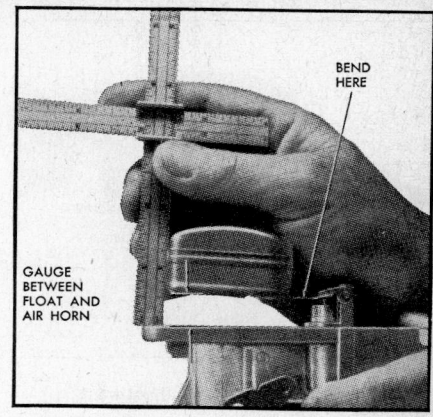

Fig. 3 YF float level adjustment

Labels: BEND HERE, GAUGE BETWEEN FLOAT AND AIR HORN

bottoms in vacuum chamber. Metering rod should contact bottom of metering rod well, and metering rod should contact lifter link at the outer end nearest the springs and at supporting lug. For models not equipped with metering rod adjusting screw, adjust by bending lip of metering rod arm to which metering rod is attached, up or down as required. For models equipped with a metering rod adjusting screw, turn the adjusting screw until metering rod just bottoms in the body casting, Fig. 5a. For final adjustment turn metering rod adjusting screw in (clockwise) one additional turn.

Idle Vent Adjustment

Fig. 6—This adjustment should be made after completing pump and metering rod adjustments. Install bowl cover and air horn assembly with gasket. With throttle valve tightly closed in carburetor bore there should be the clearance listed in the *YF Specifications Chart* between idle vent valve and inside of bowl cover. Adjust idle vent screw as required.

Fast Idle Cam Linkage Adjustment

Unit With Built-In Auto. Choke

Referring to Fig. 7, remove choke coil housing, gasket and baffle plate. Crack throttle valve (barely open) and hold choke valve firmly in closed position, then close throttle valve. This will allow the fast idle cam to revolve to the fast idle position.

Clearance on 1969-70 Ford units is measured between the throttle valve and the throttle bore (side opposite idle port). Clearance on 1971-74 Ford and 1974 American Motors units is measured between lower edge of choke plate and the carburetor bore.

With choke valve held tightly closed, and slight tension on throttle lever, refer to *YF Specifications* when adjusting units with throttle valve to throttle bore clearance settings.

NOTE: Caution: The choke trip lever must not contact the fast idle cam during adjustment. All other units should have the fast idle adjusting screw aligned with the index mark at the back side of the cam. If cam has no index mark, position the fast idle screw on the kickdown step of the fast idle cam against the shoulder of the high

step. Adjust linkage by bending the choke rod at elbow, Figs. 7 and 7a.

The 1970-73 American Motors units have engine fast idle RPM settings in place of specified carburetor to choke plate clearance. Refer to *YF Specifications Chart.* Adjustment is same as above.

Choke Unloader Adjustment

With throttle valve held wide open and choke valve held toward closed position with a rubber band, there should be the clearance listed in the *YF Specifications Chart* between lower edge of choke valve and inner air horn wall.

On Fig. 1 carburetors, adjust by bending unloader lug on choke trip lever, Fig. 8. On Fig. 2 carburetors adjust by bending unloader tang on throttle lever, Fig. 9.

NOTE: On 1974 American Motors models, the choke unloader adjustment has been eliminated. It is only necessary to check for full throttle opening when throttle is operated from inside the vehicle.

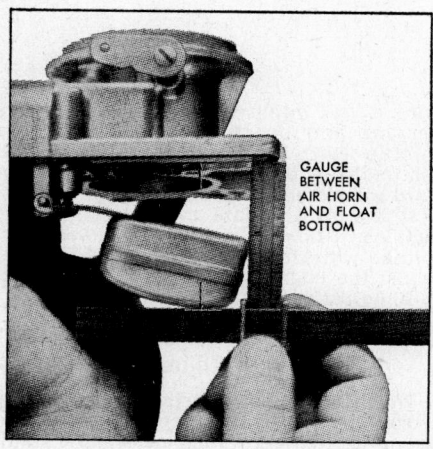

Fig. 4 YF float drop adjustment

Label: GAUGE BETWEEN AIR HORN AND FLOAT BOTTOM

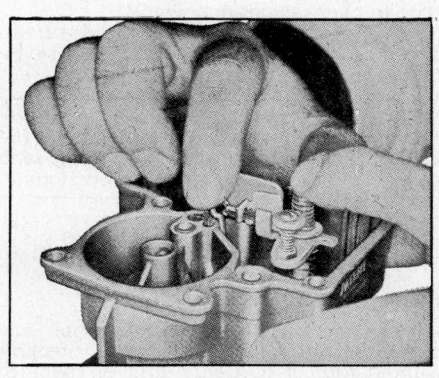

Fig. 5 YF metering rod adjustment

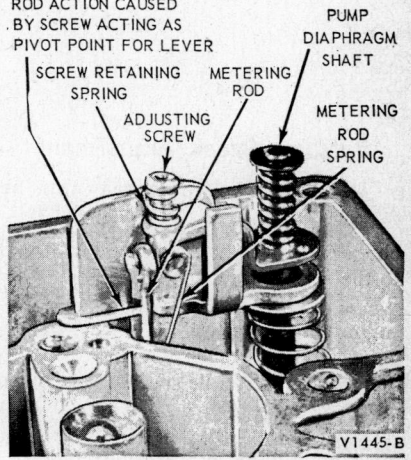

Fig. 5A YF metering rod adjustment

Labels: ROD ACTION CAUSED BY SCREW ACTING AS PIVOT POINT FOR LEVER, PUMP DIAPHRAGM SHAFT, SCREW RETAINING SPRING, METERING ROD, ADJUSTING SCREW, METERING ROD SPRING, V1445-B

Fig. 6 YF idle vent adjustment

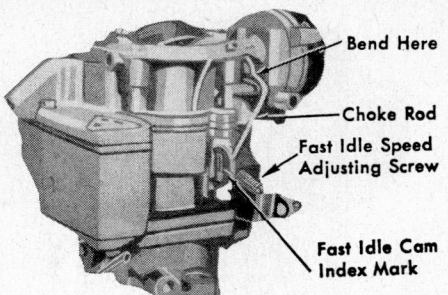

Fig. 7A YF fast idle cam linkage adjustment

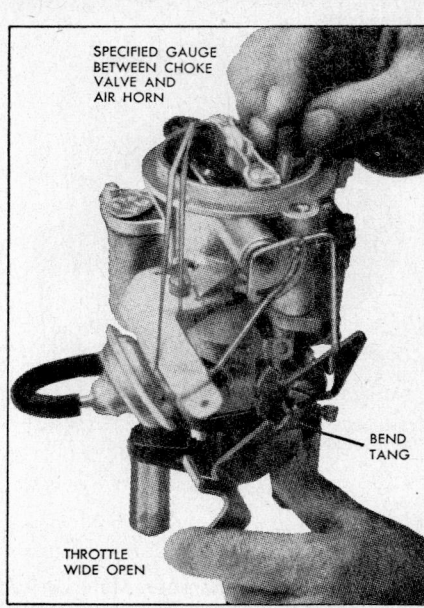

Fig. 9 YF unloader adjustment for Fig. 2 carburetors

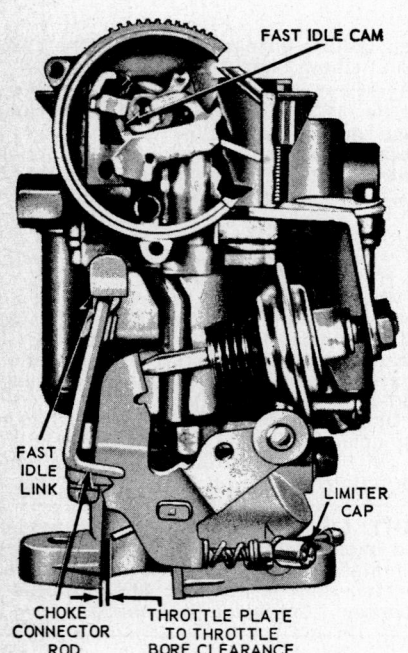

Fig. 7 YF fast idle speed adjustment for Fig. 1 carburetors

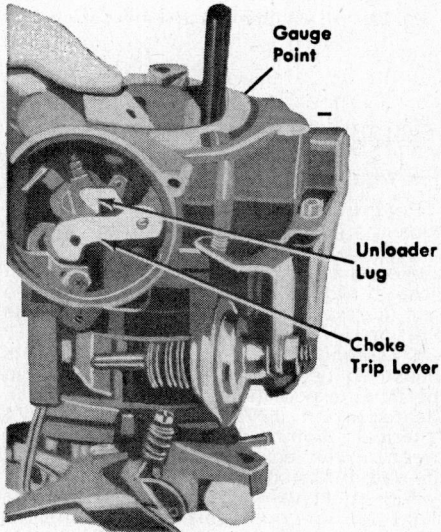

Fig. 8 YF unloader adjustment for Fig. 1 carburetors

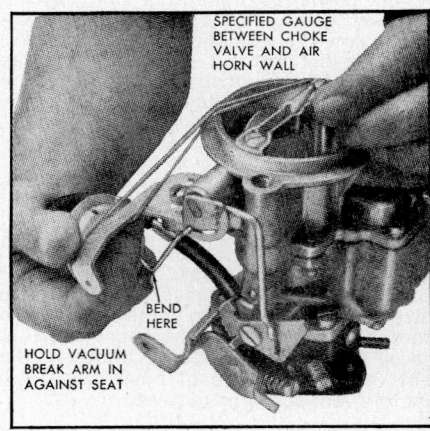

Fig. 10 YF vacuum break adjustment for Fig. 2 carburetors

Vacuum Break Adjustment

Fig. 10—With vacuum break arm held against its stop, and choke valve held toward closed position with a rubber band, bend vacuum break link to obtain the clearances listed in the *YF Specifications Chart* between lower edge of choke valve and air horn wall.

Choke Plate Pulldown Adjustment

For Fig. 1a Units

Bend a 0.026 in. diameter wire gauge at a 90 degree angle approximately 1/8-inch from one end. Insert the bent end of the gauge between the choke piston slot and the right hand slot in choke housing. Rotate the choke piston lever counterclockwise until gauge is snug in the piston slot. Exert a light pressure on choke piston lever to hold the gauge in place, then use a drill with a diameter equal to the specified pulldown clearance between the lower edge of choke plate and carburetor bore to check clearance, Fig. 11.

To adjust the choke plate pulldown clearance, bend the choke piston lever as required to obtain specified setting.

NOTE: When bending the lever, be careful not to distort the piston link. Install the choke thermostatic spring housing and gasket. Set the housing to specifications.

Dechoke Adjustment

For Fig. 1a Units

Hold the throttle plate fully open and close the choke plate as far as possible without forcing it. Use a drill of specified diameter to check the clearance between choke plate and air horn, Fig. 12. If clear-

ance is not within specification, adjust by bending arm on choke trip lever of the throttle lever. Bending the arm downward will decrease the clearance, bending it upward will increase the clearance.

If the choke plate clearance and fast idle cam linkage adjustment was performed with the carburetor on the engine, adjust the engine idle speed and fuel mixture. Adjust dashpot (if so equipped).

Dashpot Adjustment

With the engine idle speed and mixture properly adjusted, the engine at normal operating temperature, loosen the anti-stall dashpot lock nut, Fig. 13. Hold the throttle in the curb idle position and de-

Fig. 11 YF choke plate pulldown adjustment

Automatic Choke Adjustment

For Figs. 1, 1a, 2a and 2b Units

Loosen choke cover retaining screws and turn choke cover so that line or index mark on cover lines up with the specified mark listed in *YF Specifications Chart* on choke housing.

Choke Diaphragm Linkage Adjustment

For Fig. 2 Units

With vacuum diaphragm bottomed, close choke valve as far as possible without forcing. Adjust choke diaphragm connector rod to give the clearance listed in the *YF Specifications Chart* between lower edge of choke valve and inner wall of air horn. Remove connector rod to prevent damage to diaphragm.

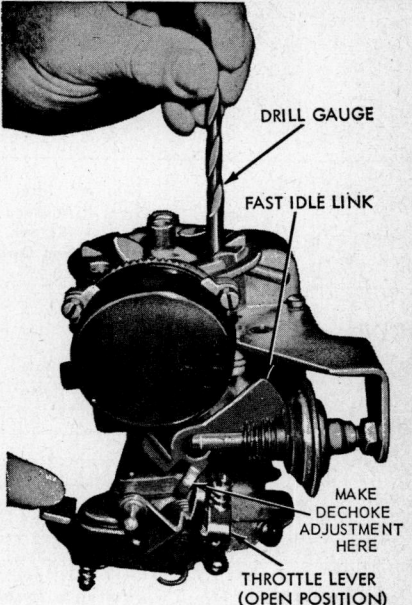

Fig. 12 YF dechoke adjustment

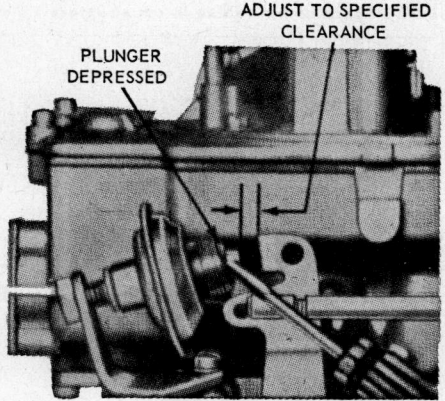

Fig. 13 YF dashpot adjustment

press the dashpot plunger. Measure the clearance between the throttle lever and plunger tip. Turn the anti-stall dashpot to provide 7/64" ± 1/64" clearance between the tip of the plunger and the throttle lever. Tighten the locknut to secure the adjustment.

CARTER BBS ADJUSTMENT SPECIFICATIONS

See Tune Up Chart in car chapter for hot idle speed.

Year	Carb. Model	Idle Mixture Screw Turns Open	Float Level	Pump Travel Inch	Bowl Vent Drill Size	Choke Unloader Drill Size	Fast Idle Cam Position Drill Size	Choke Vacuum Kick Drill Size	Automatic Choke Setting
DODGE & PLYMOUTH									
1969	4601S	1-2	¼	—	.060	3/16	48 Drill	35 Drill	2 Rich
	4602S	1-2	¼	—	.060	3/16	48 Drill	35 Drill	2 Rich
1970	4715S	①	¼	—	1/32	3/16	48 Drill	35 Drill	2 Rich
	4716S	①	¼	—	1/32	3/16	48 Drill	48 Drill	2 Rich
	4717S	①	¼	5/16	9/32	3/16	48 Drill	35 Drill	2 Rich
	4718S	①	¼	5/16	9/32	3/16	48 Drill	48 Drill	2 Rich
1971	4955S	①	¼	5/16	17/64	3/16	48 Drill	35 Drill	2 Rich
	4956S	①	¼	5/16	17/64	3/16	48 Drill	35 Drill	2 Rich

①—Air/fuel ratio or idle CO% rating is found in Tune Up Specification tables in car chapters.

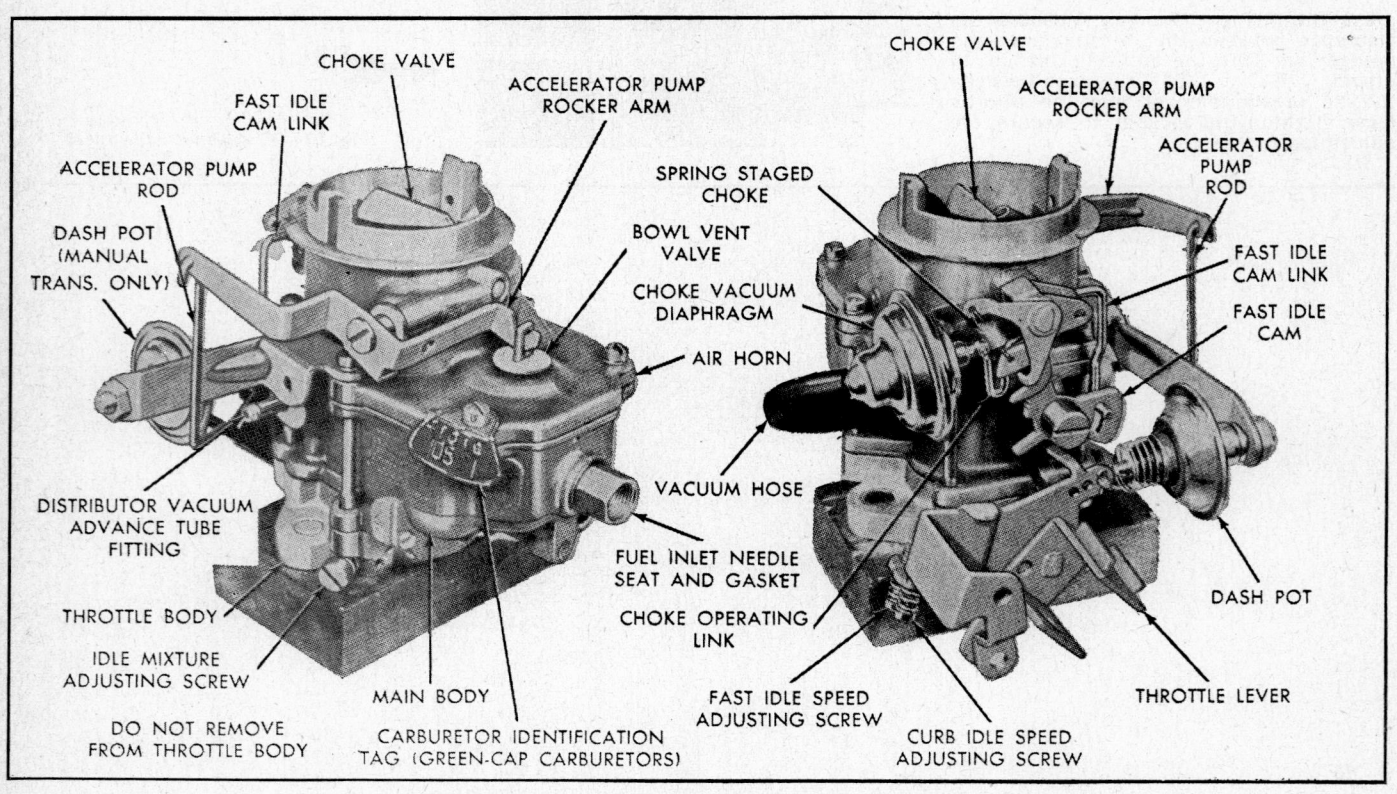

Fig. 1   Exterior of 1969 model BBS carburetor used with C.A.P. (Typical)

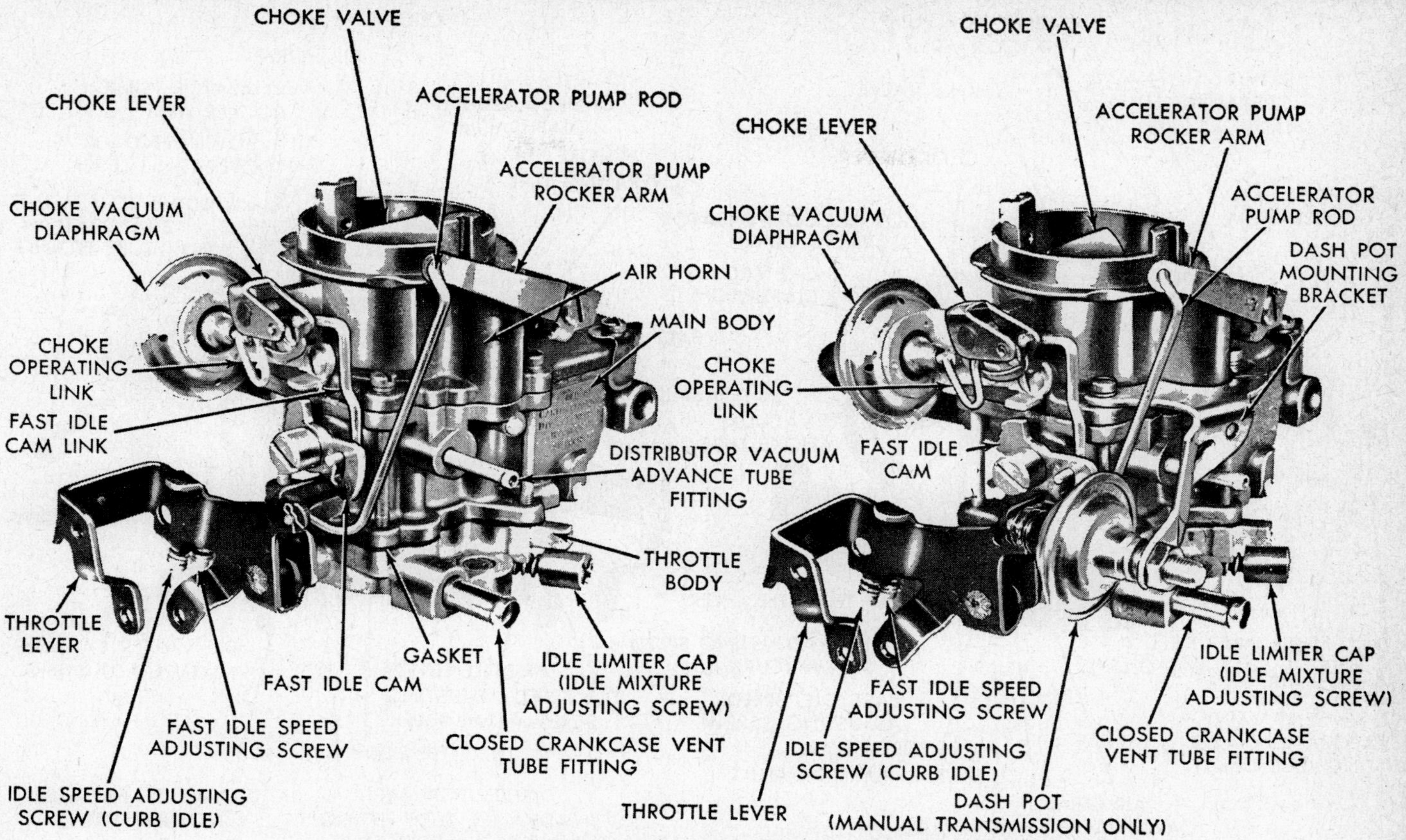

CHOKE VALVE

CHOKE LEVER

ACCELERATOR PUMP ROD

ACCELERATOR PUMP ROCKER ARM

CHOKE VACUUM DIAPHRAGM

AIR HORN

MAIN BODY

CHOKE OPERATING LINK

FAST IDLE CAM LINK

CHOKE OPERATING LINK

DISTRIBUTOR VACUUM ADVANCE TUBE FITTING

THROTTLE BODY

THROTTLE LEVER

FAST IDLE CAM

GASKET

IDLE LIMITER CAP (IDLE MIXTURE ADJUSTING SCREW)

FAST IDLE SPEED ADJUSTING SCREW

CLOSED CRANKCASE VENT TUBE FITTING

IDLE SPEED ADJUSTING SCREW (CURB IDLE)

CHOKE VALVE

CHOKE LEVER

ACCELERATOR PUMP ROCKER ARM

ACCELERATOR PUMP ROD

DASH POT MOUNTING BRACKET

CHOKE VACUUM DIAPHRAGM

FAST IDLE CAM

IDLE LIMITER CAP (IDLE MIXTURE ADJUSTING SCREW)

FAST IDLE SPEED ADJUSTING SCREW

IDLE SPEED ADJUSTING SCREW (CURB IDLE)

CLOSED CRANKCASE VENT TUBE FITTING

THROTTLE LEVER

DASH POT (MANUAL TRANSMISSION ONLY)

Fig. 2   Exterior of 1970 model BBS carburetor used with Cleaner Air System (CAS)

MODEL BBS ADJUSTMENTS

Float Level Adjustment

Fig. 4—Invert main body so that weight of floats only is forcing needle against seat. If proper gauge is not available, measure from surface of fuel bowl to crown of each float at center. Float setting should be as listed in the *BBS Specifications Chart*. If an adjustment is necessary, bend lip of float lever in or out until correct setting is obtained.

Pump & Bowl Vent Adjustment C.A.P. & C.A.S.

Fig. 5

This adjustment automatically adjusts the accelerator pump as well. The pro-

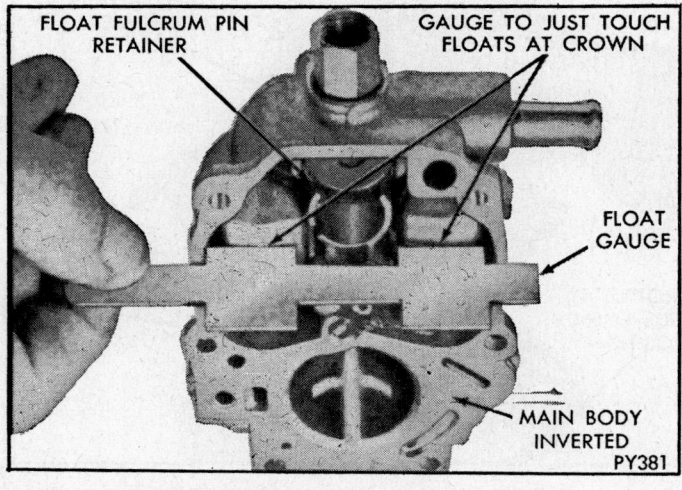

FLOAT FULCRUM PIN RETAINER

GAUGE TO JUST TOUCH FLOATS AT CROWN

FLOAT GAUGE

MAIN BODY INVERTED

PY381

Fig. 4   Checking float level. BBS carburetors

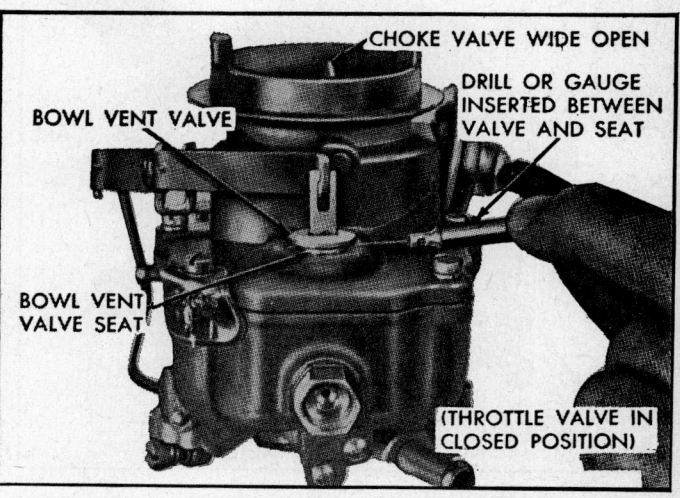

CHOKE VALVE WIDE OPEN

DRILL OR GAUGE INSERTED BETWEEN VALVE AND SEAT

BOWL VENT VALVE

BOWL VENT VALVE SEAT

(THROTTLE VALVE IN CLOSED POSITION)

Fig. 5   Bowl vent adjustment. BBS carburetors with C.A.P.

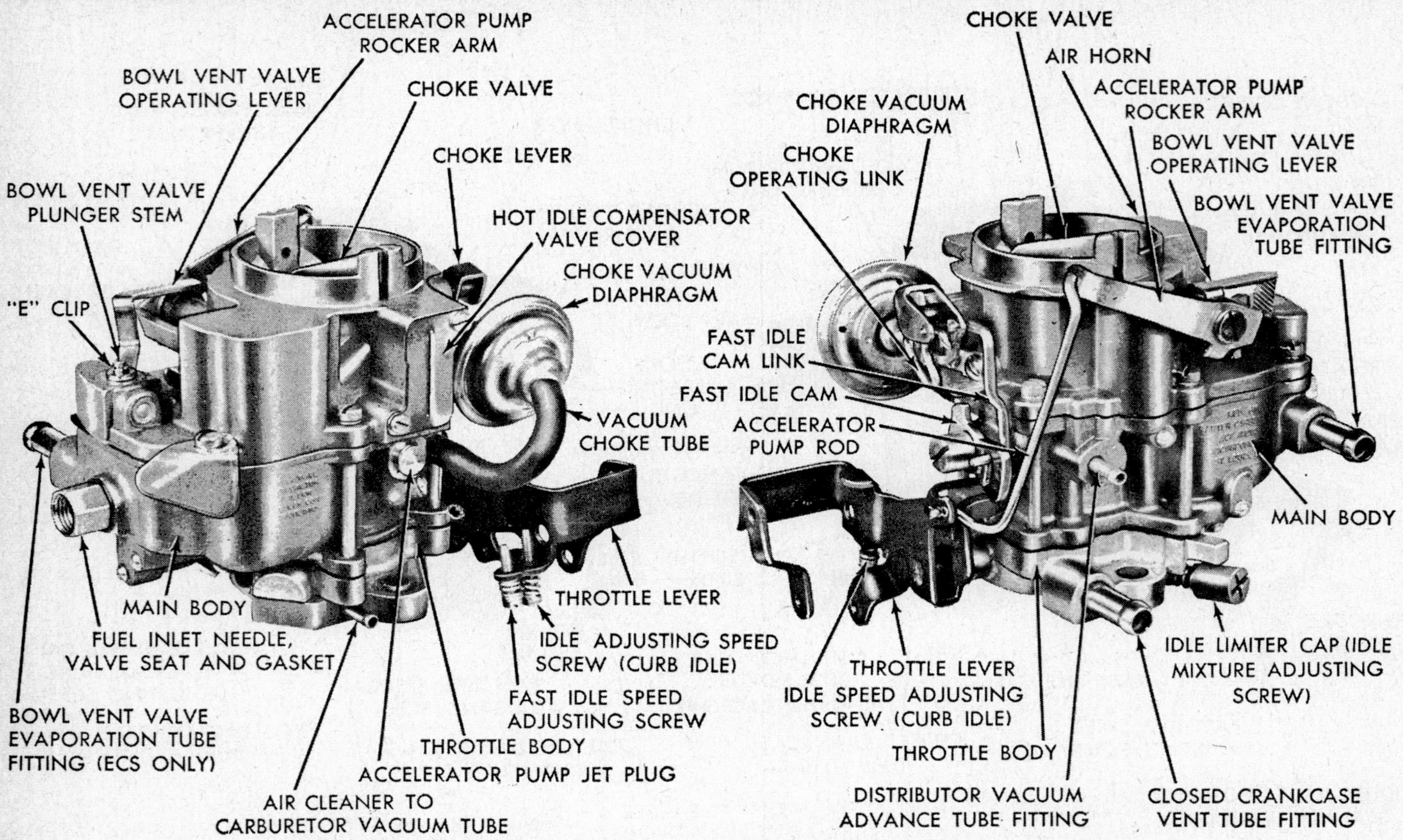

ACCELERATOR PUMP
ROCKER ARM

BOWL VENT VALVE
OPERATING LEVER

CHOKE VALVE

CHOKE LEVER

BOWL VENT VALVE
PLUNGER STEM

HOT IDLE COMPENSATOR
VALVE COVER

CHOKE VACUUM
DIAPHRAGM

"E" CLIP

VACUUM
CHOKE TUBE

MAIN BODY

FUEL INLET NEEDLE,
VALVE SEAT AND GASKET

IDLE ADJUSTING SPEED
SCREW (CURB IDLE)

BOWL VENT VALVE
EVAPORATION TUBE
FITTING (ECS ONLY)

FAST IDLE SPEED
ADJUSTING SCREW

THROTTLE LEVER

ACCELERATOR PUMP JET PLUG

AIR CLEANER TO
CARBURETOR VACUUM TUBE

CHOKE VALVE

AIR HORN

ACCELERATOR PUMP
ROCKER ARM

CHOKE VACUUM
DIAPHRAGM

CHOKE
OPERATING LINK

BOWL VENT VALVE
OPERATING LEVER

BOWL VENT VALVE
EVAPORATION
TUBE FITTING

FAST IDLE
CAM LINK

FAST IDLE CAM

ACCELERATOR
PUMP ROD

MAIN BODY

THROTTLE LEVER

IDLE SPEED ADJUSTING
SCREW (CURB IDLE)

THROTTLE BODY

DISTRIBUTOR VACUUM
ADVANCE TUBE FITTING

IDLE LIMITER CAP (IDLE
MIXTURE ADJUSTING
SCREW)

CLOSED CRANKCASE
VENT TUBE FITTING

Fig. 3 Exterior of 1970-71 model BBS carburetor used with Evaporation Control System (ECS)

cedure is as follows:
1. Back off idle speed adjusting screw. Open choke valve so that when throttle valve is closed the fast idle adjusting screw will not contact fast idle cam.
2. Be sure pump operating rod is in center hole in throttle lever and that bowl vent clip on pump stem is in center groove.
3. Close throttle valve tightly. It should be possible to insert a drill of the specified size between bowl vent and air horn.
4. If an adjustment is necessary, bend pump operating rod at the lower angle as required to obtain the correct bowl vent opening.

NOTE: This is an important adjustment

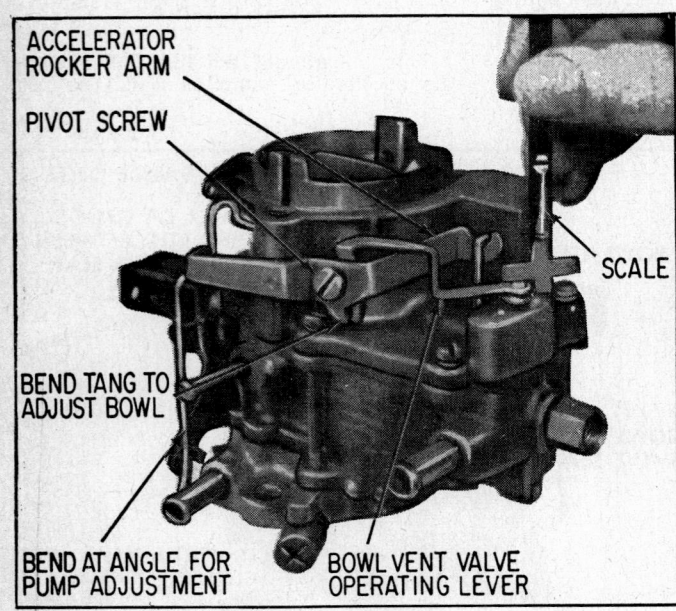

ACCELERATOR
ROCKER ARM

PIVOT SCREW

SCALE

BEND TANG TO
ADJUST BOWL

BEND AT ANGLE FOR
PUMP ADJUSTMENT

BOWL VENT VALVE
OPERATING LEVER

Fig. 6 Bowl vent adjustment. BBS carburetors with E.C.S.

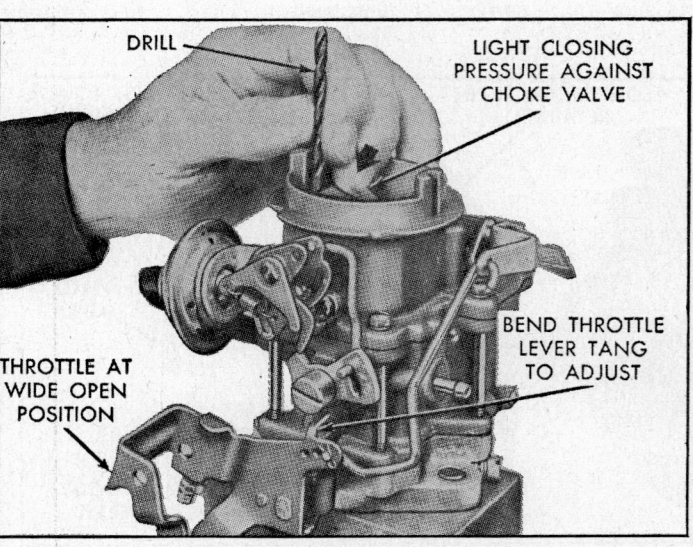

DRILL

LIGHT CLOSING
PRESSURE AGAINST
CHOKE VALVE

THROTTLE AT
WIDE OPEN
POSITION

BEND THROTTLE
LEVER TANG
TO ADJUST

Fig. 7 Checking choke unloader setting (wide open kick). BBS carburetors

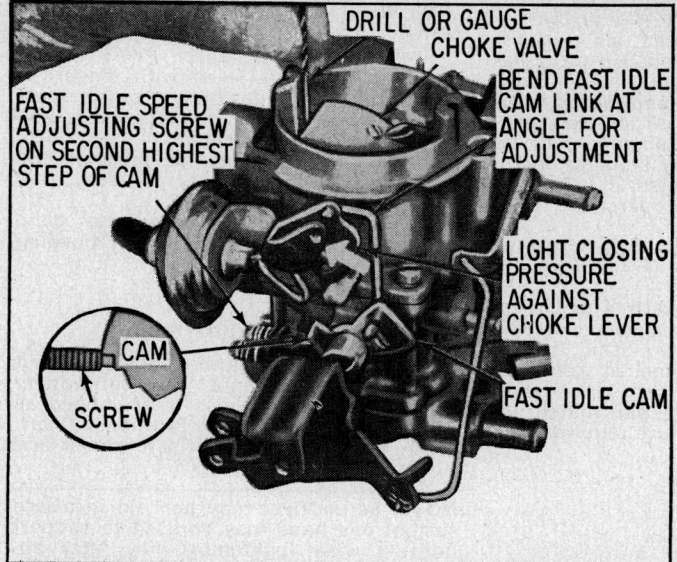

Fig. 8 Fast idle cam position. BBS carburetors

Fig. 9 Vacuum kick adjustment. BBS carburetors

since too much lift at the bowl vent will result in considerable loss in low speed fuel economy. If the pump operating rod is moved to either the short or long stroke position, a corresponding change must be made in the location of the bowl vent clip, and the amount of lift of the bowl rechecked and adjusted.

Pump and Bowl Vent Adjustments E.C.S.

Fig. 6

On the E.C.S. BBS carburetor, it is necessary to check or set the accelerator pump travel before checking the bowl vent valve opening.

Accelerator Pump Travel Adjustment

1. Be sure the accelerator pump rod is in outer hole (long stroke) of throttle lever.
2. Close throttle valve to curb idle.
3. Using a straight edge placed on flat surface (air cleaner mounting surface), measure distance between straight edge and top of accelerator pump plunger. Refer to *BBS Specification Chart*.
4. If an adjustment is necessary, bend accelerator pump rod at angle until correct pump travel has been obtained.

Bowl Vent Valve Adjustment

This adjustment to be made after accelerator pump adjustment.
1. With throttle valve at curb idle, measure distance from top of casting to top of bowl vent valve stem. Refer to *BBS Specifications Chart*.
2. If an adjustment is necessary, bend lower tang on bowl vent valve operating lever (at pivot) until correct opening has been obtained.

Choke Unloader Adjustment

Fig. 7—Hold throttle valve in wide open position. Insert a drill of the specified size between upper edge of choke valve

and inner wall of air horn. With a finger lightly pressing against choke valve, a slight drag should be felt as the drill is being withdrawn. If an adjustment is necessary, bend unloader tang on throttle lever as required.

Fast Idle Cam Position

Fig. 8

1. With fast idle speed adjusting screw contacting the second highest step on the fast idle cam, move choke valve toward closed position with light pressure on choke shaft lever.

2. Insert specified drill between choke valve and wall of air horn. If an adjustment is necessary, bend fast idle rod at upper angle until correct valve opening has been obtained.

Vacuum Kick Adjustment

Fig. 9

The choke diaphragm adjustment controls the fuel delivery while the engine is running. It positions the choke valve within the air horn by action of the linkage between the choke shaft and diaphragm. The diaphragm must be ener-

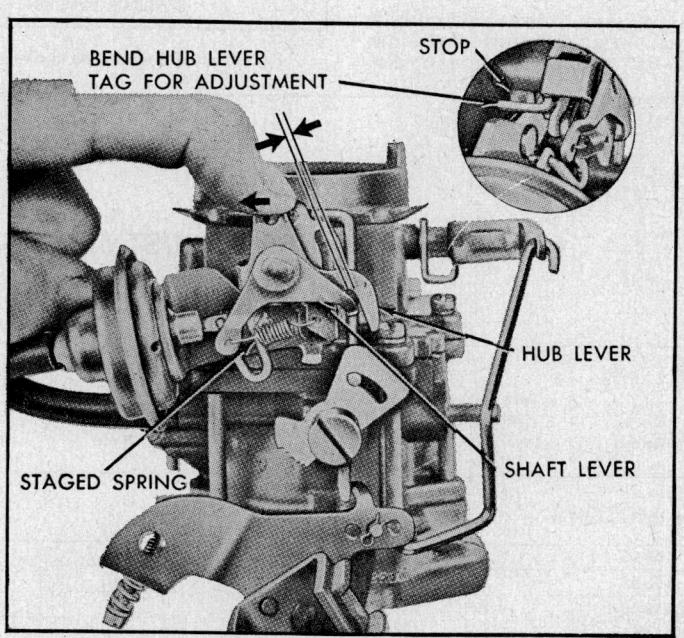

Fig. 10 Spring staged choke adjustment. BBS carburetors

gized to measure the vacuum kick adjustment. Use a vacuum source, or vacuum supplied by another vehicle. Adjust as follows:

1. If adjustment is to be made with the engine running, back off the fast idle speed screw until choke can be closed to the kick position with engine at curb idle.

NOTE: Number of screw turns required so that fast idle can be returned to original adjustment.

If an auxiliary vacuum source is to be used, open throttle valve (engine not running) and move choke to closed position. Release throttle first, then release choke.

2. When using an auxiliary vacuum source, disconnect vacuum hose from carburetor and connect it to hose from vacuum supply with a small length of tube to act as a fitting. Removal of hose from diaphragm may require forces which change the system. Apply a vacuum of 10 inches or more of mercury.

3. Insert specified drill between choke valve and wall of air horn. Apply sufficient closing pressure on lever to which choke rod attaches to provide a minimum stroke valve opening without distortion of diaphragm link. Note that cylindrical stem of diaphragm will extend as internal spring is compressed. This spring must be fully compressed for proper measurement of vacuum kick adjustment.

4. An adjustment will be necessary if a slight drag is not obtained as drill is being removed. Shorten or lengthen diaphragm link to obtain correct choke opening. Length changes should be made carefully by bending (opening or closing) the bend provided in the diaphragm link. *Do not apply twisting or bending force to diaphragm.*

5. Reinstall vacuum hose on correct carburetor fitting. Return fast idle screw to its original location if disturbed as suggested in Step 1.

6. Check the adjustment as follows: With no vacuum applied to diaphragm, *choke valve should move freely between open and closed positions.* If movement is not free, examine linkage for misalignment or interferences caused by bending operation. Repeat adjustment if necessary to provide proper link operation.

Spring Staged Choke Adjustment
Fig. 10

The spring staged choke is a device incorporated in the choke mechanism that limits the choke blade closing torque when cranking the engine at temperatures below zero. Thus the spring staging of the choke is a better match for the engine's starting mixture requirements at low temperatures.

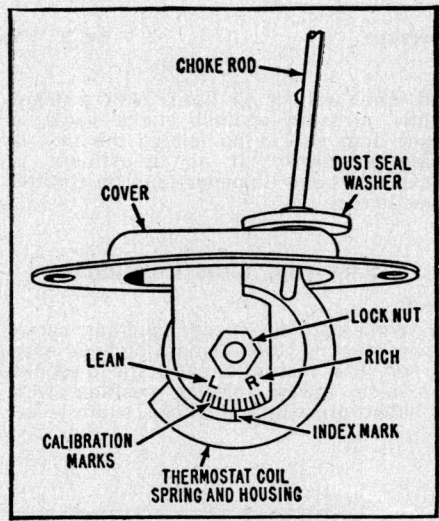

Fig. 11   BBS well-type choke setting

To check the spring staged choke for correct operating clearance, proceed as follows:

1. Push on hub lever with finger at closed choke position. A small opening should exist between shaft and hub levers as indicated.
2. Using a drill or gauge, measure the opening which should be from .010 to .040".
3. If adjustment is necessary, bend hub lever tang until correct opening is obtained.

Choke Adjustment

Fig. 11—Loosen mounting post lock nut and turn mounting post with screwdriver until index mark on disc is positioned as listed in the *BBS Specifications Chart.* Hold in this position with screwdriver and tighten lock nut.

NOTE: Screwdriver may be held in a vise so that one hand may be used to support housing while tightening nut. After adjustment is completed and coil housing and rod and carburetor are installed on engine, lift cover disc and open and close choke valve manually to see if connector rod clears sides of hole in housing cover without binding. If rod does not clear housing cover without binding, replace with a new unit since connecting rod cannot be bent without affecting calibration.

Dashpot Adjustment
Clean Air Carburetors

The dashpot is used only on cars equipped with the Cleaner Air Package and manual transmission, Figs. 1 and 2.

To adjust the dashpot, have the curb idle speed and mixture properly adjusted, and install a tachometer. Position throttle lever so that actuating tab on lever is contacting stem of dashpot but not depressing it. The tachometer should read 2000 rpm if the setting is correct. If not correct, screw dashpot in or out as required, then tighten lock nut on dashpot against the bracket.

CARTER RBS ADJUSTMENT SPECIFICATIONS

See Tune Up Chart in car chapter for hot idle speed.

Year	Carb. Model	Idle Screw (Mixture) Turns Open	Float Level	Accel. Pump	Bowl Vent	Fast Idle Cam Setting RPM	Fast Idle Throttle Plate Setting	Choke Unloader	Pulldown Setting	Choke Setting
AMERICAN MOTORS										
1969	4631S	1	9/16	1/64	5/64	2000	.035	1/8	13/64	Index
	4633S	1	9/16	1/64	5/64	2000	.035	3/16	13/64	Index
	4634S	1	9/16	1/64	5/64	2000	.035	3/16	7/32	2 Rich
	4666S	1	9/16	1/64	5/64	2000	.035	1/8	7/32	2 Rich

Continued

CARTER RBS ADJUSTMENT SPECIFICATIONS—Continued

See Tune Up Chart in car chapter for hot idle speed.

Year	Carb. Model	Idle Mixture Screw Setting	Float Level	Step-Up Rod	Accelerating Pump Stroke	Fast Idle Linkage	Fast Idle Throttle Plate Setting	Dechoke Setting	Pulldown Setting	Dashpot Setting	Choke Setting
FORD ENGINES											
1970	D0ZF-C	①	9/16	—	.400③	See Text	.040	.250	.190	—	Index
	D0ZF-D	①	9/16	—	.400③	See Text	.046	.252	.190	—	1 Rich
	D0ZF-F	①	9/16	—	.400③	See Text	—	.252	.190	7/32	1 Rich
1971	D1ZF-HA, LA	①	9/16	—	.400③	.115②	—	.250	.270	—	Index
	D1ZF-NA, KA	①	9/16	—	.400③	.115②	—	.250	.190	—	1 Rich
1972	D2OF-LA	①	9/16	—	.400③	.115②	—	.250	.300	—	Index
	D2OF-MA	①	9/16	—	.400③	.115②	—	.250	.190	—	1 Rich
	D2OF-SA	①	9/16	—	.400③	.115②	—	.250	.190	—	1 Rich
1973	D3OF-BA	①	9/16	—	.420③	.115②	—	.250	.300	—	Index
	D3OF-CA	①	9/16	—	.400③	.115②	—	.250	.190	—	Index
1974	D4DE-AAA	①	9/16	—	—	.115②	—	.250	.190	—	1 Lean
	D4DE-AB	①	9/16	—	—	.115②	—	.250	.190	—	Index
	D4DE-BB	①	9/16	—	—	.115②	—	.250	.300	—	Index
	D4DE-SB	①	9/16	—	—	.115②	—	.250	.300	—	Index
	D4DE-TA	①	9/16	—	—	.115②	—	.250	.190	—	Index

①—Air/fuel ratio or idle CO% rating is found in Tune Up Specification tables in car chapters.
②—At kickdown.
③—Closed throttle.

MODEL RBS ADJUSTMENTS

This carburetor, Fig. 1 incorporates a single aluminum casting with a pressed steel bowl. Adjustments are readily accessible and most calibration points are located in the single casting.

Fuel pickups are located near the centerline of the carburetor bore to gain the benefits of a concentric bowl carburetor, yet so located that engine heat being radiated through the bore is conducted through the casting but is not readily conducted to the fuel in the bowl. Two internal vapor vents allow rapid fuel vapor dissipation to help provide smooth idle conditions and to minimize hard starting when engine is hot. Also an external vent, mechanically controlled by the throttle, is used on 1974 California units.

A diaphragm-controlled step-up type metering rod controls the fuel supply. The accelerator pump is spring-actuated.

The carburetor is equipped with a vacuum piston automatic choke. On 1974 California units, an electric assist choke is used to open the choke plate within 1-1½ minutes after underhood temperatures reach approximately 60° F. For service procedures, refer to the "Emission Control System" chapter.

The 1973-74 RBS unit incorporates an Exhaust Gas Recirculation port, Fig. 2. The E.G.R. port connects to the primary bore and allows a metered amount of exhaust gas to be fed into the fuel-air mixture.

The carburetor model number is stamped on the side of the flange near the throttle lever.

Float Level Adjustment

Fig. 3—With carburetor inverted, bowl and bowl gasket removed, and only weight of float pressing needle into its seat, measure vertical distance from casting to the small "bump" at outer ends of float. Gauge both ends of float. If the vertical distance is not as listed in the *RBS Specifications Chart*, adjustment can be made by removing float from casting, or by

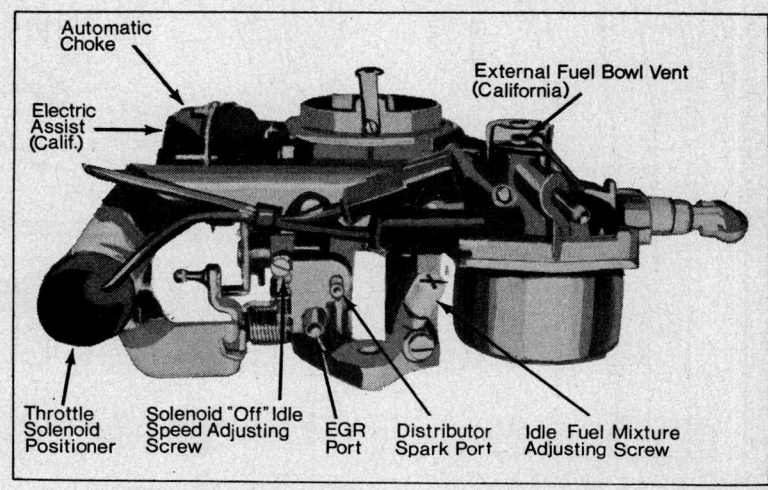

Fig. 2   Carter RBS carburetor side view. 1973-74

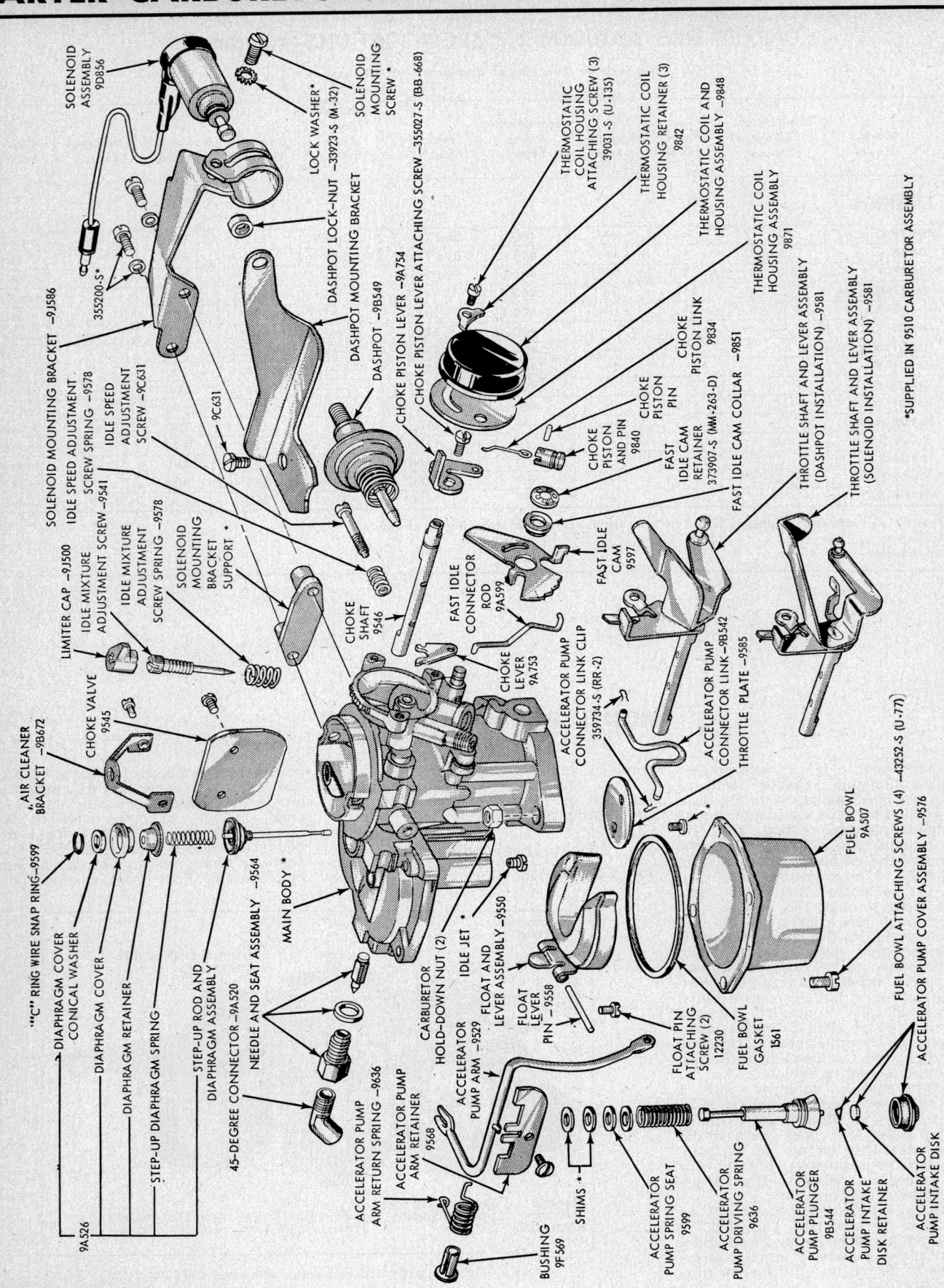

Fig. 1 Carter model RBS carburetor. 1969-74 (typical)

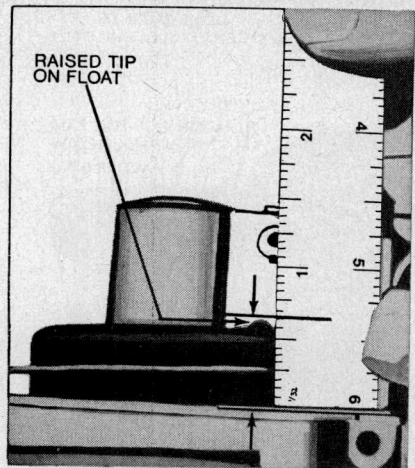

Fig. 3   RBS float level adjustment

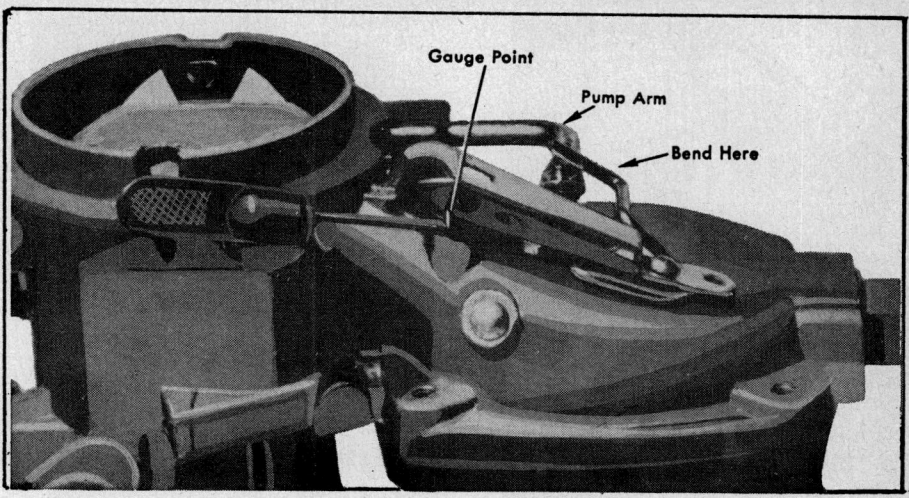

Fig. 5   Bowl vent adjustment

Fig. 4   Adjusting fuel float level

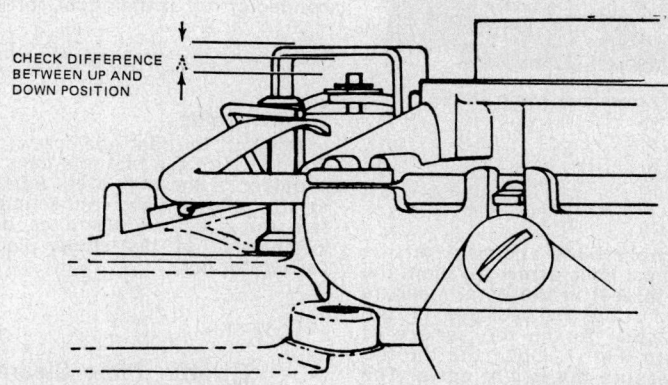

Fig. 5A   Bowl vent adjustment. 1974 California units

Bowl Vent Adjustment

1969 Units

With pump stroke adjusted properly and throttle valve fully closed, measure the clearance between the vent valve and the carburetor casting. Refer to *RBS Specifica-tions Chart*. To adjust bend the connector rod at accelerator pump end to obtain the specified clearance, Fig. 5.

1974 California Units

With accelerator pump properly adjusted, place throttle at curb idle position on the extended solenoid. Measure direction between top of vent guard and top of vent valve stem. Then, open throttle until vent valve seats and measure same distance again. The difference between the two measurements is the vent opening, Fig. 5A. Refer to Carter RBS Specification Chart. Adjust by bending link at accelerator pump arm contact point.

holding lip end of float bracket securely with needle-nose pliers. However, be sure to hold float lip away from needle when adjusting. To adjust, bend bracket at its narrowest portion, Fig. 4.

Float Drop Adjustment

1970-74

With the air horn upright and the float hanging free measure the vertical distance from the main body casting surface for the fuel bowl to the outer ends of the float on the top side. Adjust by bending tab at the end of the float arm to obtain 1.250" setting.

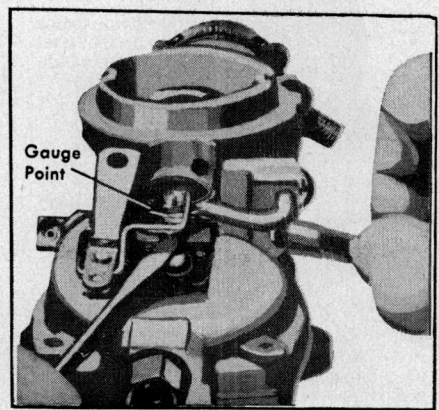

Fig. 6   Pump adjustment

Accelerator Pump Adjustment

1969 Units

Pump adjustment must be made each time carburetor is disassembled, and must be made before the bowl vent and unloader adjustment. Back out curb idle adjusting screw and hold choke valve wide open so throttle valve is fully closed. Turn pump adjusting nut to obtain the specified clearance between shoulder on pump shaft and pump arm, Fig. 6.

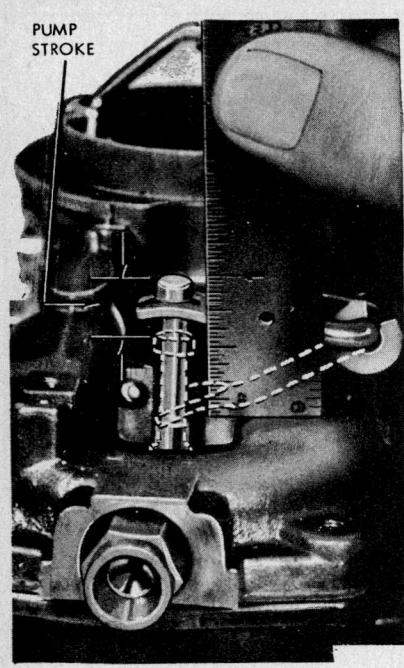

PUMP STROKE

Fig. 7   Accelerator pump stroke

1970-74 Units

Open the choke plate and back off the idle speed adjustment screw to allow the throttle plate to seat in the bore. Measure the height from the flat surface of the main body casting to the top surface of the pump stem, Fig. 7. Open the throttle wide, then measure the height again. The pump stroke is the difference between the two measurements. Refer to *RBS Specifications Chart*. To adjust the stroke to specifications, open or close the pump connector link at the offset portion, Fig. 8.

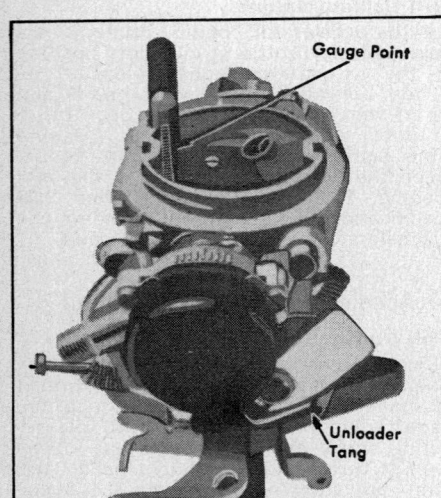

Gauge Point

Unloader Tang

Fig. 10   Unloader adjustment

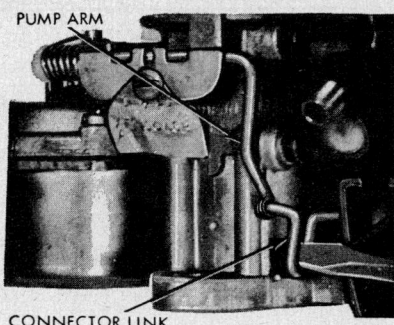

PUMP ARM

CONNECTOR LINK

Fig. 8   Adjusting accelerator pump stroke

Fast Idle Cam Adjustment

1969-70 Units

With choke valve tightly closed and choke connector rod in upper end of slot in cam, align cam index with center of fast idle tang. Adjust by bending choke connector rod at the offset portion.

1971-74 Units

Position the fast idle screw on the kick-down step of the fast idle cam against the shoulder of the high step. Adjust by bending the choke plate connecting rod to obtain the specified clearance between the lower edge of the choke plate and the carburetor bore.

Throttle Plate Clearance

Align the fast idle tang on the throttle lever with the index mark on the fast idle cam. Use a drill between the throttle plate and the throttle bore at the idle port side to check the clearance, Fig. 9. Adjust by bending tang on the throttle lever. Refer to *R.B.S. Specification Chart*.

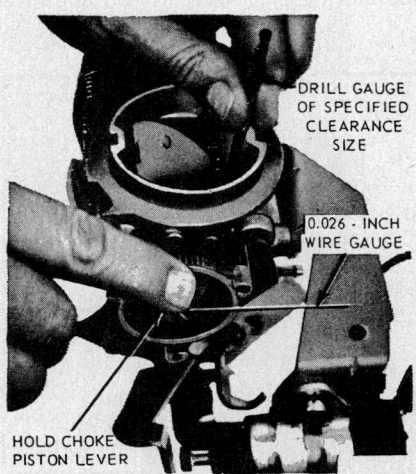

DRILL GAUGE OF SPECIFIED CLEARANCE SIZE

0.026 - INCH WIRE GAUGE

HOLD CHOKE PISTON LEVER

Fig. 11   Adjusting choke plate pulldown

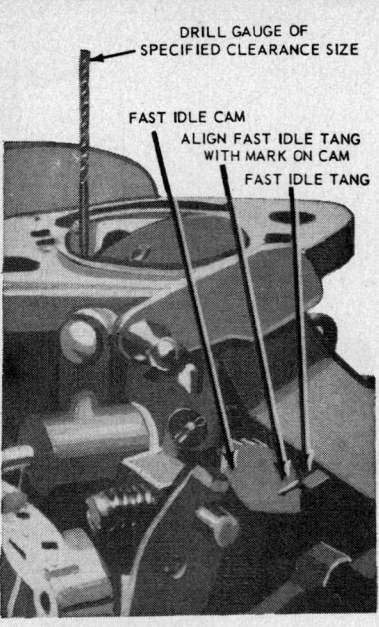

DRILL GAUGE OF SPECIFIED CLEARANCE SIZE

FAST IDLE CAM

ALIGN FAST IDLE TANG WITH MARK ON CAM

FAST IDLE TANG

Fig. 9   RBS throttle plate clearance.

Choke Unloader Adjustment

1969 American Motors Units

Fig. 10—With throttle valve wide open, there should be the clearance listed in the *RBS Specifications Chart* between top edge of choke valve and inner wall of air horn. To adjust, bend tang on throttle lever.

Choke Plate Pulldown or Piston Linkage Adjustment

Bend a .026 in. diameter wire gauge at a 90 degree angle approximately 1/8-inch from one end. Insert the bent end of the gauge between the choke piston slot and the right hand slot in choke housing. Rotate the choke piston lever counter clockwise until gauge is snug in the piston slot. Exert a light pressure on choke piston lever to hold the gauge in place, then use a drill with a diameter equal to the specified pulldown clearance between the lower edge of choke plate and carburetor bore to check clearance, Fig. 11.

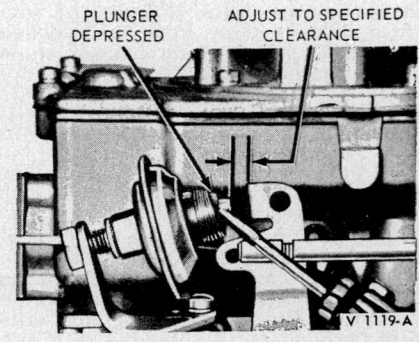

PLUNGER DEPRESSED

ADJUST TO SPECIFIED CLEARANCE

V 1119-A

Fig. 12   Typical anti-stall dashpot adjustment

To adjust the choke plate pulldown clearance, bend the choke piston lever as required to obtain specified setting. NOTE: When bending the lever, be careful not to distort the piston link. Install the choke thermostatic spring housing and gasket. Set the housing to specifications.

Dechoke Clearance

1970-74 Ford Units

Hold the throttle lever at the wide open position and close the choke plate as far as possible without forcing it. The dechoke clearance on the 1970 units is measured between the upper edge of the choke plate and the inner wall of the main body. While clearance on 1971-74 units is measured between the lower edge of the choke plate and the inner wall of the main body.

Dashpot Adjustment

Loosen the anti-stall dashpot lock nut, Fig. 12. Hold the throttle in the closed position and depress the plunger. The clearance between the throttle lever and the plunger tip for American Motors is $3/32''$ and Ford $7/32''$. Tighten the locknut to secure the adjustment.

Automatic Choke Adjustment

Loosen retainer screws and turn choke cover so that line or index mark on cover lines up with the specified mark on choke housing (see *RBS Specifications Chart*).

CARTER BBD ADJUSTMENT SPECIFICATIONS

See Tune Up Chart in car chapter for hot idle speed.

Year	Carb. Model	Initial Idle Mix. Screws Turns Open	Float Level	Pump Travel Inch	Bowl Vent Drill Size	Choke Unloader Drill Size	Choke Vacuum Kick Drill Size	Fast Idle Cam Position Drill Size	Automatic Choke Setting
CHRYSLER, DODGE & PLYMOUTH									
1969	4605S	2	1/4	—	1/16	1/4	20 Drill	41 Drill	On Index
	4606S	2	1/4	—	1/16	1/4	41 Drill	41 Drill	On Index
	4607S	1	1/4	—	1/16	1/4	20 Drill	41 Drill	On Index
	4608S	1	1/4	—	1/16	1/4	28 Drill	41 Drill	On Index
	4613S	1 1/2	5/16	1	1/16	1/4	20 Drill	30 Drill	2 Rich
	4614S	1 1/2	5/16	1	1/16	1/4	20 Drill	30 Drill	2 Rich
	4474S	1 1/2	5/16	1	1/16	1/4	20 Drill	30 Drill	2 Rich
1970	4721S	①	1/4	—	1/32	1/4	20 Drill	41 Drill	On Index
	4722S	①	1/4	—	1/32	1/4	20 Drill	41 Drill	On Index
	4723S	①	1/4	—	15/64	1/4	20 Drill	41 Drill	On Index
	4724S	①	1/4	—	15/64	1/4	20 Drill	41 Drill	On Index
	4725S	①	11/32	1	1/32	1/4	20 Drill	28 Drill	2 Rich
	4726S	①	11/32	1	1/32	1/4	28 Drill	28 Drill	2 Rich
	4727S	①	11/32	1	1/8	1/4	20 Drill	28 Drill	2 Rich
	4728S	①	11/32	1	3/16	1/4	28 Drill	28 Drill	2 Rich
	4894S	①	11/32	1	1/32	1/4	28 Drill	28 Drill	2 Rich
	4895S	①	1/4	—	1/32	1/4	20 Drill	41 Drill	On Index
1971	4957S	①	1/4	.200②	13/64	1/4	20 Drill	41 Drill	On Index
	4958S	①	1/4	.200②	13/64	1/4	20 Drill	41 Drill	On Index
	4961S	①	11/32	1	3/16	1/4	20 Drill	20 Drill	2 Rich
	4962S	①	11/32	1	3/16	1/4	28 Drill	28 Drill	2 Rich
1972	6149S	①	1/4	.225③	17/64	1/4	.149	.096	Fixed
	6150S	①	1/4	.225③	17/64	1/4	.149	.096	Fixed
	6151S	①	1/4	.225③	17/64	1/4	.149	.096	Fixed
	6152S	①	1/4	.225③	17/64	1/4	.149	.096	Fixed
1973	6316SA	①	1/4	.242③	—	1/4	.150	.095	Fixed
	6317SA	①	1/4	.242③	—	1/4	.130	.095	Fixed
	6343SA④	①	1/4	.242③	—	1/4	.150	.095	Fixed
	6344SA④	①	1/4	.242③	—	1/4	.150	.095	Fixed
1974	6464S	①	1/4	1/2③	—	.325	.150	.095	Fixed
	6465S	①	1/4	1/2③	—	.325	.110	.095	Fixed
	6466S④	①	1/4	1/2③	—	.325	.150	.095	Fixed
	6467S④	①	1/4	1/2③	—	.325	.110	.095	Fixed
1975	800S	①	1/4	1/2③	—	.280	.130	.070	Fixed
	8001S	①	1/4	1/2③	—	.310	.110	.070	Fixed
	8003S	①	1/4	1/2③	—	.310	.110	.070	Fixed
	8062S	①	1/4	1/2③	—	.310	.110	.070	Fixed
	8064S	①	1/4	1/2③	—	.310	.070	.070	Fixed
	8066S	①	1/4	1/2③	—	.280	.130	.070	Fixed

①—Air/fuel ratio or idle CO% rating is found in Tune Up Specification tables in car chapters.
②—Throttle closed.
③—At idle.
④—With California Emission package.

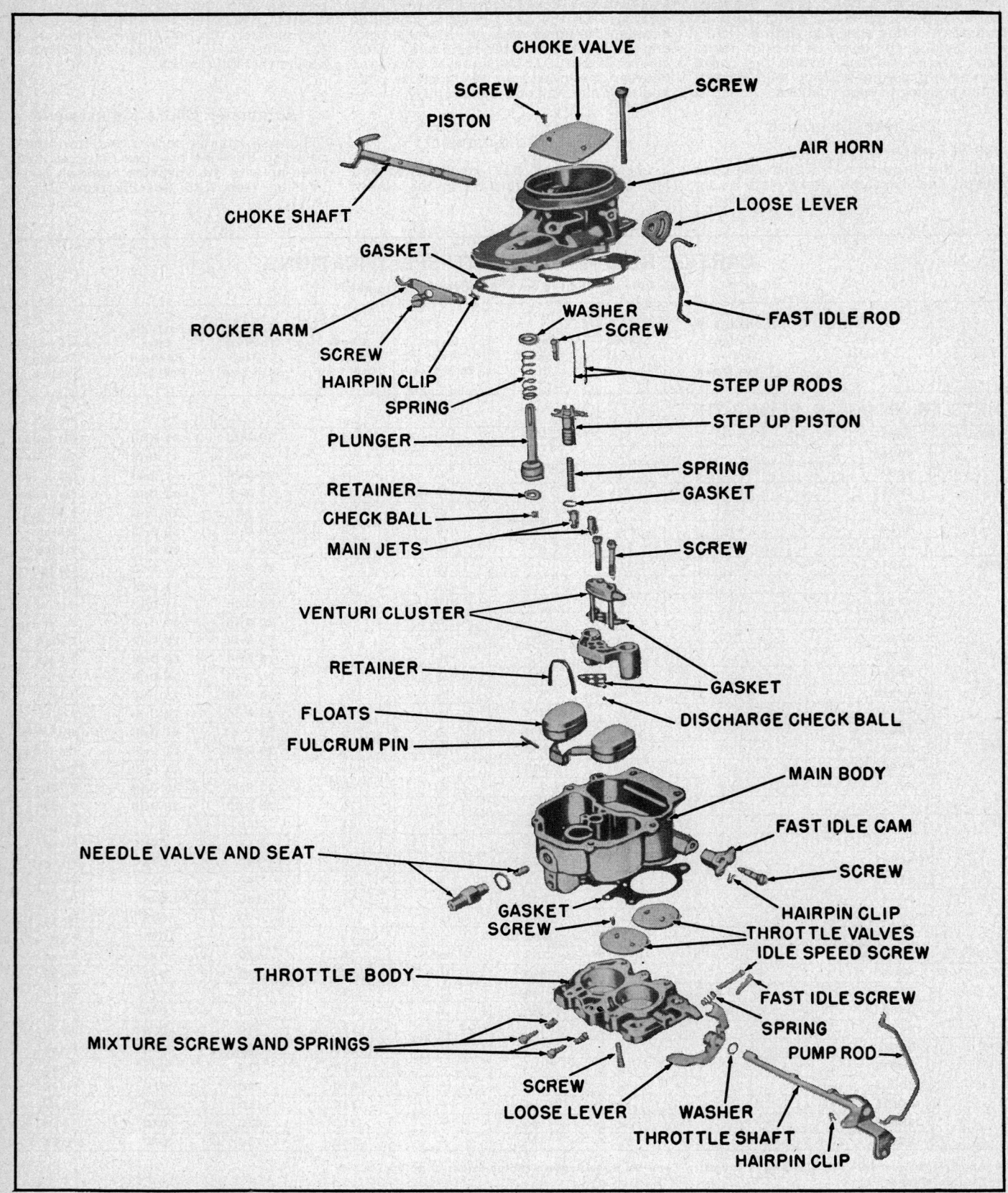

Fig. 1 Carter Model BBD two-barrel carburetor exploded

MODEL BBD ADJUSTMENTS

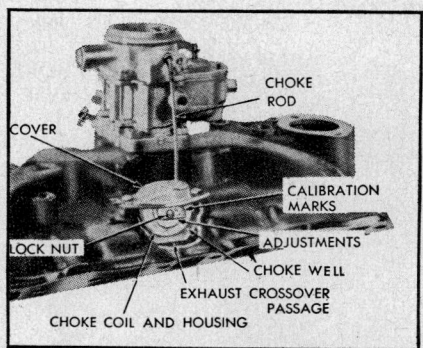

Fig. 2 Well-type automatic choke mounted on intake manifold

CHOKE ROD
COVER
CALIBRATION MARKS
LOCK NUT
ADJUSTMENTS
CHOKE WELL
EXHAUST CROSSOVER PASSAGE
CHOKE COIL AND HOUSING

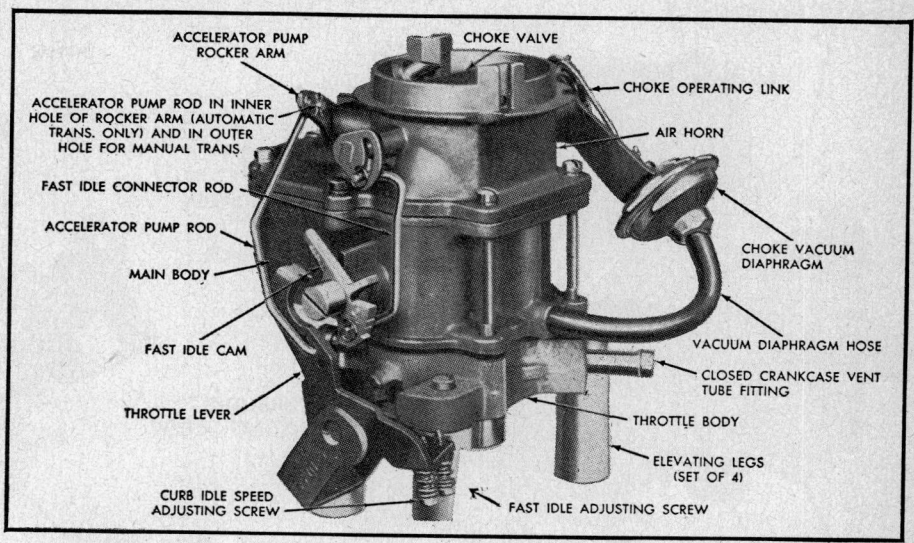

ACCELERATOR PUMP ROCKER ARM
CHOKE VALVE
ACCELERATOR PUMP ROD IN INNER HOLE OF ROCKER ARM (AUTOMATIC TRANS. ONLY) AND IN OUTER HOLE FOR MANUAL TRANS.
CHOKE OPERATING LINK
AIR HORN
FAST IDLE CONNECTOR ROD
ACCELERATOR PUMP ROD
MAIN BODY
CHOKE VACUUM DIAPHRAGM
FAST IDLE CAM
VACUUM DIAPHRAGM HOSE
CLOSED CRANKCASE VENT TUBE FITTING
THROTTLE LEVER
THROTTLE BODY
ELEVATING LEGS (SET OF 4)
CURB IDLE SPEED ADJUSTING SCREW
FAST IDLE ADJUSTING SCREW

Fig. 3 BBD 1¼" bore carburetor assembly C.A.P. equipped

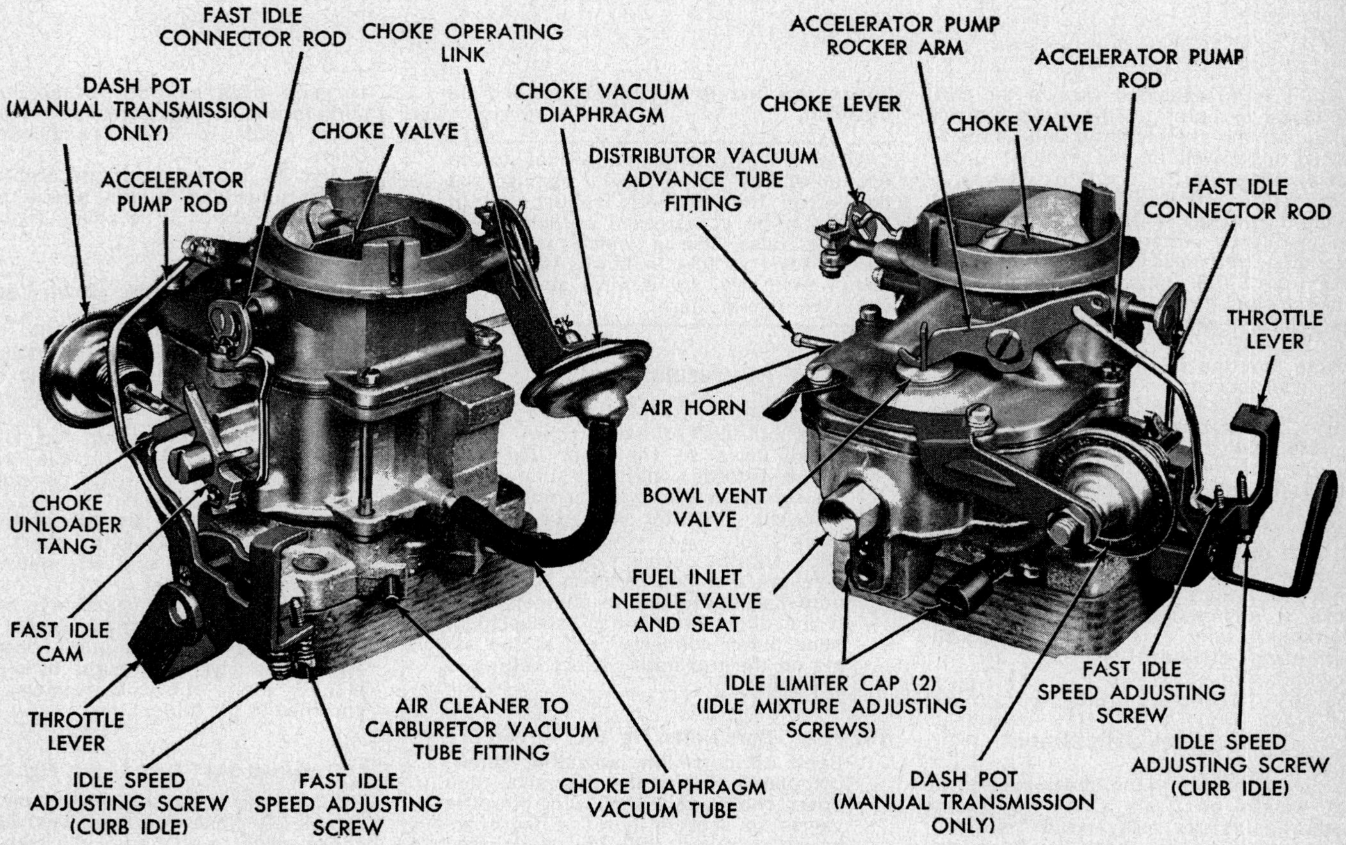

FAST IDLE CONNECTOR ROD
CHOKE OPERATING LINK
DASH POT (MANUAL TRANSMISSION ONLY)
CHOKE VALVE
CHOKE VACUUM DIAPHRAGM
ACCELERATOR PUMP ROCKER ARM
ACCELERATOR PUMP ROD
CHOKE LEVER
CHOKE VALVE
ACCELERATOR PUMP ROD
DISTRIBUTOR VACUUM ADVANCE TUBE FITTING
FAST IDLE CONNECTOR ROD
THROTTLE LEVER
CHOKE UNLOADER TANG
AIR HORN
FAST IDLE CAM
BOWL VENT VALVE
THROTTLE LEVER
FUEL INLET NEEDLE VALVE AND SEAT
IDLE SPEED ADJUSTING SCREW (CURB IDLE)
FAST IDLE SPEED ADJUSTING SCREW
AIR CLEANER TO CARBURETOR VACUUM TUBE FITTING
CHOKE DIAPHRAGM VACUUM TUBE
IDLE LIMITER CAP (2) (IDLE MIXTURE ADJUSTING SCREWS)
DASH POT (MANUAL TRANSMISSION ONLY)
FAST IDLE SPEED ADJUSTING SCREW
IDLE SPEED ADJUSTING SCREW (CURB IDLE)

Fig. 3A BBD 1¼" bore carburetor assembly C.A.S. equipped

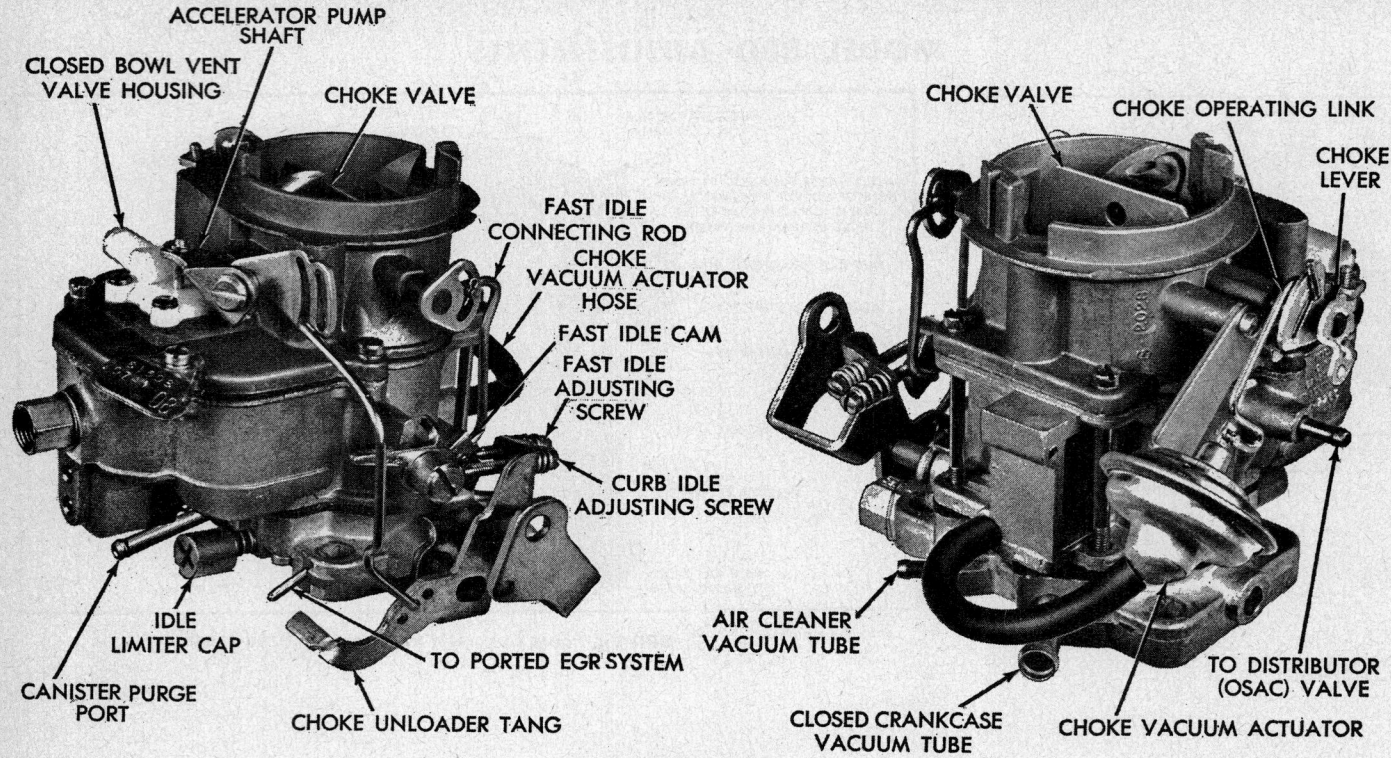

ACCELERATOR PUMP SHAFT

CLOSED BOWL VENT VALVE HOUSING

CHOKE VALVE

FAST IDLE CONNECTING ROD

CHOKE VACUUM ACTUATOR HOSE

FAST IDLE CAM

FAST IDLE ADJUSTING SCREW

CURB IDLE ADJUSTING SCREW

IDLE LIMITER CAP

CANISTER PURGE PORT

TO PORTED EGR SYSTEM

CHOKE UNLOADER TANG

CHOKE VALVE

CHOKE OPERATING LINK

CHOKE LEVER

AIR CLEANER VACUUM TUBE

CLOSED CRANKCASE VACUUM TUBE

CHOKE VACUUM ACTUATOR

TO DISTRIBUTOR (OSAC) VALVE

Fig. 3B   BBD 1¼″ bore carburetor assembly E.C.S. equipped (typical)

Fig. 1 is an exploded view of the BBD two barrel carburetor. The choke housing containing the thermostatic coil spring is located in a well at the exhaust cross-over passage, Fig. 2.

The carburetor shown in Fig. 3 is a standard model when the vehicle is equipped with either a manual shift or automatic transmission. When used with C.A.P. or C.A.S. equipment, a dashpot (slow closing throttle device) is provided for vehicles with manual transmission only, Fig. 3A.

Note that the 1973-74 E.C.S. equipped unit incorporates a Canister Purge Port, Fig. 3B.

The carburetors illustrated in Fig. 4 are used on the larger V8 engines; the one on the right is a standard model while the one at the left is used with C.A.P. or C.A.S. equipment. Note that the C.A.P. model incorporates a dashpot for use with manual shift transmissions only. Also on 1973-74 Chrysler units, an electric choke system is incorporated to open choke at approximately 63°. For service information refer to the "Emission Control System" chapter.

Float Level Adjustment

Fig. 5—With carburetor body inverted so that weight of floats ONLY is forcing needle against its seat, use a T-scale or the tool shown, and check the float level from surface of fuel bowl to crown of each float at center.

If an adjustment is necessary, hold floats on bottom of bowl and bend float

lip as required to give the specified dimension.

CAUTION: When bending the float lip, do not allow the lip to push against the needle as the synthetic rubber tip (if used) can be compressed sufficiently to cause a false setting which will affect correct level of fuel in bowl. After being compressed, the tip is very slow to recover its original shape.

Accelerator Pump

Except 1¼″ Bore Units, Fig. 6
1. Back off idle adjusting screw. Open choke valve so that fast idle cam allows throttle valves to fully close. Be sure that pump connector rod is installed in outer hole of throttle lever.
2. With throttle valves closed tightly, measure distance between top of air horn and end of pump plunger shaft. If the dimension is not as specified, bend pump connector rod at the angle on the rod until correct setting is obtained.

1974 1¼″ Bore Units, Fig. 6A
1. Back off curb idle adjusting screw, completely closing throttle valve, then open choke valve, allowing throttle valves to seat in bores. Ensure accelerator pump "S" link is located in outer hole or pump arm.
2. Turn curb idle adjusting screw until screw contacts, stop, then rotate screw two additional turns.

3. Measure distance between air horn surface and top of accelerator pump shaft. Refer to BBD Specifications Chart.
4. Adjust by loosening pump arm adjusting screw and rotating sleeve until proper dimension is obtained. Tighten adjusting screw.

Accelerator Pump and Bowl Vent

C.A.S. Equipped 1¼″ Bore Units, Fig. 7
1. Back off idle speed adjusting screw. Open choke valve so that fast idle cam allows throttle valves to close completely.
2. Be sure pump operating rod is in medium stroke hole in throttle lever, and that bowl vent clip on pump stem is on center notch.
3. With throttle valves closed tightly, it should be just possible to insert the specified gauge or drill size between bowl vent and its seat.
4. If an adjustment is necessary, bend pump operating rod at the angle. On CAP carburetors, bend pump operating rod to give the height of pump plunger stem above bowl cover as specified in the table.

E.C.S. Equipped 1¼″ Bore Units, Fig. 7A
1. Back off idle speed adjusting screw to completely close throttle valves. Open choke valve so that fast idle cam allows throttle valves to seat in bores.
2. Be sure accelerator pump operating rod is in medium stroke hole in throttle lever.

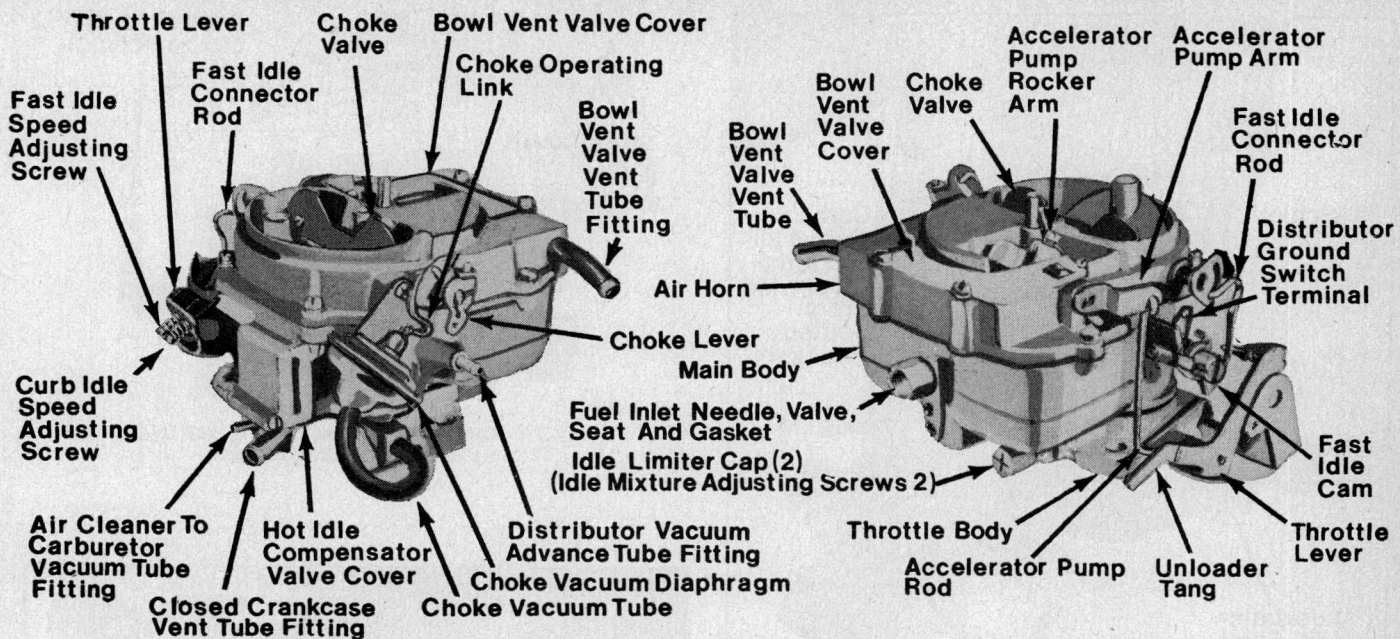

Fig. 4   BBD 1½″ bore carburetors (typical)

3. Close throttle valves tightly. Measure distance between top of vent valve plastic housing and end of pump plunger stem.

4. To adjust pump travel, bend accelerator pump operating rod at lower angle. Refer to BBD Specifications Chart.

NOTE: This is an important adjustment, since too much lift at the bowl vent will result in considerable loss in low speed fuel economy.

   Remember that if the pump operating rod is moved to either the short or long stroke position, a corresponding change must be made in the location of the bowl

vent clip, and the amount of lift of the bowl vent rechecked.

Bowl Vent Adjustment
Models with Separate Pump Fig. 7B
1½″ Bore Units

1. Open choke valve so that fast idle

cam allows valves to close, curb idle.

2. Be sure that pump operating rod is in long stroke hole in throttle lever. Remove bowl vent valve cover if not previously done.

3. On E.C.S. units, close throttle valves tightly. Using a narrow ruler, measure the distance from top of bowl vent valve (rubber tip) to top of air horn casting, Fig. 7B. Refer to Specifica-

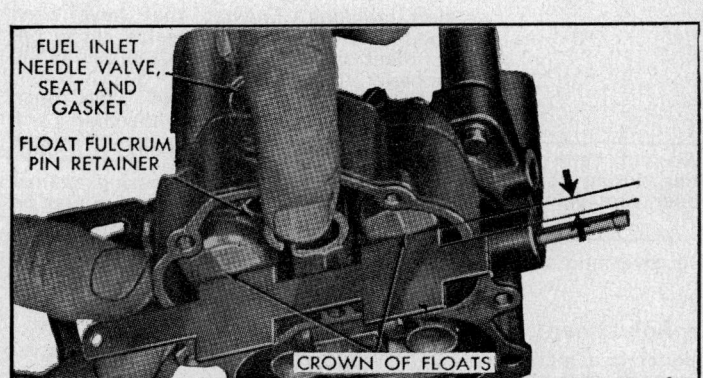

Fig. 5   Checking float level. BBD carburetors

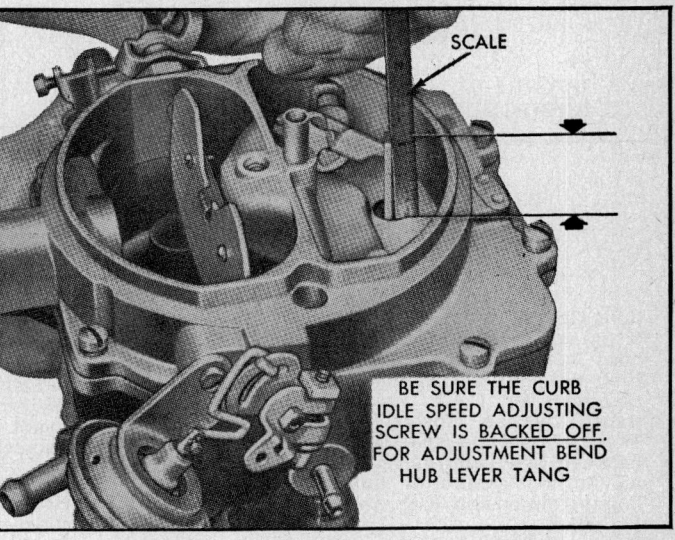

Fig. 6   Checking accelerator pump travel. BBD except 1¼″ bore carburetors

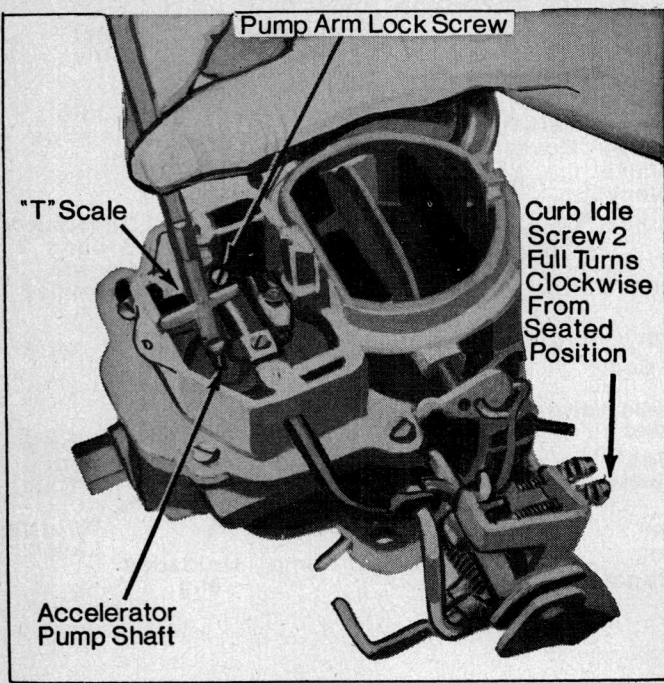

Fig. 6A   Accelerator pump setting, 1974 1¼" E.C.S. units

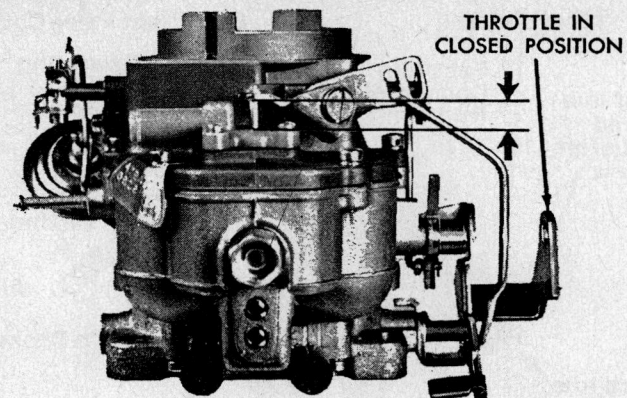

Fig. 7A   Checking bowl vent opening BBD 1¼" bore carburetors E.C.S. equipped

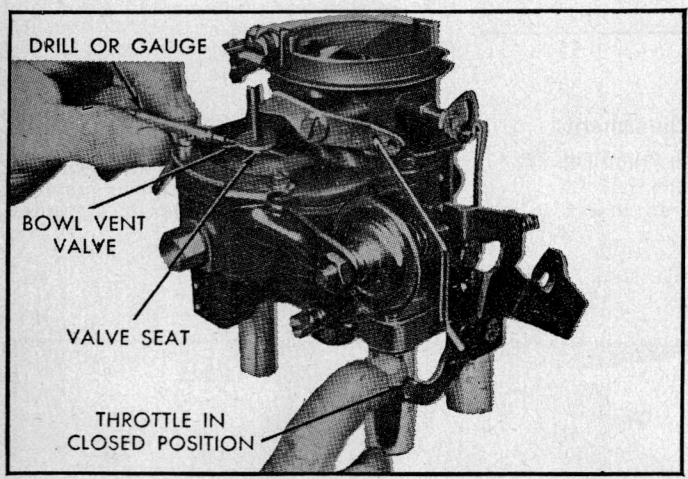

Fig. 7   Checking bowl vent opening. BBD 1¼" bore carburetors C.A.S. equipped

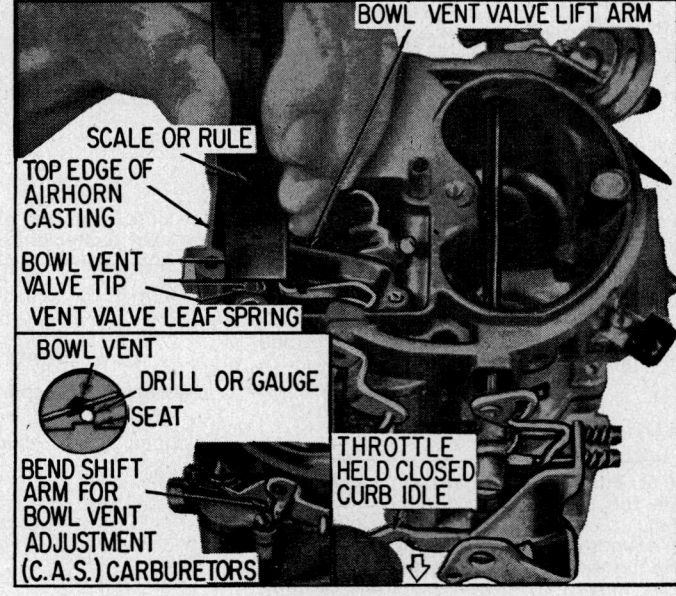

Fig. 7B   Measuring bowl vent valve opening BBD 1½" bore C.A.S. and E.C.S. carburetors

tions Chart.

If an adjustment is necessary, bend bowl vent lift arm, using a suitable tool, until correct opening has been obtained. On C.A.S. units, with the throttle valves closed, (curb idle). There should be specified clearance between bowl vent valve and seat on air horn. Measure at outermost or largest dimension with a drill shank, Fig. 7B.

If an adjustment is necessary, bend vent valve lifter arm until correct clearance has been obtained.

Note: Important: Do not bend bowl vent valve leaf spring during bending operation or improper vent valve operation will result.

Install bowl vent valve cover and secure with attaching screws.

Choke Unloader Adjustment

Fig. 8—The choke unloader is a mechanical device to partially open the choke valve at wide open throttle. It is used to eliminate choke enrichment during en-

gine cranking. Engines that have been flooded or stalled by excessive choke enrichment can be cleared by the use of the unloader. Adjust as follows:

1. Hold throttle valve in wide open position. Insert the specified drill size between upper edge of choke valve and inner wall of air horn.
2. With a finger lightly pressing against choke valve, a slight drag should be felt as the drill is being withdrawn.
3. If an adjustment is necessary, bend unloader tang on throttle lever until specified opening has been obtained.

Fast Idle Cam Position
Figs. 9 and 10

1. With fast idle adjusting screw contacting second highest step on fast

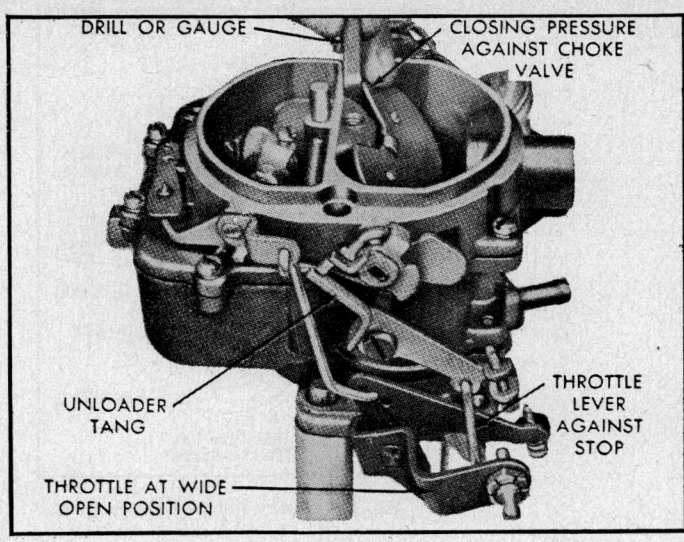

Fig. 8   Choke unloader setting. BBD carburetors

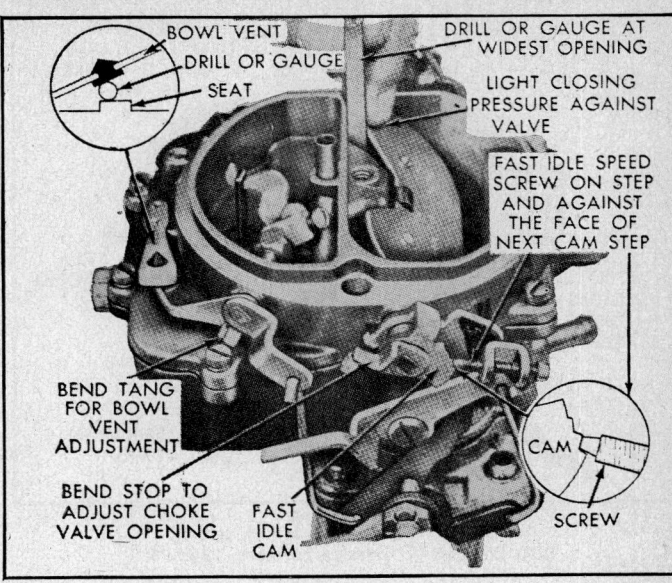

Fig. 10   Fast idle cam position adjustment.
BBD except 1¼" bore carburetors

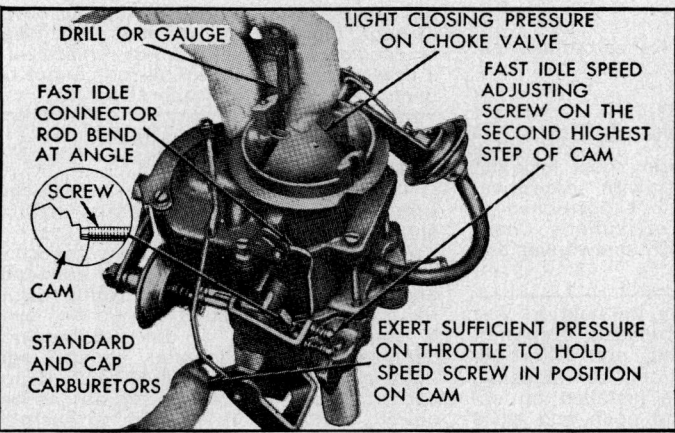

Fig. 9   Fast idle cam position adjustment.
BBD 1¼" bore carburetors

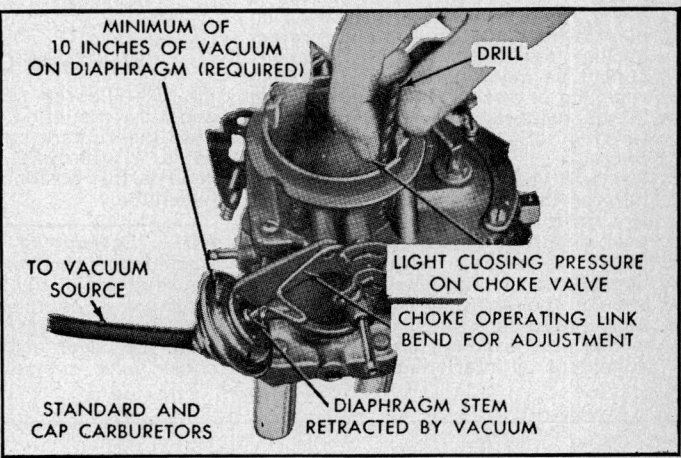

Fig. 11   Choke vacuum kick setting.
BBD 1¼" bore carburetors, 1969-74

idle cam, move choke valve toward closed position with light pressure on choke shaft lever.

2. Insert the specified size drill between choke valve and air horn wall. An adjustment will be necessary if a slight drag is not obtained as drill is being removed.

3. On all models except 1969 1½ inch bore units, adjust by bending fast idle connector rod at lower angle. On 1969 1½ inch bore units, adjust by bending stop on choke shaft.

Choke Vacuum Kick Adjustment
Figs. 11 and 12

The choke diaphragm adjustment controls the fuel delivery while the engine is running. It positions the choke valve within the air horn by action of the link-

age between choke shaft and diaphragm. The diaphragm must be energized to measure the vacuum kick adjustment. Use either a distributor test machine with a vacuum source, or vacuum supplied by another vehicle.

1. If adjustment is to be made with engine running, disconnect fast idle linkage to allow choke to close to kick position with engine at curb idle. If an auxiliary vacuum source is to be used, open throttle valves (engine not running) and move choke to closed position. Release throttle first, then release choke.

2. When using an auxiliary vacuum source, disconnect vacuum hose from carburetor and connect it to hose from vacuum supply with a small length of tube to act as a fitting.

Removal of hose from diaphragm may require forces which damage the system. On all 1969-72 units, apply a vacuum of 10 or more inches of mercury and on all 1973-74 units, apply a vacuum of 15 or more inches of mercury.

3. Insert the specified drill size between choke valve and wall of air horn. Apply sufficient closing pressure on lever to which choke rod attaches to provide a minimum choke valve opening without distortion of diaphragm link. Note that the cylindrical stem of diaphragm will extend as internal spring is compressed. This spring must be fully compressed for proper measurement of vacuum kick adjustment.

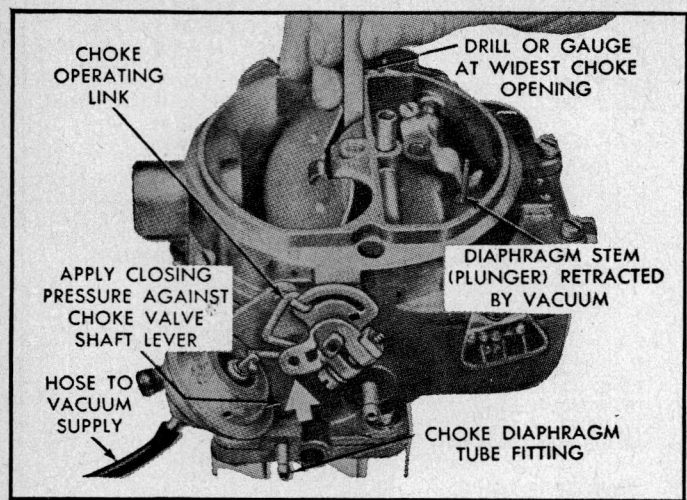

Fig. 12   Choke vacuum kick setting.
BBD except 1¼" bore carburetors, 1969-71

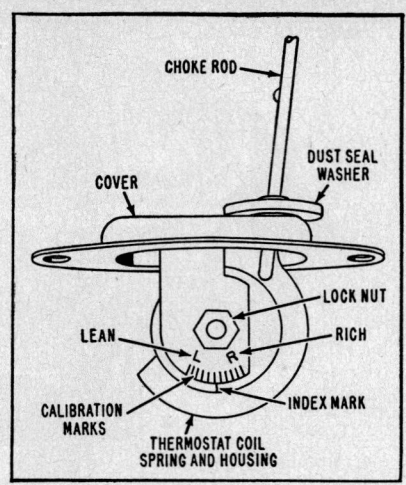

Fig. 13   BBD well-type choke setting

4. An adjustment will be necessary if a slight drag is not obtained as drill is being removed. Shorten or lengthen diaphragm link to obtain correct choke opening. Length changes should be made carefully by bending (opening or closing) the bend provided in the diaphragm link. *Do not apply twisting or bending force to diaphragm.*

5. Reinstall vacuum hose on correct carburetor fitting. Return fast idle linkage to its original condition if it has been disturbed as in Step 1.

6. Check as follows: With no vacuum applied to diaphragm, choke valve should move freely between open and closed positions. If movement is not free, examine linkage for misalignment or interferences caused by

bending operation. Repeat adjustment if necessary.

Well-Type Choke Setting

Fig. 13—Loosen mounting post lock nut and turn mounting post with screwdriver until index mark on disc is positioned as listed in the *BBD Specifications Chart*. Hold in this position with screwdriver and lock nut.

NOTE: Screwdriver may be held in vise so that one hand may be used to support housing while tightening nut. After adjustment is completed and coil housing, rod and carburetor are installed on engine, lift cover disc and open and close choke valve manually to see if connector

rod clears sides of hole in housing cover without binding. If rod does not clear housing cover without binding, replace with a new unit since connecting rod cannot be bent without affecting calibration.

Dashpot Adjustment

Cleaner Air Carburetors

The dashpot is used only on vehicles with the Cleaner Air Package and manual shift transmission, Fig. 4.

To adjust the dashpot, have the curb idle speed and mixture properly adjusted, and install a tachometer. Position throttle lever so that actuating tab on lever is contacting stem of dashpot but not depressing it. Tachometer should read 2000 rpm if the setting is correct. If not correct, screw dashpot in or out as required, then tighten lock nut on dashpot against the bracket.

CARTER WCD ADJUSTMENT SPECIFICATIONS

See Tune Up Chart in car chapter for hot idle speed.

Year	Carb. Model	Idle Mixture Screw Setting	Float Level	Pump Setting	Metering Rod	Fast Idle Setting	Choke Unloader	Dashpot Setting	Automatic Choke
AMERICAN MOTORS									
1969	4667S	1½	7/32	See Text	See Text	—	3/16	7/64	On Index
	4668S	1½	7/32	See Text	See Text	—	3/16	7/64	On Index
1970	4816S	①	7/32	See Text	See Text	.021	3/16	3/32	Index
	4817S	①	7/32	See Text	See Text	.024	3/16	3/32	Index
	4950S	①	7/32	See Text	See Text	.024	3/16	3/32	Index

① —Air/fuel ratio or idle CO% rating is found in Tune Up Specification tables in car chapters.

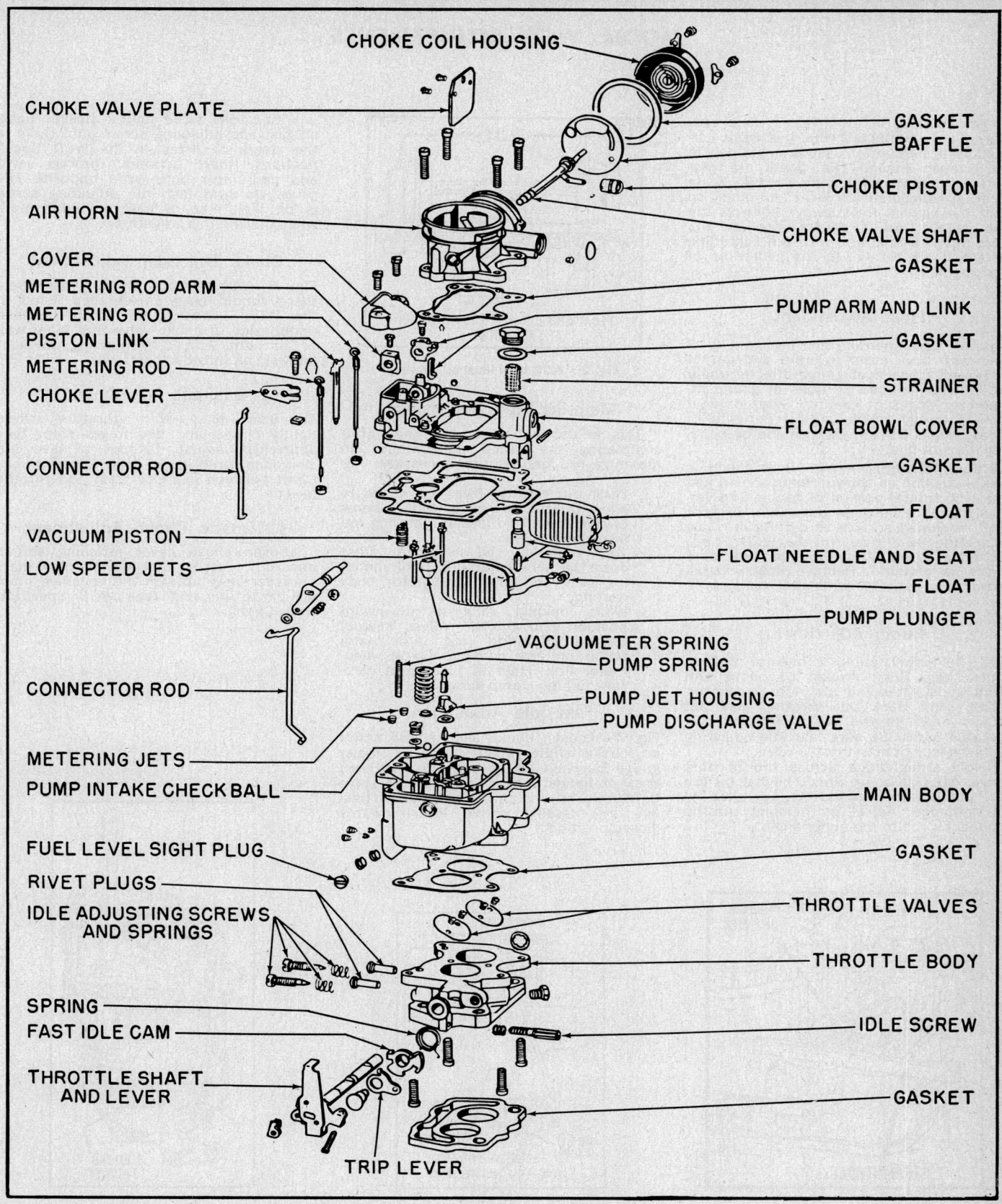

Fig. 1 Carter Model WCD two-barrel carburetor

MODEL WCD ADJUSTMENTS

The WCD carburetor, Fig. 1, is a two-barrel unit containing the five basic circuits. The carburetor uses a single needle valve even though two floats are provided. On some WCD units the two floats operate independently of each other so that the highest float always controls the fuel level. This is necessary when the carburetor is mounted with the centerline of the floats parallel to the centerline of the engine.

Float Adjustment

Lateral Adjustment—Referring to Fig. 2 and with bowl cover inverted and gasket removed, place float gauge directly under floats with notched portions of gauge fitted over edges of casting. Sides of float should barely touch vertical uprights of float gauge. Adjustment is made by bending arms of floats.

Vertical Adjustment—With float gauge in same position as shown, floats should just clear horizontal portion of gauge. The vertical distance between top center of float and machined surface of casting must be the dimension given in the *WCD Specifications Chart*. Adjust by bending float arms as required. Remove floats, install bowl cover gasket and reinstall floats.

Pump Adjustment

Fig. 3—Install pump connector link in outer hole (long stroke) of pump arm with ends extending away from countershaft arm. Back out throttle lever set screw until throttle valves seat in carburetor bores. Be sure fast idle adjusting screw does not hold throttle open.

Hold straightedge across top of dust cover boss at pump arm. The flat on top of pump arm should be parallel to straightedge. Adjust by bending throttle connector rod to the upper angle.

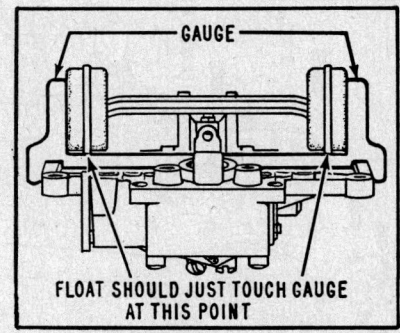

Fig. 2 WCD float level adjustment

Metering Rod Adjustment

This adjustment must be made after completing the pump adjustment. No metering rod gauges are necessary. Adjust as follows:

1. Back out throttle lever set screw to allow throttle valves to seat in bores of carburetor and loosen metering rod arm clamp screw.
2. With metering rod in place, press down on vacumeter link until metering rods bottom in carburetor body casting.
3. While holding rods in downward position and throttle valves seated, revolve metering rod arm until finger on arm contacts lip of vacumeter link. Hold in place and carefully tighten clamp screw.

Fast Idle Adjustment

Fig. 4—Loosen choke lever clamp screw on choke shaft. Insert a .010" feeler gauge between lip of fast idle cam and boss of flange casting. Hold choke valve tightly closed and take slack out of linkage by pressing choke lever towards closed position.

With choke valve tightly closed, tighten fast idle adjusting screw until there is the clearance listed in the *WCD Specifications Chart* between throttle valve and carburetor bore (side opposite idle port). Be sure fast idle adjusting screw is on high step of cam or index mark while making this adjustment.

Choke Unloader Adjustment

Fig. 5—With throttle valves wide open, there should be the clearance listed in the *WCD Specifications Chart* between upper edge of choke valve and inner wall of air horn. Adjust by bending unloader lip (ear) on throttle shaft lever.

Dashpot Adjustment

American Mtrs—With throttle valves tightly closed and diaphragm stem fully depressed, adjust dashpot to give the clearance listed in the *WCD Specifications Chart* between dashpot stem and throttle lever.

Automatic Choke Adjustment

Loosen choke cover retaining screws and turn cover so that line or index mark on cover lines up with the specified mark on choke housing (see *WCD Specifications Chart*).

Fig. 3 WCD pump adjustment

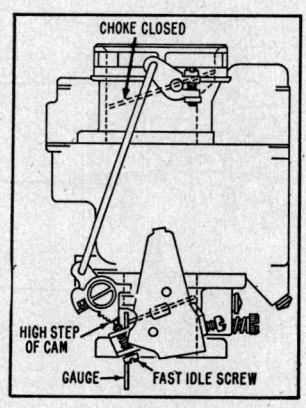

Fig. 4 WCD fast idle adjustment

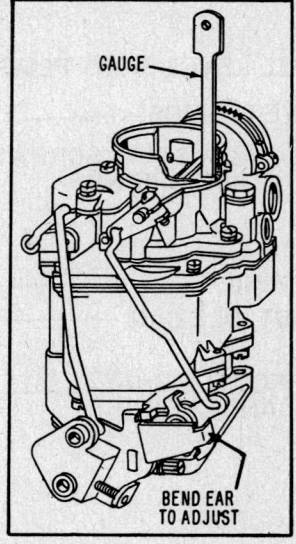

Fig. 5 WCD unloader adjustment

CARTER WGD ADJUSTMENT SPECIFICATIONS

See Tune Up Chart in car chapters for hot idle speed.

Year	Carb. Model	Air/Fuel Ratio	Float Setting	Fast Idle Throttle Valve Setting	Choke Unloader	Choke Diaphragm Linkage	Choke Coil Rod Position
PONTIAC							
1972	6311S	①	⁵⁄₁₆	.030	³⁄₁₆	⁹⁄₆₄	Center Notch

①—Air/fuel ratio or idle CO% rating is found in Tune Up Specification tables in car chapters.

MODEL WGD ADJUSTMENTS

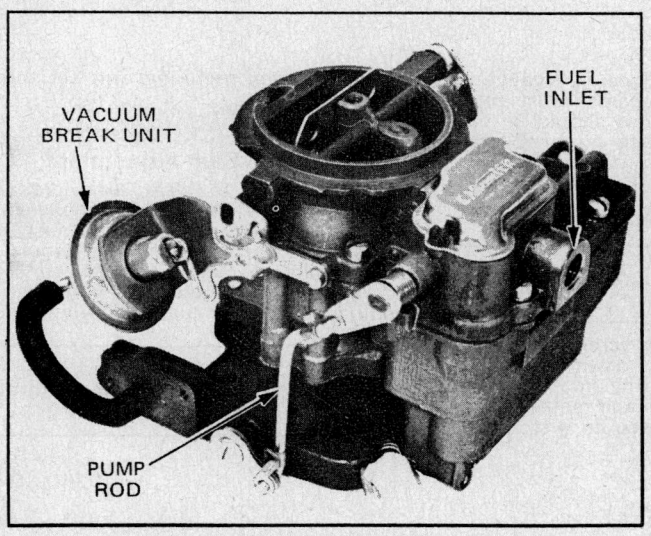

Fig. 1   Carter WGD carburetor assembly

Fig. 2   WGD float level alignment

MODEL WGD ADJUSTMENTS

The WGD carburetor, Fig. 1, is similar to the WCD model except that the WGD has only one float, a reduced overall height thermostatic coil located on the engine manifold which is connected to the choke valve by a rod and simplified adjustments.

Also a vacuum break diaphragm unit has been incorporated, this is a modified unit in that a tension spring has been added to the choke vacuum break diaphragm plunger. The purpose of the tension or bucking spring is to offset tension of the thermostatic coil in relation to atmospheric temperatures.

Float Adjustment

With air horn inverted, check to see that float is parallel with outer edge of air horn casting, Fig. 2. Adjust by bending float arm. Next, place gauge between air horn

Fig. 3   WGD checking float level adjustment

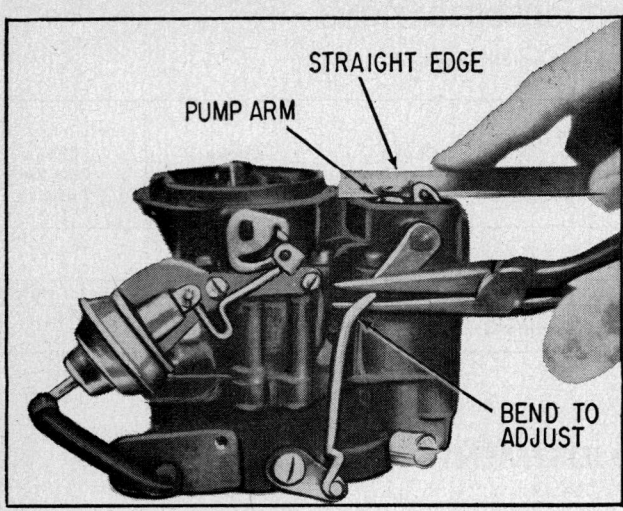

Fig. 4   WGD pump adjustment

Fig. 5   WGD metering rod adjustment

and center of float, Fig. 3. Refer to *WGD Specifications Chart.* Adjust float level by bending float arm until float touches gauge. Float should not have excessive clearance at hinge pin and must operate freely.

NOTE: When adjusting float, care must be exercised to avoid pressing the flared tip needle into the needle seat as a false setting will result. Allow only the float weight to seat needle when gauging.

Pump Adjustment

Fig. 4—Back out throttle stop screw, turn fast idle cam to "hot" position and fully close throttle valves. Place ¼" gauge or a similar straight edge across dust cover boss. The dust cover boss should be parallel with the top surface of pump arm. Adjust by bending pump rod at offset.

Metering Rod Adjustment

NOTE: This adjustment should be made after the pump adjustment. No metering rod gauges are necessary.

Back out throttle stop screw, fully close throttle valves and press down on vacuum piston link until metering rods bottom. While holding rods down and metering arm tongue against lip of vacuum piston link,

carefully tighten metering arm set screw, Fig. 5.

Fast Idle Cam Adjustment

Open throttle to clear fast idle cam and close choke valve. With choke valve held fully closed and stop on fast idle cam against the casting, there should be .005" minimum clearance between inner and outer choke levers, Fig. 6. Adjust by bending outer lever lug, as required, Fig. 7.

NOTE: With choke fully closed, tang on fast idle cam must clear stop on throttle body flange.

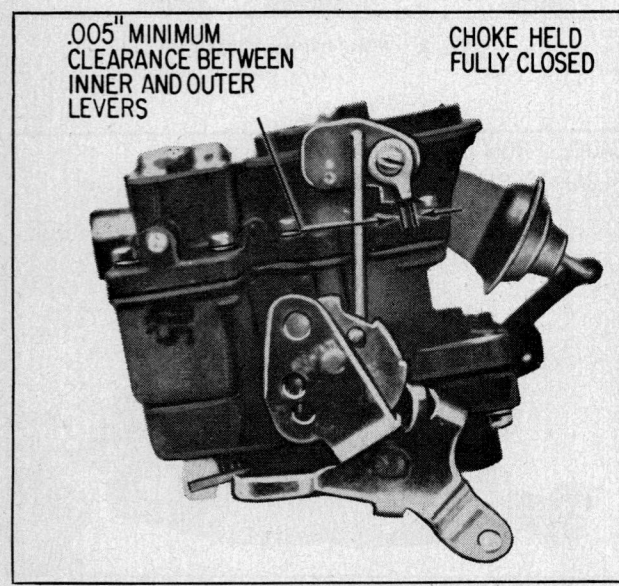

Fig. 6   WGD fast idle cam position

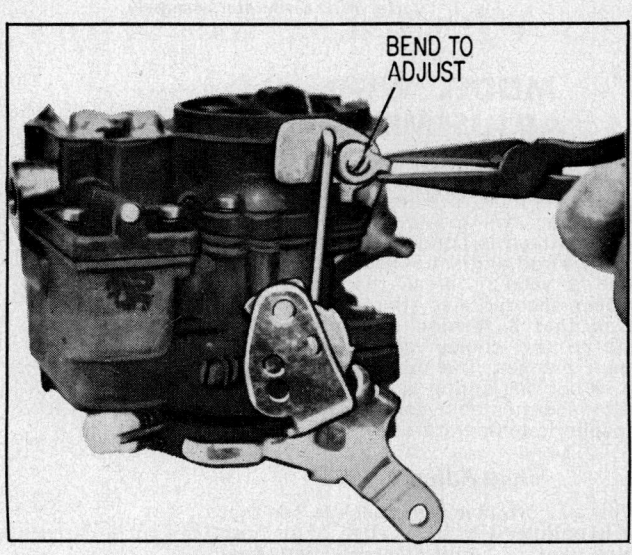

Fig. 7   WGD choke lever adjustment

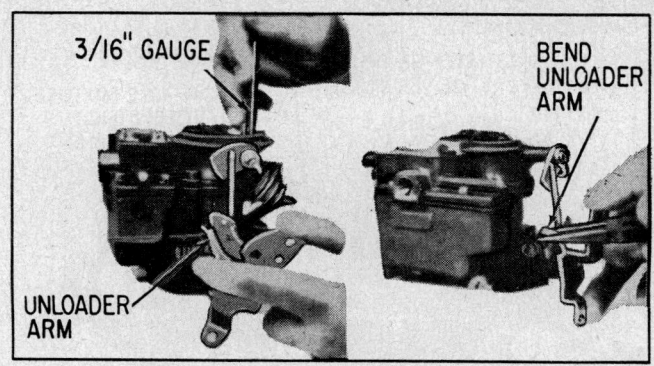

Fig. 8   WGD choke unloader adjustment

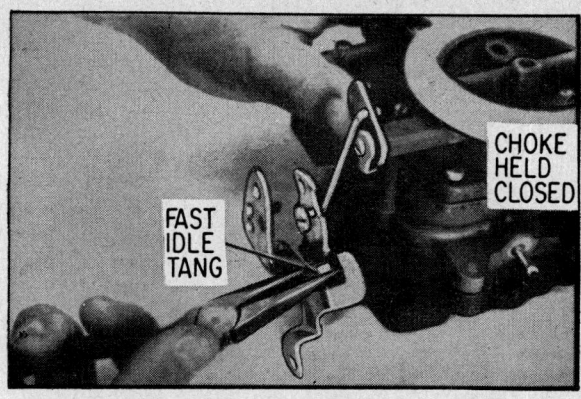

Fig. 9   WGD fast idle speed adjustment unit on engine

Unloader Adjustment

Hold choke closed lightly. Fully open throttle, forcing choke valve open. Check clearance between upper edge of choke valve and wall of air horn, Fig. 8. Refer to WGD Specifications Chart. Adjust by bending the unloader arm as required.

Fast Idle Speed Adjustment

With carburetor on engine, rotate fast idle cam until fast idle tang contacts high step of cam. With engine at normal operating temperature adjust fast idle tang to obtain engine speed of 1500 rpm, Fig. 9.

CARTER AVS ADJUSTMENT SPECIFICATIONS

See Tune Up Chart in car chapter for hot idle speed.

Year	Carb. Model	Idle Mixture Turns Open	Float Level	Float Drop	Pump Travel	Bowl Vent	Fast Idle Cam Position	Choke Vacuum Break	Secondary Throttle Lever	Secondary Throttle Lockout	Choke Setting
CHRYSLER, DODGE, PLYMOUTH, IMPERIAL											
1969	4611S	1-2	7/32	1/2	7/16	1/8	50 Drill①	35 Drill	21/64	.020	Index
	4612S	1-2	7/32	1/2	7/16	1/8	50 Drill①	50 Drill	21/64	.020	Index
	4615S	1-2	5/16	1/2	7/16	1/8	50 Drill①	35 Drill	21/64	.020	Index
	4616S	1-2	5/16	1/2	7/16	1/8	50 Drill①	50 Drill	21/64	.020	Index
	4617S	1-2	7/32	1/2	7/16	1/8	50 Drill①	25 Drill	11/32	.020	Index
	4618S	1-2	7/32	1/2	7/16	1/8	50 Drill①	35 Drill	3/8	.020	Index
	4638S	1-2	5/16	1/2	7/16	1/8	50 Drill①	50 Drill	21/64	.020	Index
	4639S	1-2	7/32	1/2	7/16	1/8	50 Drill①	50 Drill	21/64	.020	Index
	4640S	1-2	7/32	1/2	7/16	1/8	50 Drill①	35 Drill	1/8	.020	Index
	4682S	—	5/16	1/2	7/16	1/8	50 Drill①	50 Drill	21/64	.020	Index
	4711S	1-2	5/16	1/2	7/16	1/8	50 Drill①	35 Drill	21/64	.020	Index
1970	4732S	②	5/16	1/2	7/16	3/64	50 Drill①	44 Drill	19/64	.020	2 Rich
	4734S	②	5/16	1/2	7/16	3/64	50 Drill①	44 Drill	19/64	.020	2 Rich
	4736S	②	5/16	1/2	7/16	3/64	50 Drill①	44 Drill	19/64	.020	2 Rich
	4737S	②	7/32	1/2	7/16	3/64	50 Drill①	20 Drill	23/64	.020	2 Rich
	4738S	②	7/32	1/2	7/16	3/64	50 Drill①	20 Drill	23/64	.020	Index
	4739S	②	7/32	1/2	7/16	3/64	50 Drill①	20 Drill	23/64	.020	Index
	4740S	②	7/32	1/2	7/16	3/64	50 Drill①	20 Drill	23/64	.020	Index
	4741S	②	7/32	1/2	7/16	3/64	50 Drill①	20 Drill	23/64	.020	Index
	4933S	②	7/32	1/2	7/16	3/64	50 Drill①	35 Drill	19/64	.020	Index
	4934S	②	7/32	1/2	7/16	1/8	50 Drill①	50 Drill	19/64	.020	Index
	4935S	②	7/32	1/2	7/16	1/8	50 Drill①	50 Drill	19/64	.020	Index
	4936S	②	7/32	1/2	7/16	3/4	50 Drill①	35 Drill	19/64	.020	Index
	4937S	②	7/32	1/2	7/16	3/4	50 Drill①	50 Drill	19/64	.020	Index
1971	4966S	②	7/32	1/2	7/16	3/4	50 Drill①	44 Drill	23/64	.020	2 Rich
	4967S	②	7/32	1/2	7/16	3/4	50 Drill①	44 Drill	23/64	.020	2 Rich
	4968S	②	7/32	1/2	7/16	3/4	50 Drill①	44 Drill	23/64	.020	2 Rich
	6125S	②	7/32	1/2	7/16	3/4	50 Drill①	44 Drill	23/64	.020	2 Rich

①—With fast idle adjusting screw contacting second highest speed step on fast idle cam the clearance between choke valve and wall of air horn should be as specified.

②—Air/fuel ratio or idle CO% rating is found in Tune Up Specification tables in car chapters.

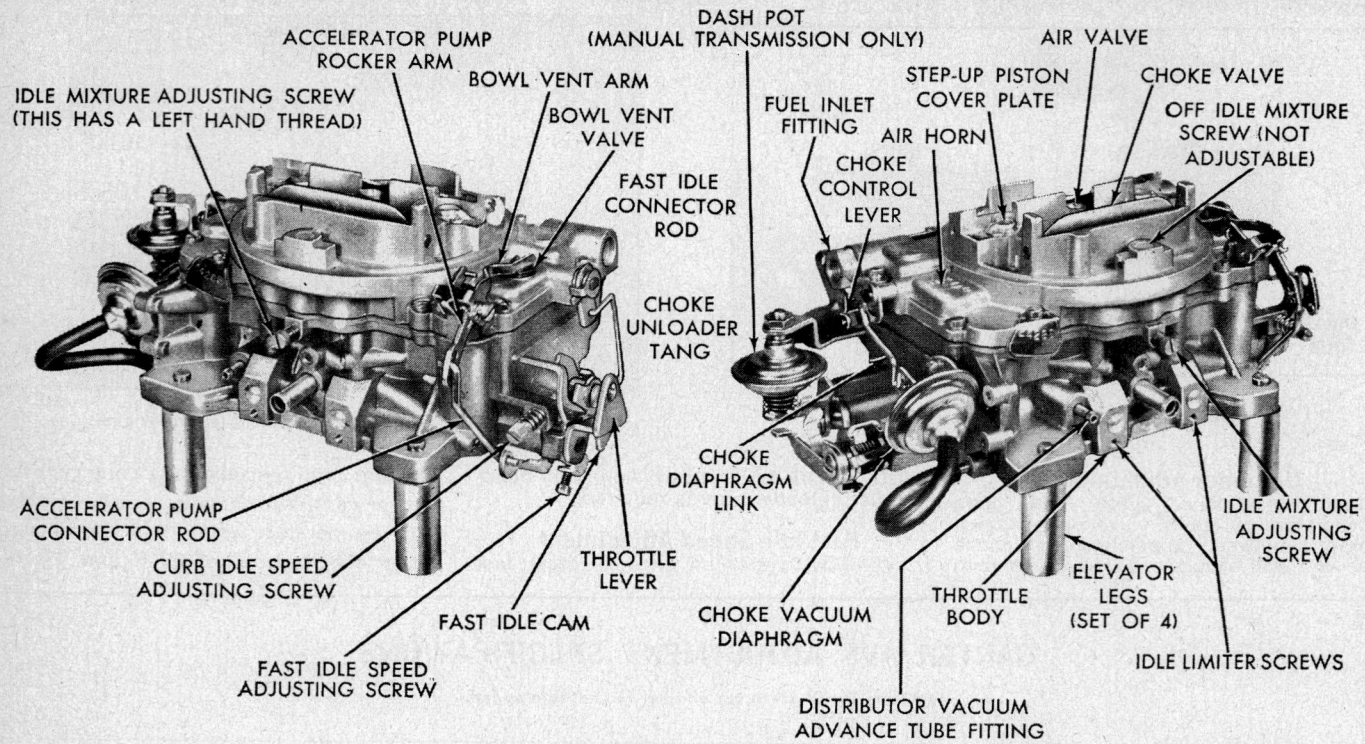

ACCELERATOR PUMP
ROCKER ARM

IDLE MIXTURE ADJUSTING SCREW
(THIS HAS A LEFT HAND THREAD)

BOWL VENT ARM

BOWL VENT
VALVE

FAST IDLE
CONNECTOR
ROD

DASH POT
(MANUAL TRANSMISSION ONLY)

FUEL INLET
FITTING

CHOKE
CONTROL
LEVER

AIR HORN

STEP-UP PISTON
COVER PLATE

AIR VALVE

CHOKE VALVE

OFF IDLE MIXTURE
SCREW (NOT
ADJUSTABLE)

CHOKE
UNLOADER
TANG

ACCELERATOR PUMP
CONNECTOR ROD

CURB IDLE SPEED
ADJUSTING SCREW

FAST IDLE CAM

FAST IDLE SPEED
ADJUSTING SCREW

THROTTLE
LEVER

CHOKE
DIAPHRAGM
LINK

CHOKE VACUUM
DIAPHRAGM

THROTTLE
BODY

ELEVATOR
LEGS
(SET OF 4)

IDLE MIXTURE
ADJUSTING
SCREW

IDLE LIMITER SCREWS

DISTRIBUTOR VACUUM
ADVANCE TUBE FITTING

Fig. 1   1969 Carter AVS four-barrel carburetor

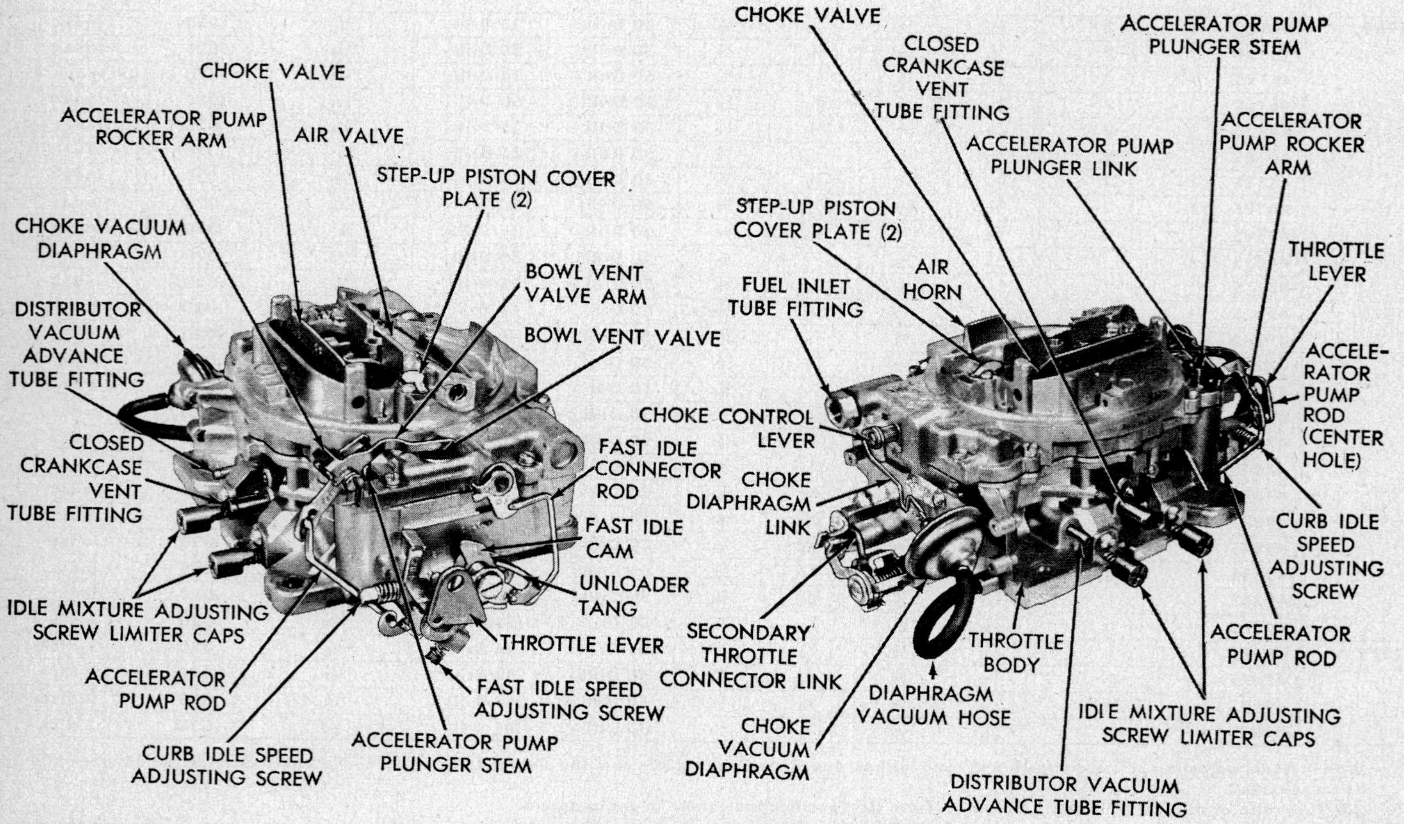

CHOKE VALVE

ACCELERATOR PUMP
ROCKER ARM

AIR VALVE

STEP-UP PISTON COVER
PLATE (2)

CHOKE VACUUM
DIAPHRAGM

DISTRIBUTOR
VACUUM
ADVANCE
TUBE FITTING

BOWL VENT
VALVE ARM

BOWL VENT VALVE

CLOSED
CRANKCASE
VENT TUBE
FITTING

FAST IDLE
CONNECTOR
ROD

FAST IDLE
CAM

UNLOADER
TANG

IDLE MIXTURE ADJUSTING
SCREW LIMITER CAPS

ACCELERATOR
PUMP ROD

CURB IDLE SPEED
ADJUSTING SCREW

ACCELERATOR PUMP
PLUNGER STEM

FAST IDLE SPEED
ADJUSTING SCREW

THROTTLE LEVER

CHOKE VALVE

CLOSED
CRANKCASE
VENT
TUBE FITTING

ACCELERATOR PUMP
PLUNGER LINK

STEP-UP PISTON
COVER PLATE (2)

ACCELERATOR PUMP
PLUNGER STEM

ACCELERATOR
PUMP ROCKER
ARM

FUEL INLET
TUBE FITTING

AIR
HORN

CHOKE CONTROL
LEVER

CHOKE
DIAPHRAGM
LINK

SECONDARY
THROTTLE
CONNECTOR LINK

DIAPHRAGM
VACUUM HOSE

CHOKE
VACUUM
DIAPHRAGM

THROTTLE
LEVER

ACCEL-
ERATOR
PUMP
ROD
(CENTER
HOLE)

CURB IDLE
SPEED
ADJUSTING
SCREW

ACCELERATOR
PUMP ROD

THROTTLE
BODY

IDLE MIXTURE ADJUSTING
SCREW LIMITER CAPS

DISTRIBUTOR VACUUM
ADVANCE TUBE FITTING

Fig. 1A   1970 Carter AVS four-barrel C.A.S. equipped

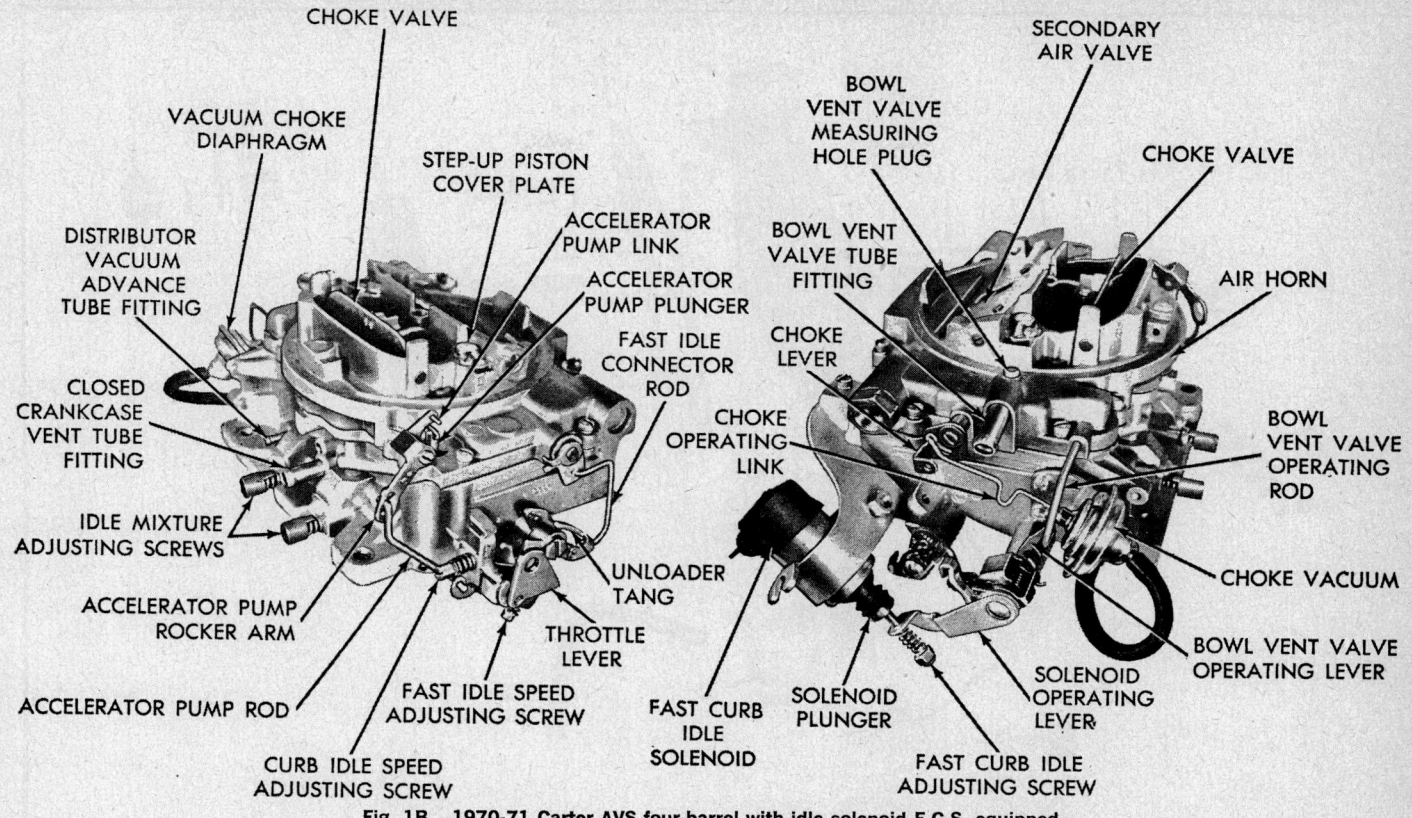

Fig. 1B   1970-71 Carter AVS four-barrel with idle solenoid E.C.S. equipped

MODEL AVS ADJUSTMENTS

The AVS carburetor, Figs. 1 thru 3, is used in conjunction with a temperature sensing choke coil mounted on the intake manifold over the exhaust crossover passage. The AVS is similar to the more familiar AFB which employs a built-in automatic choke.

AVS means "Air Valve Secondary". The spring loaded air valve, located above the secondary fuel nozzles, gives smooth response whenever the secondary throttle valves are actuated.

The primary side of the carburetor uses venturi clusters for fine fuel control in the idle and economy ranges. The use of fuel nozzles pressed into the secondary side of the fuel bowl virtually eliminates secondary bore restriction, thus giving this carburetor high air capacity in the power ranges.

A hot idle compensator, consisting of a bi-metal strip, a valve and a mounting bracket, is located between the secondary bores to supply additional air to the idle mixture during prolonged hot idle periods.

Float Alignment

Fig. 4—Sides of floats should be parallel to edge of casting with minimum clearance between lever and air horn lugs without binding. To adjust, bend float lever.

Float Level Adjustment

Fig. 5—With air horn inverted, air horn gasket in place and float needle seated, slide float gauge between top of the float (at outer end) and air horn gasket. Refer to *AVS Specifications Chart.*

Check other float in same manner. Adjust by bending float arm. After bending arm, recheck the float alignment.

Float Drop Adjustment

Fig. 6—There should be the dimension listed in the *AVS Specifications Chart* between top of floats (at outer end) and air horn gasket. To adjust, bend stop tabs on float brackets.

Pump Adjustment

Fig. 7—With throttle valves tightly closed there should be the dimension listed in the *AVS Specifications Chart* from top of air horn to top of pump plunger shaft with throttle connector rod in inner hole of pump arm. To adjust, bend throttle connector rod at angle.

Fast Idle Cam Adjustment

Fig. 8—With fast idle speed adjusting screw contacting second highest speed step on fast idle cam, move choke valve toward closed position with light pressure on choke shaft lever.

Insert drill gauge between choke valve and wall of air horn. Refer to *AVS Specifications Chart.* An adjustment will be necessary if a slight drag is not obtained as the drill is being removed. Adjust by bending fast idle connector rod at angle.

Choke Unloader Adjustment

Fig. 9—With throttle valves wide open there should be $1/4''$ clearance between upper edge of choke valve and inner wall of air horn. To adjust, bend unloader tang on fast idle cam.

Bowl Vent Adjustment

C.A.S. Equipped, Fig. 10—With throttle valves tightly closed, insert a drill gauge between air horn and valve at smallest opening. Refer to *AVS Specifications Chart.* Adjust by bending tang on pivot end of lever.

E.C.S. Equipped, Fig. 10A—Remove bowl vent valve checking hole plug in air horn. With throttle valves at closed curb idle position, insert a narrow ruler down through hole. Allow ruler to rest lightly on top of valve. Measure from top of valve to top of air horn casting at opening. Refer

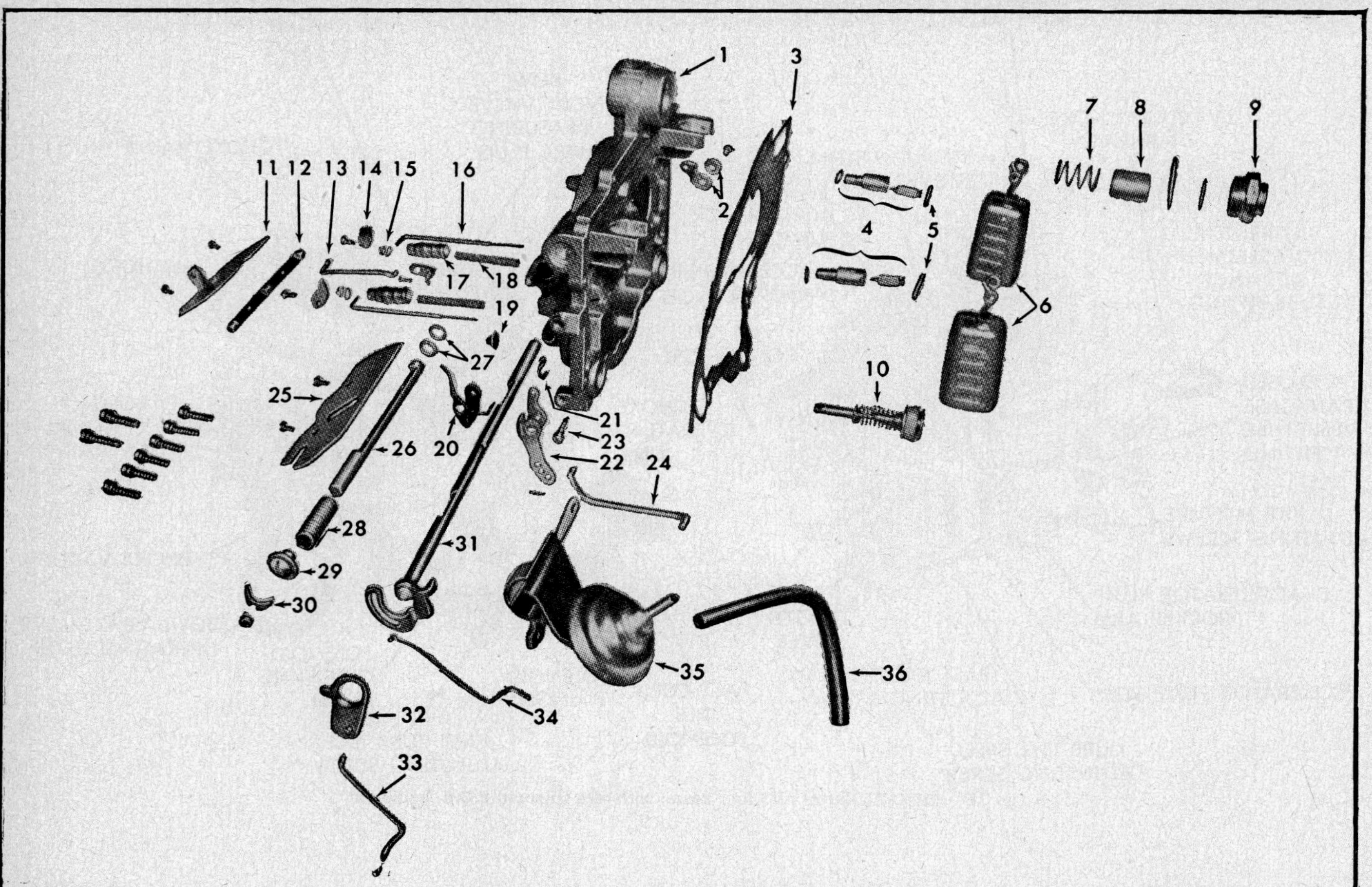

Fig. 2 AVS air horn parts exploded

1. Air Horn	11. Choke Valve	20. Vent Valve Lever	29. Air Valve Bearing
2. Choke Lever and Retainer	12. Choke Shaft	21. Pump "S" Link	30. Bearing Retainer
3. Air Horn Gasket	13. Choke Actuating Link and Lever	22. Pump Lever	31. Intermediate Choke Shaft and Lever
4. Needle and Seat Assembly	14. Power Piston Cover	23. Pump Pivot Screw	32. Choke Kick Lever
5. Float Hinge Pin	15. Metering Rod Spring	24. Pump Rod	33. Choke Rod
6. Float	16. Metering Rod	25. Air Valve	34. Vacuum Break Link
7. Fuel Filter Spring	17. Power Piston	26. Air Valve Shaft	35. Vacuum Break Assembly
8. Fuel Filter	18. Power Piston Spring	27. Shaft Bushing and Washer	36. Vacuum Break Hose
9. Fuel Inlet Fitting	19. Idle Vent Valve	28. Air Valve Spring	
10. Accelerator Pump Assembly			

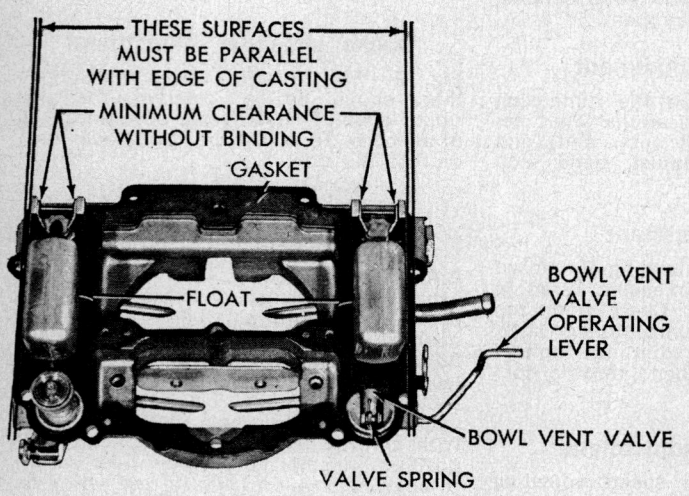

Fig. 4 AVS float alignment

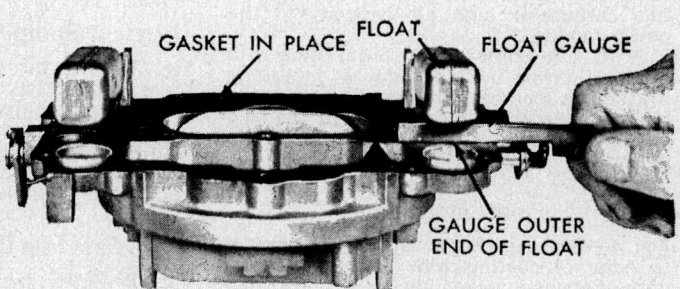

Fig. 5 AVS float level

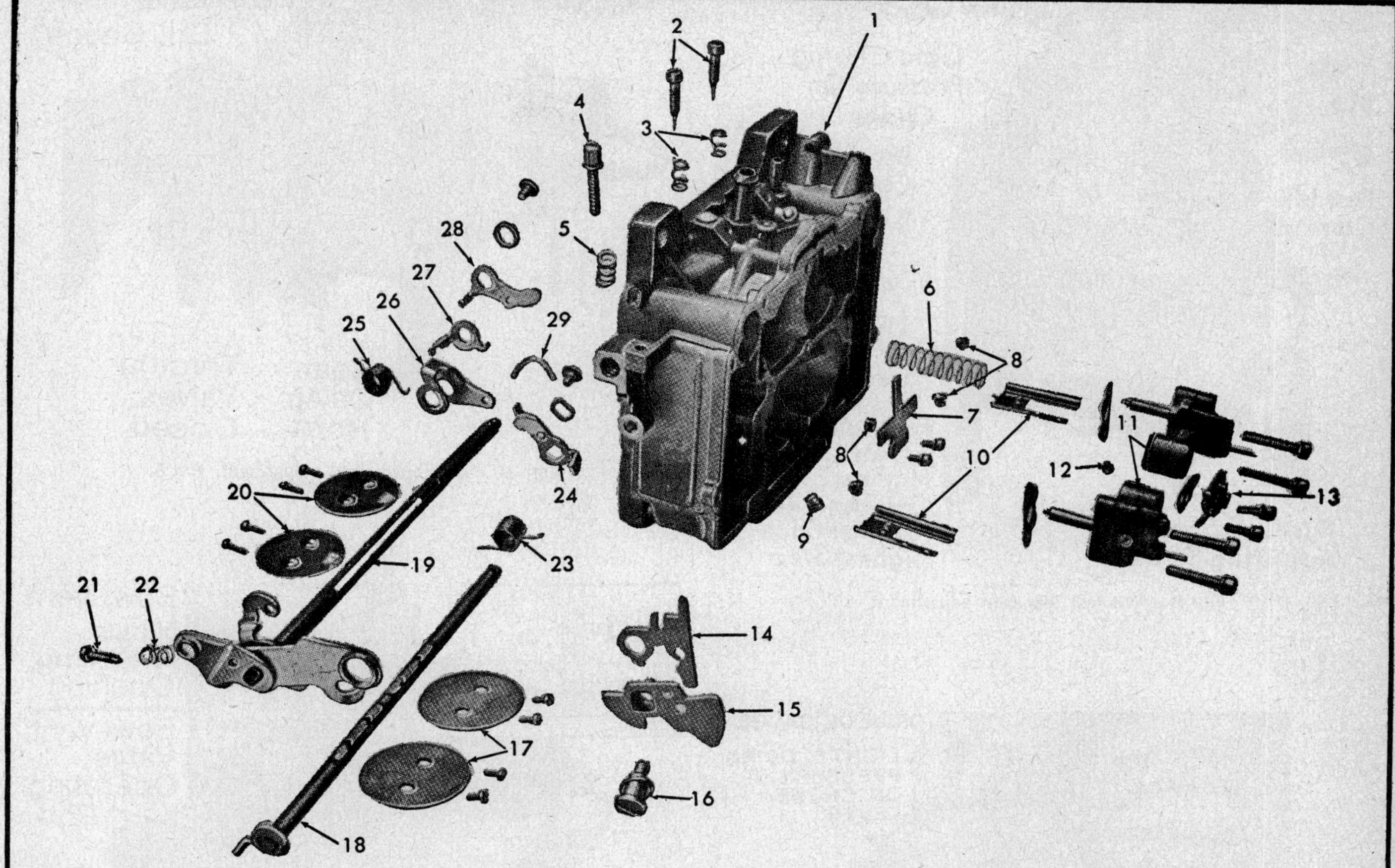

1. Main Body
2. Idle Mixture Needle
3. Idle Mixture Spring
4. Idle Speed Screw
5. Idle Speed Spring
6. Pump Return Spring
7. Hot Idle Compensator
8. Main Metering Jet
9. Pump Inlet Assembly
10. Splash Shield
11. Venturi Cluster
12. Pump Discharge Check Ball
13. Pump Nozzle
14. Lockout Dog
15. Fast Idle Cam
16. Pivot Screw
17. Secondary Throttle Valve
18. Secondary Throttle Shaft
19. Primary Throttle Shaft
20. Primary Throttle Valve
21. Fast Idle Screw
22. Fast Idle Spring
23. Secondary Throttle Shaft Spring
24. Secondary Throttle Shaft Dog Lever and Retainer
25. Primary Throttle Shaft Spring
26. Secondary Throttle Trip Lever
27. Spring Pick Up Lever
28. Primary Throttle Shaft Arm and Retainer
29. Secondary Actuating Link

Fig. 3   AVS main body parts exploded

LEVEL FLOAT POSITION

BEND STOP TABS EACH FLOAT

Fig. 6   AVS float drop

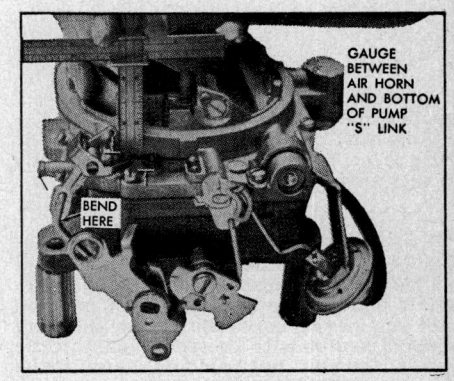

GAUGE BETWEEN AIR HORN AND BOTTOM OF PUMP "S" LINK

BEND HERE

Fig. 7   AVS pump adjustment

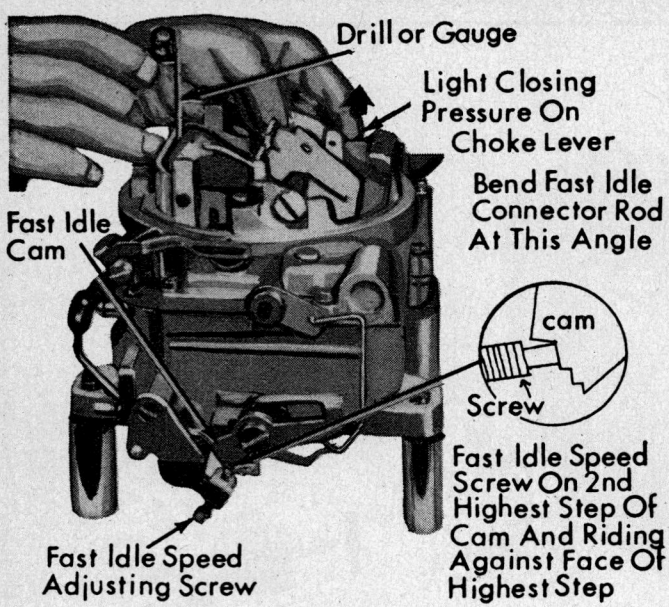

Drill or Gauge

Light Closing Pressure On Choke Lever

Bend Fast Idle Connector Rod At This Angle

Fast Idle Cam

cam

Screw

Fast Idle Speed Screw On 2nd Highest Step Of Cam And Riding Against Face Of Highest Step

Fast Idle Speed Adjusting Screw

Fig. 8 AVS fast idle cam adjustment

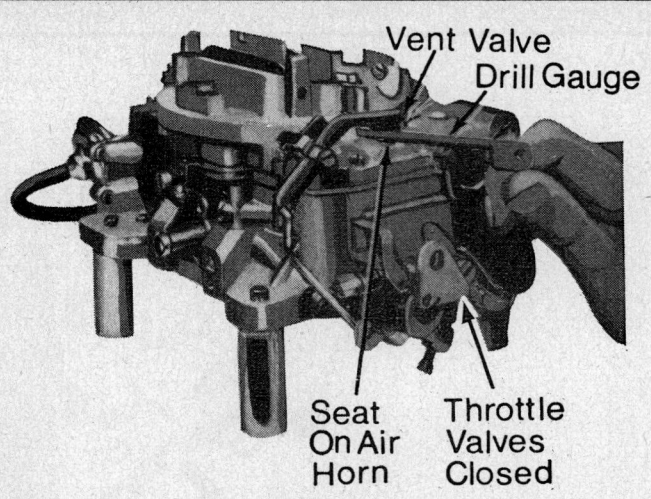

Vent Valve Drill Gauge

Seat On Air Horn

Throttle Valves Closed

Fig. 10 AVS bowl vent adjustment. C.A.S.

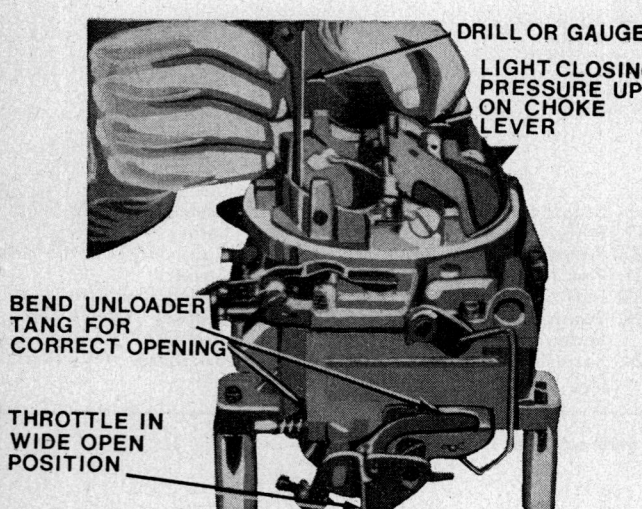

DRILL OR GAUGE

LIGHT CLOSING PRESSURE UP ON CHOKE LEVER

BEND UNLOADER TANG FOR CORRECT OPENING

THROTTLE IN WIDE OPEN POSITION

Fig. 9 AVS choke unloader adjustment

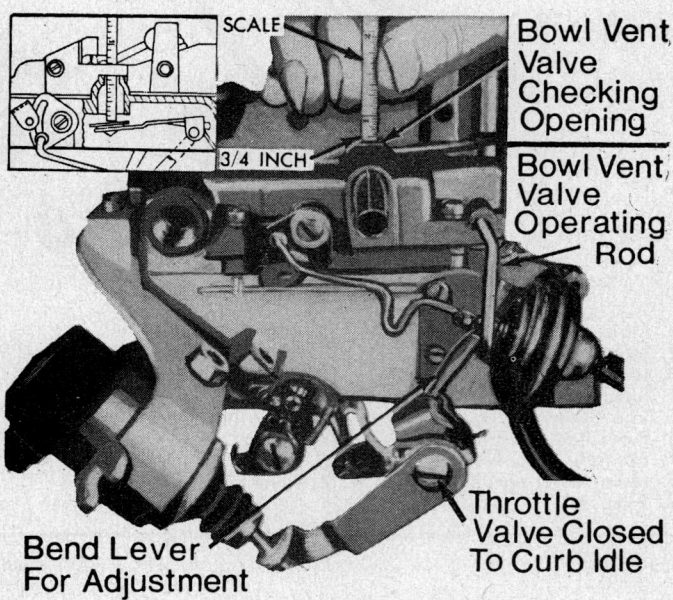

SCALE

3/4 INCH

Bowl Vent Valve Checking Opening

Bowl Vent Valve Operating Rod

Bend Lever For Adjustment

Throttle Valve Closed To Curb Idle

Fig. 10A AVS bowl vent adjustment. E.C.S.

to *AVS Specifications Chart.*

Adjust by bending bowl vent valve operating lever. Install new plug and rap lightly to seat, using a hammer.

Vacuum Kick Adjustment

Fig. 11—If adjustment is to be made with engine running, disconnect fast idle linkage to allow choke to close to kick position with engine at curb idle. If an auxiliary vacuum source is to be used, open throttle valves (engine not running) and move choke valve to closed position. Release throttle first, then release choke.

When using an auxiliary vacuum source, disconnect vacuum hose from carburetor and connect it to hose from vacuum supply with a small length of tube to act as a fitting. Removal of hose from diaphragm may require forces which damage the system. Apply a vacuum of 10 or more inches.

Insert drill gauge between choke valve and wall of air horn. Refer to *AVS Specifications Chart.* Apply sufficient closing pressure on lever to which choke rod attaches to provide a minimum choke valve opening without distortion of diaphragm link. Note that on most units, a cylindrical stem extends as an internal

spring is compressed. This spring must be fully compressed for proper measurement of vacuum kick adjustment.

An adjustment will be necessary if a slight drag is not obtained as drill is being removed. Shorten or lengthen diaphragm link to obtain correct choke opening. Adjust by carefully opening or closing the bend provided in diaphragm link. Note: Important: Do not apply twisting or bending force to diaphragm.

Reinstall vacuum hose on correct carburetor fitting. Return fast idle linkage to its original condition if disturbed. Make following check. With no vacuum applied to

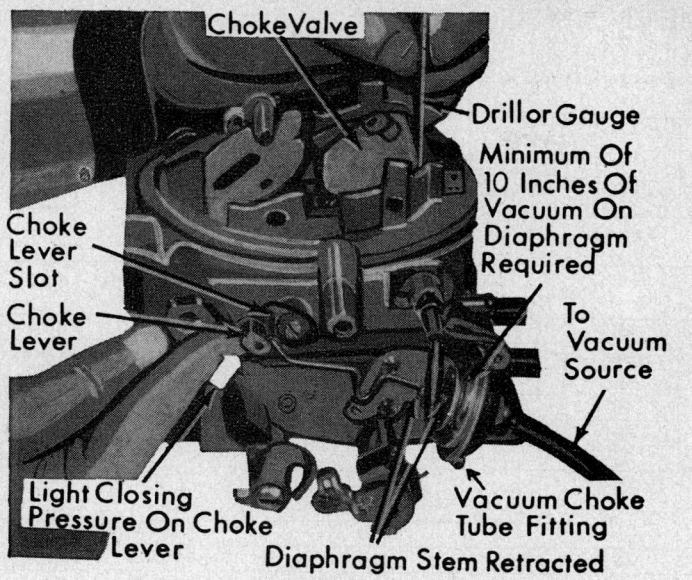

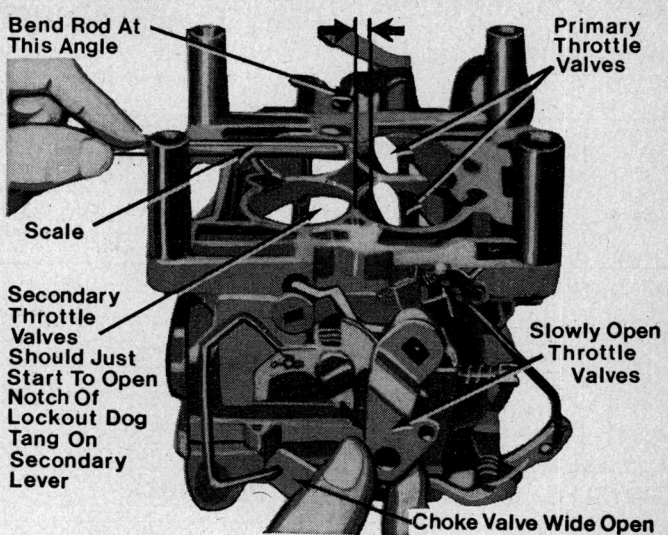

Fig. 11 AVS choke vacuum kick adjustment

Fig. 13 AVS secondary throttle opening adjustment

Fig. 12 AVS secondary
air valve adjustment

Secondary Air Valve Adjustment

Fig. 12—Loosen lock screw and allow air valve to position itself at wide open position. From wide open position, (spring barely moving valve), turn slotted sleeve two full turns counter clockwise. Hold in this position with finger, then tighten lock screw securely. Check valve for freedom of movement.

Secondary Throttle Lever Adjustment

Fig. 13—Block the choke valve in the wide open position and invert the carburetor. Slowly open the primary throttle valves until specified measurement is obtained between the lower edge of the primary valve and the bore opposite idle port. Refer to *AVS Specifications Chart*. At this measurement, the secondary valves should just start to open. Adjust by bending the secondary throttle operating rod at the angle.

Closing Shoe Adjustment

Fig. 14—With primary and secondary throttle valves closed, bend secondary closing shoe to obtain .020" clearance between positive closing shoes on primary and secondary throttle levers. To adjust, bend shoe on secondary lever.

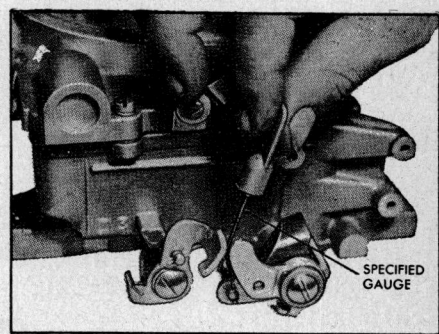

Fig. 14 AVS closing shoe adjustment

diaphragm, choke valve should move freely between open and closed positions. If movement is not free, examine linkage for misalignment or interferences caused by bending operation. Repeat adjustment if necessary to provide proper link operation.

Secondary Throttle Lockout

Fig. 13—Crack throttle valves and manually open and close choke valve. Tang on secondary throttle lever should freely engage in notch of lockout dog. To adjust, bend tang on secondary throttle lever.

CARTER CARBURETORS

CARTER AFB ADJUSTMENT SPECIFICATIONS

See Tune Up Chart in car chapters for hot idle speed.

Year	Carb. Model	Idle Mixture Turns Open	Float Level	Float Drop	Pump Travel	Fast Idle Throttle Valve or Cam Position Clearance	Choke Unloader Setting	Secondary Throttle Lever Setting	Secondary Throttle Lockout Setting	Bowl Vent Setting	Choke Piston Linkage Setting	Choke Setting
AMERICAN MOTORS												
1969	4660S	2	$^{11}/_{32}$	2	$^{21}/_{64}$	—	$^{5}/_{32}$	$^{7}/_{16}$	.015	—	$^{5}/_{64}$	2 Rich
	4661S	2	$^{11}/_{32}$	2	$^{21}/_{64}$	—	$^{5}/_{32}$	$^{7}/_{16}$	.015	—	$^{1}/_{8}$	On Index
	4662S	2	$^{11}/_{32}$	2	$^{21}/_{64}$	—	$^{5}/_{32}$	$^{7}/_{16}$	.015	—	$^{7}/_{64}$	On Index
	4663S	2	$^{11}/_{32}$	2	$^{21}/_{64}$	—	$^{5}/_{32}$	$^{7}/_{16}$	.015	—	$^{1}/_{8}$	On Index
	4664S	2	$^{11}/_{32}$	2	$^{21}/_{64}$	—	$^{5}/_{32}$	$^{7}/_{16}$	.015	—	$^{7}/_{64}$	On Index
	4665S	2	$^{11}/_{32}$	2	$^{21}/_{64}$	—	$^{5}/_{32}$	$^{7}/_{16}$	.015	—	$^{1}/_{8}$	On Index
CHRYSLER, IMPERIAL, DODGE, PLYMOUTH												
1969	4619S	—	$^{7}/_{32}$	$^{3}/_{4}$	$^{7}/_{16}$	—	—	$^{17}/_{64}$	.020	—	—	—
	4620S	1–2	$^{7}/_{32}$	$^{3}/_{4}$	$^{7}/_{16}$	50 Drill②	$^{1}/_{4}$	$^{17}/_{64}$	.020	$^{5}/_{32}$	39 Drill	2 Rich
	4621S	1–2	$^{7}/_{32}$	$^{3}/_{4}$	$^{7}/_{16}$	50 Drill②	$^{1}/_{4}$	$^{17}/_{64}$	.020	$^{5}/_{32}$	39 Drill	2 Rich
1970	4742S	③	$^{7}/_{32}$	$^{3}/_{4}$	$^{7}/_{16}$	—	—	$^{17}/_{64}$	.020	—	—	—
	4745S	③	$^{7}/_{32}$	$^{3}/_{4}$	$^{7}/_{16}$	50 Drill②	$^{1}/_{4}$	$^{17}/_{64}$	.020	$^{3}/_{4}$①	54 Drill	2 Rich
	4746S	③	$^{7}/_{32}$	$^{3}/_{4}$	$^{7}/_{16}$	50 Drill②	$^{1}/_{4}$	$^{17}/_{64}$	.020	$^{3}/_{4}$①	39 Drill	2 Rich
1971	4969S	③	$^{7}/_{32}$	$^{3}/_{4}$	$^{31}/_{64}$	—	$^{1}/_{4}$	$^{17}/_{64}$	.020	$^{3}/_{4}$①	—	—
	4970S	③	$^{7}/_{32}$	$^{3}/_{4}$	$^{31}/_{64}$	50 Drill②	$^{1}/_{4}$	$^{17}/_{64}$	.020	$^{3}/_{4}$①	—	—
	4971S	③	$^{7}/_{32}$	$^{3}/_{4}$	$^{31}/_{64}$	50 Drill②	—	$^{17}/_{64}$	.020	—	—	—

①—At curb idle.
②—With fast idle speed adjusting screw contacting second highest speed step on fast idle cam the clearance between choke valve and wall of air horn should be as specified.
③—Air/fuel ratio or idle CO% rating is found in Tune Up Specification tables in car chapters.

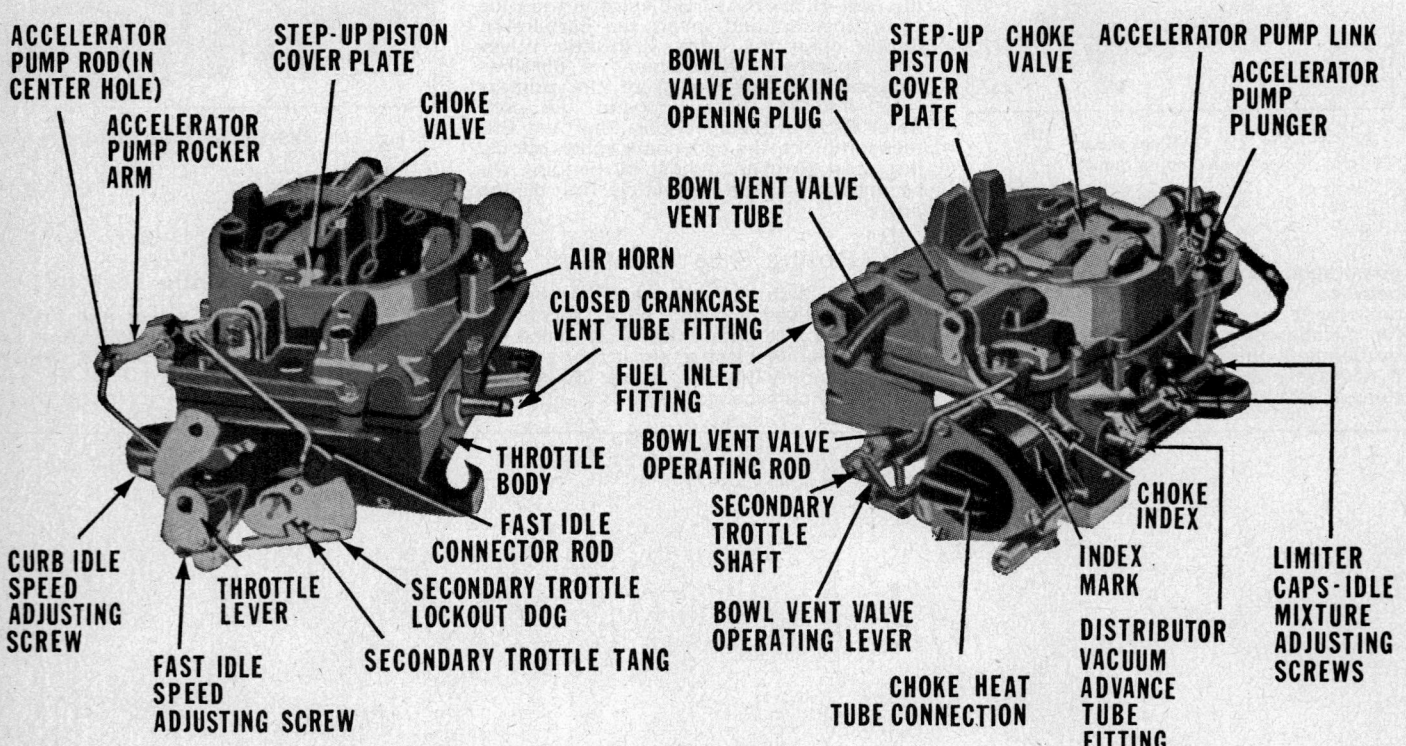

ACCELERATOR PUMP ROD(IN CENTER HOLE)
ACCELERATOR PUMP ROCKER ARM
STEP-UP PISTON COVER PLATE
CHOKE VALVE
BOWL VENT VALVE CHECKING OPENING PLUG
STEP-UP PISTON COVER PLATE
CHOKE VALVE
ACCELERATOR PUMP LINK
ACCELERATOR PUMP PLUNGER
BOWL VENT VALVE VENT TUBE
AIR HORN
CLOSED CRANKCASE VENT TUBE FITTING
FUEL INLET FITTING
THROTTLE BODY
FAST IDLE CONNECTOR ROD
BOWL VENT VALVE OPERATING ROD
SECONDARY THROTTLE SHAFT
CHOKE INDEX
INDEX MARK
CURB IDLE SPEED ADJUSTING SCREW
THROTTLE LEVER
SECONDARY TROTTLE LOCKOUT DOG
SECONDARY TROTTLE TANG
BOWL VENT VALVE OPERATING LEVER
CHOKE HEAT TUBE CONNECTION
DISTRIBUTOR VACUUM ADVANCE TUBE FITTING
LIMITER CAPS-IDLE MIXTURE ADJUSTING SCREWS
FAST IDLE SPEED ADJUSTING SCREW

Fig. 1 Typical Carter AFB carburetor assembly

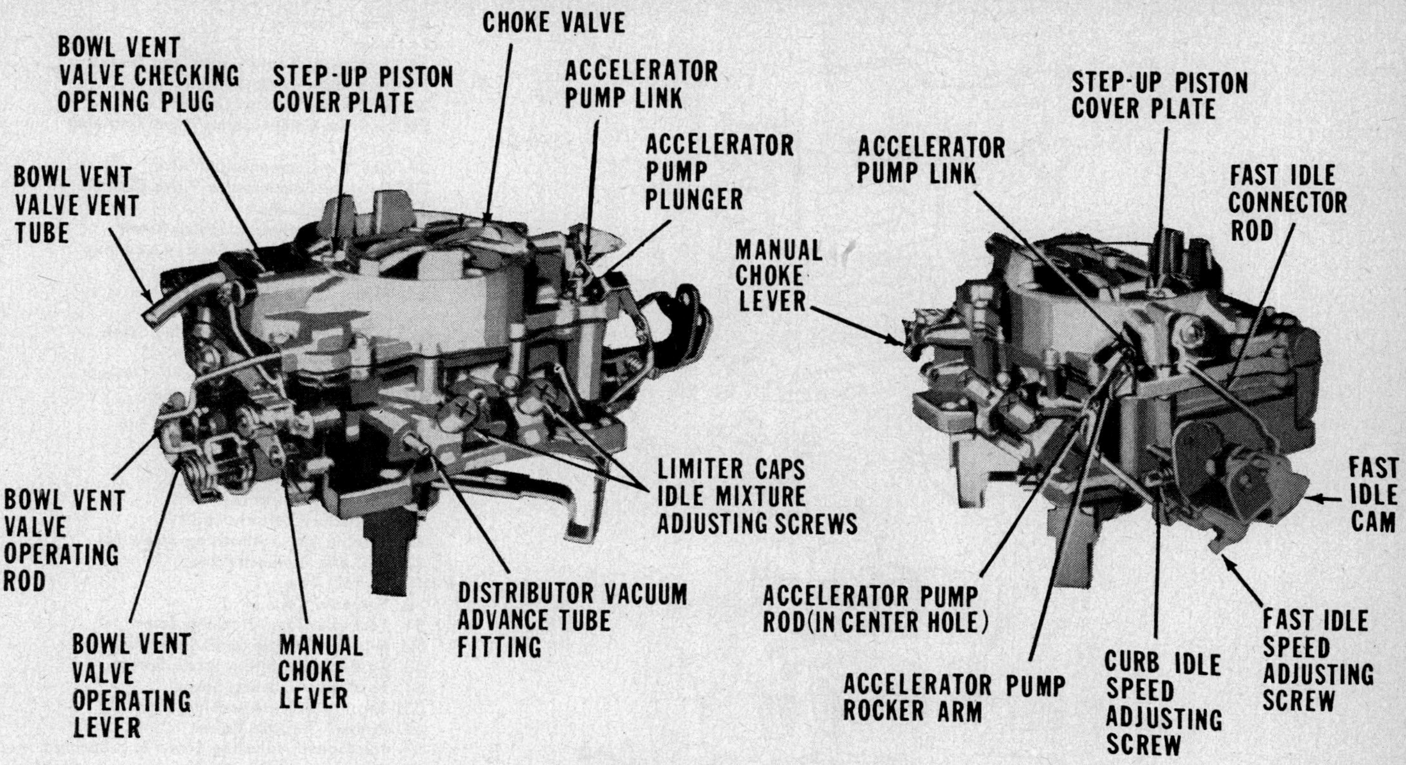

BOWL VENT
VALVE CHECKING
OPENING PLUG

BOWL VENT
VALVE VENT
TUBE

STEP-UP PISTON
COVER PLATE

CHOKE VALVE

ACCELERATOR
PUMP LINK

ACCELERATOR
PUMP
PLUNGER

MANUAL
CHOKE
LEVER

ACCELERATOR
PUMP LINK

STEP-UP PISTON
COVER PLATE

FAST IDLE
CONNECTOR
ROD

BOWL VENT
VALVE
OPERATING
ROD

BOWL VENT
VALVE
OPERATING
LEVER

MANUAL
CHOKE
LEVER

DISTRIBUTOR VACUUM
ADVANCE TUBE
FITTING

LIMITER CAPS
IDLE MIXTURE
ADJUSTING SCREWS

ACCELERATOR PUMP
ROD (IN CENTER HOLE)

ACCELERATOR PUMP
ROCKER ARM

CURB IDLE
SPEED
ADJUSTING
SCREW

FAST
IDLE
CAM

FAST IDLE
SPEED
ADJUSTING
SCREW

Fig. 1A   Carter AFB carburetor assembly, 1971 Chrysler

MODEL AFB ADJUSTMENTS

The AFB carburetor, Figs. 1 and 2, contains many features, some of which are the locations of the step-up rods and pistons. The step-up rods, pistons and springs are accessible for service without removing the air horn or the carburetor from the engine. The venturi assemblies (primary and secondary) are replaceable and contain many of the calibration points for both the high and low speed systems. One fuel bowl feeds both the primary and secondary nozzles on the right side while the other fuel bowl takes care of the primary and secondary nozzles on the left side. This provides excellent performance in cornering, quick stops and acceleration.

All the major castings of the carburetor are aluminum, with the throttle body integral with the main body. This allows an overall height reduction in the carburetor. The section containing the accelerator pump is termed the primary side of the carburetor; the rear section is the secondary.

Float Alignment

Fig. 3—Sight down side of float to determine if it is parallel to the outer edge of the air horn casting. To adjust, bend float lever by applying just enough pressure to make the adjustment. Apply the pressure on the end of the float with the fingers while supporting the float lever with the thumb.

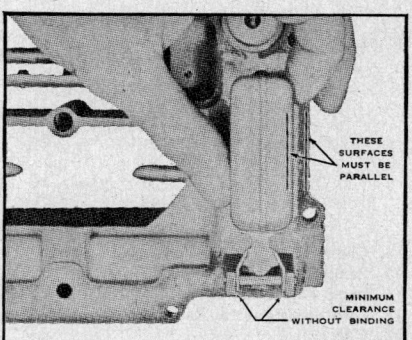

THESE
SURFACES
MUST BE
PARALLEL

MINIMUM
CLEARANCE
WITHOUT BINDING

Fig. 3   AFB float alignment

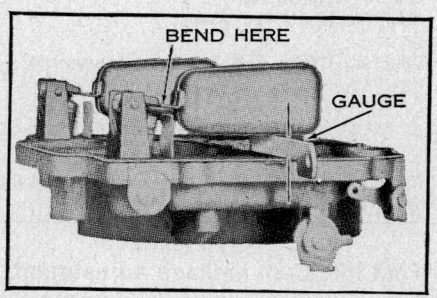

BEND HERE

GAUGE

Fig. 4   AFB float level adjustment

After aligning the float, remove as much clearance as possible between arms of float lever and lugs on air horn by bending the float lever. Arms of float lever should be as parallel to the inner surfaces of the lugs on the air horn as possible. Floats must operate freely without excess clearance on its hinge pin.

Float Level Adjustment

Fig. 4—With air horn inverted, bowl cover gasket in place and needle seated, clearance between top of float (at outer end) and air horn gasket should be as listed in the *AFB Specifications Chart*. To adjust, bend float arm. Adjust both floats and recheck float alignment.

Float Drop Adjustment

Fig. 5—With bowl cover held in upright position, measure between outer end of each float, the distance between top of floats and bowl cover gasket should be as listed in the *AFB Specifications Chart*. To adjust, bend tabs on float brackets.

Pump Adjustment

Fig. 6—Back out idle speed screw until throttle valves seat in carburetor bores. With throttle connector rod in center hole (medium stroke) of pump arm, distance from top of bowl cover to top of

CARTER CARBURETORS

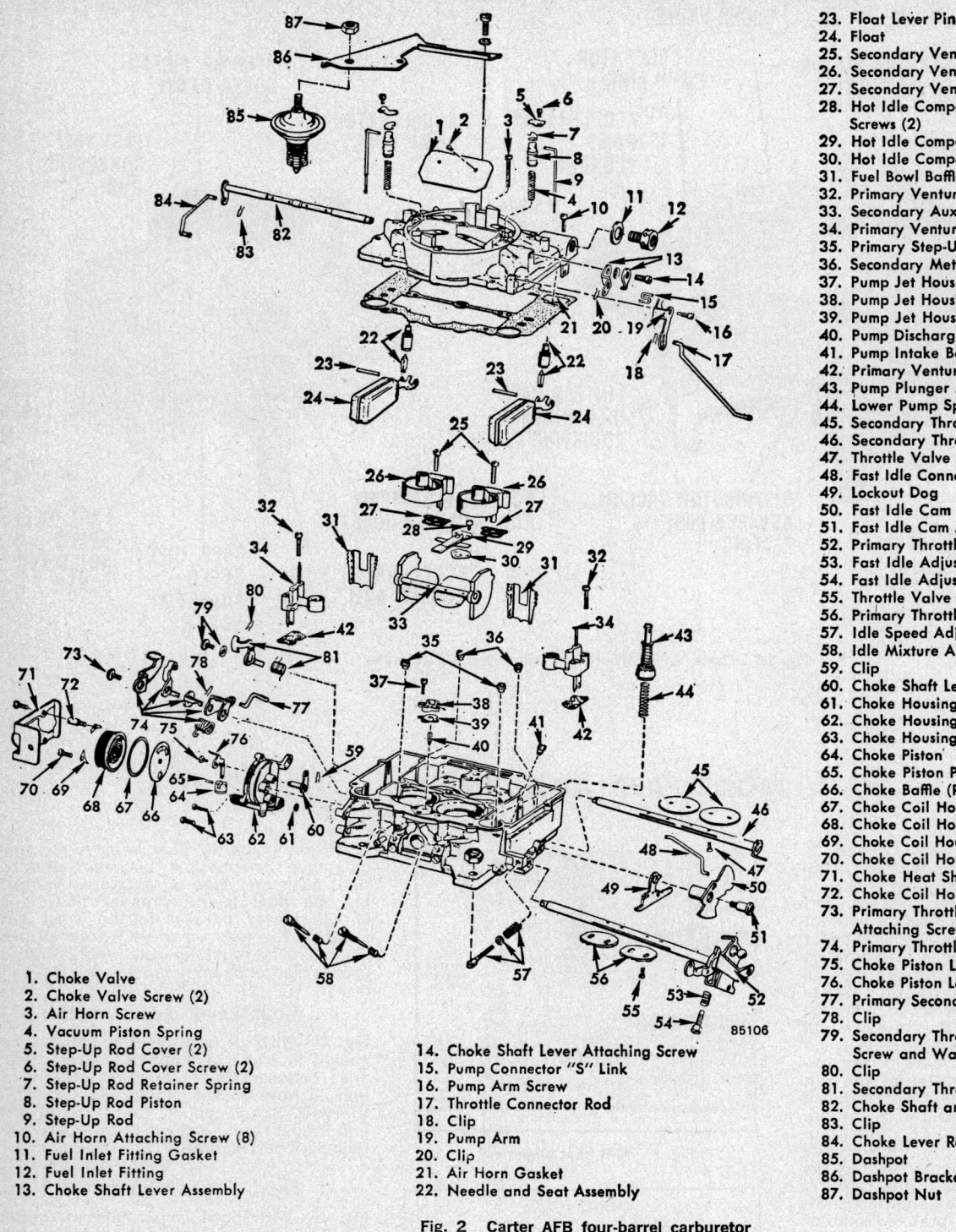

23. Float Lever Pin
24. Float
25. Secondary Venturi Retaining Screws
26. Secondary Venturi Assembly
27. Secondary Venturi Gasket
28. Hot Idle Compensator Valve Retaining Screws (2)
29. Hot Idle Compensator Valve
30. Hot Idle Compensator Valve Gasket
31. Fuel Bowl Baffle
32. Primary Venturi Attaching Screw
33. Secondary Auxiliary Valve Assembly
34. Primary Venturi Assembly
35. Primary Step-Up Rod Jets
36. Secondary Metering Jets
37. Pump Jet Housing Attaching Screw
38. Pump Jet Housing Assembly
39. Pump Jet Housing Assembly Gasket
40. Pump Discharge Check Needle
41. Pump Intake Ball Check
42. Primary Venturi Gasket
43. Pump Plunger Assembly
44. Lower Pump Spring
45. Secondary Throttle Valves
46. Secondary Throttle Shaft
47. Throttle Valve Attaching Screw (4)
48. Fast Idle Connector Rod
49. Lockout Dog
50. Fast Idle Cam
51. Fast Idle Cam Attaching Screw
52. Primary Throttle Shaft Lever Assembly
53. Fast Idle Adjusting Screw Spring
54. Fast Idle Adjusting Screw
55. Throttle Valve Attaching Screw (4)
56. Primary Throttle Valves
57. Idle Speed Adjusting Screw and Spring
58. Idle Mixture Adjustment Screws and Springs
59. Clip
60. Choke Shaft Lever
61. Choke Housing Gasket
62. Choke Housing
63. Choke Housing Attaching Screws
64. Choke Piston
65. Choke Piston Pin
66. Choke Baffle (Rotating)
67. Choke Coil Housing Gasket
68. Choke Coil Housing
69. Choke Coil Housing Retainer (3)
70. Choke Coil Housing Retainer Screw
71. Choke Heat Shield
72. Choke Coil Housing Retainer Screw (2)
73. Primary Throttle Shaft Lever Assembly Attaching Screw
74. Primary Throttle Shaft Lever Assembly
75. Choke Piston Lever Attaching Screw
76. Choke Piston Lever and Link
77. Primary Secondary Connector Rod
78. Clip
79. Secondary Throttle Lever Shoe Attaching Screw and Washer
80. Clip
81. Secondary Throttle Lever Shoe Assembly
82. Choke Shaft and Lever Assembly
83. Clip
84. Choke Lever Rod
85. Dashpot
86. Dashpot Bracket
87. Dashpot Nut

1. Choke Valve
2. Choke Valve Screw (2)
3. Air Horn Screw
4. Vacuum Piston Spring
5. Step-Up Rod Cover (2)
6. Step-Up Rod Cover Screw (2)
7. Step-Up Rod Retainer Spring
8. Step-Up Rod Piston
9. Step-Up Rod
10. Air Horn Attaching Screw (8)
11. Fuel Inlet Fitting Gasket
12. Fuel Inlet Fitting
13. Choke Shaft Lever Assembly
14. Choke Shaft Lever Attaching Screw
15. Pump Connector "S" Link
16. Pump Arm Screw
17. Throttle Connector Rod
18. Clip
19. Pump Arm
20. Clip
21. Air Horn Gasket
22. Needle and Seat Assembly

Fig. 2   Carter AFB four-barrel carburetor

pump plunger shaft should be as listed in the *AFB Specifications Chart*. Adjust by bending throttle connector rod at its offset angle.

NOTE: Some models require the throttle connector rod to be placed in either the inner hole (long stroke) or outer hole

(short stroke). In such cases the chart will indicate the proper hole connection.

Fast Idle Cam Linkage Adjustment

Exc. Chrysler Corp. Fig. 7—With choke valve tightly closed and lug on outer

choke shaft lever contacting stop on inner choke shaft lever, align center of fast idle screw with index mark on cam. To adjust, bend fast idle connector rod. On some models it may be necessary to bend stop lug on fast idle cam.

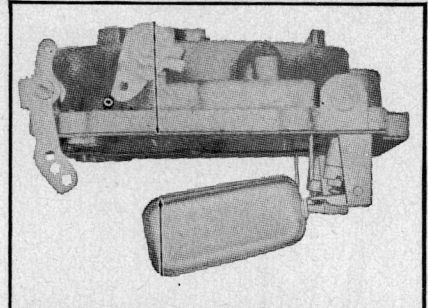

Fig. 5   AFB float drop adjustment

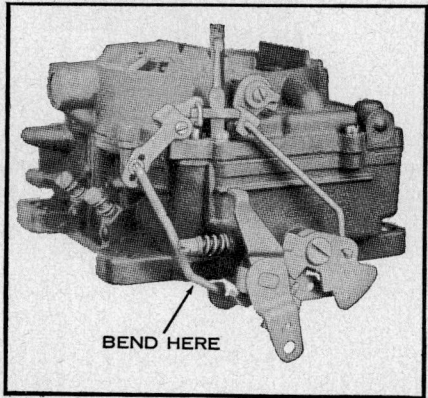

Fig. 6   AFB pump adjustment

Fast Idle Throttle Valve Clearance

Exc. Chrysler Corp. Fig. 8—With choke valve tightly closed, tighten fast idle adjusting screw on index mark on cam until the clearance between throttle valve and carburetor bore (side opposite idle port) is as listed in the *AFB Specifications Chart.*

Fast Idle Speed Cam Position Adjustment

Fig. 8A—With fast idle speed adjusting screw contacting second highest speed step on fast idle cam, move choke valve toward closed position with light pressure on choke shaft lever.

Insert drill gauge between choke valve and wall of air horn. Refer to *AFB Specifications Chart.* An adjustment is necessary if a slight drag is not obtained as the drill is being removed. Adjust by bending fast idle connector rod at angle.

Choke Unloader Adjustment

Fig. 9—With throttle wide open, clearance between upper edge of choke valve and inner wall of air horn should be as listed in the *AFB Specifications Chart.* To adjust, bend unloader tang on throttle shaft lever.

Secondary Throttle Lever Adjustment

Figs. 10 and 11—Block choke valve wide open. Secondary throttle valves should just start to open when primary throttle valves are opened to the clearance listed in the *AFB Specifications Chart* between lower edge of throttle valve and carburetor bore (side opposite idle port). To adjust, bend throttle operating rod, Fig. 10.

Primary and secondary throttle valves should reach wide open position at the same time.

With primary and secondary throttle valves tightly closed, there should be the clearance listed in the *AFB Specifications Chart* between the positive closing shoes and primary and secondary throttle levers. To adjust, bend shoe on secondary lever.

Secondary Throttle Lockout

Fig. 12—Crack throttle valves and manually open and close choke valve. Tang on secondary throttle lever should freely engage in notch of lockout dog. To adjust, bend tang on secondary throttle lever. Refer to AFB Specifications Chart.

Bowl Vent Valve Adjustment

Except ECS Equipped-Fig. 8A—With throttle valves tightly closed, insert drill gauge between air horn and valve at smallest opening. Refer to *AFB Specifications Chart.* Adjust by bending adjusting tang on pivot end of lever.

ECS Equipped Fig. 13—Remove bowl vent valve checking hole plug in air horn. With throttle valves at closed curb idle position, insert a narrow ruler down through hole. Allow ruler to rest lightly on top of valve. Measure from top of

Fig. 7   AFB fast idle linkage adjustment

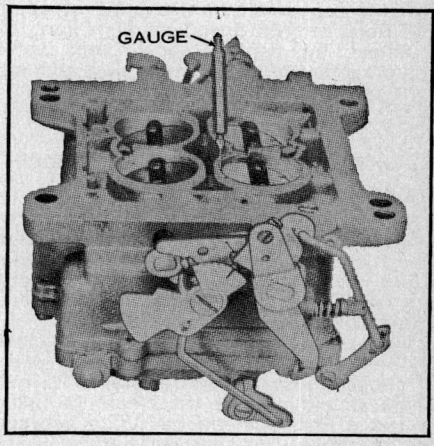

Fig. 8   AFB throttle valve clearance adjustment

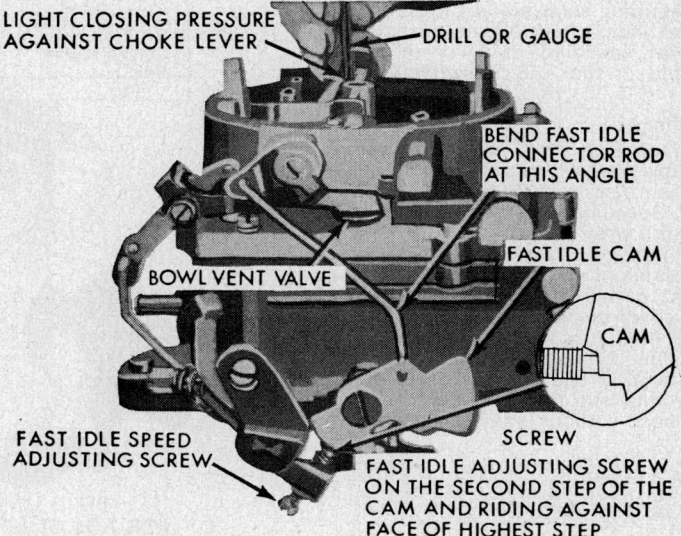

Fig. 8A   AFB fast idle cam position adjustment

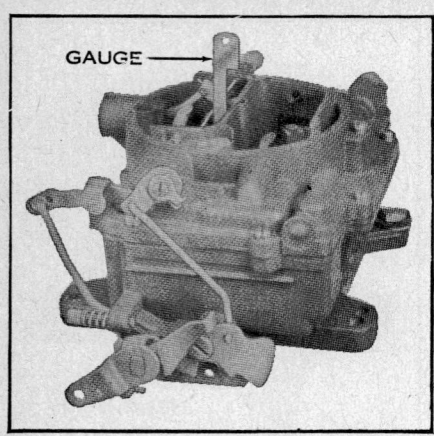

Fig. 9   AFB choke unloader adjustment

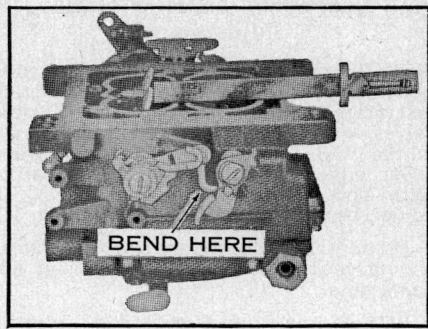

Fig. 10   AFB secondary throttle lever adjustment

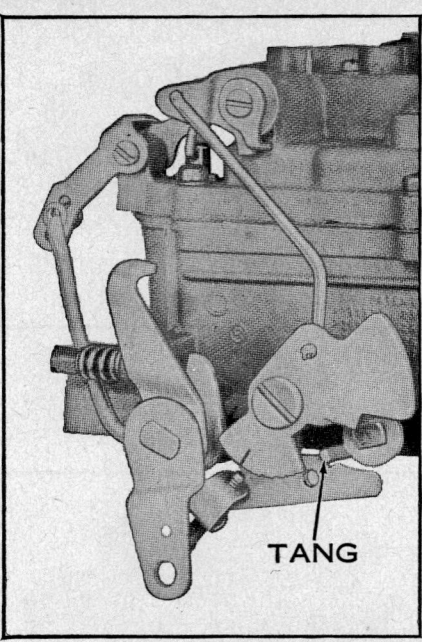

Fig. 12   AFB secondary lockout adjustment

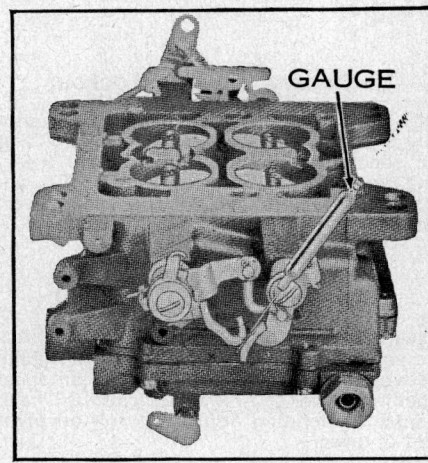

Fig. 11   AFB gauging clearance between positive closing shoes on primary and secondary throttle valves

valve to top of air horn casting at opening. Refer to *AFB Specifications Chart.*

Adjust by bending bowl vent valve operating lever. Install new plug and rap lightly to seat, using a hammer.

Choke Piston Linkage Adjustment
Fig. 14

Bend a .026" wire gauge at a 90-degree angle approximately ⅛" from its end. Open choke valve and insert the wire gauge so that bent portion is between top of slot in choke piston cylinder and bottom of slot in piston.

Hold wire gauge in position and close choke valve by pressing on piston lever in choke housing until resistance is felt. There should now be the clearance listed in the *AFB Specifications Chart* between top of choke valve and air horn wall. To adjust, bend choke connector link.

Automatic Choke Setting
Built-In Type, Fig. 15

Loosen retaining screws and turn choke cover so that index mark or line on cover lines up with specified mark on choke housing listed in the *AFB Specifications.*

Well-Type Choke

Loosen mounting post lock nut and turn mounting post with screwdriver until index mark on disc is positioned as listed in the *AFB Specifications Chart.* Hold in this position with a screwdriver and tighten lock nut, Fig. 16.

After adjustment is completed and coil housing and carburetor are installed on engine, lift cover disc and open and close choke valve manually to see if connector rod clears sides of hole in housing cover without binding. If binding exists, replace with a new unit since the connector rod cannot be bent without affecting calibration.

Dashpot Adjustment
Chrysler Line with C.A.P.

Use only on cars with manual trans-

mission, make the dashpot adjustment after the fast idle setting. Then with the fast idle screw on highest step of cam, adjust dashpot for a clearance of .052" between dashpot stem and lever. Tighten lock nut.

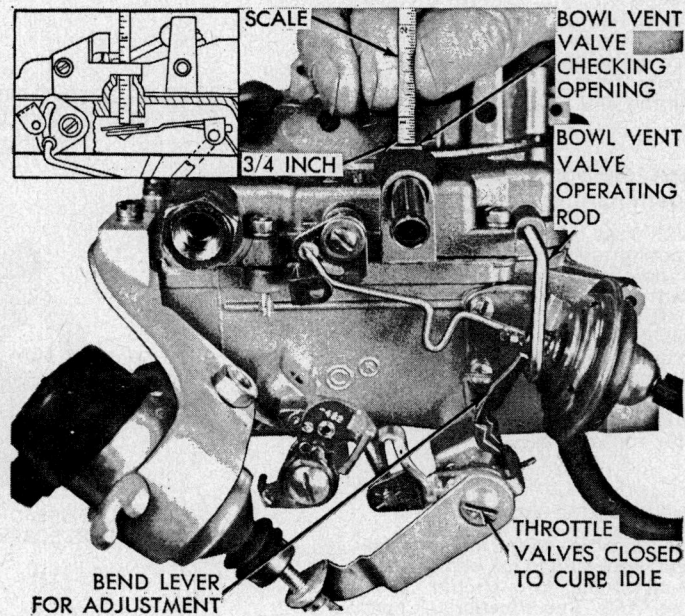

Fig. 13   AFB bowl vent valve adjustment ECS equipped

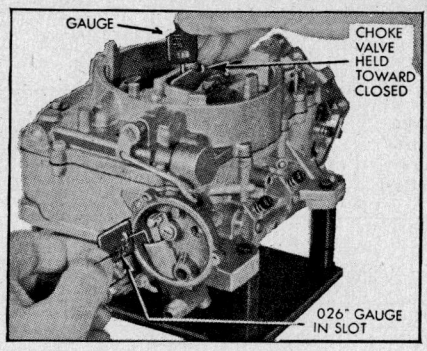

Fig. 14 AFB choke piston clearance

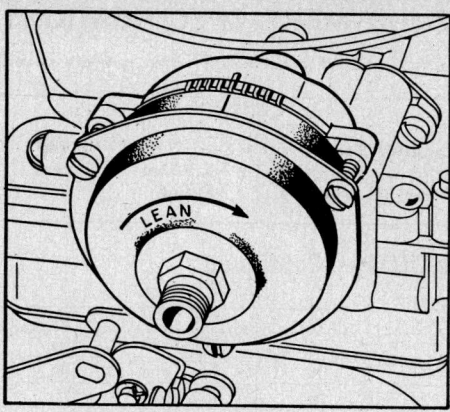

Fig. 15 AFB choke setting (built-in type)

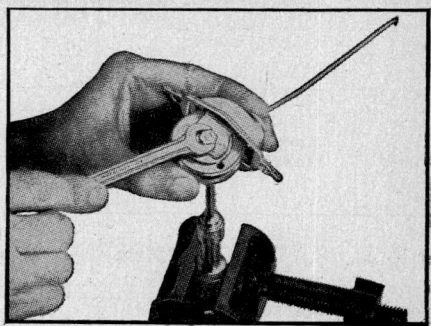

Fig. 16 AFB well-type choke setting (Chrysler line)

CARTER TQ ADJUSTMENT SPECIFICATIONS

See Tune Up Chart in car chapters for hot idle speeds.

Year	Carb. Model	Air/Fuel Ratio	Float Setting	Secondary Throttle Linkage	Secondary Air Valve Opening	Secondary Air Valve Spring	Pump Travel	Choke Control Lever (On Car)	Choke Unloader	Fast Idle R.P.M.	Choke Setting
CHRYSLER, DODGE, IMPERIAL & PLYMOUTH											
1971	4972S	①	1	11/32	31/64	1 1/4 Turn	31/64	5 41/64	11 Drill	1800	2 Rich
	4973S	①	1	11/32	31/64	1 1/4 Turn	31/64	5 41/64	11 Drill	1800	2 Rich
1972	6090S	①	1	②	31/64	1 Turn	31/64	3 3/8 ③	.190	1900	Fixed
	6138S	①	1	②	29/64	1 Turn	9/16	3 3/8 ③	.190	1900	Fixed
	6139S	①	1	②	29/64	1 Turn	31/64	3 3/8 ③	.190	1900	Fixed
	6140S	①	1	②	31/64	1 Turn	9/16	3 3/8 ③	.190	1900	Fixed
	6165S	①	1	②	31/64	1 Turn	9/16	3 3/8 ③	.190	2000	Fixed
	6166S	①	1	②	31/64	1 Turn	31/64	3 3/8 ③	.190	2100	Fixed
1973	6318S	①	1 1/16	②	29/64	1 1/4 Turn	35/64	3 3/8 ③	.190	1300	Fixed
	6319S	①	1 1/16	②	29/64	1 1/4 Turn	31/64	3 3/8 ③	.190	1800	Fixed
	6320S	①	1 1/16	②	31/64	1 1/4 Turn	35/64	3 3/8 ③	.190	1700	Fixed
	6321S	①	1 1/16	②	31/64	1 1/4 Turn	31/64	3 3/8 ③	.190	1800	Fixed
	6322S	①	1 1/16	②	31/64	1 1/4 Turn	31/64	3 3/8 ③	.190	1700	Fixed
	6324S	①	1 1/16	②	31/64	1 1/4 Turn	31/64	3 3/8 ③	.190	1700	Fixed
	6339S	①	1 1/16	②	29/64	1 1/4 Turn	35/64	3 3/8 ③	.190	1300	Fixed
	6340S④	①	1 1/16	②	29/64	1 1/4 Turn	31/64	3 3/8 ③	.190	1800	Fixed
	6341S④	①	1 1/16	②	29/64	1 1/4 Turn	35/64	3 3/8 ③	.190	1700	Fixed
	6342S④	①	1 1/16	②	29/64	1 1/4 Turn	31/64	3 3/8 ③	.190	1800	Fixed
	6410S④	①	1 1/16	②	31/64	1 1/4 Turn	31/64	3 3/8 ③	.190	1700	Fixed
	6411S④	①	1 1/16	②	31/64	1 1/4 Turn	31/64	3 3/8 ③	.190	1700	Fixed
1974	6452S	①	⑤	②	1/2	1 1/4 Turn	35/64	3 3/8 ③	.310	1900	Fixed
	6453S	①	⑤	②	1/2	1 1/4 Turn	31/64	3 3/8 ③	.310	1900	Fixed
	6454S④	①	⑤	②	1/2	1 1/4 Turn	35/64	3 3/8 ③	.310	1900	Fixed
	6455S④	①	⑤	②	1/2	1 1/4 Turn	31/64	3 3/8 ③	.310	1900	Fixed
	6456S	①	⑤	②	1/2	1 1/4 Turn	35/64	3 3/8 ③	.310	1700	Fixed
	6457S④	①	⑤	②	1/2	1 1/4 Turn	31/64	3 3/8 ③	.310	1800	Fixed
	6459S④	①	⑤	②	1/2	1 1/4 Turn	31/64	3 3/8 ③	.310	1800	Fixed
	6460S	①	⑤	②	1/2	1 1/4 Turn	31/64	3 3/8 ③	.310	1700	Fixed
	6461S④	①	⑤	②	1/2	1 1/4 Turn	31/64	3 3/8 ③	.310	1700	Fixed
	6462S	①	⑤	②	1/2	1 1/4 Turn	31/64	3 3/8 ③	.310	1700	Fixed
	6463S④	①	⑤	②	1/2	1 1/4 Turn	31/64	3 3/8 ③	.310	1700	Fixed

Continued

CARTER CARBURETORS

CARTER TQ ADJUSTMENT SPECIFICATIONS—Continued

See Tune Up Chart in car chapters for hot idle speeds.

Year	Carb. Model	Air/Fuel Ratio	Float Setting	Secondary Throttle Linkage	Secondary Air Valve Opening	Secondary Air Valve Spring	Pump Travel	Choke Control Lever (On Car)	Choke Unloader	Fast Idle R.P.M.	Choke Setting
CHRYSLER, DODGE, IMPERIAL & PLYMOUTH—Continued											
1974	6487S⑥	①	⑤	②	½	1¼ Turn	35/64	3⅜③	.310	2000	Fixed
	6488S④	①	⑤	②	½	1¼ Turn	35/64	3⅜③	.310	1800	Fixed
	6489S	①	⑤	②	½	1¼ Turn	31/64	3⅜③	.310	2000	Fixed
	6496S	①	⑤	②	½	1¼ Turn	31/64	3⅜③	.310	2000	Fixed
	6498S⑤	①	29/32	②	33/64	1¼ Turn	31/64	3⅜③	.310	1900	Fixed
	6499S④	①	29/32	②	33/64	1¼ Turn	35/64	3⅜③	.310	1900	Fixed
1975	9002S	①	29/32	②	½	1¼ Turn	35/64	3⅜	.310	1600	Fixed
	9004S	①	29/32	②	½	1¼ Turn	35/64	3⅜	.310	1600	Fixed
	9008S	①	29/32	②	½	1¼ Turn	35/64	3⅜	.310	1800	Fixed
	9009S	①	29/32	②	½	1¼ Turn	35/64	3⅜	.310	1600	Fixed
	9010S	①	29/32	②	½	1¼ Turn	35/64	3⅜	.310	1600	Fixed
	9011S	①	29/32	②	½	1¼ Turn	35/64	3⅜	.310	1600	Fixed
	9012S	①	29/32	②	½	1¼ Turn	35/64	3⅜	.310	1800	Fixed
	9046S	①	29/32	②	½	1¼ Turn	35/64	3⅜	.310	1800	Fixed
	9050S	①	29/32	②	½	1¼ Turn	35/64	3⅜	.310	1600	Fixed
	9051S	①	29/32	②	½	1¼ Turn	35/64	3⅜	.310	1600	Fixed
	9052S	①	29/32	②	½	1¼ Turn	35/64	3⅜	.310	1800	Fixed
	9053S	①	29/32	②	½	1¼ Turn	35/64	3⅜	.310	1800	Fixed

①—For Air/Fuel ratio and idle CO%, see Tune-Up charts in car chapters.
②—Adjust link so primary and secondary stops both contact at same time.
③—Off car.
④—With California Emission package.
⑤—Brass float, 1 inch; cellular plastic float, 29/32 inch.
⑥—Except California.

FORD & MERCURY

Year	Carb. Model	Air/Fuel Ratio	Float Setting	Secondary Throttle Linkage	Secondary Air Valve Opening	Secondary Air Valve Spring	Pump Travel	Choke Control Lever (On Car)	Choke Unloader	Fast Idle R.P.M.	Choke Setting
1974	D4AE-BB, BC	①	1¹/₁₆	②	.468	—	5/16③	—	.250	1250	Index

①—For Air/Fuel ratio and idle CO%, see Tune-Up charts in car chapters.
②—Adjust link so primary and secondary stops both contact at same time.
③—Measured bottom of "S" link to top of bowl cover.

MODEL TQ ADJUSTMENTS

The TQ (Thermo-Quad) carburetor, Figs. 1 thru 2, is unique in design in that it has a black main body or fuel bowl of molded phenolic resin. This acts as an effective heat insulator. Fuel is kept cooler by about 20 degrees Fahrenheit than in carburetors of all metal design. Another reason for the lower operating temperatures is its suspended design metering system. All calibration points with the exception of the idle adjusting screws, are in the upper aluminum casting or air horn and are in effect suspended in cavities in the plastic main body.

Some 1974 units incorporate cellular plastic floats. Note that the float level settings are different. Refer to TQ Specifications Chart.

Float Setting

Fig. 3—With bowl cover inverted, gasket installed and floats resting on seated needle, the dimension of each float from bowl cover gasket to bottom side of float should be as shown in *TQ Specifications Chart*.

Secondary Throttle Linkage

Fig. 4—Block choke valve in wide open position and invert carburetor. Slowly open the primary throttle valves until it is possible to measure between lower edge of primary valve and its bore. When dimension is as shown in *TQ Specifications Chart*, the secondary valves should just start to open. If necessary to adjust, bend rod until correct dimension is obtained.

Secondary Air Valve Opening

Fig. 5

1. With air valve in closed position, the opening along air valve at its long side must be at its maximum and parallel with air horn gasket surface.

2. With air valve wide open, the opening of the air valve at the short side and air horn must be as shown in *TQ Specifications Chart*. The corner of air valve is notched for adjustment. Bend the corner with a pair of pliers to give proper opening.

Secondary Air Valve Spring Tension

Fig. 6—Loosen air valve lock plug and allow air valve to position itself wide open. With a long screwdriver that will enter center of tool C-4152 positioned on air valve adjustment plug, turn plug counterclockwise until air valve contacts stop lightly, then turn additional turn as specified in *TQ Specifications Chart*. Hold plug with screwdriver and tighten lock plug securely with tool C-4152.

Accelerator Pump Stroke

Fig. 7—Move choke valve wide open to release fast idle cam. Back off idle speed

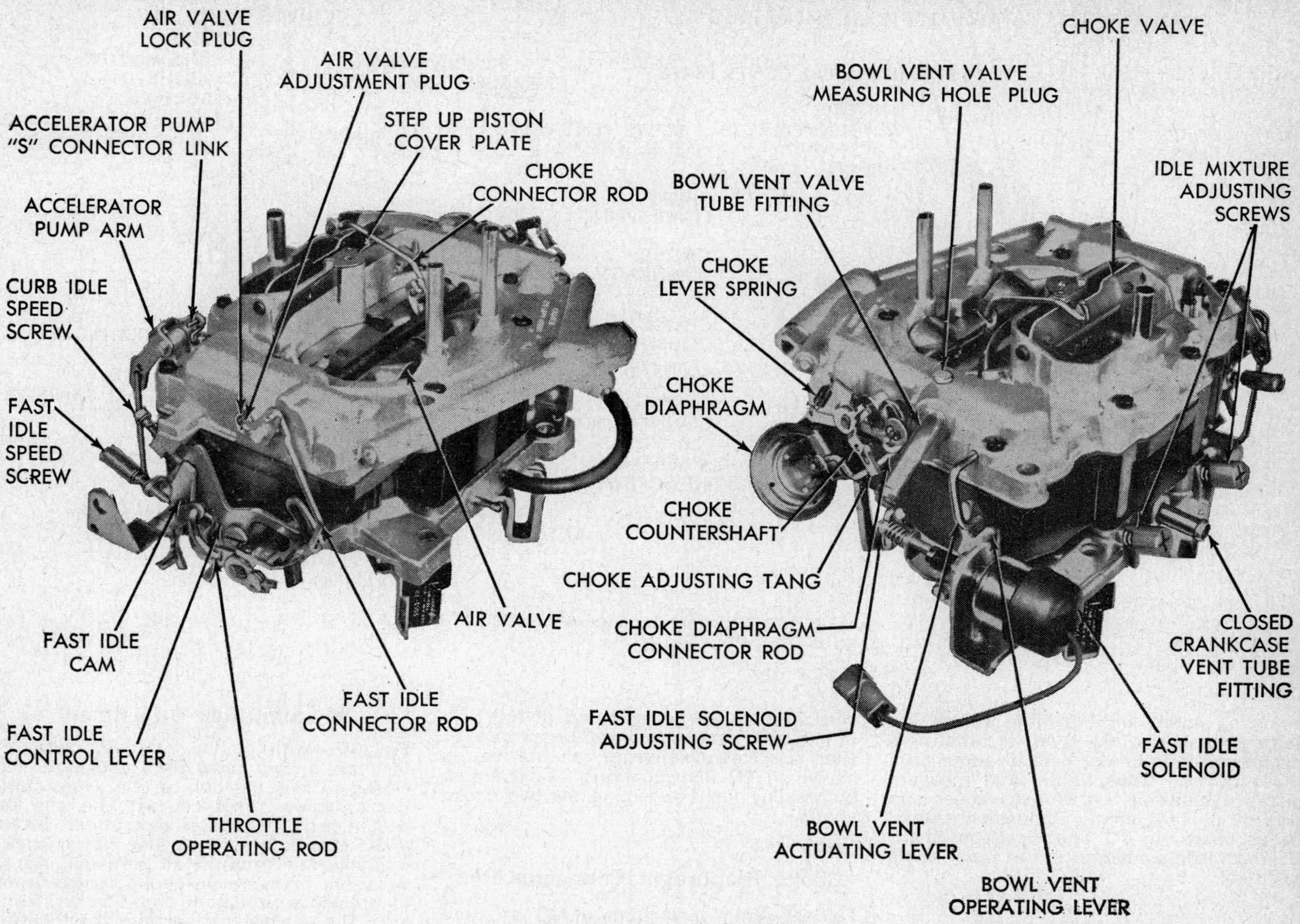

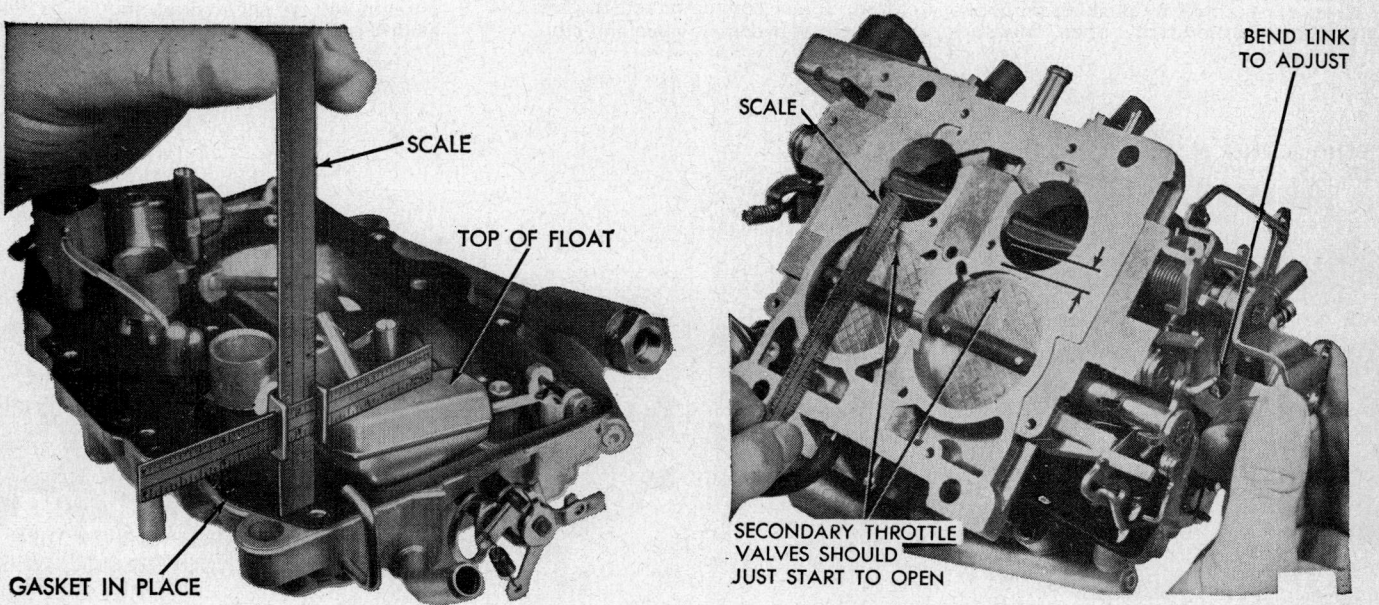

AIR VALVE
LOCK PLUG

AIR VALVE
ADJUSTMENT PLUG

ACCELERATOR PUMP
"S" CONNECTOR LINK

STEP UP PISTON
COVER PLATE

ACCELERATOR
PUMP ARM

CHOKE
CONNECTOR ROD

CURB IDLE
SPEED
SCREW

FAST
IDLE
SPEED
SCREW

FAST IDLE
CAM

FAST IDLE
CONNECTOR ROD

AIR VALVE

FAST IDLE
CONTROL LEVER

THROTTLE
OPERATING ROD

CHOKE VALVE

BOWL VENT VALVE
MEASURING HOLE PLUG

BOWL VENT VALVE
TUBE FITTING

IDLE MIXTURE
ADJUSTING
SCREWS

CHOKE
LEVER SPRING

CHOKE
DIAPHRAGM

CHOKE
COUNTERSHAFT

CHOKE ADJUSTING TANG

CHOKE DIAPHRAGM
CONNECTOR ROD

FAST IDLE SOLENOID
ADJUSTING SCREW

BOWL VENT
ACTUATING LEVER

BOWL VENT
OPERATING LEVER

CLOSED
CRANKCASE
VENT TUBE
FITTING

FAST IDLE
SOLENOID

Fig. 1 TQ carburetor assembly. 1972

SCALE

TOP OF FLOAT

GASKET IN PLACE

Fig. 3 TQ float setting

BEND LINK
TO ADJUST

SCALE

SECONDARY THROTTLE
VALVES SHOULD
JUST START TO OPEN

Fig. 4 TQ secondary throttle adjustment

CARTER CARBURETORS

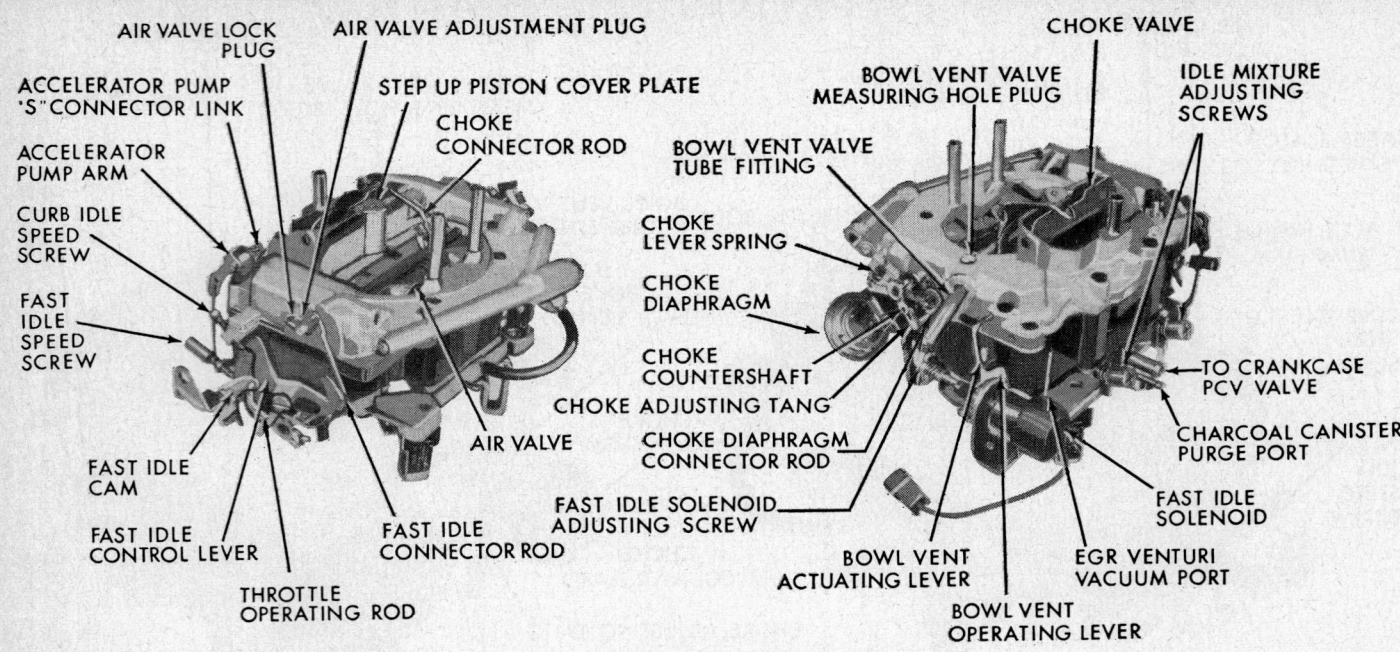

Fig. 1A   TQ carburetor assembly. 1973-74

adjusting screw until throttle valves are seated in bores. Be sure throttle connector rod is in center hole of pump arm. Close throttle valve tightly and measure distance between top of bowl cover and end of plunger shaft. Dimension should be as shown in *TQ Specifications Chart.* Bend throttle connector rod at lower angle to adjust.

Choke Control Lever

Fig. 8—Place carburetor on a flat surface and on 1973-74 Chrysler units, disconnect choke diaphragm rod at diaphragm. On all units, close choke by pushing on choke lever with throttle partly open. Measure vertical distance between top of rod hole in control lever and base of carburetor (flat surface). Dimension should be as shown in TQ Specifications Chart. Adjust by bending link connecting the two choke shafts.

Choke Diaphragm Connector Rod

Fig. 9—Apply a vacuum of 10 or more inches of Mercury to diaphragm to fully depress diaphragm stem. An auxiliary source like a distributor test machine can be used for this purpose. With air valve closed, adjust connector rod to give .040" clearance between air valve and stop.

Vacuum Kick Adjustment

Fig. 10—With engine running, back off fast idle speed screw until choke can be closed to kick position at idle. Note number of screw turns so fast idle can be turned back to original adjustment. Insert a #35 drill between long side (lower edge) of choke valve and the air horn wall. Apply sufficient pressure on choke control lever to provide a minimum choke valve opening. The spring connecting the control lever to the adjustment lever must be fully extended for proper adjustment. Bend tang as shown to change contact with end of diaphragm rod. Do not adjust diaphragm rod. A slight drag should be felt as drill is being removed.

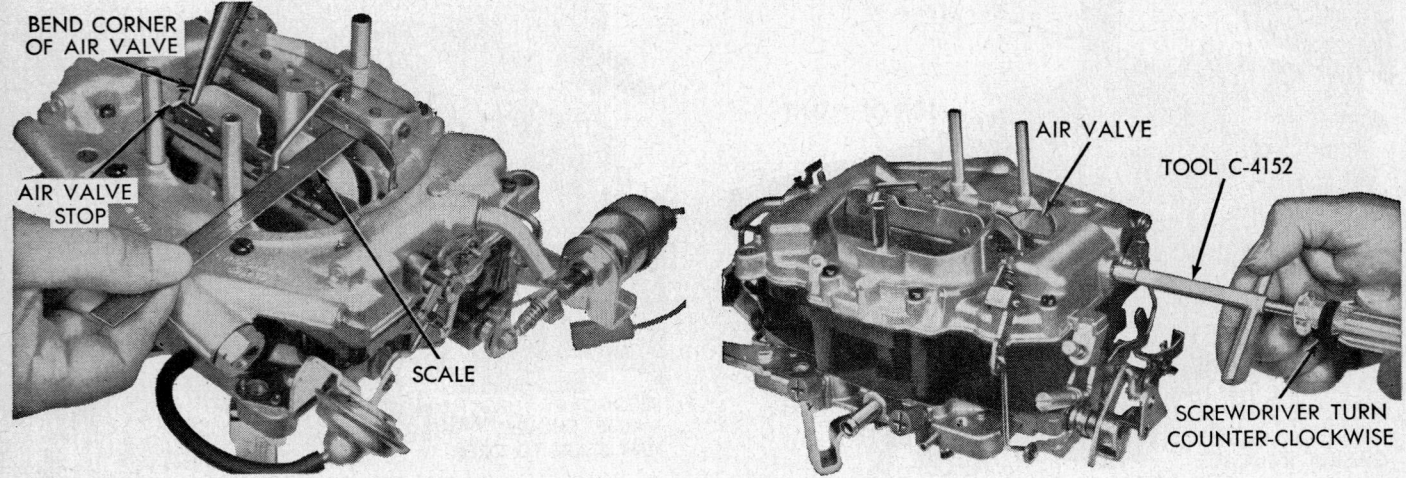

Fig. 5   TQ secondary air valve opening

Fig. 6   TQ secondary air valve spring tension

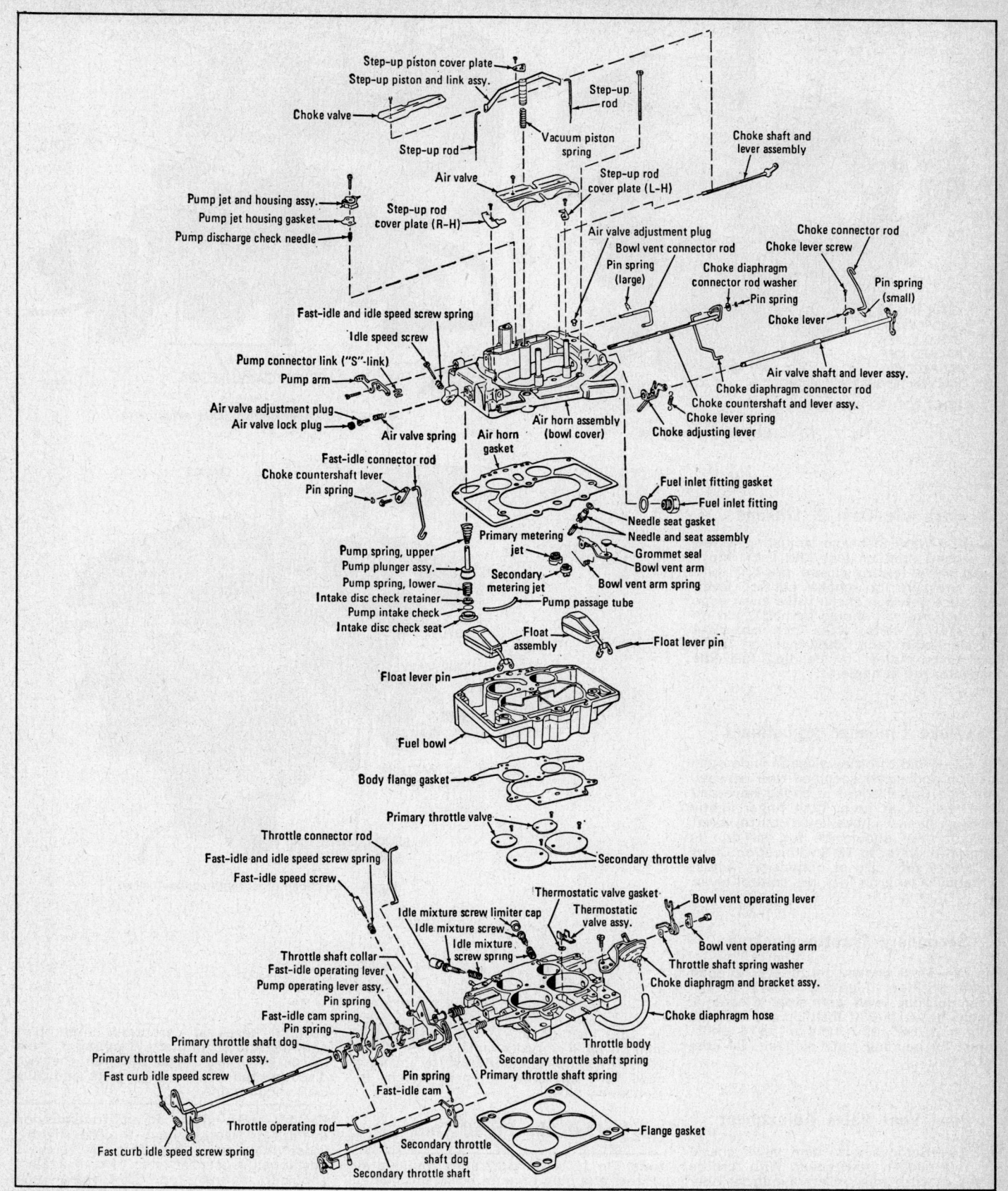

Fig. 2 Carter TQ model exploded view

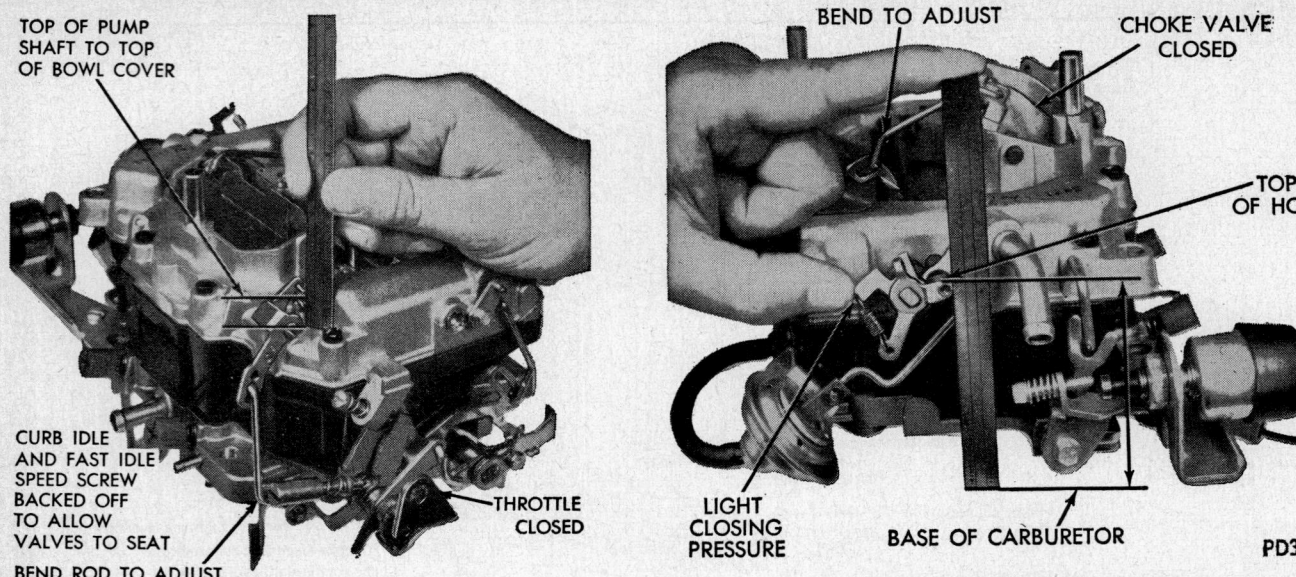

Fig. 7   TQ accelerator pump stroke

Fig. 8   TQ choke control lever adjustment

Fast Idle Cam & Linkage

Fig. 11—With fast idle adjusting screw on second step of fast idle cam, move choke valve toward closed position with light pressure on choke control lever. Clearance between choke valve lower edge and air horn wall should be .110 inch on all 1971-73 units, .100 inch on 1974 Chrysler units and .099 inch on 1974 Ford units. Adjust by bending fast idle connector rod at angle.

Choke Unloader Adjustment

Fig. 12—Hold throttle valves in wide open position and insert specified drill between long side (lower edge) of choke valve and inner wall of air horn. With finger lightly pressing against choke valve control lever, a slight drag should be felt as drill is withdrawn. Refer to TQ Specification Chart for proper drill size or dimension. Adjust by bending tang on fast idle control lever.

Secondary Throttle Lockout

Fig. 13—Move choke control lever to open choke position. Measure clearance between lockout lever and stop. Clearance should be .010-.030 inch on all 1971-73 units and .060-.090 inch on 1974 units. Adjust by bending tang on fast idle control lever.

Bowl Vent Valve Adjustment

Fig. 14—Remove bowl vent valve checking hole plug in bowl cover. With throttle valves at curb idle, insert a narrow ruler down through hole. Allow ruler to rest lightly on top of valve. Dimension should

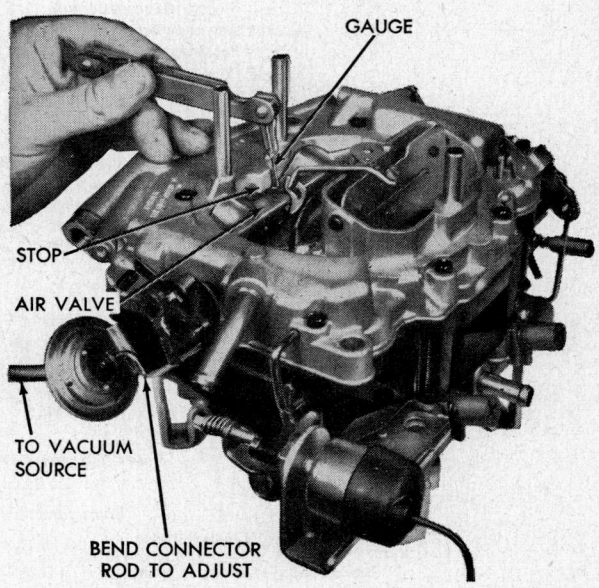

Fig. 9   TQ choke diaphragm connector rod

be .850 inch on all 1971-73 units, .812 inch on 1974 Chrysler units and .900 inch on 1974 Ford units. Adjust by bending bowl vent operating lever at notch. Install a new plug.

Fast Idle Speed Cam

Note: On 1974 Chrysler units, remove air cleaner and plug vacuum fittings to heated air control and OSAC valves. On 1974 Ford units, remove air cleaner, disconnect vacuum hoses at carburetor spark port and distributor primary diaphragm, then install a jumper hose between the two disconnected hoses. Disconnect and plug EGR vacuum line.

Fig. 15—With engine off and transmission in Park or Neutral, open throttle slightly. Close choke valve until fast idle screw is positioned on second step of cam against shoulder of first step. Start engine and stabilize RPM, then adjust fast idle speed. Refer to TQ Specification Chart.

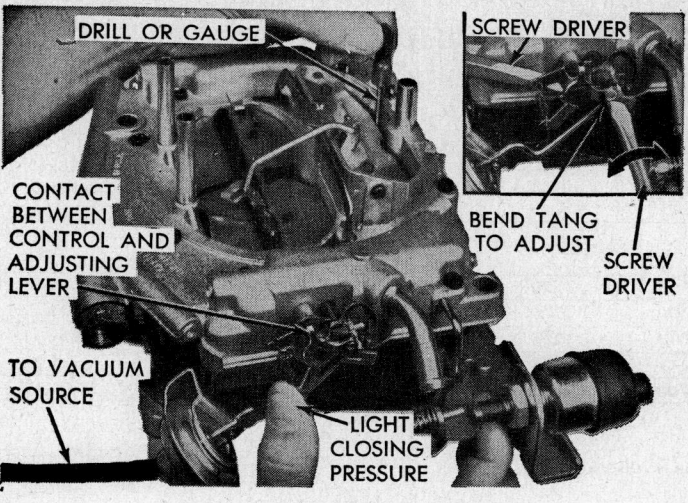

Fig. 10   TQ vacuum kick adjustment

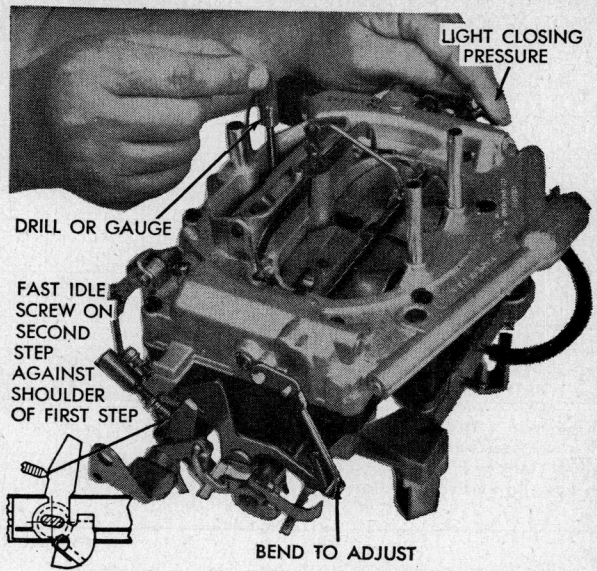

Fig. 11   TQ fast idle cam & linkage adjustment

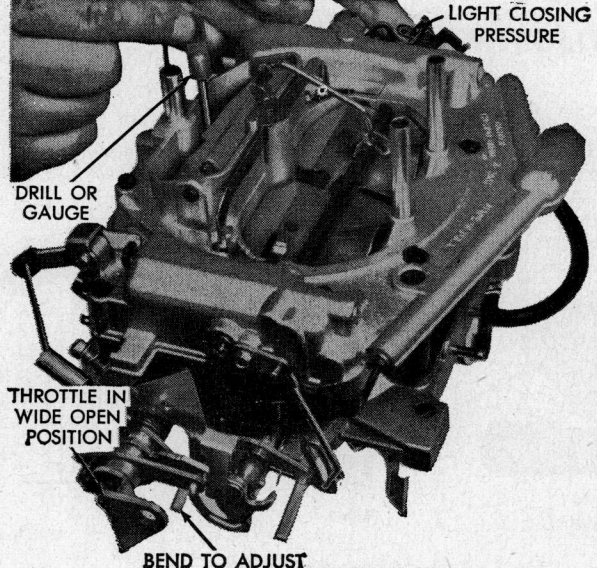

Fig. 12   TQ choke unloader adjustment

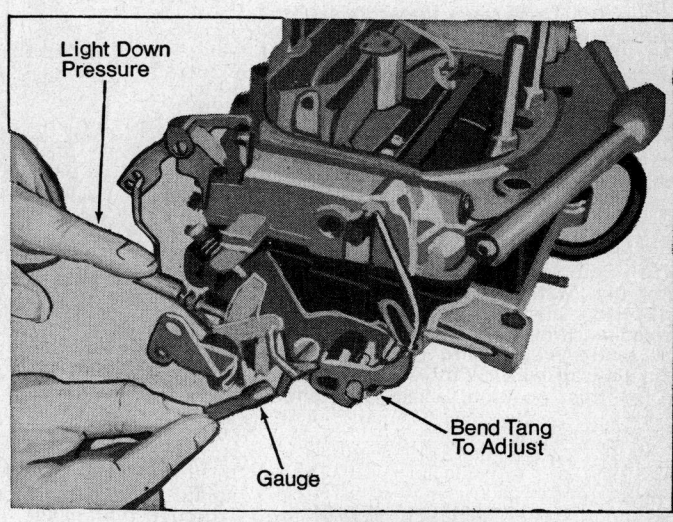

Fig. 13   TQ secondary throttle lockout

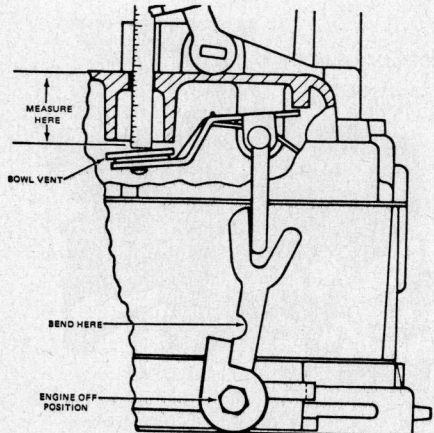

Fig. 14   TQ bowl vent valve adjustment

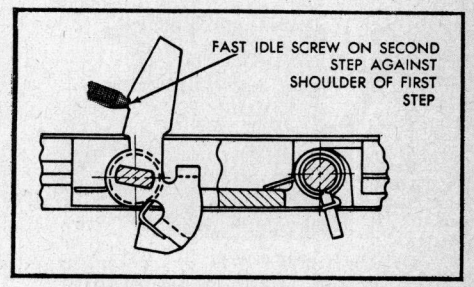

Fig. 15   TQ fast idle speed cam position

Ford Autolite/Motorcraft Carburetors

MODEL 1250-1V CARB. ADJUSTMENT SPECIFICATIONS

See Tune Up Chart in car chapters for hot idle speeds.

Year	Carb. Model (9510)	Idle Mixture Turns Open	Float Setting	Pump Stroke	Fast Idle Speed	Choke Pulldown	Dechoke Clearance	Choke Link Position	Choke Setting
PINTO									
1971	711-BDA	②	①	.085	1700	.120	.210	Outer Hole	Index
	711-BDB	②	①	.070	1700	.075	.210	Outer Hole	Index
1972	721F-KFA	②	③	.070	1700	.075	.210	Outer Hole	Index
1973	731F-KAA	②	③	.085	—	.075	—	—	Index
	731F-KEA	②	③	.085	1700	.075	.210	Outer Hole	Index

①—With body in vertical position, set at 1.16–1.20.
    With body horizontal set at 1.35–1.37 (see Fig. 2).
②—Air/fuel ratio or idle CO% rating is found in Tune Up Specification tables in car chapters.
③—With body in vertical position (dry), set at 1.20.

MODEL 1250-1V ADJUSTMENTS

Fuel & Float Level Adjust

Fig. 2—With carburetor upper body held in vertical position, measure distance between upper body gasket and bottom of float (left view in illustration). Bend tab to adjust.

Turn upper body to horizontal position and measure distance from bottom of float to gasket (right view in illustration). Bend tab to adjust.

Choke Plate Pull-Down

Fig. 3—Remove air cleaner, thermostatic spring and water housing. Depress vacuum piston until vacuum bleed port is revealed and insert a piece of wire .040" thick, suitably bent, into this port. Raise piston to trap wire. With wire and piston held in this position, close the choke

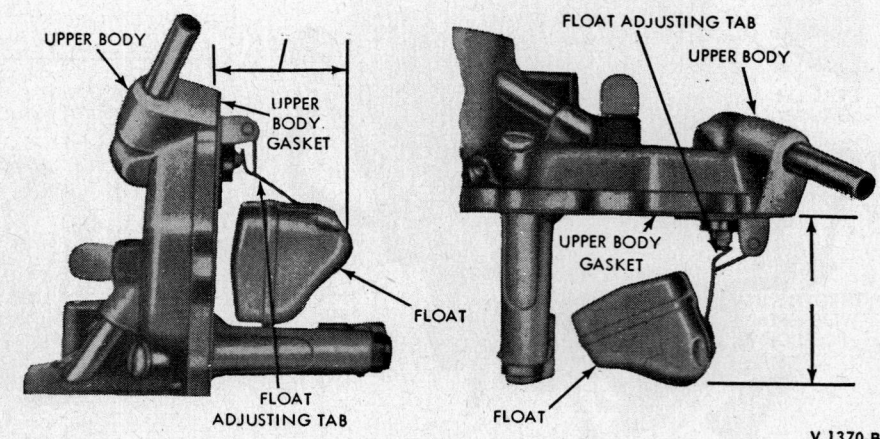

Fig. 2 Fuel and float level setting

plate until its movement is stopped through the linkage. Partially open throttle for fast idle tab to clear cam. Bottom of choke plate should now be as specified from carburetor body. If necessary, bend extension of choke thermostat lever to adjust.

Dechoke Adjustment

Fig. 4—Open throttle fully and hold it against stop. Check clearance between bottom of choke plate and carburetor body. Adjust if necessary, by bending the projection on the fast idle cam.

Accelerator Pump Adjustment

Unscrew the throttle stop screw until the throttle plate is fully closed. Depress the accelerator pump diaphragm plunger and check the clearance between the operating lever and the plunger. Refer to *1250-1V Specifications Chart.* Adjust by bending the gooseneck of the pump push rod.

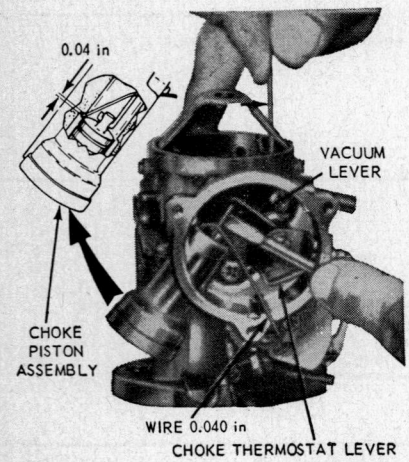

Fig. 3 Choke plate pull-down clearance

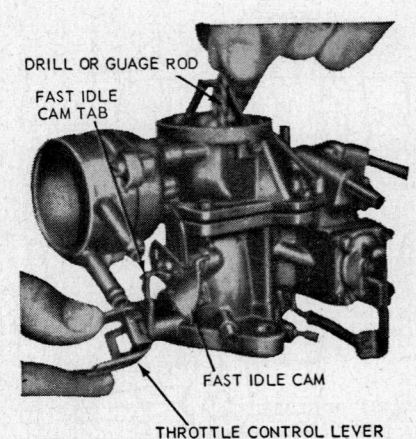

Fig. 4 De-choke adjustment

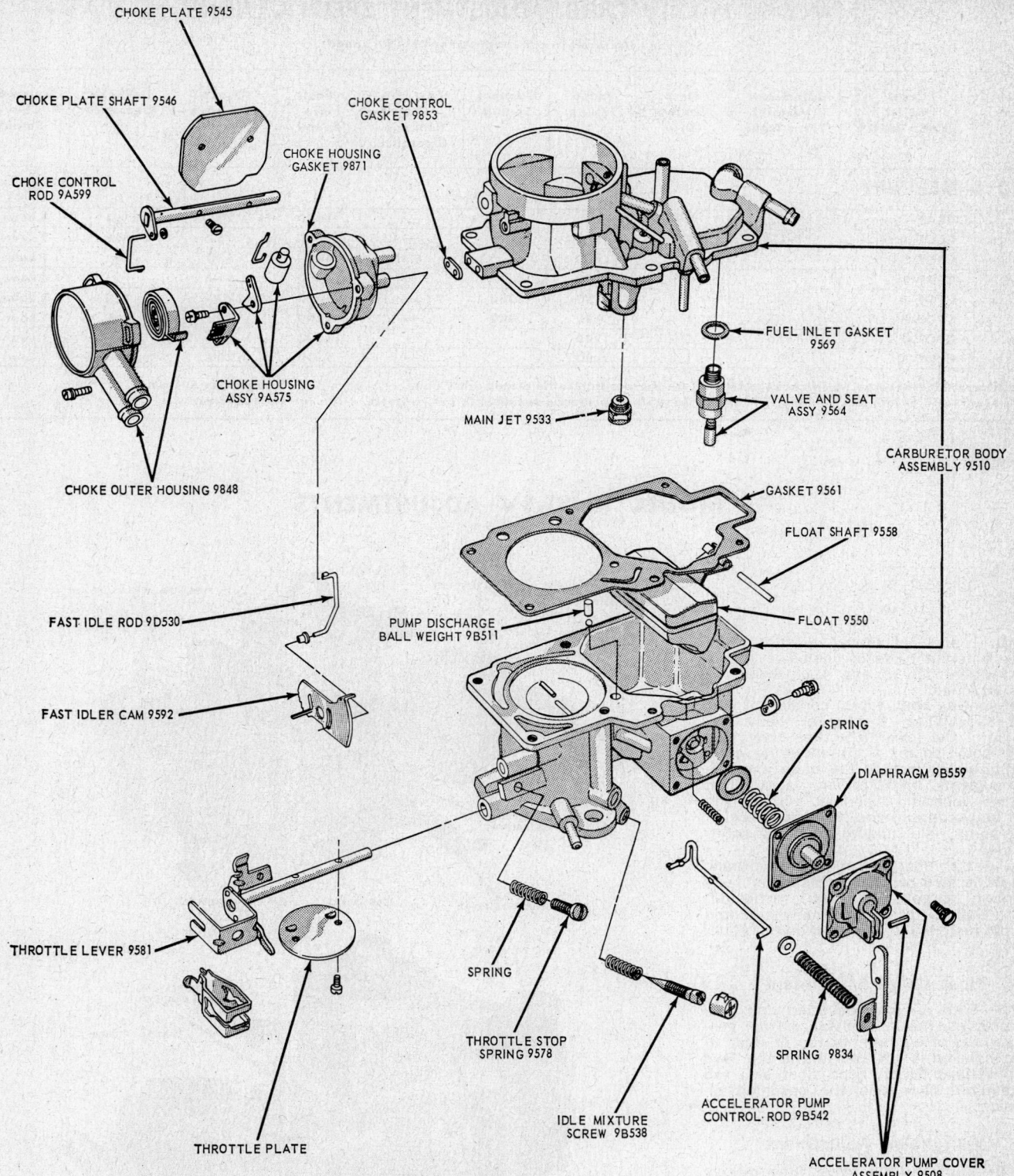

Fig. 1   Exploded view of Model 1250-IV carburetor

Fast Idle Adjustment

With the choke plate pulldown correctly adjusted and held in the pulldown position, check that the throttle lever fast idle tab is on the second step of the fast idle cam at the arrow on the fast idle cam. If necessary, bend the fast idle rod at its existing bend. Install thermostatic spring and water housing.

At normal operating temperature position the throttle lever fast idle tab on the second step of the cam and check the engine speed. Adjust if necessary by bending the tab contacting the fast idle cam.

FORD Autolite/Motorcraft CARBURETORS

MODEL 1100-1V CARB. ADJUSTMENT SPECIFICATIONS

See Tune Up Chart in car chapters for hot idle speeds.

Year	Carb. Model (Code 9510)	Idle Screw (Mixture) Turns Open	Float Setting (Dry)	Pump Setting	Dashpot Setting	Fast Idle Cam Linkage Clearance	Fast Idle Speed	Choke Pulldown Clearance	Dechoke Clearance ①	Automatic Choke Setting
FORD & MERCURY										
1969	C8AF-E④	②	1³⁄₃₂	.190	.080	—	1600	.280	¹⁵⁄₆₄	3 Lean
	C8OF-A③	1–1½	1³⁄₃₂	.190	.080	—	1400	.150	¹⁵⁄₆₄	2 Lean
	C8OF-B④	②	1³⁄₃₂	.190	2	—	1500	.130	¼	1 Lean
	C9DF-B	②	1³⁄₃₂	.150	3	—	1400	.150	¼	3 Lean
	C9OF-A	②	1³⁄₃₂	.190	.080	—	1600	.200	.160	3 Lean
	C9OF-B	②	1³⁄₃₂	.190	.080	—	1400	.200	.160	1 Lean
	C9OF-J	②	1³⁄₃₂	.190	—	—	1400	.200	.160	1 Lean
	C9OF-K	②	1³⁄₃₂	.190	—	—	1600	.200	.160	3 Lean

①—Minimum clearance between choke plate and air horn with throttle plates wide open.
②—Air/fuel ratio or idle CO% rating is found in Tune Up Specifications tables in car chapters.
③—Thermactor system.
④—Imco system.

MODEL 1100-1V ADJUSTMENTS

Figs. 1 and 2 illustrate exterior views of the different types of one-barrel carburetors while Figs. 3 and 4 illustrate the units exploded.

As shown, both types consist of two main assemblies, the upper body (air horn) and the lower (throttle) body. The upper body contains the metering components which include the main and idle fuel systems with power valve, float chamber vent and fuel inlet system. The lower body contains the fuel bowl, accelerating pump, idle mixture adjusting screw (needle).

On 1100 models a built-in hydraulic dashpot is incorporated in the lower body as shown. However, the 1101 model differs in that it has an externally mounted dashpot fastened to a bracket on the upper body.

Float Level Adjustment

Fig. 5—With air horn inverted and gasket removed, measure distance from gasket surface of air horn to top of float. If the dimension is not as listed in the *Ford Specifications Chart*, bend float arm tab as required to obtain the specified dimension.

Vent Valve Adjustment

Fig. 6—With throttle valve fully closed, groove on vent valve rod should be even with open end of vent. To adjust, bend arm on vent valve rod actuating lever (where it contacts pump lever) to align groove with edge of bore.

Pump Adjustment

Position throttle and choke valve link-

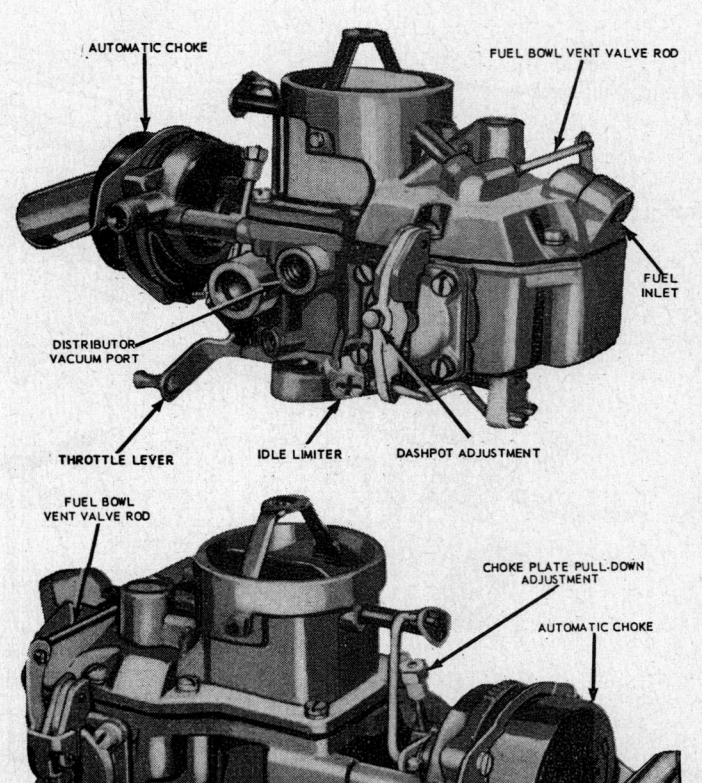

Fig. 1 Autolite 1100 carburetor with automatic choke mounted on throttle body & internal type dashpot. 1969

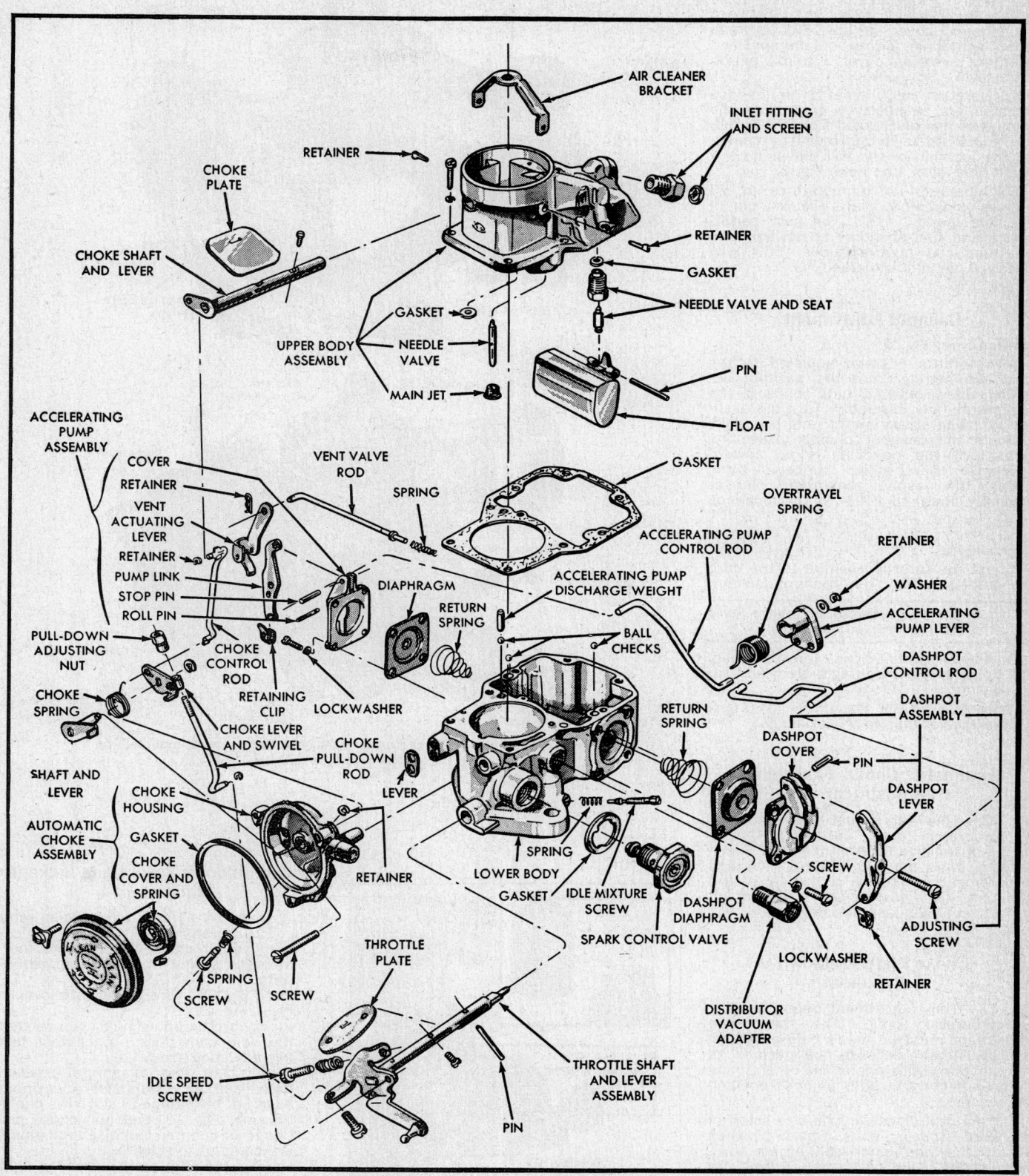

Fig. 3   Exploded view of Autolite 1100 carburetor shown in Fig. 1

age so that throttle valve will be completely closed. Hold throttle valve closed and place a gauge of the thickness listed in the *Ford Specifications Chart* between roll pin and cover surface, Fig. 7. Bend pump actuating rod to obtain specified clearance between cover and roll pin in pump lever.

Acceleration requirements in various climates are satisfied by controlling the amount of fuel discharged from the pump. The pump stroke is controlled by changing the location of the roll pin in the external type lever stop hole, Fig. 8.

For operation in temperatures of 50 degrees and below, place the roll pin in the hole marked "HI". For best performance and fuel economy at normal temperatures and high altitudes (5000 ft.) place roll pin in hole marked "LO".

Dashpot Adjustment

Internal-type, Fig. 9

With throttle position adjusted to the curb idle setting, turn the dashpot adjusting screw outward until it clears the dashpot plunger assembly. Turn the dashpot adjusting screw inward until it initially contacts the dashpot plunger assembly; then, turn the adjusting screw inward (clockwise) the specified number of turns against the dashpot diaphragm plunger assembly. Refer to *1100-1V Specifications Chart*.

External-type

Adjust the throttle position to the curb idle setting, loosen the dashpot locknut.

NOTE: Check the accelerating pump lever and stroke for proper adjustment.

On 1969 units close throttle valve and fully depress diaphragm stem and adjust dashpot.

Refer to *1100-1V Specifications Chart*. Torque the locknut to 7-10 inch lbs.

Automatic Choke Fast Idle Adjustment

Fig. 11—This adjustment refers to Fig. 1 carburetor only. Insert a gauge or drill of the size listed in the *Ford Specifications Chart* between throttle valve and carburetor bore. Close choke valve and turn fast idle adjusting screw inward until it just contacts fast idle cam.

Choke Plate Pulldown Adjustment

Fig. 12—This adjustment refers to Fig. 1 carburetor only. The fast idle adjustment must be made before making this adjustment because the position of the pulldown rod is one of the determining factors affecting throttle-to-choke opening relationship.

Place a drill or gauge of a size listed in the *Ford Specifications Chart* between choke valve and inner wall of air horn. Close choke valve on gauge or drill and hold it securely. Close throttle until fast idle screw touches fast idle cam. Adjust plastic nut to just contact swivel on choke lever.

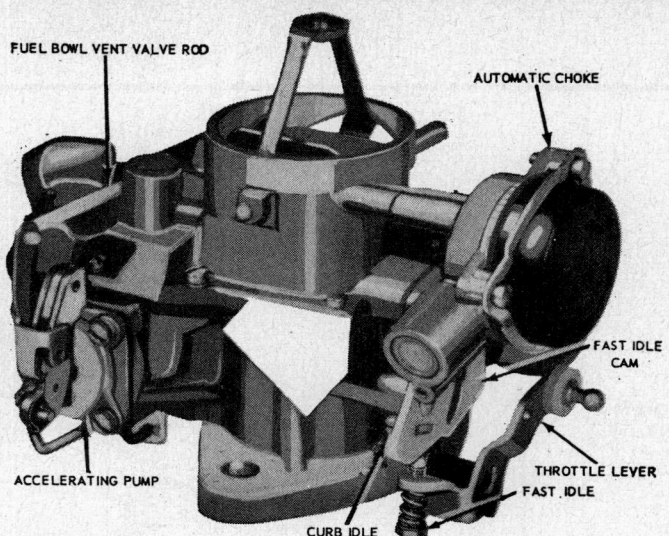

Fig. 2 Autolite 1100 carburetor with automatic choke mounted on air horn & external type dashpot. 1969

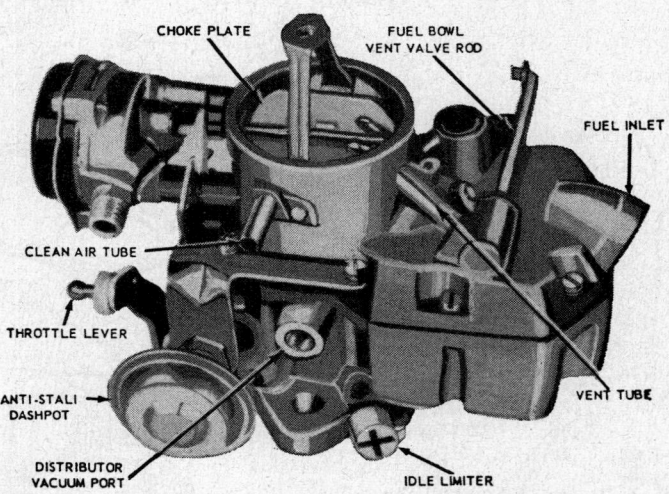

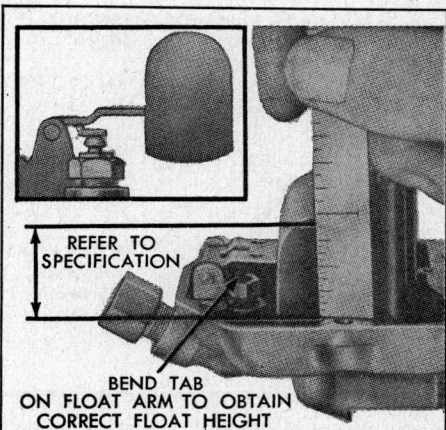

REFER TO SPECIFICATION

BEND TAB ON FLOAT ARM TO OBTAIN CORRECT FLOAT HEIGHT

Fig. 5 Float level adjustment

Choke Pulldown & Fast Idle Linkage Adjustment

Figs. 13 and 14—These adjustments refer to Fig. 1 carburetor only.
1. Remove air cleaner and choke thermostatic spring housing from carburetor.
2. Bend a .036" wire gauge as shown in inset, Fig. 13.
3. Block throttle about half open so that fast idle cam does not contact fast idle adjusting screw.
4. Insert bent end of gauge between lower end of piston slot and upper edge of right-hand slot in choke housing, Fig. 13, and pull choke piston lever counterclockwise until gauge is snug in piston slot.
5. Hold gauge in place by exerting light pressure on choke piston lever.
6. Gradually bend rod (link) between choke piston and piston lever until choke plate opens just wide enough

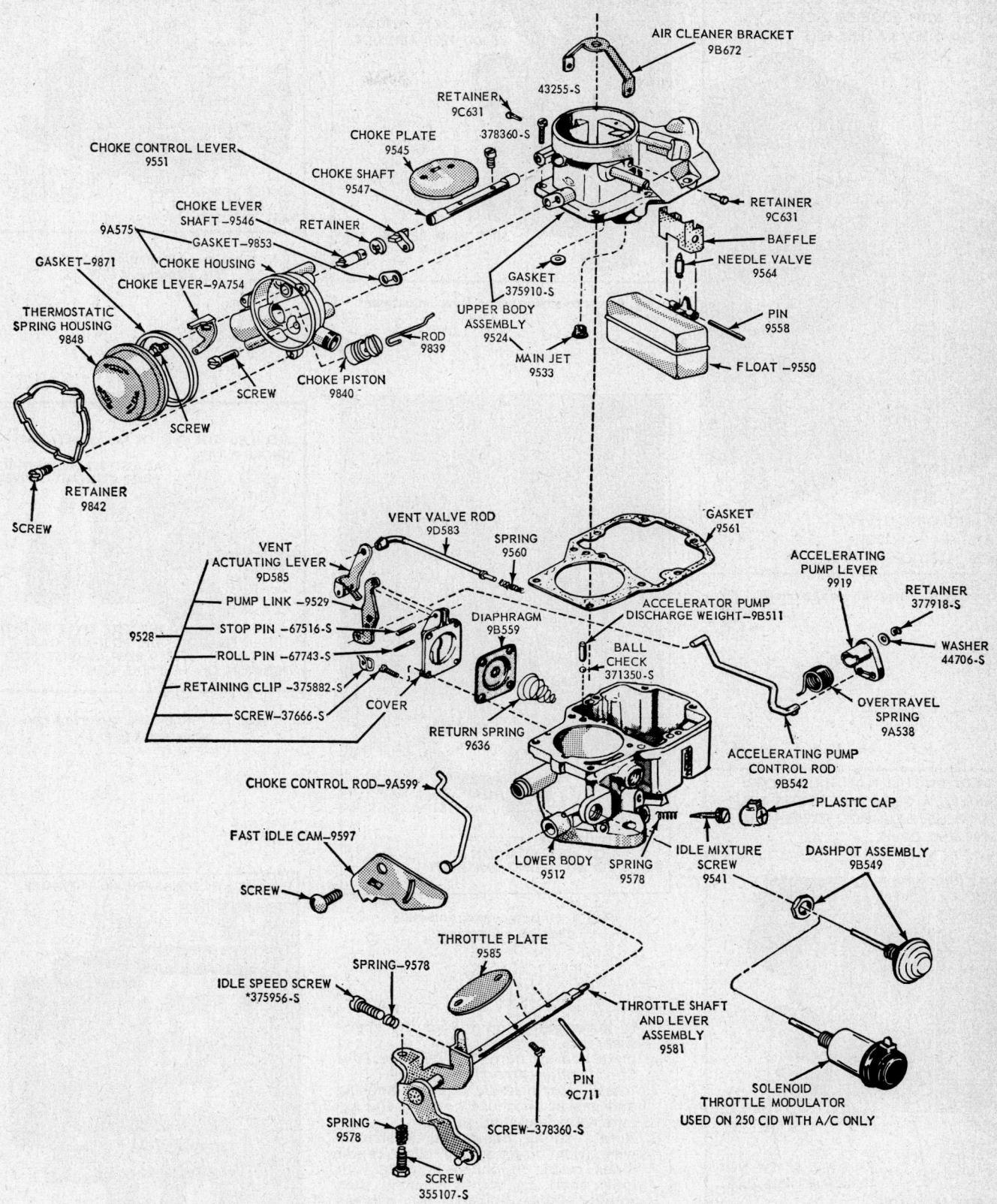

Fig. 4   Exploded view of model 1100 carburetor shown in Fig. 2

NOTCH ON VENT VALVE ROD TO ALIGN WITH EDGE OF HOLE, WITH THROTTLE IN HOT IDLE POSITION

BEND ACTUATING LEVER TO OBTAIN CORRECT ROD POSITION

Fig. 6 Vent valve adjustment

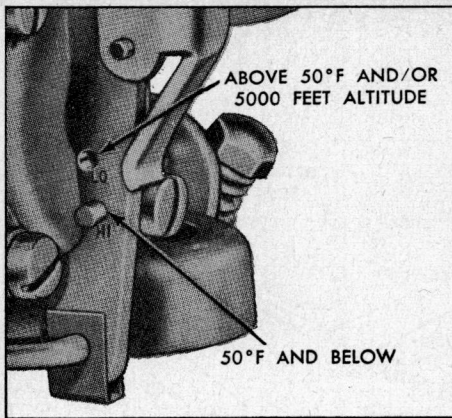

ABOVE 50°F AND/OR 5000 FEET ALTITUDE

50°F AND BELOW

Fig. 8 Accelerator pump lever adjustment

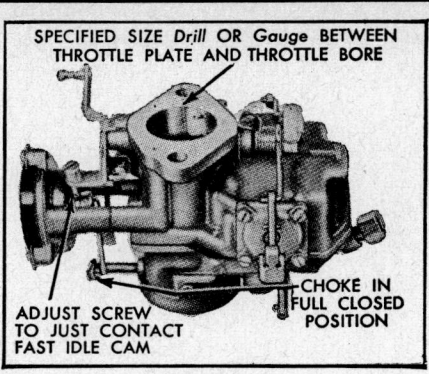

SPECIFIED SIZE *Drill* OR *Gauge* BETWEEN THROTTLE PLATE AND THROTTLE BORE

CHOKE IN FULL CLOSED POSITION

ADJUST SCREW TO JUST CONTACT FAST IDLE CAM

Fig. 11 Automatic choke fast idle adjustment (Fig. 1)

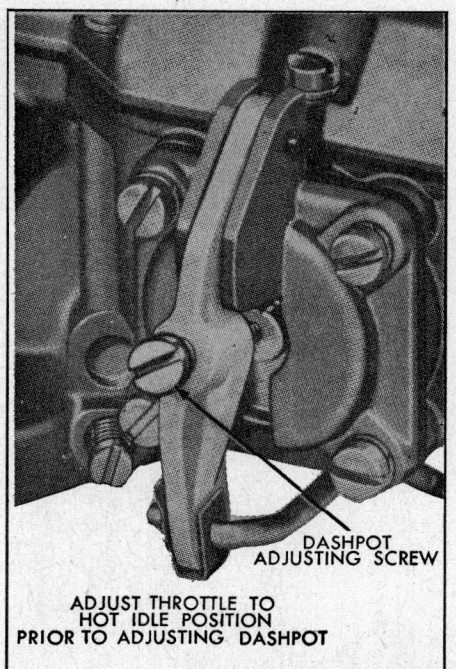

DASHPOT ADJUSTING SCREW

ADJUST THROTTLE TO HOT IDLE POSITION PRIOR TO ADJUSTING DASHPOT

Fig. 9 Internal type anti-stall dashpot adjustment

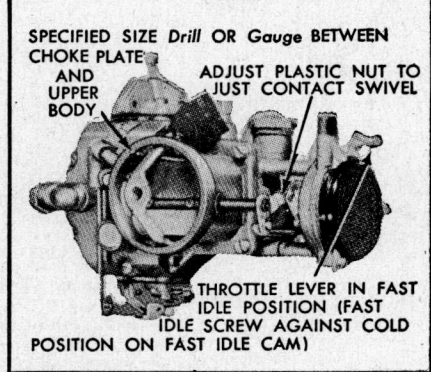

SPECIFIED SIZE *Drill* OR *Gauge* BETWEEN CHOKE PLATE AND UPPER BODY

ADJUST PLASTIC NUT TO JUST CONTACT SWIVEL

THROTTLE LEVER IN FAST IDLE POSITION (FAST IDLE SCREW AGAINST COLD POSITION ON FAST IDLE CAM)

Fig. 12 Automatic choke linkage adjustment (Fig. 1)

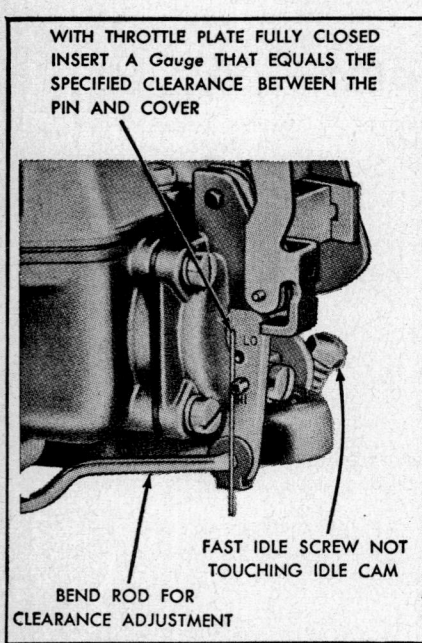

WITH THROTTLE PLATE FULLY CLOSED INSERT A *Gauge* THAT EQUALS THE SPECIFIED CLEARANCE BETWEEN THE PIN AND COVER

FAST IDLE SCREW NOT TOUCHING IDLE CAM

BEND ROD FOR CLEARANCE ADJUSTMENT

Fig. 7 Accelerator pump adjustment

to allow gauge or drill of the specified size between front of choke plate and air horn, Fig. 13 (see *Ford Specifications Chart*).
7. Install thermostatic spring housing and gasket on choke housing and secure with clamp and screws.
8. Rotate spring housing counterclockwise (rich direction) to align center index mark on choke housing with index mark on spring housing; then rotate spring housing 90 degrees counterclockwise.
9. Position fast idle adjusting screw on index mark on fast idle cam, Fig. 14.
10. Adjust fast idle cam linkage to speci-

THERMOSTATIC SPRING HOUSING INDEX MARK

CHOKE HOUSING INDEX MARK

Fig. 15 Automatic choke setting

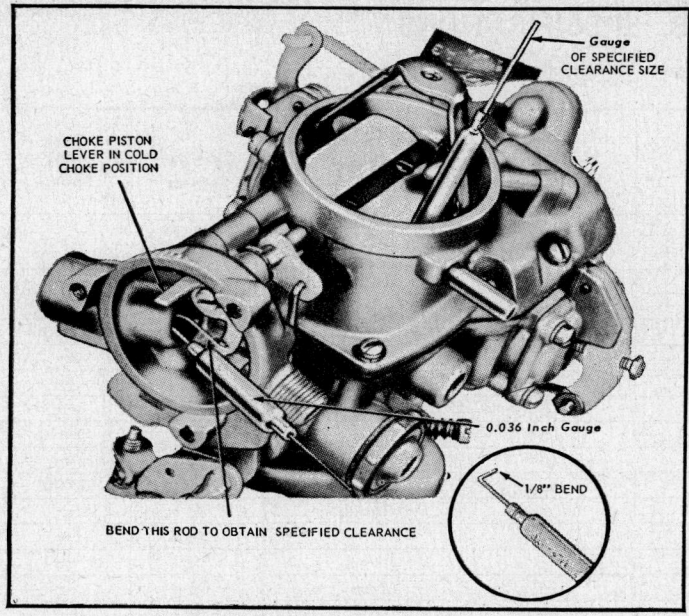

Fig. 13   Choke plate clearance adjustment (Fig. 2)

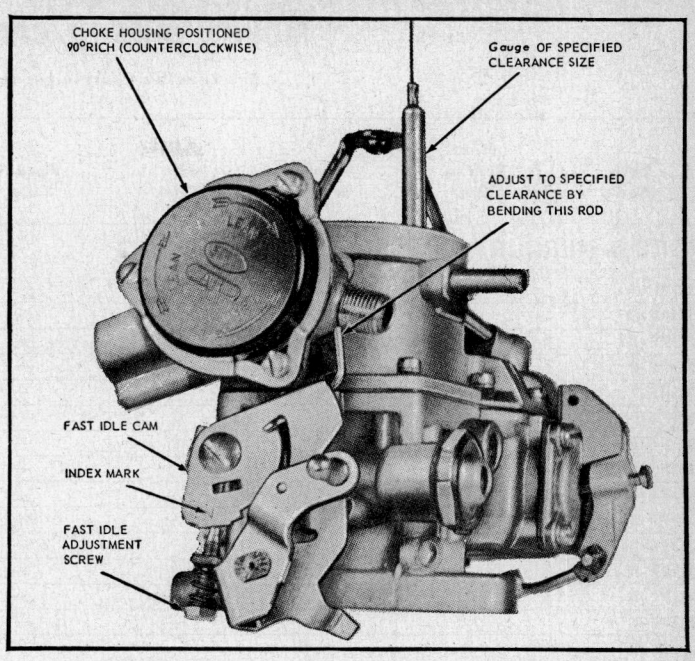

Fig. 14   Fast idle cam linkage adjustment (Fig. 2)

fication by bending choke control rod, Fig. 14, to provide the specified clearance between front of choke plate and air horn. Bend rod inward to decrease (outward to increase) clearance. Make certain fast idle screw remains on index mark of fast idle cam during adjustment procedure.

11. Set thermostatic spring housing to specified mark listed in the *Ford Specifications Chart.*

NOTE: If the foregoing adjustments were made with the carburetor installed on the engine, adjust engine idle speed and mixture, fast idle speed and dashpot as outlined above.

Automatic Choke Setting

Fig. 15—Loosen retaining screws and set thermostatic spring housing to the mark specified in the *Ford Specifications Chart* and tighten retaining screws.

MODEL 1940-1V CARB. SPECIFICATIONS

See Tune Up Chart in car chapters for hot idle speeds.

Carb. Model	Float Setting (Dry)	Pump Setting	Fast Idle Cam	Vacuum Kick	Choke Unloader	Automatic Choke Adjustment	Dashpot Setting	Fast Idle Speed
FORD & MERCURY								
DOPF-A	①	②	5/64	3/16	5/32	Index	—	2100
DOPF-C	①	②	5/64	3/16	5/32	Index	—	2100
DOPF-D	①	②	5/64	3/16	5/32	Index	3/32	2100
DOPF-E	①	②	③	—	④	—	—	—
DOPF-F	①	②	③	—	④	—	—	—
DOPF-G	①	②	③	—	④	—	3/32	—
DOPF-H	①	②	③	—	④	—	3/32	—
DOPF-J	①	②	③	—	④	—	3/32	—
DOPF-K	①	②	1/16	5/32	1/8	Index	3/32	2100
DOPF-L	①	③	1/16	5/32	1/8	Index	3/32	—
DOPF-M	①	②	—	—	—	—	3/32	—
DOPF-N	①	②	—	—	—	—	3/32	—
DOPF-R	①	②	—	—	—	—	3/32	—
DOPF-T	①	②	—	—	—	—	3/32	—

①—Toe in float, flush with gasket surface of main body.
②—27/32" from centerline of pump link hole in pump rod to edge of 5/16" boss on main body.
③—No vacuum, second step.
④—At wide open throttle.

MODEL 1940-1V ADJUSTMENTS

The model 1940-1V, Figs. 1A, 2A, 3A, is a concentric unit, that is, the fuel bowl completely surrounds the venturi, and is available with either manual or automatic choke.

Principal sub-assemblies include a bowl cover, carburetor body and throttle body. A thick gasket between the throttle body and carburetor body retards heat transfer to the fuel to resist percolation.

In addition to the usual circuits, this unit incorporates a spark valve. This is a diaphragm operated, spring loaded valves in the main body connected to the throttle bore port. When the spark valve closes off the port, spark advance vacuum is decreased, retarding the ignition timing.

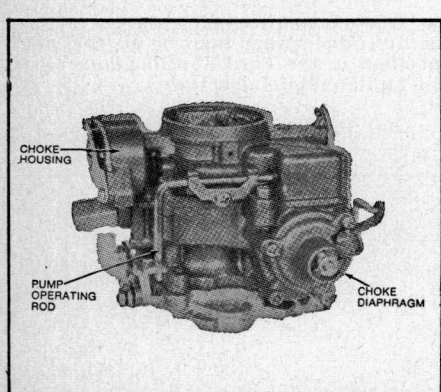

Fig. 1A   1940-1V carburetor with automatic choke

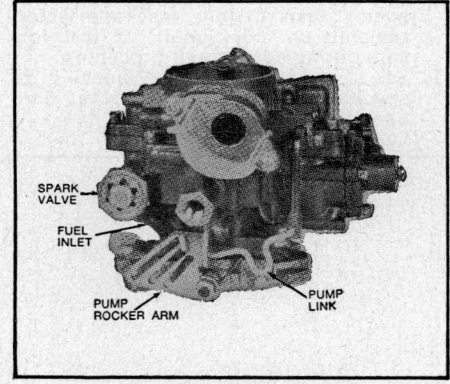

Float Level Adjustment

Fig. 4A—Install float assembly in float shaft cradle. Insert retaining spring and while holding with fingers, invert the bowl. A straight edge placed across the surface of the bowl should just touch the toes of the float. If necessary, bend the float tang to obtain this adjustment.

Pump Adjustment

Fig. 5A—With throttle in the curb idle position, the distance from the vacuum passage casting to the center of the hole in the pump operating rod should be as listed in specifications.

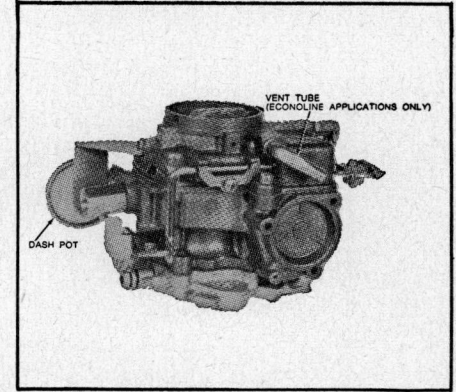

Fig. 2A   1940-1V carburetor with manual choke

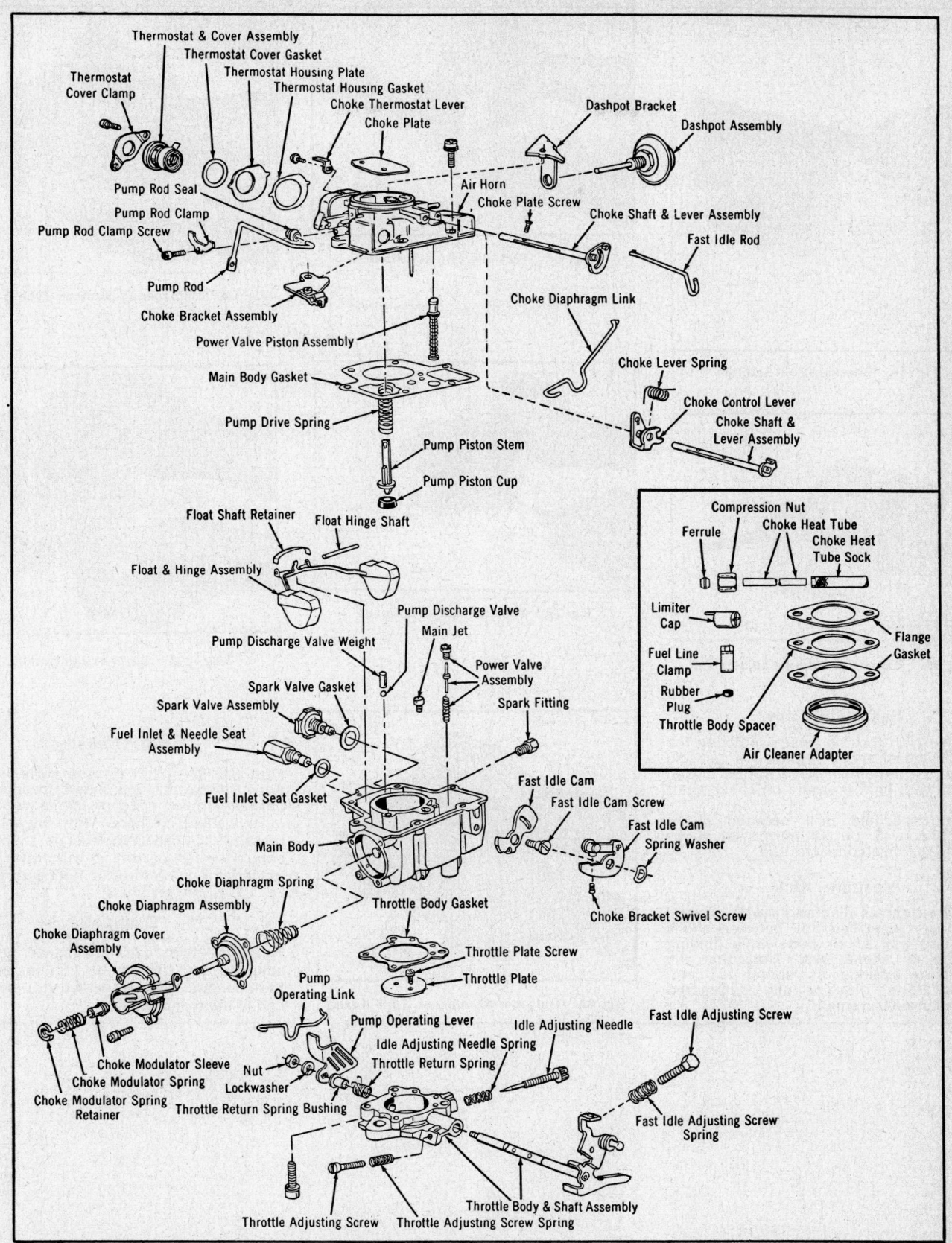

Fig. 3A 1940-1V carburetor. Exploded

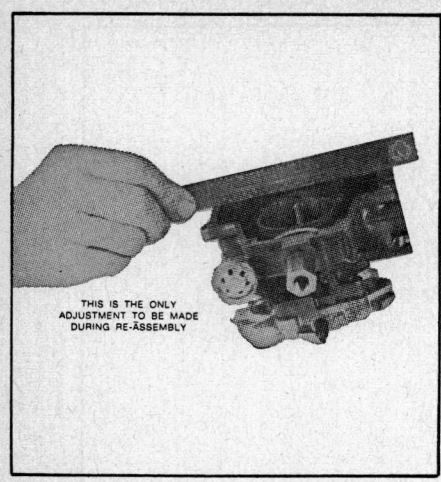

THIS IS THE ONLY ADJUSTMENT TO BE MADE DURING RE-ASSEMBLY

Fig. 4A   Checking float setting

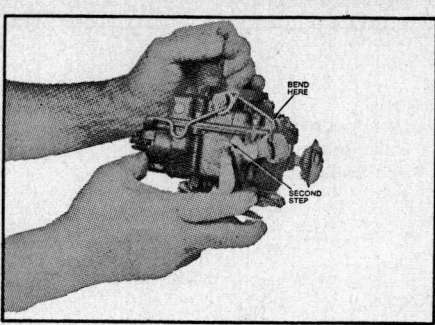

BEND HERE

SECOND STEP

Fig. 6A   Fast idle cam adjustment

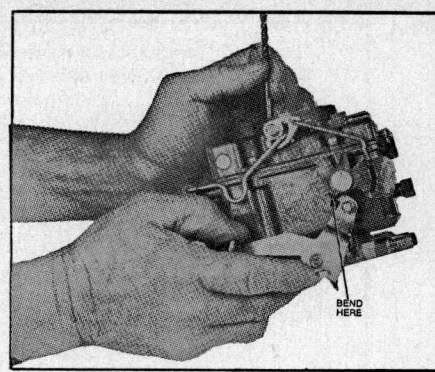

BEND HERE

Fig. 9A   Unloader adjustment. Type B tang

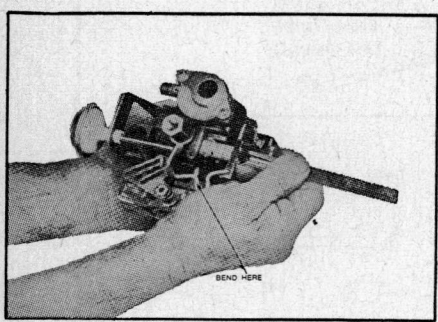

BEND HERE

Fig. 5A   Pump piston stroke adjustment

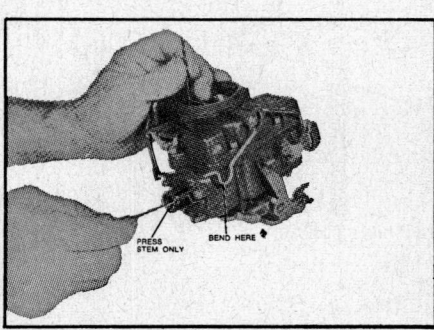

PRESS STEM ONLY

BEND HERE

Fig. 7A   Vacuum kick adjustment

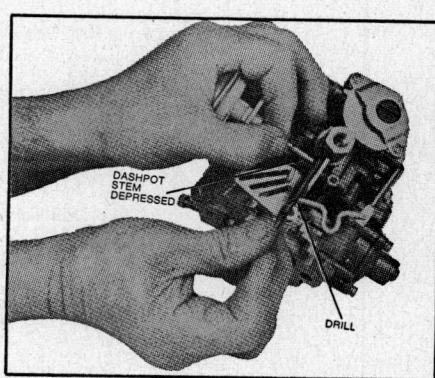

DASHPOT STEM DEPRESSED

DRILL

Fig. 10A   Dashpot adjustment

Fast Idle Cam

Fig. 6A—With throttle lever contacting the second highest speed step on the fast idle cam, move the choke valve toward closed position with light pressure on choke shaft lever.

Insert specified drill between choke valve and wall of air horn. Adjust by bending fast idle connector rod.

Vacuum Kick

Fig. 7A—Depress diaphragm with a small drift. Insert specified drill between choke valve and wall of air horn while holding pressure on choke lever. Note that the diaphragm extends as spring is compressed. Spring must be fully compressed for proper measurement.

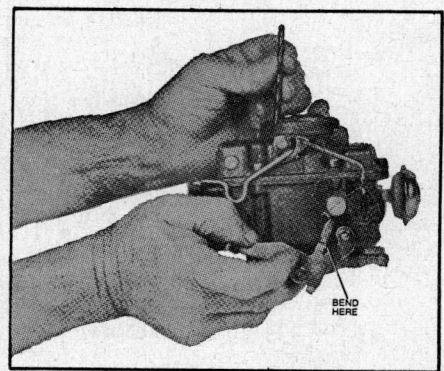

BEND HERE

Fig. 8A   Unloader adjustment. Type A tang

Choke Unloader

Figs. 8A, 9A—With throttle valve in wide open throttle position, insert specified drill between upper edge of choke valve and inner wall of air horn. With finger lightly pressing against shaft lever, a slight drag should be felt as drill is withdrawn. Bend unloader tang on throttle if necessary.

Dashpot

Fig. 10A—With curb idle speed properly adjusted and the engine at idle, depress the dashpot. Insert specified drill between end of stem and tang.

MODEL 2100, 6200-2V CARB. ADJUSTMENT SPECIFICATIONS

See Tune Up Chart in car chapters for hot idle speeds.

Year	Carb. Model (Code 9510) ①	Idle Mixture Turns Open	Float Level (Dry)	Fuel Level (Wet)	Pump Setting Hole No. ④	Choke Plate Clearance (Pull down)	Fast Idle Cam Linkage Clearance	Fast Idle Speed (Hot Engine)	Dechoke Clearance ②	Dashpot Setting	Choke Setting
AMERICAN MOTORS											
1969	9HM2	2	½	13/16	No. 3	.125	.120	1600	.080	.140	Index
	9HA2	2	½	13/16	No. 3	.140	.120	1600	.080	.140	Index
	9ZA2	2	½	13/16	No. 3	.140	.120	1600	.080	.140	Index
1970	0DA2	③	3/8	13/16	No. 3	.300	.170	1600	.200	⅛	2 Rich
	0DM2	③	3/8	13/16	No. 3	.260	.170	1600	.200	⅛	Index
	0RA2	③	3/8	13/16	No. 3	.350	.170	1600	.200	⅛	1 Rich
1971	1DA2	③	3/8	13/16	No. 3	.190	.170	1600	.200	⅛	2 Rich
	1DM2	③	3/8	13/16	No. 3	.190	.170	1600	.200	⅛	1 Rich
	1RA2	③	3/8	13/16	No. 3	.190	.170	1600	.200	⅛	2 Rich
1972	2DA2	③	3/8	3/4	No. 3A	.130	.120	1600	.200	9/64	2 Rich
	2DM2	③	3/8	3/4	No. 3A	.140	.130	1600	.200	7/64	1 Rich
	2RA2	③	3/8	3/4	No. 3A	.130	.120	1600	.200	—	2 Rich
1973	3DA2	③	3/8	3/4	No. 3A	.120	.110	1600	.250	—	2 Rich
	3DM2	③	3/8	3/4	No. 3A	.130	.130	1600	.250	9/64	1 Rich
	3RA2	③	3/8	3/4	No. 3A	.120	.110	1600	.250	—	2 Rich
1974	4DA2	③	13/32	25/32	Inboard	.140	.130	1600	.250	.140	1 Rich
	4DA2-E	③	13/32	25/32	Inboard	.140	.130	1600	.250	.140	1 Rich
	4DM2	③	13/32	25/32	Inboard	.130	.130	1600	.250	.140	2 Rich
	4RA2	⑤	13/32	25/32	Inboard	.140	.130	1600	.250	.140	1 Rich
	4RAC2	⑥	13/32	25/32	Inboard	.140	.130	1600	.250	.140	1 Rich
1975	5DAZ	③	13/32	3/4	—	.140	.130	1600⑦	.250	—	1 Rich
	5DMS	③	13/32	3/4	—	.130	.130	1600⑦	.250	.093	2 Rich
	5RAS	③	13/32	3/4	—	.140	.130	1600⑦	.250	—	1 Rich
FORD AND MERCURY											
1969	C8AF-BD	③	3/8	3/4	No. 3	.130	.110	1400	.060	⅛	2 Rich
	C9AF-A	③	3/8	3/4	No. 2	.120	.110	1600	.060	⅛	Index
	C9AF-B	③	31/64	7/8	No. 3	.210	.170	1300	.060	⅛	1 Rich
	C9AF-C	③	31/64	7/8	No. 3	.130	.100	1500	.060	⅛	2 Rich
	C9AF-J	③	31/64	7/8	No. 3	.130	.100	1500	.060	⅛	2 Rich
	C9OF-C	③	31/64	7/8	No. 3	.120	.100	1600	.060	—	2 Rich
	C9ZF-A	③	9/16	15/16	No. 3	.150	.130	1300	.060	7/64	1 Rich
	C9ZF-B	③	31/64	7/8	No. 3	.120	.100	1600	.060	—	2 Rich
	C9ZF-G	③	3/8	3/4	No. 3	.120	.110	1600	.060	⅛	Index
	C9MF-A	③	31/64	7/8	No. 2	.150	.120	1500	.060	⅛	2 Rich
1970	D0AF-C	③	7/16	13/16	No. 3	.150	.130	1400	.060	—	1 Rich
	D0AF-D	③	7/16	13/16	No. 3	.150	.130	1500	.060	⅛	1 Rich
	D0AF-E	③	7/16	13/16	No. 3	.230	.190	1300	.060	—	2 Lean
	D0AF-F	③	7/16	13/16	No. 3	.200	.170	1600	.060	⅛	2 Lean
	D0AF-G	—	7/16	13/16	No. 3	.210	.170	1400	.060	⅛	1 Rich
	D0AF-J	③	7/16	13/16	No. 3	.200	.160	1400	.060	⅛	—
	D0AF-T	③	7/16	13/16	No. 3	.200	.160	1400	.060	—	—
	D0AF-U	③	7/16	13/16	No. 3	.150	.130	1500	.060	—	1 Rich
	D0AF-V	③	7/16	13/16	No. 3	.200	.170	1600	—	—	2 Lean
	D0AF-Y	③	7/16	13/16	No. 3	.210	.170	1400	.060	—	1 Rich
	D0AF-Z	③	7/16	13/16	No. 3	.200	.160	1500	.060	⅛	—
	D0AF-AA	③	7/16	13/16	No. 3	.200	.160	1500	.060	—	—
	D0AF-AU	—	7/16	13/16	No. 3	.200	.170	1600	.060	—	2 Lean
	D0AF-AV	—	7/16	13/16	No. 3	.200	.170	1600	.060	⅛	2 Lean
	D0OF-K	③	7/16	13/16	No. 3	.220	.190	1500	—	—	Index

Continued

MODEL 2100, 6200-2V CARB. ADJUSTMENT SPECIFICATIONS—Continued

See Tune Up Chart in car chapters for hot idle speeds.

Year	Carb. Model (Code 9510) ①	Idle Mixture Turns Open ③	Float Level (Dry)	Fuel Level (Wet)	Pump Setting Hole No. ④	Choke Plate Clearance (Pull down)	Fast Idle Cam Linkage Clearance	Fast Idle Speed (Hot Engine)	Dechoke Clearance ②	Dashpot Setting	Choke Setting
FORD AND MERCURY—Continued											
1970	D0OF-L	③	7/16	13/16	No. 3	.190	.130	1500	—	1/8	1 Rich
	D0OF-M	③	7/16	13/16	No. 3	.190	.130	1500	—	—	1 Rich
	D0OF-T	—	7/16	13/16	No. 3	.190	.160	1500	.060	1/8	1 Rich
	D0OF-U	—	7/16	13/16	No. 3	.220	.190	1500	.060	—	Index
	D0OF-V	—	7/16	13/16	No. 3	.190	.160	1500	.060	—	1 Rich
1971	D1AF-BA	③	7/16	13/16	No. 2	.150	.130	1500	.060	—	Index
	D1AF-DA	③	7/16	13/16	No. 3	.170	.150	1400	.060	—	1 Rich
	D1AF-FA	③	7/16	13/16	No. 3	.220	.190	1300	.060	—	1 Rich
	D1AF-JA	③	7/16	13/16	No. 3	.190	.130	1600	.060	1/8	Index
	D1AF-KA	③	7/16	13/16	No. 3	.190	.130	1600	.060	—	Index
	D1MF-FA	③	7/16	13/16	No. 3	.200	.160	1400	.060	1/8	1 Rich
	D1MF-JA	③	7/16	13/16	No. 3	.190	.160	1500	.060	1/8	1 Rich
	D1MF-KA	③	7/16	13/16	No. 3	.190	.160	1500	.060	1/8	1 Rich
	D1OF-ABA	③	7/16	13/16	No. 3	.170	.150	1400	.060	—	1 Rich
	D1OF-PA	③	7/16	13/16	No. 3	.230	.190	1500	.060	—	Index
	D1OF-RA	③	7/16	13/16	No. 3	.200	.170	1500	.060	—	1 Rich
	D1OF-YA	③	7/16	13/16	No. 3	.200	.170	1500	.060	—	1 Rich
	D1OF-ZA	③	7/16	13/16	No. 3	.230	.190	1500	.060	—	Index
	D1YF-DA	③	7/16	13/16	No. 3	.200	.160	1500	.060	—	Index
	D1ZF-AA	③	7/16	13/16	No. 2	.150	.130	1500	.060	—	Index
	D1ZF-SA	③	7/16	13/16	No. 3	.200	.170	1500	.060	—	1 Rich
	D1ZF-UA	③	7/16	13/16	No. 3	.200	.170	1500	.060	—	1 Rich
1972	D2AF-FB	③	7/16	13/16	No. 3	.140	.130	1500	.030	1/8	Index
	D2AF-GB	③	7/16	13/16	No. 3	.140	.130	1500	.030	1/8	Index
	D2AF-HA	③	7/16	13/16	No. 2	.150	.130	1400	.060	1/8	1 Rich
	D2AF-UC	③	7/16	13/16	No. 3	.170	.150	1500	.060	—	Index
	D2GF-AA	③	7/16	13/16	No. 2	.150	.130	1400	.060	1/8	1 Rich
	D2GF-BA	③	7/16	13/16	No. 2	.150	.130	1400	.060	—	1 Rich
	D2MF-FB	③	7/16	13/16	No. 4	.180	.150	1500	.060	—	1 Rich
	D2MF-FE	③	7/16	13/16	No. 4	.170	.150	1500	.060	—	Index
	D2OF-KA	③	7/16	13/16	No. 2	.140	.130	1400	.060	—	1 Rich
	D2OF-UB	③	7/16	13/16	No. 3	.190	.160	⑤	.030	—	⑥
	D2WF-CA	③	7/16	13/16	No. 3	.190	.160	⑤	.030	—	⑥
	D2ZF-FA	③	7/16	13/16	No. 2	.150	.130	1400	.060	—	1 Rich
	D2ZF-LA	③	7/16	13/16	No. 3	.240	.210	1500	.030	—	1 Rich
1973	D3AF-CE	③	7/16	13/16	No. 2	—	—	1500	—	—	2 Rich
	D3AF-DC	③	7/16	13/16	No. 3	—	—	1500	—	—	3 Rich
	D3GF-AF	③	7/16	13/16	No. 2A	—	—	1400	—	—	3 Rich
	D3GF-BA	③	7/16	13/16	No. 2A	—	—	—	—	—	3 Rich
	D3MF-AE	③	7/16	13/16	No. 3	—	—	1500	—	—	3 Rich
	D3ZF-EA	③	7/16	13/16	No. 2A	—	—	1400	—	—	1 Rich
	D3GF-BB	③	7/16	13/16	No. 2A	—	—	1250	—	—	1 Rich
	D3AF-KA	③	7/16	13/16	No. 3	—	—	1500	—	—	3 Rich
	D3MF-BA	③	7/16	13/16	No. 3	—	—	1500	—	—	3 Rich
1974	D4AE-DA	③	7/16	13/16	No. 2A	—	—	—	—	—	1 Rich
	D4AE-EA	③	7/16	13/16	No. 2A	—	—	—	—	—	3 Rich
	D4AE-FA	③	7/16	13/16	No. 3A	—	—	—	—	—	3 Rich
	D4AE-GA	③	7/16	13/16	No. 3A	—	—	—	—	—	3 Rich
	D4AE-HB	③	7/16	13/16	No. 3A	—	—	—	—	—	3 Rich
	D4AE-KA	③	7/16	13/16	No. 2A	—	—	—	—	—	3 Rich
	D4DE-RB	③	7/16	13/16	No. 2	—	—	—	—	—	3 Rich
	D4DE-LA	③	7/16	13/16	No. 2	—	—	—	—	—	3 Rich
	D4DE-NB	③	7/16	13/16	No. 2	—	—	—	—	—	3 Rich

Continued

MODEL 2100, 6200-2V CARB. ADJUSTMENT SPECIFICATIONS—Continued

See Tune Up Chart in car chapters for hot idle speeds.

Year	Carb. Model (Code 9510) ①	Idle Mixture Turns Open	Float Level (Dry)	Fuel Level (Wet)	Pump Setting Hole No. ④	Choke Plate Clearance (Pull down)	Fast Idle Cam Linkage Clearance	Fast Idle Speed (Hot Engine)	Dechoke Clearance ②	Dashpot Setting	Choke Setting
FORD AND MERCURY—Continued											
1974	D4DE-PA	③	7/16	13/16	No. 2	—	—	—	—	—	3 Rich
	D4DE-VA	③	7/16	13/16	No. 2A	—	—	—	—	—	3 Rich
	D4OE-CA	③	7/16	13/16	No. 2	—	—	—	—	—	3 Rich
	D4OE-EA	③	7/16	13/16	No. 2	—	—	—	—	—	3 Rich
	D4OE-FA	③	7/16	13/16	No. 2A	—	—	—	—	—	3 Rich
	D4OE-PA	③	7/16	13/16	No. 2A	—	—	—	—	—	3 Rich
	D4ME-BA	③	7/16	13/16	No. 3A	—	—	—	—	—	3 Rich
	D4ME-CA	③	7/16	13/16	No. 3A	—	—	—	—	—	3 Rich

①—Stamped on left side of fuel bowl or on tag attached to bowl cover.
②—Minimum clearance between choke plate and air horn wall with throttle plates wide open.
③—Air/fuel ratio or idle CO% rating is found in Tune Up Specification tables in car chapters.
④—With link in inboard hole in pump lever.
⑤—Auto Trans. 1500; Manual Trans. 1400.
⑥—California 1 Rich; all others 2 Rich.
⑦—Hot on 2nd step of cam with TCS solenoid & EGR disconnected.

MODEL 4100-4V ADJUSTMENT SPECIFICATIONS

See Tune Up Chart in car chapters for hot idle speeds.

Year	Carb. Model (Code 9510) ①	Idle Screws (Mixture) Turns Open	Float Level (Dry)	Fuel Level (Wet)	Pump Setting (Hole No.) ④	Choke Plate Clearance (Pull down)	Fast Idle Cam Linkage Clearance	Fast Idle Speed (Hot Engine)	Secondary Throttle Plate Clearance ②	Dechoke Clearance ③	Dashpot Setting	Choke Setting
1969	C8AF-AE	⑤	⑥	⑦	No. 3	.140	.120	1350	—	.060	7/64	2 Rich

①—Stamped on left side of primary bowl cover or tag attached to blow cover.
②—Additional turns in after screw contacts lever.
③—Minimum clearance between choke plate and air horn with primary throttle plates wide open.
④—With link in inboard hole in pump lever.
⑤—Air/fuel ratio or idle CO% rating is found in Tune Up Specification tables in car chapters.
⑥—Primary floats 17/32″, secondary 11/16″.
⑦—Primary floats 29/32″, secondary 11/16″.

2100, 6200-2V & 4100-4V ADJUSTMENTS

Models 2100, 6200-2V, Figs. 1 thru 4

These carburetors have two main bodies—the air horn and throttle body. The air horn assembly, which serves as a cover for the throttle body, contains the choke plate and vents for the fuel bowl. On all 1969 units and 1972 Ford units, an external bowl vent valve is used.

A choke modulator assembly is incorporated in the 1970-74 units, Fig. 5. While a staged choke system is an added feature used on 1972 Ford installations, Fig. 2. This system, through the use of a bimetal sensor and a series of diaphragms, pulls open the choke plate within 15-60 seconds. The system operates only during times when underhood temperatures are above approximately 60 degrees F. The 1973 units have an additional port for the Exhaust Gas Recirculation (EGR) system, Fig. 3. On 1973-74 Ford units an electric choke system is incorporated which opens choke plate within 1-1½ minutes when underhood temperatures are above approximately 55° to 60°. For service information refer to the "Emission Control System" chapter.

The throttle plate, accelerating pump, power valve and fuel bowl are in the throttle body. The choke housing is attached to the throttle body.

The two bodies each contain a main and booster venturi, main fuel discharge, accelerating pump discharge, idle fuel discharge, and a throttle plate. An antistall dashpot is attached to the carburetor when

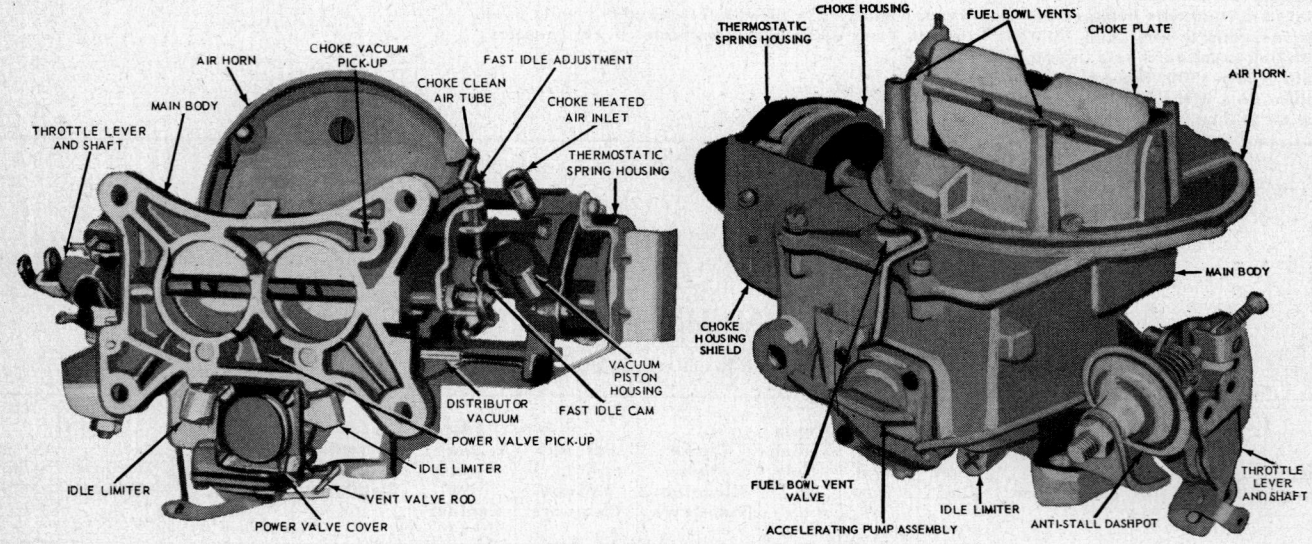

Fig. 1   Typical Autolite/Motorcraft 2100, 6200 carburetor. 1969

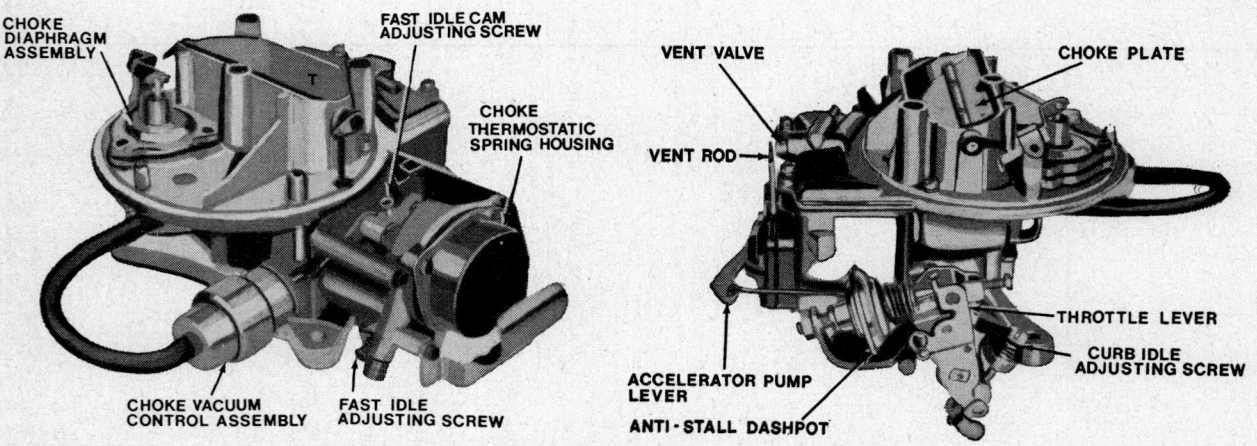

Fig. 2   Typical Autolite/Motorcraft 2100 carburetor. 1970-72

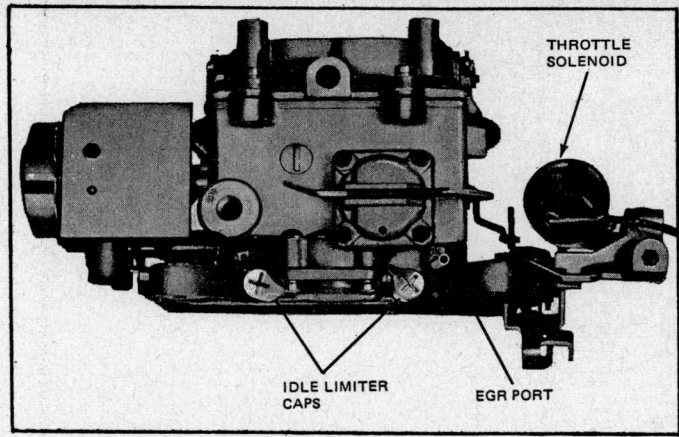

Fig. 3   Autolite/Motorcraft 2100 carburetor. 1973-74

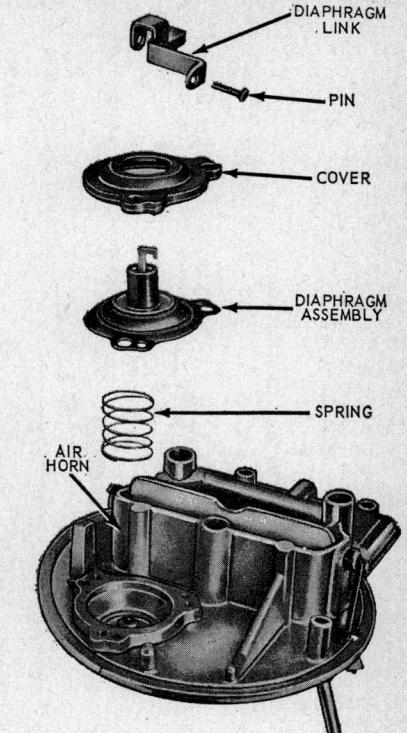

Fig. 5   Autolite/Motorcraft 2100 choke diaphragm assembly

the vehicle is equipped with an automatic transmission.

Autolite 4100-4V

In these carburetors, Figs. 6 and 7, the choke plate magnet has been eliminated but an automatic choke clean air pick-up tube has been added. A rubber hose and steel tube connects the clean air pick-up tube to the automatic choke heat chamber in the right-hand exhaust manifold.

Float Level Adjustment

2100, 6200, 4100, Fig. 8—This is a preliminary adjustment; the final adjustment must be made after the carburetor is mounted on the engine.

With air horn removed, float raised and fuel inlet needle seated, measure distance between top surface of throttle body and top surface of float. Take measurement near center of float at a point $\frac{1}{8}$" from free end of float.

If a cardboard float gauge is used, place the gauge in the corner of the enlarged end section of the fuel bowl as shown. The gauge should touch the float near the end but not on the end radius.

Depress the float tab to seat the fuel inlet needle. The float height is measured from the gasket surface of the throttle body with gasket removed. If the float height is not as listed in the *Ford Specifications Chart*, bend tab on float as required to achieve the desired setting.

Fuel Level Adjustment

Fig. 9—With vehicle on a level surface, operate engine until normal temperature is reached, then stop engine and check fuel level as follows:
1. Remove carburetor air cleaner.
2. Remove air horn retaining screws and carburetor identification tag.
3. Temporarily leave air horn and gasket in position on throttle body and start engine.

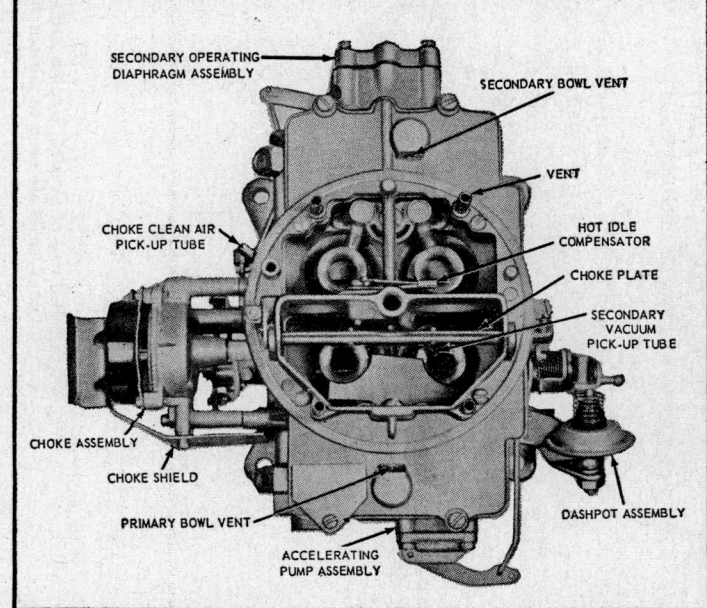

Fig. 6   Autolite 4100 carburetor showing hot idle compensator and choke clean air pick-up tube

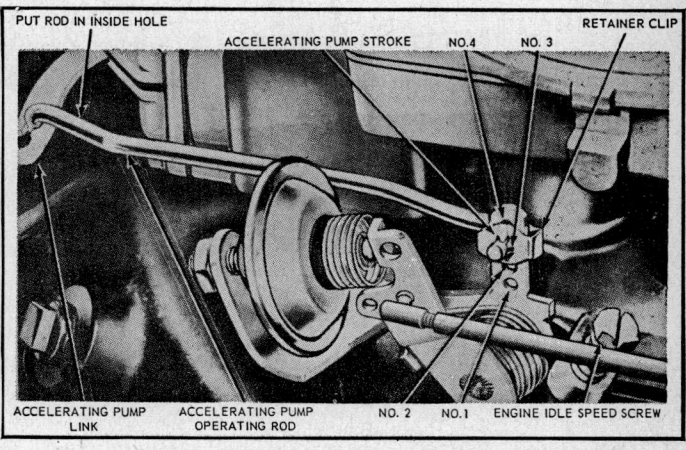

Fig. 10   Pump stroke and idle speed adjusting points. 2100, 6200, 4100

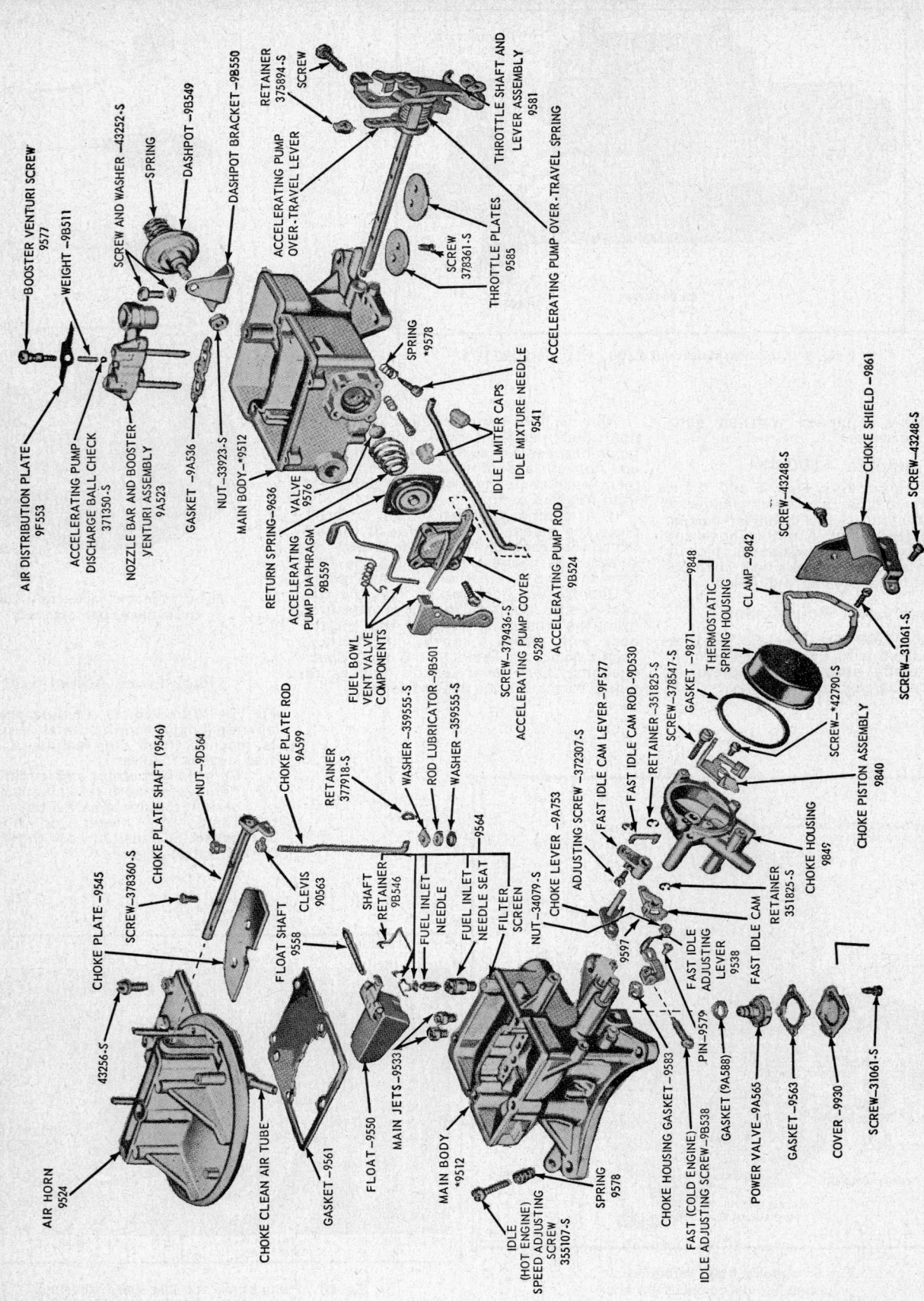

Fig. 4 Exploded view of a typical Autolite 2100, 6200 two-barrel carburetor. Note that this unit is provided with the idle limiter caps which are used to prevent an overly rich mixture adjustment on cars with exhaust emission control

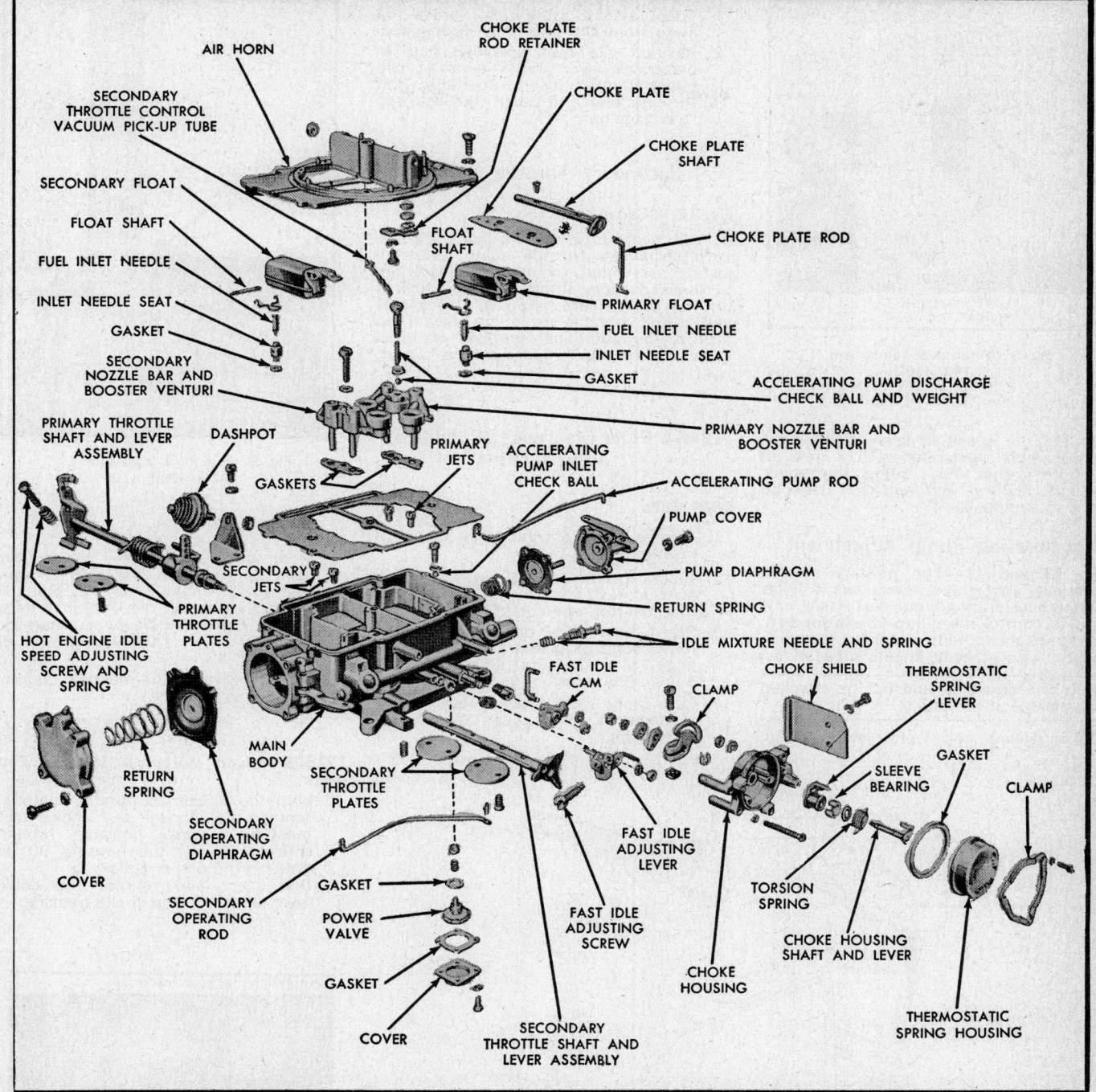

Fig. 7   Exploded view of a typical Autolite 4100 four-barrel carburetor

4. Allow engine to idle for several minutes, then rotate air horn and remove air horn gasket to gain access to float or floats.

5. While engine is idling, use a standard depth gauge to measure vertical distance from top machined surface of throttle body to level of fuel in bowl. The measurement must be made at least ¼" away from any vertical surface to assure an accurate reading.

6. If the fuel level is not as listed in the *Ford Specifications Chart*, stop the engine to avoid any fire hazard due to fuel spray when float setting is disturbed.

7. To adjust fuel level, bend float tab (contacting fuel inlet needle) up-ward in relation to original position to raise the fuel level, and downward to lower it.

8. Each time an adjustment is made to the float tab to alter the fuel level, the engine must be started and permitted to idle for at least three minutes to stabilize the fuel level. Check fuel level after each adjustment

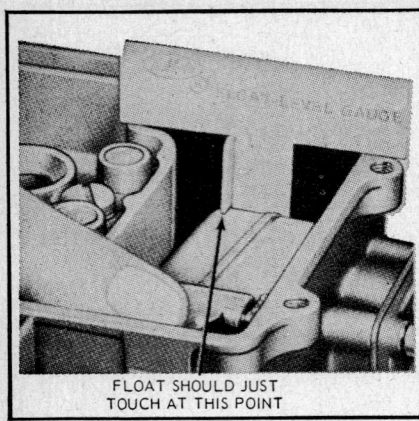

Fig. 8 Float level adjustment. 2100, 4100

press tab end of clip toward rod. Then, at the same time, press rod away from clip until it is disengaged.

2. Position clip over specified hole in overtravel lever. Press ends of clip together and insert operating rod through clip and lever. Release clip to engage rod.

Secondary Throttle Plate

Fig. 12, 4-Barrel Units

Hold secondary throttle plate closed. Turn secondary throttle shaft lever adjusting screw out (counterclockwise) until the secondary throttle plates stick in throttle bores. Turn screw in (clockwise) until it just contacts secondary lever. Then turn it the additional number of turns listed in the *Ford Specifications Chart*.

Choke Plate Clearance (Pulldown) Adjustment

1969 Units

1. Bend a .036" pin gauge as shown in inset of Fig. 13.
2. Block throttle about half-way open so that fast idle cam does not contact fast idle adjustment screw.
3. Insert bent edge of gauge between lower edge of piston slot and upper edge of right-hand slot in choke housing as shown.
4. Pull choke countershaft lever counterclockwise until gauge is snug in piston slot.

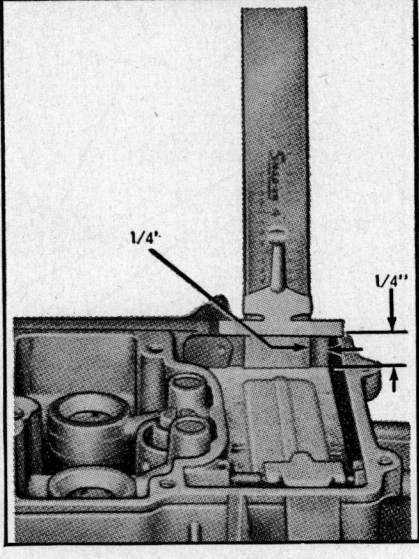

Fig. 9 Fuel level adjustment. 2100, 6200, 4100

until the specified level is achieved.

9. Assemble carburetor with a new air horn gasket. Then adjust idle speed and mixture, and anti-stall dashpot, if so equipped.

Accelerating Pump Adjustment

Figs. 10 and 11—The primary throttle shaft lever (overtravel lever) has 4 holes and the accelerating pump link has 2 or 4 holes to control the pump stroke for various atmospheric temperatures, operating conditions and specific engine applications.

NOTE: The stroke should not be changed from the specified setting.

1. To release rod from retainer clip,

5. Hold gauge in place by exerting light pressure on countershaft lever, and adjust choke plate clevis adjusting nut to obtain the clearance listed in the *Ford Specifications Chart* between front of choke plate and air horn, Fig. 13.
6. Install choke thermostatic spring housing.

1970 American Motors & 1970-72 Ford Units

1. With the engine at normal operating temperature, loosen the choke thermostatic spring housing retainer screws and set the housing 90 degrees in the rich direction.
2. Disconnect and remove the choke heat tube from the choke housing.

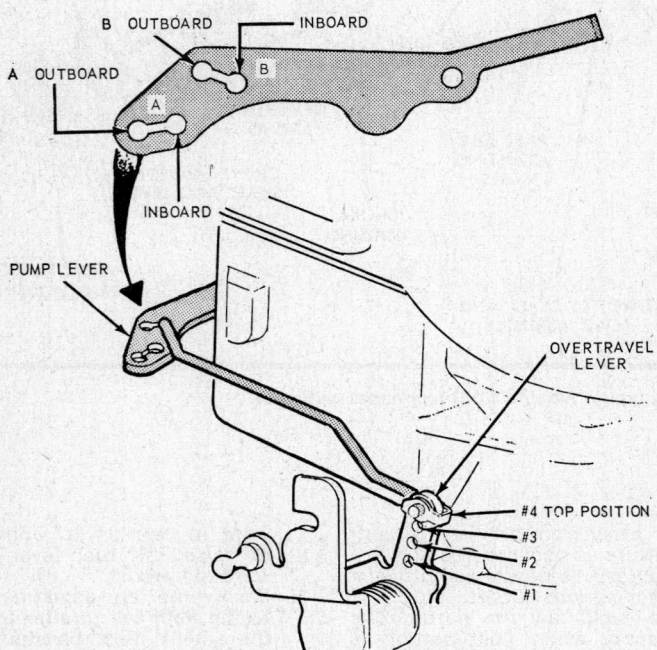

Fig. 11 Pump stroke adjusting points, 2100 with 4 holes in accelerating pump linkage

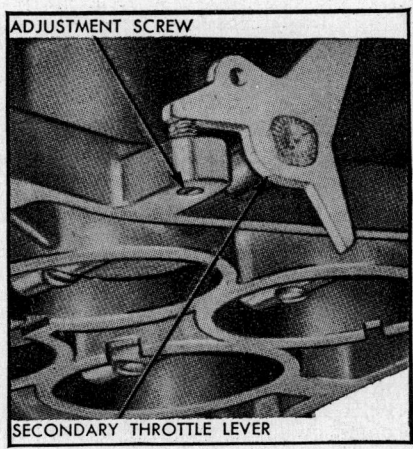

Fig. 12 Secondary throttle plate adjustment. 4100

3. Turn the fast idle adjusting screw outward one full turn.
4. Start the engine, then check clearance between the lower edge of the choke plate and the air horn wall, Fig. 14. Refer to Specifications Chart.
5. Adjust by turning the diaphragm stop screw located on the underside of the choke diaphragm housing, clockwise to decrease or counter-clockwise to increase the clearance, Fig. 14.
6. Connect the choke heat tube and set the choke thermostatic spring housing to specifications. Adjust the fast idle speed.

1971-74 American Motors Units

1. Loosen the choke cover retaining screws. Rotate the choke cover 1/4 turn counterclockwise (rich) from index and tighten the retaining screws. Disconnect the choke heat inlet tube.
2. Align the fast idle speed adjusting screw with the second step of the fast idle cam, Fig. 15.
3. Start the engine without moving the accelerator linkage. Turn the fast idle cam lever adjusting screw out counterclockwise 3 full turns.
4. Measure the clearance between the lower edge of the choke valve and the air horn wall. Refer to *2100 Specifications Chart* for the correct setting. Adjust by grasping the modulator arm securely with a pair of pliers at point "A" and twisting the arm at point "B" with a second pair of pliers. Twist toward the front of the carburetor to increase clearance and toward the rear to decrease clearance, Fig. 16.

CAUTION: Use extreme care while twisting the modulator arm to avoid damaging the nylon piston rod of the modulator assembly.

NOTE: Connect the choke heat tube. Turn

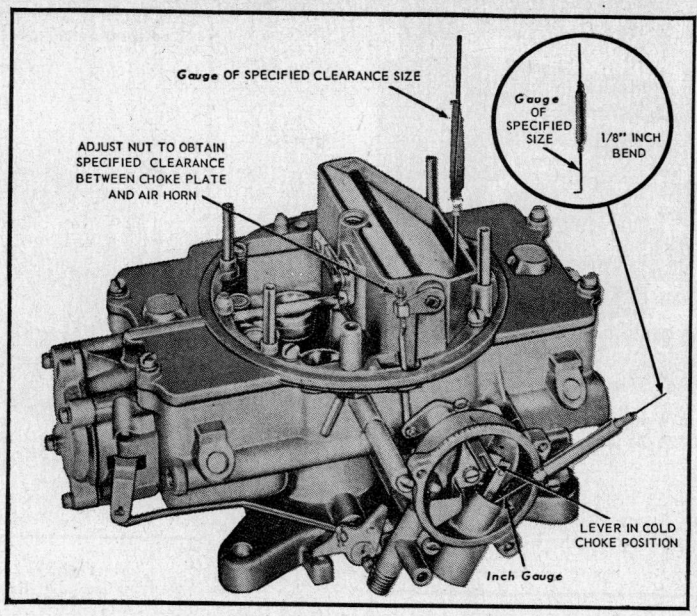

Fig. 13   Vacuum piston type choke plate clearance adjustment, 2100, 6200, 4100; 1969

the fast idle cam lever adjusting screw in (clockwise) 3 full turns. Do not reset the choke cover until the fast idle cam linkage adjustment has been performed.

1973-74 Ford Units

Since the choke plate pulldown is set in production by means of an air-fuel meter, no specific clearance is indicated for pulldown adjustment. If the vehicle shows indication of leanness during cold starting, decrease the clearance between the choke plate and the air horn wall by 0.020 inch. If the engine shows signs of an overrich

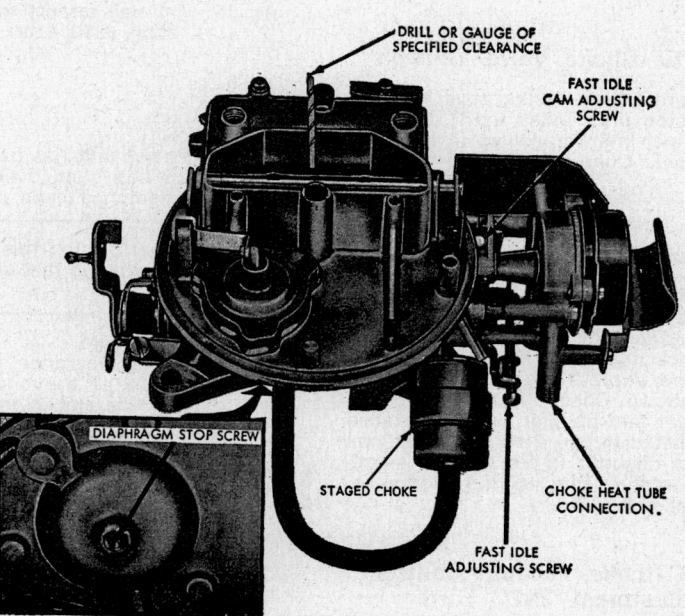

Fig. 14   Choke plate pulldown clearance 2100. 1970 American Motors and 1970-74 Ford

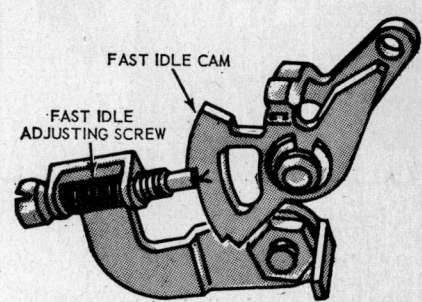

CONVENTIONAL ONE - PIECE FAST IDLE LEVER

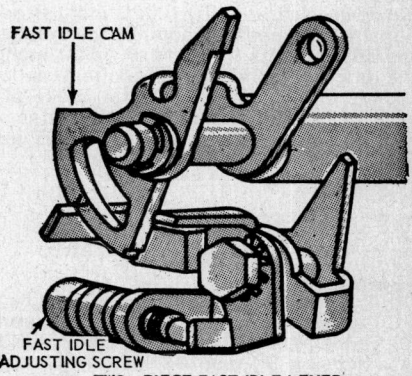

TWO - PIECE FAST IDLE LEVER

Fig. 15   Autolite/Motorcraft fast idle adjustment 2100

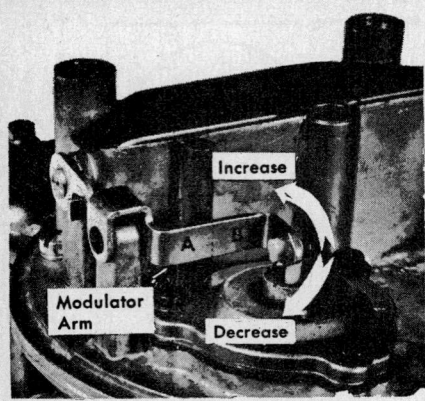

Fig. 16 Choke plate pulldown clearance 2100. 1971-74 American Motors

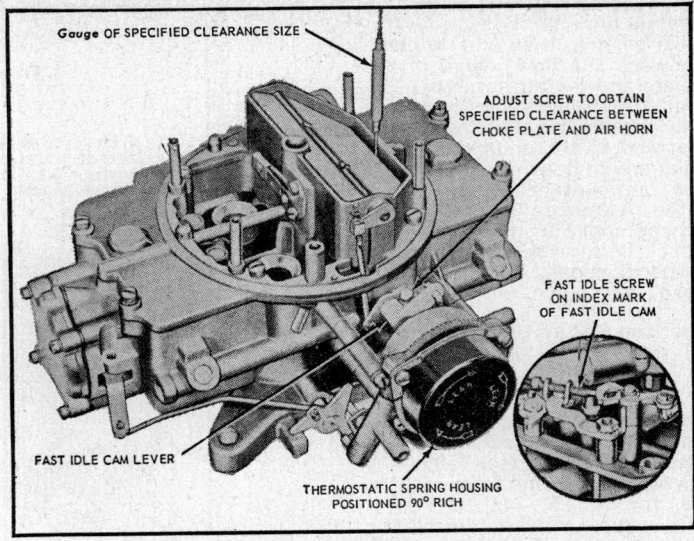

Fig. 17 Vacuum piston type choke fast idle cam linkage adjustment. 2100, 6200, 4100

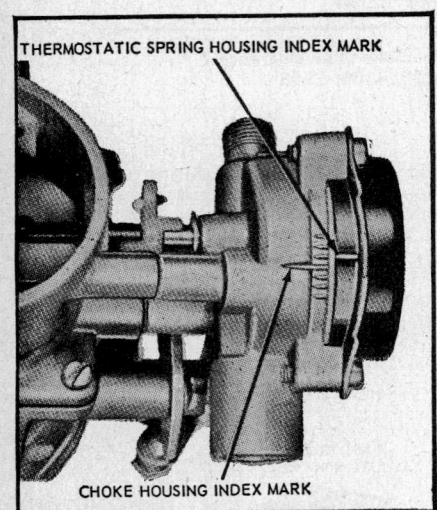

Fig. 18 Automatic choke adjustment. 2100, 6200, 4100

on most units by a V stamped on the cam, Fig. 15. When a two-piece fast idle lever is used, a tang on the top lever will align with the V mark on the cam, Fig. 15.

3. Be sure the cam is at the kickdown position while checking or adjusting the fast idle cam clearance. Check clearance between the lower edge of the choke plate and the air horn wall, Fig. 17. Refer to *2100 Specifications Chart*. Adjust clearance by turning the fast idle cam clearance adjusting screw clockwise to increase and counterclockwise to decrease the clearance.

4. Set the choke thermostatic spring housing to specifications, Fig. 18. Adjust the anti-stall dashpot, idle speed and fuel mixture.

Automatic Choke Valve Tension

Turn thermostatic spring cover against spring tension until index mark on cover is aligned with mark specified in the *Ford Specifications Chart* on choke housing, Fig. 18.

Anti-Stall Dashpot Adjustment

Fig. 19—With engine idle speed and mixture properly adjusted and with engine at normal operating temperature, loosen dashpot lock nut. Hold throttle in closed position and depress plunger with screwdriver as shown. Check clearance between throttle lever and plunger tip. If clearance is not as listed in the *Ford Specifications Chart*, turn dashpot in its bracket as required to obtain the desired clearance. Tighten lock nut.

Staged Choke Vacuum Control Adjustment 1972 Ford

NOTE: This adjustment should be made

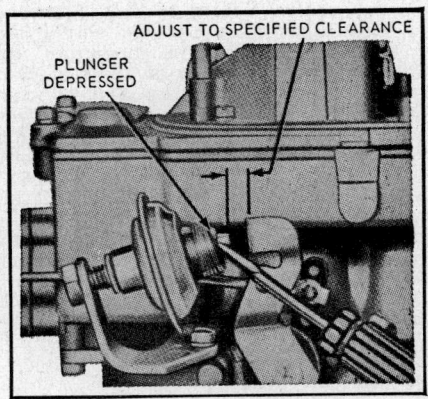

Fig. 19 Anti-stall dashpot adjustment. 2100, 6200, 4100

only if the control unit has been replaced, the carburetor has been overhauled or a choke adjustment has been made.

NOTE: Before performing this adjustment, the choke pulldown and fast idle cam must be adjusted.

1. Close choke plate.
2. Measure the clearance between the forward edge of the choke link and the edge of the slot in the choke vacuum lever, Fig. 20.

NOTE: Place C-clip in a position so that gap is visible.

3. Adjust by inserting a ¼ inch socket and drive on the nylon adjuster, Fig. 20. Hold the choke link with needlenose pliers to prevent flexing, then turn the adjuster until 1/32 inch clearance is obtained.

condition during cold starting, increase the pulldown clearance by 0.020 inch. If additional adjustment is required always make the adjustments in steps of 0.020 inch. If the original pulldown adjustment is lost, set the clearance between the choke plate and the air horn to 0.160 inch. Then adjust as required in steps of 0.020 inch, Fig. 14.

Fast Idle Cam Clearance

1969-74 Units

1. Loosen the choke thermostatic spring housing retainer screws and set the housing 90 degrees in the rich direction.
2. Position the fast idle speed screw at the kickdown step of the fast idle cam. The kickdown step is identified

Fig. 20 Autolite/Motorcraft staged choke vacuum control adjustment 2100D. 1972 Ford

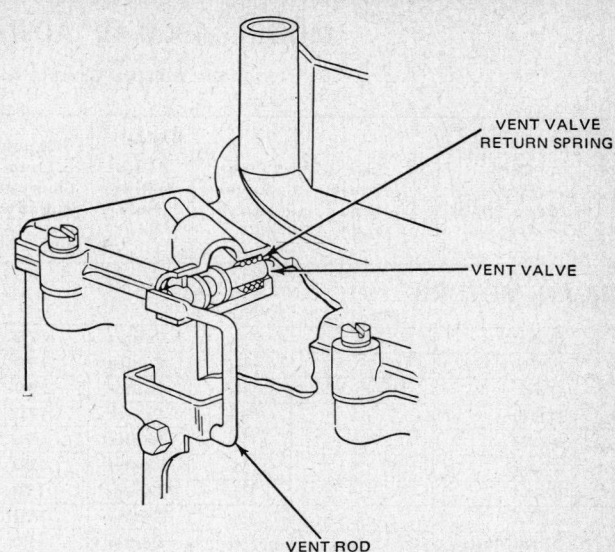

Fig. 22 Fuel bowl vent valve adjustment 2100. 1972 Ford

External Bowl Vent Valve Adjustment

NOTE: The vent valve adjustment should be performed after the accelerating pump adjustment.

The vent valve, must be closed during normal and wide-open throttle operation, and open to the specified clearance at closed throttle or idle operation.

1969 Units

1. Check clearance between bowl vent valve and air horn casting with throttle

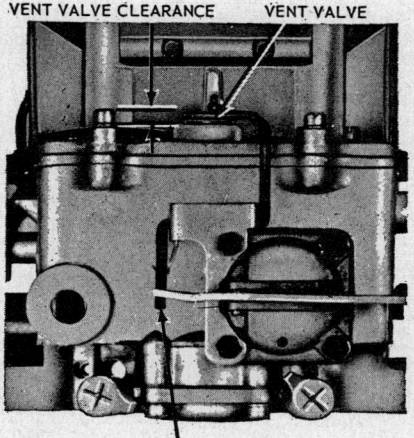

Fig. 21 Fuel bowl vent valve adjustment 2100, 6200. 1969

positioned at curb idle setting, Fig. 21.
2. Adjust by bending the vent rod at the rod attaching bracket to obtain .065 inch clearance for American Motors installation and .070 inch clearance for Ford installations.

1972 Units

1. Fully depress the vent valve into the valve bore.
2. Measure the clearance between the flat on the vent rod and the fully seated valve, Fig. 22.
3. Adjust by bending the vent rod at the point where it contacts the accelerator pump lever until 3/32 inch clearance is obtained.

FORD AUTOLITE/MOTORCRAFT CARBURETORS

MODEL 4300-4V ADJUSTMENT SPECIFICATIONS

See Tune Up Chart in car chapters for hot idle speeds.

Year	Carb. Model (Code 9510) ①	Idle Mixture Turns Open	Float Level (Dry)	Pump Setting (Hole No.)	Choke Plate Clearance (Pulldown)	Fast Idle Cam Linkage Setting	Fast Idle Speed (Hot Engine)	Auxiliary Inlet Valve Setting	Dechoke Clearance	Dashpot Setting	Choke Setting
AMERICAN MOTORS											
1970	OWA4	②	13/16	Center	.170	.190	1600	—	.300	1/8	2 Rich
	OWM4	②	13/16	Center	.190	.200	1600	—	.300	1/16	2 Rich
1971	ITA4	②	13/16	Center	.190	.200	1600	—	.300	1/8	Index
	ITM4	②	13/16	Center	.170	.190	1600	—	.300	1/16	Index
1972	2RA4	②	13/16	Center	.190	.190	1600	—	.300	9/64	1 Rich
	2TA4	②	13/16	Center	.190	.190	1600	—	.300	9/64	1 Rich
	2TM4	②	13/16	Center	.190	.190	1600	—	.300	9/64	1 Rich
1973	3TA4	②	13/16	Center	.190	.160	1600	.060	.275	9/64	2 Rich
	3TA4 Police	②	15/16	Center	.190	.160	1600	.030	.275	9/64	2 Rich
	3TM4	②	13/16	Center	.190	.160	1600	.060	.275	9/64	2 Rich
1974	4TA4	②	13/16	Center	.170	.160	1600	.050	.325	9/64	2 Rich
	4TA4 Police	②	25/32	Center	.170	.160	1600	.030	Preset	9/64	2 Rich
	4TM4	②	13/16	Center	.170	.160	1600	.050	.325	9/64	2 Rich
1975	5TA4-P③	②	25/32	—	.140	.160	1600④	—	.325	—	2 Rich

①—Tag attached to bowl cover.
②—Air/fuel ratio or idle CO% rating is found in Tune Up Specification tables in car chapters.
③—Model 4350.
④—Hot on 2nd step of cam with TCS solenoid & EGR disconnected.

FORD AND MERCURY ENGINES

Year	Carb. Model (Code 9510) ①	Idle Mixture Turns Open	Float Level (Dry)	Pump Setting (Hole No.)	Choke Plate Clearance (Pulldown)	Fast Idle Cam Linkage Setting	Fast Idle Speed (Hot Engine)	Auxiliary Inlet Valve Setting	Dechoke Clearance	Dashpot Setting	Choke Setting
1969	C8SF-H	⑤	25/32	#2	.230	.160	1300	1/16	.300	3/32	1 Rich
	C8VF-J	⑤	25/32	#2	.230	.160	1300	1/16	.300	3/32	1 Rich
	C9AF-G	⑤	25/32	#2	.270	.220	1200	1/16	.300	3/32	Index
	C9AF-R	⑤	25/32	#2	.230	.160	1300	1/16	.300	—	1 Rich
	C9OF-D	⑤	13/16	#2	.160	.100	1400	1/16	.300	—	1 Lean
	C9OF-E	⑤	13/16	#3	.250	.230	1400	1/16	.300	—	1 Lean
	C9ZF-C	⑤	13/16	#2	.170	.130	1250	1/16	.300	3/32	2 Lean
	C9ZF-D	⑤	13/16	#2	.160	.100	1400	1/16	.300	—	1 Lean
	C9ZF-E	⑤	13/16	#3	.230	.210	1300	1/16	.300	1/8	Index
	C9ZF-F	⑤	13/16	#3	.250	.230	1400	1/16	.300	—	1 Lean
1970	D0AF-K	⑤	49/64	#2	.220	.170	1300	1/16	.300	.070	Index
	D0AF-L	⑤	25/32	#2	.250	.220	1400	1/16	.300	.070	Index
	D0AF-M	⑤	1.00	#3	.160	.120	1600	1/16	.300	.080	2 Rich
	D0AF-R	⑤	1.00	#3	.160	.120	1600	1/32	.300	—	2 Rich
	D0AF-AD	⑤	1.00	#3	.160	.120	1600	1/16	.300	.080	2 Rich
	D0AF-AJ	⑤	1.00	#3	.160	.120	1600	1/16	.300	.080	2 Rich
	D0AF-AE	⑤	1.00	#3	.160	.120	1600	1/32	.300	—	2 Rich
	D0AF-AK	⑤	1.00	#3	.160	.120	1600	1/32	.300	—	2 Rich
	D0AF-AB	⑤	25/32	#2	.250	.220	1400	1/16	.300	.070	Index
	D0AF-AL	⑤	25/32	#2	.250	.220	1400	1/16	.300	.070	Index
	D0AF-AG	⑤	25/32	#2	.220	.170	1300	1/16	.300	.070	Index
	D0AF-AM	⑤	25/32	#2	.220	.170	1300	1/16	.300	.070	Index
	D0AF-AN	⑤	49/64	#2	.225	.170	1350	1/16	.300	.070	Index
	D0OF-B	⑤	13/16	#2	.180	.160	1250	1/16	.300	—	Index
	D0OF-C	⑤	13/16	#2	.200	.180	1400	1/16	.300	.080	Index
	D0OF-D	⑤	13/16	#2	.180	.160	1250	1/16	.300	—	Index
	D0OF-H	⑤	13/16	#2	.200	.180	1400	1/16	.300	—	Index

Continued

2–444

MODEL 4300-4V ADJUSTMENT SPECIFICATIONS—Continued

See Tune Up Chart in car chapters for hot idle speeds.

Year	Carb. Model (Code 9510) ①	Idle Mixture Turns Open	Float Level (Dry)	Pump Setting (Hole No.)	Choke Plate Clearance (Pulldown)	Fast Idle Cam Linkage Setting	Fast Idle Speed (Hot Engine)	Auxiliary Inlet Valve Setting	Dechoke Clearance	Dashpot Setting	Choke Setting
FORD AND MERCURY ENGINES—Continued											
1970	DOOF-Y	⑤	13/16	#2	.180	.160	1250	1/16	.300	—	Index
	DOOF-Z	⑤	13/16	#2	.180	.160	1250	1/16	.300	—	Index
	DOOF-AA	⑤	13/16	#2	.200	.180	1400	1/16	.300	—	Index
	DOOF-AB	⑤	13/16	#2	.180	.160	1250	1/16	.300	—	Index
	DOOF-AC	⑤	13/16	#2	.200	.180	1400	1/16	.300	.080	Index
	DOOF-AD	⑤	13/16	#2	.200	.180	1400	1/16	.300	—	Index
	DOOF-AE	⑤	13/16	#2	.180	.160	1250	1/16	.300	—	Index
	DOSF-A	⑤	25/32	#2	.220	.170	1300	1/16	.300	.070	Index
	DOSF-D	⑤	25/32	#2	.220	.170	1300	1/16	.300	.070	Index
	DOSF-E	⑤	25/32	#2	.220	.170	1300	1/16	.300	.070	Index
	DOVF-A, C	⑤	25/32	#2	.230	.170	1250	1/16	.300	.100	1 Rich
1971	D1AF-MA	⑤	49/64	#2	.220	—	1350	1/16	—	1/16	Index
	D1OF-AAA	⑤	13/16	#2	.200	.180	1400	1/16	—	—	Index
	D1OF-EA	⑤	13/16	#2	.180	.160	1250	1/16	—	—	Index
	D1SF-AA	⑤	49/64	#2	.220	—	1350	1/16	—	1/16	Index
	D1VF-AA	⑤	47/64	#2	.220	.170	1250	1/16	—	.100	1 Rich
	D1ZF-FA	⑤	13/16	#3	.220	.220	1200	1/16	—	—	1 Lean
	D1ZF-GA	⑤	13/16	#3	.200	.200	1200	1/16	—	—	Index
1972	D2AF-AA	⑤	49/64	#1	.220	.200	1350	—	—	—	2 Rich
	D2AF-LA	⑤	49/64	#1	.215	.190	1900	.030	—	—	Index
	D2SF-AA	⑤	49/64	#1	.220	.200	1350	—	—	—	2 Rich
	D2SF-BA	⑤	49/64	#1	.220	.200	1350	—	—	—	2 Rich
	D2VF-AA	⑤	49/64	#1	.230	.200	1250	—	—	—	Index
	D2VF-BA	⑤	49/64	#1	.230	.200	1250	—	—	—	Index
	D2ZF-AA	⑤	13/16	#1	.200	.180	1200	.030	—	—	Index
	D2ZF-BB	⑤	13/16	#1	.200	.200	1200	.030	—	—	Index
	D2ZF-DA	⑤	13/16	#1	.200	.200	1200	.030	—	—	Index
	D2ZF-GA	⑤	13/16	#1	.200	.180	1200	.030	—	—	Index
1973	D3AF-HA	⑤	3/4	#1	.210	.200	1350	1/16	—	—	Index
	D3VF-DA	⑤	3/4	#1	.210	.190	1350	1/16	—	—	Index
	D3ZF-AC	⑤	13/16	#1	.180	.180	1300	1/32	—	—	Index
	D3ZF-BC	⑤	13/16	#1	.170	.170	1300	1/32	—	—	1 Rich
	D3ZF-DC	⑤	13/16	#1	.180	.180	1300	1/32	—	—	Index
	D3AF-EB	⑤	7/8	#1	.200	.200	1900	1/32	—	—	Index
1974	D4AE-AA	⑤	3/4	#1	.230	.200	—	1/16	—	—	Index
	D4AE-NA	⑤	3/4	#1	.220	.200	—	1/16	—	—	Index
	D4OE-AA	⑤	13/16	#1	.180	.180	—	1/32	—	—	Index
	D4OE-BA	⑤	13/16	#1	.170	.170	—	1/32	—	—	Index
	D4TE-ATA	⑤	13/16	#1	.220	.180	—	1/16	—	—	Index
	D4VE-AB	⑤	3/4	#1	.220	.200	—	1/16	—	—	Index

①—Tag attached to bowl cover.

③—8-390 with Imco 2 Rich, with Thermactor 1 rich.

④—8-428 with Imco Index, with Thermactor 1 rich.

⑤—Air/fuel ratio or idle CO% rating is found in Tune Up Specification tables in car chapters.

MODEL 4300-4V ADJUSTMENTS

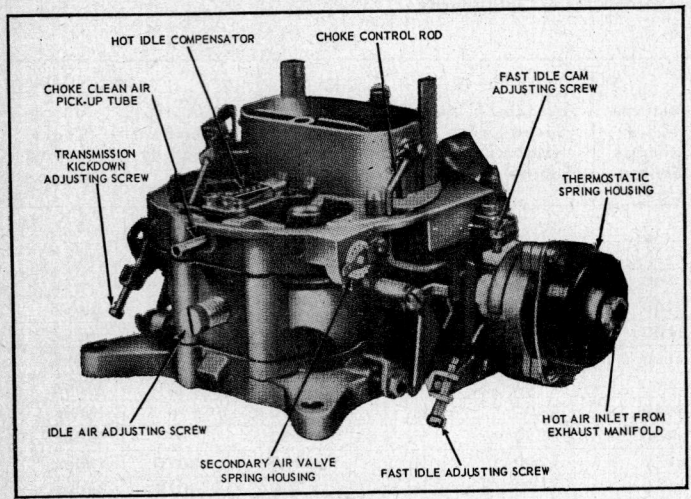

Fig. 1 Right rear view of 4300-4V carburetor

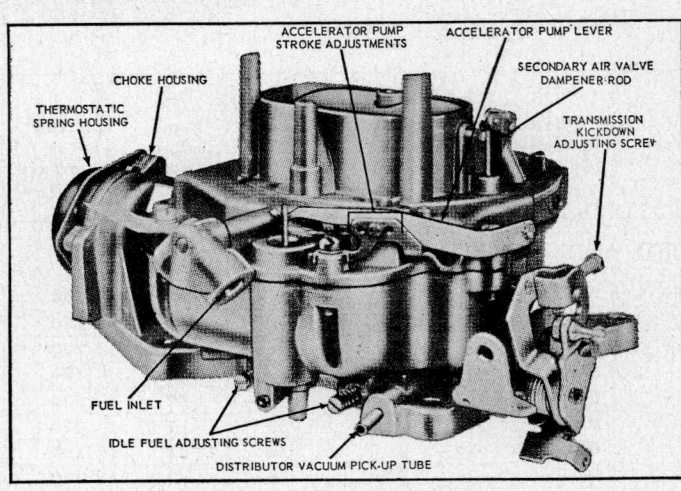

Fig. 2 Left front view of Model 4300-4V carburetor

The model 4300, Figs. 1 thru 6, is a four barrel, three piece, separately cast design consisting of air horn, main body and mounting flange. A cast-in center fuel inlet has provision for a supplementary fuel inlet system. The fuel bowl is vented by an internal balance vent and a mechanical atmospheric vent operates during idle. An idle air by-pass system is designed to provide a consistent idle and a hot idle compensator is used to help stability.

The main (primary) fuel system has booster-type venturii cast integral with the air horn, and the main venturii are cast integral with the main body. The secondary throttle plates are mechanically operated from the primary linkage. On models 4300 and 4300-A, the air valve plates are located above the main venturis, Figs. 1, 2 and 3, an integral hydraulic dashpot dampens sudden movement of the air valve plates to help prevent plate flutter and erratic engine operation. On model 4300-D the air valve plates are located above the secondary bore. Secondary fuel supply is controlled by metering rods which are attached to the air valve plates, Figs. 4 and 6.

The automatic choke system consists of a standard bimetal thermostat. On 1972 Ford units a staged choke release system is used which opens the choke plate within 15-60 seconds when underhood temperatures are above 60°, Figs. 3 and 4. On 1973-74 Ford units an electric choke system is incorporated which opens choke within 1-1½ minutes when underhood temperatures are above approximately 55° to 60°. On 1973-74 American Motors units, an electric choke system is also incorporated which opens choke when underhood temperatures are above approximately 95°. For service information refer to the "Emission Control System" chapter.

A single fuel bowl supplies both the primary and secondary fuel systems. Pontoon-type floats are used to help stabilize fuel level during cornering and hill-climbing. The accelerator pump is of the piston type. It is located in the fuel bowl for more positive displacement and a safeguard against external leaks.

Float Setting
Fig. 7
1. Adjust gauge to specified height.
2. Insert gauge into air horn outboard holes as shown.

3. Check clearance and alignment of float pontoons to gauge. Both pontoons should just touch gauge for proper setting. Align pontoons if necessary by slightly twisting pontoons.
4. If it is necessary to adjust float clearance, bend primary needle tab downward to raise float and upward to lower float.

NOTE: To raise float, insert open end of bending tool to *right* side of float lever tab and between needle and float hinge. Raise float lever off needle and bend tab downward.

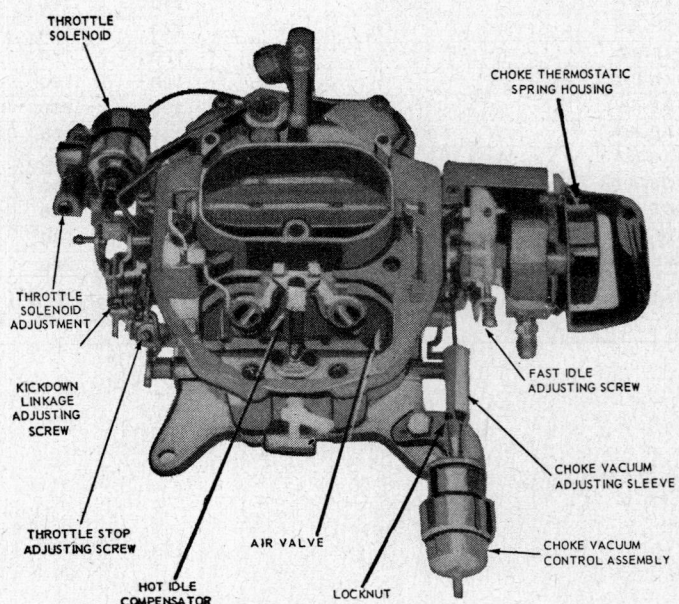

Fig. 3 4300A-4V carburetor with staged choke. 1972

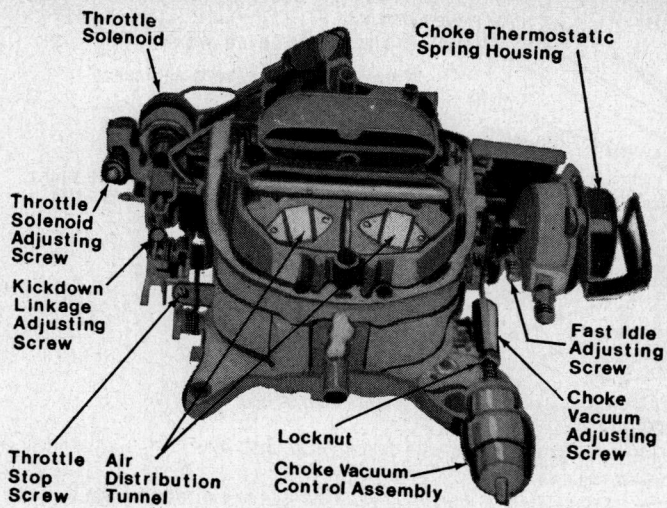

Fig. 4 4300D-4V carburetor with staged choke. 1972

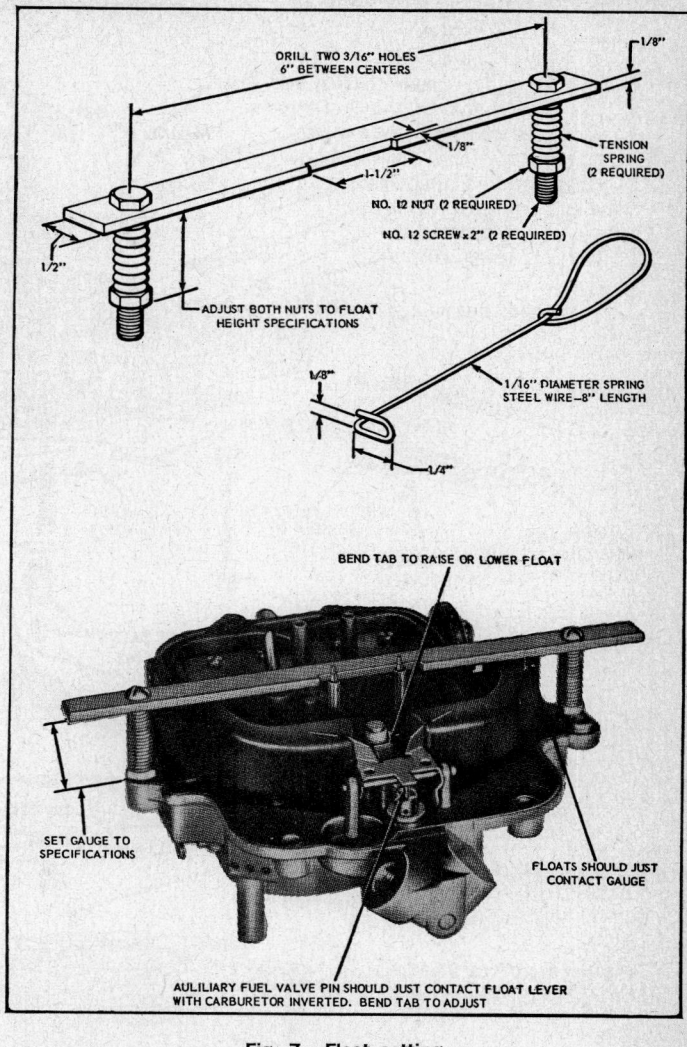

Fig. 7 Float setting

To lower float, insert open end of bending tool to *left* side of float lever tab, between needle and float hinge. Support float lever and bend tab upward.

Auxiliary Valve Setting

Fig. 8, 1969-74 Ford and 1973-74 American Motors units

1. Turn the air horn assembly upright allowing the float to hang freely.
2. Push up on the float until the primary fuel inlet needle lightly contacts its seat.
3. While holding the float in this position, measure the clearance between the float level auxiliary tab and the auxiliary inlet valve plunger.
4. Adjust by bending the tab. Refer to *4300 Specifications Chart.*

NOTE: IMPORTANT: To measure this clearance on a police fleet carburetor with a semi-articulating float, the float assembly must be positioned so that the bottom of both pontoons are same distance from gasket surface of air horn when primary fuel inlet is seated.

Fast Idle Speed Adjustment

Figs. 1 thru 4

The fast idle adjusting screw contacts one edge of the fast idle cam. Each position on the fast idle cam permits a slower idle rpm as engine temperature rises and choking is reduced.

NOTE: Make certain the curb idle speed and mixture are adjusted to specification before attempting to set the fast idle speed.

1. With the engine operating temperature normalized (hot), air cleaner removed and the tachometer attached, manually rotate the fast idle cam until the fast idle adjusting screw rests on the center step of the cam.
2. Adjust by turning the fast idle adjusting screw inward or outward as required. Refer to *4300 Specifications Chart.*

Accelerator Pump Stroke Adjustment

Fig. 9

The accelerator pump stroke has been

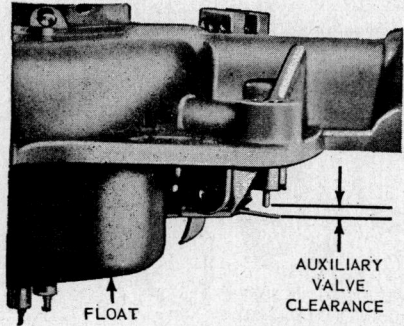

Fig. 8 Auxiliary valve setting. 1969-74 Ford and 1973-74 American Mtrs.

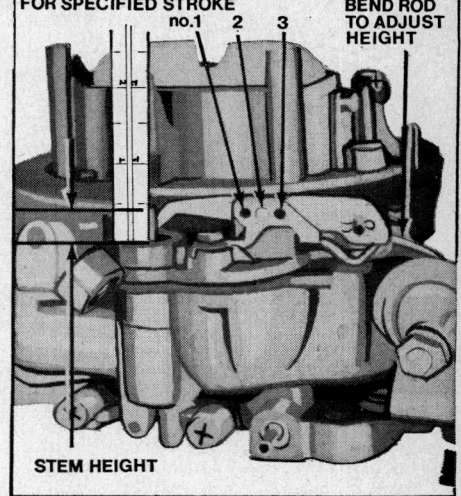

Fig. 9 Accelerator pump stroke adjustment

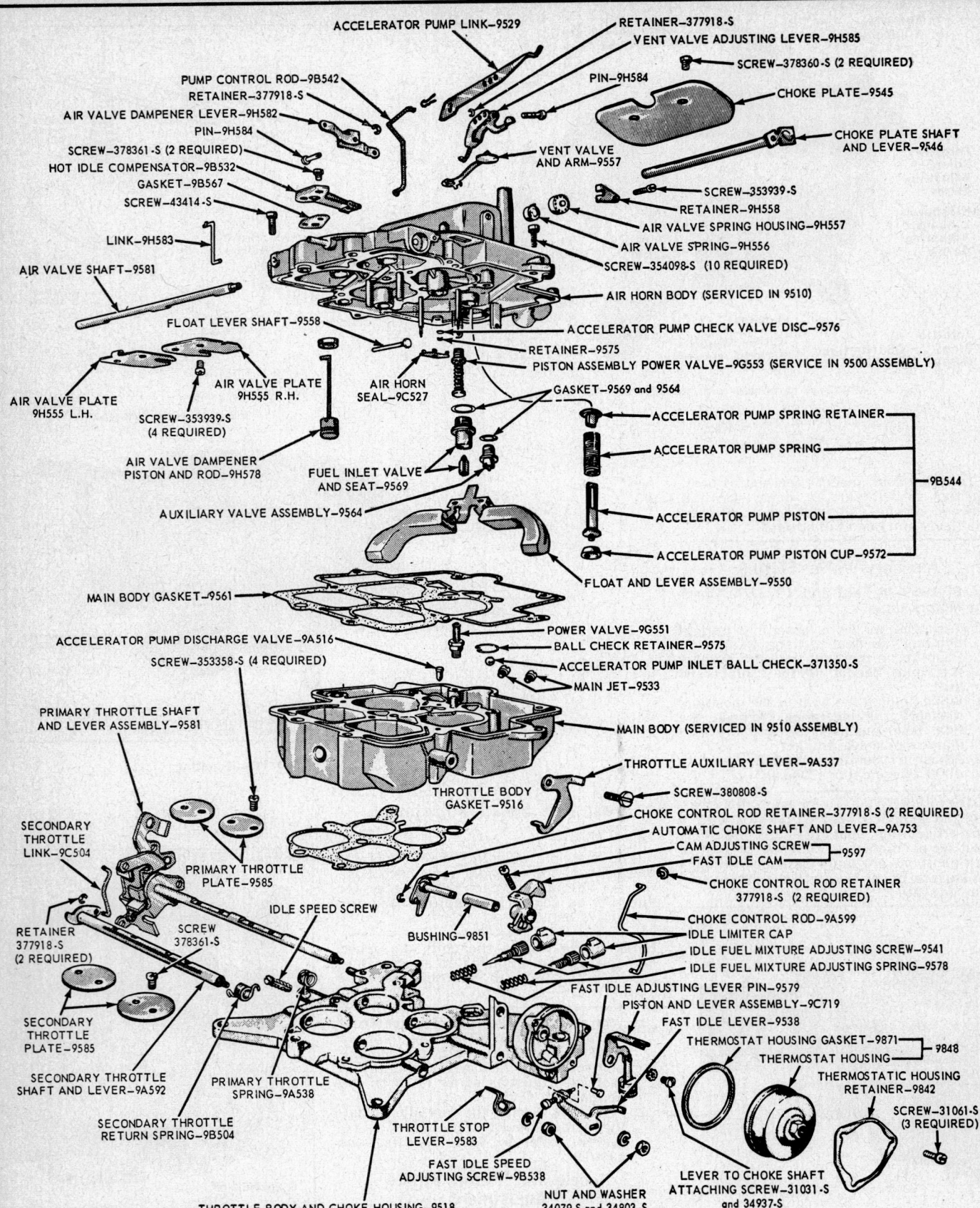

Fig. 5 Exploded view of a typical Autolite 4300A four-barrel carburetor. Note that this unit is provided with idle limiter caps which are used to prevent an overly rich mixture on cars with exhaust emission control

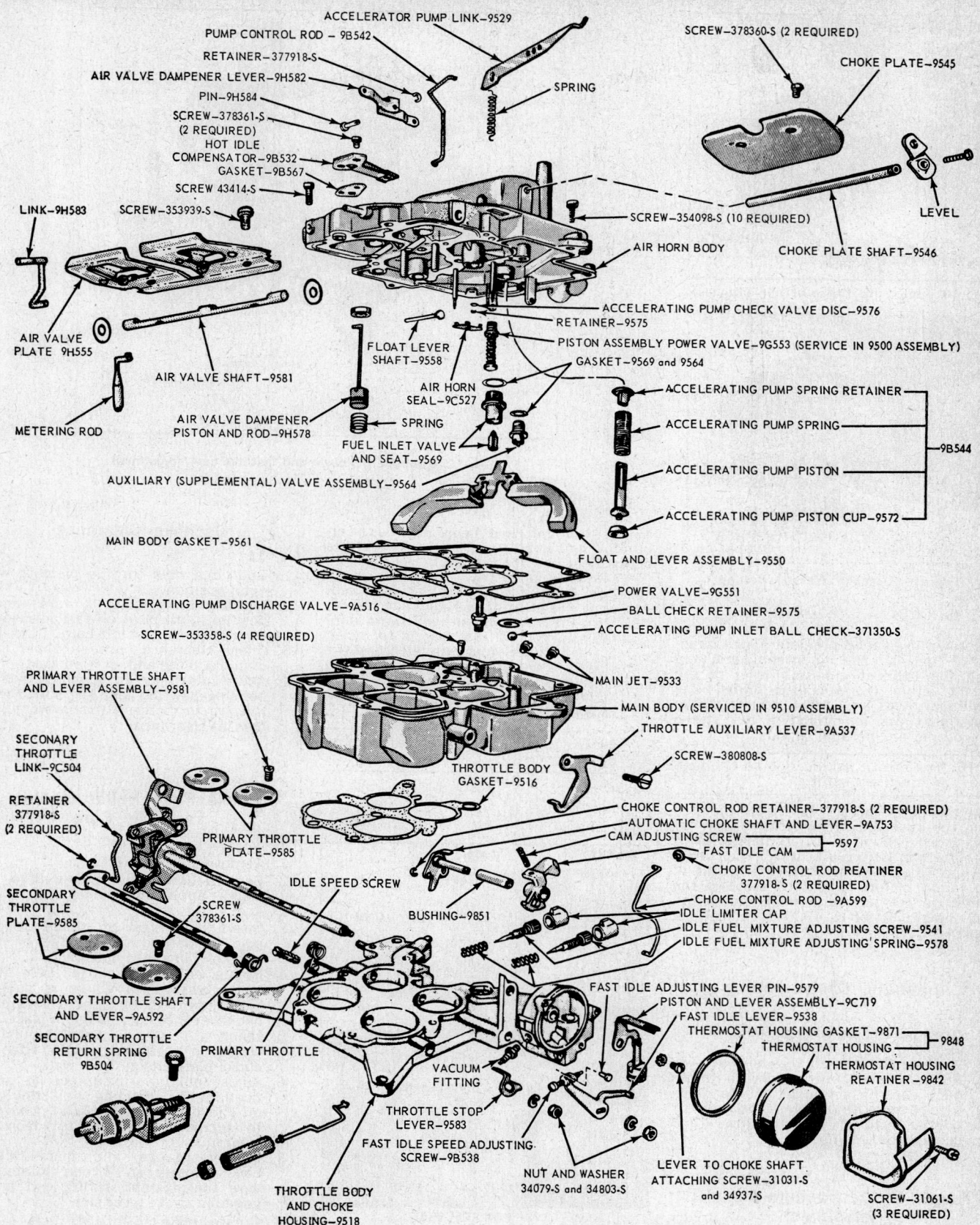

ACCELERATOR PUMP LINK-9529
PUMP CONTROL ROD - 9B542
RETAINER-377918-S
AIR VALVE DAMPENER LEVER-9H582
PIN-9H584
SCREW-378361-S (2 REQUIRED)
HOT IDLE COMPENSATOR-9B532
GASKET-9B567
SCREW 43414-S
LINK-9H583
SCREW-353939-S
SPRING
SCREW-378360-S (2 REQUIRED)
CHOKE PLATE-9545
LEVEL
SCREW-354098-S (10 REQUIRED)
AIR HORN BODY
CHOKE PLATE SHAFT-9546
AIR VALVE PLATE 9H555
AIR VALVE SHAFT-9581
METERING ROD
AIR VALVE DAMPENER PISTON AND ROD-9H578
FLOAT LEVER SHAFT-9558
AIR HORN SEAL-9C527
SPRING
FUEL INLET VALVE AND SEAT-9569
AUXILIARY (SUPPLEMENTAL) VALVE ASSEMBLY-9564
ACCELERATING PUMP CHECK VALVE DISC-9576
RETAINER-9575
PISTON ASSEMBLY POWER VALVE-9G553 (SERVICE IN 9500 ASSEMBLY)
GASKET-9569 and 9564
ACCELERATING PUMP SPRING RETAINER
ACCELERATING PUMP SPRING
ACCELERATING PUMP PISTON
ACCELERATING PUMP PISTON CUP-9572
9B544
MAIN BODY GASKET-9561
ACCELERATING PUMP DISCHARGE VALVE-9A516
SCREW-353358-S (4 REQUIRED)
FLOAT AND LEVER ASSEMBLY-9550
POWER VALVE-9G551
BALL CHECK RETAINER-9575
ACCELERATING PUMP INLET BALL CHECK-371350-S
MAIN JET-9533
MAIN BODY (SERVICED IN 9510 ASSEMBLY)
THROTTLE AUXILIARY LEVER-9A537
SCREW-380808-S
PRIMARY THROTTLE SHAFT AND LEVER ASSEMBLY-9581
SECONARY THROTTLE LINK-9C504
RETAINER 377918-S (2 REQUIRED)
PRIMARY THROTTLE PLATE-9585
SECONDARY THROTTLE PLATE-9585
IDLE SPEED SCREW
SCREW 378361-S
BUSHING-9851
THROTTLE BODY GASKET-9516
CHOKE CONTROL ROD RETAINER-377918-S (2 REQUIRED)
AUTOMATIC CHOKE SHAFT AND LEVER-9A753
CAM ADJUSTING SCREW
FAST IDLE CAM
9597
CHOKE CONTROL ROD REATINER 377918-S (2 REQUIRED)
CHOKE CONTROL ROD -9A599
IDLE LIMITER CAP
IDLE FUEL MIXTURE ADJUSTING SCREW-9541
IDLE FUEL MIXTURE ADJUSTING SPRING-9578
SECONDARY THROTTLE SHAFT AND LEVER-9A592
SECONDARY THROTTLE RETURN SPRING 9B504
PRIMARY THROTTLE
FAST IDLE ADJUSTING LEVER PIN-9579
PISTON AND LEVER ASSEMBLY-9C719
FAST IDLE LEVER-9538
THERMOSTAT HOUSING GASKET-9871
THERMOSTAT HOUSING
9848
THERMOSTAT HOUSING REATINER-9842
VACUUM FITTING
THROTTLE STOP LEVER-9583
FAST IDLE SPEED ADJUSTING SCREW-9B538
NUT AND WASHER 34079-S and 34803-S
LEVER TO CHOKE SHAFT ATTACHING SCREW-31031-S and 34937-S
SCREW-31061-S (3 REQUIRED)
THROTTLE BODY AND CHOKE HOUSING-9518

Fig. 6 Exploded view of typical 4300D-4V carburetor

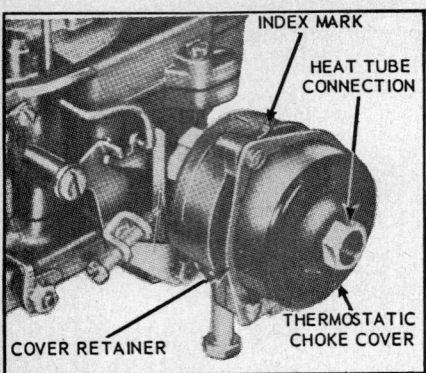

Fig. 10   Automatic choke setting (Typical)

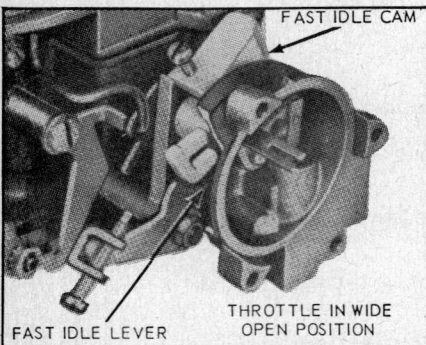

Fig. 11   Dechoke clearance setting

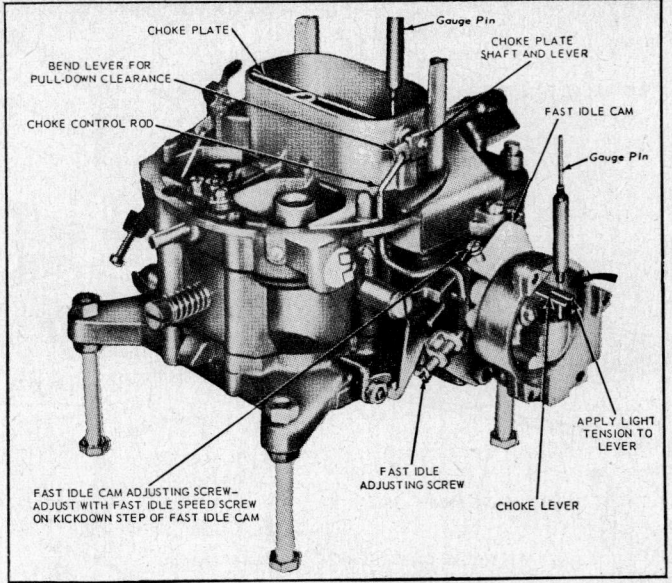

Fig. 12   Choke plate pulldown and fast idle cam adjustment

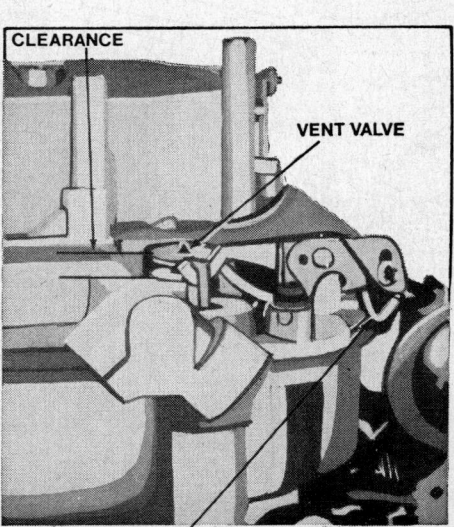

Fig. 13   Fuel bowl vent valve adjustment

calibrated to inject a pre-determined quantity of fuel into the air stream and help keep the exhaust emission level of the engine within the specified limits. The additional holes provided for pump stroke adjustment are for adjusting the stroke for specific engine applications.

NOTE: The stroke should not be changed from the specified setting.

If the pump stroke has been changed from the specified setting refer to the following instructions to correct the stroke to specification. Before adjusting the accelerator pump stroke, measure the height of the pump piston. Adjust by bending the pump control rod to correct the piston stem height. Refer to *4300 Specifications Chart.*

Automatic Choke Setting

Fig. 10
1. If carburetor is installed on engine, loosen choke heat tube nut.
2. Loosen choke cover retaining screws.
3. Rotate choke cover clockwise to reduce choking action or counterclockwise to increase choking action.
4. Tighten choke cover screws and choke heat tube nut.

Staged Choke Vacuum Control Adjustment

Figs. 3 and 4
This adjustment should be made only if

the control unit has been replaced, carburetor has been overhauled or a choke adjustment has been made.
1. Close choke plate.
2. Back off the adjusting sleeve locknut until it is clear of the adjusting sleeve.
3. Turn the adjusting sleeve inward until the choke plate just begins to move. Scribe a mark on the upper flat of the sleeve, then back off the sleeve one complete turn.
4. Tighten the locknut firmly against the sleeve to set the adjustment.

NOTE: Do not turn the diaphragm stem.

Dechoke Clearance

Fig. 11
1. Open and hold throttle plate to wide open position.
2. Rotate choke plate toward closed position until pawl on fast idle speed lever contacts fast idle cam.
3. Check clearance between upper edge of choke plate and air horn wall.
4. Adjust clearance to specifications by bending pawl on fast idle speed lever forward to increase (backward to decrease) clearance.

Choke Plate Pulldown and Fast Idle Cam

Fig. 12
1. Remove choke cover.
2. Bend a .036" wire gauge at a 90° angle, approximately 1/8" from the end.
3. Insert bent edge of gauge between piston slot and upper edge of right hand slot in choke housing.
4. Rotate automatic choke lever counterclockwise until gauge is snug in piston slot. Exert light pressure on choke lever to hold gauge in place.
5. Using a gauge pin, check pulldown clearance between lower edge of choke plate and air horn wall.
6. Adjust pulldown clearance to specifications by bending adjusting arm on choke shaft lever. Bend downward to increase (upward to decrease) clearance.
7. Remove gauge and install choke cover loosely so it can rotate. Be sure thermostatic spring end is engaged in choke lever slot.
8. Rotate choke cover to 90° rich.
9. Position fast idle adjusting screw end to kickdown step on fast idle cam

and hold in this position.

10. Using a gauge pin, check fast idle cam clearance between lower ege of choke plate and air horn wall.

11. Adjust fast idle cam clearance to specifications by turning adjusting screw clockwise to increase (coun-terclockwise to decrease) clearance.

12. Install choke cover and rotate it to specified setting, then tighten cover.

Fuel Bowl External Vent Valve
Fig. 13

1. Set throttle plates in closed position.

2. Check clearance between vent valve and valve seat.

3. If clearance is not .070 inch, bend end of vent valve lever downward to decrease and upward to increase.

MODEL 5200 ADJUSTMENT SPECIFICATIONS

See Tune Up Chart in car chapters for hot idle speeds.

Year	Carb. Model (9510) ①	Idle Mixture Turns Open	Float Level	Pump Setting (Hole)	Choke Pulldown	Dechoke Clearance	Fast Idle Speed	Fast Idle Cam Clearance	Dashpot Setting	Choke Setting
1971	D12F-AA	②	.420	Lower	.236	.256	1800	.010	—	Index
	D12F-BA	②	.420	Lower	.236	.256	1600	.010	—	Index
	D12F-CA	②	.420	Lower	.236	.256	1800	.010	—	Index
	D12F-DA	②	.420	Lower	.236	.256	1800	.010	—	1 Rich
	D12F-EA	②	.420	Lower	.236	.256	1600	.010	—	1 Rich
	D12F-FA	②	.420	Lower	.236	.256	1800	.010	—	1 Rich
1972	D22F-AB	②	.420	#3	.236	.256	1800	.156	—	1 Lean
	D22F-AC	②	.420	#3	.236	.256	1800	.156	—	1 Lean
	D22F-BB	②	.420	#2	.236	.256	1600	.079	—	1 Lean
	D22F-EB	②	.420	#3	.236	.256	1800	.156	—	Index
	D22F-CB	②	.420	#3	.236	.256	1800	.156	—	1 Lean
	D22F-DB	②	.420	#2	.236	.256	1600	.079	—	1 Lean
	D22F-EA	②	.420	#3	.236	.256	1800	.156	—	Index
	D22F-GA	②	.420	#3	.236	.256	1800	.156	—	Index
1973	D32F-AC	②	.420	#2	.158	—	—	—	—	Index
	D32F-BD	②	.420	#2	.158	.256	1600	.118	—	1 Lean
	D32F-CA	②	.420	#2	.158	.256	1800	.158	—	Index
	73TF-AA	②	.420	#2	.237	.256	1600	.118	—	Lean
	73TF-BA	②	.420	#2	.237	.256	1800	.118	—	Index
1974	D42E-AA	②	.460	#2	.280	.255	—	.1575	—	Index
	D42E-AC	②	.460	#2	.280	.255	—	.158	—	Index
	D42E-BA	②	.460	#2	.280	.255	—	.1575	—	1 Rich
	D42E-CB	②	.460	#2	.280	.255	—	.1575	—	Index
	D42E-CD	②	.460	#2	.280	.255	—	.158	—	Index
	D42E-DB	②	.460	#2	.280	.255	—	.1575	—	1 Rich
	D42F-EA	②	.460	#2	.236	.255	—	.1575	—	Index
	D42E-EB	②	.460	#2	.236	.255	—	.158	—	Index
	D42F-FA	②	.460	#2	.236	.255	—	.1575	—	Index
	D42F-GA	②	.460	#2	.236	.255	—	.1575	—	Index
	D42E-KA	②	.460	#2	.280	.255	—	.158	—	1 Rich
	D4ZE-AA	②	.430	#2	.195	.256	—	.195	—	1 Rich
	D4ZE-BA	②	.430	#2	.195	.256	—	.195	—	1 Rich
	D4ZE-BC	②	.435	#2	.195	.255	—	.195	—	1 Rich
	D4ZE-CA	②	.430	#2	.195	.256	—	.195	—	1 Rich
	D4ZE-DA	②	.430	#2	.195	.256	—	.195	—	1 Rich
	D4ZE-DC	②	.435	#2	.195	.255	—	.195	—	1 Rich

①—Tag attached to carburetor

②—Air/fuel ratio or idle CO% rating is found in Tune Up Specification tables in car chapters.

MODEL 5200 ADJUSTMENTS

This carburetor is a two stage, two venturi carburetor, Figs. 1 and 5. The primary stage or venturi is smaller than the secondary venturi. The secondary is operated by mechanical linkage.

The primary stage includes a curb idle system, accelerator pump system, idle transfer system, main metering system and power enrichment system.

The secondary stage includes a transfer system, main metering system, and power system. Both the primary and secondary systems draw fuel from a common fuel bowl.

Dry Float Setting

Fig. 2—With the bowl cover held in an inverted position and the float tang resting lightly on the spring loaded fuel inlet needle, measure the clearance between the edge of the float and the bowl cover. Adjust clearance by bending the float tang up or down as required, Fig. 3.

NOTE: Do not scratch or damage the tang. Adjust both floats equally.

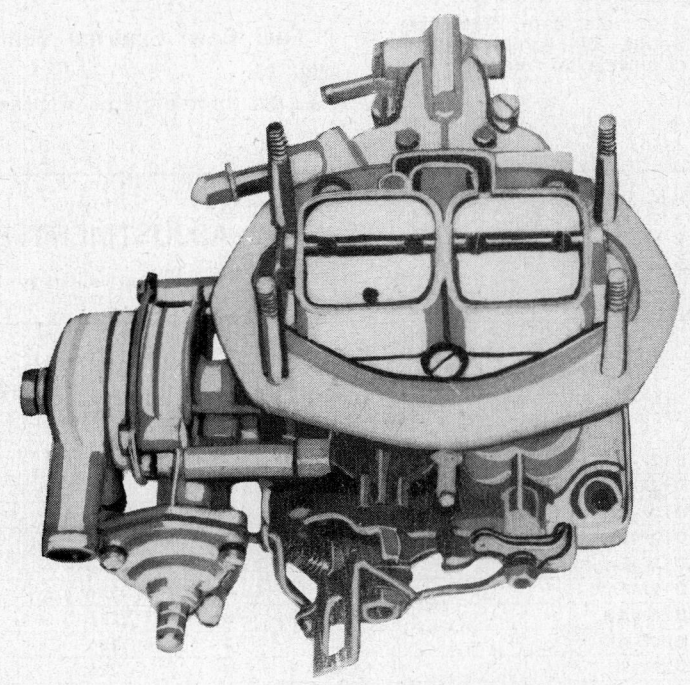

Fig. 1   Model 5200-2V carburetor

Dechoke Clearance

Fig. 4—Hold throttle lever in wide open position and take slack out of choke linkage by applying finger pressure to top edge of choke plate. Measure clearance between lower edge of choke plate and air horn wall. Adjust by bending tab on fast idle lever where it touches the fast idle cam.

Choke Plate Vacuum Pull-Down

Fig. 6—Remove three screws and ring retaining choke spring cover and pull the water cover and choke spring cover out of way. Set the fast idle cam on the top step. Push the diaphragm stem back against its stop. Place gauge rod or drill between the lower edge of the choke plate and the air horn wall. Remove the slack from the choke linkage by applying finger pressure to the top edge of the choke plate. Adjust the choke plate-to-air horn clearance by removing the plug from the diaphragm and turning the adjusting screw in or out as required.

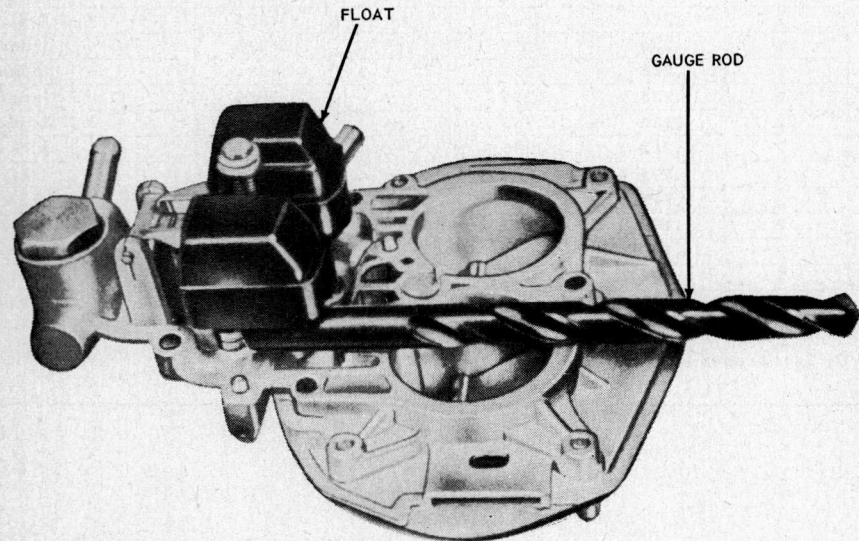

Fig. 2   Dry float setting

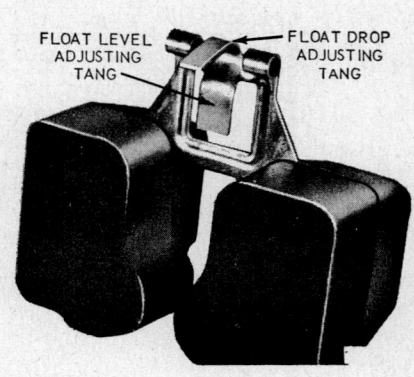

Fig. 3   Float adjusting point

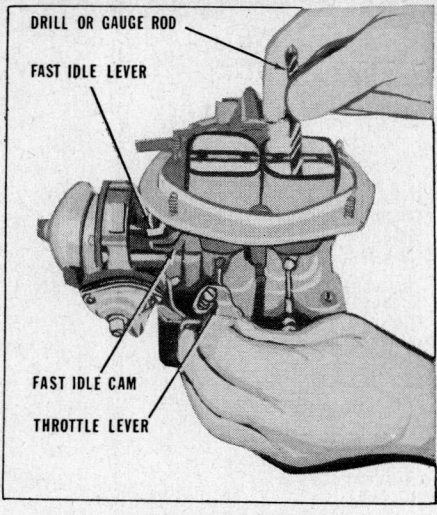

Fig. 4   De-choke adjustment

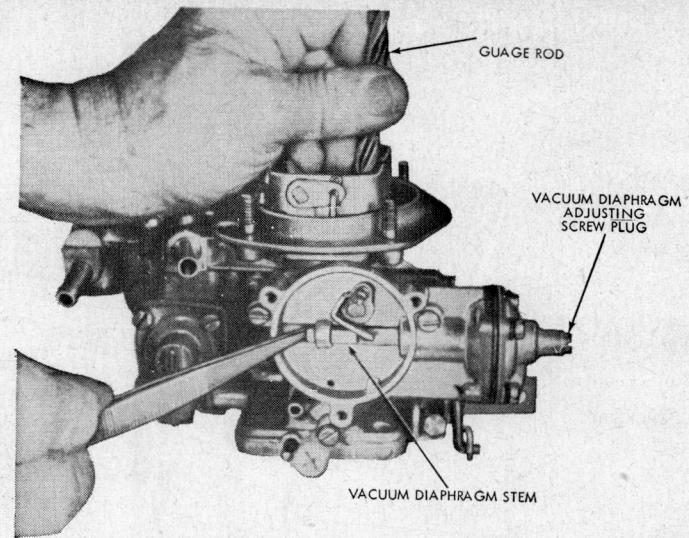

Fig. 6   Choke plate pull-down

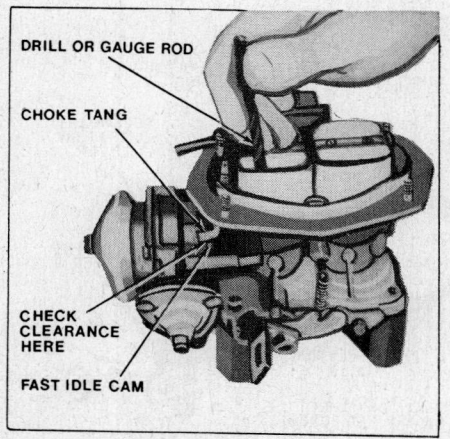

Fig. 7   Fast idle cam clearance

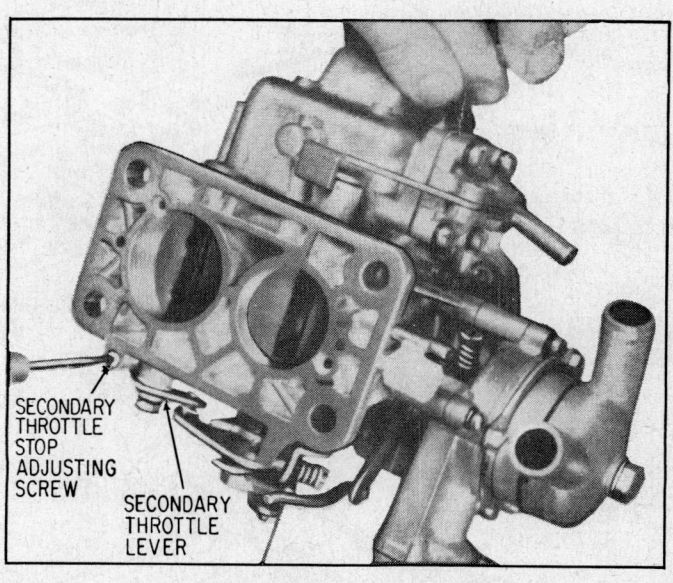

Fig. 8   Secondary throttle stop adjustment

Fast Idle Cam Clearance

Fig. 7—Insert a 5/32 inch drill between the lower edge of the choke plate and the air horn wall. With the fast idle screw held on the second step of the fast idle cam, measure the clearance between the tang of the choke lever and the arm on the fast idle cam. Adjust clearance by bending choke lever tang up or down as required. Refer to *5200 Specifications Chart.*

Secondary Throttle Stop Screw Adjustment

Fig. 8—Back off the secondary throttle stop screw until the secondary throttle plate seats in its bore. Turn the screw in until it touches the tab on the secondary throttle lever. On all units except when used on 2800 cc engines, turn the screw inward an additional 1/4 turn. On units used on 2800 cc engines, turn screw inward an additional 3/4 turn.

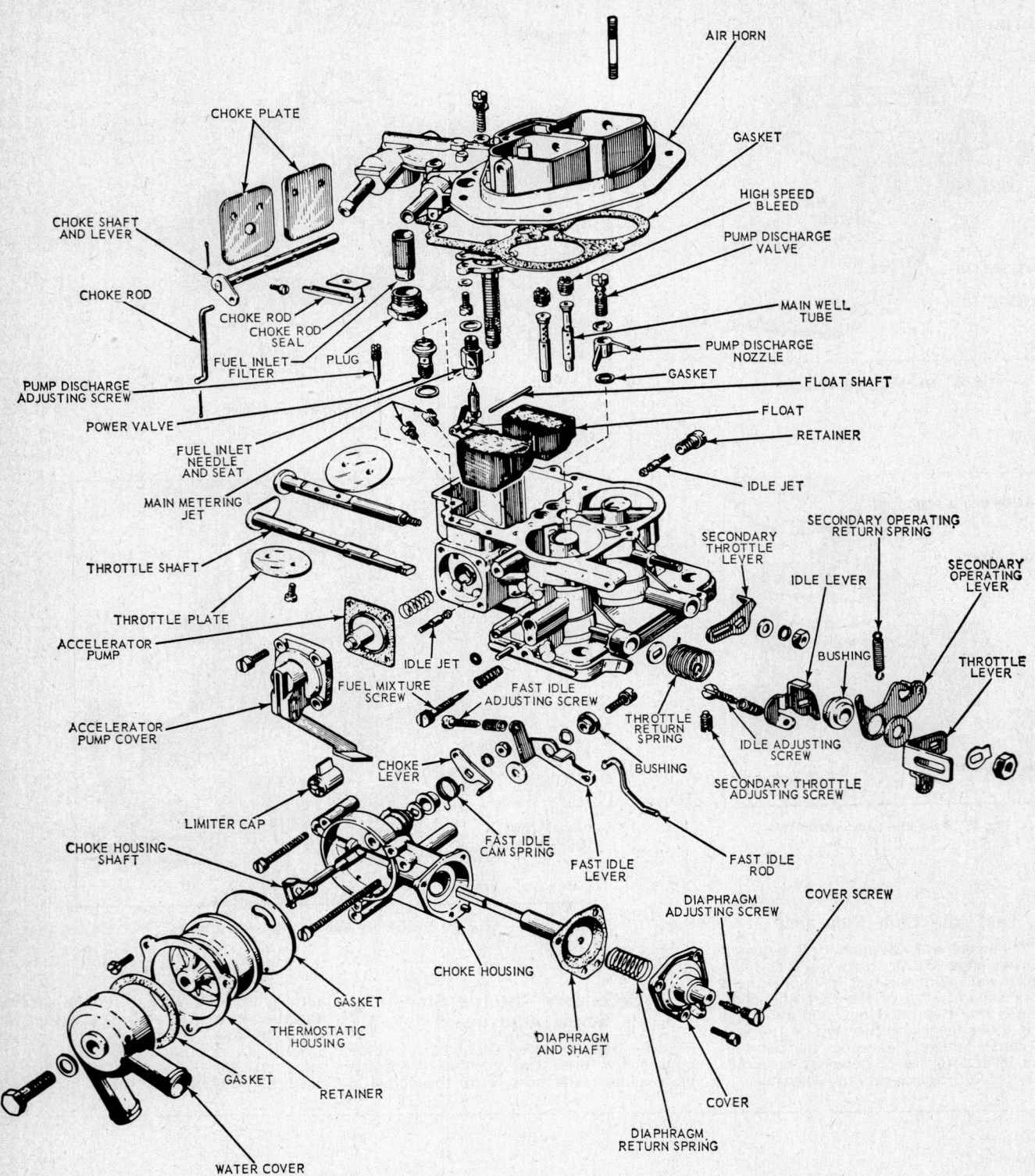

Fig. 5 Exploded view of model 5200 carburetor. All bolts and screws are Metric thread.
Early production Metric heads; later production U.S. heads

GM Delco/Rochester Carburetor Section

MODEL 2GC, 2GV CARBURETOR ADJUSTMENT SPECIFICATIONS

See Tune Up Chart in car chapters for hot idle speeds.
★Located on tag attached to or stamped on carburetor.

Year	Carb. Part No. ★	Float Level	Float Drop	Pump Rod	Idle Vent	Intermediate Choke Rod	Vacuum Break	Automatic Choke	Choke Rod	Choke Unloader	Fast Idle Speed
BUICK											
1969	7029140	15/32	1 7/32	1 11/32	.020②	—	.110	③	.055	.140	—
	7029141	15/32	1 7/32	1 11/32	.020②	—	.110	③	.055	.140	—
1970	7040142	15/32	1 7/32	1 13/32	—	—	.150	③	.080	.180	—
	7041143	15/32	1 7/32	1 15/32	—	—	.190	③	.100	.200	—
	7040446	15/32	1 7/32	1 13/32	—	—	.150	③	.080	.180	—
1971	7041143	15/32	1 7/32	1 15/32	—	—	.160④	—	.080	.200	—
	7041142	15/32	1 7/32	1 15/32	—	—	.150④	—	.080	.180	—
	7041442	15/32	1 7/32	1 15/32	—	—	.150④	—	.080	.180	—
1972	7042142	15/32	1 11/32	1 15/32	—	—	.140⑤	—	.080	.180	—
	7042143	15/32	1 11/32	1 15/32	—	—	.160④	—	.080	.180	—
	7042842	15/32	1 11/32	1 15/32	—	—	.140⑤	—	.080	.180	—
1973	7043142	15/32	1 9/32	1 15/32	—	—	.140⑤	—	.080	.180	—
	7043143	15/32	1 9/32	1 15/32	—	—	.150⑤	—	.080	.200	—
	7043144	15/32	1 9/32	1 15/32	—	—	.140⑤	—	.080	.180	—
1974	7044141	15/32	1 9/32	1 15/32	—	—	.160⑥	—	.080	.180	—
	7044142	15/32	1 9/32	1 15/32	—	—	.140⑤	—	.080	.180	—
	7044144	15/32	1 9/32	1 15/32	—	—	.140⑤	—	.080	.180	—
	7044442	15/32	1 9/32	1 15/32	—	—	.140⑤	—	.080	.180	—
	7044444	15/32	1 9/32	1 15/32	—	—	.140⑤	—	.080	.180	—
1975	7045140	15/32	1 9/32	—	—	—	.140⑤	—	.080	.180	—
	7045143	15/32	1 9/32	—	—	—	.140⑤	—	.080	.180	—
	7045145	15/32	1 9/32	—	—	—	.120⑤	—	.080	.140	—
	7045146	15/32	1 9/32	—	—	—	.120⑤	—	.080	.140	—
	7045147	15/32	1 9/32	—	—	—	.120⑤	—	.080	.140	—
	7045148	15/32	1 9/32	—	—	—	.120⑤	—	.080	.140	—
	7045149	15/32	1 9/32	—	—	—	.120⑤	—	.080	.140	—
	7045150	15/32	1 9/32	—	—	—	.120⑤	—	.080	.180	—
	7045446	15/32	1 9/32	—	—	—	.120⑤	—	.080	.140	—
	7045447	15/32	1 9/32	—	—	—	.140⑤	—	.080	.180	—
	7045448	15/32	1 9/32	—	—	—	.120⑤	—	.080	.140	—
	7045449	15/32	1 9/32	—	—	—	.120⑤	—	.080	.140	—
	7045450	15/32	1 9/32	—	—	—	.120	—	.080	.180	—
	7045451	15/32	1 9/32	—	—	—	.140	—	.080	.180	—
	7045452	15/32	1 9/32	—	—	—	.120	—	.080	.140	—
	7045453	15/32	1 9/32	—	—	—	.140	—	.080	.180	—

①—Rod is installed in lower of two lever holes.
②—At slow idle RPM vent valve should be open to specified dimension.
⑤—Secondary adjustment .120".
③—Holes in lever are marked "ALT" or "STD". Install in proper hole.
④—Secondary adjustment .140".
⑥—Secondary adjustment .130".

CHECKER MOTORS

Year	Carb. Part No. ★	Float Level	Float Drop	Pump Rod	Idle Vent	Intermediate Choke Rod	Vacuum Break	Automatic Choke	Choke Rod	Choke Unloader	Fast Idle Speed
1969	7029102	3/4	1 3/8	1 13/32	.020	—	.215	—	.085	.275	2100
	7029104	3/4	1 3/8	1 13/32	.020	—	.215	—	.085	.275	2100
	7029124	3/4	1 3/8	1 7/16	—	—	—	—	—	—	—
	7029127	3/4	1 3/8	1 13/32	.020	—	.215	—	.085	.275	2100
	7029129	3/4	1 3/8	1 13/32	.020	—	.215	—	.085	.275	2100
1970	7040114	23/32	1 3/8	1 17/32	.025	—	.200	—	.085	.325	—
	7040116	23/32	1 3/8	1 17/32	.025	—	.200	—	.085	.325	—
	7040123	23/32	1 3/8	1 17/32	.020	—	—	—	—	—	—
	7040134	25/32	1 11/32	1 17/32	.020	—	.200	—	.085	.325	—
	7040136	25/32	1 11/32	1 17/32	.020	—	.200	—	.085	.325	—
	7040414	23/32	1 3/8	1 17/32	—	—	.200	—	.085	.325	—
	7040416	23/32	1 3/8	1 17/32	—	—	.200	—	.085	.325	—
	7040434	25/32	1 11/32	1 17/32	.020	—	.215	—	.085	.325	—
	7040436	25/32	1 11/32	1 17/32	.020	—	.215	—	.085	.325	—
1971	7041114	25/32	1 5/8	1 17/32	—	—	.170	—	.100	.325	—
	7041123	23/32	1 1/8	1 17/32	.020	—	—	—	—	—	—
1972	7042114	23/32	1 9/32	1 1/2	—	—	.170	—	.100	.325	—
1973	7043114	19/32	1 9/32	1 7/16	—	—	.130	—	.245	.325	—
1974	7044114	19/32	1 9/32	1 3/16	—	—	.130	—	.245	.325	1600

Continued

GM DELCO/ROCHESTER CARBURETORS

MODEL 2GC, 2GV CARBURETOR ADJUSTMENT SPECIFICATIONS—Continued

See Tune Up Chart in car chapters for hot idle speeds.
★Located on tag attached to or stamped on carburetor.

Year	Carb. Part No. ★	Float Level	Float Drop	Pump Rod	Idle Vent	Intermediate Choke Rod	Vacuum Break	Automatic Choke	Choke Rod	Choke Unloader	Fast Idle Speed
CHEVROLET ENGINES											
1969	7029101	27/32②	1¾	1⅛	.020	—	.100	—	.060	.215	—
	7029102	¾②	1⅜	1 13/32	.020	—	.215	—	.085	.275	—
	7029103	27/32②	1¾	1⅛	.020	—	.100	—	.060	.215	—
	7029104	¾②	1⅜	1 13/32	.020	—	.215	—	.085	.275	—
	7029110	27/32②	1¾	1⅛	.020	—	.100	—	.060	.215	—
	7029112	27/32②	1¾	1⅛	.020	—	.100	—	.060	.215	—
	7029113	¾②	1⅜	1 13/32	.020	—	.200	—	.085	.275	—
	7029114	¾②	1⅜	1 13/32	.020	—	.200	—	.085	.275	—
	7029115	¾②	1⅜	1 13/32	.020	—	.200	—	.085	.275	—
	7029116	¾②	1⅜	1 13/32	.020	—	.200	—	.085	.275	—
	7029117	¾②	1¾	1 13/32	.020	—	.215	—	.085	.275	—
	7029118	¾②	1¾	1 13/32	.020	—	.215	—	.085	.275	—
	7029119	⅝②	1¾	1 13/32	.020	—	.215	—	.085	.275	—
	7029120	⅝②	1¾	1 13/32	.020	—	.215	—	.085	.275	—
	7029127	¾②	1⅜	1 13/32	.020	—	.215	—	.085	.275	—
	7029129	¾②	1⅜	1 13/32	.020	—	.215	—	.085	.275	—
1970	7040101	27/32②	1¾	1⅜	.025	—	.130	—	.060	.160	—
	7040102	23/32②	1⅜	1 7/32	.025	—	.200	—	.085	.325	—
	7040103	27/32②	1¾	1⅜	.025	—	.130	—	.060	.160	—
	7040104	23/32②	1⅜	1 7/32	.025	—	.200	—	.085	.325	—
	7040110	27/32②	1¾	1⅜	.025	—	.100	—	.060	.215	—
	7040112	27/32②	1¾	1⅜	.025	—	.100	—	.060	.215	—
	7040113	23/32②	1⅜	1 7/32	.025	—	.215	—	.085	.275	—
	7040114	23/32②	1⅜	1 7/32	.025	—	.200	—	.085	.325	—
	7040115	23/32②	1⅜	1 7/32	.025	—	.215	—	.085	.275	—
	7040116	23/32②	1⅜	1 7/32	.025	—	.200	—	.085	.325	—
	7040117	23/32②	1⅜	1 7/32	.025	—	.215	—	.085	.325	—
	7040118	23/32②	1⅜	1 7/32	.025	—	.215	—	.085	.325	—
	7040119	23/32②	1⅜	1 7/32	.025	—	.215	—	.085	.325	—
	7040120	23/32②	1⅜	1 7/32	.025	—	.215	—	.085	.325	—
	7040126	25/32②	1 11/32	1 7/32	.020	—	.200	—	.085	.325	—
	7040127	23/32②	1⅜	1 7/32	.025	—	.215	—	.085	.275	—
	7040128	25/32②	1 11/32	1 7/32	.020	—	.200	—	.085	.325	—
	7040129	23/32②	1⅜	1 7/32	.025	—	.215	—	.085	.275	—
	7040134	25/32②	1 11/32	1 7/32	.020	—	.200	—	.085	.325	—
	7040136	25/32②	1 11/32	1 7/32	.020	—	.200	—	.085	.325	—
	7040401	27/32②	1¾	1 5/16	—	—	.130	—	.060	.160	—
	7040402	23/32②	1⅜	1 7/32	—	—	.200	—	.085	.325	—
	7040403	27/32②	1¾	1 5/16	—	—	.130	—	.060	.160	—
	7040404	23/32②	1⅜	1 7/32	—	—	.200	—	.085	.325	—
	7040410	27/32②	1¾	1 5/16	—	—	.100	—	.060	.215	—
	7040412	27/32②	1¾	1 5/16	—	—	.100	—	.060	.215	—
	7040413	23/32②	1⅜	1 7/32	—	—	.215	—	.085	.275	—
	7040414	23/32②	1⅜	1 7/32	—	—	.200	—	.085	.325	—
	7040415	23/32②	1⅜	1 7/32	—	—	.215	—	.085	.275	—
	7040416	23/32②	1⅜	1 7/32	—	—	.200	—	.085	.325	—
	7040417	23/32②	1⅜	1 7/32	—	—	.215	—	.085	.325	—
	7040418	23/32②	1⅜	1 7/32	—	—	.215	—	.085	.325	—
	7040419	23/32②	1⅜	1 7/32	—	—	.215	—	.085	.325	—
	7040420	23/32②	1⅜	1 7/32	—	—	.215	—	.085	.325	—
	7040426	25/32②	1 11/32	1 7/32	.020	—	.215	—	.085	.325	—
	7040427	23/32②	1⅜	1 7/32	—	—	.215	—	.085	.275	—
	7040428	25/32②	1 11/32	1 7/32	.020	—	.215	—	.085	.325	—
	7040429	23/32②	1⅜	1 7/32	—	—	.215	—	.085	.275	—

Continued

MODEL 2GC, 2GV CARBURETOR ADJUSTMENT SPECIFICATIONS—Continued

See Tune Up Chart in car chapters for hot idle speeds.

★Located on tag attached to or stamped on carburetor.

Year	Carb. Part No. ★	Float Level	Float Drop	Pump Rod	Idle Vent	Intermediate Choke Rod	Vacuum Break	Automatic Choke	Choke Rod	Choke Unloader	Fast Idle Speed
CHEVROLET ENGINES—Continued											
1970	7040434	$\frac{25}{32}$②	$1\frac{11}{32}$	$1\frac{17}{32}$	.020	—	.215	—	.085	.325	—
	7040436	$\frac{25}{32}$②	$1\frac{11}{32}$	$1\frac{17}{32}$	.020	—	.215	—	.085	.325	—
1971	7041101	$\frac{27}{32}$②	$1\frac{3}{4}$	$1\frac{5}{16}$	—	—	.110	—	.075	.215	—
	7041102	$\frac{25}{32}$②	$1\frac{3}{8}$	$1\frac{17}{32}$	—	—	.170	—	.100	.325	—
	7041106	$\frac{9}{16}$②	$1\frac{7}{8}$	$1\frac{3}{16}$	—	—	.085	—	.080	.200	—
	7041107	$\frac{9}{16}$②	$1\frac{7}{8}$	$1\frac{3}{16}$	—	—	.100	—	.080	.200	—
	7041110	$\frac{27}{32}$②	$1\frac{3}{4}$	$1\frac{5}{16}$	—	—	.080	—	.040	.215	—
	7041113	$\frac{23}{32}$②	$1\frac{3}{8}$	$1\frac{17}{32}$	—	—	.180	—	.100	.325	—
	7041114	$\frac{25}{32}$②	$1\frac{3}{8}$	$1\frac{17}{32}$	—	—	.170	—	.100	.325	—
	7041117	$\frac{23}{32}$②	$1\frac{3}{8}$	$1\frac{17}{32}$	—	—	.170	—	.100	.325	—
	7041118	$\frac{23}{32}$②	$1\frac{3}{8}$	$1\frac{17}{32}$	—	—	.170	—	.100	.325	—
	7041127	$\frac{23}{32}$②	$1\frac{3}{8}$	$1\frac{17}{32}$	—	—	.180	—	.100	.325	—
	7041137	$\frac{23}{32}$②	$1\frac{3}{8}$	$1\frac{17}{32}$	—	—	.180	—	.100	.325	—
	7041181	$\frac{21}{32}$②	$1\frac{7}{8}$	$1\frac{3}{8}$	—	—	.120	—	.080	.180	—
	7041182	$\frac{21}{32}$②	$1\frac{7}{8}$	$1\frac{3}{8}$	—	—	.120	—	.080	.180	—
1972	7042100	$\frac{25}{32}$	$1\frac{31}{32}$	$1\frac{5}{16}$	—	—	.080	—	.040	.215	—
	7042101	$\frac{25}{32}$	$1\frac{31}{32}$	$1\frac{5}{16}$	—	—	.110	—	.075	.215	—
	7042106	$\frac{19}{32}$	$1\frac{7}{8}$	$1\frac{1}{16}$	—	—	.085	—	.060	.215	2800
	7042107	$\frac{19}{32}$	$1\frac{7}{8}$	$1\frac{1}{16}$	—	—	.100	—	.080	.215	2800
	7042111	$\frac{23}{32}$	$1\frac{9}{32}$	$1\frac{1}{2}$	—	—	.180	—	.100	.325	—
	7042112	$\frac{23}{32}$	$1\frac{9}{32}$	$1\frac{1}{2}$	—	—	.170	—	.100	.325	—
	7042113	$\frac{23}{32}$	$1\frac{9}{32}$	$1\frac{1}{2}$	—	—	.180	—	.100	.325	—
	7042114	$\frac{23}{32}$	$1\frac{9}{32}$	$1\frac{1}{2}$	—	—	.170	—	.100	.325	—
	7042118	$\frac{23}{32}$	$1\frac{9}{32}$	$1\frac{1}{2}$	—	—	.190	—	.100	.325	—
	7042122	$\frac{19}{32}$	$1\frac{7}{8}$	$1\frac{1}{16}$	—	—	.085	—	.060	.215	—
	7042125	$\frac{19}{32}$	$1\frac{7}{8}$	$1\frac{1}{16}$	—	—	.100	—	.080	.215	—
	7042820	$\frac{25}{32}$	$1\frac{31}{32}$	$1\frac{5}{16}$	—	—	.080	—	.040	.215	—
	7042821	$\frac{25}{32}$	$1\frac{31}{32}$	$1\frac{5}{16}$	—	—	.110	—	.075	.215	—
	7042826	$\frac{19}{32}$	$1\frac{7}{8}$	$1\frac{1}{16}$	—	—	.085	—	.060	.215	2800
	7042827	$\frac{19}{32}$	$1\frac{7}{8}$	$1\frac{1}{16}$	—	—	.100	—	.080	.215	2400
	7042831	$\frac{23}{32}$	$1\frac{9}{32}$	$1\frac{1}{2}$	—	—	.180	—	.100	.325	—
	7042832	$\frac{23}{32}$	$1\frac{9}{32}$	$1\frac{1}{2}$	—	—	.170	—	.100	.325	—
	7042833	$\frac{23}{32}$	$1\frac{9}{32}$	$1\frac{1}{2}$	—	—	.180	—	.100	.325	—
	7042834	$\frac{23}{32}$	$1\frac{9}{32}$	$1\frac{1}{2}$	—	—	.170	—	.100	.325	—
	7042836	$\frac{19}{32}$	$1\frac{7}{8}$	$1\frac{1}{16}$	—	—	.085	—	.060	.215	—
	7042838	$\frac{23}{32}$	$1\frac{9}{32}$	$1\frac{1}{2}$	—	—	.200	—	.100	.325	—
	7042839	$\frac{19}{32}$	$1\frac{7}{8}$	$1\frac{1}{16}$	—	—	.100	—	.080	.215	—
1973	7043100	$\frac{13}{16}$	$1\frac{9}{32}$	$1\frac{9}{32}$	—	—	.080	—	.150	.215	1600
	7043101	$\frac{13}{16}$	$1\frac{9}{32}$	$1\frac{9}{32}$	—	—	.080	—	.150	.215	1600
	7043105	$\frac{13}{16}$	$1\frac{9}{32}$	$1\frac{9}{32}$	—	—	.080	—	.150	.215	1600
	7043111	$\frac{19}{32}$	$1\frac{9}{32}$	$1\frac{1}{2}$	—	—	.140	—	.200	.250	1600
	7043112	$\frac{19}{32}$	$1\frac{9}{32}$	$1\frac{7}{16}$	—	—	.130	—	.245	.325	1600
	7043113	$\frac{19}{32}$	$1\frac{9}{32}$	$1\frac{1}{2}$	—	—	.140	—	.200	.250	1600
	7043114	$\frac{19}{32}$	$1\frac{9}{32}$	$1\frac{7}{16}$	—	—	.130	—	.245	.325	1600
	7043118	$\frac{19}{32}$	$1\frac{9}{32}$	$1\frac{7}{16}$	—	—	.130	—	.245	.325	1600
	7043120	$\frac{13}{16}$	$1\frac{9}{32}$	$1\frac{9}{32}$	—	—	.080	—	.150	.215	1600
1974	7044111	$\frac{19}{32}$	$1\frac{9}{32}$	$1\frac{21}{32}$	—	—	.140	—	.200	.250	1600
	7044112	$\frac{19}{32}$	$1\frac{9}{32}$	$1\frac{9}{16}$	—	—	.130	—	.245	.325	1600
	7044113	$\frac{19}{32}$	$1\frac{9}{32}$	$1\frac{21}{32}$	—	—	.140	—	.200	.250	1600
	7044114	$\frac{19}{32}$	$1\frac{9}{32}$	$1\frac{9}{16}$	—	—	.130	—	.245	.325	1600

Continued

MODEL 2GC, 2GV CARBURETOR ADJUSTMENT SPECIFICATIONS—Continued

See Tune Up Chart in car chapters for hot idle speeds.

★Located on tag attached to or stamped on carburetor.

Year	Carb. Part No. ★	Float Level	Float Drop	Pump Rod	Idle Vent	Intermediate Choke Rod	Vacuum Break	Automatic Choke	Choke Rod	Choke Unloader	Fast Idle Speed
CHEVROLET ENGINES—Continued											
1974	7044115	19/32	1 9/32	1 21/32	—	—	.140	—	.200	.250	1600
	7044116	19/32	1 9/32	1 9/16	—	—	.130	—	.245	.325	1600
	7044117	19/32	1 9/32	1 9/16	—	—	.140	—	.245	.325	1600
	7044118	19/32	1 9/32	1 9/16	—	—	.130	—	.245	.325	1600
	7044120	19/32	1 9/32	1 21/32	—	—	.130	—	.200	.250	1600
	7044123	19/32	1 9/32	1 21/32	—	—	.140	—	.200	.250	1600
	7044124	19/32	1 9/32	1 9/16	—	—	.130	—	.245	.325	1600
	7044126	19/32	1 9/32	1 21/32	—	—	.140	—	.200	.250	1600
	7044127	19/32	1 9/32	1 9/16	—	—	.130	—	.245	.325	1700
	7044129	19/32	1 9/32	1 21/32	—	—	.140	—	.200	.250	1600
1975	7045101	19/32	1 7/32	1 19/32	—	—	.130	—	.375	.350	—
	7045102	19/32	1 7/32	1 19/32	—	—	.130	—	—	.350	—
	7045103	19/32	31/32	1 5/8	—	—	.130	—	.380	.350	—
	7045105	19/32	1 7/32	1 19/32	—	—	.130	—	.375	.350	—
	7045106	19/32	1 7/32	1 19/32	—	—	.130	—	.380	.350	—
	7045111	21/32	31/32	1 5/8	—	—	.130	—	.400	.350	—
	7045112	21/32	31/32	1 5/8	—	—	.130	—	.400	.350	—
	7045114	21/32	31/32	1 5/8	—	—	.130	—	.400	.350	—
	7045115	21/32	31/32	1 5/8	—	—	.130	—	.400	.350	—
	7045123	21/32	31/32	1 5/8	—	—	.130	—	.400	.350	—
	7045124	21/32	31/32	1 5/8	—	—	.130	—	.400	.350	—
	7045401	21/32	1 7/32	1 19/32	—	—	.130	—	.380	.350	—
	7045402	21/32	1 7/32	1 19/32	—	—	.130	—	.375	.350	—
	7045405	21/32	1 7/32	1 19/32	—	—	.130	—	.380	.350	—
	7045406	21/32	1 7/32	1 19/32	—	—	.130	—	.380	.350	—
	7045407	19/32	1 7/32	1 5/8	—	—	.130	—	.380	.350	—
	7045408	19/32	1 7/32	1 19/32	—	—	.130	—	.380	.350	—
	7045410	21/32	31/32	1 5/8	—	—	.130	—	.400	.350	—
	7045412	21/32	31/32	1 19/32	—	—	.130	—	.400	.350	—

②—Gauge from lip at toe of float to air horn gasket.   ③—At slow idle RPM vent valve should be opened to specified dimension.

DODGE AND PLYMOUTH

Year	Carb. Part No. ★	Float Level	Float Drop	Pump Rod	Idle Vent	Intermediate Choke Rod	Vacuum Break	Automatic Choke	Choke Rod	Choke Unloader	Fast Idle Speed
1971	7041180	21/32	1 3/4	1 5/64	—	—	41 Drill	—	—	29 Drill	1800

OLDSMOBILE

Year	Carb. Part No. ★	Float Level	Float Drop	Pump Rod	Idle Vent	Intermediate Choke Rod	Vacuum Break	Automatic Choke	Choke Rod	Choke Unloader	Fast Idle Speed
1969	7029155	9/16	1 3/8	1 7/16	.025②	—	.180	1 Lean	.140	.170	900③
	7029156	9/16	1 3/8	1 7/16	.025②	—	.180	On Index	.140	.170	900③
	7029158	9/16	1 3/8	1 7/16	.025②	—	.180	On Index	.140	.170	900③
	7029159	9/16	1 3/8	1 7/16	.025②	—	.180	On Index	.140	.170	900③
1970	7040154	9/16	1 3/8	1 11/32	—	—	.160	On Index	.140	.170	900③
	7040155	9/16	1 3/8	1 11/32	—	—	.160	1 Lean	.140	.170	900③
	7040156	9/16	1 3/8	1 11/32	—	—	.160	On Index	.140	.170	900③
	7040158	9/16	1 3/8	1 11/32	—	—	.160	On Index	.140	.170	900③
	7040159	9/16	1 3/8	1 11/32	—	—	.160	On Index	.140	.170	900③
1971	7041155	17/32	1 3/8	1 11/32	—	—	.200	1 Lean	.140	.170	1000③
	7041156	17/32	1 3/8	1 11/32	—	—	.200	On Index	.140	.170	1000③
	7041159	17/32	1 3/8	1 11/32	—	—	.215	On Index	.140	.170	1000③
1972	7042155	17/32	1 3/8	1 11/32	—	—	.215	1 Lean	.160	.170	1000③
	7042156	17/32	1 3/8	1 11/32	—	—	.200	On Index	.160	.170	1000③
1973	7043152	15/32	1 9/32	1 11/32	—	—	.200	On Index	.160	.250	900③
	7043154	15/32	1 9/32	1 11/32	—	—	.200	On Index	.160	.250	900③
	7043158	15/32	1 9/32	1 11/32	—	—	.200	On Index	.160	.250	900③
1974	7044159④	15/32	1 9/32	1 11/32	—	—	.200	On Index	.160	.250	900③
	7044162④	15/32	1 9/32	1 11/32	—	—	.250	On Index	.160	.250	1000③

②—At slow idle RPM vent valve should open to specified dimension.   ③—On low step of cam.   ④—California.

MODEL 2GC, 2GV CARBURETOR ADJUSTMENT SPECIFICATIONS—Continued

See Tune Up Chart in car chapters for hot idle speeds.

★Located on tag attached to or stamped on carburetor.

Year	Carb. Part No. ★	Float Level	Float Drop	Pump Rod	Idle Vent	Intermediate Choke Rod	Vacuum Break	Automatic Choke	Choke Rod	Choke Unloader	Fast Idle Speed
PONTIAC											
1969	7028066	9/16	1 3/4	1 11/32	—	—	.170	①	.085	.180	—
	7028071	9/16	1 3/4	1 11/32	—	—	.160	①	.085	.180	—
	7029060	9/16	1 3/4	1 11/32	—	—	.150	①	.085	.180	—
	7029062	9/16	1 3/4	1 11/32	—	—	.150	①	.085	.180	—
1970	7040060	11/16	1 3/8	1 11/32	—	—	.150	①	.085	.180	—
	7040062	9/16	1 3/8	1 11/32	—	—	.150	①	.085	.180	—
	7040064	11/16	1 3/8	1 11/32	—	—	.150	①	.085	.180	—
	7040066	11/16	1 3/8	1 11/32	—	—	.170	①	.085	.180	—
	7040071	9/16	1 3/8	1 11/32	—	—	.160	①	.085	.180	—
	7040072	9/16	1 3/8	1 11/32	—	—	.150	①	.085	.180	—
	7040460	11/16	1 3/8	1 11/32	—	—	.150	①	.085	.180	—
	7040461	11/16	1 3/8	1 11/32	—	—	.150	①	.080	.180	—
	7040462	9/16	1 3/8	1 11/32	—	—	.150	①	.085	.180	—
	7040463	9/16	1 3/8	1 11/32	—	—	.150	①	.085	.180	—
	7040466	11/16	1 3/8	1 11/32	—	—	.170	①	.085	.180	—
	7040471	9/16	1 3/8	1 11/32	—	—	.160	①	.085	.180	—
1971	7041060	11/16	1 3/4	1 11/32	—	—	.125	①	.085	.180	—
	7041061	11/16	1 3/4	1 11/32	—	—	.125	①	.085	.180	—
	7041062	9/16	1 3/4	1 11/32	—	—	.105	①	.085	.180	—
	7041063	9/16	1 3/4	1 11/32	—	—	.105	①	.085	.180	—
	7041064	11/16	1 3/4	1 11/32	—	—	.130	①	.085	.180	—
	7041070	11/16	1 3/4	1 11/32	—	—	.125	①	.085	.180	—
	7041072	9/16	1 3/4	1 11/32	—	—	.105	①	.085	.180	—
	7041074	11/16	1 3/4	1 11/32	—	—	.130	①	.085	.180	—
	7041101	27/32	1 3/4	1 13/32	—	—	.110	①	.075	.200	—
	7041110	27/32	1 3/4	1 13/32	—	—	.080	①	.040	.200	—
	7041171	9/16	1 3/8	1 11/32	—	—	.160	①	.085	.180	—
1972	7042060	11/16	1 9/32	1 11/32	—	—	.150	①	.085	.180	—
	7042061	11/16	1 9/32	1 11/32	—	—	.150	①	.085	.180	—
	7042062	11/16	1 9/32	1 11/32	—	—	.130	①	.085	.180	—
	7042064	11/16	1 9/32	1 11/32	—	—	.150	①	.085	.180	—
	7042065	21/32	1 3/8	1 11/32	—	—	.157	①	.085	.180	—
	7042067	11/16	1 9/32	1 11/32	—	—	.147	①	.085	.180	—
	7042073	21/32	1 3/8	1 11/32	—	—	.130	①	.085	.180	—
	7042076	11/16	1 9/32	1 11/32	—	—	.157	①	.085	.180	—
	7042078	11/16	1 9/32	1 11/32	—	—	.147	①	.085	.180	—
	7042100	25/32	1 31/32	1 5/16	—	—	.080	①	.040	.215	—
	7042101	25/32	1 31/32	1 5/16	—	—	.100	①	.075	.215	—
1973	7043061	21/32	1 9/32	1 11/32	—	—	.180	1 Lean	.085	.180	—
	7043063	21/32	1 9/32	1 5/16	—	—	.170	1 Lean	.085	.180	—
	7043066	21/32	1 9/32	1 11/32	—	—	.180	1 Lean	.085	.180	—
	7043067	21/32	1 9/32	1 11/32	—	—	.180	1 Lean	.085	.180	—
	7043073	21/32	1 9/32	1 5/16	—	—	.180	1 Lean	.085	.180	—
1973-74	7043060	21/32	1 9/32	1 11/32	—	—	.160	1 Lean	.085	.180	—
	7043062	21/32	1 9/32	1 5/16	—	—	.170	1 Lean	.085	.180	—
	7043070	23/32	1 9/32	1 11/32	—	—	.160	1 Lean	.085	.180	—
	7043071	23/32	1 9/32	1 5/16	—	—	.200	1 Lean	.085	.180	—
	7043072	23/32	1 9/32	1 5/16	—	—	.170	1 Lean	.085	.180	—
1974	7044063	21/32	1 9/32	1 5/16	—	—	.160	1 Lean	.085	.180	—
	7044066	21/32	1 9/32	1 11/32	—	—	.180	1 Lean	.085	.180	—
	7044067	21/32	1 9/32	1 11/32	—	—	.180	1 Lean	.085	.180	—

MODEL 2GC, 2GV CARBURETOR ADJUSTMENT SPECIFICATIONS—Continued

See Tune Up Chart in car chapters for hot idle speeds.

★Located on tag attached to or stamped on carburetor.

Year	Carb. Part No. ★	Float Level	Float Drop	Pump Rod	Idle Vent	Intermediate Choke Rod	Vacuum Break	Automatic Choke	Choke Rod	Choke Unloader	Fast Idle Speed
PONTIAC—Continued											
1975	7045143	15/32	—	1 13/16	.025	—	.140③	—	.080	.180	—
	7045160	9/16	1 7/32	1 3/4	.025	—	.145③	—	.085	.180	—
	7045162	9/16	1 7/32	1 13/16	.025	—	.145④	—	.085	.180	—
	7045171	9/16	1 7/32	1 13/16	.025	—	.145④	—	.085	.180	—

①—With choke valve closed, pull upward on choke rod to the limit of its travel. The end of rod should fit the gauge notch on the choke lever.
②—Rear .120".   ③—Rear .265".   ④—Rear .260".

MODEL 2GC, 2GV ADJUSTMENTS

Models 2GC and 2GV use an automatic choke, Figs. 1 and 2.

There are two different types of automatic choke systems used on these units; 1) The carburetor mounted thermostatic coil, Fig. 3 and, 2) the well type, Fig. 4.

Float Level Adjustment

Fig. 5—Adjust float level as directed for the type of float shown in the specification listed in the *Rochester Specifications Chart.*

Float Drop Adjustment

Fig. 6—Adjust float drop as directed for the type of float shown in the specification listed in the *Rochester Specifications Chart.*

Pump Rod Adjustment

Fig. 7—Back out idle stop screw and completely close throttle valves in bore. Place proper size gauge listed in the *Rochester Specifications Chart* on top of air horn ring. Bend pump rod at lower angle to obtain specified dimension to top of pump rod.

Idle Vent Adjustment

Fig. 8—Open throttle until vent valve just closes. Place proper size gauge on top of air horn ring. Dimension to top of pump rod should be as specified in the *Rochester Specifications Chart.* Adjust by bending tang on pump lever.

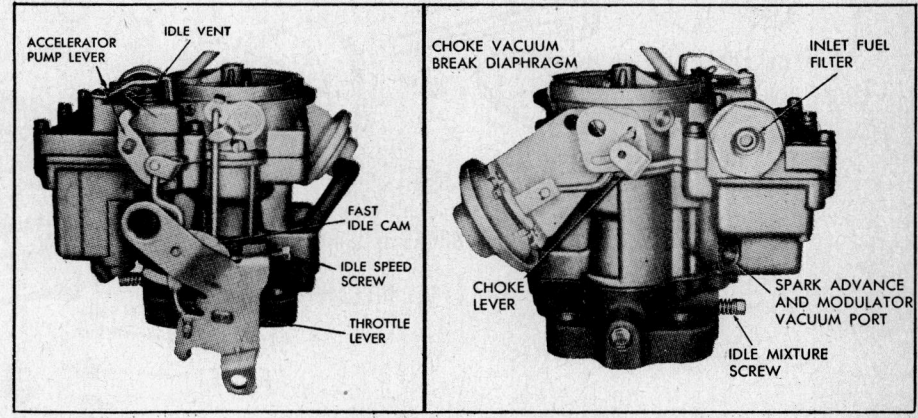

Fig. 1   Rochester Model 2GV two-barrel carburetor

Intermediate Choke Rod Adjustment

Choke Mounted on Throttle Body, Fig. 9 —Remove thermostat cover and coil assembly and inside baffle plate. Hold choke valve completely closed and bend intermediate choke rod as necessary to that end of choke piston is as specified in the *Rochester Specifications Chart* with end of choke piston bore.

Vacuum Break Adjustment

Model 2GV, Fig. 10—Push vacuum break diaphragm plunger in until it is seated and make sure choke valve is closed so that connecting rod is at end of slot in choke shaft lever. In this position, adjust rod by bending so that specified gauge will fit between upper edge of choke valve and inner wall of air horn (see *Rochester Specifications Chart*). Adjust by bending connecting rod at point shown.

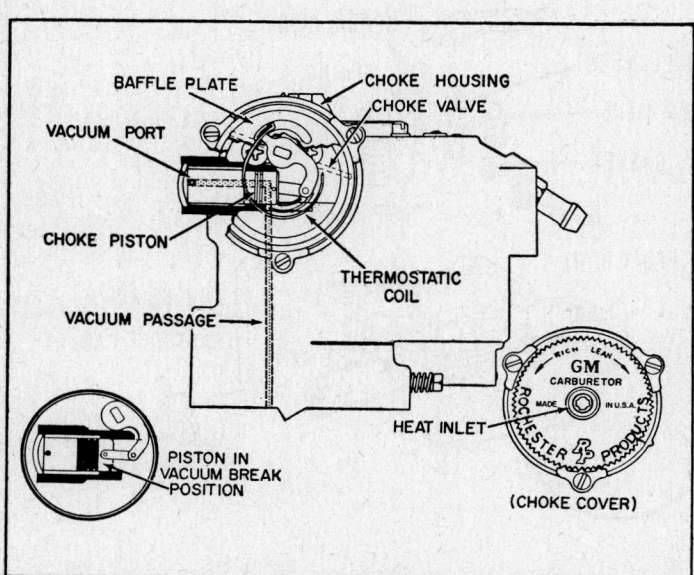

Fig. 3   Carburetor mounted automatic choke

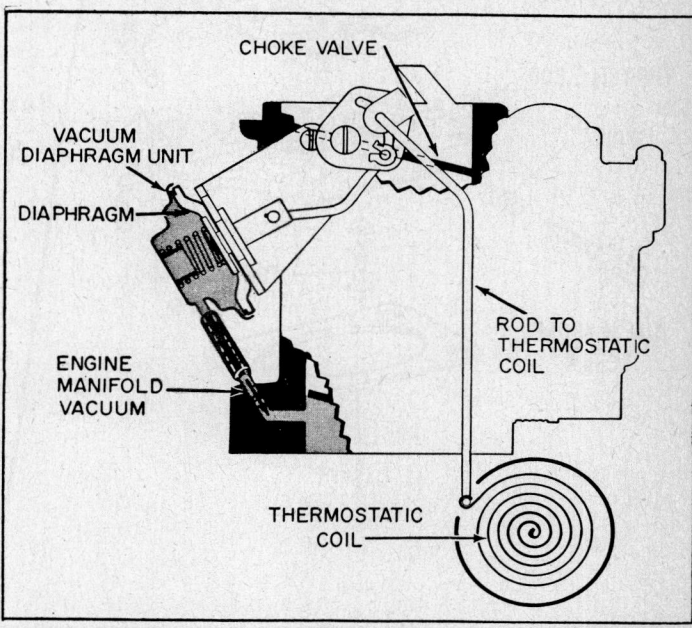

Fig. 4   Well-type choke. 2GV models

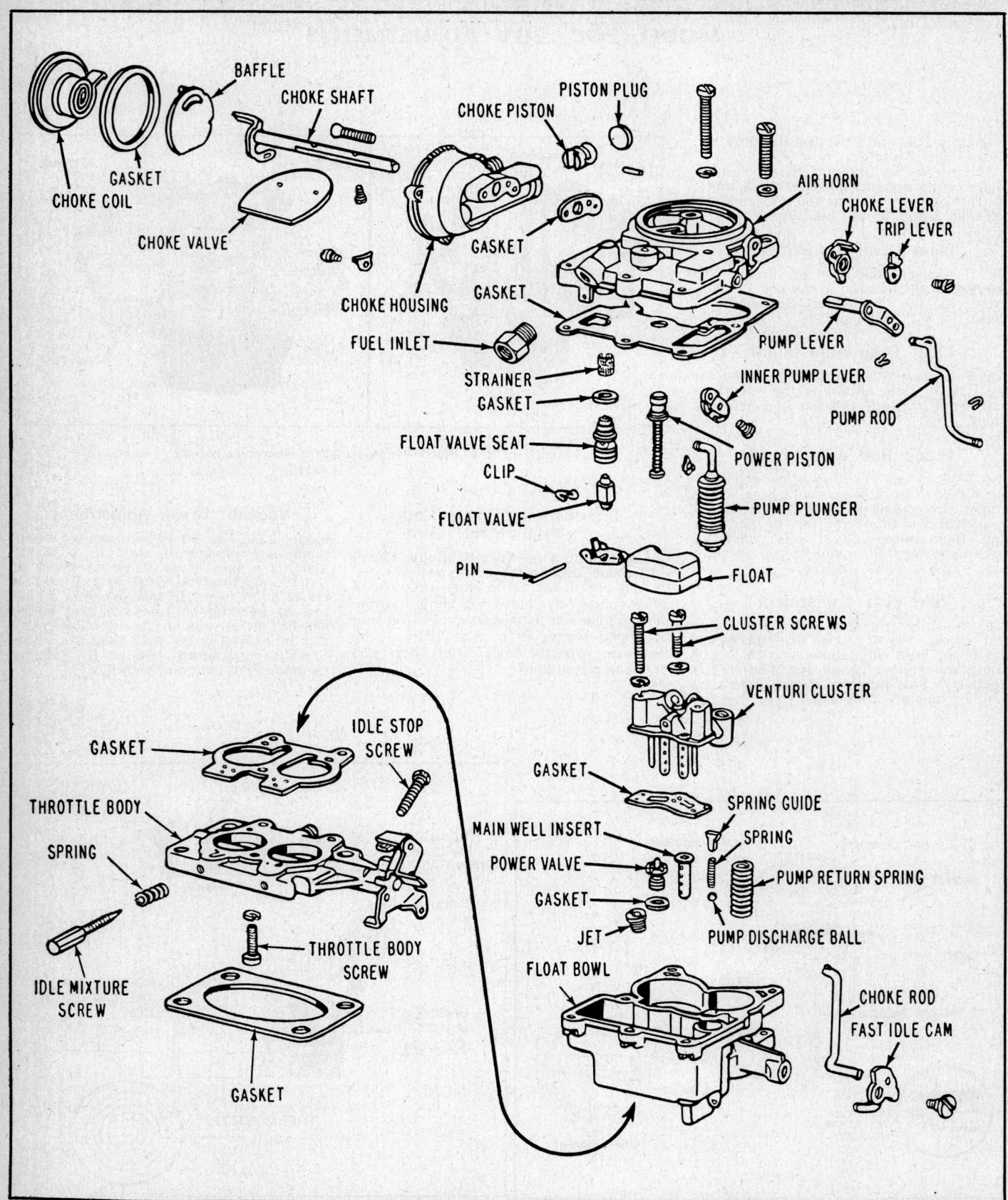

Fig. 2 Exploded view of typical Rochester two-barrel carburetor

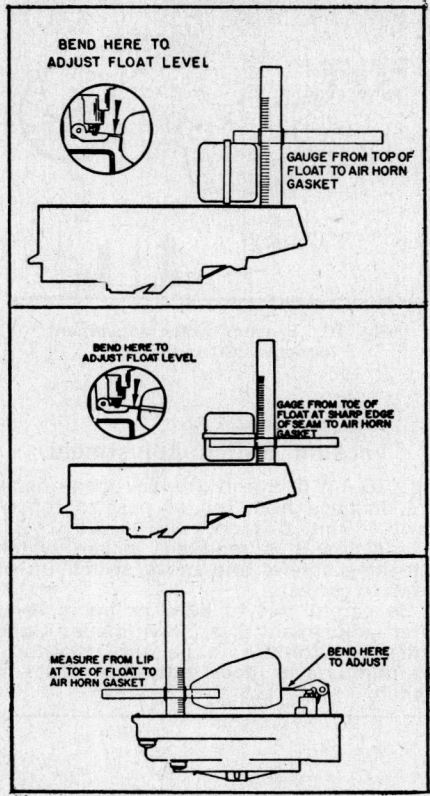

Fig. 5   Float level adjustment.
Model 2GC, 2GV

Automatic Choke Setting

Carburetor Mounted Choke, Fig. 11—
Loosen three retaining screws and rotate
choke cover against coil tension until
index mark is in line with specified point
on choke housing (see *Rochester Specifications Chart*).

Choke Rod Adjustment

Fig. 12—It is important to position both
slow idle and fast idle screws as follows

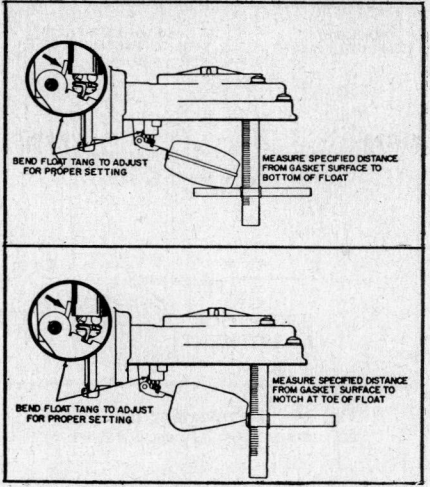

Fig. 6   Float drop adjustment.
Model 2GC, 2GV

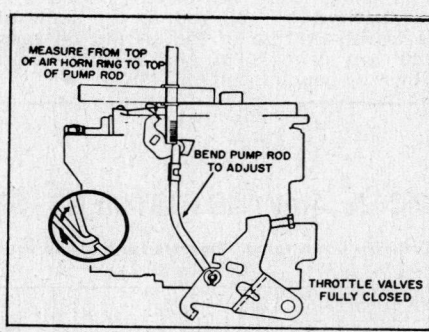

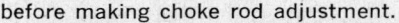

Fig. 7   Pump rod adjustment
for 2GC, 2GV carburetors

before making choke rod adjustment.
1. On models using a single idle stop
   screw, turn stop screw in until it
   just contacts bottom step of fast idle
   cam. Then turn screw in one full
   turn farther.
2. On models using both a slow idle
   and a fast idle screw, turn slow idle
   stop screw in until it just contacts
   stop. Then turn this screw in one
   full turn from this point. Next turn
   the fast idle screw in until it touches
   bottom step of fast idle cam.
3. On all models, place idle screw on

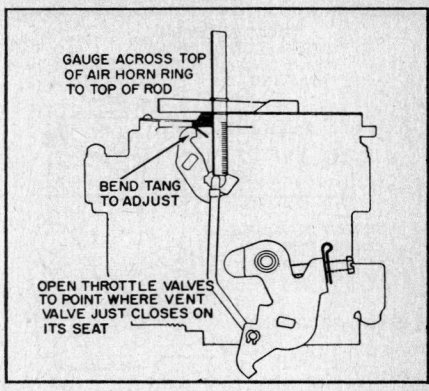

Fig. 8   Idle vent adjustment
for 2GC, 2GV carburetors

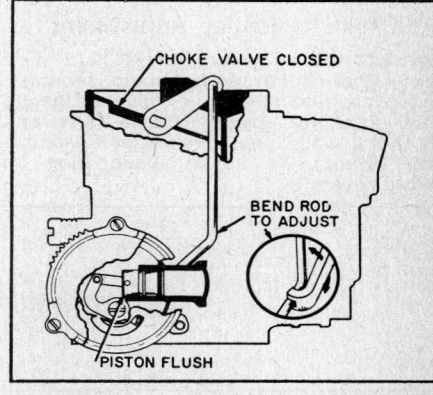

Fig. 9   Intermediate choke rod adjustment
for 2GC chokes mounted on throttle body

second step of fast idle cam against
shoulder of high step. While holding
screw in this position, check clearance between upper edge of choke
valve and air horn wall as shown.
Adjust to specified dimension by
bending tang on choke lever and collar assembly (see *Rochester Specifications Chart*).

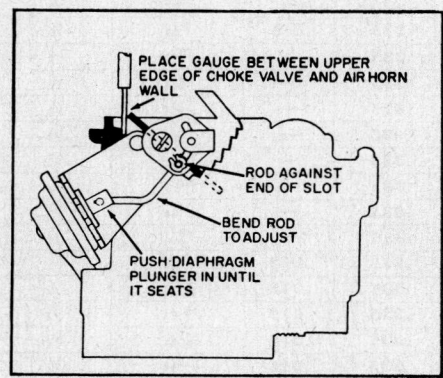

Fig. 10   Vacuum break adjustment
for 2GV carburetors

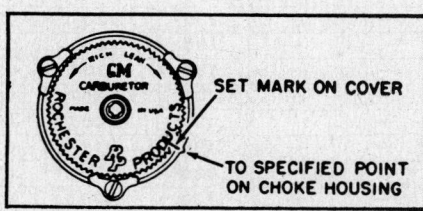

Fig. 11   Automatic choke adjustment
for 2GC carburetors

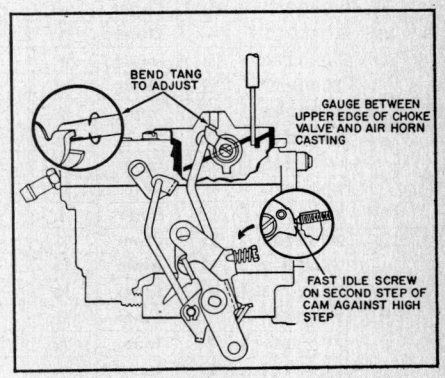

Fig. 12   Choke rod adjustment

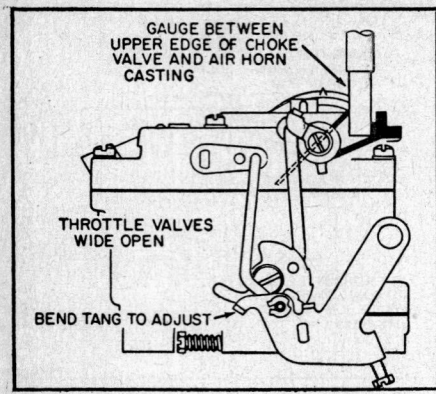

Fig. 13 Choke unloader adjustment for 2GC, 2GV carburetors

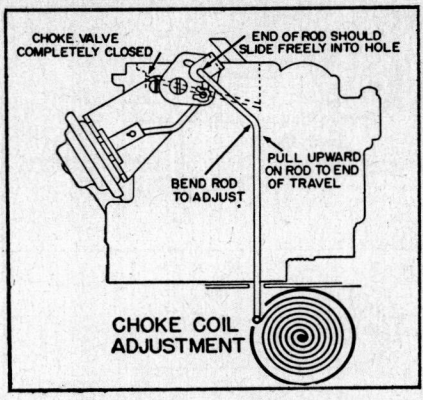

Fig. 14 Thermostatic coil rod adjustment for 2GV carburetors

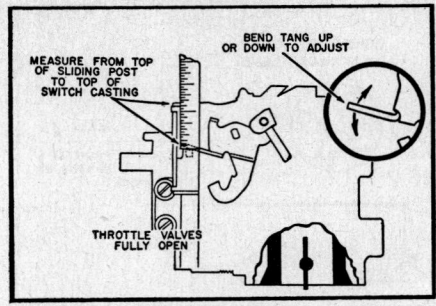

Fig. 15 Vacuum switch adjustment for some 2GC carburetors

Choke Unloader Adjustment

Fig. 13—With throttle valves held wide open, the choke valve should be open just enough to admit the specified gauge between upper edge of choke valve and air horn wall (see *Rochester Specifications Chart*). To adjust, bend tang on throttle lever.

Thermostatic Coil Rod Adjustment

Model 2GV, Fig. 14—Disconnect upper end of thermostatic coil rod from choke lever. Hold choke valve completely closed and pull upward on coil rod to the limit of its travel. Bottom of rod should be even with top of hole in choke shaft lever. Adjust by bending coil rod.

Vacuum Switch Adjustment

Fig. 15—With throttle wide open measure distance from top of post to top of switch. This distance should be $1\frac{3}{32}$". If adjustment is required, loosen switch attaching screws and move switch up or down to correct.

Be careful not to bend or bump lever after adjustment has been made. Open and close throttle to be sure that arm on pump lever does not bind post on switch.

QUADRAJET 4MC & 4MV ADJUSTMENT SPECIFICATIONS

See Tune Up Chart in car chapters for hot idle speeds.

Year	Carb. Model	Float Level	Pump Rod Hole	Pump Rod Adj.	Idle Vent	Air Valve	Fast Idle (Bench)	Choke Rod	Vacuum Break	Air Valve Dashpot	Choke Unloader	Air Valve Lockout	Secondary Metering Rods	Air-Valve Valve Spring Wind-Up
BUICK														
1969	7029240	$\frac{3}{8}$	Outer	$\frac{13}{32}$	$\frac{1}{2}$	—	—	.130	.180	.030	.325	.045	$\frac{53}{64}$	$\frac{1}{2}$
	7029241	$\frac{5}{16}$	Outer	$\frac{13}{32}$	$\frac{1}{2}$	—	—	.130	.180	.030	.325	.045	$\frac{53}{64}$	$\frac{1}{2}$
	7029242	$\frac{3}{8}$	Outer	$\frac{13}{32}$	$\frac{1}{2}$	—	—	.130	.180	.030	.325	.045	$\frac{53}{64}$	$\frac{1}{2}$
	7029243	$\frac{3}{8}$	Outer	$\frac{13}{32}$	$\frac{1}{2}$	—	—	.140	.215	.030	.325	.015	$\frac{53}{64}$	$\frac{1}{2}$
	7029244	$\frac{5}{16}$	Outer	$\frac{13}{32}$	$\frac{1}{2}$	—	2 Turns	.130	.190	.030	.325	.045	$\frac{53}{64}$	$\frac{1}{2}$
	7029245	$\frac{5}{16}$	Outer	$\frac{13}{32}$	$\frac{1}{2}$	—	2 Turns	.130	.215	.030	.325	.015	$\frac{53}{64}$	$\frac{1}{2}$
1970	7040240	$\frac{3}{8}$	Inner	$\frac{9}{32}$	—	—	—	.130	.180	.030	.335	—	$\frac{53}{64}$	$\frac{1}{2}$
	7040243	$\frac{3}{8}$	Inner	$\frac{9}{32}$	—	—	—	.130	.215	.030	.335	—	$\frac{53}{64}$	$\frac{1}{2}$
	7040244	$\frac{5}{16}$	Outer	$\frac{13}{32}$	—	—	—	.130	.170	.030	.335	.045	$\frac{53}{64}$	$\frac{1}{2}$
	7040245	$\frac{5}{16}$	Outer	$\frac{13}{32}$	—	—	—	.130	.215	.030	.335	—	$\frac{53}{64}$	$\frac{1}{2}$
	7040246	$\frac{5}{16}$	Inner	$\frac{9}{32}$	—	—	—	.130	.200	.030	.335	—	$\frac{53}{64}$	$\frac{1}{2}$
	7040247	$\frac{3}{8}$	Inner	$\frac{9}{32}$	—	—	—	.130	.160	.030	.325	—	$\frac{53}{64}$	$\frac{1}{2}$
1971	7041242	$\frac{3}{8}$	Inner	$\frac{1}{4}$	—	—	—	.130	.200⑤	.030	.335	—	$\frac{53}{64}$	$\frac{1}{2}$
	7041243	$\frac{13}{32}$	Inner	$\frac{1}{4}$	—	—	—	.130	.215⑥	.030	.335	—	$\frac{53}{64}$	$\frac{1}{2}$
	7041245	$\frac{15}{32}$	Inner	$\frac{9}{32}$	—	—	—	.130	.170①	.030	.335	—	$\frac{53}{64}$	$\frac{1}{2}$
	7041540	$\frac{3}{8}$	Inner	$\frac{1}{4}$	—	—	—	.130	.180⑤	.030	.335	—	$\frac{53}{64}$	$\frac{1}{2}$
	7041544	$\frac{15}{32}$	Inner	$\frac{9}{32}$	—	—	—	.130	.170①	.030	.335	—	$\frac{53}{64}$	$\frac{1}{2}$
1972	7042240	$\frac{3}{8}$	Inner	$\frac{1}{4}$	—	—	—	.130	.180⑤	.030	.335	.015	$\frac{53}{64}$	$\frac{1}{2}$
	7042242	$\frac{3}{8}$	Inner	$\frac{1}{4}$	—	—	—	.130	.200⑤	.030	.335	.015	$\frac{53}{64}$	$\frac{1}{2}$
	7042243	$\frac{13}{32}$	Inner	$\frac{1}{4}$	—	—	—	.130	.215⑥	.030	.335	.015	$\frac{53}{64}$	$\frac{1}{2}$
	7042244	$\frac{15}{32}$	Inner	$\frac{9}{32}$	—	—	—	.130	.170①	.030	.335	.015	$\frac{53}{64}$	$\frac{1}{2}$
	7042245	$\frac{15}{32}$	Inner	$\frac{9}{32}$	—	—	—	.130	.170①	.030	.335	.015	$\frac{53}{64}$	$\frac{1}{2}$
	7042940	$\frac{3}{8}$	Inner	$\frac{1}{4}$	—	—	—	.130	.180⑤	.030	.335	.015	$\frac{53}{64}$	$\frac{1}{2}$

Continued

QUADRAJET 4MC & 4MV ADJUSTMENT SPECIFICATIONS—Continued

See Tune Up Chart in car chapters for hot idle speeds.

Year	Carb. Model	Float Level	Pump Rod Hole	Pump Rod Adj.	Idle Vent	Air Valve	Fast Idle (Bench)	Choke Rod	Vacuum Break	Air Valve Dashpot	Choke Unloader	Air Valve Lockout	Secondary Metering Rods	Air-Valve Valve Spring Wind-Up
BUICK—Continued														
1972	7042942	$3/8$	Inner	$1/4$	—	—	—	.130	.200⑤	.030	.335	.015	$53/64$	$1/2$
	7042944	$15/32$	Inner	$9/32$	—	—	—	.130	.170①	.030	.335	.015	$53/64$	$1/2$
1973	7043240	$13/32$	Inner	$1/4$	—	—	2	.130	.215⑤	.030	.325	.015	$53/64$	$7/16$
	7043242	$13/32$	Inner	$7/16$	—	—	2	.130	.200⑤	.030	.325	.015	$53/64$	$7/16$
	7043243	$13/32$	Inner	$7/16$	—	—	2	.130	.215⑥	.030	.325	.015	$53/64$	$7/16$
	7043244	$15/32$	Outer	$3/8$	—	—	2	.130	.170①	.030	.325	.015	$53/64$	$11/16$
	7043245	$15/32$	Inner	$9/32$	—	—	2	.130	.170①	.030	.325	.015	$53/64$	$11/16$
	7043246	$15/32$	Outer	$3/8$	—	—	2	.130	.170①	.030	.325	.015	$53/64$	$11/16$
1974	7044240	$13/32$	Inner	$1/4$	—	—	2	.130	.215⑤	.030	.325	.015	$53/64$	$7/16$
	7044241	$13/32$	Inner	$1/4$	—	—	2	.130	.215⑥	.030	.325	.015	$53/64$	$7/16$
	7044242	$13/32$	Inner	$1/4$	—	—	2	.130	.200⑦	.030	.325	.015	$53/64$	$7/16$
	7044244	$15/32$	Outer	$3/8$	—	—	2	.130	.170①	.030	.325	.015	$53/64$	$11/16$
	7044246	$15/32$	Outer	$3/8$	—	—	2	.130	.170①	.030	.325	.015	$53/64$	$11/16$
	7044540	$13/32$	Inner	$1/4$	—	—	2	.130	.215⑤	.030	.325	.015	$53/64$	$7/16$
	7044544	$15/32$	Outer	$3/8$	—	—	2	.130	.170①	.030	.325	.015	$53/64$	$11/16$
	7044546	$15/32$	Outer	$3/8$	—	—	2	.130	.170①	.030	.325	.015	$53/64$	$11/16$
	7044547	$15/32$	Outer	$3/8$	—	—	2	.130	.170①	.030	.325	.015	$53/64$	$11/16$
	7044549	$15/32$	Outer	$3/8$	—	—	2	.130	.170①	.030	.325	.015	$53/64$	$11/16$
	7044551	$13/32$	Inner	$1/4$	—	—	2	.130	.215⑤	.030	.325	.015	$53/64$	$7/16$
1975	7045240	$7/16$	Inner	$9/32$	—	—	—	.095	.135⑧	—	.240	.015	—	$7/16$
	7045241	$5/16$	Outer	$15/32$	—	—	—	.095	.135⑨	—	.240	.015	—	$3/4$
	7045244	$5/16$	Outer	$15/32$	—	—	—	.095	.130⑨	—	.240	.015	—	$3/4$
	7045246	$5/16$	Outer	$15/32$	—	—	—	.095	.130⑨	—	.240	.015	—	$3/4$
	7045544	$5/16$	Outer	$15/32$	—	—	—	.095	.145⑩	—	.240	.015	—	$3/4$
	7045546	$5/16$	Outer	$15/32$	—	—	—	.095	.145⑩	—	.240	.015	—	$3/4$
	7045548	$7/16$	Inner	$9/32$	—	—	—	.095	.135⑧	—	.240	.015	—	$7/16$
	7045549	$7/16$	Inner	$9/32$	—	—	—	.095	.135⑧	—	.240	.015	—	$7/16$
	7045551	$7/16$	Inner	$9/32$	—	—	—	.095	.135⑧	—	.240	.015	—	$7/16$
	7045553	$5/16$	Outer	$15/32$	—	—	—	.095	.145⑨	—	.240	.015	—	$3/4$
	7045554	$5/16$	Outer	$15/32$	—	—	—	.095	.145⑩	—	.240	.015	—	$3/4$

①—Secondary adjustment .150".
②—Early $3/8$"; late $7/16$".
③—Early, inner; late, outer.
④—Early $9/32$"; late $13/32$".
⑤—Secondary adjustment .160".
⑥—Secondary adjustment .195".
⑦—Secondary adjustment .180".
⑧—Rear .120.
⑨—Rear .115.
⑩—Rear .130.

CADILLAC

Year	Carb. Model	Float Level	Pump Rod Hole	Pump Rod Adj.	Idle Vent	Air Valve	Fast Idle (Bench)	Choke Rod	Vacuum Break	Air Valve Dashpot	Choke Unloader	Air Valve Lockout	Secondary Metering Rods	Air-Valve Valve Spring Wind-Up
1969	7029230	$1/4$	Outer	$11/32$	—	—	1½ Turns	.090	.230	.030	.300	.015	$27/32$	$1/2$
	7029231	$1/4$	Outer	$11/32$	—	—	1½ Turns	.090	.230	.030	.300	.015	$27/32$	$1/2$
1970	7047030	$1/4$	Outer	$11/32$	—	—	1½ Turns	.090	.230	.030	.300	.015	$27/32$	$1/2$
1971	7041766	$1/4$	Outer	$11/32$	—	—	1½ Turns	.090	.300	.030	.310	.015	.840	$1/2$
	7041777	$23/64$	Outer	$11/32$	—	—	1½ Turns	.090	.300	.030	.310	.015	.840	$1/2$
1972	7047231	$15/64$	Outer	$11/32$	—	—	1½ Turns	.090	.140	.030	.310	.015	.840	$9/16$
	7047232	$23/64$	Outer	$11/32$	—	—	1½ Turns	.090	.140	.030	.310	.015	.840	$9/16$
1973	7047331	$1/4$	Outer	$11/32$	—	—	①	.090	.200	.030	.310	.015	.840	$5/16$
	7047332	$23/64$	Outer	$11/32$	—	—	①	.090	.205	.030	.310	.015	.840	$3/8$
	7043230	$1/4$	Outer	—	—	—	1½ Turns	.090	.200	—	.310	.030	—	—
	7043232	$3/8$	③	—	—	—	1½ Turns	.090	.200	—	.310	.030	—	—
	7043233	$5/16$	Outer	—	—	—	1½ Turns	.090	.180	—	.310	.030	—	—
	7043234	$1/4$	Inner	—	—	—	1½ Turns	.090	.200	—	.310	.030	—	—
	7043235	$3/8$	③	—	—	—	1½ Turns	.090	.215	—	.310	.030	—	—
1974	7044230	.250	Inner	.250	—	—	②	.110	.185	.030	.312	.015	.840	④
	7044232	.360	Inner	.250	—	—	②	.110	.200	.030	.312	.015	.840	④
	7044233	.290	Outer	.344	—	—	②	.110	.185	.030	.312	.015	.840	$3/8$
	7044234	.250	Inner	.344	—	—	②	.110	.185	.030	.312	.015	.840	$7/16$
	7044235	.360	Inner	.344	—	—	②	.110	.200	.030	.312	.015	.840	$9/16$
	7047430	.250	Inner	—	—	—	②	.110	.185	—	.310	.015	—	—
	7047431	.250	Inner	—	—	—	②	.110	.185	—	.310	.015	—	—

Continued

GM DELCO/ROCHESTER CARBURETORS

QUADRAJET 4MC & 4MV ADJUSTMENT SPECIFICATIONS—Continued

See Tune Up Chart in car chapters for hot idle speeds.

Year	Carb. Model	Float Level	Pump Rod Hole	Pump Rod Adj.	Idle Vent	Air Valve	Fast Idle (Bench)	Choke Rod	Vacuum Break	Air Valve Dash-pot	Choke Unloader	Air Valve Lockout	Secondary Metering Rods	Air-Valve Valve Spring Wind-Up
CADILLAC—Continued														
1974	7047432	.360	Inner	—	—	—	②	.110	.200	—	.310	.015	—	—
	7047433	.290	Outer	—	—	—	②	.110	.185	—	.310	.015	—	—
	7047434	.360	Inner	—	—	—	②	.110	.200	—	.310	.015	—	—
	7044530	.250	Inner	.250	—	—	②	.110	.185	.030	.312	.015	.840	⅜
	7044532	.360	Inner	.250	—	—	②	.110	.200	.030	.312	.015	.840	½
	17050631	.360	Outer	—	—	—	②	.110	.200	—	.310	.015	—	—
	17050632	.250	Outer	—	—	—	②	.110	.185	—	.310	.015	—	—
1975	7045230	¹⁵⁄₃₂	Outer	⅜	.075	—	2 Turns	.080	⑤	.030	.215	.015	—	⁷⁄₁₆
	7045530	¹⁵⁄₃₂	Outer	⅜	.075	—	2¼ Turns	.080	.230	.030	.215	.015	—	¼

①—1925 RPM on engine. ②—1200–1250 RPM on second step and A/C off. ③—Exc. Calif., Inner; California, Outer. ④—Up to 4,000 ft. altitude, ½ turn. Above 4,000 ft. altitude, ⁵⁄₁₆ turn for Eldorado, ⁷⁄₁₆ turn for all others exc. commercial vehicles and ⅜ for commercial vehicles. ⑤—Front .160″, rear .130″.

Year	Carb. Model	Float Level	Pump Rod Hole	Pump Rod Adj.	Idle Vent	Air Valve	Fast Idle (Bench)	Choke Rod	Vacuum Break	Air Valve Dash-pot	Choke Unloader	Air Valve Lockout	Secondary Metering Rods	Air-Valve Valve Spring Wind-Up
CHECKER MOTORS														
1970	7029202	⁷⁄₃₂	Inner	—	⅜	—	2 Turns	.100	.180	.015	.450	—	—	—
	7040202	¼	Inner	—	—	—	2 Turns	.100	.245	.020	.400	—	—	—
	7040502	¼	Inner	—	—	—	2 Turns	.100	.245	.020	.450	—	—	—
1972	7042202	¼	Inner	—	—	—	2 Turns	.100	.215	.020	.450	—	—	—
	7042210	³⁄₁₆	Inner	—	—	—	2 Turns	.100	.215	.020	.450	—	—	—
	7042902	¼	Inner	—	—	—	2 Turns	.100	.215	.020	.450	—	—	—
	7042910	³⁄₁₆	Inner	—	—	—	2 Turns	.100	.215	.020	.450	—	—	—
1973	7043202	¼	Inner	—	—	—	2 Turns	.430	.250	—	.450	—	—	—
1974	7044502	¼	Inner	—	—	—	—	.430	.230	—	.450	—	—	⅞
CHEVROLET ENGINES														
1969	7029202	⁷⁄₃₂	Inner	⁵⁄₁₆	⅜	—	2 Turns	.100	.180	.015	.450	.015	—	⁷⁄₁₆
	7029203	⁷⁄₃₂	Inner	⁵⁄₁₆	⅜	—	2 Turns	.100	.245	.015	.450	.015	—	⁷⁄₁₆
	7029204	¼	Inner	⁵⁄₁₆	⅜	—	2 Turns	.100	.180	.015	.450	.015	—	¹³⁄₁₆
	7029207	³⁄₁₆	Inner	⁵⁄₁₆	⅜	—	2 Turns	.100	.245	.015	.450	.015	—	¹³⁄₁₆
	7029215	¼	Inner	⁵⁄₁₆	⅜	—	2 Turns	.100	.245	.015	.450	.015	—	¹³⁄₁₆
1970	7040200	¼	Inner	⁵⁄₁₆	—	—	2 Turns	.100	.245	.020	.400	.015	—	¹³⁄₁₆
	7040201	¼	Inner	⁵⁄₁₆	—	—	2 Turns	.100	.275	.020	.450	.015	—	¹³⁄₁₆
	7040202	¼	Inner	⁵⁄₁₆	—	—	2 Turns	.100	.245	.020	.400	.015	—	⁷⁄₁₆
	7040203	¼	Inner	⁵⁄₁₆	—	—	2 Turns	.100	.275	.020	.450	.015	—	⁷⁄₁₆
	7040204	¼	Inner	⁵⁄₁₆	—	—	2 Turns	.100	.245	.020	.400	.015	—	¹³⁄₁₆
	7040205	¼	Inner	⁵⁄₁₆	—	—	2 Turns	.100	.275	.020	.450	—	—	¹³⁄₁₆
	7040207	¼	Inner	⁵⁄₁₆	—	—	2 Turns	.100	.275	.015	.450	—	—	¹³⁄₁₆
	7040500	¼	Inner	⁵⁄₁₆	—	—	2 Turns	.100	.245	.020	.450	.015	—	¹³⁄₁₆
	7040501	¼	Inner	⁵⁄₁₆	—	—	2 Turns	.100	.275	.020	.450	.015	—	¹³⁄₁₆
	7040502	¼	Inner	⁵⁄₁₆	—	—	2 Turns	.100	.245	.020	.450	.015	—	⁷⁄₁₆
	7040503	¼	Inner	⁵⁄₁₆	—	—	2 Turns	.100	.275	.020	.450	.015	—	⁷⁄₁₆
	7040505	¼	Inner	⁵⁄₁₆	—	—	2 Turns	.100	.275	.020	.450	.015	—	¹³⁄₁₆
	7040507	³⁄₁₆	—	⁵⁄₁₆	—	—	2 Turns	.100	.275	.020	.450	—	—	¹³⁄₁₆
	7040509	¼	—	⁵⁄₁₆	—	—	2 Turns	.100	.275	.020	.450	—	—	¹³⁄₁₆
	7040511	¼	—	⁵⁄₁₆	—	—	2 Turns	.100	.245	.020	.450	—	—	⁷⁄₁₆
1971	7041200	¼	—	—	—	—	—	.100	.260	.020	.450	—	—	⁷⁄₁₆
	7041201	¼	Inner	—	—	—	2 Turns	.100	.275	.020	.450	—	—	⁷⁄₁₆
	7041202	¼	Inner	—	—	—	2 Turns	.100	.260	.020	.450	—	—	⁷⁄₁₆
	7041203	¼	Inner	—	—	—	2 Turns	.100	.275	.020	.450	—	—	⁷⁄₁₆

Continued

QUADRAJET 4MC & 4MV ADJUSTMENT SPECIFICATIONS—Continued

See Tune Up Chart in car chapters for hot idle speeds.

Year	Carb. Model	Float Level	Pump Rod Hole	Pump Rod Adj.	Idle Vent	Air Valve	Fast Idle (Bench)	Choke Rod	Vacuum Break	Air Valve Dash-pot	Choke Unloader	Air Valve Lockout	Secondary Metering Rods	Air-Valve Valve Spring Wind-Up
CHEVROLET ENGINES—Continued														
1971	7041204	¼	Inner	—	—	—	2 Turns	.100	.260	.020	.450	—	—	7/16
	7041205	¼	Inner	—	—	—	2 Turns	.100	.275	.020	.450	—	—	7/16
	7041212	¼	Inner	—	—	—	2 Turns	.100	.260	.020	—	—	—	7/16
	7041213	¼	Inner	—	—	—	2 Turns	.100	.275	.020	.450	—	—	7/16
1972	7042202	¼	—	3/8	—	—	—	.100	.215	.020	.450	—	—	½
	7042203	¼	—	3/8	—	—	—	.100	.215	.020	.450	—	—	½
	7042215	¼	—	3/8	—	—	—	.100	.250	.020	.450	—	—	7/16
	7042216	¼	—	3/8	—	—	—	.100	.250	.020	.450	—	—	7/16
	7042217	¼	—	3/8	—	—	—	.100	.250	.020	.450	—	—	7/16
	7042220	¼	—	3/8	—	—	—	.100	.250	.020	.450	—	—	7/16
	7042902	¼	—	3/8	—	—	—	.100	.215	.020	.450	—	—	½
	7042903	¼	—	3/8	—	—	—	.100	.215	.020	.450	—	—	½
1973	7043200	¼	Inner	13/32	—	—	2 Turns	.430	.250	—	.450	.015	—	11/16
	7043201	¼	Inner	13/32	—	—	2 Turns	.430	.250	—	.450	.015	—	11/16
	7043202	¼	Inner	13/32	—	—	2 Turns	.430	.250	—	.450	.015	—	½
	7043203	¼	Inner	13/32	—	—	2 Turns	.430	.250	—	.450	.015	—	½
	7043212	¼	Inner	13/32	—	—	2 Turns	.430	.215	—	.450	.015	—	¾
	7043213	¼	Inner	13/32	—	—	2 Turns	.430	.215	—	.450	.015	—	¾
1974	7044201	3/8	Inner	13/32	—	—	2 Turns	.430	.250	.015	.450	—	—	7/16
	7044202	¼	Inner	13/32	—	—	2 Turns	.430	.230	.015	.450	—	—	7/8
	7044203	¼	Inner	13/32	—	—	2 Turns	.430	.230	.015	.450	—	—	7/8
	7044206	¼	Inner	13/32	—	—	2 Turns	.430	.230	.015	.450	—	—	7/8
	7044207	¼	Inner	13/32	—	—	2 Turns	.430	.230	.015	.450	—	—	7/8
	7044208	¼	Inner	13/32	—	—	2 Turns	.430	.230	.015	.450	—	—	1 Turn
	7044209	¼	Inner	13/32	—	—	2 Turns	.430	.230	.015	.450	—	—	1 Turn
	7044210	¼	Inner	13/32	—	—	2 Turns	.430	.230	.015	.450	—	—	1 Turn
	7044211	¼	Inner	13/32	—	—	2 Turns	.430	.230	.015	.450	—	—	1 Turn
	7044221	3/8	Inner	13/32	—	—	2 Turns	.430	.250	.015	.450	—	—	7/16
	7044223	3/8	Inner	13/32	—	—	2 Turns	.430	.250	.015	.450	—	—	7/16
	7044225	3/8	Inner	13/32	—	—	2 Turns	.430	.250	.015	.450	—	—	7/16
	7044500	3/8	Inner	—	—	—	2 Turns	.430	.250	.015	.450	—	—	7/16
	7044502	¼	Inner	13/32	—	—	2 Turns	.430	.230	.015	.450	—	—	7/8
	7044503	¼	Inner	13/32	—	—	2 Turns	.430	.230	.015	.450	—	—	7/8
	7044505	3/8	Inner	—	—	—	2 Turns	.430	.250	.015	.450	—	—	7/16
	7044506	¼	Inner	13/32	—	—	2 Turns	.430	.230	.015	.450	—	—	7/8
	7044507	¼	Inner	13/32	—	—	2 Turns	.430	.230	.015	.450	—	—	7/8
	7044508	3/8	Inner	13/32	—	—	2 Turns	.430	.250	.015	.450	—	—	7/16
	7044509	¼	Inner	13/32	—	—	2 Turns	.430	.230	.015	.450	—	—	7/8
1975	7045200	17/32	Inner	.275	—	—	—	.300	①	.015	.325	—	—	9/16
	7045202	15/32	Inner	.275	—	—	—	.300	②	.015	.325	—	—	7/8
	7045203	15/32	Inner	.275	—	—	—	.300	②	.015	.325	—	—	7/8
	7045204	15/32	Inner	.275	—	—	—	.325	①	.015	.325	—	—	7/8
	7045206	15/32	Inner	.275	—	—	—	.300	②	.015	.325	—	—	7/8
	7045207	15/32	Inner	.275	—	—	—	.300	②	.015	.325	—	—	7/8
	7045208	15/32	Inner	.275	—	—	—	.300	②	.015	.325	—	—	7/8
	7045209	15/32	Inner	.275	—	—	—	.300	②	.015	.325	—	—	7/8
	7045210	15/32	Inner	.275	—	—	—	.300	②	.015	.325	—	—	7/8
	7045211	15/32	Inner	.275	—	—	—	.300	②	.015	.325	—	—	7/8
	7045218	15/32	Inner	.275	—	—	—	.325	①	.015	.375	—	—	9/16
	7045222	15/32	Inner	.275	—	—	—	.300	②	.015	.325	—	—	7/8
	7045223	15/32	Inner	.275	—	—	—	.300	②	.015	.325	—	—	7/8
	7045224	15/32	Inner	.275	—	—	—	.325	②	.015	.325	—	—	¾
	7045228	15/32	Inner	.275	—	—	—	.325	②	.015	.325	—	—	¾
	7045501	15/32	Inner	.275	—	—	—	.325	②	.015	.325	—	—	9/16

Continued

QUADRAJET 4MC & 4MV ADJUSTMENT SPECIFICATIONS—Continued

See Tune Up Chart in car chapters for hot idle speeds.

Year	Carb. Model	Float Level	Pump Rod Hole	Pump Rod Adj.	Idle Vent	Air Valve	Fast Idle (Bench)	Choke Rod	Vacuum Break	Air Valve Dash-pot	Choke Unloader	Air Valve Lockout	Secondary Metering Rods	Air-Valve Valve Spring Wind-Up
CHEVROLET ENGINES—Continued														
1975	7045502	15/32	Inner	.275	—	—	—	.300	②	.015	.325	—	—	7/8
	7045503	15/32	Inner	.275	—	—	—	.300	②	.015	.325	—	—	7/8
	7045504	15/32	Inner	.275	—	—	—	.300	②	.015	.375	—	—	7/8
	7045506	15/32	Inner	.275	—	—	—	.300	②	.015	.325	—	—	7/8
	7045507	15/32	Inner	.275	—	—	—	.300	②	.015	.325	—	—	7/8
	7045509	15/32	Inner	.275	—	—	—	.300	②	.015	.325	—	—	7/8
	7045510	15/32	Inner	.275	—	—	—	.325	②	.015	.325	—	—	7/8
	7045512	15/32	Inner	.275	—	—	—	.325	②	.015	.325	—	—	7/8
	7045514	15/32	Inner	.275	—	—	—	.300	②	.015	.375	—	—	7/8

①—Front .200, Rear .550   ②—Front .180, Rear .170

Year	Carb. Model	Float Level	Pump Rod Hole	Pump Rod Adj.	Idle Vent	Air Valve	Fast Idle (Bench)	Choke Rod	Vacuum Break	Air Valve Dash-pot	Choke Unloader	Air Valve Lockout	Secondary Metering Rods	Air-Valve Valve Spring Wind-Up
FORD ENGINES														
1970-71	D0OF-A	11/32	Outer	5/16	—	—	2 Turns	.130	.140	.030	.300	.015	—	—
	D0OF-B	11/32	Outer	5/16	—	—	2 Turns	.166	.190	.030	.300	.015	—	—
	D0OF-E	11/32	Outer	5/16	—	—	2 Turns	.166	.190	.030	.300	.015	—	—
	D0OF-F	11/32	Outer	5/16	—	—	2 Turns	.130	.140	.030	.300	.015	—	—
OLDSMOBILE														
1969	7029250	1/4	Inner	5/16	—	—	2 Turns	.140	.180	.030	.200	.020	—	1/2
	7029251	1/4	Inner	5/16	—	—	2 Turns	.120	.180	.030	.200	.020	—	3/4
	7029252	1/4	Inner	5/16	—	—	2 Turns	.120	.180	.030	.200	.020	—	3/4
	7029253	1/4	Outer	3/8	—	—	—	.120	—	.050	.200	.020	—	3/4
	7029254	1/4	Inner	5/16	—	—	—	.140	—	.030	.200	.020	—	3/4
	7029255	1/4	Inner	5/16	—	—	—	.090	—	.050	.200	.020	—	3/4
1970	7040250	1/4	Inner	3/8	—	—	—	.140	.200	.030	.200	.020	—	1/2
	7040251	1/4	Inner	3/8	—	—	—	.140	.200	.030	.200	.020	—	3/4
	7040252	1/4	Inner	3/8	—	—	—	.170	.200	.030	.200	.020	—	3/4
	7040253	1/4	Inner	3/8	—	—	—	.230	.275	.030	.200	.020	—	3/4
	7040255	1/4	Inner	3/8	—	—	—	.275	.325	.030	.200	.020	—	3/4
	7040256	1/4	Inner	3/8	—	—	—	.275	.325	.030	.200	.020	—	3/4
	7040257	1/4	Inner	3/8	—	—	—	.170	.200	.030	.200	.020	—	3/4
	7040258	1/4	Inner	3/8	—	—	—	.170	.200	.030	.200	.020	—	3/4
1971	7041250	1/4	Inner	3/8	—	—	—	.140	.200	.050	.200	.035	—	1/2
	7041251	1/4	Inner	3/8	—	—	—	.140	.200	.050	.200	.035	—	3/4
	7041252	1/4	Inner	3/8	—	—	—	.170	.200	.050	.200	.035	—	3/4
	7041253	1/4	Inner	3/8	—	—	—	.230	.200	.050	.200	.035	—	3/4
	7041257	1/4	Inner	3/8	—	—	—	.170	.200	.050	.200	.035	—	3/4
1972	7042250	1/4	Inner	3/8	—	—	—	.230	.230	.050	.200	.035	—	1/2
	7042251	1/4	Inner	3/8	—	—	—	.230	.215	.050	.200	.035	—	3/4
	7042252	1/4	Inner	3/8	—	—	—	.230	.215	.050	.200	.035	—	3/4
	7042953	1/4	Inner	3/8	—	—	2 Turns	.230	.275	.050	.200	.035	—	3/4
1973	7043253	1/4	Inner	—	—	—	2 Turns	.230	.275	—	.300	.035	—	3/4
	7043257	1/4	Inner	—	—	—	2 Turns	.230	.200	—	.300	.035	—	1/2
	7043259	1/4	Inner	—	—	—	2 Turns	.230	.215	—	.300	.035	—	3/4
1973-74	7043250	1/4	Inner	—	—	—	2 Turns	.230	.200	—	.300	.035	—	1/2
	7043251	1/4	Inner	—	—	—	2 Turns	.230	.200	—	.300	.035	—	3/4
	7043252	1/4	Inner	—	—	—	2 Turns	.230	.200	—	.300	.035	—	3/4
	7043255	1/4	Inner	—	—	—	2 Turns	.230	.200	—	.300	.035	—	1/2
	7043256	1/4	Inner	—	—	—	2 Turns	.230	.200	—	.300	.035	—	1/2
	7043250	1/4	Inner	3/8	—	—	—	.230	.200	.030	.300	.035	.070	1/2
	7043251	1/4	Inner	3/8	—	—	—	.230	.200	.030	.300	.035	.070	3/4
	7043252	1/4	Inner	3/8	—	—	—	.230	.200	.030	.300	.035	.070	3/4
	7043255	1/4	Inner	3/8	—	—	—	.230	.200	.030	.300	.035	.070	1/2
	7043256	1/4	Inner	3/8	—	—	—	.230	.200	.030	.300	.035	.070	1/2
	7043259	1/4	Inner	3/8	—	—	—	.230	.200	.030	.300	.035	.070	—

Continued

QUADRAJET 4MC & 4MV ADJUSTMENT SPECIFICATIONS—Continued

See Tune Up Chart in car chapters for hot idle speeds.

Year	Carb. Model	Float Level	Pump Rod Hole	Pump Rod Adj.	Idle Vent	Air Valve	Fast Idle (Bench)	Choke Rod	Vacuum Break	Air Valve Dash-pot	Choke Unloader	Air Valve Lockout	Secondary Metering Rods	Air-Valve Valve Spring Wind-Up
OLDSMOBILE														
1974	7044152	—	—	—	—	—	—	—	.200	—	—	—	—	—
	7044557	¼	Inner	⅜	—	—	2 Turns	.230	.200	.030	.300	.035	.070	¾
	7044558	¼	Inner	⅜	—	—	2 Turns	.230	.200	.030	.300	.035	.070	¾
	7044559	¼	Inner	⅜	—	—	2 Turns	.230	.275	.030	.275	.035	.070	¾
1975	7045183	15/32	Inner	9/32	.025	—	—	.135	.190①	.030	.230	.015⑥	—	½
	7045184	15/32	Inner	9/32	.025	—	—	.135	.190①	.030	.230	.015⑥	—	¾
	7045185	15/32	Inner	9/32	.025	—	—	.135	.190①	.030	.230	.015⑥	—	¾
	7045246	5/16	Outer	⅜	.025	—	—	.095	.130②	.015	.240	.015⑥	—	¾
	7045250	15/32	Inner	9/32	.025	—	—	.170	.245③	.030	.300	.015⑥	—	½
	7045251	15/32	Inner	9/32	.025	—	—	—	.190①	.030	.230	.015⑥	—	¾
	7045264	½	Inner	9/32	.025	—	—	.130	.150⑤	.030	.230	.015⑥	—	½
	7045483	15/32	Inner	9/32	.025	—	—	.160	.275①	.030	.230	.015⑥	—	½
	7045484	15/32	Inner	9/32	.025	—	—	.135	.190①	.030	.230	.015⑥	—	¾
	7045485	15/32	Inner	9/32	.025	—	—	.160	.275③	.030	.230	.015⑥	—	¾
	7045546	5/16	Outer	⅜	.025	—	—	.095	.145④	.030	.240	.015⑥	—	¾
	7045550	15/32	Inner	9/32	.025	—	—	.160	.275③	.030	.230	.015⑥	—	½
	7045551	15/32	Inner	9/32	.025	—	—	.135	.190①	.030	.230	.015⑥	—	¾
	7045553	15/32	Inner	9/32	.025	—	—	.135	.150⑤	.030	.230	.015⑥	—	½
	7045554	15/32	Inner	9/32	.025	—	—	.160	.275③	.030	.230	.015⑥	—	½
	7045557	½	Inner	9/32	.025	—	—	.130	.150⑤	.030	.240	.015⑥	—	¾
	7045559	5/16	Outer	⅜	.025	—	—	.095	.145④	.030	.240	.015⑥	—	¾

①—Rear adjustment .140″.
②—Rear adjustment .115″.
③—Rear adjustment .180″.
④—Rear adjustment .130″.
⑤—Rear adjustment .260″.
⑥—Secondary lockout.

Year	Carb. Model	Float Level	Pump Rod Hole	Pump Rod Adj.	Idle Vent	Air Valve	Fast Idle (Bench)	Choke Rod	Vacuum Break	Air Valve Dash-pot	Choke Unloader	Air Valve Lockout	Secondary Metering Rods	Air-Valve Valve Spring Wind-Up
PONTIAC														
1969	7028270	¼	Inner	9/32	⅜	—	3 Turns	.100	.245	.030	.300	.015	53/64	½
	7028273	¼	Inner	9/32	⅜	—	3 Turns	.100	.245	.030	.300	.015	53/64	½
	7029260	3/16	Inner	9/32	⅜	—	3 Turns	.100	.150	.030	.300	.015	53/64	½
	7029261	3/16	Inner	9/32	⅜	—	3 Turns	.100	.180	.030	.300	.015	53/64	½
	7029262	9/32	Inner	9/32	⅜	—	3 Turns	.100	.245	.030	.300	.015	53/64	½
	7029263	9/32	Inner	9/32	⅜	—	3 Turns	.100	.245	.030	.300	.015	53/64	½
	7029268	9/32	Inner	9/32	⅜	—	3 Turns	.100	.245	.030	.300	.015	53/64	½
	7029270	9/32	Inner	¼	⅜	—	3 Turns	.100	.245	.030	.300	.015	53/64	½
	7029273	9/32	Inner	¼	⅜	—	3 Turns	.100	.245	.030	.300	.015	53/64	½
1970	7040262	9/32	—	—	—	—	—	.100	.400	.025	—	.015	—	7/16
	7040263	9/32	—	—	—	—	—	.100	.400	.025	—	.015	—	7/16
	7040264	9/32	—	—	—	—	—	.100	.400	.025	—	.015	—	7/16
	7040267	9/32	—	—	—	—	—	.100	.400	.025	—	.015	—	7/16
	7040268	9/32	—	—	—	—	—	.100	.400	.025	—	.015	—	7/16
	7040270	9/32	—	—	—	—	—	.100	.245	.025	—	.015	—	¾
	7040273	9/32	—	—	—	—	—	.100	.245	.025	—	.015	—	¾
	7040274	9/32	—	—	—	—	—	.100	.400	.025	—	.015	—	7/16
	7040562	9/32	—	—	—	—	—	.100	.400	.025	—	.015	—	7/16
	7040563	9/32	—	—	—	—	—	.100	.400	.025	—	.015	—	7/16
	7040564	9/32	—	—	—	—	—	.100	.400	.025	—	.015	—	7/16
	7040567	9/32	—	—	—	—	—	.100	.400	.025	—	.015	—	7/16
	7040568	9/32	—	—	—	—	—	.100	.400	.025	—	.015	—	7/16
	7040570	9/32	—	—	—	—	—	.100	.245	.025	—	.015	—	¾
	7040573	9/32	—	—	—	—	—	.100	.245	.025	—	.015	—	¾
1971	7041262	9/32	—	—	—	—	—	.100	.240	.025	—	.015	—	7/16
	7041263	9/32	—	—	—	—	—	.100	.240	.025	—	.015	—	7/16
	7041267	9/32	—	—	—	—	—	.100	.370	.025	—	.015	—	½
	7041268	9/32	—	—	—	—	—	.100	.430	.025	—	.015	—	½
	7041270	9/32	—	—	—	—	—	.100	.430	.025	—	.015	—	½
	7041271	9/32	—	—	—	—	—	.100	.240	.025	—	.015	—	7/16
	7041273	9/32	—	—	—	—	—	.100	.370	.025	—	.015	—	½

Continued

QUADRAJET 4MC & 4MV ADJUSTMENT SPECIFICATIONS—Continued
See Tune Up Chart in car chapters for hot idle speeds.

Year	Carb. Model	Float Level	Pump Rod Hole	Pump Rod Adj.	Idle Vent	Air Valve	Fast Idle (Bench)	Choke Rod	Vacuum Break	Air Valve Dash-pot	Choke Unloader	Air Valve Lockout	Secondary Metering Rods	Air-Valve Valve Spring Wind-Up
PONTIAC—Continued														
1972	7042262	13/32	Inner	13/32	—	—	2 Turns	.100	.290	.025	.310	.015	—	7/16
	7042263	13/32	Inner	13/32	—	—	2 Turns	.100	.325	.025	.310	.015	—	11/16
	7042264	13/32	Inner	13/32	—	—	2 Turns	.100	.290	.025	.310	.015	—	5/8
	7042270	13/32	Inner	7/16	—	—	2 Turns	.100	.290	.025	.310	.015	—	7/16
	7042272	13/32	Inner	13/32	—	—	2 Turns	.100	.195	.025	.310	.015	—	—
	7042273	13/32	Inner	7/16	—	—	2 Turns	.100	.325	.025	.310	.015	—	7/16
	7042274	13/32	Inner	13/32	—	—	2 Turns	.100	.195	.025	.310	.015	—	—
	7042276	13/32	Inner	13/32	—	—	2 Turns	.100	.290	.025	.310	.015	—	—
	7042278	13/32	Inner	13/32	—	—	2 Turns	.100	.290	.025	.310	.015	—	—
1973	7043262	13/32	Inner	13/32	—	—	2 Turns	.200	.260	.025	.310	.015	—	3/8
	7043263	13/32	Inner	13/32	—	—	2 Turns	.200	.290	.025	.310	.015	—	5/8
	7043264	13/32	Inner	13/32	—	—	2 Turns	.200	.260	.025	.310	.015	—	1/2
	7043265	13/32	Inner	13/32	—	—	2 Turns	.200	.290	.025	.310	.015	—	9/16
	7043266	13/32		13/32	—	—	—	.205	.260	.025	.310	.015	—	1/2
	7043270	13/32	Inner	—	—	—	2 Turns	.200	.290	—	.310	.015	—	—
	7043272	13/32	Outer	13/32	—	—	2 Turns	.200	.290	.025	.310	.015	—	3/8
	7043273	13/32	Inner	—	—	—	2 Turns	.200	.290	—	.310	.015	—	—
	7043274	13/32	Outer	13/32	—	—	2 Turns	.200	.290	.025	.310	.015	—	9/16
1974	7043263	13/32	Inner	.410	—	—	—	.205	.290	.025	.310	.015	—	5/8
	7044262	13/32	Inner	.410	—	—	2 Turns	.200	.260	.025	.300	.010	—	3/8
	7044266	13/32	Inner	.410	—	—	2 Turns	.200	.260	.025	.300	.010	—	1/2
	7044267	13/32	Inner	.410	—	—	—	.205	.260	.025	.310	.015	—	3/8
	7044268	13/32	Inner	.410	—	—	2 Turns	.200	.260	.025	.300	.010	—	1/2
	7044269	13/32	Inner	.410	—	—	2 Turns	.200	.290	.025	.300	.010	—	1/2
	7044270	13/32	Inner	.410	—	—	2 Turns	.200	.290	.025	.300	.010	—	3/4
	7044272	13/32	Outer	.315	—	—	2 Turns	.200	.290	.025	.300	.010	—	3/8
	7044273	13/32	Inner	.410	—	—	2 Turns	.200	.290	.025	.300	.010	—	3/4
	7044274	13/32	Outer	.315	—	—	2 Turns	.200	.290	.025	.300	.010	—	9/16
	7044278	25/64	Inner	.410	—	—	2 Turns	.200	.260	.025	.310	.015	—	3/4
	7044280	25/64	Inner	.410	—	—	2 Turns	.200	.260	.025	.310	.015	—	1/2
	7044560	13/32	Inner	.410	—	—	2 Turns	.200	.260	.025	.300	.010	—	3/8
	7044567	13/32	Outer	.315	—	—	2 Turns	.200	.290	.025	.300	.010	—	9/16
	7044568	13/32	Inner	.410	—	—	2 Turns	.200	.260	.025	.300	.010	—	1/2
	7044569	13/32	Inner	.410	—	—	2 Turns	.200	.260	.025	.300	.010	—	1/2
	7044570	13/32	Outer	.315	—	—	2 Turns	.200	.290	.025	.300	.010	—	3/8
	7044572	13/32	Inner	.410	—	—	2 Turns	.200	.260	.025	.300	.010	—	1/2
1975	7045246	5/16	Outer	15/32	.025	—	—	.095	.130[1]	.015	.240	.015	—	3/4
	7045260	1/2	Inner	9/32	—	—	—	.130	.150[4]	.030	.230	—	—	1/2
	7045262	1/2	Inner	9/32	—	—	—	.130	.150[4]	.030	.230	—	—	1/2
	7045263	1/2	Inner	9/32	—	—	—	.130	.150[4]	.030	.230	—	—	1/2
	7045264	1/2	Inner	9/32	—	—	—	.130	.150[4]	.030	.230	—	—	1/2
	7045266	1/2	Inner	9/32	—	—	—	.130	.150[4]	.030	.230	—	—	1/2
	7045268	1/2	Inner	9/32	—	—	—	.130	.150[4]	.030	.230	—	—	.375
	7045269	1/2	Inner	9/32	—	—	—	.130	.160[3]	.030	.230	—	—	1/2
	7045274	1/2	Inner	9/32	—	—	—	.130	.150[4]	.030	.230	—	—	1/2
	7045546	5/16	Outer	15/32	.025	—	—	.095	.145[2]	.015	.240	.015	—	3/4
	7045562	1/2	Inner	9/32	—	—	—	.130	.150[4]	.030	.230	—	—	1/2
	7045564	1/2	Inner	9/32	—	—	—	.130	.150[4]	.030	.230	—	—	1/2
	7045566	1/2	Inner	9/32	—	—	—	.130	.150[4]	.030	.230	—	—	1/2
	7045568	1/2	Inner	9/32	—	—	—	.130	.150[4]	.030	.230	—	—	1/2
	7045569	1/2	Inner	9/32	—	—	—	—	.145[3]	.030	.230	—	—	1/2
	7045571	1/2	Inner	9/32	—	—	—	—	.160[3]	.030	.230	—	—	3/4
	7045572	5/16	Outer	15/32	.025	—	—	.095	.145[4]	.015	.240	.015	—	1/2
	7045573	1/2	Inner	9/32	—	—	—	—	.160[3]	.015	.230	—	—	1/2
	7045575	5/16	Outer	15/32	.025	—	—	.095	.150[4]	.015	.230	—	—	.375

[1]—Rear .115".
[2]—Rear .130".
[3]—Rear .265".
[4]—Rear .260".

QUADRAJET 4MV, 4MC ADJUSTMENTS

The Quadrajet unit, Figs. 1, 2, has two stages in operation. The primary (fuel inlet) side has small bores with a triple venturi equipped with plain tube nozzles. The triple venturi feature, plus the smaller primary bores, give a more stable and finer fuel control in the idle and economy ranges of operation. Fuel metering in the primary side is accomplished with tapered metering rods positioned by a manifold vacuum responsive piston.

The secondary side has two very large bores which have greatly increased air capacity to meet all engine demands. The air valve principle is used in the secondary side for metering control and supplements fuel flow from the primary bores.

Using the air valve principle, fuel is metered in direct proportion to the air passing through the secondary bores.

The fuel reservoir is centrally located to avoid problems of fuel slosh causing engine turn cut-out and delayed fuel flow to the carburetor bores. The float system uses a single float pontoon for ease of service. The float needle valve is pressure balanced to overcome problems encountered with high fuel pump pressures and to permit use of a small float to control fuel "shut-off" through the large fuel inlet needle seat. It has a synthetic tip which gives added insurance against flooding problems casued by dirt.

The primary side of the carburetor has six systems of operation: float, idle, main metering, power, pump and choke. The secondary side has one metering system which supplements the primary main metering system and receives fuel from a common float chamber.

Model 4MV Choke System

Fig. 3—The choke system consists of a choke valve located in the primary air horn bore, a vacuum diaphragm unit, fast idle cam, connecting linkage, air valve lockout lever and a thermostatic coil. Some applications may use a split choke pick-up spring or a vacuum break modulating spring. The thermostatic coil is located in the engine manifold and is connected to the intermediate choke shaft and lever assembly. Choke operation is controlled by a combination of engine intake manifold vacuum, the offset choke valve, temperature and throttle position.

Model 4MC Choke System

Fig. 4—The choke consists of a choke valve located in the primary air horn bore, a choke housing and vacuum diaphragm assembly, fast idle cam, connecting linkage, air valve lockout lever, and thermostatic coil. Choke operation is controlled by a combination of intake manifold vacuum, the offset choke valve, temperature, and throttle position.

Air Valve Operation

Fig. 5—When the engine reaches a point where the primary bores cannot meet engine air and fuel demands, the primary throttle lever, through connecting linkage

to the secondary throttle shaft lever, begins to open the secondary throttle valves. As air flow through the secondary bores creates a low pressure (vacuum) beneath the air valve, atmospheric pressure on top of the air valve forces the air valve open against spring tension. This allows the required air for increased engine speed to flow past the air valve.

Air Valve Dashpot Operation

Fig. 6—The secondary air valve has an attached piston assembly which acts as a damper to prevent oscillation of the valve due to engine pulsations. The damper piston operates in a well that is filled with fuel from the float bowl. The motion of the piston is retarded by fuel which must by-pass the piston when it moves up in the fuel well. The piston is attached loosely to a plunger rod. The rod has a rubber seal which retains the damper piston to the plunger rod and also acts as a valve. The purpose of the valve is to seat on the piston when the air valve opens and the piston rod moves upward. This closes off the area through the center of the piston and slows down the air valve opening to prevent secondary discharge nozzle lag.

ADJUSTMENTS
Float Level Adjustment

Fig. 7—With adjustable T-scale, measure from top of float bowl gasket surface

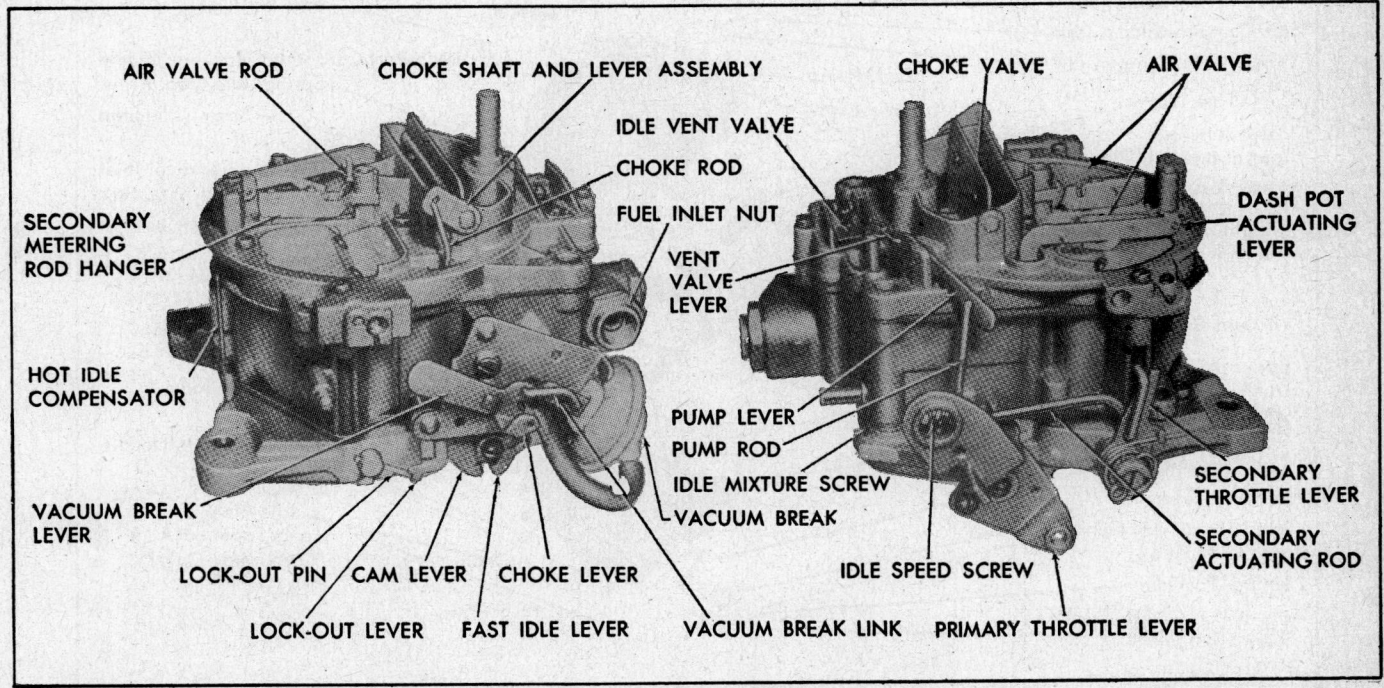

Fig. 1   Quadrajet Model 4MV carburetor

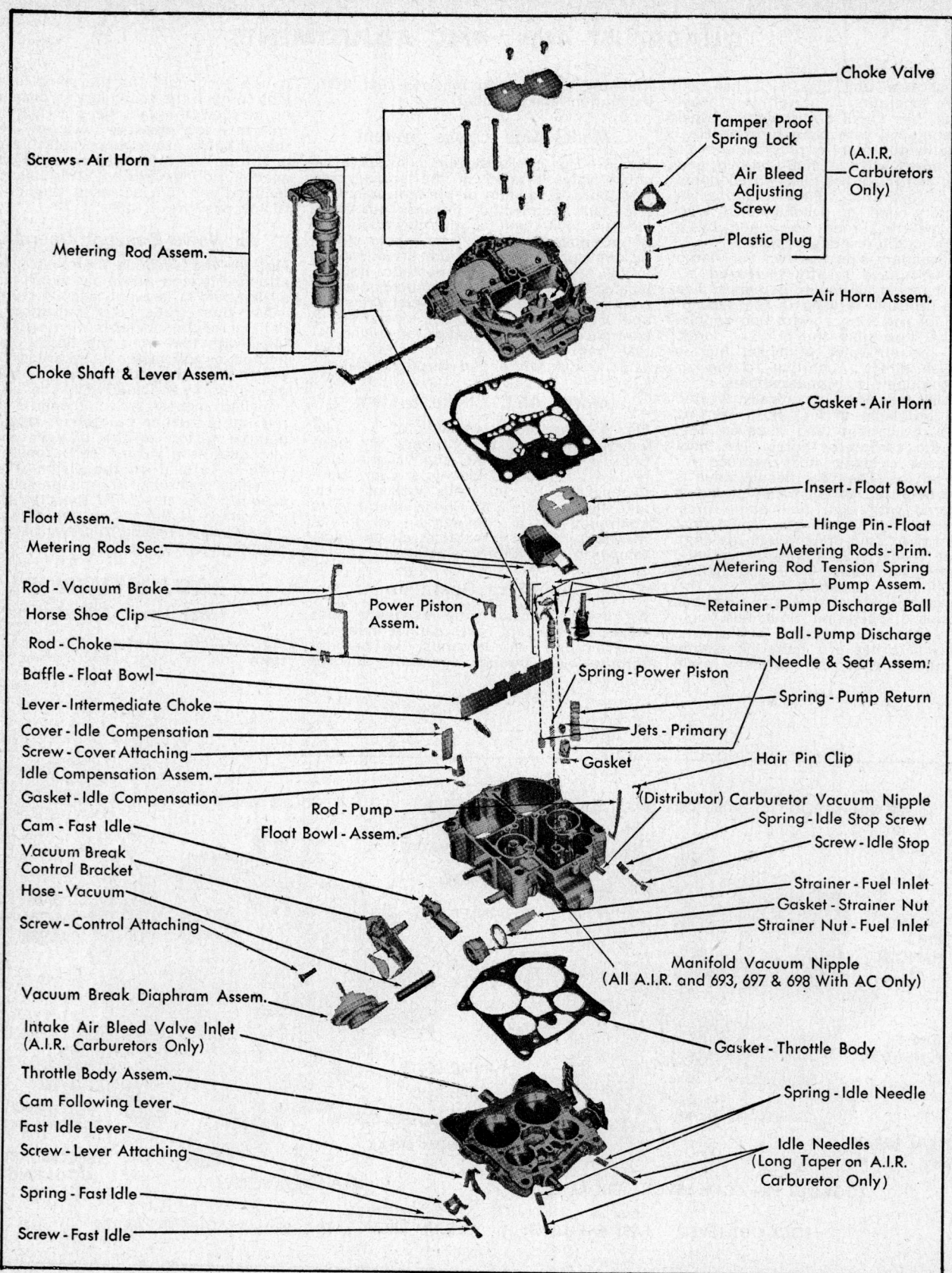

Choke Valve

Tamper Proof Spring Lock

Air Bleed Adjusting Screw

Plastic Plug

(A.I.R. Carburetors Only)

Screws - Air Horn

Metering Rod Assem.

Choke Shaft & Lever Assem.

Air Horn Assem.

Gasket - Air Horn

Insert - Float Bowl

Hinge Pin - Float

Float Assem.

Metering Rods Sec.

Metering Rods - Prim.

Metering Rod Tension Spring

Rod - Vacuum Brake

Horse Shoe Clip

Pump Assem.

Retainer - Pump Discharge Ball

Rod - Choke

Power Piston Assem.

Ball - Pump Discharge

Baffle - Float Bowl

Needle & Seat Assem.

Lever - Intermediate Choke

Spring - Power Piston

Spring - Pump Return

Cover - Idle Compensation

Screw - Cover Attaching

Jets - Primary

Idle Compensation Assem.

Gasket

Hair Pin Clip

Gasket - Idle Compensation

(Distributor) Carburetor Vacuum Nipple

Cam - Fast Idle

Rod - Pump

Spring - Idle Stop Screw

Float Bowl - Assem.

Screw - Idle Stop

Vacuum Break Control Bracket

Hose - Vacuum

Strainer - Fuel Inlet

Gasket - Strainer Nut

Screw - Control Attaching

Strainer Nut - Fuel Inlet

Manifold Vacuum Nipple (All A.I.R. and 693, 697 & 698 With AC Only)

Vacuum Break Diaphram Assem.

Intake Air Bleed Valve Inlet (A.I.R. Carburetors Only)

Gasket - Throttle Body

Throttle Body Assem.

Spring - Idle Needle

Cam Following Lever

Fast Idle Lever

Screw - Lever Attaching

Idle Needles (Long Taper on A.I.R. Carburetor Only)

Spring - Fast Idle

Screw - Fast Idle

Fig. 2   4MV Quadrajet carburetor. Typical

(gasket removed) to top of float at toe (locate gauging point 3/16″ back from toe). Adjust as directed in the illustration to the dimension listed in the *Rochester Specifications Chart*. Make sure retaining pin is held firmly in place and tang of float is seated on float needle.

Pump Rod Adjustment

Fig. 8—With throttle valves completely closed and pump rod in specified hole in pump lever, measure from top of choke valve wall (next to vent stack) to top of pump stem. Dimension should be as listed in the *Rochester Specifications Chart*. To adjust, bend pump lever as required.

Idle Vent Adjustment

Fig. 9—After pump rod adjustment has been made, open primary throttle valve to a point where the idle vent just closes. With T-scale, measure distance from top of choke valve wall (next to vent stack) to top of pump plunger stem. If dimension is not as specified in the *Rochester Specifications Chart*, bend wire tang on pump lever.

Fast Idle Adjustment

Fig. 10—With primary throttle valves completely closed, and the cam follower over the high step of the fast idle cam, adjust fast idle screw after screw makes contact with lever. Refer to *4MC and 4MV Specifications Chart*.

Choke Rod Adjustment

Fig. 11—With the fast idle adjustment made, and cam follower on second step of fast idle cam and against the high step, rotate choke valve toward closed position by pushing down on vacuum break lever (Model 4MV) or thermostatic coil tang (Model 4MC). Dimension between lower edge of choke valve (at choke lever end) should be as specified in the *Rochester Specifications Chart*. Adjust by bending choke rod on 4MV models or bending fast idle cam tang on 4MC models.

Vacuum Break Adjustment

4MV, Figs. 12 and 13

With vacuum break diaphragm stem against its seat and choke valve held toward the closed position, the dimension between lower edge of choke valve and air horn, at choke lever end, should be as specified. To adjust, bend vacuum break tang.

4MC, Fig. 14

With choke valve closed and choke rod in bottom of the slot in the upper choke lever, align the thermostatic spring pick-up tang directly over the index tab on the inside of the choke housing. After tang is aligned, adjust vacuum break tang to specifications between tang and vacuum break pin.

With vacuum break diaphragm seated and tang against vacuum break pin, the dimension between wall and lower edge of choke valve should be as specified. Make sure choke rod is in bottom of slot in choke lever when gauging. Adjust by turning screw on vacuum break cover. Refer to *4MC and 4MV Specifications Chart*.

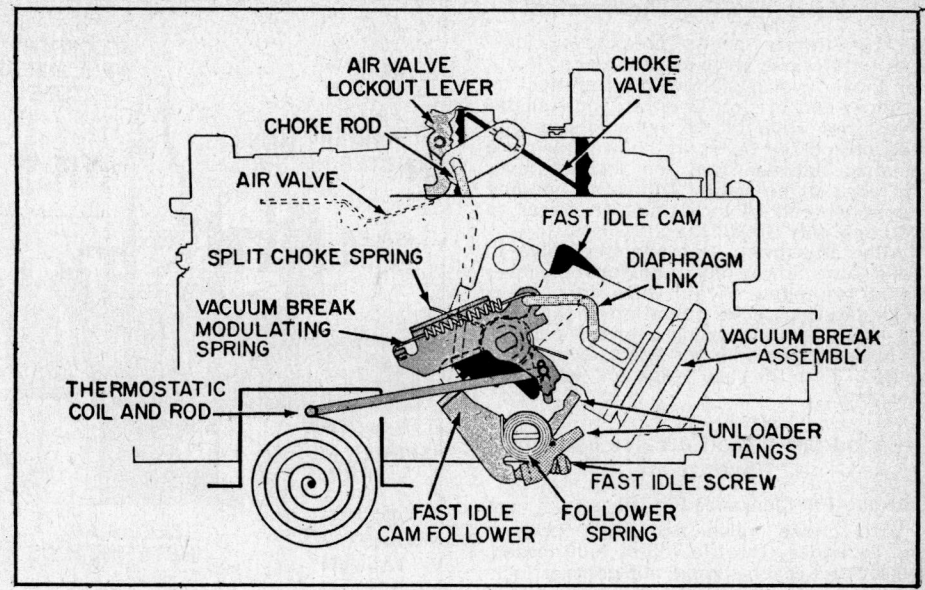

Fig. 3   Rochester Model 4MV choke system

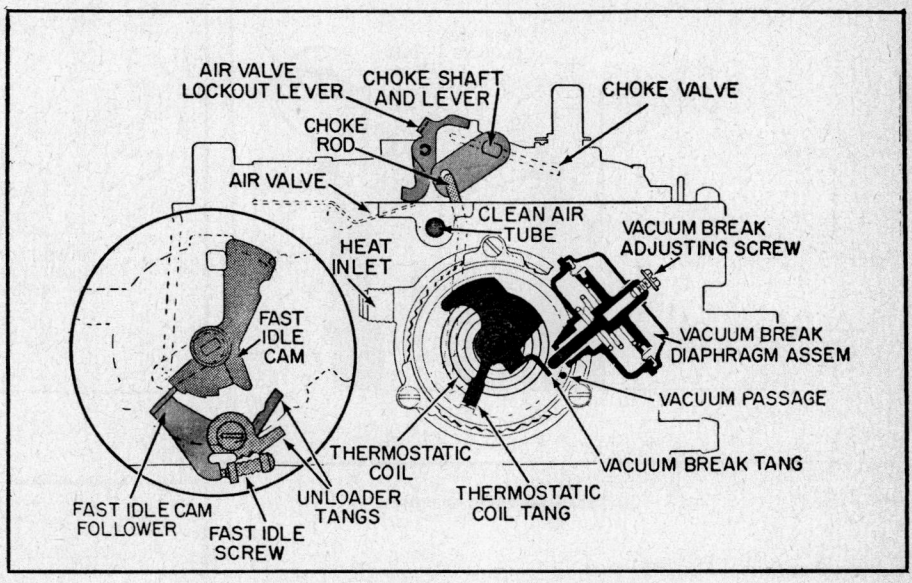

Fig. 4   Rochester Model 4MC choke system

Air Valve Dashpot Adjustment

Fig. 15—With vacuum break diaphragm seated, there must be the specified clearance between dashpot rod and end of slot in air valve lever. To adjust, bend rod at air valve end.

Split Choke Spring Adjustment

Fig. 16—With split choke spring in specified notch, (see automatic choke specifications) open choke valve by pushing upward on vacuum break lever to end of travel making sure choke rod is in upper end of slot in choke lever. Dimension between end of torsion spring and tang should be as specified in the *Rochester Specifications Chart*. Bend tang to adjust.

Choke Unloader Adjustment

Fig. 17—With choke valve held closed by means of a rubber band on vacuum break lever, open throttle valves fully. With valves in this position, dimension between lower edge of choke valve and air horn wall should be as specified. To adjust, bend tang on fast idle lever.

Air Valve Lockout Adjustment

Fig. 18—Rotate vacuum break lever clockwise until choke valve is wide open. If upper choke lever is slotted, the rod must be in upper end of slot. Open air valve slightly so that edge of air valve is opposite tang on lockout lever, as shown. Measure distance between tang on lockout lever and edge of air valve. Adjust by bending the upper end of lockout lever. Refer to *4MC and 4MV Specifications Chart.*

After adjustment, close choke valve to make sure lower edge of lockout lever clears top edge of air valve for proper locking during choke operation. If the lockout lever does not swing over top edge of air valve make sure air valve is properly seated. File the top edge of valve for clearance.

Secondary Throttle Valve Lockout Adjustment

Lockout—Pin Clearance Fig. 19

With choke valve and both primary and secondary throttle valves fully closed, the lockout lever should not contact lockout pin. Clearance must not exceed .015". Bend lockout pin to adjust.

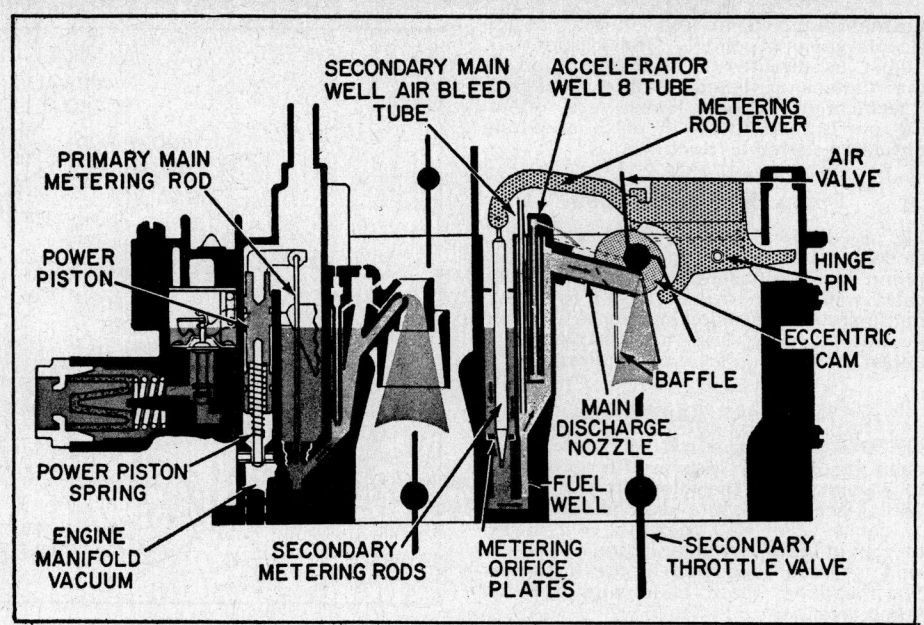

Fig. 5   Diagram of Quadrajet power system

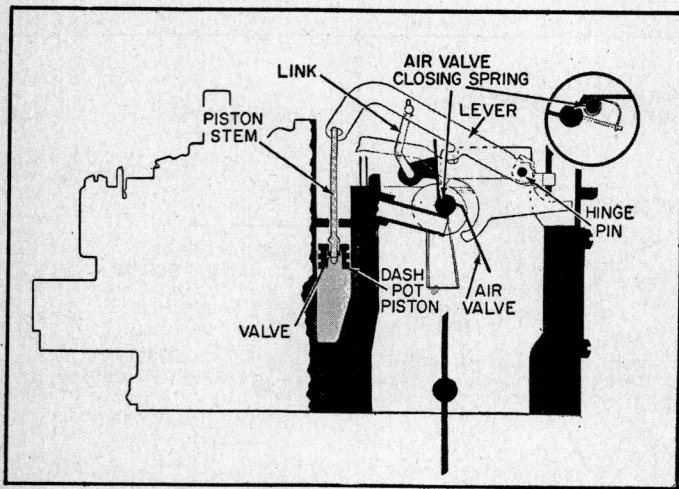

Fig. 6   Quadrajet air valve dashpot

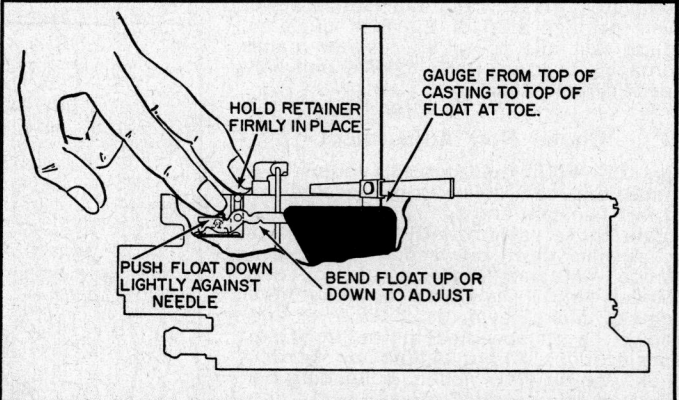

Fig. 7   Quadrajet float level adjustment

Opening Clearance, Fig. 19

Hold choke valve wide open by rotating vacuum break lever toward open choke clockwise. With secondary throttle valves held partially open measure the clearance between lockout pin and toe of lockout lever.

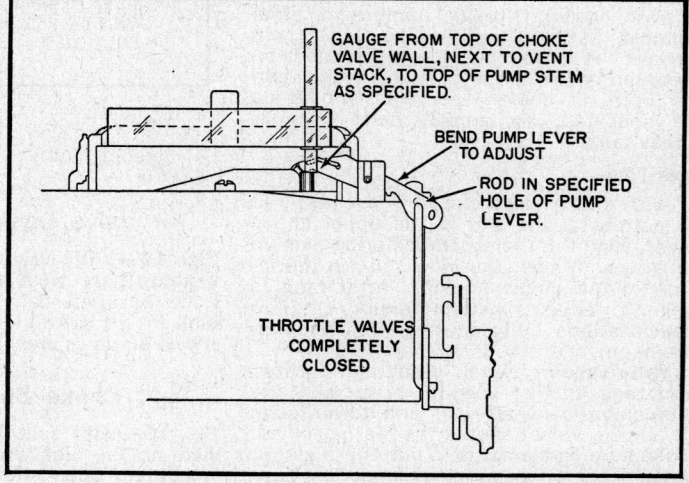

Fig. 8   Quadrajet pump rod adjustment

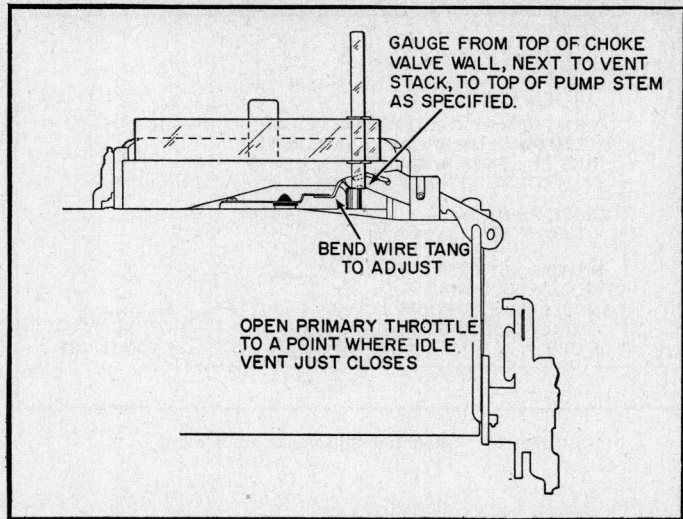

GAUGE FROM TOP OF CHOKE VALVE WALL, NEXT TO VENT STACK, TO TOP OF PUMP STEM AS SPECIFIED.

BEND WIRE TANG TO ADJUST

OPEN PRIMARY THROTTLE TO A POINT WHERE IDLE VENT JUST CLOSES

Fig. 9   Quadrajet idle vent adjustment

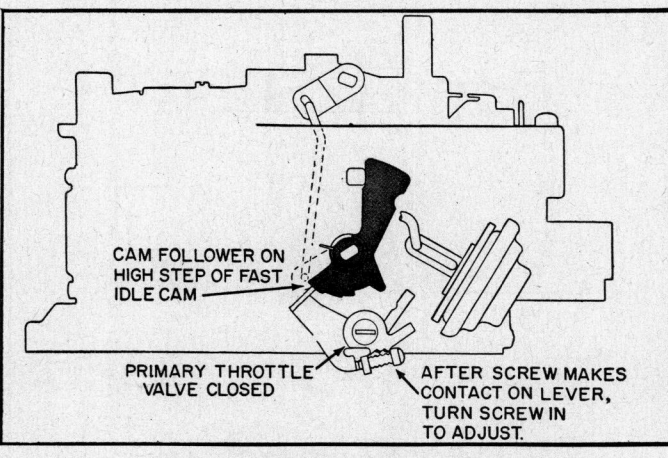

CAM FOLLOWER ON HIGH STEP OF FAST IDLE CAM

PRIMARY THROTTLE VALVE CLOSED

AFTER SCREW MAKES CONTACT ON LEVER, TURN SCREW IN TO ADJUST.

Fig. 10   Quadrajet fast idle adjustment

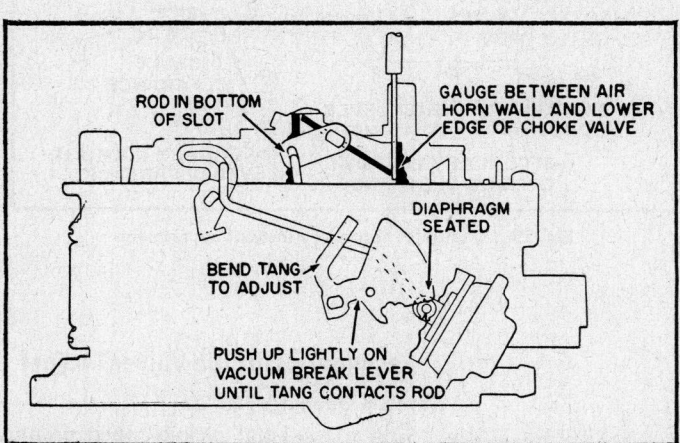

ROD IN BOTTOM OF SLOT

GAUGE BETWEEN AIR HORN WALL AND LOWER EDGE OF CHOKE VALVE

DIAPHRAGM SEATED

BEND TANG TO ADJUST

PUSH UP LIGHTLY ON VACUUM BREAK LEVER UNTIL TANG CONTACTS ROD

Fig. 12   Quadrajet vacuum break adjustment

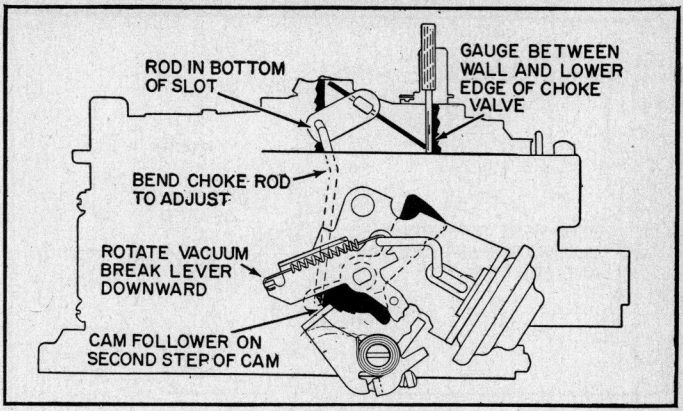

ROD IN BOTTOM OF SLOT

GAUGE BETWEEN WALL AND LOWER EDGE OF CHOKE VALVE

BEND CHOKE ROD TO ADJUST

ROTATE VACUUM BREAK LEVER DOWNWARD

CAM FOLLOWER ON SECOND STEP OF CAM

Fig. 11   4MV choke rod adjustment

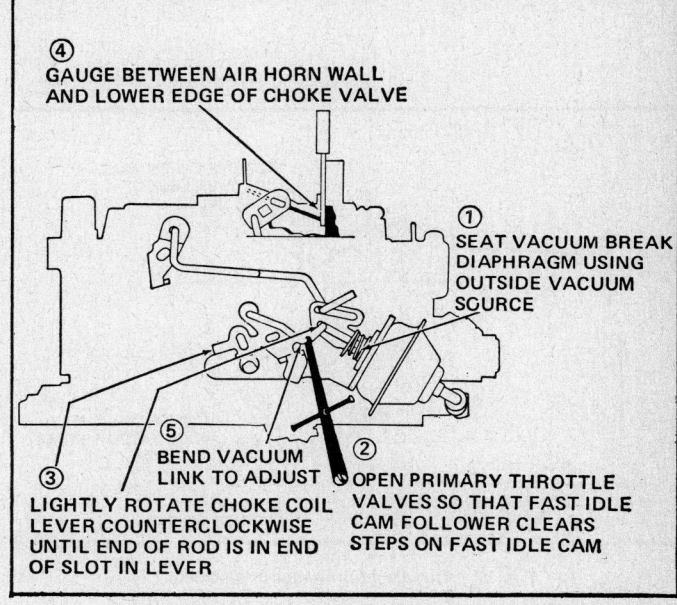

④ GAUGE BETWEEN AIR HORN WALL AND LOWER EDGE OF CHOKE VALVE

① SEAT VACUUM BREAK DIAPHRAGM USING OUTSIDE VACUUM SOURCE

⑤ BEND VACUUM LINK TO ADJUST

③ LIGHTLY ROTATE CHOKE COIL LEVER COUNTERCLOCKWISE UNTIL END OF ROD IS IN END OF SLOT IN LEVER

② OPEN PRIMARY THROTTLE VALVES SO THAT FAST IDLE CAM FOLLOWER CLEARS STEPS ON FAST IDLE CAM

Fig. 13   Quadrajet vacuum break adjustment

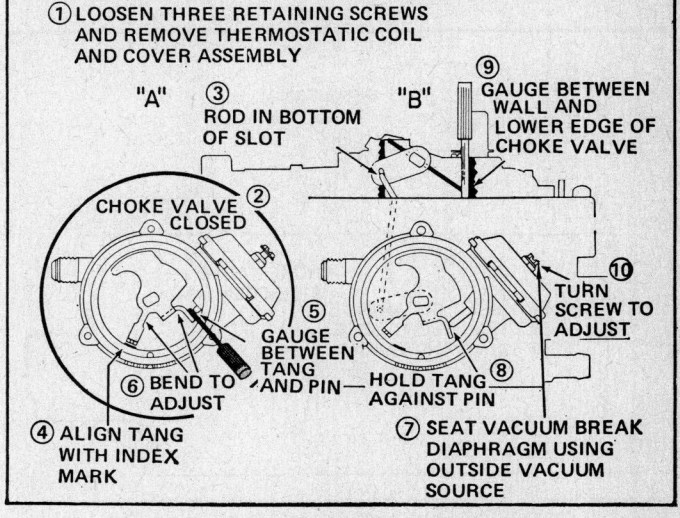

① LOOSEN THREE RETAINING SCREWS AND REMOVE THERMOSTATIC COIL AND COVER ASSEMBLY

"A"   ③ ROD IN BOTTOM OF SLOT

"B"   ⑨ GAUGE BETWEEN WALL AND LOWER EDGE OF CHOKE VALVE

CHOKE VALVE ② CLOSED

⑤ GAUGE BETWEEN TANG AND PIN

⑥ BEND TO ADJUST

⑩ TURN SCREW TO ADJUST

⑧ HOLD TANG AGAINST PIN

④ ALIGN TANG WITH INDEX MARK

⑦ SEAT VACUUM BREAK DIAPHRAGM USING OUTSIDE VACUUM SOURCE

Fig. 14   4MC vacuum break adjustment

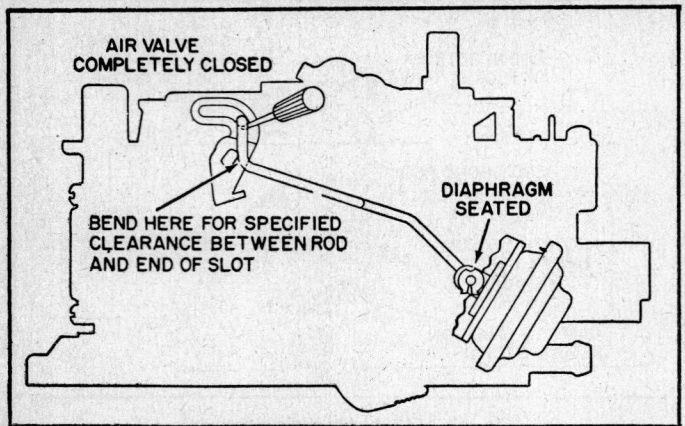

Fig. 15   Quadrajet air valve dashpot adjustment

AIR VALVE COMPLETELY CLOSED

BEND HERE FOR SPECIFIED CLEARANCE BETWEEN ROD AND END OF SLOT

DIAPHRAGM SEATED

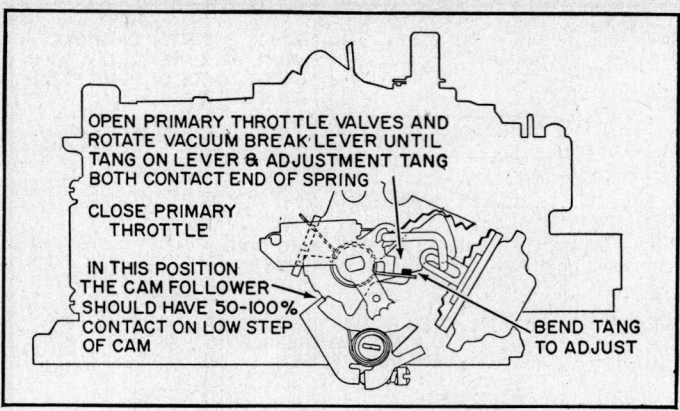

Fig. 16   Quadrajet split choke adjustment

OPEN PRIMARY THROTTLE VALVES AND ROTATE VACUUM BREAK LEVER UNTIL TANG ON LEVER & ADJUSTMENT TANG BOTH CONTACT END OF SPRING

CLOSE PRIMARY THROTTLE

IN THIS POSITION THE CAM FOLLOWER SHOULD HAVE 50-100% CONTACT ON LOW STEP OF CAM

BEND TANG TO ADJUST

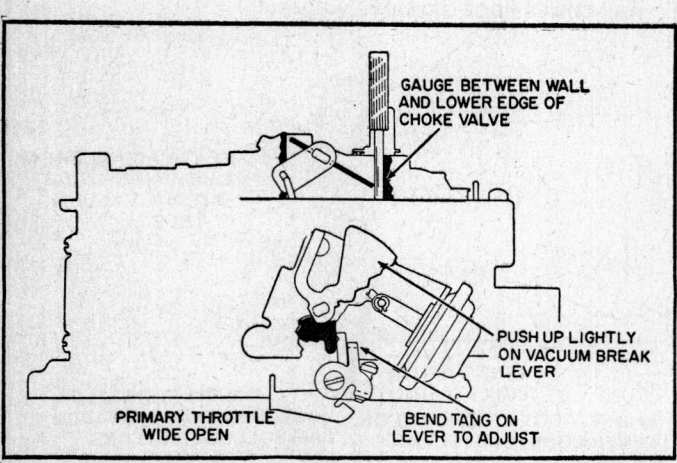

Fig. 17   Quadrajet unloader adjustment

GAUGE BETWEEN WALL AND LOWER EDGE OF CHOKE VALVE

PUSH UP LIGHTLY ON VACUUM BREAK LEVER

PRIMARY THROTTLE WIDE OPEN

BEND TANG ON LEVER TO ADJUST

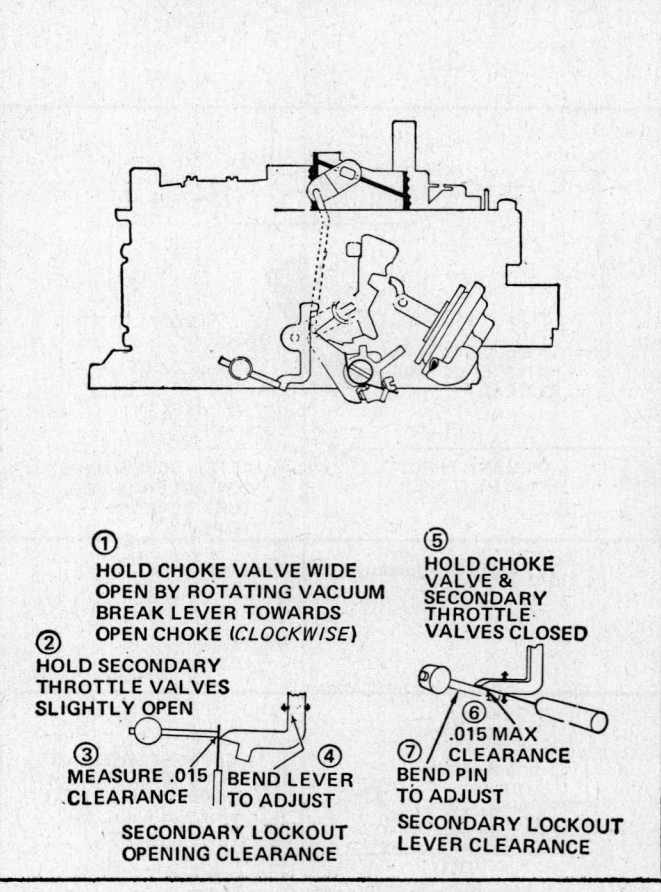

① HOLD CHOKE VALVE WIDE OPEN BY ROTATING VACUUM BREAK LEVER TOWARDS OPEN CHOKE (*CLOCKWISE*)

② HOLD SECONDARY THROTTLE VALVES SLIGHTLY OPEN

③ MEASURE .015 CLEARANCE

④ BEND LEVER TO ADJUST

SECONDARY LOCKOUT OPENING CLEARANCE

⑤ HOLD CHOKE VALVE & SECONDARY THROTTLE VALVES CLOSED

⑥ .015 MAX CLEARANCE

⑦ BEND PIN TO ADJUST

SECONDARY LOCKOUT LEVER CLEARANCE

Fig. 19   Quadrajet secondary lockout adjustment

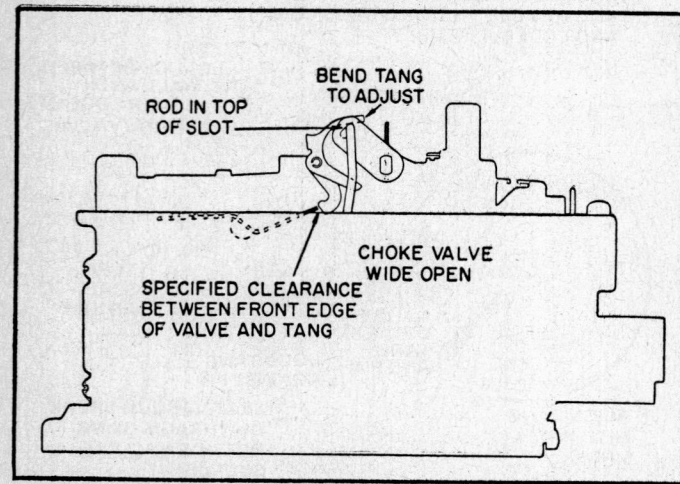

Fig. 18   Quadrajet air valve lockout adjustment

BEND TANG TO ADJUST

ROD IN TOP OF SLOT

CHOKE VALVE WIDE OPEN

SPECIFIED CLEARANCE BETWEEN FRONT EDGE OF VALVE AND TANG

Secondary Throttle Valves, Adjust

Throttle Opening, Fig. 20

With a two-point pickup, open primary throttle valves until actuating link contacts tang on secondary lever. With valves

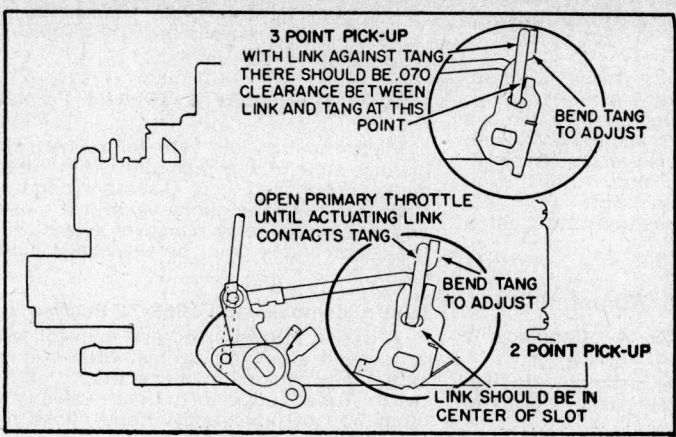

Fig. 20   Quadrajet secondary throttle valves
opening adjustment

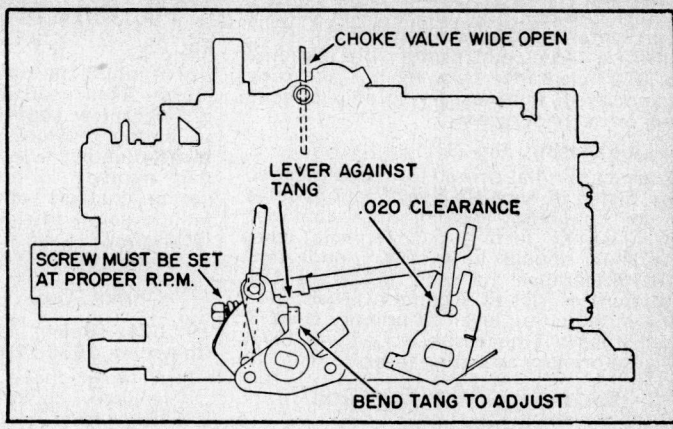

Fig. 21   Quadrajet secondary throttle valves
closing adjustment

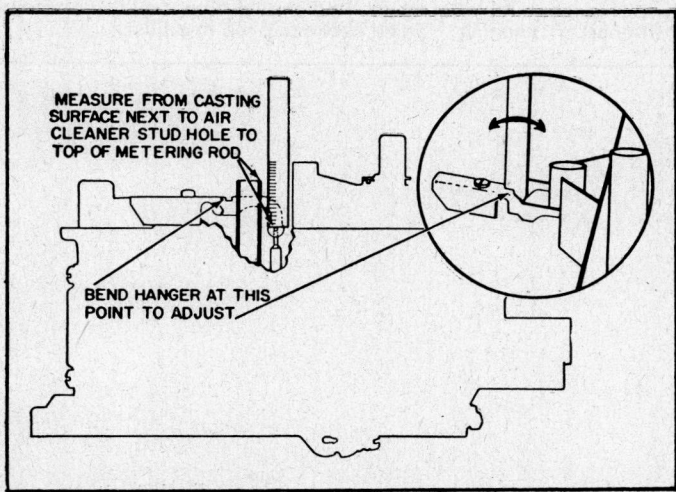

Fig. 22   Quadrajet secondary metering rod adjustment

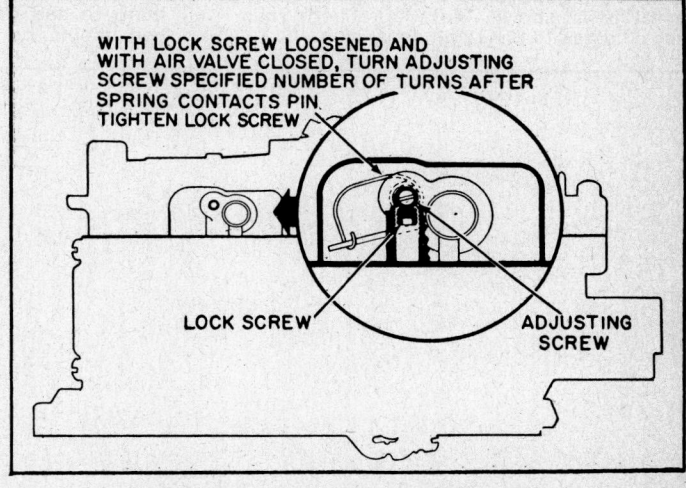

Fig. 23   Quadrajet air valve spring adjustment

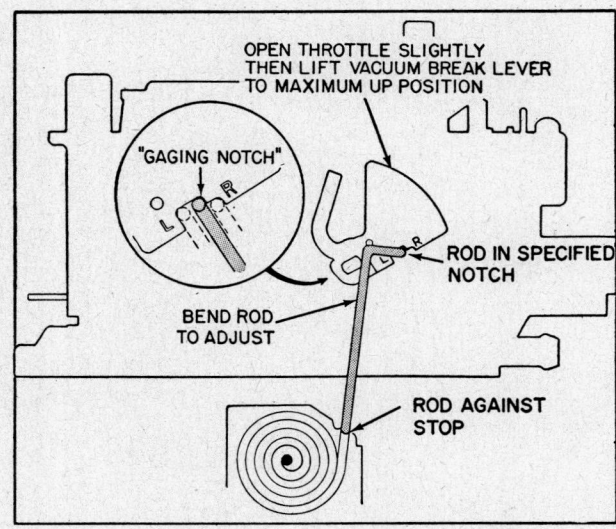

Fig. 24   Choke coil adjustment. Typical

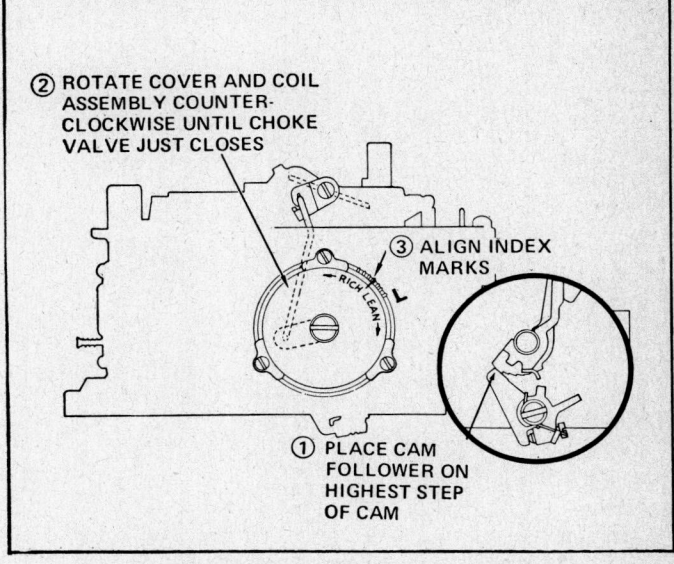

Fig. 25   4MC choke coil adjustment

in this position, bottom of link should be in center slot of secondary lever.

With a three-point pickup, there should be .070" clearance between link and tang as indicated. If necessary to adjust, bend tang on secondary lever.

Throttle Closing, Fig. 21

Set curb idle screw to recommended rpm (listed in *Tune-Up Specifications* table in car chapters), making sure cam follower is not resting on fast idle cam. The 4MV should have .020" and 4MC .070" clearance between actuating link and front of slot in secondary lever when tang of actuating lever on primary shaft is against pin. If necessary to adjust, bend tang on primary actuating lever.

Secondary Metering Rod Adjustment

Fig. 22

Measure from top of metering rod to top of air horn casting next to air cleaner stud hole. Dimension should be as specified. To adjust, bend metering rod hanger at point shown. *Make sure both rods are adjusted to the same dimension.*

Air Valve Spring Adjustment

Fig. 23

To adjust the air valve spring wind-up, loosen Allen head lockscrew and turn adjusting screw counterclockwise to remove all spring tension. With air valve closed, turn adjusting screw clockwise the specified number of turns after the torsion spring contacts pin on shaft. Hold adjusting screw in this position and tighten lock screw.

Choke Coil Rod Adjustment

1973-74 Buick, 1969-74 Cadillac & Chevrolet, 1970-71 Ford, Fig. 24

1. Remove choke coil assmebly to disengage choke rod from vacuum break lever.
2. Reinstall coil assembly but do not install rod into lever.
3. With choke valve completely closed, fast idle cam in cold start position, and vacuum break lever in maximum upward position, pull choke rod upward to end of travel. Upper end of rod should be positioned in gauging notch, Fig. 24. Bend choke rod to adjust and reassemble coil assembly, rod and lever.

1970-74 Oldsmobile & 1973-74 Pontiac, Fig. 25

Place the fast idle cam follower on the highest step of the fast idle cam. Rotate choke cover and coil assembly counterclockwise until the choke valve just closes and the index point on cover aligns with the center index point on the choke housing.

1969 Oldsmobile and 1969-72 Pontiac

With fast idle adjusted and cam follower on second step and against high step of cam, close choke and check dimension between lower edge of choke valve and inner wall of main body. Bend choke rod to adjust.

1969-72 Buick Fig. 24

With choke valve completely closed and choke rod in bottom of choke lever slot, pull or push choke coil rod to end of travel. Rod should be positioned as shown. Bend choke coil rod to adjust.

MONOJET M, MV ADJUSTMENT SPECIFICATIONS

See Tune Up Chart in car chapters for hot idle speeds.

Year	Carb. Part No. ①	Initial Idle Mix Screw Turns Open	Float Level	Metering Rod	Idle Vent	Fast Idle Off Car	Choke Rod	Vacuum Break	Unloader	Fast Idle R.P.M.
BUICK										
1969	7029014	2	¼	.070	.050	—	.170	.245	.350	620④
	7029047	2	9/32	.140	.020	—	.190	.275	.350	720④
1970	7040014	2	¼	.070	.050	—	.170	.245	.350	650④
	7040015	2	¼	.140	.050	—	.200	.275	.350	900④
	7040017	—	¼	.070	—	.100	.190	.230	.350	900④
1971	7041014	—	¼	.080	.050	—	.160	.225	.500	500④
	7041017	—	¼	.080	.050	—	.180	.225	.350	550④
1973	7043014	—	¼	.080	—	—	.245	.300	.500	1800
	7043017	—	11/32	.080	—	—	.275	.350	.500	1800
1974	7044014	—	11/32	.080	—	—	.230	.275	.500	1800
	7044017	—	11/32	.080	—	—	.275	.350	.500	1800
1975	7045012	—	11/32	.080	—	—	.160	.200⑦	.275	—
	7045013	—	11/32	.080	—	—	.275	.350⑧	.275	—
	7045314	—	11/32	.080	—	—	.230	.275⑧	.275	—
CHECKER MOTORS										
1969	7029014	1½–2	¼	.070	.050	.100	.170	.245	.350	2400
	7029015	1½–2	¼	.090	.050	.100	.200	.245	.350	2400
	7029017	1½–2	¼	.090	.050	.100	.200	.245	.350	2400
1970	7040014	—	¼	.070	—	.100	.170	.200	.350	2400
1971	7041014	—	¼	.080	—	.100	.160	.200	.350	900①
1972	7042014	—	¼	.080	—	—	.125	.190	.500	2400
	7042984	—	¼	.080	—	—	.125	.190	.500	2400
1973	7043014	—	¼	.080	—	—	.245	.300	.500	1800
1974	7044014	—	19/64	.079	—	—	.230	.275	.500	1800
	7044314	—	19/64	.073	—	—	.245	.300	.500	1800

①—Low step.

Year	Carb. Part No. ①	Initial Idle Mix Screw Turns Open	Float Level	Metering Rod	Idle Vent	Fast Idle Off Car	Choke Rod	Vacuum Break	Unloader	Fast Idle R.P.M.
CHEVROLET ENGINES										
1969	7029008	3	¼	.080	.050	.100	.150	—	—	2400⑤
	7029014	3	¼	.070	.050	.100	.170	.245	.350	2400⑤
	7029015	3	¼	.090	.050	.100	.200	.275	.350	2400⑤
	7029017	3	¼	.090	.050	.100	.200	.275	.350	2400⑤
1970	7040008	—	¼	.080	—	.100	.200	—	—	2400⑥
	7040014	—	¼	.070	—	.110	.170	.200	.350	2400⑥
	7040017	—	¼	.090	—	.100	.190	.160	.350	2400⑥
1971	7041014	—	¼	.080	—	.100	.160	.200	.350	—
	7041017	—	¼	.080	—	.100	.180	.230	.350	—
	7041023	—	1/16	—	—	.110	.120	.200	.350	—
	7041024	—	1/16	—	—	.110	.080	.140	.350	—
1972	7042014	—	¼	.080	—	—	.125	.190	.500	2400
	7042017	—	¼	.078	—	—	.150	.225	.500	2400
	7042023	—	1/8	—	—	.110	.130	.200	.350	2400
	7042024	—	1/16	—	—	.110	.070	.120	.350	2400
	7042984	—	¼	.078	—	—	.125	.190	.500	2400
	7042987	—	¼	.076	—	—	.150	.225	.500	2400
	7042993	—	1/8	—	—	.110	.130	.200	.350	2400
	7042994	—	1/16	—	—	.110	.070	.120	.350	2400

Continued

MONOJET M, MV ADJUSTMENT SPECIFICATIONS—Continued

See Tune Up Chart in car chapters for hot idle speeds.

Year	Carb. Part No. ①	Initial Idle Mix Screw Turns Open	Float Level	Metering Rod	Idle Vent	Fast Idle Off Car	Choke Rod	Vacuum Break	Unloader	Fast Idle R.P.M.
CHEVROLET—Continued										
1973	7043014	—	¼	.080	—	—	.245	.300	.500	1800
	7043017	—	11/32	.080	—	—	.275	.350	.500	1800
	7043023	—	⅛	—	—	—	.090	.140	.375	2000
	7043024	—	⅛	—	—	—	.070	.120	.375	2200
	7043033	—	11/32	—	—	—	.090	.140	.375	2000
	7043034	—	⅛	—	—	—	.070	.120	.375	2200
	7043323	—	11/32	—	—	—	.090	.140	.375	2000
	7043324	—	⅛	—	—	—	.070	.120	.375	2200
	7043333	—	11/32	—	—	—	.090	.140	.375	2000
	7043334	—	⅛	—	—	—	.070	.120	.375	2200
1974	7044014	—	11/32	.080	—	—	.230	.275	.500	1800
	7044017	—	11/32	.080	—	—	.275	.350	.500	1800
	7044023	—	⅛	—	—	—	.080	.130	.375	2000
	7044024	—	⅛	—	—	—	.080	.130	.375	2200
	7044033	—	⅛	—	—	—	.080	.130	.375	2000
	7044034	—	⅛	—	—	—	.080	.130	.375	2200
	7044314	—	11/32	.080	—	—	.245	.300	.500	1800
	7044323	—	⅛	—	—	—	.080	.130	.375	2000
	7044324	—	⅛	—	—	—	.080	.130	.375	2200
	7044333	—	⅛	—	—	—	.080	.130	.375	2000
	7044334	—	⅛	—	—	—	.080	.130	.375	2200
	7044336	—	⅛	—	—	—	.245	.300	.500	1800
	7044337	—	⅛	.080	—	—	.080	.130	.375	2000
	7044339	—	11/32	—	—	—	.245	.300	.500	1800
	7044340	—	⅛	.080	—	—	.080	.130	.375	2200
1975	7045012	—	11/32	.080	—	—	.160	.200⑦	.215	—
	7045013	—	11/32	.080	—	—	.275	.350⑧	.275	—
	7045018	—	⅛	.080	—	—	.230	.275⑧	.275	—
	7045024	—	⅛	—	—	—	.080	.100⑨	.375	—
	7045025	—	⅛	—	—	—	.080	.100⑨	.375	—
	7045027	—	⅛	—	—	—	.075	.350⑧	.375	—
	7045028	—	⅛	—	—	—	.080	.100⑨	.375	—
	7045029	—	⅛	—	—	—	.080	.100⑨	.375	—
	7045038	—	11/32	.084	—	—	.080	.100⑨	.375	—
	7045314	—	11/32	.080	—	—	.230	.275⑧	.275	—
OLDSMOBILE										
1969	7029014	⑥	¼	.070	.050	—	.170	.245	.350	750④
	7029057	⑥	5/16	.120	.030	—	.180	.260	.350	750④
1970	7040014	⑥	¼	.070	—	—	.170	.200	.350	900④
	7040017	⑥	¼	.070	—	—	.190	.225	.350	750④
1971	7043014	⑥	¼	.070	—	—	.160	.200	.350	900④
	7043017	⑥	¼	.070	—	—	.180	.225	.350	750④
1973	7043014	⑥	¼	.080	—	—	.245	.300	.500	1800
	7043017	⑥	11/32	.080	—	—	.275	.350	.500	1800
1974	7044014	⑥	11/32	.080	—	—	.230	.275	.500	1800
	7044017	⑥	11/32	.080	—	—	.275	.350	.500	1800
	7044314	⑥	11/32	.080	—	—	.245	.300	.500	1800
1975	7045012	⑥	11/32	.080	—	—	.160	.200⑦	.275	—
	7045013	⑥	11/32	.080	—	—	.275	.350⑧	.275	—
	7045314	⑥	11/32	.080	—	—	.230	.275⑧	.275	—

Continued

MONOJET M, MV ADJUSTMENT SPECIFICATIONS—Continued

See Tune Up Chart in car chapters for hot idle speeds.

Year	Carb. Part No. ①	Initial Idle Mix Screw Turns Open	Float Level	Metering Rod	Idle Vent	Fast Idle Off Car	Choke Rod	Vacuum Break	Unloader	Fast Idle R.P.M.
PONTIAC										
1969	7029165	5	9/32	.085	.040	.120	.200	.275	.450	2400⑤
	7029166	5	9/32	.085	.040	.130	.180	.260	.450	2800⑤
	7029167	5	9/32	.085	.040	.120	.200	.275	.450	2600⑤
	7029168	5	9/32	.085	.040	.130	.180	.260	.450	2800⑤
1970	7040014	⑥	1/4	.100	—	—	.170	.200	.350	—
	7040017	⑥	1/4	.100	—	—	.190	.230	.350	—
1971	7041014	⑥	1/4	.080	—	—	.160	.200	.350	—
	7041017	⑥	1/4	.078	—	—	.180	.225	.350	—
1972	7042014	⑥	1/4	.080	—	—	.160	.200	.500	2400
	7042017	⑥	1/4	.080	—	—	.180	.230	.500	2400
	7042984	⑥	1/4	.080	—	—	.160	.200	.500	2400
	7042987	⑥	1/4	.080	—	—	.180	.230	.500	2400
1973	7043014	⑥	11/32	.080	—	—	.245	.300	.500	1800
	7043017	⑥	11/32	.080	—	—	.275	.350	.500	1800
1974	7044017	⑥	11/32	.080	—	—	.275	.350	.500	1800
	7044041	⑥	11/32	.079	—	—	.230	.275	.500	1800
	7044314	⑥	11/32	.080	—	—	.245	.300	.500	1800
1975	7045012	⑥	11/32	.080	—	—	.160	.200⑨	.275	—
	7045013	⑥	11/32	.080	—	—	.275	.350⑦	.275	—
	7045314	⑥	11/32	.080	—	—	.230	.275⑦	.275	—

①—On tag attached to carburetor.
②—20 RPM above slow idle speed.
③—Turns in from slow idle position.
④—On low step of cam.
⑤—On high step of cam.
⑥—Air/fuel ratio or idle CO% rating is found in Tune Up Specification tables in car chapters.
⑦—Rear .215.
⑧—Rear .312.
⑨—Rear .450.

MONOJET M & MV ADJUSTMENTS

The Monojet carburetor is a single-bore downdraft unit with a triple venturi coupled with a refined metering system which results in a unit having superior fuel mixture control and performance.

A plain tube nozzle is used in conjuction with the multiple venturi. Fuel flow through the main metering system is controlled by a mechanically and vacuum operated variable orifice jet. This consists of a specially tapered rod which operates in the fixed orifice main metering jet and is connected directly by linkage to the main throttle shaft. A vacuum-operated enrichment system is used in conjunction with the main metering system to provide good performance during moderate to heavy accelerations.

A separate and adjustable idle system is used in conjunction with the main metering system to meet fuel mixture requirements during engine idle and low speed operation. The off-idle discharge port is of a vertical slot design which gives good transition between curb idle and main metering system operation.

The idle system incorporates a hot idle compensator on some models where necessary to maintain smooth engine idle during periods of extreme hot engine operation.

The main metering system has an adjustable flow feature which enables production to control the fuel mixture more accurately then attained heretofore.

The Monojet carburetor is designed so that a manual or automatic choke system can be used. The conventional choke valve is located in the air horn bore. On automatic choke models, the vacuum diaphragm unit is an integral part of the air horn. The automatic choke coil is manifold mounted and connects to the choke valve shaft by connecting linkage.

The choke system has a new feature to give added enrichment during cold start. This feature greatly reduces starting time and yet allows the use of low torque thermostatic coils for increased economy.

The carburetor has internally balanced venting through a vent hole in the air horn. An external idle vent valve is used on some models where necessary for improved hot engine idle and starting.

Float Level Adjustment
Fig. 2
1. Hold float retaining pin firmly in place and float arm against top of float needle by pushing downward on float arm at point between needle seat and hinge pin as shown.
2. With adjustable T-scale, measure distance from top of float at toe to float bowl gasket surface (gasket removed). Measurement should be made at a point $1/16$" in from end of flat surface at float toe (not on radius).
3. Bend float pontoon up or down at float arm junction to adjust.

Metering Rod Adjustment
Fig. 3
1. Remove metering rod by holding throttle valve wide open. Push down-

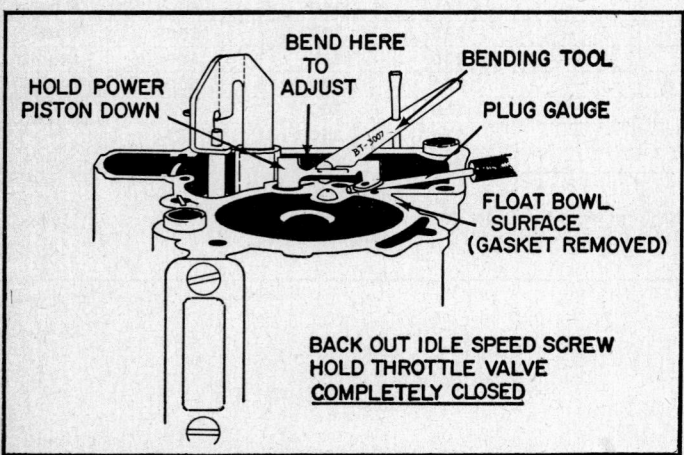

Fig. 3 Monojet metering rod adjustment

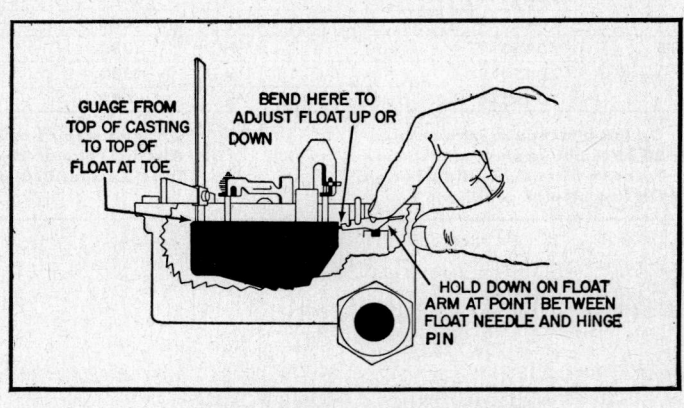

Fig. 2 Monojet float level adjustment

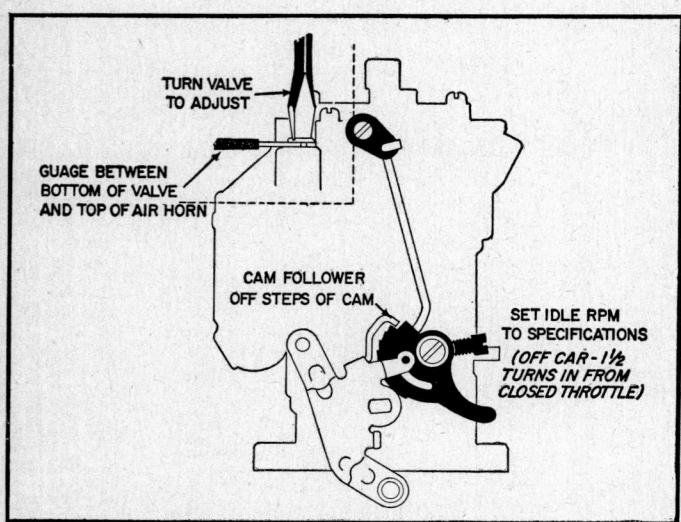

Fig. 4 Monojet idle vent adjustment

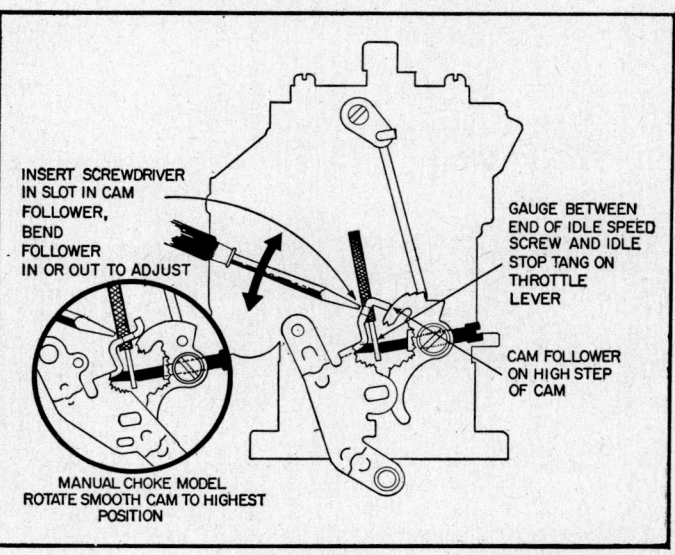

Fig. 5 Monojet fast idle adjustment (off car)

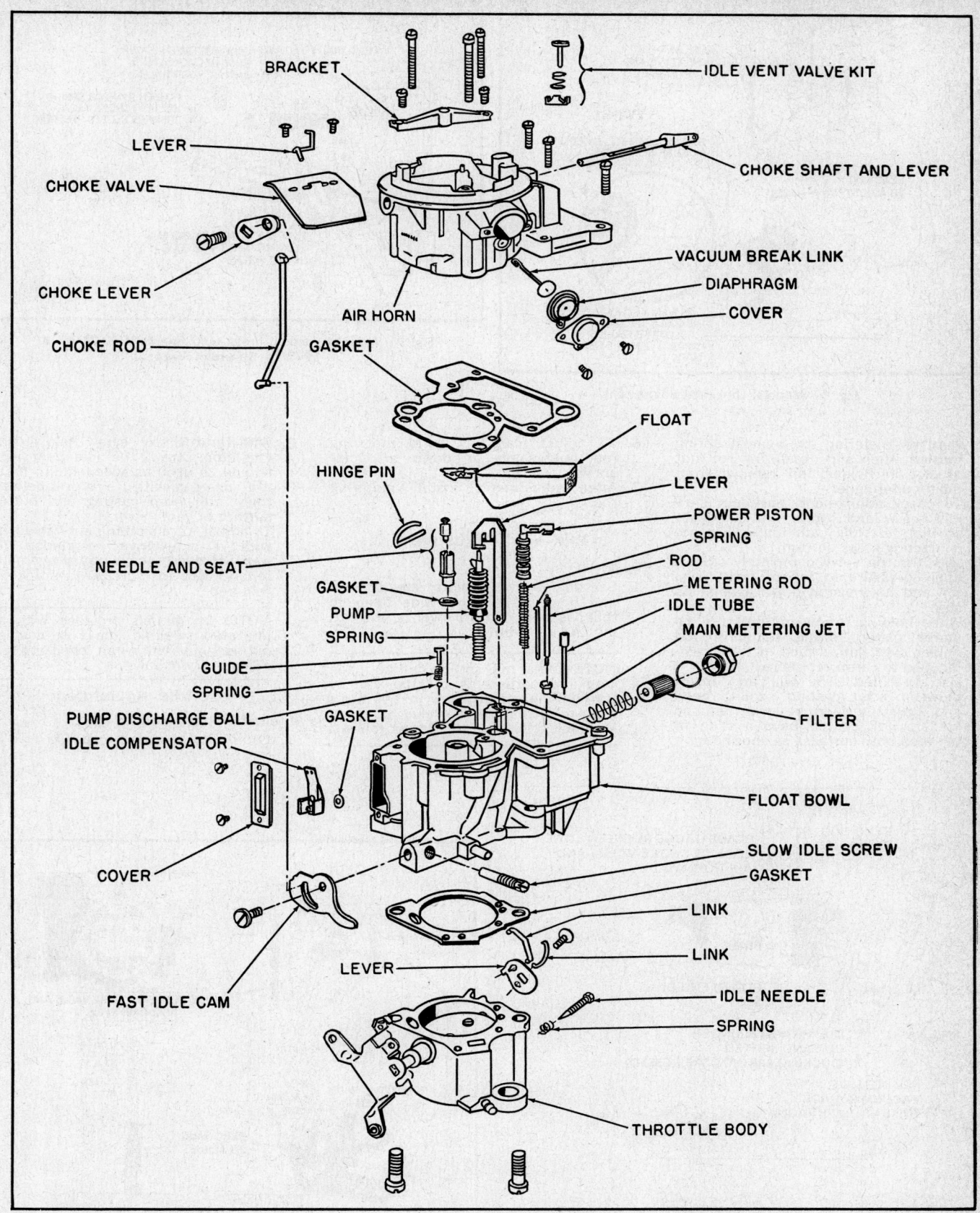

Fig. 1   Monojet Model MV carburetor. Model M has manual choke

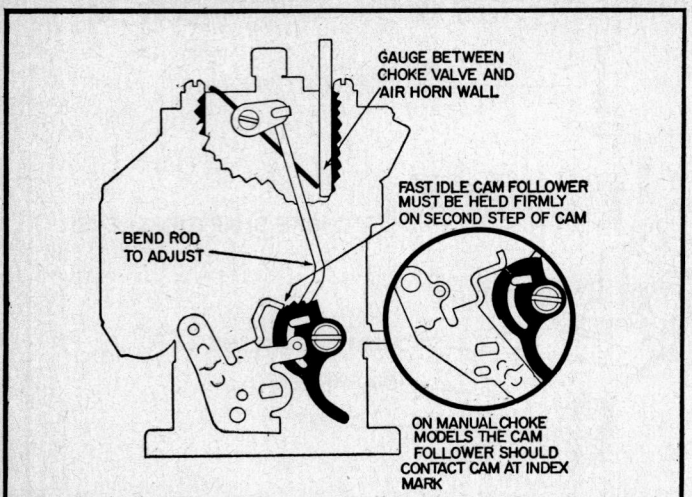

Fig. 6   Monojet choke rod adjustment

Fig. 7   Monojet vacuum break adjustment. 1969-71 All & 1971-74 Chevrolet Vega

ward on metering rod against spring tension, then slide metering rod out of slot in holder and remove from main metering jet.
2. To check adjustment, back out slow idle screw and rotate fast idle cam so that fast idle cam follower is not contacting steps on cam.
3. With throttle valve completely closed, apply pressure to top of power piston and hold piston down against its stop.
4. While holding downward pressure on power piston, swing metering rod holder over flat surface of bowl casting next to carburetor bore.
5. Use specified size drill and insert between bowl casting sealing bead and lower surface of metering rod holder. Drill should have a slide fit between both surfaces as shown.

6. To adjust, carefully bend metering rod holder up or down at point shown.
7. After adjustment, install metering rod.

Idle Vent Adjustment

Fig. 4
1. Set engine idle rpm to specification and hold choke valve wide open so that fast idle cam follower is not hitting fast idle cam.

NOTE: Initial idle setting can be made with the carburetor off the car by turning idle speed screw in 1½ turns from closed throttle valve position. Recheck setting on the car as follows:

2. With throttle stop screw held against idle stop screw, the idle vent valve should be open as specified. To measure, insert specified size drill between top of air horn casting and bottom surface of vent valve.
3. To adjust, turn slotted vent valve head with a screwdriver clockwise (inward) to decrease clearance and counterclockwise to increase clearance as required.

NOTE: On models provided with the idle stop solenoid, make sure solenoid is activated when checking and adjusting vent valve.

Fast Idle Adjustment
Automatic Choke Models, Fig. 5
1. Set normal engine idle speed.

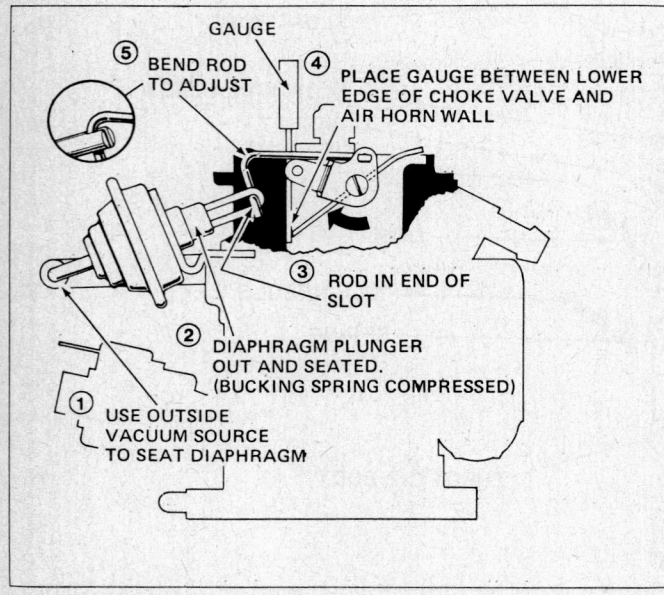

Fig. 8   Monojet vacuum break adjustment. 1972-74 All exc. Chevrolet Vega

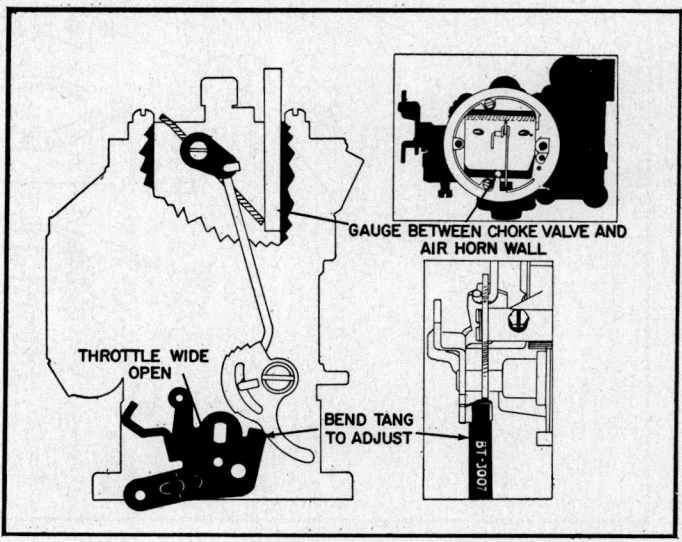

Fig. 9   Monojet unloader adjustment

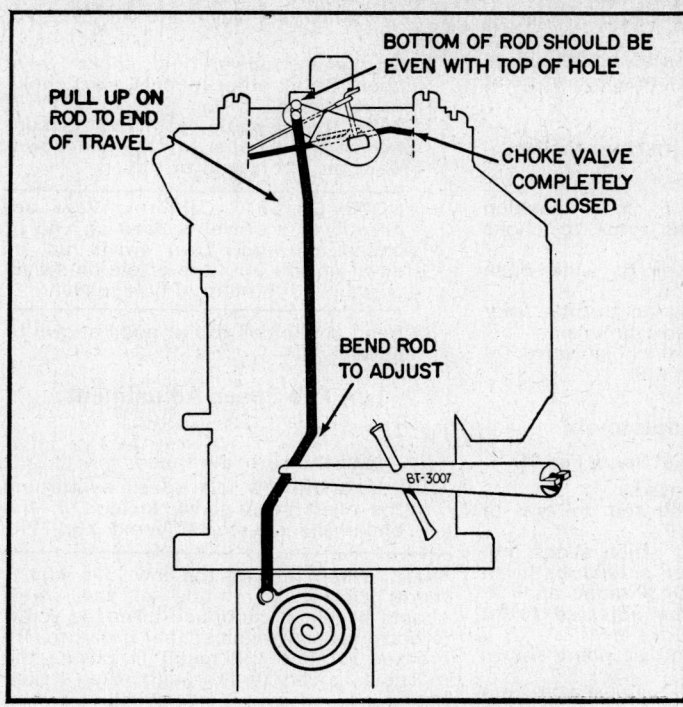

Fig. 10   Monojet choke coil adjustment. Typical

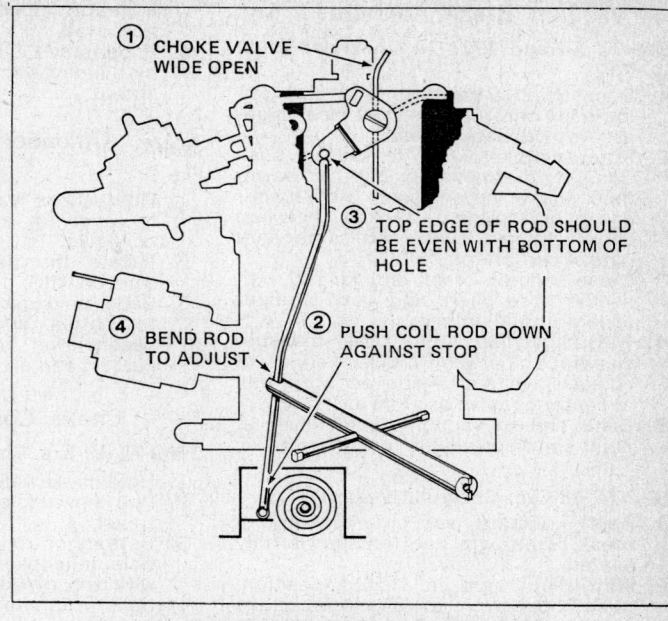

Fig. 11   Monojet choke coil adjustment. Typical

2. Place fast idle cam follower tang on highest step of cam.
3. With tang held against cam, check clearance between end of slow idle speed screw and idle stop tang on throttle lever. It should be as specified.
4. To adjust, insert screwdriver in slot provided in fast idle cam follower tang and bend inwards (towards cam) or outward to obtain specified dimension.

Manual Choke Models

Use same procedure as above except in Step 2 rotate fast idle cam clockwise to its farthest up position.

Choke Rod Adjustment

Automatic Choke Models, Fig. 6
1. With fast idle adjustment made, place fast idle cam follower on second step of fast idle cam and hold firmly against the rise to the high step.
2. Rotate choke towards direction of closed choke by applying force to choke coil lever.
3. Bend choke rod at point shown to give specified opening between lower edge of choke valve (at center of valve) and inside air horn wall.

Manual Choke Models

Use same procedure as above except in Step 1. As there are no steps on the manual choke cam, the index line on side of cam should be lined up with contact point of fast idle cam follower tang.

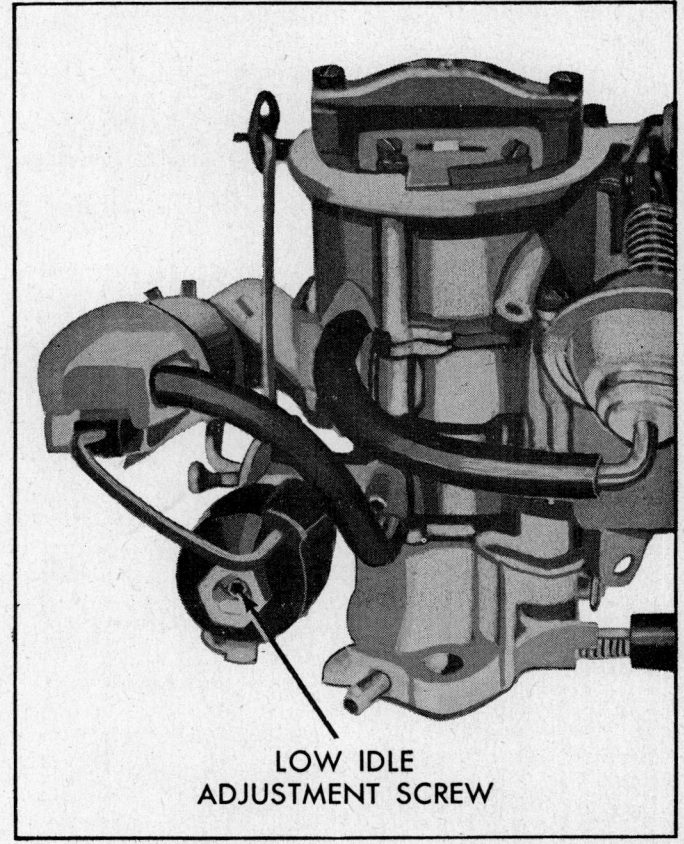

Fig. 12   Monojet low idle speed adjustment, 1972-73 Chevrolet

Vacuum Break Adjustment

1969-71 All and 1971-74 Chevrolet Vega, Fig. 7

1. Open throttle valve so that cam follower on throttle lever will clear highest step on fast idle cam.
2. Rotate choke valve to closed position. If thermostatic coil is warm, hold choke valve closed with rubber band or spring attached between choke shaft lever and stationary part of carburetor.
3. Grasp vacuum break plunger rod with needle nose pliers and push straight inward until diaphragm seats.
4. With specified drill size, measure clearance between lower edge of choke valve and inside air horn wall at center of valve as shown.
5. Bend end of vacuum break lever at point shown to adjust.

1972-74 All Exc. Chevrolet Vega, Fig. 8

1. Apply outside vacuum to vacuum break diaphragm until plunger is fully seated.
2. With diaphragm in seated position, push choke valve to the closed choke position. Vacuum break rod should be at end of slot in the diaphragm plunger and spring loaded plunger fully compressed.
3. Measure clearance between lower edge of choke valve and inside air horn wall.
4. If clearance is not as specified, adjust by bending vacuum break rod at point shown.

Unloader Adjustment

Fig. 9

1. Hold choke valve in closed position by applying a light force to choke coil lever.
2. Rotate throttle lever to wide open throttle valve position.
3. Bend unloader tang on throttle lever to obtain specified dimension between lower edge of choke valve (at center) and air horn wall.

Choke Coil Adjustment

1969-71 All Exc. Chevrolet Vega, Fig. 10

1. Hold choke valve closed.
2. Pull upward on coil rod to end of travel.
3. Bottom of rod end which slides into hole in choke lever should be even with top of hole. *On Pontiac applications rod should be adjusted to fit in notch in top of choke lever.*
4. Bend choke coil rod at point shown to adjust.
5. Connect coil rod to choke lever and install retaining clip.

1971-74 Chevrolet Vega and All 1972-74, Fig. 11

1. On Vega models, hold choke valve open. On all other models, hold choke valve closed.
2. With thermostatic coil rod disconnected from upper lever, push downward on rod to end of travel.

NOTE: On 1972 California Vega applications, a swivel is used on end of choke coil rod. Turn swivel up or down on rod until top of pin on swivel is even with bottom of hole in lever.

3. Bend choke coil rod at point shown to adjust.

Low Idle Speed Adjustment

Fig. 12

1. Adjust the curb idle speed.
2. Adjust the low idle speed by turning the allen head screw located in the end of the idle stop solenoid, Fig. 12.

NOTE: When making the low idle adjustment, clockwise rotation of the screw should never be continued after the screw is bottomed out against the armature. Increased rotation will result in raising the solenoid cover up through the staked housing.

ONE & TWO BARREL CARB. ADJUSTMENT SPECIFICATIONS

See Tune Up Chart in car chapter for hot idle speeds.

Year	Carb. Part No.①	Carb. Model	Idle Mixture Turns Open	Float Level (Dry)	Fuel Level (Wet)	Pump Setting	Bowl Vent Clearance	Fast Idle Bench	Fast Idle On Car	Choke Unloader Clearance	Anti-Stall Dashpot Clearance	Choke Setting
AMERICAN MOTORS												
1969	4294A	1931	1	5/16	—	②	1/16	—	1600⑦	15/64	—	1 Rich
CHEVROLET ENGINES												
1969–70	R4055-A	2300	1½	.350	③	.015	.085	.025	2200	.250	—	⑥
	R4056-A	2300	1½	.350	③	.015	.085	.025	2200	.250	—	⑥
	R3659-A	2300	—	.350	③							

Year	Carb. Part No.①	Carb. Model	Idle Mixture Turns Open	Float Level (Dry)	Fuel Level (Wet)	Pump Setting	Bowl Vent Clearance	Fast Idle Bench	Fast Idle On Car	Choke Unloader Clearance	Vacuum Kick Drill Size	Cam Position Drill Size	Choke Setting
CHRYSLER ENGINES													
1969	R-4161-A	1920	⑱	See Text	27/32	⑥	3/32	—	1600⑪	9/32⑮	#39	#52	2 Rich
	R-4162-A	1920	⑱	See Text	27/32	⑥	3/32	—	1800⑪	9/32⑮	#50	#52	2 Rich
	R-4163-A	1920	⑱	See Text	27/32	⑥	3/32	—	1600⑪	9/32⑮	#39	#52	2 Rich
	R-4164-A	1920	⑱	See Text	27/32	⑥	3/32	—	1800⑪	9/32⑮	#50	#52	2 Rich
	R-4165-A	1920	⑱	See Text	27/32	⑥	3/32	—	1700⑪	9/32⑮	#39	#52	—
	R-4391-A	2300	⑱	9/16	③	.015	.080–.125	.059	2200	5/32	—	—	See Text
	R-4392A	2300	⑱	9/16	③	.015	.080–.125	.059	1800	5/32	—	—	See Text
	R-4393A	2300	⑱	3/4	③	—	—	—	—	—	—	—	—
	R-4394A	2300	⑱	3/4	③	—	—	—	—	—	—	—	—
1970	R-4351A	1920	⑱	See Text	27/32	⑥	3/32	—	1600⑪	④	#39	#52	2 Rich
	R-4352A	1920	⑱	See Text	27/32	⑥	3/32	—	1800⑪	④	#50	#52	2 Rich
	R-4353A	1920	⑱	See Text	27/32	⑥	3/32	—	1600⑪	④	#39	#52	2 Rich
	R-4354A	1920	⑱	See Text	27/32	⑥	3/32	—	1800⑪	④	#50	#52	2 Rich
	R-4355A	1920	⑱	See Text	27/32	⑥	3/32	—	1700⑪	④	#39	#52	2 Rich
	R-4363A	1920	⑱	See Text	27/32	⑥	3/32	—	1700⑪	④	#39	#52	2 Rich
	R-4371A	2210	⑱	.200	—		5/64	—	1700⑪	11/64	#28	#35	2 Rich
	R-4175AF	2300	⑱	⑰	③	—	—	—	—	—	—	—	—
	R-4144A	2300	⑱	⑰	③	.015	.101	.059	1800	5/32	#50	#53	2 Rich
	R-4365AR	2300	⑱	⑰	③	—	—	—	—	—	—	—	—
	R-4374A	2300	⑱	⑰	③	.015	.101	.059	2200	5/32	#28	#53	2 Rich
	R-4375A	2300	⑱	⑰	③	.015	.101	.059	2200	5/32	#28	#53	2 Rich
	R-4376A	2300	⑱	⑰	③	.015	.101	.059	1800	5/32	#50	#53	2 Rich
	R-4382AF	2300	⑱	⑰	③	—	—	—	—	—	—	—	—
	R-4383AR	2300	⑱	⑰	③	—	—	—	—	—	—	—	—
1971	R-4655A	1920	⑱	See Text	27/32	—	1/32	.063	1600	9/32	#39	#52	2 Rich
	R-4656A	1920	⑱	See Text	27/32	—	1/32	.063	1900	5/32	#39	#52	2 Rich
	R-4659A	1920	⑱	See Text	27/32	—	1/32	.063	1800	5/32	#39	#52	2 Rich
	R-6363A	1920	⑱	See Text	27/32	—	1/64	.063	2000	9/32	—	—	2 Rich
	R-6364A	1920	⑱	See Text	27/32	—	1/64	.063	1900	9/32	—	—	2 Rich
	R-4373A	2210	⑱	.200	—	9/16	5/64	.110	1700	11/64	—	—	2 Rich
	R-4665A	2210	⑱	.200	—	9/16	.015	.110	1800	1/4	#28	#35	2 Rich
	R-4666A	2210	⑱	.200	—	9/16	.015	.110	1800	1/4	#30	#35	2 Rich
	R-4669A	2300	⑱	⑰	③	.015	.101	.059	1800	5/32	—	—	2 Rich
	R-4670A	2300	⑱	⑰	③	.015	.101	.059	1800	5/32	—	—	2 Rich
	R-4671A	2300	⑱	⑰	③	—	—	—	—	—	—	—	—
	R-4672A	2300	⑱	⑰	③	—	—	—	—	—	—	—	—
	R-4789A	2300	⑱	⑰	③	—	—	—	—	—	—	—	—

Continued

HOLLEY CARBURETORS

ONE & TWO BARREL CARB. ADJUSTMENT SPECIFICATIONS—Continued

See Tune Up Chart in car chapter for hot idle speeds.

Year	Carb. Part No.①	Carb. Model	Idle Mixture Turns Open	Float Level (Dry)	Fuel Level (Wet)	Pump Setting	Bowl Vent Clearance	Fast Idle Bench	Fast Idle On Car	Choke Unloader Clearance	Vacuum Kick Drill Size	Cam Position Drill Size	Choke Setting
CHRYSLER ENGINES—Continued													
1971	R-4790A	2300	⑱	⑰	③	—	—	—	—	—	—	—	—
	R-4791A	2300	⑱	⑰	③	.015	.101	.059	2600	5/32	#28	#53	On Index
	R-4792A	2300	⑱	⑰	③	.015	.101	.059	2800	5/32	#39	#53	On Index
1972	R-6153A	1920	⑱	See Text	27/32	—	.015	.063	2000	④	.100	.064	Fixed
	R-6154A	1920	⑱	See Text	27/32	—	.015	.063	2000	④	.100	.064	Fixed
	R-6155A	1920	⑱	See Text	27/32	—	.015	.063	2000	④	.100	.064	Fixed
	R-6156A	1920	⑱	See Text	27/32	—	.015	.063	2000	④	.100	.064	Fixed
	R-6159A	1920	⑱	See Text	27/32	—	.015	.063	1900	④	.100	.064	Fixed
	R-6363A	1920	⑱	See Text	27/32	—	.015	.063	2000	④	.100	.064	Fixed
	R-6364A	1920	⑱	See Text	27/32	—	.015	.063	1900	④	.100	.064	Fixed
	R-6365A	1920	⑱	See Text	27/32	—	.015	.063	2000	④	.100	.064	Fixed
	R-6366A	1920	⑱	See Text	27/32	—	.015	.063	2000	④	.100	.064	Fixed
	R-6162A	2210	⑱	.180	—	.285	.015	.110	1900	.170	.100	.064	Fixed
	R-6164A	2210	⑱	.180	—	.250	.015	.110	2000	.170	.100	.064	Fixed
	R-6368A	2210	⑱	.180	—	.285	.015	.110	1900	.170	.100	.064	Fixed
	R-6370A	2210	⑱	.180	—	.285	.015	.110	2000	.170	.100	.064	Fixed
	R-6404A	2300	⑱	⑰	③	.015	.015	—	1800	.150	.130	.110	Fixed
	R-6405A	2300	⑱	—	—	—	—	—	—	—	.130	.110	
	R-6406A	2300	⑱	—	—	—	—	—	—	—	.130	.110	
1973	R-6447A	1920	⑱	.260	—	—	.015	.065	2000	④	.100	.065	Fixed
	R-6448A	1920	⑱	.260	—	—	.015	.045	1700	④	.080	.045	Fixed
	R-6593A⑨	1920	⑱	.260	—	—	.015	.065	2000	④	.100	.065	Fixed
	R-6594A	1920	⑱	.260	—	—	.015	.065	1700	④	.100	.065	Fixed
	R-6595A	1920	⑱	.260	—	—	.015	.065	2000	④	.100	.065	Fixed
	R-6596A⑨	1920	⑱	.260	—	—	.015	.065	1700	④	.100	.065	Fixed
	R-6452A	2210	⑱	.180	—	.250	.015	.110	1900	.170	.150	.110	Fixed
	R-6454A	2210	⑱	.180	—	.250	.015	.110	1800	.170	.150	.110	Fixed
	R-6472A⑨	2210	⑱	.180	—	.250	.015	.110	1800	.170	.150	.110	Fixed
	R-6575A⑨	2210	⑱	.180	—	.250	.015	.110	1900	.170	.150	.110	Fixed
1974	R-6721A	1945	⑱	1/32	—	11/16	—	.080	1600	.250	.140	.080	Fixed
	R-6722A	1945	⑱	1/32	—	13/16	—	.080	1800	.250	.090	.080	Fixed
	R-6723A	1945	⑱	1/32	—	11/16	—	.080	1600	.250	.140	.080	Fixed
	R-6724A	1945	⑱	1/32	—	3/4	—	.080	1800	.250	.080	.080	Fixed
	R-6725A⑨	1945	⑱	1/32	—	11/16	—	.080	1600	.250	.140	.080	Fixed
	R-6726A⑨	1945	⑱	1/32	—	3/4	—	.080	1800	.250	.090	.080	Fixed
	R-6731A	2245	⑱	.180	—	.255	.015	.110	1800	.170	.150	.110	Fixed
	R-6737A	2245	⑱	.180	—	.255	.015	.110	1600	.170	.150	.110	Fixed
1975	R-7017A	1945	⑱	3/64	—	—	—	.080	1600	.250	.130	.080	Fixed
	R-7018A	1945	⑱	3/64	—	—	—	.080	1700	.250	.090	.080	Fixed
	R-7019A	1945	⑱	3/64	—	—	—	.080	1600	.250	.130	.080	Fixed
	R-7020A	1945	⑱	3/64	—	—	—	.080	1700	.250	.090	.080	Fixed
	R-7027A	2245	⑱	3/16	—	1/4	.015	.110	1600	.170	.150	.110	Fixed
	R-7029A	1945	⑱	3/64	—	—	—	.080	1600	.250	.130	.080	Fixed
	R-7210A	1945	⑱	3/64	—	—	—	.080	1700	.250	.090	.080	Fixed

Continued

ONE & TWO BARREL CARB. ADJUSTMENT SPECIFICATIONS—Continued

See Tune Up Chart in car chapter for hot idle speeds.

Year	Carb. Part No.①	Carb. Model	Idle Mixture Turns Open	Float Level (Dry)	Fuel Level (Wet)	Pump Setting	Bowl Vent Clearance	Fast Idle Bench	Fast Idle On Car	Choke Unloader Clearance	Vacuum Kick Drill Size	Cam Position Drill Size	Choke Setting
CHRYSLER ENGINES—Continued													
1975	R-7211A	2245	⑱	3/16	—	1/4	.015	.110	1600	.170	.150	.110	Fixed
	R-7226A	2245	⑱	3/16	—	1/4	.015	.110	1600	.170	.150	.110	Fixed
	R-7329A	1945	⑱	3/64	—	—	—	.080	1700	.250	.130	.080	Fixed

①—Located on tag attached to carburetor or on casting.
②—Seasonal setting holes in lever; long stroke for cold weather, short stroke for warm weather.
③—At lower edge of sight plug opening.
④—Unloader automatically set when fast idle cam is adjusted.
⑥—Seasonal setting; use center hole for moderate weather, long stroke hole for cold weather, and short stroke hole for warm weather.
⑦—Engine hot and screw on second step of cam.
⑧—See "Fast idle index adjustment" in text.
⑨—With California Emission package.
⑩—With headlights on A-C operating (if equipped); engine hot and screw on lowest step of cam.

⑪—Engine hot and screw on highest step of cam.
⑫—Engine hot and screw on second highest step of cam.
⑬—Lever touching screw; then tighten screw 1/4 turn.
⑭—Between throttle valve and carburetor bore.
⑮—With fast idle speed adjusting screw contacting second highest step on fast idle cam there should be 1/16" clearance between choke valve and wall of air horn. When this adjustment is correct the choke unloader clearance should be as specified in the chart.
⑯—Top of rod should be even with bottom of hole.
⑰—Center float in bowl with bowl inverted.
⑱—Air/fuel ratio or idle CO% rating is found in Tune Up chart in car chapters.

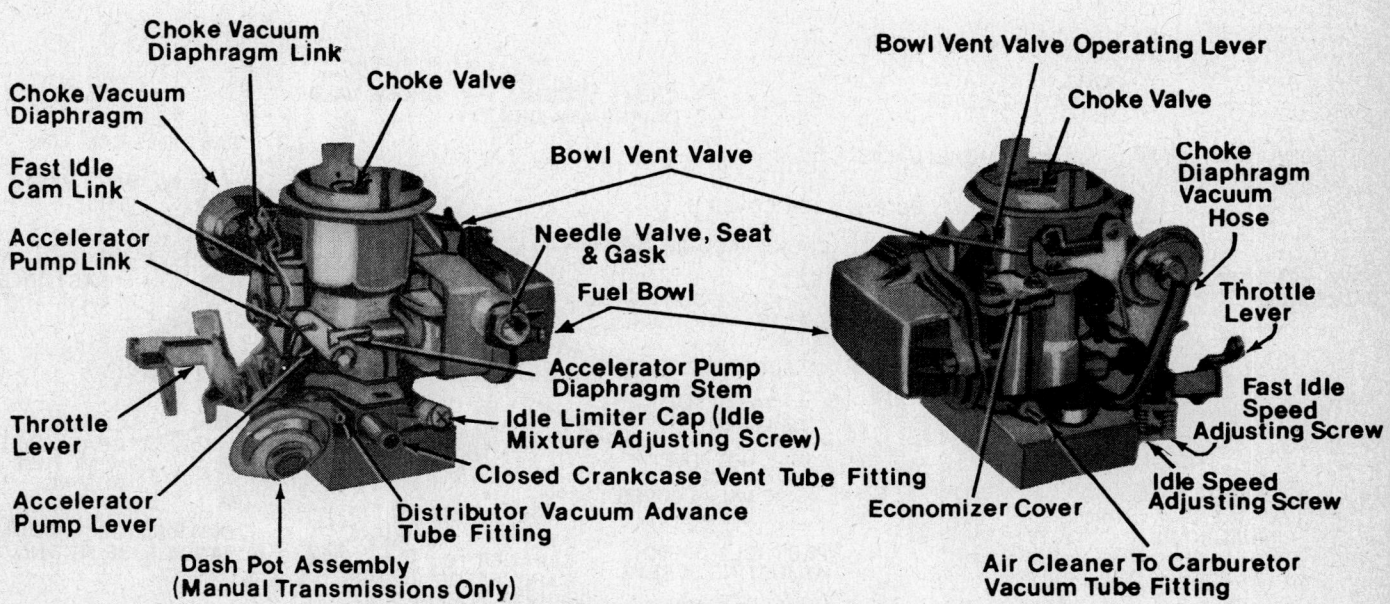

Fig. 1   Holley model 1920 single-barrel carburetor. C.A.S. equipped 1969-72 typical

ONE & TWO BARREL CARBURETOR ADJUSTMENTS

MODEL 1920

On these units, Figs. 1 thru 4, the choke valve located in the carburetor bore is connected to a well type choke.

Some models are equipped with a spring-staged choke, shown in Fig. 12, which is a device incorporated in the choke mechanism that limits the choke valve closing torque when cranking the engine at temperatures below zero. The spring-staging of the choke is suited for starting mixture requirements at both low and moderate temperatures. On 1973 Chrysler units, an electric choke system is incorporated to open choke at approximately 63°. For service information refer to the "Emission Control System" chapter.

The accelerator pump is a diaphragm, spring driven type operated by a lever connected to the throttle shaft.

A two stage power valve mounted in the metering body and actuated by manifold vacuum delivers additional fuel for full power and high speed operation.

Float Level Setting

NOTE: Do not allow float tab to contact float needle head during the adjustment procedure as the rubber tip of the needle can be compressed, giving a false reading.

1969-72 Units

Fig. 5—With carburetor inverted slide float gauge into position and test setting on "touch" leg of gauge. Float should just touch gauge. Reverse gauge and test "no touch" leg. Float should just clear gauge. To adjust, bend float tab which touches head of fuel inlet needle, using needle nose pliers.

1973 Units

Fig. 6—With the carburetor inverted, measure from the top of the float to the upper wall of the main body with the gauge against the cast rib approximately two inches from the float hinge pin. Be sure the gauge is parallel with the top of the float. Refer to *Holley Specifications Chart* for proper dry float setting. Adjust by bending the float tab which touches the head of the fuel inlet needle using needle nosed pliers.

Checking Fuel Level

Fig. 7—With engine running and vehicle on a level floor, measure fuel level through the economizer diaphragm opening. Use a 6″ scale with a depth gauge, measure distance from machined surface of the opening to the exact fuel surface. If the level is not as listed in the *Holley Specifications Chart*, adjust the float level as outlined above.

Float Bowl Vent Valve Setting

Fig. 8—With throttle valve closed, bowl vent should be adjusted so that the shank of a drill of the size listed in the *Holley Specifications Chart* can be inserted between valve and surface of carburetor body. Adjust by bending bowl vent operating lever up or down as required. Be sure vent rod does not bind in the guide after adjusting.

Fast Idle Cam Position and Choke Unloader Adjustment

Fig. 9—With fast idle speed adjusting screw contacting second highest step on fast idle cam, move choke valve toward closed position with light pressure on choke shaft lever. Insert specified gauge between top of choke valve and wall of air horn. Refer to *Holley Specifications Chart*. Adjust by bending fast idle link at angle, until correct valve opening has been obtained.

NOTE: IMPORTANT: When the correct fast idle cam position adjustment has been made, the choke unloader (wide open kick) adjustment has also been obtained. No further adjustment is required.

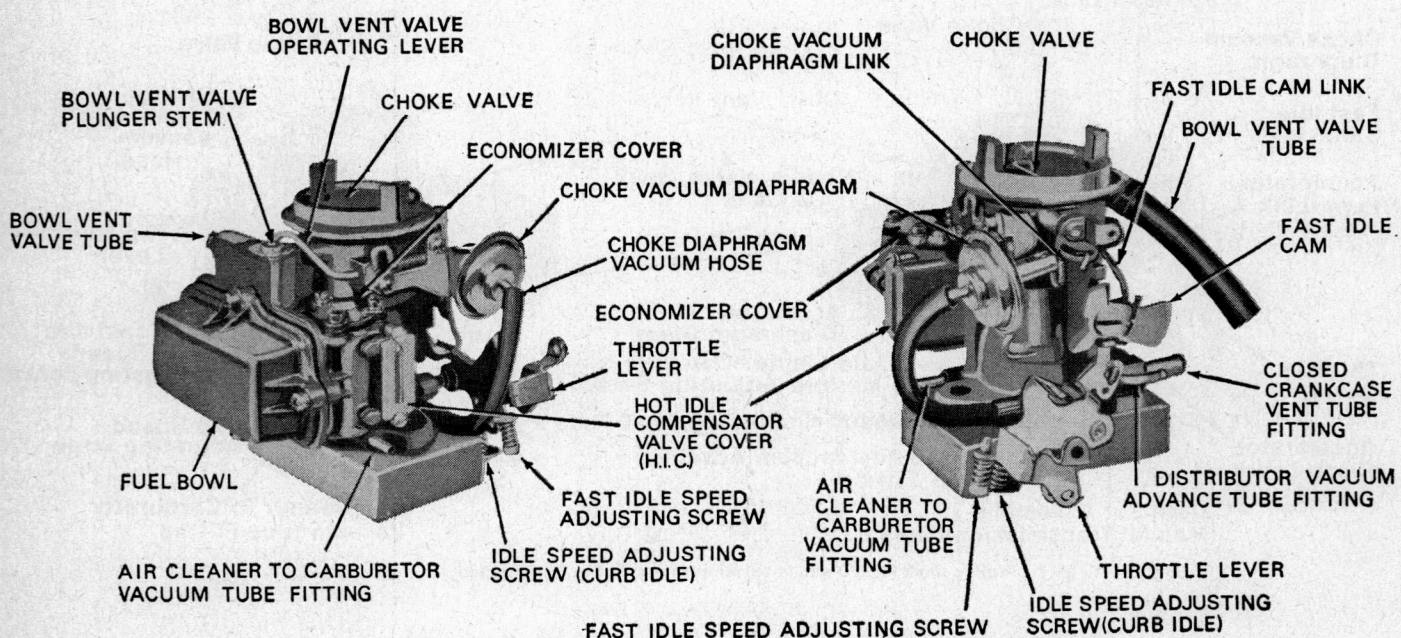

Fig. 2 Holley model 1920 single-barrel carburetor. E.C.S. equipped 1969-72 typical

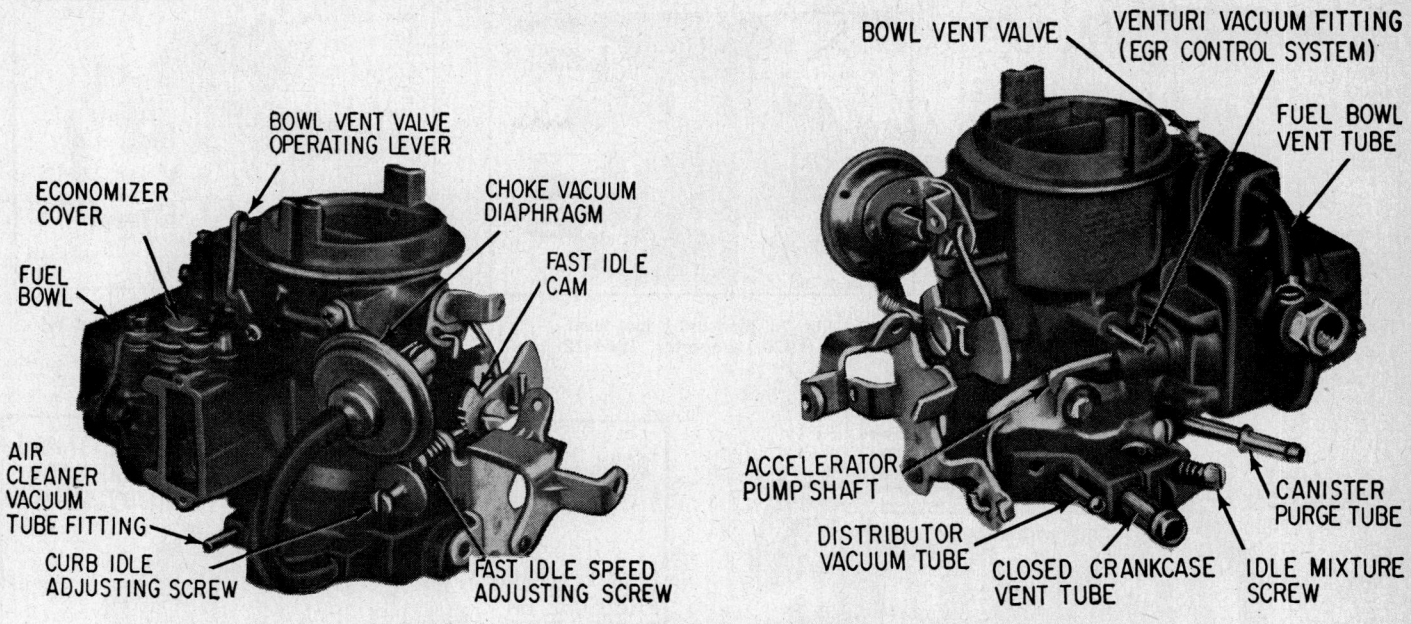

Fig. 3 Holley model 1920 single-barrel carburetor. 1973 typical

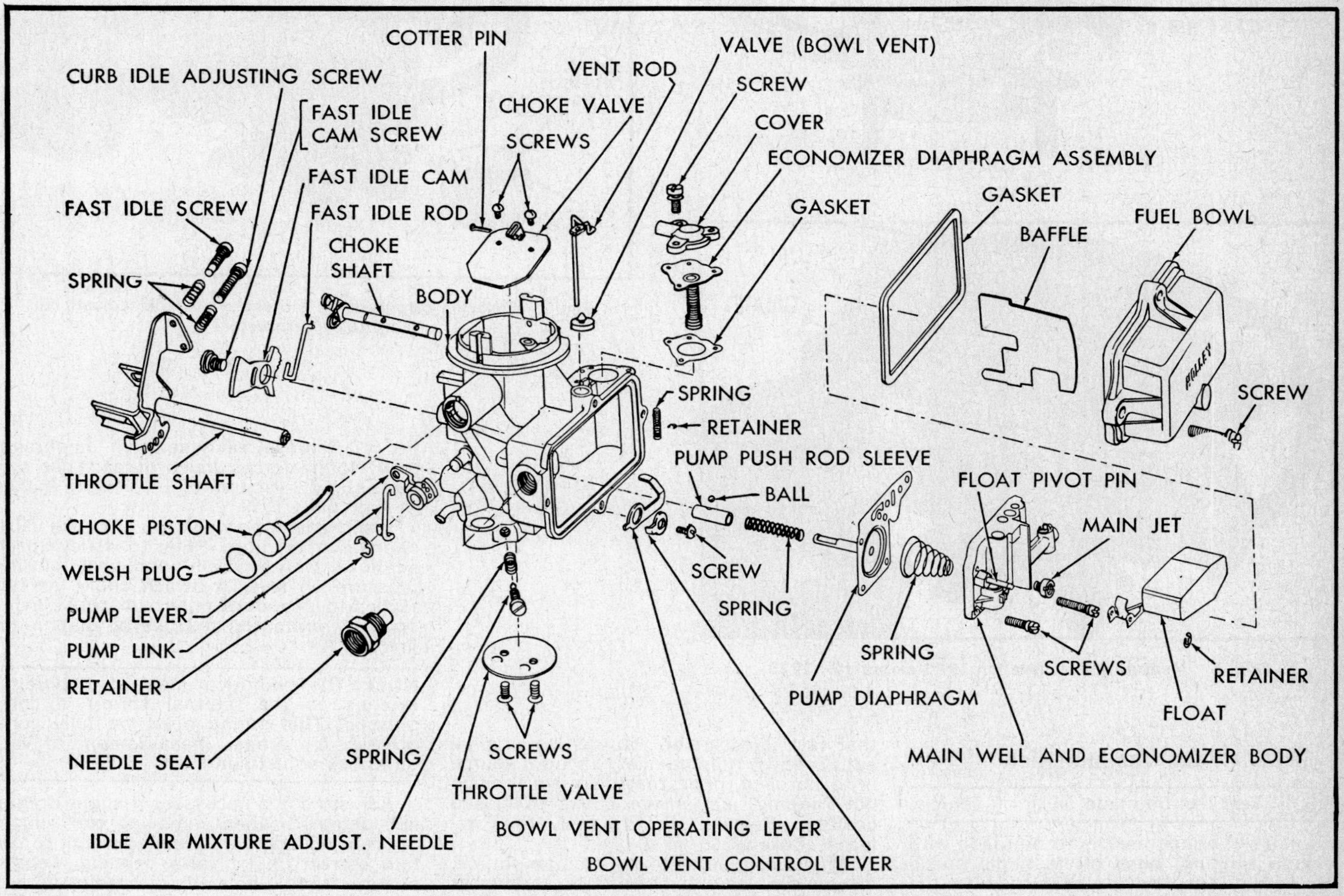

Fig. 4 Exploded view of typical Holley 1920 carburetor

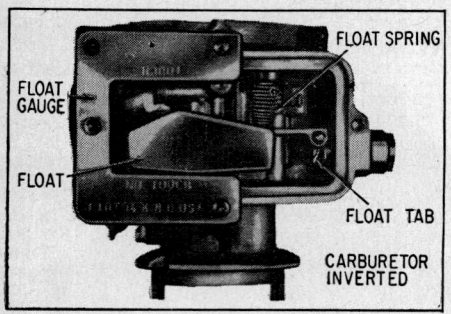

Fig. 5 Measuring float level
on 1920 carburetor, 1969-72

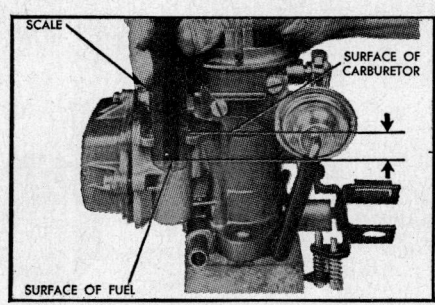

Fig. 7 Measuring fuel level
on 1920 carburetor, 1969-72

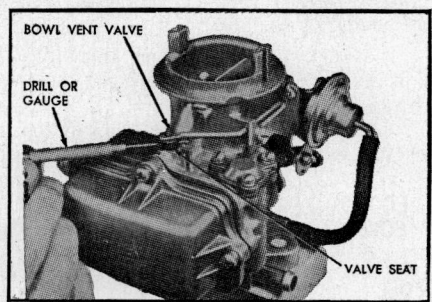

Fig. 8 Measuring bowl vent opening
on 1920 carburetor

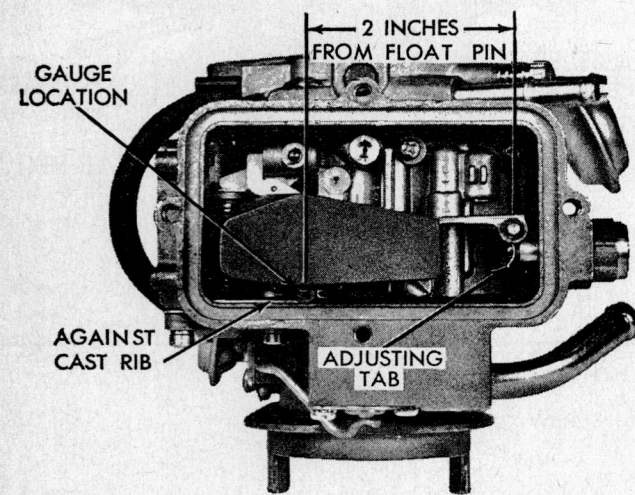

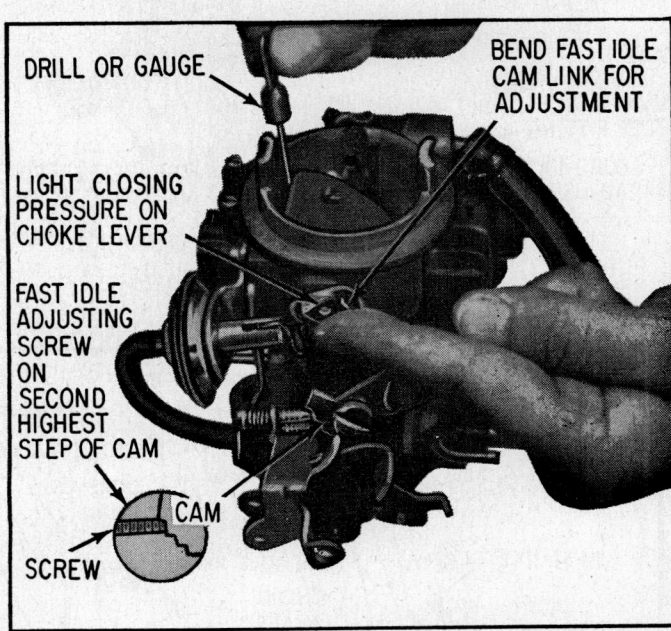

Fig. 9 Fast idle cam position and choke unloader adjustment
on 1920 carburetor

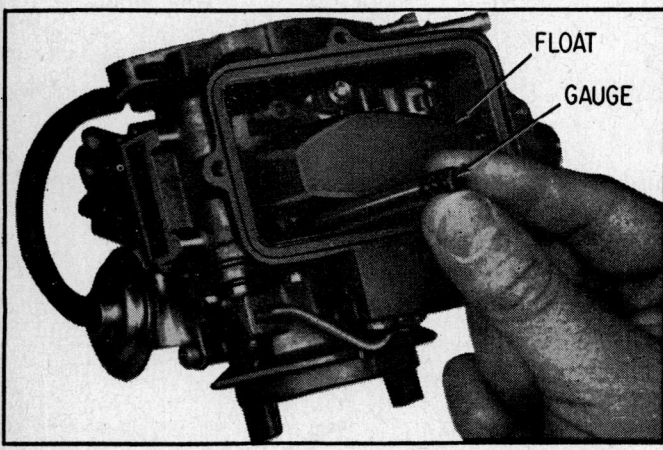

Fig. 6 Measuring float level on 1920 carburetor. 1973

Choke Vacuum Kick

NOTE: Test can be made on or off vehicle.

Fig. 10—If adjustment is to be made with engine running, back off fast idle speed screw until choke can be closed to the kick position with engine at curb idle. (Note number of screw turns required so that fast idle can be returned to original adjustment). If an auxiliary vacuum source is to be used, open throttle valve (engine not running) and move choke to closed position. Release throttle first, then release choke.

When using an auxiliary vacuum source, disconnect vacuum hose from carburetor and connect it to hose from vacuum supply with a small length of tube to act as a fitting. Removal of hose from diaphragm may require forces which damage the system. Apply a vacuum of 15 or more inches of mercury.

Insert gauge between top of choke valve and wall of air horn. Refer to *Holley Specifications Chart*. Apply sufficient closing pressure on lever to which choke rod attaches to provide a minimum choke valve opening without distortion of diaphragm link.

NOTE: The cylindrical stem of diaphragm extends as the internal spring is compressed. This spring must be fully compressed for proper measurement of vacuum kick adjustment.

Adjustment is necessary if slight drag is not obtained when removing the gauge. Shorten or lengthen diaphragm link to obtain correct choke valve opening. Length changes should be made by carefully opening or closing the U-bend provided in the link. Improper bending causes contact be-

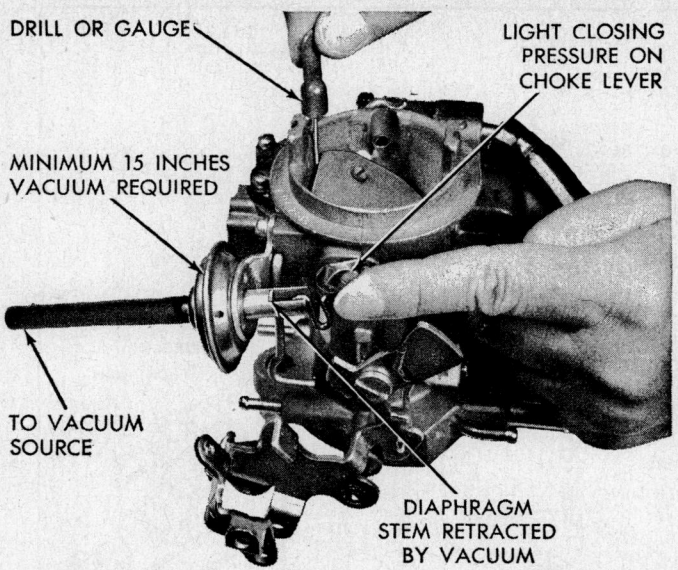

DRILL OR GAUGE

LIGHT CLOSING
PRESSURE ON
CHOKE LEVER

MINIMUM 15 INCHES
VACUUM REQUIRED

TO VACUUM
SOURCE

DIAPHRAGM
STEM RETRACTED
BY VACUUM

Fig. 10   Choke vacuum kick adjustment on 1920 carburetor

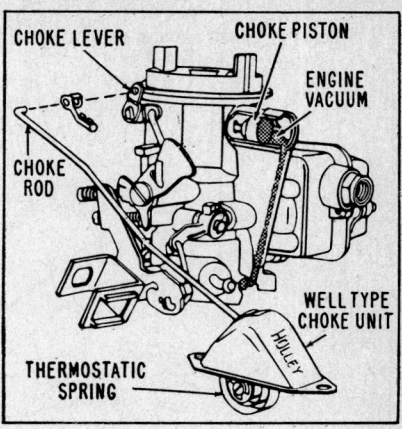

CHOKE LEVER

CHOKE PISTON

ENGINE
VACUUM

CHOKE
ROD

WELL TYPE
CHOKE UNIT

THERMOSTATIC
SPRING

Fig. 11   Well-type automatic choke
used with 1920 carburetor

tween the U-section and the diaphragm assembly.

NOTE: Do not apply twisting or bending force to diaphragm.

After completion of adjustment, reinstall vacuum hose on correct carburetor fitting. Return fast idle screw to its original location if disturbed. Make following check. With no vacuum applied to diaphragm, the choke valve should move freely between open and closed positions. If movement is not free, examine linkage for misalignment or interferences caused by bending operation.

Well-Type Automatic Choke

Fig. 11—To function properly, it is important that all parts be clean and move freely. Other than an occasional cleaning, the choke requires no attention. However, it is important that the choke control unit work freely in the well and at the choke shaft. Move the choke rod up and down to check for free movement on the pivot. If the unit binds, a new choke unit should be installed.

This type choke is serviced only as a unit. Do not attempt to repair or change the setting.

When installing the choke unit, be certain that the coil housing does not contact the sides of the well in the exhaust

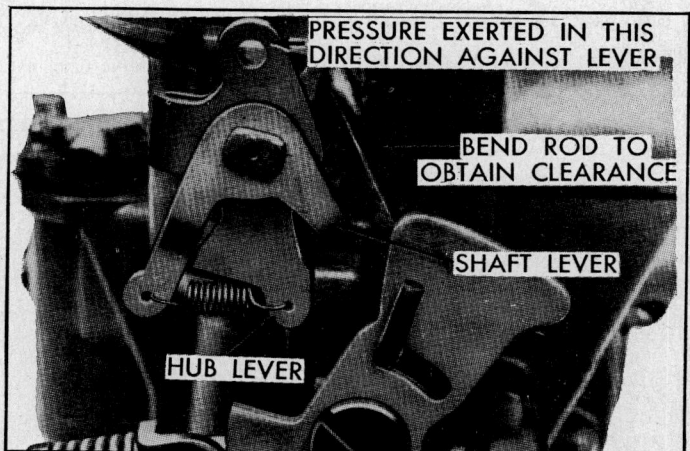

PRESSURE EXERTED IN THIS
DIRECTION AGAINST LEVER

BEND ROD TO
OBTAIN CLEARANCE

SHAFT LEVER

HUB LEVER

Fig. 12   Spring-staged choke adjustment on 1920 carburetor

manifold. Any contact at this point will affect choke operation. Do not lubricate any parts of the choke or the control unit. This causes an accumulation of dirt which will result in binding of the mechanism.

Spring Staged Choke Adjustment

To test the adjustment on carburetors equipped with the feature, press against the choke lever firmly, Fig. 12. Measure clearance between hub lever and shaft lever. If the clearance is not within .010" and .025", bend fast idle rod slightly until normal clearance is obtained. The cam position and unloader setting resulting from such bending of the choke link are satisfactory.

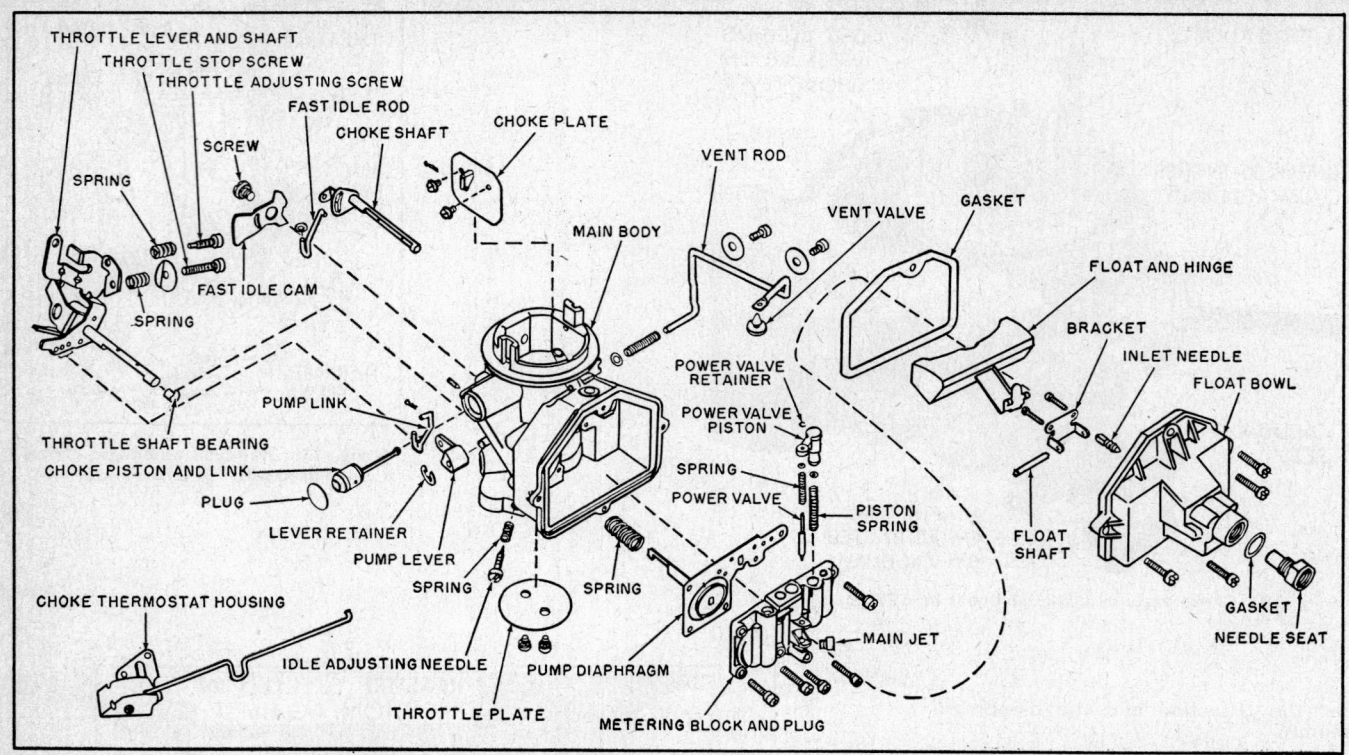

Fig. 2   Exploded view of Holley 1931 carburetor

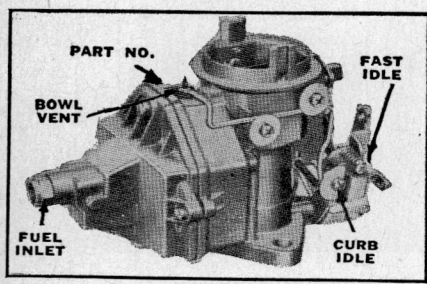

Fig. 1   Holley Model 1931 single-barrel carburetor

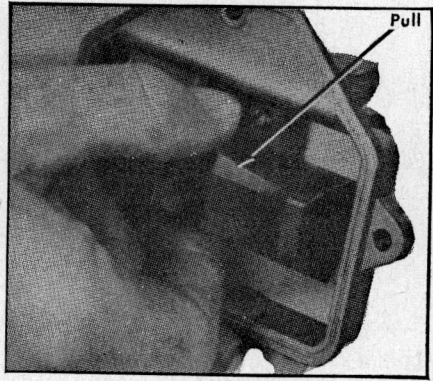

Fig. 4   Lowering float by pulling it out on 1931 carburetor

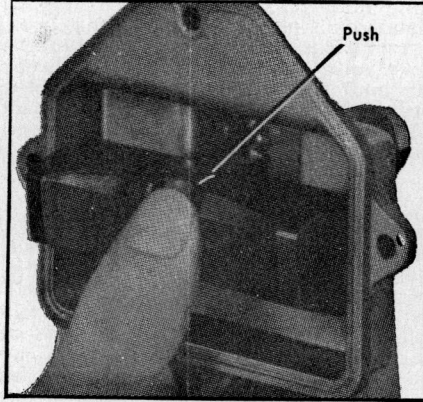

Fig. 5   Raising float by pushing it in on 1931 carburetor

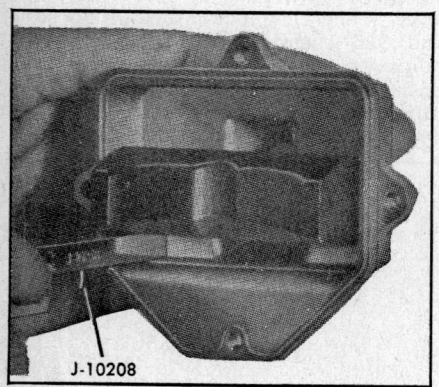

J-10208

Fig. 3   Checking float level on 1931 carburetor

MODEL 1931

This carburetor, Figs. 1 and 2, features a one-piece main body and throttle body casting together with a large capacity fuel bowl. The fuel inlet and float assembly, located in the center of the fuel bowl cover, maintains a stable fuel level for best performance on turns. The large capacity fuel bowl is designed to efficiently handle vapor loaded fuels and fuel vapors.

The automatic choke is mounted in a heat sink on the exhaust manifold and is connected to the carburetor by a choke rod.

Float Adjustment

Figs. 3, 4, 5—Invert carburetor fuel bowl cover and check float setting at both ends, Fig. 3. If float adjustment is necessary the float may be lowered by pulling on the center of the float, Fig. 4. The float may be raised by pushing on the center of the float, Fig. 5.

CAUTION: During float adjustment do not allow the float tab to contact the fuel inlet needle as the resilient tip of the needle can be damaged or compressed, resulting in an improper float setting and a leaky needle and seat.

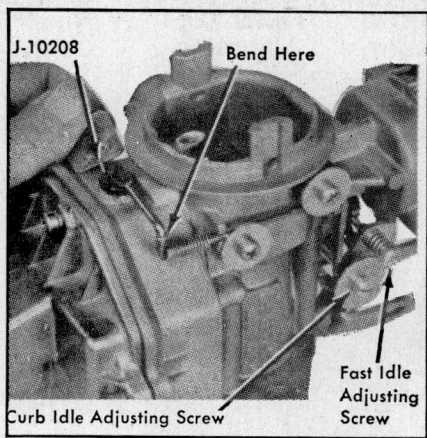

Fig. 6 Bowl vent adjustment
on 1931 carburetor

Fig. 7 Choke unloader adjustment
on 1931 carburetor

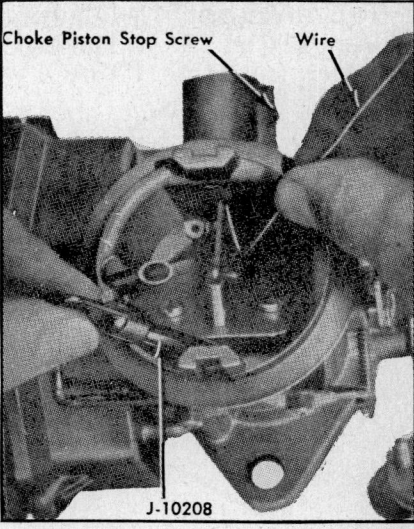

Fig. 8 Choke piston stop adjustment
on 1931 carburetor

If the proper gauge is not available, measure the distance between the roof of the float cover and top of float. If the setting is not as listed in the *Holley Specifications Chart*, adjust as required.

Bowl Vent Setting

Fig. 6—With throttle set at curb idle, clearance between vent valve and seat should be as listed in the *Holley Specifications Chart*. If an adjustment is necessary, bend vent rod at the horizontal portion above the fuel bowl. Check operation of vent rod for binding.

Accelerator Pump Setting

The accelerator link is set in the middle hole in the throttle lever for normal driving conditions. In the event a richer pump discharge is required, place the pump link in the outer hole of the throttle lever. For a leaner pump discharge, place the pump link in the inner hole of the throttle lever.

Fast Idle Adjustment

With the fast idle screw resting on second step of fast idle cam, and engine at normal operating temperature, the fast idle rpm should be as listed in the *Holley Specifications Chart*. Turning the fast idle screw in clockwise increases (counterclockwise decreases) speed.

Choke Unloader Setting

Fig. 7—With throttle valve held in wide open position and choke plate rotated toward closed position, the distance between top edge of choke plate and flat portion of air horn should be as listed in the *Holley Specifications Chart*. Adjust by bending tab on throttle lever.

Choke Piston Stop Adjustment

Fig. 8—Hold choke piston against stop screw with a wire inserted in slot above choke piston link. Rotate choke plate toward closed position until link is firm. The distance between top edge of choke plate and flat portion of air horn should be ³⁄₁₆". Adjust by turning piston stop screw in or out as required.

Automatic Choke Setting

The adjustment is made by loosening choke cover screws and rotating cover in the desired direction as indicated by an arrow on the cover. The choke should be set to the mark specified in the *Holley Specifications Chart* for all normal driving. Never set the choke more than two graduations in either direction of the specified setting.

MODEL 1945

This single barrel carburetor, Fig. 1, utilizes dual cellular plastic floats to control the fuel level, thus permitting high angularity operation during the most severe operating conditions. Also, the float construction eliminates the possibility of a malfunction due to a punctured float.

On 1974 Chrysler units, an electric choke system is incorporated to open the choke at approximately 60 degrees F. For service information, refer to the "Emission Control System" chapter.

The accelerator pump is of the piston type and is operated by a rod and a link connected to the throttle lever.

The power enrichment system on all units, consists of a power valve installed near the center of the carburetor body and a vacuum piston located in the bowl cover. On 1974 California units, in addition to the vacuum operated enrichment system, a spring loaded mechanical modulator rod opens the power valve at 80 degrees of throttle opening regardless of engine vacuum.

Dry Float Setting

Fig. 2—Hold float fulcrum retaining pin in position and invert carburetor bowl. Place a straight edge across surface of bowl, contracting float toes. Remove straight edge and measure distance float dropped from surface of fuel bowl. Refer to Holley Specifications Chart. Adjust by bending float tang to obtain proper dimension.

Fast Idle Cam Position Adjustment

Fig. 3—With fast idle speed adjusting screw contacting second highest step on fast idle cam, move choke valve toward closed position with light pressure on choke shaft lever. Insert specified gauge between top of choke valve and wall of air horn. Refer to *Holley Specifications Chart*. An adjustment will be necessary if a slight drag is not obtained as drill shank is being removed. Adjust by bending fast idle link at lower angle, until correct valve opening has been obtained.

Choke Vacuum Kick Adjustment

NOTE: Test can be made on or off vehicle.

Fig. 4—If adjustment is to be made with engine running, back off fast idle speed screw until choke can be closed to the kick position with engine at curb idle. (Note number of screw turns required so that fast idle can be returned to original adjustment). If an auxiliary vacuum source is to be used, open throttle valve (engine not running) and move choke to closed position. Release throttle first, then release choke.

When using an auxiliary vacuum source, disconnect vacuum hose from carburetor and connect it to hose from vacuum supply with a small length of tube to act as a fitting. Removal of hose from diaphragm may require forces which damage the system. Apply a vacuum of 15 or more inches of mercury.

Insert gauge between top of choke valve and wall of air horn. Refer to *Holley Specifications Chart*. Apply sufficient closing pressure on lever to which choke rod at-

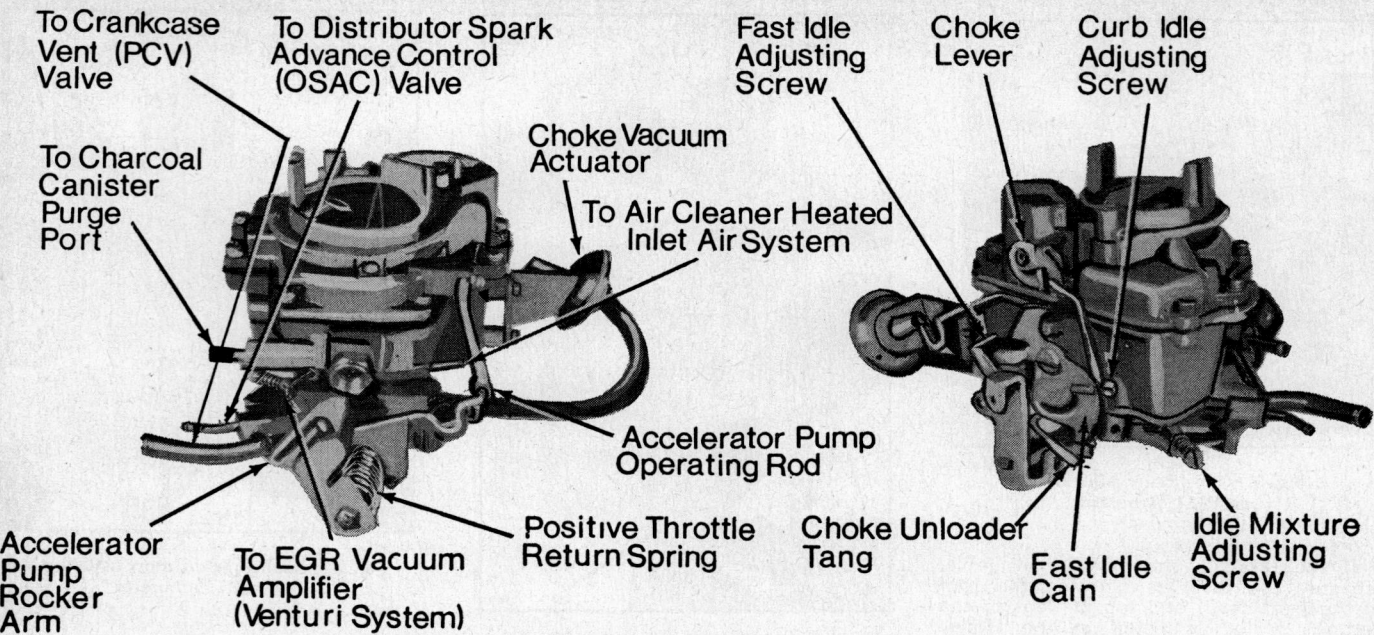

To Crankcase Vent (PCV) Valve

To Distributor Spark Advance Control (OSAC) Valve

To Charcoal Canister Purge Port

Choke Vacuum Actuator

To Air Cleaner Heated Inlet Air System

Fast Idle Adjusting Screw

Choke Lever

Curb Idle Adjusting Screw

Accelerator Pump Operating Rod

Accelerator Pump Rocker Arm

To EGR Vacuum Amplifier (Venturi System)

Positive Throttle Return Spring

Choke Unloader Tang

Fast Idle Cam

Idle Mixture Adjusting Screw

Fig. 1   Holley model 1945 single barrel carburetor

taches to provide a minimum choke valve opening without distortion of diaphragm link.

NOTE: The cylindrical stem of diaphragm extends as the internal spring is compressed. This spring must be fully compressed for proper measurement of vacuum kick adjustment.

Adjustment is necessary if slight drag is not obtained when removing the gauge. Shorten or lengthen diaphragm link to obtain correct choke valve opening. Length changes should be made by carefully opening or closing the U-bend provided in the link. Improper bending causes contact between the U-section and the diaphragm assembly.

NOTE: Do not apply twisting or bending force to diaphragm.

After completion of adjustment, reinstall vacuum hose on correct carburetor fitting. Return fast idle screw to its original location if disturbed. Make following check. With no vacuum applied to diaphragm, the choke valve should move freely between open and closed positions. If movement is not free, examine linkage for misalignment or interferences caused by bending operation.

Choke Unloader (Wide Open Kick) Adjustment

Fig. 5—With throttle valves in wide open position, insert drill gauge between upper edge of choke valve and inner wall of air horn. Refer to *Holley Specifications Chart*. With a finger lightly pressing against shaft lever, a slight drag should be felt as drill is being withdrawn. Adjust by bending unloader tang on throttle lever until correct opening has been obtained.

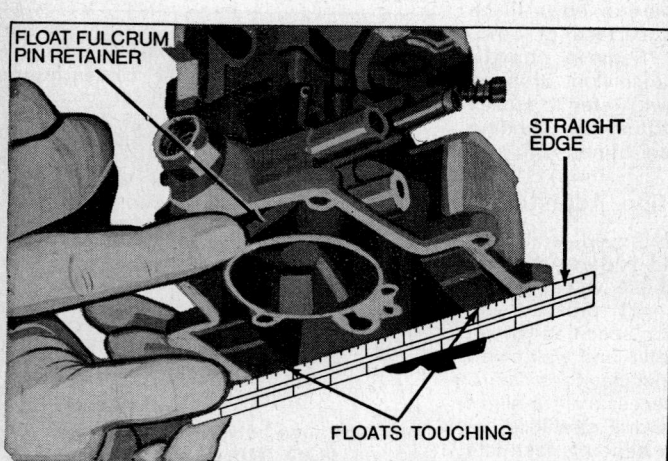

FLOAT FULCRUM PIN RETAINER

STRAIGHT EDGE

FLOATS TOUCHING

Fig. 2   Measuring float level. 1945 carburetor

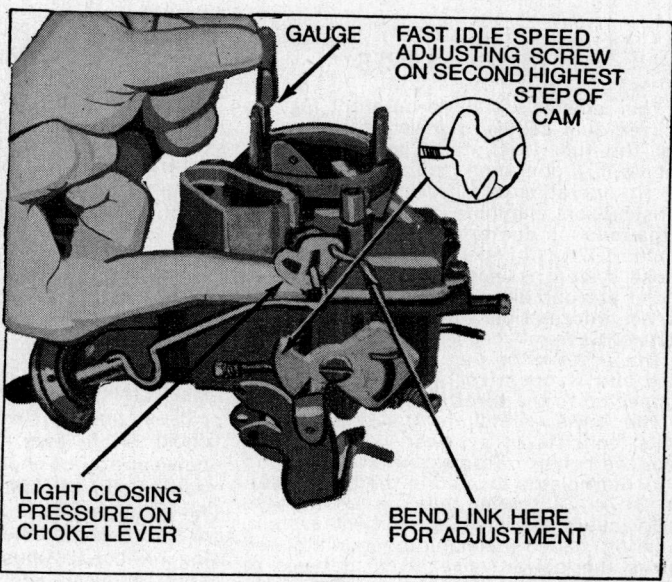

GAUGE

FAST IDLE SPEED ADJUSTING SCREW ON SECOND HIGHEST STEP OF CAM

LIGHT CLOSING PRESSURE ON CHOKE LEVER

BEND LINK HERE FOR ADJUSTMENT

Fig. 3   Fast idle cam position adjustment. 1945 carburetor

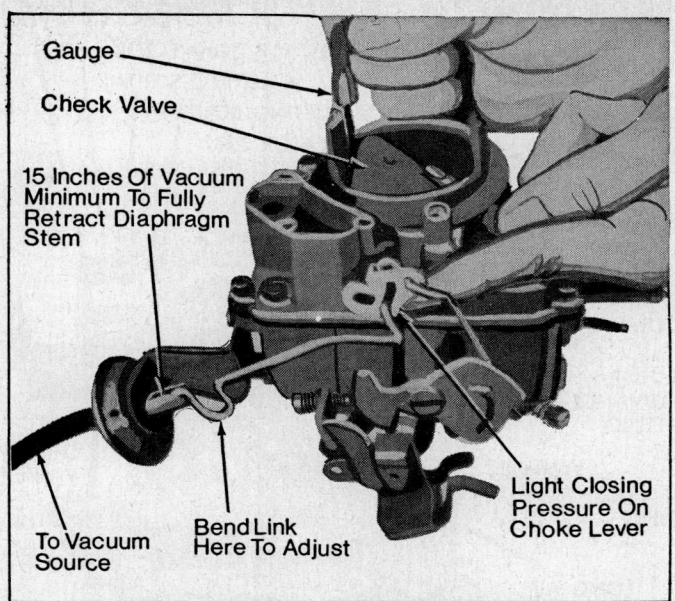

Gauge

Check Valve

15 Inches Of Vacuum
Minimum To Fully
Retract Diaphragm
Stem

Light Closing
Pressure On
Choke Lever

To Vacuum
Source

Bend Link
Here To Adjust

Fig. 4   Choke vacuum kick adjustment. 1945 carburetor

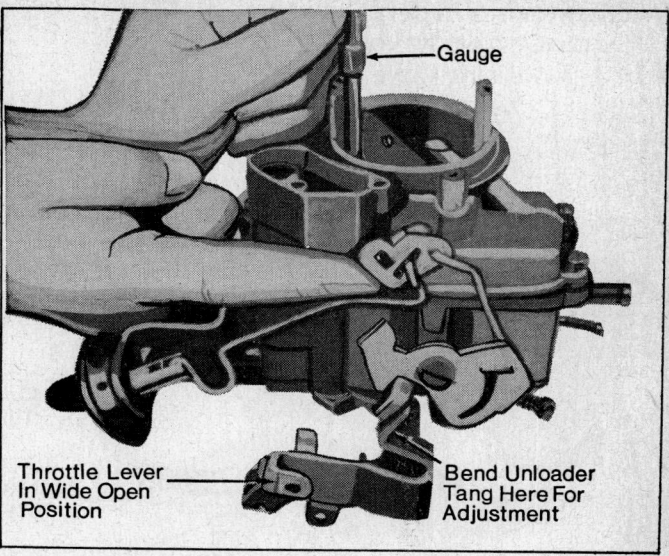

Gauge

Throttle Lever
In Wide Open
Position

Bend Unloader
Tang Here For
Adjustment

Fig. 5   Choke unloader adjustment. 1945 carburetor

Accelerator Pump Setting

Fig. 6—With throttle at curb idle position, measure distance from vacuum passage casting to outer edge of hole in pump operating rod. Refer to Holley Specifications Chart. Adjust by bending link between throttle lever and pump operating rod.

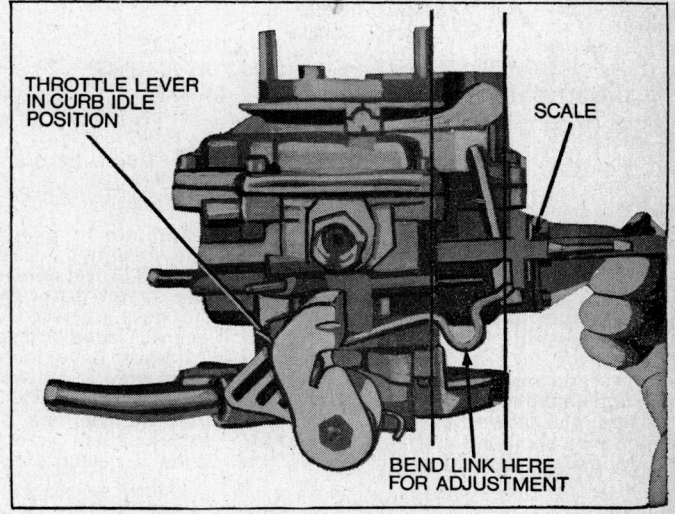

THROTTLE LEVER
IN CURB IDLE
POSITION

SCALE

BEND LINK HERE
FOR ADJUSTMENT

Fig. 6   Accelerator pump adjustment. 1945 carburetor

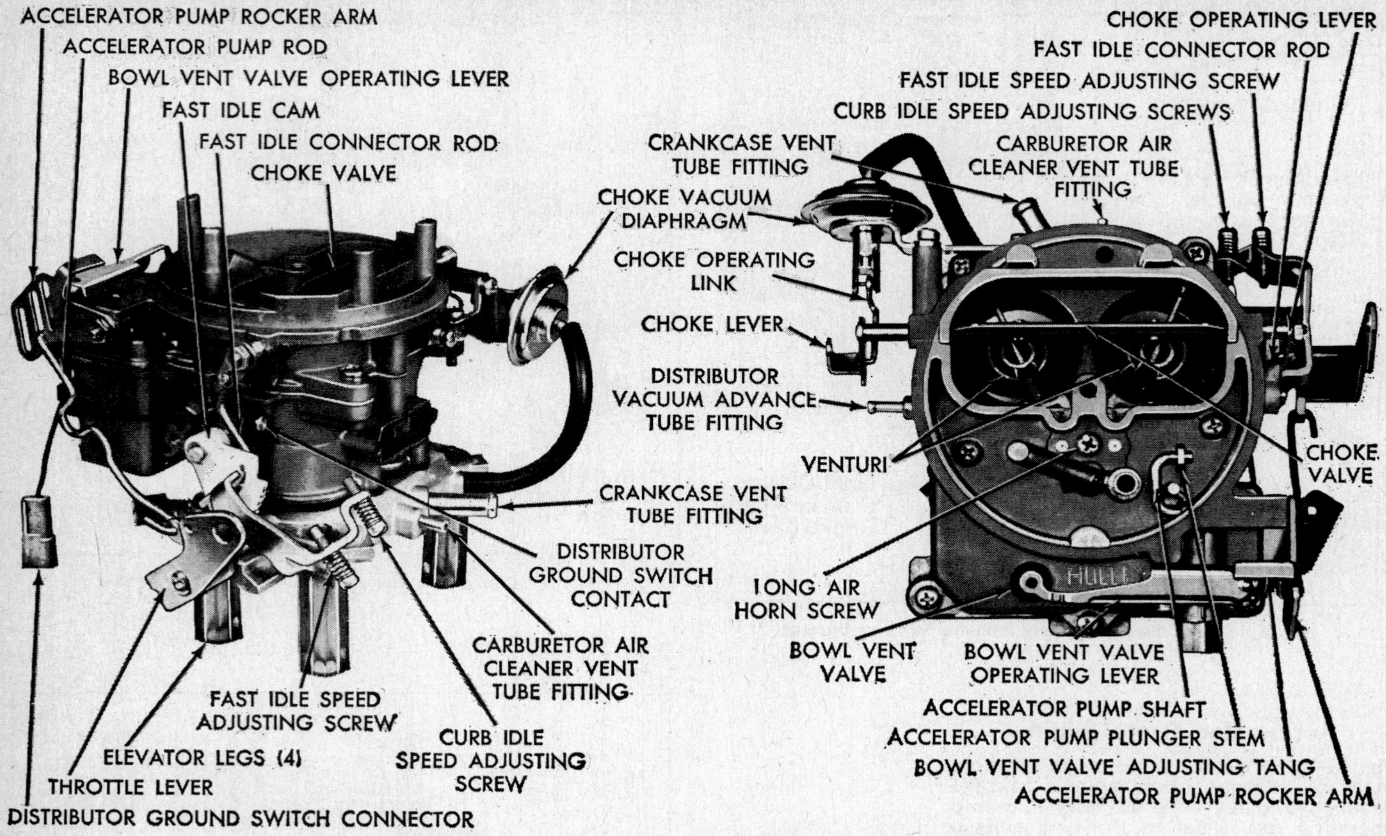

HOLLEY CARBURETORS

ACCELERATOR PUMP ROCKER ARM
ACCELERATOR PUMP ROD
BOWL VENT VALVE OPERATING LEVER
FAST IDLE CAM
FAST IDLE CONNECTOR ROD
CHOKE VALVE

CHOKE OPERATING LEVER
FAST IDLE CONNECTOR ROD
FAST IDLE SPEED ADJUSTING SCREW
CURB IDLE SPEED ADJUSTING SCREWS

CRANKCASE VENT TUBE FITTING
CHOKE VACUUM DIAPHRAGM
CHOKE OPERATING LINK
CHOKE LEVER
DISTRIBUTOR VACUUM ADVANCE TUBE FITTING

CARBURETOR AIR CLEANER VENT TUBE FITTING
CHOKE VALVE

VENTURI
LONG AIR HORN SCREW
BOWL VENT VALVE
BOWL VENT VALVE OPERATING LEVER
ACCELERATOR PUMP SHAFT
ACCELERATOR PUMP PLUNGER STEM
BOWL VENT VALVE ADJUSTING TANG
ACCELERATOR PUMP ROCKER ARM

CRANKCASE VENT TUBE FITTING
DISTRIBUTOR GROUND SWITCH CONTACT
CARBURETOR AIR CLEANER VENT TUBE FITTING

FAST IDLE SPEED ADJUSTING SCREW
ELEVATOR LEGS (4)
THROTTLE LEVER
DISTRIBUTOR GROUND SWITCH CONNECTOR
CURB IDLE SPEED ADJUSTING SCREW

Fig. 1 Holley models 2210 & 2245 two-barrel typical carburetors

MODELS 2210 & 2245

This carburetor, Fig. 1, is a two-barrel unit but can be considered as two carburetors built side by side into one unit, utilizing the same fuel and air inlets. Each throat of the carburetor has its own throttle valve and main metering systems and are supplemented by the float, accelerating, idle and power systems. The 1970 version is equipped with a distributor ground switch, Fig. 1, which retards the distributor when the carburetor is at curb idle, resulting in better emission control. The 1971 version is equipped with a hot idle compensator valve which is a thermostatically operated air bleed to relieve an overrich condition at idle, Fig. 2. The 1971-74 units have incorporated a bowl vent valve tube which works in conjunction with the vent valve. The 1973 unit has an extra port for use with the (EGR) Exhaust Gas Recirculation system. On 1973-74 Chrysler units, an electric choke system is incorporated to open choke at approximately 60° to 63°. For service information refer to the "Emission Control System" chapter.

Float Adjustment

Invert air horn so that weight of float only is forcing needle against seat. Measure the clearance between top of float and float stop, Fig. 3. Be sure drill gauge is perfectly level when measuring. Refer to *Holley Specifications Chart*. Adjust by

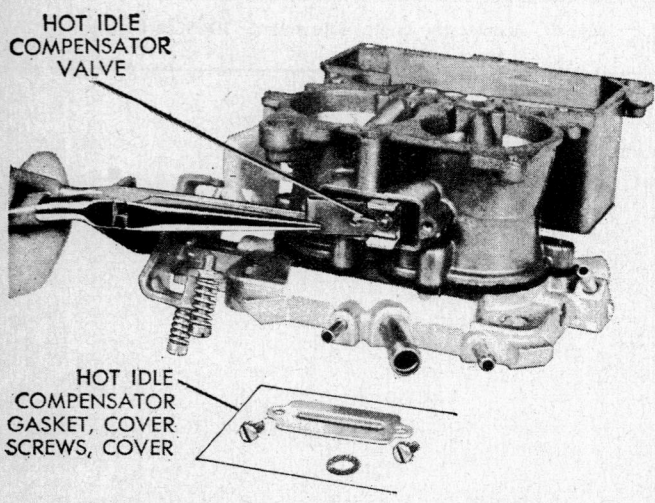

HOT IDLE COMPENSATOR VALVE
HOT IDLE COMPENSATOR GASKET, COVER SCREWS, COVER

Fig. 2 Hot idle compensator valve on 1971 units

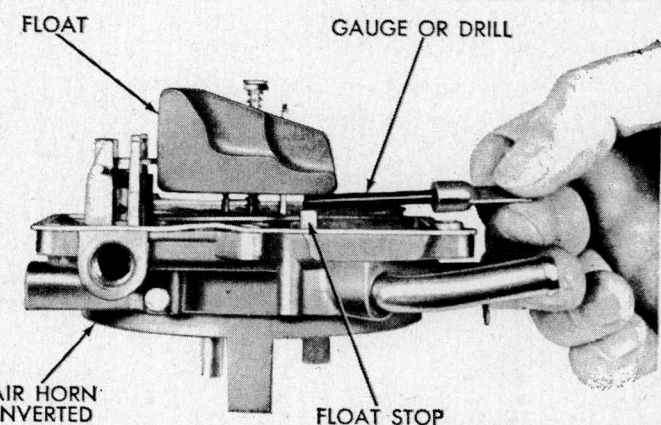

FLOAT
GAUGE OR DRILL
AIR HORN INVERTED
FLOAT STOP

Fig. 3 Checking float level on 2210 & 2245 carburetors

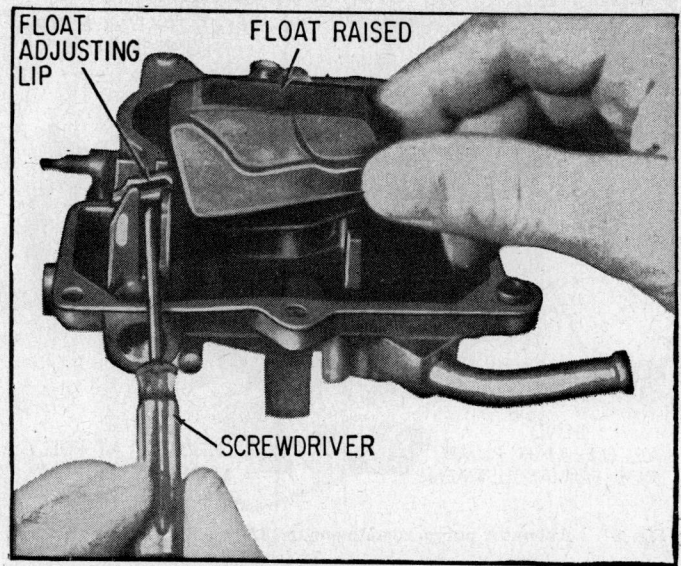

Fig. 4   Adjusting float on 2210 & 2245 carburetors

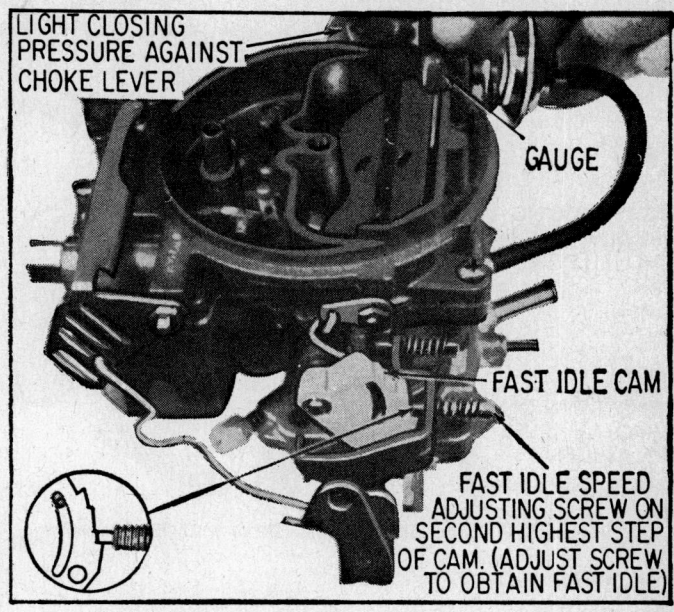

Fig. 6   Fast idle cam position adjustment on 2210 & 2245 carburetors

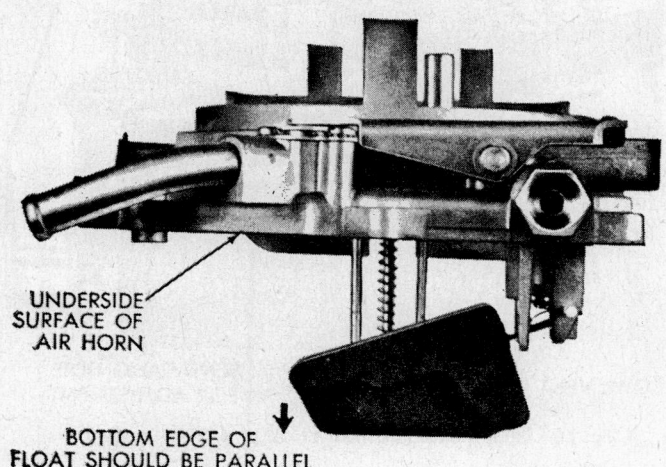

Fig. 5   Checking float drop on 2210 & 2245 carburetors

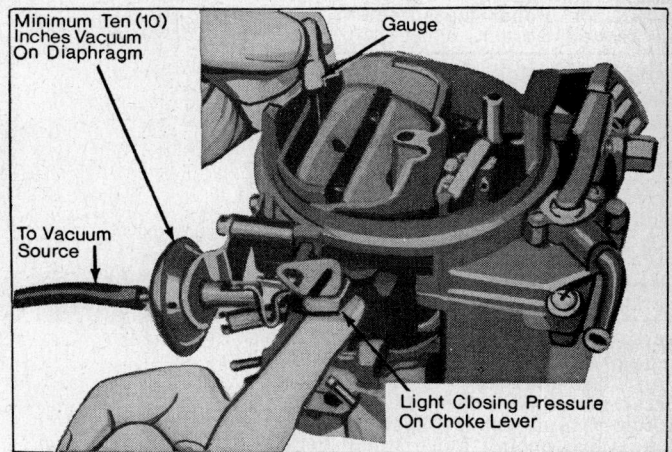

Fig. 7   Vacuum kick adjustment on 2210 & 2245 carburetors

bending float lip toward or away from needle, using a narrow blade screwdriver, Fig. 4, until correct clearance of setting has been obtained.

Float Drop Adjustment

Check float drop, by holding air horn in an upright position. The bottom edge of float should be parallel to underside surface of air horn, Fig. 5. Adjust by bending tang on float arm until parallel surfaces have been obtained.

Fast Idle Cam Position Adjustment

Fig. 6—With fast idle speed adjusting screw contacting second highest step on fast idle cam, move choke valve toward closed position with light pressure on choke shaft lever. Insert specified gauge between top of choke valve and wall of air horn. Refer to *Holley Specifications Chart.* An adjustment will be necessary if a slight drag is not obtained as drill shank is being removed. Adjust by bending fast idle link at angle, until correct valve opening has been obtained.

Choke Vacuum Kick Adjustment

NOTE: Test can be made on or off vehicle.

Fig. 7—If adjustment is to be made with engine running, back off fast idle speed screw until choke can be closed to the kick position with engine at curb idle. (Note number of screw turns required so

that fast idle can be returned to original adjustment). If an auxiliary vacuum source is to be used, open throttle valve (engine not running) and move choke to closed position. Release throttle first, then release choke.

When using an auxiliary vacuum source, disconnect vacuum hose from carburetor and connect it to hose from vacuum supply with a small length of tube to act as a fitting. Removal of hose from diaphragm may require forces which damage the system. Apply a vacuum of 10 or more inches of mercury. Insert gauge between top of choke valve and wall of air horn. Refer to *Holley Specifications Chart.* Apply sufficient closing pressure on lever to which choke rod attaches to provide a minimum choke valve opening without distortion of diaphragm link.

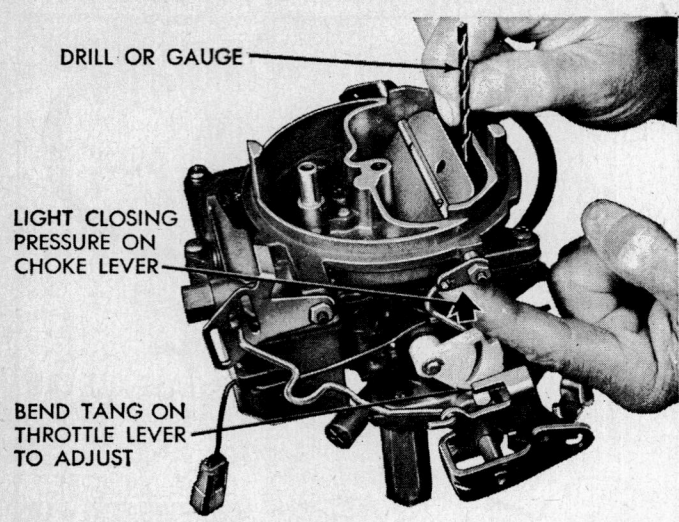

Fig. 8   Choke unloader adjustment on 2210 & 2245 carburetors

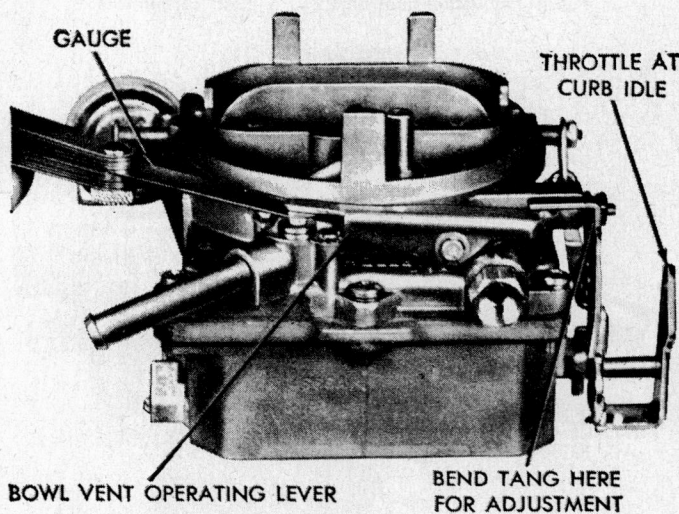

Fig. 9   Accelerator pump adjustment on 2210 & 2245 carburetors

NOTE: The cylindrical stem of diaphragm extends as the internal spring is compressed. This spring must be fully compressed for proper measurement of vacuum kick adjustment.

Adjustment is necessary if slight drag is not obtained when removing the gauge. Shorten or lengthen diaphragm link to obtain correct choke valve opening. Length changes should be made by carefully opening or closing the U-bend provided in the link. Improper bending causes contact between the U-section and the diaphragm assembly.

NOTE: Do not apply twisting or bending force to diaphragm.

After completion of adjustment, reinstall vacuum hose on correct carburetor fitting. Return fast idle screw to its original location if disturbed. Make following check. With no vacuum applied to diaphragm, the choke valve should move freely between open and closed positions. If movement is not free, examine linkage for misalignment or interferences caused by bending operation.

Choke Unloader (Wide Open Kick) Adjustment

Fig. 8—With throttle valves in wide open position, insert drill gauge between upper edge of choke valve and inner wall of air horn. Refer to *Holley Specifications Chart.* With a finger lightly pressing against shaft lever, a slight drag should be felt as drill is being withdrawn. Adjust by bending unloader tang on throttle lever until correct opening has been obtained.

Fig. 10   Bowl vent adjustment on 2210 & 2245 carburetors

Accelerator Pump Adjustment

Fig. 9—Back off curb idle speed adjusting screw. Open choke valve so that fast idle cam allows throttle valves to be completely seated in bores. Be sure that pump connector rod is installed in correct slot of accelerator pump rocker arm. First slot for manual transmissions next to attaching screw.

Close throttle valves tightly. Measure the distance between top of air horn and end of plunger shaft. Refer to *Holley Specifications Chart.* Adjust pump travel by bending pump operating rod, at loop of rod, until correct setting has been obtained.

Bowl Vent Valve Clearance Adjustment

Fig. 10—With the throttle valves at curb idle, it should be possible to insert a inch gauge between the bowl vent valve plunger stem and operating rod. Refer to *Holley Specifications Chart.* Adjust by bending the tang on pump lever to change arc of contact with throttle lever, until correct clearance has been obtained.

MODEL 2300

The 2300 carburetor, Fig. 1 and 2, is used only as a compound installation. This system utilizes two types of Holley two-barrels, primary, Fig. 1, mounted in the center and the secondarys, Fig. 2, mounted fore and aft. The Fig. 2, units contain all the regulatory systems with the exception of chokes, power enrichment valve, accelerating pump, idle system and spark advance. The throttle operation of the primary carburetor is conventional whereas the secondary units are equipped with throttle control vacuum diaphragms, Fig. 2, for the purpose of opening the secondary throttles which closes mechanically. The choke used only on the primary unit is controlled by a temperature sensing choke coil mounted on the intake manifold, over the exhaust crossover passage, Fig. 3.

The only adjustments required on the secondary units are the float level and the wet fuel level. All other adjustments are made on the primary unit.

Float Adjustment

Make a preliminary float adjustment by inverting fuel bowl and turn adjustable needle and seat until top of float is specified distance from top of fuel bowl, Fig. 4. Refer to *Holley Specifications Chart*. Do not fully tighten lock screw. Snug screw to temporarily retain adjustment.

NOTE: Final adjustment of the float is made on the vehicle.

Wet Fuel Level

Fig. 5—With car on a level floor and engine idling, remove sight plug from fuel bowl. Fuel level should be in line with threads at bottom of sight plug hole. To adjust, loosen lock screw and turn adjusting nut as required to reise or lower fuel level.

Automatic Choke Control Lever Setting

Adjustment of the choke control lever is necessary to provide correct relationship between choke valve, thermostatic coil spring and the fast idle cam. It should be checked and adjusted (if necessary), as preparation of the choke system linkage before making the Vacuum Kick, Cam Position or Unloader adjustment. These three adjustments must be made after qualification of the choke control lever.

NOTE: Improper bending of choke rod will result in binding.

Chevrolet

Close the choke rod by applying slight pressure on choke control lever, the thermostatic choke rod should be even with top of choke rod hole. Adjust by bending choke rod at upper angle.

Chrysler

Open the throttle to mid-position. Close the choke valve by applying slight pressure on choke control lever. The top of choke rod hole in control lever should be 3-49/64" above choke pad with carburetor on en-

gine, or 1-23/32" above carburetor base with carburetor on bench, Fig. 6. Adjust by bending choke shaft rod at point indicated.

Fast Idle Cam Position Adjustment

Chevrolet

Fig. 7—With throttle slightly open, close choke plate positioning fast idle lever against top step of fast idle cam. Adjust the fast idle screw to obtain the clearance listed in the *Holley Specifications Chart* between throttle valve and bore on idle trans-

fer slot side of carburetor. Adjust by bending the idle lever.

Chrysler

Fig. 8—With fast idle speed adjusting screw contacting second highest step on fast idle cam, move choke valve toward closed position with light pressure on choke shaft lever. Insert specified gauge between top of choke valve and wall of air horn. Refer to *Holley Specifications Chart*. An adjustment will be necessary if a slight drag is not obtained as drill shank is being removed. Adjust by bending cam position adjusting tang.

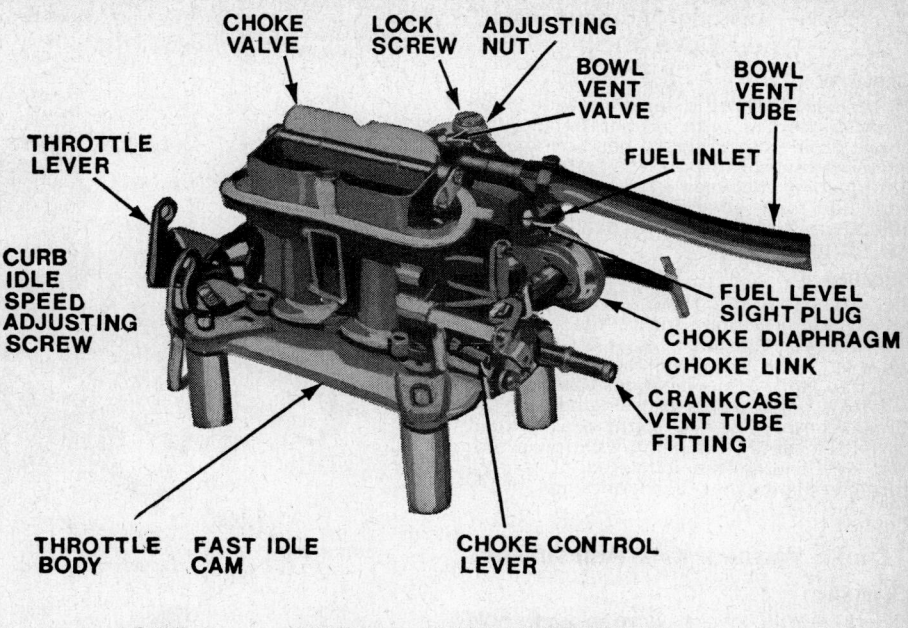

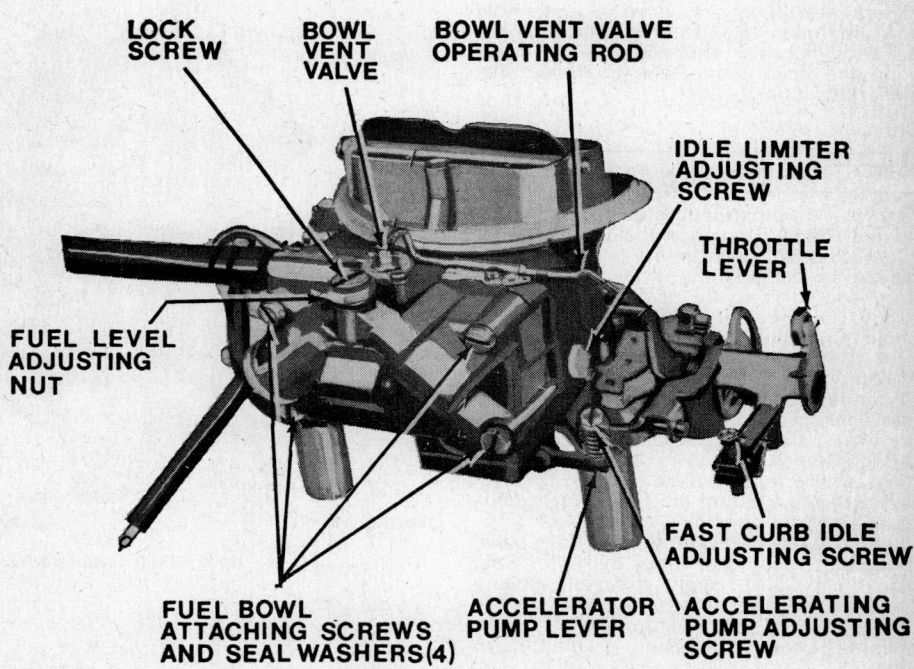

Fig. 1   Holley 2300 carburetor assembly primary center unit

Choke Unloader Adjustment
(Wide Open Kick)

Chevrolet

Fig. 9—Hold throttle lever in wide open throttle position with rubber band. Hold choke valve toward closed position against unloader tang of throttle shaft, then measure opening between choke valve lower edge and main body. Refer to *Holley Specifications Chart*. Adjust by bending choke rod (at off-set bend).

Chrysler

Fig. 10—Hold the throttle valves in the wide open position. Insert the specified drill between the upper edge of the choke valve and the inner wall of the air horn. Refer to *Holley Specifications Chart*.

With a finger lightly pressing against the choke control lever, a slight drag should be felt as the drill is being withdrawn. Adjust by bending the indicated tang until correct opening has been obtained.

Choke Vacuum Kick Adjustment

Chevrolet

Fig. 11—With choke valve closed, hold vacuum break against stop. Measure the distance between the choke valve lower edge and main body. Refer to *Holley Specifications Chart*.

Chrysler

NOTE: Test can be made on or off vehicle.

Fig. 12—If adjustment is to be made with engine running, position the fast idle tang (Cam position adjustment) to allow choke closure to kick position. If an auxiliary vacuum source is to be used, open throttle valve (engine not running) and move choke to closed position. Release throttle first, then release choke.

When using an auxiliary vacuum source, disconnect vacuum hose from carburetor and connect it to hose from vacuum supply with a small length of tube to act as a fitting. Removal of hose from diaphragm may require forces which damage the system. Apply a vacuum of 10 or more inches of mercury.

Insert gauge between top of choke valve and wall of air horn. Refer to *Holley Specifications Chart*. Apply sufficient closing pressure on lever to which choke rod attaches to provide a minimum choke valve opening without distortion of diaphragm link.

NOTE: The cylindrical stem of diaphragm extends as the internal spring is compressed. This spring must be fully compressed for proper measurement of vacuum kick adjustment.

Adjustment is necessary if slight drag is not obtained when removing the gauge. Shorten or lengthen diaphragm link to obtain correct choke valve opening. Length changes should be made by carefully opening or closing the U-bend provided in the link. Improper bending causes contact between the U-section and the diaphragm assembly.

NOTE: Do not apply twisting or bending force to diaphragm.

After completion of adjustment, reinstall

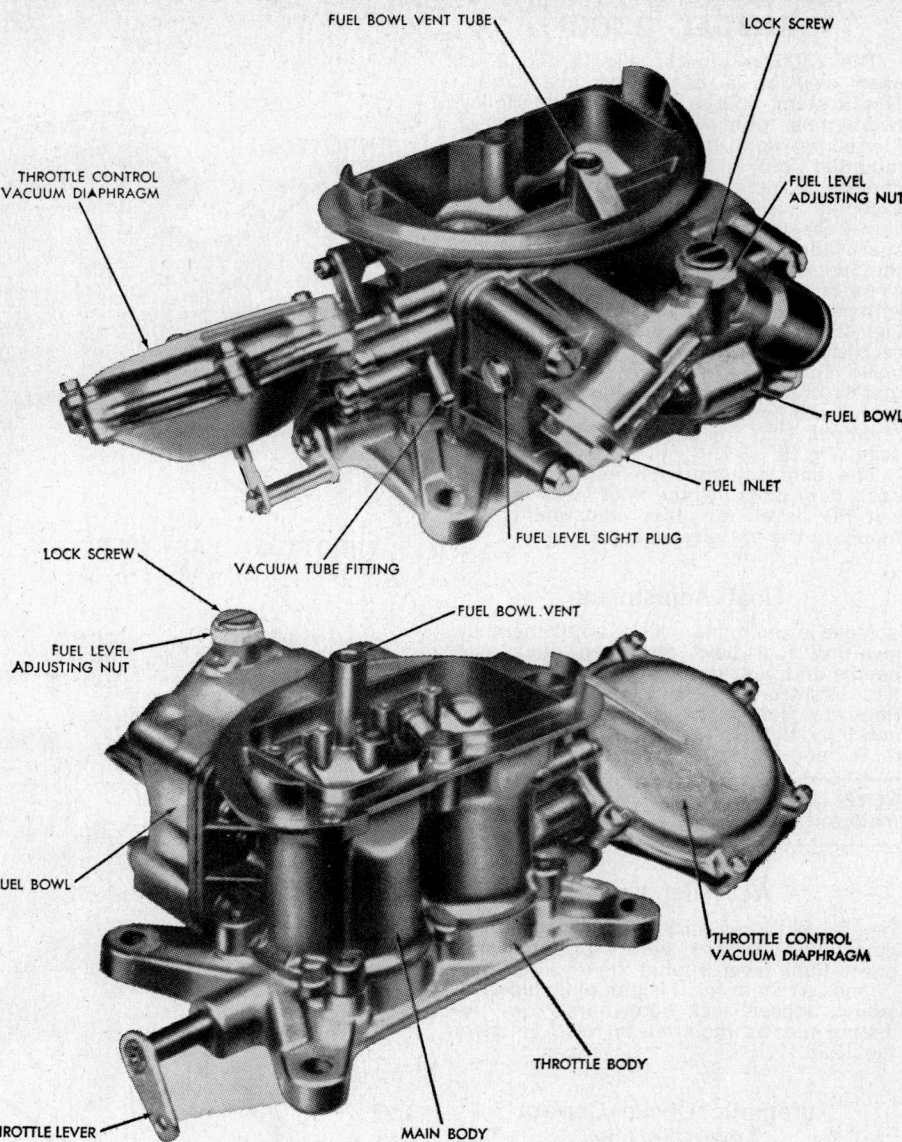

Fig. 2   Holley 2300 carburetor assembly secondary outboard front or rear

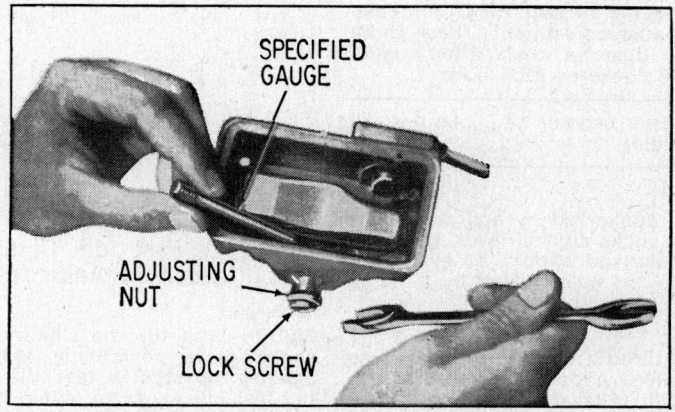

Fig. 4   Float adjustment on 2300 carburetor

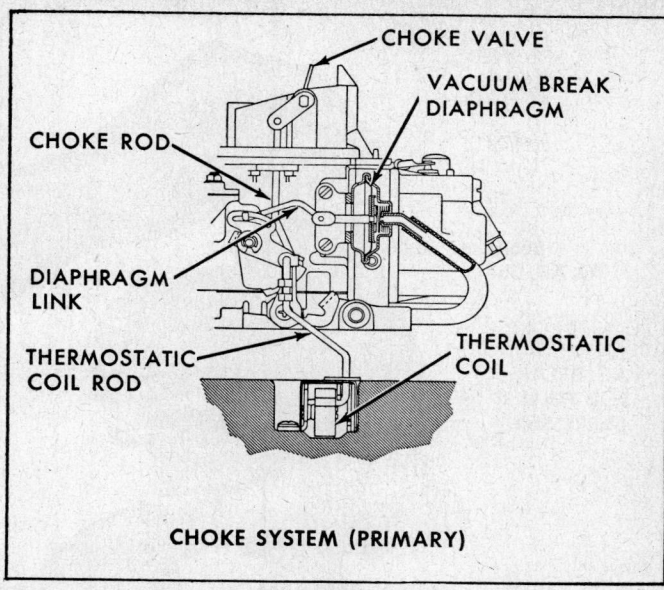

CHOKE VALVE

VACUUM BREAK DIAPHRAGM

CHOKE ROD

DIAPHRAGM LINK

THERMOSTATIC COIL ROD

THERMOSTATIC COIL

CHOKE SYSTEM (PRIMARY)

Fig. 3   Well type choke. 2300 carburetor

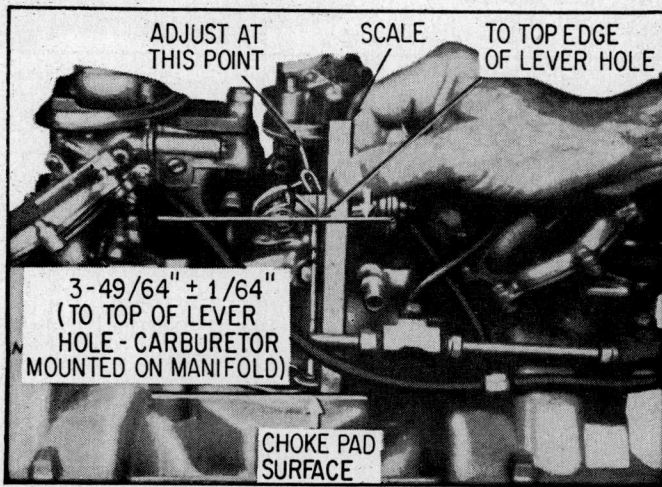

ADJUST AT THIS POINT

SCALE

TO TOP EDGE OF LEVER HOLE

3-49/64" ± 1/64"
(TO TOP OF LEVER HOLE - CARBURETOR MOUNTED ON MANIFOLD)

CHOKE PAD SURFACE

Fig. 6   Automatic choke control lever adjustment, Chrysler 2300

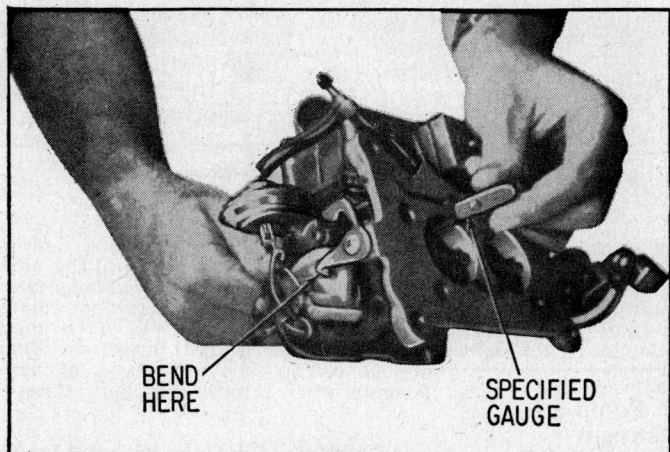

BEND HERE

SPECIFIED GAUGE

Fig. 7   Fast idle cam adjustment, Chevrolet 2300

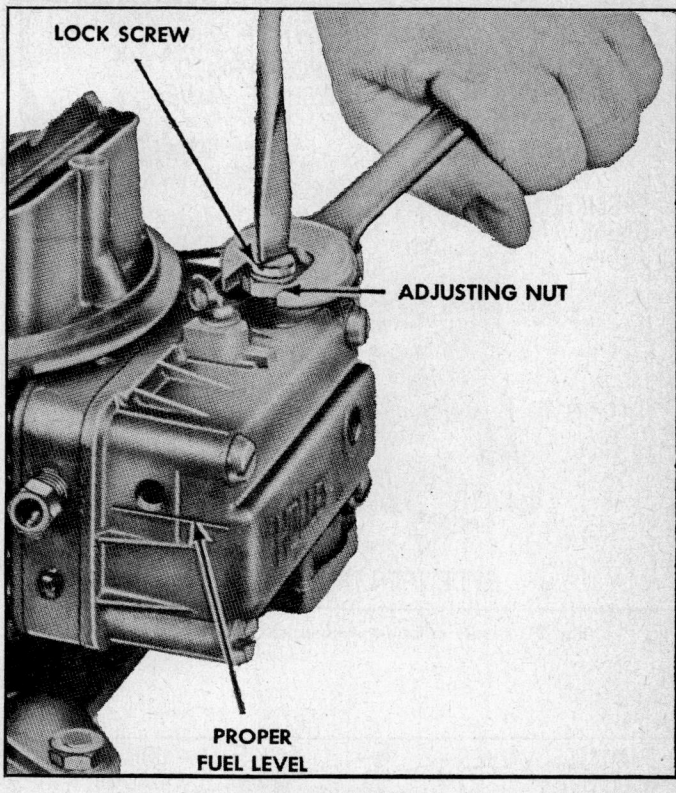

LOCK SCREW

ADJUSTING NUT

PROPER FUEL LEVEL

Fig. 5   Fuel level adjustment on 2300 carburetor

vacuum hose on correct carburetor fitting. Return fast idle screw to its original location if disturbed. Make following check. With no vacuum applied to diaphragm, the choke valve should move freely between open and closed positions. If movement is not free, examine linkage for misalignment or interferences caused by bending operation.

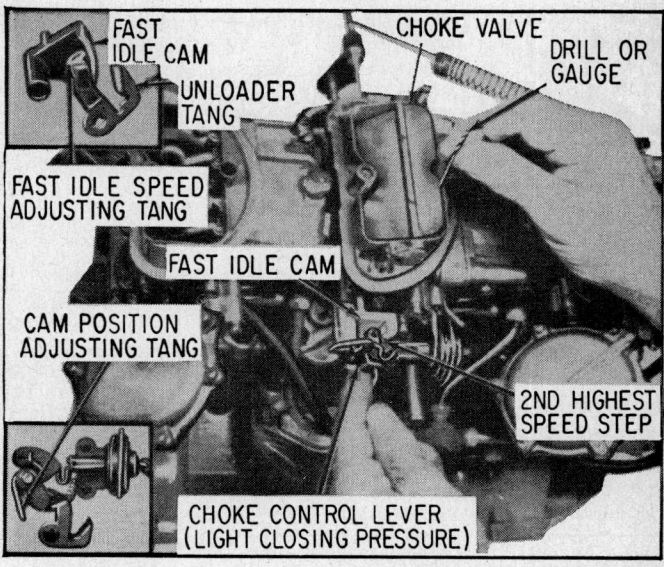

FAST IDLE CAM

CHOKE VALVE

DRILL OR GAUGE

UNLOADER TANG

FAST IDLE SPEED ADJUSTING TANG

FAST IDLE CAM

CAM POSITION ADJUSTING TANG

2ND HIGHEST SPEED STEP

CHOKE CONTROL LEVER (LIGHT CLOSING PRESSURE)

Fig. 8   Fast idle cam and speed adjustment, Chrysler 2300

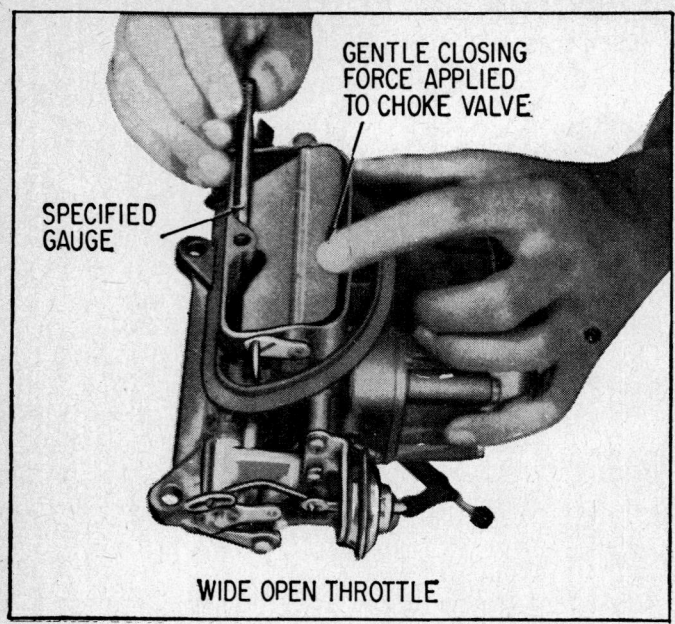

Fig. 9   Choke unloader adjustment, Chevrolet 2300

Fig. 11   Vacuum kick adjustment, Chevrolet 2300

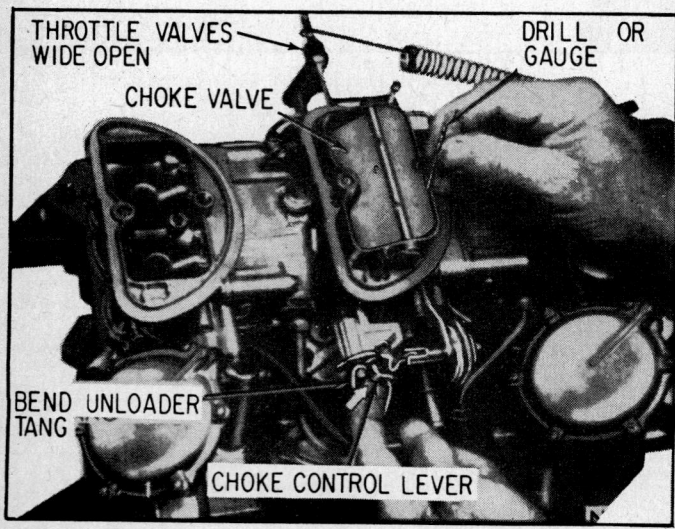

Fig. 10   Choke unloader adjustment, Chrysler 2300

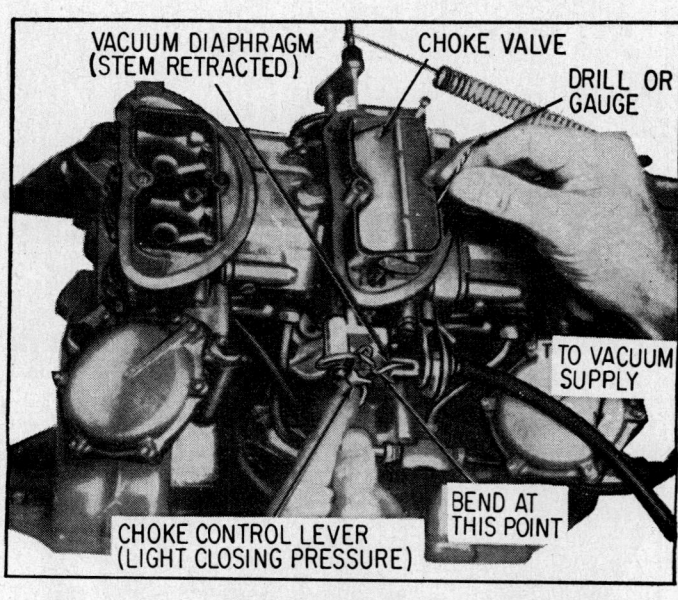

Fig. 12   Vacuum kick adjustment, Chrysler 2300

Fast Idle Adjustment
(On Vehicle)

Chrysler

Fig. 8—Close choke valve until fast idle screw tang can be positioned on the second highest-speed step of the fast idle cam. Start the engine and determine the stabilized speed. Bend the fast idle tang by use of a screwdriver placed in the tang slot to secure the specified speed. Refer to *Holley Specifications Chart*.

NOTE: Bend only in a direction perpendicular to the contact surface of the cam. Movement in any other direction changes the cam position adjustment. Bend only when tang is clear of cam. Stopping the engine between adjustments is not necessary. However, reposition the fast idle tang on the cam after each speed adjustment to provide correct throttle closing torque.

Accelerator Pump
Lever Adjustment

Fig. 13—With throttle lever in wide open position and pump lever fully compressed (down). Measure the clearance between spring adjusting nut and arm of the pump lever. Refer to *Holley Specifications Chart*. Adjust by turning nut or screw as required while holding opposite end. (The pump operating lever is not threaded). There should be no free movement of pump leverage when throttle is at curb idle.

Bowl Vent Valve Adjustment

Fig. 14—With throttle valves at fast curb

Fig. 13 Adjusting accelerator pump lever clearance

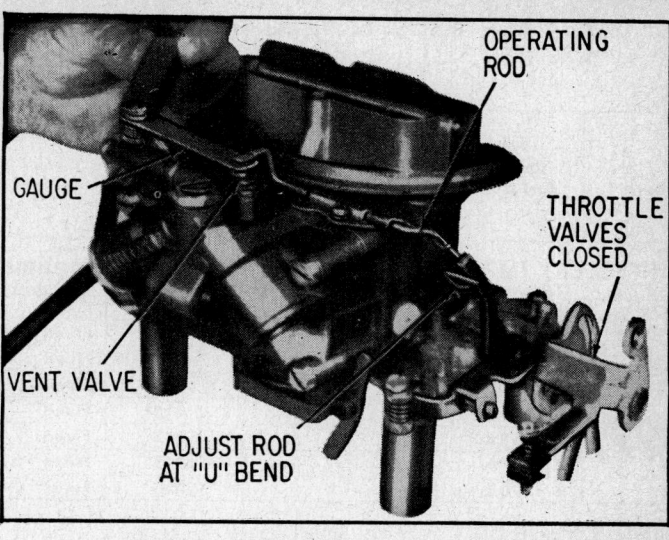

Fig. 14 Adjusting bowl vent valve clearance

idle, insert drill or gauge between the bowl vent valve and the bowl vent rod with the fast curb idle speed properly set. Refer to *Holley Specifications Chart*. Adjust by bending rod to change arc of contact with throttle lever, until correct clearance has been obtained.

4150 & 4160 CARB. ADJUSTMENT SPECIFICATIONS

See Tune Up Chart in car chapters for hot idle speeds.

Year	Carb. Part No. ①	Float Level (Dry)	Fuel Level (Wet)	Pump Lever Clearance	Choke Setting	Choke Unloader Clearance	Bowl Vent Clearance	Fast Idle		Choke Vacuum Break	Dashpot Setting
								Bench	On Car		
CHEVROLET ENGINES											
1969–70	R4053-A	⑩	④	.015	⑬	.350	—	.025	2200	.300	—
	R4296-A	⑩	④	.015	⑬	.350	—	.025	2200	.350	—
	R4346	⑩	④	.015	⑬	.350	—	.025	2200	.300	—
	R4492-A	⑩	④	.015	⑬	.350	—	.025	2200	.350	—
	R4557-A	⑩	④	.015	⑬	.350	—	.025	2200	.350	—
1971	R4800-A	②	④	.015	1.320⑤	.350	—	.025	2200	.350	—
	R4801-A	②	④	.015	1.320⑤	.350	—	.025	2200	.350	—
	R4802-A	②	④	.015	1.320⑤	.350	—	.025	2200	.350	—
	R4803-A	②	④	.015	1.320⑤	.350	—	.025	2200	.350	—
1972	R6238-A	②	④	.015	1.320⑤	.350	—	.025	2350	.350	—
	R6239-A	②	④	.015	1.320⑤	.350	—	.025	2350	.350	—
CHRYSLER, IMPERIAL, DODGE, PLYMOUTH											
1969	R-4166-A	⑪	⑨	.015	See Text	5/32	5/64	46 Drill	1400⑧	—	—
	R-4440-A	⑪	⑨	.015	See Text	5/32	5/64	46 Drill	1500⑭	—	—
1970–71	R4360-A	⑪	⑨	.015	2 Rich	25 Drill	72 Drill	53 Drill	1600	46 Drill	—
	R4366-A	⑪	⑨	.015	2 Rich	25 Drill	5/64	53 Drill	1600	46 Drill	—
1971	R4668-A	⑪	⑨	.015	2 Rich	25 Drill	.015	53 Drill	1700	46 Drill	—
	R4735-A	⑪	⑨	.015	2 Rich	25 Drill	.015	53 Drill	1700	46 Drill	—
	R6191-A	⑪	⑨	.015	2 Rich	25 Drill	.015	53 Drill	1800	18 Drill	—
	R6193-A	⑪	⑨	.015	2 Rich	25 Drill	.015	53 Drill	1800	18 Drill	—

Continued

4150 & 4160 CARB. ADJUSTMENT SPECIFICATIONS—Continued

See Tune Up Chart in car chapters for hot idle speeds.

Year	Carb. Part No. ①	Float Level (Dry)	Fuel Level (Wet)	Pump Lever Clearance	Choke Setting	Choke Unloader Clearance	Bowl Vent Clearance	Fast Idle		Choke Vacuum Break	Dashpot Setting
								Bench	On Car		
CHRYSLER, IMPERIAL, DODGE, PLYMOUTH—Continued											
1972	R-6160A	⑦	⑨	.015	Fixed	.150	.015	.060	1600	.080	—
	R-6252A	⑦	⑨	.015	Fixed	.150	.015	.060	1800	.140	—
	R-6253A	⑦	⑨	.015	Fixed	.150	.015	.060	1600	.080	—
	R-6254A	⑦	⑨	.015	Fixed	.150	.015	.060	1800	.140	—
	R-6255A	⑦	⑨	.015	Fixed	.150	.015	.060	1600	.080	—
	R-6256A	⑦	⑨	.015	Fixed	.150	.015	.060	2000	.140	—
	R-6257A	⑦	⑨	.015	Fixed	.150	.015	.060	1800	.080	—
	R-6290A	⑦	⑨	.015	Fixed	.150	.015	.060	1500	.080	—
FORD ENGINES											
1969	C9AF-M	See Text	④	No. 2⑮	2 Rich	—	.060–.090	.060	1350⑫	—	.100
	C9AF-N	See Text	④	No. 2⑮	1 Rich	—	.060–.090	.080	1550⑫	—	.100
	C9OF-H	See Text	④	No. 2⑮	1 Rich	—	.060–.090	.080	1550⑫	—	.100
1970	D0OF-N	See Text	④	—	2 Rich	—	—	—	2200	—	—
	D0OF-R	See Text	④	—	2 Rich	—	—	—	2400	—	—
	D0OF-S	See Text	④	—	—	—	—	—	—	—	—
	D0ZF-AA	See Text	④	.015	—	—	—	—	1900	—	.140
	D0ZF-AB	See Text	④	.015	—	—	—	—	2100	—	.200
	D0ZF-AC	See Text	④	.015	—	—	—	—	1900	—	—
	D0ZF-AD	See Text	④	.015	—	—	—	—	2100	—	—
	D0ZF-Z	See Text	④	—	—	—	—	—	—	—	—
1971	D1ZF-VA	See Text	④	.015	—	—	—	—	2100	—	⅛
	D1ZF-XA	See Text	④	.015	2 Rich	19/64	—	—	2400	—	—
	D1ZF-YA	See Text	④	.015	2 Rich	19/64	—	—	2200	—	7/64

① — Located on tag attached to carburetor, on casting or on choke plate flange.
② — Float centered in bowl.
③ — Primary .350″, secondary .450″.
④ — Use sight plug hole in fuel bowl as outlined in text.
⑤ — Bottom of throttle body to center of hole in operating lever.
⑥ — With lever touching screw, then tighten ¼ turn more.
⑦ — Primary .110″, secondary .204″.
⑧ — No. 5 Step on cam.
⑨ — Primary 9/16″, secondary 13/16″.
⑩ — Primary .350″, secondary .500″.
⑪ — Primary 15/64″, secondary 17/64″.
⑫ — On top step of cam.
⑬ — Top of rod even with bottom of hole.
⑭ — No. 2 Step on cam.
⑮ — Hole setting.

MODELS 4150, 4160 ADJUSTMENTS

These carburetors, Figs. 1, 2 and 3 are four barrel units whose primary sides contain all the basic systems that make up a complete carburetor. The secondary sides of these units contain a fuel transfer and by-pass system which operates when a greater quantity of fuel-air mixture is required.

As shown in Fig. 1, some late model 4150 units have a central fuel inlet whereas other 4150 and 4160 units have a side inlet.

As shown in Figs. 1 and 4, fuel inlet systems vary slightly between models. In some units, the floats are hinged in the center while in others they are hinged at the float end.

Dry Float Setting

Except Fig. 4 Units—Invert fuel bowl. Loosen lock screw enough to allow adjusting nut to rotate. Turn adjusting nut to proper setting:

On Ford units, adjust float parallel to bowl floor, Fig. 5.

On Chevrolet & Chrysler units, whether the float is hinged at the center or the end, set level to obtain specified dimension between float and bowl with bowl inverted, Fig. 5.

For Fig. 4 Units Only—Referring to Fig. 6, adjust float so that its center is an equal distance from top and bottom of fuel bowl with fuel bowl inverted. After carburetor is installed on engine, check and adjust fuel level.

Fuel Level Adjustment

Fig. 7—With car on a level floor and engine idling, fuel level should be at the level with the threads on the bottom of the sight plug hole (plus or minus $1/16''$). To adjust, loosen lock screw and turn adjusting nut as required.

Secondary Throttle Plate Adjustment

Late Model Units—Referring to Fig. 8, back the secondary throttle stop screw out until secondary throttle plates are closed in the bores. Turn screw in (clockwise) until it touches stop on secondary throttle lever; then turn it in an additional $1/2$ turn.

Accelerating Pump Adjustment

Late Model Units—Using a feeler gauge and with primary throttle plates in wide open position, there should be the clearance listed in the *Holley Specifications Chart* between pump operating lever adjusting screw and pump arm when pump arm is fully depressed manually, Fig. 9. Turn adjusting screw in to increase (out to decrease) clearance. One-half turn of adjusting screw is equal to .015".

To satisfy acceleration requirements in various climates, the pump discharge can be adjusted, Fig. 9. The bottom hole

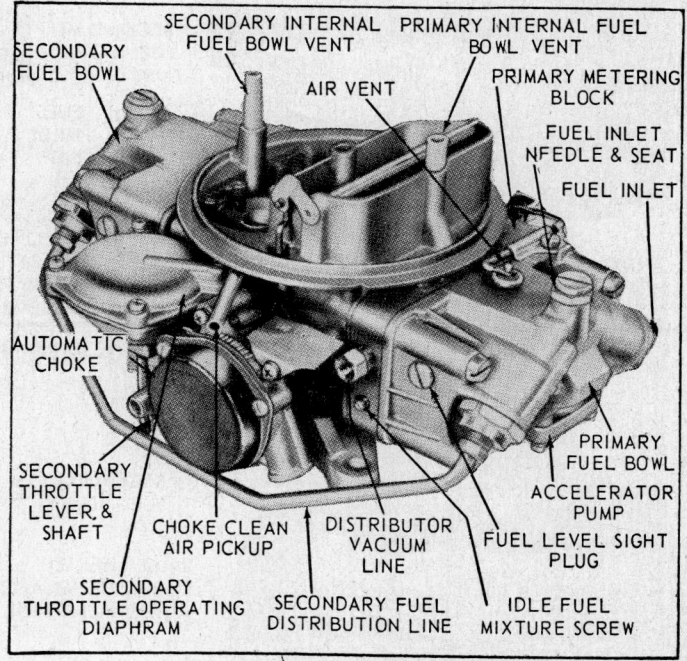

Fig. 4 Holley 4150 carburetor featuring an external fuel distributor tube connecting primary and secondary fuel inlets. These units also feature a choke clean air pick-up tube

Labels in Fig. 4: SECONDARY FUEL BOWL; SECONDARY INTERNAL FUEL BOWL VENT; PRIMARY INTERNAL FUEL BOWL VENT; AIR VENT; PRIMARY METERING BLOCK; FUEL INLET NEEDLE & SEAT; FUEL INLET; AUTOMATIC CHOKE; SECONDARY THROTTLE LEVER & SHAFT; CHOKE CLEAN AIR PICKUP; DISTRIBUTOR VACUUM LINE; PRIMARY FUEL BOWL; ACCELERATOR PUMP; FUEL LEVEL SIGHT PLUG; IDLE FUEL MIXTURE SCREW; SECONDARY THROTTLE OPERATING DIAPHRAM; SECONDARY FUEL DISTRIBUTION LINE

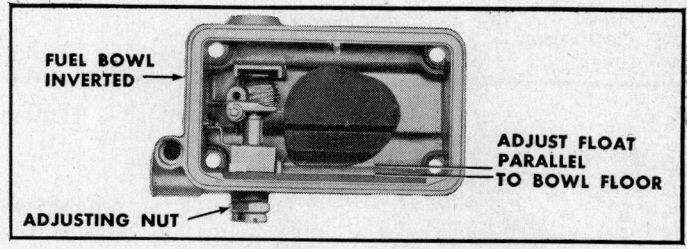

Labels in Fig. 5: FUEL BOWL INVERTED; ADJUST FLOAT PARALLEL TO BOWL FLOOR; ADJUSTING NUT

Fig. 5 Float adjustments except Fig. 4 type Ford units. On Chevrolet and Chrysler, adjust to specified dimension

(No. 2) in the cam provides a maximum pump discharge for extreme cold weather and the top hole (No. 1) provides the minimum pump discharge for warm weather operation.

Late Model Units—Referring to Fig. 10, the pump cam screw should be in the No. 1 position on the throttle lever for all normal operating conditions. For extreme cold weather the No. 2 position can be used to provide maximum pump discharge.

With throttle plates held in wide open position, there should be the clearance listed in the *Holley Specifications Chart* between the pump diaphragm actuating lever and the lower portion of the pump override spring screw.

This adjustment *must* be rechecked with the throttle plates closed to make certain that there is no lag between throttle linkage and pump lever. The slightest movement of the throttle lever must correspondingly actuate the pump lever. Should there be any lag, a stumble or flat spot will result. To eliminate the lag, lengthen the adjusting screw.

Bowl Vent Valve Adjustment

Fig. 11—The fuel bowl vent valve clearance must be adjusted whenever the accelerator pump lever and/or pump stroke

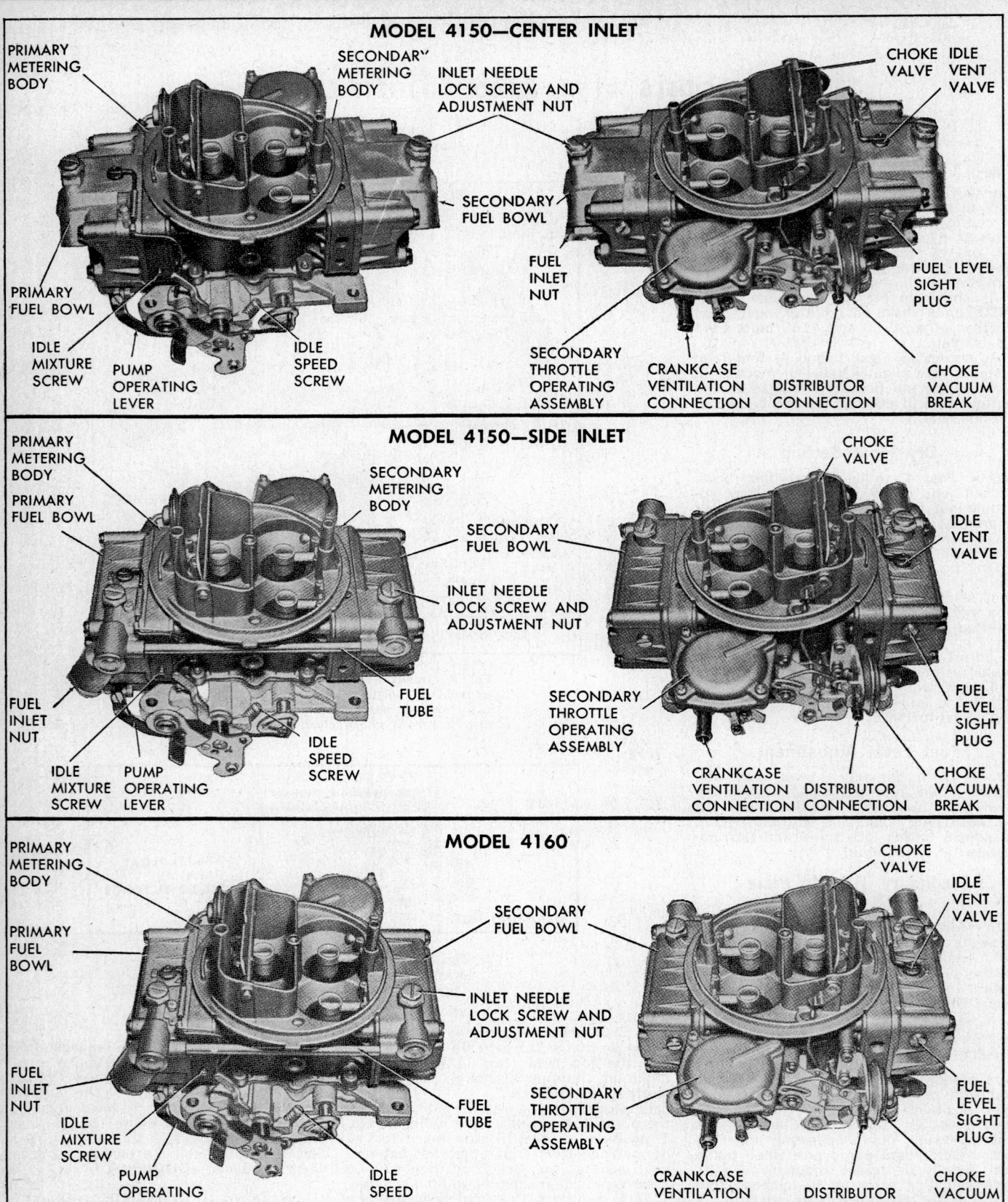

Fig. 1 Holley Models 4150 and 4160 late model four-barrel carburetors

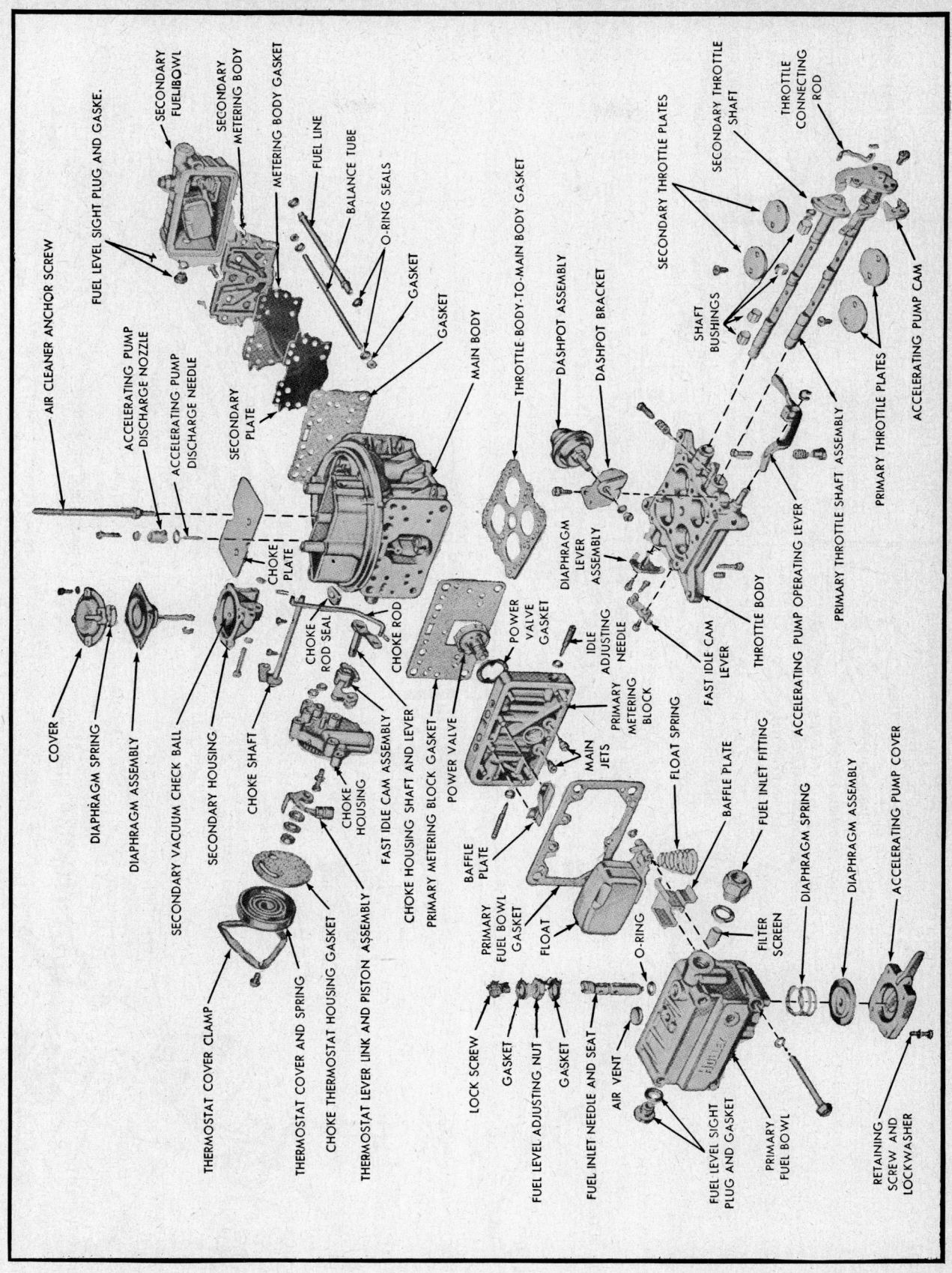

Fig. 2 Exploded view of a typical side fuel inlet 4150 and 4160 carburetor

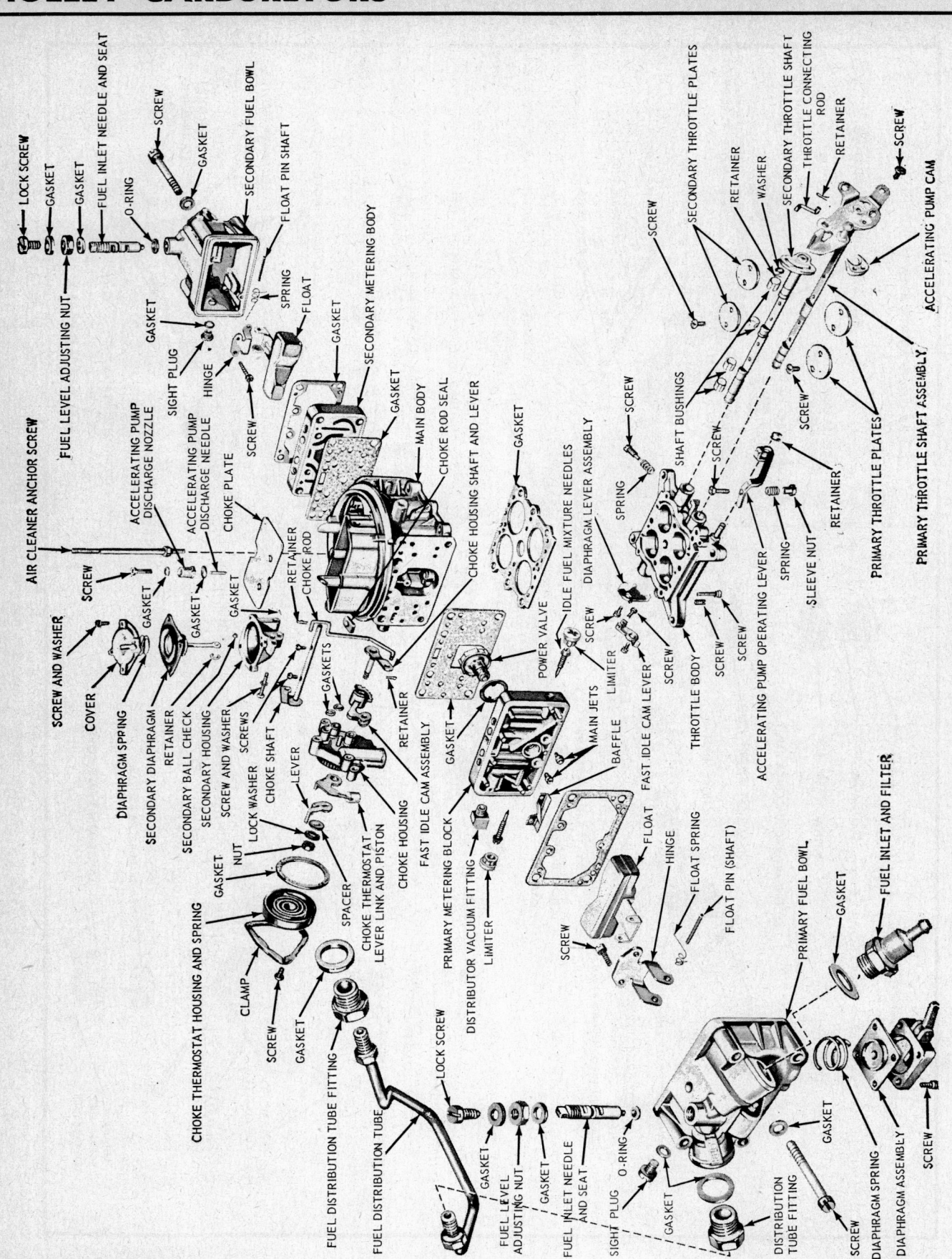

Fig. 3   Exploded view of a typical center fuel inlet 4150 carburetor

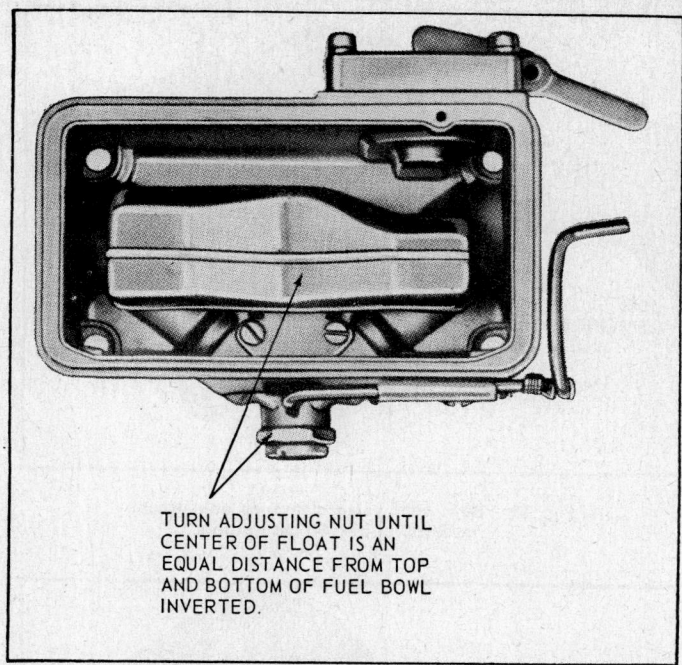

TURN ADJUSTING NUT UNTIL CENTER OF FLOAT IS AN EQUAL DISTANCE FROM TOP AND BOTTOM OF FUEL BOWL INVERTED.

Fig. 6   Float adjustment on Fig. 4 type Ford units

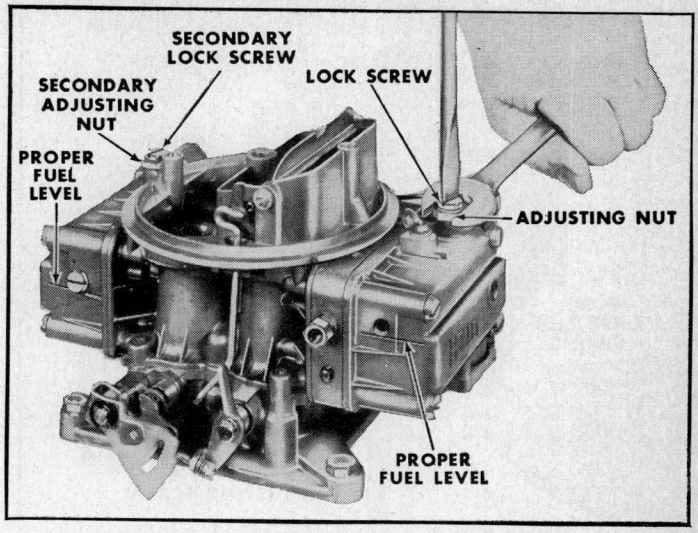

Fig. 7   Float level adjustment on all 4150 and 4160 carburetors

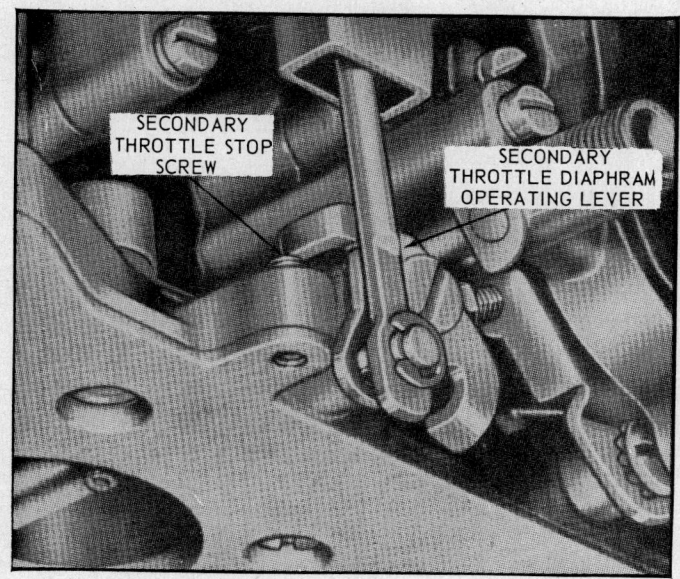

Fig. 8   Secondary throttle plate adjustment on Fig. 11 type carburetors

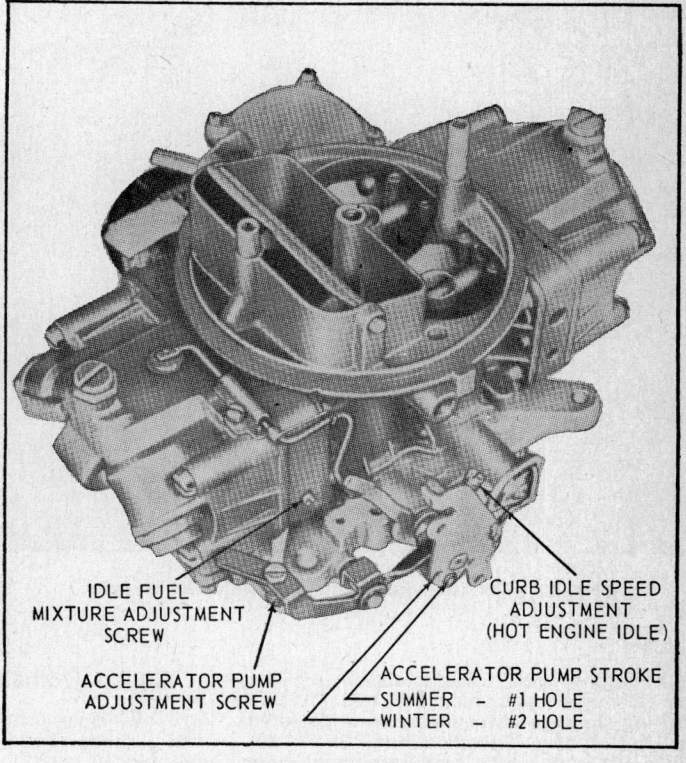

Fig. 9   Carburetor adjustment points on late type carburetors

adjustments have been changed. A change in the pump adjustments will affect the fuel bowl vent valve clearance.

With engine temperature stabilized and engine operating at curb idle speed, check clearance between bottom of vent valve and top of fuel bowl at vent opening. If clearance is not as listed in the *Holley Specifications Chart*, bend vent rod as required.

Fast Idle Speed

Units With Built-in Choke—With hot idle speed properly adjusted, set fast idle speed with transmission in neutral, engine at normal operating temperature, tachometer attached, headlamps turned on, and air conditioner operating (if so equipped). Referring to Fig. 12, align kickdown step of fast idle cam with the adjusting screw, and turn adjusting screw to obtain the specified rpm listed in the *Holley Specifications Chart*.

Units With Well Type Choke—With fast idle lever on high step of cam and choke valve wide open (engine warm) set fast idle to give the rpm listed in *Holley Specifications Chart*. Adjust fast idle screw on 4150 units or bend fast idle lever on 4160 units.

Fast Idle Cam Setting

Units With Well Type Choke—The fast

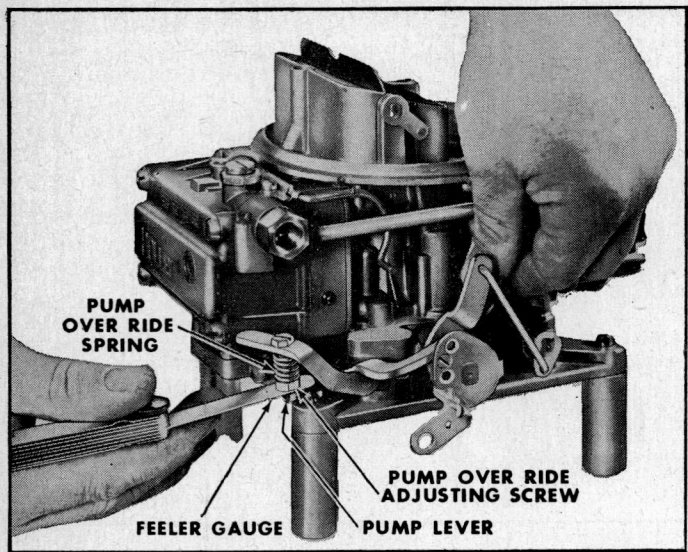

PUMP OVER RIDE SPRING

PUMP OVER RIDE ADJUSTING SCREW

FEELER GAUGE **PUMP LEVER**

Fig. 10 Pump adjustment on Fig. 9 type carburetors

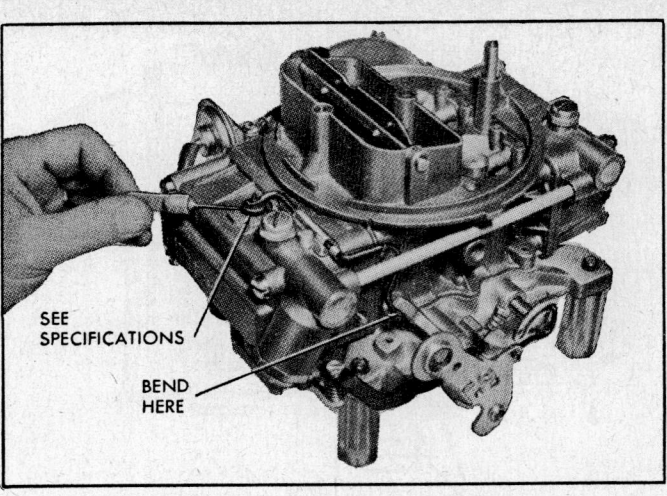

SEE SPECIFICATIONS

BEND HERE

Fig. 11 Bowl vent valve clearance adjustment on 4150 and 4160 carburetors

FAST IDLE ADJUSTMENT SCREW

Fig. 12 Fast idle adjustment. Units with built-in choke

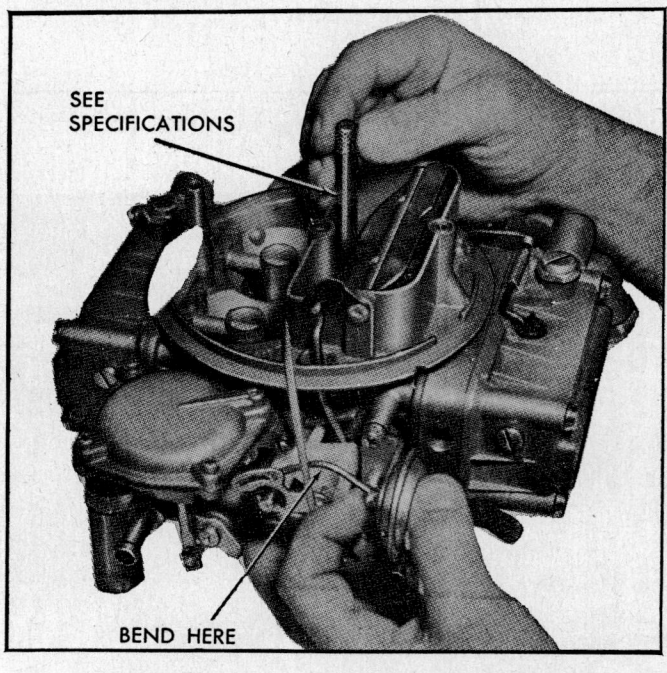

SEE SPECIFICATIONS

BEND HERE

Fig. 13 Vacuum break adjustment. Well type choke

idle setting with the carburetor off the car is made by turning the fast idle adjusting screw to obtain the clearance listed in the *Holley Specifications Chart* between throttle valve and carburetor bore (idle port side) with fast idle screw on high step of cam.

Vacuum Break Adjustment

Fig. 13—On models so equipped, hold choke valve closed with a rubber band. Hold vacuum break in against its stop. Measure distance between lower edge of choke valve and wall of air horn. If the clearance is not as listed in the *Holley Specifications Chart*, bend vacuum break link to adjust.

Choke Unloader Adjustment

Fig. 14—Hold throttle lever wide open with a rubber band. Hold choke valve toward closed position toward unloader tang of throttle shaft. Then measure opening between lower edge of choke valve and air horn wall. If the opening is not as listed in the *Holley Specifications Chart*, bend choke rod at offset angle.

Idle Mixture Adjustment
1968-69 Chrysler Corp.

The screw located next to the primary bowl vent on top of choke air horn is the only means to be used to adjust carburetor idle mixture. Unless an engine exhaust analyzer is available. Rough idle

and low speed surge on vehicles may be the result of improper idle setting balance between the right and left carburetor bores. To correct this condition:
1. Remove the cup plugs in the sides of the primary metering block. A small sharp punch is recommended for removing cup plugs.
2. With engine thoroughly warmed up, install an exhaust gas analyzer and adjust carburetor idle speed and mixture.
3. Turn the single idle adjusting screw (located on top of air horn) counterclockwise (rich direction) until it is seated, then move it ¾ turn clockwise (lean direction). Do not disturb this screw during the other steps of this procedure.

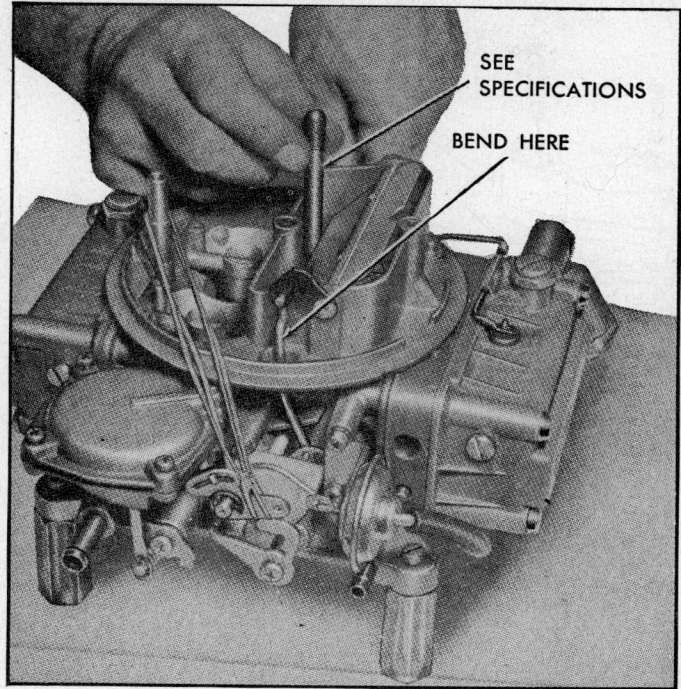

Fig. 14   Choke unloader adjustment. Well type choke

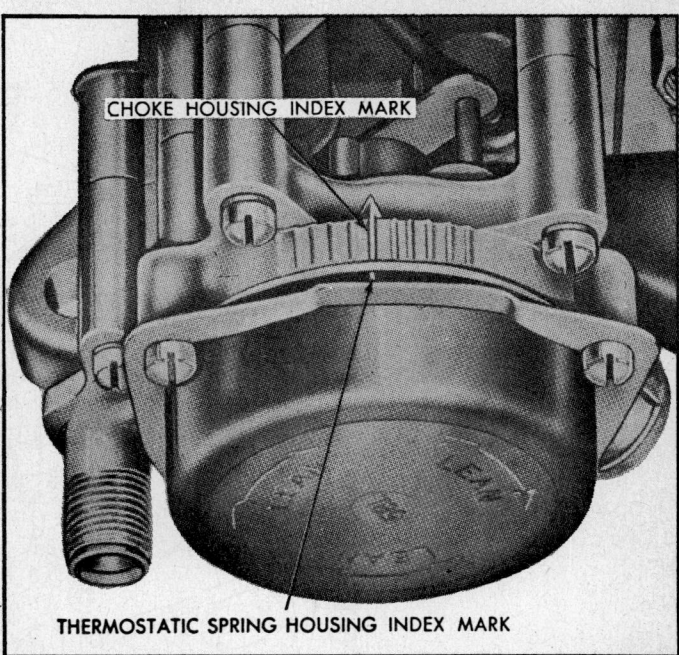

Fig. 15   Built-in automatic choke adjustment

4. With a narrow screw driver, turn the two idle limiter screws clockwise until they are both seated. These screws have prevailing torque features which may require rather high effort to turn screws. It is very important that this prevailing torque is overcome and the screws completely seat against idle discharge ports.

5. Turn both idle limiter screws 1½ to 2 turns counterclockwise as a starting point (experience will dictate more or less turns as a rough setting but both screws should be turned equally).

6. Start engine and set specified idle speed for engines with 300 or more miles. Set 75 rpm below specifications if under 50 miles or 50 rpm below specifications if 50 to 300 miles are on engine.

7. Observe air/fuel ratio reading on ex-haust gas analyser. Turn each screw 1/16 inch turn richer (counterclockwise) and note change in air/fuel meter reading.

IMPORTANT: When adjusting mixture screws to obtain air/fuel ratio specified, do not turn the mixture screw more than 1/16 turn at a time of 10 second increments. The combustion analyzer is so sensitive that the ratio must be changed in very small increments if accurate readings are to be obtained. The meters read in air/fuel ratio so that a higher reading indi-cates a leaner mixture and visa versa.

8. It is very important that both idle limiter screws be turned the same amount on each adjustment so that as finally set both screws will be the same number of turns from the seated position.

9. Install cup plugs over limiter screws.

Built-In Choke Setting

Fig. 15—Loosen retaining screws and turn choke cover so that index mark or line on choke cover lines up with speci-fied mark on choke housing. See *Holley Specifications Chart.*

Well Type Choke Adjustment

With throttle half open and choke valve closed, bend the choke rod to obtain specified clearance for Chevrolet units. On Chrysler units, follow same procedure so that the top of the choke rod hole in the control lever is 1²³/₃₂" above the bottom of the carburetor base.

HOLLEY CARBURETORS

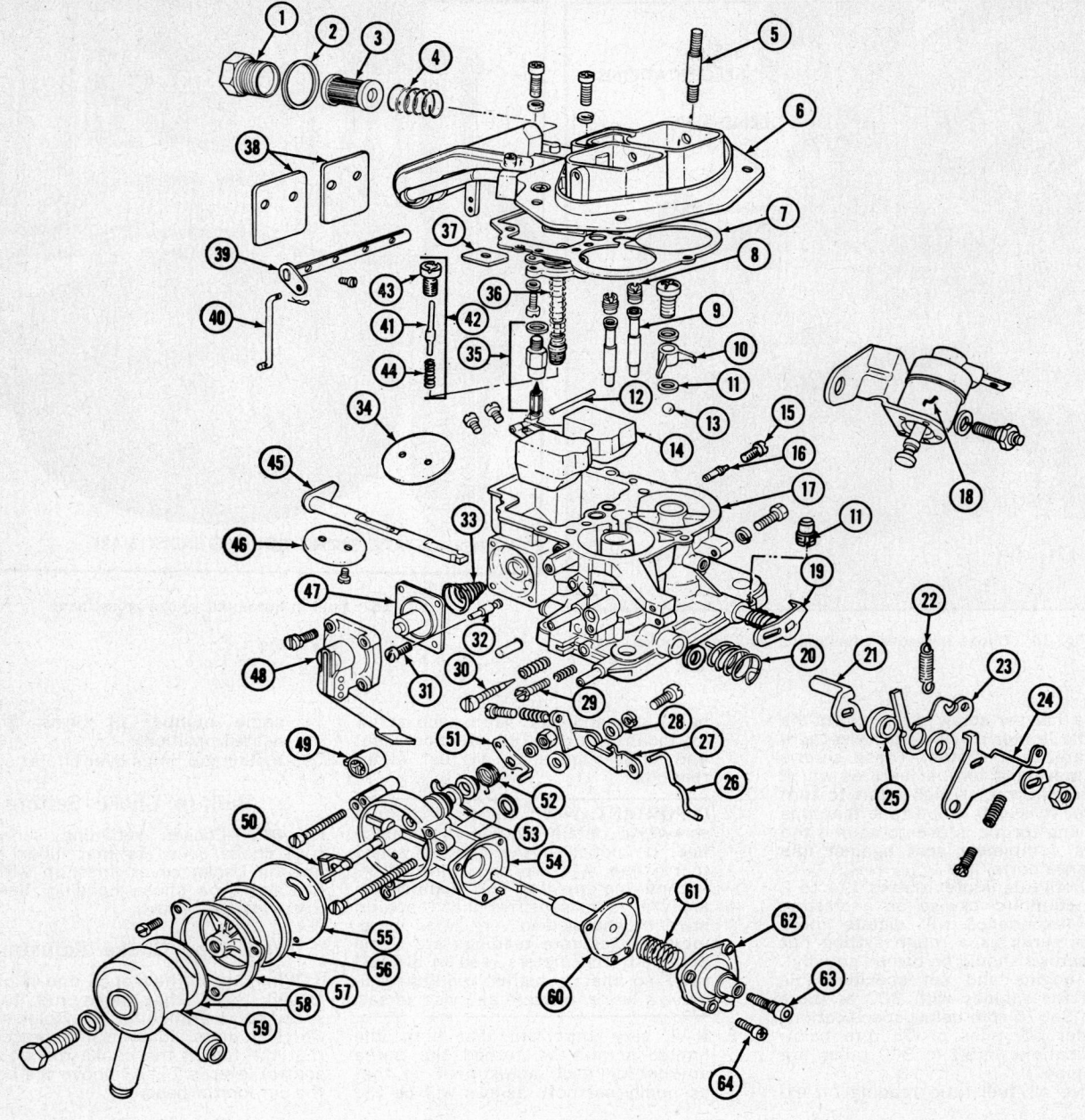

1. Fuel Inlet Nut
2. Gasket
3. Filter
4. Spring
5. Studs, Air Cleaner Attachment
6. Air Horn
7. Gasket
8. High Speed Bleed
9. Main Well Tube
10. Pump Discharge Nozzle
11. Gasket
12. Float Shaft
13. Discharge Check Ball
14. Float
15. Retainer
16. Secondary Idle Jet
17. Carburetor Body Assembly
18. Idle Stop Solenoid
19. Secondary Throttle Lever
20. Throttle Return Spring
21. Idle Lever
22. Secondary Operating Lever Return Spring
23. Secondary Operating Lever
24. Throttle Lever
25. Bushing
26. Fast Idle Rod
27. Fast Idle Lever
28. Bushing
29. Low Idle Screw
30. Fuel Mixture Screw
31. Retainer
32. Primary Idle Jet
33. Return Spring
34. Secondary Throttle Plate
35. Fuel Inlet Needle and Seat Assembly
36. Power Valve Economizer Assembly
37. Choke Rod Seal
38. Choke Plates
39. Choke Shaft and Lever
40. Choke Rod
41. Power Valve
42. Power Valve Assembly
43. Seat
44. Spring
45. Primary Throttle Shaft and Lever Assembly
46. Primary Throttle Plate
47. Accelerator Pump
48. Accelerator Pump Cover
49. Mixture Screw Limiter Cap
50. Choke Housing Shaft
51. Choke Lever
52. Fast Idle Cam Spring
53. Fast Idle Cam
54. Choke Housing
55. Gasket
56. Thermostatic Housing
57. Retainer
58. Gasket
59. Water Cover
60. Diaphragm and Shaft
61. Return Spring
62. Choke Diaphragm Cover
63. Hex Head Screw
64. Cover Screw

Fig. 2 Exploded view of a typical Holley 5210 carburetor

5210 CARB. ADJUSTMENT SPECIFICATIONS

See Tune Up Chart in car chapter for hot idle speeds, air/fuel ratio and idle CO% rating.

Year	Carb. Part No.	Carb. Model	Float Level (Dry)	Float Drop	Pump Position	Fast Idle Cam Index	Vacuum Plate Pulldown	Fast Idle Setting	Choke Setting
CHEVROLET VEGA & PONTIAC ASTRE									
1973	R-6477A	5210	.420	1"	#3	.140	.300	2000	1 Rich
	R-6478A	5210	.420	1"	#2	.140	.300	2200	2 Rich
	R-6580A	5210	.420	1"	#2	.140	.300	2200	2 Rich
	R-6581A	5210	.420	1"	#3	.140	.300	2000	1 Rich
1974	338168	5210-C	.420	1"	#2	.140	.400	2200	3½ Rich
	338170	5210-C	.420	1"	#2	.140	.400	2200	3½ Rich
	338179	5210-C	.420	1"	#3	.140	.300	2000	2½ Rich
	338181	5210-C	.420	1"	#3	.140	.300	2000	2½ Rich
1975	348659	5210-C	.420	1"	—	—	.325	1600	3 Rich
	348660	5210-C	.420	1"	#2	.110	.300	1600	4 Rich
	348661	5210-C	.420	1"	—	—	.275	1600	3 Rich
	348662	5210-C	.420	1"	#2	.110	.275	1600	4 Rich
	348663	5210-C	.420	1"	—	—	.325	1600	3 Rich
	348664	5210-C	.420	1"	#2	.110	.300	1600	4 Rich
	348665	5210-C	.420	1"	—	—	.275	1600	3 Rich
	348666	5210-C	.420	1"	#2	.110	.275	1600	4 Rich

MODEL 5210

The Holley 5210 two-barrel carburetor, Figs. 1 and 2, has a number of unique features. An automatic choke system activated by a water heated bi-metal thermostatic coil and a primary venturi smaller in size than the secondary venturi.

An Exhaust Gas Recirculation (EGR) system is used on all applications with the EGR valve located in the intake manifold.

Float Adjustment

Fig. 3—With the air horn inverted and the float tang resting lightly on the spring loaded fuel inlet needle, measure the clearance between the bowl cover and the end of each float. Refer to *Holley 5210 Specifications Chart*. Adjust by bending the float tang as required.

Fast Idle Cam Index Adjustment

Fig. 4—Place the fast idle screw on the second step of the fast idle cam and against the shoulder of the first step. Place a drill or gauge on the down stream side of the choke plate. Refer to *5210 Specifications Chart*. Adjust by bending the choke lever tang.

NOTE: The dechoke is automatically set when the fast idle cam index is adjusted.

Vacuum Plate Pulldown Adjustment

Fig. 5—Remove the three hex headed screws and ring retaining the choke bi-metal cover. Do not remove the choke water housing screw if adjusting on the car. Pull the choke water housing and bi-

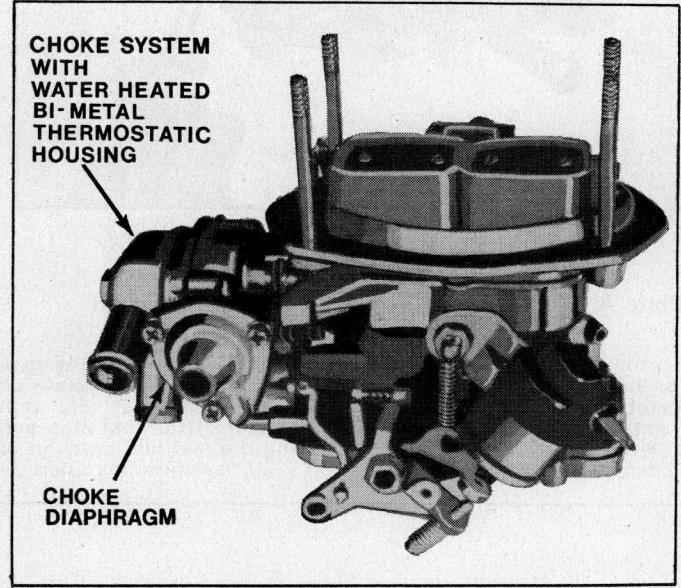

CHOKE SYSTEM WITH WATER HEATED BI-METAL THERMOSTATIC HOUSING

CHOKE DIAPHRAGM

Fig. 1   Holley 5210 2 barrel carburetor

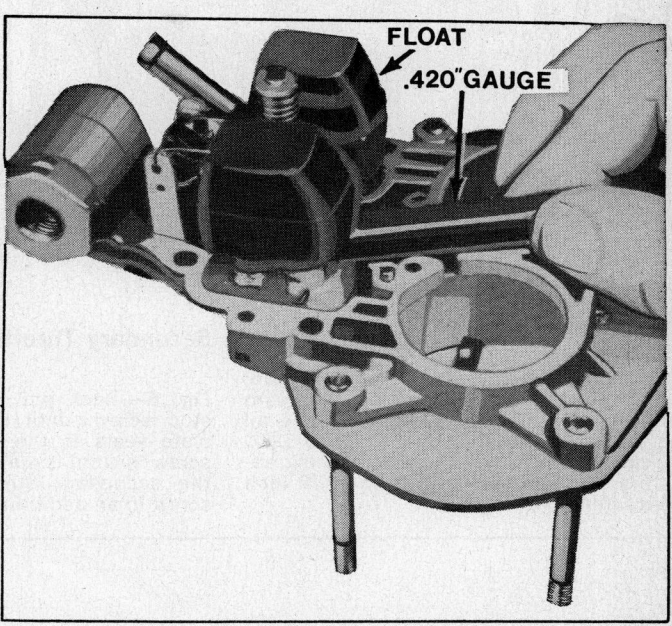

FLOAT

.420"GAUGE

Fig. 3   Checking float level on 5210 carburetor

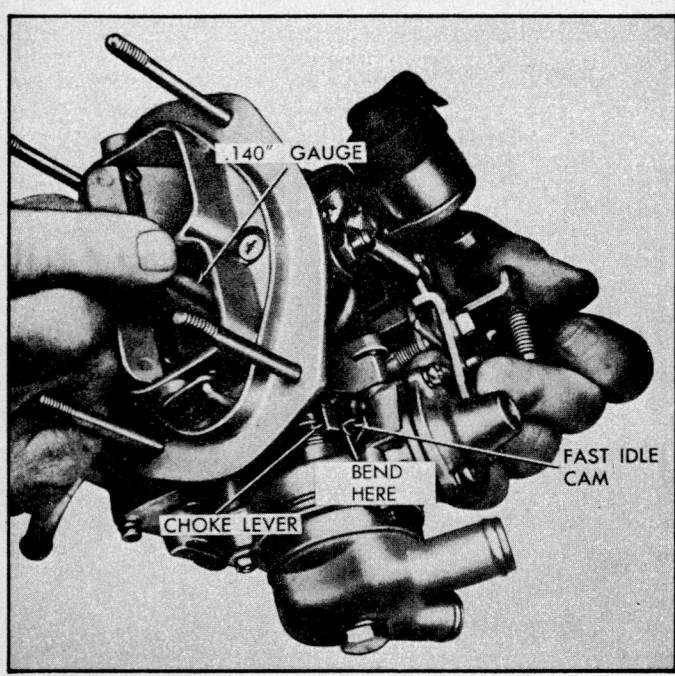

Fig. 4   Fast idle cam index adjustment 5210 Holley carburetor

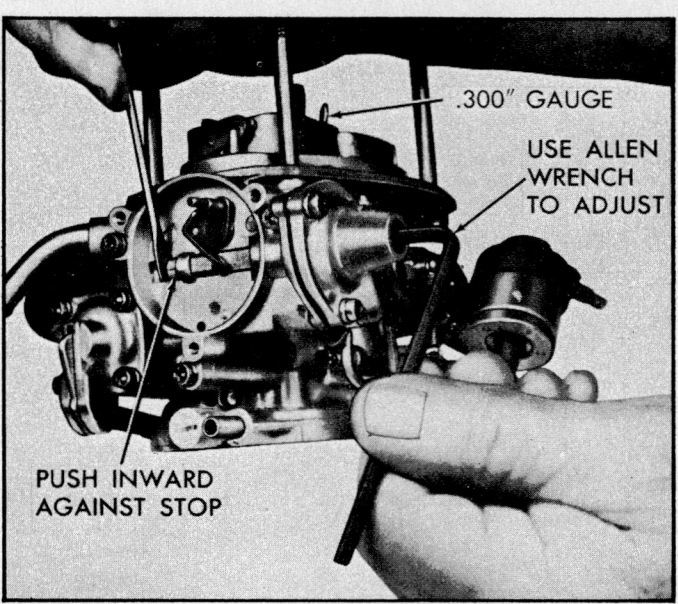

Fig. 5   Vacuum pull down adjustment 5210 Holley carburetor

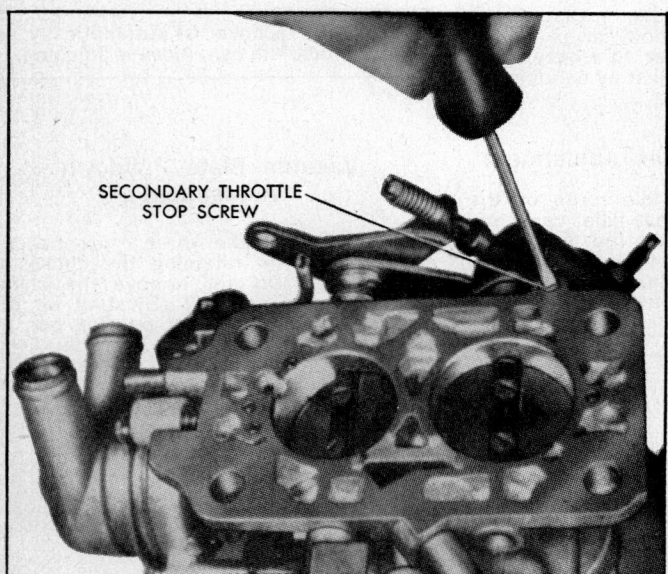

Fig. 6   Secondary throttle plate adjustment

Fig. 7   Fast idle adjustment 5210 Holley carburetor

metal cover assembly out of the way. With a screwdriver or suitable tool, push the diaphragm stem back against the stop. Place drill or gauge on the down stream side of the primary choke plate. Take all the slack out of the linkage. Refer to *5210 Specifications Chart.* Adjust by turning adjusting screw in or out with an 5/32 inch Allen wrench.

Secondary Throttle Plate Adjustment

Fig. 6—Back out the secondary throttle stop screw, until the secondary throttle plate seats in the carburetor bore. Turn screw in until it makes contact with tab on the secondary throttle lever, then turn screw in an additional ¼ turn.

Fast Idle Adjustment

Fig. 7—With the engine at operating temperature, position the fast idle screw on the second step of the fast idle cam against the shoulder of the first step and adjust by turning the fast idle screw in or out. Refer to *5210 Specifications Chart.*

TUNE UP SERVICE

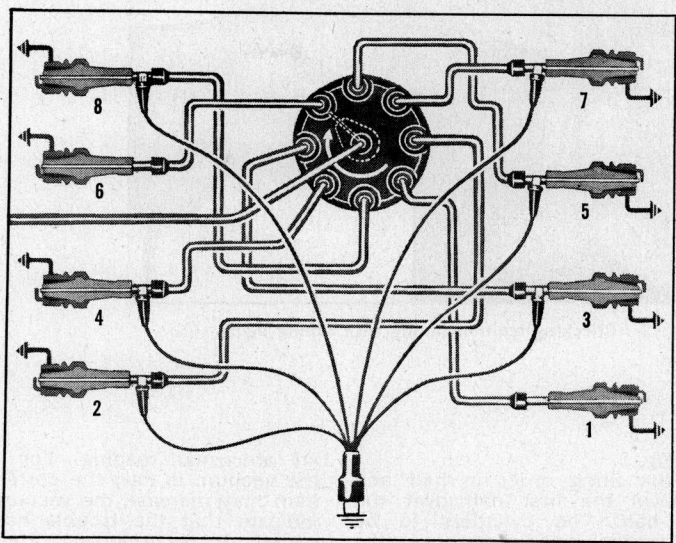

Fig. 1   Cylinder balance test connections. The firing order in this example is 1-8-4-3-6-5-7-2. Therefore, the cylinders to be tested together are 1-6, 8-5, 4-7, 3-2, using the grounding leads as shown

CONTENTS

Diagnosis & Testing 2-517
Distributors, Standard 2-525
Electronic Ignition Systems 2-535
   Chrysler 2-535
   Delco-Remy 2-537
   Ford 2-543
Ignition Coils 2-521
Ignition Resistors 2-521
Tune Up Procedure 2-517
Tune Up Service 2-518
Tune Up Service Bulletins 2-520

Tune up service has become increasingly important to the modern automotive engine with its vastly improved power and performance. Improved fuel and electrical systems and especially the exhaust emission controls with their inherently critical settings, engines have become more sensitive to usage and operating conditions, which have a decided effect on power and performance. It is important, therefore, that this service be performed on the engine every spring and fall or more often if conditions warrant.

In addition to the servicing of spark plugs, ignition points and condenser, a proper tune up includes a number of tests to check the condition of the engine and its related systems and uncover sources of future problems.

TUNE UP PROCEDURE

Since a quality tune up is dependent upon the proper operation of a number of systems, we have listed here in a logical sequence, the steps to be followed.
1. Diagnosis. This to consist of a compression test, cylinder balance test, oscilloscope check, manifold vacuum test, charging circuit and cranking voltage test.
2. Service spark plugs.
3. Service ignition system, secondary wiring, distributor and coil.
4. Check and service battery and charging system.
5. Service manifold heat valve, if used.
6. Service carburetor, linkage, fuel and air filters.
7. Check operation of various emission control devices.

Once these mechanical checks have been performed the tune up can be finalized. The final steps are:
1. Setting the dwell.
2. Setting slow idle, idle fuel mixture, choke and ignition timing.
3. Adjusting the fast idle.
4. Checking ignition output and secondary resistance.
5. Road test.

DIAGNOSIS & TESTING

Before a satisfactory tune up can be performed, the existing condition of the engine and its related systems must be determined. A tune up should not be attempted if tests indicate internal engine problems such as burnt valves, worn rings, blown head gasket, etc., until such conditions have been corrected.

Oscilloscope Test

Although oscilloscopes differ in many ways, they all display a light or "trace" on a screen which measures the voltage present at a given point and time. As the ignition system operates, its voltage creates a pattern on the screen. This pattern, when read in accordance with the manufacturers instructions for the particular unit, indicates the condition of the entire ignition system.

Compression Test

An engine cannot be tuned to develop maximum power and smooth performance unless the proper compression is obtained in each cylinder.

CAUTION: When cranking the engine for a compression test or any other reason, the coil high tension cable should be removed from the distributor cap and grounded to the engine block or the distributor primary grounded with jumper wire.

1. Remove any foreign matter from around spark plugs by blowing out plug area with compressed air. Then remove plugs.
2. Remove air cleaner and block throttle and choke in wide open position.

3. Insert compression gauge firmly in spark plug opening and crank engine through at least four compression strokes to obtain highest possible reading.
4. Test and record compression of each cylinder. Compression should read within the limits given in the *Tune Up Charts* in the car chapters.
5. If one or more cylinders read low, inject about a tablespoon of engine oil on top of pistons in the low reading cylinders. Crank engine several times and recheck compression.
6. If compression is now higher, it indicates worn piston rings. If compression does not improve, valves are sticking or seating poorly. If two adjacent cylinders show low compression and injecting oil does not improve the condition, the cause may be a head gasket leak between cylinders.

Cylinder Balance

It is sometimes difficult to locate a weak cylinder especially in an eight cylinder engine. A compression test, for example, will not locate a leaky intake manifold, a valve not opening properly due to a worn camshaft, or a defective spark plug.

With the cylinder balance test, the power output of one cylinder may be checked against another, using a set of grounding leads, Fig. 1. When the power of each cylinder is not equal, the engine will lose power and run roughly. The cylinder balance test is as follows:
1. Connect a tachometer and vacuum gauge.
2. Start engine and run it at a fast idle.
3. Ground large clip of grounding leads and connect individual leads to all spark plugs *except the pair being*

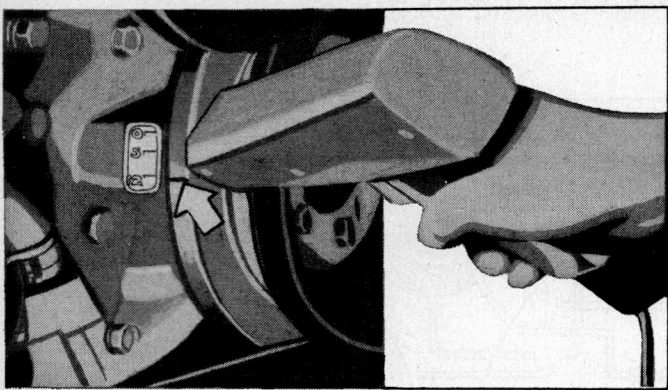

Fig. 2 Checking ignition timing with timing lights

tested, Fig. 1.

4. Divide the firing order in half and write down the first half over the second half. The cylinders to be tested together appear one over the other.

Firing Order	Pairs Tested
1-8-4-3-6-5-7-2	1-6, 8-5, 4-7, 3-2
1-2-7-8-4-5-6-3	1-4, 2-5, 7-6, 8-3
1-5-4-8-6-3-7-2	1-6, 5-3, 4-7, 8-2
1-5-4-2-6-3-7-8	1-6, 5-3, 4-7, 2-8
1-8-7-3-6-5-4-2	1-6, 8-5, 7-4, 3-2
1-3-7-2-6-5-4-8	1-6, 3-5, 7-4, 2-8
1-5-6-3-4-2-7-8	1-4, 5-2, 6-7, 3-8
1-6-5-4-3-2	1-4, 6-3, 5-2
1-5-3-6-2-4	1-6, 5-2, 3-4
1-4-5-2-3-6	1-2, 4-3, 5-6
1-3-4-2	1-4, 3-2
1-4-3-2	1-3, 4-2

5. Operate engine on each pair of cylinders in turn and note engine rpm and manifold vacuum for each pair. A variation of more than one inch of vacuum or 40 rpm between pairs of cylinders being tested indicates that the cylinders are off balance.

6. To isolate one weak cylinder, short out one bank of cylinders at a time. The bank giving the lower readings will include the weak cylinder.

Manifold Vacuum Test

NOTE: On some high performance engines, the camshaft provides such a great degree of valve overlap that vacuum at idle speed will be too low for an accurate test. For this reason, a vacuum test made on such units is of little value.

Manifold vacuum is affected by carburetor adjustment, valve timing, ignition timing, valve condition, cylinder compression, condition of positive crankcase ventilation system and leakage of manifold, carburetor, carburetor spacer or cylinder head gaskets.

Because abnormal gauge readings may indicate that more than one of the above factors are at fault, use care in analyzing

an abnormal reading. For example, if the vacuum is low, the correction of one item may increase the vacuum enough to indicate that the trouble has been corrected. It is important, therefore, that each cause of an abnormal reading be investigated and further tests conducted, where necessary, to arrive at the correct diagnosis of the trouble. To check manifold vacuum, proceed as follows:

1. Bring engine to operating temperature.
2. Connect an accurate vacuum gauge to the intake manifold.
3. Operate engine at recommended idle speed.
4. Check vacuum reading on gauge.

Test Conclusions

NORMAL READING: 18 inches or more. Allowance should be made for the effect of altitude on gauge reading.

LOW & STEADY: Loss of power in all cylinders possibly caused by late ignition or valve timing, or loss of compression.

VERY LOW: Intake manifold, carburetor spacer or head gasket leak.

NEEDLE FLUCTUATES STEADILY AS SPEED INCREASES: Partial or complete loss of power in one or more cylinders caused by a leaky head or manifold gasket, burnt valve, weak valve spring or a defect in the ignition system.

GRADUAL DROP IN READING AT IDLE SPEED: Excessive back pressure in exhaust system.

INTERMITTENT FLUCTUATION: Defect in ignition system or sticking valve.

SLOW FLUCTUATION OR DRIFTING OF NEEDLE: Improper idle mixture, carburetor, carburetor spacer, intake manifold gasket leak or restricted crankcase ventilation system.

Cranking Voltage Test

The condition of the starting circuit can be checked by connecting a voltmeter across the battery posts, grounding the coil so the engine will not fire and cranking the engine. If, during cranking, the voltage reading drops below 9.6 volts,

there is high resistance in the circuit.

Charging Circuit Test

The performance of the charging circuit should be checked during any tune-up. See specific unit section of this manual for test procedures.

Ignition Timing

The use of a timing light, Fig. 2, is recommended for checking and setting ignition timing. This setting is critical especially on units equipped with emission control systems.

NOTE: When setting timing, be sure idle speed is set lower than speed at which centrifugal advance begins. See Distributor Specifications Chart in car chapters.

NOTE: The timing light should be connected to the proper spark plug lead by the use of an adapter. The boots around the connections should not be pierced to connect the light as this can cause spark arcing and misfiring.

Lacking a timing light, the timing can be set with the engine stopped by using a jumper light. Be sure to use a light bulb that corresponds with the vehicle voltage, Fig. 3.

1. Rotate engine until No. 1 cylinder is positioned at the specified timing mark.
2. Connect jumper light between distributor ignition terminal and ground.
3. Turn on ignition switch.
4. Loosen distributor and turn it in the direction of normal rotation until the points just close (light out). Then slowly turn the distributor in the opposite direction just to the exact point that the light goes on. Tighten distributor in this position.

Combustion Efficiency Test

This test checks the carburetor air/fuel mixture by measuring the amount of various chemicals present in the engine exhaust under different conditions. By following the manufacturer's instructions for the specific unit, the carburetor idle, intermediate, high speed and accelerator pump circuits can be checked for proper operation.

This test is especially important when working on engines equipped with exhaust emission controls because of the more critical mixture adjustments on such units.

SERVICE

Spark Plugs

1. Examine firing ends of plugs for evidence of oil fouling gas fouling, burned or overheated condition. Oil fouling is usually identified by wet, sludgy deposits caused by excessive oil consumption. Gas fouling is identified by dry, black, fluffy deposits caused by incomplete combustion. Burned or overheated spark plugs are identified by white, burned or blistered insulator nose and badly

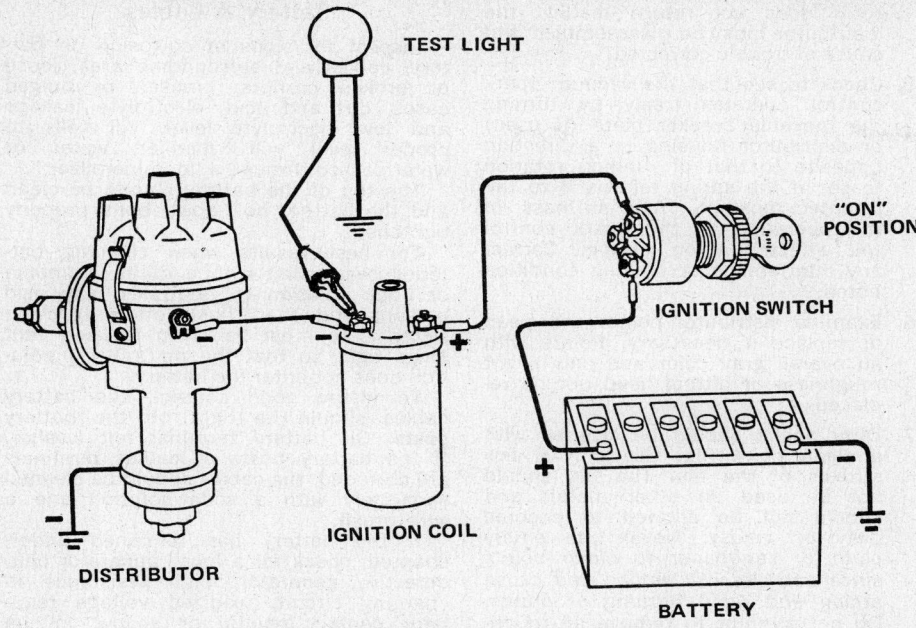

Fig. 3 Jumper light circuit for static ignition timing

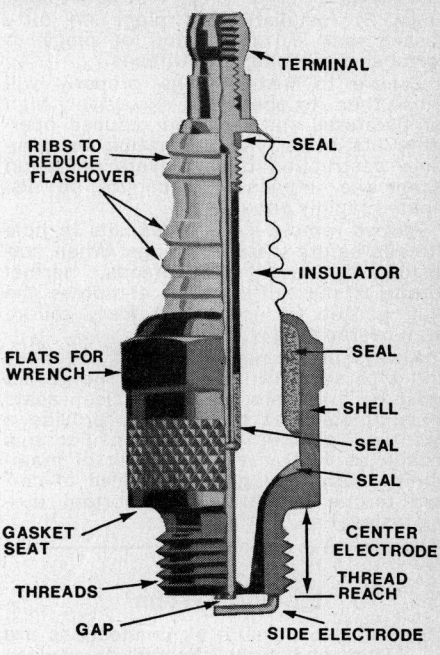

Fig. 4 Spark plug details

burned electrodes. Improper fuel, insufficient cooling or improper ignition timing normally are the cause. Normal conditions are usually identified by white powdery deposits or rusty-brown to grayish-tan powdery deposits.

2. Clean plugs with a suitable sand blast cleaner following the manufacturers instructions.
3. Remove carbon and other deposits from threads with a stiff wire brush.

NOTE: Do not use brush to clean electrodes as small pieces of wire can stick inside plug and later cause misfiring.

4. Dress electrodes with a small file to secure flat, parallel surfaces on both center and side electrodes, Fig. 4.
5. Use a round wire gauge to check the gap, Fig. 5, and adjust by bending the side (never center) electrode to the proper specifications as shown in the Tune Up Charts in the car chapters.
6. If gaskets are used, place new ones on plugs and torque plugs to specification.

IMPORTANT

Improper installation of spark plugs is one of the greatest single causes of unsatisfactory spark plug performance. Improper installation is the result of one or more of the following practices: 1) Installation of plugs with insufficient torque to fully seat the gasket; 2) excessive torque which changes gap set-

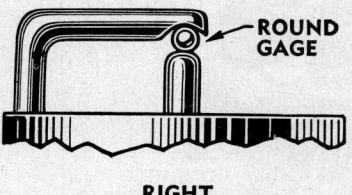

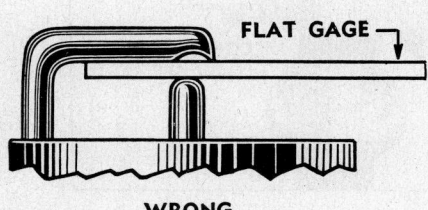

Fig. 5 Correct and incorrect spark plug gauges

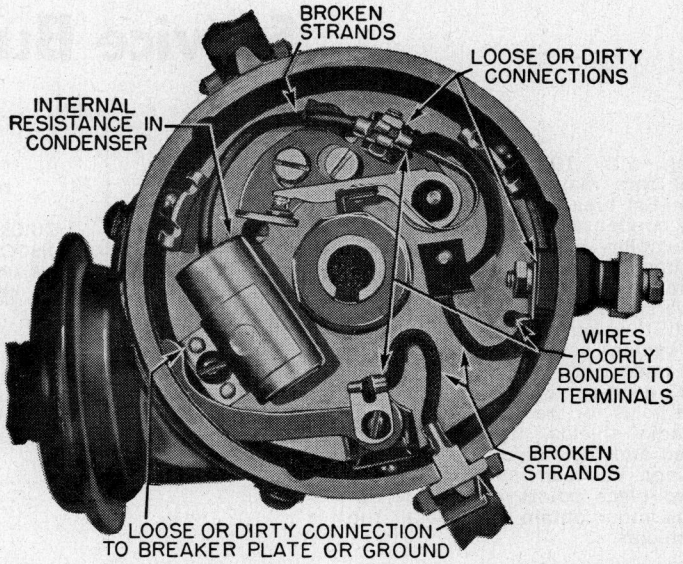

Fig. 6 What to look for when checking for high resistance in the primary circuit of the distributor. In addition to the points indicated, look for external circuit high resistance at ignition switch terminals, ammeter terminals, coil terminals and broken or poorly insulated wires in this circuit

tings; 3) installation of plugs on dirty gasket seal; 4) installation of plugs to corroded spark plug hole threads.

Failure to install plugs properly will cause them to operate at excessively high temperatures and result in reduced operating life under mild operation or complete destruction under severe operation where the intense heat cannot be dissipated rapidly enough.

Always remove carbon deposits in hole threads before installing plugs. When corrosion is present in threads, normal torque is not sufficient to compress the plug gasket (if used) and early failure from overheating will result.

Always use a new gasket (if required) and wipe seats in head clean. The gasket must be fully compressed on clean seats to complete heat transfer and provide a gas tight seal in the cylinder. For this reason as well as the necessity of maintaining correct plug gap, the use of correct torque is extremely important during installation.

Ignition System

1. Check to be sure all connections are clean and tight. Repair or replace any wires that are frayed, loose or damaged, Fig. 6. Replace brittle or damaged spark plug wires.
2. Remove distributor cap, clean and inspect for cracks, carbon tracks and burned or corroded terminals. Replace cap if necessary.
3. Clean rotor and inspect for damage or deterioration. Replace rotor if necessary.
4. Check distributor centrifugal advance mechanism (if used) by turning distributor rotor in direction of running rotation as far as possible, then release rotor to see if springs return it to its retarded position. If

rotor does not return readily, the distributor must be disassembled and cause of trouble corrected.

5. Check to see that the vacuum spark control operates freely by turning the movable breaker plate (if used) or distributor housing in a direction opposite to that of running rotation to see if the spring returns it to the retarded position. Any stiffness in the operation of the spark control will affect ignition timing. Correct any interference or binding condition noted.
6. Examine distributor points and clean or replace if necessary. Points with an overall gray color and only slight roughness or pitting need not be replaced.
7. Dirty points should be cleaned with a clean point file. Use only a few strokes of the file. The file should not be used on other metals and should not be allowed to become dirty or greasy. *Never use emery cloth or sandpaper to clean points since particles will embed and cause arcing and rapid burning of points.* Do not attempt to remove all roughness nor dress the point surfaces down smooth. Merely remove scale or dirt.
8. Replace points that are badly burned or pitted. Where burned or badly pitted points are encountered, the ignition system and engine should be checked to determine the cause of the trouble so it can be eliminated. Unless the condition causing point burning is corrected, new points will provide no better service than the old points. See *distributor* chapter for an analysis of point burning or pitting, and for proper installation of points & condenser.

Battery & Cables

Inspect for signs of corrosion on battery, cables and surrounding area, loose or broken carriers, cracked or bulged cases, dirt and acid, electrolyte leakage and low electrolyte level. Fill cells to proper level with distilled water or water passed through a "demineralizer."

The top of the battery should be clean and the battery hold-down bolts properly tightened.

For best results when cleaning batteries, wash first with a dilute ammonia or soda solution to neutralize any acid present and then flush off with clean water. Care must be taken to keep vent plugs tight so that the neutralizing solution does not enter the battery.

To insure good contact, the battery cables should be tight on the battery posts. Oil battery terminal felt washer. If the battery posts or cables terminals are corroded, the cables should be cleaned separately with a soda solution and a wire brush.

If the battery has remained undercharged, check for a loose generator belt, defective generator, high resistance in charging circuit, oxidized voltage regulator contact points, or a low voltage setting.

If the battery has been using too much water, the voltage regulator setting is too high.

Fuel System

All fuel filters and the air cleaner element should be serviced during a tune up, including the sintered bronze "stone" used in some units.

Since carburetion is dependent in several ways on both compression and ignition, it should always be checked last when tuning an engine. Refer to the Carburetor Chapter for pertinent data on specific units.

Service Bulletins

Beginning with 1972 some General Motors V-8 cars may be equipped with the new Uni-Set breaker points (one piece points and condenser), Fig. 7. Due to the limited availability of the Uni-Set for service, you should be aware of the alternatives to circumvent this problem.

1. A conversion kit is available (Part No. 1876065) which contains a breaker plate, contact set, radio shields, condenser and wick.
2. If the existing breaker plate has tapped holes for the condenser clamp and radio shields, it need not be changed and the conversion kit is not necessary. You can install the previous two piece points and condenser but you must obtain and install the radio shields.

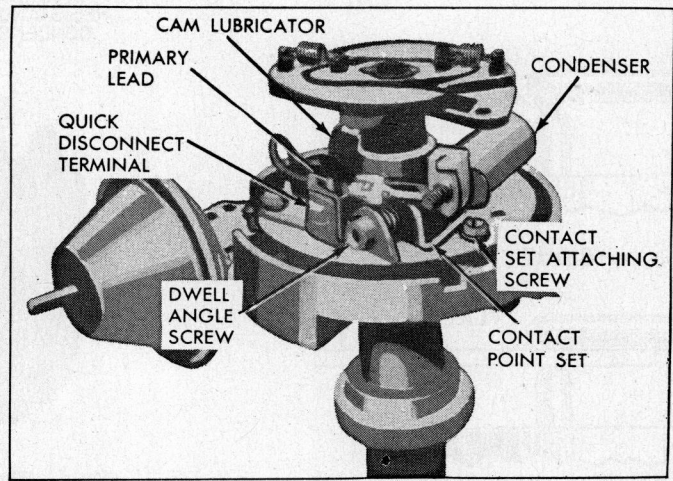

Fig. 7 Delco-Remy one-piece breaker points & condenser (Uni-Set)

Ignition Coils & Resistors

IGNITION COILS

If poor ignition performance is obtained and the coil is suspected, it may be tested on the car or it may be removed for the test.

Ignition coils are often condemned when the trouble is actually in the ignition switch. A completely defective ignition switch will produce an open primary circuit, giving the same indications as if the coil were completely dead. A partly defective ignition switch will cause a weak spark.

By cutting the ignition switch out of the circuit, it can easily be determined whether the coil is defective or the fault lies in the ignition switch.

In the absence of any testing equipment a simple check of an ignition coil can be made as follows: Turn on ignition switch with breaker points closed. Remove the high tension cable from the center socket of the distributor cap and hold it 1/4" to 3/8" away from a clean spot on the engine. If the coil and other units connected to it are in good condition a spark should jump from the wire to the engine as the points are opened. If not, use a jumper wire from the distributor terminal to the engine; if the primary is in good condition a spark will occur.

All ignition coils with metal containers can be tested for gounded windings by placing one test clip on a clean part of the metal container and touching the other clip to the primary and high tension terminals. If the lamp lights or tiny sparks appear at the points of contact, the windings are grounded and the coil should be replaced.

Coil Polarity

Most coils are marked positive and negative at the primary terminals. When installing or connecting a coil be sure to make the connections as shown in Fig. 1. A reversal of this polarity may affect the performance of the engine (or the radio).

If the coil is not marked as to its polarity, it can be checked by holding any high tension wire about 1/4" away from its spark plug terminal with the engine

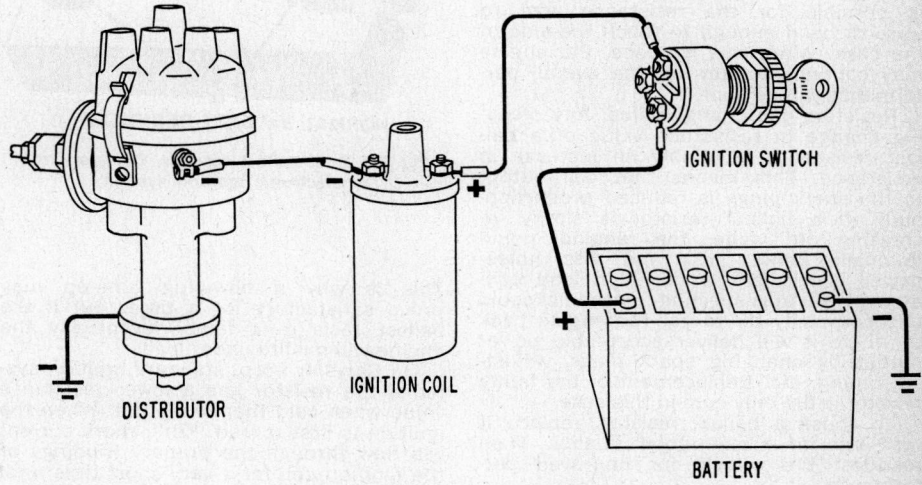

Fig. 1 Wiring connections for coil with negative grounded system

running. Insert the point of a wooden lead pencil between the spark plug and the wire, Fig. 2. If the spark flares and has a slight orange tinge on the spark plug side of the pencil, polarity is correct. If the spark flares on the cable side, coil connections should be reversed.

IGNITION RESISTORS

The ignition coils used with 12-volt systems are specially designed 6-volt coils which operate with a resistor connected in series with the primary ignition circuit. The purpose of the resistor

is to prolong the service life of the distributor breaker points.

Block Type Ballast Resistors

This type resistor came into existance with the introduction of the 12-volt battery. Its basic purpose is to allow full battery voltage to the ignition coil during engine starting, and to reduce battery voltage to the coil when the engine is running. The higher voltage during starts means easier starts. But sustained high voltage to the breaker points can cause point failure. The reduced voltage during engine operation increases break-

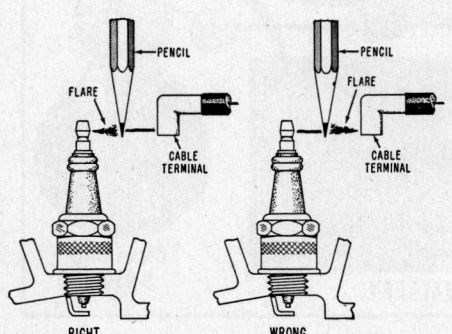

Fig. 2 Checking coil polarity

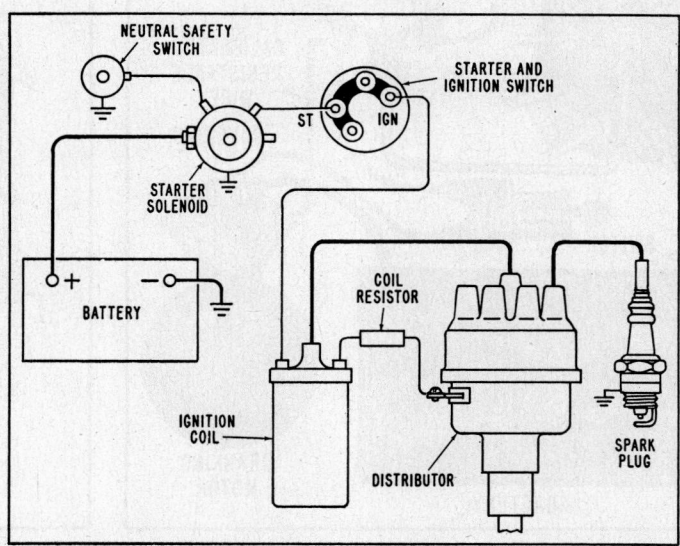

Fig. 3 Chrysler ignition circuit diagram with a temperature sensitive block-type resistor

er point life.

These resistors are normally very dependable. But if one fails, it can be one of the most difficult of all ignition malfunctions to diagnose. An open resistor means that no current reaches the coil and the engine cannot operate. It is possible for the resistance wire to warp or bend enough to touch the side of the case. When this happens, the engine may continue to run but the overall performance will be poor.

Resistors can change value. Any creeping change in resistance value of a ballast resistor is invariably an increase in resistance. This means that coil output to the spark plugs is reduced proportionately. If a ballast resistor is slowly increasing in value the engine could gradually deliver less and less horsepower, particularly under high load conditions. An unsuspecting mechanic could unsuccessfully try to get the engine back to where it will deliver acceptable power output by changing spark plugs, adjusting timing, etc. Replacement of the faulty resistor is the only cure in this case.

To check a ballast resistor, replace it with one of known good quality. Then road-test the vehicle for improved performance.

It is important to remember that new spark plugs can temporarily mask the need for resistor replacement because new plugs require less voltage to fire.

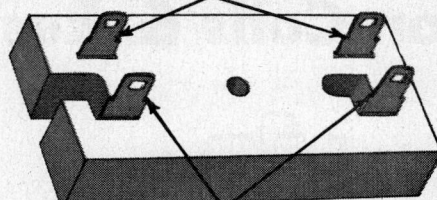

Fig. 4 Dual ballast resistor, Chrysler Corp. electronic ignition system

This is why a new-plug tune-up may prove satisfactory for a time. But if the ballast resistor is faulty, eventually the engine will misfire under load.

On Chrysler Corp. standard ignition systems, the resistor has a lower resistance value when cold than when hot. When the ignition is first turned "On", more current will flow through the primary windings of the ignition coil for a very short time until the resistor heats up.

SERVICE NOTE: If the engine fires when the ignition switch is turned on but quits when the switch is released to its running position, it indicates that the resistor is defective and must be replaced.

A dual ballast resistor, Fig. 4, is used on Chrysler Corp. vehicles equipped with electronic ignition. The normal side of the resistor is a compensating resistance in the primary circuit. At low engine speeds, current is maintained for a longer period of time in this side of the resistor, causing the unit to heat up, in turn increasing resistance. This increased resistance reduces the primary circuit voltage, protecting the ignition coil from high voltage at low engine speeds.

As engine speed increases, the period of time in which current is maintained in the normal side of the resistor is shorter, causing the unit to cool, in turn decreasing resistance. This decreased resistance permits the primary circuit voltage to increase for high speed operation.

During engine start, the normal side of the ballast resistor is by-passed, allowing full battery voltage to be applied to the primary circuit.

The auxiliary side of the ballast resistor limits voltage to the control unit, thereby protecting the unit.

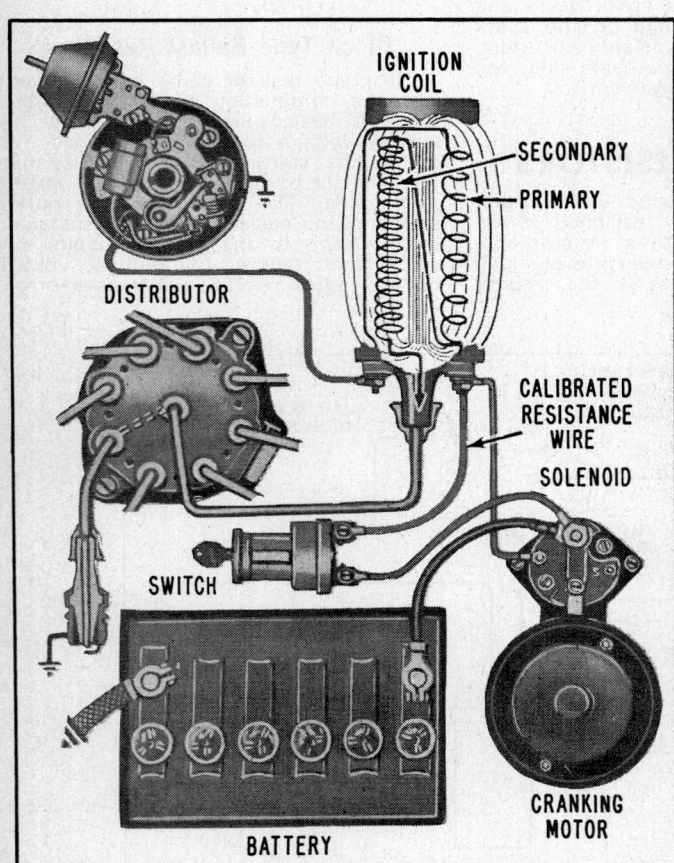

Fig. 5 Delco-Remy ignition circuit diagram with a resistance wire connected to a two-terminal ignition switch

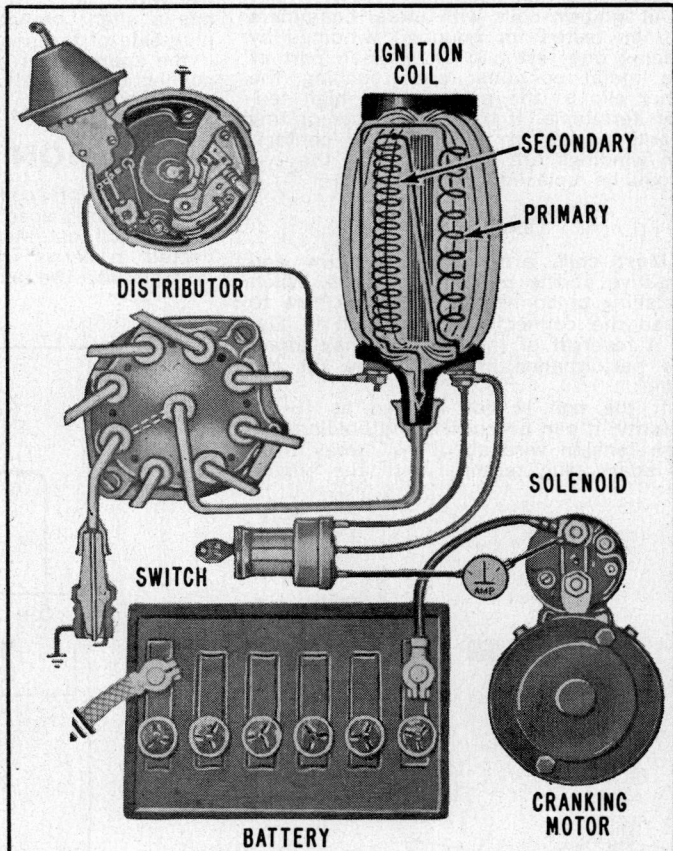

Fig. 6 Delco-Remy ignition circuit diagram with a resistance wire connected to a three-terminal ignition switch

Wire Type Resistors

The special resistance wires used with 12-volt systems are five to six feet long and contained in the regular wiring harness. The wire is made of stainless steel or special alloy, plastic-coated and covered with a glass braid. There is a relatively small temperature rise and the resistance wire is switched out of the circuit for starting and back in again for running.

On Delco-Remy systems Figs. 5 and 6, the resistor is by-passed by means of a "finger" inside the solenoid switch housing which is attached to the additional switch terminal.

On Ford systems, Fig. 7, the resistor is by-passed through a terminal on the starter relay which is connected directly to the positive terminal of the coil.

SERVICE NOTE: If the engine fires when the ignition switch is turned on but quits when the switch is released to the "run" position, it indicates that the resistance wire has lost its continuity or there is a bad connection at the resistor terminals. If the wire is defective, it must be replaced, either by a ballast type resistor or a new length of resistance wire.

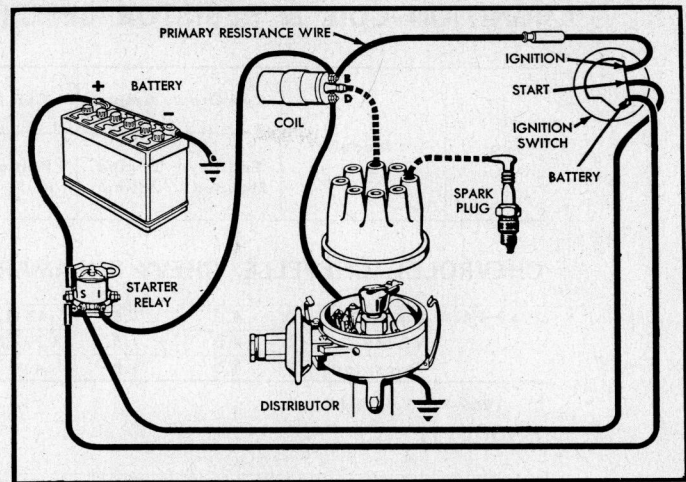

Fig. 7 Ford ignition circuit diagram with a resistance wire connected to a three-terminal ignition switch

IMPORTANT: Do not attempt to operate the engine for an extended length of time with the resistor shorted out by means of a jumper wire as the breaker points will burn up in short order.

IGNITION COIL & RESISTOR SPECIFICATIONS

Year	Model	Coil Draw, Amps.		Coil Resistance, Ohms		Ignition Resistor Ohms @ 75°F.
		Engine Stopped	Engine Idling	Primary @ 75°F.	Secondary @ 75°F.	

AMERICAN MOTORS—All Models

Year	Model	Engine Stopped	Engine Idling	Primary @ 75°F.	Secondary @ 75°F.	Ignition Resistor Ohms @ 75°F.
1969–74	6 Cyl.	3.5	1.6	1.40–1.65	3000–20000	1.80
	V8②	3.5	1.6	1.77–2.05	3000–20000	1.35
	V8④	3.5	1.6	1.64–1.80	9300–11800	1.35

②—Delco-Remy. ④—American Motors
⑧—Prestolite.

BUICK—All Models

Year	Model	Engine Stopped	Engine Idling	Primary @ 75°F.	Secondary @ 75°F.	Ignition Resistor Ohms @ 75°F.
1969–73	All	3.8	2.3	1.28–1.42	7200–9500	1.75–1.85
1973	6 Cyl.	4.0	3.9	1.4–1.65	3000–20000	1.75–1.85
1974	6 Cyl.	4.0	3.9	1.4–1.65	3000–20000	1.25–1.45
	V8	3.8	2.3	1.77–2.05	3000–20000	1.25–1.45

CADILLAC

Year	Model	Engine Stopped	Engine Idling	Primary @ 75°F.	Secondary @ 75°F.	Ignition Resistor Ohms @ 75°F.
1969–74	Exc. Below	2.4	1.25	1.77–2.01	3000–20000	1.30–1.35
1974	H.E.I.	—	—	.4–.5	8000–9500	

CHECKER MOTORS

Year	Model	Engine Stopped	Engine Idling	Primary @ 75°F.	Secondary @ 75°F.	Ignition Resistor Ohms @ 75°F.
1969–74	6 Cyl.	4.0	1.8	1.41–1.65①	3000–20000	1.80
	V8	4.0	1.8	1.77–2.05	3000–20000	1.35

①—1969-70, 1.41-1.63.

Continued

TUNE UP SERVICE

IGNITION COIL & RESISTOR SPECIFICATIONS—Continued

Year	Model	Coil Draw, Amps.		Coil Resistance, Ohms		Ignition Resistor Ohms @ 75°F.
		Engine Stopped	Engine Idling	Primary @ 75°F.	Secondary @ 75°F.	

CHEVROLET, CHEVELLE, CHEVY II, CAMARO, MONTE CARLO, VEGA

Year	Model	Engine Stopped	Engine Idling	Primary	Secondary	Ign. Resistor
1969-74	4 & 6 Cyl.	4.0	1.8	1.41-1.65①	3000-20000	1.80
	V8 Std. Ign.	4.0	1.8	1.77-2.05	3000-20000	1.35
	Trans. Ign.	4.0	1.8	.41-.51	3000-20000	.43-.68

①—1969-70, 1.41-1.63.

CORVETTE

Year	Model	Engine Stopped	Engine Idling	Primary	Secondary	Ign. Resistor
1969-74	Std. Ign.	4.0	1.8	1.77-2.05	3000-20000	1.35
	Trans. Ign.	...	...	.41-.51	3000-20000	.43-.68

CHRYSLER, DODGE, PLYMOUTH, IMPERIAL—All Models

Year	Model	Engine Stopped	Engine Idling	Primary	Secondary	Ign. Resistor
1969-72	①	3.0	1.9	1.65-1.79	9400-11700	.50-.60
	②	3.0	1.9	1.41-1.55	9200-10600	.50-.60
1973-74	①	3.0	1.9	1.60-1.79	9400-11700	.50-.60③
	②	3.0	1.9	1.41-1.55	8000-10200	.50-.60③

①Prestolite coils.   ②Essex coils.
③Auxiliary (control unit side) 4.75—5.75 ohms.

FORD, MERCURY, LINCOLN, THUNDERBIRD—All Models

Year	Model	Engine Stopped	Engine Idling	Primary	Secondary	Ign. Resistor
1969-74	Std. Ign.	4.5	2.5	1.40-1.54	7600-8800	1.30-1.40
1974	Breakerless	—	—	1.0-2.0	7000-13000	1.30-1.40

①—Engine cranking.   ②—Emitter .31-.35
Collector .41-.45
Base 7.1-7.9

OLDSMOBILE—All Models

Year	Model	Engine Stopped	Engine Idling	Primary	Secondary	Ign. Resistor
1969-70	Toronado	4.0	2.2	1.77-2.05	6500-9500	1.35
	Delmont	6.0	1.35	1.77-2.05	6500-9500	1.35
	6 Cyl.	4.0	1.8	1.45-1.63	6500-9500	1.85
	All Others	4.0	2.0	1.77-2.05	6500-9500	1.35
1971-72	6 Cyl.	4.0	1.8	1.45-1.63	6500-9500	1.85
	V8	4.0	2.2	1.77-2.05	6500-9500	1.35
1973-74	Toronado	4.0	2.2	1.77-2.05	6500-20000	1.35
	6 Cyl.	4.0	1.8	1.40-1.65	3000-20000	1.80
	V8	4.0	2.0	1.77-2.05	6500-20000	1.35

PONTIAC—All Models

Year	Model	Engine Stopped	Engine Idling	Primary	Secondary	Ign. Resistor
1969	Pontiac	3.2-3.6	1.9-2.3	1.7-2.0	3000-20000	...
	6 Cyl.	3.5	2.8	1.4-1.7	3000-20000	...
	Temp., F-Bird	3.4	2.1	1.7-2.0	3000-20000	...
1970	Six	3.4	2.1	1.4-1.7①	3000-20000	...
	V8	3.4	2.1	1.7-2.0	3000-20000	...
1971-72	Six	3.5②	2.8③	1.4-1.65	3000-20000	...
	V8	3.4	2.1	1.7-2.0	3000-20000	...
1973-74	Six	...	...	1.4-1.65	3000-20000	...
	V8	...	...	1.8-2.2	3000-20000	...
	Unitized	...	...	0-.5	6000-9000	...

①—Firebird 1.4-1.65
②—Ventura II 4.0
③—Ventura II 1.8

Standard Ignition Distributors

CONTENTS

Bosch Distributor Service 2-529
Breaker Contact Service 2-525
Centrifugal Advance Mechanism 2-527
Chrysler Distributor Service 2-529
Condenser 2-527
Delco-Remy Distributor Service 2-530
Autolite/Motorcraft Distributor Service .. 2-531
Prestolite Distributor Service 2-529
Vacuum Advance Mechanism 2-528

BREAKER CONTACT POINTS

Contact Analysis

The normal color of points should be a light gray. If the contact surfaces are black it is usually caused by oil vapor or grease from the cam. If they are blue, the cause is usually excessive heating due to improper alignment, high resistance or open condenser circuit.

If the contacts develop a crater or depression on one point and a high spot of metal on the other, the cause is an electrolytic action transferring metal from one contact to the other, Fig. 2, due to an unbalanced ignition system, which can sometimes be improved by a slight change in condenser capacity. If the mound is on the positive point, Fig. 3, install a condenser of greater capacity; if on the negative point, Fig. 4, use a condenser of lesser capacity.

One of the most common causes of point failure is the presence of oil or grease on the contact surfaces, usually from over-lubrication of the wick at the top of the cam or too much grease on the rubbing block of the breaker arm.

Breaker Point Gap

If points are set too close, arcing and burning will occur, causing hard starting and poor low speed performance. If points are set too wide, the cam angle or dwell will be too small to allow saturation of the coil at high engine speeds, resulting in weak spark.

Contact point opening has a direct bearing on cam angle or dwell which is the number of degrees that the breaker cam rotates from the time the points close until they open again, Fig. 5. The cam angle or dwell increases as point opening is decreased and vice versa. If point gap is set with a feeler gauge, the cam angle or dwell should be checked either with a portable dwell meter or by installing the distributor in a distributor tester.

Breaker Arm Spring Tension

Breaker arm spring tension is important. If the tension is too great the arm will bounce, causing an interruption of the current in the coil and misfiring. If the spring tension is too little, the rub-

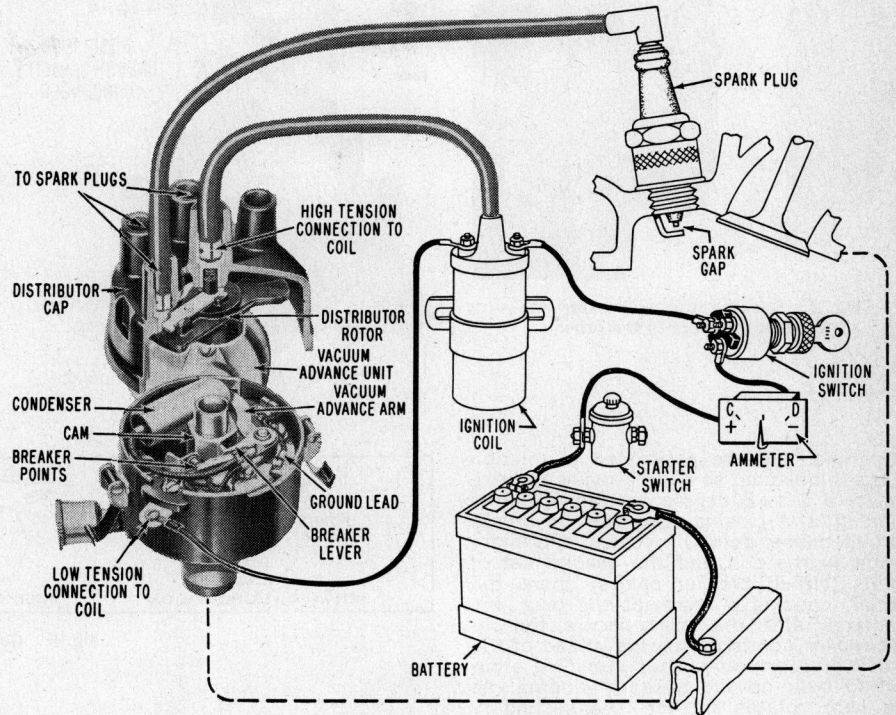

Fig. 1   Typical ignition system

bing block will not follow the cam, causing a variation in cam dwell. The spring tension should always be set at the high limit as given in the *Distributor Specifications* chart in the car chapter, as it will be reduced as the rubbing block wears.

Hook a spring scale on the breaker arm and pull in a straight line as shown in Fig. 6. Take a reading as the points start to separate under the slow and steady pull of the scale. If the tension is not within specifications, loosen the screw that holds the end of the point spring and slide the end of the spring in or out as necessary. Tighten the screw and recheck the spring tension.

Breaker Point Alignment

Check alignment of points with points closed, Fig. 7. Align new points where necessary but do not attempt to align used points. Instead, replace used points where serious misalignment is observed. After aligning points, adjust point gap.

Adjusting Breaker Gap

Specifications for breaker gap, *as measured with a feeler gauge*, are listed in the *Tune Up Specifications* in the car chapters. However, if at all possible, this should be set on a distributor tester, with a dial indicator, Fig. 8, or by hooking up

a portable dwell meter with the distributor cap and rotor removed and, while cranking the engine, setting the dwell.

NOTE: When setting the dwell with the engine cranking, be sure to ground the coil secondary lead and do not operate the starter for sustained periods at a time.

This eliminates the possibility of an incorrect gap because of rough points, Fig. 9.

The advantage of a distributor testing machine is that it not only measures cam angle or dwell but it also uncovers irregularities between cam lobes, point bounce, alignment of rubbing block with cam, alignment of contacts and breaker arm spring tension.

Setting Dual Points

The distributor used on some Chrysler Corp. and Ford Co. vehicles contain two sets of points which permit additional current build-up in the primary winding of the coil, Fig. 10. Thus, maximum voltage is induced in the secondary winding.

The two sets of points are connected

Fig. 2 Showing how metal from one contact transfers to the other

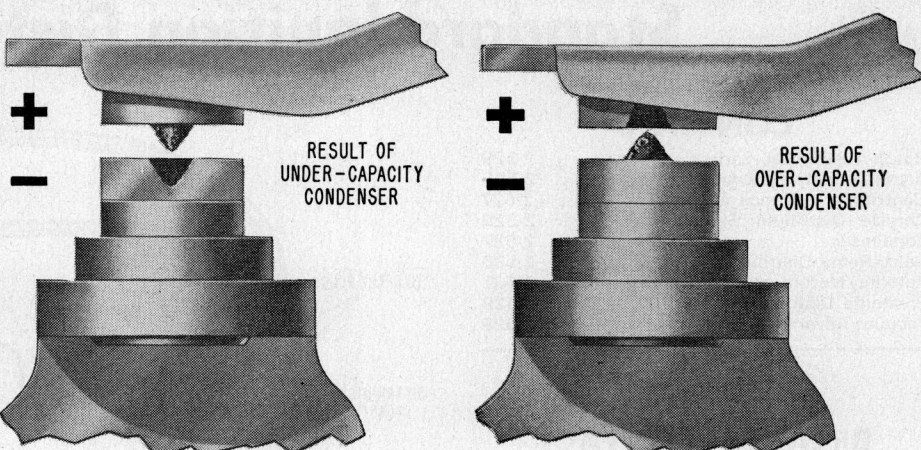

+

−

RESULT OF UNDER-CAPACITY CONDENSER

Fig. 3 Mound on positive point

+

−

RESULT OF OVER-CAPACITY CONDENSER

Fig. 4 Mound on negative point

in parallel and are positioned in relation to the 8-lobe cam so as to provide approximately a 7 to 8 degree overlap of points opening and closing. One set of points (circuit *maker* points) closes the primary circuit in the coil and the second set of points (circuit *breaker* points) opens the circuit, causing a spark at the plug. Immediately after the spark occurs, the circuit *maker* points are closed ahead of the circuit *breaker* points, thus providing a circuit to build-up the primary winding. As the cam rotates further, the secondary points close and just before the secondary points open, the primary points open 7 degrees ahead.

Since the "make" and "break" points are timed to close and open at the exact instant necessary for efficient engine operation, adjustment of the points is an important factor in correct distributor operation.

Feeler Gauge or Dial Indicator Method—Rotate the distributor shaft until the breaker arm rubbing block of one set of points is on the high spot of the cam. Then, with a screwdriver blade in the triangular opening, close or open the

POINTS CLOSE POINTS OPEN

NORMAL DWELL—NORMAL GAP

WIDE GAP SMALL DWELL

INSUFFICIENT DWELL

SMALL GAP LARGE DWELL

EXCESSIVE DWELL

Fig. 5 Cam angle or dwell

points to the proper clearance by turning the screwdriver blade against the stationary point plate. Check the clearance with a clean wire gauge or dial indi-

cator. Then turn the distributor shaft until the rubbing block of the second set of points is on the high spot of the cam and adjust the second set of points in the same manner.

Dwell Meter Method—If this method is used *block one set of points open* with a piece of wrapping paper or cardboard. Then adjust the other set of points to the correct dwell angle. Now block open the first set of points and adjust the

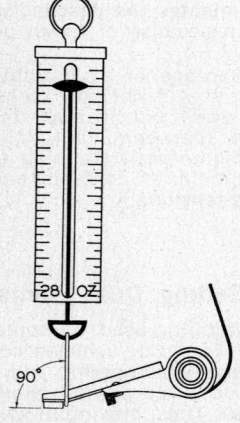

90°

Fig. 6 Measuring breaker spring tension

LATERAL MISALIGNMENT

PROPER LATERAL ALIGNMENT

CORRECT LATERAL MISALIGNMENT BY BENDING FIXED CONTACT SUPPORT **NEVER BEND BREAKER LEVER**

Fig. 7 Breaker point alignment

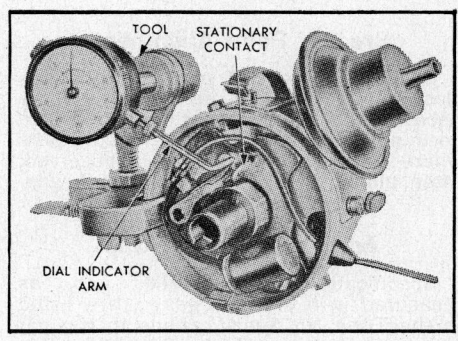

TOOL STATIONARY CONTACT

DIAL INDICATOR ARM

Fig. 8 Dial indicator for measuring breaker gap

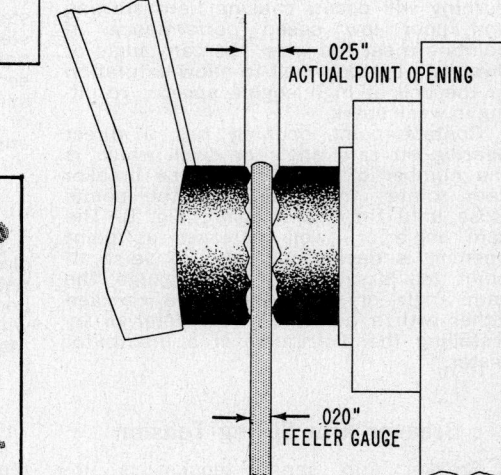

.025" ACTUAL POINT OPENING

.020" FEELER GAUGE

Fig. 9 Why flat feeler gauge will not provide accurate point spacing if points are rough

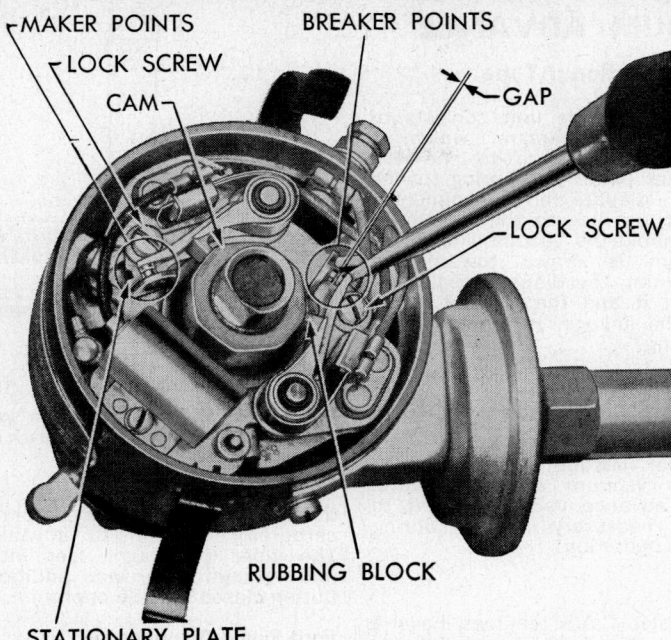

MAKER POINTS
LOCK SCREW
CAM
BREAKER POINTS
GAP
LOCK SCREW
RUBBING BLOCK
STATIONARY PLATE

Fig. 10   Prestolite dual point distributor

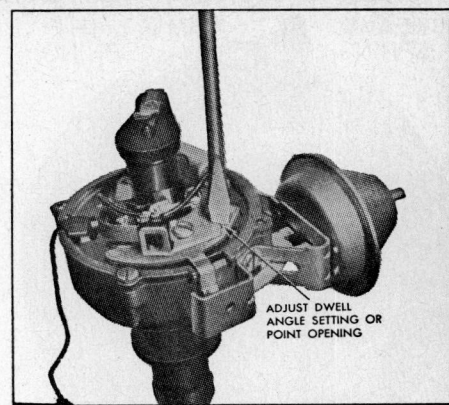

ADJUST DWELL ANGLE SETTING OR POINT OPENING

Fig. 11   Breaker point setting. Delco-Remy internally adjusted points

second set. After both sets of points have been adjusted, allow them to operate together while checking that their total dwell angle measures up to manufacturer's specifications.

Prestolite & Chrysler Single Point Set Adjustment

Adjustment of breaker gap is accomplished by loosening the lock screw in the stationary point and moving the adjusting screw as required to obtain the correct breaker gap.

Delco-Remy Internal Adjustment Breaker Points

A slot is provided in the contact point assembly which allows easy dwell angle or breaker point adjustment, Fig. 11.

Delco-Remy External Adjustment Breaker Points

With engine running at idle speed, the breaker gap is adjusted by first raising the window provided in the cap and inserting a "hex" wrench into the adjusting screw, Fig. 12. Turn the adjusting screw clockwise until the engine begins to misfire. Then give the wrench one-half turn in the opposite direction which will provide the proper breaker gap. If a cam angle meter is to be used, turn the adjusting screw until the correct angle is obtained.

Autolite/Motorcraft Breaker Points

The breaker point set is attached to the movable breaker plate. A slot in the stationary point bracket allows for easy breaker point adjustment, Fig. 13.

the piston. To provide this spark advance based on engine speed, the centrifugal governor mechanism is used.

This mechanism, Fig. 14, consists of centrifugal advance weights which throw out against spring tension as the engine speed increases. This movement imparts, through a toggle arrangement, rotational motion to the breaker cam or plate, depending on the model, causing it to rotate a number of degrees with respect to the distributor drive shaft. This causes the points to be opened and closed earlier in the cycle so the spark is delivered to the cylinder earlier.

In servicing the distributor, all weights should be removed from the hinge pins, cleaned and checked for excessive wear, either in the weights or pins, or the plate which is slotted for the movement of the pins on top of the governor weights. Replacement should be made if there is any appreciable wear in the slots, as any wear at this point would change the characteristic of the spark advance.

If these parts are in good condition, the hinge pins should be lubricated before being reassembled, by greasing the hinge pins and filling the pockets in the governor weights with grease. Do not use vaseline for this purpose as its melting point is comparatively low.

CONDENSER

A condenser should not be condemned because the points are burned or oxidized. Oil vapor, or grease from the cam, or high resistance may be the cause of such a condition.

Condensers should be tested with a good condenser tester for leakage, break-down, capacity, and resistance in series in the condenser circuit. Manufacturers of condenser testers furnish complete instructions as to their use.

CENTRIFUGAL ADVANCE

When engine speed increases, the spark must be introduced in the cylinder earlier in the cycle in order that the fuel charge can be ignited and will have time to burn and deliver its power to

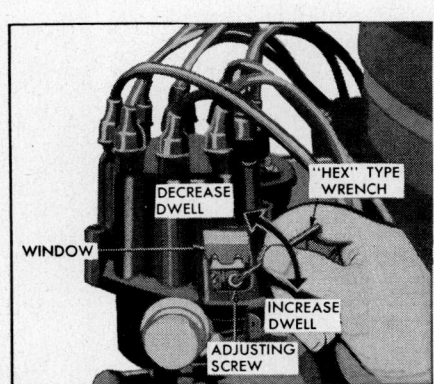

DECREASE DWELL
"HEX" TYPE WRENCH
WINDOW
INCREASE DWELL
ADJUSTING SCREW

Fig. 12   Adjust breaker point gap through window in distributor cap

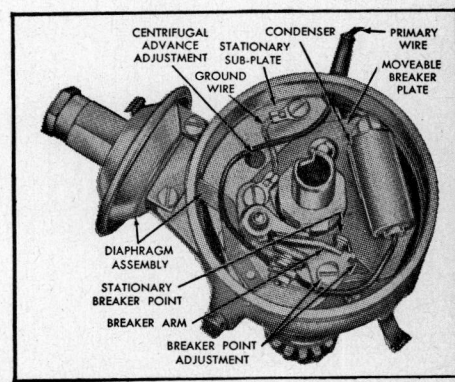

CENTRIFUGAL ADVANCE ADJUSTMENT
STATIONARY SUB-PLATE
CONDENSER
PRIMARY WIRE
GROUND WIRE
MOVEABLE BREAKER PLATE
DIAPHRAGM ASSEMBLY
STATIONARY BREAKER POINT
BREAKER ARM
BREAKER POINT ADJUSTMENT

Fig. 13   Breaker plate installation. Autolite/Motorcraft dual advance distributor (Typical)

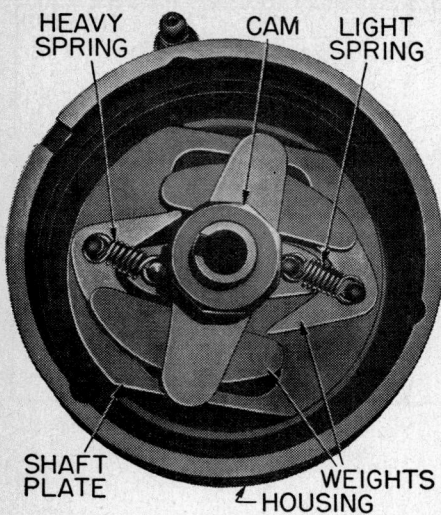

Fig. 14 Top view of Delco-Remy distributor with breaker plate removed to show centrifugal governor mechanism

When installing new centrifugal governor assemblies, it is important that the spacer washers between the housing and shaft be installed correctly. If incorrectly installed, the governor assembly will be too high, causing it to rub against the bottom of the breaker plate.

On some distributors, both springs are alike, while on others there is one heavy and one light spring, as in Fig. 14. Another combination that may be found is an additional flat spring on the outside of the outer spring posts, Fig. 15. As the governor speed is increased, the flat springs are first pulled against the posts by the eyes of the coil springs to provide a rapid spark advance of a few degrees before the coil springs pull against the spring posts.

VACUUM ADVANCE
Conventional Type

The vacuum advance unit consists of a spring loaded diaphragm, which is connected through linkage to the distributor breaker plate. The spring loaded side of the diaphragm is connected through a vacuum line to the carburetor or intake manifold. As vacuum increases, the diaphragm is drawn toward the source of vacuum, the diaphragm linkage is pulled with it and the breaker plate, attached to the linkage, is turned to advance the timing.

Exhaust Emission Control Types
Chrysler C.A.P.

The Chrysler vacuum advance units incorporate a vacuum advance control valve in the advance vacuum circuit to provide the necessary retard during closed throttle operation.

Chrysler C.A.S.

Some Chrysler C.A.S. engines have a solenoid incorporated in the distributor vacuum advance mechanism to retard the ignition timing when the throttle is closed. At closed throttle, electrical contacts on the carburetor throttle stop, with idle adjusting screw in the closed position, cause the distributor solenoid to energize. This retards the ignition timing to provide reduced exhaust emissions under hot idle conditions. Cold or part throttle starting is not penalized because the distributor solenoid is not energized unless the hot idle adjusting screw is against the throttle stop contact. Timing must be set at closed throttle to give accurate setting.

Ford Dual-Diaphragm

This unit consists of two independent diaphragms. The outer diaphragm uses carburetor vacuum to advance timing. The inner diaphragm uses intake manifold vacuum to provide additional retard during closed throttle operation.

Ford Single Diaphragm

This unit operates in the same manner as conventional units.

General Motors CCS

In this system, the advance is the ported type, that is the vacuum take-off is located above the throttle plate(s) so that during periods of closed throttle operation there is little or no vacuum reaching the advance unit and timing is retarded. As soon as the throttle is cracked, vacuum reaches the advance unit and timing is advanced.

NOTE: Some models of the Chevrolet V8-307 engine use the conventional type advance unit.

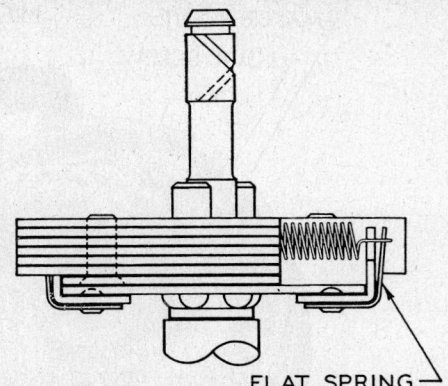

Fig. 15 Flat spring used on some governors to provide a rapid spark advance

Distributor Service

BOSCH DISTRIBUTOR SERVICE

NOTE: On 1971-74 units, replacement parts for servicing the distributor shaft, drive gear, bushing and cam are not available. In addition on 1974 units, the advance weights, advance springs and breaker plate are not serviceable since the breaker plate is permanently staked into the housing.

If distributor has been disassembled, refer to Fig. 16 at reassembly.

1. Lubricate pivot pins and install advance weights. Lubricate shaft and install cam assembly.
2. Install advance springs and advance plate, securing plate with clip and screws.
3. Insert grommet and condenser wire through hole in housing and install condenser and contact points.
4. Install vacuum advance unit. Hook vacuum advance rod over pin in advance plate and install snap ring.

PRESTOLITE & CHRYSLER DISTRIBUTOR SERVICE

Shaft & Bushing Wear Test

1. Remove distributor from vehicle and clamp distributor in a vise. Use extreme caution not to damage distributor.
2. Install a dial indicator on housing so plunger rests against moveable contact arm when rubbing block is on the highest point of a cam.
3. Place a wire loop around distributor shaft and hook a spring scale on the other end of the loop. Apply a one pound pull in line with indicator plunger and read movement on indicator. Movement must not exceed .006 inch. If movement exceeds limit, replace either housing or shaft on Chrysler distributors or bushing or shaft on Prestolite distributors to bring movement back within tolerance.

Distributor Reassembly

If the distributor has been disassembled, reassemble as follows, referring to Figs. 17 and 18 for guidance.

1. Check operation of centrifugal weights and weight springs for distortion. Lubricate governor weights.
2. Inspect all bearing surfaces and pivot pins for roughness, binding, or excessive looseness.
3. Install cam spacer (chamfered end down) on distributor shaft.
4. Slide cam and yoke on distributor

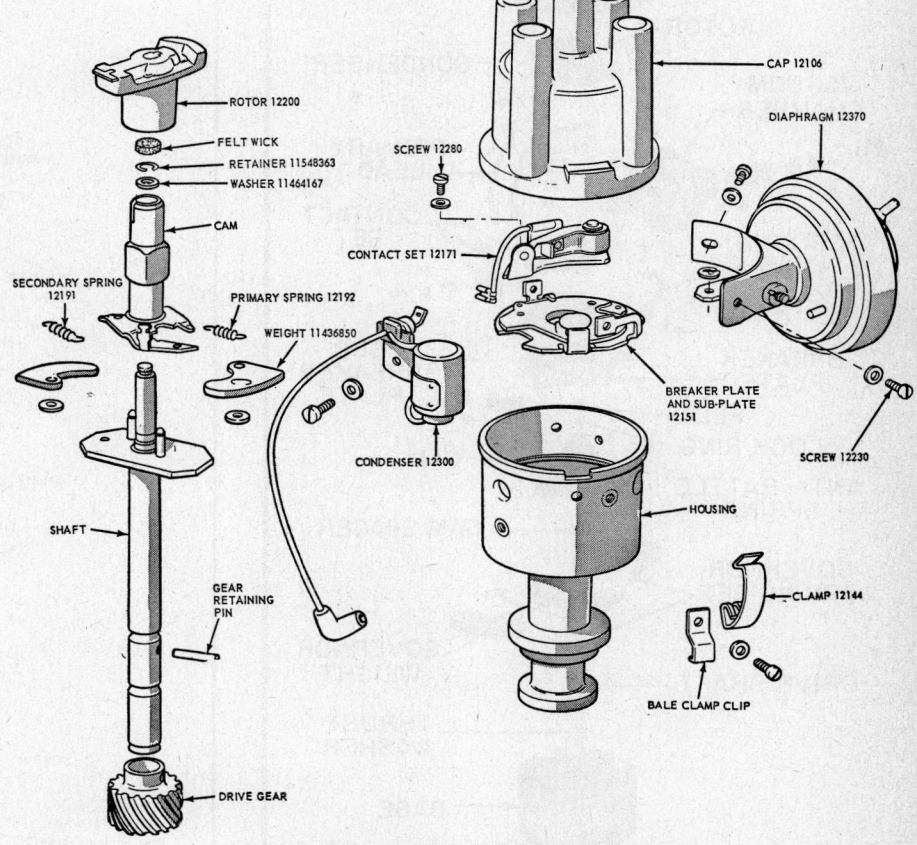

Fig. 16   Exploded view of Bosch distributor

shaft. Engage weight lugs with slots in yoke as shown in Fig. 19. Install cam retaining clip, being sure it is properly seated in distributor shaft groove.

5. Lubricate and install two concave washers for Prestolite distributors, or a single flat thrust washer for Chrysler distributors. Position washers on shaft and slide shaft into distributor body. On Chrysler six cylinder distributors, if drive gear is worn or damaged, replace as follows:
   a. Install thrust washer and old gear on shaft and install pin. Scribe a line centered between two gear teeth from center to edge of shaft and in line with center of rotor electrode.
   b. Remove pin and gear. Clean burrs from around pin hole and install new gear.
   c. Place a .007 inch feeler gauge between gear and thrust washer and drill a .124-.129 inch hole in gear and shaft about 90 degrees from old hole in shaft and with scribe line centered between gear teeth and in line with center of rotor electrode as shown in Fig. 18A.

NOTE: If new pin hole location appears to interfere with shaft oil groove, rotate gear to centerline of next pair of gear teeth and align with scribe line on shaft.

   d. Install pin.
6. Position lower thrust washer and drive collar on lower end of shaft and install retainer pin.
7. Install oiler wick and oiler.
8. Install breaker plate assembly, align condenser lead, breaker point spring, primary lead and install attaching screw.
9. Install felt wick in top of cam.
10. Attach vacuum advance unit arm to breaker plate and install retainer. Install vacuum unit attaching screws and washers.
11. Test breaker arm spring tension and adjust breaker gap.
12. Lubricate felt pad in top of distributor cam with 3 to 5 drops of light engine oil and install rotor.

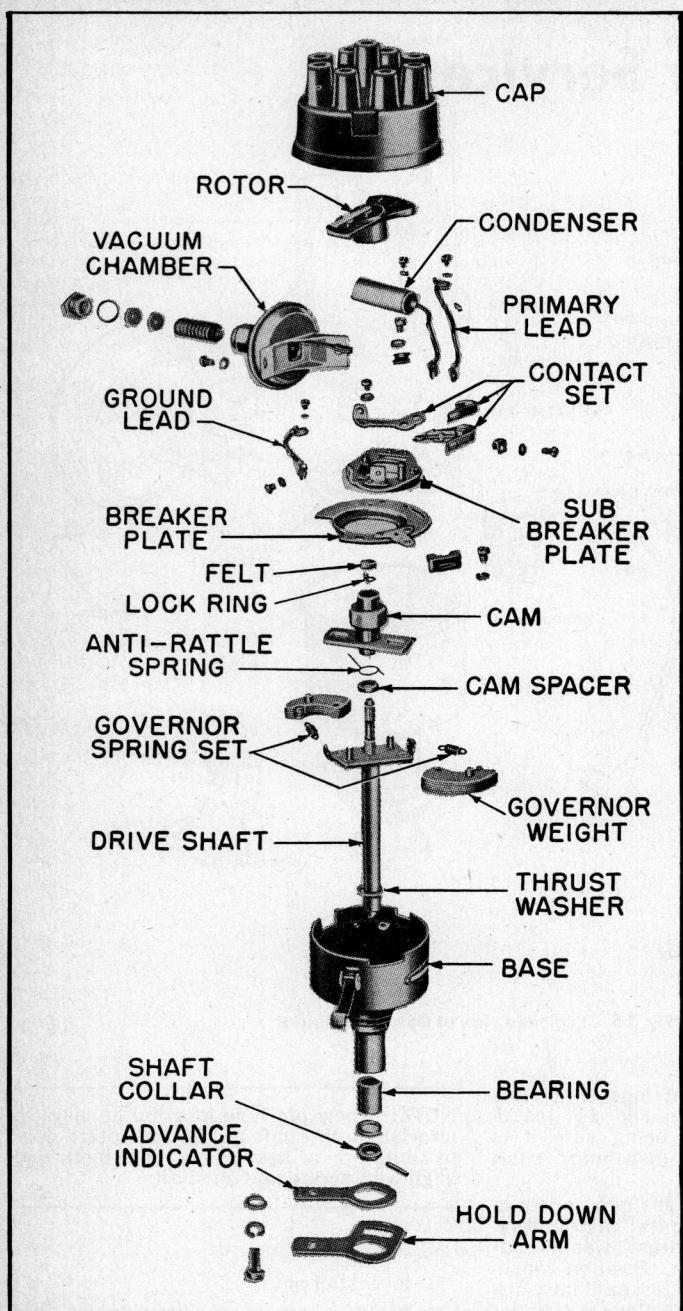

Fig. 17 Exploded view of typical Prestolite distributor

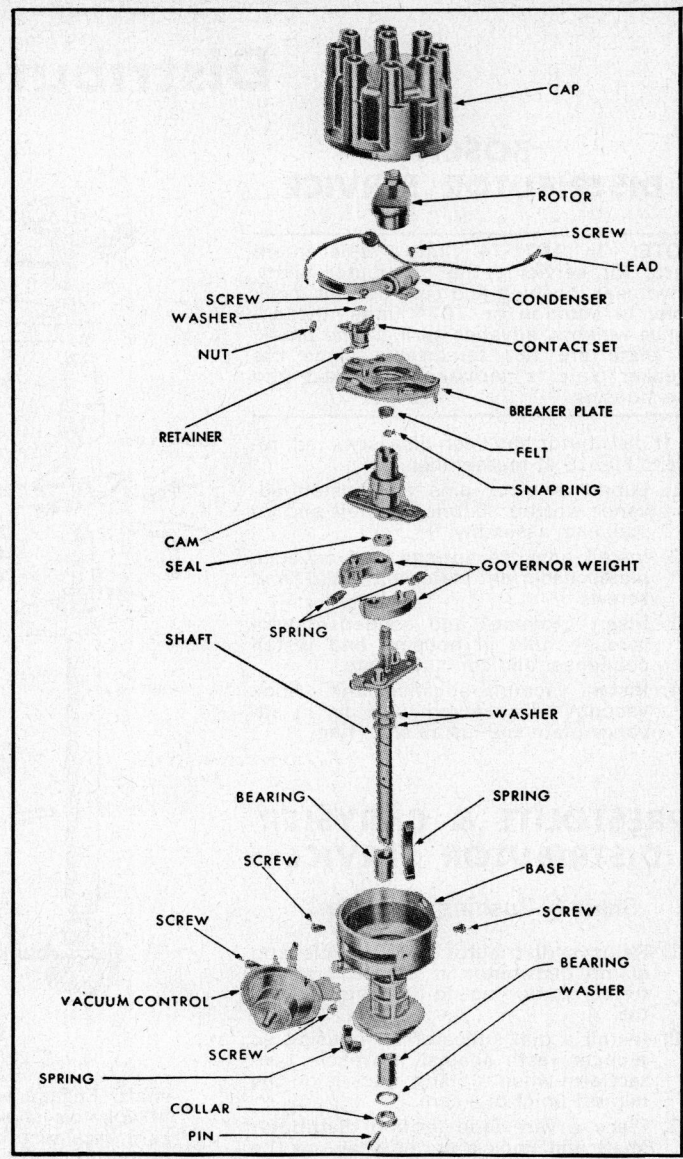

Fig. 18 Exploded view of typical Chrysler V-8 distributor

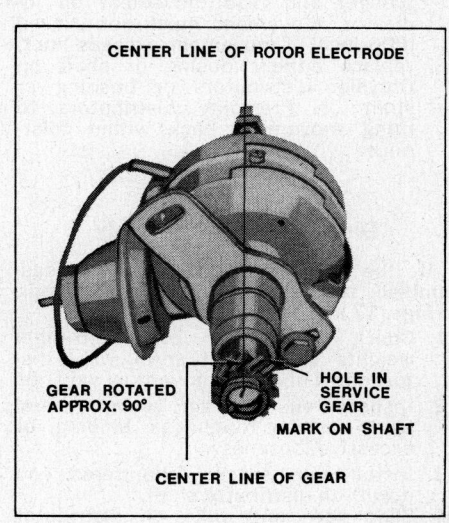

Fig. 18A Gear tooth alignment, Chrysler 6 cyl. distributor

DELCO-REMY DISTRIBUTOR SERVICE

External Adjustment Type

If the distributor has been disassembled, refer to Fig. 20 for guidance when reassembling.

1. Fill housing lubricating cavity with proper lubricant and install new plastic seal and felt washer.
2. Install vacuum advance unit, breaker plate and spring retainer on upper bushing.
3. Slide weight cam over mainshaft and install weights and springs.
4. Insert mainshaft assembly into housing, indexing assembly with drive gear and washers.

5. On Chevrolet Corvette units, install tachometer drive gear.
6. On all units, slide gear shims and drive gear over mainshaft and install retaining pin. Ensure shaft rotates freely.
7. Install breaker points and condenser.

Internal Adjustment Type

If the distributor has been disassembled, refer to Fig. 21 when reassembling. Fig. 22 shows the details of the breaker plate and attaching parts.

1. Replace cam assembly to shaft. Lubricate top end of shaft with light engine oil prior to replacing.
2. Install weights on their pivot pins. Install springs, weight cover and stop plate.
3. Lubricate shaft and install in housing.
4. Install thrust washers and driven gear to shaft and secure with roll pins. On Vega distributors, install damper cup on shaft and install pin. Check to see that shaft turns freely. Install driven gear with mark on hub in line with rotor segment.
5. Install breaker plate.
6. Attach condenser and breaker point set in proper location with appropriate attaching screws, Fib. 22. Connect primary and condenser leads to

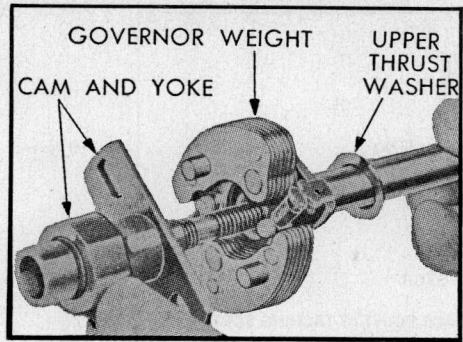

Fig. 19 Distributor shaft details

breaker point set quick disconnect terminal. *Contact point set pilot must engage matching hole in breaker plate.*
7. Attach vacuum control assembly to distributor housing, using upper mounting holes.
8. Adjust breaker arm spring tension and breaker gap.
9. Install rotor.

FORD AUTOLITE/MOTORCRAFT DISTRIBUTOR SERVICE

Dual Advance Distributor

This distributor, Fig. 23, is similar to conventional design in that both a centrifugal advance mechanism is provided to regulate ignition timing according to speed and a vacuum advance unit to regulate ignition timing according to load. However, unlike other make distributors, the centrifugal advance mechanism can be adjusted through a slot in the breaker plate.

Adjust centrifugal advance before adjusting vacuum advance. If specified centrifugal advance is not indicated on a distributor test machine, bend one spring bracket with a screwdriver through a hole in the breaker plate on all distributors except 2800 cc units, Fig. 24. On 2800 cc units, remove plug inside of distributor housing to gain access to adjustment bracket, Fig. 25. Bend bracket away from distributor shaft to decrease advance and toward shaft to increase advance. Identify bracket after adjustment is made. After an adjustment has been made to one spring, check the minimum advance point again. Then operate distributor at the specified

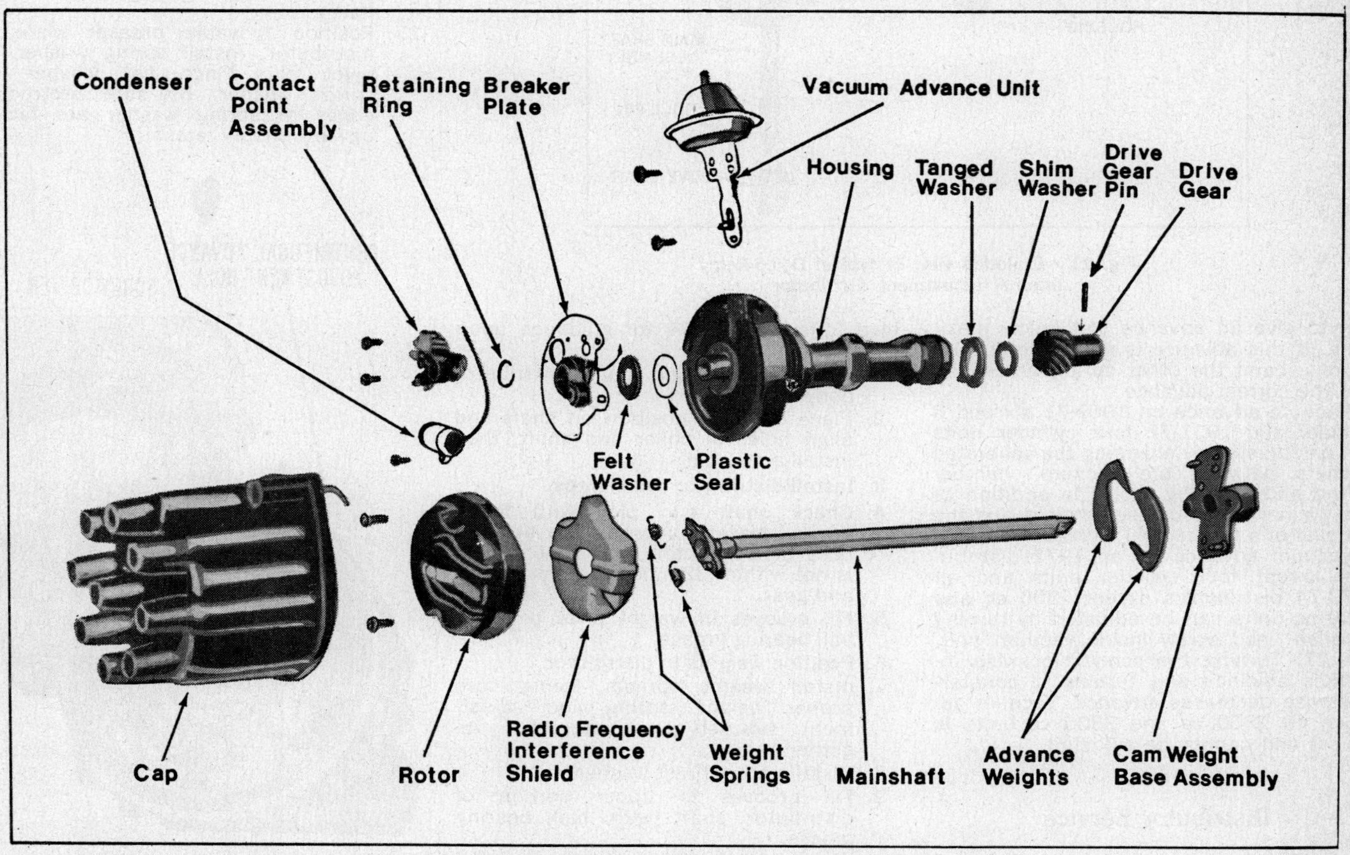

Fig. 20 Delco-Remy external adjustment distributor

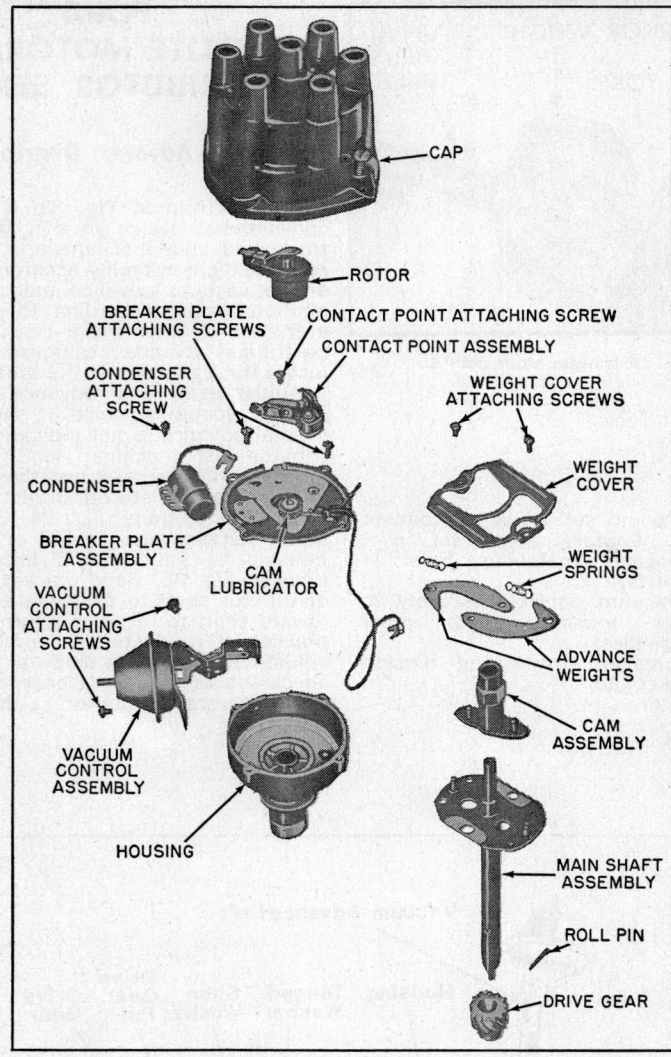

Fig. 21 Exploded view of typical Delco-Remy internal adjustment distributor

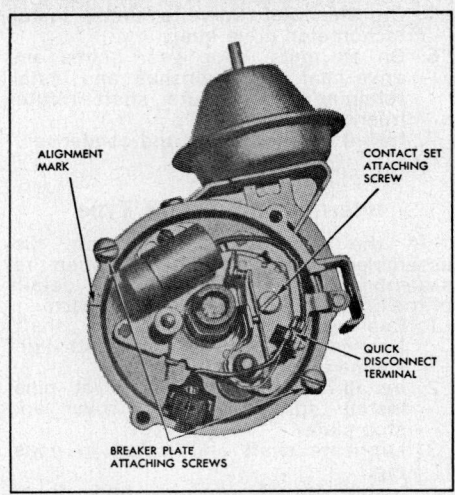

Fig. 22 Breaker plate installation. Delco-Remy internal adjustment distributor

weights.

11. Install cam retainer. Apply a light film of cam lubricant to cam lobes. Saturate wick with 10W engine oil. Install wick in cam.
12. Position stationary sub plate in distributor. Install one end of ground wire under plate retaining screw closest to diaphragm mounting flange.
13. Position movable breaker plate in distributor. Install spring washer on pivot pin. Place flat washer on spring washer. Be sure protruding edges of spring washer are facing upward. Install retainer.

rpm to give an advance just below maximum. If this advance is not up to specifications, bend the other spring bracket to give the correct advance.

Vacuum advance on 1969-71 six and 8 cylinder and 1971-72 four cylinder units can be adjusted by changing the calibrated washers between the vacuum chamber spring and nut, Fig. 26. The addition of one washer will decrease advance and the removal of a washer will increase advance.

Vacuum advance on all 1972 distributors except four cylinder units and all 1973-74 distributors except 2300 cc and 2800 cc units can be adjusted by turning an allen head screw inside vacuum unit, Fig. 27. Turning the screw clockwise increases advance and turning it counterclockwise decreases advance. Vacuum advance on 2300 cc and 2800 cc units is pre-set and cannot be adjusted.

Distributor Service

Six & V8 Units

If the distributor has been disassembled, refer to Fig. 24 for guidance upon reassembly.

1. Oil shaft and slide it into distributor body.
2. Place collar in position on shaft and align holes in collar and shaft, then install a new pin.
3. Install distributor cap clamps.
4. Check shaft end play with feeler gauge placed between collar and base of distributor. If shaft end play is not within .024-.035", replace shaft and gear.
5. Fill grooves in weight pivot pin with ball bearing grease.
6. Position weights in distributor.
7. Install weight springs, being sure proper weight, spring and adjustment bracket are assembled together.
8. Install upper thrust washer.
9. Fill grooves in upper portion of distributor shaft with ball bearing grease.
10. Install cam assembly, being sure that slots in cam engage pins in

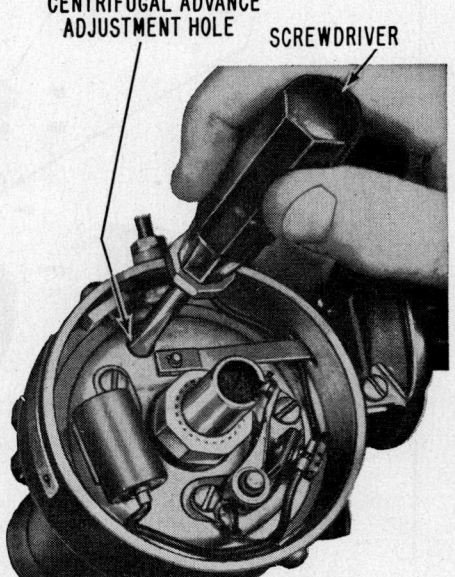

Fig. 24 Centrifugal advance adjustment all exc. 2800 cc units

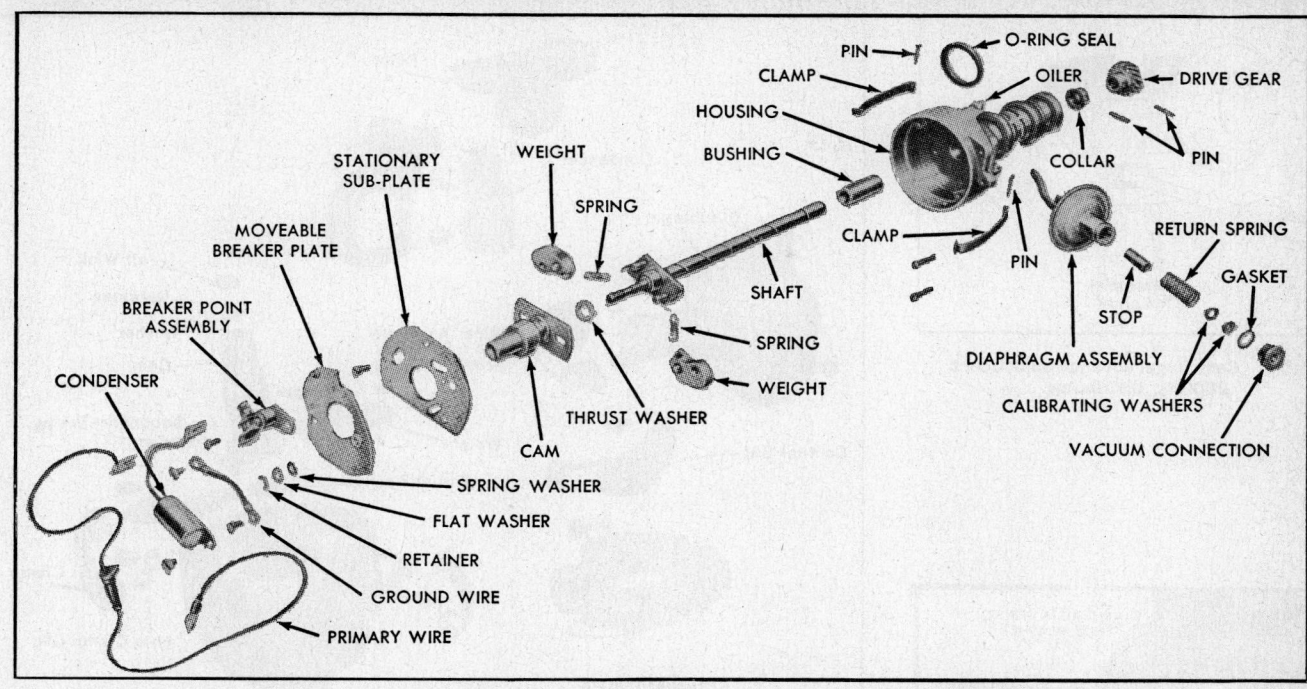

Fig. 23 Exploded view of Autolite/Motorcraft V-8 dual-advance distributor. (Typical)

14. Install new breaker point assembly. Install ground wire on breaker point attaching screw furthest from point adjustment slot.
15. Install condenser.
16. Working from inside to outside of distributor housing, pass primary wire through opening in distributor. Pull wire through opening until locating stop is flush with inside of distributor.
17. Connect condenser wire and primary wire to breaker points.
18. Position diaphragm and hook its link over pin on breaker plate. Install diaphragm attaching screws. Secure link with retainer. Install oil seal.
19. Adjust breaker arm spring tension, align and adjust breaker points and check and adjust cam dwell, centrifugal and vacuum advance.

2300 cc & 2800 cc Units

If distributor has been disassembled, refer to Figs. 28 and 29 at reassembly.
1. Lubricate top of distributor shaft and install cam assembly, then retaining ring and felt wick.
2. Lubricate pivot pins and install advance weights and on 2800 cc units, "C" clips. On all units, install advance springs.

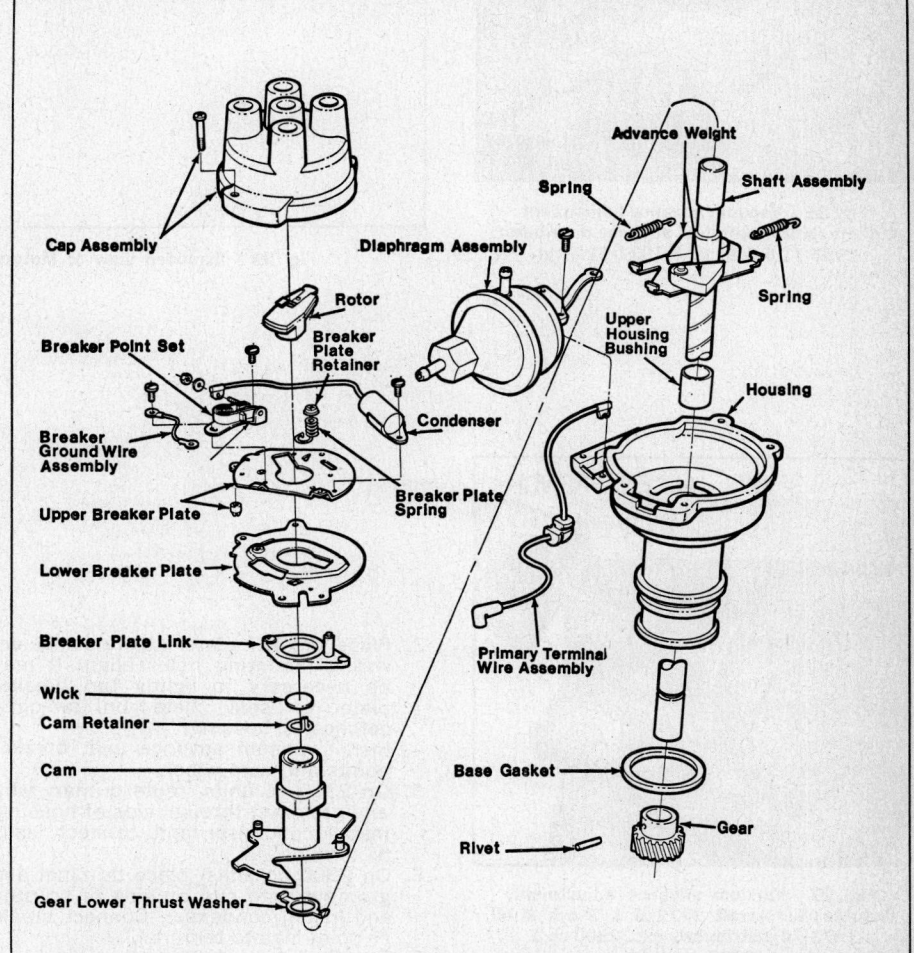

Fig. 28 Exploded view of Motorcraft 2300 cc dual advance distributor

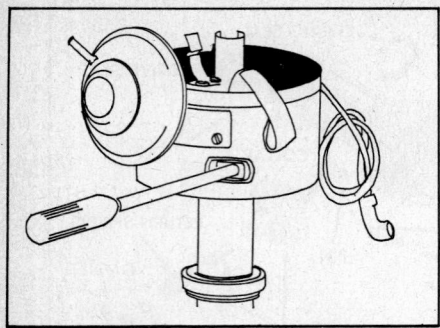

Fig. 25 Centrifugal advance adjustment. 2800 cc distributor

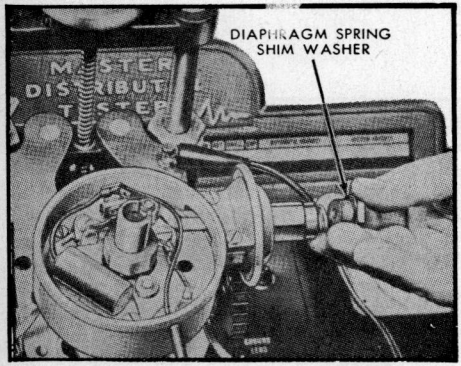

Fig. 26 Vacuum advance adjustment Autolite/Motorcraft dual advance distributor. 1969-71 6 & 8 cyl. & 1971-72 4 cyl.

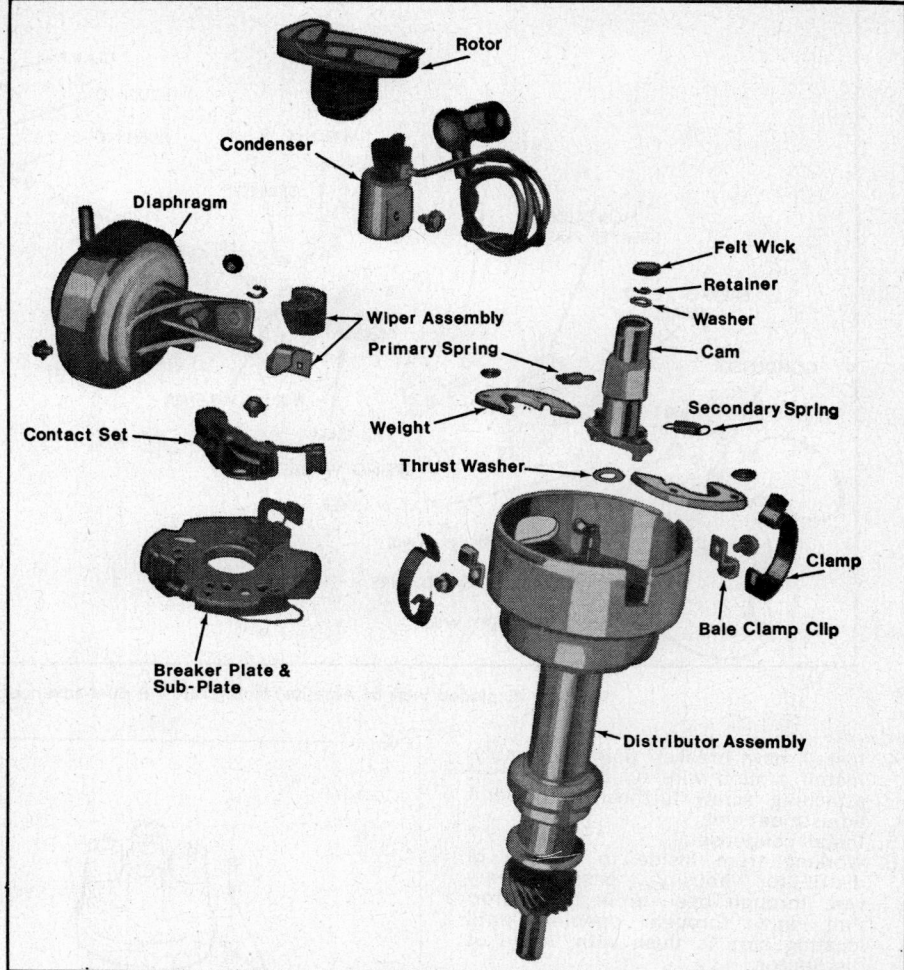

Fig. 29 Exploded view of Motorcraft 2800 cc dual advance distributor

Fig. 27 Vacuum advance adjustment. Autolite/Motorcraft 1972 6 & 8 cyl. & all 1973-74 distributors exc. 2300 cc & 2800 cc units

3. Place breaker plate into housing, ensuring mounting holes align. It may be necessary to lightly tap breaker plate to seat plate on swedged perches in housing.
4. Install vacuum advance unit, breaker points and cam wiper.
5. On 2300 cc units, route primary wire and grommet through side of housing. Install condenser and connect leads to terminal.
6. On 2800 cc units, place terminal and grommet into slot on side of housing and install condenser. Connect breaker point lead to terminal.
7. On all units, install rotor.

1600 cc Units

If distributor has been disassembled, refer to Fig. 30 at reassembly.

1. Install thrust washers onto shaft, slide shaft into housing and install thrust washer, wave washer and drive gear. Install tension pin.
2. Install cam assembly making sure advance stop is in correct slot and install snap ring. Replace felt wick.
3. Install vacuum advance unit.
4. Install advance springs to posts from which they were removed, lubricate

governor weight pivots and install governor weights with flat edge adjacent to cam spindle and install spring clips.

5. Install grommet in lower plate leaving sufficient wire to reach contact point connection. Connect ground spring to pivot post and place upper plate on lower plate, engaging the hold down spindle in keyhole slot and install the two spring washers, flat washer and large snap ring.

6. Check clearance between upper and lower plates, beneath nylon bearing nearest to the hold down pin. Maximum clearance is .010 inch. If clearance is excessive, thread nut further onto hold down screw.

7. Install contact points and condenser onto breaker plate assembly and install the assembly and secure with two screws.

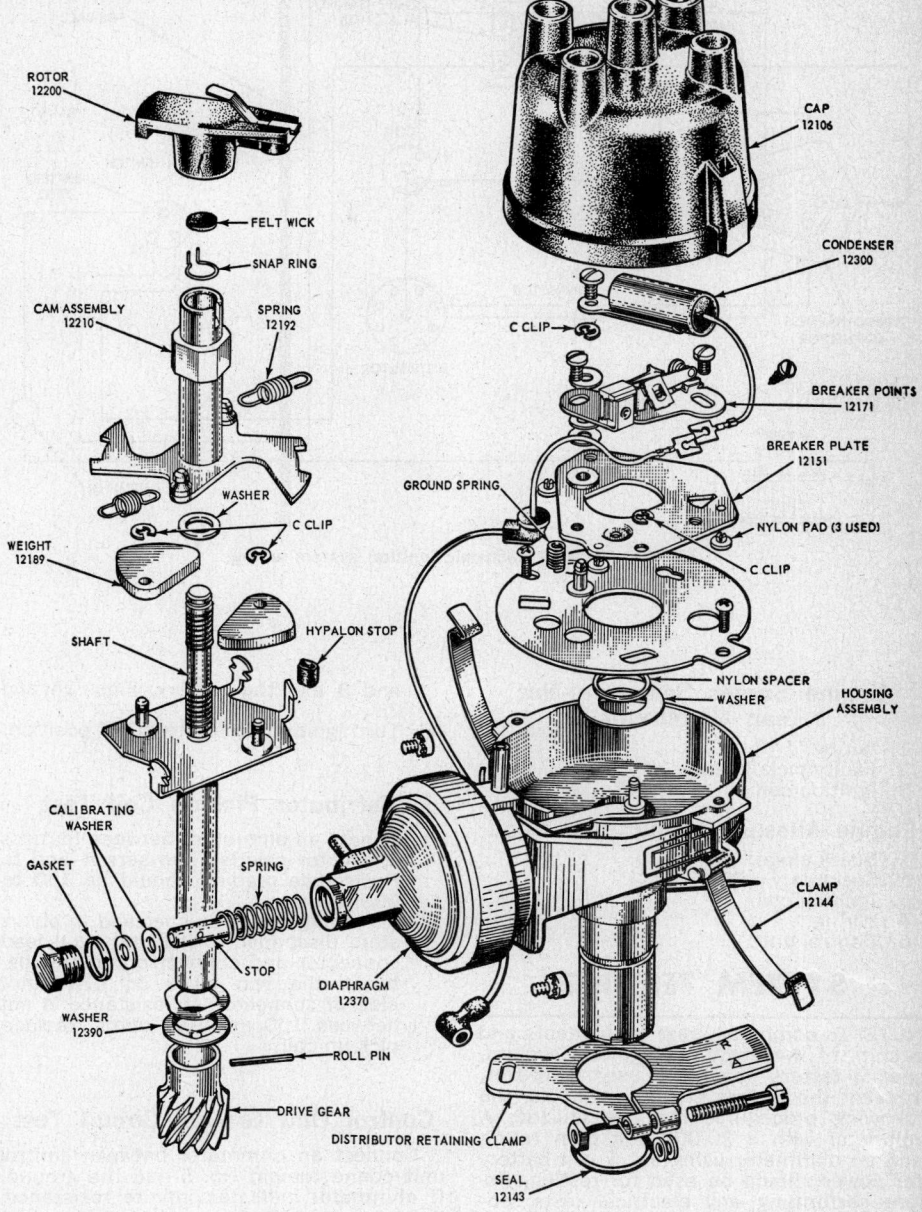

Fig. 30 Exploded view of Autolite/Motorcraft 1600 cc dual advance distributor

Electronic Ignition Systems

CHRYSLER SYSTEM

This system, Fig. 1, is composed of a magnetic distributor, an electronic control unit, a wiring harness, a production coil and a dual ballast resistor.

The distributor is essentially the same as the conventional type except the contacts have been replaced by a pickup coil and the cam by a reluctor. With a conventional contact type system, the voltage necessary to fire the spark plugs is developed by interrupting the current flowing through the primary of the ignition coil by opening a set of contacts. With the Electronic System, the voltage is produced the same way except that the current is interrupted by a transistor in the electronic control unit. This happens each time the control unit receives a "timing" pulse from the distributor magnetic pickup.

Since the magnetic pickup, reluctor and the control unit, which replace the contact points and cam, do not normally change or wear out with service, engine timing and dwell does not require periodic adjusting. This minimizes regular ignition maintenance to cleaning and replacing the spark plugs.

TROUBLE SHOOTING
Engine Will Not Start—Fuel System OK

1. Wiring harness electrical terminals covered with grease.
2. Dual ballast.
3. Faulty ignition coil.
4. Faulty pickup or improper pickup air gap.
5. Faulty wiring.
6. Faulty control unit.

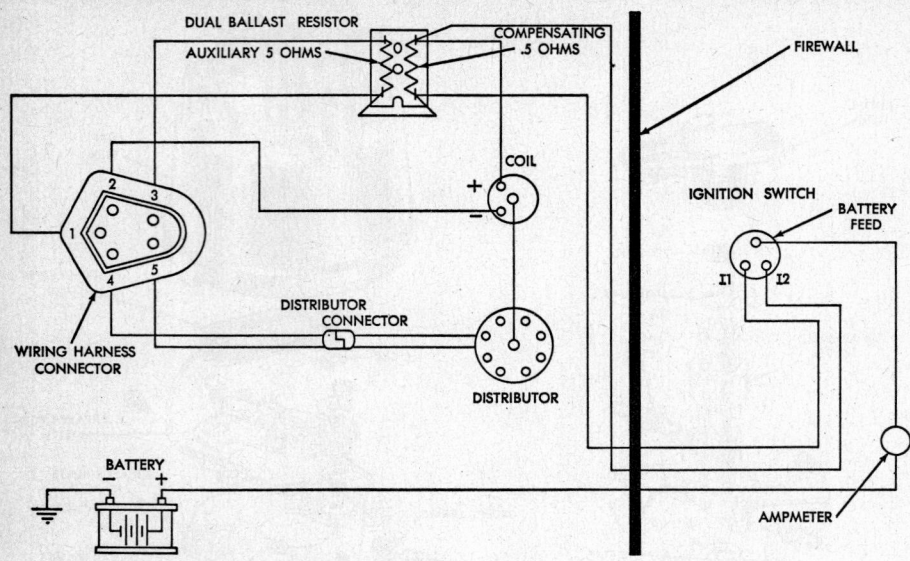

Fig. 1 Chrysler electronic ignition system wiring

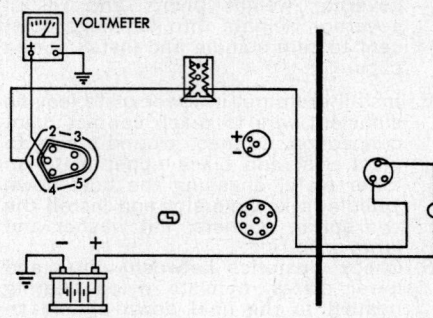

Fig. 2 Harness wiring test, No. 1 cavity

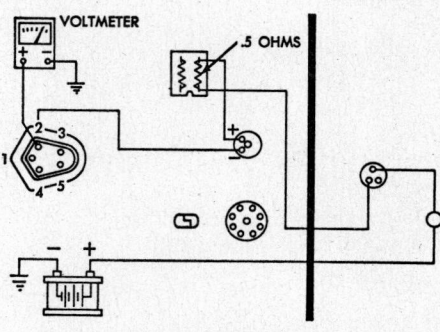

Fig. 2A Harness wiring test, No. 2 cavity

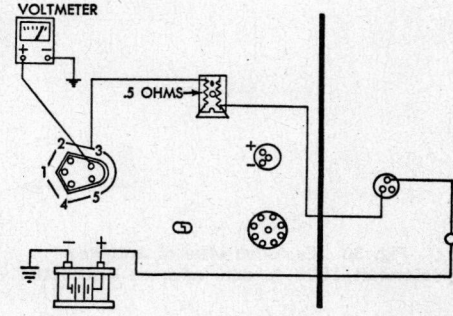

Fig. 2B Harness wiring test, No. 3 cavity

Engine Surges Severely—Not Lean Carburetor

1. Wiring.
2. Faulty pickup leads.
3. Ignition coil.

Engine Misses—Carburetion Good

1. Spark plugs.
2. Secondary cables.
3. Ignition coil.
4. Wiring.
5. Control unit.

SYSTEM TESTING

NOTE: To completely test components and circuits of the electronic ignition system, special testers should be used. However, in event the testers are not available, the following procedures may be utilized. A voltmeter with a 20,000 volt/ohm rating and an ohmmeter using a 1.5 volt battery for power should be used for testing. Before performing any electrical tests, ensure all wiring is properly connected.

Harness Wiring Test

1. Check battery voltage and note reading.
2. Disconnect harness connector from control unit.

CAUTION: Before disconnecting or connecting harness connector, ensure ignition switch is in the "Off" position.

3. Turn ignition switch to "On" position.
4. Connect the voltmeter between harness connector cavity No. 1 and the ground. Voltage reading should be within 1 volt of battery voltage earlier noted. If not, check circuit between cavity No. 1 and the battery, Fig. 2.
5. Test harness connector cavities numbers 2 and 3 in same manner. If voltage is not within specifications, check circuits between cavities numbers 2 and 3 and the battery, Figs. 2A and 2B.
6. Turn ignition switch to "Off" position.

Distributor Pick-up Coil Test

1. Conect an ohmmeter between harness connector cavities numbers 4 and 5. Resistance reading should be 150 to 900 ohms.
2. If reading is not as specified in above step, disconnect distributor dual lead connector and connect ohmmeter between the two leads on distributor side of connector. If resistance is not between 150 and 900 ohms, replace pick-up coil.

Control Unit Ground Circuit Test

Connect an ohmmeter between control unit connector pin No. 5 and the ground. If ohmmeter indicates infinite resistance, tighten bolts securing control unit to firewall and recheck resistance. If reading is still infinite, replace control unit.

Distributor Shaft & Bushing Wear Test

1. Remove distributor from vehicle and clamp distributor in a vise. Use extreme caution not to damage distributor.
2. Attach a dial indicator to housing so plunger rests against reluctor sleeve.
3. Place a wire loop around reluctor sleeve and hook a spring scale on the other end of the loop. Apply a one pound pull in line with indicator plunger and read movement on indicator. Movement must not exceed .006 inch. If movement exceeds limit, replace either housing or shaft to bring movement back within tolerance.

DISTRIBUTOR SERVICE
Distributor Disassemble

1. Remove rotor and vacuum advance unit.
2. Remove reluctor. If reluctor cannot be pulled off easily, use two screwdrivers with a 7/16 inch blade to pry up from bottom of reluctor. Use extreme caution not to damage teeth on reluctor.
3. Remove two screws from lower plate and lift out lower and upper plates and pick-up coil as an assembly.

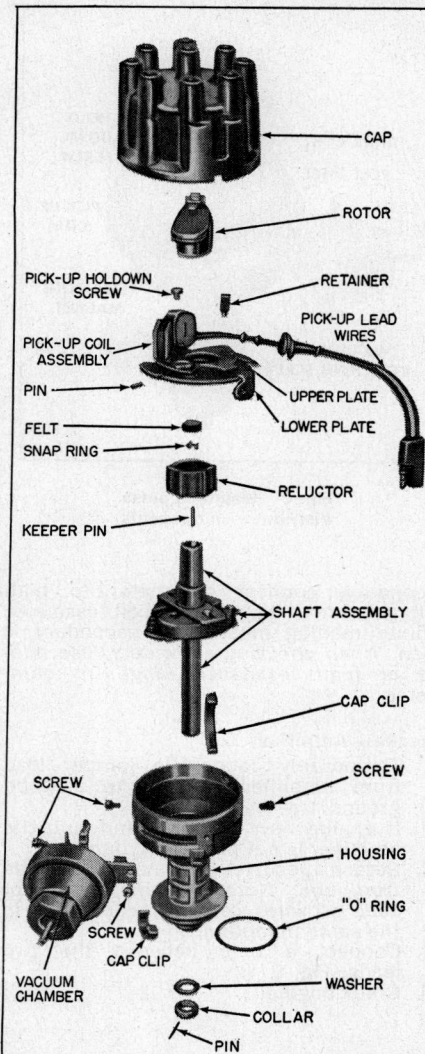

Fig. 3 Exploded view of typical Chrysler electronic distributor

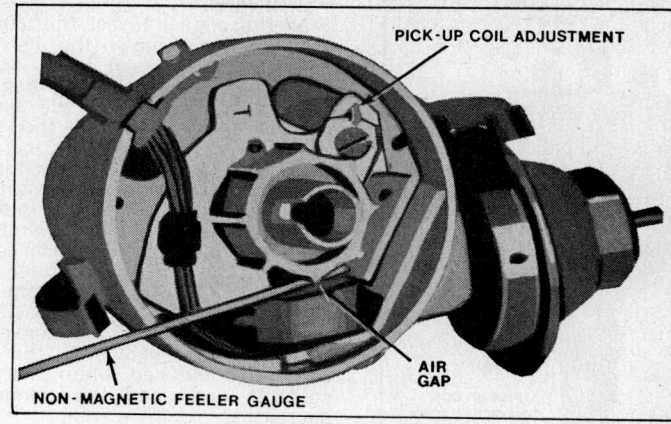

Fig. 4 Air gap adjustment

4. On six cylinder distributors, remove drive gear retaining pin and slide gear from shaft. Support gear so that gear teeth will not be damaged when pin is driven from shaft. On V8 distributors, remove shaft retaining pin and slide retainer from shaft.
5. Remove lower thrust washer by cleaning burrs from around pin hole.
6. Push up on shaft and remove through top of housing.

Distributor Assemble

1. Lubricate and test operation of governor weights. Inspect weight springs for distortion and bearing surfaces and pins for damage.
2. Lubricate upper thrust washer and install onto shaft. Install shaft into housing.

3. On six cylinder distributors, if drive gear is damaged, replace gear as outlined in the Standard Distributor section in this chapter. On V8 distributors, install shaft retainer and pin.
4. Install lower and upper plates and pick-up coil as an assembly.
5. Connect vacuum advance unit arm to pick-up plate and install vacuum unit mounting screws.
6. Place reluctor keeper pin into position on reluctor sleeve and slide reluctor downward on sleeve and press into place firmly. On V-8 distributors, the reluctor is installed with the two arrows on top.

NOTE: Distributors on V-8 engines may rotate either clockwise or counter-clockwise. The arrow at the keeper pin must point in the direction of distributor rotation. If not, remove reluctor and turn it 180 degrees and reinstall it. When removing reluctor, use care not to lose keeper pin.

7. Place 1 drop of light engine oil on felt pad on top of reluctor and install rotor.

Pick-up Replacement & Air Gap Adjustment

1. With distributor removed from vehicle, perform Steps 1 to 3 as outlined in Distributor Disassemble.
2. Remove pick-up coil and upper plate by depressing retainer clip and moving it away from mounting stud. Pick-up coil cannot be removed from upper plate.
3. Lightly lubricate upper plate pivot pin and lower plate support pins with distributor lubricant. Install upper plate pivot pin through smallest hole in lower plate and install retainer clip.

NOTE: The upper plate must ride on the support pins on the lower plate.

4. Install lower and upper plates and pick-up coil as an assembly and install distributor into vehicle.
5. To set air gap, line up one reluctor tooth with pick-up pole and install a non-magnetic .008 inch feeler gauge

between reluctor tooth and pick-up pole, Fig. 4. Rotate pick-up coil until contact is made between reluctor tooth, feeler gauge and pick-up pole. Tighten pick-up hold down screw and remove feeler gauge. Feeler gauge should be removed without force. If not, readjust gap.
6. Perform a secondary gap check with a .010 inch feeler gauge. Do not force feeler gauge between reluctor tooth and pick-up since it is possible to do so. Apply vacuum to vacuum control unit. Pick-up should not contact reluctor tooth. Readjust air gap if contact occurs.

NOTE: If pick-up contacts reluctor teeth on one side of shaft only, the distributor shaft most likely is bent and shaft replacement is required.

DELCO-REMY SYSTEMS CAPACITOR DISCHARGE (CD) & UNITIZED IGNITION

Both systems use a Magnetic Pulse Breakerless distributor. This unit, Fig. 5, resembles a conventional distributor. However, in the Magnetic Pulse unit, an iron timer core replaces the conventional breaker cam, Fig. 6. The timer core, which has equally spaced projections, one for each cylinder, rotates inside a magnetic pick-up assembly, which replaces the conventional breaker plate assembly.

The magnetic pick-up assembly consists of ceramic permanent magnet, a pole piece and a pick-up coil. The pole piece is metal plate having equally spaced internal teeth, one for each cylinder. The magnetic pick-up assembly is mounted over the main bearing on the distributor housing and is actuated by the vacuum advance unit. A conventional centrifugal advance is also used.

Ignition Pulse Amplifier

Capacitor Discharge Amplifier

This unit, Fig. 7, consists of transistors,

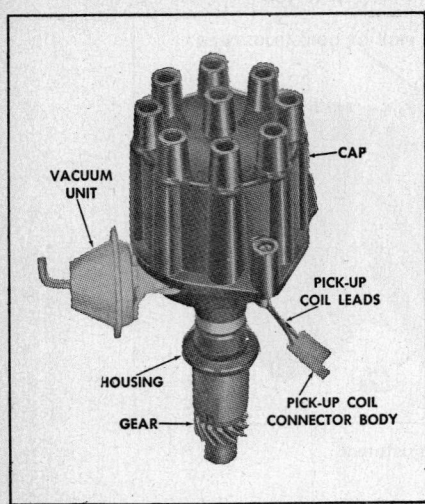

Fig. 5 Delco-Remy Magnetic Pulse distributor

mal 12 volts.

As the engine turns, the vanes on the rotating timer core in the distributor line up with the internal teeth on the pole piece. This establishes a magnetic path through the center of the pick-up coil. This voltage is amplified then applied at the gate of the thyristor, causing it to turn on. The charged capacitor then discharges through the thyristor and primary winding of the coil, inducing high voltage in the secondary winding to fire the spark plugs. This special ignition coil acts as a step up transformer to fire the spark plugs when the primary current *increases*.

This contrasts with the conventional ignition system in which the secondary voltage is induced when the distributor contacts open and the primary current *decreases*.

Trouble Shooting Procedure

Faulty engine performance usually will be evidenced by one of the following conditions: 1. Engine will not run at all. 2. Engine will start but not run. 3. Engine will miss or surge. *The special coil used cannot be tested on a conventional coil tester.*

Engine will not run at all

Hold one spark plug lead about ¼ inch from the engine block and crank the engine. If sparking occurs, the trouble most likely is not ignition. If sparking does not occur, check the ignition system. The wiring, distributor cap and rotor can be checked in the conventional manner. Only the coil requires a different procedure.

The special coil can be checked for primary and secondary winding continuity with an ohmmeter: With leads disconnected from coil, connect ohmmeter across primary terminals. If reading is infinite, winding is open. To check the

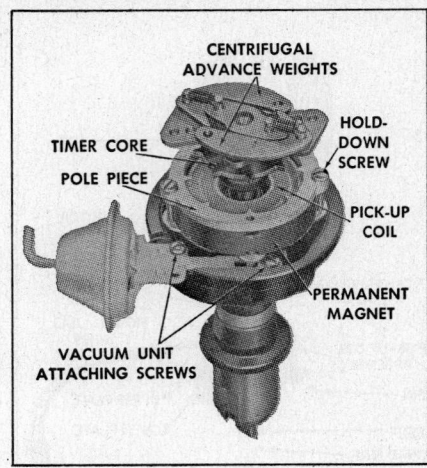

Fig. 6 Magnetic pulse distributor components

secondary, connect ohmmeter to high voltage center tower and coil case. An infinite reading means coil secondary is open. *When checking secondary, use middle or high resistance range on ohmmeter.*

Checking Amplifier:

1. Temporarily connect a jumper lead from amplifier housing to a good ground.
2. If engine now will start and run, the amplifier is not properly grounded.
3. Detach positive and negative leads from coil. *Note carefully the color code so wires can be reconnected in the same manner.*
4. Connect a bulb between the two leads, Fig. 9.
5. Crank engine.

diodes, resistors, a thyristor and a transformer. These are mounted on a printed circuit board to make the amplifier a solid state unit with no moving parts, with a capacity of delivering 30,000 volts.

The ignition coil primary is connected across a high voltage capacitor (condenser), which is charged to about 300 volts during the time the spark plugs are not firing. On impulse signal voltage from the distributor, the capacitor discharges this high voltage into the coil primary.

Due to the transformer action in the coil, the high voltage primary is increased many times to produce the high voltage secondary. Fig. 8 shows a typical circuit diagram.

Voltage is supplied to the transformer which operates through a rectifying bridge circuit of four diodes to keep the capacitor charged. A zener diode limits this charge to 300 volts. This capacitor voltage is maintained at its maximum value during cranking even though battery voltage may be well below its nor-

Fig. 7 Capacitor Discharge (CD) amplifier unit

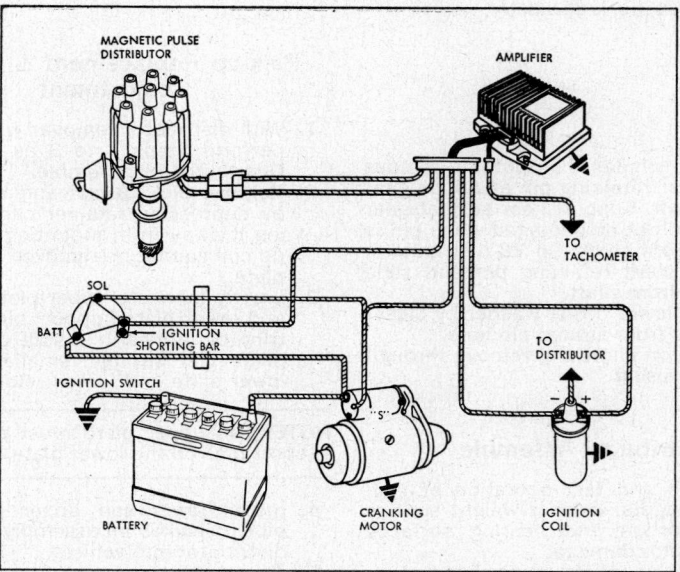

Fig. 8 CD ignition circuit (typical)

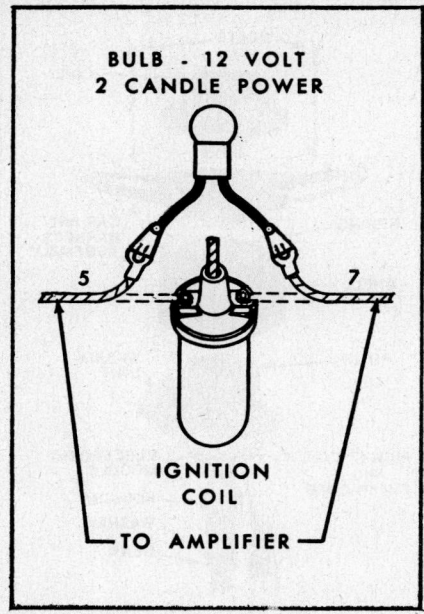

Fig. 9 Amplifier output test

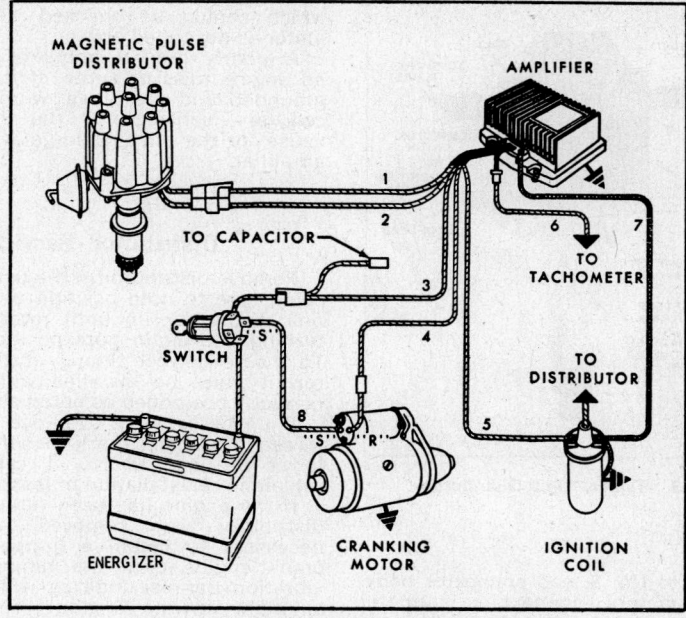

Fig. 10 Pictorial diagram of CD system

6. If bulb flickers on and off, amplifier is operating properly. In this case, recheck secondary system for the cause of "no run" condition.
7. If bulb does not flicker on and off, check distributor.

Distributor checks:

1. On CD system, be sure that the two distributor leads are connected to distributor connector body, Fig. 10.
2. With distributor connector disconnected from harness connector, connect an ohmmeter (1), Fig. 11, to the two terminals on distributor connector.
3. Connect a test stand vacuum source

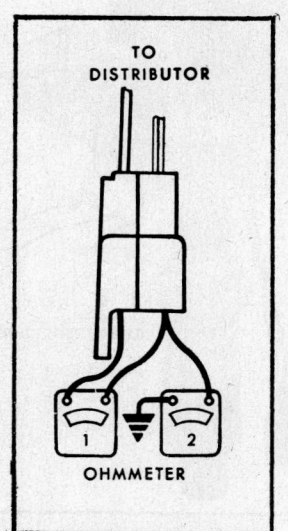

Fig. 11 Distributor test

to the distributor and observe ohmmeter reading throughout vacuum range. (Distributor need not be removed from engine.)
4. Any reading outside the 550-750 ohm range indicates a defective pick-up coil in distributor.
5. Remove one ohmmeter (2) lead, Fig. 11, from connector body and connect to ground.
6. Observe ohmmeter reading throughout vacuum range.
7. Any reading less than infinite indicates a defective pick-up coil.
8. Reconnect harness connector to distributor connector.

Continuity checks-CD system

Carefully inspect all wiring connections to be sure that they are clean and tight. If satisfactory, disconnect amplifier No.

3 and No. 4 leads, Fig. 10 from the two connectors, then proceed as follows:
1. Connect voltmeter from ground to No. 4 connector lead.
2. Turn switch to "Start" position.
3. If reading is zero, circuit is open between connector body and battery.
4. If reading is obtained, connect voltmeter from ground to No. 3 connector lead.
5. Turn switch to the run position.
6. If reading is zero, circuit is open between connector body and switch.
7. If reading is obtained, replace amplifier.

Engine will start but not run-CD System

If engine starts but then stops when switch is returned to the run position, proceed as follows:
1. Be sure that leads are properly con-

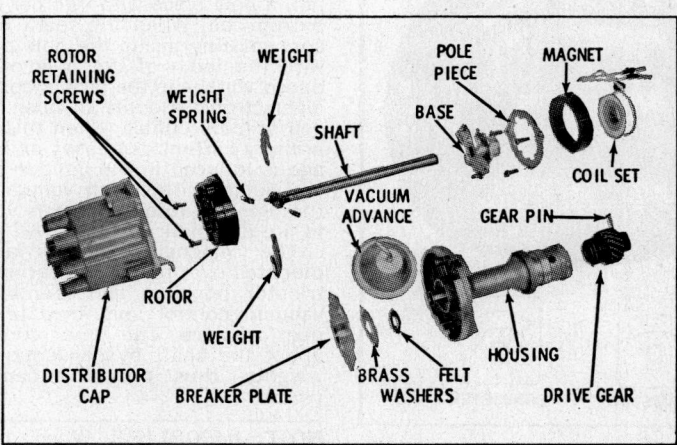

Fig. 12 Exploded view of Magnetic Pulse distributor

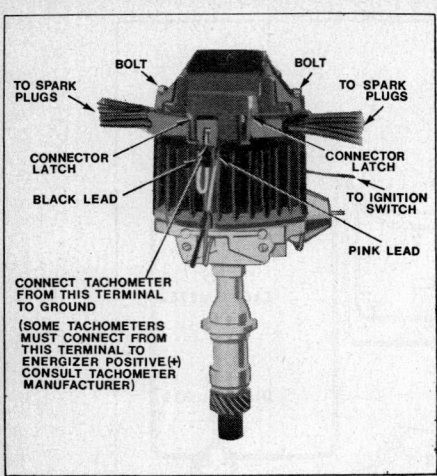

Fig. 13 Typical Unit Distributor

nected to No. 3 lead connector body.
2. If satisfactory, connect a voltmeter from ground to the terminal connector inside the connector.
3. Turn switch to run position.
4. If reading is zero, lead between connector and ignition switch is open.
5. If reading is obtained, replace amplifier.

Engine miss or surge:

The vehicle fuel system should be checked in the usual manner. If satisfactory, check the ignition system in the

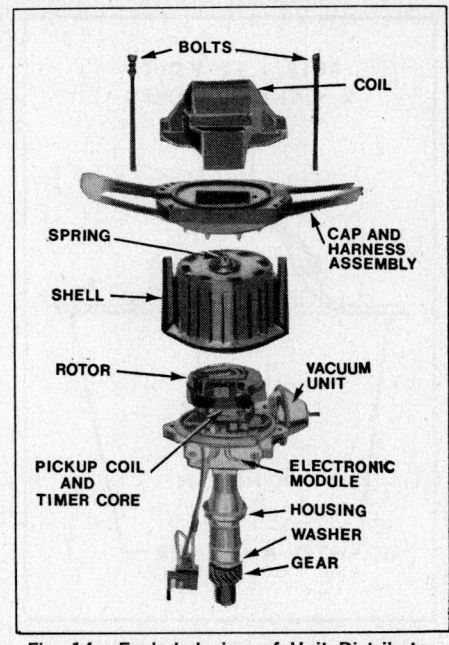

Fig. 14 Exploded view of Unit Distributor

usual manner except the special coil which should be checked with a ohmmeter as described above.

A poorly ground amplifier can cause an engine miss or surge. If it is properly grounded and the plugs, wiring, cap and coil are satisfactory, the most likely cause for the miss or surge is a defective amplifier.

Distributor Service

Remove distributor in the usual manner, being sure to note position of rotor, then pull distributor up until rotor just stops turning and again note position of rotor. To insure correct timing of the distributor, it must be installed with the rotor correctly positioned as noted above.

If necessary to remove secondary wires from cap, mark position on cap tower for lead to No. 1 cylinder. This will aid in reinstallation of leads.

If the engine has been turned after the distributor was removed, it will be necessary to install a jumper wire and crank engine until the timing mark on vibration damper indexes with the proper mark on the engine front cover. If both valves of No. 1 cylinder are closed, the piston will be on top dead center of the firing stroke.

Fig. 12 shows an exploded view of the distributor.

No adjustments can be made on either system and no periodic maintenance is required.

No periodic lubrication is required. Engine oil lubricates the lower bushing, and an oil-filled reservoir provides lubrication for upper bushing.

Unit Ignition System

The "Unit Distributor" utilizes an all-electronic module, pickup coil and timer core in place of the conventional ignition points and condenser. Point pitting and rubbing block wear resulting in retarded ignition timing, is eliminated. Since the coil is part of the Unit Distributor there is no need for distributor-to-coil primary (breaker points to coil negative lead) or secondary lead (high voltage lead).

The main features making the Unit Ignition System unique are shown in Figs. 13 and 14.

A magnetic pickup assembly - located over the shaft contains a permanent magnet, a pole piece with internal teeth, and a pickup coil. When the teeth of the timer core rotating inside the pole piece line up with the teeth of the pole piece, the induced voltage in the pickup coil signals the all-electronic module to open the ignition coil primary circuit. When this occurs, the primary current decreases and a high voltage is induced in the ignition coil secondary winding. This high voltage is directed through the rotor and high voltage leads to fire the spark plugs.

The magnetic pickup assembly is mounted over the main bearing on the distributor housing, and is rotated by the vacuum control unit, thus providing vacuum advance. The timer core is rotated about the shaft by conventional advance weights, thus providing centrifugal advance.

NOTE: *IMPORTANT*: When making compression checks, disconnect ignition switch connector from Unit Ignition System.

Trouble Diagnosis

Insure that the black and pink leads are

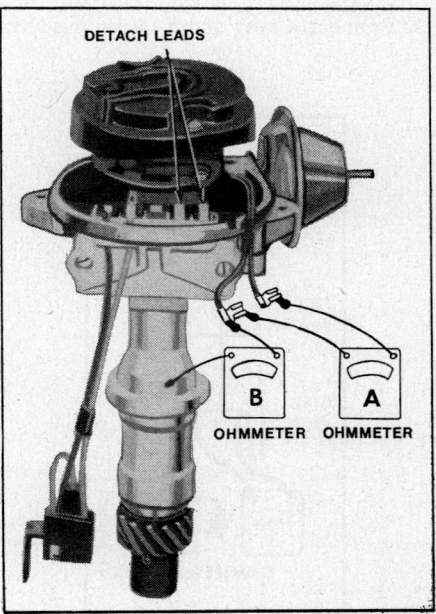

Fig. 16 Pickup coil test.
Unit Distributor

Fig. 15 Ignition Coil test.
Unit Distributor

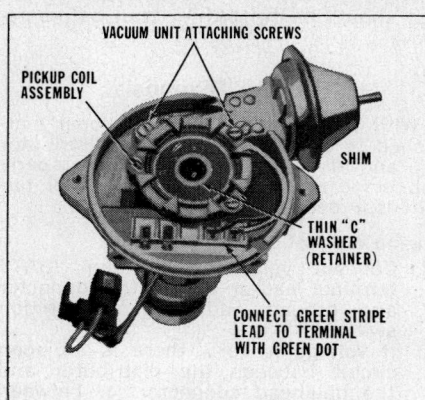

Fig. 17 Unit Distributor with shaft assembly removed

connected, Fig. 13. Tighten both bolts, Fig. 13. Loose bolts may cause poor performance and radio interference.

NOTE: Before performing extensive diagnostic operations determine if fuel system is operating properly.

On Vehicle

Engine Will Not Start

1. Disconnected or loose ignition switch connector, Fig. 13.
   a. Connect voltmeter from ignition switch connector to ground.
   b. Turn on ignition switch.
   c. If reading is zero, circuit is open between connector and ignition switch.
   d. If reading is Energizer voltage, hold one spark lead with insulated pliers about ¼" from dry area of engine

[Figure: H.E.I. distributor external components with labels:]
GROUND TERMINAL
B+TERMINAL
C-TERMINAL
BAT. TERMINAL (CONNECTED TO IGN. SWITCH)
LATCH (4)
TACH TERMINAL
CONNECT TACHOMETER FROM THIS TERMINAL TO GROUND
(SOME TACHOMETERS MUST CONNECT FROM THIS TERMINAL TO ENERGIZER POSITIVE(+). CONSULT TACHOMETER MANUFACTURER.)
CONNECTOR

Fig. 18 H.E.I. distributor external components

block while cranking engine. If a strong spark is present, ignition would appear to be trouble free. If no spark, follow "On Test Bench" procedure.

Engine Will Start, But Will Not Run. Rough Engine Operation, Miss or Surge

1. Spark plug lead arc-over, voltage leaking to ground or faulty spark plugs.
   a. If no defects are found, follow "On Test Bench" procedure.

On Test Bench

NOTE: Unit disassembled, Fig. 14

Engine Will Not Start. Engine Will Start, But Will Not Run. Rough Engine Operation, Miss or Surge.

1. Inspect coil, eight inserts, shell and rotor for arc-over or leakage.
   a. Connect ohmmeter, Fig. 15.
   b. Tests "A" and "B" should have practically a zero result. If infinite on either reading, replace coil.
   c. Test "C" should result in 6000-9000 ohms. If outside range, replace coil.
   d. Test "D" should result in infinity. If not, replace coil.
   e. Connect vacuum source to vacuum unit.
   f. Connect ohmmeter, Fig. 16 and observe ohmmeter throughout vacuum range.
   g. If test "A" reads less than 650 ohms, or more than 850 ohms at any time, replace pickup coil.
   h. If test "B" does not read infinity at any time, replace pickup coil.
2. If no defects have been found, replace electronic module.

Pickup Coil Or Vacuum Unit Replacement, Fig. 17

1. Remove unit from engine.
2. Drive retaining pin out through gear.
3. Remove rotor and shaft assembly from housing.
4. Remove shim and "C" washer.
5. Remove pickup coil or vacuum unit.

HIGH ENERGY IGNITION SYSTEM (H.E.I.)

The H.E.I. system utilizes an all-electronic module, pickup coil and timer core in place of the conventional ignition points and condenser (the condenser is used for noise suppression only). Point pitting and rubbing block wear resulting in retarded ignition timing, is eliminated.

NOTE: H.E.I. components are not interchangeable with "Unit Distributor" Components.

Since the coil is part of the H.E.I. distributor there is no need for distributor-to-coil primary (breaker points to coil negative lead) or secondary lead (high voltage lead).

The main features of H.E.I. system differentiating this system from the "Unit Ignition" system are shown in Figs. 18 and 19.

The magnetic pickup consists of a rotat-

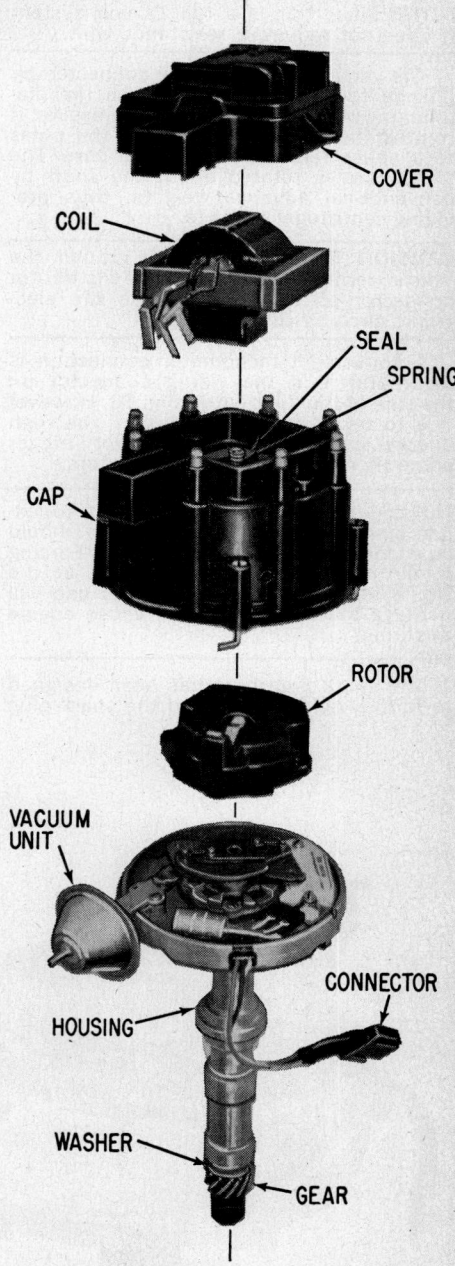

Fig. 19 H.E.I. distributor internal components

[Figure labels:] COVER, COIL, SEAL, SPRING, CAP, ROTOR, VACUUM UNIT, HOUSING, CONNECTOR, WASHER, GEAR

ing timer core attached to the distributor shaft, a stationary pole piece, permanent magnet and pickup coil.

When the distributor shaft rotates, the teeth of the timer core line up and pass the teeth of the pole piece inducing voltage in the pickup coil which signals the all-electronic module to open the ignition coil primary circuit. Maximum inductance occurs at the moment the timer core teeth are lined up with the teeth on the pole piece. At the instant the timer core teeth start to pass the pole teeth, the primary current decreases and a high voltage is induced in the ignition coil secondary winding and is directed through the rotor and high voltage leads to fire the spark plugs.

TUNE UP SERVICE

NOTE: Since this is a full 12 volt system it does not require a resistance wire.

The vacuum diaphragm is connected by linkage to the pole piece. When the diaphragm moves against spring pressure it rotates the pole piece allowing the poles to advance relative to the timer core. The timer core is rotated about the shaft by conventional advance weights, thus providing centrifugal advance.

CAUTION: Never connect to ground the "tach" terminal, Fig. 18, of the distributor connector as this will damage the electronic circuitry of the module.

A convenient tachometer connection is incorporated in the wiring connector on the side of the distributor, Fig. 18. However due to its transistorized design, the high energy ignition system will not trigger some models of engine tachometers.

NOTE: When using a timing light to adjust ignition timing, the connection should be made at the No. 1 spark plug. Forcing foreign objects through the boot at the No. 1 terminal of the distributor cap will damage the boot and could cause engine misfiring.

The spark plug boot has been designed to form a tight seal around the spark plug

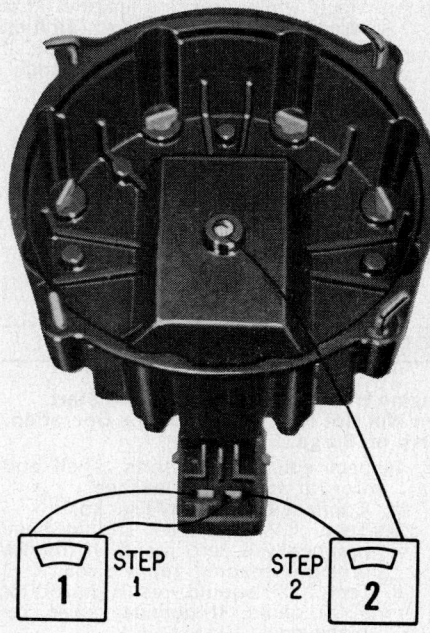

Fig. 20 H.E.I. distributor ignition coil ohmmeter test

and should be twisted ½ turn before removal.

System Diagnosis

With the wiring connector properly attached to connector at side of distributor cap and all the spark plug leads properly connected at plugs and at distributor terminals. Proceed as follows:

Engine Will Not Start

1. Connect voltmeter between "BAT" terminal lead on distributor connector and ground and turn on ignition switch.
2. If voltage is zero, there is an open circuit between the distributor and the bulkhead connector; or between the bulkhead connector and the ignition switch; or between the ignition switch and the starter solenoid. Repair as required.
3. If reading is battery voltage, hold one spark plug lead with insulated pliers approximately ¼ inch away from a dry area of engine block and crank engine. If a spark is visible, the distributor has been eliminated as source of trouble. Check spark plugs and fuel system.
4. If there is no visible spark, perform the "Component Checkout" and proceed as described further on.

Engine Starts But Runs Rough

1. Check for proper fuel delivery to carburetor.
2. Check all vacuum hoses for leakage.
3. Visually inspect and listen for sparks jumping to ground.
4. Check ignition timing.
5. Check centrifugal advance mechanism for proper operation.
6. Remove spark plugs and check for unusual defects, such as very wide gap, abnormal fouling, cracked insulators (inside and out), etc.
7. If no defects are found, perform the "Component Checkout" procedure as described below.

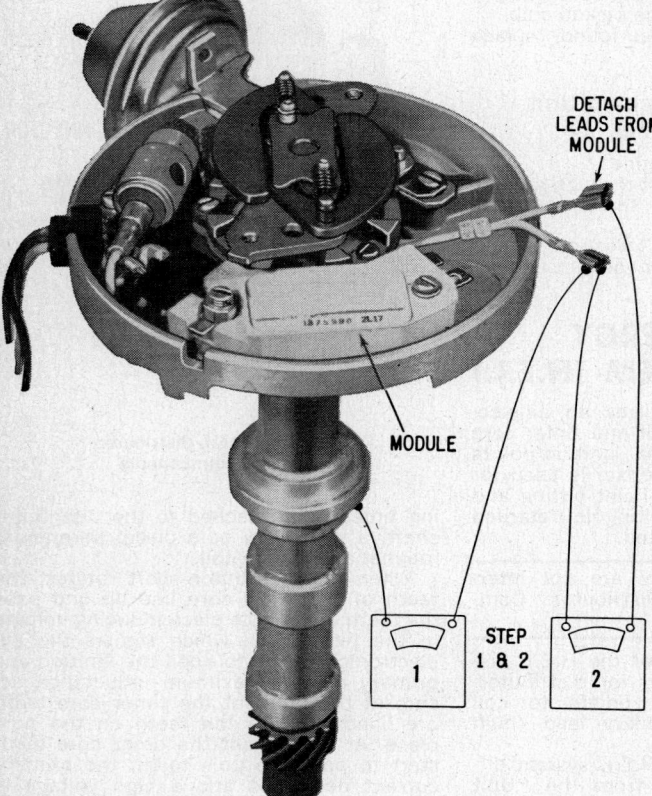

Fig. 21 Distributor pickup coil ohmmeter test

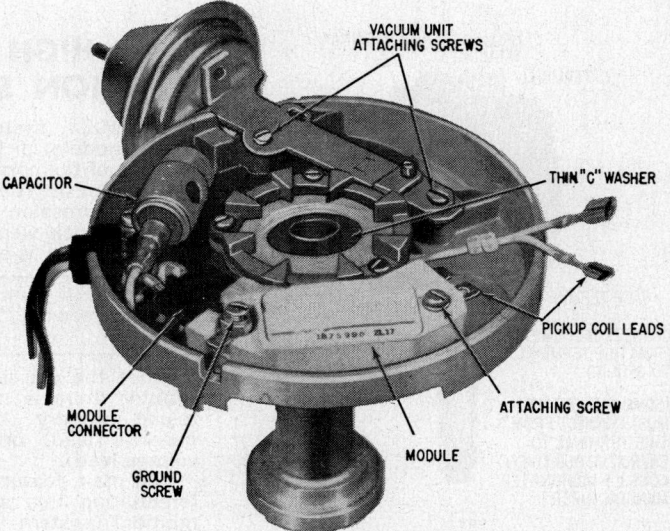

Fig. 22 H.E.I. distributor component replacement

Component Checkout

1. Remove cap and coil assembly.
2. Inspect cap, coil and rotor for spark arc-over.
3. Connect ohmmeter, Fig. 20, step 1. If ohmmeter reading is other than zero or very near to zero, the ignition coil must be replaced.
4. If no reading on ohmmeter was observed in step 1, reconnect the ohmmeter, Fig. 20, step 2. If ohmmeter reading is infinite on high scale, the ignition coil must be replaced.
5. Connect an external vacuum source to the vacuum advance unit. Replace vacuum unit if inoperative.
6. If vacuum unit is operating properly, connect ohmmeter, Fig. 21, step 1. If ohmmeter reading on middle scale is not infinite at all times, pick-up coil must be replaced.
7. With ohmmeter connected, Fig. 21, step 2, ohmmeter reading must be within 650 to 850 ohms at all times. If not replace pick-up coil.

COMPONENTS REPLACE

Ignition Coil Replacement, Fig. 19

1. Remove screws holding distributor cover to distributor cap and remove distributor cover.
2. Remove four screws holding coil to cap.
3. Remove harness connector and battery wire from side of distributor cap.
4. Push coil leads out of position in cap and remove coil.
5. Reverse procedure to install.

Module Replacement, Fig. 22

1. Disconnect wiring harness connector at side of distributor cap and remove distributor.
2. Remove rotor and disconnect wires from module terminals.
3. Remove two mounting screws and remove module.

CAUTION: At installation, coat bottom of new module with dielectric lubricant (furnished with new module) to aid in heat transfer into distributor housing. Failure to apply lubricant will cause excessive heat at module and premature module failure.

4. Reverse procedure to install.

Pole Piece, Magnet or Pick-Up Coil Replacement, Fig. 22

Removal

1. With distributor removed, disconnect wires at module terminals.
2. Remove roll pin from drive gear by driving out with ⅛ inch diameter drift punch.
3. Remove gear, shim and the tanged washer from distributor shaft. Remove any burrs that may have been caused by removal of pin.
4. Remove distributor shaft from housing.
5. Remove washer from upper end of distributor housing.

NOTE: Bushings in the housing are not serviceable.

6. Remove three screws securing pole piece to housing and remove pole piece, magnet and pick-up coil.

Installation

1. Install pick-up coil, magnet and pole piece and loosely install three screws holding pole piece.
2. With washer installed at top of housing, install distributor shaft and rotate to check for proper clearance between pole piece teeth and timer core teeth.
3. If necessary, realign pole piece to provide adequate clearance and secure properly.
4. Install tanged washer, shim and drive gear (teeth up) to bottom of shaft. Align drive gear and install new roll pin.

FORD SYSTEM

1973-74 Breakerless (B/L) Solid State Ignition System

The (B/L) ignition system does not use ignition points and is controlled by an electronic module, also a new oil filled coil is incorporated. Total diagnosis of system requires only a volt-ohmmeter tester.

The electronic module, Fig. 1, is the brain of this system and is well protected from outside elements such as heat and shock. The heat sink containing all the electronic devices is sealed in a mixture of epoxy and sand. This module can not be disassembled and must be replaced if malfunctioning.

The conventional ignition coils are not to be used with this system. The proper coil is easily identified as it is all blue and terminals are labeled differently from conventional ignition coils "BAT" (battery) and "DEC" (Distributor Electronic Control), Fig. 2.

The ignition switch energizes the module

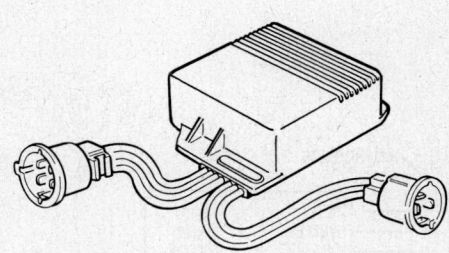

Fig. 1   Ford electronic module

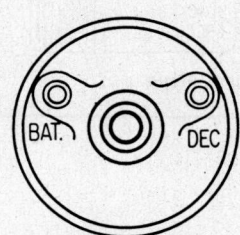

Fig. 2   Ford electronic ignition coil identification

through the white wire while engine is cranking and through the red wire when engine is running.

The distributor shaft and armature rotation, Fig. 3, causes the armature poles to pass by the core of the magnetic pick-up assembly. In turn cutting the magnetic field and signaling the electronic module, Fig. 4, through the orange and purple wires to break the primary ignition current, thus inducing secondary voltage in the coil to fire the spark plugs. The coil is then energized again by the primary circuit and ready for the next spark cycle. This primary circuit is controlled by a timing circuit in the module.

The B/L ignition system is protected against electrical current produced during normal vehicle operation and against reverse polarity or high voltage accidentally applied if vehicle is jump started.

NOTE: IMPORTANT: The ignition system will be damaged if other than volt-ohm test procedures are used to check alternator output. This alternator test procedure is outlined in the "Ford Autolite/Motorcraft Alternator" section, under "Voltmeter Test."

CAUTION: Do not use the volt-amp test procedure or any other test that utilizes a knife switch on the battery terminal.

Since the interval between the time that the module activates the primary ignition circuit and the time the distributor signal turns it off varies with engine speed. Consequently, a dwell measurement is insignificant.

System Diagnosis

If the ignition system is suspected of a malfunction inspect for loose connections and perform the "Secondary Ignition Checkout" procedure in the Trouble Shooting Chapter elsewhere in this manual. Since the secondary circuit is identical to that of a conventional ignition system.

If no spark is observed during the above test, check the ignition coil high tension wire, replace if damaged. If no damage is observed at the coil wire, disconnect the three-way and four-way connectors at the electronic module and make tests at the harness connectors.

NOTE: Do not make tests at the module terminals.

Voltage Tests At Harness Connectors, Fig. 5

NOTE: If all the following tests comply with specifications replace the module.

Key On

1. Check for battery voltage between pin #3 and engine ground. If voltage is less than specified, the voltage feed wire to the module is damaged and must be repaired.
2. Check for battery voltage between pin #5 and engine ground. If voltage is less than specified proceed as follows:
   a. Without disconnecting the coil, connect voltmeter between coil

"BAT" terminal and engine ground.

b. Connect a jumper wire between the coil "DEC" terminal and engine ground.

c. With all lights and accessories off, turn on the ignition switch.

d. A satisfactory primary circuit between the battery and the coil will register 4.9 to 7.9 volts.

e. If less than 4.9 volts register on voltmeter, check for worn primary circuit insulation, broken wire strands or loose-corroded terminals.

f. If a greater than a 7.9 voltage is registered on voltmeter, check and replace if necessary the resistance wire.

Cranking Engine

1. Check for 8 to 12 volts between pin #1 and engine ground. If voltage is not within specifications, the voltage feed wire to the module is damaged.

2. Check for 8 to 12 volts between pin #5 and ground. If voltage is not within specifications, the ignition bypass circuit is open or grounded between starter solenoid or ignition switch and pin #5. Also check primary connections at the coil.

3. Check for ½ volt oscillation (using the 2.5 volt scale) between pin #7 and pin #8. If the voltmeter does not register this oscillation proceed as follows:

a. Perform same test at the three wire pigtail (with the distributor disconnected), in turn eliminating the orange and purple wires as a cause of malfunction. If no oscillation is present at pigtail, visually inspect distributor components. Make sure that the toothed armature is not damaged, is tight on sleeve and secured properly with the alignment pin, Fig. 3. If armature is not damaged and is rotating properly when cranking the engine and voltmeter is not oscillating, replace the magnetic pickup (stator assembly).

Resistance Test At Harness Connectors, Fig. 5

Key Off

1. Check for resistances of: 400 to 800

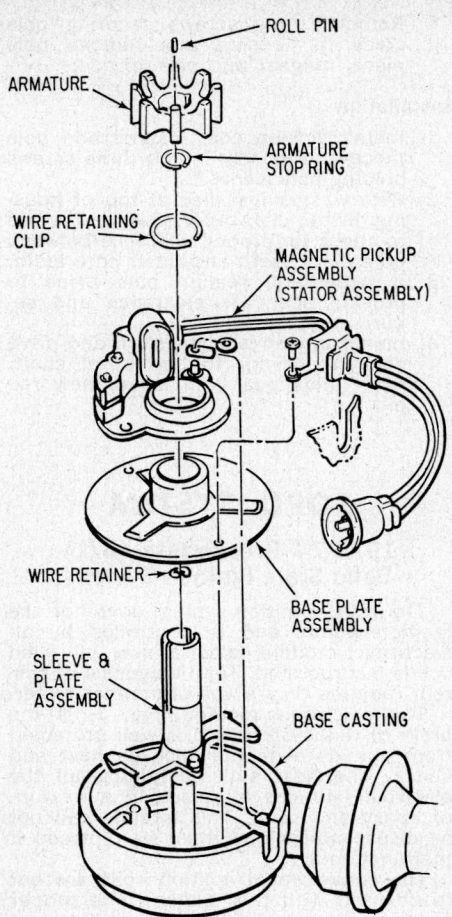

Fig. 3 Ford breakerless (B/L) distributor

ohms between pin #7 and #8, 0 ohms between pin #6 and engine ground and for 70,000 ohms or more between ground and either pin #7 or pin #8. If any of these values do not comply with specifications proceed as follows:

a. Perform same test at the three wire pigtail (with the distributor disconnected), in turn eliminating the orange and purple wires as a cause of malfunction.

b. If any of the above checks do not comply with specifications, the magnetic pick-up assembly (stator assembly) is not functioning and must be replaced.

2. Check for a resistance of 7000 to 13,000 ohms between pin #3 and coil secondary. Also check for a resistance of 1.0 to 2.0 ohms between pin #5 and pin #4. If either check is not within specifications, diagnose coil separately from rest of system. Coil primary resistance must be within 1.0 to 2.0 ohms and coil secondary resistance must be within 700 to 13,000 ohms. If not within specifications follow procedures for testing standard ignition coils as outlined in the "TUNE UP SERVICE" chapter under "Ignition Coils & Resistors."

3. Check for a resistance of more than 4.0 ohms between pin #5 and engine ground. If resistance is less than specified, locate the short to ground either at the coil "DEC" terminal or in the green wire, Fig. 4.

4. If a resistance of 1.0 to 2.0 ohms is not obtained between pins #3 and #4, replace the primary resistance wire.

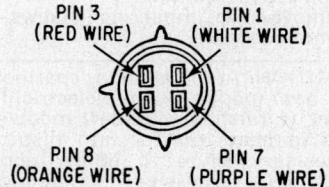

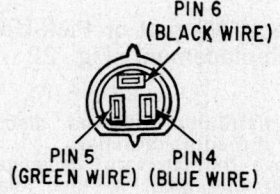

Fig. 5 Ford breakerless ignition female harness connectors (system test points)

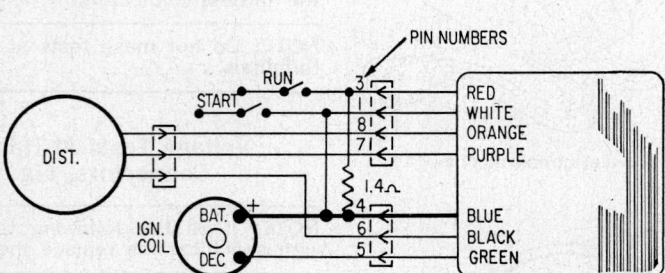

Fig. 4 Ford breakerless ignition primary circuit

EMISSION CONTROL SYSTEMS

This chapter will deal with system descriptions, operations, visual inspections and maintenance procedures not requiring special training and sophisticated testing equipment.
NOTE: A pictorial section for locating emission control system components begins on page 2-575.

CONTENTS

Domestic Car Systems

Catalytic Converters 2-569
Crankcase Ventilation (PCV) 2-546
Electric Assist Choke 2-545
Fuel Evaporative Controls 2-571

AMERICAN MOTORS

Air Guard 2-546
Engine Mod. 2-548
Exhaust Gas Recirculation 2-549
Thermostatic Air Cleaner 2-550
Trans. Controlled Spark 2-553

CHRYSLER CORP.

Air Injection 2-546
Cleaner Air Package 2-557

Cleaner Air System 2-559
Exhaust Gas Recirculation 2-561
NOx System 2-559
Orifice Spark Advance Control 2-560

FORD MOTOR CO.

Auto Therm Air Cleaner 2-550
Cold Temperature Activated Vacuum . 2-569
Decel Valve 2-567
Delay Vacuum By-Pass 2-567
Dual-Area Diaphragm 2-567
Electronic Distributor Modulator ... 2-564
Electronic Spark Control 2-564
Exhaust Gas Recirculation 2-566
High Speed EGR Modulator
    Sub-System 2-564

Improved Combustion 2-562
Spark Delay Valve 2-565
Temperature Activated Vacuum 2-568
Thermactor 2-546
Trans. Regulated Spark 2-565
Trans. Regulated Spark +1 2-565

GENERAL MOTORS CORP.

Air Injection Reactor 2-546
Combined Emission Control 2-555
Controlled Combustion System 2-551
Exhaust Gas Recirculation 2-556
Speed Controlled Spark 2-556
Thermostatic Controlled Air Cleaner . 2-550
Trans. Controlled Spark 2-554

ELECTRIC ASSIST CHOKE

Most American Motors, Chrysler and Ford vehicles are equipped for 1973-74 with an electric assist choke. This device aids in reducing the emissions of hydrocarbon (HC) and carbon monoxide (CO) during starting and warmup (choke on) period. The electric assist choke is designed to give a more rapid choke opening at temperatures of about 60° to 65° F. or greater and a slower choke opening at temperatures of about 60° to 65° F. or below.

The electric assist choke system does not change any carburetor service procedures and cannot be adjusted. If system is found out of calibration the heater control switch and/or choke unit must be replaced.

American Motors & Ford

Fig. 1—The electric choke system consists of a choke cap, thermostatic spring, a bimetal temperature sensing disc (switch), and a ceramic positive temperature coefficient (PTC) heater. The choke is powered from terminal or tap of the alternator. Current is constantly supplied to the ambient temperature switch. The system is grounded through a ground strap connected to the carburetor body. At temperatures below approximately 60 degrees, the switch opens and no current is supplied to the ceramic heater located within the thermostatic spring. Normal thermostatic spring choking action then occurs. At temperatures above approximately 60-65 degrees, the temperature sensing switch closes and current is supplied to the ceramic heater. As the heater warms, it causes the thermostatic spring to pull the choke plates open within 1-1½ minutes.

Chrysler

NOTE: The wattage of the choke heater is part of the choke calibration and may change from year to year.

Fig. 2—The control switch is connected to the ignition switch from which electrical power is obtained and transfered through electrical connection to the control switch. The 1973 switch serves two purposes:

1. Above 63° F. the control switch will energize the choke heater.
2. After a period of time, the control switch will de-energize the choke heater. The shut-down will result after the control switch warms to about 110° F. by engine heat and a small electrical heater within the switch. Since the heater control switch is mounted to the engine and near the carburetor, some winter operation may energize the choke heater. This could happen after the choke has opened without benefit of electric

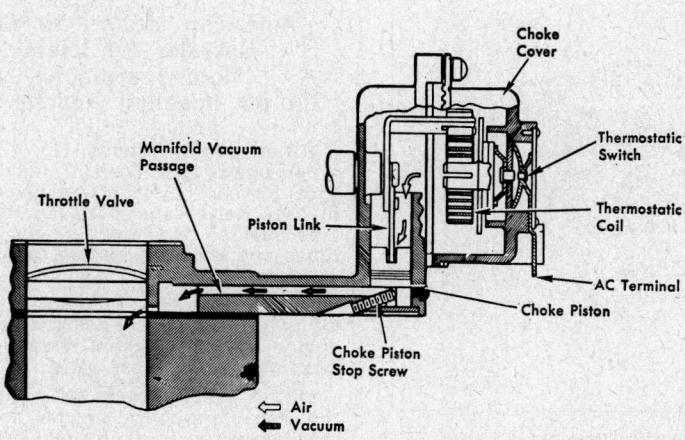

Fig. 1   American Motors and Ford electric assist choke

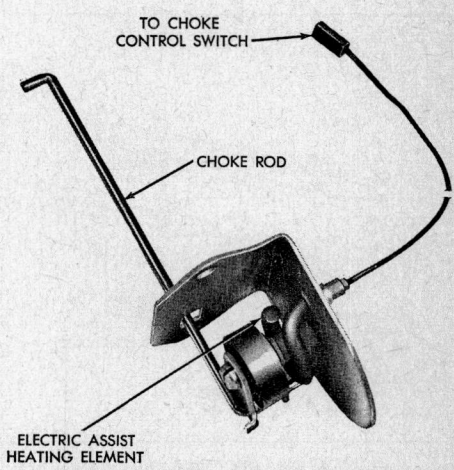

Fig. 2   Chrysler electric assist choke

heat. If this happens it will have no adverse effect on engine operation, and will soon be turned off.

The 1974 switch serves three purposes:
1. Below 58° F. the control switch will partially energize the choke heater.
2. Above 58° F. the control switch will fully energize the choke heater.
3. The control switch will de-energize the choke heater at approximately 110° F. During winter operations, engines will experience three stages of choke heat; partial heat during engine warm-up, full heat after engine warm-up and no heat well after engine warm-up. Engine starts during summer temperatures will not experience the partial heat stage.

NOTE: The heating element should not be exposed to or immersed in any fluid for any purpose. An electric short in the wiring to the heater or within the heater will be a short of the ignition system.

CRANKCASE VENTILATION

Fresh air is circulated through the engine crankcase and drawn into the intake manifold, carrying crankcase vapors with it, Fig. 3. This air flow is controlled by a spring loaded ventilation valve which is closed during high vacuum periods and opens to provide maximum ventilation as manifold vacuum drops off.

Because the hoses vent directly into the intake manifold, any malfunction in the system will have a direct effect on the carburetor mixture calibration. For this reason, the valve and hoses must be kept clear and all connections must be air tight.

The system should be checked and the valve cleaned or replaced at every tune-up and, any time there is an engine idle complaint.

SYSTEM TESTS

A quick check of the system can be made by pulling the end of the valve out of the valve cover and, with the engine

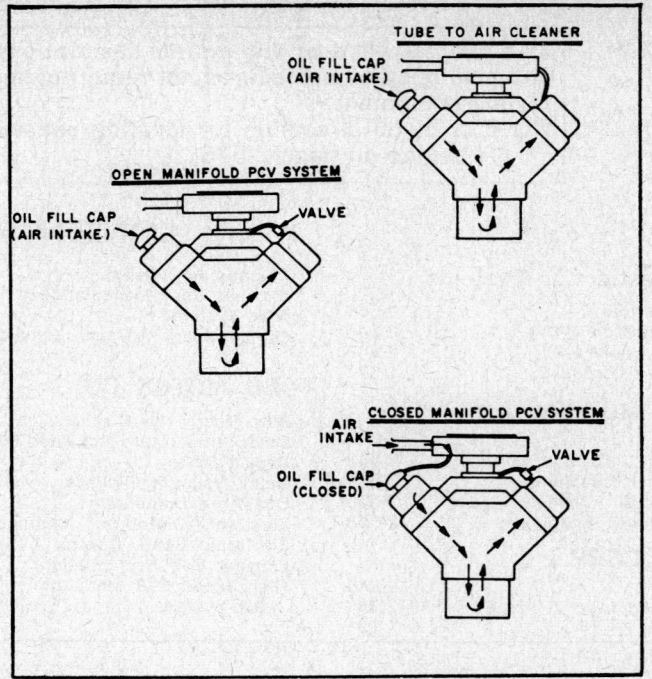

Fig. 3   Various PCV systems

idling, placing a finger over the end of the valve to block the air flow. A vacuum should be felt and the engine speed should drop approximately 50 rpm if the system is satisfactory. If there is no change in engine speed a clogged system is indicated. To isolate the problem, remove the valve from the hose. If the ventilator hoses and carburetor passages are clear, a strong vacuum will be felt and the engine idle will change drastically or the engine will stall when the end of the hose is uncovered. If this occurs, the trouble is in the valve. If the engine continues to idle approximately as it did before the hose was uncovered, the hoses or carburetor passages are blocked.

Regulator Valve Test

1. Install a regulator valve known to be

good in the crankcase ventilation system.
2. Start engine and compare engine idle condition to the prior idle condition.
3. If the loping or rough idle condition remains when the good regulator valve is installed, the crankcase ventilation system is not at fault. Further engine component diagnosis will have to be made to find the cause of the malfunction.
4. If the idle condition proves satisfactory, replace the regulator valve and clean hoses, fittings, etc.

EXHAUST EMISSION CONTROLS AIR PUMP SYSTEMS

American Motors Air Guard, Chrysler Air Injection, Ford Thermactor & GM Air Injection Reactor (A.I.R.)

All air pump systems, Fig. 4 consist of an air pump, Figs. 6 and 7, injection tubes (one for each cylinder), a diverter or air by-pass valve, check valves (one for In Line engines, two for V8s), air manifolds, tubes and hoses necessary to connect the various components.

Carburetors, distributors and diverter or air by-pass valves are designed for specific engine applications and should not be interchanged with other units.

In this system, fresh air is pumped into the exhaust system in the area of the exhaust valves, to ignite and burn the unburned portion of exhaust gases in the

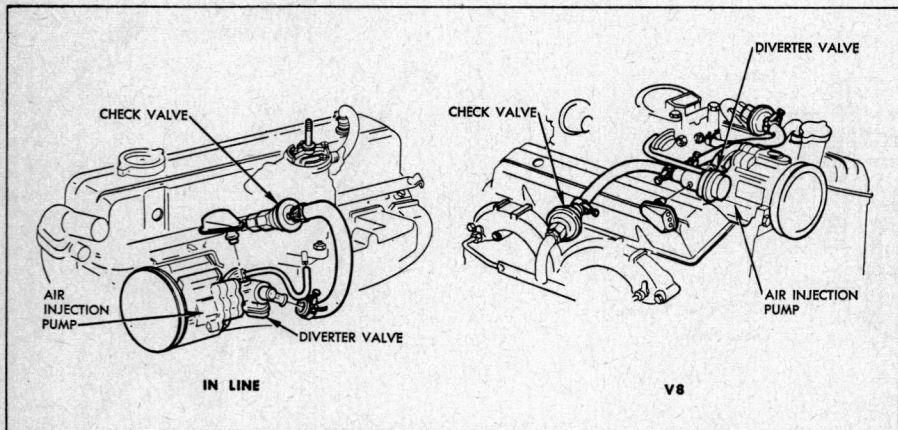

Fig. 4   Typical installation of an air pump system with a diverter valve, otherwise known as an air by-pass valve. 1969-74

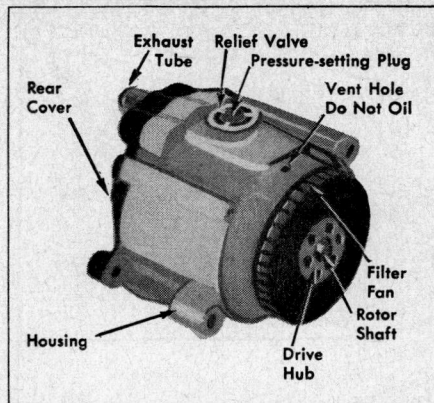

Fig. 6 Air injection pump with integral centrifugal air filter and pressure relief valve

exhaust system, thus minimizing exhaust contaminations.

The mixture control or backfire by-pass valve, Fig. 8, when triggered by a sharp increase in manifold vacuum, supplies the intake manifold with fresh air to lean out the fuel/air mixture and prevent backfire.

The diverter or air by-pass valve, Figs. 9 and 10, when triggered by a sharp increase in manifold vacuum, shuts off the injected air to the exhaust and prevents backfiring during this richer period. On engine overrun the total air supply is dumped through the muffler on the diverter or air by-pass valve. At high engine speeds the excess air is dumped through the pressure relief valve when the relief valve is part of the air pump, Fig. 6, and through the diverter or air by-pass valve when the pressure relief valve is part of the diverter or air by-pass valve, Fig. 10.

The check valve(s) prevents air pump damage due to exhaust back flow, which can occur even under normal operating conditions.

Although a properly operating system

will effectively reduce emissions, if any system component or engine component operating in conjunction with the system should malfunction, emissions may be increased.

Maintenance

Engine tune-up should be checked whenever the air pump system seems to be malfunctioning, especially items affecting air/fuel ratio.

Because of the similarity of many parts, typical illustrations and procedures are given in the following text.

Air Manifold, Hose and Tube; Fig. 11

1. Inspect all hoses and tubes for deterioration or cracks.
2. Check hose and tube routing as interference may cause wear.
3. Check all hose and tube connections.
4. Check the pressure side of the system for leaks with a soapy water solution. With the pump running, bubbles will form if a leak exists.
5. When replacing any hose or tube, note routing before removal.

CAUTION: The hoses used with this system are made of special material to withstand high temperature. No other type should be used.

Check Valves:

1. Check valves should be inspected whenever the hose is disconnected from the valve or check valve failure is suspected.

   NOTE: Any indication of exhaust gases in the air pump indicates check valve failure.

2. Orally blow through the check valve (toward air manifold) then attempt to suck back. Flow should be toward air manifold only.

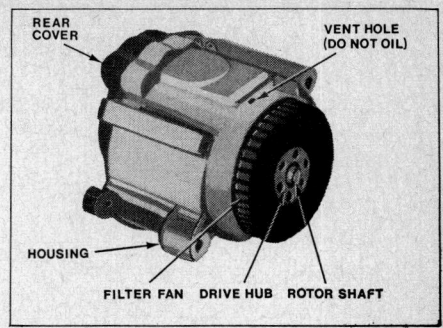

Fig. 7 Air injection pump with integral centrifugal air filter without pressure valve

3. When replacing a check valve, be careful not to bend or twist the air manifold.

Diverter or Air By-Pass Valve:

1. Check condition and routing of all lines, especially the signal line. All lines must be secure without crimps or leaks.
2. Disconnect signal line at valve. A vacuum signal must be available with engine running.
3. With engine warmed up to operating temperature and carburetor at curb idle, no air should be escaping through the valve's muffler. Manually open and quickly close the throttle; a momentary blast of air should discharge through the valve's muffler for at least one second. Defective valve should be replaced.

CAUTION: Although sometimes similar in appearance, these valves are de-

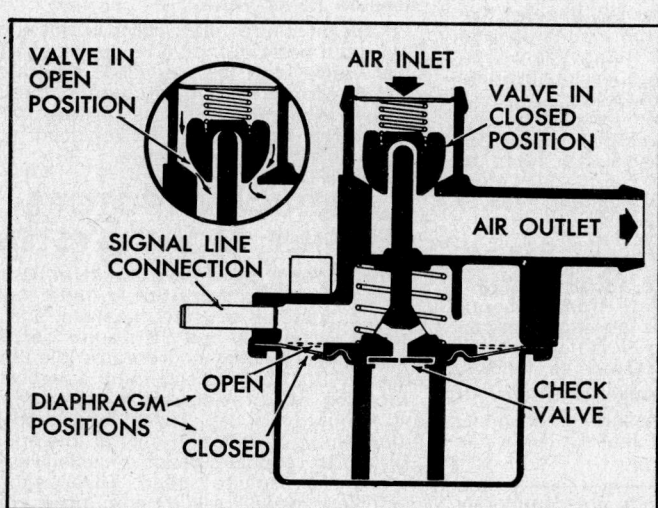

Fig. 8 Typical mixture control or backfire by-pass valve

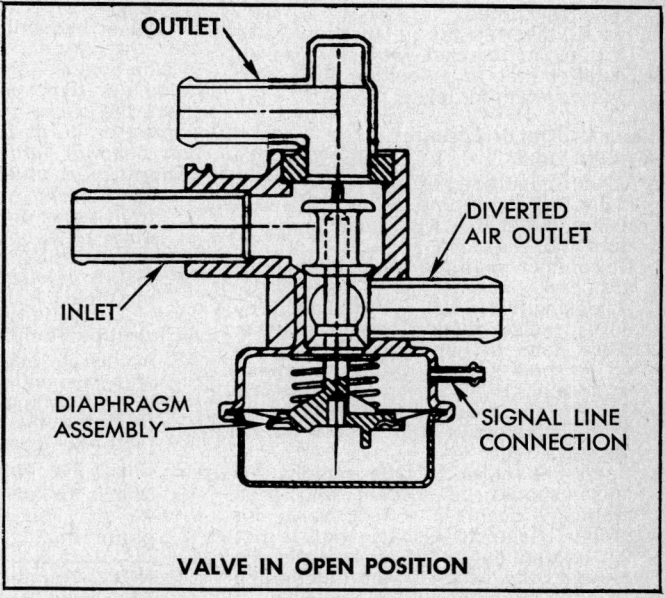

VALVE IN OPEN POSITION

Fig. 9 Typical diverter or air by-pass valve without pressure relief valve

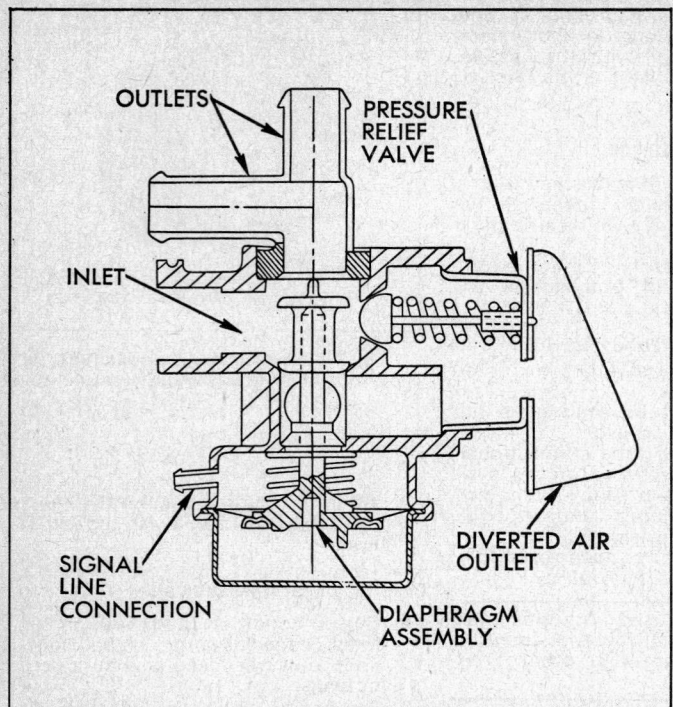

OUTLETS

PRESSURE RELIEF VALVE

INLET

SIGNAL LINE CONNECTION

DIAPHRAGM ASSEMBLY

DIVERTED AIR OUTLET

Fig. 10   Typical diverter or air by-pass valve with integral pressure relief valve

IN LINE

INJECTION TUBE

AIR MANIFOLD ASSEMBLY

CHECK VALVE

CHECK VALVE

V-8

AIR MANIFOLD ASSEMBLY

INJECTION TUBE

Fig. 11   Typical air manifold installations

signed to meet particular requirements of various engines; therefore, be sure to install the correct valve for the engine being serviced.

4. To replace a valve, disconnect vacuum signal line and valve exhaust hose(s).
5. Remove diverter or air by-pass valve from pump; also muffler from valve assembly, noting angle of attachment.
6. Install muffler to new valve at angle previously noted.
7. Install diverter or air by-pass valve to pump or bracket with new gasket.
8. Install outlet and vacuum lines and check system for leaks.

Mixture Control or Backfire By-Pass Valve:

1. Check condition of all lines, especially the signal line. A defective signal or outlet line will cause malfunctioning of the valve.
2. Disconnect pump-to-valve inlet hose at pump.
3. A leaking valve will be indicated by an air noise coming from the hose. Place palm of hand over hose; little or no pull with a gradual increase is normal. If an intermediate strong pull is felt or air noise is heard, the valve is defective and should be replaced.
4. Open and close throttle rapidly. Air noise should be evident and then gradually decrease. Check valve for proper usage. If a strong pull is not felt immediately or if air noise is not present, the valve is not functioning properly and should be replaced. A noisy valve should also be replaced.
5. To replace a valve, disconnect the sig-

nal line, air inlet and outlet hoses then remove valve.
6. Install new valve and connect air outlet, inlet and signal line hoses.

CAUTION: Although similar in appearance, these valves are designed to meet particular requirements of various engines and are not interchangeable.

Air Injection Tube:

There is no periodic service or inspection for the air injection tubes. However, whenever the cylinder head is removed from In Line engines, or whenever exhaust manifolds are removed from V8 engines, inspect the tubes for carbon build-up and warped or burnt tubes. Remove any carbon build-up with a wire brush. Warped or burnt tubes must be replaced.

1. To replace a tube, remove carbon from tubes and, using penetrating oil, work tubes out of cylinder head or exhaust manifold.
2. Install new tubes in cylinder head or manifold.

Air Injection Pump:

1. Accelerate engine to about 1500 rpm and observe air flow from hose(s). If air flow increases as engine is accelerated, the pump is operating satisfactorily. If not, proceed as follows:
2. Check for proper drive belt tension.
3. Check for leaky pressure relief valve. Air may be heard leaking with the pump running.

NOTE: The air pump is not completely noiseless. Under normal conditions noise rises in pitch as engine speed increases. To determine if excessive

noise is the fault of the system, operate the engine with the pump drive belt removed. If excessive noise does not exist with the belt removed, proceed as follows:

4. Check for proper installation of the relief valve silencer if so equipped.
5. Check for seized air pump.
6. Check hoses, tubes, air manifolds and all connections for leaks and proper routing.
7. Check carburetor air cleaner for proper installation.
8. Check air pump for proper mounting.
9. If none of the above conditions exists and the air pump has excessive noise, replace the pump.

Pressure Relief Valve

If the pressure relief valve is not functioning properly it should be replaced. The relief valve can be serviced separately only if incorporated in air pump, if relief valve is incorporated in the diverter valve the diverter valve has to be replaced.

AMERICAN MOTORS "ENGINE MOD" SYSTEM

This system controls exhaust emission levels by using composition cylinder head gaskets instead of steel gaskets and a special carburetor and distributor calibration. The carburetor incorporates idle limiters. The distributor centrifugal advance is calibrated to provide best performance and economy in the driving range and ignition timing is retarded only at idle speed (T.D.C.) to reduce exhaust emission levels at this slow engine speed. These engine modifications will result in a more complete combustion. Thermostatically controlled air cleaners are also used on most units to speed up engine warm-up.

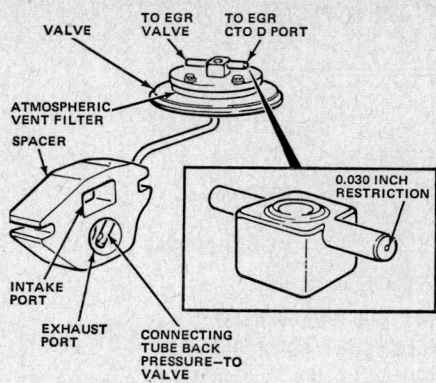

Fig. 11A Exhaust back pressure transducer sensor. (Typical)

AMERICAN MOTORS EXHAUST GAS RECIRCULATION (EGR)

NOTE: EGR valves used with exhaust back-pressure sensors have shorter and more tapered stems than those used without the sensor. The shorter stems are needed to match the EGR metering to back-pressure sensor operation.

The EGR system consists of a diaphragm actuated flow control valve (EGR valve), coolant temperature override switch, low temperature vacuum signal modulator, high temperature vacuum signal modulator and connecting hoses.

The purpose of the EGR system is to limit the formation of oxides of nitrogen (NOx) by diluting the fresh intake charge with a metered amount of exhaust gas, thereby reducing the peak temperatures of the burning gases in the engine combustion chambers.

EGR Valve

The EGR valve is mounted on a machined surace at the rear of the intake manifold on V-8 engines and on the side of the intake manifold on six cylinder en-

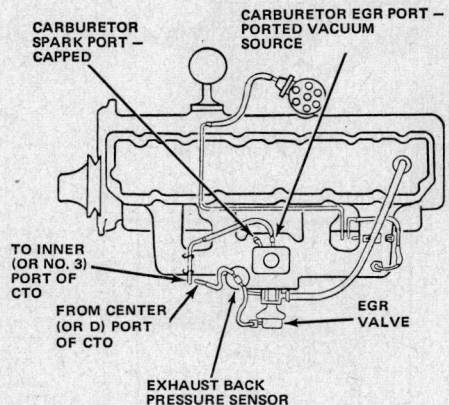

Fig. 11C EGR vacuum line routing. 6 cyl. with Air Guard

gines. The valve used with an automatic transmission is calibrated differently than the valve used with a manual transmission.

The valve is held in a normally closed position by a coiled spring located above the diaphragm. A special fitting is provided at the carburetor to route ported (above throttle) vacuum through hose connections to a fitting on the valve which is located above the diaphragm. A passage in the intake manifold directs exhaust gas from the exhaust crossover passage (V8 engine) or from below the riser area (six cylinder engine) to the EGR valve. When the diaphragm is actuated by vacuum, the valve opens and meters exhaust gas through another passage in the intake manifold to the floor of the manifold below the carburetor.

Coolant Temperature Override Switch

This switch is located at the coolant passage of the intake manifold (adjacent to oil filler tube) on a V8 engine or at the left side of the engine block (formerly the drain plug location) on a six cylinder engine. The outer part of the switch is open and not used. The inner port is connected by a hose to the EGR fitting at the carburetor. The center port is connected to the EGR valve.

When the coolant temperature is below 115° F (160° F on 304 CID with man. trans.), the center port of the switch is closed and no vacuum signal is applied to the EGR valve, therefore, no exhaust gas will flow through the valve. When the coolant temperature reaches 115° F (160° F on 304 CID with man. trans.), both the center and inner port of the switch are open and a vacuum signal is applied to the EGR valve. However, the vacuum signal to the EGR valve is subject to regulation by low and high temperature signal modulators.

Low Temperature Vacuum Signal Modulator

This unit is located at the left side of the front upper crossmember, just ahead of the radiator, on the same mounting bracket as the TCS ambient temperature override switch and is connected to the EGR vacuum signal hose. The modulator is open when ambient temperatures are below 60° F. This causes a weakened vacuum signal to the EGR valve and a resultant decrease in the amount of exhaust gas being recirculated.

High Temperature Vacuum Signal Modulator

This unit is located at the rear of the engine compartment and is connected to the EGR vacuum signal hose. The modulator opens when the underhood air temperature reaches 115° F and causes a weakened vacuum signal to the EGR valve. As a result, the amount of exhaust gas being recirculated is decreased.

Exhaust Back-Pressure Sensor

All six cylinder and some V8-304, 360 engines used on 1974 California vehicles are required to have an exhaust back-pressure sensor, Fig. 11A. This device consists of a diaphragm valve, a spacer and a metal tube. The EGR valve is mounted to the sensor spacer and is modulated by the sensor.

The EGR system, when equipped with a back-pressure sensor, obtains a vacuum signal at the carburetor spark port and not the EGR port. The vacuum signal

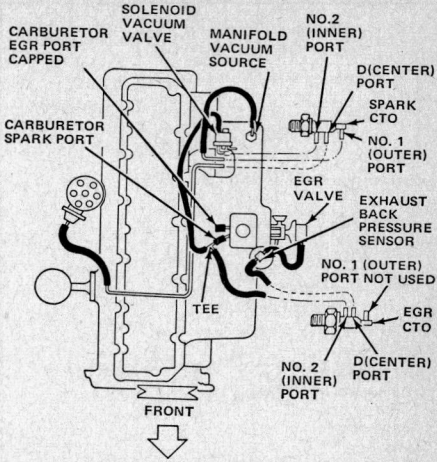

Fig. 11B EGR vacuum line routing. 6 cyl. less Air Guard

passes through the EGR CTO (Coolant Temperature Override) switch (when coolant temperature exceeds 115° F) to the valve portion of the sensor where it is modulated by exhaust back-pressure.

NOTE: The inlet nipple of the exhaust back-pressure sensor has a .030 inch restriction, Fig. 11A. The vacuum line from the EGR CTO must be connected to this nipple, Figs. 11B, 11C and 11D.

When exhaust back-pressure is relatively high, as during acceleration and some cruising conditions, exhaust back-pressure traveling through the metal tube overcomes spring tension on the diaphragm within the back-pressure sensor valve, and closes the valve atmospheric vent.

With the back-pressure sensor valve no longer vented to atmosphere, the vacuum signal now passes through the back-pressure sensor valve, and the EGR valve. When vacuum signals the EGR valve, exhaust gas recirculation commences.

When exhaust back-pressure is too low to overcome diaphragm spring tension, the vacuum signal is vented to atmosphere and does not pass through to the

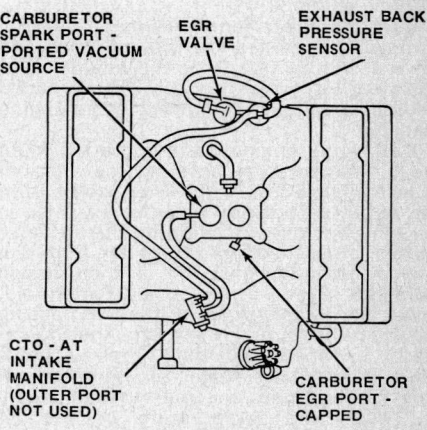

Fig. 11D EGR vacuum line routing. V8-304, 360

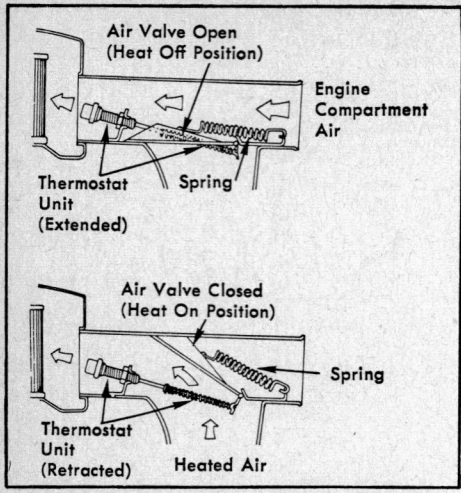

Fig. 12 Temperature operated duct and valve assembly

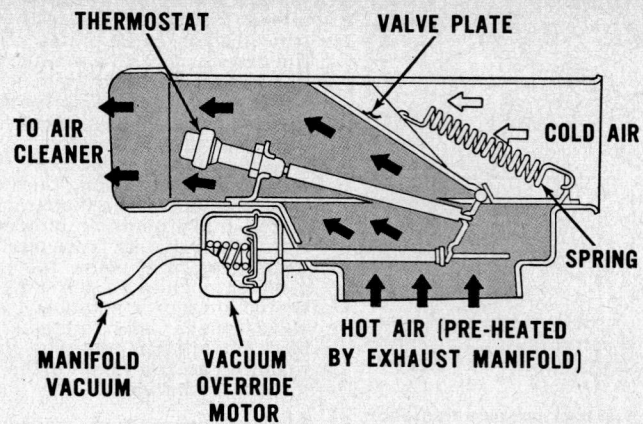

Fig. 13 Duct and valve assembly with vacuum override motor

EGR valve. With no vacuum signal applied to the EGR valve, exhaust gas does not re-circulate.

All six cylinder and some V8-304, 360 engines incorporate a steel restrictor plate under the exhaust back-pressure sensor. The restrictor plate limits the rate of EGR flow, thereby improving driveability. Note that gaskets are used on both sides of the plate.

The back-pressure sensor is not service-able and must be replaced if defective.

THERMOSTATIC CONTROLLED AIR CLEANER, TAC & AUTO-THERM AIR CLEANER SYSTEMS

American Motors Six & All Ford

Temperature Controlled

Carburetor air temperature is thermo-statically controlled by the air duct and valve assembly. Air from the engine com-partment, or heated air from the shrouded exhaust manifold is supplied to the engine Fig. 12.

During the engine warm-up period when the air temperature entering the air duct is less than 105° F, the thermostat is in the retracted position and the air valve is held in the closed position by the air valve spring, thus shutting off the air from the engine compartment. Air is then drawn from the shroud at the exhaust manifold.

As the temperature of the air passing the thermostat unit rises, the thermostat starts to open and pulls the air valve down. This allows cooler air from the en-gine compartment to enter the air clean-er. When the temperature of the air reaches 130° F, the air valve is in the open position so that only engine compartment air is allowed to enter the air cleaner.

Vacuum Controlled

Some Ford systems incorporate a vac-uum override motor, Fig. 13. This motor during cold acceleration periods provides additional air to carburetor. The decrease in intake manifold vacuum during acceler-ation causes the vacuum override motor to override the thermostat control, open-ing the system to both engine compart-ment air and heated air from the exhaust manifold shroud.

Yet another Ford application of same system uses a vacuum motor, Fig. 14, in-stalled on the perimeter of the air cleaner to take the place of the vacuum override motor. When the manifold vacuum is low, during heavy engine loading or high speed operation, a spring in the vacuum motor opens the motor valve plate into the air cleaner. This provides the maximum air supply for greater volumetric efficiency.

Thermostatically Controlled Vacuum Operated

A vacuum operated duct valve with a thermostatic bi-metal control, Fig. 15, is used on some installations. The valve in the duct assembly is in an open position when the engine is not operating. When the engine is operating at below normal operating temperature, manifold vacuum is routed through the bi-metal switch to the vacuum motor to close the duct valve allowing only heated air to enter the air cleaner. When the engine reaches normal operating temperature the bi-metal switch opens an air bleed which eliminates the vacuum and the duct valve opens allowing only cold air to enter the air cleaner. Dur-ing periods of acceleration the duct valve will open regardless of temperature due to the loss of manifold vacuum.

The Ford V8-428 Police engine incor-porates a thermostatic choke bleed valve in the air cleaner. The bleed valve allows cold air to be blended with the hot air from the choke stove at underhood tem-peratures below 50 degrees F.

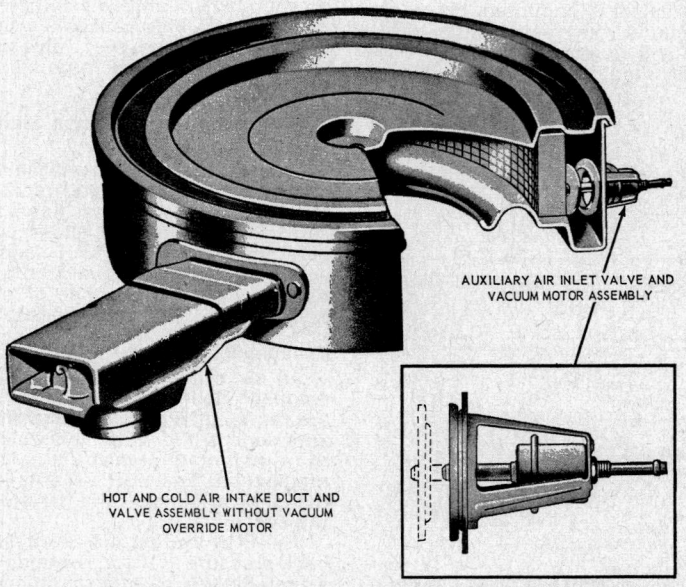

Fig. 14 Air cleaner with auxiliary air inlet valve and vacuum motor

American Motors V8 & All General Motors

Figs. 16 thru 19—Carburetor air temperature is controlled by a pair of doors, located in the air cleaner snorkel, which channel either pre-heated or under hood air to the carburetor.

Pre-heated air is obtained by passing under hood air through ducts surrounding the exhaust manifold, causing it to pick up heat from the manifold surface. The heated air is then drawn up through a pipe to the air cleaner snorkel.

Under hood air is picked up at the air cleaner snorkel in the conventional manner.

The two air mixing doors work together so that as one opens, the other closes and vice versa. When under hood temperature is below approximately 90 deg. F., the cold air door closes, causing the hot air door to open. Hot air from the exhaust manifold stove is then drawn into the carburetor. As the under hood temperature increases, the cold air door begins to open until the temperature reaches approximately 115° to 130 deg. F, at which time the cold air door is fully open and the hot air door is fully closed.

The doors are controlled by a vacuum motor mounted on the air cleaner snorkel. This motor, in turn, is controlled by a sensor inside the air cleaner which regulates the amount of vacuum present in the vacuum motor according to air cleaner temperature. Whenever manifold vacuum drops below 5-8 inches, depending on the unit, the diaphragm spring in the motor will open the cold air door wide in order to provide maximum air flow.

The vacuum motor and control door assembly in the left snorkel on outside air induction units does not have a sensor and is controlled only by manifold vacuum. This snorkel remains closed until full throttle is obtained. With manifold vacuum at 6-8 inches, the door will open, allowing maximum air flow.

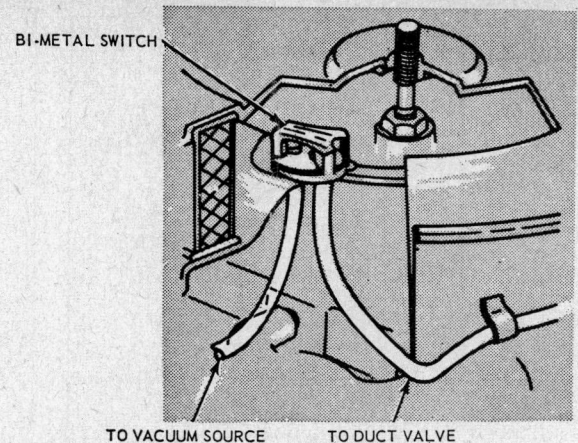

BI-METAL SWITCH

TO VACUUM SOURCE TO DUCT VALVE

Fig. 15 Vacuum operated duct and valve assembly

GENERAL MOTORS C.C.S.

Controlled Combustion System

The C.C.S. system, Fig. 16, is designed to keep the air entering the carburetor at approximately 100 deg. F. or above so that the carburetor can be calibrated to operate leaner without affecting engine performance, provide improved fuel economy, eliminate carburetor icing and improve engine warm-up.

Because of the leaner carburetor calibration, the ignition timing at idle must be retarded. This is done by means of a "ported" vacuum advance, with the vacuum take-off just above the throttle plate(s), so that there is no vacuum advance at closed throttle but there is advance as soon as the throttle is cracked slightly. Ignition timing is set at or near TDC and centrifugal advance does not start until approximately 1000 rpm.

Thermo Vacuum Switch

Because of the increased possibility of engine overheating at idle with the C.C.S. calibration, the thermo vacuum switch Fig. 20 is added to the system on some engines. This switch senses engine coolant temperature and, if temperature reaches 220 deg. F., the switch valve moves to allow manifold vacuum to reach the distributor to advance the timing and allow the engine to run cooler.

Idle Stop Solenoid

Most cars equipped with the Controlled Combustion System have an idle stop solenoid mounted on the carburetor, Fig. 21, to prevent engine operation after the engine is shut off (dieseling). Dieseling is prevalent with the CCS system, especially with automatic transmission because of

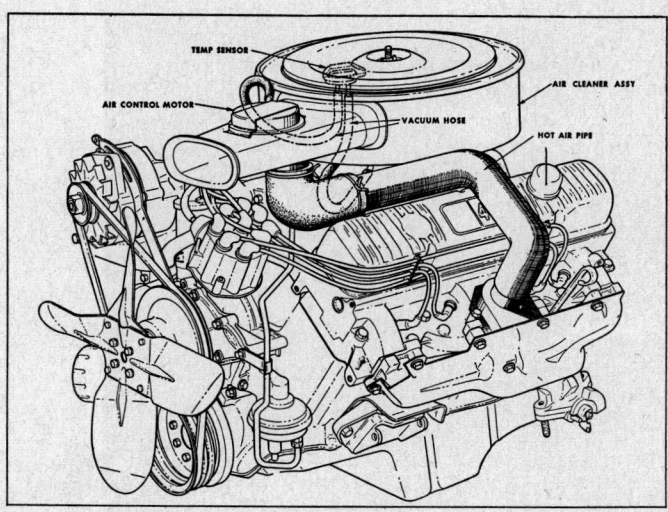

Fig. 16   Controlled Combustion System installed on a V8 engine

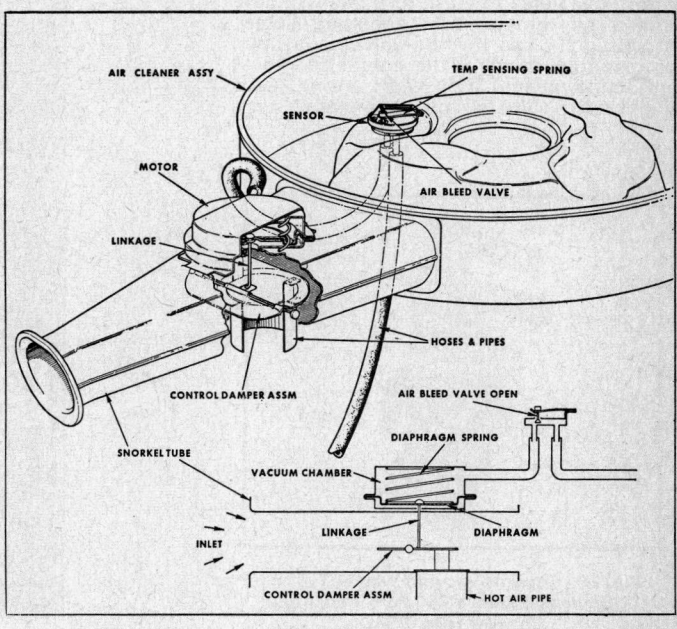

Fig. 17   Cold air door open

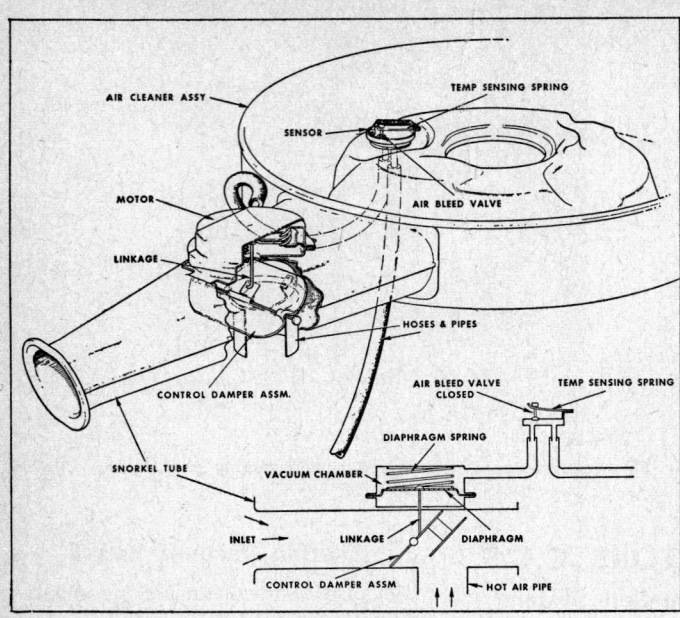

Fig. 18 Hot air door open

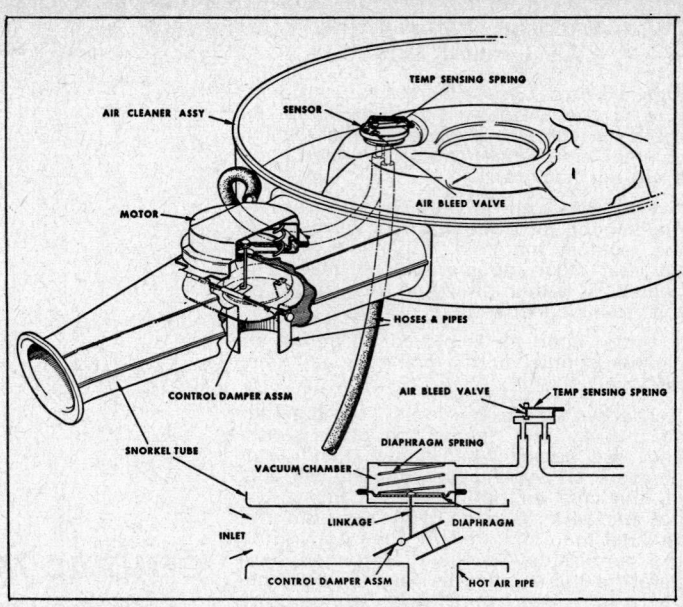

Fig. 19 Cold and hot air doors both partially open

the retarded ignition timing and higher operating temperature of the engine. Idle speed is higher with automatic transmissions.

The solenoid eliminates this dieseling by fully closing the throttle valve(s) when the ignition is turned off.

When the ignition switch is turned on, the solenoid coil is activated and the plunger is driven to its full extended position. The plunger acts on the throttle valve lever and sets the throttle valve(s) in a position to achieve specified idle rpm.

When the ignition is turned off, the solenoid is de-energized and the plunger retracts into the solenoid, causing the throttle valve(s) to close to a position controlled by the low idle adjusting screw. At this point the throttle valve(s) is open only enough to allow the engine to run at a much lower rpm. This lower setting keeps the throttle valve(s) from completely clos-

ing and scuffing the throttle bore(s).

The lower idle speed setting is made with a set screw when the solenoid is electrically disconnected. The setting for normal idle speed is adjusted, with the solenoid energized, through the hex screw in the plunger and/or by repositioning the solenoid in its mounting clamp.

NOTE: To set the solenoid while starting a hot engine, the accelerator pedal must be depressed approximately one third its

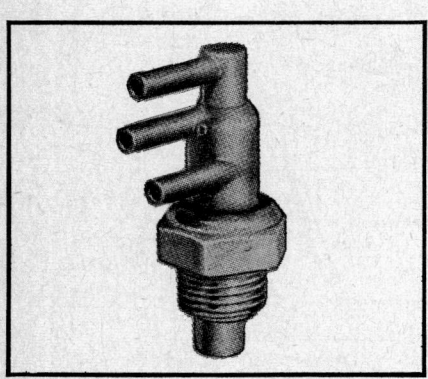

Fig. 20 Thermo vacuum switch. Typical of General Motors CCS, Ford IMCO and Chrysler NOx, OSAC (temperature sensing valve)

Fig. 21 Idle stop solenoid

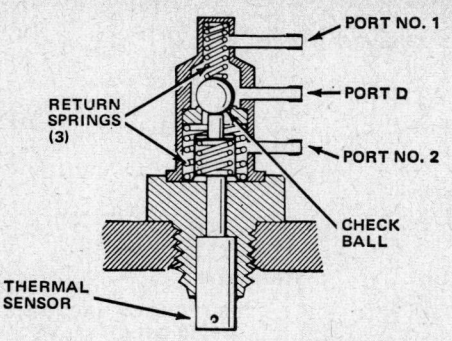

Fig. 21A Coolant temperature override switch. American Motors

travel. When starting a cold engine, however, the accelerator must be fully depressed to set both the choke and the solenoid.

CAUTION: Unburned gases emit undesirable amounts of hydro-carbons, predominantly during idle operation. One would naturally think that if the idle mixture is

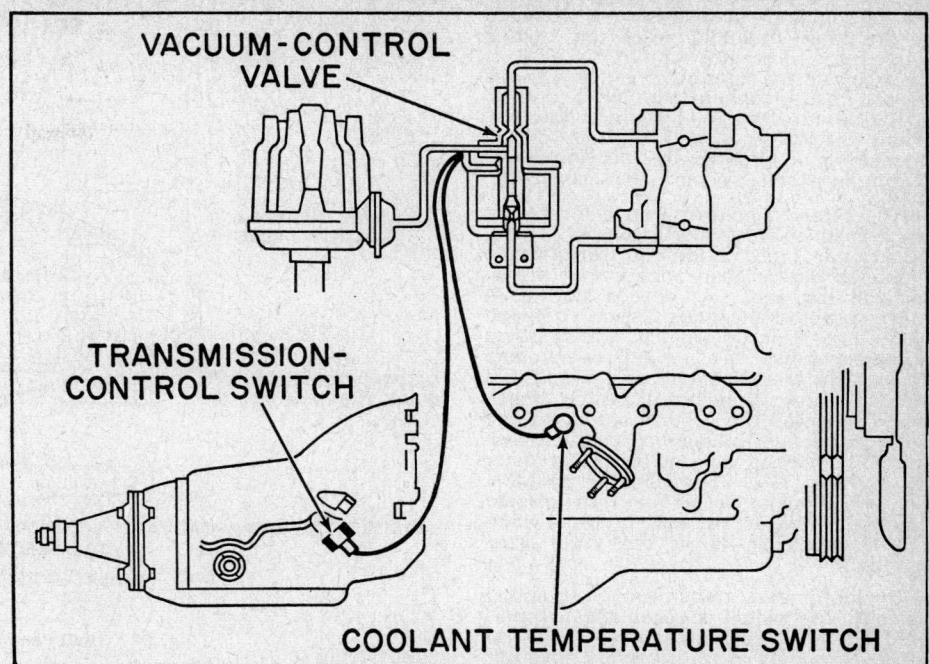

Fig. 22 Typical T.C.S. emission control

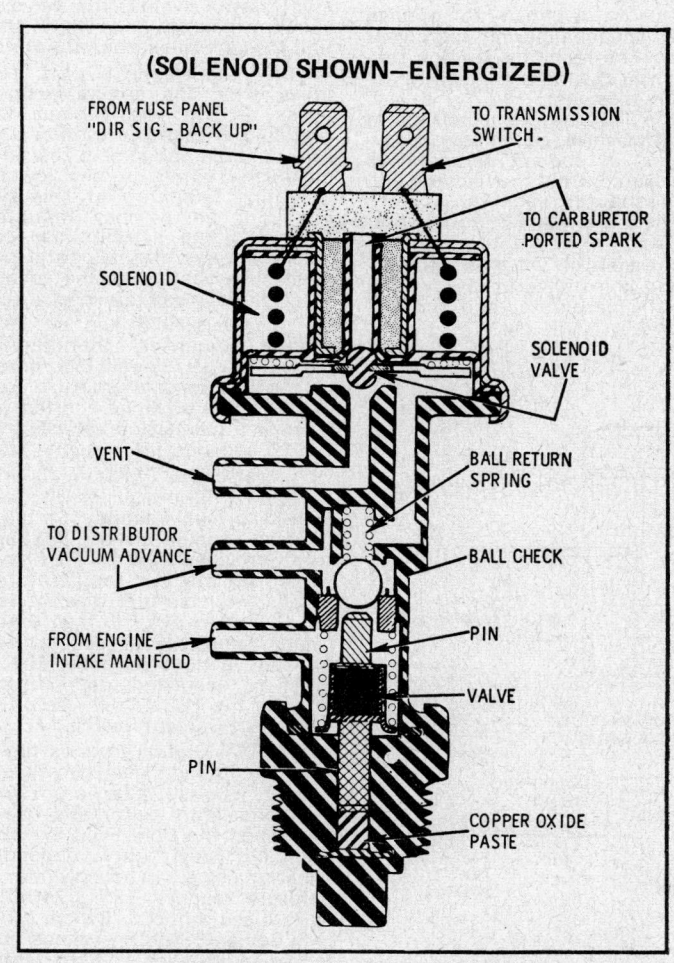

Fig. 23 TVS-TCS combination valve

made as lean as possible, exhaust emission would be reduced. This is true up to a point. However, if the idle mixture is made too lean, the hydro-carbon content may increase above acceptable limits. The amount of carbon monoxide exceeds acceptable limits when idle mixtures are too rich. Conversely, the hydro-carbon content exceeds acceptable limits if the idle mixture is too "lean". Consequently, proper idle adjustment is essential. Detailed carburetor setting instructions are given in the carburetor chapter.

TRANSMISSION CONTROLLED SPARK (TCS)

American Motors

This system is designed to provide vacuum spark advance during high gear operation and certain engine conditions. The resultant is a lower peak combustion pressure and temperature during the power stroke, significantly reducing exhaust emissions.

Basically the system incorporates an ambient temperature override switch, solenoid vacuum valve, solenoid control switch and in some systems a coolant temperature override switch.

The ambient temperature override switch, used on 1971-73 vehicles, senses ambient temperatures and completes the electrical circuit from the battery to the solenoid vacuum valve when ambient temperatures are above 63° F.

The solenoid vacuum valve is attached to the intake manifold. When the valve is energized, carburetor ported vacuum is blocked and the distributor vacuum line is vented to atmosphere through a port in the valve, resulting in no vacuum advance. When the valve is de-energized, ported vacuum is applied to the distributor resulting in normal vacuum advance.

The solenoid control switch, located at the transmission, opens or closes in relation to car speed automatic transmission equipped cars or gear range manual transmission equipped. At speeds above 34 MPH on automatic transmission equipped cars, high gear on manual transmission equipped cars, the switch opens and breaks the ground circuit to the solenoid vacuum valve. The control switch closes and completes the ground circuit to the solenoid vacuum valve on automatic transmission equipped vehicles at speeds under 25 MPH on 1971-73 models or 34 MPH on 1974 models. On manual transmission equipped vehicles, the switch closes when the transmission is in the lower gear ranges.

On automatic transmission equipped vehicles, the switch is automatically operated by the speedometer gear speed on 1971-73 models or transmission governor oil pressure on 1974 models. On manual transmission vehicles, the switch is manually operated by the shifter shaft.

The coolant temperature override switch, Fig. 21A, is threaded into the thermostat housing on V8 engines or into the left rear side of the cylinder block on six cylinder engines. Its purpose is to improve driveability during the warm-up period by providing full distributor vacuum advance until the engine coolant has reached 160° F. on V8 engines or 115° F on 1974 California six cylinder engines. The switch incorporates a thermal unit which reacts to coolant temperatures to route either intake manifold or carburetor ported vacuum to the distributor vacuum advance diaphragm.

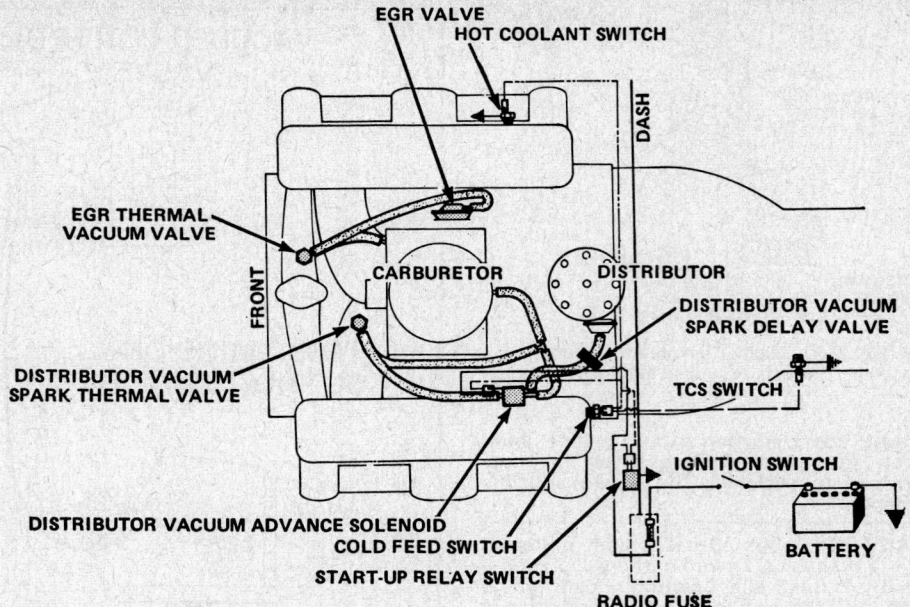

Fig. 24   1973 Pontiac mid-year TCS system

General Motors

This system is designed to provide vacuum spark advance during high gear operation only. The resulting ignition timing in the lower gears significantly reduces exhaust emissions.

Basically, the T.C.S. system consists of a vacuum control valve, transmission control switch and a coolant temperature switch. The valve controls the vacuum signal to the distributor vacuum advance unit in response to a signal from either switch, Fig. 22.

The vacuum control valve is of solenoid design and is installed in the vacuum line between the carburetor and the distributor. When energized by the transmission control switch, the valve blocks the vacuum source and vents the advance unit through the carburetor air horn.

When the engine is cold, and in some units when the engine temperature exceeds 210°F., the coolant temperature switch overrides the system and provides full manifold vacuum to the advance unit, advancing timing in turn lowering engine operating temperature. This switch operates through a relay mounted on the firewall. Some systems use combination TVS-TCS valve, Fig. 23, to provide system over-riding vacuum to the advance unit.

Figs. 24 and 24A—A TCS system change on mid-year 1973 and all 1974 Pontiac models (vehicles manufactured after March 15, 1973) will incorporate the following revisions: A Start-Up Relay Switch supplies full advance (ported advance on manual transmission vehicles) in any gear for 20 seconds after engine start.

A Distributor Vacuum Spark Thermal Valve on 1973 models or Distributor Spark-EGR Thermal Vacuum Switch on 1974 models, sensing air-fuel mixture temperature, provides full advance in any gear when the mixture temperature is below 62° F. When air-fuel mixture temperature rises above 62° F., the thermal valve closes, shutting off vacuum, in turn to provide vacuum advance, the distributor must be energized, depending on condition, by the TCS Switch, Cold Feed Switch or the Hot Coolant Switch.

The TCS Switch grounds the distributor solenoid in high gear on all applications and in reverse gear on 1974 vehicles equipped with automatic transmissions only when the Cold Feed Switch is closed. The Cold Feed Switch, depending on application, closes when cylinder head temperature reaches 125°, 140° or 155° F. Regardless of TCS Switch position, the Hot Coolant Switch grounds the distributor solenoid when coolant temperature is over 240° F.

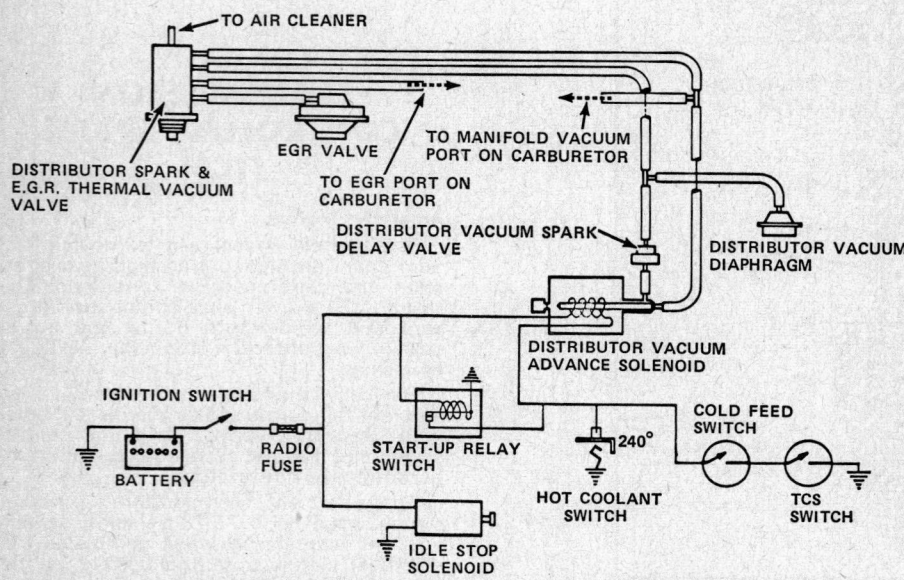

Fig. 24A   1974 Pontiac TCS-EGR system. V8 (Typical)

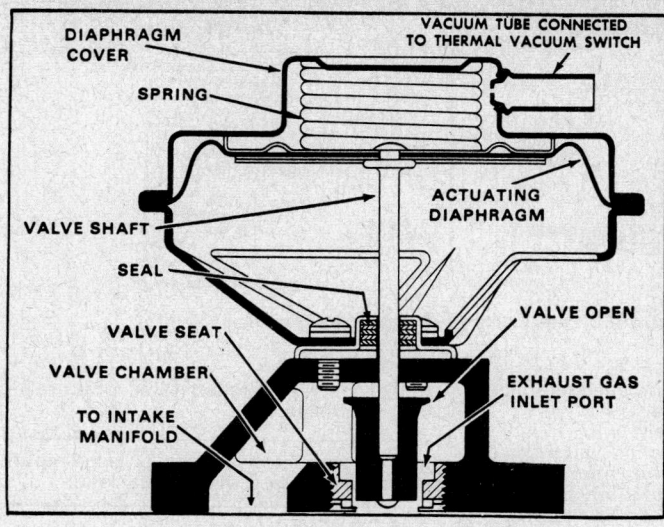

Fig. 25   Single diaphragm EGR valve cross section

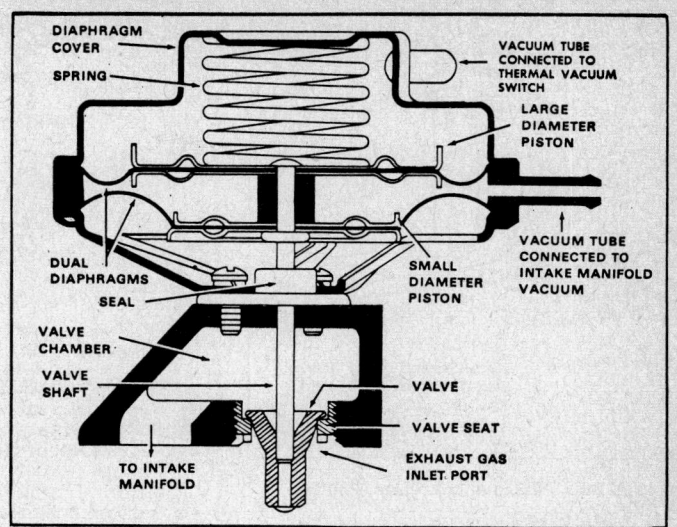

Fig. 25A   Dual diaphragm EGR valve cross section

On some models, a Distributor Vacuum Spark Delay Valve is installed between the distributor solenoid and distributor. This valve restricts the rate of initial vacuum supplied to the distributor, full vacuum will be supplied gradually.

The Time Relay is an electrical on-off type switch. When the coil is energized, it starts heating the bi-metal strip and opening the normally closed relay points within 20 seconds after the ignition switch is turned on. If for some reason the ignition key is left in the "ON" position and ve-

hicle is not started within 20 seconds and the relay completes its "countdown", vacuum advance will be block off until the relay has cooled off.

NOTE: Once the relay has run one cycle (about 20 seconds), after the key has been turned on, the relay must cool off before it will reactivate, even if the key is switched "OFF" and then turned "ON" again.

GENERAL MOTORS C.E.C.

Combined Emission Control System

This system is designed to provide vacuum spark advance during high gear operation only, as does the T.C.S. system, but the C.E.C. solenoid vacuum switch also regulates curb idle and high gear deceleration throttle positions, further reducing emissions.

The C.E.C. system consists of a vacuum control solenoid valve, transmission control switch, coolant temperature switch and a time-delay relay.

When the solenoid is in the non-energized position, vacuum to the distributor vacuum advance unit is shut off and the distributor is vented to the atmosphere through a filter at the opposite end of the solenoid. When the solenoid is energized

Fig. 25C   Exhaust back pressure transducer. Pontiac

Fig. 25B   Exhaust back pressure transducer. Oldsmobile

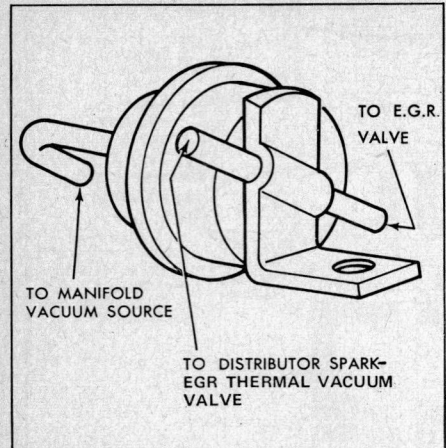

Fig. 25D   Vacuum bias valve. Pontiac

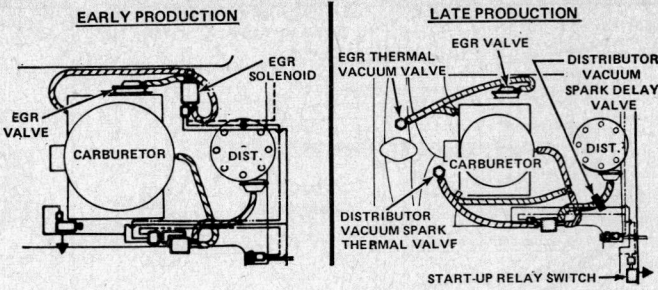

Fig. 25E   Early & late 1973 Pontiac EGR systems

by one of the switches or the relay, the vacuum port is uncovered and the plunger is seated at the opposite end, shutting off the clean air vent. This routes vacuum to the distributor. The solenoid is energized in high gear by the transmission switch. The coolant temperature switch overrides the transmission switch to energize the solenoid and provide vacuum advance below 82° F., for 1969-72 vehicles and 93° for 1973-74 vehicles. The time-delay relay is incorporated into the circuit to energize the solenoid for approximately 15 seconds on 1969-72 vehicles and 20 seconds on 1973-74 vehicles, after the ignition key is turned on.

When the solenoid plunger is in the non-energized position, it allows the throttle to close to the curb idle setting. When the solenoid plunger is in the energized position, it keeps the throttle open to the high gear deceleration position which controls hydrocarbon emission.

GENERAL MOTORS S.C.S.

Speed Controlled Spark

This system is essentially the same as the T.C.S. system except that here the vacuum spark advance is controlled by the vehicles speed rather than the gear position of the transmission.

The S.C.S. system consists of a vacuum advance solenoid valve, a speed sensing switch and a temperature switch. The vacuum control valve is installed in the vacuum line between the carburetor and the distributor. When energized, this valve cuts off vacuum to the distributor. The speed sensing switch de-energizes the vacuum control valve at speeds above 38 mph allowing normal vacuum spark advance. Abnormal operating temperatures (below 85 degrees F and above 220 degrees F) will cause the temperature switch to de-energize the vacuum control valve, over-riding the speed sensing switch.

Testing

To test the S.C.S. system, leave the distributor vacuum hose connected, be certain the engine temperature is between 95

and 230 degrees F, and proceed as follows:
1. Raise the rear wheels.
2. Start engine and shift into Drive.
3. Accelerate engine while watching the timing mark on the harmonic balancer. Timing should advance when the car speed exceeds 38 mph.

Trouble Shooting

Full Vacuum Advance at all Speeds:
1. Blown fuse.
2. Wire disconnected at vacuum control valve.
3. Wire disconnected at speed sensor.
4. Faulty speed sensor.
5. Faulty temperature switch.

No Vacuum Advance at Speeds Over 38 mph:
1. Vacuum lines reversed at vacuum control valve.
2. Foreign matter in vacuum control valve.
3. Distributor vacuum line broken or disconnected.
4. Faulty vacuum control valve.
5. Speed sensor switch or wire shorted.

GENERAL MOTORS E.G.R.

Exhaust Gas Recirculation

Figs. 25 and 25A—This system is used to reduce oxides of nitrogen emissions at the engine's exhaust. This is accomplished by introducing exhaust gases into the intake manifold at throttle positions other than idle. It consists of an E.G.R. valve mounted on a special intake manifold. The exhaust gas intake port of the E.G.R. valve is connected to the intake manifold exhaust crossover channels where it can pick up exhaust gases.

As the throttle valves are opened and the engine speeds up, vacuum is applied to a vacuum diaphragm in the E.G.R. valve through a connecting tube. When the vacuum reaches approximately 3" hg., the diaphragm moves upward against spring tension and is in the full-up position at approximately 7" to 8" hg. of vacuum. This diaphragm is connected by a shaft to a valve which closes off the exhaust gas port. As the diaphragm moves up, it opens the valve in the exhaust gas port which allows exhaust gas to be pulled into the intake manifold and enter the cylinders. The exhaust gas port must be closed during idle as the mixing of exhaust gases with the fuel air mixture at this point would cause rough running.

The dual diaphragm EGR valve, Fig. 25A, is designed to provide increased ex-

haust gas recirculation rates when engine loads increase.

NOTE: Manifold vacuum is used as the signal to indicate the engine load.

The valve is similar to the single diaphragm valve except that a second diaphragm has been added to the valve and is connected to the upper diaphragm, with a spacer thus both diaphragms move together. A manifold vacuum signal is applied to the volume between the two diaphragms. The upper diaphragm has a larger diameter piston than the lower diaphragm, therefore the load caused by the manifold vacuum between the two diaphragms aids the spring load. Thus as the engine load increases and manifold vacuum decreases the combined load of the spring and the vacuum chamber are reduced allowing the valve to open further for a given EGR vacuum signal.

Therefore, for high intake manifold vacuums (such as cruising), the opening is less than for low manifold vacuums obtained during accelerations. The valve now is capable of providing more recirculation on accelerations where loads are higher and the tendency to produce NOx is greater.

Exhaust Back Pressure Transducer Valve

Figs. 25B and 25C.—This valve, used on some 1974 California vehicles, modulates EGR flow according to engine load. The device consists of a diaphragm valve, a spacer and a metal tube.

The EGR system, when equipped with a back pressure transducer valve, obtains a vacuum signal at the carburetor spark port and not at the EGR port. This vacuum is modulated by the transducer and, in turn activates the EGR valve.

When exhaust back-pressure is relatively high, as during acceleration and some cruising conditions, exhaust back-pressure traveling through the metal tube overcomes spring tension on the diaphragm within the back-pressure transducer valve, and closes the valve atmospheric vent.

With the back-pressure transducer valve no longer vented to atmosphere, the vacuum signal now passes through the back-pressure transducer valve, and the EGR valve. When vacuum signals the EGR valve, exhaust gas recirculation commences.

When exhaust back-pressure is too low to overcome diaphragm spring tension, the vacuum signal is vented to atmosphere and does not pass through to the EGR valve. With no vacuum signal applied to the EGR valve, exhaust gas does not re-circulate.

Vacuum Bias Valve

Fig. 25D—This valve, used on some 1974 Pontiac vehicles, California models, is located between the EGR valve and the distributor spark-EGR thermal vacuum valve. At high manifold vacuum conditions (such as cruising), the VBV decreases EGR flow and in turn, acts to reduce surge. When NOx formation is high and manifold vacuum is low as during acceleration, the VBV does not reduce EGR flow.

Fig. 25E—An EGR system change on all mid-year 1973 V8 and 1974 six cylinder Pontiac models (vehicles manufactured after March 15, 1973) will incorporate a new EGR Thermal Vacuum Valve which senses engine coolant temperature. This thermal valve, located between the carburetor and EGR valve, controls vacuum to the EGR valve. When coolant temperature is below 95° F. on 1973 models or 100° F. on 1974 models, the thermal valve isolates the EGR valve from the vacuum source, therefore eliminating exhaust gas recirculation. When coolant temperature is above 95° F. on 1973 models or 100° F. on 1974 models, the thermal valve opens and allows vacuum to actuate the EGR valve, allowing ported recirculation.

Fig. 24A—On 1974 Pontiac vehicles equipped with V8 engines, the EGR Thermal Vacuum Valve and the Distributor Spark Thermal vacuum Valve is incorporated into one assembly. This Distributor Spark-EGR Thermal Vacuum Valve senses air-fuel mixture temperature. This thermal valve is located between the EGR Valve and its vacuum source. The valve prevents actuation of the EGR valve when air-fuel mixture temperature is below 62° F. When air-fuel mixture temperature exceeds 62° F., the valve opens and allows vacuum to activate the EGR valve.

The E.G.R. valve cannot be disassembled and no actual service is required on it. However, it can be checked for proper operation as follows:

All Except 1973 Mid-Year & 1974 Pontiac EGR System

1. Check the exhaust gas valve shaft for movement by opening the throttle to 1200-1500 rpm. The shaft should move upward and return to its original position when the engine speed is allowed to drop to idle.
2. An outside vacuum source can be connected to the vacuum supply port in the top of the E.G.R. valve. The valve shaft should reach the top of its travel at 7" to 10" hg. of vacuum and the vacuum should not leak down.
3. If the E.G.R. valve does not operate correctly, it must be replaced.

1973 Mid-Year & 1974 Pontiac EGR System

1. With engine at operating temperature, remove air cleaner. Open throttle part way, release throttle and observe EGR valve diaphragm movement through cut away portion on inboard side. The EGR valve should open with throttle opening.
2. If no diaphragm movement is observed, insure that vacuum hoses are properly connected. If so, using a vacuum gauge, check for vacuum at hose connected to the EGR valve. If vacuum is present, the EGR valve is faulty and must be replaced.
3. If no vacuum was present at EGR hose, check for vacuum at thermal valve side of hose running from carburetor. If vacuum is present, the interconnecting hose or the EGR valve may be plugged, if there is no obstruction.
4. If no vacuum is present at thermal valve side of hose running from carburetor, the hose between the carburetor and thermal valve may be obstructed or the carburetor is faulty.

G. M. CURB IDLE SETTING PROCEDURES

C.C.S., T.C.S., T.V.S., & C.E.C. Systems

NOTE: This adjustment must be made with the engine at normal operating temperature. This is particularly important on engines equipped with a thermo vacuum switch.

1. Disconnect fuel tank line from vapor canister.
2. Disconnect distributor vacuum hose at distributor and plug hose.
3. Set dwell and timing (in that order) at specified RPM.
4. Adjust carburetor speed screw to specified RPM in tune-up charts in car chapters. If equipped with C.E.C. *DO NOT ADJUST SOLENOID SCREW*, see Note. C.E.C. Valve adjustment is to be made only after replacement of the solenoid, major carburetor overhaul. or removal of the throttle body. In any of these cases, adjustment should be made as follows:
   a. With slow idle speed set to specified RPM, manually extend C.E.C. Valve plunger to contact throttle lever.
   b. Adjust plunger length to obtain the proper engine RPM as listed in *Tune-Up Specifications Chart*.
5. With auto. trans. in Park and manual trans. in Neutral, adjust fast idle speed. *Refer to Carburetor Specifications Charts and procedures.*

CHRYSLER C.A.P.

Cleaner Air Package

The Cleaner Air Package is in addition to the Positive Crankcase Ventilation (PCV). The PCV device is designed to control the emission of hydrocarbon vapors from the crankcase, whereas the Cleaner Air Package controls the emission of hydrocarbon vapors (unburned gasoline) and carbon monoxide in the vehicle exhaust.

The Cleaner Air Package is engineered to continuously control carburetion and ignition at the best settings for performance and combustion during all driving conditions. These adjustments keep unburned gasoline and carbon monoxide in the exhaust at a minimum concentration.

Only three special components are involved in the CAP installation, Fig. 26. The carburetor and distributor have been re-designed and a new component—the Vacuum Advance Control Valve—has been added. In addition, some cooling system components have been changed to handle the increased heat rejection at idle and low speed.

Special Carburetor and Ignition

The carburetor is specially calibrated to provide leaner mixtures at idle and low

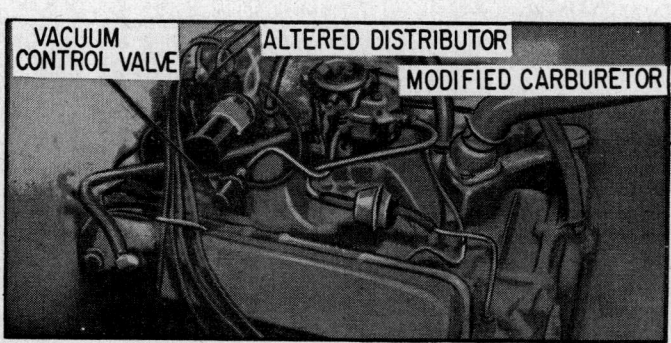

Fig. 26 Chrysler's Cleaner Air Package (CAP)

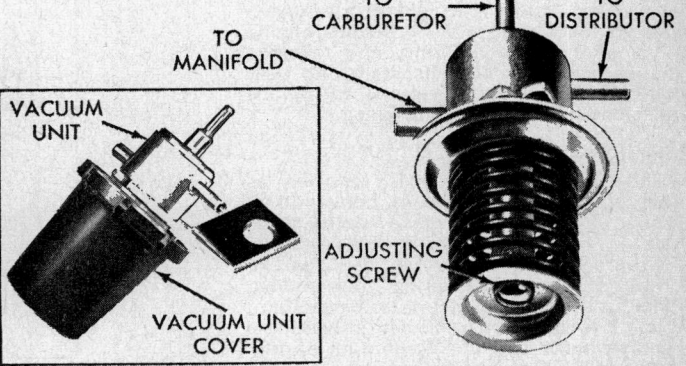

Fig. 27 Distributor vacuum advanced control valve, deceleration valve

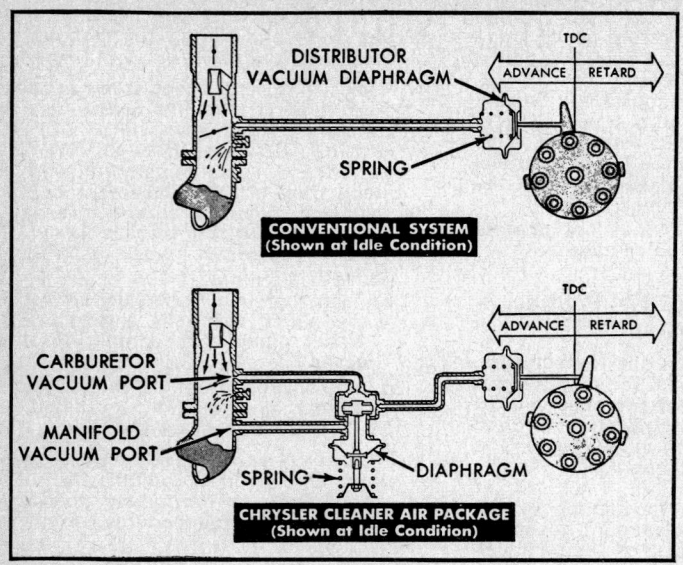

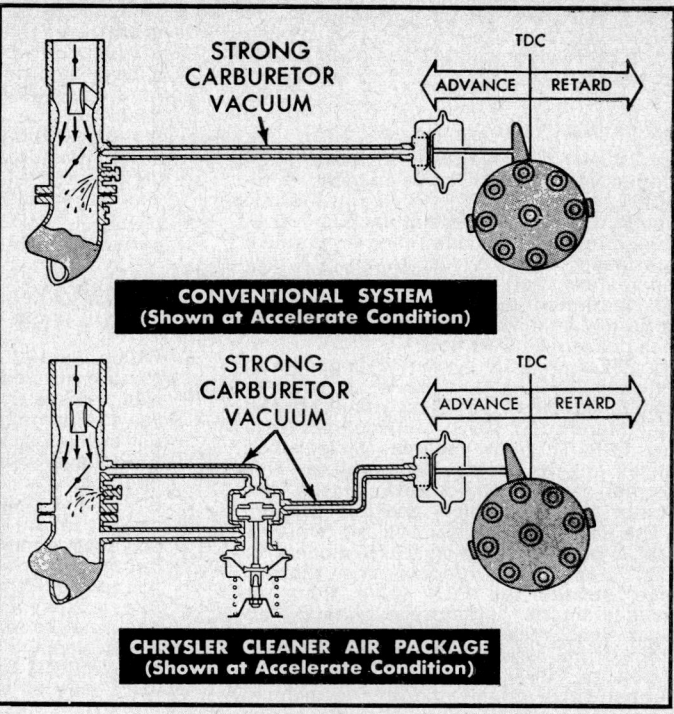

Fig. 28   Engine idle condition

Fig. 29   During acceleration

speed operation. The distributor is designed to give retarded timing at idle. The vacuum advance control valve, in conjunction with the distributor, provides advanced timing during deceleration.

CAP idle timing for all engines is retarded instead of advanced. Exhaust emission is reduced at idle by using leaner air/fuel mixtures, increased engine speed, and retarded ignition timing. The higher air flow at this idle condition approximates the desirable conditions of cruise. CAP, therefore, is designed to operate with late timing during idle, and with conventional spark advance during acceleration and cruise.

Vacuum Advance Control Valve, 1969 6-170 with Std. Trans. & 1969 V8-426 Hemi

Early ignition of the air/fuel mixture is needed during deceleration to provide the most efficient combustion and reduced exhaust emissions. The vacuum advance control valve provides that additional spark advance during deceleration. The vacuum advance control valve is connected by vacuum hoses to the carburetor, to the intake manifold, and to the distributor vacuum chamber, Fig. 27.

Carburetor vacuum and manifold vacuum act on the vacuum advance control valve. From these two signals, the vacuum advance control valve senses engine speed and load conditions, and relays a vacuum signal to the distributor to vary spark timing when necessary to reduce emissions to an acceptable level.

Engine Idle, Fig. 28

The initial idle timing is retarded as much as 15 degrees from conventional timing. The vacuum advance control valve does not affect timing at idle because the distributor vacuum chamber receives the same vacuum signal as in the conventional system, namely, carburetor vacuum. At idle it is not strong enough to overcome the distributor vacuum diaphragm spring.

Manifold vacuum acts on the vacuum control valve diaphragm, but is not strong enough to overcome the vacuum control valve spring. So the spring holds the vacuum control valve closed to manifold vacuum and open the low carburetor vacuum.

Acceleration, Fig. 29

During acceleration and cruise, manifold vacuum is not strong enough to actuate the CAP control valve. Thus the CAP system operates in the same manner as the conventional system. The throttle blade opens enough to permit the distributor vacuum advance to function, and spark timing is advanced according to the amount of vacuum created by the pumping action of the pistons.

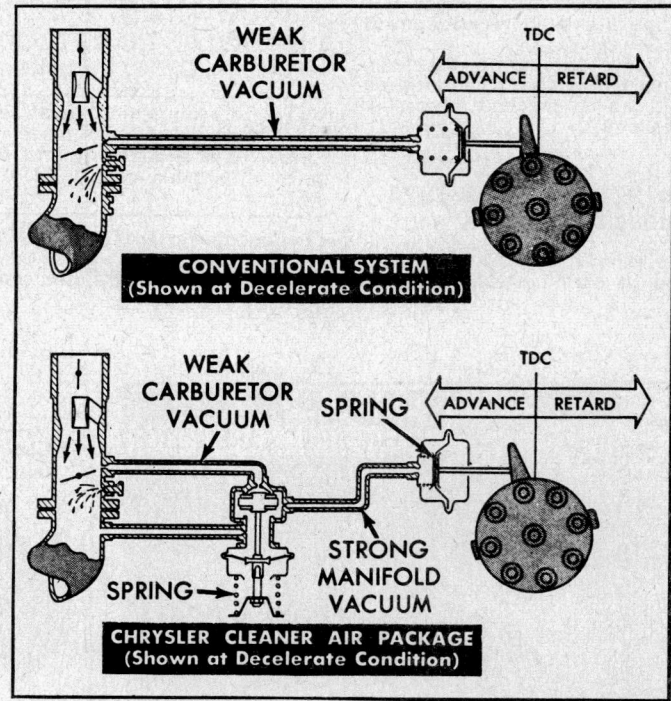

Fig. 30   During deceleration

Deceleration, Fig. 30

The conventional system provides the highest emissions under deceleration conditions. Carburetor vacuum is too weak to overcome the distributor advance diaphragm spring.

Manifold vacuum is at its strongest under deceleration conditions. Therefore, the CAP system uses manifold vacuum rather than carburetor vacuum to control spark timing.

Manifold vacuum is strong enough to overcome the vacuum advance control valve spring and the distributor vacuum diaphragm spring, moving spark timing to the maximum advance condition.

CHRYSLER C.A.S.

Cleaner Air System

This system employs higher inlet air temperature, higher idle speeds, retarded ignition timing, leaner carburetor mixtures and lower compression to reduce exhaust emissions, Fig. 31.

Heated Air System

Used on most 1970-74 Chrysler engines, this system uses a thermostatically controlled air cleaner to maintain an inlet air temperature of 95 to 105 deg. F. Temperature is controlled by intake manifold vacuum, a temperature sensor and a vacuum diaphragm which operates the heat control door in the air cleaner snorkel.

A vacuum hose connects the base of the carburetor to one side of the sensor. Another hose connects the other side of the sensor to the vacuum diaphragm.

The sensor contains a bimetallic strip which controls a small air valve. This valve controls the amount of vacuum to be applied to the diaphragm.

When the temperature at the sensor is below 95 deg. F, the valve is closed and manifold vacuum is applied to the diaphragm, lifting the heat control door. This allows heated air from the exhaust manifold stove to enter the air cleaner.

When the temperature at the sensor rises above 105 deg. F, the valve in the sensor opens and decreases the vacuum at the diaphragm and the spring in the diaphragm housing pushes the heat control down, closing off the air flow from the stove and opening the snorkel to outside air.

Since the diaphragm is opposed by a spring, it requires not less than 5"Hg. to lift the heat control door off the floor of the snorkel and not greater than 9"Hg. to raise the door to the top of the snorkel.

Under hard acceleration when intake manifold vacuum drops sharply, the spring forces the heat control door to the bottom of the snorkel, closing off the hot air and admitting cooler under hood air to eliminate any undue resistance to free breathing of the engine.

Dual Snorkel

The dual snorkel air cleaner performs at low temperature and above 105 deg. F basically like a single snorkel air cleaner except that on deep throttle acceleration, both snorkels are open (when manifold vacuum drops between 5"Hg).

The "non-heat" air snorkel is connected to manifold vacuum through a tee in the

vacuum hose between the carburetor and the sensor.

Check the second snorkel vacuum diaphragm as one with the heat connector.

Idle Speed Solenoid

Because of the high idle speeds used on some high performance engines, these engines have an electrical solenoid throttle stop which holds the throttle at the correct idle position when energized but de-energizes when the ignition is turned off, allowing the throttle blades to close more completely, thereby eliminating the possibility of "afterrun" or "dieseling".

Distributor Solenoid

Some engines have a solenoid incorporated in the distributor vacuum advance mechanism to retard the ignition timing when the throttle is closed. At closed throttle, and with the idle adjusting screw in the closed position, electrical contacts on the carburetor throttle stop cause the distributor solenoid to energize. This retards the ignition timing to reduce emissions during hot idle conditions. Cold or part throttle starting is not penalized because the distributor solenoid is not energized unless the hot idle adjusting screw is against the throttle stop contact.

NOTE: Ignition timing must be set at closed throttle to give accurate setting.

CHRYSLER NOx

Oxides of Nitrogen

The NOx system controls nitrogen oxides emissions by allowing vacuum spark advance only in high gear (manual trans-

mission), or above 30 mph (automatic transmission), and with the use of an increased overlap camshaft and a 185 degree F coolant thermostat. Vacuum to the distributor is controlled by a solenoid vacuum valve mounted in the line between the carburetor vacuum port and the distributor. When the solenoid is energized the plunger shuts off vacuum to the distributor and vents it to the atmosphere. When it is de-energized the plunger opens allowing normal vacuum spark advance. There are two separate systems employed to control the solenoid vacuum valve, one for vehicles equipped with manual transmissions and the other for those having automatic transmissions.

Manual Transmission

The NOx system for manual transmissions consists of a solenoid vacuum valve, transmission switch and in the 1971 system a thermal switch, Fig. 32. The solenoid vacuum valve is mounted and operates as explained above. The transmission switch is mounted on the transmission housing and is used to sense the transmission gear position. It remains closed ("on") in any gear below high which energizes the solenoid thereby preventing vacuum spark advance. It opens when the top gear is selected permitting normal vacuum spark advance. The thermal switch is mounted on the firewall and senses ambient air temperature. If the temperature is below 70 degrees F, this switch will be open. This breaks the circuit between the transmission switch and the solenoid valve leaving the NOx system inoperative and allowing normal vacuum spark advance in all gears.

Automatic Transmission

The NOx system for automatic transmission equipped vehicles consists of a solenoid vacuum valve, a speed switch and

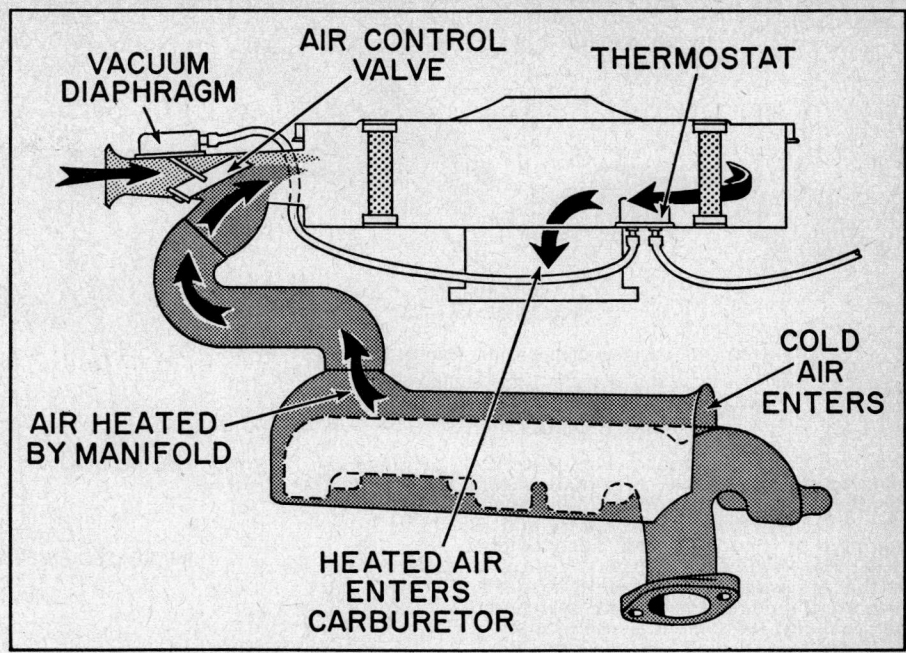

Fig. 31 Chrysler Corp. Heated Air Inlet system

EMISSION CONTROL SYSTEMS

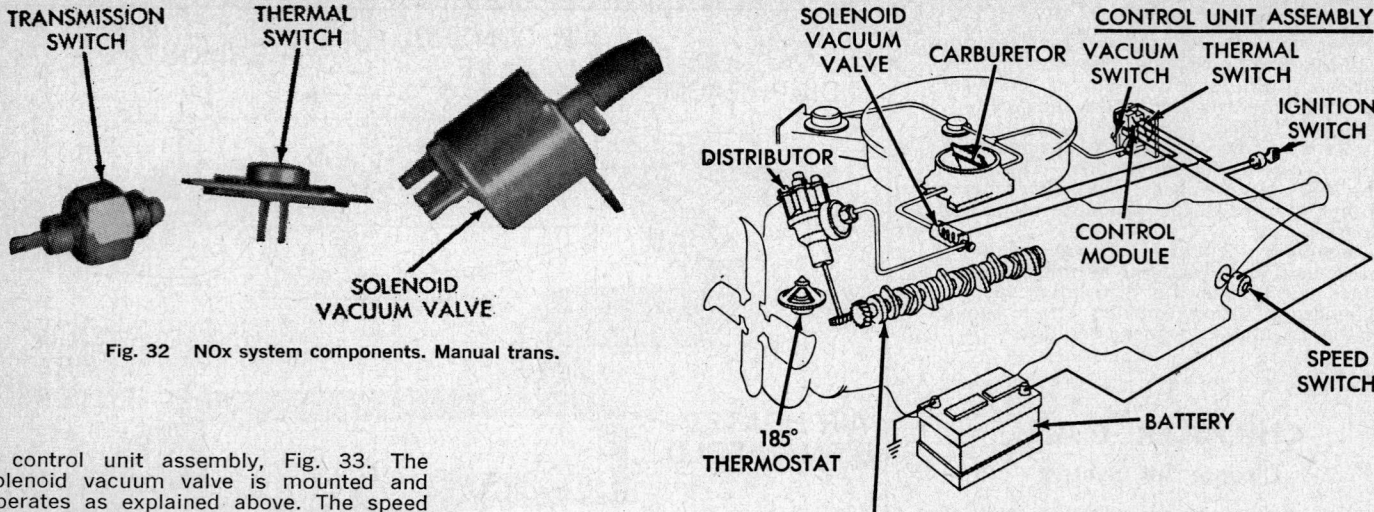

Fig. 32   NOx system components. Manual trans.

Fig. 33   NOx system. Automatic trans.

a control unit assembly, Fig. 33. The solenoid vacuum valve is mounted and operates as explained above. The speed switch senses the vehicle speed and is mounted in line with the speedometer cable. The control unit assembly mounts on the fire wall. It contains three parts, the control module, the thermal switch and the vacuum switch. It senses ambient temperature and manifold vacuum. These components work together for one purpose, to prevent vacuum spark advance under following conditions:

1. Temperature above 70 degrees F.
2. Speeds below 30 mph.
3. Acceleration necessary on 1971 vehicles only.

Whenever all conditions are present, the solenoid vacuum valve will be energized shutting off vacuum to the distributor.

CHRYSLER IGNITION

Electronic Ignition

A better control of exhaust emissions is achieved through the use of the "Electronic Ignition". By eliminating the breaker points, engine misfiring and increased emissions caused by worn or misadjusted breaker points is eliminated.

Distributor Solenoid, 1972-74

A start only solenoid is used on some distributors to provide additional spark advance during engine starting. The solenoid is located in the vacuum unit attached to the distributor housing and operates only while the ignition switch is in start position.

Use of the solenoid provides improved starting characteristics while maintaining a low level of hydrocarbon and carbon monoxide emissions at idle.

CHRYSLER ORIFICE SPARK ADVANCE CONTROL (OSAC)

Fig. 34—The OSAC system is used on all 1973-74 engines, to aid in the control of NOx (Oxides of Nitrogen). The system controls the vacuum to the vacuum advance actuator of the distributor.

A tiny orifice is incorporated in the OSAC valve which delays the change in ported vacuum to the distributor by about

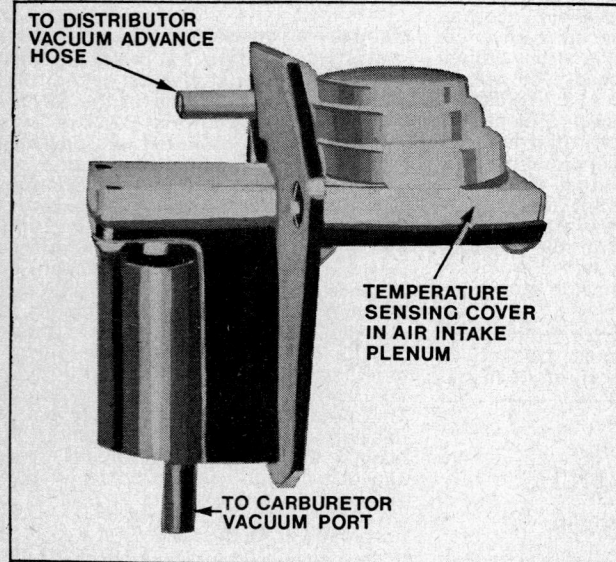

Fig. 34   Chrysler OSAC valve

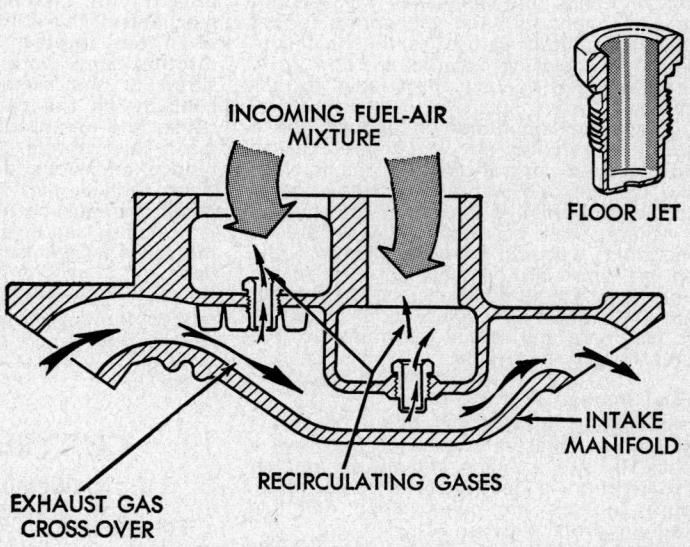

Fig. 35   EGR floor jets V-8 configuration

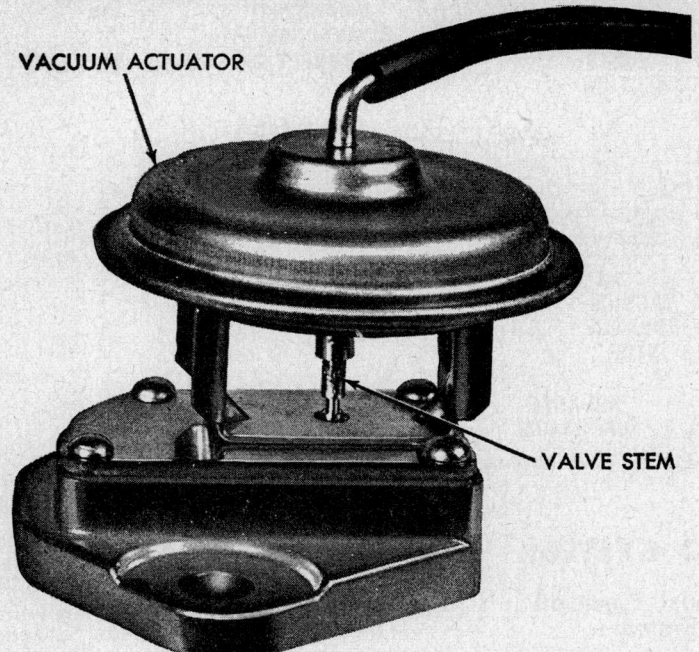

Fig. 36   Chrysler EGR control valve

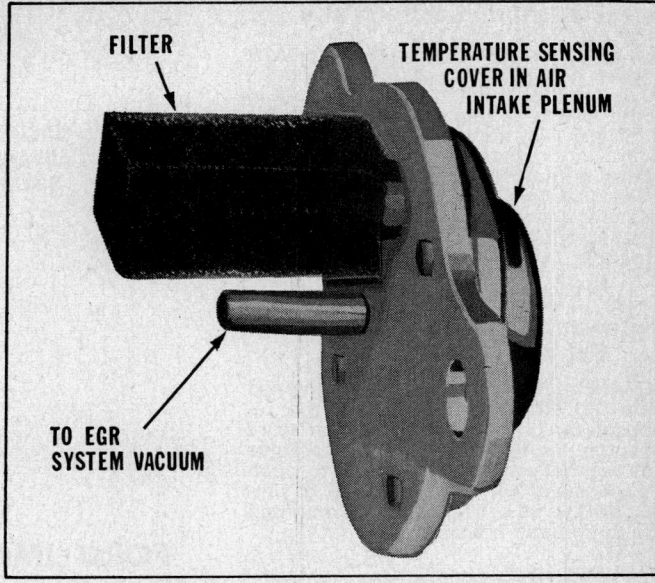

Fig. 37   Chrysler EGR temperature control valve

17 seconds (27 seconds on some 1974 applications) when going from idle to part throttle. When going from part throttle to idle, the change in ported vacuum to the distributor will be instantaneous. The valve will only delay the ported vacuum signal when the ambient temperature is about 60° F. or above. Vacuum is obtained by a vacuum tap just above the throttle plates of the carburetor. This type of tap provides no vacuum at idle, but provides manifold vacuum as soon as the throttle plates are opened slightly. Proper operation of this valve depends on air tight fittings and hoses and on freedom from sticking or plugging due to deposits.

TEMPERATURE OPERATED VACUUM BY-PASS VALVE

This vacuum by-pass or Thermal Ignition Control (TIC) valve, Fig. 20, is used on some engines to reduce the possibility of engine overheating under extremely high temperature operating conditions. When engine coolant temperature at idle reaches 225° F., the valve opens automatically and applies manifold vacuum directly to the distributor for normal vacuum spark advance. This will by-pass the NOx or OSAC system. This increases engine idle speed and provides additional engine cooling. When the engine has cooled to normal operating temperature, the NOx or OSAC system is restored to normal operation.

CHRYSLER EXHAUST GAS RECIRCULATION (EGR)

In this system, exhaust gases are circulated to dilute the incoming fuel air mixture. Dilution of the incoming mixture lowers peak flame temperatures during combustion and thus limits the formation of NOx.

Floor Jet Exhaust Gas System 1972-73

In this system the exhaust gases are introduced into the intake manifold through jets in the floor below the carburetor, Fig. 35. An orifice in each jet allows a controlled amount of exhaust gas to be drawn through by engine vacuum to dilute incoming fuel and air. In eight cylinder engines, exhaust gases are taken from the intake manifold exhaust crossover passage. While in six cylinder engines, gases are taken from the exhaust manifold "plenum" chamber located at the "hot spot" below the carburetor riser.

NOTE: In 1973-74 two additional systems are used to control the rate of exhaust gas recirculation, depending on engine model. These systems are: Ported Vacuum Control System and Venturi Vacuum Control System.

Both systems use the same type exhaust gas recirculation (EGR) control valve, Fig. 36, only the method of controlling the valve is different. The valve is a vacuum actuated, poppet type unit used to modulate exhaust gas flow from the exhaust gas crossover into the incoming air fuel mixture.

Venturi Vacuum Control System

The venturi vacuum control system utilizes a vacuum tap at the throat of the carburetor venturi to provide a control signal. This vacuum signal is amplified to the level required to operate the EGR control valve. Elimination of recycle at wide open throttle is accomplished by a dump diaphragm which compares venturi and manifold vacuum to determine when wide open throttle is achieved. At wide open throttle, the internal reservoir is "dumped", limiting output to the EGR valve to manifold vacuum. The valve opening point is set above the manifold vacuums available at wide open throttle.

NOTE: This system is dependent primarily on engine intake airflow as indicated by the venturi signal, and is also affected by intake vacuum and exhaust gas back pressure.

Ported Vacuum Control System

The ported vacuum control system utilizes a slot type port in the carburetor throttle body which is exposed to an increasing ratio of manifold vacuum as the throttle blade opens. This throttle bore port is connected through an external nipple directly to the EGR valve. The flow rate is dependent on three variables, 1) manifold vacuum, 2) throttle position, and 3) exhaust gas back pressure. Recycle at wide open throttle is eliminated by calibrating the valve opening point above manifold vacuums available at wide open throttle as port vacuum cannot exceed manifold vacuum. Elimination of wide open throttle recycle provides maximum performance.

Temperature Control Valve

The plenum mounted temperature control valve, Fig. 37, is utilized on the ported vacuum control system and the venturi vacuum control system. The valve reduces the recycle rate at low ambient temperature for improved driveability. The unit contains a temperature sensitive bimetal disc which senses plenum air temperature. The snap action of the disc unplugs a calibrated orifice to provide the bleed air. Calibration is protected by an air filter unit.

Coolant Control Exhaust Gas Recirculation (CCEGR)

1974 engines using EGR are equipped with a CCEGR valve mounted in the radiator top tank. When coolant temperature in the top tank reaches 65° F, the valve opens so that vacuum is applied to open the EGR valve. On some engines, a similar CCEGR valve set for 90° F, is mounted in the thermostat housing.

EGR Delay System

Some 1974 vehicles are equipped with an EGR Delay System, which has an electrical timer mounted on the dash panel in the engine compartment controlling an engine mounted solenoid. This solenoid which is connected with vacuum hoses to the carburetor venturi and vacuum amplifier, prevents EGR operation for about 35 seconds after engine start up.

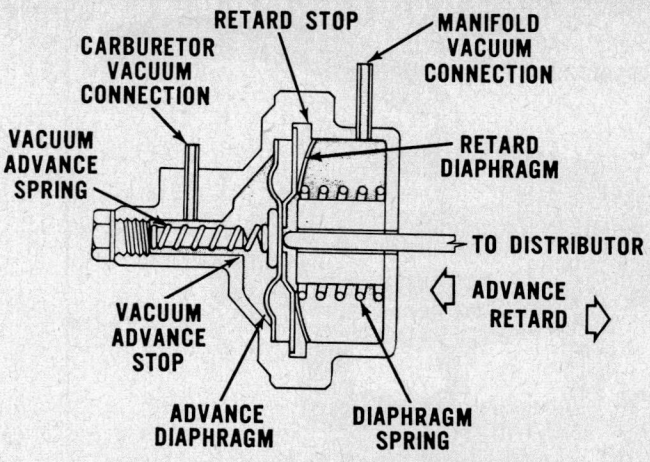

Fig. 38 Dual diaphragm vacuum advance valve

FORD IMCO SYSTEM

Improved Exhaust Emission Control System

This system combines a thermostatically controlled air cleaner and higher engine operating temperature with leaner carburetor calibration and later ignition timing under closed throttle operating conditions.

Dual Diaphragm Distributor

Fig. 38—In addition to the conventional centrifugal and vacuum advance control units, this unit uses a separate diaphragm to retard the spark timing under closed throttle conditions. The advance diaphragm is connected to the carburetor above the throttle plate(s) so that when the throttle is opened, the timing is advanced. The retard diaphragm is connected to the intake manifold so that during closed throttle operation, when manifold

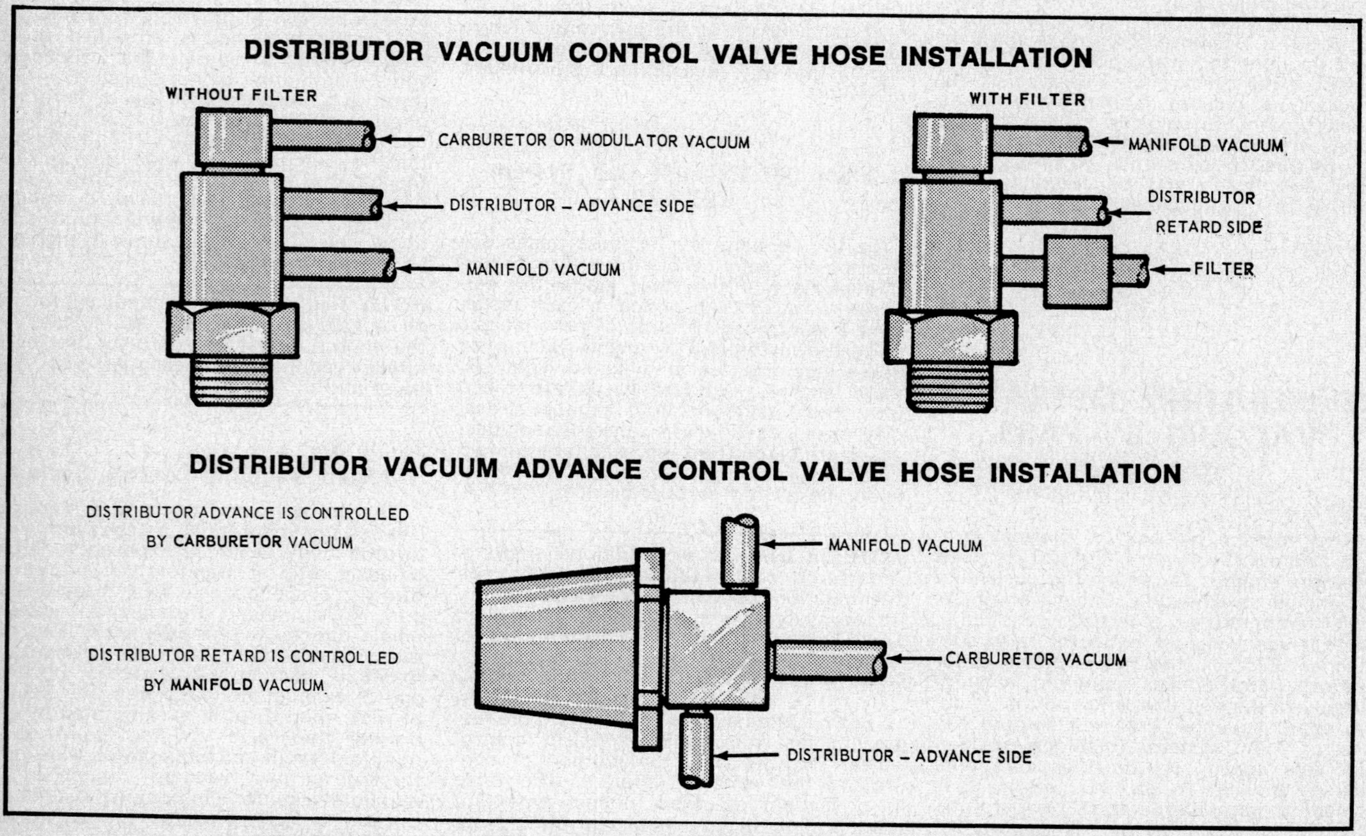

DISTRIBUTOR VACUUM CONTROL VALVE HOSE INSTALLATION

WITHOUT FILTER
← CARBURETOR OR MODULATOR VACUUM
← DISTRIBUTOR – ADVANCE SIDE
← MANIFOLD VACUUM

WITH FILTER
← MANIFOLD VACUUM
← DISTRIBUTOR RETARD SIDE
← FILTER

DISTRIBUTOR VACUUM ADVANCE CONTROL VALVE HOSE INSTALLATION

DISTRIBUTOR ADVANCE IS CONTROLLED BY **CARBURETOR** VACUUM

DISTRIBUTOR RETARD IS CONTROLLED BY **MANIFOLD** VACUUM

← MANIFOLD VACUUM
← CARBURETOR VACUUM
← DISTRIBUTOR – ADVANCE SIDE

Fig. 39 Distributor vacuum control valve and distributor vacuum advance control valve

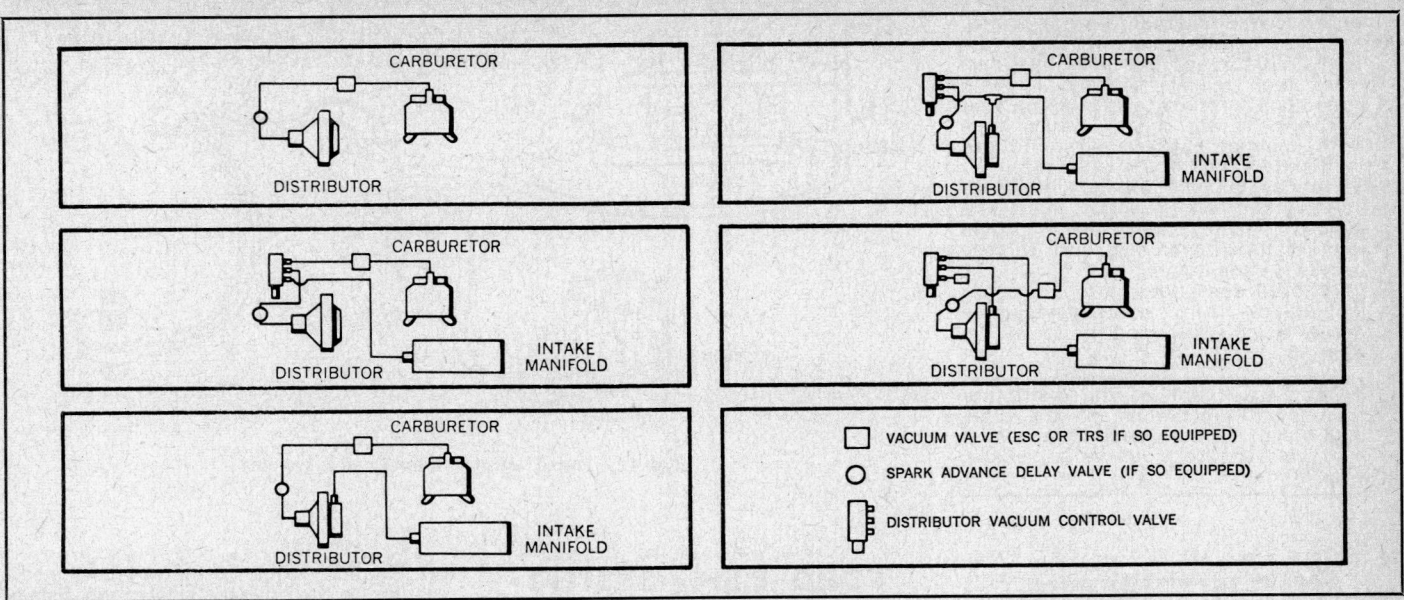

Fig. 40 Ford distributor vacuum system schematics

vacuum is high, the timing is retarded to provide more complete combustion.

Distributor Vacuum Control Valve

This valve, Fig. 39, is exposed to cooling system temperature and when coolant temperature exceeds normal limits during long idle periods, the valve opens a vacuum passage to the advance diaphragm of the distributor which speeds up the engine idle lowering the temperature.

To test the valve, proceed as follows:

1. With engine at operating temperature, connect a tachometer to the engine.
2. Note engine idle rpm with transmission in neutral.
3. Disconnect the vacuum hose from the intake manifold at the temperature sensing valve and plug the hose.
4. If idle speed does not change when hose is disconnected, the valve is acceptable to this point. If idle drops 100 rpm or move, valve must be replaced.
5. Reinstall vacuum line then cover radiator sufficiently to raise engine coolant temperature above thermostat setting.

NOTE: Be sure all-season coolant is up to specification and exercise caution so that the engine does not become unduly overheated.

6. Continue to run the engine until the high temperature lamp comes on or the temperature gauge reaches the high end of the band. At this point, the engine idle speed should increase by approximately 100 rpm. If it has not, the valve is defective and must be replaced.

Distributor Vacuum Advance Control Valve

This valve, Figs. 27 and 39, provides the necessary ignition advance during acceler-

ation periods to provide the most efficient combustion and reduce emissions. To check the valve, proceed as follows:

1. With engine at operating temperature and idle speed correctly set, connect a tachometer to the engine.
2. Remove cover from valve and slowly turn the adjusting screw counterclockwise without exerting any inward pressure. After five and no more than six turns, the idle speed should suddenly increase to approximately 1000 rpm.

NOTE: Any more than six turns out will release the compressed spring and washer.

3. If idle speed does not increase after the sixth turn, push inward on the end of the spring and release. Idle speed will increase.
4. After valve has been triggered to the higher rpm, slowly turn the adjusting screw clockwise until idle speed drops back down to proper level. Turn

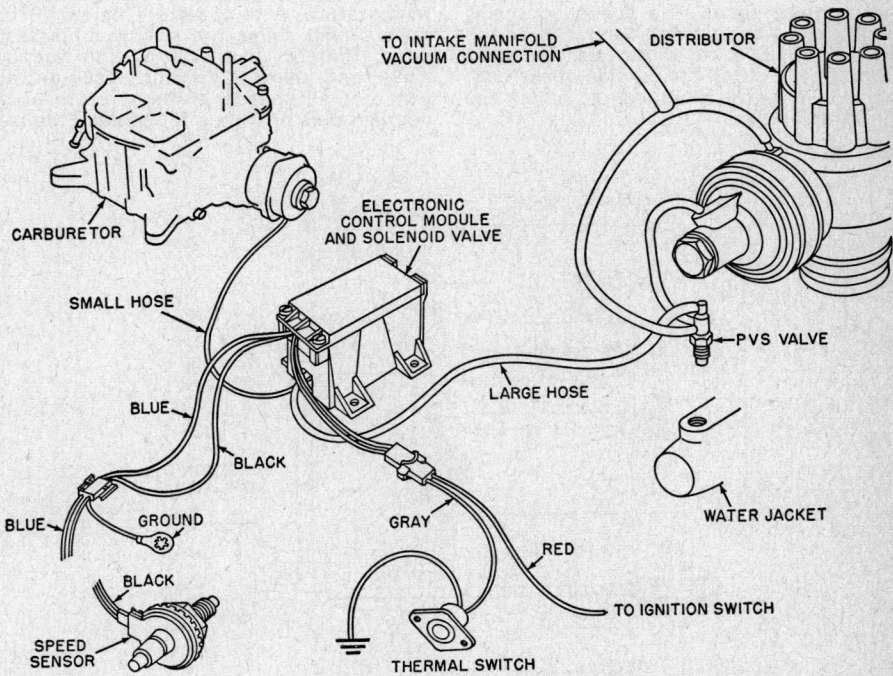

Fig. 41 Electronic Distributor Modulator

5. Increase engine speed to 2000 rpm and hold for approximately five seconds then release throttle. The engine should return to idle within four seconds. If not, check return time with dashpot backed off so it does not contact the throttle lever.

6. If the engine still will not return to idle within four seconds, turn the adjusting screw clockwise in one-quarter turn increments until throttle return is satisfactory.

7. If throttle does not return after four one-quarter turn adjustments, the valve is defective and must be replaced.

NOTE: Application of the distributor vacuum control valve and the dual-diaphragm vacuum advance mechanism will vary from vehicle to vehicle, Fig. 40.

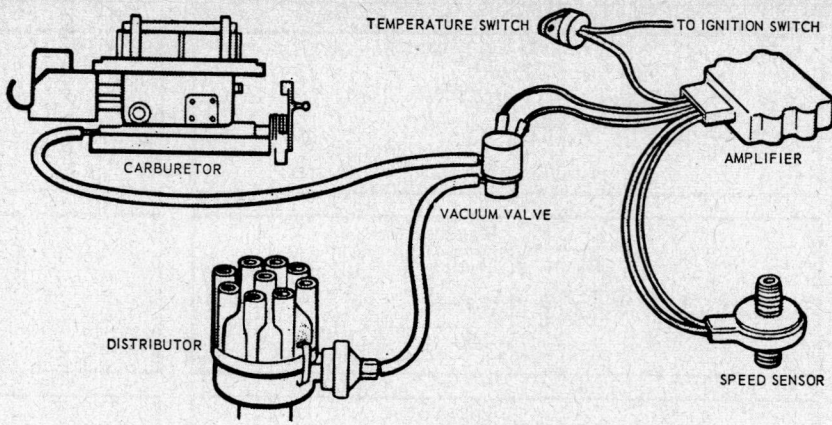

Fig. 42   Ford Electronic Spark Control system

FORD ELECTRONIC DISTRIBUTOR MODULATOR

Description

This system operates to prevent spark advance below 23 mph on acceleration and below approximately 18 mph on deceleration. Control by the modulator is canceled out if the outside air temperature is below 58 deg. F, allowing the distributor to operate through the standard vacuum control system, Fig. 41.

The modulator system consists of four components: speed sensor, thermal switch, and electrical control amplifier-solenoid valve. The control amplifier and solenoid valve are combined in one assembly and mounted in the passenger compartment on the dash panel. The speed sensor is connected to the speedometer cable. The thermal switch is mounted near the front door hinge pillar on the outside of the cowl panel. It may be mounted on either the right or left side.

FORD E.S.C. SYSTEM

Electronic Spark Control System

This system, Fig. 42, reduces the exhaust emissions of an engine by providing vacuum spark advance only at speeds above 24 to 33 mph (depending on the engine application). It consists of a speed sensor, an electronic amplifier, an outside air temperature switch and a vacuum control valve. The vacuum control valve is inserted between the carburetor vacuum advance port and the distributor primary advance connection. This valve is normally open, but when energized electrically by the electronic amplifier it closes to cut off vacuum to the primary vacuum advance unit on the distributor thus preventing vacuum spark advance. The temperature switch, which is mounted in either the right or left A-pillar, senses outside air temperature. A temperature below 49 degrees F will cause the switch contacts to open, thereby de-energizing the vacuum valve and allowing normal vacuum advance at all speeds. A temperature of 60 degrees plus or minus 5 degrees F causes

the contacts to close, thereby cutting off vacuum to the advance side of the distributor at speeds below 24 to 33 mph. On deceleration the vacuum advance cut-out speed is approximately 18 mph.

On some applications the vacuum hose connections between the carburetor and distributor may route through a PVS valve. This valve serves as a by-pass or safety override switch. When the coolant temperature reaches 230 degrees F, manifold vacuum is applied directly to the primary (advance) side of the distributor advancing the timing and thereby lowering operating temperature.

FORD HIGH SPEED EGR MODULATOR SUB-SYSTEM

The high speed EGR modulator sub-system used on some V-8 engines, Fig. 42A is basically the same in operation as the ESC system described previously. This system cuts off exhaust gas recirculation flow by stopping vacuum flow from the EGR port to the EGR valve at speeds above 64 mph, inturn improving driveability.

The vacuum solenoid valve installed in the vacuum line is normally open (not energized), allowing vacuum flow from the EGR port to the EGR valve. The EGR system remains functional when the valve is not energized.

The speed sensor driven by the speedometer cable, produces an electric signal directly proportional to vehicle road speed, signalling the amplifier to energize the vacuum solenoid valve at which time the electronic module receives the signal from the speed sensor and amplifies it to provide a usable signal to the vacuum solenoid valve.

When the vehicle speed exceeds approximately 64 mph (trigger speed of the amplifier) the circuit to the ignition switch is completed and the normally open vacuum solenoid valve is energized. The plunger moves upwards and shuts off the EGR port vacuum and the vent at the bot-

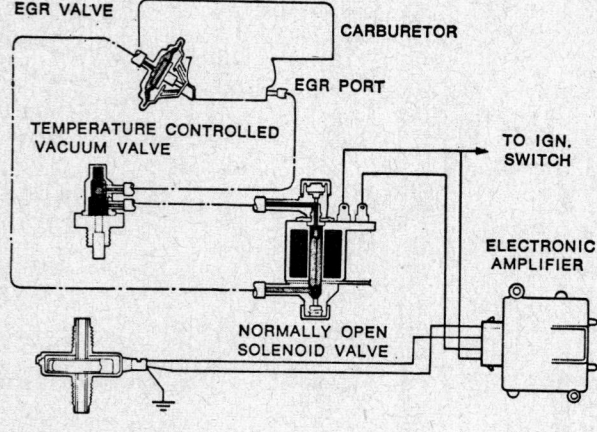

Fig. 42A   Ford high speed EGR modulator sub-system components

tom of the vacuum valve is opened, bleeding vacuum from the EGR valve and hose. Spring force closes the EGR valve which remains non functional until the vacuum solenoid valve is de-energized, at speeds below approximately 64 mph.

NOTE: There is a continuous internal vacuum bleed provided by the vent at the top of EGR valve. Whether the valve is in a closed or open position, this vent purges the vacuum supply hose from carburetor of any gasoline vapor.

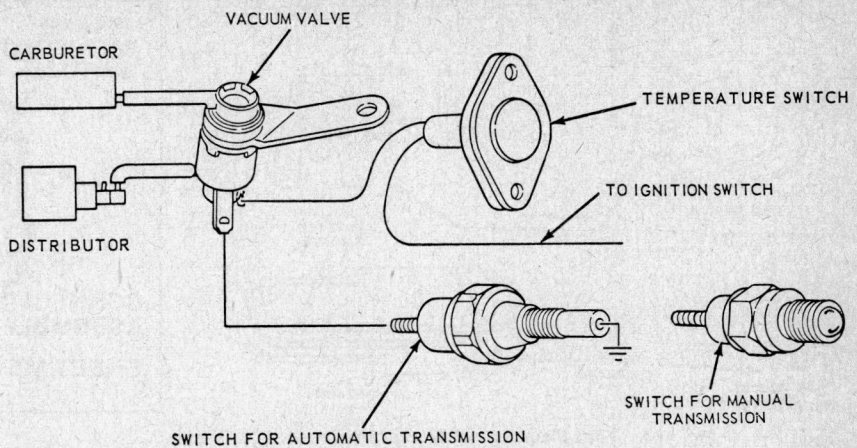

Fig. 43   Ford TRS system

FORD T.R.S. SYSTEM

Transmission Regulated Spark Control System

This system, Fig. 43, reduces the exhaust emissions of an engine by providing vacuum spark advance only in high gear. It consists of a vacuum control valve, an outside air temperature switch, and a transmission switch. The vacuum control valve is inserted between the carburetor vacuum advance port and the distributor primary advance connection. This valve is normally open, but when energized electrically by the transmission switch it closes to cut off vacuum to the primary vacuum advance unit on the distributor thus preventing vacuum spark advance. The temperature switch, which is mounted in either the right or left A-pillar, senses outside air temperature. A temperature below 49 degrees F will cause the switch contacts to open, thereby de-energizing the vacuum valve and allowing normal vacuum advance in all gears. A temperature of 60 degrees plus or minus 5 degrees F causes the contacts to close, thereby cutting off vacuum to the advance side of the distributor in all but high gear.

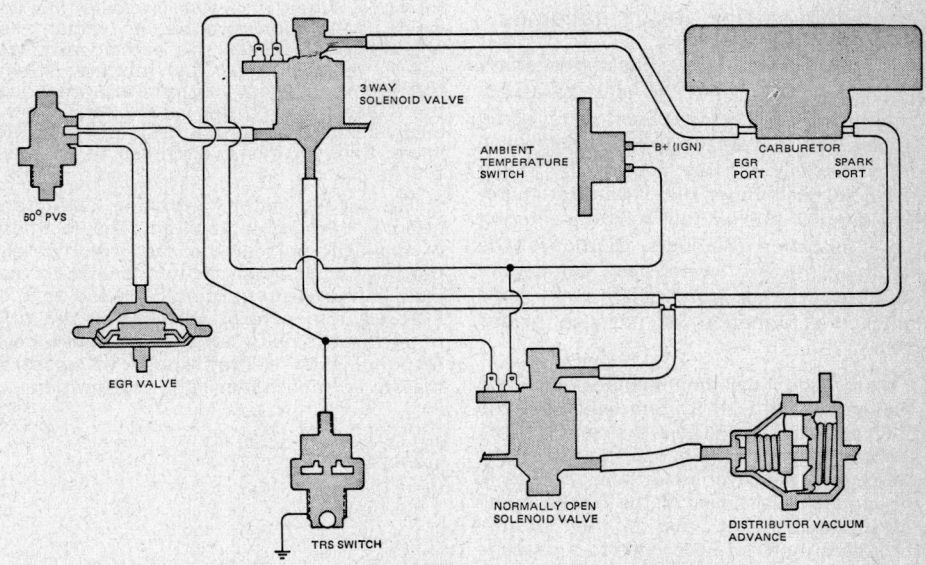

Fig. 44   Ford transmission regulated spark one system—TRS+1

FORD T.R.S. + 1

Transmission Regulated Spark +1

Fig. 44—The TRS+1 system consists of two separate vacuum control systems, that are electrically controlled by input information from a manual transmission gear selector switch, and an outside ambient air temperature switch. The TRS function of the TRS+1 system is identical to the function performed by the 1972 TRS system. The plus 1 system of the TRS+1, controls the selection of the carburetor vacuum source for the vehicle EGR system. The EGR vacuum supply source can be either carburetor spark port, or carburetor EGR port depending upon the manual transmission gear selected, and the outside ambient air temperature.

FORD SPARK DELAY VALVE

This unit is used in conjunction with

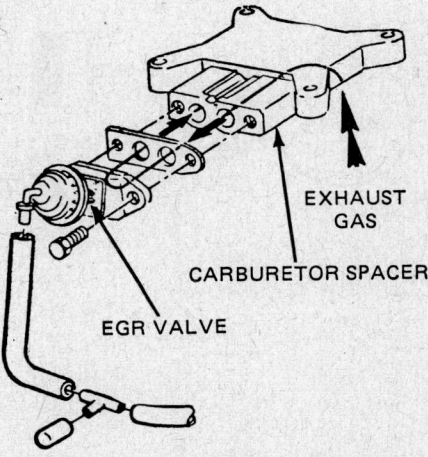

Fig. 45   Ford V8 EGR valve hook up

some of the other Ford systems. Its purpose is to further reduce emissions by delaying the spark advance during rapid acceleration and by cutting off advance immediately upon deceleration.

This plastic disc-shaped valve is installed in the carburetor vacuum line at the distributor advance diaphragm. It is a one way valve and will not operate if installed backwards. The black side of the valve must be toward the carburetor. This valve cannot be repaired or checked for proper operation.

NOTE: On all systems which employ the dual diaphragm distributor the line which has high vacuum at idle (normal operating temperature) is connected to the secondary (retard) side of the distributor vacuum advance unit. This is the connection closest to the distributor cap.

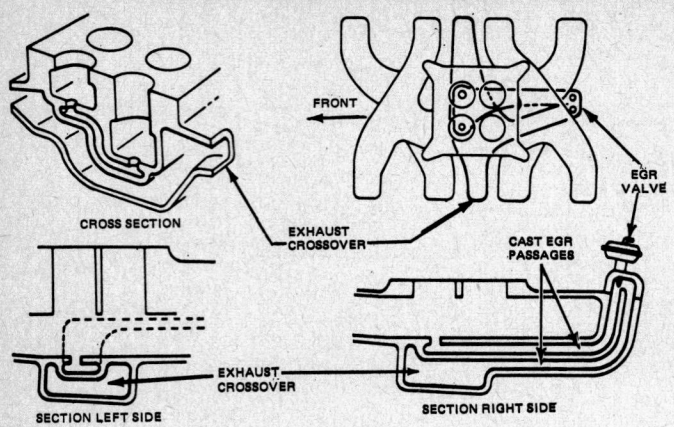

Fig. 45A   Ford Floor Entry EGR System

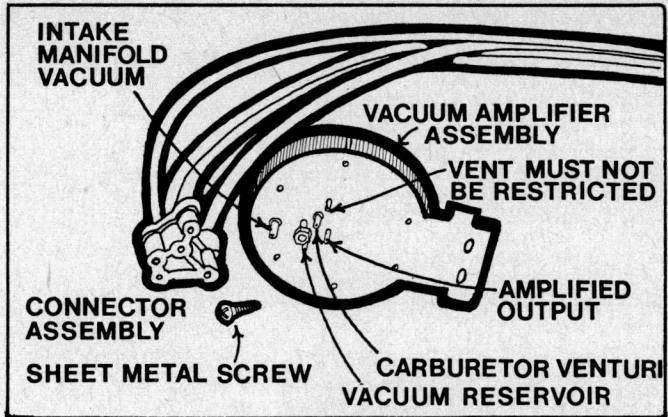

Fig. 45B   Venturi Vacuum Amplifier

FORD EGR SYSTEM

Exhaust Gas Recirculation

In this system the exhaust gases are metered through the EGR valve to a passage in the carburetor spacer, or on some 1974 eight cylinder engines, through two drilled passages in the floor of the intake manifold riser under the carburetor therefore diluting the air fuel mixture entering the combustion chambers. Dilution of the incoming mixture lowers peak flame temperatures during combustion and thus limits the formation of nitrogen oxides (NOx).

Most eight cylinder engines use the "Spacer Entry" EGR System which has the EGR valve mounted on the rear of the carburetor spacer, Fig. 45. The exhaust gases are taken from a drilled passage in the exhaust crossover of the intake manifold. The exhaust gas is then routed through a metered EGR valve to a passage in the carburetor spacer and fed into the primary bore. Some 1974 eight cylinder engines use the "Floor Entry" EGR system, which has the EGR valve mounted on the rear of the intake manifold. The EGR valve controls the exhaust gases that enter specially cast passages in the manifold from the exhaust crossover passage. When the valve opens, the exhaust crossover is then opened to the two drilled passages in the floor of the intake manifold riser under the carburetor, Fig. 45A.

On six cylinder engines, the EGR system is basically the same as the Spacer Entry EGR System except that exhaust gas is routed directly from the exhaust manifold.

Two variables control the operation of the EGR system, 1) engine coolant temperature and 2) carburetor vacuum. When engine coolant temperature is below the specified level the EGR system is locked out by a temperature controlled vacuum switch. This vacuum switch is installed in

series with the EGR valve. This valve receives vacuum from a port in the carburetor body. When the valve is closed due to lower coolant temperature, no vacuum is applied to the EGR valve and no exhaust gas is fed to the air-fuel mixture. When the engine coolant temperature reaches the specified level, the valve opens allowing vacuum to be applied to the EGR valve. Exhaust gas is then fed to the air-fuel mixture.

The second factor controlling EGR operation is carburetor vacuum. The location of the EGR port in the carburetor determines at what point vacuum is sent to the EGR valve. Vacuum should be fed to the EGR vacuum control valve when the primary throttle plate reaches a position corresponding to a road speed of approximately 20 mph under light acceleration.

A Venturi Vacuum Amplifier, Fig. 45B, used in 1974, uses a weak venturi vacuum signal to produce a strong intake manifold vacuum to operate the EGR valve, thereby achieving an accurate, repeatable and almost exact proportion between venturi airflow and EGR flow. This assists in controlling oxides of nitrogen with minimal sacrifice in driveability.

There are three types of EGR valves, the poppet type, modulating type and the tapered stem type.

NOTE: If the tapered stem valve is plugged or causes rough idle due to leakage, it should be replaced.

The poppet type valve, Fig. 46, consists of springloaded diaphragm, and a valve stem and valve operating in an enclosed

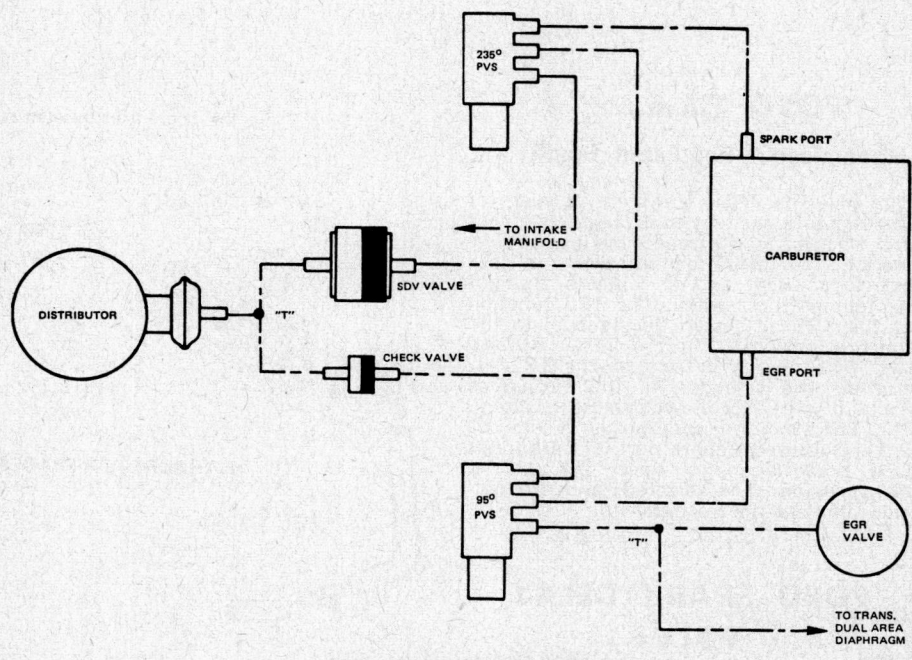

Fig. 45C   Ford EGR/CSC System

valve body. At approximately 3 inch Hg of vacuum, the valve begins to open. The valve stem is pulled forward unseating the valve and allowing exhaust gas to flow into the valve chamber. Venturi vacuum will then pull the gas from the chamber into the air-fuel flow and then into the combustion chambers. Once the valve has been unseated the only means of limiting exhaust gas flow is the size of the flow restrictor placed in the inlet port of the valve body. The size of the restrictor will vary according to engine application.

On the modulating type valve, Fig. 47, an additional disc has been added to the valve stem below the main valve. The modulating valve operates exactly like the poppet valve when vacuum is between approximately 3 in Hg and 10.5 in Hg. When vacuum reaches approximately 10.5 inches, the lower disc (high vacuum flow restrictor) approaches the shoulders of the valve seat and restricts the flow of exhaust gas. The purpose of the modulation of gas flow is to improve driveability on certain engine models.

NOTE: The EGR valve and vacuum control valve cannot be repaired and must be replaced if damaged.

Cold Start Cycle

The EGR/CSC System regulates both distributor advance and EGR valve operation according to coolant temperature by sequentially switching vacuum signals. The major system components are, a 95° F EGR-PVS (Ported Vacuum Switch) valve, a SDV (Spark Delay Valve) and a vacuum check valve, Fig. 45C.

When engine coolant temperature is below 82° F, the EGR-PVS valve admits carburetor EGR port vacuum (at about 2500 RPM) directly to the distributor advance diaphragm, through the one way check valve. At the same time, the EGR-PVS valve shuts off carburetor EGR vacuum to the EGR valve and transmission diaphragm.

When engine coolant temperature is 95°F and above, the EGR-PVS valve is actuated and directs carburetor EGR vacuum to the EGR valve and transmission diaphragm instead of the distributor. At

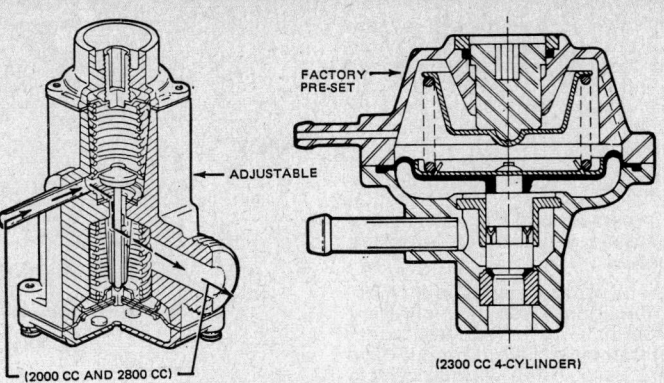

Fig. 45D Ford decel valve

temperatures between 82° and 95° F, the EGR-PVS valve may be open, closed or in mid position.

The Spark Delay Valve (SDV) delays carburetor vacuum to the distributor advance by restricting the vacuum signal through the SDV for a predetermined time. During normal acceleration, little or no vacuum is admitted to the distributor advance diaphragm until acceleration is completed and engine coolant temperature is 95° F or higher.

The check valve blocks off vacuum signal from the SDV to the EGR-PVS valve so that carburetor spark vacuum will not be dissipated when the EGR-PVS valve is actuated above 95° F.

The 235° F PVS valve which is not part of the EGR-PVS system is connected to the distributor vacuum advance to prevent engine overheating as on previous models.

DUAL-AREA DIAPHRAGM

On 1973-74 vehicles, new dual-area diaphragms are used, Fig. 48. These diaphragms offset effects of engines using the EGR system and equipped with automatic transmissions. The new diaphragms permit vehicles to function with satisfactory shift spacing and shift feel.

To test, remove the vacuum diaphragm and test unit using an outside vacuum source. Set regulator on tester to 18 in. Hg with end of vacuum hose blocked off then connect vacuum hose to vacuum diaphragm unit. If unit does not hold 18 in. Hg. reading, the diaphragm is leaking and must be replaced.

FORD DECEL VALVE

This valve, Fig 45D, used on the 1600cc, 2000cc, 2300cc and 2800cc engines, is mounted on the intake manifold adjacent to the carburetor and meters an additional amount of fuel and air during engine deceleration periods. This additional fuel and air, together with engine modifications, permits more complete combustion with the resultant being lower levels of exhaust emissions. During engine deceleration, manifold vacuum forces the diaphragm assembly against the spring in the decel

valve, which in turn raises the decel valve (open position). With the valve open, existing manifold vacuum pulls a metered amount of fuel and air from the carburetor, which travels through the decel valve body assembly into the intake manifold. The decel valve remains open and continues to feed additional air and fuel for a specifield time.

FORD DVB SYSTEM

Delay Vacuum By-Pass System

This system is designed to delay distributor vacuum advance under varying ambient temperatures and vehicle speeds. The system consists of a solenoid vacuum valve (SV), spark delay valve (SDV), and a check valve (one-way valve), Fig. 49.

The spark delay valve SDV is a two-way flow device used for controlling distributor vacuum advance. It delays the flow of vacuum in one direction through a sintered metal restrictor, yet permits an instantaneous flow in the other direction through a one-way check valve.

When the vehicle is accelerating, the direction of air flow is from the distributor toward the carburetor through the restrictor.

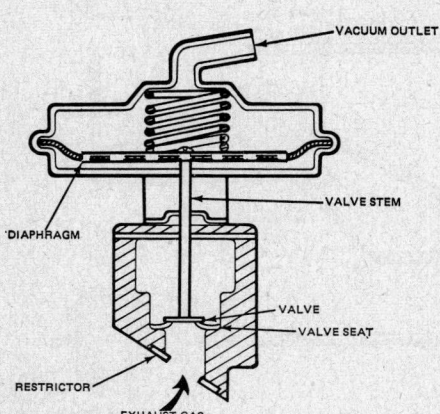

Fig. 46 Ford poppet-type EGR valve

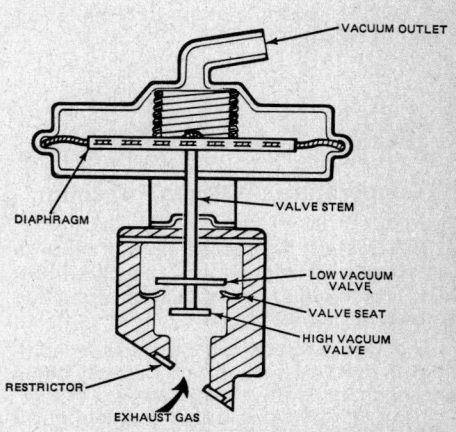

Fig. 47 Ford modulating type EGR valve

The check valve is held closed by the pressure differential between the SDV inlet and outlet connections. After a specified time period, (depending on restrictor porosity) the vacuum will bleed through the restrictor and equalize the pressure at both connections.

When the vehicle decelerates, the pressure differential is reversed, the direction of air flow is reversed, and the check valve opens, to instantly equalize air pressure across the valves.

Since different vehicle engine and transmission combinations require different time delay periods to effectively meet emission requirements. Five different type SDV valves are used in the various vehicle engine applications. Each type is color coded.

Since the SDV is not affected by ambient air temperature changes, it would act to retard the distributor spark advance during cold weather when exhaust emissions can be met normally without the retarding action. For this reason, the DVB system is also connected between the vacuum source at the carburetor spark port and the distributor primary diaphragm in parallel with the SDV system.

At temperatures of 60 degrees F and above. the normally open solenoid vacuum valve receives battery voltage from the ambient temperature switch whenever the ignition switch is on closing the solenoid valve and shutting off vacuum to the distributor. The temperature switch is open at temperatures of 49 degrees F and below and no signal is sent to the solenoid valve. Thus, the solenoid valve will remain open admitting carburetor spark port vacuum to the distributor primary vacuum diaphrgam directly through the open solenoid valve.

NOTE: The DVB system is energized only when the weather is warm and allows no direct flow of vacuum through the solenoid valve.

The DVB system check valve prevents the outlet of the SDV valve from being vented to the atmosphere to cause a loss of vacuum to the distributor resulting in no distributor advance when the DVB is energized. The check valve must be installed in the vacuum line as shown or the SDV valve will not permit the check valve to close.

FORD T.A.V. SYSTEM

Temperature Activated Vacuum

This system selects either the carburetor spark port vacuum, or the carburetor EGR port vacuum as a function of outside ambient air temperature.

The EGR system can be used in addition to the TAV system, although systems work independently of each other.

The TAV system, Fig. 50, consists of an ambient temperature switch, a three-way vacuum valve, and an external inline vacuum bleed. The three-way vacuum valve is used to select the carburetor vacuum source that is supplied to the distributor vacuum advance mechanism. The ambient temperature switch provides the switching circuit to determine which vacuum source will be selected as a function of outside air temperature. The inline vacuum bleed function is to purge the vacuum line in the TAV system of any excessive gasoline vapors.

The basic difference between a TAV system and the standard IMCO system is the selective control feature provided by TAV system for distributor vacuum advance as a function of outside air temperature.

When the ambient air temperature is above 60 degrees F the three-way vacuum valve is energized, therefore the EGR vacuum is controlling the distributor advance. When the ambient air temperature is below 49 degrees F the three-way vacuum valve is de-energized, therefore the spark port vacuum is controlling the distributor advance.

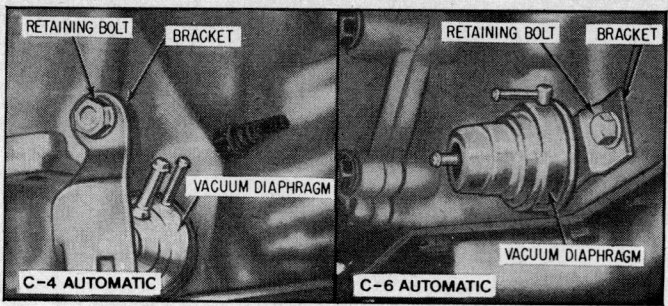

Fig. 48   1973 Dual diaphragm vacuum modulator

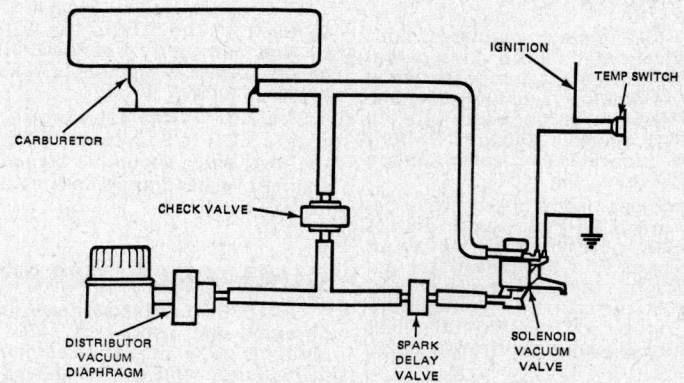

Fig. 49   Ford delay vacuum by-pass system—DVB

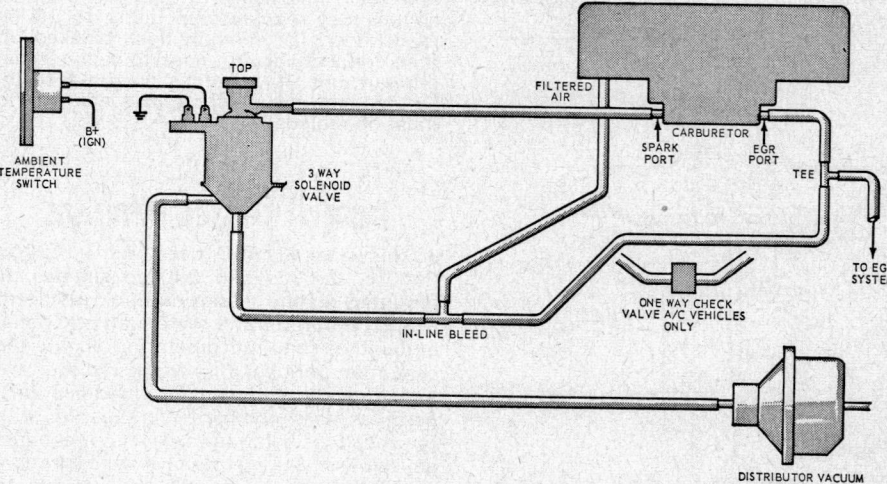

Fig. 50   Ford temperature activated vacuum system—TAV

NOTE: The TAV system controls spark advance below 49 degrees F. while the EGR system controls spark advance above 60 degrees F.

FORD CTAV SYSTEM

Cold Temperature Activated Vacuum

This system operates basically the same as the TAV system previously discussed except that a latching relay, Fig. 51, has been added. The latching relay, activated by temperature switch closing remains energized regardless of temperature switch position which prevents system cycling due to minor ambient temperature changes.

The temperature switch energizes the three-way vacuum valve and latching relay when ambient temperature is above 65° F. When ambient temperature is below 49° F, the system is inoperative and the distributor diaphragm and EGR valve receives vacuum directly from its respective carburetor ports.

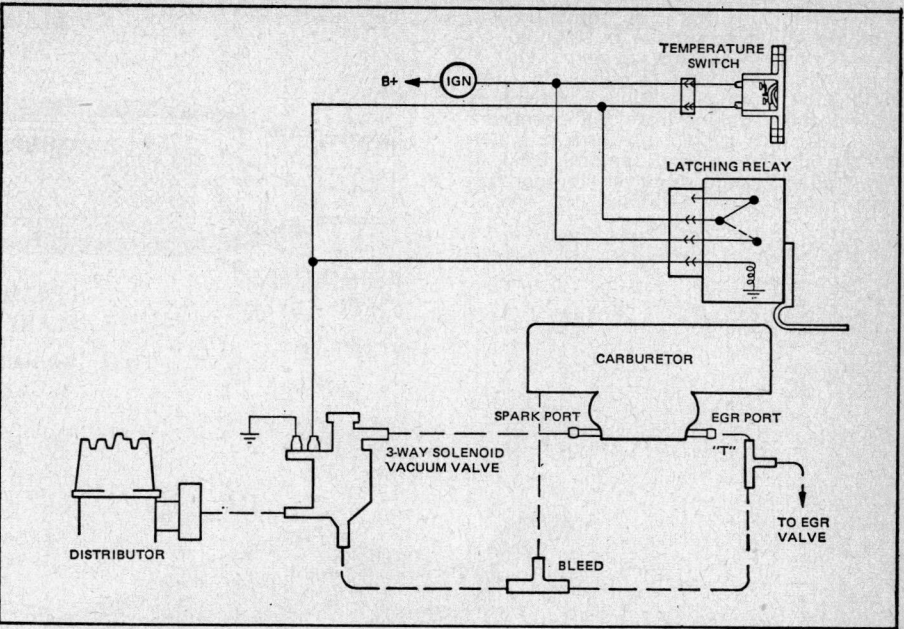

Fig. 51   Ford cold temperature activated vacuum system—CTAV

CATALYTIC CONVERTERS

The catalytic converter serves two purposes: it permits a faster chemical reaction to take place and although it enters into the chemical reaction, it remains unchanged, ready to repeat the process. The catalytic converter combines hydrocarbons (HC) and carbon monoxide (CO) with oxygen to form water (H_2O) and carbon dioxide (CO).

The catalyst is structured in the form of pellets, Fig. 1 (General Motors), or a honeycomb monolithic composition, Figs. 2 (Chrysler Corp.) and 3 (Ford). The catalyst consists of a porous substrate of an inert material, coated with platinum and other noble metals, the catalytically active materials.

This device, located in the exhaust system between the exhaust manifold and muffler, requires the use of heat shields, in some cases, due to its high operating temperatures. The heat shields are necessary to protect chassis components, passenger compartment and other areas from heat related damage.

A smaller diameter fuel tank filler tube neck is incorporated to prevent the larger service station pump nozzle, used for leaded fuels, being inserted into the filler tube, thereby preventing system contamination, Fig. 4.

CAUTION: Since the use of leaded fuels contaminates the catalysts, deteriorating its effectiveness, the use of unleaded fuels is mandatory in vehicles equipped with catalytic converters. The catalytic converter can tolerate very small amounts of leaded fuels without permanently reducing the catalyst effectiveness.

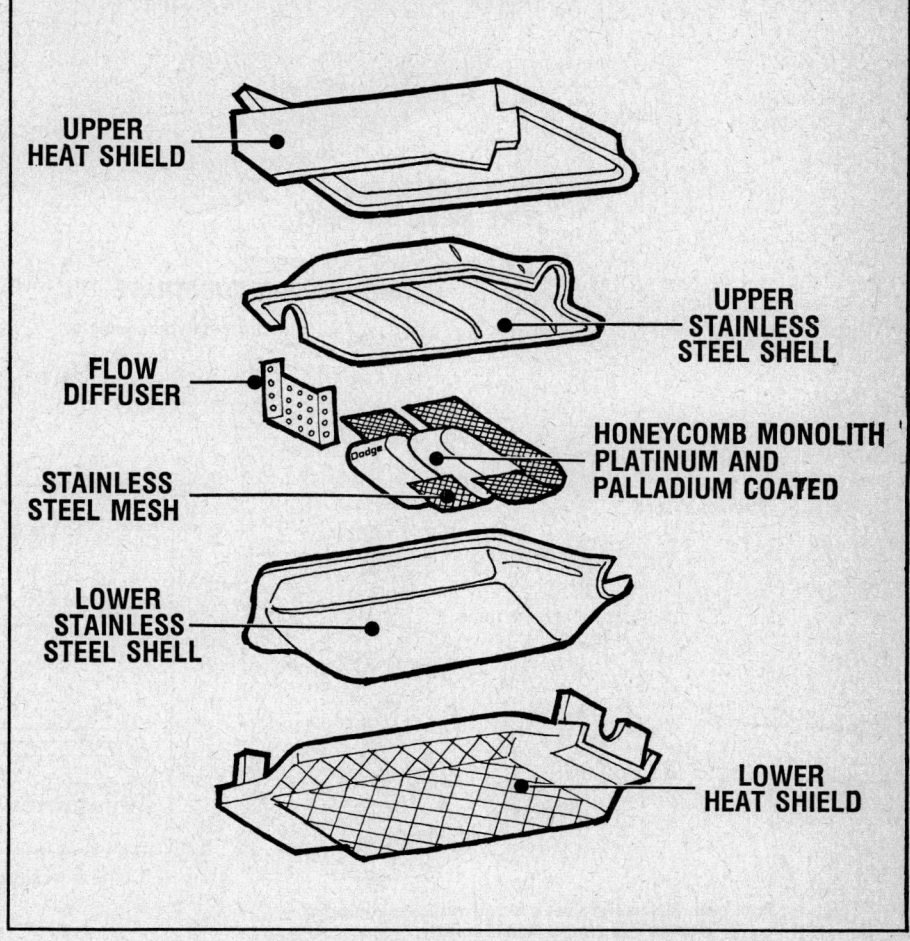

Fig. 2   Chrysler Corp. catalytic converter

EMISSION CONTROL SYSTEMS

Chrysler Corp. vehicles equipped with catalytic converters have a solenoid operated throttle control system, Fig. 5. This system maintains engine idle above 2000 RPM during certain conditions to protect the catalyst from high temperatures. Also this system prevents complete throttle closing at high engine RPM, in turn reducing the catalyst temperature under deceleration conditions.

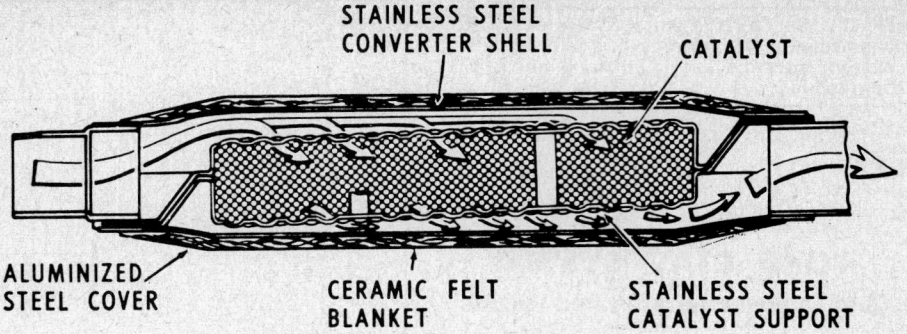

Fig. 1　General Motors catalytic converter

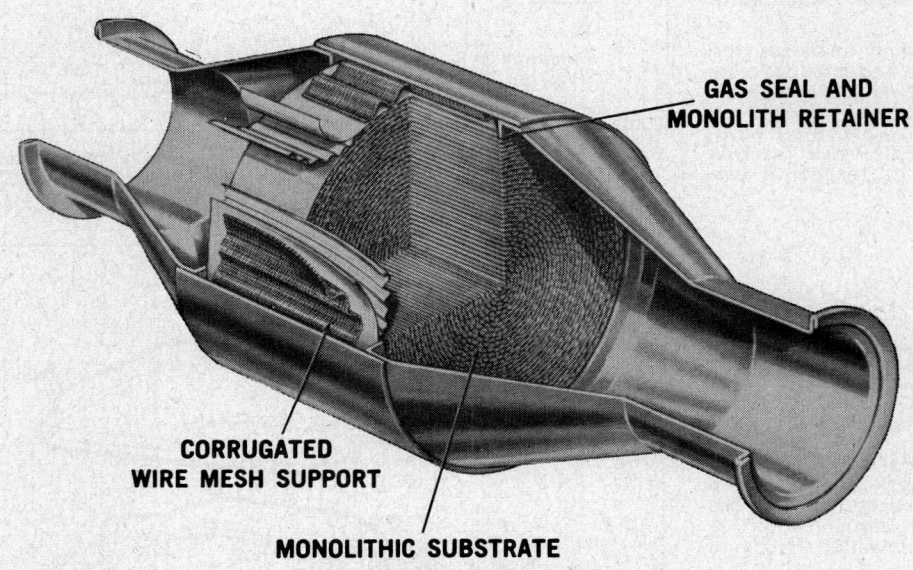

Fig. 3　Ford catalytic converter

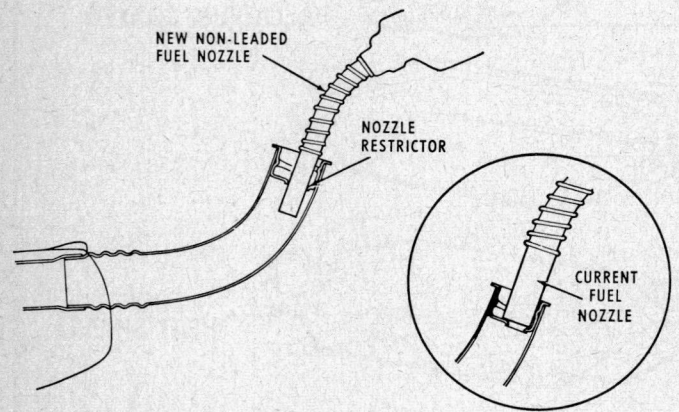

Fig. 4　Fuel tank filler safety neck for all vehicles equipped with catalytic converters (Typical)

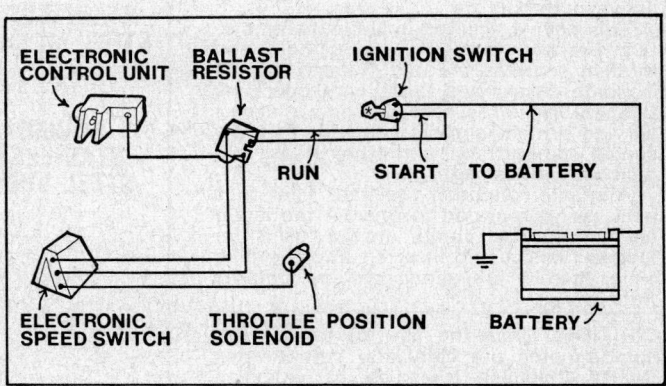

Fig. 5　Chrysler Corp. throttle control system for all vehicles equipped with catalytic converters

FUEL EVAPORATIVE EMISSION CONTROLS

CAUTION: The utmost care should be exercised when using a torch in the area of the fuel evaporation system as an open flame near these hoses may cause a fire and ultimate explosion.

NOTE: Vapor line hoses used in these systems are made from a special rubber material. Bulk service hoses are available for service and will be marked "EVAP". Ordinary fuel hoses should not be used as they are subject to deterioration and may clog system.

CAUTION: Installation of a fill cap from a non-emission fuel tank will render the system inoperative, since the non-emission fill cap is vented and the system must be sealed to function properly. Also if a nonvented fill cap is installed on a conventional tank, the result will be a serious deformation or a total collapse of the fuel tank.

to the valve cover of the engine. On V8 engines, the line is routed to the left valve cover. Vapors are then drawn into the PCV system and burned along with the normal air-fuel mixture. Most fuel tanks incorporate an integral fuel expansion tank to provide an air displacement area for normal fuel expansion, unless the tank itself is designed to provide an adequate air displacement area for fuel expansion.

The vent system routes raw fuel vapor to the engine valve cover. A check valve is included to prevent the flow of liquid fuel to the valve cover under all operating conditions.

The 1971-74 engines incorporate a "Fuel Vapor Storage (Charcoal) Canister". This canister contains activated charcoal granules which absorb and store the fuel tank vapors until they are drawn into the intake manifold through the PCV system on 1971-73 six cylinder engines or through the carburetor air cleaner on all V-8's and 1974 six cylinder engines.

The filler cap includes a two-way relief valve which is closed to atmosphere under normal operating conditions and opens only when an abnormal pressure or vacuum develops within the tank. It is normal to occasionally encounter an air pressure release when removing the filler cap.

compartment. Constant purging of vapors from the canister is accomplished through a calibrated orifice in the canister center connection to the PCV hose and/or the air cleaner snorkel.

General Motors fuel tanks include a fill limiting baffle which allows space for normal fuel expansion. To prevent damage to the tank from excessive internal or external pressure resulting from the closed system, a filler cap is used, which includes a two-way relief valve which opens only when an abnormal pressure or vacuum develops within the tank.

A liquid vapor separator is provided to prevent liquid fuel from entering the system. Liquid fuel entering the separator is spilled back into the tank while raw fuel vapor is passed into the lines.

The carbon canister provides a storage place for the raw fuel vapor when the engine is not running. When the engine is running, vapors are drawn from the canister into the engine.

Maintenance:

The only service required is that the filter mounted at the bottom of the canister be replaced at recommended intervals.

NOTE: The purge valve (used on some applications), can be repaired without replacing complete vapor canister, using repair kit, part No. 7041344. The service is NOT a routine maintenance item and should be performed if damage or parts are missing.

AMERICAN MOTORS FIG. 1

A closed fuel tank vent is used which routes the fuel vapors from the tank, through a check valve and connecting lines

GENERAL MOTORS FIG. 2

Fuel vapor is drawn from the tank, through a separator and lines, to a carbon-filled canister located in the engine

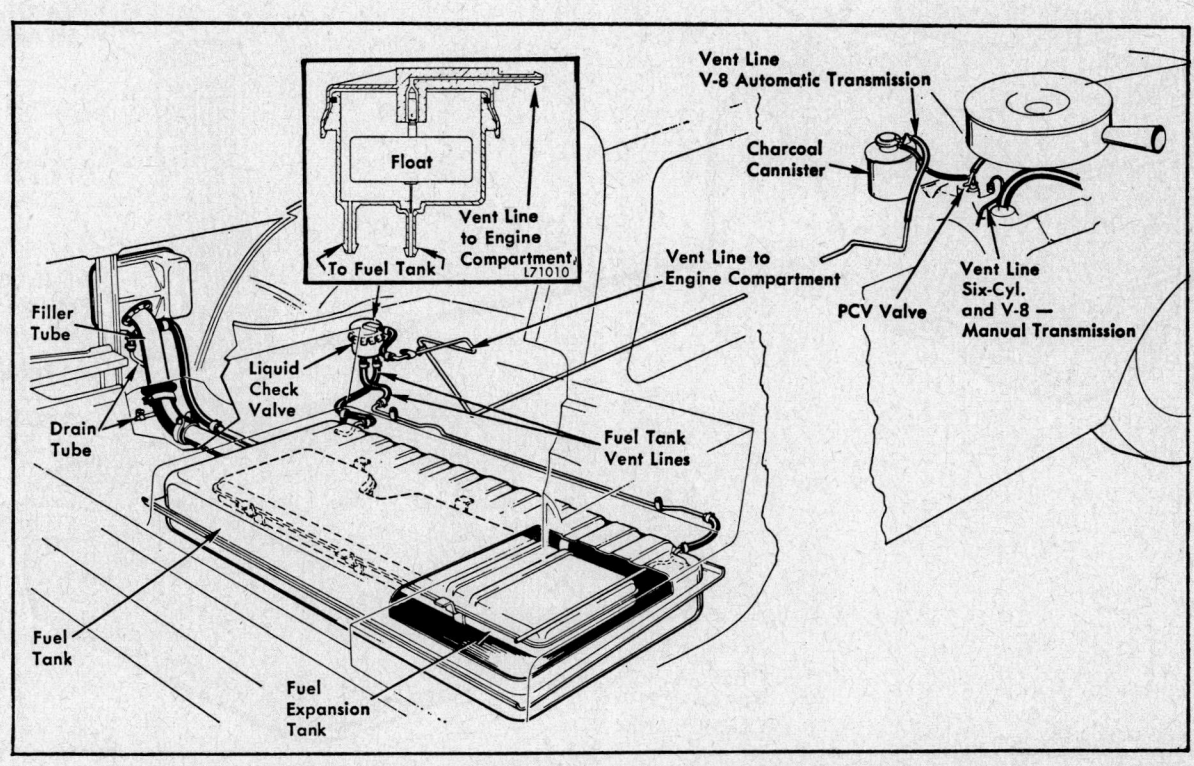

Fig. 1   Evaporative emission control system with charcoal canister. Typical American Motors

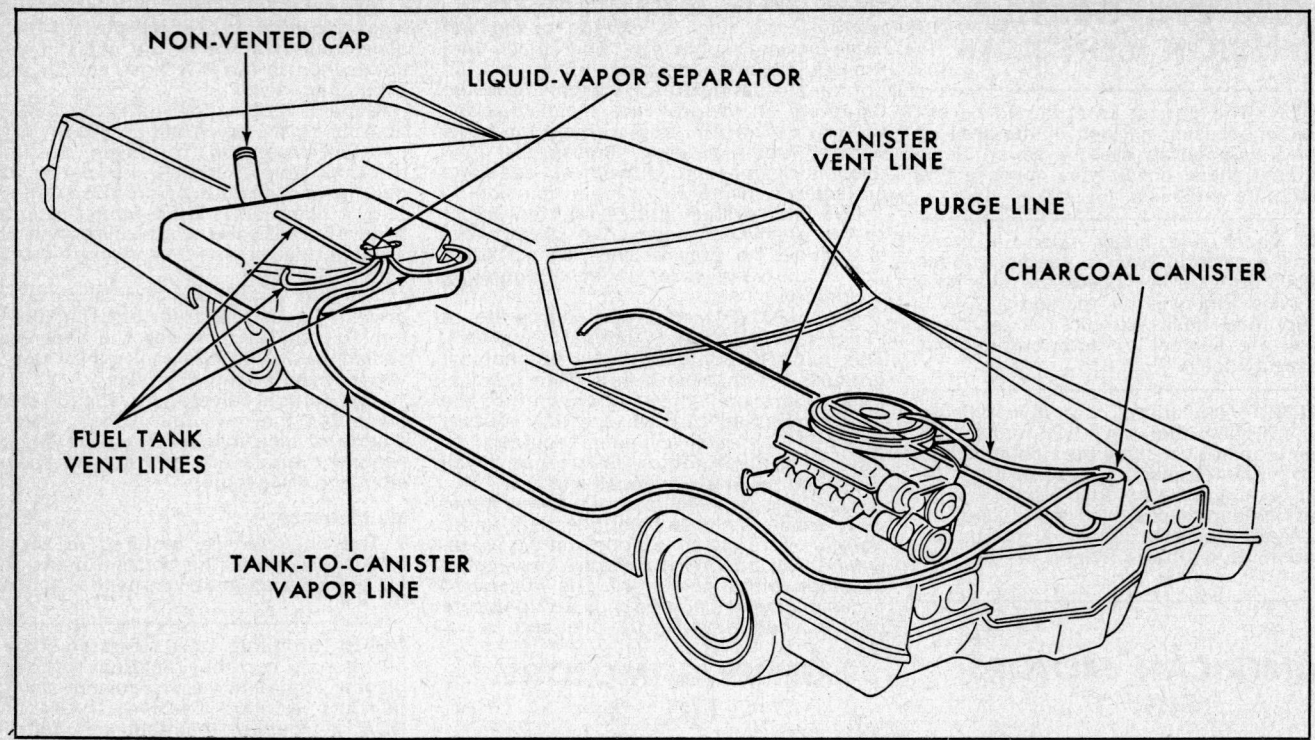

NON-VENTED CAP

LIQUID-VAPOR SEPARATOR

CANISTER VENT LINE

PURGE LINE

CHARCOAL CANISTER

FUEL TANK VENT LINES

TANK-TO-CANISTER VAPOR LINE

Fig. 2 Evaporative emission control system. General Motors (typical)

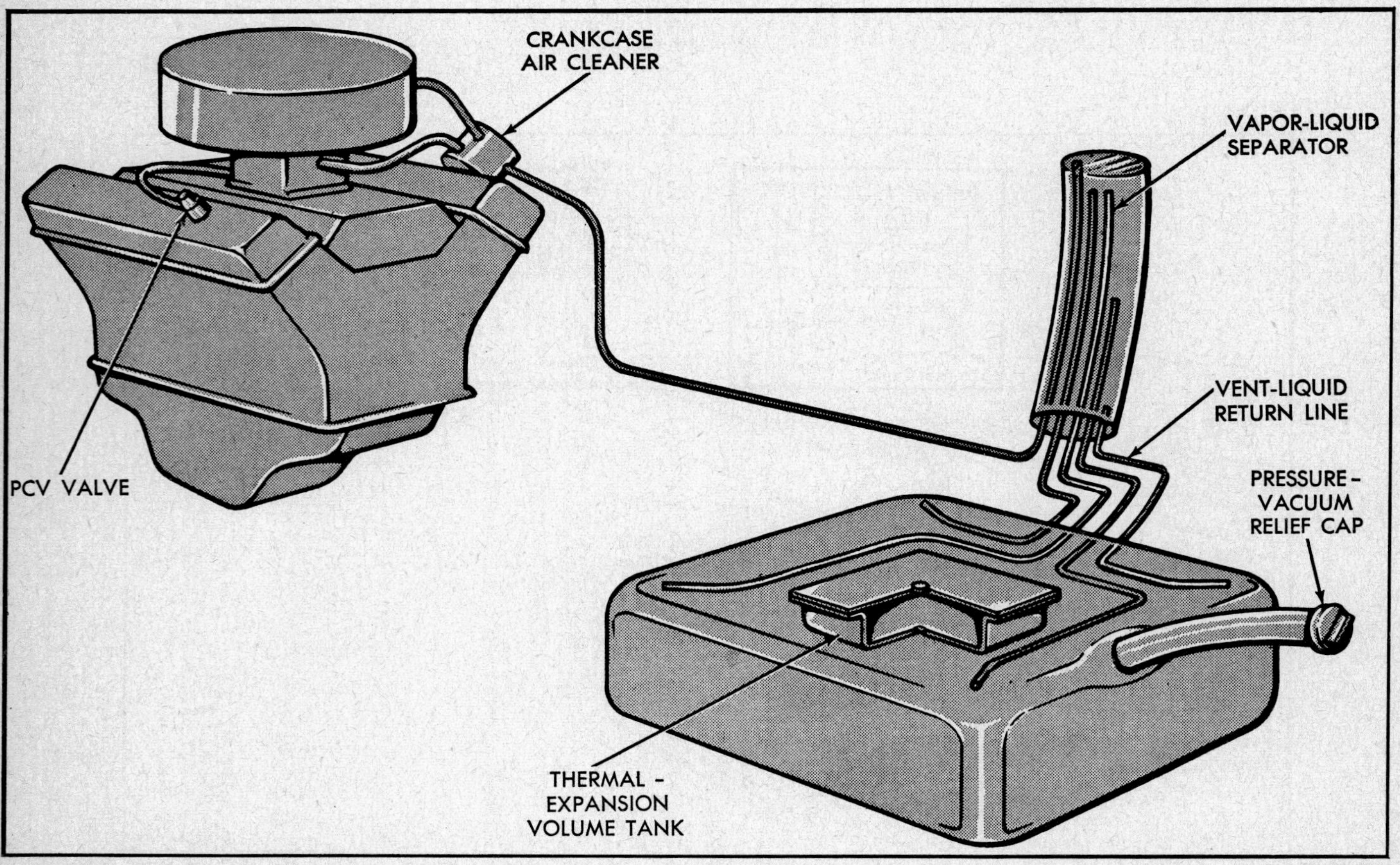

CRANKCASE AIR CLEANER

VAPOR-LIQUID SEPARATOR

VENT-LIQUID RETURN LINE

PCV VALVE

PRESSURE-VACUUM RELIEF CAP

THERMAL-EXPANSION VOLUME TANK

Fig. 3 Evaporative emission control system. Chrysler Corp., 1969-71

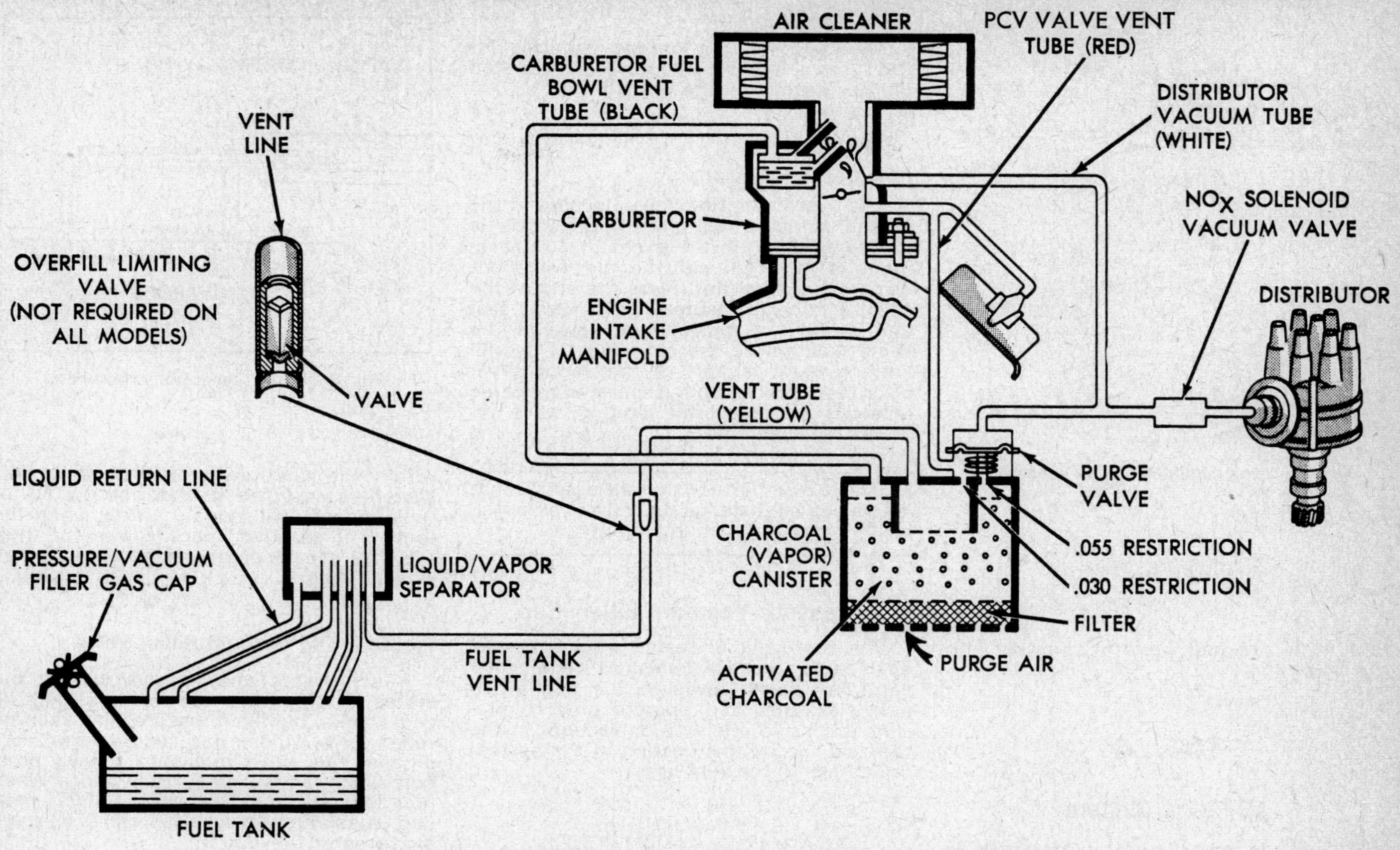

Fig. 4 Evaporative emission control system. Chrysler Corp., typical 1972-74

CHRYSLER CORP. FIG. 3

1969-71 System

This is a closed system venting fuel vapors through lines to the engine crankcase by way of the crankcase inlet air cleaner. With the engine running, the vapors are purged from the crankcase with the normal crankcase vapor.

The fuel tank incorporates an expansion tank to provide space for air displacement during normal fuel expansion. The filler cap is a special unit which incorporates a relief valve.

A liquid vapor separator is included between the tank and the vapor line to insure against liquid fuel entering the system. Liquid fuel is spilled back into the

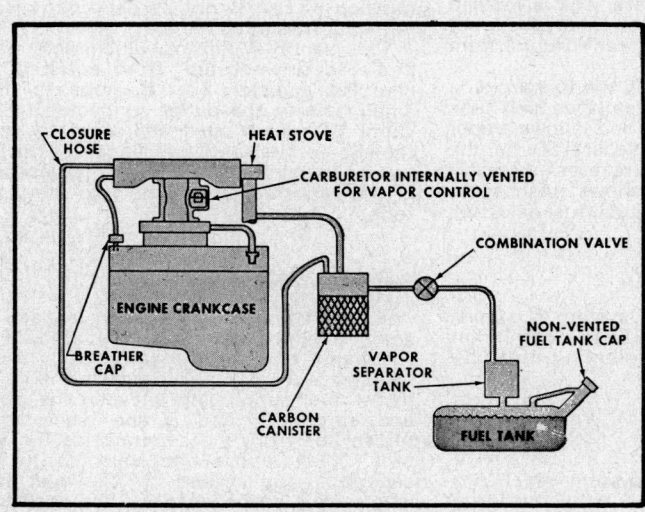

Fig. 5 Evaporative emission control system. Ford carbon storage type. 1970

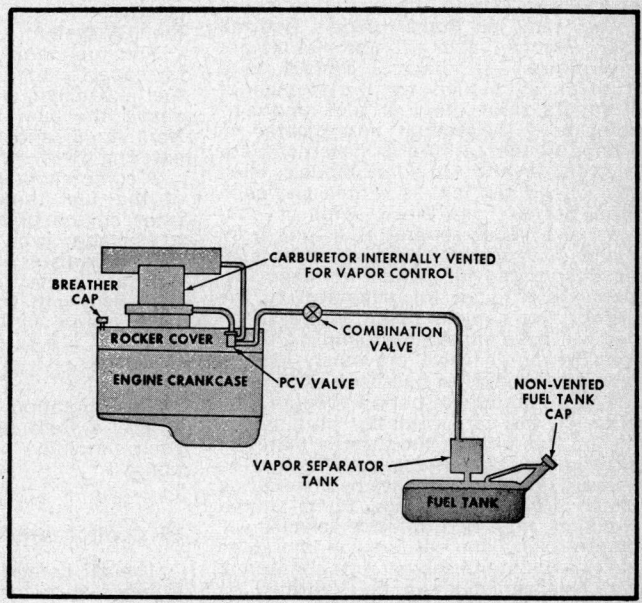

Fig. 6 Evaporative emission control system. Ford crankcase storage type. 1970

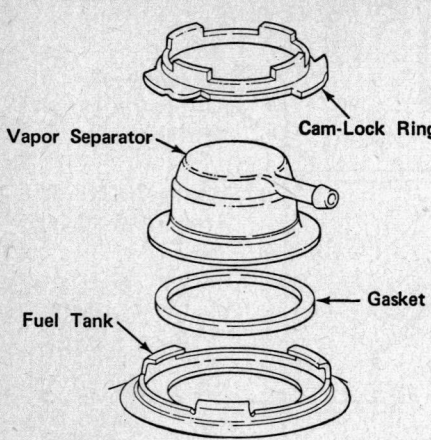

Fig. 7 Tank mounted vapor separator

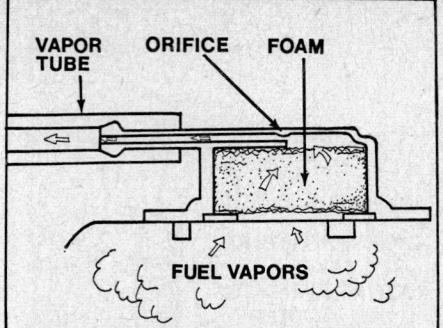

Fig. 8 Vapor separator crossection

Maintenance

The only service normally required for the system, is to replace the filter mounted in the bottom of the canister at 12,000 mile intervals.

Overfill Limiting Valve

The overfill limiting valve, located in the engine compartment on some models is not serviceable, in the event that replacement is required, cut the old valve out using a tubing cutter. Flare the end of the existing tube to insure a good vapor seal and install the replacement valve in the same position as the old valve. If overfill limiting valve is part of the vapor separator, the entire vapor separator must be replaced if the overfill limiting valve requires replacement.

NOTE: It is important that all overfill limiting valves be installed as vertical as possible, in order to function properly.

Pressure-Vacuum Filler Cap

The fuel tank is sealed with a special engineered pressure vacuum relief filler cap. The relief valves in the cap are a safety feature, and operate only to prevent excessive pressure or vacuum in the tank caused by malfunction in the system or damage to the vent lines.

FORD MOTOR CO. FIGS. 5 & 6

1970

In this system, fuel vapor is transported either to a carbon canister or the engine crankcase, depending on the engine application. It is then drawn into the engine, from the carbon canister to the air cleaner, or from the crankcase through the PCV system.

The fuel tank is designed to limit the fill capacity to provide space for normal fuel expansion. A separate tank is located above the fuel tank to separate vapor from liquid and prevent any liquid from entering the system.

A combination valve on the forward side of the fuel tank isolates the fuel tank from engine pressures and allows vapor to escape from the separator to the carbon canister. It also relieves excessive fuel tank pressure and allows fresh air to be drawn into the tank as fuel is used.

1971-74

The operation of the system is similar to the system used in 1970, but it has been simplified by the following modifications:

Fill Control Vent System

The fill control vent system which provides positive control of fuel height during fill operations is made possible by the design of the filler pipe and by vent lines

within the filler neck or fuel tank. This system is designed so that about 10% of tank capacity will remain empty when the tank is filled. This space allows for thermal fuel expansion and temporary storage of fuel vapors.

Pressure and Vacuum Relief Valve

The pressure and vacuum system operates through the use of a sealed fill cap with a built-in pressure and vacuum relief valve. Under normal operating conditions, the valve opens to relieve pressure when it exceeds $\frac{3}{4}$ to $1\frac{1}{4}$ psi. When fuel tank vacuum reaches $\frac{1}{2}$ inch mercury maximum, the valve opens allowing air to enter the system.

Vapor Vent and Storage System

This system, on vertically mounted fuel tanks consists of a vapor separator, Fig. 7, mounted on the uppermost surface of the tank. The empty space at the top of the tank provides adequate breathing space for the vapor separator. Horizontally mounted fuel tanks use a raised mounting section for the vapor separator. This raised section provides additional breathing space for the vapor separator since the space allowed for thermal expansion of fuel is not as deep as it is on vertically mounted tanks.

The vapor separator which acts as a baffle to prevent fuel from entering the charcoal canister, Fig. 8, consists of a small hole in the outlet connected to the vapor tube plus open cell foam to separate liquid fuel and fuel vapors. The fuel vapors in the tank go through the opening in the vapor separator and into the vapor tube.

Fuel Vapor Return System

A fuel vapor return system is used on some engines to reduce the amount of fuel vapor entering the carburetor. It consists of a fuel vapor separator installed in the fuel supply line between the pump and carburetor and a one piece vapor return line from the separator to the fuel tank. Fuel vapors are collected in the separator and routed to the fuel tank where they recondense or are contained by the evaporative emission control system.

tank while raw fuel vapor is admitted into the vapor line.

FIG. 4

1972-74 System

In this system when the fuel tank is filled to the base of the filler tube, vapors can no longer escape, they become trapped above the fuel. Vapor flow through the vent line is blocked by the limiting valve; and the filler tube is blocked by fuel preventing more fuel to enter the tank. At any time pressures in the tank rise above operating pressures of the limiting valve, about $\frac{1}{2}$ psi the valve opens and allows vapors to flow forward to the charcoal canister. Due to the configuration of the fuel tank on some models and all station wagons, vapor separator tanks are not required. The charcoal canister is a feature on all models for the storage of fuel vapors from the fuel tank and carburetor bowl. A vacuum port located in the base of the carburetor governs vapor flow to the engine. On some models, each corner of the fuel tank is vented and each of the hoses from these vents if connected to a vapor separator. A tube from the separator leads to the charcoal canister. Evaporated fuel vapor from the fuel tank, flows through the separator to the canister. The canister used in 1973 vehicles will have three hoses and no purge valve. The purge valve previously located on top of the canister has been eliminated by using an additional ported vacuum connection on the carburetor for purging the canister. This utilizes the throttle plates of the carburetor as purge valve. This system will improve hot idle quality by eliminating canister purging during idle. Some limited production, High Performance vehicles will continue to use the earlier type two stage canister which utilizes an integral purge valve. This canister can be identified by four hose connections while the new type canister uses only three.

COMPONENTS LOCATION

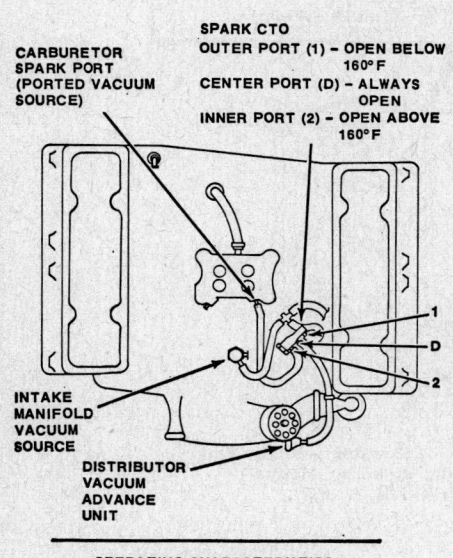

Fig. CL1 Spark CTO system vacuum hose routing. 1974 American Motors V8-401

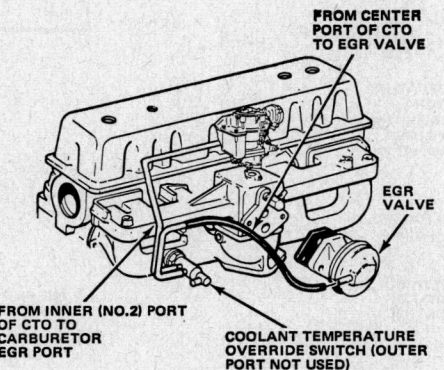

Fig. CL2 EGR system vacuum hose routing. 1974 American Motors six cylinder

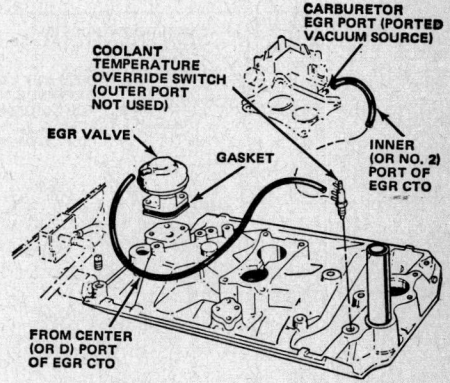

Fig. CL3 EGR system vacuum hose routing. 1974 American Motors V8

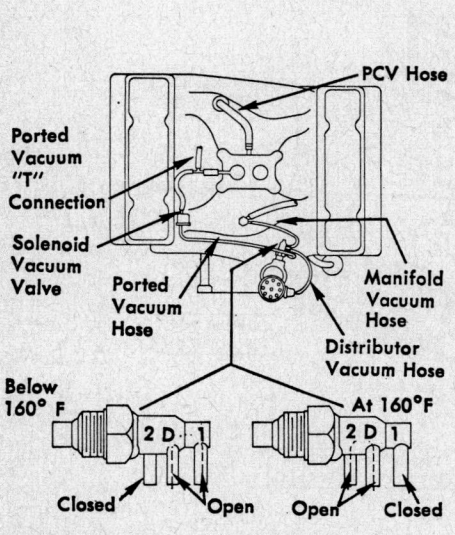

Fig. CL4 CTO system vacuum hose routing. 1972 American Motors

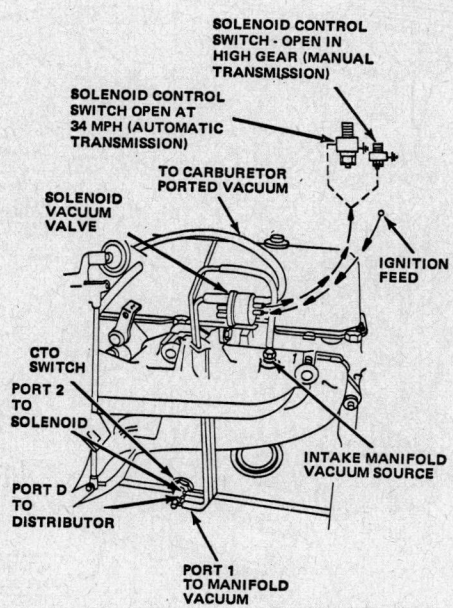

Fig. CL5 TCS system vacuum and wiring. 1972-74 American Motors 6-232

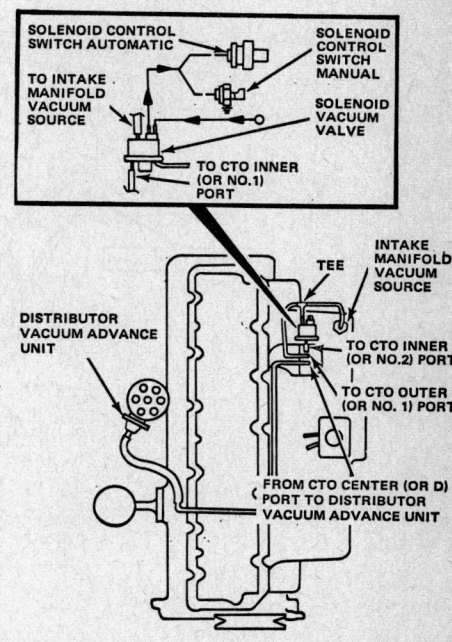

Fig. CL6 TCS system vacuum and wiring. 1972-74 American Motors Matador with 6-258

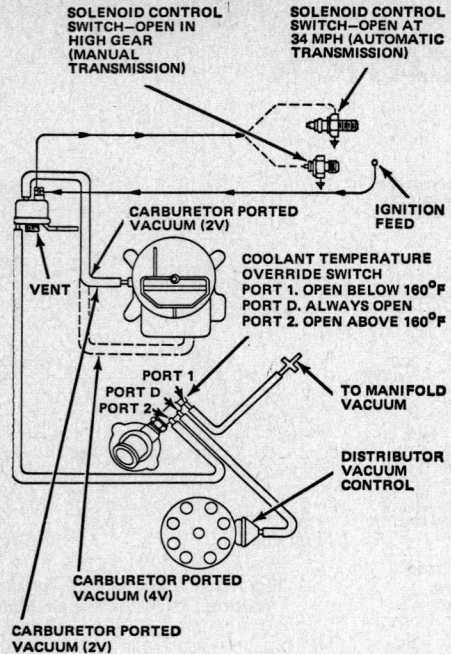

Fig. CL7 TCS system vacuum and wiring. American Motors V8-390 & 401

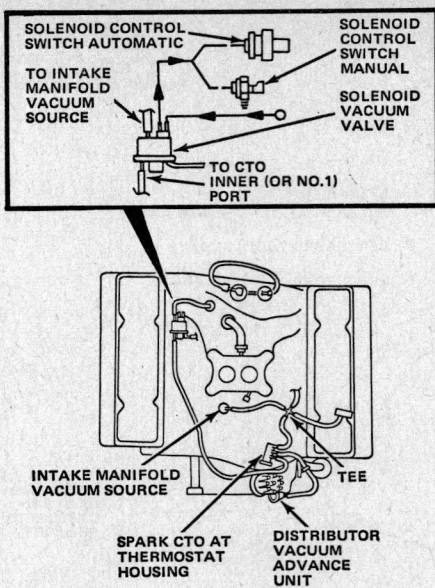

Fig. CL8 TCS system vacuum and wiring. American Motors V8-304 & 360

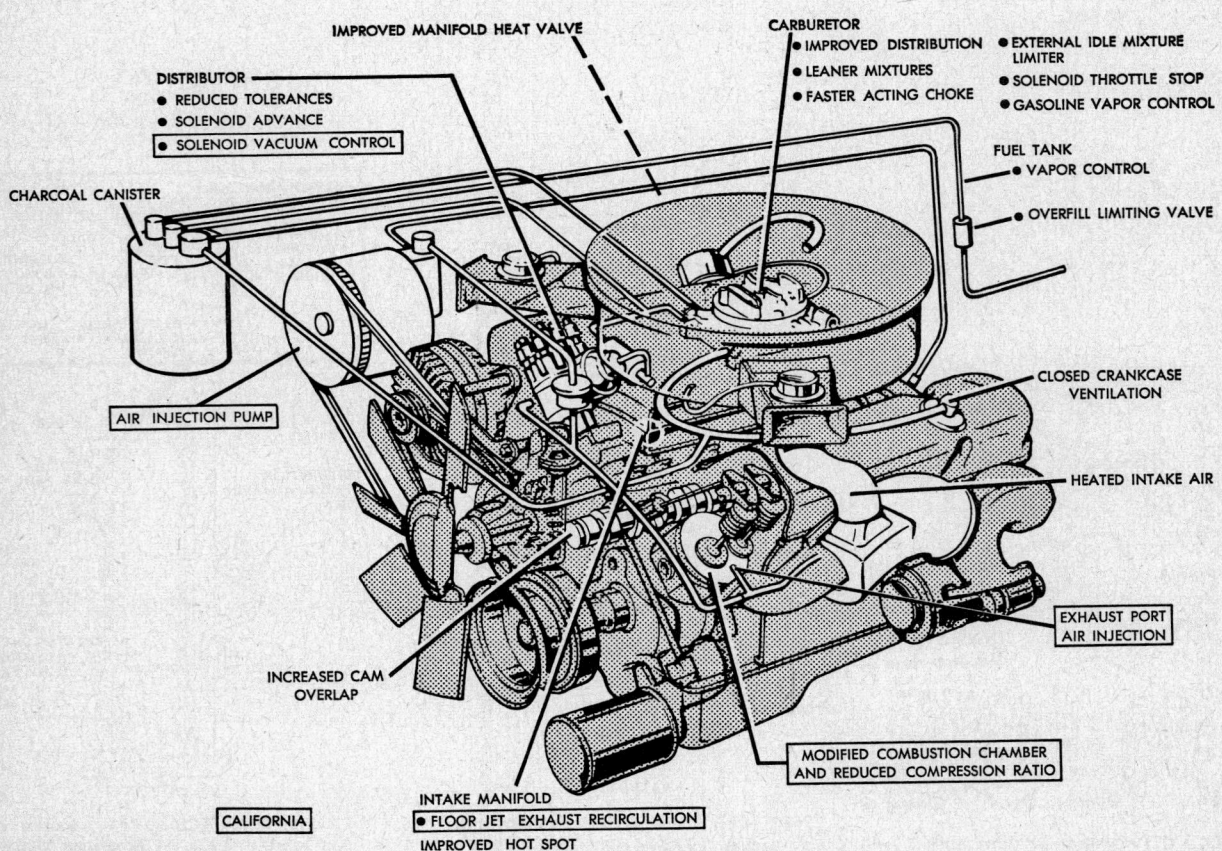

Fig. CL9 Chrysler Emission Control System. 1972

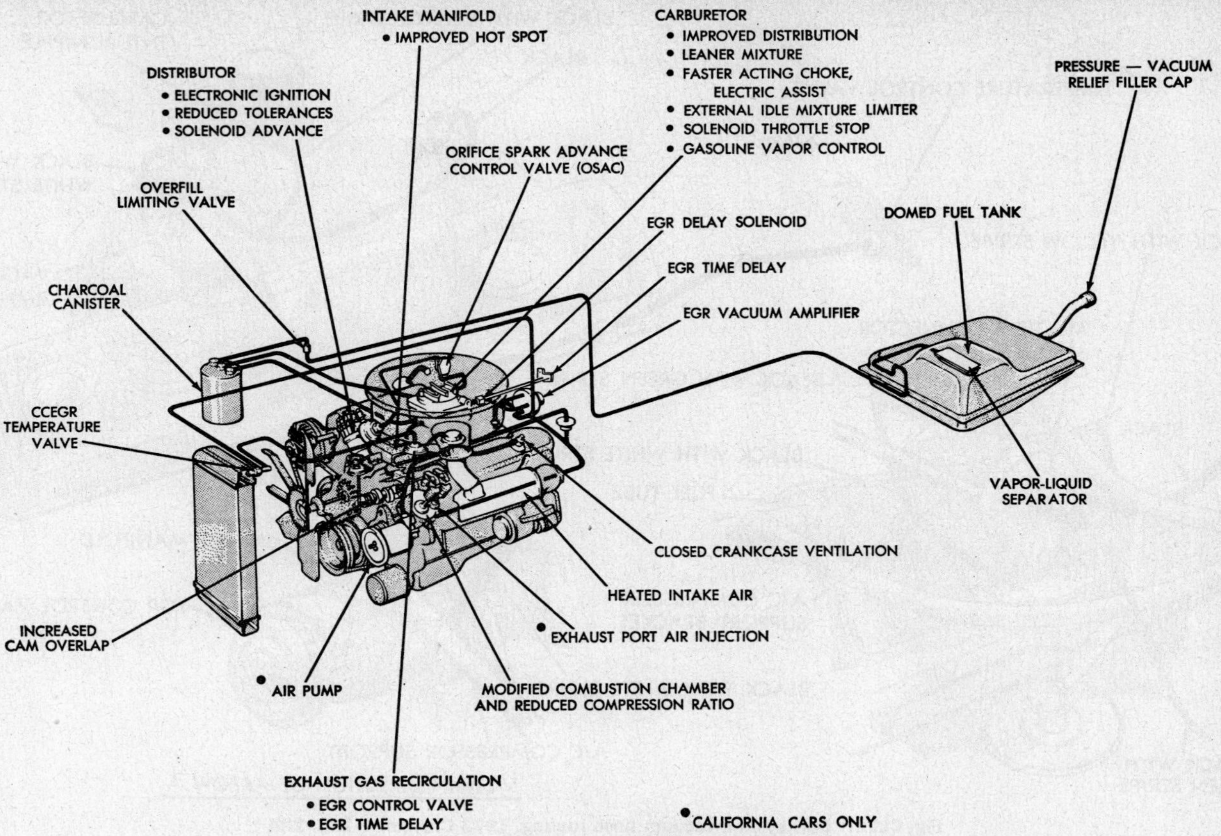

INTAKE MANIFOLD
• IMPROVED HOT SPOT

CARBURETOR
• IMPROVED DISTRIBUTION
• LEANER MIXTURE
• FASTER ACTING CHOKE,
  ELECTRIC ASSIST
• EXTERNAL IDLE MIXTURE LIMITER
• SOLENOID THROTTLE STOP
• GASOLINE VAPOR CONTROL

PRESSURE — VACUUM
RELIEF FILLER CAP

DISTRIBUTOR
• ELECTRONIC IGNITION
• REDUCED TOLERANCES
• SOLENOID ADVANCE

ORIFICE SPARK ADVANCE
CONTROL VALVE (OSAC)

OVERFILL
LIMITING VALVE

EGR DELAY SOLENOID

EGR TIME DELAY

DOMED FUEL TANK

EGR VACUUM AMPLIFIER

CHARCOAL
CANISTER

CCEGR
TEMPERATURE
VALVE

VAPOR-LIQUID
SEPARATOR

CLOSED CRANKCASE VENTILATION

HEATED INTAKE AIR

INCREASED
CAM OVERLAP

EXHAUST PORT AIR INJECTION

AIR PUMP

MODIFIED COMBUSTION CHAMBER
AND REDUCED COMPRESSION RATIO

EXHAUST GAS RECIRCULATION
• EGR CONTROL VALVE
• EGR TIME DELAY

• CALIFORNIA CARS ONLY

Fig. CL10   Chrysler Emission Control System. 1973-74

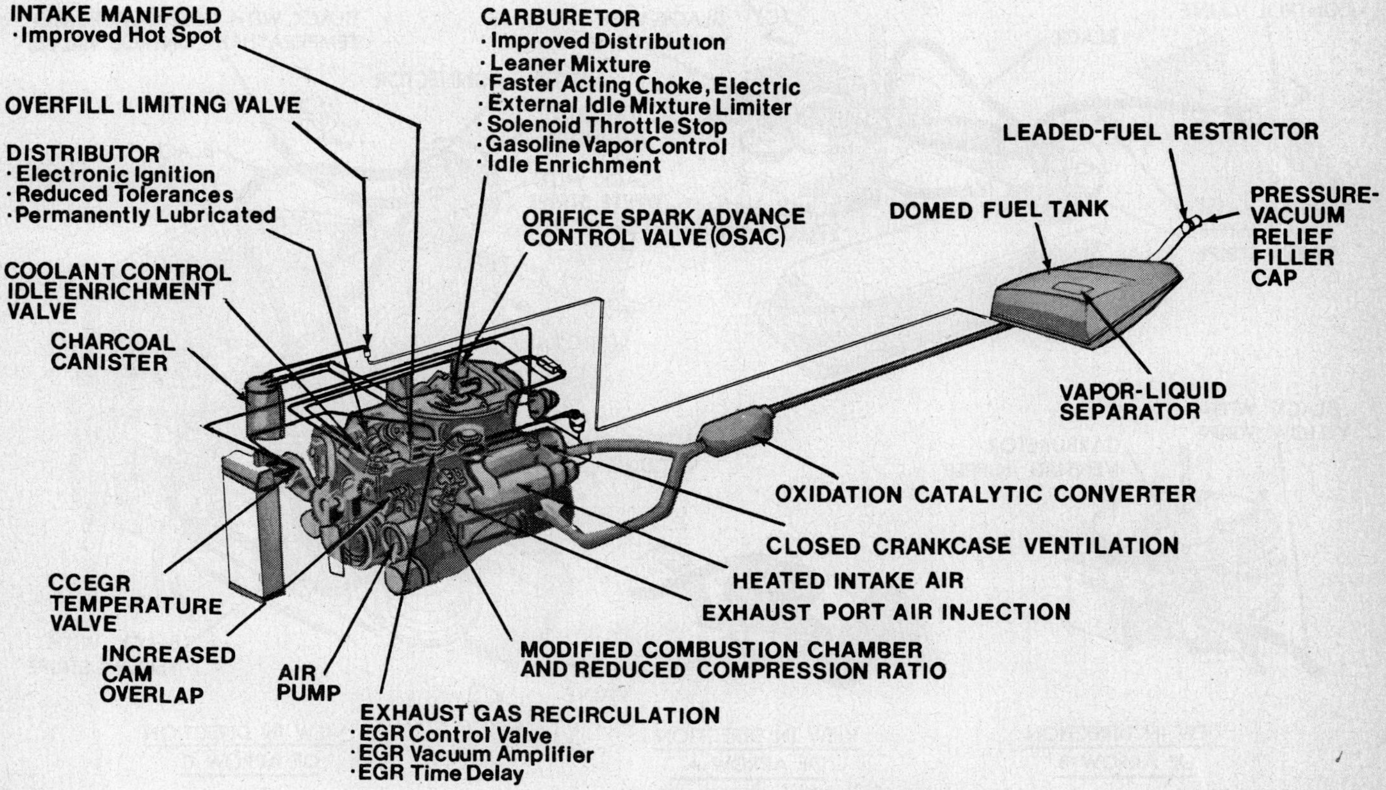

INTAKE MANIFOLD
·Improved Hot Spot

CARBURETOR
·Improved Distribution
·Leaner Mixture
·Faster Acting Choke, Electric
·External Idle Mixture Limiter
·Solenoid Throttle Stop
·Gasoline Vapor Control
·Idle Enrichment

OVERFILL LIMITING VALVE

LEADED-FUEL RESTRICTOR

DISTRIBUTOR
·Electronic Ignition
·Reduced Tolerances
·Permanently Lubricated

ORIFICE SPARK ADVANCE
CONTROL VALVE (OSAC)

DOMED FUEL TANK

PRESSURE-
VACUUM
RELIEF
FILLER
CAP

COOLANT CONTROL
IDLE ENRICHMENT
VALVE

CHARCOAL
CANISTER

VAPOR-LIQUID
SEPARATOR

CCEGR
TEMPERATURE
VALVE

OXIDATION CATALYTIC CONVERTER

CLOSED CRANKCASE VENTILATION

INCREASED
CAM
OVERLAP

AIR
PUMP

HEATED INTAKE AIR

EXHAUST PORT AIR INJECTION

MODIFIED COMBUSTION CHAMBER
AND REDUCED COMPRESSION RATIO

EXHAUST GAS RECIRCULATION
·EGR Control Valve
·EGR Vacuum Amplifier
·EGR Time Delay

Fig. CL11   Chrysler Emission Control System. 1975

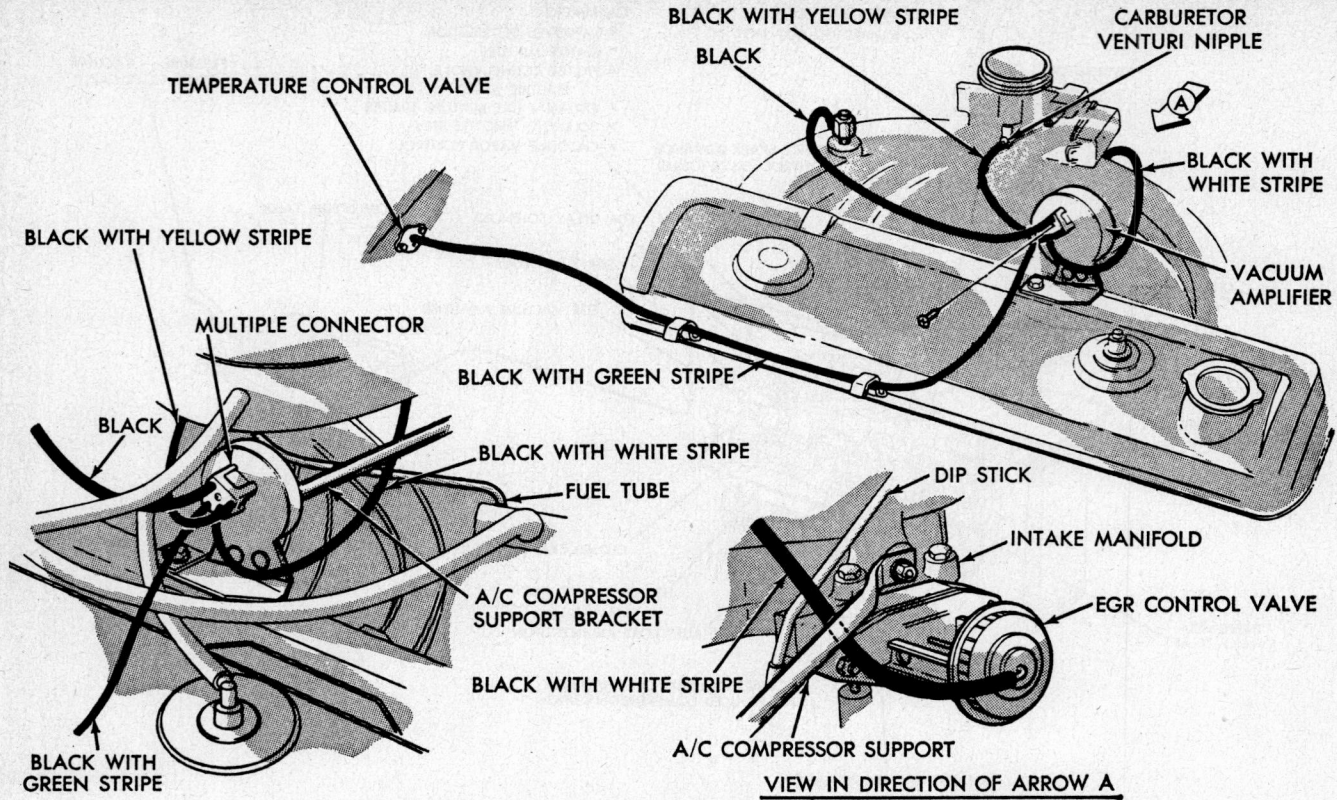

TEMPERATURE CONTROL VALVE

BLACK WITH YELLOW STRIPE

BLACK WITH YELLOW STRIPE

BLACK

MULTIPLE CONNECTOR

BLACK

CARBURETOR VENTURI NIPPLE

BLACK WITH WHITE STRIPE

VACUUM AMPLIFIER

BLACK WITH GREEN STRIPE

BLACK WITH WHITE STRIPE

FUEL TUBE

DIP STICK

INTAKE MANIFOLD

EGR CONTROL VALVE

A/C COMPRESSOR SUPPORT BRACKET

BLACK WITH WHITE STRIPE

A/C COMPRESSOR SUPPORT

BLACK WITH GREEN STRIPE

VIEW IN DIRECTION OF ARROW A

Fig. CL12   EGR system vacuum hose routing. 1973 Chrysler 6-198, 225

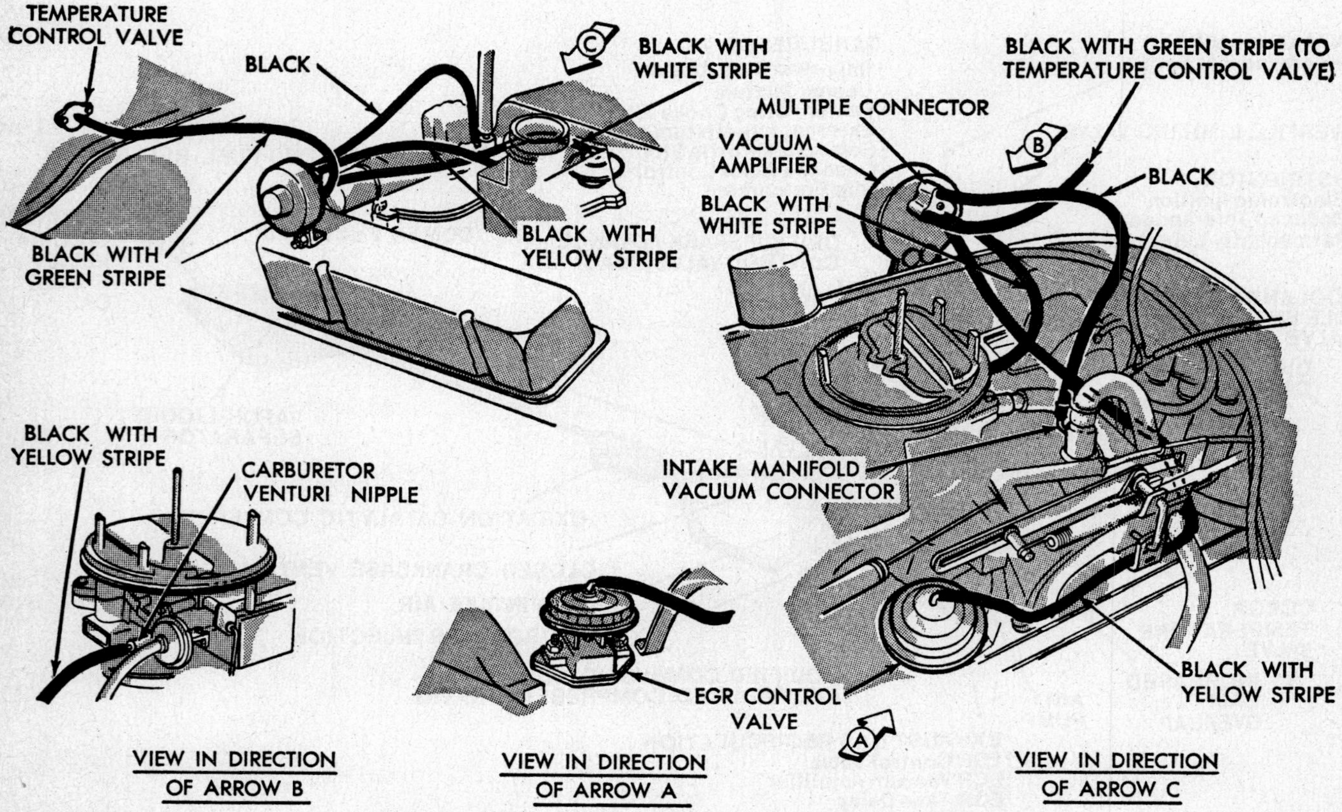

TEMPERATURE CONTROL VALVE

BLACK

BLACK WITH WHITE STRIPE

BLACK WITH GREEN STRIPE (TO TEMPERATURE CONTROL VALVE)

MULTIPLE CONNECTOR

VACUUM AMPLIFIER

BLACK WITH WHITE STRIPE

BLACK

BLACK WITH YELLOW STRIPE

BLACK WITH GREEN STRIPE

BLACK WITH YELLOW STRIPE

CARBURETOR VENTURI NIPPLE

INTAKE MANIFOLD VACUUM CONNECTOR

EGR CONTROL VALVE

BLACK WITH YELLOW STRIPE

VIEW IN DIRECTION OF ARROW B

VIEW IN DIRECTION OF ARROW A

VIEW IN DIRECTION OF ARROW C

Fig. CL13   EGR system vacuum hose routing. 1973 Chrysler V8-360

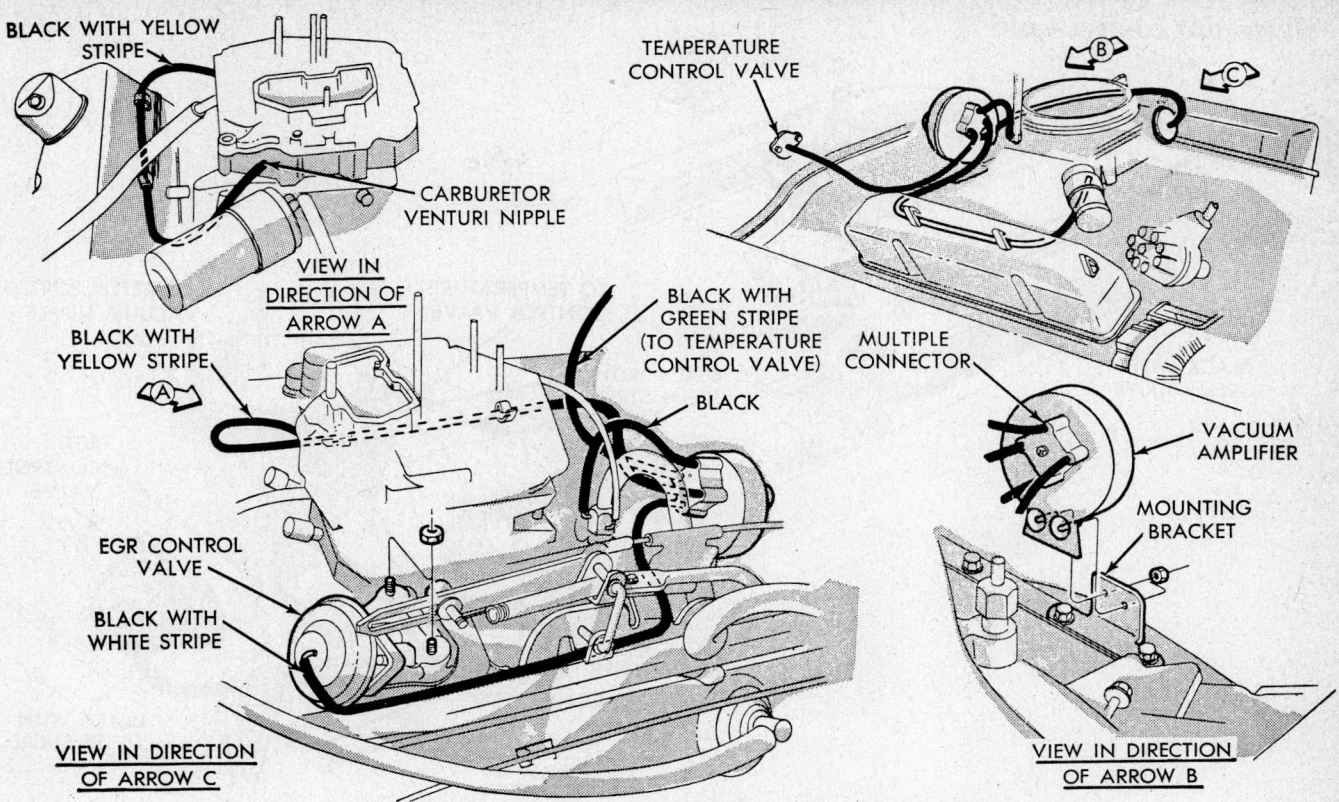

Fig. CL14   EGR system vacuum hose routing. 1973 Chrysler V8-440

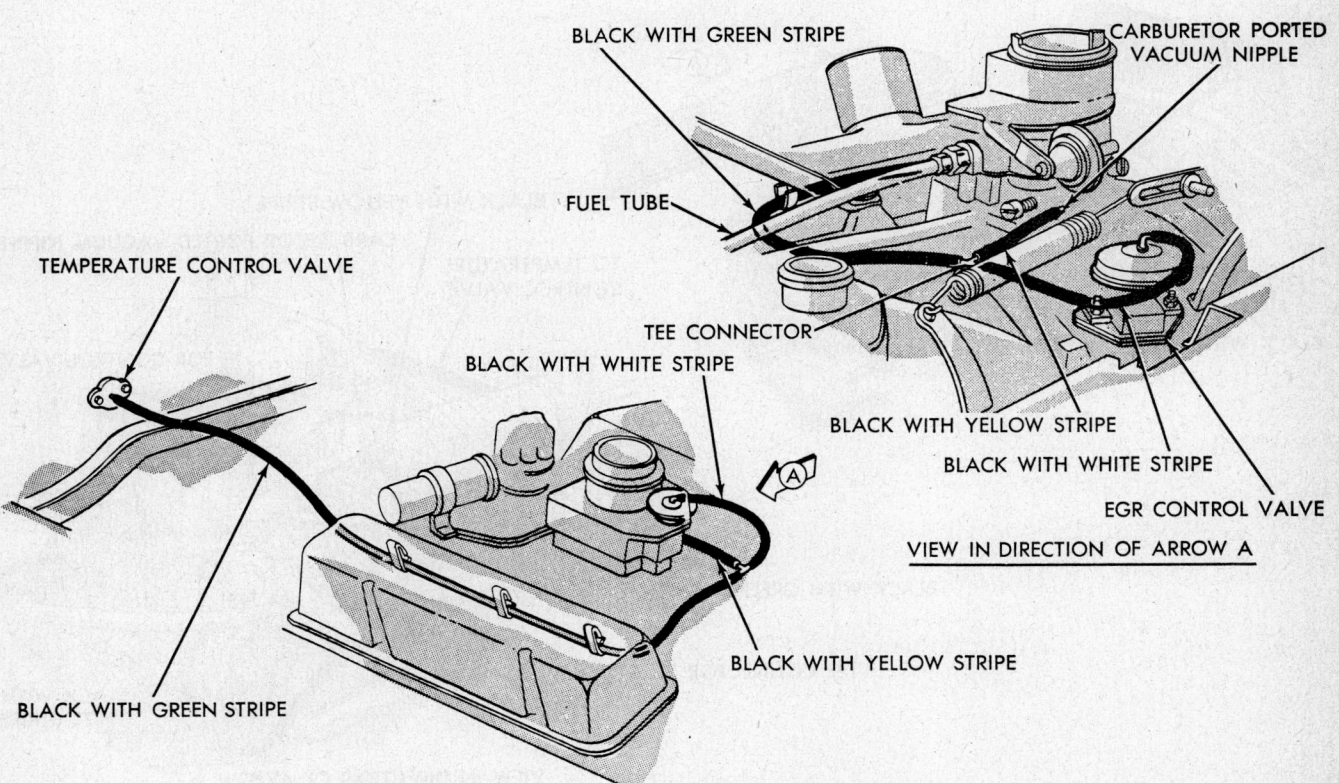

Fig. CL15   EGR system vacuum hose routing. 1973 Chrysler V8-318

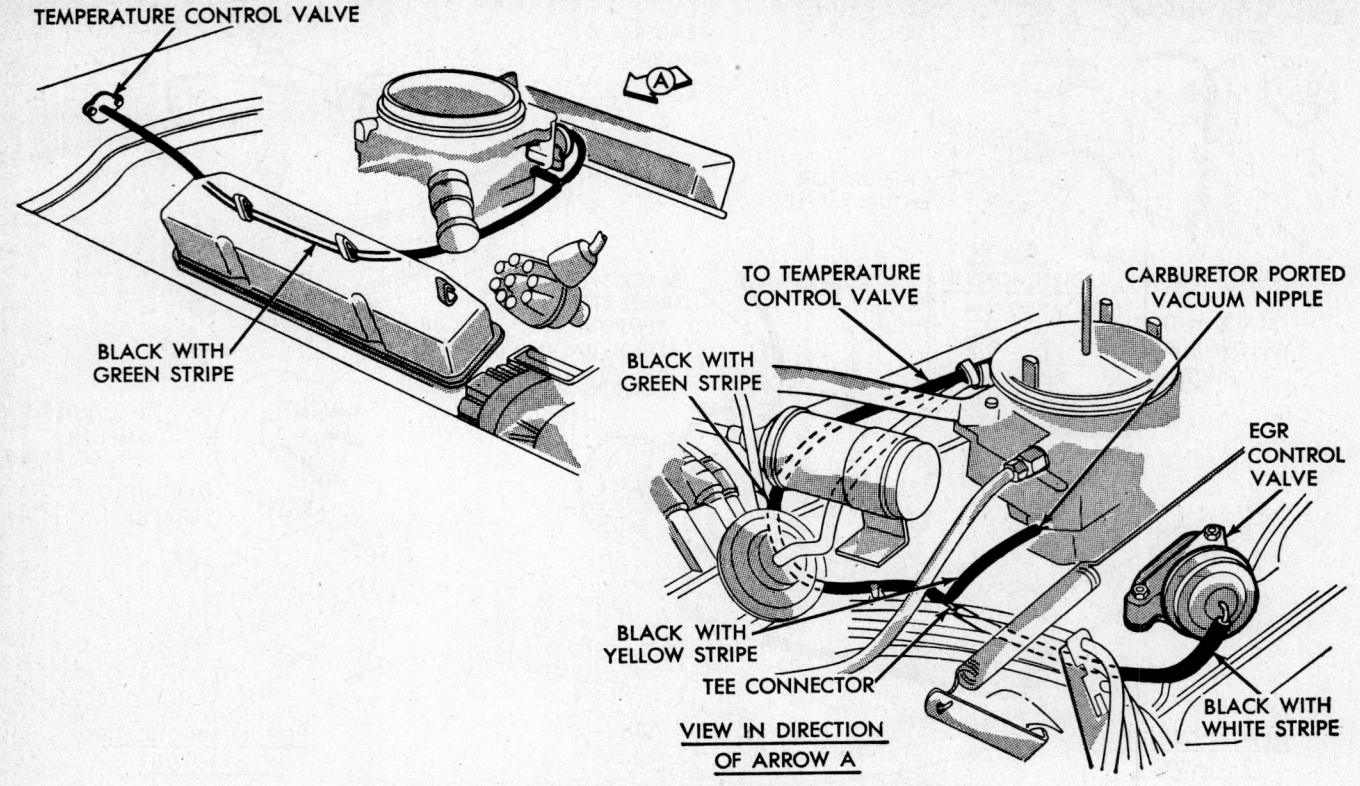

TEMPERATURE CONTROL VALVE

BLACK WITH GREEN STRIPE

TO TEMPERATURE CONTROL VALVE

CARBURETOR PORTED VACUUM NIPPLE

BLACK WITH GREEN STRIPE

EGR CONTROL VALVE

BLACK WITH YELLOW STRIPE

TEE CONNECTOR

BLACK WITH WHITE STRIPE

VIEW IN DIRECTION OF ARROW A

Fig. CL16   EGR system vacuum hose routing. 1973 Chrysler V8-400

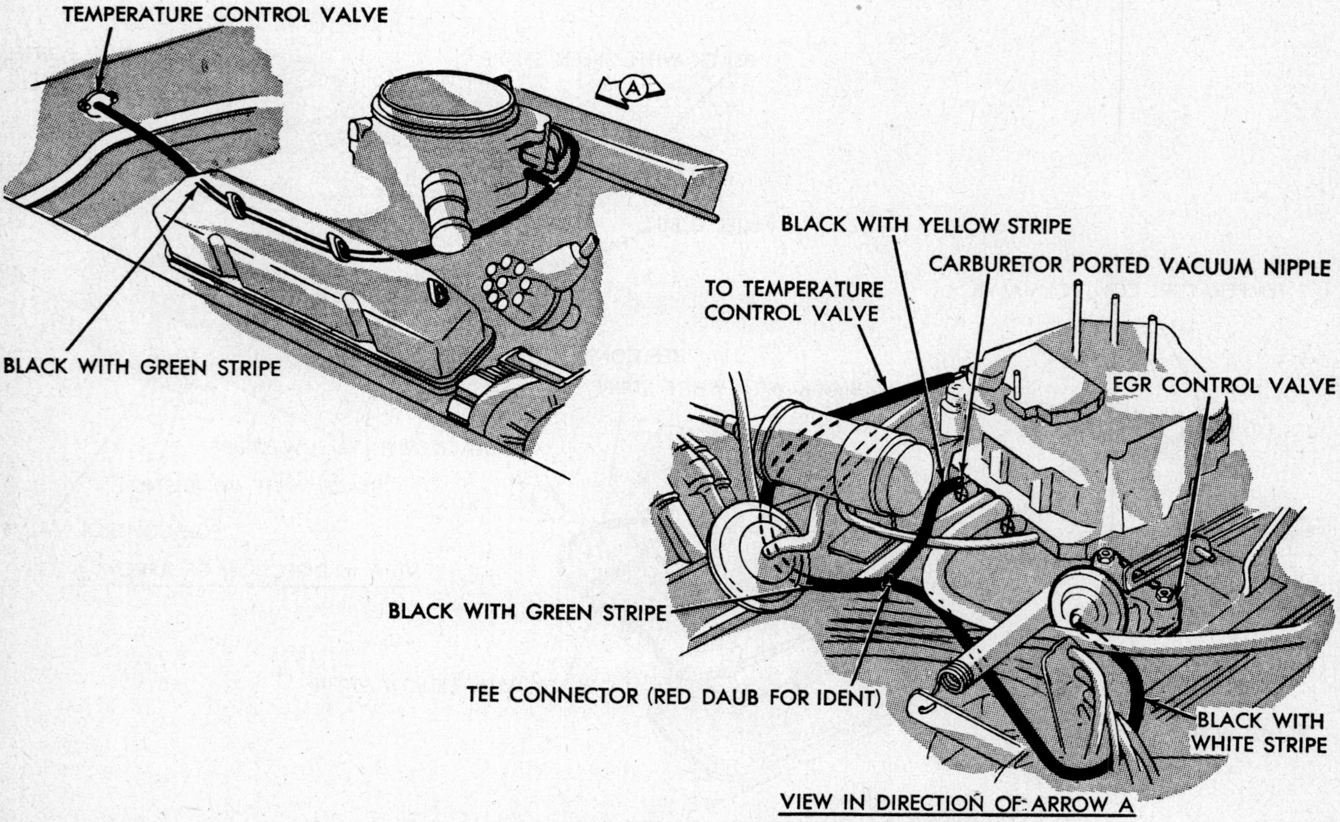

TEMPERATURE CONTROL VALVE

BLACK WITH GREEN STRIPE

BLACK WITH YELLOW STRIPE

CARBURETOR PORTED VACUUM NIPPLE

TO TEMPERATURE CONTROL VALVE

EGR CONTROL VALVE

BLACK WITH GREEN STRIPE

TEE CONNECTOR (RED DAUB FOR IDENT)

BLACK WITH WHITE STRIPE

VIEW IN DIRECTION OF ARROW A

Fig. CL17   EGR system vacuum hose routing. 1973 Chrysler V8-440 High Performance

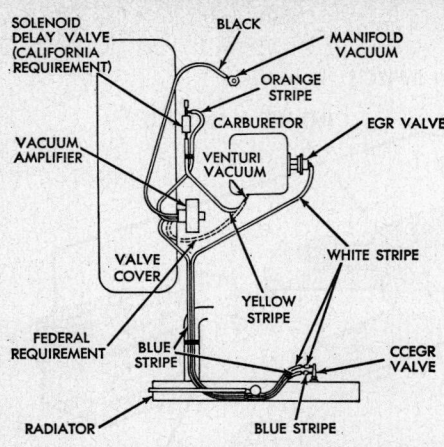

Fig. CL18 EGR system vacuum hose routing. 1974 Chrysler 6-198, 225

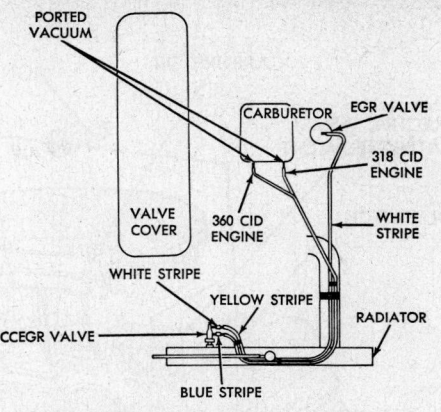

Fig. CL19 EGR system vacuum hose routing. 1974 Chrysler V8-318, 360 (ported vacuum) exc. California

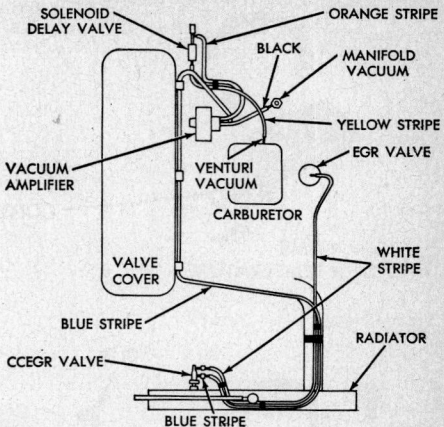

Fig. CL20 EGR system vacuum hose routing. 1974 Chrysler V8-318 (venturi system), California

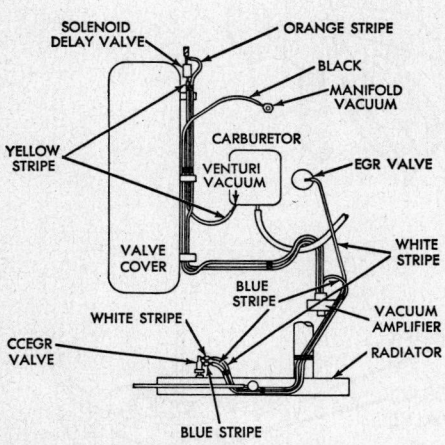

Fig. CL21 EGR system vacuum hose routing. 1974 Chrysler V8-360 (venturi system), California

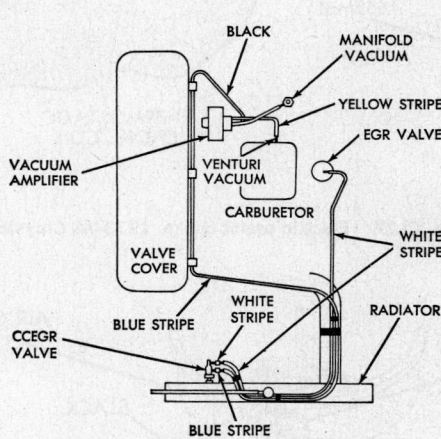

Fig. CL22 EGR system vacuum hose routing. 1974 Chrysler V8-360 (venturi system) exc. California

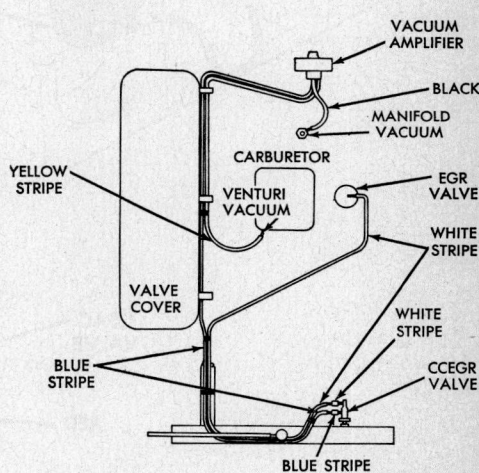

Fig. CL23 EGR system vacuum hose routing. 1974 Chrysler V8-400, 440 (venturi system) exc. California

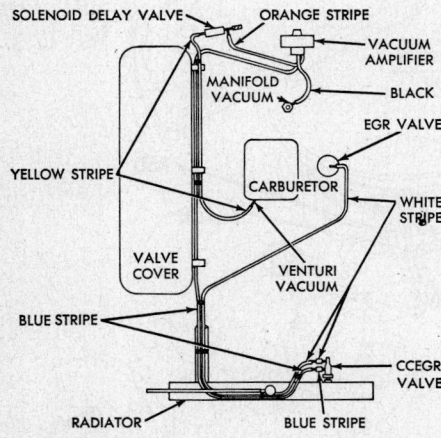

Fig. CL24 EGR system vacuum hose routing. 1974 Chrysler V8-400, 440 (venturi system), California

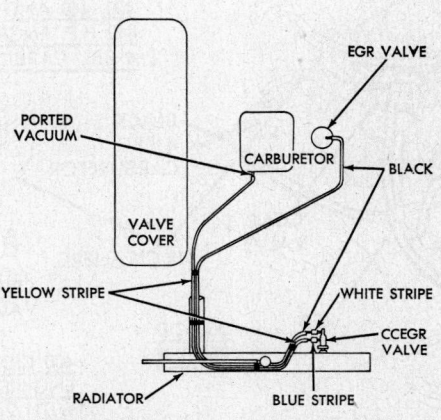

Fig. CL25 EGR system vacuum hose routing. 1974 Chrysler V8-400, 440 (ported system), exc. California

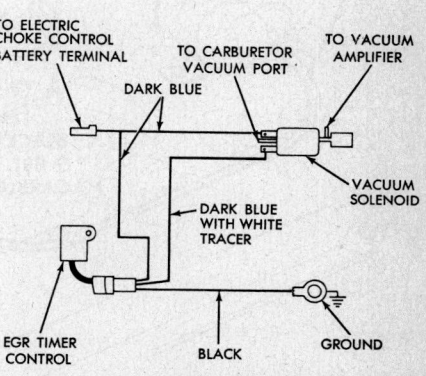

Fig. CL26 EGR Time Delay Valve system wiring. 1974 Chrysler

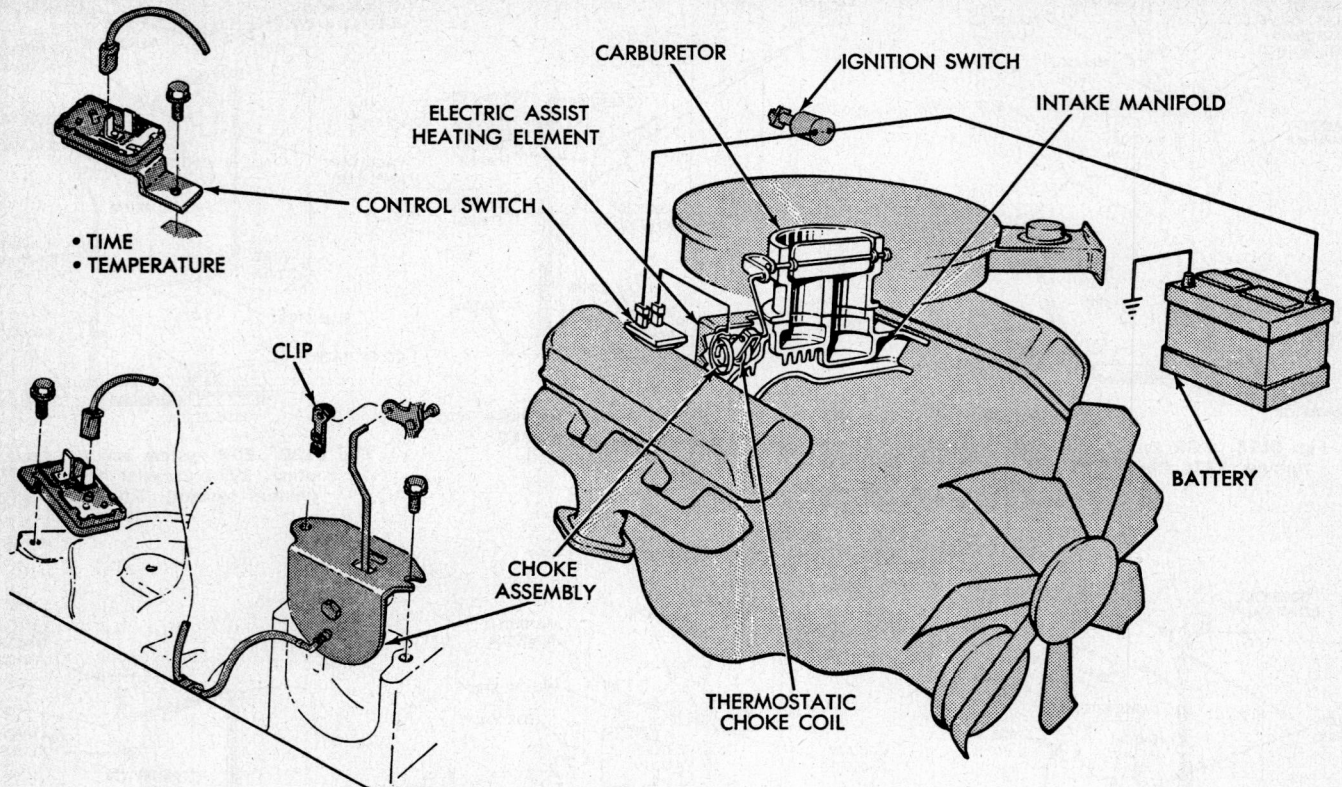

• TIME
• TEMPERATURE

CONTROL SWITCH

ELECTRIC ASSIST
HEATING ELEMENT

CARBURETOR

IGNITION SWITCH

INTAKE MANIFOLD

CLIP

CHOKE
ASSEMBLY

THERMOSTATIC
CHOKE COIL

BATTERY

Fig. CL27   Electric assist choke. 1973-74 Chrysler

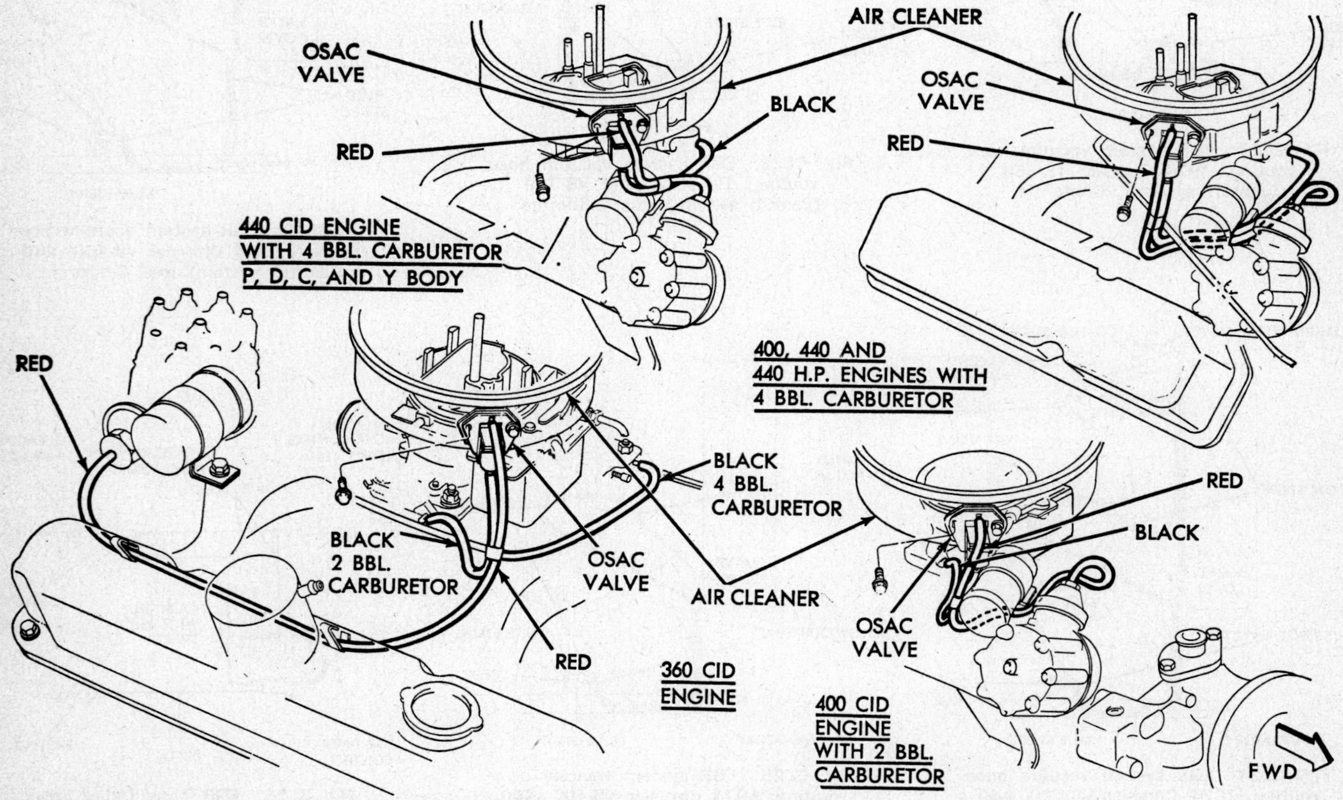

AIR CLEANER

OSAC
VALVE

RED

BLACK

OSAC
VALVE

RED

440 CID ENGINE
WITH 4 BBL. CARBURETOR
P, D, C, AND Y BODY

400, 440 AND
440 H.P. ENGINES WITH
4 BBL. CARBURETOR

RED

BLACK
4 BBL.
CARBURETOR

RED

BLACK
2 BBL.
CARBURETOR

OSAC
VALVE

AIR CLEANER

BLACK

RED

360 CID
ENGINE

OSAC
VALVE

400 CID
ENGINE
WITH 2 BBL.
CARBURETOR

FWD

Fig. CL29   OSAC valve vacuum hose routing. 1974 Chrysler V8-360, 400, 440

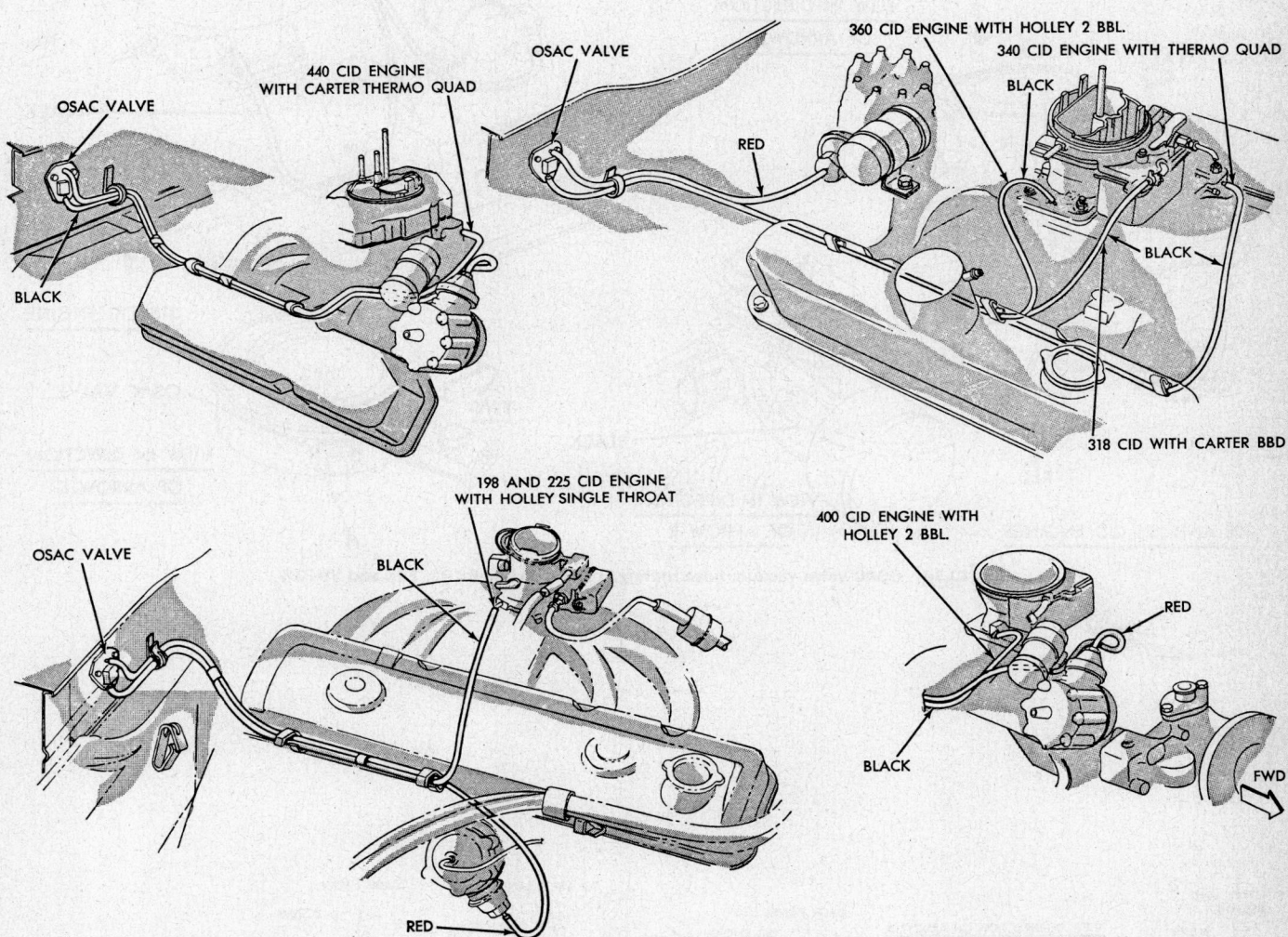

440 CID ENGINE WITH CARTER THERMO QUAD

OSAC VALVE

OSAC VALVE

BLACK

OSAC VALVE

RED

360 CID ENGINE WITH HOLLEY 2 BBL.

340 CID ENGINE WITH THERMO QUAD

BLACK

BLACK

318 CID WITH CARTER BBD

OSAC VALVE

198 AND 225 CID ENGINE WITH HOLLEY SINGLE THROAT

BLACK

RED

400 CID ENGINE WITH HOLLEY 2 BBL.

RED

BLACK

FWD

Fig. CL28   OSAC valve vacuum hose routing. 1973 Chrysler

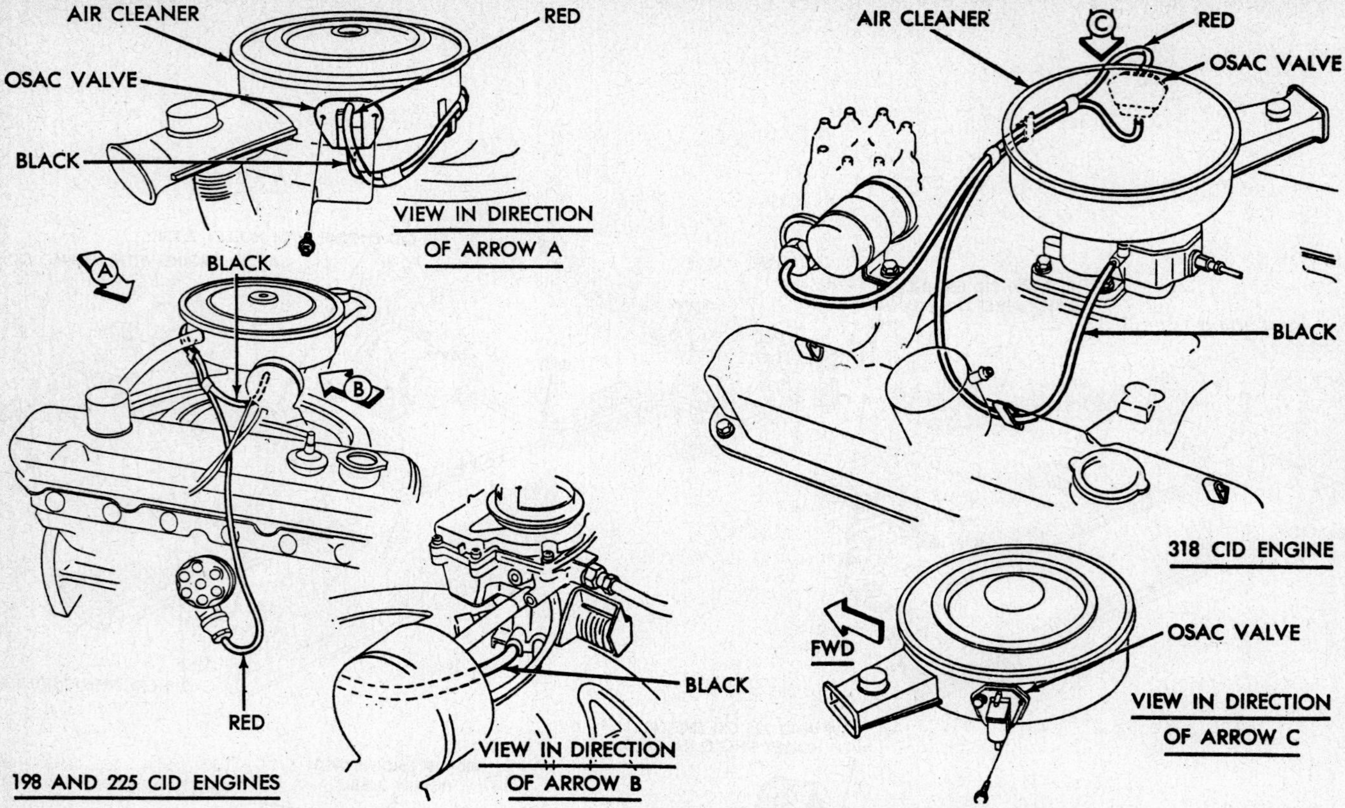

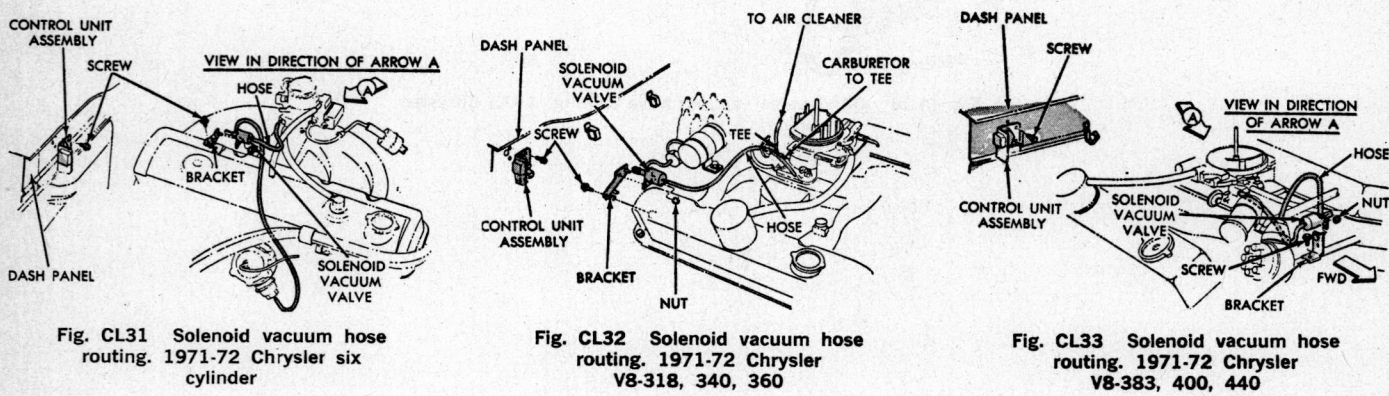

AIR CLEANER

OSAC VALVE

RED

BLACK

VIEW IN DIRECTION
OF ARROW A

BLACK

RED

198 AND 225 CID ENGINES

BLACK

VIEW IN DIRECTION
OF ARROW B

AIR CLEANER

RED

OSAC VALVE

BLACK

318 CID ENGINE

OSAC VALVE

FWD

VIEW IN DIRECTION
OF ARROW C

Fig. CL30   OSAC valve vacuum hose routing. 1974 Chrysler 6-198, 225 and V8-318

CONTROL UNIT
ASSEMBLY

SCREW

HOSE

VIEW IN DIRECTION OF ARROW A

BRACKET

DASH PANEL

SOLENOID
VACUUM
VALVE

Fig. CL31   Solenoid vacuum hose
routing. 1971-72 Chrysler six
cylinder

DASH PANEL

SOLENOID
VACUUM
VALVE

SCREW

CONTROL UNIT
ASSEMBLY

BRACKET

NUT

TO AIR CLEANER

CARBURETOR
TO TEE

TEE

HOSE

Fig. CL32   Solenoid vacuum hose
routing. 1971-72 Chrysler
V8-318, 340, 360

DASH PANEL

SCREW

VIEW IN DIRECTION
OF ARROW A

HOSE

NUT

CONTROL UNIT
ASSEMBLY

SOLENOID
VACUUM
VALVE

SCREW

BRACKET

FWD

Fig. CL33   Solenoid vacuum hose
routing. 1971-72 Chrysler
V8-383, 400, 440

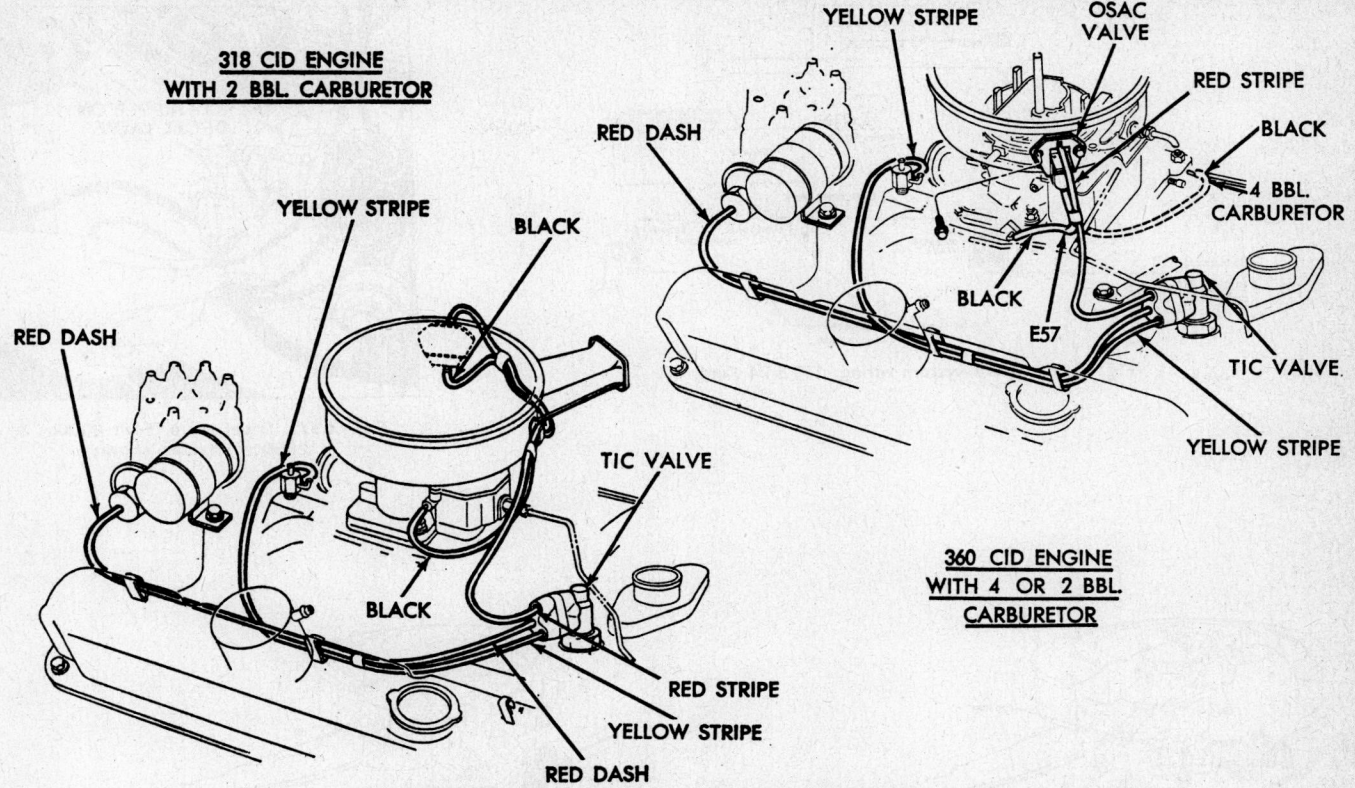

318 CID ENGINE WITH 2 BBL. CARBURETOR

YELLOW STRIPE

BLACK

RED DASH

RED DASH

TIC VALVE

BLACK

RED STRIPE
YELLOW STRIPE
RED DASH

YELLOW STRIPE

OSAC VALVE

RED STRIPE

BLACK

4 BBL. CARBURETOR

BLACK

E57

TIC VALVE

YELLOW STRIPE

360 CID ENGINE WITH 4 OR 2 BBL. CARBURETOR

Fig. CL34   TIC valve vacuum hose routing. 1974 Chrysler V8-318, 360

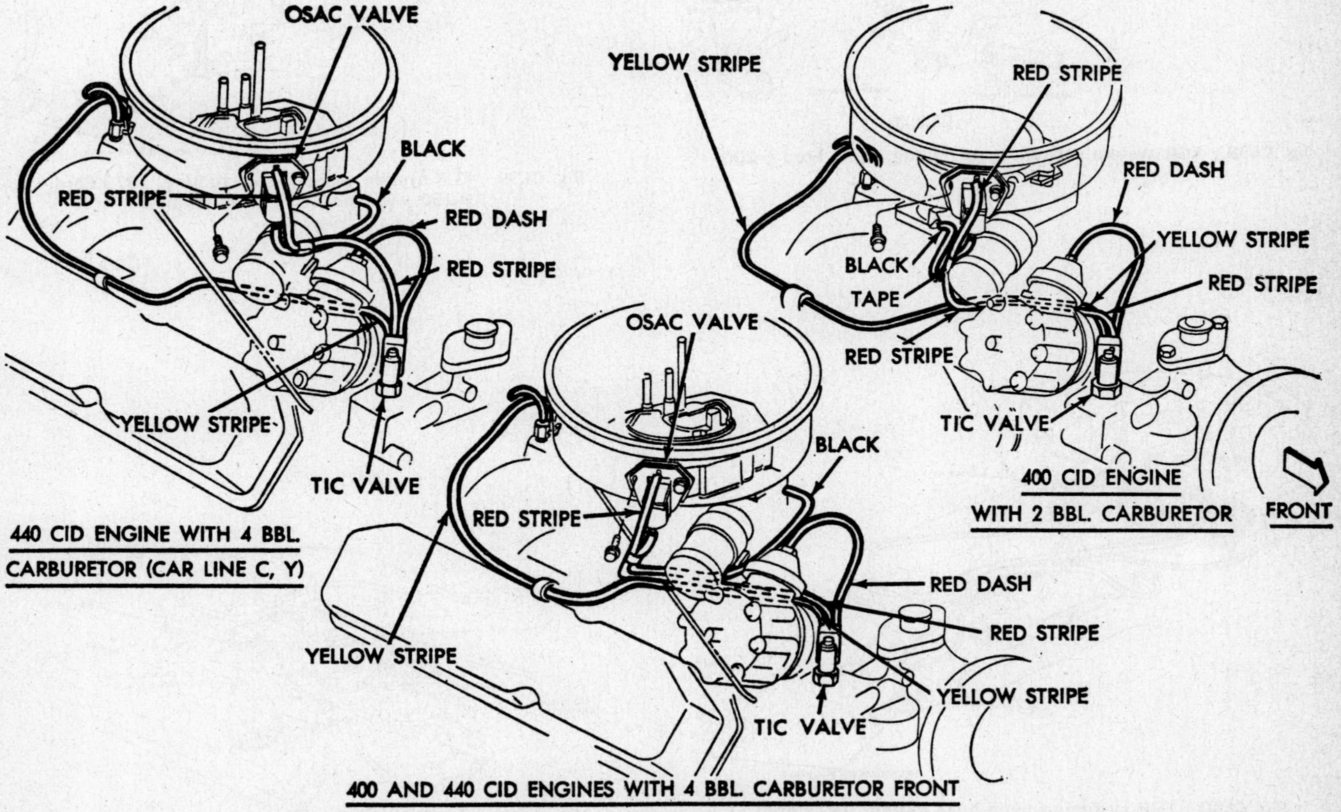

OSAC VALVE

BLACK

RED STRIPE

RED DASH

RED STRIPE

YELLOW STRIPE

TIC VALVE

440 CID ENGINE WITH 4 BBL. CARBURETOR (CAR LINE C, Y)

YELLOW STRIPE

RED STRIPE

RED DASH

BLACK

YELLOW STRIPE

RED STRIPE

RED STRIPE

TIC VALVE

400 CID ENGINE WITH 2 BBL. CARBURETOR

FRONT

OSAC VALVE

BLACK

RED STRIPE

YELLOW STRIPE

RED DASH

RED STRIPE

YELLOW STRIPE

TIC VALVE

400 AND 440 CID ENGINES WITH 4 BBL CARBURETOR FRONT

Fig. CL35   TIC valve vacuum hose routing. 1974 Chrysler V8-400, 440

EMISSION CONTROL SYSTEMS

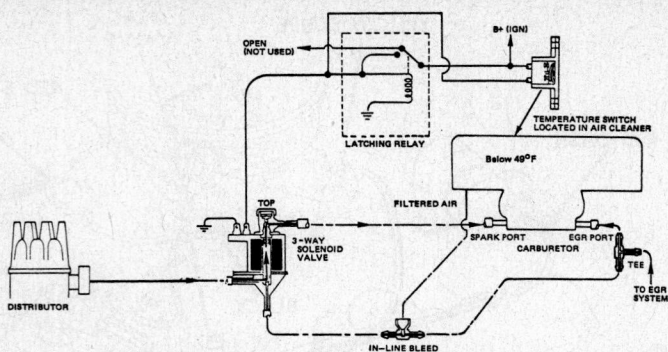

Fig. CL36   CTAV system wiring. 1973-74 Ford

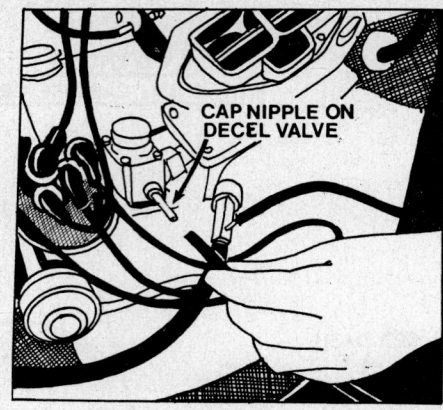

Fig. CL37   Decel valve. Ford 2000cc & 2800cc engines shown

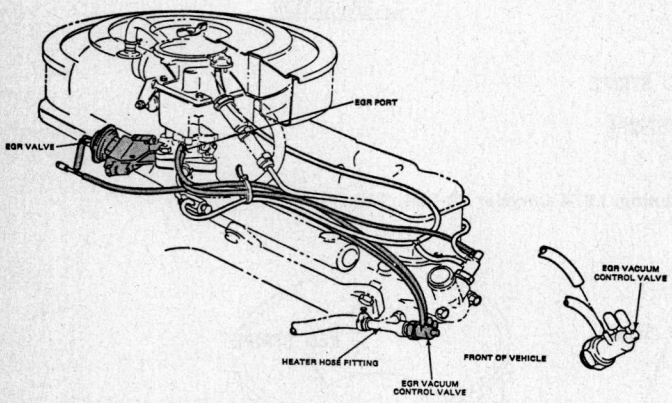

Fig. CL38   EGR system vacuum hose routing. 1973 Ford 6-200

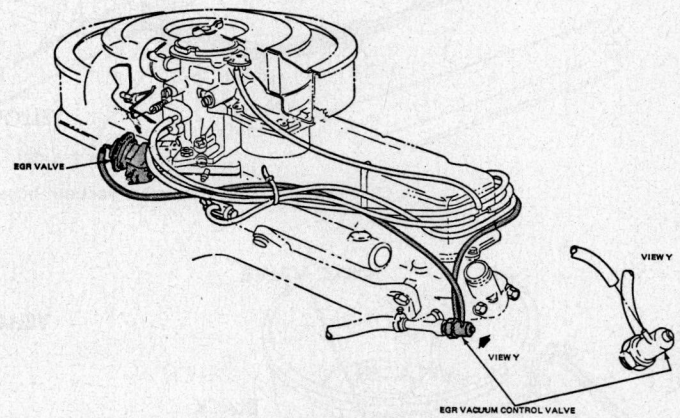

Fig. CL39   EGR system vacuum hose routing. 1973 Ford 6-250 with manual transmission

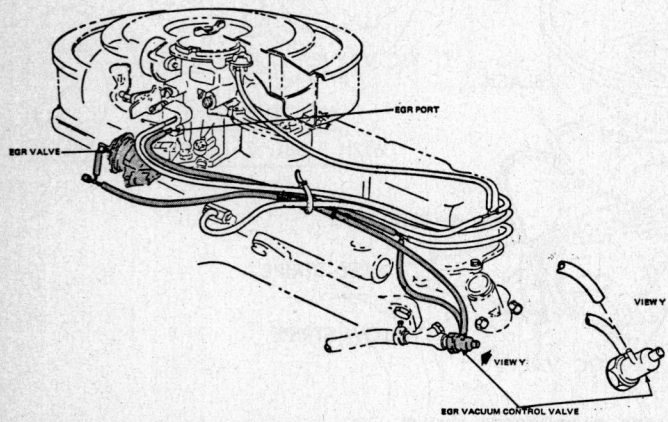

Fig. CL40   EGR system vacuum hose routing. 1973 Ford 6-250 with automatic transmission

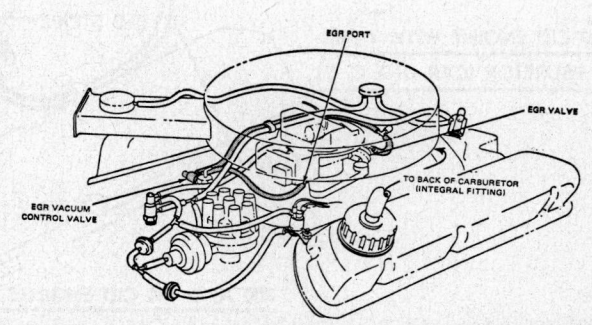

Fig. CL41   EGR system vacuum hose routing. 1973 Ford V8-302

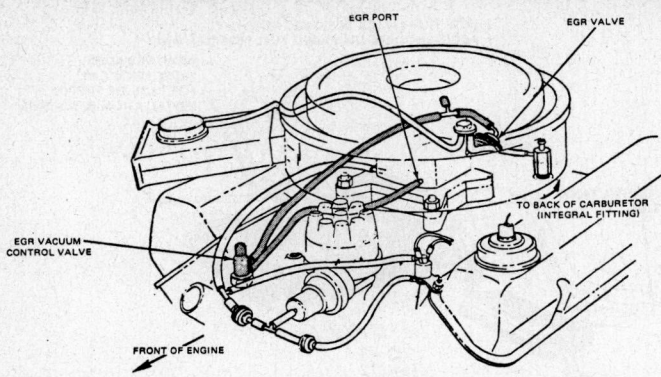

Fig. CL42   EGR system vacuum hose routing. 1973 Ford V8-351W

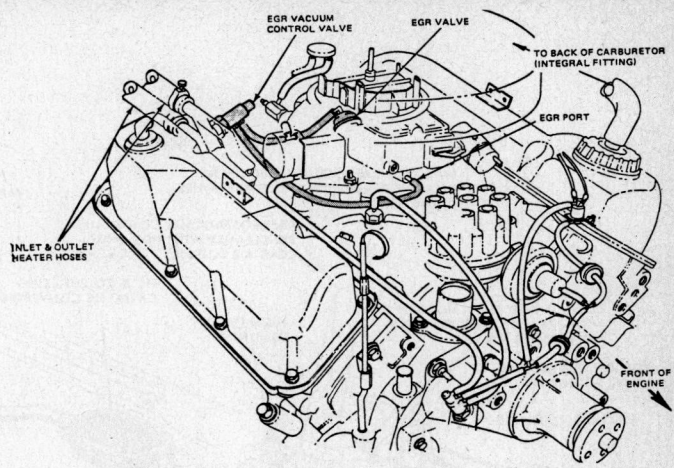

Fig. CL43   EGR system vacuum hose routing. 1973 Ford V8-351C with air conditioning

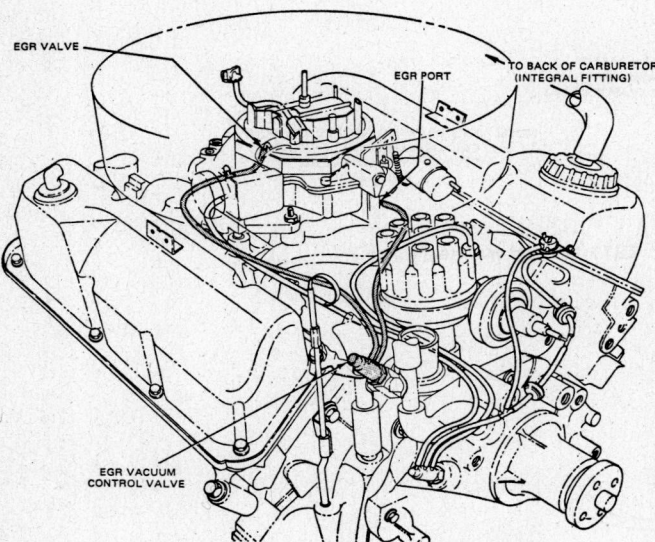

Fig. CL44   EGR system vacuum hose routing. 1973 Ford V8-351C, 400 and V8-351 CJ with air conditioning

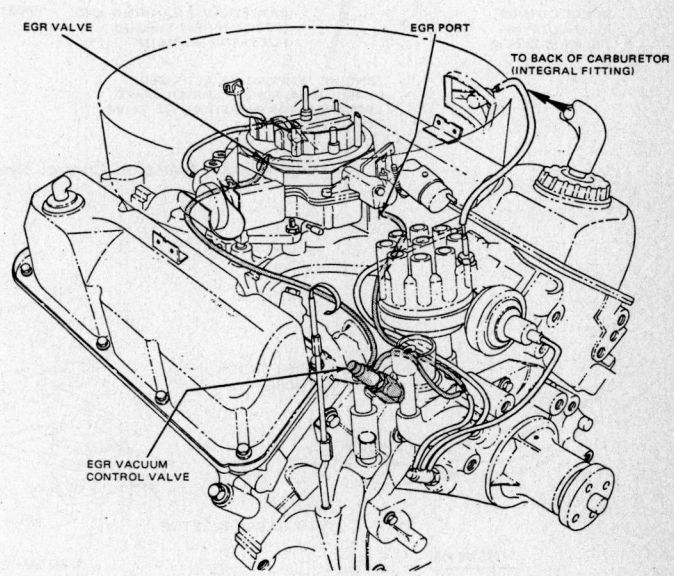

Fig. CL45   EGR system vacuum hose routing. 1973 V8-351C, 400 without air conditioning

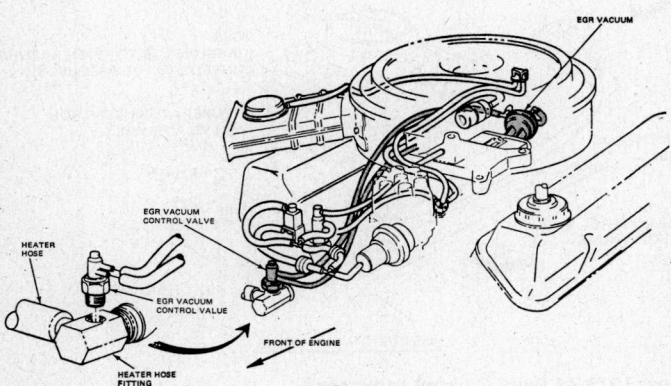

Fig. CL46   EGR system vacuum hose routing. 1973 V8-429, 460

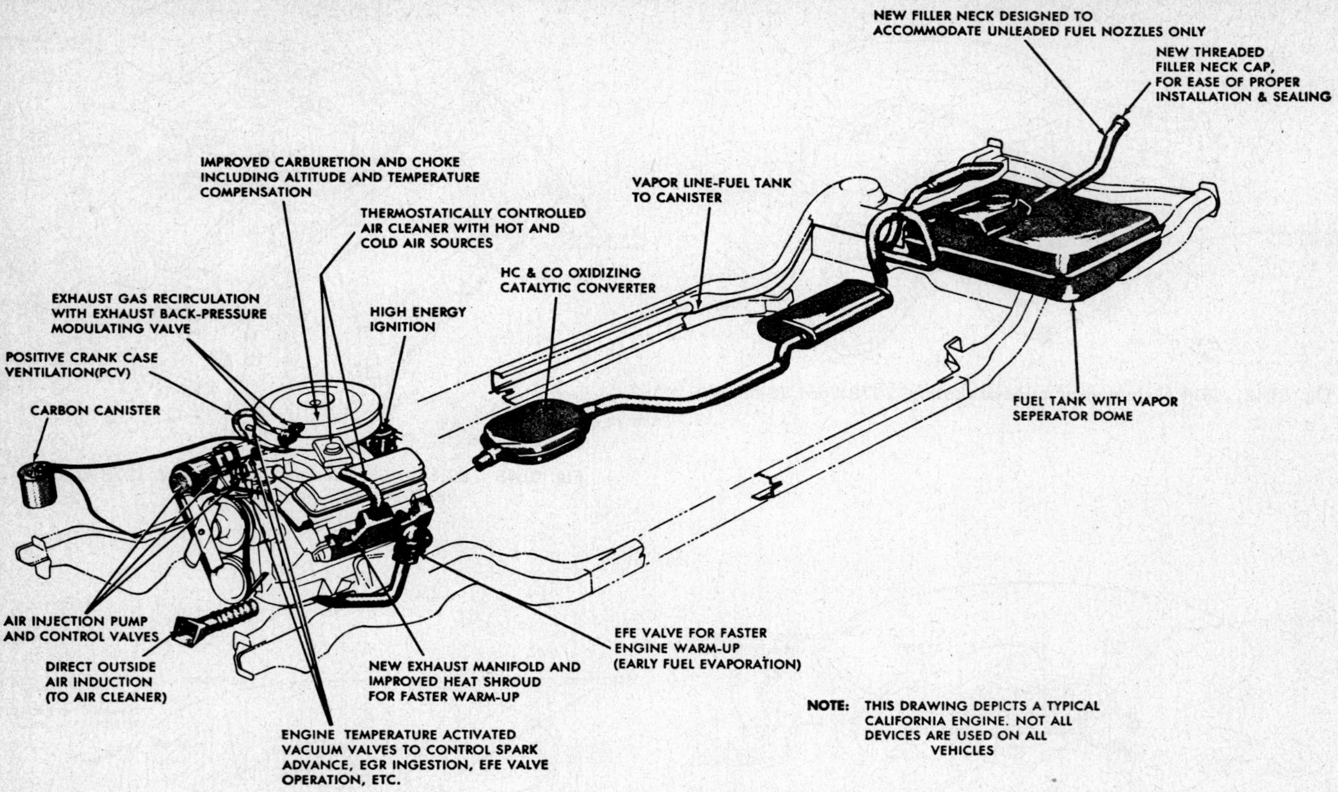

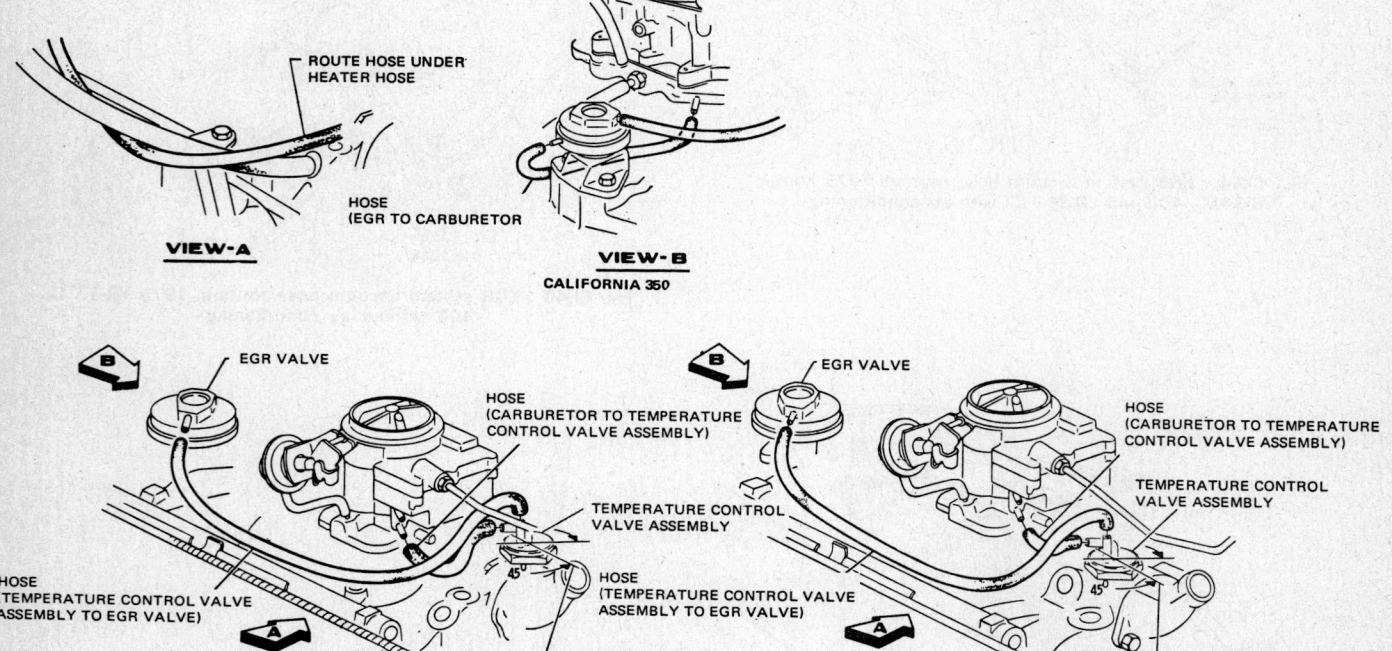

NEW FILLER NECK DESIGNED TO ACCOMMODATE UNLEADED FUEL NOZZLES ONLY

NEW THREADED FILLER NECK CAP, FOR EASE OF PROPER INSTALLATION & SEALING

IMPROVED CARBURETION AND CHOKE INCLUDING ALTITUDE AND TEMPERATURE COMPENSATION

THERMOSTATICALLY CONTROLLED AIR CLEANER WITH HOT AND COLD AIR SOURCES

VAPOR LINE-FUEL TANK TO CANISTER

HC & CO OXIDIZING CATALYTIC CONVERTER

EXHAUST GAS RECIRCULATION WITH EXHAUST BACK-PRESSURE MODULATING VALVE

HIGH ENERGY IGNITION

POSITIVE CRANK CASE VENTILATION(PCV)

CARBON CANISTER

FUEL TANK WITH VAPOR SEPERATOR DOME

AIR INJECTION PUMP AND CONTROL VALVES

DIRECT OUTSIDE AIR INDUCTION (TO AIR CLEANER)

NEW EXHAUST MANIFOLD AND IMPROVED HEAT SHROUD FOR FASTER WARM-UP

EFE VALVE FOR FASTER ENGINE WARM-UP (EARLY FUEL EVAPORATION)

ENGINE TEMPERATURE ACTIVATED VACUUM VALVES TO CONTROL SPARK ADVANCE, EGR INGESTION, EFE VALVE OPERATION, ETC.

NOTE: THIS DRAWING DEPICTS A TYPICAL CALIFORNIA ENGINE. NOT ALL DEVICES ARE USED ON ALL VEHICLES

Fig. CL47   Emission Control System. 1975 General Motors (typical)

ROUTE HOSE UNDER HEATER HOSE

HOSE (EGR TO CARBURETOR)

VIEW-A

VIEW-B
CALIFORNIA 350

EGR VALVE

HOSE (CARBURETOR TO TEMPERATURE CONTROL VALVE ASSEMBLY)

TEMPERATURE CONTROL VALVE ASSEMBLY

HOSE (TEMPERATURE CONTROL VALVE ASSEMBLY TO EGR VALVE)

HOSE (TEMPERATURE CONTROL VALVE ASSEMBLY TO EGR VALVE)

¢ OF ENGINE

350 CUBIC INCH ENGINE

EGR VALVE

HOSE (CARBURETOR TO TEMPERATURE CONTROL VALVE ASSEMBLY)

TEMPERATURE CONTROL VALVE ASSEMBLY

¢ OF ENGINE

455 CUBIC INCH ENGINE

Fig. CL48   EGR system vacuum hose routing. 1973-74 Buick 2 barrel carburetors

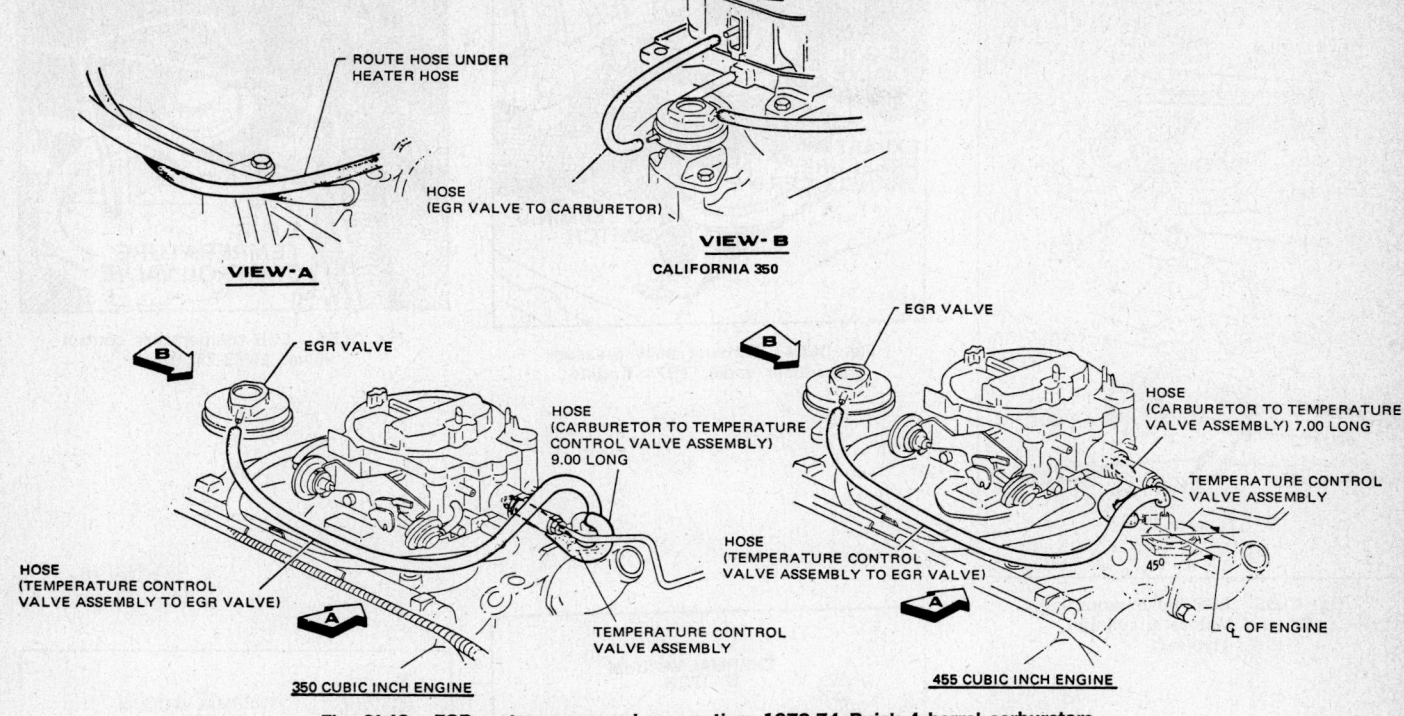

ROUTE HOSE UNDER
HEATER HOSE

HOSE
(EGR VALVE TO CARBURETOR)

VIEW-A

VIEW-B
CALIFORNIA 350

EGR VALVE

EGR VALVE

HOSE
(CARBURETOR TO TEMPERATURE
CONTROL VALVE ASSEMBLY)
9.00 LONG

HOSE
(CARBURETOR TO TEMPERATURE
VALVE ASSEMBLY) 7.00 LONG

TEMPERATURE CONTROL
VALVE ASSEMBLY

HOSE
(TEMPERATURE CONTROL
VALVE ASSEMBLY TO EGR VALVE)

HOSE
(TEMPERATURE CONTROL
VALVE ASSEMBLY TO EGR VALVE)

45°

¢ OF ENGINE

TEMPERATURE CONTROL
VALVE ASSEMBLY

350 CUBIC INCH ENGINE

455 CUBIC INCH ENGINE

Fig. CL49   EGR system vacuum hose routing. 1973-74 Buick 4 barrel carburetors

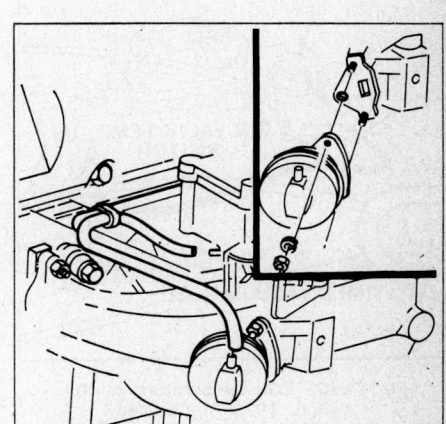

Fig. CL51   EGR valve mounting.
1973-74 Chevrolet Vega

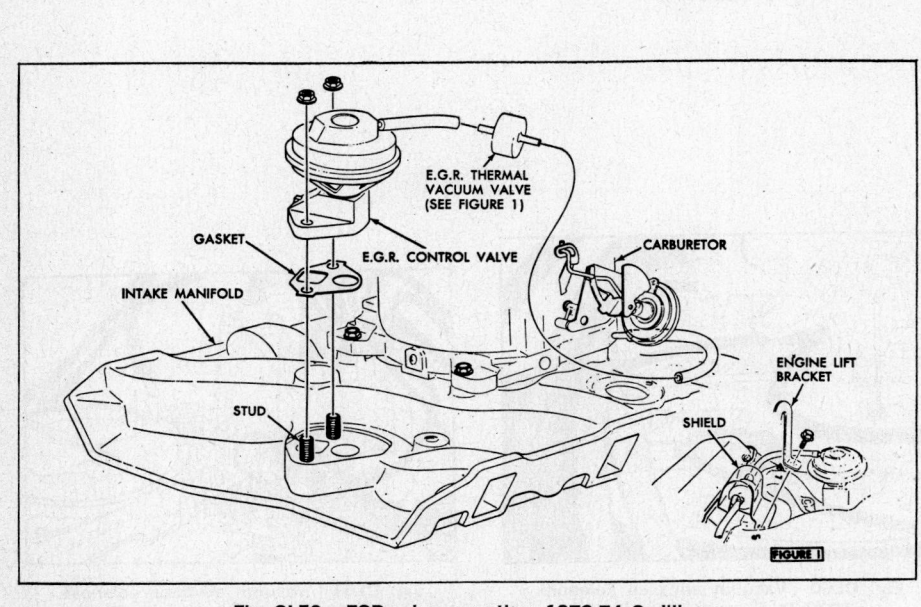

E.G.R. THERMAL
VACUUM VALVE
(SEE FIGURE 1)

GASKET

E.G.R. CONTROL VALVE

CARBURETOR

INTAKE MANIFOLD

STUD

SHIELD

ENGINE LIFT
BRACKET

FIGURE 1

Fig. CL50   EGR valve mounting. 1973-74 Cadillac

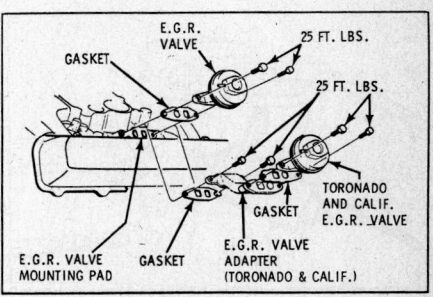

E.G.R.
VALVE

25 FT. LBS.

GASKET

25 FT. LBS.

TORONADO
AND CALIF.
E.G.R. VALVE

GASKET

E.G.R. VALVE
MOUNTING PAD

GASKET

E.G.R. VALVE
ADAPTER
(TORONADO & CALIF.)

Fig. CL52   EGR valve mounting.
1973-74 Oldsmobile

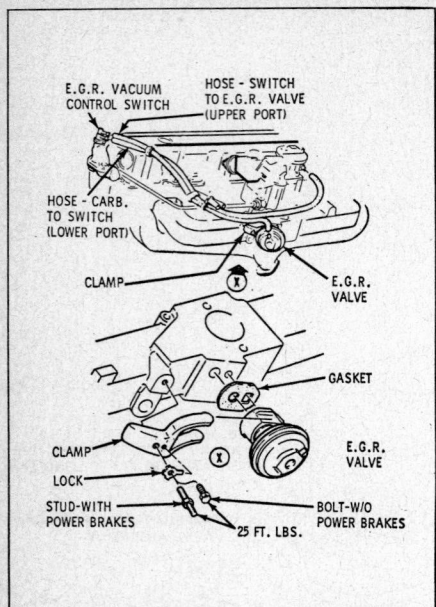

Fig. CL53 EGR valve mounting.
General Motors 6 cylinder
(typical)

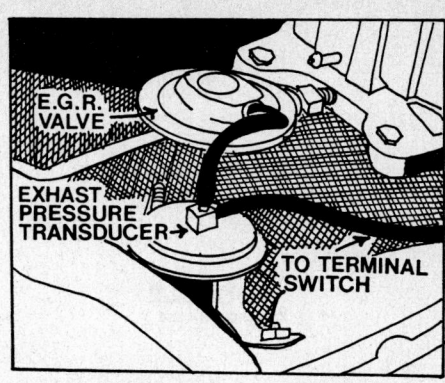

Fig. CL54 Exhaust back pressure
transducer valve. 1974 Cadillac

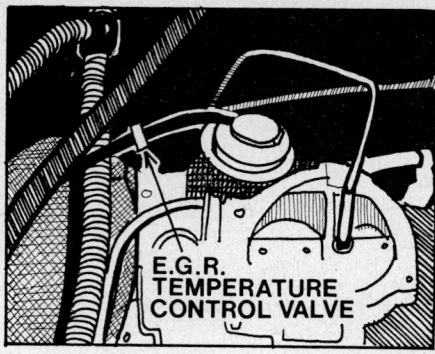

Fig. CL55 EGR temperature control
valve. 1973-74 Buick

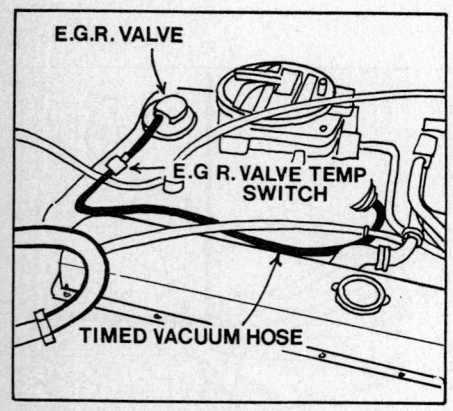

Fig. CL56 EGR temperature control
switch. 1973-74 Cadillac

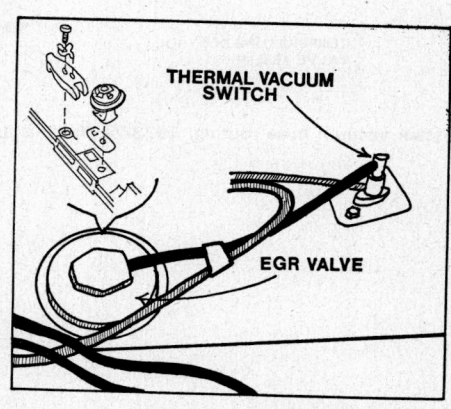

Fig. CL57 EGR & TVS location.
1973-74 Chevrolet small
V8 engines

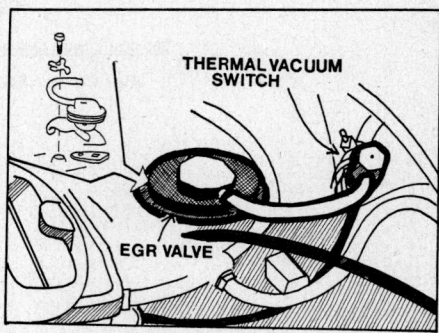

Fig. CL58 EGR & TVS location.
1973-74 Chevrolet large
V8 engines

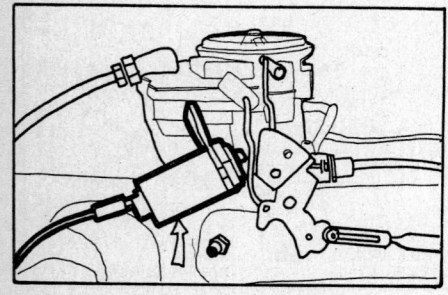

Fig. CL59 Idle stop solenoid.
General Motors (typical)

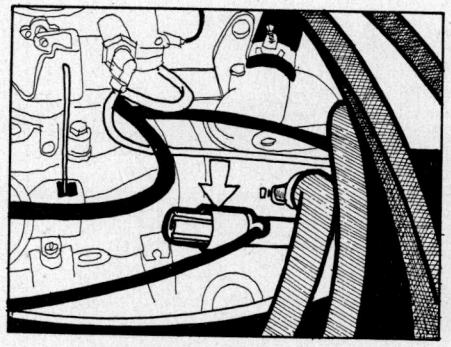

Fig. CL60 Vacuum advance solenoid.
1972-74 Chevrolet small V8

Fig. CL61 Vacuum advance solenoid.
1972-74 Chevrolet large V8

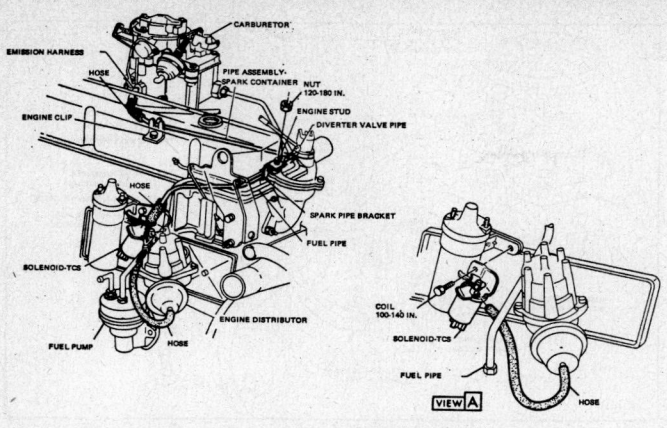

Fig. CL62 TCS vacuum hose routing. General Motors
6 cylinder (typical)

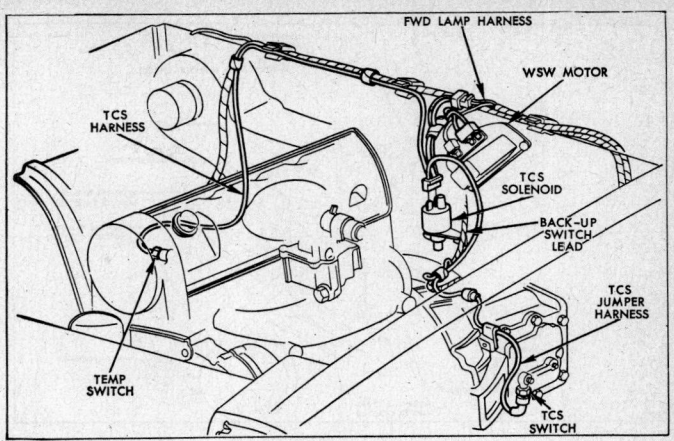

Fig. CL64 TCS wiring. 1973-74 Chevrolet Vega

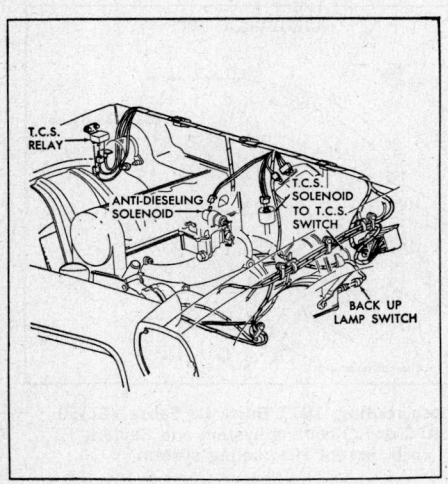

Fig. CL63 TCS wiring. 1971-72
Chevrolet Vega

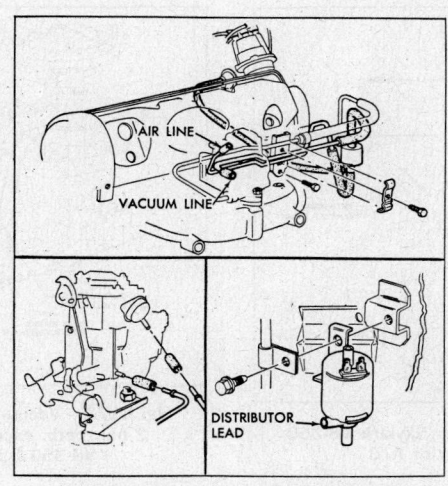

Fig. CL65 TCS vacuum hose routing.
1971-72 Chevrolet Vega

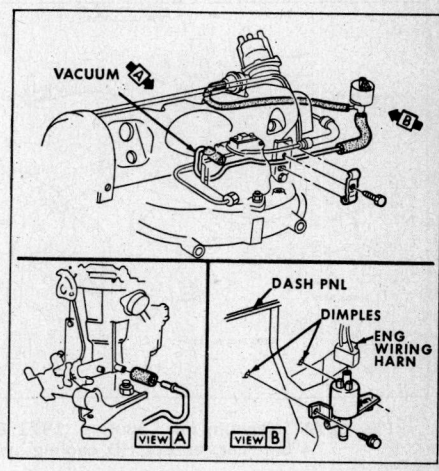

Fig. CL66 TCS vacuum hose routing.
1973-74 Chevrolet Vega

Fig. CL67 TCS location. 1971-74
Chevrolet Vega

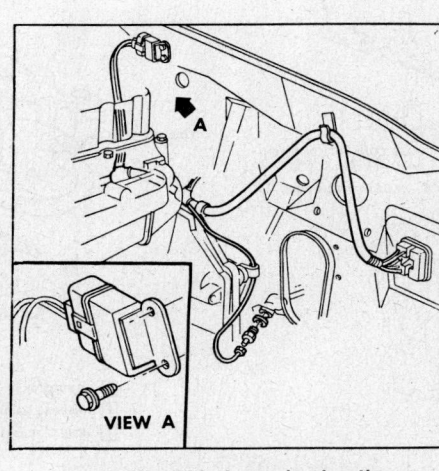

Fig. CL68 TCS time relay location.
1971-74 Chevrolet (typical)

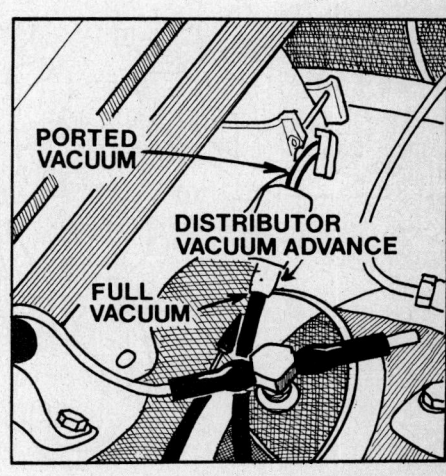

Fig. CL69 Thermo Override Switch.
1973-74 Chevrolet Corvette

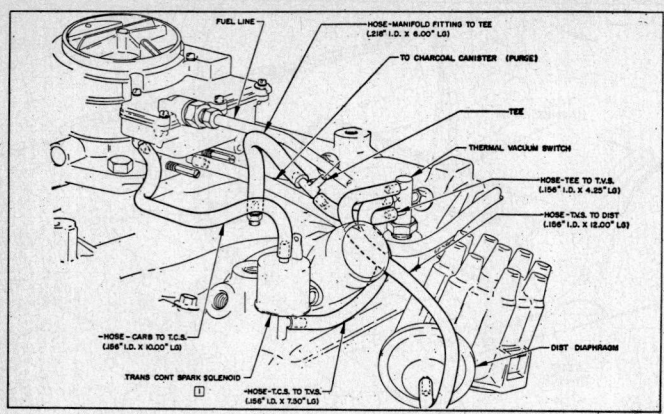

Fig. CL70   Vacuum hose routing. 1971 Buick Le Sabre
V8-350 2 bar. carb. with A/C or HD

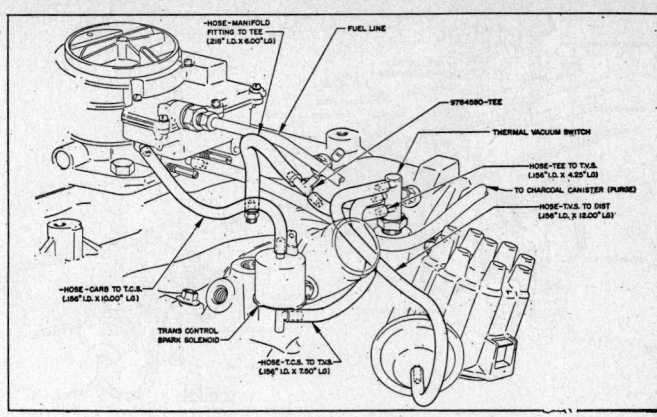

Fig. CL71   Vacuum hose routing. 1971 Buick Skylark
V8-350 2 bar. carb. with HD cooling system

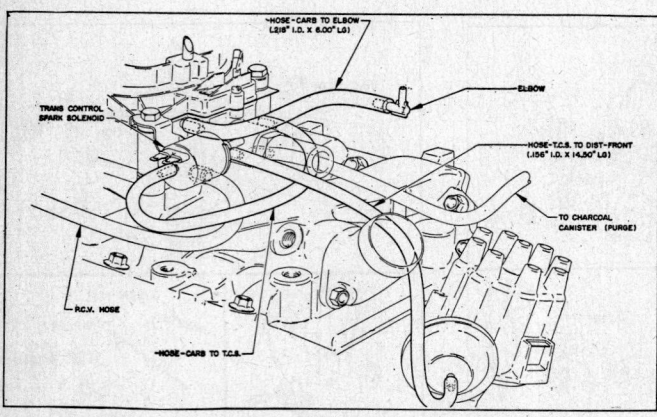

Fig. CL72   Vacuum hose routing. 1971 Buick Skylark V8-350
4 bar. car. except HD cooling system or A/C

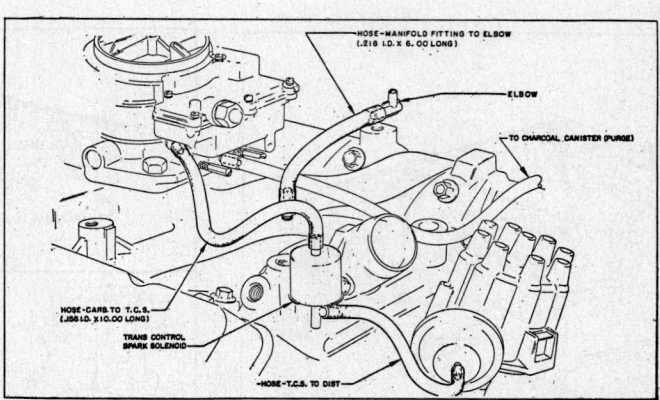

Fig. CL73   Vacuum hose routing. 1971 Buick Le Sabre V8-350
2 bar. carb. except A/C or HD cooling system and Skylark
V8-350 2 bar. carb. except HD cooling system

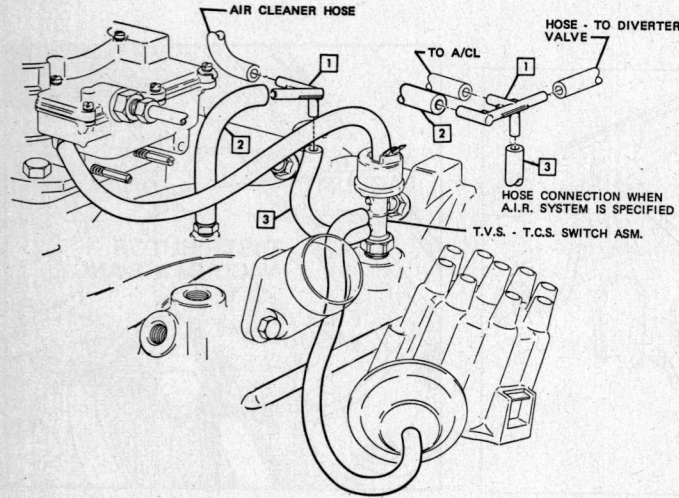

Fig. CL74   Vacuum hose routing. 1972 Buick V8-350
2 bar. carb. with A/C

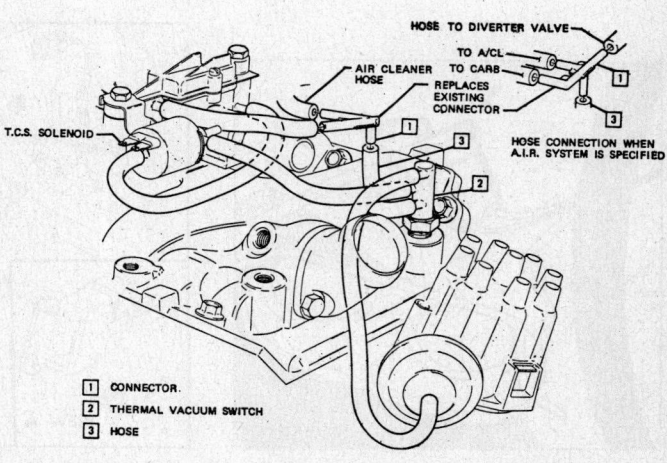

Fig. CL75   Vacuum hose routing. 1972 Buick V8-350 4 bar.
carb. with HD cooling system except A/C

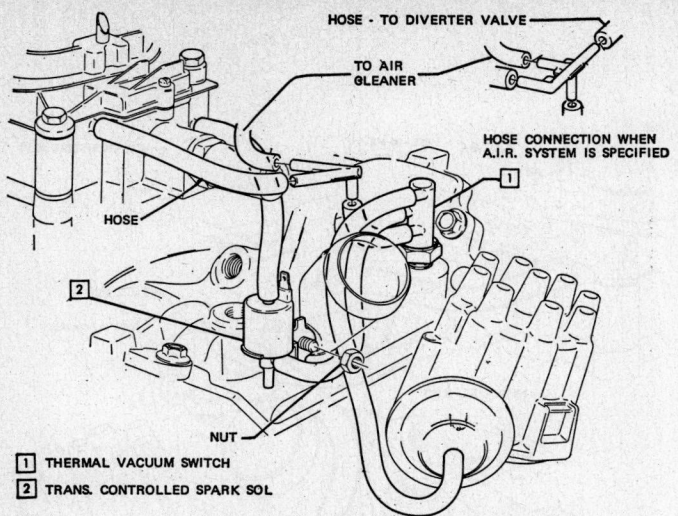

Fig. CL76   Vacuum hose routing. 1972 Buick V8-350 4 bar. carb. with A/C

1 THERMAL VACUUM SWITCH
2 TRANS. CONTROLLED SPARK SOL

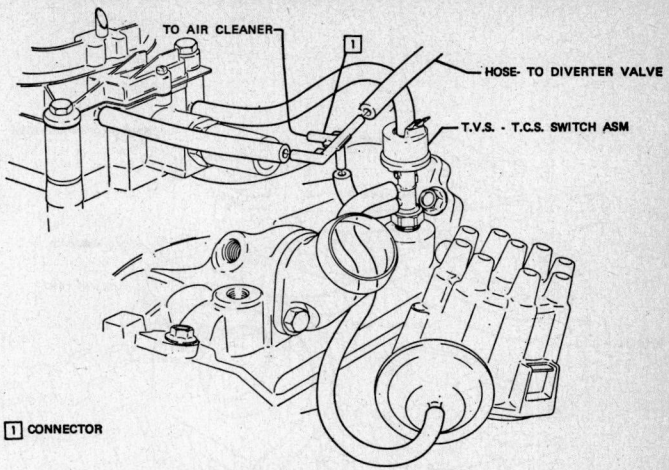

1 CONNECTOR

Fig. CL77   Vacuum hose routing. 1972 Buick Centurion, Electra, Estate Wagon, Le Sabre and Riviera V8-455 with A/C

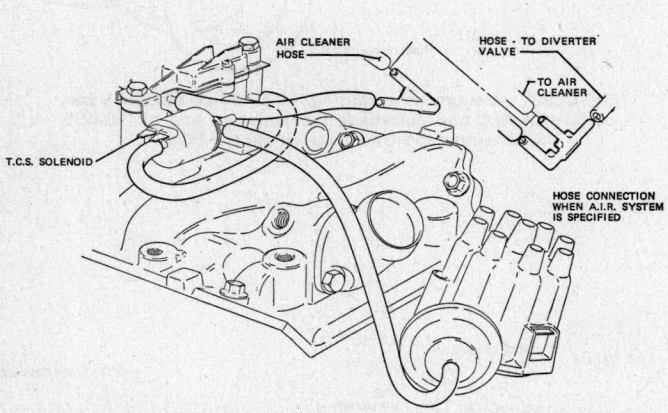

Fig. CL78   Vacuum hose routing. 1972 Buick Le Sabre and Skylark except A/C and HD cooling system

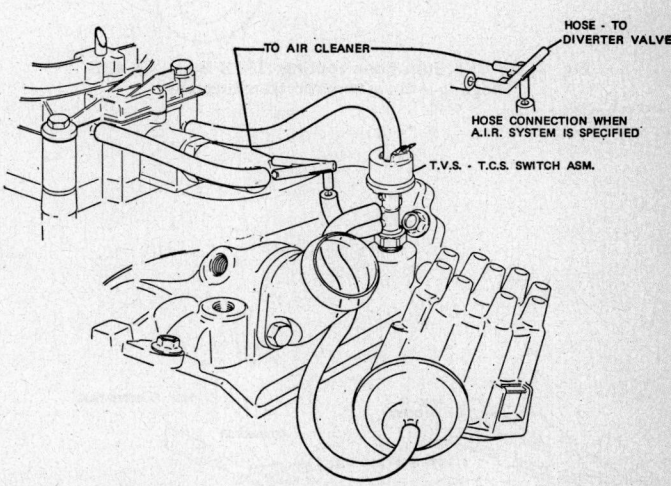

Fig. CL79   Vacuum hose routing. 1972 Buick Le Sabre & Skylark V8-350 4 bar. carb. with A/C

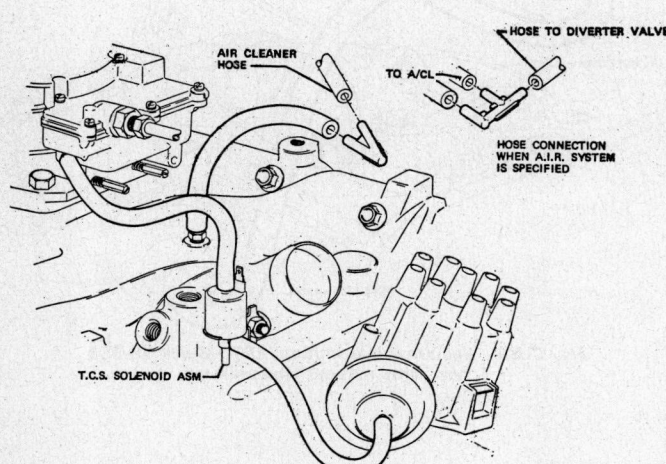

Fig. CL80   Vacuum hose routing. 1972 Buick V8-350 2 bar. carb. except A/C or HD cooling system

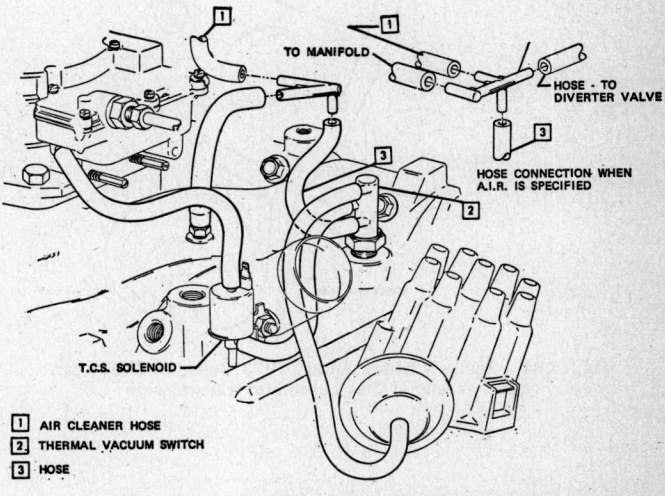

1 AIR CLEANER HOSE
2 THERMAL VACUUM SWITCH
3 HOSE

Fig. CL81   Vacuum hose routing. 1972 Buick V8-350 2 bar. carb. with HD cooling system except A/C

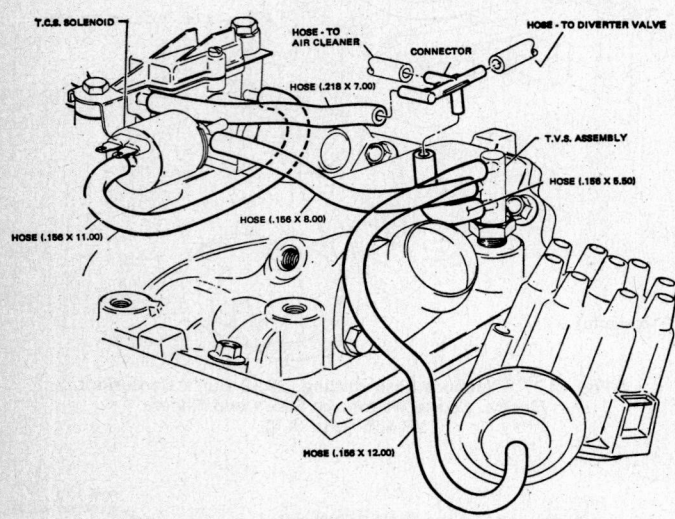

Fig. CL82 Vacuum hose routing. 1973 Buick V8-455
Stage 1 with automatic transmission

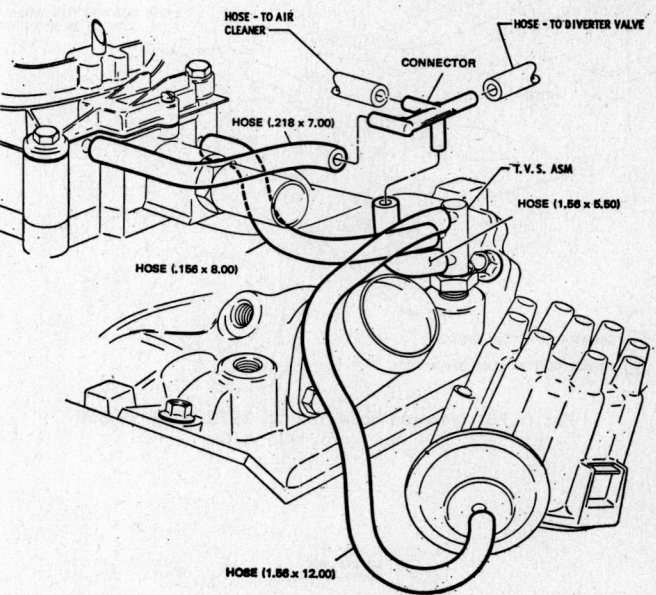

Fig. CL83 Vacuum hose routing. 1973 Buick V8-350 4 bar.
carb. with A/C and automatic transmission and all V8-455
with automatic transmission except Stage 1

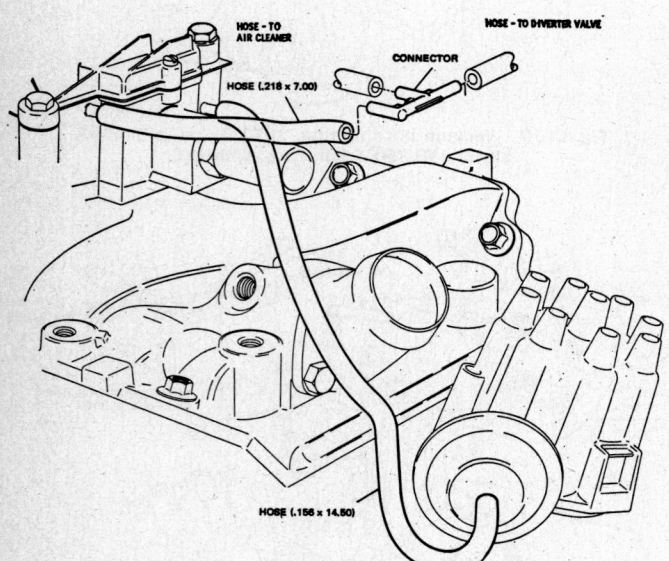

Fig. CL84 Vacuum hose routing. 1973 Buick V8-350 4 bar.
carb. except A/C or automatic transmission

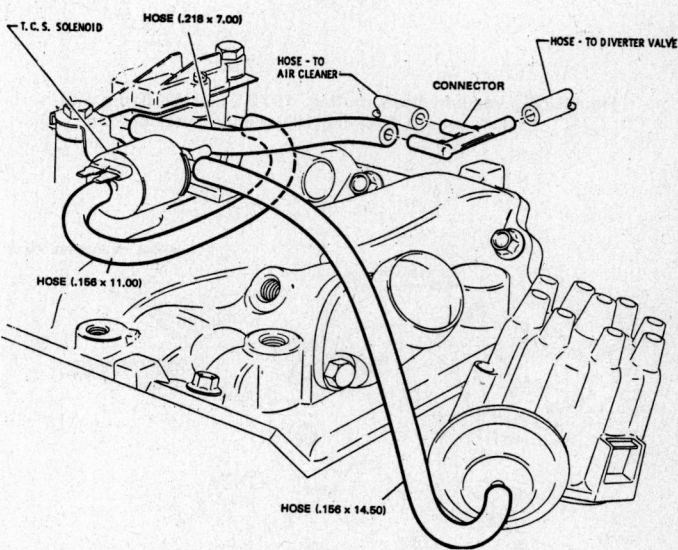

Fig. CL85 Vacuum hose routing. 1973 Buick V8-350
4 bar. with manual transmission

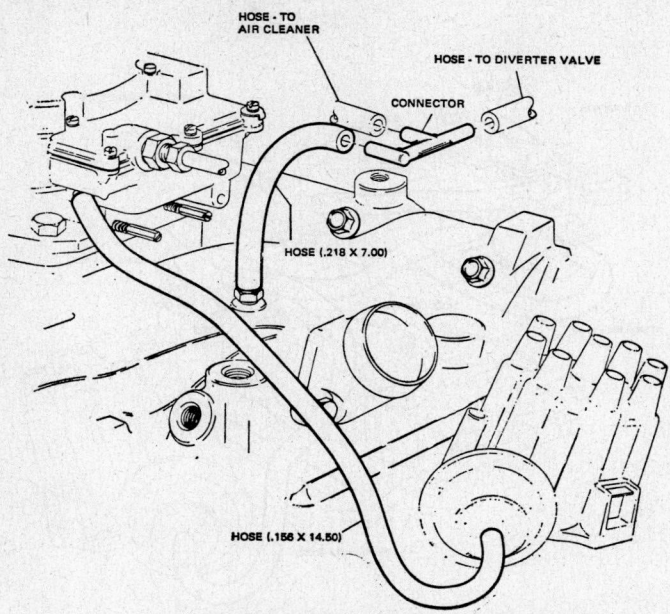

Fig. CL86   Vacuum hose routing. 1973-74 Buick V8-350 2 bar. carb. except A/C and automatic transmission

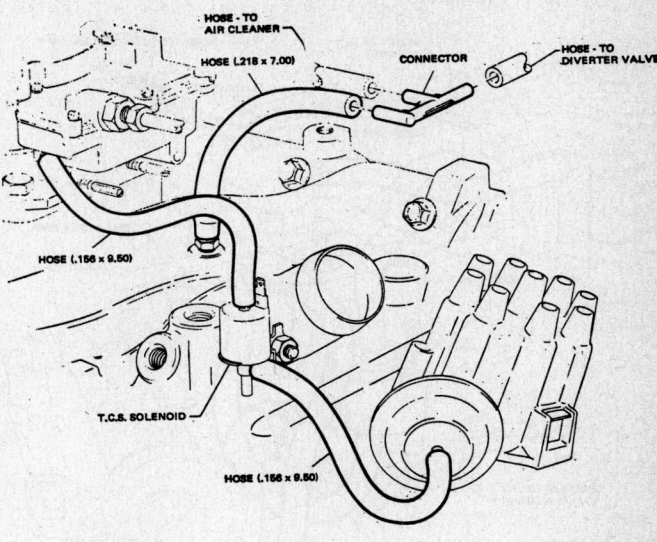

Fig. CL87   Vacuum hose routing. 1972-73 Buick V8-350 2 bar. carb. with manual transmission

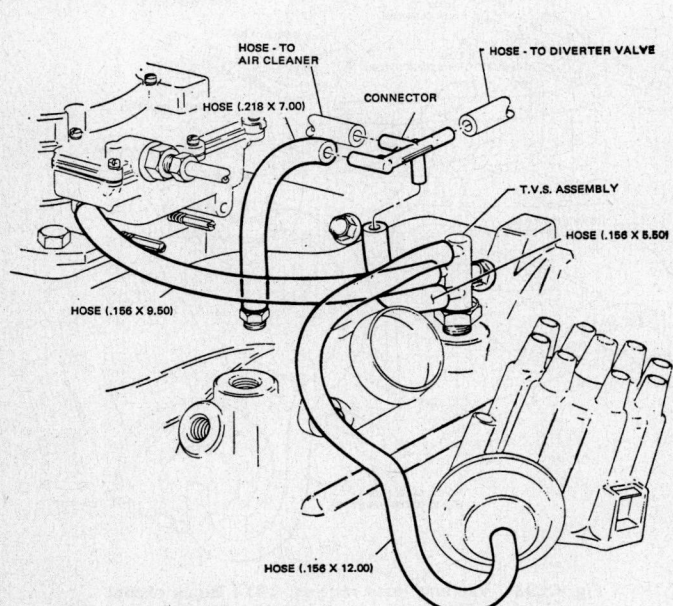

Fig. CL88   Vacuum hose routing. 1973-74 Buick V8-350 2 bar. carb. with A/C and HD cooling system

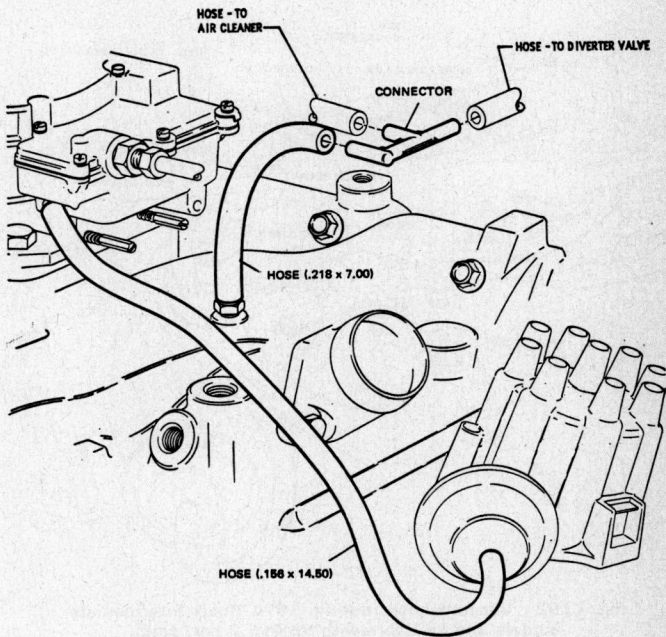

Fig. CL89   Vacuum hose routing. 1973-74 Buick V8-350 2 bar. carb. except A/C or HD cooling system

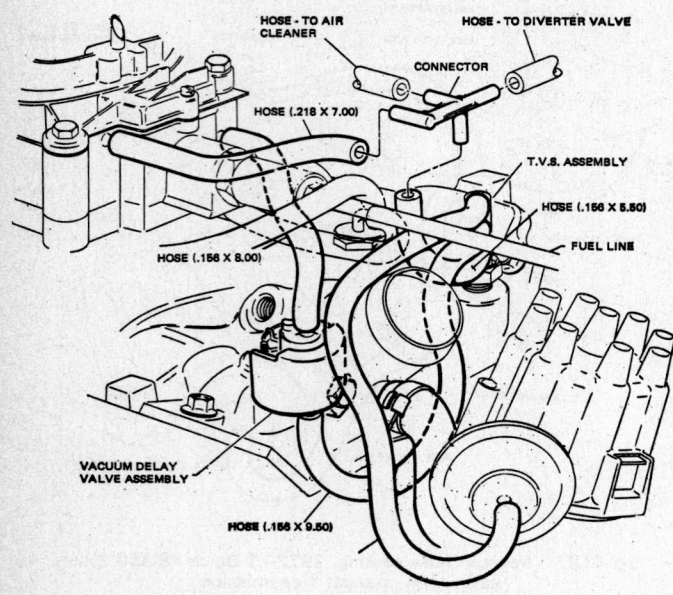

Fig. CL90 Vacuum hose routing. 1973-74 Buick V8-350 4 bar. carb.

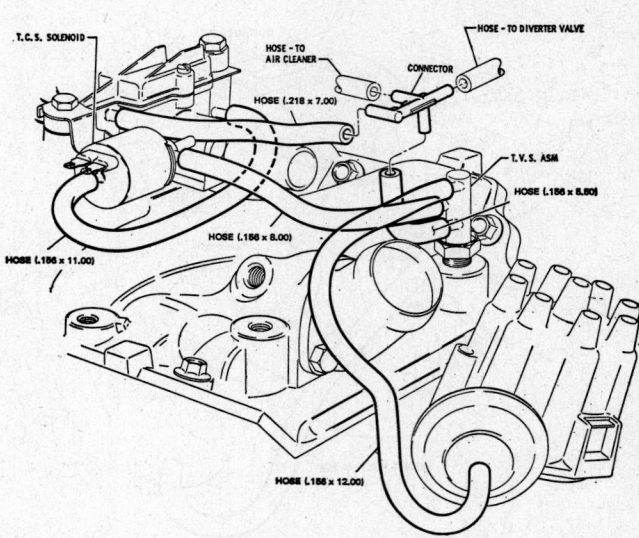

Fig. CL91 Vacuum hose routing. 1972-74 Buick intermediate models with Stage 1 engine

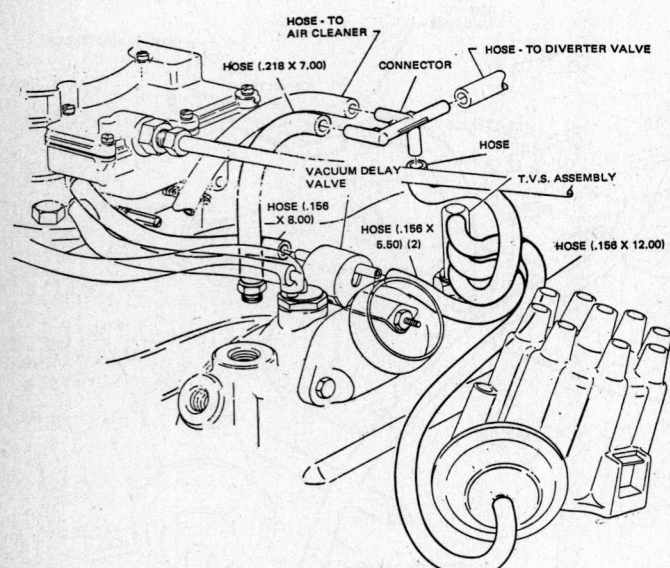

Fig. CL92 Vacuum hose routing. 1974 Buick intermediate models and Le Sabre with V8-455 2 bar. carb.

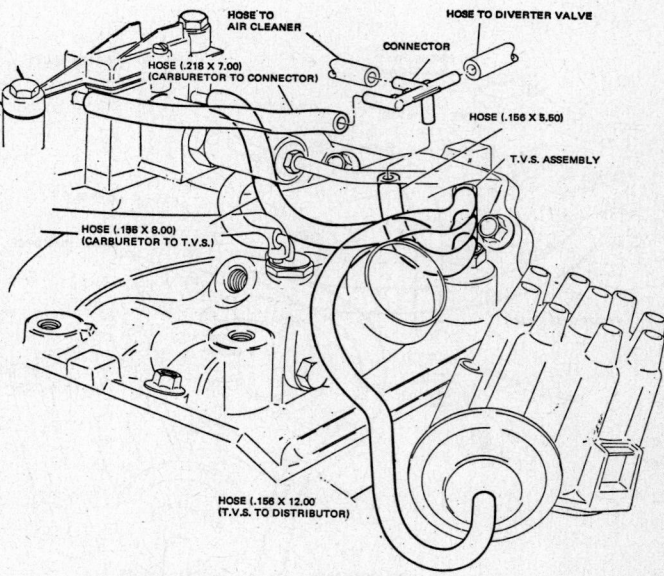

Fig. CL93 Vacuum hose routing. 1974 Buick except intermediate models with V8-455 Stage 1

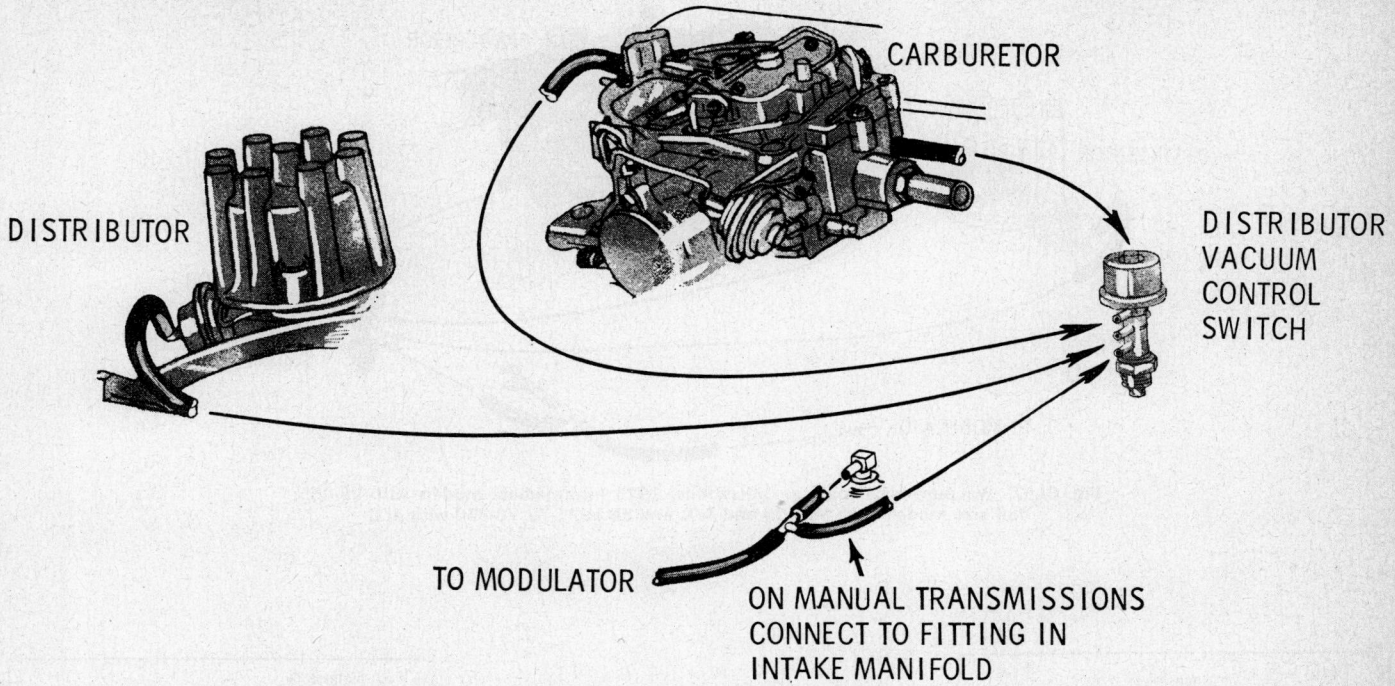

CARBURETOR

DISTRIBUTOR

DISTRIBUTOR
VACUUM
CONTROL
SWITCH

TO MODULATOR

ON MANUAL TRANSMISSIONS
CONNECT TO FITTING IN
INTAKE MANIFOLD

Fig. CL94   Vacuum hose routing. 1971-72 Oldsmobile except Toronado and V8-350 with manual transmission

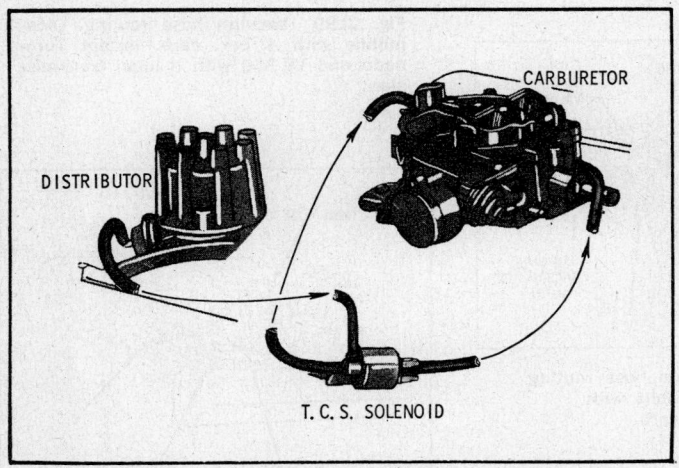

CARBURETOR

DISTRIBUTOR

T. C. S. SOLENOID

Fig. CL95   Vacuum hose routing. Oldsmobile, 1971 without
A/C and 1972 with 4 bar. carb. and manual transmission

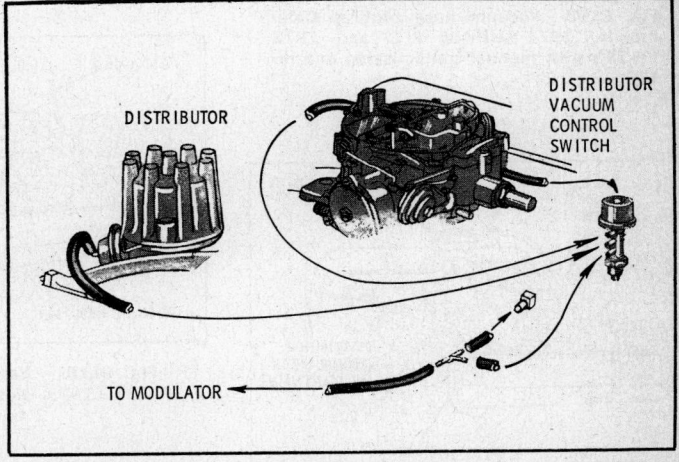

DISTRIBUTOR
VACUUM
CONTROL
SWITCH

DISTRIBUTOR

TO MODULATOR

Fig. CL96   Vacuum hose routing. 1971-72
Oldsmobile Toronado

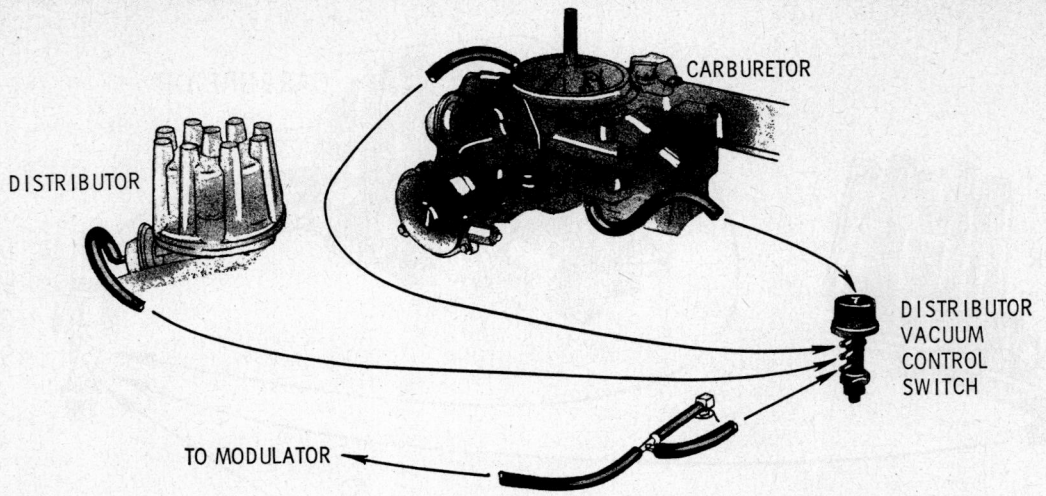

Fig. CL97 Vacuum hose routing. Oldsmobile, 1971 intermediate models with V8-455, full size models with V8-455 and A/C and all 1971-72 V8-350 with A/C

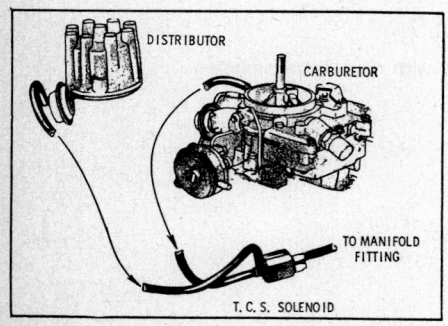

Fig. CL98 Vacuum hose routing. Oldsmobile, 1971 without A/C and 1972 V8-350 with manual transmission and no A/C

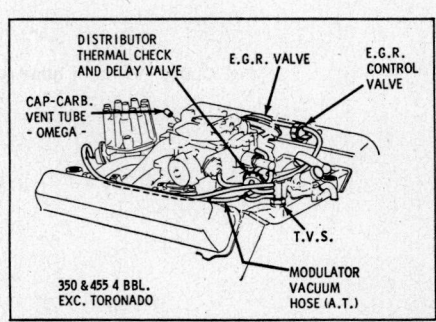

Fig. CL99 Vacuum hose routing. Oldsmobile with 4 bar. carb. except Toronado and V8-350 with manual transmission

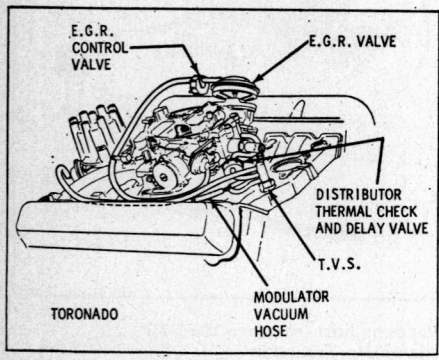

Fig. CL100 Vacuum hose routing. 1973 Oldsmobile Toronado

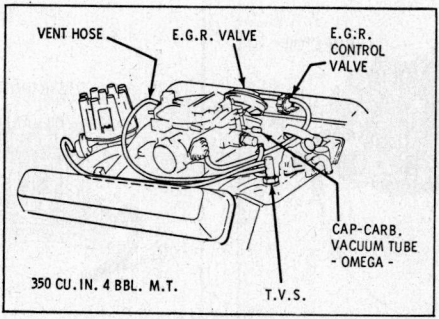

Fig. CL101 Vacuum hose routing. 1973 Oldsmobile with 2 bar. carb.

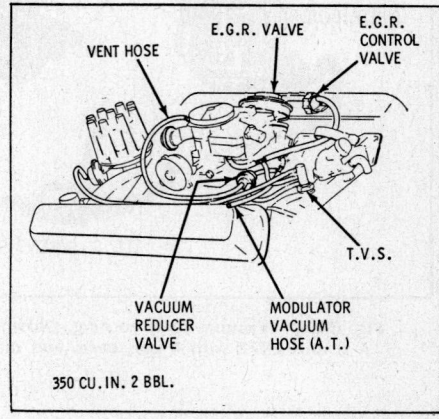

Fig. CL102 Vacuum hose routing. 1973 Oldsmobile V8-350 4 bar. carb.

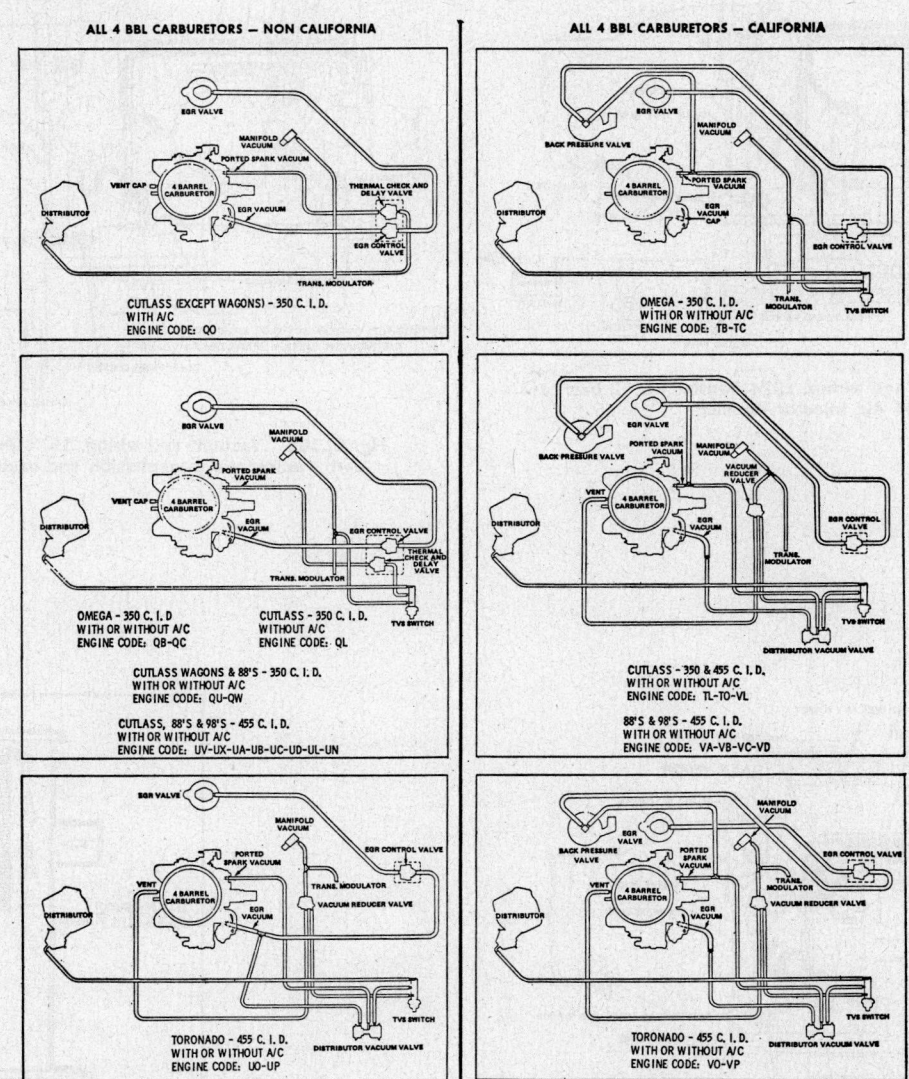

Fig. CL103   Vacuum hose routing. 1974 Oldsmobile

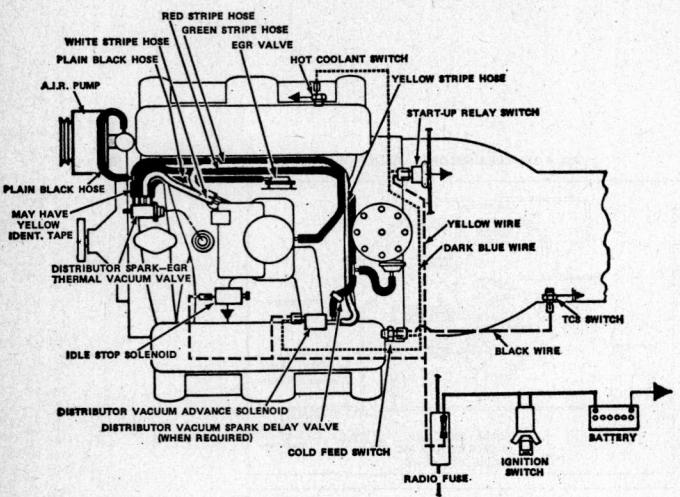

Fig. CL104   Vacuum and wiring. 1974 Pontiac with 2 bar. carb.
and Air Injector Reactor

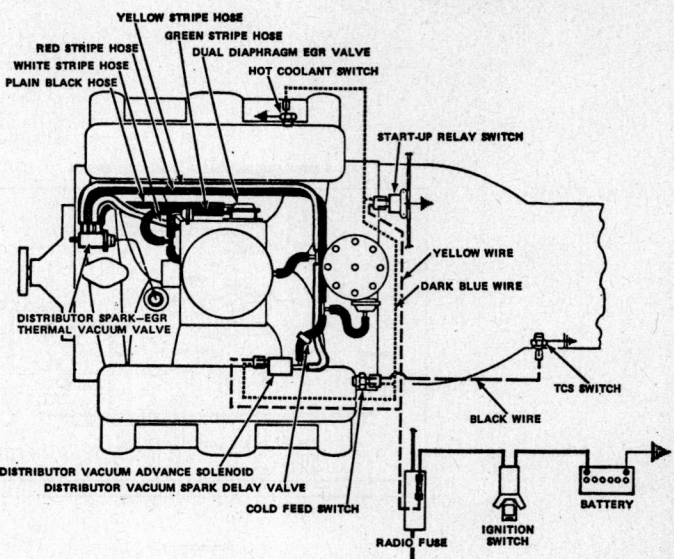

Fig. CL105   Vacuum and wiring. 1974 Pontiac with 2 bar.
carb., automatic transmission and vacuum bias valve

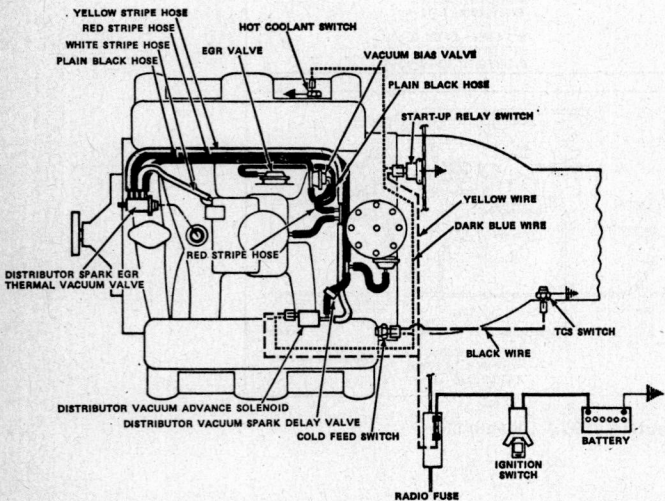

Fig. CL106   Vacuum and wiring. 1974 Pontiac with 4 bar. carb. and
automatic transmission with dual diaphragm

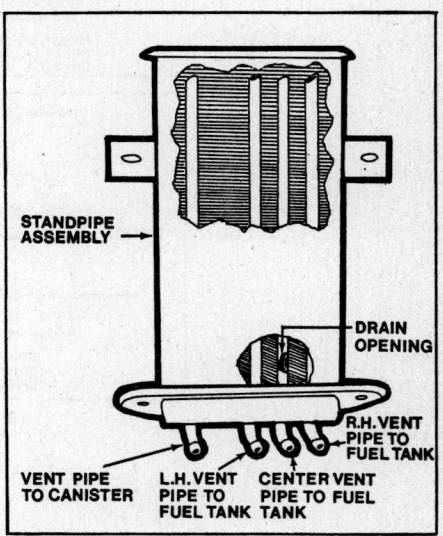

Fig. CL107   Vapor separator.
General Motors (typical)

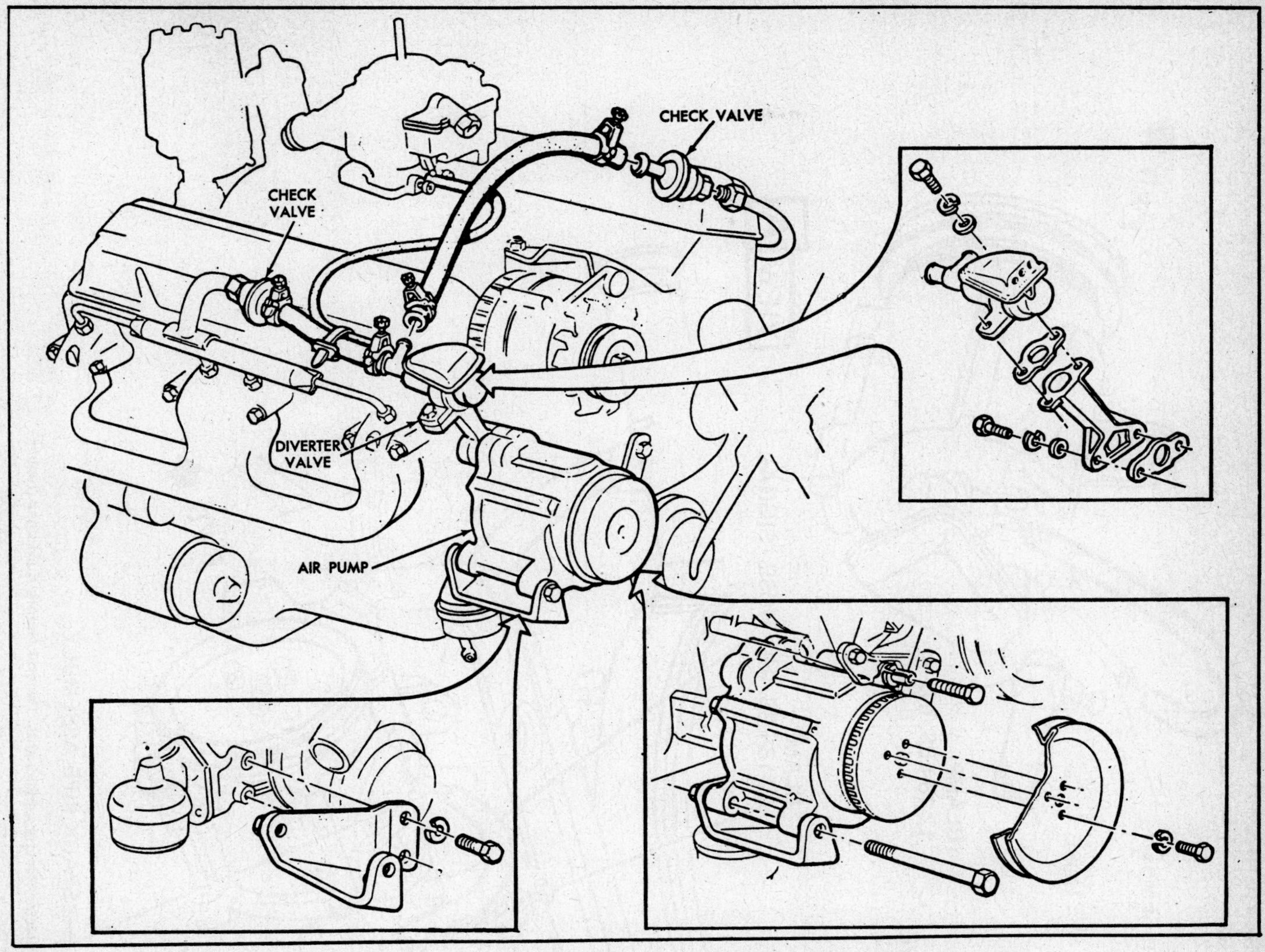

CHECK VALVE

CHECK VALVE

DIVERTER VALVE

AIR PUMP

Fig. CL108   Air Injector Reactor components. 1971-74 Chevrolet V8

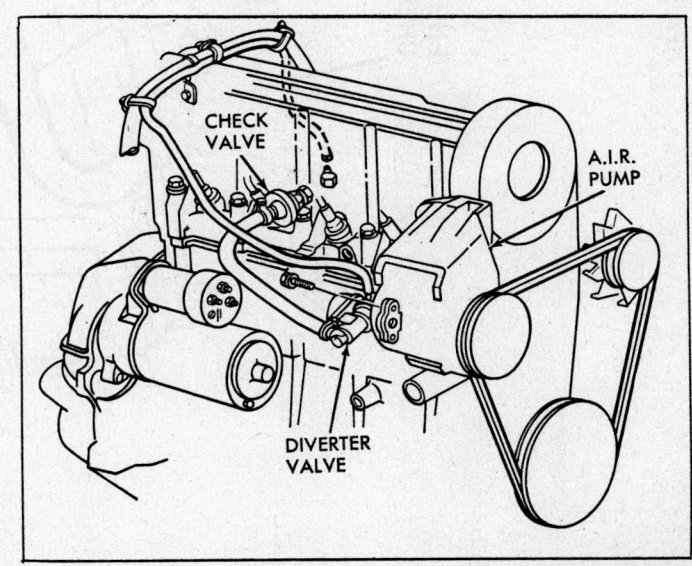

CHECK VALVE

A.I.R. PUMP

DIVERTER VALVE

Fig. CL109   Air Injector Reactor components. Chevrolet Vega

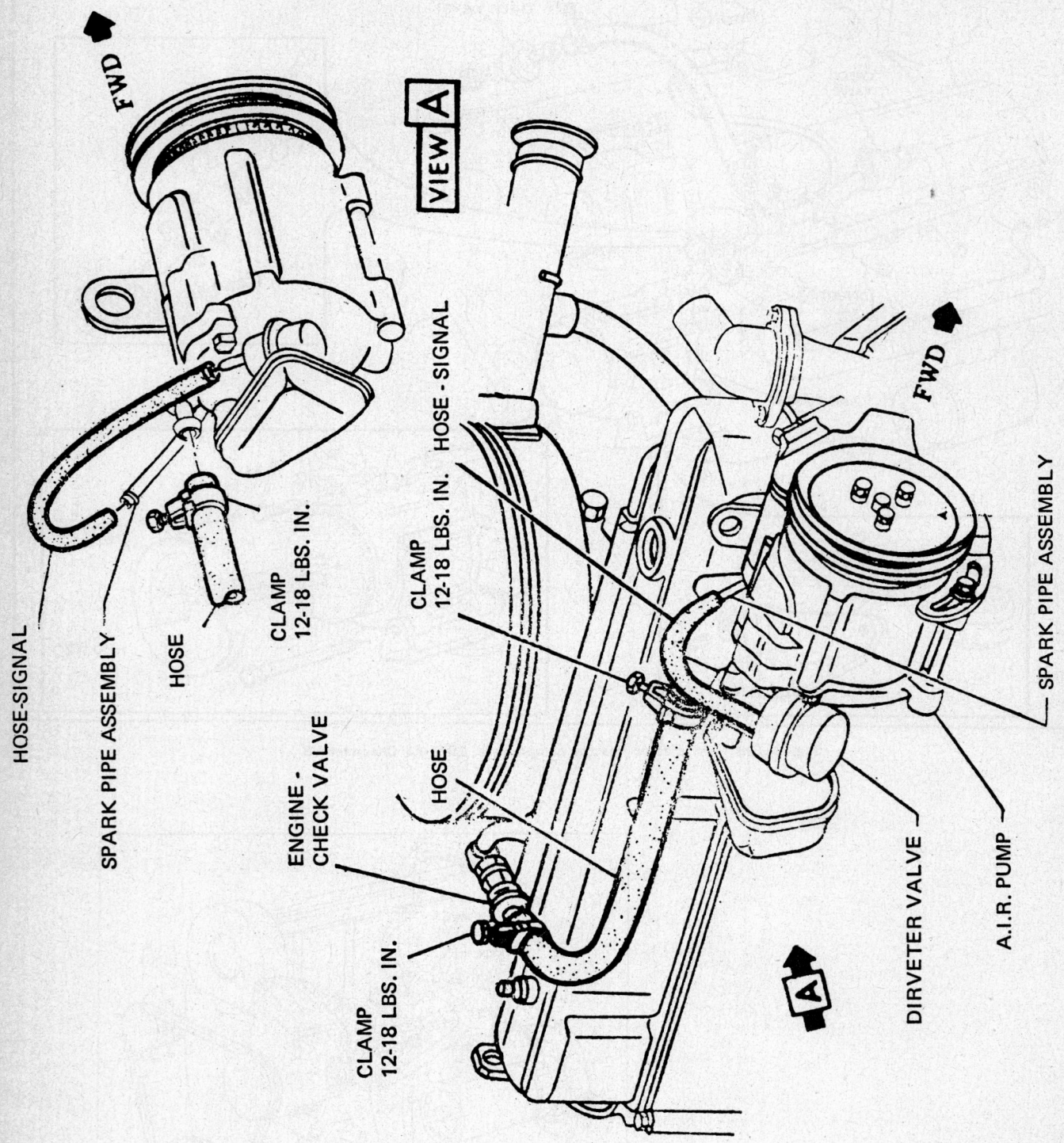

FWD

VIEW A

HOSE-SIGNAL

SPARK PIPE ASSEMBLY

HOSE

CLAMP
12-18 LBS. IN.

CLAMP
12-18 LBS. IN. HOSE - SIGNAL

ENGINE -
CHECK VALVE

HOSE

CLAMP
12-18 LBS. IN.

A

FWD

SPARK PIPE ASSEMBLY

DIRVETER VALVE

A.I.R. PUMP

Fig. CL110 Air Injector Reactor components. General Motors 6 cylinder (typical)

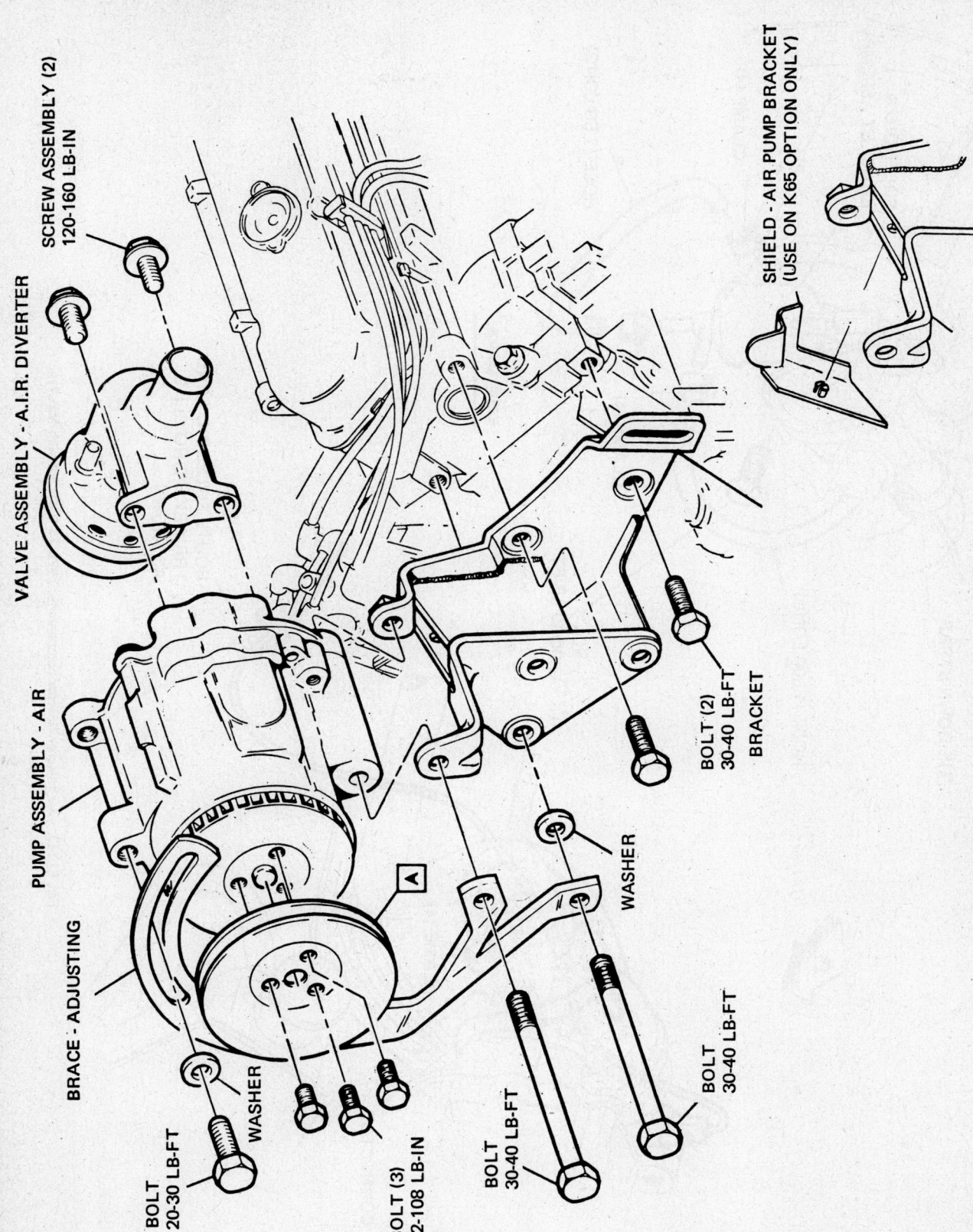

SCREW ASSEMBLY (2) 120-160 LB-IN

VALVE ASSEMBLY - A.I.R. DIVERTER

PUMP ASSEMBLY - AIR

BRACE - ADJUSTING

BOLT 20-30 LB-FT

WASHER

BOLT (3) 72-108 LB-IN

BOLT 30-40 LB-FT

BOLT 30-40 LB-FT

WASHER

BOLT (2) 30-40 LB-FT

BRACKET

WASHER

SHIELD - AIR PUMP BRACKET (USE ON K65 OPTION ONLY)

Fig. CL111 Air Injector Reactor pump mounting. 1972-74 Buick V8

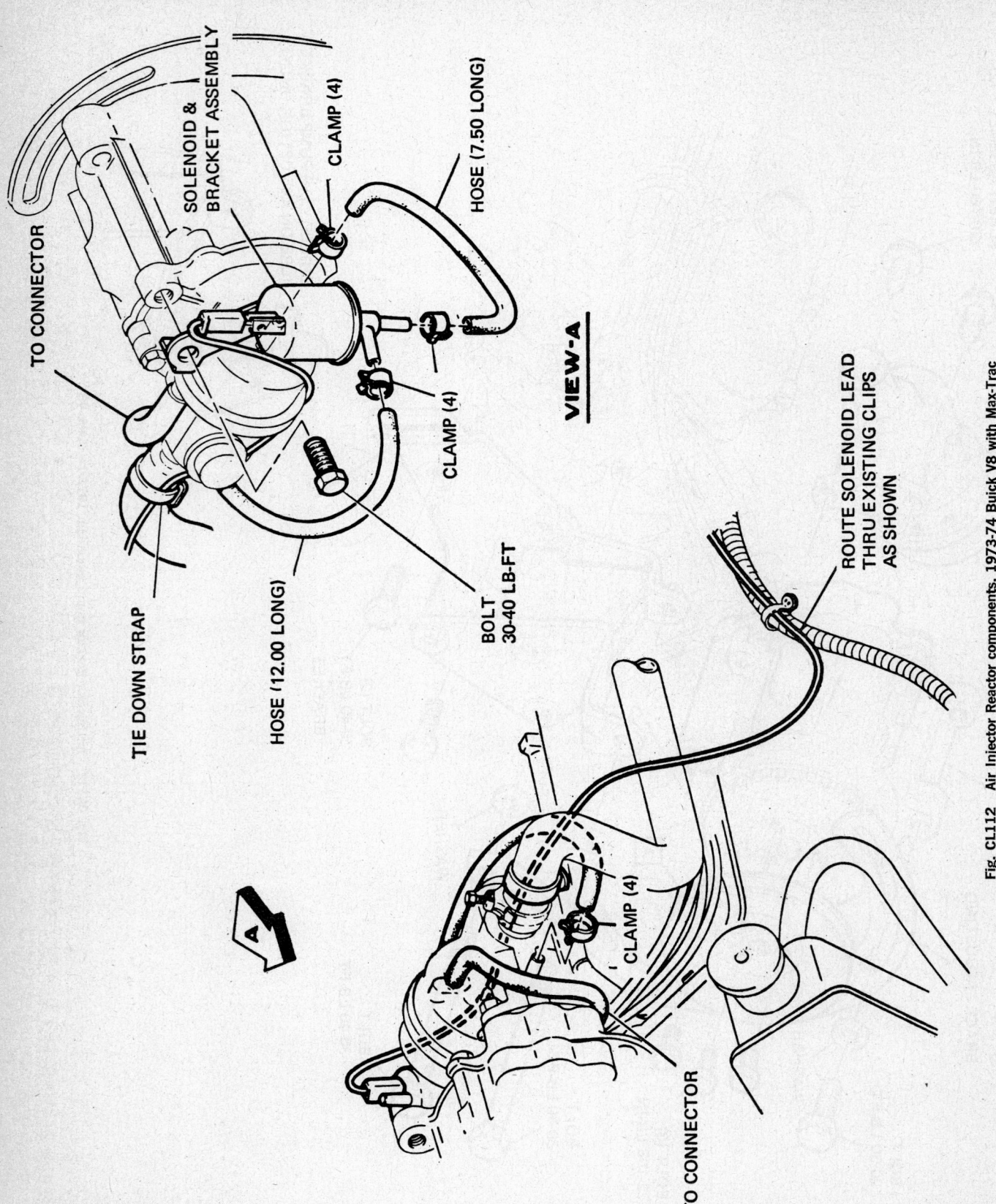

TO CONNECTOR

SOLENOID & BRACKET ASSEMBLY

CLAMP (4)

HOSE (7.50 LONG)

CLAMP (4)

VIEW-A

TIE DOWN STRAP

HOSE (12.00 LONG)

BOLT 30-40 LB-FT

ROUTE SOLENOID LEAD THRU EXISTING CLIPS AS SHOWN

CLAMP (4)

TO CONNECTOR

Fig. CL112 Air Injector Reactor components. 1973-74 Buick V8 with Max-Trac

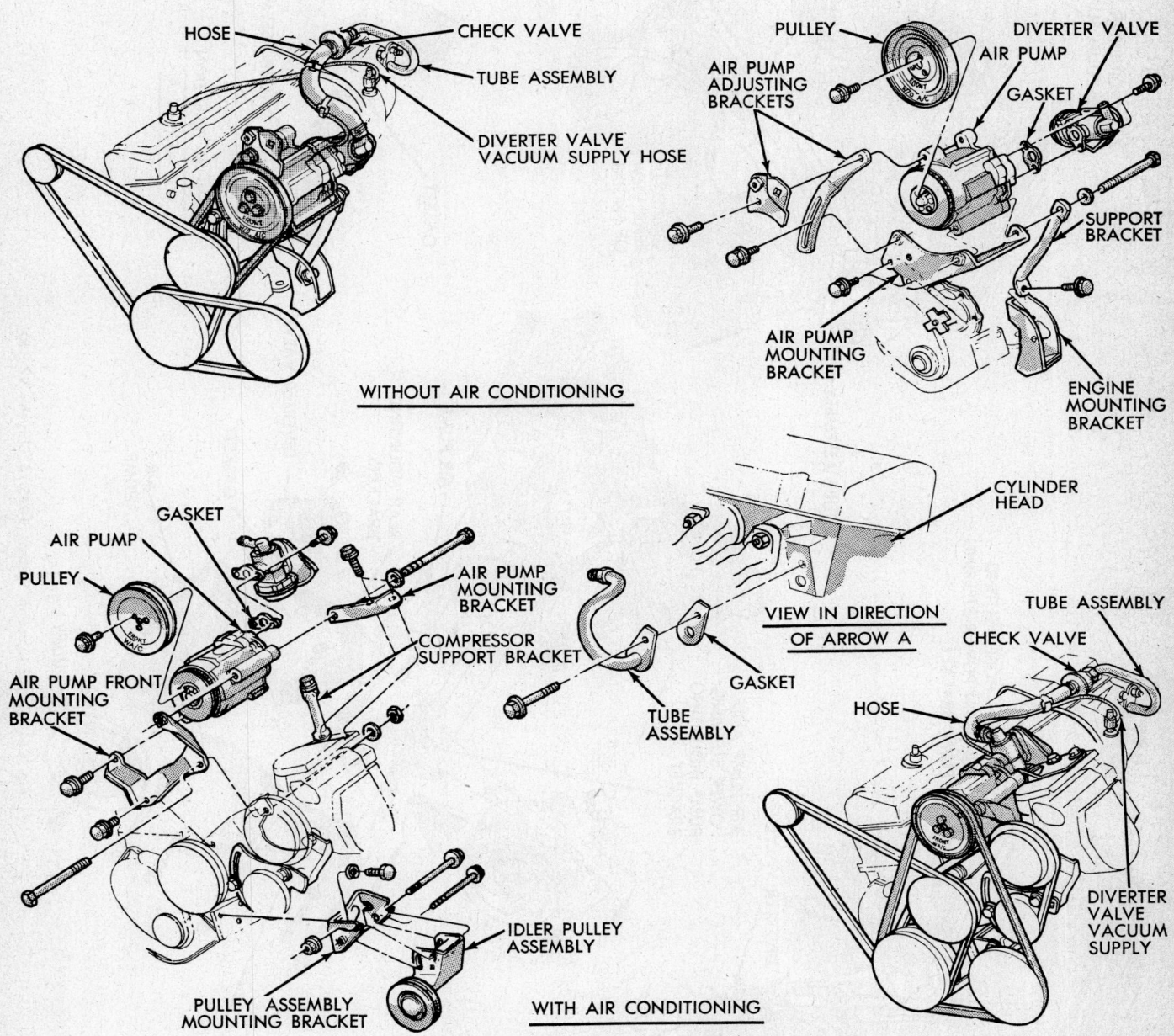

WITHOUT AIR CONDITIONING

HOSE — CHECK VALVE — TUBE ASSEMBLY — DIVERTER VALVE VACUUM SUPPLY HOSE

PULLEY — DIVERTER VALVE — AIR PUMP — GASKET — SUPPORT BRACKET — ENGINE MOUNTING BRACKET — AIR PUMP MOUNTING BRACKET — AIR PUMP ADJUSTING BRACKETS

WITH AIR CONDITIONING

AIR PUMP — GASKET — PULLEY — AIR PUMP FRONT MOUNTING BRACKET — AIR PUMP MOUNTING BRACKET — COMPRESSOR SUPPORT BRACKET — PULLEY ASSEMBLY MOUNTING BRACKET — IDLER PULLEY ASSEMBLY

CYLINDER HEAD — VIEW IN DIRECTION OF ARROW A — GASKET — TUBE ASSEMBLY

TUBE ASSEMBLY — CHECK VALVE — HOSE — DIVERTER VALVE VACUUM SUPPLY

Fig. CL113   Air Injection System. 1972-74 Chrysler 6 cylinder

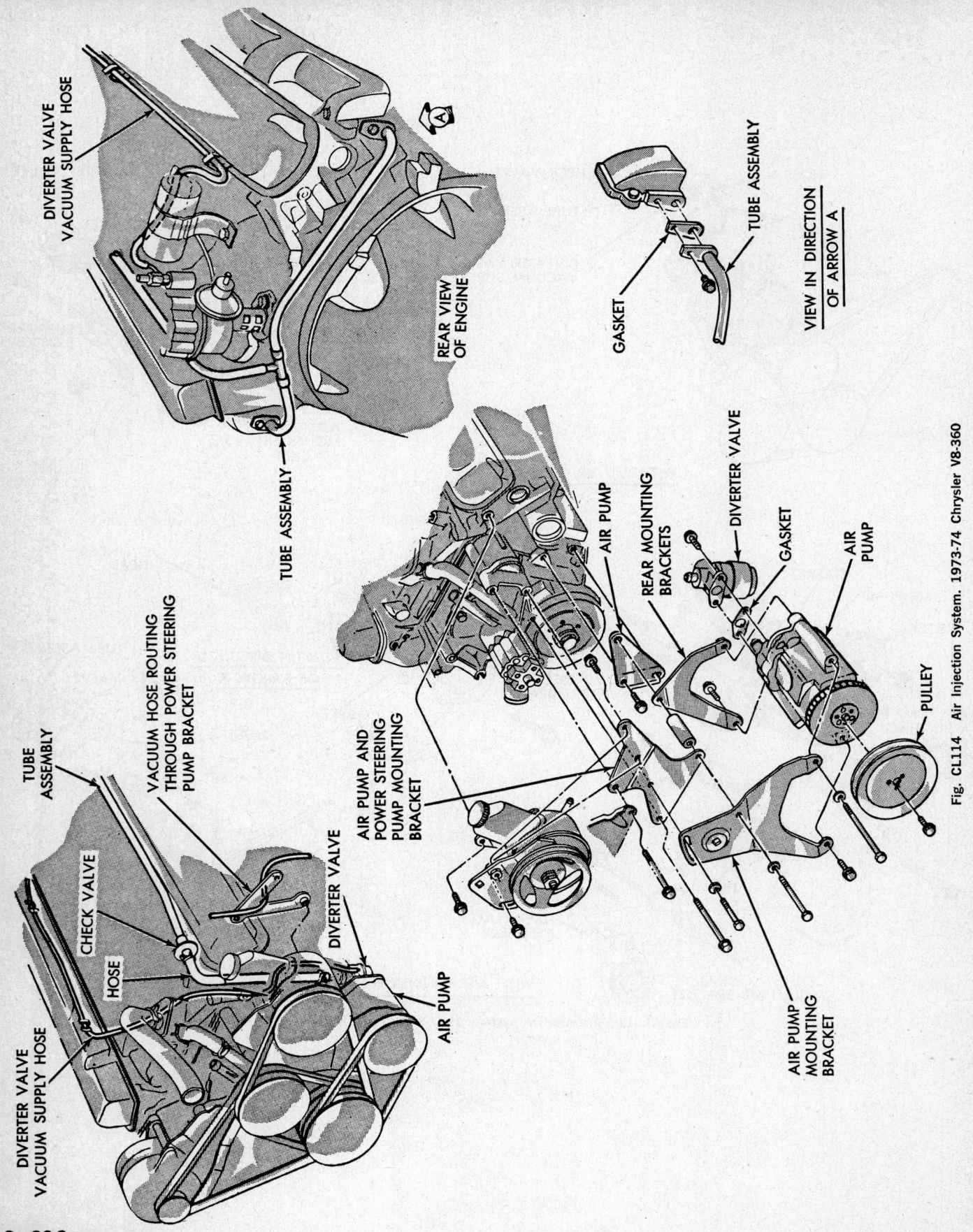

DIVERTER VALVE VACUUM SUPPLY HOSE

REAR VIEW OF ENGINE

TUBE ASSEMBLY

GASKET

TUBE ASSEMBLY

VIEW IN DIRECTION OF ARROW A

AIR PUMP

REAR MOUNTING BRACKETS

DIVERTER VALVE

GASKET

AIR PUMP

PULLEY

AIR PUMP AND POWER STEERING PUMP MOUNTING BRACKET

AIR PUMP MOUNTING BRACKET

VACUUM HOSE ROUTING THROUGH POWER STEERING PUMP BRACKET

TUBE ASSEMBLY

CHECK VALVE

HOSE

DIVERTER VALVE

DIVERTER VALVE VACUUM SUPPLY HOSE

AIR PUMP

Fig. CL114 Air Injection System. 1973-74 Chrysler V8-360

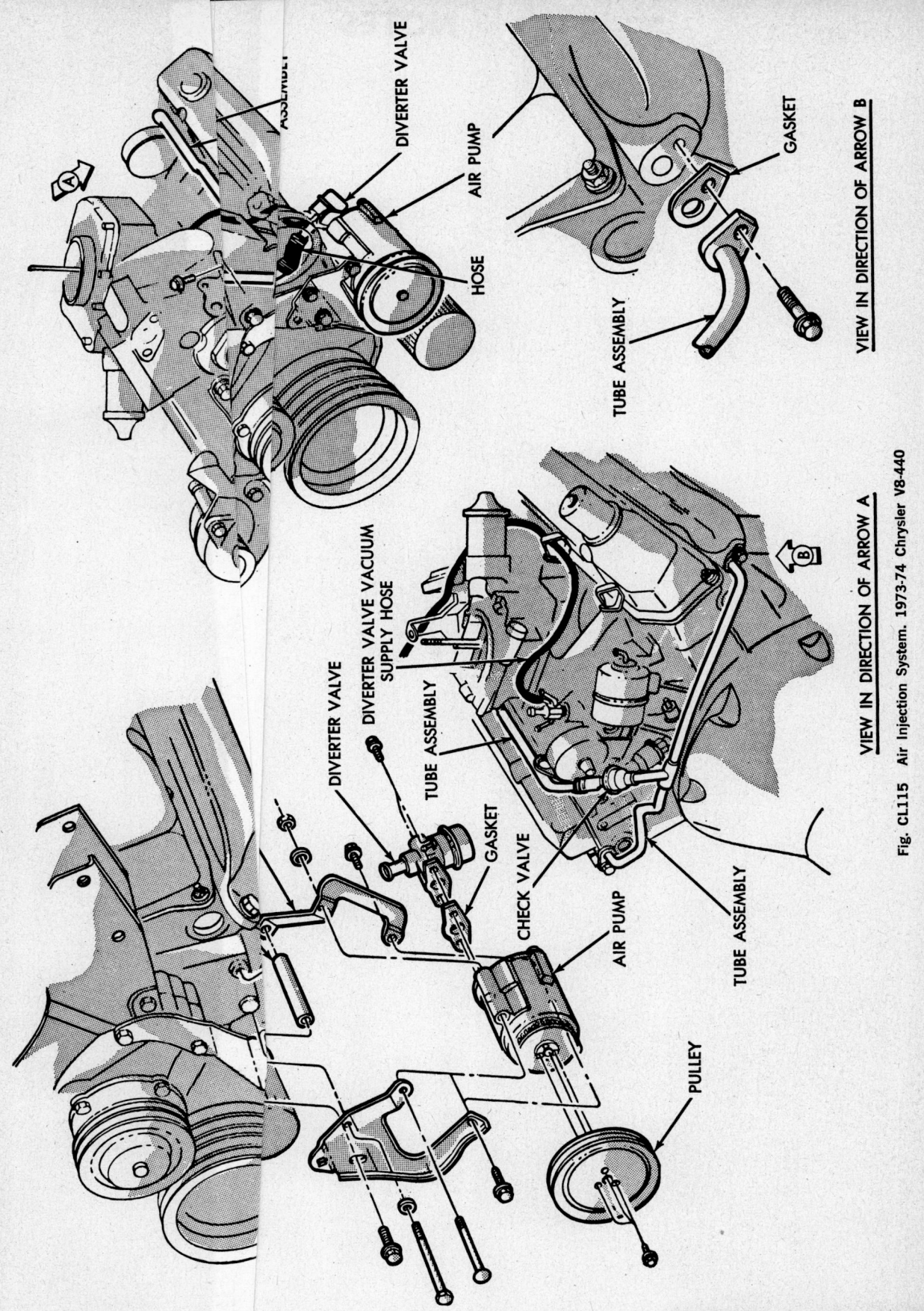

VIEW IN DIRECTION OF ARROW B

GASKET

TUBE ASSEMBLY

DIVERTER VALVE

AIR PUMP

HOSE

VIEW IN DIRECTION OF ARROW A

DIVERTER VALVE

DIVERTER VALVE VACUUM SUPPLY HOSE

TUBE ASSEMBLY

GASKET

CHECK VALVE

AIR PUMP

TUBE ASSEMBLY

PULLEY

Fig. CL115 Air Injection System. 1973-74 Chrysler V8-440

Special Service Tools

Throughout this manual references are made and illustrations may depict the use of special tools required to perform certain jobs. These special tools can generally be ordered through the dealers of the make vehicle being serviced. It is also suggested that you check with local automotive supply firms as they also supply tools manufactured by other firms that will assist in the performance of these jobs. The vehicle manufacturers special tools are supplied by:

American Motors & General Motors . . . . Service Tool Division
Kent-Moore Corporation
1501 South Jackson Street
Jackson, Michigan 49203

Chrysler Corp. . . . . Miller Special Tools
A Division of Utica Tool Co.
32615 Park Lane
Garden City, Michigan 48135

Ford Motor Co. . . . . Owatonna Tool Company
Owatonna, Minnesota 55060

How to Push and Tow Automatic Drive Cars

TOWING PRECAUTIONS

A disabled car must not be towed on the rear wheels with the transmission in any of the driving ranges as unnecessary damage to the transmission may result. Unless otherwise indicated in the chart, it may be towed for short distances only, with the control lever or push button in neutral (N) at a speed not in excess of 25 mph.

If for any reason the transmission is locked up, the car must not be towed on its rear wheels or serious damage to the transmission will result. If the car is to be towed for any extended distance, it should be done with the rear wheels off the ground or with the propeller shaft removed.

NOTE: Beginning with 1969 General Motors cars (1970 for others), except Corvair, if the ignition key is not available it will be necessary to tow the car with the front wheels off the ground and the rear wheels on a dolly or vice versa as the steering and shift mechanisms are also locked.

PUSH STARTING

As indicated in the chart below, a number of transmissions cannot be started by pushing. The oil circuits in these transmissions are such (no rear pump) that the engine cannot be driven through the transmission. If the battery will not crank the engine, a fully charged battery should be installed or a "jumper" circuit should be used from another charged battery.

IMPORTANT

Alternator equipped cars cannot be push-started when the battery is completely dead because, unlike a generator, there is no residual magnetism in the rotor (which corresponds to the field coils in a generator).

When using jumper cables on alternator equipped cars, be sure to connect positive to positive and negative to negative to prevent damage to the alternator.

Car	Transmission	Push Starting				Towing	
		Start Pushing In	Ignition On At M.P.H.	Shift At M.P.H.	Shift To	Hold Speed At or Below M.P.H.	Maximum Distance Miles
American Motors	Flashomatic⑨	Neutral	15–20	15–20	L	40	①
	Torque Command	③	③	③	③	35	100
Chrysler Corp.	Powerflite	Neutral	0	25	L	35	100
	Torqueflite, Aluminum⑧	Neutral	0	15	L	35	100
	Torqueflite, Cast Iron	Neutral	0	15–20	L	35	100
Ford Motor Co.	Cruisematic, C4 and C6	③	③	③	③	30	①
	3 Speed⑩	Neutral	30	30	L	40	12
	2 Speed	Neutral	25	25	L	30	15
Gen. Mot. Corp.	Buick Dual Path Drive	③	③	③	③	25	①
	Buick Twin Turbine	Neutral	0	15	L	35②	①
	Corvair Powerglide	Neutral	0	20–25	L	50	①
	Dual Coupling Hydra-Matic	Neutral	30–35⑥	30–35⑥	D⑥	⑤	①
	F-85 Hydra-Matic, 1961–63	③	③	③	③	30	①
	Jetaway Hydra-Matic	③	③	③	③	45	①
	Roto Hydra-Matic	③	③	③	③	30	①
	Turbo Hydra-Matic "350" & "375B"	③	③	③	③	35①	①
	Turbo Hydra-Matic "400" & "375"	③	③	③	③	45①	①
	Powerglide, Aluminum⑨	Neutral	0	25–30	L	30①	①
	Powerglide, Cast Iron	Neutral	0	25–30	L	30	①
	Super Turbine "300"	③	③	③	③	25①	①
	Super Turbine "400"	③	③	③	③	25①	①
	Tempestorque, 1961–63	Neutral	0	20–25⑦	L	30	①
	Tempestorque, 1964	③	③	③	③	25	①
	Turboglide⑥	Neutral	25	25–30	HR or GR	30④	①
Studebaker	Flightomatic	Neutral	0	20	L	40	①

①—See Towing Precautions.
②—25 M.P.H. with air suspension.
③—Not possible to start by pushing. See Push Starting above.
④—10 M.P.H. with air suspension.
⑤—Do not tow.
⑥—Not possible to push start after 1958. See Push Starting note above.
⑦—Not possible to push start after 1962. See Push Starting note above.
⑧—Not possible to push start after 1965. See Push Starting note above.
⑨—Not possible to push start after 1966. See Push Starting note above.
⑩—Not possible to push start after 1967. See Push Starting note above.